PHILOSOPHY

AND

PSYCHOLOGY

VOLUME II

HARVARD UNIVERSITY LIBRARY

WIDENER LIBRARY SHELFLIST, 43

PHILOSOPHY
AND
PSYCHOLOGY

VOLUME II

AUTHOR AND TITLE LISTING

Published by the Harvard University Library
Distributed by the Harvard University Press
Cambridge, Massachusetts
1973

SHELFLIST VOLUMES IN PRINT:

COPYRIGHT © 1973

BY THE PRESIDENT AND FELLOWS OF HARVARD COLLEGE

STANDARD BOOK NUMBER: 674–66486–8

LIBRARY OF CONGRESS CATALOGUE CARD NUMBER: 72–83389

PRINTED IN U.S.A.

Contents

VOLUME I

Preface v

Statistical Summaries ix

Classification Schedules 3

Classified Listing 29

Chronological Listing 415

VOLUME II

Author and Title Listing

WIDENER LIBRARY SHELFLIST, 43

PHILOSOPHY

AND

PSYCHOLOGY

AUTHOR AND TITLE LISTING

Phil 2490.150   A. Comte als Pädagog. (Sterzel, Georg Friedrick.) Leipzig, 1886.

Phil 336.1.15   A. Fouillée's Neue Theorie der Ideenloréfts. (Pawlicki, S.) Wien, 1893.

Phil 4210.125.10F   A. Rosmini's Stellung in der Geschichte der neueren Philosophie. (Werner, Karl.) Wien, 1884.

Phil 5240.30.2   A.B.C. of Adler's psychology. (Mairet, Philippe.) N.Y., 1929.

Phil 3120.1.125   A.E. Biedermanns Theorie...religiöse Erkenntnis. (Hennig, M.) Leipzig, 1902.

Phil 4754.1.30   A.M. Deborin. (Ahlberg, René.) Berlin, 1959.

Phil 2340.10.105   A.N. Whitehead; un philosophe de l'expérience. (Bera, M.A.) Paris, 1948.

Phil 165.60   A.R. Wadia. Bangalore, 1954.

Phil 40.15   The A.R.E. journal. (Association for Research and Enlightenment.) Virginia Beach. 1,1966+

Phil 2475.1.475   A Bergson, la patrie reconnaissante. (Milhand, Jean.) Paris, 1967.

Phil 9540.10   A critique of pure tolerance. (Wolff, Robert Paul.) Boston, 1965.

Phil 8656.40   A la busca del Dios perdido. (Balbontín, José A.) Madrid, 1969.

Phil 2725.19.90   A la recherche de Dieu. (Jolivet, R.) Paris, 1931.

Phil 960.145   A la recherche de l'unité. (Techoueyres, E.) Reims, 1934.

Phil 3450.19.465   A la rencontre de Martin Heidegger. (Dantlo, René.) Toulouse, 1969.

Phil 2805.196   A la suite de Pascal. (Valensin, A.) Saint-Felicien-en-Vivarais, 1926.

Phil 7069.31.7   Á landmaerum annars heims. (Findlay, J.A.) Reykjavik, 1934?

Phil 2475.1.208.9   À propos de Bergson. (Nicolardot, F.) Paris, 1924.

Phil 7068.98.10   A propos d'Eusapia Paladino. (Fontenay, Guillaume de.) Paris, 1898.

Phil 5247.13.32   A propósito de examen de ingenios del Dr. Huarte. (Ramis Alonso, M.) Palma de Mallorca, 1943.

Phil 6957.35   A prospective study of the incidences of mental disorder. (Hagnell, Olle.) Stockholm, 1966.

Phil 9245.115   A szczęściu. Wyd. 3. (Tatarkiewicz, W.) Warszawa, 1962.

Phil 196.20   A travers la métaphysique. (Valensin, A.) Paris, 1925.

Phil 8605.2.5   A vapore. (Zoppola, G.) Firenze, 1914.

Phil 4630.7.80   Aaberg, Bengt. Individualitet och universalitet hos Waldemar Rudin. Lund, 1968.

Phil 4515.91   Åberg, L.H. Den Boströmska verldsåsigten i sina grunddrag framstäld. Stockholm, 1882.

Phil 4655.1.80   Åberg, L.H. Carl Pontus Wikner. Sockholm, 1889.

Phil 8875.19   Åberg, L.H. Filosofisk sedelära. v.1-4. Uppsala, 1893-94.

Phil 4515.91.5   Åberg, L.H. Försök till en lärobok i allmän samhällslära. Upsala, 1879.

Phil 4655.1.80.2   Åberg, L.H. Granskning af P. Wikners kritik. Stockholm, 1882.

Phil 4513.3.33   Åberg, L.N. Fyra föreläsningar. Uppsala, 1891.

Phil 3425.119   Åberg, Lawrence H. Hegel och Boströms rättsfilosofiska grundtankar. Upsala, 1885.

Phil 585.178   Aaberg, Thorsten. Livsåskådningar. Stockholm, 1965.

Phil 10.86F   Aabo, Finland. Yliopisto. Institute of Psychology. Reports. Turku.

Phil 7055.101   Aakerblom, Lilly. Bortom mänsklig horisont. Stockholm, 1966.

Phil 5210.1   Aall, A. Psykologiens historie i Norge. Kristiania, 1911.

Phil 4500.2   Aall, Anathon. Filosofien i Norden. Kristiania, 1919.

Phil 8875.16   Aall, Anathon. Macht und Pflicht. Leipzig, 1902.

Phil 800.5   Aall, Anathon. Filosofiens historie. Oslo, 1929.

Phil 4513.6.31   Aall, H.H. Interessen som normativ idé. Kristiania, 1913.

Phil 5590.510   Aamark, Curt. Individ, persenlighet och medmänsklig miljö. Stolkholm, 1969.

Phil 337.5.5   Aandslaenker. (Grung, Frants.) Kjøbenhavn, 1886.

Phil 3120.11.96   Aanschomving en verstand. (Bolland, G.J.P.J.) Leiden, 1897.

Phil 7150.49   Aarberon, Norman. The cry for help. N.Y., 1961.

Phil 2115.149.5   Aaron, R.I. John Locke. 2nd ed. Oxford, 1955.

Phil 331.1   Aaron, R.I. The nature of knowing. London, 1930.

Phil 1870.113   Aaron, Richard I. Locke and Berkeley's commonplace book. Aberdeen, 1931. 2 pam.

Phil 5080.5   Aaron, Richard I. Our knowledge of universals. London, 1945.

Phil 2115.149A   Aaron, Richard Ithamar. John Locke. London, 1937.

Phil 2115.149.3   Aaron, Richard Ithamar. John Locke. 3rd ed. Oxford, 1971.

Phil 730.5   Aaron, Richard Ithamar. The theory of universals. Oxford, 1952.

Phil 730.5.2   Aaron, Richard Ithamar. The Theory of universals. 2nd ed. London, 1967.

Phil 720.43   Aaron, Richard Ithamar. The true and the valid. London, 1955.

Phil 8875.14   Aars, K.B.R. Gut und Böse. Christiania, 1907.

Phil 4513.2.35   Aars, K.B.R. Haben die naturgesetze Wirklichkeit? Christiania, 1907.

Phil 5240.24   Aars, K.B.R. Inledning til psychologien. Kristiania, 1898.

Phil 4513.2.31   Aars, K.B.R. Tanker og syn En liden studie. Kristiania, 1894.

Phil 175.22   Aars, K.B.R. Zur psychologischen Analyse der Welt. Leipzig, 1900.

Phil 331.4   Aars, Kristian B. Die idee zum ursprung des gedankens. Kristiania, 1911.

Phil 3482.7   Aars, Kristian Birch-Reichenwald. Die Autonomie der Moral mit besondere Berucksichtigung der Morallehre Immanuel Kants. Hamburg, 1896.

Phil 270.37   Aarsagsforestilling. (Bang, Niels H.) København, 1925.

Phil 5590.502   Aarts, Josephus Franciscus Maria Carolus. Zelfbeoordelingen. Tilburg, 1964.

Phil 4515.99   Åt minnet af C.J. Boström, 1797-1897. Festskrift. Stockholm, 1897.

Phil 4962.5   Abad Carretero, Luis. Niñez y filosofía. México, 1957.

Phil 4962.5.5   Abad Carretero, Luis. Vida y sentido. México, 1960.

Phil 7054.161   Abaddon and Mahanaim...guardian angels. (Berg. J.T.) Philadelphia, 1856.

Htn   Phil 9558.21*   Abaddon's steam engine. Philadelphia, 1817.

Phil 5590.1   Abaunza, A. Los valores psicologicos de la personalidad. Mexico, 1940.

Phil 175.19   Abauzit, Frank. L'absolutisme intellectuel. Saint-Blaise, 1909.

Phil 193.21.25   Abauzit, Frank. L'enigme du monde. Paris, 1922.

Phil 8875.8   Abbadie, J. L'Art de se connoitre soy-même. v.1-2. La Haye, 1711.

Phil 1505.5   Abbagmano, N. La filosofia medievale. Bari, 1963.

Phil 400.74   Abbagnano, N. Il nuovo idealismo inglese ed americano. Napoli, 1927.

Phil 8580.35   Abbagnano, N. La religione. Torino, 1961.

Phil 175.29   Abbagnano, N. Le sorgenti irrazionali del pensiero. Genova, 1923.

Phil 800.16   Abbagnano, N. Storia della filosofia. 2. ed. Torino, 1963. 3v.

Phil 4235.1.97   Abbagnano, Nicola. Bernardino Telesio. Milano, 1941.

Phil 1750.270.15   Abbagnano, Nicola. Critical existentialism. 1. ed. Garden City, N.Y., 1969.

Phil 85.15   Abbagnano, Nicola. Dizionario di filosofia. Torino, 1961.

Phil 1750.270   Abbagnano, Nicola. Esistenzialismo positivo; due saggi. 1. ed. Torino, 1948.

Phil 1750.270.5   Abbagnano, Nicola. Introduzione all'esistenzialismo. Torino, 1947.

Phil 1750.270.8   Abbagnano, Nicola. Introduzione all'esistenzialismo. 3. ed. Torino, 1948.

Phil 1750.270.10   Abbagnano, Nicola. Philosophie des menschlichen Konflikts. Hamburg, 1957.

Phil 4060.10.30   Abbagnano, Nicola. Scritti scelti. Torino, 1967.

Phil 175.68   Abbagnano, Nieda. Per o contro l'uomo. Milano, 1968.

Phil 4080.3.281   Abbate, Michele. La filosofia di Benedetto Croce e la crisi della società italiana. Torino, 1966.

Phil 4080.3.280   Abbate, Michele. La filosofia di Benedetto Croce e la crisi della società italiano. Torino, 1955.

Phil 410.77   Der Abbau des "Unendlich". (Mozkowski, A.) Berlin, 1925.

Phil 5425.62   The Abbé Du Bos - his advocacy of the theory of climate. (Koller, A.H.) Champaign, 1937.

Phil 8951.11.80   L'abbé Louis Bautain. (Prupard, Paul.) Tournai, 1961.

Phil 2605.5.95   L'abbé Simon Foucher. (Rabbe, Felix P.) Paris, 1867.

Phil 8580.15   Abbetmeyer, Theo. Das Gralsreich als Streiter wider den Untergang des Abendlandes. Heilbronn, 1916.

Phil 8625.2   Abbot, Ezra. Literature of the doctrine of a future life. Cambridge? 1862?

Phil 8625.2.5   Abbot, Ezra. The literature of the doctrine of a future life. N.Y., 1871.

Phil 8655.5.5   Abbot, F.E. Scientifc theism. 2. ed. Boston, 1886.

Phil 331.1   Abbot, F.E. Scientific philosophy. London, 1882.

Phil 8655.5   Abbot, F.E. Scientific theism. Boston, 1885.

Phil 1845.4.90   Abbot, F.E. Testimonials to his character. Boston, 1879.

Phil 8580.1   Abbot, F.E. The way out of agnosticism. Boston, 1890.

Phil 8580.9   Abbot, F.L. Faith built on reason. Boston, 1902.

Phil 8610.890.42   Abbot, Francis Ellingwood. The way out of agnosticism, or The philosophy of free religion. 2. ed. Ann Arbor, 1962.

Phil 1870.82.5   Abbot, T.K. Bishop Berkeley and Professor Fraser. Dublin, 1877.

Phil 1870.82A   Abbot, T.K. Sight and touch...Berkeleian theory. London, 1864.

Phil 7069.21.10   Abbott, Anne. The two worlds of attraction. Boston, 1921.

Phil 7052.7   Abbott, D.P. Behind the scenes with the mediums. Chicago, 1907.

Phil 7052.7.5   Abbott, D.P. The history of a strange case. Chicago, 1908.

Phil 1850.80A   Abbott, E.A. Francis Bacon. London, 1885.

Phil 6990.19.5   Abbott, E.A. Philomythus, an antidote against credulity. London, 1891.

Phil 175.17   Abbott, F.E. The syllogistic philosophy. Boston, 1906. 2v.

Phil 5040.21.5   Abbott, F.K. The elements of logic. London, 1947.

Phil 9160.2.15   Abbott, Jacob. The child at Howe. N.Y., 1871.

Phil 9160.2.8   Abbott, Jacob. The child at Howe. 2. ed. Boston, 1834.

Htn   Phil 9160.1.9*   Abbott, Jacob. Parental duties in the promotion of early piety. London, 1836.

Phil 9160.1.5   Abbott, Jacob. A primer of ethics. Boston, 1891.

Phil 9160.1   Abbott, Jacob. The Rollo code of morals. Boston, 1841.

Phil 9160.2.5   Abbott, Jacob. The school-girl. Boston, 1840.

Phil 9340.4   Abbott, John S. The school-boy. Boston, 1839.

Phil 5643.1   Abbott, T.K. Sight and touch. London, 1864.

Phil 177.70   Abbozzi di filosofia umana. (Cifarelli, Natale.) Bari, 1913.

Phil 3095.83   Abbt, Thomas. Alexander Gottlieb Baumgartens Leben und Charakter. Halle, 1765.

Phil 6950.5   Abby, Carl. Is anyone sane. Boston, 1935.

Phil 5242.22   ABC de psychologie. (Cuvillier, Armand.) Paris, 1923.

Phil 5258.196   ABC des Helfens. (Schmitt, Friedrich.) Stuttgart, 1965.

Phil 8419.12.5   The ABC of aesthetics. (Stein, Leo.) N.Y., 1927.

Phil 5254.2.15   The ABC of psychology. (Ogden, C.K.) Harmondsworth, 1944.

Phil 331.41   Abdil'din, Zhabaikhan M. Problema nachala v teoreticheskom poznanii. Alma-Ata, 1967.

Phil 4710.160   Abdullaev, Magomed A. Iz istorii filosofskoi i obshchestvenno-politicheskoi mysli narodov Dagestana v XIX v. Moskva, 1968.

Phil 960.155   Abegg, Emil. Indische Psychologie. Zürich, 1945.

Phil 6110.11   Abel, J.F. Einleitung in die Seelenlehre. Stuttgart, 1786.

Phil 5240.25   Abel, Jacob Friedrich von. Einleitung in die Seelenlehre. Stuttgart, 1786. 2 pam.

Phil 5240.25.5   Abel, Jacob Friedrich von. Erläuterungen wichtiger Gegenstände aus der philosophischen und christlichen Moral. Tübingen, 1790.

Phil 5240.25.10   Abel, Jacob Friedrich von. Versuch über die Seelenstärke. Tübingen, 1804.

Phil 5240.25.15   Abel, Jakob Friedrich von. Rede über das Genie. Marbach, 1955.

Phil 5240.25.20   Abel, Jakob Friedrich von. Versuch über die Natur der speculativen Vernunft zur Prüfung des Kantischen Systems. Frankfurt, 1787.

Phil 2280.7.80   Abel, Reuben. The pragmatic humanism of F.C.S. Schiller. N.Y., 1955.

Phil 8690.12   Abelé, Jean. Le christianisme se désintéressé-t-il de la science? Paris, 1960.

Phil 5240.51   Abella Gibert, D. El nostre caracter. Barcelona, 1961.

Phil 4301.2   Abellán, José Luis. Filosofia española en America, 1936-1966. Madrid, 1967.

Phil 1750.115.37   Abellio, Raymond. La structure absolue; essai de phénoménologie génétique. Paris, 1965.

Phil 5190.85   Abelson, Herbert Irving. Persuasion; how opinions and attitudes are changed. N.Y., 1959.

Phil 5240.5   Abelson, R. Mental fatigue - 1908. Leipzig, 1908.

Phil 1750.166.80   Abendländische Humanität. (Krueger, Gerhard.) Stuttgart, 1953.

Phil 3120.64.30   Die abendländische Leidenschaft. (Bense, Max.) München, 1938.

Phil 623.15   Der abendländische Rationalismus. (Ziegler, Leopold.) Jena, 1905.

Phil 1504.17.4   Die abendländische Spekulation. v.17, pt.4. (Schneider, A.) Münster, 1915.

Phil 475.1   Abendroth, Robert. Das Problem der Materie. v.1. Leipzig, 1889.

Phil 3808.237   Abendroth, Walter. Arthur Schopenhauer in Selbstzeugnissen und Bilddokumenten. Reinbek, 1967.

Author and Title Listing

Phil 974.3.170 Abendroth, Walter. Rudolf Steiner und die heutige Welt. München, 1969.
Phil 1020.9.5 Abenmasarra y su escuela. (Asian Palacios, M.) Madrid, 1914.
Phil 3310.8 Das Abenteuer des Geistes. (Glockner, Hermann.) Stuttgart, 1938.
Phil 665.44 Aber, Mary R.A. Souls. Chicago, 1893.
Phil 3450.19.103 Aber Herr Heidegger. (Ballmer, Karl.) Basel, 1933.
Phil 5240.1.12 Abercrombie, J. The culture and discipline of the mind. 6th ed. Edinburgh, 1837.
Phil 5240.1.3 Abercrombie, J. Inquiries...intellectual powers. Boston, 1835.
Phil 5240.1 Abercrombie, J. Inquiries...intellectual powers. Edinburgh, 1831.
Phil 5240.1.2 Abercrombie, J. Inquiries...intellectual powers. N.Y., 1832.
Phil 5240.1.4 Abercrombie, J. Inquiries...intellectual powers. N.Y., 1838.
Phil 6950.3 Abercrombie, J. Pathological, practical researches, diseases...brain. Philadelphia, 1831.
Phil 8875.1 Abercrombie, J. The philosophy of the moral feelings. N.Y., 1833.
Phil 8875.1.3 Abercrombie, J. The philosophy of the moral feelings. N.Y., 1839.
Phil 8655.1.6 Abernethy, J. Discourses concerning...God. Aberdeen, 1778. 2v.
Phil 8655.1.3 Abernethy, J. Discourses concerning...God. Dublin, 1743. 2v.
Phil 3552.242 Abfassungszeit von Leibnizens Unvorgreiflichen Gedanken. (Neff, L.) Durlach, 1880.
Phil 8590.35 Abgrund und Gründe. Versuch einer Philosophie christlicher Positivität. (Krieger, Evelina.) Graz, 1966.
Phil 2490.53.15 Abhandlung über den Geist des Positivismus. (Comte, Auguste.) Leipzig, 1915.
Phil 3552.56 Abhandlung über die beste philosophische Ausdrucksweise. (Leibniz, Gottfried Wilhelm.) Berlin, 1916.
Phil 303.3 Abhandlung über die Cosmogonie. (Wuttke, A.) Haag, 1850.
Phil 2493.45.4 Abhandlung über die Empfindungen. (Condillac, Etienne Bonnot.) Berlin, 1870.
Phil 2520.43 Abhandlung über die Methode. (Descartes, René.) Leipzig, 1919-20. 2 pam.
Phil 1870.40.35 Abhandlung über die Prinzipien der menschlichen Erkenntnis. (Berkeley, G.) London, 1920.
Phil 3819.45.9 Abhandlung über die Verbesserung des Verstandes. 4. Aufl. (Spinoza, Benedictus de.) Leipzig, 1922.
Phil 3425.455 Abhandlung über Leib und Seele. (Erdmann, Johann Eduard.) Leiden, 1902.
Phil 25.36 Abhandlungen aus dem Gebiete der Psychotherapie. Stuttgart. 1-15,1925-1931 15v.
Phil 8893.32 Abhandlungen aus dem Gebiete der Ethik, der Staatswissenschaft, der Asthetik und der Theologie. (Strümpell, L.) Leipzig, 1895.
Phil 182.76 Abhandlungen aus dem Gebiete der Philosophie und ihrer Geschichte. Freiburg, 1913.
Phil 175.8 Abhandlungen der Fries'schen Schule. Leipzig. 1847-1918 5v.
Phil 1200.31 Abhandlungen für die Geschichte und das Eigenthümliche der späteren stoischen Philosophie. (Conz, C.P.) Tübingen, 1794.
Phil 3850.18.15 Abhandlungen und Aufsätze. (Scheler, Max.) Leipzig, 1915. 2v.
Phil 8597.3A Abhandlungen von den vornehmsten Wahrheiten der natürlichen Religion. 6. Aufl. (Reimarus, H.S.) Hamburg, 1791.
Phil 3018.10 Abhandlungen zur Geschichte de Metaphysik, Psychologie. (Strümpell, Ludwig.) Leipzig, 1896.
Phil 10.22 Abhandlungen zur Philosophie und ihrer Geschichte. Halle. 1-52 7v.
Phil 10.22.8 Abhandlungen zur Philosophie und ihrer Geschichte. Leipzig. 1-25,1907-1916 3v.
Phil 10.72 Abhandlungen zur Philosophie und Psychologie. Dornach. 1,1951+ 2v.
Phil 10.26 Abhandlungen zur Physiologie der Gesichtsempfindungen. Leipzig. 1-5 3v.
Phil 182.4.3 Abhandlungen zur systematischen Philosophie. (Harms, F.) Berlin, 1868.
Phil 7011.2.2 Abhedānanda, Swami. The science of psychic phenomena. 2. ed. Calcutta, 1966.
Phil 7069.44.45 Abhedānanda. Life beyond death. Calcutta, 1944.
Phil 331.8 Abicht, J.H. Philosophie der Erkenntnisse. Pt.1-2. Bayreuth, 1791.
Phil 175.1 Abicht, J.H. System der Elementarphilosophie. Erlangen, 1795.
Phil 5040.17.5 Abicht, Johann H. Verbesserte Logik. Fürth, 1802.
Phil 5040.17 Abicht, Johann H. Vom dem Nutzen und der Einrichtung eines zu logischen uebingen Bestimmten Collegimus. Leipzig, 1790.
Phil 9560.62 Abicht, Johann Heinrich. Neues System einer philosophischen Tugendlehre. Leipzig, 1970.
Phil 5485.8 Abilities: their structure, growth, and action. (Cattell, Raymond Bernard.) Boston, 1971.
Phil 5258.68.5A The abilities of man; their nature and measurement. (Spearman, C.) N.Y., 1927.
Phil 5259.27 Ability and knowledge: the London school. (Thomas, Frank C.) London, 1935.
Phil 3120.8.20 Die Abkehr von Nichtrealen. (Brentano, Franz.) Bern, 1966.
Phil 5645.8 Abney, W. de W. Colour vision. London, 1895.
Phil 5645.8.5 Abney, W. de W. Researches in colour vision. London, 1913.
Phil 6328.6 Abnormal behavior. (Sando, I.J.) N.Y., 1923.
Phil 7106.10 Abnormal hypnotic phenomena, a survey of nineteenth century cases. London, 1967[1968] 4v.
Phil 6322.10 Abnormal man. (MacDonald, A.) Washington, D.C., 1893.
Phil 6967.10.2 Abnormal mental strain. (Read, C. Stanford.) London, 1920.
Phil 6332.19 The abnormal personality. 2. ed. (White, Robert.) N.Y., 1956.
Phil 6332.19.3 The abnormal personality. 3d ed. (White, Robert.) N.Y., 1964.
Phil 6312.1 Abnormal psychology. (Coriat, I.H.) London, 1911.
Phil 6312.1.3 Abnormal psychology. (Coriat, I.H.) N.Y., 1910.
Phil 6317.6.10 Abnormal psychology. (Hallingworth, H.L.) N.Y., 1930.
Phil 6322.17 Abnormal psychology. (Meyer, Max F.) Columbia, 1927.
Phil 6305.9 Pamphlet box. Abnormal psychology. German dissertations.
Phil 6312.1.5 Abnormal psychology. 2. ed. (Coriat, I.H.) N.Y., 1914.
Phil 6305.5 Pamphlet vol. Abnormal psychology. 1891-1912. 9 pam.
Phil 6332.4.3 Abnormal psychology and its educational applications. (Watts, Frank.) London, 1921.

Phil 6400.24 Abnormal speech. (Winkler, Carl.) Orange, Conn., 1932.
Phil 7069.19.150 The abolishing of death. (King, Basil.) N.Y., 1919.
Phil 8665.9.5 The abolition of God. (Koch, H.G.) Philadelphia, 1963.
Phil 7069.28.20 The abomination in our midst. (Dudley, O.F.) London, 1928.
Phil 3850.27.245 Aborra oganga. (Corah, Hakki.) Istanbul, 1967.
Phil 5780.10 Les aboulies sociales, le scrupule, la timidité, l'autoritarisme. (Dupuis, Léon.) Paris, 1940.
Phil 5254.3 About ourselves. (Overstreet, H. Allen.) N.Y., 1927.
Phil 175.54 Abraches, Cassiano. Metafisica. Braga, 1956.
Phil 3640.257 Abraham, G.E.H. Nietzsche. London, 1933.
Phil 3640.257.5 Abraham, G.E.H. Nietzsche. N.Y., 1933.
Phil 6310.2.14 Abraham, Karl. Clinical papers and essays on psychoanalysis. London, 1955.
Phil 5893.6 Abraham, Karl. Dreams and myths; a study in race psychology. N.Y., 1913.
Phil 6310.2.8 Abraham, Karl. Klinische Beitrage zur Psychoanalyse aus den Jahren 1907-1926. Leipzig, 1921.
Phil 6310.23 Abraham, Karl. On character and libido development. N.Y., 1966.
Phil 6310.2.16 Abraham, Karl. Psychoanalytische Studien zur Charakterbildung und andere Schriften. Frankfurt, 1969. 2v.
Phil 331.35 Abrahamian, Lev. Gnoseologicheskie problemy teorii znakov. Erevan, 1965.
Phil 3905.84 Abrahamsen, David. The mind and death of a genius. N.Y., 1946.
Phil 310.805 Abram Deborin/Nikolai Bucharin: Kontroversen über dialektischen und mechanistischen Materialismus. (Negt, Oskar.) Frankfurt, 1969.
Phil 5625.107 Abramian, Lev. Signal i uslovnyi refleks. Erevan, 1961.
Phil 5722.5 Abramowski, Edouard. Le subconscient normal. Paris, 1914.
Phil 4803.108.25 Abramowski, Edward. Filozofia spoleczna. Warszawa, 1965.
Phil 4803.108.1 Abramowski, Edward. Pisma. Warszawa, 1924.
Phil 5238.201 Abrams, A. Unfinished tasks in the behavioral sciences. Baltimore, 1964.
Phil 8580.10 Abranches, J. dos Santos. Questões fundamentaes. Coimbra, 1891.
Htn Phil 6990.38* Abrege de la notice sur la vie et les vertus d'Anna Maria Taigi. (Luquet, J.F.O.) Rome, 1851.
Phil 2610.7 Abregé de la philosophie de Gassendi. 2e ed. v.1-7. (Gassendi, P.) Lyon, 1684. 6v.
Htn Phil 2610.7.5* Abregé de la philosophie de Mr. Gassendi. (Gassendi, P.) Paris, 1675.
Phil 802.16 Abreges pour les aveugles. (Chartier, Emile.) Paris, 1943.
Phil 7069.60.25 Abreu Filho, Julio. Rosa dos ventos; artigos e palestras. São Paulo, 1960.
Phil 978.5.11 An abridgment by K. Hilliard of The secret doctrine. (Blavatsky, H.P.) N.Y., 1907.
Phil 2115.45.5 An abridgment of Mr. Locke's Essay concerning human understanding. (Locke, J.) Glasgow, 1744.
Phil 2115.45.2 An abridgment of Mr. Locke's Essay concerning human understanding. (Locke, J.) Boston, 1794.
Htn Phil 2115.45* An abridgment of Mr. Locke's Essay concerning human understanding. (Locke, J.) London, 1700.
Htn Phil 2115.44* An abridgment of Mr. Locke's Essay concerning humane understanding. (Locke, J.) London, 1696.
Phil 2300.30.15 An abridgment of the Light of nature pursued. (Tucker, Abraham.) London, 1807.
Phil 5058.5.9A Abriss der Algebra der Logik. (Schröder, E.) Leipzig, 1909. 2v.
Phil 803.5 Abriss der Geschichte der Philosophie. (Deter, C.J.) Berlin, 1913.
Phil 1109.2 Abriss der griechischen Philosophie. (Eckstein, F.) Frankfurt, 1955.
Phil 5042.21A Abriss der Logistik. (Carnap, Rudolf.) Wien, 1929.
Phil 3195.9.80 Abriss der Philosophie Eugen Dührings. Inaug. Diss. (Posner, S.) Breslau, 1906.
Phil 5057.12 Abriss der philosophischen Logik. (Ritter, Heinrich.) Berlin, 1824.
Phil 5057.12.4 Abriss der philosophischen Logik. 2. Aufl. (Ritter, Heinrich.) Berlin, 1829.
Phil 5244.7 Abriss der Psychologie. (Ebbinghaus, H.) Leipzig, 1908.
Phil 5252.30.9 Abriss der Psychologie. (Müller, G.E.) Göttingen, 1924.
Phil 5244.7.4 Abriss der Psychologie. 6e Aufl. (Ebbinghaus, H.) Leipzig, 1919.
Phil 3525.61 Abriss des Systemes der Logik. (Krause, K.C.F.) Göttingen, 1828.
Phil 3525.45 Abriss des Systemes der Philosophie. (Krause, K.C.F.) Göttingen, 1825.
Phil 5213.1.5 Abriss einer Geschichte der Psychologie. (Dessoir, M.) Heidelberg, 1911.
Phil 8423.6 Abriss einer Wissenschaftslehre der Ästhetik. (Wize, K.F.) Berlin, 1909.
Phil 6670.2 Abrutz, Sydney. Hypnos och suggestion. Stockholm, 1925.
Phil 5640.19 Abrutz, Sydney. Om sinnesrörelsernas fysiologi och psykologi. Upsala, 1901.
Phil 6110.13 Abrutz, Sydney. Till nervsystems dynamik. Stockholm, 1917.
Phil 3010.7 Die Absage an die Romantik in der Zeit nach den Weltkriege. (Klugen, A. von.) Berlin, 1938.
Phil 7150.85 Die Abschätzung der Suizidalität. (Poeldinger, Walter.) Bern, 1968.
Phil 8665.9 Abschaffung Tottes? (Koch, H.G.) Stuttgart, 1961.
Phil 1750.858 Abschied von der Metaphysik? Beiträge zu einer Philosophie der Endlichkeit. (Schröder, Erich Christian.) Trier, 1969.
Phil 3120.30.115 Abschied von Martin Buber. (Levin-Goldschmidt, Hermann.) Köln, 1966.
Phil 2270.107 Absi, Marcelle. La théorie de la religion chez Spencer et ses successeurs. Thèse. Beyrouth, 1952.
Phil 182.78 Das Absolute. (Heiler, Josef.) München, 1921.
Phil 4370.15 The absolute being. (Tallet, Jorge.) N.Y., 1958.
Phil 181.79 The absolute collective. (Gutkind, Eric.) London, 1937.
Phil 8665.7 Det absolute gudshegreb. (Kent, G.) Kristiania, 1886.
Phil 8626.9 Absolute idealism and immortality. (Ball, J.W.) Lincoln, 1908.
Phil 3801.474 Das Absolute in der Geschichte. (Kasper, Walter.) Mainz, 1965.
Phil 575.27 Das absolute Individuum. (Schlaf, Johannes.) Berlin, 1910.
Phil 3160.20 Die absolute Reflexion. (Cramer, Wolfgang.) Frankfurt, 1966- 2v.
Phil 187.43 Absolute relativism. (McTaggart, William.) London, 1887.
Phil 3425.62 Die absolute Religion. (Hegel, Georg Wilhelm Friedrich.) Leipzig, 1929.

Phil 3801.445.50 — Das Absolute und die Geschichte. (Habermas, J.) Bonn, 1954.

Phil 720.70 — Die absolute Ungeschichtlichkeit der Warhrheit. (Lauth, Reinhard.) Stuttgart, 1966.

Phil 8674.16 — Absolute value: a study in Christian theism. (Tvethoworn, Illtyd.) London, 1970.

Phil 8599.19.2 — Die Absolutheit des Christentums. 2. Aufl. (Troeltsch, Ernst.) Tübingen, 1912.

Phil 6311.15 — Absolution. (Barrett, E.B.) London, 1932.

Phil 8887.127 — Absolutism and relativism in ethics. (Moser, Shia.) Springfield, 1968.

Phil 175.19 — L'absolutisme intellectuel. (Abauzit, Frank.) Saint-Blaise, 1909.

Phil 400.35 — Het absoluut idealisme. (Mouw, J.A. der.) Leiden, 1905.

Phil 2050.59 — An abstract of a treatise of human nature, 1740. (Hume, David.) Cambridge, Eng., 1938.

Phil 2050.59.2 — An abstract of a treatise of human nature, 1740. (Hume, David.) Hamden, Conn., 1965.

Phil 6955.9 — Abstract of the statutes of the United States, and of the several territories relating to the custody of the insane. (Folsom, C.F.) Philadelphia, 1884.

Phil 5032.1 — Abstraction, relation, and induction. (Weinberg, Julius Rudolph.) Madison, 1965.

Phil 5360.18 — Abstraction and concept formation. (Pikas, Anatol.) Cambridge, 1944.

Phil 5360.4 — L'abstraction et son rôle dans l'éducation intellectuelle. 2e éd. (Queyrat, F.) Paris, 1907.

Phil 5400.59.2 — L'abstraction sentimentale. (Sourian, É.) Parjs, 1925.

Phil 5400.59 — L'abstraction sentimentale. Thèse. (Sourian, É.) Paris, 1925.

Phil 5400.59.5 — L'abstraction sentimentale. 2. ed. (Sourian, É.) Paris, 1951.

Phil 75.50 — Abstracts of Bulgarian scientific literature. Philosophy and pedagogics. (Bulgarska Akademiia na Naukite, Sofia. Biblioteka.) Sofia. 1958+ 4v.

Phil 5360.34 — Abstrakcia. 1. vyd. (Tenzer, Oliver.) Bratislava, 1966.

Phil 8423.21 — Abstraktion und Einfühlung. (Worringer, W.) München, 1959.

Phil 3425.706 — Abstraktion und Konkretion bei Hegel und Kierkegaard. (Hagen, Eduard von.) Bonn, 1969.

Phil 1540.19 — Die Abstraktionslehre in der Scholastik bis Thomas von Aquin. Inaug.-Diss. (Gessner, Jakob.) Tulda, 1930.

Phil 2880.8.130 — Absurdes sein? (Moeller, Joseph.) Stuttgart, 1959.

Phil 6122.53 — The absurdity of any mind-body relation. (Myers, C.S.) London, 1932.

Phil 5590.65 — Abt, L.E. Projective psychology. 1.ed. N.Y., 1950.

Phil 23.16.5 — Abteilung Charakterologie, psychologische und philosophische Anthropologie. (Neve Deutsche Forschungen.) Berlin. 1-17 4v.

Phil 23.16 — Abteilung Philosophie. (Neve Deutsche Forschungen.) Berlin. 3-37 18v.

Phil 1540.74 — Abu Ma'shar and Lah'n Aristoteliaram. (Lemny, Richard.) Beirut, 1962.

Phil 7084.36 — Abu Schirin. Das goldene ägyptisch-arabische Traumbuch. Heidenheim, 1960.

Phil 3428.84 — Die abweichungen Steinthals von Herbart. (Ivanoff, T.) Jena, 1893.

Phil 4340.15 — Academia...Madrid. Academia Española, Madrid. Discursos leídos en las recepciones públicas de la Real Academia Española. Ser. 2. Madrid, 1945- 6v.

Phil 310.185 — Academia Republicci Populare Romîne. Bucuresti, 1960.

Phil 40.11 — Academia Republici Populare Romine. Institutul de Filozofie. Arcetári filozofice. 4,1957+ 18v.

Phil 310.580 — Academia Republicii Populare Romine. Biblioteca. Materialismus dialectic si stiintele contemporane ale naturii. Bucuresti, 1963.

Phil 310.581 — Academia Republicii Populare Romine. Institut de Filosofie. Dialectica materialista. Bucuresti, 1963.

Phil 4817.5 — Academia Republicii Socialiste România, Bucharest. Philosophes roumains contemporains. Bucureşti, 1958.

Phil 4817.6 — Academia Republicii Socialiste România, Bucharest. Institutu I de Filozofie. Antologiia iz istoriiata na rumunskata progresivna misul. Sofiia, 1965.

Phil 4816.10 — Academia Republicii Socialiste România, Bucharest. Institutul de Filozofie. Istoria gîradirii sociale şi filozofice în Romînia. Bucureşti, 1964.

Phil 178.7 — Academical questions. (Drummond, W.) London, 1805.

Phil 178.7.5 — Academical questions. (Drummond, W.) London, 1805.

Phil 2805.425 — Académie des sciences, belles lettres et arts de Clermont-Ferrand. Cinq études sur Blaise Pascal. Clermont-Ferrand, 1962.

Phil 6675.4 — Académie des Sciences, Paris. Report on experiments on animal magnetism. Edinburgh, 1833.

Phil 8886.21.5 — L'Académie française. v.1-4. (La Primaudaye, P. de.) Saumur, 1613.

Htn Phil 8886.21.3* — L'Académie française. 3. ed. (La Primaudaye, P. de.) London, 1594. 2v.

Htn Phil 8886.21.2* — L'Académie française. 3. ed. (La Primaudaye, P. de.) Paris, 1582.

Phil 5241.160 — Academische redeväringen. (Buytendijk, F.J.J.) Utrecht, 1961.

Phil 9590.9 — The academy for souls. (Cosgrave, J.O.) N.Y., 1931.

Phil 4065.111 — Acanfora-Venturelli, R. Il monismo teosofico di G.B. Palermo, 1893.

Phil 4060.7 — Acari, P. Un meccanismo umano. Milano, 1909.

Phil 5374.243 — Academia...Vatican City. Pontificia Academia delle Scienze, Vatican City. Brain and conscious experience. Study Week, September 28 to October 4, 1964. N.Y., 1966.

Phil 40.7 — Pamphlet box. Accademia di filosofia italica, Genoa.

Phil 175.39 — Accambray, Leon. Un testament philosophique. Paris, 1937.

Phil 380.2.5A — Accent on form. (Whyte, Lancelot L.) N.Y., 1954.

Phil 8581.42 — Accepting the universe. (Burroughs, John.) Boston, 1920.

Phil 5643.18 — Die Accommodationsfehler des Auges. (Stellwag, K. von C.) n.p., 1855.

Phil 7085.2 — Account of Jane E. Rider somnambulist. (Belden, L.W.) Springfield, 1834.

Phil 2050.86 — Account of life...D. Hume. (Ritchie, T.E.) London, 1807.

Phil 1850.96.2 — An account of Lord Bacons Novum Organon Scientiarum. (Hoppus, J.) London, 1827. 3 pam.

Phil 1850.96.3 — An account of Lord Bacons Novum Organon Scientiarum. (Hoppus, J.) London, 1827. 3 pam.

Phil 1850.96 — An account of Lord Bacon's Novum Organon Scientiarum. (Hoppus, J.) London, 1827-28.

Phil 2115.78A — An account of Mr. Lock's religion. (Locke, J.) London, 1700.

Htn Phil 8673.14* — An account of the growth of deism in England. (Stephens, William.) London, 1696.

Htn Phil 2725.6.30* — An account of the life and writings of Mr. John LeClerc. London, 1712. 2 pam.

Phil 1870.119 — An account of the life of George Berkeley. 2nd ed. (Stock, J.) Dublin, 1777.

Htn Phil 6947.1.893* — Account of the rise and progress of the asylum. Philadelphia, 1814. 2 pam.

Htn Phil 8897.22* — An account of the societies for reformation of manners. (Woodward, Josiah.) London, 1699.

Phil 7060.83 — Accredited ghost stories. (Jarvis, T.M.) London, 1823.

Phil 4960.630 — Acerboni, Lidia. La filosofia contemporanea in Brasile. Milano, 1966.

Phil 5750.3.10 — Ach, Narziss. Analyse des Willens. Berlin, 1935.

Phil 5750.3 — Ach, Narziss. Über den Willensakt und das Temperament. Leipzig, 1910.

Phil 5750.3.2 — Ach, Narziss. Über die Willenstätigkeit und das Denken. Göttingen, 1905.

Phil 310.270 — Der Acheismus im dialektischen Materialismus. (Ehlen, Peter.) München, 1961.

Phil 8875.21 — Achelis, J. Ethik. Leipzig, 1910.

Phil 8875.21.5 — Achelis, J. Ethik. 2nd ed. Leipzig, 1900.

Phil 7076.16 — Achelis, Thomas. Die Ekstase in ihrer kulturellen Bedeutung. Berlin, 1902.

Phil 490.8 — Achêma. v.1-2,6. (Poortman, J.J.) Assen, 1954. 5v.

Phil 5548.5A — The achievement nature. (McClelland, D.C.) N.Y., 1953.

Phil 2750.11.152 — The achievement of Jacques and Raïssa Maritain. 1st ed. (Gallagher, Donald.) N.Y., 1962.

Phil 575.97 — Achievement of personality. (Stuart, C.) N.Y., 1938.

Phil 5585.82A — Achieving sanity in the modern world. (Mayo, Elton.) Cambridge, Mass., 194-?

Phil 5545.74 — Achilles, E.M. Experimental studies in recall and recognition. N.Y., 1920.

Phil 5520.305 — Achkov, P.A. Myshlenie i iazyk. Moskva, 1959.

Phil 3120.22.15 — Die Achse der Natur. (Blüher, Hans.) Hamburg, 1949.

Phil 196.11 — Acht Aufsätze zur Apologie der menschlichen Vernunft. (Varnbüler, Theodore.) Leipzig, 1878.

Phil 5245.9 — Acht psychologische Vorträge. (Fortlage, A.R.K.) Jena, 1869.

Phil 5585.2 — Die acht Sinne des Menschen. (Duttenhofer.) Nördlingen, 1858.

Phil 530.40.42 — De achtergrond der Spaansche mystiek. (Brouwer, Johan.) Zutphen, 1935.

Phil 3246.78.5 — Achtundvierzig Briefe. (Fichte, Johann Gottlieb.) Leipzig, 1862.

Phil 70.3.75 — Achtzehnte Internationale Kongress für Psychologie in Moskau, 1966. (Kussmann, Thomas.) Göttingen, 1967.

Phil 5850.502 — Aciles, P.S. Psychology at work. N.Y., 1932.

Phil 3640.291.5 — Ackerknecht, E. Friedrich Nietzsche, der Prophet der schenkenden Tugend. 2e Aufl. Stettin, 1926.

Phil 6980.14.100 — Ackerknecht, E.H. Kurge Geschichte der Psychiatrie. Stuttgart, 1957.

Phil 6980.14.102 — Ackerknecht, E.H. A short history of psychiatry. N.Y., 1959.

Phil 7060.12 — Ackermann, G. Über die Entwickelung von Wahnideen. Weimar, 1892.

Phil 3640.345 — Ackermann, O. Kant im Urteil Nietzsches. Tübingen, 1939.

Phil 5125.32 — Ackermann, Robert John. Nondeductive inference. London, 1966.

Phil 331.34 — Ackermann, Robert John. Theories of knowledge. N.Y., 1965.

Phil 5066.28.5 — Ackermann, W. Soluable cases of the decision problem. Amsterdam, 1954.

Phil 5066.28 — Ackermann, W. Ein System der typenfreien Logik. Pt.1. Leipzig, 1941-

Phil 5648.11.25 — Ackerson, Luton. A correlational analysis of proficiency in typing. N.Y., 1926.

Phil 9495.165 — Acland, Richard. Sexual morality. London, 1965.

Phil 3195.3.31 — Das Acquist der Philosophie und Briefe. (Dietzgen, Joseph.) Stuttgart, 1903.

Phil 5875.65.10 — The acquisition and development of language. (Menyuk, Paula.) Englewood Cliffs, 1971.

Phil 5520.504 — Acquisition du langage et développement de la pensée, sous-systèmes, et opérations concrètes. (Sinclair-de Zwart, Hermina.) Paris, 1967.

Phil 5241.41 — Acquisition of skill. (Batson, W.H.) Princeton, 1916.

Phil 5535.8 — Acquisition of skill. (Conference on Acquisition of Skill, New Orleans.) N.Y., 1966.

Phil 8877.78.3 — Acres of diamonds. (Conwell, Russell H.) N.Y., 1943.

Phil 9245.128 — Acres of happiness. 1st ed. (Maggal, Moshe M.) N.Y., 1967.

Phil 4000.10 — Acri, Francesco. Critica di alcune critiche di spaventa. Bologna, 1875.

Phil 4060.8.81 — Acri. (Cancarini, Itala.) Brescia, 1945.

Phil 3095.50 — Acroasis logica. (Baumgarten, A.G.) Halae, 1773.

Phil 7069.13.15 — Across the barrier. (Dallas, Helen A.) London, 1913.

Phil 585.161 — Act and agent. (Browning, Douglas.) Coral Gables, Fla., 1964.

Phil 5465.137 — The act of creation. (Koestler, Arthur.) London, 1964.

Phil 5465.137.5 — The act of creation. (Koestler, Arthur.) N.Y., 1969.

Phil 35.50 — Acta Instituti psychologici Universitatis Zagra iensis. (Zagreb. Univerzitet. Psihologijski Institut.) 1,1964+

Phil 10.101 — Acta paedopsychiatrica. Basel. 38,1971+

Phil 10.49 — Acta philosophica Fennica edidit Societas Philosophica. Helsinki. 1,1935 9v.

Phil 10.49.5 — Acta psychologica Fennica. Helsingissä. 1,1951+

Phil 10.94 — Acta psychologica Gothoburgensia. Stockholm. 1-7 2v.

Phil 10.39 — Acta psychologica Keijo. Keijo, Japan.

Phil 10.78 — Acta psychologica Taiwanica; science reports of the National Jaiwan University. Taipei. 1,1958+ 3v.

Phil 10.102 — Acta symbolica. Akron, Ohio. 1,1970+

Phil 70.19 — Actas. (Congreso Internacional de Filosofia, Barcelona.) Madrid, 1949. 3v.

Phil 70.21 — Actas. (Congreso Nacional de Filosofia.) Buenos Aires. 1-3 4v.

Phil 70.16.5 — Actas. (Interamerican Congress of Psychology.) 1,1953 2 pam.

Phil 178.46.10 — Acte et synthèse. (Decoster, Paul.) Bruxelles, 1928.

Phil 70.13.10 — Actes. (Congrès International de Philosophie des Science, Paris, 1949.) Paris, 1951. 9v.

Phil 70.3.55 — Actes. Proceedings. (International Congress of Psychology, 15th, Brussels, 1957.) Amsterdam. 1959

Phil 8400.36.4 — Actes du cinquième congrès international d'esthétique, Amsterdam, 1964. (International Congress on Aesthetics, 5th, Amsterdam, 1964.) La Haye, 1968.

Phil 2610.100 — Actes du Congrès du Tricentenaire de Pierre Gassendi. (Comité du Tricentenaire de Gassendi.) Paris, 1957.

Phil 70.13 — Actes du Congrès International. (Congrès International de Philosophie Scientifique, 1st, Paris, 1935.) Paris, 1936. 8v.

Phil 70.1.8   Actes du huitième congrés international de philosophie à Prague. (International Congress of Philosophy, 8th, Prague, 1934.) Prague. 1936

Phil 5400.159   Action, emotion and will. (Kenny, A.) London, 1963.
Phil 8876.54   L'action. (Blondel, Maurice.) Paris, 1893.
Phil 8876.54.10   L'action. (Blondel, Maurice.) Paris, 1936.
Phil 585.177.5   Action. (Brown, Donald George.) Toronto, 1968.
Phil 8885.52   Action. (Knox, Malcolm.) London, 1968.
Phil 6946.42   Action against mental disability; the report. (U.S. President's Task Force on the Mentally Handicapped.) Washington, 1970.
Phil 585.177   Action and purpose. (Taylor, Richard.) Englewood Cliffs, N.J., 1966.
Phil 6946.1.5   Action for mental health. (Joint Commission on Mental Illness and Health.) N.Y., 1961.
Phil 9530.52   The active mind. (Orage, A.R.) N.Y., 1954.
Phil 8881.38   Active principles, or Elements of moral science. (Godwin, John H.) London, 1885.
Phil 6980.351.5   Active psychotherapy. (Herzberg, Alexander.) N.Y., 1946.
Phil 5867.35   Active/passive: the crucial psychological dimension. (Fried, Edrita.) N.Y., 1970.
Phil 179.12   Activism. (Eno, Henry Lane.) Princeton, N.J., 1920.
Phil 5255.2   L'activité mentale. (Paulhan, F.) Paris, 1889.
Phil 5255.2.2   L'activité mentale. 2. éd. (Paulhan, F.) Paris, 1913.
Phil 2405.5.5   L'activité philosophique contemporaine en France. 1. éd. (Farber, Marvin.) Paris, 1950. 2v.
Phil 5259.20   L'activité psychique. (Tassy, Edme.) Paris, 1925.
Phil 5811.16   L'activité psychique chez les animaux. (Bretegnier, Louis.) Paris, 1930.
Phil 5811.16.5   L'activité psychique chez les animaux. Thèse. (Bretegnier, Louis.) Toulouse, 1930.
Phil 8880.26   L'activité réfléchie. (Fleuriau, A. de.) Paris, 1911.
Phil 5520.419   Les activités intellectuelles. (Oleron, P.) Paris, 1964.
Phil 9560.23   An activity analysis of the four cardinal virtues. Diss. (Mensing, C.) Washington, 1929.
Phil 7080.50   Activity of young children during sleep. (Garvey, Chester R.) Minneapolis, 1939.
Phil 3482.20   Acton, Harry Burrows. Kant's moral philosophy. London, 1970.
Phil 4967.15   La acusación de plagio contra el rector Frondizi. (Asociación de Egresados de la Facultad de Derecho y Ciencias Sociales de la Universidad de Buenos Aires.) Buenos Aires? 1959.
Phil 1712.24   Aczyístość i synteza. (Moniuszko, Antoni.) Warszawa, 1962.
Phil 3831.8   Ad Spinozae opera posthuma. (Leopold, J.H.) Hagae, 1902.
Phil 310.596   Adajnyk, Walter. Marxism and existentialism. 1. ed. Garden City, N.Y., 1965.
Phil 8080.14   Adalékok az estétika történetehez. (Ludács, G.) Budapest, 1953.
Phil 1700.12   Adam, Antoine. Le mouvement philosophique dan la première moitie du XVIIIe siècle. Paris, 1967.
Phil 8520.39   Adam, Antoine. Sur le problème religieux dans la première moitié du XVIIe siècle. Oxford, 1959.
Phil 2400.2   Adam, C. La philosophie en France. Paris, 1894.
Phil 2520.169   Adam, C.E. De methodo apud Cartesium, Spinozam et Leibnitium. Lutetiae, 1885.
Phil 2520.169.10   Adam, C.E. Descartes; sa vie et son oeuvre. Paris, 1937.
Phil 2520.169.15   Adam, C.E. Descartes; ses amitiés féminines. Paris, 1937.
Phil 8401.20   Adam, Charles. Essai sur le jugement. Paris, 1885.
Phil 1850.103   Adam, Charles. Philosophie de François Bacon. Paris, 1890.
Phil 6110.28   Adám, György. Interoception and behaviour. Budapest, 1967.
Phil 8580.29   Adam, J.D. Under the highest leadership. N.Y., 1918.
Phil 3000.1.2   Adam, M. Vitae germanorum philosophorum. Franefort, 1663.
Phil 3000.1   Adam, M. Vitae germanorum superiori. Franefort, 1615.
Phil 600.1   Adam, W. Inquiry into theories of history. v.1-10. London, 1862.
Phil 8702.2.9   Adam and the adamite. (McCausland, D.) London, 1872.
Phil 9345.12   Adam et Eve. (Folliet, Joseph.) Lyon, 1965.
Phil 2266.80.3   Adam Smith. (Farrer, J.A.) London, 1881.
Phil 2266.80   Adam Smith. (Farrer, J.A.) N.Y., 1881.
Phil 2266.82   Adam Smith als Moralphilosoph. (Paszkowski, W.) Halle, 1890.
Phil 2266.81   Adam Smith's Moralphilosophie. (Schubert, Johannes.) Leipzig, 1890.
Phil 2266.90   Adam Smith's science of morals. (Campbell, Thomas Douglas.) London, 1971.
Phil 281.14   Adamczyk, S. Filozofia przyrody. Lublin, 1963.
Phil 331.31   Adamczyk, S. Krytyka ludzkiego poznania. Wyd.1. Lublin, 1962.
Phil 175.50   Adamczyk, S. Matafzika ogólna czyli ontologia. Lublin, 1960.
Phil 8401.23.5   Adamian, Arshag. Stat'i ob estetike. Erevan, 1967.
Phil 8401.23   Adamian, Arshag. Stat'i ob iskusstve. Moskva, 1961.
Phil 9340.10   Adams, (Mrs.). Daily duties inculcated in a series of letters. Boston, 1835.
Phil 800.3   Adams, C. Études sur les principaux philosophes. Paris, 1903.
Phil 9490.1   Adams, C.K. The present obligations of the scholar. Madison, Wis., 1897.
Phil 5810.5   Adams, Donald K. Experimental studies of adaptive behavior in cats. Diss. Baltimore, 1929.
Phil 8401.24   Adams, E.K. The aesthetic experience: its meaning in a functional psychology. Chicago, 1907.
Phil 281.20   Adams, George. Von dem ätherischen Raume. Stuttgart, 1964.
Phil 1800.2   Adams, George P. Contemporary American philosophy. N.Y., 1930. 2v.
Phil 1800.2.5   Adams, George P. Contemporary American philosophy. N.Y., 1962. 2v.
Phil 400.38   Adams, George P. Idealism and the modern age. New Haven, 1919.
Phil 175.44   Adams, George P. Man and metaphysics. N.Y., 1948.
Phil 5210.3   Adams, Grace K. Psychology. N.Y., 1931.
Phil 5643.38   Adams, H.F. Autokinetic sensations. Chicago, 1912.
Phil 5240.23   Adams, H.F. The ways of the mind. N.Y., 1925.
Phil 4260.109   Adams, Henry P. The life and writings of Giambattista Vico. London, 1935.
Phil 8875.2   Adams, J. Elements of moral philosophy. Cambridge, 1837.
Phil 3808.177   Adams, J.S. The aesthetics of pessimism. Philadelphia, 1940.
Phil 7054.89   Adams, J.S. A rivulet from the ocean of truth. Boston, 1854.
Htn   Phil 7150.17*   Adams, John. An essay concerning self-murther. London, 1700.

Phil 5240.41   Adams, John. Everyman's psychology. 1. ed. Garden City, 1929.
Phil 7054.56   Adams, John Quincy. Twelve messages from the spirit. Boston, 1859.
Phil 8610.902.15   Adams, R.C. Good without God. N.Y., 1902.
Phil 1750.705   Adams, Robert. Better part of valor; More, Erasmus, Colet and Vives, on humanism, war, and peace. Seattle, 1962.
Phil 2050.204   Adams, William. An essay on Mr. Hume's essay on miracles. London, 1752.
Phil 1700.1   Adamson, R. The development of modern philosophy. Photoreproduction. Edinburgh, 1903 2v.
Phil 3246.80   Adamson, R. Fichte. Philadelphia, 1881.
Phil 3246.80.3   Adamson, R. Fichte. Philadelphia, 1892.
Phil 3482.1   Adamson, R. Philosophy of Kant. Edinburg, 1879.
Phil 5010.1   Adamson, R. A short history of logic. Edinburgh, 1911.
Phil 3482.1.5   Adamson, R. Über Kant's Philosophie. Leipzig, 1880.
Phil 1105.4   Adamson, Robert. The development of Greek philosophy. Edinburgh, 1908.
Phil 5850.140   L'adaption de l'homme à son métier. 1. éd. (Bonnardel, Raymond.) Paris, 1946.
Phil 5240.45   Adcock, C.J. Factorial analysis for non-mathematicians. Carlton, 1954.
Phil 2150.18.45   Addis, Laird. Moore and Ryle: two ontologists. Iowa City, 1965.
Phil 525.34   Addison, C.M. What is mysticism. N.Y., 1923.
Phil 8581.13.16   Additional observations...natural theology by H. Lord Brougham. (Wallace, T.) Dublin, 1835.
Phil 8709.2.4   Address...before British association. (Tyndall, John.) N.Y., 1875.
Phil 6674.3.5   An address...medical profession of Bristol and Bath. (Estlin, John B.) London, 1843.
Phil 8709.2   Address. (Tyndall, John.) Cambridge, 1874. 2 pam.
Phil 8709.2.9   Address. (Tyndall, John.) N.Y., 1874.
Htn   Phil 2305.2.30*   Address before...British association at Belfast. (Tyndall, John.) London, 1874.
Phil 9035.28   An address delivered before the American Whig and Cliosophic Societies. 2d ed. (Gaston, William.) Princeton, 1835.
Phil 9530.21   Address delivered before the American Whig and Cliosophic societies of the college of New Jersey, Sept. 26, 1843. (Dayton, William L.) Princeton, 1843.
Phil 5938.7   An address of the birth of Spurzheim. (Bartlett, E.) Boston, 1838.
Phil 9145.5   Address on some growing evils of the day. (Friends for Pennsylvania, New Jersey and Delaware.) Philadelphia, 1882.
Phil 9010.27   An address to persons of fashion. (Hill, Richard.) Baltimore, 1807.
Phil 9010.27.2   An address to persons of fashions. 6th ed. (Hill, Richard.) Shrewsbury, 1771.
Phil 9455.7   An address to the Phi Beta Kappa Society of Brown University, Sept. 5, 1832. (Metcalf, Thomas.) Boston, 1833.
Phil 510.7   Addresses...at and in reference to the 1st Monist congress. (Wakeman, T.B.) Cos Cob, 1913.
Phil 3246.55.12   Addresses in the German nation. Photoreproduction. (Fichte, Johann Gottlieb.) Chicago, 1923.
Phil 9344.1   Addresses on duties of youth. (Eddy, A.D.) N.Y., 1836.
Phil 6325.2A   Addresses on psycho-analysis. (Putnam, J.J.) London, 1921.
Phil 4508.7   Adelborg, Gustaf Otto. Om det personligt andliga. Stockholm, 1907.
Phil 165.392   Adelmann, Frederick. The quest for the absolute. Chestnut Hill, 1966.
Phil 5257.32   Adenoids and diseased tonsils; their effect on general intelligence. (Rogers, M.C.) N.Y., 1922.
Phil 3085.2.85   Aders, Fritz. Jacob Friedrich Abel als Philosophie. Inaug. Diss. Berlin, 1893.
Phil 2475.1.390   Ades, Albert. Ades chez Bergson. Paris, 1949.
Phil 2475.1.390   Ades chez Bergson. (Ades, Albert.) Paris, 1949.
Phil 2340.10.210   Adhin, Herman S. Whitehead en de wereld. Proefschrift. Delft, 1963.
Phil 9035.25   Adickes, E. Charakter und Weltanschauung. Tübingen, 1907.
Phil 3482.2.5   Adickes, E. German Kantian bibliography. v.1-3. Boston, 1896[1893]
Phil 3482.2   Adickes, E. Kant - Studien. Kiel, 1895. 2v.
Phil 3482.2.7   Adickes, E. Kant als Naturforscher. Berlin, 1924. 2v.
Phil 3482.2.16   Adickes, E. Kant und das Ding an sich. Berlin, 1924.
Phil 3482.2.25   Adickes, E. Kant und die als-ob-Philosophie. Stuttgart, 1927.
Phil 3482.2.12   Adickes, E. Kants Ansichten über Geschichte und Bau der Erde. Tübingen, 1911.
Phil 3482.2.30   Adickes, E. Kants Lehre von der doppelten Affektion unseres ich als Schlüssel zu seiner Erkenntnis Theorie. Tübingen, 1929.
Phil 3482.2.35   Adickes, E. Kants Systematik als Systembilden der Factor. Berlin, 1887.
Phil 3482.2.21   Adickes, E. Ein neu aufgefundenes Kollegheft nach Kants Vorlesung über Psysischegeographie. Tübingen, 1913.
Phil 3482.2.20   Adickes, E. Untersuchungen zu Kants Physischer Geographie. Tübingen, 1911.
Phil 3549.15.80   Adickes, Erich. Vier Schriften des Herrn Professor Kappes. Pt.1-2. Berlin, 1903.
Htn   Phil 5058.15*   Aditis at logicam. (Smith, Samuel.) Oxoniae, 1656-1657.
Htn   Phil 5058.15.3*   Aditus ad logicam. (Smith, Samuel.) Oxoniae, 1634.
Phil 5592.180   The adjective checklist manual. (Gough, Harrison Gould.) Palo Alto, 1965.
Phil 5040.19   Adjukiewicz, Kazimierz. Glówne zasady metodologji nauk i logiki. Warszawa, 1928.
Phil 5040.19.5   Adjukiewicz, Kazimierz. Logika pragmatyczna. Warszawa, 1965.
Phil 5262.9.30   Adjustment and mastery. (Woodworth, R.S.) Baltimore, 1933.
Phil 5590.422   Adjustment and personality. (Lazarus, Richard.) N.Y., 1961.
Phil 1145.90   Adkins, Arthur. Merit and responsibility. Oxford, 1960.
Phil 1145.90.1   Adkins, Arthur. Merit and responsibility. Oxford, 1960[1970]
Phil 860.4   Adkins, Arthur William Hope. From the many to the one: a study of personality and views of human nature in the context of ancient Greek society, values and beliefs. London, 1970.
Phil 6310.1.25A   Adler, A. The case of Miss R. N.Y., 1929.
Phil 6310.1.40   Adler, A. Heilen und Bilden. München, 1914.
Phil 6310.1.39   Adler, A. Heilen und Bilden. München, 1922.
Phil 6310.1.27A   Adler, A. The individual psychology of Alfred Adler. 1st ed. N.Y., 1956.

Phil 6310.1   Adler, A. The neurotic constitution; individualistic psychology. N.Y., 1917.

Phil 6310.1.5   Adler, A. The practice and theory of individual psychology. London, 1924.

Phil 6310.1.6   Adler, A. The practice and theory of individual psychology. N.Y., 1932.

Phil 6310.1.9   Adler, A. Praxis und Theorie der Individual-Psychologie. 2. Aufl. München, 1924.

Phil 6310.1.42   Adler, A. The problem child. N.Y., 1963.

Phil 6310.1.3   Adler, A. Problems of neurosis. London, 1930.

Phil 6310.1.20   Adler, A. The science of living. Garden City, N.Y., 1929.

Phil 6310.1.21   Adler, A. The science of living. N.Y., 1929.

Phil 6310.1.38   Adler, A. Der Sinn des Lebens. Wien, 1933.

Phil 6310.1.22   Adler, A. Social interest. London, 1938.

Phil 6310.1.45   Adler, A. Superiority and social interest. Evanston, Ill., 1964.

Phil 6310.1.11   Adler, A. Die Technik der Individual-Psychologie. Teil 1-2. München, 1928-30.

Phil 6310.1.15   Adler, A. Die Theorie der Organminderwertigkeit. Leipzig, 1908.

Phil 6310.1.36   Adler, A. What life should mean to you. Boston, 1931.

Phil 6310.1.35   Adler, A. What life should mean to you. N.Y., 1931.

Phil 6310.6   Adler, Alexandra. Guiding human misfits. N.Y., 1938.

Phil 6310.6.2   Adler, Alexandra. Guiding human misfits. N.Y., 1939.

Phil 9035.53.5   Adler, Alfred. Menschenkenntnis. 2. Aufl. Leipzig, 1928.

Phil 9035.53.6   Adler, Alfred. Menschenkenntnis. 5. Aufl. Zürich, 1947.

Phil 6110.10.10   Adler, Alfred. Über den nervösen Charakter. München, 1922.

Phil 6110.10.11   Adler, Alfred. Über den nervösen Charakter. 4. Aufl. München, 1928.

Phil 9035.53.2A   Adler, Alfred. Understanding human nature. Garden City, N.Y., 1927.

Phil 9035.53   Adler, Alfred. Understanding human nature. N.Y., 1927.

Phil 9035.53.4   Adler, Alfred. Understanding human nature. N.Y., 1928.

Phil 9035.53.10   Adler, Alfred. Understanding human nature. N.Y., 1946.

Phil 281.8   Adler, Arthur. Das heutige Weltbild. Brieg, 1922.

Phil 8615.5.9   Adler, Felix. Creed and deed. N.Y., 1894.

Phil 8615.5.10   Adler, Felix. The essentials of spirituality. N.Y., 1905.

Phil 8615.5.15   Adler, Felix. An ethical philosophy of life. N.Y., 1918.

Phil 8615.5.5   Adler, Felix. Life and destiny. N.Y., 1905.

Phil 8615.5.23   Adler, Felix. Our part in this world. N.Y., 1946.

Phil 8615.5.20   Adler, Felix. The reconstruction of the spiritual ideal. N.Y., 1924.

Phil 8615.5   Adler, Felix. The religion of duty. N.Y., 1905.

Phil 8615.5.4   Adler, Felix. Vägen till målet. Stockholm, 1925.

Phil 3625.3.105   Adler, Friedrich. Ernst Machs Überwindung des mechanischen Materialismus. Wien, 1918.

Phil 6310.1.30   Adler, Gerhard. Entdeckung der Seele. Zürich, 1934.

Phil 6310.1.106   Adler, Gerhard. The living symbol. N.Y., 1961.

Phil 6310.1.37   Adler, Gerhard. Studies in analytical psychology. London, 1948.

Phil 6310.16   Adler, Kurt. Essays in individual psychology. N.Y., 1959.

Phil 5190.21.5   Adler, M.J. Dialectic. N.Y., 1927.

Phil 5240.36.5   Adler, M.J. What man has made of man. N.Y., 1938.

Phil 3850.16.81   Adler, Max. Georg Simmels Bedeutung für die Geistesgeschichte. Wien, 1919.

Phil 440.2   Adler, Mortimer J. The idea of freedom. Garden City, N.Y., 1958-61. 2v.

Phil 175.62   Adler, Mortimer Jerome. The conditions of philosophy. 1st ed. N.Y., 1965.

Phil 8875.27   Adler, Mortimer Jerome. A dialectic of morals. Notre Dame, 1941.

Phil 585.208   Adler, Mortimer Jerome. The difference of man and the difference it makes. N.Y., 1968.

Phil 8430.46   Adler, Mortimer Jerome. Poetry and politics. Pittsburgh, 1965.

Phil 8875.27.5   Adler, Mortimer Jerome. The time of our lives. 1st ed. N.Y., 1970.

Phil 6310.1.91   Adlers psykologi. (Ganz, M.) Stockholm, 1939.

VPhil 730.31   Admec, Josef. Holismus. Praha, 1966.

Phil 6945.15   Administrative psychiatry. (Bryan, William A.) N.Y., 1936.

Phil 2520.150   Admiranda methodus novae philosophiae Renati des Cartes. (Schoock, Martin.) Waesberge, 1643.

Phil 3819.58   Adnotationes ad tractatum theologico politicum. (Spinoza, Benedictus de.) Hagae, 1802.

Phil 10.92   Adolescence. N.Y. 1,1966+ 3v.

Phil 5876.15   Adolescence: psychosocial perspectives. (Caplan, Gerald.) N.Y., 1969.

Phil 5878.10   Adolescence and the conflict of generations. (Pearson, Gerald Hamilton Jeffrey.) N.Y., 1958.

Phil 5876.30   The adolescent and his will. (Gattegno, Caleb.) N.Y., 1971.

Phil 5876.35   Adolescent development. (Bernard, Harold Wright.) Scranton, 1971.

Phil 10.93   Adolescent psychiatry. N.Y. 1,1971+

Phil 6854.12   Adolescent suicide. (Jacobs, Jerry.) N.Y., 1971.

Phil 4620.2.90   Adolf Phalén in memoriam. (Hedenius, I.) Uppsala, 1937.

Phil 3549.2.90   Adolph, H. Die Philosophie des Grafen Keyserling. Stuttgart, 1927.

Phil 3210.85   Adolph, H. Die Weltanschauung G.T. Fechners. Stuttgart, 1923.

Phil 175.37   Adolph, Heinrich. Personalistische Philosophie. Leipzig, 1931.

Phil 2475.1.294.4   Adolphe, Lydie. La dialectique des images chez Bergson. Thèse. Paris, 1951.

Phil 2475.1.294.5   Adolphe, Lydie. La dialectique des images chez Bergson. 1. éd. Paris, 1951.

Phil 2475.1.294   Adolphe, Lydie. La philosophie religieuse de Bergson. Paris, 1946.

Phil 2475.1.294.6   Adolphe, Lydie. L'univers bergsonien. Paris, 1955.

Phil 3085.4.31   Adorno, F.W. Minima Moralia. Berlin, 1951.

Phil 75.88   Adorno, Francesco. Il pensiero greco. Orientamenti bibliografici a cura di Francesco Adorno. Bari, 1969.

Phil 75.88.5   Adorno, Francesco. Il pensiero greco-romano e il cristianesimo. 1. ed. Bari, 1970.

Phil 1105.12   Adorno, Francesco. Studi sul pensiero greco. Firenze, 1966.

Phil 3425.589   Adorno, T.W. Drei Studien zu Hegel. Frankfurt, 1963.

Phil 3450.11.160   Adorno, T.W. Zur Metakritik der Erkenntnistheorie. Stuttgart, 1956.

Phil 3425.405   Adorno, Theodor W. Aspekte der Hegelschen Philosophie. Berlin, 1957.

Phil 3085.7.40   Adorno, Theodor W. Aufsätze zur Gesellschaftstheorie und Methodologie. 1. Aufl. Frankfurt, 1970.

Phil 3085.7.30   Adorno, Theodor W. Eingriffe. Frankfurt, 1963.

Phil 3085.7.1   Adorno, Theodor W. Gesammelte Schriften. 1. Aufl. Frankfurt, 1971.

Phil 3000.5   Adorno, Theodor W. Jargon der Eigentlichkeit; zur deutschen Ideologie. Frankfurt, 1967.

Phil 3085.7.45   Adorno, Theodor W. Kritik: kleine Schriften zur Gesellschaft. 1. Aufl. Frankfurt, 1971.

Phil 3085.7.80   Adorno, Theodor W. Mit Beiträgen von Kurt Oppens. Frankfurt, 1968.

Phil 3085.7.31   Adorno, Theodor W. Negative Dialektik. Frankfurt, 1966.

Phil 8401.37   Adorno, Theodor W. Ohne Leitbild. Frankfurt, 1967.

Phil 3085.7.35   Adorno, Theodor W. Stichworte. Kritische Modelle. Frankfurt, 1969.

Phil 4803.454.66   Adresse aux nations slaves sur les destinées du monde. (Hoene-Wroński, Józef Maria.) Paris, 1847.

Phil 5240.49   Adrian, E.D.A. Factors in mental evolution. Oxford, 1960.

Phil 530.35.30   Adriani, Maurilio. Italia mistica. Roma, 1968.

Phil 3450.3.90   Adriani Heereboordi. (Stearne, John.) Dublinii, 1660.

Phil 194.30.80   Adriano Tilgher. (Scalero, L.) Padova, 1962.

Phil 5240.21   Adumkiewicz, A. Die Eigenkraft der Materie. Wien, 1906.

Phil 7054.114   Advance thought. (Glass, C.E.) London, 1876.

Htn   Phil 1850.3.2*   Advancement and proficiency of learning. (Bacon, Francis.) Oxford, 1640.

Htn   Phil 1850.3.3*   Advancement and proficiency of learning. (Bacon, Francis.) Oxford, 1640.

Phil 1850.35.7A   The advancement of learning. (Bacon, Francis.) Boston, 1904.

Phil 1850.36   The advancement of learning. (Bacon, Francis.) London, 1900.

Phil 1850.35.20   The advancement of learning. (Bacon, Francis.) London, 1950.

Phil 1850.35.2A   The advancement of learning. (Bacon, Francis.) Oxford, 1869.

NEDL   Phil 1850.35.6   The advancement of learning. (Bacon, Francis.) St. Louis, 1901.

Phil 1850.35.3   The advancement of learning. v.2. (Bacon, Francis.) London, 1893-95.

Phil 1850.35.8   The advancement of learning. 1st ed. (Bacon, Francis.) London, 1901-05. 2v.

Phil 1850.35.2.3   The advancement of learning. 3rd ed. (Bacon, Francis.) Oxford, 1885.

Phil 1850.35.4   The advancement of learning. 4th ed. (Bacon, Francis.) Oxford, 1891.

Phil 1850.35.5   The advancement of learning. 5th ed. (Bacon, Francis.) Oxford, 1900.

Phil 8709.2.13   Advancement of science. (Tyndall, John.) N.Y., 1874.

Phil 8709.2.14   Advancement of science. (Tyndall, John.) N.Y., 1874.

Phil 5520.740   Advances in psycholinguistics. (Bressanone Conference on Psycholinguistics, University of Padova, 1969.) Amsterdam, 1971.

Phil 10.97   Advances in the study of behavior. N.Y. 1,1965+ 2v.

Phil 9178.7   Advantages which man derives from woman. (Stephens, John.) N.Y., 1815.

Htn   Phil 7069.11.45*   An adventure. (Moberly, C.A.E.) London, 1911.

Phil 7069.11.48   An adventure. 4th ed. (Moberly, C.A.E.) London, 1931.

Phil 9245.57   Adventure for happiness. (Cadman, Samuel P.) N.Y., 1935.

Phil 8880.18.9   An adventure in moral philosophy. (Fite, Warner.) London, 1926.

Phil 6945.35   The adventure in psychiatry. (Martin, Denis V.) Oxford, 1962.

Phil 5590.455.11   The adventure of living. (Tournier, Paul.) N.Y., 1965.

Phil 8595.22   Adventures and confessions. (Phelps, William L.) N.Y., 1926.

Phil 5425.50   Adventures in genius. (Durant, William.) N.Y., 1931.

Phil 197.40.5   Adventures in philosophy. (Wordsworth, J.C.) N.Y., 1926.

Phil 190.52   Adventures in philosophy and religion. (Pratt, James B.) N.Y., 1931.

Phil 8590.18.25   Adventures in religion. (King, Basil.) Garden City, 1929.

Phil 6328.18.10   Adventures in self discovery. (Seabury, David.) N.Y., 1938.

Phil 7069.49   Adventures in the supernormal. (Garrett, Eileen Jeanette Lyttle.) N.Y., 1949.

Phil 7069.69.20   Adventures into the psychic. (Stearn, Jess.) N.Y., 1969.

Phil 7060.250   The adventures of a modern occultist. (Bland, Oliver.) N.Y., 1920.

Phil 801.28   The adventures of human thought. (Boas, George.) N.Y., 1929.

Phil 822.8A   Adventures of ideas. (Whitehead, A.N.) N.Y., 1933.

Phil 8877.65   Adventures on the borderlands of ethics. (Cabot, Richard C.) N.Y., 1926.

Phil 7060.68.5   Adventurings in the psychical. (Bruce, Henry Addington Bayley.) Boston, 1914.

Phil 8585.27A   Adventurous religion and other essays. 1st ed. (Fosdick, Harry E.) N.Y., 1926.

Phil 338.3   The adversaries of the sceptic. (Hodder, A.) London, 1901.

Phil 9245.55A   Adversity's noblemen. (Trinkhaus, C.E.) N.Y., 1940.

Phil 3832.15   Adversus anonymun theologs-politicum. (Mansveld, R.) Amstelaedami, 1674.

Htn   Phil 9166.3.5*   Advice from a lady of quality to her children. (Glasse, S.) Boston, 1796.

Htn   Phil 9166.3*   Advice from a lady of quality to her children. 3. ed. (Glasse, S.) Newbury Port, 1778. 2v.

Htn   Phil 9340.7*   Advice to a young lord, written by his father. London, 1691.

Htn   Phil 9340.9*   Advice to the fair sex. Philadelphia, 1803.

Phil 9179.9.4   Advice to the teens. (Taylor, Isaac.) Boston, 1820.

Phil 9341.3   Advice to young man...Oxford. (Berens, E.) London, 1832.

Phil 9342.4.2   Advice to young men. (Cobbett, W.) London, 1887.

Phil 9342.4.10   Advice to young men. (Cobbett, W.) London, 1906.

Phil 9342.4.12   Advice to young men. (Cobbett, W.) London, 1926.

Phil 9342.4.15   Advice to young men. (Cobbett, W.) London, 1930.

Phil 9342.4   Advice to young men. (Cobbett, W.) N.Y., 1831.

Phil 9341.8   Advice to youth. (Blair, H.) n.p., n.d.

Phil 9070.95   Advise to a son. (Wright, L.B.) Ithaca, N.Y., 1962.

Phil 10.45   Adyar pamphlets. Adyar. 13,1912

Phil 3482.2.100   Aebi, Magdalena. Kant's Begründung der "Deutschen Philosophie". Basel, 1947.

Phil 4120.4.84   Aebischer, Max. Der Einzelne und der Staat nachtreibung Giovanni Gentile. Schweiz, 1954.

Phil 5875.120   Aebli, Hans. Über den Egozentrismus des Kindes. Stuttgart, 1968.

Phil 6110.12   Aeby, C.T. Schema des Faserverlaufes im menschlichen Gehirn und Rückenmark. Bern, 1883.

Phil 525.117   Aegerter, E. Le mysticisme. Paris, 1952.

Phil 3504.42   Aenesidem-Schulze, der Gegner Kants. Inaug. Diss. (Wiegershausen, H.) Münster, 1910.

Phil 3850.13.35   Aenesidemus. (Schulze, G.E.) Berlin, 1911.

Phil 3850.13.33   Aenesidemus öder über die Fundamenta. (Schulze, G.E.) Helmstadt, 1792.

Phil 5240.44   Aeppli, E. Psychologie des Bewussten und Unbewussten. Zürich, 1947.

Phil 3425.204   Är en practisk philosophi möjlig efter Hegels verldsåsigt? (Nyblaeus, Axel.) Lund, 1855.

Phil 5412.7   Der Ärger als dynamisches Problem. Inaug. Diss. (Dembo, Tamara.) Berlin, 1931.

Phil 4080.3.42   Aesthetic as science of expression and general linguistic. (Croce, Benedetto.) N.Y., 1953.

Phil 4080.3.42.10   Aesthetic as science of expression and general linguistic. (Croce, Benedetto.) N.Y., 1968.

Phil 8412.23.2   The aesthetic attitude. (Langfeld, Herbert Sidney.) N.Y., 1920.

Phil 8412.23.3   The aesthetic attitude. (Langfeld, Herbert Sidney.) Port Washington, N.Y., 1967.

Phil 8893.10.5   The aesthetic element in morality. (Sharp, F.C.) N.Y., 1893.

Phil 8402.40   The aesthetic experience. (Buermeyer, L.) Merion, Pa., 1924.

Phil 8412.32   The aesthetic experience. (Lechner, R.) Chicago, 1953.

Phil 8401.24   The aesthetic experience: its meaning in a functional psychology. (Adams, E.K.) Chicago, 1907.

Phil 336.2   The aesthetic experience. Its nature in epistemology. (Furry, W.D.) Baltimore, 1908.

Phil 8414.8.11   Aesthetic experience and its presuppositions. (Nahm, Milton Charles.) N.Y., 1968.

Phil 8402.57.5A   Aesthetic inquiry: essays on art criticism and the philosophy of art. (Beardsley, Monroe Curtis.) Belmont, Calif., 1967.

Phil 8416.28   Aesthetic judgment. (Prall, D.W.) N.Y., 1929.

Phil 8402.12F   Aesthetic measure. (Birkhoff, G.D.) Cambridge, 1933.

Phil 8419.11   Aesthetic motive. (Schneider, E.) N.Y., 1939.

Phil 8410.3   The aesthetic object; an introduction to the philosophy of value. (Jordan, E.) Bloomington, 1937.

Phil 8413.11   Aesthetic principles. (Marshall, Henry.) N.Y., 1895.

Phil 8413.26   The aesthetic process. (Morris, B.) Evanston, 1943.

Phil 8416.34   Aesthetic quality, a contextualistic theory of beauty. (Pepper, S.C.) N.Y., 1938.

Phil 8412.14   The aesthetic sentiment. (Lundholm, H.) Cambridge, 1941.

Phil 8407.25   Aesthetic studies: architecture and poetry. (Gilbert, K.) Durham, 1952.

Phil 3492.40.2   The aesthetic theories of Kant. (Knox, Israel.) N.Y., 1958.

Phil 2475.1.259A   The aesthetic theory of Bergson. (Szathmary, A.) Cambridge, 1937.

Phil 2045.120   The aesthetic theory of Thomas Hobbes. (Thorpe, C.D.) Ann Arbor, 1940.

Phil 8120.10.5   The aesthetic thought of the French Enlightenment. (Coleman, Francis X.J.) Pittsburgh, 1971.

Phil 8402.51   Aesthetica. (Baumgarten, A.) Bari, 1936.

Phil 8402.62A   Aesthetica. (Bense, Max.) Baden-Baden, 1965.

Phil 8402.56   Aesthetica. v.1,2-4. (Bense, Max.) Stuttgart, 1954- 2v.

Phil 8050.76   Aesthetica di silencio. (Mascello, Leonardo.) Rio de Janeiro, 1919.

Htn   Phil 4080.3.38*   Aesthetica in nuce. (Croce, Benedetto.) Napoli, 1929.

Phil 4080.3.38.3   Aesthetica in nuce. 3. ed. (Croce, Benedetto.) Laterza, 1954.

Phil 8090.5   Aestheticism. (Johnson, Robert Vincent.) London, 1969.

Phil 8402.55   Aesthetics; lectures and essays. (Bullough, E.) London, 1957.

Phil 8402.57   Aesthetics; problems in the philosophy of criticism. (Beardsley, Monroe Curtis.) N.Y., 1958.

Phil 8406.19   Aesthetics. (Feibleman, J.) N.Y., 1949.

Phil 8422.14A   Aesthetics. (Véron, Eugène.) London, 1879.

Phil 8408.7   Aesthetics: a critical theory of art. (Hartman, H.G.) Columbus, 1919.

Phil 8400.18   Aesthetics and language. (Elton, William.) Oxford, 1954.

Phil 8419.22   Aesthetics and philosophy of art criticism. (Stolnitz, Jerome.) Boston, 1960.

Phil 8402.70   Aesthetics and psychology. (Berlyne, Daniel Ellis.) N.Y., 1971.

Phil 8413.30   Aesthetics and psychology. (Mauron, C.) London, 1935.

Phil 8400.34   Aesthetics and the philosophy of criticism. (Levich, M.) N.Y., 1963.

Phil 8050.85   Aesthetics from classical Greece to the present. 1. ed. (Beardsley, Monroe Curtis.) n.p., n.d.

Phil 8092.32   The aesthetics of modernism. (Chiari, Joseph.) London, 1970.

Phil 3808.177   The aesthetics of pessimism. (Adams, J.S.) Philadelphia, 1940.

Phil 8402.5.1   Aesthetics or the science of beauty. (Bascom, J.) Boston, 1867.

Phil 8402.5.2   Aesthetics or the science of beauty. (Bascom, J.) N.Y., 1874.

Phil 8400.16   Aesthetics today. (Philipson, Morris.) Cleveland, 1961.

Phil 8416.25   Ästhetik; Belehrungen über die Wissenschaft vom Schönen und der Kunst. 3. Aufl. (Prölss, Robert.) Leipzig, 1904.

Phil 8419.4   Ästhetik, Grundzüge der Wissenschaft des Schönen und der Kunst. (Schasler, Max.) Leipzig, 1886. 2v.

Phil 8407.19   Ästhetik; kritische Philosophie des Stils. (Görland, Albert.) Hamburg, 1937.

Phil 8422.7.5   Ästhetik; oder, Wissenschaft des Schönen. (Vischer, F.T.) München, 1922-23. 6v.

Phil 8420.20   Ästhetik, oder Lehre von der Weltauschauung und Kunst. v.1-2. (Trahndorff, K.F.E.) Berlin, 1827.

Phil 8412.10   Ästhetik; Psychologie des Schönen und der Kunst. (Lipps, Theodor.) Hamburg, 1903-06. 2v.

Phil 8403.10.5   Aesthetik. (Carriere, Moriz.) Leipzig, 1859. 2v.

Phil 8403.10.2   Aesthetik. (Carriere, Moriz.) Leipzig, 1873. 2v.

Phil 8405.2.5   Ästhetik. (Ehrlich, Walter.) Chur, 1947.

Phil 8408.18   Ästhetik. (Hartmann, N.) Berlin, 1953.

Phil 3425.56.10   Ästhetik. (Hegel, Georg Wilhelm Friedrich.) Berlin, 1955.

Phil 8408.27   Ästhetik. (Huber, Kurt.) Ettal, 1954.

Phil 5400.76   Ästhetik. (Kratz, H.) Gütersloh, 1891.

Phil 8413.25   Ästhetik. (Meyer, T.A.) Stuttgart, 1923.

Phil 8413.15   Ästhetik. (Monrad, M.J.) Christiania, 1889-90. 2v.

Phil 8413.40   Ästhetik. (Mundt, Theodor.) Göttingen, 1966.

Phil 8050.40   Ästhetik. (Schulemann, G.) Breslau, 1930.

Phil 8050.77   Ästhetik. (Utitz, Emil.) Berlin, 1923.

Phil 8422.7A   Ästhetik. (Vischer, F.T.) Reutlingen, 1846-57. 3v.

Phil 8426.4   Ästhetik. (Zimmermann, R.) Wien, 1858-65. 2v.

Phil 8411.3   Aesthetik. pt.1-2. (Köstlin, K.) Tübingen, 1869.

Phil 8408.33   Ästhetik. 2. Aufl. (Hamann, R.) Leipzig, 1919.

Phil 8402.10.5   Aesthetik. 2. ed. (Bouterwek, F.) Göttingen, 1815. 2v.

Phil 8403.10.3   Aesthetik. 3. Aufl. (Carriere, Moriz.) Leipzig, 1885. 2v.

Phil 3095.82   Die Aesthetik Alex Gottlieb Baumgartens. (Ruman, Albert.) Halle, 1928.

Phil 8411.12   Ästhetik auf realistischer Grundlage. (Kirchmann, J.H. von.) Berlin, 1868. 2v.

Phil 8060.8   Ästhetik der Antike. (Krueger, J.) Berlin, 1964.

Phil 8418.11   Ästhetik des Hässlichen. (Rosenkranz, K.) Königsberg, 1853.

Phil 8404.20   Ästhetik des tätigen Geistes. (Dyroff, Adolf.) Bonn, 1948.

Phil 8423.13   Aesthetik i ømrids. (Wilkens, Claudius.) Kjøbenhavn, 1888.

Phil 8050.46   Die Ästhetik in ihrer Geschichte und als wissenschaftliches System. (Hermann, C.) Leipzig, 1876.

Phil 8402.44   Ästhetik in Umrissen. (Bayer, Josef.) Prag, 1856. 2v.

Phil 3195.2.125   Die Ästhetik Martin Deutingers. (Ettlinger, Max.) Kempten, 1914.

Phil 3640.119.10   Die Ästhetik Nietzsches. (Filser, Benno.) Passau, 1917.

Phil 8404.15   Ästhetik und allgemeine Kunstwissenschaft. (Dessoir, Max.) Stuttgart, 1923.

Phil 8404.15.2   Ästhetik und allgemeine Kunstwissenschaft in den Grundzügen dargestellt. (Dessoir, Max.) Stuttgart, 1906.

Phil 8448.5   Ästhetik und Gewalt. Gütersloh, 1970.

Phil 8430.7   Ästhetik und Sozialwissenschaft. (Burckhard, M.) Stuttgart, 1895.

Phil 8422.7.2   Ästhetik Vollständiges, Inhaltsverzeichniss, Namen und Sachregister. (Vischer, F.T.) Stuttgart, 1858.

Phil 8419.39.5   Der Ästhetiker Johann G. Sulzer. (Tumarkin, Anna.) Frauenfeld, 1933.

Phil 8411.17   Ästhetisch-literarische Arbeiten. (Katann, O.) Wien, 1918.

Phil 8400.69   Aesthetische Aufsätze. Budapest, 1966.

Phil 8422.15   Das ästhetische Bewusstsein. Photoreproduction. (Volkelt, Johannes.) München, 1920.

Phil 8893.10   Das aesthetische Element in der Moral. (Sharp, F.C.) Berlin, 1892.

Phil 8423.8.2   Ästhetische Feldzüge. (Wienbarg, Ludolf.) Berlin, 1964.

Phil 8423.8   Ästhetische Feldzüge. 2. Aufl. (Wienbarg, Ludolf.) Hamburg, 1919.

Phil 8426.2   Ästhetische Forschungen. (Zeising, Adolf.) Frankfurt, 1855.

Phil 8406.5   Aesthetische Fragen. (Frauenstädt, J.) Dessau, 1853.

Phil 8407.13   Das ästhetische Gefühl. (Göller, Adolf.) Stuttgart, 1905.

Phil 8407.10   Der ästhetische Genuss. (Groos, Karl.) Giessen, 1902.

Phil 8850.2   Ästhetische Gesichtspunkte in der englischen Ethik des 18. Jahrhunderts. (Zangenberg, Therese.) Langensalza, 1918.

Phil 8404.10   Das Ästhetische nach seinem eigenthümlichen Grundwesen. (Dittes, Friedrich.) Leipzig, 1854.

Phil 8406.9   Das aesthetische Problem. (Federn, Karl.) Hannover, 1928.

Phil 8419.67   Ästhetische Prozesse. (Schmidt, Siegfried Josef.) Köln, 1971.

Phil 8412.8.5   Ästhetische Streitfragen. (Laurila, K.S.) Helsinki, 1934.

Phil 8423.3   Das ästhetische Symbol. (Wernaer, R.M.) Leipzig, 1907.

Phil 5525.15   Der ästhetische Wert des Komischen und das Wesen des Humors. (Roetschi, Robert.) Bern, 1915.

Phil 8402.26.5A   Das ästhetische Wesen. (Burov, A.I.) Berlin, 1958.

Phil 8050.75   Die ästhetische Wirklichkeit; eine Einfuhrung. 2. Aufl. (Nohl, H.) Frankfurt, 1954.

Phil 8422.15.5   Ästhetische Zeitfragen. (Volkelt, Johannes.) München, 1895.

Phil 8411.22   Ästhetisches Erleben und kunstlerisches Schaffen. (Kuhr, Victor.) Stuttgart, 1929.

Phil 8092.5   Ästhetisches Mass und Ästhetische Information. (Gunzenhaeuser, R.) Hamburg, 1962.

Phil 8050.57.5   Aestetiske afhandlinger og recensioner. (Hauch, J.C.) Kjøbenhavn,1869. 1861.

Phil 510.1.22   Aether und Wille. (Wagner, Richard.) Leipzig, 1901.

Phil 978.64   Die ätherischen Bildekräfte in Kosmos, Erde und Mensch. (Wachsmuth, G.) Dornach, 1926.

Phil 6315.66   Die Ausserlichkeit des Lebensstils. (Frankenstein, Carl.) Amsterdam, 1959.

Phil 3494.47   Aeusserungen über Kant. (Metzger, J.D.) Königsberg, 1804.

Phil 4630.6.30   Af efterladte papirer. (Rubin, E.) København, 1956.

Phil 730.25   Afanas'ev, V.C. Problema tselostnosti v filosofii i biologii. Moskva, 1964.

Phil 310.245   Afanas'ev, V.G. Osnovy marksistskoi filosofii. Moskva, 1960.

Phil 310.507   Afanas'ev, Viktor G. Nauchnyi kommunizm. Moskva, 1966.

Phil 310.505   Afanas'ev, Viktor G. Osnovy filosofskikh znanii. 2. izd. Moskva, 1965.

Phil 310.506   Afanas'ev, Viktor G. Osnovy filosofskikh znanii. 3. izd. Moskva, 1965.

Phil 8430.92   Afasizhev, Marat Nurbievich. Freĭdizm i burzhuaznoe iskusstvo. Moskva, 1971.

VPhil 6400.31   Afazja. Wyd. 1. (Maruszewski, Mariusz.) Warszawa, 1966.

Phil 5630.10   The affairs of Dame Rumor. (Jacobson, David J.) N.Y., 1948.

Phil 5400.168   Affect, cognition, and personality. (Tomkins, Silvan Solomon.) N.Y., 1965.

Phil 5590.416   Affect, imagery, consciousness. (Tomkins, S.S.) N.Y., 1962. 2v.

Phil 3833.6   Die Affectenlehre Spinoza's. (Meniţescu, Joan.) Leipzig, 1887.

Phil 5400.83   The affective consciousness. (Britan, H.H.) N.Y., 1931.

Phil 6625.10   Affective disorders. (Greenacre, Phyllis.) N.Y., 1961.

Phil 6325.7   Affectivité et intelligence: étude psycho-pathologique. (Pagès, Louis.) Paris, 1926.

Phil 6325.7.2   Affectivité et intelligence: étude psycho-pathologique. Thèse. (Pagès, Louis.) Paris, 1926.

Phil 6951.11   Affektivität, Suggestibilität, Paranoia. (Bleuler, E.) Halle, 1906.

Phil 6951.11.2   Affektivität, Suggestibilität, Paranoia. 2. Aufl. (Bleuler, E.) Halle, 1926.

Phil 1020.21   Affifi, A.E. The mystical philosophy of Muhyid din-ibnul 'Arabi. Cambridge, 1939.

Htn   Phil 8587.15.5*   L'affinité des religions. (Higginson, T.W.) Paris, n.d.

Phil 8587.15.6   L'affinité des religions. (Higginson, T.W.) Paris, n.d.

Phil 2477.89.30   L'affirmation de Dieu. (Bruaire, Claude.) Paris, 1964.

Phil 8893.33   Les affirmations de la conscience moderne. (Séailles, G.) Paris, 1903.

Phil 8050.57   Afhandlinger og aesthetiske betragtninger. (Hauch, J.C.) Kjøbenhavn, 1855.

Phil 8050.57.10   Afhandlinger og aesthetiske betragtninger. (Hauch, J.C.) Kjøbenhavn, 1869.

Phil 8598.79.5.10   Afiny i Ierusalim. (Shestov, L.) Parizh, 1951.

Phil 150.26   Afnan, Soheil. Philosophical terminology in Arabic and Persian. Leiden, 1964.

Phil 3808.62.5   Aforismi sulla saggezza della vita. (Schopenhauer, Arthur.) Torino, 1923.

Phil 3850.5.90   African Spir. (Humanus.) Leipzig, 1892.

	Phil 3850.5.85	African Spir und die Bedeutung seiner Philosophie. Leipzig, 1881.
	Phil 3850.5.95	African Spir's Erkenntnislehre. Inaug. Diss. (Lessing, Theodor.) Giessen, 1900.
	Phil 9035.80	After all it's up to you. (Cheley, Frank H.) Boston, 1935.
	Phil 7054.22.5	After death; a personal narrative. (Stead, William T.) N.Y., 1914.
	Phil 7069.09.7	After death - what? (Lonbroso, Cesare.) Boston, 1909.
	Phil 8640.8	After death - what? (Peters, M.C.) N.Y., 1908.
	Phil 7054.174.5	After-death communications. (Bazett, L.M.) London, 1920.
	Phil 7054.22	After death or Letters from Julia. 3. ed. (Stead, William T.) Chicago, 1910.
	Phil 184.26	After-dinner philosophy. (Joad, C.E.M.) London, 1926.
	Phil 7054.4.9	After her death. (Whiting, Lilian.) Boston, 1898.
	Phil 7069.18.160	After her death. (Whiting, Lilian.) Boston, 1918.
	Phil 5643.25.2	After images. (Franz, Shepherd I.) N.Y., 1899.
	Phil 8709.19	After materialism - what? 1. ed. (Tute, Richard C.) N.Y., 1945.
	Phil 7069.44.5	After Pentecost; the Alexandrian chronicle of Cleophas. (Cummins, G.D.) London, 1944.
	Phil 3640.535	Afterphilologie. (Rohde, Erwin.) Leipzig, 1872.
	Phil 3425.203	Afzelius, F.G. Hegelska philosophien. Upsala, 1843.
	Phil 5040.11	Afzelius, F.G. Lärobok i logiken for elementar-undervisningen. Upsala, 1852.
	Phil 3801.125	Afzelius, F.G. Von Schelling's nya lara. Upsala, 1843.
	Phil 396.8	De ag ligt nog voor ons essays van humanisten. 's-Gravenhage, 1969.
	Phil 402.22	Against the self-images of the age: essays on ideology and philosophy. (MacIntyre, Alasdair Chalmers.) London, 1971.
	Phil 8963.5	Agape and Eros. (Nygren, A.) London, 1953.
	Phil 8980.126	Agapov, B.N. My ne odin na svete. Moskva, 1961.
	Phil 8690.2	Agassiz, L.J.R. The structure of animal life. N.Y., 1866.
	Phil 7054.27.5	Agassiz and spiritualism. (Putnam, A.) Boston, n.d.
	Phil 4080.3.375	Agazzi, E. Il Giovane Croce e il Marxismo. Torino, 1962.
	Phil 5190.36	Agazzi, Evandro. Introduzione ai problemi dell'assiomatica. Milano, 1961.
	Phil 5066.273	Agazzi, Evandro. La logica simbolica. Brescia, 1964.
	Phil 5465.180	Age and achievement. (Lehman, Harvey Christian.) Princeton, 1953.
	Phil 1660.5.2	The age of adventure; the Renaissance philosophers. (De Santillana, Giorgio.) Boston, 1957.
	Phil 1660.5	The age of adventure; the Renaissance philosophers. (De Santillana, Giorgio.) N.Y., 1956.
	Phil 1722.9	The age of analysis. (White, M.G.) Boston, 1955.
	Phil 1510.5	The age of belief. (Fremantle, A.J.) Boston, 1955.
	Phil 2402.7	An age of crisis. (Crocker, Lester G.) Baltimore, 1959.
	Phil 1730.27.1	The age of enlightenment. (Berlin, Isaiah.) Freeport, 1957.
	Phil 1700.7	The age of ideology. (Aiken, H.D.) Boston, 1957.
Htn	Phil 2225.3.80*	The age of infidelity...answer to the second part of The age of reason. (Williams, Thomas.) Philadelphia, 1796.
	Phil 6113.4	The age of mental virility. (Dorland, W.A.N.) N.Y., 1908.
	Phil 8595.16	Age of reason. (Paine, Thomas.) London, 1795.
	Phil 8595.15.18	The age of reason. (Paine, Thomas.) N.Y., 1896.
	Phil 8595.15.19	Age of reason. (Paine, Thomas.) N.Y., 1898.
	Phil 8595.15.23	Age of reason. (Paine, Thomas.) N.Y., 194-?
	Phil 8595.15.24	The age of reason. (Paine, Thomas.) N.Y., 1951.
Htn	Phil 2225.3.30*	The age of reason. (Paine, Thomas.) Paris, 1794.
Htn	Phil 8595.15.5*	Age of reason. Investigation of true and fabulous theology. (Paine, Thomas.) Boston, 1794. 4 pam.
	Phil 8595.15.17	Age of reason. Investigation of true and fabulous theology. (Paine, Thomas.) Boston, 1875. 2 pam.
	Phil 8595.15.9A	Age of reason. Investigation of true and fabulous theology. (Paine, Thomas.) London, 1852.
Htn	Phil 8595.15.16*	Age of reason. Investigation of true and fabulous theology. (Paine, Thomas.) n.p., n.d. 5 pam.
Htn	Phil 8595.15.8*	Age of reason. Investigation of true and fabulous theology. pt.1-2. (Paine, Thomas.) London, 1796.
	Phil 8595.15.7	Age of reason. Investigation of true and fabulous theology. pt.1-2. 2d ed. (Paine, Thomas.) London, 1795.
Htn	Phil 8595.15.6*	The age of reason. Pt.1. (Paine, Thomas.) Paris, 1794.
	Phil 8707.4	The age of the earth. (Rhind, W.) Edinburgh, 1838.
	Phil 288.10	The age of the world. (Haber, Francis.) Baltimore, 1959.
	Phil 9400.14	The aged and society. (Industrial Relations Research Association.) Champaign, 1950.
	Phil 7069.69.10	Agee, Doris. Edgar Cayce on E.S.P. 1st ed. N.Y., 1969.
	Phil 6615.2	Les agents provocateurs de l'hystérie. (Guinon, Georges.) Paris, 1889.
	Phil 801.23.9	Les âges de l'intelligence. (Brunschvicg, L.) Paris, 1934.
	Phil 801.23.11	Les âges de l'intelligence. 3. ed. (Brunschvicg, L.) Paris, 1934.
	Phil 3800.387.5	The ages of the world. (Schelling, F.W.J. von.) N.Y., 1942.
	Phil 3800.387	The ages of the world. (Schelling, F.W.J. von.) N.Y., 1942.
	Phil 8580.32	Aggebo, Anker. Jeg er nemlig ikke religiøs. København, 1959.
	Phil 5421.20.10	Aggression; a social psychological analysis. (Berkourt, L.) N.Y., 1962.
	Phil 5421.20	Aggression. (Scott, John Paul.) Chicago, 1958.
	Phil 5421.20.130	Aggression im Menschenbild. (Hollitscher, Walter.) Wien, 1970.
	Phil 5421.20.50	Der Aggression trieb und das Böse. (Czapiewski, Winfried.) Essen, 1967.
	Phil 5421.20.90	Aggression und Friedensfähigkeit in Deutschland. (Gamm, Hans-Jochen.) München, 1968.
	Phil 5421.20.110	Aggression und menschliche Natur. (Rattner, Josef.) Olten, 1970.
	Phil 5421.20.135	Aggression und Mitmenschlichkeit. (Keil, Siegfried.) Stuttgart, 1970.
	Phil 5421.20.115	Aggressionshandlungen Jugendlicher. (Schindler, Sepp.) Wien, 1969.
	Phil 5421.20.145	Aggressive man and aggressive beast. (Stokes, Allen W.) Logan, 1968?
	Phil 5350.5.10	Aging and society. (Riley, Matilda White.) N.Y., 1968. 2v.
	Phil 9400.13	Aging successfully. (Lawton, George.) N.Y., 1946.
	Phil 8610.903	Agnosticism. (Flint, Robert.) Edinburgh, 1903.
	Phil 8610.884.10	Agnosticism. 2. ed. (Momerie, A.W.) Edinburgh, 1887.
	Phil 8610.896	Agnosticism and religion. (Schurman, J.G.) N.Y., 1896.
	Phil 8624.4	Agnosticism and the future life. n.p., n.d.
	Phil 645.29	Agnosticisme. 2e éd. (Roberty, E. de.) Paris, 1893.
NEDL	Phil 193.35	An agnostic's apology. (Stephen, L.) London, 1893.
NEDL	Phil 193.35.1	An agnostic's apology. (Stephen, L.) N.Y., 1893.
X Cg	Phil 193.35.2	An agnostic's apology. 2d ed. (Stephen, L.) N.Y., 1903.
	Phil 193.35.4	An agnostic's apology and other essays. 2d. ed. (Stephen, L.) London, 1903.
	Phil 8610.964	Agnostitsizm i problema znaniia i very v burzhuaznoi filosofii. (Ekmalian, A.) Erevan, 1964.
	Phil 6980.431	La agonía del psicoanalisis. 3. ed. (López Ibor, Juan.) Madrid, 1961.
	Phil 2725.11.85	Agosti, Vittorio. La filosofia di Jules Lachelier. Torino, 1952.
	Phil 1200.50	Agostino, V. Studi sul reostoicismo. Torino, 1950.
	Phil 5246.25.80	Agostino Gemelli e la psicologia del lavoro in Italia. (Spaltro, Enzo.) Milano, 1966.
	Phil 4964.5	Agramonte y Pichardo, R. José Augustin Caballero y las origines de la conciencia cubana. La Habana, 1952.
	Phil 5240.39	Agramonte y Richardo, R. Compendio de psicología. Habana, 1939.
	Phil 5240.39.15	Agramonte y Richardo, R. Tratado de psicología general. v.1-2, pt.1. 4a ed. Habana, 1940.
	Phil 8705.7	Agreement of evolution and Christianity. (Phillips, S.L.) Washington, 1904.
	Phil 5421.20.65	Agressie en agressiviteit. (Carp, Eugène Antoine.) Utrecht, 1968.
Htn	Phil 1105.2*	Agricola, R. De inventione. Libri III. Coloniae, 1518.
Htn	Phil 1105.2.5*	Agricola, R. De inventione dialectica. pt.3. Parisiis, 1535.
	Phil 645.10	Agrippa di Nettesheym e la direzione scettica. (Rossi, G.) Torino, 1906.
Htn	Phil 3085.1.36*	Agrippa von Nettesheim, H.C. Apologia aduersus calumnias proptes declamationem. n.p., 1533.
Htn	Phil 3085.1.30*	Agrippa von Nettesheim, H.C. De nobilitate. n.p., 1532.
Htn	Phil 3085.1.32*	Agrippa von Nettesheim, H.C. De occulta philosophia. Lugduni, 1550.
Htn	Phil 3085.1.35*	Agrippa von Nettesheim, H.C. Henrici Cornelii Agrippae. Coloniae, 1575.
Htn	Phil 8875.3.4*	Agrippa von Nettesheim, Heinrich Cornelius. De incertitudine et vanitate omnium scientiarum et artium liber. Ealf, 1531.
Htn	Phil 8875.3.2*	Agrippa von Nettesheim, Heinrich Cornelius. De incertitudine et vanitate omnium scientiarum et artium liber. n.p., 1544.
	Phil 8875.3	Agrippa von Nettesheim, Heinrich Cornelius. De incertitudine et vanitate omnium scientiarum et artium liber. Lugdun Batavorum, 1643.
Htn	Phil 8875.3.8*	Agrippa von Nettesheim, Heinrich Cornelius. Della vanitate delle scienze. Venetia, 1552.
	Phil 8875.3.15	Agrippa von Nettesheim, Heinrich Cornelius. Paradoxe sur l'incertitude vanité et abus des sciences. n.p., 1603.
	Phil 8875.3.16	Agrippa von Nettesheim, Heinrich Cornelius. Paradoxe sur l'incertitude vanité et abus des sciences. n.p., 1603.
	Phil 8875.3.5	Agrippa von Nettesheim, Heinrich Cornelius. The vanity of arts and sciences. London, 1676.
	Phil 3482.9	Aguanno, G. d'. La filosofia etico-giuridica de Kant a Spencer. Pt.I. Palermo, 1895.
	Phil 4215.1.91	Aguanno, Giuseppe d'. Gian Domenico Roamgnosi filosofo e giureconsulto. Pt.2. Parma, 1906.
	Phil 3450.11.505	Aguirre, Antonio. Genetische Phänomenologie und Reduktion. Den Haag, 1970.
	Phil 8825.5	Ahlâk öprelileri. (Akarsu, Bedia.) Istanbul, 1965.
	Phil 5750.5	Ahlander, J.A. De libertate. Disquisitio. Lundae, 1852.
	Phil 5010.2	Ahlander, J.A. De prascipuis philosophorum recentioris aevi logicam tractandi rationibus. Diss. Lundae, 1849.
	Phil 4513.1.35	Ahlberg, A. Filosfi och vetenskap. Stockholm, 1919.
	Phil 4513.1.31	Ahlberg, A. Filosfiska essayer. Stockholm, 1918.
	Phil 4513.1.38	Ahlberg, A. Filosofi och dikt. Stockholm, 1924.
	Phil 800.20	Ahlberg, A. Fran antikens och medeltidens tankevärd. Stockholm, 1966.
	Phil 4513.1.40	Ahlberg, A. Det ondas problem. Stockholm, 1923.
	Phil 4513.1.42	Ahlberg, A. Tidoreflexer; filosofiska uppsatser. Stockholm, 1926.
	Phil 3808.144	Ahlberg, Alf. Arthur Schopenhauer. Stockholm, 1924.
	Phil 175.34	Ahlberg, Alf. De filosofiska grundproblemen. Stockholm, 1922.
	Phil 5750.4	Ahlberg, Alf. Viljans frihet från transcendental-filosofiens ståndpunkt. Stockholm, 1915.
	Phil 4754.1.30	Ahlberg, René. A.M. Deborin. Berlin, 1959.
	Phil 310.385	Ahlberg, René. Dialektische Philosophie und Gesellschaft in der Sowiet-Union. Berlin, 1960.
	Phil 5240.28	Ahlenstiehl, H. Über die Stellung der Psychologie im Stammbaum der Wissenschaften. Berlin, 1923.
	Phil 585.150	Ahlman, Erik. Ihmisen probleemi. Helsinki, 1953.
	Phil 1885.92	Ahmed, M. The theory of judgment in the philosophies of F.H. Bradley and John Cook Wilson. Dacca, 1955.
	Phil 5070.19	Ahmet, Nureltin. Conformisme et révolte. Thèse. Paris, 1934.
	Phil 3585.10.82	Ahrem, Maximilien. Das Problem des tragischen bei Theodor Lipps und Johannes Volkelt. Inaug. Diss. Nürnberg, 1908.
	Phil 5240.2	Ahrens, Heinrich. Cours de psychologie. v.1-2. Paris, 1836-38.
	Phil 5240.2.5	Ahrens, Heinrich. Curso de psicología. Madrid, 1873. 2v.
	Phil 310.120	Ai, Ssu-ch'i. Lektsii po dialekticheskom materializme. Moskva, 1959.
	Phil 177.19.20	Ai figli del popolo; consigli. (Conti, Augusto.) Firenze, 1914.
	Phil 8875.30	Aichen, Henry D. Reason and conduct. N.Y., 1962.
Htn	Phil 1930.3.30*	Aids to reflection. (Coleridge, S.T.) London, 1825.
	Phil 5330.1	Aiken, C. Methods for mind training. N.Y., 1889.
	Phil 5330.1.3	Aiken, C. Methods for mind training. N.Y., 1897.
	Phil 1700.7	Aiken, H.D. The age of ideology. Boston, 1957.
	Phil 2255.1.126	Aiken, L.W. Bertrand Russell's philosophy of morals. N.Y., 1963.
	Phil 4751.3.6	Aikhenval'd, Iu.I. Otdel'nyia stranitsy. Moskva, 1910.
	Phil 9340.1	Aikin, J. Letters from a father to his son. London, 1794-1800. 2v.
Htn	Phil 9340.1.2*	Aikin, J. Letters from a father to his son. Philadelphia, 1794.
Htn	Phil 9340.1.5*	Aikin, J. Letters from a father to his son. Philadelphia, 1796.
	Phil 5040.7	Aikins, H.A. The principles of logic. N.Y., 1902.
	Phil 5040.7.1	Aikins, H.A. The principles of logic. 2nd ed. N.Y., 1904.
	Phil 284.4.12	The aim and structure of physical theory. (Duhem, P.) N.Y., 1962.
	Phil 284.4.10	The aim and structure of physical theory. (Duhem, P.) Princeton, 1954.
	Phil 9352.11	The aim of life. (Moxom, P.S.) Boston, 1894.
	Phil 3450.11.117	The aims of phenomenology; the motives, methods, and impact of Husserl's thought. 1st ed. (Farber, Marvin.) N.Y., 1966.

Author and Title Listing

Phil 3640.39	Ainsi parlait Zarathustra. 29e éd. (Nietzsche, Friedrich.) Paris, 1914.
Phil 2725.35.105	Ainval, Christiane d'. Une doctrine de la présence spirituelle; la philosophie de Louis Lavelle. Louvain, 1967.
Phil 5465.56.20	L'air et les songes. (Bachelard, G.) Paris, 1943.
Phil 5414.25	Airas, Erkki. Syyllisyydentuntoon vaikuttavista tekijöistä. Helsinki, 1956.
Phil 9558.10.14	Aires Ramos da Silva de Eca, M. Reflexões sobre a vaidade dos homens. Rio de Janeiro, 1962.
Phil 9558.10.12	Aires Ramos da Silva de Eca, M. Reflexões sobre a vaidade dos homens. Saõ Paulo, 1942.
Phil 9558.10.10	Aires Ramos da Silva de Eca, M. Reflexões sobre a vaidade dos homens. Facsimile. Rio de Janeiro, 1921.
Phil 5655.9	Airkem, Inc. Odors and the sense of smell. N.Y., 1952.
Phil 9167.3	Airs d'un père à sa fille. (Hallifax, de M.) London, 1757.
Phil 5640.17	Aitken, E.H. The five windows of the soul. London, 1913.
Phil 5640.17.5	Aitken, E.H. Le va del l'anima. Torino, 1913.
Phil 45.5	Ajatus; filosofisen yhdistyksen vuosikiya. Helsinki. 1-27 10v.
Phil 4803.130.35	Ajdukiewicz, Kazimierz. Jezyk i poznanie. Wyd. 1. Warszawa, 1960-
Phil 4803.130.30	Ajdukiewicz, Kazimierz. Zagadnienia i Kierunki filozofii. W Krakowie, 1949.
Phil 960.147	Ajñana. (Malkani, G.R.) London, 1933.
Phil 310.3	Akadamiia Nauk SSSR. Institut Filosofii. Dialekticheskii materializm. Moskva, 1953.
Phil 310.7	Akadamiia Nauk SSSR. Institut Filosofii. Dialekticheskii materializm. Moskva, 1954.
Phil 310.6.15	Akadamiia Nauk SSSR. Institut Filosofii. Grundlagen der marxistischen Philosophie. Berlin, 1960.
Phil 310.6.5	Akadamiia Nauk SSSR. Institut Filosofii. Osnovy marksistskoi filosofii. Moskva, 1958.
Phil 310.6.6	Akadamiia Nauk SSSR. Institut Filosofii. Osnovy marksistskoi filosofii. Izd. 2. Moskva, 1964.
Phil 310.198	Akadamiia Nauk SSSR. Institut Filosofii. Problemy istorii filosofskoi i sotsiologicreskoi mysli XIX veka. Moskva, 1960.
Phil 310.195	Akadamiia Nauk SSSR. Institut Filosofii. Voprosy dialekticheskogo materializma. Moskva, 1960.
Phil 310.380	Akadamiia Nauk SSSR. Kafedra Filosofii. Russkie uchenye v bor'be protiv idealizma i metafiziki vozzrenii v estestvoznanii. Moskva, 1961.
Phil 331.21	Akadamiia Nauk SSSR. Kafedra Filosofii. Voprosy teorii poznaniia i logiki. Moskva, 1960.
Phil 3246.298	Akademie...Berlin. (Buhr, Manfred.) Berlin, 1962.
Phil 10.50	Die Akademie. Erlangen. 2-3,1924-1925 2v.
Phil 8050.20	Akademiia Khudozhestv SSSR. Institut Teorii i Istorii Iskusstva. Istoriia estetiki. Moskva, 1962- 5v.
Phil 8400.13	Akademiia Khudozhestv SSSR. Institut Teorii i Istorii Iskusstva. Ocherki marksistsko-leninskoi estetiki. Moskva, 1956.
Phil 8400.15	Akademiia Khudozhestv SSSR. Institut Teorii i Istorii Iskusstva. Ocherki marksistsko-leninskoi estetiki. Moskva, 1960.
Phil 5585.74	Akademiia Nauk, SSSR. Institut Filosofii. Sektsiia Psikhologii. Issledovaniia po psikhologii vospriiatiia; sbornik. Moskva, 1948.
Phil 4795.10	Akademiia nauk Azerbaidzhanskoi SSR, Baku. Sektor filosofii. Ocherki po istorii Azerbaidzhanskoi filosofii. Baku, 1966.
Phil 4780.4	Akademiia nauk BSSR, Minsk. Instytut filosofii. Iz istorii filosofskoi i obshchestvenno-politicheskoi mysli Belorussii. Minsk, 1962.
Phil 5040.27	Akademiia Nauk Kazakhskoi SSSR, Alma-Ata. Institut Literatury i Prava. Problemy logiki dialektiki poznaniia. Alma-Ata, 1963.
Phil 1695.20	Akademiia Nauk SSR. Institut Filosofii. Sovremennye religioznye filosofskie techeniia kapitalisticheskikh stran. Moskva, 1962.
Phil 800.10.10	Akademiia Nauk SSSR. Geschichte der Philosophie. Berlin, 1959- 6v.
Phil 5625.75.7	Akademiia Nauk SSSR. Arkhiv. Rukopisnye materialy I.P. Pavlova. Moskva, 1949.
Phil 5650.36	Akademiia Nauk SSSR. Biblioteka. Fiziologicheskaia akustika. Moskva, 1960.
Phil 75.66	Akademiia Nauk SSSR. Fundamental'naia Biblioteka Obshchestvennykh Nauk. Istoriia zarubezhnoi domarksistskoi filosofii, za 1917-1962 gody. Moskva, 1963.
Phil 75.75	Akademiia Nauk SSSR. Fundamental'naia Biblioteka Obshchestvennykh Nauk. Kritika burzhuaznoi i reformistskoi filosofii i sotsiologii epokhi imperializma. Moskva, 1967.
Phil 5257.69	Akademiia Nauk SSSR. Institut Filosofii, Sektor Psikologii. Protsess myshleniia i zakonomernosti analiza, Sinteza i obobshcheniia. Moskva, 1960.
Phil 3003.8	Akademiia Nauk SSSR. Institut Filosofii. Die deutsche Philosophie. Berlin, 1961.
Phil 3003.10	Akademiia Nauk SSSR. Institut Filosofii. Die deutsche Philosophie nach 1945. Berlin, 1961.
Phil 331.33	Akademiia Nauk SSSR. Institut Filosofii. Dialektika teoriia poznaniia. Moskva, 1964- 3v.
Phil 331.33.10	Akademiia Nauk SSSR. Institut Filosofii. Erkenntnistheoretische und methodologische Probleme der Wissenschaft. Berlin, 1966.
Phil 8400.47	Akademiia Nauk SSSR. Institut Filosofii. Estetika: kategorii i iskusstvo. Moskva, 1965.
Phil 8655.19	Akademiia Nauk SSSR. Institut Filosofii. Filosofskie problemy ateizma. Moskva, 1963.
Phil 6110.26	Akademiia Nauk SSSR. Institut Filosofii. Filosofskie voprosy fiziologii vysshei nervnoi deiatel'nosti. Moskva, 1963.
Phil 5040.26	Akademiia Nauk SSSR. Institut Filosofii. Filosofskie voprosy sovremennoi formal'noi logiki. Moskva, 1962.
Phil 5066.225.5	Akademiia Nauk SSSR. Institut Filosofii. Formal'naia logika i metodologiia nauki. Moskva, 1964.
Phil 310.511	Akademiia Nauk SSSR. Institut Filosofii. Formy myshleniia. Moskva, 1962.
Phil 5590.456	Akademiia Nauk SSSR. Institut Filosofii. Garmonicheskii chelovek. Moskva, 1965.
Phil 800.10	Akademiia Nauk SSSR. Institut Filosofii. Istoriia filosofii. Moskva, 1940-1941. 2v.
Phil 800.10.5	Akademiia Nauk SSSR. Institut Filosofii. Istoriia filosofii. Moskva, 1957. 7v.
Phil 8050.10	Akademiia Nauk SSSR. Institut Filosofii. Iz istorii esteticheskoi mysli drevnosti i srednevekov'ia. Moskva, 1961.
Phil 8050.15	Akademiia Nauk SSSR. Institut Filosofii. Iz istorii esteticheskoi mysli novogo vremeni. Moskva, 1959.
Phil 930.66	Akademiia Nauk SSSR. Institut Filosofii. Izbrannye proizuedeniia progeniia kitaiskikh myslitelei novogo vremeni, 1840-1898. Moskva, 1961.
Phil 5066.135	Akademiia Nauk SSSR. Institut Filosofii. Logicheskie issledovaniia. Moskva, 1959.
Phil 310.601	Akademiia Nauk SSSR. Institut Filosofii. Marksistsko-leninskaia filosofiia i sotsiologiia v SSSR i evropeiskikh sotsialisticheskikh stranakh. Moskva, 1965.
Phil 8400.8	Akademiia Nauk SSSR. Institut Filosofii. Nekotorye voprosy marksistsko-leninskoi estetiki. Moskva, 1954.
Phil 8980.131	Akademiia Nauk SSSR. Institut Filosofii. Nravstvennost' i religiia. Moskva, 1964.
Phil 4710.17A	Akademiia Nauk SSSR. Institut Filosofii. Ocherki po istorii filosoficheskoi i obshchestvenno-politicheskoi mysli narodov SSSR. Moskva, 1955. 2v.
Phil 5240.54	Akademiia Nauk SSSR. Institut Filosofii. Osnovnye napravleniia issledovanii psikhologii myshleniia v kapitalisticheskikh stranakh. Moskva, 1966.
Phil 8655.20	Akademiia Nauk SSSR. Institut Filosofii. Osnovy nauchnogo ateizma. 3. izd. Moskva, 1964.
Phil 5066.224.5	Akademiia Nauk SSSR. Institut Filosofii. Problems of the logic of scientific knowledge. Dordrecht, 1970.
Phil 8980.131.10	Akademiia Nauk SSSR. Institut Filosofii. Problemy etiki. Moskva, 1964.
Phil 5066.225	Akademiia Nauk SSSR. Institut Filosofii. Problemy logiki. Moskva, 1963.
Phil 5066.224	Akademiia Nauk SSSR. Institut Filosofii. Problemy logiki nauchnogo poznaniia. Moskva, 1964.
Phil 8875.32	Akademiia Nauk SSSR. Institut Filosofii. Protiv sovremennoi burzhuaznoi etiki. Moskva, 1965.
Phil 310.607	Akademiia Nauk SSSR. Institut Filosofii. Protiv sovremennykh burzhuaznykh fal'sifikatorov marksistsko-leninskoi filosofii. Moskva, 1964.
Phil 1700.10	Akademiia Nauk SSSR. Institut Filosofii. Sovremennaia filosofiia i sotsiologiia v stranakh Zapadnoi Evropy i Ameriki. Moskva, 1964.
Phil 5210.10	Akademiia Nauk SSSR. Institut Filosofii. Sovremennaia psikhologiia v kapitalisticheskikh stranakh. Moskva, 1963.
Phil 8709.23	Akademiia Nauk SSSR. Institut Filosofii. Uspekhi sovremennoi nauki i religiia. Moskva, 1961.
Phil 5040.23	Akademiia Nauk SSSR. Institut Filosofii. Vaprosy logiki. Moskva, 1955.
Phil 8400.10	Akademiia Nauk SSSR. Institut Filosofii. Voprosy marksistsko-leninskoi estetiki. Moskva, 1956.
Phil 310.510	Akademiia Nauk SSSR. Institut Filosofii. Zakony myshleniia. Moskva, 1962.
Phil 1700.9	Akademiia Nauk SSSR. Institut Filosofii. Sektor Sovremennoi Burzhuaznoi Filosofii i Sotisiologii Stran Zapada. Noveishie priemy zashchity starogo mira. Moskva, 1962.
Phil 8400.40	Akademiia Nauk SSSR. Institut Istorii Iskusstv. Sovremennoe iskusstvoznanie za rubezhom; ocherki. Moskva, 1964.
Phil 960.245	Akademiia Nauk SSSR. Institut Narodov Azii. Obshchestvenno-politicheskaia i filosofskaia mysl' Indii. Moskva, 1962.
Phil 270.105.5	Akademiia Nauk SSSR. Institute Filosofii. Problema prichinnost v sovremeni fizike. Moskva, 1960.
Phil 270.105	Akademiia Nauk SSSR. Institute Filosofii. Problema prichinnosti v sovremennoi biologie. Moskva, 1961.
Phil 8690.14	Akademiia Nauk SSSR. Institutii Filosofii. Dostizheniia estestvoznaniia i religiia. Moskva, 1960.
Phil 735.257	Akademiia Nauk SSSR. Kafedra Filosofii, Leningrad. Problema tsennosti v filosofii. Leningrad, 1966.
Phil 5190.40	Akademiia Nauk SSSR. Kafedra Filosofii, Leningrad. Problema vozmozhnosti i deistvitel'nosti. Leningrad, 1964.
Phil 8980.8	Akademiia nauk SSSR. Kafedra Filosofii. Moral'nye oblik stroitelia kommunizma. Moskva, 1964.
Phil 8655.18	Akademiia Nauk SSSR. Muzei Istorii Religii i Ateizma. Istoriia pravoslaviia i russkogo ateizma. Leningrad, 1960.
Phil 310.515	Akademiia Nauk SSSR. Nauchnyi Sovet po Filosofskim Voprosam Estestvoznaniia. Dialekticheskii materializm i sovremennoe estestvoznanie. Moskva, 1962.
Phil 175.61	Akademiia Nauk SSSR. Nauchnyi Sovet po Filosofskim Voprosam Estestvoznaniia. O sushchnosti zhizni. Moskva, 1964.
Phil 4710.50.25	Akademiia Nauk URSR, Kiev. Pobudova naukovoï teorii. Kyïv, 1965.
Phil 175.60	Akademiia Nauk URSR, Kiev. Institut Filosofii. Liudyna i svitohliad. Kyiv, 1963.
Phil 4710.50.10	Akademiia Nauk URSR, Kiev. Instytut Filosofii. Borot'ba mizh materializmom ta idealizmom na Ukraini. Kyïv, 1964.
Phil 4710.50.20	Akademiia Nauk URSR, Kiev. Instytut Filosofii. Narys istorii filosofii na Ukraini. Kyïv, 1966.
Phil 4710.50.5	Akademiia Nauk URSR, Kiev. Instytut Filosofii. Z istorii filosofs'koi dumki na Ukraini. Kyïv, 1962.
Phil 1020.34	Akademiia Nauk Uzbekskoi SSR, Tashkend. Otdel Filosofii i Prava. Materialy poistorii progressivnoi obshchestvennoi filosfskoi mysl v Uzbekistane. Tashkent, 1957.
Phil 5210.8.5	Akademiia Pedagogicheskikh Nauk RSFSR, Moscow. Institut Psikhologii. Ergebnisse der sowjetischen Psychologie. Berlin, 1967.
Phil 6110.24	Akademiia Pedagogicheskikh Nauk RSFSR, Moscow. Institut Psikhologii. Pogranichnye problemy psikhologii i fiziologii. Moskva, 1961.
Phil 5210.8	Akademiia Pedagogicheskikh Nauk RSFSR, Moscow. Institut Psikhologii. Psikhologicheskaia nauk a v SSSR. Moskva, 1959. 2v.
Phil 8825.5	Akarsu, Bedia. Ahlâk öprelileri. Istanbul, 1965.
Phil 4610.7.88	Akesson, Elof. Norströmiana. Stockholm, 1924.
Phil 310.250	Akhmedli, D. Svoboda i neobkhodimost'. Baku, 1960.
Phil 5585.62	Akishige, Yoshiharu. Experimentelle Untersuchungen über die Struktur des Wahrnehmungsraumens. Fukuoka, 1937.
Phil 8980.131.15	Akmambetov, Galikhan G. Problemy nravstvennogo razvitiia lichnosti. Alma-Ata, 1971.
Phil 5643.132	Ákos, Károly. The critical flicker frequency series effect. Budapest, 1966.
Phil 1135.230	Akpibeia. (Kurz, Dietrich.) Göppingen, 1970.
Phil 8430.55.2	Akróasis, die Lehre von der Harmonik der Welt. 2. Aufl. (Kayser, Hans.) Basel, 1964.
Phil 7069.19.5	Aksakov, A.N. Animus und Spsiritismus. Leipzig 1919. 2v.
Phil 7060.103.7	Aksakov, Aleksandr N. Animisme et spiritisme. Paris, 1895.

Author and Title Listing

Phil 7060.103.5 Aksakov, Aleksandr N. Animismus und spiritismus...als Entgegnung auf Dr. Ed. V. Hartmann's Werk "Der Spiritismus". Leipzig, 1890.

Phil 7060.106 Aksakov, Aleksandr N. Vorläuser des Spiritismus. Leipzig, 1898.

Phil 960.138 Aksara, a forgotten chapter in the history of Indian philosophy. Inaug. Diss. (Modi, P.M.) Baroda, 1932.

Phil 475.3 Aksel'rod, L. I. Protiv idealizma. Moskva, 1933.

Phil 4759.1.40 Aksiomy religioznago opyta. (Il'in, I.A.) Paris, 1953.

Phil 4225.8.37 Akt und Sein. 4. Aufl. (Sciacca, Michele Federico.) Freiburg, 1964.

Phil 70.1.14 Akten des XIV. (International Congress of Philosophy.) Wien. 1968 6v.

Phil 5252.73 Aktualgenetische Untersuchungen an Situationsdarstellungen. Inaug. Diss. (Mantell, U.) München, 1936.

Phil 665.28 Aktualität oder Substantialität der Seele? Inaug. Diss. (Hein, Joseph.) Paderborn, 1916.

Phil 3425.776 Aktualität und Folgen der Philosophie Hegels. (Negt, Oskar.) Frankfurt am Main, 1970.

Phil 310.752 Aktual'nye problemy dialekticheskoi logiki. (Simpozium po Dialekticheskoi Logike, Alma-Ata, 1968.) Alma-Ata, 1971.

Phil 310.556 Aktual'nye problemy istoricheskogo materializma. (Fomina, V.A.) Moskva, 1963.

Phil 8980.191 Aktual'nye problemy marksistskoi etiki. (Bandzeladze, Gela.) Tbilisi, 1967.

Phil 5590.477 Aktual'nye problemy persondogii i klinicheskoi psikhiatrii. (Zurabashvili, Avlippi.) Tbilisi, 1970.

Phil 310.682 Aktual'nye voprosy istorii marksistsko-leninskoi filosofii. Moskva, 1968.

Phil 5240.47 Aktuelle Probleme der Gestalttheorie. Bern, 1954.

Phil 8605.15 Aktuelni problemi odnosa prema religiji. (Zrvotić, Milad.) Beograd, 1961.

Phil 8401.27 Al arte por el dolor. (Antonio de la Virgen del Carmen.) Burgos, 1952.

Phil 1020.7.10 Al-Ghazáli, the mystic. (Smith, Margaret.) London, 1944.

Phil 2515.5.95 Alain. (Maurois, André.) Paris, 1950.

Phil 2515.5.91 Alain (Émile Chartier) in der Reihe der französischen Moralisten. (Hess, G.) Berlin, 1932.

Phil 2515.5.90 Alain (Émile Chartier) in der Reihe der französischen Moralisten. Inaug.-Diss. (Hess, G.) Berlin, 1931.

Phil 2515.5.92 Alain professeur par X.X., élève de roi Henri IV. Paris, 1932.

Phil 2340.21.5 Alan Watts journal. 1,1969+

Phil 182.94.80 Alarco, L.F. Nicolai Hartmann y la idea de la metafisica. Lima, 1943.

Phil 5210.20 Alarcón, Reynaldo. Panorama de la psicología en el Perú. Lima, 1968.

Phil 3085.6.80 Alardus Amstelredamus. (Traaf, B.) Amsterdam, 1958.

Phil 3085.6.85 Alardus Amstelredamus en Cornelius Crocus. (Koelker, A.) Nijmegen, 1963.

Phil 175.2 Alaux, J.E. L'analyse métaphysique. Paris, 1872.

Phil 175.2.8 Alaux, J.E. Métaphysique considérée comme science. Paris, 1879.

Phil 2496.80 Alaux, J.E. La philosophie de M. Cousin. Paris, 1864.

Phil 8875.12 Alaux, J.E. Philosophie morale et politique. Paris, 1893.

Phil 175.2.5 Alaux, J.E. La raison. Paris, 1860.

Phil 6110.8 Alaux, J.E. Théorie de l'âme humaine. Paris, 1896.

Phil 9550.5 Albee, Ernest. A history of English utilitarianism. London, 1902.

Phil 9550.5.2 Albee, Ernest. A history of English utilitarianism. London, 1957.

Phil 6980.32 Albee, George. Mental health manpower trends. N.Y., 1959.

Phil 4120.2.92 Albeggiani, F. Il sistema filosofico di Cosmo Guastella. Firenze, 1927.

Phil 2250.89 Albeggiani, F. Il sistema filosofico di Josiah Royce. Palermo, 1930.

Phil 4080.3.365 Albeggiani, Ferdinando. Inizio e svolgimento della filosofia dello spirito di Benedetto Croce. Palermo, 1960?

Phil 7072.2 Alberg, Albert. Frost flowers on the windows. Chicago, 1899.

Phil 4000.15 Alberghi, Sante. Metafisica e spiritualisti italiani contemporanei. Milano, 1960.

Phil 4960.220.5 Alberini, Coriolano. Die deutsche Philosophie in Argentinien. Berlin, 1930.

Phil 4960.220 Alberini, Coriolano. Problemas de la história de las ideas filosóficas en la Argentina. La Plata, 1966.

Phil 3850.27.260 Al'bers Shveitser - velikii gumanist XX veka. Moskva, 1970.

Phil 3482.8 Albert, Georg. Kant's transcendentale Logik. Wien, 1895.

Phil 3640.85 Albert, H. Frederic Nietzsche. Paris, 1903.

Phil 8875.33 Albert, Henri. Les dangers du moralisme. n.p., 1896?

Phil 7069.27.12 Albert Chevalier comes back. (Chevalier, F.) London, 1927.

Phil 3310.12 Albert Görlands systematische Philosophie. (Gulden, P.H.) Assen, 1943.

Phil 3850.27.117 Albert Schweitzer, life and message. (Ratter, Magnus C.) Boston, 1950.

Phil 3850.27.185 Albert Schweitzer, Mensch und Werk. Bern, 1959.

Phil 3850.27.99 Albert Schweitzer, Persönalichkeit und Denken. Inaug. Diss. (Raab, Karl.) Düsseldorf, 1937.

Phil 3850.27.235 Albert Schweitzer, prophet of freedom. (Phillips, Herbert M.) Evanston, Ill., 1957.

Phil 3850.27.215 Albert Schweitzer, sein Denken und sein Weg. (Baehr, Hans N.) Tübingen, 1962.

Phil 3850.27.16 Albert Schweitzer; the man and his mind. 6th ed. (Seaver, George.) London, 1969.

Phil 3850.27.250 Albert Schweitzer, Wirklichkeit und Legende. (Kantzenbach, Friedrich Wilhelm.) Göttingen, 1969.

Phil 3850.27.114 Albert Schweitzer. (Amadou, Robert.) Bruxelles, 1951.

Phil 3850.27.114.5 Albert Schweitzer. (Amadou, Robert.) Paris, 1952.

Phil 3850.27.116 Albert Schweitzer. (Christolles, H.) Stuttgart, 1953.

Phil 3850.27.122 Albert Schweitzer. (Feschotte, Jacques.) Paris, 1952.

Phil 3850.27.205 Albert Schweitzer. (Gittleman, D.) n.p., 1959.

Phil 3850.27.119 Albert Schweitzer. (Grabs, R.) Berlin, 1948.

Phil 3850.27.106 Albert Schweitzer. (Grabs, R.) Berlin, 1949.

Phil 3850.27.97 Albert Schweitzer. (Kraus, Oskar.) London, 1943.

Phil 3850.27.165 Albert Schweitzer. (Langfeldt, Gabriel.) London, 1960.

Phil 3850.27.166 Albert Schweitzer. (Langfeldt, Gabriel.) N.Y., 1960.

Phil 3850.27.113 Albert Schweitzer. (Lind, Emil.) Bern, 1948.

Phil 3850.27.175 Albert Schweitzer. (Mueller, Hans.) Duisburg, 1956.

Phil 3850.27.195 Albert Schweitzer. (Picht, Werner.) Hamburg, 1960.

Phil 3850.27.145 Albert Schweitzer. (Pierhal, Jean.) N.Y., 1957.

Phil 3850.27.90 Albert Schweitzer. (Regester, John D.) N.Y., 1931.

Phil 3850.27.110.2 Albert Schweitzer. (Seaver, George.) Boston, 1951.

Phil 3850.27.109 Albert Schweitzer. (Seaver, George.) London, 1947.

Phil 3850.27.132 Albert Schweitzer. (Steinitz, Benno.) Wien, 1955.

Phil 3850.27.108 Albert Schweitzer: revolutionary christian. (Seaver, George.) N.Y., 1944.

Phil 3850.27.95 Albert Schweitzer. 2. Aufl. (Kraus, Oskar.) Berlin, 1929.

Phil 3850.27.122.4 Albert Schweitzer. 4. éd. (Feschotte, Jacques.) Paris, 1958.

Phil 3850.27.110 Albert Schweitzer. 4th ed. (Seaver, George.) London, 1951.

Phil 3850.27.255 Albert Schweitzer- Pionier der Menschlichkeit. (Götting, Gerald.) Berlin, 1970.

Phil 3850.27.93 The Albert Schweitzer jubilee book. (Robock, A.A.) Cambridge, 1945.

Phil 3850.27.93.1 The Albert Schweitzer Jubilee Book. Westport, Conn., 1970.

Phil 3850.27.135 Albert Schweitzer und der Friede. (Tau, Max.) Hamburg, 1955.

Phil 3850.27.101.5 Albert Schweitzer und Karl Jaspers. (Buri, Fritz.) Zürich, 1950.

Phil 3850.27.200 Albert Schweitzer und unsere Zeit. (Buri, Fritz.) Zürich, 1947.

Phil 3850.27.220 Albert Schweitzers etisk-religiösa iderl. (Loennebo, M.) Stockholm, 1964.

Phil 3850.27.140 Albert Schweitzers Kulturkritik. (Hygen, J.B.) Göttingen, 1955.

Phil 3850.27.40 Albert Schweitzers Leben und Denken. (Schweitzer, A.) N.Y., 1949.

Phil 3850.27.225 Albert Schweitzer's of friendship. 1st ed. (Anderson, E.) N.Y., 1964.

Phil 3850.27.141 Albert Schweitzers tanker om kulturen. (Hygen, J.B.) Oslo, 1954.

Phil 1155.10 Albertelli, P. Gli eleati. Bari, 1939.

Phil 1504.12 Alberts des Grossen Verhältnis zu Palto. v.12, pt.1. (Gaul, L.) Münster, n.d.

Phil 8875.9 Albertson, Ralph. Little Jeremiads. Lewiston, 1903.

Phil 1504.14.5 Albertus Magnus, Beiträge zu seiner Würdigung. 2. Aufl. v.14, pt.5-6. (Hertling, G. von.) Münster, 1914.

Phil 1504.15 Albertus Magnus. v.15,16. (Stadler, H.J.) Münster, 1916. 2v.

Phil 3850.3.81 Alberty, Gerhard. Gotthilf Samuel Steinbart, 1738-1809. Inaug. Diss. Gotha, 1930.

Phil 5592.186 Albou, Paul. Les questionnaires psychologiques. Paris, 1968.

Phil 525.121 Albrecht, C. Psychologie des mystischen Bewusstseins. Bremen, 1951.

Phil 331.25 Albrecht, E. Beiträge zur Erkenntnistheorie und das Verhältnis von Sprache und Denken. Halle, 1959.

Phil 5040.32 Albrecht, Erhard. Die Beziehungen von Erkenntnistheorie, Logik und Sprache. Halle, 1956.

Phil 5068.14 Albrecht, Erhard. Darstellung und Kritik der erkenntnistheoretischen Grundlagen der Kausalitätsauffassung und der Ethik des Neopositivismus. Rostock, 1949.

Phil 3000.8 Albrecht, Herbert. Deutsche Philosophie heute. Bremen, 1969.

Phil 3425.490 Albrecht, Wolfgang. Hegels Gottesbeweis. Berlin, 1958.

Phil 3492.2.55 Albrecht Krause's Darstellung der Kantischen Raumtheorie und der Kantischen Lehre. (Vold, John M.) Cristiania, 1885.

Phil 800.4 Albrich, K. Im Kampf um unsere Stellung zu Welt und Leben. Leipzig, 1924.

Phil 8655.11 Albright, W.F. From the stone age to Christianity. Baltimore, 1940.

Phil 2905.1.33 Album. (Teilhard de Chardin, Pierre.) London, 1966.

Phil 8968.15.80 Alcalá, M. La etica de situación y T. Steinbüchel. Barcelona, 1963.

Phil 5049.15.10 Alcala, P. de. Petri hispani summulae logicales. Venetiis, 1572.

Phil 9160.8 Alcalde Prieto, D. Cuadros de familia. Valladolid, 1890.

Phil 75.26 Alcan, Felix. La philosophie française contemporaine. Paris, 1926.

Phil 8597.9 Alcastor. (Riddle, A.G.) n.p., 1883.

Phil 1870.30.25 Alcifrone. Dialoghi. v.1-5. (Berkeley, G.) Torino, 1932.

Htn Phil 1870.29* Alciphron. (Berkeley, G.) Dublin, 1732.

Phil 1870.30.15 Alciphron. (Berkeley, G.) Leipzig, 1915.

Htn Phil 1870.30* Alciphron. (Berkeley, G.) London, 1732. 2v.

Htn Phil 1870.30.2* Alciphron. (Berkeley, G.) New Haven, 1803.

Phil 1870.30.30 Alciphron. (Berkeley, G.) Paris, 1952.

Htn Phil 1870.30.1* Alciphron. 2d ed. (Berkeley, G.) London, 1732. 2v.

Phil 5593.45.20 Alcock, T. The Rorschach in practice. Philadelphia, 1964[1963]

NEDL Phil 9160.3.10 Alcott, W.A. The boy's guide. Boston, 1844.

Phil 9160.3.3 Alcott, W.A. The young husband. Boston, 1839.

Phil 9160.3.7 Alcott, W.A. The young wife. Boston, 1837.

Phil 9340.2.5 Alcott, William Alex. Young woman's guide to excellence. Boston, 1847.

Phil 1828.2 Alcott and the Concord school of philosophy. (Brown, Florence W.) n.p., 1926.

Phil 8404.9 Alcune considerazioni sul bello. (Daneo, G.) Torino, 1877.

Phil 5520.42 Alcune osservazioni sulle questioni di parole. (Vailati, G.) Torino, 1899.

Phil 8655.6 Alden, H.M. God in his world. N.Y., 1890.

Phil 8612.5 Alden, Henry M. A study of death. N.Y., 1895.

Phil 9590.1 Alder, V.S. The fifth dimension. London, 1940.

Phil 1050.15.5 Alderblum, N.H.H. A study of Gersonedes in his proper perspective. N.Y., 1926.

Phil 7060.77 Alderson, J. Essay on apparitions. London, 1823.

Phil 6315.2.165 Aldington, H.D. Tribute to Freud. N.Y., 1956.

Phil 8610.832 Aldred, G.A. The devil's chaplain. (Robert Taylor, 1784-1844). Glasgow, 1942.

Phil 7052.15.2 Aldrete ó Los espiritistas españoles. 2. ed. (Aldrete y Soto, Luis de.) Barcelona, 1881.

Phil 7052.15.2 Aldrete y Soto, Luis de. Aldrete ó Los espiritistas españoles. 2. ed. Barcelona, 1881.

Phil 5040.1.8 Aldrich, H. Artis logicae compendium. Oxonii, 1844.

Phil 5040.1 Aldrich, H. Artis logicae rudimenta. Oxford, 1852.

Phil 5040.1.2 Aldrich, H. Artis logicae rudimenta. Oxford, 1856.

Phil 5040.1.3 Aldrich, H. Artis logicae rudimenta. Oxford, 1862.

Phil 5040.1.7 Aldrich, H. Artis logicae rudimenta. Oxonae, 1723.

Phil 5040.1.5 Aldrich, H. Artis logicae rudimenta. 5th ed. Oxford, 1835.

Phil 5040.1.6 Aldrich, H. Artis logicae rudimenta. 6th ed. Oxford, 1850.

Phil 8580.27 Aldwinckle, M.R.F. The object of Christian worship. Thesis. Strasbourg, 1938.

Phil 9230.1 Alea, sive de curanda ludendi in pecunniam cupiditate. (Joostens, P.) Amsterodami, 1642.

Phil 4215.1.110 Alecci, Romolo. La dottrina di G.D. Romognosi intorno alla civiltá. Padova, 1966.

Phil 5403.16 La alegría. (Monedero Gil, Carmelo.) Madrid, 1970.

Phil 331.27 Alejandro, J.M. Estudios gnoseológicos. Barcelona, 1961.

Phil 5040.30 Alejandro, Jose Maria de. La lógica y el hombre. Madrid, 1970.

Phil 4972.5.55 Alejandro Korn. (Romero, Francisco.) Buenos Aires, 1940.

Phil 4972.5.56 Alejandro Korn. (Romero, Francisco.) Buenos Aires, 1956.

Phil 4972.5.53 Alejandro Korn. (Romero, Francisco.) La Plata, 1938.

Phil 4972.5.60 Alejandro Korn. (Universidad Nacional del Litoral.) Rosario, 1962.

Phil 800.13.2 Aleksandrov, G.F. A history of western European philosophy. 2d ed. New Haven, 1949.

Phil 800.12 Aleksandrov, G.F. Istoriia zapnoevropliskoi filosofii. Izd. 2. Moskva, 1946.

Phil 8875.31 Aleksandrov, R.N. Pis'ma k neizvestnomu drugu. Frankfurt, 1951.

Phil 310.230 Alekseev, M.N. Dialekticheskaia logika. Moskva, 1960.

Phil 5040.24 Alekseev, M.N. Dialektika farm myshlemiia. Moskva, 1959.

Phil 4761.1.80 Aleksei Aleksandrovich Kozlov. (Askoldov, C.) Moskva, 1912.

Phil 4080.10.88 Alemanni, V. Pietro Ceretti. Milano, 1904.

Phil 3925.11.80 Aleorta, José Ignacio. Peter Wust, filosofo espiritualista de nuestro tiempo. Bilbao, 1965.

Phil 1505.7 Alessio, Franco Paolo. Studi e ricerche di filosofia medievale. Pavia, 1961.

Phil 175.41 Alessio, Roberto de. Ensayos de filosofía prática. Montevideo, 19- .

Htn Phil 4931.2.30F* Alexander, A. In Aristotelis meteorolicus libros commentaria. n.p., 1527.

Phil 8875.4.15 Alexander, A. Outlines of moral science. N.Y., 1858.

Phil 175.3 Alexander, A. Some problems of philosophy. N.Y., 1886.

Phil 8875.4 Alexander, A. A theory of conduct. N.Y., 1890.

Phil 800.2 Alexander, A.B.D. A short history of philosophy. Glasgow, 1907.

Phil 800.2.3 Alexander, A.B.D. A short history of philosophy. 3. ed. Glasgow, 1922.

Phil 3820.5 Alexander, B. Spinoza. München, 1923.

Phil 8401.32 Alexander, C.W.J. Notes on the synthesis of form. Cambridge, 1964.

Phil 6980.33 Alexander, F. Dynamic psychiatry. Chicago, 1952.

Phil 6110.3.2 Alexander, F.M. Constructive conscious control of the individual. N.Y., 1923.

Phil 6110.3 Alexander, F.M. Man's supreme inheritance. London, 1910.

Phil 6110.3.1 Alexander, F.M. Man's supreme inheritance. N.Y., 1918.

Phil 6110.3.15 Alexander, F.M. The universal constant in living. N.Y., 1941.

Phil 6110.3.10 Alexander, F.M. The use of the self. N.Y., 1932.

Phil 6980.133 Alexander, Franz G. The history of psychiatry. N.Y., 1966.

Phil 6310.4.10 Alexander, Franz G. The medical value of psychoanalysis. N.Y., 1936.

Phil 6310.4.15.5A Alexander, Franz G. Our age of unreason. Philadelphia, 1951.

Phil 6310.4.4 Alexander, Franz G. Psychoanalyse der Gesamtpersönlichkeit. Leipzig, 1927.

Phil 6310.4.5 Alexander, Franz G. The psychoanalysis of the total personality. N.Y., 1930.

Phil 6310.4.35 Alexander, Franz G. Psychoanalytic pioneers. N.Y., 1966.

Phil 6310.4.20 Alexander, Franz G. Psychoanalytic threapy. N.Y., 1946.

Phil 6310.4.9 Alexander, Franz G. Roots of crime. N.Y., 1935.

Phil 6310.4.30 Alexander, Franz G. The scope of psychoanalysis. N.Y., 1961.

Phil 6310.4.25 Alexander, Franz G. The western mind in transition. N.Y., 1960.

Phil 8580.21.5 Alexander, H.B. God and man's destiny. 1. ed. N.Y., 1936.

Phil 175.14.5 Alexander, H.B. Nature and human nature. Chicago, 1923.

Phil 175.14 Alexander, H.B. The problem of mataphysics and the meaning of metaphysical explenation. Diss. N.Y., 1902.

Phil 175.14.2 Alexander, H.B. The problem of metaphysics and the meaning of metaphysical explenation. N.Y., 1902.

Phil 8580.21 Alexander, H.B. Truth and the faith. N.Y., 1929.

Phil 5360.25 Alexander, Hubert Griggs. Language and thinking; a philosophical introduction. Princeton, N.J., 1966.

Phil 2475.1.340 Alexander, I.W. Bergson. London, 1957.

Phil 5850.108.5 Alexander, James. Mastering your own mind. N.Y., 1931.

Phil 5850.108 Alexander, James. Thought-control in everyday life. N.Y., 1928.

Phil 9530.37 Alexander, James. Through failure to success. N.Y., 1934.

Phil 8580.20 Alexander, Mikhailovich. The religion of love. N.Y., 1929.

Phil 2138.80 Alexander, P.P. Mill and Carlyle. Edinburgh, 1866.

Phil 2035.80.17 Alexander, P.P. Moral causation, or Notes on Mr. Mill's notes to the chapter on freedom in the 3rd edition of his examination of Sir W. Hamilton's philosophy. Edinburgh, 1868.

Phil 2035.80.18 Alexander, P.P. Moral causation. Notes on Mr. Mill's examination. 2nd ed. Edinburgh, 1875.

Phil 331.30 Alexander, Peter. Sensationalism and scientific explanation. London, 1963.

Phil 6110.19 Alexander, R. The doctor alone can't cure you. Overton, 1943.

Phil 7069.54.20 Alexander, Rolf. Creative realism. 1. ed. N.Y., 1954.

Phil 7072.4 Alexander, Rolf. The power of the mind. London, 1965.

Phil 5240.33 Alexander, S. Foundations and sketch plan of a conational psychology. Cambridge, Eng., 1911.

Phil 2115.99 Alexander, S. Locke. London, 1908.

Phil 8875.5 Alexander, S. Moral order and progress. London, 1889.

Phil 672.120 Alexander, S. Space, time and deity. London, 1920. 2v.

Phil 8401.22.5 Alexander, Samuel. Art and instinct. Oxford, 1927.

Phil 8401.10 Alexander, Samuel. Art and the material. London, 1925.

Phil 8401.22 Alexander, Samuel. Artistic creation and cosmic creation. London, 1927.

Phil 8401.22.10 Alexander, Samuel. Beauty and other forms of value. London, 1933.

Phil 1845.3.95 Alexander, Samuel. Philosophical and literary pieces. London, 1939.

Phil 3820.4.5 Alexander, Samuel. Spinoza; an address...tercentenary...birth. Manchester, 1933.

Phil 3820.4 Alexander, Samuel. Spinoza and time. London, 1921.

Phil 1845.3.79 Pamphlet box. Alexander, Samuel.

Phil 9035.21.15 Alexander Faulkner Shand, 1858-1936. (Stout, G.F.) London, 1936?

Phil 3095.81 Alexander G. Baumgarten. (Poppe, B.) Borna, 1907.

Phil 3095.83 Alexander Gottlieb Baumgartens Leben und Charakter. (Abbt, Thomas.) Halle, 1765.

Phil 5252.164 Alexander Mitscherlich: Ansprachen anlässlich der Verleihung des Friedenspreises. (Boersenverein des deutschen Buchhandels, Frankfurt am Main.) Frankfurt, 1969.

Phil 3745.10.5 Alexander Pfänders phänomenologie. (Spiegelberg, H.) Den Haag, 1963.

Phil 672.120.50 Alexander's space, time and deity. (Liddell, Anna F.) Chapel Hill, 1925?

Phil 2445.4.20 Alexandre, M. En souvenir de Michel Alexandre. Paris, 1956.

Phil 3482.14 Alexandre, Michel. Lecture de Kant. Paris, 1961.

Phil 7060.147 Alexandre Bisson, J. Les phénomènes dits de matérialisation. Paris, 1914.

Phil 4967.32 Alexandre Rodrigues Ferreira: aspectos de sua vida e obra. (Fontes, Gloria Marly Duarte.) Manaus, 1966.

Phil 1150.4 Alexandria and her schools. (Kingsley, C.) Cambridge, 1854.

Phil 1150.12 Alexandrine teaching on the universe. (Tollington, R.B.) London, 1932.

Phil 281.3 Alexejeff, W.G. Mathematik als Grundlage der Weltanschauung. Jurjew, 1903.

Phil 4080.8.83 Alfani, Augusto. Della vita e delle opere. Firenze, 1906.

Phil 2725.8.85 Alfaric, Prosper. Laromiguière et son école. Paris, 1929.

Phil 3085.9.30 Alff, Wilhelm. Überlegungen; Vierzehn Essays. Heidelberg, 1964.

Phil 8088.2 Alfieri, V. L'estetica dall'illuminismo. Milano, 1957.

Phil 1105.8 Alfieri, V.E. Studi di filosofia greca. Bari, 1950.

Phil 260.11 Alfieri, Vittorio Enpo. Atomos idea. Firenzo, 1953.

Phil 800.18 Alfieri, Vittorio Enzo. Filosofia e filologia. Napoli, 1967.

Phil 4080.3.495 Alfieri, Vittorio Enzo. Pedagogia crociana. Napoli, 1967.

Phil 2805.375 Alfieri, Vittorio Enzo. Il problema Pascal. Milano, 1959.

Phil 5240.16 Alfonso, N.R. I limiti dell'esperimento in psicologia. Roma, 1905.

Phil 5040.10 Alfonso, N.R. d'. Principii di logica reale. Torino, 1894.

Phil 5710.13 Alfonso, Nicolo R. La dottrina dei temperamenti nell'antichità e ai nostri giorni. Roma, 1902.

Phil 4235.3.90 Alfonso Testa e i primordii del Kantismo in Italia. (Credaro, L.) Catania, 1913.

Phil 6310.8 Alfred Adler; a biography. (Bottome, P.) N.Y., 1939.

Phil 6310.1.93 Alfred Adler, the man and his work. (Orgler, Hertha.) London, 1939.

Phil 6310.1.103 Alfred Adler, the man and his work. 3d ed. (Orgler, Hertha.) London, 1963.

Phil 6310.1.100 Alfred Adler. (Orgler, Hertha.) Wien, 1956.

Phil 6310.1.98 Alfred Adler. (Way, Lewis M.) Harmondsworth, 1956.

Phil 6310.8.5 Alfred Adler. 3rd ed. (Bottome, P.) London, 1957.

Phil 6310.1.110 Alfred Adler oder das Elénd der Psychologie. 1. Aufl. (Sperker, Manès.) Wien, 1970.

Phil 6310.1.102 Alfred Adler zum Gedenken. (Internationale Vereinegung für Individualpsychologie, Vienna.) Wien, 1957.

Phil 2477.8.81 Alfred Binet. Thèse. (Martin, Robert.) Paris, 1924.

Phil 2477.8.83 Alfred Binet et son oeuvre. (Bertrand, F.L.) Paris, 1930.

Phil 2477.8.84 Alfred Binet et son oeuvre. Thèse. (Bertrand, F.L.) Paris, 1930.

Phil 2605.1.81 Alfred Fouillées psychischen Monismus. (Pasmanik, D.) Bern, 1899.

Phil 2340.10.25 Alfred North Whitehead; an anthology. (Whitehead, Alfred North.) N.Y., 1953.

Phil 2340.10.175 Alfred North Whitehead. (Kline, George Louis.) Englewood Cliffs, 1963.

Phil 2340.10.26 Alfred North Whitehead. (Whitehead, Alfred North.) N.Y., 1961.

Phil 2340.10.40 Alfred North Whitehead. 1st ed. (Whitehead, Alfred North.) N.Y., 1961.

Phil 2340.10.235 Alfred North Whitehead's philosophy of values. Thesis. (Weisenbeck, Jude D.) Waukesha, Wisconsin, 1969.

Phil 1020.7 Algazel. Dogmática, moral, ascética. v. 1-3. (Asin Palacios, M.) Zaragola, 1901. 2v.

Phil 5066.260 Algebra i matematicheskaia logika. Kiev, 1966.

Phil 5042.8.5A The algebra of logic. (Couturat, L.) Chicago, 1914.

Phil 5042.8 L'algèbre de la logique. 1st ed. (Couturat, L.) Paris, 1905.

Phil 5042.8.2 L'algèbre de la logique. 2e éd. (Couturat, L.) Paris, 1905.

Phil 10.41.10 Algemeen Nederlands tijdschrift voor wijstegeerte en psychologie. Assen. 15,1921+ 19v.

Phil 10.41.11 Algemeen Nederlands tijdschrift voor wijstegeerte en psychologie. Systemtisch en alfabetisch register. 1-50,1907-1958

Phil 8403.31 algemeine Ästhetik. (Cohn, Jonas.) Leipzig, 1910.

Phil 8404.13 Algemeine ästhetik. (Diez, Max.) Leipzig, 1906.

Phil 5649.36 Algemene theorie der menselijke houding en beweging als verbinding en tegenstelling van de fysiologische en de psychologische beschouwig. 3. Druk. (Buytendijk, Frederik Jacobus Johannes.) Utrecht, 1964.

Phil 8625.1.5 Alger, W.R. A critical history of the doctrine of a future life. N.Y., 1871.

Phil 8625.1 Alger, W.R. A critical history of the doctrine of a future life. Philadelphia, 1864.

Phil 8875.24 Alger, W.R. The school of life. Boston, 1881.

Phil 9515.2 Alger, W.R. The solitudes of nature and of man. 4. ed. Boston, 1867.

Phil 9515.2.5 Alger, W.R. Solitudes of nature and of man. 5th ed. Boston, 1867.

Phil 8655.15 Algermissen Konrad. Die Gottlosenbewegung der Gegenwart. 1. und 2. Aufl. Hannover, 1933.

Phil 2445.5.30 Alguié, Ferdinand. Solitude de la raison. Paris, 1966.

Phil 4303.5.5 Alguns aspétos da filosofia no Brazil. (Cruz Costa, João.) São Paulo, 1938?

Phil 5400.36 Alibert, J.L. Physiologie des passions. 2e éd. Paris, 1827. 2v.

Phil 310.445.25 Alienacja? (Jaroszewski, Tadeusz M.) Warszawa, 1965.

Phil 3425.732 L'aliénation dans la phénoménologie de l'esprit de G.W.F. Hegel. (Boey, C.) Paris, 1970.

Phil 6965.6 Aliénation mentale, chez les employés de chemins de fer et de transports publics. Thèse. (Provost, Maurice.) Paris, 1914.

Phil 600.59.5 The alienation of reason; a history of positivist thought. (Kolakowski, Leszek.) Garden City, N.Y., 1968.

Phil 6961.2 L'aliéné devant la philosophie, la morale et la societé. (Lemoine, A.) Paris, 1865.

Phil 3805.104 Alin, Folke. Studier öfrer Schleiermachers uppfattning af det evangeliska skapelsebegreppet. Lund, 1909.

Phil 510.137.5 Aliotta, A. L'éternité des esprits. Paris, 1924.

Phil 400.29.5 Aliotta, A. The idealistic reaction against science. London, 1914.

Phil 5240.29 Aliotta, A. La misura in psicologia sperimentale. Firenze, 1905.
Phil 623.21 Aliotta, A. Le origini dello irrazionalismo contemporaneo. Napoli, 1928.
Phil 510.137 Aliotta, A. Il problema di Dio e il nuovo pluralismo. Città di Castello, 1924.
Phil 400.29 Aliotta, A. La reazione idealistica contro la scienza. Palermo, 1912.
Phil 400.29.9 Aliotta, A. Relativismo e idealismo. Napoli, 1922.
Phil 4060.4.35 Aliotta, Antonio. Critica dell'esistenzialismo. 2. ed. v.2,5. Roma, 1957. 2v.
Phil 175.26.9 Aliotta, Antonio. L'esperimento nella scienza. Napoli, 1936.
Phil 175.26 Aliotta, Antonio. La guerra eterna e il dramma dell'esistenza. Napoli, 1917.
Phil 175.26.2 Aliotta, Antonio. La guerra eterna e il dramma dell'esistenza. 2a ed. Napoli, 1920.
Phil 4060.4.2 Aliotta, Antonio. Opere complete. Roma, 1947. 7v.
Phil 175.26.5 Aliotta, Antonio. La teoria di Einstein. Palmero, 1922.
Phil 4285.1.100 Aliotta, S. Un precursore della neoscolastica. Noto, 1952.
Phil 8875.34 Alisjahbana, Sutan Takdir. Values as integrating forces in personality society and culture. Kuala Lumpur, 1966.
Phil 8401.2.3 Alison, Archibald. Essays on the nature and principles of taste. Boston, 1812. 2v.
Phil 8401.2 Alison, Archibald. Essays on the nature and principles of taste. Edinburgh, 1790.
Phil 8401.2.5 Alison, Archibald. Essays on the nature and principles of taste. Hartford, 1821.
Phil 8401.2.2 Alison, Archibald. Essays on the nature and principles of taste. 2. ed. Edinburgh, 1811.
Phil 8401.2.4 Alison, Archibald. Essays on the nature and principles of taste. 4th ed. Edinburgh, 1815. 2v.
Phil 7059.12.13 All about devils. (Hull, Moses.) Chicago, 1890.
Phil 4757.2.30A All and everything. v.1-2. 1st ed. (Gurdjieff, Georges Ivanovitch.) N.Y., 1950. 2v.
Phil 6980.198 All but me and thee. (Cooke, Elliot D.) Washington, 1946.
Phil 1807.7 All coherence gone. (Harris, Victor I.) Chicago, 1949.
Phil 8402.38 Alla ricerca del tempo nell'arte. 1. ed. (Boldrini, M.) Milano, 1954.
Phil 4080.9.40 Alla ricerca di me stesso. (Carlini, Armando.) Firenze, 1951.
Phil 585.228 Alla scoperta della persona umana. (Deho, Ambrogio.) Padova, 1967.
Phil 3015.6 Alla soglia dell'étà romantica. (Pupi, A.) Milano, 1962.
Phil 8673.38 Allah neden var. (Sencer, Muammer.) Istanbul, 1970.
Phil 672.20 Allan, A. Space and personality. Edinburgh, 1913.
Phil 2005.10.80 Allan, Donald James. Guy Cromwell Field. London, 1956.
Phil 2520.346 Allard, J.L. Le mathématisme de Descartes. Ottawa, 1963.
Phil 3565.118 Der Allbeseelungsgedanke bei Lotze. (Hahn, Gustav.) Stuttgart, 1925.
Phil 492.10 Alle fonti del deismo e del materialismo moderno. (Rossi, M.M.) Firenze, 1942.
Phil 8662.20 Alle Moglichkeit liegt bei uns. (Heer, Freidrich.) Nürnberg, 1958.
Phil 1712.15 Alle origini della crisi contemporanea. (Magnino, Bianca.) Roma, 1946.
Phil 2266.157 Alle origini dell'etica contemporanea Adamo Smith. (Preti, Giulio.) Bari, 1957.
Phil 8881.48 Alle radici della morale. (Galli, E.) Milano, 1919.
Phil 181.51 Alle soglie della metafisica. (Galli, Ettore.) Milano, 1922.
Phil 7060.43.5 The alleged haunting of B-- house. (Goodrich-Freer, A.) London, 1899.
Phil 7054.21 The alleged physical phenomena of spiritualism. (Lewis, H.C.) Boston, 1887.
Phil 3110.175 Alleman, G.M. A critique of some philosophical aspects of the mysticism of Jacob Boehme. Thesis. Philadelphia, 1932.
Phil 5240.34 Allen, A.H.B. The self in psychology. London, 1935.
Phil 8110.5 Allen, B.S. Tides in English taste (1619-1800); a background for the study of literature. Cambridge, Mass., 1937. 2v.
Phil 672.166 Allen, Chalinder. The tyranny of time. N.Y., 1947.
Phil 8655.13 Allen, D.C. Doubt's boundless sea. Baltimore, 1964.
Phil 9230.20 Allen, David D. The nature of gambling. N.Y., 1952.
Phil 2750.11.95 Allen, E. Christian humanism...Jacques Maritain. London, 1950.
Phil 8951.24 Allen, E. Creation and grace...Ernie Brunner. London, 1950.
Phil 4752.2.105 Allen, E. Freedom in God...on Berdyaev. London, 1950. 4 pam.
Phil 8662.15.80 Allen, E. Jesus, our leader...Karl Heim. London, 1950.
Htn Phil 8580.3* Allen, E. Reason, the only oracle of man. Bennington, Vt., 1784.
Phil 8580.3.5 Allen, E. Reason, the only oracle of man. N.Y., 1836.
Phil 8580.3.2 Allen, E. Reason, the only oracle of man. N.Y., 1940.
Phil 1750.364 Allen, E.L. Existentialism from within. London, 1953.
Phil 5645.9 Allen, Frank. Persistence of vision in color blind subjects. n.p., 1902.
Phil 6310.9 Allen, Frederick H. Psychotherapy with children. N.Y., 1942.
Phil 5645.2 Allen, G. Colour-sense. London, 1879. 2v.
Phil 8655.4 Allen, G. Evolution of the idea of God. N.Y., 1897.
Phil 2070.155A Allen, Gay Wilson. William James; a biography. N.Y., 1967.
Phil 2070.155.1 Allen, Gay Wilson. William James. Minneapolis, 1970.
Phil 8401.18 Allen, Grant. Physiological aesthetics. N.Y., 1877.
Phil 5810.1 Allen, J.B. The associative processes of the guinea pig. Granville, Ohio, 1904.
Phil 8580.12.2 Allen, J.H. Positive religion. Boston, 1894. 5v.
Phil 6110.9.5 Allen, James. As a man thinketh. N.Y., 19- .
Phil 6110.9 Allen, James. As a man thinketh. N.Y., 19- .
Phil 6110.9.3 Allen, James. As a man thinketh. N.Y., 19- .
Phil 8875.17 Allen, James. From poverty to power. N.Y., 1907.
Phil 3475.3.105 Allen, L. The self and its hazards...K. Jaspers. London, 1950.
X Cg Phil 8709.9.5 Allen, Leslie H. Bryan and Darrow at Dayton. N.Y., 1925.
Phil 7069.43.5 Allen, Maurice. Our invisible friends. N.Y., 1943.
Phil 9160.4 Allen, N. The New England family. New Haven, 1882.
Phil 978.49.825 Allen, P.M. The writings and lectures of Rudolf Steiner. N.Y., 1956.
Phil 5592.55 Allen, Robert M. Personality assessment procedures. N.Y., 1958.
Phil 8580.4 Allen, S.M. Religion and science; the letters of "Alpha". Boston, 1875.
Phil 6990.32 Allen, Simeon C. Miracles and medicine. Boston, 1929.
Phil 525.101.10 Allen, Warner. The happy issue. London, 1948.
Phil 525.101 Allen, Warner. The timeless moment. London, 1946.
Phil 5710.12 Allendy, R. Les tempéraments. Paris, 1922.
Phil 5750.6 Allendy, René F. Le problème de la destinée. Paris, 1927.
Phil 7084.22 Allendy, René Félix. Les rêves et leur interpretation psychanalytique. Paris, 1926.
Phil 3890.8.6 Allerhand bissher Publicirte Kleine deutsche Schriften. (Thomasius, Christian.) Halle, 1701.
Phil 6315.2.114 Allers, R. The successful error; a critical study of Freudian psychoanalysis. N.Y., 1940.
Phil 6980.34 Allers, Rudolf. Existentialism and psychiatry. Springfield, 1961.
Phil 9035.61.9 Allers, Rudolf. Practical psychology in character development. N.Y., 1934.
Phil 9035.61.5 Allers, Rudolf. Psychology of character. N.Y., 1931.
Phil 9035.61.12 Allers, Rudolf. Das Werden der settlichen Person. 4. Aufl. Freiburg, 1935.
Phil 336.16 Alles und Nichts. (Fink, Eugen.) Den Haag, 1959.
Phil 5810.6 Allesch, G.J. von. Zur nichteuklidischen Struktur des Phänomenalen Raumes. Jena, 1931.
Htn Phil 1845.1.25* Allestree, Richard. The gentleman's calling. London, 1660.
Htn Phil 1845.1.30* Allestree, Richard. The ladies calling. Oxford, 1673.
Htn Phil 9340.6* Allestree, Richard. The ladies calling. Oxford, 1673.
Htn Phil 1845.1.35F* Allestree, Richard. The whole duty of man. London, 1725.
Phil 196.9 Der allgeist. Grundzüge des Panpsychismus. (Venetianer, M.) Berlin, 1874.
Phil 5645.39 Allgemein Orientierende experimental psychologische Untersuchungen über den zeitlichen Verlauf von Farbwandelspielen. Inaug. Diss. (Jerrentrup, F.) Bochum, 1936.
Phil 6317.34 Allgemeine, Tiefenpsychologie. (Heiss, Robert.) Bern, 1956.
Phil 8408.16 Allgemeine Ästhetik. (Häberlin, Paul.) Basel, 1929.
Phil 6020.5 Allgemeine Ausdruckslehre. (Kirchhoff, Robert.) Göttingen, 1957.
Htn Phil 5827.4.6* Allgemeine Betrachtungen über die Triebe der Thiere. (Reimarus, Hermann Samuel.) Hamburg, 1760.
Phil 5827.4.5 Allgemeine Betrachtungen über die Triebe der Thiere. 2. Ausg. (Reimarus, Hermann Samuel.) Hamburg, 1762.
Phil 5827.4.7 Allgemeine Betrachtungen über die Triebe der Thiere. 3. Ausg. (Reimarus, Hermann Samuel.) Hamburg, 1773. 2 pam.
Phil 184.13.7 Allgemeine der Wirklichkeit. (Jacoby, Günther.) Halle, 1925.
Phil 349.9 Allgemeine Erkenntnislehre. (Schlick, Moritz.) Berlin, 1918.
Phil 8893.22 Allgemeine Ethik. (Steinthal, H.) Berlin, 1885.
Phil 8884.16 Allgemeine Ethik. 1. und 2. Aufl. (Jodl, Friedrich.) Stuttgart, 1918.
Phil 8888.1.3 Allgemeine Ethik. 2. Aufl. (Nahlowsky, J.W.) Pleizig, 1885.
Phil 6968.13 Allgemeine Gerichtliche Psychiatrie. (Schaefer, H.) Berlin, 1910.
Phil 803.3.2 Allgemeine Geschichte der Philosophie. (Deussen, P.) Leipzig, 1907-020. 3v.
Phil 810.2.5 Allgemeine Geschichte der Philosophie. (Kinkel, W.) Osterwieck, 1920-27. 4v.
Phil 800.1 Allgemeine Geschichte der Philosophie. Berlin, 1909.
Phil 803.3 Allgemeine Geschichte der Philosophie. v.1, pts.1-3. v.2, pts.1-3. (Deussen, P.) Leipzig, 1894-1917. 7v.
Phil 803.3.1A Allgemeine Geschichte der Philosophie. v.1-2. (Deussen, P.) Leipzig, 1894-1920. 7v.
Phil 800.1.5 Allgemeine Geschichte der Philosophie. 2. Aufl. Leipzig, 1913.
Phil 192.21.15 Allgemeine Grundlegung der Philosophie. (Rickert, H.) Tübingen, 1921.
Phil 8837.3 Allgemeine kritische Geschichte der ältern und neuern Ethik. (Meiners, C.) Göttingen, 1800-01. 2v.
Phil 5041.9 Allgemeine Logik. (Bergmann, J.) Berlin, 1879.
Phil 3428.35 Allgemeine Metaphysik. (Herbart, J.F.) Königsberg, 1828-29. 2v.
Phil 3480.69.2 Allgemeine Naturgeschichte. Theorie des Himmels. (Kant, Immanuel.) Frankfurt, 1799.
Htn Phil 3480.69.1* Allgemeine Naturgeschichte. Theorie des Himmels. (Kant, Immanuel.) Königsberg, 1755.
Phil 3480.69 Allgemeine Naturgeschichte. Theorie des Himmels. (Kant, Immanuel.) Leipzig, 1890.
Phil 3480.69.3 Allgemeine Naturgeschichte. Theorie des Himmels. (Kant, Immanuel.) Zeitz, 1798.
Phil 3480.69.4 Allgemeine Naturgeschichte. Theorie des Himmels. 4. Aufl. (Kant, Immanuel.) Zeitz, 1808.
Phil 3480.69.6 Allgemeine Naturgeschichte und Theorie des Himmels. (Kant, Immanuel.) Berlin, 1955.
Phil 6323.5.3 Allgemeine Neurosenlehre. (Nunberg, Hermann.) Bern, 1959.
Phil 6323.5 Allgemeine Neurosenlehre auf psychoanalytischer Gundlage. (Nunberg, Hermann.) Bern, 1932.
Phil 4752.1.30 Allgemeine Organisationslehre Tektologie. (Malinovskii, Aleksandr A.) Berlin, 1926-28. 2v.
Phil 3428.34 Allgemeine Pädagogik. (Herbart, J.F.) Göttingen, 1806.
Phil 6117.11 Allgemeine Pathologie der Krankheiten des Nervensystems. (Huguenin, G.) Zürich, 1873.
Phil 181.39 Allgemeine Philosophie...der Natur. (Geyser, Joseph.) Münster, 1915.
Phil 8900.4 Allgemeine philosophische Ethik. (Ziller, T.) Langensalza, 1880.
Phil 3428.36 Allgemeine practische Philosophie. (Herbart, J.F.) Göttingen, 1808.
Phil 8888.1 Allgemeine praktische Philosophie. (Nahlowsky, J.W.) Leipzig, 1871.
Phil 3428.36.5 Allgemeine praktische Philosophie. 3. Ausg. (Herbart, J.F.) Hamburg, 1891.
Phil 5241.122 Allgemeine Psychologie. (Brrermann, Ernst.) Paderborn, 1958.
Phil 5253.1.5 Allgemeine Psychologie. (Natorp, P.) Tübingen, 1912.
Phil 5265.1.15 Allgemeine Psychologie. (Ziehen, Theodor.) Berlin, 1923.
Phil 5253.1.9 Allgemeine Psychologie. 2. Aufl. (Natorp, P.) Marburg, 1910.
Phil 5244.9.23 Allgemeine Psychologie. 3. Aufl. (Erismann, Theodor.) Berlin, 1962-1965. 4v.
Phil 5258.35.15 Allgemeine Psychologie auf personalistischer Grundlage. (Stern, W.) Haag, 1935.
Phil 6954.2.5 Allgemeine Psychopathologie. (Emminghaus, H.) Leipzig, 1878.
Phil 6959.4 Allgemeine Psychopathologie. (Jaspers, K.) Berlin, 1913.
Phil 5640.18 Allgemeine Sinnesphysiologie. (Kries, J. von.) Leipzig, 1923.
Phil 5244.1 Allgemeine Theorie des Denkens und Empfindens. (Eberhard, J.A.) Berlin, 1776.

Phil 6317.34.5 Allgemeine Tiefenpsychologie. (Heiss, Robert.) Bern, 1964.

Phil 3475.3.125 Allgemeine Wahrheit und existentielle Wahrheit. (Schmidhauser, N.) Bonn, 1953.

Phil 1200.39 Die Allgemeinen pädagogischen Gedanken der alten Stoa. Inaug. Diss. (Tsirimbas, Antonios.) München, 1936.

Phil 5066.16 Ein allgemeiner Kalkülbegriff. (Schröber, Karl.) Leipzig, 1941.

Phil 340.3 Allgemeiner Theil der Erkenntnislehre. (Jacob, T.) Berlin, 1853.

Phil 95.2 Allgemeines Handwörterbuch der philosophischen Wissenschaften. (Krug, Wilhelm Traugott.) Leipzig, 1827. 5v.

Phil 95.2.2A Allgemeines Handwörterbuch der philosophischen Wissenschaften. 2e Aufl. (Krug, Wilhelm Traugott.) Leipzig, 1832-38. 5v.

Phil 5850.385.87 Ein allgemeines Modell für die Skalierung von Meinungen. (Wehowski, D.) Münster? 1961.

Phil 5241.77 Allgermeine Einfuhrung in das Gesamtgebiet der Psychologie. (Baade, Walter.) Leipzig, 1928.

Phil 175.4 Allibaco, W.A. Philosophic and scientific ultimatum. N.Y., 1864.

Phil 5627.97 Allier, Raoul. La psychologie de la conversion chez les peuples noncivilisés. Paris, 1925. 2v.

Phil 3425.237.5 Allievo, G. Esame dell'Hegelianismo. Torino, 1897.

Phil 4060.3.35 Allievo, G. G. Allievo...per essere aggregato...Universita di Torino. Torino, 1858.

Phil 3808.149 Allievo, G. Giobbe e Schopenhauer. Torino, 1912.

Phil 3425.237 Allievo, G. L'Hegelianismo, la scienza e la vita. Milano, 1868.

Phil 4060.3.30 Allievo, G. Saggi filosofici. Milano, 1866.

Phil 2270.175 Allievo, Giuseppe. La psicologia di Herbert Spencer. 2a ed. Torino, 1913.

Phil 5040.2 Allihn, F.H.T. Des antibarbarus logicus. Halle, 1853.

Phil 3000.2 Allihn, F.H.T. Die Umkehr der Wissenschaft in Preussen. Berlin, 1855.

Phil 3425.269 Allihn, F.H.T. Der verderbliche Einfluss der Hegelschen Philosophie. Leipzig, 1852.

Phil 8875.15 Allihn, Friedrich H. Grundriss der Ethik. 2e Aufl. Langensalza, 1898.

Phil 4000.17 Alliney, G. I pensatori della seconda metà del secolo XIX. Milano, 1942.

Phil 8580.5 Alliott, R. Psychology and theology. London, 1855.

Phil 5592.190 Allison, Joel. The interpretation of psychological tests. N.Y., 1968.

Phil 7069.29.5 Allison, Lydia W. Leonard and Soule experiments in psychical research. Boston, 1929.

Phil 9120.10 Allmän inledning till apriorisk. (Cederschiöld, F.) Lund, 1821.

Phil 2490.54.15 Allmän öfversikt af positivismen. (Comte, Auguste.) Stockholm, 1896.

Phil 2045.113 Alloggio, Sabino. Critica della concezione dello stato in Tommaso Hobbes. Napoli, 1930.

Phil 5585.78 Allpart, F.H. Theories of perception and the concept of structure. N.Y., 1955.

Phil 575.91.5 Allport, G.W. The field of personality. n.p., n.d.

Phil 5590.70 Allport, G.W. The nature of personality. Cambridge, Mass., 1950.

Phil 5590.380 Allport, G.W. Pattern and growth in personality. N.Y., 1961.

Phil 575.91A Allport, G.W. Personality; a psychological interpretation. N.Y., 1937.

Phil 575.215A Allport, G.W. Personality and social encounter. Boston, 1960.

Phil 9035.45.15 Allport, G.W. The psychology of character by A.A. Roback. Princeton, 1927.

Phil 5630.5A Allport, G.W. The psychology of rumor. N.Y., 1947.

Phil 5630.5.2 Allport, G.W. The psychology of rumor. N.Y., 1948.

Phil 5850.349.25 Allport, G.W. Review of P.M. Symonds' Diagnosing personality. Cambridge, Mass., 1932.

Phil 5649.19A Allport, G.W. Studies in expressive movement. N.Y., 1933.

Phil 5627.189 Allport, Gordon W. The individual and his religion. N.Y., 1950.

Phil 5627.189.3 Allport, Gordon W. The individual and his religion. N.Y., 1951.

Phil 1845.5.79 Pamphlet box. Allport, Gordon W.

Phil 5240.46A Allport, Gordon Willard. Becoming. New Haven, 1955.

Phil 5240.46.2 Allport, Gordon Willard. Becoming. New Haven, 1964.

Phil 5240.46.5.2 Allport, Gordon Willard. Becoming. New Haven, 1967.

Phil 5590.71 Allport, Gordon Willard. The nature of personality. Cambridge, 1950.

Htn Phil 6123.5.2* All's right with the world. (Newcomb, C.B.) Boston, 1897.

Phil 6123.5 All's right with the world. (Newcomb, C.B.) Boston, 1897.

Phil 9320.7 Der Alltag als Übung vom Weg zur Verwandlung. 2. Aufl. (Duerckheim-Montmartin, Karlfried.) Bern, 1966.

Phil 5243.28.8 Alltagsrätsel des Seelenlebens. (Driesch, Hans.) Stuttgart, 1938.

Phil 705.25 Allure du transcendental. (Bénézé, Georges.) Paris, 1936.

Phil 705.25.5 Allure du transcendental. Thèse. (Bénézé, Georges.) Paris, 1936.

Phil 6310.14 Allwohn, Adolf. Das heilende Wort. Göttingen, 1958.

Phil 3801.134 Allwohn, Adolf. Der Mythos bei Schelling. Charlottenburg, 1927.

Phil 5750.1 Allyn, J. Philosophy of mind in volition. Oberlin, 1851.

Phil 5627.146 Alm, Ivar. Den religiösa funktionen i människosjälen. Akademisk abhandlung. Stockholm, 1936.

Phil 5810.8 Alm, O.W. The effect of habit interference upon performance in maze learning. Worcester, 1931.

Phil 2905.1.2 Almago, Romano S. A basic Teilhard-bibliography, 1955 - Apr. 1968. N.Y., 1968.

Phil 18.8.5 Almanach. (Internationaler Psychoanalytischer Verlag.) Vienna, 1926-1936 11v.

Phil 7069.20 Almasque, Jose A. Memorias de un fraile. Habana, 192-?

VPhil 9070.124 Almásy, József. A tizparancsalat a közéletben. Budapest, 1942.

Phil 175.65 Almeida, Fernando Pinho de. A essência da matéria e o sentido da vida. Coimbra, 1967.

Phil 281.9 Almeida, Theodoro de. Recreação filosofica. Lisboa, 1786-1805. 10v.

Phil 5252.175 Almen psykologi. 3. opl. v.1-2. (Madsen, K.B.) København, 1968.

Phil 4520.8.42 Almenn rökfraeð (Bjarnason, Ágúst.) Reykjavík, 1913.

Phil 4520.8.52 Almenn sálarfraeð (Bjarnason, Agúst.) Reykjavík, 1916.

Phil 2262.92 Almer, T. Studier i Shaftesburys filosofi. Lund, 1939.

Phil 4630.3.80 Almguist, Karl Gustaf. Andreas Rydelius etiska akådning. Lund, 1955.

Phil 8610.940.1 Almost an autobiography. (Cohen, C.) London, 1940.

Phil 9495.4.5 Almost fourteen. (Warren, M.A.) N.Y., 1897.

Phil 6750.220 The almosts, a study of the feeble minded. (MacMurchy, H.) Boston, 1920.

Phil 5040.13 Almquist, S. Vårt tankelif. Stockholm, 1906.

Phil 3791.125 Alois Riehl. (Siegel, Carl.) Graz, 1932.

Phil 3791.126 Alois Riehl und H. Spencer. Inaug. Diss. (Ramlow, Lilli.) Saalfeld, 1933.

Phil 4357.6.80 Alonso, Manuel. Temas filosoficos medievales. Comillas, 1959.

Phil 1750.335 Alonso-Fueyo, S. Existencialismo y existencialistas. Valencia, 1949.

Phil 1750.575 Alonso-Fueyo, Sabino. El drama del hombre actual. Valencia, 1958.

Phil 4000.16 Alorpio, F. de. Storia e dialogo. Bologna, 1962.

Phil 800.7 Alpern, Henry. The march of philosophy. N.Y., 1933.

Phil 6158.45 Alpert, Richard. LSD. N.Y., 1966.

Phil 178.4 The alpha. (Dennys, E.N.) London, 1855.

Phil 178.4.2 The alpha. (Dennys, E.N.) London, 1855.

Phil 178.4.100 The Alpha Union for freedom through truth. 4th ed. Hertfordshire, 1909.

Phil 8597.7 Alphabet of natural theology. (Rennie, J.) London, 1834.

Phil 3850.18.115 Alpheus, Karl. Kant und Scheler. Diss. Freiburg, 1936.

Phil 2520.229.2 Alquié, F. La découverte métaphysique de l'homme chez Descartes. Thèse. Paris, 1950.

Phil 2520.229 Alquié, F. La découverte métaphysique de l'homme chez Descartes. 1. éd. Paris, 1950.

Phil 2520.193.5 Alquié, F. Descartes, l'homme et l'oeuvre. Paris, 1956.

Phil 2520.193.10 Alquié, F. Descartes. Stuttgart, 1962.

Phil 2520.193 Alquié, F. Notes sur la première partie des principes de la philosophie de Descartes. Paris, 1933.

Phil 8875.25 Alquié, F. Notions de morale générale. Paris, 1933.

Phil 8875.25.5 Alquié, F. Le problème moral. Paris, 1933.

Phil 2520.229.5 Alquié, F. Science et métaphysique chez Descartes. Paris, 1965.

Phil 3482.15.5 Alquié, Ferdinand. La critique kantienne de la metaphysique. Paris, 1968.

Phil 175.43 Alquié, Ferdinand. Le désir d'éternité. 1. ed. Paris, 1943.

Phil 175.43.4 Alquié, Ferdinand. Le désir d'éternité. 4th ed. Paris, 1963.

Phil 331.12 Alquié, Ferdinand. L'expérience. Paris, 1957.

Phil 3482.15 Alquié, Ferdinand. La morale de Kant. Paris, 1965.

Phil 3820.8 Alquié, Ferdinand. Nature et vérité dans la philosophie de Spinoza. Paris, 1965.

Phil 175.43.10 Alquié, Ferdinand. La nostalgie de l'être. Paris, 1950.

Phil 175.43.11 Alquié, Ferdinand. La nostalgie de l'être. Thèse. Paris, 1950.

Phil 2445.5.35 Alquié, Ferdinand. Signification de la philosophie. Paris, 1971.

Phil 5240.31 Alrutz, S.G.L.R. Om själslifvets studium på fysiologisk grundval. Stockholm, 1899.

Phil 3903.3.97 De "Als ob" philosophie en het psychisch monisme. (Valeton, Matthée.) Amsterdam, 1923.

Phil 5627.264.25 Als zienda onzienlijke. v.1-3. (Fortmann, Henricus Martinus Maria.) Hilversum, 1964- 4v.

Phil 5810.4 Alsberg, M. Die Grundlagen des Gedächtnisses, der Vererbung und der Instinkte. München, 1906.

Htn Phil 3640.41* Also sprach Zarathustra. (Nietzsche, Friedrich.) Leipzig, 19- .

Phil 3640.41.4 Also sprach Zarathustra. (Nietzsche, Friedrich.) Leipzig, 1905?

Phil 3640.41.8A Also sprach Zarathustra. (Nietzsche, Friedrich.) Leipzig, 1909.

Phil 3640.41.15 Also sprach Zarathustra. (Nietzsche, Friedrich.) Stuttgart, 1943.

Phil 3640.17.6 Also Sprach Zarathustra. (Nietzsche, Friedrich.) Stuttgart, 1956.

Phil 5040.12 Alstedius, J.H. Logicae systema harmonicum. Herbonae Nassoviorum, 1614.

Phil 5520.418 Alston, W. Philosophy of language. Englewood Cliffs, N.J., 1964.

Phil 1695.22 Alston, W. Readings in twentieth century philosophy. N.Y., 1936.

Phil 8580.38 Alston, William P. Religious belief and philosophical thought. N.Y., 1963.

Phil 5190.23 Alstrin, Eric. Dissertatio gradualis. Upsaliae, 1725.

Phil 8875.23 Alstrin, Eric. Dissertatio philosophica. Upsala, 1723.

Phil 2520.171 Alstrin, Eric. Dissertationis academicae. Holmiae, 1727.

Phil 175.36 Alstrin, Eric. Dissertationis academicae. pt.1-2. Upsaliae, 1728.

Phil 8950.3 Alstrin, Eric. Ethica theologiae ministra. Upsaliae, 1725.

Phil 8690.5 Alstrin, Eric. Exercitium academicum. Upsaliae, 1727.

Phil 3552.285 Alstrin, Eric. Meditationes philosophicas. Upsala, 1731.

Phil 270.35 Alstrin, Eric Praeses. Dissertatio philosophica, de concursu caussaê primaê cum secundis. Upsaliae, 1732.

Phil 8580.19 Alstrin, Erico. Dissertatio philosophica. Upsaliae, 1728.

Phil 281.11 Alt, Theodor. Fundamentum Weltanschauung. Mannheim, 1920.

Phil 8401.8 Alt, Theodor. Die Grenzen der Kunst und die Buntfarbigkeit der Antike. Berlin, 1886.

Phil 525.190 Alt anden gang. (Grandjean, Louis E.) København, 1960.

Phil 3450.11.515 Altamore, Giovanni. Della fènomenologia all'ontologia. Padova, 1969.

Phil 7150.18 Altavilla, Enrico. La psicologia del suicidio. Napoli, 1910.

Phil 530.20.115 Altdeutsche und altniederländische Mystik. (Ruh, Kurt.) Darmstadt, 1964.

Phil 3778.41 Die alte Frage: was ist die Wahrheit? (Reinhold, K.L.) Altona, 1820.

Phil 978.49.165 Alte Mythen und ihre Bedeutung. (Steiner, R.) Dornach, 1937.

Phil 1200.56 Die alte Stoa und ihr Naturbegriff. (Simon, Heinrich.) Berlin, 1956.

Phil 3850.1.30 Der alte und der neue Glaube. (Strauss, D.F.) Bonn, 1873. 2v.

Phil 3850.1.29 Der alte und der neue Glaube. (Strauss, D.F.) Leipzig, 1872.

Phil 3850.1.35 Der alte und der neue Glaube. 2. Aufl. (Strauss, D.F.) Bonn, 1881.

Phil 978.49.375 Alte und neue Einweihungsmethoden. (Steiner, R.) Dornach, 1967.

Phil 8893.52 Alte und neue Tafeln. (Steudel, F.) Berlin, 1912?

Phil 3425.214 Alte Vernunft und neuer Verstand. (Bolland, G.J.P.J.) Leiden, 1902.

Phil 960.18.5 Altekar, A.S. Sources of Hindu dharma in its socio-religious aspects. Chicago, 1917.

Phil 960.17.40 Altekar, A.S. Sources of Hindu dharma in its socio-religious aspects. Shalapur, 1952?

Phil 10.37 — Altenaeum; philosophische Zeitschrift. München. 1-3,1862-1864 3v.

Phil 6311.18.5 — Alteration of personality. (Binet, Alfred.) N.Y., 1896.

Phil 6311.18 — Les altérations de la personnalité. (Binet, Alfred.) Paris, 1892.

Phil 6311.18.6 — Alterations of personality. (Binet, Alfred.) London, 1896.

X Cg Phil 1182.5 — Der altere Pythagoreismus. (Bauer, W.) Berlin, 1897.

Phil 5374.278 — Altered states of consciousness. (Tart, Charles T.) N.Y., 1969.

Phil 5241.97 — Altering frames of reference in the sphere of human behavior. (Burrow, Trigant.) N.Y., 1937.

Phil 2750.19.125 — Alternativ til det absurde. (Berg, Randi.) Oslo, 1969.

Phil 184.39 — L'alternative. (Jankélévitch, V.) Paris, 1938.

Phil 5240.19 — The alternative. London, 1882.

Phil 735.175 — Alternativen der Ordnung. (Meimberg, Rudolf.) Berlin, 1956.

Phil 672.150 — Alternitas; a Spinozistic study. (Hallett, H.F.) Oxford, 1930.

Phil 5258.7 — Altes und Neues aus dem Gebiet der innren Seelenkunde. (Schubert, G.H. von.) Leipzig, 1825-44. 5v.

Phil 5258.7.3 — Altes und Neues aus dem Gebiet der innren Seelenkunde. (Schubert, G.H. von.) Leipzig, 1817.

Phil 8875.10 — Altgeld, J.P. The cost of something for nothing. Chicago, 1904.

Phil 6110.16 — Althaus, J. On failure of brain-power. London, 1883.

Phil 8893.43.5 — L'altività pratica e la coscienza morale. (Sarlo, Francisco de.) Firenze, 1907.

Phil 3820.3.5 — Altkircli, Ernst. Maledictus und Benedictus: Spinoza. Leipzig, 1924.

Phil 3820.3 — Altkircli, Ernst. Spinoza im Porträt. Jena, 1913.

Phil 190.20.7 — L'altra metà. 3a ed. (Papini, Giovanni.) Firenze, 1919.

Phil 190.20.8 — L'altra metà. 4a ed. (Papini, Giovanni.) Firenze, 1922.

Phil 8890.23.21 — Altruism. (Palmer, George H.) N.Y., 1920.

Phil 8893.103A — Altruistic love. (Sorokin, Pitirim Aleksandrovich.) Boston, 1950.

Phil 8893.103.2 — Altruistic love. (Sorokin, Pitirim Aleksandrovich.) N.Y., 1969.

Phil 6980.36 — Altschule, Mark David. Roots of modern psychiatry. N.Y., 1957.

Phil 6980.36.2 — Altschule, Mark David. Roots of modern psychiatry. 2. ed. N.Y., 1965.

Phil 5460.11 — Alucinaciones. (Bosch, G.) Buenos Aires, 1935.

Phil 4351.4.15 — Alvarado, Francisco. Cartas criticas. Madrid, 1824-25. 5v.

Phil 4351.4.10 — Alvarado, Francisco. Cartas del filósofo rancio. Sevilla, 1811-14. 3v.

Phil 4351.4.5 — Alvarado, Francisco. Las cartas inéditas del filosofo rancio. Madrid, 1916.

Phil 4351.4.20 — Alvarado, Francisco. La maza de fraga sobre los filosofastros liberales del día. Madrid, 1812.

Phil 4351.4 — Alvarado, Francisco. Obras escogidas del filosofo rancio. Madrid, 1912.

Phil 8401.4 — Alvard, Julien. L'art moral. Paris, 1957.

Phil 281.10 — Alvarea de Queiroz, M. Historia da creação do mundo conforme as ideas de Moizes. Porto, 1762.

Phil 8875.11 — Alvarez, Agustín. Creación del mundo moral. 2a ed. Buenos Aires, 1915.

Phil 6854.16 — Alvarez, Alfred. The savage god: a study of suicide. London, 1972.

Phil 4962.10 — Alvarez, González. Introducción a una metafisica de la contingencia. Cuenca, 1959.

Phil 8580.14 — Alvarez, Joachim. Lectiones philosophiae. v.2. Vallisoleti, 1868-69. 3 pam.

Phil 8725.8 — Alvarez, Lili. El seglarismo y su integridad. Madrid, 1959.

VPhil 5401.51 — Alvarez, Martins d'. O medo no seculo XX. Rio de Janeiro, 1964.

Phil 8401.26 — Alvarez, Villar A. Filosofia del arte. Madrid, 1962.

Phil 6950.12 — Alvarez, W.C. Minds that came back. Philadelphia, 1961.

Phil 672.143 — Alvarez de Toledo, A. Le problème de l'espace. Paris, 1920.

Phil 5240.65 — Alvarez Villar, Alfonso. Psicología de los pueblos primitivos. Madrid, 1969.

Phil 5810.7.5 — Alverdes, F. The psychology of animals in relation to human psychology. London, 1932.

Phil 180.48 — Am Ende der Philosophie. (Freund, Ludwig.) München, 1930.

Phil 8693.20 — Am Rande der Dinge. 2. Aufl. (Dessauer, F.) Frankfurt, 1952.

Phil 8701.6 — Am Wendepunkt der Ideen. (Lang, O.) Wien, 1909.

Phil 4073.82 — Amabile, L. Fra Tommaso Campanella: la sua congiura. Napoli, 1882-. 3v.

Phil 175.59 — Amado Levy-Valensi, E. Les niveaux de l'être la connaissance et le mal. Paris, 1962.

Phil 2880.1.95 — Amadou, R. De l'agent inconnu au philosophe inconnu. Paris, 1962.

Phil 2880.1.85 — Amadou, R. Louis C. de Saint-Martin et le Martinisme. Paris, 1946.

Phil 3850.27.114 — Amadou, Robert. Albert Schweitzer. Bruxelles, 1951.

Phil 3850.27.114.5 — Amadou, Robert. Albert Schweitzer. Paris, 1952.

Phil 7069.54.15 — Amadou, Robert. La parapsychologie. Paris, 1954.

Phil 7069.58.5 — Amadou, Robert. La télépathie. Paris, 1958.

Phil 1190.20 — Amand de Merdito, Emmanuel. Fatalisme et liberté dans l'antique grecque. Louvain, 1945.

Phil 4170.3.82 — Amante, B. Un santo nel secolo XIX: A.C. de Meis. Lanciano, 1920.

Phil 1715.2.10 — Gli amanti de Sofia, 1902-1918. (Papini, Giovanni.) Firenze, 1942.

Phil 800.6 — Amato, F. d'. Studi di storia della filosofia. Geneva, 1931.

Phil 5066.324 — Amato, Nicolò. Logica simbolica e diritto. Milano, 1969.

Phil 7069.36.50 — An amazing experiment. (Thomas, C.D.) London, 1936.

Phil 8622.74 — Amb o sense fe; mots de conversa. Barcelona, 1968.

Phil 2150.22.125 — Ambacher, Michel. Marcuse et la critique de la civilisation américaine. Paris, 1969.

Phil 281.13 — Ambacher, Michel. Méthode de la philosophie de la nature. Paris, 1961.

Phil 281.6.15 — Ambacher, Michel. Le précurseur philosophique. Paris, 1844.

Phil 4959.205 — Ambiente filosófico de la Nueva España. (Mayagoitia, David.) México, 1945.

Phil 8877.68.5 — An ambiguity of the word "good". (Carritt, Edgar F.) London, 1937.

Phil 281.1 — Ambler, R.P. Birth of the universe. N.Y., 1853.

Phil 7059.16 — Ambler, R.P. Spiritual teacher. N.Y., 1852.

Phil 5040.25 — Ambrose, A. Logic. N.Y., 1961.

Phil 5066.32 — Ambrose, Alice. Fundamentals of symbolic logic. N.Y., 1948.

Phil 2150.18.110 — Ambrose, Alice. G.E. Moore; essays in retrospect. London, 1970.

Phil 5400.68 — Ambrosi, L. La dottrina del sentimento nella storia della filosofia. Roma, 1894.

Phil 3565.88 — Ambrosi, L. Ermanno Lotze e la sua filosofia. Milano, 1912.

Phil 5374.32 — Ambrosi, L. I principii della conoscenza. Roma, 1898.

Phil 5465.4 — Ambrosi, L. La psicologia della immaginazione. Roma, 1898.

Phil 5465.4.10 — Ambrosi, L. La psicologia dell'immaginazione nella storia della filosofia. Padova, 1959.

Phil 5465.4.5 — Ambrosi, L. Saggio sulla immaginazione. Roma, 1892.

Phil 175.25 — Ambrosi, Luigi. Il primo passo alla filosofia. v.3. 5a ed. Milano, 1915.

Phil 3245.82 — Ambrosius, J.M. Om Immanuel Hermann Fichte's teism och etik. Lund, 1882.

Phil 4769.1.97 — Ambrozaitis, K. Die Staatslehre W. Solowjews. Paderborn, 1927.

Phil 486.3 — L'âme. (Lecomte, F.D.) Paris, 1869.

Phil 5258.1 — L'âme. (Sagra, R. de la.) Paris, 1868.

Phil 5831.6 — L'âme des bêtes. (Verlaine, Louis.) Paris, 1931.

Phil 1135.159 — L'âme du monde de Platon aux Stoiciens. Thèse. (Moreau, J.) Paris, 1939.

Phil 6115.4 — L'âme est la fonction du cerveau. (Ferrière, E.) Paris, 1883. 2v.

Phil 5258.3 — L'âme et la vie. (Saisset, E.E.) Paris, 1864.

Phil 6128.29 — L'âme et le cerveau. 3. éd. (Surbled, Georges.) Paris, 1908.

Phil 6111.14 — L'ame et le corps. (Binet, A.) Paris, 1905.

Phil 6111.14.3 — L'ame et le corps. (Binet, A.) Paris, 1913.

Phil 6121.4 — L'âme et le corps. (Lemoine, A.) Paris, 1862.

Phil 6100.18 — L'âme et le corps. (Odette, Laffoneriere.) Paris, 1961.

Phil 3838.15 — L'ame et le corps d'après Spinoza. (Siwek, Paul.) Paris, 1930.

Phil 5823.1 — L'âme et l'instinct; l'homme et l'animal. (Nicolaÿ, Fernand.) Paris, 1922.

Phil 665.29 — L'âme humaine. (Baraduc, H.) Paris, 1896.

Phil 665.38 — L'âme humaine. (Coconnier, M.J.) Paris, 1890.

Phil 5262.22 — L'âme humaine. 2. série. (Waddington, Charles.) Paris, 1862.

Phil 665.96 — Ame humaine et science moderne. (Langre, Michel de.) Paris, 1963.

Phil 530.55.7 — Une âme mystique au temps prèsent. v.1-2. (Emilie, Sister.) Louvain, 1926-27.

Phil 2825.30 — Amédée Ponceau, études et témoignages. Bruges, 1966.

Phil 8952.11 — Amen, amen. (Constantino, S.A.) N.Y., 1944.

Phil 1830.52 — Amend, V.E. Ten contemporary thinkers. N.Y., 1964.

Phil 4060.9.30 — Amendala, G. Etica e biografia. Milano, 1953.

Phil 4060.9.35 — Amendola, Evakühn. Vita can Giovanni Amendola. Firenze, 1960.

Phil 2730.86 — Amendola, G. Maine de Biran. Firenze, 1911.

Phil 9178.8 — Amenities of home. (Sherwood, M.E.W.) N.Y., 1881.

Phil 2280.5.95 — America and the life of reason. (Kallen, H.M.) N.Y., 1921.

Phil 4957.50 — América como conciencia. (Zea, Leopoldo.) México, 1953.

Phil 8591.34 — Les americaines, ou La preuve de la religion chrétienne par les lumières naturelles. 1. éd. (Le Prince de Beaumont, Marie.) Lyon, 1770. 6v.

Phil 165.355 — American Academy for Jewish Research. Harry Austryn Wolfson. Jerusalem, 1965.

Phil 8875.28 — American Academy of Political and Social Science, Philadelphia. Ethical standards and professional conduct. Philadelphia, 1955.

Phil 9400.15 — American Academy of Political and Social Science, Philadelphia. Social contribution by the aging. Philadelphia, 1952.

Phil 6110.21 — American Academy of Political and Social Science. Mental health in the United States. Philadelphia, 1953.

Phil 8655.9 — The American antitheistical catechism. London, 1830?

Phil 10.62 — American Association for Applied Psychology. Directory of applied psychologists. Bloomington, Ind.

Phil 8655.8 — American Association for the Advancement of Atheism, Inc. Annual report. N.Y. 1,1926

Phil 9495.5.6 — The American boy and the social evil. (Wilson, Robert N.) Philadelphia, 1905.

Phil 9174.1.8 — American boys and girls. (Osgood, S.) N.Y., 1867.

Phil 40.8 — American Catholic Philosophical Association. Proceedings. Washington, D.C. 1,1926+ 15v.

Phil 9045.3 — American citizenship. Yale lectures. (Brewer, D.J.) N.Y., 1902.

Phil 5520.77 — American Congress on General Semantics. Papers from the second American congress on general semantics, August, 1941. Chicago, 1943.

Phil 2340.10.28 — American essays in social philosophy. (Whitehead, Alfred North.) N.Y., 1959.

Phil 6951.5.52 — American Foundation for Mental Hygiene, Inc. A mind that found itself and its author. N.Y., 193-.

Phil 9341.6 — The American gentleman. (Butler, C.) Philadelphia, 1836.

Phil 6980.58 — American handbook of psychiatry. (Arieti, Silvano.) N.Y., 1959. 3v.

Phil 8877.30 — The American hope. (Cole, W.M.) N.Y., 1910.

Phil 1750.166.5 — American humanism and the new age. (Mercier, Louis J.A.) Milwaukee, 1948.

Phil 8505.4 — American Humanist Association. (Humanist.) Yellow Springs, Ohio. 10,1950+ 7v.

Phil 9530.66 — The American idea of success. 1st ed. (Huber, Richard M.) N.Y., 1971.

Phil 10.52 — The American image. Boston. 1,1939+ 23v.

Phil 8663.3.97 — American infidel. 1. ed. (Larson, O.P.) N.Y., 1962.

Phil 40.9 — American Institute for Psychoanalysis. Curriculum. N.Y.

NEDL Phil 10.10 — American journal of insanity. Utica. 1-16,1844-1860 9v.

Phil 10.33 — The American journal of neurology and psychiatry. N.Y. 1-4,1882-1883 2v.

Phil 10.47 — The American journal of orthopsychiatry. Menasha, Wis. 1,1930+ 43v.

Phil 10.47.3 — The American journal of orthopsychiatry. Index. Menasha, Wis., 1941-1952. 2v.

Phil 10.88 — The American journal of psychoanalysis. N.Y. 23,1963+ 8v.

Phil 10.88.5 — The American journal of psychoanalysis. Cumulative index. v.1-17,1941-1957. n.p., n.d.

Phil 10.1 — American journal of psychology. Baltimore. 1,1888+ 90v.

VPhil 5205.16 — The American journal of psychology. Worcester, Mass., 1895-96.

Phil 10.1.5 — American journal of psychology. Index. N.Y. 1-50,1926-1937 2v.

Phil 10.90 American journal of psychotherapy. Lancaster, Pa. 19,1965+ 5v.

Phil 9341.6.9 The American lady. (Butler, C.) Philadelphia, 1841.

Phil 9290.1 The American mechanic. (Quill, C.) Philadelphia, 1838.

Phil 40.2 American Medico-Psychological Association. Proceedings. St. Louis. 60,1904

Phil 1815.3.5 American minds. (Persons, S.) N.Y., 1958.

Phil 5545.19 American mnemotechny. (Miles, Pliny.) N.Y., 1848.

Phil 8877.8 The American moralist. (Chipman, G.) Wrentham, Mass., 1801.

Phil 530.155 American mysticism, from William James to Zen. 1. ed. (Bridges, Leonard Hal.) N.Y., 1970.

Phil 10.68 The American nationalist. St. Louis. 1,1956+ 9v.

Phil 6951.12.10A American nervousness. (Beard, G.M.) N.Y., 1881.

Phil 2150.6.30 American patriotism and other social studies. (Münsterberg, H.) N.Y., 1913.

Phil 1830.11 American philosophers at work. (Hook, Sidney.) N.Y., 1956.

Phil 1830.5A American philosophic addresses. (Blau, Joseph L.) N.Y., 1946.

Phil 182.42 The American philosophic pragmatism. (Huizinga, A.V.C.P.) Boston, 1911.

Phil 40.6 American Philosophical Association. Proceedings. 1-25,1902-1925 4v.

Phil 40.6.3 American Philosophical Association. Proceedings and addresses. 1,1927+ 9v.

Phil 10.84 American philosophical quarterly. Pittsburgh. 1,1964+ 6v.

Phil 8520.28A American philosophies of religion. (Wieman, H.N.) Chicago, 1936.

Phil 1817.3A American philosophy. (Riley, I.W.) N.Y., 1907.

Phil 1830.15 American philosophy. (Winn, R.B.) N.Y., 1955.

Phil 1813.10 American philosophy and the future. (Norak, Michael.) N.Y., 1968.

Phil 1810.2 American philosophy today and tomorrow. (Kallen, H.M.) N.Y., 1935.

NEDL Phil 10.12.5 American phrenological journal. Philadelphia.

NEDL Phil 10.12 American phrenological journal. Philadelphia. 1838-1905 11v.

Phil 1812.12 American pragmatism. (Moore, E.C.) N.Y., 1961.

Phil 1830.35 The American pragmatists. (Kanvitz, Milton R.) N.Y., 1960.

Phil 5252.12.17 American problems. (Münsterberg, H.) N.Y., 1910.

Phil 6980.38.5 American Psychiatric Association. Application of basic science techniques to psychiatric research. Washington, 1957.

Phil 6980.40 American Psychiatric Association. Approaches to the study of human personality. Washington, 1956.

Phil 6980.38.10 American Psychiatric Association. Biographical directory of fellows and members of the American Psychiatric Association. N.Y., 1941.

Phil 6950.14 American Psychiatric Association. Comperative psycholinguistic analysis of two psychotherapeutic interviews. N.Y., 1961.

Phil 6980.38.2 American Psychiatric Association. One hundred years of American psychiatric Association, 1844-1944. N.Y., 1945.

Phil 6945.4 American Psychiatric Association. Propositions and resolutions of the Association of Medical Superintendents of American Institutions for the insane. Philadelphia, 1876.

Phil 6302.10 American Psychiatric Association. Committee on Relations with the Social Science. Proceedings...colloquium on personality investigation. 1st - 2nd, 1928-1929. Baltimore, 1929.

Phil 9380.3 American Psychiatric Association. Military Mobilization Committee. Psychiatric aspects of civilian morale. N.Y., 1942.

Phil 40.13 American Psychoanalytic Association. Bulletin. N.Y. 1-8,1937-1952 4v.

Phil 40.10 American Psychoanalytic Association. Journal. N.Y. 1,1953+ 21v.

Phil 40.10.5 American Psychoanalytic Association. Journal. Monograph series. N.Y. 1,1958+ 4v.

Phil 130.15 American Psychological Association. Biographical directory. Washington. 1968+

Phil 40.4.5 American Psychological Association. Proceedings of annual meeting. Lancaster, Pa. 26-48,1917-1940 4v.

Phil 40.4.3 American Psychological Association. Proceedings of the annual convention. Washington. 74,1966+ 5v.

Phil 40.4 Pamphlet box. American psychological association.

Phil 5240.52 American Psychological Association. Project on Scientific Information. Exchange in Psychology. Reports. Washington, 1963- 3v.

Phil 10.82 American psychologist. Lancaster. 1,1946+ 29v.

Phil 5215.3 American psychology. (Fay, J.W.) New Brunswick, N.J., 1939.

Phil 6310.20 American Psychopathological Association. Psychopathology of communication. N.Y., 1958.

Phil 8602.4 American religion. (Weiss, J.) Boston, 1871.

Phil 8505.15 American Scientific Affiliation. Journal. Mankato. 1,1949+ 6v.

Phil 9495.156A The American sex revolution. (Sorokin, P.A.) Boston, 1956.

Phil 58.3.9 American Society for Psychical Research. Journal. N.Y. 1,1907+ 52v.

Phil 58.3 American Society for Psychical Research. Proceedings. Boston. 1885-1889

Phil 58.3.5 American Society for Psychical Research. Proceedings. Boston. 1906-1927 22v.

Htn Phil 9160.7* The American spectator. A collection of essays relating to the married state. Boston, 1797.

Phil 1802.12 American thought. (Cohen, M.R.) Glencoe, Ill., 1954.

Phil 1817.3.8 American thought. (Riley, I.W.) Gloucester, 1959.

Phil 1817.3.5 American thought. (Riley, I.W.) N.Y., 1915.

Phil 1817.3.7 American thought. 2nd ed. (Riley, I.W.) N.Y., 1923.

Phil 1830.54 American thought before 1900. 1st ed. (Kurtz, Paul W.) N.Y., 1966.

Phil 1750.96.5 American thought in transition: the impact of evolutionary naturalism, 1865-1900. (Boller, Paul F.) Chicago, 1969.

Phil 6116.28 Americans view their mental health. (Gurin, Gerald.) N.Y., 1960.

Phil 193.70.5 America's progressive philosophy. (Sheldon, W.H.) New Haven, 1942.

Phil 5212.10 America's psychologists. (Clark, Kenneth.) Washington, 1957.

Phil 575.248 Americký personalismus; příspěvek k rozboru krize současného buržoazního myšlení. (Kovály, Pavel.) Praha, 1962.

Phil 1812.7A Amerikanische Philosophie. (Müller, Gustav E.) Stuttgart, 1936.

Phil 1812.7.5 Amerikanische Philosophie. 2. Aufl. (Müller, Gustav E.) Stuttgart, 1950[1936]

Phil 5247.69 Amerikanische und deutsche Psychologie. (Holzner, Burket.) Würzburg, 1958?

Phil 1812.11A Amerikanisches Philosophieren. (Marcuse, Ludwig.) Hamburg, 1959.

Phil 735.261 Amerikanskaia burzhuaznaia aksiologiia na sluzh e imperializma. (Antonovich, Ivan I.) Minsk, 1967.

VPhil 1830.55 Amerikanskie prosvetiteli. Moskva, 1968-69. 2v.

Phil 575.149 Amerikanskii personalizm-filosofiia imperialisticheskoi reaktsii. (Mel'vil', Iu.K.) Moskva, 1954.

Phil 1812.5.10 Amerikanskii pragmatizm. (Mel'vil, Iu.K.) Moskva, 1957.

Phil 4260.121 Amerio, Franco. Introduzione allo studio di G.B. Vico. Torino, 1947.

Phil 4073.100 Amerio, Romano. Campanella. Brescia, 1947.

Phil 175.5 Amersin, F. Gemeinverständliche Weisheitslehre. Triest, 1881.

Phil 175.5.5 Amersin, F. Populäre Philosophie oder leichtfassliche Einfuhrung in die Weisheitslehre. Graz, 1872.

Phil 5643.86 Ames, Adelbert. Collection of papers. n.p., n.d. 6 pam.

Phil 5643.87 Ames, Adelbert. Depth in pictorial art. N.Y., 1925.

Phil 5585.175 Ames, Adelbert. The morning notes of Adelbert Ames, Jr. New Brunswick, N.J., 1960.

Phil 5627.17 Ames, E.S. Psychology of religious experience. Boston, 1910.

Phil 8580.17.10 Ames, Edward S. Humanism. Chicago, 1931.

Phil 8580.17 Ames, Edward S. Religion. N.Y., 1929.

Phil 5593.54.10 Ames, Louise Bates. Rorschach responses in old age. 1. ed. N.Y., 1954.

Phil 1800.6 Ames, Van Meter. Zen and American thought. Honolulu, 1962.

Phil 6688.26 L'âmi de la nature, ou Manière de traiter les maladies. (Sousselier, de la Tour.) Dijon, 1784.

Phil 6310.18 Amidieu du Clos-Vinarie-Paule. Les interréactions des facteurs religieux et psychologiques en hygiène mentale. Thèse. Québec, 1958.

Phil 4851.10A Amin, Osman. Lights on contemporary Moslem philosophy. Cairo, 1958.

Phil 530.20.30 Les amis de Dieu au quatorzième siècle. (Jundt, Auguste.) Paris, 1879.

Phil 1145.51 L'amité antique d'après les moeurs populaires. Thèse. (Dugas, L.) Paris, 1894.

Phil 8876.7 Ammaestramenti degli antighi. (Bartolommeo, F.) Milan, 1808.

Phil 5520.44 Ammann, H.J.F. Die menschliche Rede. Lahr, 1925-28. 2v.

Phil 5545.173 L'amnésie continue. (Janet, Pierre.) Paris, 1893.

Phil 5627.269.15 Amon, Jesus. Prejuicio antiprotestante y religiosidad utilitaria. Madrid, 1969.

Phil 8677.13 Amor del intellectualis. (Wyneken, G.A.) Greifswald, 1898.

Phil 3640.255.5 Amor fati; Nietzsche in Italien. (Pourtalès, Guy de.) Freiburg, 1930.

Phil 8655.22 Amor Ruibal, Angel Maria. Cuatro manuscritos inéditos: Los principios de donde recibe el ente la existencia. Madrid, 1964.

Phil 8627.11 Amore, morte ed immortalità. (Chiappelli, A.) Milano, 1913.

Htn Phil 7075.11.5* Gli amori degli uomeni. (Mantegazza, P.) Milano, 1886.

Phil 8580.31 Amorim de Carvalho. Deus e o homem na poesia e na filosofia. Porto, 195-.

Htn Phil 2340.3.30* Amoris effigies. 4th ed. (Waring, Robert.) London, 1671.

Phil 4200.2.30 L'amorosa filosofia di F. Patrizzi. (Patrizzi, F.) Firenze, 1963.

Phil 4351.1.25 Amoroso Lima, A. Las edades del hombre. Buenos Aires, 1943.

Phil 1750.512.3 Amoroso Lima, Alceu. El existencialismo, filosofía de nuestro tiempo. 3. ed. Buenos Aires, 1951.

Phil 1750.166.170 Amoroso Lima, Alcew. Pelo humanismo ameaçado. Rio de Janeiro, 1965.

Phil 302.2 L'amour dans l'univers. (Vial, L.C.E.) Paris, 1896.

Phil 720.27 L'amour du vrai. (Lemaitre, C.) Louvain, 1929.

Phil 5400.91 L'amour et la haine. (Janet, Pierre.) Paris, 1932.

Phil 5421.25.25 L'amour humain. (Blais, Gerard.) Sherbrooke, 1968.

Phil 2490.94 L'amoureuse histoire d'Auguste Comte et de C. de Vaux. (Rouvre, C. de.) Paris, 1917.

Phil 175.13 Ampère, A.M. Philosophie. Paris, 1870.

Phil 1020.20 The amphibolous terms in Aristotle. (Wolfson, H.A.) Cambridge, Mass., 1938.

Phil 1050.12.3 The amphibolous terms in Aristotle. (Wolfson, Harry A.) Cambridge, Mass., 1938.

Htn Phil 8676.1* Amphitheatrum. (Vanino, G.C.) Lugdunum, 1615.

Phil 9495.163 The amplexus reservatus seen in the history of Catholic doctrine on the use of marriage. (Exner, Adam.) Ottawa, 1963.

Phil 8685.14 Amryc, C. Pantheism. n.p., 1898.

Phil 6950.4 Pamphlet box. Amsden, G.S. Minor writings.

Phil 6947.1854 Amsterdam. Valerius-Kliniek. Een halve eeuw arbeid op psychiatrisch-neurologischgen, terrein 1910-1960. Wagenin, 1960.

Phil 5627.200 Amstutz, J. Stuxen des Gebets. Bern, 1954.

Phil 2805.83 L'amulette de Pascal. (Lelut, L.F.) Paris, 1846.

Phil 9010.21 Amusement. (Vincent, Marvin.) Troy, 1867.

Phil 5811.8 Amusement philosophique sur le langage des bestes. (Boujeant, G.H.) Paris, 1739.

Phil 9010.01 Pamphlet box. Amusements.

Phil 9010.8 Amusements. (Testimony of Progressive Friends.) N.Y., 1856-59. 3 pam.

Phil 9010.24 Amusements and the Christian life. (Vaes, Lachlan.) Philadelphia, 1884.

Phil 585.142 Amussis vitae humanae. (Wölcker, Joannes.) Olomucii, 1698.

Htn Phil 8580.22.5* Amyraut, M. A treatise concerning religions. London, 1660.

Phil 3820.7 Amzalak, M.B. Spinoza. Lisboa, 1927.

Phil 3565.110 An, Ho-Sang. Hermann Lotzes Bedeutung für das Problem der Beziehung. Bonn, 1967.

Phil 3838.15.10 An coeur du Spinozisme. (Siwek, Paul.) Paris, 1952.

Phil 6316.15.5 An den Grenzen der Psychoanalyse. (Goerres, Albert.) München, 1968.

Phil 8520.13 An der Grenze der Philosophie. Photoreproduction. (Maier, Heinrich.) Tübingen, 1909.

Phil 1540.28 An der Grenze von Scholastik und Naturwissenschaft. 2. Aufl. (Maier, A.) Roma, 1952.

Htn Phil 3625.1.47* An die Freunde Lessings. (Mendelssohn, Moses.) Berlin, 1786.

Htn Phil 3625.1.55* An die Freunde Lessings. (Mendelssohn, Moses.) Berlin, 1786.

Htn Phil 5765.1* An homun bonus v. malus volens fiat. (Porzio, S.) Florentiae, 1551.

Phil 2138.107 An Millius veram mathematicorum axiomatum originem invenerit. (Millet, J.) Paris, 1867.

Htn Phil 5247.13.22* Anacrise, ou Parfait jugement et examen. (Huarte de San Juan, J.) Lyon, 1580.

Phil 8404.7 An anagram of ideas on art. (Deren, Maya.) N.Y., 1946.

Phil 70.20 Anais. (Congresso Nacional de Filosofia, Brazil.) São Paulo. 1-4 4v.

Phil 58.16 Anais. (Sociedade Brasileira de Filosofía.) Rio de Janeiro. 1-8,1939-1945+

Phil 342.15 Anaknisses and the a priori. (Lion, Alene.) Oxford, 1935.

Phil 801.6 Analecta historiae philosophicae. (Budeus, J.F.) Halle, 1706.

Phil 801.6.2 Analecta historiae philosophicae. 2. ed. (Budeus, J.F.) Halle, 1724.

Phil 3450.11.485 Analecta Husserliana; the yearbook of phenomenological research. Dordrecht. 1,1971+

Phil 11.44 Analele: seria acta logica. (Bucharest Universitătea.) 1,1958+ 3v.

Phil 11.18.10 Anales. (Buenos Aires. University Nacional. Instituto de Psicología.) Buenos Aires. 1-3,1935-1941 2v.

Phil 16.15 Anales. (Granada, Spain (City). Universidad. Cátedra Francisco Suárez.) Granada. 9,1969+

Phil 10.20 Anales de psicología. Buenos Aires. 1911

Phil 70.110 Anales del Seminario de Metafísica. (Madrid. Universidad. Seminario de Metafísica.) Madrid, 1967.

Phil 8654.118 L'analis del linguaggio teologico: il nome di Dio. Padova, 1969.

Phil 187.76 Analisi del concetto di realtà empirica. (Musatti, C.L.) Castello, 1926.

Phil 258.5 Analisi linguistica e metafisica. (Pieretti, Antonio.) Milano, 1968.

Phil 5253.20 Analisi quantitativa e programmi di ricerca in psicologia epsichiatria. (Nicoletti, Ivan.) Torino, 1968.

Phil 7082.128 El análisis de los sueños. (Otaola, J.R. de.) Barcelona, 195-?

Phil 193.46 Analisis del pensamiento racional. (Sanz del Rio, D.J.) Madrid, 1877.

Phil 7150.30 Analisis estadistico del suicidio. (Bula, C.A.) Rosario, 1934.

Phil 3640.723 Analitica e dialettica in Nietzsche. (DeFeo, Nicola M.) Bari, 1965.

Phil 5055.31 Analiticheskaia sposobnost' myshleniia. (Puzikov, Petr D.) Minsk, 1965.

Phil 4753.3 Analiz filosofskikh poniatii. (Chernov, Vladimir I.) Moskva, 1966.

Phil 310.655 Analiza i sinteza u okviru dijalektike Hegela i Marksa. (Zaječaranovič, Gligorije.) Beograd, 1966.

Phil 190.54 Analogia entis. (Przywara, Erich.) München, 1932.

VPhil 8656.42 Az analógia je lentősége a tudomángos es vallásos világismeret kialakulásában. (Békassy, Árpád.) Budapest, 1936.

Phil 250.1 Analogia microcosmi. (Nancel, N. de.) Paris, 1611.

Phil 6060.56 L'analogie des phenomenes physiques et psychiques et l'écriture. (Dubouchet, Jeanne.) Bruxelles, 1960.

Phil 5325.11 Analogie in volkstümlichen Denken. (Stern, L.W.) Berlin, 1893.

Phil 346.36 Analogie und Geschichtlichkeit. (Puntel, L.) Freiburg, 1969.

Phil 5520.461 Analogie und Metapher. (Soehingen, Gottlieb.) Freiburg, 1962.

Phil 8663.3.93 Analogy, or The theology of nature. (Homo (pseud.).) New Haven, 1885.

Phil 1900.41 The analogy of religion, natural and revealed, to the constitution and course of nature. (Butler, Joseph.) London, 1878.

Phil 1900.43 The analogy of religion, natural and revealed. 1st ed. (Butler, Joseph.) London, 1906.

Phil 1900.34 Analogy of religion. (Butler, Joseph.) Boston, 1809.

Phil 1900.35 Analogy of religion. (Butler, Joseph.) Cambridge, 1827.

Phil 1900.37.3.6 Analogy of religion. (Butler, Joseph.) Cincinnati, 1849.

Htn Phil 1900.30.2* Analogy of religion. (Butler, Joseph.) London, 1736.

Htn Phil 1900.30* Analogy of religion. (Butler, Joseph.) London, 1736.

Phil 1900.31 Analogy of religion. (Butler, Joseph.) London, 1740.

Phil 1900.33 Analogy of religion. (Butler, Joseph.) London, 1798.

Phil 1900.36 Analogy of religion. (Butler, Joseph.) London, 1834.

Phil 1900.37.15 Analogy of religion. (Butler, Joseph.) London, 1857.

Phil 1900.39 Analogy of religion. (Butler, Joseph.) London, 1860.

Phil 1900.40.2 Analogy of religion. (Butler, Joseph.) London, 1873.

Phil 1900.40 Analogy of religion. (Butler, Joseph.) London, 1884.

Phil 1900.37 Analogy of religion. (Butler, Joseph.) N.Y., 1839.

Phil 1900.37.3 Analogy of religion. (Butler, Joseph.) N.Y., 1843.

Phil 1900.38 Analogy of religion. (Butler, Joseph.) Philadelphia, 1857.

Htn Phil 1900.32.6* Analogy of religion. Bishop of Gloucester. (Butler, Joseph.) Boston, 1793.

Phil 1900.32A Analogy of religion. Bishop of Gloucester. (Butler, Joseph.) Boston, 1793.

Phil 1900.35.5 Analogy of religion. 2d ed. (Butler, Joseph.) Cambridge, 1830.

Phil 1900.37.3.5A Analogy of religion. 20th ed. (Butler, Joseph.) N.Y., 1848.

Phil 1900.39.5 Analogy of religion. 20th ed. (Butler, Joseph.) N.Y., 1860.

Phil 1900.28 Analogy of religion and ethical discourses. (Butler, Joseph.) Boston, 1860.

Phil 1900.25 Analogy of religion and sermons. (Butler, Joseph.) London, 1852.

Phil 5850.205 Analyse critique de la notion de validité. (Frankard, Paul.) Louvain, 1958.

Phil 1850.66 Analyse de la philosophie. (Bacon, Francis.) Leyde, 1756.

Phil 1850.110 Analyse de la philosophie du chancelier François Bacon avec sa vie. (Deleyre, A.) Leyde, 1778. 2v.

Phil 2750.29.30 Analyse de la révolution moderne. (Michaud, Humbert.) Paris, 1968?

Phil 5257.25.5 Analyse de l'esprit. (Russell, Bertrand Russell.) Paris, 1924.

Phil 5635.5.5 Die Analyse der Empfindungen. (Mach, Ernst.) Jena, 1900.

Phil 5635.5.6 Die Analyse der Empfindungen. 6. Aufl. (Mach, Ernst.) Jena, 1911.

Phil 3246.296 Analyse der formalen Strukturen des transzendentalen Wissens in Johann Gottlieb Fichtes. (Widmann, J.) München? 1961.

Phil 5649.21 Analyse der Handgeschicklichkeit. Inaug. Diss. (Weigand, E.) Würzburg, 1936.

Phil 5876.10 Analyse des formes prises par la socialité des adolescent dans le cadre de leurs loisis. (Piel, Jacques.) Bruxelles, 1968.

Phil 6028.7 Analyse des Gebarens. Inaug. Diss. (Streble, Hermann.) Berlin, 1934.

Phil 5750.3.10 Analyse des Willens. (Ach, Narziss.) Berlin, 1935.

Phil 5811.20 Analyse du comportement dit maternel chez la souris. (Beniest-Noirot, Eliane.) Paris, 1958.

Phil 5249.2.95 Analyse et critique des principes de la psychologie. (Ménard, A.) Paris, 1911.

Phil 5249.2.81 Analyse et critique des principes de la psychologie de W. James. (Ménard, A.) Paris, 1911.

Phil 186.143 Analyse et synthèse. (Lechat, Jean.) Paris, 1962.

Phil 5850.356.10 L'analyse hiérarchique. (Matalon, Benjamin.) Paris, 1965.

Phil 175.2 L'analyse métaphysique. (Alaux, J.E.) Paris, 1872.

Phil 5242.5 Analyse physiologique. (Collineau, J.C.) Paris, 1843-44. 2 pam.

Phil 5520.41.5 L'analyse psychologique de la fonction linguistique. (Delacroix, H.) Oxford, 1926.

Phil 5246.82 Analyse spectacle de la psychologie. (Gagey, Jacques.) Paris, 1970.

Phil 801.4.5 Analyses des ouvrages de philosophie. 3. ed. (Bouillier, F.) Paris, 1870.

Phil 1750.830.10 Analyses structurales et idéologies structuralistes. (Parain-Vial, Jeanne.) Toulouse, 1969.

Phil 10.51 Analysis. Oxford, Eng. 1,1933+ 10v.

Phil 165.30 Analysis. Oxford, England. Philosophy and analysis. N.Y., 1954.

Phil 5545.150 The analysis and cause of existence of memory and The analysis and cause of unconsciousness and sleep. pt.1-2. (Richards, Lysander.) n.p., 1920.

Phil 410.79 Analysis des Unendlichen im Psychischen und Physischen. (Latzin, H.) Wien, 1931.

Phil 8408.12.5 The analysis of beauty. (Hogarth, William.) Oxford, 1955.

Phil 8408.12 The analysis of beauty. (Hogarth, William.) Pittsfield, 1909.

Phil 5247.73 The analysis of behavior. (Holland, James G.) N.Y., 1961.

Phil 5240.60 Analysis of behavioral change. (Weick.) N.Y., 1968.

Phil 7082.196.5 The analysis of dreams. (Boss, Medard.) N.Y., 1958.

Phil 5465.85 The analysis of fantasy. (Henry, W.E.) N.Y., 1956.

Phil 6060.30 Analysis of handwriting. (Jacoby, Hans.) London, 1939.

Phil 5257.78 The analysis of human operant behavior. (Reese, Ellen P.) Dubuque, Iowa, 1966.

Phil 338.27 An analysis of knowing. (Hartland-Swann, John.) London, 1958.

Phil 353.17 The analysis of knowledge. (Wood, L.) London, 1940.

Phil 342.13.5A An analysis of knowledge and value. (Lewis, Clarence I.) La Salle, Ill., 1946.

Phil 193.141 An analysis of man and his philosophy. (Schleier, S.T.) St. Louis, 1938.

Phil 5257.25 The analysis of mind. (Russell, Bertrand Russell.) London, 1921.

Phil 5257.25.2 The analysis of mind. (Russell, Bertrand Russell.) London, 1924.

Phil 2138.88 Analysis of Mr. Miil's system of logic. (Stebbing, W.) London, 1875.

Phil 5585.81 Analysis of perception. (Smythies, J.R.) London, 1956.

Phil 5590.483 An analysis of personality theories. (Mehrabian, Albert.) Englewood Cliffs, N.J., 1968.

Phil 331.3 An analysis of process of conceptual cognition. (Avey, Albert E.) Cincinnati, 1915.

Phil 5635.5.9 The analysis of sensations. (Mach, Ernst.) Chicago, 1914.

Phil 5635.5.8 The analysis of sensations on the relation of the physical to the psychical. (Mach, Ernst.) N.Y., 1959.

Phil 2030.4 Analysis of the influence of natural religion on the temporal happiness of mankind. (Grote, George.) London, 1822.

Phil 5829.7 An analysis of the learning process in the snail. (Thompson, E.L.) Cambridge, 1917.

Phil 5252.7A Analysis of the phenomena of human mind. (Mill, J.) London, 1829. 2v.

Phil 325.7 Analysis of the problem of perception in British empiricism. Thesis. (Hartnack, J.) Copenhagen, 1950.

Phil 2340.10.95 An analysis of the thought of Alfred N. Whitehead and William E. Hocking concerning good and evil. Diss. (Thompson, E.J.) Chicago, 1935.

Phil 5850.251 The analysis of therapeutic groups. (Taylor, F.K.) London, 1961.

Phil 7069.32.10 Analysis of unusual experiences in healing relative to diseased minds. (Bull, Titus.) N.Y., 1932.

Phil 5255.2.12 Analystes et esprits synthétiques. (Paulhan, F.) Paris, 1902.

Phil 179.6 Analytic interest psychology. (Engle, J.S.) Baltimore, 1904.

Phil 258.15 Analytic philosophy; an historical introduction. (Gross, Barry R.) N.Y., 1970.

Phil 335.10 Analytic philosophy of knowledge. (Danto, Arthur Coleman.) Cambridge, Eng., 1968.

Phil 5258.27.15 Analytic psychology. (Stout, G.F.) London, 1902. 2v.

Phil 5258.27.12 Analytic psychology. (Stout, G.F.) N.Y., 1896. 2v.

Phil 5585.49 An analytic study of visual perceptions. Thesis. (Rogers, Anna Sophie.) Worcester, Mass., 1917.

Phil 8411.7.5 An analytical inquiry into the principles of taste. 2. ed. (Knight, R.P.) London, 1805.

Phil 8411.7.6 An analytical inquiry into the principles of taste. 3. ed. (Knight, R.P.) London, 1806.

Phil 8411.7.10 An analytical inquiry into the principles of taste. 4. ed. (Knight, R.P.) London, 1808.

Phil 165.332 Analytical philosophy. (Butler, R.J.) Oxford, 1962.

Phil 165.332.2 Analytical philosophy. 2nd series. (Butler, R.J.) Oxford, 1965.

Phil 8605.7 An analytical philosophy of religion. (Zuurdeeg, Willem.) N.Y., 1958.

Phil 6319.1.6 Analytical psychology. (Jung, C.G.) N.Y., 1916.

Phil 5262.17.2 Analytical psychology. (Witmer, L.) Boston, 1902.

Phil 6319.1.255 Analytical psychology: its theory and practice. (Jung, C.G.) London, 1968.

Phil 6311.31 Analytical psychology and the English mind. (Baynes, H.) London, 1950.

Phil 400.116 Analytical solipsism. (Todd, William.) The Hague, 1968.

Phil 5625.81 An analytical study of the conditioned knee-jerk. (Wendt, George R.) N.Y., 1930.

Phil 5170.8 Analytical syllogistics. (Howard, D.T.) Evanston, 1946.

Phil 3484.27 L'analytique transcendentale de Kant. (Coninck, Antoine de.) Louvain, 1955-

Phil 346.19 Analytische Erkenntnistheorie. (Pap, Arthur.) Wien, 1955.

Phil 6319.1.190   Analytische Psychologie en Godsdienst. (Hostie, Raymond.) Utrecht, 1954.

Phil 6319.1.11   Analytische Psychologie und Erziehung. (Jung, C.G.) Heidelberg, 1926.

Phil 5411.6   Analytische Untersuchungen über die Psychologie des Hasses und der Versöhnung. (Pfister, Oskar.) Leipzig, 1910.

Phil 3552.258   Die analytische Urteilslehre Leibnizens. Diss. (Jasinowski, B.) Wien, 1918.

Phil 960.16   Ánanda Achárya. Brahmadarsanam...introduction to the study of Hindu philosophy. London, 1917.

Phil 5210.5   Anan'ev, B.G. Ocherki po istorii russkoi psikhologii XVII i XIX v. Moskva, 1947.

Phil 5585.170   Anan'ev, B.G. Psikhologiia chuvstvennogo poznaniia. Moskva, 1960.

Phil 5585.170.5   Anan'ev, B.G. Psychologie der sinnlichen Erkenntnis. Berlin, 1963.

Phil 5640.135   Anan'ev, B.G. Teoriia oshchushchenii. Leningrad, 1961.
Phil 585.305   Anan'ev, Boris G. Chelovek kak predmet poznaniia. Leningrad, 1968.

Phil 5585.266   Anan'ev, Boris G. Individual'noe razvitie cheloveka i konstantnost' vospriiatiia. Moskva, 1968.

Phil 5240.42.5   Ananiew, B.G. Hamptaufgaben der sowjetischen psychologischen Wissenschaft. Berlin, 1952.

Phil 1710.4   Die Anarchie der philosophischen Systeme. (Kröner, Franz.) Leipzig, 1929.

Phil 5400.164   The anarchy of feeling. (Schneiders, A.A.) N.Y., 1963.
Phil 5850.111   Anastasi, A. Fields of applied psychology. N.Y., 1964.
Phil 5240.35.2   Anastasi, Anne. Differential psychology. N.Y., 1949.
Phil 5240.35.3   Anastasi, Anne. Differential psychology. N.Y., 1956.
Phil 5240.35   Anastasi, Anne. Differential psychology. NY., 1937.
Phil 4210.146   Anastasia, M. I principii della politica nella filosofia di Antonio Rosmini. Osimo, 1934.

Phil 8636.7   The anastasis of the dead. (Lewis, Jason.) Boston, 1860.
Phil 6128.1   Anatomia dei centri nervosi. (Scervini, P.) Napoli, 1892.
Phil 5821.10   Anatomie comparée du système nerveux. (Leuret, F.) Paris, 1839.

Phil 8419.36   Anatomie de l'âme; essai de psych-esthétique. (Sébag, Henri.) Paris, 1952. 3v.

Phil 5813.4   Anatomie des systèmes nerveux des animaux. pt.1-2. Atlas. (Desmoulins, A.) Paris, 1825. 3v.

Phil 6116.10   Anatomie du système nerveux de l'homme. (Gehuchten, Arthur van.) Louvain, 1900. 2v.

Phil 5548.103.5   The anatomy of achievement motivation. (Heckhausen, H.) N.Y., 1967.

Phil 3450.19.395   The anatomy of disillusion; Martin Heideggers notion of truth. (Macomber, William B.) Evanston, 1967.

Phil 9245.59   The anatomy of happiness. (Gumpert, M.) N.Y., 1951.
Phil 5047.13   The anatomy of knowledge. (Hooper, C.E.) London, 1906.
Phil 349.58   The anatomy of knowledge. (Study Group on the Unity of Knowledge.) Amherst, 1969.

Phil 2045.142   The anatomy of Leviathan. (McNeilly, F.S.) London, 1968.
Phil 9430.10.10   The anatomy of negation. (Saltus, Edgar.) N.Y., 1925?
Phil 6980.416   The anatomy of psychotherapy. (Lennard, H.L.) N.Y., 1960.

Htn   Phil 7080.29*   The anatomy of sleep. (Binns, E.) London, 1842.
Phil 9530.58   The anatomy of success. (Darvas, Nicolas.) Indianapolis, 1966.

Phil 7150.5   Anatomy of suicide. (Winslow, F.) London, 1840.

Htn   Phil 6100.12*   The anatomy of the brain. (Bell, C.) London, 1802.
Phil 6128.5   The anatomy of the brain. (Spurzheim, J.K.) London, 1826.
Phil 8582.45.3   The anatomy of truth. 3. ed. (Capron, F.H.) London, 1927.
Phil 8880.66   An anatomy of values; problems of personal and social choice. (Fried, Charles.) Cambridge, 1970.

Phil 8110.9   Anceschi, L. L'estetica dell'empirismo inglese. Bologna, 1959.

Phil 8080.6   Anceschi, Luciano. Autonomia ed eteronomia dell'arte. Firenze, 1936.

Phil 8401.30   Anceschi, Luciano. Autonomia ed eteronomia dell'arte. 2. ed. Firenze, 1959.

Phil 8080.9   Anceschi, Luciano. D. Hume e i presupposti empiristici della estetica kantiana. Milano, 1956.

Phil 8401.30.5   Anceschi, Luciano. Progetto di una sistematica dell'arte. Milano, 1962.

Phil 8401.30.7   Anceschi, Luciano. Progetto di una sistematica dell'arte. 2. ed. Milano, 1966.

Phil 3482.11   Anceschi, T. I presupposti storici e teorici. n.p., 1955.
Phil 197.68   Anchors to windward. (White, S.E.) N.Y., 1943.
Phil 8950.12   Anciaux, L. Le dynamisme de la morale chrétienne. Gembloux, 1968-69.

Phil 817.10   L'ancienne et la nouvelle philosophie. (Roberty, E. de.) Paris, 1887.

Phil 8591.81   Ancient beliefs and modern superstitions. (Lings, Martin.) London, 1965.

Phil 8591.83   Ancient beliefs and modern superstitions. 1. ed. (Lings, Martin.) London, 1965.

Phil 8637.15   Ancient beliefs in the immortality of the soul. (Moore, Clifford Herschel.) N.Y., 1931.

Phil 1123.4   Ancient European philosophy...Greek. (Snider, D.J.) St. Louis, Mo., 1903.

Phil 1135.164   Ancient formal logic. (Bochenski, I.M.) Amsterdam, 1951.
Phil 176.41   Ancient metaphysics. v.1-6. (Monboddo, James Barnet.) Edinburgh, 1779-99. 7v.

Phil 8591.8.5   Ancient religion and modern thought. 2. ed. (Lilly, W.S.) London, 1885.

Phil 1133.54   Ancient Western philosophy: the Hellenic emergence. (McLean, George F.) N.Y., 1971.

Phil 978.6.15   The ancient wisdom. (Besant, Annie.) London, 1897.
Phil 175.6.6   Ancillon, F. Essai sur la science. Paris, 1830.
Phil 175.6   Ancillon, F. Essais de philosophie. Paris, 1832. 4v.
Phil 175.6.2   Ancillon, F. Essais de philosophie. Paris, 1832. 4v.
Phil 175.6.20   Ancillon, F. Mélanges de littérature et de philosophie. Paris, 1809. 2v.

Phil 175.6.15   Ancillon, F. Pensées sur l'homme, ses rapports. Berlin, 1829. 2v.

Phil 175.6.9   Ancillon, F. Über Glauben und Wissen in der Philosophie. Berlin, 1824.

Phil 8875.7   Ancillon, J.P.F. Zur Vermittlung der Extreme. Berlin, 1831-38. 2v.

Phil 8655.2   Ancillon, L.F. Judicium de judiciis. Berolini, 1792.
Phil 4635.9.80   Ancker, E. Torgny Segerstedt, 1876-1945. Stockholm, 1962.
Phil 1750.330.5   Ancora sull'esistenzialismo. (Paci, Enzo.) Torino, 1956.
Phil 9340.5   Ancourt, Abbé d'. The lady's preceptor. London, 1743.
Phil 5246.78   And og sjael; symboler og symbolik. v.1-2. (Gernhammer, Vilhelm.) Silkeborg, 1968.

Phil 8626.24   And the life everlasting. (Baillie, John.) N.Y., 1933.
Phil 7069.19.225   Andatrú vorra tíma. (Vojd, Karl.) Reykjavik, 1919.
Phil 4520.8.40   Andatrúin. (Bjarnason, Ágúst.) Reykjavík, 1905.
Phil 7069.10.3   Andatrúin. (Gook, Arthur.) Akureyri, n.d.
Phil 7069.24.33   Andatrúin. (Sigurgeirsson, Oddur.) Reykjavik, 1924.

Phil 7069.18.98   Andatrúin afhjúpud (Gook, Arthur.) Akureyri, 1918.
Phil 4520.8.48   "Andatrúin" krufin. (Bjarnason, Ágúst.) Reykjavik, 1906.
Phil 7069.21.70   Anden. (Danils, H.) Stockholm, 1921.
Phil 3850.68   Der andere Zug. (Struve, Wolfgang.) Salzburg, 1969.
Phil 310.738   Anders, Georg. Wider die Fälscher der Geschichte. München, 1958.

Phil 1750.460   Anders, Günther. Die Antiquiertheit des Menschen. München, 1956.

Phil 5190.90   Andersen, Kenneth E. Persuasion: theory and practice. Boston, 1971.

Phil 5270.36   Anderson, Barry F. The psychology experiment. 2d ed. Belmont, Calif., 1971.

Phil 9160.6   Anderson, C. Book for parents. The genius and design of the domestic constitution. Boston, 1834.

Phil 6310.12   Anderson, C.M. Beyond Freud. London, 1958.
Phil 3850.27.225   Anderson, E. Albert Schweitzer's of friendship. 1st ed. N.Y., 1964.

Phil 3850.27.128   Anderson, E. The world of Albert Schweitzer. N.Y., 1955.
Phil 1850.140   Anderson, Fulton H. Francis Bacon. Los Angeles, 1962.
Phil 1850.139   Anderson, Fulton H. The philosophy of Francis Bacon. Chicago, 1948.

Phil 5627.270.5   Anderson, George Christian. Your religion: neurotic or healthy? 1st ed. Garden City, 1970.

Phil 8580.3.25   Anderson, George P. Who wrote "Ethan Allen's Bible"? n.p., 1937.

Phil 5627.138   Anderson, J.B. Applied religious psychology. Boston, 1919.

Phil 331.9   Anderson, J.F. The bond of being. St. Louis, 1949.
Phil 331.9.5   Anderson, J.F. Reflections on the analogy of being. The Hague, 1967.

Phil 8655.3   Anderson, J.H. God or no God. Osceola, Neb., 1889.
Phil 1845.15   Anderson, John. Studies in empirical philosophy. Sydney, 1962.

Phil 8950.4   Anderson, L.D. The business of living. N.Y., 1923.
Phil 175.40   Anderson, L.F. God and the cosmic order. N.Y., 1939.
Phil 175.40.5   Anderson, L.F. Logic and the cosmic order. N.Y., 1939.
Phil 5240.37   Anderson, L.F. Psychology and the cosmic order. n.p., 1939.

Phil 5040.16   Anderson, Louis. Das logische; seine Gesetze und Kategorien. Leipzig, 1929.

Phil 9075.31   Anderson, Louis F. Die Seele und das Gewissens. Leipzig, 1929.

Phil 2070.156   Anderson, Luke. The concept of truth in the philosophy of William James. Rome, 1965.

Phil 1020.11   Anderson, M.B. Arabian philosophy. n.p., n.d.
Phil 9500.3   Anderson, Maggie P. Sick-room thoughts and gleanings. Saint John, N.B., 1897.

Phil 1800.3A   Anderson, P.P. Philosophy in America. N.Y., 1939.
Phil 1800.3.5   Anderson, P.P. Platonism in the Midwest. Philadelphia, 1963.

Phil 8690.6   Anderson, Paul R. Science in defense of liberal religion. N.Y., 1933.

Phil 5520.480.5   Anderson, Richard Chase. Readings in the psychology of cognition. N.Y., 1965.

Phil 2050.261   Anderson, Robert Fendel. Hume's first principles. Lincoln, 1966.

Phil 1105.1   Anderson, W. Philosophy of ancient Greece. Edinburgh, 1791.

Phil 3480.77   En Andeskadares drömmar i ljusetay metafysikens drömmar. (Kant, Immanuel.) Lund, 1921. 10v.

Phil 178.2   Andeutung eines Systems speculativer Philosophie. (Daumer, G.F.) Nürnberg, 1831.

Phil 5828.9   Andeutungen aus dem Seelenleben der Thiere. (Schmarda, L.K.) Wien, 1846.

Htn   Phil 3801.447*   Andeutungen über Glauben und Wissen. (Hast, Johann.) Münster, 1842.

Phil 3640.158   Andler, Charles. Nietzsche, sa vie et sa pensée. Paris, 1920-31. 6v.

Phil 3640.158.4   Andler, Charles. Nietzsche, sa vie et sa pensée. Paris, 1958. 3v.

Phil 3640.158.3   Andler, Charles. Nietzsche, sa vie et sa pensée. 3. éd. Paris, 1922.

Phil 3640.158.5   Andler, Charles. Nietzsche und Jakob Burckhardt. Basel, 1926.

Phil 175.58   Ando, Takatuna. Metaphysics. Hague, 1963.
Phil 4899.255.80   Ando Sëëki, filosof, materialist XVIII veka. (Radul'-Zatulovskii, Iakov B.) Moskva, 1961.

Phil 3850.54.80   Andorn, Hans. Salomon Ludwig Steinheims "Offenbarung nach dem Lehrbegriff der Synagoge". Berlin, 1930.

Phil 4450.6   Andrade, A.A. de. Filósofos portugueses do séc. XVIII. v.1-3. Lisboa, 1957-

Phil 310.774   Andrade, Almir de. Ensaio critico sôbre os fundamentos da filosofia dialética. Rio de Janeiro, 1971.

Phil 4482.1.90   Andrade, Antonio Alberto de. Vernei a filosofia portuguesa. Braga, 1946.

Phil 4482.1.100   Andrade, António Alberto de. Vernei e a cultura do seu tempo. Coimbra, 1966.

Phil 525.215   Andrae, Tor. Islamische Mystiker. Stuttgart, 1960.
Phil 3085.5.35   Andre, H. Annäherung durch Abstand. Salzburg, 1957.
Phil 3085.5.40   Andre, H. Natur und Mysterium. Einsiedeln, 1959.
Phil 3085.5.31   Andre, H. Wunderbare Wirklichkeit. Salzburg, 1955.
Phil 2400.1   André, Y.M. Documents...l'histoire...philosophie. Caen, 1844-56. 2v.

Phil 2733.80   André, Y.M. La vie du R.P. Malebranche, Bibliothèque Oratorienne. Paris, 1886.

Phil 8401.14   André, Yves. Essai sur le beau. Amsterdam, 1760.
Phil 2445.3.1   André, Yves. Oeuvres. Paris, 1766-67. 4v.
Phil 2445.3.3   André, Yves. Oeuvres philosophiques. Paris, 1843.
Phil 8401.14.5   André Yves. Essai su le beau. Paris, 1924.
Phil 2520.80   Andrea, T. Brevis replicatia...notis Cartesii. Amstelodami, 1653.

Phil 4060.5.90   Andrea Angiulli e l'eredità dell'800. (Cordaro, Philip.) Castanissetta, 1969.

Phil 8950.1   Andreae, J.V. Civis Christianus. Lipsiae, 1706.
Phil 5240.58.2   Andreas, Burton G. Experimental psychology. 2. ed. N.Y., 1972.

Phil 7069.67.50   Andreas, Peter. Between heaven and earth, adventures in the search of the nature of man. Toronto, 1967.

Phil 2805.245   Andreas, Peter. Pascal. Strasbourg, 1946.
Phil 7069.67.50.2   Andreas, Peter. Was niemand glauben will. Berlin, 1967.
Phil 310.30   Andreas, Theodor. Zur Widerlegung des dialektische und historische Materialismus. 5. Aufl. n.p., 1954.

Phil 7082.144   Andreas-Friedrich, Ruth. Ursprung und Sinn der Träume. Zürich, 1958.

Phil 4630.3.80   Andreas Rydelius etiska åkädning. (Almquist, Karl Gustaf.) Lund, 1955.

Phil 3640.207   Andreas-Salomé, L. Friedrich Nietzsche in seinen Werken. Dresden, 1924?

Phil 6315.2.118   Andreas-Salomé, L. Mein Dank an Freud; offener Brief an S. Freud zu seinem 75. Geburtstag. Wien, 1931.

Phil 9340.12   Andreas-Salomé, Lou. Die Erotik. Frankfurt, 1910.

Phil 5040.15   Andreasi, A. Arte logica. Verona, 1882.

Phil 505.6   Andreev, Edvard P. Prostranstvo mikromira. Moskva, 1969.

Phil 310.305   Andreev, I.D. Dialekticheskii materializm. Moskva, 1960.

Phil 310.180   Andreev, I.D. Osnovnye zakony i kategorii materialisticheskoi dialektiki. Moskva, 1959.

Phil 331.20   Andreev, Ivan D. Osnovy teorii poznaniia. Moskva, 1959.

Phil 331.20.5   Andreev, Ivan D. Puti i trudnosti poznaniia. Moskva, 1968.

Phil 310.638   Andreev, Kosta. Doktor Petur Genov za marksistkata filosofiia i bolshevizma. Sofiia, 1964.

Phil 4822.8   Andreev, Kosta. Kritikata na Dimitur Blagoev na neokantianstvoto v Bulgariia po vuprosite na filosofiiata. Sofiia, 1968.

Phil 4120.4.100   Andreola, A. Giovanni Gentile a la sua scuola. Milano, 1951.

Phil 3085.5.80   Andre's Philosophie des Lebens. (Sieverth, Gustav.) Salzburg, 1959.

Phil 8625.3   Andresen, Karl. Die Unsterblichkeitsfrage. Leipzig, 1906.

Phil 8625.3.15   Andresen, Karl. Wir werden wieder geboren. Hamburg, 1894.

X Cg   Phil 7082.50   Andrésson, Fridrik. Draumur Fridriks Andréssonar. Reykjavík, 1904. (Changed to XM 1329)

Phil 2280.8.90   Andrew Seth Pringle-Pattison, 1856-1931. (Baillie, J.B.) London, 1931.

Phil 9010.29   Andrews, Charles W. Religious novels; an argument against their use. 2d ed. N.Y., 1856.

Phil 5400.42   Andrews, Cyril B. Life, emotion, and intellect. London, 1913.

Phil 5066.245   Andrews, Peter Bruce. A transfinite type theory with type variables. Amsterdam, 1965.

Phil 175.21   Andrews, S.P. Basic outlines of universology. N.Y., 1872.

Phil 5240.43   Andrews, T.G. Methods of psychology. N.Y., 1948.

Phil 8580.6   Andrews, W.S. A treatise upon theological subjects. Cambridge, 1829.

Phil 5875.100   Andriessen, H. De groei van het geweten. Zeist, 1965.

Phil 585.245   Andriessen, J.H. Naar omega. Conceptie van nieuw denken. Den Haag, 1967.

Phil 2610.84   Andrieux, L. Pierre Gassendi. Thèse. Paris, 1927.

Phil 585.410   Der androgyne Mensch. (Nornengast, Urda.) Bellnhausen, 1970.

Phil 8875.36   Androutsos, Chrestos. Systèma êthikês. Athênai, 1925.

Phil 9245.52   Andrus, F.N. The evolution of happiness. Boston, 1936.

Phil 809.10   Aneignung und Polemik. (Jaspers, Karl.) München, 1968.

Phil 192.18   Anekdota. (Ruge, Arnold.) Zürich, 1843. 2v.

Phil 1112.5   Die Anfänge der europäischen Philosophie. (Howald, E.) München, 1925.

Phil 5871.35   Die Anfänge der Geschwisterbeziehung. (Savioz, Esther.) Bern, 1968.

Phil 600.27   Die Anfänge des französischen Positivismus. Teil I. (Schinz, Max.) Strassburg, 1914.

Phil 6320.30   Die Anfänge des menschlichen Seelenlebens. (Kruse, Friedrich.) Stuttgart, 1969.

Phil 2050.66   Anfänge und Entwicklung der Religion. (Hume, David.) Leipzig, 1909.

Phil 3246.175   Die Anfänge von Fichtes Staatsphilosophie. (Strecker, Reinhard.) Leipzig, 1916.

Phil 3246.175.2   Die Anfänge von Fichtes Staatsphilosophie. (Strecker, Reinhard.) Leipzig, 1917.

Phil 1112.10   Anfanchisches Fragen; Studien zur Frühen griechischen Philosophie. (Hoelscher, Vvo.) Göttingen, 1968.

Phil 3425.624   Der Anfang der Erkenntnis. Kritische Analyse des ersten Kapitels der Hegelschen Logik. (Erdei, László.) Budapest, 1964.

Phil 192.35   Der Anfang der Philosophie. (Reiff, J.F.) Stuttgart, 1840.

Phil 8612.33.5   Anfang und Ende. (Bürgel, B.H.) Berlin, 1947.

Phil 176.95   Anfangsgründe der Philosophie. (Bauch, Bruno.) Gotha, 1920.

Phil 2275.50.10   Anfangsgründe der Philosophie über die menschliche Seele. (Stewart, D.) Berlin, 1794. 2v.

Phil 176.26.15   Angangsgründe der speculaterien Philosophie. (Bouterwek, Friedrich.) Bruxelles, 1968.

Phil 1504.7   Der angebliche Exzessive Realismus Dons Scotus. v.7, pt.1. (Minges, P.) Münster, 1908.

Phil 1190.5.5   Der angebliche Heraklitismus des Skeptikers. (Pappenheim, E.) Berlin, 1889.

Phil 3489.14   Der angebliche Mysticismus Kants. (Hoar, Robert.) Brugg, 1895.

Phil 3270.12.95   Angehelli, Ignacio. Studies on Gottlob Frege and Traditional philosophy. Dordrecht, 1967.

Phil 5241.174   Angel in armor; a post Freudian perspective on the nature of man. (Becker, Ernest.) N.Y., 1969.

Phil 7068.74.10   Angel voices from the spirit world. (Lawrence, Jas.) Cleveland, 1874.

Phil 7054.185   Angelic revelations concerning the origin, ultimation and destiny of the human spirit. (Oxley, William.) Manchester, 1875-83. 4v.

Phil 4070.1.80   Angelini, A. Ausonio Franchi. Roma, 1897.

Phil 4170.7.90   Angelini, A. Di Terenzio Mamiani filosofo. Roma, 1885. 2v.

Phil 9340.8   Angell, Frances. Compete Philadelphia, 1935.

Phil 5238.1   Angell, J.R. Chapters from modern psychology, 1911. London, 1912.

Phil 5240.6.9   Angell, J.R. An introduction to psychology. N.Y., 1918.

Phil 5300.4   Angell, J.R. A preliminary study...partial tones...of sound. Chicago, 1902.

Phil 5240.5.30   Angell, J.R. Psychology. 2. ed. N.Y., 1905.

Phil 5240.6.2   Angell, J.R. Psychology. 4. ed. N.Y., 1908.

Phil 5240.6.15   Angell, J.R. The relations of structural and functional psychology to philosophy. Chicago, 1903.

Phil 9513.9   Angell, Robert Cooley. Free society and moral crisis. Ann Arbor, 1958.

Phil 8401.36   Angelov, Valentin. Groznoto. Sofiia, 1964.

Phil 8430.8   Angels' wings. (Carpenter, Edward.) London, 1898.

Phil 5643.2   Angelucci, A. Untersuchungen über die Sehthätigkeit. Giessen, 1890.

Phil 5412.5   Anger; its religious and moral significance. (Stratton, G.M.) N.Y., 1923.

Phil 5412.20   Anger. (Madow, Leo.) N.Y., 1972.

Phil 9513.50   Angers, France (Diocese). Conferences ecclesiastiques du Diocese d'Angers. Angers, 1737.

Phil 5850.188   Angewandte Psychologie. (Erismann, T.) Berlin, 1916.

Phil 5850.347   Angewandte Psychologie. (Stern, Louis W.) n.p., 1903. 2 pam.

Phil 5850.335   Angewandte Psychologie in der Schweiz. (Schweizerische Stiftung für Angewandte Psychologie.) Bern, 1959.

Phil 600.2   Angiuli, A. La filosofia e la ricerca positiva. Napoli, 1869.

Phil 4060.5.30   Angiulli, A. La filosofia e la scuola. Napoli, 1888.

Phil 1801.11   Angle-amerikanskaia burzhuaznaia filosofiia epokhi imperializmo. (Bogomolov, A.S.) Moskva, 1964.

Phil 331.10   Anglès D'Auriac. Essai de philosophie générale. 1. ed. Paris, 1954. 2v.

Htn   Phil 2150.4.30*   Angli pro populo anglicano defensio. (Milton, Joannis.) Londini, 1651.

Phil 8950.5   Anglican and International Christian Moral Science Association. Science and the gospel. London, 1870.

Phil 8550.342.10   Anglican moods of the eighteenth century. (Curtis, Lewis P.) Hamden, Conn., 1966.

Phil 5401.32   L'angoisse. (Lyon, Josette.) Paris, 1957.

Phil 5421.10.30   Angoisse (sikinti). (Özcan, Mehmed Tevfik.) Ankara, 1966.

Phil 2805.110.5   L'angoisse de Pascal, suivi d'une étude sur les deux maisons de Pascal à Clermont-Ferrand. (Barrès, Maurice.) Paris, 1923.

Phil 2805.110   L'angoisse de Pascal. (Barrès, Maurice.) Paris, 1918.

Phil 5400.94   L'angoisse et l'émotion. (Lacroze, R.) Paris, 1938.

Phil 5400.94.5   L'angoisse et l'émotion. (Lacroze, R.) Paris, 1938.

Phil 5401.56   Angst; psychische und somatische Aspekte. Bern, 1967.

Phil 1750.769   Angst und Hoffnung in unserer Zeit. (Darmstaedter Gespräch, 8th, Darmstadt.) Darmstadt, 1965.

Phil 5401.28   Angst und Lachen. (Leroy, Paul.) Wien, 1954.

Phil 5401.22   Angst und Mut. (Wandruszka von Wanstetten, M.W.) Stuttgart, 1950.

Phil 5401.50   Angst und Schreck in klinisch psychologischer und sozialmedizinischer Sicht. (Panse, Friedrich.) Stuttgart, 1952.

Phil 5873.4   Die Angst unserer Kinder. (Zulliger, Hans.) Frankfurt, 1969.

Phil 5401.30   Die Angstneurose. (Bitter, Wilhelm.) Bern, 1948.

Phil 5590.6   Angyal, Andras. Foundations for a science of personality. N.Y., 1941.

Phil 6310.21   Angyal, András. Neurosis and treatment. N.Y., 1965.

Htn   Phil 3480.19.7*   Anhang zu den Zerstreuten Aufsatzen. (Kant, Immanuel.) Frankfurt, 1794.

Phil 8626.6.2.5   Anhang zur zweiten Auflage der Athanasia. (Bolzano, B.) Sulzbach, 1838.

Phil 175.27   Anhuth, R.O. Das wahnsinnige Bewusstsein. Halle, 1877.

Phil 960.252   Anikeev, Nikolai P. O materialisticheskikh traditsiiakh v indiiskoi filosofii. Moskva, 1965.

Phil 4870.16   Anikeev, Nikolai Petrovich. Modern ideological struggle for the ancient philosophical heritage of India. Calcutta, 1969.

Phil 5240.40   Anile, Antonio. La salute del pensiero "I libro d'oro". Bari, 1922.

Phil 4265.4.81   L'anima; saggi e guidizi. Maggio 1911. G. Vailati. Firenze, 1911.

Phil 4170.13   Anima brutorum secundum sanioris. (Monti, G.F.) Neapoli, 1742.

Phil 5402.3.15   L'anima delle cose. (Mantegazza, P.) Torino, 1921.

Phil 1714.3   L'anima dell'umanesimo e del rinascimento. (Olgiati, F.) Milano, 1924.

Phil 1140.10   Anima e intelletto. (Movia, Giancarlo.) Padova, 1968.

Phil 1719.3   L'anima moderna, da Lessing a Nietzsche. (Tonelli, L.) Milano, 1925.

Phil 665.39   L'anima nel mondo greco e romano nel medio evo e nella filosofia moderna. (Pietropaolo, F.) Roma, 1898.

Phil 8627.15   L'anima umana non muore. (Cojazzi, Antonio.) Torino, 1944.

Phil 6319.1.192   Anima und Animus in der Psychologie C.G. Jung. (Rath, Paul.) Winterthur, 1954.

Phil 3801.436   Animadversiones in constructionem materiae Schellingianam. Pt.1-4. (Grubbe, Samuel.) Upsaliae, 1818.

Htn   Phil 2115.140*   Animadversions on a late book entituled The reasonableness of Christianity. Oxford, 1697.

Phil 5828.20   Animal behavior. (Scott, J.P.) Garden City, 1963.

Phil 5822.1.15   Animal behaviour. (Morgan, C.L.) London, 1900.

Phil 5247.47A   Animal drive and the learning process. (Holt, Edwin B.) N.Y., 1931.

Phil 5832.7.5   Animal education; an experimental study on the psychological development of the white rat. (Watson, John B.) Chicago, 1903.

Phil 2280.5.30   Animal faith and spiritual life. (Santayana, George.) N.Y., 1967.

Phil 7060.92.19   Animal ghosts. (O'Donnell, Elliot.) London, 1913.

Phil 5827.1.13   Animal intelligence. (Romanes, G.J.) N.Y., 1888.

Phil 6671.7.5   Animal magnetism. (Binet, A.) N.Y., 1888.

Phil 6677.2   Animal magnetism. (Heidenhain, R.P.H.) London, 1880.

Phil 6681.9.2   Animal magnetism. (Lee, Edwin.) London, 1849.

Phil 6681.5   Animal magnetism. (Leger, J.) N.Y., 1846.

Phil 6692.1   Animal magnetism. (Ware, J.) n.p., 1851.

Phil 6681.9   Animal magnetism. 3d ed. (Lee, Edwin.) London, 1843. 2 pam.

Phil 5822.1.20   The animal mind. (Morgan, C.L.) N.Y., 1930.

Phil 5832.8   The animal mind. (Washburn, M.F.) N.Y., 1908.

Phil 5832.8.5   The animal mind. 2. ed. (Washburn, M.F.) N.Y., 1917.

Phil 5832.8.7   The animal mind. 3. ed. (Washburn, M.F.) N.Y., 1926.

Phil 5832.13.10   Animal motivation. (Warden, C.J.) N.Y., 1931.

Phil 5835.10   Animal social psychology. (Zajonc, Robert Boleslaw.) N.Y., 1969.

Phil 3850.27.55   The animal world of Albert Schweitzer. (Schweitzer, A.) Boston, 1974.

Phil 5817.2   Animals, not automata. (Hazard, R.G.) N.Y., 1875.

Phil 299.15   The animate and the inanimate. (Sidis, W.G.) Boston, 1925.

Phil 5812.3   Animaux raisonment. (Chesnel, A.) Paris, 1845.

Phil 1200.38   Animi perturbationes ex mente potissimum. (Reichard, Elias C.) Magdeburgi, 1764.

Phil 7060.103.7   Animisme et spiritisme. (Aksakov, Aleksandr N.) Paris, 1895.

Phil 3915.83   L'animismo di Guglielmo Wundt. (Cesca, Giovanni.) n.p., 1891.

Phil 7060.103.5   Animismus und spiritismus...als Entgegnung auf Dr. Ed. V. Hartmann's Werk "Der Spiritismus". (Aksakov, Aleksandr N.) Leipzig, 1890.

Phil 5841.20.8   Animus und Anima. (Jung, Emma.) N.Y., 1957.

Phil 5841.20.5   Animus und Anima. (Jung, Emma.) Zürich, 1967.

Phil 7069.19.5   Animus und Spsiritisium. (Aksakov, A.N.) Leipzig 1919. 2v.

Phil 4803.334.85   Aniol Dovgird - myslitel' epokhi Prosveshcheniia. (Doroshevich, Engel's Konstantinovich.) Minsk, 1967.

Phil 4803.334.80   Aniol Dowgird, filozof nieznany. (Kaczmarek, Stefan.) Poznań, 1963.

Phil 4803.334.81   Aniol Dowgird, filozof nieznany. (Kaczmarek, Stefan.) Warszawa, 1965.

Phil 1540.7.2   Les anis de Dieu au quatorzième siècle. Thèse. (Jundt, A.) Strasbourg, 1879.

Phil 8980.131.5   Anisimov, Sergei F. Nravstvennyi progressi religiia. Moskva, 1965.

Phil 735.284   Anisimov, Sergei F. Tseunoi real'nye i mnimye. Moskva, 1970.

Phil 525.75   Anker-Larsen, Johannes. With the door open, my experience. N.Y., 1931.

Phil 5413.14   Ankles, T.M. A study of jealousy as differentiated from envy. Boston, 1939.

Phil 3585.1.40   Anlage zur Architectonic oder Theorie. (Lambert, Johann Heinrich.) Riga, 1771. 2v.

Phil 6124.1   Anleitung beim Studium des Baues der nervösen Centralorgane. (Obersteiner, H.) Leipzig, 1888.

Phil 75.6   Anleitung der Literatur der Philosophie. (Hiszmann, M.) Göttingen, 1778.

Phil 6689.11   Anleitung zur experimentellen Untersuchung des Hypnotismus. (Tamburini, A.) Wiesbaden, 1882-85.

Phil 3778.38   Anleitung zur Kenntniss und Beurtheilung der Philosophie in ihren sämmtlichen Lehrgebäuden. (Reinhold, K.L.) Wien, 1805.

Phil 4515.33   Anmärkningar om helveteslären. 2. uppl. (Boström, C.J.) Upsala, 1864.

Phil 3428.159   Anmärkningar vid Herbarts filosofiska system. (Borelius, J.J.) Kalmar, 1866.

Phil 348.4.3   Anmerkungen zur Grundwissenschaft. 2. Aufl. (Rehmke, J.) Leipzig, 1925.

Phil 3085.5.35   Annäherung durch Abstand. (Andre, H.) Salzburg, 1957.

Phil 10.41   Annalen der critische Philosophie. Assen. 1-29,1931-1959 21v.

Phil 10.27   Annalen der Philosophie. Leipzig. 1-8,1919-1929 8v.

Phil 10.100   Annalen der Philosophie und der philosophischen Geistes von einer Gesellschaft gelehrter Männer. Reprinted 1970. Halle. 1-3,1795-1797// 2v.

Phil 51.1   Annales. (Louvain. Université. Institute Supériéuse de Philosophie.) Louvain. 1-5,1912-1924 5v.

Phil 21.18   Annales. (Lublin, Poland. Universytitu Marii Curie.) Skodowskiej. 3,1948+ 5v.

NEDL Phil 10.3   Annales de philosophie chrétienne. Paris. 1830-1913 160v.

NEDL Phil 10.3.5   Annales de philosophie chrétienne. Paris. 1884-1902

Phil 10.32   Annales des sciences psychiques. Paris. 1-7,1891-1897 7v.

Phil 10.38   Annales du magnetisme animal. Paris. 1814-1817 4v.

NEDL Phil 10.2   Annales medico-psychologiques. Paris. 1843-1929 94v.

Phil 10.2   Annales medico-psychologiques. Paris. 1930+ 73v.

NEDL Phil 10.2.5   Annales medico-psychologiques. Table 1-2. Paris. 1-2,1843-1878

Phil 10.31   Annali dello spiritismo in Italia; rivista psicologica. Torino. 1-35,1864-1898 21v.

Phil 4210.215   Annali di Antonio Rosmini Serbati. (Radice, Gianfranco.) Milano, 1967. 2v.

Phil 10.99   Annali di psicologia. Milan. 1,1968+

Phil 10.11   Annals of phrenology. Boston. 1-2,1835-1836 2v.

Phil 10.4.5   L'année philosophique, études critiques. Paris. 1-2,1867-1868 2v.

Phil 10.4   L'année philosophique. Paris. 1-24,1890-1913 24v.

Phil 10.18   L'année psychologique. Paris. 1894+ 13v.

Phil 2520.167   Les années d'apprentissage de Descartes (1596-1628). (Sirven, J.) Albi, 1928.

Phil 2520.167.2   Les années d'apprentissage de Descartes (1596-1628). v.1-2. Thèse. (Sirven, J.) Albi, 1928.

Phil 6980.45   Annell, A.L. Elementär barrpsykiatri. Stockholm, 1958.

Phil 8580.13   Annet, Peter. A collection of the tracts of a certain free thinker. London, 1739-1749.

Phil 5535.40   Annett, John. Feedback and human behavior. Baltimore, 1969.

Phil 974.4   Annie Besant, servant of humanity. (New India, Madras.) Madras, 1924.

Phil 974.4.30   Annie Besant...and the changing world. (Bhagavan Das.) Adyar, 1934.

X Cg   Phil 978.6.86   Annie Besant: an autobiography. (Besant, Annie.) London, 1908.

Phil 978.6.97   Annie Besant. 2d ed. (Prakasa, Sri.) Bombay, 1954.

Phil 4210.135.10   Anniversario della festa secolare per Antonio Rosmini. (Bettanini, A.) n.p., 1901.

Htn   Phil 2520.166*   Annotata majora in principia philosophiae R. Des Cartes. (Geulincx, A.) Dordraci, 1691.

Phil 75.74   An annotated bibliography of philosophy in Catholic thought, 1900-1964. (McLean, George F.) N.Y., 1967.

Phil 5535.38   An annotated bibliography of visual discrimination learning. (Green, Edward J.) N.Y., 1969.

Phil 2070.01A   Annotated bibliography of writings of William James. (Perry, Ralph B.) N.Y., 1920.

Phil 6903.10   Annotated list of publications, 1946-1970. (Tavistock Institute of Human Relations.) London, 1970?

Phil 2205.80   Annotations on the practical part of Dr. Paley's Principles of moral and political philosophy. (Pearson, Edward.) Ipswich, 1801.

Phil 4160.5.30   Annotaziori per un nuovo criticismo. (Lazzerini, Virgilio.) Milano, 1965.

Phil 10.5   Annuaire philisophique. (Martin, L.A.) Paris. 1-5,1864-1868 5v.

Phil 59.3   Annual convention. (Theosophical Society in America.) N.Y. 5-7,1891-1893

Phil 8655.8   Annual report. (American Association for the Advancement of Atheism, Inc.) N.Y. 1,1926

Phil 42.3.10   Annual report. (California. University. Institute of Human Development.) Berkeley. 1940+

Phil 42.6.3   Annual report. (Connecticut. Society for Mental Hygiene.) New Haven. 1912-1930

Phil 16.11   Annual report. (Group Psychotherapy of Southern California.) Los Angeles. 1-2,1953-1955

Phil 9495.9   Annual report. (Portland (Oregon). Social Hygiene Society.) Portland, Ore. 1-4

Phil 59.2   Annual report of the officers. (Thirteen Club, New York.) N.Y. 4-11,1884-1893+ 2v.

Phil 10.80   Annual review of psychology. Palo Alto, California. 1+ 34v.

Phil 5238.30   Annual survey of psychoanalysis; a comprehensive survey of current psychoanalytic theory and practice. N.Y. 1-9,1950-1958 8v.

Phil 57.10   Annuario. (Rio de Janeiro. Universidade do Brasil. Instituto de Psicologia.)

Phil 58.10.3   Annuario. (Società per gliStudi Filosofici, Palermo. Bibliotheca Filosofica.) Palermo, 1912-

Phil 9070.105   Annulus memoriae ex dictaminibus ethicis et politicis. (Weber, Johann Adam.) Salisburgi, 1679.

Phil 8655.16   Anonimnye ateisticheskie traktaty. Moskva, 1969.

Phil 6321.16   Anormalidades del caracter. (Laburu, J.A. de.) Montevideo, 1941.

Phil 70.14.3   Another, slightly variant report of the Thursday morning session. (Conference of Psychologists, Hanover, New Hanpshire.) n.p., 1925.

Phil 7060.111.19   Another grey ghost book. (Middelton, Jessie A.) London, 1915.

Phil 192.49   Anrede bey Eröffnung von Vorlesungen über Metaphysik. (Richter, H.) Leipzig, 1823.

Phil 8400.27   Anregung und metaphysische Grundlagen der Aesthetik von Alex Gottbeb Baumgarten. (Prieger, E.) Berlin, 1875. 3 pam.

Phil 5520.38   Anregungen zur psychologischen Betrachtung der Sprache. (Schmieder, A.) Langensalza, 1902.

Phil 5240.53   Anrich, Ernst. Moderne Physik und Tiefenpsychologie. Stuttgart, 1963.

Phil 3017.7   Die Ansätze zu einer Kulturantropologie in der Gegewärtigen deutschen Philosophie. (Razzug, Aśad.) Tübingen, 1963.

Phil 5790.30   Ansatz zu einer allgemeinen Verhaltenstheorie in der Sozialwissenschaften. (Langenheder, Werner.) Köln, 1968.

Phil 176.77   Anschauung und Begriff. (Brod, Max.) Leipzig, 1913.

Phil 5241.178   Anschauung und Denken. (Baeumker, Clemens.) Paderborn, 1913.

Phil 5520.32.7   Die Anschauungen Ludwig Noirés über Ursprung und Wesen von Sprache und Vernunft. Diss. (Berg, Anton.) Darmstadt, 1918.

Phil 3585.10.94   Anschütz, G. Theodor Lipps' neuere Urteilslehre. Leipzig, 1913.

Phil 5240.7   Anschütz, Georg. Die Intelligenz, eine Einführung in die Haupttatdachenfet. Harz, 1913.

Phil 5642.20   Anschütz, Georg. Kurze Einführung in die Farbe-Ton-Forschung. Leipzig, 1927.

Phil 5240.7.10   Anschütz, Georg. Psychologie. Hamburg, 1953.

Phil 5240.7.5   Anschütz, Georg. Über die Erforschung der Denkvorgänge. Osterwieck, 1913.

Phil 2138.123   Anschutz, R.P. The philosophy of J.S. Mill. Oxford, 1953.

Phil 1845.14.2   Anscombe, G.E.M. Intention. Oxford, 1958.

Phil 165.290   Anscombe, G.E.M. Three philosophers. Ithaca, N.Y., 1961.

Phil 418.10   Anscombe, Gertrude Elizabeth Margaret. Intention. Oxford, 1957.

Phil 3925.16.265   Anscombe, Gertrude Elizabeth Margaret. An introduction to Wittgenstein's Tractatus. London, 1959.

Phil 3270.4.80   Anselm von Feuerbach der Jurist, als Philosoph. Inaug. Diss. (Fleischmann, M.) München, 1906.

Phil 1504.18.2   Anselms von Laon systematische Sentenzen. v.18, pt.2-3. (Bliemetzrieder, P.) Münster, n.d.

Phil 8870.13   Anshen, R.N. Moral principles of action. 1st ed. N.Y., 1952.

Phil 296.1   Ansicht der Welt. (Petöcz, M.) Leipzig, 1838.

Phil 3499.26   Ansichten aus Immanuel Kant's Leben. (Rink, Friedrich T.) Königsberg, 1805.

Phil 1135.69   Ansichten der griechischen Philosophen. (Apelt, O.) Eisen, 1901.

Phil 3823.2   Die Ansichten Spinozas. (Dörffling, M.) Leipzig, 1873.

Phil 193.15   Ansichten von der Nachseite der Naturwissenschaft. (Schubert, G. von.) Dresden, 1840.

Phil 5421.10.25   Ansietà e carenze affettive. (Marchisa, Ernestina.) Napoli, 1968.

Phil 3808.115   Anspach, F.W. Schopenhauer und Chamfort. Göttingen, 1914.

Phil 7069.47.35   Anspacher, L.K. Challenge of the unknown. N.Y., 1947.

Phil 3030.4   Der Anspruch der Vernunft. (Buhr, Manfred.) Berlin, 1968.

Phil 5049.26   Die Ansprüche der Logistiker. (Jacoby, G.) Stuttgart, 1962.

Phil 6119.12   The answer is...your nerves. (Jackson, A.S.) Madison, Wis., 1942.

Phil 8599.4.97   An answer to a book intituled, Christianity as old as the creation. 2. ed. (Leland, John.) London, 1740. 2v.

Phil 8599.4.95   An answer to a late book intituled, Christianity as old as the creation. (Leland, John.) Dublin, 1733. 2v.

Phil 7068.56   Answer to charges of belief in modern revelations. (Newton, Alonzo E.) Boston, 1856. 2 pam.

Phil 8693.2   Answer to Hugh Miller and theoretic geologists. (Davies, T.A.) N.Y., 1860.

Phil 8589.20.3   Answer to Job. (Jung, Carl Gustav.) Cleveland, 1964.

Htn   Phil 2115.83*   Answer to Mr. Locke's letter. (Stillingfleet, E.) London, 1697.

Htn   Phil 2115.83.3*   Answer to Mr. Locke's second letter. (Stillingfleet, E.) London, 1698.

Htn   Phil 2280.3.30*   An answer to some cases of conscience. (Stoddard, Solomon.) Boston, 1722.

Phil 8880.37.3   Antäus. (Freyer, Hans.) Jena, 1922.

Phil 181.19   Antäus. (Gruppe, O.F.) Berlin, 1831.

Phil 3499.6.18   Antäus. (Romundt, H.) Leipzig, 1882.

Phil 3960.10   Antal, Geza von. Die holländische Philosophie im neunzehnten Jahrhundert. Utrecht, 1888.

Phil 5520.399   Antal, Laszló. Questions of meaning. The Hague, 1963.

Phil 4316.1   Antecedentes de la escuela filosófica Catalana del siglo XIX. (Parpal y Marques, C.) Barcelona, 1914.

Phil 2555.1.80   Antécédents de l'hégélianisme...Dom Deschamps. (Beaussire, E.) Paris, 1865.

Phil 2520.139   Les antécédents historique du "Je pense, donc je suis". (Blanchet, Léon.) Paris, 1920.

Phil 310.562   Les antécédents idéologiques du matérialisme historique. (Molnár, Erik.) Budapest, 1965.

Phil 5875.50   The antecedents of self-esteem. (Coopersmith, Stanley.) San Francisco, 1967.

Phil 3640.57A   L'antéchrist. (Nietzsche, Friedrich.) Paris, 1931.

Phil 3640.56   L'antéchrist. (Nietzsche, Friedrich.) Paris, 1967.

Phil 4630.2.43   Anteckningar i filosofi och historia. (Rein, J.) Helsingfors, 1889.

Phil 4655.1.25   Anteckningar till filosofiens historia efter P. Wikners kollegium af K.S. (Wikner, Pontus.) Upsala, 18- .

Phil 165.16   Anteile. Frankfurt am Main, 1950.

Phil 2998.1   Anthologie aus F.W.J. von Schelling's Werken. Berlin, 1844-57. 8 pam.

Htn   Phil 3800.51*   Anthologie aus Schelling's Werken. (Schelling, F.W.J. von.) Berlin, 1844.

Phil 1700.2   Anthologie der neueren Philosophie. Berlin, 1919.

Phil 2430.2   Anthologie des philosophes français. (Cuvillier, Armand.) Paris, 1962.

Phil 2400.4.5   Anthologie des philosophes français contemporains. 2e éd. Paris, 1931.

Phil 4210.11   Anthologie philosophique. (Rosmini-Serbati, Antonio.) Lyon, 1954.

Phil 3850.27.21   An anthology. (Schweitzer, A.) N.Y., 1947.

	Phil 1717.11	Anthology of recent philosophy. (Robinson, D.S.) N.Y., 1929.
	Phil 1717.11.5	Anthology of recent philosophy. (Robinson, D.S.) N.Y., 1931.
	Phil 8690.4	Anthony, H.D. Relativity and religion. London, 1927.
	Phil 6310.10	Anthony, Joseph. The invisible curtain. N.Y., 1957.
	Phil 5240.27	Anthony, R. Réflexions d'un biologiste sur l'objet...de la psychologie. Paris, 1925.
	Phil 1930.5.80	Anthony Collins; the man and his works. (O'higgins, James.) The Hague, 1970.
	Phil 978.49.697	Anthoposophie. 3. Aufl. (Steiner, R.) Dornach, 1968.
	Phil 3480.40	Anthropologie. (Kant, Immanuel.) Königsberg, 1820.
	Phil 193.34.3	Anthropologie. (Steffens, H.) Breslau, 1822. 2v.
	Phil 5259.4	Anthropologie. (Tissot, C.J.) Paris, 1843. 2v.
	Phil 3245.35	Anthropologie: von der menschlichen Seele. (Fichte, Immanuel Hermann.) Leipzig, 1860.
	Phil 2730.85	L'anthropologie de Maine de Biran. (Tisserand, Pierre.) Paris, 1909.
	Phil 3745.1.50	Anthropologie für Ärzte und Weltweise. (Platner, E.) Leipzig, 1772.
	Phil 3480.40.4	Anthropologie in pragmatischer Hinsicht. (Kant, Immanuel.) Leipzig, 1833.
	Phil 3480.40.13	Anthropologie in pragmatischer Hinsicht. (Kant, Immanuel.) Leipzig, 1899.
	Phil 3480.40.5	Anthropologie in pragmatischer Hinsicht. (Kant, Immanuel.) Paris, 1863.
Htn	Phil 3480.40.2*	Anthropologie in pragmatischer Hinsicht. 2. Aufl. (Kant, Immanuel.) Königsberg, 1800.
	Phil 3480.40.15	Anthropologie in pragmatischer Hinsicht. 5. Aufl. (Kant, Immanuel.) Leipzig, 1912.
	Phil 3480.40.16	Anthropologie in pragmatischer Hinsicht. 6. Aufl. (Kant, Immanuel.) Leipzig, 1922.
	Phil 3480.40.3	Anthropologie in pragmatischer Hinsicht Abgefasst. (Kant, Immanuel.) Frankfurt, 1799.
	Phil 2730.111	Die Anthropologie Maine de Birans. (Buol, J.) Winterthur, 1961.
	Phil 2805.221	Die Anthropologie Pascals. (Lohde, Richard.) Halle, 1936.
	Phil 182.43.5	Anthropologie philosophique. (Häberlin, Paul.) Paris, 1943.
	Phil 9150.19	L'anthropologie philosophique. Thèse. (Folkmar, D.) Paris, 1899.
	Phil 5252.54	Anthropologie und Psychologie. (Michelet, C.L.) Berlin, 1840.
	Phil 5255.4	Anthropologie und Psychologie. (Planck, K.C.) Leipzig, 1874.
	Phil 575.190	Anthropologisch-historische benadering van het moderne subjectgevoel. (Huibregtse, Kornelis.) Haarlem, 1950.
	Phil 8892.86	Anthropologische Ethik. (Reyer, Wilhelm.) Köln, 1963.
	Phil 4753.2.35	Das anthropologische Prinzip. (Chernyshevskii, N.G.) Berlin, 1956.
	Phil 5247.7	Anthropologische Vorträge. (Henle, F.G.J.) Braunschweig, 1876-80.
	Phil 3007.1	Der Anthropologismus. (Harms, F.) Leipzig, 1845.
	Phil 1135.76	The anthropology of the Greeks. (Sikes, E.E.) London, 1914.
	Phil 10.98	Anthropos. Ljubljana. 1969+
	Phil 978.49.465	Anthroposophie, Psychosophie, Pneumatosophie. (Steiner, R.) Dornach, 1965.
	Phil 200.3	Anthroposophie. (Zimmermann, R.) Wien, 1882.
	Phil 978.49.767	Anthroposophie. 2. Aufl. (Steiner, R.) Dornach, 1970.
	Phil 974.3.105	Die Anthroposophie Rudolf Steiners und die moderne Geisleswissenschaft. Diss. (Hoffmann, K.) Giessen, 1928.
	Phil 974.3.75	Die Anthroposophie Steiners und Indien. (Schomerus, H.W.) Leipzig, 1922.
	Phil 978.96	Die Anthroposophie und die Zukunft des Christentums. (Lauer, Hans Erhard.) Stuttgart, 1966.
	Phil 978.49.650	Anthroposophische Gemeinschaftsbildung. (Steiner, R.) Dornach, 1965.
	Phil 978.49.130	Anthroposophy. (Steiner, R.) n.p., n.d. 5 pam.
	Phil 3001.14	Anti-Cartesianismus; deutsche Philosophie im Widerstand. (Bohne, F.) Leipzig, 1938.
	Phil 8702.5	Anti-evolution: Girardeau vs. Woodrow. (Martin, J.L.) Memphis, Tenn.? 1888.
	Phil 510.1.27	Anti-Haeckel. 3rd ed. (Loofs, F.) London, 1904.
	Phil 3425.91.28	Anti-Hegel. (Bachmann, C.F.) Jena, 1835.
	Phil 2045.102	Anti-Hobbes. (Feuerbach, P.J.A.) Erfurt, 1798.
	Phil 1707.9	Anti-intellectualism in present philosophy. Diss. (Hammond, A.L.) Baltimore, 1926.
	Phil 3483.12	Anti-Kant. (Baumann, J.) Gotha, 1905.
	Phil 3500.57.10	Anti-Kant. (Stattler, B.) München, 1788. 2v.
	Phil 3483.7	Anti-Kant oder. (Bolliger, A.) Basel, 1882.
	Phil 497.3	Anti-Materialismus. v.1-2, 3. (Weis, L.) Berlin, 1871-73. 2v.
	Phil 22.16	The anti-mesmerist. London. 1-10
	Phil 2805.490	L'anti-Pascal di Voltaire. (Sina, Mario.) Milano, 1970.
	Phil 6320.25	Anti-pensée et monde des conflits. (Kalmar, Jacques M.) Neuchâtel, 1967.
	Phil 2422.8	The anti-philosophers; a study of philosophers in eighteenth century France. (White, Reginald James.) London, 1970.
	Phil 193.80	Anti-pragmatism. (Schinz, Albert.) Boston, 1909.
	Phil 2115.4F	Anti-scepticism: or notes upon...Mr. Lock's essay. (Lee, Henry.) London, 1702.
	Phil 3801.431.2	Anti-Sextus, oder über der absolute Erkenntniss von Schelling. (Goetz, Johann K.) Heidelberg, 1807.
Htn	Phil 3801.431*	Anti-Sextus, oder über der absolute Erkenntniss von Schelling. (Goetz, Johann K.) Heidelberg, 1807.
	Phil 8660.4.5	Anti-theistic theories. (Baird lectures for 1877). (Flint, R.) Edinburgh, 1879.
	Phil 3640.211	Anti-Zarathustra. (Henne am Rhyn, O.) Altenburg, 1899.
	Phil 3640.211.5	Anti-Zarathustra. 2e Aufl. (Henne am Rhyn, O.) Altenburg, 1901?
	Phil 930.46	Antica filosofia cinese. v.1-2. Milano, 1956.
	Phil 8842.8	L'antica morale filosofia. (Romagnosi, G.D.) Prato, 1838.
	Phil 8060.4	Antichnye mysliteli ob iskusstve. 2. izd. (Asmus, V.F.) Moskva, 1938.
	Phil 3640.53.5	Der Antichrist. 2. Aufl. (Nietzsche, Friedrich.) Berlin, 1940.
	Phil 8896.14	Anticipations à une morale du risque. (Vesper, Noël.) Paris, 1914.
Htn	Phil 2145.65*	Antidote against atheisme. (More, Henry.) London, 1653.
Htn	Phil 9510.5*	An antidote against swearing. (Boreman, R.) London, 1662.
	Phil 8875.18	Antieh, José. Egoismo y altruismo. Barcelona, 1906.
	Phil 281.12	Antieke en moderne kosmologie. Arnhem, 1941.
	Phil 1135.170	Antieke wijsgerige opvattingen in het christelijk denkleven. (Robbers, Joannes Henricus.) Roermond, 1959.
	Phil 3450.19.180	El antiguo y el nuevo Heidegger y un dialogo con el. (Llambías de Azevedo, Juan.) Montevideo, 1958.
	Phil 1195.7	Antik och modern sofistik. (Liljeqvist, Efraim.) Göteborg, 1896.
	Phil 6127.11	Antik Schriften über Seelenheilung und Seelenleitung. (Rabbow, Paul.) Leipzig, 1914.
	Phil 8062.7	Antike Ästhetik. (Perpeet, Wilhelm.) Freiburg, 1961.
	Phil 3801.637	Die antike Dialektik in der Spätphilosophie Schellings. (Oeser, Erhard.) Wein, 1965.
	Phil 1145.97	Die antike Ethik in ihrer geschichtlichen Entwicklung als Einleitung in die Geschichte der christlichen Moral. (Luthardt, C.E.) Leipzig, 1887.
	Phil 1135.33	Antike Humanität in moderner Beleuchtung. (Stettner, E.) Bieletz, 1912.
	Phil 5545.266	Die antike Mnemotechnik. Thesis. (Blum, Herwig.) Hildesheim, 1969.
	Phil 1400.10	Antike Philosophie und byzan tinisches Mittelalter. (Olhler, Klaus.) München, 1969.
Htn	Phil 6685.10.5*	L'antimagnétisme, ou origine. (Paulet, J.J.) Loudres, 1784.
	Phil 2750.11.84	Antimoderne. (Maritain, Jacques.) Paris, 1922.
	Phil 3487.26	Das Antinomenproblem im Entstehungsgang der Transzendentalphilosophie. (Fang, Joong.) Münster, 1957.
	Phil 720.62	L'antinomia del mentitore nel pensiero contemporaneo da Peirce a Tarski. (Rivetti Barbo, Francesca.) Milano, 1961.
	Phil 4215.3.30	Le antinomie dello spirito. (Rensi, Giuseppe.) Piacenza, 1910.
	Phil 3549.26	Antinomie und Dialektik. (Kulenkampff, Arend.) Stuttgart, 1970.
	Phil 5050.24	Die Antinomien der Logik. (Kutschera, Franz von.) Freiburg, 1964.
	Phil 3499.18	Die Antinomien Kants. (Rauschenberger, W.) Berlin, 1923.
	Phil 8643.38	Antiphädon. (Spazier, Karl.) Berlin, 1961.
	Phil 1750.157	Antipolitique. (Simond, D.) Lausanne, 1941.
	Phil 1750.460	Die Antiquiertheit des Menschen. (Anders, Günther.) München, 1956.
Htn	Phil 3800.100*	Antiquissimi de prima malorum humanorum origine. (Schelling, F.W.J. von.) Tubingae, 1792.
	Phil 735.112	Antirelativismus. (Spiegelberg, H.) Zürich, 1935.
	Phil 3497.15	Antischrift zur Vertheidigung der Vernunft und Religion. (Promnitz, C.F.) Berlin, 1796.
	Phil 3925.16.245	Antiseri, Dario. Dopo Wittgenstein. Roma, 1967.
	Phil 2733.96	Le antitesi...in ispecie nella dottrina...di Malebranche. (Turbiglio, S.) Roma, 1877.
	Phil 3120.21	Antithesen. (Beerling, Reinier Franciscus.) Haarlem, 1935.
	Phil 2475.1.210	De antithesen in de philosophie van Henri Bergson. (Van Paassen, C.R.) Haarlem, 1923.
	Phil 9230.6	Antithesis de sorte. (Gataker, T.) Lugdunum Batavorum, 1659-60. 3 pam.
	Phil 5360.32	Das antithetische Kamptbild. Inaug. Diss. (Reumann, Kurt.) Berlin, 1966.
	Phil 5374.23	Die antithetische Struktur des Bewusstseins. (Hofmann, Paul.) Berlin, 1914.
	Phil 8950.7	Antnenko, V.H. Sotsialistychnyi humanizm i khrystianskyi bubov do blyzhiv'oho. Kyïv, 1961.
	Phil 4970.1.20	Antología; su pensamiento en sus mejores páginas. (Ingenieros, José.) Buenos Aires, 1961.
	Phil 4957.805	Antología de la filosofía americana contemporánea. (Zea, Leopoldo.) México, 1968.
	Phil 4019.1	Antologia dei filosofi italiani del dopoguerra. 2. ed. (Tilgher, A.) Modena, 1937.
	Phil 4961.65	Antología del pensamiento filosófico en Colombia. (García Bacca, J.D.) Bogotá, 1955.
	Phil 4961.915	Antología del pensamiento filosófico venezolano. (García Bacca, Juan David.) Caracas, 1954.
	Phil 4960.625.5	Antologia do pensamento social e político no Brasil, seleção e notas. (Vita, Luís Washington.) São Paulo, 1968.
	Phil 1111.7	Antologia filosofica; la filosofia griega. (Gaos, José.) México, 1940.
	Phil 177.126	Antología filosófica. (Caso, Antonio.) México, 1957.
	Phil 4960.240	Antología filosófica argentina del siglo XX. (Vázquez, Juan Adolfo.) Buenos Aires, 1965.
	Phil 3480.28.30	Antologia Kantiana. (Kant, Immanuel.) Torino, 1925.
	Phil 4210.14	Antologia pedagogica. 1. ed. (Rosmini-Serbati, Antonio.) Brescia, 1955.
	Phil 5520.370	Antologia semantica. (Bunge, Mario.) Buenos Aires, 1960.
	Phil 4260.104	Antologia vichiana. (Caramella, S.) Messina, 1930.
	Phil 4806.2	Antologie z dějin československé filosofie. (Československá akademie věd.) Praha, 1963.
	Phil 4817.6	Antologiia iz istoriiata na rumunskata progresivna misul. (Academia Republicii Socialiste România, Bucharest. Institutu I de Filozofie.) Sofiia, 1965.
	Phil 6110.1	Anton, G. Bau, Leistung und Erkrankung des menschlichen Stirnhirnes. T.1. Graz, 1902.
	Phil 1105.14	Anton, John Peter. Essays in ancient Greek philosophy. Albany, 1971.
	Phil 165.426	Anton, John Peter. Naturalism and historical understanding. Albany, 1967.
	Phil 3310.1.125	Anton Günther. (Knoodt, Peter.) Wien, 1881. 2v.
	Phil 3625.9.80	Anton Marty; sein Leben und seine Werke. (Kraus, Oskar.) Halle, 1916.
	Phil 4225.66.80	Antonaci, Antonio. Francesco Storella. Galatina, 1966.
	Phil 1195.12	Antonelli, M. Figures di sofisti in Platon. Torino, 1948.
	Phil 4225.8.85	Antonelli, M.T. Studi in onore di M.F. Sciacca. Milano, 1959.
	Phil 8401.25	Antoni, Carlo. Chiose all'estetica, con un profile dell'autore a cura di G. Calogero. Roma, 1960.
	Phil 4080.3.260	Antoni, Carlo. Commento a Croce. 1. ed. Venezia, 1955.
	Phil 3425.317	Antoni, Carlo. Considerazioni su Hegel e Marx. Napoli, 1946.
	Phil 8401.25.5	Antoni, Carlo. Scritti di estetica. Napoli, 1968.
	Phil 4060.9.40	Antoni, Giuseppe. Pensiero ed esistenza. Padova, 1965.
	Phil 2805.213	Antoniadis, S. Pascal traducteur de la Bible. Thèse. Leyde, 1930.
	Phil 4070.7.90	Antonio Banfi e il pensiero contemporaneo. (Convegno di Studi Banfiani, Reggio Emilia.) Firenze, 1969.
	Phil 4357.1.81	Antonio de Gouveia e o Aristotelismo la renascenca. (Carvalho, Joaquim de.) Coimbra, 1916.
	Phil 8401.27	Antonio de la Virgen del Carmen. Al arte por el dolor. Burgos, 1952.
	Phil 4114.90	Antonio Genovesi. (Corpaci, Francesco.) Milano, 1966.
	Phil 4114.80	Antonio Genovesi. (Racioppi, G.) Napoli, 1871.
	Phil 4210.170	Antonio Rosmini, uomo di pensiero, di azione, di virtu. (Pusineri, Giovanni.) Milano, 1956.
	Phil 4210.151	Antonio Rosmini. (Brunello, Bruno.) Milano, 1945.
	Phil 4210.153.5	Antonio Rosmini. (Donati, B.) Modena, 1941.
	Phil 4210.84	Antonio Rosmini. (Garelli, V.) Torino, 1861.

Phil 4210.159 — Antonio Rosmini. (Garioni Bertolatti, G.) Torino, 1957.
Phil 4210.149.3 — Antonio Rosmini. (Morando, Dante.) Brescia, 1958.
Phil 4210.136 — Antonio Rosmini. (Stopppani, Pietro.) Milano, 1905.
Phil 4210.93.15 — Antonio Rosmini. (Tommaseo, N.) Domodossola, 1958.
Phil 4210.134 — Antonio Rosmini all'estero. (Sernagiotto, L.) Venezia, 1889.
Phil 4210.152 — Antonio Rosmini come uomo del risorgimento italiano. (Callovini, C.) Roma, 1953.
Phil 4210.118 — Antonio Rosmini e il suo monumento in Milano. (Cornelio, A.M.) Torino, 1896.
Phil 4210.81 — Antonio Rosmini ed i gesuiti. (Nardi, P. de.) Torino, 1882.
Phil 4210.166 — Antonio Rosmini nel primo centenario della morte. (Riva, Clemente.) Firenze, 1958.
Phil 4210.161 — Antonio Rosmini nella cultura del sus tempo. (Gambaro, Angiolo.) Torino, 1955?
Phil 4210.147 — Antonio Rosmini nella restaurazione. (Bulferetti, Luigi.) Firenze, 1942.
Phil 4210.120 — Antonio Rosmini o il filosofo cristiano. (Bianciardi, S.) Firenze, 1858.
Phil 3482.12 — Antonopoulos, Georg. Der Menschen als Bürger zweier Welten. Bonn, 1958.
Phil 5130.4 — Antonov, Georgii V. Ot formal'noi logiki k dialektike. Moskva, 1971.
Phil 735.261 — Antonovich, Ivan I. Amerikanskaia burzhuaznaia aksiologiia na sluzh e imperializma. Minsk, 1967.
Phil 585.375 — Antonovich, Ivan I. Sovremennaia "Anlosofskaia antropoligiia". Minsk, 1970.
Phil 5821.16 — Antriebe tierischen und menschlichen Verhaltens. (Lovenz, Konrad Zacharias.) München, 1968.
Phil 585.422 — Antropoligia filosofica. (Groethuysen, Bernhard.) Napoli, 1969.
Phil 4210.26 — Antropologia. (Rosmini-Serbati, Antonio.) Novara, 1847.
Phil 585.355 — Antropologia filosfica e occultamente ideologico. (Bosio, Franco.) Urbino, 1968.
Phil 585.222 — Antropología filosófica. (Farré, Luis.) Madrid, 1968.
Phil 585.400 — Antropología metafisica. (Marías Aguilera, Julián.) Madrid, 1970.
Phil 4210.131 — L'antropologia soprannaturale di A. Rosmini. (Calzi, Carlo.) Firenze, 1885.
Phil 4753.2.30 — Antropologicheskii printsip v filosofii. (Chernyshevskii, N.G.) Moskva, 1943.
Phil 8881.53 — L'antropologie. (Girini Corio, Gioseffo.) n.p., 1761. 2v.
Phil 5545.215 — Antsyferova, L.I. O zakonomernostiakh elementarnoi poznavatel'noi deiatel'nosti. Moskva, 1961.
Phil 5750.9 — Antweiler, A. Das Problem der Willensfreiheit. Freiburg, 1955.
Phil 3245.80 — Antwort an...Dr. Immanuel Hermann Fichte. (Zeller, E.) Berlin, 1876.
Htn — Phil 3625.1.160* — Antwort an den herrn Moses Mendelssohn zu Berlin. (Lavater, J.C.) Berlin, 1770.
Phil 8589.20 — Antwort auf Hiob. (Jung, Carl Gustav.) Zürich, 1952.
Phil 978.122 — Antwort auf Lebensrätsel. (Hagmann, Diego.) Zürich, 1968.
Phil 8589.30 — Antwort auf Wort. (Jordan, Placidus.) München, 1969.
Phil 2045.150 — Die Antwort des Leviathan; Thomas Hobbes' politische Theorie. (Willms, Bernard.) Neuwied, 1970.
Phil 2150.22.80 — Antworten auf Herbert Marcuse. Frankfurt, 1968.
Phil 52.12 — Anuario de filosofia. (Mexico City.) Universidad Nacional. Facultad de Filosofía y Letras.)
Phil 10.96 — Anuario filosofico. Pamplona. 1,1968+ 2v.
Phil 22.62 — Anuario psicologia. (Mexico City.) Universidad Nacional. Facultad de Filosofía y Letras.) Mexico. 1-3,1962-1964//
Phil 5590.563 — Anufriev, Evgenii A. Sotsial'naia vol' i aktivnost' lichnosti. Moskva, 1971.
Htn — Phil 3246.49.2* — Die Anweisung zum seeligen Leben. (Fichte, Johann Gottlieb.) Berlin, 1806.
Phil 3246.49A — Die Anweisung zum seeligen Leben. (Fichte, Johann Gottlieb.) Berlin, 1828.
Phil 3246.49.5 — Die Anweisung zum seeligen Leben. (Fichte, Johann Gottlieb.) Hamburg, 1954.
Htn — Phil 3480.40.49* — Anweisung zur Menschen und Weltkenntniss. 4. Aufl. (Kant, Immanuel.) Leipzig, 1831.
Phil 978.49.720 — Anweisungen für eine esoterische Schulung: aus den Inhalten der Esoterischen Schule. (Steiner, R.) Dornach, 1968.
Phil 5627.111 — Die Anwendung der Psychoanalyse auf Mythologie und Religionsgeschichte. (Clemen, Carl.) Leipzig, 1928.
Phil 356.2 — Das Anwendungsproblem. (Zilsel, Edgar.) Leipzig, 1916.
Phil 6311.16 — L'anxiété. (Boven, William.) Neuchâtel, 1934.
Phil 5401.44 — Anxiety and magic thinking. (Odier, Charles.) N.Y., 1956.
Phil 3120.30.110 — Anzenbacher, Arno. Die Philosophie Martin Bubers. Wien, 1965.
Phil 5592.145 — Anzieu, D. Les méthodes projectives. Paris, 1960.
Phil 5592.148 — Anzieu, D. Les méthodes projectives. 3e éd. Paris, 1970.
Phil 6315.2.260 — Anzieu, Didier. L'auto-analyse. Paris, 1959.
Phil 5210.11 — Anzieu, Didier. Esquisse de la psychologie française. Paris, 1962?
Phil 8520.9 — Anzoletti, Luisa. La fede nel soprannaturale. Milano, 1894.
Phil 8690.3 — Anzoletti, Luisa. Per un nuovo patto fra la scienze e la religione. Milano, 1899.
Phil 585.125 — Aolliet, Joseph. L'homme social. Paris, 1942.
Phil 5460.15 — APA-AAAS Symposium on Hallucinations. Hallucinations. N.Y., 1962.
Phil 974.3.110 — Apel, Max. Geheimwissenschaft. Charlettenburg, 1922.
Phil 3482.5 — Apel, Max. Immanuel Kant. Berlin, 1904.
Phil 3482.5.7 — Apel, Max. Kants Erkenntnistheorie und seine Stellung zur Metaphysik. Berlin, 1895.
Phil 3482.5.5 — Apel, Max. Kommentar zu Kants Prologomena. Leipzig, 1923.
Phil 3482.5.3 — Apel, Max. Kommentar zu Kants "Prologomena". Schöneberg, 1908.
Phil 85.5 — Apel, Max. Philosophisches Wörterbuch. 4. Aufl. Berlin, 1953.
Phil 331.6 — Apel, Paul. Geist und Materie. Berlin, 1905. 2v.
Phil 475.2 — Apel, Paul. Die Überwindung des Materialismus. 3e Aufl. Berlin, 1921.
Phil 1105.5 — Apell, Otto. Beiträge zur Geschichte der griechischen Philosophie. Leipzig, 1891.
Phil 3085.3.31 — Apelt, E.F. Metaphysik. Leipzig, 1857.
Phil 5125.1 — Apelt, E.F. Die Theorie der Induction. Leipzig, 1854.
Phil 1135.69 — Apelt, O. Ansichten der griechischen Philosophen. Eisen, 1901.
Phil 5374.6 — L'aperception du corps humain. (Bertrand, A.) Paris, 1880.
Phil 4825.10 — Aperçu de la philosophie contemporaine en Yougoslavie. (Nedeljkovič, Dušan.) Beograd, 1934.
Phil 4803.454.105 — Aperçu de la philosophie de Wroński. (Brawn, Jérzy Bronislaw.) Rome, 1969?

Phil 9035.40 — Apfelbach, H. Der Aufbau des Charakters. Wien, 1924.
Phil 5240.26 — Apfelbach, Hans. Das Denkgefühe, eine Untersuchung über den emotionalen Charakter der Denkprozesse. Wien, 1922.
Phil 5049.17 — Apharismi e logica transcendali quas praeside Samuel Grubbs. (Johanson, Johan.) Upsaliae, 1815.
Phil 6400.16 — Aphasia. (Weisenburg, T.) N.Y., 1935.
Phil 6400.18 — Aphasia: a guide to retraining. (Granich, L.) N.Y., 1947.
Phil 6400.14 — Aphasia and kindred disorders of speech. (Head, Henry.) Cambridge, Eng., 1926. 2v.
Phil 6400.6 — Der aphasische Symptomencomplex. Photoreproduction. (Wernicke, C.) Breslau, 1874.
Phil 3483.45.5 — Aphorismen den Freunden der Vernunftkritik nach Kantischer Lehre. (Bouterwek, F.) Gottingen, 1793.
Phil 9070.114 — Aphorismen zur Ethik. (Margolius, Hans.) Heidelberg, 1957.
Phil 3808.25.7 — Aphorismen zur Lebensweisheit. (Schopenhauer, Arthur.) Leipzig, 1920.
Phil 3808.25.5 — Aphorismen zur Lebensweisheit. (Schopenhauer, Arthur.) Stuttgart, 1924.
Phil 510.9.6 — Aphorismen zur monistischen Philosophie. 2. ed. (Noiré, Ludwig.) Mainz, 1884.
Phil 194.32 — Aphorismen zur Philosophie. (Tittmann, F.W.) Dresden, 1859.
Phil 8405.2 — Aphorismen zur Philosophie der Kunst. (Ehrlich, Walter.) Tübingen, 1962.
Phil 6682.3.10 — Aphorismes de Mesmer. 3. éd. (Mesmer, F.A.) Paris, 1785.
Phil 4630.3.39 — Aphorismi philosophici de moderamine libertatis philosophicae. Diss. (Rydelius, Anders.) Lundini, 1726.
Phil 585.300 — Aphorismoí kaí dialogismoí. v.1-2. (Tsatsos, Könstantinos.) Athens, 1965-68.
Phil 8876.6 — Aphorisms. (Bartlett, J.) Boston, 1823.
Htn — Phil 8876.6.4* — Aphorisms. (Bartlett, J.) Portsmouth, 1810.
Phil 8876.6.3 — Aphorisms. (Bartlett, J.) Portsmouth, 1810.
Htn — Phil 8886.6* — Aphorisms on man. (Lavater, J.C.) Boston, 1790.
Phil 270.17.5 — Aphoristische Betrachtungen über das Kausalproblem. (Lang, Albert.) Köln, 1909.
Phil 8586.60 — Aphoristische Darstellung der Religion. (Grillo, Friedrich.) Bruxelles, 1968.
Phil 3001.16 — Apokalyse der deutschen Seele. (Balthasar, H.U.) Salzburg, 1937-39. 3v.
Phil 8430.53 — Apollineo e dionisiaco nella storia del classicismo. (Pesce, Domenico.) Napoli, 1968.
Phil 3640.720 — Apollinisch und Dionysisch; Geschichte eines genialen Irrtuums. (Vogel, Martin.) Regensburg, 1966.
Phil 8401.28 — Apollonio, M. Ontologia dell'arte. Brescia, 1961.
Phil 3640.790 — Apollos Wiederkehr; eine Untersuchung der Rolle des Kreises in Nietzsches Denken. (Bulhof-Rutgers, Ilse Nina.) 's-Gravenhage, 1969.
Phil 8585.24 — Apologetica. (Fernandes de Santanna, Manuel.) Lisboa, 1901.
Phil 8605.8 — Apologetika. 2. izd. (Zen'kovskii, V.V.) Parizhe, 195-? 3 pam.
Phil 2805.335 — L'apologétique de Pascal. (Lacombe, R.E.) Paris, 1958.
Phil 2477.6.155 — L'apologétique philosophique. (Saint-Jean, Raymond.) Paris, 1966.
Htn — Phil 3085.1.36* — Apologia aduersus calumnias proptes declamationem. (Agrippa von Nettesheim, H.C.) n.p., 1533.
Phil 4260.86 — Apologia del genere umano. Venezia, 1768.
Phil 8672.13 — Apologia dell'ateismo. (Rensi, G.) Roma, 1925.
Phil 645.22.12 — Apologia dello scetticismo. (Rensi, Giuseppe.) Roma, 1926.
Phil 4073.52 — Apologia di Galileo. (Campanella, Tommaso.) Torino, 1968.
Phil 8886.22 — Apologia diffidentis. (Leith, W.C.) London, 1908.
Htn — Phil 4265.1.90* — Apologia J. Caesare Vanino neapolitano. (Arpe, P.F.) Csmomopoli, 1712.
Htn — Phil 2175.1.30* — Apologia pro vita sua. pt.1-7. (Newman, John H.) London, 1864. 3 pam.
Phil 1750.143 — L'apologie de la guerre dans la philosophie contemporaine. Thèse. (Juganaru, P.) Paris, 1933.
Phil 3838.11 — Apologie de Spinoza et du s'isme. (Sabatier, A. de Castres.) Altona, 1805.
Phil 8968.13 — Apologie der katholischen Moral. (Schilling, Otto.) Paderborn, 1936.
Htn — Phil 2805.205* — Apologie des lettres provinciales de Louis de Montalte. (Petit-Didier, M.) Delft, 1697-98.
Htn — Phil 2805.205.5* — Apologie des lettres provinciales de Louis de Montalte. Pt.1-4. (Petit-Didier, M.) Delft, 1697-98. 2v.
Phil 3425.91.5 — Apologie Hegel's gegen Dr. R. Haym. (Rosenkranz, K.) Berlin, 1858.
Phil 3270.1.31 — Die Apologie meiner Lehre. (Fischer, Kuno.) Mannheim, 1854.
Phil 8595.16.27.10 — Apologies for Christianity and the Bible. (Watson, R.) London, 1824.
Htn — Phil 8595.16.24* — An apology for Christianity. (Watson, R.) Philadelphia, 1796.
Htn — Phil 8595.16.27.3* — Apology for Christianity. 1st American ed. (Watson, R.) Providence, 1794.
Phil 8595.16.24.2 — An apology for Christianity. 2. ed. (Watson, R.) Cambridge, 1777.
Htn — Phil 2050.89* — An apology for life and writings of D. Hume. (Pratt, Samuel J.) London, 1777.
Phil 8595.16.23 — An apology for the Bible. (Watson, R.) Cambridge, 1828.
Phil 8595.16.26.5 — An apology for the Bible. (Watson, R.) London, 1796.
Htn — Phil 8595.16.27* — Apology for the Bible. (Watson, R.) N.Y., 1796.
Phil 8595.16.28.5 — An apology for the Bible. (Watson, R.) N.Y., 1835. 8 pam.
Phil 8595.16.27.25 — An apology for the Bible. (Watson, R.) Nashville, 1855.
Phil 8595.16.27.5 — Apology for the Bible. 2. ed. (Watson, R.) Philadelphia, 1796.
Phil 8595.16.26 — Apology for the Bible. 7. ed. (Watson, R.) London, 1796.
Phil 6110.15 — Apoplexie und ihre Vererbung. (Arnason, A.) Kopenhagen, 1935.
Phil 8598.135.15 — Aporie und Glaube. (Schlette, Heinz Robert.) München, 1970.
Phil 4957.15 — Aportes a una bibliografía anotada de historia de las ideas en América. (Montevideo. Universidad. Facultad de Humanidades y Ciencias.) Montevideo, 1964.
Phil 331.15 — Apostel, Léo. Logique apprentissage et probabilité. Paris, 1959.
Phil 4752.2.110 — An apostle of freedom. (Vallon, Michell A.) N.Y., 1960.
Phil 6132.25 — An apostle of healing...Pastor Richard Howton. (Waylen, H.) London, 1928.
Phil 4843.6 — Apostolopoulos, Ntimēs. Syntomē historia tēs neoellenikēs philosophias. Athena? 1949.

Phil 193.134.10 — Apotheoz pespohveiossiti. (Shestov, L.) Sankt Peterburg, 1905.

Phil 6990.3.15 — L'apparition...grotté de Lourdes en 1858. (Fourcade, M. l'abbé.) Tarbes, 1862.

Phil 7060.37.15 — Apparitions; a narrative of facts. 2. ed. (Savile, B.W.) London, 1880.

Phil 7060.87 — Apparitions. (Crosland, N.) London, 1873.

Phil 7060.11 — Apparitions. (Taylor, J.) London, 1815.

Phil 7069.42.10 — Apparitions. (Tyrrell, George N.M.) London, 1942?

Phil 7069.42.12 — Apparitions. (Tyrrell, George N.M.) London, 1953.

Phil 7069.39.4 — Apparitions and haunted houses. (Bennett, E.N.) London, 1939.

Phil 7069.58.2 — Apparitions and precognition. (Jaffe, Aniela.) New Hyde Park, N.Y., 1963.

Phil 7068.94.10 — Apparitions and thought-transference. (Podmore, Frank.) London, 1894.

Phil 6990.14 — Apparitions de la St. Vierge à deux jeunes enfants. (LaVausserie.) Paris, 1873.

Phil 6990.3.35 — Les apparitions de Lourdes. (Estrade, J.B.) Tours, 1899.

Phil 6990.3.110 — Les apparitions de Lourdes. (Laurentin, René.) Paris, 1966.

Phil 5460.14.10 — Les appartenances du délirant. (Faure, Henri.) Paris, 1965.

Phil 2193.30 — An appeal to common sense in behalf of religion. (Oswald, J.) Edinburgh, 1766-72. 2v.

Phil 2193.30.2 — An appeal to common sense in behalf of religion. (Oswald, J.) London, 1768-72. 2v.

Phil 343.23 — The appeal to immediate experience. (Mack, R.D.) N.Y., 1945.

Phil 348.25 — The appeal to the given. (Ross, Jacob Joshua.) London, 1970.

Phil 8582.25.5 — An appeal to the real leaders of men. (Carson, Capshaw, (pseud.).) Chicago, 1918.

Phil 1885.37 — Appearance and reality. (Bradley, Francis H.) London, 1893.

Phil 1885.37.3 — Appearance and reality. (Bradley, Francis H.) London, 1899.

Phil 1885.37.15 — Appearance and reality. (Bradley, Francis H.) Oxford, 1930.

Phil 1885.37.20 — Appearance and reality. (Bradley, Francis H.) Oxford, 1968.

Phil 1885.37.5A — Appearance and reality. 2d ed. (Bradley, Francis H.) London, 1902.

Phil 1885.37.7 — Appearance and reality. 2d ed. (Bradley, Francis H.) London, 1908.

Phil 5252.47 — The appearance of mind. (McKerrow, J.C.) London, 1923.

Phil 5258.140.5 — Appecciafuoco, Romolo. La psicologia sperimentale di Sante de Panctis. Roma, 1946.

Phil 1505.1 — Appel, H. Lehre der Scholastiker von der Synteresis. Rostock, 1891.

Phil 6690.1 — Appel à tous les partisans et amis du magnétisme. 2e éd. (L'union Protectrice.) Paris, 1850.

Phil 2490.57 — Appel aux conservateurs. (Comte, Auguste.) Paris, 1855.

Phil 665.92 — L'appel de l'esprit. (LaNoé, François de.) Paris, 1960.

Phil 3246.71.20A — Appellation an das Publikum über...atheistischen. (Fichte, Johann Gottlieb.) Jena, 1799.

Phil 4001.4.9 — Appendice alla filosofia delle scuole italiane. 2. ed. (Bonavino, C.) Milano, 1866.

Phil 8896.1 — The appendix to volumes I. and II. of the moral system, or Law of human nature. (Vincent, G.) London, 1850.

Htn Phil 665.1.5* — Appendix to 1st pt. An enquiry into nature of human soul. v.3. (Baxter, A.) London, 1750.

Phil 5374.7.5 — Apperception. (Lange, K.M.) Boston, 1893.

Phil 5374.7.6 — Apperception. (Lange, K.M.) Boston, 1894.

Phil 3552.297 — Der Apperceptionsbegriff bei Leipzig und dessen Nachfolgern. (Capesius, J.) Hermannstadt, 1894.

Phil 8401.16 — Appin, Adolph. L'oeuvre d'art vivant. Genève, 1921.

Phil 7069.68.15 — Appleman, John A. Your psychic powers and immortality. N.Y., 1968.

Phil 175.20 — Appleton, J.H. Doctor Charles E.C.B. Appleton: his life and literary relics. London, 1881.

Phil 5810.2 — Appleton, L.E. A comparative study of the play activities of adult savages and civilized children. Chicago, 1910.

Phil 1105.6 — Appleton, R.B. The elements of Greek philosophy from Thales to Aristotle. London, 1922.

Phil 5210.15 — Appley, Mortimertt. Psychology in Canada. Ottawa, 1967.

Phil 5247.72 — Applicability of factor analysis in the behavioral science. (Henrysson, Sten.) Stockholm, 1957.

Phil 5257.47 — Applicability of the probable error formulae to psychological data. Diss. (Russell, J.T.) Chicago, 1934.

Phil 6980.38.5 — Application of basic science techniques to psychiatric research. (American Psychiatric Association.) Washington, 1957.

Phil 8952.1 — Application of Christianity to...ordinary affairs of life. (Chalmers, T.) Glasgow, 1820.

Phil 8952.1.2 — Application of Christianity to...ordinary affairs of life. (Chalmers, T.) Glasgow, 1821.

Phil 8952.1.5 — Application of Christianity to...ordinary affairs of life. (Chalmers, T.) N.Y., 1821.

Phil 8952.1.6 — Application of Christianity to...ordinary affairs of life. 3d American ed. (Chalmers, T.) Hartford, 1821.

Phil 5058.22.19 — The application of logic. (Sidgwick, A.) London, 1910.

Phil 6536.5 — The application of the auditory memory test to two thousand institut'l epileptics. (Ninde, F.W.) West Chester, 1924?

Phil 5593.46 — The application of the Rorschach test to young children. (Ford, Mary E.N.) Minneapolis, 1946.

Phil 5057.13 — The applications of logic. (Robinson, A.T.) N.Y., 1912.

Phil 5850.277 — Applications of psychology. (Moss, F.A.) Boston, 1929.

Phil 8892.15.2 — Applied ethics being one of the Wm.B. Noble lectures for 1910. (Roosevelt, T.) Cambridge, 1911.

Phil 8892.15 — Applied ethics being one of the Wm.B. Noble lectures for 1910. (Roosevelt, T.) Cambridge, 1911.

Phil 6060.23 — Applied graphology. (Smith, Albert J.) N.Y., 1920.

Phil 5465.59 — Applied imagination. (Osborn, A.F.) N.Y., 1953.

Phil 5051.33 — Applied logic. (Little, W.W.) Boston, 1955.

Phil 5254.6 — Applied mental efficiency. (Orr, T.V.) Chicago, 1913.

Phil 8953.3 — Applied philosophy. (Dawbarn, C.Y.C.) London, 1923.

Phil 186.111 — Applied philosophy. (Lodge, R.C.) London, 1951.

Phil 6313.14.5 — Applied psychoanalysis. (Deutsch, Felix.) N.Y., 1949.

Phil 5850.314 — Applied psychology; its principles and methods. (Poffenberger, A.T.) N.Y., 1927.

Phil 5850.145.50 — Applied psychology. (Burtt, H.E.) N.Y., 1948.

Phil 5850.191.5 — Applied psychology. (Ewer, B.C.) N.Y., 1925.

Phil 5850.230 — Applied psychology. (Hollingworth, H.L.) N.Y., 1923.

Phil 5850.232 — Applied psychology. (Husband, R.W.) N.Y., 1934.

Phil 5850.145.50.5 — Applied psychology. 2. ed. (Burtt, H.E.) Englewood Cliffs, 1957.

Phil 10.55 — Applied psychology monographs of American association for applied psychology. Stanford, Cal. 1-17,1943-1948 5v.

Phil 5627.138 — Applied religious psychology. (Anderson, J.B.) Boston, 1919.

Phil 200.17.5 — Appollon et Dionysos. (Zafiropulo, Jean.) Paris, 1961.

Phil 7069.27.10 — Appolonius. (Bennett, E.N.) London, 1927?

Phil 4303.6 — Apports hispaniques à la philosophie chrétienne. (Carreras y Artau, J.) Louvain, 1962.

Phil 5590.110 — Appraising personality. 1. ed. (Harrower, M.R.) N.Y., 1952.

Phil 8419.12 — Appreciation: painting, poetry and prose. (Stein, Leo.) N.Y., 1947.

Phil 2490.109 — Appréciation générale du positivisme. (Cirra, Émile.) Paris, 1898.

Phil 2630.11.5 — Apprendre à vivre et à penser. (Guitton, Jean.) Paris, 1957.

Phil 5435.12 — L'apprentissage du mouvement et l'automatisme. (Veldt, Jacobus van der.) Louvain, 1928.

Phil 5625.101.5 — Apprentissage et activités psychologiques. (Le Ny, Jean François.) Paris, 1967.

Phil 6112.43 — An approach to community mental health. (Caplan, Gerald.) N.Y., 1961.

Phil 2520.400 — An approach to Descartes' meditations. (Broadie, Frederick.) London, 1970.

Phil 194.45 — The approach to metaphysics. (Tomlin, E.W.F.) London, 1947.

Phil 182.105 — Approach to philosophy. (Hawkins, D.J.B.) London, 1938.

Phil 190.18A — The approach to philosophy. (Perry, R.B.) N.Y., 1905.

Phil 197.55 — The approach to philosophy. (Walfenden, J.F.) London, 1932.

Phil 5627.65.5 — An approach to the psychology of religion. (Flower, John C.) London, 1927.

Phil 960.166 — Approaches de l'Inde. (Masui, J.) Tours? 1949.

Phil 2750.11.75 — Approaches to God. 1st ed. (Maritain, Jacques.) N.Y., 1954.

Phil 5222.3.10 — Approaches to personality. (Murphy, Gardner.) N.Y., 1932.

Phil 5520.415 — Approaches to semiotics. (Conference on Paralinguistics and Kinesics.) The Hague, 1964.

Phil 6400.22 — Approaches to the study of aphasia. (Osgood, Charles E.) Urbana, 1963.

Phil 6980.40 — Approaches to the study of human personality. (American Psychiatric Association.) Washington, 1956.

Phil 7068.52 — The approaching crisis. (Davis, A.J.) N.Y., 1852.

Phil 8707.27 — Approche contemporaine d'une affirmation de Dieu. (Robert, M.D.) Bruges, 1962.

Phil 1750.99 — Approches phénoménologiques de l'idée d'être. (Breton, Stanislas.) Paris, 1959.

Phil 3820.6 — Appuhn, C. Spinoza. Paris, 1927.

Phil 1870.73.7 — Gli appunti (commonplace book). (Berkeley, G.) Bologna, 1924.

Phil 180.27 — Appunti critici di filosofia contemporanea. (Fabbricotti, Carlo A.) Firenze, 1918.

Phil 178.54 — Appunti di filosofia. v.1-3. (Dandolo, G.) Messina, 1903-1909.

Phil 178.54.3 — Appunti di filosofia. 3. ed. (Dandolo, G.) Padova, 1894.

Phil 402.12 — Appunti sull'ideologia. (Cofrancesco, Dino.) Milano, 1968.

Phil 4365.1.5 — Aprendizaje y heroismo. (Ors y Rovira, E. d'.) Madrid, 1915.

Phil 6325.24 — Après Freud. (Pontalis, J.B.) Paris, 1965.

Phil 7068.91.4 — Après la mort. (Dénis, Léon.) Paris, 1891.

Phil 8626.20 — L'après-mort. (Barbarin, Georges.) Paris, 1958.

Phil 8401.35 — Apresian, Grant Z. Cheloveku byt' khudozhnikom. Moskva, 1965.

Phil 8171.5.5 — Apresian, Grant Z. Esteticheskaia mysl' narodov Zakavkaz'ia. Moskva, 1968.

Phil 8171.5 — Apresian, Grant Z. Krasota i dobro. Moskva, 1966.

Phil 8030.6 — Apresian, Z.G. Estetika; bibliografiia, 1956-60. Moskva, 1963.

Phil 8401.34.5 — Apresian, Zorii Grantovich. Freedom and the artist. Moscow, 1968.

Phil 8401.34 — Apresian, Zorii Grantovich. Svoboda khudozhestvennogo tvorchestva. Moskva, 1965.

Phil 2750.13.80 — Aproximaçoa do pensamento concerto de Gabriel Marcel. (Tavares, M. de la Salette.) Lisboa, 1948.

Phil 5274.6 — Apter, Michael John. The computer simulation of behavior. London, 1970.

Phil 6032.8 — Aptitudes et caractère par la physiognomonie. (Weber, F.) Genève, 1970.

Phil 5635.17.5 — Les aptitudes rythmiques. (Hiriartborde, Edmond.) Paris, 1968.

Phil 182.67.80 — Apuntes dispersos sobre fenomenologia. (Pierola, Raul A.) Santa Fe, 1957.

Phil 600.7.100 — Aquarone, Stanislas. The life and works of Émile Littré. Leyden, 1958.

Phil 800.8 — Aquilanti, F. Linei fondamentali di storia della filosofia. v.1-3. Milano, 1938-40. 2v.

Phil 1105.3 — Aquilianiis, S. Placitis philosophorum. Lipsiae, 1756.

Phil 10.76 — Aquinas; rivista di filosofia. Roma. 1,1958+ 9v.

Phil 1700.6 — Aquinas and Kant. (Ardley, Gavin.) London, 1950.

Phil 9495.166.5 — Aquinas Institute of Philosophy and Theology. Institute of Spiritual Theology. Sex, love and the life of the spirit. Chicago, 1966.

Phil 2610.95 — Aquirre, Francisco Solano de. El atomismo de Gassendi. Barcelona, 1956.

Phil 175.31 — Aquisto, B. d'. Elementi di filosofia fondamentale. Palermo, 1857.

Phil 1020.30 — The Arab genius in science and philosophy. 2d ed. (Farrukh, O.A.) Washington, 1954.

Phil 1020.11 — Arabian philosophy. (Anderson, M.B.) n.p., n.d.

Phil 1020.14A — Arabic thought and its place in history. (O'Leary, DeLacy.) London, 1922.

Phil 1020.14.5 — Arabic thought and its place in history. (O'Leary, DeLacy.) London, 1939.

Phil 5040.20.5 — Aragón, G.A. Lógica elemental. 4a ed. Habana, 1926.

Phil 6110.20 — Arai, T. Mental fatique. N.Y., 1912.

Phil 8580.18 — Araiztegui, R.M. Bosquejo de un paralelo de la relation catholica. Habana, 1872.

VPhil 5125.34 — Arandjelović, Jovan T. Uloga indukcije u naučnom istraživanju. Beograd, 1967.

Phil 7069.29.100 — Árangur reynslu minnar í dulraenum afnum. (Pórdrdóttir, Théódóra.) Akureyri, 1929.

Phil 4365.1.15 — Aranguren, José. La filosofia di Eugenio d'Ors. Milano, 1953.

Phil 8401.12 — Aranio, Ruiz. Umanità dell'arte. Firenze, 1954.

Phil 4872.242.85 — Arapura, John G. Radhakrishnan and integral experience. London, 1966.

Phil 5465.173	Arasteh, A. Reza. Creativity in the life-cycle. Leiden, 1968-
Phil 5590.460	Arasteh, A. Reza. Final integration in the adult personality. Leiden, 1965.
Phil 8580.34	Arata, C. Persona ed evidenza nella prospettiva classica. Milano, 1963.
Phil 2138.149	Arata, Fidia. La logica di J. Stuart Mill e la problematica eticosociale. Milano, 1964.
Phil 8400.12	Arata, Rodolfo. I fondamenti del giudizio estetico. Bologna, 1960.
Phil 6320.10.5	Die Arbeit am Charakter. (Künkel, Fritz.) Schwerin, 1939.
Phil 5525.31	Eine Arbeit über das Lachen und des Komische. (Wallerstein, M.) Wien, 1925.
Phil 6117.36	Arbeit und Wille. pt.1-2. (Hallervorden, E.) Würzburg, 1897.
Phil 5850.214.10	Arbeits- und Berufspsychologie. (Giese, Fritz.) Halle, 1928.
Phil 5850.221.10	Arbeitsfreude - Leistungsanstrengungen. (Goersdorf, Kurt.) München, 1958.
Phil 5528.2	Arbeitsschen, eine psychologischpädagogische Studie. (Sperisen, Walter.) Bern, 1946.
Phil 4582.2.31	Arbetets ära kulturhistorisk undersökning. (Hofstedt, A.) Stockholm, 1900.
Phil 9245.28.10	Arbetsglädje-livsglädje. (Marden, Orison S.) Stockholm, 1912.
Phil 5628.10.15	Arbman, Ernst. Ecstasy or religious trance. Stockholm, 1963-70. 3v.
Phil 4352.1.160	Arboleya y Martinéz, Maximiliane. Balmes politico. Barcelona, 1911.
Phil 2475.1.320	Arbour, Romeo. Henri Bergson et les lettres françaises. Paris, 1955.
Phil 2490.142	Arbouss-Bastide, Paul. La doctrine de l'éducation universelle dans la philosophie d'Auguste Comte. v.1-2. Paris, 1957.
Phil 8580.28	Arbousse-Bastide, A.F. Le christianisme et l'esprit moderne. Paris, 1862.
Phil 2490.142.2	Arbouse-Bastide, Paul. La doctrine de l'éducation universelle dans la philosophie d'Auguste Comte. Paris, 1957. 2v.
Phil 7054.116.2	Arcana of nature. (Tuttle, H.) London, 1909.
Phil 7054.116.7	Arcana of spiritualism. (Tuttle, H.) Chicago, 1934.
Phil 7069.00.40	Arcana of spiritualism. (Tuttle, Hudson.) Manchester, 1900.
Phil 4075.45	Arcana politica. (Cardano, Girolamo.) Lugduni, 1635.
Phil 6110.14	The Arcane formulas, or Mental alchemy. Chicago, 1909.
Phil 4260.84	Arcari, P. Processi...di scienza nuova in G.B. Vico. Friburgo, 1911.
Phil 40.11	Arcetári filozofice. (Academia Republici Populare Romine, Bucurest. Institutut de Filozofie.) 4,1957+ 18v.
Phil 175.33	Arch, Robert. Whence, whither, and why. London, 1926.
Phil 850.2	Archaeologiae philosophicae. v.1-2. (Burnett, T.) London, 1728-33.
Phil 8642.8	Archaeology. (Richmond, I.) London, 1950.
Phil 8599.52	Die archaische Verborgenheit. (Theill-Wunder, Hella.) München, 1970.
Phil 3425.112	Archambault, P. Hegel. Paris, n.d.
Phil 3552.108	Archambault, P. Leibniz. Paris, n.d.
Phil 2805.103	Archambault, P. Pascal. Paris, n.d.
Phil 2840.83A	Archambault, P. Renouvier. Paris, 1911.
Phil 2138.92	Archambault, P. Stuart Mill. Paris, n.d.
Phil 2477.6.85	Archambault, P. Vers un realisme integral...Blondel. Paris, 1928.
Phil 8582.37	L'arche d'alliance. 2. éd. (Cherix, Robert B.) Paris, 1923.
Phil 1135.152	Hē archē tēs ōeri metempsykōseōs doxēs tōn Hellēnōn philosophōn. (Boreas, Theophilos.) Athens, 1913.
Phil 8677.9.80	Archer, William. God and Mr. Wells. N.Y., 1917.
Phil 7082.74	Archer, William. On dreams. London, 1935.
Phil 9352.7.15	Architects of fate. (Marden, O.S.) Boston, 1895.
Phil 10.65	Archiv für Begriffsgeschichte; Bausteine zu einem historischen Wörterbuch der Philosophie. Bonn. 1,1955+ 11v.
Phil 10.53	Archiv für den thierischen Magnetismus. Altenberg. 1-12,1817-1824 6v.
Phil 10.13	Archiv für die gesamte Psychologie. Leipzig. 1,1903+ 107v.
Phil 10.13.12	Archiv für die gesamte Psychologie. Erganzungsband. Leipzig. 1-4,1929-1937 5v.
Phil 10.13.5	Archiv für die gesamte Psychologie. Register. Leipzig. 1-75,1925-1931 2v.
Phil 10.6	Archiv für Geschichte der Philosophie. Berlin. 1,1887+ 43v.
Phil 10.6.5	Archiv für Geschichte der Philosophie. Register. Berlin. 1-20 2v.
Phil 10.61.5	Archiv für mathematische Logik und Grundlagenforschung. Stuttgart. 5-7
Phil 10.61	Archiv für Philosophie. Stuttgart. 4,1950+ 8v.
NEDL Phil 10.7	Archiv für Psychiatrie. Berlin. 1868-1929 27v.
Phil 10.7	Archiv für Psychiatrie. Berlin. 1929-1942 12v.
NEDL Phil 10.7.15	Archiv für Psychiatrie und Nervenkrankheiten. General Register. Berlin. 1-45,1898-1909 2v.
Phil 10.7.5	Archiv für Psychiatrie und Nervenkrankheiten vereinigt mit Zeitschrift für die gesamte Neurologie und Psychiatrie. Berlin. 179,1947+ 31v.
Phil 10.24	Archiv für Religionspsychologie. Tübingen. 1914+ 4v.
Phil 10.58	Archiv für spiritualistische Philosophie und ihre Geschichte. Amsterdam.
Phil 10.8	Archiv für systematische Philosophie. Berlin. 1-34,1895-1931 27v.
Phil 10.8.5	Archiv für systematische Philosophie. Register. Berlin. 1-15
Phil 58.15	Archives. (Société Belge de Philosophie.) Bruxelles. 1-5,1928-1933
NEDL Phil 10.9	Archives de neurologie. Paris. 1880-1929 11v.
Phil 10.9	Archives de neurologie. Paris. 1930-1946 11v.
Phil 10.30	Archives de philosophie. Paris. 1,1923+ 47v.
Phil 10.30.3	Archives de philosophie. Tables generales. 1937
Phil 10.14	Archives de psychologie. Genève. 1,1902+ 38v.
Phil 10.21	Archives du magnétisme animal. Paris. 1-4 2v.
Phil 10.34	Archives of neurology and psycho-pathology. Utica, N.Y. 1-3 6v.
Phil 10.19.5	Archives of psychology. (Columbia University.)
Phil 10.19	Archives of psychology. (Columbia University.) N.Y. 1907-1945 37v.
Phil 10.74	Archivio de psicologia, neurologia e psichiotrea. Milano. 5,1944+ 19v.

Phil 175.45	Archivio di Filosofia. Il compito della fenomenologia. Padova, 1957.
Phil 165.19	Archivio di Filosofia. Il compito della Metafisica. Milano, 1952.
Phil 735.136	Archivio di Filosofia. La crisi dei valori. Roma, 1945.
Phil 8580.33.5	Archivio di Filosofia. Demitizzazione e immagine. Padova, 1962.
Phil 165.66	Archivio di Filosofia. La diaristica filosofica. Padova, 1959.
Phil 1750.371	Archivio di Filosofia. Esistenzialismo cristiano. Padova, 1949.
Phil 1750.115.20	Archivio di Filosofia. Fenomenologia e sociologia. Padova, 1951.
Phil 5238.165	Archivio di Filosofia. Filosofia della alienazione e analisi esistenziale. Padova, 1961.
Phil 8400.4	Archivio di Filosofia. Filosofia dell'arte. Roma, 1953.
Phil 165.65	Archivio di Filosofia. Filosofia e simbolismo. Roma, 1956.
Phil 3552.350	Archivio di Filosofia. Leibniz. Il congresso internazionale di filosofia, Roma, 1946. Roma, 1947.
Phil 165.67	Archivio di Filosofia. Metafisica ed esperienza religiosa. Roma, 1956.
Phil 8580.33	Archivio di Filosofia. Il problema della demitizzazione. Padova, 1961.
Phil 8624.100	Archivio di Filosofia. Il problema dell'immortalità. Roma, 1946.
Phil 400.115	Archivio di Filosofia. Il solipsismo. Padova, 1950.
Phil 8400.4.5	Archivio di Filosofia. Surrealismo e simbolismo. Padova, 1965.
Phil 70.96	Archivio di Filosofia. Tecnica e casistica. Padova, 1964.
Phil 672.197	Archivio di Filosofia. Il tempo. Padova, 1958.
Phil 672.198	Archivio di Filosofia. Tempo e eternità. Padova, 1959.
Phil 672.199	Archivio di Filosofia. Tempo e intenzionalità. Padova, 1960.
Phil 4030.5	Archivio di Filosofia. Testi umanistici inediti sul De anima. Padova, 1951.
Phil 1630.5	Archivio di Filosofia. Testi umanistici su l'ermetismo. Roma, 1955.
Phil 1630.10	Archivio di Filosofia. Umanesimo e esoterismo. Padova, 1960.
Phil 10.40	Archivio di filosofia. Roma. 1-11,1931-1941 17v.
Phil 10.43	Archivio di storia della filosofia. Roma. 1-8,1932-1939 5v.
Phil 10.16	Archivo de historia de la filosofía. Madrid. 1-2,1905-1907 2v.
Phil 5520.150	Archivio di Filosofia. Semantica. Roma, 1955.
Phil 42.13	Archivos. (Chile. Universidad, Santiago. Instituto Central de Psicología.) Santiago. 2,1963+
Phil 10.17	Archivos de psiquiatría y criminología. Buenos Aires. 6-12,1907-1913
Phil 41.4	Archivos del laboratorio de facultad de filosofia y letras psicologicas. (Buenos Aires. Universidad Nacional. Facultad de Filosofía y Letras.) Buenos Aires, 1931.
Phil 10.23	Archivos italiano di psicologia. Torino. 1-19,1920-1941 8v.
Phil 10.70	Archiwum historii filozofii i myśli spolecznej. Warszawa. 1-13 6v.
Phil 3235.89	Ardab'ev, A.I. Ateizm Ludviga Feierbakha. Moskva, 1963.
Phil 2050.263	Ardal, Páll S. Passion and value in Hume's Treatise. Edinburgh, 1966.
Phil 4963.3	Ardao, Arturo. Battle y Ordoñez y el positivismo filosófico. Montevideo, 1951.
Phil 4961.805.5	Ardao, Arturo. Espiritualismo y positivismo en el Uruguay. México, 1950.
Phil 4961.805.10	Ardao, Arturo. La filosofía en el Uruguay en el siglo XX. México, 1956.
Phil 4961.805	Ardao, Arturo. Filosofía pre-universitaria en el Uruguay. Montevideo, 1945.
Phil 4983.1.90	Ardao, Arturo. Introducción a Vaz Ferreira. Montevideo, 1961.
Phil 4961.805.15	Ardao, Arturo. Racionalismo y liberalismo en el Uruguay. Montevideo, 1962.
Phil 2270.126	Ardigó, R. La dottrina Spenceriana dell'inconoscible. Roma, 1899.
Phil 4200.1.83	Ardigò, R. Pietro Pomponazzi. Mantova, 1869.
Phil 4060.1.40	Ardigo, Roberto. L'idealismo e la scienza. Roma, 1919.
Phil 4060.1.30	Ardigo, Roberto. An inconsistent preliminary objection against positivism. Cambridge, 1910.
Phil 4060.1.35	Ardigo, Roberto. Natura naturans. Ostiglia, 1918.
Phil 4060.1.2	Ardigo, Roberto. Opere filosofiche. Padova, 1901-13. 11v.
Phil 4060.1.23	Ardigo, Roberto. Pagine scelte. Genova, 1913.
Phil 4060.1.25	Ardigo, Roberto. Scritti vari. Firenze, 1920.
Phil 4060.1.91	Ardigò. (Troilo, Erminio.) Milano, 1926.
Phil 1700.6	Ardley, Gavin. Aquinas and Kant. London, 1950.
Phil 1870.170	Ardley, Gavin W.R. Berkeley's renovation of philosophy. The Hague, 1968[1969]
Phil 8701.20	Are science and religion at strife? (Lee, John H.) Evanston, 1945.
Phil 8637.8	Are souls immortal? 3rd ed. (Miller, J.) Princeton, N.J., 1887.
Phil 6679.3	Are the cominform countries using hypnotic techniques to elicit confessions. (Janis, I.L.) Santa Monica, Calif., 1949.
Phil 7069.09.20	Are the dead alive? (Rider, Fremont.) N.Y., 1909.
Phil 8882.24.15	Are you human? (Hyde, W. De W.) N.Y., 1916.
Phil 535.30	Arendt, Dieter. Nihilismus. Köln, 1970.
Phil 3640.295	Arevalo Martinez, R. Nietzsche und conquistador. Guatemala, 1943.
Phil 2270.134	Arfvidsson, H.D. Religion och vetenskap...Spencers. Diss. Lund, 1894.
Phil 5642.18	Argelander, A. Das Farbenhören und der synäthetische Faktor der Wahrnehmung. Jena, 1927.
Phil 175.9.5	Argens, J.B. The impartial philosopher. London, 1749. 2v.
Phil 175.9.8	Argens, J.B. Philosophical dissertations. London, 1753. 2v.
Phil 175.9.2	Argens, J.B. La philosophie du Bon-Sens. La Haye, 1755. 3v.
Phil 175.9	Argens, J.B. La philosophie du Bon-Sens. La Haye, 1765. 2v.
Phil 75.36	Argentine Republic. Comisión Nacional de Cooperación Intelectual. Bibliografía argentina de publicaciones filosóficas, años 1937 a 1943. Buenos Aires, 1943.
Phil 8658.10	The argument for a finitist theology. Diss. (Dotterer, R.H.) Lancaster, Pa., 1917.
Phil 5525.44	Argument of laughter. (Monro, David Hector.) Carlton, Victoria, 1951.

Author and Title Listing

Phil 5525.44.5 Argument of laughter. (Monro, David Hector.) Notre Dame, 1963.
Phil 165.360 Argumentationen. (Delius, Harald.) Göttingen, 1964.
Htn Phil 8624.3* Arguments and replies. (Layton, Henry.) London, 1703. 7 pam.
Phil 8666.7 Les arguments de l'athéisme. (La Paquerie, J.) Paris, 1909.
Htn Phil 8662.2* Arguments to prove the being of God. (Hancock, J.) London, 1707.
Phil 5590.462 Argyle, Michael. The psychology of interpersonal behavior. Harmondsworth, 1967.
Phil 5627.258 Argyle, Michael. Religious behavior. London, 1958.
Phil 8582.3.2 Argyll, G.D.C. The reign of law. London, 1871.
Phil 8582.3.5 Argyll, G.D.C. The reign of law. 4. ed. London, 1867.
Phil 8582.3.1 Argyll, G.D.C. The reign of law. 5. ed. N.Y., 1869.
Phil 8582.3.6 Argyll, G.D.C. The unity of nature. London, 1884.
Phil 8582.3.7 Argyll, G.D.C. The unity of nature. N.Y., 1884.
Phil 720.1.2 Argyll, G.D.C. What is truth? N.Y., 1889.
Phil 3640.79.50 Ariadne; Jahrbuch der Nietzsche-Gesellschaft. München. 1925
Htn Phil 8950.2* Ariadne mystica. Monachij, 1698. 2 pam.
Phil 4983.1.80 Arias, Alejandro. Vaz Ferreira. 1. ed. México, 1948.
Phil 4351.2.5 Arias, Alejandro C. Estudios literarios y filosóficos. Montevideo, 1941.
Phil 4351.2 Arias, Alejandro C. Sobre la cultura. Montevideo, 1943.
Phil 3805.220 Ariebel, Horst. Die Bedeutung des Bösen für die Entwiklung. Ratingen, 1961.
Phil 5240.55 Ariete, Silvano. The intrapsycic self. N.Y., 1967.
Phil 6950.7.6 Arieti, S. Interpretation of schizophrenia. N.Y., 1955.
Phil 6950.7 Arieti, S. Interpretation of schizophrenia. N.Y., 1955.
Phil 6980.58 Arieti, Silvano. American handbook of psychiatry. N.Y., 1959. 3v.
Phil 7055.205 Arigó, desafio à ciência. (Serrano, Geraldo.) Rio de Janeiro, 1967.
Phil 7055.205.7 Arigó: vida, mediunidade e martírio. 2. ed. (Pires, José.) São Paulo, 1966.
Phil 5627.190 Arin. (Jung, C.G.) Zürich, 1951.
Phil 960.26 Arische Weltanschauung. 3. Aufl. (Chamberlain, Houston.) München, 1916.
Htn Phil 8587.9* Aristée ou de la divinité. (Hemsterhuis, F.) Paris, 1778-79. 2 pam.
Phil 3488.14 Aristoteles und Kant bezüglich der idee der theoretischen Erkenntnis. (Görland, A.) Giessen, 1909.
Phil 40.1 Aristotelian Society. Proceedings. London. 1,1887+ 70v.
Phil 40.1.5 Aristotelian Society. Supplementary volume. London. 1,1918+ 43v.
Phil 40.1.3 Aristotelian Society. Synoptic index, 1900-49. Oxford, 1949. 2v.
Phil 165.180 Aristotelian Society for the Systematic Study of Philosophy. Concepts of continuity. v.4. London, 1924.
Phil 2280.16.80 Aristotelian Society for the Systematic Study of Philosophy, London. Philosophical studies; essays in memory of L. Susan Stebbing. London, 1948.
Phil 270.51 The Aristotelian-Thomistic concept of chance. (Junkersfeld, M.J.) Indiana, 1945.
Phil 353.25 Aristotelische Erkenntnislehre bei Whately und Newman. (Willam, Franz.) Freiburg, 1960.
Phil 1540.15 Der aristotelische Realismus in der Frühscholastik. Inaug.-Diss. (Reiners, Josef.) Bonn, 1907.
Phil 5047.24.5 Den aristoteliska logiken jämförd med modern logik. (Hjelmérus, Alfred.) Umea, 1918.
Phil 1540.47 L'aristotelismo della scolastica nella storia. 3. ed. (Talamo, Salvatore.) Siena, 1881.
Phil 1535.18.5 Die aristotellisch-thomistische Philosophie. (Gredt, Joseph.) Freiburg, 1935. 2v.
Phil 1523.12.10 Aristotle in the West. (Steenberghen, F.) Louvain, 1955.
Phil 5425.11 Arithmetical prodigies. (Scripture, E.W.) Worcester, 1891.
Phil 5066.12.5 Arithmétique. (Peano, G.) Turin, 1898.
Phil 5066.12 Aritmetica generale e algebra elementare. (Peano, G.) Torino, 1902.
Phil 8625.4 Arjuna. The single eye. N.Y., 1921.
Phil 8980.159 Arkhangel'skii, Leonid M. Kategorii marksistskoi etiki. Moskva, 1963.
Phil 8980.159.5 Arkhangel'skii, Leonid M. Lektsii po marksistskoi etiki. v.1-. Sverdlovsk, 1969.
Phil 10.63 Arkhé; revista de metafísica. Cordoba. 1-3,1952-1954 2v.
Phil 310.685 Arkhiptsev, Fedor T. V.I. Lenin o nauchnom poniatii materii. Moskva, 1957.
Phil 10.29 Arkiv för psykologi och pedagogik. Stockholm. 1-8,1922-1929 2v.
Phil 6315.2.305 Arlow, J.A. The legacy of Sigmund Freud. N.Y., 1956.
Phil 8580.40 Armaner, Neda. Inanç ve hareket bütünlüğü bakimindan din terbiyesi. Istanbul, 1967.
Phil 1700.5 Armani, T. Da G. Bruno e da A. Gentile allo Spencer e all' Ardigò. Camerino, 1904.
Phil 3475.3.145 Armbruster, Ludwig. Objekt und Transzendenz bei Jaspers. Innsbruck, 1957.
Phil 177.19.15 L'armonia delle cose. (Conti, Augusto.) Firenze, 1888. 2v.
Phil 3552.450 L'armonia prestabilita in Leibniz. (Vitale, Ignazio.) Padova, 1959.
Phil 720.80 Armour, Leslie. The concept of truth. Assen, 1969.
Phil 175.56 Armour, Leslie. The rational and the real. The Hague, 1962.
Phil 8413.5 Armour for aphrodite. (Moore, T.S.) London, 1929.
Phil 175.15 Armstrong, A.C. Transitional eras in thought. N.Y., 1904.
Phil 1845.12 Armstrong, A.E. In the last analysis. N.Y., 1956.
Phil 850.21A Armstrong, A.H. An introduction to ancient philosophy. London, 1947.
Phil 850.21.5 Armstrong, A.H. An introduction to ancient philosophy. 2d ed. London, 1949.
Phil 850.21.10 Armstrong, A.H. An introduction to ancient philosophy. 3d ed. London, 1957.
Phil 850.21.11 Armstrong, A.H. An introduction to ancient philosophy. 3d ed. Westminster, Md., 1959.
Phil 1133.43 Armstrong, Arthur Hilary. The Cambridge history of later Greek and early medieval philosophy. London, 1967.
Phil 1870.142 Armstrong, D.M. Berkeley's theory of vision. Victoria, 1960.
Phil 1845.17 Armstrong, David M. A materialist theory of the mind. London, 1968.
Phil 573.2 Armstrong, David M. Perception and the physical world. London, 1961.
Phil 5635.46 Armstrong, David Malet. Bodily sensations. London, 1962.
Phil 5465.95 Armstrong, Frank A. Idea-tracking. N.Y., 1960.
Phil 5525.32.5 Armstrong, M. Laughing: an essay. London, 1928.
Phil 5525.32 Armstrong, M. Laughing: an essay. N.Y., 1928.
Phil 1540.77 Armstrong, O.H. Christian faith and Greek philosophy. N.Y., 1964.
Phil 8655.10 Armstrong, R.A. Man's knowledge of God. London, 1886.
Phil 325.22 Armstrong, Robert L. Metaphysics and British empiricism. Lincoln, 1970.
Phil 5240.32 Armstrong-Jones, K. The growth of the mind. Edinburgh, 1929?
Phil 85.1 Arnaiz y Alcalde, N. Diccionario manual de filosofía. Madrid, 1927.
Phil 2840.82 Arnal, A. La philosophie religieuse de C. Renouvier. Paris, 1907.
Phil 6110.15 Árnason, A. Apoplexie und ihre Vererbung. Kopenhagen, 1935.
Phil 2490.184.5 Arnaud, Pierre. La pensée d'Auguste Comte. Paris, 1969.
Phil 2490.184 Arnaud, Pierre. Sociologie de Comte. Paris, 1969.
Phil 720.22 Arnauld, A. Des vrayes et des fausses idées. Cologne, 1683.
Phil 5040.3.25 Arnauld, Antoine. L'art de penser; la logique de Port Royal. v.1-3. Stuttgart, 1965- 2v.
Phil 5040.3.20 Arnauld, Antoine. The art of thinking. Indianapolis, 1964.
Phil 5040.4.4 Arnauld, Antoine. Logic, or The art of thinking. Edinburgh, 1850.
Phil 5040.4.2 Arnauld, Antoine. Logic, or The art of thinking. London, 1717.
Phil 5040.4.3 Arnauld, Antoine. Logic, or The art of thinking. London, 1723.
Phil 5040.4 Arnauld, Antoine. Logik, or The art of thinking. London, 1702.
Phil 5040.4.4.7 Arnauld, Antoine. La logique, ou L'art de penser. Paris, 1965.
Phil 5040.3.5 Arnauld, Antoine. Logique de Port Royal. Paris, 1854.
Phil 5040.3.9 Arnauld, Antoine. Logique de Port Royal. Paris, 1861.
Phil 5040.3.12 Arnauld, Antoine. Logique de Port Royal. Paris, 1869.
NEDL Phil 5040.3.15 Arnauld, Antoine. Logique de Port Royal. Paris, 1878.
Phil 5040.3.18 Arnauld, Antoine. Logique de Port-Royal. Facsimile. Lille, 1964.
Phil 2438.17 Arnauld, Antoine. Oeuvres de Messire Antoine Arnauld. v.1-43. Paris, 1964. 38v.
Phil 2438.15 Arnauld, Antoine. Oeuvres philosophiques. Paris, 1843.
Phil 2438.16 Arnauld, Antoine. Oeuvres philosophiques. Paris, 1843.
Phil 5040.4.5 Arnauld, Antoine. The Port Royal logic. Edinburgh, 1861.
Phil 175.18 Arndt, Julius. Des Bewusstwerden der Menschheit. Halle, 1850.
Phil 6110.6 Arnett, L.D. The soul, a study of past and present beliefs. n.p., 1904.
Phil 2280.5.109 Arnett, W.E. Santayana and the sense of beauty. Bloomington, Ind., 1955.
Phil 8401.40.5 Arnheim, Rudolf. Art and visual perception. Berkeley, 1965.
Phil 8401.40 Arnheim, Rudolf. Toward a psychology of art. Berkeley, 1967.
Phil 8401.40.10 Arnheim, Rudolf. Visual thinking. Berkeley, 1969.
Phil 1350.8 Arnold, E.V. Roman stoicism. Cambridge, 1911.
Phil 8625.5.15 Arnold, Edwin. Death and afterwards. London, 1907.
Phil 8625.5.17 Arnold, Edwin. Death and afterwards. N.Y., 1901.
Phil 5330.11 Arnold, F. Attention and interest...study in psychology. N.Y., 1910.
Phil 5325.5 Arnold, Felix. The psychology of association. N.Y., 1906.
Phil 5325.5.2 Arnold, Felix. The psychology of association. N.Y., 1906.
Phil 5240.4 Arnold, G.F. Psychology applied to legal evidence. Calcutta, 1906.
Phil 7054.14 Arnold, H. Wie errichtet und leitet man spiritistische Zirkel in der Familie? Leipzig, 1894.
Phil 7140.128 Arnold, Hans. Schulmedizin und Wunderkuren. Leipzig, 1892.
Phil 7059.9 Arnold, L.M. History of the origin of all things. n.p., 1852.
Phil 5590.130 Arnold, M.B. The human person. N.Y., 1954.
Phil 5374.69 Arnold, Magda. Story sequence analysis. N.Y., 1962.
Phil 5400.145 Arnold, Magda B. Emotion and personality. N.Y., 1960. 2v.
Phil 3808.231 Arnold, Otto. Schopenhauer padägogische. Leipzig, 1906.
Phil 175.16 Arnold, R.B. Scientific fact and metaphysical reality. London, 1904.
Phil 6950.1 Arnold, T. Observation...insanity, lunacy or madness. v.1-2. Leicester, 1782-86.
Phil 5210.2 Arnold, V.H. La psychologie de réaction en Amérique. Thèse. Paris, 1926.
Phil 5590.230 Arnold, Wilhelm. Person, Charakter, Persönlichkeit. Göttingen, 1957.
Phil 7082.112.1 Arnold-Forster, Mary Story-Maskelyne. Studies in dreams. London, 1921.
Phil 7082.112 Arnold-Forster, Mary Story-Maskelyne. Studies in dreams. N.Y., 1921.
Phil 3280.60 Arnold Geulincs collegium oratorium i. e. nova methodus omnis generis orationes. (Geulincx, A.) Amsterdam, 1968.
Phil 3280.84 Arnold Geulincx' Erkenntnisstheorie und Occasionalismus. (Grimm, Edward.) Jena, 1875.
Phil 3280.86 Arnold Geulincx te Leiden. (Land, J.P.N.) Amsterdam, 1887.
Phil 3280.85 Arnold Geulincx und seine Philosophie. (Land, J.P.N.) Haag, 1895.
Phil 2855.6.82 Arnold Reymond. Torino, 1956.
Phil 3482.3.5 Arnoldt, Emil. Kant's transcendentale idealität des Raumes und der zeit. Pt.1-5. Königsberg, 1870-72.
Phil 3482.3 Arnoldt, Emil. Kritische excurse im Gebiete der Kant-Forschung. Köningsburg, 1894.
Htn Phil 4112.83* Arnone, N. Pasquale Galluppi giacobino. Napoli, 1912.
Phil 9575.1 Arnot, W. The race for riches. Philadelphia, 1853.
Phil 9070.60 Arnoux, André. La voie du bonheur. Paris, 1957.
Phil 3910.125 Arnsperger, W. Christians Wolff's Verhältnis zu Lubniz. Weimar, 1897.
Phil 5655.6 Aromatics and the soul. (McKenzie, Dan.) London, 1923.
Phil 2880.8.275 Aron, Raymond. Marxism and the existentialists. N.Y., 1970.
Phil 2490.145 Aron, Raymond. War and industrial society. London, 1958.
Phil 7069.51.10 Aron, Robert. Mors et vita. Paris, 1951.
Phil 2250.87 Aronson, M.J. La philosophie morale de Josiah Royce. Paris, 1927.
Phil 2250.87.2 Aronson, M.J. La philosophie morale de Josiah Royce. Thèse. Paris, 1927.
Htn Phil 4265.1.90* Arpe, P.F. Apologia J. Caesare Vanino neapolitano. Csmomopoli, 1712.
Phil 6053.2.1 Arpentigny, Casimir Stanislas d'. La science de la main. The science of the hand. London, 1886.

Author and Title Listing

Phil 10.60 Arquivos brasileiros de psicotéchica. 1,1949+ 19v.

Phil 5545.1 Arréat, L. Mémoire et imagination. Paris, 1895.

Phil 8401.6 Arréat, Lucien. Art et psychologie individuelle. Paris, 1906.

Phil 1700.4 Arréat, Lucien. Dix années de philosophie. Paris, 1901.

Phil 8950.6.2 Arregui, Antonio M. Summarium theologiae morales. Bilbao, 1919.

Phil 8950.6 Arregui, Antonio M. Summarium theologiae morales. Bilbao, 1922.

Phil 8950.8 Arrese y Ontiveros, Pedro Alexandro de. Modo para vivir eternamento. Madrid, 1710.

Phil 281.4.5A Arrhenius, S. World's in the making. London, 1908.

Phil 9530.32 L'arrivisme. (Laurie, Ossip.) Paris, 1929.

Phil 4962.20 Arroyave Calle, J.C. El ser del hombre. Medellín, 1952.

Htn Phil 3552.55* Ars Combinatoria. (Leibniz, Gottfried Wilhelm.) Francofurti, 1690.

Phil 525.97.5 Arsen'ev, N.S. Ostkirche und Mystik. 2. Aufl. München, 1943.

Phil 4751.1.32 Arsen'ev, N.S. Pravoslavie, katolichestvo, protestantizm. Parizh, 1948.

Phil 4751.1.30 Arsen'ev, N.S. Zhazhda podlinnago Bytiia. Berlin, n.d.

Phil 2805.194 Arsovitch, R. Pascal et l'expérience du Puy-de-Dome. Thèse. Montpellier, 1925.

Phil 8406.15 Art, esthétique, idéal. (Figari, Pedro.) Paris, 1920.

Phil 8413.16 Art, form, and civilization. (Mundt, Ernest.) Berkeley, 1952.

Phil 70.94.6 Art, mind, and religion; proceedings. (Oberlin Colloquium in Philosophy, 6th, Oberlin College, 1965.) Pittsburgh. 1967

Phil 8692.24 Art, science, and religion. (Coggin, Philip.) London, 1962.

Phil 8404.8 Art, the critics and you. (Ducasse, Curt.) N.Y., 1944.

Phil 8425.2 Art: its constitution and capacities. (Young, E.) Bristol, 1854.

Phil 8092.13.5 Art against ideology. (Fischer, Ernst.) London, 1969.

Phil 8418.20.10 Art and alienation: the role of the artist in society. (Read, Herbert.) London, 1967.

Phil 8402.32 Art and analysis. (Ballard, Edward.) The Hague, 1957.

Phil 8423.24 Art and anarchy, and other essays. (Wind, Edgar.) London, 1963.

Phil 8419.45 Art and beauty. (Schoen, Max.) N.Y., 1932.

Phil 8430.70 Art and belief. (Bolam, David Whielden.) N.Y., 1970.

Phil 8092.26 Art and existence: a phemomenological aesthetics. (Kalelin, Eugene Francis.) Lewisburg, Pa. 1971.

Phil 8406.24 Art and existentialism. (Fallico, A.B.) Englewood Cliffs, 1962.

Phil 8050.70 Art and freedom; a historical and biographical interpretation. (Kallen, H.M.) N.Y., 1942. 2v.

Phil 8401.22.5 Art and instinct. (Alexander, Samuel.) Oxford, 1927.

Phil 8404.17 Art and morality. (De Selincourt, O.) London, 1935.

Phil 8400.46 Art and philosophy. (New York University. Institute of Philosophy, 7th, 1964.) N.Y., 1966.

Phil 2750.11.89 Art and poetry. (Maritain, Jacques.) N.Y., 1943.

Phil 8414.7 Art and reality. (Nolte, Fred O.) Lancaster, 1942.

Phil 8413.33 Art and scholasticism. (Maritain, J.) N.Y., 1962.

Phil 8416.11.22 Art and social life. (Plekhanov, Georgii Valentinovich.) London, 1953.

Phil 8416.11.20 Art and society. (Plekhanov, Georgii Valentinovich.) N.Y., 1936.

Phil 8410.8 Art and the human enterprise. (Jenkins, I.) Cambridge, 1958.

Phil 8430.24 Art and the intellect. (Taylor, Harold.) N.Y., 1960.

Phil 8401.10 Art and the material. (Alexander, Samuel.) London, 1925.

Phil 8430.32 Art and the social order. (Gotshalk, D.W.) Chicago, 1947.

Phil 8420.12 Art and the unconscious; a psychological approach to a problem of philosophy. (Thorburn, J.M.) London, 1925.

Phil 8416.21 Art and truth. (Purser, J.W.R.) Glasgow, 1937.

Phil 8401.40.5 Art and visual perception. (Arnheim, Rudolf.) Berkeley, 1965.

Phil 8404.19A Art as experience. (Dewey, J.) N.Y., 1934.

Phil 4352.1.33 Art d'arriver au vrai. (Balmes, Jaime.) Paris, 1852.

Phil 6681.2 L'art de magnétiser. (Lafontaine, C.) Paris, 1886.

Phil 5040.3.25 L'art de penser; la logique de Port Royal. v.1-3. (Arnauld, Antoine.) Stuttgart, 1965- 2v.

Phil 5243.34.15 L'art de penser. (Dimnet, E.) Paris, 1930.

Phil 8896.16 L'art de perfectionner l'homme. (Virey, J.J.) Paris, 1808. 2v.

Phil 8875.8 L'Art de se connoitre soy-même. v.1-2. (Abbadie, J.) La Haye, 1711.

Phil 7082.78 L'art de se rendre heureux par les songes. Francfort, 1746.

Phil 8419.68 L'art de sentir et de juger en matière de goût. v.1-2. (Séran de la Tour.) Genève, 1970.

Phil 8887.71.5 Un art de vivre. (Maurois, André.) Paris, 1939.

Phil 8416.11.25 L'art et de vie sociale (quatorze études). (Plekhanov, Georgii Valentinovich.) Paris, 1950.

Phil 6682.22 L'art et hypnose. (Magnia, E.) Genève, 1905?

Phil 8403.27.5 L'art et la beauté. (Challaye F.) Paris, 1929.

Phil 8430.18 L'art et la morale. (Lalo, C.) Paris, 1922.

Phil 8403.4 L'art et la nature. (Cherbuliez, V.) Paris, 1892.

Phil 8877.16 L'art et la vie. (Collignon, A.) Metz, 1866.

Phil 8412.6.10 L'art et la vie. (Lalo, Charles.) Paris, 1946-47. 3v.

Phil 8408.22 L'art et l'âme. (Huyghe, René.) Paris, 1960.

Phil 8416.27 L'art et le reel; essai de metaphysique fondée sur l'esthétique. (Perès, Jean.) Paris, 1897.

Phil 6998.8 Art et magie chez l'enfant. (Aubin, Henri.) Toulouse, 1971.

Phil 8401.6 Art et psychologie individuelle. (Arréat, Lucien.) Paris, 1906.

Phil 2418.3 Art et science dans la philosophie française contemporaine. (Segond, J.) Paris, 1936.

Phil 2750.11.85 Art et scolastique. 3. éd. (Maritain, Jacques.) Paris, 1935.

Phil 2750.11.85.4 Art et scolastique. 4. éd. (Maritain, Jacques.) Paris, 1965.

Phil 8407.44.5 L'art et ses problèmes. (Grenier, Jean.) Lausanne, 1970.

Phil 8408.19 Art experience. (Hiriyanna, M.) Mysore, 1954.

Htn Phil 6012.6.5* The art how to know men. (Cureau de la Chambre, Marin.) London, 1665.

Phil 8430.39 Art in human affairs. (Meier, N.C.) N.Y., 1942.

Phil 978.49.125 Art in the light of mystery wisdom. (Steiner, R.) N.Y., 1935.

Phil 8418.5.2 Art in theory; an introduction to the study of comparative aesthetics. 2. ed. (Raymond, G.L.) N.Y., 1909.

Phil 8407.20 L'art invincible. (Guillou, R.) Paris, 1948.

Phil 8401.4 L'art moral. (Alvard, Julien.) Paris, 1957.

Phil 8897.61 The art of behaviour. (Winsor, F.) Boston, 1932.

Phil 9245.36.5 The art of being easy at all times and in all places. (Deslandes, A.F.B.) London, 1724.

Phil 9245.1 The art of being happy. (Droz, F.X.J.) Boston, 1832.

Phil 9245.1.5 The art of being happy. (Droz, F.X.J.) London, 18- ?

Phil 5520.102 The art of clear thinking. 1. ed. (Flesch, R.F.) N.Y., 1951.

Phil 3808.30 Art of controversy. (Schopenhauer, Arthur.) London, 1896.

Phil 5242.35.10 The art of creation. (Carpenter, Edward.) London, 1904.

Phil 5110.5 The art of deception. (Capaldi, Nicholas.) N.Y., 1971.

Phil 6155.8 The art of ecstasy. (Marshall, William.) Don Mills, 1967.

Phil 9245.42 The art of employing time to the greatest advantage. London, 1822.

Htn Phil 9005.1* The art of excelling. (Burges, T.) Providence, 1799.

Phil 5400.88 The art of feeling. (Wyatt, H.G.) Boston, 1932.

Phil 9400.9 The art of growing old. (Poweys, J.C.) London, 1944.

Phil 9245.50.5 The art of happiness. (Powys, J.C.) N.Y., 1935.

Phil 1158.27 Art of happiness. (Sedgwick, H.D.) Indianapolis, 1933.

Phil 3549.2.45 The art of life. (Keyserling, Hermann.) London, 1937.

Phil 3808.28 Art of literature. (Schopenhauer, Arthur.) London, 1891.

Phil 8876.101 The art of living. (Borle, Charles A.) Boston, 1936.

Phil 8893.14.15 The art of living. (Smiles, Samuel.) Boston, 1887.

Phil 8887.71 The art of living. 5. ed. (Maurois, André.) N.Y., 1940.

Phil 9070.20 The art of living in wartime. (Greenbie, M.L.B.) N.Y., 1943.

Phil 5042.80 The art of logic, 1654. (Coke, Zachary.) Menston, Eng., 1969.

Phil 5058.106.1 The art of logic. 1628. Facsimile. (Spencer, Thomas.) Menston, Eng., 1970.

Phil 5041.52.6 The art of logike. Facsimile. (Blundeville, Thomas.) Menston, 1967.

Phil 5057.36 The art of making sense. (Ruby, Lionel.) London, 1956.

Phil 5545.29 The art of memory. (Fuller, H.H.) St. Paul, Minn., 1898.

Phil 5545.171 The art of memory. (Murden, J.R.) N.Y., 1818.

Phil 5545.95 The art of memory. (Yates, Frances Amelia.) London, 1966.

Phil 5545.26 Art of memory. London, 1823.

Phil 5627.180.5 The art of mental prayer. (Frost, Bede.) London, 1935.

Phil 8956.22 The art of moral judgement. (Greet, Kenneth.) London, 1970.

Phil 7080.21 The art of natural sleep. (Powell, S.P.) N.Y., 1908.

Phil 2255.1.38 The art of philosophizing. (Russell, Bertrand Russell.) N.Y., 1968.

Phil 5062.35 The art of practical thinking. (Weil, R.) N.Y., 1940.

Phil 5053.1 The art of reasoning. (Neil, Samuel.) London, 1853.

Phil 5242.48 The art of straight thinking. (Clarke, Edwin L.) N.Y., 1929.

Phil 5242.47 The art of straight thinking. (Clarke, Edwin L.) N.Y., 1932.

Phil 5040.3.20 The art of thinking. (Arnauld, Antoine.) Indianapolis, 1964.

Phil 5243.34.10 The art of thinking. (Dimnet, E.) London, 1929.

Phil 5243.34.3 The art of thinking. (Dimnet, E.) N.Y., 1929.

Phil 5243.34.9A The art of thinking. (Dimnet, E.) N.Y., 1929.

Phil 5243.34.5A The art of thinking. (Dimnet, E.) N.Y., 1929.

Phil 182.18.5 The art of thinking. (Henton, J.) London, 1879.

Phil 5062.36 The art of thought. (Wallas, G.) London, 1926.

Phil 5850.385 The art of thought. (Wallas, Graham.) N.Y., 1926.

Phil 5241.101 The art of understanding. (Baker, H.J.) Boston, 1940.

Phil 8418.6.10 An art philosopher's cabinet. (Raymond, G.L.) N.Y., 1915.

Phil 6980.772 L'art pyschopathologique. (Volmat, R.) Paris, 1956.

Phil 8419.47 Art reconstructed, a new theory of aesthetics. (Shaw, T.L.) Boston, 1937.

Phil 8418.5 Art theory; an introduction to the study of comparative aesthetics. (Raymond, G.L.) N.Y., 1894.

Phil 6980.398.20 Art therapy in a children's community. (Kramer, Edith.) Springfield, 1958.

Phil 8980.162 Artač, Marija. Gradiva za pouk temeljev socialistične morale. Ljubljana, 1969.

Phil 8430.43 Arte, ciências e trópico. (Freyre, G.) São Paulo, 1962.

Phil 3450.19.300 Arte, verdad y ser en Heidegger. (Cerezo Galan, Pedro.) Madrid, 1963.

Phil 4080.3.285 Arte. 1. ed. (Montano, Rocco.) Napoli, 1951.

Phil 8406.4.5 L'arte come comunicazione. (Formaggio, Dino.) Milano, 1953.

Phil 8415.6 L'arte come conoscenza degli individuali. (Ozzòla, L.) Roma, 1928.

Phil 5242.35 L'arte della creazione. (Carpenter, Edward.) Roma, 1909.

Phil 5190.10.15 L'arte di persuadere. (Prezzalini, G.) Firenze, 1907.

Phil 8140.5 Arte e architettura in regime fascista. (Napoli, Paolo.) Roma, 1938.

Phil 8418.15 Arte e libertá e altri saggi. (Russo, S.) Padova, 1960.

Phil 8403.26 Arte e sentimento. (Capasso, Aldo.) Firenze, 1957.

Phil 3450.19.420 Arte e verità nel pensiero di Martin Heidegger. (Vottimo, Gianni.) Torino, 1966.

Phil 8430.18.5 L'arte et la vie sociale. (Lalo, C.) Paris, 1921.

Phil 8418.16 L'arte et le arti. (Russi, Antonio.) Pisa, 1960.

Phil 5040.15 Arte logica. (Andreasi, A.) Verona, 1882.

Phil 8406.21 L'arte nella vita dell'uomo. (Fasola, Giusta Nicco.) Pisa, 1956.

Htn Phil 5041.52.5* The arte of logicke. (Blundeville, Thomas.) London, 1619.

Htn Phil 5051.19* The arte of reason. (Lever, Ralph.) London, 1573.

Phil 8430.13 El arte y las masas, ensayos sobre una nueva teoría della actividad estética. (Castelnuovo, E.) Buenos Aires, 1935.

Phil 4351.1.33 Arteaga, E. La belleza ideal. Madrid, 1943.

Phil 530.50.10 Arters, Stephanus. La spiritualité des Pays-Bas. Louvain, 1948.

Phil 3808.108.5 Arthur Schopenhauer; de philosophie. (Scheffer, Wessel.) Leiden, 1870.

Phil 3808.152 Arthur Schopenhauer, een levensbeeld. (Francken, C.J. Wijnaendts.) Haarlem, 1905.

Phil 3808.76.50 Arthur Schopenhauer; Mensch und Philosoph in seinen Briefen. (Schopenhauer, Arthur.) Wiesbaden, 1960.

Phil 3808.144 Arthur Schopenhauer. (Ahlberg, Alf.) Stockholm, 1924.

Phil 3808.80 Arthur Schopenhauer. (Asher, D.) Berlin, 1871.

Phil 3808.81 Arthur Schopenhauer. (Busch, O.) Heidelberg, 1877.

Phil 3808.186 Arthur Schopenhauer. (Copleston, Frederick.) London, 1946.

Phil 3808.160 Arthur Schopenhauer. (Cornill, Adolph.) Heidelberg, 1856.

Phil 3808.145 Arthur Schopenhauer. (Damm, O.F.) Leipzig, 1912.

Phil 3808.155 Arthur Schopenhauer. (Eymer, Karl.) n.p., 1915.

Phil 3808.234 Arthur Schopenhauer. (Frankfurt am Main. Stadt- und Universitätsbibliothek.) Frankfurt, 1960.

Phil 3808.84 Arthur Schopenhauer. (Frommann, H.) Jena, 1872.

Phil 3808.86 Arthur Schopenhauer. (Gwinner, W.) Leipzig, 1862.

Phil 3808.86.3 Arthur Schopenhauer. (Gwinner, W.) Leipzig, 1922.

Phil 3808.148 Arthur Schopenhauer. (Haym, R.) Berlin, 1864.

Phil 3808.169 Arthur Schopenhauer. (Hübscher, Arthur.) Leipzig, 1938.

Phil 3808.194 Arthur Schopenhauer. (Kurth, K.O.) Kitzingen, 1952.

Phil 3808.93 Arthur Schopenhauer. (Lindner, E.O.) Berlin, 1863.

Phil 3808.171 Arthur Schopenhauer. (Michaelis, G.) Leipzig, 1937.
Phil 3808.24.14 Arthur Schopenhauer. (Schopenhauer, Arthur.) n.p., n.d.
Phil 3808.113 Arthur Schopenhauer. (Seillière, E.) Paris, 1911.
Phil 3808.136 Arthur Schopenhauer. (Stern, I.) Zürich, 1883.
Phil 3808.103 Arthur Schopenhauer. (Volkelt, J.) Stuttgart, 1901.
Phil 3808.230 Arthur Schopenhauer. (Wolff, H.M.) Bern, 1960.
Phil 3808.98 Arthur Schopenhauer. (Zimmern, H.) London, 1876.
Phil 3808.215 Arthur Schopenhauer. Berlin, 1955.
Phil 3808.142 Arthur Schopenhauer als Psychologie. (Hohenemser, Richard.) Leipzig, 1924.
Phil 3808.237 Arthur Schopenhauer in Selbstzeugnissen und Bilddokumenten. (Abendroth, Walter.) Reinbek, 1967.
Phil 3808.147 Arthur Schopenhauer seine wirklichen und vermeintlichen Krankheiten. (Ebstein, W.) Stuttgart, 1907.
Phil 3808.121.5 Arthur Schopenhauer und die menschliche Willensfreiheit. (Penzig, Rudolph.) Halle, 1879.
Phil 3808.109A Arthur Schopenhauer und seine Weltanschauung. (Kowaleski, A.) Halle, 1908.
Phil 3808.95.5 Arthur Schopenhauer's Lehre von der Schuld in ethischer Beziehung. Inaug. Diss. (Crämer, Otto.) Heidelberg, 1895.
Phil 7082.6 Arthurs, André. Répertoire des images et symboles oniriques rencontrés au cours des analyses psychotherapiques. Genève, 1967.
Phil 3484.20 Arti e pensiero nelle laro istanze metafisiche. (Caracciolo, A.) Roma, 1953.
Phil 5270.18 Artifact in behavioral research. (Rosenthal, Robert.) N.Y., 1969.
Phil 8404.3.20 Artificio e natura. (Dorfles, Gillo.) Torino, 1968.
Phil 5040.1.8 Artis logicae compendium. (Aldrich, H.) Oxonii, 1844.
Phil 5040.1 Artis logicae rudimenta. (Aldrich, H.) Oxford, 1852.
Phil 5040.1.2 Artis logicae rudimenta. (Aldrich, H.) Oxford, 1856.
Phil 5040.1.3 Artis logicae rudimenta. (Aldrich, H.) Oxford, 1862.
Phil 5040.1.7 Artis logicae rudimenta. (Aldrich, H.) Oxonae, 1723.
Phil 5040.1.5 Artis logicae rudimenta. 5th ed. (Aldrich, H.) Oxford, 1835.
Phil 5040.1.6 Artis logicae rudimenta. 6th ed. (Aldrich, H.) Oxford, 1850.
Phil 8414.8 The artist as creator; an essay of human freedom. (Nahm, Milton Charles.) Baltimore, 1956.
Phil 8404.22 The artist in society. (Dunham, Barrows.) N.Y., 1960.
Phil 5465.142 The artist in society. (Hatterer, Lawrence J.) N.Y., 1965.
Phil 6060.48 Los artistas escriben. 1. ed. (Ras, M.) Madrid, 1954.
Phil 8418.25 L'artiste et la société. (Rouart, Eugène.) Paris, 1902.
Phil 8401.22 Artistic creation and cosmic creation. (Alexander, Samuel.) London, 1927.
Phil 5465.145 Artistic productivity and mental health. (Fried, Edrita.) Springfield, Ill., 1964.
Phil 8140.4 Artistic theory in Italy, 1450-1600. (Blunt, A.) Oxford, 1956.
Phil 8050.54 Artists and thinkers. (Flaccus, L.W.) N.Y., 1916.
Phil 4073.37 Artiveneti. (Campanella, Tommaso.) Firenze, 1945.
Phil 8420.9 The arts, artists and thinkers. (Todd, John.) London, 1959.
Phil 8412.36 Les arts de l'espace. 3. éd. (Lier, Henri.) Tournai, 1963.
Phil 70.75.4 Arts liberaux et philosophie au moyen âge. (Congrès International de Philosophie Médiévale, 4th, Montreal, 1967.) Montreal. 1969
Phil 8876.67 The arts of life. (Bowker, R.R.) Boston, 1900.
Phil 8407.41.5 The arts of the beautiful. (Gilson, Etienne.) N.Y., 1965.
Phil 3808.168 Arturo Schopenhauer. (Padovani, Umberto A.) Milano, 1934.
Phil 960.36 Arunáchalam, P. Light from the East. London, 1927.
Phil 175.63 Arvasi, S. Ahmet. Insan ve insanötesi. Istanbul, 1970.
Phil 5440.27 Arvelighed og moral. (Gjellerup, Karl.) Kjøbenhavn, 1881.
Phil 8092.20 Arvon, Henri. L'esthétique marxiste. Paris, 1970.
Phil 3235.118 Arvon, Henri. Ludwig Feuerbach. 1. éd. Paris, 1957.
Phil 3000.6 Arvon, Henri. La philosophie allemande. Paris, 1970.
Phil 9290.8 Arvon, Henri. La philosophie du travail. Paris, 1961.
Phil 10.54 Arya; a philosophical review. Pondicherry, India. 6-7,1920-1921
Phil 10.42 Aryan path. Bombay. 1,1930+ 45v.
Phil 270.110 Arystolelesowska i tomistyczna teoria przyczyry sprawczej na tle pojęcia bytu. (Jaworski, M.) Lublin, 1958.
Phil 3492.43 Arzt und Arztliches bei Kant. (Koenig, Ernst.) Kitzingen, 1954.
Phil 6110.9 As a man thinketh. (Allen, James.) N.Y., 19- .
Phil 6110.9.3 As a man thinketh. (Allen, James.) N.Y., 19- .
Phil 6110.9.5 As a man thinketh. (Allen, James.) N.Y., 19- .
Phil 6112.2.2 As a matter of course. (Call, A.P.) Boston, 1894.
Phil 960.134 As above, so below. (Tombleson, J.B.) London, 1928.
Phil 8954.4 As I was saying. (Elliot, W.H.) London, 1944?
Phil 193.135 As ideák problémája. (Somogyi, Jozsef.) Budapest, 1931.
Phil 197.25.5 As if; a philosophical phantasy. (Williams, C.L.) San Francisco, 1914.
Phil 7069.34.62 As in a mirror. (Wells, Helen B.) N.Y., 1934. 2 pam.
Phil 7069.00.20 As it is to be. (Daniels, Cora L.) Exeter, 1900.
Phil 7068.92.25 As it is to be. 5. ed. (Daniels, Cora Linn Morrison.) Franklin, Mass., 1892.
Phil 2070.76.5A As William James said: extracts from the published writings. (James, William.) N.Y., 1942.
Phil 5241.117.5 Ascendant psychology. (Brill, Albert.) Guilford, Conn., 1959.
Phil 978.77.6 Ascended master discourses. (King, G.R.) Chicago, 1937.
Phil 978.77.7 Ascended master light. (King, G.R.) Chicago, 1938.
Phil 8697.16 The ascent of faith. (Harrison, A.J.) N.Y., 1894.
Phil 365.55 The ascent of life. (Gondge, Thomas A.) Toronto, 1961.
Phil 8593.25 Ascent of the mountain. 1. ed. (Novak, Michael.) N.Y., 1971.
Phil 665.10 The ascent of the soul. (Bradford, A.H.) N.Y., 1902.
Phil 8622.72 Ascent to faith. 1st ed. (Kanellopoulos, Panagiótēs.) N.Y., 1966.
Phil 252.5 Ascent to the absolute: metaphysical papers and lectures. (Findlay, John Niemayer.) London, 1970.
Phil 8705.22 Ascèse et science. (Pégand, Georges.) Paris, 1963.
Phil 530.35.25 Ascesi e mistica trecentesca. (Petrocchi, Giorgio.) Firenze, 1957.
Phil 8890.37.5 Ascetica. (Petrone, Igino.) Milano, 1918.
Htn Phil 1845.2.30* Ascham, Roger. The scholemaster. London, 1571.
Phil 4065.65.5 Das Aschermitt Wochsmahl. (Bruno, Giordano.) Frankfurt, 1904.
Phil 3425.128 Aschkenasy, H. Hegels Einfluss auf die Religionsphilosophie in Deutschland. Berlin, 1907.
Phil 8404.3.5 Le ascillazioni del gusto. (Dorfles, Gillo.) Milano, 1958.
Phil 4080.3.155 Ascoli, M. Intorno alla concezione del diritto nel sistema di Benedetto Croce. Roma, 1925.

Phil 1700.8 Aseev, I.A. Osnovnye napravleniia burzhuaznoi filosofii i sotsiologii XX veka. Leningrad, 1961.
Phil 4600.8 Asfelin, G. Studier Aillägnade Efraim Liljequish. Lund, 1930. 2v.
Phil 8980.165 Ash, William F. Marxism and moral concepts. N.Y., 1964.
Phil 6670.1 Ashburner, J. Notes and studies... philosophy of animal magnetism. London, 1867.
Phil 6110.22 Ashby, William R. Design for a brain. N.Y., 1952.
Phil 6110.22.2 Ashby, William R. Design for a brain. 2. ed. N.Y., 1960.
Phil 510.129 Ashcroft, E.A. The world's desires. London, 1905.
Phil 3808.80 Asher, D. Arthur Schopenhauer. Berlin, 1871.
Phil 3808.80.2 Asher, D. Das Endergebniss der Arthur Schopenhauer Philosophie. Leipzig, 1885.
Phil 8580.11 Asher, David. Der religiöse Glaube. Leipzig, 1860.
Phil 5115.5 Ashley, M.L. The nature of hypothesis. Chicago, 1903.
Phil 9560.35 Ashley, Robert. Of honour. San Marino, 1947.
Phil 9070.59 Ashley Montagu, M.F. How to find happiness and keep it. 1st ed. Garden City, 1942.
Phil 2280.5.145 Ashmore, Jerome. Santayana, art, and aesthetics. Cleveland, 1966.
Phil 9070.47.5 Ashton, M.O. To whom it may concern. 2. ed. Salt Lake City, 1946.
Phil 3640.42 Asi hablaba Zarathustra. (Nietzsche, Friedrich.) Valencia, 19- ?
Phil 1020.9.5 Asian Palacios, M. Abenmasarra y su escuela. Madrid, 1914.
Phil 5222.16 Asian psychology. (Murphy, Gardner.) N.Y., 1968.
Phil 1020.7 Asin Palacios, M. Algazel. Dogmática, moral, ascética. v. 1-3. Zaragola, 1901. 2v.
Phil 1020.7.3 Asin Palacios, M. La espiritualidad de Algozel y su sentido cristiano. Madrid, 1935-41.
Phil 1020.7.2 Asin Palacios, M. Obras escogidas. Madrid, 1946.
Phil 5627.116 Die Askese; eine religionspsychologische Untersuchung. (Schjelderup, K. von.) Berlin, 1928.
Phil 672.237 Askin, Iakov F. Problema vremeni. Moskva, 1966.
Phil 8602.47.5 Asking them questions. Second series. (Wright, Ronald S.) London, 1938.
Phil 8602.47.10 Asking why. (Wright, Ronald S.) London, 1939.
Phil 5876.5.5 Asklund, Lis. Brytningstid, en bok om ungdom och samlernad. 5. uppl. Stockholm, 1964.
Phil 4761.1.80 Askoldov, C. Aleksei Aleksandrovich Kozlov. Moskva, 1912.
Phil 8881.26.18 Aslan, G. La morale selon Guyau. Paris, 1906.
Phil 175.10 Asmus, P. Das Ich. Halle, 1873.
Phil 8060.4 Asmus, V.F. Antichnye mysliteli ob iskusstve. 2. izd. Moskva, 1938.
Phil 3482.10 Asmus, V.F. Dialektika Kanta. Moskva, 1929.
Phil 5040.22 Asmus, V.F. Logika. Moskva, 1947.
Phil 8125.40 Asmus, V.F. Nemetskaia estetika XVIII veka. Moskva, 1962.
Phil 3482.13 Asmus, V.F. Die Philosophie Kants. Berlin, 1960.
Phil 331.32 Asmus, V.F. Problema intuitsii v filosofii i matematike. Moskva, 1963.
Phil 5040.22.5 Asmus, V.V. Uchenie logiki o dokazatel'stvi oprovrrzheniia. Moskva, 1954.
Phil 8170.10 Asmus, Valenti F. Voprosy teorii i istorii esteiki. Moskva, 1968.
Phil 1105.10 Asmus, Valentin F. Istoriia antichnoi filosofii. Moskva, 1965.
Phil 4751.4.25 Asmus, Valentin F. Izbrannye filosofskie trudy. v.1- Moskva, 1969- 2v.
Phil 310.1.8 Asmus, Valentin F. Ocherki istorii dialektiki v novoi filosofii. 2. izd. Moskva, 1929. 2 pam.
Phil 4610.9.80 Asmussen, E. Entwicklungsund grundprobleme der philosophie Rasmus Nielsens. Inaug. Diss. Flensburg, 1911.
Phil 4967.15 Asociación de Egresados de la Facultad de Derecho y Ciencias Sociales de la Universidad de Buenos Aires. La acusación de plagio contra el rector Frondizi. Buenos Aires? 1959.
Phil 4513.4.31 Asp, Matthia. Disputatio gradualis de philosopho curioso. Upsaliae, 1730.
Phil 4513.4.41 Asp, Matthia. Dissertatio academica de caussis obscuritatis philosophorum. Upsaliae, 1733.
Phil 4513.4.47 Asp, Matthia. Dissertatio academica de syncretismo philosophico. Upsaliae, 1737.
Phil 4513.4.33 Asp, Matthia. Dissertatio academica potiores antiquorum. Upsaliae, 1732.
Phil 4513.4.45 Asp, Matthia. Dissertatio gradualis de usu philosophiae in convertendis gentilibus. Upsaliae, 1737.
Phil 4513.4.35 Asp, Matthia. Dissertatio gradualis de vera perfectionis idea. Upsaliae, 1732.
Phil 4513.4.37 Asp, Matthia. Exercitium academicum de philosophia parabolica. Upsaliae, 1733.
Phil 4513.4.43 Asp, Matthia. Mexethma philosophicum de subordinatione veritatum. Upsaliae, 1733.
Phil 4513.4.39 Asp, Matthia. Stylus character animi. Upsaliae, 1732.
Phil 672.180 Aspecten van de tijd. Assen, 1950.
Phil 9575.9 Un aspecto del orden cristiano. (Gallegas Rocafull, J.M.) México, 1943.
Phil 5520.270 Aspectos de filosofia da linguagen. (Vieira de Almeida, F.) Coimbra, 1959.
Phil 4065.107.5 Les aspects de Dieu dans la philosophie de Giordano Bruno. (Namer, Emile.) Paris, 1926.
Phil 4065.107 Les aspects de Dieu dans la philosophie de Giordano Bruno. Thèse. (Namer, Emile.) Paris, 1926.
Phil 5190.17 Aspects de la dialectique. Paris, 1956.
Phil 5643.96 Les aspects de l'image visuelle. (Duret, René.) Paris, 1936.
Phil 5850.326.12 Aspects of applied psychology and crime. (Roback, A.A.) Cambridge, 1964.
Phil 6360.14 Aspects of autism. London, 1968.
Phil 8581.71 Aspects of belief. (Bezzant, J.S.) N.Y., 1938.
Phil 1803.15 Aspects of contemporary American philosophy. (Donnell, Franklin H.) Würzburg, 1965.
Phil 8615.5.50 Aspects of ethical religion; essays in honor of Felix Adler...fiftieth anniversary...Ethical movement, 1876. (Bridges, Horace J.) N.Y., 1926.
Phil 380.2.10 Aspects of form. (Whyte, Lancelot L.) London, 1951.
Phil 3007.5 Aspects of German culture. (Hall, G.S.) Boston, 1881.
Phil 960.260 Aspects of Indian thought. (Gopinatha, Kaviraja.) Burdwan, 1966.
Phil 5039.20 Aspects of inductive logic. (Hintikka, Kaarlo Jaakko J.) Amsterdam, 1966.
Phil 5545.227 Aspects of learning and memory. (Richter, Derek.) N.Y., 1966.
Phil 5041.58.8 Aspects of modern logic. (Beth, Evert Willem.) Dordrecht, 1970.
NEDL Phil 8697.1 Aspects of religious and scientific thought. (Hutton, R.H.) London, 1899.

Phil 1702.13 Aspects of the modern European mind. (Cruickshank, John.) Harlow, 1969.

Phil 1512.10 Aspects of the new scholastic philosophy. (Hart, C.A.) N.Y., 1932.

Phil 8635.8 Aspects of theism. (Knight, W.A.) London, 1893.

Phil 735.200 Aspects of value. (Gruber, Frederick C.) Philadelphia, 1959.

Phil 5401.58 Aspekte der Angst. (Starnberger Gespräche.) Stuttgart, 1965.

Phil 3425.405 Aspekte der Hegelschen Philosophie. (Adorno, Theodor W.) Berlin, 1957.

VPhil 5057.43 Aspekti odnosa izmedju Hegelove i Marxove dijalektike. (Rodin, Davor.) Beograd, 1967.

Phil 2150.6.83 Aspelin, G. Utgångspunkterna för Münsterbergs värdelära. Lund, 1929.

Phil 4513.8.31 Aspelin, Gunnar. Lek och allvar. Lund, 1968.

Phil 1505.4 Aspelin, Gunnar. Ur medeltidens tankevärld. Stockholm, 1959.

Phil 402.6 Aspelin, Gunnar. Världsbilder och livsidal. Lund, 1968.

Phil 1717.26 Aspetti della rivoluzione scientifica. (Rossi, Paolo.) Napoli, 1971.

Phil 8592.49 Aspirations from the inner, the spiritual life. (McCormac, H.) London, 1860.

Phil 8587.5 Aspirations of nature. (Hecker, I.T.) N.Y., 1857.

Phil 3585.26 Asser-Kramer, G. Neue nege zu Frieden und Freiheit. Pähl/Oberbayern, 1962.

Phil 187.98 Assertiones ex universa philosophia. (Markovics, J.M.) Pestini, 1802? 2 pam.

Phil 2475.1.257 Les assertions bergsoniennes. (Fénart, Michel.) Paris, 1936.

Phil 5548.50 Assessment of human motives. (Lindzey, Gardner.) N.Y., 1958.

Phil 5548.50.2 Assessment of human motives. (Lindzey, Gardner.) N.Y., 1964.

Phil 7068.87.5 Assier, Adolphe d'. Posthumous humanity. London, 1887.

Phil 5545.38 Assimilative memory. (Loisette, A.) N.Y., 1896.

Phil 7150.48 Assistenza medico sociale ai tenfati suicide. (Fondazione Piero Varenna, Milan.) Milano, 1959.

Phil 5238.188 Association de Psychologie Scientifique de la Langue Française. Les attitudes; symposium, Bordeaux. Paris, 1961.

Phil 5238.188.10 Association de Psychologie Scientifique de Langue Française. Le comportement, symposium de l'association de psychologie...(Rome, 1967). Paris, 1968.

Phil 5625.95 Association de Psychologie Scientifique de Langue Française. Le conditionnement et l'apprentissage. Strasbourg, 1956.

Phil 5545.260 Association de Psychologie Scientifique de Langue Française. La Mémoire. 1. éd. Paris, 1970.

Phil 5590.463 Association de Psychologie Scientifique de Langue Française. Les modèles de la personnalité en psychologie. 9e symposium de l'association de psychologie scientifique de langue française. Paris, 1965.

Phil 5548.65 Association de Psychologie Scientifique de Langue Française. La motivation. 1. éd. Paris, 1959.

Phil 5585.80 Association de Psychologie Scientifique de Langue Française. La perception. Paris, 1955.

Phil 5238.67 Association de Psychologie Scientifique de Langue Française. Les problèmes de la mesure en psychologie. Paris, 1962.

Phil 5520.409 Association de Psychologie Scientifique de Langue Française. Problèmes de psycholinguistique. Paris, 1963.

Phil 5435.16 Association de Psychologie Scientifique de Langue Française. Les processus d'adaptation; Xe symposium, Marseille, 1965. 1. éd. Paris, 1967.

Phil 5325.23 L'association des idées. (Claparède, Édouard.) Paris, 1903.

Phil 6951.19 Association des idées chez les idiots. (Boulenger.) Gand, 1906.

Phil 5325.19 L'association des idées obéitelles à des lois? Thèse. (Pétrovitch, D.) Caen, 1920.

Phil 40.15 Association for Research and Enlightenment. The A.R.E. journal. Virginia Beach. 1,1966+

Phil 6110.17 Association for Research in Nervous and Mental Diseases. The hypothalamus and central levels of autonomic function. Baltimore, 1940.

Phil 6110.18 Association for Research in Nervous and Mental Diseases. The interrelationship of mind and body. Baltimore, 1939.

Phil 1505.3 Association Guiellaume Bodé. Quelques aspects de l'humanisme médiéval. Paris, 1943.

Phil 1540.26 Association Guillaume Bude, Paris. Quelques aspects de l'humanisme médiéval. Paris, 1943.

Phil 1750.153 Association Guillaume Budé. L'humanisme en Alsace. Paris, 1939.

Phil 5325.1.2 Pamphlet box. Association of ideas.
Phil 5325.1 Pamphlet vol. Association of ideas. 1900-12. 11 pam.
Phil 5325.50 The association of ideas and critical theory in eighteenth-century England. (Kallich, Martin.) The Hague, 1970.

Phil 70.55 Association pour l'Étude Scientifique du Symbolisme. Congrès. Paris. 6,1957+ 3v.

Phil 40.20 Association Psychanalytique de France. Bulletin. Neully-sur-Seine. 4,1968+

Phil 5325.26 Association theory today. (Robinson, E.S.) N.Y., 1932.
Phil 3552.270 Der Associationsbegriff bei Leibniz. (Frenzel, Bernhard.) Leipzig, 1898.

Phil 8402.4 Das Associationsprincip und der Anthropomorphismus in der Asthetik. (Biese, Alfred.) Kiel, 1890.

Phil 5810.1 The associative processes of the guinea pig. (Allen, J.B.) Granville, Ohio, 1904.

Phil 40.12.5 Associazione Filosofica Ligure. Atti. Milano. 2,1955+
Phil 40.12 Associazione Filosofica Ligure. Relazione e discussione. Milano. 1951-1952

Phil 4080.22.31 Assoluto e relativo. 1. ed. (Coresi, Vincenzo.) Bergamo, 1959.

Phil 2270.131 L'assoluto inconoscibile di H. Spencer. (Nardi, P. de.) Forlì, 1904.

Phil 5325.24 Assoziationspsychologie und Erkenntnis. (Kern, B.) Berlin, 1913.

Phil 8587.6.15 Assumed authority:...Hedge's address. (Bowen, D.) Boston, 1864.

Phil 8401.29.10 Assunto, Rosario. L'automobile di Mallarmé e altri ragionamenti intorno, alla vocazione odierna delle arti. Roma, 1968. 10v.

Phil 3801.168 Assunto, Rosario. Estetica dell'identita. Urbino, 1962.

Phil 8401.33 Assunto, Rosario. Guidizio estetico critica e censura. Firenze, 1963.

Phil 8401.29 Assunto, Rosario. L'integrazione estetica, studi e ricerche. Milano, 1959.

Phil 8088.6 Assunto, Rosario. Stagione ragioni nell'estetica del settecento. Milano, 1967.

Phil 8092.4 Assunto, Rosario. Teoremi e problemi di estetica contemporanea. Milano, 1960.

Phil 3425.647 L'assunzione hegeliana. (Incardona, Nunzio.) Palermo, 1965.

Phil 8630.9.10 The assurance of immortality. (Fosdick, H.E.) N.Y., 1916.
Phil 8401.31.5 Astakhov, I.B. Estetika. Moskva, 1971.
Phil 8401.31 Astakhov, I.B. Iskusstvo i problema prekrasnogo. Moskva, 1963.

Phil 8400.44 Astakhov, Ivan B. Estetika i sovremennost'. Moskva, 1965.
Phil 5040.28 Astat'ev, Vsevdod K. Zakony myshleniia v formal'noi i dialketicheskoi logike. L'vov, 1968.

Phil 1105.7 Aster, E. Geschichte der antiken Philosophie. Berlin, 1920.

Phil 1800.1 Aster, E. Geschichte der englischen Philosophie. Bielefeld, 1927.

Phil 6310.3 Aster, E. Die Psychoanalyse. Berlin, 1930.
Phil 2520.160 Aster, E. von. Einführung in die Philosophie Descartes. München, 1921.

Phil 3000.4 Aster, E. Von. Die Philosophie der Gegenwart. Leiden, 1935.

Phil 3482.6.2 Aster, Ernst. Immanuel Kant. 2. Aufl. Leipzig, 1918.
Phil 5240.17.2 Aster, Ernst von. Einführung in die Psychologie. 2. Aufl. Leipzig, 1919.

Phil 331.5.10 Aster, Ernst von. Geschichte der neueren Erkenntnistheorie. Berlin, 1921.
Phil 800.14.14 Aster, Ernst von. Geschichte der Philosophie. 14. Aufl. Stuttgart, 1963.

Phil 331.5 Aster, Ernst von. Prinzipien der Erkenntnislehre. Leipzig, 1913.

Phil 3805.55 Asthetik. (Schleiermacher, Friedrich.) Berlin, 1931.
Phil 3425.425 L'asthétique de Hegel. (Teyssèdre, Bernard.) Paris, 1958.
Phil 6122.47 The Astor lectures. (Murray, William J.) N.Y., 1917.
Phil 6957.4 Astounding disclosures. (Hunt, J.H.) n.p., 1851.
Phil 7054.69 Astounding facts from the spirit world. (Gridley, J.A.) South Hampton, 1854.

Phil 5068.52 Astrada, C. Dialéctica y positivismo lógico. Tucumán, 1961.

Phil 8875.26 Astrada, C. La ética formal. La Plata, 1938.
Phil 1750.749 Astrada, C. Existencialismo y crisis de la filosofía. 2. ed. Buenos Aires, 1963.

Phil 1750.373 Astrada, C. La revolución existencialista. n.p., 1952.
Phil 4351.5 Astrada, Carlos. Ensayos filosoficos. Bahia Blanca, 1963.
Phil 400.92 Astrada, Carlos. Idealismo fenomenológico y metafísica existencial. Buenos Aires, 1936.

Phil 960.146 Astreya, B.L. The elements of Indian logic. 2d ed. Benares, 1934.

Phil 8658.4.5 Astro-theology. (Derham, W.) Hamburg, 1728.
Htn Phil 8658.4* Astro-theology. (Derham, W.) London, 1715.
Phil 8658.4.2 Astro-theology. (Derham, W.) London, 1719.
Phil 8610.857 The astronomico-theological lectures. (Taylor, Robert.) Boston, 1857.

Phil 8696.25 L'astronomie et le sentiment religieux. (Giret, André.) Paris, 1965.

Phil 8677.3 Astronomy and general physics, considered with reference to natural theology. (Whewell, William.) London, 1833.
Phil 8677.3.2 Astronomy and general physics, considered with reference to natural theology. (Whewell, William.) London, 1834.
Phil 8677.3.3 Astronomy and general physics, considered with reference to natural theology. (Whewell, William.) N.Y., 1841.
Phil 8677.3.6 Astronomy and general physics, considered with reference to natural theology. 7. ed. (Whewell, William.) London, 1852.

Phil 3450.9.30 Astrov, V. Rudolf Maria Holzapfel. Jena, 1928.
Phil 5465.202 Astruc, Louis. Créativité et sciences humaines. Paris, 1970.

Phil 3425.356 Asveld, Paul. La pensée, religieuse du jeune Hegel. Louvain, 1953.

Phil 6946.1.15 Asylums. (Goffman, E.) Garden City, 1961.
Phil 6946.1.16 Asylums: essays on the social situation of mental patients and other inmates. (Goffman, Erving.) Chicago, 1970.

Phil 6945.8 The asylums of Europe. (Beard, G.M.) Cambridge, 1881.
Phil 8879.4 At our best. (Ellis, S.S.) Boston, 1873.
Phil 978.59.5 At the feet of the master. (Krishnamurti, J.) Chicago, 1927?

Phil 9070.100 At vaere ung. (Moeller, Orla.) København, 1962.
Phil 4825.12 Atanasijevič, Ksenija. Penseurs yougoslaves. Belgrade, 1937.

Phil 4065.106 Atanasijević, Ksenija, 1894. (Atanassievitch, K.) Belgrade, 1923.

VPhil 175.66 Atanasijević, Ksenija. Smisao i vrednost eqzistencije. Beograd, 1968.

Phil 4065.106 Atanassievitch, K. Atanasijević, Ksenija, 1894. Belgrade, 1923.

Phil 308.2 Atbert, Hans. Traktat über kritische Vernunft. Tübingen, 1968.

Phil 4650.1.33 Ateism contra teism. (Vannérus, Allen.) Stockholm, 1903.
Phil 8655.14 L'ateismo contemporaneo. Torino, 1967- 4v.
Phil 8657.30 L'ateismo contemporaneo [l'aberrante avventura dello spirito] relazioni, studi, esperienze. (Coseglia, Raffaele.) Napoli, 1965.

Phil 8670.24 El ateismo de las masas. (Pita Carpenter, Tomás.) Madrid, 1969.

Phil 8661.40 L'ateismo nella filosofia italiana contemporanea. (Giannini, Giorgio.) Roma, 1969.

Phil 8655.24 L'ateismo oggi. 1. ed. (Aubry, Joseph.) Torino, 1968.
Phil 3235.89 Ateizm Ludviga Feierbakha. (Ardab'ev, A.I.) Moskva, 1963.
Phil 8626.6 Athanasia oder Gründe für die Unsterblichkeit der Seele. (Bolzano, B.) Sulzbach, 1827.

Phil 8667.13 Un athée. (Monod, W.) Neuchâtel, 1904.
Phil 8667.10 Atheism and the value of life. (Mallock, William H.) London, 1884.

Htn Phil 8658.3* Atheism defined and confuted. (Dove, J.) London, 1656.
Phil 182.8 Atheism in philosophy. (Hedge, F.H.) Berlin, 1884.
Phil 8709.15 The atheism of astronomy. (Teller, Woolsey.) N.Y., 1938.
Phil 8663.5 L'athéisme. (Information Catholiques Internationales.) Paris, 1963.

Phil 8666.6.5 L'athéisme. (Le Dantec, Felix.) Paris, 1912.
Phil 8655.2 L'athéisme contemporain. Genève, 1956.
Phil 8677.11 L'athéisme déraciné de la science...démocratie. (Weill, Alexandre.) Paris, 1878.

Phil 8672.12 L'athéisme dogmatique en sociologie religieuse. (Richard, Gaston.) Strasbourg, 1923.

Phil 2880.8.180 L'athéisme d'un chrétien; ou Un chrétien à l'écoute de Sartre. (Patte, Daniel.) Paris, 1965.

Phil 2419.5 Der Atheismus der französischen Materialisten des 18. Jarhunderts. 1. Aufl. (Tsebenko, M.D.) Berlin, 1956.
Phil 8656.46.2 Atheismus im Christentum? 2. Aufl. (Ratschow, Carl Heinz.) Gütersloh, 1971.
Phil 8664.10 Atheismus in West und Ost. 1. Aufl. (Jüchen, Aurel von.) Berlin, 1968.
Phil 8667.25 Der Atheismus und seine Geschichte im Abendlande. (Mauthner, F.) Stuttgart, 1922-23. 4v.
Phil 3903.3.50 Der Atheismusstreit gegen die Philosophie des Als Ob. (Vaihinger, Hans.) Berlin, 1916.
Phil 8590.33 Atheistischer Humanismus und christliche Existenz in der Gegenwart. (Kasch, Wilhelm.) Tübingen, 1964.
Phil 8673.20.5 The atheist's handbook. n.p., 196-.
Phil 8672.25 An atheist's values. (Robinson, R.) Oxford, 1964.
Phil 978.100 Athen und Ephesus. (Wulf, Berthold.) Freiburg, 1965.
Phil 10.36 Athenaeum; kiadja a filozofiai társaság. Budapest. 12-28,1926-1942 5v.
Phil 8598.79.5 Athènes et Jerusalem. (Shestov, L.) Paris, 1938.
Phil 8598.79.5.15 Athens and Jerusalem. (Shestov, L.) Athens, 1966.
Phil 3525.80 Atienza y Medrano, A. El Krausismo. Madrid, 1877.
Phil 1523.12 Atistote en Occident. (Steenberghen, F.) Louvain, 1946.
Phil 8580.16.10 Atkins, Gaius G. Modern religious cults. N.Y., 1923.
Phil 8580.16 Atkins, Gaius G. Pilgrims of the lonely road. N.Y., 1913.
Phil 1865.190.7 Atkinson, Charles. Jeremy Bentham. N.Y., 1969.
X Cg Phil 1865.82 Atkinson, Charles M. Jeremy Bentham. London, 1905.
Phil 5240.3.2 Atkinson, H.G. Letters...laws of man's nature. Boston, 1851.
Phil 281.2 Atkinson, J. Universe powers of nature revealed. London, 1856.
Phil 5548.108.5 Atkinson, John W. The dynamics of action. N.Y., 1970.
Phil 5548.85.5 Atkinson, John W. An introduction to motivation. Princeton, 1964.
Phil 5548.85A Atkinson, John W. Motives in fantasy, action, and society. Princeton, 1958.
Phil 5548.85.2 Atkinson, John W. Motives in fantasy, action, and society. Princeton, 1968.
Phil 5548.108 Atkinson, John W. A theory of achievement motivation. N.Y., 1966.
Phil 7059.15 Atkinson, Lulu Hurst. Lulu Hurst...writes her biography. Rome, Ga., 1897.
Phil 5238.197 Atkinson, R.C. Studies in mathematical psychology. Stanford, 1964.
Phil 5535.1 Atkinson, Richard G. An introduction to mathematical learning theory. N.Y., 1965.
Phil 960.33 Atkinson, W.W. A series of lessons on the inner teachings of the philosophies and religions of India. Chicago, 1908.
Phil 7069.01.10 Atkinson, W.W. Thought-force in business and everyday life. 2. ed. Chicago, 1901.
Phil 1700.3 Atkinson, William W. The crucible of modern thought. Chicago, 1910.
Phil 5240.22 Atkinson, William W. Your mind and how to use it. Holyoke, Mass., 1911.
Phil 5240.3 Atkinson H.G. Letters...laws of man's nature. London, 1851.
NEDL Phil 5300.1 Atlante della espressione del dolore. (Mantegazza, P.) Firenze, 1876.
Phil 3625.5.45 Atlas, S. From critical to speculative idealism. The Hague, 1964.
Phil 3625.5.60 Atlas, S. Geschichte des eigenen Lebens. Berlin, 1935.
Phil 3625.5.40 Atlas, S. Kritische Untersuchungen über den menschlichen Geist. Leipzig, 1797.
Phil 3625.5.78.2 Atlas, S. Lebensgeschichte. Berlin, 1792-93. 2 pam.
Phil 3625.5.78 Atlas, S. Lebensgeschichte. München, 1911.
Phil 6116.24PF Atlas of electroencephalography. (Gibbs, F.A.) Cambridge, Mass., 1941.
Phil 665.82 Atom und Seele. (Sausgruber, Kurt.) Freiburg, 1958.
Phil 3475.3.76 Die Atombombe und die Zükunft des Menschen. (Jaspers, Karl.) München, 1960.
Phil 3210.35 Atomenlehre. (Fechner, G.T.) Leipzig, 1864.
Phil 7012.2 Atomic-consciousness. (Bathurst, James.) Exeter, 1892.
Phil 7012.2.5 Atomic consciousness reviewed. (Bathurst, James.) Bristol, 190-?
Phil 260.3 Atomic philosophy. (Welling, J.C.) Washington, 1884.
Phil 332.22 Atomism, empiricism, and scepticism. Abstract of thesis. (Bowers, David F.) Princeton, 1941.
Phil 260.16 Atomism in England from Hariot to Newton. (Kargon, Robert.) Oxford, 1966.
Phil 2610.95 El atomismo de Gassendi. (Aquirre, Francisco Solano de.) Barcelona, 1956.
Phil 260.1.5 Atomistik und Kriticismus. (Sasswitz, K.) Braunschweig, 1878.
Phil 260.11 Atomos idea. (Alfieri, Vittorio Enpo.) Firenzo, 1953.
Phil 8708.27 Atoms, men and God. (Sabine, P.E.) N.Y., 1953.
Phil 8969.10 Die Atomwaffe als Frage an die christliche Ethik. (Thielicke, Helmut.) Tübingen, 1958.
Phil 8702.18 Atraction universelle et religion naturelle. (Metzger, H.) Paris, 1938. 3v.
Phil 5241.172 Attachment and loss. (Bowlby, John.) London, 1969.
Phil 176.83 Attardés et précurseurs. (Boll, Marcel.) Paris, 1921.
Phil 6012.2 Attempt to establish physiognomy upon scientific principles. (Cross, John.) Glasgow, 1817.
Phil 8662.1 An attempt to prove the existance...of the supreme unoriginated being. (Hamilton, Hugh.) London, 1785.
Phil 10.57 The attendant. Philadelphia. 1-3,1944-1946
Phil 5651.9 Attention, arousal, and the orientation reaction. 1. ed. (Lynn, Richard.) Oxford, 1966.
Phil 5330.01 Pamphlet box. Attention.
Phil 5330.7.7 Attention. (Pillsbury, W.B.) London, 1921.
Phil 5330.26 L'attention. (Reynax.) Paris, 1930.
Phil 5330.5 Attention. (Uhl, L.L.) Baltimore, 1890.
Phil 5330.05 Pamphlet vol. Attention. German dissertations. 6 pam.
Phil 2733.112 L'attention à Dieu selon Malebranche. (Blanchard, Pierre.) Paris, 1956.
Phil 5330.11 Attention and interest...study in psychology. (Arnold, F.) N.Y., 1910.
Phil 5330.36 Attention et incertitude dans les travaux de surveillance et d'inspection. (Leplat, Jacques.) Paris, 1968.
Phil 5535.30 Attention in discrimination learning; a point of view and a theory. (Lovejoy, Elijah.) San Francisco, 1968.
Phil 5330.9 L'attention spontanée et volontaire. (Roehrich, E.) Paris, 1907.
Phil 5330.34 Attentiviteit als psychodiagnosticum. Proefschrift. (Rutten, Josephus W.H.M.) Maastricht, 1964.
Phil 175.35 Atterbom, P.D.A. Inledning till philosphiens system. Upsala, 1835.
Phil 40.12.5 Atti. (Associazione Filosofica Ligure.) Milano. 2,1955+
Phil 70.10 Atti. (Congresso Nazionale de Filosofia.) Milano. 16-18 8v.
Phil 70.32 Atti. (Convegno degli Psicolozi Italiani.) Firenze. 9-11,1951-1956 3v.
Phil 70.1.12 Atti. Actes. (International Congress of Philosophy, 12th, Venice, 1958.) Firenze. 1958-1961 12v.
Phil 70.38 Atti del congresso di studi metodologici promosso del centro di studi metodologici. (Congresso di Studi Metodologici, Turin, 1952.) Torino, 1954.
Phil 4210.160 Atti del congresso internazionale di filosofia Antonio Rosmini. (Congresso Internazionale di Filosofia Antonio Rosmini, Stresa and Rovereto, 1955.) Firenze, 1957. 2v.
Phil 70.22 Atti del convegno. (Centro di Studi Filosofici di Gallarate.) Brescia. 1,1945+ 21v.
Phil 70.1.5 Atti del v. congresso internazionale. (International Congress of Philosophy, 5th, Naples, 1924.) Napoli. 1925
Phil 70.3.10 Atti del V Congresso internazionale di psicologia. (International Congress of Psychology, 5th, Rome, 1905.) Roma. 1905
Phil 8825.10 Attisam, Adelchi. Saggi di etica e di filosofia del diritto. Napoli, 1970.
Phil 4080.3.265 Attisani, A. Interpretazioni crociane. Messina, 1953.
Phil 179.25 Attiskt. (Ekelund, V.) Stockholm, 1919.
Phil 5335.10 Attitude and attitude change. (Triandis, Harry C.) N.Y., 1971.
Phil 3425.734 L'attitude Hégélienne devant l'existence. (Grégoire, Franz.) Louvain, 1953.
Phil 5400.110 The attitude theory of emotion. (Bull, Nina.) N.Y., 1951.
Phil 5238.188 Les attitudes; symposium, Bordeaux. (Association de Psychologie Scientifique de la Langue Française.) Paris, 1961.
Phil 5649.26 Attitudes et mouvements. (Buyteuddigk, Frederik J.J.) Paris, 1957.
Phil 400.106 Les attitudes idéalistes. (Blanchi, R.) Paris, 1949.
Phil 5585.233 Attitudes intellectuelles et spatiales dans le dessin. (Chateau, Jean.) Paris, 1965.
Phil 5242.2.5 L'attività psichica. (Cesca, G.) Messina, 1904.
Phil 4225.4 Atto e valore. (Sacheli, C.A.) Firenze, 1938.
Phil 4225.8.36 Atto ed essere. 2. ed. (Sciacca, Michele Federico.) Milano, 1958.
X Cg Phil 8631.11 Attractions of heaven. (Graves, Hiram A.) Boston, 1846?
Phil 8660.10 The attributes of God. (Farnell, Lewis R.) Oxford, 1925.
Phil 1135.195 Les attributs de l'ephectisme grec et leur survivance dans une cosmologie racinienne. (Chicoteau, Marcel.) Cardiff, 1943?
Phil 400.85.5 L'attualismo considerazioni. (Papafava, N.) Milano, 1932.
Phil 8580.30A Attwater, D. Modern Christian revolutionaries. N.Y., 1947.
Phil 5040.6.2 Atwater, L.H. Manual of elementary logic. Philadelphia, 1867.
Phil 5040.6 Atwater, L.H. Manual of elementary logic. Philadelphia, 1867.
Phil 9575.8 Atwood, Albert W. The mind of the millionaire. N.Y., 1926.
Phil 6321.12.15 Au dela du scientisme. (Laforgue, R.) Genève, 1963.
Phil 680.50 Au-delà du structuralisme. (Lefebvre, Henri.) Paris, 1971.
Phil 348.14 Au den Quellen unseres Denkens. (Raretz, Karl von.) Wien, 1937.
Phil 6316.8.15 Au fond de l'homme cela. (Groddeck, Georg.) Paris, 1963.
Phil 8711.2 Au sauffle de l'esprit créatur. (Vignon, Paul.) Paris, 1946.
Phil 5627.6.95A Au sujet de la conversion...théorie de Wm. James. (Porret, J.A.) Genève, 1907.
Phil 5643.3 Aubert, H.R. Physiologie der Netzhaut. Breslau, 1865.
Phil 5651.1 Aubert, H.R. Physiologische Studien...Orientierung. Tübingen, 1888.
Phil 8580.37 Aubert, Jean-Marie. Philosophie de la nature. Paris, 1965.
Phil 1300.5 Aubertin, C. De sapientiae doctoribusqui, a ciceronis morte ad neronis principatum. Parisiis, 1857.
Phil 6998.8 Aubin, Henri. Art et magie chez l'enfant. Toulouse, 1971.
Phil 5525.42 Aubouin, Elie. Les genres du risible. Marseille, 1948.
Phil 5525.42.2 Aubouin, Elie. Les genres du risible. Thèse. Marseille, 1948.
Phil 5525.42.10 Aubouin, Elie. Technique et psychologie du comique. Thèse. Marseille, 1948.
Phil 8655.24 Aubry, Joseph. L'ateismo oggi. 1. ed. Torino, 1968.
Phil 6980.43 Aucelin Schoetzenberger, Anne. Précis de psychodrame, introduction. 1. éd. Paris, 1966.
Phil 8893.83.15 Auch die Aufklärung hat ihre Gefahren. (Salat, Jakob.) München, 1801.
Phil 8893.83.15.5 Auch ein paar Worte über die Fräge. (Salat, Jakob.) München, 1802.
Phil 193.190 Auch ein Weg zur Philosophie. (Schneider, Erich.) Berlin, 1947.
Phil 8836.2.80 Auchmuty, J.J. Lecky. London, 1945.
Phil 6950.2 Audiffrent, G. Des maladies du cerveau. Paris, 1874.
Phil 5650.11 L'audition. (Bonnier, Pierre.) Paris, 1901.
Phil 5642.9 Audition colorée. (Millet, J.) Paris, 1892.
Phil 5642.7 L'audition colorée. 2. éd. (Suarez de Mendoza, Ferdinand.) Paris, 1899.
Phil 5642.13 Audition colorée et phénomènes connexes. (Lemaitre, A.) Paris, 1901.
Phil 2880.8.165 Audry, Colette. Sartre et la réalité humaine. Paris, 1966.
Phil 1540.75 Auer, J. Die Entwicklung der Grandenlehre in der Hochscholastik. v.2. Freiburg, 1951.
Phil 8580.24A Auer, J.A.C.F. Humanism states its case. Boston, 1933.
Phil 5750.8 Auer, Johannes. Die menschliche Willensfreiheit im Lehrsystem des Thomas von Aquin und Johannes Duns Scotus. München, 1938.
Phil 3820.1.8 Auerbach, B. Spinoza; ein Denkerleben. Berlin, 1911.
Phil 3820.1 Auerbach, B. Spinoza. Mannheim, 1854.
Phil 281.7 Auerbach, Felix. Ektropismen en ny teori om livets bevarande i varldsprocessen. Stockholm, 1913.
NEDL Phil 281.4.9 Auerbach, Felix. Werden der Welten. Leipzig, 1913.
Phil 175.24 Auerbach, Mathias. Einfälle und Betrachtungen. Dresden, 1904.
Phil 3552.262 Auerbach, S. Zur Entwickelungsgeschichte der leibnitzschen Monadenlehre. Diss. Dessau, 1884.
Phil 5046.16.5 Auf dem Kampffelde der Logik. (Geyser, J.) Freiburg, 1926.
Phil 8894.17.5 Auf dem Wege zur Wahrheit. (Trine, Ralph W.) Stuttgart, 1909.
Phil 6680.1.30 Auf den Spuren der Seheim. (Sopp, Erich.) Sersheim, 1953.
Phil 8693.20.10 Auf den Spuren der Unendlichkeit. (Dessauer, F.) Frankfurt, 1954.

Phil 8092.13.10   Auf den Spuren der Wirklichkeit. (Fischer, Ernst.) Reinbek, 1968.

Phil 9070.136   Auf der Suche nach dem eigenen Ich. (Frank, Hannelore.) Stuttgart, 1969.

Phil 720.61   Auf der Suche nach Wahrheit. (Jenny, Guido.) Zürich, 1961.

Phil 974.3.83   Auf Geisteswegen. (Steffen, Albert.) Dornach, 1942.
Phil 6060.29.5   Auf Spuren des Menschen. (Pulver, Max.) Zürich, 1942.
Phil 525.66   Auf Wegen der Mystik. (Schwarz, Hermann.) Erfurt, 1924.
Phil 5645.33.5   Der Aufbau der Farbwelt. 2. Aufl. (Katz, David.) Leipzig, 1930.

Phil 8423.19F   Der Aufbau der form beim natürlichen Werden und kunstlerischen Schoffen. Atlas. (Wyneken, Karl.) Freiburg, 1903-

Phil 8423.19   Der Aufbau der Form beim naturlichen Werden und kunstlerischen Schoffen. (Wyneken, Karl.) Freiburg, 1903- 2v.

Phil 5258.62   Aufbau der höheren geistigen Entwicklung. (Staak, Hermann.) Rostock, 1921.

Phil 5250.4.5   Die Aufbau der menschlichen Seele. (Kroell, H.) Leipzig, 1900.

Phil 3483.49   Der Aufbau der Persönlichkeit von Kant. (Breysig, Kurt.) Stuttgart, 1931.

Phil 5590.95.6   Aufbau der Person. 6. Aufl. (Lersch, Philipp.) München, 1954.

Phil 5590.95.7   Aufbau der Person. 7. Aufl. (Lersch, Philipp.) München, 1956.

Phil 5590.95.9   Aufbau der Person. 9. Aufl. (Lersch, Philipp.) München, 1964.

Phil 6311.10   Der Aufbau der Psychose. (Birnbaum, Karl.) Berlin, 1923.
Phil 182.94.19   Der Aufbau der realen Welt. 2. Aufl. (Hartmann, N.) Meisenheim, 1949.

Phil 181.52   Der Aufbau der Systeme. (Groos, Karl.) Leipzig, 1924.
Phil 4260.103   Der Aufbau der Weltgeschichte bei Giambattista Vico. (Peters, Richard.) Stuttgart, 1929.

Phil 9035.40   Der Aufbau des Charakters. (Apfelbach, H.) Wien, 1924.
Phil 5590.95   Der Aufbau des Charakters. (Lersch, Philipp.) Leipzig, 1938.

Phil 5590.95.3   Der Aufbau des Charakters. 3. Aufl. (Lersch, Philipp.) Leipzig, 1948.

Phil 3120.45.50   Der Aufbau des Seins; System der Philosophie. (Brandenstein, Béla.) Tübingen, 1950.

Phil 5585.226   Der Aufbau figural-optischer Phänomene bei sukzessiver Reizung. (Mueller, Kurt.) Frankfurt, 1963.

Phil 3246.232   Der Aufbruch der Freiheit. (Weischedel, W.) Leipzig, 1939.

Phil 3007.16   Aufbruch in die Illusion. 1. Aufl. (Heise, Wolfgang.) Berlin, 1964.

Phil 3450.25   Der Aufbruch zum Paradies; Sätze. (Hiller, Kurt.) München, 1922.

Phil 5643.90   Aufdeckung latenter eidetischer Anlagen und des integrierton Typus mit der Intermittenz-Methode. Inaug. Diss. (Schmaläin, Wilhelm.) Marburg, 1927.

Phil 1710.2   Die auferstandene Metaphysik. (Kerler, D.H.) Ulm, 1921.
Phil 3022.4   Die Auferstehung Metaphysik. (Wust, Peter.) Leipzig, 1920.

Phil 5545.233   Auffassung und Gedächtnis. (Katzenberger, Lothar Friedrich.) München, 1967.

Phil 3790.8.85   Die Auffassung vom Wesen der Religion bei A. Ritschl. Diss. (Hack, Valentin.) Leipzig, 1911.

Phil 978.49.40   Die Aufgabe der Geisteswissenschaft und deren Bau in Dornach. (Steiner, R.) Berlin, 1921.
Phil 5228.12   Aufgabe der Psychologie. (Schiller, P. von.) Wien, 1948.
Phil 179.13   Die Aufgabe einer Psychologie der Deutung als Vorarbeit für die Geisteswissenschaften. (Elsenhans, T.) Giessen, 1904.

Phil 5520.10   Die Aufgabe und Gliederung der Sprachwissenschaft. (Finck, F.N.) Halle, 1905.

Phil 8408.5   Aufgaben der Kunstphysiologie. (Hirth, Georg.) München, 1891.

Phil 1750.615   Die Aufhebung des Irrationalismus. (Marck, Siegfried.) Wilhelmshaven, 1958.

Phil 1760.15A   Die Aufklärung, in ausgewählten Texten Dargestellt. (Funke, Gerhard.) Stuttgart, 1963.

Phil 5421.20.35   Aufklärung über Aggression: Kant, Darwin, Freud, Lorenz. (Denker, Rolf.) Stuttgart, 1966.

Phil 5421.20.37   Aufklärung über Aggression: Kant, Darwin, Freud, Lorenz. 2. Aufl. (Denker, Rolf.) Stuttgart, 1968.

Phil 7060.10.80   Aufklärung und Erweckung. (Geiger, M.) Zürich, 1963.
Phil 2520.355   Aufklärung und Metaphysik. Die Neubegründung des Wissens durch Descartes. (Schmidt, Gerhart.) Tübingen, 1965.

Phil 848.6   Die Auflösung der klassischen Substanzkonzeption und ein Versuch Rehabilitierung. Inaug. Diss. (Fertig, Hermann.) München, 1965.

Phil 5330.22   Die Aufmerksamkeit. (Henning, H.) Berlin, 1925.
Phil 5330.29   Die Aufmerksamkeit. (Kreibig, Josef C.) Wien, 1897.
Phil 7068.96.35   Aufrichtige Unterhaltungen über den Spiritismus. (Pribytkov, V von.) Leipzig, 1896?

Phil 3085.7.40   Aufsätze zur Gesellschaftstheorie und Methodologie. 1. Aufl. (Adorno, Theodor W.) Frankfurt, 1970.
Phil 193.185.5   Aufsätze zur Sozialphilosophie. (Silva-Tarouca, Amadeo.) Wien, 1970.

Phil 349.94   Aufsätze zur Wissenschaftstheorie. (Stegmueller, Wolfgang.) Darmstadt, 1970.

Phil 5850.247   Aufsätze zur Zeitgeschichte. (Jung, Carl G.) Zürich, 1946.

Phil 193.142.5   Aufsatzentürufe. 3e Aufl. (Straub, L.W.) Leipzig, 1897.
Phil 8406.30   Der Aufstand der Abstrakt-Konkreten. (Farner, Konrad.) Neuwied, 1970.

Phil 1717.17.7   Der Aufstieg der wissenschaftlichen Philosophie. (Reichenbach, Hans.) Braunschweig, 1968.
Phil 192.67.22   Der Aufstieg im Geiste. 2. Aufl. (Rintelen, Fritz J. von.) Frankfurt, 1968.

Phil 400.66   Der Aufstieg von Kant zu Goethe. (Lippa, L. von.) Berlin, 1921.

Phil 5643.43.5   Augentauschungen. (Bader, Paul.) Leipzig, 1907.
Phil 585.188.2   Auger, Pierre. L'homme microscopique. 2e éd. Paris, 1966.
Phil 8580.36   Augereau, Joseph. La chance suprême de l'homme. Paris, 1964.

Phil 5500.10   Augier, E. De l'action à la connaissance. Paris, 1924.
Phil 5545.175   Augier, E. La mémoire et la vie. Paris, 1939.
Phil 7054.90.5   Auguez, Paul. Spiritualisme; faits curieux. Paris, 1858.
Phil 2490.124   August Comtes Verhältnis zur Kunst. (Kühnert, H.) Leipzig, 1910.

Phil 8583.11.90   August Dorners Religionsphilosophie. Inaug. Diss. (Lau, Paul.) Königsberg, 1928.

Phil 3450.14.80   August Ludwig Hülsen und der Bund der freien Männer. (Flitner, Willy.) Naumberg, 1913.

Phil 2490.136A   Auguste Comte; sa vie, son oeuvre, avec un exposé de sa philosophie. (Cresson, André.) Paris, 1941.
Phil 2490.79   Pamphlet box. Auguste Comte.
Phil 2490.93   Auguste Comte. (Ostwald, W.) Leipzig, 1914.
Phil 2490.112   Auguste Comte. (Seillière, E.) Paris, 1924.
Phil 2490.84.20   Auguste Comte and positivism. (Mill, John Stuart.) Ann Arbor, 1965.

Phil 2490.84.15   Auguste Comte and positivism. (Mill, John Stuart.) London, 1908?

Phil 2490.180   Auguste Comte and the making of sociology: delivered on November 4, 1965 at the London School of Economics. (Fletcher, Ronald.) London, 1966.

Phil 2490.83.2   Auguste Comte et la philosophie positive. (Littré, M.P.E.) Paris, 1864.

Phil 2490.94.10   Auguste Comte et le catholicisme. (Rouvre, C. de.) Paris, 1928.

Phil 2490.84.10   Auguste Comte et le positivisme. 2. éd. (Mill, John Stuart.) Paris, 1879.

Phil 2490.65   Auguste Comte méconnu. Extraits de son oeuvre finale (1851-1857). (Comte, Auguste.) Paris, 1898.

Phil 2490.117   Auguste Comte thinker and lover. (Style, Jane M.) London, 1928.

Phil 2490.127   Auguste Comtes Bild vom Menschen. Inaug.-Diss. (Peter, J.) Stuttgart, 1936.

Phil 2920.3.30   Auguste Valensin. (Valensin, Auguste.) Paris, 1961.
Phil 3640.433   Augustin, G. Nietzsches religiöse Entwicklung. Stuttgart, 1936.

Phil 4809.796.80   Augustin Smetana. (Michňáková, Irena.) Praha, 1963.
Htn   Phil 4931.1.30*   Augustinus, S. Of the citie of God. London, 1610.
Phil 4265.3.80   Augusto Vera. (Mariano, R.) Napoli, 1887.
Phil 4352.1.130   Auhofer, H.J. La sociologia de Jaime Balmes. Madrid, 1959.

Phil 9513.48   Aukrust, Tor. Mennesket i samfunnet. En sosialetikk. Oslo, 1965-

Phil 8950.10   Aula, Olari. Kristikunnan kouluss. Porvoo, 1964.
Phil 175.11   Aulard, A. Éléments de philosophie. Paris, 1869.
Phil 9035.65   Aulich, Werner. Untersuchungen über das charakterologische Rhythmusproblem. Inaug. Diss. Halle, 1932.

Htn   Phil 2555.3.30*   Aulicus inculpatus. (DuRefuge, E.) Amsterdam, 1644.
Phil 185.52.15   Aum, the cosmic silence. (King, Mrs. E.D.) Los Angeles, 1918. 2 pam.

Phil 331.40   Aune, Bruce. Knowledge, mind and nature. N.Y., 1967.
Phil 325.18   Aune, Bruce. Rationalism, empiricism, and pragmatism: an introduction. N.Y., 1970.

Phil 9182.4   Auprès du foyer. (Wagner, Charles.) Paris, 1898.
Phil 8612.11.2   Aurelj, T. La vita e la morte. 2. ed. Roma, 1904.
Phil 4112.88   Auria, Renata d'. Il Galluppi. Roma, 1942.
Phil 3640.30.5   Aurora. (Nietzsche, Friedrich.) Valencia, 1910?
Phil 3640.30.9   Aurore. 7e éd. (Nietzsche, Friedrich.) Paris, 1912.
Phil 3110.50.10   L'aurore naissante. (Böhme, J.) Milan, 1927.
Htn   Phil 3110.50*   L'aurore naissante. (Böhme, J.) Paris, 1800. 2v.
Phil 3808.20   Aus A. Schopenhauer's handschriftlichen Nachlass. (Schopenhauer, Arthur.) Leipzig, 1864.

Phil 5811.5.10   Aus dem Geistesleben der Thiere oder Staaten und Thaten der Kleinen. (Büchner, L.) Berlin, 1876.
Phil 5811.5.12   Aus dem Geistesleben der Tiere. (Büchner, L.) Leipzig, 18- ?

Phil 974.3.119.5   Aus dem Leben von Marie Steiner von Silvers. (Wiesberger, Halla.) Dornach, 1956.

Phil 978.49.410   Aus dem mitteleuropäschen Geisteleben. (Steiner, R.) Dornach, 1962.

Phil 106.1.25   Aus dem philosophischen Wörterbuch. (Voltaire, Francois Marie Arouet de.) Frankfurt, 1967.

Phil 6689.9   Aus dem Reiche des Hellsehwunders. (Tartaruga, U.) Pfullingen, 1924.

Phil 5828.11.5   Aus dem Seelenleben höherer Tiere. (Sokolowsky, A.) Leipzig, 1910.

Phil 6315.2.8.40A   Aus den Anfänger der Psychoanalyse. (Freud, Sigmund.) London, 1950.

Phil 3486.16   Aus den grossen Tagen der deutschen Philosophie. (Eck, Samuel.) Tübingen, 1901.

Phil 3625.21   Aus den Papieren eines bejahrten Philosophie-Studenten. (Marcuse, L.) München, 1964.

Phil 3494.19.35   Aus den Tiefen der Erkennens...Kants. (Marcus, Ernst.) München, 1925.

Phil 7082.132   Aus den Tiefen des Traumlebens. (Giessler, Carl Max.) Halle-Saale, 1890.

Phil 978.49.692.4   Aus der Akasha-Chronik. 4. Aufl. (Steiner, R.) Dornach, 1969.

Phil 978.49.694   Aus der Akasha-Forschung: Das Fünfte Evangelium. (Steiner, R.) Dornach, 1963.

Phil 3450.19.40A   Aus der Erfahrung des Denkens. (Heidegger, Martin.) Pfullingen, 1954.

Htn   Phil 6315.2.74*   Aus der Geschichte einer infantilen Neurose. (Freud, Sigmund.) Leipzig, 1924.

Phil 8591.43   Aus der Gotterkenntnis meinerwerke. (Ludendorff, Mathilde S.) München, 1935.

Phil 5640.23   Aus der Innenwelt. (Rubinstein, S.) Leipzig, 1888.
Phil 184.25   Aus der Lehre vom Ganzen. (Jacob, T.) Berlin, 1855.
Phil 4710.25.5   Aus der philosophischen Riffamationsliteratur. (Pelikán, Ferdinand.) Prag, 1934.

Phil 197.18.10   Aus der Werkstatt der philosophia perennis. (Willmann, O.) Freiburg, 1912.

Phil 184.16   Aus der Werkstatt der Philosophie. (Jodl, F.) Wien, 1911.
Phil 3805.80   Aus F.D.E. Schleiermacher's Leben. Berlin, 1858-63. 4v.

Phil 978.49.815   Aus Gesprächen mit Rudolf Steiner. (Boos-Hamburger, H.) Basel, 1954.

Phil 3425.91.7   Aus Hegels Leben. (Rosenkranz, K.) Leipzig, 1845.
Phil 176.2.10   Aus J. Bäggesen's Briefwechsel mit K.L. Reinhold. (Bäggesen, Jen.) Leipzig, 1931. 2v.

Phil 2490.108   Aus jeunes gens un maitre: Auguste Comte; une direction: le positivisme. (Deherme, G.) Paris, 1921.

Phil 6319.1.270   Aus Leben und Werkstatt von C.G. Jung. (Jaffé, Aniela.) Zürich, 1968.

Phil 6327.12.9   Aus Leiden Freuden. (Reik, Theodor.) London, 1940.
Phil 3120.15.10   Aus meinem Tagebuch. 2. Aufl. (Brunner, Constantin.) Stuttgart, 1967.

Phil 3745.5.85   Aus meinen Leben. (Paulsen, Friedrich.) Jena, 1909.
Phil 8419.51   Aus Meiner Malerwerkstatt. (Schneiderfranken, J.A.) Basel, 1932.

Phil 365.11   Aus Natur- und Menschenleben. (Preyer, W.) Berlin, 1885.
Phil 176.33   Aus Natur und Wissenschaft. (Büchner, L.) Leipzig, 1874.
Phil 3800.720   Aus Schellings Leben. In briefe. v.1, 2-3. (Schelling, F.W.J. von.) Leipzig, 1869-70. 2v.

Phil 978.49.300   Aus Schicksals fragender Zeit. (Steiner, R.) Dornach, 1959.

Phil 3805.161   Aus Schleiermacher's Hause: Jugender'en seiner Stiefsohnes. (Willich, E. von.) Berlin, 1909.

Phil 3805.75   Aus Schleiermacher's Leben. (Schleiermacher, Friedrich.) Berlin, 1860. 2v.

Phil 8630.14   Ausblicke ins Paradies. (Foerst-Crato, Ilse.) München, 1958.

Phil 5400.19.2   Der Ausdruck der Gemüthsbewegungen bei dem Menschen und de Thieren. 4. Aufl. (Darwin, Charles.) Stuttgart, 1884.

Phil 6000.3   Der Ausdruck der Gemütsbewegungen. (Rudolph, H.) Dresden, 1903. 2v.

Phil 5400.192   Ausdruck und Konvention. Habilitationsschrift. (Franke, Joachim.) Göttingen, 1967.

Phil 6015.2   Ausdruck und Persönlichkeit. (Fischer, G.H.) Leipzig, 1934.

Phil 6020.3   Ausdrucksbewegung von Gestaltungskraft. (Klages, L.) Leipzig, 1923.

Phil 6011.5   Ausdruckstheorie. (Bühler, Karl.) Jena, 1933.

Phil 5400.140   Ausdrucksverstehen im Erlebensaspekt. Inaug. Diss. (Holzkamp, Klaus.) Berlin, 1956.

Phil 5374.38   Ein Ausflug in das Gebiet des Bewusstseins. (Heisler, N.) Basel, 1892.

Phil 3552.90   Ausfuhrlicher...Historie der leibnitzischen Philosophie. (Ludovici, C.G.) Leipzig, 1737. 2v.

Phil 1517.8   Ausgehedes Mittelalter. (Maier, A.) Roma, 1964. 2v.

Phil 3480.28.35   Ausgewählt und Bearbeitet von L. Weis. (Kant, Immanuel.) Hamburg, 1906.

Phil 3480.126   Ausgewählte Kleine Schriften. (Kant, Immanuel.) Hamburg, 1965.

Phil 3480.19.13   Ausgewählte Kleine Schriften. (Kant, Immanuel.) Leipzig, 1919.

Phil 3210.25   Ausgewählte Schriften. (Fechner, G.T.) Berlin, 1907.

Phil 4195.10   Ausgewählte Schriften. (Pico della Mirandola, Giovanni.) Jena, 1905.

Phil 3195.3.10   Ausgewählte Schriften. 1. Aufl. (Dietzgen, Joseph.) Berlin, 1954.

Phil 2648.62   Ausgewählte Texte. (Holbach, Paul Henri T.) Berlin, 1959.

Phil 978.92   Ausgewählte theosophische Werke. (Hartmann, F.) Calw-Wimberg, Württ, 1959.

Phil 3120.27.30   Ausgewählte Vorträge und Aufsätze. (Binswanger, L.) Bern, 1947. 2v.

Phil 3120.27.25   Ausgewählte Vorträge und Aufsätze. (Binswanger, L.) Bern, 1961. 2v.

Phil 3415.15   Ausgewählte Werke. (Hartmann, Eduard von.) Leipzig, 1888. 12v.

Phil 3635.6   Ausgewählte Werke. (Möbius, Paul.) Leipzig, 1905-11. 8v.

Phil 4769.1.10   Ausgewählte Werke. (Solov'ev, V.S.) Jena, 1914-16. 2v.

Phil 3235.77   Ausgewahlte Briefe von und an L. Feuerbach. v.1-2. (Feuerbach, Ludwig.) Leipzig, 1904.

Phil 1133.19.10   Der Ausklang der antiken Philosophie und das Erwachen einer neuen Zeit. (Kafka, Gustav.) n.p., n.d.

Phil 9560.66   Auskunft über die Tugenden. (Pieper, Josef.) Zürich, 1970.

Phil 4070.1.80   Ausonio Franchi. (Angelini, A.) Roma, 1897.
Phil 4070.1.93   Ausonio Franchi. (Romano, P.) Savona, 1896.
Phil 3120.15.97.15

Phil 5643.51   Aussen und Innen. (Bickel, Lothar.) Zürich, 1960.
   Die Aussengrenzen des Gesichtsfeldes für weisse und farbige Objecte beim normalen Auge. Inaug. Diss. (Drott, Anton.) Breslau, 1894?

Phil 6127.6   Aussenwelt und Innenwelt, Leib und Seele. (Rehmke, J.) Griefswald, 1898.

Phil 8587.43   Auslesene Briefe über verschiedne Gegenstände aus der Sittenlehre und Religion. (Hervey, Jacob.) Hamburg, 1762.

Phil 5374.42   Das ausserpersönliche Unbewusste. (Giése, Fritz.) Braunschweig, 1924.

Phil 5241.188   Die ausserpsychologische Voraussetzungen der Tiefenpsychologie. (Biran, Sigmund.) München, 1966.

Phil 7076.24   Aussersinnliche Wahrnehmung. (Pagenstecher, Gustav.) Halle, 1924.

Phil 3235.28   Aussprüche aus seinen Werken. (Feuerbach, Ludwig.) Leipzig, 1879.

Phil 85.10   Austeda, F. Kleines Worterbuch der Philosophie. Frankfurt, 1954.

Phil 5238.28   Austen Riggs Center, Stockbridge, Massachusetts. Psychoanalytic psychiatry and psychology. N.Y. 1,1954

Phil 8865.342   Austin, Eugene M. The ethics of the Cambridge Platonists. Philadelphia, 1935.

Phil 331.29   Austin, J.L. Sense and sensibilia. Oxford, 1962.
Phil 9340.3   Austin, J.M. Voice to youth. N.Y., 1847.
Phil 175.52.5   Austin, John L. How to do things with words. Cambridge, 1962.

Phil 175.52   Austin, John L. Philosophical papers. Oxford, 1961.
Phil 175.52.2   Austin, John L. Philosophical papers. 2d ed. Oxford, 1970.

Phil 5425.67   Austin, Mary Hunter. Everyman's genius. Indianapolis, 1925.

Phil 7082.56   Austmann, S.J. Sögur af ýmsu tagi. Winnipeg, 1915.
Phil 40.5   Australasian Association of Psychology and Philosophy. Monograph series. Sidney.

Phil 10.28   Australasian journal of psychology and philosophy. Sydney. 1,1923+ 29v.

Phil 10.59   Australian journal of psychology. Victoria. 1,1949+ 11v.

Phil 10.59.5   Australian journal of psychology. Cumulative index, 1-10,1949-1958. Melbourne, n.d.

Phil 10.95   Australian psychologist. Queensland, Australia. 1,1956+
Phil 5545.42   Austriacus, J. De memoria artificios a lebellus. Argentorati, 1603.

Phil 735.94   The Austrian theory of value. (Eaton, Howard O.) Norman, 1930.

Phil 4520.8.30   Austurlönd. (Bjarnason, Ágúst.) Reykjavík, 1908.
Phil 801.27   Austurlönd. (Bjarnason, A.) Reykjavik, 1908.
Phil 5870.107   Ausubel, David Paul. Theory and problems of child development. 2nd ed. N.Y., 1970.

Phil 3890.8.40   Ausübung der Sittenlehre. (Thomasius, Christian.) Hildesheim, 1968.

Phil 3890.8.45.1   Ausübung der Vernunftlehre. (Thomasius, Christian.) Hildesheim, 1968.

Phil 3120.55.45   Auswahl aus seinen Schriften. (Bloch, Ernst.) Frankfurt, 1967.

Phil 3499.2.5   Auswahl der besten Aufsätze über die Kantische Philosophie. (Reinhold, K.L.) Frankfurt, 1790.

Phil 3778.6   Auswahl vermischter Schriften. (Reinhold, K.L.) Jena, 1796-97. 2v.

Phil 3625.8.62   Auszug aus der Vernunftlehre. (Meier, Georg Friedrich.) Halle, 1752.

Phil 1122.4   Les auteurs philosophiques, grecs. (Payot, E.) Paris, 1898.

Phil 6990.29   Authentic documents relative to the cure of Winefrid White. 3. ed. (Milner, John.) London, 1806.

Phil 978.59.7   Authentic notes of discussions and talks given by Kris at Ojai and Sarabia. (Krishnamurti, J.) Hollywood, 1940.

Phil 5590.315   Authoritarianism and temperament. (Gelbmann, Frederick J.) Washington, 1958.

Phil 1517.6   Authority and reason in the early middle ages. (Macdonald, A.J.) London, 1933.

Phil 8598.61   The authority of Christian experience. (Strachan, Robert H.) London, 1929.

Phil 6315.2.260   L'auto-analyse. (Anzieu, Didier.) Paris, 1959.
Htn Phil 1865.65*   Auto-icon. (Bentham, Jeremy.) London, 1842?
Phil 4114.20   Autobiografia, lettere e altri scritti. (Genovesi, Antonio.) Milano, 1962.

Phil 4260.17.16   Autobiografia. 1. ed. (Vico, G.B.) Torino, 1965.
Phil 9171.6   Autobiografia di un padre di famiglia. (Levi, G.) Firenze, 1868.

Phil 4260.17.15   Autobiografia e scienza nuova. (Vico, G.B.) Torino, 1932.
Phil 978.6.85   Autobiographical sketches. Photoreproduction. (Besant, Annie.) London, 1885.

Phil 6315.2.79   An autobiographical study. (Freud, Sigmund.) London, 1935.

Phil 6315.2.79.5   An autobiographical study. 2d ed. (Freud, Sigmund.) London, 1946.

Phil 2270.79.10   Eine Autobiographie. (Spencer, Herbert.) Stuttgart, 1905. 2v.

NEDL Phil 1855.80   Autobiography. (Bain, Alexander.) London, 1904.
Phil 1930.8.88A   An autobiography. (Collingwood, Robin George.) London, 1964.

Phil 4080.3.78   An autobiography. (Croce, Benedetto.) Oxford, 1927.
Phil 3625.5.79   Autobiography. (Maimon, Salomon.) London, 1954.
Htn Phil 2138.79.4*   Autobiography. (Mill, John S.) London, 1873.
X Cg Phil 2138.79.6   Autobiography. (Mill, John S.) N.Y., 1874.
Phil 2138.79.10.3   Autobiography. (Mill, John S.) N.Y., 1887.
Phil 2138.79.8.4   Autobiography. (Mill, John S.) N.Y., 1944.
Phil 2138.79.8.5   Autobiography. (Mill, John S.) N.Y., 1957.
Phil 2138.79.8.6   Autobiography. (Mill, John S.) N.Y., 1969.
Phil 2270.79A   An autobiography. (Spencer, Herbert.) N.Y., 1904. 2v.

Phil 6328.2.31   Autobiography. (Stekel, Wilhelm.) N.Y., 1950.
Phil 2138.79.10.5   Autobiography. Early draft. (Mill, John S.) Urbana, 1961.
Phil 7068.94.35   Autobiography by Jesus of Nazareth. (Pettis, O.G.) Washington, 1894.

Phil 2225.7.85A   The autobiography of a philosopher. (Ayer, Alfred Jules.) Boston, 1930.

Phil 2225.7.87   The autobiography of a philosopher. (Ayer, Alfred Jules.) Boston, 1930.

Phil 9400.7   Autobiography of an elderly woman. (Vorse, M.H. (Mrs.).) Boston, 1911.

Phil 2255.1.15   The autobiography of Bertrand Russell, 1872-1914. 1st American ed. (Russell, Bertrand Russell.) Boston, 1967. 3v.

Phil 6953.16.3   The autobiography of David. London, 1946.
Phil 4260.17.7   The autobiography of Giambattista Vico. (Vico, G.B.) Ithaca, 1944.

Phil 8674.9   The autobiography of God. (Trattner, Ernest R.) N.Y., 1930.

Phil 8620.22   Autobiography of Satan. (Beard, J.R.) London, 1872.
Phil 5374.15   The autobiography of the I or ego. (Wheeler, C.K.) Boston, 1903.

Phil 4260.91   Autografi e documenti vichiani inediti o dispersi. (Donati, Benvenuto.) Bologna, 1921.

Phil 5643.38   Autokinetic sensations. (Adams, H.F.) Chicago, 1912.
Phil 6022.4.5   Autokraten und Demokraten. (Märker, Friedrich.) Erlenbach, 1931.

Phil 3425.221   Die Autolatrie oder Selbstanbetung. (Reichlin-Meldegg, Karl A.) Pforzheim, 1943.

Phil 5247.2   Autology...mental science. (Hamilton, D.H.) Boston, 1873.
Phil 7068.96.15   Automatic or spirit writing, with other psychic experiences. (Underwood, Sara A.) Chicago, 1896.
Phil 7069.05.30   Automatic speaking and writing. (Bennett, E.T.) London, 1905.

Phil 7069.30.15   Automatic writing. (Mühl, Anita M.) Dresden, 1930.
Phil 5625.128   Automatisation du comportement et commutation. (Baumstimler, Yves.) Paris, 1969.

Phil 6671.5.9   Automatisme et suggestion. (Bernheim, H.) Paris, 1917.
Phil 6959.1   L'automatisme psychologique. (Janet, Pierre.) Paris, 1889.

Phil 6959.1.3   L'automatisme psychologique. 2. ed. (Janet, Pierre.) Paris, 1894.

Phil 8401.29.10   L'automobile di Mallarmé e altri ragionamenti intorno, alla vocazione odierna delle arti. (Assunto, Rosario.) Roma, 1968. 10v.

Phil 9010.32   L'automobiliste et la morale chrétienne. (Renard, Hubert.) Paris, 1967.

Phil 5751.17   L'autonomia della volontà. (Bianca, Giovanni.) Firenze, 1937.

Phil 8080.6   Autonomia ed eteronomia dell'arte. (Anceschi, Luciano.) Firenze, 1936.

Phil 8401.30   Autonomia ed eteronomia dell'arte. 2. ed. (Anceschi, Luciano.) Firenze, 1959.

Phil 6320.1   The autonomic functions and the personality. (Kempf, E.J.) N.Y., 1918.

Phil 5625.86.5   Autonomic imbalance and the hypothalamus. (Gellhorn, Ernst.) Minneapolis, 1957.

Phil 6120.14   The autonomic nervous system. (Kuntz, A.) Philadelphia, 1934.

Phil 5625.86   Autonomic regulations. (Gellhorn, Ernst.) N.Y., 1943.
Phil 3482.7   Die Autonomie der Moral mit besonderer Berucksichtigung der Morallehre Immanuel Kants. (Aars, Kristian Birch-Reichenwald.) Hamburg, 1896.

Phil 735.82   Die Autonomie der Werte. (Kühn, Lenore.) Berlin, 1926-31. 2v.

Phil 8080.24   Die Autonomie des Ästhetischen in der neuren Philosophie. (Kreis, Friedrich.) Tübingen, 1922.

Phil 2045.160   Autonomie und Autorität; Rousseau in den Spuren von Hobbes? (Mayer-Tasch, Peter Cornelius.) Neuwied, 1968.

Phil 705.37   Autonomismus und Transzendenzphilosophie. (Hengstenberg, H.E.) Heidelberg, 1950.

Phil 8894.36   Autonomous man. (Turner, Dean.) St. Louis, 1970.
Phil 6951.5.10   The autopathography of C.W. Beers. (Farrar, C.B.) n.p., 1908.

Phil 5145.6   Autopsie du hasard. (Boursin, Jean Louis.) Paris, 1970.
Phil 5335.8   Autoritarismus und politische Apathie. (Freyhold, Michaela von.) Frankfurt, 1971.

Phil 181.71.5   Autorité spirituelle et pouvoir temporel. (Guénon, R.) Paris, 1929.

Phil 7149.2   Autosuggestion and its personal application. (Duckworth, J. Herbert.) N.Y., 1922.

Phil 1930.8.87   An autotbiography. (Collingwood, Robin George.) London, 1951.

Phil 530.20.40   Autour de la docte ignorance. (Vansteenberghe, E.) Munster en Westphalie, 1914?

Phil 1504.14.2   Autour de la "Docte Ignorance." v.14, pt.2-4. (Vansteenberghe, E.) Münster, 1915.

Phil 1750.147   Autour de l'humanisme d'Erasme à Pascal. (Brémond, Henri.) Paris, 1937.

Phil 5374.65   Autour des fondements de l'être et du connaître selon l'analyse psychologique. (Latour, M.) Paris, 1949. 2v.

Phil 8591.20.5   Autour d'un petit livre. (Loisy, Alfred.) Paris, 1903.

Phil 8591.20.12   Autres mythes à propos de la religion. (Loisy, Alfred.) Paris, 1938.

Phil 8082.4   Autunno del Rinascimento. (Ossola, Carlo.) Firenze, 1971.

Phil 365.9   Auvard, Alfred. L'evoluisme. Paris, 1914.

Phil 8580.25   Auvergne, D. Regards catholiques sur le monde. Paris, 1938.

Phil 7069.65.20   Aux fontières de l'irrationnel. (Maudiut, Jacques A.) Paris, 1965.

Phil 7069.39.57   Aux frontières de l'au-dela. (Labadié, Jean.) Paris, 1939.

Phil 5640.43   Aux sources de la connaissance la sensation. 3. éd. (Piéron, Henri.) Paris, 1945.

Phil 4770.5   Avaliani, S.Sh. Filosofskie vzgliady I.R. Tarkhnishvili. Tbilisi, 1957.

Phil 3640.611   L'avant dernière pensée de Nietzsche. (Wahl, J.A.) Paris, 1961.

Phil 2477.8.90   Avanzini, Guy. La contribution de Binet à l'élaboration d'une pédagogie scientifique. Paris, 1969.

Phil 9558.5   L'avarice. (Rogues de Fursac, J.) Paris, 1911.

Phil 3160.15.5   Avé-Lallemant, E. Der kategoriale Ort des Seelischen in der Naturwirklichkeit. München, 1959.

Phil 7108.388   Avé-Lallemant, F.C.B. Der Magnetismus mit seinen mystischen Verirrungen. Leipzig, 1881.

Phil 5810.3.2   Avebury, John L. On the senses, instincts, and intelligence of animals. 2nd ed. London, 1889.

Phil 5810.3.3   Avebury, John L. Die Sinne und das geistige Leben der Thiere. Leipzig, 1889.

Phil 9245.9.55   Avebury, John Lubbock. Le bonheur de vivre. v.1-2. Paris, 1897-98.

Phil 9245.9.50   Avebury, John Lubbock. Duty of happiness. Philadelphia, 1896.

Phil 9245.9.75   Avebury, John Lubbock. Peace and happiness. N.Y., 1909.

Phil 9245.9.2.3   Avebury, John Lubbock. The pleasures of life. London, 1889.

Phil 9245.9.7   Avebury, John Lubbock. The pleasures of life. London, 1893.

Phil 9245.9.1   Avebury, John Lubbock. The pleasures of life. N.Y., 1887.

Phil 9245.9.3   Avebury, John Lubbock. The pleasures of life. N.Y., 1893.

Phil 9245.9.4   Avebury, John Lubbock. The pleasures of life. v.1-2. London, 1913-14.

Phil 8886.12.5   Avebury, John Lubbock. The use of life. N.Y., 1900.

Phil 2905.1.515   Avec Teilhard de Chardin, vues ardentes. (Mortier, Jeanne M.) Paris, 1967.

Phil 8887.30.5   Aveling, E.B. "The value of this earthly life": a reply. London, 1884.

Phil 5240.8   Aveling, Francis. On the consciousness of the universal. Thesis. London. 1912.

Phil 5750.7   Aveling, Francis. Personality and will. N.Y., 1931.

Phil 720.23   Aveling, Francis. The psychological approach to reality. London, 1929.

Phil 4301.1   Avelino, Andres. Prolegomenos a la unica metafisica posible. Ciudad Trujillo, 1941.

Phil 4301.1.5   Avelino, Andres. Une lettre à Jacques Maritain. Ciudad Trujillo, 1944.

Phil 331.2.21   Avenarius, R. L'empiriocriticismo. Roma, 1909.

Phil 331.2   Avenarius, R. Kritik der Reinen Erfahrung. Leipzig, 1888.

Phil 331.2.5   Avenarius, R. Kritik der Reinen Erfahrung. Leipzig, 1907.

Phil 175.12   Avenarius, R. Der menschliche Weltbegriff. Leipzig, 1891.

Phil 331.2.12   Avenarius, R. Philosophie als Denken der Welt Gemäss dem Prinzip des kleinsten Kraftmasses. Leipzig, 1876.

Phil 331.2.13   Avenarius, R. Philosophie als Denken der Welt Gemäss dem Prinzip des kleinsten Kraftmasses. 3. Aufl. Berlin, 1917.

Phil 3820.2   Avenarius, R. Ueber die...Spinozischen Pantheismus. Leipzig, 1868.

Phil 331.2.10   Avenarius, R. Zur Terminalfunktion. Berlin, 1913.

Phil 331.2.30   Avenarius and the stand point of pure experience. (Bush, W.T.) N.Y., 1905.

Phil 1504.1.2   Avencebrolis fons vitae. v.1, pt.2-3. (Baeumker, C.) Münster, 1892. 2v.

NEDL Phil 1504.1.2   Avencebrolis fons vitae. v.1, pt.4. (Baeumker, C.) Münster, 1892.

Phil 1200.20   Avenel, J. Le stoïcisme et les stoïciens. Paris, 1886.

Phil 180.19.5   L'avenir de la metaphysique fondée sur l'experience. (Fouillée, Alfred.) Paris, 1889.

X Cg Phil 1701.7   Avenir de la philosophie. (Berr, Henri.) Paris, 1899.

Phil 2475.1.179   L'avenir de la philosophie Bergsonienne. (Seillière, E.) Paris, 1917.

Phil 365.47.10   L'avenir de l'esprit. (Lecomte du Noüy, Pierre.) Gallimard, 1941.

Phil 365.47.15   L'avenir de l'esprit. (Lecomte du Noüy, Pierre.) N.Y., 1943.

Phil 8419.48   L'avenir de l'esthétique essai sur l'objet d'une science naissante. (Souriau, E.) Paris, 1929.

Phil 2490.96   L'avenir de l'intelligence. 2e éd. (Maurras, Charles.) Paris, 1917.

Phil 7060.129   L'avenir des sciences psychiques. (Boirac, Émile.) Paris, 1917.

Phil 600.15   L'avenir d'intelligence. (Maurras, C.) Paris, 1909.

Phil 5407.7   L'aventure, l'ennui, le sérieux. (Jankélévitch, Vladimir.) Paris, 1963.

Phil 2825.20   L'aventure de l'esprit dans les espèces. (Pradines, M.) Paris, 1955.

Phil 1540.32   L'aventure de l'humanisme européen au moyen-âge. (Renucci, P.) Clermont-Ferrand, 1953.

Phil 193.241   L'aventure philosophique. (Sauvage, Micheline.) Paris, 1966.

Phil 310.16.5   Les aventures de la dialectique. (Merlean-Ponty, Maurice.) Paris, 1961.

Phil 2905.1.108   Un aventurier de l'esprit, Pierre Teilhard de Chardin. (Martin-Deslias, Noël.) Paris, 1963.

Phil 8626.19   The avenue of beeches. (Budgett, H.M.) London, 1930.

Phil 75.1   Averra, Adolfo. Bibliografia delle Scienze Filosofiche. Torino, 1891.

Htn Phil 1020.4.1*   Averroës. Destructio destructionú. Lugduni, 1529.

Phil 1020.4.30   Averroes y Lulio. (Reyes, A.) Caracas, 1940.

Phil 1020.4.40   Averroïsme bolonais au XIVe siècle. (Kuksewicz, Zdzislaw.) Wroclaw, 1965.

Phil 1020.4.25   Der Averroismus in der christlich-peripatetischen Psychologie des späteren Mittelalters. (Werner, Karl.) Wien, 1881.

Phil 1020.4.5   Averrose et l'Averroisme. (Renan, E.) Paris, 1852.

Phil 5625.123   Aversive conditioning and learning. (Brush, Franklin Robert.) N.Y., 1971.

Phil 5625.124   Aversive stimulation. (Miami Symposium on the Prediction of Behavior.) Coral Gables, Fla., 1968.

Phil 8877.24.5   Aves recte vivendi. (Curtis, G.W.) N.Y., 1899.

Phil 5040.14   Avey, A.E. The function and forms of thought. N.Y., 1927.

Phil 175.28.2   Avey, A.E. Readings in philosophy. N.Y., 1924.

Phil 165.3   Avey, A.E. Readings in philosophy. N.Y., 1936.

Phil 331.3   Avey, Albert E. An analysis of process of conceptual cognition. Cincinnati, 1915.

Phil 2400.3   Avezac-Lavigne, C. Saint-Simonisme-Positivisme. Paris, 1905.

Phil 3480.80.80   Avhandlingar om fred och rätt. (Kant, Immanuel.) Stockholm, 1915.

Phil 1020.8   Avicenne. (Carra de Vaux.) Paris, 1900.

Phil 1020.8.19   Avicenne et le point de départ de Duns Scot. (Gilson, Etienne.) Paris, 1927.

Phil 4210.87   Avogadro della Motta, Emiliano. La filosofia dell'abate Antonio Rosmini esaminata. 4a ed. Napoli, 1877.

Phil 4210.87.5   Avogadro della Motta, Emiliano. Sul valore scientifico e sulle pratiche consequenze. Napoli, 1853.

Phil 2880.7   Avoir une âme. (Sourian, E.) Paris, 1938.

Phil 8980.180   Avraamov, D. Kommunist nravstvennost'. Moskva, 1963.

Phil 8401.41   Avramov, Dimitur. Estetika na modernoto izkustvo. Sofiia, 1969.

Phil 8413.17   Avviamento alla critica d'arte. (Mormone, R.) Napoli, 1954.

Phil 4080.9.33   Avviamento allo studio della filosofia. 3a ed. (Carlini, Armando.) Firenze, 1921.

Phil 5643.148   The awakened eye. 1. ed. (Parmenter, Ross.) Middletown, Conn., 1968.

Phil 7069.35.25   The awakening of the sixth sense; a look into the great unknown. (Spivey, T.S.) Shawneetown, Ill., 1935.

Phil 7069.43   Awareness. (Garrett, Eileen Jeanette Lyttle.) N.Y., 1943.

Phil 5325.28   Awareness. (Herrick, C.J.) Philadelphia, 1939.

Phil 5374.284   Awareness: exploring, experimenting, experiencing. (Stevens, John O.) Lafayette, Calif., 1971.

Phil 2445.6.30   Axelos, Kôstas. Le jeu du monde. Paris, 1969.

Phil 800.15   Axelos, Kostas. Vers la pensée planétaire. Paris, 1964.

Phil 735.280   Axiological ethics. (Findlay, Niemeyer.) London, 1970.

Phil 5252.10   Das Axiom der Psychophysik. (Müller, F.A.) Marburg, 1882.

Htn Phil 193.32*   Axiomata philosophica. (Stahli, D.) London, 1651.

Phil 192.92   Axiomatik alles möglichen Philosophierens. (Rogge, E.) Meisenheim, 1950.

Phil 4260.117   Die Axiomatik bei Giambattista Vico. (Luginbühl, Johannes.) Bern, 1946.

Phil 6310.22   Axline, Virginia Mae. Dibs: in search of self. Boston, 1965.

Phil 6998.4.2   Axline, Virginia Mae. Play therapy. N.Y., 1969.

Phil 3425.306   Axmann, Walter. Zur Frage nach dem Ursprung des dialektischen Denkens bei Hegel. Inaug. Diss. Würzburg, 1939.

Phil 1540.60   Axters, Stephanus. Scholastick Lexicon. Antwerpen, 1937.

Phil 281.6.10   Ayais, H. Constitution de l'univers. Paris, 1840.

Phil 281.6.5   Ayais, H. Explication universelle. Paris, 1826. 2v.

Phil 1800.5   Ayer, A.J. British empirical philosophers. London, 1952.

Phil 5068.6   Ayer, A.J. Foundations of empirical knowledge. London, 1940.

Phil 331.11   Ayer, A.J. The problem of knowledge. London, 1956.

Phil 175.38.4   Ayer, Alfred J. Language, truth and logic. London, 1938.

Phil 175.38.15A   Ayer, Alfred J. Language, truth and logic. N.Y., 1952.

Phil 2225.7.87   Ayer, Alfred Jules. The autobiography of a philosopher. Boston, 1930.

Phil 2225.7.85A   Ayer, Alfred Jules. The autobiography of a philosopher. Boston, 1930.

Phil 1845.11.5   Ayer, Alfred Jules. The concept of a person. N.Y., 1963.

Phil 396.5   Ayer, Alfred Jules. The humanist outlook. London, 1968.

Phil 1845.10.5   Ayer, Alfred Jules. Metaphysics and common sense. London, 1969.

Phil 2225.5.155   Ayer, Alfred Jules. The origins of pragmatism: studies in the philosophy of Charles Sanders Peirce and William James. London, 1968.

Phil 1845.10   Ayer, Alfred Jules. Philosophical essays. London, 1954.

Phil 1845.11   Ayer, Alfred Jules. Philosophy and language. Oxford, 1960.

Phil 2255.1.170   Ayer, Alfred Jules. Russell and Moore: the analytical heritage. Cambridge, 1971.

Phil 1900.87   Ayer, Joseph Cullen. Versuch einer Darstellung der Ethik Joseph Butlers. Inaug. Diss. Leipzig, 1893.

Phil 2255.10.36   The Ayn Rand letter. N.Y. 1,1971+

Phil 8875.13   Ayres, Clarence E. The nature of the relationship between ethics and economics. Chicago, Ill., n.d.

Phil 5750.12   Ayres, Michel Richard. The refutation of determinism. London, 1968.

Phil 8893.14.9   Aýudate! Self-help. 5. ed. (Smiles, Samuel.) Paris, 1900.

Phil 9060.1   Azaïs, P.H. Des compensations dans destinées humaines. Paris, 1825. 3v.

Phil 9060.1.2   Azaïs, P.H. Des compensations dans les destinées humaines. Paris, 1846.

Phil 175.30   Azais, H. Cours de philosophie générale. Paris, 1824. 8v.

Phil 5920.1   Azais, P.H. De la phrénologie. Paris, 1839. 2v.

Phil 2445.1.30   Azaïs, Pierre H. Manuel du philosophe. Paris, 1816.

Phil 2445.1.79   Pamphlet box. Azaïs, Pierre H.

Phil 9035.1   Azam, E. Le caractère. Paris, 1887.

Phil 1750.166.275   Azevedo, Fernando de. Na batalho do humanismo. 2. ed. São Paulo, 1967.

Phil 8876.54.5   L'azione. (Blondel, Maurice.) Firenze, 1921. 2v.

Phil 4225.77.30   L'azione creatice di Sergio Sarti. (Sarti, Sergio.) Brescia, 1959.

Phil 2477.6.95   L'azione e il pensiero. (Scivittaro, F.) Roma, 1936.

Phil 4710.170   Aznaurov, Artem A. Ocherki po etike velikikh russikh revoliutsionnykh demokratov. Baku, 1964.

Phil 5750.10   Azzalini, Mario. La necessità del volere e la reattività sociale. Padova, 1931.

Phil 6046.55   Azzi, G. L'idea del futuro rappresentato dalle linee della mano. Lucca, 1655.

Phil 7054.178   Azzi, Gaetano. Idea vera dello spiritismo. Torino, 1895.

Phil 410.6   B. Bolzano's Paradoxien des Unendlichen. (Přihonsky, F.) Berlin, 1889.

Phil 5241.77 Baade, Walter. Allgermeine Einfuhrung in das Gesamtgebiet der Psychologie. Leipzig, 1928.
Htn Phil 6671.14* Baader, F. Über die Extase oder das Verzücktseyn der magnetischen Schlafredner. Leipzig, 1817.
Phil 3090.31 Baader, Franz von. Beiträge zur dinamischen Philosophie im Gegensaze der Mechanischen. Berlin, 1809.
Phil 3090.42 Baader, Franz von. Fermenta cognitionis. pt. 1-6. Berlin, 1822-25. 5v.
Phil 3090.24.5 Baader, Franz von. Gesellschaftslehre. München, 1957.
Phil 3090.25 Baader, Franz von. Kleine Schriften. Würzburg, 1847.
Phil 3090.27 Baader, Franz von. Leben und theosophische Werke. v.1-2. Stuttgart, 1886-87.
Phil 3090.62 Baader, Franz von. Lettres inédites. Paris, 1942-51. 4v.
Phil 3090.61 Baader, Franz von. Lettres inédites de Franz von Baader. Thèse. Paris, 1942.
Phil 3090.20 Baader, Franz von. Philosophische Schriften und Aufsätze. v.1-2. Münster, 1831-33.
Phil 3090.10 Baader, Franz von. Sämmtliche Werke. Leipzig, 1851-60. 16v.
Phil 3090.22 Baader, Franz von. Sätze ans der erotischen Philosophie und andere Schriften. Frankfurt, 1966.
Phil 3090.23 Baader, Franz von. Schriften. Leipzig, 1921.
Phil 3090.24 Baader, Franz von. Schriften zur Gesellschaftsphilosophie. Jena, 1925.
Phil 3090.65 Baader, Franz von. Seele und Welt. Berlin, 1928.
Phil 3090.35 Baader, Franz von. Sur la notion du tems. Munic, 1818.
Phil 3090.40 Baader, Franz von. Über das Verhalten des Wissens zum Glauben. Münster, 1833.
Phil 3090.30 Baader, Franz von. Über den Begriff des Gut-Oderpositiv und der Richtgut-Oder-Negative-Gewordnen. Luzern, 1829.
Phil 8876.166 Baader, Franz von. Über die Begründung der Ethik durch die Physik und andere Schriften. Stuttgart, 1969.
Phil 3090.38 Baader, Franz von. Über die Freiheit der Intelligenz. München, 1826.
Phil 3090.64 Baader, Franz von. Über die Nothwendigkeit einer Revision der Wissenschaft natürlicher. Erlanzen, 1841.
Phil 3090.28 Baader, Franz von. Über Liebe. München, 1953.
Phil 3090.24.10 Baader, Franz von. Vom Sinn der Gesellschaft. Köln, 1966.
Phil 3090.39 Baader, Franz von. Von Segen und Fluch der Creatur. Strassburg, 1826.
Phil 3090.37 Baader, Franz von. Vorlesungen...über religiöse Philosophie. München, 1827.
Phil 3090.41 Baader, Franz von. Vorlesungen über speculative Dogmatik. pt. 1-5. Stuttgart, 1828-38.
Phil 3090.86 Baader und Kant. (Sauter, J.) Jena, 1928.
Phil 3483.21 Baake, Wilhelm. Kants Ethik bei den englischen Moralphilosophen des 19. Jahrhunderts. Leipzig, 1911.
Phil 140.50 Baan, P.A.H. Psychiatrie in de maatschappij. Groningen, 1957. 8 pam.
Phil 1750.166.125 Baanbrekers van het humanisme. (Zuidema, S.U.) Franeker, 1959.
Phil 5241.76 Baar, Jacob. Psychology. N.Y., 1928.
Phil 2750.10.90 Baas, George. A critical analysis of the philosophy of Emile Meyerson. Baltimore, 1930.
Phil 5203.18 Baatz, Walter. Geistes und naturwissenschaftliche Abhandlungen der Mitglieder des Wiener Arbeitskreises. Wien, 1957.
Phil 5041.89 Babaiants, M.S. Zakon iskheichennogo tret'ego. Moskva, 1962.
Phil 8581.10.9 Babbage, C. The ninth Bridgewater treatise. 2. ed. London, 1838.
Phil 8581.11 Babbage, C. The ninth Bridgewater treatise. 2. ed. London, 1838.
Phil 6111.38 Babbitt, E.D. Human culture and cure. pt.3-4. Los Angeles, 1898.
Phil 6671.1 Babbitt, E.D. Vital magnetism. N.Y., n.d.
Phil 8402.28.10 Babbitt, Irving. The new Laocoon; an essay on the confusion of the arts. Boston, 1913.
Phil 8402.28.5 Babbitt, Irving. The new Laocoon. Boston, 1910.
Phil 8402.28 Babbitt, Irving. The new Laocoon. Boston, 1910.
Phil 6951.28 Babcock, H. Dementia praecox. N.Y., 1933.
Phil 9530.22 Babcock, M.D. The success of defeat. N.Y., 1905.
Phil 3850.27.125 Babel, Henry. Que pense Albert Schweitzer? Genève, 1953.
Phil 3850.27.127 Babel, Henry. Schweitzer tel qu'il fut. Boudry-Neuchâtel, 1966.
Phil 3120.30.120 Babolin, Albino. Essere e alterità in Martin Buber. Padova, 1965.
Phil 310.560 Babosov, E.M. Dialektika analiza i sinteza v nauchnom poznanii. Minsk, 1963.
Phil 8691.34 Babosov, Evgenii M. Nauckno-tekhnicheskaia revoliutsiia i modernizatsiia katolitsizma. Minsk, 1971.
Phil 2905.1.635 Babosov, Evgenii M. Teiiardizm. Minsk, 1970.
Phil 8951.8 Babrovnitzki, I. Sushchestvennyia cherty pravoslavnago. Elisavetgrad, 1897.
Phil 9530.41 Babson, Roger Ward. Storing up triple reserves. N.Y., 1929.
Phil 5520.495 Bacchin, Giovanni Romano. I fondamenti della filosofia del linguaggio. Assisi, 1965.
Phil 176.234 Bacchin, Giovanni Romano. L'immediato e la sua negazione. Perugia, 1967.
Phil 6985.25 Bach, George Robert. Intensive group psychotherapy. N.Y., 1954.
Phil 6990.61 Bach, H. Mirakelbücker bayerischer Wallfahrtsorte. Möhrendorf, 1963.
Phil 5585.236 Bach, Marcus. The power of perception. Garden City, 1966.
Phil 8691.15 Bach, W.H. Big Bible stories. Lilly Dale, N.Y., 1897.
Phil 3092.1.5 Bach ofen und die Zukunft des Humanismus. (Kerényi, Karoly.) Zürich, 1945.
Phil 2262.78.5 Bacharach, A. Shaftesburys Optimismus und sein Verhältnis zum Leibnizschen. Inaug. Diss. Thann, 1912.
Phil 5465.56.20 Bachelard, G. L'air et les songes. Paris, 1943.
Phil 5465.56 Bachelard, G. L'eau et les rêves. Paris, 1942.
Phil 5041.42 Bachelard, G. Essai sur la connaissance approchée. Thèse. Paris, 1927.
Phil 5465.56.42 Bachelard, G. La flamme d'une chandelle. 2. éd. Paris, 1962.
Phil 623.25 Bachelard, G. Le rationalisme appliqué. Paris, 1949.
Phil 5465.56.10 Bachelard, G. La terre et les rêveries de la volonté. Paris, 1948.
Phil 5465.56.30 Bachelard, G. La terre et les rêveries du repos. Paris, 1948.
Phil 672.155.10 Bachelard, Gaston. La dialectique de la durée. Paris, 1936.
Phil 2477.15.32 Bachelard, Gaston. Le droit de rêver. 2. éd. Paris, 1970.
Phil 2477.15.35 Bachelard, Gaston. Études. Paris, 1970.
Phil 332.19 Bachelard, Gaston. La formation de l'esprit scientifique. Photoreproduction. Paris, 1938.
Phil 672.155 Bachelard, Gaston. L'intuition de l'instant. Paris, 1932.
Phil 672.239 Bachelard, Gaston. L'intuition de l'instant. Paris, 1966.
Phil 2477.15 Bachelard, Gaston. Le matérialisme rationnel. Paris, 1953.
Phil 2477.15.22 Bachelard, Gaston. On poetic imagination and reverie; selections from the works of Gaston Bachelard. Indianapolis, 1971.
Phil 2477.15.8 Bachelard, Gaston. The poetics of reverie. N.Y., 1969.
Phil 2477.15.6 Bachelard, Gaston. The poetics of space. N.Y., 1964.
Phil 2477.15.10 Bachelard, Gaston. La poétique de la rêverie. Paris, 1960.
Phil 2477.15.13 Bachelard, Gaston. La poétique de la rêverie. 3. éd. Paris, 1965.
Phil 2477.15.5 Bachelard, Gaston. La poétique de l'espace. 1. éd. Paris, 1957.
Phil 2477.15.5.2 Bachelard, Gaston. La poétique de l'espace. 2. éd. Paris, 1958.
Phil 6311.48 Bachelard, Gaston. La psychanalyse du feu. Paris, 1965.
Phil 3450.11.190 Bachelard, Suzanne. La logique de Husserl. Paris, 1957.
Phil 3450.11.191 Bachelard, Suzanne. A study of Husserl's formal and transcendental logic. Evanston, 1968.
Phil 2477.15.80 Bachelard. (Quillet, Pierre.) Paris, 1964.
Phil 2477.15.110 Bachelard. (Voisin, Marcel.) Bruxelles, 1967.
Phil 5041.75 Bachhuber, A.H. Introduction to logic. N.Y., 1957.
Phil 3425.91.28 Bachmann, C.F. Anti-Hegel. Jena, 1835.
Phil 5041.1 Bachmann, C.F. System der Logik. Leipzig, 1828.
Phil 3425.91.30 Bachmann, C.F. Über Hegel's System und die Nothwendigkeit. Leipzig, 1833.
Phil 3805.90 Bachmann, F. Entwickelung der Ethik Schleiermachers. Leipzig, 1892.
Phil 3092.1 Bachofen, J.J. Selbstbiographie undAntrittsrede. Halle, 1927.
Phil 6329.12 Bachofen-Freud. (Turel, Adrien.) Bern, 1939.
Phil 3640.240.5 Bachofen und Nietzsche. (Baeumler, Alfred.) Zürich, 1929.
Phil 5241.165 Bachrach, Arthur. Experimental foundations of clinical psychology. N.Y., 1962.
Phil 3850.18.113 Bachus, A. Enzelmensch Familie und Staat in der Philosophie Max Schelers. Inaug. Diss. Düsseldorf, 1936.
Phil 6132.16 Back numbers Wilmans express, condensed. (Wilmans, Helen.) n.p., 18- ?
Phil 6120.21 Back to life. (Kupper, H.I.) N.Y., 1945.
Phil 8592.41 Back to realities. (Mellone, S.H.) London, 1928.
Phil 7054.179 Back to the father's house. London, 18- . 2v.
Phil 9510.2 Backbiting. (Tonna, C.E.B.P.) N.Y., 1842. 2 pam.
Phil 9343.11 Backbone; the development of character. (Drury, Samuel S.) N.Y., 1923.
Phil 176.101 Backer, S. de. Disputationes metaphysicae. Fasc.1-3. Paris, 1920-1923.
Phil 5599.85.5 Backes-Thomas, Madeleine. Le test des trois personnages. Neuchâtel, 1969.
Phil 8419.30 A background for beauty. (Silcock, Arnold.) London, 1951.
Phil 182.112 Background to modern thought. (Hardie, C.D.) London, 1947.
Phil 1819.10 Backgrounds of romanticism. (Trawick, Leonard Moses.) Bloomington, 1967.
Phil 5525.10 Backhaus, W.E. Das Wesen des Humors. Leipzig, n.d.
Phil 6750.17 The backward baby. (Sheffield, Herman B.) N.Y., 1915.
NEDL Phil 9430.1 Bacmeister, A. Der Pessimismus und die Sittenlehre. Gütersloh, 1882.
VPhil 1850.1F Bacon, F. Opera omnia. Frankfort, 1664-68.
VPhil 1850.1.2F Bacon, F. Opera omnia. Frankfort, 1665.
VPhil 1850.1.7F Bacon, F. Opera omnia. Hafniae, 1694.
VPhil 1850.1.8F Bacon, F. Opera omnia. Lipsiae, 1694.
Phil 1850.1.4F Bacon, F. Opera omnia. London, 1730. 2v.
VPhil 1850.1.3F Bacon, F. Opera omnia. London, 1730 4v.
Htn Phil 1850.1.10* Bacon, F. Operum moralium et civilium tomus. London, 1638.
Phil 1850.160 Bacon, F.V. The philosophy of Francis Bacon. Liverpool, 1964.
Htn Phil 1850.3.2* Bacon, Francis. Advancement and proficience of learning. Oxford, 1640.
Htn Phil 1850.3.3* Bacon, Francis. Advancement and proficience of learning. Oxford, 1640.
Phil 1850.35.7A Bacon, Francis. The advancement of learning. Boston, 1904.
Phil 1850.36 Bacon, Francis. The advancement of learning. London, 1900.
Phil 1850.35.20 Bacon, Francis. The advancement of learning. London, 1950.
Phil 1850.35.2A Bacon, Francis. The advancement of learning. Oxford, 1869.
NEDL Phil 1850.35.6 Bacon, Francis. The advancement of learning. St. Louis, 1901.
Phil 1850.35.3 Bacon, Francis. The advancement of learning. v.2. London, 1893-95.
Phil 1850.35.8 Bacon, Francis. The advancement of learning. 1st ed. London, 1901-05. 2v.
Phil 1850.35.2.3 Bacon, Francis. The advancement of learning. 3rd ed. Oxford, 1885.
Phil 1850.35.4 Bacon, Francis. The advancement of learning. 4th ed. Oxford, 1891.
Phil 1850.35.5 Bacon, Francis. The advancement of learning. 5th ed. Oxford, 1900.
Phil 1850.66 Bacon, Francis. Analyse de la philosophie. Leyde, 1756.
Phil 1850.34.2 Bacon, Francis. The books of Lord Verulam. London, 1825.
Htn Phil 1850.55* Bacon, Francis. A collection of some principall rules and maximes of the common laws of England. London, 1630.
Htn Phil 1850.72* Bacon, Francis. The confession of faith. London, 1641.
Htn Phil 1850.32.5* Bacon, Francis. De augmentis scientiarum. Libri IX. Amsterdam, 1662.
Htn Phil 1850.32* Bacon, Francis. De augmentis scientiarum. Libri IX. Lugdunum, 1652.
Phil 1850.32.8 Bacon, Francis. De dignitate et augmentis scientarum. Libri IX. Argentorari, 1654.
Phil 1850.41 Bacon, Francis. De dignitate et augmentis scientiarum. Wirceburgi, 1779-80. 2v.
Htn Phil 1850.31.15* Bacon, Francis. De dignitate et augmentis scientiarum. Libri IX. Paris, 1624.
Htn Phil 1850.56* Bacon, Francis. De Verulamio summi angliae. London, 1620.
Htn Phil 1850.39* Bacon, Francis. The essayes or counsels. London, 1625.
Phil 1850.40.4 Bacon, Francis. Essays. 2nd ed. London, 1857.
Phil 1850.40 Bacon, Francis. Essays. 3rd ed. London, 1857.
Phil 1850.40.2 Bacon, Francis. Essays. 3rd ed. London, 1858.
Htn Phil 1850.29.10* Bacon, Francis. Essays or counsels, civil and moral...and discourse of the wisdom of the ancients. London, 1701.
Htn Phil 1850.29* Bacon, Francis. Essays or counsels, civil and moral...where unto is added the wisdom of the ancients. London, 1673.

Author and Title Listing

Htn Phil 1850.27.10* Bacon, Francis. Essais politiques et moraux. Paris, 1621.
X Cg Phil 1850.59.10 Bacon, Francis. Exemplum tractatus de justitia universali. Metz, 1806. (Changed to XM 1503)
Phil 9220.7 Bacon, Francis. For friendship's sake. N.Y., 1900.
Phil 1850.16.15 Bacon, Francis. Francis Bacon. The great instauration. Garden City, 1937.
Htn Phil 1850.1.11F* Bacon, Francis. Francisci Baconi operum moralium. Londini, 1638. 2 pam.
Phil 1850.25.5 Bacon, Francis. François Bacon. Paris, 1926.
Phil 1850.28 Bacon, Francis. Grosskanzlers von England moralische, politische und ökonomische Versuche. Breslau, 1762.
Htn Phil 1850.75.5* Bacon, Francis. Histoire naturelle. Paris, 1631.
Htn Phil 1850.75* Bacon, Francis. Historia naturalis et experimentalis de ventis. Amstelodami, 1662. 3 pam.
Htn Phil 1850.74* Bacon, Francis. Historia naturalis et experimentalis de ventis. Lugdunum Batavorum, 1638.
Htn Phil 1850.65* Bacon, Francis. Historia vitae et mortis. Amstelodami, 1663.
Htn Phil 1850.63* Bacon, Francis. Historia vitae et mortis. Lugdunum Batavorum, 1636.
Htn Phil 1850.64* Bacon, Francis. Historia vitae et mortis. Lugdunum Batavorum, 1637.
Htn Phil 1850.64.5* Bacon, Francis. Historie of life and death. London, 1638.
Htn Phil 1850.57* Bacon, Francis. The historie of the raigne of...Henry VII. London, 1622.
Htn Phil 1850.64.7* Bacon, Francis. History naturall and experimentall, of life and death. London, 1638.
Htn Phil 1850.74.5* Bacon, Francis. The naturall and experimentall history of winds. London, 1653.
Phil 1850.50.8 Bacon, Francis. Neues Organon. J.H. Kirchmann. Berlin, 1870.
Htn Phil 1850.38* Bacon, Francis. Neuf livres de la dignité et de l'accroissement des sciences. Paris, 1632.
Phil 1850.51 Bacon, Francis. The novum organon. Oxford, 1855.
Phil 1850.50.10 Bacon, Francis. Novum organum. Glasguae, 1803.
Phil 1850.50.25 Bacon, Francis. Novum organum. Lanciani, 1928.
Phil 1850.50.13A Bacon, Francis. Novum organum. London, 1905.
Htn Phil 1850.50.6* Bacon, Francis. Novum organum. Lugdunum Batavorum, 1650. 2 pam.
Phil 1850.50.11 Bacon, Francis. Novum organum. Oxonii, 1813.
Phil 1850.50.12 Bacon, Francis. Novum organum. St. Louis, 1901.
Phil 1850.50.9 Bacon, Francis. Novum organum. Wirceburgi, 1779.
Phil 1850.50.5A Bacon, Francis. Novum organum. Rev. A. Johnson. London, 1859.
Phil 1850.50.2 Bacon, Francis. Novum organum. T. Fowler. Oxford, 1878.
Phil 1850.50.3 Bacon, Francis. Novum organum. T. Fowler. Oxford, 1878.
Phil 1850.50.4 Bacon, Francis. Novum organum. T. Fowler. 2nd ed. Oxford, 1889.
Htn Phil 1850.50.7* Bacon, Francis. Novum organum. 2a ed. Amsterdam, 1660.
Phil 1850.50.26 Bacon, Francis. Nuovo organo. Firenze, 1938.
Phil 1850.50.23 Bacon, Francis. Nuovo organo delle scienze. Bassano, 1788.
Phil 1850.23 Bacon, Francis. Oeuvres. Dijon, 1800. 3v.
Htn Phil 1850.27.5* Bacon, Francis. Les oeuvres morales et politiques. Paris, 1633. 2v.
Htn Phil 1850.27* Bacon, Francis. Les oeuvres morales et politiques. Paris, 1637.
Htn Phil 1850.27.3* Bacon, Francis. Les oeuvres morales et politiques. Paris, 1637.
Phil 1850.26.5 Bacon, Francis. Oeuvres philosophiques, morales et politiques. Paris, 1811.
Phil 1850.25 Bacon, Francis. Oeuvres philosophiques. Paris, 1834. 3v.
Phil 1850.26 Bacon, Francis. Oeuvres philosophiques et morales. Paris, 1797. 2v.
Htn Phil 1850.33.5* Bacon, Francis. Of the advancement and proficiencie of learning. London, 1674.
Phil 1850.35.12 Bacon, Francis. Of the advancement of learning. 5th ed. Oxford, 1920.
Phil 1850.34.3 Bacon, Francis. Of the proficience and advancement of learning. London, 1828.
Phil 1850.34.5 Bacon, Francis. Of the proficience and advancement of learning. London, 1838.
Phil 1850.35A Bacon, Francis. Of the proficience and advancement of learning. London, 1851.
Phil 1850.35.1 Bacon, Francis. Of the proficience and advancement of learning. London, 1861.
Htn Phil 1850.76* Bacon, Francis. Opuscula varia posthuma, philosophica, civilia, et theologica. Londini, 1658.
Phil 1850.10 Bacon, Francis. Philosophical works. London, 1737. 3v.
Htn Phil 1850.37* Bacon, Francis. Les progrez et avancement aux sciences divines et humaines. Paris, 1624.
Htn Phil 1850.18* Bacon, Francis. Remaines, being essayes and severall letters. London, 1648.
Htn Phil 1850.75.10* Bacon, Francis. Resuscitatio, or Bringing into public light. London, 1657.
Htn Phil 1850.5.2F* Bacon, Francis. Resuscitatio. 2nd ed. London, 1661.
Phil 1850.30 Bacon, Francis. Scripta in naturali...philosophia. Amsterdam, 1653.
Htn Phil 1850.5.5F* Bacon, Francis. The second part of the Resuscitatio. London, 1670.
Phil 1850.59.50 Bacon, Francis. Sermones fideles, ethici, politici, o economici, sive interiora rerum. Lugdunum Batavorum, 1659.
Htn Phil 1850.60* Bacon, Francis. Sermones fidelis. Amsterdam, 1662.
Htn Phil 1850.71* Bacon, Francis. Sylva Sylvarum. London, 1627.
Htn Phil 1850.62* Bacon, Francis. True peace; or A moderate discourse. London, 1663.
Htn Phil 1850.31* Bacon, Francis. The two books of proficience and advancement of learning. London, 1605.
Phil 1850.41.7 Bacon, Francis. Über die Würde und den Fortgang der Wissenschaften. Darmstadt, 1966.
Htn Phil 1850.59* Bacon, Francis. The use of the law. London, 1629.
Htn Phil 1850.61* Bacon, Francis. A wise and moderate discourse concerning church affaires. n.p., 1641.
VPhil 1850.1.15F Bacon, Francis. Works. London, 1740. 4v.
VPhil 1850.2F Bacon, Francis. Works. London, 1753. 3v.
VPhil 1850.2.1F Bacon, Francis. Works. London, 1765. 5v.
Phil 1850.2.2F Bacon, Francis. Works. London, 1778. 5v.
Phil 1850.11 Bacon, Francis. Works. London, 1802-7. 12v.
Phil 1850.2.5 Bacon, Francis. Works. London, 1803. 10v.
Phil 1850.12.5 Bacon, Francis. Works. London, 1818. 12v.
Phil 1850.12.20 Bacon, Francis. Works. London, 1824. 10v.
Phil 1850.15.5 Bacon, Francis. Works. London, 1870-72. 7v.
Phil 1850.15.3 Bacon, Francis. Works. Faksimile-Neudruck. Stuttgart, 1963. 14v.
Phil 1850.15.2 Bacon, Francis. Works. v.1,3-15. Paris, 1860-65. 14v.

Phil 1850.14 Bacon, Francis. Works. v.1-7, 9-14. London, 1857-74. 13v.
Phil 1850.15A Bacon, Francis. Works. v.1-8, 10-15. Boston, 1861-64. 14v.
Phil 1850.13 Bacon, Francis. Works. v.1-16. London, 1825-34. 17v.
Phil 1850.12 Bacon, Francis. Works. v.2. London, 1815.
Phil 1850.21 Bacon, Francis. The works of Lord Bacon. London, 1838. 2v.
Phil 1850.79 Pamphlet box. Bacon, Francis.
Htn Phil 1850.73* Bacon, Francois. Historia naturalis. Londini, 1622.
Phil 1850.100A Bacon; his writings and his philosophy. (Craik, G.L.) London, 1846.
Phil 1850.100.7 Bacon; his writings and his philosophy. (Craik, G.L.) London, 1862.
Phil 1850.100.5 Bacon; his writings and his philosophy. v.1-3. (Craik, G.L.) London, 1860.
Phil 8615.13 Bacon, S.F. An evaluation of the philosophy and pedagogy of ethical culture. Diss. Washington, 1933.
Phil 1850.81 Bacon. (Church, R.W.) London, 1884.
Phil 1850.81.3 Bacon. (Church, R.W.) London, 1896.
Phil 1850.81.9 Bacon. (Church, R.W.) London, 1908.
Phil 1850.81.4 Bacon. (Church, R.W.) N.Y., 1884.
Phil 1850.81.6 Bacon. (Church, R.W.) N.Y., 1899.
Phil 1850.81.5 Bacon. (Church, R.W.) N.Y., 1901.
Phil 1850.83A Bacon. (Fowler, J.) N.Y., 1881.
Phil 1850.87 Bacon. (Nichol, J.) Philadelphia, 1888-89. 2v.
Phil 1850.88 Bacon. (Rémusat, Charles de.) Paris, 1858.
Phil 1850.121 Bacon und die Naturphilosophie. (Frost, Walter.) München, 1927.
Phil 1850.92 Bacon Verulamius. (Janet, P.) Angers, 1889.
Phil 1850.151 Bacon von Verulam und seine Stellung in der Geschichte der Philosophie. (Pamer, C.) Triest, 1888.
Phil 1850.131 Baconee Locke. (Tinivella, G.) Milano, 1939.
Phil 4803.186.30 Baczko, Bronisław. Człowiek i światopoglądy. Warszawa, 1965.
Phil 4065.140 Badaloni, Nicola. La filosofia di Giordano Bruno. Firenze, 1955.
Phil 4260.140 Badaloni, Nicola. Introduzione a G.B. Vico. Milano, 1961.
Phil 4073.117 Badaloni, Nicola. Tommaso Campanella. 1. ed. Milano, 1965.
Phil 5520.355 Badania eksperymentalne nad rozumieniem zdán. (Szewczuk, W.) Kraków, 1960.
Phil 5241.67 Badareu, D. Essai sur la pensée. Thèse. Paris, 1924.
Phil 4818.298.80 Badareu, Dan. Un système matérialiste métaphysique au XIXe siècle: la philosophie de Basile Conta. Paris, 1924.
Phil 7060.70 Badaud, U.N. Coup d'oeil sur la magie au XIXe siècle. Paris, 1891.
Phil 8612.70 Badawi, Abdurrahmân. Le problème de la mort dans la philosophie existentielle. Le Claire, 1964.
Phil 1020.85 Badawi, Abdurrahman. Le transmission de la philosophie grecque au monde arabe. Paris, 1968.
Phil 9560.40 Baden, H.J. Ende und Anfang der Humanität. Gütersloh, 1955.
Phil 3110.180 Baden, Hans J. Das religiöse Problem der Gegenwart bei Jakob Böhme. Leipzig, 1939.
Phil 5643.43.5 Bader, Paul. Augentauschungen. Leipzig, 1907.
Phil 5241.82 Badley, John H. The will to live. London, 1931.
Phil 176.79 Badoureau, A. Causeries philosophiques. Paris, 1920.
Htn Phil 9351.12* Baecalaureate address. (Lindsley, Philip.) Nashville, 1827.
Phil 3625.1.185 Baeck, Leo. Mendelssohn Gedenkfeier der Jüdischen Gemeinde zu Berlin am 8, Sept. 1929. Berlin, 1929.
Phil 3821.14 Bäck, Leo. Spinozas Erste Einwirkungen auf Deutschland. Berlin, 1895.
Phil 7082.170 Baege, Max Hermann. Naturgeschichte des Traums. Leipzig, 1928.
Phil 176.2.10 Bäggesen, Jen. Aus J. Bäggesen's Briefwechsel mit K.L. Reinhold. Leipzig, 1931. 2v.
Phil 176.2 Bäggesen, Jens. Philosophischer Nachlasz. Zürich, 1858. 2v.
Phil 3850.27.215 Baehr, Hans N. Albert Schweitzer, sein Denken und sein Weg. Tübingen, 1962.
Phil 8402.66 Baekkelund, Kjell. Kunst eller kaos? Oslo, 1969.
Phil 3585.1.80 Baensch, Otto. Johann Heinrich Lamberts Philosophie und seine Stellung zu Kant. Inaug. Diss. Magdeburg, 1902.
Phil 8050.49 Baer, Hans. Grundriss eines Systems. Strassburg, 1913.
Phil 3808.107 Baer, J. Schopenhauer - Bibliothek. Frankfurt, 1905.
Phil 3821.27 Baer, Joseph. Spinoza. Frankfurt, 191-?
Phil 176.1 Bärenbach, F. Grundlegung der kritischen Philosophie. Leipzig, 1879.
Phil 8735.10 Baerenbach, Friedrich von. Gedanken über die Teleologie in der Natur. Berlin, 1878.
Phil 3565.127 Baerwald, Leo. Die Entwicklung der Lotzeschen Psychologie. Berlin, 1905.
Phil 7069.25.3 Baerwald, R. Die intellektuellen Phänomene. Berlin, 1925.
Phil 7069.26.80 Baerwald, R. Okkultismus und Spiritismus. Berlin, 1926.
Phil 7140.127 Baerwald, Richard. Psychologie der Selbstverteidigung in Klampf-, Not- und Krankheitzeiten. Leipzig, 1927.
Phil 8876.63 Baets, Maurice de. Les bases de la morale et du droit. Paris, 1892.
Phil 1504.1.2 Baeumker, C. Avencebrolis fons vitae. v.1, pt.2-3. Münster, 1892. 2v.
NEDL Phil 1504.1.2 Baeumker, C. Avencebrolis fons vitae. v.1, pt.4. Münster, 1892.
Phil 1504.2.6 Baeumker, C. Die Impossibilia. v.2. pt.6. Münster, 1898.
Phil 1135.68 Baeumker, C. Das Probleme der Materie in der griechischen Philosophie. Münster, 1890.
Phil 1504.3.2 Baeumker, C. Witelo. v.3, pt.2. Münster, 1908.
Phil 5241.178 Baeumker, Clemens. Anschauung und Denken. Paderborn, 1913.
Phil 1506.4 Baeumker, Clemens. Platonismus in Mittelalter. München, 1916.
Phil 1504.13.6 Baeumker, F. Das Inevitable des Honorius Augustodunensis. v.13, pt.6. Münster, 1914.
Phil 1504.10.6 Baeumker, F. Die Lehre Anselms von Canterbury. v.10, pt.6. Münster, 1912.
Phil 3001.13 Baeumler, A. Studien zur dutschen Geistesgeschichte. Berlin, 1937.
Phil 3640.240.5 Baeumler, Alfred. Bachofen und Nietzsche. Zürich, 1929.
Phil 3483.28.5 Baeumler, Alfred. Das Irrationalitätsproblem in der Asthetik und Logik. 2. Aufl. Darmstadt, 1967.
NEDL Phil 3483.28 Baeumler, Alfred. Kant's Kritik der Urteilskraft. Halle, 1923.
Phil 3640.240A Baeumler, Alfred. Nietzsche der Philosoph und Politiker. Leipzig, 1931.
Phil 3640.240.3 Baeumler, Alfred. Nietzsche der Philosoph und Politiker. 3e Aufl. Leipzig, 1937.

Phil 8637.24.2 — Bag død og grav. 2. udg. (Muderspach, L.) København, 1927.

Phil 6390.4 — Bagby, English. The psychology of personality. N.Y., 1928.

Phil 5125.22 — Bagchi, S. Inductive reasoning. Calcutta, 1953.

Phil 1701.18 — Bagdasar, N. Filosofia contemporana a istorici. București, 1930.

Phil 2270.135 — Bager-Sjögren, J. Herbert Spencer och utvecklingsfilosofien. Lund, 1893.

Phil 8612.26 — Baghdigian, B.K. The forgotten purpose. Kansas City, 1934.

Phil 310.718 — Bagirov, Z.N. V.I. Lenin i dialekticheskoe ponimanie otritsaniia. Baku, 1969.

Phil 270.30 — Baglioni, B. Il principio di causalità. Perugia, 1908.

Phil 8876.1 — Bagshaw, W. On man. London, 1833. 2v.

Phil 8626.1.10 — Baguenault de Puchesse, F. A immortalidade, a morte e a vida. Porto, 1903.

Phil 8626.1 — Baguenault de Puchesse, F. L'immortalité, la mort et la vie. Paris, 1868.

Phil 2493.83 — Baguenault de Puchesse, Gustave. Condillac; sa vie, sa philosophie, son influence. Paris, 1910.

Phil 420.2 — Bahm, Archie J. Types of intuition. Albuquerque, 1960[1961]

Phil 5593.60 — Bahm, Ewald B. Psychodiagnostisches Vademecum. Bern, 1960.

Phil 176.3 — Bahnsen, J. Beitrage zur Charakterologie. Leipzig, 1867. 2v.

Phil 176.3.9 — Bahnsen, J. Das tragische als Weltgesetz und der Humor. Lauenburg, 1877.

Phil 176.3.10 — Bahnsen, J. Das tragische als Weltgesetz und der Humor. Leipzig, 1931.

Phil 5041.27 — Bahnsen, J. Der Widerspruch im Wessen und Wesen der Welt. Berlin, 1880-82. 2v.

Phil 176.3.7 — Bahnsen, J. Wie ich Wurde was ich Ward. Leipzig, 1931.

Phil 176.3.5 — Bahnsen, J. Wie ich Wurde was ich Ward. München, 1905.

Phil 176.3.3 — Bahnsen, J. Zum Verhältniss Zwischen Wille und Motiv. Lauenburg, 1870.

Phil 3808.248 — Bahr, Hans Dieter. Das gefesselte Engagement; zur Ideologie der Kontemplativen Asthetik Schopenhauer. Bonn, 1970.

Phil 9515.3.80 — Bahrat, Karl F. Mit dem Herrn [von] Zimmermann. n.p., 1790.

Phil 9045.2 — Bahrdt, C.F. Handbuch der Moral für den Bürgerstand. Halle, 1790.

Phil 8876.117 — Baier, Kurt. The moral point of view. Ithaca, 1958.

Phil 8876.117.2 — Baier, Kurt. The moral point of view. N.Y., 1967.

Phil 525.84 — Bailey, A.A. From intellect to intuition. N.Y., 1932.

Phil 978.74.30 — Bailey, A.A. (Mrs.). The consciousness of the atom. 2d ed. N.Y., 1922.

Phil 978.74.35 — Bailey, A.A. (Mrs.). The destiny of the nations. N.Y., 1949.

Phil 978.74.45 — Bailey, A.A. (Mrs.). Education in the new age. 1st ed. N.Y., 1954.

Phil 978.74.20 — Bailey, A.A. (Mrs.). Initiation, human and solar. 3d. ed. N.Y., 1926.

Phil 978.74.25 — Bailey, A.A. (Mrs.). Letters on occult meditation. 2d ed. N.Y., 1926.

Phil 5241.81 — Bailey, A.A. (Mrs.). The soul and its mechanism (the problem of psychology). N.Y., 1930.

Phil 978.74.5 — Bailey, A.A. (Mrs.). A treatise on cosmic fire. 2d ed. N.Y., 1930[1925]

Phil 978.74.15 — Bailey, A.A. (Mrs.). A treatise on the seven rays. N.Y., 1936-42. 4v.

Phil 978.74.10 — Bailey, A.A. (Mrs.). A treatise on white magic. N.Y., 1934.

Phil 978.74.40 — Bailey, A.A. (Mrs.). Unfinished autobiography. N.Y., 1951.

Phil 1158.25.2 — Bailey, Cyril. The Greek atomists and Epicurus. N.Y., 1964.

Phil 1158.25A — Bailey, Cyril. The Greek atomists and Epicurus. Oxford, 1928.

Phil 9050.4.5 — Bailey, L.H. The outlook to nature. N.Y., 1911.

Phil 6311.21 — Bailey, Pearce. Diseases of the nervous system resulting from accident and injury. N.Y., 1906.

Phil 6315.2.355 — Bailey, Percival. Sigmund the unserene. Springfield, Ill., 1965.

Phil 5135.1 — Bailey, S. Essays...opinions. London, 1826.

Phil 5135.1.3 — Bailey, S. Essays...opinions. London, 1831.

Phil 5135.1.5 — Bailey, S. Essays on opinions and truth. Boston, 1854.

Phil 5135.1.4 — Bailey, S. Essays on the formation and publication of opinions. London, 1837.

Phil 176.4A — Bailey, S. Essays on the pursuit of truth. London, 1829.

Phil 176.4.3 — Bailey, S. Essays on the pursuit of truth. London, 1831.

Phil 5241.1 — Bailey, S. Letters...philosophy...human mind. London, 1855.

Phil 5241.1.2 — Bailey, S. Letters...philosophy...human mind. London, 1858.

Phil 1870.83 — Bailey, S. Review of Berkeley's theory of vision. London, 1842.

Phil 5041.2.5 — Bailey, Samuel. The theory of reasoning. London, 1851.

Phil 5041.2 — Bailey, Samuel. The theory of reasoning. London, 1852.

Phil 2520.81 — Baillet, A. La vie de Monsieur Des-Cartes. Paris, 1691.

Htn — Phil 2520.81.2* — Baillet, A. La vie de Monsieur Des-Cartes. Paris, 1691. 2v.

Htn — Phil 2520.81.5* — Baillet, A. La vie de Monsieur Des-Cartes. Paris, 1692.

Phil 2520.81.6 — Baillet, A. La vie de Monsieur Des-Cartes. Paris, 1706.

Phil 2520.81.15 — Baillet, A. Vie de Monsieur Descartes. Paris, 1946.

Phil 2280.8.90 — Baillie, J.B. Andrew Seth Pringle-Pattison, 1856-1931. London, 1931.

Phil 3425.103 — Baillie, J.B. The origin and significance of Hegel's logic. London, 1901.

Phil 1905.23 — Baillie, J.B. Reflections on life and religion. London, 1952.

Phil 176.78 — Baillie, J.B. Studies in human nature. London, 1921.

Phil 8581.80 — Baillie, James. Spiritual religion. London, 1940.

Phil 8626.24 — Baillie, John. And the life everlasting. N.Y., 1933.

Phil 8581.52.10 — Baillie, John. The interpretation of religion. N.Y., 1928.

Phil 8581.52.20 — Baillie, John. Invitation to pilgrimage. London, 1942.

Phil 8581.52 — Baillie, John. The roots of religion in the human soul. London, 1926.

Phil 8581.52.30 — Baillie, John. The sense of the presence of God. London, 1962.

Phil 332.7 — Baillie, T.B. An outline of the idealistic construction of experience. London, 1906.

Phil 2477.1.140 — Baillot, A. Emile Boutroux et la pensée religieuse. Paris, 1957.

Phil 3808.151.2 — Baillot, A. Influence de la philosophie de Schopenhauer en France. Thèse. Paris, 1927. 2 pam.

Phil 801.34 — Baillot, A.F. La notion d'existence. Paris, 1954.

Phil 2905.1.150 — Bailly, Thomas de. Quodlibets. Paris, 1960.

Phil 5241.2.10 — Bain, A. The emotions and the will. London, 1865.

Phil 5241.2.13 — Bain, A. The emotions and the will. N.Y., 1886.

Phil 5241.2.10.15 — Bain, A. The emotions and the will. 3. ed. N.Y., 1875.

Phil 5241.2.15 — Bain, A. Le émotions et la volonté. 3e éd. Paris, 1885.

Phil 6111.1.20 — Bain, A. L'esprit et le corps. Paris, 1878.

Phil 6111.1.9 — Bain, A. Geist und Körper. 2. Aufl. Leipzig, 1881.

Phil 2138.81A — Bain, A. John Stuart Mill. London, 1882.

Phil 2138.81.5 — Bain, A. John Stuart Mill. N.Y., 1882.

Phil 5241.2 — Bain, A. Mental science. N.Y., 1868.

Phil 5241.2.2 — Bain, A. Mental science. N.Y., 1873.

Phil 5241.2.5 — Bain, A. Mental science. N.Y., 1880.

Phil 6111.1 — Bain, A. Mind and body. London, 1873.

Phil 6111.1.2 — Bain, A. Mind and body. N.Y., 1873.

Phil 6111.1.5 — Bain, A. Mind and body. N.Y., 1874.

NEDL Phil 8876.2 — Bain, A. Moral science. N.Y., 1869.

Phil 9035.2 — Bain, A. On the study of character. London, 1861.

Phil 5241.2.20 — Bain, A. The senses and the intellect. London, 1855.

Phil 5241.2.22 — Bain, A. The senses and the intellect. N.Y., 1879.

Phil 5241.2.21.5 — Bain, A. The senses and the intellect. 3. ed. N.Y., 1872.

Phil 5241.2.27 — Bain, A. The senses and the intellect. 4th ed. N.Y., 1894.

NEDL Phil 1855.80 — Bain, Alexander. Autobiography. London, 1904.

Phil 1855.30 — Bain, Alexander. Dissertaions on leading philosophical topics. London, 1903.

Phil 5041.3 — Bain, Alexander. Logic. London, 1870. 2v.

Phil 5041.3.5 — Bain, Alexander. Logic deductive and inductive. N.Y., 1887.

Phil 5041.3.10 — Bain, Alexander. Logique déductive et inductive. 3e éd. Paris, 1894. 2v.

Phil 1855.60 — Bain, Alexander. Practical essays. London, 1884.

Phil 525.28 — Bain, James L.M. The Christ of the Holy Grail. London, 1909.

Phil 5241.2.21 — Bain, S. The senses and the intellect. 2. ed. London, 1864.

Phil 7069.44.35 — Baird, A.T. One hundred cases for survival after death. N.Y., 1944.

Phil 5645.11A — Baird, J.W. The color sensitivity of the peripheral retina. Washington, 1905.

Phil 5585.310 — Baird, John C. Psychophysical analysis of visual space. 1. ed. Oxford, 1970.

Phil 5465.28 — Baitch, Baïa. La psychologie de la rêverie. Thèse. Paris, 1927.

VPhil 8400.49 — Bakalov, Georgi. Izkustvo i kritika. Sofiia, 1906.

Phil 5402.36 — Bakan, David. Disease, pain and suffering. Chicago, 1968.

Phil 5627.266.10 — Bakan, David. The duality of human existence. Chicago, 1966.

Phil 5270.6 — Bakan, David. On method: toward a reconstruction of psychological investigation. 1st ed. San Francisco, 1967.

Phil 6315.2.230 — Bakan, David. Sigmund Freud and the Jewish mystical tradition. Princeton, N.J., 1958.

Phil 5041.97 — Bakanialze, Mamiie I. Problema subordinatsii logicheskikh form. Alma-Ata, 1968.

Phil 1900.88 — Baker, A.E. Bishop Butler. London, 1923.

Phil 801.20 — Baker, A.E. How to understand philosophy. N.Y., 1926.

Phil 8581.89 — Baker, A.E. Prophets for a day of judgment. London, 1944.

Phil 6311.12 — Baker, A.E. Psychoanalysis explained and criticized. London, 1926.

Phil 8691.27 — Baker, Albert E. Science, Christianity and truth. London, 1943.

Phil 176.82 — Baker, Arthur. Outlines of logic, psychology and ethics. London, 1891.

Phil 6327.21.80 — Baker, Elsworth. Man in the trap. N.Y., 1967.

Phil 5645.10 — Baker, Emma S. Experiments on tne aesthetics of light and colour. Toronto, 1903.

Phil 1905.20A — Baker, H.C. The dignity of man. Cambridge, 1947.

Phil 1801.8A — Baker, H.C. The wars of truth. Cambridge, 1952.

Phil 5241.101 — Baker, H.J. The art of understanding. Boston, 1940.

Phil 672.156 — Baker, John Tull. An historical and critical examination of English space and time theories. Thesis. Bronxville, N.Y., 1930.

Phil 5241.128 — Baker, Lawrence. General experimental psychology. N.Y., 1942.

Phil 6111.59 — Baker, R.S. New ideals in healing. N.Y., 1909.

Phil 8656.24 — Baker, Rannie B. Concept of a limited God. Washington, 1934.

Phil 7150.15 — Baker, W.E. Diary of a suicide. N.Y., 1913.

Phil 1106.1A — Bakewell, C.M. Source book in ancient philosophy. N.Y., 1907.

Phil 1106.1.5 — Bakewell, C.M. Source book in ancient philosophy. N.Y., 1907.

Phil 1106.1.7 — Bakewell, C.M. Source book in ancient philosphy. N.Y., 1940.

Phil 8626.2 — Bakewell, F.C. Natural evidence of a future life. London, 1835.

Phil 6951.1 — Bakewell, T. The domestic guide in cases of insanity. Newcastle, 1809.

Phil 1106.15 — Bakhuizen Van Den Brink, R.C. Varias lectiones ex historia philosophiae antiquae. Lugduni-Batavorum, 1842.

Phil 1750.115.120 — Bakker, Reinout. De geschiedenis van het fenomenologisch denken. Antwerp, 1964.

Phil 2750.20.95 — Bakker, Reinout. Merleau-Ponty. Bearn, 1965.

Phil 3160.9.90 — Bakker, Reinout. Het wijsgerig en psychologisch denken van Carl Gustav Carus in het licht van zijn Godsbeschouwing. Assen, 1954.

Phil 5068.30 — Baknadze, K.S. Sub"ektivnyi idealizm. Tbilisi, 1955.

Phil 630.56 — Bakoš, Mik. O socialistickom realizme. Bratislava, 1952.

Phil 1701.45 — Bakradze, K.S. Ocherki po istorii noveishei i sovremennoi burzhuaznoi filosofii. Tbilisi, 1960.

Phil 3425.505 — Bakradze, K.S. Sistema i metod filosofii Gegelia. Tbilisi, 1958.

Phil 282.28.2 — Balaban, Grigorii Iu. Real'nyi mir v svete uni persal'noi seorii podoishnogo ravnovesiia. 2. izd. Hamilton, 1970.

Phil 1870.121 — Baladi, Naguit. La pensée religieuse de Berkeley. La Caire, 1945.

Phil 186.83 — La balance naturelle, ou Essai sur une loi universelle appliquée aux sciences. (LaSalle, A. de.) Londres, 1788. 2v.

Phil 5400.12 — Balance of emotion and intellect. (Waldstein, C.) London, 1878.

Phil 8708.17 — Balance the fundamental verity. (Smith, Orlando Jay.) Boston, 1904.

Phil 5590.17 — Balanced personality. (Magoun, F.A.) N.Y., 1943.

Phil 4115.93 — Balbino, G. Il primato d'un popolo; Fichte e Gioberti. Catania, 1916.

Phil 8656.40 — Balbontín, José A. A la busca del Dios perdido. Madrid, 1969.

Htn Phil 9560.17* — Baldacchini, F. Dyalogo de patientia. Perosia, 1525.

Phil 4065.135 — Baldi, E. Giordano Bruno. Firenze, 1955.

Phil 2115.235 — Baldini, Artemio Enzo. Il pensiero giovanile di John Locke. Milano, 1969.

Phil 176.123 — Baldini, Bernardino. Dialogi duo in quorum altero agitur de multitudine rerum. Mediolani, 1558. 3 pam.

Phil 1135.182 — Baldry, Harold Capame. The unity of mankind in Greek thought. Cambridge, Eng., 1965.

Phil 5870.95 — Baldwin, Alfred Lee. Behavior and development in childhood. N.Y., 1955.

Phil 365.6 — Baldwin, J.M. Development and evolution. N.Y., 1902.

Phil 86.3.5 — Baldwin, J.M. Dictionary of philosophy. v.1,3. N.Y., 1911. 3v.

NEDL Phil 86.3A — Baldwin, J.M. Dictionary of philosophy. v.1. London, 1901-05.

Phil 86.3.10 — Baldwin, J.M. Dictionary of philosophy. v.2. N.Y., 1940.

Phil 5241.3.15 — Baldwin, J.M. Elements of psychology. N.Y., 1893.

Phil 176.45 — Baldwin, J.M. Fragments in philosophy and science. N.Y., 1902.

Phil 5041.29.2 — Baldwin, J.M. Genetic theory of reality. N.Y., 1915.

Phil 5241.3 — Baldwin, J.M. Hand book of psychology. Senses and intellect. 1. ed. N.Y., 1889.

Phil 5241.3.2 — Baldwin, J.M. Handbook of psychology...feeling and will. N.Y., 1891.

Phil 5241.3.3 — Baldwin, J.M. Handbook of psychology. Senses and intellect. N.Y., 1890.

Phil 5211.2A — Baldwin, J.M. History of psychology. N.Y., 1913. 2v.

Phil 176.45.5 — Baldwin, J.M. Imitation. n.p., 1894-1904. 8 pam.

Phil 5241.3.30A — Baldwin, J.M. The individual and society. Boston, 1911.

Phil 5241.3.9 — Baldwin, J.M. Interpretation sociale et morale des principes du développement mental. Paris, 1899.

Phil 5241.3.8 — Baldwin, J.M. Mental development. 2. ed. N.Y., 1897.

Phil 5211.2.5 — Baldwin, J.M. Sketch of the history of psychology. Lancaster, 1905.

Phil 5241.3.5A — Baldwin, J.M. Social and ethical interpretations. Mental development. N.Y., 1897.

Phil 5241.3.6 — Baldwin, J.M. Social and ethical interpretations. Mental development. N.Y., 1902.

Phil 5241.3.6.10 — Baldwin, J.M. Social and ethical interpretations. Mental development. 5. ed. N.Y., 1913.

Phil 5241.3.28 — Baldwin, J.M. The story of the mind. N.Y., 1898.

Phil 5241.3.24 — Baldwin, J.M. The story of the mind. N.Y., 1901.

Phil 5041.29 — Baldwin, J.M. Thought and things. London, 1906-11. 3v.

Phil 165.7 — Baldwin, R.C. An introduction to philosophy through literature. N.Y., 1950.

Phil 9045.15 — Baldwin, S.E. The relations of education to citizenship. New Haven, 1912.

Phil 8876.14.2 — Baldwin, W. The sayings of the wise. London, 1908.

Htn Phil 8876.14.8* — Baldwin, W. A treatise of morall philosophie. London, n.d.

Htn Phil 8876.14.5* — Baldwin, W. A treatise of morall philosophie. London, 1640.

Htn Phil 8876.14.3* — Baldwin, W. A treatise of morall phylosophye. London, n.d.

Phil 8402.18 — Balet, Leo. Synthetische Kunstwissenschaft. Stuttgart? 1938.

Phil 8402.22 — Balfour, A.J. Criticism and beauty. Oxford, 1910.

Phil 176.5 — Balfour, A.J. Defence of philosophic doubt. London, 1879.

Phil 176.5.13 — Balfour, A.J. Familiar belief and transcendent reason. London, n.d.

Phil 176.5.8 — Balfour, A.J. Foundations of belief. London, 1901.

Phil 176.5.5 — Balfour, A.J. Foundations of belief. N.Y., 1895.

Phil 8656.13.3 — Balfour, A.J.B. L'idée de Dieu et l'esprit humain. 4. éd. Paris, 1916.

Phil 8656.13 — Balfour, A.J.B. Theism and humanism. N.Y., 1915.

Phil 8656.13.5 — Balfour, A.J.B. Theism and thought. London, 1923.

Phil 8656.13.7 — Balfour, A.J.B. Theism and thought. N.Y., 1924.

Phil 600.3 — Balfour, A.T. Religion of humanity. Edinburgh, 1888.

Phil 600.3.2 — Balfour, A.T. Religion of humanity. London, 1888.

Phil 7069.20.10 — Balfour, Gerald W. The ear of Dionysius. N.Y., 1920.

Phil 8876.3 — Balfour, J. A delineation...nature. Obligations. Morality. Edinburgh, 1753.

Phil 8876.3.2 — Balfour, J. A delineation of the nature and obligation of morality. Edinburgh, 1763.

Phil 176.118 — Balfour, James. Philosophical essays. Edinburgh, 1768.

Phil 630.41 — The Balfour lectures on realism. (Seth Pringle Pattison, Andrew.) Edinburgh, 1933.

Phil 8581.18 — Balguy, J. A letter to a deist. London, 1730-38. 7 pam.

Phil 4368.4 — Baliñas, Carlos A. El pensamiento de Amor Ruibal. Madrid, 1968.

Phil 4803.799.95 — Baliński, Michał. Pamiętniki o Janie Śniadeckim. Wilno, 1865. 2v.

Phil 6311.36 — Balint, Michael. Primary love, and psycho-analytic technique. London, 1952.

Phil 6311.36.2 — Balint, Michael. Primary love, and psycho-analytic technique. N.Y., 1965.

Phil 5241.119 — Balint, Michael. Problems of human pleasure and behavior. London, 1957.

Phil 6311.40 — Balint, Michael. Thrills and regressions. London, 1959.

Htn Phil 7075.10* — Ball, B. La folie erotique. Paris, 1888.

Phil 6951.2 — Ball, B. La morphinomanie. Paris, 1888.

Phil 1905.25 — Ball, Frank N. Intellectual calculus. Ipswich, 1957.

Phil 8626.9 — Ball, J.W. Absolute idealism and immortality. Lincoln, 1908.

Phil 3450.42 — Ball, Thomas. Paul Leopold Hoffner als Philosophie. Mainz? 194-?

Phil 5041.4 — Ballantine, W.G. Inductive logic. Boston, 1896.

Phil 5125.17 — Ballantine, William G. The basis of belief, proof by inductive reasoning. N.Y., 1930.

Phil 5241.4 — Ballantyne, J. An examination of the human mind. Edinburgh, 1828.

Phil 8581.23 — Ballard, A. From talk to text. N.Y., 1964.

Phil 8402.32 — Ballard, Edward. Art and analysis. The Hague, 1957.

Phil 5751.8 — Ballard, F. Determinism: false and true. London, 1911.

Phil 510.1.20 — Ballard, Frank. Haeckel's monism false. London, 1905.

Phil 5241.32 — Ballard, J.H. Some phases of the psychology of puzzle learning. N.Y., 1915.

Phil 4210.139 — Ballarini. Principj della scuola Rosminiana. Milano, 1850. 2v.

Phil 5241.5.3 — Ballauf, L. Die Grundlehren der Psychologie und ihre Anwendung auf die Lehre. Cöthen, 1890.

Phil 3428.85 — Ballauff, F. Entstehung und Bedeutung; Herbarts. Aurich, 1898.

Phil 5241.5 — Ballauff, L. Die Elemente der Psychologie. Cöthen, 1877.

Phil 165.8 — Ballauff, T. Das gnoseologische Problem. Göttingen, 1949.

Phil 3483.65 — Ballauff, Theodor. Vernünftiger Wille und gläubige Liebe. Meisenheim, 1957.

Phil 8968.15.85 — Balle, Theo. Dialogische Existenz. Bamberg, 1967.

Phil 8951.13 — Ballerini, A. Opus theologicum morale in Busernbaum Medullam. 3.ed. Prati, 1898-1901. 7v.

Phil 4710.142 — Ballestrem, Karl G. Russian philosophical terminology. Dordrecht, 1964.

Phil 4710.155 — Ballestrem, Karl G. Die sowjetische Erkenntnismetaphysik und ihr Verhältnis zu Hegel. Dordrecht, 1968.

Phil 6400.1.3 — Ballet, G. Die innerliche Sprache und die verschiedenen Formen der Aphasie. Leipzig, 1890.

Phil 6400.1 — Ballet, G. Le langage intérieur. Paris, 1886.

Phil 3450.19.103 — Ballmer, Karl. Aber Herr Heidegger. Basel, 1933.

Phil 978.110 — Ballmer, Karl. Deutschtum und Christentum in der Theosophie des Goetheanismus. Besazio, 1966.

Phil 978.49.885 — Ballmer, Karl. Ernst Haeckel und Rudolf Steiner. Besazio, 1965.

Phil 978.108 — Ballmer, Karl. Der Macher bim Ich. Besazio, 1967.

Phil 8080.7 — Ballo, Guido. I miti delle Poetiche. Milano, 1959.

Phil 7054.105 — Ballou, Adin. An exposition of views...spirit manifestations. Boston, 1852.

Phil 7054.105.2 — Ballou, Adin. An exposition of views...spirit manifestations. 2. ed. Boston, 1853.

Phil 8656.23 — Ballou, Moses. The divine character vindicated. N.Y., 1854.

Phil 8581.73 — Ballou, Robert O. The glory of God. N.Y., 1938.

Phil 7150.61 — Balluseck, Lothar von. Selbstmord. Bad Godesberg, 1965.

Phil 6315.2.270 — Bally, Gustav. Einführung in die Psychanalyse Sigmund Freuds. Hamburg, 1961.

Phil 5811.19.12 — Bally, Gustav. Vom Spielraum der Freiheit. 2. Aufl. Basel, 1966.

Phil 5811.19 — Bally, Gustav. Vom Ursprung und von den Grenzen der Freiheit. Basel, 1945.

Phil 4352.1.110 — Balmes, el buen amigo de la verdad. (Prados y Lopez, M.) Madrid, 1954?

Phil 1535.1.15 — Balmes, Giacomo. Corso di filosofia elementare. v.1-4. Firenze, 1854.

Phil 1535.1.10 — Balmes, Giacomo. La filosofia fondamentale. v.1-2. Napoli, 1851.

Phil 4352.1.33 — Balmes, Jaime. Art d'arriver au vrai. Paris, 1852.

Phil 8610.846 — Balmes, Jaime. Cartas á un escéptico en materia de religion. Barcelona, 1846.

Phil 1535.1.35 — Balmes, Jaime. El criterio. Madrid, 1929.

Phil 4352.1.35 — Balmes, Jaime. Curso de filosofia elemental. v.1-4. Barcelona, 1911.

Phil 4352.1.50 — Balmes, Jaime. Elements of logic. N.Y., 1880.

Phil 4352.1.45 — Balmes, Jaime. Filosofia elemental. Madrid, 1935.

Phil 1535.1.5 — Balmès, Jaime. Filosofía fundamental. Paris, 18- . 2v.

Phil 4352.1.40 — Balmes, Jaime. Filosofia fundamental. 2. ed. Barcelona, 1848. 4v.

Phil 1535.1.40 — Balmes, Jaime. Habla Balmes. Barcelona, 1958.

Phil 1535.1.25 — Balmes, Jaime. Lehrbuch der Elemente der Philosophie. v.1-4. Regensburg, 1861.

Phil 4352.1.55 — Balmes, Jaime. Obras completas. Madrid, 1948- 8v.

Phil 1535.1 — Balmès, Jaime. Philosophie fondamentale. Paris, 1852. 3v.

Phil 176.228 — Balmes, Raymond. Leçons de philosophie. Paris, 1965-66. 2v.

Phil 4352.1.140 — Balmes. (Casanovas, J.) Barcelona, 1932. 3v.

Phil 4352.1.95 — Balmes apologista. (Ruano y Corbo, J.M.) Santiago, 1911.

Phil 4352.1.112 — Balmes i Casanovas. (Batelari, Miguel.) Barcelona, 1959.

Phil 4352.1.160 — Balmes politico. (Arboleya y Martinéz, Maximiliane.) Barcelona, 1911.

Phil 4352.1.60 — Balmes y el nacionalismo espanol. (Baucells Serra, Ramón.) Vich, 1940.

Phil 8581.32 — Balmforth, R. The new reformation...moral and social problems. London, 1893.

Phil 525.220 — Baloković, J.B. Towards the center. N.Y., 1956.

Phil 2475.1.109A — Balsillie, D. An examination of Professor Bergson's philosophy. London, 1912.

Phil 8876.61 — Balsillie, David. The ethic of nature and its practical bearings. Edinburgh, 1889.

Phil 3001.12 — Balthasar, H.U. Apokalyfse der deutschen Seele. Salzburg, 1937-39. 3v.

Phil 3001.16.5 — Balthasar, H.U. Prometheus. Heidelburg, 1947.

Phil 3120.30.90 — Balthasar, Hans von. Einsame Zinesprache; Martin Buber und das Christentum. Köln, 1958.

Phil 3120.30.91 — Balthasar, Hans von. Martin Buber and Christianity. London, 1961.

Phil 176.227 — Balthasar, Nicolas J.J. Mon moi dans l'être. Louvain, 1946.

Phil 720.37 — Balthasar, Hans. Wahrheit. Einsiedeln, 1947.

Phil 2805.196.5 — Balthazar. (Valensin, A.) Paris, 1934.

Phil 2805.196.7 — Balthazar. (Valensin, A.) Paris, 1954.

Phil 974.3.128 — Baltz, Karl von. Rudolf Steiners musikalische Inpulse. Dornach, 1961.

Phil 3821.1 — Baltzer, A. Spinoza's Entwicklungsgang. Kiel, 1888.

Phil 2520.232 — Balz, A.G.A. Cartesian studies. N.Y., 1951.

Phil 2520.235 — Balz, A.G.A. Descartes and the modern mind. New Haven, 1952.

Phil 2045.94 — Balz, Albert G.A. Idea and essence in the philosophies of Hobbes and Spinoza. N.Y., 1918.

Phil 5041.47.7 — Balzano, Bernard. Grundlegung der Logik. Ausgewählte Paragraphen aus der Wissenschaftslehre. Hamburg, 1963.

Phil 5041.47.5 — Balzano, Bernard. Wissenschaftslehre. Leipzig, 1929-31. 4v.

Phil 7069.20.20 — Bamber, L. Kelway. Claude's second book. N.Y., 1920.

Phil 735.88 — Bamberger, F. Untersuchungen zur Entstehung der Wertproblems in der Philosophie des 19. Jahrhunderts. Halle, 1924.

Phil 3808.166 — Bamberger, Herz. Das Tier in der Philosophie Schopenhauer's. Inaug. Diss. Wirzburg, 1897.

Phil 281.4 — Bamberger, L. Die Vorstellung von Weltebäude im Wandel du Zeit. Leipzig, 1908.

Phil 5211.7 — Bamborough, J.B. The little world of man. London, 1952.

Phil 5625.104 — Ban, Thomas A. Conditioning and psychiatry. Chicago, 1964.

Phil 8402.65 — Banach, Andrzej. O kiczu. Wyd. 6. Kraków, 1968.

Phil 5627.130.10 — Le banc des pénitents. (Swarts, G.) Paris, 1931.

Phil 5627.130.12 — Le banc des pénitents. Thèse. (Swarts, G.) Paris, 1931.

Phil 2733.118 — Banchetti, A. Il pensiero e l'opera di Nicola Malebranche. Milano, 1963.

Phil 1145.100 — Banchetti, Silvestro. La persona umana nella morale dei Greci. Milano, 1966.

Phil 4260.132 — Banchetti, Silvestro. Il significato morale dell'estetica vichiana. Milano, 1957.

Phil 5850.127 — Band, Francis. La science des caractères. Paris, 1944.

Phil 8656.30 — Bandeira de Mello, L.M. Próva matemático da existencia de Deus. Leopoldina, 1942.

Phil 8581.90 — Bandeira de Mello, L.M. Teoria do destino. Gazeta de Leopoldina, 1944.

Phil 2262.90 — Bandini, L. Shaftesbury; etica e religione, la morale del sentimento. Bari, 1930.

Phil 1135.28.15 — Bandry, J. Le problème de l'origine et de l'eternité du monde. Thèse. Paris, 1931.

Phil 5590.427 — Bandura, A. Social learning and personality development. N.Y., 1963.

Phil 8980.191 — Bandzeladze, Gela. Aktual'nye problemy marksistskoi etiki. Tbilisi, 1967.

Phil 8980.191.5 — Bandzeladze, Gela. Opyt izlozheniia sistemy marksistskoi etiki. Tbilisi, 1963.

Phil 1905.33.30 — Banerje, N.V. Language. London, 1963.

Phil 1955.6.225 — Banerjee, Gour Moham. The theory of democratic education; a critical exposition of John Dewey's philosophy of education. Calcutta, 1961.

Phil 176.195 — Banerjee, N.V. Concerning human understanding. London, 1958.

Phil 70.114 — Banff Conference on Theoretical Psychology, 1st, 1965. Toward unification in psychology. Toronto, 1970.

Phil 476.8 — Banfi, A. Storia del materialismo nei secoli XVI e XVII. v.1-2. Milano, 1951-53.

Phil 4070.7.55 — Banfi, Antonio. La crisi. Milano, 1967.

Phil 3483.92 — Banfi, Antonio. Esegesi e letture kantiane. Urbino, 1969. 2v.

Phil 5627.267.15 — Banfi, Antonio. Esperienza religiosa e coscienza religiosa e coscienza filosofica. Urbino, 1967.

Phil 4070.7.35 — Banfi, Antonio. Filosofi contemporanei. v.1-2. Milano, 1961.

Phil 1740.10 — Banfi, Antonio. La filosofia degli ultimi cinquanta anni. Milano, 1957.

Phil 4070.7.45 — Banfi, Antonio. Filosofia dell'arte; scelta. Roma, 1962.

Phil 3425.420 — Banfi, Antonio. La filosofia di G.G.F. Hegel. Milano, 1956.

Phil 4070.7.10 — Banfi, Antonio. La filosofia e la vita spirituale. Roma, 1967.

Phil 705.19 — Banfi, Antonio. Immanenza e trascendenza. Alessandria, 1924.

Phil 3425.422 — Banfi, Antonio. Inconfro con Hegel. Urbino, 1965.

Phil 4070.7.5 — Banfi, Antonio. Principi di una teoria della ragione. Milano, 1960.

Phil 4070.7.50 — Banfi, Antonio. I problemi di una estetica filosofica. Milano, 1961.

Phil 4070.7.30 — Banfi, Antonio. La ricerca della realta. Firenze, 1959. 2v.

Phil 4070.7.40 — Banfi, Antonio. Studi sulla filosofia del novecento. Roma, 1965.

Phil 4070.7.60 — Banfi, Antonio. L'uomo copernicano. Milano, 1965.

Phil 8402.24 — Banfi, Antonio. Vita dell'arte. Milano, 1947.

Phil 8876.73 — Bang, N.H. Begrebet moral; analyse og kritik. København, 1897.

Phil 270.37 — Bang, Niels H. Aarsagsforestillingen. København, 1925.

Phil 4803.465.86 — Bańka, Józef. Narodziny filozofii nauki o pracy w Polsce. Wyd. 1. Warszawa, 1970.

Phil 575.290 — Ban'ka, Józef. Współczesne problemy filosofii aechniki. Poznań, 1971.

Phil 6111.62 — Bankoff, G.A. The conquest of brain mysteries. London, 1947.

Phil 510.27 — Der Bankrott der Darwin-Haeckel'schen Entwicklungstheories und die Krönung des monistischen Gebäudes. (Loewenthal, Eduard.) Berlin, 1900.

Phil 5238.208 — Banks, Charlotte. Stephanos. London, 1965.

Phil 7069.62 — Banks, Frances. Frontiers of revelation. London, 1962.

Phil 4803.879.90 — Bańku, Józef. Poglądy filozoficzno-społeczne Michała Wiszniewskiego. Wyd. 1. Warszawa, 1967.

Phil 8876.160 — Banner, William Augustus. Ethics: an introduction to moral philosophy. N.Y., 1968.

Phil 11.5 — Banner of light. Cambridge. 1907

Phil 3450.11.100 — Bannes, Joachim. Versuch einer Darstellung und Beurteilung der Grundlagen der Philosophie E. Husserls. Inaug. Diss. Breslau, 1930.

Phil 3450.11.99 — Bannes, Joachim. Versuch einer Darstellung und Beurteilung der Grundlagen der Philosophie E. Husserls. Breslau, 1930.

Phil 9070.33 — Banning, M.C. Conduct yourself accordingly. N.Y., 1944.

Phil 8826.7 — Banning, Willem. Typen van zedelee. Haarlem, 1965.

Phil 5590.514 — Bannister, Donald. The evaluation of personal constructs. London, 1968.

Phil 5590.514.5 — Bannister, Donald. Perspectives in personal construct theory. London, 1970.

Phil 9070.128 — Banowsky, William Slater. It's a playboy world. Old Tappan, 1969.

Phil 5585.270 — Bánfeti Fuchs, Károly Miklás. Problemen der subliminale perceptie. Assen, 1964.

Phil 7060.92.47 — The Banshee. (O'Donnell, Elliot.) London, 1920.

Phil 1955.6.170 — Bansola, Adriano. L'etica di John Dewey. Milano, 1960.

Phil 5241.126 — Banterwek, Heinrich. Charakter als Naturgesetz. Ulm, 1959.

Phil 575.135 — Bañuelos García, M. Personalidad y caracter. Madrid, 1942.

Phil 3450.15.80 — Barach, C.S. Hieronymus Hirnhaim. Wien, 1864.

Phil 1506.1 — Barach, C.S. Zur Geschichte des Nominalis von Roscellin. Wien, 1866.

Phil 176.75 — Barach, Carl S. Kleine philosophische Schriften. Wien, 1878.

Phil 665.29 — Baraduc, H. L'âme humaine. Paris, 1896.

Phil 6671.22.5 — Baragnon, Petrus. Étude magnétisme animal sous le point de vue d'une exacte pratique. 2. éd. Paris, 1853.

Phil 6980.93 — Barahona Fernandes, Henrique João de. Filosofia e psiquiatria. Coimbra, 1966.

Phil 5241.115 — Barakin, E.W. Quantitative theory on human behavior. Santa Monica, 1952.

Phil 3640.316 — Baranger, William. La pensée de Nietzsche. Paris, 1946.

Phil 3483.52 — Bárány, Gerö. Kant Immanuel; halálának századik évfordulójára. Kolozsvár, 1904.

Phil 2050.219 — Baratono, A. Hume e l'illuminismo inglese. 2a ed. Milano, 1944.

Phil 8402.36 — Baratono, A. Il monda sensbile. Milano, 1934.

Phil 5241.45 — Baratono, Adelchi. I fatti psichici elementari. Torino, 1900.

Phil 1701.16 — Baratono, Adelchi. Filosofia in margine. Milano, 1930.

Phil 5241.45.5 — Baratono, Adelchi. Fondamenti di psicologia sperimentale. Torino, 1906.

Phil 282.6 — Baratsch, W. Kosmologische Gedanken. Leipzig, 1911.

Phil 282.6.2 — Baratsch, W. Kosmologische Gedanken. 2. ed. Leipzig, 1912.

Phil 3450.11.475 — Baratta, Giorgio. L'idealismo fenomenologico di Edmund Husserl. Urbino, 1969.

Phil 4829.344.20 — Barba ideja. (Dvorniković, Vladimir.) Beograd, 1937.

Phil 5241.85 — Barbado, M. Introducción a la psicología experimental. Madrid, 1928.

Phil 5520.360 — Barbara, Dominick A. Psychological and psychiatric aspects of speech and hearing. Springfield, 1960.

Phil 5628.54.4 — Barbara Pfister, eine pfälzische Stigmatisierte. 4. Aufl. (Lauer, Nikolaus.) Speyer, 1964.

Phil 900.4 — Barbaricae philosophiae. (Heurnius, O.) Lugdunum Batavorum, 1600.

Phil 8626.20 — Barbarin, Georges. L'après-mort. Paris, 1958.

Phil 9495.148 — Barbarism and sexual freedom. (Comfort, A.) London, 1948.

Phil 3640.208 — Barbat, V.J. Nietzsche, tendances et problèmes. Zürich, 1911.

Phil 6990.3.55 — Barbé, Daniel. Lourdes: hier, aujourd'hui, demain. Paris, 1893.

Phil 6990.3.54 — Barbé, Daniel. Lourdes: yesterday, today and tomorrow. Baden, 1893.

Phil 1506.9 — Barbedette, D. Manière d'enseigner la philosophie scolastique. Paris, 1936.

Phil 2401.15 — Barber, W.H. Leibniz in France. Oxford, 1955.

Phil 6990.44.20 — Barbet, Jean. La dame plus belle que tout. Paris, 1957.

Phil 9230.5 — Barbeyrac, J. Traité du jeu. Amsterdam, 1737. 3v.

Phil 2750.11.210 — Barbiellini Amidei, Gaspare. Dopo Maritain. Torino, 1967.

Phil 8876.62.3 — Barbier, Louise. La loi morale fondée sur l'etude comparée des deux natures de l'homme. Paris, 1884.

Phil 2730.94 — Barbillion, G. De l'idée de dieu dans la philosophie de Maine de Biran. Thèse. Grenoble, 1927. 2 pam.

Phil 6642.5 — Barbizet, Jacques. Pathologie de la mémoire. 1. éd. Paris, 1970.

Htn Phil 2115.153* — Barbon, N. A discourse...in answer to Mr. Lock. London, 1696.

Phil 7055.388 — Barbosa, Elia. No mundo de Chico Xavier. São Paulo, 1968.

Phil 8656.44 — Barbotin, Edmond. Humanité de Dieu. Paris, 1970.

Phil 585.390 — Barbotin, Edmond. Humanité de l'homme. Paris, 1970.

Phil 6311.13 — Barbour, C.E. Sin and the new psychology. London, 1931.

Phil 8951.4.5 — Barbour, G.F. Essays and addresses. Edinburgh, 1949.

Phil 8656.12 — Barbour, G.F. Ethical approach to theism. Edinburgh, 1913.

Phil 8951.4 — Barbour, G.F. Philosophical study of Chrisian ethics. Edinburgh, 1911.

Phil 2905.1.325 — Barbour, George Brown. In the field with Teilhard de Chardin. N.Y., 1965.

Phil 8691.33 — Barbour, Ian G. Issues in science and religion. Englewood Cliffs, N.J., 1966.

Phil 8876.115 — Barbour, R.R.P. Ethical theory. Adelaide, 1933.

Phil 8876.110 — Barboza, E. Etica. Lima, 1936.

Phil 5241.107 — Barboza, Enrique. Psicologia. Lima, 1940.

Phil 5011.5 — Barbu, Z. Le développement de la pensée dialectique. Paris, 1947.

Phil 4352.1.125 — Barcelona. Biblioteca Central. Catálogo de la exposicion bibliográfica. Barcelona, 1948.

Phil 3001.1 — Barchou, A.T.H. Histoire de la philosophie allemande. Paris, 1836. 2v.

Phil 3552.80 — Barchudarian, J. Inwiefern ist Leibniz in der Psychologie ein Vorgänger Herbarts. Jena, 1889.

Phil 8656.1 — Barclay, J. Without faith, without God. London, 1836.

Phil 8876.92 — Barclay, Thomas. The wisdom of Lang-Sin. N.Y., 1927.

Phil 6111.56 — Barcroft, J. The brain. New Haven, 1938.

Phil 6111.56.10 — Barcroft, Joseph. The dependence of the mind on its physical environment. Newcastle upon Tyne? 1938?

Phil 801.31 — Bardili, C.G. Epochen der Vorzüglichsten philosophischen Begriffe. Halle, 1788. 2 pam.

Phil 5041.5 — Bardili, C.G. Grundriss der ersten Logik. Stuttgart, 1800.

Phil 176.125 — Bardili, C.G. Sophylus oder Sittlichkeit und Natur. Stuttgart, 1794.

Phil 5325.25 — Bardili, C.G. Über die Geseze der Ideenassoziation. Tübingen, 1796.

Phil 176.91 — Bardonnet, L. L'univers-organisme. Paris, 1923. 4v.

Phil 282.9 — Bardonnet, L. L'universe-organisme. Paris, 1912. 2v.

Phil 6671.2 — Barety, A. Le magnetisme animal. Paris, 1887.

Phil 978.95 — Barfield, Owen. Romanticism comes of age. 1st American ed. Middletown, Conn., 1967[1966]

Phil 5520.486 — Barfield, Owen. Speaker's meaning. 1. ed. Middletown, 1967.

Phil 1857.1 — Barfield, Owen. Unancestral voice. London, 1965.

Phil 1857.2 — Barfield, Owen. Worlds apart; a dialogue of the 1960's. 1st American ed. Middletown, Conn., 1964.

Phil 165.80 — Bari (City). Università. Istituto di Storia della Filosofia. Contributi di A. Corsana. Trani, 1955.

Phil 3483.48 — Barié, G.E. Oltre la critica. Milano, 1929.

Phil 3552.303 — Barié, G.E. La spiritualità dell'essere e Leibniz. Padova, 1933.

Phil 8092.12 — Barilli, Renato. Per un'estetica mondana. Bologna, 1964.

Phil 7060.119 — Baring-Gould, S. Book of ghosts. London, 1904.

Phil 310.634 — Barion, Jakob. Ideologie, Wissenschatt, Philosophie. Bonn, 1966.

Phil 2905.1.305 — Barjon, L. La carrière scientifique de Pierre Teilhard de Chardin. Monaco, 1964.

Phil 2520.348 — Barjonet-Huraux, Marcelle. Descartes. Paris, 1963.

Phil 2520.84 — Bark, F. Descartes' Lehre von den Leidenschaften. Rostock, 1893.

Phil 3110.163 — Barker, C.J. Pre-requisites for the study of Jakob Böhme. London, 1920.

Phil 9120.170 — Barker, E. The values of life. Glasgow, 1939.

Phil 7069.19.10 — Barker, Elsa. Last letters from the living dead man. N.Y., 1919.

Phil 7069.18.10 — Barker, Elsa. Letters from a living dead man. N.Y., 1918.

Phil 7069.15.10 — Barker, Elsa. War letters from the living dead man. N.Y., 1915.

Phil 5190.75 — Barker, John A. A formal analysis of conditionals. Carbondale, 1969.

Phil 5401.52 — Barker, John Charles. Scared to death; an examination of fear. London, 1968.

Phil 5041.34 — Barker, Johnson. A digest of deductive logic for the use of students. London, 1897.

Phil 6111.51 — Barker, L.F. A description of the brains...of two brothers dead of hereditary ataxia. Chicago, 1903.

Phil 6111.26 — Barker, L.F. The nervous system and its constituent neurones. N.Y., 1899.

Phil 6311.24 — Barker, L.F. Psychotherapy. N.Y., 1940.

Phil 5440.34 — Barker, Roger Garlock. Ecological psychology. Stanford, Calif., 1968.

Phil 5041.91 Barker, Stephen Francis. The elements of logic. N.Y., 1965.

Phil 705.21 Barkman, H. Bidrag till denTransscendentala kategoriläran. Uppsala, 1901.

Phil 3483.25 Barkman, H. Kategorilära enligt Kantiska principer. Akademisk afhandling. Upsala, 1901.

Phil 5425.114.1 Barlow, F. Mental prodigies. N.Y., 1969.

Phil 5241.6 Barlow, J. Connection. Physiology. Intellectual philosophy. 2. ed. Philadelphia, 1846.

Phil 9430.7 Barlow, J.W. The ultimatum of pessimism. London, 1882.

Phil 332.24 Barlow, K.E. The state of public knowledge. London, 1946.

Phil 2475.1.440 Barlow, Michel. Henri Bergson. Paris, 1966.

Phil 2750.22.130 Barlow, Michel. Le socialisme d'Emmanuel Mounier. Toulouse, 1971.

Htn Phil 8951.6* Barlow, Thomas. Several miscellaneous and mighty cases of conscience. London, 1692.

Phil 5870.17 Barn av samma stam. (Söderling, Bertil.) Stockholm, 1967.

Phil 5241.110 Barnard, Chester Irving. Mind in everyday affairs. Princeton, 1936.

Phil 8626.25 Barnes, C.T. The duration of mind. Salt Lake City, 1955.

Phil 8691.24.2 Barnes, E.W. Scientifc theory and religion. N.Y., 1934.

Phil 8691.24 Barnes, E.W. Scientific theory and religion. Cambridge, Eng., 1933.

Phil 8581.39 Barnes, Earl. Where knowledge fails. N.Y., 1907.

Phil 8581.87 Barnes, H.E. The twilight of Christianity. N.Y., 1929.

Phil 1750.790 Barnes, Hazel Estella. An existentialist ethics. 1st ed. N.Y., 1967.

Phil 1750.555.6 Barnes, Hazel Estella. Humanistic existentialism; the literature of possibility. Lincoln, 1967.

Phil 5649.7 Barnes, J.C. Voluntary isolation of control in a natural muscle group. Diss. Princeton, 1916.

Phil 7069.45 Barnes, M.S. Long distance calling. N.Y., 1945.

Phil 176.156 Barnes, W. The philosophical predicament. London, 1950.

Phil 6671.13.5 Barnes, W.A. Personal influence. Boston, 1906.

Phil 6671.13 Barnes, W.A. Personal magnetism and clairvoyance. 4th ed. Boston, 1900.

Phil 6671.13.7 Barnes, W.A. Psychology, hypnotism, personal magnetism and clairvoyance. Boston, 1898.

Phil 5041.6 Barnes, William. An outline of Rede-Craft (Logic). London, 1880.

Phil 5867.15 Barnesprog. (Thetmark, J.C.) København, 1964.

Phil 2075.7.80 Barnett, George. Corporate society and education. Ann Arbor, 1962.

Phil 960.12 Barnett, L.D. Brahma-knowledge, outline of philosophy of the Vedânta. London, 1907.

Phil 8876.96 Barnett, M.J. The five redeemers. Boston, 1890.

Phil 1905.24 Barnhart, F.J.C. Principles of the infinite philosophy. N.Y., 1955.

Phil 8876.4 Barni, J. La morale dans la démocratie. Paris, 1868.

Phil 3483.9 Barni, J. Philosophie de Kant. Examen de la Critique du jugement. Paris, 1850.

Phil 3483.9.10 Barni, J. Philosophie de Kant. Examen des fondements de la métaphysique des moeurs. Paris, 1851.

Phil 130.4 Barni, Jules. Les martyrs de la libre pensée. 2. éd. Paris, 1880.

Phil 3120.3.30 Barnick, Johannes. Vierfaltigkeit in Logik und Welt oder die vier Bücher vom Sinn des Ganzen. Berlin, 1969.

Phil 176.119 Baron, K. Metaphysica generalis. Londini, 1657?

Phil 1930.10.80 Baron, S.W. Freedom and reason. Glencoe, Ill., 1951.

Phil 2648.92 Baron d'Holbach; a prelude to the French Revolution. (Wickwar, William H.) London, 1935.

Phil 2648.91 Baron d'Holbach. (Cushing, M.P.) N.Y., 1914.

Phil 8587.32.112 Baron von Hügel, man of God. (Hügel, Friedrich.) London, 1947.

Phil 3552.360 Barone, F. Leibniz e la logica formale. Torino, 1955.

Phil 3925.16.80 Barone, Francesco. Wittgenstein inedito. Torino, 1953.

Phil 3450.18.170 Barone, Francesco. Nicolai Hartmann nella filosofia del novecento. Torino, 1957.

Phil 3640.650 Baroni, C. Nietzsche éducateur. Paris, 1961.

Phil 5871.80 Baroni, Christophe. Les parents, les inconnus. Genève, 1969.

Phil 801.19 Barr, Knut. Världsförklaringar och lifsåskådningar. Stockholm, 1910.

Phil 1145.95 Barr, S. The three worlds of man. Columbia, 1963.

Phil 9495.168.30 Barra, Giovanni. Castità: problema o liberazione? Torino, 1964.

Phil 2905.1.330 Barral, Louis Marie. Éléments du bâti scientifique Teilhardien. Monaco, 1964.

Phil 2750.20.100 Barral, Mary Rose. Merleau-Ponty. Pittsburgh, 1965.

Phil 8876.5 Barratt, A. Physical ethics. London, 1869.

Phil 282.1 Barratt, A. Physical metempiric. London, 1883.

Phil 5421.10.35 Barraud, Jean. L'homme et son angoisse. Paris, 1969.

Phil 190.102 Barraud, Jean. Le message d'Amédée Ponceau. Paris, 1962.

Phil 176.207 Barraud, Jean. Philosophie de la qualité. Paris, 1956.

Phil 8620.64 Barreau, Jean Claude. Où est le mal? Paris, 1969.

Phil 4351.6.85 Barreiro Gomez, José. Sistematización de lo personal y lo sobrenatural. Lugo, 1969.

Phil 5241.116 Barrell, Joseph. A philosophical study of the human mind. N.Y., 1954.

Phil 4225.15.80 Barrello, O. L'estetica di M. Spirito. Lugano, 1958.

Phil 2630.6.80 Barrenechea, M.A. Un idealismo estético; la filosofía de Jules de Gaultier. Buenos Aires, 1921.

Phil 3425.113 Barrès, M. De Hegel aux cantines du nord. Paris, n.d.

Phil 2805.110.5 Barrès, Maurice. L'angoisse de Pascal, suivi d'une étude sur les deux maisons de Pascal à Clermont-Ferrand. Paris, 1923.

Phil 2805.110 Barrès, Maurice. L'angoisse de Pascal. Paris, 1918.

Phil 4963.6 Barreto, Luís Pereira. Obras filosóficas. São Paulo, 1967.

Phil 8876.94 Barrett, C.L. Ethics; an introduction to the philosophy of moral values. N.Y., 1933.

Phil 400.84 Barrett, Clifford. Contemporary idealism in America. N.Y., 1932.

Phil 176.135 Barrett, Clifford. Philosophy. N.Y., 1935.

Phil 8400.45 Barrett, Cyril. Collected papers on aesthetics. N.Y., 1966.

Phil 6311.15 Barrett, E.B. Absolution. London, 1932.

Phil 9560.38 Barrett, E.B. The guest of honour. Dublin, 1954.

Phil 8951.25 Barrett, E.B. Life begins with love. Dublin, 1953.

Phil 5751.3 Barrett, Edward Boyd. Strength of will. N.Y., 1915.

Phil 7068.95.10 Barrett, Harrison D. Life work of Mrs. Cora L.V. Richmond. Chicago, 1895.

Phil 5241.86.5 Barrett, J.F. Elements of psychology. 2. ed. Milwaukee, 1931.

Phil 8876.106 Barrett, J.W. How to overcome your 7 deadly enemies. N.Y., 1939.

Phil 8661.8.35 Barrett, R.H. A refutation of Mr. U.H. Gillespie's argument a priori for the existence of a great first cause. London, 1968.

Phil 270.1 Barrett, T.S. Examination of Gillespie's "First Cause". London, 1869.

Phil 270.2.5 Barrett, T.S. A new view of causation. London, 1871.

Phil 270.2 Barrett, T.S. Philosophy of science...on cause and effect. London, 1872.

Phil 176.113 Barrett, Thomas S. An introduction to the study of logic and metaphysics. London, 1875.

Phil 7069.26.2 Barrett, W. Death-bed visions. London, 1926.

Phil 7060.82.5 Barrett, W.E. On the threshold of the unseen. 3. ed. London, 1918.

Phil 7060.82.4 Barrett, W.F. On the threshold of the unseen. London, 1917.

Phil 1750.167.5 Barrett, William. Irrational man. Garden City, 1958.

Phil 1695.15 Barrett, William. Philosophy in the twentieth century. N.Y., 1962. 4v.

Phil 1750.167 Barrett, William. What is existentialism? N.Y., 1947.

Phil 1750.167.2 Barrett, William. What is existentialism? N.Y., 1947.

Phil 1750.167.3A Barrett, William. What is existentialism? N.Y., 1964.

Phil 7069.19.15 Barrett, William F. On the threshold of the unseen. N.Y., 1919.

Phil 7069.11.10 Barrett, William F. Psychical research. N.Y., 1911.

Htn Phil 8581.19* Barrington, J.S. A discourse of natural and revealed religion. n.p., n.d.

Phil 332.15 Barron, J.T. Elements of epistemology. N.Y., 1931.

Phil 1801.5 Barron, J.T. The idea of the absolute in modern British philosophy. Thesis. Washington, D.C., 1929.

Phil 5041.8 Barron, William. Elements of logic. N.Y., 1856.

Phil 4963.5 Barros, Roque Spencer Maciel de. A evolução do pensamento de Pereira Barreta. São Paulo, 1967.

Phil 8581.58 Barrow, George A. The validity of the religious experience. Boston, 1917.

Phil 9510.4 Barrow, I. Sermons on evil-speaking. N.Y., 1887.

Phil 7140.10 Barrows, C.M. Suggestion instead of medicine. Boston, 1900.

Phil 6985.45 Barrucand, Dominique. La catharsis dans le théâtre. Paris, 1970.

Phil 2477.3.31 Barruel, Augustine. Les Helviennes. 5. éd. Paris, 1812. 4v.

Phil 2477.3.33 Barruel, Augustine. Les Helviennes. 7e éd. Paris, 1830. 4v.

Phil 8622.66 Barruffo, Antonio. Dinamismo e maturità della fede. Roma, 1968.

Phil 6951.7 Barrus, C. Nursing the insane. N.Y., 1908.

Phil 8876.78 Barry, John D. Intimations. San Francisco, 1913.

Phil 8691.19 Barry, W. The triumph of life. London, 1928.

Phil 2750.11.145 Bars, Henry. Maritain en notre temps. Paris, 1959.

Phil 2750.11.146 Bars, Henry. La politique selon Jacques Maritain. Paris, 1961.

Phil 176.7 Barsalou-Fromenty, Gustave. La philosophie terrestre. Geneva, 1876.

Phil 6111.70.5 Barsley, Michael. Left-handed man in a right-handed world. London, 1970.

Phil 6111.70 Barsley, Michael. The other hand; an investigation into the sinister history of left-handedness. 1st ed. N.Y., 1967.

Phil 9070.62 Bartek, Edward. A treasury of parables. N.Y., 1959.

Phil 3270.12.80 Bartelett, J.M. Funktion und Gegenstand. München, 1961.

Phil 3565.128 Bartell, Fr., pastor. Lotze's religionsphilosophische Gedanken im Lichte der göttlichen Offenbarung. Hannover, 1884.

Phil 3549.8.105 Bartels, Enno. Ludwig Klages seine Lebenslehre und das Vitalismusproblem. Meisenheim, 1953.

Phil 282.26 Barth, Aron. The creation in the light of modern science. Jerusalem, 1968.

Phil 176.151 Barth, Hans. Wahrheit und Ideologie. Zürich, 1945.

Phil 176.151.2 Barth, Hans. Wahrheit und Ideologie. 2. Aufl. Erlenbach, 1961.

Phil 2520.114.11 Barth, Heinrich. Descartes' Begründung der Erkenntnis. Bern, 1913.

Phil 3120.66.30 Barth, Heinrich. Erkenntnis der Existenz. Basel, 1965.

Phil 332.25.2 Barth, Heinrich. Philosophie der Erscheinung. 2. Aufl. Basel, 1966-

Phil 3483.42 Barth, Heinrich. Philosophie der praktischen Vernunft. Tübingen, 1927.

Phil 332.25 Barth, Heinrich. Philosophie Erscheinung. Basel, 1947. 2v.

Phil 176.185 Barth, Heinrich. Das Sein der Dinge. Wien, 1956.

Phil 1200.10 Barth, P. Die Stoa. Stuttgart, 1903.

Phil 1200.10.6 Barth, P. Die Stoa. 5. Aufl. Stuttgart, 1941.

Phil 1200.10.7 Barth, P. Die Stoa. 6. Aufl. Stuttgart, 1946.

Phil 3425.232 Barth, Paul. Die Geschichtsphilosophie Hegels und der Hegelianer bis auf Marx und Hartman. 2. Aufl. Photoreproduction. Leipzig, 1925.

Phil 3425.232.5 Barth, Paul. Die Geschichtsphilosophie Hegels und der Hegelianer bis auf Marx und Hartman. Darmstadt, 1967.

Phil 2520.183 Barthel, A. Descartes' Leben und Metaphysik. Inaug.-Diss. Erlangen, 1885.

Phil 705.6 Barthel, E. Elemente der transzendentalen Logik. Strassburg, 1913.

Phil 5645.4.27 Barthel, Ernst. Goethes Relativitätstheorie der Farbe. Bonn, 1923.

Phil 8581.102 Barthel, Ernst. Der Mensch und die ewigen Hintergründe. München, 1939.

Phil 5241.83 Barthel, Ernst. Vorstellung und Denken. München, 1931.

Phil 176.121 Barthel, Ernst. Die Welt als Spannung und Rhythmus. Leipzig, 1928.

Phil 8581.1 Barthel, N. Religion scientifique de l'humanité. Paris, 1859.

Phil 3850.27.98 Barthelemy, Guy. Chez le Docteur Schweitzer. Laussane, 1953.

Phil 1150.1 Barthélemy, H.J. De l'école d'Alexandrie. Paris, 1845.

Phil 2475.1.435 Barthélemy-Madaule, Madeleine. Bergson, adversaire de Kant. Paris, 1966.

Phil 2475.1.437 Barthélemy-Madaule, Madeleine. Bergson. Paris, 1967.

Phil 2905.1.200 Barthélemy-Madaule, Madeleine. Bergson et Teilhard de Chardin. Paris, 1963.

Phil 2905.1.200.5 Barthélemy-Madaule, Madeleine. La personne et le drame humain chez Teilhard de Chardin. Paris, 1967.

Phil 8691.18 Barthélemy-Saint-Hilaire, J. La philosophie dans ses rapports avec les sciences et la religion. Paris, 1889.

Phil 2445.2.6 Barthélemy-Saint-Hilaire, J. Philosophie des deux Ampère. Paris, 1866.

Phil 1850.111 Barthélemy-Sainte-Hilaire, Jules. Étude sur François Bacon. Paris, 1890.

Phil 1750.9 Barthoemiss, C. Histoire critique des doctrines religieuses et philosophiques. Paris, 1855. 2v.

Phil 4235.1.80 Bartholmes, C. De Bernardino Telesio. Paris, 1849.

Phil 2651.82 Bartholmess, B.J.W. Huet, évêque d'Avranches. Paris, 1850.

Phil 4065.80 Bartholmess, C. Jordano Bruno. Paris, 1846-47. 2v.

Phil 4065.80.5 Bartholmess, C. Jordano Bruno. Paris, 1846-47. 2v.

Phil 3001.4 Bartholmiss, C.J.W. Histoire philosophique de l'academie de Prusse. Paris, 1850. 2v.

Phil 9400.27 Bartholody, E Mendelssohn. Der Lebensabend. 1. Aufl. Gütersloh, 1958.

Phil 3160.2.87 Bartholomäus Carneri, der Ethiker des Darwinismus. (Steiner, R.) Dresden, 1900.

Phil 3160.2.75 Bartholomäus von Carneri's Briefwechsel mit E. Häckel und F. Jodl. (Carneri, B.) Leipzig, 1922.

Phil 9150.26 Bartholomew, I.G. The cause of evil. London, 1927.

Phil 9070.7 Bartlett, A.C. Find your own frontier. Boston, 1940.

Phil 5938.7 Bartlett, E. An address of the birth of Spurzheim. Boston, 1838.

Phil 8402.16 Bartlett, E.M. Types of aesthetic judgment. London, 1937.

Phil 5650.21 Bartlett, F.C. The problem of noise. Cambridge, 1934.

Phil 5545.174.5 Bartlett, F.C. Remembering. Cambridge, Eng., 1964.

Phil 5545.174 Bartlett, F.C. Remembering. N.Y., 1932.

Phil 5520.205 Bartlett, F.C. Thinking. London, 1958.

Phil 6315.2.112 Bartlett, Francis H. Sigmund Freud. Photoreproduction. London, 1938.

Phil 7054.43.3A Bartlett, G.C. The Salem seer. N.Y., n.d.

Phil 7054.43 Bartlett, G.C. The Salem seer. N.Y., 1891.

Phil 8876.6 Bartlett, J. Aphorisms. Boston, 1823.

Phil 8876.6.3 Bartlett, J. Aphorisms. Portsmouth, 1810.

Htn Phil 8876.6.4* Bartlett, J. Aphorisms. Portsmouth, 1810.

Phil 1900.80 Bartlett, T. Memoirs...Joseph Butler D.C.L. London, 1839.

Phil 5643.103 Bartley, S. Howard. Vision. N.Y., 1941.

Phil 5585.120 Bartley, S.H. Principles of perception. N.Y., 1958.

Phil 6111.61.1 Bartley, Samuel Howard. Fatigue and impairment in man. 1. ed. N.Y., 1947.

Phil 623.40 Bartley, William W. The retreat to commitment. 1st ed. N.Y., 1962.

Phil 3483.51 Bartling, Dirk. De structuur van het aesthetisch a priori bij Kant Proef. Assen, 1931.

Phil 4215.1.83 Bartolomei, A. Del significato e del valore delle dottrine di Romagnosi per il criticismo contemporaneo. Roma, 1901.

Phil 400.100 Bartolomeis, F. de. Idealismo ed esistenzialismo. Napoli, 1944.

Phil 2115.198 Bartolomeis, Francesco de. John Locke. Il pensiero filosofico e pedagogico. Firenze, 1967.

Phil 8876.7 Bartolommeo, F. Ammaestramenti degli antighi. Milan, 1808.

Phil 1106.17 Bartolone, Félippi. L'origine dell'intellettualismo. Palermo, 1959.

Phil 176.226 Bartolone, Filippo. Struttura e significato nella storia della filosofia. Bologna, 1964.

Phil 1750.744.5 Bartolone, Filippo. Valenze esistenziali del cristianesimo. Messina, 1968.

Phil 9530.43 Barton, Bruce. More power to you. N.Y., 1917.

Phil 8980.193 Barton, William Ernest. The moral challenge of Communism. London, 1966.

Phil 9030.7 Bartoš, Jaromír. Kategorie nahodilého v dějinách filosofického myšlení. Praha, 1965.

Phil 3425.56.35 Bartsch, Heinrich. Register zu Hegel's Vorlesungen über die Ästhetik. Mainz, 1844.

Phil 3425.56.36 Bartsch, Heinrich. Register zu Hegel's Vorlesungen über die Ästhetik. Stuttgart, 1964.

Phil 3450.32.80 Bártschi, Lina. Der Berner Philosoph Carl Hebler. Bern, 1944.

Phil 3640.707 Bartuschat, Wolfgang. Nietzsche. Heidelberg? 1964.

Phil 960.40.4 Barua, B.M. A history of pre-Buddhistic Indian philosophy. Calcutta, 1921.

Phil 960.40.5 Barua, B.M. A history of pre-Buddhistic Indian philosophy. Delhi, 1970.

Phil 960.40 Barua, B.M. Prolegomena to a history of Buddhist philosophy. Calcutta, 1918.

Phil 3838.9 Baruch de Spinoza. (Starcke, C.N.) København, 1923.

Phil 3841.8 Baruch de Spinoza in Selbstzeugnissen und Bilddokumenten. (Vries, Theun de.) Reinbek, 1970.

Phil 3845.4 Baruch Spinoza. (Zweig, Arnold.) Darmstadt, 1968.

Phil 3823.12 Baruch Spinoza and western democracy. (Dunner, J.) N.Y., 1955.

Phil 3825.7.2A Baruch Spinoza's Leben und Charakter. (Fischer, Kuno.) Heidelberg, 1946.

Phil 3825.7 Baruch Spinoza's Leben und Charakter. (Fischer, Kuno.) Mannheim, 1865.

Phil 3841.1.2 Baruch d'Espinoza. (Vloten, J. van.) Amsterdam, 1865.

Phil 6311.35 Baruk, Henri. La désorganisation de la personnalité. Paris, 1952.

Phil 310.764 Barulin, Vladimir S. Otnoshenie material'nogo i ideal'nogo v obshchestve kak problema istoricheskogo materializma. Barnaul, 1970.

Phil 3552.112.5 Baruzi, Jean. Leibniz et l'organisation religieuse. Paris, 1907.

Phil 3552.112 Baruzi, Jean. La pensée chretienne...Leibniz. Paris, 1909.

Phil 2401.8 Baruzi, Jean. Philosophes et savants français du XXe siècle. Paris, 1926. 3v.

Phil 5751.16 Barwis, J. Three dialogues. London, 1776.

Phil 4110.4.98 Barzellotti, G. Commemorazione dell'accademico Luigi Ferri. Roma, 1895.

Phil 4080.8.85 Barzellotti, G. Due filosofi italiani. Roma, 1908.

Phil 600.23 Barzellotti, G. The ethics of positivism. N.Y., 1878.

Phil 2885.80 Barzellotti, G. Hippolito Taine. Roma, 1895.

Phil 4110.4.99 Barzellotti, G. Luigi Ferri. Roma, 1895.

Phil 2885.80.5 Barzellotti, G. La philosophie de H. Taine. Paris, 1900.

Phil 176.57.2 Barzellotti, G. Santi, solitari e filosofi. 2nd ed. Bologna, 1886.

Phil 189.6 Basal concepts in philosophy. (Ormond, A.T.) N.Y., 1894.

Phil 960.235 Basanta Kumar Mallik. London, 1961.

Phil 4963.4 Basave Fernandez del Valle, A. Ideario filosófico, 1953-1961. Monterrey, 1961.

Phil 3483.6 Basch, V. Essai critique sur L'esthétique de Kant. Paris, 1896.

Phil 3483.6.2 Basch, V. Essai critique sur L'esthétique de Kant. 2. éd. Paris, 1927.

Phil 3425.239 Basch, Victor. Les doctrines politiques des philosophes de l'Allemagne; Leibniz, Kant, Fichte, Hegel. Paris, 1927.

Phil 176.133 Basch, Victor. Essais d'esthétique, de philosophie et de littérature. Paris, 1934.

Phil 8402.5.1 Bascom, J. Aesthetics or the science of beauty. Boston, 1867.

Phil 8402.5.2 Bascom, J. Aesthetics or the science of beauty. N.Y., 1874.

Phil 8581.20 Bascom, J. Philosophy of religion. N.Y., 1876.

Phil 5241.7 Bascom, J. The principles of psychology. N.Y., 1869.

Phil 176.9 Bascom, J. Science, philosophy and religion. N.Y., 1871.

Phil 5241.7.2 Bascom, J. The science of mind. N.Y., 1881.

Phil 801.11 Bascom, John. An historical interpretation of philosophy. N.Y., 1893.

Phil 1905.11.78 Bascom, John. Things learned by living. N.Y., 1913.

NEDL Phil 5811.1 Bascomb, J. Comparative psychology. N.Y., 1878.

Phil 4967.20 A base physica do espirito. (Farias Brito, Raymundo de.) Rio de Janeiro, 1912.

Phil 350.4 La base trofica de la inteligencia. (Turró, R.) Madrid, 1918.

Phil 8581.2.10 Basedow, J.B. Examen in der allernatürlichsten Religion. Leipzig, 1784.

Phil 8581.2 Basedow, J.B. Neue Aussichten in die Wahrheiten und Religion der Vernunft. Altona, 1764. 2v.

Phil 8876.8 Basedow, J.B. Practische Philosophie für alle Stande. v.1-2. Dessau, 1777.

Phil 8876.63 Les bases de la morale et du droit. (Baets, Maurice de.) Paris, 1892.

Phil 2270.74.20 Les bases de la morale évolutionniste. 8e éd. (Spencer, Herbert.) Paris, 1905.

Phil 6060.1.17 Les bases fondamentales de la graphologie. (Crepieux-Jamin, J.) Paris, 1921.

Phil 8400.23 Bases of artistic creation essays by Maxwell Anderson, Rhys Carpenter and Roy Harris. New Brunswick, 1942.

Phil 8599.10.6 Bases of religious belief. (Tyler, Charles Mellen.) N.Y., 1897.

Phil 8890.41.10 Les bases psychologiques de la vie morale. (Parodi, D.) Paris, 1928.

Phil 8876.9.5 Basford, J.L. Seven seventy seven sensations. Boston, 1897.

Phil 8876.9 Basford, J.L. Sparks from the philosophers stone. London, 1882.

Phil 8581.114 Başgil, Ali Fuad. Din ve Lâiklik. Istanbul, 1962.

Phil 4710.135 Bashilov, B. Pravye i levye, blizkie i dal'nie. Buenos Aires, 194-?

Phil 2270.76.5 Le basi della morale. 3a ed. (Spencer, Herbert.) Piacenza, 1920.

Phil 4210.90 Le basi della psicologia e della biologia secondo il Rosmini. (Sarlo, Francesco de.) Roma, 1893.

Phil 194.13 Le basi dell'umanismo. (Trojano, P.R.) Torino, 1907.

Phil 3552.342 Le basi fisico-metafische della filosofia di Leibniz. (Ottaviano, C.) Padova, 1952.

Phil 8967.7 Basic Christian ethics. (Ramsey, Paul.) N.Y., 1950.

Phil 5520.9.5 The basic law of vocal utterance. (Sutro, Emil.) N.Y., 1894.

Phil 175.21 Basic outlines of universology. (Andrews, S.P.) N.Y., 1872.

Phil 1522.6 Basic principles and problems of philosophy. (Ryan, J.K.) Washington, 1939.

Phil 310.751.6 The basic principles of dialectical and historical materialism. (Spirkin, Aleksandr G.) Moscow, 1971.

Phil 5258.123 Basic problems of behavior. (Sherman, M.) N.Y., 1941.

Phil 165.6 Basic problems of philosophy. (Bronstein, D.J.) N.Y., 1947.

Phil 5242.55.5 Basic psychology. (Carmichael, L.) N.Y., 1957.

Phil 6118.9 Basic readings in neuropsychology. (Isaacson, R.L.) N.Y., 1964.

Phil 2905.1.2 A basic Teilhard-bibliography, 1955 - Apr. 1968. (Almago, Romano S.) N.Y., 1968.

Phil 6332.18 Basic theory of psychoanalysis. (Waelder, Robert.) N.Y., 1960.

Phil 2255.1.52 Basic writings, 1903-1959. (Russell, Bertrand Russell.) N.Y., 1961.

Phil 6319.1.5.10 Basic writings. (Jung, C.G.) N.Y., 1959.

Phil 2250.15 The basic writings of Josiah Royce. (Royce, Josiah.) Chicago, 1969. 2v.

Phil 930.74 Basic writings of Mo Tzu, Hsün Tzu and Han Fei Tzu. N.Y., 1967.

Phil 3640.46 Basic writings of Nietzsche. (Nietzsche, Friedrich.) N.Y., 1968.

Phil 6315.2.53 The basic writings of Sigmund Freud. (Freud, Sigmund.) N.Y., 1938. 3v.

Phil 8581.112 Basilius, Harold Albert. Contemporary problems in religion. Detroit, 1956.

Phil 5125.17 The basis of belief, proof by inductive reasoning. (Ballantine, William G.) N.Y., 1930.

Phil 8416.34.5 The basis of criticism in the arts. (Pepper, S.C.) Cambridge, 1945.

Phil 6536.8 The basis of epilepsy. (Tracy, Edward A.) Boston, 1930.

Phil 3494.11.10 The basis of freedom: a study of Kant's theory. (Miller, E.M.) Sydney, 1924.

Phil 5545.230 The basis of memory. (Bousfield, William Robert.) N.Y., 1928.

Phil 3808.71 The basis of morality. (Schopenhauer, Arthur.) London, 1903.

Phil 3808.71.2 The basis of morality. 2nd ed. (Schopenhauer, Arthur.) London, 1915.

Phil 177.98 A basis of opinion. (Coates, Adrian.) London, 1938.

Phil 8592.12 The basis of religion. (Momerie, A.W.) Edinburgh, 1886.

Phil 8656.31 Baskfield, G.T. The idea of God in British and American personal idealism. Thesis. Washington, 1933.

Phil 1801.10 Baskin, M.P. Filosofiia amerikanskogo prosveshcheniia. Moskva, 1955.

Phil 801.37 Baskin, M.P. Filosofiia i zhizn'. Moskva, 1961.

Phil 3235.120 Baskin, M.P. Filosofiia Ludviga Feierbakha. Moskva, 1957.

Phil 176.13 Baskin, M.P. Krizis burzhuaznogo soznaniia. Moskva, 1962.

Phil 310.17 Baskin, M.P. Materializm i religiia. Moskva, 1955.

Phil 400.120 Baskin, M.P. Sovremennyi sub"ektivnyi idealizm. Moskva, 1957.

Phil 8400.42 Baskin, Mark P. Protiv sovremennogo abstraktsionizma i formalizma. Moskva, 1964.

Phil 5520.552 Başlan-gicindan bugüne erdem açisindan düsünce. 2. b. (Hançerlioglu, Oshan.) Istanbul, 1966.

Phil 9245.142 Başlangicidan bugüne mutluluk düsüncesi. (Hancerlioğlu, Orhan.) Istanbul, 1969.

Phil 5590.552 Başlangicindan bugüne erdem açisindan düşünce. (Hançerlioğlu, Orhan.) Istanbul, 1966.

Phil 6111.49 Bassett, Clara. Mental hygiene in the community. N.Y., 1934.

Phil 4170.16.5 Bassi, Enrico. Rodolfo Mondolfo nella vita e nel pensiero socialista. Bologna, 1968.

RRC Phil 5722.81 Bassin, Filipp. Problema bessoznatel'nogo. Moskva, 1968.

Phil 2050.78.80 Basson, A.H. David Hume. Harmondsworth, 1958.

Phil 5066.58   Basson, A.H. Introduction to symbolic logic. London, 1953.

Phil 5066.58.2   Basson, A.H. Introduction to symbolic logic. 2nd ed. London, 1957.

Phil 4520.4.31   Bastholm, Christopher. Philosophie för olarde. Lund, 1795.

Phil 332.8   Bastian, Adolf. Die Lehre von Denken zur Ergänzung. v.1-3. Berlin, 1902-05.

Phil 665.54   Bastian, Adolf. Die Seele indischer und hellenischer Philosophie in den Gespenstern moderner Geistereseherei. Berlin, 1886.

Phil 8826.4   Bastian, Adolf. Zur ethnischen Ethik. Berlin, 1889.

Phil 6111.10.2   Bastian, H.C. The brain as an organ of mind. N.Y., 1880.

Phil 6111.10.5   Bastian, H.C. Le cerveau organe de la pensée chez l'homme et chez les animaux. 2. ed. Paris, 1888.

Phil 6111.10.3   Bastian, H.C. Das Gehirn als Organ des Geistes. Leipzig, 1882.

Phil 6400.13   Bastian, H.C. The Lumleian lectures on some problems in connection with aphasia and new speech defects. n.p., 1897.

Phil 5649.12   Bastian, H.C. The "muscular sense". London, 1887.

Phil 6951.18   Bastian, H.C. On paralysis from brain disease. N.Y., 1875.

Phil 6111.10.15   Bastian, H.C. On the neural processes underlying attention and volition. London, 1893.

Phil 6615.4   Bastian, Henry Charlton. Various forms of functional paralysis. London, 1893.

Phil 9075.50   Bastide, G. Meditations pour une éthique de la personne. 1st éd. Paris, 1953.

Phil 176.146   Bastide, George. De la condition humaine. Thèse. Paris, 1939.

Phil 8876.155   Bastide, Georges. Traite de l'action morale. Paris, 1961. 2v.

Phil 6111.33   Bastide, Jules. La pensée et le cerveau. Paris, 1886.

Phil 525.70   Bastide, Roger. Les problèmes de la vie mystique. Paris, 1931.

Phil 6951.32   Bastide, Roger. Soziologie des maladies mentales. Paris, 1965.

Phil 2475.1.235   Basu, P.S. Bergson et le Vedanta. Montpellier, 1930.

Phil 525.241   Bataille, Georges. L'expérience intérieure. 4. éd. Paris, 1954.

Phil 3640.320   Bataille, Georges. Sur Nietzsche. Paris, 1945.

Phil 2520.255.20   La bataille du "cogito". 1. éd. (Lefèvre, Roger.) Paris, 1960.

Phil 8656.16   Batailles d'idées sur les problèmes de Dieu, du bien, du vrai. (Bouyssonie, A.) Paris, 1923.

Phil 7060.116   Batchel, R. The stoneground ghost tales. Cambridge, Eng., 1912.

Phil 9341.10A   Batchelder, S. The young men of America. N.Y., 1858.

Phil 9513.4   Batchelor, George. Social equilibrium. Boston, 1887.

Phil 4352.1.112   Batelari, Miguel. Balmes i Casanovas. Barcelona, 1959.

Phil 7069.27.5   Bateman, A.B. Christianity and spiritualism. London, 1927.

Phil 9050.1   Bates, E. Rural philosophy. London, 1803.

Phil 9050.1.2   Bates, E. Rural philosophy. London, 1804.

Phil 9050.1.3   Bates, E. Rural philosophy. Philadelphia, 1807.

Phil 7069.17.10   Bates, Emily K. Our living dead. London, 1917.

Phil 7012.2   Bathurst, James. Atomic-consciousness. Exeter, 1892.

Phil 7012.2.5   Bathurst, James. Atomic consciousness reviewed. Bristol, 190-?

Phil 4340.10   Batlori, Miguel. Il pensiero delea rinascenza in Spagna e Portogallo. Milano, 1964.

Phil 5241.41   Batson, W.H. Acquisition of skill. Princeton, 1916.

Phil 8402.59   Battaglia, F. Il valore estetico. Brescia, 1963.

Phil 3450.19.410   Battaglia, Felice. Heidegger e la filosofia di valori. Bologna, 1967.

Phil 4065.116   Battaglini, F. Giordano Bruno e il Vaticano. Roma, 1889.

Phil 2515.4.92   Battanelli, E.P. Cournot métaphysicien de la connaissance. Thèse. Paris, 1913.

Phil 5850.127.5   Battegay, Raymond. Der Mensch in der Gruppe. Bern, 1967-3v.

Phil 2045.110   Battelli, G. Le dottrine politiche dell'Hobbes e dello Spinoza. Firenze, 1904.

Phil 6111.50   Batten, L.W. The relief of pain by mental suggestion. N.Y., 1917.

Phil 7069.30.2   Battersby, Henry F.P. Psychic certainties. London, 1930.

Phil 282.4.5   Batteux, C. Geschichte der Meynungen...Grundursachen. Leipzig, 1773.

Phil 282.4   Batteux, C. Histoire des causes premières. Paris, 1769.

Phil 8402.34   Batteux, Charles. Les beaux arts reduits. Paris, 1747.

Phil 8402.25.3   Batteux, Charles. Einschränkung des schonen Künste auf einen einzigen Grundsatz. 3. Aufl. Leipzig, 1770.

Phil 6951.31   Battie, William. A treatise on madness. London, 1962.

Phil 1955.6.128   Battle, J.J. The metaphysical presuppositions of the philosophy of John Dewey. Thesis. Fribourg, 1951.

Phil 5627.107.15   Battle for the mind. (Sargant, W.W.) Melbourne, 1957.

Phil 2030.5A   Battle in the sea. (Guérard, A.L.) Cambridge, 1954.

Phil 5262.21.15   The battle of behaviorism. (Watson, John B.) London, 1928.

Phil 9075.40   The battle of the conscience. (Bergler, Edmund.) Washington, D.C., 1948.

Phil 2035.81   Battle of the two philosophies. London, 1866.

Phil 4963.3   Battle y Ordoñez y el positivismo filosófico. (Ardao, Arturo.) Montevideo, 1951.

Phil 7054.61.12   The battleground of the spiritual reformation. (Brittan, Samuel B.) N.Y., 1882.

Phil 332.37   Battro, Antonio M. Dictionnaire d'epistémologie génétique. Dordrecht, 1966.

Phil 176.40   Batz, P. Philosophie der Erlösung. Berlin, 1876-86. 2v.

Phil 176.40.5   Batz, P. Die Philosophie der Erlösung. 2e Aufl. Berlin, 1879.

Phil 6110.1   Bau, Leistung und Erkrankung des menschlichen Stirnhirnes. T.1. (Anton, G.) Graz, 1902.

Phil 6113.5   Der Bau der Spinalganglien des Menschen und der Säugetiere. (Dogiel, A.S.) Jena, 1908.

Phil 6111.22   Bau und Leben des Gehirns. (Burdach, K.F.) Leipzig, 1819-26. 3v.

Phil 6127.3   Bau und Verrichtungen des Gehirns. (Rohon, J.V.) Heidelburg, 1887.

Phil 4352.1.60   Baucells Serra, Ramón. Balmes y el nacionalismo espanol. Vich, 1940.

Phil 1135.105   Bauch, B. Das Substanzproblem in der griechischen Philosophie bis zur Blütezeit. Heidelberg, 1910.

Phil 176.95   Bauch, Bruno. Anfangsgründe der Philosophie. Gotha, 1920.

Phil 3246.275   Bauch, Bruno. Fichte und der deutsche Staatsgedanke. Beyer, 1925.

Phil 3246.204.2   Bauch, Bruno. Fichte und unsere Zeit. 2. Aufl. Erfurt, 1921.

Phil 3483.8   Bauch, Bruno. Geschichte der Philosophie. v.5. Leipzig, 1911.

Phil 8876.98   Bauch, Bruno. Grundzüge der Ethik. Stuttgart, 1935.

Phil 332.11   Bauch, Bruno. Die Idee. Leipzig, 1926.

Phil 3483.8.8   Bauch, Bruno. Immanuel Kant. Berlin, 1917.

Phil 3483.8.9   Bauch, Bruno. Immanuel Kant. 2. Aufl. Berlin, 1921.

Phil 3483.8.3   Bauch, Bruno. Immanuel Kant. 3. Aufl. Berlin, 1920.

Phil 3001.10   Bauch, Bruno. Jena und die Philosophie des deutschen Idealismus. Jena, 1922.

Phil 3483.8.5   Bauch, Bruno. Luther und Kant. Berlin, 1904.

Phil 1701.8   Bauch, Bruno. Neuere Philosophie bis Kant. 3. Aufl. Berlin, 1919.

Phil 720.21   Bauch, Bruno. Wahrheit, Wert und Wirklichkeit. Leipzig, 1923.

Phil 8402.33   Baudauin, Paul. La beauté et la vie. Paris, 1959.

Phil 7068.98.5   Baudidi Vesme, C. Geschichte des Spiritismus. Leipzig, 1898-1900.

Phil 8876.100   Baudin, E. Cours de philosophie morale. Paris, 1936.

Phil 5241.42.5   Baudin, E. Cours de psychologie. 5e éd. Paris, 1927.

Phil 176.112   Baudin, E. Introduction générale à la philosophie. Paris, 1927.

Phil 5041.53   Baudin, E. Précis de logique des sciences. Paris, 1938.

Phil 2805.247A   Baudin, Émile. Études historiques et critiques sur la philosophie de Pascal. v.1-3. Neuchâtel, 1946-47. 4v.

Phil 4265.1.81   Baudouin, A. Histoire critique de Jules César Vanini. Toulouse, n.d.

Phil 7140.116.55   Baudouin, C. Der Couéismus. Darmstadt, 1926.

Phil 7140.116.51   Baudouin, C. Emile Coué and his life-work. N.Y., 1923.

Phil 5241.57.10   Baudouin, C. Makten i vår själ. Stockholm, 1925.

Phil 6319.1.220   Baudouin, C. L'oeuvre de Jung. Paris, 1963.

Phil 5241.57   Baudouin, C. The power within us. N.Y., 1923.

Phil 6311.6.5   Baudouin, C. Studies in psychoanalysis. N.Y., 1922.

Phil 6311.6   Baudouin, C. Studies in psychoanalysis. London, 1922.

Phil 7140.115   Baudouin, C. Suggestion and autosuggestion. London, 1920.

Phil 7140.115.3   Baudouin, C. Suggestion and autosuggestion. London, 1921.

Phil 7140.115.5   Baudouin, C. Suggestion and autosuggestion. N.Y., 1921.

Phil 7140.115.20   Baudouin, C. Suggestion et autosuggestion. 5. ed. Neuchâtel, 1938.

Phil 7140.115.15   Baudouin, C. Suggestion und autosuggestion. Dresden, 1924.

Phil 2805.385   Baudouin, Charles. Blaise Pascal. Paris, 1962.

Phil 575.139   Baudouin, Charles. Découverte de la personne, esquisse d'un personnalisme analytique. Paris, 1940.

Phil 7082.80   Baudouin, Charles. Introduction à l'analyse des rêves. Genève, 1945.

Phil 7082.80.1   Baudouin, Charles. Introduction à l'analyse des rêves. Paris, 1950.

Phil 5811.13   Baudouin, Charles. Das Lernen des Hundes. Inaug. Diss. Berlin, 1909.

Phil 5627.257.5   Baudouin, Charles. Psychanalyse du symbole religieux. Paris, 1957.

Phil 8876.10   Baudrillart, H. Études de philosophie morale. Paris, 1858. 2v.

Phil 1701.35   Baudry, Bernard. Point de vue sur l'Occident. Paris, 1958.

Phil 5041.48   Baudry, L. Petit traité de logique formelle. Paris, 1929.

Phil 5751.18   Baudry, L. La querelle des futurs contingents. Paris, 1950.

Phil 9075.15   Bauer, Arthur. La conscience collective et la morale. Paris, 1912.

Phil 3565.87   Bauer, C. Programm der Realschule zu Meerane. n.p., 1885.

Phil 3050.2   Bauer, Edgar. Bibliothek der deutschen Aufklärer des achtzehnten Jahrhunderts. Darmstadt, 1963. 2v.

Phil 176.114   Bauer, G.F. Die Welt als Subjekt-Objekt. Berlin, 1923.

Phil 2880.8.250   Bauer, George Howard. Sartre and the artist. Chicago, 1969.

Phil 1020.13   Bauer, H. Die Psychologie Alhazens. Münster, 1911.

Phil 1504.10.5   Bauer, H. Die Psychologie Alhazens. v.10, pt.5. Münster, n.d.

Phil 2750.11.235   Bauer, Hans Ludwig. Schopferische Erkenntnis. München, 1968.

Phil 3850.16.110   Bauer, Isidora. Die Tragik in der Existenz des modernen Menschen bei Georg Simmel. München, 1961.

Phil 3850.16.112   Bauer, Isidora. Die Tragik in der Existenz des modernen Menschen bei Georg Simmel. Berlin, 1961.

Phil 8581.59   Bauer, Joachim M. The modern notion of faith. Diss. Washington, 1930.

Phil 5241.114   Bauer, R.A. The new man in Soviet psychology. Cambridge, Mass., 1952.

Phil 5238.177   Bauer, Raymond A. Some views on Soviet psychology. Washington, 1962.

X Cg   Phil 1182.5   Bauer, W. Der altere Pythagoreismus. Berlin, 1897.

Phil 801.1   Bauer, W. Geschichte der Philosophie. Halle, 1863.

Phil 9390.12   Bauer, W. Eid und Frieden. Stuttgart, 1956.

Phil 176.200   Bauernfeind, O. Die Suingebung des Daseins. Meisenheim, 1957.

Phil 5590.405   Baughman, E.E. Personality. Englewood Cliffs, N.J., 1962.

Phil 8581.61   Bauhofer, O. Das Metareligiöse. Leipzig, 1930.

Phil 185.40   Die Bauhütte. (Kolbenheyer, E.G.) München, 1925.

Phil 5811.12   Bauke, Leopold. Ist das tier Unvernünftig? 31. Aufl. Stuttgart, 191-?

Phil 5811.12.10   Bauke, Leopold. Tierfabeln und andere Irrtümer in der Tierkunde. 19. Aufl. Stuttgart, 19- ?

Phil 5811.12.5   Bauke, Leopold. Unterscheidet das tier Mann und Frau? Berlin, 1908.

Phil 3460.92   Baum, Guenther. Vernunft und Erkenntnis. Bonn, 1969.

Phil 5590.24   Baumann, Emilio. Psico-cinesia, ovvero L'arte di formare il carattere. Pte. 1. Roma, 1900.

Phil 270.100   Baumann, Evert D. De harmonie der dingen. Leiden, 1933.

Phil 5628.10.10   Baumann, Evert Dirk. De goddelijke waanzin. Assen, 1932.

Phil 3483.12   Baumann, J. Anti-Kant. Gotha, 1905.

Phil 801.16   Baumann, J. Gesamtgeschichte der Philosophie. 2. Aufl. Gotha, 1903.

Phil 801.16.5   Baumann, J. Geschichte der Philosophie nach Ideengehalt und Beweisen. Gotha, 1890.

Phil 8581.92   Baumann, J. Die Grundfrage der Religion. Stuttgart, 1895.

Phil 510.1.14   Baumann, J. Häckels Welträthsel nach ihren starken und ihren schwachen Seiten. Leipzig, 1900.

Phil 8581.38   Baumann, J. Religionsphilosophie auf modernwissenschaftlicher Grundlage. Leipzig, 1886.

Phil 332.6   Baumann, J. Der Wissensbegriff. Heidelberg, 1908.

Phil 672.1   Baumann, J. Die Lehren von Raun, Zeit, und Mathematik. v.1-2. Berlin, 1868-69.

Phil 1701.10   Baumann, Julius. Deutsche und ausserdeutsche Philosophie. Gotha, 1903.

Phil 2520.178   Baumann, Julius. Doctrina Cartesiana de vero et falso explicata atque examinata. Berolini, 1860?
Phil 8876.11.5   Baumann, Julius. Handbuch der Moral. Leipzig, 1879.
Phil 8876.11.10   Baumann, Julius. Realwissenschaftliche Begründung der Moral. Leizpig, 1898.
Phil 8876.11   Baumann, Julius. Sechs Vorträge aus dem Gebiete der praktischen Philosophie. Leipzig, 1874.
Phil 176.10.5   Baumann, Julius J. Elemente der Philosophie. Leipzig, 1891.
Phil 176.10.11   Baumann, Julius J. Die grundlegenden Thatsachen. 2e Aufl. Stuttgart, 1902.
Phil 176.10   Baumann, Julius J. Philosophie. Leipzig, 1872.
Phil 176.10.10   Baumann, Julius J. Welt- und Lebensansichte in Ihren. Gotha, 1906.
Phil 5257.3.25   Baumann. Rehmke, Joh: Lehrbuch der allgemeinen Psychologie. Göttingen, 1894.
Phil 176.11   Baumeister, F.C. Elementa philosophiae. Leipzig, 1755.
Phil 3910.77.10   Baumeister, F.C. Historiam doctrinae recentius controversae de mundo optimo. Lipsiae, 1741.
Phil 176.11.5   Baumeister, F.C. Institutiones metaphysicae. Wittebergae, 1775.
Phil 176.11.3   Baumeister, F.C. Institutiones metaphysicae. Wittenbergae, 1749.
Phil 3910.77.15   Baumeister, F.C. Institutiones philosophiae naturalis. Olomueii, 1774.
Phil 3910.77.3   Baumeister, F.C. Institutiones philosophiae rationalis methodo Wolfii conscriptae. 5. ed. Vitembergae, 1741.
Phil 3910.77   Baumeister, F.C. Philosophia definitiva. Vitembergae, 1767.
Phil 176.11.10   Baumeister, F.C. Philosophia recens controversa complexa definitiones theoremata. Vratislaviae, 1766.
Phil 645.45   Baumer, Franklin. Religion and the rise of scepticism. 1st ed. N.Y., 1960.
Phil 1701.48   Baumer, Franklin Le van. Intellectual movements in modern European history. N.Y., 1965.
Phil 6111.88   Baumer, Franz. Vom Zauberkult zur Psychoanalyse. München, 1970.
Phil 176.12   Baumgärtner, H. Die Weltzellen. Leipzig, 1875.
Phil 3090.83   Baumgardt, D. Franz von Baader und die philosophische Romantik. Halle, 1927.
Phil 8826.6   Baumgardt, D. Der Kampf um den Lebenssinn den Vorläufern der modernen Ethik. Leipzig, 1933.
Phil 1865.184.2   Baumgardt, David. Bentham and the ethics of today. N.Y., 1966.
Phil 1865.184   Baumgardt, David. Bentham and the ethics of today. Princeton, 1952.
Phil 8402.51   Baumgarten, A. Aesthetica. Bari, 1936.
Phil 310.40   Baumgarten, A. Bemerkungen zur Erkenntnistheorie des dialektischen und historischen Materialismus. Berlin, 1957.
Phil 801.32   Baumgarten, A. Die Geschichte der abendländischen Philosophie eine Geschichte des geistigen Fortschritts der Menscheit. Genève, 1945.
Phil 3095.50   Baumgarten, A.G. Acroasis logica. Halae, 1773.
Phil 3095.52   Baumgarten, A.G. Initia philosophiae practicae primae acroamatice. Halae, 1760.
Phil 3095.51   Baumgarten, A.G. Meditationes philosophicae de nonnullis ad poema pertinentibus. Halae, 1735.
Phil 3095.35.5   Baumgarten, A.G. Metaphysica. Halae, 1739.
Phil 3095.35   Baumgarten, A.G. Metaphysica. Halae, 1757.
Phil 3095.40   Baumgarten, A.G. Metaphysica. 7th ed. Halae, 1779.
Phil 3095.45   Baumgarten, A.G. Metaphysik. Halle, 1766.
Phil 3095.30   Baumgarten, A.G. Philosophia generalis. Halae, 1770.
Phil 3095.51.10   Baumgarten, A.G. Reflections on poetry. Berkeley, 1954.
Phil 332.12   Baumgarten, Arthur. Erkenntnis, Wissenschaft, Philosophie. Tübingen, 1927.
Phil 5041.57   Baumgarten, Arthur. Logik als Erfahrungswissenschaft. Kaunas, 1939.
Phil 8876.95   Baumgarten, Arthur. Der Weg des Menschen. Tübingen, 1933.
Phil 1801.4   Baumgarten, E. Die geistigen Grundlagen des amerikanischen Gemeinwesens. Frankfurt, 1936-8. 2v.
Phil 5238.16   Baumgarten, F. Progress de la psycotechnique. Bern, 1949-
Phil 2730.87   Baumgarten, Franz. Die Erkenntnislehre von Maine de Biran. Krakau, 1911.
Phil 8876.80   Baumgarten, O. Praktische Sittenlehre. Tübingen, 1921.
Phil 3246.310   Baumgartner, Hans Michael. Johann Gottlieb Fichte; Bibliographie. Stuttgart, 1968.
Phil 3450.18.140   Baumgartner, Hans Michael. Die Unbedingtheit des Sittlichen. München, 1962.
Phil 1504.2   Baumgartner, M. Die Erkenntnislehre. v.2, pt.1. Münster, 1895.
Phil 5241.61   Baumgartner, M. Grundriss der Psychologie. Dillingen, 1906.
Phil 5041.35   Baumgartner, M. Logik und Erkenntnistheorie. Facsimile. n.p., 1905-06.
Phil 1504.2.4   Baumgartner, M. Die Philosophie. v.2, pt.4. Münster, 1896.
Phil 9075.88   Baumhauer, Otto. Das Vor-Urteil des Gewissens. Limburg, 1970.
Phil 1195.3   Baumhauer, T.C.M. Disputatio literaria. Rhenum, 1844.
Phil 1100.7   Baumhauer, Theodor C.M. Disputatia literaria. Trajuti ad Rhinum, 1844. 4 pam.
Phil 5625.128   Baumstimler, Yves. Automatisation du comportement et commutation. Paris, 1969.
Phil 5592.10   Der Baumtest. 2. Aufl. (Koch, Karl.) Bern, 1954.
Phil 5592.10.3   Der Baumtest. 3. Aufl. (Koch, Karl.) Bern, 1957.
Phil 1504.4.2   Baur, L. Gundissalinus de divisione philosophiae. v.4, pt.2-3. Münster, n.d. 2v.
Phil 1504.18.4   Baur, L. Die Philosophie des Robert Grosseteste. v.18, pt.4-6. Münster, n.d.
Phil 1504.9   Baur, L. Die philosophischen Werke des Robert Grosseteste. v.9. Münster, 1912.
Phil 176.140.5   Baur, Ludwig. Metaphysik. 3. Aufl. München, 1935.
Phil 6980.130   Baur, Pierre. Le psychodrame et la vie. Paris, 1968.
Phil 9560.31   Baurmann, W. Vertu. Berlin, 1939.
Phil 3120.8.165   Bausola, Adriano. Conoscenza e moralità in Franz Brentano. Milano, 1968.
Phil 4080.3.456   Bausola, Adriano. Etica e politica. Milano, 1966.
Phil 4080.3.455   Bausola, Adriano. Filosofia e storia nel pensiero crociano. Milano, 1965.
Phil 1701.54   Bausola, Adriano. Indagini di storia della filosofia. Milano, 1969.
Phil 3801.194   Bausola, Adriano. Metafiscia e rivelazione nella filosofia positiva di Schelling. Milano, 1965.
Phil 3801.194.5   Bausola, Adriano. Lo svolgimento del pensiero di Schelling. Milano, 1969.
Phil 8412.21   Bausteine zu einer Asthetik der inneren Form. (Lippold, F.) München, 1920.

Phil 3903.3.102   Bausteine zu einer Philosophie des "Als-Ob". München. 1-14,1922-1927 13v.
Phil 6315.1.16   Bausteine zur Psychoanalyse. (Ferenczi, Sandor.) Leipzig, 1927-39. 4v.
Phil 9075.1   Bautain, L.E.M. La conscience. Paris, 1861.
Phil 5241.9.5   Bautain, L.E.M. L'esprit humain et ses facultés. Paris, 1859. 2v.
Phil 8876.12   Bautain, L.E.M. Manuel de philosophie morale. Paris, 1866.
Phil 8876.12.5   Bautain, L.E.M. Philosophie morale. Paris, 1842. 2v.
Phil 5241.9   Bautain, L.E.M. Psychologie experimentale. Strasbourg, 1839. 2v.
Phil 8951.11   Bautain, Louis E. La morale de l'évangile comparée. Paris, 1855. 2 pam.
Phil 8951.11.5   Bautain, Louis E. Philosophie du Christianisme. Paris, 1835. 2v.
Phil 8626.18   Bavan, Edwyn R. The hope of a world to come underlying Judaism and Christianity. London, 1930.
Phil 8691.22   Bavink, B. Science and God. London, 1933.
Phil 5241.23   Bawden, H.H. A syllabus of psychology. Poughkeepsie, N.Y., 1902.
Phil 176.136   Bawden, Henry H. The principles of pragmatism. Boston, 1910.
Phil 176.14   Bax, E.B. Problem of reality. London, 1892.
Phil 176.14.10   Bax, E.B. The real, the rational and the alogical. London, 1920.
Phil 176.14.5   Bax, E.B. The roots of reality. London, 1907.
Htn   Phil 665.1.5*   Baxter, A. Appendix to 1st pt. An enquiry into nature of human soul. v.3. London, 1750.
Htn   Phil 665.1.2*   Baxter, A. An enquiry into nature of human soul. London, 1745. 2v.
Phil 8626.4   Baxter, A. The evidence of reason in proof of the immortality of the soul. London, 1779.
Phil 282.5.5   Baxter, A. Matho, or, The cosmotheoria puerilis. London, 1745. 2v.
Phil 282.5   Baxter, A. Matho; sive, Cosmotheoria puerilis. London, 1746.
Phil 5710.10   Baxter, M.F. An experimental study of...temperaments. Diss. Ithaca, N.Y., 1927.
Phil 6315.2.345   Bayen, Jeanne Françoise. Sigmund Freud. Paris, 1964.
Phil 4769.1.94   Bayer, J.J.M. Solowiew. Den Haag, 1964.
Phil 8402.44   Bayer, Josef. Asthetik in Umrissen. Prag, 1856. 2v.
Phil 3246.210   Bayer, Karl. Zu Fichte's Gedächtniss. Ansbach, 1835.
Phil 332.28   Bayer, R. Épistémalogie et logique depuis Kant jusqu'a nos jours. 1. éd. Paris, 1954.
Phil 8092.6   Bayer, R. L'esthétique mondiale au XXe siècle. Paris, 1961.
Phil 8402.8.20   Bayer, Raymond. Essais sur la méthode en esthétique. Paris, 1953.
Phil 8402.8.15   Bayer, Raymond. L'esthétique de la grâce. Paris, 1933. 2v.
Phil 8402.8.10   Bayer, Raymond. L'esthétique de la grâce. Paris, 1933. 2v.
Phil 8402.8   Bayer, Raymond. Traité d'esthétique. Paris, 1956.
Phil 8402.8.5   Bayer, Raymond. Von der Methode der Asthetik. Darmstadt, 1960.
Phil 8610.959   Bayet, Albert. Histoire de la libre-pensée. Paris, 1959.
Phil 8876.51.5   Bayet, Albert. L'ideé de bien. Paris, 1908.
Phil 8876.51.9   Bayet, Albert. Le mirage de la vertu. Paris, 1912.
Phil 8826.5   Bayet, Albert. La morale des gaulois. Paris, 1930.
Phil 8876.51.19   Bayet, Albert. La morale laïque et ses adversaires. 4e éd. Paris, 1925.
Phil 8826.5.10   Bayet, Albert. La morale paienne a l'époque gallo-romaine. Paris, 1931.
Phil 8876.51   Bayet, Albert. La morale scientifique. 2e ed. Paris, 1907.
Phil 2805.209   Bayet, Albert. Les provinciales de Pascal. Paris, 1929.
Phil 2805.209.5   Bayet, Albert. Les provinciales de Pascal. Paris, 1946.
Phil 8876.51.13   Bayet, Albert. La science des faits moraux. Paris, 1925.
Phil 7150.21.2   Bayet, Albert. Le suicide et la morale. Thèse. Paris, 1922.
Phil 6951.8   Bayle, A.L.J. Traité des maladies du cerveau. Paris, 1826.
Phil 2450.80   Bayle et Jurien. (Denis, J.) Caen, 1886.
Phil 3552.460   Bayle's og Leibniz' drøftelse af theodicé-problemet; en idéhistorisk redegørelse. v.1-2. (Nedergaard-Hansen, Leif.) København, 1965.
Phil 7069.67.5   Bayless, Raymond. The enigma of the poltergeist. West Nyack, 1967.
Phil 8876.119   Baylis, C.A. Ethics. N.Y., 1958.
Phil 6111.30   Baylor, Courtenay. Remaking a man...mental refitting. N.Y., 1919.
Phil 8691.31   Bayne, Stephen. Space age to Christianity. N.Y., 1963.
Phil 6311.31   Baynes, H. Analytical psychology and the English mind. London, 1950.
Phil 8656.10   Baynes, H. The idea of God...in the light of language. London, 1895.
Phil 6480.160   Baynes, H.G. Mythology of the soul. Baltimore, 1940.
NEDL   Phil 5041.7   Baynes, T.S. Essay...new analytic. Logical forms. Edinburgh, 1850.
Phil 176.99   Bayrhoffer, K.T. Die Grundprobleme der Metaphysik. Marburg, 1835.
Phil 801.30   Bayrhoffer, K.T. Die Idee und Geschichte der Philosophie. Marburg, 1838.
Phil 5070.13   Bazaillas, A. La crise de la croyance. Paris, 1901.
Phil 575.72   Bazaillas, Albert. La vie personnelle. Paris, 1905.
Phil 4974.65   Bazán, Armando. Vida y obra del maestro Enrique Molina. Santiago, 1954.
Phil 7054.174.5   Bazett, L.M. After-death communications. London, 1920.
Phil 7069.20.30   Bazter, Francis K. Does telepathy explain spiritualism? N.Y., 1920.
Phil 6311.20   Be glad you're neurotic. (Bisch, L.E.) N.Y., 1936.
Phil 575.147   Be not afraid. (Mounier, E.) London, 1957.
Phil 8581.33   Beach, D.N. The newer religious thinking. Boston, 1893.
Phil 9341.17   Beale, Dorothea. A few words to girls at school. n.p., 18- .
Phil 8581.3   Beale, L.S. Life theories. London, 1871.
NEDL   Phil 9161.1   Bean, James. The Christian minister's affectionate advice to a new married couple. London, 1814.
X Cg   Phil 9161.1.3   Bean, James. The Christian minister's affectionate advice to a new married couple. London, 1814.
Phil 978.49.729   Die Beantwortung von Welt- und Lebensfragen durch Anthroposophie. (Steiner, R.) Dornach, 1970.
Phil 6951.12.10A   Beard, G.M. American nervousness. N.Y., 1881.
Phil 6945.8   Beard, G.M. The asylums of Europe. Cambridge, 1881.

42

Phil 2270.87   Beard, G.M. Herbert Spencer on American nervousness. N.Y., 1883.

Phil 6951.12.5   Beard, G.M. Die Nervenschwäche. 2. Aufl. Leipzig, 1883.

Phil 6951.12.15   Beard, G.M. Neurasthenia (nerve exhaustion), with remarks on treatment. n.p., 1879?

Phil 6951.12.4   Beard, G.M. Practical treatise on nervous exhaustion. 2. ed. N.Y., 1880.

Phil 6951.12.3   Beard, G.M. Practical treatise on nervous exhaustion. 2. ed. N.Y., 1880.

Phil 6951.12   Beard, G.M. Psychology of the Salem witchcraft...1697. Photoreproduction. N.Y., 1882.

Phil 5811.7   Beard, G.M. Trance and trancoidal states in the lower animals. N.Y., 1881.

Phil 8620.22   Beard, J.R. Autobiography of Satan. London, 1872.

Phil 8581.4   Beard, J.R. Letters on the grounds and objects of religious knowledge. London, 1856. 2v.

Phil 7069.66.30   Beard, Paul. Survival of death: for and against. London, 1966.

Phil 5585.115   Beardslee, D.C. Readings in perception. Princeton, 1958.

Phil 5041.60   Beardsley, M.C. Pratical logic. N.Y., 1950.

Phil 8402.57.5A   Beardsley, Monroe Curtis. Aesthetic inquiry: essays on art criticism and the philosophy of art. Belmont, Calif., 1967.

Phil 8402.57   Beardsley, Monroe Curtis. Aesthetics; problems in the philosophy of criticism. N.Y., 1958.

Phil 8050.85   Beardsley, Monroe Curtis. Aesthetics from classical Greece to the present. 1. ed. n.p., n.d.

Phil 176.223   Beardsley, Monroe Curtis. Philosophical thinking. N.Y., 1965.

Phil 8876.164   Beardsmore, R.W. Moral reasoning. London, 1969.

Phil 1140.5   Beare, J.G. Greek theorie of elementary cognition. Oxford, 1906.

Phil 8665.4   The bearing of the evolutionary theory on the conception of God. Thesis. (Kawaguchi, U.) Menasha, Wis., 1916.

Phil 8876.45   Beary, H.R. Individual development of man. N.Y., 1909.

Phil 5241.10   Beasley, F. A search of truth. Philadelphia, 1822.

Htn   Phil 1860.40*   Beattie, James. Dissertations moral and critical. Dublin, 1783. 2v.

Phil 1860.40.2   Beattie, James. Dissertations moral and critical. London, 1783.

Phil 1860.10   Beattie, James. Dissertations moral and critical. Works 1-3. Philadelphia, 1809. 3v.

Phil 1860.60   Beattie, James. Elements of moral science. Philadelphia, 1792-94. 2v.

Phil 1860.60.5   Beattie, James. Elements of moral science. v.1-2. Baltimore, 1813.

Phil 1860.10.3   Beattie, James. Elements of moral science. Works 7-9. Philadelphia, 1809. 3v.

Phil 1860.50.2   Beattie, James. Essay on the nature and immutability of truth. Dublin, 1773.

Htn   Phil 1860.50*   Beattie, James. Essay on the nature and immutability of truth. Edinburgh, 1770.

Phil 1860.50.5   Beattie, James. Essay on the nature and immutability of truth. Edinburgh, 1777.

Phil 1860.50.6   Beattie, James. Essay on the nature and immutability of truth. Edinburgh, 1805.

Phil 1860.50.3   Beattie, James. Essay on the nature and immutability of truth. London, 1773.

Phil 1860.50.4   Beattie, James. Essay on the nature and immutability of truth. London, 1774.

Phil 1860.50.13   Beattie, James. Essay on the nature and immutability of truth. London, 1823.

Phil 1860.50.7   Beattie, James. Essay on the nature and immutability of truth. Philadelphia, 1809.

Phil 1860.10.2   Beattie, James. Essays. Works 4-6. Philadelphia, 1809. 3v.

Phil 1860.10.4   Beattie, James. The minstrel. Works 10. Philadelphia, 1809.

Phil 1860.45   Beattie, James. Neue philosophische Versuche. Leipzig, 1779-80. 2v.

Phil 7069.29.7   Beatty, Mabel. Man made perfect. Lonodon, 1929.

Phil 5650.20   Beatty, R.T. Hearing in man and animals. London, 1932.

Phil 8050.51   Le beau et son histoire. (Gauckler, T.G.) Paris, 1873.

Phil 1750.166.220   Beaujon, Edmond. Némésis; ou, La limite. Paris, 1965.

Phil 6111.2   Beaunie, H.E. Recherches...l'activité cérébrale. v.1-2. Paris, 1884-86.

Phil 6671.16   Beaunis, H. Der künstlich Hervorgerufene Somnambulismus. Leipzig, 1889.

Phil 5635.18   Beaunis, H. Les sensations internes. Paris, 1889.

Phil 9245.34   Beausobre, Louis de. Essai sur le bonheur. Berlin, 1758.

Phil 2555.1.80   Beaussire, É. Antécédents de l'hégélianisme...Dom Deschamps. Paris, 1865.

Phil 8876.57   Beaussire, Emile. Les principes de la morale. Paris, 1885.

Phil 8402.33   La beauté et la vie. (Baudauin, Paul.) Paris, 1959.

Phil 2805.241.5   Beauté poétique. (Tourneur, Zacharie.) Muln, 1933.

Phil 2115.27   The beauties of Locke. (Locke, J.) London, n.d.

Phil 8880.1.15   The beauties of Owen Felltham. (Feltham, O.) N.Y., 1803.

Phil 8110.11   The beautiful, the sublime, and the picturesque in eighteenth-century British aesthetic theory. (Hipple, W.J.) Carbondale, 1957.

Phil 8413.11.5   The beautiful. (Marshall, Henry.) London, 1924.

Phil 978.27   The beautiful necessity. (Bragdon, C.) Rochester, N.Y., 1910.

Phil 8602.37   The beautiful sunset of life. (Waggoner, John G.) Boston, 1928.

Phil 8416.24   Beauty; an interpretation of art and the imaginative life. 1st ed. (Parkhurst, H.H.) N.Y., 1930.

Phil 8403.42   Beauty and human nature. (Chandler, A.R.) N.Y., 1934.

Phil 8401.22.10   Beauty and other forms of value. (Alexander, Samuel.) London, 1933.

Phil 8413.21   Beauty and the beast; an essay in evolutionary aesthetic. (McDowall, S.A.) Cambridge, Mass., 1920.

Phil 8662.9   The beauty of God. (Hood, John.) Baltimore, 1908.

Phil 9560.29   The beauty of kindness. (Miller, J.R.) N.Y., 1905.

Phil 1750.240   Beauvoir, S. de. L'existentialisme et la sagesse des nations. Paris, 1948.

Phil 8876.108   Beauvoir, Simone de. The ethics of ambiguity. N.Y., 1949.

Phil 8876.108.5A   Beauvoir, Simone de. Pour une morale de l'ambiguité. Paris, 1947.

Phil 8876.108.7   Beauvoir, Simone de. Pour une morale de l'ambiguité suivi de Pyrrus et Cinéas. Paris, 1944.

Phil 8402.34   Les beaux arts reduits. (Batteux, Charles.) Paris, 1747.

Phil 9530.36.5   Beaverbrook, W.M.A. Success. 2. ed. London, 1921.

Phil 9530.36.8   Beaverbrook, W.M.A. The three keys to success. N.Y., 1956.

Phil 801.26   Beccari, Arturo. Storia della filosofia e della scienza. Torino, 1928.

Phil 6111.19   Becher, E. Gehirn und Seele. Heidelberg, 1911.

Phil 3001.11   Becher, Erich. Deutsche Philosophen. München, 1929.

Phil 176.107   Becher, Erich. Einführung in die Philosophie. München, 1926.

Phil 176.107.5   Becher, Erich. Einführung in die Philosophie. 2. Aufl. Berlin, 1949.

Phil 8735.15   Becher, Erich. Die fremddienliche Zweckmässigkeit der Pflanzengallen und dieHypothese eines überindividuellen Seelischen. Leipzig, 1917.

Phil 8876.56   Becher, Erich. Die Grundfrage der Ethik. Köln, 1908.

Phil 282.7.19   Becher, Erich. Grundlagen und Grenzen des Naturerkennens. München, 1928.

Phil 3483.47   Becher, Erich. Immanuel Kant. München, 1924.

Phil 282.7.16   Becher, Erich. Metaphysik und Naturwissenschaften. München, 1926.

Phil 282.7   Becher, Erich. Naturphilosophie. Leipzig, 1914.

Phil 282.7.11   Becher, Erich. Weltgebäude, Weltgesetze, Weltentwicklung. Berlin, 1915.

Phil 332.27   Bechert, R. Eine Semiphilosophie im Grundriss Dargestellt. München, 1941.

Phil 5520.40   Bechtel, F. Über die Bezeichnungen der sinnlichen Wahrnehmungen. Weimar, 1879.

Phil 6111.16   Bechterew, W. von. Die Funktionen der Nervencentra. Jena, 1908. 3v.

Phil 6111.16.5   Bechterew, W. von. Die Leitungsbahnen im Gehirn und Rückenmark. Leipzig, 1899.

Phil 6111.16.12   Bechterew, W. von. Psyche und Leben. Wiesbaden, 1908.

Phil 6625.8   Beck, Aaron T. Depression: clinical, experimental, and theoretical aspects. N.Y., 1967.

Phil 5520.39   Beck, Ernst H.F. Die Impersonalien in sprachpsychologischer, logischer und linguistischer Hinsicht. Leipzig, 1922.

Phil 9161.7   Beck, Frank O. Marching manward. N.Y., 1913.

Phil 3790.4.85   Beck, Friedrich. Heinrich Rickert und der philosophische transzendente subjektivismus. Inaug. Diss. Erlangen, 1925.

Phil 3450.18.150   Beck, Heinrich. Möglichkeit und Notwendigkeit. Pullach, 1961.

Phil 3483.1   Beck, J.S. Erläuternder Auszug. Riga, 1793-96. 3v.

Phil 3483.1.15   Beck, J.S. Grundriss der critischen Philosophie. Halle, 1796.

Phil 3483.1.10   Beck, J.S. The principles of critical philosophy. London, 1797.

Phil 5241.55.10   Beck, Joseph. Grundriss der empirischen Psychologie und Logik. 7. Aufl. Stuttgart, 1887.

Phil 2520.238   Beck, L.J. The method of Descartes. Oxford, 1952.

Phil 2655.3.93   Beck, L.J. Manual skills and the measurement of handedness. Worcester, 1936.

Phil 2655.3.93   Beck, Leslie J. La méthode synthétique d'Hamelin. Paris, 1935.

Phil 2520.350   Beck, Leslie John. The metaphysics of Descartes. Oxford, 1965.

Phil 8581.105   Beck, Lewis W. Six secular philosophers. 1. ed. N.Y., 1960.

Phil 3483.75   Beck, Lewis White. A commentary on Kant's Critique of practical reason. Chicago, 1960.

Phil 3001.22   Beck, Lewis White. Early German philosophy: Kant and his predecessors. Cambridge, 1969.

Phil 3483.85.5   Beck, Lewis White. Kant studies today. La Salle, 1969.

Phil 176.168.5   Beck, Lewis White. Philosophic inquiry. Englewood Cliffs, N.J., 1958.

Phil 176.168   Beck, Lewis White. Philosophic inquiry. N.Y., 1953.

Phil 3483.85   Beck, Lewis White. Studies in the philosophy of Kant. 1st ed. Indianapolis, 1965.

Phil 900.10   Beck, Lily M.A. The story of Oriental philosophy. N.Y., 1928.

Phil 5241.102   Beck, M. Psychologie. Leiden, 1938.

Phil 3120.28.25   Pamphlet vol. Beck, M. A collection of reprints. 5 pam.

Phil 176.104   Beck, Maximillian. Wesen und Wert. Berlin, 1925. 2v.

Phil 7076.18   Beck, Paul. Die Ekstase. Bad Sachsa, 1906.

Phil 5850.128   Beck, Samuel. Reflexes to intelligence. Glencoe, 1959.

Phil 6951.10   Beck, Theodric R. An inaugural dissertation on insanity. Thesis. N.Y., 1811.

Phil 3245.85   Beckedorf, H. Die Ethik Immanuel Hermann Fichtes. Inaug. Diss. Hannover, 1912.

Phil 3640.253   Beckenhaupt, D. Nietzsche und das gegenwärtige Geistesleben. Leipzig, 1931.

Phil 176.110   Becker, Carl. Die moderne Weltanschauung. Berlin, 1911.

Phil 176.110.5   Becker, Carl. Vom geistigen Leben und Schaffen. Berlin, 1912.

Phil 1750.152.10   Becker, Carl Lotus. The heavenly city of the eighteenth-century philosophers. New Haven, 1968.

Phil 5585.95   Becker, Egon. Mengenvergleich und Übung. Frankfurt, 1957.

Phil 5241.174   Becker, Ernest. Angel in armor; a post Freudian perspective on the nature of man. N.Y., 1969.

Phil 585.140   Becker, Ernest. The birth and death of meaning. N.Y., 1962.

Phil 585.140.2   Becker, Ernest. The birth and death of meaning. 2. ed. N.Y., 1971.

Phil 585.140.5   Becker, Ernest. The structure of evil. N.Y., 1968.

Phil 5252.18.60   Becker, F. Die Instinkt-Psychologie William McDougalls. Reichenberg, 1933.

Phil 3925.9.90   Becker, J. Die Religionsphilosophie Karl Werners. Inaug. Diss. Bonn, 1935.

Phil 8826.1   Becker, J.H. Ursprung...Sittlichkeit. Leipzig, 1888.

Phil 5590.40   Becker, Josef. Einfuhrung in die Charakterkunde. Nurnberg, 1947.

Phil 176.219   Becker, O. Dasein und Dawesen. Pfullingen, 1963.

Phil 5041.61   Becker, O. Einführung in die Logistik. Meisenheim, 1951.

Phil 5066.48   Becker, O. Untersuchungen über den Modalkalkül. Meinsenheim/Glan, 1952.

Phil 6311.54   Becker, Raymond de. Bilan de la psychologie des profondeurs. Paris, 1968.

Phil 6480.200.5   Becker, Raymond de. Les machinations de la nuit. Paris, 1965.

Phil 7084.48   Becker, Raymond de. Rêve et sexualité. Paris, 1965.

Phil 7082.178   Becker, Raymond de. Les songes. Paris, 1958.

Phil 3425.738   Becker, Werner. Hegels Begriff der Dialektik und das Prinzip des Idealismus. Stuttgart, 1969.

Phil 310.732   Becker, Werner. Idealistische und materialistische Dialektik; das Verhältnis von Herrschaft und Knechtschaft bei Hegel und Marx. Stuttgart, 1970.

Htn   Phil 3801.197*   Becker, Hubert. F.W.J. von Schelling. München, 1855.

Htn   Phil 3801.197.16*   Beckers, Hubert. Historisch-kritische Erläuterungen zu Schelling's Abhandlungen über die Quelle der ewigen Wahrheiten. München, 1858.

Htn Phil 3801.197.30*A Beckers, Hubert. Schelling's Geistesentwicklung in Ihrem inneren Zusammenhang. München, 1875.

Htn Phil 3801.197.10*A Beckers, Hubert. Über die Bedeutung des Schelling'schen Metaphysik. München, 1861.

Htn Phil 3801.197.25* Beckers, Hubert. Über die Wahre und bleibende Bedeutung der Naturphilosophie Schelling's. München, 1864.

Phil 3801.197.20 Beckers, Hubert. Die Unsterblichkeitslehre Schelling's im ganzen Zusammenhange ihrer Entwicklung. München, 1865.

Phil 8656.2 Beckett, E. The origin of the laws of nature. London, 1879.

Phil 8691.25.2 Beckett, Lucile C. Everyman and the infinite. London, n.d.

Phil 8691.25 Beckett, Lucile C. The world breath. London, 1935.
Phil 1135.168 Beckmann, F. Humanitas. Münster, 1952.
Phil 3805.215 Beckmann, Klaus. Der Begriff der Häresie bei Schleiermacher. München, 1959.

Phil 5068.32 Beckwith, B.P. Religion. N.Y., 1957.
Phil 5240.46A Becoming. (Allport, Gordon Willard.) New Haven, 1955.
Phil 5240.46.2 Becoming. (Allport, Gordon Willard.) New Haven, 1964.
Phil 5240.46.5.2 Becoming. (Allport, Gordon Willard.) New Haven, 1967.

Htn Phil 3801.734* Bedenken eines süddeutschen Krebsfeindes über Schellings erste Vorlesung in Berlin. (Reichlin-Meldegg, C.A. von.) Stuttgart, 1842.

Phil 176.172 Bedetti, A. Filosofia della vita. Cremons, 1952.
Phil 3625.1.111 Die Bedeuterung Moses Mendelssohn. Inaug. Diss. (Goldstein, L.) Konigsberg, 1897.

Phil 978.49.170 Bedeutsames aus dem äusseren Geistesleben um die Mitte des XIX Jahrhunderts. (Steiner, R.) Dornach, 1939.
Phil 3450.11.410 Bedeutung, Sim, Gegenstand. Thesis. (Orth, Ernst Wolfgang.) Bonn, 1967.

Phil 978.49.260 Die Bedeutung der Anthroposophie im Geistesleben der Gegenwart. (Steiner, R.) Dornach, 1957.

Phil 9150.22 Die Bedeutung der Entwickelungsgeschichte. (Lingle, T.W.) Leipzig, 1899.

Phil 6676.7 Die Bedeutung der hypnotischen Suggestion als Heilmittel. (Grossmann, J.) Berlin, 1894.

Phil 335.4 Die Bedeutung der Logik. (Ehrat, P.) Zittau, 1896.
Phil 5055.5A Die Bedeutung der Logik. (Prantl, C.) München, 1849.
Phil 3428.89 Die Bedeutung der Metaphysik Herbarts. (Flügel, Otto.) Langensalza, 1902.

Phil 338.23 Die Bedeutung der modernen Physik für die Theorie der Erkenntnis. (Hermann, G.) Leipzig, 1937.

Phil 3425.224 Die Bedeutung der person Jesu...Hegel. (Schmidt-Japing, J.W.) Göttingen, 1924.

Phil 5214.4 Die Bedeutung der Philosophie für die Entwicklung der Psychologie zur Einzelwissenschaft. Inaug. Diss. (Ebert, Manfred.) München, 1966.

Phil 185.37 Die Bedeutung der Philosophie für die Erfahrungswissenschaften. (Kreyenbühl, J.) Heidelberg, 1885.

Phil 3425.191 Die Bedeutung der Philosophie Hegels. (Hammacher, Emil.) Leipzig, 1911.

Phil 6327.4 Die Bedeutung der Psychoanalyse. (Rank, Otto.) Wiesbaden, 1913.

Phil 5257.57 Die Bedeutung der Psychologie für die Wissenschaft. (Révész, Géza.) Bern, 1947.

Phil 6316.2 Die Bedeutung der Reize für Pathologie und Therapie. (Goldscheider, A.) Leipzig, 1898.

Phil 1195.17 Die Bedeutung der Sophistik. (Grieder, H.) Basel, 1962.
Phil 7140.105 Die Bedeutung der Suggestion. (Bekhterev, W.M.) Wiesbaden, 1905.

Phil 3805.220 Die Bedeutung des Bösen für die Entwiklung. (Ariebel, Horst.) Ratingen, 1961.

Phil 3120.19.95 Die Bedeutung des hypothetischen Imperativs in der Ethik Bruno Bauchs. (Strasser, Johano.) Bonn, 1967.

Phil 3488.41 Die Bedeutung des Terminus transzendental in Immanuel Kants Kritik der reinen Vernunft. Inaug. Diss. (Gerresheim, E.) Köln, 1962.

Phil 6319.1.47 Die Bedeutung des Vaters für das Schicksal des Einzelnen. 4. Aufl. (Jung, C.G.) Zürich, 1962.

Phil 5520.7 Die Bedeutung des Wortes. (Erdmann, Karl O.) Leipzig, 1900.

Phil 5520.7.2 Die Bedeutung des Wortes. 2. Aufl. (Erdmann, Karl O.) Leipzig, 1910.

Phil 1145.10 Bedeutung des 7 Jahrhunderts. (Holstein, R.) Stettin, 1903.

Phil 5520.580.5 Bedeutung und Begriff. (Schmidt, Siegfried J.) N.Y., 1969.

Phil 7082.192 Bedeutung und Deutung des Traumes in der Psychotherapie. (Graevenitz, Jutta von.) Darmstadt, 1968.

Phil 5651.77 Die Bedeutung unserer Sinne für die Orientierung in Luftraume. (Garten, S.) Leipzig, 1917.

Phil 3450.11.300 Die Bedingungen der Möglichkeit der Transzendentalphilosophie. (Seebohm, W.T.) Bonn, 1961.

Phil 8587.32.115 Bedoyere, M. de la. The life of Baron von Hügel. London, 1951.

Phil 3110.32 Bedrachtingh vande goddelycke openbaringh. (Böhme, J.) n.p., 1642.

VPhil 3640.760 Bedřich Nietzsche. (Borský, Lev.) Praha, 1912.
Phil 5402.19 Beebe-Center, J.G. The psychology of pleasantness and unpleasantness. N.Y., 1932.

Phil 6420.2 Beech, H.R. Research and experiment in Stuttering. Oxford, 1968.

Phil 8581.5.7 Beecher, C.E. Common sense applied to religion. N.Y., 1857.

Phil 9341.1 Beecher, C.E. Duty of American women to their country. N.Y., 1845.

Phil 7054.60.5 Beecher, Charles. A review of the spiritual manifestations. London, 1853.

Phil 7054.60.4 Beecher, Charles. A review of the spiritual manifestations. N.Y., 1853.

Phil 8656.14 Beecher, E. The conflict of the ages. 5. ed. Boston, 1854.

Phil 8626.23 Beecher, E. History of opinions on the scriptural doctrine of retribution. N.Y., 1878.

X Cg Phil 8691.2 Beecher, H.W. Evolution and religion. pt.1. N.Y., 1885.
Phil 9558.2 Beecher, H.W. Industry and idleness. Philadelphia, 1850.
Phil 9558.2.5 Beecher, H.W. Industry and idleness. Philadelphia, 1896.
Phil 9341.2.2 Beecher, H.W. Lectures to young men. Boston, 1850.
Phil 9341.2.10 Beecher, H.W. Lectures to young men. Edinburgh, 1887.
Phil 9341.2.6 Beecher, H.W. Lectures to young men. N.Y., 1856.
Phil 9341.2.5 Beecher, H.W. Lectures to young men. Salem, 1846.
Phil 5875.170 Beeinflussung des Verhaltens durch den Schuleintritt. (Grotloh-Amberg, Heidi.) Bern, 1971.

Phil 3120.30.95 Beek, Martinus Adrianus. Martin Buber. Baarn, 1964.

Phil 3120.30.95.5 Beek, Martinus Adrianus. Martin Buber: personalist and prophet. Westminster, 1968.

Phil 5722.50 Beelden uit het onbewuste. (Helsdingen, R.J. van.) Arnhem, 1957.

Phil 1504.17 Beemelmans, F. Zeit und Ewigkeit nach Thomas von Aquino. v.17, pt.1. Münster, 1914.

Phil 3808.153 Beer, Margrieta. Schopenhauer. London, 1914.
Phil 1905.21 Beer, Samuel. The city of reason. Cambridge, 1949. 2v.

Phil 3625.3.91 Beer, Theodor. Die Weltanschauung eines modernen Naturforschers. Dresden, 1903.

Phil 2805.108 Beerens, J.F. De casuïstiek in Pascal. Utrecht, 1909.
Phil 3425.495 Beerling, R.F. De list de rede in de geschiedenisfilosofie van Hegel. Arnhem, 1959.

Phil 176.162 Beerling, R.F. Onsocratische gesprekken. Amsterdam, 1949.
Phil 1750.169 Beerling, Reimer. Het existentialisme. 's Gravenhage, 1947.

Phil 3450.11.430 Beerling, Reiner F. De transcendentale vreemdeling. Hilversum, 1965.

Phil 3120.21 Beerling, Reinier Franciscus. Antithesen. Haarlem, 1935.
Phil 3120.21.5 Beerling, Reinier Franciscus. Heden en verleden. Arnhem, 1962.

Phil 3120.21.10 Beerling, Reinier Franciscus. Ideeën en idolen. Arnhem, 1968.

Phil 6951.5.15 Beers, C.W. The mental hygiene movement. N.Y.? 1921.
Phil 6951.5.5.7 Beers, C.W. A mind that found itself. Garden City, 1925.
Phil 6951.5.6 Beers, C.W. A mind that found itself. Garden City, 1929.
Phil 6951.5.7 Beers, C.W. A mind that found itself. Garden City, 1933.
Phil 6951.5.8 Beers, C.W. A mind that found itself. Garden City, 1937.
Phil 6951.5.3 Beers, C.W. A mind that found itself. N.Y., 1908.
NEDL Phil 6951.5.2 Beers, C.W. A mind that found itself. 2. ed. N.Y., 1912.
Phil 6951.5.5 Beers, C.W. A mind that found itself. 4. ed. N.Y., 1921.
Phil 6951.5.17 Beers, C.W. A new project; the first International Congress on Mental Hygiene. N.Y., 1924.

Phil 6951.5.4.2 Beers C.W. A mind that found itself. 4. ed. N.Y., 1920.
Phil 1107.4 Before and after Socrates. (Cornford, F.M.) Cambridge, Eng., 1932.

Phil 1107.4.3 Before and after Socrates. (Cornford, F.M.) Cambridge, Eng., 1960.

Phil 3507.8 Der Befreier; eine Begegnung mit Kant. (Zimmermann, Heinz.) München, 1930.

Phil 11.27 Befreiung; Zeitschrift für kritisches Denken. Aaran. 1-3,1953-1955 3v.

Phil 8876.120 Befreiung und Erfüllung. (Brock, Erich.) Zürich, 1958.
Phil 5425.58 Begabung im Lichte der Eugenik. (Somogyi, J.) Leipzig, 1936.

Phil 5627.15.11 Begbie, H. Life changers. N.Y., 1927.
Phil 5627.15.9 Begbie, H. More twice-born men. N.Y., 1923.
Phil 5627.15.3 Begbie, H. Souls in action. N.Y., 1911.
Phil 5627.15 Begbie, H. Twice-born men, a clinic in regeneration. N.Y., 1909.

Phil 3120.30.39.10 Begegnung. (Buber, Martin.) Stuttgart, 1960.
Phil 978.49.890 Die Begegnung Max Heindel mit Rudolf Steiner. (Vallmer, Georg.) Darmstadt, 1965.

Phil 6315.58 Die Begegnung mit dem kranken Menschen. (Friedemann, Adolf.) Bern, 1967.

Phil 1750.350.2 Begegnung mit dem Nichts. (Kuhn, H.) Tübingen, 1950.
Phil 978.49.820 Begegnungen mit Rudolf Steiner. (Steffen, A.) Dornach, 1955.

Phil 974.3.80 Begegnungen mit Rudolf Steiner. (Steffen, Albert.) Zürich, 1926.

Phil 1707.17 Begegnungen und Auseinandersetzungen mit Denkern und Dichtern der Neuzeit. (Haensel, Ludwig.) Wien, 1957.

Phil 3120.30.140 Der begegnungscharakter der Wirklichkeit...Martin Bubers. (Grünfeld, Werner.) Ratingen, 1965.

Phil 843.5.5 Die Begegnungsphilosophie. (Boeckenhoff, J.) Freiburg, 1970.

Phil 8125.32 Begennu, Siegfried. Zur Theorie des Schönen. Berlin, 1956.

Phil 8050.47 Begg, W.P. The development of taste, and other studies in aesthetics. Glasgow, 1887.

Phil 400.64 Beggerow, H. Die Erkenntnis der Wirklichkeiten. Halle, 1927.

Phil 1750.640 Begiashvili, A.F. Metod analiza v sovremennoi burzhuaznoi filosofii. Tbilisi, 1960.

Phil 332.38 Begiashvili, Archie F. Problema nachala poznaniia v B. Rassela i E. Gusserlia. Tbilisi, 1969.

Phil 5520.444 Begiashvili, Archil. Sovremennaia angliiskaia lingvisticheskaia filosofiia. Tbilisi, 1965.

Phil 285.8 The beginning. (Ehrhardt, Arnold.) N.Y., 1968.
Phil 802.4A A beginner's history of philosophy. (Cushman, H.E.) Boston, 1910-11. 2v.

Phil 802.4.3 A beginner's history of philosophy. (Cushman, H.E.) Boston, 1918-19.

Phil 802.4.2A A beginner's history of philosophy. (Cushman, H.E.) Boston, 1918-20. 2v.

Phil 5043.22 Beginners' logic. (Dotterer, Ray H.) N.Y., 1924.
Phil 5043.22.5 Beginners' logic. (Dotterer, Ray H.) N.Y., 1938.
Phil 5259.5.18 A beginner's psychology. (Titchener, E.B.) N.Y., 1916.
Phil 5259.5.19 A beginner's psychology. (Titchener, E.B.) N.Y., 1924.
Phil 4752.2.33A The beginning and the end. (Berdiaev, Nikolai Aleksandrovich.) London, 1952.

Phil 7054.126 The beginning of man and what becomes of him. (Richards, L.S.) Boston, 1815.

Phil 9380.10 Beginnings of a bibliography on psychological factors in morale. (Hurvich, L.M.) n.p., n.d.

Phil 193.29 Beginnings of a new school of metaphysics. (Smart, Benjamin Humphrey.) London, 1839.

Phil 9150.30 The beginnings of Darwinian ethics: 1859-1871. (Gantz, K.F.) Chicago, 1939.

Phil 8877.48 The beginnings of ethics. (Cutler, Carroll.) N.Y., 1889.
Phil 7060.253 The beginnings of seership. (Turvey, Vincent N.) London, 1911.

Phil 5041.96.3 Beginselen der logica. 3. druk. (Berg, Innocentius Jozefus Marie van den.) Bilthaven, 1963.

Phil 5261.10.2 Beginselen der Zielkunde. 2e. Druk. (Verluys, J.) Amsterdam, 1899.

Phil 2885.111 Begouëm, Henry. Quelques souvenirs sur H. Taine. Toulouse, 1923.

Phil 8885.18.20 Begrebet "det etiske". (Koröman, Kristian.) København, 1903.

Phil 8876.73 Begrebet moral; analyse og kritik. (Bang, N.H.) København, 1897.

Phil 5253.7.5 Begrebet som psykologisk element. (Naesgaard, S.) København, 1924.

Phil 5058.43 Begriff, Urteil, Schluss. (Stammler, G.) Halle, 1928.

Phil 5011.3   Begriff, Urteil und Schluss in ihrer gemeinsamen Wurze. pt.1-2. (Binde, Robert.) Glogan, 1886-87.

Phil 8895.1   Begriff, Wesen...Darstellung der Ethik. (Uloth, L.) Göttingen, 18- .

Phil 705.54.5   Begriff. (Lauth, Reinhard.) München, 1967.

Phil 350.3   Der Begriff. (Tauschinski, Hippolyt.) Wien, 1865.

Phil 8590.14   Der Begriff a priori in der modernen Religionsphilosophie. (Köhler, R.) Leipzig, 1920.

Phil 4580.66   Der Begriff der Analogie. (Høffding, Harald.) Leipzig, 1924.

Phil 3425.664.2   Der Begriff der Arbeit bei Hegel. 2. Aufl. (Lim, Sok-Zin.) Bonn, 1966.

Phil 5190.4.5   Der Begriff der Definition. (Rethwisch, E.) Berlin, 1880.

Phil 3018.17   Der Begriff der Dialektik und die Anthropologie. (Sannwald, A.) München, 1931.

Phil 3805.170   Der Begriff der Eigentümlichkeit oder Individualität bei Schleiermacher. (Frahne, A.) Halle, 1884.

Phil 2070.143   Der Begriff der Erfahrungskontinuität bei William James. (Schmidt, Hermann.) Heidelberg, 1959.

Phil 3552.300   Der Begriff der ewigen Wahrheiten bei Leibniz. Inaug. Diss. (Pflugbeil, R.) Leipzig, 1902.

Phil 9220.9   Der Begriff der Freundschaft in der Philosophie. Inaug. Diss. (Eglinger, Ruth.) Basel, 1916.

Phil 3489.21   Der Begriff der Ganzheit und die Kantische Philosophie. (Heyse, Hans.) München, 1927.

Phil 3485.22   Der Begriff der Gesellschaft bei Kant. (Doerpinghaus, Wilhelm.) Köln? 1959?

Phil 3805.215   Der Begriff der Häresie bei Schleiermacher. (Beckmann, Klaus.) München, 1959.

Phil 5250.21   Der Begriff der Intuition. (König, Josef.) Halle, 1926.

Phil 349.20.25   Der Begriff der Maschine bei Julius Schultz. Inaug. Diss. (Ditz, Erwin.) Leipzig, 1935.

Phil 3552.97   Der Begriff der Materie bei Leibniz. (Wernick, G.) Jena, 1893.

Phil 525.24   Der Begriff der Mystik. (Zielinski, C.) Jena, 1913.

Phil 3492.50.5   Der Begriff der Pflicht in Kants vorkritischen Schriften. (Küpenberg, Max.) Innsbruck, 1927.

Phil 3493.35   Der Begriff der reflektierenden Urteilskraft in Kants Kritik der reinen Vernunft. (Liedtke, Max.) Hamburg, 1964.

Phil 3552.263   Der Begriff der Repräsentation bei Leibniz. (Köhler, Paul.) Bern, 1913.

Phil 3915.150   Der Begriff der Seele und die Idei der Unsterblichkeit. (Heinzelmann, G.) Tübingen, 1910.

Phil 600.42   Der Begriff der Tatsache in der positivistischen Philosophie des 19. Jahrhunderts. (Grunicke, Lucia.) Halle, 1930.

Phil 3487.12   Der Begriff der Urteilskraft bei Kant. (Frost, Walter.) Halle, 1906.

Phil 5068.24   Der Begriff der Wissenschaft im logischen Positivismus. (Haeberli, Hans.) Bern, 1955.

Phil 672.22   Der Begriff der Zeit. (Eyfferth, Max.) Berlin, 1870.

Phil 2475.1.139.5   Der Begriff der Zeit bei Henri Bergson. (Florian, M.) Greifswald, 1914.

Phil 3450.18.160   Der Begriff des a priori in Nicolai Hartmanns Erkenntnismetaphysik und Ontologie. (Grabes, H.) Köln, 1962.

Phil 9550.4   Der Begriff des Absolut Wertvollen. (Krueger, F.) Leipzig, 1898.

Phil 8885.29   Der Begriff des absolut Wertvollen. (Krueger, Felix.) Leipzig, 1898.

Phil 8583.44   Der Begriff des Absoluten. (Dallago, Carl.) Innsbruck, 1964.

Phil 4080.3.54   Der Begriff des Barock. (Croce, Benedetto.) Zürich, 1925.

Phil 182.98.5   Der Begriff des Begriffes. (Horn, E.) München, 1932.

Phil 182.98   Der Begriff des Begriffes. Inaug. Diss. (Horn, E.) München, 1931.

Phil 3497.11   Der Begriff des Bösen in Kants Kritizismus. (Petras, Otto.) Leipzig, 1913.

Phil 3120.10.81   Der Begriff des Daseins bei Julius Bergmann. Inaug. Diss. (Eckstein, Ernst.) Erlangen, 1902.

Phil 341.10   Der Begriff des Dinges in der Philosophie der Gegenwart. Inaug. Diss. (Kastenholz, Joseph.) Bonn, 1916.

Phil 3195.6.81   Der Begriff des Geistes bei Dilthey. (Stein, Arthur.) Bern, 1913.

Phil 3486.6   Begriff des höchsten Gutes bei Kant und Schleiermacher. (Elsmann, W.) Leipzig, 1887.

Phil 5835.1.3   Der Begriff des Instinktes einst und jetzt. 3. Aufl. (Ziegler, H.E.) Jena, 1920.

Phil 2490.116   Der Begriff des Kulturzeitalters bei Comte. Diss. (Borchert, H.) Halle, 1927.

Phil 672.27   Der Begriff des Raumes. (Ulrich, Georg.) Berlin, 1907.

Phil 8423.16.80   Der Begriff des Schönen bei Winckelmann. (Spengler, Walter Eckehart.) Göppingen, 1970.

Phil 5867.10   Der Begriff des Spieles und das ästhetische Weltbild in der Philosophie der Gegenwart [play]. (Heidemann, Ingeborg.) Berlin, 1968.

Phil 8125.6   Der Begriff des Tragischen. (Vorholz, Gerhard.) Halle, 1932.

Phil 3195.6.84   Der Begriff des Verstehens bei Dilthey. 2. Aufl. (Stein, Arthur.) Tübingen, 1926.

Phil 3195.10.130   Der Begriff des Werdens und der Entwicklung bei Driesch. (Teufel, Herbert.) München, 1960.

Phil 3850.18.155   Der Begriff des Wertpersontypus bis Scheler und Spranger. (Doerry, Gerd.) Berlin, 1958.

Phil 3832.7   Der Begriff die sittlichen Unvollkommenheit bei Descartes und Spinoza. (Müller, J.) Leipzig, 1890.

Phil 5080.3   Begriff und Beziehung. (Burkamp, W.) Leipzig, 1927.

Phil 3850.18.95   Begriff und Theorie vom Geist bei Max Scheler. Diss. (Herzfeld, Hans.) Leipzig, 1930.

Phil 3489.15   Der Begriff Wissenschaft im Kantischen Sinne. (Huch, Lilly.) Berlin, 1917.

Phil 3489.17   Die Begriffe Phänomenon und Noumenon. (Hicks, G.D.) Leipzig, 1897.

Phil 5360.5   Begriffsbildung: eine psychologische Untersuchung. (Willwoll, A.) Leipzig, 1926.

Phil 1504.19.2   Die Begründung der Erkenntnis. v.19, pt.2-3. (Hessen, J.) Münster, 1916.

Phil 804.6   Begründung der Geschichte der Philosophie als Wissenschaft. (Einhorn, D.) Wien, 1919.

Phil 3500.67   Die Begründung der Notwehr in der Philosophie von Kant und Hegel. (Sander, J.) Bleicherode, 1939.

Phil 193.244   Die Begründung der Wissenschaften durch Philosophie und Kybernetik. (Schneider, Peter K.) Stuttgart, 1966.

Phil 3504.12.10   Die Begründung des deutschen Idealismus durch I. Kant. (Wernieke, A.) Braunschweig, 1910.

Phil 3900.1.85   Begründung des Realismus. (Berger, Herbert.) Bonn, 1958.

Phil 8125.18   Die Begrundung der deutschen Ästhetik durch...Baumgarten und...Meier. (Betgmann, Ernst.) Leipzig, 1911.

Phil 5400.77   Begtrup, Julius. Some prominent characteristics of human nature and a new conception of God. London, 1929.

Phil 2475.1.269   Béguin, Albert. Henri Bergson. Essais et témoignages inédits recueilles. Neuchâtel, 1941.

Phil 6325.1.35   Die Behandlung schwer erziehlbarer und abnormer Kinder. (Pfister, Oskar.) Bern, 1921.

Phil 7140.107   Die Behandlung und kranken durch Suggestion. (Brügelmann, W.) Leipzig, 1906.

Phil 5627.107.20   Behanna, Gertrude Florence. The late Liz. N.Y., 1957.

Phil 5627.107.20.5   Behanna, Gertrude Florence. The late Liz. N.Y., 1968.

Phil 5255.11.9   Das Beharren und die Gegensätzlichkeit des Erlebens. (Pikler, Gyula.) Stuttgart, 1908.

Phil 5241.93   Behavior, knowledge, fact. (Bentley, A.F.) Bloomington, 1935.

Phil 5832.9   Behavior. (Watson, John B.) N.Y., 1914.

Phil 5832.9.2A   Behavior. (Watson, John B.) N.Y., 1914.

Phil 5374.225   Behavior and awareness. (Eriksen, Charles.) Durham, 1962.

Phil 5374.280   Behavior and conscious experience. (Smith, Kendon Rasey.) Athens, 1969.

Phil 5870.95   Behavior and development in childhood. (Baldwin, Alfred Lee.) N.Y., 1955.

Phil 5238.90   Behavior and evolution. (Roe, Anne.) New Haven, 1958.

Phil 5252.81A   Behavior and neurosis. (Masserman, J.H.) Chicago, 1943.

Phil 5252.81.2   Behavior and neurosis. (Masserman, J.H.) N.Y., 1964.

Phil 5259.40.5   Behavior and psychological man. (Tolman, Edward C.) Berkeley, 1958.

Phil 5780.25   Behavior control. 1. ed. (London, Perry.) N.Y., 1969.

Phil 5850.259   Behavior in a selling group. (Lombard, G.F.F.) Boston, 1955.

Phil 5500.35   Behavior in uncertainty and its social implications. (Cohen, J.) London, 1964.

Phil 5820.5   Behavior mechanisms in monkeys. (Klüver, H.) Chicago, 1933.

Phil 6360.2   Behavior modification in child treatment. (Browning, Robert Mitchell.) Chicago, 1971.

Phil 7140.131   The behavior of health. (Ferri, N.A.) Boston, 1937.

Phil 5258.120   Behavior of organisms. (Skinner, Burrhus F.) N.Y., 1938.

Phil 5625.114   Behavior principles. (Ferster, Charles B.) N.Y., 1968.

Phil 11.46   Behavior research and therapy. Oxford. 4,1966+ 4v.

Phil 5205.32   Behavior Research Fund, Chicago. A community's adventure. Chicago, 1931? 5 pam.

Phil 5625.92   Behavior theory and conditioning. (Spence, K.W.) New Haven, 1956.

Phil 5258.195   Behavior theory and learning; selected papers. (Spence, Kenneth Wartenbee.) Englewood Cliffs, 1960.

Phil 5238.32   Behavior theory and social science. New Haven, 1955.

Phil 6980.413   Behavior therapy and beyond. (Lazarus, Arnold A.) N.Y., 1971.

Phil 6980.780.10   Behavior therapy techniques. (Wolpe, Joseph.) Oxford, 1966.

Phil 5238.232   Behavioral and Social Sciences Survey Committe. Psychology. Englewood Cliffs, N.J., 1970.

Phil 5585.210   The behavioral basis of perception. (Taylor, James.) New Haven, 1962.

Phil 5440.38   Behavioral genetics; method and research. N.Y., 1969.

Phil 5590.430   Behavioral individuality in early childhood. (Thomas, Alexander.) N.Y., 1963.

Phil 11.33   Behavioral science. Ann Arbor. 1,1956+ 15v.

Phil 5262.21.6   Behaviorism. (Watson, John B.) N.Y., 1925.

Phil 5262.21.5   Behaviorism. (Watson, John B.) N.Y., 1925.

Phil 5262.21.7   Behaviorism. (Watson, John B.) N.Y., 1930.

Phil 5238.198   Behaviorism and phenomenology. (Wann, T.W.) Chicago, 1964.

Phil 5257.28   Behaviorism and psychology. (Roback, A.A.) Cambridge, 1935.

Phil 5257.28.30   Behaviorism at twenty-five. (Roback, A.A.) Cambridge, Mass., 1937.

Phil 5259.32   Le behaviorisme. Thèse. (Tilquin, A.) Paris, 1942-45.

Phil 5241.150   Behaviour. 1. ed. (Broadlunt, Donald Eric.) N.Y., 1961.

Phil 6314.11   Behaviour therapy and the neuroses. (Eysenck, Hans J.) Oxford, 1960.

Phil 5250.26   Behaviourism; a symposium by Josiah Morse. (King, W.P.) London, 1930.

Phil 5850.304   Behavorial change in the clinic. (Pascal, Gerald.) N.Y., 1959.

Phil 6961.4   Behind the bars. (Lunt, Adeline T.P.) Boston, 1871.

Phil 5257.62   Behind the scenes with ourselves. (Ramus, Carl.) N.Y., 1931.

Phil 7052.7   Behind the scenes with the mediums. (Abbott, D.P.) Chicago, 1907.

Phil 181.18   Behind the veil. (Griffith, J.) London, 1876.

Phil 1540.90   Behler, Ernst. Die Ewigkeit der Welt. München, 1965.

Phil 530.11.18   The Behmenists and the Philadelphians. Inaug.-Diss. (Thune, Nils.) Uppsala, 1948.

Phil 2520.280   Behn, Irene. Der Philosoph und die Königin. Freiburg, 1957.

Phil 530.40.50   Behn, Irene. Spanische Mystik. Düsseldorf, 1957.

Phil 801.29.5   Behn, Siegfried. The eternal magnet, a history of philosophy. N.Y., 1929.

Phil 8910.2   Behn, Siegfried. Ethik; ein Repetitorium. Bonn, 1948.

Phil 5041.45   Behn, Siegfried. Romantische oder klassische Logik? Münster, 1925.

Phil 5593.50   De Behn-Rorschach-test. (Broek, P. van den.) 's Gravenhage, 1950.

Phil 7069.30   Behr, Hermann. Letters from eternity. N.Y., 1930.

Htn   Phil 3808.70*   Die beiden Grundprobleme der Ethik. (Schopenhauer, Arthur.) Frankfurt, 1841.

Phil 3808.70.10   Die beiden Grundprobleme der Ethik. (Schopenhauer, Arthur.) Leipzig, 1860.

Phil 3808.70.12A   Die beiden Grundprobleme der Ethik. (Schopenhauer, Arthur.) Leipzig, 1881.

Phil 3808.70.5   Die beiden Grundprobleme der Ethik. 5. Aufl. (Schopenhauer, Arthur.) Leipzig, 1908.

Phil 3450.46   Die beiden Labyrinthe der Philosophie. (Heintel, Erich.) Wien, 1968.

Phil 3483.58   Beier, Franz. Kants Apriorismus. Pfullingen, 1933.

Phil 1540.96   Beierwaltes, Werner. Platonismus in der Philosophie des Mittelalters. Darmstadt, 1969.

Phil 5115.2   Beigefügt sind Beiträge zur Lehre vom hypothetischen Urtheile. (Sigwart, C.) Tübingen, 1871.

Phil 5238.215   Being, becoming and behavior; the psychological sciences. (Matson, Floyd W.) N.Y., 1967.

Phil 3450.19.296   Being, man and death: a key to Heidegger. (Demske, James M.) Lexington, 1970.

Phil 5059.22   Being, negation, and logic. (Toms, Eric.) Oxford, 1962.

Phil 8665.1	The being and attributes of God. (Knight, H.) London, 1747.
Phil 182.105.5	Being and becoming. (Hawkins, D.J.B.) N.Y.,1954.
Phil 349.34	Being and being known. (Swabey, William C.) N.Y., 1937.
Phil 8612.56	Being and death. (Ferrater Mora, José.) Berkeley, Calif., 1965.
Phil 187.93.10	Being and having. (Marcel, Gabriel.) Westminster, 1949.
Phil 2880.8.56.3A	Being and nothingness. (Sartre, Jean Paul.) N.Y., 1956.
Phil 2880.8.56.2	Being and nothingness. (Sartre, Jean Paul.) N.Y., 1965.
Phil 181.73.5	Being and some philosophers. (Gilson, E.) Toronto, 1949.
Phil 181.73.7	Being and some philosophers. 2. ed. (Gilson, E.) Toronto, 1952.
Phil 3450.19.32	Being and time. (Heidegger, Martin.) London, 1962.
Phil 3120.27.40	Being in the world. (Binswanger, L.) N.Y., 1963.
Phil 559.4	Being nothing and God; a philosophy of appearance. (Seidel, George Joseph.) Assen, 1970.
Phil 4883.2	Beisembiev, Kasym Beisembievich. Ideino-politicheskie techeniia v Kazakhstane Kontsa XIX-nachala XX veka. Alma-Ata, 1961.
Phil 4883.2.5	Beisembiev, Kasym Beisembievich. Progressivno-demokraticheskaia i marksistskaia mysl' v Kazakhstane nachala XX veka. Alma-Ata, 1965.
Phil 165.370	Beispiela. (Landgrebe, Ludwig.) Den Haag, 1965.
Phil 5045.3	Beispiele zur Logik. (Freyer, Paul.) Berlin, 1889.
Phil 5228.1.5	Beiträge...Psychologie. (Siebeck, H.) Giessen, 1891.
Phil 5238.24	Beiträge aus der Sowjetpsychologie. Berlin, 1952.
Phil 70.120	Beiträge der bulgarischen Teilnehmer an dem XIV. (International Congress of Philosophy.) Wien, 1968.
Phil 3821.17	Beiträge über die Verhältnis Schopenhauers zu Spinoza. (Brockdorff, C.) Hildesheim, 1900.
Phil 11.16	Beiträge und Psychologie. Stuttgart. 1-11,1928-1932 11v.
Phil 165.210	Beiträge zer Philosphie und Wissenschaft. (Höfling, Helmut.) München, 1960.
Phil 5640.24	Beiträge zu einer exacten Psycho-Physiologie. (Dreher, E.) Halle, 1880.
Phil 178.34.5	Beiträge zu einer exacten Psycho-Physiologie. (Dreher, Eugen.) n.p., 1880-91. 4 pam.
Phil 5520.25	Beiträge zu einer Kritik der Sprache. 2. Aufl. (Mauthner, Fritz.) Stuttgart, 1906.
Phil 3504.8	Beiträge zum Verständniss Kant's. (Witte, J.H.) Berlin, 1874.
Phil 1135.41	Beiträge zur...Ananke und Heimarmene. (Gundel, Wilhelm.) Giessen, 1914.
Phil 8407.10.10	Beiträge zur Ästhetik. (Groos, Karl.) Tübingen, 1924.
Phil 8404.15.5	Beiträge zur allgemeinen Kunstwissenschaft. (Dessoir, Max.) Stuttgart, 1929.
Phil 5635.5.4	Beiträge zur Analyse de Empfindungen. (Mach, Ernst.) Jena, 1886.
Phil 1705.3.5	Beiträge zur Charakteristik der neueren Philosophie. (Fichte, T.H.) Sulzbach, 1829.
Phil 1705.3	Beiträge zur Charakteristik der neueren Philosophie. (Fichte, T.H.) Sulzbach, 1841.
Phil 11.20	Beiträge zur christlichen Philosophie. Mainz. 1-6,1947-1950
Phil 2905.1.580	Beiträge zur Deutung von Teilhard de Chardin. (Klohr, Olof.) Berlin, 1966.
Phil 3090.31	Beiträge zur dynamischen Philosophie im Gegensaze der Mechanischen. (Baader, Franz von.) Berlin, 1809.
Phil 8876.74	Beiträge zur Dogmatik und Ethik. (Bolliger, Adolf.) Aaran, 1890.
Phil 187.28.13	Beiträge zur einer optimistischen Weltauffassung. (Mechnikov, I.I.) München, 1908.
Phil 3004.1.2	Beiträge zur Einführung in die Geschichte der Philosophie. 2. Aufl. (Eucken, Rudolf.) Leipzig, 1906.
Phil 3500.16	Beiträge zur Entwicklung der Kant'schen Ethik. Inaug. Diss. (Schmidt, Karl.) Marburg, 1900.
Phil 3500.16.5	Beiträge zur Entwicklung der Kant'schen Ethik. Inaug. Diss. (Schmidt, Karl.) Marburg, 1900.
Phil 5047.34	Beiträge zur Erkenntnistheorie uhd Methodenlehre. (Hönigswald, R.) Leipzig, 1906.
Phil 331.25	Beiträge zur Erkenntnistheorie und das Verhältnis von Sprache und Denken. (Albrecht, E.) Halle, 1959.
Phil 3483.50	Beiträge zur Erläuterung und Prüfung des Kantischen Sistems in sechs Abhandlungen. Gotha, 1794.
Phil 5252.12	Beiträge zur experimentellen Psychologie. (Münsterberg, H.) Freiberg, 1888-92.
Phil 5045.10	Beiträge zur Förderung der Logik. (Friedrich, E.F.) Leipzig, 1864.
Phil 5238.65	Beiträge zur genetischen Charakterologie. Bern. 1-3
Phil 3480.30.6.5	Beiträge zur Geschichte...Anhang zur. 5. Aufl. (Erdmann, B.) Berlin, 1900.
Phil 1504.25	Beiträge zur Geschichte. Supplement. Münster. 2-3,1923-1935 3v.
Phil 1105.5	Beiträge zur Geschichte der griechischen Philosophie. (Apell, Otto.) Leipzig, 1891.
Phil 1127.1	Beiträge zur Geschichte der griechischen Philosophie. (Wendland, Paul.) Berlin, 1895.
Phil 530.20.20	Beiträge zur Geschichte der Mystik in der Reformationszeit. (Hegler, A.) Berlin, 1906.
Phil 809.1.2	Beiträge zur Geschichte der Philosophie. (Joel, M.) Breslau, 1885.
Phil 809.1	Beiträge zur Geschichte der Philosophie. Bd.1-2. (Joel, M.) Breslau, 1876.
Phil 1504.20	Beiträge zur Geschichte der Philosophie des Mittelalters. Münster. 20+ 60v.
Phil 971.6	Beiträge zur Geschichte der Weisheitsreligion. (Negner, Helena.) Pforzheim, 1960.
Phil 5022.2	Beiträge zur Geschichte des Induktionsproblems. (Meckies, H.) Münster, 1933.
X Cg Phil 490.4.3	Beiträge zur Geschichte des Materialismus. 3. Aufl. (Plekhanov, G.V.) Stuttgart, 1921.
Phil 493.10	Beiträge zur Geschichte des vormarxistischen Materialismus. 1. Aufl. (Stiehler, G.) Berlin, 1961.
Phil 3493.54	Beiträge zur Geschichte und Interpretation der Philosophie Kants. (Lehmann, Gerhard.) Berlin, 1969.
Phil 493.4	Beiträge zur Geschichte und Kritik des Materialismus. (Schilling, G.) Leipzig, 1867.
Phil 5374.232	Beiträge zur Grundlegung der Elementaranalytik des Bewusstseins. (Wildangel, G.) Köln, 1962.
Phil 3425.108.7	Beiträge zur Hegelforschung. (Lasson, G.) Berlin, 1919-21. 2v.
Phil 1020.19.5	Beiträge zur islamischen Atomenlehre. (Pines, Salomon.) Berlin, 1936.
Phil 1020.19	Beiträge zur islamischen Atomenlehre. Inaug Diss. (Pines, Salomon.) Berlin, 1936.

Phil 930.36F	Beiträge zur Kosmologischen Spekulation der Chinesen der Han - Zert. Inaug. Diss. (Eberhard, Wolfram.) Berlin, 1933.
Phil 974.3.70	Beiträge zur Kritik der anthroposophischen Welt- und Lebensanschauung. Inaug. Diss. (Hovels, Karl.) Rheinland, 1926.
Phil 5643.50	Beiträge zur Lehre vom optischen Zeitsinn. Inaug. Diss. (Pauwels, Friedrich.) Frieburg, 1911?
Phil 5814.5	Beiträge zur Lehre von der Tierseele und ihrer Entwicklung. (Ettlinger, Max.) Münster, 1925.
Phil 282.14	Beiträge zur Lehre von Ding und Gesetz. (Bommersheim, P.) Leipzig, 1927.
Phil 5055.7	Beiträge zur Logik der Urtheile und Schlüsse. (Pokorny, T.) Leipzig, 1901.
Phil 5585.44.2	Beiträge zur Phänomenologie der Wahrnehmung. (Schapp, W.) Erlangen, 1925.
Phil 5585.44	Beiträge zur Phänomenologie der Wahrnehmung. (Schapp, W.) Halle, 1910.
Phil 5066.220	Beiträge zur Philosophie. (Nelson, Leonard.) Frankfurt, 1959.
Phil 11.3	Beiträge zur Philosophie. Heidelberg. 1-32,1912-1938+ 32v.
NEDL Phil 11.9	Beiträge zur Philosophie des deutschen Idealismus. Erfurt. 1918-1927
Phil 5245.19.5	Beiträge zur Philosophie des Gefühls. (Feldegg, F.) Leipzig, 1900.
Phil 8598.15	Beiträge zur Philosophie und Geschichte der Religion und Sittenlehre überhaupt und verschiedenen Glaubensarten und kirchen Insbesondere. (Stäudlin, C.F.) Lübeck, 1797-98. 4v.
Phil 5643.11	Beiträge zur Physiologie. v.1-5. (Hering, E.) Leipzig, 1861-
Phil 5592.110	Beiträge zur Psychodiagnostik. (Doebeli, Peter.) Zürich, 1959.
Phil 5245.9.10	Beiträge zur Psychologie. (Fortlage, A.R.K.) Leipzig, 1875.
Phil 11.8	Beiträge zur Psychologie der Aussage. Leipzig. 1903-1906 2v.
Phil 5250.7.10	Beiträge zur Psychologie der Gestalt. (Koffka, K.) Leipzig, 1919.
Phil 5590.360	Beiträge zur Psychologie der Persönlichkeit. Berlin, 1959.
Phil 5520.200	Beiträge zur Psychologie der Sprache und des Denkens. Berlin, 1955.
Phil 5643.79	Beiträge zur Psychologie des Sehens. (Berger, E.) München, 1925.
Phil 5238.2	Beiträge zur Psychologie und Philosophie. (Martius, Götz.) Leipzig, 1905.
Phil 5850.311	Beiträge zur psychologischen Methodologie der wirtschaftlichen Berufseignung. (Piorkowski, C.) Leipzig, 1915.
Phil 6962.9	Beiträge zur psychologischen Theorie der Geistesstörungen. (Meyerhof, O.) Göttingen, 1910.
Phil 5627.9	Beiträge zur religiösen Psychologie. (Vorbrodt, G.) Leipzig, 1904.
Phil 8586.24	Beiträge zur Spekulativen philosophie. (Goeschel, C.F.) Berlin, 1838.
Phil 8090.10	Beiträge zur Theorie der Künste im 19. Jahrhundert. (Koopmann, Helmut.) Frankfurt, 1971-
Phil 3915.52	Beiträge zur Theorie der Sinneswahrnehmung. (Wundt, Wilhelm.) Leipzig, 1862.
Phil 6127.15.5	Ein Beitrag zur Anatomie des Sprach-Centrums. (Rüdinger, N.) Stuttgart, 1882.
Phil 971.10	Ein Beitrag zur anthroposophischen Hochschulfrage. (Leiste, Heinrich.) Dornach, 1970.
Phil 2493.80	Ein Beitrag zur Beurteilung Condillacs. (Burger, K.) Altenburg, 1885.
Phil 3018.16	Beitrag zur Geschichte der Philosophie. (Schram, J.) Bonn, 1836.
Phil 3425.287.5	Ein Beitrag zur Geschichte des Hegelianismus in Russland. (Iakovenko, B.-V.) Prag, 1934.
Phil 3425.287	Ein Beitrag zur Geschichte des Hegelianismus in Russland. (Iakovenko, B.-V.) Prag, 1934.
Phil 1200.40	Beitrag zur Kenntnis der Sozial- und Staats-philosophischen Anschauungen der Hauptvertreter der neueren Stoa. Inaug. Diss. (Mann, W.) Halle (Saale), 1936.
Phil 3483.19	Ein Beitrag zur Kritik der Kantschen Ethik. Inaug. Diss. (Brennekam, M.) Greefswald, 1895.
Phil 5643.72	Beitrag zur Lehre von den Geschichtsempfindungen. Inaug. Diss. (Karplus, S.) Berlin, 1902.
Phil 5643.32	Beitrag zur physiologischen Optik. (Listing, J.B.) Leipzig, 1905.
Phil 525.20.5	Beitrag zur Problematik von Mystik und Glaube. (Salomon, Gotfried.) Strassburg, 1916.
Phil 6688.22	Ein Beitrag zur therapeutischen Verwertung des Hypnotismus. (Schrenck von Notzing, A.) n.p., 1888-97. 18 pam.
Phil 176.3	Beiträge zur Charakterologie. (Bahnsen, J.) Leipzig, 1867. 2v.
Phil 8080.14.5	Beiträge zur Geschichte der Ästhetik. (Ludács, G.) Berlin, 1954.
Phil 346.12	Beiträge zur Klärung des Begriffs. (Phalén, Adolf.) Uppsala, 1913.
Phil 8885.23	Beiträge zur Theorie der sittlichen Erkenntnis. (Kellerwessel, Josef.) Münster, 1919.
VPhil 8656.42	Beizmann, Cécile. Livret de cotation des formes dans le Rorschach d'après une compilation des cotations de H. Rorschach. Paris, 1966.
Phil 4803.537.40	Békassy, Oszkar. Az analógia je lentősége a tudomángos vallásos világismeret kialakulásában. Budapest, 1936.
Phil 5650.38	Eine Bekehrung. (Lutosławski, Wincenty.) Kempten, 19- .
Phil 5640.140	Békésy, Georg von. Experiments in hearing. N.Y., 1960.
Phil 5241.30.15	Békésy, Georg von. Sensory inhibition. Princeton, 1967.
	Bekhterev, V. General principles of human reflexology. London, 1933.
Phil 5241.30	Bekhterev, V. La psychologie objective. Paris, 1913.
Phil 7140.105	Bekhterev, W.M. Die Bedeutung der Suggestion. Wiesbaden, 1905.
Phil 803.14	Beknopte geschiedenis der wijshegeerte. (Delfgaauw, B.M.O.) Baarn, 1954. 2v.
Phil 1123.16	Beknopte geschiedenis van de antieke filosofie. (Strycker, Emile de.) Antwerpen, 1967.
Phil 7069.26.70	Beknopte Handleiding bei psychical research. (Tenhaeff, W.H.C.) 's Gravenhage, 1926. 3v.
Phil 3640.190.5	Bélart, Hans. Friedrich Nietzsches Ethik. Berlin, 1907.
Phil 3640.190	Bélart, Hans. Friedrich Nietzsches Ethik. Leipzig, 1901.
Phil 3640.190.20	Bélart, Hans. Friedrich Nietzsches Freundschafts-Tragödie mit Richard Wagner und Cosime Wagner-Liszt. Dresden, 1912.

Phil 3640.190.11   Bélart, Hans. Friedrich Nietzsches Leben. 2. Aufl. Berlin, 1910?

Phil 3640.190.30   Bélart, Hans. Nietzsches Metaphysik. Berlin, 1904.

Phil 5485.2   Belastung und Regression. (Lienert, Gustav Adolf.) Meisenheim am Glan, 1964.

Phil 150.25   Belaval, Y. Les philosophes et leur langage. Paris, 1952.

Phil 3552.400   Belaval, Yvon. Leibniz critique de Descartes. Paris, 1960.

Phil 3552.336.5   Belaval, Yvon. Leibniz; initiation à sa philosophie. Paris, 1962.

Phil 3552.336   Belaval, Yvon. Pour connaître la pensée de Leibniz. Paris, 1952.

Phil 6951.17   Belbèze, Raymond. La neurasthénie ruale. Paris, 1911.

Phil 7085.2   Belden, L.W. Account of Jane E. Rider somnambulist. Springfield, 1834.

Phil 3821.26   Belen'kii, M.S. Spinoza. Moskva, 1964.

Htn   Phil 3801.774*   Beleuchtung der neuen Schellingschen Lehre. (Schmidt, A.) Berlin, 1843.

Phil 5592.60   Beleving en verbeelding in het tekenen. (Lennep, Johanna Elisabeth van.) Amsterdam, 1958.

Phil 9161.2   Beleze, G.L.G. Livre de lecture courante des devoirs des enfants. Paris, 1855.

Phil 6671.17   Belfiore, Giulio. Magnetismo e ipnotismo. 2. ed. Milano, 1903.

Phil 2050.255   Belgion, Montgomery. David Hume. London, 1965.

Phil 1750.129.5   Belgion, Montgomery. The human parrot and other essays. London, 1931.

Phil 1750.129   Belgion, Montgomery. Our present philosophy of life. London, 1929.

Phil 720.31   Belgodere, F.J.A. La verdad, la ciencia y la filosofía. México, 1939.

Phil 2520.130   Belharz, Alfons. Descartes, Hume und Kant. Wiesbaden, 1910.

Phil 5070.30   Belief, existence, and meaning. (Martin, Richard Milton.) N.Y., 1969.

Phil 5070.28   Belief: the Gifford lectures delivered at the University of Aberdeen in 1960. (Price, Henry Habberley.) London, 1969.

Phil 8405.3   Belief and art. (Evans, W.V.) Chicago, 1939.

Phil 3745.14.15   Belief and faith. (Pieper, Josef.) N.Y., 1963.

Phil 8610.955   Belief and unbelief since 1850. (Wood, Herbert.) Cambridge, 1955.

Phil 8667.50   Belief in God; a study in the epistemalogy of religion. (Mavrodes, George I.) N.Y., 1970.

Phil 8667.6   Belief in God. (Momerie, A.W.) Edinburgh, 1888.

Phil 8673.10   Belief in God. 2. ed. (Savage, M.J.) Boston, 1881.

Phil 8636.2   The belief in God and immortality. (Leuba, James H.) Boston, 1916.

Phil 8630.5A   Belief in immortality. (Frazer, J.G.) London, 1913-24. 3v.

Phil 8631.2   The belief in immortality. (Gross, J.B.) Philadelphia, 1882.

Phil 8632.19   The belief in personal immortality. (Haynes, E.S.P.) N.Y., 1913.

Phil 8592.45.6   Belief unbound. (Montague, W.P.) Freeport, N.Y., 1970.

Phil 8592.45   Belief unbound. (Montague, W.P.) New Haven, 1930.

Phil 5335.2   Beliefs, attitudes and human affairs. (Bem, Daryl J.) Belmont, Calif., 1970.

Phil 5627.268.18   Beliefs, attitudes and values; a theory of organization and change. (Rokeach, Milton.) San Francisco, 1970.

Phil 5627.270.10   Beliefs and values. (Scheibe, Karl Edward.) N.Y., 1970.

Phil 8581.53   Beliefs that matter. (Brown, William A.) N.Y., 1928.

Phil 3120.30.56.40   A believing humanism: my testament 1902-1965. (Buber, Martin.) N.Y., 1967.

Phil 8402.60   Belik, Aleksandr P. Estetika i sovremennost'. Moskva, 1963.

Phil 8402.60.2   Belik, Aleksandr P. Estetika i sovremennost'. Izd. 2. Moskva, 1967.

Phil 2401.1   Belin, J.P. Le mouvement philosophique, 1748-1789. Paris, 1913.

Phil 4807.2   Bělka, František. Kapitaly z dějin českého revolučniho myšlení. Vyd. 1. Havlíčkův Brod, 1960.

Phil 8691.17   Bell, A.J. Whence comes man; from nature or from God? London, 1888.

Phil 6849.4   Bell, Alan P. The personality of a child molester. Chicago, 1971.

Phil 8581.57   Bell, Bernard I. Beyond agnosticism, a book for tired mechanists. N.Y., 1929.

Htn   Phil 6100.12*   Bell, C. The anatomy of the brain. London, 1802.

Phil 8581.10.4.5   Bell, Charles. Bridgewater treatises [4]. The hand, its mechanism and vital endowments. N.Y., 1840.

Phil 8581.10.4.10   Bell, Charles. Bridgewater treatises [4]. The hand, its mechanism and vital endowments. 7. ed. London, 1865.

Phil 6111.42   Bell, Charles. Idee einer neuen Hirnanatomie (1811). Leipzig, 1911.

Phil 7069.04.10   Bell, Clark. Spiritism, hypnotism and telepathy. 2. ed. N.Y., 1904.

Phil 8581.75   Bell, E.T. Man and his lifebelts. N.Y., 1938.

Phil 8876.97   Bell, F.O. The minor moralist. London, 1903.

Phil 9341.5   Bell, J.D. A man. Philadelphia, 1860.

Phil 8403.24.5   Il bell nel vero o estetic. 4. ed. (Conti, Auguso.) Firenze, 1901. 2v.

Phil 8876.81   Bellaigue, A. La science morale. Paris, 1904.

Phil 6980.102   Bellak, L. Contemporary European psychiatry. N.Y., 1961.

Phil 8581.81A   Bellamy, E. The religion of solidarity. Yellow Springs, 1940.

Phil 3821.12   Bellangé, C. Spinoza et la philosophie moderne. Paris, 1912.

Phil 7060.133   The Belledoon mysteries, 1830-40. 3. ed. (McDonald, Neil T.) Wallaceburg, Ont., n.d.

Phil 672.2   Bellermann, G. Beweis aus der neueren Raumtheorie. Berlin, 1889.

Phil 8581.115   Bellet, Maurice. Essai d'une critique de la foi. Paris, 1968.

Phil 2280.5.107   Belleza, arte y poesía en la estética de Santayana. (Lida, R.) Tucumán, 1943.

Phil 4351.1.33   La belleza ideal. (Arteaga, E.) Madrid, 1943.

Phil 4265.2.31   Le bellezze della fede ni misteri. (Mariano, R.) Milano, 1867. 3v.

Phil 5400.138   Bellingroth, Friedhelm. Triebwirkung des Films auf Jugendliche. Bern, 1958.

Phil 4075.84   Bellini, Angelo. Girolamo Cardano e il suo tempo. Milano, 1947.

Phil 6980.102.5   Bellman, Richard. A simulation of the initial psychiatric interview. Santa Monica, Calif., 1966.

Phil 8418.30.2   Il bello. 2. ed. (Ruvo, Vincenzo de.) Napoli, 1965.

Phil 8403.24   Il bello nel vero o estetica. (Conti, Augusto.) Firenze, 1872. 2v.

Phil 4260.130   Bellofiore, L. La dottrina del diritto naturale in G.B. Vico. Milan, 1954.

Phil 4260.130.5   Bellofiore, L. La dottrina providenza in G.B. Vico. Padova, 1962.

Phil 176.102   Bellomia Barone, F. Il problema fondamentale dell'essere. Ortona a Mare, 1909.

Phil 960.30   Belloni-Filippi, F. I maggiori sistemi filosofici indiani. Milano, 1914.

Phil 8958.7   Beloe inochestvo. (Ioann, Bishop of San Francisco.) Berlin, 1932.

Phil 6111.64   Beloff, John. The existence of mind. London, 1962.

Phil 5548.142   Belohnung und Bestrafung im Lernexperiment. (Bloeschl, Lilian.) Weinheim, 1969.

Phil 8876.44   Belot, G. Études de morale positive. Paris, 1907.

Phil 8876.44.2   Belot, G. Études de morale positive. 2e éd. Paris, 1921. 2v.

Phil 8876.44.5   Belot, G. Études sur philosophie morale au XIXeme siècle. Paris, 1904.

Phil 4769.6.81   Belov, P.T. Materializm I.M. Sechenova. Moskva, 1963.

Phil 6328.2.5   The beloved ego. (Stekel, Wilhelm.) London, 1921.

Phil 176.16   Belsham, T. Elements of the philosophy of the mind. London, 1801.

Phil 5425.82   Belt, W.R. The infirmities of genius. London, 1952.

Phil 3246.206   Belthusen, J.C. Einige Fragen, veranlasst Durch. Helmstädt, 1799.

Phil 4961.905   Beltrán Guerrero, Luis. Introducción al positivismo venezolano. Caracas, 1956?

Phil 960.43   Belvalkar, S.K. History of Indian philosophy. v.2,7. Poona, 1927-33. 2v.

Phil 960.43.2   Belvalkar, S.K. An outline scheme for a history of Indian philosophy. Poona, 1919. 2v.

Phil 3425.215   Belysning och granskning af Hegelska philosophiens. (Genberg, P.) Lund, 1846.

Phil 705.40   Belzer, G. Das Problem der Transzendenz in der Geschichte der neueren Philosophie. Amsterdam, 1952.

Phil 4765.1   Bem, A.L. Zhizn' i smert'; sbornik pamiatniki N.E. Osipova. Praga, 1936.

Phil 5335.2   Bem, Daryl J. Beliefs, attitudes and human affairs. Belmont, Calif., 1970.

Phil 4580.82   Bemaerkninger om den Høffdingske filosofi. (Schiodte, C.) København, 1900.

Phil 3500.17.15   Bemerkungen ueber den Kantischen Begriff...metaphysischen Rechtslehre. (Schwab, J.C.) Bruxelles, 1968.

Phil 3500.13   Bemerkungen über Kant's Philosophie Religion. (Storr, D.G.C.) Tübingen, 1794.

Phil 8062.6   Bemerkungen zur altgriechischen Kunsttheorie. (Utitz, Emil.) Berlin, 1959.

Phil 310.40   Bemerkungen zur Erkenntnistheorie des dialektischen und historischen Materialismus. (Baumgarten, A.) Berlin, 1957.

Phil 3120.30.155   Ben-Chorin, Schalom. Zwiesprache mit Martin Buber. München, 1966.

Phil 1106.2   Benard, Charles. La philosophie ancienne. Paris, 1885.

Phil 176.17   Bénard, Charles. Précis de philosophie. Paris, 1845.

Phil 176.17.2   Bénard, Charles. Précis de philosophie. Paris, 1857.

Phil 176.17.5   Bénard, Charles. Questions de philosophie. Paris, 1869.

Phil 410.81   Benardete, José A. Infinity. Oxford, 1964.

Phil 8430.6   Benaz, Manuel. Lo bello y la buena a la luz. Buenos Aires, 1933.

Phil 1750.295   Bence, Max. Technische Existenz, Essays. Stuttgart, 1949.

Phil 5421.25.5   Benda, Clemen Ernst. The image of love. N.Y., 1961.

Phil 5751.14   Benda, Clemens E. Der Wille zum Geist. Berlin, 1932.

Phil 5414.45   Benda, Clemens Ernst. Gewissen und Schuld. Stuttgart, 1970.

Phil 623.26   Benda, J. La crise du rationalisme. Paris, 1949.

Phil 2401.9   Benda, J. De quelques constantes de l'esprit humain. Paris, 1950.

Phil 1750.235   Benda, J. Tradition de l'existentialisme. Paris, 1947.

Phil 1701.22   Benda, J. Trois idoles romantique. Genève, 1948.

Phil 2475.1.197   Benda, Julien. Le bergsonisme. 5e éd. Paris, 1917.

Phil 5241.113   Benda, Julien. Du style d'idées. Paris, 1948.

Phil 176.111.25   Benda, Julien. Essai d'un discours cohérent sur les rapports de Dieu et du monde. Paris, 1931.

Phil 1750.126.3   Benda, Julien. The great betrayal. London, 1928.

Phil 176.111   Benda, Julien. Lettres à Mélisande. Paris, 1926.

Phil 3483.55   Benda, Julien. El pensamiento vivo de Kant. Buenos Aires, 1939.

Phil 2475.1.192   Benda, Julien. Une philosophie pathétique. Paris, 1913.

Phil 2475.1.192.5   Benda, Julien. Une philosophie pathétique. Paris, 1914.

Phil 2475.1.191   Benda, Julien. Sur le succès du Bergsonisme. Paris, 1914.

Phil 1750.126.8   Benda, Julien. La trahison des clercs. Paris, 1958.

Phil 1750.126.8.2   Benda, Julien. La trahison des clercs. Paris, 1965.

Phil 1750.126.6A   Benda, Julien. The treason of the intellectuals. N.Y., 1928.

Phil 8402.46   Bendavid, L. Beytrage zur Kritik des Geschmacks. Wien, 1797.

Phil 332.16   Bendavid, L. Über den Ursprung unserer Erkenntniss. Berlin, 1802.

Phil 8402.45   Bendavid, L. Versuch einer Geschmackslehre. Berlin, 1799.

Phil 5402.18   Bendavid, L. Versuch über das Vergnügen. Wien, 1794.

Phil 3483.33.5   Bendavid, L. Vorlesungen über die Critik der practischen Vernunft. Wien, 1796.

Phil 3483.33.10   Bendavid, L. Vorlesungen über die Critik der reinen Vernunft. Wien, 1795.

Phil 3483.33   Bendavid, L. Vorlesungen über die Critik des Urtheilskraft. Wien, 1796.

Phil 1870.123.5   Bender, Frans. George Berkeley. Baarn, 1966.

Phil 1870.123   Bender, Frans. George Berkeley's philosophy re-examined. Amsterdam, 1946.

Phil 7010.5.1   Bender, Hans. Parapsychologie; ihre Ergebnisse und Probleme. Bremen, 1970.

Phil 7010.5   Bender, Hans. Parapsychologie. Entwicklung, Ergebnisse, Probleme. Darmstadt, 1966.

Phil 7012.4   Bender, Hans. Unser sechster Sinn. Stuttgart, 1971.

Phil 176.82.5   Bender, Hedwig. Philosophie, Metaphysik und Einzelforschung. Leipzig, 1897.

Phil 8876.58   Bender, Hedwig. Über das Wesen der Sittlichkeit. Halle, 1891.

Phil 176.81   Bender, Hedwig. Zur Lösung des metaphysischen Problems. Berlin, 1886.

Phil 5585.65   Bender, L. A visual motor gestalt test. N.Y., 1938.

Phil 1106.13   Bender, W. Mythologie und Metaphysik. Die Entstehung der Weltanschauungen im greichisch Altertums. Stuttgart, 1899.

Phil 3805.83   Bender, W. Schleiermachers Theologie. v.1-2. Nördlingen, 1876-78.

Phil 8581.6   Bender, W. Das Wesen der Religion. Bonn, 1886.

Phil 8581.6.4   Bender, W. Das Wesen der Religion. 4. Aufl. Bonn, 1888.

Author and Title Listing

Phil 75.84	Bendfeldt Rojas, Lourdes. Bibliografía filosófica de publicaciones de las Universidades de Costa Rica y San Carlos de Guatemala y de autores guatemaltecos que exhibió la Biblioteca Nacional. Guatemala, 1964.
Phil 525.239	Bendiscioli, Mario. Der Quietismus zwischen Häresie und Orthodoxie. Wiesbaden, 1964.
Phil 7069.44.17	Bendit, L.J. Paranormal cognition in human psychology. London, 1944.
Phil 7069.49.15	Bendit, Phoebe Daphne Payne. The psychic sense. N.Y., 1949.
Phil 3483.34	Bendixson, A. Kritiska studier till Kants transcendentala ästetik. Upsala, 1885.
Phil 3549.8.100	Benduk, Hugo. Der Gegensatz vom Seele und Geist bei Ludwig Klages. Werli, 1935.
Phil 4110.8.30	Il bene e la libertà. (Fedi, Remo.) Milano, 1944.
Phil 5203.14	Benedek, László. Magyar pszichológiai irodalom 1945-66. Budapest, 1967.
Phil 4080.3.505	Benedetti, Ulisse. Benedetto Croce e il fascismo. Roma, 1967.
Phil 4080.3.350	Benedetto Croce, critico dei contemporanei. (Gandolfo, Antonio.) Padova, 1958.
Phil 4080.3.290	Benedetto Croce. (Buenos Aires. Universidad Nacional.) Buenos Aires, 1954.
Phil 4080.3.430	Benedetto Croce. (Caprariis, Vittorio de.) Milano, 1963.
Phil 4080.3.121	Benedetto Croce. (Castellano, G.) Napoli, 1924.
Phil 4080.3.340	Benedetto Croce. (Giordano-Orsini, Gian Napoleon.) Carbondale, 1961.
Phil 4080.3.255	Benedetto Croce. (Letterature Moderne.) Milano, 1953.
Phil 4080.3.385	Benedetto Croce. (Murray, G.) London, 1953.
Phil 4080.3.410	Benedetto Croce. (Nicolini, F.) Roma, 1954.
Phil 4080.3.170	Benedetto Croce. (Nicolini, Fausto.) Napoli, 1944.
Phil 4080.3.172	Benedetto Croce. (Nicolini, Fausto.) Torino, 1962.
Phil 4080.3.485	Benedetto Croce. (Ricci, Angelo.) Pôrto Alegre, 1966.
Phil 4080.3.180	Benedetto Croce. (Sgoi, Carmelo.) Messina, 1947.
Phil 4080.3.135	Benedetto Croce. (Spirito, Ugo.) Roma, 1929.
Phil 4080.3.210	Benedetto Croce. (Sprigge, Cecil Jackson Squire.) Cambridge, Eng., 1952.
Phil 4080.3.211	Benedetto Croce. (Sprigge, Cecil Jackson Squire.) New Haven, 1952.
Phil 4080.3.515	Benedetto Croce. Napoli, 1967.
Phil 4080.3.160.2	Benedetto Croce. 2. ed. (Cione, Edmondo.) Milano, 1953.
Phil 4080.3.121.5	Benedetto Croce. 2a ed. (Castellano, G.) Bari, 1936.
Phil 4080.3.465	Benedetto Croce als Kritiker seiner Zeit. (Lönne, Karl-Egon.) Tübingen, 1967.
Phil 4080.3.225	Benedetto Croce e gli studi contemporanei d'estetica e storia. (Vettori, V.) Firenze, 1952.
Phil 4080.3.505	Benedetto Croce e il fascismo. (Benedetti, Ulisse.) Roma, 1967.
Phil 4080.3.395	Benedetto Croce e il seicento. (Grandi, M.) Milano, 1962.
Phil 4080.3.458	Benedetto Croce e il suo mondo. (Feo, Italo de.) Torino, 1966.
Phil 4080.3.472	Benedetto Croce e la fondazione del concetto di libertà. (Roggerone, Giuseppe A.) Milano, 1966.
Phil 4080.3.540	Benedetto Croce e la politica italiana. (Colapietra, Raffaele.) Bari, 1969.
Phil 4080.3.240	Benedetto Croce e lo storicismo. (Olgiati, F.) Milano, 1953.
Phil 4080.3.435	Benedetto Croces literarisches und politisches Interesse an der Geschichte. (Mager, Wolfgand.) Koln, 1965.
Phil 3839.4	Benedetto Spinoza. v.3. (Turbiglio, S.) Roma, 1874.
Phil 672.134.5	Benedicks, Carl. Space and time. London, 1924.
Phil 7069.33.10	Benedict, Anna Louise. Continuity of life. Boston, 1933.
Phil 6111.47	Benedict, F.G. Mental effort. Washington, 1933.
Phil 8876.48	Benedict, W.R. World views and their ethical implications. Cincinnati, 1902.
Phil 3827.12	Benedict de Spinoza. (Hallett, H.F.) London, 1957.
Phil 3842.2	Benedict de Spinoza. (Willis, R.) London, 1870.
Phil 3821.18	Benedict Spinoza. (Bröchner, Hans.) Kjøbenhavn, 1857.
Phil 3826.7	Benedict Spinoza. (Gunn, J.A.) Melbourne, 1925.
Phil 3831.4	Benedict von Spinoza. (Loewenhardt, S.E.) Berlin, 1872.
Phil 3841.1.15	Benedictus de Spinoza. 2. Aufl. (Vloten, J. van.) Schiedam, 1871.
Phil 3819.10.14	Benedictus de Spinoza's Sämmtliche Werke. (Spinoza, Benedictus de.) Stuttgart, 1871. 2v.
Phil 3831.5	Benedictus Spinoza. (Linde, A. van der.) Gravenhage, 1871.
Phil 8951.7.9	Benedictus XIV. Casus conscientiae de mandato. Augustae Vindelicorum, 1772.
Phil 8951.7.10	Benedictus XIV. Casus conscientiae de mandato. Appendix. v.1-5. Augustae Vindelicorum, 1772. 3v.
Phil 5241.37	Benedikt, M. Die Seelenkunde des Menschen als eine Erfahrungswissenschaft. Leipzig, 1895.
Phil 4829.203.80	Benedikt Benković. (Brida, Marija.) Beograd, 1967.
Phil 270.10	Beneficence design in problem of evil...causation. (Journeyman (pseud.).) N.Y., 1849.
Phil 3483.46	Beneke, F. Eduard. Kant und die philosophische Aufgabe unserer Zeit. Berlin, 1832.
Phil 3100.55	Beneke, F.E. The elements of psychology. London, 1871.
Phil 3100.52	Beneke, F.E. Erfahrungsseelenlehre als Grundlage alles Wissens in ihren Hauptzügen Dargestellt. Berlin, 1820.
Phil 3100.42	Beneke, F.E. Grundlegung zur Physik der Sitten. Berlin, 1822.
Phil 3100.60	Beneke, F.E. Grundlinien des natürlichen System der praktischen Philosophie. Berlin, 1837-41. 2v.
Phil 3100.46	Beneke, F.E. Lehrbuch der pragmatischen Psychologie. Berlin, 1853.
Phil 3100.50	Beneke, F.E. Lehrbuch der Psychologie. Berlin, 1861.
Phil 3100.50.2	Beneke, F.E. Die neue Psychologie. 2. Aufl. Berlin, 1845.
Phil 3100.50.4	Beneke, F.E. Die neue Psychologie. 4. Aufl. Berlin, 1877.
Phil 3100.51	Beneke, F.E. Neue Seelenlehre. Bautzen, 1854.
Phil 3100.45	Beneke, F.E. Pragmatische Psychologie. v.1-2. Berlin, 1850.
Phil 3100.65	Beneke, F.E. Psychologische Skizzen. Göttingen, 1825-27. 2v.
Phil 3100.43	Beneke, F.E. Schutzschrift für meine Grundlegung zur Physik der Sitten. Leipzig, 1823.
Phil 3100.70	Beneke, F.E. Syllogismorum analyticorum origines et ordinem naturalem. Berolini, 1839.
Phil 3100.40	Beneke, F.E. System der Logik. Berlin, 1842. 2v.
Phil 3100.30	Beneke, F.E. System der Metaphysik and Religionsphilosophie. Berlin, 1840.
Phil 3100.53	Beneke, F.E. Das Verhältniss von Seele und Leib. Göttingen, 1826.
Phil 3552.115	Beneke, H.F. Leibniz als Ethiker. Erlangen, 1891.
Phil 6113.6	Beneke oder die Seelenlehre als Naturwissenschaft. (Dressler, J.G.) Bautzen, 1840.
Phil 3100.81	Benekes religions Philosophie im Zusammenhang seines Systems, seine Gottes- und Unsterblickkeitslehre. (Kempen, Aloys.) Münster, 1914.
Phil 2520.198	Beneš, J. Descartesova metoda ve vědách a ve filosofii. V Praze, 1936.
Phil 9150.10	Benett, W. Ethical aspects of evolution. Oxford, 1908.
Phil 8581.40	Benett, W. Religion and free will. Oxford, 1913.
Phil 8876.60	Benett, William. Freedom and liberty. London, 1920.
Phil 332.17	Bénézé, G. Critique de la mesure. Paris, 1937.
Phil 705.25	Bénézé, Georges. Allure du transcendental. Paris, 1936.
Phil 705.25.5	Bénézé, Georges. Allure du transcendental. Thèse. Paris, 1936.
Phil 735.109	Bènèzè, Georges. Valeur. Paris, 1936.
Phil 735.109.5	Bènèzè, Georges. Valeur. Thèse. Paris, 1936.
Phil 1524.3	Benezetö a közepkori keresztény hölcselet tortenelmehe. (Trikál, Josef.) Budapest, 1913.
Phil 4600.4.85	Bengt Lidforss. (Beyer, Nils.) Stockholm, 1968.
Phil 4600.4.45	Bengt Lidforss i urral. (Lidforss, Bengt.) Stockholm, 1965.
Phil 6049.00.7	Benham, W.G. The laws of scientific hand reading. N.Y., 1912.
Phil 6051.21	Benham, William G. The law of scientific hand reading. N.Y., 1901.
Phil 5811.20	Beniest-Noirot, Eliane. Analyse du comportement dit maternel chez la souris. Paris, 1958.
Phil 6957.9	Benign stupors. (Hoch, August.) N.Y., 1921.
Phil 5241.43	Benigni, Edvige. Elementi di psicologia sperimentale positiva. Torino, 1900.
Phil 3821.25	Benincá, A. La libertà umana. Caravate, 1952.
Phil 1750.570	Benitez, Claros. Une philosophie pour notre temps. Beirut? 1961.
Phil 8581.41	Benitez de Lugo, A. El cristianismo y la filosofia. Sevilla, 1882.
Phil 2255.1.90	Benjamin, A.C. The logical atomism of Bertrand Russell. Diss. Champaign, Ill., 1927?
Phil 9500.4	Benjamin, F.N. (Mrs.). The sunny side of shadow. Boston, 1887.
Phil 176.149	Benjamin, Harold. Man, the problem-solver. Boston, 1930.
Phil 4575.95	Benjamin Höijer. (Liljekrantz, B.) Lund, 1912.
Phil 4575.93	Benjamin Höijer. Akademisk afhandling. (Bygdén, Anders L.) Upsala, 1872.
Phil 6967.3.25	Benjamin Rush and American psychiatry. (Mills, Charles K.) n.p., 1886.
Phil 1106.3.9	Benn, A.W. Early Greek philosophy. London, 1908.
Phil 1106.3.10	Benn, A.W. Early Greek philosophy. N.Y., n.d.
Phil 1106.3.11	Benn, A.W. Early Greek philosophy. N.Y., 1909?
Phil 1106.3	Benn, A.W. The Greek philosophers. London, 1882. 2v.
Phil 1106.3.2A	Benn, A.W. The Greek philosophers. London, 1914.
Phil 1106.3.15	Benn, A.W. History of ancient philosophy. London, 1912.
Phil 623.9	Benn, A.W. The history of English rationalism in the nineteenth century. London, 1906. 2v.
Phil 623.9.5	Benn, A.W. The history of English rationalism in the nineteenth century. N.Y., 1962. 2v.
Phil 1701.6	Benn, A.W. History of modern philosophy. London, 1912.
Phil 1701.6.25	Benn, A.W. History of modern philosophy. London, 1930.
Phil 1106.3.5	Benn, A.W. The philosophy of Greece. London, 1898.
Phil 176.87	Benn, Alfred W. Revaluations. London, 1909.
Phil 3625.11.90	Benndorf, H. Persönliche Erinnerungen an Alexius Meinong. Graz, 1951.
Phil 3425.622	Benner, Dietrich. Theorie und Praxis. System theoretische Betrachtungen zu Hegel und Marx. Wien, 1966.
Phil 6319.1.212	Bennet, E.A. C.G. Jung. N.Y., 1962.
Phil 5041.55	Bennett, A.A. Formal logic. N.Y., 1939.
Phil 8876.55	Bennett, Arnold. How to live on 24 hours a day. N.Y., 1910.
Phil 8876.55.7	Bennett, Arnold. How to make the best of life. N.Y., 1923.
Phil 8876.55.20	Bennett, Arnold. The human machine. London, 1920.
Phil 8876.55.13A	Bennett, Arnold. The human machine. N.Y., 1911.
Phil 9341.12	Bennett, Arnold. Mental efficiency. N.Y., 1911.
Phil 9341.12.5	Bennett, Arnold. Mental efficiency and other hints to men and women. London, 1912.
Phil 8876.55.5	Bennett, Arnold. The reasonalbe life, being hints for men and women. London, 1907.
Phil 6951.16	Bennett, C. The modern malady. London, 1890.
Phil 525.63	Bennett, C.A. A philosophical study of mysticism. New Haven, 1923.
Phil 525.63.5	Bennett, C.A. A philosophical study of mysticism. New Haven, 1931.
Phil 8581.63	Bennett, Charles A. The dilemma of religious knowledge. New Haven, 1931.
Phil 8610.881.10	Bennett, D.M. An infidel abroad. N.Y., 1881.
Phil 8610.876.10	Bennett, D.M. Thirty discussions, Bible stories, essays and lectures. N.Y., 1876.
Phil 7069.39.4	Bennett, E.N. Apparitions and haunted houses. London, 1939.
Phil 7069.27.10	Bennett, E.N. Appolonius. London, 1927?
Phil 7069.05.30	Bennett, E.T. Automatic speaking and writing. London, 1905.
Phil 7069.08.10	Bennett, E.T. The direct phenomena of spirtualism. London, 1908.
Phil 8626.16	Bennett, F.S.M. Expecto, an essay towards a biology of the world to come. Chester, 1926.
Phil 5241.58	Bennett, H.E. Psychology and self-development. Boston, 1923.
Phil 8951.23	Bennett, J. Christian ethics and social policy. N.Y., 1946.
Phil 9341.7.5	Bennett, J. Letters to a young lady. London, 1803. 2v.
Phil 9341.7	Bennett, J. Letters to a young lady. Philadelphia, 1818.
Phil 5520.410	Bennett, J.F. Rationality. London, 1964.
Phil 176.212	Bennett, J.G. The dramatic universe. London, 1956-61. 2v.
Phil 6671.3	Bennett, J.H. The mesmeric mania. Edinburgh, 1851.
Phil 525.225	Bennett, John G. Witness. London, 1962.
Phil 3483.86	Bennett, Jonathan Francis. Kant's analytic. Cambridge, 1966.
Phil 7076.2.2	Benneville, George de. Some remarkable passages in the life of Dr. George de Benneville. Germantown, Pa., 1870.
Phil 5642.17	Benoist, Émilien. Contribution à l'étude de l'audition colorée. Paris, 1899.
Phil 2115.103	Benoit, G. von. Darstellung der Locke'schen Erkenntnisstheorie. Bern, 1869.
Phil 6311.46	Benoit, Hubert. Métaphysique et psychanalyse. 2. éd. Paris, 1964.
Phil 3822.3	Benoit de Spinoza. (Couchond, P.L.) Paris, 1902.
Phil 3821.6	Benôit Spinoza. (Borrell, Philippe.) Paris, 1911.

	Phil 2401.3.5	Benrubi, Isaac. Contemporary thought of France. London, 1926.
	Phil 2401.3.12	Benrubi, Isaac. Philosophische Strömungen der Gegenwart in Frankreich. Leipzig, 1928.
	Phil 2401.3.15A	Benrubi, Isaac. Les sources et les courants de la philosophie contemporaine en France. Paris, 1933. 2v.
	Phil 2475.1.290	Benrubi, Isaak. Bergson. Buenos Aires, 1942.
	Phil 2475.1.280	Benrubi, Isaak. Souvenirs sur Henri Bergson. Neuchâtel, 1942.
	Phil 1535.25	Bensa, A.M. Manuel de logique. Paris, 1855.
	Phil 3001.15	Bense, M. Vom Wesen deutscher Denker. München, 1938.
	Phil 3120.64.30	Bense, Max. Die abendländische Leidenschaft. München, 1938.
	Phil 8402.62A	Bense, Max. Aesthetica. Baden-Baden, 1965.
	Phil 8402.56	Bense, Max. Ästhetica. v.1,2-4. Stuttgart, 1954- 2v.
	Phil 176.160.5	Bense, Max. Einleitung in die Philosophie. München, 1941.
	Phil 3425.324	Bense, Max. Hegel und Kierkegaard. Köln, 1948.
	Phil 176.160	Bense, Max. Literaturmetaphysik. 1. Aufl. Stuttgart, 1950.
	Phil 1701.24	Bense, Max. Die Philosophie. Frankfurt a.M., 1951.
	Phil 1750.295.5	Bense, Max. Rationalismus und Sensibilität. Krefeld, 1956.
	Phil 5520.551	Bense, Max. Semiotik. Baden-Baden, 1967.
	Phil 8402.56.5	Bense, Max. Ungehorsam der Ideen. Köln, 1965.
	Phil 5627.134.40	Benson, C.I. The eight points of the Oxford Group. Melbourne, 1936.
	Phil 6990.3.19	Benson, R.H. Lourdes. St. Louis, 1914.
	Phil 3483.23	Bensow, O. Till Kants lära om tinget i och för sig. Lund, 1896.
	Phil 801.22	Bensow, Oscar. Grunddragen af filosofiens historia. Stockholm, 1916. 2v.
	Phil 3246.97	Bensow, Oscar. Zu Fichtes Lehre von Nicht- ich. Bern, 1898.
	Phil 5041.95	Bentham, Edward. An introduction to logick, 1773. Menston, 1967.
Htn	Phil 5041.37*	Bentham, G. Outline of a new system of logic. London, 1827.
	Phil 9550.15A	Bentham, J. Utilitarianism. London, 1890.
Htn	Phil 1865.65*	Bentham, Jeremy. Auto-icon. London, 1842?
	Phil 1865.25A	Bentham, Jeremy. Benthamiana. Edinburgh, 1843.
	Phil 1865.176	Bentham, Jeremy. Bentham's theory of fictions. London, 1932.
	Phil 1865.176.2	Bentham, Jeremy. Bentham's theory of fictions. N.Y., 1932.
Htn	Phil 1865.40.2*	Bentham, Jeremy. The book of fallacies. London, 1824.
	Phil 1865.195	Bentham, Jeremy. The correspondence of Jeremy Bentham. London, 1968. 3v.
	Phil 1865.30.30	Bentham, Jeremy. Deontologia. Torino, 1925.
	Phil 1865.30.35	Bentham, Jeremy. Deontologia. Torino, 1930.
Htn	Phil 1865.30.2*	Bentham, Jeremy. Deontology. London, 1834. 2v.
	Phil 1865.30	Bentham, Jeremy. Deontology. v.1-2. London, 1834.
Htn	Phil 1865.29*	Bentham, Jeremy. A fragment on government. London, 1776.
Htn	Phil 1865.49*	Bentham, Jeremy. An introduction to the principles of morals and legislation. London, 1789.
Htn	Phil 1865.50.1*	Bentham, Jeremy. Introduction to the principles of morals and legislation. London, 1823. 2v.
	Phil 1865.51A	Bentham, Jeremy. An introduction to the principles of morals and legislation. N.Y., 1948.
	Phil 1865.51.10	Bentham, Jeremy. An introduction to the principles of morals and legislation. Oxford, 1907.
	Phil 1865.50	Bentham, Jeremy. Introduction to the principles of morals and legislation. v.1-2. London, 1823.
	Phil 1865.22	Bentham, Jeremy. The limits of jurisprudence defined. N.Y., 1945.
	Phil 1865.60	Bentham, Jeremy. Not Paul, but Jesus. Camden, 1917.
Htn	Phil 1865.60.5*	Bentham, Jeremy. Not Paul, but Jesus. London, 1823.
	Phil 1865.28	Bentham, Jeremy. Of laws in general. London, 1970.
	Phil 1865.53	Bentham, Jeremy. Official aptitude maximized. London, 1830.
Htn	Phil 1865.35*	Bentham, Jeremy. Panopticon. Dublin, 1791.
	Phil 1865.19	Bentham, Jeremy. Panopticon. London, 1812-17. 4 pam.
	Phil 1865.18	Bentham, Jeremy. Principios de la ciencia social. Salamanca, 1821.
Htn	Phil 1865.50.5*	Bentham, Jeremy. Principles of legislation. Boston, 1830.
	Phil 1865.42	Bentham, Jeremy. The rationale of reward. London, 1830.
	Phil 1865.66	Bentham, Jeremy. La religion naturelle...d'apres les papiers de J. Bentham. Paris, 1875.
Htn	Phil 1865.55*	Bentham, Jeremy. A table of the springs of action. London, 1815.
	Phil 1865.43	Bentham, Jeremy. Theorie des peines et des récompenses. v.1-2. London, 1811.
	Phil 1865.10	Bentham, Jeremy. Works. Edinburgh, 1843. 11v.
	Phil 1865.12	Bentham, Jeremy. The works of Jeremy Bentham. N.Y., 1962. 11v.
	Phil 1865.05	Pamphlet box. Bentham, Jeremy. Political pamphlets, 1821-1825.
	Phil 1865.51.15	Bentham, Jeromy. An introduction to the principles of morals and legislation. London, 1970.
	Phil 1865.190	Bentham. (Hart, H.L.A.) London, 1962?
	Phil 1865.184.2	Bentham and the ethics of today. (Baumgardt, David.) N.Y., 1966.
	Phil 1865.184	Bentham and the ethics of today. (Baumgardt, David.) Princeton, 1952.
	Phil 1865.193	Bentham i jcgo system ctyczny. (Maślińska, Hallna.) Warszawa, 1964.
	Phil 1865.194	Bentham in the twentieth century. (Robbins, Lionel.) London, 1965.
	Phil 1865.25A	Benthamiana. (Bentham, Jeremy.) Edinburgh, 1843.
	Phil 1865.176	Bentham's theory of fictions. (Bentham, Jeremy.) London, 1932.
	Phil 1865.176.2	Bentham's theory of fictions. (Bentham, Jeremy.) N.Y., 1932.
	Phil 5241.93	Bentley, A.F. Behavior, knowledge, fact. Bloomington, 1935.
	Phil 5241.59	Bentley, I.M. The field of psychology. N.Y., 1924.
	Phil 5241.59.15	Bentley, I.M. The new field of psychology. N.Y., 1934.
	Phil 5241.59.5	Bentley, I.M. The psychology of mental arrangement. Worcester, 1902.
	Phil 176.145	Bentley, J.E. Visual outline of philosophy. N.Y., 1939.
	Phil 8876.83	Bentley, Joseph. How to sleep on a windy night. Philadelphia, 1928.
	Phil 8610.713.40	Bentley, Richard. La friponnerie laïque des pretendus esprits forts d'Angleterre. Amsterdam, 1738.
Htn	Phil 8610.713.20*	Bentley, Richard. Remarks upon a late discourse of free-thinking. London, 1713. 3 pam.
	Phil 8610.713.30	Bentley, Richard. Remarks upon a late discourse of free-thinking. pt.3. 8th ed. Cambridge, Eng., 1743.
	Phil 3839.5	Bento de Spinoza. (Tak, W.G. van der.) 's Gravenhage, 1928.
	Phil 3475.3.185F	Bentz, Hans Wille. Karl Jaspers in Übersetzungen. Frankfurt, 1961.
	Phil 6315.2.290F	Bentz, Hans Willi. Sigmund Freud in Übersetzungen. Frankfurt, 1961.
	Phil 6671.20	Benussi, V. La suggestione e l'ipnosi come mezzi di analisi psichisa reale. Bologna, 1925.
	Phil 5585.27	Benussi, Vittorio. Psychologie der Zeitauffassung. Heidelberg, 1913.
	Phil 176.46	Benvenuti, F. Saggi filosofici. Firenze, 1863.
	Phil 3110.177	Benz, E. Der Vollkommene Mensch nach Böhme. Stuttgart, 1937.
	Phil 3001.19	Benz, Ernst. Las sources mystiques de la phlosophie romantique allemande. Paris, 1968.
	Phil 3640.485	Benz, Ernst. Nietzsches Ideen zur Geschichte des Christentum wider der Kirche. Leiden, 1956.
	Phil 8594.16.80	Benz, Ernst. Rudolf Otto's Bedeutung für die Religionswissenschaft und die Theologie. Leiden, 1971.
	Phil 3801.203	Benz, Ernst. Schelling. Zürich, 1955.
	Phil 365.58	Benz, Ernst. Schöpfungsglaube und Endzeiterwartung. München, 1965.
	Phil 2805.228	Benzécri, E. L'esprit humain selon Pascal. Paris, 1939.
	Phil 176.150	Benzecri, E. Essai sur la nature et la portee d l'attitude metaphysique. Alcan, 1939.
	Phil 3915.162	Benzoni, R. Esposizione analitica del sistema di filosofia di Guglielmo Wundt. Palermo, 1890.
	Phil 5125.7	Benzoni, Roberto. L'induzione. Pt.1-3. Genova, 1894.
	Phil 6960.2	Beobachtungen...des Irrseyns. (Knight, P.S.) Koln, 1829.
Htn	Phil 3480.82.1*	Beobachtungen über das Gefühl des Schönen und Erhabenen. (Kant, Immanuel.) Königsberg, 1764.
	Phil 3480.82.6	Beobachtungen über das Gefühl des Schönen und Erhabenen. (Kant, Immanuel.) Berlin, 1910.
	Phil 3480.82.4	Beobachtungen über das Gefühl des Schönen und Erhabenen. (Kant, Immanuel.) Grätz, 1797.
Htn	Phil 3480.82*	Beobachtungen über das Gefühl des Schönen und Erhabenen. (Kant, Immanuel.) Riga, 1771.
	Phil 5828.11	Beobachtungen über die Psyche. (Sokolowsky, A.) Frankfurt, 1908.
	Phil 3496.4	Beobachtungen über die Quelle der Metaphysik. (Obereit, J.H.) Meiningen, 1791.
	Phil 5250.13.20	Beobachtungen über zweiklänge. (Krueger, Felix.) Leipzig, 1900-08. 10 pam.
	Phil 6968.8	Beobashtungen über den Wahnsinn. (Spurzheim, J.K.) Hamburg, 1818.
	Phil 3640.293	Beonio-Brocchieri, V. Federico Nietzsche. Roma, 1926.
	Phil 5500.20	Het beoordelen in de psychologie. (Dijkhuis, J.H.M.) Utrecht, 1960.
	Phil 2340.10.105	Bera, M.A. A.N. Whitehead; un philosophe de l'expérience. Paris, 1948.
	Phil 7082.24.5	Beradt, Charlotte. The third Reich of dreams. Chicago, 1968.
	Phil 978.59.125	Bercou, Lydia. Krishnamurti, sa vie, sa parole. n.p., 1969.
	Phil 5241.180	Berdelle, Philipp. Kleine Theorie des praktischen Denkens. Mainz, 1969.
	Phil 4752.2.115	Berdiaeff. (Porret, Eugene.) Neuchâtel, 1951.
	Phil 4752.2.130	Berdiaeff. (Segundo, J.L.) Paris, 1963.
	Phil 282.8	Berdiaev, N. Smysl tvorchestva. Moskva, 1916.
	Phil 8876.91.15	Berdiaev, N.A. De la destination de l'homme. Paris, 1935.
	Phil 8876.91.12A	Berdiaev, N.A. The destiny of man. London, 1959.
	Phil 8876.91.11	Berdiaev, N.A. The destiny of man. N.Y., 1960.
	Phil 665.72	Berdiaev, N.A. Dukh i real'nost'. Paris, 1941-.
	Phil 8581.69.3	Berdiaev, N.A. Filosofiia svobodnogo dukha. v.1-2. Parizh, 1927.
	Phil 8581.69.5	Berdiaev, N.A. God, man and the church. London, 1937.
	Phil 575.142.10	Berdiaev, N.A. Ia i mir ob"ektov. Paris, 193-?
	Phil 8581.94	Berdiaev, N.A. Khristianstvo i aktivnaia uslovnost'. Parizh, 194-.
	Phil 8610.929.40	Berdiaev, N.A. Marksizm i religiia. Paris, 1929.
	Phil 8876.91	Berdiaev, N.A. O naznachenii cheloveka. Parizh, 1931.
	Phil 575.142	Berdiaev, N.A. O rabstve i svobode cheloveka. Paris, 194-.
	Phil 7150.34	Berdiaev, N.A. O samoubiistvie. Paris, 1931.
	Phil 8581.69.7	Berdiaev, N.A. Samopoznanie: opyt filosofskoi avtobiografii. Parizh, 1949.
	Phil 4710.66	Berdiaev, N.A. Sofiia; problemy dukhovnoi kul'tury i religioznoi filosofii. Berlin, 1923-
	Phil 7150.46	Berdiaev, N.A. Le suicide. Paris, 1953?
	Phil 8876.91.5	Berdiaev, N.A. Von der Bestimmung des Menschen. Bern, 1935.
	Phil 176.138.20	Berdiaev, Nikolai A. Essai de metaphysique eschatologique. Paris, 1946.
	Phil 176.138	Berdiaev, Nikolai A. Méditations sur l'existence. Paris, 1936.
	Phil 176.138.15	Berdiaev, Nikolai A. Slavery and freedom. London, 1943.
	Phil 176.138.16	Berdiaev, Nikolai A. Slavery and freedom. N.Y., 1944.
	Phil 176.138.5	Berdiaev, Nikolai A. Solitude and society. London, 1938.
	Phil 176.138.8	Berdiaev, Nikolai A. Solitude and society. London, 1947.
	Phil 4752.2.33A	Berdiaev, Nikolai Aleksandrovich. The beginning and the end. London, 1952.
	Phil 4752.2.79	Berdiaev, Nikolai Aleksandrovich. Christian existentialism. London, 1965.
	Phil 4752.2.78	Berdiaev, Nikolai Aleksandrovich. Christianity and anti Semitism. Aldington, 1952.
	Phil 4752.2.78.2	Berdiaev, Nikolai Aleksandrovich. Christianity and anti-Semitism. N.Y., 1954.
	Phil 4752.2.68	Berdiaev, Nikolai Aleksandrovich. De l'esprit bourgeois. Neuchâtel, 1949.
	Phil 4752.2.40	Berdiaev, Nikolai Aleksandrovich. Dialectique existentielle du divin et de l'humain. Paris, 1947.
	Phil 4752.2.45	Berdiaev, Nikolai Aleksandrovich. The divine and the human. London, 1949.
	Phil 4752.2.55	Berdiaev, Nikolai Aleksandrovich. Dream and reality. London, 1950.
	Phil 4752.2.43	Berdiaev, Nikolai Aleksandrovich. Ekzistentsial'naia dialektika bozhestvennogo i chelovecheskogo. Parizh, 1952.
	Phil 4752.2.63	Berdiaev, Nikolai Aleksandrovich. Essai d'autobiographie spirituelle. Paris, 1958.
	Phil 4752.2.65	Berdiaev, Nikolai Aleksandrovich. Das Ich und die Welt der Objekte. Darmstadt, 195-?
	Phil 4752.2.60	Berdiaev, Nikolai Aleksandrovich. Khristianstvo i antisimitizm. Parizh, 1946.
	Phil 4752.2.72	Berdiaev, Nikolai Aleksandrovich. The meaning of the creative act. N.Y., 1955.
	Phil 4752.2.38	Berdiaev, Nikolai Aleksandrovich. Nicolas Berdiaeff ou la Révolte contre l'objectivation. Paris, 1967.

Phil 4752.2.70 Berdiaev, Nikolai Aleksandrovich. The realm of spirit and the realm of Caesar. London, 1952.
Phil 4752.2.75 Berdiaev, Nikolai Aleksandrovich. Royaume de l'esprit et royaume de César. Neuchâtel, 1951.
Phil 4752.2.35 Berdiaev, Nikolai Aleksandrovich. Russkaia ideia. Parizh, 1946.
Phil 4752.2.73 Berdiaev, Nikolai Aleksandrovich. Le sens de la création. Paris, 1955.
X Cg Phil 4752.2.30 Berdiaev, Nikolai Aleksandrovich. Sub specie aeternitatis. Sankt Peterburg, 1907.
Phil 4752.2.77A Berdiaev, Nikolai Aleksandrovich. Truth and revelation. London, 1953.
Phil 4752.2.50 Berdiaev, Nikolai Aleksandrovich. Tsarstvo dukha i tsarstvo kesaria. Parizh, 1951.
Phil 4752.2.125 Berdiaev en Russie. (Caín, Lucienne.) Paris, 1962.
Phil 4752.2.155 Berdiaev i Rossia. (Poltoratskii, Nikolai P.) N.Y., 1967.
Phil 8581.69.10 Berdiajew, N.A. Von der Würde des Christentums und der Unwürde der Christen. 4. Aufl. Luzern, 1937.
Phil 8581.69A Berdyaev, N.A. Freedom and the spirit. N.Y., 1935.
Phil 4752.2.150 Berdyaev's philosoophy. (Nucho, Fuad.) London, 1967.
Phil 4752.2.185 Berdyaev's philosophy of history. (Richardson, David B.) The Hague, 1968.
Phil 3821.5 Berendt, M. Spinoza's Erkenntnisslehre. Berlin, 1881.
Phil 9341.3 Berens, E. Advice to young man...Oxford. London, 1832.
Phil 2005.3.80 Beresford, J.D. W.E. Ford: a biography. London, 1917.
Phil 2005.3.81 Beresford, J.D. W.E. Ford: a biography. N.Y., 1917.
Phil 8400.17 Berestnev, V.F. Osnovy marksistsko-leninskoi estetiki. Moskva, 1960.
Phil 8402.48 Berestnev, V.F. Problemy estetiki. Moskva, 1958.
Phil 5520.32.7 Berg, Anton. Die Anschauungen Ludwig Noirés über Ursprung und Wesen von Sprache und Vernunft. Diss. Darmstadt, 1918.
Phil 6311.30.5 Berg, Charles. Deep analysis. 1st American ed. N.Y., 1947.
Phil 5241.155 Berg, Charles. Mankind. London, 1962.
Htn Phil 3801.198* Berg, Franz. Sextus oder über die absolute Erkenntniss von Schelling. Würzburg, 1804.
Phil 5041.96.3 Berg, Innocentius Jozefus Marie van den. Beginselen der logica. 3. druk. Bilthaven, 1963.
Phil 5627.264 Berg, J.H. Psychologie en theologische antropologie. Nijkerk, 1964.
Phil 1750.50 Berg, J.H. van der. The phenomenological approach to psychiatry. Springfield, Ill., 1955.
Phil 75.68 Berg, Jan. Selektiv bibliografi i teoretisk filosofi. Stockholm, 1960.
Phil 5241.145 Berg, Jan Hendrik van den. The changing nature of man. 1. ed. N.Y., 1961.
Phil 5241.145.5.2 Berg, Jan Hendrik van den. De dingen. 2. druk. Nijkerk, 1966.
Phil 7042.8.2 Berg, Jan Hendrik van den. Leven in meervoud. 2. druk. Nijkerk, 1963.
Phil 3120.69.30 Berg, Jan Hendrik van den. Metabletica van de materie. Nijkerk, 1968-
Phil 9500.8 Berg, Jan Hendrik van den. The psychology of the sickbed. Pittsburgh, 1966.
Phil 5241.182 Berg, Jan Hendrik van den. De zuilen van het Panthéon en andere studies. Nijkerk, 1969.
Phil 9513.19 Berg, Ludwig. Sozialethik. München, 1959.
Phil 2750.19.125 Berg, Randi. Alternativ til det absurde. Oslo, 1969.
Phil 9558.35 Berg, Robert Frederik. Liegen met en zonder opzet. Utrecht, 1961.
Phil 7054.161 Berg. J.T. Abaddon and Mahanaim...guardian angels. Philadelphia, 1856.
Phil 4210.79.10 Bergamaschi, Cirillo. Bibliografia rosminiana. Milano, 1967. 2v.
Htn Phil 6671.24* Bergasse, N. Lettre d'un médicin. Bordeaux, 1784.
Phil 7106.2 Bergasse, Nicolas. Considérations sur le magnétisme animal. La Hague, 1784.
Phil 3246.216 Bergbom, F. De ortu et indole idealismi Fichtii. Diss. Aboae, 1822.
Phil 8876.145 Berge, André. Les maladies de la vertu. Paris, 1960.
Phil 6980.105.10 Berge, André. Les psychothérapies. 1. éd. Paris, 1968.
Phil 8876.52 Berge, Vincent. La vraie morale basée sur l'étude de la nature. 3. ed. Paris, 1913.
VPhil 9590.34 Bergel, Bernard. Von der Krankheit und Genesung des Seienden, oder Der zweite Sündenfall. Tel-Aviv, 1966.
Phil 3745.1.80 Bergemann, P. Ernst Platner als Moralphilosophe. Halle, 1891.
Phil 8876.75 Bergemann, Paul. Ethik als Kulturphilosophie. Leipzig, 1904.
Phil 5643.79 Berger, E. Beiträge zur Psychologie des Sehens. München, 1925.
Phil 1050.16.5 Berger, Emil. Das Problem der Erkenntnis in der Religions-Philosophie Jehuda Hallevis. Inaug-Diss. Berlin, 1915.
Phil 1750.245 Berger, G. Existentialism and literature in action. Buffalo, 1948.
Phil 2477.19.30 Berger, G. Phénoménologie du temps et prospective. Paris, 1964.
Phil 3450.11.119 Berger, Gaston. Le cogito dans la philosophie de Husserl. Paris, 1941.
Phil 332.23 Berger, Gaston. Recherches sur les conditions de la connaissance. Paris, 1941.
Phil 5241.27 Berger, H. Über die körperlichen Äusserungen psychologischen Zustände. Jena, 1904. 2v.
Phil 3900.1.85 Berger, Herbert. Begründung des Realismus. Bonn, 1958.
Phil 282.24 Berger, Herman. Op zoek naar identiteit. Nijmegen, 1968.
Phil 585.385 Berger, Herman. De progressieve en de conservatieve mens in hermeneutisch perspectief. Nijmegen, 1969.
Phil 585.386 Berger, Herman. Progressive and conservative man. Pittsburgh, Pa., 1971.
Phil 3270.9.80 Berger, Hermann. Julius Frauenstädt, sein Leben, seine Schriften und seine Philosophie. Inaug. Diss. v.8. Rostock, 1911.
Phil 176.19 Berger, J.E. Grundzuge zur Wissenschaft. Altona, 1817. 4v.
Phil 176.19.5 Berger, J.E. Philosophische Darstellung der Harmonien des Weltalls. Altona, 1808.
Phil 5649.30 Bergès, Jean. Les gestes et la personnalité. Paris, 1967.
Phil 476.1 Bergier, N.S. Examen du matérialisme. Paris, 1771. 2v.
Phil 3483.31 Bergk, J. Briefe über Immanuel Kant's metaphysische Anfangsgründe der Rechtslehre. Leipzig, 1797.
Phil 3483.90 Bergk, Johann Adam. Reflexionen über I. Kant's Metaphysische Anfangsgründe der Tugendlehre. Bruxelles, 1968.
Phil 6951.27 Bergler, E. Money and emotional conflicts. 1. ed. Garden City, 1951.
X Cg Phil 7075.132 Bergler, E. Die psychische Importenz des Mannes. Bern, 1937.
Phil 9075.40 Bergler, Edmund. The battle of the conscience. Washington, D.C., 1948.
Phil 5525.54 Bergler, Edmund. Laughter and the sense of humor. N.Y., 1956.
Phil 5470.5 Bergler, Edmund. The psychology of gambling. N.Y., 1957.
Phil 6311.26.5 Bergler, Edmund. The superego. N.Y., 1952.
Phil 6311.26 Bergler, Edmund. Talleyrand, Napoleon, Stendhal, Grabbe, psychoanalytisch-biographishe essays. Wien, 1935.
Phil 5690.2 Bergler, Reinhold. Psycologie stereotyper Systeme. Bern, 1966.
Phil 165.240 Bergman, S. Studies in philosophy. Jerusalem, 1960.
Phil 3625.8.95 Bergmann, E. Georg Friedrich Meier als mitbegründer der deutschen Äthetik unter Benutzung ungedruckter Quellen. Leipzig, 1910.
Phil 8050.36 Bergmann, E. Geschichte der Ästhetik und Kunstphilosophie. Leipzig, 1914.
Phil 801.25 Bergmann, E. Weltanschauung. Breslau, 1926. 2v.
Phil 3745.1.153 Bergmann, Ernst. Ernst Platner und die Kunstphilosophie. Leipzig, 1913.
Phil 3246.173 Bergmann, Ernst. Fichte, der Erzieher zum Deutschtum. Leipzig, 1915.
Phil 3246.173.10 Bergmann, Ernst. Fichte und Carl Christian Erhard Schmid. Leipzig, 1926?
Phil 3246.173.5 Bergmann, Ernst. Fichte und der Nationalsozialismus. Breslau, 1933.
Phil 1735.8 Bergmann, Ernst. Der Geist des XIX. Jahrhunderts. Breslau, 1922.
Phil 1735.8.2 Bergmann, Ernst. Der Geist des XIX. Jahrhunderts. 2. Aufl. Breslau, 1927.
Phil 3246.173.2 Bergmann, Ernst. Johann Gottlieb Fichte der Erzieher. 2. Aufl. Leipzig, 1928.
Phil 2630.2.122 Bergmann, Ernst. Die Philosophie Guyaus. Leipzig, 1912.
Phil 2705.83 Bergmann, Ernst. Die Satiren des Herrn Maschine. Leipzig, 1913.
Phil 5068.18.10 Bergmann, Gustav. Logic and reality. Madison, 1964.
Phil 5068.18.5 Bergmann, Gustav. Meaning and existence. Madison, 1960.
Phil 5068.18.2 Bergmann, Gustav. The metaphysics of logical positivism; papers. 2. ed. Madison, 1967.
Phil 3120.8.145 Bergmann, Gustav. Realism; a critique of Brentano and Meinong. Madison, 1967.
Phil 3120.2.80 Bergmann, H. Das philosophische Werk Bernard Bolzanos. n.p., 1909.
Phil 3625.5.95 Bergmann, Hugo. The philosophy of Salomon Maimon. Jerusalem, 1967.
Phil 5041.9 Bergmann, J. Allgemeine Logik. Berlin, 1879.
Phil 801.15 Bergmann, J. Geschichte der Philosophie. Berlin, 1892-93. 2v.
Phil 332.1 Bergmann, J. Grundlinien einer Theorie des Bewusstseins. Berlin, 1870.
Phil 176.20 Bergmann, J. Sein und Erkennen. Berlin, 1880.
Phil 400.17 Bergmann, J. System des objectiven Idealismus. Marburg, 1903.
Phil 8876.86 Bergmann, J. Über das Richtige. Berlin, 1883.
Phil 8402.6 Bergmann, J. Über das Schöne. Berlin, 1887.
Phil 176.20.5 Bergmann, J. Vorlesungen über Metaphysik. Berlin, 1886.
Phil 9550.10 Bergmann, Julius. Über den Utilitarianismus. Marburg, 1883.
Phil 6951.14 Bergmann, W. Die Seelenleiden der Nervösen. 2. und 3. Aufl. Freiburg, 1922.
Phil 3246.265 Bergner, Dieter. Neue Bemerkungen zu Johann Gottlieb Fichte. Berlin, 1957.
Phil 5545.248 Bergon, Annie van. Task interruption. Amsterdam, 1968.
Phil 2475.1.370 Bergonismo y política. 1. ed. (Quintanilla, Louis.) México, 1953.
Phil 2475.1.435 Bergson, adversaire de Kant. (Barthélemy-Madaule, Madeleine.) Paris, 1966.
Phil 2475.1.266 Bergson, exposición de sus ideas fundamentales. (Figueroa, E.L.) La Plata, 1930.
X Cg Phil 5374.8 Bergson, H. Essai sur les données immédiates de la conscience. 2. éd. Paris, 1898.
NEDL Phil 5374.8.5 Bergson, H. Essai sur les données immédiates de la conscience. 2. èd. Paris, 1898.
Phil 176.51.29 Bergson, H. La filosofia dell'intuizione. Lanciano, 1922.
NEDL Phil 176.51.20 Bergson, H. Intuition og rerdensanskueke oversat af Knud Terlov. Kobenhavn, 1914.
X Cg Phil 2401.6 Bergson, H. La philosophie. Paris, 1915.
NEDL Phil 176.51.25 Bergson, H. Den skabende udvikling. Kobenhavn, 1914.
Phil 2475.1.37 Bergson, Henri. Le bon sens et études classiques. Clermont, 1947.
Phil 2475.1.103 Bergson, Henri. Choix de texte avec étude du...R. Gillouin. Paris, 1918.
Phil 2475.1.51.4 Bergson, Henri. Creative evolution. London, 1954.
Phil 2475.1.51.8 Bergson, Henri. Creative evolution. N.Y., 1911.
Phil 2475.1.51.6 Bergson, Henri. Creative evolution. N.Y., 1911.
Phil 2475.1.51.2 Bergson, Henri. Creative evolution. N.Y., 1911.
Phil 2475.1.51 Bergson, Henri. Creative evolution. N.Y., 1944.
Phil 2475.1.30 Bergson, Henri. The creative mind. N.Y., 1946.
Phil 2475.1.38.4 Bergson, Henri. Les deux sources. Paris, 1932.
Phil 2475.1.38.2 Bergson, Henri. Les deux sources de la morale et de la religion. Genève, 1945.
Phil 2475.1.38 Bergson, Henri. Les deux sources de la morale et de la religion. 14 éd. Paris, 1933.
Phil 2475.1.71 Bergson, Henri. Discours de réception. Paris, 1918.
Phil 2475.1.35 Bergson, Henri. Discours sur la politesse. Paris, 1945.
Phil 2475.1.66.5 Bergson, Henri. Dreams. N.Y., 1914.
Phil 2475.1.39.10 Bergson, Henri. Duration and simultaneity. Indianapolis, 1965.
Phil 2475.1.39 Bergson, Henri. Durée et simultanéité. 2e éd. Paris, 1923.
Phil 2475.1.39.5 Bergson, Henri. Durée et sumultanéité à propos de la théorie d'Einstein. Paris, 1922.
Phil 2475.1.78 Bergson, Henri. Écrits et paroles. Paris, 1957. 3v.
Phil 2475.1.57 Bergson, Henri. Einführung in die Metaphysik. Jena, 1909.
Phil 2475.1.45 Bergson, Henri. L'énergie spirituelle. 5. éd. Paris, 1920.
Phil 2475.1.40.6 Bergson, Henri. Essai sur les données immédiates de la conscience. Genève, 1945.
Phil 2475.1.40 Bergson, Henri. Essai sur les données immédiates de la consciènce. Paris, 1889.
Phil 2475.1.40.10 Bergson, Henri. Essai sur les données immédiates de la conscience. Paris, 1961.
Phil 2475.1.40.2 Bergson, Henri. Essai sur les données immédiates de la conscièńce. 9. éd. Paris, 1911.
Phil 2475.1.40.4 Bergson, Henri. Essai sur les données immédiates de la conscience. 43. éd. Paris, 1944.
Phil 2475.1.50.10 Bergson, Henri. L'évolution créatrice. Genève, 1945.

Phil 2475.1.50   Bergson, Henri. L'évolution créatrice. 4. éd.
                        Paris, 1908.
Phil 2475.1.50.2A   Bergson, Henri. L'évolution créatrice. 5. éd.
                        Paris, 1909.
Phil 2475.1.50.4   Bergson, Henri. L'évolution créatrice. 9. éd.
                        Paris, 1912.
Phil 2475.1.50.6   Bergson, Henri. L'évolution créatrice. 10. éd.
                        Paris, 1912.
Phil 2475.1.50.8   Bergson, Henri. L'évolution créatrice. 52. éd.
                        Paris, 1940.
Phil 2475.1.56.2   Bergson, Henri. An introduction to metaphysics.
                        London, 1913.
Phil 2475.1.56   Bergson, Henri. An introduction to metaphysics.
                        N.Y., 1912.
Phil 2475.1.69.6   Bergson, Henri. Laughter. London, 1911.
NEDL Phil 6111.12.15   Bergson, Henri. Materie und Gedächtnis. Jena, 1919.
Phil 2475.1.60.6   Bergson, Henri. Matière et mémoire. Genève, 1946.
X Cg   Phil 6111.12   Bergson, Henri. Matière et mémoire. Paris, 1900.
Phil 2475.1.60   Bergson, Henri. Matière et mémoire. 7. éd. Paris, 1911.
Phil 2475.1.60.2   Bergson, Henri. Matière et mémoire. 8. éd. Paris, 1912.
Phil 2475.1.60.4   Bergson, Henri. Matière et mémoire. 36. éd. Paris, 1941.
Phil 2475.1.61.4A   Bergson, Henri. Matter and memory. London, 1919.
Phil 2475.1.61   Bergson, Henri. Matter and memory. N.Y., 1911.
Phil 2475.1.61.2   Bergson, Henri. Matter and memory. N.Y., 1912.
Phil 2475.1.63   Bergson, Henri. The meaning of the war. London, 1915.
Phil 2475.1.76   Bergson, Henri. Memoire et vie. 1e éd. Paris, 1957.
Phil 2475.1.46   Bergson, Henri. Mind energy. London, 1920.
Phil 2475.1.5   Bergson, Henri. Oeuvres. 1e éd. Paris, 1959.
Phil 2475.1.8   Bergson, Henri. Oeuvres. 3. éd. Paris, 1970.
Phil 2475.1.65.4   Bergson, Henri. La pensée et le mouvant. Genève, 1946.
Phil 2475.1.65   Bergson, Henri. La pensée et le mouvant. 5. éd.
                        Paris, 1934.
Phil 2475.1.65.2   Bergson, Henri. La pensée et le mouvant. 12. éd.
                        Paris, 1941.
Phil 2475.1.67   Bergson, Henri. La perception du changement.
                        Oxford, 1911.
Phil 2475.1.69.7   Bergson, Henri. Le rire. Genève, 1945.
Phil 2475.1.69.5   Bergson, Henri. Le rire. Paris, 1928.
NEDL Phil 5525.11.10   Bergson, Henri. Le rire. 5. éd. Paris, 1908.
Phil 2475.1.69   Bergson, Henri. Le rire. 57. éd. Paris, 1941.
NEDL Phil 5525.11.5   Bergson, Henri. Il riso, saggio sul significato del
                        comico. Bari, 1916.
Phil 2475.1.73   Bergson, Henri. Schöpferische Entwicklung. Jena, 1921.
Phil 2475.1.42   Bergson, Henri. Time and free will; an essay on the
                        immediate data of consciousness. London, 1959.
Phil 2475.1.41   Bergson, Henri. Time and free will; an essay on the
                        immediate data of consciousness. N.Y., 1960.
Phil 2475.1.38.6   Bergson, Henri. The two sources of morality and religion.
                        N.Y., 1935.
Phil 8581.66.15   Bergson, Henri. The two sources of morality and religion.
                        N.Y., 1946.
Phil 2475.1.66   Bergson, Henri. The world of dreams. N.Y., 1958.
Phil 2475.1.75   Bergson, Henri. Zeit und Freiheit. Jena, 1920.
Phil 2475.1.79   Pamphlet box. Bergson, Henri.
Phil 2475.1.249   Bergson, mon maître. 6e éd. (Maire, Gilbert.)
                        Paris, 1935.
Phil 2475.1.286A   Bergson; sa vie, son oeuvre, avec un exposé de sa
                        philosophie. (Cresson, André.) Paris, 1941.
Phil 2475.1.340   Bergson. (Alexander, I.W.) London, 1957.
Phil 2475.1.437   Bergson. (Barthélemy-Madaule, Madeleine.) Paris, 1967.
Phil 2475.1.290   Bergson. (Benrubi, Isaak.) Buenos Aires, 1942.
Phil 2475.1.219   Bergson. (Caramella, S.) Milano, 1925.
Phil 2475.1.227   Bergson. (Challaye, F.) Paris, 1929.
Phil 2475.1.302.5   Bergson. (Challaye, F.) Paris, 1947.
Phil 2475.1.222   Bergson. (Chevalier, Jacques.) Paris, 1926.
Phil 2475.1.430   Bergson. (Giusso, Lorenzo.) Milano, 1949.
Phil 2475.1.263   Bergson. (Jankélévitch, V.) Paris, 1931.
Phil 2475.1.350   Bergson. (Mathieu, Vittorio.) Torino, 1954.
Phil 2475.1.310   Bergson. (Mossé-Bastide, R.M.) Paris, 1955.
Phil 2475.1.207   Bergson. (Pentimalli, G.H.) Torino, 1920.
Phil 2475.1.81   Bergson. (Solomon, J.) London, 1911.
Phil 2475.1.445   Bergson. (Wahl, Jean André.) Paris, 1965.
Phil 2475.1.410   Bergson: sa vie, son oeuvre, avec un exposé de sa
                        philosophie. (Cresson, André.) Paris, 1964.
Phil 2475.1.204   Bergson and future philosophy. (Hamilton, George R.)
                        London, 1921.
Phil 2475.1.202   Bergson and his philosophy. (Gunn, John Alex.)
                        London, 1920.
Phil 2475.1.201   Bergson and personal realism. (Flewelling, Ralph.)
                        N.Y., 1920.
Phil 2475.1.165   Bergson and religion. (Miller, L.H.) N.Y., 1916.
Phil 2475.1.135   Bergson and romantic evolutionism. (Lovejoy, A.O.)
                        Berkeley, 1913.
Phil 2475.1.500   Bergson and the evolution of physics. 1st ed. (Gunter,
                        Pete Addison Y.) Knoxville, 1969.
Phil 2475.1.119   Bergson and the modern spirit. (Dodson, G.R.)
                        Boston, 1913.
Phil 2475.1.325   Bergson e il suo umanismo integrale. (Montiani, Oddino.)
                        Padova, 1957.
Phil 2475.1.214   Bergson e lo spiritualismo. (Serini, P.) Genova, 1923.
Phil 2475.1.400   Bergson et le Christ des évangiles. (Gouhier, Henri.)
                        Paris, 1961.
Phil 2475.1.239   Bergson et le Judaïsme. (Pallière, Aimé.) Paris, 1933.
Phil 2475.1.235   Bergson et le Vedanta. (Basu, P.S.) Montpellier, 1930.
Phil 2475.1.425   Bergson et les niveaux de réalité. (Mourélos, Giorgos.)
                        Paris, 1964.
Phil 2475.1.360   Bergson et Plotin. 1. éd. (Mossé-Bastide, Rose Marie.)
                        Paris, 1959.
Phil 2475.1.360.5   Bergson et Plotin. 1. éd. Thèse. (Mossé-Bastide, Rose
                        Marie.) Paris, 1959.
Phil 2905.1.200   Bergson et Teilhard de Chardin. (Barthélemy-Madaule,
                        Madeleine.) Paris, 1963.
Phil 2475.1.85   Bergson for beginners. (Kitchin, D.B.) London, 1913.
Phil 2475.1.330   Bergson on morality. (Copleston, F.C.) London, 1956.
Phil 2475.1.241   Bergson und die deutsche Romantik. (Dryssen, Carl.)
                        Marburg, 1922.
Phil 2475.1.395   The Bergsonian heritage. (Hanna, T.) N.Y., 1962.
Phil 2475.1.128   Bergsonian philosophy and Thomism. (Maritain, Jacques.)
                        N.Y., 1955.
Phil 2475.1.300   Le Bergsonisme. (Iliev, Alhanasso.) Sofia, 193-?
Phil 2475.1.299   Le Bergsonisme. (Politzer, Georges.) Paris, 1947.
Phil 2475.1.197   Le bergsonisme. 5e éd. (Benda, Julien.) Paris, 1917.
Phil 2475.1.209   Bergsonisme et moralité. (Rodrigues, G.) Paris, 1921.
Phil 2475.1.206   Bergson's doctrine of intuition. (Luce, A.A.)
                        London, 1922.
Phil 2475.1.253   Bergson's Einfluss auf die französische Schriftsprache.
                        Inaug. Diss. (Sommer, Erika.) München, 1935.

Phil 2475.1.243   Bergson's idea of creation. (Stallknecht, N.P.)
                        Princeton, N.J., 1934?
Phil 2475.1.315   Bergson's mysticism. Thesis. (Kelley, J.J.)
                        Fribourg, 1954.
Phil 8581.47   Bergstedt, C.F. Hvad vi veta, hvad vi tro och hvad vi
                        vilja. Stockholm, 1878.
Phil 9070.104F   Bergstroem, L. Imperatives and ethics. Stockholm, 1962.
Phil 5241.96   Bergström, J.A. An experimental study of some of the
                        conditions of mental activity. Worcester, 1894.
Phil 735.1   Berguer, G. La notion de valeur. Genève, 1908.
Phil 5627.178   Berguer, Georges. Traité de psychologie de la religion.
                        Lausanne, 1946.
Phil 8400.36   Bericht. (International Congress on Aesthetics, 1st,
                        Berlin, 1913.) Stuttgart, 1913.
Phil 70.9   Bericht. (Kongress für Experimentelle Psychologie.) Jena.
                        10,1927
Phil 5249.13.30   Bericht über das Berliner Seminar. (Jung, Carl G.)
                        Berlin, 1933.
Phil 70.1.3   Bericht über den III International Kongress.
                        (International Congress of Philosophy, 3rd, Heidelberg,
                        1908.) Heidelberg. 1909
Phil 70.9.25   Bericht über den Kongress. (Deutsche Gesellschaft für
                        Psychologie.) Jena. 14,1934
Phil 1135.174   Die Berichte über die Sukressionen der Philosophen.
                        (Kienle, W.) Berlin, 1961.
Phil 3489.29.10   Berichtigung der Urtheile des Publikums über Kant und seine
                        Philosophie. (Heynig, J.G.) Cölln, 1797.
Phil 6671.4.5   Bérillon, E. De la suggestion. Paris, 1886.
Phil 6671.4.9   Bérillon, E. Historie de l'hypnotisme expérimental.
                        Paris, 1902.
Phil 6671.4   Bérillon, E. Hypnotisme experimental. Paris, 1884.
Phil 5625.112   Beritashvili, Ivan S. Neural mechanisms of higher
                        vertebrate behavior. 1st English ed. Boston, 1965.
Phil 4791.4   Beritashvili, Ivan Solomonovich. Uchenie o prirode
                        cheloveka v drevnei Gruzii. Tbilisi, 1961.
Phil 5204.24   Berka, M. Kleines psychologisches Lexicon. Wien, 1949.
Phil 5066.80   Berkeley, E.C. Symbolic logic. N.Y., 1955.
Phil 1870.40.35   Berkeley, G. Abhandlung über die Prinzipien der
                        menschlichen Erkenntnis. London, 1920.
Phil 1870.30.25   Berkeley, G. Alcifrone. Dialogli. v.1-5. Torino, 1932.
Htn   Phil 1870.29*   Berkeley, G. Alciphron. Dublin, 1732.
Phil 1870.30.15   Berkeley, G. Alciphron. Leipzig, 1915.
Htn   Phil 1870.30*   Berkeley, G. Alciphron. London, 1732. 2v.
Htn   Phil 1870.30.2*   Berkeley, G. Alciphron. New Haven, 1803.
Phil 1870.30.30   Berkeley, G. Alciphron. Paris, 1952.
Htn   Phil 1870.30.1*   Berkeley, G. Alciphron. 2d ed. London, 1732. 2v.
Phil 1870.73.7   Berkeley, G. Gli appunti (commonplace book).
                        Bologna, 1924.
Htn   Phil 1870.95.2*   Berkeley, G. Berkeley and Percival. Cambridge, 1914.
Phil 1870.95   Berkeley, G. Berkeley and Percival. Cambridge, 1914.
Phil 1870.73   Berkeley, G. Commonplace book. London, 1930.
Phil 1870.45.25   Berkeley, G. Dialoghi tra Hylas e Filonous. Bari, 1939.
Phil 1870.45.6   Berkeley, G. The dialogues between Hylas and Philonous.
                        N.Y., 1954.
Phil 1870.45.10   Berkeley, G. Dialogues entre Hylas et Philonous.
                        Paris, 1920.
Htn   Phil 1870.72*   Berkeley, G. A discourse addressed to magistrates and men
                        in authority. Dublin, 1738.
Phil 1870.45.21   Berkeley, G. Drei Dialoge zwischen Hylas und Philonous.
                        Berlin, 1955.
Phil 1870.45.20   Berkeley, G. Drei Dialoge zwischen Hylas und Philonous.
                        Leipzig, 1926.
Phil 1870.60.1.2   Berkeley, G. Essay towards a new theory. Dublin, 1709.
Htn   Phil 1870.60*   Berkeley, G. Essay towards a new theory of vision.
                        Dublin, 1709.
Htn   Phil 1870.60.1*   Berkeley, G. Essay towards a new theory of vision. 2d ed.
                        Dublin, 1709.
Htn   Phil 1870.65.9*   Berkeley, G. Extrait des recherches sur les vertus de
                        l'eau de goudron. Amsterdam, 1749.
Phil 1870.73.5   Berkeley, G. Le journal philosophique. Commonplace book.
                        Paris, 1908.
Phil 1870.75   Berkeley, G. Memoirs. 2nd ed. London, 1784.
Phil 1870.70   Berkeley, G. Miscellany containing several tracts on
                        various subjects. London, 1752.
Phil 1870.60.3A   Berkeley, G. A new theory of vision. London, 1906.
Phil 1870.73.18   Berkeley, G. Philosophical commentaries generally called
                        the commonplace book. London, 1944.
Phil 1870.22   Berkeley, G. Philosophical writings. Edinburgh, 1952.
Phil 1870.15   Berkeley, G. Philosophische Werke. Leipzig, 192-.
                        3v.
Phil 1870.73.13   Berkeley, G. Philosophisches Tagebuch (commonplace book).
                        Leipzig, 1926.
Phil 1870.40.25   Berkeley, G. Les principes de la connaissance humaine.
                        Paris, 1920.
Phil 1870.40.50   Berkeley, G. Principi della conoscenza umana.
                        Bologna, 1925.
Phil 1870.40.22   Berkeley, G. The principles of human knowledge.
                        London, 1942.
Phil 1870.65.5   Berkeley, G. Recherches sur les vertus de l'eau de
                        goudron. Amsterdam, 1745.
Phil 1870.65.8   Berkeley, G. Recherches sur les vertus de l'eau de
                        goudron. Genève, 1748.
Phil 1870.20A   Berkeley, G. Selections. Oxford, 1874.
Phil 1870.20.3   Berkeley, G. Selections (Fraser). 3rd ed. Oxford, 1884.
Phil 1870.20.4   Berkeley, G. Selections annotated. 5th ed. Oxford, 1899.
Phil 1870.65.15   Berkeley, G. Siris. Leipzig, 1915.
Phil 1870.66.5   Berkeley, G. La siris. Paris, 1920.
Htn   Phil 1870.65*   Berkeley, G. Siris: a chain of...reflexions.
                        Dublin, 1744.
Phil 1870.60.2   Berkeley, G. The theory of vision vindicated.
                        Cambridge, 1860.
Phil 1870.45.3   Berkeley, G. Three dialogues...Hylas and Philonous.
                        Chicago, 1901.
Htn   Phil 1870.45.1*   Berkeley, G. Three dialogues...Hylas and Philonous.
                        London, 1713.
Phil 1870.40.45   Berkeley, G. Tratto dei principii della cognoscenza umana
                        e tre dialogui. Bari, 1923.
Htn   Phil 1870.40.1*   Berkeley, G. Treatise...principles of human knowledge.
                        Dublin, 1710.
Htn   Phil 1870.40.2*   Berkeley, G. Treatise...principles of human knowledge.
                        London, 1734.
Phil 1870.40.3   Berkeley, G. Treatise...principles of human knowledge.
                        London, 1776.
Phil 1870.40.9   Berkeley, G. Treatise concerning the principles of human
                        knowledge. Chicago, 1878.
Phil 1870.40.13   Berkeley, G. A treatise concerning the principles of human
                        knowledge. Chicago, 1904.

Phil 1870.40.12 — Berkeley, G. A treatise concerning the principles of human knowledge. Philadelphia, 1881.

Phil 1870.60.15 — Berkeley, G. Versuch einer neuen Theorie der Gesichtswahrnehmung. Leipzig, 1912.

Phil 1870.10 — Berkeley, G. Works. London, 1820. 3v.

Phil 1870.11.5 — Berkeley, G. Works. London, 1853. 2v.

Phil 1870.10.5 — Berkeley, G. Works. London, 1908. 3v.

Phil 1870.17 — Berkeley, G. Works. London, 1948-53. 9v.

Phil 1870.12A — Berkeley, G. Works. Oxford, 1871. 4v.

Phil 1870.13A — Berkeley, G. Works. Oxford, 1901.

Phil 1870.79.5 — Pamphlet box. Berkeley, G.

Phil 1870.79 — Pamphlet box. Berkeley, G. German dissertations.

Phil 1870.93 — Berkeley. (David, M.) Paris, n.d.

Phil 1870.99 — Berkeley. (Didier, Jean.) Paris, 1911.

Phil 1870.84.1 — Berkeley. (Fraser, Alexander Campbell.) Edinburgh, 1881.

NEDL Phil 1870.84 — Berkeley. (Fraser, Alexander Campbell.) Philadelphia, 1881.

Phil 1870.84.2.3 — Berkeley. (Fraser, Alexander Campbell.) Philadelphia, 1899.

Phil 1870.130 — Berkeley. (Guéroult, Martial.) Paris, 1956.

Phil 1870.112 — Berkeley. (Hicks, G.D.) London, 1932.

Phil 1870.126 — Berkeley. (Warnock, G.J.) London, 1953.

Phil 1880.28 — Berkeley and his philosophy. (Bowen, F.) Cambridge, 1838-57. 5 pam.

Phil 1870.115 — Berkeley and Malebranche. (Luce, Arthur A.) London, 1934.

Htn Phil 1870.95.2* — Berkeley and Percival. (Berkeley, G.) Cambridge, 1914.

Phil 1870.95 — Berkeley and Percival. (Berkeley, G.) Cambridge, 1914.

Phil 1870.102 — Berkeley's Abhandlung über Principien der menschlichen Erkenntnis. (Ueberweg, F.) Berlin, 1869.

Phil 1870.111 — Berkeley's American sojourn. (Rand, Benjamin.) Cambridge, 1932.

Phil 1870.180 — Berkeley's analysis of preception. (Stack, George J.) The Hague, 1970.

Phil 1870.120A — Berkeley's argument about material substance. (Broad, C.D.) London, 1942.

Phil 1870.115.10 — Berkeley's immaterialism. (Luce, Arthur A.) London, 1945.

Phil 1870.170 — Berkeley's renovation of philosophy. (Ardley, Gavin W.R.) The Hague, 1968[1969]

Phil 1870.94 — Berkeleys System. (Cassirer, E.) Giessen, 1914.

Phil 1870.142 — Berkeley's theory of vision. (Armstrong, D.M.) Victoria, 1960.

Phil 5421.20.10 — Berkourt, L. Aggression; a social psychological analysis. N.Y., 1962.

Phil 3120.30.105 — Berkovits, Eliezer. A Jewish critique of the philosophy. N.Y., 1962.

Phil 5421.20.75 — Berkowitz, Leonard. Roots of aggression. 1. ed. N.Y., 1969.

Phil 1730.27.1 — Berlin, Isaiah. The age of enlightenment. Freeport, 1970.

Phil 2138.145 — Berlin, Isaiah. John Stuart Mill and the ends of life. London, 1960?

Phil 8876.123 — Berlin, Isaiah. Two concepts of liberty. Oxford, 1958.

Phil 5105.30.30 — Berlin, Isaiah. Two concepts of liberty. Oxford, 1959.

Phil 3246.299 — Berlin. Deutsche Staats Bibliothek. Johann Gottlieb Fichte, 1762-1962. Berlin, 1962.

Phil 176.221 — Berlin. Freie Universität. Freiheit als Problem der Wissenschaft. Berlin, 1962.

Phil 2520.240 — Berlin. Freie Universität. Gedenkfeier anlässlich des drei hundertjährigen Todestagen des Philosophen René Descartes. Berlin, 1950.

Phil 8980.15 — Berlin. Institut für Gesellschaftswissenschaften. Neues Leben. 1. Aufl. Berlin, 1957.

Phil 3425.28.5 — Berliner Schriften. (Hegel, Georg Wilhelm Friedrich.) Hamburg, 1956.

Phil 8612.37 — Berlinger, R. Das Nichts und der Tod. Frankfurt, 1954.

Phil 1701.30 — Berlinger, Rudolph. Das Werk der Freiheit. Frankfurt, 1959.

Phil 5520.429 — Berlyne, Daniel E. Structure and direction in thinking. N.Y., 1965.

Phil 8402.70 — Berlyne, Daniel Ellis. Aesthetics and psychology. N.Y., 1971.

Phil 5241.72 — Berman, Louis. The religion called behaviorism. N.Y., 1927.

Phil 5751.12 — Bermann, G. El determinismo en la ciencia y en la vida. Buenos Aires, 1920.

Phil 4359.1.83 — Bermann, G. José Ingenieros. Buenos Aires, 1926.

Phil 6990.3.38 — Bernadette and Lourdes. (Saint-Pierre, M. de.) N.Y., 1954.

Phil 6990.3.105 — Bernadette and Lourdes. (Stafford, Ann (pseud.).) London, 1967.

Phil 6990.44 — Bernadette of Lourdes. (Blanton, M.G.) London, 1939.

Phil 6990.3.60 — Bernadette Soubirous. (Groneman, William.) Leuven, 1933.

Phil 5241.106 — Bernal del Riesgo, A. Iniciación en la psicología. v.1-2. La Habana, 1936.

Phil 8402.20 — Bernard, Charles. Esthétique et critique. Paris, 1946.

Phil 2477.9.84 — Bernard, Claude. Philosophie, manuscrit inédit. Paris, 19- .

Phil 2477.9.84.2 — Bernard, Claude. Philosophie. Paris, 1954.

Phil 6400.2 — Bernard, D. De l'aphasie. Paris, 1885.

Phil 6400.2.2 — Bernard, D. De l'aphasie. Paris, 1889.

Phil 5876.35 — Bernard, Harold Wright. Adolescent development. Scranton, 1971.

Phil 9550.7 — Bernard, L.L. Transition to an objective standard of social control. Chicago, 1911.

Phil 2750.13.90 — Bernard, M. La philosophie religieuse de Gabriel Marcel. Le Puy, 1952.

Phil 9400.1.4 — Bernard, T. Comforts of old age. London, 1820.

Htn Phil 9400.1.3* — Bernard, T. Comforts of old age. N.Y., 1818.

Phil 9400.1 — Bernard, T. Spurrina...comforts of old age. London, 1816.

Phil 960.157 — Bernard, Theos. Philosophical foundations of India. London, 1945.

Phil 3821.21 — Bernard, Walter. The philosophy of Spinoza and Brunner. N.Y., 1934.

Phil 3120.2.110 — Bernard Bol'tsano. (Kolman, E.) Moskva, 1955.

Phil 3120.2.95 — Bernard Bolzano. (Fels, Heinrich.) Leipzig, 1929.

Phil 3120.2.101 — Bernard Bolzano. (Franzis, Emerich.) Münster, 1933.

Phil 3120.2.112 — Bernard Bolzano. (Kolman, E.) Berlin, 1963.

Phil 3120.2.20 — Bernard Bolzano - Gesamtausgabe. (Bolzano, Bernard.) Stuttgart, 1969.

Phil 3120.2.98 — Bernard Bolzano und sein Kreis. (Winter, E.) Leipzig, 1933.

Phil 1905.10.75 — Bernard Bosanquet and his friends. (Bosanquet, B.) London, 1935.

Phil 1905.10.90 — Bernard Bosanquet's philosophy of the state. Inaug.-Diss. (Pfannenstill, Bertil.) Lund, 1936.

Htn Phil 4932.2.30F* — Bernard de Clairvaux, St. Opera. n.p., 1508.

Phil 2128.85 — Bernard de Mandeville et la "Fable des Abeilles". Thèse. (Grégoire, F.) Nancy, 1947.

Phil 2128.83 — Bernard de Mandeville und die Bienenfabel. (Sakmann, Paul.) Freiburg, 1897.

Phil 2128.40A — Bernard de Mandeville's Bienenfabel. Diss. (Mandeville, B.) Halle, 1886. 2v.

Phil 4235.1.97 — Bernardino Telesio. (Abbagnano, Nicola.) Milano, 1941.

Phil 4235.1.85 — Bernardino Telesio. (Gentile, G.) Bari, 1911.

Phil 4235.1.90 — Bernardino Telesio. (Troilo, E.) Modena, 1910.

Phil 4235.1.82 — Bernardino Telesio ossia studi storici su l'idea della natura nel risorgimento italiano. (Fiorentino, Francesco.) Firenze, 1872-74. 2v.

Phil 2280.1.93 — Bernays, Paul. Das Moralprinzip bei Sidgwick und bei Kant. Göttingen, 1910.

Phil 7069.00.65 — Berndt, G.H. Das Buch der Wunder und der Geheimwissenschaften. 2. Aufl. v.1-2. Leipzig, 1900.

Phil 6980.105 — Berne, Eric. The mind in action. N.Y., 1947.

Phil 6985.40 — Berne, Eric. Principles of group treatment. N.Y., 1966.

Phil 6980.105.5 — Berne, Eric. Transactional analysis in psychotherapy. N.Y., 1961.

Phil 3450.32.80 — Der Berner Philosoph Carl Hebler. (Bártschi, Lina.) Bern, 1944.

Phil 176.50 — Bernès, M. Cours élémentaire de philosophie. Paris, n.d.

Phil 5241.80 — Bernhard, E.A. Philosophische und naturwissenschaftliche Grundlagen der Psychologie. Berlin, 1930.

Phil 3483.41 — Bernhardi, A.B. Gemeinfassliche Darstellung der Kantischen Lehren über Sittlichkeit, Freyheit, Gottheit und Unsterblichkeit. v.1-2. Freyberg, 1796-97.

Phil 525.54.5 — Bernhardische und Eckhartische Mystik. (Bernhart, J.) Kempten, 1912.

Phil 525.54.5 — Bernhart, J. Bernhardische und Eckhartische Mystik. Kempten, 1912.

Phil 525.54 — Bernhart, J. Die philosophische Mystik des Mittelalters. München, 1922.

Phil 6671.5.9 — Bernheim, H. Automatisme et suggestion. Paris, 1917.

Phil 6671.5.5 — Bernheim, H. De la suggestion. Paris, 1884.

Phil 6671.5 — Bernheim, H. Hypnotisme. Paris, 1891.

Phil 6671.5.3 — Bernheim, H. Hypnotisme and suggestion. Paris, 1910.

Phil 6671.5.4 — Bernheim, H. Die Suggestion und ihre Heilwirkung. Leipzig, 1888.

Phil 6400.7 — Bernheim, Hippolyte. Doctrine de l'aphasie. Paris, 1907.

Phil 8402.54 — Bernheimer, Richard. The nature of representation. N.Y., 1961.

Phil 3483.82 — Berni, M. Il criticismo kantiano. Verona, 1960.

Phil 8626.10 — Bernies, V. Spiritualité et immortalité. Paris, 1901.

Phil 5649.28 — Berning, A. Experimentelle Untersuchungen von Bewegungsstilen. Inaug. Diss. Bonn, 1960.

Phil 3850.51 — Berning, V. Das Denken Herman Schells. Essen, 1964.

Phil 282.17 — Bernoulli, C. Romantiske Naturphilosophie. Jena, 1926.

Phil 3640.90.5 — Bernoulli, Carl A. Franz Overbeck und Friedrich Nietzsche. Jena, 1908. 2v.

Phil 3640.90.7 — Bernoulli, Carl A. Nietzsche und die Schweiz. Leipzig, 1922.

Phil 5640.2 — Bernstein, J. Five senses of man. N.Y., 1876.

Phil 5640.2.4 — Bernstein, J. Five senses of man. N.Y., 1890.

Phil 5640.2.3 — Bernstein, J. Die fünf Sinne des Menschen. Leipzig, 1875.

Phil 5640.2.5 — Bernstein, J. Les sens. 5e éd. Paris, 1893.

Phil 6671.28.6 — Bernstein, Morey. The search for Bridey Murphy. Garden City, N.Y., 1965.

Phil 6671.28 — Bernstein, Morey. The search for Bridey Murphy. London, 1956.

Phil 6671.28.5 — Bernstein, Morey. The search for Bridey Murphy. 1. ed. Garden City, N.Y., 1956.

Phil 1955.6.210 — Bernstein, Richard. John Dewey. N.Y., 1966.

Phil 2225.5.125 — Bernstein, Richard J. Perspectives on Peirce. New Haven, 1965.

Phil 1750.866 — Bernstein, Richard Jacob. Praxis and action. Philadelphia, 1971.

Phil 3915.154 — Bernstein, Xenja. Die Kunst nach Wilhelm Wundt. Nürnberg, 1914.

Phil 7112.5 — Bernstien, Abraham Emmanuel. Explorations of a hypnotist. London, 1959.

Phil 5751.20 — Berofsky, Bernard. Free will and determinism. N.Y., 1966.

Phil 990.25 — Beroukhim, Moussa. La pensée iranienne à travers l'histoire. Thèse. Paris, 1938.

X Cg Phil 1701.7 — Berr, Henri. Avenir de la philosophie. Paris, 1899.

Phil 2610.105 — Berr, Henri. Du scepticisme de Gassendi. Paris, 1960.

Phil 1701.7.5 — Berr, Henri. La synthèse des connaissances et l'histoire. Thèse. Paris, 1898.

Phil 8626.12 — Berry, J.B.N. Some assurances of immortality. N.Y., 1909.

Phil 6111.44.5 — Berry, Richard J.A. Your brain and its story. London, 1939.

Phil 4260.125 — Berry, Thomas. The historical theory of Giambattista Vico. Washington, 1949.

Phil 8876.150 — Bersandius, J. Venatio hominum. Francofonte, 1677.

Phil 3552.313 — Berse, Max. Über Leibniz: Leibniz und seine Ideology. Jena, 1946.

Phil 8876.15 — Bersot, D.P.E. Un moraliste. Paris, 1882.

Phil 8685.21 — Bersot, E. Du spiritualisme et de la nature. Paris, 1846.

Phil 176.21.5 — Bersot, P.E. Essais de philosophie et de morale. Paris, 1864. 2v.

Phil 176.21 — Bersot, P.E. Libre philosophie. Paris, 1868.

Phil 6671.6 — Bersot, P.E. Mesmer, le magnétism animal. Paris, 1879.

Phil 1506.11 — Bertala, E. Saggi e studi di filosofia medievale. Padova, 1951.

Phil 5241.170 — Bertalanffy, Ludwig von. Robots, men, and minds; psychology in the modern world. N.Y., 1967.

Phil 8876.85 — Bertauld, Alfred. L'ordre social et l'ordre moral. Paris, 1874.

Phil 270.3 — Bertauld, P.A. Introduction à la recherche des causes premières. Paris, 1876.

Phil 3790.10.91 — Bertele, H. Paul Rée's Lehre vom Gewissen. Thesis. München, 1927.

Phil 3552.254 — Bertereau, A. Leibnitz considéré comme historien de la philosophie. Thèse. Paris, 1843.

Phil 4001.1 — Berthé de Besaucèle, Louis. Les Cartériens d'Italie. Thèse. Paris, 1920.

Phil 8402.61 — Berthelemy, J. Traité d'esthétique. Paris, 1964.

Phil 8951.28 — Berthélemy, Jean. Structure et dimensions de la liberté. Paris, 1956.

Phil 7060.105 — Berthelen, K.A. Die Klopf- und Spussgeister. Zittau, 1914.

Phil 645.15 — Berthelot, M. Science et libre pensée. 2e éd. Paris, 1905.

Phil 176.55 — Berthelot, René. Un romantisme utilitaire. Paris, 1911. 3v.

Phil 8610.883.10 — Berthet, André. Les débats de la conscience, catéchisme laïque. Paris, 1883.

X Cg Phil 2295.80 — Berthold, G. John Toland und der Monismus der Gegenwart. Heidelberg, 1876.

Phil 801.24   Berthre de Bowinisseaux, P.V.J. La charlatanisme philosophique de tous les âges dévoilé. Paris, 1807.

Phil 4065.82   Berti, D. Giordano Bruno da Nola. Torino, 1889.
Htn   Phil 4073.81*   Berti, D. Nuovi documenti su T. Campanella. Roma, 1881.
Phil 525.113   Bertin, G. I mistice medievali. Milano, 1944.
Phil 365.26   Bertinaria, F. La dottrina dell'evoluzione e la fil. Genova, 1876.
Phil 5247.35.5   Bertinaria, F. La psicologia fisica ed iperfisica di Hoenato Wronski. Torino, 1877.
Phil 4001.2   Bertinaria, F. Sull'indole e le vicende della filosofia italiana. Torino, 1846.
Phil 5850.135.15   Bertine, Eleanor. How to interview. N.Y., 1931.
Phil 5850.135.20   Bertine, Eleanor. How to interview. 2. ed. N.Y., 1934.
Phil 5850.131   Bertine, Eleanor. Human relationships. 1. ed. N.Y., 1958.
Phil 6319.1.240   Bertine, Eleanor. Jung's contribution to our time. N.Y., 1968.
Phil 6311.38   Bertine, Eleanor. Menschliche Beziehungen. Zürich, 1957.
Phil 1701.12   Bertini, G. Maria. Storia della filosofia moderna. pt.1. Torino, 1881.
Phil 176.128   Bertini, G.M. Idea di una filosofia della vita. Firenze, 1933.
Phil 5041.38   Bertini, G.M. La logica. Roma, 1880.
Phil 476.6   Bertini, G.M. Schiarimenti sulla controversia fra spiritualismo e materialismo. Torino, 1870.
Phil 4070.4.30   Bertini, Giovanni M. Scritti filosofici. Milano, 1942.
Phil 1106.10   Bertling, Oskar. Geschichte der alten Philosophie. Leipzig, 1907.
Phil 8876.156   Bertocci, Peter. Personality and the good. N.Y., 1963.
Phil 8656.27   Bertocci, Peter Anthony. The empirical argument for God in late British thought. Cambridge, 1938.
Phil 8656.27.5   Bertocci, Peter Anthony. The person God is. N.Y., 1970.
Phil 9075.86   Bertola, Ermenegildo. Il problema della coscienza nella téologia Monastica del XII secolo. Padova, 1970.
Phil 7068.64   Bertolacci, W.R. Christian spiritualism. London, 1864.
Phil 2725.50   Bertoni, Italo. Il neoilluminismo etico di André Lalande. Milano, 1965.
Phil 1106.18   Bertozzi, A. Saggi sul pensiero antico. Padova, 1960.
Phil 3640.121.4   Bertram, Ernst. Nietzsche; essai de mythologie. Paris, 1932.
Phil 3640.121.3   Bertram, Ernst. Nietzsche; Versuch einer Mythologie. Berlin, 1929.
Phil 3640.121.2   Bertram, Ernst. Nietzsche. Berlin, 1918.
Phil 3640.121.3.5   Bertram, Ernst. Nietzsche. Bonn, 1965.
Phil 5374.6   Bertrand, A. L'aperception du corps humain. Paris, 1880.
Phil 6669.1   Bertrand, A. Du magnetisme animal en France. Paris, 1826.
Phil 86.1   Bertrand, A. Lexique de philosophie. Paris, 1892.
Phil 176.86   Bertrand, A. Principes de philosophie. Paris, 1893.
Phil 7085.7   Bertrand, A. Traité du somnabulisme. Paris, 1823.
Phil 7076.12   Bertrand, Alexandre Jacques François. Extase. Paris, 1826.
Phil 2477.8.83   Bertrand, F.L. Alfred Binet et son oeuvre. Paris, 1930.
Phil 2477.8.84   Bertrand, F.L. Alfred Binet et son oeuvre. Thèse. Paris, 1930.
Phil 2805.88   Bertrand, J.L.F. Blaise Pascal. Paris, 1891.
Phil 1750.425   Bertrand, Jean. L'énergie spirituelle et la destinée humaine. Lyon, 1956.
Phil 282.20   Bertrand, René. Le mystère de vivre. Monaco, 1957.
Phil 5241.65.10   Bertrand-Barraud, D. De la nature affective de la conscience. Paris, 1927.
Phil 325.4   Bertrand-Barraud, D. Des bases critique d'un empirisme psychologique. Paris, 1926.
Phil 5241.65   Bertrand-Barraud, D. Les valeurs affectives et l'exercice discursif de la pensée. Paris, 1924.
Phil 5241.65.5   Bertrand-Barraud, D. Les valeurs affectives et l'exercice discursif de la pensée. Thèse. Paris, 1924.
Phil 6111.3   Bertrand de Saint-Germain, Guillaume Scipion. Des manifestations de la vie et de l'intelligence. Paris, 1848.
Phil 2255.1.190   Bertrand Russell; a collection of critical essays. 1st ed. Garden City, 1972.
Phil 165.393   Bertrand Russell, philosopher of the century. (Schoenman, Ralph.) London, 1967.
Phil 2255.1.112   Bertrand Russell. (Dorward, Alan.) London, 1951.
Phil 2255.1.110   Bertrand Russell. (Leggett, H.W.) London, 1949.
Phil 2255.1.111   Bertrand Russell. (Leggett, H.W.) N.Y., 1950.
Phil 2255.1.160   Bertrand Russell. (Watling, John.) Edinburgh, 1970.
Phil 2255.1.118   Bertrand Russell. (Wood, Alan.) London, 1957.
Phil 2255.1.128   Bertrand Russell: a life. (Gottschalk, Herbert.) London, 1965.
Phil 2255.1.95   Bertrand Russell: philosopher and humanist. (Lewis, John.) London, 1968.
Phil 2255.1.130A   Bertrand Russell and the British tradition in philosophy. (Pears, David Francis.) London, 1967.
Phil 2255.1.35   The Bertrand Russell case. (Dewey, John.) N.Y., 1941.
Phil 2255.1.127   Bertrand Russell on education. (Park, J.) Columbus, 1963.
Phil 2255.1.58A   Bertrand Russell speaks his mind. 1st ed. (Russell, Bertrand Russell.) Cleveland, 1960.
Phil 2255.1.115   Bertrand Russell's construction of the external world. (Fritz, C.A.) London, 1952.
Phil 2255.1.150   Bertrand Russell's philosophy of language. (Clark, Robert J.) The Hague, 1969.
Phil 2255.1.126   Bertrand Russell's philosophy of morals. (Aiken, L.W.) N.Y., 1963.
Phil 2255.1.113   Bertrand Russell's theories of causation. Inaug. Diss. (Götlind, E.) Uppsala, 1952.
Phil 2255.1.155   Bertrand Russell's theory of knowledge. (Eames, Elizabeth Ramsden.) London, 1969.
Phil 4225.1.95   Bertrando Spaventa. (Gentile, Giovanni.) Firenze, 1920.
Phil 8663.3.85   Bertron, Ottilie. Review of Col. Ingersoll's attacks upon Christianity. Philadelphia, 1889.
Phil 176.63   Bertz, Eduard. Weltharmonie monistische Betrachtungen. Dresden, 1908.
Phil 1540.85   Bérubé, Camille. La connaissance de l'individuel au Moyen Âge. Montréal, 1964.
Phil 9075.24   Die Berührung und Verwerthung der Gewissens. (Hasenclever, K.H.) Karleruhe, 1877.
Phil 6122.5.3   Der Beruf des Körpers in Beziehung auf den Geist. (Moore, G.) Leipzig, 1850.
Phil 5548.146   Der Berufserfolg als Motivationsphänomen. (Stückmann, Günther.) Berlin, 1968.
Phil 5520.650   Bervi, Vasilii V. Kritika osnovnykh idei estestvoznaniia. Photoreproduction. Sankt-Peterburg, 1904.
Phil 974.2.25   Besant, A. The theosophical society and H.P.B. Three articles. London, 1891?
Phil 978.6   Pamphlet box. Besant, A. Minor writings.
Phil 978.6.15   Besant, Annie. The ancient wisdom. London, 1897.
X Cg   Phil 978.6.86   Besant, Annie. Annie Besant: an autobiography. London, 1908.

Phil 978.6.85   Besant, Annie. Autobiographical sketches. Photoreproduction. London, 1885.
Phil 978.6.30   Besant, Annie. Birth and evolution of the soul. 2nd ed. London, 1903.
Phil 978.6.9   Besant, Annie. The building of the kosmos. London, 1894.
Phil 978.6.50   Besant, Annie. The changing world. Chicago, 1910.
Phil 978.6.63.5   Besant, Annie. Death - and after? London, 1893.
Phil 978.6.63   Besant, Annie. Death - and after? London, 1898.
Phil 978.6.25   Besant, Annie. Esoteric christianity. N.Y., 1902.
Phil 978.6.13   Besant, Annie. Essays and addresses. v.2-4. London, 1912-13. 3v.
Phil 978.6.20   Besant, Annie. Evolution of life and form. 2nd ed. London, 1900.
Phil 978.6.64   Besant, Annie. Karma. (Theosophical manual IV). London, 1897.
Phil 978.6.3   Besant, Annie. On the nature and the existence of God. London, 1875.
Phil 978.6.62   Besant, Annie. Reincarnation (Theosophical manual II). London, 1897.
Phil 978.6.60   Besant, Annie. The seven principles of man. London, 1892.
Phil 978.6.61   Besant, Annie. The seven principles of man. London, 1892.
Phil 978.6.61.5   Besant, Annie. The seven principles of man. 15th ed. London, 189-?
Phil 978.6.35   Besant, Annie. Some problems of life. 2nd ed. London, 1904.
Phil 978.6.70   Besant, Annie. The sphinx of theosophy. London, 189-?
Phil 978.6.45   Besant, Annie. Study in consciousness. London, 1904.
Phil 978.6.40   Besant, Annie. Theosophy and new psychology. London, 1904.
Phil 978.6.88   Besant, Annie. Theosophy and the theosophical society. Adyar, 1913.
Phil 978.6.72   Besant, Annie. Thought-forms. Wheaton, Ill., 1969.
Phil 978.6.44A   Besant, Annie. Thought power; its control and culture. London, 1901.
Phil 978.6.43   Besant, Annie. Thought power; its control and culture. London, 1906.
Phil 978.6.4   Besant, Annie. Why I became a theosophist. N.Y., 1890.
Phil 978.6.5   Besant, Annie. Why I became a theosophist. N.Y., 1891.
Phil 165.340A   Besch, L. Menschenbild und Lebensführung. München, 1963.
Phil 4210.194   Beschin, G. La comunicazione delle persone nella filosofia. Milano, 1964.
Phil 2725.35.87   Beschin, Giuseppe. Il tempo e la libertà in L. Lavelle. Milano, 1964.
Phil 6955.17   Beschouwingen over Psychopathenstrafrecht. (Feber, G.H.A.) Zwolle, 1932.
Phil 5520.580   Die Beschreibung des Zusammenhangs von Sprache und Denken in der Sprachphilosophie von Locke bis Wittgenstein. (Schmidt, Siegfried J.) n.p., 1965.
Phil 5204.8.2   Beschrijvend en verklarend woordenboek der psychologie. 2. Druk. (Essen, Jac van.) Haarlem, 1953.
Phil 8980.346.5   Besedy o kommunisticheskoi morali. (Dzhafarli, Teimuraz M.) Moskva, 1970.
Phil 8402.37   Besenbruch, Walter. Zum Problem des Typischen in der Kunst. Weimar
Phil 6990.18   Die Besessenen im neuen Testament. (Nanz, C.F.) Reutlingen, 1840.
Phil 8644.3   Beside the new-made grave. (Turner, F.H.) Boston, 1906.
Phil 665.43.2   Beskow, B. von. Om själens helsa. 2e uppl. Stockholm, 1867.
Phil 665.43   Beskow, B. von. Om själens helsa. 4e uppl. Stockholm, 1880.
Phil 9120.8   Le besoin et la devoir religieux. (Sérol, Maurice.) Paris, 1908.
Phil 6400.5.5   Eine besondere Art der Wortblindhut, Dyslehre. (Bulin, René.) Wiesbaden, 1887.
Phil 6016.1.5   Besonderephysiognomische und chromantische Anmerkungen. (Goclenius, R.) Hamburg, 1692.
Phil 2477.12   Bespaloff, R. Cheninement et carrefours. Paris, 1938.
Phil 3483.84   Besse, Guy. La morale selon Kant et selon Marx. Paris, 196-.
Phil 3483.2   Bessel-Hagen, F. Die Grabstätte Immanuel Kants. Königsberg, 1880.
Phil 5635.33   Besser, L. Was ist Empfindung? Bonn, 1881.
Phil 5751.9   Bessmer, Julius. Das menschliche Wollen. Freiburg, 1915.
Htn   Phil 5041.31*   Best, William. A concise system of logics. N.Y., 1796.
Phil 8894.28   The best life; an address. (Thwing, C.F.) N.Y., 1898.
Phil 7069.24.50   Besterman, T. Crystal-gazing: a study in the history, distribution, theory, and practice of scrying. London, 1924.
Phil 7069.34.5   Besterman, T. Inquiry into the unknown. London, 1934.
Phil 974.4.25   Besterman, T. Mrs. Annie Besant. London, 1934.
Phil 7069.30.1   Besterman, T. Some modern mediums. London, 1930.
Phil 2648.96   Besthern, Rudolf. Textkritische Studien zum Werk Holbachs. Berlin, 1969.
Phil 3246.35   Die Bestimmung der Menschen. (Fichte, Johann Gottlieb.) Berlin, 1825.
Phil 3246.34.2   Die Bestimmung der Menschen. (Fichte, Johann Gottlieb.) Frankfurt, 1800.
Htn   Phil 3246.34*   Die Bestimmung des Menschen. (Fichte, Johann Gottlieb.) Berlin, 1800.
Phil 3246.35.3A   Die Bestimmung des Menschen. (Fichte, Johann Gottlieb.) Leipzig, 1879.
Phil 3246.35.8   Die Bestimmung des Menschen. (Fichte, Johann Gottlieb.) Leipzig, 1944.
Phil 3246.35.10   Die Bestimmung des Menschen. (Fichte, Johann Gottlieb.) Stuttgart, 1966.
Phil 3246.35.7   Die Bestimmung des Menschen. 2. Aufl. (Fichte, Johann Gottlieb.) Berlin, 1801.
Phil 3246.35.8.5   Die Bestimmung des Menschen. 2. Aufl. (Fichte, Johann Gottlieb.) Leipzig, 1944.
Phil 8951.1   Bestmann, H.J. Geschichte der christlichen Sitte. Nödling, 1880-85. 2v.
Phil 176.240   Betancur, Cayetano. Filosofos y filosofias. Bogota, 1969.
Phil 3425.201   De beteekenis van de Hegel-studie voor onzen tijd. (Boer, J. de.) Baarn, 1915.
Phil 2262.80   De beteekenis van Shaftesbury in de Engelsche ethiek. Proefschrift. (Bierens de Haan, J.D.) Utrecht, 1891.
Phil 5400.130   De betekenis van de gelaatsexpressie. (Frijda, N.H.) Amsterdam, 1956.
Phil 8125.18   Betgmann, Ernst. Die Begrundung der deutschen Ästhetik durch...Baumgarten und...Meier. Leipzig, 1911.
Phil 5066.195   Beth, Evert W. Formal methods. Dordrecht, 1962.
Phil 5041.58.8   Beth, Evert Willem. Aspects of modern logic. Dordrecht, 1970.
Phil 3120.32.30   Beth, Evert Willem. Door wetenschap tot wijsheid. Assen, 1964.
Phil 5011.7   Beth, Evert Willem. Geschiedenis der logica. Den Haag, 1948.

Phil 5041.58.7   Beth, Evert Willem. Moderne logica. 2. druk. Assen, 1967.

Phil 3120.32.21   Beth, Evert Willem. Science a road to wisdom: collected philosophical studies. Dordrecht, 1968.

Phil 5041.58   Beth, Evert Willem. Summulae logicales. Groningen, 1942.

Phil 1801.7.2A   Bethell, S.L. The cultural revolution of the seventeenth century. N.Y., 1951.

Phil 3625.8.31   Betrachtung über den Fehler der menschlichen Tugenden. (Meier, Georg Friedrich.) Halle, 1755.

Phil 182.97   Betrachtungen aus der Spekulativen Weltweisheit. (Herz, M.) Königsberg, 1771.

Htn   Phil 3801.488*   Betrachtungen über den gegenwartigen Zustand der Philosophie...Schellingsche Philosophie. (Klein, Georg M.) Nürnberg, 1813.

Phil 8587.14   Betrachtungen über die Religion. v.1-2. (Heydenreichs, K.H.) Leipzig, 1904.

Phil 8589.2   Betrachtungen über die vornehmsten Wahrheiten der Religion. 5. Aufl. (Jerusalem, J.F.W.) Braunschweig, 1776-91. 3v.

Phil 5822.3   Betrachtungen über Wirbelthiere. (Matthes, B.) Dresden, 1861.

Phil 6687.2   Betrachtungen und der animal Magnetismus. (Richter, J.A.L.) Leipzig, 1817.

Phil 3549.2.60   Betractungen der Stille und Besinnlichkeit. (Keyserling, Hermann.) Jena, 1942.

Phil 8587.14.3   Berücksichtigen über die Philosophie. (Heydenreichs, K.H.) Leipzig, 1790-91. 2 pam.

Phil 805.2.5   Beträge zur Geschichte der Philosophie. (Fries, J.F.) Heidelberg, 1819.

Phil 805.25   Beträge zur Geschichte der Philosophie. pt.1-12. (Fuelleborn, Georg Gustav.) Bruxelles, 1968. 5v.

Phil 2115.128   Betraktelse af Lockes. (Rosell, Anton.) Upsala, 1857.

Phil 4515.90   Betraktelser i samhällslären med granskning af Boströmska statslaräns grundinier. (Theorell, Sven L.) Stockholm, 1860.

Phil 493.3   Betraktelseröfver den materialistiska och idealistiska verldsäsigten. (Svenson, S.G.) Stockholm, 1871.

Phil 5249.6.25   The betrayal of intelligence. (Jastrow, J.) N.Y., 1938.

Phil 4210.135.10   Bettanini, A. Anniversario della festa secolare per Antonio Rosmini. n.p., 1901.

Phil 5871.40   Bettelheim, Bruno. The children of the dream. N.Y., 1969.

Phil 6980.106   Bettelheim, Bruno. The empty fortress. N.Y., 1967.

Phil 5832.25   Das Betteln der Zoo-Tiere. (Winkelstraeter, K.H.) Bern, 1960.

Phil 1750.705   Better part of valor; More, Erasmus, Colet and Vives, on humanism, war, and peace. (Adams, Robert.) Seattle, 1962.

Phil 9182.4.15   The better way. (Wagner, Charles.) N.Y., 1903.

Phil 6990.3.116   Bettez, Norbert Marie. Lourdes et Fatima. Montréal, 1967.

Phil 9230.14   Betting and gambling. (Green, Peter.) London, 1927.

Phil 5465.7   Betts, G.H. The distribution and functions of mental imagery. N.Y., 1909.

Phil 8622.2.5   Between faith and thought: reflections and suggestions. (Kroner, Richard.) N.Y., 1966.

Phil 9220.12   Between friends. (Price, W.J.) Norwood, Mass., 1934.

Phil 7069.67.50   Between heaven and earth, adventures in the search of the nature of man. (Andreas, Peter.) Toronto, 1967.

Phil 3120.30.72   Between man and man. (Buber, Martin.) London, 1947.

Phil 5068.8   Between physics and philosophy. (Frank, P.) Cambridge, 1941.

Phil 7069.64.20   Between two worlds. (Fodor, Nandor.) West Nyack, 1966.

Phil 5520.310   Betydningsproblemer. (Nordisk Sommeruniversitet.) Oslo, 1954.

Phil 5648.22   Betz, Dieter. Untersuchungen im haptischen Raum. Diss. Hamburg, 1964.

Phil 332.9   Betz, H.J. Ervaringswijsbegeerte. 's-Gravenhage, 1881.

Phil 3821.7   Betz, H.J. Levenschets van Baruch de Spinoza. 's Gravenhage, 1876.

Phil 3821.7.7   Betz, H.J. Spinoza en de vrijheid. 's Gravenhage, 1877.

Phil 3821.7.5   Betz, H.J. Spinoza en Kant. 's Gravenhage, 1883.

Phil 5241.47   Betz, W. Psychologie des Denkens. Leipzig, 1918.

Phil 9035.96   Betzendahl, Walter. Der menschliche Charakter in Wertung und Forschung. Paderborn, 1956.

Phil 4200.1.81   Betzendörfer, Walter. Die Lehre von der zweifachen Wahrheit bei Petrus Pomponatius. Inaug. Diss. Tübingen, 1919.

Phil 5850.130   Beuesch, H. Wissenschaft der Menschenbehandlung. Heidelberg, 1958.

Htn   Phil 5041.11*   Beurhusius, F. In P. Rami. London, 1581.

Phil 3850.24.90   Beuschlein, K. Die Möglichkeit der Gotteserkenntnis in der Philosophie Gideon Spickers. Diss. Würzburg, 1914.

Phil 1200.14.5   Bevan, E.R. Stoïciens et sceptiques. Paris, 1927.

Phil 1200.14   Bevan, E.R. Stoics and sceptics. Oxford, 1913.

Phil 8581.72   Bevan, E.R. Symbolism and belief. London, 1938.

Phil 6111.29   Bevan, J.O. The genesis and evolution of the individual soul. London, 1909.

Phil 801.12   Bevan, J.O. Handbook of history and development of philosophy. London, 1916.

Phil 8876.43   Beveridge, A.J. Work and habits. Philadelphia, 1908.

Phil 9341.16   Beveridge, Albert J. The young man and the world. N.Y., 1906.

Htn   Phil 2295.86*   Beverley, Thomas. Christianity the great mystery; answer to a late treatise. Dondon, 1696.

Phil 5374.31.5   Bevidsthedens form. (Nasgaard, S.) Kóbenhavn, 1922.

Phil 4462.1.30   Bevilaqua, Clovis. Esboços e fragmentos. Rio de Janeiro, 1899.

Phil 3850.22.95   Die Bewahrung der Vernunft. Inaug. Diss. (Herzog, Reinhart.) München, 1967.

Phil 7069.38.30   Beware familiar spirits. (Mulholland, J.) N.Y., 1938.

Phil 3625.8.57   Beweis: dass' keine Materie dencken könne. 2e Aufl. (Meier, Georg Friedrich.) Halle, 1751. 7 pam.

Phil 672.2   Beweis aus der neueren Raumtheorie. (Bellermann, G.) Berlin, 1889.

Phil 3625.8.58   Beweis dass die menschliche Seele ewig Lebt. (Meier, Georg Friedrich.) Halle, 1751.

Phil 8599.6   Beweis dass Gott die menschen bereits durch seine Offenbarung in der Natur zur seligkeit führt. (Töllner, J.G.) Züllichau, 1766.

Phil 8662.12   Der Beweis vom dasein Gottes. (Huhn, Friedrich.) Berlin, 1927.

Phil 8635.6   Die Beweise für die Unsterblichkeit der Seele. (Kneib, P.) Freiburg, 1903.

Phil 3625.8.55   Beweiss: das keine Materie dencken Könne. (Meier, Georg Friedrich.) Halle, 1742.

Phil 3494.19.40   Die Bewersführung in der Kritik der reinen Vernunft. (Marcus, Ernst.) Essen, 1914.

Phil 8832.8   The bewildered age. (Held, Virginia.) N.Y., 1962.

Phil 978.118   Bewisstseinsfragen des Erziehers. (Heuser, Annie.) Dornach, 1966.

Phil 8581.79   Bewkes, E.G. Experience, reason and faith. N.Y., 1940.

Phil 5500.2.5   Die bewusste Beziehung. (Schrader, E.) Leipzig, 1893.

Phil 6319.1.30   Bewusstes und Unbewusstes. (Jung, C.G.) Frankfurt, 1957.

Phil 5722.20   Bewusstsein, Unbewusstes, Unterbewusstes. (Grau, Kurt Joachim.) München, 1922.

Phil 5374.26   Das Bewusstsein. (Fischer, J.C.) Leipzig, 1874.

Phil 5374.17   Das Bewusstsein. (Rehmke, J.) Heidelberg, 1910.

Phil 5374.25   Das Bewusstsein. (Schlegel, Emil.) Stuttgart, 1891.

Phil 5374.156   Bewusstsein als Verhangnis. (Seidel, A.) Bonn, 1927.

Phil 335.1.5   Das Bewusstsein der Aussenwelt. (Eisler, Rudolf.) Leipzig, 1901.

Phil 341.2   Das Bewusstsein der Transcendenz. (Koch, Max.) Halle an der Saale, 1895.

Phil 1750.75   Bewusstsein und Existenz. (Brecht, Franz Josef.) Bremen, 1948.

Phil 5374.11.3   Das Bewusstsein und sein Object. (Wolff, J.) Berlin, 1889.

Phil 5374.16   Bewusstsein und Unbewusstes. (Herbertz, R.) Köln, n.d.

Phil 8643.27   Bewusstsein und Unsterblichkeit. (Schleich, Carl L.) Berlin, 1922.

Phil 5251.21   Der Bewusstseinsmechanismus. (Langwieser, Karl.) Leipzig, 1897.

Phil 341.8   Das Bewusstseinsproblem. (Kehr, Theodor.) Tübingen, 1916.

Phil 575.28   Das Bewusstseinsproblem. (Schulz, Bernhard.) Wiesbaden, 1915.

Phil 3935.1.30   Bewusstseinsstellung und Geschichte. (Yorck von Wartenburg, Paul.) Tübingen, 1956.

Phil 6317.9.5   Bewusstseinstypen und ihre Beziehung zur Psychopathologie. (Hoop, J.H. van der.) Bern, 1937.

Phil 5640.22   Bewusstseinsvorgang und Gehirnprozess. (Semon, R.) Wiesbaden, 1920.

Phil 3425.619   De bewustwording; beschouwingen bij de fenomenologie van de geest van Hegel. (Flam, Leopold.) Bruxelles, 1966.

Phil 176.93   Bexell, Carl E. Samvetet i forhallaude till natur. Jönköping, 1840.

Phil 5520.78   Beyer, Alfred. Der Sieg des Denkens. Berlin, 192-.

Phil 1925.83   Beyer, Joseph. Ralph Cudworth als Ethiker, Staats-Philosoph und Usthetiker auf Grund des gedruckten Schriften. Inaug. Diss. Bottrop, 1935.

Phil 4600.4.85   Beyer, Nils. Bengt Lidforss. Stockholm, 1968.

Phil 3425.595.7   Beyer, W.R. Georg Wilhelm Friedrich Hegel in Nürnberg 1808-1816. Nürnberg, 1966.

Phil 3425.595.2   Beyer, W.R. Hegel-Bilder; Kritik der Hegel-Deutungen. 2. Aufl. Berlin, 1967.

Phil 3425.595   Beyer, W.R. Hegel-Bilder. Berlin, 1964.

Phil 3425.380   Beyer, W.R. Zwischen Phänomenologie und Logik. Frankfurt, 1955.

Phil 1740.20   Beyer, Wilhelm Raimund. Vier Kritiken. Heidegger, Sartre, Adorno, Lukácz. Köln, 1970.

Phil 7069.29.50   Beyond, a continuation of the seekers. (Lascelles, (pseud.) London, 1929.

Phil 7068.96.30   Beyond. (Hubbard, H.S.) Boston, 1896.

Phil 8581.57   Beyond agnosticism, a book for tired mechanists. (Bell, Bernard I.) N.Y., 1929.

Phil 535.35   Beyond belief and unbelief. (Leon, Philip.) London, 1965.

Phil 9495.168   Beyond birth control; the Christian experience of sex. (Callahan, Sidney Cornelia.) N.Y., 1968.

Phil 9075.36   Beyond conscience. (Smith, T.V.) N.Y., 1934.

Phil 192.67.15   Beyond existentialism. (Rintelen, Fritz J. von.) London, 1961.

Phil 5258.120.20A   Beyond freedom and dignity. 1st ed. (Skinner, Burrhus F.) N.Y., 1971.

Phil 6310.12   Beyond Freud. (Anderson, C.M.) London, 1958.

Phil 3640.31.5A   Beyond good and evil. (Nietzsche, Friedrich.) Chicago, 1949.

Phil 3640.31A   Beyond good and evil. (Nietzsche, Friedrich.) N.Y., 1907.

Phil 3640.31.3   Beyond good and evil. (Nietzsche, Friedrich.) N.Y., 1917.

Phil 3640.31.9   Beyond good and evil. (Nietzsche, Friedrich.) N.Y., 1917.

Phil 3640.31.4   Beyond good and evil. (Nietzsche, Friedrich.) N.Y., 1924.

Phil 1750.145   Beyond humanism. (Hartshore, Charles.) Chicago, 1937.

Phil 7069.38.59   Beyond mortal cognition. (Thomas, J.F.) Boston, 1937.

Phil 7069.37.12   Beyond life's sunset. (Thomas, Charles D.) London, 194-.

Phil 7069.30.32   Beyond our ken. (Stallard, C.L.) London, 1930.

Phil 8666.16.5   Beyond personality; the Christian idea of God. (Lewis, Clive Staples.) London, 1945.

Phil 8583.28.20   Beyond politics. (Dawson, Christopher H.) London, 1939.

Phil 6327.4.23A   Beyond psychology. (Rank, Otto.) Camden, 1941.

Phil 630.50   Beyond realism and idealism. (Urban, W.M.) London, 1949.

Phil 2120.13   Beyond scepticism and realism. (Laszlo, Ervin.) The Hague, 1966.

Phil 5249.26   Beyond sense perception. 1. ed. (Jeffrey, Melville.) Los Angeles, 1953.

Phil 7069.67.75   Beyond space and time. (Ebon, Martin.) N.Y., 1967.

Phil 176.42.15   The beyond that is within. (Boutroux, E.) London, 1912.

Phil 7069.10.30   Beyond the borderline of life. (Myers, Gustavus.) Boston 1910.

Phil 6128.50   Beyond the clinical frontiers. (Strecker, E.A.) N.Y., 1940.

Phil 8712.26   Beyond the horizon of science. (Williston, A.L.) Boston, 1944.

Phil 6315.2.70   Beyond the pleasure principle. (Freud, Sigmund.) N.Y., 1924.

Phil 6315.2.59.10   Beyond the pleasure principle. (Freud, Sigmund.) N.Y., 1950.

Phil 6158.10   The beyond within; the LSD story. (Cohen, Sidney.) N.Y., 1965.

Phil 332.13   Beysens, J.T. Criteriologie of de leer over waarheid en zekerheid. 2. druk. Leiden, 1911.

Phil 8876.72   Beysens, J.T. Ethiek of natuurlijke zedenleer. Leiden, 1913.

Phil 8951.14   Beysens, J.T. Hoofdstukken uit de bijzondere ethiek. v.1-5. Bussum, 1917-19-.

Phil 5041.44   Beysens, J.T. Logica of Denkleer. 3e druk. Hilversum, 1923?

Phil 8656.19   Beysens, J.T. Theodicee of natuurlijke godsleer. 2. druk. Bussum, 1919.

Phil 3778.32   Beyträge zur Berichtigung bisheriger Missverständnisse der Philosophen. (Reinhold, K.L.) Jena, 1790. 2v.

Phil 3778.30   Beyträge zur leichtern Übersicht des Zustandes der Philosophie. v.1-6. (Reinhold, K.L.) Hamburg, 1802. 2v.

Phil 5262.1   Beytráge zur philosophischen Anthropologie. (Wagner, M.) Wien, 1794-96. 2v.

Phil 8402.46   Beytrage zur Kritik des Geschmacks. (Bendavid, L.) Wien, 1797.

Phil 5421.15.30   Bezembinder, Thomas G.G. Een experimentele methode om de juistheid van interpersonale perceptie zuiver te bepalen. Proefschrift. Groningen, 1961.

Phil 6960.8   Beziehungen das Dämonen- und Hexenwesens zur deutschen Irrenpflege. (Kirehhoff.) Berlin, 1888.

Phil 6325.13   Die Beziehungen der Psychologie zur Medizin. (Peters, W.) Würzburg, 1913.

Phil 6319.1.49   Die Beziehungen der Psychotherapie zur Seelsorge. (Jung, C.G.) Zürich, 1932.

Phil 5040.32   Die Beziehungen von Erkenntnistheorie, Logik und Sprache. (Albrecht, Erhard.) Halle, 1956.

Phil 5722.18   Die Beziehungen zwischen dem ich und dem Unbewussten. (Jung, C.G.) Darmstadt, 1928.

Phil 5722.18.5   Die Beziehungen zwischen dem ich und dem Unbewussten. (Jung, C.G.) Zürich, 1935.

Phil 3270.17.50   De bezinning. (Falm, Leopold.) Amsterdam, 1968.

Phil 8831.8   De bezinning over goed en kwaad in de geschiedenis van het menselijk denken. (Graaf, Johannes de.) Utrecht, 1957-3v.

Phil 4710.1   Bezobrazova, M. Handschriftliche...Philosophie in Russland. Leipzig, 1892.

Phil 5650.2   Bezold, Friedrich. þer die funktionelle Prüfung des menschlichen Gehörorgans. Wiesbaden, 1897.

Phil 8980.208   Bezuglov, A.A. Eto kasaetsia usekh. Moskva, 1956.

Phil 8581.71   Bezzant, J.S. Aspects of belief. N.Y., 1938.

Phil 960.276   Bhagavad Datta. The story of creation as seen by the seers. Delhi, 1968.

Phil 5400.39.3   Bhagavan, Das. La science des émotions. Bruxelles, 1921.

Phil 5400.39   Bhagavan, Das. The science of the emotions. London, 1900.

Phil 5400.39.9   Bhagavan, Das. The science of the emotions. 3rd ed. Adyar, 1924.

Phil 974.4.30   Bhagavan Das. Annie Besant...and the changing world. Adyar, 1934.

Phil 176.205   Bhattacharya, H.M. The principles of philosophy. Calcutta, 1948.

Phil 5751.17   Bianca, Giovanni. L'autonomia della volontà. Firenze, 1937.

Phil 400.102   Bianca, Giovanni. Essenza ed esistenza, idealità e realtà. Catania, 1946.

Phil 4260.157   Bianca, Giovanni A. Il concetto di poesia in Giambattista Vico. Messina, 1967.

Phil 8402.64   Bianca, Giovanni A. Discussioni sull'arte e sulla condizione dell'uomo. Messina, 1965.

Phil 2115.165   Bianca, Giuseppe G. La credenza come fondamento. Padova, 1950.

Phil 6111.45   Bianchi, L. Foundations of mental health. N.Y., 1930.

Phil 6111.35   Bianchi, L. The mechanism of the brain. Edinburgh 1922.

Phil 6400.8   Bianchi, Leonardo. Licções sobre as localisações cerebraes. Rio de Janeiro, 1899.

Phil 282.23   Bianchi, Ugo. Teogonie e cosmogonie. Roma, 1960.

Phil 6111.54   Bianchini, M.L. La igiene mentale ed it potenziamento della stirpe. Roma, 1937.

Phil 4210.120   Bianciardi, S. Antonio Rosmini o il filosofo cristiano. Firenze, 1858.

Phil 8092.14   Bianco, Giovanni A. Il rifiuto del mondo nell'arte comtemporanea. Bari, 1964.

Phil 3640.230   Bianquis, G. Nietzsche en France; l'influence de Nietzsche sur la pensée française. Paris, 1929.

Phil 3640.555   Bianquis, Genevieve. Nietzsche devant ses contemporains. Monaco, 1959.

Phil 5272.14   Bias in prediction; on correction methods. (Rydberg, Sven.) Uppsala, 1963.

Phil 5241.186   Biasutti, Bruno. Critica della società competitiva. Roma, 1968.

Phil 3492.32   Die Bibel bei Kant. (Kügelgen, C.W. von.) Leipzig, 1904.

Phil 8715.2   Bibel und Naturwissenschaft. (Zart, G.) Berlin, 1878.

Phil 8583.16.8   Bibelns filosofi. (Deussen, Paul.) Stockholm, 1916.

Phil 4520.2.34   Biberg, N.F. Commentationem Stoicarum. Diss. Upsaliae, 1815-1821.

Phil 4520.2.30   Biberg, N.F. In jus natuarae recentiorum stricturae. Diss. Upsaliae, 1818.

Phil 4520.2.32   Biberg, N.F. Notionum ethicarum quas formales dicunt, dialexis critica. Diss. Pt.1-2. Upsaliae, 1823-24.

Phil 4520.2.3   Biberg, N.F. Samlade skrifter. Upsala, 1828-30. 3v.

Phil 8715.1   Bible, science and faith. (Zahm, John Augustine.) Baltimore, 1895.

Phil 7068.61   Bible. New Testament. English. New Testament of our Lord...as revised and corrected by the spirits. N.Y., 1861.

Phil 8709.1   The Bible and other ancient literature in the nineteenth century. (Townsend, L.T.) N.Y., 1888.

Phil 6128.22   Bible authority for metaphysical healing. (Sankey, Dora J.) Boston, 1912.

Phil 8610.899.55   The Bible God, Bible teachings. (Turner, M.M. (Mrs.).) N.Y., 1899.

Phil 8610.888.10   The Bible handbook of freethinkers and inquiring Christians. (Foote, G.W.) London, 1900.

Phil 7054.27.11   Bible marvel workers. (Putnam, A.) Boston, 1873.

Phil 8692.6   The bible on the side of science. (Crosby, H.) N.Y., 1875.

Phil 8610.892   Bible studies. (Wheeler, J.M.) London, 1892.

Phil 75.14   Bibliografía. (Valverde Téllez, E.) México, 1907.

Phil 75.64.5   Bibliografía argentina de filosofía. La Plata.

Phil 75.64   Bibliografía argentina de filosofía y ciencias de la educación. La Plata.

Phil 75.36   Bibliografía argentina de publicaciones filosóficas, años 1937 a 1943. (Argentine Republic. Comisión Nacional de Cooperación Intelectual.) Buenos Aires, 1943.

Phil 4352.1.79   Bibliografía balmesiana. (Dios Mendoza, J. de.) Barcelona, 1961.

Phil 4080.3.160.5   Bibliografía crociana. 1. ed. (Cione, Edmondo.) Roma, 1956.

Phil 4983.1.79   Bibliografía de Carlos Vaz Ferreira. (Montevideo. Universidad. Facultad de Humanidades y Ciencias.) Montevideo, 1962.

Phil 4965.4   Bibliografía de las obras del Dr. Dn. Alejandro O. Deustua. Lima, 1939.

Phil 4006.5.80   Bibliografia degli scritti di Eugenio Garin. Bari, 1969.

Phil 4073.97   Bibliografia degli scritti di Tommaso Campanella. (Firpo, Luigi.) Torino, 1940.

Phil 7150.6   Bibliografia del suicidio. (Motta, Emilio.) Bellinzona, 1890.

Phil 4210.78   Bibliografia delle opere di A. Rosmini. (Caviglione, C.) Torino, 1925.

Htn   Phil 4065.01*   Bibliografia delle opere di Giordano Bruno. (Salvestrini, V.) Pisa, 1926.

Phil 75.1   Bibliografia delle Scienze Filosofiche. (Averra, Adolfo.) Torino, 1891.

Phil 4065.02   Bibliografia di Giordano Bruno. 2. ed. (Salvestrini, V.) Firenze, 1958.

Phil 4225.8.79   Bibliografia di M.F. Sciacca. (Ottonello, Pier Paolo.) Milano, 1969.

Phil 75.62   Bibliografía filosófica. (Martínez Gómez, Luis.) Barcelona, 1961.

Phil 75.84   Bibliografía filosófica de publicaciones de las Universidades de Costa Rica y San Carlos de Guatemala y de autores guatemaltecos que exhibió la Biblioteca Nacional. (Bendfeldt Rojas, Lourdes.) Guatemala, 1964.

Phil 75.16   Bibliografia filosofica italiana, 1914-15. (Levi, Alessandro.) Roma, 1917.

Phil 75.41   Bibliografia filosofica italiana. Milano. 1949+ 17v.

Phil 75.42   Bibliografia filosofica italiana dal 1900 al 1950. (Instituto di Studi Filosofici.) Roma, 1950. 4v.

Phil 75.89   Bibliografía filosófica mexicana. México. 1,1968+

Phil 75.69   Bibliografia filozofickéj Knižnej tvorby na Slovensku. (Matica Slovenská, Turčiansky sv. Martin. Bibliografický Odbor.) Martin, 1965.

Phil 75.46   Bibliografia filozofii polskiej [1750-1830]. v.1,3. (Polska Akademia Nauk. Komitet Filozoficzny.) Warszawa, 1955. 2v.

Phil 75.42.5   Bibliografia ragionata delle riviste filosofiche italiane dal 1900 al 1955. (Istituto di Studi Filosofici.) Roma, 1963.

Phil 4210.79.10   Bibliografia rosminiana. (Bergamaschi, Cirillo.) Milano, 1967. 2v.

Phil 4260.05   Bibliografia vichiana. (Croce, Benedetto.) Napoli, 1904-10.

Phil 4260.05.5   Bibliografia vichiana. Quinto supplemento. (Croce, Benedetto.) Napoli, 1932.

Phil 5593.58   Bibliografica italiana. (Chiari, Silvano.) Firenze, 1958.

Phil 5003.10   Bibliografiia po logike. (Primakovskii, A.P.) Moskva, 1955.

Phil 2520.2   Bibliographia cartesiana. (Sebba, G.) The Hague, 1964.

Phil 6060.52   Bibliographia graphologica. (Wintermantel, F.) Stuttgart, 1958.

Phil 3585.1.45F   Bibliographia Lambertiana. (Steck, Max.) Berlin, 1943.

Phil 5003.12   Bibliographia logica. (Risse, Wilhelm.) Hildesheim, 1965.

Phil 75.43   Bibliographia philosophica. (Bril, G.A. de.) Rhenum, 1950. 2v.

Phil 8610.889.15   A bibliographical dictionary of freethinkers of all ages and nations. (Wheeler, Joseph Mazzini.) London, 1889.

Phil 2477.6.108   Bibliographie blondelienne. (Hayen, A.) Bruxelles, 1953.

Phil 4843.1   Bibliographie critique de la philosophie grecque...1453-1953. (Boumblinopoulos, Georgios E.) Athènes, 1966.

Phil 3552.01   Bibliographie de la philosophie de Leibniz. Thèse. (Ravier, E.) Caen, 1927.

Phil 2733.84   Bibliographie de Malebranche. (Blampignon, Emile Antoine.) Montbéliard, n.d.

Phil 3450.19.160   Bibliographie der Heidegger. Literatur, 1917-1955. (Lüble, Hermann.) Meisenheim am Glan, 1957.

Phil 210.10   Bibliographie der Hermeneutik und ihrer Anwendungs Gereiche seit Schleiermacher. (Henrichs, Norbert.) Düsseldorf, 1968.

Phil 2050.01   Bibliographie der Hume-Literatur. (Metz, Rudolf.) Erfurt, 1928.

NEDL Phil 75.18   Bibliographie der Philosophie und Psychologie. Leipzig. 1920

Phil 5203.1   Bibliographie der Psycho-Physiologischen. Hamburg, 1890.

Phil 5203.24   Bibliographie der psychologischen Literatur der sozialistischen Länder. Berlin. 3,1960+ 5v.

Phil 5203.34   Bibliographie der psychologischen Literatur der 16. Jahrhunderts. (Schueling, H.) Hildesheim, 1967.

Phil 3090.01   Bibliographie der Schriften Franz v. Baaders. (Jost, J.) Bonn, 1926.

Phil 75.59   Bibliographie der sowjetischen Philosophie. Freiburg. 1-4 2v.

Phil 974.3.116   Bibliographie der Werke Rudolf Steiners in die Geburt. (Wachsmuth, G.) Dornach, 1942.

Phil 7103.2   Bibliographie des modernen Hypnotismus. (Dessoir, Max.) Berlin, 1888.

Phil 178.17.10   Bibliographie des modernen Hypnotismus. (Dessoir, Max.) n.p., 1888-1913. 25 pam.

Phil 7103.2.1   Bibliographie des modernen Hypnotismus. Nachtrag. (Dessoir, Max.) Berlin, 1890.

Phil 3552.02   Bibliographie des oeuvres de Leibniz. (Ravier, E.) Paris, 1937.

Phil 7150.23   Bibliographie des Selbstmords. (Rost, Hans.) Augsburg, 1927.

Phil 2880.1.88   Bibliographie du Martinisme. (Chateautien, G.) Lyon, 1939.

Phil 3850.46   Bibliographie Eduard Spranger. (Neu, Theodor.) Tübingen, 1958.

Phil 3270.18.1   Bibliographie Eugen Fink. (Herrmann, Friedrich Wilhelm von.) Den Haag, 1970.

Phil 6834.3   Bibliographie Freundschaftseros; einschliesslich Homoerotik, Homosexualität und der verwandten und vergleichenden Gebiete. (Welter, Ernst Günther.) Frankfurt, 1964.

Phil 2805.78   Bibliographie générale des oeuvres de Blaise Pascal. (Maire, Albert.) Paris, 1925-27. 5v.

Phil 2905.1.1   Bibliographie générale des oeuvres et articles sur Pierre Teilhard de Chardin parus jusqu'a fin decémbre 1969. (Jarque i Jutglar, Joan E.) Fribourg, 1970.

Phil 1811.2.5   Bibliographie méthodique du pragmatisme américain. Thèse. (Leroux, E.) n.p., 1922.

Phil 75.78   Bibliographie Philosophie. Berlin. 2,1968 4v.

Phil 75.78.2   Bibliographie Philosophie. Beiheft. 1,1967+

Phil 3195.6.01   Bibliographie Wilhelm Dilthey. (Herrmann, Ulrich.) Berlin, 1969.

Phil 75.39   Bibliographische Einführungen in das Studium der Philosophie. Bern. 1948

Phil 75.52   Bibliographischer Wegweiser der philosophischen Literatur. (Totok, Wilhelm.) Frankfurt, 1959.

Phil 75.4   Bibliographisches Handbuch der philosophischer Literatur. (Geissler, C.A.) Leipzig, 1850.

Phil 6123.8   Bibliography. Mental hygiene in industry. (National Committee for Mental Hygiene, Inc. Division on Rehabilition.) N.Y., 1945.

Phil 630.37   Bibliography and genetic study of American realism. (Harlow, V.E.) Oklahoma City, 1931.

Phil 7003.2   A bibliography and index of psychic research and related topics. Chicago. 1962-1964//

Phil 2045.02   A bibliography by H. MacDonald and M. Hargreaves. (Hobbes, Thomas.) London, 1952.

Phil 5650.30   A bibliography in audition. v.1-2. (Harvard University. Psycho-Acoustic Laboratory.) Cambridge, 1950.

Phil 8030.5   A bibliography of aesthetics and of the philosophy of the fine arts from 1900-1932. (Hammond, W.A.) N.Y., 1934.

Phil 9035.45.5   A bibliography of character. (Roback, A.A.) Cambridge, Mass., 1927.

Phil 75.74.5   A bibliography of Christian philosophy and contemporary issue. (McLean, George F.) N.Y., 1967.

Phil 5465.144   Bibliography of creativity; studies and related areas. (Razik, Jaher A.) Buffalo, 1965.

Phil 2050.02   A bibliography of David Hume. (Jessop, T.E.) London, 1938.

Phil 8030.2   A bibliography of experimental aesthetics, 1865-1932. (Chandler, A.R.) Columbus, 1933.

Phil 1870.78   A bibliography of George Berkeley. (Jessop, T.E.) London, 1934.

Phil 75.55   Bibliography of humanism. (Kwee, Swan Liat.) Utrecht, 1957.

Phil 960.278   A bibliography of Indian philosophy. 1. ed. (Ramaswami Aiyas C.P. Research Endowment Committee.) Madras, 1963-2v.

Phil 1955.6.01   A bibliography of John Dewey. (Thomas, Milton H.) N.Y., 1929.

Phil 1955.6.05A   Bibliography of John Dewey. 2d ed. (Thomas, Milton H.) N.Y., 1939.

Phil 2218.90   A bibliography of Joseph Priestley, 1733-1804. (Crook, Ronald E.) London, 1966.

Phil 7003.5   Bibliography of parapsychology. (Zorab, George.) N.Y., 1957.

Phil 75.10   Pamphlet vol. Bibliography of philosophy.

Phil 75.70   The bibliography of philosophy. (Higgins, Charles L.) Ann Arbor, 1965.

Phil 75.76   Bibliography of philosophy. Paris, 1966? 2 pam.

Phil 5203.31   A bibliography of psychological research and writings on Africa. (Klingelhofer, Edward L.) Uppsala, 1967.

Phil 8030.3   A bibliography of psychology and experimental aesthetics, 1864-1937. (Chandler, A.R.) Berkeley, 1938.

Phil 75.29   Bibliography of recent French philosophy, 1920. (Renoir, Edmund.) n.p. n.d.

Phil 5640.136.5   Bibliography of sensory deprivation and social isolation. (Sváb, L.) Prague, 1966.

Phil 5066.14.10   A bibliography of symbolic logic. (Church, Alonzo.) Monasha, Wisconsin, 1936.

Phil 2138.02A   Bibliography of the published writings of J.S. Mill. (Mill, John S.) Evanston, Ill., 1945.

Phil 5627.50   Bibliography of Theodore Schroeder on the psychology of religion. (Sankey-Jones, N.E.) Cos Cob, Conn., 1934.

Phil 2055.7.80A   The bibliography of William E. Hocking. (Gilman, R.C.) Waterville, Me., 1951.

Phil 5650.25   Bibliography on hearing. (Harvard University. Psycho-Acoustic Laboratory.) Cambridge, 1955.

Phil 5203.9   A bibliography on psychology. (Estey, H.G.) Gardner, 1926.

NEDL Phil 58.17   Biblioteca. (San Miguel, Buenos Aires. Facultades de Filosofía y Teología.) San Miguel.

Phil 11.25   Biblioteca de filosofía mexicana. Mexico. 1-10,1942-1943 2v.

Phil 75.12   Bibliotheca philosophica. (Cosentini, F.) Sassari, 1895.

Phil 25.6.5   Bibliotheca platonica. Osceola.

Phil 5203.3   Bibliotheca psychologica. (Grässe, J.G.T.) Leipzig, 1848.

Phil 75.9   Bibliothecae philosphicae. (Struve, B.G.) Göttingen, 1740.

Phil 3050.2   Bibliothek der deutschen Aufklärer des achtzehnten Jahrhunderts. (Bauer, Edgar.) Darmstadt, 1963. 2v.

Phil 11.4   Bibliothek für Philosophie. Berlin. 1-21+ 4v.

Phil 70.1   Bibliothèque. (International Congress of Philosophy, 1st, Paris, 1900.) Paris. 1900-1903

Phil 11.35   Bibliotheque d'anthropotechnie. Paris. 1+ 2v.

Phil 10.38.5   Bibliotheque du magnetisme animal. Paris. 1-8,1817-1819 4v.

Phil 2805.397   Bibliothèque Nationale, Paris. Blaise Pascal, 1623-1662. Paris, 1962

Phil 2475.1.365   Bibliothèque Nationale, Paris. Henri Bergson; exposition. Paris, 1959.

Phil 6132.14   Biblische Anthropologie. (Wörner, Ernst.) Stuttgart, 1887.

Phil 8707.38   Die biblische Schöpfungsgesichte und ihr Verhältniss zu den Ergebnissen der Naturforschung. (Reusch, Franz Heinrich.) Bonn, 1877.

Phil 4260.07   Biblografia vichiana. (Croce, Benedetto.) Napoli, 1947-48. 2v.

Phil 2648.64   Bicentenaire du Système de la nature. (Holbach, Paul Henri T.) Paris, 1970.

Phil 3120.15.97.15   Bickel, Lothar. Aussen und Innen. Zürich, 1960.

Phil 3120.15.97.5   Bickel, Lothar. Kultur. Zürich, 1956.
Phil 3120.15.97.10

Phil 3120.15.97   Bickel, Lothar. Das Leben - eine Aufgabe. Zürich, 1959.

Phil 3120.15.97   Bickel, Lothar. Wirklichkeit und Wahrheit des Denkens. Zürich, 1953.

Phil 6111.24.5   Bidder, Friedrich. Die Selbständigkeit des sympathischen Nervensystems. Leipzig, 1842.

Phil 6111.24.9   Bidder, Friedrich. Untersuchungen über die Textur des Rückenmarks. Leipzig, 1857.

Phil 6111.24   Bidder, Friedrich. Zur Lehre von dem Verhältniss der Ganglienkörper zu den Nerwenfasern. Leipzig, 1847.

Phil 3821.23   Bidney, David. Psychology and ethics of Spinoza. New Haven, 1940.

Phil 3821.23.2   Bidney, David. The psychology and ethics of Spinoza. 2nd ed. N.Y., 1962.

Phil 5403.5   Bidrag til nydelsernes fysiologi som grundlag for en rationel aestetik. (Lange, C.G.) Kjobenhavn, 1899.

Phil 801.18   Bidrag til opfattelsen of philosophiens historisk Udvikling. (Bróchner, Hans.) Kjøbenhavn, 1869.

Phil 705.21   Bidrag till denTransscendentala kategoriläran. (Barkman, H.) Uppsala, 1901.

Phil 4515.81.5   Bidrag till en karakteristik af den Boströmska filosofien. (Nybláeus, A.) Lund, 1892.

Phil 822.5   Bidrag till filosofiens historia. (Wolff, M.) Stockholm, 1882.

Phil 3425.251   Bidrag till granskning af den Hegelska dialektiken och dess princip "Motsägelsen". (Nyblaeus, Axel.) Upsala, 1851.

Phil 2050.177   Bidrag till kännedomen af David Humes filosofiska betydelse. (Henschen, W.A.) Upsala, 1863.

Phil 4570.1.20   Bidrag till utredandet af samhällslärans grundbegrepp. 1. delen. (Grubbe, Samuel.) Upsala, 1826.

Phil 5535.18   Bidrag till zäknefärdighetens psykologi akademisk. (Wictorin, Mauritz.) Göteborg, 1952.

Phil 1850.94   Biechy, A. Essai sur la méthode de Bacon. Toulon, 1855.

Phil 5125.2   Biéchy, A. L'induction. Paris, 1869.

Phil 3640.223   Biedenkapp, Georg. Friedrich Nietzsche und Friedrich Naumann als Politiker. Göttingen, 1901.

Phil 176.22   Biederman, G. Wissenschaft des Geistes. Leipzig, 1858.

Phil 3001.2   Biedermann, F.C. Die deutsche Philosophie. Leipzig, 1842. 2v.

Phil 1535.21   Biedermann, G. Natur-Philosophie. Prag, 1887-89. 3v.

Phil 1535.21.2   Biedermann, G. Philosophie des Geistes. Prag, 1886.

Phil 5041.12   Biedermann, Gustav. Zur logischen Frage. Prag, 1870.

Htn   Phil 3801.210*   Biedermann, K. Degenetica philosophandi ratione et methods praesertim Fichti, Schellingii, Hegelii. Lipsiae, 1835.

Phil 8876.64   Biedermann, Karl. Zeit- und Lebensfragen aus dem Gebiete der Moral. Breslau, 1899.

Phil 5592.115   Biedma, Carlos. Die Sprache der Zeichnung. Bern, 1959.

Phil 8520.36   Bieler, Ludwig. Theios. Wien, 1935-36. 2v.

Phil 1050.4.20   Bieler, Majer. Der göttliche Wille (Logosbegriff) bei Gabirol. Breslau, 1933.

Phil 3483.43   Biéma, Émile van. L'espace et les temps chez Leibnizet chez Kant. Paris, 1908.

Phil 3450.19.107A   Biemel, W. Le concept de inonde chez Heidegger. Louvain, 1950.

Phil 8892.23   Le bien et la loi morale; éthique. (Royer, Clémence.) Paris, 1881.

Phil 6111.57   Bier, A. Die Seele. 3. Aufl. München, 1939.

Phil 176.61   Bierbower, A. Principles of a system of philosophy. N.Y., 1870.

Phil 2520.85   Bierendempfel, G. Descartes als Gegner des Sensualismus und Materialismus. Wolfenbüttel, 1884.

Phil 1701.15   Bierens de Haan, J. Hoofdfiguren der geschiedenis van het urjsgeerig denden. 2e druk. Haarlem, 1927.

Phil 5811.18   Bierens de Haan, J.A. Die tierpsychologische Forschung, ihre Ziele und Wege. Leipzig, 1935.

Phil 2262.80   Bierens de Haan, J.D. De beteekenis van Shaftesbury in de Engelsche ethiek. Proefschrift. Utrecht, 1891.

Phil 176.115.9   Bierens de Haan, J.D. Idee - studies. 3e druk. Amsterdam, 1920.

Phil 3120.40.55   Bierens de Haan, J.D. Innerlijk perspectief. Assen, 1966.

Phil 3821.8   Bierens de Haan, J.D. Levensleer naar de beginselen van Spinoza. 's Gravenhage, 1900.

Phil 176.115.50   Bierens de Haan, J.D. Menschengeest. Amsterdam, 1926.

Phil 3120.40.45   Bierens de Haan, J.D. Het rijk van den geest. Zeist, 1938.

Phil 3808.172   Bierens de Haan, J.D. Schopenhauer. 's Gravenhage, 1933.

Phil 3120.40.40   Bierens de Haan, J.D. De strijd tusschen idealisme en naturalisme in de 19. eeuw. Haarlem, 1929.

Phil 3120.40.30   Bierens de Haan, J.D. Het tragische schuld noodlot en bevrijding. Leiden, 1933.

Phil 176.115.2   Bierens de Haan, J.D. De verborgen harmonie. 2e druk. Amsterdam, 1918.

Phil 176.115.15   Bierens de Haan, J.D. Vergezichten. Studies. Amsterdam, 1921.

Phil 176.115.35   Bierens de Haan, J.D. De weg tot het inzicht. Amsterdam, 1920.

Phil 176.115.45   Bierens de Haan, J.D. Wereldorde engeestesleven. 2e Aufl. Amsterdam, 1922.

Phil 176.115.8   Bierens de Haan, J.D. Wysgeerige studies. 's-Gravenhage, 1904.

Phil 3120.40.35   Bierens de Haan, J.D. De zin van het komische. Leiden, 1930.

Phil 5241.39   Bierens de Haan, P. Hoofdlijnen eener psychologie met metafysischen grondslag. Amsterdam, 1897.

Phil 3120.40.50   Bierens de Haan. J.D. De norm der waarheid is in ons-zelf. Utrecht, 1897.

Phil 8581.31   Bierer, E. The evolution of religions. N.Y., 1906.

Phil 525.268   Bieri, Edgard L. Un concetto dell'aldilà. Roma, 1970.

Phil 5041.90   Bierman, Arthur Kalmer. Logic: a dialogue. San Francisco, 1964.

Phil 5211.5   Bierviet, J.J. van. La psychologie d'aujourd'hui. Paris, 1927.

Phil 6111.36   Bierviet, J.J. L'homme droit et l'homme gauche. Gand, 1901.

Phil 5465.37   Biervliet, J.J. van. La part de l'imagination. Paris, 1937.

Phil 5545.2.6   Biervliet, J.J. von. Esquisse d'une éducation de la mémoire. 2. éd. Gand, 19- .

Phil 5545.2   Biervliet, J.J. von. La mémoire. Gand, 1893.

Phil 5241.48   Biervliet, Jules Jean van. Eléments de psychologie humaine. Gand, 1895.

Phil 5241.48.5   Biervliet, Jules Jean van. La psychologie quantitative. Gand, 1907.

Phil 8402.4   Biese, Alfred. Das Associationsprincip und der Anthropomorphismus in der Asthetik. Kiel, 1890.

Phil 176.152   Biese, Alfred. Die Philosophie des Metaphorischen. Hamburg, 1893.

Phil 176.97   Biese, Franz. Philosophie Propädeutik für Gymnasien und höhere Bildungsanstalten. Berlin, 1845.

Phil 3483.30   Biese, Reinhold. Die Erkenntnislehre des Aristoteles und Kant's. Berlin, 1877.

Phil 2520.270   Bievre, C. de. Descartes und Pascal. Brasschaet, 1956.

Phil 8691.15   Big Bible stories. (Bach, W.H.) Lilly Dale, N.Y., 1897.

Htn   Phil 4363.2.81*   Bigelow, John. Molinos the quietist. N.Y., 1882.

Phil 4363.2.80A   Bigelow, John. Molinos the quietist. N.Y., 1882.

Phil 7080.16   Bigelow, John. The mystery of sleep. N.Y., 1903.

Phil 7080.16.5   Bigelow, John. Mystery of sleep. N.Y., 1924.

Phil 8633.1.11   Bigg, C. Neoplatonism. London, 1895.

Phil 1170.6A   Biggs, John Burville. Information and human learning. Melbourne, 1968.

Phil 5535.26

Phil 8092.22   Bignami, Ariel. Notas para la polémica sobre realismo. Buenos Aires, 1969.

Phil 2480.88   Bigoni, Angelo. Vero rapporto del fisico e del morale dell'uomo. Padova, 1813.

Phil 8597.10   Bigotry, superstition, hypocrasy...Atheism. (Robles, M.) London, 1742.

Phil 176.242   Bihari, Péter. A philosophiai tudamányok encyclopaediája. Budapest, 1875.

Phil 3549.8.125   De bijdrage von Ludwig Klages tot de algemene psychologie. (Bruhers, E.M.J.) Roermond, 1941.

Phil 11.52   Bijdragen tot de psychologie. Assen. 2,1968+ 9v.

Phil 5241.166   Bijkerk, R.J. Psycho-logica. Amsterdam, 1962.

Phil 6311.54   Bilan de la psychologie des profondeurs. (Becker, Raymond de.) Paris, 1968.

Phil 1750.625   Bilancio della fenomenologia. (Garin, Eugenio.) Padova, 1960.

Phil 3246.231   Das Bild des Menschen in der Philosophie Fichtes. (Steinbeck, W.) München, 1939.

Phil 3808.24.17   Das Bild des Menschen in Schopenhauers Philosophie. (Schopenhauer, Arthur.) Berlin, 1932.

Phil 3120.45.40 Das Bild des Menschen und die Idee des Humanismus. (Brandenstein, Béla.) Bregenz, 1948.
Phil 5592.181 Der Bild-Test. Inaug. Diss. (Kempf, H.E.) Marburg, 1964?
Phil 6320.13 Das Bild vom Ander. (Kaminski, Gerhard.) Berlin, 1959.
Phil 6328.59 Bilder und Urbilder; Erscheinungsformen des Arrhetypus. (Seifert, Friedrich.) München, 1965.
Phil 3120.30.45 Bilder von Gut und Böse. (Buber, Martin.) Köln, 1952.
Phil 3310.8.30 Bilderbuch meiner Jugend; Erinnerungen. (Glockner, Hermann.) Bonn, 1970. 2v.
Phil 6965.18 Bildnerei der Geisteskranken. (Prinzhorn, H.) Berlin, 1922.
Phil 3925.16.115 Die Bildtheorie der Sprache. (Burkhardt, Jörg R.) München, 1965.
Phil 5258.10 Die Bildung der menschlichen Geistes. (Schultz-Schultzenstein, K.H.) Berlin, 1855.
Phil 5772.2.4 Die Bildung des Willens. (Wiese, L.) Berlin, 1879.
Phil 8612.58.1 Bildung und Erziehung angesichts der Endlichkeit des Menschen. (Zoepfl, Helmut.) Donauwörth, 1967.
Phil 3850.18.10 Bildung und Wissen. (Scheler, Max.) Frankfurt, 1947.
Phil 3425.364 Der Bildungsbegriff des Jungen Hegel. (Fusch, Carl-Ludwig.) Weinheim, 1953.
Phil 9170.1 Bildungslehre...zum ehelichen Glücke. (K., J.P.A.) Düsseldorf, 1807.
Phil 3640.575 Das Bildungsproblem in der Philosophie Nietzsches. (Hotter, Karl.) München, 1958.
Phil 3120.4.31 Bilfinger, G.B. Dilucidationes philosophicae de Deo. 3. ed. Tubingae, 1746.
Phil 3552.82 Bilfingeri, G.B. Harmonia...praestabilita...Leibnitii. Tubingae, 1741.
Phil 351.7 Bilgi ve değer. (Ülken, Hilmi Ziya.) Ankara, 1965.
Phil 5241.34 Bilharz, A. Neue Denklehre. Wiesbaden, 1908.
Phil 176.76 Bilharz, Alfons. Metaphysik als Lehre vom Vorbewussten. Bd.I. Wiesbaden, 1897.
Phil 176.76.5 Bilharz, Alfons. Philosophie als Universalwissenschaft. Wiesbaden, 1912.
Phil 3483.14 Bilharz, Altons. Erläuterungen zu Kant's Kritik der reinen Vernunft. Wiesbaden, 1884.
Phil 75.2 Biliotheca philosophica. (Büchring, Adolph.) Nordhausen, 1867.
Phil 365.38.5 Bill, Annie C.B. The conquest of death; an imminent step in evolution. Boston, 1935.
Phil 365.38 Bill, Annie C.B. Questions and answers on conscious evolution. N.Y., 1933.
Phil 5871.108 Biller, Henry B. Father, child, and sex role. Lexington, 1971.
Phil 176.67 Pamphlet box. Billia, L.M. Miscellaneous pamphlets.
Phil 5241.46 Billia, Lorenzo M. Has the psychological laboratory proved helpful. Chicago, 1909.
Phil 5170.5 Billia, Lorenzo M. Quatres règles inexactes du syllogisme. Heidelberg, 1908?
Phil 8620.46 Billicsich, F. Das Problem des Übels in der Philosophie. Wien, 1952. 3v.
Phil 4710.15 Billig, Joseph. Der russische Idealismus der 30er Jahre und seine Überwindung. Inaug. Diss. Berlin, 1930.
Phil 5241.100 Billings, E.G. Handbook of elementary psychology. N.Y., 1939.
Phil 6671.21 Billot, G.P. Recherches psychologiques...magnétisme vital. v.1-2. Paris, 1839.
Phil 5241.103 Bills, A.G. General experimental psychology. N.Y., 1934.
Phil 6111.60 Bills, A.G. The psychology of efficiency. N.Y., 1943.
Phil 5041.65 Bilsky, Manuel. Logic and effective argument. N.Y., 1956.
Phil 3625.1.85 Biltz, Otto. Der Phädo Platos und Mendelssohns. Inaug. Diss. Berlin, 1897.
Phil 5011.3 Binde, Robert. Begriff, Urteil und Schluss in ihrer gemeinsamen Wurze. pt.1-2. Glogan, 1886-87.
Phil 3640.179 Binder, Elsa. Malwida vom Meysenburg und Friedrich Nietzsche. Berlin, 1917.
Phil 5041.51 Binder, Frank. Dialectic, or The tactics of thinking. London, 1932.
Phil 3640.580 Binder, J. Nietzsches Raatsauffassung. Göttingen, 1925.
Phil 8951.10 Bindi, Enrico. Religione e morale, scritti varii. Firenze, 1904.
Phil 5627.265 Bindl, Maria Frieda. Das religiöse Erleben im Spiegel der Bildgestaltung. Freiburg, 1965.
Phil 6140.15 Bindman, Arthur J. Perspectives in community mental health. Chicago, 1969.
Phil 5548.60 Bindra, Dalbir. Motivation. N.Y., 1959.
Phil 3640.416 Bindschedler, M.B. Nietzsche und die poetische Lüge. Basel, 1954.
Phil 6111.14 Binet, A. L'ame et le corps. Paris, 1905.
Phil 6111.14.3 Binet, A. L'ame et le corps. Paris, 1913.
Phil 6671.7.5 Binet, A. Animal magnetism. N.Y., 1888.
Phil 6671.7 Binet, A. Le magnétisme animal. Paris, 1887.
Phil 6111.14.6 Binet, A. The mind and the brain. London, 1907.
Phil 5545.77 Binet, A. Psychologie des grands calculateurs et joueurs d'échecs. Paris, 1894.
Phil 5620.1A Binet, A. La psychologie du raisonnement. Paris, 1886.
Phil 5620.1.5 Binet, A. The psychology of reasoning. Chicago, 1899.
Phil 5620.1.7 Binet, A. The psychology of reasoning. Chicago, 1907.
Phil 7140.4 Binet, A. La suggestibilité. Paris, 1900.
Phil 6311.18.5 Binet, Alfred. Alteration of personality. N.Y., 1896.
Phil 6311.18 Binet, Alfred. Les altérations de la personnalité. Paris, 1892.
Phil 6311.18.6 Binet, Alfred. Alterations of personality. London, 1896.
Phil 5241.54 Binet, Alfred. L'étude expérimentale de l'intelligence. Photoreproduction. Paris, 1922.
Phil 5241.54.5 Binet, Alfred. The experimental psychology of Alfred Binet; selected papers. N.Y., 1969.
Phil 6750.216 Binet, Alfred. The intelligence of the feeble-minded. Baltimore, 1916.
Phil 7042.4 Binet, Alfred. On double consciousness. Chicago, 1890.
Phil 7042.4.1 Binet, Alfred. On double consciousness. Chicago, 1896.
Phil 7042.4.2 Binet, Alfred. On double consciousness. Chicago, 1905.
Phil 6060.10 Binet, Alfred. Les révélations de l'écriture d'après un controle scientifique. Paris, 1906.
Phil 5627.22 Binet-Sangle, Charles. Les lois psychophysiologique du développement des religions. Paris, 1907.
Phil 6980.112.10 Binger, C.A.L. More about psychiatry. Chicago, 1949.
Phil 6659.2 Binger, Carl A.L. Personality in arterial hypertension. N.Y., 1945.
Phil 6980.112 Bingham, J. The inside story. 1. ed. N.Y., 1953.
Phil 5850.135 Bingham, W.V. Psychology applied. n.p., 1923.
Phil 5241.87 Bingham, Walter V. Psychology today. Chicago, 1932.
Phil 5850.135.30 Bingham, Walter van Dyke. How to interview. 3. ed. N.Y., 1941.
Phil 5850.135.10 Bingham memorial lecture. Pittsburgh. 1961
Phil 8876.140 Binkley, Luther J. Contemporary ethical theories. N.Y., 1961.

Htn Phil 7080.29* Binns, E. The anatomy of sleep. London, 1842.
Phil 5850.136 Binois, René. La psychologie appliquée. 3. éd. Paris, 1952.
Phil 3120.27.30 Binswanger, L. Ausgewählte Vorträge und Aufsätze. Bern, 1947. 2v.
Phil 3120.27.25 Binswanger, L. Ausgewählte Vorträge und Aufsätze. Bern, 1961. 2v.
Phil 3120.27.40 Binswanger, L. Being in the world. N.Y., 1963.
Phil 5241.64 Binswanger, L. Einführung in die Probleme der allgemeinen Psychologie. Berlin, 1922.
Phil 3120.27.32 Binswanger, L. Grundformen und Erkenntnis menschlichen Daseins. 2. Aufl. Zürich, 1953.
Phil 6980.112.20 Binswanger, L. Der Mensch in der Psychiatrie. Pfullingen, 1957.
Phil 6867.30 Binswanger, Ludwig. Drei Formen missglückten : Verstiegenheit, Verschrobenheit, Maineriertheit. Tübingen, 1956.
Phil 6976.30 Binswanger, Ludwig. Drei Formen missglückten Daseins: Verstiegenheit, Verschrobenheit, Manieriertheit. Tübingen, 1956.
Phil 6315.2.226 Binswanger, Ludwig. Erinnerungen an Sigmund Freud. Bern, 1956.
Phil 6978.12.15 Binswanger, Ludwig. Melancholie und Manie. Pfullingen, 1960.
Phil 6951.30 Binswanger, Ludwig. Schizophrenie. Pfullingen, 1957.
Phil 6315.2.225A Binswanger, Ludwig. Sigmund Freud. N.Y., 1957.
Phil 6951.30.5 Binswanger, Ludwig. Wahn; Beiträge zu seiner phanomenologischen und daseinsanalytischen Erforschung. Pfullingen, 1965.
Phil 4972.22 Bio-perspectivas. (Kehl, Renato.) Rio de Janeiro, 1938.
Phil 193.73.5 The biocomos...life psychologically ordered. (Snider, Denton J.) St. Louis, 1911.
Phil 4260.185 La biografia di G.B. Vico. (Falco, Enrico de.) Roma, 1968.
Phil 4215.1.97 Biografia di G.D. Romagnosi e catalogo delle sue opere. (Giorgi, A. de.) Parma, 1874.
Htn Phil 130.1*A Biographia philosophica. (Martin, Benjamin.) London, 1764.
Phil 5643.52A Biographic clinics. (Gould, George M.) Philadelphia, 1903-05. 6v.
Phil 2005.2.81 Biographica philosophica. 2d ed. (Fraser, A.C.) Edinburgh 1905.
Phil 623.16 A biographical dictionary of modern rationalists. (McCabe, Joseph.) London, 1920.
Phil 130.15 Biographical directory. (American Psychological Association.) Washington. 1968+
Phil 6980.38.10 Biographical directory of fellows and members of the American Psychiatric Association. (American Psychiatric Association.) N.Y., 1941.
Phil 811.3.2 A biographical history of philosophy. (Lewes, G.H.) London, 1857.
Phil 811.3.5 The biographical history of philosophy. (Lewes, G.H.) London, 1875.
Phil 811.3.6 The biographical history of philosophy. (Lewes, G.H.) N.Y., 1859.
Phil 811.3 A biographical history of philosophy. v.1-4. (Lewes, G.H.) London, 1845-46. 2v.
Phil 3090.80 Biographie Franz von Baader's. (Hoffmann, F.) Leipzig, 1857.
Phil 6958.5 Biographieen Geisteskranker. (Ideler, K.W.) Berlin, 1841.
Phil 978.49.690 Biographien und biographische Skizzen, 1894-1905. 1. Aufl. (Steiner, R.) Dornach, 1967.
Phil 8610.858.5 Biographies of ancient and modern celebrated freethinkers. (Bradlaugh, Charles.) Boston, 1877.
Phil 3195.6.79.6 Biographisch-literarischer Grundriss der allgemeinen Geschichte der Philosophie. 6. Aufl. (Dilthey, Wilhelm.) Trebnitz, 189-.
Phil 3270.4.79 Biographischer Nachlass. v.1-2. (Feuerbach, P.J.A.) Leipzig, 1853.
Phil 8602.1.5 The biography of God as men have told it. (Ward, D.J.H.) Denver, 1924?
Phil 7054.138 Biography of Mrs. Samantha Mettler. (Green, Frances H.) N.Y., 1853.
Phil 7060.52 A biography of the brothers Davenport. (Nichols, T.L.) London, 1864.
X Cg Phil 9495.11 Biological, physiological and sociological reproduction, also sexual hygiene. 14. ed. (Hall, W.S.) Chicago, 1913.
Phil 6118.8 Biological and biochemical basis of behavior. (Symposium on Interdisciplinary Research, University of Wisconsin.) Madison, Wis., 1958.
Phil 6317.25 Biological approach to the problem of abnormal behavior. (Harrington, M.) Lancaster, Pa., 1938.
Phil 5590.45.15 The biological basis of personality. (Eysenck, Hans Jurgen.) Springfield, 1967.
Phil 5627.57 The biological foundations of belief. (Wells, W.R.) Boston, 1921.
Phil 8888.7.10 La biologie de l'éthique. (Nordau, Max.) Paris, 1930.
Phil 5425.54 Biologie de l'invention. (Nicolle, Charles.) Paris, 1932.
Phil 5425.59 Biologie deutscher Dichter und Denker. (Hamann, Otto.) Zürich, 1923.
Phil 346.17.5 Biologie et connaissance, essai sur les relations entre les régulations organiques et les processus cognitifs. (Piaget, Jean.) Paris, 1967.
Phil 8702.32 Biologie et réflexion chrétienne. (Moretti, Jean.) Paris, 1967.
Phil 3790.1.90 Der biologisch-psychologische Gottesbeweis bei Herman S. Reimarus. (Scherer, C.C.) Würzburg, 1899.
Phil 8842.5 Das biologische Prinzip in den moralphilosophischen Anschauungen W. Rolph's, M. Guyau's und Fr. Nietzsches. (Reybekiel, A.) Krakau, 1906.
Phil 8892.3 Biologische Probleme. (Rolph, W.H.) Leipzig, 1882.
Phil 8892.3.3 Biologische Probleme. 2. Aufl. (Rolph, W.H.) Leipzig, 1884.
Phil 5251.64 Biologische Psychologie. (Leonhard, Karl.) Leipzig, 1962.
Phil 5402.15 Die biologische Theorie der Lust und Unlust. (Nádejde, D.C.) Leipzig, 1908.
Phil 5822.14 The biology of art. (Morris, Desmond.) London, 1962.
Phil 5822.14.5 The biology of art. (Morris, Desmond.) N.Y., 1962.
Phil 5400.175 Biology of emotions::new understanding derived from biological multidisciplinary investigation. (Jacobson, Edmund.) Springfield, 1967.
Phil 6311.22 The biology of human conflict. (Burrow, T.) N.Y., 1937.
Phil 6957.22 The biology of schizophrenia. 1. ed. (Hoskins, Roy G.) N.Y., 1946.
Phil 6980.112.50 Bion, Wilfred R. Experiences in groups. London, 1961.
Phil 5627.261.5 Bionome Geschlechtsentfaltung. (Schulz, Johannes Josef.) München, 1961.
Phil 6312.20 Bios, Psyche, Person. (Caruso, Igor A.) Freiburg, 1957.

Phil 177.60.5   Bios und Psyche. (Conrad-Martius, Hedwig.) Hamburg, 1949.
Phil 8885.40   Biosophy and spiritual democracy. (Kettner, F.) N.Y., 1954.
Phil 11.19   Biosphical series. N.Y.
Phil 585.50   Biot, René. Poussière vivante. Paris, 1957.
Phil 3450.11.420   Biral, Alessandro. L'unità del sapere in Husserl. Padova, 1967.
Phil 5241.188   Biran, Sigmund. Die ausserpsychologische Voraussetzungen der Tiefenpsychologie. München, 1966.
Phil 6978.12.20   Biran, Sigmund. Melancholie und Todestriebe. München, 1961.
Phil 3195.6.157   Birand, Kâmiran. Dilthey ve Rickert'te manevi ilimlerin temellendirilmesi. Ankara, 1954.
Phil 850.40   Birand, Kámiran. Ilk cağ felsefesi torihi. Ankara, 1958.
Phil 8951.17   Birchard, Ford G. Out of the rut, a layman's point of view. Boston, 1931.
Phil 3483.80   Bird, G. Kant's theory of knowledge. London, 1962.
Phil 7069.28.4   Bird, J. Malcolm. The Margery mediumship. N.Y., 1928.
Phil 7069.25.5A   Bird, J. Malcolm. "Margery" the medium. Boston, 1925.
Phil 310.583   Biriukov, B.V. Dialekticheskii materializm. Moskva, 1964.
Phil 5066.264   Biriukov, Boris Vl. Krushenie metafizicheskoi kontseptsii univeral'nosti predmetnoi oblasti v logike. Moskva, 1963.
Phil 6315.2.480   Birk, Kasimir. Sigmund Freud und die Religion. Münsterschwarzach, 1970.
Phil 3195.8.80   Birkenbihl, M. Georg Friedrich Daumer. Inaug. Diss. Aschaffenburg, 1905.
Phil 8402.12F   Birkhoff, G.D. Aesthetic measure. Cambridge, 1933.
Phil 8402.12.5   Birkhoff, G.D. Medida estetica. Rosario, 1945.
Phil 3805.221   Birkner, Hans J. Schleiermachers christliche Sittenlehre, im Zusammenhang seines philosophisch-theologischen Systems. Berlin, 1964.
Phil 8876.17   Birks, T.R. First principles of moral science. London, 1873.
Phil 2270.80   Birks, T.R. Modern physical fatalism. London, 1876.
Phil 9550.1   Birks, T.R. Modern utilitarianism. London, 1874.
Phil 2218.82   Birmingham, England. Priestley memorial. Photoreproduction. London, 1875.
Phil 6311.10   Birnbaum, Karl. Der Aufbau der Psychose. Berlin, 1923.
Phil 6311.10.15   Birnbaum, Karl. Handwörterbuch der medizinischen Psychologie. Leipzig, 1930.
Phil 5241.140   Birnbaum, W. Organisches Denken. Tübingen, 1960.
Phil 5838.261   Birney, Robert C. Instinct, an enduring problem in psychology. Princeton, 1961.
Phil 5478.14   Birney, Robert Charles. Fear of failure. N.Y., 1969.
Phil 2070.136   Biró, B. A tudatalatti világ: William James lélektanában. Szeged, 1929.
Phil 3905.82   Biró, Paul. Die Sittlichkeitsmetaphysik Otto Weiningers. Wien, 1927.
Phil 3905.82.2   Biró, Paul. Die Sittlichkeitsmetaphysik Otto Weiningers. Diss. Wien, 1927.
Phil 8581.27   Biroth, H. Tolerance in religion; liberal thoughts of modern thinkers. Rome, 1913.
Phil 8876.157   Biroud, K. Manevi limler metadu olorok anlama. Ankara, 1960.
Phil 5350.5A   Birren, James E. The psychology of aging. Englewood Cliffs, N.J., 1964.
Phil 5886.15   Birren, James Emmett. Handbook of aging and the individual. Chicago, 1960.
Phil 1701.26   Birro, Cela. The ways of enjoyment. N.Y., 1957.
Phil 8125.28   Birt, Theodor. Laienurtheil über bildende Kunst bei den Alten. Marburg, 1902.
Phil 585.140   The birth and death of meaning. (Becker, Ernest.) N.Y., 1962.
Phil 585.140.2   The birth and death of meaning. 2. ed. (Becker, Ernest.) N.Y., 1971.
Phil 978.6.30   Birth and evolution of the soul. 2nd ed. (Besant, Annie.) London, 1903.
Phil 6317.20.15   The birth of institute. (Hendrick, Ives.) Freeport, 1961.
Phil 5520.455   The birth of language; the case history of a non-verbal child. (Kastein, Shulamith.) Springfield, 1966.
Phil 193.49.12   The birth of reason and other essays. (Santayana, G.) N.Y., 1968.
Phil 6316.12.15   The birth of the ego; a nuclear hypothesis. (Glover, Edward.) N.Y., 1968.
Phil 281.1   Birth of the universe. (Ambler, R.P.) N.Y., 1853.
Phil 3640.58.20   The birth of tragedy. (Nietzsche, Friedrich.) N.Y., 1967.
Phil 3640.79.10   The birth of tragedy and The genealogy of morals. 1. ed. (Nietzsche, Friedrich.) Garden City, N.Y., 1956.
Phil 5250.72   Birth to maturity. (Kagan, J.) N.Y., 1962.
Phil 9178.6.5   A birthday present. (Somerville, E.) Boston, 1803.
Phil 9178.6.6   A birthday present. (Somerville, E.) Boston, 1805.
Phil 5421.20.80   Bis hierher und nicht weiter. (Mitscherlich, Alexander.) München, 1969.
Phil 3808.210   Biscardo, R. Il pessimismo romantico nel mondo di Schopenhauer. 1.ed. Bolzano, 1955.
Phil 6311.20   Bisch, L.E. Be glad you're neurotic. N.Y., 1936.
Phil 6311.20.5   Bisch, L.E. Why be shy? N.Y., 1941.
Phil 5400.103   Bisch, L.E. Your nerves. N.Y., 1945.
Phil 9070.23   Bisch, Louis Edward. The conquest of self. Garden City, 1923.
Phil 3255.87   Bischof, Hermann. Sebastian Franck von deutsche Geschichtsschreibung. Tübingen, 1857.
Phil 5590.438   Bischof, Ledford J. Interpreting personality theories. N.Y., 1964.
Phil 6111.21   Bischoff, T.L.W. von. Das Hirngewicht des Menschen. Bonn, 1880.
Phil 4080.3.520   Biscione, Michele. Interpreti do Croce. Napoli, 1968.
Phil 3640.681   Biser, Eugen. Gott ist tot. München, 1962.
Phil 5041.54   Biser, I. A general scheme for natural systems. Philadelphia, 1938.
Phil 5241.12   Bishop, D. An introduction...study...mind. London, 1849.
Phil 5241.12.5   Bishop, D. An introduction...study...mind. London, 1857.
Phil 9400.3   Bishop, E.M. Seventy years young. N.Y., 1907.
Phil 6990.68   Bishop, George Victor. Faith healing; God or fraud? . Los Angeles, 1967.
Phil 2805.219   Bishop, M. Pascal. N.Y., 1930.
Phil 6158.35   Bishop, Malden Grange. The discovery of love; a psychedelic experience with LSD-25. N.Y., 1963.
Phil 1870.110   Bishop Berkeley. (Hone, J.M.) London, 1931.
Phil 1870.82.5   Bishop Berkeley and Professor Fraser. (Abbot, T.K.) Dublin, 1877.
Phil 1900.92   Bishop Butler, moralist and divine. (Norton, William J.) New Brunswick, 1940.
Phil 1900.88   Bishop Butler. (Baker, A.E.) London, 1923.
Phil 1900.83   Bishop Butler. (Pynchon, T.R.) N.Y., 1889.
Phil 1900.94   Bishop Butler. (Spooner, W.A.) London, 1901.
Phil 1900.82   Bishop Butler and his critics. (Eaton, J.R.T.) Oxford, 1877.

Phil 1900.91   Bishop Butler and the age of reason. (Mossner, E.C.) N.Y., 1936.
Phil 6122.40   Bismarck, Nietzsche, Scheffel, Mörike; der Einfluss nervöser Zustände auf ihr Leben und Schaffen. (Müller, A.) Bonn, 1921.
Phil 7060.59   Bissel, J. Incolorum alterius mundi phenoemena. Dillingen, 1685.
Phil 3910.132   Bissinger, Anton. Die Stuktur der Gotteserkenntnis. Bonn, 1970.
Phil 310.653   Bit i suvremenost. (Sutlič, Vanja.) Sarajevo, 1967.
Phil 8125.10   Bite-Palevitch. Essai sur les tendances critiques. Paris, 1925.
Phil 3625.5.86   Bitte, I.H. Salomon Maimon. Berlin, 1876.
Phil 5627.261   Bitter, W. Zur Rettung des Menschlichen in unserer Zeit. Stuttgart, 1961.
Phil 5401.30   Bitter, Wilhelm. Die Angstneurose. Bern, 1948.
Phil 6980.114   Bitter, Wilhelm. Magie und Wunder in der Heilkunde. Stuttgart, 1959.
Phil 8980.213   Bittighoefer, Bernd. Moral und Gesellschaft. Berlin, 1968.
Phil 8980.213.5   Bittighoefer, Bernd. Die Rind dir andere neben Dir. Berlin, 1965.
Phil 5241.108   Bittle, Alestine N.C. The whole man. Milwaukee, 1945.
Phil 3450.48.80   Bittner, Gerhard. Sachlichkeit und Bildung; kritische Studie...Hans-Eduard Hengstenberg. München? 1965?
Phil 6980.113   Bittner, Günther. Psychoanalyse und soziale Erziehung. München, 1967.
Phil 176.96   Biunde, F.X. Fundamental-Philosophie. Trier, 1838.
Phil 5465.9   Biuso, C. La fantasia. Catania, 1903.
Phil 282.10   Bixby, J.T. The open secret; a study of life's deeper forces. Boston, 1912.
Phil 8691.3   Bixby, J.T. Similarities of physical and religious knowledge. N.Y., 1876.
Phil 9150.9.2   Bixby, James T. The crisis in morals. Boston, 1891.
Phil 9150.9.3   Bixby, James T. The ethics of revolution. Boston, 1900.
Phil 8581.78.5   Bixler, J.S. Conversations with an unrepentant liberal. New Haven, 1946.
Phil 8581.78   Bixler, J.S. Religion for free minds. N.Y., 1939.
Phil 176.144   Pamphlet box. Bixler, J.S. Minor works.
Phil 8633.1.31   Bixler, Julius S. Immortality and the present mood. Cambridge, 1931.
Phil 2070.126   Bixler, Julius S. Religion in the philosophy of William James. Boston, 1926.
Phil 8876.79   Bizyenos, Georgios. Psychologikai meletai apo tou kalou. Athens, 1885.
Phil 8402.58   Bizzarri, R. Il problema estetico. Brescia, 1954.
Phil 801.27   Bjarnason, A. Austurlönd. Reykjavik, 1908.
Phil 801.27.5   Bjarnason, A. Hellas. Reykjavik, 1910.
Phil 801.27.20   Bjarnason, A. Nitjánda äldin. Reykjavik, 1906.
Phil 801.27.15   Bjarnason, A. Vesturlönd. Reykjavik, 1815.
Phil 4520.8.42   Bjarnason, Ágúst. Almenn rökfraeđ Reykjavík, 1913.
Phil 4520.8.52   Bjarnason, Ágúst. Almenn sálarfraeđ Reykjavík, 1916.
Phil 4520.8.40   Bjarnason, Ágúst. Andatrúin. Reykjavík, 1905.
Phil 4520.8.48   Bjarnason, Ágúst. "Andatrúin" krufin. Reykjavík, 1906.
Phil 4520.8.30   Bjarnason, Ágúst. Austurlönd. Reykjavík, 1908.
Phil 4520.8.32   Bjarnason, Ágúst. Drauma-joi, sannar sagnir. Reykjavík, 1915.
Phil 4520.8.34   Bjarnason, Ágúst. Hellas. Reykjavík, 1910.
Phil 2630.2.131   Bjarnason, Ágúst. Jean-Marie Guyau. Kobenhavn, 1911.
Phil 4520.8.36   Bjarnason, Ágúst. Níjtánda öldin. Reykjavík, 1906.
Phil 4520.8.44   Bjarnason, Ágúst. Siđraeđ Reykjavík, 1924.
Phil 4520.8.46   Bjarnason, Ágúst. Upphaf kristninnar og...Jesús Kristur. Reykjavík, 1904.
Phil 4520.8.38   Bjarnason, Ágúst. Vesturlönd. Reykjavík, 1915.
Phil 7082.62   Bjarnason, Halldór. Draumur. Reykjavik, 1879.
Phil 9495.167.5   Bjerg, Kresten. Moralpsykologi og sexualmoral. København, 1967.
Phil 6311.2.2   Bjerre, P. The history and practice of psychanalysis. Boston, 1920.
Phil 6311.2   Bjerre, P. The history of psychanalysis. Boston, 1919.
Phil 6311.2.5   Bjerre, P. Von der Psychoanalyse zur Psychosynthese. Halle, 1925.
Phil 5311.2.5   Bjerre, P. Von der Psychoanalyse zur Psychosynthese. Halle, 1925.
Phil 6311.2.10   Bjerre, P. Wie deine Seele geheilt wird. Halle, 1925.
Phil 7084.20   Bjerre, Paul. Das Träumen als Heilungsweg der Seele. Zürich, 1936.
Phil 3640.196   Bjerre, Poul. Det geniala vansinnet. Göteborg, 1903.
Phil 5241.60   Bjerre, Poul. Studier i själstäkekonst. Stockholm 1914.
Phil 5627.266.25   Bjoerkhen, John. Människan och makterna. Stockholm, 1966.
Phil 4520.6.2   Björklund, G. Skrifter. Upsala, 1924.
Phil 8626.8   Björklund, Gustaf. Death and resurrection. London, 1910.
Phil 8626.8.5   Björklund, Gustaf. Om döden och uppstandeken fran cellärans synpunkt. London, 1910.
Phil 8626.24   Björkman, E.A. Det bortkastade helvetet. Stockholm, 1864.
Phil 4520.3.31   Björkman, N.O. Om det absoluta förnuftet. Stockholm, 1888.
Phil 6111.15   Björnson, B. Wise-Kunst. N.Y., 1909.
Phil 6671.25   Björnström, F.J. Hypnotism. N.Y., 1889.
Phil 176.52   Bjorkman, E. Is there anything new under the sun? N.Y., 1911.
Phil 7159.8   Bjornstad, James. Twentieth century prophecy: Jeane Dixon, Edgar Cayce. Minneapolis, 1969.
Phil 5041.28.3   Black, George A. Problem; science-analysis. N.Y., 1911.
Phil 5041.28   Black, George A. Problem; science (function) analysis. N.Y., 1905.
Phil 8876.47   Black, Hugh. Culture and restraint. N.Y., 1901.
Phil 5520.97A   Black, M. Language and philosophy. Ithaca, 1949.
Phil 165.13   Black, M. Philosophical analysis. Ithaca, 1950.
Phil 3925.16.110   Black, Max. A companion to Wittgenstein's Tractatus. Ithaca, 1964.
Phil 5041.59.2   Black, Max. Critical thinking. N.Y., 1947.
Phil 5041.59.5   Black, Max. Critical thinking. 2nd ed. N.Y., 1954.
Phil 5520.514   Black, Max. The labyrinth of language. N.Y., 1968.
Phil 1905.32.30   Black, Max. Models and metaphores. N.Y., 1962.
Phil 1830.53   Black, Max. Philosophy in America. London, 1965.
Phil 165.13.5A   Black, Max. Problems of analysis. Ithaca, 1954.
Phil 5878.5   Black and white identity formation: studies in the psychosocial development of lower socioeconomic class adolescent boys. (Hauser, Stuart T.) N.Y., 1971.
Phil 5893.4   Black child, white child; the development of racial attitudes. (Porter, Judith Deborah Revitch.) Cambridge, 1971.
Phil 7069.30.10   "Black objects". (Kernaham, C.) London, 1930.
Phil 623.37   Black ship to hell. 1. American ed. (Brophy, B.) N.Y., 1962.
Phil 7150.98   Black suicide. (Hendin, Herbert.) N.Y., 1969.
Phil 7060.30   Blackburn, D. Thought-reading. London, 1884.

Phil 6100.14 Blackburn, I.W. Illustrations of the gross morbid anatomy of the brain in the insane. Washington, 1908.
Phil 5241.109 Blackburn, J.M. Psychology and the social pattern. London, 1945.
Htn Phil 2045.95.2* Blackburne, Richard. Magni philosophi Thomae Hobbes malmesburiensis vita. London, 1682.
Htn Phil 2045.95* Blackburne, Richard. Thomae Hobbes angli malmesburiensis vita. Carolopoli, 1681.
Phil 1750.166.35.5 Blackham, H.J. The human tradition. Boston, 1953.
Phil 1750.166.35.7 Blackham, H.J. The human tradition. Boston, 1954.
Phil 1750.166.35 Blackham, H.J. Living as a humanist. London, 1957.
Phil 1750.166.145 Blackham, H.J. Objections to humanism. London, 1963.
Phil 1750.362 Blackham, H.J. Six existentialist thinkers. London, 1952.
Phil 8826.2.5 Blackie, J.S. Four phases of morals; Socrates, Aristotle, Christianity, Utilitarianism. 2nd ed. Edinburgh, 1874.
Phil 8826.2 Blackie, J.S. Four phases of morals. Edinburgh, 1871.
Phil 8656.3 Blackie, J.S. The natural history of atheism. London, 1877.
Phil 8656.3.2 Blackie, J.S. The natural history of atheism. N.Y., 1878.
Phil 8402.7 Blackie, J.S. On beauty; three discourses delivered in the University of Edinburgh. Edinburgh, 1858.
Phil 2053.92 Blackstone, William T. Francis Hutcheson and contemporary ethical theory. Athens, Ga., 1965.
Phil 176.44 Blackwell, A.B. The philosophy of individuality. N.Y., 1893.
Phil 8626.7 Blackwell, A.B. Physical basis of immortality. N.Y., 1876.
Phil 176.44.5 Blackwell, A.B. Studies in general science. N.Y., 1869.
Phil 9352.5 The blade and the ear. (Muzzey, A.B.) Boston, 1865.
Phil 8626.11 Blades, Franklin. Is the life of man eternal? N.Y., 1911.
Phil 3549.2.20 Blätter der Schule der Weisheit; eine Chronik der Weiterentwicklung der Schule der Weisheit für die Mitglieder des Vereins der Freunde des Keyserling-Archivs. v.1-2. Innsbruck, 1948-49.
Phil 11.15 Blätter für deutsche Philosophie. Berlin. 1-16,1927-1943 16v.
Phil 11.7 Blätter für freies religiöses Leben. Philadelphia. 1-19,1857-1875+ 9v.
Phil 3483.88 Blaha, Ottokar. Die Ontologie Kants. Ihr Grundriss in der Transzendentalphilosophie. Habilitationsschrift. Salzburg, 1967.
Phil 8656.14.27 Blain, Jacob. A review, giving the main ideas in E. Beecher's Conflict of ages. Buffalo, 1856.
Phil 801.9 Blainville, H. de. Historie des sciences de l'organisation. Paris, 1845. 3v.
Phil 176.59 Blair, D. The master-key. Wimbledon, 1914.
Phil 9341.8 Blair, H. Advice to youth. n.p., n.d.
Phil 9161.6 Blair, H. On the duties of the young. London, 1794.
Phil 8581.65 Blair, P. Thoughts on nature and religion. London, 1774.
Phil 5421.25.25 Blais, Gerard. L'amour humain. Sherbrooke, 1968.
Phil 2805.397 Blaise Pascal, 1623-1662. (Bibliothèque Nationale, Paris.) Paris, 1962
Phil 2805.385 Blaise Pascal. (Baudouin, Charles.) Paris, 1962.
Phil 2805.88 Blaise Pascal. (Bertrand, J.L.F.) Paris, 1891.
Phil 2805.192.15 Blaise Pascal. (Brunschvicg, L.) Paris, 1953.
Phil 2805.430 Blaise Pascal. (Gouhier, Henri.) Paris, 1966.
Phil 2805.435 Blaise Pascal. (Hoven, Pieter van der.) Baarn, 1964.
Phil 2805.265 Blaise Pascal. (Jaccard, L.F.) Neuchâtel, 1951.
Phil 2805.99 Blaise Pascal. (Jordan, H.R.) London, 1909.
Phil 2805.185 Blaise Pascal. (Langenskjold, Agnes.) Uppsala, 1922.
Phil 2805.345 Blaise Pascal. (Mortimer, Ernest.) London, 1959.
Phil 2805.253 Blaise Pascal. (Peters, F.E.) Hamburg, 1946.
Phil 2805.112.10 Blaise Pascal. (Stewart, Hugh F.) London, 1942.
Phil 2805.186 Blaise Pascal. v.1-2. (Bohlin, J.) Stockholm, 1920-21.
Phil 2805.242 Blaise Pascal. 2. Aufl. (Buchholz, E.) Göttingen, 1942.
Phil 2805.214 Blaise Pascal et sa soeur Jacqueline. (Mauriac, F.) Paris, 1931.
Phil 2805.90.5 Blaise Pascal études d'histoire morale. (Giraud, V.) Paris, 1910.
Phil 5585.72 Blake, R.R. Perception. N.Y., 1951.
Phil 4710.110.5 Blakeley, Thomas J. Soviet philosophy; a general introduction to contemporary Soviet thought. Dordrecht, 1964.
Phil 4710.110 Blakeley, Thomas J. Soviet scholasticism. Dordrecht, 1961.
Phil 4710.110.10 Blakeley, Thomas J. Soviet theory of knowledge. Dordrecht, 1964.
Phil 7060.25 Blakeman. R. Philosophical essay on credulity and superstition. N.Y., 1849.
Phil 8876.18 Blakey, R. An essay...good and evil. Edinburgh, 1831.
Phil 5011.1 Blakey, R. Historical sketch of logic. London, 1851.
Phil 8826.3 Blakey, R. History of moral science. Edinburgh, 1836. 2v.
NEDL Phil 801.3 Blakey, R. History of the philosophy of the mind. London, 1848. 4v.
Phil 801.3.2 Blakey, R. History of the philosophy of the mind. London, 1850. 4v.
Phil 5041.13 Blakey, Robert. Essay towards...system of logic. London, 1834.
Phil 8581.22 Blamires, W.L. Studies and speculation in natural history. London, 1901.
Phil 2733.84 Blampignon, Emile Antoine. Bibliographie de Malebranche. Montbéliard, n.d.
Phil 2733.81 Blampignon, Emile Antoine. Étude sur Malebranche. Paris, 1862.
Phil 86.7 Blanc, Elie. Dictionnaire de philosophie ancienne. Paris, 1906.
Phil 1506.2 Blanc, Elie. Manuale philosophiae scholasticae. Lugduni, 1901. 2v.
Phil 2270.102 Blanc, Elie. Les nouvelles bases de la morale d'après Herbert Spencer. Lyon, 1881.
Phil 1506.2.5 Blanc, Elie. Traité de philosophie scolastique. Lyon, 1909. 3v.
Phil 7068.65.2 Blanc, H. Le merveilleux dans le Jansénisme, le magnétisme, le méthodisme et le baptisme américains. Paris, 1865.
Phil 8581.127 Blanc de Saint-Bonnet, Antoine Joseph Elisée Adolphe. De l'affaiblissement de la raison et de la décadence en Europe. 2. éd. Paris, 1854.
Phil 2905.1.160 Blanchard, Julien P. Méthode et principes du père Teilhard de Chardin. Paris, 1961.
Phil 8876.104 Blanchard, Mme. Common sense. N.Y., 1916.
Phil 8876.105 Blanchard, Mme. Timidity. N.Y., 1916.
Phil 2733.112 Blanchard, Pierre. L'attention à Dieu selon Malebranche. Paris, 1956.
Phil 8581.70 Blanchard, Pierre. Catéchisme de la nature, ou religion et morale naturelles. Paris, n.d.
Phil 8626.3 Blanche, C.I. Le surnaturel. Paris, 1872.
Phil 5041.78 Blanché, Robert. Introduction à la logique contemporaine. Paris, 1957.
Phil 5241.94 Blanché, Robert. La notion de fait psychique. Thèse. Paris, 1934.
Phil 5041.93.10 Blanché, Robert. Raison et discours, dépense de la logique réflexive. Paris, 1967.
Phil 2340.9.94 Blanché, Robert. Le rationalisme de Whewell. Paris, 1935.
Phil 2340.9.93 Blanché, Robert. Le rationalisme de Whewell. Thèse. Paris, 1935.
Phil 5041.93 Blanché, Robert. Structures intellectuelles. Paris, 1966.
Phil 4352.1.85 Blanche-Raffin, A. de. Jacques Balmes, sa vie et ouvrages. Paris, 1849.
Phil 2520.139 Blanchet, Léon. Les antécédents historique du "Je pense, donc je suis". Paris, 1920.
Phil 4073.84 Blanchet, Léon. Campanella. Paris, 1920.
Phil 5811.24 Blancheteau, Marc. L'orientation spatiale chez l'animal, ses indices et ses repères. Paris, 1969.
Phil 400.106 Blanchi, R. Les attitudes idéalistes. Paris, 1949.
Phil 3640.304 Blanco, Julio E. Homenaje a Friedrich Nietzsche en el primer centenario de su nacimiento. Baranquilla, 1944.
Phil 7060.250 Bland, Oliver. The adventures of a modern occultist. N.Y., 1920.
Phil 7059.11.2 Bland, T.A. In the world celestial. 2. ed. Chicago, 1902.
Phil 6951.3 Blandford, G.F. Insanity and its treatment. Edinburgh, 1892.
Phil 1750.552 Blankart, Franz André. Zweiheit, Bezug und Vermittlung. Zürich, 1966.
Phil 1905.15 Blanshard, B. The nature of thought. N.Y., 1940. 2v.
Phil 176.170 Blanshard, B. On philosophical style. Bloomington, 1954.
Phil 623.42 Blanshard, Brand. Reason and analysis. La Salle, Ill., 1962.
Phil 8876.135A Blanshard, Brand. Reason and goodness. London, 1961.
Phil 6990.44 Blanton, M.G. Bernadette of Lourdes. London, 1939.
Phil 9400.30 Blanton, S. Now or never. Englewood Cliffs, N.J., 1959.
Phil 6420.32 Blanton, Smiley. For stutterers. N.Y., 1936.
Phil 8597.3.15 Blasche, J.C. Kurze auch dem Laien verstandliche Verantwortung wider die Beschuldigungen. Jena, 1778.
Phil 1106.9 Blass, F. Ideale und materielle Lebensauschauung. Kiel, 1889.
Phil 8656.17 Blatchford, R. God and my neighbor. Chicago, 1919.
Phil 8656.17.5 Blatchford, R. God and my neighbor. London, 1904.
Phil 6946.38 Blatt, Burton. Exodus from pandemonium; human abuse and a reformation of public policy. Boston, 1970.
Phil 1830.5A Blau, Joseph L. American philosophic addresses. N.Y., 1946.
Phil 2070.128 Blau, Théodore. William James. Thèse. Paris, 1933.
Phil 978.5.11 Blavatsky, H.P. An abridgement by K. Hilliard of The secret doctrine. N.Y., 1907.
Phil 978.5.1 Blavatsky, H.P. Collected writings. 1st American ed. v.5-8. Los Angeles, 1950. 4v.
Phil 978.5.5 Blavatsky, H.P. Isis unveiled. v.1-2. Point Loma, California, 1919. 4v.
Phil 978.5.24 Blavatsky, H.P. The key to theosophy. London, 1889.
Phil 978.5.26 Blavatsky, H.P. The key to theosophy. Los Angeles, 1920.
Phil 978.5.25 Blavatsky, H.P. The key to theosophy. 2nd American ed. N.Y., 1896.
Phil 978.5.27 Blavatsky, H.P. The key to theosophy. 4th ed. Point Loma, Calif., 1923.
Phil 978.5.7 Blavatsky, H.P. Personal memoirs of H.P. Blavatsky. London, 1937.
Phil 978.5.9 Blavatsky, H.P. The secret doctrine. v.1-2. Point Loma, Calif., 1925. 4v.
Phil 978.5.6 Blavatsky, H.P. The secret doctrine. v.3. London, 1888-97.
Phil 978.5.85 Blavatsky, H.P. Some unpublished letters. London, 1929.
Phil 978.5.30 Blavatsky, H.P. Studies in occultism. 2nd ed. Boston, 1897.
Phil 978.5.28A Blavatsky, H.P. The theosophical glossary. London, 1892.
Phil 978.5.12 Blavatsky, H.P. The voice of the silence. N.Y., 1889.
Phil 978.5.13 Blavatsky, H.P. The voice of the silence. N.Y., 1889.
Phil 978.5.22 Blavatsky, H.P. The voice of the silence. Peking, 1927.
Phil 978.5.20 Blavatsky, H.P. The voice of the silence. 4th ed. Point Loma, 1920.
Phil 978.5.15 Blavatsky, H.P. The voice of the silence. 5th ed. London, 1896.
Phil 978.5.18 Blavatsky, H.P. The voice of the silence. 6th ed. London, 1903.
Phil 735.12 Blechman, Nathan. The philosophic function of value. Boston, 1918.
Phil 8620.1 Bledsoe, A.T. A theodicy. N.Y., 1856.
Phil 8876.130 Blegvad, Mogeus. Den naturalistiske sejlslutning. København, 1959.
Phil 3486.2.9 Bleibendes und Vergängliches in der Philosophie Kants. (Erhardt, Franz.) Leipzig, 1926.
Phil 5425.36 Bleibtreu, K. Letzte Wahrheiten. Leipzig, 1894.
Phil 5241.49 Bleibtreu, K. Zur Psychologie der Zukunft. Leipzig, 1890.
Phil 176.23 Blein, A. Essais philosophiques. Paris, 1843.
Phil 282.22 Bleksley, A.E. The problems of cosmology. Johannesburg, 1956.
Phil 3821.19 Blessed Spinoza. (Browne, Lewis.) N.Y., 1932.
Phil 3450.29.80 Blessing, Eugen. Theodor Haecker. Nürnberg, 1959.
Phil 6951.11 Bleuler, E. Affeklivität, Suggestibilität, Paranoia. Halle, 1906.
Phil 6951.11.2 Bleuler, E. Affektivität, Suggestibilität, Paranoia. 2. Aufl. Halle, 1926.
Phil 6951.11.5 Bleuler, E. Textbook of psychiatry. N.Y., 1924.
Phil 5643.16 Bleuler, E. Zwangsmässige Lichtemfindungen. Leipzig, 1881.
Phil 5241.84 Bleuler, Eugen. Naturgeschichte der Seele und ihres Bewusst-Werdens. Berlin, 1921.
Phil 176.47A Blewett, G.J. Study of nature...with other essays. Toronto, 1907.
Phil 1955.6.160 Blewett, John. John Dewey. N.Y., 1960.
Phil 978.5.90 Bleyi lotos. Burbank, Calif. 1958-1959 3v.
Phil 3640.235.30 Ein Blick in Notizbücher Nietzsches. (Podach, Erich F.) Heidelberg, 1963.
Phil 3001.6 En blick pa den newarande filosofien i Tyshland. (Borelius, J.J.) Stockholm, 1879.
Phil 3001.6.5 Blicke auf den Gegenwärtigen Standpunkt der Philosophie in Deutschland und Frankreich. (Borelius, J.J.) Berlin, n.d.
Htn Phil 3801.776* Blicke auf die Schellingsch- Jacobi'sche Streitsache. (Schaffroth, J.A.G.) Stuttgart, 1812.
Phil 8707.1 Blicke in das Leben der Gegenwart. (Reichenbach, H.G.L.) Dresden, 1856.

Phil 194.34.10 Blicke in das Wesen des Menschen. (Troxler, I.P.V.) Aarau, 1812.
Phil 8585.13.15 Blicke in die intellectuelle, physische und moralische Welt. (Frauestädt, C.M.J.) Leipzig, 1869.
Phil 176.36 Blicke ins Leben. v.1-4. (Burdach, K.F.) Leipzig, 1842. 2v.
Phil 3260.82 Bliedner, E. Philosophie der Mathematik. Jena, 1904.
Phil 1504.18.2 Bliemetzrieder, P. Anselms von Laon systematische Sentenzen. v.18, pt.2-3. Münster, n.d.
Phil 2880.8.96 Bligbeder, Marc. L'homme Sartre. Paris? 1947.
Phil 8876.46 Bligh, S.M. The desire for qualities. London, n.d.
Phil 9530.18.4 Bligh, Stanley M. The direction of desire. London, 1910.
Phil 6750.14 The blight of the feeble-minded. (Munro, Caroline S.G.) Boston, 191-?
Phil 176.24 Blignières, C. Exposition de la philosophie. Paris, 1857.
Phil 5643.102 The blind sport of Mariotte. (Brøns, J.) Copenhagen, 1939.
Phil 9347.8 Bliss of marriage; or How to get a rich wife. (Hall, S.S.) New Orleans, 1858.
Phil 6980.712.100 Blisten, D.R. The social theories of Harry Stack Sullivan. N.Y., 1953.
Phil 476.5 Bliven, Eliza M. Materialism. n.p., n.d.
Phil 3890.8.110 Bloch, E. Christian Thomasius. Berlin, 1953.
Phil 165.40.5 Bloch, Ernest. Wissen und Hoffen. Berlin, 1955.
Phil 3120.55.45 Bloch, Ernst. Auswahl aus seinen Schriften. Frankfurt, 1967.
Phil 176.69 Bloch, Ernst. Geist der Utopie. München, 1918.
Phil 3120.55.20 Bloch, Ernst. Gesamtausgabe. Frankfurt, 1961. 15v.
Phil 3790.4.87 Bloch, Ernst. Kritische Erörterungen über Rickert. Diss. Ludwigshafen, 1909.
Phil 3120.55.25 Bloch, Ernst. Die Kunst, Schiller zu sprechen und andere literarische Aufsätze. Frankfurt, 1969. 14v.
Phil 8581.120 Bloch, Ernst. Man on his own. N.Y., 1970.
Phil 3120.55.30 Bloch, Ernst. Das Morgen im Heute; eine Auswahl. Frankfurt, 1960.
Phil 3120.55.60 Bloch, Ernst. Pädagogica. 1.Aufl. Frankfurt, 1971.
Phil 176.69.15 Bloch, Ernst. Philosophische Grundfragen. Frankfurt, 1961.
Phil 3120.55.50 Bloch, Ernst. A philosophy of the future. N.Y., 1970.
Phil 176.69.10 Bloch, Ernst. Spuren. Berlin, 1930.
Phil 176.69.12 Bloch, Ernst. Spuren. Berlin, 1960.
Phil 176.69.12.5 Bloch, Ernst. Spuren. 5. Aufl. Frankfurt, 1967.
Phil 3425.334 Bloch, Ernst. Subjekt-Objekt; Erläuterungen zu Hegel. Berlin, 1951.
Phil 176.69.5 Bloch, Ernst. Tübinger Einleitung in die Philosophie. Berlin, 1923.
Phil 3120.55.55 Bloch, Ernst. Tübinger Einleitung in die Philosophie I. Frankfurt, 1963.
Phil 3425.756 Bloch, Ernst. Über Methode und System bei Hegel. Frankfurt am Main, 1970.
Phil 3120.55.35 Bloch, Ernst. Verfremdungen. Frankfurt, 1962. 2v.
Phil 3120.55.40 Bloch, Ernst. Wegzeichen der Hoffnung. Frankfurt, 1967.
X Cg Phil 7075.9 Bloch, Iwan. Le Marquis de Sade et son temps. Berlin, 1901.
X Cg Phil 7075.9.5 Bloch, Iwan. Neue Forschungen über den Marquis de Sade. Berlin, 1904.
X Cg Phil 9495.125 Bloch, Iwan. The sexual life of our time. London, 1910?
Phil 2610.100.5 Bloch, Olivier René. La philosophie de Gassendi. La Haye, 1971.
Phil 2070.82.5 Bloch, Werner. Der Pragmatismus von James und Schiller. Leipzig, 1913.
Phil 5853.8 Blocher, Donald H. Developmental counseling. N.Y., 1966.
Phil 5594.161 Block, J. The Q-sort method in personality assessment. Springfield, Ill., 1961.
Phil 5592.155.5 Block, Jack. The challenge of response sets. N.Y., 1965.
Phil 8612.20.5 Block, Oscar. Döden; populär framställning. Stockholm, 1904. 2v.
Phil 8612.20 Block, Oscar. Om døden; en almenfattelig fremstelling. København, 1903. 2v.
Phil 5548.142 Bloeschl, Lilian. Belohnung und Bestrafung im Lernexperiment. Weinheim, 1969.
Phil 4520.1.31 Blomquist, G. Lyckovägar. Stockholm, 1916.
Phil 176.134 Blondeau, Cyrille. Propositions de philosophie. Paris, 1932.
NEDL Phil 6951.17 Blondel, C. La conscience morbide. Thèse. Paris, 1913.
Phil 6311.8 Blondel, C. La psychanalyse. Paris, 1924.
Phil 7150.29 Blondel, Charles. Le suicide. Strasbourg, 1933.
Phil 2800.1.88 Blondel, M. Léon Ollé-Laprune. Paris, 1923.
Phil 5241.90 Blondel, M. La pensée. Paris, 1934. 2v.
Phil 5241.90.5 Blondel, M. La pensée. 4. éd. Paris, 1948.
Phil 8876.54 Blondel, Maurice. L'action. Paris, 1893.
Phil 8876.54.10 Blondel, Maurice. L'action. Paris, 1936.
Phil 8876.54.5 Blondel, Maurice. L'azione. Firenze, 1921. 2v.
Phil 2477.6.45 Blondel, Maurice. Blondel et Teilhard de Chardin. Paris, 1965.
Phil 2477.6.32 Blondel, Maurice. Carnets intimes, 1883-1894. Paris, 1961.
Phil 2477.6.20 Blondel, Maurice. Correspondance, 1899-1912. Paris, 1957. 3v.
Phil 2477.6.180 Blondel, Maurice. Correspondance de Maurice Blondel et Joannès Wehrlé; extraits. Paris, 1969. 2v.
Phil 2477.6.34 Blondel, Maurice. Correspondance philosophique. Paris, 1961.
Phil 3552.123 Blondel, Maurice. De vinculo substantiali. Thesis. Paris, 1893.
Phil 176.129.10 Blondel, Maurice. Dialogues avec les philosophes, Descartes, Spinoza. Paris, 1966.
Phil 3552.123.5 Blondel, Maurice. Une énigme historique, le "vinculum substantiali" d'après Leibniz. 1. éd. Paris, 1930.
Phil 176.129.5 Blondel, Maurice. L'être et les êtres. Paris, 1935.
Phil 176.129.6 Blondel, Maurice. L'être et les êtres. Paris, 1963.
Phil 8581.95.10 Blondel, Maurice. Exigences philosophiques du christianisme. 1. éd. Paris, 1950.
Phil 2477.6.40 Blondel, Maurice. Lettres philosophiques. Paris, 1961.
Phil 8581.95 Blondel, Maurice. La philosophie et l'esprit chrétien. Paris, 1944.
Phil 2477.6.30 Blondel, Maurice. Les premiers écrits de Maurice Blondel. 1. éd. Paris, 1956.
Phil 176.129 Blondel, Maurice. Le problème de la philosophie catholique. Paris, 1932.
Phil 2477.6.135 Blondel et le christianisme. (Bouillard, Henri.) Paris, 1961.
Phil 2477.6.45 Blondel et Teilhard de Chardin. (Blondel, Maurice.) Paris, 1965.
Phil 2477.6.160 The Blondelian synthesis; a study of the influence of German philosophical sources on the formation of Blondel's method and thought. (McNeill, John J.) Leiden, 1966.
Phil 2477.6.92 Le blondelisme. (Taymans d'Eypernon, F.) Louvain, 1933.
Phil 5926.1.18 Blondell, Charles. La psycho-physiologie de Gall. Thèse. Paris, 1913.
Phil 8581.64 Blood, B.P. Optimism, the lesson of ages. Boston, 1860.
Phil 176.70 Blood, B.P. Pluriverse. Boston, 1920.
Phil 5590.578.1 Bloom, Benjamin Samuel. Stability and change in human characteristics. N.Y., 1966.
Phil 5710.11 Bloor, Constance. Temperament, a survey of psychological theories. London, 1928.
Phil 176.166 Bloskhurst, J.B. Body, mind and creativity. N.Y., 1954.
Phil 6958.1 The blot upon the brain. (Ireland, W.W.) Edinburgh, 1885.
Phil 6958.1.3 The blot upon the brain. (Ireland, W.W.) N.Y., 1886.
Htn Phil 6990.40* Blount, Charles. Miracles, no violations of the law of nature. London, 1683.
Phil 8980.220 Bludov, Iakov S. Prostota i skromnost'. Kiev, 1968.
Phil 3120.22.15 Blüher, Hans. Die Achse der Natur. Hamburg, 1949.
Phil 3120.22 Blüher, Hans. Empedokles, oder das Sakrament des freien Todes. n.p., 1918.
Phil 3120.22.5 Blüher, Hans. Gesammelte Aufsätze. Jena, 1919.
Phil 3120.22.25F Blüher, Hans. In medias res. Jena, 1920.
Phil 3120.22.10 Blüher, Hans. Philosophie auf Posten, Schriften 1916-21. Heidelberg, 1928.
Phil 3120.22.40 Blüher, Hans. Traktat über die Heilkunde. Jena, 1928.
Phil 3120.22.20 Blüher, Hans. Werke und Tage. München, 1953.
Phil 3120.22.35 Blüher, Hans. Die Wiedergeburt der platonischen Akademie. Jena, 1920. 4 pam.
Phil 3120.22.30 Pamphlet vol. Blüher, Hans. Prien, 1920. 4 pam.
Phil 6311.23 Bluemel, C.S. The troubled mind. Baltimore, 1938.
Phil 6311.23.5 Bluemel, C.S. War, politics, and insanity. Denver, 1948.
Phil 6420.12 Bluemel, Charles Sidney. Stammering and cognate defects of speech. N.Y., 1913. 2v.
Phil 8402.35 Blümner, Hugo. Laokoon-studien. Freiburg, 1881-82.
Phil 2128.81 Bluet. An enquiry whether a general practice of virtue tends to the wealth or poverty...of a people. London, 1725.
Phil 3110.60 Blüthen aus Jakob Böhme's Mystik. (Böhme, J.) Stuttgart, 1838.
Phil 3022.3.15 Die Blüthezeit der deutschen Philosophie. (Windlband, Wilhelm.) Leipzig, 1880.
Phil 6111.63 Blum, Gerald S. A model of the mind. N.Y., 1961.
Phil 5545.266 Blum, Herwig. Die antike Mnemotechnik. Thesis. Hildesheim, 1969.
Phil 6158.40 Blum, Richard H. Utopiates; the use and users of LSD-25. N.Y., 1966.
Phil 6420.12.5 Blumel, Charles Sidney. Stammering and allied disorders. N.Y., 1935.
Phil 5520.62 Blumenfeld, W. Sinn und Unsinn. München, 1933.
Phil 8876.162 Blumenfeld, Walter. Vom sittlichen Bewusstsein. Bonn, 1968.
Phil 5520.728 Blumenthal, Arthur L. Language and psychology. N.Y., 1970.
Phil 3552.365 Blumenthal, Erwin. Herders Auseinandersetzung mit der Philosophie Leibnitzens. Diss. Hamburg, 1934.
Phil 6990.27 Blumhardt, C.G. Vertheidigungsschrift. Reutlingen, 1850.
Phil 3640.404 Blunck, R. Friedrich Nietzsche. München, 1953.
Phil 176.89 Blundell, A. Idealism, possible and impossible. London, 1911.
Phil 5041.52.6 Blundeville, Thomas. The art of logike. Facsimile. Menston, 1967.
Htn Phil 5041.52.5* Blundeville, Thomas. The arte of logicke. London, 1619.
Phil 8140.4 Blunt, A. Artistic theory in Italy, 1450-1600. Oxford, 1956.
Phil 4060.1.80 Bluwstein, J. Die Weltauschauung Roberto Ardigo. Leipzig, 1911.
Phil 5041.70 Blyth, J.W. A modern introduction to logic. Boston, 1957.
Phil 2340.10.100 Blyth, J.W. Whitehead's theory of knowledge. Providence, R.I., 1941.
Phil 5722.72 Blyznychenko, Leonid A. Vvod i zakreplenre informatsii v pamiati cheloveka vo vremia estestvennogo sna. Kiev, 1966.
Htn Phil 9345.5* Boarding school. (Foster, H. (Webster).) Boston, 1829.
Phil 8965.2 The Boardman Lectureship in Christian ethics. (University of Pennsylvania.) Philadelphia, 1900.
Phil 801.28 Boas, George. The adventures of human thought. N.Y., 1929.
Phil 630.32 Boas, George. The datum as essence in contemporary philosophy. Niort, 1927.
Phil 1701.17.5 Boas, George. Dominant themes of modern philosophy. N.Y., 1957.
Phil 2401.2 Boas, George. French philosophies of the romantic period. Baltimore, 1925.
Phil 2401.2.10 Boas, George. The happy beast in French thought of the 17th century. Baltimore, 1933.
Phil 8402.52.5 Boas, George. The heaven of invention. Baltimore, 1962.
Phil 176.210 Boas, George. The limits of reason. London, 1961.
Phil 801.28.5 Boas, George. The major traditions of European philosophy. N.Y., 1929.
Phil 1701.17 Boas, George. Our new ways of thinking. N.Y., 1930.
Phil 8402.52A Boas, George. A primer of cities. Baltimore, 1937.
Phil 1135.173 Boas, Georje. Rationalism in Greek philosophy. Baltimore, 1961.
Phil 6311.11 Boas, J.M. La défense psychique. Thèse. Paris, 1924.
Phil 6311.11.2 Boas, J.M. La défense psychique. Thèse. Paris, 1924.
Phil 282.2 Boase, H.S. Few words on evolution and creation. London, 1882.
Phil 1701.52 Bobbio, Norberto. Da Hobbes a Marx; saggi di storia della filosofia. Napoli, 1965.
Phil 3483.70 Bobbio, Norberto. Diritto e stato nel pensiero di Emanuele Kant. Torino, 1957.
Phil 1750.205 Bobbio, Norberto. The philosophy of decadentism; a study in existentialism. Oxford, 1948.
Phil 1500.2 Bobenstuber, P.L. Philosophia thomistica salisburgensis. Augusta Vindelicorum, 1724.
Phil 5039.26 Bober, Juraj. Problémy dialektiky. 1. vyd. Bratislava, 1968.
Phil 2477.5.30 Boberil, Roger. Essais philosophiques. Rennes, 1910. 2 pam.
Phil 6060.26 Bobertag, Otto. Ist die Graphologie zuverlässig? Heidelberg, 1929.
Phil 5274.3 Bobneva, Margarita I. Tekhnicheskaia psikhologiia. Moskva, 1966.
Phil 8402.42 Bobrik, Eduard. Freie vorträge über Ästhetik. Zürich, 1834.
Phil 5041.14 Bobrik, Eduard. Neues praktisches System der Logik. Zürich, 1838.
Phil 8402.42.5 Bobriks Ästhetik; Beiträge zur Lehre des ästhetischen Formalismus. (Fiebig, Ernst.) Bonn, 1930.
Phil 4710.16 Bobrov, E.A. Filosofiia v Rossii; materialy. Kazan, 1899.
Phil 5400.9 Bobtschew, N. Die Gefühlslehre...von Kant bis auf unsere Zeit. Leipzig, 1888.

Phil 86.5   Boccalaro, M.A. Dizionario filosofico. Bologna, 1951.
Phil 5241.40   Bocci, Balduino. I primi teoremi di psicologia.
                   Siena, 1915.
Phil 8656.26   Bocheńske, I.M. De cognitione existential Dei per niam
                   causalitatis relate ad fidem catholicam. Poznań, 1936.
Phil 5041.63   Bochenski, I. Mario. Die zeitgenossischen Denkmethoden.
                   München, 1954.
Phil 1135.164   Bochénski, I.M. Ancient formal logic. Amsterdam, 1951.
Phil 5011.6   Bochénski, I.M. Formale Logik. Freiburg, 1956.
Phil 5011.6.6   Bochénski, I.M. A history of formal logic. Notre Dame,
                   Ind., 1961.
Phil 5011.6.10   Bochénski, I.M. Logico-philosophical studies.
                   Dordrecht, 1962.
Phil 5011.6.5   Bochénski, I.M. Logisch-philosophische Studien.
                   Freiburg, 1959.
Phil 5066.10   Bochénski, I.M. Noue lezioni di logica simbolica.
                   Roma, 1938.
Phil 176.214   Bochénski, I.M. Philosophy; an introduction.
                   Dordrecht, 1963.
Phil 5066.10.5   Bochénski, I.M. Précis de logique mathématique.
                   Bussum, 1948.
Phil 5066.10.7   Bochénski, I.M. A precis of mathematical logic.
                   Dordrecht, 1959.
Phil 5520.446   Bocheński, Innocentius M. The logic of religion.
                   N.Y., 1965.
Phil 5041.92   Bochénski, Innocentius M. The methods of contemporary
                   thought. Dordrecht, 1965.
Phil 730.10A   Bocheński, Innocentius M. The problem of universals.
                   Notre Dame, 1956.
Phil 5041.87   Bocheński, Innocentius M. Die zeitgenossischen
                   Denkmethoden. 2. Aufl. Bern, 1959.
Phil 1701.20.10 Bochénski, J.M. Contemporary European philosophy. 2d ed.
                   Berkeley, 1956.
Phil 1701.20   Bochénski, J.M. Europäische Philosophie der Gegenwart.
                   Bern, 1947.
Phil 1701.20.5   Bochénski, J.M. Europäische Philosophie der Gegenwart. 2.
                   Aufl. München, 1951.
Phil 1701.20.7   Bochénski, J.M. La philosophie contemporaine en Europe. 2.
                   éd. Paris, 1951.
Phil 3235.124   Bochmuell, Klaus. Leiblichkeit und Gesellschaft.
                   Göttingen, 1961.
Phil 5211.10   Bochorishvili, A.t. Prints'pial'nye voprosy psikhologii.
                   Tbilisi, 1957- 2v.
Phil 5722.70   Bochorishvili, A.T. Problema bessoznatel'nogo v
                   psikhologii. Tbilisi, 1961.
Phil 974.3.126   Bock, Emil. Rudolf Steiner. Stuttgart, 1961.
Phil 3450.19.375 Bock, Irmgard. Heideggers Sprachdenken. München, 1964.
Phil 5272.12   Bock, R. Darrell. The measurement and prediction of
                   judgment and choice. San Francisco, 1968.
Phil 978.105   Bockemnehl, Jochen. Naturwissenshaftliche Grundfragen.
                   Dornach, 1964.
Phil 5751.1.5   Bockshammer, G.F. Die Freyheit des menschlichen Willens.
                   Stuttgart, 1821.
Phil 5751.1   Bockshammer, G.F. On the freedom of the human will.
                   Andover, 1835.
Phil 5850.138.5 Bodalev, Aleksei A. Formirovanie poniatiia o drugom
                   cheloveke kak lichnosti. Leningrad, 1970.
Phil 6311.56   Bodamer, Joachim. Der gefährdete Mensch. Freiburg, 1968.
Phil 3425.700   Bodanmer, Theodor. Hegel Deutung der Sprache.
                   Hamburg, 1969.
Phil 3483.54   Bodansky, Siegfried. Kants Dissertation vom Jahre 1770 und
                   ihre Beziehung zur Kritik der Reinen Vernunft.
                   Friedele, 1911-13.
Phil 5041.30   Bode, B.H. An outline of logic. N.Y., 1910.
Phil 3552.110.5 Bodemann, E. G.W. Leibniz. Hannover, 1876.
Phil 9515.3.83   Bodemann, E. J.G. Zimmermann. Hannover, 1878.
Phil 3552.110   Bodemann, E. Die Leibniz-Handschriften. Hannover, 1895.
Htn Phil 8876.19.6* Bodenham, John. Politeuphuia, wits common-wealth.
                   London, 1650.
Htn Phil 8876.19.7* Bodenham, John. Politeuphuia, wits common-wealth.
                   London, 1653.
Htn Phil 8876.19.2* Bodenham, John. Politeuphuia, wits common-wealth.
                   London, 1655.
Htn Phil 8876.19.13* Bodenham, John. Politeuphuia, wits common-wealth.
                   London, 1674.
Htn Phil 8876.19*   Bodenham, John. Politeuphuia, wits common-wealth.
                   London, 1688.
Htn Phil 8876.19.5* Bodenham, John. Politeuphuia. London, 1598.
Htn Phil 8876.19.3* Bodenham, John.. Wits commonwealth. London, 1722.
Phil 8402.53   Bodensohn, A. Über das Wesen des Asthetischen.
                   Frankfurt, 1961.
Phil 8599.19.115 Bodenstein, Walter. Neige des Historismus.
                   Gütersloh, 1959.
Phil 5400.31.9   Bodily changes in pain, hunger, fear and rage. 2d ed.
                   (Cannon, W.B.) N.Y., 1929.
Phil 5635.46   Bodily sensations. (Armstrong, David Malet.)
                   London, 1962.
Phil 6122.75   Bodily structure and the will. (MacConaill, Michael A.)
                   London, 1960.
Phil 7069.55.25 Bodin, Edward Longstreet. Upper purgatory. Daytona Beach,
                   Fla., 1955.
Phil 6315.2.95   Bodin, Jean. Contre Freud. Paris, 1926.
Phil 525.258   Bodmershof, Wilhelm. Geistige Versenkung. Zürich, 1965.
Phil 8876.40   Bodnai, Zsigmond. Az orkölcsi törvény alkalmazása.
                   Budapest, 1896.
Phil 4815.223.35 Bodnár, Zsigmond. Az erkölcsi világ. Budapest, 1896.
Phil 4815.223.30 Bodnár, Zsigmond. Szellemi haladásunk törvénye.
                   Budapest, 1892.
Phil 310.6.12   Bodrenski, J.M. The dogmatic principles of Soviet
                   philosophy. Dordrecht, Holland, 1963.
Phil 310.6.10   Bodrenski, J.M. Die dogmatischen Grundlagen der
                   sowjetischen Philosophie. Dordrecht, Holland, 1959.
Phil 801.17   Bodrero, E. I limiti della storia della filosofia.
                   Roma, 1919.
Phil 1200.65   Bodson, Arthur. La Morale sociale des derniers stoïciens,
                   Sénèque, Epictète et Marc Aurèle. Paris, 1967.
Phil 176.166   Body, mind and creativity. (Bloskhurst, J.B.) N.Y., 1954.
Phil 665.95   Body, mind and death. (Flew, Antony.) N.Y., 1964.
Phil 6132.4.13   Body, mind and spirit. (Worcester, Elwood.) Boston, 1931.
Phil 6125.31   Body, soul, spirit; a survey of the body-mind problem.
                   (Peursen, Cornelis Anthonie van.) London, 1966.
Phil 6113.21   Body, soul and spirit. (Dulley, William.) London, 1923.
Phil 6115.30   Body and mature behavior. (Feldenkrais, M.) N.Y., 1949.
Phil 6122.1   Body and mind. (Maudsley, H.) London, 1870.
Phil 6122.1.3   Body and mind. (Maudsley, H.) N.Y., 1871.
Phil 6122.1.5   Body and mind. (Maudsley, H.) N.Y., 1873.
Phil 6122.1.4   Body and mind. (Maudsley, H.) N.Y., 1895.
Phil 6122.13.5   Body and mind. (McDougall, William.) N.Y., 1911.

Phil 6122.13.11 Body and mind. 4th ed. (McDougall, William.)
                   London, 1918.
Phil 6122.13.13 Body and mind. 6th ed. (McDougall, William.)
                   London, 1923.
Phil 5227.8   Body and mind in Western thought. (Reeves, Joan Wynn.)
                   Harmondsworth, 1958.
Phil 5374.61   Body and self, one and inseparable. (Campbell, Percy A.)
                   San Francisco, 1942.
Phil 6127.2   Body and soul. (Redford, G.) London, 1847.
Phil 6126.5   Body and spirit. (Quackenbos, J.D.) N.Y., 1916.
Phil 5762.1   Body and will. (Maudsley, H.) London, 1883.
Phil 6115.32.5   Body experience in fantasy and behavior. (Fisher,
                   Seymour.) N.Y., 1970.
Phil 6115.32   Body image and personality. (Fisher, Seymour.) Princeton,
                   N.J., 1958.
Phil 181.79.5   The body of God. (Gutkind, Eric.) N.Y., 1969.
Phil 3483.29   Böckel, C.G.A. Die Todtenfeyer Kant's. 1. Aufl.
                   Königsberg, 1804.
Phil 3246.320   Boeckelmann, Frank. Die Schriften zu Johann Gottlieb
                   Fichtes Atheismus-Streit. München, 1969.
Phil 843.5.5   Boeckenhoff, J. Die Begegnungsphilosophie.
                   Freiburg, 1970.
Phil 8870.29   Boeckle, Franz. Moral zwischen Anspruch und Verantwortung.
                   Düsseldorf, 1964.
Phil 8951.32   Boeckman, Peter Wilhelm. Liv, fellesskap, tjeneste.
                   Oslo, 1970.
Phil 585.213   Boehler, Walther. Der mensch zwischen Übernatur und
                   Unternatur. Nürnberg, 1966.
Phil 3552.309   Boehm, A. Le "vinculum substantiale" chez Leibniz.
                   Paris, 1938.
Phil 7084.44   Boehm, Arthur. Rätsel des Traumes und des Zufalls.
                   Leipzig, 1920.
Phil 1750.127   Boehm, Benno. Sokrates im achtzehnten Jahrhundert.
                   Leipzig, 1929.
Phil 1750.127.2 Boehm, Benno. Sokrates im achtzehnten Jahrhundert.
                   Leipzig, 1929.
Phil 577.2   Boehm, Gottfried. Studien zur Perspektivität. Thesis.
                   Heidelberg, 1969.
Phil 3450.11.460 Boehm, Rudolf. Vom Gesichtspunkt des Phänomenologie. Den
                   Haag, 1968[1969]
Phil 5241.130   Boehme, Edwin. Das Gedankenleben und seine Beherrschung.
                   Cöln, 1959.
Phil 176.238   Boehme, Guenther. Der pädagogische Beruf der Philosophie.
                   München, 1968.
Phil 3110.50.10 Böhme, J. L'aurore naissante. Milan, 1927.
Htn Phil 3110.50*   Böhme, J. L'aurore naissante. Paris, 1800. 2v.
Phil 3110.32   Böhme, J. Bedrachtingh vande goddelycke openbaringh.
                   n.p., 1642.
Phil 3110.60   Böhme, J. Blüthen aus Jakob Böhme's Mystik.
                   Stuttgart, 1838.
Phil 3110.47   Böhme, J. Clef, ou Explication des divers points et termes
                   principaux. Paris, 1826.
Htn Phil 3110.40*   Böhme, J. Concerning the election of grace. London, 1655.
Htn Phil 3110.35*   Böhme, J. Concerning the three principles of divine
                   essence. London, 1648.
Phil 3110.35.5   Böhme, J. Concerning the three principles of divine
                   essence. London, 1910.
Phil 3110.45.10 Böhme, J. Confessions. N.Y., 1954.
Phil 3110.45   Böhme, J. The confessions of Jacob Böhme. London, 1920.
Phil 3110.31   Böhme, J. De electione gratiae et quaestiones
                   theosophicae. London, 1930.
Phil 3110.38   Böhme, J. De la signature des choses. Paris, 1908.
Phil 3110.55   Böhme, J. Der weeg zu Christo. Amsterdam, 1682.
Htn Phil 3110.23*   Böhme, J. Epistles. London, 1649-50.
Phil 3110.55.30 Böhme, J. Glaube und Tat. Berlin, 1957.
Htn Phil 3110.36.2* Böhme, J. High and deep searching out. London, 1656.
Phil 3110.36.5   Böhme, J. High and deep searching out. London, 1909.
Phil 3110.24   Böhme, J. Die Lehre des deutschen Philosophen J. Böhme.
                   München, 1844.
Phil 3110.55.35 Böhme, J. Die lochteure Pforte. Berlin, 1921.
Htn Phil 3110.39*   Böhme, J. Musterium magnum. London, 1654.
Phil 3110.39.5   Böhme, J. Mysterium magnum. Amsterdam, 1682.
Htn Phil 3110.30*   Böhme, J. Questions concerning the soul. London, 1647.
Htn Phil 3110.15*   Böhme, J. Remainder of books. London, 1662.
Phil 3110.11   Böhme, J. Sämmtliche Werke. v.1-7. Leipzig, 1860.
                   6v.
Phil 3110.11.2   Böhme, J. Sämmtliche Werke. v.1-7. Leipzig, 1922.
                   6v.
Phil 3110.13   Böhme, J. Sämtliche Schriften. Stuttgart, 1942.
                   10v.
Phil 3110.28.2   Böhme, J. Schriften. Leipzig, 1920.
Phil 3110.12   Böhme, J. Schriften. Leipzig, 1938.
Phil 3110.28   Böhme, J. Schriften Jakob Böhme. Leipzig, 1923.
Phil 3110.26   Böhme, J. Sein Leben und seine theosophischen Werke.
                   Stuttgart, 1885.
Phil 3110.27.10 Böhme, J. Sex puncta theosophica. Leipzig, 1921.
Phil 3110.37.4   Böhme, J. The signature of all things, with other
                   writings. London, 1926.
Phil 3110.37.5   Böhme, J. The signature of all things, with other
                   writings. London, 1934.
Phil 3110.27   Böhme, J. Six theosophic points, and other writings.
                   London, 1919.
Phil 3110.43   Böhme, J. Über die Umkehr und die Einsicht. Wien, 1953.
Phil 3110.36.30 Böhme, J. Vom dreifachen Leben des Menschen.
                   Hamburg, 1924.
Phil 3110.42   Böhme, J. Vom Lebendigen Glauben. Gütersloh, 1960.
Phil 3110.55.25 Böhme, J. Vom übersinlichen Leben. Hamburg, 1954.
Phil 3110.41   Böhme, J. Von der Genaden-Wahl. Amsterdam, 1682.
Phil 3110.55.5   Böhme, J. The way to Christ. 1st ed. N.Y., 1947.
Phil 3110.55.15 Böhme, J. The way to Christ discovered. Manchester, 1752.
X Cg Phil 3110.55.20 Böhme, J. The way to Christ discovered. N.Y., 1850.
                   (Changed to XM 710, 1971)
Phil 3110.22   Böhme, J. Works. Glasgow, 1886.
Htn Phil 3110.10.2* Böhme, J. Works. London, 1764- 4v.
Phil 3110.79   Pamphlet box. Böhme, J.
Phil 8876.59   Böhmer, Gustav. Ein Buch von der deutschen Gesinnung fünf
                   ethische Essays. München, 1897.
Phil 5585.1   Böhmer, H. Die Sinneswahrnehmung. Erlangen, 1868.
Phil 476.2.5   Böhner, A.N. Du matérialisme. Genève, 1861.
Phil 476.2   Böhner, A.N. Naturforschung und Kulturleben.
                   Hannover, 1859.
Phil 1540.30   Böhner, P. Medieval logic. Chicago, 1952.
Phil 1540.30.2   Böhner, P. Medieval logic. Manchester, 1952.
Phil 1511.3.20   Boehner, Philotheus. Christliche Philosophie von ihren
                   Anfängen bis Nikol von Cues. 3e Aufl. Paderborn, 1954.
Phil 3483.36   Böhringer, A. Kant's erkenntnis-theoretischer Idealismus.
                   Freiburg, 1888.
Phil 530.20.10   Böhringer, F. Die deutschen Mystiker. Zürich, 1855.

Phil 9245.134 Boelen, Bernard J. Eduaimonie en het wezen der ethiek. Leuven, 1949.

Phil 1750.798 Boelen, Bernard Jacques Marie. Existential thinking. Pittsburgh, 1968.

Phil 3120.31.30 Boem, W. Über die Möglichkeit systematischer Kulturphilosophie. Saale, 1927.

Phil 3425.201 Boer, J. de. De beteekenis van de Hegel-studie voor onzen tijd. Baarn, 1915.

Phil 5590.428 Boer, J. de. A system of characterology. Assen, 1963.

Phil 1020.3.6 Boer, T.J. de. The history of philosophy in Islam. London, 1961.

Phil 3450.11.225 Boer, Theodorus de. De ontwikkelingsgang in het denken van Husserl. Assem, 1966.

Phil 1020.17.5 Boer, Tjitze de. Die Widersprüche der Philosophie nach al Gozzali und ihr Ausgleich durch Ibn Rosd. Strassburg, 1894.

Phil 1020.17 Boer, Tjitze de. De wijsbegeerte in den Islam. Haarlem, 1921.

Phil 3549.8.80 Börlin, E. Darstellung und Kritik der Charakterologie von Ludwig Klages. Giessen, 1929.

Phil 2053.81 Boerma, N.W. De Leer van den Zedelijken zin bij Hutcheson. n.p., n.d.

Phil 3475.1.80 Börner, W. Friedrich Jodl - eine Studie. Stuttgart, 1911.

Phil 8876.107 Börner, W. Politische Zeitfragen in ethischer Beleuchtung. Wien, 1935.

Phil 8876.107.5 Börner, W. Zur ethischen Lebensgestaltung. Wien, 1937?

Phil 978.94 Boernsen, Hans. Naturwissenschaft an der Schwelle. Stuttgart, 1964.

Phil 5252.164 Boersenverein des deutschen Buchhandels, Frankfurt am Main. Alexander Mitscherlich: Ansprachen anlässlich der Verleihung des Friedenspreises. Frankfurt, 1969.

Phil 8876.22 Bösch, I.M. Das menschliche Mitgefühl. Winterthur, 1891.

Phil 5585.52 Böse, Karl G. Über Sinneswahrnehmung und deren Entwicklung zur Intelligenz. Braunschweig, 1872.

Phil 8620.50 Das Böse. (Häberlin, P.) Bern, 1960.

Phil 4520.5.34 Boethius, Daniel. De modo inculcandi veritates morales in concione publica. Diss. Upsaliae, 1800.

Phil 4520.5.25 Boethius, Daniel. Dissertatio philosophica, de angustis rationis humanae limitibus. Upsaliae, 1774.

Phil 4520.5.32 Boethius, Daniel. Dissertatio philosophica de morali ordine in eventu rerum jure postulato. Upsaliae, 1790.

Phil 4520.5.30 Boethius, Daniel. Dissertatio philosophica de origine atque indole nimiae divitiarum aestimationis. Upsaliae, 1788.

Phil 3483.37 Boette, Werner. Kants religion. Langensalza, 1920.

Phil 3246.225 Boettger, Fritz. Ruf zur Tat; Johann Gottlieb Fichte. 1. Aufl. Berlin, 1956.

Phil 6951.13 Böttger, H. Die Nahrungsverweigerung der Irren. Leipzig, 1878.

Phil 3483.83 Boeversen, F. Die Idee der Freiheit in der Philosophie Kants. Heidelberg, 1962.

Phil 3425.732 Boey, C. L'aliénation dans la phénoménologie de l'esprit de G.W.F. Hegel. Paris, 1970.

Phil 8657.14.20 Bóg i palingenezya. (Cieszkowski, August D.) Poznań, 1912.

Phil 4710.172.3 Bogatov, Vitalii V. Istoriia filosofii narodov SSSR. Izd. 3. Moskva, 1970.

Phil 310.500 Bogdanov, I.A. Sushchnost' i iavlenie. Kiev, 1962.

Phil 6980.124 Bogdanovich, L.A. Carnets d'une psychiatre soviétique. Paris, 1963.

Phil 3120.23.81 Bogdanski, A.A. The significance of Clemens Baeumker in neo-scholastic philosophy. Milwaukee, 1942.

Phil 5649.18 Bogen, H. Gang und Charakter. Leipzig, 1931.

Phil 5850.138 Bogen, Helmuth. Psychologische Grundlegung der praktischen Berufsberatung. Langensalza, 1927.

Phil 6760.5 Bogen om Jesper. (Gjedde, Georg.) København, 1971.

Phil 850.29 Bogliolo, Luigi. La filosofia antica. Torino, 1955.

Phil 176.232 Bogliolo, Luigi. Nuovo corso di filosofia a norma del Concilio Vaticano II. Roma, 1969- 2v.

Phil 1506.13 Bogliolo, Luigi. Il problema della filosofia cristiana. Brescia, 1959.

Phil 1695.34 Bogomdov, Aleksei S. Iz istorii zarubezhno filosofii XIX-XX vehov. Moskva, 1967.

Phil 1801.11 Bogomolov, A.S. Angle-amerikanskaia burzhuaznaia filosofiia epokhi imperializmo. Moskva, 1964.

Phil 365.56 Bogomolov, A.S. Ideia razvitiia v burzhuaznoifilas, XIX i XV vekov. Moskva, 1962.

Phil 1870.150 Bogomolov, A.S. Kritika subektivno-idealisticheskoi filosofii D. Berkli. Moskva, 1959.

Phil 3001.20 Bogomolov, A.S. Nemetskaia burzhuaznaia filosofiia posle 1865 goda. Moskva, 1969.

Phil 3819.57.25 Bogoslovsko-politicheskii traktat. (Spinoza, Benedictus de.) Moskva, 1935.

Phil 5041.39.2 Bogoslovsky, B.B. The technique of controversy. London, 1928.

Phil 5041.39 Bogoslovsky, B.B. The technique of controversy. N.Y., 1928.

Phil 1020.49 Bogoutdinov, Alautin M. Ocherki po istorii tadzhikskoi filosofii. Stalinabad, 1961.

Phil 6420.16.9 Bogue, Benjamin N. Stammering; its cause and correction. Indianapolis, 1939.

Phil 6420.16.5 Bogue, Benjamin N. Stammering; its cause and cure. Indianapolis, 1926.

Phil 2401.16 Boguslavskii, Veniamin M. U istokov frantsuzskogo ateizma i materializma. Moskva, 1964.

Phil 3483.53 Bohatec, J. Die Religionsphilosophie Kants. Hamburg, 1938.

Phil 2520.170 Bohatec, Josef. Die cartesianische Scholastik. Leipzig, 1912.

Phil 2255.3 A Bohemian philosopher at Oxford in the 17th century. (Young, Robert F.) London, 1925.

Phil 3821.10 Bohin, Vilhelm. Spinoza. Berlin, 1894.

Phil 8876.68 Bohlin, F. Das Grundproblem der Ethik. Uppsala, 1923.

Phil 2805.186 Bohlin, J. Blaise Pascal. v.1-2. Stockholm, 1920-21.

Phil 1750.166.55 Bohlin, T.B. Debatt med profanhumanisten. Stockholm, 1951.

Phil 5593.57 Bohm, E.B. Lehrbuch der Rorschach-Psychodiagnostik. 2. Aufl. Bern, 1957.

Phil 5811.10.10 Bohn, Georges. Die Entstehung des Denkvermögens. Leipzig, 1911?

Phil 5811.10.7 Bohn, Georges. La naissance de l'intelligence. Paris, 1920.

Phil 5811.10.5 Bohn, Georges. Die neue Tierpsychologie. Leipzig, 1912.

Phil 5811.10 Bohn, Georges. La nouvelle psychologie animale. Paris, 1911.

Phil 6311.9 Bohn, W. Ein Fall von doppeltem Bewusstsein. Inaug. Diss. Breslau, 1923.

Phil 3001.14 Bohne, F. Anti-Cartesianismus; deutsche Philosophie im Widerstand. Leipzig, 1938.

Phil 5627.103 Bohne, G. Die religiöse Entwicklung der Jugend in der Reifezeit. Leipzig, 1922.

Phil 3120.25 Bohnenblust, Gottfried. Vom Adel des Geistes; gesammelte Reden. Zürich, 1943.

Phil 6930.7 Boieldiev, M.J.A. Discours sur la mélancolie. Paris, 1808.

Phil 6111.65 Boiko, E. Studies in higher neurodynamics as related to problems of psychology. Jerusalem, 1961.

Phil 3552.255 Boirac, Aemilius. De spatio apud Leibnitium. Thesis. Paris, 1894.

Phil 7060.129 Boirac, Émile. L'avenir des sciences psychiques. Paris, 1917.

Phil 176.68 Boirac, Émile. L'idée du Phénomène. Thèse. Paris, 1894.
Phil 7069.17.13 Boirac, Émile. Our hidden forces. N.Y., 1917.
Phil 7069.18.21 Boirac, Émile. Psychic science. London, 1918.
Phil 7060.129.9 Boirac, Émile. La psychologie inconnue. 2. ed. Paris, 1912.

Phil 7069.18.20 Boirac, Émile. The psychology of the future. N.Y., 1918.
Phil 2477.11.105 Boirel, R. Brunschvicg; sa vie, son oeuvre avec un exposé de la philosophie. Paris, 1964.

Phil 8581.44 Bois, Henri. De la connaissance religieuse. Paris, 1894.
Phil 1135.131 Bois, Henri. Le dogme grec. Paris, 1893.
Phil 1050.9 Bois, Henri. Essai sur les origines se la philosophie. Paris, 1890.

Phil 5627.7.5 Bois, Henri. Sentiment religieux et sentiment moral. Paris, 1903.

Phil 5520.175 Bois, Joseph S. Explorations in awareness. N.Y., 1957.
Phil 7069.07.9 Bois, Jules. Le miracle moderne. 4. ed. Paris, 1907.
Htn Phil 6990.3.27* Boissaire, P.G. Lourdes depuis 1858 jusqu'à nos jours. Paris, 1894.

Phil 6990.3.25 Boissarie, P.G. Lourdes und seine Geschichte vom medizinischen Standpunkte. 2. ed. Augsburg, 1892.

Phil 2705.84 Boissier, Raymond. La Mettrie. Paris, 1931.
Phil 2705.84.2 Boissier, Raymond. La Mettrie. Thèse. Paris, 1931.
Phil 8893.100 Boissière, P. La morale fouillée dans ses fondements. Paris, 1866.

Phil 5525.43 Bojové poslanie humoru a satiry. (Kalina, J.) Bratislava, 1953.

Phil 9590.19 Bok, E.W. Dollars only. N.Y., 1926.
Phil 9435.2 Bok, Edward. Why I believe in poverty. Boston, 1915.
Phil 176.142 Bolaffio, C. Colui che si chiama "Io sono". Modena, 1936.
Phil 8430.70 Bolam, David Whielden. Art and belief. N.Y., 1970.
Phil 11.48 Bölcseleti közlemények. Budapest. 1-4,1935-1938
Htn Phil 2115.141* Bold, S. A collection of tracts. London, 1706.
Phil 8402.38 Boldini, M. Alla ricerca del tempo nell'arte. 1. ed. Milano, 1954.

Phil 974.3.20 Boldt, Ernst. Rudolf Steiner: ein kämpfer Gegen seine Zeit. München, 1923.

Phil 974.3.25 Boldt, Ernst. Rudolf Steiner und das Epigonenturn. München, 1923.

Phil 974.3.11 Boldt, Ernst. Von Luther bis Steiner. München, 1921.
Phil 3483.26 Boldt, Georg. Protestantismens idé och Immanuel Kant. Helsingfors, 1900.

Phil 332.18 Boldt, Karl. Die Einheit des Erkenntnisproblems. Leipzig, 1937.

Phil 332.18.5 Boldt, Karl. Die Erkenntnisbeziehung. Tübingen, 1937.
Phil 8980.10 Boldyrev, N.I. Vospitanie kommunistecheskoi morali u shkol nikov. Izd. 2. Moskva, 1956.

Phil 2225.5.88 Boler, J.F. Charles Peirce and scholastic realism. Seattle, 1963.

Phil 57.12 Boletim; revista de estudos psicológicos. (Rio de Janeiro. Universidade do Brasil. Instituto de Psicologia.) 7,1957+ 2v.

NEDL Phil 22.35 Boletin bibliografico. (México (city). Universidad Nacional. Facultad de Filosofia y Estudios Superiores. Centro de Estudios Filosoficos.) Mexico.

Phil 5751.10 Bolin, W. Problemet om viljans frihet, kritiskt och logiskt undersökt. Helsingfors, 1868.

Phil 3483.38 Bolin, W. Undersökning af läran om viljans frihet - Kants behandling af problemet. Helsingfors, 1868.

Phil 3552.133 Bolin, Wilhelm. Leibnitz ett förebud till Kant. Akademisk afhandling. Helsingfors, 1864.

Phil 3235.84 Bolin, Wilhelm. Ludwig Feuerbach. Stuttgart, 1891.
Phil 3826.10 Bolin, Wilhelm. Spinoza. 2. Aufl. Darmstadt, 1927.
Phil 3235.84.10 Bolin, Wilhelm. Über Ludwig Feuerbach's Briefwechsel und Nachlass. Helsingfors, 1877.

Phil 176.83 Boll, Marcel. Attardés et précurseurs. Paris, 1921.
Phil 5041.85 Boll, Marcel. Les étapes de la logique. 4. éd. Paris, 1957.

Phil 5011.4 Boll, Marcel. La logique. Paris, 1935.
Phil 5590.250 Boll, Marcel. La personnalité; sa structure. Paris, 1958.
Phil 600.33 Boll, Marcel. La science et l'esprit positif chez les penseurs contemporains. Paris, 1921.

Phil 3120.11.96 Bolland, G.J.P.J. Aanschomving en verstand. Leiden, 1897.
Phil 3425.214 Bolland, G.J.P.J. Alte Vernunft und neuer Verstand. Leiden, 1902.

Phil 3120.13.9 Bolland, G.J.P.J. Briefwechsel mit E. von Hartmann. 's Gravenhage, 1937.

NEDL Phil 3120.11.90 Bolland, G.J.P.J. Collegium logicum. 2. druk. Amsterdam, 1931. 2v.

Phil 5041.43 Bolland, G.J.P.J. G.J.P.J. Bolland's colleges uitgegeven door Ester vas Hunes. Haarlem, 1923.

Phil 282.16 Bolland, G.J.P.J. Hat wereldraadsel. Leiden, 1896.
Phil 3120.11.97 Bolland, G.J.P.J. De natuur. Leiden, 1915.
Phil 3120.35.30 Bolland, G.J.P.J. Natuurbegrip en leuen. Leiden, 1917. 2 pam.

Phil 1106.12 Bolland, G.J.P.J. De oorsprong der grieksche wijsbegeerte. 3e uitg. Leiden, 1921.

Phil 3120.11.95 Bolland, G.J.P.J. Open brief aan den heer K.J.A.M. Schaepman. Leiden, 1899.

Phil 3120.11.94 Bolland, G.J.P.J. Het schoone en de kunst of de naaste en onmiddellijke zelfbevrediging van absolute geestelijkheid in het kort besproken. Amsterdam, 1906.

Phil 3821.13 Bolland, G.J.P.J. Spinoza. Leiden, 1899.
Phil 3120.11.98 Bolland, G.J.P.J. Spreuken. 's Gravenhage, 1962.
Phil 3120.11.93 Bolland, G.J.P.J. Verslag van de rede. Leiden, 1906.
Phil 8581.55 Bolland, G.J.P.J. Wijsbegeerte van den godsdienst bewerkt naar dictaten. Amsterdam, 1923.

Phil 3120.11.92 Bolland, G.J.P.J. Zuivere rede. Leiden, 1904.
Phil 3801.222 Bolland, G.J.P.L. Schelling, Hegel, Fechner en de nieuwere theosophie. Leiden, 1910.

Phil 3120.13.90 Bolland. (Wigersma, I.B.) Amsterdam, 1927.
Phil 1750.96.5 Boller, Paul F. American thought in transition: the impact of evolutionary naturalism, 1865-1900. Chicago, 1969.

Phil 11.17 Bollettino filosofico. Roma. 1-4,1935-1938 2v.
Phil 4210.55 Bollettino rosminiano. Rovereto. 1,1886

Phil 5627.129   Bolley, Alphons. Gebetsstimmung und Gebet. Düsseldorf, 1930.

Phil 3483.7   Bolliger, A. Anti-Kant oder. Basel, 1882.

Phil 8581.49   Bolliger, A. Drei ewige Lichter. Berlin, 1903.

Phil 8876.74   Bolliger, Adolf. Beiträge zur Dogmatik und Ethik. Aaran, 1890.

Phil 5751.5   Bolliger, Adolf. Die Willensfreiheit. Berlin, 1903.

Phil 5865.4   Bollinger, Heinz. Das Werden der Person. München, 1967.

Phil 332.26   Bollnou, Atto. Das Verstechen. Mainz, 1949.

Phil 1750.179.10   Bollnow, O.F. Deutsche Existenzphilosophie. Bern, 1953.

Phil 3195.6.101   Bollnow, O.F. Dilthey, eine Einführung in seine Philosophie. Leipzig, 1936.

Phil 3195.6.102   Bollnow, O.F. Dilthey. 2. Aufl. Stuttgart, 1955.

Phil 1750.179   Bollnow, O.F. Existenzphilosophie. 2e Aufl. Stuttgart, 1942?

Phil 1750.179.5A   Bollnow, O.F. Existenzphilosophie. 3. Aufl. Stuttgart, 1949.

Phil 1750.179.20   Bollnow, O.F. Existenzphilosophie. 4e Aufl. Stuttgart, 1955.

Phil 1750.179.15   Bollnow, O.F. Neue Geborgenheit. Stuttgart, 1955.

Phil 9560.50   Bollnow, O.F. Wasen und Wandel der Tugenden. Frankfurt, 1958.

Phil 5400.128   Bollnow, O.F. Das Wesen der Stimmungen. 3. Aufl. Frankfurt, 1956.

Phil 745.12   Bollnow, Otto F. Die Lebensphilosophie. Berlin, 1958.

Phil 3120.62.30   Bollnow, Otto Fredrich. Mass und Vermesserheit des Menschen. Göttingen, 1962.

Phil 8876.118.2   Bollnow, Otto Friedrich. Einfache Sittlichkeit. 2. Aufl. Göttingen, 1957.

Phil 1750.560.15   Bollnow, Otto Friedrich. Franzosischer Existentialismus. Stuttgart, 1965.

Phil 332.44   Bollnow, Otto Friedrich. Philosophie der Erkenntnis; das Vorverständnis und die Erfahrung des Neuen. Stuttgart, 1970.

Phil 332.29   Bologna, Italo. Il pensiero filosofico ed il suo fondamento. Milano, 1957.

Phil 41.10   Bologna. Universita. Instituto di Filosofia. Sgione Teoretica. Ricerche filosofiche. 1,1959+ 5v.

Phil 310.11   Bol'shukhin, A.A. Oroli narodnogo max i lichnosti v istorii. Gor'kii, 1951.

Phil 974.7   Bolt, Ernst. Die Philosophie der Liebe. v.1-2. Berlin, 1927.

Phil 2035.89   Bolton, M.P.W. Examination of the principles of the Scoto-Oxonian philosophy. London, 1869.

Phil 8876.20   Bolton, R. On the employment of time. London, 1754.

Phil 8626.6.2.5   Bolzano, B. Anhang zur zweiten Auflage der Athanasia. Sulzbach, 1838.

Phil 8626.6   Bolzano, B. Athanasia oder Gründe für die Unsterblichkeit der Seele. Sulzbach, 1827.

Phil 410.6.10.2   Bolzano, B. Paradoxes of the infinite. London, 1950.

Phil 410.6.10   Bolzano, B. Paradoxes of the infinite. New Haven, 1950.

Phil 410.6.5   Bolzano, B. Paradoxien des Unendlichen. Leipzig, 1920.

Phil 3120.2.20   Bolzano, Bernard. Bernard Bolzano - Gesamtausgabe. Stuttgart, 1969.

Phil 3120.2.61   Bolzano, Bernard. Bolzano-Brevier. Wien, 1947.

Phil 3120.2.3   Bolzano, Bernard. Gesammelte Schriften. 2. Ausg. Wien, 1882.

Phil 3120.2.35   Bolzano, Bernard. O nejlepšim státé. Praha, 1952.

Phil 3120.2.30   Bolzano, Bernard. O pokroku a dobročinnosti. Praha, 1951.

Phil 3120.2.45   Bolzano, Bernard. Was ist Philosophie? Amsterdam, 1969.

Phil 3120.2.40   Bolzano, Bernard. Wissenschaft und Religion in Vormärz. Berlin, 1965.

Phil 3120.2.61   Bolzano-Brevier. (Bolzano, Bernard.) Wien, 1947.

Phil 3120.2.84   Bolzano Lehre vom "Satz an Sich". (Gotthardt. J.) Berlin, 1909.

Phil 3120.2.125   Bolzano und die Sorben. (Zeil, Wilhelm.) Bautzen, 1967.

Phil 3120.2.98.5   Der Bolzanoprozess. (Winter, E.) Brünn, 1944.

Phil 3120.2.99   Bolzano's Begründung des objektivismus in der theoretischen und praktischen Philosophie. (Waldschmitt, L.) Giessen, 1937.

Phil 1801.9A   Boman, Lars. Criticism and construction in the philosophy of the America new realism. Stockholm, 1955.

Phil 600.29   Bombard, Émile. La marche de l'humanité et les grands hommes d'après la doctrine positive. Paris, 1900.

Phil 3475.3.73   La bombe atomique et l'avenir de l'homme. (Jaspers, Karl.) Paris, 1958.

Phil 5651.4   Bomier, Pierre. L'orientation. Paris, 1900.

Phil 282.14   Bommersheim, P. Beiträge zur Lehre von Ding und Gesetz. Leipzig, 1927.

Phil 735.98   Bommersheim, Paul. Wertrecht und Wertmacht. Berlin, 1931.

Phil 332.4   Bon, F. Die Dogmen der Erkenntnistheorie. Leipzig, 1902.

Htn   Phil 332.4.9*   Bon, F. Die Grundlagen der Logik und Mathematik. n.p., 193-. 2v.

Phil 332.20A   Bon, F. Von den Begriffen, den Urteilen und der Wahrheit. Leipzig, 1913.

Phil 8876.39.5   Bon, Fred. Grundzüge der wissenschaftlichen und technischen Ethik. Leipzig, 1896.

Phil 8876.39   Bon, Fred. Über das Sollen und das Gute. Leipzig, 1898.

Phil 2648.39.2   Le bon-sens, ou idées naturelles. (Holbach, Paul Henri T.) Londres, 1774.

Phil 177.13   Le bon sens. (Clemente, A.) Paris, 1878. 2v.

Phil 2648.39   Le bon-sens. (Holbach, Paul Henri T.) London, 1782.

Htn   Phil 2648.39.3*   Le bon-sens. (Holbach, Paul Henri T.) Londres, 1772.

Phil 2648.39.4   Le bon-sens. (Holbach, Paul Henri T.) Londres, 1772. 2 pam.

Phil 2648.39.5   Le bon-sens. (Holbach, Paul Henri T.) Londres, 1789.

Phil 2648.39.6   Le bon-sens. (Holbach, Paul Henri T.) Rome, 1792.

Phil 2648.34.2   Le bon sens du Curé Meslier. (Holbach, Paul Henri T.) Paris, 1802.

Phil 2648.34   Le bon sens du Curé Meslier. (Holbach, Paul Henri T.) Paris, 1802.

Phil 2648.34.3   Le bon sens du Curé Meslier. (Holbach, Paul Henri T.) Paris, 1802.

Phil 2475.1.37   Le bon sens et études classiques. (Bergson, Henri.) Clermont, 1947.

Phil 7060.92.29   Bona-fide adventures with ghosts. (O'Donnell, Elliot.) Bristol, 1908.

Phil 1701.58   Bonafede, Giulio. Interpretazioni della filosofia moderna. Palermo, 1965.

Phil 8591.70   Bonafede, Giulio. Luciano Laberthomière. Palermo, 1958.

Phil 1506.12   Bonafede, Giulio. Saggi sulla filosofia medievale. Torino, 1951.

Phil 1506.12.5   Bonafede, Giulio. Storia della filosofia medievale. 2. ed. Roma, 1957.

Phil 2477.4.30   Bonald, L.G.A. Recherches philosophiques sur les premiers objets des connaissances morales. Paris, 1818. 2v.

Phil 3808.181   Bonanno, S. La "Volanta" in Arturo Schopenhauer. Torino, 1903.

Phil 4073.124   Bonansea, Bernardino M. Tommaso Campanella. Washington, 1969.

Phil 6311.34.10   Bonaparte, M. Psychanalyse et biologie. 1. éd. Paris, 1952.

Phil 6311.34   Bonaparte, Marie. Introduction à la théorie des instincts. 1. éd. Paris, 1951.

Phil 6311.34.5   Bonaparte, Marie. Psychanalyse et anthropologie. Paris, 1952.

Phil 6311.34.12   Bonaparte, Marie. Stratioikoi kai koinōnikoi polemoi. Manchester, N.H., 1929.

Phil 6311.34.6   Bonaparte, Marie. Treis dialexeis eisagōgēs eis tēn psychanalēsē. Athenai, 1950.

Phil 8876.89   Bonar, J. Moral sense. London, 1930.

Phil 623.2.15   Bonarino, Cristoforo. Le rationalisme. Bruxelles, 1855.

Phil 176.74.5   Bonatelli, F. La coscienza e il meccanesimo interiore. Padova, 1872.

Phil 176.74.2F   Pamphlet box. Bonatelli, Francesco. Miscellaneous pamphlets.

Phil 176.74   Pamphlet box. Bonatelli, Francesco. Miscellaneous pamphlets.

Phil 8876.84   Bonatelli, Paolo. Spunti di dottrina etica. Bologna, 1928.

Phil 6311.32   Bonaventura, E. La psicoanalisi. 4. ed. Milano, 1950.

Phil 176.71   Bonaventura, E. Le qualità del mondo fisico. Firenze, 1916.

Phil 672.149   Bonaventura, Enzo. Il problema psicologico del tempo. Milano, 1929.

Htn   Phil 1535.15*   Bonaventura, St., Cardinal. Cursus philosophicus. n.p., 1742.

Phil 1535.15.5   Bonaventura, St., Cardinal. Summa totius philosophiae Aristotelicae. pt.1-2. Romae, 1635. 2v.

Phil 4001.4.9   Bonavino, C. Appendice alla filosofia delle scuole italiane. 2. ed. Milano, 1866.

Phil 4001.4.5   Bonavino, C. La filosofia delle scuole italiane. Capolago, 1852.

Phil 4001.4.6   Bonavino, C. La filosofia delle scuole italiane. 2. ed. Firenze, 1863.

Phil 4001.4   Bonavino, C. L'introduzione alla filosofia delle scuole italiane. Italia, 1852.

Phil 2733.98   Bonavino, C. Malebranche. Milano, 1926.

Phil 4070.1.65   Bonavino, Cristoforo. Il razionalismo del popolo dei Ausonio Franchi. 3a ed. corretta et aumentata. Milano, 1864.

Phil 4070.1.50   Bonavino, Cristoforo. Saggi di critica e polemica per Ausonio Franchi (pseud.). Milano, 1871-72. 3v.

Phil 4070.1.35   Bonavino, Cristoforo. Studi filosofici e religiosi; del sentimento. 1. ed. Torino, 1854.

Phil 4070.1.36   Bonavino, Cristoforo. Studi filosofici e religiosi; del sentimento. 2. ed. Torino, 1854.

Phil 4070.1.45   Bonavino, Cristoforo. Su la teoria del giudizio. Milano, 1871. 2v.

Phil 4070.1.60   Bonavino, Cristoforo. Ultima critica. Milano, 1889-93. 3v.

Phil 8620.41   Bond, C.J. The nature and meaning of evil. London, 1937.

Phil 6980.127   Bond, Earl Clanford. One mind. N.Y., 1958.

Phil 7069.20.40   Bond, Frederick B. The gate of remembrance. 3. ed. Boston, 1920.

Phil 7069.20.42   Bond, Frederick B. The gate of remembrance. 4th ed. N.Y., 1921.

Phil 8691.21   Bond, Walter G. Three things that matter; religion, philosophy, science. London, 1931.

Phil 331.9   The bond of being. (Anderson, J.F.) St. Louis, 1949.

Phil 282.21   Bondi, Hermann. Cosmology. 2. ed. Cambridge, Eng., 1960.

Phil 282.21.5   Bondi, Hermann. The universe at large. Garden City, 1960.

Phil 2401.4   Bondi, P. Etudes littéraires: essais sur les philosophes. Florence, 1918.

Phil 5241.95   Bone, H. Une étude du préjugé au moyen des tests. Thèse. Paris, 1934.

Phil 8876.53   Bonet-Maury, G. L'unité morale des religions. Paris, 1913.

Phil 1540.23   Bonfarri, G. Lo studio della natura nell'umanesimo. Mantova, 1937.

Phil 3821.30   Bonfi, Antonio. Spinoza e il suo tempo. Firenze, 1969.

Phil 7054.177   Bonfiglioli, Casimiro. Lo spiritismo nella unianità. Bologna, 1888.

Phil 5545.98   Bongard, Mikhail M. Problema uznavaniia. Moskva, 1967.

Phil 176.131   Bonghi, Ruggiero. Delle relazioni della filosofia colla società; prolusione. Milano, 1859.

Phil 8610.911.4   Bongini, V. Il pregiudizio religioso. Roma, 1911.

Phil 8725.1   Bonham, J. Secularism; its progress and morals. N.Y., 1894.

Phil 9245.3   Le bonheur. (Gasparin, A.E.) Paris, 1874.

Phil 9245.64   Le bonheur considéré comme l'un des beaux-arts. (Polin, Raymond.) Paris, 1965.

Phil 9245.9.55   Le bonheur de vivre. v.1-2. (Avebury, John Lubbock.) Paris, 1897-98.

Phil 665.62   Le bonheur est en nous-mêmes. (Laborier-Tradens, A.) Paris, 1931.

Phil 5403.11   Bonheur et civilisation. (Cazeneuve, Jean.) Paris, 1966.

Phil 5241.105   Le bonheur s'apprend. 2. éd. (Boris, J.S. Anselme.) Montreal, 1941.

Phil 4070.5.30   Boni, Guido. L'essere nella spontaneità creativa e nella riffessione razionale. Roma, 1953.

Phil 1602.2   Bonicatti, Maurizio. Studi sull'Umanesimo. Secoli XIV-XVI. Firenze, 1969.

Phil 2477.6.120   Bonicelli, B.M. La logica morale in Maurice Blondel. Torino, 1950.

Phil 2255.1.125   Bonifacino, V. Ensayos beligerantes: Bertrand Russell, James Joyce. Montevideo, 1960.

Phil 332.35   Bonilla, Abelardo. Conocimiento, verdad y belleza. San Salvador, 1958.

Phil 4302.4   Bonilla y San Martin, A. Historia de la filosofía española. Madrid, 1908.

Phil 4302.4.5   Bonilla y San Martin, A. Historia de la filosofía española. Madrid, 1911.

Phil 4372.1.85   Bonilla y San Martin, D.A. Luis Vives y la filosofía del renacimiento. Madrid, 1903.

Phil 3890.1.81   Bonitz, Hermann. Zur Erinnerung an Friedrich Adolf Trendelenburg. Boston, 1872.

Phil 176.84   Bonlnois, Helen. The law of being. London, 1920.

Phil 5627.145   Bonnaire, L. de. Examen critique, physique et théologique des convulsions. n.p., 1733.

X Cg   Phil 8876.21   Bonnaire, L. de. Les leçons de la sagesse. Paris, 1750-51. 3v.

Phil 8876.65   Bonnaire, L. de. La regle des devoirs. Paris, 1758. 3v.

Phil 6990.4.2   Bonnaire, Louis de. Observations. n.p., 1773. 2 pam.

Phil 2401.7 — Bonnard, A. Le mouvement antipositiviste contemporain en France. Thèse. Paris, 1936.

Phil 2750.10.105 — Bonnard, A. La notion d'irrationnel chez Emile Meyerson. Thèse. Paris, 1936.

Phil 2840.85 — Bonnard, Edmond. Le criticisme de M. Renouvier. Thèse. Lausanne, 1890.

Phil 9590.4 — Bonnard, L.C. Entufhrôn. Paris, 1933.

Phil 5850.140 — Bonnardel, Raymond. L'adaption de l'homme à son métier. 1. éd. Paris, 1946.

Phil 8581.26 — Bonnefon, C. Dialogue sur la vie et sur la mort. 3. éd. Paris, 1911.

Phil 1200.33 — Bonnell, Karl E. Programm. Berlin, 1864.

Phil 8626.21 — Bonner, H.B. (Mrs.). The Christian hell. London, 1913.

Phil 5592.177 — Bonner, Hubert. On being mindful of man, essay toward a proactive psychology. Boston, 1965.

Phil 5590.423 — Bonner, Hubert. Psychology of personality. N.Y., 1961.

Phil 8610.919 — Bonner, Hypatia Bradlaugh (Mrs.). Christianity and conduct. London, 1919.

Phil 2465.30 — Bonnet, Charles. Essai analytique sur les facultés de l'âme. Copenhagen, 1760.

Phil 2465.30.5 — Bonnet, Charles. Essai analytique sur les facultés de l'âme. v.1-2. 3e éd. Copenhagen, 1775.

Phil 2465.85 — Bonnet, Charles. Mèmoires autobiographiques de Charles Bonnet de Genève. Thèse. Paris, 1948.

Phil 2465.33 — Bonnet, Charles. Psychologischer Versuch. Lemgo, 1773.

Phil 2465.79 — Pamphlet box. Bonnet, Charles.

Phil 2465.82 — Bonnet, Georges. Charles Bonnet (1720-1793). Thèse. Paris, 1929.

Phil 2725.17.90 — Bonnet, Georges. La morale de Félix Le Dantec (1869-1917). Thèse. Poitiers, 1930.

Phil 4115.90 — Bonnetty, A. Examen critique de la philosophie de Gioberti. Paris, 1847-49. 2 pam.

Phil 8691.9 — Bonney, T.G. Christian doctrines and modern thought. London, 1892.

Phil 5650.11 — Bonnier, Pierre. L'audition. Paris, 1901.

Phil 6990.3.31 — Bonnières, L. de. Dans la lumière de Lourdes. Paris, 1920.

Phil 8620.14 — Bonniot, P.J. de. Le problème du mal. 3. éd. Paris, 1911.

Phil 5041.49 — Bonnot, Lucien. Logique positive; essai d'un théorie nouvelle de la connaissance. Dijon, 1930.

Phil 8430.94 — Bono, Pierluigi. La morale dell'artista. Milano, 1969.

Phil 2750.20.125 — Bonomi, Andrea. Esistenza e struttura. Milano, 1967.

Phil 2648.34.5 — Le bons sens du Curé Jean Meslier. (Holbach, Paul Henri T.) Hildesheim, 1970.

Phil 5241.69 — Bonsfield, Paul. The mind and its mechanism. London, 1927.

Phil 6315.2.89 — Bonsfield, William A. A neglected complex and its relation to Freudian psychology. London, 1924.

Phil 5241.14 — Bonstetten, C.V. de. Etudes de l'homme. Genève, 1821. 2v.

Phil 5465.1 — Bonstetten, K.V. von. Recherches sur la nature et les lois de l'imagination. Genève, 1807. 2v.

Phil 176.141 — Bontadini, G. Saggio di una metafisica dell'esperienza. Milano, 1938.

Phil 282.15 — Bontecou, Daniel J. A chart of nature. Chicago, 1928.

Phil 8876.82 — Bonucci, A. L'orientazione psicologica dell'etica e della filosofia del diritto. Perugia, 1907.

Phil 720.12 — Bonucci, A. Verità e realtà. Modena, 1911.

Phil 282.12 — Boodin, J.E. Cosmic evolution. N.Y., 1925.

Phil 282.12.10 — Boodin, J.E. God and creation. N.Y., 1934. 2v.

Phil 332.5.5 — Boodin, J.E. A realistic universe. N.Y., 1916.

Phil 332.5.10 — Boodin, J.E. A realistic universe. N.Y., 1931.

Phil 8581.85 — Boodin, J.E. Religion of tomorrow. N.Y., 1943.

Phil 1905.26 — Boodin, J.E. Studies in philosophy. Los Angeles, 1957.

Phil 332.5 — Boodin, J.E. Truth and reality. N.Y., 1911.

Phil 575.278 — The book; on the taboo against knowing who you are. (Watts, Alan Wilson.) N.Y., 1966.

Phil 5648.11 — Book, W.F. The psychology of skill. Missoula, Mont., 1908.

Phil 5648.11.5 — Book, W.F. The psychology of skill. N.Y., 1925.

Phil 9172.4.2 — A book about boys. 2. ed. (Moncrieff, A.H.) Edinburgh, 1868.

Phil 9160.6 — Book for parents. The genius and design of the domestic constitution. (Anderson, C.) Boston, 1834.

Phil 7054.112 — A book for skeptics being communications from angels. (Everett, J.J.) Columbus, 1853.

Phil 2255.7.15 — A book of contemplation. (Runes, Dagobert D.) N.Y., 1957.

Phil 7068.97.5 — The book of dreams and ghosts. (Lang, Andrew.) London, 1897.

Htn   Phil 1865.40.2* — The book of fallacies. (Bentham, Jeremy.) London, 1824.

Phil 7060.119 — Book of ghosts. (Baring-Gould, S.) London, 1904.

Phil 9035.22 — The book of human character. (Bucke, Charles.) London, 1837. 2v.

Phil 7060.23 — Book of human nature. (Sunderland, L.) N.Y. 1853.

Phil 7069.45.30 — The book of Johannes, by Peter Fripp. (Dowden, Hester.) London, 1945.

Phil 8893.91.90 — The book of life. (Sinclair, Upton.) Chicago, 1921.

Phil 8893.92A — The book of life. 4th ed. v.1-2. (Sinclair, Upton.) Long Beach, 1926.

Htn   Phil 2268.1.30* — The book of Mormon. (Smith, Joseph.) Palmyra, 1830.

Phil 4075.79.20A — The book of my life. (Cardano, Girolamo.) N.Y., 1930.

X Cg   Phil 8893.24 — The book of nature. (Stewart, J.) London, n.d.

Htn   Phil 6045.22.21* — The book of palmestry and physiognomy. (Indagine, Joannes.) London, 1683.

Phil 7060.23.5 — Book of psychology. (Sunderland, L.) N.Y. 1853.

Phil 9530.26 — A book of rejoicing, big business. (Parlette, R.A.) Chicago, 1917.

Phil 178.12.18 — A book of secrets. (Dresser, H.W.) N.Y., 1902.

Phil 7054.153 — The book of spirits. n.d.

Phil 7069.28.12 — The book of spiritual wisdom by "Cuno". (Haynes, Frederick H.) London, 1928.

Phil 6049.65 — The book of the hand. (Gettings, Fred.) London, 1965.

Phil 7069.07.35 — Book of the Psychic Society. (Edgerly, Webster.) Washington, 1907.

Phil 7082.108 — A book of true dreams. (Monteith, Mary E.) London, 1929.

Phil 8610.914 — The book of truth. (Griggs, H.S.) Brooklyn, 1914.

Phil 4075.55 — The book on games of chance. (Cardano, Girolamo.) N.Y., 1961.

Phil 7082.124 — A book on the interpretation of dreams. (Richardson, Phelps.) Worcester, 1904-05.

Phil 7054.24 — A book written by the spirits of the so-called dead. (Helleberg, C.E.) Cincinnati, 1883.

Phil 5203.11.10 — Books in psychology. v.1-2. (Harvard University. Department of Psychology.) Cambridge, 1938.

Phil 1850.34.2 — The books of Lord Verulam. (Bacon, Francis.) London, 1825.

Phil 5041.15.6 — Boole, George. An investigation of the laws of thought. N.Y., 1951.

Phil 5041.15.2 — Boole, George. The laws of thought. Chicago, 1916.

Phil 5041.15.3 — Boole, George. The laws of thought. Chicago, 1940.

Htn   Phil 5041.15.1* — Boole, George. The laws of thought. London, 1854.

Phil 5041.15 — Boole, George. The laws of thought. London, 1854.

Phil 5066.34 — Boole, George. The mathematical analysis of logic. Oxford, 1948.

Phil 5041.15.4 — Boole, George. Studies in logic and probability. London, 1952.

Phil 5246.9.8A — Boole, M.E. The mathematical psychology of Gratry and Boole. London, 1897.

Phil 8691.23 — Boorman, W.R. Independent young thinkers. Boston, 1933.

Phil 1801.6 — Boorstin, D.J. The lost world of Thomas Jefferson. N.Y., 1948.

Phil 978.49.815 — Boos-Hamburger, H. Aus Gesprächen mit Rudolf Steiner. Basel, 1954.

Phil 8691.32 — Booth, E.P. Religion ponders science. 1. ed. N.Y., 1964.

Phil 179.3.99 — Booth, Meyrick. Rudolf Eucken; his philosophy. London, 1914.

Phil 6311.7 — Bopp, L. Modern Psychoanalyse, katholische, beichte und pädagogik. Kempten, 1923.

Phil 8120.9 — Bopp, Léon. Philosophie de l'art; ou, Alchimie contre histoire. Paris, 1954.

Phil 8400.50 — Bor'ba idei v estetike. (Internationale Hegelkongress, 5th, Salzburg, 1964.) Moskva, 1966.

Phil 4752.1.35 — Bor'ba Lenina protiv Bogdanovskoi revizii marksizma. (Shcheglov, A.V.) Moskva, 1937.

Phil 310.435 — Bor'ba marksistsko-leninskoi filosofii v SSSR. (Suvorov, L.M.) Moskva, 1961.

Phil 310.215 — Bor'ba marksizma-leninizma protiv sovremennogo filosofskogo revizionizma. (Novikov, A.I.) Leningrad, 1959.

Phil 310.585 — Bor'ba marksizma-leninizma s ideologiei anarkhizma i sovremennost'. (Kosichev, A.D.) Moskva, 1964.

Phil 4710.83 — Bor'ba materializma i idealizma v russkoi psikhologicheskoi nauke. (Budilova, E.A.) Moskva, 1960.

Phil 310.150 — Bor'ba v SSSR protiv mekhanitsizma. (Mal'tsev, V.I.) Moskva, 1959.

Phil 4755.1 — Bor'ba za Logos. (Ern, Vladimir F.) Moskva, 1911.

Phil 974.2.65 — Borborka, Geoffrey A. H.P. Blavatsky, Tibet and Tulka. Madras, 1966.

Phil 3808.188 — Borch, Rudolf. Schopenhauer. Boston, 1941.

Phil 2138.127 — Borchard, Ruth. John Stuart Mill. London, 1957.

Phil 2490.116 — Borchert, H. Der Begriff des Kulturzeitalters bei Comte. Diss. Halle, 1927.

Phil 2520.82 — Bordas-Demoulin, J.B. Le Cartésianisme. Paris, 1843. 2v.

Phil 2477.2.25 — Bordas-Demoulin, J.B. Oeuvre posthumes. Paris, 1861. 2v.

Phil 176.25 — Bordas-Demoulin, Jean B. Mélanges philosophiques. Paris, 1846.

Phil 2520.145 — Bordas-Demoulin. Les cartésianisme. Paris, 1874.

Phil 1915.83 — Borden Parker Browne's treatment of the problem of change and identity. (Fránquiz Ventura, José Antonio.) Rio Piedras, 1942.

Phil 7068.94.50 — Borderland; a quarterly review and index. London. 1893-1897 3v.

Phil 6957.12.7 — The borderland, some of the problems of insanity. (Hyslop, T.B.) N.Y., 1925.

Phil 7069.06.10 — Borderland of psychical research. 2. ed. (Hyslop, James Hervey.) Boston, 1906.

Phil 6972.7 — The borderlands of insanity. (Wynter, A.) N.Y., 1875.

Phil 6972.7.2 — The borderlands of insanity (with 5 new chpaters). (Wynter, A.) London, 1877.

Phil 6312.12 — Borderlands of psychiatry. (Cobb, S.) Cambridge, 1943.

Phil 8592.108 — The borderlands of theology. (MacKinnon, D.M.) Cambridge, Eng., 1961.

Phil 525.170 — Bordet, Louis. Religion et mysticisme. Paris, 1959.

Phil 8612.82 — Bordoni, Marcello. Dimensioni antropologiche della morte. Roma, 1969.

Phil 1135.152 — Boreas, Theophilos. Hē archē tēs ōeri metempsykōseōs doxēs tōn Hellēnōn philosophōn. Athens, 1913.

Phil 282.13 — Boreas, Theophilos. Tis filosofias i ipothesis ke i epitqnvion ropi. Athens, 1913.

Phil 410.11 — Borel, Émile. Les paradoxes de l'infini. Paris, 1946.

Phil 930.34 — Borel, Henri. De chinesche filosofi. 3. druk. Amsterdam, 1896-97. 2v.

Phil 3428.159 — Borelius, J.J. Anmärkningar vid Herbarts filosofiska system. Kalmar, 1866.

Phil 3001.6 — Borelius, J.J. En blick pa den newarande filosofien i Tyshland. Stockholm, 1879.

Phil 3001.6.5 — Borelius, J.J. Blicke auf den Gegenwärtigen Standpunkt der Philosophie in Deutschland und Frankreich. Berlin, n.d.

Phil 4514.1.35 — Borelius, J.J. Den dogmatiska rationismens strid mot den spekulativa filosofien. Stockholm, 1872.

Phil 3425.200 — Borelius, J.J. Det hegelska systemet och den spekulativa ethiken. Lund, 1853.

Phil 3425.200.5 — Borelius, J.J. I hvad afseende är Hegel Pantheist? Upsala, 1851.

Phil 4515.96 — Borelius, J.J. Kritik öfver den Boströmska filosofien. v.1-2. Stockholm, 1859-60.

Phil 5041.36.5 — Borelius, J.J. Lärobok i den formella logiken. 4. Uppl. Lund, 1882.

Phil 4514.1.40 — Borelius, J.J. Menniskans naturlif i dess förhållande till det andliga lifvet. Stockholm, 1855.

Phil 3425.200.10 — Borelius, J.J. Om filosofiens supremati enligt Hegelska systemet. Lund, 1852.

Phil 9230.30 — Borély, Joseph. Discours prononcé devant la cour royale d'Aix à l'audience solennelle de rentrée. Aix, 1836.

Htn   Phil 9510.5* — Boreman, R. An antidote against swearing. London, 1662.

Phil 5525.72 — Borev, Iurii B. Komicheskoe. Moskva, 1970.

Phil 8402.63 — Borev, Iurii B. Vvedenie v estetiku. Moskva, 1965.

Phil 5590.498 — Borgatta, Edgar. Handbook of personality theory and research. Chicago, 1968.

Phil 5270.26 — Borger, Robert. Explanation in the behavioral sciences. Cambridge, Eng., 1970.

Phil 4080.3.75 — La Borghesia. (Croce, Benedetto.) Bari, 1945.

Phil 8626.28 — Borgia, Anthony V. Life in the world unseen. London, 1956.

Phil 8626.28.5 — Borgia, Anthony V. More about life in the world unseen. London, 1958.

Phil 3925.16.215 — Borgis, Ilona. Index zu Ludwig Wittgensteins "Tractatus logico-philosophicus" und Wittgenstein - Bibliographie. Frieburg, 1968.

Phil 5241.112 — Boring, E.G. Foundations of psychology. N.Y., 1948.

Phil 5241.92.20 — Boring, E.G. History, psychology and science. N.Y., 1963.

Phil 5211.4A — Boring, E.G. A history of experimental psychology. N.Y., 1929.

Phil 5211.4.5 — Boring, E.G. A history of experimental psychology. 2. ed. N.Y., 1950.

Phil 5374.57 — Boring, E.G. The physical dimensions of consciousness. N.Y., 1933.

Phil 1905.14.100 — Boring, E.G. Psychologist at large. N.Y., 1961.

Phil 5241.92A — Boring, E.G. Psychology; a factual textbook. N.Y., 1935.

Phil 5241.92.10 — Boring, E.G. The relation of the attributes of sensation to the dimensions of the stimulus. Baltimore, 1935. 3 pam.

Phil 5211.4.20 — Boring, E.G. Sensation and perception in the history of experimental psychology. N.Y., 1942.

Phil 5648.17 — Boring, Edwin G. Cutaneous sensation after nerve-division. London, 1916.

Phil 5211.4.7A — Boring, Edwin Garrigues. A history of experimental psychology. 2. ed. N.Y., 1957.

Phil 5241.105 — Boris, J.S. Anselme. Le bonheur s'apprend. 2. éd. Montreal, 1941.

Phil 5360.27 — Borisov, Vadim N. Urovni logicheskogo protsessa i osnovnye napravleniia ikh issledovaniia. Novosibirsk, 1967.

Phil 3195.6.107 — Bork, A. Diltheys Auffassung des griechischen Geistes. Berlin, 1944.

Phil 1701.19 — Borkenan, Franz. Der Übergang vom Feudalen zum bügerlichen Weltbild. Paris, 1934.

Phil 176.25.10 — Borland, Hal Glen. Countyman: a summary of belief. 1st ed. Philadelphia, 1965.

Phil 8876.101 — Borle, Charles A. The art of living. Boston, 1936.

Phil 7069.09.2 — Bormann, W. Der Schotte Home. Leipzig, 1909.

Phil 6671.23 — Bormes, Baron de. Lettre de M.L.B.D.B....sur l'existence du magnétisme animal. Genève, 1784.

Phil 332.40 — Born, Friedrich Gottlab. Versuch über die ursprünglichen Grundlagen des menschlichen Denkens und die davon Abhängigen Schranken unserer Erkenntniss. Bruxelles, 1969.

Phil 2805.414 — Borne, Étienne. De Pascal à Teilhard de Chardin. Clermont-Ferrand, 1963.

Phil 8656.37 — Borne, Étienne. Dieu n'est pas mort. Paris, 1959.

Phil 720.64 — Borne, Étienne. Passion de la vérité. Paris, 1962.

Phil 8620.48 — Borne, Étienne. Le problème du mal. 1. éd. Paris, 1958.

Phil 3745.6.90 — Borne, G. von dem. Karl Christian Plancks Anthropologie auf der Grundlage seiner Logik des reinen Denkens. Inaug. Diss. Winnendens, 1930.

Phil 2805.203 — Bornhausen, K. Pascal. Basel, 1920.

Phil 3110.91 — Bornkamm, H. Luther und Böhme. Bonn, 1925.

Phil 8612.86 — Bornscheuer, Lothar. Miseriae regum. Diss. Berlin, 1968.

Phil 8656.20 — Bornträger, J.C.F. Über das Daseyn Gottes in Beziehung auf Kantische und Mendelssonnsche Philosophie. Hannover, 1788.

Phil 3483.87 — Borodai, I.M. Voobrazhenie i teoriia poznaniia. Moskva, 1966.

Phil 8612.52.5 — Boros, Ladislaus. L'homme et son ultime option, Mysterium mortis. Paris, 1966.

Phil 8612.57 — Boros, Ladislaus. The moment of truth. London, 1965.

Phil 8612.52 — Boros, Ladislaus. Mysterium mortis. Olten, 1962.

Phil 4710.50.55 — Borot'ba filosofs'kykh techii na zakhidnoukraïns'kykh zemliak u 20-30kh rokakh XX st. (Oleksiuk, Myroslav M.) L'viv, 1970.

Phil 4710.50.10 — Borot'ba mizh materializmom ta idealizmom na Ukraini. (Akademiia Nauk URSR, Kiev. Instytut Filosofii.) Kyïv, 1964.

Phil 1750.757 — Borowitz, Eugene B. A layman's introduction to religious existentialism. Philadelphia, 1965.

Phil 720.24 — Borowne, S.S.S. A pragmatist theory of truth and reality. Thesis. Princeton, 1930.

Phil 8951.29 — Borowski, A. Teologia moralna. Wyd. 2. Lublin, 1960.

Phil 3483.15.5 — Borowski, L.E. Darstellung des Lebens und Charakters Immanuel Kants. Königsberg, 1804.

Phil 3483.15 — Borowski, L.E. Immanuel Kant. 2. Aufl. Halle, 1907.

Phil 5412.15 — Borra, Edoardo. Quando gli uomini perdono le staffe. Roma, 1959.

Phil 3821.6 — Borrell, Philippe. Benôit Spinoza. Paris, 1911.

Phil 1750.415 — Borrello, Oreste. L'estetica dell'esistenzialismo. Messina, 1956.

Phil 2880.8.200 — Borrello, Oreste. Studi su Sartre. Bologna, 1964.

Phil 8691.14 — Borrero Echeverria, E. La vieja ortodoxia y la ciencia moderna. Habana, 1879.

Phil 3483.44 — Borries, Kurt. Kant als Politiker. Leipzig, 1928.

Phil 8691.13 — Borrows, Samuel Jure. Science and immortality. Boston, 1887.

Phil 4080.3.445 — Borsari, Silvano. L'opera di Benedetto Croce. Napoli, 1964.

VPhil 3640.760 — Borský, Lev. Bedřich Nietzsche. Praha, 1912.

Phil 585.412 — Borsodi, Ralph. Seventeen problems of man and society. 1. ed. Anand, 1968.

Phil 6109.2 — Borst, Clive Vernon. The mind-brain identity theory. N.Y., 1970.

Phil 8626.14 — Det bortkastade helvetet. (Björkman, E.A.) Stockholm, 1864.

Phil 7055.101 — Bortom mänsklig horisont. (Aakerblom, Lilly.) Stockholm, 1966.

Phil 4225.1.100 — Bortot, Renato. L'hegelismo di Bertrando Spaventa. Firenze, 1968.

Phil 1701.50 — Borzaga, Reynold. Contemporary philosophy; phenomenological and existential currents. Milwaukee, 1966.

Phil 1750.595 — Bos, Julius G. Existentiële zin en onzim. Den Haag, 1960.

Phil 1905.10.75 — Bosanquet, B. Bernard Bosanquet and his friends. London, 1935.

Phil 630.6 — Bosanquet, B. Distinction between mind and its objects. Manchester, 1913.

Phil 176.56.2A — Bosanquet, B. Essays and addresses. London, 1891.

Phil 5041.16.5 — Bosanquet, B. The essentials of logic. London, 1895.

Phil 5041.16.9 — Bosanquet, B. The essentials of logic. London, 1914.

Phil 8050.38 — Bosanquet, B. A history of aesthetic. London, 1892.

Phil 8050.38.5 — Bosanquet, B. A history of aesthetic. London, 1922.

Phil 5041.16.15 — Bosanquet, B. Implication and linear inference. London, 1920.

Phil 5041.20.8 — Bosanquet, B. Knowledge and reality. London, 1885.

Phil 5041.16 — Bosanquet, B. Logic, or The morphology of knowledge. Oxford, 1888. 2v.

Phil 5041.16.2A — Bosanquet, B. Logic, or The morphology of knowledge. Oxford, 1911. 2v.

Phil 575.18A — Bosanquet, B. The principle of individuality and value. London, 1912.

Phil 5241.24.2A — Bosanquet, B. Psychology of the moral self. London, 1904.

Phil 176.56.7 — Bosanquet, B. Science and philosophy and other essays. London, 1927.

Phil 8876.50 — Bosanquet, B. Some suggestions in ethics. London, 1918.

Phil 5241.24.5A — Bosanquet, B. Three chapters on the nature of the mind. London, 1923.

Phil 8402.13 — Bosanquet, B. Three lectures on aesthetic. London, 1915.

Phil 575.18.5 — Bosanquet, B. Value and destiny of the individual. London, 1913.

Phil 1701.11 — Bosanquet, Bernard. The meeting of extremes in contemporary philosophy. London, 1921.

Phil 8581.62 — Bosanquet, Bernard. What religion is. London, 1920.

Phil 1905.10.79 — Pamphlet box. Bosanquet, Bernard.

Phil 5041.17 — Bosanquet, S.R. A new system of logic. London, 1839.

Phil 5460.11 — Bosch, G. Alucinaciones. Buenos Aires, 1935.

Phil 3821.32 — Boschavini, Emilia Giancotti. Lexicon Spinozanum. La Haye, 1970.

Phil 176.180 — Bosco, Giovanni. Ricerche filosofiche. Napoli, 1953.

Phil 310.644 — Bosenko, Valerii A. Dialektika kak teoriia razvitiia. Kiev, 1966.

Phil 585.355 — Bosio, Franco. Antropologia filosofica e occultamento ideologico. Urbino, 1968.

Phil 3450.11.440 — Bosio, Franco. Fondazione della logica in Husserl. Milano, 1966.

Phil 8581.91.10 — Bosley, Harold A. A firm faith for today. 1. ed. N.Y., 1950.

Phil 8581.91 — Bosley, Harold A. The philosophical heritage of the Christian faith. Chicago, 1944.

Phil 8581.113 — Bošnjak, Branko. Filozofija i krščanstvo. Zagreb, 1966.

Phil 1750.766 — Bošnjak, Branko. Humanizam i socijalizam. Zagreb, 1963.

Phil 8581.113.5 — Bošnjak, Branko. Marksist i krščanin. Zagreb, 1969.

Phil 8580.18 — Bosquejo de un paralelo de la relation catholica. (Araiztegui, R.M.) Habana, 1872.

Phil 6951.25 — Boss, M. Körperliches Kranksein als Folge seelescher Gleichgewichtsstörungen. Bern, 1940.

Phil 7082.196.5 — Boss, Medard. The analysis of dreams. N.Y., 1958.

Phil 7082.196 — Boss, Medard. Des Traum und seine Auslegung. Bern, 1953.

Phil 6311.37 — Boss, Medard. Psychoanalyse und Daseinsanalytik. Bern, 1957.

Phil 6311.37.5 — Boss, Medard. Psychoanalysis and daseinsanalysis. N.Y., 1963.

Phil 5921.3F — Bossard, H. Practische Phrenologie. Berlin, 1851.

Phil 7082.18 — Bossard, Robert. Psychologie des Traumbewusstseins. Zürich, 1951.

Phil 3808.116.3 — Bossert, Adolphe. Schopenhauer. 3. éd. Paris, 1912.

Phil 3808.116.10 — Bossert, Adolphe. Schopenhauer als Mensch und Philosoph. Dresden, 1905.

Htn Phil 5751.11* — Bossuet, J.B. Traitez du libre-arbitre. Paris, 1731.

Phil 5374.51 — Bostock, John. The neural energy constant. London, 1930.

Phil 9035.81 — Boston. The will to win. Boston, 1938.

Phil 7054.83 — Boston Courier report of the proceedings of professed spiritual agents and mediums. (Lunt, George.) Boston, 1859. 2 pam.

Phil 5465.140 — Boston Institute. Conference on creativity as a process. Boston, 1957-58.

Phil 8610.870.25 — Boston lectures, 1870-1871. Christianity and scepticism. Boston, 1871. 2v.

Phil 6111.52 — Boston Mental Hygiene Survey. Report of the Boston mental hygiene survey, 1930. Boston, 1930.

Phil 5921.5 — Boston Phrenological Society. A catalogue of specimens. Boston, 1835.

Phil 4515.33 — Boström, C.J. Anmärkningar om helveteslären. 2. uppl. Upsala, 1864.

Phil 4515.48 — Boström, C.J. De nexu rerum cum Deo ex ratione pantheismi positiones. Upsaliae, 1827.

Phil 4515.45 — Boström, C.J. Dissertatio de notionibus religionis. Upsala, 1841.

Phil 4515.40 — Boström, C.J. Föreläsningar i etiken. Upsala, 1897.

Phil 4515.35 — Boström, C.J. Föreläsningar i religionsfilosofi. Stockholm, 1885.

Phil 4515.34 — Boström, C.J. Grundlinier eines philosophischen Systems. Leipzig, 1923.

Phil 4515.31 — Boström, C.J. Grundlinier till philosophiska civil- och criminalrätten. Stockholm, 1903.

Phil 4515.31.3 — Boström, C.J. Grundlinier till philosophiska civil- och criminalrätten. Upsala, 1883.

Phil 4515.32.5 — Boström, C.J. Grundlinier till philosophiska statslärans propaedeutik. Upsala? 1859?

Phil 4515.32.2 — Boström, C.J. Grundlinier till philosophiska statslärans propaedeutik. 2. uppl. Upsala, 1884.

Phil 4515.32.3 — Boström, C.J. Grundlinier till philosophiska statslärans propaedeutik. 3. uppl. Stockholm, 1901.

Phil 4515.50 — Boström, C.J. Om religion, vishet och dygd. Stockholm, 1943.

Phil 4515.36 — Boström, C.J. Philosophy of religion. New Haven, 1962.

Phil 4515.30.2 — Boström, C.J. Satser om lag och lagstiftning med tillägg och anmärkningar å nyo utgifne. 2e uppl. Upsala, 1871.

Phil 4515.10 — Boström, C.J. Skrifter af C.J. Boström utgifna af H. Edfeldt. v.1-3. Upsala, 1883-1901. 2v.

Phil 4514.1.80 — Boström, C.J. Den speculativa philosophen Johann Jacob Borelius Calmar. Upsala, 1860.

Phil 3483.4 — Boström, G. Kritisk framställning of Kants frihetslära. Lund, 1897.

Phil 4515.85.5 — Boströms äldsta latinska dissertationer. Thesis. (Liljeqvist, Efraim.) Lund, 1915.

Phil 4515.86 — Boströms lära om guds ideer. (Leander, P.J.H.) Lund, 1886.

Phil 4515.91 — Den Boströmska verldsåsigten i sina grunddrag framstäld. (Åberg, L.H.) Stockholm, 1882.

Phil 1106.11 — Boswell, F.P. A primer of Greek thought. Geneva, 1923.

Phil 176.154 — Botelho, Pero de. Da filosofia. 1. ed. Candeia, 1949.

Phil 5643.91 — Botelho de Oliveyra, B. Escudo apologetico, physico, optico occidental. Lisboa, 1720.

Phil 5649.34 — Both, Jan Jacob. Manuele varrdigheid; cen oriëntatie. Proefschrift. Groningen, 1967.

Phil 7069.09.40 — Both sides of the veil. (Robbins, A.M.) Boston, 1909.

Phil 7060.91 — Both sides of the veil. (Robbins, Anne M.) Boston, 1911.

Phil 7069.68.35 — Botschaft aus dem Jenseits. (Federmann, Reinhard.) Tübingen, 1968.

Phil 3120.30.87 — Die Botschaft Martin Bubers. (Goldstein, Walter Benjamin.) Jerusalem, 1952-56. 3v.

Phil 6327.42 — Botsende Generaties. (Ree, Frank van.) Assen, 1968.

Phil 1750.166.17 — Bottai, Giuseppe. Verteidigung des Humanismus. 2. Aufl. Berlin, 1942.

Phil 6671.9 — Bottey, F. Le magnétisme animal. Paris, 1886.

Phil 7054.119 — The bottom facts...science of spiritualism. (Truesdell, J.W.) N.Y., 1883.

Phil 7068.84 — The bottom facts concerning the science of spiritualism. (Truesdell, J.W.) N.Y., 1884.

Phil 6310.8 — Bottome, P. Alfred Adler; a biography. N.Y., 1939.

Phil 6310.8.5 — Bottome, P. Alfred Adler. 3rd ed. London, 1957.

Phil 5520.411 — Bottotini, Gianfranco. Il segno dalla fino al cinema. Milano, 1963.

Phil 1135.57 — Bouché-Leclerq, A. Placita Graecorum. Paris, 1871.

Phil 7060.74 — Boucher, J. Une séance de spiritisme. Niort, 1908.

Phil 5545.3 — Boucher, J. Des idées innées de la mémoire. Paris, 1867.

Phil 5241.26 — Boucher, J. Psychologie. Paris, 1908.

Phil 3549.2.87 — Boucher, M. La philosophie de H. Keyserling. 6. éd. Paris, 1927.

Phil 1750.166.10 — Boucher, Maurice. Goethescher Geist und zwanzigstes Jahrhundert. Mainz, 1947.

Phil 3850.22.93 — Boucher, Maurice K.N.F. Solger; esthétique et philosophie de la présence. Thèse. Paris, 1934.

Phil 6049.17 — Bouchet, G. Cosmogonie humaine. Vichy, 1917.

Phil 176.155 — Bouchet, Henri. Introduction à la philosophie de l'individu. Paris, 1949.

Phil 2725.2.68 — Bouchitté, Louis Herve. Réfutation de la doctrine. Paris, 1821.

Phil 2880.5.90 — Boudeau, J.M.L. Ernest Seillière. Paris, 1925.

Phil 3640.805 — Boudot, Pierre. Nietzsche et l'au-delà de la liberté; Nietzsche et les écrivains français de 1930 à 1960. Paris, 1970.

Phil 3640.845 — Boudot, Pierre. L'ontologie de Nietzsche. Paris, 1971.

Phil 8876.99 — Bouffleis, Stanislas de. Discours sur la vertu. 2e éd. Paris, 1800.

Phil 5751.13 — Boufflers, S. Le libre arbitre. Paris, 1808.

Phil 2610.83 — Bougerel, J. Vie de Pierre Gassendi. Paris, 1737.

Phil 735.16 — Bougle, Celestin C. Leçons de sociologie sur l'évolution des valeurs. Paris, 1922.

Phil 2477.6.135 — Bouillard, Henri. Blondel et le christianisme. Paris, 1961.

Phil 6111.4.2 — Bouiller, F. De l'unité de l'ame pensante et du principe vital. Paris, 1858.

Phil 6111.4 — Bouiller, F. Du principe vital. Paris, 1862.

Phil 176.98 — Bouiller, D.R. Discours philosophiques. Amsterdam, 1759.

Phil 801.4.5 — Bouiller, F. Analyses des ouvrages de philosophie. 3. ed. Paris, 1870.

Phil 5402.8 — Bouiller, F. Du plaisir et de la douleur. Paris, 1865.

Phil 5402.8.3 — Bouiller, F. Du plaisir et de la douleur. 3e ed. Paris, 1885.

Phil 2520.83.5 — Bouiller, F. Histoire de la philosophie Cartésienne. Paris, 1854. 2v.

Phil 2520.83.6 — Bouiller, F. Histoire de la philosophie Cartésienne. Paris, 1868. 2v.

Phil 801.4 — Bouiller, F. Manuel de l'histoire de la philosophie. Paris, 1845.

Phil 2733.99 — Bouiller, F. Mémoire sur la vision en Dieu de Malebranche. Orleans, 1852?

Phil 8876.69 — Bouiller, F. Questions de morale pratique. Paris, 1889.

Phil 176.26 — Bouiller, F. Theorie de la raison impersonnelle. Paris, 1844.

Phil 5241.21 — Bouiller, F.C. Études familières de psychologie et de morale. Paris, 1884.

Phil 5241.21.5 — Bouiller, F.C. Nouvelles études familières de psychologie et de morale. Paris, 1887.

Phil 9075.2 — Bouiller, F.C. La vraie conscience. Paris, 1882.

Phil 9341.15 — Bouilly, J.N. Conseils à ma fille. Paris, 18- ?

Phil 5360.12 — Bouisson, R. Essai sur l'abstraction. Gap, 1942.

Phil 5811.8 — Boujeant, G.H. Amusement philosophique sur le langage des bestes. Paris, 1739.

Phil 2805.233 — Boulan, Émile. De Pascal à Victor Hugo. Groningue, 1946.

Phil 3450.2.80 — Boulan, Émile. François Hemsterhuis, le Socrate hollandais. Groningue, 1924.

Phil 282.19 — Boulding, K.E. The image. Ann Arbor, 1956.

Phil 6951.19 — Boulenger. Association des idées chez les idiots. Gand, 1906.

Phil 5811.2 — Boullier, D.R. Essai philosophique sur l'âme des bêtes. Amsterdam, 1728.

Phil 5811.2.2 — Boullier, D.R. Essai philosophique sur l'âme des bêtes. Amsterdam, 1737. 2v.

Phil 5635.40 — Boulogne, C.D. My friends. N.Y., 1953.

Phil 4065.101 — Boulting, William. Giordano Bruno, his life, thought and martyrdom. London, 1916.

Phil 4065.101.2 — Boulting, William. Giordano Bruno. London, 1914.

Phil 5590.504 — Bouman, Jan C. Psykologi för Erl. Stockholm, 1968.

Phil 3821.16 — Boumann, L. Explicatio spinozismi. Diss. Berlin, 1828.

Phil 4843.1 — Boumblinopoulos, Georgios E. Bibliographie critique de la philosophie grecque...1453-1953. Athènes, 1966.

Phil 3500.98 — The bounds of sense: an essay on Kant's 'Critique of pure reason'. (Strawson, Peter Frederick.) London, 1966.

Phil 176.175 — Bounet, G. Introduction à tous les cours de philosophie. Paris, 1952.

Phil 8581.51 — Bouquet, A.C. The Christian religion and its competitors today. Cambridge, Eng., 1925.

Phil 7054.78 — The bouquet of spiritual flowers. (Child. A.B.) Boston, 1856.

Phil 5811.3 — Bourbon del Monte, J.B.F. L'homme et les animaux. Paris, 1877.

Phil 9430.2 — Bourchenin, D. La trace du pessimisme dans la société. Paris, 1892.

Phil 176.58 — Bourdeau, J. La philosophie affective. Paris, 1912.

Phil 176.49 — Bourdeau, J. Pragmatisme et modernisme. Paris, 1909.

Phil 8612.12.2 — Bourdeau, L. Le problème de la mort. 2. éd. Paris, 1896.

Phil 176.64 — Bourdeau, L. Problème de la vie, essai de sociologie générale. Paris, 1901.

Phil 5241.68 — Bourdon, B. L'intelligence. Paris, 1926.

NEDL Phil 5643.26 — Bourdon, B. La perception visuelle de l'espace. Paris, 1902.

Phil 2555.10.81 — Boureau-Deslandes, ein Materialist der Frühaufklärung. 1. Aufl. (Geissler, Rolf.) Berlin, 1967.

Phil 3425.758 — Bourgeois, Bernard. Hegel à Francfort; ou Judaisme, christianisme, hégélianisme. Paris, 1970.

Phil 3425.688 — Bourgeois, Bernard. La pensée politique de Hegel. Paris, 1969.

Phil 5590.185 — Bourjade, Jean. Principes de caractérologie. Neuchâtel, 1955.

Phil 8951.27 — Bourke, V.J. Ethics. N.Y., 1959.

Phil 5751.19 — Bourke, Vernon. Will in Western thought. N.Y., 1964.

Phil 8826.8 — Bourke, Vernon Joseph. History of ethics. Garden City, 1968.

Phil 9341.13.5 — Bourn, Benjamin. A sure guide to hell, in seven sections. London, 1785.

Phil 2115.91A — Bourne, H.R.F. The life of John Locke. London, 1876. 2v.

Phil 2115.91.2A — Bourne, H.R.F. The life of John Locke. N.Y., 1876. 2v.

Phil 5520.714 — Bourne, Lyle Eugene. The psychology of thinking. Englewood Cliffs, N.J., 1971.

Phil 5628.51.5 — Bourneville, Désiré Magloire. Science and miracle. Louise Lateau ou la stigmatisée belge. Paris, 1875.

Phil 1750.126.10 — Bourquin, Constant. Itinéraire de Sirius à Jérusalem. Paris, 1931.

Phil 6671.8 — Bourru, H. La suggestion mentale. Paris, 1887.

Phil 5145.6 — Boursin, Jean Louis. Autopsie du hasard. Paris, 1970.

Phil 126.1 — Bouscaillou, R.P. Precis de philosophie. Paris, 1873.

Phil 5402.16 — Bousfield, P. Pleasure and pain. London, 1926.

Phil 6311.5 — Bousfield, Paul. The elements of practical psychoanalysis. London, 1920.

Phil 6311.5.5 — Bousfield, Paul. The omnipotent self. London, 1923.

Phil 5545.230 — Bousfield, William Robert. The basis of memory. N.Y., 1928.

Phil 1701.25 — Bousquet, J. Les capitals; ou De Jean Duns Scot à Jean Paulhan. Paris, 1955.

Phil 8876.23 — Boussinesq, J. Conciliation du véritable déterminisme mécanique. Paris, 1878.

Phil 2880.8.88 — Boutang, P. Sartre, est-il un possédé? Paris, 1947.

Phil 2880.8.88.5 — Boutang, P. Sartre, est-il un possédé? Paris, 1950.

Phil 8402.10.5 — Bouterwek, F. Aesthetik. 2. ed. Göttingen, 1815. 2v.

Phil 3483.45.5 — Bouterwek, F. Aphorismen den Freunden der Vernunftkritik nach Kantischer Lehre. Gottingen, 1793.

Phil 176.53.15 — Bouterwek, F. Idee einer Spodiktik. Halle, 1799. 2v.

Phil 8402.10 — Bouterwek, F. Ideen zur Metaphysik des Schönen. Leipzig, 1807.

Phil 3483.45 — Bouterwek, F. Immanuel Kant. Hamburg, 1799.

Phil 176.53 — Bouterwek, F. Kleine schriften philosophischen. Bd.1. Göttingen, 1818.

Phil 176.53.7 — Bouterwek, F. Lehrbuch der philosophischen Vorkenntnisse. Göttingen, 1820.

Phil 176.53.2 — Bouterwek, F. Lehrbuch der philosophischen Wissenschaften. Göttingen, 1820. 2v.

Phil 8876.90 — Bouterwek, F. Praktische Aphorismen. Leipzig, 1808.

Phil 176.26.15 — Bouterwek, Friedrich. Angangsgründe der speculaterien Philosophie. Bruxelles, 1968.

Phil 176.26.10 — Bouterwek, Friedrich. Die Epochen der Vernunft nach der Idee einer Apoditik. Bruxelles, 1968.

Phil 5465.33 — Bouthoul, G. L'invention. Paris, 1930.

Phil 176.42.15 — Boutroux, E. The beyond that is within. London, 1912.

Phil 1750.113 — Boutroux, E. De l'idée de la loi naturelle. Paris, 1913.

Phil 801.10 — Boutroux, E. Études d'histoire de la philosophie. Paris, 1908.

Phil 801.10.5 — Boutroux, E. Historical studies in philosophy. London, 1912.

Phil 2401.5 — Boutroux, E. Nouvelles études d'histoire de la philosophie. Paris, 1927.

Phil 2805.92.7 — Boutroux, E. Pascal. Manchester, 1902.

Phil 2805.92 — Boutroux, E. Pascal. Paris, 1900.

Phil 2805.92.3 — Boutroux, E. Pascal. 3. éd. Paris, 1903.

Phil 2805.92.9 — Boutroux, E. Pascal. 5. éd. Paris, 1912.

Phil 2270.106 — Boutroux, E. La religion selon Herbert Spencer. Paris, 1905.

Phil 8691.6.5 — Boutroux, E. Science et religion in contemporary philosophy. London, 1909.

NEDL Phil 8691.6.1 — Boutroux, E. Science et religion. Paris, 1908.

Phil 2070.111.5 — Boutroux, E. William James. Leipzig, 1912.

Phil 2070.111A — Boutroux, E. William James. Paris, 1911.

Phil 8691.6.10 — Boutroux, E. Wissenschaft und Religion in der Philosophie unserer Zeit. Leipzig, 1910.

Phil 2477.1.66 — Boutroux, Émile. Certitude et vérité. London, 1915.

Phil 2477.1.25 — Boutroux, Émile. Choix de textes. Paris, 1910.

Phil 2477.1.34 — Boutroux, Émile. The contingency of the laws of nature. Chicago, 1916.

Phil 2477.1.30 — Boutroux, Émile. De la contingence des lois de la nature. Thèse. Paris, 1874.

Phil 2477.1.32 — Boutroux, Émile. De la contingence des lois de la nature. 3. éd. Paris, 1898.

Phil 2477.1.40 — Boutroux, Émile. De l'idée de loi naturelle dans la science et la philosophie contemporaines. Paris, 1895.

Phil 2477.1.41 — Boutroux, Émile. De l'idée de loi naturelle dans la science et la philosophie contemporaines. Paris, 1949.

Phil 2520.134 — Boutroux, Émile. De veritatibus aeternis apud Cartesium. Thesis. Parisiis, 1874.

Phil 2070.147.5 — Boutroux, Émile. Décès de M. William James. Paris, 1910.

Phil 2520.134.5 — Boutroux, Émile. Des vérités éternelles chez Descartes. Paris, 1927.

Phil 2477.1.44 — Boutroux, Émile. Natural law in science and philosophy. London, 1914.

Phil 2477.1.55 — Boutroux, Émile. La nature et l'esprit. Paris, 1926.

Phil 2477.1.06 — Boutroux, Émile. Philosophical pamphlets, 1888-1909. Paris, 1888-1909.

Phil 2477.1.07 — Boutroux, Émile. Philosophical pamphlets. Paris, 1904-05. 2 pam.

Phil 3552.287 — Boutroux, Émile. La philosophie allemande au XVII siècle. Paris, 1929.

Phil 3483.35 — Boutroux, Émile. La philosophie de Kant. Paris, 1926.

Phil 2477.1.63 — Boutroux, Émile. Philosophy and war. London, 1916.

Phil 2477.1.64 — Boutroux, Émile. Philosophy and war. N.Y., 1916.

Phil 2477.1.50 — Boutroux, Émile. Questions de morale et d'éducation. Paris, 1895?

Phil 179.3.81.7 — Boutroux, Émile. Rudolf Euckens Kampf um einen neuen Idealismus. Leipzig, 1911.

Phil 2070.127 — Boutroux, Émile. William James. 2d ed. N.Y., 1912.

Phil 2477.1.08 — Pamphlet box. Boutroux, Émile. Minor writings.

Phil 2520.101 — Boutroux, P. L'imagination et les Math Selon Descartes. Paris, 1900.

Phil 8951.3 — Boutteville, M.L. La morale de l'église et la morale naturelle. Paris, 1866.

Phil 5041.18 — Bouttier, M.Z. Essai de philosophie française. Paris, 1844.

Phil 6951.15 — Bouveret, L. La neurasthénie. 2. éd. Paris, 1891.

Phil 6311.52 — Bouvet, Maurice. Oeuvres psychanalytiques. Paris, 1967-68. 2v.

Phil 3625.3.85 — Bouvier, Robert. La pensée d'Ernst Mach. Paris, 1923.

Phil 176.222 — Bouwsma, O.K. Philosophical essays. Lincoln, Nebraska, 1965.

Phil 585.230 — Bouwstenen voor een filosofische anthropologie. (Strasser, Stephan.) Hilversum, 1965.

Phil 1020.15 — Bouyges, P.M. Notes sur les philosophes arabes. Beyrouth, 1921.

Phil 8656.16 — Bouyssonie, A. Batailles d'idées sur les problèmes de Dieu, du bien, du vrai. Paris, 1923.

Phil 2725.2.105 — Bovard, René. Drame de conscience. Paris, 1961.

Phil 1706.1.25 — Bovarysm. (Gaultier, Jules de.) N.Y., 1970.

Phil 1706.1.23 — Le Bovarysme. 3. éd. Photoreproduction. (Gaultier, Jules de.) Paris, 1902.

Phil 8876.24.5 — Bovee, C.N. Intuitions and summaries of thought. Boston, 1862. 2v.

Phil 8876.24 — Bovee, C.N. Thoughts, feelings, and fancies. N.Y., 1857.

Phil 6311.16 — Boven, William. L'anxiété. Neuchâtel, 1934.

Phil 9035.63 — Boven, William. La science du caractère. Neuchâtel, 1931.

Phil 7069.68.55 — De bovenzinnelijke wereld. (Piccardt, Karel.) Amsterdam, 1968.

Phil 8691.30 — Boveri, Walter. Ethik und Atomzeitalter. Zürich, 1958.

Phil 5421.20.15 Bovet, Pierre. L'instinct combatif; problèmes de psychologie et d'éducation. 3. éd. Neuchâtel, 1961.

Phil 6834.5 Bovet, Théodore. Sinnerfülltes Anders-sein. Tübingen, 1959.

Phil 5425.16 Bovio, G. Il genio. Milano, 1900.

Phil 5643.21 Bowditch, H.P. Optical illusions of motion. Cambridge, 1882.

Phil 1850.158 Bowen, Catherine. Francis Bacon. 1st ed. Boston, 1963.

Phil 8587.6.15 Bowen, D. Assumed authority:...Hedge's address. Boston, 1864.

Phil 1880.28 Bowen, F. Berkeley and his philosophy. Cambridge, 1838-57. 5 pam.

Phil 1880.25 Bowen, F. Critical essays. Boston, 1842.

Phil 1880.25.5 Bowen, F. Critical essays. 2nd ed. Boston, 1845.

Phil 1880.30 Bowen, F. Gleanings from a literary life 1830-80. N.Y., 1880.

Phil 1880.50.2 Bowen, F. The idea of cause. N.Y., 1879.

Phil 1880.50 Bowen, F. The idea of cause. N.Y., 1879.

Phil 1880.43.2 Bowen, F. Lowell lectures...metaphysics...science. Boston, 1849.

Phil 1880.43 Bowen, F. Lowell lectures...metaphysics...science. Boston, 1849.

Phil 1701.1.2 Bowen, F. Modern philosophy. N.Y., 1877.

Phil 1701.1 Bowen, F. Modern philosophy. N.Y., 1877.

Phil 1701.1.3 Bowen, F. Modern philosophy. 2nd ed. N.Y., 1877.

Phil 1880.40 Bowen, F. Principles of metaphysical and ethical science. Boston, 1855.

Phil 1880.46 Bowen, F. Treatise on logic. Cambridge, 1864.

Phil 1880.46.4 Bowen, F. Treatise on logic. 4th ed. Cambridge, 1866.

Phil 1880.46.8 Bowen, F. Treatise on logic. 8th ed. Boston, 1880.

Phil 1880.23 Pamphlet vol. Bowen, F. On the origin of species...Darwin. 8 pam.

Phil 2038.80 Bower, G.S. Hartley and James Mill. London, 1881.

Phil 2038.80.5 Bower, G.S. Hartley and James Mill. N.Y., 1881.

Phil 5425.74 Bowerman, Walter. Studies in genius. N.Y., 1947.

Phil 332.22 Bowers, David F. Atomism, empiricism, and scepticism. Abstract of thesis. Princeton, 1941.

Phil 5627.263 Bowers, M.K. Conflicts of the clergy. Edinburgh, 1963.

Phil 1195.21 Bowersock, Glen Warren. Greek sophists in the Roman empire. Oxford, 1969.

Phil 8876.121 Bowes, Pratima. The concept of morality. London, 1959.

Phil 9415.14 Bowker, John. Problems of suffering in religions of the world. Cambridge, 1970.

Phil 8876.67 Bowker, R.R. The arts of life. Boston, 1900.

Phil 8581.21 Bowker, R.R. Of religion. Boston, 1903.

Phil 5241.172 Bowlby, John. Attachment and loss. London, 1969.

Phil 6311.27 Bowlby, John. Personality and mental illness, psychiatric diagnosis. N.Y., 1942.

Phil 6111.48 Bowman, A. Mind and brain in thought and reason process. London, 1930.

Phil 1905.13 Bowman, A.A. A sacramental universe. Princeton, 1939.

Phil 8581.74 Bowman, Archibald Allan. Studies in the philosophy of religion. London, 1938. 2v.

Phil 5585.300 Bowman, Jan C. The figure-ground phenomenon in experimental and phenomenological psychology. Thesis. Stockholm, 1968.

Phil 6111.46 Bowman, Karl M. Personal problems for men and women. N.Y., 1931.

Phil 5241.15 Bowne, B.P. Introduction to psychological theory. N.Y., 1887.

Phil 3483.10A Bowne, B.P. Kant and Spencer. Boston, 1912.

Phil 176.27.5 Bowne, B.P. Metaphysics. N.Y., 1882.

Phil 176.27 Bowne, B.P. Metaphysics. N.Y., 1882.

Phil 176.27.2 Bowne, B.P. Metaphysics. N.Y., 1898.

Phil 176.27.12 Bowne, B.P. Personalism. Boston, 1908.

Phil 2270.90 Bowne, B.P. The philosophy of Herbert Spencer. N.Y., n.d.

Phil 2270.90.2 Bowne, B.P. The philosophy of Herbert Spencer. N.Y., 1881.

Phil 8656.8.5 Bowne, B.P. Philosophy of theism. N.Y., 1887.

Phil 8876.25 Bowne, B.P. The principles of ethics. N.Y., 1892.

Phil 8876.25.5 Bowne, B.P. The principles of ethics. N.Y., 1893.

Phil 8656.8 Bowne, B.P. Studies in theism. N.Y., 1879.

Phil 8656.8.7 Bowne, B.P. Theism. N.Y., 1902.

Phil 332.2 Bowne, B.P. Theory of thought and knowledge. N.Y., 1897.

Phil 8581.37 Bowne, Borden P. Essence of religion. Boston, 1910.

Phil 8581.37.5 Bowne, Borden P. Studies in Christianity. Boston, 1909.

Phil 2270.90.5 Bowne, Borden Parker. The philosophy of Herbert Spencer; being an examination of the first principles of his system. New York, 1881. Photoreproduction. Ann Arbor, Michigan, 1970.

Phil 5011.8 Bowne, G.D. The philosophy of logic, 1880-1908. The Hague, 1966.

Phil 5599.95 Bowyer, Laura Ruth. The Lowenfeld world technique. 1. ed. Oxford, N.Y., 1970.

Phil 801.2 Box, E.B. Handbook...history of philosophy. London, 1886.

Phil 801.2.5 Box, E.B. Handbook...history of philosophy. London, 1908.

Phil 8656.25 Box, Hubert S. The world and God. Thesis. London, 1934.

Phil 9530.12 The boy! How to help him succeed. (Fowler, M.C.) Boston, 1902.

Phil 5938.12.5 The boy - what will he become? (Phrenological Institution, Brighton.) Hove, 1929.

Phil 9530.24 Boy wanted. (Waterman, Nixon.) Chicago., 1906.

Phil 4065.50.15 Boyanov, Slavi. Filosofiiata na Dzhordano Bruno. Sofiia, 1969.

Phil 7069.19.20 Boyce, Adam. The great beyond and its inhabitants. London, 1919.

Phil 8876.26 Boyd, J.R. Eclectic moral philosophy. N.Y., 1846.

Phil 6111.37 Boyd, T.P. The voice eternal. 2nd ed. San Francisco, 1912-14.

Phil 7076.5 Boyer, Onesimas Alfred. She wears a crown of thorns; Marie Rose Perron, 1902-1936. N.Y., 1951.

Phil 2490.102 Boyer de Sainte-Suzanne, Raymond de. Essai sur la pensée religieuse d'Auguste Comte. Paris, 1923.

Phil 4757.2.110 Boyhood with Gurdjieff. (Peters, Arthur A.) N.Y., 1964.

Phil 5865.5.35 Boyle, D.G. A student's guide to Piaget. 1st ed. Oxford, 1969.

Phil 6990.45 Boyle, J.L. A pictorial history of Lourdes. Philadelphia, 1940.

Htn Phil 2520.103* Boyle, Pierre. Recueil de quelques...philosophie de Descartes. Amsterdam, 1684.

Htn Phil 8735.2* Boyle, R. A disquisition...final causes of natural things. London, 1688.

Htn Phil 8691.5* Boyle, R. Some considerations about the reconcileablness of reason and religion. London, 1675.

Phil 1535.2 Boylesve, M. de. Cursus philosophiae. Paris, 1855.

Phil 5241.98 Boynton, P.L. Intelligence, its manifestations and measurement. N.Y., 1933.

Phil 9160.3.10 The boy's guide. (Alcott, W.A.) Boston, 1844.

Phil 1955.6.245 Boyston, JoAnn. John Dewey; a checklist of translations, 1900-1967. Carbondale, 1969.

Phil 1200.28 Boza Masvidal, A.A. El estoicismo. Tesis. Habana, 1922.

Phil 4829.491.80 Božidar Knežević. (Grubačić, Kosta.) Sarajevo, 1962.

Phil 7069.38.4 Bozzano, E. Discarnate influence. London, 1938.

Phil 7069.19.27 Bozzano, E. Les phénomènes de hantise. Paris, 1920.

Phil 7069.30.2.15 Bozzano, Ernesto. Letteratura d'Oltretomba. Città della Pieve, 1930.

Phil 4070.9.1 Bozzetti, Giuseppe. Opere complete: saggi, scritti inediti, opere minori, recensioni. Milano, 1966. 3v.

Phil 4210.140 Bozzetti, Giuseppe. Rosmini nell'ultima critica di Ausonio Franchi. Firenze, 1917.

Phil 6120.8.25 Braat, J.P. De experimenteele psychologie en Kretschmer's constitutietypen. Amsterdam, 1934.

Phil 6327.28.80 Braaten, Leif Johan. Klient-sentrert rådgivning og terapi...Carl R. Rogers' psykologi. Oslo, 1967.

Phil 6951.24 Braatøy, T. Männer zwischen 15 und 25. Oslo, 1934.

Phil 5627.125 Brabant, F.H. Religion and the mysterious. London, 1930.

Phil 5374.180 Brach, Jacques. Conscience et connaissance. Paris, 1957.

Phil 3890.10.100 Brachmann, W. Ernst Troeltschs historische Weltanschauung. Halle, 1940.

Phil 1870.136.5 Bracken, Harry M. The early reception of Berkeley's immaterialism, 1710-1733. The Hague, 1965.

Phil 1870.136 Bracken, Harry M. The early reception of Berkeley's immaterialism. The Hague, 1959.

Phil 5241.25 Brackenbury, L. Primer of psychology. London, 1907.

Phil 6111.27.2 Brackett, Anna C. The technique of rest. N.Y., 1893.

Phil 7068.86.40 Brackett, E.A. Materialized apparitions. Boston, 1886.

Phil 7069.08.12 Brackett, E.A. Materialized apparitions. Boston, 1908.

Phil 9245.117 Bradburn, Norman Marshall. Reports on happiness. Chicago, 1965.

Phil 9245.136 Bradburn, Norman Marshall. The structure of psychological well-being. Chicago, 1969.

Phil 1506.7 Brade, W.R.V. From Plotinus to St. Thomas Aquinas. London, 1926.

Phil 6111.66 Braden, C.S. Spirits in rebellion. Dallas, 1963.

Phil 6158.15 Braden, William. The private sea; LSD and the search for God. Chicago, 1967.

Phil 665.10 Bradford, A.H. The ascent of the soul. N.Y., 1902.

Phil 5440.1 Bradford, A.H. Heredity and Christian problems. N.Y., 1895.

Phil 705.9 Bradford, Alden. Human learning favorable to true religion. Boston, 1841.

Phil 176.108 Bradford, Gamaliel. Life and I. Boston, 1928.

Phil 8610.889.5 Bradlaugh, C. Humanity's gain from unbelief. London, 1889.

Phil 8610.889.7 Bradlaugh, C. Humanity's gain from unbelief. London, 1929.

Phil 8610.858.5 Bradlaugh, Charles. Biographies of ancient and modern celebrated freethinkers. Boston, 1877.

Phil 8610.891.5 Bradlaugh, Charles. Doubts in dialogue. London, 1909.

Phil 8620.23 Bradlaugh, Charles. A few words about the devil. N.Y., 1874.

Phil 8610.870.10 Bradlaugh, Charles. Theological essays. London, 1883.

Phil 8610.933 Bradlaugh and Ingersoll. (Cohen, C.) London, 1933.

Phil 7069.67.30 Bradley, Dorothy Bomar. Psychic phenomena, revelations and experiences. West Nyack, 1967.

Phil 2280.1.90 Bradley, F.H. Mr. Sidgwick's hedonism. London, 1877.

Phil 5041.20 Bradley, F.H. Principles of logic. London, 1883.

Phil 5041.20.3 Bradley, F.H. Principles of logic. N.Y., 1912.

Phil 5041.20.5A Bradley, F.H. Principles of logic. 2nd ed. London, 1922. 2v.

Phil 1885.37 Bradley, Francis H. Appearance and reality. London, 1893.

Phil 1885.37.3 Bradley, Francis H. Appearance and reality. London, 1899.

Phil 1885.37.15 Bradley, Francis H. Appearance and reality. Oxford, 1930.

Phil 1885.37.20 Bradley, Francis H. Appearance and reality. Oxford, 1968.

Phil 1885.37.5A Bradley, Francis H. Appearance and reality. 2d ed. London, 1902.

Phil 1885.37.7 Bradley, Francis H. Appearance and reality. 2d ed. London, 1908.

Phil 1885.15 Bradley, Francis H. Collected essays. Oxford, 1935. 2v.

Phil 1885.35 Bradley, Francis H. Essays on truth and reality. Oxford, 1914.

Htn Phil 1885.30* Bradley, Francis H. Ethical studies. London, 1876.

Phil 8876.27.12 Bradley, Francis Herbert. Ethical studies. N.Y., 1951.

Phil 8876.27.15 Bradley, Francis Herbert. Ethical studies. 2nd ed. London, 1969.

Phil 8876.27.7 Bradley, Francis Herbert. Ethical studies. 2nd ed. Oxford, 1927.

Phil 8876.27.16A Bradley, Francis Herbert. Ethical studies. 2nd ed. Oxford, 1967.

Phil 58.2.25 Bradley, Herbert Dennis. An indictment of the present administration of the Society for Psychical Research. London, 1931.

Phil 5722.7 Bradley, M.K. The logic of the unconscious mind. London, 1920.

Phil 5170.18 Bradley, Raymond. Logic, physics and metaphysics. Auckland, 1967.

Phil 1885.86A Bradley and Bergson. (Loomba, R.M.) Lucknow, 1937.

Phil 1885.89 Bradley's dialectic. (Church, Ralph Withington.) London, 1942.

Phil 1885.97 Bradley's metaphysics and the self. (Vander Veer, Garrett L.) New Haven, 1970.

Phil 8581.84 Bradshaw, M.J. Philosophical foundations of faith. N.Y., 1941.

Phil 850.32 Brady, Ignatius. A history of ancient philosophy. Milwaukee, 1959.

Phil 510.150 Bräuer, E.W. Überwindung der Materie. Leipzig, 1925.

Phil 176.143 Bräuer, Ernst Wasa. Metaphysik als beobachtende Wissenschaft. Berlin, 1934.

Phil 5465.194 Braeuer, Gottfried. Das Finden als Moment des Schöpferischen. Tübingen, 1966.

Phil 3552.81 Braeutigam, L. Leibniz und Herbart über die Freiheit des menschlichen Willens. Heidelberg, 1882.

Phil 310.646 Braga, J. Crítica do materialismo dialéctico. Lisboa, 1966.

Phil 978.27 Bragdon, C. The beautiful necessity. Rochester, N.Y., 1910.

Phil 978.80.10 Bragdon, C.F. The new image. N.Y., 1928.

Phil 978.80 Bragdon, C.F. Old lamps for new. N.Y., 1925.

Phil 672.172 Bragdon, C.F. A primer of higher space. Rochester, 1913.

Phil 672.172.5 Bragdon, C.F. A primer of higher space. 2nd ed. N.Y., 1923.

Phil 8691.26 Bragg, W. Science and faith. London, 1941.

Htn Phil 9420.1* Bragge, F. A practical treatise...regulation...passions. London, 1708.

Phil 575.60.5 Braham, Ernest G. Ourselves and reality. London, 1929.

Phil 575.60 | Braham, Ernest G. Personality and immortality in post Kantian thought. London, 1926.

Phil 3120.40.80 | Brahell Brujs, W.R. van. Ter herdenling van Dr. J.D. Bierens de Haan. Naarden, 1944.

Phil 270.47 | Brahma, N.K. Causality and science. London, 1939.

Phil 960.12 | Brahma-knowledge, outline of philosophy of the Vedânta. (Barnett, L.D.) London, 1907.

Phil 960.16 | Brahmadarsanam...introduction to the study of Hindu philosophy. (Ananda Achárya.) London, 1917.

Phil 960.142 | Brahman: a study in the history of Indian philosophy. (Griswold, Hervey De Witt.) N.Y., 1900.

Phil 3483.20 | Brahn, Max. Die Entwicklung des Seelenbegriffes bei Kant. Inaug. Diss. Leipzig, 18- ?

Phil 3640.128.2 | Brahn, Max. Friedrich Nietzsches Meinung über Staaten und Kriege. 2e Aufl. Leipzig, 1915.

Htn Phil 7230.1* | Braid, J. Observations on trance. London, 1850.

Htn Phil 6671.10* | Braid, James. Electro-biological phenomena. Edinburgh, 1851.

Phil 6671.10.10 | Braid, James. Magic, witchcraft, animal magnetism. London, 1852.

Phil 6671.10.20 | Braid, James. Neurypnologie. Paris, 1883.

X Cg Phil 6671.10.15 | Braid, James. Neurypnology. London, 1899.

Htn Phil 6671.10.5* | Braid, James. Power of the mind over the body. London, 1846.

Phil 8876.76 | Braileanu, T. Die Grundlegung zur einer Wissenschaft der Ethik. Wien, 1919.

Phil 978.33 | Brailsford-Bright, J. Theosophy and modern socialism. London, 1889.

Phil 6117.31.10 | Brain, mind and the external signs of intelligence. (Hollander, Bernard.) London, 1931.

Phil 5585.75 | Brain, W.R. Mind, perception and science. Oxford, 1951.

Phil 332.30 | Brain, W.R. The nature of experience. London, 1959.

Phil 5241.167 | Brain, Walter. Science and man. London, 1966.

Phil 6400.30.2 | Brain, Walter Russell. Speech disorders; aphasia, apraxia and agnosia. 2d ed. London, 1965.

Phil 6111.56 | The brain. (Barcroft, J.) New Haven, 1938.

Phil 6128.7 | The brain. (Swedenborg, E.) London, 1882-87.

NEDL Phil 11.14 | Brain. N.Y. 1-52,1878-1929 82v.

Phil 11.14 | Brain. N.Y. 53,1930+ 83v.

Phil 5238.234 | Brain and behaviour. (Pribram, Karl H.) Harmondsworth, Middlesex, Eng., 1969. 4v.

Phil 6132.10 | Brain and body: the nervous system. 2d ed. (Wilson, A.) London, 1900.

Phil 5374.243 | Brain and conscious experience. Study Week, September 28 to October 4, 1964. (Accademia...Vatican City.) Pontificia Academia delle Scienze, Vatican City.) N.Y., 1966.

Phil 6117.46 | Brain and intelligence. (Halstood, W.C.) Chicago, 1947.

Phil 6121.7 | The brain and its functions. (Luys, J.) N.Y., 1882.

Phil 6123.2 | The brain and its physiology. (Noble, D.) London, 1846.

Phil 6128.78 | Brain and mind. (Smythies, John Raymond.) London, 1965.

Phil 6129.1.4 | Brain and personality. (Thomson, W.H.) N.Y., 1906.

Phil 6129.1.8 | Brain and personality. (Thomson, W.H.) N.Y., 1914.

Phil 6117.8A | The brain and spinal cord. (Horsley, V.) London, 1892.

Phil 6128.40.6 | The brain and the mind. (Sunner, Paul.) N.Y., 1926.

Phil 6132.36 | The brain as an organ. (Wertham, F.) N.Y., 1934.

Phil 6111.10.2 | The brain as an organ of mind. (Bastian, H.C.) N.Y., 1880.

Phil 5252.87 | Brain capacity and intelligence. (Miller, Edmond M.) Sydney, 1926.

Phil 6112.8 | Brain exhaustion. (Corning, J.L.) N.Y., 1884.

Phil 6124.4 | The brain from ape to man. (Tilney, Frederick.) N.Y., 1928. 2v.

Phil 6112.21 | Brain in relation to mind. (Christison, J.S.) Chicago, 1899.

Phil 6128.6 | The brain in relation to the mind. (Swan, J.) London, 1854.

Phil 6121.39A | Brain mechanisms and intelligence. (Lashley, Karl S.) N.Y., 1963.

Phil 6112.2.15 | Brain power for business men. (Call, A.P.) Boston, 1911.

Phil 6112.8.5 | Brain rest. (Corning, J.L.) N.Y., 1885.

Phil 5592.170 | The brain watchers. (Gross, Martin L.) N.Y., 1962.

NEDL Phil 6132.33 | Brain-work. (Wood, H.) Philadelphia, 1880.

Phil 6132.2 | Brain-work and overwork. (Wood, H.C.) Philadelphia, 1885.

Phil 5817.15.3 | Brains of rats and men. (Herrick, C. Judson.) Chicago, 1930.

Phil 6951.26 | Brainstorm. (Brown, Carlton.) N.Y., 1944.

Phil 5780.15 | Brainwashing. (Hunter, Edward.) N.Y., 1956.

Phil 5780.15.2 | Brainwashing. (Hunter, Edward.) N.Y., 1960.

Phil 8581.9 | Braithwaite, H.T. Esse and posse. London, 1872.

Phil 9560.32.5 | Braithwaite, R.B. Theory of games. Cambridge, Eng., 1963.

Phil 9560.32 | Braithwaite, R.B. Theory of games as a tool for the moral philosopher. Cambridge, Eng., 1955.

Phil 3821.20 | Brakell Buys, W.R. de V. van. Het Godsbegrip bij Spinoza. Utrecht, 193-?

Phil 4065.120 | Brambilla, E. Studi letterari. Sugli eroici furori di G. Bruno. Milano, 1892.

Phil 2045.105 | Bramhall, J. Castigations of Mr. Hobbes. London, 1658.

Phil 5241.31 | Bramshausen, N. Einführung in die experimentelle Psychologie. Leipzig, 1915.

Phil 6671.15.6 | Bramwell, J.M. Hypnotism: its history, practice, and theory. N.Y., 1956.

Phil 6671.15 | Bramwell, J.M. Hypnotism. 2nd ed. London, 1906.

Phil 4210.245 | Brancaforte, Antonio. Discussioni rosminiane. Catania, 1968.

Phil 1750.756 | Brancatisano, F. Per un umanesimo scientifico. Firenze, 1963.

Phil 4260.180 | Brancato, Francesco. Vico nel risorgimento. Palermo, 1969.

Phil 1750.115.200 | Brand, Gerd. Die Lebenswelt. Berlin, 1971.

Phil 3450.11.150 | Brand, Gerd. Welt. Den Haag, 1955.

Phil 5590.165 | Brand, Howard. The study of personality. N.Y., 1954.

Phil 6315.2.420 | Brandell, Gunnar. Freud; enfant de son siècle. Paris, 1967.

Phil 5858.5 | Branden, Nathaniel. The psychology of self-esteem. Los Angeles, 1969.

Phil 3120.45.50 | Brandenstein, Béla. Der Aufbau des Seins; System der Philosophie. Tübingen, 1950.

Phil 3120.45.40 | Brandenstein, Béla. Das Bild des Menschen und die Idee des Humanismus. Bregenz, 1948.

Phil 3120.45.45 | Brandenstein, Béla. Grundlegung der Philosophie. Halle, 1926[1970] 6v.

Phil 182.94.85 | Brandenstein, Béla. Teleologisches Denken. Bonn, 1960.

Phil 3120.45.30 | Brandenstein, Béla. Vom Sinn der Philosophie und ihrer Geschichte. Bonn, 1957.

Phil 3120.45.35 | Brandenstein, Béla. Wahrheit und Wirklichkeit. Meisenheim, 1965.

Phil 7082.68 | Brander, Robert. Der Schlaf und das Traumleben. Leipzig, 1884.

Phil 972.12 | Brander-Pracht, K. Der neue Mensch. Berlin, 1920.

Phil 1106.4 | Brandes, C.A. Handbuch der Geschichte der griechisch-römischen Philosophie. Berlin, 1835-60. 5v.

Phil 3640.107.5 | Brandes, G. Friedrich Nietzsche. London, 1914.

Phil 3640.107 | Brandes, G. Friedrich Nietzsche. N.Y., 1909.

Phil 315.4 | Brandes, Georg. Dualismen i vor nyeste philosophie. Kjobenhavn, 1866.

Htn Phil 3801.234* | Brandis, Christian A. Gedächtnissrede auf Friedrich Wilhelm Joseph von Schelling. Berlin, 1856.

Phil 8876.28 | Brandis, J.D. Überhumanes Leben. Schleswig, 1825.

Phil 5875.65.5 | Brandis, Walter. Social class language and communication. London, 1970.

Phil 6111.34 | Brandler-Pracht, Karl. Geheime Seelenkräfte. Berlin, 1921.

Phil 672.226 | Brandon, Samuel George Frederick. History, time and deity. Manchester, 1965.

Phil 4065.124 | Brandt, C. Giordano Bruno. Buenos Aires, 1940.

Phil 3821.24 | Brandt, C. Spinoza y el panteismo. Buenos Aires, 1941.

Phil 5520.499 | Brandt, Elmar. Der theoretische Bedeutungbegriff. Inaug. Diss. München, 1964.

Phil 5041.41 | Brandt, F. Formel logik. København, 1927.

Phil 5041.41.5 | Brandt, F. Formel logik til brug ved filosofikum. 3e udg. København, 1930.

Phil 5241.104 | Brandt, F. Psykoligi. v.1-2. København, 1934-40.

Phil 5645.55 | Brandt, Frithiof. Form kolarisme. København, 1958.

Phil 2045.108 | Brandt, Frithiof. Den mekaniske naturopfattelse hos Thomas Hobbes. København, 1921.

Phil 2045.108.5 | Brandt, Frithiof. Thomas Hobbes' mechanical conception of nature. Copenhagen, 1928.

Phil 2045.83 | Brandt, G. Grundlinien der Philosophie von T. Hobbes. Kiel, 1895.

Phil 5643.107 | Brandt, Herman F. The psychology of seeing. N.Y., 1945.

Phil 7069.23.5 | Brandt, J.v.W. The red octopus. London, 1923?

Phil 3805.183 | Brandt, R.B. The philosophy of Schleiermacher. N.Y., 1941.

Phil 8876.125 | Brandt, Richard. Ethical theory. Englewood Cliffs, N.J., 1959.

Phil 176.132 | Branford, B. Eros and Psyche. London, 1934.

Phil 5041.21.10 | Braniss, C.J. Grundriss der Logik. Breslau, 1830.

Phil 5041.21 | Braniss, C.J. Die Logik...Verhaltniss zur philosophische Geschichte betrachter. Berlin, 1823.

Phil 176.100 | Braniss, C.J. System der Metaphysik. Breslau, 1834.

Phil 3805.158 | Braniss, C.J. Über Schleiermachers Glaubenslehre. Berlin, 1824.

Phil 1701.2 | Braniss, C.J. Übersecht des Entwicklungsganges der Philosophie. Breslau, 1842.

Phil 3640.238 | Brann, H.W. Nietzsche und die Frauen. Leipzig, 1931.

Phil 130.3 | Brasch, M. Die Klassiker der Philosophie. Leipzig, 1884-85. 3v.

Phil 3001.3 | Brasch, M. Leipziger Philosophen. Leipzig, 1894.

Phil 3900.1.80 | Brasch, M. Welt- und Lebensanschauung Friedrich Ueberweg. Leipzig, 1889.

Phil 1701.14 | Brasch, Moritz. Die Philosophie der Gegenwart. Leipzig, 1888.

Phil 3821.15 | Brasch, Moritz. Spinoza's System der Philosophie. Berlin, 1870.

Phil 4001.3 | Braschi, C. I filosofi italiani dal XVIII al XIX secolo. Milano, 1916.

Phil 176.65 | Brass, T. Chapter from story of Pauline Parsons. Ashland, 1916.

Phil 3640.710 | Brassard, Werner à. Untersuchungen zum Problem des Übermenschen bei Friedrich Nietzsche. Freiburg, 1962.

Phil 3120.16.30 | Brastberger, G.U. Philosophische Briefe an meine Schwester. Halle, 1779.

Phil 3483.39 | Brastberger, G.U. Untersuchungen über Kants Critik der practischen Vernunft. Tübingen, 1792.

Phil 3483.39.5 | Brastberger, G.U. Untersuchungen über Kants Critik der reinen Vernunft. Halle, 1790.

Phil 176.190 | Brates, Georg. Du und die Philosophie. Berlin, 1955.

Phil 6980.132 | Bratz, Emil. Humor in der Neurologie und Psychiatrie. Berlin, 1930.

Phil 5585.23 | Braude, M. Die Elemente der Reinen Wahrnehmung. Lemberg, 1899.

Phil 3425.576 | Braum, Hermann. Realität und Reflexion. Heidelberg, 1960.

Phil 165.390 | Braum, Cornelis Gerardus Franciscus. Filia. Wijsgerige opstellen in vriendschap aangeboden aan Prof. Dr. J.H. Robbers. Nijmegen, 1966.

Phil 2045.140 | Braun, Dietrich. Der sterbliche Gott oder Leviathan gegen Behemoth. Thesis. Zürich, 1963.

Phil 176.72 | Braun, Edmond. La logique de l'absolu. Paris, 1887.

Phil 8951.22 | Braun, K. Justice and the law of love. London, 1950.

Phil 2630.1.84 | Braun, Ludwig L. Gratrys Theorie der religiosen Erkenntnis. Strassburg, 1914.

Phil 3415.93 | Braun, Otto. Eduard von Hartmann, von Otto Braun. Stuttgart, 1909.

Phil 3801.233 | Braun, Otto. Hinauf zum Idealismus! Schelling-Studien. Leipzig, 1908.

Phil 179.3.109 | Braun, Otto. Rudolf Euckens Philosophie und das Bildungsproblem. Leipzig, 1909.

Phil 3801.233.8 | Braun, Otto. Schellings geistige Wandlungen in den Jahren 1800-1810. Leipzig, 1906.

Phil 3801.233.5 | Braun, Otto. Schellings geistige Wandlungen in den Jahren 1800-1810. Inaug. Diss. Leipzig, 1906.

Phil 450.12 | Braun-Urban, Heiner. Wandlung der Welt durch Wandlung des Bewusstseins. München, 1969.

Phil 5330.6.5 | Braunschweiger, D. Die Lehre von der Aufmerksamkeit. Leipzig, 1899.

Phil 176.90 | Brausewetter, A. Die Weltanschauung als Erlebnis. Heft 3-4. Leipzig, 1920. 2v.

Phil 6315.2.79.30 | Brautbriefe. (Freud, Sigmund.) Frankfurt, 1968.

Phil 3625.1.42A | Brautbriefe. (Mendelssohn, Moses.) Berlin, 1936.

Phil 2905.1.610 | Bravo, Francisco. Teilhard de Chardin, su concepción de la historia. 1. ed. Barcelona, 1970.

Phil 4803.454.105 | Brawn, Jérzy Bronislaw. Apercu de la philosophie de Wroński. Rome, 1969?

Phil 5751.7.3 | Bray, Charles. The philosophy of necessity. 3. ed. London, 1889.

Phil 8402.47 | Bray, Lucien. Du beau. Paris, 1902.

Phil 2905.1.290 | Braybrook, N. Teilhard de Chardin. N.Y., 1964.

Phil 1870.122 | Brayton, Alice. George Berkeley in Apulia. Boston, 1946.

Phil 1870.122.5 | Brayton, Alice. George Berkeley in Newport. Newport, R.I., 1954.

Phil 3425.722 | Brazill, William J. The young Hegelians. New Haven, 1970.

Phil 2630.8.35 | Breakdown of morals and Christian education. (Gilson, Etienne.) n.p., 1952?

Phil 7072.22.5 | Breakthrough. (Raudive, Konstantins.) N.Y., 1971.

Phil 5865.5.16 | Brearley, Molly. A guide to reading Piaget. N.Y., 1967.

Phil 8626.22   Brecher, G. Die Unsterblichkeitslehre des israelitischen Volkes. Leipzig, 1857.

Phil 3450.19.94A   Brecht, F.J. Heidegger und Jaspers. Wuppertal, 1948.

Phil 5241.120   Brecht, F.J. Vom menschlichen Denken. Heidelberg, 1955.

Phil 1750.75   Brecht, Franz Josef. Bewusstsein und Existenz. Bremen, 1948.

Phil 810.16   Brechungen. (Kempski, Jürgen von.) Reinbek, 1964.

Phil 1750.115.40   Breda, H.L. Problémes actuels de la phénoménologie. Paris, 1952.

Phil 2050.90   Brede, W. Der Unterschied der lehren Humes. Halle, 1896.

Phil 2050.214   Brede, Wilhelm. Der Unterschied der Lehren Humes im Treatise und im Inquiry. Halle, 1896.

Phil 1133.37   Breden, Heribert. Grund und Gegenwart als Frageziel der frühgriechischen Philosophie. Den Haag, 1962.

Phil 3805.187   Bredow, G. Wertanalysen zu Schleiermachers. Diss. Würzburg, 1941.

Phil 5545.97   Breer, Paul E. Task experience as a source of attitudes. Homewood, 1965.

Phil 5241.35.2   Breese, B.B. Psychology. N.Y., 1921.

Phil 7069.31.55   Bréf frá Ingu. (Jónsdóttir, J.) Winnipeg, 1931.

Phil 5238.230   Breger, Louis. Clinical-cognitive psychology. Englewood Cliffs, N.J., 1969.

Phil 801.33.5   Bréhier, É. La filosofia e il suo passato. Napoli, 1965.

Phil 801.21   Bréhier, É. Histoire de la philosophie. Paris, 1926. 9v.

Phil 801.21.6   Bréhier, É. Histoire de la philosophie. Paris, 1963. 3v.

Phil 801.21.6.1   Bréhier, É. Histoire de la philosophie. Paris, 1969.

Phil 801.21.5A   Bréhier, É. The history of philosophy. v.1-3,5-7. Chicago, 1963. 7v.

Phil 801.33   Bréhier, E. La philosophie et son passé. Paris, 1940.

Phil 2401.10   Bréhier, E. Transformation de la philosophie française. Paris, 1950.

Phil 1106.16   Bréhier, Émile. Etudes de philosophie antique. Paris, 1955.

Phil 1701.23.5   Bréhier, Émile. Études de philosophie moderne. Paris, 1965.

Phil 3001.5   Bréhier, Émile. Histoire de la philosophie allemande. Paris, 1921.

Phil 3001.5.3   Bréhier, Émile. Histoire de la philosophie allemande. 3. ed. Paris, 1954.

Phil 1750.144A   Bréhier, Émile. La notion de renaissance dans l'histoire de la philosophie. Oxford, 1934.

Phil 3801.232   Bréhier, Émile. Schelling. Paris, 1912.

Phil 2477.13   Bréhier, Émile. Science et humanisme. Paris, 1947.

Phil 1701.23.3   Bréhier, Émile. Les thèmes actuels de la philosophie. Paris, 1954.

Phil 1701.23   Bréhier, Émile. Les thèmes actuels de la philosophie. 1. éd. Paris, 1951.

Phil 1200.18   Bréhier, Émile. La théorie des incorporels dans l'ancien stoïcisme. Thèse. Paris, 1908.

Phil 1200.18.5   Bréhier, Émile. La théorie des incorporels dans l'ancien stoïcisme. 2e éd. Paris, 1928.

Phil 5325.35   Brehm, Jack W. Explorations in cognitive dissonance. N.Y., 1962.

Phil 5751.21   Brehm, Jack Williams. A theory of psychological reactance. N.Y., 1966.

Phil 1506.10   Brehser, Emile. La philosophie du moyen âge. Paris, 1949.

Phil 1750.700   Breisach, Ernst. Introduction to modern existentialism. N.Y., 1962.

Phil 7069.32.20   Breitfield, R. Your psychic self. N.Y., 1932.

Phil 5241.78   Breitwieser, Joseph V. Psychological experiments. Colorado Springs, 1914.

Phil 188.12.80   Brelage, Manfred. Fundamentalanalyse und Regionalanalyse. Köln, 1957.

Phil 705.57   Brelage, Manfred. Studien zur Transzendentalphilosophie. Berlin, 1965.

Phil 9220.15   Brelting, Rudolf. Die Freundschaft. Düsseldorf, 1956.

Phil 2805.188   Bremond, H. En prière avec Pascal. Paris, 1923.

Phil 8581.77A   Brémond, H. Introduction à la philosophie de la prière. Paris, 1929.

Phil 1750.147   Brémond, Henri. Autour de l'humanisme d'Erasme à Pascal. Paris, 1937.

Phil 8581.34   Bremond, Henri. L'inquiétude religieuse. 2nd series. Paris, 1909. 2v.

Phil 2750.20.130   Brena, Gian Luigi. La struttura della percezione. Milano, 1969.

Phil 525.92   Brenes Mesen, R. El misticismo como instrumento de investigación de la verdad. San José de Costa Rica, 1921.

Phil 5811.17   Brenes Mesén, Roberto. La voluntad en los microorganismos. Costa Rica, 1905.

Phil 525.29   Brenier de Montmorand, Antoine F.J.H.L.M. Psychologie des mystiques catholiques orthodoxes. Paris, 1920.

Phil 2070.150   Brennan, Bernard P. The ethics of William James. N.Y., 1961.

Phil 2070.150.5A   Brennan, Bernard P. William James. N.Y., 1968.

Phil 5041.80   Brennan, Joseph Gerard. A handbook of logic. N.Y., 1957.

Phil 5041.80.2   Brennan, Joseph Gerard. A handbook of logic. 2nd ed. N.Y., 1961.

Phil 5241.99   Brennan, R.E. General psychology. N.Y., 1932.

Phil 5211.6   Brennan, R.E. History of psychology. N.Y., 1945.

Phil 3483.19   Brennekam, M. Ein Beitrag zur Kritik der Kantschen Ethik. Inaug. Diss. Greefswald, 1895.

Phil 8581.28   Brent, C.H. Presence. N.Y., 1914.

Phil 8876.42   Brent, C.H. The splendor of the human body. N.Y., 1904.

Phil 176.215   Brent, Duncan. Of the seer and the vision. Amsterdam, 1967.

Phil 5425.35A   Brentano, F. Das Genie. Leipzig, 1892.

Phil 8876.112   Brentano, F. Grundlegung und Anfban der Ethik. Bern, 1952.

Phil 5075.4   Brentano, F. Kategorienlehre. Leipzig, 1933.

Phil 3120.8.20   Brentano, Franz. Die Abkehr von Nichtrealen. Bern, 1966.

Phil 5241.17.17   Brentano, Franz. La classificazione delle attivitapsichiche. Lanciano, 1913.

Phil 3120.8.50   Brentano, Franz. Grundzüge der Asthetik. Bern, 1959.

Phil 3120.8.60F   Brentano, Franz. Index. Highland Park, Illinois, 1959.

Phil 3120.8.45   Brentano, Franz. Die Lehre vom Nrichtigen Urteil. Bern, 1956.

Phil 3120.8.31   Brentano, Franz. Meine Letzten wünsche für Oesterreich. Stuttgart, 1895.

Phil 8876.41   Brentano, Franz. Origin of knowledge of right and wrong. London, 1902.

Phil 5241.17.23   Brentano, Franz. Psychologie du point de vue empirique. Paris, 1944.

Phil 5241.17.25A   Brentano, Franz. Psychologie vom empirischen Standpunkt. Hamburg, 1955.

Phil 5241.17.5   Brentano, Franz. Psychologie vom empirischen Standpunkt. Leipzig, 1924-25. 2v.

Phil 3120.8.35   Brentano, Franz. Religion und Philosophie. Bern, 1954.

Phil 332.14.12   Brentano, Franz. The true and the evident. London, 1966.

Phil 3120.8.40   Brentano, Franz. Über die Zukunft der Philosophie. Leipzig, 1929.

Phil 5635.37   Brentano, Franz. Untersuchungen zur Sinnespsychologie. Leipzig, 1907.

Phil 332.14   Brentano, Franz. Versuch über die Erkenntnis. Leipzig, 1925.

Phil 332.14.2   Brentano, Franz. Versuch über die Erkenntnis. 2. Aufl. Hamburg, 1970.

Phil 3120.8.32   Brentano, Franz. Die vier Phasen der Philosophie und ihr augenblicklicher Stand. Leipzig, 1926.

Phil 8656.21   Brentano, Franz. Vom Dasein Gottes. Leipzig, 1929.

Phil 5241.17.20   Brentano, Franz. Vom sinnlichen und noetischen Bewusstsein. Leipzig, 1928.

Phil 8876.41.9   Brentano, Franz. Vom Ursprung sittlicher Erkenntnis. Hamburg, 1955.

Phil 8876.41.6   Brentano, Franz. Vom Ursprung sittlicher Erkenntnis. Leipzig, 1889.

Phil 8876.41.7A   Brentano, Franz. Vom Ursprung sittlicher Erkenntnis. 2e Aufl. Leipzig, 1921.

Phil 5241.17.13A   Brentano, Franz. Von der Klassifikation der psychischen Phänomene. Leipzig, 1911.

Phil 332.14.11   Brentano, Franz. Wahrheit und Evidenz. Hamburg, 1962.

Phil 332.14.10   Brentano, Franz. Wahrheit und Evidenz. Leipzig, 1930.

Phil 3120.8.30   Brentano, Franz. Was für ein Philosoph manchmal Epoche macht. Wien, 1876.

Htn   Phil 5041.23*   Brerewood, E. Tractatus guidam logici. Oxoniae, 1631. 3 pam.

Phil 6317.22.85   Brés, Yvon. Freud et la psychanalyse américaine Karen Horney. Paris, 1970.

Phil 6060.82   Bresard, Suzanne. Empreintes. Neuchâtel, 1968.

Phil 3910.80   Breslau. Prussia Magdalinisch-Gymnas. Christian ven Wolf. Breslau, 1831.

Phil 5520.740   Bressanone Conference on Psycholinguistics, University of Padova, 1969. Advances in psycholinguistics. Amsterdam, 1971.

Phil 7069.27.11   Bret, Thomas. Précis de métapsychic. Paris, 1927. 2v.

Phil 5811.16   Bretegnier, Louis. L'activité psychique chez les animaux. Paris, 1930.

Phil 5811.16.5   Bretegnier, Louis. L'activité psychique chez les animaux. Thèse. Toulouse, 1930.

Phil 1135.13   Breton, G. Essai sur la poésie philosophique en Grèce. Paris, 1882.

Phil 3450.18.155   Breton, S. L'être spirituel recherches sur la philosophie de N. Hartmann. Lyon, 1962.

Phil 1750.99   Breton, Stanislas. Approches phénoménologiques de l'idée d'être. Paris, 1959.

Phil 3450.11.170   Breton, Stanislas. Conscience et intentionalité. Paris, 1956.

Phil 2477.17.30   Breton, Stanislas. Essence et existence. Paris, 1962.

Phil 8581.30.4   Bretschneider, K.G. Die religiöse Glaubenslehre. 4. ed. Halle, 1846.

Phil 623.6   Bretschneider, K.G. Sendschreiben an einen Staatsmann über die Frage...Rationalismus. Leipzig, 1830.

Phil 5211.1   Brett, G.S. History of psychology. London, 1912-21. 3v.

Phil 5211.1.5   Brett, G.S. History of psychology. London, 1953.

Phil 2070.82.8   Brett, George Sidney. William James and American ideals. Toronto? 1937.

Phil 2262.94   Brett, R.L. The third earl of Shaftesbury. London, 1951.

Phil 1845.3.105   Brettschneider, B.D. The philosophy of Samuel Alexander. N.Y., 1964.

Htn   Phil 6720.6*A   Breuer, Josef. Studien über Hysterie. Leipzig, 1895.

Htn   Phil 6720.6.10*   Breuer, Josef. Studien über Hysterie. Leipzig, 1909.

Phil 6615.20.7   Breuer, Josef. Studies in hysteria. Boston, 1961.

Phil 6615.20.5   Breuer, Josef. Studies on hysteria. London, 1956.

Phil 6615.20.6   Breuer, Josef. Studies on hysteria. N.Y., 1957.

Phil 575.51.42   Breukers, Eugenio Marie Josephine. Levensvormen. Roermond, 1947.

Phil 4610.7.85   Brev, 1889-1916. (Norström, V.) Stockholm, 1923.

Phil 4080.3.34.5   Brevario de estetica. (Croce, Benedetto.) Lisboa, 1914.

Phil 8416.18   Brevario della nuova estetica. (Propris, A. de.) Roma, 1951.

NEDL   Phil 4080.3.34   Brevario di estetica. (Croce, Benedetto.) Laterza, 1913.

Phil 4210.15   Breve esposizione della filosofia di Melchiorre Gioja. (Rosmini-Serbati, Antonio.) Milano, 1840. 8 pam.

Phil 4363.3.90   Breve relacion de la muerte. (Cardenas, Juan.) Sevilla, 1732.

Phil 1717.18   Breve schizzo dei sistemi di filosofia moderna e del proprio sistema. (Rosmini Serbati, Antonio.) Napoli, 1952.

Phil 1717.18.4   Breve schizzo dei sistemi di filosofia moderna e del proprio sistema. 4e ed. (Rosmini Serbati, Antonio.) Firenze, 1964.

Phil 802.25   Breve storia della filosofia. (Carlini, Armando.) Firenze, 1957.

Phil 817.8.15   Breve storia della filosofia ad uso delle scuole. (Ruggiero, Guido de.) Bari, 1955. 3v.

Phil 4080.3.37   Breviaire d'esthétique. (Croce, Benedetto.) Paris, 1923.

Phil 4080.3.34.12   Breviario di estetica; quattro lezioni. 12. ed. (Croce, Benedetto.) Bari, 1954.

Phil 11.26   Breviarium litterarum. Berlin, 1-5 5v.

Phil 3640.77.10   Brevier. 2. Aufl. (Nietzsche, Friedrich.) Wien, 1951.

Phil 5011.2   Brevis ad artem cogitandi. London, 1776.

Phil 2520.80   Brevis replicatia...notis Cartesii. (Andrea, T.) Amstelodami, 1653.

Phil 5257.34   The brevity book on psychology. (Ruckmick, C.A.) Chicago, 1920.

Phil 9045.3   Brewer, D.J. American citizenship. Yale lectures. N.Y., 1902.

Phil 6990.33.5   Brewer, E.C. Dictionary of miracles. Philadelphia, 188-?

Phil 6990.33   Brewer, E.C. A dictionary of miracles. Philadelphia, 1884.

Phil 9590.11   Brewster, E.T. The understanding of religion. Boston, 1923.

Phil 8656.15   Brewster, F.C. God; revelation by Christianity and astronomical science. Newport, 1922.

Phil 3483.49   Breysig, Kurt. Der Aufbau der Persönlichkeit von Kant. Stuttgart, 1931.

Phil 5627.261.10   Brezzi, Paolo. L'experienza della preihera. Firenze, 1961.

Phil 5649.29   Brichcín, Milan. Teoretické a metodologické problémy výzkumů průběhu volních pohybu. Praha, 1966.

Phil 4200.2.15   Brickman, Benjamin. An introduction to Francesco Patrizi's Nova de universis philosophia. Thesis. N.Y., 1941.

Phil 6111.75 — Brickner, Richard Max. The intellectual functions of the frontal lobes. N.Y., 1936.
Phil 6978.10 — Bricout, Jacques. L'homme et la douleur. Paris, 1969.
Phil 7069.23.2 — Brid, J. Malcolm. My psychic adventures. London, 1923.
Phil 4829.203.80 — Brida, Marija. Benedikt Benković. Beograd, 1967.
X Cg Phil 9182.5 — Bridal greetings: a marriage gift. (Wise, D.) N.Y., 1852.
Phil 3483.5 — Bridel, P. La philosophie de la religion. Lausanne, 1876.
Phil 2733.102 — Bridet, L. La théorie de la connaissance dans la philosophie de Malebranche. Paris, 1929.
Phil 2733.102.5 — Bridet, L. La théorie de la connaissance dans la philosophie de Malebranche. Thèse. Paris, 1929.
Phil 7054.148 — The bridge between two worlds. (Judson, Abby A.) Minneapolis, 1894.
Phil 806.39.5 — The bridge of criticism. 1st ed. (Gay, Peter.) N.Y., 1970.
Phil 978.70 — The bridge of the gods in Gaelic mythology. (Pinchin, Edith F.) London, 1934.
Phil 6311.28 — Bridger, A.E. Minds in distress. London, 1913.
Phil 8581.35 — Bridges, H.J. Criticisms of life. Boston, 1915.
Phil 8615.5.50 — Bridges, Horace J. Aspects of ethical religion; essays in honor of Felix Adler...fiftieth anniversary...Ethical movement, 1876. N.Y., 1926.
Phil 600.31.9 — Bridges, J.H. Essays and addresses. London, 1907.
Phil 8581.48 — Bridges, J.H. Five discourses on positive religion. London, 1882.
Phil 600.31.5 — Bridges, J.H. Illustrations of positivism. Chicago, 1915.
Phil 2490.80 — Bridges, J.H. The unity of Comte's life and doctrine. London, 1866.
Phil 6311.3 — Bridges, J.W. An outline of abnormal psychology. Columbus, 1919.
Phil 6311.3.2 — Bridges, J.W. An outline of abnormal psychology. 2d ed. Columbus, 1921.
Phil 6311.3.3 — Bridges, J.W. An outline of abnormal psychology. 3rd ed. Columbus, 1925.
Phil 5241.79.10 — Bridges, J.W. Personality, many in one. Boston, 1932.
Phil 5241.79 — Bridges, J.W. Psychology, normal and abnormal. N.Y., 1930.
Phil 530.155 — Bridges, Leonard Hal. American mysticism, from William James to Zen. 1. ed. N.Y., 1970.
Phil 8581.10 — Bridgewater treatises [1,8]. On the power, wisdom, and goodness of God. (Chalmers, T.) Philadelphia, 1836.
Phil 8581.10.2 — Bridgewater treatises [2]. On the adaptation of external nature to the physical condition of man. (Kidd, J.) Philadelphia? 1836?
Phil 8581.10.4.5 — Bridgewater treatises [4]. The hand, its mechanism and vital endowments. (Bell, Charles.) N.Y., 1840.
Phil 8581.10.4.10 — Bridgewater treatises [4]. The hand, its mechanism and vital endowments. 7. ed. (Bell, Charles.) London, 1865.
Phil 8581.10.5 — Bridgewater treatises [5]. Animal, vegetable physiology. (Roget, P.M.) Philadelphia, 1836. 2v.
Phil 8581.10.6 — Bridgewater treatises [6]. Geology and mineralogy. (Buckland, W.) Philadelphia, 1837. 2v.
Phil 8581.10.7 — Bridgewater treatises [7]. On the power...God. (Kirby, W.) Philadelphia, 1837.
Phil 8581.10.8 — Bridgewater treatises [8]. Chemistry, meteorology. (Prout, William.) London, 1855.
Phil 5545.192 — Bridoux, André. Le souvenir. 2. éd. Paris, 1956.
Phil 1200.64 — Bridoux, André. Le stoïcisme et son influence. Paris, 1966.
Phil 3425.116.5 — Brie, S. Der Volksgeist bei Hegel. Berlin, 1909.
Phil 6990.21.3 — A brief disclosure to the people of England of the liberality of the Irish Roman Catholics. London, 1824.
Phil 5046.40 — A brief English tract of logick, 1677. Facsimile. (Good, Thomas.) Leeds, 1967.
Phil 930.33 — A brief history of early Chinese philosophy. 2. ed. (Suzuki, Daisetz T.) London, 1914.
Phil 1106.6 — Brief history of Greek philosophy. (Burt, B.C.) Boston, 1889.
Phil 1707.1.19A — A brief history of modern philosophy. (Höffding, H.) N.Y., 1912.
Phil 1717.4 — A brief introduction to modern philosophy. (Rogers, A.K.) N.Y., 1899.
Phil 3805.33.20 — Brief outline of the study of theology. (Schleiermacher, Friedrich.) Edinburgh, 1850.
Phil 187.96 — Brief readings in philosophy. (McDonald, M.F.) Brooklyn, 1931.
Phil 8877.43 — A brief text-book of moral philosophy. (Coppens, Charles.) N.Y., 1895.
Phil 2262.57 — Ein Brief über den Enthusiasmus. Die Moralisten, eine philosophische Rhapsodie. (Shaftesbury, A.A.C.) Leipzig, 1909.
Phil 2115.70.7 — Ein Brief über Toleranz. (Locke, J.) Hamburg, 1957.
Phil 3925.11.28 — Brief und Aufsätze. (Wust, Peter.) Münster, 1958.
Htn Phil 2045.84.2* — A brief view and survey of the...errors...in Mr. Hobbes's book, entitled Leviathan. (Clarendon, Edward Hyde.) Oxford, 1676.
Htn Phil 2045.84* — A brief view and survey of the...errors...in Mr. Hobbes's book, entitled Leviathan. (Clarendon, Edward Hyde.) Oxford, 1676.
Phil 1133.9 — Brief view of Greek philosophy. (Cornwallis, C.F.) London, 1844.
Phil 1133.9.3 — Brief view of Greek philosophy. (Cornwallis, C.F.) Philadelphia, 1846.
Phil 3246.78 — Briefe, Ausgewahlt und Herausgegeben von E. Bergmann. (Fichte, Johann Gottlieb.) Leipzig, 1919.
Phil 3940.2.45 — Briefe, 1901-1958. (Ziegler, L.) München, 1963.
Phil 3910.75 — Briefe...aus 1719-1753. (Wolff, Christian von.) St. Petersburg, 1860.
Phil 3160.3.92 — Briefe. (Cohen, Hermann.) Berlin, 1939.
Phil 3480.92.5 — Briefe. (Kant, Immanuel.) Göttingen, 1970.
Phil 3625.1.43 — Briefe. (Mendelssohn, Moses.) Berlin, 1892.
Phil 3805.76 — Briefe. (Schleiermacher, Friedrich.) Berlin, 1923.
Phil 3808.76.15 — Briefe. (Schopenhauer, Arthur.) Leipzig, 1893.
Phil 3640.76A — Briefe. v.1-5. 3rd ed. (Nietzsche, Friedrich.) Berlin, 1902. 6v.
Phil 3500.5.30 — Briefe ästhelischen Inhalts. (Schmidt-Phiseldek, C.) Altona, 1797.
Phil 3890.8.95 — Briefe an Christian Thomasius. (Pufendoy, Samne.) München, 1897.
Phil 8415.7.4 — Briefe an eine Jungfrau über dieHauptgegenstände der Asthetik. 4. Aufl. (Oeser, C.) Leipzig, 1852.
Phil 8415.7.13 — Briefe an eine Jungfrau über dieHauptgegenstände der Asthetik. 13. Aufl. (Oeser, C.) Leipzig, 1872.
Phil 3925.11.25 — Briefe an Freunde. (Wust, Peter.) Münster, 1955.
Phil 3925.11.26 — Briefe an Freunde. 2. Aufl. (Wust, Peter.) Münster, 1956.
Phil 3460.75 — Briefe an Friedrich Bouterwek. (Jacobi, F.H.) Göttingen, 1868.

Phil 3640.76.15 — Briefe an Peter Gast. (Nietsche, Friedrich.) Leipzig, 1908.
Phil 3450.11.60 — Briefe an roman ingarden. (Husserl, Edmund.) Den Haag, 1968.
Phil 3487.14 — Briefe über den moralischen Erkenntnisgrund der Religion überhaupt. (Flatt, Johann F.) Tübingen, 1789.
Phil 3808.82 — Briefe über des Schopenhauerische Philosophie. (Frauenstädt, C.M.J.) Leipzig, 1854.
Phil 3499.2 — Briefe über die Kantische Philosophie. (Reinhold, K.L.) Leipzig, 1790-92. 2v.
Phil 3499.2.3 — Briefe über die Kantische Philosophie. (Reinhold, K.L.) Leipzig, 1924.
Phil 3528.58 — Briefe über die Wissenschaftslehre. (Krug, Wilhelm Traugott.) Bruxelles, 1968.
Phil 3800.135 — Briefe über Dogmatismus und Kritizismus. (Schelling, F.W.J. von.) Leipzig, 1914.
Phil 3310.6.90 — Briefe über Garve's Schriften und Philosophie. (Schelle, K.G.) Leipzig, 1800.
Phil 5258.78 — Briefe über genetische Psychologie. (Schultz, J.) Berlin, 1902.
Phil 8673.36 — Briefe über Gott und Unsterblichkeit. (Seidlitz, Carl Siegmund von.) Bruxelles, 1968.
Phil 3483.31 — Briefe über Immanuel Kant's metaphysische Anfangsgründe der Rechtslehre. (Bergk, J.) Leipzig, 1797.
Phil 8585.13 — Briefe über natürliche Religion. (Fauenstädt, C.M.J.) Leipzig, 1858.
Phil 3800.730 — Briefe und Dokumente. (Schelling, F.W.J. von.) Bonn, 1962.
Phil 3425.14 — Briefe von und an Hegel. (Hegel, Georg Wilhelm Friedrich.) Hamburg, 1952-53. 4v.
Phil 3270.3.83 — Briefe von und über Jakob Frohschammer. (Münz, Bernhard.) Leipzig, 1897.
Phil 6315.2.66 — Briefe 1873-1939. (Freud, Sigmund.) Frankfurt, 1960.
Phil 6315.2.66.10 — Briefe 1873-1939. 2. Aufl. (Freud, Sigmund.) Frankfurt, 1968.
Phil 6315.2.69 — Briefe 1907-1926. Sigmund Freud and Karl Abraham. (Freud, Sigmund.) Frankfurt, 1965.
Phil 6315.2.66.5 — Briefe 1909-39. (Freud, Sigmund.) Frankfurt, 1963.
Phil 5252.69.10 — A briefer general psychology. (Murphy, Gardner.) N.Y., 1935.
Phil 3808.76 — Brieftasche, 1822-1823. (Schopenhauer, Arthur.) Berlin, n.d.
Phil 978.49.645 — Briefwechel und Dokumente, 1901-1925. 1. Aufl. (Steiner, R.) Dornach, 1967.
Phil 3819.70 — Briefwechsel; Einleitung. (Spinoza, Benedictus de.) Leipzig, 1876.
Phil 3819.70.5 — Briefwechsel; Übertragen und mit Einleitung. (Spinoza, Benedictus de.) Leipzig, 1914.
Phil 3246.78.9A — Briefwechsel. (Fichte, Johann Gottlieb.) Leipzig, 1925. 2v.
Phil 6315.2.26 — Briefwechsel. (Freud, Sigmund.) Frankfurt, 1968.
Phil 3480.90 — Briefwechsel. (Kant, Immanuel.) Leipzig, 1922.
Phil 3480.92 — Briefwechsel. (Kant, Immanuel.) Leipzig, 1924. 2v.
Phil 3480.91 — Briefwechsel. (Kant, Immanuel.) München, 1912. 3v.
Phil 3552.77 — Der Briefwechsel. (Leibniz, Gottfried Wilhelm.) Hannover, 1889.
Phil 3120.13.9 — Briefwechsel mit E. von Hartmann. (Bolland, G.J.P.J.) 's Gravenhage, 1937.
Phil 3640.77A — Briefwechsel mit Franz Overbeck. (Nietzsche, Friedrich.) Leipzig, 1916.
Phil 3805.78 — Briefwechsel mit J.C. Gass. (Schleiermacher, Friedrich.) Berlin, 1852.
Phil 3800.722 — Briefwechsel mit Niethammer von seiner Berufung nach Jena. (Schelling, F.W.J. von.) Leipzig, 1913.
Phil 3805.76.9 — Briefwechsel mit seiner Braut. 2. Aufl. (Schleiermacher, Friedrich.) Gotha, 1920.
Phil 3819.73 — Der Briefwechsel Spinozas. (Spinoza, Benedictus de.) Halle, 1919. 2v.
Phil 3808.76.20 — Briefwechsel und andere Dokumente; Ausgewählt und Herausgegeben von Mar Brahn. (Schopenhauer, Arthur.) Leipzig, 1911.
Phil 3819.72 — Briefwechsel und andere Dokumente. (Spinoza, Benedictus de.) Leipzig, 1916.
Phil 3819.72.5 — Briefwechsel und andere Dokumente. (Spinoza, Benedictus de.) Leipzig, 1923.
Phil 3890.9.85 — Der Briefwechsel zwischen Ignoz Paul Vital Troxler. (Troxler, I.P.V.) Aran, 1953.
Phil 3235.76 — Briefwechsel zwischen L. Feuerbach und C. Kapp, 1832-1848. (Feuerbach, Ludwig.) Leipzig, 1876.
Phil 3552.78 — Briefwechsel zwischen Leibniz, Arnould, und dem Landgrafen Earnst von Hessen-Rheinfels. (Leibniz, Gottfried Wilhelm.) Hannover, 1846.
Phil 3195.6.33 — Briefwechsel zwischen Wilhelm Dilthey und den Grafen Paul York von Watenburg. (Dilthey, Wilhelm.) Halle, 1923.
Phil 8876.102 — Briel, C. L'homme moral, ou Règles de conduite prises dans sa propre nature. Sens, 179-
Phil 9161.5 — Brière, L. de la. La jeune mariée. Paris, 1896.
Phil 4891.10.2 — Brière, O. Fifty years of Chinese philosophy, 1898-1848. N.Y., 1965.
Phil 4891.10 — Brière, O. Fifty years of Chinese philosophy, 1898-1950. London, 1956.
Phil 8581.24.5 — Brierley, J. Ourselves and the universe. N.Y., 1905.
Phil 8581.24 — Brierley, J. Religion and experience. N.Y., 1906.
Phil 8581.24.18 — Brierley, J. Själslifvet. Stockholm, 1904.
Phil 8581.24.20 — Brierley, J. Vårt gemensamma lif. Stockholm, 1907.
Phil 8581.24.25 — Brierley, J. Vi och världsalltet. Stockholm, 1903.
Phil 6311.33 — Brierley, Marjorie Ellis. Trends in psycho-analysis. London, 1951.
Phil 5241.52 — Brierley, S.S. (Mrs.). An introduction to psychology. London, 1921.
Phil 7060.14.3 — Brierre de Boismont, A. Des hallucinations, ou histoire raisonnée. 3. ed. Paris, 1862.
Phil 7060.14.5 — Brierre de Boismont, A. Des hallucinations. 2. ed. Paris, 1852.
Phil 7060.14.9 — Brierre de Boismont, A. Hallucinations. 1st American ed. Philadelphia, 1853.
Phil 7150.1 — Brierre de Boismont, A.J.F. Du suicide. Paris, 1856.
Phil 7150.1.2 — Brierre de Boismont, A.J.F. Du suicide et la folie suicide. 2. éd. Paris, 1865.
Phil 3819.74 — Brieven,,,vertoog over het zuivere denken. (Spinoza, Benedictus de.) Amsterdam, 1897.
Phil 5241.50 — Briffault, Robert. Psyche's lamp. London, 1921.
Phil 6111.5 — Brigham, Amariah. Remarks on the influence of mental cultivation upon health. Hartford, 1832.
Phil 6111.5.2 — Brigham, Amariah. Remarks on the influence of mental cultivation upon health. Boston, 1833.
Phil 9400.8 — Brigham, H. The youth of old age. Boston, 1934.
Phil 6625.6 — Bright, Timothy. A treatise of melancholie. N.Y., 1940.

Phil 8626.13   Brightman, E.S. Immortality in post-Kantian idealism. Cambridge, 1925.

Phil 176.94   Brightman, E.S. An introduction to philosophy. N.Y., 1925.

Phil 8876.93   Brightman, E.S. Moral laws. N.Y., 1933.

Phil 8581.67.10   Brightman, E.S. Nature and values. N.Y., 1945.

Phil 8581.67   Brightman, E.S. Personality and religion. N.Y., 1934.

Phil 400.71   Brightman, E.S. A philosophy of ideals. N.Y., 1928.

Phil 8581.67.5   Brightman, E.S. A philosophy of religion. N.Y., 1940.

Phil 8656.22   Brightman, E.S. The problem of God. N.Y., 1930.

Phil 8581.86   Brightman, E.S. The spiritual life. N.Y., 1942.

Phil 176.94.5   Brigtman, E.S. Person and reality. N.Y., 1958.

Phil 9070.113   Brihat, Denise. Risque et prudence. Paris, 1966.

Phil 75.43   Bril, G.A. de. Bibliographia philosophica. Rhenum, 1950. 2v.

Phil 5590.3   Brill, A. Individual ascendency. N.Y., 1938.

Phil 6315.2.124   Brill, A.A. Freud's contribution to psychiatry. N.Y., 1944.

Phil 6311.1.5   Brill, A.A. Fundamental conceptions of psychoanalysis. N.Y., 1921.

Phil 6311.1.2   Brill, A.A. Psychanalysis; its theories. Philadelphia, 1914.

Phil 6311.1.3   Brill, A.A. Psychanalysis. 2. ed. Philadelphia, 1917.

Phil 6980.135   Brill, Abraham A. Lectures on psychoanalytic psychiatry. N.Y., 1946.

Phil 5241.117.5   Brill, Albert. Ascendant psychology. Guilford, Conn., 1959.

Phil 5241.117   Brill, Albert. Fundamental fundamentals. N.Y., 1955.

Phil 270.70   Brill, John. The chance character of human existence. N.Y., 1956.

X Cg   Phil 5653.6   Brillat-Savarin, A. Physiologie des Geschmacks. Leipzig, 18- .

Phil 5590.415   Brim, Orville Gilbert. Personality and decision processes. Stanford, 1962.

Phil 8610.899.25   Brimstone ballads and other verse. (Mackenzie, G.L.) London, 1899.

Phil 3640.340   Brin, Slata G.R. Kollektivistisches in der Philosophie Nietzsches. Basel, 1948.

Phil 8120.10   Brincourt, A. Les oeuvres et les lumières. Paris, 1955.

Phil 3483.24   Bring, Gustaf. Immanuel Kants förhallande till den filosofiska teologien. Lund, 1876.

Phil 8954.4.5   Bring me my bow. (Elliot, W.H.) London, 1946.

Phil 8402.49   Brinkmann, D. Natur und Kunst. Zürich, 1938.

Phil 5722.27   Brinkmann, Donald. Probleme des Unbewussten. Zürich, 1943.

Phil 9045.8   Brinley, C.A. Citizenship. Philadelphia, 1893.

Phil 3640.282.1   Brinton, Clarence Crane. Nietzsche. 1. ed. N.Y., 1965.

Phil 165.230   Brinton, Crane. The fate of man. N.Y., 1961.

Phil 4065.94A   Brinton, D.G. Giordano Bruno. Philadelphia, 1890.

Phil 8581.12   Brinton, D.G. The religious sentiment. N.Y., 1876.

Phil 9245.11.3   Brinton, Daniel G. The pursuit of happiness. Philadelphia, 1893.

Phil 3110.174   Brinton, H. The mystic will. N.Y., 1930.

Phil 4352.1.101   Briones Ortún, Juan. En torno a Balmes. Bilboa, 1933.

Phil 2905.1.435   Briones Toledo, Hernán. Pierre Teilhard de Chardin y otros ensayos. Santiago de Chile, 1966.

Phil 176.30   Brisor de Warville, Jean Pierre. De la vérité. Neuchatel, 1782.

Phil 5520.744   Brisset, Jean Pierre. La grammaire logique. Paris, 1970.

Phil 8402.68   Brissoni, Armando. Pagine di estetica. Padova, 1968.

Phil 3425.714   Brissoni, Armando. Ricerche sull'estetica di Hegel. Padova, 1968.

Phil 5400.83   Britan, H.H. The affective consciousness. N.Y., 1931.

Phil 1822.8   British analytical philosophy. (Williams, Bernard.) London, 1966.

Phil 8581.109   British Broadcasting Corporation. Religion and humanism. London, 1964.

Phil 9495.166   British Council of Churches. Sex and morality: a report to the British Council of Churches. London, 1966.

Phil 1800.5   British empirical philosophers. (Ayer, A.J.) London, 1952.

Phil 41.1   Pamphlet box. British institute of philosophical studies.

Phil 8002.3   British journal of aesthetics. London. 2,1962+ 9v.

Phil 11.12   British journal of psychical research. London. 1-2,1926-1929

X Cg   Phil 11.2   The British journal of psychology. Cambridge. 1,1904

Phil 11.2   The British journal of psychology. Cambridge. 2,1905+ 49v.

Phil 11.2.8   The British journal of psychology. Medical section. Cambridge. 1,1920+ 26v.

Phil 11.2.5   The British journal of psychology. Monograph supplement. Cambridge. 1,1911 11v.

Phil 11.2.10   The British journal of psychology. Statistical section. London. 1,1947+ 9v.

Phil 11.42   The British journal of social and clinical psychology. London. 1,1962+ 8v.

Phil 11.2.11   British journal of statistical psychology. Cumulative index, 1-14. n.p., n.d.

Phil 8870.31   British moralists, 1650-1800. (Raphael, David Daiches.) Oxford, 1969. 2v.

Phil 8843.2.2   British moralists. v.1-2. (Selby-Bigge, L.A.) Indianapolis, 1964.

Phil 8843.2   British moralists. v.1-2. (Selby-Bigge, L.A.) Oxford, 1897.

Phil 1812.8   British philosophers. (Matthews, K.) London, 1943.

Phil 1817.10   British philosophers. (Ritchie, A.D.) London, 1950.

Phil 1830.20   British philosophy in the mid-century. (Mace, Cecil Alec.) London, 1957.

Phil 1830.20.2   British philosophy in the mid-century. 2nd ed. (Mace, Cecil Alec.) London, 1966.

Phil 41.12   The British Psychological Society, 1901-1961. (British Psychological Society.) London, 1901-1961.

Phil 41.12   British Psychological Society. The British Psychological Society, 1901-1961. London, 1901-1961.

Phil 11.39   British Psychological Society. Bulletin. London. 11,1951+ 8v.

Phil 1812.3   British thought and thinkers. (Morris, G.S.) Chicago, 1880.

Phil 176.220   Brito, Antonio J. Estudos de filosofia. Lisboa, 1962.

Phil 5465.6   Brittain, H.L. A study in imagination. n.p., 1907.

Phil 6111.6.2   Brittan, S.B. Man and his relations:...influence of the mind on the body. N.Y., 1864.

Phil 6111.6   Brittan, S.B. Man and his relations:...influence of the mind on the body. N.Y., 1868.

Phil 7054.61   Brittan, S.B. A review of Rev. Charles Beecher's report. N.Y., 1853.

Phil 7054.61.12   Brittan, Samuel B. The battleground of the spiritual reformation. N.Y., 1882.

Phil 7054.61.5   Brittan, Samuel B. A discussion of the facts of...ancient and modern spiritualism. N.Y., 1853.

Phil 7054.61.3   Brittan, Samuel B. The tables turned. N.Y., 1854.

Phil 7054.61.7   Brittan, Samuel B. The telegraph's answer. N.Y., 1855.

Phil 7054.123.5   Britten, Emma H. Ghostland. Boston, 1876.

NEDL   Phil 7054.123   Britten, Emma H. Modern American spiritualism. N.Y., 1870.

Phil 7054.123.2   Britten, Emma H. Modern American spiritualism. 4th ed. N.Y., 1870.

Phil 5520.69   Britton, Karl. Communication. London, 1939.

Phil 176.230   Britton, Karl. Philosophy and the meaning of life. London, 1969.

Phil 5241.71   Britz, Carl August. Eine theoretische und experimentelle Untersuchung über den psychologischen der Klarheit. Diss. Saarlouis, 1913.

Phil 2480.85   Brive, France. Mussée Ernest Rupin. Cabanis, médecin, philosophe et l'époque révolutionaire. Brive, 1957.

Phil 5520.642   Brkić, Jovan. Norm and order; an investigation into logic, semantics, and the theory of law and morals. N.Y., 1970.

Phil 6112.40.12   Bro, Harmon Hartzell. Dreams in the life of prayer: the approach of Edgar Cayce. 1st ed. N.Y., 1970.

Phil 6112.40.10   Bro, Harmon Hartzell. Edgar Cayce on dreams. N.Y., 1968.

Phil 2050.245   Broad, C. D. Hume's doctrine of space. London, 1961.

Phil 1870.120A   Broad, C.D. Berkeley's argument about material substance. London, 1942.

Phil 5751.15   Broad, C.D. Determinism, indetermination, and libertarianism. Cambridge, Eng., 1934.

Phil 1905.22A   Broad, C.D. Ethics and the history of philosophy. London, 1952.

Phil 8876.88   Broad, C.D. Five types of ethical theory. London, 1930.

Phil 8876.88.5   Broad, C.D. Five types of ethical theory. London, 1951.

Phil 5241.66.5   Broad, C.D. The mind and its place. N.Y., 1927.

Phil 5241.66   Broad, C.D. The mind and its place in nature. London, 1925.

Phil 1850.118   Broad, C.D. The philosophy of Francis Bacon. Cambridge, Eng., 1926.

Phil 1905.22.10.2A   Broad, C.D. Religion, philosophy and physical research. London, 1953.

Phil 1905.22.10   Broad, C.D. Religion, philosophy and physical research. N.Y., 1953.

Phil 2150.7.99   Broad, Charles D. Examination of McTaggart's philosophy. Cambridge, Eng., 1933. 3v.

Phil 2150.7.90   Broad, Charles D. John McTaggart Ellis McTaggart, 1866-1925. London, 1928.

Phil 630.12A   Broad, Charles D. Perception, physics and reality. Cambridge, 1914.

Phil 7069.62.15   Broad, Charlie. Lectures on physical research. London, 1962.

Phil 575.185   Broad, Charlie P. Personal identity and survival. London, 1958.

Phil 5650.34   Broadbent, D.E. Perception and communication. N.Y., 1958.

Phil 5352.20   Broadbent, Donald Eric. Decision and stress. London, 1971.

Phil 2520.400   Broadie, Frederick. An approach to Descartes' meditations. London, 1970.

Phil 5241.150   Broadlunt, Donald Eric. Behaviour. 1. ed. N.Y., 1961.

Phil 720.14.2   Brochard, V. De l'erreur. 2e éd. Paris, 1897.

Phil 176.54A   Brochard, V. Etudes de philosophie ancienne et de philosophie moderne. Paris, 1912.

Phil 1200.22   Brochard, Victor. De assensione Stoici quid Senserint. Thesis. Parisiis, 1879.

Phil 1190.6.5   Brochard, Victor. Les sceptiques grecs. Paris, 1959.

Phil 1190.6   Brochard, Victor. Les sceptiques grecs. Paris, 1887.

Phil 8581.46   Brochner, Hans. Om det religiöse i dets enhed met det humane. Kjöbenhavn, 1869.

Phil 8876.120   Brock, Erich. Befreiung und Erfüllung. Zürich, 1958.

Phil 3001.12   Brock, Werner. An introduction to contemporary German philosophy. Cambridge, 1935.

Phil 3640.232   Brock, Werner. Nietzsches Idee der Kultur. Bonn, 1930.

Phil 3425.754   Brockard, Hans. Subjekt; Versuch zur Ontologie bei Hegel. München, 1970.

Phil 3821.17   Brockdorff, C. Beiträge über die Verhältnis Schopenhauers zu Spinoza. Hildesheim, 1900.

Phil 3001.9   Brockdorff, C. Die deutsche Auflslärungsphilosophie. München, 1926.

Phil 1801.3   Brockdorff, C. Die englische aufklärungs Philosophie. München, 1924.

Phil 801.13   Brockdorff, C. von. Die Geschichte der Philosophie. Hildesheim, 1906.

Phil 801.13.2   Brockdorff, C. von. Die Geschichte der Philosophie. Osterwick, 1908.

Phil 2475.1.158   Brockdorff, Cary. Die Wahrheit über Bergson. Berlin, 1916.

Phil 575.12.5   Brockdorff, Cay. Die wissenschaftliche Selbsterkenntnis. Stuttgart, 1906.

Phil 5241.74   Brockdorff, Cay L.G.C. Die philosophischen Anfangsgründe der Psychologie. Heldesheim, 1905.

Phil 2520.157   Brockdorff, Cay von. Descartes und die Fortbildung der kartesianischen Lehre. München, 1923.

Phil 2045.100   Brockdorff, Cay von. Hobbes im Lichte seiner didaktischen und pädagogischen Bedeutung. Kiel, 1919.

Phil 2045.116   Brockdorff, Cay von. Die Urform der "Computatio sive logica" des Hobbes. Kiel, 1934.

Phil 960.1   Brockie, W. Indian thought. Sunderland, 1876.

Phil 525.89   Brockington, A.A. Mysticism and poetry. London, 1934.

Phil 6998.3   Brockton Symposium and Workshop on Behavior Therapy. Proceedings. Nutley, N.J. 1,1970+

Phil 8581.43.2   Brod, M. Heidentum, Christentum, Judentum. München 1921. 2v.

Phil 8581.43   Brod, M. Heidentum, Christentum, Judentum. München, 1922. 2v.

Phil 8581.43.3   Brod, M. Paganism, Christianity, Judaism; a confession of faith. University, 1970.

Phil 176.77   Brod, Max. Anschauung und Begriff. Leipzig, 1913.

Phil 3120.26.30   Brod, Max. Diesseits und Jenseits. Winterthur, 1947. 2v.

Phil 9240.36   Brod, Viktor. Die Ich-du-Beziehung als Erfahrungsgrundlage der Ethik. München, 1967.

Phil 332.3   Brodbick, A. Das Wesen des Wissens. Stuttgart, 1884.

Phil 6111.7   Brodie, B. Mind and matter. N.Y., 1857.

Phil 5241.16   Brodie, B.C. Psychological inquiries. London, 1854.

Phil 5241.16.2   Brodie, B.C. Psychological inquiries. London, 1856.

Phil 5241.16.4   Brodie, B.C. Psychological inquiries. London, 1862.

Phil 960.258   Brodov, Vasilii V. Indiiskaia filosofiia novogo vremeni. Moskva, 1967.

Phil 6951.29   Brody, E.B. Psychotherapy with schizophrenia. N.Y., 1952.

Phil 3821.18 — Bröchner, Hans. Benedict Spinoza. Kjøbenhavn, 1857.
Phil 801.18 — Bröchner, Hans. Bidrag til opfattelsen of philosophiens historisk Udvikling. Kjøbenhavn, 1869.
Phil 801.18.3 — Bröchner, Hans. Philosophiens historie i Grundrids. Kjøbenhavn, 1873-74.
Phil 3640.696 — Broecker, W. Das was kommt gesehen von Nietzsche und Hölderlin. Pfullingen, 1963.
Phil 600.53 — Broecker, Walter. Dialektik, Positivismus, Mythologie. Frankfurt, 1958.
Phil 1133.46 — Broecker, Walter. Die Geschichte der Philosophie vor Sokrates. Frankfurt, 1965.
Phil 3483.94 — Broecker, Walter. Kant über Metaphysik und Erfahrung. Frankfurt, 1970.
Phil 5593.50 — Broek, P. van den. De Behn-Rorschach-test. 's Gravenhage, 1950.
Phil 3450.11.305 — Broekman, J.M. Phänomenologie und Egologie. Den Haag, 1963.
Phil 8691.28 — Broekman, R.W. Het vraagteken achter de horizon van ons Leven. Assen, 1957.
Phil 9400.45 — Brøndsted, Holger Valdemar. Tanker til overvejelse for os aeldre. København, 1969.
Phil 9161.10 — Broendum, L.C. Familielivets etik. København, 1963.
Phil 3640.95 — Broene, J. Philosophy of Friedrich Nietzsche. n.p., n.d.
Phil 5643.102 — Brøns, J. The blind sport of Mariotte. Copenhagen, 1939.
Phil 6060.60 — Broeren, Wilhelm. Über die Zuverlässigkeit der Beschreibung von Sprechstimme und Handschrift. Inaug. Diss. n.p., 1964.
Phil 7054.152 — Brofferio, Angelo. Per lo spiritismo. 2. ed. Milano, 1893.
Phil 4210.126 — Brogialdi, Adolfo. Elogio di Antonio Rosmini letto l'11 giugno 1863 all'Accademia degli Eutelet. Firenze, 1863.
Phil 8622.59 — Broglic, Guy de. Pour une théorie rationnelle de l'acte de foi. Paris, 1963. 2v.
Phil 600.4 — Broglie, A.T.P. La réaction contre le positivisme. Paris, 1894.
Phil 8581.108 — Broglie, Guy de. Les signes de crédibilité de la révélation chrétienne. Paris, 1964.
Phil 8951.12 — Broglie, L'abbé de. La morale sans Dieu. Paris, 1903.
Phil 8581.68.20 — Broglie, Paul. Les conditions modernes. Paris, 1910.
Phil 8581.68.10 — Broglie, Paul. La définition de la religion. Paris, 1882.
Phil 8581.68.15 — Broglie, Paul. Les fondements intellectuels de la foi chrétienne. Paris, 1905.
Phil 8876.66 — Broglie, Paul. Instruction morale. 10e éd. Paris, 18- .
Phil 600.4.5 — Broglie, Paul. Le positivisme et la science expérimentale. Paris, 1880-81. 2v.
Phil 8581.68.5 — Broglie, Paul. Religion et critique. 3. éd. Paris, 1906.
Phil 8691.16 — Broglie, Paul. La science et la religion. Paris, 1885.
Phil 2050.262 — Broiles, R. David. The moral philosophy of David Hume. The Hague, 1964.
Phil 8582.35.5 — Broken lights; an inquiry into the present condition and future prospects of religious faith. (Cobbe, F.P.) London, 1864.
Phil 8582.35 — Broken lights; an inquiry into the present condition and future prospects of religious faith. (Cobbe, F.P.) London, 1864.
Phil 8626.17 — Bromberg, F.G. Man's immortality proved by study of his natural constitution. Mobile, Ala., 1929.
Phil 5850.143 — Bromberg, R. Toegepaste psychologie. Leiden, 1926.
Phil 6951.23 — Bromberg, W. The mind of man. N.Y., 1937.
Phil 6315.2.405 — Brome, Vincent. Freud and his early circle; the struggles of psychoanalysis. London, 1967.
Phil 5871.85 — Bronfenbrenner, Urie. Two worlds of childhood: U.S. and U.S.S.R. N.Y., 1970.
Phil 4803.846.80 — Bronisław Trentowski (1808-1869). (Horodyski, Władysław.) Kraków, 1913.
Phil 1701.40 — Bronowski, Jacob. The Western intellectual tradition. N.Y., 1960.
Phil 165.6 — Bronstein, D.J. Basic problems of philosophy. N.Y., 1947.
Phil 930.56 — Bronzovij vek. (Kuo, Mo-jo.) Moskva, 1959.
Phil 9010.30 — Brooke, Iris. Pleasures of the past. London, 1955.
Htn Phil 720.11* — Brooke, R.G. Nature of truth. London, 1640.
Phil 8876.103 — Brooklyn Ethical Association. Life and the conditions of survival. Chicago, 1895.
Phil 8610.902 — Brooklyn Philosophical Association. Facts worth knowing. N.Y., 1902.
Phil 7140.116.71 — Brooks, C.H. The practice of autosuggestion by the method of Emile Coué. London, 1922.
Phil 7140.116.73A — Brooks, C.H. The practice of autosuggestion by the method of Emile Coué. N.Y., 1922.
Phil 7140.116.72 — Brooks, C.H. The practice of autosuggestion by the method of Emile Coué. N.Y., 1922.
Phil 7140.116.70 — Brooks, C.H. The practice of autosuggestion by the method of Emile Coué. N.Y., 1922.
Phil 5241.22 — Brooks, H.J. The elements of mind. London, 1902.
Phil 510.131 — Brooks, H.J. The riddle of the universe scientifically interpreted. n.p., 1924.
Phil 8691.10 — Brookshire, E.V. The law of human life; scriptures in the light of science. N.Y., 1916.
Phil 2805.419 — Brooms, Jack Howard. Pascal. N.Y., 1966.
Phil 623.37 — Brophy, B. Black ship to hell. 1. American ed. N.Y., 1962.
Phil 365.39 — Brorskabets religion. (Collin, C.) Kristiania, 1912.
Phil 3140.82 — Brosch, P. Die Ontologie des J. Clauberg. Greifswald, 1926.
Phil 6329.22 — Brother animal; the story of Freud and Tausk. 1st ed. (Roazen, Paul.) N.Y., 1969.
Phil 1535.26 — Brothers of the Christian Schools. Elementary course of Christian philosophy. N.Y., 1893.
Phil 3483.32 — Brotherus, K.R. Immanuel Kants Philosophie der Geschichte. Helsingfors, 1905.
Phil 86.4 — Brothier, L. Ebauche d'un glossaire du langage philosophique. Paris, 1863.
Phil 801.14 — Brothier, Léon. Histoire populaire de la philosophie. Paris, 1861.
Phil 801.14.3 — Brothier, Léon. Histoire populaire de la philosophie. 3. ed. Paris, 1907.
Phil 5241.63 — Brough, J. The study of mental science. London, 1903.
Phil 5811.4 — Brougham, H. Dialogues on instinct. London, 1844.
Phil 5811.4.2 — Brougham, H. Dialogues on instinct. Philadelphia, 1845.
Phil 8581.13 — Brougham, H. A discourse of natural theology. Philadelphia, 1835.
Phil 8581.13.3 — Brougham, H. A discourse of natural theology. 4. ed. London, 1835.
Phil 8581.13.5 — Brougham, H. Dissertations on the subjects of science. London, 1839. 2v.
Phil 1801.1 — Brougham, H. Lives of philosophers of the time of George III. London, 1855.

Phil 2205.30.8 — Brougham and Vaux, Henry Brougham. Discourse of natural theology. London, 1835.
Phil 5921.1 — Broussais, F.J.V. Cours de phrénologie. Paris, 1836.
Phil 6951.6.5 — Broussais, F.J.V. De l'irritation et de la folie. Paris, 1839. 2v.
Phil 6951.6 — Broussais, F.J.V. In irritation and insanity. Columbia, 1831.
Phil 5921.1.5 — Broussais, F.J.V. Lectures on phrenology. London, 1847.
Phil 530.40.42 — Brouwer, Johan. De achtergrond der Spaansche mystiek. Zutphen, 1935.
Phil 530.40.40 — Brouwer, Johan. Psychologie der Spaansche mystiek. Amsterdam, 1931.
Phil 176.109 — Brouwer, L.E.J. Wiskunde, waarheid, werkkeijkheid. Gröningen, 1919.
Phil 52.9A — Brown, A.W. The metaphysical society. N.Y., 1947.
Phil 6750.1 — Brown, B. Treatment, cure, cretins, idiots. Boston, 1847-62. 4 pam.
Phil 9341.9.20 — Brown, C.R. What is your name? New Haven, 1931.
Phil 8581.88 — Brown, C.R. A working faith. Chapel Hill, 1926.
Phil 9341.9.5 — Brown, C.R. Yale talks. New Haven, 1919.
Phil 9341.9 — Brown, C.R. The young man's affairs. N.Y., 1909.
Phil 6951.26 — Brown, Carlton. Brainstorm. N.Y., 1944.
Phil 8951.20 — Brown, Charles R. Dreams come true. N.Y., 1944.
Phil 6111.53.2 — Brown, Charles R. Faith and health. 2. ed. N.Y., 1910.
Phil 8633.1.20 — Brown, Charles R. Living again. Cambridge, 1920.
Phil 8581.36 — Brown, Charles R. Modern man's religion. N.Y., 1911.
Phil 5270.22 — Brown, Clarence William. Scientific method in psychology. N.Y., 1955.
Phil 585.177.5 — Brown, Donald George. Action. Toronto, 1968.
Phil 1828.2 — Brown, Florence W. Alcott and the Concord school of philosophy. n.p., 1926.
Phil 6951.22 — Brown, H.C. A mind mislaid. N.Y., 1937.
Phil 8876.29 — Brown, H.S. Lectures for the people. Philadelphia, 1859.
Htn Phil 2262.79.1* — Brown, J. Essays on the characteristics. London, 1751.
Phil 2262.79.2 — Brown, J. Essays on the characteristics. London, 1752.
Phil 2262.79 — Brown, J. Essays on the characteristics. 2d ed. London, 1751.
Phil 6315.2.285 — Brown, J.A.C. Freud and the post-Freudians. Baltimore, 1961.
Phil 5190.38 — Brown, J.A.C. Techniques of persuasion. Baltimore, 1963.
Phil 5645.29 — Brown, J.H. Spectropia. 3. ed. London, 1864.
Phil 5548.80 — Brown, J.S. The motivation of behavior. N.Y., 1961.
Phil 8876.30 — Brown, John. An estimate of the manners and principles of the times. v.1-2. London, 1758.
Htn Phil 8876.30.5* — Brown, John. An estimate of the manners and principles of the times. 2nd ed. London, 1757.
Phil 7054.149 — Brown, John. Mediumistic experiences of John Brown. 3. ed. San Francisco, 1897.
Phil 2045.136 — Brown, Keith C. Hobbes. Cambridge, 1965.
Phil 4080.3.450 — Brown, Merle Elliott. Neo-idealistic aesthetics. Detroit, 1966.
Phil 6311.39 — Brown, Norman Oliver. Life against death. 1st ed. Middletown, Conn., 1959.
Phil 6311.47 — Brown, Norman Oliver. Love's body. N.Y., 1966.
Phil 8581.83 — Brown, Oswald E. God and the new knowledge. Nashville, 1926.
Phil 4912.5 — Brown, Robert. Contemporary philosophy in Australia. London, 1969.
Phil 7054.25 — Brown, Robert. Demonology and witchcraft. London, 1889.
Phil 5520.225 — Brown, Roger William. Words and things. Glencoe, Ill., 1958.
Phil 5520.225.2 — Brown, Roger William. Words and things. N.Y., 1958.
Phil 7074.10 — Brown, Rosemary. Unfinished symphonies; voices from the beyond. N.Y., 1971.
Phil 7052.20 — Brown, Slater. The heyday of spiritualism. N.Y., 1970.
Phil 1890.40.2 — Brown, T. Inquiry into relation of cause and effect. Andover, 1822.
Phil 1890.30.2 — Brown, T. Lectures on philosophy of human mind. Andover, 1822. 3v.
Phil 1890.30.4 — Brown, T. Lectures on philosophy of human mind. Edinbrugh, 1846. 4v.
Phil 1890.30 — Brown, T. Lectures on philosophy of human mind. Edinburgh, 1820. 4v.
Phil 1890.30.3.5 — Brown, T. Lectures on philosophy of human mind. Hallowell, 1831.
Phil 1890.30.5 — Brown, T. Lectures on philosophy of human mind. London, 1860.
Phil 1890.30.3 — Brown, T. Lectures on philosophy of human mind. Philadelphia, 1824. 3v.
Phil 1890.30.7 — Brown, T. Sketch of a system of human mind. Edinburgh, 1820.
Phil 1890.30.6 — Brown, T. Treatise on the philosophy of human mind. Cambridge, 1827. 2v.
Phil 8876.31 — Brown, T. Redivivus. An exposition of vulgar and common errors. Philadelphia, 1846.
Phil 5241.28.25 — Brown, W. College psychology. N.Y., 1950.
Phil 5241.28 — Brown, W. Essentials of mental measurement. Cambridge, 1911.
Phil 5241.28.2A — Brown, W. Essentials of mental measurement. 2. ed. Cambridge, Eng., 1921.
Phil 5241.28.3 — Brown, W. Essentials of mental measurement. 3. ed. Cambridge, Eng., 1925.
Phil 5241.28.4 — Brown, W. Essentials of mental measurement. 4. ed. Cambridge, Eng., 1940.
Phil 5241.28.13 — Brown, W. Mind and personality. London, 1926.
Phil 5241.28.20 — Brown, W. Personality and religion. London, 1946.
Phil 5241.28.10 — Brown, W. Psychology and psychotherapy. London, 1922.
Phil 5241.28.7 — Brown, W. Psychology and the sciences. London, 1924.
Phil 5241.28.17 — Brown, W. Science and personality. New Haven, 1929.
NEDL Phil 8656.4 — Brown, W. An essay on the existence...supreme creator. Aberdeen, 1816. 2v.
Phil 8876.32 — Brown, W.L. An essay on the natural equality of men. London, 1794.
Phil 5435.7 — Brown, Warner. Habit interference in sorting cards. Berkeley, 1914.
Phil 5640.33 — Brown, Warner. The judgment of very weak sensory stimuli. Berkeley, 1914.
Phil 6311.19 — Brown, William. Mind, medicine and metaphysics. London, 1936.
Phil 5850.145 — Brown, William. Oxford essays on psychology. London, 1948.
Phil 6311.4.2 — Brown, William. Psychological methods of healing. London, 1938.
Phil 6671.19.3 — Brown, William. Suggestion and mental analysis. 3. ed. London, 1923.
Phil 6111.41 — Brown, William. Talks on psychotherapy. London, 1923.
Phil 8581.53 — Brown, William A. Beliefs that matter. N.Y., 1928.
Phil 8581.53.5 — Brown, William A. Pathways to certainty. N.Y., 1930.

Phil 8951.9   Brown, William L. Comparative view of Christianity. Edinburgh, 1826. 2v.

Phil 6111.9.5   Brown-Séquard, C.E. Course...physiology and pathology of central nervous system. Philadelphia, 1860.

Phil 6111.9   Brown-Séquard, C.E. Experimental and clinical researches. Richmond, 1855.

Phil 5649.9   Browne, George H. The esthetics of motion. New Ulm, 1917.

Phil 8876.38   Browne, I.H. Essays on subjects of important enquiry. London, 1822.

Phil 8626.5   Browne, I.H. The immortality of the soul. Cambridge, 1795.

Phil 3821.19   Browne, Lewis. Blessed Spinoza. N.Y., 1932.

Phil 8581.14.5   Browne, Peter. A letter in answer to a book...entitled Christianity not mysterious. London, 1697.

Phil 8581.14.9   Browne, Peter. The procedure, extent and limits of human understanding. London, 1728.

Phil 8581.14.10   Browne, Peter. The procedure, extent and limits of human understanding. London, 1737.

Phil 8581.14   Browne, Peter. Things divine and supernatural. London, 1733.

Htn   Phil 176.31*   Browne, R. Liber...vetaribus rarum principia. London, 1678.

Phil 672.29.3   Browne, Robert T. The mystery of space. N.Y., 1919.

Htn   Phil 8951.2*   Browne, T. Christian morals. 2. ed. London, 1756.

Htn   Phil 6990.40.5*   Browne, T. Miracles work's. London, 1683.

Phil 8581.93   Brownell, B. Earth is enough. N.Y., 1933.

Phil 176.148   Brownell, B. The philosopher in chaos. N.Y., 1941.

Phil 5640.138   Brownfield, Charles A. Isolation; clinical and experimental approaches. N.Y., 1965.

Phil 585.161   Browning, Douglas. Act and agent. Coral Gables, Fla., 1964.

Phil 165.384   Browning, Douglas. Philosophers of process. N.Y., 1965.

Phil 6360.2   Browning, Robert Mitchell. Behavior modification in child treatment. Chicago, 1971.

Phil 7054.57.5   Brownson, O.A. The spirit-rapper, an autobiography. Detroit, 1884.

Phil 7054.57   Brownson, O.A. The spirit-rapper. Boston, 1854.

Phil 5241.122   Brrermann, Ernst. Allgemeine Psychologie. Paderborn, 1958.

Phil 2477.89.30   Bruaire, Claude. L'affirmation de Dieu. Paris, 1964.

Phil 3425.606   Bruaire, Claude. Logique et religion chrétienne dans la philosophie de Hegel. Paris, 1964.

Phil 6111.85   Bruaire, Claude. Philosophie du corps. Paris, 1968.

Phil 8656.9.2   Bruce, A.B. The moral order of the World. N.Y., 1899.

Phil 6111.18.5   Bruce, H.A. Nerve control and how to gain it. N.Y., 1918.

Phil 575.12   Bruce, H.A. Riddle of personality. N.Y., 1908.

Phil 575.12.2   Bruce, H.A. Riddle of personality. N.Y., 1915.

Phil 6111.18   Bruce, H.A. Scientific mental healing. Boston, 1911.

Phil 7080.26   Bruce, H.A. Sleep and sleeplessness. Boston, 1915.

Phil 7060.68.5   Bruce, Henry Addington Bayley. Adventurings in the psychical. Boston, 1914.

Phil 7060.68   Bruce, Henry Addington Bayley. Historic ghosts and ghost hunters. N.Y., 1908.

Phil 8876.33   Bruce, J. Elements of the science of ethics. London, 1786.

Phil 8951.15   Bruce, William S. Social aspects of Christian morality. London, 1905.

Phil 8951.5   Bruch, J.F. Lehrbuch der christlichen Sittenlehre. v.1-2. Strassburg, 1829-32.

Phil 3483.96   Bruch, Jean Louis. La philosophie religieuse de Kant. Thèse. Paris, 1968.

Phil 665.94   Bruch, Johann Friedrich. Die Lehre von der Präexistenz der Menschlichen Seelen. Strassburg, 1859.

Phil 5520.8   Bruchmann, K. Psychologische Studien. Leipzig, n.d.

Phil 3528.37   Bruchstücke aus meiner Lebensphilosophie. v.1-2. (Krug, Wilhelm Traugott.) Berlin, 1800-01.

Phil 3850.20.80   Bruck, Reinhard. Heinrich Steffens. Diss. Borna, 1906.

Phil 801.5.3   Brucker, J. Historia critica philosophiae. Lipsiae, 1867. 6v.

Phil 801.5.2   Brucker, J. Historia critica philosophiae. Lipsiae, 1867. 6v.

Phil 801.5.7   Brucker, J. Institutiones historiae philosophicae. Lipsiae, 1747.

Phil 801.5.15   Brucker, J. Kurtze Fragen aus der philosophischen Historie. Ulm, 1731-36. 7v.

Phil 801.5.20   Brucker, J. Miscellanea historiae philosophicae literariae criticae. Augustae Vindelicorum, 1748.

Phil 332.10   Brucker, Jacob. Historia philosophica doctrinae de ideis. Augustae Vindelicorum, 1723.

Phil 801.5   Brucker J. Historia critica philosophiae. Lipsiae, 1742-67. 6v.

Phil 1709.3   Brudshjkher ar filosofiens historii. (Jørgensen, J.) København, 1917.

Phil 3850.16.31   Brüche und Tür. (Simmel, Georg.) Stuttgart, 1957.

Phil 5650.12   Brücke, Ernst. Über die Wahrnehmung. Wien, 1884.

Phil 3483.40   Brückmann, R. Immanuel Kant: sein Leben und sein Lehre. v.1-2. Königsberg, 1918-19.

Phil 5593.63.5   Brückner, Peter. Konflikt und Konfliktschicksal. Bern, 1963.

Phil 735.260   Bruederlin, Kurt. Zur Phänomenologie des Werterlebens. Winterthur, 1962.

Phil 7140.107   Brügelmann, W. Die Behandlung und kranken durch Suggestion. Leipzig, 1906.

Phil 3246.303   Brueggen, Michael. Der Gang des Denkens in der Philosophie Johann Gottlieb Fichtes. München, 1964.

Phil 5640.6.25   Brühl, P.N. Die specifischen Sinnesenergien nach John Müller. Fulda, 1915.

Phil 5627.100   Bruehn, W. Religionspsychologie. Breslau, 1926.

Phil 334.14.10   Bruemmer, Vincent. Transcendental criticism and Christian philosophy. Franeker, 1961.

Phil 11.50   Bruenn. Universita. Knihovna. Přehled nové časopisecké literatury z oblasti. filosofie, estetiky, sociologie. Brno. 1965+

Phil 4115.79   Bruers, A. Gioberti. (Guide bibliografiche). Roma, 1924.

Phil 600.5   Brütt, M. Der Positivismus. Hamburg, 1889.

Phil 75.38   Brugger, Ilse. Filosofía alemana traducida al español. Buenos Aires, 1942.

Phil 75.38.5   Brugger, Ilse. Filosofía alemana traducida al español. Supplement. Pt.1. Buenos Aires, 1942.

Phil 86.6   Brugger, Walter. Philosophisches Wörterbuch. 5. Aufl. Freiburg 1953.

Phil 5241.73   Brugmans, H.J. Psychologische methoden en begrippen. Haarlem, 1922.

Phil 2070.83   Brugmans, H.J.F.W. Waarheidstheorie van William James. Groningen, 1913.

Phil 3549.8.125   Bruhers, E.M.J. De bijdrage von Ludwig Klages tot de algemene psychologie. Roermond, 1941.

Phil 8402.41   Bruhn, Karl. De växandes estetiska liv. Vasa, 1720-21. 2v.

Phil 176.117   Bruhn, Wilhelm. Einführung in das philosophische Denken für Anfanger und Alleinlermende. Leipzig, 1923.

Phil 8691.20   Bruhn, Wilhelm. Glauben und Wissen. Leipzig, 1921.

Phil 978.24.5   Bruhn, Wilhelm. Theosophie und Anthroposophie. Leipzig, 1921.

Phil 978.24   Bruhn, Wilhelm. Theosophie und Theologie. Glückstadt, 1907.

Phil 8581.56   Bruhn, Wilhelm. Der Vernunftcharakter der Religion. Leipzig, 1921.

Phil 3425.192   Bruijn, J.C. Hegel's phaenomenologie I-II, proeve van tekstverklaring. Proefschrift. Amsterdam, 1923.

Phil 3001.8   Bruleg, Lucien. Holländische Philosophie. Breslau, 1926.

Phil 2555.5.90   Brulez, L. Delboeufs Bedeutung für die Logik. Diss. Berlin, 1919.

Phil 3960.14   Brulez, Lucien. Holländische Philosophie. Breslau, 1926.

Phil 5751.6   Brulez, Lucien. Het vrijheidsbegrip. 's Gravenhage, 1920.

Phil 6480.236   Bruller, Jean. Ce que tout rêveur doit savoit de la méthode psychanalytique d'interprétation des rêves. Paris, 1934.

Phil 1106.19   Brumbaugh, Robert S. The philosophers of Greece. N.Y., 1964.

VPhil 8951.31   Brumen, Vinko. Iskanja. Buenos Aires, 1967.

Phil 3450.2.85   Brummel, L. Frans Hemsterhuis, een philosofenleven. Haarlem, 1925.

Phil 6111.67   Brun, J. La main et l'esprit. Paris, 1963.

Phil 840.2   Brun, Jean. Les conquêtes de l'homme et la séparation ontologique. Thèse. Paris, 1961.

Phil 1158.37   Brun, Jean. L'épicurisme. Paris, 1959.

Phil 1200.60   Brun, Jean. Le stoïcisme. Paris, 1958.

Phil 5811.11   Brun, Rudolf. Die Raumorientierung der Ameisen. Jena, 1914.

Phil 4070.3   Brunello, B. Lineamenti di filosofia dell'azione. Modena, 1938.

Phil 4210.193   Brunello, B. Rosmini. Bologna, 1963.

Phil 4210.151   Brunello, Bruno. Antonio Rosmini. Milano, 1945.

Phil 5650.5   Bruner, A.G. The hearing of primitive peoples. N.Y., 1908.

Phil 176.60   Bruner, J.J. La experiencia y la especulación. Santiago de Chile, 1886.

Phil 332.36   Bruner, J.S. On knowing. Cambridge, 1962.

Phil 5241.118   Bruner, J.S. A study of thinking. N.Y., 1956.

Phil 2477.16.30   Brunet, Christian. Prolégomenes a une esthétique intégrale. Paris, 1962.

Phil 2805.370.5   Brunet, Georges. Le Pari de Pascal. Paris, 1956.

Phil 2805.370   Brunet, Georges. Un prétendu traité de Pascal. Paris, 1959.

Phil 2050.264   Brunet, Oliver. Philosophie et esthétique chez David Hume. Paris, 1965.

Phil 2750.8.89   Brunet, Pierre. Maupertuis. Paris, 1929. 2v.

Phil 2750.8.87   Brunet, Pierre. Maupertuis. Thèse. Paris, 1929. 2 pam.

Phil 9150.13   Bruneteau, E. La doctrine morale de l'évolution. Paris, 1911.

Phil 600.18   Brunetière, F. Sur les chemins de la croyance. Paris, 1912.

Phil 2050.258   Brunetto, Filippo. La questione della vera causa in David Hume. Bologna, 1965.

Phil 8951.30   Brungs, Robert A. Building the city. N.Y., 1967.

Phil 165.265   Brunhold, C. De Montaigne à Luis de Broglie. 8. ed. Paris, 1963?

Phil 1506.8.10   Bruni, Gerardo. Progressive scholasticism. Saint Louis, Mo., 1929.

Phil 1506.8   Bruni, Gerardo. Riflessioni sulla scolastica. Roma, 1927.

Phil 585.75   Bruning, Walther. Philosophische Anthropologie. Stuttgart, 1960.

Phil 8402.39   Brunius, Teddy. Estetik. Stockholm, 1961.

Phil 2150.18.85   Brunius, Teddy. G.E. Moore's analyses of beauty. Uppsala, 1964[1965].

Phil 8110.10   Brunius, Teddy. Pionjärer och fullföjare. Stockholm, 1952.

Phil 8402.39.5   Brunius, Teddy. Theory and taste. Uppsala, 1969.

Phil 176.158.5   Brunner, August. Die Grundragen der Philosophie. 4. Aufl. Freiburg, 1956.

Phil 8581.100   Brunner, August. Die Religion. Freiburg, 1956.

Phil 176.158   Brunner, August. Der Stufenbau der Welt. 1. Aufl. München, 1950.

Phil 1701.21   Brunner, Auguste. La personne incarnée, étude sur la phénoménologie et la philosophie existentialiste. Paris, 1947.

Phil 3120.15.47   Brunner, Constantin. Aus meinem Tagebuch. 2. Aufl. Stuttgart, 1967.

Phil 3120.15.33   Brunner, Constantin. Der entlarvte Mensch. Haag, 1951.

Phil 3120.15.30   Brunner, Constantin. Kunst, Philosophie, Mystik, Gesammelte Anfsätze. Zürich, 1940.

Phil 176.73.2   Brunner, Constantin. Die Lehre von den Geistigen und vom Volk. 2. Aufl. Potsdam, 1927. 2v.

Phil 176.73.3   Brunner, Constantin. Die Lehre von den Geistigen und vom Volk. 3. Aufl. Stuttgart, 1962. 2v.

Phil 176.73   Brunner, Constantin. Die Lehre von den Geistigen und vom Volke. Berlin, 1908. 2v.

Phil 3120.15.35   Brunner, Constantin. Materialismus und Idealismus. Köln, 1959.

Phil 3120.15.40   Brunner, Constantin. Science, spirit, superstition; a new enquiry into human thought. Toronto, 1968.

Phil 3821.11   Brunner, Constantin. Spinoza Gegen Kant und die Sache der geistigen Wahrheit. Berlin, 1910.

Phil 3120.15.31   Brunner, Constantin. Unser Charakter, oder Ich bin der Richtige! Zürich, 1939.

Phil 3120.15.50   Brunner, Constantin. Vom Einsiedler Constantin Brunner. Potsdam, 1924.

Phil 3552.340   Brunner, F. Études sur la signification historique de la philosophie de Leibniz. Thèse. Paris, 1950[1951]

Phil 8951.21A   Brunner, Heinrich E. Justice and the social order. London, 1945.

Phil 8581.96   Brunner, Heinrich Emil. Christianity and civilisation. N.Y., 1949. 2v.

Phil 8581.96.2   Brunner, Heinrich Emil. Christianity and civilization. N.Y., 1949.

Phil 8612.53   Brunner, S. Büchlein gegen die Todesfurcht. Wien, 1856.

Phil 3640.380   Brunngraber, Rudolf. Was zu Kommen hat. Wien, 1947.

Phil 4065.105.15   Brunnhofer, H. Giordano Bruno's Lehre vom Kleinsten als die Quelle der prastabilirten Harmonie des Leibnitz. 2. Aufl. Leipzig, 1899.

Phil 4065.105   Brunnhofer, H. Giordano Bruno's Weltanschauung. Leipzig, 1882.

Phil 2520.226   Bruno, A. Cartesio e l'illuminismo. Bari, 1949.

Phil 4080.3.325 — Bruno, Antonino. Economia ed etica nello svolgimento. Siracusa, 1958.

Phil 8402.29 — Bruno, F. Il problema estetica contemporanea. Lanclano, 1928.

Phil 4065.65.5 — Bruno, Giordano. Das Aschermitt Wochsmahl. Frankfurt, 1969.

Htn Phil 4065.35* — Bruno, Giordano. Camoeracensis acrotismus. Vitebergae, 1588.

Phil 4065.31 — Bruno, Giordano. Caudelaio. Strasburgo, n.d.

Phil 4065.50.10 — Bruno, Giordano. Cause, principe et unité. Paris, 1930.

Phil 4065.50.12 — Bruno, Giordano. Cause, principle, and unity. N.Y., 1964.

Phil 4065.65 — Bruno, Giordano. La cena de le cenerè. Torino, 1955.

Htn Phil 4065.58* — Bruno, Giordano. De gl'heroici furori. Parigi, 1585.

Phil 4065.61 — Bruno, Giordano. De gl'heroici furori. Torino, 1928.

Phil 4065.52 — Bruno, Giordano. De la causa. Padova, 1941.

Htn Phil 4065.55* — Bruno, Giordano. De monade, numero et figura. Franco, 1591.

Phil 4065.32 — Bruno, Giordano. De umbris idearum. Berolini, 1868.

Htn Phil 4065.32.5* — Bruno, Giordano. De umbris idearum. Paris, 1582.

Phil 4065.62 — Bruno, Giordano. Des fureurs héroïques. Paris, 1954.

Phil 4065.14A — Bruno, Giordano. Dialoghi italiani. Firenze, 1958.

Phil 4065.70 — Bruno, Giordano. Due dialoghi sconosciuti e due dialoghi noti. Roma, 1957.

Phil 4065.60.30 — Bruno, Giordano. Eroici furori, Übersetzt von L. Kuhlenbeck. Leipzig, 1898.

Phil 4065.43 — Bruno, Giordano. L'éthique et le deuxième dialogue du spaccio. Paris, 1919.

Phil 4065.45.5 — Bruno, Giordano. The expulsion of the triumphant beast. New Brunswick, 1964.

Phil 4065.15 — Bruno, Giordano. Gesammelte Werke. Leipzig, 1904-09. 6v.

Phil 4065.27 — Bruno, Giordano. Giordano Bruno. 2. ed. Milano, 1944.

Phil 4065.25 — Bruno, Giordano. Giordano-Bruno-Buch. Bad Oldesloe, 1927.

Phil 4065.50.4 — Bruno, Giordano. Giordano Bruno von der Ursache dem Prinzip und dem Einen. 4e aufl. Leipzig, 1923.

Phil 4065.60 — Bruno, Giordano. The heroic enthusiasts. pt.1-2. London, 1887-1889. 2v.

Phil 4065.75 — Bruno, Giordano. Heroische Leidenschaften und individuelles Leben. Hamburg, 1957.

Phil 4065.32.20 — Bruno, Giordano. Le ombre delle idee. Catania, 1901.

Phil 4065.12A — Bruno, Giordano. Opera latine. v. 1-3. Neapoli, 1879-91. 6v.

Phil 4065.11 — Bruno, Giordano. Opere. Gottinga, 1888. 2v.

Phil 4065.10A — Bruno, Giordano. Opere. Lipsia, 1830. 2v.

Phil 4065.28 — Bruno, Giordano. Opere di G. Bruno e di T. Campanella. Milano, 1956.

Phil 4065.13 — Bruno, Giordano. Opere italiane. Bari, 1907. 2v.

Htn Phil 4065.30* — Bruno, Giordano. Philothei Jordani. Paris, 1582.

Phil 4065.41 — Bruno, Giordano. Reformation des Himmels. Leipzig, 1889.

Phil 4065.40 — Bruno, Giordano. Spaccio de la bestia trionfante. Roma, 1888.

Phil 4065.45 — Bruno, Giordano. Spaccio della bestia trionfante. v.1-2. Lanciano, 1920.

Phil 4065.50.2 — Bruno, Giordano. Von der Ursache, dem Princip und dem Einen. 2. Ausg. Heidelberg, 1889.

Phil 4210.89 — Pamphlet box. Bruno, Giordano.

Bruno, J.F. Rosmini's contribution to ethical philosophy. N.Y., 1916.

Htn Phil 3800.200* — Bruno. (Schelling, F.W.J. von.) Berlin, 1802.

Phil 3800.200.7 — Bruno. (Schelling, F.W.J. von.) Hamburg, 1954.

Phil 3800.200.17 — Bruno. (Schelling, F.W.J. von.) Leipzig, 1928.

Phil 3800.200.20 — Bruno. (Schelling, F.W.J. von.) Paris, 1845.

Htn Phil 3800.200.5* — Bruno. (Schelling, F.W.J. von.) Reutlingen, 1834.

Phil 3800.200.30 — Bruno. (Schelling, F.W.J. von.) Torino, 1906.

Phil 3800.200.11A — Bruno. 2. Aufl. (Schelling, F.W.J. von.) Berlin, 1842.

Phil 3800.99.2 — Bruno. 2e Aufl. (Kuhlenbeck, L.) Leipzig, 1899.

Htn Phil 3800.200.10* — Bruno. 2e Aufl. (Schelling, F.W.J. von.) Berlin, 1842.

Phil 3120.12.80 — Bruno Bauers Übergang von der hegelschen Rechten zum Radikalismus. Inaug. Diss. (Kegel, Martin.) Leipzig, 1908.

Phil 4065.108 — Bruno e Hegel. (Maturi, Sebastiano.) Firenze, 1926.

Phil 5520.67 — Bruns, L. Metaphysik des Wortes. Inaug. Diss. Bonn, 1937.

Phil 801.23.9 — Brunschvicg, L. Les âges de l'intelligence. Paris, 1934.

Phil 801.23.11 — Brunschvicg, L. Les âges de l'intelligence. 3. ed. Paris, 1934.

Phil 2805.192.15 — Brunschvicg, L. Blaise Pascal. Paris, 1953.

Phil 2805.192 — Brunschvicg, L. Le génie de Pascal. Paris, 1924.

Phil 176.85.13 — Brunschvicg, L. L'idéalisme contemporain. Paris, 1905.

Phil 176.85.15 — Brunschvicg, L. L'idéalisme contemporain. 2e éd. Paris, 1921.

NEDL Phil 176.85.3 — Brunschvicg, L. Introduction à la vie de l'esprit. 3e éd. Paris, 1920.

Phil 176.85.10 — Brunschvicg, L. Nature et liberté. Paris, 1921.

Phil 2725.11.83 — Brunschvicg, L. Notice sur la vie et les travaux de Jules Lachelier. Paris, 1921.

Phil 2805.192.10A — Brunschvicg, L. Pascal. Paris, 1932.

Phil 176.85.20 — Brunschvicg, L. La philosophie de l'esprit. 1. éd. Paris, 1949.

Phil 801.23.15 — Brunschvicg, L. La physique du vingtième siècle et la philosophie. Paris, 1936.

Phil 801.23 — Brunschvicg, L. Le progrès de la conscience dans la philosophie. Paris, 1927. 2v.

Phil 2520.200A — Brunschvicg, L. René Descartes. Paris, 1937.

Phil 3821.3.3 — Brunschvicg, L. Spinoza, et ses contemporaines. 3. éd. Paris, 1923.

Phil 3821.3 — Brunschvicg, L. Spinoza. 2. éd. Paris, 1894.

Phil 5374.55 — Brunschvicg, Léon. De la connaissance de soi. Paris, 1931.

Phil 8581.98 — Brunschvicg, Léon. De la vraie et de la fausse conversion. 1. éd. Paris, 1951.

Phil 2477.11.30 — Brunschvicg, Léon. Écrits philosphiques. 1. éd. Paris, 1951- 3v.

Phil 5500.7 — Brunschvicg, Léon. La modalité du jugement. Thèse. Paris, 1897.

Phil 5500.7.3 — Brunschvicg, Léon. La modalité du jugement. 3.éd. Paris, 1964.

Phil 8581.98.5 — Brunschvicg, Léon. La raison et la religion. Paris, 1964.

Phil 1182.10 — Brunschvicg, Léon. Le rôle du pythagorisme dans l'évolution des idées. Paris, 1937.

Phil 2477.11.105 — Brunschvicg; sa vie, son oeuvre avec un exposé de la philosophie. (Boirel, R.) Paris, 1964.

Phil 5041.72 — Brunstaed, Friedrich. Logik. München, 1933.

Phil 5400.72 — Brunswick, D. The effects of emotional stimuli on the gastro-intestinal tone. Baltimore, 1924.

Phil 5585.59 — Brunswick, E. Wahrnehmung und Gegenstandswelt. Leipzig, 1934.

Phil 5241.53 — Brunswig, A. Einführung in die Psychologie. München, 1921.

Phil 3483.11 — Brunswig, A. Das Grundproblem Kants. Leipzig, 1914.

Phil 3552.265 — Brunswig, A. Leibniz. Wien, 1925.

Phil 5357.1 — Brunswig, A. Vergleichen und die Relationserkenntnis. Leipzig, 1910.

Phil 5545.164 — Brunswig, Alfred. Das Gedächtnis und seine Erziehung. Berlin, 1926.

Phil 3425.253 — Brunswig, Alfred. Hegel. München, 1922.

Phil 9070.102 — Brunswik, E. Wunsch und Pflicht im Auflau des menschlichen Lebens. Wien, 1937.

Phil 5640.42 — Brunswik, Egon. Experimentelle Psychologie in Demonstrationen. Wien, 1935.

Phil 5625.123 — Brush, Franklin Robert. Aversive conditioning and learning. N.Y., 1971.

Phil 5520.722 — Brushlinskii, Andrei V. Psikhologiia myshleniia i kibernetika. Moskva, 1970.

Phil 5520.315 — Brutian, G.A. Teoriia poznaniia obshchei semantiki. Erevan, 1959.

Phil 5870.35 — Bruun, Ulla-Britta. Förskoleålderns psykologi. Göteborg, 1968.

Phil 8050.58 — Bruyne, E. de. Geschiedenis van de aesthetica. Antwerpen, 1951. 5v.

Phil 8402.30 — Bruyne, Edgar. Esquisse d'une philosphie de l'art. Bruxelles, 1930.

Phil 8070.2.10 — Bruyne, Edgar de. The esthetics of the Middle Ages. N.Y., 1969.

Phil 8070.2 — Bruyne, Edgar de. Études d'esthétique médiévale. Brugge, 1946. 3v.

Phil 8620.21 — Bruyssel, Ernest van. Mal et ses origines. Paris, 1911.

Phil 6980.141 — Bry, Adelaide. Inside psychotherapy. N.Y., 1972.

Phil 5627.117 — Bry, Carl Christian. Verkappte Religionen. Gotha, 1925.

Phil 9590.5 — Bryan, G.B. Psychic dictatorship in America. Los Angeles, 1940.

Phil 176.147 — Bryan, W.L. Wars of families of minds. New Haven, 1940.

Phil 6945.15 — Bryan, William A. Administrative psychiatry. N.Y., 1936.

Phil 7069.18.40 — Bryan, William J. The truth about spiritualism. N.Y., 1918.

X Cg Phil 8709.9.5 — Bryan and Darrow at Dayton. (Allen, Leslie H.) N.Y., 1925.

Phil 5425.92 — Bryant, J.E. Genius and epilepsy. Concord, Mass., 1953.

Phil 9035.44 — Bryant, S.W. Short studies in character. London, 1894.

Phil 3425.348 — Bryant, W. McK. Hegel's educational ideas. N.Y., 1896.

Phil 9045.6 — Bryce, J. The hindrances to good citizenship. New Haven, 1909.

Phil 9045.6.2 — Bryce, J. The hindrances to good citizenship. New Haven, 1909[1919]

Htn Phil 8876.13* — Bryskett, Lodowick. Discourse of civil life. London, 1606.

Phil 9290.4 — Bryson, Lyman. The use of the radio in leisure time. N.Y., 1935?

Phil 1701.47 — Brytninger i tidens tankelin. Oslo, 1960.

Phil 5876.5.5 — Brytningstid, en bok um ungdom och samlernad. 5. uppl. (Asklund, Lis.) Stockholm, 1964.

Phil 3640.645 — Brzozowski, S.L. Fryderyk Nietzsche. Stanisławów, 1907.

Phil 4803.241.30 — Brzozowski, Stanisław L. Idee. Lwów, 1910.

Phil 3120.30.39.10 — Buber, Martin. Begegnung. Stuttgart, 1960.

Phil 3120.30.56.40 — Buber, Martin. A believing humanism: my testament 1902-1965. N.Y., 1967.

Phil 3120.30.72 — Buber, Martin. Between man and man. London, 1947.

Phil 3120.30.45 — Buber, Martin. Bilder von Gut und Böse. Köln, 1952.

Phil 3120.30.63 — Buber, Martin. Dialogisches Leben. Zürich, 1947.

Phil 3120.30.73 — Buber, Martin. Eclipse of God. N.Y., 1957.

Phil 5628.10.5.1 — Buber, Martin. Ekstatische Konfessionen. Leipzig, 1921.

Phil 3120.30.39.5 — Buber, Martin. Ereignisse und Begegnungen. Berlin, 193-?

Phil 3120.30.39 — Buber, Martin. Ereignisse und Begegnungen. Leipzig, 1925.

Phil 3120.30.51 — Buber, Martin. Die Frage an den Einzelnen. Berlin, 1936.

Phil 3120.30.75 — Buber, Martin. Good and evil. N.Y., 1953.

Phil 3120.30.35 — Buber, Martin. Gottesfinsterrns. Zürich, 1953.

Phil 3120.30.62 — Buber, Martin. Hin Weise. Zürich, 1953.

Phil 3120.30.44 — Buber, Martin. I and thou. Edinburg, 1958.

Phil 3120.30.44.3 — Buber, Martin. I and thou. N.Y., 1970.

Phil 3120.30.44.5 — Buber, Martin. I and thou. 2. ed. N.Y., 1958.

Phil 3120.30.42 — Buber, Martin. Ich und Du. Heidelberg, 1958.

Phil 3120.30.43.5 — Buber, Martin. Ich und Du. Köln, 1966.

Phil 3120.30.43 — Buber, Martin. Ich und Du. Leipzig, 1923.

Phil 3120.30.74 — Buber, Martin. Images of good and evil. London, 1952.

Phil 3120.30.78 — Buber, Martin. Israel and the world. 2. ed. N.Y., 1963.

Phil 3120.30.79 — Buber, Martin. The knowledge of man. N.Y., 1965.

Phil 3120.30.76 — Buber, Martin. Logos. Heidelberg, 1962.

Phil 3120.30.71 — Buber, Martin. Martin Buber, philosophe de la relation. Paris, 1968.

Phil 3120.30.37 — Buber, Martin. Der Mensch und sein Gebild. Heidelberg, 1955.

Phil 3120.30.56 — Buber, Martin. Nachlese. Heidelberg, 1965.

Phil 3120.30.32 — Buber, Martin. On Judaism. N.Y., 1967.

Phil 3120.30.38 — Buber, Martin. On the Bible; eighteen studies. N.Y., 1968.

Phil 3120.30.70 — Buber, Martin. Pointing the way. London, 1951.

Phil 3120.30.41 — Buber, Martin. Das Problem des Menschen. Heidelberg, 1948.

Phil 3120.30.49 — Buber, Martin. Die Rede. 2. Aufl. Leipzig, 1920.

Phil 3120.30.55 — Buber, Martin. Rede über das Erzieherische. Berlin, 1926.

Phil 3120.30.53 — Buber, Martin. Reden über Erziehung. Heidelberg, 1953.

Phil 3120.30.60 — Buber, Martin. Die Schriften über das dialogische Prinzip. Heidelberg, 1954.

Phil 3120.30.64 — Buber, Martin. Schuld und Schuldgefühle. Heidelberg, 1958.

Phil 3120.30.57 — Buber, Martin. Die Stunde und die Erkenntnis. Berlin, 1936.

Phil 3120.30.68A — Buber, Martin. Two types of faith. London, 1951.

Phil 3120.30.30 — Buber, Martin. Urdistanz und Beziehung. Heidelberg, 1951.

Phil 3120.30.22A — Buber, Martin. Volker, Staaten und Zion. Berlin, 1917.

Phil 3120.30.20 — Buber, Martin. The way of response. N.Y., 1966.

Phil 3120.30.15 — Buber, Martin. Werke. München, 1962. 3v.

Phil 3120.30.7 — Buber, Martin. Writings. N.Y., 1958.

Phil 3120.30.47 — Buber, Martin. Zwei Glaubensweisen. Zürich, 1950.

Phil 3120.30.77 — Buber, Martin. Zwischen Gesellschaft und Staat. Heidelberg, 1952.

Phil 3120.30.210 — Buber and Buberism. (Edwards, Paul.) Lawrence, 1971.

Phil 3640.205 — Bubnoff, N. von. Friedrich Nietzsches Kulturphilosophie und Umwertungslehre. Leipzig, 1924.

Phil 4710.37 — Bubnov, Nikolai M. Russische Religionsphilosophen. Heidelberg, 1956.

Phil 5241.19 — Buccola, G. La legge del tempo. Milano, 1883.

Phil 8599.16.80 — Das Buch De tribus impostoribus. (Presser, Jacob.) Amsterdam, 1926.

Phil 3549.10 — Buch der Erinnerung. (Kassner, Rudolf.) Leipzig, 1938.

Phil 3195.11.35 Buch der Erinnerung. 2. Aufl. (Dessoir, Max.) Stuttgart, 1947.

Phil 3549.10.2 Buch der Erinnerung. 2. Aufl. (Kassner, Rudolf.) Erlenbach, 1954.

Phil 6128.28 Das Buch der Erziehung an Leib und Seele. 2. ed. (Schreber, D.G.M.) Leipzig, 1882.

Phil 1504.5.3 Buch der Ringsteine Alfârâbis. v.5, pt.3. (Horten, M.) Münster, 1906.

Phil 7082.140 Das Buch der Träume. (Ježower, Ignaz.) Berlin, 1928.

Phil 7069.00.65 Das Buch der Wunder und der Geheimwissenschaften. 2. Aufl. v.1-2. (Berndt, G.H.) Leipzig, 1900.

Phil 6400.21 Das Buch Emanuel. (Forsboom, Bernhard.) München, 1957.

Phil 6316.8.8 Das Buch vom Es; psychoanalytische Briefe an eine Freuden. 3. Aufl. (Groddeck, Georg.) Leipzig, 1934.

Phil 6316.8.12 Das Buch vom Es. (Groddeck, Georg.) Wiesbaden, 1961.

Phil 3549.2.47 Das Buch vom persönlichen Leben. (Keyserling, Hermann.) Stuttgart, 1936.

Phil 3549.2.40 Das Buch vom Ursprung. (Keyserling, Hermann.) Baden-Baden, 1947.

Phil 8876.59 Ein Buch von der deutschen Gesinnung fünf ethische Essays. (Böhmer, Gustav.) München, 1897.

Phil 1020.5.5 Das Buch von der Erkenntniss der Wahrheit. (Dayser, C.) Strassburg, 1893.

Phil 1020.5 Das Buch von der Erkenntniss der Wahrheit. (Kayser, C.) Leizig, 1889.

Phil 5811.9 Buchan, P. Scriptural and philosophical arguments. Peterhead, 1834.

Phil 6671.11 Buchanan, A. On darlingism, misnamed electro-biology. London, 1851.

Phil 8656.5 Buchanan, J. Faith in God. London, 1857. 2v.

Phil 7059.6 Buchanan, J.R. Manual of psychometry. Boston, 1885.

Phil 5921.4 Buchanan, J.R. Sketches of Buchanan's discoveries in neurology. Louisville, 1842.

Phil 5241.20 Buchanan, Joseph. The philosophy of human nature. Richmond, 1812.

Phil 5241.20.2 Buchanan, Joseph. The philosophy of human nature. Weston, Mass., 1970.

Phil 176.106.10 Buchanan, S.M. Poetry and mathematics. N.Y., 1929.

Phil 176.106 Buchanan, S.M. Possibility. London, 1927.

Phil 176.106.2 Buchanan, S.M. Possibility. N.Y., 1927.

Phil 11.10 Buchanan's journal of man. Cincinnati. 1,1849 3v.

Phil 11.10.2 Buchanan's journal of man. Cincinnati. 1849-1850

Phil 11.44 Bucharest Universitātea. Analele: seria acta logica. 1,1958+ 3v.

Phil 1750.848 Buchdahl, G. Metaphysics and the philosophy of science. Oxford, 1969.

Phil 530.15.30 Buche, Joseph. L'école mystique de Lyon, 1776-1847. Paris, 1935.

Phil 3483.18.5 Buchenau, A. Grundprobleme der Kritik der reinen Vernunft. Leipzig, 1914.

Phil 3483.18 Buchenau, A. Kants Lehre vom kategorischen Imperativ. Leipzig, 1913.

Phil 3483.18.2 Buchenau, A. Kants Lehre vom kategorischen Imperativ. 2. Aufl. Leipzig, 1923.

Phil 176.32 Buchez, P.T.B. Traité de philosophie. Paris, 1838. 3v.

Phil 3120.60.30 Buchheim, Karl. Logik der Tatsachen. München, 1959.

Phil 2805.242 Buchholz, A. Blaise Pascal. 2. Aufl. Göttingen, 1942.

Phil 2225.5.80 Buchler, J. Charles Peirce's empiricism. N.Y., 1939.

Phil 176.217 Buchler, J. The concept of method. N.Y., 1961.

Phil 5500.14.5 Buchler, J. Nature and judgment. N.Y., 1955.

Phil 5500.14 Buchler, J. Toward a general theory of human judgment. N.Y., 1951.

Phil 1905.34 Buchler, Justus. Metaphysics of natural complexes. N.Y., 1966.

Phil 5627.134.32 Buchman, Frank. Remaking the world. London, 1961.

Phil 5627.134.33 Buchman, Frank. Remaking the world. N.Y., 1949.

Phil 3483.22 Buchner, E.F. A study of Kant's psychology. N.Y., 1893.

Phil 4710.50.30 Buchvarov, Mikhail D. Ukraïns'ko-bolgars'ki filosofs'ki zv'iazki. Kyïv, 1966.

Phil 1630.40 Buck, August. Die humanistische Tradition in der Romania. Hamburg, 1968.

Phil 5535.64 Buck, Günther. Lernen und Erfahrung. Stuttgart, 1967.

Phil 5241.33 Buck, J.D. Constructive psychology. Chicago, 1908.

Phil 978.46 Buck, J.D. The nature and aim of theosophy. Cincinnati, 1889.

Phil 9035.22 Bucke, Charles. The book of human character. London, 1837. 2v.

Phil 8876.34 Bucke, R.M. Man's moral mature. N.Y., 1879.

Phil 5627.232 Bucke (R.M.) Memorial Society for the Study of Religious Experience. Newsletter-review. Montreal. 1,1966+

Phil 7230.7 Bucke (R.M.) Memorial Society for the Study of Religious Experience. Trance and possession states. Montreal? 1968.

Phil 525.53 Buckham, J.N. Mysticism and modern life. N.Y., 1915.

Phil 315.8 Buckham, J.W. Dualism or duality? n.p., 1913.

Phil 8581.82 Buckham, J.W. The inner world...philosophy of Christianity. N.Y., 1941.

Phil 575.22.5 Buckham, John W. Christianity and personality. N.Y., 1936.

Phil 575.22 Buckham, John W. Personality and the Christian ideal. Boston, 1909.

Phil 8581.10.6 Buckland, W. Bridgewater treatises [6]. Geology and mineralogy. Philadelphia, 1837. 2v.

Phil 8656.6.5 Buckland, W. Geologie und Mineralogie. Neufchatel, 1838-39. 2v.

Phil 8656.6 Buckland, W. Geology and mineralogy...natural theology. London, 1837. 2v.

Phil 8656.6.2 Buckland, W. Geology and mineralogy...natural theology. Philadelphia, 1841. 2v.

Phil 8691.7 Buckland, William. Vindiciae geologicae. Oxford, 1820.

Phil 9400.16 Buckley, J.C. The retirement handbook. 1st ed. N.Y., 1953.

Phil 6311.29 Buckley, James M. Faith-healing. N.Y., 1900.

Phil 5330.31 Buckner, D. Vigilance. Los Angeles, 1963.

Phil 6951.4.5 Bucknill, J.C. A manual psychological medicine...insanity. London, 1858.

Phil 6951.4.6 Bucknill, J.C. A manual psychological medicine...insanity. London, 1858.

Phil 2225.5.130 Buczyńska, Hanna. Peirce. Warszawa, 1965.

Phil 3450.19.121 Buddeberg, Else R. Denken und Dichten des Seins. Stuttgart, 1956.

Phil 3450.19.120 Buddeberg, Else R. Heidegger und die Dichtting. Stuttgart, 1953.

Phil 3110.5 Buddecke, W. Die Jakob Böhme-Ausgaben. Göttingen, 1937. 2v.

Phil 3110.78 Buddecke, W. Verzeichnis von Jakob Böhme-Handschreften. Göttingen, 1934.

Phil 176.103 Buddeus, J.F. Elementa philosophiae instrumentalis. Halae Saxonum, 1724-25.

Phil 176.103.3 Buddeus, J.F. Elementa philosophiae instrumentalis. v.1-2. Halae-Saxonum, 1719-20.

Phil 176.103.5 Buddeus, J.F. Elementa philosophiae instrumentalis. v.1-2. Halae Saxonum, 1724-25.

Phil 176.103.10 Buddeus, J.F. Elementa philosophiae practicae. Halaeo Magdeburgical, 1724.

Phil 8951.18 Buddeus, J.F. Institutiones theologiae moralis. Lipsiae, 1719.

Phil 1050.1 Buddeus, J.F. Introductio ad historia philosophiae ebraeorum. Halae, 1702.

Phil 8656.7.20 Buddeus, J.F. Lehr-Sätze von der Atheisterey und dem Aberglauben mit gelehrten Anmerckungen erläutert. 2. Aufl. Jena, 1723.

Phil 8656.7 Buddeus, J.F. Theses theologicae de atheismo. Traiecti ad Rhenum, 1737.

Phil 8656.7.10 Buddeus, J.F. Traité de l'athéisme et de la superstition. Amsterdam, 1740.

Phil 8591.84 Buddha, Marx, and God: some aspects of religion in the modern world. (Ling, Trevor Oswald.) N.Y., 1966.

Phil 8633.1.11 Buddhism and immortality. (Bigelow, W.S.) Boston, 1908.

Phil 910.2 Buddhist ethics: essence of Buddhism. (Saddhatissa, Hammalaiva.) London, 1970.

Phil 525.57 Buddhist mysticism. Thèse. (Maw, M.B.) Bordeaux, 1924.

Phil 960.141 The Buddhist philosophy of universal flux. (Mookerjee, S.) Calcutta, 1935.

Phil 801.6 Budeus, J.F. Analecta historiae philosophicae. Halle, 1706.

Phil 801.6.2 Budeus, J.F. Analecta historiae philosophicae. 2. ed. Halle, 1724.

Phil 8626.19 Budgett, H.M. The avenue of beeches. London, 1930.

Phil 4710.83 Budilova, E.A. Bor'ba materializma i idealizma v russkoi psikhologicheskoi nauke. Moskva, 1960.

Phil 4769.6.83 Budilova, E.A. Uchenie I.M. Sechenova ob oshchushchenii i myshlenii. Moskva, 1924.

Phil 7054.169 Budington, Henry A. Death is birth. Springfield, Mass., 1897.

Phil 4683.37.30 Buduls, Hermanis. Cilvēks dzīves spoguli. Stockholm, 1954.

Phil 8612.53 Büchlein gegen die Todesfurcht. (Brunner, S.) Wien, 1856.

Phil 3210.67 Das Büchlein vom Leben nach dem Tode. (Fechner, G.T.) Dresden, 1836.

Phil 3210.67.2 Das Büchlein vom Leben nach dem Tode. 3. Aufl. (Fechner, G.T.) Hamburg, 1887.

Phil 3210.67.3 Das Büchlein vom Leben nach dem Tode. 6. Aufl. (Fechner, G.T.) Hamburg, 1906.

Phil 3210.67.4 Das Büchlein vom Leben nach dem Tode. 8. Aufl. (Fechner, G.T.) Leipzig, 1922.

Phil 2555.2.80 Büchner, A. Un philosophe amateur, essai biographique sur Léon Dumont. Paris, 1884.

Phil 5811.5.10 Büchner, L. Aus dem Geistesleben der Thiere oder Staaten und Thaten der Kleinen. Berlin, 1876.

Phil 5811.5.12 Büchner, L. Aus dem Geistesleben der Tiere. Leipzig, 18-?

Phil 176.33 Büchner, L. Aus Natur und Wissenschaft. Leipzig, 1874.

Phil 476.3.3 Büchner, L. Force et matière. Paris, 1863.

Phil 176.33.10 Büchner, L. Fremdes und Eignes. Leipzig, 1890.

Phil 476.3.11 Büchner, L. El hombre segum la ciencia. Barcelona, 1869.

Phil 476.3.6 Büchner, L. L'homme selon la science. Paris, 1870.

Phil 476.3.2.10 Büchner, L. Der Humor in Kraft und Stoff. Darmstadt, 1856.

Phil 176.33.15 Büchner, L. Im Dienste der Wahrheit. Giessen, 1900.

Phil 476.3.4.10 Büchner, L. Kraft och materia. Stockholm, 1869.

Phil 476.3.1 Büchner, L. Kraft und Stoff. Frankfurt, 1855.

Phil 476.3.2.5 Büchner, L. Kraft und Stoff. Frankfurt, 1858.

Phil 476.3 Büchner, L. Kraft und Stoff. Frankfurt, 1859.

Phil 476.3.2.4 Büchner, L. Kraft und Stoff. Frankfurt, 1898.

Phil 476.3.2 Büchner, L. Kraft und Stoff. Leipzig, 1867.

Phil 5811.5.5 Büchner, L. Liebe und Leibes- Leben in der Thierwelt. Berlin, 1879.

Phil 476.3.7 Büchner, L. Man in the past, present and future. London, 1872.

Phil 476.3.9 Büchner, L. Man in the past, present and future. N.Y., 1894.

Phil 476.3.5 Büchner, L. Mind in animals. London, 1880.

Phil 5811.5 Büchner, L. Natur und Geist. Frankfurt, 1857.

Phil 476.3.20 Büchner, L. Natur und Geist. 2e Aufl. Hamm, 1865.

Phil 476.3.15 Büchner, L. Science et nature. v.1-2. Paris, 1866.

Phil 176.33.5 Büchner, L. La vie psychique des bêtes. Paris, 1881.

Phil 5811.5.20 Büchring, Adolph. Biliotheca philosophica. Nordhausen, 1867.

Phil 75.2 Bühler, Charlotte M. Der menschliche Lebenslauf als psychologisches Problem. Leipzig, 1933.

Phil 5241.88 Bühler, Charlotte M. Der menschliche Lebenslauf als psychologisches Problem. 2. Aufl. Göttingen, 1959.

Phil 5241.88.5 Bühler, Charlotte M. Psychologie im Leben unserer Zeit. München, 1962.

Phil 5241.88.3 Bühler, Charlotte M. Psychologische Probleme unserer Zeit. Stuttgart, 1968.

Phil 5241.88.10 Bühler, Charlotte M. Psychology for contemporary living. 1st American ed. N.Y., 1969.

Phil 5241.88.3.5 Bühler, K. Studien über Henry Home. Bonn, 1905.

Phil 2055.1.80 Bühler, Karl. Ausdruckstheorie. Jena, 1933.

Phil 6011.5 Bühler, Karl. Das Gestaltprinzip im Leben des Menschen und der Tiere. Bern, 1960.

Phil 5241.70.5 Bühler, Karl. Handbuch der Psychologie. Jena, 1922.

Phil 5241.70 Bühler, Karl. Die Kirse der Psychologie. 2. Aufl. Jena, 1929.

Phil 5211.3.2 Buehler, W. Meditation als Erkenntnisweg. Stuttgart, 1962.

Phil 978.49.870 Buell, C.S. Essentials of psychology. Boston, 1898.

Phil 5241.38 Bülow, F. Die Entwicklung der Hegelschen Sozialphilosophie. Leipzig, 1920.

Phil 3425.210 Bülow, G. Des dominicus gundissalinus. v.2, pt.3. Münster, 1897.

Phil 1504.2.3 Bueno, Miguel. Conferencias. 1. ed. México, 1959.

Phil 176.225 Bueno, Miguel. Las grandes direcciones de la filosofía. México, 1957.

Phil 801.35 Bueno, Miguel. Prolegómenos filosóficos. México, 1963.

Phil 801.35.5 Bueno, Miquel. Ensayos liminares. México, 1962.

Phil 801.35.10 Bueno Martinez, Gustavo. El papel de la filosofía en el conjunto del saber. Madrid, 1970.

Phil 176.236 Buenos Aires. Colegio Máximo. Nuestra bibliográfica de la filosofía católica. Buenos Aires, 1939.

Phil 75.34 Buenos Aires. Universidad. Instituto de Filosofía. Descartes. Buenos Aires, 1937. 3v.

Phil 2520.201

Phil 41.8 — Buenos Aires. Universidad. Instituto de Filosofía. Sección de Psicología. Monógrafias psicológicas.

Phil 4080.3.290 — Buenos Aires. Universidad Nacional. Benedetto Croce. Buenos Aires, 1954.

Phil 4260.122 — Buenos Aires. Universidad Nacional. Vico y Herder. Buenos Aires, 1948.

Phil 41.4 — Buenos Aires. Universidad Nacional. Facultad de Filosofía y Letras. Archivos del laboratorio de facultad de filosofía y letras psicologicas. Buenos Aires, 1931.

Phil 41.6 — Buenos Aires. Universidad Nacional. Instituto de filosofía. Cuadernos de filosofía. Buenos Aires. 1,1948+ 4v.

Phil 41.3 — Buenos Aires. Universidad Nacional. Instituto de Filosofía. Publicaciónes de clasicos de la filosofía. Buenos Aires. 3v.

Phil 41.5 — Buenos Aires. Universidad Nacional. Instituto de Filosofía. Publicaciones de ensayos filosoficos. Buenos Aires. 1-4,1942-1945 2v.

Phil 11.18.5 — Buenos Aires. University Nacional. Facultad de Filosofía y Letras. Publicaciones de filosofia argentina. Buenos Aires. 1-5 3v.

Phil 11.18 — Buenos Aires. University Nacional. Facultad de Filosofía y Letras. Publicaciones de filosofia contemporanea. Buenos Aires. 1-4,1938-1945

Phil 11.18.10 — Buenos Aires. University Nacional. Instituto de Psicología. Anales. Buenos Aires. 1-3,1935-1941 2v.

Phil 8612.33.5 — Bürgel, B.H. Anfang und Ende. Berlin, 1947.
Phil 8612.33 — Bürgel, B.H. Saat und Ernte. Berlin, 1942.
Phil 282.18 — Bürgel, B.H. Die Weltanschauung des modernen Menschen. Berlin, 1932.

Phil 6906.15 — Bürger und Irre. (Doerner, Klaus.) Frankfurt, 1969.
Phil 9590.25.5 — Die bürgerliche Moralinwaffe der imperialistischen Reaktion. (Shishkin, A.F.) Berlin, 1952.

Phil 3425.698 — Bürgerlicher Optimismus im Niedergang. (Hahn, Manfred.) München, 1969.

Phil 6111.43 — Bürker, Karl. Neueres über die Zentralisation der Funktionen. Giessen, 1926.

Phil 6350.2 — Buerli, Alois. Indikation zur analytischen Psychotherapie mit Hilfe des "Experimentellen Triebdiagnostik". Bern, 1970.

Phil 8402.40 — Buermeyer, L. The aesthetic experience. Merion, Pa., 1924.

Phil 3120.61.30 — Bueschel, Johann Gabriel Bernhard. Über die Charlatanerie der Gelehrten seit Menken. Leipzig, 1971.

Phil 1106.14 — Büsching, A.F. Vergleichung der griechischen Philosophie mit der Neuern. Berlin, 1785.

Phil 6615.18 — Buess, Heinrich. Die Wandlungen des Psychogenie-Begriffs. Inaug. Diss. Hölstein, 1940.

Phil 3120.55.80 — Buetow, H.G. Philosophie und Gesellschaft im Denken Ernst Blochs. Berlin, 1963.

Phil 5585.19 — Büttner, A. Zweierlei Denken. Leipzig, 1910.
Phil 3790.1.97 — Büttner, Wilhelm. Hermann S. Reimarus als Metaphysiker. Inaug. Diss. Paderborn, 1909.

Phil 5590.486 — Bueva, Liudmila P. Sotsial'naia sreda i soznanie lichnosti. Moskva, 1968.

Phil 176.34.9F — Buffier, Claude. Cours de science. Paris, 1732.
Phil 176.34.5 — Buffier, Claude. First truths. London, 1780.
Phil 176.34 — Buffier, Claude. Oeuvres philosophiques. Paris, 1843.
Phil 5041.33 — Buffier, Claude. Les principis du raisonment exposez en deux logiques nouvéles. Paris, 1714.

Phil 974.3.155 — Bugaev, Boris N. Rudolf Steiner i gete v mirovozzrenii sovremennosti. Moskva, 1917.

Phil 3552.236 — Bugarski, G.M. Die Natur des Willens bei Leibniz. Leipzig, 1897.

Phil 1905.27.30 — Bugbee, H.G. The inward morning. State College, Pa., 1958.

Phil 3001.24 — Buggenhagen, Erich Arnold von. Contribuições à historia da filosofia alemã. São José, 1965.

Phil 4960.660 — Buggenhagen, Erich Arnold von. Pensamento filosófico brasileiro na atualidade. São Paulo, 1968.

Phil 7069.18.110 — The bugle. (Hicks, Betsey B.) N.Y., 1918.
Phil 5041.24 — Buhle, J.G. Einleitung in die allgemeine Logik und die Kritik der reinen Vernunft. Göttingen, 1795.

Phil 1701.3 — Buhle, J.G. Geschichte der neueren Philosophie. Göttlieb, 1800-1804. 6v.

Phil 1701.3.5 — Buhle, J.G. Histoire de la philosophie moderne. Paris, 1816. 6v.

Phil 801.8 — Buhle, T.G. Lehrbuch der Geschichte der Philosophie. Göttingen, 1796-1804. 8v.

Phil 8622.56 — Buhr, H. Der Glaube - was ist das? Pfullingen, 1963.
Phil 3246.298 — Buhr, Manfred. Akademie...Berlin. Berlin, 1962.
Phil 3030.4 — Buhr, Manfred. Der Anspruch der Vernunft. Berlin, 1968.
Phil 3246.298.5 — Buhr, Manfred. Revolution und Philosophie. Berlin, 1965.
Phil 3120.68.79 — Buhr, Manfred. Wilhelm Raimund Beyer, eine Bibliographie. Wien, 1967.

Phil 575.240 — Bui-Kim-Duong, J.B. L'épanouissement de la personnalité humaine par la conformité au Christ. Fribourg/Suisse, 1960.

Phil 9070.27 — The builder. (Lansing, Florence.) N.Y., 1936.
Phil 1722.6 — Builders of delusion. (Ward, Charles H.) Indianapolis, 1931.

Phil 9035.6 — Building a character. (Peabody, A.P.) Boston, 1887.
Phil 9380.4 — Building morale. (Nash, Jay Bryan.) N.Y., 1942.
Phil 978.6.9 — The building of the kosmos. (Besant, Annie.) London, 1894.

Phil 8951.30 — Building the city. (Brungs, Robert A.) N.Y., 1967.
Phil 2905.1.67 — Building the earth. (Teilhard de Chardin, Pierre.) London, 1965.

Phil 2905.1.65 — Building the earth. 1st American ed. (Teilhard de Chardin, Pierre.) Wilkes-Barre, Pa., 1965.

Phil 2075.10 — Building the human. (Johann, Robert O.) N.Y., 1968.
Phil 8691.11 — Buisson, F. La religion, la morale, et la science...quatre conference. 3. éd. Paris, 1904.

Phil 5649.24 — Bujeau, L.V. Le schematisme, psychologie de l'action. Paris, 1941.

Phil 8581.29 — Bukaty, A. Polska w apostazii cryli wtak zwanym russo-sławianismie. Paryż, 1842.

Phil 4803.454.100 — Bukaty, Antoni. Hoene-Wroński i jego udział w rozwinięciu ostatecznem wiedzy ludzkiej. Paryz, 1844.

Phil 5627.269.5 — Bukin, Viktor R. Psikhologiia veruiushchikh i ateisticheskoe vospitanie. Moskva, 1969.

Phil 7150.30 — Bula, C.A. Analisis estadistico del suicidio. Rosario, 1942.

Phil 4210.147 — Bulferetti, Luigi. Antonio Rosmini nella restaurazione. Firenze, 1942.

Phil 365.48 — Bulford, S. Man's unknown journey. London, 1941.
Phil 8581.54.5 — Bulgakov, C. Dva grada. Moskva, 1911.
Phil 8581.54 — Bulgakov, S. Sviet nevechernii. Moskva, 1917.
Phil 8656.35 — Bulgakov, S.N. Filosofiia imeni. Parizh, 1953.

Phil 176.116 — Bulgakov, S.N. Die Tragödie der Philosophie. Darmstadt, 1927.

Phil 4210.133 — Bulgarini, G.B. La storia della questione rosminiana. Milano, 1888.

Phil 165.295 — Bulgarska Akademiia na Naukite, Sofia. Vuprosi na dialekticheskiia materializum i na chastnite kauki. Sofiia, 1961.

Phil 75.50 — Bulgarska Akademiia na Naukite, Sofia. Biblioteka. Abstracts of Bulgarian scientific literature. Philosophy and pedagogics. Sofia. 1958+ 4v.

Phil 310.600 — Bulgarska Akademiia na Naukite, Sofia. Institut po Filosofiia. Sektsiia po Dialekticheski Materializum i Logika. Problemi na zakonite i kategoriite na dialektikata i logikata. Sofiia, 1965.

Phil 11.37 — Bulgarska Akademiiana naukite, Sofiia. Institut po Filosofiia. Izvestiia. Sofia. 1+ 14v.

Phil 3640.790 — Bulhof-Rutgers, Ilse Nina. Apollos Wiederkehr; eine Untersuchung der Rolle des Kreises in Nietzsches Denken. 's-Gravenhage, 1969.

Phil 6400.5.5 — Bulin, René. Eine besondere Art der Wortblindhut, Dyslexie. Wiesbaden, 1887.

Phil 9161.4 — Bulkeley, H.W. A word to parents. Philadelphia, 1858?
Phil 5400.110 — Bull, Nina. The attitude theory of emotion. N.Y., 1951.
Phil 7069.32.10 — Bull, Titus. Analysis of unusual experiences in healing relative to diseased minds. N.Y., 1932.
Phil 6311.17 — Bull, Titus. The imperative conquest. N.Y., 1936.
Phil 7069.33.15 — Bull, Titus. Nature, man and destiny. N.Y., 1933.
Phil 5520.96.80 — Bulla de Villaret, H. Une nouvelle orientation. Paris, 1965.

Phil 2655.1.82 — Bulle, F. Franziskus Hemsterhuis und der deutsche Irrationalismus. Jena, 1911.

Phil 58.6 — Bulletin, 1901-1914. (Société Française de Philosophie.) Paris. 1,1901+ 33v.

Phil 40.13 — Bulletin. (American Psychoanalytic Association.) N.Y. 1-8,1937-1952 4v.

Phil 40.20 — Bulletin. (Association Psychoanalytique de France.) Neully-sur-Seine. 4,1968+

Phil 11.39 — Bulletin. (British Psychological Society.) London. 11,1951+ 8v.

Phil 15.11 — Bulletin. (France. Centre d'Études et Recherches Psycho-Techniques.) Paris. 5,1956+ 9v.

Phil 15.5.10 — Bulletin. (Freethinker of America.) N.Y. 1,1937+ 5v.

Phil 48.10 — Bulletin. (Institut Général Psychologique, Paris.) Paris. 1-33,1900-1933 22v.

Phil 48.12 — Bulletin. (International Association of Applied Psychology.) Paris. 1,1952+ 3v.

Phil 48.7 — Bulletin. (International Institute for Psychical Research, Ltd.) London.

Phil 51.5 — Bulletin. (London. University. Council for Psychical Research.) London.

Phil 52.7.5 — Bulletin. (Massachusetts. Society for Social Hygiene.) Boston. 1-15,1931-1945

Phil 52.7 — Bulletin. (Massachusetts. Society for Social Hygiene.) Boston. 1918-1920

Phil 52.10 — Bulletin. (Menninger Clinic.) Topeka, Kan. 15,1951+ 19v.

Phil 9495.42 — Bulletin. (Oregon Social Hygiene Society.) Portland.
Phil 54.3 — Bulletin. (Oriental Esoteric Society, Washington, D.C.) Washington. 11-16,1915-1920 4v.

Phil 25.137 — Bulletin. (Philadelphia Associates for Psychoanalysis.) Philadelphia. 15,1965+ 7v,

Phil 3640.698 — Bulletin. (Société Française d'Études Nietzschéennes.) Paris.

Phil 58.20 — Bulletin. (Société Internationale pour l'Étude de la Philosophie Mediévale.) Louvain. 1,1959+ 4v.

Phil 53.4 — Bulletin. Philosophical series. (New Mexico. University.) Albuquerque. 1

Phil 62.2 — Bulletin. 2. ed. no.1-3. (Wyoming. University. Department of Psychology.) Laramie, Wyoming. 1919-

Phil 11.30 — Bulletin de psychologie édité par le Groupe d'études de psychologie de l'Université de Paris. Paris. 7,1953+ 19v.

Phil 15.65 — Bulletin mensuel de correspondance des groupes et adhérents fédérés. (Fédération française de la libre pensée.) Paris. 1890-1893

Phil 4080.3.345 — Bulletin of Croce studies in U.S. Madison, Wis. 1-5,1959-1964//

Phil 7150.90 — Bulletin of suicidology. Washington. 1,1967+
Phil 530.11.6 — Bullett, G.W. The English mystics. London, 1950.
Phil 3425.236 — Bullinger, A. Hegels Lehre vom Widerspruch. Dillingen, 1884.

Phil 8876.87 — Bullock, Arthur B. The supreme human tragedy and other essays. London, 1920.

Htn Phil 1930.5.95* — Bullock, T. The reasoning of Christ and his Apostles...sermons...Nov. and Dec., 1724. London, 1725.

Phil 4302.5 — Bullón y Fernández, E. Los precursores españoles de Bacon y Descartes. Salamanca, 1905.

Phil 8402.55 — Bullough, E. Aesthetics; lectures and essays. London, 1957.

Phil 5241.135 — Bulyne, D.E. Conflict. N.Y., 1960.
Phil 5440.31 — Bumke, O. Kultur und Ertartung. Berlin, 1922.
Phil 5722.14 — Bumke, O. Das Unterbewusstsein, eine Kritik. Berlin, 1922.

Phil 5722.14.2 — Bumke, O. Das Unterbewusstsein, eine Kritik. 2. Aufl. Berlin, 1926.

Phil 6311.14 — Bumke, Oswald. Die Psychoanalyse; eine Kritik. Berlin, 1931.

Phil 5241.51 — Bumke, Oswald. Psychologische Vorlesungen für Hörer aller Fakultälen. Wiesbaden, 1919.

Phil 5241.51.2 — Bumke, Oswald. Psychologische Vorlesungen für Hörer aller Fakultälen. 2. Aufl. München, 1923.

Phil 3483.16 — Bund, Hugo. Kant als Philosophie des Katholizismus. Berlin, 1913.

Phil 9343.7 — A bundle of letters to busy girls. (Dodge, Grace H.) N.Y., 1887.

Phil 7074.20.10 — The bundle of life. 1st ed. (Burke, Jane R.) N.Y., 1934.
Phil 5465.32 — Bundy, Murray W. The theory of imagination in classical and mediaeval thought. Urbana, 1927.

Phil 5241.44 — Bunge, Carlos O. Estudios filosóficos. Buenos Aires, 1919.

Phil 5241.44.5 — Bunge, Carlos O. Principes de psychologie. Paris, 1903.
Phil 8876.49 — Bunge, E.O. Il diritto. 3. ed. Torino, 1909.
Phil 745.3 — Bunge, Gustav von. Vitalismus und Mechanismus. Leipzig, 1886.

Phil 7069.68.50 — Bunge, H. Meesters van het verborgene. Amsterdam, 1968.
Phil 165.343 — Bunge, M. The critical approach to sciences and philosophy. N.Y., 1964.

Phil 5520.370 Bunge, Mario. Antologia semantica. Buenos Aires, 1960.
Phil 270.90 Bunge, Mario. Causality. Cambridge, 1959.
Phil 176.218 Bunge, Mario. The myth of simplicity. Englewood Cliff, N.J., 1963.
Phil 6060.42 Bunker, M.N. What handwriting tells about yourself. Cleveland, 1951.
Phil 5247.49 Bunkless psychology. (Hungerford, H.) Washington, 1933.
Phil 310.800 Bŭnkov, Angel I. Dialekticheskaia logika. Sofiia, 1971.
Phil 4822.4 Bunkov, Angel Iliev. Prinos kum istoriiata na bulgarskata filosofska misul'. Sofiia, 1943.
Phil 4822.4.5 Bunkov, Angel Iliev. Razvitie na filosofskata misul v Bulgariia. Sofiia, 1966.
Phil 176.35 Bunot, Albert Louis. Eléments de philosophie chretienne. Paris, 1869.
Phil 4803.496.30 Bunt na kolanach. (Kossak, Jerzy.) Warszawa, 1960.
Phil 2730.111 Buol, J. Die Anthropologie Maine de Birans. Winterthur, 1961.
Phil 4215.3.80 Buonaiui, E. Giuseppe Rensi. Roma, 1945.
Phil 525.67 Buonaiuti, E. Il misticismo medioevale. Pinerolo, 1928.
Phil 8581.45.15 Buonaiuti, Ernesto. Escursioni spirituali. Roma, 1921.
Phil 8581.45.20 Buonaiuti, Ernesto. Pellegrino di Roma. Bari, 1964.
Phil 8581.45.10 Buonaiuti, Ernesto. La religione nella vito dello spirito. Roma, 1926.
Phil 8581.45 Buonaiuti, Ernesto. Verso la luce. Foligno, 1924.
Phil 1540.20 Buonamici, G. La dottrina della conoscenza secondo Aristotele e la scuola. pt.1. Pisa, 1903.
Phil 4080.8.31 Il buono nel vero. Libri quattro. (Conti, Augusto.) Firenze, 1873. 2v.
Phil 615.1 Buozyńska, Hanna. Wartość i fakt. Wyd. 1. Warszawa, 1970.
Phil 2250.112 Buranelli, V. Josiah Royce. N.Y., 1964.
Phil 1506.14 Burch, G.B. Early medieval philosophy. N.Y., 1951.
Phil 3195.10.99 Burchard, H. Der entelechiebegriff bei Aristoteles und Driesch. Inaug. Diss. Quakenbrück, 1928.
Phil 5325.16 Burchardt, F. Die Vorstellungsreihe. Meissen, 1888.
Phil 8430.7 Burckhard, M. Ästhetik und Sozialwissenschaft. Stuttgart, 1895.
Phil 5590.225 Burckhardt, Georg. Charakter und Umwelt. München, 1956.
Phil 176.80.5 Burckhardt, Georg E. Individuum und Welt als Werk. München, 1920.
Phil 176.80 Burckhardt, Georg E. Was ist Individualismus? Leipzig, 1913.
Phil 176.80.10 Burckhardt, Georg E. Weltanschauungskrisis. v.1-2. Leipzig, 1925-26.
Phil 3483.60 Burckhardt, W. Kant's objectiver Idealismus. Naumburg, 1898.
Phil 6111.22 Burdach, K.F. Bau und Leben des Gehirns. Leipzig, 1819-26. 3v.
Phil 176.36 Burdach, K.F. Blicke ins Leben. v.1-4. Leipzig, 1842. 2v.
Phil 9010.19 Burder, George. Lawful amusements. London, 1805.
Phil 6671.18 Burdin, C. Historie académique du magnétisme animal. Paris, 1841.
Phil 8980.248 Burdiva, Alla I. Formuvannia komunistychnoi idei nosti osoby. Kyïv, 1970.
Phil 176.43 Burdon, W. Materials for thinking. London, 1820. 2v.
Phil 41.2 Pamphlet box. Bureau for Scientific Investigation Demonstration of Psychic Phenomena.
Phil 5500.40 Bureaucratic structure and decision-making. (Downs, Anthony.) Santa Monica, 1966.
Phil 3160.10.90 Burg, Josef. Konstitution und Gegenstand im logistischen Neupositivismus Rudolf Carnaps. Inaug. Diss. Leipzig, 1933.
Phil 3552.440 Burgelin, Pierre. Commentaire du Discourse de métaphysique de Leibniz. Paris, 1959.
Phil 672.165 Burgelin, Pierre. L'homme et le temps. Photoreproduction. Paris, 1945.
Phil 3483.13 Burger, D. Kants wipbegeerte, kortelijk verklaard. 's Gravenhage, 1881.
Phil 2115.125 Burger, D. Locke's bewijs voor het bestaan van God. Amersfoort, 1872.
Phil 8050.48 Burger, Fritz. Weltanschaungsprobleme und Lebenssysteme in der Kunst der Vergangenheit. München, 1918.
Phil 2493.80 Burger, K. Ein Beitrag zur Beurteilung Condillacs. Altenburg, 1885.
Htn Phil 3120.3.35* Burgeridicii, F. Idea philosophiae. Oxonii, 1667.
Htn Phil 3120.3.30* Burgeridicii, F. Institutionum logicarum. Cantabrigiae, 1647. 2 pam.
Htn Phil 3120.3.31* Burgeridicii, F. Institutionum logicarum. Libri duo. Cantabrigiae, 1660.
Phil 2340.10.180 Burgers, Johannes Martinus. Experience and conceptual activity. Cambridge, Mass., 1965.
X Cg Phil 176.37 Burgersdijck, F.P. Collegium physicum disputationibus XXXII absolutum. Lugdunum Batavorum, 1642.
Phil 176.37.10 Burgersdijck, F.P. Instituionum metaphysicarum libri II. n.p., 1647.
X Cg Phil 176.37.5 Burgersdijck, F.P. Institutionum metaphyricarum libri II. Hagae Comitis, 1657.
Phil 176.37.6 Burgersdijck, F.P. Institutionum metaphyricarum libri II. Lugdunum Batavorum, 1642.
Htn Phil 5041.25.2* Burgersdijck, Franco. Institutionum logicarum. Cantabrigiae, 1647-80. 3 pam.
Htn Phil 5041.25.3* Burgersdijck, Franco. Institutionum logicarum. Cantabrigiae, 1668-1670. 3 pam.
Htn Phil 5041.25* Burgersdijck, Franco. Institutionum logicarum. Lugdunum Batavorum, 1642-60. 2 pam.
Htn Phil 5041.25.4* Burgersdijck, Franco. Institutionum logicarum libri duo. Cantabrigiae, 1680. 3 pam.
Htn Phil 5041.26* Burgersdijck, Franco. Monitio logica, or An abstract and translation of Burgersdicius his Logick. London, 1697.
Htn Phil 8876.35* Burgersdyck, F. Idea philosophiae tum moralis. Oxoniae, 1631.
Phil 8876.35.3 Burgersdyck, F. Idea philosophiae tum moralis. 2a ed. Lugduni, 1629.
Htn Phil 9005.1* Burges, T. The art of excelling. Providence, 1799.
Htn Phil 9515.1* Burges, T. Solitude and society contrasted. Providence, 1797.
Phil 5400.1 Burgess, S.W. Historical illustrations of the origin and progress of the passions. London, 1825. 2v.
Htn Phil 8876.36.4* Burgh, J. The dignity of human nature. Boston, 1794.
Htn Phil 8876.36.5* Burgh, J. The dignity of human nature. Hartford, 1802.
Phil 8876.36 Burgh, J. The dignity of human nature. London, 1754.
Phil 8876.36.3 Burgh, J. The dignity of human nature. London, 1767. 2v.
Phil 8876.36.6 Burgh, J. The dignity of human nature. N.Y., 1812.
Phil 9341.11 Burgh, J. Directions prudential, moral, religious. London, 1755.
Phil 332.21 Burgh, W.G. Knowledge of the individual. London, 1939.
Phil 8878.57 Burgh, W.G. de. From morality to religion. London, 1938.

Phil 176.153 Burgmüller, H. Zur Klärung der Begriffe. 1. Aufl. München, 1947.
Phil 8400.14A Burgum, E.B. The new criticism; an anthology of modern aesthetics. N.Y., 1930.
Phil 3850.27.101.5 Buri, Fritz. Albert Schweitzer und Karl Jaspers. Zürich, 1950.
Phil 3850.27.200 Buri, Fritz. Albert Schweitzer und unsere Zeit. Zürich, 1947.
Phil 3850.27.101 Buri, Fritz. Christentum und Kulture bei Albert Schweitzer. Beru, 1941.
Phil 8622.68 Buri, Fritz. Denkender Glaube. Bern, 1966.
Phil 8610.958.5 Buri, Fritz. Die Substanz des christlichen Glaubens, ihr Verlust und ihre Neugewinnung. Tübingen, 1960.
Phil 5080.3 Burkamp, W. Begriff und Beziehung. Leipzig, 1927.
Phil 5041.50 Burkamp, W. Logik. Berlin, 1932.
Phil 176.124 Burkamp, Wilhelm. Die Struktur der Ganzheiten. Berlin, 1929.
Phil 3120.20 Burkamp, Wilhelm. Wirklichkeit und Sinn. v.1-2. Berlin, 1938.
Phil 8581.60 Burkart, Anna D. The person in religion. Thesis. Philadelphia, 1930.
Phil 7069.70.15 Burke, Clara Baker. The ghosts about us. Philadelphia, 1969.
Phil 8402.14.2 Burke, E. A philosophical enquiry into the origin of our ideas. 3rd ed. London, 1761.
Phil 8402.14A Burke, E. A philosophical enquiry into the origin of our ideas of the sublime and beautiful. 6th ed. London, 1770.
Phil 8402.14.7 Burke, E. A philosophical enquiry into the origin of our ideas of the sublime and beautiful. Philadelphia, 1806.
Phil 8402.14.5 Burke, E. A philosophical enquiry into the origin of our ideas of the sublime and beautiful. N.Y., 1829.
Phil 8402.14.10 Burke, E. A philosophical enquiry into the origin of our ideas of the sublime and beautiful. Baltimore, 1833.
Phil 8402.14.20 Burke, E. A philosophical inquiry into the origin of our ideas of the sublime and beautiful. London, 1958.
Phil 8402.14.15 Burke, E. Philosophische Untersuchungen über den Ursprung unsrer Begriffe vom Erhaben und Schönen. Riga, 1773.
Phil 176.122.10 Burke, J.B. The emergence of life. London, 1931.
Phil 176.122 Burke, J.B. The mystery of life. London, 1931.
Phil 7074.20.10 Burke, Jane R. The bundle of life. 1st ed. N.Y., 1934.
Phil 7074.20.6 Burke, Jane R. Let us in. N.Y., 1931.
Phil 7074.20.5 Burke, Jane R. Let us in. 1st ed. N.Y., 1931.
Phil 7074.20 Burke, Jane R. The one way. N.Y., 1922.
Phil 7074.20.1 Burke, Jane R. The one way. N.Y., 1923.
Phil 7057.8.15 Burke, Jane Revere. Messages on healing understood to have been received by William James. N.Y., 1936.
Phil 8581.106A Burke, K. The rhetoric of religion. Boston, 1961.
Phil 5520.80 Burke, Kenneth. A grammar of motives. N.Y., 1945.
Phil 176.137A Burke, Kenneth. Permanence and change. N.Y., 1935.
Phil 176.137.2 Burke, Kenneth. Permanence and change. 2nd ed. Los Altos, Calif., 1954.
Phil 1182.52 Burkert, Walter. Weisheit und Wissenschaft. Nürnberg, 1962.
Phil 2200.5.80 Burkhardt, F. The cleavage in our culture. Boston, 1952.
Phil 585.190 Burkhardt, Hans. Dimensionen menschlicher Wirklichkeit. Schweinfurt, 1965.
Phil 3925.16.115 Burkhardt, Jörg R. Die Bildtheorie der Sprache. München, 1965.
Phil 1135.63 Burle, C. Nostion de droit naturel. Trevoux, 1908.
Htn Phil 1106.5.5* Burley, W. Liber de vita et moribus philosophorum. Tübingen, 1886.
Htn Phil 1106.5.6* Burley, W. Vita omnium philosophorum et poetarum. n.p., n.d.
Htn Phil 1106.5* Burley, W. Von dem Leben, sitten und freyen Sprüchen der alten Philosophie. Ausburg, 1519.
Htn Phil 5000.1* Burley, Walter. Expositio super artem veterem Porphyrii et Aristotelis. Pts.1,2. Manuscripts. n.p., 1442?
Phil 8581.50 Burlingame, E.L. Current discussion. N.Y., 1878. 2v.
Phil 5400.118 Burloud, A. Psychologie de la sensibilité. Paris, 1954.
Phil 9035.86 Burloud, Albert. Le caractère. Paris, 1942.
Phil 5241.75.12 Burloud, Albert. La pensée conceptuelle. Thèse. Paris, 1927.
Phil 5241.75 Burloud, Albert. La pensée d'après les recherches experimentales de H.J. Watt, de Messer et de Bühler. Paris, 1927.
Phil 5241.75.2 Burloud, Albert. La pensée d'après les recherches experimentales de H.J. Watt, de Messer et de Bühler. Thèse. Paris, 1927.
Phil 5241.75.15 Burloud, Albert. Principles d'une psychologie des tendances. Paris, 1938.
Phil 5402.17 Burlton Allen, A.H. Pleasure and instinct. London, 1930.
Phil 3425.305 Burman, E.O. Hegels rättsfilosofi. Uppsala, 1939.
Phil 8656.18 Burman, E.O. Om teismen. Upsala, 1886.
Phil 3246.187 Burman, E.O. Die Transscendentalphilosophie Fichte's und Schelling's. Upsala, 1891.
Phil 9341.4 Burnap, G.W. Lectures on the sphere and duties of woman. Baltimore, 1841.
Phil 9341.4.5 Burnap, G.W. Lectures to young men. Baltimore, 1840.
Phil 176.88 Burne, C.D. The contact between minds. London, 1923.
Phil 176.88.10 Burne, C.D. The horizon of experience. N.Y., 1934.
Phil 1106.8 Burnet, J. Greek philosophy. pt. 1. London, 1914.
Phil 1106.8.4 Burnet, J. Greek philosophy. pt.1. London, 1928.
Phil 1133.1.12A Burnet, John. Early Greek philosophers. 4th ed. London, 1952.
X Cg Phil 1133.1.2 Burnet, John. Early Greek philosophy. London, 1892.
Phil 8626.15.7 Burnet, Thomas. Burnett's state of the dead. London, 1725-28. 4 pam.
Phil 8626.15.5 Burnet, Thomas. De statu mortuorum et resurgentium tractatus of the state of the dead. London, 1728. 5 pam.
Htn Phil 2115.129* Burnet, Thomas. Remarks upon an essay concerning humane understanding. London, 1697. 3 pam.
Phil 8691.8.9 Burnet, Thomas. The sacred theory of the earth. Glasgow, 1753. 2v.
Phil 8691.8.4 Burnet, Thomas. The sacred theory of the earth. London, 1719. 2v.
Phil 8691.8.7 Burnet, Thomas. The sacred theory of the earth. London, 1722-26. 2v.
Phil 8691.8.15 Burnet, Thomas. The sacred theory of the earth. London, 1965.
Phil 8691.8.12 Burnet, Thomas. The sacred theory of the earth. 7. ed. London, 1759. 2v.
Htn Phil 8691.8.5* Burnet, Thomas. Telluris theoria sacra. v.1-2. London, 1681-89.
Htn Phil 8691.8F* Burnet, Thomas. The theory of the earth. v.1-4. London, 1684-90.

Htn Phil 8691.8.2F* Burnet, Thomas. The theory of the earth. 2. ed. London, 1690-91. 4 pam.

Phil 8626.15.9 Burnet, Thomas. A treatise concerning the state of the departed souls. London, 1633.

Phil 8626.15.12 Burnet, Thomas. A treatise concerning the state of the departed souls. 2. ed. London, 1739.

Phil 6111.17 Burnett, C.M. Philosophy of spirits in relation to matter. London, 1850.

Phil 5645.1 Burnett, S.M. Theories of color-perception. Philadelphia, 1884.

Phil 850.2 Burnett, T. Archaeologiae philosophicae. v.1-2. London, 1728-33.

Phil 850.2.5 Burnett, T. Doctrina antigua. London, 1736. 3 pam.
Phil 585.10 Burnett, Whit. The spirit of man. 1st ed. N.Y., 1958.
Phil 165.70 Burnett, Whit. This is my philosophy. 1st ed. N.Y., 1957.
Phil 8626.15.7 Burnett's state of the dead. (Burnet, Thomas.) London, 1725-28. 4 pam.

Phil 176.126 Burnham, James. Introductioon to philosophical analysis. N.Y., 1932.

Phil 5645.59 Burnham, R.W. Color. N.Y., 1963.
Phil 1750.788.2 Burnier, Michel Antoine. Choice of action; the French existentialists on the political front line. 1st American ed. N.Y., 1968.

Phil 1750.788 Burnier, Michel Antoine. Les existentialistes et la politique. Paris, 1966.

Phil 5520.124A The burning fountain. (Wheelwright, Phillip Ellis.) Bloomington, 1954.

Phil 5520.124.2 The burning fountain. (Wheelwright, Phillip Ellis.) Bloomington, 1964.

Phil 5520.124.3 The burning fountain. (Wheelwright, Phillip Ellis.) Bloomington, 1968.

Phil 176.38 Burnouf, E.L. La vie et la pensée. Paris, 1886.
Phil 1701.5 Burns, C. Delisle. The growth of modern philosophy. London, 1909.

Phil 1865.188 Burns, J.H. Jeremy Bentham and University College. London, 1962.

Phil 3910.130 Burns, John V. Dynamism in the cosmology of Christian Wolf. 1st ed. N.Y., 1966.

Phil 5650.50 Burns, William. Noise and man. London, 1968.
Phil 5465.188 Burnshaw, Stanley. The seamless web; language thinking. N.Y., 1970.

Phil 5500.37 Buron, Robert. Decision-making in the development field. Paris, 1966.

Phil 4210.116.20 Buroni, Giuseppe. Della nuova dichiarazione quasi ultima della S. Congregazione dell'Indice. Torino, 1882.

Phil 4210.116F Buroni, Giuseppe. Dell'essere e del conoscere. Torino, 1877.

Phil 4210.116.5 Buroni, Giuseppe. Nozioni di ontologia. 2a ed. Torino, 1878.

Phil 4210.116.10 Buroni, Giuseppe. Risposta 1a al padre Cornoldi in difesa delle nozioni di ontologia. Torino, 1878.

Phil 8402.26.5A Burov, A.I. Das ästhetische Wesen. Berlin, 1958.
Phil 8402.26 Burov, A.I. Esteticheskaia sushchnost' iskusstva. Moskva, 1956.

Phil 5627.31 Burr, Anna Robeson. Religious confessions and confessants. Boston, 1914.

Phil 6951.9 Burr, Colonel Bell. Handbook of psychology and mental disease. 4. ed. Philadelphia, 1915.

Phil 6951.9.5 Burr, Colonel Bell. Practical psychology and psychiatry. 5. ed. Philadelphia, 1922.

Phil 8691.4 Burr, E.F. Pater mundi. 1st series. Boston, 1870.
Phil 8691.4.2 Burr, E.F. Pater mundi. 2nd series. Boston, 1873.
Phil 585.143 Burr, Harold S. The nature of man and the meaning of existence. Springfield, 1962.

Phil 5241.91 Burridge, William. A new physiological psychology. London, 1933.

Phil 8581.25 Burris, M.A. Creation's way. Smithville, Ohio, 1911.
Phil 8581.42 Burroughs, John. Accepting the universe. Boston, 1920.
Phil 5643.36 Burrow, N.J. The determination of the position. Baltimore, 1909.

Phil 6311.22 Burrow, T. The biology of human conflict. N.Y., 1937.
Phil 6311.22.5 Burrow, T. Preconscious foundations of human experience. N.Y., 1964.

Phil 6951.20 Burrow, T. The structure of insanity. London, 1932.
Phil 5241.97 Burrow, Trigant. Altering frames of reference in the sphere of human behavior. N.Y., 1937.

Phil 5241.97.10 Burrow, Trigant. The neurosis of man. London, 1949.
Phil 5241.97.5 Burrow, Trigant. Science and man's behavior. N.Y., 1953.
Phil 5241.97.15 Burrow, Trigant. A search for man's sanity. N.Y., 1958.
Phil 5374.45.2 Burrow, Trigant. The social basis of consciousness. N.Y., 1927.

Phil 1106.6 Burt, B.C. Brief history of Greek philosophy. Boston, 1889.

Phil 1701.4 Burt, Bery C. History of modern philosophy. Chicago, 1892. 2v.

Phil 5274.8 Burt, Cyril. The factors of the mind. London, 1940.
Phil 5241.111 Burt, Cyril. Intelligence and fertility. London, 1947.
Phil 176.224 Burth, Edwin Arthur. In search of philosophic understanding. N.Y., 1966.

Htn Phil 1905.9.9* Burthogge, R. An essay upon reason. London, 1694. 3 pam.

Phil 1905.9.30 Burthogge, R. Of the soul of the world of particular souls. London, 1699.

Phil 1905.9.6 Burthogge, R. The philosophical writings. Chicago, 1921.
Htn Phil 2115.107* Burthogge, Richard. An essay upon reason and the nature of spirits. London, 1694-1755. 3 pam.

Phil 6980.148 Burton, A. Case histories in clinical and abnormal psychology. v.2. N.Y., 1947.

Phil 6311.45 Burton, Arthur. Case studies in counseling and psychotherapy. Englewood Cliffs, N.J., 1959.

Phil 176.66 Burton, Asa. Essays. Portland, 1824.
Phil 7069.35.7 Burton, Eva. A natural bridge to cross. N.Y., 1935.
Phil 1865.80 Burton, J.H. Introduction to study of Bentham's works. Edinburgh, 1843.

Phil 2050.80.9A Burton, J.H. Letters of eminent persons to Hume. Edinburgh, 1849.

Phil 2050.80A Burton, J.H. Life and correspondence of Hume. Edinburgh, 1846. 2v.

Phil 7069.44 Burton, Jean. Heyday of a wizard. 1. ed. N.Y., 1944.
Phil 5875.60 Burton, Lindy. Vulnerable children; three studies of children in conflict. London, 1968.

Phil 8620.20 Burton, Marion LeRoy. The problem of evil. Chicago, 1909.
Phil 8620.2 Burton, W. Cheering views of man and providence. Boston, 1832.

Phil 8402.9 Burton, W. The scenery-shower, with word-paintings of the beautiful. Boston, 1844.

Phil 8581.76 Burtt, Edwin A. Types of religious philosophy. 1. ed. N.Y., 1939.

NEDL Phil 5041.40 Burtt, Edwin Arthur. Principles and problems of right thinking. N.Y., 1928.

Phil 5041.40.5 Burtt, Edwin Arthur. Principles and problems of right thinking. N.Y., 1931.

Phil 5041.40.10 Burtt, Edwin Arthur. Principles and problems of right thinking. N.Y., 1938.

Phil 5041.40.20 Burtt, Edwin Arthur. Right thinking. 3rd ed. N.Y., 1946.
Phil 5850.145.50 Burtt, H.E. Applied psychology. N.Y., 1948.
Phil 5850.145.50.5 Burtt, H.E. Applied psychology. 2. ed. Englewood Cliffs, 1957.

Phil 8610.913A Bury, J.B. A history of freedom of thought. N.Y., 1913.
Phil 8610.913.5A Bury, J.B. A history of freedom of thought. 2. ed. London, 1952.

Phil 665.73 Bury, R.G. The devil's puzzle. Dublin, 1949.
Phil 9590.25 Burzhuaznaia moral' - oruzhie imperialisticheskoi reaktsii. (Shishkin, A.F.) Moskva, 1951.

Phil 176.130 Buscalioni, C.M. Carolus Michael Buscalioni Monregalensis ut philosophiae rationalis professor crearetur. Turin? 1848.

Phil 1535.3 Buscarini, G. Discussioni di filosofia razionale. Milano, 1857. 2v.

Phil 8951.19.5 Busch, F. Découvertes d'un bibliophile. 2. éd. Strassburg, 1843.

Phil 8951.19.2 Pamphlet vol. Busch, F. Découvertes d'un bibliophile. 5 pam.

Phil 3808.190 Busch, Hugo. Das Testament Arthur Schopenhauer. Wiesbaden, 1950.

Phil 5627.6.20A Busch, K.A. William James als Religionsphilosoph. Göttingen, 1911.

Phil 3808.81 Busch, O. Arthur Schopenhauer. Heidelberg, 1877.
Phil 801.7 Buschings, A.F. Grundriss einer Geschichte de Philosophie. Berlin, 1772-4. 2v.

Phil 9495.135.5 Buschke, A. Sex habits. N.Y., 1933.
Phil 282.11 Busco, Pierre. Les cosmogonies modernes. Paris, 1924.
Phil 282.11.5 Busco, Pierre. Les cosmogonies modernes. Thèse. Paris, 1924.

Phil 6750.259 Busemann, Adolf. Psychologie der intelligenz defekte. München, 1959.

Phil 6750.259.2 Busemann, Adolf. Psychologie der intelligenz Defekte. München, 1963.

Phil 5592.192 Busemann, Adolf. Weltanschauung in psychologischer Sicht. München, 1967.

Phil 6671.12 Bush, G. Mesmer and Swedenborg. N.Y., 1847.
Phil 5535.2 Bush, Robert Ray. Stochastic models for learning. N.Y., 1964.

Phil 5535.2.5 Bush, Robert Ray. Studies in mathematical learning theory. Stanford, 1959.

Phil 331.2.30 Bush, W.T. Avenarius and the stand point of pure experience. N.Y., 1905.

Phil 6990.25 Bushenskii, N. Kniga chudes. Pesch', 1860.
Phil 5811.6 Bushnan, J.S. The philosophy of instinct and reason. Edinburgh, 1837.

Phil 8581.16 Bushnell, H. Nature and the supernatural. N.Y., 1858.
Phil 8581.16.2 Bushnell, H. Nature and the supernatural. N.Y., 1859.
Phil 9375.5 Business. (Platt, J.) London, 1876.
Phil 8950.4 The business of living. (Anderson, L.D.) N.Y., 1923.
Phil 165.438 The business of reason. (MacIntosh, John James.) London, 1969.

Phil 5850.278.15 Business psychology. (Münsterberg, H.) Chicago, 1915.
Phil 5585.245 Business Research Limited, Bangkok. Esthetic perception of villagers in Northeast Thailand, a pilot study. Bangkok? 1965.

Phil 3821.4 Busolt, Georg. Grundzuge der Erkenntnisztheorie Spinozas. Berlin, 1875.

Phil 5421.20.95 Buss, Arnold H. The psychology of aggression. N.Y., 1961.
Phil 6976.10 Buss, Arnold H. Theories of schizophrenia. N.Y., 1969.
Phil 6111.13 Busse, L. Geist und Körper, Seele und Leib. Leipzig, 1903.

Phil 6111.13.2 Busse, L. Geist und Körper, Seele und Leib. 2. Aufl. Leipzig, 1913.

Phil 1701.9.5 Busse, Ludwig. Die Weltanschauungen der grossen Philosophie der Neuzeit. 6e Aufl. Leipzig, 1917.

Phil 3425.264 Busse, Martin. Phänomenologie des Geistes und der Staat. Berlin, 1931.

Phil 3552.295 Bussenius, Karl. Über die Theodicee des Leibniz. Halle, 1876.

Phil 5751.4 Bussey, Gertrude C. Typical recent conceptions of freedom. Thesis. Greenfield, 1917.

Phil 5628.10.20 Busson, Claude Ignace. Premières [-secondes] lettres sur l'extatique de Niéderbronn et sur ses révélations. Besançon, 1849.

Phil 623.23.10A Busson, Henri. De Petrarque á Descartes. Paris, 1957.
Phil 623.24A Busson, Henri. La pensée religieuse française de Charron à Pascal. Paris, 1933.

Phil 623.23.5 Busson, Henri. Les sources et le développement du rationalisme dans la littérature française de la Renaissance. Paris, 1922.

Phil 623.23 Busson, Henri. Les sources et le développement du rationalisme dans la littérature française de la Renaissance. Thèse. Paris, 1922.

Phil 1750.772 Bustos, Ismael. El sentido existencial de la política. Santiago de Chile, 1956.

Phil 730.30 Butchvarov, Panayot. Resemblance and identity. Bloomington, 1966.

Phil 8505.8.5 Butinova, M.S. Estestvoznanie i religiia. Moskva, 1957.
Phil 9530.1 Butler, B.F. How to get rich. Boston, 1888.
Phil 9341.6 Butler, C. The American gentleman. Philadelphia, 1836.
Phil 9341.6.9 Butler, C. The American lady. Philadelphia, 1841.
Phil 525.35 Butler, Cuthbert. Western mysticism. London, 1922.
Phil 525.35.8 Butler, Cuthbert. Western mysticism: the teaching of Augustine, Gregory and Bernard. 3rd ed. London, 1967.

Phil 525.35.5 Butler, Cuthbert. Western mysticism. 2d ed. London, 1927.
Phil 6111.32.5 Butler, Hiram Erastus. Practical methods to insure success. 31st ed. Applegate, Calif., 1915.

Phil 6111.32 Butler, Hiram Erastus. Practical methods to insure success. 33rd ed. Applegate, Calif., 1920.

Phil 176.157 Butler, J. Four philosophies. N.Y., 1951.
Phil 5241.89 Butler, J.R. Human nature. N.Y., 1933.
Phil 5241.89.10 Butler, J.R. Human psychology. N.Y., 1936.
Phil 5274.10 Butler, John M. Quantitative naturalistic research. Englewood Cliffs, 1963.

Phil 1900.41 Butler, Joseph. The analogy of religion, natural and revealed, to the constitution and course of nature. London, 1878.

Phil 1900.43 Butler, Joseph. The analogy of religion, natural and revealed. 1st ed. London, 1906.

Phil 1900.34 Butler, Joseph. Analogy of religion. Boston, 1809.

	Phil 1900.35	Butler, Joseph. Analogy of religion. Cambridge, 1827.
	Phil 1900.37.3.6	Butler, Joseph. Analogy of religion. Cincinnati, 1849.
Htn	Phil 1900.30*	Butler, Joseph. Analogy of religion. London, 1736.
Htn	Phil 1900.30.2*	Butler, Joseph. Analogy of religion. London, 1736.
	Phil 1900.31	Butler, Joseph. Analogy of religion. London, 1740.
	Phil 1900.33	Butler, Joseph. Analogy of religion. London, 1798.
	Phil 1900.36	Butler, Joseph. Analogy of religion. London, 1834.
	Phil 1900.37.15	Butler, Joseph. Analogy of religion. London, 1857.
	Phil 1900.39	Butler, Joseph. Analogy of religion. London, 1860.
	Phil 1900.40.2	Butler, Joseph. Analogy of religion. London, 1873.
	Phil 1900.40	Butler, Joseph. Analogy of religion. London, 1884.
	Phil 1900.37	Butler, Joseph. Analogy of religion. N.Y., 1839.
	Phil 1900.37.3	Butler, Joseph. Analogy of religion. N.Y., 1843.
	Phil 1900.38	Butler, Joseph. Analogy of religion. Philadelphia, 1857.
	Phil 1900.32A	Butler, Joseph. Analogy of religion. Bishop of Gloucester. Boston, 1793.
Htn	Phil 1900.32.6*	Butler, Joseph. Analogy of religion. Bishop of Gloucester. Boston, 1793.
	Phil 1900.35.5	Butler, Joseph. Analogy of religion. 2d ed. Cambridge, 1830.
	Phil 1900.37.3.5A	Butler, Joseph. Analogy of religion. 20th ed. N.Y., 1848.
	Phil 1900.39.5	Butler, Joseph. Analogy of religion. 20th ed. N.Y., 1860.
	Phil 1900.28	Butler, Joseph. Analogy of religion and ethical discourses. Boston, 1860.
	Phil 1900.25	Butler, Joseph. Analogy of religion and sermons. London, 1852.
	Phil 1900.70	Butler, Joseph. Ethical discourses. Philadelphia, 1855.
	Phil 1900.69	Butler, Joseph. Fifteen sermons. London, 1836.
	Phil 1900.60.4	Butler, Joseph. Fifteen sermons and six sermons. 4th ed. London, 1749.
	Phil 1900.60.5	Butler, Joseph. Fifteen sermons and six sermons. 5th ed. London, n.d.
	Phil 1900.60.2.6	Butler, Joseph. Fifteen sermons and six sermons. 6th ed. London, 1792.
	Phil 1900.60	Butler, Joseph. Fifteen sermons preached at the Rolls Chapel. London, 1726.
	Phil 1900.62	Butler, Joseph. Five sermons preached at the Rolls Chapel. N.Y., 1950.
	Phil 1900.60.15	Butler, Joseph. Sermons. Cambridge, 1827.
	Phil 1900.76	Butler, Joseph. Sermons I, II, III upon human nature. Edinburgh, 1888.
	Phil 1900.75	Butler, Joseph. Six sermons on moral subjects. Cambridge, 1849.
	Phil 1900.15	Butler, Joseph. Whole works. London, 1847.
	Phil 1900.19	Butler, Joseph. Whole works. London, 1900. 2v.
	Phil 1900.9	Butler, Joseph. Works. Edinburgh, 1804. 2v.
	Phil 1900.10	Butler, Joseph. Works. Oxford, 1807. 2v.
	Phil 1900.9.5	Butler, Joseph. Works. Oxford, 1844. 2v.
	Phil 1900.9.9	Butler, Joseph. Works. Oxford, 1849-50. 2v.
	Phil 1900.11	Butler, Joseph. Works. Oxford, 1896. 2v.
	Phil 1900.9.2	Butler, Joseph. Works. v.1-2. Cambridge, 1827.
	Phil 176.48	Butler, N.M. Philosophy. N.Y., 1908.
	Phil 176.48.3	Butler, N.M. Philosophy. N.Y., 1938.
	Phil 165.332	Butler, R.J. Analytical philosophy. Oxford, 1962.
	Phil 165.332.2	Butler, R.J. Analytical philosophy. 2nd series. Oxford, 1965.
	Phil 2280.5.110A	Butler, Richard. The mind of Santayana. Chicago, 1955.
Htn	Phil 5545.4*	Butler, S. Unconscious memory. London, 1880.
	Phil 5722.3A	Butler, S. Unconscious memory. N.Y., 1911.
Htn	Phil 8656.11*	Butler, Samuel. God the known and God the unknown. London, 1909.
	Phil 1106.7	Butler, W.A. Lectures on the history of ancient philosophy. Cambridge, 1856. 2v.
	Phil 1106.7.5	Butler, W.A. Lectures on the history of ancient philosophy. Philadelphia, 1857. 2v.
	Phil 1900.81.3	Butler. (Collins, W.L.) Edinburgh, 1881.
	Phil 1900.81	Butler. (Collins, W.L.) Philadelphia, 1881.
	Phil 1900.98	Butler and Hume on religion. (Jeffner, Anders.) Stockholm, 1966.
	Phil 1900.96	Butler's ethics. (Carlsson, P.A.) The Hague, 1964.
	Phil 1900.95	Butler's moral philosophy. (Duncan-Jones, A.) Harmondsworth, 1952.
	Phil 3160.10.95	Butrick, Richard. Carnap on meaning and analyticity. The Hague, 1970.
	Phil 7069.44.20	Butterworth, G.W. Spiritualism and religion. London, 1944.
	Phil 6111.40	Butts, Bryan J. Hints on metaphysics. Boston, 1885.
	Phil 8050.24	Buyer, Raymond. Histoire de l'esthétique. Paris, 1961.
	Phil 8876.37	Buys, J. De statibus hominum. Moguntiae, 1613.
	Phil 5520.54	Buyssens, T. Langage et pensée, vie et matière. Brasschaat, 1928.
	Phil 5241.160	Buytendijk, F.J.J. Academische redeväringen. Utrecht, 1961.
	Phil 585.45	Buytendijk, F.J.J. Das Menschliche. Stuttgart, 1958.
	Phil 5649.36	Buytendijk, Frederik Jacobus Johannes. Algemene theorie der menselijke houding en beweging als verbinding en tegenstelling van de fysiologische en de psychologische beschouwig. 3. Druk. Utrecht, 1964.
	Phil 5811.15.25	Buytendijk, Frederik Jacobus Johannes. Mensch und Tier. Hamburg, 1958.
	Phil 5811.15.10A	Buytendijk, Frederik Jacobus Johannes. The mind of the dog. Boston, 1936.
	Phil 6111.80.5	Buytendijk, Frederik Jacobus Johannes. Prolegomena einer antropologischen Physiologie. Salzburg, 1967.
	Phil 6111.80	Buytendijk, Frederik Jacobus Johannes. Prolegomena van een antropologische fysiologie. Utrecht, 1965.
	Phil 5811.15	Buytendijk, Frederik Jacobus Johannes. Psychologie der dieren. Haarlem, 1920.
	Phil 5811.15.5	Buytendijk, Frederik Jacobus Johannes. Psychologie des animaux. Paris, 1928.
	Phil 5811.15.15	Buytendijk, Frederik Jacobus Johannes. Wege zum Verständnis der Tiere. Zürich, 1940?
	Phil 5811.15.20	Buytendijk, Frederik Jacobus Johannes. Wesen und Sinn des Spiels. Berlin, 1933.
	Phil 5649.26	Buyteuddigk, Frederik J.J. Attitudes et mouvements. Paris, 1957.
	Phil 8402.2	Buzin, Germain. Le crépuscule des images. Paris, 1946.
	Phil 6111.58	Buzzard, E.F. An outline of neurology and its outlook. London, 1929.
	Phil 4963.1	Buzzi, E. De donde venimos. Lima, 1942.
	Phil 9182.4.5	By the fireside. (Wagner, Charles.) N.Y., 1904.
	Phil 5627.153	By the grace of God. London, 1937.
	Phil 7060.92.20	By ways of ghost-land. (O'Donnell, Elliot.) London, 1911.
	Phil 332.42	Bychko, Ihor Valentynovych. Poznanie i svoboda. Moskva, 1969.
	Phil 8980.252.3	Bychkova, N.V. Moral' kak ee ponimaiut kommunisty. Izd. 3. Moskva, 1966.
	Phil 8980.252	Bychkova, N.V. Moral'kak ee ponimaiut kommunisty. Moskva, 1962.
	Phil 8980.252.2	Bychkova, N.V. Moral'kak ee ponimaiut kommunisty. 2. izd. Moskva, 1960.
	Phil 11.53	Bydgoskie Towarzystwo naukowe. Wydział nauk Humanistycznych. Komisja Filozofii i Pedagogiki. Prace. Bydgoszcz. 1,1969+
	Phil 176.139	Byers, R.P. Superuniversity studies. Boston, 1936.
	Phil 705.17	Byers, R.P. Transcendental values. Boston, 1925.
	Phil 9161.8	Byford, W.H. The philosophy of domestic life. Boston, 1869.
	Phil 4575.93	Bygdén, Anders L. Benjamin Höijer. Akademisk afhandling. Upsala, 1872.
	Phil 8402.43	Byk, S. Physiologie des Schönen. Leipzig, 1878.
	Phil 1133.15	Byk, S.A. Die vorsokratische Philosophie der Griechen. Leipzig, 1876-77. 2v.
	Phil 1870.182	Bykhovskii, Bernard E. Dzhordzh Berkli. Moskva, 1970.
	Phil 3235.128	Bykhovskii, Bernard E. Liudvig Feierbakh. Moskva, 1967.
	Phil 930.67	Bykov, Fedor S. Zarozhdenie obshchestvenno-politicheskoi i filosofskoi mysli v kitae. Moskva, 1966.
	Phil 8581.17	Byles, J.B. Foundations of religion in the mind and heart of man. London, 1875.
	Phil 7009.145.1	Byrd, Elizabeth. A strange and seeing time. London, 1971.
	Phil 5590.453	Byrne, Donn Erwin. Personality research; a book of readings. Englewood Cliffs, N.J., 1966.
	Phil 5145.4	Byrne, Edmund F. Probability and opinion. The Hague, 1968.
	Phil 7069.65.37	Byrne, Patrick. Irish ghost stories. Cork, 1968.
	Phil 8980.346	Byt' chelovekom na zemle. (Dzhafarli, Teimuraz M.) Moskva, 1968.
	Phil 4768.2.5	Bytie i soznanie o meste psikhologii. (Rubinshtein, Sergei L.) Moskva, 1957.
	Phil 5135.7.5	Bzhalava, Iosif T. Psikhologiia ustanovki i kibernetika. Moskva, 1966.
	Phil 5135.7	Bzhalava, Iosif T. Vospriiatie i ustanovka. Tbilisi, 1965.
	Phil 282.4.9	C. Batteux von seine nachahmungs Theorie in Deutsch. (Schenker, M.) Leipzig, 1909.
	Phil 2150.21.80	C.A. Mace: a symposium. (Carver, Vida.) London, 1962.
	Phil 6319.1.212	C.G. Jung. (Bennet, E.A.) N.Y., 1962.
	Phil 5249.13.28	C.G. Jung: psychological reflections. (Jung, Carl G.) Princeton, 1970.
	Phil 6319.1.225	C.G. Jung and Hermann Hesse. (Serreano, Miguel.) London, 1966.
	Phil 6319.1.265	C.G. Jung in Selbstzeugnissen und Bilddokumenten. (Wehr, Gerhard.) Reinbek, 1969.
	Phil 5249.13.99	C.G. Jung's Philosophie auf der Grundlage seiner Tiefenpsychologie. Inaug. Diss. (Kellner, Kurt.) Düren, 1937.
	Phil 5249.13.95	C.G. Jung's Psychologie im Abriss. (Corrie, Joan.) Zürich, 1929.
	Phil 3460.84	C.G.J. Jacobi und Helmholtz auf dem Gymnasium. (Kusch, E.) Potsdam, 1896.
	Phil 4515.89	C.J. Boström och hans filosofi. Örebro, 1859.
	Phil 4353.15	Caba, Pedro. Sintesis de su obra filosofica: antroposofica y metafisica de la presencia. Mexico, 1959.
	Phil 5425.49	Cabanès, Auguste. Grands Névropathes. Paris, 1930-31. 3v.
	Phil 2480.85	Cabanis, médecin, philosophe et l'époque révolutionnaire. (Brive, France. Mussée Ernest Rupin.) Brive, 1957.
	Phil 2480.20A	Cabanis, P.J.G. Choix de textes. Paris, n.d.
	Phil 2480.10	Cabanis, P.J.G. Oeuvres. Paris, 1823. 5v.
	Phil 2480.15	Cabanis, P.J.G. Oeuvres philosophiques. 1. éd. Paris, 1956. 2v.
	Phil 2480.30	Cabanis, P.J.G. Rapports du physique et du moral de l'homme. Paris, 1802. 2v.
	Phil 2480.30.2	Cabanis, P.J.G. Rapports du physique et du moral de l'homme. Paris, 1805.
	Phil 2480.30.5	Cabanis, P.J.G. Rapports du physique et du moral de l'homme. Paris, 1824. 3v.
	Phil 2480.31	Cabanis, P.J.G. Rapports du physique et du moral de l'homme. Paris, 1843.
	Phil 2480.31.5	Cabanis, P.J.G. Rapports du physique et du moral de l'homme. 8e éd. Paris, 1844.
	Phil 8403.32	Cabat, Walter. The place of beauty in American life. N.Y., 1911.
	Phil 4215.1.85	Caboara, L. La filosofia del diritto di G.D. Romagnosi. Citta, 1930.
	Phil 4215.1.86	Caboara, L. La filosofia politica di Romagnosi. Roma, 1936.
Htn	Phil 1980.2.80*	Cabot, J.E. Memoir of Ralph Wlado Emerson. Boston, 1887. 2v.
	Phil 8615.19	Cabot, P. The conversion of a sinner. Boston, 1923.
	Phil 8633.1.24	Cabot, Philip. The sense of immortality. Cambridge, 1924.
	Phil 9495.138	Cabot, R.C. The Christian approach to social morality. N.Y., 1913.
	Phil 9495.138.5	Cabot, R.C. Christianity and sex. N.Y., 1937.
	Phil 8827.5	Cabot, R.C. What men live by. Boston, 1914.
	Phil 8877.65	Cabot, Richard C. Adventures on the borderlands of ethics. N.Y., 1926.
	Phil 8877.65.20A	Cabot, Richard C. The meaning of right and wrong. N.Y., 1933.
	Phil 8877.65.22	Cabot, Richard C. The meaning of right and wrong. N.Y., 1936.
	Phil 8877.65.30	Cabot, Richard C. Prescriptions. Boston, 1915.
	Phil 8877.65.8	Cabot, Richard C. What men live by. Boston, 1914.
	Phil 4482.1.95	Cabral de Moncada, L. Um iluminista portugues do século XVIII; Luiz Antonio Verney. Coimbra, 1941.
	Phil 4983.8.90	Cabrera, Francisco de A. Razón contra razón...de Enrique José de Varona. 3. ed. Habana, 1893.
	Phil 8403.17	Cabrisas y Madero. El sentido del dolor en el arte. La Habana, 1937.
	Phil 5871.110	Cacciagierra, Francesco. I sentimenti del fanciullo nell'ambito familiare. Milano, 1968.
	Phil 4803.727.80	Cáceres, Alfredo. La obra psicológica de Radecki, 1910-35. Montevideo, 1936.
	Phil 5190.41	Cackowski, Zdzisław. Problemy i pseudoproblemy. Warszawa, 1964.
	VPhil 8877.96	Čáda, F. Cádova etika individualní. Praha, 1920.
	Phil 2515.17	Cadences. (Chevalier, J.) Paris, 1939- 2v.
	Phil 4466.5.30	Cadernos de filosofia. (Feijó, Diogo Antonio.) São Paulo, 1967.
	Phil 5465.40	Cadman, S. Parkes. Imagination. N.Y., 1930.
	Phil 1802.5	Cadman, S.P. Charles Darwin and other English thinkers. Boston, 1911.
	Phil 8582.42	Cadman, S.P. Imagination and religion. N.Y., 1926.
	Phil 9245.57	Çadman, Samuel P. Adventure for happiness. N.Y., 1935.
	VPhil 8877.96	Čádova etika individualní. (Cáda, F.) Praha, 1920.

Phil 5545.158 Les cadres sociaux de la mémoire. (Halbwachs, Maurice.) Paris, 1925.

Phil 7069.17.20 Cadwallader, Mary E. Hydesville in history. Chicago, 1917.

Phil 7054.187 Cadwallader, Mary E. Mary S. Vanderbilt, a twentieth century seer. Chicago, 1921.

Phil 4065.170 La caemologie de Giordano Bruno. (Michel, Paul.) Paris, 1962.

Phil 477.1 Cahagnet, A. Études sur le matérialisme. Argenteuil, 1869.

Phil 6672.9.5 Cahagnet, L. Celestial telegraph. 1. American ed. N.Y., 1855.

Htn Phil 6672.9.17* Cahagnet, L. Magnetic magic. n.p., 1898.

Phil 6672.9 Cahagnet, L. Magnétisme, arcanes de vie future. Paris, 1848.

Phil 6672.9.15 Cahagnet, L. Magnétisme; encyclopédie magnétique. v.1-6. Paris, 1854-62. 3v.

Phil 189.13 Cahier d'études philosophiques. v.1-2. (Ouy, A.) Paris, 1924-1925.

Phil 2672.40 Le cahier vert; comment les dogmes finissent. Lettres inédites. (Jouffroy, Théodore S.) Paris, 1924.

Phil 5245.17 Cahiers de psychologie rationnelle. v.1-4. (Falinski, E.) Paris, 1926.

Phil 12.60 Cahiers internationaux de symbolisme. Genève. 1-6+ 3v.

Phil 2905.1.20 Cahiers Pierre Teilhard de Chardin. Paris. 1-5+ 6v.

Phil 12.110 Cahiers pour l'analyse. Paris. 1,1966+ 2v.

Phil 12.135 Les cahiers rationalistes. Paris. 108,1950+

Phil 3425.300 Cahiers sur la dialectique de Hegel. (Lenin, V.I.) Paris, 1938.

Phil 5752.12 Cahn, Steven. Fate, logic, and time. New Haven, 1967.

Phil 1135.34 Caiazzo, D. L'idea di giustizia nel pensiero greco. Roma, 1958.

Phil 8430.10 Caillais, Roger. Meduse et cie. Paris, 1960.

Phil 2805.226 Cailliet, E. The clue to Pascal. London, 1944.

Phil 5590.170 Cailliet, E. The dawn of personality. 1. ed. Indianapolis, 1955.

Phil 2805.226.5 Cailliet, E. Pascal; genius in the light of scripture. Philadelphia, 1945.

Phil 2805.226.6 Cailliet, E. Pascal. N.Y., 1961.

Phil 8582.55 Cailliet, Émile. The life of the mind. N.Y., 1942.

Phil 525.86 Cailliet E. Mysticisme. Cahors, 1937.

Phil 5465.149 Caillois, Roger. Images, images, essais sur le rôle et les pouvoirs de l'imagination. Paris, 1966.

Phil 7082.22.5 Caillois, Roger. L'incertitude qui vient des rêves. Paris, 1956.

Phil 7082.22 Caillois, Roger. Le rêve et les sociétés humaines. Paris, 1967.

Phil 6312.22 Cain, Jacques. Le problème des névroses experimentales. Paris, 1959.

Phil 4752.2.125 Caín, Lucienne. Berdiaev en Russie. Paris, 1962.

Phil 2750.19.100 Cain, Seymour. Gabriel Marcel. London, 1963.

Phil 5640.148 Cain, William S. Stimulus and sensation; readings in sensory psychology. Boston, 1971.

Phil 3484.1 Caird, E. A critical account of the philosophy of Kant. Glasgow, 1877.

Phil 3484.1.3A Caird, E. A critical account of the philosophy of Kant. Glasgow, 1889. 2v.

Phil 3484.1.2 Caird, E. A critical account of the philosophy of Kant. London, 1877.

Phil 3484.1.5 Caird, E. A critical account of the philosophy of Kant. v.2. N.Y., 1889.

Phil 400.26 Caird, E. Idealism and theory of knowledge. London, 1903.

Phil 177.1.5 Caird, Edward. Essays on literature and philosophy. Glasgow, 1892. 2v.

Phil 177.1 Caird, Edward. Essays on literature and philosophy. N.Y., 1892. 2v.

Phil 1135.20.5 Caird, Edward. The evolution of theology in the Greek philosophers. Glasgow, 1923.

X Cg Phil 3425.80.3A Caird, Edward. Hegel. Edinburgh, 1883.

Phil 3425.80.7 Caird, Edward. Hegel. Edinburgh, 1891.

Phil 3425.212 Caird, Edward. Hegel. Milano, 191-

X Cg Phil 3425.80 Caird, Edward. Hegel. Philadelphia, 1883.

NEDL Phil 3425.80.5 Caird, Edward. Hegel. Philadelphia, 1896.

Phil 2490.98.7 Caird, Edward. Philosophie sociale et religion d'Auguste Comte. Paris, 1907.

Phil 2490.98A Caird, Edward. The social philosophy...of Comte. 2nd ed. Glasgow, 1893.

Phil 2490.98.1 Caird, Edward. The social philosophy and religion of Comte. Glasgow, 1885.

Phil 1135.20 Caird, Edward. Volution of theology in Greek philosophers. Glasgow, 1904. 2v.

Phil 1930.6.80 Pamphlet box. Caird, Edward. Biography.

Phil 8582.1.5 Caird, J. The fundamental ideas of Christianity. Glasgow, 1899. 2v.

Phil 8582.1.2 Caird, J. An introduction to the philosophy of religion. N.Y., 1880.

Phil 8582.64 Caird, John. An introduction to the philosophy of religion. N.Y., 1881.

Phil 3822.1.10 Caird, John. Spinoza. Edinburgh, 1902.

Phil 3822.1 Caird, John. Spinoza. Philadelphia, 1888.

Phil 8610.881 Cairns, John. Unbelief in the eighteenth century as contrasted with its earlier and later history. Edinburgh, 1881.

Phil 4080.20.30 Cairola, G. Scritti. Torino, 1954.

Phil 5242.41 Calabresi, R. La determinazione del presente psichico. Firenze, 1930.

Phil 3195.6.195 Calabrò, Gaetano. Dilthey e il diritto naturale. Napoli, 1968.

Phil 1740.26 Calabró, Gaetano. La società fuori tutela. Napoli, 1970.

Phil 3808.138 Calas, T. Schopenhauer; pessimisme-athéisme. Thèse. Montauban, 1909.

Phil 802.12 Calcagni, Gaetano. Compendio di storia della filosofia. Arce, 1931. 2v.

Phil 8430.14 Calcara, A. Discorsi di letteratura e d'arte. Marcianise, 1961.

Phil 4115.87.10 Calcaterra, C. Polemica giobertiana. Torino, 1923.

Phil 6672.1 Calcutta Mesmeric Hospital. Second half-yearly report. London, 1850.

Phil 1980.3.100 Calde-Marshall, A. Havelock Ellis. London, 1959.

Phil 8520.8 Caldecott, Alfred. The philosophy of religion in England and America. N.Y., 1901.

X Cg Phil 9245.44 Calder, Alexander. The man of the future. London, 1872.

Phil 4060.8.30 Calderaro, Francesco. Francesco Arri e il suo spiritualismo. Roma, 1941.

Phil 8403.40 Calderaro, José. La dimensión estetica del hombre. Buenos Aires, 1961.

Phil 1350.13 Calderini, A. Virtù romana. Milano, 1936.

Phil 365.13 Calderoni, G. L'evoluzione e i suoi limiti. Roma, 1907.

Phil 600.24 Calderoni, Giuseppe. Il positivismo. Roma, 1900.

Phil 177.57 Calderoni, M. Il pragmatismo a cura di Giovanni Papini. Lanciano, 1920.

Phil 333.11 Calderoni, M. La previsione nella teoria della conoscenza. Milano, 1907.

Phil 2050.92A Calderwood, H. David Hume. Edinburgh, n.d.

Phil 8877.1.2 Calderwood, H. Handbook of moral philosophy. London, 1872.

Phil 8877.1 Calderwood, H. Handbook of moral philosophy. London, 1884.

Phil 8877.1.5 Calderwood, H. Handbook of moral philosophy. London, 1895.

Phil 8877.1.3 Calderwood, H. Handbook of moral philosophy. 6th ed. London, 1879.

Phil 410.1.2 Calderwood, H. The philosophy of the infinite. Cambridge, 1861.

Phil 410.1 Calderwood, H. The philosophy of the infinite. Edinburgh, 1854.

Phil 6112.1 Calderwood, H. The relations of mind and brain. London, 1879.

Phil 6112.1.3 Calderwood, H. The relations of mind and brain. 3d ed. London, 1892.

Phil 5922.1 Caldwell, C. Phrenology vindicated and antiphrenology unmasked. N.Y., 1838.

Phil 177.38 Caldwell, W. Pragmatism and idealism. London, 1913.

Phil 3808.105 Caldwell, W. Schopenhauer's system...philosophical significance. Edinburgh, 1896.

Phil 6983.2 Caldwell, William Vernon. LSD psychotherapy; an explosion of psychedelic and psycholytic therapy. N.Y., 1968.

Phil 52.8 Calendar. (Metaphysical Club, Boston.) Boston, n.d.

Phil 1712.12 A calendar of doubts and faiths. (Malisoff, William M.) N.Y., 1930.

Phil 4752.2.145 Calian, Carnegie Samuel. The significance of eschatology in the thoughts of Nicolas Berdiaev. Leiden, 1965.

Phil 42.3.10 California. University. Institute of Human Development. Annual report. Berkeley. 1940+

Phil 5520.108 California. University. Philosophical Union. Meaning and interpretation. Berkeley, 1950.

Phil 42.3 California. University. Publications. Philosophy. Berkeley. 1-30,1904-1957 15v.

Phil 42.3.5 California. University. Publications. Psychology. Berkeley. 1-6,1910-1950 4v.

Phil 6112.42 California. University Medical Center. Man and civilization: control of the mind. N.Y., 1961.

Phil 6480.265 Caligor, Leopold. Dreams and symbols. N.Y., 1969.

Phil 177.3 Calinich, E.A.E. Philosophische Propädeutik. Dresden, 1847.

Phil 177.2 Calker, F. Propädeutik der Philosophie. Bonn, 1821.

Phil 177.2.5 Calker, F. Urgesetzlehre der wahren Guten und Schöne. Berlin, 1820.

Phil 5042.1 Calker, J.F.A. Denklehre oder Logik und Dialektik...Geschichte und Literatur. Bonn, 1822.

Phil 5242.13.5 Calkins, M.W. Der doppelte Standpunkt...Psychologie. Leipzig, 1905.

Phil 5242.13.9 Calkins, M.W. A first book in psychology. N.Y., 1910.

Phil 5242.13.10 Calkins, M.W. A first book in psychology. 2. ed. N.Y., 1911.

Phil 5242.13.12 Calkins, M.W. A first book in psychology. 4. ed. N.Y., 1914.

Phil 5242.13 Calkins, M.W. An introduction to psychology. N.Y., 1901.

Phil 8877.44.5 Calkins, Mary W. The good man and the good. N.Y., 1928.

Phil 177.33.7 Calkins, Mary Whiton. The persistent problems of philosophy. N.Y., 1936.

Phil 177.33.3 Calkins, Mary Whiton. The persistent problems of philosophy. 3d ed. N.Y., 1912.

Phil 177.33.10 Pamphlet vol. Calkins, Mary Whiton. Statistics of dreams. 14 pam.

VPhil 5205.12 Pamphlet box. Calkins on association.

Phil 6112.2.2 Call, A.P. As a matter of course. Boston, 1894.

Phil 6112.2.15 Call, A.P. Brain power for business men. Boston, 1911.

Phil 6112.2.9 Call, A.P. Freedom of life. Boston, 1905.

Phil 6112.2.11 Call, A.P. How to live quietly. Boston, 1914.

Phil 6112.2.4 Call, A.P. Power through repose. Boston, 1891.

Phil 6112.2.5 Call, A.P. Power through repose. Boston, 1893.

Phil 6112.2.8.7 Call, A.P. Power through repose. Boston, 1934.

Phil 8735.1 Call, W.M.W. Final causes. London, 1891.

Phil 2475.1.505 Callagher, Idella J. Morality in evolution: the moral philosophy of Henri Bergson. The Hague, 1970.

Phil 1135.161 Callahan, John F. Four views of time in ancient philosophy. Cambridge, 1948.

Phil 9495.168 Callahan, Sidney Cornelia. Beyond birth control; the Christian experience of sex. N.Y., 1968.

Phil 9342.16 Callet, P. L'écolier chretien. Lyon, 1776.

Phil 8877.33.5 Callieres, F. de. The knowledge of the world and the attainments. Dublin, 1774.

Phil 2402.9.5 Callot, E. La philosophie de la vie au XVIIIe siècle. Paris, 1965.

Phil 2402.9 Callot, E. Six philosophes français du XVIIIe siècle. Annecy, 1963.

Phil 1630.24 Callot, Emile. Doctrines et figures humanistes. Paris, 1963.

Phil 2520.85.30 Callot, Emile. Problèms du Cartesianisme. Annecy, 1956.

Phil 2725.13.95 Callot, Emile. Propos sur Jules Lequier. Paris, 1962.

Phil 4210.152 Callovini, C. Antonio Rosmini come uomo del risorgimento italiano. Roma, 1953.

Phil 5400.166 Callwood, J. Love, hate, fear, anger and the other lively emotions. Garden City, 1964.

Phil 6132.7.15 Calm yourself. (Walton, G.L.) Boston, 1913.

Phil 6952.1 Calmeil, J.L.F. De la folie. Paris, 1845. 2v.

Phil 7068.37 Calmet, Augustin. Des benediktiner-abtes zu Senones. München. 1837.

Phil 7067.46.20 Calmet, Augustin. Disertazioni sopra le apparizioni de spiriti. Venezia. 1770.

Phil 7067.46.5 Calmet, Augustin. Dissertations sur les apparitions. Paris, 1746.

Phil 7067.46.18 Calmet, Augustin. Dissertazioni sopra le apparizioni de spiriti. Venezia, 1756.

Phil 7067.46.15 Calmet, Augustin. Gelehrte Verhandlung der Materi von Erscheinungen der Geisteren. 3. Aufl. Augspurg. 1751.

Phil 7067.46.16 Calmet, Augustin. Gelehrte Verhandlung der Materi von Erscheinungen der Geisteren. 3. Aufl. Augspurg. 1757.

Phil 7067.46.25 Calmet, Augustin. The phantom world. London, 1850.

Phil 7067.46.26 Calmet, Augustin. The phantom world. Philadelphia. 1850.

Phil 7060.5.5 Calmet, Augustin. Recueil de dissertations...sur les apparitions. Avignon, 1751. 2v.

Htn Phil 7067.46.10* Calmet, Augustin. Traité sur les apparitions des esprits. Paris, 1751. 2v.

Phil 7067.46.10 Calmet, Augustin. Traité sur les apparitions des esprits. Paris, 1751. 2v.
Phil 177.76 Calò, G. Maestri e problemi di filosofia. Torino, 1924. 2v.
Phil 645.19 Calo, Giovanni. Il problema della libertà nel pensiero contemporaneo. Milano, 1906.
Phil 177.105.10 Calogero, G. Filosofia del dialogo. Milano, 1962.
Phil 4265.6.95 Calogero, G. La filosofia di Bernardino Varisco. Messina, 1950.
Phil 177.105.2 Calogero, G. Lezioni di filosofia. Torino, 1960. 3v.
Phil 177.105 Calogero, G. Lezioni di filosofia. v.2-3. Roma, 1946. 2v.
Phil 4080.3.141 Calogero, G. Studi crociani. Rieti, 1930.
Phil 1135.184.5 Calogero, Giudo. Storia della logica antica. Bari, 1967-
Phil 4080.18 Calogero, Guido. La conclusione della filosofia del conoscere. Firenze, 1938.
Phil 4080.18.10 Calogero, Guido. Quaderno laico. Bari, 1967.
Phil 4080.18.5 Calogero, Guido. Scritti. Firenze, 1960. 2v.
Phil 283.10 Calter, A.C. Cosmologia. Boston, 1931.
Htn Phil 5922.2* Calvert, G.H. Illustrations of phrenology. Baltimore, 1832.
Phil 177.82 Calvet, Adolphe. Le discontinu dans la philosophie et dans les sciences exactes. Paris, 1923.
Phil 2905.1.405 Calvet, Jean. Réflexions sur le "Phénomène humain" de Pierre Teilhard de Chardin. Paris, 1966.
Phil 1750.353 Calvinisme en existentie-philosophie. (Spier, J.M.) Kampen, 1951.
Phil 4210.80 Calza, G. Esposizione ragionata della filosofia. Intra, 1878-79. 2v.
Phil 4210.131 Calzi, Carlo. L'antropologia soprannaturale di A. Rosmini. Firenze, 1885.
Phil 186.54.5 Camaldolensische Gespräche. (Landino, C.) Jena, 1927.
Phil 5003.5 Cambridge. University. Library. Catalog of a collection of books on logic. Cambridge, 1889.
Phil 8505.3 Pamphlet box. Cambridge Conferences. Announcements.
Phil 2340.15.30 Cambridge conversations. (Watmough, J.R.) Cambridge, 1949.
Phil 1133.43 The Cambridge history of later Greek and early medieval philosophy. (Armstrong, Arthur Hilary.) London, 1967.
Phil 8595.23A The Cambridge Platonists; a study. (Powicke, F.J.) London, 1926.
Phil 8582.18A The Cambridge Platonists. (Campagnac, E.T.) Oxford, 1901.
Phil 8595.23.5A The Cambridge Platonists. (Powicke, F.J.) Cambridge, 1926.
Htn Phil 6672.11* Cambry, Jacques. Traces du magnétisme. La Haye, 1784. 2 pam.
Phil 177.86.10 Camera, Ugo. Problemi filosofici. Roma, 1931. 2 pam.
Phil 177.86 Camera, Ugo. Saggio di una sistema di filosofia busato sulla suggestione. Aquila, 1920.
Phil 4803.454.70 Caméralistique; économie politique et finances. (Hoene-Wroński, Józef Maria.) Paris, 1884.
Phil 3822.2 Camerer, T. Die Lehre Spinoza's. Stuttgart, 1877.
Phil 3822.2.10 Camerer, T. Die Lehre Spinozas. 2. Aufl. Stuttgart, 1914.
Phil 3822.2.5 Camerer, T. Spinoza und Schleiermacher. Stuttgart, 1903.
Phil 8403.16 Cameron, Charles. Two essays. London, 1835.
Phil 6312.11.5 Cameron, Donald E. Objective and experimental psychiatry. 2. ed. N.Y., 1941.
Phil 1828.2.5 Cameron, Kenneth Walter. Concord harvest:publications of the Concord school of philosophy and literature. Hartford, 1970.
Phil 7069.18.50 Cameron, Margaret. The seven purposes. N.Y., 1918.
Phil 7069.19.30 Cameron, Margaret. Twelve lessons from the seven purposes. N.Y., 1919.
Phil 6312.16.5 Cameron, N. Personality development and psychopathology. Boston, 1963.
Phil 6312.16 Cameron, N. The psychology of behavior disorders. Boston, 1947.
Htn Phil 283.8* Camilla, G. Enthosiasmo, de'misterii e maravigliose cause della compositione del mondo. Vinegia, 1564.
Phil 806.35 Il cammino del pensiero. (Guiliano, Balbino.) Firenze, 1962.
Htn Phil 4065.35* Camoeracensis acrotismus. (Bruno, Giordano.) Vitebergae, 1588.
Phil 8403.36 Camón, Aznar J. El arte desde su esencia. Zaragoza, 1940.
Phil 8403.2 Camón Aznar, J. El tiempo en el arte. Madrid, 1958.
Phil 8582.18A Campagnac, E.T. The Cambridge Platonists. Oxford, 1901.
Phil 9495.37.15 Campaigns of peace. (National Council of Public Morals for Great and Greater Britain.) N.Y., 1919.
Phil 2150.18.80 Campanale, D. Filosofia ed etica scientifica. Bari, 1962.
Phil 4080.38 Campanale, Domenico. Fondamento e problemi della metafisica. Bari, 1968-
Phil 3925.16.82 Campanale, Domenico. Studi su Wittgenstein. Bari, 1956.
Phil 4073.52 Campanella, Tommaso. Apologia di Galileo. Torino, 1968.
Phil 4073.37 Campanella, Tommaso. Artiveneti. Firenze, 1945.
Phil 4073.67 Campanella, Tommaso. Cosmologia, inediti; theologicorum liber III. Roma, 1964.
Phil 4073.72 Campanella, Tommaso. Le creature sovrannaturali. Roma, 1970.
Phil 4073.50 Campanella, Tommaso. Cristologia. Roma, 1958. 2v.
Phil 4073.33 Campanella, Tommaso. De antichristo. Roma, 1965.
Phil 4073.58 Campanella, Tommaso. De dictis Christi. Roma, 1969.
Phil 4073.65 Campanella, Tommaso. De homine. Roma, 1960.
Phil 4073.65.2 Campanella, Tommaso. De homine. Roma, 1961.
Phil 4073.40 Campanella, Tommaso. De sancta mono triade. Roma, 1958.
Phil 4073.30 Campanella, Tommaso. Del senso delle cose e delle magia. Bari, 1925.
Phil 4073.55 Campanella, Tommaso. Della grazia gratificante. Roma, 1959.
Phil 4073.42 Campanella, Tommaso. Della necessita di una filosofia cristiana. Torino, 1953.
Phil 4073.60 Campanella, Tommaso. Dio e la predestinazione. Firenze, 1949-51. 2v.
Phil 4073.32A Campanella, Tommaso. Epilogo magno (fisiologia italiana). Roma, 1939.
Phil 4073.70 Campanella, Tommaso. Escatologia. Roma, 1969.
Phil 4073.34 Campanella, Tommaso. Legazioni ai Maomettani. Firenze, 1960.
Phil 4073.75 Campanella, Tommaso. Lettere. Bari, 1927.
Htn Phil 4073.35* Campanella, Tommaso. Ludovico iusto XIII; Atheismus Tsiumphatus. Parisiis, 1636.
Phil 4073.39.5 Campanella, Tommaso. Magia e grazia. Roma, 1957.
Phil 4073.62F Campanella, Tommaso. Metaphysica. Torino, 1961.
Phil 4073.36 Campanella, Tommaso. Monarchia Messiae. Torino, 1960.
Phil 4073.39 Campanella, Tommaso. Opuscali inediti. Firenze, 1951.
Phil 4073.43 Campanella, Tommaso. Il peccato originale. Roma, 1960.
Phil 4073.45 Campanella, Tommaso. La prima e la seconda resurrezione. Roma, 1955.
Phil 4073.66 Campanella, Tommaso. I sacri segni, inediti. Roma, 1965. 6v.
Phil 4073.31 Campanella, Tommaso. Telogia. Milano, 1936.
Phil 4073.20 Campanella, Tommaso. Tommaso Campanella, poeta. Salerno, 1957.
Phil 4073.68 Campanella, Tommaso. Vita Christi. Roma, 1962. 2v.
Phil 4073.79 Pamphlet box. Campanella, Tommaso.
Phil 4073.100 Campanella. (Amerio, Romano.) Brescia, 1947.
Phil 4073.84 Campanella. (Blanchet, Léon.) Paris, 1920.
Phil 2750.22.115 Campanini, Giorgio. La rivoluzione cristiana. Brescia, 1968.
Phil 4112.84 Campari, A. Galluppi e Kant nella dottrina morale. Conegliano, 1907.
Phil 8877.22 Campbell, A. An enquiry...original of moral virtue. London, 1734.
Phil 8582.2 Campbell, A. The necessity of revelation. London, 1739.
Phil 6952.21.5 Campbell, C.M. Delusion and belief. Cambridge, 1926.
Phil 6952.21.6 Campbell, C.M. Delusion and belief. Cambridge, 1927.
Phil 6952.21.15 Campbell, C.M. Destiny and disease in mental disorders. N.Y., 1935.
Phil 575.86 Campbell, C.M. Human personality and the environment. N.Y., 1934.
Phil 6952.21A Campbell, C.M. A present-day conception of mental disorders. Cambridge, 1924.
Phil 6952.21.10 Campbell, C.M. Towards mental health. Cambridge, 1933.
Phil 645.31.5A Campbell, Charles A. Scepticism and construction. London, 1931.
Phil 8877.94 Campbell, Charles Arthur. In defense of free will. London, 1967.
Phil 720.1 Campbell, G.D. What is truth? Edinburgh, 1889.
Phil 6980.157 Campbell, John D. Everyday psychiatry. Philadelphia, 1945.
Phil 7069.68.40 Campbell, John Lorne. Strange things: the story of Fr. Allan McDonald, Ada Goodrich Freer, and the Society for Psychical Research's enquiry into Highland second sight. London, 1968.
Phil 5374.58 Campbell, P.A. Consciousness, brain-child. East Cleveland, 1933.
Phil 5242.16 Campbell, P.A. The game of mind. N.Y., 1913.
Phil 5374.61 Campbell, Percy A. Body and self, one and inseparable. San Francisco, 1942.
Phil 1750.470 Campbell, Robert. L'esistenzialismo. Napoli, 1955.
Phil 2880.8.80 Campbell, Robert. Jean Paul Sartre; ou une littérature philosophique. Paris, 1945.
Phil 2880.8.81 Campbell, Robert. Jean Paul Sartre. Paris, 1946.
Phil 2266.90 Campbell, Thomas Douglas. Adam Smith's science of morals. London, 1971.
Phil 7054.147 Campbell, Z. The spiritual telegraphic opposition line. Springfield, 1853.
Phil 9342.17.5 Campe, J.H. Vaterlicher Rath für meine Tochter. 2. Aufl. Tübingen, 1789.
Phil 5242.21 Campion, George G. Elements in thought and emotion. London, 1923.
Phil 4983.1.85 Campo, Aníbal del. El problema de la creencia y el intelectualismo de Vaz Ferreira. Montevideo, 1959.
Phil 3484.24 Campo, M. La genesi del criticismo kantiano. v.1-2. Varese, 1953-
Phil 3484.24.10 Campo, M. Schizzo storico della esegesi e critica kantiana. Varese, 1959.
Phil 1702.9 Campo, M. Variazioni sulla storia della filosofia moderna. Brescia, 1946.
Phil 8877.67 Campos Gimenez, J. La voz de la virtud. Habana, 1868.
Phil 1117.8.5 La camprensione del soggeho. 1. ed. (Mondolfo, Rodolfo.) Firenze, 1958.
Phil 9240.10.5 Camus, Albert. L'homme révolté. 94. éd. Paris, 1952.
Phil 8657.7 Can I believe in God the Father. (Clarke, W.N.) N.Y., 1899.
Phil 7069.02.20 Can telepathy explain? (Savage, Minot J.) N.Y., 1902.
Phil 7069.20.150 Can the dead communicate with the living? (Haldeman, Isaac M.) N.Y., 1920.
Phil 5520.710 Can there be a private language? (Smerud, Warren B.) The Hague, 1970.
Phil 8886.66 Can we agree? (Leake, C.D.) Austin, 1950.
Phil 8627.7 Can we be sure of mortality? (Cheney, William A.) N.Y., 1910.
Phil 8643.14.5 Can we believed in immortality. (Snowden, J.F.) N.Y., 1919.
Phil 6132.32 Can we live forever? (Welsh, F.G. (Mrs.).) Chicago, 1938.
Phil 9070.40 Can you take it? (Katterhenry, E.A.) St. Louis, Mo., 1944.
Phil 12.105 Canadian journal of behavioral science. Toronto. 1,1969+
Phil 12.150 Canadian journal of philosophy. Edmonton. 1,1971+
Phil 12.40 Canadian journal of psychology. Toronto. 1,1947+ 14v.
Phil 4060.8.81 Cancarini, Itala. Acri. Brescia, 1945.
Phil 4260.220 Candela, Mercurio. Diritto e umanità in G.B. Vico. Empoli, 1968.
Phil 4260.190 Candela, Silvestro. L'unità e la religiosità del pensiero di Giambattista Vico. Napoli, 1969.
Phil 8672.5 A candid examination of theism. (Romanes, J.) London, 1878.
Htn Phil 2915.50* Candide ou L'optimisme. n.p., 1759.
Phil 177.52 Candidus, L. Das Weltstreben. München, 1913.
Phil 5242.60 Candland, D.K. Exploring behavior. 1. ed. N.Y., 1961.
Phil 8610.889.10 The candle from under the bushel. (Hart, William.) N.Y., 1889.
Phil 1980.4.11 Candle in the dark. (Edman, Irwin.) N.Y., 1939.
Phil 8583.32 The candle of the Lord. (De Pauley, W.C.) London, 1937.
Phil 8657.12 Candlish, J.S. The kingdom of God. Edinburgh, 1884.
Phil 5425.13 Candolle, A. de. Histoire des sciences et des savants. Genève, 1885.
Phil 5425.13.15 Candolle, A. de. Zur Geschichte der Wissenschaften und der Gelehrten. Leipzig, 1911.
Phil 87.3 Candou, José M. Diccionario manual de filosofía. Madrid, 1946.
Phil 5850.148.5 Caner, George C. It's how you take it. N.Y., 1946.
Phil 333.21 Canfield, J.V. Readings in the theory of knowledge. N.Y., 1964.
Phil 8735.58 Canfield, John V. Purpose in nature. Englewood Cliffs, N.J., 1966.
Phil 1930.16.30 Canger, Georg P. Synoptic naturalism. Minneapolis, 1960.
Phil 5625.90 Canguilhem, G. La formation du concept de reflexe aux XVII et XVIII siècles. Paris, 1955.
Phil 8403.13 Canitt, Edgar. An introduction to aesthetics. London, 1949.
Phil 8403.13.5 Canitt, Edgar. The theory of beauty. London, 1914.
Phil 8403.13.10 Canitt, Edger. What is beauty. Oxford, 1932.
Phil 2725.14.92 Canivez, André. Jules Lagneau. Paris, 1965. 2v.
Phil 2520.215 Cannabrava, E. Descartes e Bergson. São Paulo, 1942?

Phil 4963.2 Cannabrava, Euryalo. A cultura brasileira e seus equivocos. Rio de Janeiro, 1955.
Phil 1702.10 Cannabrava, Euryalo. Ensaios filosóficos. Rio de Janeiro, 1957.
Phil 4963.2.5 Cannabrava, Euryalo. Estética da crítica. Rio de Janeiro, 1963.
Phil 7069.46.5 Cannon, A. The shadow of destiny. London, 1946?
Phil 6672.14A Cannon, A. Sleeping through space. 1st ed. N.Y., 1939.
Phil 978.76 Cannon, Alex. The power of karma in relation to destiny. London, 193-.
Phil 7069.34.7 Cannon, Alexander. Powers that be (the Mayfair lectures). London, 1934.
Phil 7069.34.8 Cannon, Alexandre. Powers that be (the Mayfair lectures). N.Y., 1935.
Phil 5400.31.9 Cannon, W.B. Bodily changes in pain, hunger, fear and rage. 2d ed. N.Y., 1929.
Phil 5400.167 Canolland, D.K. Emotion::bodily change, an enduring problem in psychology. Princeton, 1962.
Phil 9495.27 Cansinos Assens, Rafael. Ética y estética de los sexos. Madrid, 1920.
Phil 3484.7 Cantecor, G. Kant. Paris, n.d.
Phil 600.21 Cantecor, Georges. Le positivisme. Paris, 1904.
Phil 2905.1.650 Canteni, Agostino. Il problema Teilhard de Chardin. Milano, 1969.
Phil 42.12 Canterbury. University College, Christchurch, New Zealand. Department of Psychology. Psychological report.
Phil 3492.10 Cantii, Schellingii, Fichtii de filio divino sententiam. Diss. (Kalich, Karl.) Lipsiae, 1870.
Phil 4260.128 Cantone, Carlo. Il concetto filosofico di diritto in Giambattista Vico. Mazara, 1952.
Phil 177.4 Cantoni, C. Corso elementare di filosofia. Milan, 1870.
Phil 177.4.12 Cantoni, C. Corso elementare di filosofia. Milan, 1901.
Phil 9550.11.5 Cantoni, C. Una critica dell'utilitarismo. Roma, 1876.
Phil 4260.80 Cantoni, C. G.B. Vico. Torino, 1867.
Phil 3484.10 Cantoni, Carlo. Emanuele Kant. v.1,3. Milano, 1879-84. 2v.
Phil 3484.10.2 Cantoni, Carlo. Emanuele Kant. 2. ed. Milano, 1907.
Phil 4110.5.90 Cantoni, Carlo. Giuseppe Ferrari. Milano, 1878.
Phil 4080.3.305 Cantoni, Carlo. In memoria di Carlo Cantoni. Pavia, 1908.
Phil 4110.4.93 Cantoni, Carlo. Luigi Ferri. Roma, 1895.
Phil 585.70.5 Cantoni, Remo. Il problema antropologico nella Filosofia Contemporanea. Milano, 1963.
Phil 585.70.10 Cantoni, Remo. Scienze umane e antropologia filosofica. Milano, 1966.
Phil 8444.2 Cantoni, Remo. Il significato del tragico. Milano, 1970.
Phil 585.174 Cantoni, Remo. Società e cultura. Milano, 1964.
Phil 585.70.15 Cantoni, Remo. Storicismo e scienze dell'uomo. Milano, 1967.
Phil 4080.26 Cantoni, Remo. Tragico e senso comune. Cremona, 1963.
Phil 585.70 Cantoni, Remo. Umano e disumano. 1. ed. Milano, 1958.
Phil 4080.26.10 Cantoni, Remo. La vita quotidiana. Milano, 1966.
Phil 410.2 Cantor, Georg. Grundlagen einer allgemeinen Monnichfaltigkeitslehre. Leipzig, 1883.
Phil 87.4 Cantoro, Umberto. Vocabulario filosófico. Bologna, 1955.
Phil 5242.52 Cantrie, H. The "why" of man's experience. N.Y., 1950.
Phil 5380.90.5 Cantril, H. The invasion from Mars. Princeton, 1947.
Phil 5238.115 Cantril, Hadley. Reflections on the human venture. N.Y., 1960.
Phil 4215.1.95 Cantù, Cesare. Notizia di G.D. Romagnosi. 2a ed. Prato, 1840.
Phil 177.25 Canz, Israel Gottlieb. Meditationes philosophicae. Tubingae, 1750.
Phil 177.25.30 Canz, Israel Gottlieb. Theologia naturalis thetico-polemica. Dresdae, 1742.
Phil 177.25.10 Canz, Israle Gottlieb. Philosophicae Leibnitianae. Francofurti, 1749.
Htn Phil 9359.5* A cap of gray hairs for a green head. (Trenchfield, C.) London, 1688.
Phil 6315.62 The capacity for emotional growth. (Zetzel, Elizabeth R.) London, 1970.
Phil 5110.5 Capaldi, Nicholas. The art of deception. N.Y., 1971.
Phil 4080.3.440 Capanna, Francesco. La religione in Benedetto Croce. Bari, 1964.
Phil 8403.26 Capasso, Aldo. Arte e sentimento. Firenze, 1957.
Phil 4365.1.82 Capdevila, José Maria. Eugeni d'Ors. Barcino, 1965.
Phil 8877.4 Capel, A. Excellent contemplations divine and moral. London, 1683.
Phil 1107.3 Capelle, Wilhelm. Die griechische Philosophie. Berlin, 1922-34. 3v.
Phil 5938.7.15 Capen, N. Reminiscences of Dr. Spurzheim and George Combe. N.Y., 1881.
Phil 6672.8 Caperu, T. Mighty curative powers of mesmerism. London, 1851.
Phil 1200.3 Capes, W.W. Stoicism. London, 1880.
Phil 3552.297 Capesius, J. Der Apperceptionsbegriff bei Leipzig und dessen Nachfolgern. Hermannstadt, 1894.
Phil 3428.80 Capesius, J. Die Metaphysik Herbarts. Leipzig, 1878.
Phil 1701.25 Les capitals; ou De Jean Duns Scot à Jean Paulhan. (Bousquet, J.) Paris, 1955.
Phil 8657.32 Capizzi, Antonio. Dall'ateismo all'umanismo. Roma, 1967.
Phil 5752.14 Capizzi, Antonio. La difesa del libero arbitrio da Erasmo a Kant. 1. ed. Firenze, 1963.
Phil 5876.15 Caplan, Gerald. Adolescence: psychosocial perspectives. N.Y., 1969.
Phil 6112.43 Caplan, Gerald. An approach to community mental health. N.Y., 1961.
Phil 2402.5 Capone Braga, G. La filosofia francese e italiana del settecento. 3a ed. v.1-2. Padova, 1947.
Phil 802.11 Capone Braga, G. Il mondo delle idee. pt. 1a, 2a. Città di Cástello, 1928-33. 2v.
Phil 4210.138 Capone-Braga, G. Saggio su Rosmini il mondo delle idee. Milano, 1914.
Phil 4260.129 Caponigri, A.R. Time and idea. London, 1953.
Phil 4340.20 Caponigri, Aloysius Robert. Contemporary Spanish philosophy; an anthology. Notre Dame, 1967.
Phil 1182.50 Capparelli, Vincenzo. Il contributo pilagorico alla scienza. Padova, 1955.
Phil 177.124 Cappellani, G. Dalla materia allo spirito. Mazara, 1959.
Phil 7060.94 Capper, Alfred. A rambler's recollections and reflections. London, 1915.
Phil 7080.1 Cappie, J. Causation of sleep. Edinburgh, 1872.
Phil 6112.24 Cappie, James. Intra-cranial circulation and its relation to physiology of brain. Edinburgh, 1890.
Phil 5585.355 Cappon, Daniel. Technology and perception. Springfield, 1971.
Phil 5850.149.5 Capps, Ora L. Controlling your circumstances and affairs of life. Denver, 1932.

Phil 5850.149 Capps, Ora L. Developing and using your inner powers. Denver, 1932.
Phil 4080.3.430 Caprariis, Vittorio de. Benedetto Croce. Milano, 1963.
Phil 7054.115.5 Capron, Eliab W. Explanation and history of the mysterious communion with spirits. 2. ed. Auburn, N.Y., 1850.
Phil 7054.115 Capron, Eliab W. Modern spiritualism: its facts and fanaticisms. Boston 1855.
Phil 8582.45.3 Capron, F.H. The anatomy of truth. 3. ed. London, 1927.
Phil 8692.13.8 Capron, F.H. The conflict of truth. 8. ed. London, 1927.
Phil 8582.34 Carabellese, P. L'essere e il problema religioso. Bari, 1914.
Phil 4080.17 Carabellese, P. L'idealismo italiano. Napoli, 1938.
Phil 4210.113 Carabellese, P. La teoria della percezione intellettiva. Bari, 1907.
Phil 3002.5 Carabellese, Pantaleo. Il problema della filosofia da Kant a Fichte (1781-1801). Palermo, 1929.
Phil 9560.11 Caraccioli, L. De la gaieté. Paris, 1782.
Phil 3484.20 Caracciolo, A. Arti e pensiero nelle laro istanze metafisiche. Roma, 1953.
Phil 4080.21 Caracciolo, A. La persona e il tempo. 1. ed. pt. 1. Arona, 1955.
Phil 8582.72 Caracciolo, Alberto. La religione come struttura e come modo autonomo della coscienza. Milano, 1965.
Phil 3475.3.170 Caracciolo, Alberto. Studi Jaspersiani. Milano, 1958.
Phil 4215.9.80 Caracciolo, C. L'idealismo e i suoi limiti nel pensiero di Antonio Renda. Palermo, 1960.
Phil 2515.18 Caraco, Albert. Huit essais sur le mal. Neuchâtel, 1963.
Phil 2515.18.5 Caraco, Albert. La luxure et la mort. Lausanne, 1968.
Phil 9495.170.10 Caraco, Albert. L'ordre et le sexe. Lausanne, 1970.
Phil 9035.7.13 El carácter; version española. (Smiles, S.) Paris, 1892.
Phil 9035.83 El caracter. (Muñoz, Juan A.) México, 1912.
Phil 9035.1 Le caractère. (Azam, E.) Paris, 1887.
Phil 9035.86 Le caractère. (Burloud, Albert.) Paris, 1942.
Phil 9035.26 Le caractère. (Malapert, P.) Paris, 1902.
Phil 9035.41 Le caractère à l'homme. (Perez, Bernard.) Paris, 1892.
Phil 2805.321 Le caractère de Pascal. (Jerphagnon, L.) Paris, 1962.
Phil 5400.3 Caractère des passions. (Vernier, I.) Paris, 1807. 2v.
Phil 325.2 Caractére empirique et la personne. (Prat, Louis.) Paris, 1906.
Phil 9035.71 Caractère et personnalité. (Peillaube, E.) Paris, 1935.
Phil 575.9 Les caractères. (Paulham, F.) Paris, 1902.
Phil 9361.1 Les caracteres de l'honneste homme et de l'homme chrestien. (Vincent.) Paris, 1690.
Phil 6021.4 Caractères des passions. (LeClerc, S.) Paris, n.d.
Phil 5590.180 Caractères et visages. 1. éd. (Mucchielli, R.) Paris, 1954.
Phil 12.21 La caractérologie. Paris. 1,1960+ 2v.
Phil 5590.350 La caractérologie à l'âge scientifique. (Mucchielli, R.) Neuchâtel, 1961.
Phil 5592.105 La caracterologie d'Heymans. (Gauchet, F.) Paris, 1959.
Phil 4357.8 Caragorri, P. La paradoja del filósofo. Madrid, 1959.
NEDL Phil 2402.1 Caraman, V.A.C. Histoire des révolutions de la philosophie. Paris, 1845-48. 3v.
Phil 2465.80 Caraman, V.A.C.R. Charles Bonnet. Paris, 1859.
Phil 4260.104 Caramella, S. Antologia vichiana. Messina, 1930.
Phil 2475.1.219 Caramella, S. Bergson. Milano, 1925.
Phil 802.13 Caramella, S. Disegno storico della filosofia. Messina, 1931.
Phil 4115.88 Caramella, S. La formazione della filosofia giobertiana. Genova, 1926.
Phil 177.97 Caramella, S. Introduzione alla filosofia e dottrina della practica. Messina, 1936.
Phil 8582.47 Caramella, S. Religione, teosofia e filosofia. Messina, 1931.
Phil 3484.22 Caramella, Santino. Commentarii alla ragion pura. Palermo, 1956-57.
Phil 3488.13 Il carattere formale della filosofia giuridica Kantiana. (Goretti, Cesare.) Milano, 1922.
Phil 2115.137 Caratteri della filosofia di Giovanni Locke. (Nardi, Pietro de.) Firenze, 1889.
Phil 5590.480 La caratterologia di G. Heymans e di R. LeSenne. (Galli, Norberto.) Zürich, 1965.
Phil 6952.28 Caravedo, B. Tratamiento social de los enfermos de la mente. Lima, 1943.
Phil 8403.37.5 Carbonara, C. Del bello e dell'arte. 2. ed. Napoli, 1953
Phil 2655.3.90 Carbonara, C. L'idealismo di O. Hamelin. Napoli, 1927?
Phil 2477.11.90 Carbonara, C. Léon Brunschvicg. Napoli, 1930.
Phil 8403.37 Carbonara, C. Ricerche per un'estetica del contenuto. Napoli, 1960.
Phil 9513.25 Carbonara, Cleto. L'esperienza e la prassi. Napoli, 1964.
Phil 1107.7 Carbonara, Cleto. La filosofia greca. Napoli, 1951. 2v.
Phil 1107.7.2 Carbonara, Cleto. La filosofia greca: Aristotele. 2. ed. Napoli, 1967.
Phil 1107.7.3 Carbonara, Cleto. La filosofia greca. Platone. 2. ed. Napoli, 1969.
Phil 3425.760 Carbonara, Cleto. Hegel e Marx nella polemica del diritto pubblico. Napoli, 1967.
Phil 2520.224.5 Carbonara, Cleto. Renato Cartesio. Napoli, 1965.
Phil 2520.224 Carbonara, Cleto. Renato Cartesio e la tradizione ontologica. Torino, 1945.
Phil 4002.8 Carbonara, Cleto. Il secolo XV. Milano, 1943.
Phil 1135.193 Carbonara Naddei, Mirella. Note sul realismo nel pensiero dei Greci. Napoli, 1965.
Phil 5042.75 Carbonard, Cleto. Psicologia, logica, dialettica. Napoli, 1963.
Phil 4070.7.85 Carbonare, Cleto. L'estetica filosofica di Antonio Banfi. Napoli, 1966.
Phil 848.2 Carbonare, Cleto. La filosofia dell' espirenza e la fondazione dell' umanesims. 2. restampa. Napoli, 1961.
Phil 848.2.3 Carbonare, Cleto. La filosofia dell'espirenza e la fondazione del Umanesimo. 3. ed. Napoli, 1969.
Phil 802.8.10 Carbonel, Pierre. Essai de philosophie classique. Paris, 1876.
Phil 802.8.2 Carbonel, Pierre. Histoire de la philosophie depuis les temps les plus reculés jusqu'à nos jours. 2e éd. Avignon, 1882.
Phil 5100.10 Carcaterra, Gaetano. Il problema della fallacia naturalistica. Milano, 1969.
Phil 4357.12.2 Carcía Hoz, Victor. El nacimiento de la intimidad, y otros estudios. 2. ed. Madrid, 1970.
Phil 177.5 Cardaillac, M. Etudes élémentaires de philosophie. Paris, 1830. 2v.
Phil 4075.45 Cardano, Girolamo. Arcana politica. Lugduni, 1635.
Phil 4075.79.20A Cardano, Girolamo. The book of my life. N.Y., 1930.
Phil 4075.55 Cardano, Girolamo. The book on games of chance. N.Y., 1961.

Htn Phil 4075.31* Cardano, Girolamo. De consolatione. Venetijs, 1542.
Htn Phil 4075.40* Cardano, Girolamo. De libris propriis, eorumque ordinis et usu. Lugduni, 1557.
Htn Phil 4075.79* Cardano, Girolamo. De propria vita liber. Parisiis, 1643.
Htn Phil 4075.51* Cardano, Girolamo. De utililate-ex adversis capienda libri. Amsterdam, 1672.
Phil 4075.79.15 Cardano, Girolamo. Des Girolamo Cardano von Mailand (Buergers von Bologna) eigene Lebenbeschreibung. Jena, 1914.
Phil 4075.79.16 Cardano, Girolamo. Des Girolamo Cardano von Mailand eigene Lebensbeschreibung. München, 1969.
Phil 4075.78 Cardano, Girolamo. Hieronymi Cardani mediolanensis. Amstelaedami, 1654.
Phil 4075.79.25 Cardano, Girolamo. Ma vie. Paris, 1936.
Phil 6012.5F Cardano, Girolamo. Metoposcopia libris tredecim. Lutetiae, 1658.
Phil 4075.1F Cardano, Girolamo. Opera. Lugduni, 1663. 10v.
Phil 4075.45.15 Cardano, Girolamo. La science du monde. 4e ed. Paris, 1661.
Phil 4075.79.10 Cardano, Girolamo. Vita di Girolamo Cardano. Milano, 1821.
Phil 4075.85 Cardano, the gambling scholar. (Ore, Oystein.) Princeton, 1953.
Phil 4363.3.90 Cardenas, Juan. Breve relacion de la muerte. Sevilla, 1732.
Phil 1695.48 Cardiel Reyes, Raul. Los filósofos modernos en la independencia latino-americana. 1. ed. México, 1964.
Phil 8882.24.9 The cardinal virtues. (Hyde, W. De W.) N.Y., 1902.
Phil 3090.81.5 Die Cardinalpunkte der F. Baader'schen Philosophie. (Hamberger, Julius.) Stuttgart, 1855.
Phil 5242.20 Cardols, Joseph. Éléments de psychologie. Namur, 1890.
Phil 177.96 Cardone, D.A. Il problema del sovraumano. Firenze, 1936.
Phil 585.35 Cardone, Domenico Antonio. Il divenire e l'uomo. v.1-3. 2. ed. Palmi, 1956-57.
Phil 4080.40.5 Cardone, Domenico Antonio. La filosofia nella storia civile del mondo. Roma, 1966.
Phil 4080.40 Cardone, Domenico Antonio. L'ozio, la contemplazione, il giuoco, la tecnica. Roma, 1968.
Phil 4112.90 Cardone, Elsa. La teologia razionale di P. Galluppi. Palmi, 1959.
Phil 4476.2.30 Cardoso Rangel de Souza Coelho, Maria Luiza. A filosofia de Silvestre Penheiro Ferreira. Braga, 1958.
Phil 585.295 Care, Norman S. Readings in the theory of action. Bloomington, 1968.
Phil 9362.20 Career girl, watch your step (Wylie, Max.) N.Y., 1964.
Phil 1717.21 The career of philosophy. (Randall, John.) N.Y., 1962. 2v.
Phil 8610.878.10 Career of religious ideas. (Tuttle, Hudson.) N.Y., 1878.
Htn Phil 1980.1.30* A careful...enquiry. (Edwards, Jonathan.) Boston, 1754.
Htn Phil 5754.1.6* A careful and strict enquiry...freedom of will. (Edwards, Jonathan.) Albany, 1804.
Phil 5754.1.4 A careful and strict enquiry...freedom of will. (Edwards, Jonathan.) Glasgow, 1790.
Phil 5754.1.12 Careful and strict enquiry into the modern...freedom. (Edwards, Jonathan.) N.Y., 1828.
Htn Phil 5754.1.10* Careful and strict enquiry into the modern...freedom of will. (Edwards, Jonathan.) Boston, 1754.
Phil 5754.1.8 Careful and strict enquiry into the modern...freedom of will. (Edwards, Jonathan.) Boston, 1762.
Phil 5754.1.2 A carefull and strict enquiry...freedom of will. 3. ed. (Edwards, Jonathan.) London, 1768.
Phil 4060.1.85 Carelle, Antonio. Naturalismo italiano. Padova, 1911.
Phil 4080.34 Carena, Giacinto. Essai d'un parallèle entre les forces physiques et les forces morales. Turin, 1817.
Phil 8403.30 Carey, Arthur. The majority report on art. Newport, R.I., 1927.
Phil 177.6 Carey, H.C. The unity of law. Philadelphia, 1872.
Phil 2905.1.600 Cargas, Harry J. The continuous flame. St. Louis, 1969?
Phil 1930.11.30 Cargill, S.T. The philosophy of analogy and symbolism. London, 1946?
Phil 2905.1.655 Cari Gustav Jung et Pierre Teilhard de Chardin. (Lecourt, Jacques.) Goële, 1970.
Phil 4080.13.30 Caria, G.M. de. Identità o contraddizione? Palermo, 1925.
Phil 70.70 Caribbean Conference for Mental Health. Proceedings. San Juan. 2-3 2v.
X Cg Phil 7075.146 The caricature of love. (Cleckley, H.M.) N.Y., 1957.
Phil 645.65 Cariddi, Walter. Filosofi della scepsi. Lecce, 1968.
Phil 7069.45.45 Carington, Whately. Telepathy. 2. ed. London, 1945.
Phil 7069.46.25 Carington, Whately. Thought transference. N.Y., 1946.
Phil 5853.14 Carkhuff, Robert R. Helping and human relations. N.Y., 1969. 2v.
Phil 3850.26.90 Carl Christian Ehrhard Schmid und sein Verhältnis zu Fichte. Inaug. Diss. (Semewald, L.) Leipzig, 1929.
Phil 3160.9.87 Carl Gustav Carus und die romantische Weltanschauung. (Wäsche, E.) Dusseldorf, 1933.
Phil 4655.1.80 Carl Pontus Wikner. (Åberg, L.H.) Sockholm, 1889.
Phil 4655.1.82.2 Carl Pontus Wikner. (Kjellberg, Elis.) Stockholm, 1902.
Phil 4655.1.82 Carl Pontus Wikner. (Kjellberg, Elis.) Upsala, 1888.
Phil 6315.2.144 Carlemans, A. Development of Freud's conception of anxiety. Amsterdam, 1949.
Phil 2905.1.300 Carles, Jules. Teilhard de Chardin. Paris, 1964.
Phil 5752.1 Carleton, H. Liberty and necessity. Philadelphia, 1857.
Phil 5242.32 Carlill, H.F. Socrates, or The emancipation of mankind. London, 1927.
Phil 1702.6 Carlini, A. Orientamenti della filosofia conteporanea. Roma, 1931.
Phil 4080.9.40 Carlini, Armando. Alla ricerca di me stesso. Firenze, 1951.
Phil 4080.9.33 Carlini, Armando. Avviamento allo studio della filosofia. 3a ed. Firenze, 1921.
Phil 802.25 Carlini, Armando. Breve storia della filosofia. Firenze, 1957.
Phil 4080.9.45 Carlini, Armando. Dalla vita dello spirito al mito del realismo. Firenze, 1959.
Phil 2040.80 Carlini, Armando. Herbert di Cherbury e la scuola di Cambridge. Roma, 1917.
Phil 4080.9.39 Carlini, Armando. Il mito del realismo. Firenze, 1936.
Phil 2520.225 Carlini, Armando. Il problema di Cartesio. Bari, 1948.
Phil 4080.9.35 Carlini, Armando. La vita dello spirito. Firenze, 1921.
Phil 9342.13 Carlisle, Isabella (Byron) Howard. Thoughts in the forms of maxims. London, 1790.
Phil 4080.5.90 Carlo, E. di. Simone Corleo. Palermo, 1924.
Phil 4120.2.90 Carlo, Eugenio di. Cosmo Guastella. Palermo, 1923.
Phil 1930.19.30 Carlo, William E. The ultimate reductibility of essence to existence in existential metaphysics. The Hague, 1966.
Phil 8877.70 Carlos, M. Moral e economia politica. Rio de Janeiro, 1941.
Phil 4351.5.80 Carlos Astrada. (Llanos, Alfredo.) Buenos Aires, 1962.
Phil 3552.131 Carlotti, G. Il sistema die Leibniz. Messina, 1923.
Phil 1802.3 Carlson, J.S. Om filosofien i Amerika. Upsala, 1895.
Phil 5242.50 Carlsson, N.G. Dimensions of behaviour. Lund, 1949.
Phil 1900.96 Carlsson, P.A. Butler's ethics. The Hague, 1964.
Htn Phil 1930.1.30* Carlyle, Thomas. Sartor Resartus. Boston, 1836.
Phil 8422.8 Carmella, S. I problemi del gusto e dell'arte nella mente di Pietro Verri. Napoli, 1926.
Phil 4440.2 Carmen Rovira, María del. Eclécticos portugueses del siglo XVIII y algunas de sus. Mexico, 1958.
Phil 8627.12 Carmichael, A. An essay...man's ultimate destination. Dublin, 1830.
Phil 5938.7.20 Carmichael, A. A memoir of the life and philosophy of Spurzheim. 1st American ed. Boston, 1833.
Phil 5242.55.5 Carmichael, L. Basic psychology. N.Y., 1957.
Phil 5242.55 Carmichael, L. The making of modern mind. Houston, 1956.
Phil 5870.85.3 Carmichael, Leonard. Carmichael's manual of child psychology. 3rd ed. N.Y., 1970. 2v.
Phil 5643.108 Carmichael, Leonard. Reacting and visual fatigue. Boston, 1947.
Phil 5042.22A Carmichäel, R.D. The logic of discovery. Chicago, 1930.
Phil 5870.85.3 Carmichael's manual of child psychology. 3rd ed. (Carmichael, Leonard.) N.Y., 1970. 2v.
Phil 5042.21A Carnap, Rudolf. Abriss der Logistik. Wien, 1929.
Phil 5042.21.20 Carnap, Rudolf. The continuum of inductive methods. Chicago, 1952.
Phil 5066.8.5 Carnap, Rudolf. Einführung in die symbolische Logik. Wien, 1954.
Phil 5066.8.6 Carnap, Rudolf. Einfuhrung in die symbolische Logik mit besonderer Berucksichtigung. Wien, 1960.
Phil 5042.60 Carnap, Rudolf. Induktive Logik und Wahrscheinlichkeit. Wien, 1959.
Phil 5066.8 Carnap, Rudolf. Introduction to semantics. Cambridge, 1942.
Phil 5066.8.2 Carnap, Rudolf. Introduction to semantics and formalization of logic. Cambridge, 1959.
Phil 5066.8.10 Carnap, Rudolf. Introduction to symbolic logic and its applications. N.Y., 1958.
Phil 5125.24.6 Carnap, Rudolf. Logical foundations of probability. 2nd ed. Chicago, 1962.
Phil 333.12.2 Carnap, Rudolf. The logical structure of the world. Berkeley, 1967.
Phil 5042.21.14.5A Carnap, Rudolf. The logical syntax of language. London, 1954.
Phil 5042.21.14.10 Carnap, Rudolf. The logical syntax of language. London, 1967.
Phil 5042.21.14 Carnap, Rudolf. The logical syntax of language. N.Y., 1937.
Phil 333.12 Carnap, Rudolf. Der logische Aufbau der Welt. Berlin, 1928.
Phil 5042.21.9A Carnap, Rudolf. Logische Syntax der Sprache. Wien, 1934.
Phil 5520.121.2 Carnap, Rudolf. Meaning and necessity. Chicago, 1964.
Phil 5042.21.17 Carnap, Rudolf. Notes for symbolic logic. Chicago, 1937.
Phil 5042.21.15 Carnap, Rudolf. Philosophy and logical syntax. London, 1935.
Phil 333.12.5A Carnap, Rudolf. Scheinprobleme in der Philosophie. Berlin, 1928.
Phil 5520.120 Carnap, Rudolf. Testability and meaning. New Haven, 1950.
Phil 5066.270 Carnap and Goodman: two formalists. (Hausman, Alan.) Iowa City, 1967.
Phil 3160.10.95 Carnap on meaning and analyticity. (Butrick, Richard.) The Hague, 1970.
Phil 177.93 Carneades, D. Matter, spirit and living intellect. London, 1936.
Phil 9530.2 Carnegie, A. How to win fortune. N.Y., 1890.
Phil 9530.38.15 Carnegie, Dale. How to win friends and influence people. N.Y., 1937.
Phil 9530.38.28 Carnegie, Dale. How to win friends and influence people. 28th ed. N.Y., 1937.
Phil 3160.2.75 Carneri, B. Bartholomäus von Carneri's Briefwechsel mit E. Häckel und F. Jodl. Leipzig, 1922.
Phil 8877.62 Carneri, B. Entwicklung und Glückseligkeit. Stuttgart, 1886.
Phil 8877.62.12 Carneri, B. Grundlegung der Ethik. Stuttgart, 19- .
Phil 9150.6 Carneri, B. Sittlichkeit und Darwinismus. Wien, 1871.
Phil 510.17 Carneri, Bartolomäus von. Empfindung und Bewusstsein. Bonn, 1893.
Phil 510.17.5 Carneri, Bartolomäus von. Empfindung und Bewusstsein. 2e Aufl. Stuttgart, 1906.
Phil 177.51 Carneri, Bartolomeo. Der Mensch als Selbstjweck. Wien, 1877.
Phil 2750.11.62 Carnet de notes. (Maritain, Jacques.) Paris, 1965.
Phil 186.105 Les carnets. 1. ed. (Lévy-Bruhe, L.) Paris, 1949.
Phil 6980.124 Carnets d'une psychiatre soviétique. (Bogdanovich, L.A.) Paris, 1963.
Phil 2477.6.32 Carnets intimes, 1883-1894. (Blondel, Maurice.) Paris, 1961.
Phil 2905.1.190 Carnets Teilhard. Paris. 1-18 13v.
Phil 4080.3.150 Carnevale, Luigi. Il concetto puro della filosofia dello spirito e la storia del secolo XIX di B. Croce. Varese, 1934.
Phil 5917.168 Carnicer, Ramón. Entre la ciencia y la magia. 1. ed. Barcelona, 1969.
Phil 6952.2A Carnochan, J.M. Cerebral localization...insanity. N.Y., 1884.
Phil 2880.1.80 Caro, E.M. Essai sur la vie et la doctrine de St. Martin. Paris, 1852.
Phil 8827.3 Caro, E.M. Études morales sur le temps présent. Paris, 1855.
Phil 8827.3.2 Caro, E.M. Études morales sur le temps présent. Paris, 1869.
Phil 8657.1 Caro, E.M. L'idée de Dieu. Paris, 1868.
Phil 8657.1.2 Caro, E.M. L'idée de Dieu et ses nouveaux critiques. Paris, 1864.
Phil 477.2 Caro, E.M. Le matérialisme et la science. Paris, 1867.
Phil 477.2.5 Caro, E.M. Le matérialisme et la science. 2e éd. Paris, 1868.
Phil 8827.3.7 Caro, E.M. Nouvelles études morales sur le temps présent. Paris, 1869.
Phil 9430.3.2 Caro, E.M. El pesimismo en el siglo XIX. Madrid, 1878.
Phil 9430.3.1 Caro, E.M. Le pessimisme au XIX siècle. 2. éd. Paris, 1880.
Phil 9430.3 Caro, E.M. Le pessimisme au XIX siècle. 4. éd. Paris, 1889.
Phil 9430.3.10 Caro, E.M. Pessimismen i nittonde arhundradet. Stockholm, 1880.
Phil 2402.2 Caro, E.M. Philosophie et philosophes. Paris, 1888.

Phil 600.7.95 — Caro, Elme. M. Littré et le positivisme. Paris, 1883.
Phil 176.130 — Carolus Michael Buscalioni Monregalensis ut philosophiae rationalis professor crearetur. (Buscalioni, C.M.) Turin? 1848.
Phil 2402.3 — Carove, F.M. Philosophie in Frankreich. Göttingen, 1827. 2v.
Phil 5421.20.65 — Carp, Eugène Antoine. Agressie en agressiviteit. Utrecht, 1968.
Phil 6312.28 — Carp, Eugène Antoine Desiré Émile. De dubbelganger. Utrecht, 1964.
Phil 665.15 — Carpenter, A. Pseuchographia anthropomagica. London, 1652.
Phil 8430.8 — Carpenter, Edward. Angels' wings. London, 1898.
Phil 5242.35.10 — Carpenter, Edward. The art of creation. London, 1904.
Phil 5242.35 — Carpenter, Edward. L'arte della creazione. Roma, 1909.
Phil 8952.20 — Carpenter, Edward. Common sense about Christian ethics. London, 1961.
Phil 6834.2 — Carpenter, Edward. Intermediate types among primitive folk. N.Y., 1914.
Phil 9220.4.3 — Carpenter, Edward. Ioläus; anthology of friendship. 3d ed. London, 1915.
Phil 8430.8.5 — Carpenter, Edward. The religious influence of art. Cambridge, 1870.
Phil 8627.14 — Carpenter, Joseph E. The place of immortality in religious belief. London, 1898.
Phil 9045.10 — Carpenter, L. Discourse on Christian patriotism. London, 1838.
Htn Phil 177.53* — Carpenter, Nathaniel. Philosophia libera. Ed. 2a. Oxoniae, 1622.
Phil 283.1 — Carpenter, S.H. Philosophy of evolution. Madison, 1874.
Phil 8877.32 — Carpenter, T.E. The doctrines of life. Boston, 1913.
Phil 8692.7 — Carpenter, W.B. Doctrine of evolution in its relation to theism. London, 1882.
Phil 6112.4.20 — Carpenter, W.B. The doctrine of human automatism. London, 1875.
Phil 8877.35 — Carpenter, W.B. Life's tangled thread. London, 1912.
Phil 177.7 — Carpenter, W.B. Nature and man. London, 1888.
Phil 6112.4.2 — Carpenter, W.B. Principles of mental psychology. London, 1881.
Htn Phil 6112.4.3* — Carpenter, W.B. Principles of mental psychology. London, 1881.
Phil 6112.4.3.5 — Carpenter, W.B. Principles of mental psychology. N.Y., 1874.
Phil 6112.4.9 — Carpenter, W.B. Principles of mental psychology. 4th ed. N.Y., 1887.
Phil 7068.77.1 — Carpenter, William B. Mesmerism, spiritualism,...historically and scientifically considered. London, 1877.
Phil 7068.77 — Carpenter, William B. Mesmerism, spiritualism,...historically and scientifically considered. N.Y., 1877.
Phil 510.127.10 — Carr, H. Wildon. Cogitans cogitata. Los Angeles, 1930.
Phil 510.127 — Carr, H. Wildon. A theory of monads. London, 1922.
Phil 5585.60 — Carr, H.A. An introduction to space perception. N.Y., 1935.
Phil 2475.1.90 — Carr, H.W. Henri Bergson; the philosophy of change. London, 1911.
Phil 5350.2.8A — Carr, H.W. Henry Bergson: philosophy of change. London, 1911.
Phil 3552.279 — Carr, H.W. Leibniz. London, 1929.
Phil 9590.26 — Carr, H.W. Life and finite individuality. London, 1918.
Phil 720.8 — Carr, H.W. The problem of truth. London, n.d.
Phil 177.65 — Carr, H.W. The scientific approach to philosophy. London, 1924.
Phil 177.65.5 — Carr, H.W. The unique status of man. N.Y., 1928.
Phil 5643.33.2 — Carr, Harvey. A visual illusion of motion during eye closure. Lancaster, 1906.
Phil 8582.43 — Carr, Herbert W. Changing backgrounds in religion and ethics. N.Y., 1927.
Phil 5752.6 — Carr, Herbert W. The freewill problem. London, 1928.
Phil 2475.1.185.5 — Carr, Herbert W. Henri Bergson; the philosophy of change. London, 1919.
Phil 2475.1.185 — Carr, Herbert W. The Philosophy of change. London, 1914.
Phil 400.41 — Carr, Herbert Wildon. The new idealist movement in philosophy. London, 1918.
Phil 4080.3.80 — Carr, Herbert Wildon. The philosophy of Benedetto Croce. London, 1917.
Phil 4080.3.81 — Carr, Herbert Wildon. The philosophy of Benedetto Croce. N.Y., 1969.
Htn Phil 9162.1* — Carr, Roger. A godlie forme of household government. London, 16- ?
Htn Phil 9162.1.5* — Carr, Roger. A godly forme of household government. London, 1621.
Phil 9035.85 — Carr, Wells. Know thyself. N.Y., 1944.
Phil 177.94 — Carra, J.L. Systême de la raison. 3e éd. Paris, 1791.
Phil 1020.7.5 — Carra de Vaux, Le Bon. Gazali. Photoreproduction. Paris, 1902.
Phil 1020.8 — Carra de Vaux. Avicenne. Paris, 1900.
Phil 9550.11 — Carran, Ludovic. La morale utilitaire. Paris, 1875.
Phil 1535.29 — Carrasquilla, R.M. Lecciones de metafísica y ética. 2. ed. Bogotá, 1918.
Phil 177.95 — Carrasquilla R., Humberto. El hombre. Medellin, 1934.
Phil 1850.116 — Carrau, L. De sermonibus fidelibus F. Baconi Verulamii. Argentorat, 1870.
Phil 1802.1 — Carrau, L. La philosophie religieuse en Angleterre. Paris, 1888.
Phil 9420.6 — Carrau, L. Théorie des passions. Strasbourg, 1870.
Phil 9075.20 — Carrau, Ludovic. La conscience psychologique et morale. Paris, 1888.
Phil 365.1 — Carrau, V.M.J.L. Études sur la théorie de l'evolution. Paris, 1879.
Phil 177.120 — Carré, Jean Raoul. Le point d'appui pris sur le néant. 1. éd. Paris, 1915.
Phil 6990.1 — Carre, L.B. La verité des miracles. n.p., 1737-41. 2v.
Phil 6990.1.2 — Carré, L.B. La verité des miracles. Utrecht, 1737-41.
Phil 1802.6 — Carré, M.H. Phrases of thought in English. Oxford, 1949.
Phil 630.48 — Carré, Meyrick H. Realists and nominalists. London, 1946.
Phil 6990.3.65 — Carrel, A. The voyage to Lourdes. 1. ed. N.Y., 1950.
Phil 9070.52 — Carrel, Alexis. Réflexions sur la conduite de la vie. Paris, 1950.
Phil 6990.3.114 — Carrel et Zola devant le miracle à Lourdes. (Cassagnard, Jean Marie.) Lourdes, 1958.
Phil 4303.6 — Carreras y Artau, J. Apports hispaniques à la philosophie chrétienne. Louvain, 1962.
Phil 4303.7 — Carreras y Artau, J. Estudios filosóficos. v.1-2. Barcelona, 1966-1968.
Phil 4303.1.5 — Carreras y Artau, T. Estudios sobre médicos-filosófos españoles del siglo XIX. Barcelona, 1952.
Phil 4303.1 — Carreras y Artau, T. Introduccio a la història del pensament filosofic a Catalunya. Barcelona, 1931.
Phil 5627.260.13 — Carrier, Hervé. Psycho-sociologie de l'appartenance religieuse. 3. ed. Rome, 1966.
Phil 8582.66 — Carrier, Hervé. The sociology of religious belonging. N.Y., 1965.
Phil 3160.4.3 — Carriere, M. Gesammelte Werke. v.1-14. Leipzig, 1886-94. 12v.
Phil 8403.10.5 — Carriere, Moriz. Aesthetik. Leipzig, 1859. 2v.
Phil 8403.10.2 — Carriere, Moriz. Aesthetik. Leipzig, 1873. 2v.
Phil 8403.10.3 — Carriere, Moriz. Aesthetik. 3. Aufl. Leipzig, 1885. 2v.
Phil 8520.15.3 — Carriere, Moriz. Die philosophische Weltanschauung. 2. Aufl. Leipzig, 1887. 2v.
Phil 2905.1.305 — La carrière scientifique de Pierre Teilhard de Chardin. (Barjon, L.) Monaco, 1964.
Phil 4957.40 — Carrillo Narváez, Alfredo. La tragectoria del pensamiento filosófico en Latinoamérica. Quito, 1959.
Phil 7069.51 — Carrington, H. Haunted people. 1. ed. N.Y., 1951.
Phil 7069.39.9 — Carrington, H. Laboratory investigations into psychic phenomena. Philadelphia, 1939.
Phil 7069.20.365 — Carrington, H. The psychic world. N.Y., 1937.
Phil 7060.75.5 — Carrington, H. True ghost stories. N.Y., 1915.
Phil 7069.08.15 — Carrington, Hereward. The coming science. Boston, 1908.
Phil 7069.20.50 — Carrington, Hereward. The coming science. N.Y., 1920.
Phil 7069.13.5 — Carrington, Hereward. Death, its causes and phenomena. 2. ed. London, 1913.
Phil 7069.09.3 — Carrington, Hereward. Eusapia Palladino and her phenomena. N.Y., 1909.
Phil 7069.19.40 — Carrington, Hereward. Modern psychical phenomena. N.Y., 1919.
Phil 7069.07.10 — Carrington, Hereward. The physical phenomena of spiritualism. Boston, 1907.
Phil 7069.08.16 — Carrington, Hereward. The physical phenomena of spiritualism. Boston, 1908.
Phil 7069.07.12 — Carrington, Hereward. The physical phenomena of spiritualism. 2. ed. Boston, 1908.
Phil 7069.07.13 — Carrington, Hereward. The physical phenomena of spiritualism. 3. ed. N.Y., 1920.
Phil 7069.14.5 — Carrington, Hereward. The problems of psychical research. London, 1914.
Phil 7069.19.45 — Carrington, Hereward. Psychical phenomena. N.Y., 1919.
Phil 7069.20.53A — Carrington, Hereward. Your psychic powers and how to develop them. N.Y., 1920.
Phil 87.14 — Carrión, Joaquin. Diccionario de sinónimos ó sea la propiedad del lenguage filosófico. Madrid, 1873.
Phil 8400.3A — Carritt, E.F. Philosophies of beauty, from Socrates to R. Bridges. N.Y., 1931.
Phil 8877.68.5 — Carritt, Edgar F. An ambignity of the word "good". London, 1937.
Phil 8877.68.10 — Carritt, Edgar F. Ethical and political thinking. Oxford, 1947.
Phil 8877.68.15 — Carritt, Edgar F. The theory of beauty. London, 1962.
Phil 8877.68 — Carritt, Edgar F. Theory of morals. London, 1928.
Phil 5425.90 — Carroll, H.A. Genius in the making. N.Y., 1940.
Phil 5520.423 — Carroll, John B. Language and thought. Englewood Cliffs, N.J., 1964.
Phil 6112.20 — Carroll, Robert S. The mastery of nervousness based upon self-reeducation. N.Y., 1917.
Phil 6112.20.2 — Carroll, Robert S. The mastery of nervousness based upon self-reeducation. 2nd ed. N.Y., 1918.
Phil 6112.20.5 — Carroll, Robert S. Our nervous friends. N.Y., 1919.
Htn Phil 2115.80* — Carroll, William. A dissertation upon the tenth chapter of the fourth book of Mr. Locke's Essay concerning human understanding. London, 1706.
Phil 5203.12 — Carron, René. Guide de l'étudiant en psychologie. Paris, 1953.
Phil 2050.230 — Carsi, M. Natura e società in David Hume. 1. ed. Firenze, 1953.
Phil 8582.25.5 — Carson, Capshaw, (pseud.). An appeal to the real leaders of men. Chicago, 1918.
Phil 8582.25 — Carson, Capshaw, (pseud.). A witness testifies. Chicago, 1918.
Phil 331.2.8 — Carstanjen, F. Richard Avenarius' Biomechanische Grundlegung. München, 1894.
Phil 5400.180 — Carstens, Erik. HAD. Kóbenhavn, 1967.
Phil 2750.11.230 — Carta a Jacques Maritain sobre la colaboración de los católicos con los movimientos de tipo fascista. (Pico, Cesar E.) Buenos Aires, 1937.
Phil 193.235 — Carta a Sartre, y otros ensayos. (Seijas, Rodolfo.) Buenos Aires, 1962.
Phil 8403.29 — Cartalano, F. La filosofia dell'arte. Torino, 1875.
Phil 4983.5.22 — Cartas a Elpidio (Selección). (Varela, Félix.) Habana, 1960.
Phil 4983.5.85 — Cartas a Elpidio sobre la impiedad. v.1-2. (Varela, Félix.) Habana, 1944.
Phil 2648.43.25 — Cartas á Eugenia. (Holbach, Paul Henri T.) Paris, 1810.
Phil 9175.4 — Cartas a mi esposa. (Pacheco, R.) Santiago de Chile, 1878.
Phil 9351.14 — Cartas a mi hijo. (Llonu, Lastenia Lurriva de.) Lima, 1919.
Phil 8610.846 — Cartas á un escéptico en materia de religion. (Balmes, Jaime.) Barcelona, 1846.
Phil 4351.4.15 — Cartas criticas. (Alvarado, Francisco.) Madrid, 1824-25. 5v.
Phil 4351.4.10 — Cartas del filósofo rancio. (Alvarado, Francisco.) Sevilla, 1811-14. 3v.
Phil 2805.36 — Cartas escritas a un provincial. (Pascal, Blaise.) Paris, 1849.
Phil 4363.5.31 — Cartas filosoficas a Attico. (Macedo, J.A. de.) Lisboa, 1815.
Phil 4369.7 — Cartas ineditas. (Sanz del Rio, Julián.) Madrid, 1873?
Phil 4351.4.5 — Las cartas inéditas del filosofo rancio. (Alvarado, Francisco.) Madrid, 1916.
Phil 2515.16 — Cartaud de la Villate. (Krauss, W.) Berlin, 1960. 2v.
Phil 5242.25 — Cartault, A. L'intellectuel. Paris, 1914.
Phil 5440.53 — Cartault, A. Les sentiments généraux. Paris, 1912.
Phil 7069.20.61 — Carter, Huntly. Spiritualism, its present-day meaning. Philadelphia, 1920.
Phil 6112.13 — Carter, R.B. Influence of education and training in preventing diseases of nervous system. London, 1855.
Phil 4001.1 — Les Cartériens d'Italie. Thèse. (Berthé de Besaucèle, Louis.) Paris, 1920.
Phil 2520.385 — Cartesiaanse uitzichten. (Wegelingh, William.) Lochem, 1966.

Author and Title Listing

Phil 2520.405   Cartesian essays; a collection of critical studies. (Magnus, Bernd.) The Hague, 1969.

Phil 5520.449A   Cartesian linguistics. (Chomsky, Noam.) N.Y., 1966.

Phil 3450.40   Cartesian meditations. (Husserl, Edmund.) The Hague, 1960.

Phil 3450.11.40A   Cartesian meditations. (Husserl, Edmund.) The Hague, 1960.

Phil 2520.120   The Cartesian philosophy before Descartes. (Martin, W.A.P.) Peking, 1888.

Phil 2520.232   Cartesian studies. (Balz, A.G.A.) N.Y., 1951.

Phil 2520.170   Die cartesianische Scholastik. (Bohatec, Josef.) Leipzig, 1912.

Phil 2520.82   Le Cartésianisme. (Bordas-Demoulin, J.B.) Paris, 1843. 2v.

Phil 2520.145   Les cartésianism. (Bordas-Demoulin.) Paris, 1874.

Phil 4463.5   Cartesianismo em Portugal: Antonio Cordeiro. (Moraes, Manuel.) Braga, 1966.

Phil 2520.214   Cartesianismo ideal e cartesianismo real. (Sergio, Antonio.) Lisboa, 1937.

Phil 2520.181   Cartesio. (Giuli, Guido de.) Firenze, 1933.

Phil 2520.320   Cartesio. (Oggione, Emilio.) Bologna, 1959.

Phil 2520.186   Cartesio. (Olgiati, Francesco.) Milano, 1934.

Phil 2520.226   Cartesio e l'illuminismo. (Bruno, A.) Bari, 1949.

Phil 2520.86.3   Cartesio nel terzo centenario nel "Discorso del metodo." Milano, 1937.

Phil 4022.1.5   Die cartesische-malebranche'sche Philosophie in Italien. Pt.1-2. (Werner, K.) Wien, 1883.

Phil 2520.155   Cartesius. (Fog, B.J.) Kjøbenhavn, 1856.

Phil 2520.128   Cartesius. (Zoozoomer, C.W.) Amsterdam, 1861.

NEDL Phil 2520.90   Cartesius und seine Gegner. (Hock, C.F.) Wien, 1835.

Phil 4303.10   Cartezon Alvarez, Daniel. De la saudade y sus formas. Nueva York, 1960.

Phil 5421.20.25   Carthy, John D. The natural history of aggression. London, 1964.

Phil 2477.6.130   Cartier, Albert. Existence et vérité. Paris, 1955.

Phil 9560.14.20   Cartojan, N. Fiore di virtù dans la litterature roamaine. n.p., n.d.

Phil 9560.14.18   Cartojan, N. Fiore di virtù in literature româneasca. Bucarsti, 1928.

Phil 283.2   Carus, C.G. Natur und Idee. Wien, 1861.

Phil 333.1   Carus, C.G. Organon der Erkenntniss. Leipzig, 1856.

Phil 5242.1.5   Carus, C.G. Psychologie zur Entwicklungsgeschichte der Seele. Pforzheim, 1846.

Phil 5242.1   Carus, C.G. Vorlesungen über Psychologie. Leipzig, 1831.

Phil 5812.5   Carus, Carl Gustav. Vergleichende Psychologie. Wien, 1866.

Phil 8620.13A   Carus, D.P. History of the devil and idea of evil. Chicago, 1900.

Phil 5212.1   Carus, F.A. Geschichte der Psychologie. Leipzig, 1808.

Phil 177.36   Carus, F.A. Ideen zur Geschichte der Philosophie. Leipzig, 1809.

Phil 5242.53.2   Carus, K.G. Vorlesungen über Psychologie. Darmstadt, 1958.

Phil 5242.53   Carus, K.G. Vorlesungen über Psychologie. Erlerbach, 193-?

Phil 6012.7   Carus, Karl G. Über Grund und Bedeutung der verschiedenen formenen der hand in verschiedenen Personen. Berlin, 1927.

Phil 5425.14   Carus, Karl G. Über ungleiche Befähigung der verschiedenen Menschheitsstämme. Leipzig, 1849.

Phil 3160.9.30   Carus, Karl Gustav. Karl Gustav Carus und Carl Fr. Ph. von Martins. Halle, 1939.

Phil 3160.9   Carus, Karl Gustav. Lebens Erinnerungen und Denkwürdigkeiten. Weimar, 1966. 2v.

Phil 9070.134   Carus, Karl Gustav. Die Lebenskunst nach den Inschriften des Tempels zu Delphi. Stuttgart, 1968.

Phil 930.1   Carus, P. Chinese philosophy. Chicago, 1898.

Phil 930.1.5   Carus, P. Chinese philosophy. 2d ed. Chicago, 1902.

Phil 930.1.2   Carus, P. Chinese thought. Chicago, 1907.

Phil 22.6.5   Carus, P. Monism: its scope and review of The Monist. Chicago, 1890-1891.

Phil 510.6A   Carus, P. Monism and meliorism. N.Y., 1885.

Phil 575.17   Carus, P. Personality. Chicago, 1911.

Phil 75.15   Carus, P. Philosophy as a science. Chicago, 1909.

Phil 6112.10   Carus, P. The soul of man. Chicago, 1891.

Phil 720.6   Carus, P. Truth on trial. Chicago, 1910.

Phil 8692.10   Carus, Paul. The dawn of a new era. Chicago, 1899.

Phil 8877.41   Carus, Paul. The ethical problem. Chicago, 1890.

Phil 8877.42   Carus, Paul. The ethical problem. 3rd ed. Chicago, 1910.

Phil 177.8   Carus, Paul. Fundamental problems. Chicago, 1889.

Phil 177.8.3   Carus, Paul. Fundamental problems. 2nd ed. Chicago, 1891.

Phil 3484.5   Carus, Paul. Kant and Spencer. Chicago, 1899.

Phil 3640.120A   Carus, Paul. Nietzsche. Chicago, 1914.

Phil 177.8.15   Carus, Paul. Philosophie als Wissenschaft. Chicago, 1911.

Phil 177.8.25   Carus, Paul. The point of view: an anthology. Chicago, 1927.

Phil 177.8.12A   Carus, Paul. Primer of philosophy. Chicago, 1893.

Phil 8403.15   Carus, Paul. The principles of art. Boston, 1886.

Phil 8692.10.15   Carus, Paul. The religion of science. Chicago, 1893.

Phil 177.8.5   Carus, Paul. The surd of metaphysics. Chicago, 1903.

Phil 177.8.9   Carus, Paul. Ursache Grund und Zweck. Dresden, 1883.

Phil 6312.20   Caruso, Igor A. Bios, Psyche, Person. Freiburg, 1957.

Phil 6312.20.5   Caruso, Igor A. Existential psychology. N.Y., 1964.

Phil 5790.2.20   Caruso, Igor A. Die Trennung der Liebenden. Bern, 1968.

Phil 680.10   Caruso, Paolo. Conversazioni con Claude Lévi-Straws, Michel Foucault, Jacques Lacan. Milano, 1969.

Phil 4060.2.80   Carvalho, Joaquim de. Leão Hebreu, filósofo. Coimbra, 1918.

Phil 4357.1.81   Carvalho, Joaquim de. Antonio de Gouveia e o Aristotelismo la renascenca. Coimbra, 1916.

Phil 510.156   Carvalho, Rubens di Souza. Filosofia universitária. Rio de Janeiro, 1964.

Phil 8620.15   Carver, T.N. The economic basis of the problem of evil. Cambridge, 1908.

Phil 8582.19   Carver, T.N. The religion worth having. Boston, 1912.

Phil 8582.19.2A   Carver, T.N. The religion worth having. Boston, 1912.

Phil 8582.19.5   Carver, T.N. The religion worth having. Los Angeles, 1940.

Phil 2150.21.80   Carver, Vida. C.A. Mace: a symposium. London, 1962.

Phil 9342.9   Cary, V. (Mrs.). Letters on female character. Richmond, 1830.

Phil 8952.12   Cary-Elwes, C.F. Law, liberty and love. N.Y., 1951.

Phil 2905.1.420   Le cas Teilhard de Chardin. (Hugedé, Norbert.) Paris, 1966.

Phil 6315.2.200   Casa de la Cultura Ecuatoriana. Sigmund Freud; homenaje. Cuenca, 1956.

Phil 8877.91   Casamayor, Louis. La justice, l'homme et la liberté. Paris, 1964.

Phil 4352.1.140   Casanovas, J. Balmes. Barcelona, 1932. 3v.

Phil 3450.11.155   Casaubon, Juan A. Germenes de idealismo en las investigaciones logicas de Husserl. Buenos Aires? 1956?

Htn Phil 177.15*   Casaubon, M. Letter...concerning natural experimental philosophy. Cambridge, 1669.

Htn Phil 5405.6*   Casaubon, M. A treatise concerning enthusiasme. 2. ed. London, 1656.

Phil 5405.6.2   Casaubon, M. A treatise conserning enthusiasme (1655). 2. ed. Gainsville, 1970.

Phil 2050.178   Casazza, G. Hume, Kant e lo scetticismo filosofico. Roma, 1913.

Phil 630.14.501   Case, Thomas. Physical realism. London, 1888.

Phil 5590.120   Case, V.S. Your personality. N.Y., 1946.

Phil 8677.16   The case against theism. (Whitehead, George.) London, 1922.

Phil 6332.31   Case book in abnormal psychology. (Weinberg, Henry.) N.Y., 1964.

Phil 7069.26.13A   The case for and against psychical belief. (Murchison, C.) Worcester, 1927.

Phil 8591.44.10   The case for Christianity. (Lewis, Clive Staples.) N.Y., 1944.

Phil 8591.44.11   The case for Christianity. (Lewis, Clive Staples.) N.Y., 1945.

Phil 665.75A   The case for modern man. 1st ed. (Frankel, Charles.) N.Y., 1956.

Phil 6980.148   Case histories in clinical and abnormal psychology. v.2. (Burton, A.) N.Y., 1947.

Phil 6315.2.155   The case history of Sigmund Freud. 1. ed. (Natenberg, M.) Chicago, 1955.

Phil 7069.24.35   The case of Lester Coltman. (Walbrook, L.) London, 1924.

Phil 6972.4   The case of Luigi Buranelli. (Winslow, F.) London, 1855.

Phil 6310.1.25A   The case of Miss R. (Adler, A.) N.Y., 1929.

Phil 6968.11   Case of moral insanity. (Stedman, H.R.) Boston, 1904.

Phil 7069.16.63   The case of Patience Worth. (Prince, W.F.) Boston, 1927.

Phil 5628.55.15   The case of Therese Neumann. (Graef, Hilda Charlotte.) Cork, 1950.

Phil 3640.70   The case of Wagner. Photoreproduction. (Nietzsche, Friedrich.) Nietzsche, 1896.

Phil 6311.45   Case studies in counseling and psychotherapy. (Burton, Arthur.) Englewood Cliffs, N.J., 1959.

Phil 1135.145   Casel, Otto. De philosophorum graecorum silentis mystics. Giessen, 1919.

Phil 2138.122   Casellato, S. Giovanni Stuart Mill e l'utilitarismo inglese. Padova, 1951.

Phil 720.44   Casellato, Sante. Di alcune considerazioni intorno alla verità e all'errore. Padova, 1958.

Phil 5722.29   Casey, D.M. La théorie du subconscient de Morton Prince. Paris, 1945.

Phil 802.18   Casey, F. Thinking. London, 1922.

Phil 8877.100   Casey, John. Morality and moral reasoning; five essays in ethics. London, 1971.

Phil 177.92   Casey, Joseph T. The primacy of metaphysics. Diss. Washington, D.C., 1936.

Phil 2402.6   Caso, A. Filósofos y moralistas franceses. México, 1943.

Phil 2750.10.106   Caso, A. Myerson y la física moderna. México, 1939.

Phil 600.48   Caso, A. Positivismo, neopositivismo y fenomenologia. México, 1941.

Phil 177.126   Caso, Antonio. Antología filosófica. México, 1957.

Phil 177.37.5   Caso, Antonio. La existencia como economía como desinterés y como caridad. México, 1919.

Phil 8877.37   Caso, Antonio. Filósofos y doctrinas morales. Mexico, 1915.

Phil 177.37   Caso, Antonio. Problemas filosóficos. México, 1915.

Phil 3640.702   El caso Nietzsche. (Vincenzi, M.) San Juan, 1963.

Phil 3450.33.13   Caspar, Caspar Toni. Grundlagen der Ontologie Nicolai Hartmanns. Tübingen, 1955.

Phil 1153.5   Caspari, A. De cynicis. Chemnitz, 1896.

Phil 333.2   Caspari, O. Grundprobleme der Erkenntniss. Berlin, 1876-79. 2v.

Phil 3565.80   Caspari, O. Hermann Lotze. Breslau, 1883.

Phil 3565.80.5   Caspari, O. Hermann Lotze. 2. Aufl. Breslau, 1895.

Phil 1107.2   Caspari, Otto. Die Irrthümer der altclassischen Philosophie. Heidelberg, 1868.

Phil 3552.267   Caspari, Otto. Leibniz' Philosophie. Leipzig, 1870.

Phil 177.30   Caspari, Otto. Zusammenhang der Dinge. Breslau, 1881.

Phil 3002.7   Casper, Bernhard. Das dialogische Denken. Freiburg, 1967.

Phil 310.758   Cassa, Marco. Ragione dialettica prassi marxista e profezia cristiana. Milano, 1966.

Phil 6990.3.114   Cassagnard, Jean Marie. Carrel et Zola devant le miracle à Lourdes. Lourdes, 1958.

Phil 510.140   Cassaigneau, M. Monisme vitaliste. Paris, 1925.

Phil 2750.11.115   Cassata, M.L. La pedagogia di Jacques Maritain. Palermo, 1953.

Phil 8598.59.5   Cassels, W.R. Supernatural religion. London, 1874-77. 3v.

Phil 8598.59.10   Cassels, W.R. Supernatural religion. London, 1879. 3v.

Phil 802.17   Casserley, J.V.L. The Christian in philosophy. London, 1949.

Phil 8877.80   Casserley, J.V.L. Morals and man in the social sciences. London, 1951.

Phil 1603.2   Cassier, E. The indivudual and the cosmos in Renaissance philosophy. N.Y., 1963.

Phil 7080.52   Cassina, U. Congetture su i sogni. Parma, 1783.

Phil 6950.6   Cassinelli, B. Histoire de la folie. Paris, 1939.

Phil 1870.94   Cassirer, E. Berkeleys System. Giessen, 1914.

Phil 2520.208.5   Cassirer, E. Descartes, Corheille, Christine de Suede. Paris, 1942.

Phil 2520.208   Cassirer, E. Descartes. Stockholm, 1939.

Phil 3552.111   Cassirer, E. Leibniz' System. Marburg, 1902.

Phil 1802.10   Cassirer, E. The platonic renaissance in England. Edinburgh, 1953.

Phil 333.5   Cassirer, Ernst. Das Erkenntnisproblem in der Philosophie. Berlin, 1906-57. 4v.

Phil 333.5.3   Cassirer, Ernst. Das Erkenntnisproblem in der Philosophie. 2. Aufl. Berlin, 1911. 2v.

Phil 333.5.15   Cassirer, Ernst. An essay on man. New Haven, 1944.

Phil 333.5.17   Cassirer, Ernst. An essay on man. New Haven, 1948.

Phil 333.5.18   Cassirer, Ernst. An essay on man. New Haven, 1962.

Phil 3002.3   Cassirer, Ernst. Freiheit und Form. 2e Aufl. Berlin, 1918.

Phil 3484.11   Cassirer, Ernst. Kants Leben und Lehre. Berlin, 1921.

Phil 3160.12.40   Cassirer, Ernst. The logic of the humanities. New Haven, 1961.

Phil 1750.141A   Cassirer, Ernst. Die Philosophie der Aufklärung. Tübingen, 1932.

Phil 333.5.9   Cassirer, Ernst. Philosophie der symbolischen Formen. Berlin, 1923-29. 3v.

Phil 333.5.10 — Cassirer, Ernst. Philosophie der symbolischen Formen. Index. Berlin, 1931.

Phil 333.5.12A — Cassirer, Ernst. The philosophy of symbolic forms. New Haven, 1953- 3v.

Phil 1750.141.3A — Cassirer, Ernst. The philosophy of the enlightenment. Princeton, N.J., 1951.

Phil 333.5.20 — Cassirer, Ernst. The problem of knowledge. New Haven, 1950.

Phil 4002.9 — Cassirer, Ernst. The Renaissance philosophy of man. Chicago, 1948.

Phil 4002.9.5 — Cassirer, Ernst. The Renaissance philosophy of man. Chicago, 1956.

Phil 1750.141.7A — Cassirer, Ernst. Rousseau, Kant, Goethe; two essays. Princeton, 1947.

Phil 333.5.8A — Cassirer, Ernst. Substance and function and Einstein's theory of relativity. N.Y., 1953.

Phil 333.5.5 — Cassirer, Ernst. Substansbegriff und Funktionsbegriff. Berlin, 1910.

Phil 3160.12.30 — Cassirer, Ernst. Wesen und Wirkung des Symbolbegriffs. Oxford, 1956.

Phil 3160.12.42 — Cassirer, Ernst. Zur Logik der Kulturwissenschaften. 2. Aufl. Darmstadt, 1961.

Phil 3484.18 — Cassirer, H.W. A commentary on Kant's Critique of judgement. London, 1938.

Phil 3484.18.5 — Cassirer, H.W. Kant's first critique. London, 1954.

Phil 5374.235.10 — Castaneda, Carlos. A separate reality; further conversations with Don Juan. N.Y., 1971.

Phil 5374.235.5 — Castaneda, Carlos. The teachings of Don Juan; a yaqui way of knowledge. Berkeley, 1968.

Phil 8870.24 — Castaneda, H. Morality and the language of conduct. Detroit, 1963.

Phil 177.88 — Castaner, C. Soul and matter. London, 1933.

Phil 1750.166.205 — Castanos, Stelios. Réponse à Heidegger sur l'humanisme. Paris, 1966.

Phil 8403.25 — Castelfranco, G. Lineamenti di estetica. 1. ed. Firenze, 1950.

Phil 2138.115 — Castell, A. Mill's logic of the moral sciences. Diss. Chicago, 1936.

Phil 5042.27 — Castell, Alburey. A college logic; an introduction to the study of argument and proof. N.Y., 1935.

Phil 1702.7 — Castell, Alburey. An introduction to modern philosophy. N.Y., 1943.

Phil 585.164 — Castell, Alburey. The self in philosophy. N.Y., 1965.

Phil 8877.86 — Castell, Alhurey. An elementary ethics. Englewood Cliffs, 1955.

Phil 7069.59.35 — Castellan, Yvonne. Le spiritisme. 2. ed. Paris, 1959.

Phil 6315.2.120 — Castellano, Filemón. El psicoanalisis de Freud. Buenos Aires, 1941.

Phil 4080.3.121 — Castellano, G. Benedetto Croce. Napoli, 1924.

Phil 4080.3.121.5 — Castellano, G. Benedetto Croce. 2a ed. Bari, 1936.

Phil 4080.3.120 — Castellano, G. Introduzione allo studio...B. Croce. Bari, 1920.

Phil 4080.3.121.20 — Castellano, G. Ragazzate letteraris: appunti...Croce. Napoli, 1919.

Phil 4080.12.45 — Castelli, Enrico. L'enquête quotidienne. Paris, 1959.

Phil 1750.372.5 — Castelli, Enrico. Esistenzialismo teologico. Roma, 1966.

Phil 1750.372 — Castelli, Enrico. Existentialisme théologique. Paris, 1948.

Phil 1750.372.2 — Castelli, Enrico. Existentialisme théologique. 2e éd. Paris, 1966.

Phil 4080.12.30 — Castelli, Enrico. Filosofia della vita. Roma, 1924.

Phil 8582.46 — Castelli, Enrico. Filosofia e apologetica. Roma, 1929.

Phil 4080.12.35 — Castelli, Enrico. Introduction à une phenomenologie de notre epoque. Paris, 1949.

Phil 2477.6.89 — Castelli, Enrico. Lettres reçues à propos de la communication de M. Blondel. Marseille, 1933.

Phil 4080.12.65 — Castelli, Enrico. I paradossi del senso comune. Padova, 1970.

Phil 4080.12.62 — Castelli, Enrico. Il tempo esaurito. 2. ed. Milano, 1954.

Phil 4080.12.50 — Castelli, Enrico. Le temps Larcelant. Paris, 1952.

Phil 8877.49 — Castellotti, G. de. Saggi di etica e di diritto. Ser. 1-2,3-5. Ascoli Piceno, 1903-06. 2v.

Phil 8430.13 — Castelnuovo, E. El arte y las masas, ensayos sobre una nueva teoría della actividad estética. Buenos Aires, 1935.

Phil 5402.13 — Castez, G. La douleur physique. Paris, 1905.

Phil 2045.105 — Castigations of Mr. Hobbes. (Bramhall, J.) London, 1658.

Phil 6952.3 — Castiglioni, C. Sulle alterazioni delle pupile nei pazzi. Milano, 1863-65. 2 pam.

Phil 3640.215A — Castiglioni, M. Il poema eroico di F. Nietzsche. Torino, 1924.

Phil 2050.260 — Castignone, Silvana. Giustizia e bene comune in David Hume. Milano, 1964.

Htn Phil 4080.4.30* — Castilio, Baldessa. The courtier. London, 1588.

Phil 5545.75 — Castilio, A.F. de. Tratado demnemonica. Lisboa, 1851.

Phil 477.3 — Castillon, J. de. Observations sur le livre "Système de la nature". Berlin, 1771.

Phil 9495.168.30 — Castità: problema o liberazione? (Barra, Giovanni.) Torino, 1968.

Phil 4668.40.30 — Castrén, Zacharias. Uskonnonfilosofian käsitteestä ja metoodista. Helsingissä, 1899.

Phil 4340.5 — Castro y Rossi, Adolf de. Obras escogidas de filósofos. Madrid, 1953.

Phil 2805.108 — De casuïstiek en Pascal. (Beerens, J.F.) Utrecht, 1909.

Phil 3484.23.5 — Casula, Mario. L'illuminismo critico. Milano, 1967.

Phil 2750.23.80 — Casula, Mario. Maréchal e Kant. Roma, 1955.

Phil 3484.23 — Casula, Mario. Studi kantiani sul trascendente. Milano, 1963.

Phil 8965.17 — Casus conscientiae. (Palazzini, Pietro.) Torino, 1958. 2v.

Phil 8965.17.2 — Casus conscientiae. 2. ed. (Palazzini, Pietro.) Torino, 1964. 2v.

Phil 8951.7.9 — Casus conscientiae de mandato. (Benedictus XIV.) Augustae Vindelicorum, 1772.

Phil 8951.7.10 — Casus conscientiae de mandato. Appendix. v.1-5. (Benedictus XIV.) Augustae Vindelicorum, 1772. 3v.

Phil 8956.8.15 — Casus conscientiae propositi ac soluti. 6. ed. (Genicot, Edouard.) Louvain, 1928.

Phil 1850.125 — Catalano, E. Il naturalismo e l'individualismo di F. Bacone. Napoli, 1931.

Phil 5003.5 — Catalog of a collection of books on logic. (Cambridge. University. Library.) Cambridge, 1889.

Phil 4352.1.125 — Catálogo de la exposicion bibliográfica. (Barcelona. Biblioteca Central.) Barcelona, 1948.

Phil 4372.1.90 — Catálogo de la exposición bibliográfica celebrada con motivo del IV centenario de la muerte de Luis Vives. (Mateu y Llopez, F.) Barcelona, 1940.

Phil 75.30 — Catalogo della Biblioteca filosofica. Text and supplement. (Florence. Biblioteca Filosofica.) Firenze, 1910.

Phil 2725.2.82 — Catalogue de livres rares et precieux provenant de la bibliothèque de M.F. de la Mennais. (Lamennais, F.R. de.) Paris, 1836.

Phil 2520.01 — Catalogue des ouvrages de Descartes. (Paris. Bibliothèque National. Département des Imprimés.) Paris, 1909.

Phil 1850.155 — Catalogue of exhibition organized by the St. Albans City Council in the Council Chamber. (Saint Albans, England. City Council.) St. Albans, 1961.

Htn Phil 2115.77.5F* — Catalogue of Locke's library. Ms. photostat. (Locke, J.) n.p., n.d.

Phil 1870.134 — Catalogue of manuscripts. (Dublin. University. Trinity College. Library.) Dublin, 1953.

Phil 75.33 — A catalogue of Renaissance philosophers. (Riedl, J.O.) Milwaukee, 1940.

Phil 5921.5 — A catalogue of specimens. (Boston Phrenological Society.) Boston, 1835.

Phil 1865.185.2 — Catalogue of the manuscripts of Jeremy Bentham in the Library of University College. (London. University. University College Library.) London, 1937.

Phil 1865.185 — Catalogue of the manuscripts of Jeremy Bentham in the Library of University College. 2nd ed. (London. University. University College Library.) London, 1962.

Htn Phil 2115.77F* — Catalogus librorum. Ms. photostat. (Locke, J.) n.p., n.d.

Phil 4235.4.81 — Catania. R. Scuola Normale Maschile Superiore. Per le solenni onoranze al filosofo Vincenzo Tedeschi Paterno Castello. Catania, 1892.

Phil 177.9 — Catara-Lettieri, Antonio. L'omu nun l'usu di la ragiuni. Messina, 1869.

Phil 177.9.5 — Catara-Lettieri, Antonio. Sull' uomo; pensieri. Messina, 1869.

Phil 8593.3.2 — A catechism of natural theology. (Nichols, I.) Boston, 1831.

Phil 8593.3.3 — A catechism of natural theology. (Nichols, I.) Boston, 1839.

Phil 8593.3 — A catechism of natural theology. (Nichols, I.) Portland, 1829.

X Cg Phil 2490.56 — Catechism of positive religion. (Comte, Auguste.) London, 1858.

Phil 8581.70 — Catéchisme de la nature, ou religion et morale naturelles. (Blanchard, Pierre.) Paris, n.d.

Phil 8610.798 — Le catéchisme des Christicoles. Paris, 1798.

Phil 2490.55 — Catèchisme positiviste. (Comte, Auguste.) Paris, 1852.

Phil 2490.55.2 — Catèchisme positiviste. (Comte, Auguste.) Paris, 1874.

Phil 8610.875 — Catéchisme religieux des libres penseurs. (Ménard, Louis.) Paris, 1875.

Phil 3488.47 — Categoria e oggetto in Kant. 1. ed. (Gattulo, Mario.) Firenze, 1966.

Phil 5075.8 — Categorial frameworks. (Koerner, Stephan.) Oxford, 1970.

Phil 2055.16.30 — Categorical analysis. (Hall, E.W.) Chapel Hill, 1964.

Phil 3497.19.5 — The categorical imperative. (Paton, Herbert J.) London, 1946.

Phil 5075.1 — The categories. (Stirling, J.H.) Edinburgh, 1903.

Phil 2555.8.35 — Les categories de la modalité. 1. éd. (Darbon, André.) Paris, 1956.

Phil 310.598 — Les categories du materialisme dialectique. (Planty-Bonjour, Guy.) Dordrecht, 1965.

Phil 2225.5.97 — The categories of Charles Peirce. Diss. (Freeman, Eugene.) Chicago, 193-.

Phil 310.598.2 — The categories of dialectical materialism. (Planty-Bonjour, Guy.) Dordrecht, 1967.

Phil 349.30 — The category of relation. (Salomaa, J.E.) Helsink:, 1929.

Phil 6315.19.35 — Catemario, A. La società malata. Napoli, 1962.

Phil 6985.45 — La catharsis dans le théâtre. (Barrucand, Dominique.) Paris, 1970.

Phil 8715.1.10 — The Catholic church and modern science. (Zahm, John Augustine.) Notre Dame, Ind., 1886.

Phil 2150.14.30 — A Catholic looks at the world. (McMahon, T.E.) N.Y., 1945.

Phil 8962.13 — Catholic morality. (Massimi, Massimo.) Paterson, 1943.

Phil 42.8 — Catholic University of America. Studies in psychology and psychiatry. Washington. 1,1927+ 9v.

Phil 8520.50 — Catholic University of America. Workshop on Christian Philosophy and Religious Renewal, 1964. Christian philosophy in the college and seminary. Washington, 1966.

Phil 365.19.60 — A Catholic view of holism. (Kolbe, F.C.) N.Y., 1928.

Phil 8725.2 — Catholicisme et laïcite. (Coulet.) Paris, 1932.

Phil 8685.2 — Catholicity and pantheism. pt.1. (DeConcilio, J.) N.Y., 1874.

Phil 2415.8 — Catholics and unbelievers in eighteenth century France. (Palmer, R.R.) Princeton, 1939.

Phil 5222.13 — Catholics in psychology. (Misiak, Henryk.) N.Y., 1954.

Phil 8877.50.5 — Cathrein, Victor. Die Einheit des sittlichen Bewusstseins der Menschheit. Freiburg, 1914. 3v.

Phil 8877.50.15 — Cathrein, Victor. Moralphilosophie. Leipzig, 1924. 2v.

Phil 8952.14 — Cathrein, Victor. Philosophia moralis in usum scholarum. Friburgi, 1959.

Phil 2045.98 — Catlin, George E.G. Thomas Hobbes as philosopher, publicist and man of letters. Oxford, 1922.

Phil 6112.3 — Catlow, P. On the principles of aesthetic medicine. London, 1867.

Phil 5520.311 — Caton, Charles. Philosophy and ordinary language. Urbana, Ill., 1963.

Phil 4265.1.85 — Cattaneo, G. Idee di G.C. Vanini sull...evoluzione. Milano, 1885.

Phil 6619.6 — Cattani, Giuseppe. Isterismo e sentimento. 19. ed. Milano, 1894.

Htn Phil 283.9* — Cattani da Diacceto, F. L'essamerone. Florenza, 1563.

Phil 8952.13 — Cattani de Menasce, Giovanni. Saggi di analisi dell'atto morale. Roma, 1957.

Phil 5212.2 — Cattell, J.M. The progress of psychology. N.Y., 1893?

Phil 1930.13.30 — Cattell, James M. James McKeen Cattell. Lancaster, Pa., 1947. 2v.

Phil 5242.46 — Cattell, R.B. General psychology. Cambridge, Mass., 1941.

Phil 5590.100 — Cattell, R.B. An introduction to personality study. London, 1950.

Phil 5548.35 — Cattell, R.B. Personality and motivation structure and measurement. Yonkers-on-Hudson, N.Y., 1957.

Phil 5242.46.5 — Cattell, R.B. Personality and social psychology. San Diego, 1964.

Phil 6312.24 — Cattell, Raymond. The meaning and measurement of neuroticism and anxiety. N.Y., 1961.

Phil 5590.446 — Cattell, Raymond. The scientific analysis of personality. Chicago, 1966.

Phil 5590.32 — Cattell, Raymond B. Description and measurement of personality. Yonkers-on-Hudson, 1946.

Phil 5485.8 Cattell, Raymond Bernard. Abilities: their structure, growth, and action. Boston, 1971.
Phil 6805.6 Cattell, Raymond Bernard. Crooked personalities in childhood and after. N.Y., 1940.
Phil 6327.21.95 Cattier, Michel. La vie et l'oeuvre der docteur Wilhelm Reich. Lausanne, 1969.
Phil 2250.100A Catton, J.B. Royce on the human self. Cambridge, 1954.
Phil 4960.245 Caturelli, Alberto. La filosofía en Argentina actual. Córdoba, 1963.
Phil 4957.30 Caturla Brú, Victoria de. Cuáles son los grandes temas de la filosofía latinoamericana? México, 1959.
Phil 4065.31 Caudelaio. (Bruno, Giordano.) Strasburgo, n.d.
Phil 8403.35 Caudwell, H. The creative impulse in writing and painting. London, 1951.
Phil 8582.21 Caulfield. An essay on the immateriality and immortality of the soul. London, 1778.
Phil 8582.4 Caumont, G. Jugements d'un mourant sur la vie. Paris, 1876.
Phil 4120.1.50 La causa di Dio e degli uomini difesa dagl'insulti degli empj e dalle pretensioni dei fanatici. (Gioja, Melchiorre.) Lugano, 1834.
Phil 284.9 La causa e la legge. (Dandolo, G.) Padova, 1901.
Phil 1850.90 Causa finalis. Eine Bakostudie. (Jung, E.) Giessen, 1893.
Phil 270.38 La causa trinitaria unica sostanza del cosmo. (Faggiotto, A.) Padova, 1929.
Phil 2150.6.82F Die Causalbetrachtung in den Geisteswissenschaften. (Ritschl, Otto.) Bonn, 1901.
Phil 2733.119 Causalità divina e libertà umana nel pensiero di Malebranche. (Nicolosi, Salvatore.) Padova, 1963.
Phil 8735.40.5 Causalità e finalità. (Fondazione Giorgio Cini, Venice. Centro de Cultura e Civiltà.) Firenze, 1959.
Phil 270.140 Causalità e indeterminismo. (Selvaggi, Filippo.) Roma, 1964.
Phil 1630.30 Causalità e infinità nella scuola padovana dal 1480 al 1513. (Poppi, Antonino.) Padova, 1906.
Phil 270.63 La causalità nel razionalismo moderno. (Giacon, Carlo.) Milano, 1954.
Phil 270.8 Causalitäs-Gesetz in der Socialwissen. (Houten, S. van.) Harlem, 1888.
Phil 270.5 Causalität und Entwicklung. (Christinnecke, J.) Jena, 1891.
Phil 2050.112 Das Causalitätsproblem bei Malebranche und Hume. (Keller, Anton.) Rastatt, 1899.
Phil 5585.211 Causalité, permanence et réalité phénoménales. (Michotte, Albert.) Louvain, 1962.
Phil 270.18 La causalité efficiente. Thèse. (Fonsegrive, G.L.) Paris, 1891.
Phil 270.146 Causaliteit. (Zwart, P.J.) Assen, 1967[1968]
Phil 270.90 Causality. (Bunge, Mario.) Cambridge, 1959.
Phil 270.9 Causality. (Jamieson, G.) London, 1872.
Phil 270.42 Causality. (Silberstein, L.) London, 1933.
Phil 270.45 Causality and implication. (Hawkins, D.J.B.) London, 1937.
Phil 270.47 Causality and science. (Brahma, N.K.) London, 1939.
NEDL Phil 4372.1.35 Causas de la decadencia de las artes. (Vives, Juan Luis.) Buenos Aires, 1948.
Phil 270.44 Causation, freedom, and determinism. (Taube, M.) London, 1936.
Phil 6968.10 The causation...reflex insanity in women. (Storer, H.R.) Boston, 1871.
Phil 270.7.10 Causation and freedom in willing. (Hazard, R.G.) Boston, 1889.
Phil 270.26 Causation and the types of necessity. (Ducasse, Curt J.) Seattle, 1924.
Phil 6968.12.7 The causation and treatment of psychopathic diseases. (Sidis, Boris.) Boston, 1916.
Phil 7080.1 Causation of sleep. (Cappie, J.) Edinburgh, 1872.
Phil 5756.1 Causational and free will. (Guthrie, M.) London, 1877.
Phil 4065.50.10 Cause, principe et unité. (Bruno, Giordano.) Paris, 1930.
Phil 4065.50.12 Cause, principle, and unity. (Bruno, Giordano.) N.Y., 1964.
Phil 270.131 Cause and effect. (Hayden Colloquium on Scientific Method and Concept. Massachusetts Institute of Technology.) N.Y., 1965.
Phil 8735.12 Cause efficiente et cause finale. (Domet de Vorges, E.) Paris, 1888.
Phil 9150.26 The cause of evil. (Bartholomew, I.G.) London, 1927.
Phil 8735.21 La cause première d'après les données experimentales. (Ferrière, Émile.) Paris, 1897.
Phil 2520.207 Causeries cartésiennes à porpos du troisième centenaire du discours de la méthode. Paris, 1938.
Phil 2070.40 Causeries pédagogiques. 4th ed. (James, William.) Lausanne, 1917.
Phil 176.79 Causeries philosophiques. (Badoureau, A.) Paris, 1920.
Phil 5242.44 Causeries psychologiques. (Claparède, Édouard.) Genève, 1933.
Phil 5242.44.5 Causeries psychologiques. Ser. 2. (Claparède, Édouard.) Genève, 1935.
Phil 5246.10 Les causes...phénomènes de l'âme. (Gruyer. L.A.) Paris, 1844.
Phil 6314.11.10 The causes and cures of neurosis. (Eysenck, Hans J.) London, 1965.
Phil 6750.3.7 Causes and prevention of idiocy. (Howe, S.G.) Boston, 1874.
Phil 4200.1.30 Les causes des merveilles de la nature, ou Les enchantements. (Pomponazzi, Pietro.) Paris, 1930.
Phil 7150.26 Les causes du suicide. (Halbwachs, M.) Paris, 1930.
Phil 2668.50 Les causes finales. (Janet, Paul A.R.) Paris, 1876.
Htn Phil 9342.8* Cautious lady, or Religion the chief happiness in a married state. London, 1760.
Phil 3450.19.535 Cauturier, Fernand. Monde et être chez Heidegger. Montréal, 1971.
Phil 2880.8.295 Cavaciuti, Santino. L'ontologia di Jean Paul Sartre. Milano, 1969.
Phil 3484.25 Cavagna, G.B. La soluzione kantiana. Bologna, 1962.
Phil 2475.1.450 Cavagna, Giordano Bruno. La dottrina della conoscenza in Enrico Bergson. Napoli, 1965.
Phil 4525.3.30 Cavallin, P. Identiska och syntetiska satser. Lund, 1894.
Phil 7082.114 Cavallin, Paul. Dröm och vaka. Stockholm, 1901.
Phil 5752.8 Cavallo, V. La libertà umana nella filosofia contemporanea. Napoli, 1933.
Phil 9400.23 Cavan, R.S. Personal adjustments in old age. Chicago, 1949.
Phil 7150.24 Cavan, R.S. Suicide. Chicago, 1928.
Phil 7069.23.9 Cavanagh, M.R. A strange manuscript. N.Y., 1923.
Phil 2475.1.303 Cavarnos, C.P. A dialogue between Bergson. Cambridge, 1949.
Phil 665.106 Cavarnos, Constantine. Modern Greek philosophers on the human soul. Belmont, 1967.
Phil 4843.2 Cavarnos, Constantine Peter. Modern Greek thought. Belmont, Mass., 1969.
Phil 8582.58 Cave, S. The Christian estimate of man. London, 1944.
Phil 1930.20 Cavell, Stanley. Must we mean what we say? N.Y., 1969.
Phil 6315.13 The caveman within us. (Fielding, W.J.) N.Y., 1922.
Phil 6312.6 The Cavendish lecture on dreamy mental states. (Crichton-Brown, J.) London, 1895.
Phil 3484.15 Cavicchi, G. de. Saggio Culle contraddizioni di Emanuele Kant. Catania, 1929.
Phil 4210.78 Caviglione, C. Bibliografia delle opere di A. Rosmini. Torino, 1925.
Phil 4210.112 Caviglione, C. Il Rosmini vero. Voghera, 1912.
Phil 365.18.5 Cavling, Viggo. The collective spirit; an idealistic theory of evolution. N.Y., 1926.
Phil 177.87 Cavour, G.B. de. Fragments philosophiques. Turin, 1841.
Phil 177.87.5 Cavour, G.B. di. Discorso. Torino, 1861.
Phil 2477.15.90 Caws, Mary Ann. Surrealism and the literary imagination; a study of Breton and Bachelard. The Hague, 1966.
Phil 7069.69.25 Cayce, Edgar. The Edgar Cayce reader. N.Y., 1969.
Phil 6112.40.20 Cayce, Edgar Evans. The outer limits of Edgar Cayce's power. 1. ed. N.Y., 1971.
Phil 7069.64.35 Cayce, Hugh Lynn. Venture inward. N.Y., 1964.
Phil 4369.2.80 Cazac, H.P. Le lieu d'origine, du philosophe Francisco Sanchez. Bordeaux, 1903.
Phil 365.10 Cazalles, Emile. Outline of the evolution-philosophy. N.Y., 1875.
Phil 177.103 Cazals de Fabel, Gabriel. Précis de philosophie à l'usage des candidats au baccalaureat. Toulouse, 1937.
Phil 5722.65 Cazaux, Jean. Surréalisme et psychologie. Paris, 1958.
Phil 2725.46 Cazeneuve, J. Lucien Lévy-Bruhl, sa vie, son oeuvre. Paris, 1963.
Phil 5403.11 Cazeneuve, Jean. Bonheur et civilisation. Paris, 1966.
Phil 5403.9 Cazeneuve, Jean. Psychologie de la joie. Paris, 1952.
Phil 2855.3.83 Cazeneuve, Jean. Ravaisson et les médecins animistes et vitalistes. Paris, 1957.
Phil 8657.6 Cazenove, J.G. Historic aspects...being attributes of God. London, 1886.
Phil 2805.470 Ce que croyait Pascal. (Garrone, Gabriel Marie.) Tours, 1969.
Phil 7082.190.5 Ce que disent les rêves. (Teillard, Ania.) Paris, 1970.
Phil 7140.116.9 Ce que j'ai fait. (Coué, Émile.) Nancy, 1924.
Phil 6480.236 Ce que tout rêveur doit savoit de la méthode psychanalytique d'interprétation des rêves. (Bruller, Jean.) Paris, 1934.
Phil 3425.109.5 Ce qui est vivant et ce qui est mort de la philosophie de Hegel. (Croce, B.) Paris, 1910.
Phil 1050.8 Cearus, F.A. Psychologie der Hebräer. Leipzig, 1809.
Phil 9045.1 Ceba, A. The citizen of a republic. N.Y., 1845.
Phil 8692.12 Ceballos Dosamantes, J. Ciencia y religion del porvenir. México, 1897.
Phil 177.71 Ceballos Dosamantes, J. El perfeccionismo absoluto. México, 1888.
Phil 6312.13 Cebola, Luiz. As grandes crises do homen ensaio de psicopatologia individual e colectiva. Lisboa, 1945.
Phil 6952.25 Cebold, Luis. Psiquiatria social. Lisboa, 1931.
Phil 177.138 Ceccato, Silvio. Un tecnico fra i filosofi. Padova, 1964- 2v.
Phil 9120.10 Cederschiöld, F. Allmän inledning till apriorisk. Lund, 1821.
Phil 9120.10.5 Cederschiöld, F. Menniskors aprioriska. Lund, 1828.
Phil 2805.35 Las celebres cartas provinciales. (Pascal, Blaise.) Madrid, 1846.
Phil 2725.14.100 Célèbres leçons et fragments. 2. éd. (Lagneau, Jules.) Paris, 1964.
Phil 4080.14.2 Celesia, Paolo. Opere. v.1-7. Roma, 1923-30. 8v.
Phil 8598.11 The celestial magnet. (Slack, David B.) Providence, R.I., 1820-21. 2 pam.
Phil 7069.02.5 A celestial message. (Gaffield, E.C.) Boston, 1902.
Phil 6672.9.5 Celestial telegraph. 1. American ed. (Cahagnet, L.) N.Y., 1855.
Phil 177.47 Cellarier, Felix. La métaphysique et sa méthode. Paris, 1914.
Phil 6990.58 Celma, Bernal. Curaciones milagrosas. Zaragoza, 1961.
Phil 4065.65 La cena de le cenerè. (Bruno, Giordano.) Torino, 1955.
Phil 4353.10 Cencillo, J.L. Experiencia profunda del ser. Madrid, 1959.
Phil 8956.8 Cenicot, Edouard. Institutiones theologiae moralis quas in Collegio Lovaniensi Societatis Jesu. 12. ed. Louvain, 1931.
Phil 4210.88.5 Cenni biografici di Antonio Rosmini. (Stresa, Italy. Istituto della Carità.) Firenze, 1924.
Phil 4210.88.2 Cenni biografici di Antonio Rosmini. 2a ed. (Stresa, Italy. Istituto della Carità.) Milano, 1857.
Phil 4110.5.95F Cenno su Giuseppe Ferrari e le sul dottrine. (Ferri, Luigi.) Roma, 1877.
Htn Phil 2520.91* Censura philosophiae Cartesianae. (Huetii, P.D.) Paris, 1689.
Phil 2490.165 Le centenaire d'Auguste Comte et la nouvelle constitution française. (Clavel, Marcel.) Fontenay-sous-Bois, 1958.
Phil 5238.7 Centenaire de T. Ribot, jubilé de la psychologie scientifique française, 1839-1939. Agen, 1939.
Phil 4352.1.115 Centenario de Jaime Balmes. (Instituto de España.) Madrid, 1949.
Phil 6158.50 The center of the cyclone. (Lilly, John Cunningham.) N.Y., 1972.
Phil 8708.31 Center of the storm. (Scopes, John Thomas.) N.Y., 1967.
Phil 2725.25 Centineo, E. René LeSenne. Palermo, 1952.
Phil 2050.215 The central problem of David Hume's philosophy. (Salmon, C.V.) Halle , 1929.
Phil 4265.1.95 Centralne kategorie filosofii Vaniniego. Wyd. 1. (Nowicki, Andrzej.) Warszawa, 1970.
Phil 4065.172 Centralne Kategorie filozofii Giordana Bruna. (Nowicki, A.) Warszawa, 1962.
Phil 1600.15 Céntre d'Études Supérieure. Courants religieux et humanisme à la fin de XVième et au début du XVIième siècle. Paris, 1959.
Phil 5465.33.10 Centre International de Synthèse, Paris. Neuvième semaine internationale de synthèse. L'invention. Paris, 1938.
Phil 70.25 Centre International de Synthèse, Paris. Valeur philosophique de la psychologie. Paris, 1951.
Phil 5525.58 The centre of hilarity. (Mason, Michael.) London, 1959.
Phil 5520.738 Centre Regional de Documentation, Pedagogique de Poitiers. Textes et communications sur le thème: philosophie et langage, 24 avril, 1969. Photoreproduction. Paris, 1969?
Phil 70.22.5 Centro di Studi Filosofici Cristiani, Gallarate. Il movimento di Gallarate. Padova. 1955

Phil 5520.453   Centro di Studi Filosofici de Gallarate. 9. Convegno Annuale. Il problema filosofico del linguaggio. Padova, 1965.

Phil 70.22   Centro di Studi Filosofici di Gallarate. Atti del convegno. Brescia. 1,1945+ 21v.

Phil 440.6   Centro di Studi Filosofici di Gallarate. Libertà e responsabilità. Padova, 1967.

Phil 6312.30   Centro di Studi Filosofici di Gallarate. Psicanalisi e filosofia. Padova, 1968.

Phil 70.22.10   Centro di Studi Filosofici di Gallarate. Senso e valore del discorso metafisico. Padova, 1966.

Phil 680.40   Centro di studi filosofici di gallarate. Strutturalismo filosofico. Padova, 1970.

Phil 5039.30   Centro di Studi Filosofici di Gallarate. Teoria della demostrazione. Padova, 1963.

Phil 1600.20   Centro di studi umanistici di Montepulciano. Il pensiero italiano del Rinascimento e il tempo Nostro. Firenze, 1970.

Phil 7150.65   Centro Nazionale di Prevenzione e Difesa Sociale. Suicidio e tentato suicidio. Milano, 1967.

Phil 2420.1   A century for freedom; a survey of the French philosophers. (Urwin, Kenneth.) London, 1946.

Phil 4365.2.45   Cepeda Calzada, Pablo. La doctrina de la sociedad en Ortega y Gasset. Valladolid, 1968.

Phil 6053.8   Cerchiari, G. Luigi. Chiromanzia e tatuaggio. Milano, 1903.

Phil 2520.205   Cercle Philosophique, Lorrain. Tricentenaire de la parution du discours de la méthode, 1637-1937. Metz, 1937.

Phil 6114.2   Cerebral convolutions of man. (Ecker, A.) N.Y., 1873.

Phil 6957.2   Cerebral hyperaemia. (Hammond, W.A.) N.Y., 1878.

Phil 6952.2A   Cerebral localization...insanity. (Carnochan, J.M.) N.Y., 1884.

Phil 5640.45   Cerebral mechanisms in behavior. (Jeffress, Lloyd A.) N.Y., 1951.

Phil 4080.10.60   Ceretti, Pietro. Opere postume. Torino, 1890.

Phil 4080.10.35   Ceretti, Pietro. Saggio circa la ragione logica di tutte le cose (Pasaelogices specimen). v.1-5. Torino, 1888-1905. 7v.

Phil 3450.19.300   Cerezo Galan, Pedro. Arte, verdad y ser en Heidegger. Madrid, 1963.

Phil 4210.145   Ceriani, G. L'ideologia rosminiana nei rapporti con la gnoseologia agostiniano-tomistica. Milano, 1937.

Phil 310.602   Černík, Václav. Dialektický vedecký zákon. Bratislava, 1964.

Phil 177.136   Cernuschi, Alberto. Teoría del autodeísmo. Buenos Aires, 1962.

Phil 8627.20   Cerný, Ladislav. The day of Yahweh and some relevant problems. Praha, 1943.

Phil 2475.1.375   Çerný, V. Ideové kořeny současného umění. Praha, 1929.

Phil 1750.685   Cerný, Václav. Proní sešit o existencialismii. Phraha, 1948.

Phil 9050.9   A certain blind man. (Fitch, R.E.) N.Y., 1944.

Phil 5585.51   Certain factors in the development of a new spatial co-ordination. Thesis. (Wooster, Margaret.) Princeton, 1923.

Phil 8586.1   The certainty and necessity of religion. (Gastrell, F.) London, 1697.

Phil 8586.1.2   The certainty and necessity of religion. (Gastrell, F.) London, 1703.

Phil 184.6   La certitude. (Javary, L.A.) Paris, 1847.

Phil 2477.1.66   Certitude et vérité. (Boutroux, Emile.) London, 1915.

Phil 5070.23   Certitude et volonté. (Lebacqz, Joseph.) Bruges, 1962.

Phil 5090.4   La certitude philosophique. (Gréard, Mlle.) Paris, 1883.

Phil 6115.2.2   Le cerveau, l'âme et les facultés. (Farges, A.) Paris, 1890.

Phil 2668.45   Le cerveau et la pensée. (Janet, Paul A.R.) Paris, 1867.

Phil 6125.18   Le cerveau et la pensée. (Piéron, Henri.) Paris, 1923.

Phil 6121.7.3   Le cerveau et ses fonctions. (Luys, J.) Paris, 1876.

Phil 6111.10.5   Le cerveau organe de la pensée chez l'homme et chez les animaux. 2. ed. (Bastian, H.C.) Paris, 1888.

Phil 6112.9   Le cervelet et ses fonctions. (Courmont, F.) Paris, 1891.

Phil 6112.9.4   Le cervelet et ses fonctions. (Courmont, F.) Paris, 1894.

Phil 3235.127   Cesa, C. Il giovane Feuerbach. Bari, 1963.

Phil 3801.272   Cesa, Claudio. La filosofia politica di Schelling. Bari, 1969.

Phil 177.81   Cesalpino, Andrea. Questions péripatéliciennes. Paris, 1929.

Phil 5752.11   Cesari, P. Les déterminismes et les êtres. Thèse. Paris, 1938.

Phil 735.185   Césari, Paul. La valeur. 1. ed. Paris, 1957.

Phil 5242.2.5   Cesca, G. L'attività psichica. Messina, 1904.

Phil 3484.14   Cesca, G. La "cosa in se". Torino, 1887.

Phil 3246.198   Cesca, G. L'idealismo soggetivo di I.G. Fichte. Padova, 1895.

Phil 5242.2   Cesca, G. Le teorie nativistiche e genetiche della localizzazione spaziale. Verona, 1883.

Phil 3915.83   Cesca, Giovanni. L'animismo di Guglielmo Wundt. n.p., 1891.

Phil 802.5   Cesca, Giovanni. I fattori della evoluzione filosofica. Padova, 1892.

Phil 177.46.5   Cesca, Giovanni. La filosofia della vita. Messina, 1903.

Phil 177.46   Cesca, Giovanni. La filosofia dell'azione. Milano, 1907.

Phil 630.14   Cesca, Giovanni. Il nuovo realismo contemporaneo. Verona, 1883.

Phil 4807.6F   Česká akademie věd a uměni. Památník na oslavu padesátiletého panovnického jubilea jeho veličenstva císaře a krále Františka Josefa I. Praha, 1898.

Phil 8176.2   Çeská estetika. (Novák, Mirko.) Praha, 1941.

Phil 12.8   Çeská mysl; časopis filosofický. Praha, 1900-1947 31v.

Phil 4806.2   Československá akademie věd. Antologie z dějin československé filosofie. Praha, 1963.

Phil 4805.5   Československá filosofie. (Král, Josef.) Praha, 1937.

Phil 12.50   Československá psychologie; časopis pro psychologickou teorii i praxi. Praha. 1,1957+ 13v.

Phil 2340.10.126   Cesselin, Felix. La philosophie organique de Whitehead. Thèse. 1e éd. Paris, 1950.

Phil 2340.10.125   Cesselin, Felix. La philosophie organique de Whitehead. 1e éd. Paris, 1950.

Phil 2805.243   Cet effrayant génie...l'oeuvre scientifique de Pascal. (Humbert, Pierre.) Paris, 1947.

Phil 8403.33   Cevallos García, G. Del arte actual y de su existencia. Cuenca, 1950.

Phil 12.100   The Ceylon rationalist ambassador. Colombo. 1,1968+ 4v.

Phil 5722.4.5   Chabaneix, P. Essai sur le subconscient dans les oeuvres. Bordeaux, 1897.

Phil 2905.3.80   Chabanis, Christian. Gustave Thibon, témoin de la lumière. Paris, 1967.

Phil 8877.60.10   Chabot, Charles. Morale théorique et notions historiques. 10e éd. Paris, 1925.

Phil 8877.60   Chabot, Charles. Nature et moralité. Paris, 1896.

Phil 5400.27   Chabrier. Les émotions et les états organiques. Paris, 1911.

Phil 2630.7.98   Chacornac, Paul. La vie simple de René Guenon. Paris, 1958.

Phil 5812.1.2   Chadbourne, P.A. Instinct. 2nd ed. N.Y., 1872.

Phil 5812.1   Chadbourne, P.A. Instinct. 2nd ed. N.Y., 1883.

Phil 8582.5   Chadbourne, P.A. Lectures on natural theology. N.Y., 1867.

Phil 5630.3   Chadwick, Thomas. The influence of rumour on human thought and action. Manchester, 1932.

Phil 310.687   Chagin, Boris A. Sub"ektivnyi faktor. Moskva, 1968.

Phil 2805.395   Chaigne, Louis. Pascal. Paris, 1962.

Phil 8403.28   Chaignet, A. Les principes de la science du beau. Paris, 1860.

Phil 1140.1   Chaignet, A.E. Histoire de la Psychologie des Grecs. Paris, 1887-93. 5v.

Phil 177.50   Chainey, George. Times garland of grace. San Diego, 1918.

Phil 177.112   Chaix-Reys, Jules. Les dimensions de l'être et du temps. Paris, 1953.

Phil 4260.120   Chaix-Ruy, Jules. La formation de la pensée philosophique de G.B. Vico. Gap, 1943.

Phil 4260.116.5   Chaix-Ruy, Jules. J.B. Vico et l'illuminisme athée. Paris, 1968.

Phil 2805.210   Chaix-Ruy, Jules. Le jansénisme; Pascal et Port-Royal. Paris, 1930.

Phil 4260.116   Chaix-Ruy, Jules. Vie de J.B. Vico. Gap, 1943.

Phil 960.167   Chakravarti, A. Humanism and Indian thought. Madras, 1937.

Phil 1750.730   Chalin, M.L. Filosofiia otohaianiia i strakha. Moskva, 1962.

Phil 2475.1.227   Challaye, F. Bergson. Paris, 1929.

Phil 2475.1.302.5   Challaye, F. Bergson. Paris, 1947.

Phil 8877.58.15   Challaye, F. Cours de morale, a l'usuge des écoles primaires superieures. Paris, 1927.

Phil 8403.27   Challaye, F. Esthétique. Paris, 1929.

Phil 3640.366   Challaye, F. Nietzsche. Paris, 1950.

Phil 802.14   Challaye, F. Petite histoire des grandes philosophies. Paris, 1942.

Phil 8877.58.5   Challaye, F. Philosophie scientifique et philosophie morale. 3. ed. Paris, 1927.

Phil 8877.58   Challaye, F. Les principes généraux de la science et de la morale. Paris, 1925.

Phil 5242.31   Challaye, F. Psychologie et métaphysique. Paris, 1925.

Phil 960.200   Challaye, Felicien. Les philosophes de l'Inde. 1. ed. Paris, 1956.

Phil 8403.27.5   Challaye F. L'art et la beauté. Paris, 1929.

Phil 8897.73.5   Challenge and response. (Wellman, Carl.) Carbordale, 1971.

Phil 2340.16.30   Challenge eternal. (Weems, B.F.) N.Y., 1955.

Phil 1750.400A   The challenge of existentialism. (Wild, John.) Bloomington, 1955.

Phil 1750.133A   Challenge of humanism. (Mercier, L.J.A.) N.Y., 1933.

Phil 187.127   The challenge of life. (Moore, C.F.) N.Y., 1925.

Phil 7069.61A   Challenge of psychical research. 1. ed. (Murphy, Gardner.) N.Y., 1961.

Phil 5592.155.5   The challenge of response sets. (Block, Jack.) N.Y., 1965.

Phil 672.215   The challenge of the passing years. (MacIver, Robert Morrison.) N.Y., 1u962.

Phil 8598.34   Challenge of the universe. (Shebbeare, Charles J.) London, 1918.

Phil 7069.47.35   Challenge of the unknown. (Anspacher, L.K.) N.Y., 1947.

Phil 8630.7.9   The challenge of the war. (Frank, Henry.) Boston, 1919.

Phil 9358.14   The challenge of youth. (Stearns, Alfred E.) Boston, 1923.

Phil 5932.1   A challenge to phrenologists. London, 1939.

Phil 2750.11.20   Challenges and renewals. (Maritain, Jacques.) Notre Dame, 1966.

Phil 8952.1   Chalmers, T. Application of Christianity to...ordinary affairs of life. Glasgow, 1820.

Phil 8952.1.2   Chalmers, T. Application of Christianity to...ordinary affairs of life. Glasgow, 1821.

Phil 8952.1.5   Chalmers, T. Application of Christianity to...ordinary affairs of life. N.Y., 1821.

Phil 8952.1.6   Chalmers, T. Application of Christianity to...ordinary affairs of life. 3d American ed. Hartford, 1821.

Phil 8581.10   Chalmers, T. Bridgewater treatises [1,8]. On the power, wisdom and goodness of God. Philadelphia, 1836.

Phil 8657.2   Chalmers, T. The power, wisdom and goodness of God. N.Y., 1834.

Phil 8691.12.5.5   Chalmers, Thomas. On the power, wisdom and goodness of God. London, 1839. 2v.

Phil 8691.12.5   Chalmers, Thomas. On the power, wisdom and goodness of God. London, 1865.

Phil 8692.5.12   Chalmers, Thomas. Series of discourses on the Christian revelation, viewed in connexion with modern astronomy. N.Y., 18- .

Phil 8692.5.3   Chalmers, Thomas. Series of discourses on the Christian revelation, viewed in connexion with modern astronomy. N.Y., 1817.

Phil 8692.5.7   Chalmers, Thomas. Series of discourses on the Christian revelation, viewed in connexion with modern astronomy. Hartford, 1818.

Phil 8692.5.5   Chalmers, Thomas. Series of discourses on the Christian revelation, viewed in connexion with modern astronomy. N.Y., 1818. 2 pam.

Phil 8692.5.15   Chalmers, Thomas. Series of discourses on the Christian revelation, viewed in connexion with modern astronomy. 12th ed. Glasgow, 1834.

Phil 1075.5   Chaloian, V.K. Istoriia armians boi filosofii. Erevan, 1959.

Phil 177.10   Chalybäur, H.M. Fundamental Philosophie. Kiel, 1861.

Phil 3002.1.6   Chalybäus, H. Historical development of speculative philosophy. Edinburgh, 1854.

Phil 3002.1.7   Chalybäus, H. Historical survey of speculative philosophy. Andover, 1854.

Phil 3002.1.5   Chalybäus, H. Historical survey of speculative philosophy. London, 1854.

Phil 3002.1   Chalybäus, H. Historie entwickelischen der speculativen Philosophie. Leipzig, 1860.

Phil 3002.1.9   Chalybäus, H. Phänomenologische Blätter. Kiel, 1840.

Phil 8582.7   Chalybäus, H.M. Philosophie und Christenthum. Kiel, 1853.

Phil 8877.53 — Chalybäus, Heinrich. System der speculativen Ethik. Leipzig, 1850. 2v.

Phil 2805.182 — Chamaillard, E. Pascal, mondain et amoureux. Paris, 1923.
Phil 9070.44 — Chamberlain, F.E. The lighted pathway. Los Angeles, Calif., 1945.

Phil 3484.6.5 — Chamberlain, H.S. Immanuel Kant. London, 1914. 2v.
Phil 3484.6 — Chamberlain, H.S. Immanuel Kant. Die Persönlichkeit...in das Werke. München, 1905.

Phil 3484.6.3 — Chamberlain, H.S. Immanuel Kant. Die Persönlichkeit...in das Werke. 3. Aufl. München, 1916.

Phil 3484.6.4 — Chamberlain, H.S. Immanuel Kant. Die Persönlichkeit...in das Werke. 4. Aufl. München, 1921.

Phil 8582.56 — Chamberlain, H.S. Mensch und Gott. München, 1921.
Phil 960.26 — Chamberlain, Houston. Arische Weltanschauung. 3. Aufl. München, 1916.
Phil 3235.115 — Chamberlain, W.B. Heaven wasn't his destination; the philosophy of Ludwig Feuerbach. London, 1941.
Phil 3484.6.18 — Chamberlain gegen Schopenhauer. (Curtiner, Egon B.) Düsseldorf, 1910.
Phil 1930.7.80 — Chamberlin, R.V. Life and philosophy. Salt Lake City, 1925.
Phil 8627.9 — Chambers, A. Man and the spiritual world. Philadelphia, 1900.
Phil 8627.9.3 — Chambers, A. Our life after death. Philadelphia, 1902.
Phil 8627.9.9 — Chambers, A. Ourself after death. Chicago, 191-.
Phil 8627.9.7 — Chambers, A. Problems of the spiritual. Philadelphia, 1907.
Phil 8627.9.5 — Chambers, A. Thoughts of the spiritual. London, 1905.
Phil 8050.28.5 — Chambers, Frank. Cycles of taste. Cambridge, 1928.
Phil 8050.28 — Chambers, Frank. The history of taste. N.Y., 1932.
Phil 573.4 — Chambers, Frank P. Perception, understanding and society. London, 1961.
Phil 6952.4 — Chambers, J. A mad world and its inhabitants. N.Y., 1877.
Phil 585.188 — Chambliss, Rollin. Meaning for man. N.Y., 1966.
Phil 4803.799.90 — Chamcówna, Mirosława. Jan Śniadecki. Kraków, 1963.
Phil 5055.29.15 — Le champ de l'argumentation. (Perelman, Chaim.) Bruxelles, 1970.
Phil 2880.8.128 — Champigny, Robert. Stages on Sartre's way. Bloomington, 1959.
Phil 8877.5.2 — Champlin, J.T. First principles of ethics. N.Y., n.d.
Phil 5242.4 — Champlin, J.T. Text-book in intellectual philosophy. Boston, 1860.
Phil 4891.1 — Chan, Wing-tsit. Chinese philosophy, 1949-1963; an annotated bibliography of mainland China publications. Honolulu, 1966-67.
Phil 75.44 — Chan, Wing-Tsit. An outline and a bibliography of Chinese philosophy. Hanover, N.H., 1953.
Phil 930.44 — Chan, Wing-tsit. An outline and a bibliography of Chinese philosophy. Hanover, 1955.
Phil 930.44.2 — Chan, Wing-tsit. An outline and annotated bibliography of Chinese philosophy. New Haven, 1961.
Phil 2225.5.30 — Chance, love, and logic. (Peirce, C.S.) N.Y., 1923.
Phil 2225.5.35 — Chance, love, and logic. (Peirce, C.S.) N.Y., 1949.
Phil 270.75.5 — Chance, skill, and luck. (Cohen, John.) Baltimore, 1960.
Phil 270.70 — The chance character of human existence. (Brill, John.) N.Y., 1956.
Phil 270.54 — La chance ou la destinée. (Foissac, Pierre.) Paris, 1876.
Phil 8580.36 — La chance suprême de l'homme. (Augereau, Joseph.) Paris, 1964.
Phil 9450.60 — Chance und Dilemma der politischen Ethik. (Schmölz, Franz Martin.) Köln, 1966.
Phil 365.5 — Chances of death...studies in evolution. (Pearson, K.) London, 1897. 2v.
Phil 8633.1.32 — The chances of surviving death. (Montague, W.P.) Cambridge, 1934.
Phil 8827.7 — Chandavarkar, G.A. A manual of Hindu ethics. 3rd ed. Poona, 1925.
Phil 8403.42 — Chandler, A.R. Beauty and human nature. N.Y., 1934.
Phil 8030.2 — Chandler, A.R. A bibliography of experimental aesthetics, 1865-1932. Columbus, 1933.
Phil 8030.3 — Chandler, A.R. A bibliography of psychology and experimental aesthetics, 1864-1937. Berkeley, 1938.
Phil 8582.27 — Chandler, Arthur. Faith and experience. 2. ed. London, 1912.
Phil 3450.19.79.5 — Chandra, Subhash. Das Phänomen des Todes im Denken Heideggers und in der Lehre Buddhas. Köln, 1965.
Phil 3450.19.79 — Pamphlet box. Chandra, Subhash. Heidegger.
Phil 2515.2.90 — Chanet, P. Considérations sur la Sagesse de Charron. Paris, 1643.
Phil 8877.6 — Chaney, G.L. Every day life and every day morals. Boston, 1885.
Phil 930.50 — Chang, Carsun. China and Gandhian India. Calcutta, 1956.
Phil 510.149 — Chang, T.S. Epistemological pluralism. Shanghai? 1932?
Phil 3425.218.5 — Chang, W.S. The development, significance and some limitatioms of Hegel's ethical teaching. Shanghai, 1926.
Phil 3425.218 — Chang, W.S. Hegel's ethical teaching. Shanghai, 1925.
Phil 2725.23.90 — Chang Chi Chang. La morale...de M. Lucien Levy-Bruhl. Lyon, 1937.
Phil 5330.27 — Change of interest with age. (Strong, E.K.) Palo Alto, 1931.
Phil 177.11 — Changeux, P.J. Traiti des extrêmes. Amsterdam, 1767. 2v.
Phil 8582.43 — Changing backgrounds in religion and ethics. (Carr, Herbert M.) N.Y., 1927.
Phil 5350.8 — Changing human behavior. (Mann, John Harvey.) N.Y., 1965.
Phil 5241.145 — The changing nature of man. 1. ed. (Berg, Jan Hendrik van den.) N.Y., 1961.
Phil 585.275 — Changing perspectives on man. Chicago, 1968.
Phil 978.6.50 — The changing world. (Besant, Annie.) Chicago, 1910.
Phil 8582.51 — Chaning-Pearce, Melville. Religion and reality. London, 1937.
Phil 8582.51.10 — Chaning-Pearce, Melville. The terrible crystal; studies in Kierkegaard and modern Christianity. London, 1940.
Phil 6952.5 — Channing, W. The mental status of guiteau. Cambridge, 1882.
Htn — Phil 1930.2.30* — Channing, William E. A discourse on religion. Boston, 1821.
Phil 5627.109 — Chansou, J. Étude de psychologie religieuse sur...la prière. Thèse. Toulouse, 1927. 2 pam.
Phil 575.1 — Chantepie, E. Le presonnage humain. Paris, 1874.
Phil 410.90 — Chany, Robert de. Sur les confins du fini, métaphysique, physique, mathématiques et religion. Paris, 1968.
Phil 2475.1.385 — Chanyshev, A.N. Filosfiia Anri Bergsona. Moskva, 1960.
Phil 1133.55 — Chanyshev, Arsenii N. Egeiskaia predfilosofiia. Moskva, 1970.
Phil 287.4 — Das Chaos als objektive Weltregion. (Grave, F.) Berlin, 1924.

Phil 338.22 — Das Chaos im kosmischer Auslese. (Hausdorff, Felix.) Leipzig, 1898.
Phil 288.3 — Chaos or cosmos? (Heermance, E.L.) N.Y., 1922.
Phil 3425.603.1 — Chapelle, A. Hegel et la religion. Paris, 1964.
Phil 3425.603 — Chapelle, A. Hegel et la religion. Paris, 1964.
Phil 3425.603.2 — Chapelle, A. Hegel et la religion. Annexes. Nanur, 1967.
Phil 3450.19.265 — Chapelle, Albert. L'ontologie phénoménologique de Heidegger. Paris, 1962.
Phil 9075.60 — Chaperd, Marc. La révolution originelle. Paris, 1958.
Phil 9342.1 — Chapin, E.H. Duties of young men. Boston, 1846.
NEDL — Phil 9342.1.5 — Chapin, E.H. Duties of young men. Boston, 1848.
Phil 9342.1.10 — Chapin, E.H. Duties of young women. Boston, 1850.
Phil 9050.6 — Chapin, E.H. Moral aspects of city life. 2d ed. N.Y., 1854.
Phil 6962.16 — Un chapitre oublié de la pathologie mentale. (Moreau, J.J.) Paris, 1850.
Phil 5212.20.2 — Chaplin, James Patrik. Systems and theories of psychology. 2. ed. N.Y., 1968.
Phil 5590.494 — Chapman, Arthur Harry. Put-offs and come-ons. London, 1968.
Phil 5042.24 — Chapman, Frank M. The fundamentals of logic. N.Y., 1933.
Phil 9342.2.12 — Chapone, H. (Mrs.). Letters on the improvement of the mind. Boston, 1809.
Phil 9342.2.9 — Chapone, H. (Mrs.). Letters on the improvement of the mind. London, 1815.
Phil 9342.2.10 — Chapone, H. (Mrs.). Letters on the improvement of the mind. London, 1819.
Phil 9342.2.4 — Chapone, H. (Mrs.). Letters on the improvement of the mind. London, 1822.
Phil 9342.2 — Chapone, H. (Mrs.). Letters on the improvement of the mind. London, 1830.
Phil 9342.2.8 — Chapone, H. (Mrs.). Letters on the improvement of the mind. N.Y., 1827.
Htn — Phil 9342.2.7* — Chapone, H. (Mrs.). Letters on the improvement of the mind. Philadelphia, 1786.
X Cg — Phil 9342.2.6 — Chapone, H. (Mrs.). Letters on the improvement of the mind. Philadelphia, 1816.
Htn — Phil 9342.2.11* — Chapone, H. (Mrs.). Letters on the improvement of the mind. Portland, 17- ?
Htn — Phil 9342.2.3* — Chapone, H. (Mrs.). Letters on the improvement of the mind. v.1-2. Hagerstown, 1819.
Htn — Phil 9342.2.2* — Chapone, H. (Mrs.). Letters on the improvement of the mind. v.1-2. N.Y., 1793.
Phil 9342.2.5 — Chapone, H. (Mrs.). Letters on the improvement of the mind. 2. ed. London, 1773. 2v.
Phil 6112.31 — Chappell, M.N. In the name of common sense. N.Y., 1938.
Phil 333.20 — Chappell, Vere C. The philosophy of mind. Englewood Cliffs, 1962.
Phil 2050.266 — Chappell, Vere Claiborne. Hume. 1st ed. Garden City, N.Y., 1966.
Phil 5520.555 — Chappell, Vere Claiborne. Ordinary language; essays in philosophical method. Englewood Cliffs, N.J., 1964.
Phil 1885.84 — Chappuis, A. Der theoretische Weg Bradley's. Paris, 1933.
Phil 176.65 — Chapter from story of Pauline Parsons. (Brass, T.) Ashland, 1916.
Phil 5238.1 — Chapters from modern psychology, 1911. (Angell, J.R.) London, 1912.
Phil 5258.66.3 — Chapters in general psychology. (Smith, Stevenson.) Seattle, 1921.
Phil 5832.5 — Chapters on man...comparative psychology. (Walse, C.S.) London, 1868.
X Cg — Phil 6117.7 — Chapters on mental physiology. (Holland, H.) London, 1852.
Phil 9035.01 — Pamphlet box. Character.
Phil 9035.7.5 — Character. (Smiles, S.) Chicago, 1890.
Phil 9035.7 — Character. (Smiles, S.) N.Y., 1880?
Phil 6327.21.10 — Character analysis. 3. ed. (Reich, Wilhelm.) N.Y., 1949.
Phil 6327.21.13 — Character analysis. 3. ed. (Reich, Wilhelm.) N.Y., 1970.
Phil 575.57 — Character and inhibition. (Roback, A.A.) n.p., 1925.
Phil 193.49.18.5 — Character and opinion in the United States. (Santayana, G.) Garden City, 1956.
Phil 193.49.15 — Character and opinion in the United States. (Santayana, G.) N.Y., 1920.
Phil 193.49.16 — Character and opinion in the United States. (Santayana, G.) N.Y., 1921.
Phil 193.49.18 — Character and opinion in the United States. (Santayana, G.) N.Y., 1934.
Phil 12.15 — Character and personality. Durham, N.C. 1,1932+ 38v.
Phil 9035.16.5 — Character and temperament. (Jastrow, J.) N.Y., 1915.
Phil 9035.49 — Character and the conduct of life. (McDougall, W.) N.Y., 1927.
Phil 6317.9A — Character and the unconscious. (Hoop, J.H. van der.) London, 1923.
Phil 9035.4 — Character as seen in body and parentage. (Jordan, F.) London, 1890.
Phil 9035.12 — Character building. (Washington, B.S.) N.Y., 1902.
Phil 9035.9 — Character essential to success in life. (Taylor, S.) Canandaigua, 1821.
Phil 9070.140 — Character guidance discussion topics; duty, honor, country. (United States. Department of the Army.) Washington. 1951+ 2v.
Phil 9035.30 — Character in the making. (Jones, A.J.) London, 1913.
Phil 8610.821 — The character of a priest. (Philanthropos [pseud.].) London, 1821. 2 pam.
Phil 575.146.10 — The character of man. (Mounier, E.) London, 1956.
Phil 9351.3 — Character of the gentleman. (Lieber, F.) Philadelphia, 1864.
Phil 6015.1.5 — Character qualities outlined and related. (Fosbroke, Gerald Eltac.) N.Y., 1923.
Phil 9590.10 — Character reading. (Symes, (Mrs.).) Akron, O., 1903.
Phil 6015.1 — Character reading through analysis of the features. (Fosbroke, Gerald Eltac.) N.Y., 1914.
Phil 2262.33 — Characteristicks. (Shaftesbury, A.A.C.) Basel, 1790. 3v.
Htn — Phil 2262.45* — Characteristicks. (Shaftesbury, A.A.C.) Leipzig, 1768.
Htn — Phil 2262.29* — Characteristicks. (Shaftesbury, A.A.C.) London, 1711. 3v.
Phil 2262.30 — Characteristicks. (Shaftesbury, A.A.C.) London, 1723. 3v.
Phil 2262.30.7 — Characteristicks. (Shaftesbury, A.A.C.) London, 1732. 3v.
Htn — Phil 2262.32.5* — Characteristicks. (Shaftesbury, A.A.C.) London, 1749. 3v.
Phil 2262.35.3A — Characteristicks. (Shaftesbury, A.A.C.) N.Y., 1900. 2v.
Phil 2262.34 — Characteristicks. v.1. (Shaftesbury, A.A.C.) London, 1870.

Phil 2262.30.3   Characteristicks. v.2,3. (Shaftesbury, A.A.C.) London, 1727. 2v.

Phil 2262.30.2   Characteristicks. v.3. (Shaftesbury, A.A.C.) London, 17-

Htn Phil 2262.29.5*   Characteristicks. 2nd ed. (Shaftesbury, A.A.C.) London, 1714. 3v.

Phil 2262.30.4   Characteristicks. 4th ed. (Shaftesbury, A.A.C.) n.p., 1727. 3v.

Htn Phil 2262.30.5*   Characteristicks. 5th ed. (Shaftesbury, A.A.C.) Birmingham, 1773. 3v.

Phil 2262.31.2   Characteristicks. 5th ed. (Shaftesbury, A.A.C.) London, 1732. 3v.

Phil 2262.32   Characteristicks. 6th ed. (Shaftesbury, A.A.C.) London, 1737. 3v.

Phil 2262.35.4   Characteristics of men, manners, opinions, times. (Shaftesbury, A.A.C.) Gloucester, Mass., 1963. 2v.

Phil 2262.35.5   Characteristics of men. v.1-2. (Shaftesbury, A.A.C.) Indianapolis, 1964.

Phil 12.10   Characterologische Jahrbücher. Berlin.

Phil 5242.66   Charakchiev, Asen. Deistvenostta na misleneto. Sofiia, 1961.

Phil 5710.15   Charakter, Blutgruppe und Konstitution. (Schaer, K.F.) Zürich, 1941.

Phil 12.30   Charakter; eine Vierteljahresschrift für psychodiagnostische Studien und verwandte Gebiete. London. 1-2,1932-1933

Phil 9035.59.15   Charakter, Einzelmensch und Gruppe. (Künkel, Fritz.) Leipzig, 1933.

Phil 9035.59.9   Charakter, Wachstum und Erziehung. 2. Aufl. (Künkel, Fritz.) Leipzig, 1934.

Phil 9035.42   Der Charakter. (Häberlin, Paul.) Basel, 1925.
Phil 9035.59.20   Charakter. (Künkel, Fritz.) Leipzig, 1932.
Phil 9035.82   Charakter. (Piwowarczyk, W.) Kielce, 1938.
Phil 5241.126   Charakter als Naturgesetz. (Banterwek, Heinrich.) Ulm, 1959.

Phil 5255.58   Charakter człowieka. (Pastuszka, J.) Lublin, 1959.
Phil 5255.58.5   Charakter człowieka. (Pastuszka, J.) Lublin, 1962.
Phil 9344.8   Der Charakter und die Bestimmung des Mannes. (Ehrenberg, F.) Leipzig, 1808.

Phil 6320.3   Charakter und Nervosität. (Kollarits, Jenö.) Berlin, 1912.

Phil 9035.79   Charakter und Schicksal. (Nohl, Herman.) Frankfurt, 1938.
Phil 5590.225   Charakter und Umwelt. (Burckhardt, Georg.) München, 1956.
Phil 9035.47.5   Charakter und Umwelt. (Hoffmann, H.) Berlin, 1928.
Phil 9035.25   Charakter und Weltanschauung. (Adickes, E.) Tübingen, 1907.

Phil 9035.31   Charakterbildung. (Ekenhans, Theodor.) Leipzig, 1908.
Phil 5590.508   Charakterentwicklung. (Salber, Wilhelm.) Wuppertal, 1969.
Phil 3003.5   Charakteristik der philosophischen Systeme seit Kant. (Drechsler, Adolf.) Dresden, 1863.

Phil 3552.233   Charakteristik des Leibnitz. (Eberhard, J.A.) Leipzig, n.d.

Phil 978.49.180   Charakteristisches zur Kennzeichnung der gegenwart Wirklichkeits-Entfremdung. (Steiner, R.) Dornach, 1939.

Phil 9035.78.5   Charakterlogie. 2. Aufl. (Helwig, Paul.) Stuttgart, 1951.
Phil 9035.78   Charakterologie. (Helwig, Paul.) Leipzig, 1936.
Phil 9035.43   Charakterologie. (Utitz, Emil.) Charlottenburg, 1925.
Phil 3120.11.84   Die Charakterologie von Julius Bahnsen. Diss. (Leiste, Heinrich.) Köln, 1928.

Phil 6325.27   Charakterstudien. (Petrilowitsch, Nikolaus.) Basel, 1969.
Phil 193.113   Der charakterwolle und der begriffliche Gegenstand. (Schweizer, Robert.) Leipzig, 1927.

Phil 4803.879.06   Charaktery rozumów ludzkich. (Wiszniewski, Michał.) Warszawa, 1876. 2 pam.

Phil 2905.1.235   Charbonneau, B. Teilhard de Chardin, prophète d'un âge totalitaire. Paris, 1963.

Phil 4065.95   Charbonnel, J.R. L'éthique de Giordano Bruno. Paris, 1919.

Phil 4002.1   Charbonnel, J.R. La pensée italienne au XVIe siècle. Paris, 1919.

Phil 8582.33.5   Charbonnel, Victor. The victory of will. Boston, 1907.
Phil 8582.33.2   Charbonnel, Victor. La volonté de vivre. 2. éd. Paris, 1898.

Phil 5628.50.10   Charbonnier, Nestor. Maladies et facultés diverses des mystiques. Bruxelles, 1875.

Phil 6952.23.20   Charcot, J.M. Clinique des maladies du système nerveaux. Paris, 1892-93. 2v.

Phil 6952.23.10   Charcot, J.M. Étude critique et clinique de la doctrine des localisations motrices. Paris, 1883.

Phil 6112.5.5   Charcot, J.M. La foi qui guérit. Paris, 1897.
Phil 6952.23   Charcot, J.M. Leçons sur les localisations dans les maladies du cerveau. Paris, 1876.

Phil 6952.23.5   Charcot, J.M. Lectures on localization in diseases of the brain. N.Y., 1878.

Phil 6672.2   Chardel, C. Esquisse de la nature humaine. Paris, 1826.
Phil 5242.3   Chardel, C. Essai de psychologie. Paris, 1838.
Phil 8892.36   Charges, and extracts of charges on moral and religious subjects. (Rush, Jacob.) Philadelphia, 1803.

Phil 165.285   Charisteria; rozprawy filozoficzne, złozone w darze Władysławowi Tatarkiewiczowi. Warszawa, 1960.

Phil 9145.8   A charitable remonstrance. (Estienne, Antoine Minim.) Edinburgh, 1887.

Phil 6535.7   Charity Organization Society, London. The epileptic and crippled child and adult. Photoreproduction. London, 1893.

Phil 801.24   La charlatanisme philosophique de tous les âges dévoilé. (Berthre de Bowinisseaux, P.V.J.) Paris, 1807.

Phil 177.45   Charles, Émile. Éléments de philosophie. Paris, 1884-85. 2v.

Phil 8627.3   Charles, R.H. A critical history of the doctrine of a future life in Israel. London, 1899.

Phil 8627.3.5   Charles, R.H. A critical history of the doctrine of a future life in Israel. 2. ed. London, 1913.

Phil 8627.3.10   Charles, R.H. Eschatology. N.Y., 1963.
Phil 2465.80   Charles Bonnet. (Caraman, V.A.C.R.) Paris, 1859.
Phil 2465.82   Charles Bonnet (1720-1793). Thèse. (Bonnet, Georges.) Paris, 1929.

Phil 2465.81   Charles Bonnet de Genève. Thèse. (Lemoine, Albert.) Paris, 1850.

Phil 1802.5   Charles Darwin and other English thinkers. (Cadman, S.P.) Boston, 1911.

Phil 1955.7.90   Charles Frederick D'Arcy, 1859-1938. (Luce, A.A.) London, 1949.

Phil 5821.1.15   Charles Georges Leroy und seine "Lettres philosophiques." (Marx, Moses.) Strassburg, 1898.

Phil 2655.2.80   Charles Henry et l'idéalisme scientifique. (Mirabaud, R.) Paris, 1926.

Phil 2150.17.90   Charles Morris. 1st ed. (Rossi-Landi, Ferruccio.) Roma, 1953.

Phil 2225.5.115   Charles Peirce. (Knight, Thomas Stanley.) N.Y., 1965.
Phil 2225.5.88   Charles Peirce and scholastic realism. (Boler, J.F.) Seattle, 1963.

Phil 2225.5.80   Charles Peirce's empiricism. (Buchler, J.) N.Y., 1939.
Phil 2225.5.165   Charles Peirce's theory of scientific method. (Reilly, Francis E.) N.Y., 1970.

Phil 2840.93.5   Charles Renouvier; hans liv og hans tanker. (Hansen, Valdemar.) København, 1962.

Phil 2840.97   Charles Renouvier. (Prat, Louis.) Ariège, 1937.
Phil 2840.93   Charles Renouvier og frihedsproblemet. (Hansen, Valdemar.) København, 1928.

Phil 2225.5.150   Charles S. Peirce on norms and ideals. (Potter, Vincent G.) Amherst, 1967.

Phil 2225.5.140   Charles S. Pierce Society. Transactions. Amherst. 1,1965+ 2v.

Phil 2880.2.80   Charles Secrétan: sa vie et son oeuvre. (Secrétan, L.) Lausanne, 1911.

Phil 1750.95.10   Charlesworth, Maxwell John. Philosophy and linguistic analysis. Pittsburgh, 1959.

Htn Phil 8657.18*   Charleton, W. The darkness of atheism dispelled by the light of native. London, 1652.

Htn Phil 8627.10*   Charleton, W. The immortality of the human soul. London, 1657.

Htn Phil 5400.2*   Charleton, W. Natural history of the passions. London, 1674.

Htn Phil 5242.18.2*   Charleton, Walter. Two discourses. 2. ed. London, 1675.
Phil 600.55   Charlton, D.G. Positivist thought in France. Oxford, 1959.

Phil 2402.8   Charlton, D.G. Secular religions in France, 1815-1870. London, 1963.

Phil 5520.86   Charl'z Darvin o proiskhozhdenii rechi. (Dobrogaev, S.M.) Leningrad, 1945.

Phil 2225.5.160   Charlz Pirs i pragmatizm. (Mel'vil', Iurii K.) Moskva, 1968.

Phil 9358.15.5   The charm of fine manners. (Starrett, H.E. (Mrs.).) Philadelphia, 1921.

Phil 8877.7   Charma, A. Essai...bases...développmens de la moralité. Paris, 1834.

Phil 5042.16   Charma, A. Leçons de logique. Paris, 1840.
Phil 177.12   Charma, Antoine. Réponses aux questions de philosophie. Paris, 1841.

Phil 9342.11   Charpentier, Louis. Décence em elle-même. Paris, 1767.
Phil 2520.126   Charpentier, T.V. Essai sur la méthode de Descartes. Thèse. Paris, 1869.

Phil 2750.22.100   Charpentreau, Jacques. L'esthétique personnaliste d'Emmanuel Mounier. Paris, 1966.

Phil 6672.10   Charpignon, J. Physiologie, médecine et métaphysique. Paris, 1848.

Phil 2515.2.39   Charron, P. Charron on wisdom. London, 1707. 2v.
Phil 2515.2.36   Charron, P. Charron on wisdom. London, 1729. 3v.
Htn Phil 2515.2.34*   Charron, P. Charron on wisdom. London? n.d.
Htn Phil 2515.2.27*   Charron, P. De la sagesse, trois livres. 3e éd. Paris, 1614.

Htn Phil 2515.2.32*   Charron, P. De la sagesse. Amsterdam, 1662.
Htn Phil 2515.2.49*   Charron, P. De la sagesse. Bordeaux, 1601.
Htn Phil 2515.2.30*   Charron, P. De la sagesse. Leide, 1646.
Htn Phil 2515.2.31*   Charron, P. De la sagesse. Leide, 1658?
Phil 2515.2.53   Charron, P. De la sagesse. Paris, 1820-24. 3v.
Phil 2515.2.55   Charron, P. De la sagesse. Paris, 1827. 3v.
Htn Phil 2515.2.48*   Charron, P. De la sagesse. Rouen, 1614.
Htn Phil 2515.2.47*   Charron, P. De la sagesse. v.1-3. Paris, 1604.
Htn Phil 2515.2.40*   Charron, P. Of wisdom, three books. London, 1651.
Htn Phil 2515.2.33*   Charron, P. Of wisdome. London, 1630.
Htn Phil 2515.2.41*   Charron, P. Of wisdome. London, 1670.
Phil 2515.2.35*   Charron, P. A la sagesse de Charron. Paris, 1672.
Phil 2515.2.42   Charron, P. A treatise on wisdom. N.Y., 1891.
Htn Phil 2515.2.45*   Charron, P. Les trois veritez. 2e éd. Bordeaux, 1595.
Phil 2515.2.50   Charron, P. Die wahre Weisheit. v.2. München, 1779.
Phil 2515.2.39   Pamphlet box. Charron, P.
Phil 2515.2.39   Charron on wisdom. (Charron, P.) London, 1707. 2v.
Phil 2515.2.36   Charron on wisdom. (Charron, P.) London, 1729. 3v.
Htn Phil 2515.2.34*   Charron on wisdom. (Charron, P.) London? n.d.
Phil 2515.2.125   Charron und sien Werk, "de la Sagesse". (Liebscher, H.) Leipzig, 1890.

Phil 282.15   A chart of nature. (Bontecou, Daniel J.) Chicago, 1928.
Phil 2520.164   Chartier, A. Étude sur Descartes. Paris, 1928.
Phil 8582.50   Chartier, E. Les dieux. Paris, 1934.
Phil 8582.50.5   Chartier, E. Propos sur la religion. Paris, 1938.
Phil 9245.54.5   Chartier, É. Propos sur le bonheur. 18e éd. Paris, 1928.
Phil 802.16   Chartier, Émile. Abreges pour les aveugles. Paris, 1943.
Phil 177.68.20   Chartier, Émile. Éléments de philosophie. Paris, 1949.
Phil 177.68.10   Chartier, Émile. Idées; Platon, Descartes, Hegel. Paris, 1932.

Phil 3484.19   Chartier, Emile. Lettres à Sergio Solmi sur la philosophie de Kant. Paris, 1946.

Phil 2515.5.97   Chartier, Émile. Lettres sur la philosophie première. 1. éd. Paris, 1955.

Phil 8403.23.5   Chartier, Émile. Préliminaires à l'esthétique. Paris, 1939.

Phil 177.68.25   Chartier, Émile. Propos sur des philosophes. Paris, 1961.
Phil 8403.23.10   Chartier, Émile. Propos sur l'esthetique. paris, 1923.
Phil 177.68   Chartier, Émile. Quatre-vingt et un chapitres sur l'esprit et les passions. Paris, 1921.

Phil 177.68.15   Chartier, Émile. Sentiments, pasiions et signes. 2e éd. Paris, 1935.

Phil 2725.14.90   Chartier, Émile. Souvenirs concernant Jules Lagneau. 2. éd. Paris, 1925.

Phil 2725.14.93   Chartier, Émile. Souvenirs concernant Jules Lagneau. 5e éd. Paris, 1925.

Phil 8403.23   Chartier, Émile. Système des beaux-arts. Paris, 1926.
Phil 3822.6.5   Chartier, Emile A. Spinoza. 5. éd. Paris, 19- .
Phil 170.1   Chase, P.E. Intellectual symbolism. Philadelphia, 1863.
Phil 5520.68.10   Chase, Stuart. Danger: man talking! N.Y., 1969.
Phil 5042.40   Chase, Stuart. Guides to straight thinking. 1st ed. N.Y., 1956.

Phil 5520.68.7   Chase, Stuart. Power of words. 1. ed. N.Y., 1954.
Phil 5520.68.3   Chase, Stuart. The tyranny of words. N.Y., 1938.
Phil 7054.46   Chase, W. The gist of spiritualism. 3. ed. Boston, 1867.
Phil 7068.65.4   Chase, Warren. The gist of spiritualism. 4th ed. Boston, 1865.

Phil 6952.17   Chaslin, Philippe. La confusion mentale primitive. Paris, 1895.

Phil 8952.10   Chassanis. La morale universelle. Paris, 1791.
Phil 9162.4   Chassay, F.E. Les devoirs des femmes dans la famille. Paris, 1852.

Phil 9495.16   La chasteté. (Colom, P.M.) Paris, 1847.
Phil 5242.54   Château, J. Psychologie et métaphysique. Paris, 1949.

Phil 5585.233 Chateau, Jean. Attitudes intellectuelles et spatiales dans le dessin. Paris, 1965.
Phil 2880.1.88 Chateautien, G. Bibliographie du Martinisme. Lyon, 1939.
Phil 3425.662 Chatelet, François. Hegel. Paris, 1968.
Phil 582.6 Chatterjee, Margaret. Our knowledge of other selves. Bombay, 1963.
Phil 960.165.5 Chatterjee, S. The fundamentals of Hinduism. Calcutta, 1950.
Phil 960.165 Chatterjee, S. An introduction to Indian philosophy. 4th ed. Calcutta, 1950.
Phil 177.106 Chatterjee, S. The problems of philosophy. Calcutta, 1949.
Phil 3640.104 Chatterton-Hill, G. Philosophy of Nietzsche. London, 1912.
Phil 1750.115.65 Chatteyee, Margaret. Our knowledge of other selves. Bombay, 1963.
Phil 585.157 Chauchard, P. L'homme normal. Paris, 1963.
Phil 6112.35 Chauchard, P. L'influx nerveux et la psychologie. Paris, 1950.
Phil 8952.21 Chauchard, P. Morale du cerveau. Paris, 1962.
Phil 5374.200 Chauchard, P. Physiologie de la conscience. 4. éd. Paris, 1959.
Phil 5545.258 Chauchard, Paul. Connaissance et maîtrise de la mémoire. Verviers, 1970.
Phil 8692.22 Chauchard, Paul. La création évolutive. Paris, 1957.
Phil 5812.10 Chauchard, Paul. Des animaux a l'homme. Paris, 1961.
Phil 2905.1.95 Chauchard, Paul. L'être humain selon Teilhard de Chardin. Paris, 1959.
Phil 2905.1.340 Chauchard, Paul. Man and cosmos. N.Y., 1965.
Phil 2905.1.97 Chauchard, Paul. La pensée scientifique de Teilhard. Paris, 1965.
Phil 5812.10.5 Chauchard, Paul. Psychisme humain et psychisme animal. 2e ed. Paris, 1961.
Phil 2905.1.96 Chauchard, Paul. Teilhard de Chardin. Paris, 1964?
Phil 9075.55 Chauchard, Paul. Les mécanismes cerebraux de la prise de conscience. Paris, 1956.
Phil 8403.39.5 Chaudhury, P.J. Studies in aesthetics. Calcutta, 1964.
Phil 8403.39 Chaudhury, P.J. Studies in comparative aesthetics. Santiniketan, 1953.
Phil 2340.18.80 Chauncey Wright and the foundations of pragmatism. (Madden, E.) Seattle, 1963.
Phil 5042.55 Chauveneau, Jean. La logique moderne. 1. éd. Paris, 1957.
Phil 8582.54 Chauvet-Dusoul, F. Philosophie et religion. Paris, 1941-43. 5v.
Phil 9495.40 Chauvin, A. De la préservation morale de l'enfant. Paris, 1912.
Phil 2630.1.86 Chauvin, A. Le père Gratry, 1805-1872. Paris, 1911.
Phil 80.1 Chauvin, E. Lexicon rationale. Rotterdam, 1692.
Phil 87.15 Chauvin, Étienne. Lexicon philosophicum. 2. Aufl. Dusseldorf, 1967.
Phil 5812.9 Chauvin, R. Le comportement social chez les animaux. Paris, 1961.
Phil 8692.19 Chauvin, Rémy. God of the scientists. Baltimore, 1960.
Phil 2520.354 Chauvois, Louis. Descartes, sa ''Méthode'' et ses erreurs en physiologie. Paris, 1966.
Phil 4353.5 Chavarri B., Misael. Diez y siete divagaciones. Santiago de Chile, 1940. 2v.
Phil 4964.10 Chaves, Osvaldo. História y filosofía. Buenos Aires, 1958.
Phil 177.90 Chávez, E.A. Dios, el universo y la libertad. Barcelona, 1935.
Phil 5242.36 Chavigny, P. L'esprit de contradiction. Paris, 1927.
Phil 6672.3 Chazarain, L.T. Découverte de la polarité humaine. Paris, 1886.
Phil 8419.2 Che cos è l'arte. (Sacchetti, E.) Firenze, 1961.
Phil 8430.63 Che cosa è l'estetica sovietica. (Plebe, Armando.) Roma, 1969.
Phil 2150.22.90 Che cosa ha veramente detto Marcuse. (Perlini, Tito.) Roma, 1968.
Phil 2880.8.265 Che cosa ha veramente detto Sartre. (Rovatti, Pier Aldo.) Roma, 1969.
Phil 3480.67.10 Che cosa significa orientarsi nel pensare. (Kant, Immanuel.) Lanciano, 1930.
Phil 8416.23 Che cos'é il bello? Schema d'un estetica psicologica. (Porena, M.) Milano, 1905.
Phil 5850.157.5 Cheatham, T.A. I believe in life. Pinehurst, N.C., 1941.
Phil 978.5.9.25 A check list of some books and authors. (Hyat, T.P.) Stanford, 1940.
Phil 8582.65 Chédel, André. Pour un humanisme laïc. Neuchâtel, 1963.
Phil 672.244 Cheek, John M. The perception of time. Charlotte, N.C.? 1891.
Phil 8620.2 Cheering views of man and providence. (Burton, W.) Boston, 1832.
Phil 6048.94.5 Cheiro's language of the hand. (Hamon, Louis.) N.Y., 1894.
Phil 6048.94.7 Cheiro's language of the hand. (Hamon, Louis.) N.Y., 1895.
X Cg Phil 6048.94.9 Cheiro's language of the hand. 9th ed. (Hamon, Louis.) N.Y., 1897.
Phil 6053.12 Cheiro's memoirs. (Hamon, Louis.) Philadelphia, 1912.
Phil 6049.01 Cheirosophy, the hand. (Smith, R.C.) London, 1901.
Phil 9035.80 Cheley, Frank H. After all it's up to you. Boston, 1935.
Phil 193.150.5 Chelo-vecheskoe ''ia'' i kul'tura. (Spakovski, A.) Novyi Sad, 1936.
Phil 291.12 Chelovck i priroda. (Khudushin, Fedor S.) Moskva, 1966.
Phil 190.107 Chelovek, ego zhizn' i bessmertie. (Pantskhava, Il'ia D.) Moskva, 1967.
Phil 8980.276 Chelovek budushchego rozhdaetsia segodnia. Moskva, 1959.
Phil 8980.275 Chelovek budushchego rozhdaetsia segodnia. Novosibirsk, 1962.
Phil 585.166 Chelovek i epokha. (International Congress of Philosophy, 13th, Mexico, 1963. Delegation from the USSR.) Moskva, 1964.
Phil 310.726 Chelovek i istoriia. (Khotiakova, Valentina Alekseevna.) Moskva, 1970
Phil 8980.501 Chelovek i moral'. (Krutova, Ol'ga Natanouna.) Moskva, 1970.
Phil 585.396 Chelovek kak filosofskaia problema. (Kakabadze, Zurab M.) Tbilisi, 1970.
Phil 585.305 Chelovek kak predmet poznaniia. (Anan'ev, Boris G.) Leningrad, 1968.
Phil 8401.35 Cheloveku byt' khudozhnikom. (Apresian, Grant Z.) Moskva, 1965.
Phil 8980.481 Cheloveku nado verit. (Khmara, V.V.) Moskva, 1960.
Phil 4753.1.35 Chelpanov, G. Uchebnik logiki. Kharbin, 1921.
Phil 4753.1.30 Chelpanov, G. Vvedenie v filosofiiu. Riga, 1923.
Phil 6155.10 Chemical ecstasy. (Clark, Walter Houston.) N.Y., 1969.

Phil 9320.10 Les chemins de la sagesse. (Desjardins, Arnaud.) Paris, 1969- 2v.
Phil 3450.19.96.12 Chemins et impusses de l'ontologie Heideggerienne. (Waelhens, A. de.) Louvain, 1953.
Phil 8595.10 Chemistry, meteorology...natural theology. (Prout, W.) London, 1855.
Phil 8670.7.2 Chemistry, meteorology and the function of digestion considered with reference to natural theology. (Prout, W.) Philadelphia, 1834.
Phil 8670.7 Chemistry, meteorology and the function of digestion considered with reference to natural theology. (Prout, W.) London, 1834.
Phil 8585.10.2 Chemistry as exemplifying the wisdom and benefience of God. (Fownes, G.) London, 1849.
Phil 8585.10 Chemistry as exemplifying the wisdom and benefience of God. (Fownes, G.) N.Y., 1844.
Phil 930.41 Chen, Li-Fu. Philosophy of life. N.Y., 1948.
Phil 6112.26.5 Cheney, A.C.P. (Mrs.). What it is that heals. London, 1912.
Phil 525.95 Cheney, Sheldon. Men who have walked with God. N.Y., 1945.
Phil 8627.7 Cheney, William A. Can we be sure of mortality? N.Y., 1910.
Phil 2477.12 Cheninement et carrefours. (Bespaloff, R.) Paris, 1938.
Phil 960.225 Chennahesavan, Sarasvate. The concept of mind in Indian philosophy. London, 1960.
Phil 8403.4 Cherbuliez, V. L'art et la nature. Paris, 1892.
Phil 720.78 Chercher la vérité, 5-12 mars 1969. (Semaine des Intellectuels Catholiques, 1969.) Paris, 1969.
Phil 2490.125 Cherfils, C. L'esthétique positiviste. Paris, 1909.
Phil 8582.37 Cherix, Robert B. L'arche d'alliance. 2 é. Paris, 1923.
Phil 400.110 Cherkashin, P.P. O reaktsionnoi sushchnosti idealizma. Moskva, 1953.
Phil 400.123 Cherkasin, P.P. Gnoseologicheskie korni idealizma. Moskva, 1961.
Phil 310.430 Cherkesov, V.I. Materialisticheskaia dialektika kak logika i teoria poznaniia. Moskva, 1962.
Phil 5520.622 Chernokov, Petr V. Osnovnye edinitsy iazyka i myshleniia. Rostov-na-Donu, 1966.
Phil 4753.3 Chernov, Vladimir I. Analiz filosofskikh poniatii. Moskva, 1966.
Phil 4753.4 Chernovolenko, Vilen F. Mirovozzronie i nauchnoe poznanie. Kiev, 1970.
Phil 4753.2.35 Chernyshevskii, N.G. Das anthropologische Prinzip. Berlin, 1956.
Phil 4753.2.30 Chernyshevskii, N.G. Antropologicheskii printsip v filosofii. Moskva, 1943.
Phil 8403.12 Chernyshevskii, N.G. Esteticheskie otnosheniia iskusstva k deistvitel'nosti. Moskva, 1945.
Phil 4753.2.40 Chernyshevskii, N.G. Estetika. Moskva, 1958.
Phil 8403.12.5 Chernyshevskii, N.G. N.G. Chernyshevski ob iskusstve. Moskva, 1950.
Phil 8403.12.10 Chernyshevskii, N.G. Stat'i po estetike. Moskva, 1938.
Phil 6672.16 Chertok, León. Hypnosis. 1st ed. Oxford, 1966.
Phil 1535.32 Cherubini, F. Cursus philosophicus. Romae, 1904. 2v.
Phil 5812.3 Chesnel, A. Animaux raisonment. Paris, 1845.
Phil 310.555.3 Chesnokov, Dimitrii I. Historical materialism. Moscow, 1969.
Phil 310.555 Chesnokov, Dimitrii I. Istoricheskii materializm. Moskva, 1964.
Phil 310.555.2 Chesnokov, Dimitrii I. Istoricheskii materializm. izd. 2. Moskva, 1965.
Phil 5042.70 Chesnokov, P.V. Logicheskaia fraza i predlozhenie. Rostov-na-Donu, 1961.
Htn Phil 9346.6.7* Chesterfield, Philip Dormer Stanhope. Principles of politeness. Portsmouth, N.H., 1786.
Phil 960.272 Chethimattam, John B. Consciousness and reality. Bangalore, 1967.
Phil 960.272.5 Chethimattam, John B. Patterns of Indian thought. Maryknoll, N.Y., 1971.
Phil 4210.143 Cheula, Pietro. Rapporti fra Kant e Rosmini. Milano, 1934.
Phil 4070.2.80 Cheula, Pietro. Saggio su la filosofia di Francesco Bonatelli. Milano, 1934.
Phil 575.220 Chevalier, Charles. La confidence et la personne humaine. Paris, 1960.
Phil 7069.27.12 Chevalier, F. Albert Chevalier comes back. London, 1927.
Phil 2515.17 Chevalier, J. Cadences. Paris, 1939- 2v.
Phil 2520.135 Chevalier, J. Descartes. Paris, 1921.
Phil 5435.9 Chevalier, J. L'habitude, essai de métaphysique scientifique. Paris, 1929.
Phil 2805.177.5A Chevalier, J. Pascal. N.Y., 1930.
NEDL Phil 2805.177 Chevalier, J. Pascal. Paris, 1921.
Phil 5627.92 Chevalier, J. Pour une science de l'individuel. Paris, 1923.
Phil 8877.79 Chevalier, J. La vie morale et l'audelà. Paris, 1938.
Phil 2475.1.222 Chevalier, Jacques. Bergson. Paris, 1926.
Phil 2475.1.222.15
Phil 2475.1.222.5A Chevalier, Jacques. Entretiens avec Bergson. Paris, 1959.
Phil 2475.1.222.10 Chevalier, Jacques. Henri Bergson. N.Y., 1928.
Phil 802.22 Chevalier, Jacques. Henri Bergson. Paris, 1928.
Chevalier, Jacques. Histoire de la pensée. v.1-3. Paris, 1955- 2v.
Phil 630.40 Chevalier, Jacques. L'idée et le sens. Grenoble, 1932.
Phil 1135.93 Chevalier, Jacques. Notion du Necessaire chez Aristote. Paris, 1915.
Phil 177.77 Chevalier, Jacques. Trois conférences d'Oxford. Paris, 1928.
Phil 177.77.5 Chevalier, Jacques. Trois conférences d'Oxford. 2. ed. Paris, 1933.
Phil 8980.275.10 Chevkashyn, D.S. Kommunistychnyi ideal i diisnist'. Kharkiv, 1970.
Phil 7069.22.3 Chevreuil, L. Le spiritisme dans l'église. Paris, 1922.
Phil 7069.20.70 Chevreuil, L. Proofs of the spirit world. N.Y., 1920.
Phil 2885.89 Chevrillon, A. Taine; formation de sa pensée. Paris, 1932.
Phil 2045.92 Chevrillon, André. Qui fuerint saeculo XVII imprimis apud Hobbesium Anglicae solutae orationis progressus. Insulae, 1893.
Phil 8582.8 Cheyne, G. Philosophical principles of religion. v.1-2. London, 1915-16.
Phil 3850.27.98 Chez le Docteur Schweitzer. (Barthelemy, Guy.) Laussame, 1953.
Phil 7069.23.20 Chez Victor Hugo. Les tables tournantes de Jersey. (Simon, Gustave.) Paris, 1923.

Phil 672.176   Chiacchierata sul concetto di spazio. (Venturini, Saul.) Milano, 1951.

Phil 400.63   Chiapelli, A. Dottrina della realtá del mondo esterno. Parte prima. Firenze, 1886.

Phil 4080.2.79   Pamphlet box. Chiapelli, Alessandro.

Phil 8627.11   Chiappelli, A. Amore, morte ed immortalità. Milano, 1913.

Phil 1702.2.5   Chiappelli, A. La crisi del pensiero moderno. Citta di Castello, 1920.

Phil 400.24.5   Chiappelli, Alessandro. Dalla critica al nuovo idealismo. Milano, 1910.

Phil 2490.92   Chiappini, T. Les idées politiques d'Auguste Comte. Paris, 1913.

Phil 6952.14   Chiara, D. Les diables de morzine en 1861. n.p., 1861.

Phil 8092.32   Chiari, Joseph. The aesthetics of modernism. London, 1970.

Phil 8403.38   Chiari, Joseph. Realism and imagination. London, 1960.

Phil 5593.58   Chiari, Silvano. Bibliografica italiana. Firenze, 1958.

Phil 5593.58.5   Chiari, Silvano. Introduzione alla psicodiagnosi di Rorschach. Firenze, 1958.

Phil 9450.59   Chiavacci, Enrico. Etica politica. Roma, 1964.

Phil 4080.19   Chiavacci, G. La ragione poetica. Firenze, 1947.

Phil 5242.45   Chiavacci, G. Saggio sulla natura dell'uomo. Firenze, 1936.

Phil 6312.10   Chicago. Institute for Psychoanalysis. Five-year report. Chicago, 1937. 2v.

Phil 42.4   Chicago. University. Contributions to philosophy. Chicago. 1,1904+ 3v.

Phil 42.4.5   Chicago. University. Philosophic studies. Chicago. 1-10 2v.

Phil 5465.50   Chicago. University. Committee on Social Thought. The works of the mind. Chicago, 1947.

Phil 1817.22   The Chicago pragmatists. (Rucker, Darnell.) Minneapolis, 1969.

Phil 125.1   Chicchitti-Suriani. Nozioni elementari di logica. Torino, 1887.

Phil 600.61   Chicherin, Boris A. Polozhitel'naia filosofiia i edinstvo nauki. Moskva, 1892.

Phil 4769.1.65   Chicherin, Boris N. Mistitsizm v nauke. Moskva, 1880.

Phil 8692.27   Chicherin, Boris N. Nauka i religiia. Moskva, 1817.

Phil 8692.17   Chicherin, Boris N. Nauka i religiia. Moskva, 1901.

Phil 1135.195   Chicoteau, Marcel. Les attributs de l'ephectisme grec et leur survivance dans une cosmologie racinienne. Cardiff, 1943?

Phil 3549.8.135   Chidani, Shichiro. Mein Weg zu Ludwig Klages. Hamburg, 1967.

Phil 1750.21   Chide, A. Le mobilisme moderne. Paris, 1908.

Phil 1703.12   The chief currents of contemporary philosophy. (Datta, D.M.) Calcutta, 1950.

Phil 1703.12.2   The chief currents of contemporary philosophy. 2nd ed. (Datta, D.M.) Calcutta, 1961.

Phil 3819.14.10   Chief works. (Spinoza, Benedictus de.) N.Y, 1955[1951] 2v.

Phil 3819.14.5   Chief works. v.2. (Spinoza, Benedictus de.) London, 1919.

Phil 2775.2.30   Les chiens de garde. (Nizan, Paul.) Paris, 1960.

Phil 3425.560   Chiereghin, F. L'influenza dello Spinozismo nella formazione. Padova, 1961.

Phil 3425.640   Chiereghin, Franco. Hegel e la metafisica classica. Padova, 1966.

Phil 3425.641   Chiereghin, Franco. L'unità del sapere in Hegel. Padova, 1963.

Phil 4225.8.67.2   La chiesane la civiltà moderna. 2. ed. (Sciacca, Michele Federico.) Milano, 1969.

Phil 3475.3.235   Chiffer und Dogma. (Hommel, Claus Uwe.) Zürich, 1968.

Phil 3475.3.57   Chiffren der Transzendenz. (Jaspers, Karl.) München, 1970.

Phil 9240.28   Child, A. Bemis. Whatever is, is right. 2d ed. Boston, 1861.

Phil 7054.78   Child. A.B. The bouquet of spiritual flowers. Boston, 1856.

Phil 5870.100   The child and reality. (Ratcliffe, Tom A.) London, 1970.

Phil 9160.2.15   The child at Howe. (Abbott, Jacob.) N.Y., 1871.

Phil 9160.2.8   The child at Howe. 2. ed. (Abbott, Jacob.) Boston, 1834.

Phil 333.16   Childe, Vere G. Society and knowledge. 1st ed. N.Y., 1956.

Phil 5870.80.2   Childhood and adolescence. 2nd ed. (Stone, Lawrence Joseph.) N.Y., 1968.

Phil 6128.57A   Childhood experience and personal destiny. (Silverberg, W.V.) N.Y., 1952.

Phil 6956.16   Childhood schizophrenia. (Goldfarb, W.) Cambridge, 1961.

Phil 5865.5.40   Children and adolescents. (Elkind, David.) N.Y., 1970.

Phil 5870.50   Children as individuals. (Fordham, Michael Scott Montague.) London, 1969.

Phil 5871.116   Children in Africa: a review of psychological research. (Evans, Judith L.) N.Y., 1970.

Phil 8882.28   The children of good fortune. (Henderson, C.H.) N.Y., 1905.

Phil 5871.40   The children of the dream. (Bettelheim, Bruno.) N.Y., 1969.

Phil 5871.75   Children under stress. (Wolff, Sula.) London, 1969.

Phil 7084.8   Children's dreams. (Kimmins, Charles William.) London, 1920.

Phil 5525.48   Children's humor. (Wolfenstein, M.) Glencoe, Ill., 1954.

Phil 5875.5   Children's views of foreign peoples. (Lambert, Wallace E.) N.Y., 1966.

Phil 8877.82   Childs, M.W. Ethics in a business society. 1st ed. N.Y., 1954.

Phil 5865.5.22   The child's conception of time. (Piaget, Jean.) London, 1969.

Phil 5867.40   Child's play. (Herron, R.E.) N.Y., 1971.

Phil 42.13   Chile. Universidad, Santiago. Instituto Central de Psicologia. Archivos. Santiago. 2,1963+

Phil 4110.3.92   Chimirri, Bruno. Inaugurazione del monumento a Francesco Fiorentino in Sambiase, 15 novembre 1908. Catanzaro, 1908.

Phil 5834.1.13   Chimpanzee intelligence. (Yerkes, R.M.) Baltimore, 1925.

Phil 5834.1.25   Chimpanzees; a laboratory colony. (Yerkes, R.M.) New Haven, 1943.

Phil 5212.15   Chin, Robert. Psychological research in Communist China, 1949-1966. Cambridge, Mass., 1969.

Phil 5212.5   Chin, Robert. Psychology in America. N.Y., 1929.

Phil 930.50   China and Gandhian India. (Chang, Carsun.) Calcutta, 1956.

Phil 2805.432   Chinard, Gilbert. En lisant Pascal. Lille, 1948.

Phil 930.34   De chinesche filosofi. 3. druk. (Borel, Henri.) Amsterdam, 1896-97. 2v.

Phil 930.30.10   Chinesche wijsgeeren. (Hackmann, H.) Amsterdam, 1930. 2v.

Phil 12.17   Chinese journal of psychology. Peiping.

Phil 930.70   The Chinese mind. (East-West Philosophers Conference.) Honolulu, 1967.

Phil 930.40   The Chinese mind. (Wong, Gung-Hsing.) N.Y., 1946.

Phil 930.25   Chinese moral sentiments before Confucius. Diss. (Rudd, H.F.) Chicago? 1915?

Phil 4891.1   Chinese philosophy, 1949-1963; an annotated bibliography of mainland China publications. (Chan, Wing-tsit.) Honolulu, 1966-67.

Phil 930.1   Chinese philosophy. (Carus, P.) Chicago, 1898.

Phil 930.1.5   Chinese philosophy. 2d ed. (Carus, P.) Chicago, 1902.

Phil 930.01   Pamphlet box. Chinese philosophy pamphlets.

Phil 930.25.2   Chinese social organs. (Rudd, H.F.) Chicago, 1928.

Phil 12.120   Chinese studies in philosophy. White Plains, N.Y. 1,1969+

Phil 930.1.2   Chinese thought. (Carus, P.) Chicago, 1907.

Phil 930.42   Chinese thought from Confucuis to Mao Tse-tung. (Creel, H.G.) Chicago, 1953.

Phil 930.30   Chinesische Philosophie. (Hackmann, H.) München, 1927.

Phil 930.35   Chinesische Philosophie. (Wilhelm, R.) Breslau, 1929.

Phil 4080.3.122   Chiocchetti, E. La filosofia di Benedetto Croce. 2a ed. Milano, 1920.

Phil 4080.3.123   Chiocchetti, E. La filosofia di Benedetto Croce. 3a ed. Milano, 1924.

Phil 4260.108   Chiocchetti, E. La filosofia di Giambattista Vico. Milano, 1935.

Phil 4120.4.81   Chiocchetti, E. La filosofia di Giovanni Gentile. Milano, 1922.

Phil 8582.38   Chiocchetti, E. Religione e filosofia. Milano, 1921.

Phil 177.66   Chiocchetti, Emilio. Il pragmatismo. Milano, 1926.

Phil 1750.560   Chiodi, Pietro. L'esistenzialismo. Torino, 1957.

Phil 3450.19.108   Chiodi, Pietro. L'esistenzialismo di Heidegger. Torino, 1947.

Phil 3450.19.108.3   Chiodi, Pietro. L'esistenzialismo di Heidegger. 3e ed. Torino, 1965.

Phil 1750.560.10   Chiodi, Pietro. Esistenzialismo e fenomenologia. Milano, 1963.

Phil 3484.26   Chiodí, Pietro. Il pensiero di Immanuel Kant. Torino, 1963.

Phil 1750.560.5   Chiodi, Pietro. Il pensiero esistenzialista. Milano, 1959.

Phil 2880.8.210   Chiodi, Pietro. Sartre il marxismo. 1. ed. Milano, 1965.

Phil 3450.19.109   Chiodi, Pietro. L'ultimo. 1e ed. Torino, 1952.

Phil 3450.19.109.2   Chiodi, Pietro. L'ultimo Heidegger. 2e ed. Torino, 1960.

Phil 8401.25   Chiose all'estetica, con un profile dell'autore a cura di G. Calogero. (Antoni, Carlo.) Roma, 1960.

Phil 8877.8   Chipman, G. The American moralist. Wrentham, Mass., 1801.

Phil 5242.42   Chircoulesco, D. Essai sur les principes d'une psychologie évolutive. Bucarest, 1929.

Phil 6025.4.15   La chirofisonomia overo di quelle parte della humana fisonomia. (Porta, G.B.) Napoli, 1677.

Phil 6060.11   Die Chirogrammatonamtie. (Henze, A.) Leipzig, 1862.

Phil 6046.57   La chiromance. (Peruchio.) Paris, 1657.

Phil 6046.57.5   La chiromance. (Peruchio.) Paris, 1663.

Htn   Phil 6045.61.7*   La chiromance. (Tricasso, Patricio.) Paris, 1583.

Htn   Phil 6045.61.5*   La chiromance. (Tricasso, Patricio.) Paris, 1583.

Htn   Phil 6045.22.35*   La chiromance et phisiognomie. (Indagine, Joannes.) Rouen, 1638.

Phil 6045.22.40   La chiromance et phisionomie. (Indagine, Joannes.) Paris, 1662?

Htn   Phil 6045.22.25*   Chiromance et physiognomonie. (Indagine, Joannes.) Lyon, 1549.

Phil 6046.65   La chiromancie medicinale. (Mey, Philipp.) La Haye, 1665.

Phil 6048.59.5   Chiromancie nouvelle...les mystères de la main, revélés et expliqués. 14e ed. (Desbarrolles, A.) Paris, 186-.

Phil 6045.22.9   Chiromantia. (Indagine, Joannes.) Argentorati, 1531.

Htn   Phil 6045.22.7*   Chiromantia. (Indagine, Joannes.) Paris, 1543.

Htn   Phil 6045.22.13*   Chiromantia. (Indagine, Joannes.) Paris, 1547.

Htn   Phil 6045.95*   Chiromantiae. (Rothmann, J.) Erphordiae, 1595.

Phil 6053.8   Chiromanzia e tatuaggio. (Cerchiari, G. Luigi.) Milano, 1903.

Phil 2255.1.135   Chisholm, John Edward. The theory of knowledge of Bertrand Russell. Rome, 1967.

Phil 5585.90   Chisholm, R.M. Perceiving. Ithaca, 1957.

Phil 630.55   Chisholm, R.M. Realism and the background of phenomenology. Glencoe, 1961.

Phil 4710.55   Chizhevskii, D. Narysy z istorii filosofii na Ukraïni. Praga, 1931.

Phil 4710.50   Chizhevskii, O. Filosofiia na Ukraïni. Vyd. 2. Praga, 1928.

Phil 210.70.1   Chladenius, Johann Martin. Einleitung zur richtigen Auslegung vernünftiger Reden und Schriften. Düsseldorf, 1969.

Phil 3425.81   Chlebik, F. Kraft und Stoff...Hegel'schen Prämissen. Berlin, 1873.

Phil 5352.18   Choice, strategy and utility. (Siegel, Sidney.) N.Y., 1964.

Phil 5058.102   Choice and chance; an introduction to inductive logic. (Skyrms, Brian.) Belmont, Calif., 1968.

Phil 5767.14   Choice and chance. (Rankin, K.) Oxford, 1961.

Phil 1750.788.2   Choice of action; the French existentialists on the political front line. 1st American ed. (Burnier, Michel Antoine.) N.Y., 1968.

Phil 5850.219   Choice points. (Glidewell, John C.) Cambridge, Mass., 1970.

Phil 5242.27   Choisnard, P. L'éducation psychologique à propos de la grande guerre. Paris, 1920.

Phil 5812.6   Choisnard, Paul. Introduction à la psychologie comparée. Paris, 1924.

Phil 177.75   Choisnard, Paul. La loi de relation et l'erreur séparatiste en science et en philosophie. Paris, 1923.

Phil 525.245   Choisy, Maryse. L'être et le silence. Genève, 1965.

Phil 6312.32   Choisy, Maryse. Mais la terre est sacrée. Genève, 1968.

Phil 6315.2.300   Choisy, Maryse. Sigmund Freud. N.Y., 1963.

Phil 1750.255   Le choix, le monde, l'existence. Grenoble, 1947.

Phil 735.121   Le choix. (Grenier, Jean.) Paris, 1941.

Phil 2520.35.50   Choix commenté du Discours de la méthode. (Descartes, René.) Geneve, 1952.

Phil 2880.8.82   Le choix de Jean Paul Sartre. (Troisfontaines, Roger.) Paris, 1945.

Phil 2880.8.82.2   Le choix de Jean Paul Sartre. 2. éd. (Troisfontaines, Roger.) Paris, 1946.

Phil 2475.1.103   Choix de texte avec étude du...R. Gillouin. (Bergson, Henri.) Paris, 1918.

Phil 2477.1.25   Choix de textes. (Boutroux, Émile.) Paris, 1910.

Phil 2480.20A   Choix de textes. (Cabanis, P.J.G.) Paris, n.d.

Phil 9045.12   Chojeckiego, E. Patrjotyzm i objawy Jego u niektórych narodów. Paryz, 1870.

Phil 1200.8   Chollet, A. La morale stoicienne. Paris, n.d.
Phil 5520.449A   Chomsky, Noam. Cartesian linguistics. N.Y., 1966.
Phil 5520.449.5   Chomsky, Noam. Linguistica cartesiana. Madrid, 1969.
Phil 333.28   Chomsky, Noam. Problems of knowledge and freedom: the Russell lectures. 1st ed. N.Y., 1971.
Phil 940.5   Chŏng, Chin-sŏk. Istoriia koreiskoi filosofii. Moskva, 1966.
Phil 9070.118   Choose life. (Mandelbaum, Bernard.) N.Y., 1968.
Phil 6854.14   Choran, Jacques. Suicide. N.Y., 1972.
Phil 177.26.5   Choraux, C. L'ombre de Socrate. Paris, 1878.
Phil 177.26   Choraux, C. La pensée et l'amour. Paris, 1869.
Phil 930.60   Chow, Yih-ching. La philosophie chinoise. 2. ed. Paris, 1961.
Phil 8877.61   Christ, Paul. Die sittliche Weltordnung. Leiden, 1894.
Phil 1020.4.15   Christ, Paul S. The psychology of the active intellect of Averroes. Thesis. Philadelphia, 1926.
Phil 8586.52   Christ and Freud. (Guirdham, A.) London, 1959.
Phil 5402.22.15   Christ and human suffering. (Jones, Eli Stanley.) N.Y., 1933.
Phil 8692.1   Christ and modern thought. (Cook, J.) Boston, 1881.
Phil 3640.347   Christ and Nietzsche. (Knight, George W.) London, 1948.
Phil 8967.6   Christ and the present crisis. (Reid, A.C.) Wake Forest, 1936.
Phil 978.49.700   Christ and the spiritual world. (Steiner, R.) London, 1963.
Phil 178.12.47   The Christ ideal. (Dresser, H.W.) N.Y., 1901.
Phil 8952.5   The Christ ideal for world peace. (Crawford, F.G.) San Francisco, 1925.
Phil 7069.19.55   Christ in you. N.Y., 1919.
Phil 525.28   The Christ of the Holy Grail. (Bain, James L.M.) London, 1909.
Phil 8430.35   Der Christ und das Schöne. 1. Aufl. (Vogel, Heinrich.) Berlin, 1955.
Phil 8587.51.5   Der Christ und die Geschichte. (Haecker, T.) Leipzig, 1935.
Phil 8964.6   Der Christ und die Weltwirklichkeit. (Oesterreichisches Seelsorge-Institut. Weihnachts-Seelsorgertagung, 1959.) Wien, 1960.
Phil 8725.14   Christelijk bestaan in een seculaire cultuur. Roermond, 1969.
Phil 3310.17.80   Het christelijk humanisme. (Faber, Heije.) Assen, 1963.
Phil 8598.74   Christen-Staat. (Sekendorf, V.L. von.) Leipzig, 1716.
Phil 8697.28   Die Christenheit im Atomzeitalter. (Howe, Günter.) Stuttgart, 1970.
Phil 9450.9   Christensen, A. Politics and crowd-morality. London, 1915.
Phil 9450.9.5   Christensen, A. Politik og massemoral. København, 1911.
Phil 1200.61   Christensen, J. An essay of the unity of Stoic philosophy. Copenhagen, 1962.
Phil 4525.1.31   Christensen, S. Indad. København, 1918.
Phil 5841.12   Christenson, Cornelia Vos. Kinsey, a biography. Bloomington, 1971.
Phil 8610.881.25   Christenthum ist Heidenthum. (Rodenhausen, C.) Hamburg, 1881.
Phil 8594.7   Das Christentum im Freilichte. (Opitz, H.G.) Leipzig, 1911.
Phil 8587.29   Das Christentum im Weltanschauungskampf. 3. Aufl. (Hunzinger, A.W.) Leipzig, 1919.
Phil 5627.168   Das Christentum und die Angst; eine religions-psychologische, historische und religionshygienische Untersuchung. (Pfister, Oskar.) Zürich, 1944.
Phil 8602.43   Das Christentum und die monistische Religion. (Werner, Max.) Berlin, 1908.
Phil 8590.26.5   Das Christentum und die Philosophie. 3. Aufl. (Kaftan, Julius.) Leipzig, 1896.
Phil 3850.27.45   Das Christentum und die Welterligionen. (Schweitzer, A.) München, 1949.
Phil 8587.13.90   Christentum und Geschichte bei W. Herrmann. (Herrmann, R.) Leipzig, 1914.
Phil 3246.197   Christentum und Geschichte in Fichtes Philosophie. (Hirsch, E.) Tübingen, 1920.
Phil 8587.51   Christentum und Kultur. (Haecker, T.) München, 1927.
Phil 3850.27.101   Christentum und Kulture bei Albert Schweitzer. (Buri, Fritz.) Beru, 1941.
Phil 8598.55.2   Christentum und moderne Weltanschauung. (Stange, Carl.) Leipzig, 1913-14. 2v.
Phil 3640.243   Das Christentum und Nietzsches Herremoral. (Kaftan, Julius.) Berlin, 1897.
Phil 8962.2   Christentum und Weltmoral. (Maushach, J.) Münster, 1897.
Phil 5520.412   Christian, W.A. Meaning and truth in religion. Princeton, 1964.
Phil 2340.10.150   Christian, William A. An interpretation of Whitehead's metaphysics. New Haven, 1959.
Phil 9240.9   The Christian answers to the problem of evil. 2. ed. (Whale, J.S.) London, 1948.
Phil 9495.138   The Christian approach to social morality. (Cabot, R.C.) N.Y., 1913.
Phil 3160.6.81   Christian August Crusius als Metaphysiker. (Festner, Carl.) Halle, 1892.
Phil 8961.13   Christian behaviour. (Lewis, Clive Staples.) London, 1943.
Phil 8961.13.10   Christian behaviour. (Lewis, Clive Staples.) N.Y., 1944.
Phil 8597.46   Christian belief and practice. (Richardson, Robert D.) London, 1940.
Phil 8677.10   Christian belief in God. (Wobbermin, George.) New Haven, 1918.
Phil 8597.51   The Christian challenge and philosophy. (Reade, W.H.V.) London, 1951.
Phil 978.8.2   The christian creed. 2nd ed. (Leadbeater, C.W.) London, 1904.
Phil 8657.7.6   The Christian doctrine of God. (Clarke, W.N.) N.Y., 1910.
Phil 8691.9   Christian doctrines and modern thought. (Bonney, T.G.) London, 1892.
Phil 8640.14   Christian eschatology and social thought. (Petry, Ray C.) N.Y., 1956.
Phil 8582.58   The Christian estimate of man. (Cave, S.) London, 1944.
Phil 8969.3.5   Christian ethicks. (Traherne, Thomas.) Ithaca, 1968.
Phil 8953.2   Christian ethics. (Davidson, William L.) London, 1899.
Phil 8956.3   Christian ethics. (Gregory, Daniel.) Philadelphia, 1875.
Phil 8957.12   Christian ethics. (Hildebrand, D. von.) N.Y., 1953.
Phil 8957.1   Christian ethics. (Hovey, A.) Boston, 1875.
Phil 8962.1   Christian ethics. (Martensen, H.L.) Edinburgh, 1873.
Phil 8962.1.5   Christian ethics. (Martensen, H.L.) Edinburgh, 1881. 2v.
Phil 8964.3   Christian ethics. (Osborne, A.R.) London, 1940.
Phil 8968.8   Christian ethics. (Sanderson, R.) London, 1833.
Phil 8968.4   Christian ethics. (Smyth, N.) N.Y., 1892.

Phil 8972.2   Christian ethics. (Wardlaw, R.) London, 1833.
Phil 8972.2.2   Christian ethics. (Wardlaw, R.) N.Y., 1835.
Phil 8972.1.5   Christian ethics. (Wuttke, K.F.A.) Boston, 1873. 2v.
Phil 8952.7   Christian ethics. Philadelphia, 1927.
Phil 8955.14   Christian ethics: a historical and systematic analysis of its dominant ideas. (al Faruqi, Ismàil Ragi A.) Montreal, 1967.
Phil 8958.2   Christian ethics and modern problems. (Inge, W.R.) London, 1930.
Phil 8951.23   Christian ethics and social policy. (Bennett, J.) N.Y., 1946.
Phil 8972.9   Christian ethics in history and modern life. (Widgery, A.G.) N.Y., 1940.
Phil 4752.2.79   Christian existentialism. (Berdiaev, Nikolai Aleksandrovich.) London, 1965.
Phil 574.6   The Christian existentialist. (Haering, Bernhard.) N.Y., 1968.
Phil 8633.1.23   The Christian faith and eternal life. (Horr, George E.) Cambridge, 1923.
Phil 1540.77   Christian faith and Greek philosophy. (Armstrong, O.H.) N.Y., 1964.
Phil 8430.5   Christian faith and the contemporary arts. (Eversople, Finley.) N.Y., 1962.
Phil 8707.7   Christian faith in an age of science. (Rice, William N.) N.Y., 1903.
Phil 8626.21   The Christian hell. (Bonner, H.B. (Mrs.).) London, 1913.
Phil 3925.3.80   Christian Hermann Weisse. (Seydel, Rudolf.) Leipzig, 1866.
Phil 8644.11   The Christian hope of immortality. (Taylor, Alfred E.) London, 1938.
Phil 9182.1   The Christian household. (Weaver, G.S.) Boston, 1856.
Phil 2750.11.95   Christian humanism...Jacques Maritain. (Allen, E.) London, 1950.
Phil 8964.1   Christian ideas and ideals. (Ottley, Robert L.) London, 1916.
Phil 802.17   The Christian in philosophy. (Casserley, J.V.L.) London, 1949.
Phil 8582.24   Christian instincts and modern doubt. (Craufurd, A.H.) London, 1897.
Phil 349.48   The Christian intellect and the mystery of being. (Sikora, Joseph John.) The Hague, 1966.
Phil 9010.25   The Christian law of amusements. (Corning, James L.) Buffalo, 1859.
Phil 8965.11   The Christian life in the modern world. (Peabody, F.G.) N.Y., 1914.
Phil 818.2   Christian metaphysics. (Smyth, C.B.) London, 1851.
X Cg   Phil 9161.1.3   The Christian minister's affectionate advice to a new married couple. (Bean, James.) London, 1814.
NEDL   Phil 9161.1   The Christian minister's affectionate advice to a new married couple. (Bean, James.) London, 1814.
Phil 8957.10   Christian morality; natural, developing, final. (Henson, Herbert H.) Oxford, 1936.
Phil 8965.10   Christian morals. (Peabody, A.P.) Boston, 1886.
Phil 8968.1   Christian morals. (Sewell, W.) London, 1841.
Htn   Phil 8962.4.5*   Christian morals. 1st American ed. (More, Hannah.) N.Y., 1813.
Htn   Phil 8951.2*   Christian morals. 2. ed. (Browne, T.) London, 1756.
Htn   Phil 8962.4.6*   Christian morals. 2nd American ed. (More, Hannah.) N.Y., 1813.
Phil 525.90   Christian mysticism. (Collins, J.B.) Baltimore, 1940.
Htn   Phil 8595.16.25*   Christian panoply. (Watson, R.) Sheperdstown, 1797. 2 pam.
Phil 8693.1   The Christian philosopher. (Dick, T.) N.Y., 1827.
Htn   Phil 8667.4*   The Christian philosopher. (Mather, C.) London, 1721.
Phil 8585.22   Christian philosophy. (Frothingham, E.L.) Baltimore, 1888-1890. 2v.
Phil 8595.55   Christian philosophy and intellectual freedom. (Pegis, Anton C.) Milwaukee, 1960.
Phil 181.44   Christian philosophy discussed under the topics of absolute values. (Gurnhill, James.) London, 1921.
Phil 8520.50   Christian philosophy in the college and seminary. (Catholic University of America. Workshop on Christian Philosophy and Religious Renewal, 1964.) Washington, 1966.
Phil 8583.17.5   Christian practice. (Delany, Selden P.) N.Y., 1920.
Phil 5627.28   Christian psychology. 3. ed. (Stalker, James.) N.Y., 1914.
Phil 8591.44.45   Christian reflections. (Lewis, Clive Staples.) London, 1967.
Phil 8663.3.32   The Christian religion. (Ingersol, Robert G.) n.p., 1851?
Phil 8663.3.33   The Christian religion. (Ingersoll, Robert G.) Manchester, 1882.
Phil 8663.3.40   The Christian religion. (Ingersoll, Robert G.) N.Y., 1882.
Phil 8581.51   The Christian religion and its competitors today. (Bouquet, A.C.) Cambridge, Eng., 1925.
Phil 6132.4.7   Christian religion as a healing power. (Worcester, Elwood.) N.Y., 1909.
Phil 7068.64   Christian spiritualism. (Bertolacci, W.R.) London, 1864.
Phil 8674.3   Christian theism. (Thompson, R.A.) N.Y., 1856.
Phil 8602.45   Christian theology. (Wiley, H.O.) Kansas City, 1940-41. 2v.
Phil 8610.872   Christian theology and modern scepticism. (Somerset, Edward Adolphhus.) London, 1872.
Phil 8610.872.2   Christian theology and modern scepticism. (Somerset, Edward Adolphhus.) N.Y., 1872.
Phil 3890.8.110   Christian Thomasius. (Bloch, E.) Berlin, 1953.
Phil 3890.8.101   Christian Thomasius und der Pietismus. (Kayser, R.) Hamburg, 1900.
Phil 3890.8.105   Christian Thomasius und seine Beziehungen zum Pietismus. Inaug. Diss. (Neisser, Liselotte.) München, 1928.
Phil 8599.19.21   Christian thought, its history and application. (Troeltsch, Ernst.) London, 1923.
Phil 8592.66   Christian truth in history. (Miller, Hugh.) N.Y., 1941.
Phil 8951.26   Christian values and economic life. 1st ed. N.Y., 1954.
Phil 3910.80   Christian ven Wolf. (Breslau. Prussia Magdalinisch-Gymnas.) Breslau, 1831.
Phil 8594.15   The Christian view of God and the world. 8. ed. (Orr, J.) N.Y., 1907.
Phil 7069.16.50   Christian wisdom. (Parker, Frank E.) Cambridge, Mass., 1916.
Phil 3910.126   Christian Wolff als Staatsdenker. (Frauendienst, W.) Berlin, 1927.
Phil 6112.22   Christiani, A. Zur Physiologie des Gehirnes. Berlin, 1885.
Phil 2733.92   Le Christianisme dans la philosophie de Malebranche. (Vidgrain, J.) Paris, n.d.

Phil 2733.90 — Le christianisme dans la philosophie de Malebranche. Thèse. (Vidgrain, Joseph.) Paris, 1923.

Phil 2648.52.6 — Le christianisme dévoilé. (Holbach, Paul Henri T.) Herblay, 1961.

Htn Phil 2648.52.2* — Le christianisme dévoilé. (Holbach, Paul Henri T.) Londres, 1767.

Phil 2648.52 — Le christianisme dévoilé. (Holbach, Paul Henri T.) Londres, 1767.

Phil 2648.52.3 — Le christianisme dévoilé. (Holbach, Paul Henri T.) Paris, 1767.

Phil 2648.52.5 — Le christianisme dévoilé. (Holbach, Paul Henri T.) Suisse, 1796.

Phil 1540.36 — Christianisme et culture phillosophique au cinquième siècle. (Fortin, E.L.) Paris, 1959.

Phil 2750.11.58 — Christianisme et démocratie. (Maritain, Jacques.) N.Y., 1943.

Phil 1170.8 — Le christianisme et la fin de la philosophie antique. (Corbière, C.) Paris, 1921.

Phil 8520.37 — Le christianisme et les philosophies. (Sertillanges, R.P.) Paris, 1939-41. 2v.

Phil 8580.28 — Le christianisme et l'esprit moderne. (Arbousse-Bastide, A.F.) Paris, 1862.

Phil 181.73 — Christianisme et philosophie. (Gilson, E.) Paris, 1936.

Phil 8690.12 — Le christianisme se désintéresse-t-il de la science? (Abelé, Jean.) Paris, 1960.

Phil 8589.5.20 — Christianity, the logic of creation. (James, H.) N.Y., 1857.

Phil 8592.2 — Christianity. (McConnell, S.) N.Y., 1912.

Phil 8598.94 — Christianity after Freud. (Sanders, B.G.) London, 1949.

Phil 8610.889 — Christianity and agnosticism. N.Y., 1889.

Phil 4752.2.78 — Christianity and anti Semitism. (Berdiaev, Nikolai Aleksandrovich.) Aldington, 1952.

Phil 4752.2.78.2 — Christianity and anti-Semitism. (Berdiaev, Nikolai Aleksandrovich.) N.Y., 1954.

Phil 8581.96 — Christianity and civilisation. (Brunner, Heinrich Emil.) N.Y., 1949. 2v.

Phil 8581.96.2 — Christianity and civilization. (Brunner, Heinrich Emil.) N.Y., 1949.

Phil 8610.919 — Christianity and conduct. (Bonner, Hypatia Bradlaugh (Mrs.).) London, 1919.

Phil 2750.11.58.5 — Christianity and democracy. (Maritain, Jacques.) N.Y., 1944.

Phil 8962.14 — Christianity and economic problems. (Munby, D.L.) London, 1956.

Phil 1750.744 — Christianity and existentialism; essays. Evanston, Ill., 1963.

Phil 1750.353.5 — Christianity and existentialism. (Spier, J.M.) Philadelphia, 1953.

Phil 850.10 — Christianity and Greek philosophy. (Cocker, B.F.) N.Y., 1870.

Phil 1135.22 — Christianity and Greek philosophy. (Cocker, B.F.) N.Y., 1875.

Phil 1135.22.4 — Christianity and Greek philosophy. (Cocker, B.F.) N.Y., 1879.

Phil 400.7.2 — Christianity and idealism. (Watson, J.) N.Y., 1897.

Phil 400.7 — Christianity and idealism. (Watson, J.) N.Y., 1897.

Phil 8587.10.15 — Christianity and infidelity. (Hennell, S.S.) London, 1857.

Phil 8610.877.5 — Christianity and infidelity. (Humphrey, G.H.) N.Y., 1877.

Phil 8586.22 — Christianity and modern thought. (Gabriel, R.H.) New Haven, 1924.

Phil 8897.69 — Christianity and morals. (Westermarck, E.) N.Y., 1939.

Phil 8708.13 — Christianity and naturalism. (Shafer, Robert.) New Haven, 1926.

Phil 575.22.5 — Christianity and personality. (Buckham, John W.) N.Y., 1936.

Phil 2125.62.5 — Christianity and positivism. (McCosh, James.) N.Y., 1871.

Phil 2125.62 — Christianity and positivism. (McCosh, James.) N.Y., 1874.

Phil 8952.4 — Christianity and problems of today. N.Y., 1922.

Phil 8592.71 — Christianity and reason. (Myers, E.D.) N.Y., 1951.

Phil 8696.6 — Christianity and science. (Gulliver, John P.) Andover, 1880.

Phil 8610.853.10 — Christianity and secularism. (Grant, B.) London, 1853.

Phil 9495.138.5 — Christianity and sex. (Cabot, R.C.) N.Y., 1937.

Phil 9495.146 — Christianity and sex. (Dawson, C.) London, 1930.

Phil 9495.39.5 — Christianity and sex problems. (Northcote, Hugh.) Philadelphia, 1906.

Phil 9495.39 — Christianity and sex problems. 2d ed. (Northcote, Hugh.) Philadelphia, 1916.

Phil 7069.27.5 — Christianity and spiritualism. (Bateman, A.B.) London, 1927.

Phil 1750.430 — Christianity and the existentialists. (Michalson, Carl.) N.Y., 1956.

Phil 8602.27.10 — Christianity and the nature of history. (Wood, Herbert G.) Cambridge, Eng., 1934.

Phil 8584.5.5 — Christianity and the new idealism. (Eucken, Rudolf.) London, 1909.

Phil 8952.8 — Christianity and the present moral unrest. London, 1926.

Htn Phil 8599.4* — Christianity as old as the creation. (Tindall, M.) London, 1730. 2v.

Phil 8599.4.2 — Christianity as old as the creation. (Tindall, M.) London, 1732.

Phil 8610.941 — Christianity cross-examined. (Floyd, W.) N.Y., 1941.

Phil 8952.2 — Christianity judged by its fruits. (Croslegh, C.) London, 1884.

Phil 2295.36 — Christianity not mysterious. (Toland, John.) Stuttgart, 1964.

Htn Phil 2295.34* — Christianity not mysterious. v.1-3. (Toland, John.) London, 1696.

Htn Phil 2295.35* — Christianity not mysterious. 2nd ed. (Toland, John.) London, 1696.

Phil 8591.45 — Christianity reborn. (Leh, L.L.) N.Y., 1928.

Htn Phil 2295.86* — Christianity the great mystery; answer to a late treatise. (Beverley, Thomas.) Dondon, 1696.

Phil 8595.16.35 — Christianity the only true theology. London, 179-?

Phil 8595.2 — Christianity the religion of nature. (Peabody, A.P.) Boston, 1864.

Htn Phil 8595.16.5* — Christianity the true theology. (Patten, William.) Warren, 1795.

Phil 6321.30.10 — Christians and Jews. (Loewenstein, R.) N.Y., 1951.

Phil 3910.125 — Christians Wolff's Verhältnis zu Lubniz. (Arnsperger, W.) Weimar, 1897.

Phil 3484.16 — Christiansen, B. Kritik der Kantischen Erkenntnislehre. Hanau, 1911.

Phil 2520.106 — Christiansen, B. Das Urteil bei Descartes. Hanau, 1902.

Phil 177.101 — Christiansen, Broder. Das Gesicht unserer Zeit. München, 1931.

Phil 8657.19 — Christiansen, Broder. Der neue Gott. München, 1934.

Phil 665.25 — Christiansen, Broder. Vom Selbstbewusstsein. Berlin, 1912.

Phil 177.42 — Christiansen, H. MeineLösung der Welträtsel. Wiesbaden, 1914.

Phil 6520.14 — Christiany, L. Eva von Buttler die Messaline und Muckerin...Mysterien des Pietismus. Stuttgart, 1870.

Phil 7069.32.12 — Christie, Anne. The opening of the door. Boston, 1932.

Phil 270.5 — Christinnecke, J. Causalität und Entwicklung. Jena, 1891.

Phil 6112.21 — Christison, J.S. Brain in relation to mind. Chicago, 1899.

Phil 1730.24 — Der christliche Bürger und die Aufklärung. (Goldmann, Lucien.) Neuwied, 1968.

Phil 8961.18 — Christliche Ethik. (Lemme, Ludwig.) Berlin, 1905. 2v.

Phil 8968.8.20 — Christliche Ethik. (Soe, N.H.) München, 1949.

Phil 8962.21 — Die christliche Ethik im Lichte der Ethnologie. (Mohr, R.) München, 1954.

Phil 3805.32.15 — Der christliche Glaube; nach den Grundsätzen. (Schleiermacher, Friedrich.) Berlin, 1960. 2v.

Phil 3805.32 — Der christliche Glaube. Bd.1-2. (Schleiermacher, Friedrich.) Reutlingen, 1828.

Phil 3805.32.5 — Der christliche Glaube. 2. Aufl. (Schleiermacher, Friedrich.) Berlin, 1830-31. 2v.

Phil 3805.32.10 — Der christliche Glaube. 5. Aufl. (Schleiermacher, Friedrich.) Berlin, 1861. 2v.

Phil 8595.36 — Christliche Lebensphilosophie. 20. bis 22. Aufl. (Pesch, T.) Freiburg, 1923.

Phil 1712.25 — Das christliche Menschenbild und die Weltanschauungen der Neuzeit im Breiszau. (Mueller, Max.) Freiburg, 1945.

Phil 8586.42 — Christliche Metaphysik und das Schicksal des modernen Bewusstseins. (Gunther, G.) Leipzig, 1937.

Phil 978.49.525 — Das christliche Mysterium. (Steiner, R.) Dornach, 1968.

Phil 525.41 — Die christliche Mystik. (Helfferich, A.) Gotha, 1842. 2v.

Phil 525.12.7 — Die christliche Mystik. (Noack, Ludwig.) Königsberg, 1853.

Phil 525.42 — Die christliche Mystik. Bd.1-2,3,4[1],4[2]. (Gorres, J.) Regensburg, 1836-42.

Phil 8592.115 — Christliche Philosophie. (Muck, Otto.) Kevelaer, 1964.

Phil 1522.1 — Die christliche Philosophie. (Ritter, A.H.) Göttingen, 1858-9.

Phil 1508.2.12 — Christliche Philosophie. 2. Aufl. (Dempf, Alois.) Bonn, 1952.

Phil 1511.3.20 — Christliche Philosophie von ihren Anfängen bis Nikol von Cues. 3e Aufl. (Boehner, Philotheus.) Paderborn, 1954.

Phil 9035.69 — Die christliche Religion in ihrer Bedeutung für die Charaktererziehung. (Lichtenfels, H.) Kallmünz, 1934.

Phil 8598.58.5 — Christliche Religionsphilosophie. Pt.1-2. (Steffens, H.) Breslau, 1839. 2v.

Phil 8957.8 — Christliche Sittenlehre. (Heppe, H.) Elberfeld, 1882.

Phil 8968.10 — Christliche Sittenlehre nach evangesischlutherischer Auffassung. (Scharling, C. Henrik.) Bremen, 1892.

Phil 8955.7 — Christliche und marxistische Ethik. (Fuchs, Emil.) Leipzig, 1958. 2v.

Phil 3640.530 — Christlicher Glaube und intellektuelle Redlichkeit. (Grau, Gerd Günther.) Frankfurt, 1958.

Phil 2805.220 — Christliches Bewusstsein...Pascal. (Guardini, R.) Leipzig, 1935.

Phil 8602.80 — Christliches Glauben und christliche Glaubenslosigkeit. (Waldmann, Günter.) Tübingen, 1968.

Phil 8582.59 — Christlieb, M.L. How can I bear suffering? London, 1944.

Phil 5635.48 — Christman, Raymond John. Sensory experience. Scranton, 1971.

Phil 8692.9 — Christmas, H. The world of matter and its testimony. London, 1848.

Phil 8615.1.20 — Christmas from an ethical standpoint. (Salter, W.M.) Chicago, 1888.

Phil 3450.11.425 — Christoff, Daniel. Husserl; ou, Le retour aux choses. Paris, 1966.

Phil 5780.17 — Christoff, Daniel. Recherche de la liberté. 1. éd. Paris, 1957.

Phil 3850.27.116 — Christolles, H. Albert Schweitzer. Stuttgart, 1953.

Phil 8893.12.15 — Christoph Sigwarts Beiträge zu Grundlegung und Aufbau der Ethik. (Flaig, Josef.) Stuttgart, 1912.

Phil 8583.28 — Christopher Dawson and the modern political crisis. (Schlesinger, Bruno P.) Notre Dame, 1949.

Phil 4515.93 — Christopher Jacob Boström Sveriges Platon. (Ljunghoff, Johannes.) Uppsala, 1916.

Phil 2115.143 — Christophersen, H.O. John Locke, en filosofis forberedelse og grunnleggelse (1632-1689). Oslo, 1932.

Phil 4605.1.80 — Christophersen, Halfdan. Marcus Jacob Monrad. Oslo, 1959.

Phil 974.3.121 — Die Christosophie Rudolf Steiners. (Stieglitz, K. von.) Witten, 1955.

Phil 5440.16 — Christ's teaching concerning heredity. (Harris, George.) n.p., 1887.

Phil 8592.69 — Christus-Religion oder philosophische Religion? (Matthes, H.) Göttingen, 1925.

Phil 978.49.320 — Christus und die menschliche Seele. (Steiner, R.) Dornach, 1946.

Phil 8582.60 — Christus und die Zeit. (Cullmann, Oscar.) Zollikon-Zürich, 1946.

Phil 705.23 — Christy, Arthur. The Orient in American transcendentalism. N.Y., 1932.

Phil 705.23.2 — Christy, Arthur. The Orient in American transcendentalism. N.Y., 1963.

Phil 6967.15 — Chronic disease and psychological individualism. (Ruesch, Jurgen.) N.Y., 1946.

Phil 6955.18 — Chronic schizophrenia. (Freeman, Thomas.) London, 1958.

Phil 8610.878 — Chronicles of Simon Christianus and his manifold and wondrous adventures in the land of Cosmos. N.Y., 1878.

Phil 3822.7A — Chronicon Spinozanum. Hagae, 1921-27. 8v.

Phil 8003.2 — Chronika aisthetikes. Athena. 1,1962+ 2v.

Phil 1930.9 — Pamphlet box. Chroust, Anton Hermann.

Phil 4803.799.85 — Chrzanowski, Ignacy. Jan Sniadecki jako nauczyciel narodu. Kraków, 1914.

Phil 8980.580 — Chto chitat' o kommunisticheskoi morali. (Moscow. Gosudavstvennaia Bibiblioteka SSSR. Imeni V.I. Lenina.) Moskva, 1955.

Phil 310.70 — Chto chitat' po filosofii. (Moscow. Gosudarstvennaia Biblioteka SSSR imeni V.I. Lenina.) Moskva, 1958.

Phil 8672.24 — Chto takoe ateizm. (Riazantsev, N.I.) Moskva, 1961.

Phil 310.370 — Chto takoe dialekticheskii i istoricheskii materializm. (Podosetnik, V.M.) Moskva, 1961.

Phil 4768.1.5 — Chto takoe marksistskaia teoriia poznaniia. (Rozental', M.M.) Moskva, 1955.

Phil 5066.234 — Chto takoe matematicheskala logika. (Kaluzhnin, Lev A.) Moskva, 1964.

Phil 8595.41 Chto takoe religiia; besedy. (Pavelkin, P.A.) Moskva, 1956.

Phil 8615.15 Chubb, Percival. On the religious frontier. N.Y., 1931.

Phil 3552.471 Chuchmarev, Vladimir I. G.W. Leibnits i russkaia kul'tura. Moskva, 1968.

Phil 4710.115 Chupakhin, I.Ia. Voprosy teorii poniatiia. Leningrad, 1961.

Phil 5066.14.10 Church, Alonzo. A bibliography of symbolic logic. Monasha, Wisconsin, 1936.

Phil 5066.14.5A Church, Alonzo. Introduction to mathematical logic. Princeton, 1956.

Htn Phil 8657.15.3* Church, Henry. Miscellanea philo-theologica, or God and man. London, 1638.

Htn Phil 8657.15* Church, Henry. Miscellanea philo-theologica, or God and man. London, 1937.

Phil 5520.351 Church, Joseph. Language and the discovery of reality; a developmental psychology of cognition. N.Y., 1961.

Phil 1850.81 Church, R.W. Bacon. London, 1884.
Phil 1850.81.3 Church, R.W. Bacon. London, 1896.
Phil 1850.81.9 Church, R.W. Bacon. London, 1908.
Phil 1850.81.4 Church, R.W. Bacon. N.Y., 1884.
Phil 1850.81.6 Church, R.W. Bacon. N.Y., 1899.
Phil 1850.81.5 Church, R.W. Bacon. N.Y., 1901.
Phil 2050.205 Church, R.W. Hume's theory of the understanding. London, 1935.

Phil 8403.20 Church, Ralph. An essay on critical appreciation. London, 1938.

Phil 2733.103 Church, Ralph W. A study in the philosophy of Malebranche. London, 1931.

Phil 1885.89 Church, Ralph Withington. Bradley's dialectic. London, 1942.

Phil 8592.67 The church and her prophets. (Marvin, D.E.) N.Y., 1909.
Phil 5228.7 The church and modern psychology. (Streeter, B.H.) Evanston, Ill., 1934.

Phil 8962.16 The church and modern science. (McLaughlin, P.J.) N.Y., 1957.

Phil 7069.20.350 The church and psychical research. (Wright, George E.) London, 1920.

Phil 6328.26 The church and psychotherapy. (Stolz, Karl R.) N.Y., 1943.

Phil 8598.85 The church can save the world. (Shoemaker, S.M.) N.Y., 1938.

Phil 8595.32 The churches and modern thought. (Philips, Vivian.) London, 1906.

Phil 9035.38 Churchill, L.A. The magnet. N.Y., 1903.
Phil 7069.16.10 Churchill, Lida A. The truth about our dead told by those who know. 1st ed. N.Y., 1916.
Phil 8582.53 Churchill, W. The uncharted way. Philadelphia, 1940.
Phil 5042.30 Churchman, C.W. Elements of logic. Phildelphia, 1940.
Phil 5066.18 Churchman, C.W. Towards a general logic of propositions. Thesis. Philadelphia, 1942.

Phil 5500.48 Churchman, Charles West. Prediction and optimal decision. Englewood Cliffs, 1961.

Phil 2515.10.15 La chute dans le temps. (Cioran, Émile M.) Paris, 1964.
Phil 5251.23.5 Chuvstvennaia, intellektual'naia i misticheskaia intuitsiia. (Losskii, N.O.) Paris, 1938.
Phil 333.22 Chuvstvennoe poznanie. Moskva, 1965.
Phil 530.20.105 Chuzeville, Jean. Les mystiques allemands du XVII au XIX siècle. Paris, 1935.
Phil 530.35.20 Chuzeville, Jean. Les mystiques italiens. Paris, 1942.
Phil 680.45 Chvotík, Květoslav. Strukturalismus a avantgarda. 1. vyd. Praha, 1970.
Phil 5042.35 Chwistek, Leon. The limits of science. London, 1948.
Phil 4803.281.20 Chwistek, Leon. Pisma filozoficzne i logiczne. Warszawa, 1961-63. 2v.

Phil 510.1.19 Chwolson, O.D. Hegel, Haeckel, Kossuth und das zwölfte Gebot. Braunschweig, 1906.

Htn Phil 6045.17F* Chyromantie ac physionomie anastasis. (Cocles, B.) Bononiae, 1517.

Phil 3425.303 Chyzhevs'kyi, Dmytro. Gegel' v Rossii. Parizh, 1939.
Phil 3425.303.5 Chyzhevs'kyi, Dmytro. Hegel bei den Slaven. 2. Aufl. Darmstadt, 1961.
Phil 3425.303.2 Chyzhevs'kyi, Dmytro. Hegel bei den Slaven 2. Aufl. Bad Homburg, 1961.

Phil 477.8 Cía y Alvarez, J.M. La función espiritual. Madrid, 1924.
Phil 8403.14 Ciaccio, G. Il vera interiore. Sarzana, 1921.
Phil 802.19 Ciardo, M. Filosofia dell'arte e filosofia come totalità. Bari, 1953.
Phil 1702.12 Ciardo, Manlio. Il dramma della metafisica nell'età contemporanea. Bologna, 1967.
Phil 4080.28 Ciardo, Manlio. Esteticità della dialettica nella vita dello spirito. Pisa, 1965.
Phil 400.136 Ciardo, Manlio. Un fallito tentativo di riforma dello hegelismo. Bari, 1948.
Phil 4065.165 Ciardo, Manlio. Giordano Bruno tra l'umanesimo e lo stoicismo. Bologna, 1960.
Phil 1702.8 Ciardo, Manlio. Le quattro epoche dello storicismo. Bari, 1947.
Phil 8827.10 Ciarletta, Nicola. Eticità e cultura. 1. ed. Milano, 1960.
Phil 6980.182 Ciba Foundation. Ciba foundation symposium [on] transcultural psychiatry. Boston, 1965.
Phil 5238.110 Ciba Foundation. Ciba Foundation symposium on the neurological basis of behaviour. Boston, 1958.
Phil 7069.56.10 Ciba Foundation. Symposium on extrasensory perception. London, 1956.
Phil 6980.182 Ciba foundation symposium [on] transcultural psychiatry. (Ciba Foundation.) Boston, 1965.
Phil 5238.110 Ciba Foundation symposium on the neurological basis of behaviour. (Ciba Foundation.) Boston, 1958.
Phil 177.62.5 Cicala, F.B. Filosofia e diritto. v.1-4. Città di Castello, 1924.
Phil 177.62 Cicala, F.B. Introduzione alla teoria dell'essere le relazioni ontotetiche. Città di Castello, 1923.
Phil 400.58 Cicala, F.B. Punto di partenza e punti di arrivo dell' "idealismo attuale". Firenze, 1924.
Phil 802.1 Cicchitti-Suriani, F. Sinossi della storia di filosofia. Torino, 1886.
Phil 1540.25 Cicero und der Humanismus; formale Untersuchungen über Petrarca und Erasmus. (Rüegg, Walter.) Zürich, 1946.
Phil 3552.488 Cichowicz, Stanislaw. Filosof i istnienie. Wyd. 1. Warszawa, 1970.
Phil 4080.23 Cicinato, Dante. Verso il trascendimento. Palmi, 1959.
Phil 4065.128 Cicuttini, L. Giordano Bruno. Milano, 1950.
Phil 8631.14 Le ciel, séjour des élus. (Ghyvelde, F. de.) Montréal, 1912.
Phil 7054.37.30 El cielo y el infierno. 4. ed. (Rivail, H.L.D.) Barcelona, 1871.

Phil 8661.33 Cien españoles y Dios. 3. ed. (Gironella, José María.) Barcelona, 1969.
Phil 190.66 Ciencia, filosofia y laicismo. (Paullier, W.) Buenos Aires, 1937. 2v.
Phil 346.26 Ciencia. (París, Carlos.) Santiago, 1957.
Phil 8707.19 La ciencia confirma a Cristo. (Riba Elichabe, R.) Rosario, 1939.
Phil 4365.1.80 La ciencia de la cultura, teoría históriologica de Eugenio d'Ors. (Rojo Perez, E.) Barcelona, 1963.
Phil 8692.12 Ciencia y religion del porvenir. (Ceballos Dosamantes, J.) México, 1897.
Phil 8657.14.20 Cieszkowski, August D. Bóg i palingenezya. Poznań, 1912.
Phil 8657.14.5 Cieszkowski, August D. Notre Père. Paris, 1906.
Phil 8657.14 Cieszkowski, August D. Ojcze-nasz. Paryż, 1848.
Phil 8657.14.15 Cieszkowski, August D. Ojcze-nasz. Poznań, 1899-1906. 4v.
Phil 8657.14.10 Cieszkowski, August D. Ojcze-nasz. v.1-3. Poznań, 1922-23.
Phil 177.70 Cifarelli, Natale. Abbozzi di filosofia umana. Bari, 1913.
Phil 5066.262 Ciger, Juraj. Základy infinitezimálnej logiky a jej axiómy. Bratislava, 1949.
Phil 1540.72 Cilento, V. La forma Aristotelica in una "Quaestio" medievale. Napoli, 1961.
Phil 1507.9 Cilento, Vicenzo. Medioevo monastico e scolastico. Milano, 1961.
Phil 850.34 Cilento, Vincenzo. Primessa storica al pensiero antico. Bari, 1963.
Phil 4683.37.30 Cilvēks dzives spogulī. (Buduls, Hermanis.) Stockholm, 1954.
Phil 8582.80 Ćimić, Esad. Drama ateizacije. Religija, ateizam i odgoj. Sarajevo, 1971.
Phil 4960.225 Cincuenta años de filosofía en Argentina. (Farré, Luis.) Buenos Aires, 1958.
Phil 4080.25 Cini, Giovanni. Senso e natura. Firenze, 1959?
Phil 4967.5.5 El cinismo. (Francovich, Guillermo.) Puebla, 1963.
Phil 2805.425 Cinq études sur Blaise Pascal. (Académie des sciences, belles lettres et arts de Clermont-Ferrand.) Clermont-Ferrand, 1962.
Phil 2530.80A Cinq leçons sur Diderot. (Dieckmann, Herbert.) Genève, 1959.
Phil 6315.2.9 Cinq leçons sur la psychoanalyse. (Freud, Sigmund.) Paris, 1923.
Phil 6990.52 Les cinquant-quatre miracles de Lourdes au jugement du drait canon. (Meist, Paul.) Paris, 1958.
Phil 2070.35.15 Cinquantenaire de la psychologie religieuse de William James. (Études Théologiques et Religieuses.) Montpellier, 1953.
Phil 930.68 Cínská filosofie v novověké evropské filosofii. (Zempliner, Artur.) Praha, 1966.
Phil 3425.109.4 Ciò che è vivo e ciò che è morto della filosofia di Hegel. (Croce, B.) Bari, 1907.
Phil 5752.9 Cioffari, Vincenzo. Fortune and fate from Democritus to St. Thomas Aquinas. N.Y., 1935.
Phil 4080.3.160.2 Cione, Edmondo. Benedetto Croce. 2. ed. Milano, 1953.
Phil 4080.3.160.5 Cione, Edmondo. Bibliografia crociana. 1. ed. Roma, 1956.
Phil 3552.449 Cione, Edmondo. Leibniz. Napoli, 1964.
Phil 4080.3.160 Cione, Edmondo. L'opera filosofica...di Benedetto Croce. Bari, 1942.
Phil 2515.10.15 Cioran, Émile M. La chute dans le temps. Paris, 1964.
Phil 2515.10.16 Cioran, Émile M. The fall into time. Chicago, 1970.
Phil 2515.10.10 Cioran, Émile M. Le Mauvais démiurge. Paris, 1969.
Phil 2515.10.5 Cioran, Émile M. The temptation to exist. Chicago, 1968.
Phil 2515.10 Cioran, Émile M. La tentation d'exister. 2. éd. Paris, 1956.
Phil 5262.43.5 The circle of life. (Walker, Kenneth M.) London, 1942.
Phil 4018.2.10 La Circolarità del pensiero europeo. (Spaventa, Bertrando.) Palermo, 1964.
Phil 42.10 Circolo Giovanile Romano di Filosofia. Quaderni. 1-4,1953-1955
Phil 7080.24 The circulation and sleep. Text and atlas. (Shepard, J.F.) N.Y., 1914. 2v.
Phil 487.1.10 La circulation de la vie. (Moleschott, J.) Paris, 1866.
Phil 8622.35 Cirne-Lima, Carlos. Der personale Glaube. Innsbruck, 1959.
Phil 2490.109 Cirra, Émile. Appréciation générale du positivisme. Paris, 1898.
Phil 2045.118 La cité de Hobbes. (Vialatoux, J.) Paris, 1935.
Phil 2805.204 La cité de Pascal. (Droulers, C.) Paris, 1928.
NEDL Phil 9513.1 The citizen and the neighbor. (Dole, C.F.) Boston, 1884.
Phil 9045.4 Citizen in relation in his relationship to the industrial situation. (Potte, Henry Codman.) N.Y., 1902.
Phil 9045.1 The citizen of a republic. (Ceba, A.) N.Y., 1845.
X Cg Phil 7075.139 A citizen's handbook of sexual abnormalities and the mental hygiene approach to their prevention. (Hartwell, S.W.) Washington, 1951.
Phil 9045.8 Citizenship. (Brinley, C.A.) Philadelphia, 1893.
Phil 9045.13 Le citoyen. (Defoy, H.) Paris, 1912.
Phil 5650.23 City noise. (New York (City). Noise Abatement Commission.) N.Y., 1930.
Phil 187.106 The city of perfection. (Masson, T.L.) N.Y., 1927.
Phil 1905.21 The city of reason. (Beer, Samuel.) Cambridge, 1949. 2v.
Phil 1750.680 Civera, Marin. El hombre. México, 1956.
Phil 1812.20 Civil disobedience and moral law in nineteenth century American philosophy. (Madden, Edward Harry.) Seattle, 1968.
Phil 9380.5A Civilian morale. (Society for the Psychological Study of Social Issues.) N.Y., 1942.
Phil 6315.2.113.2 Civilisation. (Freud, Sigmund.) London, 1953.
Phil 8585.23.5 Civilisation at the cross roads. (Figgis, J.N.) N.Y., 1912.
Phil 990.20 Civilisation et synthèse. (Foroughir, A.H.) Paris, 1936.
Phil 8879.6.5 Civilitas morum. (Erasmus, D.) Goslariae, 1733.
Htn Phil 9162.5* La civilité puerile et honneste pour l'instruction des enfans. Troyes, 1677.
Phil 6315.2.51 Civilization and its discontents. (Freud, Sigmund.) N.Y., 1930.
Phil 6315.2.51.5A Civilization and its discontents. (Freud, Sigmund.) N.Y., 1962.
Phil 1750.80 Civilization du travail? Paris, 1956.
Phil 12.12 Civiltà e idee. Torina. 1-20 2v.
Phil 8950.1 Çivis Christianus. (Andreae, J.V.) Lipse, 1706.
Phil 8692.26 Čížek, Fr. Od víry k vědě. Praha, 1961.
Htn Phil 177.16* CJ.A. Physicae. Amsterdaam, 1645.
Phil 2880.1.83 Claassen, J. Ludwig von Saint-Martin. Stuttgart, 1891.
Phil 3450.11.320 Claesges, Ulrich. Edmund Husserls Theorie. Köln, 1962.

Author and Title Listing

Phil 3450.11.322 Claesges, Ulrich. Edmund Husserls Theorie der Raumkonstitution. Den Haag, 1964.
Phil 802.9 Claeson, Gustaf. Filosofiens historia i sammandrag. n.p., n.d.
Phil 4525.2.5 Claeson, Krist. Skrifter. Stockholm, 1860. 2v.
Phil 585.406.2 Claessens, Dieter. Instinkt, Psyche, Geltung. 2. Aufl. Köln, 1970.
Phil 177.140 Claeys, R.H. Inleiding tot de metafysica. Gent, 1968.
Phil 8870.20 Clair, F.F. The ultimate defense. 1st ed. Rutland, 1959.
Phil 2630.11.25 Le clair et l'obscur. (Guitton, Jean.) Paris, 1962.
Phil 6681.14 Clairvoyance. 2d ed. (Leadbeater, C.W.) London, 1903.
Phil 6688.10 Clairvoyance and crystal gazing. (Stephenson, Charles Y. (Mrs.).) London, 1918.
Phil 7069.24.22 Clairvoyance and materialisation, a record of experiments. (Geley, Gustave.) London, 1927.
Phil 9240.4 Clamageran, J.J. La lutte contre le mal. Paris, 1897.
Phil 2422.3 The Clandestine organization and diffusion of philosophic ideas in France from 1700 to 1750. (Wade, Ira O.) Princeton, 1938.
X Cg Phil 8877.10 Clap, T. An essay...nature. Foundation. Moral virtue. New Haven, 1765.
Phil 5585.24 Claparède, É. Expériences collectives sur le...confrontation. Genève, 1906.
Phil 2465.31 Claparède, E. La psychologie animale de Charles Bonnet. Genève, 1909.
Phil 5242.9 Claparède, E. Rapport sur la terminologie psychologique. Genève, 1909.
Phil 5325.23 Claparède, Édouard. L'association des idées. Paris, 1903.
Phil 5242.44 Claparède, Édouard. Causeries psychologiques. Genève, 1933.
Phil 5242.44.5 Claparède, Édouard. Causeries psychologiques. Ser. 2. Genève, 1935.
Phil 9450.23 Claparède, Édouard. Morale et politique. Neuchâtel, 1947.
Phil 6672.13 Claparède, Édouard. Recherches expérimentales sur guelques processus psychiques simples dans un cas d'hypnose. Genève, 1909.
Phil 3850.5.94 Claparède-Spir, H. Evocation. Genève, 1944.
Phil 3850.5.93 Claparède-Spir, H. Un pprécurseur. Lausanne, 1920.
Phil 3800.390.10 Clara. (Schelling, F.W.J. von.) München, 1948.
Htn Phil 3800.390* Clara. (Schelling, F.W.J. von.) Stuttgart, 1862.
Htn Phil 3800.390.5* Clara. 2e Aufl. (Schelling, F.W.J. von.) Stuttgart, 1865.
Phil 8582.28 Claraz, Jules. La faillité des religions. Paris, 1912.
Phil 5812.8 Claremont, C.A. The innumerable instincts of man. London, 1940.
Phil 5242.37 Claremont, C.A. Intelligence, and mental growth. N.Y., 1928.
Htn Phil 2045.84* Clarendon, Edward Hyde. A brief view and survey of the...errors...in Mr. Hobbes's book, entitled Leviathan. Oxford, 1676.
Htn Phil 2045.84.2* Clarendon, Edward Hyde. A brief view and survey of the...errors...in Mr. Hobbes's book, entitled Leviathan. Oxford, 1676.
Phil 7040.40 Claridge, Gordon S. Personality and arousal; a psychophysiological study of psychiatric disorder. Oxford, 1967.
Phil 5520.402 Clarity is not enough. (Lewis, Hywel D.) London, 1963.
Phil 5520.402.2 Clarity is not enough. (Lewis, Hywel D.) N.Y., 1963.
Phil 8692.28 Clark, Cecil Henry Douglas. The scientist and the supernatural: a systematic examination of the relation between Christianity and humanism. London, 1966.
Phil 8582.48 Clark, E.H. This world and the next. Boston, 1934.
Phil 5627.164 Clark, E.T. The psychology of religious awakening. N.Y., 1929.
Phil 165.4 Clark, G.H. Selections from Hellenistic philosophy. N.Y., 1940.
Phil 5627.108 Clark, Glenn. Fishers of men. Boston, 1928.
Phil 5627.108.25 Clark, Glenn. I will lift up mine eyes. 9. ed. N.Y., 1937.
Phil 5627.108.15 Clark, Glenn. The soul's sincere desire. Boston, 1926.
Phil 1955.6.165 Clark, Gordon H. Dewey. Philadelphia, 1960.
Phil 8877.71 Clark, Gordon H. Reading in ethics. N.Y., 1931.
Phil 8877.71.15 Clark, Gordon H. Reading in ethics. 2nd ed. N.Y., 1943.
Phil 802.21 Clark, Gordon Haddon. Thales to Dewey. Boston, 1957.
Phil 3850.27.210 Clark, Henry. The ethical mysticism of Albert Schweitzer. Boston, 1962.
Phil 7069.45.5 Clark, Ida C.G. Men who wouldn't stay dead. N.Y., 1945.
Phil 5643.24 Clark, J.H. Sight and hearing. N.Y., 1856.
Phil 530.20.90 Clark, J.M. The great German mystics. Oxford, 1949.
Phil 6952.7.30 Clark, James. A memoir of John Conolly. London, 1869.
Phil 165.205 Clark, John A. The student seeks an answer. Waterville, Me., 1960.
Phil 5012.2A Clark, Joseph. Conventional logic and modern logic. Woodstock, 1952.
Phil 5212.10 Clark, Kenneth. America's psychologists. Washington, 1957.
Phil 6952.15 Clark, L.P. Neurological and mental diagnosis. N.Y., 1908.
Phil 9010.22 Clark, Martha. Victims of amusements. Philadelphia, n.d.
Phil 3484.12 Clark, Norman. An introduction to Kant's philosophy. London, 1925.
Phil 7069.34.9 Clark, R. A spiritual spiritualism. London, 1934.
Phil 2255.1.150 Clark, Robert J. Bertrand Russell's philosophy of language. The Hague, 1969.
Phil 5042.65 Clark, Romane. Introduction to logic. Princeton, N.J., 1962.
Phil 5520.34 Clark, Ruth S. An experimental study of silent thinking. N.Y., 1922.
Phil 177.84.5 Clark, S.C. Key-notes for daily harmonies. Boston, 1898.
Phil 177.84 Clark, S.C. The melody of life. N.Y., 1902.
Phil 978.56 Clark, S.C. Short lessons in theosophy. Boston, 1892.
Phil 8877.11 Clark, S.D. The faithful steward. Boston, 1853.
Phil 6112.17 Clark, Susie C. A look upward. Boston, 1899.
Phil 8877.26 Clark, T.M. Lectures on the formation of character. Hartford, 1852.
Phil 7054.162 Clark, Uriah. Plain guide to spiritualism. Boston, 1863.
Phil 8633.1.34 Clark, W.E. Indian conceptions of immortality. Cambridge, 1934.
Phil 5627.259.20 Clark, W.H. The psychology of religion. N.Y., 1959.
Phil 6155.10 Clark, Walter Houston. Chemical ecstasy. N.Y., 1969.
Phil 5242.17 Clark, William. The formation of opinion. Cambridge, 1888?
Phil 2805.179 Clark, William. Pascal and the Port Royalists. Edinburgh, 1902.
Phil 5242.15 Clark University, Worcester, Mass. Lectures and addresses before departments of psychology and pedagogy...20 anniversary. Worcester, 1910.
Phil 5520.130 Clark University, Worcester, Massachusetts. Conference on Expressive Language Behavior. On expressive language. Worcester, Mass., 1955.
Phil 5520.477 Clarke, Bowman L. Language and natural theology. The Hague, 1966.
Phil 7060.16 Clarke, E.H. Visions: study of false sight. Boston, 1878.
Phil 5242.48 Clarke, Edwin L. The art of straight thinking. N.Y., 1929.
Phil 5242.47 Clarke, Edwin L. The art of straight thinking. N.Y., 1932.
Phil 6112.32 Clarke, Eric K. Mental hygiene for community nursing. Minneapolis, 1942.
Phil 8877.73 Clarke, F. (Mrs.). Give yourself a new deal. Boston, 1933.
Phil 1915.77 Clarke, J. Defence of Dr. Clarke's...attributes. v.1-3. London, 1732-33.
Phil 8657.8 Clarke, J.C.C. Man and his Divine Father. Chicago, 1900.
Phil 8582.40 Clarke, M. Traités de l'existence et des attributs de Dieu, des devoirs de la religion naturelle. n.p., 1744. 3v.
Phil 1300.15 Clarke, M.L. The Roman mind. Cambridge, Mass., 1956.
Phil 1300.10A Clarke, M.L. The Roman mind. London, 1956.
Phil 735.93 Clarke, Mary E. A study in the logic of value. London, 1929.
Phil 4752.2.90 Clarke, O.G. Introduction to Berdyaev. London, 1950.
Phil 5752.2.15 Clarke, S. Remark on philosophical inquiry...human liberty. London, 1717. 2 pam.
Phil 1915.60.4 Clarke, Samuel. Discourse...attributes of God. London, 1706. 2 pam.
Phil 1915.60.5 Clarke, Samuel. Discourse...attributes of God. London, 1711. 2 pam.
Phil 1915.60 Clarke, Samuel. Discourse...attributes of God. London, 1719. 2 pam.
Phil 1915.60.2 Clarke, Samuel. Discourse...attributes of God. London, 1719.
Phil 1915.60.3 Clarke, Samuel. Discourse...attributes of God. London, 1728.
Phil 1915.60.7 Clarke, Samuel. Discourse...attributes of God. 6th ed. London, 1725. 2 pam.
Phil 1915.63.2 Clarke, Samuel. An exposition of the church catechism. 2d ed. London, 1730.
Phil 1915.63.6 Clarke, Samuel. An exposition of the church catechism. 6th ed. London, 1756.
Phil 3552.375A Clarke, Samuel. The Leibniz-Clarke correspondence. Manchester, 1956.
Htn Phil 1915.70* Clarke, Samuel. Letter to Dodwell. London, 1708-13. 9 pam.
Phil 1915.70.5 Clarke, Samuel. Letters to Mr. Dodwell. London, 1731.
Phil 1915.14 Clarke, Samuel. Oeuvres philosophiques. Paris, 1843.
Phil 1915.61 Clarke, Samuel. The scripture-doctrine of the Trinity. London, 1712.
Phil 1915.61.2 Clarke, Samuel. The scripture-doctrine of the Trinity. 2d ed. London, 1719.
Phil 1915.61.3 Clarke, Samuel. The scripture-doctrine of the Trinity. 3d ed. London, 1732.
Phil 1915.20 Clarke, Samuel. Sermons on several subjects and occasions. 8th ed. London, 1756. 8v.
Htn Phil 1915.10.2F* Clarke, Samuel. Works. London, 1738. 2v.
VPhil 1915.10F Clarke, Samuel. Works. London, 1738. 4v.
Phil 1915.12F Clarke, Samuel. Works. London, 1742. 2v.
Phil 1915.25 Clarke, Samuel. XVIII sermons. 3rd ed. London, 1734.
Htn Phil 1915* Clarke, Samuel. Miscellaneous pamphlets on Dr. Clarke. London, 1686-1834. 4 pam.
Phil 8657.7 Clarke, W.N. Can I believe in God the Father. N.Y., 1899.
Phil 8657.7.6 Clarke, W.N. The Christian doctrine of God. N.Y., 1910.
Phil 8627.8 Clarke, W.N. Immortality. New Haven, 1920.
Phil 1730.28 Clartés et ombres du siècle des lumières. Études sur le 18e siècle littéraire. (Mortier, Roland.) Genève, 1969.
Phil 4330.15 Clascar, Federico. Estudi sobre la filosofia a Catalunya en el siglo XVIII. Barcelona, 1918.
Phil 6112.38 Clased ranks. (Cumming, Elaine.) Cambridge, 1957.
Phil 3484.17F Clasen, Karl H. Kant-Bildnisse. Königsberg, 1924.
Phil 3552.120.10 Class, Gustav. Der Determinismus von Leibnitz. Tübingen, 1874.
Phil 8877.52 Class, Gustav. Ideale und Güter; Untersuchungen zur Ethik. Erlangen, 1886.
Phil 3552.120.5 Class, Gustav. Die metaphysischen Voraussetzungen. Tübingen, 1874.
Phil 8586.9 The class-book of natural theology. 2nd ed. (Gallaudet, T.H.) Hartford, 1837.
Phil 178.74 Classe de philosophie. (Daval, Simone.) Paris, 1962. 2v.
Phil 5643.5 Classen, A. Physiologie des Gesichtssinnes. Braunschweig, 1876.
Phil 5643.4 Classen, A. Über das Schlussverfahren der Sehactes. Rostock, 1863.
Phil 3484.8 Classen, August. Über den Einfluss Kants auf die Theorie der Sinneswahrnehmung. Leipzig, 1886.
Phil 5066.36.20 Classes, relations et nombres. (Piaget, Jean.) Paris, 1942.
Phil 1805.5 Classic American philosophers. (Fisch, M.H.) N.Y., 1951.
Phil 7069.22.17 The classic of spiritism. (Milburn, L.M.) N.Y., 1922.
Phil 5625.105 Classical conditioning, a symposium. (Prokasy, William Frederick.) N.Y., 1965.
Phil 5227.3A The classical psychologists. (Rand, B.) Boston, 1912.
Phil 1750.552.10 Classics and the philosophy of existence. (Hijmans, Benjamin Lodwijk.) Winnipeg, 1965.
Phil 5039.4 Classics in logic. (Runes, Dagobert D.) N.Y., 1962.
Phil 165.195 Classics in philosophy and ethics. N.Y., 1960.
Phil 5238.155 Classics in psychology. (Shipley, T.) N.Y., 1961.
Phil 5520.432 Classics in semantics. (Hayden, Donald E.) N.Y., 1965.
Phil 6750.10 The classification...feeble minded, imbecile and idiotic. (Davis, C.H.S.) N.Y., 1883.
Phil 2270.60.10 Classification des sciences. (Spencer, Herbert.) Paris, 1888.
Phil 1050.12.5 The classification of sciences on mediaeval Jewish philosophy. (Wolfson, Harry A.) Chicago, 1925.
Phil 2490.86 The classification of the sciences...philosophy of M. Comte. (Spencer, Herbert.) London, 1871.
Htn Phil 2270.60* The classification of the sciences. (Spencer, Herbert.) London, 1864.
Phil 2270.60.3 The classification of the sciences. (Spencer, Herbert.) N.Y., 1864.
Phil 5640.37 Classification universelle systématique et coordonnée des connaissances humaines. (Phusis, Maurice (pseud.).) Paris, 1934.
Phil 5241.17.17 La classificazione delle attivitapsichiche. (Brentano, Franz.) Lanciano, 1913.

Phil 5042.12   Clauberg, Johann. Logica vetus et nova. 2a ed. Amsterdam, 1658.

Phil 3140.1   Clauberg, Johann. Opera omnia philosophica. Reprint. Hildesheim, 1968. 2v.

Phil 87.1   Clauberg, K.N. Systematisches Wörterbuch der Philosophie. Leipzig, 1923.

Phil 8582.10   Claubergii, J. De cognitione dei et nostri. Franequerae, 1685.

Phil 3140.81   Claubergstudien. (Göpfert.) Meiningen, 1898.
Phil 2636.85   Claude Helvetius. (Horowitz, I.L.) N.Y., 1954.
Phil 7069.20.20   Claude's second book. (Bamber, L. Kelway.) N.Y., 1920.
Phil 6112.37   Clausen, John A. Sociology and the field of mental health. N.Y., 1956.

Phil 5870.90   Clauser, Günter. Die moderne Elternschule. Freiburg, 1969.

Phil 5520.466   Clauss, Karl. General semantics. pt.1. Berlin, 1966. 2v.

Phil 6112.11   Clavel, Adolphe. Le corps et l'ame. Paris, 1851.
Phil 600.30   Clavel, Adolphe. La morale positive. Paris, 1873.
Phil 2490.165   Clavel, Marcel. Le centenaire d'Auguste Comte et la nouvelle constitution française. Fontenay-sous-Bois, 1958.

Phil 1750.856   Clavel, Maurice. Qui est aliéné? Critique et métaphysique sociale de l'Occident. Paris, 1970.

Phil 5258.142   Clavier psychologigue. (Streletski, C.) Paris, 1942.
Phil 1930.4.35   Clavis universalis. (Collier, Arthur.) Chicago, 1909.
Htn   Phil 1930.4.31*   Clavis universalis. (Collier, Arthur.) Edinburgh, 1836.
Htn   Phil 1930.4.30*   Clavis universalis. (Collier, Arthur.) London, 1713. 2 pam.

Phil 5545.210   Clavis universalis. (Rossi, Paolo.) Milano, 1960.
Phil 5242.51   Clawson, J. Psychology in action. N.Y., 1946.
Phil 8403.22   Clay, Felix. The origin of the sense of beauty. London, 1908.

Phil 283.5   Clay, J. Schets eener kritische geschiedenis van het begrip natuurwet. Leiden, 1915.

Phil 6945.16   Clayton, J.M. Speech on the veto message of the President on the bill for the benefit of the indigent insane. Washington, 1854.

Phil 5049.25   Clear thinking. 4th ed. (Jepson, R.W.) London, 1948.
Phil 974.2.7   Cleather, A.L. (Mrs.) H.P. Blavatsky, a great betrayal. Calcutta, 1922.

Phil 974.2.5   Cleather, A.L. (Mrs.) H.P. Blavatsky, her life and work for humanity. Calcutta, 1922.

Phil 974.2.9   Cleather, A.L. (Mrs.) H.P. Blavatsky as I knew her. Calcutta, 1923.

Phil 974.2.10   Cleather, A.L. (Mrs.) H.P. Blavatsky as I knew her. N.Y., 1923. 3 pam.

Phil 2200.5.80   The cleavage in our culture. (Burkhardt, F.) Boston, 1952.

X Cg   Phil 7075.146   Cleckley, H.M. The caricature of love. N.Y., 1957.
Phil 6825.2.2   Cleckley, Hervey Milton. The mask of sanity. 2. ed. St. Louis, 1950.

Phil 3110.47   Clef, ou Explication des divers points et termes principaux. (Böhme, J.) Paris, 1826.
Phil 5042.28.5   La clef des sciences et des beaux arts, ou La logique. (Cochet, J.) Paris, 1757.

Phil 9560.33   Cleghorn, S.N. The seamless robe; the religion of loving kindness. N.Y., 1945.

Phil 6112.23   Cleland, J. The relation of brain to mind. Glasgow, 1882.
Htn   Phil 9342.15*   Cleland, James. Erö-paideia, or The institution of a young noble man. Oxford, 1607.

Phil 5627.111   Clemen, Carl. Die Anwendung der Psychoanalyse auf Mythologie und Religionsgeschichte. Leipzig, 1928.

Phil 525.59   Clemen, Carl. Die Mystik nach Wesen, Entwicklung und Bedeutung. Bonn, 1923.

Phil 177.79A   Clemenceau, G. In the evening of my thought. Boston, 1929. 2v.

Phil 2280.5.101   Clemens, C. George Santayana; an American philosopher in exile. Webster Groves, 1937.

Phil 177.74   Clemens, F. Das Manifest der Vernunft. 3e Aufl. Berlin, 1875.

Phil 4065.81   Clemens, F.J. Giordano Bruno und Nicolaus von Cusa. Bonn, 1847.

Phil 8590.27.10   Clemens, Franz J. Die Wahrheit in dem von J. von Kuhn in Tübingen. Münster, 1860.

Phil 177.13   Clemente, A. Le bon sens. Paris, 1878. 2v.
Phil 6112.14   Clements, J. Metaphysics of the nature and in the conception of the soul. Boston, 1909.

Phil 7113.5   Clements, John. Hypnotism; masterpiece of myths. Manchester, 1966.

Phil 450.2   Clements, Tad S. Science and man; the philoosophy of scientific humanism. Springfield, Illinois, 1968.

Phil 8877.59   Clemmens, H.W. Moralische Betrachtungen. Stuttgart, 1761.
Phil 8582.62   Cleobury, F.H. God, man and the absolute. London, 1947?
Phil 6312.14   Clerambault, G.G. Oeuvre psychiatrique. v.1-2. Paris, 1942. 2v.

Phil 5242.43   Clergué, G. Essai de psychologie critique sur la nature première. Thèse. Paris, 1914.

Phil 7054.32   Clerk, A.M. Spiritism; the keystone of Christianity. London, 1894.

Phil 2805.409   Clermont-Ferrand. Musée du Ranquet. Pascal, sa ville et son temps. Clermont-Ferrand, 1962.

Phil 4225.8.42   La clessidra. 3. ed. (Sciacca, Michele Federico.) Milano, 1960.

Phil 6842.2.5   Cleugh, James. The Marquis and the Chevalier. London, 1951.

X Cg   Phil 7075.135   Cleugh, James. The marquis and the chevalier. London, 1951.

Phil 720.30   Cleugh, M.F. Time and its importance to modern thought. London, 1937.

Phil 1133.40   Cleve, Felix M. The giants of pre-sophistic Greek philosophy. The Hague, 1965.

Phil 1133.40.2   Cleve, Felix M. The giants of pre-sophistic Greek philosophy. 2nd ed. The Hague, 1969. 2v.

Phil 3822.8   Cleve, Z.J. De cognitionis generibus Spinozae. Thesis. Helsingforsiae, 1850.

Phil 177.67   Cleve, Z.J. De principio philosophiae. Helsingfors, 1848.
Phil 9045.5   Cleveland, G. Good citizenship. Philadelphia, 1908.
Phil 9530.3   Cleveland, G. The self-made man. N.Y., 1897.
Phil 5812.2   Clevenger, S.V. Comparative physiology and psychology. Chicago, 1885.

Phil 5825.2.5   Clever Hans; the horse of Mr. von Osten. (Pfungst, Oskar.) N.Y., 1965.

Phil 6327.28   Client-centered therapy. (Rogers, Carl Ransom.) Boston, 1951.

Phil 177.14A   Clifford, W.K. Lectures and essays. London, 1879. 2v.

X Cg   Phil 177.14.2   Clifford, W.K. Lectures and essays. 2nd ed. London, 1886.
Phil 5643.41   Clifford, W.K. Seeing and thinking. London, 1879.

Phil 8877.75.5   Clifford, William K. The ethics of belief. London, 1947.
Phil 8877.75   Clifford, William K. The scientific basis of morals, and other essays. N.Y., 1884.

Phil 5525.29   A clinic on the comic. (Gilman, Bradley.) Nice, 1926.
Phil 5247.68   Clinical and counseling psychology. 1. ed. (Hadley, John M.) N.Y., 1958.

Phil 6325.8.15   Clinical and experimental studies in personality. (Prince, Morton.) Cambridge, Mass., 1929.

Phil 6325.8.16   Clinical and experimental studies in personality. (Prince, Morton.) Cambridge, Mass., 1939.

Phil 5500.44   Clinical and social judgment: the discrimination of behavioral information. N.Y., 1968.

Phil 6321.12.5   Clinical aspects of psychoanalysis. (Laforgue, R.) London, 1938.

Phil 5238.230   Clinical-cognitive psychology. (Breger, Louis.) Englewood Cliffs, N.J., 1969.

Phil 6122.49.3   The clinical examination of the nervous system. 3d ed. (Monrad-Krohn, G.) London, 1926.

Phil 5258.175   Clinical inference and cognitive theory. (Sarbin, Theodore.) N.Y., 1960.

Phil 5593.54.15   The clinical interaction (with specific reference to Rorschach). (Sarason, S.B.) N.Y., 1954.

Phil 6313.14   The clinical interview. v.1-2. (Deutsch, Felix.) N.Y., 1955. 2v.

Phil 6952.6A   Clinical lectures on mental diseases. (Clouston, T.S.) Philadelphia, 1884.

Phil 6310.2.14   Clinical papers and essays on psychoanalysis. (Abraham, Karl.) London, 1955.

Phil 6960.5.5   Clinical psychiatry. (Kraepelin, E.) N.Y., 1902.
Phil 6960.5.7   Clinical psychiatry. (Kraepelin, E.) N.Y., 1904.
Phil 6328.55   Clinical psychology. (Sundberg, N.D.) N.Y., 1962.
Phil 6313.13   Clinical studies in psychopathology. (Dicks, H.V.) London, 1939.

Phil 6420.34   Clinical studies in speech therapy. (McAllister, Anne H.) London, 1937.

Phil 6325.30   The clinical study of social behavior. (Peterson, Donald Robert.) N.Y., 1968.

Phil 6952.23.20   Clinique des maladies du système nerveaux. (Charcot, J.M.) Paris, 1892-93. 2v.

Phil 8421.3   Clio, or A discourse on taste. 2. ed. (Usher, James.) London, 1769.

Phil 7069.17.23   Clodd, Edward. The question: "If a man die, shall he live again?" London, 1917.

Phil 7069.18.60   Clodd, Edward. The question: "If a man die, shall he live again?" N.Y., 1918.

Phil 600.9   The clothes of religion. (Ward, W.) London, n.d.
Phil 530.11.12   Cloud of Unknowing. The cloud of unknowing. London, 1959.
Phil 530.11.12   The cloud of unknowing. (Cloud of Unknowing.) London, 1959.

Phil 530.11.10   The cloud of unknowing. London, 1924.
Phil 530.11.7   Cloud of unknowing. A book of contemplation. London, 1912.
Phil 530.11.9   Cloud of unknowing. A book of contemplation. 4. ed. London, 1946.

Phil 7069.20.110   A cloud of witnesses. (De Koven, Anna F.) N.Y., 1920.
Phil 6952.6A   Clouston, T.S. Clinical lectures on mental diseases. Philadelphia, 1884.

Phil 6112.25.6   Clouston, T.S. Hygiene of mind. 6th ed. London, 1912.
VPhil 585.167   Člověk, kto si? (International Congress of Philosophy, 13th, Mexico, 1963.) Bratislava, 1965.

Phil 310.650.3   Člověk, svět a filosofie. Vyd. 3. (Kubeš, Miloslav.) Praha, 1968.

VPhil 585.167.5   Člověk a moderní doba. (Filipec, Jindřich.) Praha, 1966.
Phil 5627.262.15   Člověk a světový názor. (Cvekl, Jiří.) Praha, 1962.
Phil 9162.3   Clowes, John. The golden wedding ring...marriage. Boston, 1823.

Phil 12.55   Club Voltaire. München. 1,1963+ 4v.
Htn   Phil 6012.4*   Clubbe, J. Physiognomy. London, 1763.
Phil 2805.226   The clue to Pascal. (Cailliet, E.) London, 1944.
Phil 7150.38   Clues to suicide. (Shneidman, Edwin S.) N.Y., 1957.
Phil 665.63   Clymer, R.S. The science of the soul. Quakertown, 1922.
Phil 1535.31   Clypeus philosophiae Thomisticae. (Guerinois, J.C.) Venetiis, 1729. 7v.

Phil 630.54   Co je realismus? (Zykmund, V.) Praha, 1957.
Phil 8980.472   Co je zmyslom našho života? (Kánský, Jiří.) Bratislava, 1961.

VPhil 585.192   Co řeší filosofická antropologie. Vyd. 1. (Šindelář, Jan.) Praha, 1966.

Phil 177.83   Coaley, C.H. Life and the student. N.Y., 1927.
Phil 5535.16   Coalitie formatie in triades. (Wilde, Henricus Andreas Maria.) Rotterdam, 1968.

Phil 8582.22   Coan, T.M. Topics of the time. Questions of belief. N.Y., 1883.

Phil 1802.4   Coates, A. Sceptical examination of contemporary British philosophy. London, 1929.

Phil 177.98   Coates, Adrian. A basis of opinion. London, 1938.
Phil 177.102   Cobb, Henry V.Z. Man's way, a first book in philosophy. 1st ed. London, 1942.

Phil 6312.12   Cobb, S. Borderlands of psychiatry. Cambridge, 1943.
Phil 6952.24.15   Cobb, Stanley. Foundations of neuropsychiatry. 2. ed. Baltimore, 1941.

Phil 6952.24   Cobb, Stanley. An outline of neuropathology for students of general medicine. Cambridge, 1929.

Phil 525.33   Cobb, Stanwood. The essential mysticism. Boston, 1918.
Phil 1750.166.130   Cobban, Alfred. In search of humanity. London, 1960.
Phil 1750.166.132   Cobban, Alfred. In search of humanity. N.Y., 1960.
Phil 8582.35   Cobbe, F.P. Broken lights; an inquiry into the present condition and future prospects of religious faith. London, 1864.

Phil 8582.35.5   Cobbe, F.P. Broken lights; an inquiry into the present condition and future prospects of religious faith. London, 1864.

Phil 9342.12.5   Cobbe, F.P. The duties of women. Boston, 1881.
NEDL   Phil 8877.12   Cobbe, F.P. An essay on intuitive morals. London, 1855-57. 2v.

Phil 8877.12.2   Cobbe, F.P. An essay on intuitive morals. pt.1. Boston, 1859.

Phil 8627.2.2   Cobbe, F.P. The hope of the human race. London, 1874.
Phil 8627.2   Cobbe, F.P. The hope of the human race. London, 1880.
Phil 8582.35.9   Cobbe, F.P. The peak in Darien...an octave of essays. Boston, 1882.

Phil 8582.35.15   Cobbe, F.P. The religious demands of the age. Boston, 1863.

Phil 9342.4.2   Cobbett, W. Advice to young men. London, 1887.
Phil 9342.4.10   Cobbett, W. Advice to young men. London, 1906.
Phil 9342.4.12   Cobbett, W. Advice to young men. London, 1926.
Phil 9342.4.15   Cobbett, W. Advice to young men. London, 1930.
Phil 9342.4   Cobbett, W. Advice to young men. N.Y., 1831.

Phil 2218.85.5 — Cobbett, William. Observations on the emigration of Joseph Priestley. Philadelphia, 1794.
Phil 4260.95 — Cochery, M. Les grandes lignes de la philosophie historique et juridique de Vico. Paris, 1923.
Phil 5042.28.5 — Cochet, J. La clef des sciences et des beaux arts, ou La logique. Paris, 1757.
Phil 2477.11.95 — Cochet, M.A. Commentaire sur la conversion spirituelle dans la philosophie de L. Branschvicg. Bruxelles, 1937.
Phil 2515.7 — Cochet, M.A. Le congrès Descartes...reflexions. Bruges, 1938.
Phil 2555.7.90 — Cochet, M.A. La métaphysique de Paul Decoster et la science. Bruges, 1937.
Phil 2520.114 — Cochin, D. Descartes. Paris, 1913.
Phil 177.27 — Cochin, D. La monde extérieur. Paris, 1895.
Phil 8403.34 — Cochofel, J.J. Iniciação estética. Lisboa, 1958.
Phil 7068.94.5 — Cock Lane and common-sense. (Lang, Andrew.) London, 1894.
Phil 8877.13 — Cockburn, C. Works. London, 1751. 2v.
Phil 8693.5.70 — Cockburn, S. The laws of nature...reply to Professor Drummond. London, 1886.
Phil 850.10 — Cocker, B.F. Christianity and Greek philosophy. N.Y., 1870.
Phil 1135.22 — Cocker, B.F. Christianity and Greek philosophy. N.Y., 1875.
Phil 1135.22.4 — Cocker, B.F. Christianity and Greek philosophy. N.Y., 1879.
Phil 8657.4 — Cocker, B.F. The theistic conception of the world. N.Y., 1875.
Phil 8575.12 — Cockshut, Anthony Oliver John. Religious controversies of the nineteenth century: selected documents. London, 1966.
Htn Phil 6045.17F* — Cocles, B. Chyromantie ac physionomie anastasis. Bononiae, 1517.
Htn Phil 6045.46* — Cocles, B. Le compendium et brief enseignement de physiognomie et chiromancie. Paris, 1546.
Htn Phil 6045.55* — Cocles, B. Physiognomiae et chiromantiae compendium. Argentorati, 1555.
Htn Phil 6012.9* — Cocles, Bartolommeo della Rocca. In disem Biechlin wurt erfunden von Coplexion der Menschen. Strassburg, 1516.
Phil 665.38 — Coconnier, M.J. L'âme humaine. Paris, 1890.
Phil 8430.9 — Coculesco, P. Esthétique. Paris, 1953.
Phil 8403.18 — Coculesco, P. Principes d'esthétique. Paris, 1935.
Phil 270.60 — Coculeseo, P. Hasard et probabilités. Paris, 1949.
Phil 9450.32 — Code de morale politique. (Union Internationale d'Études Sociales.) Bruxelles, 1957.
Phil 5627.26.5 — Coe, George A. The psychology of religion. Chicago, 1917.
Phil 5627.26 — Coe, George A. The spiritual life; studies in the science of religion. Chicago, 1914.
Phil 5627.26.2 — Coe, George A. The spiritual life; studies in the science of religion. N.Y., 1900.
Phil 177.69 — Coellen, L. Von der Selbstoffenbarung des göttlichen Lebens. Darmstadt, 1924.
Phil 8403.19 — Coen, Augusto. L'estetica sperimentale. Roma, 1920.
Phil 6316.32 — Coeppert, Hans. Das Ich. München, 1968.
Phil 5850.161 — Coetsier, Leo. Toegepaste psychologie. Gent, 1965.
Phil 2805.211 — Le coeur humain, inhumain, surhumain de Blaise Pascal. (Orliac, Jehanne d'.) Paris, 1931.
Phil 9530.47 — Coffee, John R. Personal achievements. N.Y., 1932.
Phil 5042.11 — Coffey, P. The science of logic. London, 1912. 2v.
Phil 333.7.2 — Coffey, Peter. Epistemology. Gloucester, Mass., 1958. 2v.
Phil 177.91 — Coffey, Peter. Ontology; or The theory of being. London, 1914.
Phil 8877.36 — Coffin, J.H. The socialized conscience. Baltimore, 1913.
Phil 665.53 — Coffin, Joseph H. The soul comes back. N.Y., 1929.
Phil 8657.23 — Coffy, Robert. Dieu des athées: Marx, Sartre, Camus. Lyon, 1965.
Phil 2905.1.430 — Coffy, Robert. Teilhard de Chardin et le socialisme. Lyon, 1966.
Phil 402.12 — Cofrancesco, Dino. Appunti sull'ideologia. Milano, 1968.
Phil 8877.14 — Cogan, T. Ethical questions. London, 1817.
Phil 9420.2.9 — Cogan, T. An ethical treatise...passions. Bath, 1807-10. 2v.
Phil 9420.2.5 — Cogan, T. Philosophical treatise...passions. v.1-2. Bath, 1802.
Phil 9420.2.7 — Cogan, T. Philosophical treatise...passions. v.1-2. Boston, 1821.
Phil 9420.2.6 — Cogan, T. Philosophical treatise...passions. v.1-2. London, 1813.
Phil 9420.2 — Cogan, T. A treatise on the passions and affections of the mind. v.2-5. v.1 lost. London, 1813. 4v.
Phil 8692.24 — Coggin, Philip. Art, science, and religion. London, 1962.
Phil 7054.100 — Coggshall, W.T. The signs of the times. Cincinnati, 1851.
Phil 510.127.10 — Cogitans cogitata. (Carr, H. Wildon.) Los Angeles, 1930.
Phil 8595.5 — Cogitationum rationalium. (Poiret, P.) Amsterdam, 1715.
Phil 2520.231 — Cogito cartésien et réflexion thomiste. Thèse. (Finance, J. de.) Paris, 1946[1945].
Phil 3450.11.119 — Le cogito dans la philosophie de Husserl. (Berger, Gaston.) Paris, 1941.
Phil 530.15.45 — Cognet, Louis. Crépuscule des mystiques. Tournai, 1958.
Phil 1540.94 — Cognet, Louis. Introduction aux mystiques rhéno-flamands. Paris, 1968.
Phil 525.185 — Cognet, Louis. Post-Reformation spirituality. London, 1959.
Phil 8735.22 — Cogni, G. Lo spirito assoluto. Firenze, 1937.
Phil 1135.183 — Cogniot, Georges. Le materialisme gréco-romain. Paris, 1964.
Phil 343.32 — Cognition: theory, research, promise. (Martin Scheerer Memorial Meetings on Cognitive Psychology. University of Kansas, 1962.) N.Y., 1964.
Phil 5520.630A — Cognition and the development of language. N.Y., 1970.
Phil 5257.75 — Cognition and thought. (Reitman, Walter Ralph.) N.Y., 1965.
Phil 5535.54 — The cognitive bases of human learning. (Saltz, Eli.) Homewood, 1971.
Phil 5325.48 — The cognitive control of motivation: the consequences of choice and dissonance. (Zimbardo, Philip G.) Glenville, Ill., 1969.
Phil 5520.734 — Cognitive development and epistemology. N.Y., 1971.
Phil 5238.203 — The cognitive processes. (Harper, Robert J.C.) Englewood Cliffs, N.J., 1964.
Phil 5252.50.10 — Cognitive psychology. (Moore, T.V.) Chicago, 1939.
Phil 5374.252 — Cognitive psychology. (Neisser, Ulric.) N.Y., 1967.
Phil 12.130 — Cognitive psychology. N.Y. 1,1970+
Phil 12.145 — Cognitive studies. N.Y. 1,1970+ 2v.
Phil 186.160 — The cognitivity paradox. (Lange, John.) Princeton, 1970.
Phil 531.4 — Cogny, Pierre. Le naturalisme. Paris, 1953.
Phil 3120.30.82 — Cohen, A.A. Martin Buber. London, 1957.
Phil 3120.30.82.1 — Cohen, A.A. Martin Buber. N.Y., 1957.
Phil 8610.940.1 — Cohen, C. Almost an autobiography. London, 1940.
Phil 8610.933 — Cohen, C. Bradlaugh and Ingersoll. London, 1933.
Phil 8877.51 — Cohen, C. An outline of evolutionary ethics. London, 1896.
Phil 5752.7 — Cohen, Chapman. Determinism or free-will? London, 1919.
Phil 8610.923 — Cohen, Chapman. Essays in freethinking. Series 1. London, 1923.
Phil 8610.927.20 — Cohen, Chapman. Essays in freethinking. 2. series. London, 1927.
Phil 8610.929.25 — Cohen, Chapman. Four lectures on freethought and life. London, 1929.
Phil 8692.15 — Cohen, Chapman. God and evolution. London, 1925.
Phil 8610.921 — Cohen, Chapman. A grammar of freethought. London, 1921.
Phil 477.9 — Cohen, Chapman. Materialism: has it been exploded?...debate. London, 1928.
Phil 477.9.5 — Cohen, Chapman. Materialism re-stated. London, 1927.
Phil 8627.13 — Cohen, Chapman. The other side of death. London, 1922.
Phil 5627.55.5 — Cohen, Chapman. Religion and sex. London, 1919.
Phil 8657.20 — Cohen, Chapman. Socialism, atheism and Christianity. London, 1908.
Phil 8657.16 — Cohen, Chapman. Theism or atheism. London, 1921.
Phil 7069.67.20 — Cohen, Daniel. Myths of the space age. N.Y., 1967.
Phil 75.22 — Cohen, F. Philosphie. Antiquarists-Katalog 159/160. Bonn, 1927.
Phil 7082.76 — Cohen, G. Das Wesen der Träume. Dresden, 1925.
Phil 3484.2.25 — Cohen, H. Kant's Begrundung der Aesthetik. Berlin, 1889.
Phil 3484.2.5A — Cohen, H. Kant's Begrundung der Ethik. Berlin, 1877.
Phil 3484.2.8 — Cohen, H. Kant's Einfluss auf die deutsche Kultur. Berlin, 1883.
Phil 3484.2 — Cohen, H. Kant's Theorie der Erfahrung. Berlin, 1871.
Phil 3484.2.2 — Cohen, H. Kant's Theorie der Erfahrung. 2. Aufl. Berlin, 1885.
Phil 3484.2.3 — Cohen, H. Kant's Theorie der Erfahrung. 3. Aufl. Berlin, 1918.
Phil 3484.2.15 — Cohen, H. Kommentar zu Immanuel Kant's Kritik. Leipzig, 1907.
Phil 3484.2.16A — Cohen, H. Kommentar zu Immanuel Kant's Kritik. 2. Aufl. Leipzig, 1917.
Phil 3484.2.17 — Cohen, H. Kommentar zu Immanuel Kant's Kritik. 3. Aufl. Leipzig, 1920.
Phil 333.3 — Cohen, H. Das Princip der Infinitesimal-Methode und seine Geschichte. Berlin, 1883.
Phil 3484.2.30 — Cohen, H. Die systematischen Begriffe. Berlin, 1873.
Phil 3160.3.92 — Cohen, Hermann. Briefe. Berlin, 1939.
Phil 177.28A — Cohen, Hermann. Logik der reinen Erkenntnis. Berlin, 1902. 3v.
Phil 5500.35 — Cohen, J. Behavior in uncertainty and its social implications. London, 1964.
Phil 5238.200 — Cohen, J. Readings in psychology. London, 1964.
Phil 6992.2 — Cohen, Jacques J. Psychotherapy. London, 1936.
Phil 270.75.5 — Cohen, John. Chance, skill, and luck. Baltimore, 1960.
Phil 5242.56.5 — Cohen, John. Homs psychologicus. London, 1970.
Phil 5242.56 — Cohen, John. Humanistic psychology. London, 1958.
Phil 270.75 — Cohen, John. Risk and gambling. London, 1956.
Phil 5520.385 — Cohen, Laurence Jonathan. The diversity of meaning. London, 1962.
Phil 5520.385.2 — Cohen, Laurence Jonathan. The diversity of meaning. 2. ed. London, 1966.
Phil 5125.40 — Cohen, Laurence Jonathan. The implications of induction. London, 1970.
Phil 1802.12 — Cohen, M.R. American thought. Glencoe, Ill., 1954.
Phil 1930.10.10 — Cohen, M.R. A dreamer's journey. (Autobiography). Boston, 1949.
Phil 5042.25 — Cohen, Morris R. Introduction to logic and scientific method. N.Y., 1934.
Phil 5042.25.2 — Cohen, Morris R. Introduction to logic and scientific method. N.Y., 1936.
Phil 5042.25.5A — Cohen, Morris R. A preface to logic. N.Y., 1944.
Phil 1930.10.35 — Cohen, Morris R. Studies in philosophy and science. N.Y., 1949.
Phil 5643.170 — Cohen, Ronald L. Problems in motion perception. Uppsala, 1964.
Phil 5500.70 — Cohen, Rudolf. Systematische Tendenzen bei Persönlichkeitsbeurteilungen. Bern, 1969.
Phil 6158.10 — Cohen, Sidney. The beyond within; the LSD story. N.Y., 1965.
Phil 5590.375 — Cohen, Yehudi A. Social structure and personality. N.Y., 1961.
Phil 1930.10.30 — Cohen Morris, R. The faith of a liberal. Selected essays. N.Y., 1946.
Phil 177.28.10 — Cohens, Hermann. Schriften zur Philosophie und Zeitgeschichte. Berlin, 1928. 2v.
Phil 720.59 — The coherence theory of truth. (Khachaturian, Haig.) Beirut, 1961.
Phil 735.106 — Cohn, Aron. Hauptprobleme der Wertphilosophie. Wien, 1934.
Phil 8827.6 — Cohn, Frederick. Evolutionism and idealism in ethics. Thesis. Omaha, Nebr., 1909.
Phil 8877.63 — Cohn, Georg. Etik og sociologi. Kjøbenhavn, 1913.
Phil 8403.31 — Cohn, Jonas. algemeine Asthetik. Leipzig, 1910.
Phil 3002.4 — Cohn, Jonas. Der deutsche Idealismus. Leipzig, 1923.
Phil 177.44 — Cohn, Jonas. Führende Denker. Leipzig, 1907.
Phil 177.44.5 — Cohn, Jonas. Gefühlston und Sättigung der Farben. n.p., 1899-1915. 16 pam.
Phil 410.10 — Cohn, Jonas. Geschichte des Unendlichkeitsproblems im abendländischen Denken bis Kant. Leipzig, 1896.
Phil 177.43 — Cohn, Jonas. DerSinn der gegenwärtigen Kultur. Leipzig, 1914.
Phil 5042.18 — Cohn, Jonas. Theorie der Dialektik. Leipzig, 1923.
Phil 333.8 — Cohn, Jonas. Voraussetzungen und Ziele des Erkennens. Leipzig, 1908.
Phil 735.101 — Cohn, Jonas. Wertwissenschaft. Stuttgart, 1932.
Phil 3160.13 — Cohn, Jonas. Wirklichkeit als Aufgabe. Stuttgart, 1955.
Phil 5242.19 — Cohn, Max. Über das Denken. Berlin, 1910.
Phil 3640.276 — Cohn, Paul. Um Nietzsches Untergang; Beiträge zum Verständnis des Genies. Hannover, 1931.
Phil 2475.1.95 — Coignet, C. De Kant à Bergson. Paris, 1911.
Phil 8877.19 — Coignet, C. La morale indépendante. Paris, 1869.
Phil 812.40 — Coincidentia oppositorum. (Metzke, Erwin.) Witten, 1961.
Htn Phil 177.78* — Cointha, Jean des Boulez. Paradoxo ou Sentença, philosophica contra opinão do vulgo. Lixboa, 1866.
Phil 9450.8 — Coit, S. Ethical democracy. London, 1900.
Phil 8870.5 — Coit, Stanton. The message of man. London, 1905.
Phil 8615.9.2 — Coit, Stanton. The spiritual nature of man. Bayswater, 1910.
Phil 8627.15 — Cojazzi, Antonio. L'anima umana non muore. Torino, 1944.
Phil 8657.5 — Coke, H. Creeds of the day. London, 1883. 2v.
Phil 5070.11 — Coke, Henry J. The domain of belief. London, 1910.

Phil 5042.80   Coke, Zachary. The art of logic, 1654. Menston, Eng., 1969.

Phil 8663.3.91   Col. Robert G. Ingersoll as he is. (McDonald, E.M.) N.Y., 1910?

Phil 4002.4   Colangelo, F. Storia dei filosofi e dei matematici napolitani. v.1-3. Napoli, 1833-34.

Phil 4080.3.540   Colapietra, Raffaele. Benedetto Croce e la politica italiana. Bari, 1969.

Phil 8582.44   Colas, Émile. La mystique et la raison. Paris, 1922.

Phil 5242.39   Cole, Lawrence W. Factors of human psychology. Boulder, 1926.

Phil 5242.39.4   Cole, Lawrence W. Factors of human psychology. Boulder, 1930[1935]

Phil 7069.37   Cole, M.A. Isaiah as read by a clairvoyant. Boston, 1937.

Phil 5238.226   Cole, Michael. Handbook of contemporary Soviet psychology. N.Y., 1969.

Phil 8877.30   Cole, W.M. The American hope. N.Y., 1910.

Phil 9070.22   Cole, Walton E. Standing up to life. Boston, 1943.

Phil 9070.22.5   Cole, Walton E. The three R's of religion. Boston, 1945.

Phil 9495.155.15   Cole, William G. Sex in Christianity and psychoanalysis. N.Y., 1955.

NEDL Phil 960.2   Colebrooke, H.T. Essais sur la philosophie des Hindous. Paris, 1833.

Phil 960.2.5   Colebrooke, H.T. Essays on the religion and philosophy of the Hindus. London, 1858.

Phil 802.23   Coleburt, Russell. An introduction to Western philosophy. N.Y., 1957.

Phil 735.205   Coleburt, Russell. The search for values. London, 1960.

Phil 4080.7.31   Colecchi, O. Sopra alcune quistioni...della filosofeia. Napoli, 1843.

Phil 5545.6   Colegrove, F.W. Memory. N.Y., 1900.

Phil 8120.10.5   Coleman, Francis X.J. The aesthetic thought of the French Enlightenment. Pittsburgh, 1971.

Phil 9513.5   Coleman, George William. Searchlights. Boston, 1910.

Phil 9513.5.5   Coleman, George William. This business of living. Boston, 1936.

Phil 9513.5.6   Coleman, George William. This business of living. Boston, 1936.

Phil 5242.58   Coleman, J.C. Personality dynamics and effective behavior. Chicago, 1960.

Phil 5350.6   Coleman, James Samuel. Models of change and response uncertainty. Englewood Cliffs, N.J., 1964.

Phil 5242.33   Coleman, L.R. Psychology; a simplification. N.Y., 1927.

Phil 5135.4   Coleridge, J.D. Thinking for ourselves. v.1-2. London, 1890.

Htn Phil 1930.3.30*   Coleridge, S.T. Aids to reflection. London, 1825.

Phil 3822.4.10   Colerus, Johannes. Korte, dog waaragtige levens-beschrijving van Benedictus de Spinoza. Amsterdam, 1705[1910]

Phil 3822.4.15   Colerus, Johannes. Das Leben des Benedict von Spinoza. Frankfurt, 1733.

Phil 3822.4.25   Colerus, Johannes. Das Leben des Benedict von Spinoza. Heidelberg, 1952.

Htn Phil 3822.4.5*   Colerus, Johannes. The life of Benedict de Spinoza. London, 1706.

Phil 3822.4.6A   Colerus, Johannes. The life of Benedict de Spinoza. London, 1706.

Phil 3822.4   Colerus, Johannes. La vie de Benoit de Spinoza. La Haye, 1706.

Phil 5244.34   Coles, Robert. Erik H. Erikson; the growth of his work. 1st ed. Boston, 1970.

Phil 8877.76   Colesanti, Giulio. Esiste una morale? Catania, 1937.

Phil 8877.76.5   Colesanti, Giulio. La morale supérieure. Paris, 1940.

Phil 1802.14   Colie, Rosalie L. Light and enlightenment. Cambridge, 1957.

Phil 8582.75   Colish, Marcia L. The mirror of language. New Haven, 1968.

Phil 4002.6   La collaboration philosophique. Bologna, 1958.

Phil 3425.225   Collan, F. De notione necessitatis Hegeliana. Diss. Helsingforsiae, 1850.

Phil 4210.2   Collana di studi filosofici Rosminiani. Milano. 1-12,1951-1956 4v.

Phil 2415.7   Collapse of the scholastic hierarchy in 17th century France. (Pickman, Edward M.) Boston, 1931.

Phil 5042.2   Collard, John. The essentials of logic. London, 1796.

Phil 5042.2.5   Collard, John. A praxis of logic. London, 1799.

Phil 1885.15   Collected essays. (Bradley, Francis H.) Oxford, 1935. 2v.

Phil 184.3.35   Collected essays and reviews. (James, W.) N.Y., 1920.

Phil 978.9.25   Collected fruits of occult teaching. (Sinnett, A.P.) London, 1919.

Phil 3915.3   Collected papers; articles. (Wundt, Wilhelm.) n.p., n.d.

Phil 6315.16.8   Collected papers. (Fenichel, Otto.) N.Y., 1953-54. 2v.

X Cg Phil 6315.22   Collected papers. (Franz, Shepherd I.) n.p., 1911-13.

Phil 6315.2.8.30A   Collected papers. (Freud, Sigmund.) London, 1949. 5v.

Phil 6315.2.34   Collected papers. (Freud, Sigmund.) London, 1957-69. 4v.

Phil 6315.2.35   Collected papers. (Freud, Sigmund.) N.Y., 1924-5.

Phil 6315.2.8.31   Collected papers. (Freud, Sigmund.) N.Y., 1959. 5v.

Phil 2120.18   Collected papers. (Lewis, Clarence Irving.) Stanford, 1970.

Phil 21.16   Collected papers. (London. University. University College Psychological Laboratory.) London. 1-10 5v.

Phil 2225.5.10A   Collected papers. (Peirce, C.S.) Cambridge, 1931. 8v.

Phil 2280.21.5   Collected papers. (Schutz, Alfred.) The Hague, 1962. 3v.

Phil 2225.5.50A   Collected papers. v.1-6. (Peirce, C.S.) Cambridge, 1960. 3v.

Phil 5259.40A   Collected papers in psychology. (Tolman, Edward C.) Berkeley, 1951.

Phil 525.7.15   Collected papers of Evelyn Underhill. (Underhill, Evelyn.) London, 1946.

Phil 6315.2.350   The collected papers of Sigmund Freud. (Studies in parapsychology, v.10). (Freud, Sigmund.) N.Y., 1963.

Phil 8400.45   Collected papers on aesthetics. (Barrett, Cyril.) N.Y., 1966.

Phil 6319.1.5A   Collected papers on analytical psychology. (Jung, C.G.) London, 1916.

Phil 6319.1.5.5   Collected papers on analytical psychology. (Jung, C.G.) London, 1922.

Phil 6328.32   Collected papers on psycho-analysis. (Sharpe, E.F.) London, 1950.

Phil 6968.35   Collected papers on schizophrenia and related subjects. (Searles, Harold F.) London, 1965.

Phil 6321.6   Collected papers on the psychology of phantasy. (Long, C.E.) N.Y., 1921.

Phil 8676.3.10   Pamphlet box. Collected sermons.

Phil 6980.712.1   Collected works. (Sullivan, Harry Stack.) N.Y., 1965. 2v.

Phil 6319.1.5.7A   Collected works. v.1,3-5,7-9,11-17. (Jung, C.G.) N.Y., 1953-63. 14v.

Phil 6319.1.5.8   Collected works. v.1,3-17. (Jung, C.G.) London, 1953-63. 15v.

Phil 2275.11   Collected works. v.1-4, 6-10, and supplement. (Stewart, D.) Edinburgh, 1854-60. 10v.

Phil 2138.11   Collected works. v.2,3, 4(2), 5(2), 10,12,13. (Mill, John S.) Toronto, 1963. 9v.

X Cg Phil 2275.11   Collected works. v.5. (Stewart, D.) Edinburgh, 1854-60.

Phil 6319.1.5.6   Collected works. v.7. 2nd ed. (Jung, C.G.) N.Y., 1966. 2v.

Phil 2275.12   Collected works. 2nd ed. (Stewart, D.) Edinburgh, 1877. 11v.

Phil 978.5.1   Collected writings. 1st American ed. v.5-8. (Blavatsky, H.P.) Los Angeles, 1950. 4v.

Phil 5261.14   Collectief-psychologische omtrekken. (Visser, H.L.A.) Haarlem, 1920.

Htn Phil 2145.1*   Collection...philosophical writings. (More, Henry.) London, 1662.

Htn Phil 2145.2.2*   Collection...philosophical writings. (More, Henry.) London, 1712.

Phil 2145.2   Collection...philosophical writings. 4th ed. (More, Henry.) London, 1712.

Phil 5066.40   Collection de logique mathématique. Serie A. Paris. 1-23 10v.

Phil 5238.5   Collection de psychologie experimentale et de métapsychie. Paris. 1-22,1908-1912 18v.

Phil 1145.3   Collection des moralistes anciens. Paris, 1782-83. 12v.

Phil 7069.33.54   Collection mimeographs. (Wells, Helen B.) N.Y., 1933. 8 pam.

Phil 1850.17   The collection of books used by James Spedding as his working library in preparing his...works of Sir F. Bacon. (Spedding, James.) London, 19- ?

Phil 978.11   Collection of lectures on theosophy and archaic religions. (Olcott, H.S.) Madras, 1883.

Phil 5247.3.300   A collection of miscellaneous papers. (Hartmann, George W.) n.p., n.d.

Phil 5545.269   A collection of moments; a study of involuntary memories. (Salaman, Esther Polianowsky.) N.Y., 1972.

Phil 5643.86   Collection of papers. (Ames, Adelbert.) n.p., n.d. 6 pam.

Htn Phil 3552.71.1*   A collection of papers. (Leibniz, Gottfried Wilhelm.) London, 1717.

Phil 3552.71   A collection of papers. (Leibniz, Gottfried Wilhelm.) London, 1717.

Phil 182.5.5   A collection of philosophical and psychological essays; extracts from periodicals. (Harris, W.T.) n.p., n.d.

Phil 8663.3.12   Collection of Robert G. Ingersoll's famous speeches. (Ingersoll, Robert G.) N.Y., 1906.

Htn Phil 2115.25*   Collection of several pieces. (Locke, J.) London, 1720.

Phil 2295.10   Collection of several pieces. (Toland, John.) London, 1726. 2v.

Htn Phil 1850.55*   A collection of some principall rules and maximes of the common laws of England. (Bacon, Francis.) London, 1630.

Phil 5942.3F   The collection of the Boston Phrenological Society, a retrospect. (Warren, J.C.) N.Y., 1921.

Phil 8580.13   A collection of the tracts of a certain free thinker. (Annet, Peter.) London, 1739-1749.

Htn Phil 2115.141*   A collection of tracts. (Bold, S.) London, 1706.

Phil 193.108   The collective mind. (Smith, H.B.) Columbus, 1924.

Phil 365.18.5   The collective spirit; an idealistic theory of evolution. (Cavling, Viggo.) N.Y., 1926.

Phil 530.11.22   Colledge, Eric. The mediaeval mystics of England. N.Y., 1961.

Phil 5042.27   A college logic; an introduction to the study of argument and proof. (Castell, Alburey.) N.Y., 1935.

Phil 42.7   College of the Pacific, Stockton, California. Publications in philosophy. Stockton. 1-3,1934-1934

Phil 42.7.5   College of the Pacific. Pacific Philosophy Institute. Publication. 1,1951+ 2v.

Phil 5241.28.25   College psychology. (Brown, W.) N.Y., 1950.

NEDL Phil 3120.11.90   Collegium logicum. 2. druk. (Bolland, G.J.P.J.) Amsterdam, 1931. 2v.

Phil 165.352   Collegium Philosophicum; Studien Joachim Ritter zum 60. Geburtstag. Basel, 1965.

X Cg Phil 176.37   Collegium physicum disputationibus XXXII absolutum. (Burgersdijck, F.P.) Lugdunum Batavorum, 1642.

Phil 2805.81   Collet, F. Fait inédit de la vie de Pascal. Paris, 1848.

Phil 8662.5.25   Collet, S.D. George Jacob Holyoake and modern atheism. London, 1855.

Phil 179.3.15   Colleted essays. (Eucken, R.) London, 1914.

Phil 2475.1.465   Colletti, Giovanni. I fondamenti logico-metafisici del bergsonismo e altri scritti. Padova, 1963.

Phil 3425.716   Colletti, Lucio. Il marxismo e Hegel. Bari, 1969.

Phil 5520.675   Colli, Giorgio. Filosofia dell'espressione. Milano, 1969.

Phil 665.2   Colliber, S. Free thoughts concerning souls. London, 1734.

Phil 8582.11   Colliber, S. An impartial enquiry. v.1-2. London, 1728-29.

Phil 6327.42.5   Colliding generations. (Ree, Frank van.) Varanasi, 1970.

Phil 1930.4.35   Collier, Arthur. Clavis universalis. Chicago, 1909.

Htn Phil 1930.4.31*   Collier, Arthur. Clavis universalis. Edinburgh, 1836.

Htn Phil 1930.4.30*   Collier, Arthur. Clavis universalis. London, 1713. 2 pam.

Phil 9230.12.5   Collier, Jeremy. An essay upon gaming. Edinburgh, 1885.

Htn Phil 9230.12*   Collier, Jeremy. An essay upon gaming. London, 1713. (Transferred to Houghton Library 14/1/72)

Phil 8877.15   Collier, Jeremy. Essays upon several moral subjects. v.1-4. London, 1702-09. 3v.

Phil 8877.15.2   Collier, Jeremy. Essays upon several moral subjects. 5th ed. pt. 1-2. London, 1703.

Phil 8877.15.4   Collier, Jeremy. Essays upon several moral subjects. 7th ed. pt. 1-2. London, 1732.

Htn Phil 8877.15.5*   Collier, Jeremy. Miscellanies in five essays. London, 1694.

Phil 283.13   Collier, K.B. Cosmogonies of our fathers. N.Y., 1934.

Phil 283.12   Colligan, J.J. Cosmology. N.Y., 1936.

Phil 8877.16   Collignon, A. L'art et la vie. Metz, 1866.

Phil 365.39   Collin, C. Brorskabets religion. Kristiania, 1912.

Phil 283.15   Collin, R. The theory of celestial influence. London, 1954.

Phil 5242.5   Collineau, J.C. Analyse physiologique. Paris, 1843-44. 2 pam.

Phil 585.156   Collingwood, F.J. Man's physical and spiritual nature. N.Y., 1963.

Phil 283.20 Collingwood, Francis. Philosophy of nature. Englewood Cliffs, N.J., 1961.
Phil 177.85.2 Collingwood, R.G. An essay on metaphysics. Oxford, 1940.
Phil 177.85 Collingwood, R.G. An essay on philosophical method. Oxford, 1933.
Phil 177.85.10 Collingwood, R.G. The new leviathan, or Man, society, civilization and barbarism. Oxford, 1942.
Phil 177.85.5 Collingwood, R.G. Speculum mentis. Oxford, 1924.
Phil 1930.8.88A Collingwood, Robin George. An autobiography. London, 1964.
Phil 1930.8.87 Collingwood, Robin George. An autotbiography. London, 1951.
Phil 8582.26.5 Collingwood, Robin George. Faith and reason. Chicago, 1968.
Phil 283.14.5 Collingwood, Robin George. The idea of nature. Oxford, 1964.
Phil 8403.21 Collingwood, Robin George. The principles of art. Oxford, 1938.
Phil 8403.21.7 Collingwood, Robin George. The principles of art. Oxford, 1967.
Phil 8582.26 Collingwood, Robin George. Religion and philosophy. London, 1916.
Phil 1930.8.125 Collingwood and the reform of metaphysics; a study in the philosophy of mind. (Rubinoff, Lionel.) Toronto, 1970.
Phil 5752.2A Collins, A. Philosophical inquiry...human liberty. London, 1717.
Phil 5752.2.3 Collins, A. Philosophical inquiry...human liberty. London, 1735.
Phil 5752.2.10 Collins, A. Philosophical inquiry...human liberty. London, 1890.
Htn Phil 8610.713.10* Collins, Anthony. Discours sur la liberté de penser. Londres, 1714.
Phil 8610.713.5 Collins, Anthony. A discourse of free-thinking. Stuttgart, 1965.
Htn Phil 8610.713* Collins, Anthony. A discourse of free thinking occasioned by the rise and growth of a sect call'd free-thinker. London, 1713. 3 pam.
Htn Phil 1930.5.30* Collins, Anthony. A discourse of the grounds and reasons of the Christian religion. London, 1724-37.
Phil 1930.5.35 Collins, Anthony. A discourse of the grounds and reasons of the Christian religion. London, 1737. 2 pam.
Htn Phil 1930.5.37* Collins, Anthony. A discourse of the grounds and reasons of the Christian religion. London, 1737. 2 pam.
Htn Phil 1930.5.29* Collins, Anthony. A discourse of the grounds and reasons of the Christian religion. v.1-2. London, 1724.
Phil 1930.5.25 Collins, Anthony. Essai sur la nature de l'âme humaine. Londres, 1769.
Htn Phil 8582.30* Collins, Anthony. Examen des prophéties qui servient de fondement de la religion chrétienne. Londres, 1768.
Htn Phil 1930.5.50* Collins, Anthony. The scheme of literal prophecy considered. London, 1727.
Phil 1930.5.51 Collins, Anthony. The scheme of literal prophecy considered. London, 1727.
Phil 5627.76 Collins, F.P. My religious experience. Kansas City, Mo., 1901.
Phil 6312.5.10 Collins, J. The doctor looks at life and death. N.Y., 1931.
Phil 6312.5 Collins, J. Letters to a neurologist. 2nd series. N.Y., 1910.
Phil 525.90 Collins, J.B. Christian mysticism. Baltimore, 1940.
Phil 1750.355A Collins, J.D. The existentialists. Chicago, 1952.
Phil 8657.21 Collins, J.D. God in modern philosophy. Chicago, 1959.
Phil 177.129 Collins, J.D. The lure of wisdom. Milwaukee, 1962.
Phil 165.200 Collins, James. Readings in ancient and medieval philosophy. Westminster, 1960.
Phil 2050.265 Collins, James Daniel. The emergence of philosophy of religion. New Haven, 1967.
Phil 1702.11 Collins, James Daniel. A history of modern European philosophy. Milwaukee, 1961.
Phil 7080.45 Collins, Joseph. Insomnia, how to combat it. N.Y., 1930.
Phil 5627.107.10 Collins, Joyce. The sparrow hath found herself a house. Dublin, 1943.
Phil 5645.26 Collins, Mary. Colour-blindness. London, 1925.
Phil 5242.30 Collins, Mary. Experimental psychology. London, 1926.
Phil 5242.30.5 Collins, Mary. A first laboratory guide in psychology. London, 1926.
Phil 5242.30.7 Collins, Mary. A first laboratory guide in psychology. London, 1926.
Phil 5850.162 Collins, Mary. Psychology and practical life. London, 1936.
Phil 5242.6 Collins, T.W. Humanics. N.Y., 1860.
Phil 1900.81.3 Collins, W.L. Butler. Edinburgh, 1881.
Phil 1900.81 Collins, W.L. Butler. Philadelphia, 1881.
Phil 177.122 Collins, William B. Metaphysics and man. Dubuque, 1959.
Phil 525.232 Colloque de Strasbourg, 1961. La mystique rhénane. Colloque de Strasbourg, 16-19 mai, 1961. Paris, 1963.
Phil 3450.11.215 Colloque International de Phénoménologie. Husserl et la pensée moderne. La Haye, 1959.
Phil 5274.2 Colloque International sur les Modèles et la Formalisation du Comportement, Paris, 1965. Les modèles et la formalisation du comportement. Paris, 1967.
Phil 8622.64 Colloque International sur Mythe et Foi, Rome, 1966. Mythe et foi. Paris, 1966.
Phil 3640.717 Colloque Philosophique International de Royaumont, 7th, 1964. Nietzsche. Paris, 1967.
Phil 4080.3.300 Colloqui con Benedetto Croce. (Galati, Vito Giuseppe.) Brescia, 1957.
Htn Phil 3200.1.30* Colloquia. (Erasmus, D.) Lugdunum Batavorum, 1636.
Phil 5938.5 Colloquies. Imaginary conversations between a phrenologist and the shade of Dugald Stewart. (Slade, J.) London, 1838.
Phil 7069.09.10 Colloquies with an unseen friend. (Paget, Walburga v.H.) London, 1909.
Phil 4225.8.102 Colloquio con Michele Federico Sciacca. (Nobile-Ventura, Attilio.) Milano, 1966.
Phil 9342.5 Collyer, R. Talks to young men. Boston, 1888.
Phil 283.18 Colmoyer, Ciro. Due contributi di filosofia scientifica. Roma, 1967.
Htn Phil 9171.7.5* Colo os matrimoniales. (Luján, Pedro de.) Toledo, 1563.
Phil 9495.16 Colom, P.M. La chasteté. Paris, 1847.
Phil 3450.19.365 Colombo, Arrigo. Martin Heidegger. Bologna, 1964.
Phil 583.10 Colombo, Arrigo. Sulla fenomenologie e la rivelazione delle cose. Bologna, 1968.
Phil 2905.1.315 Colomer, Eusebi. Pierre Teilhard de Chardin. Barcelona, 1961.
Phil 9510.6 Colonéri, L.J. La dénonciation et les dénonciateurs. 4. éd. Paris, 1948.

Phil 1818.12 The colonial origins of American thought. (Savelle, Max.) Princeton, 1964.
Phil 4210.200 Colonna, Salvatore. L'educazione religiosa nella pedagogia di A. Rosmini. Lecce, 1963.
Phil 5645.59 Color. (Burnham, R.W.) N.Y., 1963.
Phil 5645.5 Color blindness. (Head, J.F.) Boston, 1881.
Phil 5645.6.10 Color blindness. (Jeffries, B.J.) Boston, 1878. 3 pam.
Phil 5645.6 Color blindness. (Jeffries, B.J.) Boston, 1879.
Phil 5645.42 Color light and vision. (Honoré, Paul.) Detroit, 1938.
Phil 5645.6.15 Color-names, color-blindness. (Jeffries, B.J.) Boston, 1882.
Phil 5645.7 Color-perception. (Hall, G.S.) n.p., 1878.
Phil 5645.11A The color sensitivity of the peripheral retina. (Baird, J.W.) Washington, 1905.
Phil 5645.56 Color vision. (Teevan, R.C.) Princeton, 1961.
Phil 5238.3 Colorado. College. Publication. Education and psychology. Colorado Springs. 1,1919
Phil 42.11 Colorado. University. University of Colorado studies. Series in philosophy. Boulder.
Phil 333.17.1 Colorado. University. Psychology Department. Contemporary approaches to cognition. Cambridge, 1968.
Phil 9347.10 The colored girl beautiful. (Hackley, E.A. (Mrs.).) Kansas City, 1916.
Phil 4080.3.143 Colorni, E. L'estetica di Benedetto Croce. Milano, 1932.
Phil 5645.47 Colors and their characters. (Rouwer, B.) The Hague, 1949.
Phil 5645.32.2 Colour and colour theories. (Franklin, Christine L.) London, 1929.
Phil 5645.26 Colour-blindness. (Collins, Mary.) London, 1925.
Phil 5645.2 Colour-sense. (Allen, G.) London, 1879. 2v.
Phil 5645.8 Colour vision. (Abney, W. de W.) London, 1895.
Phil 5645.38 Colour vision. (Peddie, William.) London, 1922.
Phil 8412.42 Colours, forms and art. Studies in differential aesthetic psychology. Akademisk avhandling. (Leijonhiel, Christer.) Stockholm, 1967.
Phil 6672.4 Colquhoun, J.C. Isis Revelata: an inquiry into animal magnetism. London, 1836. 2v.
Phil 6750.2 Colquhoun, L. Report of the proceedings...of idiotry. Edinburgh, 1837.
Phil 5242.7 Colsenet, E. La vie inconsciente. Paris, 1880.
Phil 3822.5 Colsenet, Edmond. De mentis essentia Spinoza quid senserit. Thesis. Parisiis, 1880.
Phil 8877.77 Coltman, J. Everyman's monitor. Philadelphia, 1815.
Phil 7060.63 Colton, C. Sampford ghost. Tiverton, 1810.
Phil 7068.10 Colton, C.C. Sampford ghost. Tiverton, 1810.
Phil 176.142 Colui che si chiama "Io sono". (Bolaffio, C.) Modena, 1936.
Phil 6312.25 Columbia. University. Psychoanalytic Clinic for Training and Reaserch. New perspectives in psychoanalysis. N.Y., 1965.
Phil 5042.15A Columbia Association in Philosophy. An introduction to reflective thinking. Boston, 1923.
Phil 42.1 Columbia College. Contributions to philosophy. N.Y. 1-12,1894-1903 12v.
Phil 42.1.5 Columbia College. Studies in the history of ideas. N.Y. 1-3,1918-1935 3v.
Phil 12.25 Columbia studies in philosophy. N.Y. 1-10,1941-1948 8v.
Phil 10.19.5 Columbia University. Archives of psychology.
Phil 10.19 Columbia University. Archives of psychology. N.Y. 1907-1945 37v.
NEDL Phil 2475.1.77 Columbia University. Library. A contribution to a bibliography of Henri Bergson. N.Y., 1913.
Phil 2475.1.77 Columbia University. Library. A contribution to a bibliography of Henri Bergson. N.Y., 1913.
Phil 9035.76 Columbia University. Teachers College. Character Education Inquiry. Studies in the nature of character. v.2. N.Y., 1929.
Phil 4260.135 Columbu, Mario. Giambattista Vico. Trani, 1957.
Phil 1850.108 The Columbus of literature. (Wigston, William F.) Chicago, 1892.
Phil 9035.35 Colville, N.J. Fate mastered, destiny fulfilled. London, 1903.
Phil 6112.19.5 Colville, W.W.J. Glints of wisdom. N.Y., 1910.
Phil 6112.19 Colville, W.W.J. Spiritual therapeutics. Chicago, 1890.
Phil 7069.14.10 Colville, William J. Light and colors. N.Y., 1914.
Phil 7069.13.10 Colville, William J. Mystic light essays. 1st ed. N.Y., 1913.
Phil 3808.101 Colvin, S.S. Schopenhauer's doctrine of the Thing-in-itself. Providence, 1897.
Phil 4065.121 Comandini, A. Per Giordano Bruno dal 1876 al 1889. Roma, 1889.
Phil 5921.2.5 Combe, A. Observations on Dr. Barclay's ojections. Edinburgh, 1823.
Phil 6112.15.5 Combe, G. On the functions of the cerebellum. Edinburgh, 1838.
Phil 5922.4.6 Combe, George. The constitution of man. Boston, 1829.
Phil 5922.4.12 Combe, George. The constitution of man. Boston, 1839.
Phil 5922.4.14 Combe, George. The constitution of man. Hartford, 1847. 6 pam.
Phil 5922.4.9 Combe, George. The constitution of man. N.Y., 1845.
Phil 5922.4.6.5 Combe, George. The constitution of man. 5. American ed. Boston, 1835.
Phil 5922.4.11 Combe, George. The constitution of man. 11th American ed. Boston, 1841.
Phil 5922.4.13 Combe, George. The constitution of man. 15. American ed. Boston, 1847.
Phil 5922.4.25 Combe, George. Elements of phrenology. Philadelphia, 1826.
Phil 5922.4.5 Combe, George. Essays on phrenology. Philadelphia, 1822.
Phil 5922.4.40 Combe, George. Lectures on moral philosophy. Boston, 1836.
Phil 5922.4.41 Combe, George. Lectures on moral philosophy. Boston, 1840.
Phil 5922.4 Combe, George. Lectures on phrenology. N.Y., 1839.
Phil 5922.4.3 Combe, George. Lectures on phrenology. 3. ed. N.Y., 1847.
Phil 5922.4.15 Combe, George. Letter...Francis Jeffrey. Edinburgh, 1826-29. 2 pam.
Phil 5922.4.51 Combe, George. The suppressed documents. Glasgow, 1836.
Phil 5922.3.7 Combe, George. A system of phrenology. Boston, 1835.
Phil 5922.3.3 Combe, George. A system of phrenology. Boston, 1838.
Phil 5922.3.5 Combe, George. A system of phrenology. N.Y., 1841.
Phil 5922.4.20 Combe, George. Testimonials. Boston, 1836. 3 pam.
Phil 6990.3.85 Combes, André. Pilerinage spirituel à Lourdes. Paris, 1959.
Phil 2905.1.590 Combes, André. Teilhard de Chardin et la sainte èvolution. Paris, 1969.

Phil 2520.325   Cómbès, J. Le dessein de la sagesse cartésienne. Lyon, 1960.

Phil 1158.9   Combes, M. Les vies d'Epicure de Platon et de Pythagore. Amsterdam, 1752.

Phil 7082.64   Combes, Marguerite. Le rêve et la personnalité. Paris, 1932.

Phil 5080.8   Combès, Michel. Le concept de concept formel. Toulouse, 1969.

Phil 5650.6   Combination tones and other related auditory phenomena. (Peterson, J.) Chicago, 1908.

Phil 5066.120   Combinatory logic. (Curry, Haskell Brooks.) Amsterdam, 1958.

Phil 58.4   Combined index. (Society for Psychical Research, London.) London, 1904. 3v.

Phil 5585.305   Combs, Arthur Wright. Florida studies in the helping professions. Gainesville, 1969.

Phil 9361.3.6   Come devo compotarmi? 6. ed. (Vertua-Gentile, Anna.) Milano, 1909.

Phil 5257.36   Come funziona la nostra intelligenza. (Rignano, E.) Bologna, 1922.

Phil 181.164.2   Come si pone il problema meta fisico. 2. ed. (Gentile, Marino.) Padova, 1965.

Phil 4225.8.38   Come si vince a Waterloo. (Sciacca, Michele Federico.) Milano, 1957.

Phil 811.8   The comedy of human philosophy. (Leon, M.) Boston, 1932.

Phil 177.16.9   Comenius, J.A. Natural philosophie reformed by divine light. London, 1651.

Phil 3450.19.215   Comentarios a la esencia de la poesia de Heidegger. (Garcia Bacca, Juan David.) Caracas, 1956.

Phil 6112.6   A comentary...mind and the emotions. (Cooke, W.) Philadelphia, 1853.

Phil 9495.148   Comfort, A. Barbarism and sexual freedom. London, 1948.
Phil 9400.1.4   Comforts of old age. (Bernard, T.) London, 1820.
Htn   Phil 9400.1.3*   Comforts of old age. (Bernard, T.) N.Y., 1818.
Phil 6048.94.10   Comfort's palmistry guide by Cheiro (pseud.) palmist. (Hamon, Louis.) Augusta, 1894.

Phil 5525.12.5   Il comico. (Leir, Giulio A.) Genova, 1913.
Phil 9035.105   Coming into existence. (Rogers, Raymond.) Cleveland, 1967.

Phil 193.137   The coming of Karuna. (Shahani, R.G.) London, 1934.
Phil 7069.08.15   The coming science. (Carrington, Hereward.) Boston, 1908.
Phil 7069.20.50   The coming science. (Carrington, Hereward.) N.Y., 1920.
Phil 2270.77.10   The coming slavery and other essays. (Spencer, Herbert.) N.Y., 1888.

Phil 8952.23   Comitato Cattolico Docenti Universitari. Il problema morale, oggi. Bologna, 1969.

Phil 2610.100   Comité du Tricentenaire de Gassendi. Actes du Congrès du Tricentenaire de Pierre Gassendi. Paris, 1957.

Phil 4210.135   Commemorazione del primo centenario dalla nascita di A. Rosmini. (Rovereto. Comitato Centrale per la Commemorazione di A. Rosmini.) Milano, 1897.

Phil 4115.107   Commemorazione della personalità e del pensiero filosofico. (Ercole, Pasquale d'.) Torino, 1901.

Phil 4110.4.98   Commemorazione dell'accademico Luigi Ferri. (Barzellotti, G.) Roma, 1895.

Phil 4110.3.89   Commemorazione di Francesco Fiorentino. (Ferrari, G.M.) Roma, 1891.

Phil 3552.440   Commentaire du Discourse de métaphysique de Leibniz. (Burgelin, Pierre.) Paris, 1959.

Phil 2477.11.95   Commentaire sur la conversion spirituelle dans la philosophie de L. Branschvicg. (Cochet, M.A.) Bruxelles, 1937.

Phil 3425.257.10   Commentaires de la logique de Hegel. (Wahl, Jean A.) Paris, 1959.

Phil 3507.5.2   Commentar über Kant's Kritik der reinen Vernunft. (Zwanziger, J.C.) Leipzig, 1792.

Phil 3507.5   Commentar über Kant's Kritik der reinen Vernunft. (Zwanziger, J.C.) Leipzig, 1794.

Phil 3503.1   Commentar zu Kants Kritik der reinen Vernunft. (Vaihinger, H.) Stuttgart, 1881. 2v.

Phil 978.59.42   Commentaries on living. (Krishnamurti, J.) London, 1957.
Phil 978.59.40   Commentaries on living. (Krishnamurti, J.) London, 1959.
Phil 978.59.41   Commentaries on living. (Krishnamurti, J.) N.Y., 1956.
Phil 978.59.44   Commentaries on living. 1st ed. (Krishnamurti, J.) N.Y., 1960.

Phil 3484.22   Commentarii alla ragion pura. (Caramella, Santino.) Palermo, 1956-57.

Phil 2835.80   Commentarii in P. Rami Dialecticam. (Downame, G.) Francofurti, 1610.

Phil 181.25.5   Commentarios e pensamentos. (Gonçalvez de Magalhães, J.G.) Rio de Janeiro, 1880.

Phil 5628.50   Commentarius iuridicus ad L. Stigmata, C. de Fabricensibus. (Ostermann, Petrus.) Coloniae Agripinae, 1629.

Phil 3425.100.9   A commentary on Hegel's logic. (McTaggart, John McTaggart Ellis.) Cambridge, 1910.

Phil 3450.19.10.5   A commentary on Heidegger's Being and time. (Gelven, Michael.) N.Y., 1970.

Phil 3487.1.5   Commentary on Kant's Critick of pure reason. (Fischer, Kuno.) London, 1866.

Phil 3484.18   A commentary on Kant's Critique of judgement. (Cassirer, H.W.) London, 1938.

Phil 3483.75   A commentary on Kant's Critique of practical reason. (Beck, Lewis White.) Chicago, 1960.

Phil 3500.27   Commentary to Kant's Critique of pure reason. (Smith, N.K.) London, 1918.

Phil 3500.60.5A   A commentary to Kant's "Critique of pure reason". 2d ed. (Smith, Norman K.) London, 1923.

Phil 190.14   Commentationes philosophicae selectiores. (Ploucquet, W.G.) Trajecti ad Rhenum, 1781.

Phil 4520.2.34   Commentationum Stoicarum. Diss. (Biberg, N.F.) Upsaliae, 1815-1821.

Phil 4080.3.260   Commento a Croce. 1. ed. (Antoni, Carlo.) Venezia, 1955.
Phil 5055.27.3   Commento alla logica sintetica. (Pavese, Roberto.) Padova, 1963.

Phil 4260.123   Commento storico alla seconda Scienza nuova. (Nicolini, F.) Roma, 1949- 2v.

Phil 177.41   Commer, E. System der Philosophie. v.1-4. Münster, 1883.
Phil 5042.14   Commer, Ernst. Logik. Paderborn, 1897.
Htn   Phil 9495.38*   Le commerce dangereux entre les deux sexes. (Drouet de Maupertuy, J.) Bruxelles, 1715.

Phil 3552.362   Commercii epistolici Leibnitiani. (Gruber, J.D.) Hanoverae, 1745. 2v.

Phil 2520.360   Commercium mentis et corporis. (Specht, Rainer.) Stuttgart, 1966.

Phil 6958.6   Commitment, detention care, and treatment of the insane. (International Congress of Charities, Corrections and Philanthrophy, Chicago, 1893.) Baltimore, 1894.

Phil 8583.25   A common faith. (Dewey, John.) New Haven, 1934.

Phil 6116.3.5   Common mind troubles. (Granville, J.M.) Salem, 1879.
Phil 6967.7   The common neuroses, their treatment by psychotherapy. (Ross, T.A.) London, 1923.

Phil 6327.17.5   The common neuroses. 2. ed. (Ross, Thomas Arthur.) London, 1942.

Phil 6314.7   Common neuroses of children and adults. (English, Oliver Spurgeon.) N.Y., 1937.

Htn   Phil 2115.64*   A common-place book to the Holy Bible. (Locke, J.) London, 1697.

Phil 2115.64.20   A common-place book to the Holy Bible. 3d ed. (Locke, J.) London, 1725.

Phil 2115.64.25   A common-place book to the Holy Bible. 4th ed. (Locke, J.) London, 1738.

Phil 5252.61.2   Common principles in psychology and physiology. (MacCurdy, J.T.) Cambridge, 1928.

Phil 5252.61   Common principles in psychology and physiology. (MacCurdy, J.T.) N.Y., 1928.

Phil 8876.104   Common sense. (Blanchard, Mme.) N.Y., 1916.
Phil 8582.23.3   Common sense. Philadelphia, 1795.
Phil 8952.20   Common sense about Christian ethics. (Carpenter, Edward.) London, 1961.

Phil 2240.82   Der "common sense" als Princip der Gewissheit. (Kappes, M.) München, 1890.

Phil 8670.13   Common sense and God. (Petty, Orville A.) New Haven, 1936.

Phil 5425.41   Common sense and its cultivation. (Hankin, Ernest H.) London, 1926.

Phil 2255.1.63   Common sense and nuclear warfare. (Russell, Bertrand Russell.) London, 1959.

Phil 182.56.2   Common sense and the rudiments of philosophy. 2d ed. (Hooper, Charles.) London, 1920.

Phil 8581.5.7   Common sense applied to religion. (Beecher, C.E.) N.Y., 1857.

Phil 5500.36   Common sense decision-making. (Fulcher, Gordon Scott.) Evanston, Ill., 1965.

Phil 8884.18   Common-sense ethics. (Joad, Cyril E.M.) N.Y., 1921.
Phil 180.82   The common sense from Heraclitus to Pierce. (Foxe, Arthur N.) N.Y., 1962.

Phil 340.5   "Common sense" in ePistemology. Thesis. (Jacoby, P.J.) NOtre Dame, 1942.

Phil 630.19.7   Common sense theology. (Joad, Cyril Edwin.) London, 1922.
Phil 2150.18.40   Commonplace book, 1919-1953. (Moore, George Edward.) London, 1962.

Phil 1870.73   Commonplace book. (Berkeley, G.) London, 1930.
Phil 2115.65   A commonplace book to the Holy Bible. (Locke, J.) London, 1824.

Phil 2115.65.25   A commonplace book to the Holy Bible. 5th London ed. (Locke, J.) N.Y., 18- ?

Phil 1750.166.85.5   Communauté des hommes. 4e éd. (Laloup, Jean.) Tournai, 1957.

Phil 3488.26.5   La communauté humaine et l'univers chez Kant. (Goldmann, L.) Paris, 1948.

Phil 5520.69   Communication. (Britton, Karl.) London, 1939.
Phil 5520.578   La communication. 1.éd. (Lévy-Valensi, Eliane Amado.) Paris, 1967.

Phil 5400.170   The communication of emotional meaning. (Davitz, Joel Robert.) N.Y., 1964.

Phil 8633.1.35   The communion of saints. (Dodd, Charles H.) Cambridge, 1936.

Phil 8510.9   Pamphlet vol. Communism and religion. Serbocroatian and Slovenian. 4 pam.

Phil 310.536   Communisme et science. (Simard, É.) Québec, 1963.
Phil 8980.1   Pamphlet vol. "Communist ethics". 4 pam.
Phil 8980.03   Pamphlet vol. "Communist ethics". 6 pam.
Phil 8980.02   Pamphlet vol. "Communist ethics". 4 pam.
Phil 8980.126.10   Pamphlet vol. "Communist ethics". 8 pam.
Phil 8980.01   Pamphlet box. Communist ethics.
Phil 8980.07   Pamphlet vol. "Communist ethics". Russian. 4 pam.
Phil 8980.05   Pamphlet vol. "Communist ethics". Russian. 6 pam.
Phil 8980.04   Pamphlet vol. "Communist ethics". Russian. 6 pam.
Phil 8980.06   Pamphlet vol. "Communist ethics". Russian. 3 pam.
Phil 8980.610F   Communist ethics and Chinese tradition. (Nivison, A. S.) Cambridge, Mass., 1954.

Phil 5780.15.10   Communist psychological warfare. (United States. Congress. House.) Washington, 1958.

Phil 2880.8.70   The communists and peace, with a reply to Claude Lefort. (Sartre, Jean Paul.) N.Y., 1968.

Phil 6953.20   Community and schizophrenia. (Dunham, Henry Warren.) Detroit, 1965.

Phil 6327.30   Community as doctor. (Rapoport, Robert N.) London, 1960.
Phil 6140.20   Community dynamics and mental health. (Klein, Donald Charles.) N.Y., 1968.

Phil 6140.25   Community life for the mentally ill; an alternative to institutional care. Chicago, 1969.

Phil 6140.6   Community mental health; an international perspective. (Research Seminar on the Evaluation of Community Mental Health Programs.) San Francisco, 1968.

Phil 12.75   Community mental health journal. Lexington, Mass. 1,1965+ 5v.

Phil 585.184   The community of communities. (Mukerjee, Radhakamal.) Bombay, 1966.

Phil 9450.22   Community of the free. (Simon, Yves.) N.Y., 1947.
Phil 5205.32   A community's adventure. (Behavior Research Fund, Chicago.) Chicago, 1931? 5 pam.

Phil 5066.11.30   Commutative Boolean functions. (Quine, Willard van Orman.) Santa Monica, 1949.

Phil 5592.95   Como informar sobre la personalidad propria. (Palmés, F.M.) Barcelona, 1958.

Phil 165.235   Comoth, R. Philosophes du dix neuvième siècle. Bruxelles, 1960.

Phil 4080.3.275   Comoth, René. Introduction à la philosophie politique de Benedetto Croce. Liège, 1955.

Phil 4210.81.15   La compagnia di Gesu e la recente condanna di A. Rosmini. (Nardi, P. de.) Intra, 1888. 5 pam.

Phil 1750.103   Compagnin, Jean. La philosophie scolastique au XXe siècle. Critique néo-scotiste du Thomisme. Paris, 1916.

Phil 2523.31.2   Compagnoni, G. Saggio di un trattato di morale. Milano, 1819.

Phil 3925.16.110   A companion to Wittgenstein's Tractatus. (Black, Max.) Ithaca, 1964.

Phil 7069.27.25   Companions still. (Speer, W.H.) London, 1927?
Phil 8705.8   A comparative estimate of the mineral and mosaical geology. (Penn, G.) London, 1822.

Phil 6990.62   Comparative miracles. (Smith, Robert D.) St. Louis, 1965.
Phil 812.9.5   Comparative philosophy. (Masson-Oursel, Paul.) N.Y., 1926.

Phil 6027.1   Comparative physiognomy. (Redfield, J.W.) N.Y., 1852.

Phil 5812.2 Comparative physiology and psychology. (Clevenger, S.V.) Chicago, 1885.

Phil 5821.4.5 Comparative physiology of the brain and comparative psychology. (Loeb, J.) N.Y., 1900.

NEDL Phil 5811.1 Comparative psychology. (Bascomb, J.) N.Y., 1878.
Phil 5832.13.15 Comparative psychology. (Warden, C.J.) N.Y., 1935-40. 3v.

Phil 5812.7A Comparative psychology. N.Y., 1934.
Phil 5809.00.-.99 Pamphlet box. Comparative psychology. Chronological file.
Phil 5808.00.-.99 Pamphlet box. Comparative psychology. Chronological file.
Phil 5812.7.10 Comparative psychology. 3rd ed. N.Y., 1951.
Phil 9035.5 Comparative psychology and universal analogy. Vegetable portraits of character. (Lazarus, M.E.) N.Y., 1851.

Phil 12.5 Comparative psychology monographs. Baltimore. 1-21,1922-1951 10v.

Phil 5832.15A Comparative psychology of mental development. (Werner, Heinz.) N.Y., 1940.
Phil 5832.15.5 Comparative psychology of mental development. (Werner, Heinz.) N.Y., 1948.
Phil 5832.15.10 Comparative psychology of mental development. (Werner, Heinz.) N.Y., 1957.
Phil 5832.15.12 Comparative psychology of mental development. (Werner, Heinz.) N.Y., 1966.

Phil 5821.12 A comparative study of certain incentives in the learning of the white rat. Diss. (Ligon, Ernest M.) Baltimore, 1929.

Htn Phil 7060.96* The comparative study of ghost stories. n.p., n.d.
Phil 2270.150 A comparative study of St. Thomas Aquinas and Herbert Spencer. Diss. (Shepperson, J.) Pittsburgh, 1923.

Phil 5810.2 A comparative study of the play activities of adult savages and civilized children. (Appleton, L.E.) Chicago, 1910.

Phil 6127.7 Comparative study of the sensory areas. Human cortex. (Ramón y Cajal, S.) n.p., 1899?

Phil 5816.1.2 A comparative view...man...animal world. (Gregory, J.) London, 1765.
Phil 5816.1 A comparative view...man...animal world. (Gregory, J.) London, 1766.

Phil 8951.9 Comparative view of Christianity. (Brown, William L.) Edinburgh, 1826. 2v.

Phil 8587.10.5 Comparativism. (Hennell, S.S.) London, 1869.
Phil 1870.109A A comparison of Kant's idealism with that of Berkeley. (Joseph, H.W.B.) London, 1929.

Phil 5254.5 A comparison of reactions to personality and achievement test items. Diss. (Osborn, John K.) Ann Arbor, 1936.

Phil 1955.6.109 A comparison of the philosophies of F.C.S. Schiller and John Dewey. Thesis. (White, Stephen, S.) Chicago, 1940.

Phil 2050.109 Compayré, Gabriel. La philosophie de David Hume. Paris, 1873.

Phil 8877.18.10 Compayré, J.G. Cours de morale theorique et pratique. 19th ed. Paris, n.d.
Phil 8877.18 Compayré, J.G. Éléments d'instruction morale et civique. Paris, 1882.
Phil 8877.18.2 Compayré, J.G. Lectures morales et civiques. Paris, 1883.
Phil 8411.5.5 Compendio de estética traducido del aleman. (Krause, K.C.F.) Sevilla, 1874.

Phil 270.95 Compendio de la fortuna. (Cordoba, Martín de.) Madrid, 1958.

Phil 5240.39 Compendio de psicología. (Agramonte y Richardo, R.) Habana, 1954.
Phil 5251.24 Compendio de psicologia contemporanea. (Liqueno, Jose M.) Córdoba, 1919.
Phil 2070.112 Compendio dei principii di psicologia. (Tarozzi, G.) Milano, 1911.
Phil 4210.35 Compendio di etica e breve storia di essa. (Rosmini-Serbati, Antonio.) Roma, 1907.
Phil 5055.27 Compendio di logica sintetica. (Pavese, Roberto.) Padova, 1914.
Phil 802.12 Compendio di storia della filosofia. (Calcagni, Gaetano.) Arce, 1931. 2v.
Phil 805.6.3 Compendio di storia della filosofia. vol. 1-2, pt.1. (Fiorentino, F.) Firenze, 1921-22. 2v.
Phil 1707.1.25 Compendio di storia della filosofia moderna. (Höffding, H.) Torino, 1923.
Phil 4170.7.30 Compendio e sintesi della propriafilosofia. (Mamiani della Rovere, Terenzio.) Torino, 1876.
Phil 3895.50 Compendium der Logik. (Ulrici, H.) Leipzig, 1860.
Phil 3895.53 Compendium der Logik. 2. Aufl. (Ulrici, H.) Leipzig, 1872.
Phil 5643.14 Compendium der physiologische Optik. (Kaiser, H.) Wiesbaden, 1872.
Phil 5262.28 Compendium der Psychologie und Logik. (Wentzke, J.A.) Leipzig, 1868.
Phil 1535.37 Compendium dialecticae, critical et ontologial. (Marxuach, F.) Barcinone, 1926.
Htn Phil 6045.46* Le compendium et brief enseignement de physiognomie et chiromancie. (Cocles, B.) Paris, 1546.
Phil 184.10 Compendium logicae et metaphysicae. (Jouin, R.P.L.) N.Y., 1884.
Phil 197.41 Compendium metaphysicae. (Wallerius, N.) Stockholmiae, 1755.
Phil 5062.24 A compendium of logic. 2nd ed. (Wesley, John.) London, 1756.
Phil 5050.5.3 Compendum einer allgemeinen Logik. (Kiesewetter, J.G.C.C.) Berlin, 1796.
Phil 6950.14 Comperative psycholinguistic analysis of two psychotherapeutic interviews. (American Psychiatric Association.) N.Y., 1961.
Phil 9340.8 Compete (Angell, Frances.) Philadelphia, 1935.
Phil 175.45 Il compito della fenomenologia. (Archivio di Filosofia.) Padova, 1957.
Phil 4170.10.30 Il compito della filosofia e altri saggi inediti ed editi.- 1. ed. (Martinetti, P.) Torino, 1951.
Phil 165.19 Il compito della Metafisica. (Archivio di Filosofia.) Milano, 1952.
Phil 5257.39.2 Complacency; the foundation of human behavior. (Raup, R.B.) N.Y., 1925.
Htn Phil 9346.12* The compleat gentleman. (Gailhard, J.) Savoy, 1678.
Htn Phil 2225.4.30* The compleat gentleman. (Peacham, Henry.) London, 1622.
Phil 9355.2.5 The compleat gentleman. (Peachman, Henry.) London, 1906.
Phil 7060.136 The compleat wizzard. London, 1770.
Phil 3808.43 Complete essays. v.1-7. (Schopenhauer, Arthur.) N.Y., 1942.
Phil 9355.2.7 The complete gentleman. (Peacham, Henry.) N.Y., 1962.
Phil 6677.17 Complete illustrated course of twenty lessons in magnetic healing. (Harraden, L.A.) n.p., 1899.
Phil 6051.7 The complete palmist. (Oxenford, I.) Chicago, 1902.
Phil 5066.17 Complete sets of logical functions. Thesis. (Wernick, William.) N.Y., 1942.

Phil 5066.90 Complete theories. (Robinson, A.) Amsterdam, 1956.
Phil 3640.15.5 Complete works. (Nietzsche, Friedrich.) N.Y., 1964. 18v.
Phil 3640.15 Complete works. v.1,3,7,9-10,13,18. (Nietzsche, Friedrich.) Edinburgh, 1910-13. 7v.
NEDL Phil 3640.15 Complete works. v.2,4-6,8,11,14-15,17. (Nietzsche, Friedrich.) Edinburgh, 1910-13. 9v.
Phil 3640.15.2 Complete works. v.11,16. (Nietzsche, Friedrich.) London, 1913. 2v.
Phil 3640.15.3 Complete works. 3. ed. v.11. (Nietzsche, Friedrich.) N.Y., 1914.
Phil 6319.1.181.2 Complex, archetype. (Jacobi, Jolan.) N.Y., 1959.
Phil 6319.1.181.3 Complex, archtype. (Jacobi, Jolan.) London, 1959.
Phil 12.9 Complex; the magazine of psychoanalysis. N.Y. 2-8,1950-1952
Phil 5258.194 Complex human behavior. (Staats, A.W.) N.Y., 1964.
Phil 335.6 Le complexe significabile. (Elie, H.) Paris, 1936.
Phil 335.6.2 Le complexe significabile. Thèse. (Elie, H.) Paris, 1936.
Phil 9450.30 The complexity of legal and ethical experience. 1. ed. (Northrop Filmer, Stuart C.) Boston, 1959.
Phil 5238.188.10 Le comportement, symposium de l'association de psychologie...(Rome, 1967). (Association de Psychologie Scientifique de Langue Française.) Paris, 1968.
Phil 5262.66 Le comportement humain. (Witvrouw, Marcel.) Bruxelles, 1966.
Phil 5812.9 Le comportement social chez les animaux. (Chauvin, R.) Paris, 1961.
Phil 5274.18 Les composantes de l'intelligence d'après les recherches factorielles. (Oléron, Pierre.) Paris, 1957.
Phil 8644.4 The composition of matter and the evolution of the mind. (Taylor, D.) London, 1912.
Htn Phil 5245.7* The composition of mind. (Fiske, J.) N.Y., 1872. 3 pam.
Phil 3484.21 Composto, R. La quarta critica kantiana. Palermo, 1954.
Phil 6321.51.15 Comprendre Jacques Lacan. (Fages, Jean Baptiste.) Toulouse, 1971.
Phil 585.220 Comprendre l'homme. (Jolif, Jean Y.) Paris, 1967-
Phil 9065.2 Het compromis als zedelijk vraagstuk. Academie proefachaft. (Sikken, William.) Assen, 193-.
Phil 70.3.4 Compte rendu des séances et texte des mémoires. (International Congress of Psychology, 4th, Paris, 1900.) Paris. 1901
Phil 6672.5 Comptes rendue. (Congrès Internationale de L'Hypnotisme.) Paris, 1889.
Phil 5593.65 Comptes rendus. (International Congress of Rorschach and Projective Methods.) Paris, 1967-68. 4v.
Phil 177.99 Compton, A.H. Human meaning of science. Chapel Hill, 1940.
Phil 5752.10 Compton, Arthur H. The freedom of man. New Haven, 1935.
Phil 2070.142 Compton, C.H. William James. N.Y., 1957.
Phil 6968.17 Compulsion and doubt. (Stekel, Wilhelm.) N.Y., 1949.
Phil 5780.18 The compulsion to confess. (Reik, Theodor.) N.Y., 1959.
Phil 5274.6 The computer simulation of behavior. (Apter, Michael John.) London, 1970.
Phil 5590.39 Computer simulation of personality. (Tomkins, Silvan S.) N.Y., 1963.
Phil 7069.30.5 Comrades on the homeward way. (Dallas, Helen A.) Lonodon, 1930.
Phil 7069.18.70 Comstock, William C. Thought for help from those who know men's need. Boston, 1918.
Phil 7069.14.20 Comstock, William C. Will higher of God and free will of life. Boston, 1914.
Phil 2490.73 Comte, Aguste. Lettres d'Auguste Comte à M. Valat. Paris, 1870.
Phil 2490.53.15 Comte, Auguste. Abhandlung über den Geist des Positivismus. Leipzig, 1915.
Phil 2490.54.15 Comte, Auguste. Allmän öfversikt af positivismen. Stockholm, 1896.
Phil 2490.57 Comte, Auguste. Appel aux conservateurs. Paris, 1855.
Phil 2490.65 Comte, Auguste. Auguste Comte méconnu. Extraits de son oeuvre finale (1851-1857). Paris, 1898.
X Cg Phil 2490.56 Comte, Auguste. Catechism of positive religion. London, 1858.
Phil 2490.55 Comte, Auguste. Catèchisme positiviste. Paris, 1852.
Phil 2490.55.2 Comte, Auguste. Catèchisme positiviste. Paris, 1874.
Phil 2490.71 Comte, Auguste. Correspondance inédite. Paris, 1903-04. 4v.
Htn Phil 2490.30* Comte, Auguste. Cours de philosophie positive. Paris, 1830-42. 6v.
Phil 2490.31 Comte, Auguste. Cours de philosophie positive. Paris, 1869. 6v.
Phil 2490.31.5 Comte, Auguste. Cours de philosophie positive. 8. éd. Paris, 1946.
Htn Phil 2490.51* Comte, Auguste. Discours sur l'ensemble du positivisme. Paris, 1848.
Phil 2490.53A Comte, Auguste. Discours sur l'esprit positif. Paris, 1844.
Phil 2490.155 Comte, Auguste. Early essays on social philosophy. London, 1911.
Phil 2490.59 Comte, Auguste. Écrits de jeunesse, 1816-1828. Suivis du Mémoire sur la cosmogonie de Laplace, 1835. Paris, 1970.
Phil 2490.54.20 Comte, Auguste. Framställning öfver den positive anden. Stockholm 1875.
X Cg Phil 2490.51.15 Comte, Auguste. A general view of positivism. N.Y., 1957.
Phil 2490.51.7 Comte, Auguste. A general view of positivism. 2d ed. London, 1880.
Phil 2490.32 Comte, Auguste. L'islamisme au point de vue social. Paris, 1911.
Phil 2490.78 Comte, Auguste. Lettres à des positivistes anglais. London 1889. 2v.
Phil 2490.78.10 Comte, Auguste. Lettres à Richard Congreve. London, 1889.
Phil 2490.72 Comte, Auguste. Lettres d'Auguste Comte à divers. v.1-2. Paris, 1902-05. 3v.
Phil 2490.74 Comte, Auguste. Lettres d'Auguste Comte à J.S. Mill. Paris, 1877.
Phil 2490.76.15 Comte, Auguste. Lettres inédites à C. de Blignières. Paris, 1932.
Phil 2490.52 Comte, Auguste. La méthode positive en seize leçons. Paris, 1917.
Phil 2490.70 Comte, Auguste. Nouvelles lettres inédites. Paris, 1939.
Phil 2490.29 Comte, Auguste. Oeuvres choisis. Paris, 1943.
Phil 2490.12 Comte, Auguste. Opuscules de philosophie sociale. Paris, 1883.
Phil 2490.63 Comte, Auguste. Pensées et préceptes. Paris, 1924.
Phil 2490.41.5 Comte, Auguste. La philosophie positive. Paris, 1880-81. 2v.
Phil 2490.41.4 Comte, Auguste. Die positive Philosophie. v.1-2. Heidelberg, 1884.

Phil 2490.41.1.5 Comte, Auguste. The positive philosophy. N.Y., 1853. 2v.

Phil 2490.41.1 Comte, Auguste. The positive philosophy. N.Y., 1855.
Phil 2490.41.2.4A Comte, Auguste. The positive philosophy. 2. ed. London, 1875. 2v.

Phil 2490.41.3 Comte, Auguste. The postive philosophy. London, 1896. 3v.

Phil 2490.41.12A Comte, Auguste. Principes de philosophie positive. Paris, 1868.

Phil 2490.41.9 Comte, Auguste. Principios de filosofía positiva. Santiago, 1875.

Phil 2490.27 Comte, Auguste. Le prolétariat dans la societe moderne. Paris, 1946.

Phil 2490.53.20 Comte, Auguste. Rede über den Geist des Positivismus. Hamburg, 1956.

Phil 2490.58.5 Comte, Auguste. Religión universal, el amor por principio. Santiago de Chile, 1944.

Phil 2490.58 Comte, Auguste. La religión universal. Santiago de Chile, 1938.

Phil 2490.76 Comte, Auguste. Six lettres inédites à Romeo Pouzin. Paris, 1914.

Phil 2490.60 Comte, Auguste. Synthèse subjective. Paris, 1856.
Phil 2490.77 Comte, Auguste. Testament. Paris, 1884.
Phil 2490.77.2 Comte, Auguste. Testament d'Auguste Comte, avec les documents qui s'y rapportent. Paris, 1896.

Phil 2490.06 Pamphlet box. Comte, Auguste. Minor writings.
Phil 197.2 Comte, Mill, and Spencer, an outline of philosophy. (Watson, J.) Glasgow, 1895.

Phil 2490.129 Comte, the founder of sociology. (Marvin, F.S.) London, 1936.

Phil 2490.90 Comte and Mill. (Whittaker, T.) London, 1908.
Phil 8586.12 Le Comte de Valmont ou les égaremens de la raison. (Gérard, Philippe Louis.) Paris, 1775.

Phil 2490.107 Comte's moralphilosophische Methode. (Spielfogel, R.) Zürich, 1909.

Phil 2490.81 Comte's philosophy of the sciences. (Lewes, G.H.) London, 1853.

Phil 2490.81.5 Comte's philosophy of the sciences. (Lewes, G.H.) London, 1871.

Phil 4210.194 La comunicazione delle persone nella filosofia. (Beschin, G.) Milano, 1964.

Phil 8092.28 Comunicazione e struttura nell'analisi di alcumi linguaggi artistici. (Dorfles, Gillo.) Milano, 1970.

Phil 3246.304 La comunitá come fondamento. (Masullo, Aldo.) Napoli, 1965.

Phil 3495.20.2 La comunità estetica in Kant. 2. ed. (Negri, Antimo.) Bari, 1968.

Phil 2840.91 Concato, E. Introduzione alla filosofia del Renouvier. Marostica Vicenza, 1921.

Phil 6321.10 Concentric method in the diagnosis of psychoneurotics. (Laignel-Lavastine, Maxime.) London, 1931.

Phil 5255.34 Le concept, le jugement et l'attention. (Prengowski, P.) Paris, 1930.

Phil 2225.11.10 Concept and quality; a world hypothesis. (Pepper, Stephen Coburn.) La Salle, 1967.

Phil 4580.66.10 Le concept d'analogie. (Høffding, Harald.) Paris, 1931.
Phil 5080.8 Le concept de concept formel. (Combès, Michel.) Toulouse, 1969.

Phil 3450.19.107A Le concept de inonde chez Heidegger. (Biemel, W.) Louvain, 1950.

Phil 8418.17.5 Le concept du beau; essaie d'une théorie. (Reimers, N.A.) Paris, 1930.

Phil 5360.16.1 Concept learning. (Hunt, Earl Busby.) N.Y., 1966.
Phil 8656.24 Concept of a limited God. (Baker, Rannie B.) Washington, 1934.

Phil 1845.11.5 The concept of a person. (Ayer, Alfred Jules.) N.Y., 1963.

Phil 8735.11 The concept of control. (Elkus, S.A.) N.Y., 1907.
Phil 8664.6 The concept of deity. (James, E.O.) London, 1950.
Phil 5238.125 The concept of development. (Harris, Dale B.) Minneapolis, 1957.

Phil 5585.46 The concept of duration as key to the logical forms of reason. Thesis. (Weber, Christian.) Lincoln, 1925.

Phil 1750.864 The concept of expression. (Tormey, Alan.) Princeton, N.J., 1971.

Phil 5590.442 The concept of identity. (Levita, David Joël de.) Paris, 1965.

Phil 5467.4 The concept of imitation. Part of thesis. (Lejins, Peter P.) Chicago, 1942.

Phil 9558.23 The concept of ingratitude in renaissance English moral philosophy. These. (Dunn, Ellen Catherine.) Washington, D.C., 1946.

Phil 418.16 The concept of intentionality. (Mohanty, Jitendra Nath.) St. Louis, 1971.

Phil 5520.290 The concept of language. (Wilson, Neil.) Toronto, Canada, 1959.

Phil 585.80 The concept of man. (Radhakrishnan, Sarvepalli.) London, 1960.

Phil 585.80.2 The concept of man. (Radhakrishnan, Sarvepalli.) London, 1960.

Phil 930.72 The concept of man in early China. (Munro, Donald J.) Stanford, 1969.

Phil 165.337 The concept of matter. (McMullin, Ethan.) Notre Dame, Indiana, 1963.

Phil 165.337.5 The concept of matter in Greek and medieval philosophy. (McMullin, Ethan.) Notre Dame, 1965.

Phil 960.163 The concept of Maya. (Devanandan, P.D.) London, 1950.
Phil 176.217 The concept of method. (Buchler, J.) N.Y., 1961.
Phil 6127.26 The concept of mind. (Ryle, Gilbert.) London, 1949.
Phil 6127.26.5 The concept of mind. (Ryle, Gilbert.) London, 1963.
Phil 960.225 The concept of mind in Indian philosophy. (Chennahesavan, Sarasvate.) London, 1960.

Phil 8876.121 The concept of morality. (Bowes, Pratima.) London, 1959.
Phil 8882.75 The concept of morality. (Hytten, E.) Stockholm, 1959.
Phil 8893.94 The concept of morals. (Stoce, W.J.) N.Y., 1937.
Phil 5548.30 The concept of motivation. (Peters, R.S.) London, 1958.
Phil 5548.30.2 The concept of motivation. 2. ed. (Peters, R.S.) London, 1967.

Phil 568.2 The concept of order. Seattle, 1968.
Phil 188.28 The concept of philosophy. (Newell, Robert.) London, 1967.

Phil 6962.28 The concept of schizophrenia. (McAuley, W.F.) N.Y., 1954.
Phil 575.288 The concept of self. (Gergen, Kenneth J.) N.Y., 1971.
Phil 400.98 Concept of self in British and American idealism. (Tallon, H.J.) Washington, 1939.

Phil 3504.55 The concept of the categorical imperative. (Williams, T.C.) Oxford, 1968.

Phil 672.158 The concept of time. Photoreproduction. (Heath, L.R.) Chicago, 1936.

Phil 720.80 The concept of truth. (Armour, Leslie.) Assen, 1969.
Phil 2070.156 The concept of truth in the philosophy of William James. (Anderson, Luke.) Rome, 1965.

Phil 735.3 The concept standard. (Nicholson, Anne M.) N.Y., 1910.
Phil 2880.8.235 La conception de la liberté chez Jean-Paul Sartre et chez Maurice Merleau-Ponty. (Gahamanyi, Célestin.) Fribourg? 1967.

Phil 4065.180 La conception de la nature chez Giordano Bruno. (Védrine, Hélène.) Paris, 1967.

Phil 720.16 La conception de la vérité. Thèse. (Lelesz, H.) Paris, 1921.

Phil 186.89.5 La conception inductive de la vie. (Lolli, R.) Paris, 1937.

Phil 960.25 The conception of freedom in Hegel, Bergson and Indian philosophy. (Shastri, Prabhu D.) Calcutta, 1914.

Phil 8672.6 The conception of God. (Royce, J.) Berkeley, 1895.
Phil 8672.6.5 The conception of God. (Royce, J.) N.Y., 1894.
Phil 8672.6.4A The conception of God. (Royce, J.) N.Y., 1898.
Phil 8672.6.6 The conception of God. (Royce, J.) N.Y., 1902.
Phil 2250.92 The conception of God in the philosophy of Josiah Royce. (Dykhuizen, George.) Chicago, 1936.

Phil 8633.1.4 The conception of immortality. (Royce, J.) Boston, 1900.
Phil 2225.5.110 The conception of law. (Haas, W.P.) Fribourg, 1964.
Phil 8890.26 Conception of moral goodness. (Perry, R.B.) n.p., 1907.
Phil 5590.540 Conception of personality; theories and research. (Levy, Leon Harris.) N.Y., 1970.

Phil 410.5 Conception of the infinite. (Fullerton, G.S.) Philadelphia, 1887.

Phil 5374.12 Conceptions and misconceptions of conciousness. (Perry, R.B.) N.Y., 1904.

Phil 338.17.9 Les conceptions de la vie. (Höffding, H.) Paris, 1928.
Phil 1135.156 Les conceptions de l'enthousiasme chez les philosophes presocratiques. (Delatte, A.) Paris, 1934.

Phil 8406.25 Conceptos estéticos mitos guaraníes. (Fariña Nuñez, Eloy.) Buenos Aires, 1926.

Phil 5360.22 Concepts and the structure of memory. (Symposium on Cognition, 2d, Pittsburgh, 1966.) N.Y., 1967.

NEDL Phil 299.4.2 Concepts and theories of modern physics. (Stallo, J.B.) N.Y., 1882.

Phil 4325.2 Concepts e imágenes en pensadores. (Yamuni, Tabush.) México, 1951.

Phil 8408.3 The concepts of aesthetics. (Hawkins, Denis John B.) London, 1962.

Phil 5374.18 The concepts of consciousness. (Halt, E.B.) London, 1914.
Phil 165.180 Concepts of continuity. v.4. (Aristotelian Society for the Systematic Study of Philosophy.) London, 1947.

Phil 8900.8 The concepts of ethics. (Zink, Sidney.) N.Y., 1962.
Phil 6953.19 Concepts of insanity in the United States, 1789-1865. (Dain, Norman.) New Brunswick, N.J., 1964.

Phil 510.130 Concepts of monism. (Worsley, A.) London, 1907.
Phil 5590.434 The concepts of personality. (Wepman, J.M.) London, 1964.
Phil 189.6.5 Concepts of philosophy. (Ormond, A.T.) N.Y., 1906.
Phil 6317.22.80 The concepts of self acceptance and self respect in Karen Horney's theory of neurosis. (Murray, M.) n.p., n.d.

Phil 6315.2.255 The concepts of Sigmund Freud. (Stoodley, Bartlett.) Glencoe, 1959.

Phil 5790.35.5 Conceptual models of human behavior in disaster. (Stoddard, Ellwyn R.) El Paso, 1968.

Phil 5080.6 Conceptual thinking. (Koerner, S.) Cambridge, Eng., 1955.
Phil 6957.20 Conceptual thinking in schizophrenia. (Hanfmann, E.) N.Y., 1942.

Phil 8413.19 Concerning beauty. (Mather, F.J.) Princeton, 1935.
Phil 9075.17 Concerning conscience. (Jeffs, Harry.) London, 1912.
Phil 5243.15.20 Concerning fluctuating and inaudible sounds. (Dunlap, K.) n.p., 1908-1916. 15 pam.

Phil 176.195 Concerning human understanding. (Banerjee, N.V.) London, 1958.

Phil 349.33 Concerning knowledge. (Sanford, H.W.) N.Y., 1935. 2v.

Phil 525.88 Concerning mysticism. Guilford, 1938.
Phil 8595.32.7 Concerning progressive revelation. (Philips, Vivian.) London, 1936.

Phil 8595.32.5 Concerning progressive revelation. (Philips, Vivian.) London, 1936.

Phil 7068.71.8 Concerning spiritualism. (Massey, G.) London, 1871.
Htn Phil 3110.40* Concerning the election of grace. (Böhme, J.) London, 1655.

Phil 525.7.20 Concerning the inner life, with The house of the soul. (Underhill, Evelyn.) London, 1947.

Htn Phil 3110.35* Concerning the three principles of divine essence. (Böhme, J.) London, 1648.

Phil 3110.35.5 Concerning the three principles of divine essence. (Böhme, J.) London, 1910.

Phil 4120.4.125 Il concetto moderno della scienza e il problema universitario. (Gentile, Giovanni.) Roma, 1921.

Phil 672.126 Il concetto del tempo. (Levi, Adolfo.) Milano, 1919.
Phil 180.41 Concetto della filosofia. (Ferro, A.A.) Savona, 1902.
Phil 5771.3 Il concetto della indeterminazione. (Vivanti, L.) Firenze, 1938.

Phil 525.268 Un concetto dell'aldilà. (Bieri, Edgard L.) Roma, 1970.
Phil 665.57 Il concetto dell'anima nella psicologia contemporanea. (Sarlo, Francesco de.) Firenze, 1900.

Phil 1955.6.133 Il concetto dell'arte in Dewey e in Berensoni. 1. ed. (Pesce, Domenico.) Firenze, 1956.

Phil 4260.157 Il concetto di poesia in Giambattista Vico. (Bianca, Giovanni A.) Messina, 1967.

Phil 4260.128 Il concetto filosofico di diritto in Giambattista Vico. (Cantone, Carlo.) Mazara, 1952.

Phil 4080.3.55 Il concetto moderno della storia. (Croce, Benedetto.) Bari, 1947.

Phil 4080.3.150 Il concetto puro della filosofia dello spirito e la storia del secolo XIX di B. Croce. (Carnevale, Luigi.) Varese, 1934.

Phil 2250.86 Il concetto sintetico del reale e la sua evoluzione nel pensiero di Josiah Royce. (Raccuglia, Pietro.) Palermo, 1920.

Phil 1135.177 La concezione dell'essere nella filosofia. (Napoli, G.) Milano, 1953.

Phil 4120.4.115 La concezione estetico-filosofica di Giovanni Gentile. (Puglisi, Filippo.) Catania, 1955.

Phil 1750.115.150 Conci, Domenico. La conclusione della filosofia categoriale. Roma, 1967.

Phil 8876.23 Conciliation du véritable déterminisme mécanique. (Boussinesq, J.) Paris, 1878.

Phil 8583.5 Conciliation rationnelle du droit et du devoir. (Disdier, H.) Genève, 1859. 2v.

Author and Title Listing

Phil 8400.2 — Concinnitas. Basel, 1944.

Htn Phil 2050.78* — Concise and genuine account of dispute between Mr. Hume and Mr. Rousseau. (Hume, David.) London, 1766.

Phil 107.5 — A concise dictionary of existentialism. (Winn, R.B.) N.Y., 1960.

Phil 105.5 — The concise encyclopaedia of Western philosophy and philosophers. (Urmson, J.O.) London, 1960.

Phil 5028.2.10 — Concise history of logic. (Scholz, Heinrch.) N.Y., 1961.

Htn Phil 805.1.3* — A concise history of philosophy. (Formey, J.H.S.) London, 1766.

Phil 805.1.5 — A concise history of philosophy and philosophers. (Formey, J.H.S.) Glasgow, 1767.

Htn Phil 5041.31* — A concise system of logics. (Best, William.) N.Y., 1796.

Htn Phil 8890.24* — Conclusion: an essay. (Pater, W.) N.Y., 1898.

Phil 1750.115.150 — La conclusione della filosofia categoriale. (Conci, Domenico.) Roma, 1967.

Phil 4080.18 — La conclusione della filosofia del conoscere. (Calogero, Guido.) Firenze, 1938.

Htn Phil 4195.30* — Conclusiones nongentae. (Pico della Mirandola, Giovanni.) n.p., 1532.

Phil 4365.2.33A — Concord and liberty. 1st. ed. (Ortega y Gasset, José.) N.Y., 1946.

Phil 1828.2.5 — Concord harvest:publications of the Concord school of philosophy and literature. (Cameron, Kenneth Walter.) Hartford, 1970.

Phil 177.17 — Concord lecturer on philosophy. Cambridge, 1883.

Phil 1822.3 — The Concord school of philosophy. (Warren, Austin.) n.p., 1929.

Htn Phil 3801.764* — Concordancia das sciencas naturaes. (Saldanha, J.C. de S. de B.D. de.) Vienna, 1845.

Phil 7054.43.15 — Concordancia del espiritismo con la ciencia. v.1-2. (Senillosa, Felipe.) Buenos Aires, 1891.

Phil 12.125 — Concurrence; a review for the encounter of commitments. Basle. 1,1969+

Phil 5520.452 — Condemned to meaning. 1. ed. (Smith, Huston.) N.Y., 1965.

Phil 5850.332F — Condensed outline of "The laws of life". (Sasha, A.W.) Oakland, Cal., 1932.

Phil 4195.90 — Condier, Pierre Marie. Jean Pic de la Mirandole. Paris, 1957.

Phil 2493.45.4 — Condillac, Étienne Bonnot. Abhandlung über die Empfindungen. Berlin, 1870.

Phil 2493.45.30 — Condillac, Étienne Bonnot. Condillac's treatise on the sensations. Los Angeles, 1930.

Phil 2493.40.10 — Condillac, Étienne Bonnot. Essai sur l'origine des connaissances humaines. Paris, 1798.

Phil 2493.40 — Condillac, Étienne Bonnot. Essai sur l'origine des connaissances humaines. v.1-2. Amsterdam, 1788.

Phil 2493.40.3 — Condillac, Étienne Bonnot. Essai sur l'origine des connaissances humnaines. Paris, 1924.

Phil 2493.30.6 — Condillac, Étienne Bonnot. The logic of Condillac. Philadelphia, 1809.

Phil 2493.30.20 — Condillac, Étienne Bonnot. La lógica, o Los primeros elementos del arte de pensar. Caracas, 1959.

Phil 2493.30 — Condillac, Étienne Bonnot. La lógica. Caracas, 1812.

Phil 2493.30.10 — Condillac, Étienne Bonnot. La logique. Paris, 1789.

Phil 2493.30.2 — Condillac, Étienne Bonnot. Logique. Paris, 1821.

Phil 2493.30.15 — Condillac, Étienne Bonnot. Logique de Condillac à l'usage des élèves des prytanées. v.1-2. Paris, 1802. 2v.

Phil 2493.10 — Condillac, Étienne Bonnot. Oeuvres. Paris, 1798. 23v.

Phil 2493.21 — Condillac, Étienne Bonnot. Oeuvres philosophiques. Paris, 1795. 2v.

Phil 2493.22 — Condillac, Étienne Bonnot. Oeuvres philosophiques. Paris, 1947-51. 3v.

Phil 2493.30.3 — Condillac, Étienne Bonnot. Segunda edición de la Lógica puesta. Madrid, 1800.

Phil 2493.35 — Condillac, Étienne Bonnot. Traité des animaux. Amsterdam, 1755.

Phil 2493.35.2 — Condillac, Étienne Bonnot. Traité des animaux. Amsterdam, 1766.

Phil 2493.45.3 — Condillac, Étienne Bonnot. Traité des sensations. Premiére partie. Photoreproduction. Paris, 1886.

Htn Phil 2493.45* — Condillac, Étienne Bonnot. Traité des sensations. v.1-2. Londres, 1754.

Phil 2493.45.2 — Condillac, Étienne Bonnot. Traité des sensations. v.1-2. Londres, 1788.

Phil 2493.51 — Condillac, Étienne Bonnot. Traité des sistêmes. Amsterdam, 1771.

Phil 2493.50 — Condillac, Étienne Bonnot. Traité des sistêmes. La Haye, 1749.

Phil 2493.45.20 — Condillac, Étienne Bonnot. Trattato delle sensazioni. Bologna, 1927.

Phil 2493.83 — Condillac; sa vie, sa philosophie, son influence. (Baguenault de Puchesse, Gustave.) Paris, 1910.

Phil 2493.89 — Condillac. (Lenoir, Raymond.) Paris, 1924.

Phil 2493.84 — Condillac. (Réthoré, François.) Paris, 1864.

Phil 2493.81 — Condillac et la psychologie anglaise contemporaine. (Dewaule, L.) Paris, 1892.

Phil 2493.45.30 — Condillac's treatise on the sensations. (Condillac, Étienne Bonnot.) Los Angeles, 1930.

Phil 585.158 — Conditio humana. (Plessner, H.) Pfullingen, 1964.

Phil 8599.42 — La condition de la raison philosophique. (Thévenaz, Pierre.) Neuchâtel, 1960.

Phil 2750.17.30 — Condition de l'homme. (Mieville, Henri L.) Genève, 1959.

Phil 8592.113 — The condition of the Christian philosopher. (Mehl, R.) London, 1963.

Phil 5625.75.3 — Conditioned reflexes. (Pavlov, Ivan P.) London, 1928.

Phil 5625.75A — Conditioned reflexes. (Pavlov, Ivan P.) Oxford, 1927.

Phil 5625.126 — Conditioned reinforcement. Homewood, Ill., 1969.

Phil 5625.82 — Conditioned responses in children. Thesis. (Razran, G.H.S.) N.Y., 1933.

Phil 5625.104 — Conditioning and psychiatry. (Ban, Thomas A.) Chicago, 1964.

Phil 6980.780.5 — The conditioning therapies. (Wolpe, Joseph.) N.Y., 1964.

Phil 5625.101 — Le conditionnement. (Le Ny, Jean François.) Paris, 1961.

Phil 5625.95 — Le conditionnement et l'apprentissage. (Association de Psychologie Scientifique de Langue Française.) Strasbourg, 1956.

Phil 5243.37 — Conditions and consequences of human variability. (Dodge, Raymond.) New Haven, 1931.

Phil 1750.600 — Les conditions de la liberté. (Naville, Pierre.) Paris, 1947.

Phil 9245.62 — Les conditions du bonheur. (Rencontres Internationales, Genève, 1961.) Neuchâtel, 1961.

Phil 9245.20 — Les conditions du bonheur. (Souriau, Paul.) Paris, 1908.

Phil 270.137 — Les conditions d'une perception de la causalité. (Grabbé, Geneviéve.) Paris, 1967.

Phil 356.5.3 — Conditions for description. (Zinkernagel, Peter.) London, 1962.

Phil 8581.68.20 — Les conditions modernes. (Broglie, Paul.) Paris, 1910.

Phil 5643.77 — Les conditions objectives de la perception visuelle. Thèse. (Déjean, Renée.) Paris, 1926. 2 pam.

Phil 349.40 — The conditions of knowing. (Sinclair, W.A.) London, 1951.

Phil 6328.2.4A — Conditions of nervous anxiety. (Stekel, Wilhelm.) London, 1923.

Phil 175.62 — The conditions of philosophy. 1st ed. (Adler, Mortimer Jerome.) N.Y., 1965.

Phil 735.225 — Conditions of rational inquiry. (Pole, David.) London, 1961.

Phil 6117.1.5 — Les conditions physiques de la conscience. (Herzen, A.) Genève, 1886.

Phil 5585.255 — Condizioni dell'esperienza e fondazione della psicologia. (Musatti, Cesare L.) Firenze, 1964.

Phil 2494.36 — Condorcet, M.J.A.N. Entwurf einer historischen Darsteillung. Frankfurt a.M., 1963.

Phil 2494.31 — Condorcet, M.J.A.N. Esquisse d'un tableau historique. n.p., 1795.

Phil 2494.30 — Condorcet, M.J.A.N. Esquisse d'un tableau historique. Paris, 1798.

Phil 2494.32 — Condorcet, M.J.A.N. Esquisse d'un tableau historique. 2e éd. Paris, 1866.

Phil 2494.35 — Condorcet, M.J.A.N. Esquisse d'un tableau historique des progrès de l'esprit humain. Paris, 1933.

Phil 2494.37 — Condorcet, M.J.A.N. Esquisse d'un tableau historique des progrès de l'esprit humain. Paris, 1966.

Phil 2494.42 — Condorcet, M.J.A.N. Outlines...historical...progress...human mind. Baltimore, 1802.

NEDL Phil 2494.41 — Condorcet, M.J.A.N. Outlines...historical...progress...human mind. Philadelphia, 1796.

Htn Phil 2494.31.5* — Condorcet, N.J.A.N. Esquisse d'un tableau historique. Paris, 1795.

Phil 2494.82A — Condorcet. (Séverac, J.B.) Paris, n.d.

Phil 2494.80 — Condorcet's "Esquisse d'un tableau historique". (Niedlich, J.K.) Sorai, 1907.

Phil 8881.10 — Conduct as a fine art. (Gilman, N.P.) Boston, 1891.

Phil 177.35.25 — The conduct of life. (Croce, Benedetto.) N.Y., 1924.

Phil 9070.51.5A — The conduct of life. 1st ed. (Mumford, Lewis.) N.Y., 1951.

Phil 2115.50 — The conduct of the understanding. (Locke, J.) Boston, 1825.

Phil 2115.50.10 — The conduct of the understanding. (Locke, J.) Cambridge, 1781.

Phil 2115.51.7 — The conduct of the understanding. (Locke, J.) N.Y., 1966.

Phil 2115.51A — The conduct of the understanding. (Locke, J.) Oxford, 1881.

Phil 2115.50.2 — The conduct of the understanding. v.1-2. (Locke, J.) Boston, 1828.

Phil 2115.50.3 — The conduct of the understanding. v.1-2. (Locke, J.) Boston, 1831.

Phil 2115.51.6 — The conduct of the understanding. 5th ed. (Locke, J.) Oxford, 1901.

Phil 9070.33 — Conduct yourself accordingly. (Banning, M.C.) N.Y., 1944.

Phil 6121.14.5 — The conduction of the nervous impulse. (Lucas, Keith.) London, 1917.

Phil 70.14 — Conference of Psychologists, Hanover, New Hanpshire, 1925. Conference of psychologists called by Laura Spelman Rockefellar Memorial. n.p., 1925. 2v.

Phil 70.14.3 — Conference of Psychologists, Hanover, New Hanpshire. Another, slightly variant report of the Thursday morning session. n.p., 1925.

Phil 70.14 — Conference of psychologists called by Laura Spelman Rockefellar Memorial. (Conference of Psychologists, Hanover, New Hanpshire, 1925.) n.p., 1925. 2v.

Phil 5535.8 — Conference on Acquisition of Skill, New Orleans. Acquisition of skill. N.Y., 1966.

Phil 575.272 — Conference on Comparative Philosophy and Culture. East-West studies on the problem of the self. The Hague, 1968.

Phil 5592.178 — Conference on Contemporary Issues in Thematic Apperceptive Methods. Contemporary issues in thematic apperceptive methods. Springfield, Ill., 1961.

Phil 5465.140 — Conference on creativity as a process. (Boston Institute.) Boston, 1957-58.

Phil 70.12 — Conference on Individual Psychological Differences. Proceedings, Washington, D.C., May 9-10, 1930. Washington, D.C., 1930.

Phil 5545.94 — Conference on Learning, Remembering and Forgetting. Learning, remembering, and forgetting. Palo Alto, 1965-

Phil 5520.415 — Conference on Paralinguistics and Kinesics. Approaches to semiotics. The Hague, 1964.

Phil 70.77 — Conference on Psychological Scaling, Princeton, New Jersey. Psychological scaling: theory and applications. N.Y., 1960.

Phil 5625.122 — Conference on Punishment. Punishment and aversive behavior. N.Y., 1969.

Phil 70.92 — Conference on Science, Philosophy and Religion. Symbols and values; an initial study. N.Y., 1954.

Htn Phil 6021.6* — Conference sur l'expression générale et particuliere des passions. (Le Brun, Charles.) Verone, 1751.

Phil 9513.50 — Conferences ecclesiastiques du Diocese d'Angers. (Angers, France (Diocese).) Angers, 1737.

Phil 176.225 — Conferencias. 1. ed. (Bueno, Miguel.) México, 1959.

Phil 5261.5 — Conferencias filosoficas. (Varona, Enrique José.) Havana, 1888.

Phil 4983.8.6 — Conferencias filosóficas. Ser.1, 3. (Varona, Enrique.) Habana, 1880. 2v.

Phil 8896.6 — Conferencias sobre el fundamento de la moral. (Varona, E.J.) N.Y., 1913.

Phil 4363.6.10 — Confesión filosófica y llamado de superación a la América Hispana. (Molina, E.) Santiago, 1942.

Phil 3552.430 — Confessio philosophi. (Leibniz, G.W.) Paris, 1961.

Phil 3552.52 — Confessio philosophi. (Leibniz, Gottfried Wilhelm.) Paris, 1961.

Phil 3552.431 — Confessio philosophi. Ein Dialog. (Leibniz, G.W.) Frankfurt, 1967.

Phil 2750.11.49A — Confession de foi. (Maritain, Jacques.) N.Y., 1941.

Htn Phil 1850.72* — The confession of faith. (Bacon, Francis.) London, 1641.

Phil 4170.7.33 — Confessioni di un metafisico. (Mamiani della Rovere, Terenzio.) Firenze, 1865. 2v.

Phil 3110.45.10 — Confessions. (Böhme, J.) N.Y., 1954.

Phil 525.105.5 — Confessions d'un mystique contemporain. (Marquette, Jacques de.) Paris, 1965.

Phil 8411.32 — Confessions esthétiques. (Kahnweiller, D.) Paris, 1963.

Phil 7060.92.55   Confessions of a ghost hunter. (O'Donnell, Elliot.) London, 1928.

Phil 7069.36.10   Confessions of a ghost-hunter. (Price, Harry.) London, 1936.

Phil 6688.11   "Confessions of a magnetiser" exposed. (Sunderland, La Roy.) Boston, 1845.

NEDL Phil 7068.82.5   Confessions of a medium. London, 1882.

Phil 7055.341   Confessions of a psychic. (Smith, Susy.) N.Y., 1971.

Phil 3110.45   The confessions of Jacob Böhme. (Böhme, J.) London, 1920.

Phil 575.220   La confidence et la personne humaine. (Chevalier, Charles.) Paris, 1960.

Phil 2515.12   La confidence et la personne humaine. (LeChevalier, Charles.) Aubier, 1960.

Phil 9495.3.2   Confidential talks with young men. (Sperry, L.B.) N.Y., 1892.

Phil 8702.12.5   Les confins de la science et de la foi. (Moreux, T.) Paris, 1925. 2v.

Phil 5500.31   Conflict, decision and dissonance. (Festinger, L.) Stanford, 1964.

Phil 5241.135   Conflict. (Bulyne, D.E.) N.Y., 1960.

Phil 7084.26   Conflict and dream. (Rivers, William Halse Rivers.) London, 1923.

Phil 5545.200   Conflict and mood. (Kendall, Patricia L.) Glencoe, Ill., 1954.

Phil 3850.16.41   The conflict in modern culture and other essays. (Simmel, Georg.) N.Y., 1968.

Phil 8890.5   Conflict in nature and life. (Patterson, J.S.) N.Y., 1883.

Phil 8870.12   Conflict of loyalties. (Institute for Religious Studies, Jewish Theological Seminary of America.) N.Y., 1952.

Phil 8656.14   The conflict of the ages. 5. ed. (Beecher, E.) Boston, 1854.

Phil 8692.13.8   The conflict of truth. 8. ed. (Capron, F.H.) London, 1927.

Phil 8693.4.6   Los conflictos entre la ciencia y la religion. (Draper, J.W.) Madrid, 1876.

Phil 8587.44   Conflicts in religious thought. (Harkness, George E.) N.Y., 1929.

Phil 8886.52   Conflicts of principle. (Lowell, Abbot L.) Cambridge, 1932.

Phil 8610.881.30   The conflicts of the age. N.Y., 1881.

Phil 5627.263   Conflicts of the clergy. (Bowers, M.K.) Edinburgh, 1963.

Phil 186.76.15   Le conflit. 6e ed. (Le Dantec, Félix.) Paris, 1913.

Phil 1750.166.100   Le conflit actuel des humanismes. (Etcheverry, A.) Paris, 1955.

Phil 1750.166.101   Le conflit actuel des humanismes. (Etcheverry, A.) Roma, 1964.

Phil 3480.86.25   Le conflit des facultes en trois sections, 1798. (Kant, Immanuel.) Paris, 1935.

Phil 210.55   Le conflit des interprétations; essais d'herméneutique. (Ricoeur, Paul.) Paris, 1969.

Phil 6321.13   Conflits sociaux et psychoses. (Leconte, M.) Paris, 1938.

Phil 5070.19   Conformisme et révolte. Thèse. (Ahmet, Nureltin.) Paris, 1934.

Htn Phil 8612.23*   Il confortatore. (Tasso, Ercole.) Bergamo, 1595.

Phil 6952.17   La confusion mentale primitive. (Chaslin, Philippe.) Paris, 1895.

Phil 8677.5   A confutation of the reason and philosophy of atheism. (Wise, Thomas.) London, 1706. 2v.

Phil 8610.896.5   Confutazione degli argomenti teologici. (Roselli, G.) Foggia, 1896.

Phil 8657.22   Congar, M.J. Le mystère du temple. 2. éd. Paris, 1963.

Phil 177.64   Conger, G.P. A course in philosophy. N.Y., 1924.

Phil 333.13   Conger, George P. The horizons of thought. Princeton, 1933.

Phil 505.5.1   Conger, George Perrigo. Theories of macrocosms and microcosms in the history of philosophy. N.Y., 1967.

Htn Phil 5545.52*   Congestorium artificiose. (Romberch, J.) Venetijs, 1533.

Phil 7080.52   Congetture su i sogni. (Cassina, U.) Parma, 1783.

Phil 70.55   Congrès. (Association pour l'Étude Scientifique du Symbolisme.) Paris. 6,1957+ 3v.

Phil 70.7   Congrès des société philosophique américaine, anglaises, belge, italienne. (Congrès des Sociétés Philosophiques, 1921.) Paris, 1926.

Phil 720.72   Congrès des Sociétés de Philosophie de Langue Française, 12th, Brussels et Louvain, 1964. La vérité. Louvain, 1964-65. 7v.

Phil 310.728   Congrès des Sociétés de Philosophie de Langue Française, 14th, 1969. La dialectique. 1. éd. Paris, 1969.

Phil 165.338   Congrès des Sociétés de Philosophie de Langue Française, 11th, Montpellier, 1961. Existence et nature. Paris, 1962.

Phil 70.18   Congrès des Sociétés de Philosophie de Langue Française, 4th, Neuchâtel, 1949. La liberté; actes. Neuchâtel. 1949

Phil 70.18.10   Congrès des Sociétés de Philosophie de Langue Française, 5th, Bordeaux, 1950. Les sciences et la sagesse. Paris. 1950

Phil 70.18.15   Congrès des Sociétés de Philosophie de Langue Française, 7th, Grenoblé, 1954. La vie, la pensée. Paris. 1954

Phil 70.7   Congrès des Sociétés Philosophiques, 1921. Congrès des société philosophique américaine, anglaises, belge, italienne. Paris, 1926.

Phil 2515.7   Le congrès Descartes...reflexions. (Cochet, M.A.) Bruges, 1938.

Phil 70.13.10   Congrès International de Philosophie des Science, Paris, 1949. Actes. Paris, 1951. 9v.

Phil 70.75.1   Congrès International de Philosophie Médiévale, 1st, Louvain and Brussels, 1958. L'homme et son destin, d'après les penseurs du moyen âge. Louvain. 1960

Phil 70.75.2A   Congrès International de Philosophie Médiévale, 2d, Cologne, 1961. Die Metaphysik im Mittelalter, ihr Ursprung und ihre Bedeutung. Berlin. 1963

Phil 70.75.3   Congrès International de Philosophie Médiévale, 3rd, Passo della Mendola (Trento), 1964. La filosofia della natura nel medioevo. Milano. 1966

Phil 70.75.4   Congrès International de Philosophie Médiévale, 4th, Montreal, 1967. Arts liberaux et philosophie au moyen âge. Montreal. 1969

Phil 70.13   Congrès International de Philosophie Scientifique, 1st, Paris, 1935. Actes du Congrès International. Paris, 1936. 8v.

Phil 70.3   Congrès international de psychologie physiologique. (International Congress of Psychology.) Paris. 1890

Phil 525.270   Congrès international de psychologie religieuse, 7th, Avon, 1950. Mystique et continence. Bruges, 1952.

Phil 6672.5   Congrès Internationale de L'Hypnotisme. Comptes rendue. Paris, 1889.

Phil 70.11   Congrés Polonais de Philosophie. Rapports et comptes rendus. Varsovie.

Phil 8610.880.14   Congrès Universel de la Libre Pensée, 14th, Prague, 1907. Světový kongres volné myšlenky v Praze 8,9,10,11 a 12 září 1907. Podrobná Zpráva. Praha, 1908.

Phil 8610.880.18   Congrès Universel de la Libre Pensée, 18th, Prague, 1920. XVIII. Světový kongres volné myšlenky v Praze od 5-9 září, 1920. Přípravy. Praha, 1920?

Phil 70.19   Congreso Internacional de Filosofia, Barcelona. Actas. Madrid, 1949. 3v.

Phil 70.21   Congreso Nacional de Filosofia. Actas. Buenos Aires. 1-3 4v.

Phil 70.3.1   Congress international de psychologie physiologique. (Internatonal Congress of Psychology, 1st, Paris, 1889.) Paris. 1889

Phil 70.38   Congresso di Studi Metodologici, Turin, 1952. Atti del congresso di studi metodologici promosso del centro di studi metodologici. Torino, 1954.

Phil 70.45   Congresso Internacional de Filosofia. Congresso Internacional de Filosofia. São Paulo, 1956.

Phil 70.45   Congresso Internacional de Filosofia. (Congresso Internacional de Filosofia.) São Paulo, 1956.

Phil 1507.6   Congresso Internationale di Studi Umanistici, Rome. Umanesimo e scienza politica. Milano, 1951.

Phil 4210.160   Congresso Internazionale di Filosofia Antonio Rosmini, Stresa and Rovereto, 1955. Atti del congresso internazionale di filosofia Antonio Rosmini. Firenze, 1957. 2v.

Phil 70.20   Congresso Nacional de Filosofia, Brazil. Anais. São Paulo. 1-4 4v.

Phil 70.10   Congresso Nazionale di Filosofia. Atti. Milano. 16-18 8v.

Phil 1507.8   Congressus Scholasticus Internationalis, Rome. Scholastico ratione historico-critica instaurada. Romae, 1951.

Phil 585.420   Congressus Thomisticus Internationalis, v.1- Romae, 1970.

Phil 2750.22.95   Conilh, Jean. Emmanuel Mounier, sa vie, son oeuvre, avec un exposé de sa philosophie. Paris, 1966.

Phil 333.15   Coninces, A. L'unité de la connaissance humaine. Bruges, 1943.

Phil 3484.27   Coninck, Antoine de. L'analytique transcendentale de Kant. Louvain, 1955-

Phil 346.27.5   Conjectures and refutations. (Popper, Karl Raimund.) N.Y., 1962.

Phil 346.27.8   Conjectures and refutations: the grouth of scientific knowledge. 3. ed. (Popper, Karl Raimund.) London, 1969.

Phil 8592.42   Conjunto de las doctrinas y filosofías del siglo comparadas con los conocimientos modernos. (Medina.) Madrid, 1872.

Phil 9530.57   Conklin, Bob. The power of a magnetic personality. West Ryack, N.Y., 1965.

Phil 5242.62   Conklin, Edmund Smith. Introductory psychology for students of education. N.Y., 1939.

Phil 1750.149   Connais-toi toi-même. (Philippard, L.) Paris, 1937.

Phil 2605.12.30   Connaissance de l'être, traité d'ontologie. (Finance, Joseph de.) Paris, 1966.

Phil 1750.346   La connaissance de l'homme on XVe siècle. (Rencontres Internationales.) Neuchâtel, 1952.

Phil 1540.85   La connaissance de l'individuel au Moyen Âge. (Bérubé, Camille.) Montréal, 1964.

Phil 2750.16.30   La connaissance dialectique et l'expérience existentielle. (Molle, G. van.) Liège, 1945.

Phil 8664.12   Connaissance et inconnaissance de Dieu. (Journet, Charles.) Paris, 1969.

Phil 343.4.5   La connaissance et l'erreur. (Mach, E.) Paris, 1908.

Phil 4756.1.45   La connaissance et l'être. (Frank, Semen L.) Paris, 1935.

Phil 5545.258   Connaissance et maîtrise de la mémoire. (Chauchard, Paul.) Verviers, 1970.

Phil 343.15   La connaissance scientifique. (Mochi, Alberto.) Paris, 1927.

Phil 5643.98   La connaissance sensorielle et les problèmes de la vision. (Piéron, Henri.) Paris, 1936.

Phil 346.15   Connaissance spéculative et connaissance pratique. (Pétrin, Jean.) Ottawa, 1948.

Phil 7069.23.10   La connaissance supra-normale. (Osty, Eugène.) Paris, 1923.

Phil 177.115   Connally, F.G. Science versus philosophy. N.Y., 1957.

Phil 42.6.3   Connecticut. Society for Mental Hygiene. Annual report. New Haven. 1912-1930

Phil 42.6   Connecticut. Society for Mental Hygiene. Publications. Pamphlet box.

Phil 42.6.5   Connecticut society for mental hygiene.

Phil 5241.6   Connection. Physiology. Intellectual philosophy. 2. ed. (Barlow, J.) Philadelphia, 1846.

Phil 477.14   Connell, Richard J. Matter and becoming. Chicago, 1966.

Phil 8882.21.3   The connexion between taste and morals. (Hopkins, M.) Boston, 1841.

Phil 8882.21.2   The connexion between taste and morals. (Hopkins, M.) Boston, 1841.

Phil 8882.21   The connexion between taste and morals. (Hopkins, M.) Boston, 1842.

Phil 333.24   Connolly, William. Political science and ideology. st ed. N.Y., 1967.

Phil 332.35   Conocimiento, verdad y belleza. (Bonilla, Abelardo.) San Salvador, 1958.

Phil 4357.14.80   El conocimiento de Dios en la filosofía de Guillermo Rubió. (Rubert Candau, José María.) Madrid, 1952?

Phil 6946.1.25   Conolly, John. The construction and government of lunatic asylums. London, 1968.

Phil 6952.7.5   Conolly, John. An inquiry concerning the indications of insanity. London, 1964.

Phil 6952.7   Conolly, John. The treatment of the insane without mechanical restraints. London, 1856.

Phil 196.8.3   La conoscenza. (Varisco, B.) Pavia, 1904.

Phil 8412.37   Conoscenza e arte. (Librizzi, Carmelo.) Padova, 1962.

Phil 3120.8.165   Conoscenza e moralità in Franz Brentano. (Bausola, Adriano.) Milano, 1968.

Phil 3499.30   Conoscenza e moralita in Kant. (Renda, A.) Palermo, 1944.

Phil 8413.4   La conoscenza sensibile nel razionalismo moderno. (Martano, Guiseppe.) Napoli, 1960.

Phil 4080.3.270   La conoscenza storica. (Raggiunti, R.) Firenze, 1955.

Phil 1715.16   Conoscenza storica e coscienza morale. (Piovani, Pietro.) Napoli, 1966.

Phil 6320.10   Conquer yourself. (Künkel, Fritz.) N.Y., 1936.

Phil 6111.62   The conquest of brain mysteries. (Bankoff, G.A.) London, 1947.

Phil 365.38.5   The conquest of death; an imminent step in evolution. (Bill, Annie C.B.) Boston, 1935.

Phil 9170.2   The conquest of death. (Kinney, A.) N.Y., 1893.

Phil 8590.18.3   The conquest of fear. (King, Basil.) Garden City, 1921.

Phil 9245.43.2   The conquest of happiness. (Russell, B.A.W.) London, 1930.
Phil 9245.43A   The conquest of happiness. (Russell, B.A.W.) N.Y., 1930.
Phil 9245.43.1   The conquest of happiness. (Russell, B.A.W.) N.Y., 1930.
Phil 6112.33   The conquest of nerves. (Courtney, J.W.) N.Y., 1919.
Phil 9070.23   The conquest of self. (Bisch, Louis Edward.) Garden City, 1923.
Phil 9245.33   La conquête du bonheur. (Payot, Jules.) Paris, 1921.
Phil 840.2   Les conquêtes de l'homme et la séparation ontologique. Thèse. (Brun, Jean.) Paris, 1961.
Phil 5780.9   Conrad, H. Psychologie und Besteuerung. Stuttgart, 1928.
Phil 5585.320   Conrad, Theodor. Zur Wesenlehre des psychischen Lebens und Erlebens. Den Haag, 1968.
Phil 665.88   Conrad-Martius, H. Die Geistseele des Menschen. München, 1960.
Phil 672.178   Conrad-Martius, H. Die Zeit. 1. Aufl. München, 1954.
Phil 177.60.5   Conrad-Martius, Hedwig. Bios und Psyche. Hamburg, 1949.
Phil 177.60   Conrad-Martius, Hedwig. Metaphysiche Gespräche. Halle, 1921.
Phil 3160.15.10   Conrad-Martius, Hedwig. Schriften zur Philosophie. München, 1963-64. 3v.
Phil 3160.15   Conrad-Martius, Hedwig. Das Sein. München, 1957.
Phil 5440.14   Consanguineous marriages; their effect upon offspring. (Withington, C.F.) Boston, 1885.
Phil 1900.90   Conscience, self love and benevolence in the system of Bishop Butler. Thesis. (Tomkins, S.S.) Philadelphia, 1934.
Phil 9075.1   La conscience. (Bautain, L.E.M.) Paris, 1861.
Phil 5585.220   La conscience. (Ey, Henri.) Paris, 1963.
Phil 9075.5   La conscience. (Labbé, J.) Paris, 1868.
Phil 9075.6   The conscience. (Maurice, J.F.D.) London, 1872.
Phil 9075.7   Conscience. (Robertson, J.D.) London, 1894.
Phil 9075.3.5   La conscience. 3. éd. (Gasparin, A.E.) Paris, 1873.
Phil 8967.3   Conscience and Christ; six lectures. (Rashdall, H.) London, 1916.
Phil 8890.33   Conscience and fanaticism. (Pitt-Rivers, Goerge.) London, 1919.
Phil 8960.4   Conscience and its problems. (Kirk, Kenneth E.) London, 1927.
Phil 9075.70   Conscience and its right to freedom. (D'Arcy, Eric.) N.Y., 1961.
Phil 9075.15   La conscience collective et la morale. (Bauer, Arthur.) Paris, 1912.
Phil 5374.46   La conscience comme principe spirituel. (Saint Prix, J. de.) Paris, 1927.
Phil 585.240   Conscience de le conscience. (Gattgno, Caleb.) Neuchâtel, 1967.
Phil 2725.35.60   La conscience de soi. (Lavelle, Louis.) Paris, 1933.
Phil 2750.14   Conscience et amour. (Madinier, Gabriel.) Paris, 1938.
Phil 5374.180   Conscience et connaissance. (Brach, Jacques.) Paris, 1957.
Phil 3450.11.170   Conscience et intentionalité. (Breton, Stanislas.) Paris, 1956.
Phil 9075.18   La conscience et la foi. (Coquerel, A.) Paris, 1867.
Phil 5374.60   La conscience et le corps. (Ruyer, Raymond.) Paris, 1937.
Phil 582.4   La conscience et l'être. (Moreau, Joseph.) Paris, 1958.
Phil 188.25   Conscience et logos. (Nédoncelle, Maurice.) Paris, 1961.
Phil 2750.15   Conscience et mouvement. (Madinier, Gabriel.) Paris, 1938.
Phil 2750.15.1   Conscience et mouvement. Thesis. (Madinier, Gabriel.) Paris, 1938.
Phil 5520.114   Conscience et signification. 1. éd. (Madinier, G.) Paris, 1953.
Phil 1705.10   La conscience malheureuse. (Fondane, B.) Paris, 1936.
Phil 9075.45   La conscience morale. (Madinier, G.) Paris, 1954.
NEDL   Phil 6951.17   La conscience morbide. Thèse. (Blondel, C.) Paris, 1913.
Phil 5850.356.5   La conscience ouvrière. Thèse. (Touraine, Alain.) Paris, 1966.
Phil 9075.20   La conscience psychologique et morale. (Carrau, Ludovic.) Paris, 1888.
Phil 8707.29   Conscience religieuse et mentalité technique. (Rotureau, G.) Paris, 1962.
Phil 3494.58   La conscience transcendentale. (Muralt, André.) Paris, 1958.
Phil 7140.116.11   Conscious auto-suggestion. (Coué, Émile.) London, 1924.
Phil 7140.116.13   Conscious auto-suggestion. (Coué, Émile.) N.Y., 1924.
Phil 5246.17   The conscious cross-section. (Givler, Robert C.) Seattle, 1915.
Phil 478.1   Conscious matter. (Duncan, W.S.) London, 1881.
Phil 6317.9.10   Conscious orientation. (Hoop, J.H. van der.) London, 1939.
Phil 5374.58   Consciousness, brain-child. (Campbell, P.A.) East Cleveland, 1933.
Phil 672.125   Consciousness, life and the fourth dimension. (Eriksen, R.) London, 1923.
Phil 5374.1.2   Pamphlet box. Consciousness.
Phil 5374.43   Consciousness. (Marshall, H.R.) London, 1909.
Phil 177.18   Consciousness. Boston, 1864.
Phil 5374.1   Pamphlet vol. Consciousness. 1866,1902-15. 10 pam.
Phil 5374.22   Consciousness a form of energy. (Montague, W.P.) N.Y., 19-? 2 pam.
Phil 6112.36   Consciousness and behavior. (Culbertson, J.T.) Dubuque, 1950.
Phil 960.272   Consciousness and reality. (Chethimattam, John B.) Bangalore, 1967.
Phil 1750.90.2   Consciousness and society. (Hughes, Henry Stuart.) N.Y., 1961.
Phil 6117.39   Consciousness and the purpose. (Hollen, Aura May.) Hollywood, 1931.
Phil 5627.55   The consciousness of communion with God. (Pennock, Gilbert L.) New Brunswick, N.J., 1919.
Phil 978.74.30   The consciousness of the atom. 2d ed. (Bailey, A.A. (Mrs.).) N.Y., 1922.
Phil 9341.15   Conseils à ma fille. (Bouilly, J.N.) Paris, 18-?
Phil 9349.5   Conseils aux jeunes de France après la victoire. 2e éd. (Jamin, F.) Paris, 1921.
Phil 9179.5   Conseils aux mères. (Théry, A.F.) Paris, 1859. 2v.
Phil 4235.1.30   Consentini de rerum. (Telesius, B.) Neapoli, 1570.
Phil 4080.16   Consentino, A. Temps, espace devenir, moi. Paris, 1938.
Phil 9550.22   Consequences of utilitarianism. (Hodgson, D.H.) Oxford, 1967.
Htn   Phil 5058.23*   Consequentie. (Strode, R.) Venice, 1493.
Phil 3640.635   Considerações sobre Frederico Nietzsche. (Melo, R. de.) Coimbra, 1961.
Phil 5627.14.2   A consideration of prayer. (Strong, A.L.) Chicago, 1908.
Phil 8591.1   Considerations...theory of religion. (Law, E.) Cambridge, 1755.

Phil 8591.1.2   Considerations...theory of religion. (Law, E.) Cambridge, 1765.
Phil 8591.1.3   Considerations...theory of religion. (Law, E.) Cambridge, 1765.
Phil 5722.32   Considerations for research in a sleep-learning program. (Simon, C.W.) Santa Monica, 1954.
Phil 5722.32.2   Considerations for research in a sleep-learning program. (Simon, C.W.) Santa Monica, 1954.
Phil 6115.6.8   Considerations on Flechsig's "Gehirn und Seele". (Jacobi, M.P. (Mrs.).) N.Y., 1897.
Phil 2138.53   Considerations on representative government. (Mill, John S.) N.Y., 1958.
Phil 192.5   Considerations sur la nature de l'homme. (Redern, S.E. de.) Paris, 1835. 2v.
Phil 2515.2.90   Considérations sur la Sagesse de Charron. (Chanet, P.) Paris, 1643.
Phil 7106.2   Considérations sur le magnétisme animal. (Bergasse, Nicolas.) La Hague, 1784.
Phil 2725.2.81   Considérations sur le système philosophique de M. de Lamennais. (Lacordaire, H.) Paris, 1834.
Htn   Phil 2750.6.30*   Considérations sur les causes de la grandeur des Romains et de leur décadence. (Montesquieu, Charles Louis de Secondat.) Amsterdam, 1734.
Phil 5216.1   Considérations sur les divers systèmes de psychologie. (Gilardin, Alphonse.) Paris, 1883.
Phil 8893.30   Considérations sur l'esprit et les moeurs. (Senac de Meilhan, G.) London, 1787.
Phil 8893.30.3   Considérations sur l'esprit et les moeurs. (Senac de Meilhan, G.) Paris, 1905.
Phil 346.6   Considerazioni filosofiche sulla dottrina della conoscenza. (Paoli, Giulio C.) Milano, 1911.
Phil 4112.55.3   Considerazioni filosofiche sull'idealismo transcendentale. 3a ed. (Galluppi, Pasquale.) Torino, 1857.
Phil 3450.19.510   Considerazioni intorno alla prima sezione di Sein und Zeit. (Guzzoni, Giorgio.) Urbino, 1969.
Phil 3425.317   Considerazioni su Hegel e Marx. (Antoni, Carlo.) Napoli, 1946.
Phil 4080.3.50   Considerazioni sul problema morale del tempo nostro. (Croce, Benedetto.) Bari, 1945.
Phil 9179.11   Consigli ai giovani. (Tommaséo, N.) Milano, 1869.
Phil 8612.90   Consolatio; Studien zur mittellateinischen Trostliteratur über den Tod und zum Problem der christlichen Trauer. (Moos, Peter von.) München, 1971-
Phil 8615.14.5   Consolations. (Martin, Alfred W.) N.Y., 1931.
Phil 8878.5.8   Consolations in travel. (Davy, H.) London, 1830.
Phil 8878.5.5   Consolations in travel. (Davy, H.) London, 1851.
Phil 8878.5.7   Consolations in travel. (Davy, H.) Philadelphia, 1830.
Phil 8878.5   Consolations in travel. (Davy, H.) Philadelphia, 1831.
Phil 8878.5.4   Consolations in travel. 4th ed. (Davy, H.) London, 1838.
Phil 8643.5   The consolations of science. (Straub, J.) Chicago, 1884.
Phil 177.73   Constable, F.C. I am. London, 1928.
Phil 177.73.5   Constable, F.C. Myself and dreams. N.Y., 1918.
Phil 5425.2.7   Constable, F.C. Poverty and hereditary genius (criticism of Galton's theory). London, 1905.
Phil 7060.142   Constable, Frank C. Telergy, the communion of souls. London, 1918.
Phil 3963.4   Constandse, Anton Levien. Geschiedenis van het humanisme in Nederland. Den Haag, 1967.
Phil 6952.8   Constans, A. Relation sur un épidémie d'hystéro-démonopathie en 1861. Paris, 1863.
Phil 978.36.5   Constant, L. Unpublished writings. Calcutta, 1883.
Phil 3120.15.90   Constantin Brunners Lehre, das Evangelium. (Moebius, A.) Berlin, 1910.
Phil 7054.90   Constantine, T.C. Modern spiritualism. Manchester, 1858.
Phil 8952.11   Constantino, S.A. Amen, amen. N.Y., 1944.
Phil 3480.64.50   Constitutio principii metaphysicae morum zwantziger. (Kant, Immanuel.) Lipsiae, 1796.
Phil 8892.4   Constitution de l'éthique. (Roberty, E. de.) Paris, 1900.
Phil 281.6.10   Constitution de l'univers. (Ayais, H.) Paris, 1840.
Phil 5922.4.6   The constitution of man. (Combe, George.) Boston, 1829.
Phil 5922.4.12   The constitution of man. (Combe, George.) Boston, 1839.
Phil 5922.4.14   The constitution of man. (Combe, George.) Hartford, 1847. 6 pam.
Phil 5922.4.9   The constitution of man. (Combe, George.) N.Y., 1845.
Phil 5922.4.6.5   The constitution of man. 5. American ed. (Combe, George.) Boston, 1835.
Phil 5922.4.11   The constitution of man. 11th American ed. (Combe, George.) Boston, 1841.
Phil 5922.4.13   The constitution of man. 15. American ed. (Combe, George.) Boston, 1847.
Phil 5066.312   Constructable sets with applications. (Mostowski, Andrzej.) Warszawa, 1969.
Phil 178.38.35   Construction and criticism. (Dewey, John.) N.Y., 1930.
Phil 6946.1.25   The construction and government of lunatic asylums. (Conolly, John.) London, 1968.
Phil 5242.65   Construction of a simulation process for initial psychiatric interviewing. Santa Monica, 1964.
Phil 5272.6.5   Construction of preference spaces. (Delbeke, L.) Louvain, 1968.
Phil 200.20   The construction of reality; lectures on the philosophy on science. (Zanstra, H.) N.Y., 1962.
Phil 735.75   The construction of the world. (Walker, Cyril T.H.) Oxford, 1919.
Phil 5401.46   Constructive aspects of anxiety. (Hiltner, S.) N.Y., 1963.
Phil 6110.3.2   Constructive conscious control of the individual. (Alexander, F.M.) N.Y., 1923.
Phil 8827.1   Constructive ethics. (Courtney, W.L.) London, 1886.
Phil 9070.3   Constructive human relationship. (Smith, G.W.) Kutztown, Pa., 1940.
Phil 5066.310   Constructive order types. (Crossley, John N.) London, 1969.
Phil 5241.33   Constructive psychology. (Buck, J.D.) Chicago, 1908.
Phil 960.35A   A constructive survey of Upanishadic philosophy. (Ranade, R.D.) Poona, 1926.
Phil 210.25   Consultation on Hermeneutics. Interpretation: the poetry of meaning. 1st ed. N.Y., 1967.
Phil 5853.6   La consultation pastorale d'orientation Rogérienne. (Saint-Arnaud, Yves.) Paris, 1969.
Phil 4818.298.15   Conta, Vasile. Opera filozofice. Bucureşti, 1967.
Phil 176.88   The contact between minds. (Burne, C.D.) London 1923.
Phil 6319.1.205   Contact with Jung. (Fordham, M.S.M.) London, 1963.
Phil 7069.19.147   Contact with the other world. (Hyslop, James H.) N.Y., 1919.
Phil 7140.119   Le contagion mentale. (Vigouroux, A.) Paris, 1905.
Phil 2648.45   La contagion sacrée. v.1-2. (Holbach, Paul Henri T.) Londres, 1768.

Phil 2648.45.2   La contagion sacrée. v.1-2. (Holbach, Paul Henri T.) Paris, 1796-97.

Htn   Phil 283.6*   Contarini, N. De perfectione rerum, libri sex. Venetiis, 1576.

Htn   Phil 8637.9.3*   Contemplatio mortis, and immortalitatis. (Montagu, H.) London, 1631.

Htn   Phil 8637.9*   Contemplatio mortis, and immortalitatis. (Montagu, H.) London, 1638.

Htn   Phil 194.2*   Contemplatio philosophica. (Taylor, B.S.) London, 1793.

Phil 525.61.5   La contemplation chrétienne. (Louismet, S.) Paris, 1923.

Phil 8408.20   The contemplative activity; a study in aesthetics. (Haezrahi, P.) N.Y., 1956.

Phil 1800.2   Contemporary American philosophy. (Adams, George P.) N.Y., 1930. 2v.

Phil 1800.2.5   Contemporary American philosophy. (Adams, George P.) N.Y., 1962. 2v.

Phil 1800.2.10   Contemporary American philosophy: second series. London, 1970.

Phil 179.24.5   The contemporary and his soul. (Edman, Irwin.) N.Y., 1931.

Phil 333.17.1   Contemporary approaches to cognition. (Colorado. University. Psychology Department.) Cambridge, 1968.

Phil 5465.124   Contemporary approaches to creative thinking. (Gruber, Howard E.) N.Y., 1962.

Phil 187.63   Contemporary British philosophy. 1st Ser. (Muirhead, J.H.) N.Y., 1924.

Phil 187.63.5   Contemporary British philosophy. 2nd ser. (Muirhead, J.H.) N.Y., 1925.

Phil 187.63.8A   Contemporary British philosophy. 3rd ser. (Muirhead, J.H.) London, 1956.

Phil 672.157   Contemporary concepts of time and the idea of God. (Ramige, E.A.) Boston, 1935.

Phil 8520.34.3   Contemporary continental theology. 2. ed. (Horton, Walter M.) N.Y., 1938.

Phil 8842.3   Contemporary English ethics. (Rees, D.) Leipzig, 1892.

Phil 8520.34   Contemporary English theology; an American interpretation. (Horton, Walter M.) N.Y., 1936.

Phil 8876.140   Contemporary ethical theories. (Binkley, Luther J.) N.Y., 1961.

Phil 8882.66A   Contemporary ethical theories. (Hill, Thomas E.) N.Y., 1950.

Phil 1701.20.10   Contemporary European philosophy. 2d ed. (Bochénski, J.M.) Berkeley, 1956.

Phil 6980.102   Contemporary European psychiatry. (Bellak, L.) N.Y., 1961.

Phil 1740.14   Contemporary European thought and Christian faith. (Dondeyne, Albert.) Pittsburgh, 1958.

Phil 8580.7.15   The contemporary evolution of religious thought in England. (Goblet d'Alviella, E.) London, 1885.

Phil 1750.759   Contemporary existentialism and Christian faith. (Williams, John Rodman.) Englewood Cliffs, N.J., 1965.

Phil 2418.6   Contemporary French philosophy. (Smith, C.) N.Y., 1964.

Phil 3017.10   Contemporary German philosophy and its background. (Rintelen, Fritz-Joachim von.) Bonn, 1970.

Phil 400.84   Contemporary idealism in America. (Barrett, Clifford.) N.Y., 1932.

Phil 4870.10   Contemporary Indian philosophers. (Ray, Benoy Gopal.) Allahabad, 1947.

Phil 4871.5   Contemporary Indian philosophy. (Radhakrishnan, Sarvepalli.) London, 1936.

Phil 4870.14   Contemporary Indian philosophy. (Srivastava, Rama Shanker.) Delhi, 1965.

Phil 4871.5.2   Contemporary Indian philosophy. 2nd ed. (Radhakrishnan, Sarvepalli.) London, 1952.

Phil 5592.178   Contemporary issues in thematic apperceptive methods. (Conference on Contemporary Issues in Thematic Apperceptive Methods.) Springfield, Ill., 1961.

Phil 4897.10.5   Contemporary Japanese philosophical thought. (Piovesana, Gino K.) N.Y., 1969.

Phil 4957.20.5   Contemporary Latin-American philosophy. (Sanchez Reulet, Aníbal.) New Mexico, 1954.

Phil 8897.90   Contemporary moral philosophy. (Warnock, Geoffrey James.) N.Y., 1967.

Phil 8955.5   Contemporary moral theology. (Ford, J.C.) Westminster, Md., 1958-63. 2v.

Phil 1760.10   Contemporary philosophic problems, selected readings. (Krikorien, Yervant H.) N.Y., 1959.

Phil 70.116   Contemporary philosophic thought. Albany, 1970. 4v.

Phil 720.101   Contemporary philosophical alternatives and the crisis of truth; a critical study of positivism, existentialism and Marxism. (Rauche, Gerhard Albin.) The Hague, 1970.

Phil 1701.50   Contemporary philosophy; phenomenological and existential currents. (Borzaga, Reynold.) Milwaukee, 1966.

Phil 5068.22   Contemporary philosophy. (Copleston, F.C.) London, 1956.

Phil 1722.4.5   Contemporary philosophy. (Wardell, R.J.) London, 1913.

Phil 1695.45   Contemporary philosophy. A survey. Firenze, 1968- 4v.

Phil 4912.5   Contemporary philosophy in Australia. (Brown, Robert.) London, 1969.

Phil 8952.22.5   Contemporary problems in moral theology. (Curran, Charles E.) Notre Dame, 1970.

Phil 5585.351   Contemporary problems in perception. (NATO Advanced Study Institute, University of Thessaloniki, 1968.) London, 1970.

Phil 8581.112   Contemporary problems in religion. (Basilius, Harold Albert.) Detroit, 1956.

Phil 12.70   Contemporary psychoanalysis. N.Y. 1,1964+ 3v.

Phil 5261.3.5   Contemporary psychology. (Villa, G.) London, 1903.

Phil 12.7   Contemporary psychology. Washington. 1,1956+ 11v.

Phil 6329.8   Contemporary psychopathology. (Tomkins, S.S.) Cambridge, 1943.

Phil 6980.707   Contemporary psychotherapies. (Stein, Morris.) N.Y., 1961.

Phil 5039.6.5   Contemporary readings in logical theory. (Copi, Irving M.) N.Y., 1967.

Phil 5590.410   Contemporary research in personality. (Sarason, Irwin G.) Princeton, 1962.

Phil 5232.5A   Contemporary schools of psychology. (Woodworth, R.S.) N.Y., 1931.

Phil 5232.5.10   Contemporary schools of psychology. (Woodworth, R.S.) N.Y., 1936.

Phil 5232.5.15A   Contemporary schools of psychology. (Woodworth, R.S.) N.Y., 1948.

Phil 5232.5.17   Contemporary schools of psychology. 3. ed. (Woodworth, R.S.) N.Y., 1967.

Phil 4340.20   Contemporary Spanish philosophy; an anthology. (Caponigri, Aloysius Robert.) Notre Dame, 1967.

Phil 5262.53   Contemporary theories and systems in psychology. (Wolman, Benjamin B.) N.Y., 1960.

Phil 338.34   Contemporary theories of knowledge. (Hill, T.E.) N.Y., 1961.

Phil 5643.150   Contemporary theory and research in visual perception. (Haber, Ralph Norman.) N.Y., 1968.

Phil 12.95   Contemporary thought in guidance and counseling. Washington. 1,1967+

Phil 2401.3.5   Contemporary thought of France. (Benrubi, Isaac.) London, 1926.

Phil 3009.2   Contemporary thought of Germany. (Jones, W.T.) N.Y., 1931. 2v.

Phil 4002.3   Contemporary thought of Italy. (Crespi, Angelo.) London, 1926.

Phil 4890.10   Contemporary thought of Japan and China. (Tsuchida, Kyoson.) London, 1927.

Phil 4890.10.2   Contemporary thought of Japan and China. (Tsuchida, Kyoson.) N.Y., 1927.

Phil 6480.213   The content analysis of dreams. (Hall, Calvin Springer.) N.Y., 1966.

Phil 8592.52.5   The contents of the history of ancient paganism. (Mason, Francis.) London, 1747.

Phil 190.27   Contes pour les métaphysiciens. (Prat, Louis.) Paris, 1910.

Phil 7068.83.12   Contestatión a los detractores del espiritismo. (Sociedad de Estudios Espiritistas de Key West.) Key West, 1883.

Phil 8403.24.5   Conti, Auguso. Il bell nel vero o estetic. 4. ed. Firenze, 1901. 2v.

Phil 177.19.20   Conti, Augusto. Ai figli del popolo; consigli. Firenze, 1901.

Phil 177.19.15   Conti, Augusto. L'armonia delle cose. Firenze, 1888. 2v.

Phil 8403.24   Conti, Augusto. Il bello nel vero o estetica. Firenze, 1872. 2v.

Phil 4080.8.31   Conti, Augusto. Il buono nel vero. Libri quattro. Firenze, 1873. 2v.

Phil 4080.8.40   Conti, Augusto. Dio e il male. Prato, 1866.

Phil 177.19   Conti, Augusto. Evidenza, amore e fede. Florence, 1858. 2v.

Phil 177.19.5   Conti, Augusto. Filosofia elementare. Firenze, 1913.

Phil 802.6.5   Conti, Augusto. Histoire de la philosophie. Paris, n.d. 2v.

Phil 4080.8.35   Conti, Augusto. Nuovi discorsi del tempo o famiglia, patria e Dio. Firenze, 1896-97. 2v.

Phil 4002.2   Conti, Augusto. La philosophie italienne contemporaine. Paris, 1865.

Phil 802.6   Conti, Augusto. Storia della filosofia; lezioni. 6a ed. Roma, 1908-09. 2v.

Phil 177.19.10   Conti, Augusto. Il vero nell'ordine o Ondologia e logica. 2a ed. Firenze, 1891. 2v.

Phil 4080.8.79   Pamphlet vol. Conti, Augusto. 5 pam.

Phil 4225.15.85   Conti, O. Polemica sull'immanenza in Ugo Spirito. Milano, 1963.

Phil 1135.220   Conti, Rosario. Cosmogonie oriéntali e filosofia presocraṭica. Roma, 1967.

Htn   Phil 2493.40.5*   Contillac, Étienne Bonnot. An essay on the origin of human knowledge. London, 1756.

Phil 5760.9   Contingence, liberté et la personnalité humaine. (Konczewska, H.) Paris, 1937.

Phil 5760.9.5   Contingence, liberté et la personnalité humaine. Thèse. (Konczewska, H.) Paris, 1937.

Phil 2403.7   Contingence et nationalisme. (Dauriac, L.) Paris, 1924.

Phil 5625.120   Contingencies of reinforcement. (Skinner, B.F.) N.Y., 1969.

Phil 2477.1.34   The contingency of the laws of nature. (Boutroux, Émile.) Chicago, 1916.

Phil 4080.3.510   Contini, Bian Franco. L'influenza culturale di Benedetto Croce. Milano, 1967.

Phil 2218.50   A continuation of the letters to the philosophers and politicians of France. (Priestley, Joseph.) Salem, 1795.

Phil 2225.5.90   Continuity, the form of forms in Charles Peirce. (Hartshorne, Charles.) n.p., 1929.

Phil 7069.33.10   Continuity of life. (Benedict, Anna Louise.) Boston, 1933.

Phil 2905.1.600   The continuous flame. (Cargas, Harry J.) St. Louis, 1969?

Phil 5042.21.20   The continuum of inductive methods. (Carnap, Rudolf.) Chicago, 1952.

Phil 8610.890.10   Contra el altar y el trono; artículos varios, publicados en "El Progreso" de 1884-85 por su director, R. Verea. N.Y., 1890.

Phil 5045.18   Contradiction et totalité. (Fougeyrollas, Pierre.) Paris, 1964.

Phil 2115.88   Contradictions in Locke's theory of knowledge. (Manly, G.W.) Leipzig, 1885.

Htn   Phil 7075.8*   Die conträre Sexualempfindung. (Moll, Albert.) Berlin, 1891.

X Cg   Phil 7075.8.3   Die conträre Sexualempfindung. (Moll, Albert.) Berlin, 1899.

Phil 8881.1   The contrast: duty and pleasure, right and wrong. (G., W.A.) London, 1890.

Phil 8430.23   Contrasts: the arts and religion. (Robertson, A.) London, 1947.

Phil 6315.2.95   Contre Freud. (Bodin, Jean.) Paris, 1926.

Phil 186.76   Contre la métaphysique; questions de méthode. (Le Dantec, Félix.) Paris, 1912.

Phil 3425.301   Contri, S. Tetralogia Hegeliana. Bologna, 1938-39. 2v.

Phil 4002.5   Contri, Siro. La filosofia scolastica in Italia nell'ora presente. Bologna, 1931.

Phil 3425.370   Contri, Siro. Punti di trascendenza nell'immanentismo hegeliano alla luce della momentalita storiosofica. Milano, 1954.

Phil 22.30   Contribuciones. (México (city). Colegio de México a la Historia del Pensamiento Hispano-Americano.) Mexico. 2-3 2v.

Phil 4960.605   Contribuição à história das idéias no Brasil. (Cruz Costa, João.) Rio de Janeiro, 1956.

Phil 4960.605.2   Contribuição à história das idéias no Brasil. 2. ed. (Cruz Costa, João.) Rio de Janeiro, 1967.

Phil 3001.24   Contribuições à historia da filosofia alemã. (Buggenhagen, Erich Arnold von.) São José, 1956.

Phil 22.56   Contributi. (Milan. Università Cattolica del Sacro Cuore. Institutadi filosofia.) Milano. 1,1969+

Phil 5238.4   Contributi. (Milan. Università Cattolica del Sacro Cuore. Laboratorio di Psicologia di Biologia.) Milano. 1-29 26v.

Phil 8415.9   Contributi all'analisi estetica. (Oberti, Elisa,) Milano, 1962.

Phil 165.80   Contributi di A. Corsana. (Bari (City). Università. Istituto di Storia della Filosofia.) Trani, 1955.

Phil 57.3   Contributi psicologia dell' Instituto. (Rome. Rome Universitas. Istituto di Psicologia Sperimentale.) Roma. 1-6,1910-1933 6v.

Phil 525.43   Contribution à la pathologie des mystiques. (Costa Guimaraes, Francisco da.) Paris, 1908.

Phil 7080.35   Contribution à la pathologie du sommeil. Le sommeil automatique. Thèse. (Poyer, G.P.) Paris, 1914.

Phil 5585.216   Contribution à la théorie de la causalité perceptive. (Thinès, G.) Louvain, 1962.

Phil 6128.16   Contribution à l'étude de certaines facultés cérébrales méconnues. (Sermyn, W.C. de.) Sawsanne, 1910.

Phil 6112.34   Contribution à l'étude de l'action vasomotrice. Thèse. (Cuny, Louis.) Paris, 1942.

Phil 5642.17   Contribution à l'étude de l'audition colorée. (Benoist, Émilien.) Paris, 1899.

Phil 6958.3   Contribution à l'étude du rôle des emotions. Thèse. (Imianitoff, Mme.) Paris, 1917.

Phil 5592.125   Contribution à l'étude pratique. (Sormani, Jacques.) Marseille, 1958.

Phil 2477.8.90   La contribution de Binet à l'élaboration d'une pédagogie scientifique. (Avanzini, Guy.) Paris, 1969.

Phil 8972.8   The contribution of Christianity to ethics. (Webb, C.J.) Calcutta, 1932.

NEDL Phil 2475.1.77   A contribution to a bibliography of Henri Bergson. (Columbia University. Library.) N.Y., 1913.

Phil 2475.1.77   A contribution to a bibliography of Henri Bergson. (Columbia University. Library.) N.Y., 1913.

Phil 3890.1.75   Contribution to history of the word person. (Trendelenburg, A.) Chicago, 1910. 2 pam.

Phil 5062.25   A contribution to the psychology of logic. (Waller, A.D.) London, 1912.

Phil 7082.90   A contribution towards a science of dreams. (Spiller, Gustav.) London, 1934.

Phil 5252.18.30   A contribution towards an improvement in psychological method. (McDougall, William.) n.p., 1898-1914. 8 pam.

Phil 55.1.10   Contributions. (Pennsylvina. University. Laboratory of Neuropathology.) Philadelphia, 1905. 5v.

Phil 11.6   Contributions. (Psychopathic Hospital, Boston, Mass.) 1-63,1913-1914+

Phil 47.1.9   Contributions from Massachusetts General Hospital. (Harvard Medical School. Department of Neurology.) Boston. 1,1906

Phil 24.3   Contributions in psychology. (Ohio. State University. Department of Psychology.) 8-12,1927-1934

Phil 8894.2   The contributions of Q.Q. (Taylor, Jane.) Philadelphia, 1830.

Phil 8894.2.5   The contributions of Q.Q. to a periodical work. 6. ed. (Taylor, Jane.) London, 1831.

Phil 5548.101   Contributions to a general normalogy, or Theory of purpose-setting. (Langkjaer, Asger.) København, 1961.

Phil 5249.13.20   Contributions to analytical psychology. (Jung, Carl G.) London, 1928.

Phil 165.351   Contributions to logic and methodology in honor of J.M. Bochenski. (Tymieniecka, Anna Teresa.) Amsterdam, 1965.

Phil 5066.280   Contributions to mathematical logic; proceedings of the logic colloquium, Hannover, 1966. (Logic Colloquium, 11th, Hannover, 1966.) Amsterdam, 1968.

Phil 6967.5   Contributions to mental pathology. (Ray, Isaac.) Boston, 1873.

Phil 3245.70.5   Contributions to mental philosophy. (Fichte, Immanuel Hermann.) London, 1860.

Phil 42.4   Contributions to philosophy. (Chicago. University.) Chicago. 1,1904+ 3v.

Phil 42.1   Contributions to philosophy. (Columbia College.) N.Y. 1-12,1894-1903 12v.

Phil 6320.11.19   Contributions to psycho-analysis, 1921-1945. (Klein, M.) London, 1968.

Phil 6315.1   Contributions to psycho-analysis. (Ferenczi, Sandor.) Boston, 1916.

Phil 6320.11.17A   Contributions to psycho-analysis. (Klein, M.) London, 1950.

Phil 12.19   Contributions to psychological theory. Durham, N.C. 1

Phil 5635.5.2   Contributions to the analysis of the sensations. (Mach, Ernst.) Chicago, 1897.

Phil 5635.5.10   Contributions to the analysis of the sensations. (Mach, Ernst.) Chicago, 1910.

Phil 7068.98.20   Contributo di fatti pella soluzione del problema di psicologia. (Falcomer, M.T.) Selessandria, 1898.

Phil 1182.50   Il contributo pilagorico alla scienza. (Capparelli, Vincenzo.) Padova, 1955.

Phil 6952.32   Contro la psichiatria. 1.ed. (Cotti, Edelweiss.) Firenze, 1970.

Phil 6119.6   Control of body and mind. (Jewett, F.G.) Boston, 1908.

Phil 8897.43   The control of ideals. (Van Wesep, H.B.) N.Y., 1920.

Phil 5402.29   The control of pain. (Prescott, Frederick.) N.Y., 1965.

Phil 5850.354.5   The control of the mind. (Thouless, R.H.) London, 1928.

Phil 5585.18   Control processes in modified hand-writing. (Downey, June Etta.) Chicago? 1908?

Phil 6120.6   Le contrôle psychique. (Kenilworth, W.W.) Paris, 1914.

Phil 5258.115   Controlling human behavior. (Starch, Daniel.) N.Y., 1936.

Phil 5850.149.5   Controlling your circumstances and affairs of life. (Capps, Ora L.) Denver, 1932.

Phil 260.6   Die Controverse und der Beharren der Elemente. (Pfeifer, X.) Dellingen, 1879.

Phil 2805.249.5   Controverses pascaliennes. (Lafuma, Louis.) Paris, 1952.

Phil 8701.14   The controversy over evolution in New England, 1859-1873. (Loewenberg, B.J.) n.p., 1935.

Phil 4080.3.470   Convegno Crociano, Bari. Interpretazioni crociane di R. Assunto. Bari, 1965.

Phil 70.32   Convegno degli Psicolozi Italiani. Atti. Firenze. 9-11,1951-1956 3v.

Phil 4070.7.90   Convegno di Studi Banfiani, Reggio Emilia. Antonio Banfi e il pensiero contemporaneo. Firenze, 1969.

Phil 4195.110   Convegno di Studi Pichiani per il V Centenario della Nascita di Giovanni Pico della Mirandola. Studi pichiani; atti e memorie del Convegno di studi pichiani per il V centenario della nascita di Giovanni Pico della Mirandola, Mondena, Mirandola, 25-26 maggio, 1963. Modena, 1965.

Phil 7150.65.10   Convegno di Studio su Suicidio eTentato Suicidio in Italia, Milan, 1967. Suicidio e tentato suicidio in Italia. Milano, 1968.

Phil 4195.106A   Convegno Internazionale per il V Centenario della Nascita di Giovanni Pico della Mirandola, Mirandola, 1963. L'opera e il pensiero di Giovanni Pico della Mirandola nella storia dell'umanesimo. Firenze, 1965.

Phil 5520.571   Convention; a philosophical study. (Lewis, David Kellogg.) Cambridge, 1969.

Phil 48.9   Convention proceedings. (International Metaphysical League.) Boston.

Phil 5012.2A   Conventional logic and modern logic. (Clark, Joseph.) Woodstock, 1952.

Phil 165.135   Conversaciones filosóficas interamericanas. (Sociedad Cubana de Filosofía.) Habana, 1955.

Phil 5520.106   Conversation and communication. (Meerloo, A.M.) N.Y., 1952.

Phil 6319.1.230   Conversation with Carl Jung and reactions from Ernest Jones. (Evans, Richard Isadore.) Princeton, 1964.

Phil 2733.61.2   Conversations chrétiennes. (Malebranche, Nicolas.) Paris, 1702.

Phil 2733.61.7   Conversations chrétiennes. (Malebranche, Nicolas.) Paris, 1929.

Phil 2733.61   Conversations chrétiennes. (Malebranche, Nicolas.) Rotterdam, 1685.

Phil 2733.61.5   Conversations chrétiennes dans lesquelles on justifie la vérité de la religion. Thèse. (Malebranche, Nicolas.) Paris, 1929.

Phil 8657.10   Conversations on the attributes of God. Boston, 1831.

Phil 181.131.5   Conversations on the good uses of freedom. 1. American ed. (Grenier, J.) Cambridge, 1967.

Phil 8581.78.5   Conversations with an unrepentant liberal. (Bixler, J.S.) New Haven, 1946.

Phil 7069.30.8   Conversations with the other world. (Grant, Isabel.) London, 1930.

Phil 4080.3.220   Conversazioni con Benedetto Croce su alcuni libri della sua biblioteca. (Marra, Dara.) Milano, 1952.

Phil 680.10   Conversazioni con Claude Lévi-Straws, Michel Foucault, Jacques Lacan. (Caruso, Paolo.) Milano, 1969.

Phil 5190.10.10   Conversazioni contedine. (Dolce, Danilo.) Milano, 1966.

Phil 8416.8.15   Conversazioni di estetica. (Pareyson, Luigi.) Milano, 1966.

Phil 5627.107.5   Conversion: Christian and non-Christian. (Underwood, A.C.) N.Y., 1925.

Phil 5627.69   Conversion and religious experience. (Kriebel, O.S.) Pennsburg, Pa., 1907.

Phil 8615.19   The conversion of a sinner. (Cabot, P.) Boston, 1923.

Phil 5627.134.65   The conversion of the church. (Shoemaker, S.M.) N.Y., 1932.

Phil 2477.19.82   Conversion spirituelle et engagement prospectif, essai pour une lecture de Gaston Berger. (Ginisty, Bernard.) Paris, 1966.

Phil 2730.100   Les conversions de Maine de Biran. (Gouhier, Henri.) Paris, 1947.

Phil 7069.30.12   Conviction of survival. (Lodge, Oliver Joseph.) London, 1930.

Phil 8887.64   Convictionism versus non-convictionism. (MacKaye, James.) n.p., 1928.

Phil 12.35   Convivium; estudios filosoficos. Barcelona. 1-2,1956-1957

Phil 9230.2   Convocation of the Province of York. Report of the committee on betting and gambling. London, 1890.

Phil 6536.13   Convulsive seizures; how to deal with them. 2d. ed. (Putnam, T.J.) Philadelphia, 1945.

Phil 8877.78.3   Conwell, Russell H. Acres of diamonds. N.Y., 1943.

Htn Phil 8599.4.7*   Conybeare, J. A defence of revealed religion against the exceptions of a late writer in his book intituled, Christianity as old as the creation. London, 1732.

Phil 1200.31   Conz, C.P. Abhandlungen für die Geschichte und das Eigenthümliche der späteren stoischen Philosophie. Tübingen, 1794.

Phil 310.756   Conz, Gianni. Introduzione a una dialettica dei complementari. Padova, 1970.

Phil 5042.26   Conze, E. Der Satz vom Widerspruch. Hamburg, 1931.

Phil 7069.31.5   Cook, Ellen A.P. The voice triumphant, the revelations of a medium. N.Y., 1931.

Phil 5648.10   Cook, H.D. Die taktile Schätzung von Ausgefüllten und leeren Strecken. Leipzig, 1910.

Phil 8692.1   Cook, J. Christ and modern thought. Boston, 1881.

Phil 7084.30.2   Cook, John. A true relation of Mr. Justice Cook's passage by sea from Wexforel to Kinsaile, and of the great storm. 2d ed. London, 1652?

Phil 978.15.4   Cook, M.C. Light on the path. Boston, 1889.

Phil 978.15.2   Cook, M.C. Light on the path. Chicago, Ill., n.d.

Phil 978.15.4.5   Cook, M.C. Light on the path. N.Y., 18- .

Phil 978.15.3   Cook, M.C. Light on the path. N.Y., 1886?

Phil 978.15   Cook, M.C. Light on the path. Point Loma, California, 1897.

Phil 978.15.5   Cook, M.C. Through the gates of gold. Boston, 1901.

Phil 9450.14   Cook, Silas A. The essence and the ethics of politics. N.Y., 1915.

Phil 7069.17.24   Cook, Walter. Reflections on "Raymond". London, 1917.

Phil 6980.198   Cooke, Elliot D. All but me and thee. Washington, 1946.

Phil 8520.11   Cooke, George W. The social evolution of religion. Boston, 1920.

Phil 8877.38   Cooke, H.P. Maurice, the philosopher. Cambridge, 1912.

Phil 7054.175.15   Cooke, I. The return of Arthur Conan Doyle. 2. ed. Liss, 1963.

Phil 8692.2.1   Cooke, J.P. The credentials of science, the warrant of faith. 2. ed. N.Y., 1888.

Phil 8692.2.2   Cooke, J.P. The credentials of science the warrent of faith. N.Y., 1893.

Phil 8692.2.4   Cooke, J.P. Religion and chemistry. N.Y., 1864.

Phil 8692.2.5   Cooke, J.P. Religion and chemistry. N.Y., 1880.

Phil 7054.76   Cooke, P. Necromancy; or a rap for the rappers. Boston, 1857 .

Phil 6012.3   Cooke, Thomas. A practical and familiar view of science of physiognomy. London, 1819.

Phil 6112.6   Cooke, W. A comentary...mind and the emotions. Philadelphia, 1853.

Phil 5425.10   Cooley, C.H. Genius, fame and the comparison of races. Philadelphia, 1897.

Phil 5066.9   Cooley, J.C. An outline of formal logic. Pt.1. Cambridge, 1934.

Phil 5066.9.5A   Cooley, J.C. A primer of formal logic. N.Y., 1942.

Phil 8610.900   Cooley, P.J. Evolution; an exposition of Christian dogmas and pagan myths. N.Y., 1900.

Phil 177.34   Cooley, W.F. The individual. N.Y., 1909.

Phil 5242.64   Cooley, William. Multivariate procedures for the behavorial sciences. N.Y., 1962.

Phil 672.168   Coomaraswamy, A. Time and eternity. Ascona, 1947.

Phil 8403.41   Coomaraswamy, A.K. Figures of speech or figures of thought. London, 1946.

Phil 8190.2   Coomaraswamy, Ananda. The transformation of nature in art. Cambridge, Mass., 1934.

Phil 5272.4   Coombs, Clyde. A theory of data. N.Y., 1967.

Phil 2120.5   Cooper, B.S. The philosophy of Sir Oliver Lodge. Thesis. Nashville, 1934.

Phil 978.60.15 Cooper, I.S. Theosophy simplified. 3d ed. Hollywood, 1919.

Phil 978.60.2 Cooper, Irving S. Reincarnation, the hope of the world. 2d ed. Chicago, 1927.

Phil 8403.6.4 Cooper, John. Letters concerning taste. 4th ed. London, 1771.

Phil 8403.6 Cooper, John G. Letters concerning taste. 3. ed. London, 1757.

Phil 9528.6 Cooper, John M. Religion outlines for colleges. Washington, D.C., 1928.

Phil 7054.141.5 Cooper, Robert. Spiritual experiences. London, 1867.

Phil 7069.14.30 Cooper, William E. Where two worlds meet. London, 1914.

Phil 7069.00.10 Cooper, William Earnshaw. Spiritual manifestations. Exeter, 19- .

Phil 5875.50 Coopersmith, Stanley. The antecedents of self-esteem. San Francisco, 1967.

Phil 6140.2 Coordinate index reference guide to community mental health. (Golann, Stuart E.) N.Y., 1969.

Phil 8877.84 Coornhert, D.V. Zedekunst. Leiden, 1942.

Phil 51.2 Coover, J.E. Experiments in psychical research at Stanford Junior University. Stanford, 1917.

Phil 5545.58 Coover, J.E. Formal discipline...experimental psychology. Thesis. Princeton, 1916.

Phil 7069.17.25 Coover, John Edgar. Experiments in psychical research at Leland Stanford Jr. University. n.p. 1917.

Phil 8877.47 Cope, Henry F. The friendly life. N.Y., 1909.

Phil 2030.1.85 Cope, Jackson I. Joseph Glanvill. St. Louis, 1956.

Phil 8877.69 Copeland, Edwin B. Natural conduct. Stanford, Calif., 1928.

Phil 4960.205 Copelli y Marroni, Francisco. Esencialismo. 1. ed. Buenos Aires, 1957.

Phil 5039.6.5 Copi, Irving M. Contemporary readings in logical theory. N.Y., 1967.

Phil 5039.6 Copi, Irving M. Readings on logic. N.Y., 1965.

Phil 5066.54.2 Copi, Irving M. Symbolic logic. 2nd ed. N.Y., 1965.

Phil 3925.16.96 Copi, Irving Marmer. Essays on Wittgenstein's Tractatus. London, 1966.

Phil 3640.292 Copleston, F. Friedrich Nietzsche. London, 1942.

Phil 802.15.5 Copleston, F. A history of philosophy. Westminster, 1960. 8v.

Phil 802.15 Copleston, F. A history of philosophy. v.1,4-8. London, 1946-50. 6v.

Phil 2475.1.330 Copleston, F.C. Bergson on morality. London, 1956.

Phil 5068.22 Copleston, F.C. Contemporary philosophy. London, 1956.

Phil 1507.7 Copleston, F.C. Medieval philosophy. London, 1952.

Phil 1507.7.2 Copleston, F.C. Medieval philosophy. N.Y., 1952.

Phil 3808.186 Copleston, Frederick. Arthur Schopenhauer. London, 1946.

Phil 5042.4 Coppée, Henry. Elements of logic. Philadelphia, 1858.

Phil 5042.4.2 Coppée, Henry. Elements of logic. Philadelphia, 1860.

Phil 8877.43 Coppens, Charles. A brief text-book of moral philosophy. N.Y., 1895.

Phil 9075.18 Coquerel, A. La conscience et la foi. Paris, 1867.

Phil 8582.52 Coqueret, H. Théosophie ou science de Dieu. Paris, 1803.

Phil 3850.27.245 Corah, Hakki. Aborra oganga. Istanbul, 1967.

Phil 177.54 Corbeil, S. La normalienne en philosophie. Montreal, 1914.

Phil 402.2 Corbett, Patrick. Ideologies. N.Y., 1966.

Phil 978.22 Corbett, S. Extracts from the Vâhan. London, 1904.

Phil 1170.8 Corbière, C. Le christianisme et la fin de la philosophie antique. Paris, 1921.

Phil 1020.48 Corbin, H. Histoire de la philosophie islamique. Paris, 1964.

Phil 4060.5.90 Cordaro, Philip. Andrea Angiulli e l'eredità dell'800. Castanissetta, 1969.

Phil 525.77 Cordelier, John. The path of the eternal wisdom. 2d ed. London, 1912.

Phil 2515.20 Cordemoy, Géraud de. Oeuvres philosophiques, avec une étude bio-bibliographique. Paris, 1968.

Phil 4958.510 Cordero, Armando. Panorama de la filosofía en Santo Domingo. Santo Domingo, 1962.

Phil 4968.4.80 Cordiel Reyes, Raúl. Del modernismo al liberalismo. México, 1967.

Phil 5042.13 Cordier, Paul. Les problèmes de la logique. Paris, 1916.

Phil 2475.1.251 Córdoba, Argentina. Universidad Nacional. Instituto de Filosofía. Homenaje a Bergson. Córdoba, 1936.

NEDL Phil 42.5 Córdoba, Argentina (City). Universidad Nacional. Centro de Estudios de Filosofía y Humanidades. Estudios de filosofía. Córdoba.

Phil 270.95 Cordoba, Martín de. Compendio de la fortuna. Madrid, 1958.

Phil 2515.14 Cordonnier, V. Le sacre de la liberté. Paris, 1958.

Phil 8582.39 Cordovani, M. Rivelazione e filosofia. Milano, n.d.

Phil 6312.4 Core, D.E. Functional nervous disorders. Bristol, 1922.

Phil 4080.22.31 Coresi, Vincenzo. Assoluto e relativo. 1. ed. Bergamo, 1959.

Phil 3425.350 Coreth, Emerich. Das dialektische Sein in Hegel's Logik. Wien, 1952.

Phil 210.72 Coreth, Emerich. Grundfragen der Hermeneutik. Freiburg, 1969.

Phil 177.128.2 Coreth, Emerich. Metaphysics. N.Y., 1968.

Phil 177.128 Coreth, Emerich. Metaphysik. Innsbruck, 1961.

Phil 665.19 Corey, J.W. The soul; its organ and development. Los Angeles, 1913.

Phil 6312.1 Coriat, I.H. Abnormal psychology. London, 1911.

Phil 6312.1.3 Coriat, I.H. Abnormal psychology. N.Y., 1910.

Phil 6312.1.5 Coriat, I.H. Abnormal psychology. 2. ed. N.Y., 1914.

Phil 6312.1.7 Coriat, I.H. Repressed emotions. N.Y., 1920.

Phil 6420.24 Coriat, Isador H. Stammering; a psychoanalytic interpretation. N.Y., 1928.

Phil 7082.72.15 Coriat, Isador Henry. The meaning of dreams. Boston, 1915.

Phil 4080.5.31 Corleo, Simone. Filosofia universale. Palermo, 1860-63. 2v.

Phil 4080.5.32 Corleo, Simone. Il sistema della filosofia universale. Roma, 1879.

Phil 6012.8 Corman, Louis. Visages et caractères. Paris, 1932.

Phil 1210.15 Cornaeus, Melchior. Curriculum philosophiae peripateticae. v.1-2. Herbipoli, 1657.

Phil 4210.118 Cornelio, A.M. Antonio Rosmini e il suo monumento in Milano. Torino, 1896.

Phil 5627.21 Cornelison, I.A. The natural history of religious feeling. N.Y., 1911.

Phil 2496.87 Cornelius, Alfred. Die Geschichtslehre Victor Cousins. Genève, 1958.

Phil 177.29 Cornelius, H. Einleitung in die Philosophie. Leipzig, 1903.

Phil 177.29.2 Cornelius, H. Einleitung in die Philosophie. 2e Aufl. Leipzig, 1919.

Phil 5242.8 Cornelius, H. Psychologie. Leipzig, 1897.

Phil 3484.13 Cornelius, Hans. Kommentar zu Kant's Kritik der reinen Vernunft. Erlangen, 1926.

Phil 333.10 Cornelius, Hans. Transcendentale Systematik. Teil 1-2. München, 1916.

Phil 5500.8 Cornelius, Hans. Versuch einer Theorie der Existentialurteile. München, 1894.

Phil 6112.7 Cornelius, K.S. Über die Wechselwirkung zwischen Leib und Seele. Halle, 1875.

Phil 6112.7.5 Cornelius, K.S. Zur Theorie der Wechselwirkung zwischen Leib und Seele. Halle, 1880.

Phil 42.2 Cornell University. Studies in philosophy. N.Y. 1-17,1900-1925 3v.

Phil 2070.134.5 Cornesse, Marie. L'idée de Dieu chez William James. Thèse. Grenoble, 1933.

Phil 2070.134 Cornesse, Marie. Le rôle des images dans la pensée de William James. Thèse. Grenoble, 1933.

Phil 1107.4 Cornford, F.M. Before and after Socrates. Cambridge, Eng., 1932.

Phil 1107.4.3 Cornford, F.M. Before and after Socrates. Cambridge, Eng., 1960.

Phil 8582.20 Cornford, F.M. From religion to philosophy. London, 1912.

Phil 1133.30 Cornford, F.M. From religion to philosophy. N.Y., 1957.

Phil 1135.157 Cornford, F.M. The laws of motion in ancient thought. Cambridge, Eng., 1931.

Phil 1107.4.5 Cornford, F.M. Principium sapientiae. Cambridge, Eng., 1952.

Phil 600.51 Cornforth, M. Science and idealism. N.Y., 1947.

Phil 310.2 Cornforth, M.C. Dialectical materialism. London, 1952. 3v.

Phil 310.2.2 Cornforth, M.C. Dialectical materialism. London, 1955-56. 3v.

Phil 310.2.3 Cornforth, M.C. Dialectical materialism. v.1-3. 3d ed. London, 1961.

Phil 310.2.5 Cornforth, M.C. Historical materialism. N.Y., 1954.

Phil 1930.14.30 Cornforth, Maurice Campbell. In defence of philosophy against positivism and pragmatism. London, 1950.

Phil 1930.14.31 Cornforth, Maurice Campbell. In defence of philosophy against positivism and pragmatism. N.Y., 1950.

Phil 5520.436.5 Cornforth, Maurice Campbell. Marxism and the linguistic philosophy. London, 1965.

Phil 5520.436 Cornforth, Maurice Campbell. Marxism and the linguistic philosophy. N.Y., 1965.

Phil 1930.12.32 Cornforth, Maurice Campbell. Science versus idealism. N.Y., 1962.

Phil 333.26 Cornforth, Maurice Campbell. The theory of knowledge. N.Y., 1955.

Phil 3808.160 Cornill, Adolph. Arthur Schopenhauer. Heidelberg, 1856.

Phil 7069.26.4 Cornillier, P.E. La prédiction de l'avenir. Paris, 1926.

Phil 7069.21.20 Cornillier, PE. The survival of the soul and its evolution after death. London, 1921.

Phil 6112.8 Corning, J.L. Brain exhaustion. N.Y., 1884.

Phil 6112.8.5 Corning, J.L. Brain rest. N.Y., 1885.

Phil 9010.25 Corning, James L. The Christian law of amusements. Buffalo, 1859.

Phil 7054.113 Corning, W.H. The infidelity of the times. Boston, 1854.

Phil 5068.56.5 Cornman, James W. Metaphysics, reference, and language. New Haven, 1966.

Phil 4210.119 Cornoldi, G.M. Il rosminianismo. Roma, 1881.

Phil 1133.9 Cornwallis, C.F. Brief view of Greek philosophy. London, 1844.

Phil 1133.9.3 Cornwallis, C.F. Brief view of Greek philosophy. Philadelphia, 1846.

Phil 177.20 Cornwallis, C.F. Philosophical theories. Philadelphia, 1846.

Phil 2840.86 Cornwell, I. Les principes du droit dans la philosophie de C. Renouvier. Thèse. Paris, 1922?

Phil 4114.90 Corpaci, Francesco. Antonio Genovesi. Milano, 1966.

Phil 4073.112 Corpano, Antonio. Tommaso Campanella. Bari, 1961.

Phil 8434.5 Il corpo umano. (Tea, Eva.) Brescia, 1949.

Phil 2075.7.80 Corporate society and education. (Barnett, George.) Ann Arbor, 1962.

Phil 6112.11 Le corps et l'ame. (Clavel, Adolphe.) Paris, 1851.

Phil 300.15.5 Le corps et le monde. (Tollenaere, M. de.) Bruges, 1967.

Phil 8905.25 Le corps humain dans la pensée de Dieu. (Hudon, Louis-Nazaire.) Alma, 1967.

Phil 4510.35 Corpus philosophorum danicorum medii aevi. Hauniae, 1955-1963. 4v.

Phil 177.133 Corradi, Gemma. Philosophy and co-existence. Leyden, 1966.

Phil 6420.36.1 Correcting nervous speech disorders. (Gifford, Mabel F.) N.Y., 1940.

Phil 5648.11.25 A correlational analysis of proficiency in typing. (Ackerson, Luton.) N.Y., 1926.

Phil 1504.1 Correns, Paul. Die dem Boethius. v.1, pt.1. Münster, 1891.

Phil 8550.420 Correntes da filosofia religiosa em Braga dos séculos IV-VII. (Martins, Mário.) Porto, 1950.

Phil 1702.4 Correnti di filosofia contemporanea, a cura di circolo filosofico di Genova. Genova, 1913.

Phil 2477.6.20 Correspondance, 1899-1912. (Blondel, Maurice.) Paris, 1957. 3v.

Phil 2672.75 Correspondance. (Jouffroy, Théodore S.) Paris, 1901.

Phil 2520.78.35 Correspondance avec Arnaud et Marus. (Descartes, René.) Paris, 1953.

Phil 3552.77.20 Correspondance de Leibniz avec l'électrice Sophie de Brunswick-Lunebourg. (Leibniz, Gottfried Wilhelm.) Hanovre, 1874. 3v.

Phil 2477.6.180 Correspondance de Maurice Blondel et Joannès Wehrlé; extraits. (Blondel, Maurice.) Paris, 1969. 2v.

Phil 2840.75 Correspondance de Renouvier et Secrétan. (Renouvier, C.B.) Paris, 1910.

Phil 8430.42.1 La correspondance des arts, éléments d'esthétique comparée. (Souriau, Étienne.) Paris, 1969.

Phil 8430.42 La correspondance des arts. (Souriau, Étienne.) Paris, 1947.

Phil 2490.71 Correspondance inédite. (Comte, Auguste.) Paris, 1903-04. 4v.

Phil 2880.1.79 La correspondance inédite de L.C. Saint-Martin dit le philosophe inconnu et Kirchberger. (Saint-Martin, L.C.) Amsterdam, 1862.

Phil 3552.78.15 Correspondance Leibnitz-Clarke présentée d'après les manuscrits originaux des bibliothèques de Hanovre et de Londres. 1. éd. (Leibniz, Gottfried Wilhelm.) Paris, 1957.

Phil 2477.6.34 Correspondance philosophique. (Blondel, Maurice.) Paris, 1961.

Phil 1020.6   Correspondance philosophique d'Ibn Sab'in. (Mehren, A.F.) Florence, 1879.

Phil 2520.78.30   Correspondance publiée avec une introduction et des notes par C. Adam et G. Milhaud. 1. éd. (Descartes, René.) Paris, 1936-51. 8v.

Phil 4580.20   Correspondence entre H. Høffding et G. Meyerson. (Høffding, Harald.) Copenhague, 1939.

Phil 2520.78.25F   Correspondence of Descartes and Constantyn Huygeno, 1635-1647. (Descartes, René.) Oxford, 1926.

Phil 1865.195   The correspondence of Jeremy Bentham. (Bentham, Jeremy.) London, 1968. 3v.

Phil 2115.75.9   The correspondence of John Locke and Edward Clarke. (Locke, J.) Cambridge, 1927.

Phil 2115.75.10   The correspondence of John Locke and Edward Clarke. (Locke, J.) London, 1927.

Htn   Phil 2115.75.11*   Correspondence of John Locke and Edward Clarke. Editor's ms. for Cambridge edition. (Locke, J.) n.p., n.d.

Phil 3819.76   The correspondence of Spinoza. (Spinoza, Benedictus de.) London, 1928.

Phil 8610.881.35   Corresspondance d'un sceptique et d'un croyant. Genève, 1881.

Phil 5249.13.95   Corrie, Joan. C.G. Jung's Psychologie im Abriss. Zürich, 1929.

Phil 4960.210.2   Las corrientes filosóficas en la vida de México. 2. ed. (Lombardo Toledano, Vicente.) México, 1963.

Phil 2218.80   Corry, J. The life of Joseph Priestley. Birmingham, 1804.

Phil 5752.3.2   Corry, W. Reflections upon liberty and necessity. London, 1759-63. 5 pam.

Phil 5752.3   Corry, W. Reflections upon liberty and necessity. London, 1761.

Phil 3552.344   Corsano, A. G.W. Leibniz. Napoli, 1952.

Phil 4002.7   Corsano, A. Il pensiero religioso italiano dall'umanesino al giurisdizionalismo. Bari, 1937.

Phil 4260.110.5   Corsano, Antonio. Giambattista Vico. Bari, 1956.

Phil 4260.110   Corsano, Antonio. Umanesino e religione in G.B. Vico. Bari, 1935.

Phil 4080.3.215   Corsi, Mario. Le origini del pensiero di Benedetto Croce. 1. ed. Firenze, 1951.

Phil 4200.1.32   Corsi inediti dell'insegnamento padovano. (Pomponazzi, Pietro.) Padova, 1966.

Phil 4080.24   Corsini, Edoardo. Institutiones philosophicae. Venetius, 1743.

Phil 6312.18   Corsini, R.J. Methods of group psychotherapy. N.Y., 1957.

Phil 5640.142   Corso, John F. The experimental psychology sensory behavior. N.Y., 1967.

Phil 1535.1.15   Corso di filosofia elementare. v.1-4. (Balmes, Giacomo.) Firenze, 1854.

Phil 8875.20   Corso di filosofia morale. 2. ed. (D'Acquisto, P.B.) Palermo, 1855.

Phil 187.78   Corso di lezioni di filosofia razionale. (Maugeri, P. Antonino.) Catania, 1865-1866. 2v.

Phil 1111.14   Corso di storia della filosofia; I sofisti. Socrate, Alcuni dialoghi platonici. (Galli, Gallo.) Torino, 1954.

Phil 177.4   Corso elementare di filosofia. (Cantoni, C.) Milan, 1870.

Phil 177.4.12   Corso elementare di filosofia. (Cantoni, C.) Milan, 1901.

Phil 179.9   Corso elementare di filosofia. (Eusebietti, Pietro.) Milano, 1912. 3v.

Phil 187.117   Corso elementare di filosofia. (Morando, G.) Milano, 1898-1899. 3v.

Phil 7069.19.50   Corson, Hiram. Spirit messages. Boston, 1919.

Phil 2750.13   Corte, Marcel de. La philosophie de Gabriel Marcel. Paris, 1937.

Phil 2515.9.30   Corte, Marcel de. Philosophis des moeurs contemporaines. Bruxelles, 1945.

Phil 8657.17   Corte, P.A. Elementi di filosofia. v.2. 4. ed. Torino, 1862.

Phil 8952.9   Corte, P.A. Primi elementi di antropologia e di scienza morale. Torino, 1867.

Phil 333.19   Cortesi, Luigi. Le vie del sapere. Milano, 1959.

Phil 2115.123   Corti, S. La teoria della conoscenza in Locke e Leibnitz. Siena, 1908.

Phil 400.72   Corti, Settimio. La rivincita dell'idealismo. Rieti, 1920.

Phil 9070.80   Corts Grau, José. El hombre en vilo. Madrid, 1958.

Phil 1750.166.210   Corts Grau, José. Los humanismos y el hombre. Madrid, 1967.

Phil 4352.1.155   Corts Grau, José. Ideario político de Balmes. Madrid, 1934.

Phil 2905.1.360   Corvez, Maurice. De la science à la foi. Tours, 1964.

Phil 8582.78   Corvez, Maurice. L'être et la conscience morale. Louvain, 1968.

Phil 3450.19.260   Corvez, Maurice. La philosophie de Heidegger. Paris, 1961.

Phil 680.20   Corvez, Maurice. Les structuralistes: les linguistes, Michel Foucault, Claude Lévi-Strauss, Jacques Lacan, Louis Althusser, les critiques littéraires. Paris, 1969.

Phil 6045.19   Corvi, Andreas. Ein schönes Büchlin der kunst Chiromantia dess Wolgelrten Magistri Andree Corvi von Mivandula. Strassburg, 1964.

Phil 2280.5.125   Cory, D. Santayana: the later years. N.Y., 1963.

Phil 177.21   Cory, Isaac P. Metaphysical inquiry. London, 1833-37.

Phil 3484.14   La "cosa in se". (Cesca, G.) Torino, 1887.

Phil 333.9   Cosalini, Alessandro. Studi filosofici sulla cognizione. Roma, 1914.

Phil 8887.62   Coscienza, volontà, libertà. (Masci, F.) Lanciano, 1884.

Phil 176.74.5   La coscienza e il meccanesimo interiore. (Bonatelli, F.) Padova, 1872.

Phil 8406.22   La coscienza estetica. (Fanciulli, G.) Torino, 1906.

Phil 7080.37   La coscienza nel sonno. (Dandolo, G.) Padova, 1889.

Phil 9075.32.10   La coscienza quale dev'essere. (Marchal, Victor.) Torino, 1932.

Phil 8657.30   Coseglia, Raffaele. L'ateismo contemporaneo [l'aberrante avventura dello spirito] relazioni, studi, esperienze. Napoli, 1965.

Phil 75.12   Cosentini, F. Bibliotheca philosophica. Sassari, 1895.

Phil 802.10   Cosentini, F. I grandi filosofi e i grandi sistemi filosofici. Torino, 1925.

Phil 3850.16.118   Coser, Lewis A. Georg Simmel. Englewood, 1965.

Phil 5520.670   Coseriu, Eugenio. Die Geschichte der Sprachphilosophie von der Antike bis zur Gegenwart. Stuttgart, 1969.

Phil 9590.9   Cosgrave, J.O. The academy for souls. N.Y., 1931.

Phil 4225.8.52   Cosi mi parlano le cose muti. (Sciacca, Michele Federico.) Milano, 1962.

Phil 194.22   Cosmic ethics. (Thomas, William C.) London, 1896.

Phil 282.12   Cosmic evolution. (Boodin, J.E.) N.Y., 1925.

Phil 298.23   Cosmic humanism. (Reiser, Oliver Leslie.) Cambridge, 1966.

Phil 575.20   Cosmic inquiry pertaining to origin and development of individuality. (Frew, D.I.) Salt Lake City, 1907.

Phil 187.27.13   Cosmic problems. (Mackenzie, J.S.) London, 1931.

Phil 7069.19.140   The cosmic relations and immortality. (Holt, Henry.) Boston, 1914. 2v.

Phil 8584.15A   Cosmic religion. (Einstein, Albert.) N.Y., 1931.

Phil 6327.21.35   Cosmic superimposition. (Reich, Wilhelm.) Rangeley, Me., 1951.

Phil 6128.45   Cosmicology. (Simmons, D.A.) N.Y., 1931?

Phil 4120.2.90   Cosmo Guastella. (Carlo, Eugenio di.) Palermo, 1923.

Phil 6049.17   Cosmogonie humaine. (Bouchet, G.) Vichy, 1917.

Phil 1135.220   Cosmogonie orïentali e filosofia presocratica. (Conti, Rosario.) Roma, 1967.

Phil 282.11   Les cosmogonies modernes. (Busco, Pierre.) Paris, 1924.

Phil 282.11.5   Les cosmogonies modernes. Thèse. (Busco, Pierre.) Paris, 1924.

Phil 283.13   Cosmogonies of our fathers. (Collier, K.B.) N.Y., 1934.

Phil 8693.2.5   Cosmogony, or The mysteries of creation. (Davies, T.A.) N.Y., 1857?

Phil 285.5   Cosmogony. (Ehrenfels, C.F.) N.Y., 1948.

Phil 3480.69.5   Cosmogony. (Kant, Immanuel.) Glasgow, 1900.

Phil 303.4   Cosmography. (Winslow, C.F.) Boston, 1853.

Phil 4073.67   Cosmologia, inediti; theologicorum liber III. (Campanella, Tommaso.) Roma, 1964.

Phil 283.10   Cosmologia. (Calter, A.C.) Boston, 1931.

Phil 288.15   Cosmologia. 5. ed. (Hoenen, Peter.) Romae, 1956.

Phil 3497.28   Cosmologia e civilta. (Papi, Fulvio.) Urbino, 1969.

Phil 3910.58   Cosmologia generalis methodo scientifica. (Wolff, Christian von.) Francofurti, 1737.

Htn   Phil 8500.1*   Cosmologia sacra. (Grew, N.) London, 1701.

Phil 287.10   Cosmología y ciencia ficcion. (Ghirardi, Olsen A.) Córdoba, Argentina, 1970.

Phil 293.33   Cosmologie du XXe siècle. (Merleau-Ponty, Jacques.) Paris, 1965.

Phil 292.6   Cosmologie rationnelle. (LeBel, J.A.) Le Mans, 1925.

Phil 295.2   Cosmology; an introduction to the philosophy of matter. (O'Neill, John.) London, 1923.

Phil 283.12   Cosmology. (Colligan, J.J.) N.Y., 1936.

Phil 140.14   Pamphlet vol. Cosmology. Epistemology. Psychology. 9 pam.

Phil 282.21   Cosmology. 2. ed. (Bondi, Hermann.) Cambridge, Eng., 1960.

Phil 193.73   Cosmos and diacosmos...nature psychologically treated. (Snider, Denton J.) St. Louis, 1909.

Phil 285.6.2   Cosmos and history. (Eliade, Mircea.) N.Y., 1970.

Phil 8702.8   The cosmos and the creeds. (Moore, W.U.) London, 1903.

Phil 300.13   Le cosmos et l'imagination. (Tuzet, Hélène.) Paris, 1965.

Phil 292.10   La cosmosphie. (Lecouturier, H.) Paris, 1850.

Phil 8080.8   Cossio del Pomar, F. Critica de arte de Baudelaire à Malraux. México, 1956.

Phil 8735.4   Cossmann, P.N. Elemente der empirischen Teleologie. Stuttgart, 1899.

Phil 2725.55   Cossu, Maria. Il pensiero estetico di Charles Lalo. Cagliari, 1965.

Phil 8952.3   The cost of living; a personal reflection and its outcome. n.p., 1919.

Phil 8875.10   The cost of something for nothing. (Altgeld, J.P.) Chicago, 1904.

Phil 177.58   Costa, Alessandro. Filosofia e buddhismo. Torino, 1913.

Phil 3808.170   Costa, Alessandro. Il pensiero religioso di Arturo Schopenhauer. Roma, 1935.

Phil 75.40   Costa, M.G. Ineditos de filosofia em Portgal. Porto, 1949.

Phil 5242.10   Costa, P. Del modo di comporre l'idee. Firenze, 1837. 2 pam.

Phil 8610.922   Costa, U. da. Die Schriften. Amsterdam, 1922.

Phil 672.223   Costa de Beauregard, Olivier. Le second principe de la science du temps. Paris, 1963.

Phil 672.232   Costa de Beauregard, Olivier. La théorie physique et la notion de temps. Bordeaux, 1963.

Phil 525.43   Costa Guimaraes, Francisco da. Contribution à la pathologie des mystiques. Paris, 1908.

Phil 3552.395   Costabel, Pierre. Leibniz et la dynamique. Paris, 1960.

Phil 2605.1.85   Costanzi, T.M. Il pensiero di Alfredo Fouillée. Napoli, 1936.

Phil 7068.93.26   Coste, A. Les phénomèmes psychiques occultes. 2. ed. Montpellier, 1895.

Phil 400.39   Coste, Adolphe. Dieu et l'âme. Paris, 1880.

Phil 6672.6   Coste, P. Marie Léon. L'inconscient étude sur l'hypnotisme. Paris, 1889.

Phil 8877.102   Coste, René. Une morale pour un monde en mutation. Gembloux, 1969.

Phil 177.107   Costello, H.T. A philosophy of the real and the possible. N.Y., 1954.

Phil 2250.106   Costello, Harry. Josiah Royce's seminar, 1913-1914. New Brunswick, 1963.

Phil 6312.7   Coster, Geraldine. Psycho-analysis for normal people. London, 1926.

Phil 6312.7.5   Coster, Geraldine. Psycho-analysis for normal people. 3. ed. N.Y., 1924.

Phil 6315.2.335   Costigan, Giovanni. Sigmund Freud, a short biography. N.Y., 1965.

Phil 5520.397   La costruzione interpretative del mondo analizzata dal l'epistenrologia genetica. (Riverso, Emmanuele.) Napoli, 1956.

Phil 6952.9   Cotard, J. Etudes sur les maladies cérébrales et mentales. Paris, 1919.

Phil 1750.97   Cotereau, Jean. Que l'homme soit! Paris, 1959.

Phil 4080.3.545   Cotroneo, Girolamo. Croce e l'illuminismo. Napoli, 1970.

Phil 8886.13   Cottage dialogues. (Leadbeater, M.) Richmond, 1811.

Phil 5592.15   Cotte, S. Utilisation du dessin comme test psychologique chez les enfants. 3. éd. Marseille, 1951.

Phil 5042.23.8   Cotter, Anthony C. Logic and epistemology. Boston, 1940.

Phil 5042.23.5   Cotter, Anthony C. Logic and epistemology. 2nd ed. Boston, 1931.

Phil 8692.8   Cotterill, H. On true relations of scientific thought and religious belief. London, 1878.

Phil 6952.32   Cotti, Edelweiss. Contro la psichiatria. 1.ed. Firenze, 1970.

Phil 8657.34   Cottier, Georges. Horizons de l'athéisme. Paris, 1969.

Phil 600.12   Cottin, P. Positivisme et anarchie. Paris, 1908.

Phil 8692.14   Cotton, Edward. Has science discovered God? N.Y., 1931.

Phil 6952.20   Cotton, Henry A. The defective delinquent and insane. Princeton, 1921.

Phil 4065.112   Cotugno, R. Giordano Bruno e le sue opere. Trani, 1907.

Phil 4260.102.10   Cotugno, R. Giovambattista Vico. Il suo secolo e le sue opere. Pt.1. Trani, 1890.

Phil 4260.102   Cotugno, R. La sorte di G.B. Vico e le polemiche...della fine del XVII alla metà del XVIII secolo. Bari, 1914.
Phil 2730.82   Couailhac, M. Maine de Biran. Paris, 1905.
Phil 6980.704   The couch and the circle. (Spotnitz, Hyman.) N.Y., 1961.
Phil 3822.3   Couchond, P.L. Benoit de Spinoza. Paris, 1902.
Phil 8877.64   Coudenhove-Kalergi, R.N. Ethik und Hyperethik. Leipzig, 1923.
Phil 8877.64.5   Coudenhove-Kalergi, R.N. Krise der Weltanschauung. Wien, 1923.
Phil 477.11   Coudenhove-Kalergi, R.N. Los von Materialismus! Wien, 1931.
Phil 7140.116.9 Coué, Émile. Ce que j'ai fait. Nancy, 1924.
Phil 7140.116.11 Coué, Émile. Conscious auto-suggestion. London, 1924.
Phil 7140.116.13 Coué, Émile. Conscious auto-suggestion. N.Y., 1924.
Phil 7140.116.7 Coué, Émile. How to practice suggestion and autosuggestion. N.Y., 1923.
Phil 7140.116.5 Coué, Émile. My method. Garden City, 1923.
Phil 7140.116   Coué, Émile. Selfmastery through conscious autosuggestion. N.Y., 1922.
Phil 7140.116.15 Coué, Émile. The world's greatest power. pt.3-6. London, 192-. 2 pam.
Phil 7140.116.55 Der Couéismus. (Baudouin, C.) Darmstadt, 1926.
Phil 7140.116.75 Der Couéismus. Diss. (Seeling, Otto.) Giessen, 1926.
Phil 8610.915   Coughlin, D.R. Review of the Bibles. East Aurora, N.Y., 1915.
Phil 8725.2   Coulet. Catholicisme et laïcite. Paris, 1932.
Phil 5645.54   Les couleurs. (Rosseau, René L.) Paris, 1959.
Phil 974.2   Coulomb, E. Some account of my intercourse with Mme. Blavatsky. London, 1885.
Phil 978.71   Coulomb, E.J. Le secret de l'absolu. Paris, 1892.
Phil 8692.20A   Coulson, C.A. Science and Christian belief. Chapel Hill, 1955.
Phil 8905.5   Coulson, Charles Alfred. Faith and technology; being the inaugural lecture of the Luton Industrial College. London, 1969.
Phil 1507.4   Coulton, G.G. Studies in medieval thought. London, 1940.
Phil 8877.20   Counsel, E. Maxims. Melbourne, 188-?
Phil 8877.20.2   Counsel, E. Maxims. 2nd ed. Melbourne, 1892.
Phil 6127.22   Counseling and psychotherapy; newer concepts in practice. (Rogers, Carl R.) Boston, 1942.
Phil 6980.575   Counseling and psychotherapy. (Patterson, Charles H.) N.Y., 1959.
Phil 12.115   The counseling psychologist. St. Louis. 1,1969+
Phil 6127.22.10A Counseling with returned servicemen. 1. ed. (Rogers, Carl R.) N.Y., 1946.
Htn Phil 9343.12* Counsellor Manners, his last legacy to his son. (Dare, Josiah.) London, 1673.
Phil 9343.12.5   Counsellor Manners, his last legacy to his son. (Dare, Josiah.) London, 1710.
Htn Phil 8972.7* Counsels and directions of Ebenezer Wales to his children. (Wales, Ebenezer.) Boston, 1813.
Phil 3808.25.30 Counsels and maxims. (Schopenhauer, Arthur.) London, 1890.
Phil 3808.26   Counsels and maxims. (Schopenhauer, Arthur.) London, 1891.
Phil 9352.12   The counsels of a worldly godmother. (Mather, Persis (pseud.).) Boston, 1905.
Phil 8589.17.10 Counter attack from the East. (Joad, Cyril E.M.) London, 1933.
Phil 8589.17.15A Counter attack from the East. 1. Indian ed. (Joad, Cyril E.M.) Bombay, 1951.
Phil 5238.195   Counterpoint. (Gaskill, H.S.) N.Y., 1963.
Phil 7069.45.10 The country beyond; a study of survival and rebirth. (Sherwood, Jane.) London, 1945.
Phil 176.25.10   Countyman: a summary of belief. 1st ed. (Borland, Hal Glen.) Philadelphia, 1965.
Phil 7060.70   Coup d'oeil sur la magie au XIXe siècle. (Badaud, U.N.) Paris, 1891.
Phil 5628.50.15 Coup d'oeil sur les thaumaturges et les médiums du XIXe siècle. (Marin, Paul.) Paris, 1891.
Phil 5401.14   Courage; an anthology. 5e ed. (Lunn, H.K.) London, 1939.
Phil 6332.50   The courage to love. (Weigert, C. Edith.) New Haven, 1970.
Phil 5401.6   Courage today and tomorrow. (Marks, J.) N.Y., 1919.
Phil 2402.4   Les courants de la pensée philosophique française. (Cresson, A.) Paris, 1927. 2v.
Phil 1600.15   Courants religieux et humanisme à la fin de XVième et au début du XVIème siècle. (Céntre d'Études Supérieure.) Paris, 1959.
Phil 8877.56   Courcelle-Seneuil, J.G. Précis de morale rationnelle. Paris, 1875.
Phil 1200.30   Courdaveaux, V. De l'immortalité de l'âme dans le stoïcisme. Paris, 1857.
Phil 5525.3   Courdaveaux, V. Études sur la comique. Le rire. Paris, 1875.
Phil 6112.9   Courmont, F. Le cervelet et ses ionctions. Paris, 1891.
Phil 6112.9.4   Courmont, F. Le cervelet et ses fonctions. Paris, 1894.
Phil 177.22.15   Cournot, A.A. Critique philosophique. 1. ed. Paris, 1958.
Phil 177.22.5A   Cournot, A.A. Essai sur les fondations de nos connaissances. Paris, 1851. 2v.
Phil 177.22.10   Cournot, A.A. An essay on the foundations of our knowledge. N.Y., 1956.
Phil 477.6   Cournot, A.A. Matérialisme, vitalisme, rationalisme. Paris, 1875.
Phil 477.6.5   Cournot, A.A. Matérialisme, vitalisme, rationalisme. Paris, 1923.
Phil 177.22   Cournot, A.A. Traité des idées fondamentales. Paris, 1861.
Phil 2515.4.90   Cournot et la psychologie vitaliste. Thèse. (Segond, J.) Paris, 1910.
Phil 2515.4.92   Cournot métaphysicien de la connaissance. Thèse. (Battanelli, E.P.) Paris, 1913.
Phil 12.140   Le courrier rationaliste. Paris. 12,1965+
Phil 3910.82   Cours abrégé de la philosophie Wolffienne. (Des Champs, J.) Amsterdam, 1743-47. 3v.
Phil 192.4   Cours complet de philosophie. (Rattier, M.S.) Paris, 1843-1844. 4v.
Phil 2672.31   Cours de droit naturel. (Jouffroy, Théodore S.) Paris, 1835. 3v.
Phil 2672.31.5   Cours de droit naturel. 4. éd.v.2. (Jouffroy, Théodore S.) Paris, 1866.
Phil 1702.1.2   Cours de l'histoire de la philosophie, XVIIIe siècle. (Cousin, Victor.) Paris, 1841. 2v.
Phil 802.2.3   Cours de l'histoire de la philosophie. (Cousin, V.) Paris, 1841.
Phil 1702.1.3   Cours de l'histoire de la philosophie moderne. (Cousin, Victor.) Paris, 1841.
Phil 6682.16   Cours de magnétisme. (Reymond, Mine. Vve.) Paris, 1886.

Phil 6673.4.11   Cours de magnétisme animal. (Du Potet, J. de S.) Paris, 1834.
Phil 6673.4.10   Cours de magnétisme en sept leçons. (Du Potet, J. de S.) Paris, 1840.
Phil 8877.58.15 Cours de morale, a l'usage des écoles primaires superieures. (Challaye, F.) Paris, 1927.
Phil 8890.29   Cours de morale. 9. ed. (Payot, Jules.) Paris, 1914.
Phil 8963.1   Cours de morale religieuse. (Necker, J.) Paris, 1800. 3v.
Phil 8877.18.10 Cours de morale theorique et pratique. 19th ed. (Compayré, J.G.) Paris, n.d.
Phil 8878.34   Cours de morale thérique et pratique. v.1-2. (Dugas, L.) Paris, 1905-06.
Phil 8878.2   Cours de philosophie, morale. (Damiron, P.) Paris, 1834.
Phil 4115.31   Cours de philosophie, 1841-1842. (Gioberti, V.) Milano, 1947.
Phil 2496.40   Cours de philosophie...Du Vrai, Du Bean, Du Bien. (Cousin, Victor.) Paris, 1836.
Phil 802.2.2   Cours de philosophie. (Cousin, V.) Paris, 1828.
Phil 5243.1   Cours de philosophie. (Damiron, J.P.) Paris, 1837. 2v.
Phil 5043.1   Cours de philosophie. (Damiron, M.J.P.) Paris, 1836.
Phil 178.1   Cours de philosophie. (Damiron, P.) Bruxelles, 1834. 3v.
Phil 178.11   Cours de philosophie. (Drious, C.J.) Paris, 1883.
Phil 178.45   Cours de philosophie. (Durand, Eugène.) Paris, 1909-21. 2v.
Phil 180.1   Cours de philosophie. (Fabre, J.) Paris, 1870.
Phil 5245.1   Cours de philosophie. (Fabre d'Envieu, J.) Paris, 1863-1866. 2v.
Phil 180.68.15   Cours de philosophie. (Foulquié, Paul.) Paris, 1961.
Phil 181.7   Cours de philosophie. (Géruzez, E.) Paris, 1840.
Phil 181.8   Cours de philosophie. (Gibon, A.E.) Paris, 1842. 2v.
Phil 181.46   Cours de philosophie. (Gille, E.) Paris, 1876.
Phil 181.112   Cours de philosophie. v.3. (Gignoux, Victor.) Paris, 1950.
Phil 187.25   Cours de philosophie. 3e éd. v.1. (Mercier, D.) Louvain, 1902.
Phil 187.25.2   Cours de philosophie. 3e éd. v.2. (Mercier, D.) Louvain, 1902.
Phil 187.25.4   Cours de philosophie. 4e éd. v.4. (Mercier, D.) Louvain, 1900.
Phil 187.25.3   Cours de philosophie. 6e éd. v.3. (Mercier, D.) Louvain, 1903.
Phil 184.9.5   Cours de philosophie. 7. ed. (Joly, H.) Paris, 1882.
Phil 2725.10.30 Cours de philosophie. 23e éd. (Lahr, Charles.) Paris, 1920. 2v.
Phil 2675.1.31   Cours de philosophie adapté au programme du baccalauréat ès lettres. (Jaffre, F.A.) Lyon, 1878.
Phil 175.30   Cours de philosophie générale. (Azais, H.) Paris, 1824. 8v.
Phil 8876.100   Cours de philosophie morale. (Baudin, E.) Paris, 1936.
Htn Phil 2490.30* Cours de philosophie positive. (Comte, Auguste.) Paris, 1830-42. 6v.
Phil 2490.31   Cours de philosophie positive. (Comte, Auguste.) Paris, 1869. 6v.
Phil 2490.31.5   Cours de philosophie positive. 8. éd. (Comte, Auguste.) Paris, 1946.
Phil 194.25.5   Cours de philosophie pour les classes de philosophie A et B. 5e éd. (Thomas, P.F.) Paris, 1921.
Phil 186.66   Cours de philosophie première. (Laffitte, Pierre.) Paris, 1889-1894. 2v.
Phil 293.7   Cours de philosophie scientifique. (Montagu, A.) Paris, 1879.
Phil 293.7.2   Cours de philosophie scientifiques et ses conséquences sociales. 2. ed. (Montagu, A.) Paris, 1881.
Phil 5921.1   Cours de phrénologie. (Broussais, F.J.V.) Paris, 1836.
Phil 5245.15.5   Cours de psychologie. (Foucault, Marcel.) Paris, 1926.
Phil 5240.2   Cours de psychologie. v.1-2. (Ahrens, Heinrich.) Paris, 1836-38.
Phil 5241.42.5   Cours de psychologie. 5e éd. (Baudin, E.) Paris, 1927.
Phil 176.34.9F   Cours de science. (Buffier, Claude.) Paris, 1732.
Phil 3425.56   Cours d'esthétique. (Hegel, Georg Wilhelm Friedrich.) Paris, 1840-43. 2v.
Phil 8410.7.5   Cours d'esthétique. 2. éd. (Jouffroy, T.S.) Paris, 1863.
Phil 8410.7   Cours d'esthétique suivi de la thèse de l'art. 1. éd. (Jouffroy, T.S.) Paris, 1843.
Phil 802.2.1   Cours d'histoire de la philosophie. (Cousin, V.) Paris, 1828?
NEDL Phil 8827.2 Cours d'histoire de la philosophie morale au dix-huitième siècle. (Cousin, V.) Paris, 1839-42. 3v.
Phil 8886.51.5   Cours élémentaire de morale. (Levesque, M.) Paris, 1801.
Phil 176.50   Cours élémentaire de philosophie. (Bernès, M.) Paris, n.d.
Phil 194.6   Cours élémentaire de philosophie. (Tissot, C.J.) Dijon, 1840.
Phil 194.6.2   Cours élémentaire de philosophie. (Tissot, C.J.) Paris, 1847.
Phil 8886.31   Cours élémentaire de philosophie morale. 2. ed. (La Hautière, E. de.) Paris, 18- .
Phil 2725.2.15   Cours philosophique sur l'histoire générale de l'humanité; discours d'ouverture, ordre et progrès. (Laffitte, Pierre.) Paris, 1859.
Phil 6673.6   Cours théorique et C. de Braidisme. (Durand, J.P.) Paris, 1860.
Phil 333.6   Coursault, J.H. The learning process. Theory of knowledge. N.Y., 1907.
Phil 6111.9.5   Course...physiology and pathology of central nervous system. (Brown-Séquard, C.E.) Philadelphia, 1860.
Phil 5850.326.5F Course in business psychology assignment. v.1-8. (Roback, A.A.) n.p., n.d.
Phil 5258.4.3   Course in experimental psychology. (Sanford, E.C.) Boston, 1894.
Phil 5258.4   Course in experimental psychology. (Sanford, E.C.) Boston, 1895.
Phil 5258.4.4   Course in experimental psychology. (Sanford, E.C.) Boston, 1901.
Phil 177.64   A course in philosophy. (Conger, G.P.) N.Y., 1924.
Phil 8878.12   A course of lectures...pneumatology, ethics. (Doddridge, P.) London, 1794.
Phil 8882.3   A course of lectures...study, moral philosophy. (Hampden, R.D.) London, 1835.
Phil 186.29   A course of philosophy. 4. ed. (Louage, Augustin.) N.Y., 1895.
Phil 8897.24   Course of popular lectures. (Wright, F.) N.Y., 1829.
Phil 8897.24.5   Course of popular lectures. v.2. (Wright, F.) Philadelphia, 1836.

	Phil 1702.1.9	Course of the history of modern philosophy. (Cousin, Victor.) N.Y., 1853. 2v.
	Phil 1702.1.8	Course of the history of modern philosophy. (Cousin, Victor.) N.Y., 1854. 2v.
	Phil 2750.11.42A	Court traité de l'existence et de l'existent. (Maritain, Jacques.) Paris, 1947.
	Phil 9560.10	Courtenay, Charles. The empire of silence. N.Y., 1916.
Htn	Phil 4080.4.30*	The courtier. (Castilio, Baldessa.) London, 1588.
Htn	Phil 8892.40.5*	The courtiers academie. (Romei, A.) London, 1598.
Htn	Phil 9162.2*	Courtin, A. de. Traité de la jalousie. Paris, 1685.
	Phil 623.17*	Courtney, J.E. Freethinkers of the nineteenth century. London, 1920.
	Phil 6112.33	Courtney, J.W. The conquest of nerves. N.Y., 1919.
	Phil 8827.1	Courtney, W.L. Constructive ethics. London, 1886.
	Phil 177.23	Courtney, W.L. Studies in philosophy. London, 1882.
	Phil 2138.82.5	Courtney, W.S. Life of John Stuart Mill. London, 1889.
	Phil 2138.82.7A	Courtney, W.S. Life of John Stuart Mill. London, 1889.
	Phil 2138.82	Courtney, W.S. Metaphysics of John Stuart Mill. London, 1879.
	Phil 7054.92	Courtney, W.S. A review of J.B. Dods...theory of spiritual manifestations. N.Y., 1855.
	Phil 5272.24	Courts, Frederick A. Psychological statistics. Homewood, Ill., 1966.
	Phil 802.2.3	Cousin, V. Cours de l'histoire de la philosophie. Paris, 1841.
	Phil 802.2.2	Cousin, V. Cours de philosophie. Paris, 1828.
	Phil 802.2.1	Cousin, V. Cours d'histoire de la philosophie. Paris, 1828?
NEDL	Phil 8827.2	Cousin, V. Cours d'histoire de la philosophie morale au dix-huitième siècle. Paris, 1839-42. 3v.
	Phil 2520.86	Cousin, V. Fragments de philosophie Cartésienne. Paris, 1845.
	Phil 802.2.5	Cousin, V. Histoire générale de la philosophie. 8e éd. Paris, 1867.
	Phil 802.2.5.11	Cousin, V. Histoire générale de la philosophie. 11e éd. Paris, 1884.
	Phil 802.2.8	Cousin, V. Introduction to the history of philosophy. Boston, 1832.
	Phil 3484.3	Cousin, V. Philosophie de Kant. Paris, 1857.
	Phil 2115.102.4	Cousin, V. Philosophie de Locke. 4e éd. Paris, 1861.
	Phil 1802.2	Cousin, V. Philosophie écossaise. 3e éd. Paris, 1857. 2 pam.
	Phil 1750.12	Cousin, V. Philosophie sensualiste au XVIIIe siècle. Paris, 1866.
	Phil 3484.3.5	Cousin, V. Philosophy of Kant. London, n.d.
	Phil 1702.1.2	Cousin, Victor. Cours de l'histoire de la philosophie, XVIIIe siècle. Paris, 1841. 2v.
	Phil 1702.1.3	Cousin, Victor. Cours de l'histoire de la philosophie moderne. Paris, 1841.
	Phil 2496.40	Cousin, Victor. Cours de philosophie...Du Vrai, Du Bean, Du Bien. Paris, 1836.
	Phil 1702.1.9	Cousin, Victor. Course of the history of modern philosophy. N.Y., 1853. 2v.
	Phil 1702.1.8	Cousin, Victor. Course of the history of modern philosophy. N.Y., 1854. 2v.
	Phil 2496.45.3	Cousin, Victor. Défense de l'université et de la philosophie. Paris, 1844.
	Phil 2496.45.2	Cousin, Victor. Défense de l'université et de la philosophie. 2e éd. Paris, 1844.
	Phil 2496.45.4	Cousin, Victor. Defense de l'université et de la philosophie. 4e éd. Paris, 1845.
	Phil 2805.80	Cousin, Victor. Des pensées de Pascal. Paris, 1843.
	Phil 2805.80.2	Cousin, Victor. Des pensées de Pascal. Paris, 1844.
	Phil 8403.8	Cousin, Victor. Du vrai, du beau et du bien. Paris, 1853.
	Phil 8403.8.6	Cousin, Victor. Du vrai, du beau et du bien. 18. éd. Paris, 1873.
	Phil 2496.50.5	Cousin, Victor. Elements of psychology. Hartford, 1834.
	Phil 2496.50	Cousin, Victor. Elements of psychology. N.Y., 1838.
	Phil 2496.50.4	Cousin, Victor. Elements of psychology. N.Y., 1855.
	Phil 2496.50.3	Cousin, Victor. Elements of psychology. N.Y., 1856.
X Cg	Phil 2496.50.2	Cousin, Victor. Elements of psychology. 3e éd. N.Y., 1842.
	Phil 2805.80.7	Cousin, Victor. Études sur Pascal. Paris, 1876.
	Phil 2496.32	Cousin, Victor. Fragments de philosophie moderne. Paris, 1856.
	Phil 2496.30	Cousin, Victor. Fragments philosophiques. Paris, 1838. 2v.
	Phil 1107.1	Cousin, Victor. Fragments philosophiques. Paris, 1840.
	Phil 2496.40.6	Cousin, Victor. Lectures on the true, the beautiful, and the good. N.Y., 1855.
	Phil 2496.40.10	Cousin, Victor. Lectures on the true, the beautiful and the good. N.Y., 1854.
	Phil 2496.40.5	Cousin, Victor. Lectures on the true, the beautiful and the good. N.Y., 1854.
	Phil 2496.31	Cousin, Victor. Nouveaux fragmens philosophiques. Paris, 1828.
	Phil 2496.5	Cousin, Victor. Oeuvres de Victor Cousin. Bruxelles, 1840-41. 3v.
	Phil 2496.35	Cousin, Victor. Philosophie populaire. Paris, 1848.
	Phil 2496.40.15	Cousin, Victor. The philosophy of the beautiful. London, 1848.
	Phil 8403.8.10	Cousin, Victor. The philosophy of the beautiful. N.Y., 1849.
	Phil 2496.55.3	Cousin, Victor. Premiers essais de philosophie. 3e éd. Paris, 1855.
	Phil 3002.6	Cousin, Victor. Über französische und deutsche Philosophie. Stuttgart, 1834.
Htn	Phil 3801.293*	Cousin, Victor. Über französische und deutsche Philosophie...Nebst einer Beurtheilen der Vorrede des...Schelling. Stuttgart, 1834.
	Phil 2496.79	Pamphlet box. Cousin, Victor.
	Phil 3850.27.170	Cousins, Norman. Dr. Schweitzer of Lambaréné. N.Y., 1960.
	Phil 8403.45	Coutinho, Afrânio. Por uma crítica estética. Rio de Janeiro, 1954.
	Phil 8692.3	Coutts, John. The divine wisdom...nature, man and bible. London, 1907.
	Phil 8692.3.9	Coutts, John. The harmony and unity of the kingdom of God. London, 1922.
	Phil 8692.3.7	Coutts, John. Homely thoughts on the city of God and way to find it. London, 1921.
	Phil 8692.3.5	Coutts, John. Old lamps and new light of science. London, 1911.
	Phil 8692.3.10	Coutts, John. A prospective view of the new age. London, 1923.
	Phil 5042.8.5A	Couturat, L. The algebra of logic. Chicago, 1914.
	Phil 5042.8	Couturat, L. L'algèbre de la logique. 1st ed. Paris, 1905.
	Phil 5042.8.2	Couturat, L. L'algèbre de la logique. 2e éd. Paris, 1905.
NEDL	Phil 3552.106	Couturat, L. La logique de Leibniz. Paris, 1901.
	Phil 5649.23	Covaciu-Ulmeanu. Effort volontaire et chronaxie. Thèse. Paris, 1936.
	Phil 6112.44	Coval, Samuel Charles. Scepticism and the first person. London, 1966.
	Phil 6315.2.129	Cové, M. L'oeuvre paradoxale de Freud. 1. éd. Paris, 1945.
	Phil 735.274	Čovek i vrednost. (Životić, Miladin.) Beograd, 1969.
	Phil 177.100	Coviello, A. Crítica bibliográfica y análisis cultural. Tucumán, 1938.
	Phil 3195.10.117	Coviello, A. El filósofo Hans Driesch. Tucumán, 1942.
	Phil 2475.1.277	Coviello, A. El proceso filosófico de Bergson y su bibliografía. 2. ed. Tucumán, 1941.
	Phil 4964.67	Coviello, Alfredo. Una página de historía en la naciente filosofía argentina y otros ensayos criticos. Tucumán, 1942.
	VPhil 310.163	Čovjek i historija. (Vranicki, Predrag.) Sarajevo, 1966.
	Phil 1107.6	Covotti, Aurelio. Da Aristotele ai Bizantini. Napoli, 1935.
	Phil 3808.112.13	Covotti, Aurelio. La metafisica del bello e dei costumi di...Schopenhauer. Napoli, 1934.
	Phil 1107.5	Covotti, Aurelio. I piesocratici; saggi. Napoli, 1934.
	Phil 3808.112.9	Covotti, Aurelio. La vita e il pensiero di Arturo Schopenhauer. Milano, 1910.
	Phil 5647.5	Cowan, Edwina Abbott. The effect of adaptation on the temperature difference linien. Thesis. Princeton, N.J. 1914.
	Phil 5402.37	Cowan, Joseph Lloyd. Pleasure and pain: a study in philosophical psychology. London, 1968.
	Phil 5520.634	Cowan, Joseph Lloyd. Studies in thought and language. Tucson, 1970.
Htn	Phil 477.4*	Coward, W. Grand essay. London, 1704.
Htn	Phil 665.3.3*	Coward, William. Just scrutiny...modern notions of the soul. London, 1705?
Htn	Phil 665.3*	Coward, William. Second thoughts concerning human souls. London, 1704.
	Phil 8877.21.2	Cowdery, M.F. Elementary moral lessons. Philadelphia, 1856.
	Phil 8877.21	Cowdery, M.F. Elementary moral lessons. Sandusky, 1855.
	Phil 6952.10	Cowles, E. Insistent and fixed ideas. Baltimore, 1888.
	Phil 6952.10.2	Cowles, E. Neurasthenia and its mental symptoms. Boston, 1891.
	Phil 6952.10.25	Pamphlet box. Cowles, E. Minor writings.
	Phil 325.16	Cowley, Fraser. A critique of British empiricism. London, 1968.
	Phil 2138.146	Cowling, M. Mill and liberalism. Cambridge, Eng., 1963.
	Phil 5627.259	Cox, David. Jung and St. Paul. N.Y., 1959.
	Phil 7080.31	Cox, E. William. A monograph on sleep and dream. London, 1878.
	Phil 5242.11	Cox, E.W. The mechanism of man. London, 1876. 2v.
	Phil 7060.107	Cox, E.W. Spiritualism answered by science. London, 1871.
	Phil 7068.71.2	Cox, E.W. Spiritualism answered by science. N.Y., 1872.
	Phil 8877.54	Cox, George C. The public conscience. N.Y., 1922.
	Phil 974.2.42	Cox, H.R.W. Who wrote the March-hare attack on the Mahatma letters? Victoria, 1936.
	Phil 8955.8.80	Cox, Harvey G. The situation ethics debate. Philadelphia, 1968.
	Phil 6952.11	Cox, J.M. Practical observations on insanity. London, 1806.
	Phil 6952.11.2	Cox, J.M. Practical observations on insanity. Philadelphia, 1811.
	Phil 5649.20	Cox, John William. Manual skill. Cambridge, Eng., 1934.
	Phil 5922.5	Cox, R. Selections from the Phrenological Journal. Edinburgh, 1836.
	Phil 2115.172	Cox, Richard H. Locke on war and peace. Oxford, 1960.
	Phil 9162.7	Cox, S. Friendly counsel for girls. N.Y., 1868.
	Phil 8582.29	Coxe, A. Cleveland. Holy writ and modern thought. N.Y., 1892.
	Phil 9342.14	Coxe, Margaret. The young lady's companion. Columbus, 1839.
	Phil 8582.13	Crabbe, G. An outline of a system of natural theology. London, 1840.
	Phil 3808.95.5	Crämer, Otto. Arthur Schopenhauer's Lehre von der Schuld in ethischer Beziehung. Inaug. Diss. Heidelberg, 1895.
	Phil 7040.39	Craft, Michael. Ten studies into psychopathic personality. Bristol, 1965.
	Phil 1802.8	Cragg, G.R. Reason and authority in the 18th century. Cambridge, Eng., 1964.
	Phil 5066.130	Crahay, Franz. Le formalisme logic-mathématique et le problème du non-sens. Paris, 1957.
	Phil 177.130	Craig, Hardin. New lamps for old. Oxford, 1960.
	Phil 7082.168	Craig, Katherine Taylor. The fabric of dreams. N.Y., 1918.
	Phil 1850.100A	Craik, G.L. Bacon; his writings and his philosophy. London, 1846.
	Phil 1850.100.7	Craik, G.L. Bacon; his writings and his philosophy. London, 1862.
	Phil 1850.100.5	Craik, G.L. Bacon; his writings and his philosophy. v.1-3. London, 1860.
	VPhil 1920.1.32	Craik, Kenneth James Williams. The nature of explanation. Cambridge, Eng., 1952.
	Phil 1920.1.30	Craik, Kenneth James Williams. The nature of explanation. Cambridge, 1943.
	Phil 1920.1.35	Craik, Kenneth James Williams. The nature of psychology. Cambridge, Eng., 1966.
Htn	Phil 5042.17*	Crakanthorp, R. Logicae, libri quinque. London, 1622.
	Phil 5042.17.3	Crakanthorp, R. Logicae libri quinque. 3a ed. Oxoniae, 1670.
	Phil 3805.98	Cramaussel, E. La philosophie religieuse de Schleiermacher. Genève, 1909.
	Phil 5242.34	Cramaussel, E. Psychologie expérimentale. Paris, 1925.
	Phil 8663.3.96	Cramer, C.H. Royal Bob. 1. ed. Indianapolis, 1952.
	Phil 5325.44	Cramer, Phede. Word association. N.Y., 1968.
	Phil 9162.6	Cramer, W.M.A. Unterhaltungen zur Beförderung der häuslichen Glückseligkeit. Berlin, 1781.
	Phil 3160.20	Cramer, Wolfgang. Die absolute Reflexion. Frankfurt, 1966- 2v.
	Phil 510.153	Cramer, Wolfgang. Die Monade. Stuttgart, 1954.
	Phil 7069.25.11.5	Crandon, Le R.G. The Margery mediumship. n.p., 1930.
	Phil 177.31	Crane, A. The new philosophy. San Francisco, 1904.
	Phil 5242.14.12	Crane, A.M. Right and wrong thinking. Boston, 1914.
	Phil 8582.36	Crane, A.M. A search after ultimate truth. Boston, 1910.
	Phil 8877.66	Crane, Anker. Lykkens smil. København, 1922.
	Phil 5115.7	Crane, Esther. The place of the hypothesis in logic. Chicago, 1924.
	Phil 8877.31	Crane, F. Human confessions. Chicago, 1911.
	Phil 5850.166	Crane, G.W. Psychology applied. Chicago, 1933.
	Phil 9010.26.2	Crane, J.T. Popular amusements. Cincinnati, n.d.

Phil 720.68 A cranium shake-up and a new philosophy to alter the war spirit in man. (Kittinger, Kenneth C.) Los Angeles, 1967.
Phil 2115.168 Cranston, M.W. John Locke. London, 1957.
Phil 2138.132 Cranston, M.W. John Stuart Mill. London, 1958.
Phil 2115.168.5 Cranston, M.W. Locke. London, 1961.
Phil 5649.40 Cratty, Bryant J. Psychology and physical activity. Englewood Cliffs, 1968.
Phil 5649.42 Cratty, Bryant J. Social dimensions of physical activity. Englewood Cliffs, 1967.
Phil 8582.24 Craufurd, A.H. Christian instincts and modern doubt. London, 1897.
Phil 8877.27 Craufurd, A.H. Enigmas of the spiritual life. London, 1888.
Phil 5243.37.10 The craving for superiority. (Dodge, Raymond.) New Haven, 1931.
Phil 3460.85 Crawford, A.W. The philosophy of F.H. Jacobi. N.Y., 1905.
Phil 8582.57 Crawford, Benjamin F. The political faith of our fathers. Carnegie, Pa., 1943.
Phil 8952.5 Crawford, F.G. The Christ ideal for world peace. San Francisco, 1925.
Phil 2138.94 Crawford, J.F. The relation of inference to fact in Mill's logic. Chicago, 1916.
Phil 2138.119 Crawford, John F. The relation of inference to fact in Mill's logic. Chicago, 1916.
Phil 2477.1.135 Crawford, L.S. The philosophy of Emil Boutroux. Thesis. Charlotteville, 1924.
Phil 7069.15.20 Crawford, Mary MacDermont. Peeps into the psychic world. Philadelphia, 1915.
Phil 5465.147 Crawford, Robert Platt. The techniques of creative thinking. 1. ed. N.Y., 1954.
Phil 7060.132 Crawford, W. J. The reality of psychic phenomena. N.Y., 1918.
Phil 7069.19.60 Crawford, William J. Experiments in psychical science. N.Y., 1919.
Phil 7069.18.80 Crawford, William J. Hints and observations for those investigating the phenomena of spiritualism. N.Y., 1918.
Phil 7069.19.65 Crawford, William J. The reality of psychic phenomena, raps, levitations. N.Y., 1919.
Phil 7072.20 Crawford, William Jackson. The psychic structures at the Goligher Circle. London, 1921.
Phil 8582.41 Crawford-Frost, W.A. The philosophy of integration. Boston, 1906.
Phil 5242.40 Crawley, Sumner Lee. Syllabus for the first course in experimental psychology. N.Y., 1930.
Phil 665.70 Crawshaw, William H. The indispensable soul. N.Y., 1931.
Phil 5042.50 Crawshay-Williams, Rupert. Methods and criteria of reasoning. London, 1957.
Phil 2255.1.185 Crawshay-Williams, Rupert. Russell remembered. London, 1970.
Phil 8875.11 Creación del mundo moral. 2a ed. (Alvarez, Agustín.) Buenos Aires, 1915.
Phil 281.5 La creacioun dou mounde. (Fourviéro, Savié de.) Avignoun, 1891. 2v.
Phil 8877.95 Creasey, John. Good, God and man; an outline of the philosophy of self-ism. London, 1967.
Phil 3827.12.5 Creation, emanation and salvation; a Spinozistic study. (Hallett, H.F.) The Hague, 1962.
Phil 8696.5 Creation. (Guyot, Arnold.) N.Y., 1884.
Phil 8702.24 La création. (Mouiren, Trophine.) Paris, 1961.
Phil 830.5 Creation and cosmology. (James, Edwin Oliver.) Leiden, 1969.
Phil 8951.24 Creation and grace...Ernie Brunner. (Allen, E.) London, 1950.
Phil 8692.22 La création évolutive. (Chauchard, Paul.) Paris, 1957.
Phil 282.26 The creation in the light of modern science. (Barth, Aron.) Jerusalem, 1968.
Phil 8693.8 Creation or biblical cosmogony. (Dana, J.D.) Oberlin, 1885.
Phil 8880.53 Création ou consentement. (Fruchon, Pierre.) Paris, 1963.
Phil 8423.25 Création picturale et ordre cérébral. (Wahl, Marcelle.) Paris, 1964.
Phil 8581.25 Creation's way. (Burris, M.A.) Smithville, Ohio, 1911.
Phil 5520.376 Creative analysis. (Upton, Albert.) Whittier, Calif., 1961.
Phil 186.57 Creative effort. 1. ed. (Lindsay, Norman.) London, 1924.
Phil 2475.1.51.4 Creative evolution. (Bergson, Henri.) London, 1954.
Phil 2475.1.51.2 Creative evolution. (Bergson, Henri.) N.Y., 1911.
Phil 2475.1.51.8 Creative evolution. (Bergson, Henri.) N.Y., 1911.
Phil 2475.1.51.6 Creative evolution. (Bergson, Henri.) N.Y., 1911.
Phil 2475.1.51 Creative evolution. (Bergson, Henri.) N.Y., 1944.
Phil 2750.19.32 Creative fidelity. (Marcel, Gabriel.) N.Y., 1964.
Phil 187.71 Creative freedom. (Mason, J.W.T.) N.Y., 1926.
Phil 193.146 The creative I and the Divine. (Schmidt, Karl.) N.Y., 1937.
Phil 5465.143 The creative imagination. (Ruitenbeek, Hendrik M.) Chicago, 1965.
Phil 8403.35 The creative impulse in writing and painting. (Caudwell, H.) London, 1951.
Phil 177.39 Creative intelligence: Essays in pragmatic attitude. N.Y., 1917.
Phil 197.25 Creative involution. (Williams, C.L.) N.Y., 1916.
Phil 193.132.10 Creative man. (Samuel, Herbert S.) Oxford, 1947.
Phil 2475.1.30 The creative mind. (Bergson, Henri.) N.Y., 1946.
Phil 5465.31.5 Creative mind. (Spearman, Charles.) Cambridge, Eng., 1931.
Phil 5465.31 Creative mind. (Spearman, Charles.) London, 1930.
Phil 8892.54 Creative morality. (Reid, L.A.) London, 1937.
Phil 9400.12 Creative old age. (De Gruchy, C.) San Francisco, 1946.
Phil 180.39 Creative personality. (Flewelling, R.) N.Y., 1926.
Phil 365.51 Creative personality. (Porter, C.) N.Y., 1950.
Phil 5465.192.1 The creative process; a symposium. (Ghiselin, Brewster.) N.Y., 1955.
Phil 194.21.5 The creative process in the individual. (Troward, Thomas.) London, 1910.
Phil 182.65 Creative psychics, the art of regeneration. (Henkel, Fred.) Los Angeles, 1917.
Phil 7069.54.20 Creative realism. 1. ed. (Alexander, Rolf.) N.Y., 1954.
Phil 645.33 Creative sceptics. (Smith, T.V.) Chicago, 1934.
Phil 2055.9.40 Creative synthesis and philosophic method. (Hartshorne, Charles.) London, 1970.
Phil 6328.25.5 The creative unconscious. (Sachs, Hanns.) Cambridge, 1942.
Phil 341.14.5 Creative understanding. (Keyserling, H. Graf von.) N.Y., 1929.
Phil 8407.31 Creative vision in artist and audience. (Guggenheimer, R.H.) N.Y., 1950.
Phil 8423.5 The creative will, studies in the philosophy and syntax of aesthetics. (Wright, W.H.) N.Y., 1916.

Phil 5465.202 Créativité et sciences humaines. (Astruc, Louis.) Paris, 1970.
Phil 5465.139 Creativity, progress and potential. (Taylor, C.W.) N.Y., 1964.
Phil 5465.198 Creativity. (Nobel Conference, 6th, Gustavus Adolphus College, 1970.) Amsterdam, 1970.
Phil 5465.200 Creativity: selected readings. (Vernon, Philip Ewart.) Harmondsworth, 1970.
Phil 5465.196 Creativity and conformity. (Moustakas, Clark E.) N.Y., 1967.
Phil 5465.172 Creativity and eternization. (Meerloo, Joost Abraham Maurits.) Assen, 1967.
Phil 5465.90 Creativity and its cultivation. (Interdisciplinary Symposium on Creativity, Michigan State University of Agriculture.) N.Y., 1959.
Phil 5465.155 Creativity and learning. (Kagan, Jerome.) Boston, 1967.
Phil 5465.100 Creativity and the individual. (Stein, Morris.) Glencoe, 1960.
Phil 5465.100.2 Creativity and the individual. (Stein, Morris.) Glencoe, 1964.
Phil 5465.173 Creativity in the life-cycle. (Arasteh, A. Reza.) Leiden, 1968-
Phil 8660.6 The creator and the creature. (Faber, F.W.) London, 1889.
Phil 8597.36 The creator spirit. (Raven, Charles E.) Cambridge, 1927.
Phil 8622.4 Creators of the modern spirit. (Waylen, B.) N.Y., 1951.
Phil 4073.72 Le creature sovrannaturali. (Campanella, Tommaso.) Roma, 1970.
Phil 8705.17 La creazione. (Perego, Angelo S.J.) Brescia, 1958.
Phil 4215.1.105 Credali, A. G.D. Romagnosi. Modena, 1935.
Phil 4235.3.90 Credaro, L. Alfonso Testa e i primordii del Kantismo in Italia. Catania, 1913.
Phil 8661.35.5 Credenti e non credenti per un mondo nuovo. (Girardi, Giulio.) Firenze, 1969.
Phil 8692.2.1 The credentials of science, the warrant of faith. 2. ed. (Cooke, J.P.) N.Y., 1888.
Phil 8692.2.2 The credentials of science the warrent of faith. (Cooke, J.P.) N.Y., 1893.
Phil 2115.165 La credenza come fondamento. (Bianca, Giuseppe G.) Padova, 1950.
Phil 8709.1.5 Credo. (Townsend, L.T.) Boston, 1870.
Phil 8588.35 Creed, J.M. Religious thought in the eighteenth century. Cambridge, Eng., 1934.
Phil 8615.5.9 Creed and deed. (Adler, Felix.) N.Y., 1894.
Phil 193.83.5 A creed for sceptics. (Strong, C.A.) London, 1936.
Phil 600.11 The creed of a layman. (Harrison, F.) London, 1907.
Phil 600.11.2 The creed of a layman. (Harrison, F.) N.Y. 1907.
Phil 8586.37 The creed of Christendom. (Greg, William R.) London, 1851.
Phil 8586.37.10 The creed of Christendom. 5th ed. (Greg, William R.) London, 1877. 2v.
Htn Phil 2045.107* The creed of Mr. Hobbes examined. (Tenison, Thomas.) London, 1670.
Phil 8586.5 The creed of science, religious, moral and social. (Graham, W.) London, 1881.
Phil 8598.38 A creedless Gospel and the Gospel creed. (Satterlee, Henry Y.) N.Y., 1895.
Phil 8657.5 Creeds of the day. (Coke, H.) London, 1883. 2v.
Phil 1930.15.30 Creegon, R.F. The shocky existence. Cambridge, 1954.
Phil 930.42 Creel, H.G. Chinese thought from Confucius to Mao Tse-tung. Chicago, 1953.
Phil 5520.445 Creelman, Marjorico Broer. The experimental investigation of meaning. N.Y., 1966.
Phil 5465.133 Créer. (Przyluski, J.) Paris, 1943.
Phil 5435.1 Creighton, C. Illustrations of unconscious memory in disease. London, 1886.
Phil 5042.7 Creighton, J.E. An introductory logic. N.Y., 1898.
Phil 5042.7.2 Creighton, J.E. An introductory logic. N.Y., 1900.
Phil 5042.29 Creighton, J.E. An introductory logic. N.Y., 1938.
Phil 5042.7.3 Creighton, J.E. An introductory logic. 3rd ed. N.Y., 1909.
Phil 5042.29.5 Creighton, J.E. An introductory logic. 4th ed. N.Y., 1923.
Phil 5042.7.10 Creighton, J.E. An introductory logic. 4th ed. N.Y., 1927.
Phil 177.40.5 Creighton, J.E. Studies in speculative philosophy. N.Y., 1925.
Phil 8610.964.5 Crekshut, A.O.J. The unbelievers. London, 1964.
Phil 8877.25 Crell, J. Ethica aristotelica. Selenoburgi, n.d.
Phil 8582.31 Cremer, Herman. Das Wesen des Christentums. 3. Aufl. Gütersloh, 1902.
Phil 6060.1.17 Crepieux-Jamin, J. Les bases fondamentales de la graphologie. Paris, 1921.
Phil 6060.1.4 Crepieux-Jamin, J. L'ecriture et le caractère. 6e ed. Paris, 189-?
Phil 6060.1.15 Crepieux-Jamin, J. Les éléments de l'écriture descanailles. Paris, 1923.
Htn Phil 6060.1.10* Crepieux-Jamin, J. La graphologie en exemples. Paris, 1899.
Phil 6060.1.25 Crepieux-Jamin, J. The psychology of the movements of handwriting. London, 1926.
Phil 6060.1 Crepieux-Jamin, J. Traite de graphologie. Paris, 1885.
Phil 1715.2 Il crepuscolo dei filosofi. (Papini, Giovanni.) Milano, 1906.
Phil 2750.11.45A Le crépuscule de la civilisation. (Maritain, Jacques.) Montreal, 1941.
Phil 180.72.5 Le crépuscule des dieux et l'avenir de l'homme. (Flam, Leopold.) Paris, 1966.
Phil 8402.2 Le crépuscule des images. (Buzin, Germain.) Paris, 1946.
Phil 623.46 Le crépuscule des magiciens. 2. éd. (Galifret, Yves.) Paris, 1965.
Phil 530.15.45 Crépuscule des mystiques. (Cognet, Louis.) Tournai, 1958.
Phil 1715.2.5 Le crepuscule des philosophes. (Papini, Giovanni.) Paris, 1922.
Phil 3640.166 Le crépuscule d'une idole, Nietzsche, nietzschéisme, nietzscheens. (Pallarès, V. de.) Paris, 1910.
Phil 1050.14.2 Crescas on problem of divine attributes. (Wolfson, Harry A.) Philadelphia, 1916.
Phil 4115.106 Crescenzo, G. de. Pietro Luciani e il giobertismo. Napoli, 1960.
Phil 1828.6.20 Crescenzo, Giovanni de. Patrick Romanelli e l'odierno naturalismo statunitense. 1. ed. Firenze, 1966.
Phil 5068.56.15 Crescini, Angelo. Le origini del metodo analitico. Udine, 1965.
Phil 4080.27 Crescini, Angelo. Per una metafisica concreta. Padova, 1963.
Phil 4002.3 Crespi, Angelo. Contemporary thought of Italy. London, 1926.

Phil 2905.1.176   Crespy, Georges. De la science à la théologie. Neuchâtel, 1965.

Phil 2905.1.177   Crespy, Georges. From science to theology. Nashville, 1968.

Phil 2905.1.175   Crespy, Georges. La pensée théologique de Teilhard de Chardin. Paris, 1961.

Phil 2402.4   Cresson, A. Les courants de la pensée philosophie française. Paris, 1927. 2v.

Phil 2050.225   Cresson, A. David Hume. 1. éd. Paris, 1952.

Phil 2515.3.32   Cresson, A. L'invérifiable; les problèmes de la métaphysique. 2e éd. Paris, 1920.

Phil 5585.63   Cresson, A. La représentation. Paris, 1936.

Phil 2490.136A   Cresson, André. Auguste Comte; sa vie, son oeuvre, avec un exposé de sa philosophie. Paris, 1941.

Phil 2475.1.286A   Cresson, André. Bergson; sa vie, son oeuvre, avec un exposé de sa philosophie. Paris, 1941.

Phil 2475.1.410   Cresson, André. Bergson: sa vie, son oeuvre, avec un exposé de sa philosophie. Paris, 1964.

Phil 3552.253   Cresson, André. De liberate apud Leibnitium. Thesis. Paris, 1903.

Phil 2520.217   Cresson, André. Descartes; sa vie, son oeuvre, avec un exposé de sa philosophie. 1e éd. Paris, 1942.

Phil 3425.400   Cresson, André. Hegel. Paris, 1955.

Phil 3484.9.5   Cresson, André. Kant; sa vie, son oeuvre, avec un exposé de sa philosophie. Paris, 1941.

Phil 3484.9.10   Cresson, André. Kant; sa vie, son oeuvre, avec un exposé de sa philosophie. 5. éd. Paris, 1959.

Phil 3552.253.5   Cresson, André. Leibniz, sa vie, son oeuvre. Paris, 1946.

Phil 3552.253.8   Cresson, André. Leibniz, sa vie, son oeuvre. 3. éd. Paris, 1958.

Phil 3484.9   Cresson, Andre. La morale de Kant. Paris, 1904.

Phil 8877.29   Cresson, Andre. La morale de la raison theorique. Paris, 1903.

Phil 3640.306   Cresson, André. Nietzsche; sa vie, son oeuvre, avec un exposé de sa philosophie. 1e éd. Paris, 1942.

Phil 2805.229.5   Cresson, André. Pascal; sa vie, son oeuvre, avec un exposé de sa philosophie. 2e éd. Paris, 1942.

Phil 2805.229.8   Cresson, André. Pascal; sa vie, son oeuvre, avec un exposé de sa philosophie. 5. éd. Paris, 1962.

Phil 1107.8   Cresson, André. La philosophie antique. 4e ed. Paris, 1957.

Phil 1702.3   Cresson, André. La position actuelle des problèmes philosophiques. Paris, 1924.

Phil 8827.8   Cresson, André. Le problème moral et les philosophes. Paris, 1933.

Phil 5242.38   Cresson, André. Les réactions intellectuelles élémentaires. Paris, 1922.

Phil 3808.184.3   Cresson, André. Schopenhauer. Paris, 1957.

Phil 3808.184   Cresson, André. Schopenhauers a vie, son oeuvre. Paris, 1946.

Phil 177.80   Cresson, André. Les septèmes philosophiques. Paris, 1929.

Phil 3822.10   Cresson, André. Spinoza. Paris, 1940.

Phil 3822.10.4   Cresson, André. Spinoza. 4. éd. Paris, 1959.

Phil 4872.109.80   Crî Aurobindo, philosophe du yoga intégral. (Sailley, Robert.) Paris, 1970.

Phil 6952.12   Crichton, A. An inquiry...nature, origin, mental derangement. London, 1798. 2v.

Phil 6312.6   Crichton-Brown, J. The Cavendish lecture on dreamy mental states. London, 1895.

Phil 7054.71   Cridge, A. Epitome of spirit-intercourse. Boston, 1854.

Phil 3002.2   Crile, G.W. The fallacy of the German state philosophy. Garden City, 1918.

Phil 5812.14   Crile, George J. A naturalistic view of man. N.Y., 1969.

Phil 5400.32   Crile, George W. The origin and nature of the emotions. Philadelphia, 1915.

Phil 8610.804   Les crimes de la philosophie. (Piestre, J.L.) Paris, 1804.

Phil 8876.54.25   Crippa, R. Profilo della critica blondeliana. Milano, 1962.

Phil 2477.6.115   Crippà, Romeo. Rassegna di bibliografia blondeliana. Torino, 1952.

Phil 2477.6.118   Crippà, Romeo. Il realismo integrale di M. Blondel. Milano, 1954.

Phil 9075.65   Crippa, Romeo. Studi nella coscienza etica e religiosa del seicento. Brescia, 1960. 3v.

Phil 5070.13   La crise de la croyance. (Bazaillas, A.) Paris, 1901.

Phil 4769.1.75   Crise de la philosophie occidentale. (Solov'ev, V.S.) Paris, 1947.

Phil 5250.6   La crise de la psychologie expérimentale. (Kostyleff, N.) Paris, 1911.

Phil 1750.754   La crise de la raison dans la pensée contemporaine. Bruges, 1960.

Phil 1750.161   La crise de l'humanisme. (Fiolle, Jean.) Paris, 1937.

Phil 623.26   La crise du rationalisme. (Benda, J.) Paris, 1949.

Phil 8893.56   A crise em seus aspectos morals. (Silva Cordeira, J.A. da.) Coimbra, 1896.

Phil 815.34   Crise filosófica do século atual. (Pacini, Dante.) Rio de Janeiro, 1969.

Phil 8886.38.8   La crise morale. (Loisy, Alfred.) Paris, 1937.

Phil 2409.1   La crise philosophique. (Janet, P.) Paris, 1865.

Phil 4070.7.55   La crisi. (Banfi, Antonio.) Milano, 1967.

Phil 735.136   La crisi dei valori. (Archivio di Filosofia.) Roma, 1945.

Phil 1750.590   La crisi del concetto filosofico. (Marchello, Giuseppe.) Milano, 1959.

Phil 1702.2.5   La crisi del pensiero moderno. (Chiappelli, A.) Citta di Castello, 1920.

Phil 600.28   La crisi del positivismo...filosofico. (Marchesini, G.) Torino, 1898.

Phil 1614.5   La crisi del Rinascimento e il dubbio cortesiano. (Nardi, Bruno.) Roma, 1950-51.

Phil 4225.8.80   Crisi dell'uomo e conquista. (Nobile-Ventura, Attilio.) Milano, 1958.

Phil 8090.8   Crisi dell'estetica romantica. (Volpe, Galvo della.) Roma, 1963.

Phil 400.69   La crisi dell'idealismo attuale. (Redanò, Ugo.) Roma, 1924.

Phil 4006.6.30   La crisi dell'immanentismo. (Garilli, G.) Palermo, 1953.

Phil 4110.14.30   Crisi e valori, ed altri saggi. (Fichera, G.) Padova, 1958.

Phil 12.6   Crisis; revista española de filosofia. Madrid. 1,1954+ 15v.

Phil 8599.46   La crisis del pensamiento cristiano en el siglo XVI. (Toro, Antonio del.) Madrid, 1961.

Phil 9150.9.2   The crisis in morals. (Bixby, James T.) Boston, 1891.

Phil 7069.65.5   The crisis in parapsychology. (Gerloff, Hans.) Tittmoning, 1965.

Phil 7069.65.6   The crisis in parapsychology. 2. supplement. (Gerloff, Hans.) Tittmoning, 1966.

Phil 7069.65.7   The crisis in parapsychology. 3. supplement. (Gerloff, Hans.) Bayerisch Gmain, 1967.

Phil 6980.482   The crisis in psychiatry and religion. (Mowrer, O.H.) Princeton, N.J., 1961.

Phil 5243.28   The crisis in psychology. (Driesch, Hans.) Princeton, 1925.

Phil 5465.146   The crisis of creativity. (Seidel, George Joseph.) Notre Dame, 1966.

Phil 3450.11.62   The crisis of European sciences and transcendental phenomenology. (Husserl, Edmund.) Evanston, 1970.

Phil 2150.1.130   The crisis of opinion. (Mott, F.J.) Boston, 1944.

Phil 2630.13.80   Crispini, Franco. Lo strutturalismo dialettico di Lucien Goldmann. Napoli, 1970.

Phil 4080.30   Cristaldi, Giuseppe. Filosofia e verità; saggi e note. Milano, 1965.

Phil 4210.205   Cristaldi, Giuseppe. Prospettive rosminiane. Milano, 1965.

Phil 4210.240   Cristaldi, Mariano. Rosmini antiromantico. Catania, 1967.

Phil 3925.16.250   Cristaldi, Mariano. Wittgenstein; l'ontologia inibita. Bologna, 1970.

Phil 4080.7.80   Cristallini, Alessandro. Ottario Colecchi, un filosofo da riscoprire. Padova, 1968.

Phil 4140.80   Cristallini, Alessandro. Il pensiero filosofico de Donato Jaja. Padova, 1970.

Phil 8583.46   Cristianesimo-marxismo. (Damiani, Raoul.) Milano, 1969.

Phil 3552.348   Il cristianesimo universale di G.W. Leibniz. 1. ed. (Preti, G.) Roma, 1953.

Phil 2905.1.82   Cristiani, Léon. Pierre Teilhard de Chardin. London, 1960.

Phil 2905.1.80   Cristiani, Léon. La vie et l'âme de Teilhard de Chardin. Paris, 1957.

Phil 8581.41   El cristianismo y la filosofia. (Benitez de Lugo, A.) Sevilla, 1882.

Phil 4265.2.90   Cristofoli, A. Il pensiero religioso di P.G. Ventura. Milano, 1927.

Phil 4073.50   Cristologia. (Campanella, Tommaso.) Roma, 1958. 2v.

Phil 1535.1.35   El criterio. (Balmes, Jaime.) Madrid, 1929.

Phil 4372.1.82   Criterio social de Luis Vives. (Gomis, J.B.) Madrid, 1946.

Phil 332.13   Criteriologie of de leer over waarheid en zekerheid. 2. druk. (Beysens, J.T.) Leiden, 1911.

Phil 308.6   Critica, oggetto e logica. (Migliorini, Ermanno.) Firenze, 1968.

Phil 12.90   Critica; revista hispano-americana de filosofia. Mexico. 1,1967+

Phil 352.8.5.3   Critica. 3. ed. recognita et aucto. (Vries, Joseph de.) Barcinone, 1964.

Phil 343.45.5   Critica. 5. ed. (Morandini, Francesco.) Romae, 1963.

Phil 334.8.5   Critica. 9. ed. (Donat, J.) Monachü, 1945.

Phil 177.100   Critica bibliográfica y análisis cultural. (Coviello, A.) Tucumán, 1920.

Phil 187.180   Crítica cosmológica da física quântica. (Machado Bandeira de Mello, Lydio.) Belo Horizonte, 1969.

Phil 8080.8   Critica de arte de Baudelaire à Malraux. (Cossio del Pomar, F.) México, 1956.

Phil 2750.19.80   Critica de la objetividad en el existencialism de Gabriel Marcel. (Rebollo Peña, A.) Burgos, 1954.

Phil 8735.60   La critica del finalismo nella cultura cartesiana. (De Angelis, Enrico.) Firenze, 1967.

Phil 3480.51.30   Critica del giudizio. (Kant, Immanuel.) Bari, 1907.

Phil 2045.113   Critica della concezione dello stato in Tommaso Hobbes. (Alloggio, Sabino.) Napoli, 1930.

Phil 3480.46.23   Critica della ragion pratica. (Kant, Immanuel.) Bari, 1909.

Phil 3480.46.25   Critica della ragion pratica. 3. ed. (Kant, Immanuel.) Bari, 1924.

Phil 3480.31.8   Critica della raigon pura. v.1-2. (Kant, Immanuel.) Bari, 1910.

Phil 3480.31.9   Critica della raigon pura. 2. ed. (Kant, Immanuel.) Bari, 1919-21. 2v.

Phil 5241.186   Critica della società competitiva. (Biasutti, Bruno.) Roma, 1968.

Phil 4170.7.43   Critica delle rivelazioni. (Mamiani della Rovere, Terenzio.) Roma, 1873.

Phil 4060.4.35   Critica dell'esistenzialismo. 2. ed. v.2,5. (Aliotta, Antonio.) Roma, 1957. 2v.

Phil 8419.57   Critica dell'estetica. (Spirito, Ugo.) Firenze, 1964.

Phil 3425.395   Critica dell'idea di progresso. (Tinivella, Giovanni.) Milano, 1955.

Phil 400.94   Critica dell'idealismo. (Ottaviano, C.) Napoli, 1936.

Phil 400.94.3   Critica dell'idealismo. 3. ed. (Ottaviano, C.) Padova, 1960.

Phil 187.74   Critica dell'identita. (Mignosi, Pietro.) Palermo, 1926.

Phil 402.10   Critica dell'ideologia contemporanea. (Volpe, Galvano della.) Roma, 1967.

Phil 8892.32.5   Critica dello morale. (Rensi, Giuseppe.) Catania, 1935.

Phil 4070.1.85   Critica dell'Ultima critica di Cristoforo Bonavino. (Galletti, B.) Palermo, 1889.

Phil 9550.11.5   Una critica dell'utilitarismo. (Cantoni, C.) Roma, 1876.

Phil 4000.10   Critica di alcune critiche di spaventa. (Acri, Francesco.) Bologna, 1875.

Phil 4080.3.90   La critica di Benedetto Croce. (Settimelli, Emilio.) Bologna, 1912.

Phil 310.646   Crítica do materialismo dialéctico. (Braga, Joaquim.) Lisboa, 1966.

Phil 3425.748   Critica e letteratura in tre hegeliani di Napoli. (Dell'Aquila, Michele.) Bari, 1969.

Phil 3480.32.60   Critica ratiunii pure. (Kant, Immanuel.) Bucuresti, 1930.

Phil 8586.29   Critica religiosa e filosofia lettere e saggi. (Giovanni, V. di.) Palermo, 1897. 5v.

Phil 3500.5   Criticae ratien. Purae expositio systematica. (Schmidt-Phiseldek, C.) Hafniae, 1796.

Phil 3484.1   A critical account of the philosophy of Kant. (Caird, E.) Glasgow, 1877.

Phil 3484.1.3A   A critical account of the philosophy of Kant. (Caird, E.) Glasgow, 1889. 2v.

Phil 3484.1.2   A critical account of the philosophy of Kant. (Caird, E.) London, 1877.

Phil 3484.1.5   A critical account of the philosophy of Kant. v.2. (Caird, E.) N.Y., 1889.

Phil 3565.82.5   A critical account of the philosophy of Lotze. (Jones, Henry.) Glasgow, 1895.

Phil 3565.82   A critical account of the philosophy of Lotze. (Jones, Henry.) N.Y., 1895.

Phil 9045.75   A critical analysis of patriotism as an ethical concept. (Reidenbach, Clarence.) Indianpolis? 1920.

Phil 2750.10.90   A critical analysis of the philosophy of Emile Meyerson. (Baas, George.) Baltimore, 1930.

Phil 165.343　The critical approach to sciences and philosophy. (Bunge, M.) N.Y., 1964.

Phil 1750.580　A critical bibliography of existentialism (the Paris School). (Douglas, Kenneth.) New Haven, 1950.

Phil 8413.6　A critical dissertation on nature and principles of taste. (M'Dermot, Martin.) London, 1823.

Phil 1870.103　A critical essay on Berkeley's theory of perception. (Ikbal Kishen, Shargha.) Allababad, n.d.

Phil 1880.25　Critical essays. (Bowen, F.) Boston, 1842.
Phil 1880.25.5　Critical essays. 2nd ed. (Bowen, F.) Boston, 1845.
Phil 6327.35　Critical essays on psychoanalysis. (Rochman, S.) N.Y., 1963.

Phil 1900.175　A critical examination of Butler's analogy (Hughes, Henry.) London, 1898.

Phil 6332.7　A critical examination of psycho-analysis. (Wohlgemuth, A.) N.Y., 1923.

Phil 1750.270.15　Critical existentialism. 1. ed. (Abbagnano, Nicola.) Garden City, N.Y., 1969.

Phil 2475.1.82　A critical exposition of Bergson's philosophy. (Stewart, J.W.K.) London, 1911.

Phil 3552.104.2　A critical exposition of the philosophy of Leibniz. 2d ed. (Russell, Bertrand Russell.) London, 1967.

Phil 5643.132　The critical flicker frequency series effect. (Ákos, Károly.) Budapest, 1966.

Phil 1123.5　Critical history of Greek philosophy. (Stace, W.T.) London, 1920.

Phil 8080.4　A critical history of modern aesthetics. (Listowel, William Francis Hare.) London, 1933.

Phil 193.62　Critical history of philosophical theories. (Schuyler, A.) Boston, n.d.

Phil 623.7.5　Critical history of rationalism in Germany. 2nd ed. (Saintes, A.) London, 1849.

Phil 8625.1.5　A critical history of the doctrine of a future life. (Alger, W.R.) N.Y., 1871.

Phil 8625.1　A critical history of the doctrine of a future life. (Alger, W.R.) Philadelphia, 1864.

Phil 8627.3　A critical history of the doctrine of a future life in Israel. (Charles, R.H.) London, 1899.

Phil 8627.3.5　A critical history of the doctrine of a future life in Israel. 2. ed. (Charles, R.H.) London, 1913.

Phil 814.6　A critical history of Western philosophy. (O'Connor, Daniel J.) N.Y., 1964.

Phil 8897.65　A critical introduction to ethics. (Wheelwright, P.) Garden City, N.Y., 1935.

Phil 8897.65.5　A critical introduction to ethics. (Wheelwright, P.) N.Y., 1949.

Htn　Phil 5425.1.5*　Critical observations. (Duff, W.) London, 1770.
Phil 3504.36　The critical philosophy of Kant. (Weir, Archibald.) London, 1881.

Phil 630.46　Critical realism. (Hicks, G.D.) London, 1938.
Phil 630.9　Critical realism. (Sellars, R.W.) N.Y., 1916.
Phil 8404.14　Critical reflections on poetry. (Dubos, Jean B.) London, 1748. 3v.

Phil 5068.68　A critical study in method. (Khachaturian, Haig.) The Hague, 1967.

Phil 960.175.5　A critical survey of Indian philosophy. (Sharma, C.) London, 1960.

Phil 5041.59.2　Critical thinking. (Black, Max.) N.Y., 1947.
Phil 5620.33　Critical thinking. (Shurter, Robert.) N.Y., 1966.
Phil 5041.59.5　Critical thinking. 2nd ed. (Black, Max.) N.Y., 1954.
Phil 730.20　The critical value of concepts and universal ideas. 2. ed. (Dalos, Patrick M.) Rome, 1960.

Phil 3488.40　Las críticas de Kant. (Gaos, José.) Caracas, 1962.
Phil 8402.22　Criticism and beauty. (Balfour, A.J.) Oxford, 1910.
Phil 1801.9A　Criticism and construction in the philosophy of the America new realism. (Boman, Lars.) Stockholm, 1955.
Phil 338.24　The criticism of experience. (Hawkins, D.J.B.) London, 1945.

Phil 2125.45.7　A criticism of the critical philosophy. (McCosh, James.) N.Y., 1884.

Phil 2475.1.226　Criticism of the philosophy of Bergson. (MacWilliam, J.) Edinburgh, 1928.

Phil 2520.255.10　Le criticisme de Descartes. 1. éd. (Lefèvre, Roger.) Paris, 1958.

Phil 2840.85　Le criticisme de M. Renouvier. Thèse. (Bonnard, Edmond.) Lausanne, 1890.

Phil 192.57　Il criticismo: fondamenti etico-religiosi. (Renda, Antonio.) Palermo, 1927.

Phil 3483.82　Il criticismo kantiano. (Berni, M.) Verona, 1960.
Phil 8581.35　Criticisms of life. (Bridges, H.J.) Boston, 1915.
Phil 8610.837　Criticisms on current theology as they appeared in the 18th century. London, 1837. 4 pam.
Phil 3480.32　Critick of pure reason. (Kant, Immanuel.) London, 1838.
Phil 3480.44.3　Critik der practischen Vernunft. (Kant, Immanuel.) Frankfurt, 1791.

Phil 3480.44.5　Critik der practischen Vernunft. (Kant, Immanuel.) Frankfurt, 1795.

Phil 3480.44.8　Critik der practischen Vernunft. (Kant, Immanuel.) Grätz, 1796.

Phil 3480.45.5　Critik der practischen Vernunft. (Kant, Immanuel.) Leipzig, 1827.

Htn　Phil 3480.44*　Critik der practischen Vernunft. (Kant, Immanuel.) Riga, 1788.

Htn　Phil 3480.45*　Critik der practischen Vernunft. (Kant, Immanuel.) Riga, 1797.

Htn　Phil 3480.45.3*　Critik der practischen Vernunft. 5. Aufl. (Kant, Immanuel.) Leipzig, 1818.

Phil 3480.30.17　Critik der reinen Vernunft, 1781. 1. Aufl. (Kant, Immanuel.) Riga, 1905.

Htn　Phil 3480.29*　Critik der reinen Vernunft. (Kant, Immanuel.) Riga, 1781.
Phil 3500.4.5　Critik der reinen Vernunft. (Schmid, K.C.E.) Jena, 1784.
Phil 3480.30.03　Critik der reinen Vernunft. Neueste Aufl. (Kant, Immanuel.) Frankfurt, 1794.

Phil 3480.30.07　Critik der reinen Vernunft. v.1-2,3-4. (Kant, Immanuel.) Grätz, 1795. 2v.

Phil 3480.29.4　Critik der reinen Vernunft. 2. Aufl. (Kant, Immanuel.) Riga, 1787.

Htn　Phil 3480.29.2*　Critik der reinen Vernunft. 2. Aufl. (Kant, Immanuel.) Riga, 1787.

Phil 3480.30.01　Critik der reinen Vernunft. 3. Aufl. (Kant, Immanuel.) Frankfurt, 1791.

Htn　Phil 3480.30*　Critik der reinen Vernunft. 3. Aufl. (Kant, Immanuel.) Riga, 1790.

Htn　Phil 3480.30.02*　Critik der reinen Vernunft. 4. Aufl. (Kant, Immanuel.) Riga, 1794.

Phil 3480.30.05　Critik der reinen Vernunft. 4. Aufl. (Kant, Immanuel.) Riga, 1794.

Phil 3480.30.1　Critik der reinen Vernunft. 5. Aufl. (Kant, Immanuel.) Leipzig, 1799.

Phil 3480.30.2.10　Critik der reinen Vernunft. 6. Aufl. (Kant, Immanuel.) Leipzig, 1818.

Phil 3480.30.2　Critik der reinen Vernunft. 7. Aufl. (Kant, Immanuel.) Leipzig, 1828.

Htn　Phil 3480.48*　Critik der Urtheilskraft. (Kant, Immanuel.) Berlin, 1790.
Phil 3480.48.2　Critik der Urtheilskraft. (Kant, Immanuel.) Berlin, 1790. 2 pam.

Htn　Phil 3480.50*　Critik der Urtheilskraft. (Kant, Immanuel.) Berlin, 1793.
Phil 3480.50.05　Critik der Urtheilskraft. (Kant, Immanuel.) Frankfurt, 1794.

Phil 3480.50.1　Critik der Urtheilskraft. (Kant, Immanuel.) Grätz, 1797. 2v.

Htn　Phil 3480.50.2*　Critik der Urtheilskraft. (Kant, Immanuel.) Grätz, 1799.
Phil 3480.50.4　Critik der Urtheilskraft. (Kant, Immanuel.) Hamburg, 1884.

Phil 3549.22　Critique; its nature and function. (Kwant, R.C.) Pittsburgh, 1967.

Phil 8830.3　Critique; systèmes de morale contemporaine. (Fouillée, A.) Paris, 1883.

Phil 193.3　Critique...de la philosophie. (Saisset, E.E.) Paris, 1865.

Phil 2475.1.515　La critique bergsonienne du concept. Thèse. (Theau, Jean.) Toulouse, 1967.

Phil 3495.4　Critique de Kant. (Nolen, D.) Paris, 1875.
Phil 3499.8　Critique de la doctrine de Kant. (Renouvier, C.) Paris, 1906.

Phil 332.17　Critique de la mesure. (Bénézé, G.) Paris, 1937.
Phil 1890.85　Critique de la philosophie de Thomas Brown. (Réthoré, François.) Paris, 1863.

Phil 2240.80　Critique de la philosophie de Thomas Reid. (Garnier, A.) Paris, 1840.

Phil 2880.8.57A　Critique de la raison dialectique. (Sartre, Jean Paul.) Paris, 1960.

Phil 3480.46　Critique de la raison pratique. (Kant, Immanuel.) Paris, 1848.

Phil 3480.46.5　Critique de la raison pratique. 2. éd. (Kant, Immanuel.) Paris, 1902.

Phil 3480.31.2　Critique de la raison pure. (Kant, Immanuel.) Paris, 1869. 2v.

Phil 3480.31.20　Critique de la raison pure. (Kant, Immanuel.) Paris, 1927.

Phil 3480.31.1　Critique de la raison pure. 1. éd. (Kant, Immanuel.) Paris, 1835. 2v.

Phil 3480.31　Critique de la raison pure. 2. éd. (Kant, Immanuel.) Paris, 1845. 2v.

Phil 3480.31.5　Critique de la raison pure. 3. éd. (Kant, Immanuel.) Paris, 1864. 2v.

Htn　Phil 2733.32*　Critique de la recherche de la verité. (Foucher, Simon.) Paris, 1675.

Phil 2725.37.35A　Critique de la vie quotidienne. 2e éd. (Lefebvre, Henri.) Paris, 1958-68. 3v.

Phil 400.43　Critique de l'idéalisme et du criticisme. (Ott, Auguste.) Paris, 1883.

Phil 8890.34　Critique des conditions de l'action. (Pardines, Maurice.) Paris, 1909. 2v.

Phil 3493.15　Critique des eléments fondamentaux de la doctrine Kantienne. (Lubnichi, Naum.) Paris, 1929.

Phil 5255.37　Critique des fondements de la psychologie. (Politzer, Georges.) Paris, 1928.

Phil 2840.100　La critique du christianisme chez Renouvier. Thèse. (Méry, Marcel.) Paris, 1952. 2v.

Phil 3480.51　Critique du jugement. (Kant, Immanuel.) Paris, 1846. 2v.

Phil 2050.193　La critique et la religion chez David Hume. (Leroy, André.) Paris, 1931.

Phil 2050.193.5　La critique et la religion chez David Hume. Thèse. (Leroy, André.) Paris, 1929.

Phil 8583.41　Critique et religion. (Duméry, Henry.) Paris, 1957.
Phil 3482.15.5　La critique kantienne de la metaphysique. (Alquié, Ferdinand.) Paris, 1968.

Phil 325.16　A critique of British empiricism. (Cowley, Fraser.) London, 1968.

Phil 8520.1　A critique of design-arguments. (Hicks, L.E.) N.Y., 1883.
Phil 3425.372　Critique of Hegel's 'Philosophy of right.' (Marx, Karl.) Cambridge, Eng., 1970.

Phil 1750.130　The critique of humanism; a symposium. (Grattan, Clinton H.) N.Y., 1930.

Phil 1750.130.5A　The critique of humanism. (Grattan, Clinton H.) N.Y., 1930.

Phil 2880.8.122　A critique of Jean Paul Sartre's ontology. (Natanson, M.) Lincoln, 1951.

Phil 3480.52.12　The critique of judgement. (Kant, Immanuel.) Oxford, 1961.

Phil 3480.52.13A　The critique of judgement. (Kant, Immanuel.) Oxford, 1964.

Phil 3480.52.2　The critique of judgement. 2d ed. (Kant, Immanuel.) London, 1914.

Phil 3480.52.10　Critique of judgment. (Kant, Immanuel.) N.Y., 1951.
Phil 5520.685　A critique of linguistic philosophy. (Rundle, Clement William Kennedy.) Oxford, 1970.

Phil 5068.12　A critique of logical positivism. (Joad, C.E.M.) London, 1950.

Phil 5100.3　The critique of poor reason. (Kamiat, A.H.) N.Y., 1936.
Phil 3480.47.15　Critique of practical reason. (Kant, Immanuel.) Chicago, 1950.

Phil 3480.47.20　Critique of practical reason. (Kant, Immanuel.) N.Y., 1956.

Phil 8888.6.1　Critique of practical reason. (Nelson, Leonard.) Scarsdale, 1970?

Phil 3480.47.7A　Critique of practical reason. 6th ed. (Kant, Immanuel.) London, 1959.

Phil 3504.11　Critique of pure Kant. (Wheeler, C.K.) Boston, 1911.
Phil 3480.32.9　Critique of pure reason. (Kant, Immanuel.) Edinburgh, 1881.

Phil 3480.32.2　Critique of pure reason. (Kant, Immanuel.) London, 1855.
Htn　Phil 3480.32.3*　Critique of pure reason. (Kant, Immanuel.) London, 1855.
Phil 3480.32.5　Critique of pure reason. (Kant, Immanuel.) London, 1869.
Phil 3480.32.6　Critique of pure reason. (Kant, Immanuel.) London, 1878.
Htn　Phil 3480.32.8.2*　Critique of pure reason. (Kant, Immanuel.) London, 1881. 2v.

Phil 3480.32.8A　Critique of pure reason. (Kant, Immanuel.) London, 1881. 2v.

Phil 3480.32.8.9　Critique of pure reason. (Kant, Immanuel.) London, 1887.
Phil 3480.32.20　Critique of pure reason. (Kant, Immanuel.) London, 1929.
Phil 3480.32.21　Critique of pure reason. (Kant, Immanuel.) London, 1933.
Phil 3480.32.10　Critique of pure reason. (Kant, Immanuel.) N.Y., 1882.

Phil 3480.32.7.5   Critique of pure reason. (Kant, Immanuel.) N.y., 1900.
Phil 3480.32.26A   Critique of pure reason. (Kant, Immanuel.) N.Y., 1961.
Phil 3480.32.17   Critique of pure reason. 2. ed. (Kant, Immanuel.) N.Y., 1927.
Phil 3504.44.5   Critique of pure reason. 2nd ed. (Weldon, Thomas D.) Oxford, 1958.
Phil 185.72   Critique of religion and philosophy. 1. ed. (Kaufmann, Walter Arnold.) N.Y., 1958.
Phil 3110.175   A critique of some philosophical aspects of the mysticism of Jacob Boehme. Thesis. (Alleman, G.M.) Philadelphia, 1932.
Phil 3480.52.9   Critique of teleological judgment. (Kant, Immanuel.) Oxford, 1928.
Phil 720.32   A critique of the postulational theory of the a priori. Diss. (Ruja, H.) Princeton, 1940.
Phil 5325.10   Critique of word association reactions; an experimental study. (Sutherland, A.H.) Menasha, Wisc., 1913.
Phil 5325.10.2   Critique of word association reactions. (Sutherland, A.H.) n.p., 191-.
NEDL Phil 12.1   La critique philosophique, politique, scientifique, littéraire. Paris. 1872-1889 36v.
Phil 177.22.15   Critique philosophique. 1. ed. (Cournot, A.A.) Paris, 1958.
Phil 2805.224   La critique philosophique de Pascal au XVIIIe siècle. Diss. (Finch, D.) Philadelphia, 1940.
NEDL Phil 12.1.5   La critique religieuse. (La critique philosophique. Suppleme.) Paris. 1878-1885 7v.
Phil 8953.10   Critiques; á la bona consciència dels christians. (Demoulin, Jérôme.) Barcelona, 1963.
Phil 8419.26   Crito, or A dialogue on beauty. (Spence, Joseph.) Edinburgh, 1885.
Phil 8419.26.1   Crito, or A dialogue on beauty. (Spence, Joseph.) Edinburgh, 1885.
Phil 3425.109.5   Croce, B. Ce qui est vivant et ce qui est mort de la philosophie de Hegel. Paris, 1910.
Phil 3425.109.4   Croce, B. Ciò che è vivo e ciò che è morto della filosofia di Hegel. Bari, 1907.
Phil 4260.85.2   Croce, B. La filosofia di Giambattista Vico. 2a. ed. Bari, 1922.
Phil 4260.85.5   Croce, B. Le fonti della gnoseologia Vichiana. Napoli, 1912.
Phil 4260.146   Croce, B. Giambattista Vico, primo scopritore della scienza estetica. Napoli, 1901.
Phil 3425.109   Croce, B. Lebendiges und Totes in Hegels Philosophie. Heidelberg, 1909.
Phil 5042.10.5   Croce, B. Logic as the science of the pure concept. London, 1917.
Phil 5042.10   Croce, B. Logica come scienza del concetto puro. Bari, 1909.
Phil 5042.10.4   Croce, B. Logica come scienza del concetto puro. 4a ed. Bari, 1920.
Phil 5042.10.3   Croce, B. Logica come scienza del concetto puro. 5a ed. Bari, 1928.
Phil 5042.10.6   Croce, B. Logica come scienza del concetto puro. 7. ed. Bari, 1947.
Phil 3425.109.15   Croce, B. Una pagina sconosciuta degli ultimi mesi della vita di Hegel. Bari, 1950.
Phil 4260.85   Croce, B. The philosophy of Giambattista Vico. London, 1913.
Phil 4260.85.8   Croce, B. The philosophy of Giambattista Vico. N.Y., 1964.
Phil 4170.3.84   Croce, B. Ricerche e documenti Desanctisiani. Dal carteggio inedito di A.C. de Meis. Napoli, 1915.
Phil 3425.109.10   Croce, B. Saggio sullo Hegel. Bari, 1913.
Phil 3425.109.14A   Croce, B. What is living and what is dead of the philosophy of Hegel. London, 1915.
Phil 4080.3.42   Croce, Benedetto. Aesthetic as science of expression and general linguistic. N.Y., 1953.
Phil 4080.3.42.10   Croce, Benedetto. Aesthetic as science of expression and general linguistic. N.Y., 1968.
Htn   Phil 4080.3.38*   Croce, Benedetto. Aesthetica in nuce. Napoli, 1929.
Phil 4080.3.38.3   Croce, Benedetto. Aesthetica in nuce. 3. ed. Laterza, 1954.
Phil 4080.3.78   Croce, Benedetto. An autobiography. Oxford, 1927.
Phil 4080.3.54   Croce, Benedetto. Der Begriff des Barock. Zürich, 1925.
Phil 4260.05   Croce, Benedetto. Bibliografia vichiana. Napoli, 1904-10.
Phil 4260.05.5   Croce, Benedetto. Bibliografia vichiana. Quinto supplemento. Napoli, 1932.
Phil 4260.07   Croce, Benedetto. Bibliografia vichiana. Napoli, 1947-48. 2v.
Phil 4080.3.75   Croce, Benedetto. La Borghesia. Bari, 1945.
Phil 4080.3.34.5   Croce, Benedetto. Brevario de estetica. Lisboa, 1914.
NEDL Phil 4080.3.34   Croce, Benedetto. Brevario di estetica. Laterza, 1913.
Phil 4080.3.37   Croce, Benedetto. Breviaire d'esthétique. Paris, 1923.
Phil 4080.3.34.12   Croce, Benedetto. Breviario di estetica; quattro lezioni. 12. ed. Bari, 1954.
Phil 4080.3.55   Croce, Benedetto. Il concetto moderno della storia. Bari, 1947.
Phil 177.35.25   Croce, Benedetto. The conduct of life. N.Y., 1924.
Phil 4080.3.50   Croce, Benedetto. Considerazioni sul problema morale del tempo nostro. Bari, 1945.
Phil 8877.34   Croce, Benedetto. Cultura e vita morale. Bari, 1914.
Phil 8877.34.2   Croce, Benedetto. Cultura e vita morale. 2a ed. Bari, 1926.
Phil 4080.3.23   Croce, Benedetto. Epistolario. v.2. Napoli, 1967.
Phil 4080.3.36   Croce, Benedetto. The essence of aesthetic. London, 1921.
Phil 4080.3.31.10   Croce, Benedetto. Estetica come scienza dell'espressione e linguista generale. 10. ed. Bari, 1958.
Phil 4080.3.31   Croce, Benedetto. Estetica come scienza dell'espressione e linguistica generale. Milano, 1902.
Phil 4080.3.31.3   Croce, Benedetto. Estetica come scienza dell'espressione e linguistica generale. 3a ed. Bari, 1908.
Phil 4080.3.31.4   Croce, Benedetto. Estetica come scienza dell'espressione e linguistica generale. 4a ed. Bari, 1912.
Phil 177.35.30   Croce, Benedetto. Eternitá storicitá della filosofia. Rieti, 1930.
Phil 4080.3.25   Croce, Benedetto. Etica e politica. Bari, 1931.
Phil 4080.3.28   Croce, Benedetto. Etica e politica. 3. ed. Bari, 1945.
Phil 8877.34.5   Croce, Benedetto. Filosofia della pratica; economia ed etica. 2a ed. Bari, 1915.
Phil 8877.34.6   Croce, Benedetto. Filosofia della pratica; economia ed etica. 6. ed. Bari, 1950.
Phil 8877.34.4   Croce, Benedetto. Filosofia della pratica; economica ed etica. Bari, 1909.
Phil 4080.3.65   Croce, Benedetto. Filosofia e storiografia. Bari, 1949.
Phil 8877.34.9   Croce, Benedetto. Fragmente zur Ethik; Übersetzt von J. Schlosser. Zürich, 1922.
Phil 8877.34.8   Croce, Benedetto. Frammenti di etica. Bari, 1922.

Phil 4080.3.10   Croce, Benedetto. Gesammelte philosophische Schriften in deutscher Ubertragung. v.1 (no.1-4), v.2 (no. 1-3). Tübingen, 1927-1930. 7v.
Phil 4080.3.70   Croce, Benedetto. Intorno alla dialettica. v.1-2. Bari, 1952.
Phil 4080.3.58   Croce, Benedetto. Liberismo e liberalismo. Milano, 1957.
Phil 4080.3.60   Croce, Benedetto. My philosophy. London, 1949.
Phil 4080.3.47   Croce, Benedetto. Nuove pagini sparse. Napoli, 1948-49. 2v.
Phil 4080.3.47.2   Croce, Benedetto. Nuove pagini sparse. 2. ed. Bari, 1966. 2v.
Phil 4080.3.48.2   Croce, Benedetto. Nuovi saggi di estetica. 2. ed. Bari, 1926.
Phil 4080.3.45   Croce, Benedetto. Pensieri vari (ristampa). Bari, 1944.
Phil 4080.3.40   Croce, Benedetto. Perche non possiamo non derci cristiani. Bari, 1944.
Phil 177.35.5   Croce, Benedetto. Philosophie de la pratique. Paris, 1911.
Phil 177.35.9   Croce, Benedetto. Philosophy of the practical. London, 1913.
Phil 4080.3.30   Croce, Benedetto. Il presupposto filosofico della concezione liberale Nota. Napoli, 1927.
Phil 4080.3.35   Croce, Benedetto. La prima forma della estetica e della logica. Messina, 1900.
Phil 4080.3.33   Croce, Benedetto. Problemi di estetics e contributi alla storia dell'estetica italiana. Bari, 1910.
Phil 4080.3.20   Croce, Benedetto. Punti di orientamento della filosofia moderna. Bari, 1931.
Phil 177.35   Croce, Benedetto. Saggi filosofici. Bari, 1910-52. 14v.
Phil 177.35.22   Croce, Benedetto. Saggi filosofici. v. 1,3-5,11. Bari, 1948-54. 5v.
Phil 8050.22   Croce, Benedetto. Storia dell'estetica per saggi. Bari, 1942.
Phil 4080.3.15   Croce, Benedetto. Tre saggi filosofici. Palermo, 1932.
Phil 177.35.40   Croce, Benedetto. Ultimi saggi. 2. ed. Bari, 1948.
Phil 4080.3.79   Pamphlet box. Croce, Benedetto.
Phil 4080.3.12   Pamphlet vol. Croce, Benedetto. 4 pam.
Phil 4080.3.1   Pamphlet box. Croce, Benedetto. Works.
Phil 4080.3.132   Croce. (Flora, F.) Milano, 1927.
Phil 4080.3.315   Croce. (Vinceguerra, Mario.) Napoli, 1957.
Phil 4080.3.405   Croce critico e prosatore. (Puppo, Mario.) Torino, 1953.
Phil 4080.3.405.10
Phil 4080.3.250   Croce e d'annunzio, e altri saggi. (Puppo, Mario.) Firenze, 1964.
Phil 4080.3.480   Croce e Gentile. (Guzzo, A.) Lugano, 1953.
Phil 4080.3.545   Croce e Gramsci. (Lentini, Giacinto.) Palermo, 1967.
Croce e l'illuminismo. (Cotroneo, Girolamo.) Napoli, 1970.
Phil 4080.3.295   Croce etico-politico e filosofo. (Sartori, G.) Firenze, 1956.
Phil 4080.3.475   Croce in Francia; ricerche sulla fortuna dell'opera crociana. (Pagliano Ungari, Graziella.) Napoli, 1967.
Phil 4080.3.137   Il Croce interprete del Vico. (Righi, Gaetano.) Bologna, 1931.
Phil 4080.3.460   Croce interprete di Hegel e altri saggi filosofici. (Franchini, Raffaello.) Napoli, 1964.
Phil 4080.3.400   Il Croce minore. (Nicolini, F.) Milano, 1963.
Phil 4080.3.165   Croce versus Gentile. (Romarell, Patrick.) N.Y., 1946.
Phil 8827.9   Crocker, L. Nature and culture. Baltimore, 1963.
Phil 2402.7   Crocker, Lester G. An age of crisis. Baltimore, 1959.
Phil 7069.20.80   Crockett, Albert Stevens. Revelations of Louise. N.Y., 1920.
Phil 6672.7   Crocq, Jean J. L'hypnotisme scientifique. Paris, 1896.
Phil 2205.82   Croft, G. A short commentary, with strictures on certain parts of the moral writings of Dr. Paley and Mr. Gisborne. Birmingham, 1797.
Phil 8692.4   Crofton, D. Genesis and geology. Boston, 1857.
Phil 8952.15   Crofts, Ambrose M. Moral philosophy. Dublin, 1960.
Phil 8715.5   Croisto y nosotros. (Zum Felde, Alberto.) Montevideo, 1959.
Phil 5042.9   Croke, J.L.O. Logic. London, 1906.
Phil 600.6   Croly, D.G. A positivist primer. N.Y., 1871.
Phil 5752.4   Crombie, A. Essay on philosophical necessity. London, 1893.
Phil 8582.14   Crombie, A. Natural theology. London, 1829. 2v.
Phil 4006.5.55   Cronache di filosofia italiana, 1900-1943. (Garin, Eugenio.) Bari, 1966.
Phil 4006.5.45   Cronache di filosofia italiana. (Garin, Eugenio.) Bari, 1955.
Phil 4006.5.50   Cronache di filosofia italiana. 2. ed. (Garin, Eugenio.) Bari, 1959.
Phil 8877.55   Cronin, Michael. The science of ethics. Dublin, 1909.
Phil 8877.55.2   Cronin, Michael. The science of ethics. 2nd ed. Dublin, 1920-22. 2v.
Phil 2115.161   Crons, E. Die religions philosophischen lehren Lockes. Halle, 1910.
Phil 2218.90   Crook, Ronald E. A bibliography of Joseph Priestley, 1733-1804. London, 1966.
Phil 6805.6   Crooked personalities in childhood and after. (Cattell, Raymond Bernard.) N.Y., 1940.
Phil 7068.74.26   Crookes, W. Researches in the phenomena of spiritualism. London, 1874.
Phil 7068.74.26.5   Crookes, W. Researches in the phenomena of spiritualism. London, 1874.
Phil 7060.108.5   Crookes, William. Recherches sur les phénomènes du spiritualisme. Paris, 1886.
Phil 7060.108   Crookes, William. Researches in the phenomenena of spiritualism. London, 1874.
Phil 7068.84.15   Crookes, William. Der Spiritualismus und die Urssenschaft. 2. Aufl. Leipzig, 1898.
Phil 3640.263   Crookshank, F.G. Individual psychology and Nietzsche. London, 1933.
Phil 5640.127   The Croonian lectures. (Hurst, A.F.) London, 1920.
Phil 6115.3   The Croonian lectures on cerebral localisation. (Ferrier, D.) London, 1890.
Phil 484.2   Croonian lectures on matter and force. (Jones, H.B.) London, 1868.
Phil 5242.26   Cros, A. Les fonctions supérieures du système nerveux. Paris, 1874.
Phil 477.7   Cros, Antoine. Les nouvelles formules du matérialisme. Paris, 1897.
Phil 8692.6   Crosby, H. The bible on the side of science. N.Y., 1875.
Phil 7060.87   Crosland, N. Apparitions. London, 1873.
Phil 7054.70   Crosland, N. Light in the valley: my experience of spiritualism. London, 1857.
Phil 8952.2   Croslegh, C. Christianity judged by its fruits. London, 1884.

Phil 3425.290   Cross, G.J. Prologue and epilogue to Hegel. Oxford, 1935.

Phil 6012.2   Cross, John. Attempt to establish physiognomy upon scientific principles. Glasgow, 1817.

Phil 1955.6.125   Crosser, P.K. The nihilism of John Dewey. N.Y., 1955.

Phil 8582.15   Crosskey, H.W. A defense of religion. London, 1854.

Phil 5066.310   Crossley, John N. Constructive order types. London, 1969.

Htn Phil 8657.11*   Croswell, A. A letter to the Rev. A. Cumming attempting to show him that it is not blasphemy to say, no man can love God. Boston, 1831. 2 pam.

Phil 2750.11.110   Croteau, Jacques. Les fondements thornistes du personnalisme de Maritain. Ottawa, 1955.

Phil 8633.1.7   Crothers, S.M. The endless life. Boston, 1905.

Phil 8877.72   Crothers, S.McC. Three lords of destiny. Boston, 1913.

Phil 1180.5F   Crousaz, J.P. Examen du Pyrrhonisme. La Haye, 1733.

Phil 5042.5.5   Crousaz, J.P. de. La logique. 2e éd. Amsterdam, 1720. 3v.

Phil 5042.5   Crousaz, J.P. de. New treatise...art of thinking. London, 1724. 2v.

Phil 8403.46   Crousaz, Jean Pierre de. Traité du beau, où l'on montre en quoi consiste ce que l'on nomme ainsi, Amsterdam, 1715. Genève, 1970.

Phil 7069.65.25   Crouzet, Jean-Philippe. Les merveilles du spiritualisme. Paris, 1965.

Phil 6312.17   Crow, Lester D. Understanding our behavior. 1st ed. N.Y., 1956.

Phil 7060.36.5   Crowe, C.S. Nacht Seite der Natur. v.1-2. Stuttgart, 1849.

Phil 7060.36   Crowe, C.S. Night side of nature. London, n.p.

Phil 7060.36.7   Crowe, C.S. The night-side of nature. N.Y., 1853.

Phil 177.55   Crowell, Frank. Man - God's masterpiece. N.Y., 1916.

Phil 3494.10   Crowning phase of critical philosophy...Kant. (Macmillan, R.A.C.) London, 1912.

Phil 630.8   Croyance et réalité. (Dauriac, L.) Paris, 1889.

Phil 5070.12   Croyance religieuse et croyance intellectuelle. (Lowrié, Ossip.) Paris, 1908.

Phil 178.3   Croyances philosophiques. (Dejean de Fonroque, Numd.) Paris, 1872.

Phil 802.3   Crozier, F.B. History of intellectual development. v.1,3. London, 1897. 2v.

Phil 9558.20   La cruauté. (Guyon, René.) Paris, 1927.

Phil 5242.67   Cruchon, Georges E. Dynamic psychology. N.Y., 1965.

Phil 1717.11.20   Crucial issues in philosophy. (Robinson, D.S.) Boston, 1955.

Phil 1707.16   Crucial problems of modern philosophy. (Hawkins, D.J.B.) London, 1957.

Phil 1707.16.5   Crucial problems of modern philosophy. (Hawkins, D.J.B.) Notre Dame, 1962.

Phil 1700.3   The crucible of modern thought. (Atkinson, William W.) Chicago, 1910.

Phil 6952.16   Cruden, Alexander. The London-citizen...sent...to...madhouse. 2. ed. London, 17-

Phil 5242.24   Crüger, J. Grundritz der Psychologie. 2. Aufl. Leipzig, 1902.

Phil 2523.85   Cruet, Jean. La philosophie morale et sociale de Destutt de Tracy, 1754-1836. Tours, 1909.

Phil 1702.13   Cruickshank, John. Aspects of the modern European mind. Harlow, 1969.

Htn Phil 7060.73*   Cruikshank, G. Discovery concerning ghosts. 2d ed. London, 1864.

Phil 5042.20   Crumley, T. Logic, deductive and inductive. N.Y., 1926.

Phil 978.66   Crump, Basil. Evolution as outlined in the Archaic Eastern records. Peking, 1930.

Phil 600.43   A crusade for humanity. (McGee, John Edwin.) London, 1931.

Phil 8702.16.5   Crusade for life. (Mather, K.F.) Chapel Hill, N.C., 1949.

Phil 2733.82   Cruse, P.J. Malebranche en Zijne Bestrijders. Utrecht, 1891.

Phil 3160.6.30   Crusius, Christian August. Die philosophischen Hauptwerke. v.1-3. Hildesheim, 1964- 3v.

Phil 6952.27   Crutcher, H.B. Foster home care for mental patients. N.Y., 1944.

Phil 575.78   Crutcher, Roberta. Personality and reason. London, 1931.

Phil 4303.5.5   Cruz Costa, João. Alguns aspétos da filosofia no Brazil. São Paulo, 1938?

Phil 4960.605   Cruz Costa, João. Contribuição à história das idéias no Brasil. Rio de Janeiro, 1956.

Phil 4960.605.2   Cruz Costa, João. Contribuição à história das idéias no Brasil. 2. ed. Rio de Janeiro, 1967.

Phil 4369.2.82   Cruz Costa, João. Ensaio sobre a vida e a obra do filósofo Francisco Sanchez. São Paulo, 1942.

Phil 4960.605.20   Cruz Costa, João. Esbozo de una historia de las ideas en el Brasil. México, 1957.

Phil 4352.2.5   Cruz Costa, Joao. Farias Brito on uma adventura do esprito. Sao Paulo, 1942.

Phil 4960.605.10   Cruz Costa, João. A filosofia no Brasil. Pôrto Alegre, 1945.

Phil 4960.605.5   Cruz Costa, João. A history of ideas in Brazil. Berkeley, 1964.

Phil 4960.605.25   Cruz Costa, João. Panorama of the history of philosophy in Brazil. Washington, 1962.

Phil 4960.605.15   Cruz Costa, João. O positivismo na república. São Paulo, 1956.

Phil 1020.32.10   Cruz Hernández, Miguel. La filosofía arabe. Madrid, 1963.

Phil 1020.32   Cruz Hernández, Miguel. Historia de la filosofía española. Madrid, 1957. 2v.

Phil 177.132   Cruz Malpica, M. Una filosofia da cultura. Porto, 1962.

Phil 5407.6   Cruz Malpique, Manuel da. Psicologia do tédio. Porto, 1963.

Phil 8667.11   La cruzada del error. (Medina, Juan J.) Sevilla, 1879.

Phil 7150.49   The cry for help. (Aarberon, Norman.) N.Y., 1961.

Phil 6689.5   Crystal gasping. (Thomas, Northcote W.) London, 1905.

Phil 7069.24.50   Crystal-gazing: a study in the history, distribution, theory, and practice of scrying. (Besterman, T.) London, 1924.

Phil 6682.10.2   Crystal-gazing and the wonders of clairvoyance. (Melvelle, John.) London, 1910.

Phil 6682.10   Crystal-gazing and the wonders of clairvoyance. (Melvelle, John.) London, 1910.

Phil 2215.80   Cua, Antonio S. Reason and virtue; a study in the ethics of Richard Price. Athens, 1966.

Phil 41.6   Cuadernos de filosofía. (Buenos Aires. Universidad Nacional. Instituto de filosofía.) Buenos Aires. 1,1948+ 4v.

Phil 59.5   Cuadernos de filosofía. (Tucumán. Universidad Nacional. Facultad de Filosofía y Letras.) Tucumán. 1,1942+ 7v.

Phil 30.9   Cuadernos filosóficos. (Universidad Nacional del Litoral. Santa Fe, Argentina. Instituto de Filosofía.) Rosario.

Phil 12.65   Cuadernos uruguayos de filosofia. Montevideo. 3,1964+ 3v.

Phil 9160.8   Cuadros de familia. (Alcalde Prieto, D.) Valladolid, 1890.

Phil 8592.39   Cuadros disolventes. (Medina, Juan J.) Sevilla, 1881.

Phil 4957.30   Cuáles son los grandes temas de la filosofía latinoamericana? (Caturla Brú, Victoria de.) México, 1959.

Phil 735.254   Cuando valen los valores? (Kempff Mercado, Manfredo.) Maracaibo, 1965.

Phil 5520.280   Cuatrecasas, Juan. Psicobiologia del lenguage. 2. ed. Buenos Aires, 1958.

Phil 187.93.30   Cuatro lecciones sobre metafísica. (Vassallo, Angel.) Buenos Aires, 1938.

Phil 8655.22   Cuatro manuscritos inéditos: Los principios de donde recibe el ente la existencia. (Amor Ruibal, Angel Maria.) Madrid, 1964.

Phil 8897.55   Cubes and spheres in human life. (Wiggin, F.A.) Boston, 1899.

Phil 1020.70   Çubukçu, I.A. Islâm felsefesinde Allah'in varliǧinin delilleri. Ankara, 1967.

Phil 4210.202   Cuciuffo, Michele. Morale e politica in Rosmini. Milano, 1967.

Htn Phil 1925.55*   Cudworth, R. Eternal and immutable morality. London, 1731.

Phil 1925.65   Cudworth, R. A sermon preached before the House of Commons, March 31, 1647. N.Y., 1930.

Phil 1925.50   Cudworth, R. Systema intellectuale. Lugduni Batavorum, 1773. 2v.

VPhil 1925.49F   Cudworth, R. Systema intellectuale huius universi. Jenae, 1733.

Phil 5752.5   Cudworth, R. A treatis of freewill. London, 1838.

Phil 1925.31   Cudworth, R. The true intellectual system of the universe. Andover, 1837-38. 2v.

Phil 1925.1   Cudworth, R. True intellectual system of the universe. London, 1678.

Htn Phil 1925.1.3*   Cudworth, R. True intellectual system of the universe. London, 1678.

Htn Phil 1925.1.2*   Cudworth, R. True intellectual system of the universe. London, 1678.

Phil 1925.31.55   Cudworth, R. The true intellectual system of the universe. London, 1820. 4v.

Phil 1925.32   Cudworth, R. The true intellectual system of the universe. London, 1845. 3v.

Htn Phil 1925.30.2*   Cudworth, R. The true intellectual system of the universe. 2d ed. London, 1743. 2v.

Phil 1925.82   Cudworth und der Platonismus. Diss. (Schmitz, Kurt J.) Bonn, 1919.

Phil 8587.24   Cué bono? or What shall it profit. (Huntington, H.) London, 1912.

Phil 4570.1.85   Cuelberg, John. Samuel Grubbe; en studie i transcendental religionsfilosofi. Upsala, 1929.

Phil 2905.1.195   Cuénot, Claude. Lexique Teilhard de Chardin. Paris, 1963.

Phil 2905.1.195.5   Cuénot, Claude. Nouveau lexique Teilhard de Chardin. Paris, 1968.

Phil 2905.1.173   Cuénot, Claude. Science and faith in Teilhard de Chardin. London, 1967.

Phil 2905.1.172   Cuénot, Claude. Teilhard de Chardin. London, 1965.

Phil 2905.1.170   Cuénot, Claude. Teilhard de Chardin. Paris, 1962.

Phil 2905.1.196.5   Cuénot, Claude. Teilhard de Chardin e il pensiero cattolico. Firenze, 1966.

Phil 2905.1.196   Cuénot, Claude. Teilhard de Chardin et la pensée catholique: colloque de Venise sous les auspices de Pax Romana. Paris, 1965.

Phil 3195.6.91   Cüppers, Clemens. Die erkenntnistheoretischen Grundgedanken Wilhelm Diltheys. Leipzig, 1933.

Phil 3195.6.92   Cüppers, Clemens. Die erkenntnistheoretischen Grundgedanken Wilhelm Diltheys. Inaug. Diss. Leipzig, 1933.

Phil 5259.25.5   Cuestiones de psicologiá racional. 2. ed. (Trejos, J.) San José de Costa Rica, 1935.

Phil 5545.162   Cuff, N.B. The relation of over-learning to retention. Nashville, 1927.

Phil 5042.6   Cuffelaer, A.J. Specimen artes ratiocinandi. v.1-3. Hamburgi, 1684.

Phil 2070.113   Cugini, U. L'empirismo radicale di William James. Genova, 1925.

Phil 2475.1.306   Cuisa, Niso. Inchiesta sul Bergsonismo. Sassari, 1953.

Phil 6112.36   Culbertson, J.T. Consciousness and behavior. Dubugue, 1950.

Phil 12.45   Culegere de studiü de psihologie. Bucuresti. 4 2v.

Phil 5325.8   Culler, A.J. Interference and adaptability. N.Y., 1912.

Phil 6672.12   Cullere, A. Magnétisme et hypnotisme. Paris, 1886.

Phil 8582.60   Cullmann, Oscar. Christus und die Zeit. Zollikon-Zürich, 1946.

Phil 5058.14   Culmination of the science of logic. (Smith, J.C.) Brooklyn, 1888.

Phil 8877.39   Culp, C.J. The ethical ideal of renunciation. Thesis. N.Y., 1914.

Phil 6312.3   Culpin, Millais. Psychoneuroses of war and peace. Cambridge, Eng., 1920.

Phil 7069.20.82   Culpin, Millais. Spiritualism and the new psychology. London, 1920.

Phil 7158.715   The cult of the seer in the ancient Middle East. (MacDermot, Violet.) Berkeley, 1971.

Phil 8740.3   Le culte. Thèse. (Will, Robert.) Strasbourg, 1925.

Phil 8667.52   Culte et loix d'une societé d'hommes sans Dieu. (Maréchal, Pierre.) Paris, 1967.

Phil 6674.7.15   Cultivation of personal magnetism. 11. ed. (Edgerley, W.J.) Meriden, Conn., 1923.

Phil 5762.20   Cultivez votre volonté. (Maillant, Claude.) Paris, 1960.

Phil 8410.4   El culto di lo bello. (Julianez Islas, L.) La Plata, 1916.

Phil 4265.2.91   Cultrera, Paolo. Della vita e delle opere del Rev. P.D. Geovachino Ventura. Palermo, 1877.

Phil 4963.2   A cultura brasileira e seus equivocos. (Cannabrava, Euryalo.) Rio de Janeiro, 1955.

Phil 8695.5.3   A cultura das sciencias e os ensinamentos da igreja. (Ferreira da Silva, A.J.) Porto, 1908.

Phil 8595.33.5   Cultura e cristianesimo. (Padovani, U.A.) Milano, 1964.

Phil 8877.34   Cultura e vita morale. (Croce, Benedetto.) Bari, 1914.

Phil 8877.34.2   Cultura e vita morale. 2a ed. (Croce, Benedetto.) Bari, 1926.

Phil 12.4   La cultura filosofica. Firenze. 1-11,1907-1917 11v.

Phil 4309.1   La cultura filosófica en España. (Ingenieros, José.) Madrid, 1916.

Phil 4959.210.5 — Cultura mexicana moderna en el siglo XVIII. 1. ed. (Navarro, Bernabé.) México, 1964.

Phil 1750.774 — La cultura y el hombre de nuestros días. (Zea, Leopoldo.) México, 1959.

Phil 6980.775.20 — Cultural aspects of delusion. (Weinstein, E.A.) N.Y., 1962.

Phil 5590.19.1 — The cultural background of personality. (Linton, Ralph.) N.Y., 196-?

Phil 1801.7.2A — The cultural revolution of the seventeenth century. (Bethell, S.L.) N.Y., 1951.

Phil 12.23 — The cultural world. Los Angeles. 2-3,1931-1932

Phil 5240.1.12 — The culture and discipline of the mind. 6th ed. (Abercrombie, J.) Edinburgh, 1837.

Phil 5590.395 — Culture and personality. (Wallace, Anthony F.C.) N.Y., 1961.

Phil 8876.47 — Culture and restraint. (Black, Hugh.) N.Y., 1901.

Phil 8897.4.2 — Culture by self-help in a literary, an academic or an oratorical career. (Waters, R.) N.Y., 1909.

Phil 8878.40 — La culture morale. 8e éd. (Dugard, Marie.) Paris, 1919.

Phil 8878.24 — The culture of justice. (DuBois, P.) N.Y., 1907.

Phil 575.33 — The culture of personality. (Randall, J.H.) N.Y., 1912.

Phil 8597.21 — The culture of the soul. (Rámanthán, P.) N.Y., 1906.

Phil 7150.60 — Cultures of violence; a study of the tragic man in society. (Porterfield, Austin Larimore.) Fort Worth, Texas, 1965.

Htn Phil 8582.16* — Culverwel, N. An elegant and learned discourse...light of nature. London, 1652.

Phil 8582.17 — Culverwel, N. Of the light of nature. Edinburgh, 1857.

Htn Phil 1928.30* — Cumberland, R. De legibus naturae. Dublin, 1720.

Phil 1928.30.2 — Cumberland, R. De legibus naturae. London, 1672.

Htn Phil 1928.30.5* — Cumberland, R. De legibus naturae. 3d ed. Lubecae, 1694.

Phil 1928.31.2 — Cumberland, R. Loix de la nature. Leiden, 1757.

Phil 1928.35 — Cumberland, R. A philosophical enquiry into the laws of nature. Dublin, 1750.

Phil 1928.31 — Cumberland, R. Traité philosophique des loix naturelles. Amsterdam, 1744.

Htn Phil 1928.33* — Cumberland, R. A treatise of the laws of nature. London, 1727.

Phil 7068.88.10 — Cumberland, Stuart. A thought-reader's thoughts. London, 1888.

Phil 6112.38 — Cumming, Elaine. Clased ranks. Cambridge, 1957.

Phil 2636.90 — Cumming, Ian. Helvetius. London, 1955.

Phil 6980.210 — Cumming, John. Ego and milieu. N.Y., 1962.

Phil 9342.7 — Cummings, A.I. Lady's present. Boston, 1856.

Phil 7069.44.5 — Cummins, G.D. After Pentecost; the Alexandrian chronicle of Cleophas. London, 1944.

Phil 7069.30.4 — Cummins, G.D. Paul in Athens (the scripts of Cleophas). London, 1930.

Phil 7074.16 — Cummins, Geraldine Dorothy. Swan on a black sea: a study in automatic writing, the Cummins-Willet scripts. London, 1970.

Phil 4075.83 — Cumston, Charles Greene. Notes on life and writings of Gironimo Cardano. Boston, 1902.

Phil 5258.155A — Cumulative record. (Skinner, Burrhus F.) N.Y., 1959.

Phil 5258.155.5A — Cumulative record. (Skinner, Burrhus F.) N.Y., 1961.

Phil 5242.29 — Cunningham, G.W. Five lectures on the problem of mind. Austin, 1925.

Phil 400.86 — Cunningham, G.W. The idealistic argument in recent British and American philosophy. N.Y., 1933.

Phil 177.63.5 — Cunningham, G.W. Problem of philosophy. N.Y., 1935.

Phil 2475.1.157 — Cunningham, G.W. A study in the philosophy of Bergson. N.Y., 1916.

Phil 177.49 — Cunningham, H.E. An introduction to philosophy. Boston, 1920.

Phil 5042.19 — Cunningham, H.E. Textbook of logic. N.Y., 1924.

Phil 8952.25 — Cunningham, Robert L. Situationism and the new morality. N.Y., 1970.

Phil 8952.6 — Cunningham, W. The gospel of work. Cambridge, 1902.

Phil 9342.18 — Cunningham, W. True womanhood. N.Y., 18- .

Phil 2520.87 — Cunningham, William. The influence of Descartes on metaphysical speculation in England. London, 1876.

Phil 8582.32 — Cunow, Heinrich. Ursprung der Religion und des Gottesglaubens. Berlin, 1913.

Phil 5812.12 — Cuny, Hilaire. Sur la psychologie animale. Paris, 1966.

Phil 6112.34 — Cuny, Louis. Contribution à l'étude de l'action vasomotrice. Thèse. Paris, 1942.

Phil 177.56 — Cunyngham, H. Short talks upon philosophy. London, 1923.

Phil 802.7 — Cunz, T. Geschichte der Philosophie in gemeinverständlicher Darstellung. Marburg, 1911.

Phil 1507.1 — Cupély. Esprit de la philosophie scolastique. Paris, 1867.

Phil 6954.1 — The curability of insanity. (Earle, P.) Philadelphia, 1887.

Phil 6990.58 — Curaciones milagrosas. (Celma, Bernal.) Zaragoza, 1961.

Phil 6159.5 — Curandera; les champignons hallucinogènes. (Solier, René de.) Paris, 1965.

Phil 8877.28 — Curbipet. Fragments of the elements and principles of the life of man. Bombay, 1904.

Phil 8592.122.15 — Le curé Meslier, athée. (Dommanget, Maurice.) Paris, 1965.

Htn Phil 6012.6.5* — Cureau de la Chambre, Marin. The art how to know men. London, 1665.

Phil 5242.70 — Curi, Umberto. Il problema dell'unità del sapere nel comportamentismo. Padova, 1967.

Phil 7069.44.30 — Curiosities of psychical research. (Seymour, C.J.) London, 1944.

Phil 6327.12.55 — Curiosities of the self. (Reik, Theodor.) N.Y., 1965.

Phil 5385.5 — Curiosity. (Nemberg, Herman.) N.Y., 1961.

Phil 5385.6 — Curiosity and exploratory behavior. (Fowler, Harry.) N.Y., 1965.

Htn Phil 2050.89.10* — Curious particulars and genuine anecdotes respecting the late Lord Chesterfield and David Hume. (Pratt, Samuel J.) London, 1788.

Phil 3822.12 — Curley, E.M. Spinoza's metaphysics. Cambridge, 1969.

Phil 8952.22.5 — Curran, Charles E. Contemporary problems in moral theology. Notre Dame, 1970.

Phil 8952.22 — Curran, Charles E. A new look at Christian morality. Notre Dame, 1968.

Phil 6119.14 — Current concepts of positive mental health. (Jahoda, Marie.) N.Y., 1959.

Phil 8581.50 — Current discussion. (Burlingame, E.L.) N.Y., 1878. 2v.

Phil 165.378 — Current philosophical issues; essays in honor of Curt John Ducasse. (Dommeyer, Frederick C.) Springfield, Illinois, 1966.

Phil 5221.1 — Current psychologies. (Levine, A.J.) Cambridge, 1940.

Phil 5535.14 — Current research in hypnopaedia; a symposium of selected literature. (Rubin, Frederick.) London, 1968.

Phil 5548.106 — Current research in motivation. (Haber, Ralph Norman.) N.Y., 1966.

Phil 5548.3 — Current theory and research in motivation, a symposium. (Nebraska. University. Department of Psychology.) Lincoln. 1954+ 15v.

Phil 5238.26 — Current trends. Pittsburgh, 1952.

Phil 70.4 — Current trends in analytical psychology. (International Congress for Analytical Psychology, 1st, Zurich, 1958.) London, 1961.

Phil 5222.7 — Current trends in British psychology. (Mace, C.A.) London, 1953.

Phil 5238.10.2 — Current trends in psychological theory. Pittsburgh, 1961.

Phil 5238.10A — Current trends in psychology. Pittsburgh, 1947.

Phil 5238.80 — Current trends in the description and analysis of behavior. Pittsburgh, 1958.

Phil 1210.15 — Curriculm philosophiae peripateticae. v.1-2. (Cornaeus, Melchior.) Herbipoli, 1657.

Phil 40.9 — Curriculum. (American Institute for Psychoanalysis.) N.Y.

Phil 1507.3 — Currie, F.J. Universal scholastic philosophy publicly defended. n.p., 1928.

Phil 5066.120 — Curry, Haskell Brooks. Combinatory logic. Amsterdam, 1958.

Phil 5066.122 — Curry, Haskell Brooks. Foundations of mathematical logic. N.Y., 1963.

Phil 5465.42 — Curry, S.S. Imagination and dramatic instinct. Boston, 1896.

VPhil 9245.125 — Curry, Samuel Silas. The smile. Boston, 1915.

Phil 4112.86 — Cursi, C.M. Onori funebri che alla memoria di Pasquale Galluppi. Napoli, 1847.

Phil 4352.1.35 — Curso de filosofia elemental. v.1-4. (Balmes, Jaime.) Barcelona, 1911.

Phil 187.25.5 — Curso de philosophia. v.1. Logica. v.3. Psychologia. (Mercier, D.) Vizeu, 1904. 2v.

Phil 5240.2.5 — Curso de psicología. (Ahrens, Heinrich.) Madrid, 1873. 2v.

Phil 5261.5.5 — Curso de psicologia. Fascimile 2. (Varona, Enrique José.) Havana, 1906.

Phil 5052.4 — Cursos de lojica y etica segun la escuela de Edinburgo. (Mora, J.J. de.) Lima, 1832.

Phil 5245.21.7 — Cursus brevior psychologiae speculativae in usum scholarum. (Fröbes, Joseph.) Parisiis, 1933.

Phil 3195.9.75 — Cursus der Philosophie als streng wissenschaftlicher Weltanschauung und Lebensgestaltung. (Dühring, E.) Leipzig, 1875.

Phil 3455.2 — Cursus logicus systematicus et agonisticus. (Isendoorn, Gisbert.) Francofurti, 1666.

Phil 1512.11 — Cursus philosophiae thomistica. 3. éd. v.1-6. (Hugon, Edward.) Paris, 1928. 3v.

Htn Phil 1535.15* — Cursus philosophicus. (Bonaventura, St., Cardinal.) n.p., 1742.

Phil 1535.32 — Cursus philosophicus. (Cherubini, F.) Romae, 1904. 2v.

Phil 1535.33 — Cursus philosophicus ad usum seminariorum. (La Scala, Puis.) Parisiis, 1910. 2v.

NEDL Phil 177.61 — Cursus philosophicus in usum scholarum auctoribus pluribus philosophiae professoribus in collegiis Valkenburgenci et Stonyhurstensi S.J. Friburgi Brisgoviae. 1-6,1915-1919 4v.

Phil 1535.2 — Cursus philosophie. (Boylesve, M. de.) Paris, 1855.

Phil 2115.148 — Curti, M. The great Mr. Locke, America's philosopher, 1783-1861. n.p., 19- .

Phil 3484.6.18 — Curtiner, Egon B. Chamberlain gegen Schopenhaur. Düsseldorf, 1910.

Phil 6112.29 — Curtis, A.M. Of meditation and health. London, 1910.

Phil 525.15.5 — Curtis, Adela M. The new mysticism. 3d ed. London, 1913.

Phil 2775.4.80 — Curtis, D.E. Progress and eternal recurrence in the work of Gabriel Naudé, 1600-1650. Hull, 1967.

Phil 8877.24.5 — Curtis, G.W. Aves recte vivendi. N.Y., 1899.

Phil 9490.3 — Curtis, G.W. The public duty of educated men. Albany, N.Y., 1878.

Phil 8627.5 — Curtis, L.Q. Immortal life. N.Y., 1901.

Phil 8550.342.10 — Curtis, Lewis P. Anglican moods of the eighteenth century. Hamden, Conn., 1966.

Phil 2115.104 — Curtis, M.M. An outline of Locke's ethical philosophy. Leipzig, 1890.

Phil 177.24 — Curtis, M.M. Philosophy and physical science. Cleveland, 1892.

Phil 1507.5 — Curtis, S.J. A short history of western philosophy in middle ages. London, 1950.

Phil 978.40 — Curtiss, F.H. Letters from the teacher. Denver, 1909?

Phil 978.28 — Curtiss, H.A. The voice of Isis. Los Angeles, 1912.

Phil 7069.19.70 — Curtiss, Harriette A. Realms of the living dead. N.Y., 1919.

Phil 1145.50 — Curtius, E. Der Freundschafts begriff der Alten. Göttingen, 1863.

Phil 6945.5 — Curwen, J. A manual for attendants in hospitals for the insane. Philadelphia, 1851.

Phil 4215.1.01 — Cusani Confalonieri, L.G. G.D. Romagnosi. Carate Brianza, 1928.

Phil 2648.91 — Cushing, M.P. Baron d'Holbach. N.Y., 1914.

Phil 7069.18.90 — Cushman, Emma Crow. Insight. Boston, 1918.

Phil 802.4A — Cushman, H.E. A beginner's history of philosophy. Boston, 1910-11. 2v.

Phil 802.4.3 — Cushman, H.E. A beginner's history of philosophy. Boston, 1918-19.

Phil 802.4.2A — Cushman, H.E. A beginner's history of philosophy. Boston, 1918-20. 2v.

Phil 8877.74 — Cushman, H.E. Ten lessons in ethics. Newton, 1924.

Phil 6952.29 — Custance, J. Wisdom, madness, and folly. N.Y., 1952.

Phil 333.14PF — Custard, Harry L. The unity of knowledge and the organization of thought. Washington, D.C., 1940.

Phil 8886.90 — Custom, law, and morality: conflict and continuity in social behavior. 1st ed. (Loiser, Burton M.) Garden City, 1969.

Phil 8894.19.5 — Custom. (Tönnies, Ferdinand.) N.Y., 1961.

Phil 5648.17 — Cutaneous sensation after nerve-division. (Boring, Edwin G.) London, 1916.

Phil 8877.48 — Cutler, Carroll. The beginnings of ethics. N.Y., 1889.

Phil 5627.16 — Cutten, G.B. The psychological phenomenon of Christianity. N.Y., 1908.

Phil 5242.28 — Cutten, George. Mind; its origin and goal. New Haven, 1925.

Phil 5628.5 — Cutten, George Barton. Speaking with tongues, historically and psychologically considered. New Haven, 1927.

Phil 6112.12 — Cutter, G.B. Three thousand years of mental healing. N.Y., 1911.

Phil 7082.66   Cutting, Mary Stewart. What dreams mean to you. London, 1928.
Phil 3450.9.79   Pamphlet vol. Cuttings and notes on R.M. Holzapfel.
Phil 2733.110   Cuvillier, A. Essai sur la mystique de Malebranche. Paris, 1954.
Phil 165.341   Cuvillier, A. Textes choisis des auteurs philosophiques. v.2. Paris, 1961.
Phil 5242.22   Cuvillier, Armand. ABC de psychologie. Paris, 1923.
Phil 2430.2   Cuvillier, Armand. Anthologie des philosophes français. Paris, 1962.
Phil 177.110.5   Cuvillier, Armand. La dissertation philosophique. Paris, 1958-62. 2v.
Phil 87.12.5   Cuvillier, Armand. Kücük felsefesözlügü. Ankara, 1944.
Phil 177.72   Cuvillier, Armand. Manuel de philosophie. Paris, 1927. 2v.
Phil 87.13   Cuvillier, Armand. Nouveau vocabulaire philosophique. 2. éd. Paris, 1957.
Phil 177.72.5   Cuvillier, Armand. Partis pris sur l'art. Paris, 1956.
Phil 87.12   Cuvillier, Armand. Petit vocabulaire de la langue philosophique. Paris, 1925.
Phil 177.110   Cuvillier, Armand. Précis de philosophie: classe de philosophie. Paris, 1954. 2v.
Phil 283.4   Cuyás, F.G. Unidad del universo. Habana, 1874.
Phil 6012.1   Cuyer, E. La mimique. Paris, 1902.
Phil 12.80   Cuyo. Mendoza. 1,1965+
Phil 5627.262.15   Cvekl, Jiří. Človĕk a svĕtový názor. Praha, 1962.
Phil 310.796.2   Cvekl, Jiří. Filosofie a současnost. 2. vyd. Praha, 1969.
Phil 310.415   Cvekl, Jiří. Lid a osobnost v dĕjrhách. Praha, 1961.
Phil 310.415.5   Cvekl, Jiří. O zákonech dĕjin. Praha, 1957.
Phil 5722.24.5   Le cycle de l'inconscient. (Lubac, Emile.) Paris, 1934.
Phil 1133.17   Le cycle mystique. (Diès, Auguste.) Paris, 1909.
Phil 5070.10   Cycles of personal belief. (Forbes, Waldo.) Boston, 1917.
Phil 8050.28.5   Cycles of taste. (Chambers, Frank.) Cambridge, 1928.
Phil 182.110   The cylindriad. (Humphreys, H.S.) Evansville, 1942.
Phil 1153.10   Cynic hero and cynic king. (Höistad, R.) Uppsala, 1948.
Phil 5300.3   Cyon, E. de. Recherches éxperimentales sur les fonctions des canaux semi-circulaires. Thèse. Paris, 1878.
Phil 8657.9   Cyon, E. von. Gott und Wissenschaft. v.1-2. Leipzig, 1912.
Phil 8692.11   Cyon, Elie de. Dieu et science. 2. éd. Paris, 1912.
Phil 5585.25   Cyon, Elie von. Das Ohrlabyrinth als Organ der mathematischen Sinne fur Raum und Zeit. Berlin, 1908.
Phil 5242.12   Cyples, W. An inquiry into the process of human experience. London, 1880.
Phil 4073.80   Cyprian, E. Vita T. Campanella. Amstelodami, 1722.
Phil 8877.90   Cysarz, Herbert. Individuelle und collektive Ethik. Tübingen, 1958.
Phil 177.104   Cysarz, Herbert. Das Schöpferische. Halle, 1943.
Phil 3160.11.10   Cysarz, Herbert. Das seiende Sein. Wien, 1948.
Phil 3160.11.5   Cysarz, Herbert. Das Unsterbliche. Halle, 1940.
Phil 2115.154   Czajkowski, C.J. The theory of private property in John Locke's political philosophy. Notre Dame, 1941.
VPhil 5627.215.15   Czakó, Ambrosius. A vallás lelektana, irta Czakó Ambró. Pécs, 1915.
Phil 5421.20.50   Czapiewski, Winfried. Der Aggression trieb und das Böse. Essen, 1967.
Phil 5130.6   Czayka, Lothar. Grundzüge der Aussagenlogik. München, 1971.
Phil 5042.45   Czech, Albert. Grundkurs der Logik. Bonn, 1970.
Phil 4809.779.80   A Czech philosopher on the Cotswolds...Francis Sedlák. (Shaw, Nellie.) London, 1940.
Phil 349.22   Czernovitz. Gymnasium. Xenia Czernowiciensia. Czernowitz, 1900.
Phil 4803.313.20   Czezowski, Tadeusz. Filozofia na rozdrozu. Wyd. 1. Warszawa, 1965.
Phil 4803.313.35   Czezowski, Tadeusz. O naukach humanistycznych. Toruń, 1946.
Phil 4803.313.30   Czezowski, Tadeusz. O uniwersytecie i studiach uniwersyteckick. Toruń, 1946.
Phil 4803.186.30   Człowiek i światopoglady. (Baczko, Bronisław.) Warszawa, 1965.
Phil 333.4.5   Czolbe, H. Die Grenzen und der Ursprung der menschlichen Erkenntniss. Jena, 1865.
Phil 333.4   Czolbe, H. Grundzüge einer extensionalen Erkenntnisstheorie. Plauen, 1875.
Phil 477.5   Czolbe, H. Neue Darstellung des Sensualismus. Leipzig, 1855.
Phil 5374.34   Czolbe, Heinrich. Entstehung des Selbstbewusstseins. Leipzig, 1856.
Phil 5545.53   D., T.W. Mnemonics. N.Y., 1844.
Phil 8080.9   D. Hume e i presupposti empiristici della estetica kantiana. (Anceschi, Luciano.) Milano, 1956.
Phil 7054.45.5   D.D. Home, his life and mission. (Home, Daniel Dunglas (Mrs.).) London, 1888.
Phil 8708.29.5   D-days at Dayton. (Tompkins, Jerry R.) Baton Rouge, La., 1965.
Phil 4012.7.5   Da Ardigò a Gramsci. (Mondolfo, Rodolfo.) Milano, 1962.
Phil 1107.6   Da Aristotele ai Bizantini. (Covotti, Aurelio.) Napoli, 1935.
Phil 1540.70   Da Dante ad Erasmo. (Vallese, Giulia.) Napoli, 1962.
Phil 176.154   Da filosofia. 1. ed. (Botelho, Pero de.) Candeia, 1949.
Phil 1700.5   Da G. Bruno e da A. Gentile allo Spencer e all' Ardigò. (Armani, T.) Camerino, 1904.
Phil 1517.5.5   Da Guglielmo d'Auvergne. 2. ed. (Masnovo, Amato.) Milano, 1946. 3v.
Phil 1517.5   Da Guglielmo d'Auvergne a San Tomaso d'Aquino. (Masnovo, Amato.) Milano, 1930. 2v.
Phil 3425.740   Da Hegel a Marx. (Rossi, Mario.) Milano, 1970- 2v.
Phil 1701.52   Da Hobbes a Marx; saggi di storia della filosofia. (Bobbio, Norberto.) Napoli, 1965.
Phil 5400.49   Da natureza da affecção. (Sergio, Antonio.) Rio de Janeiro, 1913.
Phil 1718.37   Da Schelling a Merkau-Ponty. (Semerarí, Giuseppe.) Bologna, 1969.
Phil 803.16   Da talete all'esistenzialismo. (Dolci, Alfredo.) Milano, 1958.
Phil 7150.12   Dabadie, F. Les suicidés illustrés. Paris, 1859.
Phil 6834.8   Dacguino, Giacomo. Diario di un omosessuale. Milano, 1970.
Phil 8875.22   D'Acol. La reduction de toutes les sciences en la connaissance de l'homme. Paris, 1668.
Phil 3195.14.45   Dacqué, Edgar. Leben als Symbol. München, 1928.
Phil 3195.14.34   Dacqué, Edgar. Urwelt, Sage und Menschheit, eine naturhistori-metaphysische Studie. 4. Aufl. München, 1927.
Phil 3195.14.40   Dacqué, Edgar. Das verlorene Paradies. 4. Aufl. München, 1953.
Phil 3195.14.50   Dacqué, Edgar. Vom Sinn der Erkenntnis. München, 1932.

Phil 8875.20   D'Acquisto, P.B. Corso di filosofia morale. 2. ed. Palermo, 1855.
Phil 4060.6.90   D'acquisto e la filosofia della creazione in Sicilia. (Giovanni, V. di.) Firenze, 1868.
Phil 8693.12.5   Dadson, Arthur J. Evolution, and its bearing on religions. London, 1901.
Phil 8693.12   Dadson, Arthur J. Evolution and religion. London, 1893.
Phil 3450.18.100   Daehler, J. Zur Freiheitslehre von Nicolai Hartmann. Inaug. Diss. Freiburg, 1952.
Phil 1150.5   Dähne, A.F. Geschichtliche Darstellung der jüdisch-alexandrinischen Religions-Philosophie. Halle, 1834. 2v.
Phil 705.49   Dämonie und Transzendenz. (Metzger, Arnold.) Pfullingen, 1964.
Phil 5238.95   Däumling, Adolf. Seelenleben und Menschenbild. München, 1958.
Phil 3552.244   Dafert, F.W. Gottfried Wilhelm Leibnitz als Deutscher. Wien, 1883.
Phil 3640.297   Daffner, H. Friedrich Nietzsches Randglassen zu Bizets Carmen. Regenburg, 1938.
Phil 2477.15.85   Dagognet, François. Gaston Bachelard. Paris, 1965.
Phil 4600.4.30   Dagsbilder. (Lidforss, Bengt.) Malmö, 1917.
Phil 5592.155   Dahistrom, W.G. An MMPI handbook. Minneapolis, 1960.
Phil 5599.93   Dahl, Gerhard. Übereinstimmungsvalidität des HAWE und Entwicklung einer reduzierten Testform. Meisenheim am Glan, 1968.
Phil 3485.15   Dahl, J. Ernstes und Heiteres über Kant. Cottbus, 1933.
Phil 7069.31.6   Dahl, Ludwig. We are here. London, 1931.
Phil 5043.24   Dahlbäck, Carl J. Om logikens studium vid elementarläroverken. Umea, 1864.
Phil 260.8   Dahlbäck, Carl J. Om atomismen. Stockholm, 1857.
Phil 310.712   Dahm, Helmut. Meuterei auf den Knien. Olten, 1969.
Phil 4769.1.140   Dahm, Helmut. Vladimir Solov'ev und Max Scheler. München, 1971.
Phil 2050.101.5   Daiches, Sally. Über das Verhältnis der Geschichtsschreibung David Hume's zu seiner praktischen Philosophie. Leipzig, 1903.
Phil 5066.250   Daigneault, Aubert. Théorie des modèles en logique mathématique. Montréal, 1963.
Phil 9340.10   Daily duties inculcated in a series of letters. (Adams, (Mrs.).) Boston, 1835.
Phil 8887.72   Daily meditations. (Mukenje, D.G.) N.Y., 1933.
Phil 7069.27.19   Daily News, London. Ghosts in the Great War. London, 1927.
Phil 7069.27.18   Daily News, London. Uncanny stories. London, 1927.
Phil 7069.27.17   Daily News, London. Warnings from beyond. London, 1927.
Phil 6953.19   Dain, Norman. Concepts of insanity in the United States, 1789-1865. New Brunswick, N.J., 1964.
Phil 5627.85   Daisy Dryden. 3. ed. (Dryden, S.H.) Boston, 1909.
Phil 178.60   Dakin, John E. Rhythmic affinity, a philosophic hypothesis. N.Y., 1929.
Phil 8587.32.95   Dakiri, A.H., Jr. Von Hügel and the supernatural. London, 1934.
Phil 4006.2.7   Dal Genovesi al Galuppi. (Gentile, G.) Napoli, 1903.
Phil 1511.6   Dal medioevo al rinascimento. (Garin, E.) Firenze, 1950.
Phil 4225.15.40   Dal mito alla scienza. (Spirito, Ugo.) Firenze, 1966.
Phil 1614.10   Dal rinascimento all'illuminismo. (Napoli, Giovanni di.) Roma, 1969.
Phil 1730.34   Dal rinascimento all'illuminismo. Studi e ricerche. (Garin, Eugenio.) Pisa, 1970.
Phil 6315.2.111   Dalbiez, R. La méthode psychanalytique et la doctrine freudienne. v.1-2. Thèse. Paris, 1936.
Phil 6315.2.111.5   Dalbiez, R. Psychoanalytical method and the doctrine of Freud. v.1. v.2 lost. N.Y., 1941.
Phil 4683.55.31   Dăle, Pauls. Vērojumi un pārdomas par cilvēku un gara kultūru. Chicago, 1952.
Phil 8693.9   Dale, T. Nelson. The outskirts of physical science. Boston, 1884.
Phil 8693.13   Dalin, C.O. Infor de stora varldsproblemen. Stockholm, 1919.
Phil 705.4   Dall, C.H. Transcendentalism in New England. Boston, 1897.
Phil 400.24.5   Dalla critica al nuovo idealismo. (Chiappelli, Alessandro.) Milano, 1910.
Phil 575.141   Dalla dialettica alla apodittica. (Giordani, Roberto.) Roma, 1946.
Phil 177.124   Dalla materia allo spirito. (Cappellani, G.) Mazara, 1959.
Phil 525.37   Dalla percezione sensible all'intuizione mistica. (Maréchal, J.) Firenze, 1913.
Phil 8667.35   Dalla religione degli dei alla religione dell'uomo. (Masi, Giorgio.) Milano, 1967.
Phil 3493.24   Dalla religione naturale prekantiani alla religione morale di Kant. (Lazzarini, Renato.) Roma, 1942.
Phil 4080.9.45   Dalla vita dello spirito al mito del realismo. (Carlini, Armando.) Firenze, 1959.
Phil 8583.44   Dallago, Carl. Der Begriff des Absoluten. Innsbruck, 1964.
Phil 178.63   Dallago, Carl. Der grosse Universende. Innsbruck, 1924.
Phil 3905.88   Dallago, Carl. Otto Weiningers und sein Werk. Innsbruck, 1912.
Phil 6313.20   Dallard, John. Personality and psychotherapy. 1st. ed. N.Y., 1950.
Phil 2270.114   Dallari, Gino. Il pensiero filosofico di Herbert Spencer. Torino, 1904.
Phil 7069.27.15   Dallas, H.A. Leaves from a psychic note-book. London, 1908.
Phil 7069.13.15   Dallas, Helen A. Across the barrier. London, 1913.
Phil 7069.30.5   Dallas, Helen A. Comrades on the homeward way. London, 1930.
Phil 7069.19.80   Dallas, Helen A. Death the gate of life? N.Y., 1919.
Phil 8657.32   Dall'ateismo all'umanismo. (Capizzi, Antonio.) Roma, 1967.
Phil 6953.1   Dallemagne, J. Dégénérés et déséquilibrés. Bruxelles, 1895.
Phil 5753.6   Dallemagne, Jules. Physiologie de la volonté. Paris, 1898.
Phil 1750.330.10   Dall'esistenzialismo al relazionismo. (Paci, Enzo.) Messina, 1957.
Phil 1750.525   Dall'essere all'esistente. (Fabro, Cornelio.) Brescia, 1957.
Phil 4225.8.70   Dallo spiritualismo critico allo spiritualismo cristiano, 1939-1951. (Sciacca, Michele Federico.) Milano, 1965. 2v.
Phil 8878.31   Dalmau y Gratacós, F. Elementos de filosofia. Barcelona, 1911.
Phil 1721.8   Dalori, Paolo. Il pensiero filosofico odierno. Roma, 1959.

Phil 730.20 Dalos, Patrick M. The critical value of concepts and universal ideas. 2. ed. Rome, 1960.

Phil 5590.370 Dalton, R.H. Personality and social interaction. Boston, 1961.

Phil 2750.11.185 Daly, Mary F. Natural knowledge of God in the philosophy of Jacques Maritain. Rome, 1966.

Phil 8878.44 Dam, Axel. Livets vardiproblemer. København, 1921.

Phil 5043.23 Dam, Axel. Logik til brug under laereruddannelsen paa seminarierne. København, 1915.

Phil 5243.26 Dam, Axel. Om muligheden af formel opdragelse af de intellektuelle evner. København, 1912.

Phil 178.48 Dam, Axel. Opdragelsens hovedopgaver. 3. udg. Kobenhavn, 1923.

Phil 5243.74 D'Amato, Michael Richard. Experimental psychology. N.Y., 1970.

Phil 6953.13 Damaye, Henri. Psychiatrie et civilisation. Paris, 1934.

VPhil 178.79 Dambska, Izydora. O narzedziach i przedmiotach poznania. Wyd. 1. Warszawa, 1967.

Phil 6990.44.20 La dame plus belle que tout. (Barbet, Jean.) Paris, 1957.

Phil 8878.1 Dameth, C.M.H. Le juste et l'utile. Paris, 1859.

Phil 8583.46 Damiani, Raoul. Cristianesimo-marxismo. Milano, 1969.

Phil 5243.1 Damiron, J.P. Cours de philosophie. Paris, 1837. 2v.

Phil 2403.1 Damiron, J.P. Essai sur l'histoire...philosophie en France. Paris, 1846. 2v.

Phil 2403.1.10 Damiron, J.P. Essai sur l'histoire...philosophie en France au dix-neuvième siècle. Paris, 1828. 2v.

Phil 2403.1.11 Damiron, J.P. Essai sur l'histoire...philosophie en France au XIXe siècle. Paris, 1834. 2v.

Phil 8658.1.5 Damiron, J.P. Memoire sur Naigeon et accessoirement sur Sylvain Maréchal et Delalande. Paris, 1857.

Phil 2403.1.5 Damiron, J.P. Memoires pour servir á l'histoire...philosophie au XVIIIe siècle. Paris, 1858. 2v.

Phil 8658.1 Damiron, J.P. Petits traites...de la providence. Paris, 1849.

Phil 8583.1 Damiron, J.P. Souvenirs de vingt ans d'enseignement. Paris, 1859.

Phil 5043.1 Damiron, M.J.P. Cours de philosophie. Paris, 1836.

Phil 8878.2 Damiron, P. Cours de philosophie, morale. Paris, 1834.

Phil 178.1 Damiron, P. Cours de philosophie. Bruxelles, 1834. 3v.

Phil 4872.55.220 Damle, Prabhakar R. Philosophical essays. Bombay, 1954.

Phil 5243.19 Damm, Hermann. Korrelative Beziehungen zwischen Elementarenvergleichsleistungen. Inaug. Diss. Leipzig, 1914.

Phil 3808.145 Damm, O.F. Arthur Schopenhauer. Leipzig, 1912.

Phil 3808.123 Damm, Oscar. Schopenhauers Ethik im Verhaltnis zu seiner Erkenntnislehre und Metaphysik. Annaberg, 1898.

Phil 8092.15 Damnjanović, Milan. Strujanja u savremenoj estetici. Zagreb, 1966.

Phil 972.17 Damodar and the pioneers of the theosophical movement. (Eek, Sven.) Adyar, 1965.

Phil 960.257 Damodaran, K. Indian thought; a critical survey. Bombay, 1967.

Phil 1750.55 Damur, Carl. Das Test der Seele. Bern, 1947.

Phil 178.25 Dana, A.H. Inductive inquiries in physiology, ethics, and ethnology. N.Y., 1873.

Htn Phil 5754.1.19* Dana, J. Examination...Edward's...freedom of will. Boston, 1770.

Htn Phil 5754.1.20* Dana, J. Examination...Edward's...freedom of will. New Haven, 1773.

Phil 8693.8 Dana, J.D. Creation or biblical cosmogony. Oberlin, 1885.

Phil 8701.2.7 Dana, J.D. Science and the bible, a review of the Six days of creation. Andover, 1856.

Phil 179.17 The dance of life. (Ellis, Havelock.) Boston, 1923.

Phil 179.17.5 The dance of life. (Ellis, Havelock.) Boston, 1926.

Phil 179.17.15 The dance of life. (Ellis, Havelock.) Boston 1929.

Phil 179.17.4 The dance of life. (Ellis, Havelock.) N.Y., 1923.

Phil 179.17.18 The dance of life. (Ellis, Havelock.) N.Y., 1929.

Phil 179.17.20 The dance of life. (Ellis, Havelock.) N.Y., 1929.

Phil 5834.1 The dancing mouse. (Yerkes, R.M.) N.Y., 1907.

Phil 178.54 Dandolo, G. Appunti di filosofia. v.1-3. Messina, 1903-1909.

Phil 178.54.3 Dandolo, G. Appunti di filosofia. 3. ed. Padova, 1894.

Phil 284.9 Dandolo, G. La causa e la legge. Padova, 1901.

Phil 7080.37 Dandolo, G. La coscienza nel sonno. Padova, 1889.

Phil 5585.41 Dandolo, G. Le integrazioni psichiche e la percezione. Padova, 1898.

Phil 5753.10 Dandolo, G. Le integrazioni psichiche e la volontà. Padova, 1908.

Phil 284.10 Dandolo, G. Intorno al valore della scienza. Padova, 1908.

Phil 178.54.5 Dandolo, G. L'obbietto della filosofia e la verità. Padova, 1908.

Phil 5545.69 Dandolo, Giovanni. La dottrina della "memoria", tedesco. Padova, 1893.

Phil 5545.69.15 Dandolo, Giovanni. La dottrina della memoria. Réggio nell'Emilia, 1891.

Phil 5545.69.5 Dandolo, Giovanni. La memoria. Messina, 1903.

Phil 960.121 Dandoy, G. An essay on the doctrine of the unreality of the world in the Advaita. Calcutta, 1919.

Phil 4872.55.20 D'Andrade, Joseph C.P. Philosophy and life and other papers. Bombay, 1952.

Phil 8404.9 Daneo, G. Alcune considerazioni sul bello. Torino, 1877.

Phil 9070.29 Danforth, William Henry. I dare you! Four fold development. 8. ed. St. Louis, Mo., 1938.

Phil 5753.17 D'Angelo, Edward. The problem of freedom and determinism. Columbia, 1968.

Phil 5520.68.10 Danger: man talking! (Chase, Stuart.) N.Y., 1969.

Phil 9375.4 Dangers and duties of the merchantile profession. (Hillard, G.S.) Boston, 1850.

Phil 6681.11 Les dangers du magnétisme animal. (Lombard, A.) Paris, 1819.

Phil 8875.33 Les dangers du moralisme. (Albert, Henri.) n.p., 1896?

Phil 7069.06.20 The dangers of spiritualism. 2. ed. (Raupert, John G.) London, 1906.

Phil 2805.101.25 Daniel, Gabriel. The discourses of Cleander and Eudoxe. London, 1704.

Phil 2805.101.15 Daniel, Gabriel. Entretiens de Cléandre et d'Eudoxe sur les lettres au provincial. 10. éd. Pierre Marteau, 1697.

Phil 2520.88.25 Daniel, Gabriel. Iter per mundum Cartesii. Amesteledami, 1694.

Phil 2805.402 Daniel, Gabriel. Lettre de Mr. l'abbé...à Eudoxe. Cologne, 1698-99.

Phil 2520.88.30 Daniel, Gabriel. Nouvelles difficultez proposees par un peripateticien. Paris, 1693.

Phil 2805.101 Daniel, Gabriel. Réponse aux lettres provinciales. Amsterdam, 1697.

Phil 2805.101.5 Daniel, Gabriel. Réponse aux lettres provinciales. Bruxelles, 1698.

Phil 2805.101.8 Daniel, Gabriel. Réponse aux lettres provinciales. La Haye, 1716.

Htn Phil 2520.88.5* Daniel, Gabriel. Voiage du monde de Descartes. Paris, 1690.

Phil 2520.88.7 Daniel, Gabriel. Voiage du monde de Descartes. Paris, 1691.

Phil 2520.88 Daniel, Gabriel. Voyage du monde de Descartes...Suite du voyage du monde de Descartes. Amsterdam, 1713.

Phil 2520.88.2 Daniel, Gabriel. Voyage du monde de Descartes. Paris, 1702.

Phil 2520.88.9 Daniel, Gabriel. Voyage du monde de Descartes. Paris, 1703.

Phil 2520.88.10 Daniel, Gabriel. Voyage du monde de Descartes. v.1-2. Amsterdam, 1706.

Htn VPhil 2520.88.20* Daniel, Gabriel. Voyage to the world of Cartesius. London, 1694.

Phil 7069.23.6 Daniel. (Dumanjó, L.) Habana, 1923.

Phil 2725.30 Daniel-Rops, Henry. Edouard LeRoy et son fauteuil. Paris, 1956.

Phil 530.15.28 Daniel-Rops, Henry. Mystiques de France. Paris, 1941.

Phil 2805.257 Daniel-Rops, Henry. Pascal et notre coeur. 6. éd. Strasbourg, 1949.

Phil 8980.316 Danielian, Mal'feda. Nekotorye voprosy marksistisko-leninskoi etiki. Erevan, 1962.

Phil 8685.1 Danièlo, J. Du panthéisme. Paris, 1848.

Phil 1504.8 Daniels, A. Quellenbeitrage und Untersuchungen zur Geschichte. v.8, pt.1-2. Münster, 1909.

Phil 5627.77 Daniels, A.H. The new life. Worcester, 1893.

Phil 7069.00.20 Daniels, Cora L. As it is to be. Exeter, 1900.

Phil 7068.92.25 Daniels, Cora Linn Morrison. As it is to be. 5. ed. Franklin, Mass., 1892.

Phil 365.64 Daniels, George H. Darwinism comes to America. Waltham, Mass., 1968.

Phil 7054.139 Daniels, J.W. Spiritualism versus Christianity. N.Y., 1856.

Phil 310.360 Danilenko, D.I. Dialekticheskii materializm. Moskva, 1961.

Phil 310.13 Danilenko, D.I. Marksistskii filosofskii materializm. Moskva, 1953.

Phil 7069.21.70 Danils, H. Anden. Stockholm, 1921.

Phil 13.20 Danish yearbook of philosophy. Copenhagen. 1,1964+

Phil 178.47 Danmar, W. World cognition. N.Y., 1923.

Phil 7069.25.4 Danmar, William. Geisterkenntnis. Leipzig, 1925.

Phil 7054.118.5 Danmar, William. Modern nirvanaism. Jamaica, 1921.

Phil 7054.118 Danmar, William. Modern nirvanaism. N.Y., 1914.

Phil 5753.16 Danner, Manfred. Gibt es einen freein Willen? Hamburg, 1967.

Phil 6990.3.31 Dans la lumière de Lourdes. (Bonnières, L. de.) Paris, 1920.

Phil 2805.290 Dans Pascal. (Demorest, Jean.) Paris, 1953.

Phil 7054.101 La danse des tables. (Rouband, F.) Paris, 1853.

Phil 4580.30 Danske filosofer. (Høffding, Harald.) København, 1909.

Phil 7054.2 Danskin, W.A. How and why I became a spiritualist. 4th ed. Baltimore, 1869.

Phil 6953.10 Dantas, J. Pintores e poetas de Rilhafolles. Liboa, 1900.

Phil 5247.13.80 Dantin Gallego, J. La filosofia natural de Huarte de San Juan. Madrid, 1952.

Phil 3450.19.465 Dantlo, René. A la rencontre de Martin Heidegger. Toulouse, 1969.

Phil 335.10 Danto, Arthur Coleman. Analytic philosophy of knowledge. Cambridge, Eng., 1968.

Phil 3640.706 Danto, Arthur Coleman. Nietzsche as philosopher. N.Y., 1965.

Phil 5590.564 Dantov, Tasbolat M. Lichnost' kak sotsiologicheskaia problema. Alma-Ata, 1970.

Phil 8404.2 Danz, Louis. The psychologist looks at art. London, 1937.

Phil 960.28 Daqupta, S. A history of Indian philosophy. v. 2-5. Cambridge, Eng., 1922-49. 4v.

Phil 960.28.5 Daqupta, S. Philosophical essays. Calcutta, 1941.

Phil 5620.30 Dar, B.A. Studies in reason and faith. Lahore, 1957.

Phil 730.26 Dar, B.A. Studies in the nature of universals. Lahore, 1958.

Phil 8900.7 Dar svobody. (Zen'kovskii, V.V.) Paris, 193-?

Phil 3823.10 Darbon, A.D. Etudes Spinozistes. Paris, 1946.

Phil 2555.8.35 Darbon, André. Les categories de la modalité. 1. éd. Paris, 1956.

Phil 2555.8.30 Darbon, André. Philosophie de la volonté. 1. éd. Paris, 1951.

Phil 8658.6 D'Arcy, C.F. Idealism and theology. London, 1899.

Phil 284.13 D'Arcy, C.F. Providence and the world-order. London, 1932.

Phil 8878.60 D'Arcy, E. Human acts. Oxford, 1963.

Phil 9075.70 D'Arcy, Eric. Conscience and its right to freedom. N.Y., 1961.

Phil 8583.35.5 D'Arcy, M.C. The meeting of love and knowledge. 1. ed. N.Y., 1957.

Phil 8583.35 D'Arcy, M.C. Mirage and truth. N.Y., 1935.

Phil 8622.30 d'Arcy, M.C. The nature of belief. Dublin, 1958.

Phil 8735.25 D'Arcy, M.C. The pain of this world and the providence of God. London, 1952.

Phil 8953.8.6 D'Arcy, Martin Cyrile. La double nature de l'amour. Paris, 1948.

Phil 8953.8.3 D'Arcy, Martin Cyrile. The mind and heart of love, lion and unicorn. London, 1954.

Phil 8953.8.2 D'Arcy, Martin Cyrile. The mind and heart of love, lion and unicorn. N.Y., 1947.

Phil 8953.8 D'Arcy, Martin Cyrile. The mind and heart of love. London, 1945.

Htn Phil 9343.12* Dare, Josiah. Counsellor Manners, his last legacy to his son. London, 1673.

Phil 9343.12.5 Dare, Josiah. Counsellor Manners, his last legacy to his son. London, 1710.

Phil 187.56.4 Dare to be wise. (McTaggart, J.M.E.) London, 1910.

Phil 9343.2.2 Darell, W. Gentleman instructed. London, 1707. 2v.

Phil 9343.2 Darell, W. Gentleman instructed. London, 1723.

Phil 8878.19 Darell, W. The gentleman instructed. London, 1738.

Phil 9343.2.3 Darell, W. A supplement to the first part of the G.I. London, 1708.

Phil 284.7 Dario, J.M. Praelectiones cosmologiae. Paris, 1923.

Phil 193.93.10 D'Aristote à Marx. (Sorel, Georges.) Paris, 1935.

Phil 2475.1.420 Darkaoui, Assad Arabi. Essai sur l'idée de pureté chez Bergson. Damas, 1963.

Phil 8610.912 The darkness, the dawn and the day. (Thomas, J.C.) London, 1912.

Htn Phil 8657.18* The darkness of atheism dispelled by the light of native. (Charleton, W.) London, 1652.

Htn Phil 3800.230*A Darlegung der wahren Verhältnisses der Naturphilosophie. (Schelling, F.W.J. von.) Tübingen, 1806.

Phil 3800.59 Darlegung des wahren Verhältnisses der Naturphilosophie zu der verbesserten Fichte'schenLehre. (Schelling, F.W.J. von.) n.p., n.d. 4 pam.

Phil 2115.119 Darlegung und Kritik der Lokeschen Lehre vom empirischen Ursprung der sittlichen Grundsätze. Inaug.-Diss. (Winter, Hermann.) Bonn, 1883.

Phil 978.47 Darlès, Jean. Glossaire raisonné de la théosophie du qnosticisme et de l'ésotérisme. Paris, 1910.

Phil 6673.12 Darly, Joseph. Day visions and clairvoyant night dreams. London, 1892.

Phil 1750.769 Darmstaedter Gespräch, 8th, Darmstadt. Angst und Hoffnung in unserer Zeit. Darmstadt, 1965.

Phil 70.93 Darmtaedter, Gespräch. Die Herausforderung. München, 1963.

Phil 3415.115 Darnoi, D.N.K. The unconcious and Eduard von Hartmann; a historico-critical monograph. The Hague, 1968.

Phil 7108.372 Darnton, Robert. Mesmerism and the end of the Enlightenment in France. Cambridge, 1968.

Phil 2490.138 Darp, Jan van. De ethik van Auguste Comte. Utrecht, 1910.

Phil 8610.929.20 Darrow, C. Infidels and heretics. Boston, 1929.

Phil 3890.1.80 Darstellung...Trendelenburgs. (Veeck, O.) Gotha, 1888.

Phil 3246.88 Darstellung der Ethik Johann Gottlieb Fichtes. (Ivanoff, C.) Leipzig, 1899.

Phil 5645.3 Darstellung der Farbenlehre. (Dove, H.W.) Berlin, 1853.

Phil 3494.33.5 Darstellung der Hauptimomente der Elementarlehre der Kantischen Kritik der reinen Vernunft. Pt. 1-2. (Metz, Andreas.) Bamberg, 1802.

Phil 3489.5 Darstellung der Kantischen Erkenntnisstheorie. (Hölder, Alfred.) Tübingen, 1873.

Phil 2115.103 Darstellung der Locke'schen Erkenntnisstheorie. (Benoit, G. von.) Bern, 1869.

Phil 3790.6.31 Darstellung der Philosophie. (Rauscher, J.O.) Salugan, 1891.

Phil 2493.82 Darstellung der Psychologie bei Condillac und Bonnet. (Mülhaupt, P.) Cassel, 1874.

Phil 3492.34.4 Darstellung der wichtigsten Wahrheiten der kritischen Philosophie. (Kiesewetter, J.G.K.C.) Berlin, 1824.

Phil 3246.44.5 Darstellung der Wissenschaftslehre aus dem Jahre 1801, 1804. v.1-2. (Fichte, Johann Gottlieb.) Leipzig, 1922.

Phil 4195.95 Darstellung des Inhalts der Disputationes in astrologiam. (Remé, Richard W.) Hamburg, 1933.

Phil 3483.15.5 Darstellung des Lebens und Charakters Immanuel Kants. (Borowski, L.E.) Königsberg, 1804.

Phil 185.48 Darstellung des Wesens der Philosophie. (Köppen, Friedrich.) Nürnberg, 1810.

Phil 2725.40 Darstellung einiger Grundzüge des literarischen Werks von Pierre de la Primaudaye. (Drochner, Karl Heinz.) Berlin, 1960.

Phil 3500.2 Darstellung Kantscher Philosophie. (Schaller, J.) Halle, 1846.

Phil 3503.7 Darstellung und Beurtheilung der Kant'schen und Hegel'schen Christologie. (Vogt, Carl.) Marburg, 1878.

Phil 3500.35 Darstellung und Erläuterung I. Kant Critik. v.1-2. (Snell, E.W.D.) Mannheim, 1791.

Phil 3460.83 Darstellung und Hauptgedanken F.H. Jacobi. (Delius, J.F.) Halle, 1878.

Phil 3808.95 Darstellung und Kritik. (Sommerlad, F.) Offenbach, 1895.

Phil 3549.8.80 Darstellung und Kritik der Charakterologie von Ludwig Klages. (Börlin, E.) Giessen, 1929.

Phil 5068.14 Darstellung und Kritik der erkenntnistheoretischen Grundlagen der Kausalitätsauffassung und der Ethik des Neopositivismus. (Albrecht, Erhard.) Rostock, 1949.

Phil 3552.283 Darstellung und Kritik der Lehre Leibniz' von der menschlichen Wahlfreiheit. Inaug. Diss. (Nithack, A.) Halle, 1893.

Phil 4815.672.80 Darstellung und Kritik der logischen Grundbegriffe der Naturphilosophie Melchior Palagyis. (Wurmb, Albert.) Weisswasser, 1931.

Phil 3160.7.85 Darstellung und Kritik der naturalistischen Weltanschauung H. Czolbes. Inaug. Diss. (Friedmann, P.) Berlin, 1905.

Phil 3235.113 Darstellung und Kritik der Philosophie Ludwig Feuerbach's. (Schaller, Julius.) Leipzig, 1847.

Phil 3625.8.85 Darstellung und Kritik der Thierpsychologie Georg Friedrich Meier's. Inaug. Diss. (Spitzer, David.) Györ, 1903.

Phil 3425.93 Darstellung und Kritik des Hegelschen Systems. (Staudenmaier, F.) Mainz, 1844.

Phil 3500.45 Darstellung und Kritik des Kantischen Lehre von der Willensfreiheit. (Salits, Peter.) Rostock, 1898.

Phil 3552.128 Darstellung und Kritik des leibnitzischen Optimismus. Inaug.-Diss. (Engler, Otto.) Jena, 1883.

Phil 4580.118 Darstellung und Würdigung der Ethik Harald Høffdings. Inaug. Diss. (Meis, Hans.) Obersassel, 1928.

Phil 2555.12.30 Dartan, Jacques. Franchir le Rubicon. Paris, 1968.

Phil 8610.898 D'Arusmont, Frances Wright. Six lectures on the nature of knowledge, free enquiry, the more important divisions and essentials of knowledge, religion, morals, opinions. London, 1898.

Phil 9530.58 Darvas, Nicolas. The anatomy of success. Indianapolis, 1966.

Phil 5400.19.2 Darwin, Charles. Der Ausdruck der Gemüthsbewegungen bei dem Menschen und den Thieren. 4. Aufl. Stuttgart, 1884.

X Cg Phil 5400.18.50 Darwin, Charles. The expression of the emotions in man and animals. London, 1872.

Phil 5400.19 Darwin, Charles. The expression of the emotions in man and animals. N.Y., 1873.

Phil 5400.19.3.5 Darwin, Charles. The expression of the emotions in man and animals. N.Y., 1894.

Phil 5400.19.3.10 Darwin, Charles. The expression of the emotions in man and animals. N.Y., 1894.

Phil 5400.19.7 Darwin, Charles. The expression of the emotions in man and animals. N.Y., 1896.

Phil 5400.19.4 Darwin, Charles. The expression of the emotions in man and animals. N.Y., 1897.

Htn Phil 1955.1.30* Darwin, Charles. The expression of the emotions in man and animals. N.Y., 1899.

Phil 1955.1.30* Darwin, Charles. On the origin of species. London, 1859.

Phil 8689.100 Darwin, evolution, and creation. (Zimmerman, Paul A.) Saint Louis, 1959.

Phil 192.10A Darwin and Hegel. (Ritchie, D.G.) London, 1893.

Phil 8696.21 Darwin and the modern world view. (Greene, J.C.) Baton Rouge, 1961.

Phil 3160.2.85 Darwin in der Ethik. (Harpf, Adolf.) Leoben, 1901.

Phil 365.64 Darwinism comes to America. (Daniels, George H.) Waltham, Mass., 1968.

Phil 3415.50 Le Darwinisme. (Hartmann, Eduard von.) Paris, 1877.

Phil 8712.19 Darwinismus, Religion, Sittlichkeit. (Weygoldt, G.P.) Leiden, 1878.

Phil 9150.17 Die Darwin'sche Theorie und ihre Stellung. (Jaeger, Gustav.) Stuttgart, 1869.

Phil 5190.70 Das, Adhar Chandra. Negative fact, negation and truth. Calcutta, 1942.

Phil 3485.18 Das, Ras-Vihari. A handbook to Kant's Critique of pure reason. Bombay, 1949.

Phil 2340.10.97A Das, Ras-Vihari. The philosophy of Whitehead. London, 1938.

Phil 8878.54 Das, Ras-Vihari. The self and the ideal. Calcutta, 1935.

Phil 5520.690 Das Jagannath, Prasad. Verbal conditioning and behavior. 1. ed. Oxford, 1969.

Phil 182.118 Das leuchten des dunckels. (Herk, Konrad.) Antwerpen, 1960.

Phil 4352.1.89 Das palabras sobre centenario de Balmes. (Menendez y Pelayo, D.M.) Vich, 1910.

Phil 175.27 Das wahnsinnige Bewusstsein. (Anhuth, R.O.) Halle, 1877.

Phil 182.60 Das Dasein als Lust, Leid, und Liebe. (Hubbe-Schleiden, Wilhelm.) Braunschweig, 1891.

Phil 3565.51.50 Das Dasein der Seele. (Lotze, Hermann.) Leipzig, 1929?

Phil 3450.19.101 Das Dasein des Menschen. (Hoberg, C.A.) Zeuleuroda, 1937.

Phil 3450.19.102 Das Dasein des Menschen. Inaug. Diss. (Hoberg, C.A.) Zeuleuroda, 1937.

Phil 185.9 Das Dasein Gottes. (Krönig, Prof.) Berlin, 1874.

Phil 3475.3.135 Das Dasein in der Philosophie von Karl Jaspers. Diss. (Räber, T.) Freiburg, 1954.

Phil 176.219 Dasein und Dawesen. (Becker, O.) Pfullingen, 1963.

Phil 672.268 Dasein und Raum. Habilitationsschrift. (Goelz, Walter.) Tübingen, 1970.

Phil 184.28.5 Dasein und Wirklichkeit. (Janssen, O.) München, 1938.

Phil 530.105 Dasgupta, S.N. Hindu mysticism. Chicago, 1927.

Phil 400.87 Dasgupta, S.N. Indian idealism. Cambridge, Eng., 1933.

Phil 960.248.2 Dasgupta, Surama. Development of moral philosophy in India. N.Y., 1965.

Phil 960.28.2 Dasgupta, Surendra Nath. A history of Indian philosophy. Cambridge, 1963.

Phil 5243.36.12 Dashiell, J.F. An experimental manual in psychology. Boston, 1931.

Phil 5243.36.10 Dashiell, J.F. Fundamentals of general psychology. Boston, 1937.

Phil 5243.36 Dashiell, J.F. Fundamentals of objective psychology. Boston, 1928.

Phil 5243.36.15 Dashiell, J.F. Manual to accompany Fundamentals of general psychology. Boston, 1931.

Phil 735.5 Dashiell, J.F. Philosophical status of values. N.Y., 1913.

Phil 960.119 Dass, Satya. Self-expression and the Indian social problem. Lahore, 1937.

Phil 5272.7 Data analysis. (Wike, Edward L.) Chicago, 1971.

Phil 2270.74.5 Data of ethics. (Spencer, Herbert.) London, 1879.

Phil 2270.30.5 Data of ethics. (Spencer, Herbert.) London, 1887.

Phil 2270.74.1.5 Data of ethics. (Spencer, Herbert.) N.Y., 1879.

Phil 2270.74 Data of ethics. (Spencer, Herbert.) N.Y., 1879.

Phil 2270.74.4 Data of ethics. (Spencer, Herbert.) N.Y., 1883.

Phil 2270.74.12 Data of ethics. (Spencer, Herbert.) NY., 189-?

Phil 2270.77 Data of ethics. Pt. IV. Justice. (Spencer, Herbert.) N.Y., 1891.

Phil 2270.74.7 Data of ethics. 3rd ed. (Spencer, Herbert.) London, 1881.

Phil 5545.25 Dates by name. (Ward, G.W.) Baltimore, 1892.

Phil 4260.89 Dati psicologici nella dottrina giuridica. (Vadalà-Papale, G.) Roma, 1889.

Phil 1703.12 Datta, D.M. The chief currents of contemporary philosophy. Calcutta, 1950.

Phil 1703.12.2 Datta, D.M. The chief currents of contemporary philosophy. 2nd ed. Calcutta, 1961.

Phil 5243.32 Dattino, Giovanni. La psicologia dei testimoni. Napoli, 1909.

Phil 630.32 The datum as essence in contemporary philosophy. (Boas, George.) Niort, 1927.

Phil 8620.3 Daub, C. Judas Ischariot. v.1-2. Heidelberg, 1816-18.

Phil 5753.9 Daub, Carl. Des Dr. C. Daub Darstellung und Beurtheilung des Hypothesen in Betreff dei Willensfreiheit. Altona, 1834.

Phil 178.24.5 Daub, Carl. Philosophische und theologische Vorlesungen. v.1-7. Berlin, 1838-44. 8v.

Phil 3485.30 Daub, Carl. Predigten nach Kantischen Grundsätzen. Bruxelles, 1968.

Phil 178.24 Daub, E. Studien. Frankfurt, 1805. 6v.

Phil 5643.57 Daublebsky, Storneck von. Der Sehraum auf grund der Erfahrung. Leipzig, 1907.

Phil 5465.21 Daudet, Léon. Le monde des images; suite de l'hérédo. Paris, 1919.

Phil 7082.172 Daudet, Léon. Le rêve éveillé. Paris, 1926.

Phil 575.71 Daudet, Léon A. L'hérédo; essai sur le drame intérieur. Paris, 1916.

Phil 5753.14 Daudin, H. La liberté de la volonté. 1. éd. Paris, 1950.

Phil 3808.238 Dauer, Dorothoa W. Schopenhauer as transmitter of buddhist ideas. Berne, 1969.

Phil 165.367 Daues, Vincent F. Wisdom in depth. Milwaukee, 1966.

Phil 9344.3 Daughters of England. (Ellis, S.S.) N.Y., 1843.

Htn Phil 9352.2* Daughters of Zion. (Mather, C.) n.p., 1691?

Phil 9343.3 Daughter's own book. Philadelphia, 1891.

Phil 5243.66 Daujat, J. Psychologie contemporaine et pensée chrétienne. Tournai, 1962.

Phil 178.2 Daumer, G.F. Andeutung eines Systems speculativer Philosophie. Nürnberg, 1831.

Phil 2880.8.94 Dauphin, E.J. Ekecrate; dialogue sur l'existentialisme. Montpellier, 1947.

Phil 3805.265 Daur, Martin. Die eine Kirche und das zweifache Recht. Thesis. München, 1970.

Phil 7069.68.60 Daurado, Alzira Guanaes. Igrejas reunidas, plano divino. 1. ed. Rio de Janeiro, 1968.

Phil 6990.24 Daurelle. Etude des manifestations surnaturelles au XIX siècle. Rome, 1878.

Phil 2403.7 Dauriac, L. Contingence et nationalisme. Paris, 1924.

Phil 630.8 Dauriac, L. Croyance et réalité. Paris, 1889.

Phil 478.2 Dauriac, L. Des notions de matière et de force. Paris, 1878.

Phil 4260.205 Daus, Hans-Jürgen. Selbstverständnis und Menschenbild in den Selbstdarstellungen Giambattista Vicos und Pietro Giannones. Thesis. Genève, 1962.

Phil 7069.14.40 D'Aute-Hooper, T. Spirit-psychometry and trance communications by unseen agencies. London, 1914.

Phil 5066.22 Daval, R. Le raisonnement mathématique. Paris, 1945.

Phil 2403.8 Daval, Roger. Histoire des idées en France. 2e éd. Paris, 1956.

Phil 3485.19.2 Daval, Roger. La métaphysique de Kant. Thèse. Paris, 1950.

Phil 3485.19 Daval, Roger. La métaphysique de Kant. 1. éd. Paris, 1950.

Phil 178.74 Daval, Simone. Classe de philosophie. Paris, 1962. 2v.

Phil 5243.52 Daval, Simone. Psychologie. Paris, 1956. 2v.

NEDL Phil 5627.7.8 Davenport, F.M. Primitive traits in religious revivals. N.Y., 1905.

Phil 7054.7.5 Davenport, R.B. The death blow to spiritualism...true story of the Fox sisters. N.Y., 1888.

Phil 8658.13 Davenport, S.F. Immanence and incarnation. Cambridge, 1925.

Phil 7060.52.5 The Davenport brothers...spiritual mediums. Boston, 1869.

Phil 8583.2 Davesiès de Pontès, L. Études morales et religieuses. Paris, 1869.

Phil 6673.8 Davey, William. The illustrated practical mesmerist. 6th ed. London, 1862?

Phil 5926.1.28 David, A. Le petit Docteur Gall. Paris, 1869?

Phil 6021.2.50 David, Alexandre. Le petit Lavater français. Paris, 1857.

Phil 6313.23 David, H.P. International resources in clinical psychology. N.Y., 1964.

Phil 5590.340.5 David, Henry Philip. Perspectives in personality research. N.Y., 1960.

Phil 1870.93 David, M. Berkeley. Paris, n.d.

Phil 6307.408 David, Michel. La psicoanalisi nella cultura italiana. Torino, 1966.

Phil 6314.8 David Eder; memoirs of a modern pioneer. (Hobman, J.B.) London, 1945.

Phil 3850.1.98 David Frédéric Strauss, la vie et l'oeuvre. (Lévy, Albert.) Paris, 1910.

Phil 3850.1.86 David Friedrich Strauss. (Harraeus, K.) Leipzig, n.d.

Phil 3850.1.93 David Friedrich Strauss. (Zeller, Eduard.) London, 1874.

Phil 3850.1.87 David Friedrich Strauss. (Ziegler, T.) Strassburg, 1908. 2v.

Phil 3850.1.91 David Friedrich Strauss. 2. Aufl. (Zeller, Eduard.) Bonn, 1874.

X Cg Phil 3850.1.96 David Friedrich Strauss als Denker und Erzieher. (Kohut, Adolph.) Leipzig, 1908.

Phil 2050.272 David Hume, filosofo della religione. (Sabetti, Alfredo.) Napoli, 1965.

Phil 2050.78.80 David Hume. (Basson, A.H.) Harmondsworth, 1958.

Phil 2050.255 David Hume. (Belgion, Montgomery.) London, 1965.

Phil 2050.92A David Hume. (Calderwood, H.) Edinburgh, n.d.

Phil 2050.196 David Hume. (Greig, John Y.T.) London, 1931.

Phil 2050.217 David Hume. (Heinemann, Fritz.) Paris, 1940.

Phil 2050.203 David Hume. (Laing, B.M.) London, 1932.

Phil 2050.93 David Hume. (Lechartier, G.) Paris, 1900.

Phil 2050.223 David Hume. (MacNabb, Donald George Cecil.) London, 1951.

Phil 2050.253.5 David Hume. (Pears, D.F.) London, 1966.

Phil 2050.256.5 David Hume. (Price, John Valdimir.) N.Y., 1969.

Phil 2050.251 David Hume. (Snethlage, J.L.) Den Haag, 1963.

Phil 2050.179 David Hume. (Wijnaendts Francken, C.J.) Haarlem, 1907.

Phil 2050.188 David Hume: Leben und Philosophie. (Metz, Rudolf.) Stuttgart, 1929.

Phil 2050.72 David Hume: philosophical historian. (Hume, David.) Indianapolis, 1965.

Phil 2050.98 David Hume: sein Leben und seine Philosophie. (Thomsen, A.) Berlin, 1912.

Phil 2050.225 David Hume. 1. éd. (Cresson, A.) Paris, 1952.

Phil 2050.229 David Hume. 1. éd. (Leroy, A.L.) Paris, 1953.

Phil 2050.223.2 David Hume. 2nd ed. (MacNabb, Donald George Cecil.) Oxford, 1966.

Phil 2050.192 David Hume als Religionsphilosoph. Inaug. Diss. (Meinardus, H.) Coblenz, 1897.

Phil 2050.101.3A David Hume and his influence on philosophy and theology. (Orr, James.) Edinburgh, 1903.

Phil 2050.101 David Hume and his influence on philosophy and theology. (Orr, James.) N.Y., 1903.

Phil 2050.184 David Hume and the miraculous. (Taylor, A.E.) Cambridge, Eng., 1927.

Phil 2050.244 David Hume politico e storico. (Giarrizzo, G.) Torino, 1962.

Htn Phil 2050.189* David Hume über den Glauben. (Jacobi, F.H.) Breslau, 1787.

Phil 2050.191 David Humes Kausalitätstheorie. Inaug. Diss. (Jahn, Franz.) Leipzig, 1895.

Phil 2050.106 David Hume's kenleer en ethiek. (Sopper, A.J.) Leiden, 1907.

Phil 2050.186 David Hume's Lehre vom Wissen. Diss. (Linke, Paul.) Leipzig, 1901.

Phil 2050.270 David Humes politische Philosophie in ihrem Zusammenhang mit seiner gesamten Lehre. Inaug. Diss. (Wenzel, Leonhard.) Köln? 1959.

Phil 2050.108 David Humes religionsphilosophische Anschauungen. (Lüers, Adolf.) Berlin, 1901.

Phil 2050.104 David Hume's Skepsis. (Masaryk, T.G.) Wien, 1884.

Phil 5753.15 Davidovich, Vsevolod E. Problemy chelovechskoi svobody. L'vov, 1967.

Phil 5590.14 Davidson, Helen H. Personality and economic background. N.Y., 1943.

Phil 3428.88 Davidson, John. New interpretation of Herbart's psychology. Edinburgh, 1906.

Phil 5753.13 Davidson, M. The free will controversy. London, 1942.

Phil 8693.17 Davidson, M. The heavens and faith. London, 1936.

X Cg Phil 1200.17 Davidson, W.L. The stoic creed. Edinburgh, 1907.

Phil 1200.17 Davidson, W.L. The stoic creed. Edinburgh, 1907.

Phil 8658.8 Davidson, W.L. Theism as grounded in human nature. London, 1893.

Phil 8953.2 Davidson, William L. Christian ethics. London, 1899.

Phil 5043.21 Davidson, William L. The logic of definition. London, 1885.

Phil 8878.25 Davies, A.E. The moral life; a study in genetic ethics. Baltimore, 1909.

Phil 5043.19 Davies, A.E. A text-book of logic. Columbus, 1915.

Phil 7054.127 Davies, Charles M. The great secret, and its unfoldment in occultism. 2. ed. London, 1896.

Phil 165.345 Davies, H.S. The English mind. Cambridge, Eng., 1964.

Phil 5243.2 Davies, J. An estimate of the human mind. London, 1828. 2v.

Htn Phil 8878.4.5* Davies, J.L. Order and growth. London, 1891.

Phil 8878.4A Davies, J.L. Theology and morality. London, 1873.

Phil 5923.3 Davies, John D. Phrenology. New Haven, 1955.

Phil 6750.223.15 Davies, S.P. The mentally retarded in society. N.Y., 1959.

Phil 6750.223 Davies, S.P. Social control of the feebleminded. N.Y., 1923.

Phil 6750.223.10 Davies, S.P. Social control of the mentally deficient. N.Y., 1930.

Phil 8693.2 Davies, T.A. Answer to Hugh Miller and theoretic geologists. N.Y., 1860.

Phil 8693.2.5 Davies, T.A. Cosmogony, or The mysteries of creation. N.Y., 1857?

Phil 8878.35 Davies, William. The pilgrim of the infinite. London, 1894.

Phil 3552.114 Davillé, L. Leibniz historien. Paris, 1909.

Phil 7068.52 Davis, A.J. The approaching crisis. N.Y., 1852.

Phil 7054.6.35 Davis, A.J. The fountain. 1st ed. Boston, 1870.

Phil 8610.854.2 Davis, A.J. Free thoughts concerning religion. 2. ed. Boston, 1854.

Phil 7054.6.9 Davis, A.J. The great harmonia. 4th ed. Boston, 1870. 5v.

Phil 7054.6.55 Davis, A.J. The harmonial man. Boston, 1853.

Phil 7054.6.50 Davis, A.J. Introduction to the writings of Andrew J. Davis. Boston, 1930.

NEDL Phil 7054.6.3 Davis, A.J. The magic staff; an autobiography. N.Y., 1857.

Phil 7054.6.18 Davis, A.J. The penetralia, being harmonial answers. 3. ed. Boston, 1857.

Phil 8658.2 Davis, A.J. The philosophy of special providences. Boston, 1856.

Phil 7054.6.5 Davis, A.J. The philosophy of spiritual intercourse. N.Y., 1851.

Phil 7054.6.6 Davis, A.J. The present age and inner life. N.Y., 1855.

Phil 7054.6.8 Davis, A.J. The present age and inner life. 3d ed. Boston, 1870.

Phil 7054.6.30 Davis, A.J. The principles of nature, her divine revelations. 12. ed. N.Y., 1855.

Phil 7068.47 Davis, A.J. The principles of nature. 3. ed. N.Y., 1847.

Phil 7054.6.05 Pamphlet box. Davis, A.J. Minor writings.

Phil 7069.20.90 Davis, Andrew J. A stellar key to the summer land. 6th ed. Los Angeles, 1920.

Phil 6750.10 Davis, C.H.S. The classification...feeble minded, imbecile and idiotic. N.Y., 1883.

Phil 1955.10.30 Davis, Charles G. The philosophy of live. 2nd ed. Chicago, 1906.

Phil 8953.7 Davis, H. Moral and pastoral theology. 3. ed. N.Y., 1938. 4v.

Phil 5813.2 Davis, H.B. The raccoon: a study in animal intelligence. London, 1907.

Phil 7060.130 Davis, H.P. Expose of Newburyport excentricities. n.p., 1873.

Phil 6953.14 Davis, J.E. Principles and practice of recreational theraphy for the mentally ill. N.Y., 1936.

Phil 6953.14.5 Davis, J.E. Principles and practice of rehabilatation. N.Y., 1943.

Phil 5039.28 Davis, J.W. Philosophical logic. Dordrecht, 1969.

Phil 6113.33 Davis, James Allen. Education for positive mental health. Chicago, 1965.

Phil 5043.2.5 Davis, N.K. Elements of inductive logic. N.Y., 1895.

Phil 5243.27 Davis, N.K. Elements of psychology. N.Y., 1892.

Phil 5043.2 Davis, N.K. The theory of thought. N.Y., 1880.

Phil 8878.21 Davis, Noals K. Elements of ethics. Boston, 1900.

Phil 7069.56.20 Davis, S.E. Man being revealed. 1. ed. N.Y., 1956.

Phil 9343.5 Davis, William. Friendly advice to industrious persons. 4th ed. London, 1817.

Phil 5400.170 Davitz, Joel Robert. The communication of emotional meaning. N.Y., 1964.

Phil 5400.198 Davitz, Joel Robert. The language of emotion. N.Y., 1969.

Phil 8878.6 Davy, C.W. The maxims...of Agogos. Boston, 1844.

Phil 2045.124 Davy, G. Thomas Hobbes et Jean-Jacques Rousseau. Oxford, 1953.

Phil 8878.5.8 Davy, H. Consolations in travel. London, 1830.

Phil 8878.5.5 Davy, H. Consolations in travel. London, 1851.

Phil 8878.5.7 Davy, H. Consolations in travel. Philadelphia, 1830.

Phil 8878.5 Davy, H. Consolations in travel. Philadelphia, 1831.

Phil 8878.5.4 Davy, H. Consolations in travel. 4th ed. London, 1838.

Phil 4752.2.140 Davy, M.M. Nicolas Berdiaev, l'homme du huitième jour. Paris, 1964.

Phil 8404.23 Davydov, Iurii N. Iskusstvo i elita. Moskva, 1966.

Phil 8953.3 Dawbarn, C.Y.C. Applied philosophy. London, 1923.

Phil 7054.170 Dawbarn, Charles. The science of spirit return. Springfield, Mass., 188-.

Phil 75.77 Dawe, Harold G.A. Philosophy in South Africa, 1950-1962. Cape Town, 1964.

Phil 6842.2 Dawes, C.R. The marquis de Sade. London, 1927.

Phil 13.25 Dawes Hicks lecture on philosophy. London, 1970+

Phil 525.18 Dawkins, M.B. Mysticism, an epistemological problem. New Haven, 1915.

Phil 8637.17 The dawn beyond the sunset. (McDonald, N.T.) London, 1929.

Phil 7069.45.55 The dawn of a new day, a revelation. (Keith, Cassius C.) Kansas City, Mo., 1945.

Phil 8692.10 The dawn of a new era. (Carus, Paul.) Chicago, 1899.

Phil 1712.11 The dawn of modern thought. (Mellone, S.H.) London, 1930.

Phil 5590.170 The dawn of personality. 1. ed. (Cailliet, E.) Indianapolis, 1955.

Phil 850.23.2 The dawn of philosophy. (Misch, G.) Cambridge, 1951.

Phil 850.23 The dawn of philosophy. (Misch, G.) London, 1950.

Phil 5832.6 The dawn of reason. (Weir, J.) N.Y., 1899.

Phil 7069.20.190 Dawn of the awakened mind. (King, John S.) N.Y., 1920.

Phil 9495.146 Dawson, C. Christianity and sex. London, 1930.

Phil 8583.28.20 Dawson, Christopher H. Beyond politics. London, 1939.

Phil 8583.28.5 Dawson, Christopher H. The judgment of the nations. N.Y., 1942.

Phil 8583.28.2 Dawson, Christopher H. Religion and the modern state. London, 1935.

Phil 8583.28.4 Dawson, Christopher H. Religion and the modern state. London, 1935.

Phil 3805.224 Dawson, Jerry F. Friedrich Schleiermacher: the evolution of a nationalist. Austin, 1966.

Phil 9150.23 Dawson, M. Nineteenth century evolution and after. N.Y., 1923.

Phil 3485.24 Daxer, Georg. Über die Anlage. Hamburg, 1897.

Phil 930.64 Day, A.B. The philosophers of China. N.Y., 1962.

Phil 7060.90.11 Day, Clarence S. Remarkable apparitions and ghost-stories. N.Y., 1848.

Phil 5243.3 Day, Henry. Elements of psychology. N.Y., 1876.

Phil 8404.5 Day, Henry. The science of aesthetics. New Haven, 1872.

Phil 5043.3 Day, Henry N. Elements of logic. N.Y., 1867.

Phil 5043.3.10 Day, Henry N. Logical praxis. N.Y., 1876.

X Cg Phil 5753.4 Day, Jeremiah. An inquiry...power of the will. New Haven, 1838. 4v.

Phil 5066.180.5 Day, John P. Inductive probability. London, 1961.

Phil 5066.180 Day, John P. Inductive probability. N.Y., 1961.

Phil 8627.20 The day of Yahweh and some relevant problems. (Cerný, Ladislav.) Praha, 1943.

Phil 6673.12   Day visions and clairvoyant night dreams. (Darly, Joseph.) London, 1892.

Phil 1020.5.5   Dayser, C. Das Buch von der Erkenntniss der Wahrheit. Strassburg, 1893.

Phil 8658.11   Dayton, A.C. Emma Livingston, infidel's daughter. Nashville, Tenn., 1861.

Phil 9530.21   Dayton, William L. Address delivered before the American Whig and Cliosophic societies of the college of New Jersey, Sept. 26, 1843. Princeton, 1843.

Phil 8880.28   De actibus humanis. (Frins, Victor.) Friburgi Brisgoviae, 1897-1911.

Htn   Phil 4265.1.30*   De admirandis naturae reginae deaeque mortalium arcanis. (Vanini, Lucilio, afterwards Giulio Cesare.) Lutetieae, 1616.

Htn   Phil 5262.16*   De anima Brutorum. (Willis, T.) Oxonii, 1672.
Phil 4372.1.40   De anima et vita. (Vives, Juan Luis.) Torino, 1959.
Phil 8896.2A   De animi tranquillitate dialogus. (Voluseno, F.) Edinburg, 1751.

Phil 4073.33   De antichristo. (Campanella, Tommaso.) Roma, 1965.
Phil 4260.44   De antiquissima Italorum sapientia. (Vico, Giovanni Battista.) Roma, 1969.

Phil 7060.39   De apparitionibus. (Schelwig, Samuel.) Lipziae, 1709.
Phil 7060.7   De apparitionibus spirituum tractatus duo. (Thyraeus, Petrus.) Coloniae Agrippinae, 1600.

Phil 1190.18   De arcesilae successoribus disputatio. (Geffers, A.) Göttingen, 1845.

Phil 1200.22   De assensione Stoici quid Senserint. Thesis. (Brochard, Victor.) Parisiis, 1879.

Phil 3428.40   De attentionis. (Herbart, J.F.) Regiomonti, 1822.
Htn   Phil 1850.32.5*   De augmentis scientiarum. Libri IX. (Bacon, Francis.) Amsterdam, 1662.

Htn   Phil 1850.32*   De augmentis scientiarum. Libri IX. (Bacon, Francis.) Lugdunum, 1652.

Phil 2750.11.37.5   De Bergson à Thomas d'Aquin. (Maritain, Jacques.) N.Y., 1944.

Phil 2750.11.37   De Bergson à Thomas d'Aquin. (Maritain, Jacques.) Paris, 1944.

Phil 4235.1.80   De Bernardino Telesio. (Bartholmes, C.) Paris, 1849.
Phil 2520.144   De Beweise für das dasein Gottes. (Liedtke, V.) Heidelberg, 1893.

Phil 2805.286   De Blaise Pascal à Henry Hammond. (Jansen, Paule.) Paris, 1954.

Phil 9495.159.2   De castitate et ordine sexuali. 2nd ed. (Fuchs, Josef Jesuit.) Roma, 1960.

Htn   Phil 2040.31*   De causis errorum. (Herbert, E.) London, 1645.
Phil 8735.18   De causis finalibus. (Lasson, A.) Berolini, 1876.
Phil 2045.61.35   De cive; or, The citizen. (Hobbes, Thomas.) N.Y., 1949.
Phil 8879.6.6   De civilitate morum. (Erasmus, D.) Rostochi, 1632.
Phil 8582.10   De cognitione dei et nostri. (Claubergii, J.) Franequerae, 1685.

Phil 8656.26   De cognitione existential Dei per niam causalitatis relate ad fidem catholicam. (Bocheńske, I.M.) Poznań, 1936.

Phil 3822.8   De cognitionis generibus Spinozae. Thesis. (Cleve, Z.J.) Helsingforsiae, 1850.

Phil 9075.30   De conscientia theses morales. Diss. (Hassel, H.) Aboae, 1738.

Htn   Phil 4075.31*   De consolatione. (Cardano, Girolamo.) Venetijs, 1542.
Phil 1153.5   De cynicis. (Caspari, A.) Chemnitz, 1896.
Phil 2050.103   De Davidis Humii philosophia. Inaug. Diss. (Kahle, C.M.) Berolini, 1832?

Phil 2412.6   De Descartes à Marcel Proust. (Muller, Maurice.) Neuchâtel, 1943.

Phil 8615.8   De "Deutsche Gesellschaft für ethische Kultur". (Mourik Broekman, M.C. von.) n.p., 1909.

Phil 4073.58   De dictis Christi. (Campanella, Tommaso.) Roma, 1969.
Phil 8120.11   De Diderot à Valéry. (Traz, Georges.) Paris, 1960.
Phil 8658.16   De Dieu. Par M***. Paris, 1811.
Htn   Phil 3801.419*   De differentia, quae inter Plotini et Schellingii doctrinam de numine summo intercedit. Thesis. (Gerlach, G.W.) Vitebergae, 1811.

Phil 1850.32.8   De dignitate et augmentis scientarum. Libri IX. (Bacon, Francis.) Argentorari, 1654.

Phil 1850.41   De dignitate et augmentis scientiarum. (Bacon, Francis.) Wirceburgi, 1779-80. 2v.

Htn   Phil 1850.31.15*   De dignitate et augmentis scientiarum. Libri IX. (Bacon, Francis.) Paris, 1624.

Phil 4195.37   De dignitate hominis. (Pico della Mirandola, Giovanni.) Bad Homburg, 1968.

Phil 4225.5.2   De diritti dell'uomo libri 6. (Spedalieri, Nicola.) Assisi, 1791.

Htn   Phil 8896.3*   De disciplinis. (Vives, Juan Luis.) Lugdunum Batavorum, 1636.

Phil 4963.1   De donde venimos. (Buzzi, E.) Lima, 1942.
Phil 705.49.5   De Einzelne und der Einsame. (Metzger, Arnold.) Pfullingen, 1967.

Phil 3110.31   De electione gratiae and quaestiones theosophicae. (Böhme, J.) London, 1930.

Phil 1200.34   De es quad stoici naturae comienienter vivendum esse, principium ponunt. (Gidionsen, W.) Lipsiae, 1852.

Phil 3805.174   De ethice a Schleiermachero propositae fundamento. Pt.1-2. (Hartenstein, G.) Lipsiae, 1837.

Phil 4200.1.15   De fato. (Pomponazzi, Pietro.) Lucani, 1957.
Htn   Phil 5768.9*   De fato i libris arbitrio libero tres. (Sepulveda, J.G.) Roma, 1526.

Phil 9245.41   De felicitate. (Miltenberger, W.F.) Washington, D.C., 1914.

Htn   Phil 190.7*   De Formarum origine. (Pemble, W.) Cantabrigia, 1631.
Phil 6315.2.82.15   De Freud à Lacan. (Hesnard, Angelo.) Paris, 1970.
Htn   Phil 4065.58*   De gl'heroici furori. (Bruno, Giordano.) Parigi, 1585.
Phil 4065.61   De gl'heroici furori. (Bruno, Giordano.) Torino, 1928.
Htn   Phil 4170.1.30*   De gli elementi. (Manuzio, Paolo.) Venetia, 1557.
Phil 9540.5   De haeretico comburendo. (Trevelyan, G.M.) Cambridge, Eng., 1914.

Htn   Phil 250.2*   De harmonia mundi totius. (Giorgio, F.) Venice, 1525.
Phil 3425.113   De Hegel aux cantines du nord. (Barrès, M.) Paris, n.d.
Phil 3425.216   De Hegeliana philosophiam juris tractandi ratione. (Lagus, R.E.) Helsingforsiae, 1852.

Phil 1195.8   De historicae doctrinae apud sophistas maiores vesligus. Inaug. Diss. (Rascher, Wilhelm.) Gottingae, 1838.

Htn   Phil 2520.34.2*   De homine, figuris, et latinitate donatus. (Descartes, René.) Lugduni Batavorum, 1662.

Htn   Phil 2520.34.3*   De homine...Schuye a Florentio Schuye. (Descartes, René.) Lugduni Batavorum, 1664.

Phil 4073.65   De homine. (Campanella, Tommaso.) Roma, 1960.
Phil 4073.65.2   De homine. (Campanella, Tommaso.) Roma, 1961.
Phil 585.120   De homine. (Landmann, Michael.) Freiburg, 1962.
Phil 13.22   De homine. Roma. 2,1962+ 12v.

Phil 9245.39   De hominis felicitate libri treo. (Nobile, Flamineo.) Lucae, 1563.

Phil 3837.6   De hrimauae mentis aeternitate apud Spinoza. (Ricardou, A.) Lutet, 1890.

Htn   Phil 6025.4*   De humana physiognomia libri. (Porta, G.B.) Hanoviae, 1593.

Htn   Phil 6000.1*   De humana physiognomonia. (Porta, G.B.) Francofurti, 1586.

Phil 185.10.30   De humanitate in philosophando rite servanda. (Krug, W.T.) Vitebergae, 1800.

Phil 1750.115.62   De Husserl à Merleau-Ponty. (Thevenaz, Pierre.) Neuchâtel, 1966.

Phil 6956.8   De hygiene mental e sua importancia em mosso meio. (Guimares, A.) San Paulo, 1926.

Phil 1870.106   De idealismi aprud Berkeleium. (Gerard, J.) Sancti Clodoaldi, 1874.

Phil 400.82   De idealismo, seu philosophia ideali. Diss. (Mussmann, J.G.) Berolini, 1826.

Phil 1504.8.6   Le "de Ignota Litteratura." v.8, pt.6-7. (Vansteenberghe, E.) Münster, 1910.

Phil 8640.1.10   De immortalite animae. (Pomponazzi, P.) Messina, 1925.
Htn   Phil 8875.3.4*   De incertitudine et vanitate omnium scientiarum et artium liber. (Agrippa von Nettesheim, Heinrich Cornelius.) Ealf, 1531.

Htn   Phil 8875.3.2*   De incertitudine et vanitate omnium scientiarum et artium liber. (Agrippa von Nettesheim, Heinrich Cornelius.) n.p., 1544.

Phil 8875.3   De incertitudine et vanitate omnium scientiarum et artium liber. (Agrippa von Nettesheim, Heinrich Cornelius.) Lugduni Batavorum, 1643.

Phil 3552.124   De infinito apud Leibnitium. Thesis. (Penjon, Auguste.) Paris, 1878.

Htn   Phil 2733.30.6*   De inquirenda veritate. (Malebranche, Nicolas.) Genevae, 1685.

Phil 2115.29.125F   De intellectu humano. Ed. 4a. (Locke, J.) London, 1701.
Htn   Phil 1105.2*   De inventione. Libri III. (Agricola, R.) Coloniae, 1518.
Htn   Phil 1105.2.5*   De inventione dialectica. pt.3. (Agricola, R.) Parisiis, 1535.

Phil 1750.165   De J.P. Sartre à L. Lavelle. (Truc, G.) Paris, 1946.
Phil 7080.17   De jure circa somnum et somnia. (Thomasius, C.) Regiomonti, 1712.

Phil 2475.1.95   De Kant à Bergson. (Coignet, C.) Paris, 1911.
Phil 1706.1   De Kant à Nietzsche. (Gaultier, Jules de.) Paris, 1900.
Phil 1706.1.6   De Kant à Nietzsche. 6e éd. (Gaultier, Jules de.) Paris, 19-.

Phil 3499.17   De Kanti antinomüs. Thesis. (Reiche, L.P.A.) Gottingae, 1847.

Phil 487.1   De Kreislauf des Lebens. (Moleschott, J.) Mainz, 1857.
Phil 5790.5   De la banalité. (Jerphagnon, Lucien.) Paris, 1965.
Phil 8413.31   De la bellesa. v.5. (Mirabent, F.) Barcelona, 1936.
Phil 4065.52   De la causa. (Bruno, Giordano.) Padova, 1941.
Phil 5090.5   De la certitude. (Franck, A.) Paris, 1847.
Phil 187.23   De la certitude. (Mercier, E.) Paris, 1844.
Phil 645.4   De la certitude et des formes recontes du scepticisme. (Robert, Louis.) Paris, 1880.

Phil 8889.1   De la certitude morale. (Ollé-Laprune, L.) Paris, 1880.
Phil 176.146   De la condition humaine. Thèse. (Bastide, George.) Paris, 1939.

Phil 343.15.5   De la connaissance à l'action. (Mochi, Alberto.) Paris, 1928.

Phil 8654.100   De la connaissance de Dieu. Paris, 1958.
Phil 8661.9.2   De la connaissance de Dieu. 2. éd. (Gratry, A.) Paris, 1854. 2v.

Phil 8661.9   De la connaissance de Dieu. 9. éd. (Gratry, A.) Paris, 1918. 2v.

Phil 5246.9   De la connaissance de l'âme. (Gratry, A.J.A.) Paris, 1857. 2v.

Phil 5374.55   De la connaissance de soi. (Brunschvicg, Léon.) Paris, 1931.

Phil 5251.38   De la connaissance de soi-même. (Loomans, Charles.) Bruxelles, 1880.

Phil 8581.44   De la connaissance religieuse. (Bois, Henri.) Paris, 1894.

Phil 2477.1.30   De la contingence des lois de la nature. Thèse. (Boutroux, Émile.) Paris, 1874.

Phil 2477.1.32   De la contingence des lois de la nature. 3. éd. (Boutroux, Émile.) Paris, 1898.

Phil 5070.5   De la croyance. (Payot, J.) Paris, 1896.
Htn   Phil 2648.32.80*   De la cruauté religieuse. (Holbach, Paul Henri T.) Londres, 1769.

Phil 2648.33   De la cruauté religieuse. (Holbach, Paul Henri T.) Paris, 1826.

Phil 8595.8   De la déomanie au XIXe siècle. (Prevost, J.M.C.) Toulouse, 1860.

Phil 8876.91.15   De la destination de l'homme. (Berdiaev, N.A.) Paris, 1935.

Phil 8701.8   De la discipline intellectuelle. (Loisy, Alfred.) Paris, 1919.

Phil 3525.23   De la doctrine de Krause. (Tiberghien, G.) Bruxelles, 1855.

Phil 2725.2.33   De la famille et de la propriété. (Lamennais, F.R. de.) Paris, 1848.

Phil 181.132   De la filosofia. (Gaos, José.) Mexico, 1962.
Phil 4958.210   De la filosofía en la Habana. (Mestre, José Manuel.) Habana, 1862.

Phil 6952.1   De la folie. (Calmeil, J.L.F.) Paris, 1845. 2v.
Phil 6953.7   De la folie au point de vue philosophique. (Despine, Prosper.) Paris, 1875.

Phil 2725.1.81   De la Forges Psychologie. (Wolff, E.) Jena, 1893.
Phil 2750.23.85   De la forme à l'acte...Joseph Maréchal. (Dirven, Edouard.) Paris, 1965.

Phil 336.8   De la forme a l'idée. (Fondard, L.) Marseille, 1937.
Phil 9560.11   De la gaieté. (Caracciolli, L.) Paris, 1782.
Phil 5520.520   De la gammatologie. (Derrida, Jacques.) Paris, 1967.
Phil 2750.11.41   De la grâce et de l'humanité de Jèsus. (Maritain, Jacques.) Bruges, 1967.

Phil 3808.50   De la guadruple racine du principe de la raison suffisante. (Schopenhauer, Arthur.) Paris, 1882.

Phil 5413.15   De la jalousie. (Delpierre, Guy.) Paris, 1954.
Phil 5753.1   De la liberté et des lois de la nature. (Desdouits, T.) Paris, 1868.

Phil 978.84   De la liéte à l'auge. (Demarquette, Jacques.) Paris, 1937.

Phil 8832.1   De la littérature didactique du Moyen Age. Photoreproduction. (Hentsch, Alice Adele.) Halle, 1903.

Phil 3425.312   De la médiation dans la philosophie de Hegel. (Niel, Henri.) Paris, 1945.

Phil 3425.316   De la médiation dans la philosophie de Hegel. Thèse. (Niel, Henri.) Madrid, 1945.

Phil 5400.20   De la méthode dans la psychologie des sentiments. (Rauh, F.) Paris, 1899.

Phil 310.790   De la méthodologie à la dialectique. (Marc, Alexandre.) Paris, 1970.

Phil 525.71   De la mística. (Gentilini, B.) Santiago de Chile, 1926.

Phil 1145.11   De la morale avant les philosophes. (Ménard, L.) Paris, 1860.

Phil 1145.12   De la morale avant les philosophes. 2e éd. (Ménard, L.) Paris, 1863.

Phil 1145.8   De la morale dans l'Antiquité. (Garnier, A.) Paris, 1865.

Phil 9450.10   De la morale politique. (Pensa, Henri.) Paris, 1910.

Phil 6962.6   De la mortalité et de la folie. (Moreau-Christopie, L.M.) Paris, 1839.

Phil 2672.81   De la mutilation d'un écrit posthume de Théodore Jouffroy. (Leroux, Pierre.) Paris, 1843.

Phil 2855.7.30   De la nature. (Robinet, Jean Baptiste René.) Amsterdam, 1761.

Phil 2855.7.32   De la nature. v.1-2. (Robinet, Jean Baptiste René.) Amsterdam, 1763.

Phil 5241.65.10   De la nature affective de la conscience. (Bertrand-Barraud, D.) Paris, 1927.

Phil 178.6   De la nature humaine. (Dollfus, C.) Paris, 1868.

Phil 6320.5   De la névropathie cérebro-cardiaque. (Krishaber, M.) Paris, 1873.

Phil 8672.30   De la notion de Dieu d'après la méthode sentimentale. (Ritti, Jean Marie Paul.) Paris, 1930.

Phil 575.66   De la personnalité. (Fernandez, R.) Paris, 1928.

Phil 3017.1   De la philosophie allemande. (Rémusat, C. de.) Paris, 1845.

Phil 2750.11.43.5   De la philosophie chrétienne. (Maritain, Jacques.) Paris, 1933.

Phil 6673.18   De la philosophie corpusculaire. (Delaudine, Antoine François.) Paris, 1785.

Phil 8878.7   De la philosophie de la nature. (Delisle de Sales, J.B.C.I.) London, 1777. 6v.

Phil 2725.9.86   De la philosophie de l'abbé de Lignac. (LeGoff, François.) Paris, 1863.

Phil 8878.7.10   De la philosophie du bonheur. (Delisle de Sales, J.B.C.I.) Paris, 1796. 2v.

Phil 1520.4   De la philosophie du moyen âge. (Patru, G.A.) Paris, 1848.

Phil 8878.43   De la philosophie morale. 2e éd. (Droz, J.) Paris, 1824.

Phil 600.7   De la philosophie positive. v.1-2. (Littré, Émile.) Paris, 1845.

Phil 1512.1   De la philosophie scolastique. (Haureau, B.) Paris, 1850. 2v.

Phil 5920.1   De la phrénologie. (Azais, P.H.) Paris, 1839. 2v.

Phil 5925.1.5   De la phrénologie et des études vraies sur la cerveau. (Flourens, M.J.) Paris, 1863.

Phil 6021.3   De la physiognomie et de parole. (Lemoine, A.) Paris, 1865.

Phil 5425.42   De la precocité intellectuelle. (Duche, Émile.) Paris, 1901.

Phil 9495.40   De la préservation morale de l'enfant. (Chauvin, A.) Paris, 1912.

Phil 6980.710.63   De la psychoanalyse à la psychosynthese. (Stocker, Arnold.) Paris, 1957.

Phil 8591.16   De la psychologie des religions. (La Grasserie, R. de.) Paris, 1899.

Phil 189.18   De la raison. (Ott, Auguste.) Paris, 1873.

Phil 5245.23   De la raison du genié et...folie. (Flourens, Pierre.) Paris, 1861.

Phil 340.1.2   De la réalite du monde sensible. (Jaures, J.) Paris, 1891.

Phil 340.1   De la réalite du monde sensible. (Jaures, J.) Paris, 1902.

Phil 2733.29   De la recherche de la vérité. (Malebranche, Nicolas.) Paris, 1676-78. 3v.

Phil 2733.29.30   De la recherche de la vérité. (Malebranche, Nicolas.) Paris, 1935. 2v.

Phil 2733.30.4   De la recherche de la vérité. (Malebranche, Nicolas.) Paris, 1945. 2v.

Phil 2733.29.35   De la recherche de la vérité. (Malebranche, Nicolas.) Paris, 1962. 2v.

NEDL Phil 2733.30.2   De la recherche de la vérité. v.2. (Malebranche, Nicolas.) Paris, 1886.

Phil 2733.30   De la recherche de la vérité. (Malebranche, Nicolas.) Paris, 1886.

Phil 2733.29.20   De la recherche de la vérité. 2e éd. (Malebranche, Nicolas.) Paris, 1675. 2v.

Phil 2733.29.10   De la recherche de la vérité. 4e éd. v.1-2. (Malebranche, Nicolas.) Amsterdam, 1688.

Phil 2733.29.3   De la recherche de la vérité. 7e éd. v.1-2. (Malebranche, Nicolas.) Paris, 1721.

Htn Phil 2515.2.27*   De la sagesse, trois livres. 3e éd. (Charron, P.) Paris, 1614.

Htn Phil 2515.2.32*   De la sagesse. (Charron, P.) Amsterdam, 1662.
Htn Phil 2515.2.49*   De la sagesse. (Charron, P.) Bordeaux, 1601.
Htn Phil 2515.2.30*   De la sagesse. (Charron, P.) Leide, 1646.
Htn Phil 2515.2.31*   De la sagesse. (Charron, P.) Leide, 1658?
Phil 2515.2.53   De la sagesse. (Charron, P.) Paris, 1820-24. 3v.
Phil 2515.2.55   De la sagesse. (Charron, P.) Paris, 1827. 3v.
Htn Phil 2515.2.48*   De la sagesse. (Charron, P.) Rouen, 1614.
Htn Phil 2515.2.47*   De la sagesse. v.1-3. (Charron, P.) Paris, 1604.

Phil 4303.10   De la saudade y sus formas. (Cartezon Alvarez, Daniel.) Nueva York, 1960.

Phil 2905.1.360   De la science à la foi. (Corvez, Maurice.) Tours, 1964.

Phil 2905.1.176   De la science à la théologie. (Crespy, Georges.) Neuchâtel, 1965.

Phil 293.2   De la science et de la nature. (Magy, F.) Paris, 1865.

Phil 6625.4   De la sensibilité générale et de ses altérations dans les affections mélancaliques. (Semal.) Paris, 1875.

Phil 3110.38   De la signature des choses. (Böhme, J.) Paris, 1908.

Phil 287.10   De la signification du cosmos. (Guitton, Jean.) Paris, 1966.

Phil 8887.2   De la solidarité morale. (Marion, H.) Paris, 1880.
Phil 6671.4.5   De la suggestion. (Bérillon, E.) Paris, 1886.
Phil 6671.5.5   De la suggestion. (Bernheim, H.) Paris, 1884.
Phil 6684.1   De la suggestion mentale. (Ochorowicz, J.) Paris, 1887.
Phil 2805.216.5   De la théologie à la prière de Pascal. Thèse. (Réguron, Paule.) Grenoble, 1934.

Htn Phil 3552.64*   De la tolérance des religions. (Leibniz, Gottfried Wilhelm.) Paris, 1692.

Phil 176.30   De la vérité. (Brisor de Warville, Jean Pierre.) Neuchatel, 1782.

Phil 3004.6   De la vida a la existencia en la filosofía contemporanea. (Esliu, Emilio.) La Plata, 1964.

Phil 2750.11.56   De la vie d'oraison. (Maritain, Jacques.) Paris, 1947.

Phil 5245.23.5   De la vie et de l'intelligence. 2. éd. (Flourens, Pierre.) Paris, 1858.

Phil 8581.98   De la vraie et de la fausse conversion. 1. éd. (Brunschvicg, Léon.) Paris, 1951.

Phil 189.10   De l'absolu. (Olivier, Aimé.) Paris, 1887.
Phil 2725.35.55   De l'acte. (Lavelle, Louis.) Paris, 1937.
Phil 5825.9   De l'actinie à l'homme. (Piéron, Henri.) Paris, 1958. 2v.

Phil 5500.10   De l'action à la connaissance. (Augier, E.) Paris, 1924.
Phil 5252.74   De l'action à la pensée. (Malgand, W.) Paris, 1935.
Phil 343.17   De l'activité purement immanente. Thèse. (Marcel, Victor.) Nancy, 1932.

Phil 8581.127   De l'affaiblissement de la raison et de la décadence en Europe. 2. éd. (Blanc de Saint-Bonnet, Antoine Joseph Elisée Adolphe.) Paris, 1854.

Phil 8887.8.5   De l'affaiblissement des idées. (Matter, J.) Paris, 1841.
Phil 2880.1.95   De l'agent inconnu au philosophe inconnu. (Amadou, R.) Paris, 1962.

Phil 5262.22.2   De l'âme humaine. 2. série. (Waddington, Charles.) Paris, 1862.

Phil 2725.2.103   De Lamennais à Maritain. (Meinvielle, Jules.) Paris, 1956.

Phil 481.1   De l'analyse de la force. v.1-3. (Galitzine, E.) Paris, 1845. 2v.

Phil 192.55   De l'analyse réflexive. Thèse. (Robef, Euthyme.) Paris, 1925.

Phil 7076.20   De l'angoisse à l'extase. (Janet, Pierre.) Paris, 1926-28. 2v.

Phil 5817.6.5   De l'animal a l'enfant. (Hachet-Souplet, P.) Paris, 1913.
Phil 6400.2   De l'aphasie. (Bernard, D.) Paris, 1885.
Phil 6400.2.2   De l'aphasie. (Bernard, D.) Paris, 1889.
Phil 6400.15   De l'aphasie. Thèse. (Legrow, A.) Paris, 1875.
Phil 6400.9   De l'aphasie sensorielle. (Mirallie, C.) Paris, 1896.
Phil 7085.1   De l'automatisme. (Mesnet, E.) Paris, 1874.
Phil 6953.5   De l'automatisme psychologique. (Dupuy, Paul.) Bordeaux, 1894.

Phil 1750.27   De l'eclectisme. (Nicolas, M.) Paris, 1840.
Phil 1150.1   De l'ecole d'Alexandrie. (Barthélemy, H.J.) Paris, 1845.
Phil 9171.1.9   De l'éducation des jeunes gens. (De Lambert, A.T. de M. de C.) Paris, 1896.

Htn Phil 1928.30*   De legibus naturae. (Cumberland, R.) Dublin, 1720.
Phil 1928.30.2   De legibus naturae. (Cumberland, R.) London, 1672.
Htn Phil 1928.30.5*   De legibus naturae. 3d ed. (Cumberland, R.) Lubecae, 1694.

Phil 2750.11.38   De l'Église du Christ; la personne de l'Église et son personnel. (Maritain, Jacques.) Paris, 1970.

Phil 3552.278   De Leibnitii studiis Aristotelicis. (Jacoby, Daniel.) Berolini, 1867.

Phil 5620.5   De l'entendement de la raison. (Thurot, J.F.) Paris, 1830. 2v.

Phil 720.14.2   De l'erreur. 2e éd. (Brochard, V.) Paris, 1897.
Phil 2636.25.5   De l'esprit, de l'homme. 4e éd. (Helvétius, C.A.) Paris, 1909.

Phil 2636.41   De l'esprit, or Essays on the mind. (Helvétius, C.A.) London, 1759.

Phil 2636.41.2   De l'esprit, or Essays on the mind. 2. ed. (Helvétius, C.A.) London, 1810.

Htn Phil 2636.40*   De l'esprit. (Helvétius, C.A.) Amsterdam, 1758.
Htn Phil 2636.40.1*   De l'esprit. (Helvétius, C.A.) Paris, 1759.
Phil 2636.40.6   De l'esprit. (Helvétius, C.A.) Paris, 1843.
Phil 2636.25.6   De l'esprit. (Helvétius, C.A.) Paris, 1959.
Phil 2636.40.2   De l'esprit. v.1-4. (Helvétius, C.A.) Paris, 1793. 2v.

Phil 4752.2.68   De l'esprit bourgeois. (Berdiaev, Nikolai Aleksandrovich.) Neuchâtel, 1949.

Phil 5400.8   De l'essence des passions. (Maillet, E.) Paris, 1877.
Phil 2825.25   De l'esthétique à la métaphysique. (Piguet, Jean Claude.) La Haye, 1959.

Phil 2725.35.50   De l'être. (Lavelle, Louis.) Paris, 1928.
Phil 575.251   De l'être à la personne. 1. éd. (Lahbabi, Mohamed Aziz.) Paris, 1954.

Phil 337.3   De l'étude des phénomènes du point de vue de leur probleme particular. (Gaillard, Gaston.) Paris, 1903.

Phil 9230.11   De l'exception de jeu. (Labrousse, Louis.) Paris, 1897.
Phil 2730.21   De l'existence, textes inédits. (Maine de Biran, Pierre.) Paris, 1966.

Phil 2750.13.95   De l'existence à l'être. (Troisfontaines, R.) Namur, 1953. 2v.

Phil 5435.4.5   De l'habitude. (Ravaisson-Mollien, Felix.) Paris, 1927.
Phil 5435.4   De l'habitude. (Ravaisson-Mollien, Felix.) Paris, 1938.
Phil 5435.4.2   De l'habitude. 2. éd. (Ravaisson-Mollien, Felix.) Paris, 1957.

Htn Phil 2636.32*   De l'homme. (Helvétius, C.A.) London, 1773. 2v.
Phil 2636.34   De l'homme. (Helvétius, C.A.) London, 1776.
Phil 1905.10.80.5   De l'humanisme à l'absolutisme. (Huang, Chia-cheng.) Paris, 1954.

Phil 2515.2.81   De l'humanisme au rationalisme. Pierre Charron. (Sabrié, J.B.) Paris, 1913.

Htn Phil 8591.4*   De l'humanité. (Leroux, Pierre.) Paris, 1860. 2v.
Phil 3552.253   De liberate apud Leibnitium. Thesis. (Cresson, André.) Paris, 1903.

Htn Phil 5771.2.5*   De libero arbitrio. (Valla, Lorenzo.) Basileae, 1518.
Phil 5771.2   De libero arbitrio. (Valla, Lorenzo.) Firenze, 1934.
Phil 5750.5   De libertate. Disquisitio. (Ahlander, J.A.) Lundae, 1852.
Htn Phil 4075.40*   De libris propriis, eorumque ordinis et usu. (Cardano, Girolamo.) Lugduni, 1557.

Phil 400.37   De l'idéal. Etude philosophique. (Ricardon, A.) Paris, 1890.

Phil 2885.33   De l'ideal dans l'art. (Taine, Hippolyte Adolphe.) Paris, 1867.

Phil 2730.94   De l'idée du dire dans la philosophie de Maine de Biran. Thèse. (Barbillion, G.) Grenoble, 1927. 2 pam.

Phil 1750.113   De l'idée de la loi naturelle. (Boutroux, É.) Paris, 1913.

Phil 2477.1.40   De l'idée de loi naturelle dans la science et la philosophie contemporaines. (Boutroux, Émile.) Paris, 1895.

Phil 2477.1.41   De l'idée de loi naturelle dans la science et la philosophie contemporaines. (Boutroux, Emile.) Paris, 1949.

Phil 2475.1.480   De l'identique au multiple. (Lebacqz, Joseph.) Québec, 1968.

Phil 2477.15.100   De l'imagination poétique dans l'oeuvre de Gaston Bachelard. (Pire, François.) Paris, 1967.

Phil 8633.5   De l'immortalité de l'âme. (Ismard, M.) Paris, 1802.

Phil 1200.30   De l'immortalité de l'âme dans le stoïcisme. (Courdaveaux, V.) Paris, 1857.

Phil 6319.1.210   De l'inconscient à Dieu. (Winckel, Erna van de.) Paris, 1959.

Phil 5374.149   De l'inconscient au conscient. (Geley, Gustave.) Paris, 1919.

Phil 7140.118.2   De l'influence: étude psychologique, métaphysique, pédagogique. (Thamiry, E.) Lille, 1922.

Phil 7140.118   De l'influence: étude psychologique. Thèse. (Thamiry, E.) Lille, 1921.

Phil 2411.1   De l'influence de la philosophie du XVIIIe siècle. (Lerminier, E.) Paris, 1833.

Phil 6113.8.20   De l'influence de l'esprit sur le corps. 9. éd. (Dubois, Paul.) Berne, 1910.

Phil 3640.376   De l'influence de Nietzsche sur la pensée politique allemande. Thèse. (Farré, R.) Baden-Baden, 1947.

Phil 9450.2   De l'influence des moeurs sur le lois. (Matter, J.) Paris, 1832.

Htn   Phil 5400.4.2*   De l'influence des passions. (Stael-Holstein, Anne Louise G.) Lausanne, 1796.

Phil 5817.12   De l'instinct et de l'intelligence. (Hement, Felix.) Paris, 1880.

Phil 5815.2   De l'instinct et de l'intelligence des animaux. 4e éd. (Flourens, Pierre.) Paris, 1861.

NEDL   Phil 2885.30   De l'intelligence. (Taine, Hippolyte Adolphe.) Paris, 1878. 2v.

Phil 2885.30.5   De l'intelligence. 2. éd. v.1-2. (Taine, Hippolyte Adolphe.) Paris, 1870. 2v.

Phil 2885.30.8   De l'intelligence. 13. éd. (Taine, Hippolyte Adolphe.) Paris, 1914. 2v.

Phil 5828.12   De l'intelligence chez l'animal. (Sorel, C.L.F.) Paris, 19- .

Phil 8896.7   De l'intention morale. (Vallier, C.A.) Paris, 1883.

Phil 6315.2.365   De l'interprétation. (Ricoeur, Paul.) Paris, 1965.

Phil 2725.35   De l'intimité spirituelle. (Lavelle, Louis.) Paris, 1955.

Phil 5253.4   De l'intuition. (Netter, S.) Strasbourg, 1879.

Phil 5115.3   De l'invention dans les arts. (Joyau, E.) Paris, 1879.

Phil 6951.6.5   De l'irritation et de la folie. (Broussais, F.J.V.) Paris, 1839. 2v.

Phil 4363.6   De lo espiritual. (Molina, E.) Concepcion, 1937.

Phil 3831.6   De logica Spinozae. (Lesbazeilles, P.) Paris, 1883.

Phil 811.26   De Lucrèce à Camus, littérature et philosophie comme réflexion sur l'homme. (Louisgrand, Jean.) Paris, 1970.

Phil 6111.4.2   De l'unité de l'ame pensante et du principe vital. (Bouiller, F.) Paris, 1858.

Phil 178.46.15   De l'unité métaphysique. (Decoster, Paul.) Bruxelles, 1934.

Phil 5400.196   De l'usage des passions. (Senault, Jean Francois.) Paris, 1964.

Phil 2415.3   De l'usage et de l'abus de l'esprit philosophique durant le XVIIE siècle. (Portalis, J.E.M.) Paris, 1834. 2v.

Phil 5062.1.5   De l'utilité des études logiques. (Waddington, C.) Paris, 1851.

Phil 193.93.2   De l'utilité du pragmatisme. 2e ed. (Sorel, Georges.) Paris, 1928.

Phil 6692.6.5   De magnetismi animalis efficacia rite diiudicanda. (Wendler, C.A.) Lipsiae, 1818.

Phil 6692.6   De magnetismis animali. Diss. (Wendler, C.A.) Lipsiae, 1805.

Phil 9558.30   De materia gravi in furto apud theologos saeculorum XVI et XVII. (Larrañaga, T.) Romae, 1960.

Phil 3552.250   De materiae apud Leibnitium notione et ad monadas relatione. (Hartenstein, G.) Lipsiae, 1846.

Phil 5545.42   De memoria artificios a lebellus. (Austriacus, J.) Argentorati, 1603.

Phil 2520.335   De mens Descartes. (Waltheunis, O.) Brussel, 1960.

Phil 3822.5   De mentis essentia Spinoza quid senserit. Thesis. (Colsenet, Edmond.) Parisiis, 1880.

Phil 2520.169   De methodo apud Cartesium, Spinozam et Leibnitium. (Adam, C.E.) Lutetiae, 1885.

Phil 4265.2.32   De methodo philosphandi. (Ventura, J.) Romae, 1828.

Phil 4520.5.34   De modo inculcandi veritates morales in concione publica. Diss. (Boethius, Daniel.) Upsaliae, 1800.

Htn   Phil 4065.55*   De monade, numero et figura. (Bruno, Giordano.) Franco, 1591.

Phil 165.265   De Montaigne à Luis de Broglie. 8. ed. (Brunhold, C.) Paris, 1958?

Phil 2404.4   De Montaigne à Teilhard de Chardin via Pascal et Rousseau. (Emery, Leon.) Lyon, 1965.

Phil 9470.3   De morali responsabilitate. (Oliveira Guimarães, José Joaquim d'.) Conimbrigae, 1901.

Phil 303.5   De mundo dialogi tres quibus. (White, T.) Paris, 1642.

Phil 4200.1.34.1   De naturalium effectuum causis, sive, De incantationibus. (Pomponazzi, Pietro.) Hildesheim, 1970.

Phil 2555.4.31   De necessitate legum naturalium. Thesis. (Derepas, Gustave.) Lutetiae, 1883.

Phil 4515.48   De nexu rerum cum Deo ex ratione pantheismi positiones. (Boström, C.J.) Upsaliae, 1827.

Phil 3640.270   De Nietzsche à Hitler. (Nicolas, M.P.) Paris, 1936.

Htn   Phil 3085.1.30*   De nobilitate. (Agrippa von Nettesheim, H.C.) n.p., 1532.

Htn   Phil 9347.16*   De noncommutando sexus habitu. (Hassen, Martin.) Vitembergae, 1714.

Phil 3425.225   De notione necessitatis Hegeliana. Diss. (Collan, F.) Helsingforsiae, 1850.

Phil 9560.8   De obstinatione. (Stearne, J.) Dublin, 1672.

Htn   Phil 3085.1.32*   De occulta philosophia. (Agrippa von Nettesheim, H.C.) Lugduni, 1550.

Htn   Phil 2150.5.30*   De optimo reipublicae statu, deque nova insula Utopia. (More, Thomas.) Basileae, 1518.

Phil 8620.7.8   De origine mali. (King, Gulielmo.) Dublinii, 1702.

Phil 3246.216   De ortu et indole idealismi Fichtii. Diss. (Bergbom, F.) Aboae, 1822.

Phil 8960.20   De parvitate materiae in sexto. (Kleber, Karl-Heinz.) Regensburg, 1971.

Phil 8520.17   De Pascal à Chateaubriand. (Monod, Albert.) Paris, 1916.

Phil 2805.414   De Pascal à Teilhard de Chardin. (Borne, Étienne.) Clermont-Ferrand, 1963.

Phil 2805.233   De Pascal à Victor Hugo. (Boulan, Émile.) Groningue, 1946.

Phil 3552.274   De perfectione apud Leibnitium. Thesim. (Mabilleau, L.) Paris, 1861.

Htn   Phil 283.6*   De perfectione rerum, libri sex. (Contarini, N.) Venetiis, 1576.

Phil 623.23.10A   De Petrarque á Descartes. (Busson, Henri.) Paris, 1957.

Phil 2520.173   De philosophia Cartesii observationes. Diss. (Grubbe, S.) Upsaliae, 1807.

Phil 3425.227   De philosophia juris Hegeliana. Thesis. (Quist, C.J.) Helsingforsiae, 1853.

Phil 1135.145   De philosophorum graecorum silentis mystics. (Casel, Otto.) Giessen, 1919.

Phil 1190.10   De philosophorum scepticorum successionibus. Inaug. Diss. (Haas, Leander.) Wurciburgi, 1875.

Phil 3552.116.5   De possibilibus apud Leibnitium. Thesis. (Vallier, Charles A.) Burdigalae, 1882.

Phil 3801.320   De posteriore Schellingii philosophia. Thesim. (Delbos, Victor.) Lutetiae, 1902.

Phil 3494.40   De potiori vi quam ad commutandam. (Marheinecke, P.) Erlangae, 1805.

Phil 5010.2   De prascipuis philosophorum recentioris aevi logicam tractandi rationibus. Diss. (Ahlander, J.A.) Lundae, 1849.

Phil 3805.190   De preeken von Schleiermacher Praefschrift. (Vogelsang, A.A.) Leiden, 1916.

Phil 9150.18   De principe de la morale. Thèse. (Massebieau, Eugéne.) Alençon, 1886.

Phil 3831.14   De principiis philosophiae practicae Spinozae. (Lénström, C.J.) Gevaliae, 1843.

Phil 2725.20   De principiis rerum. (Lamy, G.) Paris, 1669.

Phil 177.67   De principio philosophiae. (Cleve, Z.J.) Helsingfors, 1848.

Phil 8881.54   De principio philosophiae moralis. Diss. (Genberg, Paul.) Lundae, 1846.

Phil 3502.4   De priore et posteriore forma Kantianae critices. (Ueberweg, F.) Berolini, 1862.

Phil 5029.1   De progressibus desciplinae logicae. Diss. (Tellbom, J.P.) Upsaliae, 1830.

Htn   Phil 4075.79*   De propria vita liber. (Cardano, Girolamo.) Parisiis, 1643.

Phil 4021.1   De quelques caractères du mouvement philosophique contemporain en Italie. (Vailati, Giovanni.) Paris, 1907.

Phil 2401.9   De quelques constantes de l'esprit humain. (Benda, J.) Paris, 1950.

Phil 5620.11   De rationis autoritate. (Vacherot, Étienne.) Cadomi, 1836.

Phil 5046.44   De re dialectica libellus. (Georgius, Trapezuntius.) Frankfurt, 1966.

Htn   Phil 1535.14*   De rebus naturalibus. (Zabarella, J.) Coloniae, 1597.

Htn   Phil 3801.435*   De recentissimae philosophiae vanitate. (Grohmann, J.C.A.) Vitebergae, 1803.

Phil 2040.35.2   De religione gentilium. (Herbert, E.) Amsterdam, 1700.

Phil 5190.4.15F   De rerum definitionibus liber unus. (Piccolomineus, F.) Venetiis, 1600.

Phil 4235.1.35   De rerum natura. (Telesius, B.) Modena, 1910. 3v.

Phil 2725.11.90   De Rosmini à Lachelier. (Jolivet, Régis.) Paris, 1953.

Phil 4972.5.20   De San Agustín a Bergson. (Korn, Alejandro.) Buenos Aires, 1959.

Phil 4073.40   De sancta mono triade. (Campanella, Tommaso.) Roma, 1958.

Phil 1300.5   De sapientiae doctoribusqui, a ciceronis morte ad neronis principatum. (Aubertin, C.) Parisiis, 1857.

Phil 75.7   De scriptoribus historiae philosophicae. (Jonsius, Johannes.) Jena, 1716.

Phil 1850.116   De sermonibus fidelibus F. Baconi Verulamii. (Carrau, L.) Argentorat, 1870.

Phil 1020.4.41   De siger de Bredant à Jacques de Plaisance. (Kuksewicz, Zdzislaw.) Wroclaw, 1968.

Phil 7082.120   De somniis observationes et cogitationes. Thesis. (Foucault, Marcel.) Paris, 1901.

Phil 3552.255   De spatio apud Leibnitium. Thesis. (Boirac, Aemilius.) Paris, 1894.

Htn   Phil 7060.2*   De spectris. (Lavater, L.) Genevae, 1580.

Phil 7060.2.2   De spectris. (Lavater, L.) Lugduni Batavorum, 1659.

Phil 7060.2.3   De spectris. (Lavater, L.) Lugduni Batavorum, 1687.

Phil 3826.2   De Spinoza. (Godfernaux, A.) Paris, 1894.

Phil 3837.3   De Spinozae philosophia dissertatio. (Rosenkranz, C.) Halae, 1828.

Phil 3832.6   De Spinozae politica. Thesis. (Malapert, P.) Paris, 1897.

Phil 3837.18   De Spinozismi fonte orientali. Diss. (Rietz, J.E.) Lundae, 1816.

Phil 3833.3   De Spinozismi initiis aphorismi. (Nordwall, A.L.) Upsaliae, 1818.

Phil 8876.37   De statibus hominum. (Buys, J.) Moguntiae, 1613.

Phil 8626.15.5   De statu mortuorum et resurgentium tractatus of the state of the dead. (Burnet, Thomas.) London, 1728. 5 pam.

Phil 1350.12   De stoicorum romanorum. (Nemanic, D.) Görz, 1880.

Phil 2138.101   De Stuarti Millii individualismo. Thesis. (Michel, Henry.) Parisiis, 1895.

Phil 2405.3   De Taine à Régny. L'évolution des idées. (Fonsegrive, G.) Paris, 1917.

Phil 803.10   De Thales à Bergson. (Devaux, P.) Liége, 1955.

Phil 8599.16.10   De tribus impostoribus. (De Tribus Impostoribus.) Berlin, 1960.

Htn   Phil 8599.16.5*   De tribus impostoribus. (De Tribus Impostoribus.) Paris, 1861.

Phil 8599.16.6   De tribus impostoribus. (De Tribus Impostoribus.) Paris, 1861.

Phil 8599.16.9   De tribus impostoribus. 2. Aufl. (De Tribus Impostoribus.) Heilbronn, 1876.

Phil 1810.1   De tribus impostoribus magnis liber. (Kortholti, C.) Hamburgi, 1701.

Phil 3450.15.85   De typho generis humani. (Hirnhaim, H.) Prague, 1676.

Phil 4065.32   De umbris idearum. (Bruno, Giordano.) Berolini, 1868.

Htn   Phil 4065.32.5*   De umbris idearum. (Bruno, Giordano.) Paris, 1582.

Htn   Phil 4075.51*   De utilitate-ex adversis capienda libri. (Cardano, Girolamo.) Amsterdam, 1672.

Phil 8402.41   De växandes estetiska liv. (Bruhn, Karl.) Vasa, 1720-21. 2v.

Phil 181.1.15   De verae philosophiae erga religionem Christianam pietate. (Gabler, G.A.) Berolini, 1836.

Phil 2520.66   De Verhandeling van den Mensch, en de Makinge van de Vrugt. (Descartes, René.) Middelburg, 1682.

Phil 4180.1   De veris principiis et vera ratione philosophandi contra pseudophilosophos. (Nizzoli, Mario.) Roma, 1956. 2v.

Phil 2040.30.15   De veritate. (Herbert, E.) Bristol, 1937.

Htn   Phil 2040.30.2*   De veritate. (Herbert, E.) London, 1633.

Htn   Phil 2040.30.3*   De veritate. (Herbert, E.) London, 1633.

Htn   Phil 2040.30*   De veritate. (Herbert, E.) Paris, 1624.

Phil 4372.1.45   De veritate fidei christianae libri quinque. (Vives, Juan Luis.) Lupluni, 1551.

Phil 2520.134   De veritatibus aeternis apud Cartesium. Thesis. (Boutroux, Émile.) Parisiis, 1874.

Htn   Phil 1850.56*   De Verulamio summi angliae. (Bacon, Francis.) London, 1620.

Phil 5170.4   De vi propria syllogismi. Thesis. v.1-2. (Rodier, G.) Parisiis, 1891.

Phil 3552.123   De vinculo substantiali. Thesis. (Blondel, Maurice.) Paris, 1893.

Phil 3280.31   De virtute et primis ejus proprietatilius. (Geulincx, A.) Pretoria, 1961.

Htn   Phil 4934.1.30*   De vita et moribus philosophorum. (Diogenes Laertius.) Basiliae, 1524.

Phil 1850.109   De vita et philosophia F. Baconi. (Welhelmy, Gerrit.) Groningae, 1843.

Phil 4265.1.83   De vita et scriptis...Julii Caesaris Vanini. 2. ed. (Schramm, J.M.) Ciistrini, 1715.

Htn   Phil 4946.1.30*   De vita Mosis. (Philo Iudaeus.) Paris, 1554.

Htn   Phil 3790.11.87*   De vita sua commentarius. (Reimarus, J.A.H.) Hamburgi, 1815.

Phil 3499.20   De voce "a priori" in philosophia Kantii. Diss. (Roeder, E.) Bonnae, 1866.

Phil 720.39   De Wahrheitsbegriff in der...Sprachen. Photostat. (Tarski, Alfred.) Leopoli, 1935.

Phil 8610.890.35   La dea ragione. Milano, 1890.

Phil 7069.17.32   The dead have never died. (Randall, Edward Caleb.) N.Y., 1917.

Phil 7069.19.190   The dead have never died. (Randall, Edward Caleb.) N.Y., 1919.

Phil 8884.5   Deafness and cheerfulness. (Jackson, A.W.) Boston, 1901.

Phil 5467.5   Deahl, J.N. Imitation in education. N.Y., 1900.

Phil 5643.6   Déal, J.N. Nouvel essai sur la lumière et les couleurs. Paris, 1827.

Phil 5923.2   Dean, Amos. Lectures on phrenology. Albany, 1834.

Phil 178.29   Dean, Amos. Philosophy of human life. Boston, 1839.

Phil 6113.14F   Dean, J. Microscopic anatomy...of the spinal cord. Cambridge, 1861.

Phil 5813.1   Dean, R. An essay on the future life of brute creatures. v.1-2. London, 1768.

Phil 8735.60   De Angelis, Enrico. La critica del finalismo nella cultura cartesiana. Firenze, 1967.

Phil 1730.14   DeAngelis, Eurico. Il metodo geometrico nella filosofia del Seicento. Pisa, 1964.

Phil 2255.1.64   Dear Bertrand Russell: a selection of his correspondence with the general public, 1950-1968. (Russell, Bertrand Russell.) London, 1969.

Phil 178.28   Pamphlet box. Dearborn, G.V.M. Minor writings.

Phil 178.28.1   Pamphlet box. Dearborn, G.V.M. Minor writings.

Phil 6113.7   Dearborn, G.V.N. Influence of joy. Boston, 1916.

Phil 5753.3   Dearborn, G.V.N. Neurology of Apraxia. Boston, 1911.

Phil 5403.1.3   Dearborn, Gran N. The emotion of joy. N.Y., 1899.

Phil 5243.46   Dearborn, W.F. Predicting the child's development. Cambridge, Mass., 1941.

Phil 5243.46.2   Dearborn, W.F. Predicting the child's development. 2d rev. ed. Cambridge, Mass., 1963.

Phil 5243.33.3   Dearden, H. Understanding ourselves. N.Y., 1926.

Phil 7069.20.100   Dearmer, Nancy K. The fellowship of the picture. N.Y., 1920.

Phil 7069.13.5   Death, its causes and phenomena. 2. ed. (Carrington, Hereward.) London, 1913

Phil 8612.62   Death, sacrifice, and tragedy. (Foss, Martin.) Lincoln, 1966.

Phil 8612.6   Death; the meaning and result. (Wilson, J.K.) N.Y., 1901.

Phil 978.6.63.5   Death - and after? (Besant, Annie.) London, 1893.

Phil 978.6.63   Death - and after? (Besant, Annie.) London, 1898.

Phil 8625.5.15   Death and afterwards. (Arnold, Edwin.) London, 1907.

Phil 8625.5.17   Death and afterwards. (Arnold, Edwin.) N.Y., 1901.

Phil 8612.55   Death and identity. (Fulton, Robert Lester.) N.Y., 1965.

Phil 8612.68.5   Death and immortality. (Pieper, Josef.) N.Y., 1969.

Phil 7069.21.30   Death and its mystery. pt.1,3. (Flammarion, Camille.) N.Y., 1921-23. 2v.

Phil 8647.11   Death and life. (Ware, Mary G.C.) Boston, 1864.

Phil 6306.5   The death and rebirth of psychology. (Progoff, Ira.) N.Y., 1956.

Phil 8626.8   Death and resurrection. (Björklund, Gustaf.) London, 1910.

Phil 7069.26.2   Death-bed visions. (Barrett, W.) London, 1926.

Phil 7054.7.5   The death blow to spiritualism...true story of the Fox sisters. (Davenport, R.B.) N.Y., 1888.

Phil 7054.169   Death is birth. (Budington, Henry A.) Springfield, Mass., 1897.

Phil 8725.5   The death of God. (Vahanian, G.) N.Y., 1961.

Phil 7069.19.80   Death the gate of life? (Dallas, Helen A.) N.Y., 1919.

Phil 8633.1.42   Death's illumination of life. (Steere, Douglas. V.) Cambridge, 1942.

Phil 7060.27.5   The debatable land between this world and the next. (Owen, R.D.) N.Y., 1872.

Phil 8710.1   The debate between the church and science. (Upham, F.W.) Andover, 1860.

Phil 8610.883.10   Les débats de la conscience, catéchisme laïque. (Berthet, André.) Paris, 1883.

Phil 1750.166.55   Debatt med profanhumanisien. (Bohlin, T.B.) Stockholm, 1951.

Phil 5592.182   Debaty, Pol. La mésure des attitudes. Paris, 1967.

Phil 7085.11.5   Debay, A. Mystères du sommeil et du magnétisme. 4. ed. Paris, 1845.

Phil 5813.5   Debblee, George B. Instinct and intuition. London, 1929.

Phil 1955.6.220   Debdalle, Gerald. L'idée d'expérience dans la philosophie de John Dewey. Thèse. Paris, 1966.

Phil 9120.4.13   El deber; versión española. (Smiles, S.) Paris, 1898.

Phil 5875.110   Debienne, Marie Claire. Le dessin chez l'enfant. Paris, 1968.

Phil 8878.55   DeBoer, Cecil. The if's and ought's of ethics. Grand Rapids, Mich., 1936.

Phil 5875.62.5   De Bono, Edward. The dog exercising machine. London, 1970.

Phil 5500.50   De Bono, Edward. The five-day course in thinking. N.Y., 1967.

Phil 5520.588   De Bono, Edward. The mechanism of mind. N.Y., 1969.

Phil 5520.493   De Bono, Edward. The use of lateral thinking. London, 1968.

Phil 310.320   Deborin, A.M. Filosofiia i politika. Moskva, 1961.

Phil 310.4.10   Deborin, A.M. Vvedemie v filosofii dialekticheskogo materializma. Moskva, 1922.

Phil 310.624   Deborin, Abram M. Dialektika i estestvoznanie. Izd. 3. Moskva, 1929.

Phil 310.625   Deborin, Abram M. Filosofiia i marksizm. Moskva, 1926.

Phil 9495.33   Debreyne, P.J.C. Moechialogie, traité des péchés contre les sixième et neuvième commandements du décalogue. 4th ed. Paris, 1868.

Phil 2520.112   Debricon, L. Descartes. Paris, n.d.

Phil 4003.1   Debrit, M. Histoire des doctrines philosophiques dans l'Italie. Paris, 1859.

Phil 9560.1   De Britaine, W. Human prudence. Dedham, 1806.

Phil 1955.8.30   DeBurgh, William G. The life of reason. London, 1949.

Phil 2042.5   DeBurgh, William George. George Dawes Hicks. London, 1944.

Phil 8583.29   De Burgh, William George. The relations of morality to religion. London, 1935.

Phil 8583.29.5   De Burgh, William George. Towards a religious philosophy. London, 1937.

Phil 5249.21   Les débuts de l'intelligence. (Janet, Pierre.) Paris, 1935.

Phil 6957.30   A decade later: a follow-up of social class and mental illness. (Myers, Jerome Keeley.) N.Y., 1968.

Phil 2075.5.30   Decadence. (Joad, Cyril E.W.) London, 1948.

Phil 2075.5.31   Decadence. (Joad, Cyril E.W.) N.Y., 1949.

Phil 8894.6.10   Décadence du sentiment moral et religieux. (Tissot, Joseph.) Paris, 1878.

Htn   Phil 2045.70*   Decameron physiologicum. (Hobbes, Thomas.) London, 1678.

Phil 5545.61   DeCamp, J.E. Study of retroactive inhibition. Thesis. Princeton, 1915.

Phil 8708.29.10   De Camp, Lyon Sprague. The great monkey trial. 1. ed. Garden City, 1968.

Phil 3823.8   De Casseres, B. Spinoza, liberator of God and man, 1632-1932. N.Y., 1932.

Phil 3450.19.515   De Cecchi Duso, Gianna. L'interpretazione heideggeriana dei presocratici. Padova, 1970.

Phil 9342.11   Décence em elle-même. (Charpentier, Louis.) Paris, 1767.

Phil 2070.147.5   Décès de M. William James. (Boutroux, Emile.) Paris, 1910.

Phil 5548.115   DeCharms, Richard. Personal causation. N.Y., 1968.

Phil 5871.15   Dechêne, Hans C. Geschwisterkonstellation und psychische Fehlentwicklung. München, 1967.

Phil 193.134.15   Déchet, Ferruccio. L'itinerario filosofico di Leone Sestov. Milano, 1964.

Phil 4752.2.195   Déchet, Ferruccio. L'ottavo giorno della creazione. Saggio su N. Berdjaev. Milano, 1969.

Phil 5755.9   La décision; essai d'analyse psychologique. Thèse. (Forti, E.) Paris, 1926.

Phil 5620.36   Decision, theory and human behavior. (Lee, Wayne.) N.Y., 1971.

Phil 5238.135   Decision, values and groups; report from the Interdisciplinary Conference in the Behavioral Science Division. N.Y. 1,1960+ 2v.

Phil 5500.34   Decision and choice. (Siegel, S.) N.Y., 1964.

Phil 5352.20   Decision and stress. (Broadbent, Donald Eric.) London, 1971.

Phil 5760.14   Decision and the condition of man. (Kurtz, Paul W.) Seattle, 1965.

Phil 5500.18   Decision-making. (Wasserman, Paul.) Ithaca, 1958.

Phil 5500.37   Decision-making in the development field. (Buron, Robert.) Paris, 1966.

Phil 5500.26   The decision-making problem in development. (Klein, Burton Harold.) Santa Monica, 1960.

Phil 5500.28   Decision-making under uncertainty and problem solving. (Jordan, Nehemiah.) Santa Monica, 1960.

Phil 9035.14.5   Decision of character. (Foster, John.) N.Y., 19- .

Phil 334.9   Decker, H.C. Das Denken in Begriffen als Kriterium (der Menschwerdung). Oosterhout, 1963.

Phil 7060.120   Decker, Johann H. Spectrologia, h. e. Discursus ut plurimum philosophicus de spectris. Hamburgi, 1690.

Phil 2905.1.680   Deckers, Marie Christine. Le vocabulaire de Teilhard de Chardin. Gembloux, 1968.

Phil 3485.34   Declève, Henri. Heidegger et Kant. La Haye, 1970.

Phil 2750.19.30   Le declin de la sagesse. (Marcel, Gabriel.) Paris, 1954.

Phil 8647.13   The decline of hell. (Walker, Daniel P.) London, 1964.

Phil 8592.60   The decline of religion. (Martin, Cecil Percy.) London, 1940.

Phil 2750.19.31   The decline of wisdom. (Marcel, Gabriel.) London, 1954.

Phil 8685.2   DeConcilio, J. Catholicity and pantheism. pt.1. N.Y., 1874.

VPhil 9590.30   De Condé, Minerva E. Forever into the past and future. Boston, 196-.

Htn   Phil 8583.26*   De Costa, J.H. Reason and faith. Philadelphia, 1791.

Phil 178.46.10   Decoster, Paul. Acte et synthèse. Bruxelles, 1928.

Phil 178.46.15   Decoster, Paul. De l'unité métaphysique. Bruxelles, 1934.

Phil 178.46.5   Decoster, Paul. La réforme de la conscience. Bruxelles, 1919.

Phil 178.46   Decoster, Paul. Le règne de la pensée. Bruxelles, 1922.

Phil 1170.10   Decoster, V. Des antécédents du Néoplatonisme. Bruxelles, 1872.

Phil 575.139   Découverte de la personne, esquisse d'un personnalisme analytique. (Baudouin, Charles.) Paris, 1940.

Phil 6672.3   Découverte de la polarité humaine. (Chazarain, L.T.) Paris, 1886.

Phil 5374.63   La découverte de soi. Thèse. 1. éd. (Gusdorf, G.) Paris, 1948.

Phil 2520.229.2   La découverte métaphysique de l'homme chez Descartes. Thèse. (Alquié, F.) Paris, 1950.

Phil 2520.229   La découverte métaphysique de l'homme chez Descartes. 1. éd. (Alquié, F.) Paris, 1950.

Phil 8951.19.5   Découvertes d'un bibliophile. 2. éd. (Busch, F.) Strassburg, 1843.

Phil 2905.1.415   Decoux, René. L'énergie dans la cosmogenèse de Pierre Teilhard de Chardin. Cran-Annecy, 1964?

Phil 130.7   Decurtins, C. Kleines Philosophenlexikon. Affoltern, 1952.

Phil 8628.1   Dedekind, G.E.W. Dokimion, oder praktischen Versuch über ein reales Verhältniss der Geister der Verstorbenen. Hannover, 1797.

Phil 8628.1.5   Dedekind, G.E.W. Über Geisternähe und Geisterwirkung oder über die Wahrscheinlichkeit das die Geister der Verstorbenen den Lebenden sowohl nahe seyn, als auch auf sie wirken können. Hannover, 1797.

Phil 2530.19   Dederot's early philosophical works. (Diderot, Denis.) Chicago, 1916.

Phil 7069.35.70   Dedication; being later letters from the writer of "Reality". (Parkman, Frances.) Boston, 1935.

Phil 3503.9   La déduction transcendentale dans l'oeuvre de Kant. v.1-2,3. (Vleeschauwer, H.J.) Antwerp, 1934-36. 2v.

Phil 5046.7   Deduction and Induction. (Gneisse, K.) Strassburg, 1899.

Phil 5066.175   Dedukcja naturalna i logistyczna. (Iwanicki, J.) Warszawa, 1949.

Phil 9343.6   Deems, C.F. What now? N.Y., 1852.

Phil 5650.19   Deenik, Arie. Het onderscheidingsvermogen voor toonintensiteiten. Leiden, 1906.

Phil 6311.30.5   Deep analysis. 1st American ed. (Berg, Charles.) N.Y., 1947.

Phil 978.29.10   The deeper mysteries. (Farnsworth, E.C.) Portland, Maine, 1921.

Phil 6990.3.75   Deery, Joseph. Our Lady of Lourdes. Dublin, 1958.

Phil 5325.42　Deese, James. The structure of association in language and thought. Baltimore, 1966.

Phil 5520.626　Deese, James Earle. Psycholinguistics. Boston, 1970.

Phil 5850.171　Defares, Peter Bernard. Grondvormen van menselijke relaties. Assen, 1963.

Phil 6750.27　Pamphlet vol. Defective and delinquent classes. 32 pam.

Phil 6952.20　The defective delinquent and insane. (Cotton, Henry A.) Princeton, 1921.

Phil 1915.77　Defence of Dr. Clarke's...attributes. v.1-3. (Clarke, J.) London, 1732-33.

Phil 400.33　A defence of idealism. (Sinclair, May.) N.Y., 1917.

Phil 974.2.50　Defence of Madame Blavatsky. (Hastings, B. (Mrs.).) Worthing, 1937. 2v.

Htn　Phil 8595.16.15*　Defence of Old Testament. (Levi, David.) N.Y., 1797.

Phil 176.5　Defence of philosophic doubt. (Balfour, A.J.) London, 1879.

Phil 186.145　A defence of philosophy. (Lea, Frank A.) London, 1962.

Phil 190.18.15A　A defence of philosophy. (Perry, R.B.) Cambridge, 1931.

Phil 182.28.5　A defence of prejudice. (Hibben, J.G.) N.Y., 1911.

Htn　Phil 8599.4.7*　A defence of revealed religion against the exceptions of a late writer in his book intituled, Christianity as old as the creation. (Conybeare, J.) London, 1732.

Htn　Phil 8595.16.11*　A defence of revelation. (Winchester, E.) N.Y., 1796.

Phil 8597.11.8　A defence of the eclipse of faith. (Rogers, H.) Boston, 1856.

Phil 8597.11.7　A defence of the eclipse of faith. (Rogers, H.) London, 1854.

Phil 665.93　Defensa del espíritu. (Maeztu, Ramiro de.) Madrid, 1958.

Phil 2805.113F　Défense de Blaise Pascal. (Faugère, Armand P.) Paris, 1868.

Phil 196.26　Defense de la vie. (Vialle, L.) Paris, 1938.

Phil 2725.2.66　Défense de l'essai sur l'indifférence. (Lamennais, F.R. de.) Paris, 1828.

Phil 2496.45.3　Défense de l'université et de la philosophie. (Cousin, Victor.) Paris, 1844.

Phil 2496.45.2　Défense de l'université et de la philosophie. 2e éd. (Cousin, Victor.) Paris, 1844.

Phil 2496.45.4　Défense de l'université et de la philosophie. 4e éd. (Cousin, Victor.) Paris, 1845.

Phil 2805.93　Défense de Pascal...est-il un faussaire? (Lefranc, A.) Paris, 1906.

Phil 2733.95　Défense du sentiment du P. Malebranche. (Gerdil, G.S.) Turin, 1748.

Phil 8878.7.25　Defense d'un homme. (Delisle de Sales, J.B.C.I.) n.p., 1802.

Phil 8878.7.27　Defense d'un homme. (Delisle de Sales, J.B.C.I.) Paris, 1803.

Phil 7060.104.5　A defense of modern spiritualism. (Wallace, A.R.) Boston, 1874.

Phil 8582.15　A defense of religion. (Crosskey, H.W.) London, 1854.

Phil 6311.11.2　La défense psychique. Thèse. (Boas, J.M.) Paris, 1924.

Phil 6311.11　La défense psychique. Thèse. (Boas, J.M.) Paris, 1924.

Phil 3640.723　DeFeo, Nicola M. Analitica e dialettica in Nietzsche. Bari, 1965.

Phil 1750.810　DeFeo, Nicola Massimo. Kierkegaard, Nietzsche, Heidegeger. Milano, 1964.

Phil 5190.4.25　Definition. (Robinson, R.) Oxford, 1950.

Phil 188.11.5　La définition de la philosophie. (Naville, Ernest.) Genève, 1894.

Phil 8581.68.10　La définition de la religion. (Broglie, Paul.) Paris, 1882.

Phil 9240.6　The definition of good. (Ewing, Alfred C.) N.Y., 1947.

Phil 8870.34　The definition of morality. (Wallace, Gerald.) London, 1970.

Phil 5220.4　The definition of psychology. (Keller, F.S.) N.Y., 1937.

Phil 5252.71　The definition of the psychical. (Mead, George H.) Chicago, 1903.

Phil 9410.8　La definizione del bene in relazione al problema dell'ottimismo. (Nutrimento, L.) Padova, 1936.

Phil 8405.12　La definizione dell'arte. (Eco, Umberto.) Milano, 1968.

Htn　Phil 7060.64*　Defoe, D. Essay on the history...of apparitions. London, 1727.

Phil 9163.1　De Foe, D. Religious courtship. London, 1762.

Phil 7060.64.5　Defoe, D. The secrets of the invisible world laid open. London, 1770.

Phil 6315.1.80　De Forest, Izette. The leaven of love. Hamden, Conn., 1954.

Phil 6315.1.14　De Forest, Izette. The leaven of love. London, 1926.

Phil 8413.27　La deformazione estetica. (Martini, Miro.) Milano, 1955.

Phil 9045.13　Defoy, H. Le citoyen. Paris, 1912.

Phil 8404.25　Defrenza, Giuseppe. Il problema della bellezza e dell'arte. Roma, 1967.

Phil 3195.6.89　Degener, Alfons. Dilthey und das Problem der Metaphysik. Bonn, 1933.

Phil 5425.7.10　Degeneration. 2. ed. (Nordau, M.) N.Y., 1895.

Phil 5425.7.12　Degeneration. 4. ed. (Nordau, M.) N.Y., 1895.

Phil 5425.7.12.5　Degeneration. 5. ed. (Nordau, M.) London, 1895.

Phil 5425.7.13　Degeneration. 6. ed. (Nordau, M.) London, 1895.

NEDL　Phil 5425.37　Les dégénérés. (Legrain, M.) Paris, 1895.

Phil 6953.1　Dégénérés et déséquilibrés. (Dallemagne, J.) Bruxelles, 1895.

Phil 5425.7.5　Dégénérescence. (Nordau, M.) Paris, 1894. 2v.

Phil 5425.33　Degenerescencia. Diss. inaug. (Pacheco, Albino Augusto.) Coimbra, 1901.

Htn　Phil 3801.210*　Degenetica philosophandi ratione et methods praesertim Fichti, Schellingii, Hegelii. (Biedermann, K.) Lipsiae, 1835.

Phil 4080.3.360　DeGennaro, Angelo A. The philosophy of Benedetto Croce. 1st ed. N.Y., 1961.

Phil 8870.28　De George, Richard T. Ethics and society. Garden City, 1966.

Phil 310.636　DeGeorge, Richard T. Patterns of Soviet thought. Ann Arbor, 1966.

Phil 8980.320A　De George, Richard T. Soviet ethics and morality. Ann Arbor, 1969.

Phil 4210.92　Degli errori filosofici di Antonio Rosmini. (Gioberti, Vincenzo.) Napoli, 1845.

Phil 4210.92.2　Degli errori filosofici di Antonio Rosmini. 2a ed. (Gioberti, Vincenzo.) Capolago, 1846. 3v.

Phil 4210.115　Degli universali secondo la teoria rosminiana. (Ferré, Pietro M.) Casale, 1880-86. 11v.

Phil 2651.80　DeGournay, M.F.A. Huet. Caen, 1854.

Phil 2490.103　DeGrange, McQuilkin. The science of individuality. Thesis. Lyon, 1923.

Phil 2750.11.48.10　The degree of knowledge. (Maritain, Jacques.) N.Y., 1938.

Phil 848.10　DeGrood, David H. Philosophies of essence; an examination of the category of essence. Groningen, 1970.

Phil 9400.12　De Gruchy, C. Creative old age. San Francisco, 1946.

Phil 2490.108　Deherme, G. Aus jeunes gens un maitre: Auguste Comte; une direction: le positivisme. Paris, 1921.

Phil 600.32　Deherme, G. Le positivisme dans l'action. Paris, 1923.

Phil 585.228　Deho, Ambrogio. Alla scoperta della persona umana. Padova, 1967.

Phil 5585.55　Dehove, H. La perception exterieure. Lille, 1931.

Phil 3525.86.5　Dei Briefwechsel Karl Christian Friedrich Krauses. (Krause, K.C.F.) Leipzig, 1903.

Phil 1135.97　Deichmann, C. Das Problem des Raumes in der griechischen Philosophie bis Aristoteles. Halle, 1893.

Phil 5635.26　Deichmann, Ludwig. Erregung secundärer Empfindungen im Gebiete der Sinnesorgane. Inaug. Diss. Greifswald, 1889.

Phil 18.21　De idee; orgaan van het Bolliano. Genootschap voor zuivore Rede. Utrecht. 1-19,1923-1941 18v.

Phil 3480.22　Deines Lebens Sinn. (Kant, Immanuel.) Wien, 1951.

Phil 3480.22.2　Deines Lebens Sinn. 2. Aufl. (Kant, Immanuel.) Wien, 1953.

Phil 365.60　D'Einstein à Teilhard. (George, Nicolas.) Paris, 1964.

Phil 8661.23　Deism, an anthology. (Gay, Peter.) Princeton, 1968.

Htn　Phil 3824.3*　Deism examin'd and confuted in...Tractatus Theologico Politicus. (Earbery, Matthias.) London, 1697.

Phil 8667.20　Deism in eighteenth century America. (Morais, H.M.) N.Y., 1934.

Phil 8667.20.5　Deism in eighteenth century America. (Morais, H.M.) N.Y., 1960.

Phil 8591.6　Deisme et christianisme. (Levallois, J.) Paris, 1866.

Htn　Phil 8661.13*　The deist's manual. (Gildon, Charles.) London, 1705.

Phil 5242.66　Deistvenostta na misleneto. (Charakchiev, Asen.) Sofiia, 1961.

Phil 8615.14　Deity, duty, destiny; selections from addresses. (Martin, Alfred W.) N.Y., 1916.

Phil 5643.77　Déjean, Renée. Les conditions objectives de la perception visuelle. Thèse. Paris, 1926. 2 pam.

Phil 5643.77.5　Déjean, Renée. La perception visuelle. Paris, 1926.

Phil 178.3　Dejean de Fonroque, Numd. Croyances philosophiques. Paris, 1872.

Phil 6953.11　Dejerine, J. L'hérédité dans les maladies du système nerveux. Paris, 1886.

Phil 1122.25　Dějiny filosofie. (Ráde, Emanuel.) Praha, 1932-33. 2v.

Phil 4110.4.95　Dejob, Charles. Notice sur Luigi Ferri. Versailles, 1896.

Phil 6313.26　Dejung, Beat. Regressionen im Verhalten des Menschen. Zürich, 1967.

Phil 3801.319　Dekker, Gerbrand J. Die Rückwendung zum Mythos. München, 1930.

Phil 7069.20.110　De Koven, Anna F. A cloud of witnesses. N.Y., 1920.

Phil 1704.4　Del arte a la historia en la filosofía moderna. (Estiú, Emilio.) La Plata, 1962?

Phil 8403.33　Del arte actual y de su existencia. (Cevallos García, G.) Cuenca, 1950.

Phil 8407.9.5　Del bello. 2. ed. (Gioberti, V.) Firenze, 1845.

Phil 8403.37.5　Del bello e dell'arte. 2. ed. (Carbonara, C.) Napoli, 1953

Phil 4115.30　Del buono, del bello. (Gioberti, V.) Firenze, 1850.

Phil 4115.30.2　Del buono, del bello. (Gioberti, V.) Firenze., 1853.

Phil 4115.30.5　Del buono. (Gioberti, V.) Napoli, 1848.

Phil 4215.1.89　Del carattere meglio determinante la filosofia di Romagnosi. (Levi, G.) Parma, 1885.

Phil 4260.93　Del criterio della verita nella scienza e nella storia secondo G.B. Vico. (Galasso, Antonio.) Milano, 1877.

Phil 4120.1.35　Del merito e delle ricompenae. (Gioja, Melchiorre.) Torino, 1853. 2v.

Phil 4120.1.32F　Del merito e delle ricompense; trattato storico e filosofico. v. 1-2. 2. ed. (Gioja, Melchiorre.) Lugano, 1830.

Phil 4120.1.33　Del merito e delle ricompense. (Gioja, Melchiorre.) Lugano, 1839. 2v.

Phil 4968.4.80　Del modernismo al liberalismo. (Cordiel Reyes, Raúl.) México, 1967.

Phil 5242.10　Del modo di comporre l'idee. (Costa, P.) Firenze, 1837. 2 pam.

Phil 1825.1　Del neohegelianismo al neorealismo. (Zulen, P.S.) Lima, 1924.

Phil 346.18　Del origen a la escencia del conocimiento. (Pardo, R.) Buenos Aires, 1954.

Phil 4961.910　Del pensar venezolano. (Granell Muñiz, Manuel.) Caracas, 1967.

Phil 4012.1　Del rinnovamento della filosofia antica italiana. (Mamiani di Rovere, T.) Milano, 1836.

Phil 4012.1.3　Del rinnovamento della filosofia antica italiana. (Mamiani di Rovere, T.) Parigi, 1834.

Phil 4012.1.4　Del rinnovamento della filosofia antica italiana. 3. ed. (Mamiani di Rovere, T.) Firenze, 1836.

Phil 2115.137.5　Del rinnovamento delle dottrine di Gall e...di Locke. (Nardi, Pietro de.) Firenze, 1890.

Phil 4073.30　Del senso delle cose e delle magia. (Campanella, Tommaso.) Bari, 1925.

Phil 4215.1.83　Del significato e del valore delle dottrine di Romagnosi per il criticismo contemporaneo. (Bartolomei, A.) Roma, 1901.

Phil 9550.14　Del sistema che fonda la morale sull utilità. (Manzoni, A.) Firenze, 1925.

Phil 7150.13　Del suicidio massime In Italia nel quinquennio 1866-70. (Taverni, Romeo.) Roma, 1873.

Phil 6673.1　Delaage, M.H. Le monde prophétique. Paris, 1853.

Phil 5635.1　Delabarre, E.B. Uber Bewegungsempfindungen. Freiburg, 1891.

Phil 2750.8.85　De la Beaumelle, Laurent A. Vie de Maupertuis. Paris, 1856.

Phil 5520.41.5　Delacroix, H. L'analyse psychologique de la fonction linguistique. Oxford, 1926.

Phil 525.45.5　Delacroix, H. Essai sur le mysticisme spéculatif. Paris, 1900.

Phil 525.45　Delacroix, H. Études d'histoire et de psychologie du mysticisme. Paris, 1908.

Phil 5520.41　Delacroix, H. Le langage et la pensée. Paris, 1924.

Phil 5520.41.3　Delacroix, H. Le langage et la pensée. 2. éd. Paris, 1930.

Phil 5627.61　Delacroix, H. La religion et la foi. Paris, 1922.

Phil 5243.42　Delacroix, Henri. Les grandes formes de la vie mentale. Paris, 1934.

Phil 8404.11　Delacroix, Henri. Psychologie de l'art. Paris, 1927.

Phil 7082.164　Delage, Yves. Le rêve. Paris, 1924.

Phil 9171.1.9　De Lambert, A.T. de M. de C. De l'éducation des jeunes gens. Paris, 1896.

Phil 9171.1.5　De Lambert, A.T. de M. de C. A mother's advice to her son and daughter. Haverhill, 1814.

Phil 9171.1   De Lambert, A.T. de M. de C. A mother's advice to her son and daughter. London, 1800.

Phil 9171.1.2   De Lambert A.T. de M. de C. A mother's advice to her son and daughter. Boston, 1814.

Phil 1828.6   Delaney, Cornelius F. Mind and nature; a study of the naturalistic philosophies of Cohen. Notre Dame, Ind., 1969.

Phil 8658.22   Delanglade, Jean. Le probleme de Dieu. Paris, 1960.

Phil 7054.157.5   Delanne, Gabriel. L'évolution animique. Paris, 1897.

Phil 7054.157   Delanne, Gabriel. Le phénomène spirite. 5. ed. Paris, 1897.

Phil 8583.17.5   Delany, Selden P. Christian practice. N.Y., 1920.

Phil 8583.17   Delany, Selden P. The ideal of Christian worship. Milwaukee, 1909.

Phil 5243.4   Delaperche, H. Essai de philosophie analytique. Paris, 1872.

Phil 1135.156   Delatte, A. Les conceptions de l'enthousiasme chez les philosophes presocratiques. Paris, 1934.

Phil 2070.132   Delattre, F. William James Bergsonien. Paris, 192-.

Phil 6673.18   Delaudine, Antoine François. De la philosophie corpusculaire. Paris, 1785.

Phil 178.81   Delavigne, A. Manual de filosophie. Bucuresti, 1846.

Phil 6440.5   Delay, Jean. Les maladies de la mémoire. 5e ed. Paris, 1970.

Phil 5243.48   Delay, Jean P.L. Les ondes cérébrales et la psychologie. Paris, 1942.

Phil 5545.90   Delay, Jean Paul Louis. Les dissolutions de la mémoire. Paris, 1942.

Phil 5545.181.5   Delay, Jean Paul Louis. Les maladies de la mémoire. 3. éd. Paris, 1961.

Phil 5817.7   The delayed reaction in animals and children. (Hunter, W.S.) Cambridge, n.d.

Phil 5272.6.5   Delbeke, L. Construction of preference spaces. Louvain, 1968.

Phil 3823.6.5   Delblos, Victor. Le problème moral dans la philosophie de Spinoza. Paris, 1893.

Phil 3823.6   Delblos, Victor. Le spinozisme. Paris, 1916.

Phil 2150.22.130   Delbo, Charlotte. La théorie et la pratique, dialogue imaginaire mais non tout à fait apocryphe entre Herbert Marcuse et Henri Lefebvre. Paris, 1969.

Phil 5043.4   Delboéuf, J. Essai de logique scientifique. Liége, 1865.

Phil 6673.17.10   Delboeuf, J. Le magnétine animal. Paris, 1889.

Phil 6673.17   Delboeuf, J. Magnétiseurs et médecins. Paris, 1890.

Phil 5243.5.10   Delboeuf, J.R.L. Étude psychophysique. Belgium, 1873.

Phil 5243.5   Delboeuf, J.R.L. Examen critique de la loi psychophysique. Paris, 1883.

Phil 5243.5.5   Delboeuf, J.R.L. La psychologie. Paris, 1876.

Phil 5635.2   Delboeuf, J.R.L. Théorie générale de la sensibilité. Bruxelles, 1876.

Phil 7080.27   Delboeuf, Joseph. Le sommeil et les rêves. Paris, 1885.

Phil 2555.5.90   Delboeufs Bedeutung für die Logik. Diss. (Brulez, L.) Berlin, 1919.

Phil 3801.320   Delbos, Victor. De posteriore Schellingii philosophia. Thesim. Lutetiae, 1902.

Phil 3003.4   Delbos, Victor. L'esprit philosophique de l'Allemagne et la pensée française. Paris, 1915.

Phil 178.32   Delbos, Victor. Figures et doctrines des philosophes. 4e éd. Paris, 1918.

Phil 2730.95   Delbos, Victor. Maine de Biran. Paris, 1931.

Phil 3485.7   Delbos, Victor. La philosophie pratique de Kant. Paris, 1905.

Phil 6313.1   Delbrück, A. Gerichtliche psychopathologie. Leipzig, 1897.

Phil 6313.1.5   Delbrück, A. Die pathologische Lüge und die psychisch abnormen Schwindler. Stuttgart, 1891.

Phil 1750.315   Deledalle, G. L'existentiel, philosophies et littératures de l'existence. Paris, 1949.

Phil 1803.10   Deledalle, G. Histoire de la philosophie américaine. 1e éd. Paris, 1954.

Phil 2403.10   Deledalle, Gérard. Les philosophes français d'aujourd'hui par eux-mêmes. Paris, 1964?

Phil 3485.23   Delekat, Friedrich. Immanuel Kant. Heidelberg, 1963.

Phil 3485.23.2   Delekat, Friedrich. Immanuel Kant. 2. Aufl. Heidelberg, 1966.

Phil 9245.63   Delessert, Benjamin Guron. Le guide du bonheur. 2. éd. Paris, 1840.

Phil 274.4   Deleuze, Gilles. Différence et répétition. Thèse. Paris, 1968.

Phil 3823.18   Deleuze, Gilles. L'idée de expression dans la philosophie de Spinoza. Thèse. Paris, 1968.

Phil 3640.708   Deleuze, Gilles. Nietzsche; sa vie, son oeuvre. Paris, 1965.

Phil 3640.670   Deleuze, Gilles. Nietzsche et la Philosophie. Paris, 1962.

Phil 3823.18.1   Deleuze, Gilles. Spinoza et le problème de l'expression. Paris, 1968.

Phil 6673.2.3   Deleuze, J.P.F. Histoire critique du magnétisme animal. Paris, 1813. 2v.

Phil 6673.2   Deleuze, J.P.F. Histoire critique du magnétisme animal. Paris, 1819. 2v.

Phil 6673.2.5   Deleuze, J.P.F. Instruction pratique sur le magnétisme animal. Paris, 1825.

Phil 6673.2.15   Deleuze, J.P.F. Lettre à l'auteur d'un ouvrage intitulé: superstitions et prestiges des philosophies du dix-huitième siècle. Paris, 1818.

Phil 6673.2.8   Deleuze, J.P.F. Practical instruction in animal magnetism. Providence, 1837.

Phil 1850.110   Deleyre, A. Analyse de la philosophie du chancelier François Bacon avec sa vie. Leyde, 1778. 2v.

Phil 178.44.10   Delff, Heinrich K.H. Die Hauptprobleme der Philosophie und Religion. Leipzig, 1886.

Phil 178.44   Delff, Heinrich K.H. Philosophie des Gemüths. Husum, 1893.

Phil 178.44.5   Delff, Heinrich K.H. Über den Weg, zum Wissen und zur Gewissheit zu Gesangen. Leipzig, 1882.

Phil 2905.1.115.5   Delfgaauw, B.M.I. Evolution; the theory of Teilhard de Chardin. London, 1969.

Phil 2905.1.115   Delfgaauw, B.M.I. Teilhard de Chardin. Baarn, 1961.

Phil 1750.195   Delfgaauw, B.M.I. Wat is existentialisme? Amsterdam, 1948.

Phil 803.14   Delfgaauw, B.M.O. Beknopte geschiedenis der wijshegeerte. Baarn, 1954. 2v.

Phil 1740.8   Delfgaauw, Bernardus M.I. De wijsbegeerts va di 20. eeuw. Baarn, 1957.

Phil 5243.39   Delgadio, H.F. Psicología. Lima, 1933.

Phil 6315.2.96   Delgado, H. Sigmund Freud. Lima, 1926.

Phil 5590.20   Delgado, Honoria. La personalidad y el carácter. Lima, 1943.

Phil 6953.6   Delgado, Honorio F. La psiquiatría psicológica. Lima, 1919.

Phil 5398.5   Delgado, José M.R. Physical control of the mind. N.Y., 1969.

Phil 8628.15   Delgado Varela, J.M. Supervivencia del hombre. Madrid, 1966.

Phil 4351.6.80   Delgado Varela, José M. La gracia divina en el correlativismo. Madrid, 1961.

Phil 5243.5.50   Delgrado, Honario. El tiempo y la vida animica normal. Lima, 1944.

Phil 1508.3   Delhaye, Philippe. La philosophie chrétienne au Moyen Âge. Paris, 1959.

Phil 2475.1.307   Delhomme, J. Vie et conscience de la vie. Thèse. Paris, 1954.

Phil 178.78   Delhomme, Yeanne. La pensée et le réel, antique de l'ontologie. Paris, 1967.

Phil 8413.23   La délicatesse dans l'art. (Martha, C.) Paris, 1884.

Phil 8405.6   Delight, the soul of art. (Eddy, Arthur.) Philadelphia, 1902.

Phil 8876.3   A delineation...nature. Obligations. Morality. (Balfour, J.) Edinburgh, 1753.

Phil 8876.3.2   A delineation of the nature and obligation of morality. (Balfour, J.) Edinburgh, 1763.

Phil 5050.4   A deliniation, primary principal reasoning. (Kidd, R.B.) London, 1856.

Phil 6962.1.10   Le délire chronique à évolution systématique. (Magnan, V.) Paris, 1892.

Phil 6968.5.15   Le délire des négations. (Séglas, J.) Paris, 189-.

Phil 6315.2.62.10   Délire et rêves dans la "gradiva" de Jenson. 8. éd. (Freud, Sigmund.) Paris, 1949.

Phil 1980.3.94   Delisle, Françoise Roussel. Friendship's odyssey. London, 1946.

Phil 1980.3.104   Delisle, Françoise Roussel. The return of Havelock Ellis, or Limbo or the dove? London, 1968.

Phil 8878.7   Delisle de Sales, J.B.C.I. De la philosophie de la nature. London, 1777. 6v.

Phil 8878.7.10   Delisle de Sales, J.B.C.I. De la philosophie du bonheur. Paris, 1796. 2v.

Phil 8878.7.25   Delisle de Sales, J.B.C.I. Defense d'un homme. n.p., 1802.

Phil 8878.7.27   Delisle de Sales, J.B.C.I. Defense d'un homme. Paris, 1803.

Phil 8878.7.20   Delisle de Sales, J.B.C.I. Memoire en faveur de Dieu. Paris, 1802.

Phil 1145.45   Delitto e pena nel pensiero dei Greci. (Levi, A.) Torino, 1903.

Phil 8583.33.15   Delitzsch, Friedrich. Whose son is Christ? Boston, 1908.

Phil 8583.33   Delitzsch, Friedrich. Zur Weiterbildung der Religion. Stuttgart, 1908.

Phil 165.360   Delius, Harald. Argumentationen. Göttingen, 1964.

Phil 5520.505   Delius, Harald. Untersuchungen zur Problematik der sogenannten synthetischen Sätze apriori. Göttingen, 1963.

Phil 3460.83   Delius, J.F. Darstellung und Hauptgedanken F.H. Jacobi. Halle, 1914.

Phil 178.53   Delius, Rudolf von. Urgesetze des Lebens. Darmstadt, 1922.

Phil 5640.16   Dell, J.A. The gateways of knowledge. Cambridge, 1912.

Phil 8962.10   Della carita cristiana in quanto essa è amore del prossimo. (Muratori, L.A.) Venezia, 1736.

Phil 334.3   Della certitude des connaissance humaines. Londres, 1741.

Phil 1535.5.10   Della conoscenza intellectuale. 2e ed. (Liberatore, M.) Roma, 1873-74. 2v.

Phil 8050.52   Della critica. (Fasola, Guista Nicco.) Firenze, 1947.

Phil 5051.20   Della dialettica. v.1-2. (Labanca, B.) Firenze, 1874.

Phil 4114.45   Della diceosina o sia della filosofia sul religione. (Genovesi, Antonio.) Napoli, n.d. 3v.

Phil 4260.101   Della dottrina di B. Spinoza e di G.B. Vico. (Sarchi, Carlo.) Milano, 1877.

Phil 3450.11.515   Della fenomenologia all'ontologia. (Altamore, Giovanni.) Padova, 1969.

Phil 4235.3.31   Della filosofia della mente. (Testa, Alfonso.) Piacenza, 1836.

Phil 4115.51   Della filosofia della rivelazione. (Gioberti, V.) Torino, 1856.

Phil 4006.3.15   Della filosofia moderna in Sicilia libri due. (Giovanni, V.) Palermo, 1868.

Phil 8893.2   Della filosofia morale. (Sandona, G.) Firenze, 1847. 2v.

Htn   Phil 296.10*   Della filosofia naturale. (Piccolomini, A.) Venetia, 1585. 2v.

Phil 4160.1.33   Della filosofia razionale. 2a ed. (Labanca, Baldassare.) Firenze, 1868. 2v.

NEDL   Phil 6025.4.8   Della fisonomia dell'huomo. (Porta, G.B.) Venetia, 1644.

Htn   Phil 6025.4.6.5*   Della fisonomia dell'huomo. (Porta, G.B.) Vicenza, 1615.

Htn   Phil 6025.4.6F*   Della fisonomia dell'huomo. Libri quattro. (Porta, G.B.) Napoli, 1598.

Phil 6025.4.7   Della fisonomia di tutto il corpo humano. (Porta, G.B.) Roma, 1637.

Htn   Phil 9030.5.5*   Della fortuna libri sei. (Garimberto, G.) Vinetia, 1550.

Phil 5465.2.5   Della forza della fantasia umana. (Muratori, L.A.) Venezia, 1740.

Phil 4073.55   Della grazia gratificante. (Campanella, Tommaso.) Roma, 1959.

Phil 2115.51.20   Della guida dell'intelligenza nella ricerca della verità. (Locke, J.) Lanciano, 1927.

Phil 180.25F   Della idea del vero e...dell'essere. (Ferri, Luigi.) Roma, 1887.

Phil 8647.5   Della immortalita dell'anima. (Florenzi Waddington, M.) Firenzi, 1868.

Htn   Phil 8890.22.10*   Della institutione di tutta la vita. (Piccolomini, A.) Vinegia, 1552.

Htn   Phil 8890.21*   Della institutione morale, libri XII. (Piccolomini, A.) Venetia, 1560. (Transferred to Houghton Library 31/1/72)

Htn   Phil 8890.21.5*   Della institutione morale, libri XII. (Piccolomini, A.) Venetia, 1594. (Transferred to Houghton Library 31/1/72)

Htn   Phil 8890.22*   Della institutione morale. (Piccolomini, A.) Venetia, 1575. (Transferred to Houghton Library 31/1/72)

Phil 196.19   Della intelligenza nell'espressione. (Vivante, L.) Roma, 1922.

Phil 5831.1.3   Della legge fondamentale dell'intelligenza nel regno animali. (Vignoli, Tito.) Milano, 1877.

Htn   Phil 8893.73.5*   Della metamorfosi...del virtuoso. (Selva, Lorenzo.) Firenze, 1583.

Htn   Phil 8893.73.10*   Della metamorfosi...del virtuoso. (Selva, Lorenzo.) Firenze, 1615.

Htn   Phil 8893.73*   Della metamorfosi...del virtuoso. (Selva, Lorenzo.) Orvieto, 1582.

128

Author and Title Listing

Phil 8881.57.5 Della miseria dell'uomo. (Giambioni, Bono.) Firenze, 1836.
Phil 8881.57 Della miseria dell'uomo. (Giambioni, Bono.) Milano, 1847.
Phil 4073.42 Della necessita di una filosofia cristiana. (Campanella, Tommaso.) Torino, 1953.
Phil 4210.116.20 Della nuova dichiarazione quasi ultima della S. Congregazione dell'Indice. (Buroni, Giuseppe.) Torino, 1882.
Phil 4115.40 Della protologia. (Gioberti, V.) Torino, 1857-58. 2v.
Phil 3494.27 Della psicologia di Kant. (Mamiani, T.) Roma, 1877.
Phil 8591.33 Della religione e della filosofia cristiana. Pt.2. (Labanca, B.) Torino, 1888.
Phil 4170.7.40 Della religione positiva e perpetua. (Mamiani della Rovere, Terenzio.) Milano, 1880.
Htn Phil 8875.3.8* Della vanitate delle scienze. (Agrippa von Nettesheim, Heinrich Cornelius.) Venetia, 1552.
Phil 4265.2.30 Della vera e della falsa filosofia. (Ventura da Raulica, G.) Napoli, 1854.
Phil 4210.82 Della vita di Antonio Rosmini-Serbati. (Paoli, F.) Torino, 1880-84. 2v.
Phil 4080.8.83 Della vita e delle opere. (Alfani, Augusto.) Firenze, 1906.
Phil 4265.2.91 Della vita e delle opere del Rev. P.D. Geovachino Ventura. (Cultrera, Paolo.) Palermo, 1877.
Phil 4120.6.90 Della vita e delle opere di Vincenzo de Grazia. (Fiorentino, F.) Napoli, 1877.
Phil 3425.748 Dell'Aquila, Michele. Critica e letteratura in tre hegeliani di Napoli. Bari, 1969.
Phil 4215.1.81 Delle censure dell'abate A. Rosmini-Serbati contro la dottrina religiosa di G.D Romagnosi. (Nova, Alessandro.) Milano, 1842.
Phil 176.131 Delle relazioni della filosofia colla società; prolusione. (Bonghi, Ruggiero.) Milano, 1859.
Phil 4114.31 Delle scienze metafisiche. (Genovesi, Antonio.) Napoli, 1791.
Phil 4114.30 Delle scienze metafisiche. (Genovesi, Antonio.) Venezia, 1782.
Phil 8880.54 Dell'egoismo. (Ferraro, L.) Novara, 1963.
Phil 5090.8 Dellepiane, A. Les sciences et la méthode reconstructives. Paris, 1915.
Phil 4210.116F Dell'essere e del conoscere. (Buroni, Giuseppe.) Torino, 1877.
Phil 9560.7.7 Dell'onore dialoghi tre. (Pescetti, Orlando.) Verona, 1624.
Phil 4170.7.35 Dell'ontologia e del metodo. (Mamiani della Rovere, Terenzio.) Parigi, 1841.
Phil 4170.7.36 Dell'ontologia e del metodo. 2a ed. (Mamiani della Rovere, Terenzio.) Firenze, 1843.
Phil 4170.7.37 Dell'ontologia e del metodo. 2a ed. (Mamiani della Rovere, Terenzio.) Firenze, 1848.
Phil 8878.42 Del Mar, E. The divinity of desire. N.Y., 1906.
Phil 6313.7 Delmas, F. Achille. La personalité humaine. Paris, 1925.
Phil 8411.36.2 "Delo vkusa". Izd. 2. (Kassil', Lev A.) Moskva, 1964.
Phil 3838.29 Delouit. Lettre d'un ami du sens commun à un Hollandois. Utrecht, 1809.
Phil 3450.19.98 Delp, A. Trogische Existenz; zur Philosophie Martin Heideggers. Freiburg, 1935.
Phil 5413.15 Delpierre, Guy. De la jalousie. Paris, 1954.
Phil 900.14 Deltanschauung des indogermanischen Asiens. (Negelein, J.) Erlangen, 1924.
Phil 4080.1.85 Del Torre, Maria A. Studi su Cesare Cremonini. Padova, 1968.
Phil 2403.3 DeLuc, J.F. Observations sur les Savans incredules. Genève, 1762.
Phil 6952.21.5 Delusion and belief. (Campbell, C.M.) Cambridge, 1926.
Phil 6952.21.6 Delusion and belief. (Campbell, C.M.) Cambridge, 1927.
Phil 6315.2.62.7 Delusion and dream, and other essays. (Freud, Sigmund.) Boston, 1968.
Phil 6315.2.62.5 Delusion and dream. (Freud, Sigmund.) N.Y., 1917.
Phil 8404.12 Delville, Jean. La mission de l'art. Bruxelles, 1900.
Phil 8878.59 Delvolvé, J. La fonchion morale. Paris, 1951.
Phil 623.3 Delvolvé, J. Rationalisme et tradition. Paris, 1910.
Phil 9075.10 Delvolve, Jean. L'organisation de la conscience morale. Paris, 1906.
Phil 2490.122 Delvolvé, Jean. Réflexions sur la pensée comtienne. Paris, 1932.
Phil 3488.48 Dem Andenken Kants. Berlin 1804. (Grohmann, Johann Christian August.) Bruxelles, 1969.
Phil 1504.1 Die dem Boethius. v.1, pt.1. (Correns, Paul.) Münster, 1891.
Phil 2520.203 Dem Gedächtnis au René Descartes. Berlin, 1937.
Phil 2805.215 Demahis, E. La pensée politique de Pascal. Thèse. St. Amand, 1931.
Phil 4114.85 Demarco, Domenico. Quello che è vivo del pensiero economico di Antonio Genovesi. Napoli, 1957.
Phil 978.84 Demarquette, Jacques. De la liête á l'auge. Paris, 1937.
Phil 7082.180 De Martino, Manfred F. Dreams and personality dynamics. Springfield, 1959.
Phil 1540.24 DeMatteis, F. L'occasionalismo e il suo sviluppo nel pensiero de N. Malebranche. Napoli, 193-.
Phil 5585.205 Dember, William Norton. The psychology of perception. N.Y., 1961.
Phil 5585.205.5 Dember, William Norton. Visual perception: the nineteenth century. N.Y., 1964.
Phil 5243.72 Dembicki, Leo. Psychologie: Modell und Wirklichkeit. Bodman/Bodensee, 1969.
Phil 5412.7 Dembo, Tamara. Der Ärger als dynamisches Problem. Inaug. Diss. Berlin, 1931.
Phil 4803.320.30 Dembowski, Bronisław. Spór o metafizyke. Warszawa, 1969.
Phil 6962.23 La démence. (Mallet, Raymond.) Paris, 1935.
Phil 6962.14 La demence. (Marie, A.) Paris, 1906.
Phil 6951.28 Dementia praecox. (Babcock, H.) N.Y., 1933.
Phil 6954.4 Dementia praecox. (Evensen, Hans.) Kristiania, 1904.
Phil 5753.7.2 Demeny, Georges. L'éducation de l'effort psychologie-physiologie. 2. éd. Paris, 1916.
Phil 2490.99 Un demifou de génie. (Grasset, Joseph.) Montpelier, 1911.
Phil 6956.5.2 Demifous et demiresponsables. 2. éd. (Grasset, Joseph.) Paris, 1908.
Phil 6313.15 De Mille, A. Introduction to scientology. 2d ed. Los Angeles, 1953.
Phil 8830.4 La démission de la morale. (Faquet, Émile.) Paris, 1910.
Phil 8580.33.5 Demitizzazione e immagine. (Archivio di Filosofia.) Padova, 1962.
Phil 585.155 Democracy: a man-search. (Sullivan, L.H.) Detroit, 1961.
Phil 2075.4.30 Democracy and civilization. (Jones, G.V.) London, 1946.
Phil 8171.100.5 Demokraticheskaia estetika Belorussii (1905-1917 gg). (Konan, Uladzimir M.) Minsk, 1971.
Phil 7069.04.60 The demonism of the ages. (Peebles, J.M.) Battle Creek, Mich., 1904.
Phil 6972.12 Demonism verified and analyzed. (White, H.W.) Shanghai, 1922.
Phil 7054.25 Demonology and witchcraft. (Brown, Robert.) London, 1889.
Phil 2520.410 Demons, dreamers, and madmen. (Frankfurt, Harry G.) Indianapolis, 1970.
Htn Phil 8628.3.5* Demonstratio immortalitatis animae. (Digby, K.) Francofurti, 1664.
Htn Phil 8628.3.8F* Demonstratio immortalitatis animae. (Digby, K.) Parisiis, 1651.
Phil 70.86.10 Démonstration, vérification, justification. (International Institute of Philosophy.) Liège, 1968.
Phil 5090.11 Demonstration and logical truth. 1st ed. (Sengupta, Pradip Kumar.) Calcutta, 1968.
Htn Phil 8667.8* A demonstration of God in his workes. (More, G.) London, 1598.
Phil 8595.21 A demonstration of the divine authority of the law of nature. (Parker, S.) London, 1681.
Phil 8659.2 A demonstration of the existence and providence of God. (Edwards, John.) London, 1696.
Htn Phil 8592.59* A demonstration that true philosophy has no tendency to undermine divine revelation. (Morgan, Caesar.) Cambridge, 1787.
Htn Phil 8628.3.9F* Demonstratos immortalitatis animae rationalis. (Digby, K.) Paris, 1655.
Phil 2805.290 Demorest, Jean. Dans Pascal. Paris, 1953.
Phil 2805.291 Demorest, Jean. Pascal écrivain. Paris, 1937.
Phil 5043.5 DeMorgan, Augustus. Formal logic. London, 1847.
Htn Phil 1955.2.30* De Morgan, Augustus. Formal logic. London, 1847.
Phil 5043.5.3 DeMorgan, Augustus. Formal logic (1847). London, 1926.
Phil 5170.15 DeMorgan, Augustus. On the syllogism, and other logical writings. London, 1966.
Phil 5043.5.5A DeMorgan, Augustus. Syllabus of a proposed system of logic. London, 1860.
Phil 7054.81.19 De Morgan, Sophia Elisabeth. From matter to spirit. London, 1863.
Phil 8878.27 DeMotte, J.B. The secret of character building. Chicago, 1893.
Phil 8953.10 Demoulin, Jérôme. Critiques; á la bona consciència dels christians. Barcelona, 1963.
Phil 1508.2.12 Dempf, Alois. Christliche Philosophie. 2. Aufl. Bonn, 1952.
Phil 8828.4 Dempf, Alois. Ethik des Mittelalters. München, 1927.
Phil 1508.2 Dempf, Alois. Die Hauptform mittelalterlicher Weltanschanung. München, 1925.
Phil 803.12 Dempf, Alois. Kritik der historischen Vernunft. Wien, 1957.
Phil 1540.43 Dempf, Alois. Metafísica de la Edad Media. Madrid, 1957.
Phil 1540.40 Dempf, Alois. Metaphysik des Mittelalters. München, 1930.
Phil 3801.320.10 Dempf, Alois. Schelling; zwei Reden. München, 1955.
Phil 178.68 Dempf, Alois. Selbstkritik der Philosophie und vergleichende Philosophiegeschichte im Umriss. Wien, 1947.
Phil 1508.2.5 Dempf, Alois. Das Unendliche in der mittelalterlichen Metaphysik und in der Kantischendialektik. Münster, 1925.
Phil 1703.7 Dempf, Alois. Weltordnung und Heilsgeschichte. Einsiedeln, 1958.
Phil 6313.16 Dempsey, P.J.R. Freud. Cork, 1956.
Phil 3450.19.296 Demske, James M. Being, man and death: a key to Heidegger. Lexington, 1970.
Phil 3450.19.295 Demske, James M. Sein, Mensch und Tod. Freiburg, 1963.
Htn Phil 192.82* Den amsteldamsen diogenes. (Roas, A.) Utrecht, 1684.
Phil 3640.221 Den Manen Friedrich Nietzsches. (Oehler, Max.) München, 1921.
Phil 3485.17 Denckmann, G. Kants Philosophie des Ästhetischen. Heidelberg, 1947.
Phil 7060.24 Dendy, W.B. Philosophy of mystery. London, 1841.
Phil 7060.24.5 Dendy, W.B. Philosophy of mystery. N.Y., 1845.
Phil 7082.158 Dendy, Walter Cooper. On the phenomena of dreams. London, 1832.
Phil 3485.11 Deneffe, A. Kant und die catholische Wahrheit. Freiburg, 1922.
Htn Phil 4931.3.80* Dénes, Lajos. Emlekkönyv Alexander Bernat hatvanadík születése napjára. Budapest, 1910.
Phil 5650.52 Denes, Peter B. The speech chain; the physics and biology of spoken language. Baltimore? 1968.
Phil 530.20.51 Denifle, H. Die deutschen Mystiker des 14. Jahrhunderts. Freiburg in der Schweiz, 1951.
Phil 530.20.50 Denifle, H. Das geistliche Leben. 7. Aufl. Graz, 1920.
Phil 2450.80 Denis, J. Bayle et Jurien. Caen, 1886.
Phil 1145.5 Denis, J. Histoire des theories...dans l'Antiquité. Paris, 1856. 2v.
Phil 1145.6 Denis, J. Histoire des theories...dans l'Antiquité. Paris, 1879. 2v.
Phil 2428.15 Denis, Jacques. Sceptiques ou libertins de la première moitié du XVIIe siècle. Genève, 1970.
Phil 7068.91.4 Dénis, Léon. Après la mort. Paris, 1891.
Phil 7069.19.90 Denis, Léon. Life and destiny. N.Y., 1919.
Phil 7059.20 Denis, Léon. Pourquoi la vie! Paris, 1892.
Phil 6013.3 Denis, Robert. Le visage de l'homme. Paris, 1961.
Phil 575.74 Denison, J.H. The enlargement of personality. N.Y., 1930.
Phil 2520.425 Denissoff, Élie. Descartes, premier théoricien de la physique mathematique. Louvain, 1970.
Phil 8125.8 Denk, Ferdinand. Das Kunstschone und chacaktivstische von Winckelmann bis Friedrich Schlegel. Inaug. Diss. München, 1925.
Phil 5520.438 Denken. (Graumann, Carl F.) Köln, 1965.
Phil 338.19 Das Denken. (Honecker, M.) Berlin, 1925.
Phil 3450.19.205 Das Denken des Martin Heideggers. (Kauthack, Katherina.) Berlin, 1959.
Phil 3270.17.30 Denken en existeren. (Flam, Leopold.) Amsterdam, 1964.
Phil 3850.51 Das Denken Herman Schells. (Berning, V.) Essen, 1964.
Phil 334.9 Das Denken in Begriffen als Kriterium (der Menschwerdung). (Decker, H.C.) Oosterhout, 1963.
Phil 3450.19.121 Denken und Dichten des Seins. (Buddeberg, Else R.) Stuttgart, 1956.
Phil 5252.38 Das Denken und die Phantasie. (Müller-Freienfels, R.) Leipzig, 1916.
Phil 349.46 Denken und Erkennen im kybernetischen Modell. (Stachowiak, Herbert.) Wien, 1965.
Phil 3850.27.50 Denken und Fat. (Schweitzer, A.) Hamburg, 1950.
Phil 342.17 Denken und Sein. (Litt, Theodor.) Stuttgart, 1948.
Phil 3450.19.220 Denken und Sein. (Ott, Heinrich.) Zollikon, 1959.
Phil 352.8 Denken und Sein. (Vries, Joseph de.) Freiburg, 1937.
Phil 720.41 Denken und Sein. v.1. (Erismann, T.) Wien, 1950.
Phil 5258.37 Das Denken und sein Gegenstand. (Stern, N.) München, 1909.

Htn Phil 193.31.5* Denken und Wirklichkeit. (Spir, A. von.) Leipzig, 1877. 2v.

Phil 193.31.6 Denken und Wirklichkeit. v.1-2. (Spir, A. von.) Leipzig, 1873.

Phil 193.31 Denken und Wirklichkeit. v.1-4. (Spir, A. von.) Leipzig, 1884-1885. 3v.

Phil 193.31.7 Denken und Wirklichkeit. 4e aufl. (Spir, A. von.) Leipzig, 1908.

Phil 8622.68 Denkender Glaube. (Buri, Fritz.) Bern, 1966.

Phil 1707.11 Denkendes Europa; ein Gang durch die Philosophie der Gegenwart. (Hartmann, Hans.) Berlin, 1936.

Phil 5421.20.35 Denker, Rolf. Aufklärung über Aggression: Kant, Darwin, Freud, Lorenz. Stuttgart, 1966.

Phil 5421.20.37 Denker, Rolf. Aufklärung über Aggression: Kant, Darwin, Freud, Lorenz. 2. Aufl. Stuttgart, 1968.

Phil 1730.22 Denker, Rolf. Grenzen liberaler Aufklärung bei Kant und Anderen. Stuttgart, 1968.

Phil 1133.25 Denker der hellenischen Frühzeit. (Nassauer, Kurt.) Frankfurt, 1948.

Phil 4007.1 Denker der italienischen Renaissance; Gestalten und Probleme. (Hönigswald, R.) Basel, 1938.

Phil 1818.9 Die Denker und Kämpfer der englischen Aufklärung. (Sakmann, Paul.) Stuttgart, 1946.

Phil 130.6.5 Denker unserer Zeit. (Hubscher, Arthur.) München, 1956-57. 2v.

Phil 1750.123.5 Denkers over zeil en leven. Amsterdam, 1917.

Phil 1703.10 Denkers van deze fijd. 2. druk. Francker, 1954-55. 3v.

Phil 1750.123 Denkers van onzen tijd. (Groot, J.V. de.) Uitgevers, 1918.

Phil 186.77.5 Denkfibel; der Gegensatz als Richtmass. 2e Aufl. (Ludovici, August.) München, 1929.

Phil 186.50.10 Denkfibel; die Lehre vom organischen Gegensatz. (Ludovici, A.) München, 1927.

Phil 186.67 Denkformen. (Leisegang, H.) Berlin, 1928.

Phil 186.67.3 Denkformen. 2. Aufl. (Leisegang, H.) Berlin, 1951.

Phil 5262.56 Denkformen und Denktechnik. (Waffenschmidt, Walter.) Meisenheim, 1961.

Phil 5255.12 Die Denkfunktion der Verneinung. (Petrescu, Nicolaus.) Leipzig, 1914.

Phil 5240.26 Das Denkgefühe, eine Untersuchung über den emotionalen Charakter der Denkprozesse. (Apfelbach, Hans.) Wien, 1922.

Phil 5051.4 Die Denkkunde oder die Logik. (Lindemann, H.S.) Solothurn, 1846.

Phil 5042.1 Denklehre oder Logik und Dialektik...Geschichte und Literatur. (Calker, J.F.A.) Bonn, 1822.

Htn Phil 3800.260* Denkmal der Schrift von den göttlichen Dingen des Herrn F.H. Jacobi. (Schelling, F.W.J. von.) Tübingen, 1812.

Phil 8583.20 Denkmann, D.K. Metaphysik der Geschichte. Leipzig, 1914.

Phil 5246.21 Denkökonomie und Energieprinzip. (Gabius, P.) Berlin, 1913.

Phil 3808.86.15 Denkrede auf Arthur Schopenhauer. (Gwinner, W.) Leipzig, 1888.

Phil 4605.1.49 Denkrichtungen der neueren Zeit. (Monrad, M.J.) Bonn, 1879.

Phil 5217.6 Denkschrift zur Lage der Psychologie. (Hoyos, C.G.) Wiesbaden, 1964.

Phil 5374.245.2 Denkstil. Beschreibung und Deutung der Denkformen. 2. Aufl. (Schueling, Hermann.) Düsseldorf, 1967.

Phil 3246.160 Das Denksystem Fichtes. (Hielscher, H.) Berlin, 1913.

Phil 3450.19.290 Der Denkweg Martin Heideggers. (Poeggeler, Otto.) Pfullingen, 1963.

Phil 6307.452 Denmark. Statens Andssvageforsorg. Ti ars andssvageforsorg, 1, oktober, 1969. København, 1969.

Phil 3210.87 Dennert, E. Fechner als Naturphilosoph und Christ. Gütersloh, 1902.

Phil 8583.34 Dennert, E. Klassiker du religiösen Weltanschauung. Bd.1. Hamburg, 1909.

Phil 510.1.33 Dennert, E. Die Wahrheit über Ernst Haeckel und seine "Welträtsel". Halle, 1920.

Phil 284.11 Dennert, E. Die Weltanschauung des modernen Naturforschers. Stuttgart, 1907.

Phil 531.6 Dennes, William R. Some dilemmas of naturalism. N.Y., 1960.

X Cg Phil 9495.127.15 Dennett, M.W. (Mrs.). The sex side of life; an explanation for young people. Astoria, 1928.

Phil 9495.127 Dennett, M.W. (Mrs.). Who's obscene? N.Y., 1930.

Phil 7060.26 Dennis, J. Subversion of materialism. Bath, n.d.

Htn Phil 2128.82* Dennis, John. Vice and luxury publick mischiefs. London, 1724.

Phil 178.4 Dennys, E.N. The alpha. London, 1855.

Phil 178.4.2 Dennys, E.N. The alpha. London, 1855.

Phil 4114.32 Denoihnsion stoixeia, metafisikis. (Genovesi, Antonio.) Vienna, 1806.

Phil 295.6 Les dénominations du monde chez les premiers auteurs chrétiens. (Orban, A.P.) Nijmegen, 1970.

Phil 9510.6 La dénonciation et les dénonciateurs. 4. éd. (Colonéri, L.J.) Paris, 1948.

Phil 8583.37 Dent, Phyllis. The growth of the spiritual life. London, 1944.

Phil 4073.85 Dentice di Accadia, C. Tommaso Campanella. Firenze, 1921.

Phil 3805.153 Dentice di Accadia, Cecilia. Schleiermacher. Milano, 1918.

Phil 9343.14 Dentico, Salvatore. Gioventu atea! Palermo, 1967.

Phil 7068.63.25 Denton, W. Nature's secrets or psychometric researches. Photoreproduction. London, 1863.

Phil 7059.7 Denton, William. The soul of things. Boston, 1863.

Phil 4215.1.115 Dentone, Adriana. Il problema morale in Romagnosi e Cattaneo. Milano, 1968.

Phil 4225.8.105 Dentone, Adriana. La problematica morale nella filosofia della integralita. 2. ed. Milano, 1966.

Phil 3485.9 Dentrice di Accadia, C. Il razionalismo religioso di E. Kant. Bari, 1920.

Phil 8583.45.2 Denzinger, Heinrich. Vier Bücher von der religiösen Erkenntniss. Frankfurt, 1967. 2v.

Phil 5069.8 Deontic logic: introductory and systematic readings. (Hilpinen, Risto.) Dordrecht, 1971.

Phil 8980.529 Deontik, Planung und Leitung der moralischen Entwicklung. (Loeser, Franz.) Berlin, 1966.

Phil 1865.30.30 Deontologia. (Bentham, Jeremy.) Torino, 1925.

Phil 1865.30.35 Deontologia. (Bentham, Jeremy.) Torino, 1930.

Htn Phil 1865.30.2* Deontology. (Bentham, Jeremy.) London, 1834. 2v.

Phil 1865.30 Deontology. v.1-2. (Bentham, Jeremy.) London, 1834.

Phil 8583.32 De Pauley, W.C. The candle of the Lord. London, 1937.

Phil 8881.37 La dépendance de la morale et l'indépendance des moeurs. (Gaultier, Jules de.) Paris, 1907.

Phil 6111.56.10 The dependence of the mind on its physical environment. (Barcroft, Joseph.) Newcastle upon Tyne? 1938?

Phil 6805.2 La dépersonnalisation. (Dugas, Laurent.) Paris, 1911.

Phil 8740.5 De Pierrefeu, Elsa (Tudor). Unity in the spirit. Rindge, N.H., 1955.

Phil 6625.8 Depression: clinical, experimental, and theoretical aspects. (Beck, Aaron T.) N.Y., 1967.

Phil 5643.87 Depth in pictorial art. (Ames, Adelbert.) N.Y., 1925.

Phil 6328.2.15 The depth of the soul. (Stekel, Wilhelm.) London, 1921.

Phil 6332.22.2 Depth psychology, a critical history. (Wyss, Dieter.) N.Y., 1966.

Phil 8888.14.1 Depth psychology and a new ethic. (Neumann, Erich.) London, 1969.

Phil 6322.40 Depth psychology and education. (Matthew, A.V.) Kolhapur, 1944.

Phil 5255.56 Depth psychology and modern man. (Progoff, Ira.) N.Y., 1959.

Phil 8597.44 Der antichrist. (Roth, J.) Amsterdam, 1934.

Phil 1155.5 Der eleatische satz vom widerspruch. (Ranulf, Svend.) København, 1924.

Phil 5655.5.2 Der Geruch. 2e Aufl. (Henning, H.) Leipzig, 1924.

Phil 1750.354 Der moderne deutsche und französische Existentialismus. 2e Aufl. (Lenz, Joseph.) Trier, 1951.

Phil 6688.25 Der principes et des procédés du magnetisme animal. (Sarrazin de Montferrier, A.A.V.) Paris, 1819. 2v.

Phil 3428.66 Der principio logico exclusi medii. (Herbart, J.F.) Gottingae, 1833.

Phil 3110.55 Der weeg zu Christo. (Böhme, J.) Amsterdam, 1682.

Phil 5780.12 Der Wille in der Handschrift. (Trey, M. de.) Bern, 1946.

Phil 165.130 Derathé, Robert. La justice et la violence. Paris, 1958.

Phil 165.225 Derbolav, Josef. Erkenntnis und Verantwortung. Düsseldorf, 1960.

Phil 6953.3 Derby, J.B. Life among lunatics. Boston, 1839.

Phil 6113.28.5 Dercum, F.X. The psychology of mind. 2. ed. Philadelphia, 1925.

Phil 1930.10.90 Deregibus, A. Il razionalismo di Morris R. Cohen. Torino, 1960.

Phil 2655.3.105 Deregibus, Arturo. La metafisica critica di Octave Hamelin. Torino, 1968.

Phil 3823.14 Deregilris, Arturo. La filosofia etico-politica di Spinoza. Torino, 1963.

Phil 8404.7 Deren, Maya. An anagram of ideas on art. N.Y., 1946.

Htn Phil 6953.2* DeRenne, G.W.J. Theory concerning the nature of insanity. Wormsloe, 1847.

Phil 2555.4.31 Derepas, Gustave. De necessitate legum naturalium. Thesis. Lutetiae, 1883.

Phil 8658.4.5 Derham, W. Astro-theology. Hamburg, 1728.

Htn Phil 8658.4* Derham, W. Astro-theology. London, 1715.

Phil 8658.4.2 Derham, W. Astro-theology. London, 1719.

Phil 8658.4.6 Derham, W. Physico-theology. London, 1714.

Phil 8658.4.7 Derham, W. Physico-theology. London, 1716.

Phil 8658.4.9 Derham, W. Physico-theology. 7. ed. London, 1727.

Phil 4080.3.200 Derisi, Octavio N. La filosofía del espíritu. Madrid, 1947.

Phil 1750.24 Derisi, Octavio N. Filosofía moderna y filosofía tomista. Buenos Aires, 1941.

Phil 178.84 Derisi, Octavio Nicolas. Los fundamentos metafisicos del orden moral. 3. ed. Madrid, 1969.

Phil 5400.204 Dermon, Emiir. Sinirlenmeden yaşayeniz. Izmir, 1970.

Phil 2840.70 Les derniers entretiens, recueillis par Louis Prat. (Renouvier, C.B.) Paris, 1904.

Phil 2840.70.3 Les derniers entretiens, recueillis par Louis Prat. (Renouvier, C.B.) Paris, 1930.

Phil 2805.102 Les derniers jours de Blaise Pascal. (Gazier, A.) Paris, 1911.

Phil 3640.94.9 Dernoscheck, G.A. Das problem des egoistischen Perfektionismus in der Ethik Spinozas und Nietzsches. Annaberg, 1905.

Phil 2490.100 Deroisin, Hippolyte P. Notes sur Auguste Comte. Paris, 1909.

Phil 5465.162 De Ropp, Robert S. The master game; pathways to higher consciousness beyond the drug experience. N.Y., 1968.

Phil 2750.20.120 Derossi, Giorgio. Maurice Merleau-Ponty. Torino, 1965.

Phil 365.30 Derr, Ezra Z. Evolution versus involution. N.Y., 1885.

Phil 2725.2.110 Derre, Jean R. Lamennais, ses amis et le mouvement des idées à l'époque romantique, 1824-1834. Paris, 1962.

Phil 5520.520 Derrida, Jacques. De la gammatologie. Paris, 1967.

Phil 3450.11.400 Derride, Jacques. La voix et le phénomène, introduction au problème du signe dans la phénoménologie de Husserl. Paris, 1967.

Phil 8956.20.80 Derungs, Ursicin. Der Moraltheologe Joseph Geishüttner (1763-1805), I. Kant und J.G. Fichte. Regensburg, 1969.

Htn Phil 7075.5.2* Des aberrations du sens génésique. 2. ed. (Moreau, P.) Paris, 1880.

Phil 6121.7.9 Des actions réflexes du cerveau. (Luys, J.) Paris, 1874.

Phil 1504.4 Des Adelard von Bath Traktat. v.4, pt.1. (Willner, H.) Münster, 1903.

Phil 6619.2.5 Des anesthésies hystériques. (Pitres, Albert.) Bordeaux, 1887.

Phil 5812.10 Des animaux a l'homme. (Chauchard, Paul.) Paris, 1961.

Phil 1170.10 Des antécédents du Néoplatonisme. (Decoster, V.) Bruxelles, 1872.

Phil 5040.2 Des antibarbarus logicus. (Allihn, F.H.T.) Halle, 1853.

Phil 2520.365 Des Aufbau des philosophischen Wissens nach René Descartes. (Mahnke, Detlef.) München, 1967.

Phil 325.4 Des bases critique d'un empirisme psychologique. (Bertrand-Barraud, D.) Paris, 1926.

Phil 7068.37 Des benediktiner-abtes zu Senones. (Calmet, Augustin.) München. 1837.

Phil 175.18 Des Bewusstwerden der Menschheit. (Arndt, Julius.) Halle, 1850.

Phil 6971.2 Des causes...maladies mentales. (Voisin, F.) Paris, 1826.

Phil 5525.26 Des causes du rire. (Dumont, L.) Paris, 1862.

Phil 1504.3.6 Des Chalcidius Kommentar zu Platos Timaeus. v.3, pt.6. (Switalski, B.W.) Münster, 1902.

Phil 8657.25 Des chrétiens interrogent l'athéisme. Paris, 1967-2v.

Phil 3415.61.3 Die des Christenthums. 3. Aufl. (Hartmann, Eduard von.) Leipzig, 1888.

Phil 9060.1 Des compensations dans destinées humaines. (Azaïs, P.H.) Paris, 1825. 3v.

Phil 9060.1.2 Des compensations dans les destinées humaines. (Azaïs, P.H.) Paris, 1846.

Phil 510.5 Des Daseins und Denkens Mechanik und Metamechanik. (Ruckhaber, Erich.) Hirschberg, 1910.

Phil 5480.1 Des dispositions innées de l'âme. (Gall, F.J.) Paris, 1811.

Phil 1504.2.3 Des dominicus gundissalinus. v.2, pt.3. (Bülow, G.) Münster, 1897.

	Phil 5753.9	Des Dr. C. Daub Darstellung und Beurtheilung des Hypothesen in Betreff dei Willensfreiheit. (Daub, Carl.) Altona, 1834.
Htn	Phil 2880.1.33*	Des erreurs et de la vérité. (Saint-Martin, L.C.) Edimbourg, 1775.
	Phil 2880.1.30	Des erreurs et de la vérité. (Saint-Martin, L.C.) Edimbourg, 1782.
	Phil 4065.62	Des fureurs héroiques. (Bruno, Giordano.) Paris, 1954.
	Phil 4075.79.15	Des Girolamo Cardano von Mailand (Buergers von Bologna) eigene Lebenbeschreibung. (Cardano, Girolamo.) Jena, 1914.
	Phil 4075.79.16	Des Girolamo Cardano von Mailand eigene Lebensbeschreibung. (Cardano, Girolamo.) München, 1969.
	Phil 525.50.5	Des graces d'oraison. 5e éd. (Poulain, A.) Paris, 1906.
	Phil 7060.14.3	Des hallucinations, ou histoire raisonnée. 3. ed. (Brierre de Boismont, A.) Paris, 1862.
	Phil 7060.14.5	Des hallucinations. 2. ed. (Brierre de Boismont, A.) Paris, 1852.
Htn	Phil 3890.3.30F*	Des heilige Lerers Predigfast. (Tauler, J.) Basel, 1621.
	Phil 6956.7	Des idées de grandeur dans le délire des persécutions. (Garnier, P.E.) Paris, 1878.
	Phil 5545.3	Des idées innées de la mémoire. (Boucher, J.) Paris, 1867.
	Phil 7060.80.9	Des Indes à la planète Mars. (Flournoy, J.) Paris, 1900.
	Phil 2750.9.30	Des limites de la philosophie. (Merten, O.) Paris, 1896.
	Phil 6950.2	Des maladies du cerveau. (Audiffrent, G.) Paris, 1874.
	Phil 6955.1	Des maladies mentales. (Falret, J.P.) Paris, 1864.
	Phil 6954.3.5	Des maladies mentales. v.1,2 and atlas. (Esquirol, Etienne.) Paris, 1838. 3v.
	Phil 6111.3	Des manifestations de la vie et de l'intelligence. (Bertrand de Saint-Germain, Guillaume Scipion.) Paris, 1848.
	Phil 5043.15.2	Des méthodes dans les sciences de raisonnement. pt.1. (Duhamel, J.M.C.) Paris, 1865.
	Phil 5043.15	Des méthodes dans les sciences de raisonnement. v.1-5. (Duhamel, J.M.C.) Paris, 1865-73. 3v.
	Phil 5585.8	Des modes accidentels de nos perceptions. (Redern, S.E. de.) Paris, 1818.
	Phil 8887.28	Des mysteres de la vie humaine. v.1-2. (Montlosier, F.D. de R.) Bruxelles, 1829. 2v.
	Phil 478.2	Des notions de matière et de force. (Dauriac, L.) Paris, 1878.
	Phil 5655.1	Des odeurs. (Duméril, A.H.A.) Paris, 1843.
	Phil 9420.9	Des passions. (Thiroux d'Arconville, M.) Londres, 1764.
	Phil 2805.80	Des pensées de Pascal. (Cousin, Victor.) Paris, 1843.
	Phil 2805.80.2	Des pensées de Pascal. (Cousin, Victor.) Paris, 1844.
	Phil 5642.11	Des phénomènes de synopsie. (Flournoy, T.) Paris, 1893.
	Phil 5360.9	Des premières perceptions du concret à la conception de l'abstrait. Thèse. (Pellet, R.) Lyon, 1938.
	Phil 978.49.490	Des Prinzip der spirituellen Ökonomie im Zusammenhang mit Wiederverkörperungsfragen; 22 Vorträge. (Steiner, R.) Dornach, 1965.
	Phil 7068.66.80	Des sciences occultes et du spiritisme. (Tissandier, J.B.) Paris, 1866.
	Phil 8892.35	Des sciences physiques aux sciences morales. (Renard, G.) Paris, 1922.
	Phil 8892.28	Des sciences physiques aux sciences morales. (Rueff, Jacques.) Paris, 1922.
	Phil 5246.5	Des signes et de l'art de penser. (Gerando, J.M. de.) Paris, 1800. 4v.
Htn	Phil 7060.6*	Des spectres ou apparitions et visions. (Le Loyer, P.) Angers, 1586.
	Phil 6968.6	Des symptomes intellectuels de la folie. (Sémérie, E.) Paris, 1867.
	Phil 1504.14	Des Theodor Abû Kurra Traktat. v.14, pt.1. (Graf, G.) Münster, n.d.
	Phil 7082.196	Des Traum und seine Auslegung. (Boss, Medard.) Bern, 1953.
	Phil 6968.5.5	Des troubles du langage...aliénés. (Séglas, J.) Paris, 1892.
	Phil 8421.2	Des Ulricus Engelberti von Strassburg O. Pr. (+1277) Abhandlung de Pulchro. (Ulricus Engelberti, Argentinensis.) München, 1926.
	Phil 5722.60	Des Unbewusste als Keimstätte des Schöpferischen. (Kankeleit, Otto.) München, 1959.
	Phil 2520.134.5	Des vérités éternelles chez Descartes. (Boutroux, Émile.) Paris, 1927.
	Phil 2733.105	Des vérités éternelles selon Malebranche. (LeMoine, A.) Paris, 1936.
	Phil 2733.105.5	Des vérités éternelles selon Malebranche. Thèse. (LeMoine, A.) Marseille, 1936.
	Phil 720.22	Des vrayes et des fausses idées. (Arnauld, A.) Cologne, 1683.
	Phil 2880.8.118	Desan, Wilfred. The tragic finale. Cambridge, Mass., 1954.
	Phil 585.130	Desan, Wilfrid. The planetary man. Washington, 1961.
	Phil 1660.5.2	De Santillana, Giorgio. The age of adventure; the Renaissance philosophers. Boston, 1957.
	Phil 1660.5	De Santillana, Giorgio. The age of adventure; the Renaissance philosophers. N.Y., 1956.
	Phil 193.250	De Santillana, Giorgio. Reflections on men and ideas. Cambridge, 1968.
	Phil 4318.2	El desarrollo de la razón en la cultura española. (Rodriguez Aranda, Luis.) Madrid, 1962.
	Phil 4959.405	Desarrollo de las ideas filosóficas en Costa Rica. (Láscaris Comneno, Constantino.) Costa Rica, 1964.
	Phil 8980.795	Desat prikazani. (Slovak, Emil.) Bratislava, 1968.
	Phil 2475.1.111	Desaymard, J. La pensée de Henri Bergson. Paris, 1912.
	Phil 6048.59.5	Desbarrolles, A. Chiromancie nouvelle...les mystères de la main, revélés et expliqués. 14e ed. Paris, 186-.
	Phil 6060.9	Desbarrolles, A. Les mystères de l'écriture; art de juger les hommes. Paris, 1872.
	Phil 5865.5.10	Desbiens, Jean Paul. Introduction à un examen philosophique de la psychologie de l'intelligence chez Jean Piaget. Québec, 1968.
	Phil 2805.225	Desbruyères, P. Face à l'épreuve avec Pascal. Lyon, 1941.
	Phil 8583.22	Descamps, E. Le génie des religions. Paris, 1923.
	Phil 2520.35.39	Descarter, René. Discours de la méthode. Paris, 1937.
	Phil 2520.35.47	Descarter, René. Discours de la méthode. 2. ed. Manchester, 1961.
	Phil 2520.370	Descartes; a collection of critical essays. 1st ed. (Doney, Willis.) Notre Dame, 1968.
	Phil 2520.375	Descartes; a study of his philosophy. (Kenny, Anthony.) N.Y., 1968.
	Phil 2520.208.5	Descartes, Corheille, Christine de Suede. (Cassirer, E.) Paris, 1942.
	Phil 2520.78	Descartes, directeur spirituel. (Swarte, V. de.) Paris, 1904.
	Phil 2520.109A	Descartes, his life and times. (Haldane, E.S.) London, 1905.
	Phil 2520.130	Descartes, Hume und Kant. (Belharz, Alfons.) Wiesbaden, 1910.
	Phil 2520.102	Descartes, la princesse Elizabeth et la reine Christine. (Foucher de Careil, A.) Paris, 1879.
	Phil 2520.102.2	Descartes, la princesse Elizabeth et la reine Christine. (Foucher de Careil, A.) Paris, 1909.
	Phil 2520.193.5	Descartes, l'homme et l'oeuvre. (Alquié, F.) Paris, 1956.
	Phil 2520.118	Descartes; Methode des richtigen Vernunftgebrauches 1637. (Gröber, G.) Strassburg, 1914.
	Phil 2520.196.10	Descartes, ou Le combat pour la vérité. (Mesnard, Pierre.) Paris, 1966.
	Phil 2475.1.238.15	Descartes, Pascal, Bergson. (Rideau, Émile.) Paris, 1937.
	Phil 2520.425	Descartes, premier théoricien de la physique mathematique. (Denissoff, Élie.) Louvain, 1970.
Htn	Phil 2520.65*	Descartes, R. Excellent compendium of musik. London, 1653.
	Phil 2520.43	Descartes, René. Abhandlung über die Methode. Leipzig, 1919-20. 2 pam.
	Phil 2520.35.50	Descartes, René. Choix commenté du Discours de la méthode. Geneve, 1952.
	Phil 2520.78.35	Descartes, René. Correspondance avec Armaud et Marus. Paris, 1953.
	Phil 2520.78.30	Descartes, René. Correspondance publiée avec une introduction et des notes par C. Adam et G. Milhaud. 1. éd. Paris, 1936-51. 8v.
	Phil 2520.78.25F	Descartes, René. Correspondence of Descartes and Constantyn Huygeno, 1635-1647. Oxford, 1926.
Htn	Phil 2520.34.2*	Descartes, René. De homine, figuris, et latinitate donatus. Lugduni Batavorum, 1662.
Htn	Phil 2520.34.3*	Descartes, René. De homine...Schuye a Florentio Schuye. Lugduni Batavorum, 1664.
	Phil 2520.66	Descartes, René. De Verhandeling van den Mensch, en de Makinge van de Vrugt. Middeleburg, 1682.
	Phil 2520.219A	Descartes, René. Descartes, 1596-1650. Genève, 1946.
	Phil 2520.70	Descartes, René. Descartes, 1596-1650. Genève, 1948.
	Phil 2520.69	Descartes, René. Descartes. Paris, 1947.
	Phil 2520.64	Descartes, René. Descartes. Paris, 1969.
	Phil 2520.78.40	Descartes, René. Descartes par lui-meme. Paris, 1956.
	Phil 2520.45.12	Descartes, René. Il discorso del metodo. Assisi, 1911.
	Phil 2520.45.5	Descartes, René. Il discorso del metodo. Milano, 19- .
	Phil 2520.35.52	Descartes, René. Discorso sul metodo. Firenze, 1962.
	Phil 2520.45.25	Descartes, René. Discorso sul metodo. Napoli, 1937.
	Phil 2520.45.18	Descartes, René. Il discorso sul metodo. Torino, 1926.
	Phil 2520.45	Descartes, René. Discorso sul metodo e meditazioni. Bari, 1912. 2v.
	Phil 2520.35.37	Descartes, René. Discours de la méthode. (Ouvrages de l'esprit). Manchester, 1941.
	Phil 2520.35.15	Descartes, René. Discours de la méthode. Cambridge, Eng., 1923.
	Phil 2520.35.21	Descartes, René. Discours de la méthode. Evreux, 1927.
	Phil 2520.35.14	Descartes, René. Discours de la méthode. Londres, 1913.
	Phil 2520.35.16	Descartes, René. Discours de la méthode. Paris, 1925.
	Phil 2520.35.17	Descartes, René. Discours de la méthode. Paris, 1926.
	Phil 2520.35.19	Descartes, René. Discours de la méthode. Paris, 1927.
	Phil 2520.35.26	Descartes, René. Discours de la méthode. Paris, 1932.
	Phil 2520.35.25	Descartes, René. Discours de la méthode. Paris, 1932.
	Phil 2520.35.45	Descartes, René. Discours de la méthode. Paris, 1950.
	Phil 2520.35.40	Descartes, René. Discours de la méthode. Paris, 1951.
	Phil 2520.35.48	Descartes, René. Discours de la méthode. Paris, 1961.
	Phil 2520.35.9	Descartes, René. Discours de la méthode pour bien conduire sa raison et chercher la vérité dans les sciences. Strasbourg, n.d.
Htn	Phil 2520.35.1*	Descartes, René. Discours de la méthode pour bien conduire sa raison et chercher la vérité dans les sciences. Leyde, 1637.
Htn	Phil 2520.35.13*	Descartes, René. Discours de la méthode pour bien conduire sa raison et chercher la vérité dans les sciences. Paris, 1668.
Htn	Phil 2520.35.12*	Descartes, René. Discours de la méthode pour bien conduire sa raison et chercher la vérité dans les sciences. Paris, 1668.
	Phil 2520.35.3	Descartes, René. Discours de la méthode pour bien conduire sa raison et chercher la vérité dans les sciences. Paris, 1668.
	Phil 2520.35.6	Descartes, René. Discours de la méthode pour bien conduire sa raison et chercher la vérité dans les sciences. Paris, 1876.
	Phil 2520.35.8	Descartes, René. Discours de la méthode pour bien conduire sa raison et chercher la vérité dans les sciences. Paris, 1886.
	Phil 2520.35.4	Descartes, René. Discours de la méthode pour bien conduire sa raison et chercher la vérité dans les sciences. Paris, 1894.
Htn	Phil 2520.35.10*	Descartes, René. A discours of a method. London, 1649.
	Phil 2520.37	Descartes, René. Discourse on method. Chicago, 1899.
	Phil 2520.37.10	Descartes, René. Discourse on method. London, 1901.
	Phil 2520.38	Descartes, René. Discourse on the method of rightly conducting the reason. Edinburgh, 1850.
	Phil 2520.54	Descartes, René. Entretien avec Burman. Paris, 1937.
Htn	Phil 2520.77*	Descartes, René. Epistola...ad celeberrimum virum D. Gisbertum Voetium. Amsterodami, 1643.
	Phil 2520.13.16	Descartes, René. Epistolae, Pars prima-tertia. Amsterdam, 1682-83. 3v.
	Phil 2520.75	Descartes, René. Epistolae. Amstelodami, 1682-83.
	Phil 2520.75.2	Descartes, René. Epistolae. Francofurti ad Moenum, 1692.
Htn	Phil 2520.75.3*	Descartes, René. Epistolae. v.1-2. Amstelodami, 1668.
	Phil 2520.75.15	Descartes, René. Epistolae. v.1-2. Amstelodami, 1714.
Htn	Phil 2520.75.5*	Descartes, René. Epistolae. v.1-2. Londini, 1668.
	Phil 2520.13.12	Descartes, René. Geometria. 3a ed. Amsterdam, 1683. 2v.
	Phil 2520.21.5	Descartes, René. Hauptschriften zur Grundlegung seiner Philosophie. Heidelberg, 1930.
Htn	Phil 2520.34.10*	Descartes, René. L'homme de René Descartes et la formation du Foetus. Paris, 1677.
Htn	Phil 2520.34*	Descartes, René. L'homme et un traitte de la formation du Foetus. Paris, 1664.
	Phil 2520.76.55	Descartes, René. Lettres de Descartes. Paris, 1724-25. 6v.
Htn	Phil 2520.76.3*	Descartes, René. Lettres ou sont traitées les plusieurs belles questions de la morale. Paris, 1657.
Htn	Phil 2520.76*	Descartes, René. Lettres ou sont traitées les plusieurs belles questions touchant la morale. Paris, 1663. 2v.
Htn	Phil 2520.76.5*	Descartes, René. Lettres ou sont traitées les plusieurs belles questions touchant la morale. v.1-3. Paris, 1666-67.

Phil 2520.76.65 Descartes, René. Lettres sur la morale. Paris, 1935.
NEDL Phil 2520.51 Descartes, René. Life and meditations. London, 1878.
Phil 2520.52.70 Descartes, René. The living thoughts of Descartes. Philadelphia, 1947.
Phil 2520.53.10 Descartes, René. Meditações metafísicas. Coimbra, 1930.
Phil 2520.52.80 Descartes, René. Meditationen über die erste Philosophie. Hamburg, 1956.
Phil 2520.53.4 Descartes, René. Meditationen über die Grundlagen der Philosophie. 4e Aufl. Leipzig, 1915.
Phil 2520.13.14 Descartes, René. Meditationeo de prima philosophia. Amsterdam, 1685.
Phil 2520.52.20 Descartes, René. Meditationes de prima philosophia. Amstelodami, 1644.
Phil 2520.52.25 Descartes, René. Meditationes de prima philosophia. Amstelodami, 1650. 3 pam.
Phil 2520.52.26 Descartes, René. Meditationes de prima philosophia. Amstelodami, 1654.
Phil 2520.52.27 Descartes, René. Meditationes de prima philosophia. Amstelodami, 1678.
Phil 2520.52.28 Descartes, René. Meditationes de prima philosophia. Amstelodami, 1698. 3 pam.
Phil 2520.52.60 Descartes, René. Meditationes de prima philosophia. Amsterdam, 1657. 5 pam.
Phil 2520.14 Descartes, René. Meditationes de prima philosophia. Amsterdam, 1685.
Phil 2520.14.9 Descartes, René. Meditationes de prima philosophia. München, 1901.
Phil 2520.52.32 Descartes, René. Meditationes de prima philosophia. Paris, 1944.
Htn Phil 2520.52.17* Descartes, René. Meditationes de prima philosophia. 2a ed. Amstelodami, 1642. 2 pam.
Phil 2520.14.2 Descartes, René. Meditationes de prima philosophia. 2e. Aufl. München, 1912.
Phil 2520.52.8 Descartes, René. Les méditationes métaphysiques. 2e éd. Paris, 1661.
Phil 2520.52.10 Descartes, René. Les méditationes métaphysiques. 3e éd. Paris, 1673.
Phil 2520.50.5 Descartes, René. The meditations, and selections from the Principles of René Descartes. n.p., 1968.
Phil 2520.52.75 Descartes, René. Méditations. 4. éd. Paris, 1952.
Htn Phil 2520.52.7* Descartes, René. Les méditations métaphysics. Paris, 1647.
Phil 2520.52.35 Descartes, René. Les méditations métaphysiques. Paris, 1724. 2v.
Phil 2520.52.50 Descartes, René. Meditazioni filosofiche. Torino, 1927.
Phil 2520.36 Descartes, René. The method, meditation and selections. Edinburgh, 1897.
Htn Phil 2520.62.5* Descartes, René. Le monde. Paris, 1664.
Phil 2520.16 Descartes, René. Oeuvres. Paris, 1824-26. 11v.
Phil 2520.19.4 Descartes, René. Oeuvres. Paris, 1844.
Phil 2520.19.4.5 Descartes, René. Oeuvres. Paris, 1850.
Phil 2520.19.3 Descartes, René. Oeuvres. Paris, 1860.
Phil 2520.19.5 Descartes, René. Oeuvres. Paris, 1865.
Phil 2520.19.7 Descartes, René. Oeuvres. Paris, 1868.
Phil 2520.32.15 Descartes, René. Oeuvres. v.1,2,6,8 (pt.1-2), 9 (pt.1-2), 10-11. Paris, 1964. 11v.
Htn Phil 2520.19.9* Descartes, René. Oeuvres choisies. Paris, 1865.
Phil 2520.19.11 Descartes, René. Oeuvres choisies. Paris, 1865.
Phil 2520.26.2 Descartes, René. Oeuvres choisies. Paris, 1876.
Phil 2520.26 Descartes, René. Oeuvres choisies. Paris, 1877.
Phil 2520.19 Descartes, René. Oeuvres de Descartes. Paris, 1897. 12v.
Phil 2520.19.2 Descartes, René. Oeuvres de Descartes. Suppl. Index général. Paris, 1913.
Phil 2520.31 Descartes, René. Oeuvres et lettres. Paris, 1937.
Phil 2520.17 Descartes, René. Oeuvres morales et philosophiques. Paris, n.d.
Phil 2520.17.5 Descartes, René. Oeuvres morales et philosophiques. Paris, 1879.
Phil 2520.15 Descartes, René. Oeuvres philosophiques. Paris, 1835. 4v.
Phil 2520.32.10 Descartes, René. Oeuvres philosophiques. Paris, 1963- 2v.
Phil 2520.18A Descartes, René. Oeuvres philosophiques publiées. Paris, 1852.
Phil 2520.13.20 Descartes, René. Opera omnia, novem tomis comprehensa. Amstelodami, 1692. 9v.
X Cg Phil 2520.11 Descartes, René. Opera philosophica. Francofurti, 1656-58.
Phil 2520.10.25 Descartes, René. Opera philosophica. Francofurti, 1692.
Phil 2520.10.8 Descartes, René. Opera philosophica. 4a ed. Amsterdam, 1664.
Htn Phil 2520.10.9* Descartes, René. Opera philosophica. 4a ed. Amsterdam, 1664.
Phil 2520.10.10 Descartes, René. Opera philosophica. 4a ed. Amsterdam, 1664.
Htn Phil 2520.10.16* Descartes, René. Opera philosophica. 5a ed. Amsterdam, 1672.
Htn Phil 2520.10.15* Descartes, René. Opera philosophica. 5a ed. Amsterdam, 1672.
Phil 2520.10.20 Descartes, René. Opera philosophica. 5a ed. Amsterdam, 1677-78. 2v.
Phil 2520.30 Descartes, René. Opuscula posthuma. Amsterdam, 1701.
Phil 2520.218 Descartes, René. Les pages immortelles de Descartes. Paris, 1942.
Phil 2520.218.5 Descartes, René. Les pages immortelles de Descartes. Paris, 1961.
Htn Phil 2520.60* Descartes, René. Passiones animae. Amstelodami, 1650.
Htn Phil 2520.60.1* Descartes, René. Passiones animae. Amstelodami, 1650.
Htn Phil 2520.60.5* Descartes, René. Passiones animae. Amstelodami, 1664.
Phil 2520.61.15 Descartes, René. Les passions de l'âme. Paris, 1726.
Phil 2520.61.16 Descartes, René. Les passions de l'âme. Paris, 1955.
Htn Phil 2520.61.12* Descartes, René. Les passions de l'âme. Rouen, 1651.
Phil 2520.27.5 Descartes, René. Pensées, choisies. Paris, 1944.
Phil 2520.27 Descartes, René. Pensées de Descartes sur la religion et la morale. Paris, 1811.
Phil 2520.78.45 Descartes, René. Philosophical letters. Oxford, 1970.
Phil 2520.22 Descartes, René. Philosophical works. N.Y., 1955. 2v.
Phil 2520.22.5 Descartes, René. The philosophical works of Descartes. London, 1967. 2v.
Phil 2520.44 Descartes, René. Philosophical writings. Edinburgh, 1954.
Phil 2520.23A Descartes, René. Philosophical writings. N.Y., 1958.
Phil 2520.32 Descartes, René. Philosophische Werke. v.1-2. n.p., n.d.
Phil 2520.28A Descartes, René. Philosophy in extracts from his writings. N.Y., 1892.
Htn Phil 2520.39.8* Descartes, René. Les principes de la philosophie. Paris, 1647.

Htn Phil 2520.39* Descartes, René. Les principes de la philosophie. Paris, 1651.
Htn Phil 2520.39.10* Descartes, René. Les principes de la philosophie. Paris, 1659.
Phil 2520.39.3 Descartes, René. Les principes de la philosophie. Paris, 1668.
Phil 2520.11.13 Descartes, René. Les principes de la philosophie. Paris, 1723.
Phil 2520.39.5 Descartes, René. Les principes de la philosophie. Paris, 1724.
Phil 2520.39.6 Descartes, René. Les principes de la philosophie. Paris, 1724.
Phil 2520.39.16 Descartes, René. Les principes de la philosophie. Paris, 1950.
Phil 2520.39.12 Descartes, René. Les principes de la philosophie. Rouen, 1698.
Phil 2520.39.9 Descartes, René. Les principes de la philosophie. Rouen, 1706.
Phil 2520.11.5 Descartes, René. Les principes de la philosophie. 2e éd. Paris, 1660.
Phil 2520.11.10 Descartes, René. Les principes de la philosophie. 4e éd. Paris, 1681.
Phil 2520.67 Descartes, René. Principia philosophiae. Amstelodami, 1692.
Htn Phil 2520.10.5* Descartes, René. Principia philosophiae. Amsterdam, 1644. 2 pam.
Htn Phil 2520.10* Descartes, René. Principia philosophiae. Amsterdam, 1650.
Phil 2520.13.11 Descartes, René. Principia philosophiae. Amsterdam, 1685. 3 pam.
Phil 2520.39.20 Descartes, René. I principii della filosofia. Bari, 1914.
Phil 2520.39.30 Descartes, René. Principii di filosofia. Napoli, 1937.
Phil 2520.11.24 Descartes, René. Die Prinzipien der Philosophie. 3. Aufl. Leipzig, 1908.
Phil 2520.11.25 Descartes, René. Die Prinzipien der Philosophie. 4e Aufl. Leipzig, 1922.
Phil 2520.55.10 Descartes, René. Règles pour la direction de l'esprit. Paris, 1945.
Phil 2520.68 Descartes, René. Regln zur des Geistes. Leipzig, 1906.
Phil 2520.55.12 Descartes, René. Regulae ad directionem ingenii. La Haye, 1966.
Phil 2520.55 Descartes, René. Regulae ad directionem ingenii. Torino, 1943.
Phil 2520.29A Descartes, René. Selections. N.Y., 1927.
Htn Phil 2520.52.15* Descartes, René. Six metaphysical meditations. London, 1680.
Phil 2520.35.2 Descartes, René. Specimina philosophiae. Amsterdam, 1656.
Phil 2520.61.5 Descartes, René. Tractat von den Leidenschafften der Seele. Franckfurth, 1723.
Phil 2520.34.5 Descartes, René. Tractatus de homine et de formatione Foetus. Amsterdam, 1677.
Phil 2520.13.15 Descartes, René. Tractatus de homine et de formatione foetus. Amsterdam, 1686.
Phil 2520.61.19 Descartes, René. Traité des passions. Paris, 1928.
Phil 2520.61.20 Descartes, René. Traité des passions suivi de la correspondance avec la princess Elisabeth. Paris, 1965.
Phil 2520.13.15.5 Descartes, René. Treatise of man. Cambridge, 1972.
Phil 2520.61.7 Descartes, René. Über die Leidenschaften der Seele. 3e Aufl. Leipzig, 1911.
Phil 2520.53.2 Descartes, René. Unstersuchungen über die Grundlagen der Philosophie. 2e Aufl. Heidelberg, 1908.
Phil 2520.354 Descartes, sa "Méthode" et ses erreurs en physiologie. (Chauvois, Louis.) Paris, 1966.
Phil 2520.217 Descartes; sa vie, son oeuvre, avec un exposé de sa philosophie. 1e éd. (Cresson, André.) Paris, 1942.
Phil 2520.169.10 Descartes; sa vie et son oeuvre. (Adam, C.E.) Paris, 1937.
Phil 2520.242 Descartes, selon l'ordre des raisons. (Gueroult, Martial.) Paris, 1953. 2v.
Phil 2520.169.15 Descartes; ses amitiés féminines. (Adam, C.E.) Paris, 1937.
Phil 2520.95.5 Descartes; son histoire depuis 1637. (Millet, J.) Paris, 1876.
Phil 2520.105A Descartes, Spinoza...new philosophy. (Iverach, James.) N.Y., 1904.
Phil 2520.105.2 Descartes, Spinoza and the new philosophy. (Iverach, James.) Edinburgh, 1904.
Phil 4017.1 Descartes, Spinoza et la pensée italienne. (Rava, Adolfo.) Paris, 1927.
Phil 2520.219A Descartes, 1596-1650. (Descartes, René.) Genève, 1946.
Phil 2520.70 Descartes, 1596-1650. (Descartes, René.) Genève, 1948.
Phil 2520.193.10 Descartes. (Alquié, F.) Stuttgart, 1962.
Phil 2520.348 Descartes. (Barjonet-Huraux, Marcelle.) Paris, 1963.
Phil 2520.201 Descartes. (Buenos Aires. Universidad. Instituto de Filosofía.) Buenos Aires, 1937. 3v.
Phil 2520.208 Descartes. (Cassirer, E.) Stockholm, 1939.
Phil 2520.135 Descartes. (Chevalier, J.) Paris, 1921.
Phil 2520.114 Descartes. (Cochin, D.) Paris, 1913.
Phil 2520.112 Descartes. (Debricon, L.) Paris, n.d.
Phil 2520.69 Descartes. (Descartes, René.) Paris, 1947.
Phil 2520.64 Descartes. (Descartes, René.) Paris, 1969.
Phil 2520.121 Descartes. (Dimier, Louis.) Paris, 1917.
Phil 2520.89 Descartes. (Fouillée, A.) Paris, 1893.
Htn Phil 2520.148* Descartes. (Ganguli, S.) Bombay, 1900.
Phil 2520.250 Descartes. (Hagmann, Moritz.) Winterthur, 1955.
Phil 2520.187 Descartes. (Keeling, Stanley V.) London, 1934.
Phil 2520.165 Descartes. (Launay, Louis de.) Paris, 1923.
Phil 2520.228 Descartes. (Lefebvre, H.) Paris, 1947.
Phil 2520.93 Descartes. (Mahaffy, J.P.) Edinburgh, 1880.
Phil 2520.93.2.5 Descartes. (Mahaffy, J.P.) Edinburgh, 1884.
Phil 2520.93.3 Descartes. (Mahaffy, J.P.) Philadelphia, 1887.
Phil 2520.220 Descartes. (Mateu y Llopis, Felipe.) Barcelona, 1945.
Phil 2520.191 Descartes. (Merrylees, W.A.) Melbourne, 1934.
Phil 2520.212 Descartes. (Monteiro de Barros Lius, Ivan.) Rio de Janeiro, 1940.
Phil 2520.227 Descartes. (Paris. Bibliotheque Nationale.) Paris, 1937.
Phil 2520.347 Descartes. (Roed, Wolfgang.) München, 1964.
Phil 2520.343 Descartes. (Sassen, F.) Den Haag, 1963.
Phil 2520.233 Descartes. (Scholz, H.) Münster, 1951.
Phil 2520.79.10 Descartes. (Serrurier, C.) Paris, 1951.
Phil 2520.78.5 Descartes. Paris, 1957.
Phil 2520.187.2 Descartes. 2d ed. (Keeling, Stanley V.) London, 1968.
Phil 2520.93 Descartes. 5e éd. (Liard, Louis.) Paris, 1911.
Phil 2520.136 Descartes. 5e éd. (Landormy, Paul.) Paris, 1917?
Phil 2520.85 Descartes als Gegner des Sensualismus und Materialismus. (Bierendempfel, G.) Wolfenbüttel, 1884.
Phil 2520.300 Descartes and his philosophy. (Sebba, Gregor.) Athens, Ga., 1959.

Phil 2520.235   Descartes and the modern mind. (Balz, A.G.A.) New Haven, 1952.

Phil 2520.114.11   Descartes' Begründung der Erkenntnis. (Barth, Heinrich.) Bern, 1913.

Phil 2520.245   Descartes Dioptrik. (Leisegang, G.) Meisenheim am Glan, 1954.

Phil 2520.86.5   Descartes' discourse on method. (Roth, Leon.) Oxford, 1937.

Phil 2520.215   Descartes e Bergson. (Cannabrava, E.) São Paulo, 1942?

Phil 2520.133   Descartes' Erkenntnisslehre. Inaug.-Diss. (Oprescu, Georg.) Göttingen, 1889.

Phil 2520.107   Descartes' Erkenntnisstheorie. (Natorp, P.) Marburg, 1882.

Phil 2520.116.10   Descartes et la métaphysique scolastique. (Gilson, E.) Bruxelles, 1924.

Phil 2520.222   Descartes et la princesse Elisabeth. (Néel, Marguerite.) Paris, 1946.

Phil 2520.435   Descartes et la princesse Elisabeth. (Petit, Léon.) Paris, 1969.

Phil 2520.102.5   Descartes et la princesse palatine. (Foucher de Careil, A.) Paris, 1862.

Phil 2520.234A   Descartes et le cartésianisme hollandais. Paris, 1950[1951].

Phil 2520.275.10   Descartes et le rationalisme. (Rodis-Lewis, Geneviève.) Paris, 1966.

VPhil 2520.390   Descartes etikája. (Kalocsai, Dezso.) Budapest, 1964.

Phil 2520.250.2   Descartes in der Auffassung durch die Historiker der Philosophie. (Hagmann, Moritz.) Winterthur, 1955.

Phil 2520.174   Descartes le philosophie au masque. (Leroy, Maxime.) Paris, 1929. 2v.

Phil 2520.119.15.5   Descartes' Leben, Werke und Lehre. 5e Aufl. (Fischer, Kuno.) Heidelberg, 1912.

Phil 2520.183   Descartes' Leben und Metaphysik. Inaug.-Diss. (Barthel, A.) Erlangen, 1885.

Phil 2520.177   Descartes leer en leven. (Serrurier, C.) 's-Gravenhage, 1930.

Phil 2520.142   Descartes' Lehre von den angeborenen Ideen. Inaug.-Diss. (Grimm, E.) Jena, 1873.

Phil 2520.84   Descartes' Lehre von den Leidenschaften. (Bark, F.) Rostock, 1892.

Phil 2520.78.40   Descartes par lui-meme. (Descartes, René.) Paris, 1956.

Phil 2520.415   Descartes politico o della ragionevole ideologia. (Negri, Antonio.) Milano, 1970.

Phil 2520.163.5   Descartes' Prinzipien der Philosophie. (Spinoza, B. de.) Leipzig, 1922.

Phil 2520.138   Descartes savant. (Milhaud, G.S.) Paris, 1921.

Phil 2520.174.5   Descartes social. (Leroy, Maxime.) Paris, 1931.

Phil 2520.157   Descartes und die Fortbildung der kartesianischen Lehre. (Brockdorff, Cay von.) München, 1923.

Phil 2520.202   Descartes und die Philosophie. (Jaspers, Karl.) Berlin, 1937.

Phil 2520.202.5   Descartes und die Philosophie. 2. Aufl. (Jaspers, Karl.) Berlin, 1948.

Phil 2520.143   Descartes und die Renaissance. (Meier, M.) München, n.d.

Phil 2520.161   Descartes und die Scholastik. (Koyré, A.) Bonn, 1923.

Phil 2520.270   Descartes und Pascal. (Bievre, C. de.) Brasschaet, 1956.

Phil 2520.175   Descartes y el idealismo subjetivista moderno. (Palau, J.Y.) Barcelona, 1927.

Phil 2520.211   Descartes y su vida, su obra, su pensamiento. (Landermy, P.C.R.) México, 1940.

Phil 2520.198   Descartesova metoda ve vědách a ve filosofii. (Beneš, J.) V Praze, 1936.

Phil 2520.260   Descartes's Rules for the direction of the mind. (Joachim, H.H.) London, 1957.

Phil 2520.141   Descates' lära om känslan. Akademisk afhaudling. (Nordlindh, Arvid.) Upsala, 1897.

Phil 2496.85   Deschamps, A.F. Reflexions sur l'instruction synodale de Mgr. l'évêque de Poitiers. Paris, 1855.

Phil 6313.6   Deschamps, Albert. Les maladies de l'esprit et les asthénies. Paris, 1919.

Phil 3910.82   Des Champs, J. Cours abrégé de la philosophie Wolffienne. Amsterdam, 1743-47. 2v.

Phil 6060.2   Deschamps, L. La philosophie de l'écriture. Paris, 1892.

Phil 2555.1.86   Deschamps, L.M. Le vrai système. Genève, 1963.

Phil 2555.1.85   Deschamps, L.M. Le vrai système. Paris, 1939.

Phil 9450.12   Deschamps, Louis. Principes de morale sociale. Paris, 1903.

Phil 2805.227   Deschanel, E.A.E.M. Pascal, La Rochefoucauld, Bossuet. Paris, 1885.

Phil 5590.60   Deschoux, M. Essai sur la personnalité. 1. éd. Paris, 1949.

Phil 178.69   Deschoux, M. Initiation à la philosophie. 1. éd. Paris, 1951.

Phil 178.69.5   Deschoux, M. Itinéraire philosophique. Paris, 1964-1971. 5v.

Phil 2477.11.94   Deschoux, Marcel. Léon Brunschvicg ou l'idéalisme à hauteur d'homme. Paris, 1969.

Phil 2477.11.93   Deschoux, Marcel. La philosophie de Léon Brunschvicg. Paris, 1949.

Phil 2477.11.98   Deschoux, Marcel. La philosophie de Léon Brunschvicg. Thèse. Paris, 1949.

Phil 5845.2   Descloitres, Claudine. La psychologie applique en Afrique; bibliographie. Aix-en-Provence, 1968.

Phil 1170.26   Descombes, Vincent. Le platonisme. Paris, 1971.

Phil 1522.5.15   Descoqs, P. Thomisme et scolastique à propos de M. Rougier. 2e éd. Paris, 1935.

Phil 178.52   Descoqs, Paul. Institutiones metaphysicae generalis; éléments d'ontologie. Paris, 1925.

Phil 8658.15   Descoqs, Pedro. Praelectiones theologiae naturalis. Paris, 1932. 2v.

Phil 284.8   Descoqus, P. Essai critique sur l'hytemorphisme. Paris, 1924.

Phil 6953.4   Descourtis, G. Du fractionnement des opérations cérébrales. Paris, 1882.

Phil 6953.4.2   Descourtis, G. Du fractionnement des opérations cérébrales. Paris, 1882.

Phil 5590.32   Description and measurement of personality. (Cattell, Raymond B.) Yonkers-on-Hudson, 1946.

Phil 6111.51   A description of the brains...of two brothers dead of hereditary ataxia. (Barker, L.F.) Chicago, 1903.

Phil 6134.3A   Descriptive outline. 9th ed. (Yogananda, Swami.) Los Angeles, 1928.

Phil 5251.1.20   Descriptive psychology. (Ladd, G.T.) N.Y., 1898.

Phil 8882.68.10   Descriptivism. (Hare, Richard Mervyn.) London, 1965?

Phil 8735.5   Desdouits, M. L'homme et la création. 2. ed. Paris, 1846.

Phil 5753.1   Desdouits, T. De la liberté et des lois de la nature. Paris, 1868.

Phil 3485.6   Desdouits, T. La philosophie de Kant. Paris, 1876.

Phil 130.10   De Selincourt, Audrey. Six great thinkers. London, 1958.

Phil 8404.17   De Selincourt, O. Art and morality. London, 1935.

Phil 8328.2.2   Desenvolvimento e cultura. 2. ed. (Mello, Mario Vieira de Mello.) Rio de Janeiro, 1970.

Phil 7068.95.27   Desertis, V.C. Psychic philosophy as the foundation of a religion of natural law. 2. ed. London, 1901.

Phil 4983.74.31   Desesperación y rebeldía en la conciencia contempóranea. (Virasoro, M.A.) Bahia Blanca, 1959.

Phil 5635.13   De Seze, V. Recherches...sur la sensibilité. Paris, 1786.

Phil 8628.10   Des Georges, A. La réincarnation des âmes selon les traditions orientales et occidentales. Paris, 1966.

Phil 2805.217   Desgrippes, George. Études sur Pascal de l'automatisme a la foi. Paris, 19- .

Phil 6313.18   Deshaies, Gabriel. Psychopathologie générale. Paris, 1959.

Phil 8878.36   Deshumbert, Marius. An ethical system based on the laws of nature. Chicago, 1917.

Phil 8878.36.8   Deshumbert, Marius. Morale fondée sur les lois de la nature. 3e éd. Paris, 191-.

Phil 960.130   Desia, Shantaram Anant. A study of Indian philosophy. Bombay, 1976.

Phil 551.1   Desiat' ispovedi. (Kichanova, Inga M.) Moskva, 1971.

Phil 5594.156A   Design and analysis of experiments in psychology and education. (Lindquist, Everet F.) Boston, 1956.

Phil 8598.34.5   The design argument reconsidered. (Shebbeare, Charles J.) London, 1923.

Phil 8598.34.6   The design argument reconsidered. (Shebbeare, Charles J.) London, 1923.

Phil 6110.22   Design for a brain. (Ashby, William R.) N.Y., 1952.

Phil 6110.22.2   Design for a brain. 2. ed. (Ashby, William R.) N.Y., 1960.

Phil 5627.134.54   Design for dedication. (Howard, Peter.) Chicago, 1964.

Phil 5520.145.10   Design for escape; world education through modern media. 1. ed. (Richards, Ivor Armstrong.) N.Y., 1968.

Phil 5520.375   Design for thinking. (Upton, Albert.) Stanford, 1961.

Phil 5520.374   Design for thinking. (Upton, Albert.) Whittier, Calif, 1948.

Phil 8668.9   Le désir de Dieu. (Nabert, Jean.) Paris, 1966.

Phil 175.43   Le désir d'éternité. 1. ed. (Alquié, Ferdinand.) Paris, 1943.

Phil 175.43.4   Le désir d'éternité. 4th ed. (Alquié, Ferdinand.) Paris, 1963.

Phil 5261.19   Le désir du néant. (Vialle, L.) Paris, 1933.

Phil 5261.19.5   Le désir du néant. Thèse. (Vialle, L.) Paris, 1932.

Phil 365.36   Desire and creation. (Monsarrat, K.W.) Liverpool, 1932.

Phil 193.88   Desire and reason. (Spalding, K.J.) London, 1922.

Phil 8876.46   The desire for qualities. (Bligh, S.M.) London, n.d.

Phil 9320.10   Desjardins, Arnaud. Les chemins de la sagesse. Paris, 1969- 2v.

Phil 8615.7   Desjardins, P. The present duty. Philadelphia, 1893.

Phil 5068.56.10   Deskription, Analytizität und Existenz. (Weingartner, Paul.) Salzburg, 1966.

Phil 9245.36.5   Deslandes, A.F.B. The art of being easy at all times and in all places. London, 1724.

Phil 803.1   Deslandes, A.F.B. Histoire critique de la philosophie. London, 1742. 3v.

Phil 803.1.5   Deslandes, A.F.B. Historie critique de la philosophie. Amsterdam, 1756. 4v.

Phil 2835.89   Desmaze, Charles. P. Ramus, professeur au Collège de France. Sa vie. Genève, 1970.

Phil 7069.44.25   Desmond, S. Love after death. London, 1944.

Phil 8628.8   Desmond, Shaw. How you live when you die. London, 1942.

Phil 7069.46.15   Desmond, Shaw. Spiritualism. London, 1946?

Phil 5813.4   Desmoulins, A. Anatomie des systèmes nerveux des animaux. pt.1-2. Atlas. Paris, 1825. 3v.

Phil 2430.6   Desné, Roland. Les materialistes français de 1750 à 1800. Paris, 1965.

Phil 6311.35   La désorganisation de la personnalité. (Baruk, Henri.) Paris, 1952.

Phil 6673.7   Despine, P. Étude scientifique sur le somnambulisme. Paris, 1880.

Phil 5243.6   Despine, P. Psychologie naturelle. Paris, 1868. 3v.

Phil 6953.7   Despine, Prosper. De la folie au point de vue philosophique. Paris, 1875.

Phil 1135.179   Des Places, E. Syngeneia. Paris, 1964.

Phil 4829.160.80   Despot, Branko. Filozofija Djue Arnolda. Zagreb, 1970.

Phil 8583.30   Desquiron de Saint Agnan, A.T. Dieu, la nature et la loi. Paris, 1814.

Phil 8878.41   Dessaignes, J.P. Études de l'homme moral. Paris, 1882. 3v.

Phil 8693.20   Dessauer, F. Am Rande der Dinge. 2. Aufl. Frankfurt, 1952.

Phil 8693.20.10   Dessauer, F. Auf den Spuren der Unendlichkeit. Frankfurt, 1954.

Phil 8693.14   Dessauer, F. Leben, Natur, Religion. 2. Aufl. Bonn, 1926.

Phil 8693.20.5   Dessauer, F. Religion im Lichte der heutigen Naturwissenschaft. 3. Aufl. Frankfurt, 1952.

Phil 9240.18   Dessauer, F.J. Prometheus und die Weltübel. Frankfurt, 1959.

Phil 3195.18.30   Dessauer, Friedrich. Durch die Tore der neuen Zeit. Göttingen, 1961.

Phil 284.15   Dessauer, Friedrich. Naturwissenschaftliches Erkennen. Frankfurt, 1958.

Phil 3625.1.103   Dessauer, M. Der deutsche Plato. Berlin, 1879.

Phil 3823.1   Dessauer, M. Der Sokrates der Neuzeit...Spinoza's. Cöthen, 1877.

Phil 3823.1.5   Dessauer, M. Spinoza and Hobbes. Breslau, 1868.

Phil 8583.43.5   Dessauer, Philipp. Meditation im christlichen Dasein. München, 1968.

Phil 8583.43   Dessauer, Philipp. Die naturale Meditation. München, 1961.

Phil 2520.325   Le dessein de la sagesse cartésienne. (Cómbes, J.) Lyon, 1960.

Phil 5875.110   Le dessin chez l'enfant. (Debienne, Marie Claire.) Paris, 1968.

Phil 8404.15   Dessoir, Max. Ästhetik und allgemeine Kunstwissenschaft. Stuttgart, 1923.

Phil 5213.1.5   Dessoir, M. Abriss einer Geschichte der Psychologie. Heidelberg, 1911.

Phil 5213.1   Dessoir, M. Geschichte der neueren deutschen Psychologie. Berlin, 1897.

Phil 5213.1.9A   Dessoir, M. Outline...history of psychology. N.Y., 1912.

Phil 8404.15.2   Dessoir, Max. Ästhetik und allgemeine Kunstwissenschaft in den Grundzügen dargestellt. Stuttgart, 1906.

Phil 8404.15.5   Dessoir, Max. Beiträge zur allgemeinen Kunstwissenschaft. Stuttgart, 1929.

Phil 7103.2   Dessoir, Max. Bibliographie des modernen Hypnotismus. Berlin, 1888.

Phil 178.17.10   Dessoir, Max. Bibliographie des modernen Hypnotismus. n.p., 1888-1913. 25 pam.

Phil 7103.2.1   Dessoir, Max. Bibliographie des modernen Hypnotismus. Nachtrag. Berlin, 1890.

Phil 3195.11.35   Dessoir, Max. Buch der Erinnerung. 2. Aufl. Stuttgart, 1947.

Phil 7042.2   Dessoir, Max. Das Doppel-Ich. Leipzig, 1890.

Phil 7042.2.2   Dessoir, Max. Das Doppel-Ich. 2e Aufl. Leipzig, 1896.

Phil 178.17.15   Dessoir, Max. Einleitung in die Philosophie. Stuttgart, 1936.

Phil 178.17.17   Dessoir, Max. Einleitung in die Philosophie. 2. Aufl. Stuttgart, 1946.

Phil 178.17   Dessoir, Max. Philosophisches Lesebuch. Stuttgart, 1903.

Phil 178.17.3   Dessoir, Max. Philosophisches Lesebuch. Stuttgart, 1910.

Phil 5243.25.5   Dessoir, Max. Psychologische Briefe. Berlin, 1948.

Phil 5257.21   Dessoir, Max. Psychologische Skizzen, von Edmund W. Rells. Leipzig, 1893.

Phil 5243.25   Dessoir, Max. Vom Diesseits der Seele. Leipzig, 1923.

Phil 6313.4.3   Dessoir, Max. Vom Jenseits der Seele. 3. Aufl. Stuttgart, 1919.

Phil 665.26   Il destarsi delle anime. (Melegari, Dora.) Milano, 1915.

Phil 4803.454.40   Le destin de la France, de l'Allemagne, et de la Russie, comme prolégomènes du messianisme. (Hoene-Wroński, Józef Maria.) Paris, 1842.

Phil 3450.19.450   Le destin de la pensée et la mort de Dieu selon Heidegger. (Laffoucrière, Odette.) La Haye, 1968.

Phil 3246.35.9   Destination de l'homme. (Fichte, Johann Gottlieb.) Paris, 1832.

Phil 3246.35.5   Destination of man. (Fichte, Johann Gottlieb.) London, 1846.

Phil 8640.7.2   La destinée de l'homme. 2. éd. (Piat, A.) Paris, 1912.

Phil 2725.25.5   Destinée et valeur. (Pirlot, J.) Namur, 1950?

Phil 5440.30   Il destino del dinastie. (Revda, A.) Torino, 1904.

Phil 8610.963   El destino humano en el realismo introspectivo. (Lahoz Lainez, Bienvenido.) Madrid, 1963.

Phil 6952.21.15   Destiny and disease in mental disorders. (Campbell, C.M.) N.Y., 1935.

Phil 8876.91.12A   The destiny of man. (Berdiaev, N.A.) London, 1959.

Phil 8876.91.11   The destiny of man. (Berdiaev, N.A.) N.Y., 1960.

Phil 8630.3   The destiny of man. (Fiske, J.) Boston, 1884.

Phil 192.66   The destiny of modern thought. (Rothschild, R.) N.Y., 1930.

Phil 1750.40   The destiny of the mind. (Haas, William S.) N.Y., 1956.

Phil 978.74.35   The destiny of the nations. (Bailey, A.A. (Mrs.).) N.Y., 1949.

Htn   Phil 1020.4.1*   Destructio destructionú. (Averroës.) Lugduni, 1529.

Phil 3011.6.5   La destruction de la raison. (Lukács, G.) Paris, 1958-59. 2v.

Phil 5170.7   The destructive hypothetical syllogism in Greek logic and in Attic oratory. (Wilcox, Stanley.) n.p., 1938.

Phil 2523.30   Destutt de Tracy, A.L.C. Élémens d'idéologie. Paris, 1817-18. 4v.

Phil 2523.32   Destutt de Tracy, A.L.C. Élémens d'idéologie. Paris, 1825-27. 5v.

Phil 2523.31   Destutt de Tracy, A.L.C. Elementi d'ideologia. Milano, 1817-19. 10v.

Phil 2523.45   Destutt de Tracy, A.L.C. Principes logiques. Paris, 1817. 2 pam.

Phil 2523.50   Destutt de Tracy, A.L.C. Principes logiques. Paris, 1817.

Phil 2523.80   Pamphlet box. Destutt de Tracy, A.L.C.

Phil 3485.32   Destutt de Tracy, Antoine Louis Claude. La métaphysique de Kant. Bruxelles, 1968.

Phil 7140.11   Die Desuggestion; ihre Bedeutung und Auswertung. (Tietjens, E.) Berlin, 1928.

Phil 7140.11.5   Desuggestion for the attainment of health. (Tietjens, E.) London, 1931.

Phil 5635.15   Desvaux, Antoine. Introduction à une étude du courant de chaleur. Thèse. Paris, 1914.

Phil 3011.10   Det organiska livet i tysk debatt, 1795-1845. Thesis. (Liedman, Sven Eric.) Land, 1966.

Phil 2255.1.131   A detailed catalogue of the archives of Bertrand Russell. (Russell, Bertrand Russell.) London, 1967.

Phil 803.5   Deter, C.J. Abriss der Geschichte der Philosophie. Berlin, 1913.

Phil 9344.6   Deterioration of the Puritan stock. (Ellis, John.) N.Y., 1884.

Phil 735.150.2   Les déterminants de la théorie générale de la valeur et ses applications en esthétique, en religion, en morale, en économie et en politique. 2e éd. (Glansdorff, Maxime.) Bruxelles, 1966.

Phil 5643.36   The determination of the position. (Burrow, N.J.) Baltimore, 1909.

Phil 384.15   Determination und Freiheit. 1. Aufl. (Welte, Bernhard.) Frankfurt, 1969.

Phil 3450.18.180   Determination und Freiheit bei Nicolai Hartmanns. (Theisen, Hans.) Köln, 1962.

Phil 9150.34   Determinatsaia evoliutsionnogo professor. (Volkova, Emma V.) Minsk, 1971.

Phil 9250.34   Determinatsiia evoliutsionnogo protsessa. (Volkova, Emma V.) Minsk, 1971.

Phil 5242.41   La determinazione del presente psichico. (Calabresi, R.) Firenze, 1930.

Phil 384.10   Determinism, free will, and moral responsibility. (Dworkin, Gerald.) Englewood Cliffs, 1970.

Phil 5751.15   Determinism, indeterminism, and libertarianism. (Broad, C.D.) Cambridge, Eng., 1934.

Phil 5751.8   Determinism: false and true. (Ballard, F.) London, 1911.

Phil 70.40   Determinism and freedom in the age of modern science. (Hook, Sidney.) N.Y., 1958.

Phil 5755.13   Determinism from Hobbes to Hume. Inaug. Diss. (Fruit, John P.) Leipzig, 1895.

Phil 5752.7   Determinism or free-will? (Cohen, Chapman.) London, 1919.

Phil 186.76.5   Le déterminisme biologique et la personnalité consciente. (Le Dantec, Félix.) Paris, 1897.

Phil 5761.16   Le déterminisme des lois de la nature et la réalité. Thèse. (Leenhardt, Henry.) Montpellier, 1924.

Phil 504.2   Déterminisme et indéterminisme. 1. éd. (Février, Paulette.) Paris, 1955.

Phil 3552.306   Le déterminisme monadique. (Rolland, E.) Paris, 1935.

Phil 3552.306.5   Le déterminisme monadique. Thèse. (Rolland, E.) Paris, 1935.

Phil 2050.194   Determinismen eller Hume imod Kant. (Howitz, Franz G.) Kjøbenhavn, 1824.

Phil 5756.8   Determinismen og dens konsekvenser. (Gjersjø, O.) Kristiania, 1907.

Phil 5752.11   Les déterminismes et les êtres. Thèse. (Cesari, P.) Paris, 1938.

Phil 5751.12   El determinismo en la ciencia y en la vida. (Bermann, G.) Buenos Aires, 1920.

Phil 5760.2   Determinismus und Strafe. (Klippel, T.) Berlin, 1890.

Phil 3552.120.10   Der Determinismus von Leibnitz. (Class, Gustav.) Tübingen, 1874.

Phil 310.658   Determinizm dialekticheskogo materializma. (Parniuk, Mikhail A.) Kiev, 1967.

Phil 270.115   Determinizm i indet w aspekcie fizykalrym i filozoficznym. (Mazierski, S.) Lublin, 1961.

Phil 1182.53   Detienne, M. La notion de daimôn dans le pythagorisme ancien. Paris, 1963.

Phil 1108.6   Detienne, Marcel. Les maîtres de vérité dans le Grèce archaique. Paris, 1967.

NEDL   Phil 9510.1.5   Detraction displayed. (Opie, A.A. (Mrs.).) N.Y., 1828.

Phil 9510.1   Detraction displayed. (Opie, A.A. (Mrs.).) Philadelphia, 1828.

Phil 3640.256   Détresses de Nietzsche. (Vialle, Louis.) Paris, 1932.

Phil 3640.256.5   Détresses de Nietzsche. Thèse. (Vialle, Louis.) Paris, 1932.

Phil 8599.16.10   De Tribus Impostoribus. De tribus impostoribus. Berlin, 1960.

Phil 8599.16.6   De Tribus Impostoribus. De tribus impostoribus. Paris, 1861.

Htn   Phil 8599.16.5*   De Tribus Impostoribus. De tribus impostoribus. Paris, 1861.

Phil 8599.16.9   De Tribus Impostoribus. De tribus impostoribus. 2. Aufl. Heilbronn, 1876.

Phil 3195.5.81   Deubler, Konrad. Tagebücher...Bauernphilosophen. Leipzig, 1886. 2v.

Phil 13.5   Deucalion; cahiers de philosophie. Paris. 1-6 3v.

Phil 3823.16   Deugd, Cornelis de. The significance of Spinoza's first kind of knowledge. Assen, 1966.

Phil 8670.19   Deus, pensamento e universo. (Pinto, Raphael de Souza.) Curitiba, 1959.

Phil 8580.31   Deus o o homem na poesia e na filosofia. (Amorim de Carvalho.) Porto, 195-.

Phil 803.3.2   Deussen, P. Allgemeine Geschichte der Philosophie. Leipzig, 1907-020. 3v.

Phil 803.3   Deussen, P. Allgemeine Geschichte der Philosophie. v.1, pts.1-3. v.2, pts.1-3. Leipzig, 1894-1917. 7v.

Phil 803.3.1A   Deussen, P. Allgemeine Geschichte der Philosophie. v.1-2. Leipzig, 1894-1920. 7v.

Phil 803.4.15   Deussen, P. Discours de la méthode pour bien étudier l'histoire de la philosophie. Paris, n.d.

Phil 178.5.2   Deussen, P. Die Elemente der Metaphysik. Aachen, 1877.

Phil 178.5   Deussen, P. Elemente der Metaphysik. 2. Aufl. Leipzig, 1890.

Phil 178.5.3   Deussen, P. Die Elemente der Metaphysik. 6e Aufl. Leipzig, 1919.

NEDL   Phil 178.5.5   Deussen, P. Elements of metaphysics. London, 1894. (Changed to KD 25702)

Phil 960.3.2   Deussen, P. On the philosophy of the Vedânta in its relations to occidental metaphysics. Bombay, 1893.

Phil 960.3.4.5   Deussen, P. Outline of the Vedânta system of philosophy. Cambridge, 1906.

Phil 960.3.4A   Deussen, P. Outline of the Vedânta system of philosophy. 2d ed. N.Y., 1906.

Phil 960.3.9   Deussen, P. Outlines of Indian philosophy. Berlin, 1907.

Phil 1108.2   Deussen, P. Philosophie der Griechen. Leipzig, 1911.

Phil 960.3.7   Deussen, P. The philosophy of the Upanishads. Edinburgh, 1906.

Phil 960.3.8   Deussen, P. The philosophy of the Upanishads. Edinburgh, 1908.

Phil 960.3.8.5   Deussen, P. The philosophy of the Upanishads. N.Y., 1966.

Phil 960.3   Deussen, P. System des Vedânta. Leipzig, 1883.

Phil 960.3.8   Deussen, P. System of the Vedânta. Chicago, 1912.

Phil 960.3.15   Deussen, P. Vedânta, Platon und Kant. 2. Aufl. Wien, 1917.

Phil 960.3.19   Deussen, P. Vedânta und Platonismus im Lichte der kantischen Philosophie. Berlin, 1922.

Phil 8583.16.8   Deussen, Paul. Bibelns filosofi. Stockholm, 1916.

Phil 3640.169   Deussen, Paul. Erinnerungen an Friedrich Nietzsche. Leipzig, 1901.

Phil 3110.151   Deussen, Paul. Jakob Böhme. Leipzig, 1911.

Phil 3485.1   Deussen, Paul. Der kategorische Imperativ. Kiel, 1891.

Phil 3485.1.5   Deussen, Paul. Der kategorische Imperativ. 2. Aufl. Kiel, 1903.

Phil 3195.7.80   Deussen, Paul. Mein Leben. Leipzig, 1922.

Phil 8583.16   Deussen, Paul. Die Philosophie der Bibel. 2. Aufl. Leipzig, 1919.

Phil 1508.1.2   Deussen, Paul. Die Philosophie des Mittelalters. 2. Aufl. Leipzig, 1919.

Phil 5243.44.5   Deut, John Y. The human machine. N.Y., 1937.

Phil 5243.44   Deut, John Y. Reactions of the human machine. London, 1936.

Phil 7060.62   Deuteroskopia; or, A brief discourse concerning the second sight. (Frazer, John.) Edinburgh, 1820

Phil 3195.2.85   Deutinger, Martin. Martin Deutinger. München, 1938.

Phil 6945.17.2   Deutsch, Albert. The mentally ill in America. 2. ed. N.Y., 1960.

Phil 6945.17.3   Deutsch, Albert. The mentally ill in America. 2. ed. N.Y., 1962.

Phil 6945.30   Deutsch, Albert. The shame of the States. 1. ed. N.Y., 1948.

Phil 6313.14.5   Deutsch, Felix. Applied psychoanalysis. N.Y., 1949.

Phil 6313.14   Deutsch, Felix. The clinical interview. v.1-2. N.Y., 1955. 2v.

Phil 6113.32   Deutsch, Felix. On the mysterious leap from the mind to the body. N.Y., 1959.

Phil 6313.8.10   Deutsch, Helene. Neuroses and character types. London, 1965.

Phil 6313.8   Deutsch, Helene. Psycho-analysis of the neuroses. London, 1932.

Phil 6313.8.5   Deutsch, Helene. Psychoanalyse der Neurosen. Wien, 1930.

Phil 5243.55   Deutsch, Jaroslav A. The structural basis of behavior. Chicago, 1960.

Phil 5876.10.10   Deutsch, Thelene. Selected problems of adolescence; with special emphasis on group formation. N.Y., 1967.

Phil 8125.12   Die deutsche Asthetik der Gegenwart. (Moos, Paul.) Berlin, 1919.

Phil 8125.12.5   Die deutsche Asthetik der Gegenwart. (Moos, Paul.) Berlin, 1931.

Phil 3001.9   Die deutsche Auflslärungsphilosophie. (Brockdorff, C.) München, 1926.

Phil 13.7   Deutsche Beiträge zur Philosophie der Zeit. München. 1,1948

Phil 1750.179.10 Deutsche Existenzphilosophie. (Bollnow, O.F.) Bern, 1953.
Phil 3013.2 Deutsche Geisteswelt. (Noack, H.) Darmstadt, 1955. 2v.
Phil 70.9.25 Deutsche Gesellschaft für Psychologie. Bericht über den Kongress. Jena. 14,1934
Phil 3002.4 Der deutsche Idealismus. (Cohn, Jonas.) Leipzig, 1923.
Phil 400.65 Der deutsche Idealismus und das Christentum. (Groos, H.) München, 1927.
Phil 3007.10.5 Das deutsche in der deutschen Philosophie. 2. Aufl. (Haering, Theodor Lorenz.) Stuttgart, 1942.
Phil 3005.7 Deutsche Klassik und Reformation. (Franz, Erich.) Halle, 1937.
Phil 3006.9.5 Der deutsche Materialismus am Ausgang des 18. Jahrhunderts. (Gulyga, A.V.) Berlin, 1966.
Phil 6990.39 Deutsche Mirakelbücher. (Schreiber, G.) Dusseldorf, 1938.
Phil 530.20.15 Die deutsche Mystik. (Greith, Carl.) Freiburg, 1861.
Phil 530.20.45 Die deutsche Mystik. (Schellenberg, E.L.) Berlin, 1919.
Phil 530.20.85 Die deutsche Mystik unter besonderer Berücksichtigung des "cherubinischen Wandersmannes" Johann Schefflers. (Neuwinger, R.) Bleicherode am Harz, 1937.
Phil 530.20.93 Deutsche Mystik zwischen Mittelalter und Neuzeit. 2. Aufl. (Wentzlaff-Eggebert, F.W.) Tübingen, 1947.
Phil 530.20.93.3 Deutsche Mystik zwischen Mittelalter und Neuzeit. 3. Aufl. (Wentzlaff-Eggebert, F.W.) Berlin, 1969.
Phil 530.20.65 Deutsche Mystiker. (Scholz, W. von.) Berlin, 1927.
Phil 530.20.5 Deutsche Mystiker des vierzehnten Jahrhunderts. (Pfeiffer, Franz.) Leipzig, 1845. 2v.
Phil 530.20.9 Deutsche Mystiker des vierzehnten Jahrhunderts. v.2. (Pfeiffer, Franz.) Göttingen, 1914.
Phil 530.20.7 Deutsche Mystiker des vierzehnten Jahrhunderts. 2e Aufl. (Pfeiffer, Franz.) Göttingen, 1907. 2v.
Phil 530.20.86 Deutsche Mystikerbriefe. (Oehl, W.) München, 1931.
Phil 530.20.87 Deutsche Mystikertexte des Mittelalters. (Quint, J.) Bonn, 1929.
Phil 3001.11 Deutsche Philosophen. (Becher, Erich.) München, 1929.
Phil 3018.38 Deutsche Philosophen: von Eckhart his Heidegger. (Sauer, Ernst Friedrich.) Göttingen, 1968.
Phil 3003.8 Die deutsche Philosophie. (Akademiia Nauk SSSR. Institut Filosofii.) Berlin, 1961.
Phil 3001.2 Die deutsche Philosophie. (Biedermann, F.C.) Leipzig, 1842. 2v.
Phil 1703.2.15 Die deutsche Philosophie der Gegenwart. (Drews, Arthur.) Berlin, 1922.
Phil 3012.3 Die deutsche Philosophie des 20. Jahrhunderts. (Moog, Willy.) Stuttgart, 1922.
Phil 3000.8 Deutsche Philosophie heute. (Albrecht, Herbert.) Bremen, 1969.
Phil 4960.220.5 Die deutsche Philosophie in Argentinien. (Alberini, Coriolano.) Berlin, 1930.
Phil 3014.1A Die deutsche Philosophie inder zweiten Halfte des neunzehnten Jahrhund. (Oesterreich, K.) Tübingen, 1910.
Phil 3003.10 Die deutsche Philosophie nach 1945. (Akademiia Nauk SSSR. Institut Filosofii.) Berlin, 1961.
Phil 3015.2 Deutsche Philosophie v.2. (Przygodda, Paul.) Berlin, 1916.
Phil 75.21 Deutsche Philsophische Gesellschaft. Literarische Berichte. Erfurt. 8-26 19v.
Phil 3625.1.103 Der deutsche Plato. (Dessauer, M.) Berlin, 1879.
Phil 13.1 Deutsche Psychologie. Langensolza. 1-7,1918-1932+ 5v.
Phil 3552.23.5 Deutsche Schriften. (Leibniz, Gottfried Wilhelm.) Berlin, 1838-40. 2v.
Phil 3552.23 Deutsche Schriften. (Leibniz, Gottfried Wilhelm.) Leipzig, 1916. 2v.
Phil 3003.1 Die deutsche Spekulation seit Kant. (Drews, A.) Berlin, 1893. 2v.
Phil 3018.15 Deutsche systematische Philosophie nach ihren Gestaltern. (Schwarz, H.) Berlin, 1931-34. 2v.
Phil 1701.10 Deutsche und ausserdeutsche Philosophie. (Baumann, Julius.) Gotha, 1903.
Phil 3007.10 Die deutsche und die europäische Philosophie. (Haering, Theodor Lorenz.) Stuttgart, 1943.
Phil 735.81 Deutsche Wertphilosophie der Gegenwart. (Messer, August.) Leipzig, 1926.
Phil 13.9 Deutsche Zeitschrift für Philosophie. Berlin. 1,1953+ 30v.
Phil 13.9.2 Deutsche Zeitschrift für Philosophie. Beiheft. Berlin. 1,1953+
Phil 530.20.10 Die deutschen Mystiker. (Böhringer, F.) Zürich, 1855.
Phil 530.20.51 Die deutschen Mystiker des 14. Jahrhunderts. (Denifle, H.) Freiburg in der Schweiz, 1951.
Phil 3018.22 Deutschen Philosophen des 19. Jahrhunderts. (Schneider, P.) Berlin, 1927.
Phil 3011.3.15 Die deutschen Philosophie der Gegenwart. (Lehmann, G.) Stuttgart, 1943.
Phil 70.26 Deutscher Kongress für Philosophie, 3rd, Brenen, 1950. Symphilosophein. München. 1952
Phil 70.26.6 Deutscher Kongress für Philosophie, 6th, München, 1960. Das Problem der Ordnung. Meisenheim. 1962
Phil 70.26.7 Deutscher Kongress für Philosophie, 7th, Münster, 1962. Die Philosophie und die Frage nach dem Fortschritt. München. 1964
Phil 70.26.8 Deutscher Kongress für Philosophie, 8th, Heidelberg, 1966. Das Problem der Sprache. München. 1967
Phil 43.1 Deutscher Monistenbund. Flugschriften. Brackwede. 3-30,1906-1914 16v.
Phil 3003.6 Deutschlands Denker seit Kant. Dessan, 1851.
Phil 3003.2 Deutschthümler, W. Ueber Schopenhauer zu Kant; ein Kleines Geschichtsbild. Wien, 1899.
Phil 3246.240 Deutschtum und Christentum bei Fichte. (Gehlen, Arnold.) Berlin, 1935.
Phil 978.110 Deutschtum und Christentum in der Theosophie des Goetheanismus. (Ballmer, Karl.) Besazio, 1966.
Phil 3488.27 Deutung und Darstellung der theoretischen Philosophie Kants. (Groyeff, F.) Hamburg, 1951.
Phil 5247.26 Die Deutungen des psychophysischen Gesetzes. (Hering, Ewald.) Tübingen, 1909.
Phil 192.78.5 Les deux chemins. (Rivier, W.) Bruxelles, 1951.
Phil 287.2 Les deux creations. (Giera, Jules.) Paris, 1872.
Phil 2672.91 Deux études sur Jouffroy et son temps. (Pommier, J.J.M.) Paris, 1930.
Phil 2477.6.80.5 Deux études sur "La pensée de M. Blondel". (Tonquedec, J. de.) Paris, 1936.
Phil 178.19.5 Les deux idéalismes. (Dunan, Charles.) Paris, 1911.
Phil 178.58 Les deux ordres, psychique el material. (Dewe, Joseph A.) Paris, 1929.
Phil 178.58.5 Les deux ordres, psychique et materiel. Thèse. (Dewe, Joseph A.) Paris, 1929.

Phil 2805.65 Deux pièces imparfaites sur la grâce et le concile de trente. (Pascal, Blaise.) Paris, 1947.
Phil 5520.64 Les deux pôles de l'esprit. (Mannoury, G.) Amsterdam, 1932.
Phil 8905.22 Les deux sources, consciente et inconsciente, de la vie morale. 2. éd. (Odier, Charles.) Neuchâtel, 1968.
Phil 2475.1.38.4 Les deux sources. (Bergson, Henri.) Paris, 1932.
Phil 9070.49.5 Les deux sources consciente et inconsciente de la vie morale. 2d éd. (Odier, Charles.) Neuchâtel, 1947.
Phil 2475.1.38.2 Les deux sources de la morale et de la religion. (Bergson, Henri.) Genève, 1945.
Phil 2475.1.38 Les deux sources de la morale et de la religion. 14 éd. (Bergson, Henri.) Paris, 1933.
Phil 293.29 Deux thèmes de la cosmologie grecque. (Mugler, Charles.) Paris, 1953.
Phil 8400.36.2 Deuxième congrès international d'esthétique. (International Congress on Aesthetics, 2nd, Paris, 1937.) Paris, 1937. 2v.
Phil 960.163 Devanandan, P.D. The concept of Maya. London, 1950.
Phil 5252.74.5 Devant la réalité. 1. éd. (Malgand, W.) Paris, 1953.
Phil 803.10 Devaux, P. De Thales à Bergson. Liége, 1955.
Phil 2120.4.90 Devaux, P. Le pragmatisme conceptuel de Clarence Irwing Lewis. Paris, 1934.
Phil 1845.3.90 Devaux, P. Le système d'Alexander. Paris, 1929.
Phil 5850.149 Developing and using your inner powers. (Capps, Ora L.) Denver, 1932.
Phil 3425.218.5 The development, significance and some limitatioms of Hegel's ethical teaching. (Chang, W.S.) Shanghai, 1926.
Phil 18.7.11 Development...psycho-analytical theory of psychosis, 1893-1926. (Richman, John.) London, 1928.
Phil 6405.2 Development and disorders of written language. (Myklebust, Helmer R.) N.Y., 1965.
Phil 365.6 Development and evolution. (Baldwin, J.M.) N.Y., 1902.
Phil 8350.2 The development and philosophy of Australian aestheticism. (Rankin, D.H.) Melbourne, 1949.
Phil 365.25 Development and purpose. (Hobhouse, L.T.) London, 1913.
Phil 365.25.2 Development and purpose. (Hobhouse, L.T.) London, 1927.
Phil 5535.20 Development in learning. (Lunzer, Eric Anthony.) London, 1968- 3v.
Phil 5251.60 Development in mathematical psychology. (Luce, Robert D.) Glencoe, 1960.
Phil 165.2A The development of American philosophy. (Muelder, Walter G.) Boston, 1940.
Phil 165.2.5 The development of American philosophy. 2. ed. (Muelder, Walter G.) Boston, 1960.
Phil 5027.3.5 The development of Arabic logic. (Rescher, N.) Pittsburgh, 1964.
Phil 5875.130 Development of audiolinguistic skills in children. (Mecham, Merlin J.) St. Louis, 1969.
Phil 1870.100 The development of Berkeley's philosophy. (Johnston, G.A.) London, 1923.
Phil 1822.1 The development of British thought. (Waddington, M.) Toronto, 1919.
Phil 9035.34 The development of character. (Newfang, Oscar.) N.Y., 1921.
Phil 6315.2.144 Development of Freud's conception of anxiety. (Carlemans, A.) Amsterdam, 1949.
Phil 1105.4 The development of Greek philosophy. (Adamson, Robert.) Edinburgh, 1908.
Phil 2138.114.2 Development of John S. Mill's system of logic. (Kubitz, O.A.) Urbana, 1932.
Phil 2138.114 Development of John S. Mill's system of logic. Thesis. (Kubitz, O.A.) Urbana, 1932.
Phil 3503.9.10 Development of Kantian thought. (Vleeschauwer, H.J.) London, 1962.
Phil 5020.5 The development of logic. (Kneale, William Calvert.) Oxford, 1962.
Phil 5020.5.10 The development of logic. (Kneale, William Calvert.) Oxford, 1968.
Phil 930.28A Development of logical method in China. (Hu, Suh.) Shanghai, 1922.
Phil 5023.1 The development of mathematical logic. (Nidditch, Peter.) London, 1962.
Phil 990.1.3 The development of metaphysics in Persia. (Igbal, S.M.) Lahore, 19- .
Phil 990.1.2 The development of metaphysics in Persia. (Igbal, S.M.) London, 1908.
Phil 1700.1 The development of modern philosophy. Photoreproduction. (Adamson, R.) Edinburgh, 1903 2v.
Phil 960.248.2 Development of moral philosophy in India. (Dasgupta, Surama.) N.Y., 1965.
Phil 2225.5.104 The development of Peirce's philosophy. (Murphey, M.G.) Cambridge, 1961.
Phil 935.5 The development of philosophy in Japan. (Kishinami, T.) Princeton, 1915.
Phil 6315.1.17 The development of psychoanalysis. (Ferenczi, Sandor.) N.Y., 1925.
Phil 8590.7 The development of religion. (King, I.) N.Y., 1910.
Phil 8050.47 The development of taste, and other studies in aesthetics. (Begg, W.P.) Glasgow, 1887.
Phil 5585.291 The development of the concept of space in the child. (Laurondeau, Monique.) N.Y., 1970.
Phil 6321.49.2 The development of the mind. (Lampl de Groot, Jeanne.) London, 1966.
Phil 6321.49 The development of the mind. (Lampl de Groot, Jeanne.) N.Y., 1965.
Phil 310.24 The development of the monist view of history. (Plekhanov, G.V.) Moscow, 1956.
Phil 5585.150 Development of the perceptual world. (Solley, Charles.) N.Y., 1960.
X Cg Phil 7075.127 The development of the sexual impulses. (Money-Kyrle, R.E.) London, 1932.
Phil 5853.8 Developmental counseling. (Blocher, Donald H.) N.Y., 1966.
Phil 5875.150 Developmental patterns in reactions to frustration. (Pareek, Udai Narain.) N.Y., 1965.
Phil 5246.46 Developmental psychology. (Goodenough, Florence L.) N.Y., 1934.
Phil 5865.8 Developmental psychology. (Nash, John.) Englewood Cliffs, N.J., 1970.
Phil 13.23 Developmental psychology. Washington. 1,1969+
Phil 5246.46.5 Developmental psychology. 2. ed. (Goodenough, Florence L.) N.Y., 1945.
Phil 6327.25 Developments in psycho-analysis. (Reviere, Joan.) London, 1952.
Phil 5593.54 Developments in the Rorschach technique. (Klapfer, Bruno.) Yonkers-on-Hudson, 1954. 2v.
Phil 3018.4 Developmnt from Kant to Hegel. (Seth, A.) London, 1882.

Phil 5011.5 Le développement de la pensée dialectique. (Barbu, Z.) Paris, 1947.
Phil 8090.3 Le développement de l'esthétique sociologique en France et en Angleterre au XIX siècle. (Needham, Harold.) Paris, 1926.
Phil 5650.54 Le développement génétique de la perception musicale. (Zenatti, Arlette.) Paris, 1969.
Phil 5875.75 Développement neuro-psychique du nourrisson. 1. ed. (Koupernir, Cyrille.) Paris, 1968.
Phil 5870.120.5 Le développement social de l'enfant et de l'adolescent. 5. ed. (Reymond-Rivier, Berthe.) Bruxelles, 1965.
Phil 5255.18.15 Le développment mental et l'intelligence. (Piéron, Henri.) Paris, 1929.
Phil 5400.107 Le devenir de l'intelligence. (Zazzo, Revné.) Paris, 1946.
Htn Phil 8583.3* DeVere, Aubrey. Proteus and Amadeus. London, 1878.
Phil 8583.3.5 DeVere, Aubrey. The subjective difficulties in religion. n.p., n.d.
Phil 6980.222 Devereaux, G. Reality and dream. N.Y., 1951.
Phil 5270.10 Devereux, George. From anxiety to method in the behavioral sciences. The Hague, 1968.
Phil 5043.6 Devey, Joseph. Logic; or The science of inference. London, 1854.
Phil 2340.14.30 Deviation into sense. (Wauchope, Oswald S.) London, 1948.
Phil 5627.25 Deviations morbides du sentiment religieux. (Garban, Louis.) Paris, 1911.
Phil 70.3.90 Deviatnadtsatyi mezhdnnarodnyi psikhologicheskii Kongress, 27 iialia - 2 avgusta 1969 g., London, Angliia. (International Congress of Psychology, 19th, London, 1969.) Moskva, 1970.
Phil 9590.8 The devil laughs. (Spallazani, L.) Boston, 1937.
Phil 3640.155 De Villers, Sireyx. La faillite du surhomme et la physologie de Nietzsche. Paris, 1920.
Phil 8610.832 The devil's chaplain. (Robert Taylor, 1784-1844). (Aldred, G.A.) Glasgow, 1942.
Phil 8610.831.3 The devil's pulpit. (Taylor, Robert.) Boston, 1866.
Phil 8610.831.20 The devil's pulpit. (Taylor, Robert.) London, 1882. 2v.
Phil 8610.831.5 The devil's pulpit. v.1, no.1-15,17-23; v.2, no.1. (Taylor, Robert.) London, 1879.
Phil 665.73 The devil's puzzle. (Bury, R.G.) Dublin, 1949.
Phil 8620.43.7 The devil's share. 2. ed. (Rougemont, Denis de.) N.Y., 1945.
Phil 5520.758 DeVito, Joseph A. Psycholinguistics. Indianapolis, 1971.
Phil 5520.702 De Vito, Joseph A. The psychology of speech and language. N.Y., 1970.
Phil 8878.61 Devlin, Patrick. The enforcement of morals. London, 1965.
Phil 6113.23 De Voe, W. Healing currents from the battery of life. 2. ed. Chicago, 1905.
Phil 9120.162 Le devoir. (Le Senne, René.) Paris, 1930.
Phil 9120.3 Le devoir. (Simon, J.) Paris, 1854.
Phil 9120.3.2 Le devoir. (Simon, J.) Paris, 1855.
Phil 8897.36 Devoir et durée. (Wilbois, J.) Paris, 1912.
Phil 9162.4 Les devoirs des femmes dans la famille. (Chassay, F.E.) Paris, 1852.
Htn Phil 7230.4.2* Devotional somnium. N.Y., 1815.
Phil 7077.3 Devotional somnium. N.Y., 1815.
Phil 5243.49 Devoto, Andrea. Saggio sulla psicologia contemporanea. Firenze, 1959.
Phil 8878.8 Dewar, D. Elements of moral philosophy. London, 1826. 2v.
Phil 8693.15 Dewart, E.H. (Mrs.). The march of life. Boston, 1929.
Phil 8658.25 Dewart, Leslie. The future of belief; theism in a world come of age. N.Y., 1966.
Phil 2493.81 Dewaule, L. Condillac et la psychologie anglaise contemporaine. Paris, 1892.
Phil 178.58 Dewe, Joseph A. Les deux ordres, psychique el material. Paris, 1929.
Phil 178.58.5 Dewe, Joseph A. Les deux ordres, psychique et materiel. Thèse. Paris, 1929.
Phil 7054.93 Dewey, D.M. History of the strange sounds or rappings. Rochester, 1850.
Phil 8404.19A Dewey, J. Art as experience. N.Y., 1934.
Phil 5043.16.5 Dewey, J. Essays in experimental logic. Chicago, 1916.
Phil 3552.83.5 Dewey, J. Leibniz's new essays concerning the human understanding. Chicago, 1902.
Phil 5043.16.3A Dewey, J. Logic; the theory of inquiry. N.Y., 1938.
Phil 5043.16A Dewey, J. Studies in logical theory. Chicago, 1903.
Phil 6113.13.3 Dewey, J.H. The way, the truth and the life...Christian theosophy. 3d ed. NY., 1888.
Phil 2255.1.35 Dewey, John. The Bertrand Russell case. N.Y., 1941.
Phil 8583.25 Dewey, John. A common faith. New Haven, 1934.
Phil 178.38.35 Dewey, John. Construction and criticism. N.Y., 1930.
Phil 1955.6.55 Dewey, John. The early works, 1882-1898. v.2,4. Carbondale, 1967- 2v.
Phil 1955.6.45 Dewey, John. Essays in experimental logic. N.Y., 1953.
Phil 8878.11.9A Dewey, John. Ethics. N.Y., 1908.
Phil 8878.11.20A Dewey, John. Ethics. N.Y., 1932.
Phil 8878.11.8 Dewey, John. Ethics [lecture]. N.Y., 1908.
Phil 178.38.5A Dewey, John. Experience and nature. Chicago, 1925.
Phil 178.38.7A Dewey, John. Experience and nature. Chicago, 1926.
Phil 1955.6.20 Dewey, John. Freedom and culture. N.Y., 1939.
Phil 3003.3A Dewey, John. German philosophy and politics. N.Y., 1915.
Phil 3003.3.5 Dewey, John. German philosophy and politics. N.Y., 1942.
Phil 1955.6.35 Dewey, John. The influence of Darwin on philosophy. N.Y., 1951.
Phil 1955.6.22 Dewey, John. Intelligence in the modern world. N.Y., 1939.
Phil 1955.6.24 Dewey, John. John Dewey. 1st ed. Indianapolis, 1955.
Phil 1955.6.200 Dewey, John. John Dewey and Arthur F. Bentley. New Brunswick, 1964.
Phil 1955.6.32A Dewey, John. Knowing and the known. Boston, 1949.
Phil 1955.6.33 Dewey, John. Knowing and the known. Boston, 1960.
Phil 8878.11.13 Dewey, John. Logical conditions of a scientific treatment of morality. Chicago, 1903.
Phil 8878.11.2 Dewey, John. Outlines of a critical theory of ethics. N.Y., 1957.
Phil 8878.11.3 Dewey, John. Outlines of a critical theory of ethics. N.Y., 1969.
Phil 1955.6.50 Dewey, John. Philosophy, psychology and social practice. N.Y., 1963.
Phil 178.38.40 Dewey, John. Philosophy and civilization. N.Y., 1931.
Phil 178.38.10 Dewey, John. The philosophy of John Dewey. N.Y., 1928.
Phil 1955.6.30 Dewey, John. Problems of men. N.Y., 1946.
Phil 5243.7 Dewey, John. Psychology. N.Y., 1887.
Phil 5243.7.2 Dewey, John. Psychology. N.Y., 1889.
NEDL Phil 5243.7.3 Dewey, John. Psychology. 3d ed. N.Y., 1896.
Phil 5243.7.16 Dewey, John. Psychology and social practice. Chicago, 1909.
Phil 178.38.16 Dewey, John. The quest for certainty. N.Y., 1929.
Phil 178.38.15A Dewey, John. The quest for certainty. N.Y., 1929.
Phil 178.38.4 Dewey, John. Reconstruction in philosophy. Boston, 1948.
Phil 8878.11.7 Dewey, John. The study of ethics, a syllabus. Photoreproduction. Ann Arbor, 1897.
Phil 1955.6.40A Dewey, John. The wit and wisdom of J. Dewey. Boston, 1949.
Phil 1955.6.02 Pamphlet box. Dewey, John.
Phil 8878.9 Dewey, O. Moral views of commerce, society and politics. N.Y., 1838.
Phil 8972.2.8 Dewey, Orville. A review on the Calvinistic views of moral philosophy. N.Y., 1835.
Phil 8870.23 Dewey, Robert E. Problems of ethics. N.Y., 1961.
Phil 1955.6.165 Dewey. (Clark, Gordon H.) Philadelphia, 1960.
Phil 8878.11.12 Dewey and Tufts. Ethics. N.Y., 1929.
Phil 1955.6.3 The Dewey newsletter. Carbondale, Ill. 1,1967+
Phil 1955.6.205 Dewey y el pensamiento americano. (Mañach, Jorge.) Madrid, 1959.
Htn Phil 1955.6.90F* Dewey's suppressed psychology. (Klyce, S.) Winchester, Mass., 1928.
Phil 178.31 Dewing, A.S. Life as reality. N.Y., 1910.
Phil 1703.1 Dewing, Arthur Stone. Introduction to History of modern philosophy. Philadelphia, 1903.
Phil 6113.3.5 Dexter, E.G. Weather influences. N.Y., 1904.
Phil 5243.45 Dexter, E.S. Introduction to the fields of psychology. N.Y., 1938.
Phil 5853.12 Dexter, Lewis Anthony. Elite and specialized interviewing. Evanston, 1970.
Phil 3460.81 Deyks, F. F.H. Jacobi im Verhaltniss zu seinen Zeitgenossen. Frankfurt, 1848.
Phil 8583.24 Deyo, M.L. A modern conception of religion. Binghamton, 1933.
Phil 8693.7 Deyo, M.L. Spiritual evolution. Binghamton, N.Y., 1913.
Phil 4003.5 Dezza, Paolo. I neotomisti italiani del XIX secolo. Milano, 1942-44. 2v.
Phil 7068.99.4 Dheur, P. Les hallucinations volontaires. Paris, 1899.
Phil 2648.90 D'Holbach et ses amis. (Hubert, René.) Paris, 1928.
Phil 2648.25 D'Holbach portatif. (Holbach, Paul Henri T.) Paris, 1967.
Phil 2648.93 D'Holbach's moral philosophy. (Topazio, V.W.) Geneva, 1956.
Phil 978.61.5 Dhopeshwarkar, A.D. The divine vision. London, 1928.
Phil 978.61.10 Dhopeshwarkar, A.D. First principles of theosophy. 3d ed. Adyar, Madras, 1923.
Phil 978.59.120 Dhopeshwarkar, A.D. J. Kishnamurti and awareness in action. Bombay, 1967.
Phil 978.59.115 Dhopeshwarkar, A.D. Krishnamurti and the experience. Bombay, 1956.
Phil 720.44 Di alcune considerazioni intorno alla verità e all'errore. (Casellato, Sante.) Padova, 1958.
Phil 4210.81.12F Di Antonio Rosmini-Serbati reformatore. (Nardi, P. de.) Forli, 1894.
Phil 4170.7.90 Di Terenzio Mamiani filosofo. (Angelini, A.) Roma, 1885. 2v.
Phil 6952.14 Les diables de morzine en 1861. (Chiara, D.) n.p., 1861.
Phil 2270.140 Diaconide, Elias. Étude critique sur la sociologie de Herbert Spencer. Paris, 1938.
Phil 5400.33 Diätetik der Seele. 2e Aufl. (Klencke, P.F.H.) Leipzig, 1873.
Phil 6328.3 Die Diätetik des Geistes. (Scholz, F.) Leipzig, 1887.
Phil 5590.570.2 Diagnose der Person. 2. Aufl. (Huth, Albert.) Bern, 1963.
Phil 4170.7.93 Diagnosi comparativa della filosofia di Rosmini e di Mamiani. (Mamini, C.) Bologna, 1860.
Phil 5850.349 Diagnosing personality and conduct. (Symonds, P.M.) N.Y., 1931.
Phil 6967.2 The diagnosis of diseases. (Reynolds, J.R.) London, 1855.
Phil 5262.43 Diagnosis of man. (Walker, Kenneth M.) London, 1942.
Phil 5465.216 The diagnosis of mental imagery. Thesis. (Fernald, Mabel Ruth.) Princeton, N.J., 1912.
Phil 6980.631 Diagnostic psychological testing. (Rapaport, David.) Chicago, 1945. 2v.
Phil 13.15 Diagnostica. Göttingen. 1,1955+ 8v.
Phil 6328.46 Diagnosties psychologiques. (Sechehaye, Marguerte Albert.) Berne, 1949.
Phil 5421.20.60 Diagnostik der Aggressivität. Habilitationsschrift. (Selg, Herbert.) Göttingen, 1968.
Phil 6319.1.16 Diagnostische Assoziationsstudien. v.1-2. (Jung, C.G.) Leipzig, 1915.
Phil 5592.173 Diagnostische Möglichkeiten der Intelligenz-Beurteilung. (Mields, J.) Heidelberg, 1962.
Htn Phil 187.54.9F* Diagram of the celestial city. (Motion, George.) n.p., n.d.
Phil 5066.277 Diagrammy Venna. (Kuzichev, Aleksandr S.) Moskva, 1968.
Phil 6060.44 Diagrams of the unconscious. (Wolff, Wermer.) N.Y., 1948.
Phil 187.149.5 Dialectic; a way into and within philosophy. (Mueller, G.E.) N.Y., 1953.
Phil 5041.51 Dialectic, or The tactics of thinking. (Binder, Frank.) London, 1932.
Phil 5190.21.5 Dialectic. (Adler, M.J.) N.Y., 1927.
Phil 1870.115.15 The dialectic of immaterialism. (Luce, Arthur A.) London, 1963.
Phil 8875.27 A dialectic of morals. (Adler, Mortimer Jerome.) Notre Dame, 1941.
Phil 13.2 Dialectica. Neuchâtel. 1,1947+ 10v.
Phil 5043.30 Dialectica. Neuchâtel. Pouvoir de l'esprit sur le réel. Neuchâtel, 1948.
Phil 310.631 La dialéctica comunista a la luz de la ciencia. (González Duran, Guillermo.) La Paz, 1965.
Phil 672.202 La dialéctica del espacio. (Samuells, Roberto.) Madrid, 1952.
Phil 310.581 Dialectica materialista. (Academia Republicii Populare Romine. Institut de Filosofie.) Bucuresti, 1963.
Phil 5068.52 Dialéctica y positivismo lógico. (Astrada, C.) Tucumán, 1961.
Htn Phil 2835.30* Dialecticae libri duo. (Ramus, P.) London, 1669.
Phil 310.550 Pamphlet vol. Dialectical materialism. 5 pam.
Phil 310.1 Pamphlet vol. Dialectical materialism. 4 pam.
Phil 310.1.4 Pamphlet vol. Dialectical materialism. 5 pam.
Phil 310.1.7 Pamphlet vol. Dialectical materialism. 3 pam.
Phil 310.1.2 Pamphlet vol. Dialectical materialism. 4 pam.
Phil 310.1.3 Pamphlet vol. Dialectical materialism. 5 pam.
Phil 310.1.6 Pamphlet vol. Dialectical materialism. 5 pam.
Phil 310.1.1 Pamphlet vol. Dialectical materialism. 6 pam.
Phil 310.1.9 Pamphlet vol. Dialectical materialism. 4 pam.
Phil 310.2 Dialectical materialism. (Cornforth, M.C.) London, 1952. 3v.

Phil 310.2.2 — Dialectical materialism. (Cornforth, M.C.) London, 1955-56. 3v.

Phil 310.1.10 — Pamphlet vol. "Dialectical materialism". (Russian). 5 pam.

Phil 310.2.3 — Dialectical materialism. v.1-3. 3d ed. (Cornforth, M.C.) London, 1961.

Phil 2655.3.100 — Dialectique. (Sesmat, A.) Paris, 1955.

Phil 310.728 — La dialectique. 1. éd. (Congrès des Sociétés de Philosophie de Langue Française, 14th, 1969.) Paris, 1969.

Phil 2835.35 — Dialectique (1555). (La Ramée, P. de.) Genève, 1964.

Phil 2825.15.80 — La dialectique de la conscience chez Jacques Paliard. (Masset, Pierre.) Paris, 1959.

Phil 672.155.10 — La dialectique de la durée. (Bachelard, Gaston.) Paris, 1936.

Phil 2750.21 — Dialectique de l'affirmation. (Marc, André.) Paris, 1952.

Phil 2475.1.294.4 — La dialectique des images chez Bergson. Thèse. (Adolphe, Lydie.) Paris, 1951.

Phil 2475.1.294.5 — La dialectique des images chez Bergson. 1. éd. (Adolphe, Lydie.) Paris, 1951.

Phil 5585.32 — La dialectique du monde sensible. (Lavelle, Louis.) Strasbourg, 1921.

Phil 5585.32.3 — La dialectique du monde sensible. Thèse. (Lavelle, Louis.) Strasbourg, 1921. 2 pam.

Phil 5075.6 — Dialectique du XX siècle. (Fuerstengerg, Hans.) Paris, 1956.

Phil 2725.15.30 — La dialectique et le rythme de l'univers. (Lasbax, E.) Paris, 1925.

Phil 5016.2 — Dialectique et sociologie. (Gurvitch, Georges.) Paris, 1962.

Phil 4752.2.40 — Dialectique existentielle du divin et de l'humain. (Berdiaev, Nikolai Aleksandrovich.) Paris, 1947.

Phil 310.645 — Dialejesta-Dialektik voy Homer bis Aristoteles. (Sichirollo, Livio.) Hildesheim, 1966.

Phil 310.230 — Dialekticheskaia logika. (Alekseev, M.N.) Moskva, 1960.

Phil 310.800 — Dialekticheskaia logika. (Bŭnkov, Angel I.) Sofiia, 1971.

Phil 310.535 — Dialekticheskii i istoricheskii materializm. (Sarab'ianov, V.N.) Moskva, 1934.

Phil 310.520 — Dialekticheskii i istoricheskii materializm. (Voitko, V.I.) Kiev, 1962.

VPhil 310.656 — Dialekticheskii i istoricheskii materializm. Moskva, 1967.

Phil 310.656.2 — Dialekticheskii i istoricheskii materializm. Izd. 4. Moskva, 1971.

Phil 310.235 — Dialekticheskii materializm, ideinoe oruzoiie bor'by za Kommunizm. (Moroz, K.V.) Moskva, 1960.

Phil 310.3 — Dialekticheskii materializm. (Akadamiia Nauk SSSR. Institut Filosofii.) Moskva, 1953.

Phil 310.7 — Dialekticheskii materializm. (Akadamiia Nauk SSSR. Institut Filosofii.) Moskva, 1954.

Phil 310.305 — Dialekticheskii materializm. (Andreev, I.D.) Moskva, 1960.

Phil 310.583 — Dialekticheskii materializm. (Biriukov, B.V.) Moskva, 1964.

Phil 310.360 — Dialekticheskii materializm. (Danilenko, D.I.) Moskva, 1961.

Phil 310.205 — Dialekticheskii materializm. (Makarov, A.D.) Moskva, 1960.

Phil 310.75 — Dialekticheskii materializm. (Pantskhava, I.D.) Moskva, 1958.

Phil 310.175 — Dialekticheskii materializm. (Rutkevich, M.N.) Moskva, 1959.

Phil 310.617 — Dialekticheskii materializm. (Sheptulin, Aleksandr P.) Moskva, 1965.

Phil 310.480 — Dialekticheskii materializm i chastnye nauki. (Iurova, I.L.) Moskva, 1962.

Phil 310.551 — Dialekticheskii materializm i meditsina. (Tsaregorodtsev, Gennadi I.) Moskva, 1963.

Phil 310.551.2 — Dialekticheskii materializm i meditsina. 2. Izd. (Tsaregorodtsev, Gennadi I.) Moskva, 1966.

Phil 310.3.15 — Dialekticheskii materializm i nekotorye problemy fiziki i khimii. (Shakhparonov, M.I.) Moskva, 1958.

Phil 310.355 — Dialekticheskii materializm i nekotorye voprosy darvinizma. (Zakharov, F.I.) Moskva, 1961.

Phil 310.295 — Dialekticheskii materializm i psikhofiziologicheskaia problema. (Orlov, V.V.) Perm, 1960.

Phil 310.515 — Dialekticheskii materializm i sovremennoe estestvoznanie. (Akademiia Nauk SSSR. Nauchnyi Sovet po Filosofskim Voprosam Estestvoznaniia.) Moskva, 1962.

Phil 310.584 — Dialekticheskii materializm i sovremennoe estestvoznanie. (Vserossiiskii Seminar pre Poda Vatelei po Voprosam Sovet Estestvozaniia.) Moskva, 1964.

Phil 310.5.5 — Dialekticheskii materializm i sovremennoe estestvozznanie. Moskva, 1957.

Phil 310.770 — Dialekticheskii materializm i voprosy estestvosnaniia. Perm', 1969.

Phil 310.60 — Dialekticheskii materializm i voprosy estestvoznaniia. (Fataliev, K.M.) Moskva, 1958.

Phil 310.450 — Dialekticheskii materializm i voprosy genetiki. (Platonov, G.V.) Moskva, 1961.

Phil 310.622 — Dialekticheskii materializm kak metodologiia estestvennonauchnogo poznaniia. (Stepanov, V.I.) Minsk, 1965.

Phil 310.525 — Dialekticheskii materializm o poniatii. (Kursanov, G.A.) Moskva, 1963.

Phil 310.4.3 — Dialekticheskii materializm o zakonakh nauki. (Kovalgin, V.M.) Minsk, 1962.

Phil 4710.12 — Dialekticheskii materializm v SSSR. (Losskii, N.O.) Paris, 193-?

Phil 5068.94 — Dialekticheskoe protivorechie i logika poznaniia. (Narskii, Igor S.) Moskva, 1969.

Phil 310.365 — Dialekticheskogo materializm. (Kalatskii, V.P.) Moskva, 1961.

Phil 310.586 — Dialektické rozpory a jejich zakonitosti. (Tlustý, V.) Praha, 1962.

Phil 310.602 — Dialektický vedecký zákon. (Černík, Václav.) Bratislava, 1964.

Phil 600.53 — Dialektik, Positivismus, Mythologie. (Broecker, Walter.) Frankfurt, 1958.

Phil 310.766.2 — Dialektik, Wissenschaft und Waffe. 2. Aufl. (Steininger, Herbert.) Berlin, 1967.

Phil 3805.22 — Dialektik. (Schleiermacher, Friedrich.) Berlin, 1903.

Phil 3450.28.10 — Dialektik der Aufklärung. (Horkheimer, Max.) Amsterdam, 1947.

Phil 310.740 — Dialektik der Entwicklung objektiver Systeme. 1. Aufl. (Pawelzig, Gerd.) Berlin, 1970.

Phil 3425.366 — Die Dialektik im System Hegels. Inaug. Diss. (Schlawin, H.) Bern, 1953.

Phil 5022.1 — Die Dialektik in der Philosophie der Gegenwart. v.1-2. (Marck, Siegfried.) Tübingen, 1929-31.

Phil 3425.596 — Die Dialektik in Hegels Phänomenologie des Geistes. (Stiehler, G.) Berlin, 1964.

Phil 5238.189 — Dialektik und Dynamik der Person. (Hiltmann, H.) Köln, 1963.

Phil 3801.445 — Dialektik und Einbildungskraft. (Habluetzel, Rudolf.) Basel, 1954.

Phil 1750.367.5 — Dialektik und Politik. 1e Aufl. (Hommes, Jakob.) Köln, 1968.

Phil 310.665.5 — Dialektik und Praxis. (Stiehler, Gottfried.) Berlin, 1968.

Phil 310.560 — Dialektika analiza i sinteza v nauchnom poznanii. (Babosov, E.M.) Minsk, 1963.

Phil 730.27 — Dialektika chasti i tselogo. (Iugai, Geragim A.) Alma-Ata, 1965.

Phil 310.647 — Dialektika človeka, misli v sveta. (Rus, Vojan.) Ljubljana, 1967.

Phil 5040.24 — Dialektika farm myshlemiia. (Alekseev, M.N.) Moskva, 1959.

Phil 310.624 — Dialektika i estestvoznanie. Izd. 3. (Deborin, Abram M.) Moskva, 1929.

Phil 310.744 — Dialektika i sovremennol estestvoznanie. Moskva, 1970.

Phil 310.335 — Dialektika kak logika. (Kopnin, P.V.) Kiev, 1961.

Phil 310.644 — Dialektika kak teoriia razvitiia. (Bosenko, Valerii A.) Kiev, 1966.

Phil 3482.10 — Dialektika Kanta. (Asmus, V.F.) Moskva, 1929.

Phil 310.599.2 — Dialektika konkrétního. 2. Vyd. (Kosík, Karel.) Praha, 1965.

VPhil 3552.476 — A dialektika Leibniz filozófiá. (Simonovits, Istvánné.) Budapest, 1965.

Phil 310.350 — Dialektika neobkhodimosti i sluchainosti. (Shirokanov, D.I.) Minsk, 1960.

Phil 310.565 — Dialektika olecného a zuláštního. (Javůrek, Zdenck.) Praha, 1962.

Phil 341.34 — Dialektika protsessa poznaniia. (Kurazhkovskaia, E.A.) Moskva, 1960.

Phil 5625.115 — Dialektika reflektornykh protsessov. (Petrushevskii, Stefan A.) Moskva, 1967.

Phil 310.618 — Dialektika sovremennoi epokhi. (Fedoseev, Petr.) Moskva, 1966.

Phil 331.33 — Dialektika teoriia poznaniia. (Akademiia Nauk SSSR. Institut Filosofii.) Moskva, 1964- 3v.

Phil 310.592 — Dialektika v naukakh o nezhivoi prirode. (Omel'ianovskyi, M.E.) Moskva, 1964.

Phil 310.768.2 — Dialektikk og samfunnsvitenskap. 2. oppl. (Enerstvedt, Regi Th.) Oslo, 1970.

Phil 310.582.5 — Dialektiko-materialisticheskii analiz osnovnykh poniatii biologii i meditsiny. Kiev, 1968.

Phil 310.780 — Das dialektische Gesetz. 1. vyd. Bratislava, 1964.

Phil 310.50 — Der dialektische Materialismus. (Gropp, Rugard Otto.) Leipzig, 1958.

Phil 310.165 — Der dialektische Materialismus die theoretische Grundlage der Politik der SED. 3. Aufl. (Hager, Kurt.) Berlin, 1959.

Phil 310.385 — Dialektische Philosophie und Gesellschaft in der Sowiet-Union. (Ahlberg, René.) Berlin, 1960.

Phil 3425.350 — Das dialektische Sein in Hegel's Logik. (Coreth, Emerich.) Wien, 1952.

Phil 310.155.1 — Dialektische Untersuchungen. (Goldmann, Lucien.) Neuwied, 1966.

Phil 190.50 — Der dialektische Ursprung der Glückseligkeit. (Paret, Hans.) Berlin, 1925.

Phil 3425.266 — Der dialektische Widerspruch in Hegels Philosophie und das Paradoxon des Christentums. (Nadler, Käte.) Leipzig, 1931.

Phil 310.665.2 — Der dialektische Widusprud. 2. Aufl. (Stiehler, Gottfried.) Berlin, 1967.

Phil 3552.476.5 — Dialektisches Denken in der Philosophie von Gottfried Wilhelm Leibniz. (Simonovits, Istvánné.) Budapest, 1968.

Phil 310.490 — Dialektychnyi materializm pro katenoriiu prychynnosti. (Nichyk, V.M.) Kyiv, 1960.

Phil 197.65.5 — Die Dialelitik des Geistes. (Wust, Peter.) Augsburg, 1928.

Phil 1630.35 — La dialettica e la retorica dell'Umanesimo. (Vasoli, Cesare.) Milano, 1968.

Phil 288.22 — Dialog des Abendlandes. (Heimendahl, Eckart.) München, 1966.

Phil 5238.222 — Dialog über den Menschen. Stuttgart, 1968.

Phil 6321.43 — Le dialoge psychanalytique. (Lévy-Valensi, E.) Paris, 1962.

Phil 2050.68.15 — Dialoge über natürliche Religion. 3e Aufl. (Hume, David.) Leipzig, 1905.

Phil 192.37.10 — Dialoge über Religionsphilosophie. (Richter, Raoul.) Leipzig, 1911.

Phil 4060.2.40 — Dialoghi d'amore. (Leo Hebraeus.) Bari, 1929.

Phil 4060.2.42 — Dialoghi d'amore. (Leo Hebraeus.) Heidelberg, 1929.

Phil 4065.118 — I dialoghi del Bruno. (Guzzo, Augusto.) Torino, 1932.

Htn Phil 4060.2.33* — Dialoghi di amore. (Leo Hebraeus.) Vinegia, 1552.

Phil 4170.7.46 — Dialoghi di scienza prima. (Mamiani della Rovere, Terenzio.) Parigi, 1846.

Phil 4065.14A — Dialoghi italiani. (Bruno, Giordano.) Firenze, 1958.

Phil 1870.45.25 — Dialoghi tra Hylas e Filonous. (Berkeley, G.) Bari, 1939.

Phil 176.123 — Dialogi duo in quorum altero agitur de multitudine rerum. (Baldini, Bernardino.) Mediolani, 1558. 3 pam.

Phil 811.20 — Dialogik; Philosophie auf dem Boden der Neuzeit. (Levin-Goldschmidt, Hermann.) Frankfurt, 1964.

Phil 3002.7 — Das dialogische Denken. (Casper, Bernhard.) Freiburg, 1967.

Phil 8968.15.85 — Dialogische Existenz. (Balle, Theo.) Bamberg, 1967.

Phil 3120.30.63 — Dialogisches Leben. (Buber, Martin.) Zürich, 1947.

Htn Phil 4120.7.30* — Dialogo. (Galilei, Galileo.) Fiorenza, 1632.

Phil 2477.6.145 — Dialogo con M. Blondel. (Sciacca, M.E.) Milano, 1962.

Htn Phil 9560.30* — Dialogo dell'honore. (Possevino, G.B.) Venice, 1553.

Phil 4190.3.30 — Dialogo e silenzio. (Ottonello, Pier Paolo.) Milano, 1967.

Phil 3450.19.100 — Dialogo existencial. (Erro, C.A.) Buenos Aires, 1937.

Htn Phil 5545.79* — Dialogo nel quale si ragiona del modo di accrescere e conservar la memoria. (Dolce, Lodovico.) Venetia, 1586.

Phil 4003.6 — Il dialogo prospettive filosofiche. Bologna, 1964.

Phil 4060.2.55 — Dialogos de amor. (Leo Hebraeus.) Madrid, 1949. 2v.

Htn Phil 4060.2.35* — Los dialogos de amor. (Leo Hebraeus.) Venetia, 1568.

Htn Phil 4060.2.37* — Los dialogos de amor. (Leo Hebraeus.) Venetia, 1572.

Phil 4060.2.38 — Diálogos de amor. 1. ed. (Leo Hebraeus.) Romano, 1953.

Phil 193.49.25.5 — Diálogos en el limbo. (Santayana, G.) Buenos Aires, 1941.

Phil 978.57 — A dialogue. (Stuart, C.) n.p., 1901.

Phil 13.19 — Dialogue. Kingston, Ont. 1,1962+ 8v.

Phil 2805.475 — Dialogue avec Blaise Pascal. Théâtre. (Eydoux, Emmanuel.) Basel, 1968.

Phil 2630.11.20 — Dialogue avec les précurseurs. (Guitton, Jean.) Aubier, 1962.

Phil 2475.1.303 — A dialogue between Bergson. (Cavarnos, C.P.) Cambridge, 1949.

Phil 8661.35 — Dialogue et révolution. (Girardi, Giulio.) Paris, 1969.

Phil 2280.5.115 — Dialogue on George Santayana. (Lamont, Corliss.) N.Y., 1959.

Phil 1955.6.145 — Dialogue on John Dewey. (Lamont, Corliss.) N.Y., 1959.

Phil 8581.26 — Dialogue sur la vie et sur la mort. 3. éd. (Bonnefon, C.) Paris, 1911.

Phil 6315.19.45 — Dialogue with Erich Fromm. 1. ed. (Evans, Richard Isadore.) N.Y., 1966.

Phil 6980.464 — Dialogue with Sammy; a psycho-analytical contribution to the understanding of a child psychosis. (McDougall, Joyce.) London, 1969.

Phil 2905.1.120 — Dialogue with Teilhard de Chardin. (Rabut, Oliver A.) London, 1961.

Phil 176.129.10 — Dialogues avec les philosophes, Descartes, Spinoza. (Blondel, Maurice.) Paris, 1966.

Phil 1870.45.6 — The dialogues between Hylas and Philonous. (Berkeley, G.) N.Y., 1954.

Phil 2050.68 — Dialogues concerning natural religion. (Hume, David.) Edinburgh, 1907.

Phil 2050.68.3 — Dialogues concerning natural religion. (Hume, David.) N.Y., 1948.

Phil 2050.67A — Dialogues concerning natural religion. 2nd ed. (Hume, David.) London, 1779.

Phil 1870.45.10 — Dialogues entre Hylas et Philonous. (Berkeley, G.) Paris, 1925.

Phil 8412.11 — Dialogues from Delphi. (Loewenberg, J.) Berkeley, 1949.

Phil 193.49.25 — Dialogues in limbo. (Santayana, G.) N.Y., 1925.

Phil 193.49.25.15 — Dialogues in limbo. (Santayana, G.) N.Y., 1926.

Phil 193.49.25.10A — Dialogues in limbo. (Santayana, G.) N.Y., 1948.

Phil 2340.10.35A — Dialogues of Alfred North Whitehead. 1st ed. (Whitehead, Alfred North.) Boston, 1954.

Phil 5811.4 — Dialogues on instinct. (Brougham, H.) London, 1844.

Phil 5811.4.2 — Dialogues on instinct. (Brougham, H.) Philadelphia, 1845.

Phil 2733.36.10 — Dialogues on metaphysics and on religion. (Malebranche, Nicolas.) London, 1923.

Phil 2050.67.10 — Dialogues sur la religion naturelle. (Hume, David.) Paris, 1964.

Phil 5525.28 — Dialogus pulcherrimus et utilissimus. (Laurentius, A.P.) Marpurgi, 1606.

Phil 13.18 — Dialoog; tydschrift voor wijsbegeerte. Antwerpen. 1,1960+ 9v.

Phil 3120.30.83 — Diamand, Malcolm L. Martin Buber, Jewish existentialist. N.Y., 1960.

Phil 7082.14 — Diamond, Edwin. The science of dreams. 1st ed. Garden City, 1962.

Phil 5477.12 — Diamond, Solomon. Inhibition and choice. N.Y., 1963.

Phil 6836.2 — Diana; a strange autobiography. (Frederics, Diana.) N.Y., 1939.

Phil 1200.36 — Dianeamma Stoikės philesophks. (Thereianos.) Tergeoiė, 1892.

Phil 6317.32.2 — Dianetics. (Hubbard, L. Ron.) Johhannesburg, 1958.

Phil 6317.32 — Dianetics. (Hubbard, L. Ron.) N.Y., 1950.

Phil 8404.6 — Diano, Carlo. Linee per una fenomenologia dell'arte. Venezia, 1956.

Phil 13.14 — Dianoia; anuario de filosofia. Mexico. 1955+ 15v.

Phil 5592.50 — Der Diapositiv-Z-Test. (Zulliger, Hans.) Bern, 1955?

Phil 6834.8 — Diario di un omosessuale. (Dacguino, Giacomo.) Milano, 1970.

Phil 165.66 — La diaristica filosofica. (Archivio di Filosofia.) Padova, 1959.

Phil 7150.15 — Diary of a suicide. (Baker, W.E.) N.Y., 1913.

Phil 2750.22.120 — Diaz, Carlos. Personalismo oberero. Madrid, 1969.

Phil 2403.9 — Diaz, F. Filosofia e politica nel Settecento francese. Torino, 1962.

Phil 3195.6.130 — Diaz de Cerio Ruiz, Franco. W. Dilthey y el problema del mundo historico. Barcelona, 1959.

Phil 4965.2 — Diaz de Gamarra y Dávalos, J.B. Elementos de filosofía moderna. México, 1963.

Phil 8654.120 — Dibattito sull'ateismo. Brescia, 1967.

Phil 5043.38 — DiBernardo, Giuliano. Logica, norme, azione. Trento, 1969.

Phil 3960.18 — Dibon, Paul. La philosophie néerlandaise au siècle d'ov. Paris, 1954.

Phil 2450.81.5A — Dibon, Paul. Pierre Bayle. Amsterdam, 1959.

Phil 6310.22 — Dibs: in search of self. (Axline, Virginia Mae.) Boston, 1965.

Phil 75.82 — Diccionario bio-bibliográfico de filósofos. (Menchaca, José.) Bilbao, 1965.

Phil 90.4 — Diccionario de filosofía. (Ferrater Mora, José.) México, 1941.

Phil 100.5 — Diccionario de filosofía. 1. ed. (Pallares, Eduardo.) México, 1964.

Phil 90.4.10 — Diccionario de filosofía. 2. ed. (Ferrater Mora, José.) México, 1944.

Phil 90.4.15 — Diccionario de filosofía. 3. ed. (Ferrater Mora, José.) Buenos Aires, 1951.

Phil 90.4.16 — Diccionario de filosofía. 4. ed. (Ferrater Mora, José.) Buenos Aires, 1958.

Phil 90.4.17 — Diccionario de filosofía. 5. ed. (Ferrater Mora, José.) Buenos Aires, 1965.

Phil 87.14 — Diccionario de sinónimos ó sea la propiedad del lenguage filosófico. (Carrión, Joaquin.) Madrid, 1873.

Phil 85.1 — Diccionario manual de filosofía. (Arnaiz y Alcalde, N.) Madrid, 1927.

Phil 87.3 — Diccionario manual de filosofía. (Candou, José M.) Madrid, 1946.

Phil 90.2.3 — Diccionnaire des sciences philosophiques. 2e éd. (Franck, Adolphe.) Paris, 1875.

Phil 5548.104 — Dichter, E. Handbook of consumer motivations. N.Y., 1964.

Phil 6688.4 — Der Dichter ein Seher. (Steinbeck, F.A.) Leipzig, 1856.

Phil 3640.266 — Die Dichtung Nietzsches. (Klein, Johannes.) München, 1936.

Phil 1870.85 — Dick, S.M. The principle of synthetic unity in Berkeley and Kant. Lowell, 1898.

Phil 6980.224 — Dick, Samuel. Psychotherapy. Minneapolis? 1909.

Phil 8693.1 — Dick, T. The Christian philosopher. N.Y., 1827.

Phil 8583.4.2 — Dick, T. On the improvement of society by the diffusion of knowledge. Glasgow, 1833.

Phil 8583.4.3 — Dick, T. On the improvement of society by the diffusion of knowledge. N.Y., 1836.

Phil 8628.2 — Dick, T. The philosophy of a future state. N.Y., 1829.

Phil 8628.2.5 — Dick, T. The philosophy of a future state. N.Y., 1831.

Phil 8628.2.2 — Dick, T. The philosophy of a future state. Philadelphia, 1843.

Phil 8693.1.2 — Dick, T. The philosophy of a future state. Philadelphia, 1845. 2 pam.

Phil 8583.4 — Dick, T. The philosophy of religion. Brookfield, Mass., 1829.

Phil 8583.4.18 — Dick, T. The philosophy of religion. v.1-2. Philadelphia, 1845.

Phil 8583.4.5.-.9 — Dick, T. Works. Philadelphia, 1836. 5v.

Phil 8583.4.15 — Dick, T. Works. v.1-4. Hartford, 1839.

Phil 8583.4.16 — Dick, T. The works of Thomas Dick. Hartford, 1851.

Phil 8633.1.12 — Dickinson, G.L. Is immortality desirable? Boston, 1909.

Phil 2150.7.95 — Dickinson, G.L. John McTaggart Ellis McTaggart. Cambridge, Eng., 1931.

Phil 8878.23.4 — Dickinson, G.L. The meaning of good. 4th ed. N.Y., 1907.

Phil 8583.10A — Dickinson, G.L. Religion, a criticism and a forecast. N.Y., 1905.

Phil 8628.7.5 — Dickinson, G.L. Religion and immortality. Boston, 1911.

Phil 8628.7 — Dickinson, G.L. Religion and immortality. London, 1911.

Phil 5066.233 — Dickoff, James. Symbolic logic and language. N.Y., 1965.

Phil 3640.770 — Dickopp, Karl-Heinz. Nietzsches Kritik des Ich-denke. Bonn, 1965.

Phil 6313.13 — Dicks, H.V. Clinical studies in psychopathology. London, 1939.

Phil 9245.22 — Dickson, Henry S. An oration...before...Phi Beta Kappa Society. New Haven, 1842.

Phil 4803.454.79 — Dickstein, Samuel. Katalog dzieł i rekopisów Hoene-Wrońskiego. Kraków, 1896.

Phil 2255.1.65 — Dictionary of mind, matter and morals. (Russell, Bertrand Russell.) N.Y., 1952.

Phil 6990.33.5 — Dictionary of miracles. (Brewer, E.C.) Philadelphia, 188-?

Phil 6990.33 — A dictionary of miracles. (Brewer, E.C.) Philadelphia, 1884.

Phil 102.5.14 — A dictionary of philosophy. (Rozental, Mark Moiseevich.) Moscow, 1967.

Phil 102.6A — The dictionary of philosophy. (Runes, D.D.) N.Y., 1942.

Phil 86.3.5 — Dictionary of philosophy. v.1,3. (Baldwin, J.M.) N.Y., 1911. 3v.

NEDL Phil 86.3A — Dictionary of philosophy. v.1. (Baldwin, J.M.) London, 1901-05.

Phil 86.3.10 — Dictionary of philosophy. v.2. (Baldwin, J.M.) N.Y., 1940.

Phil 104.3 — A dictionary of philosophy in the words of philosophers. 2nd ed. (Thomson, J.R.) London, 1892.

Phil 6315.2.78 — Dictionary of psychoanalysis. (Freud, Sigmund.) N.Y., 1950.

Phil 5207.10 — Dictionary of psychology. (Warren, Howard Crosby.) N.Y., 1934.

Phil 5066.286 — Dictionary of symbols of mathematical logic. (Feys, Robert.) Amsterdam, 1969.

Phil 102.6.5 — Dictionary of thought. (Runes, D.D.) N.Y., 1959.

Phil 90.8 — Dictionnaire de la langue philosophique. (Foulquié, Paul.) Paris, 1962.

Phil 86.7 — Dictionnaire de philosophie ancienne. (Blanc, Elie.) Paris, 1906.

Phil 332.37 — Dictionnaire d'epistémologie génétique. (Battro, Antonio M.) Dordrecht, 1966.

Phil 1703.17 — Dictionnaire des idées contemporaines. Paris, 1964.

Phil 90.2 — Dictionnaire des sciences philosophiques. (Franck, Adolphe.) Paris, 1844. 6v.

Phil 90.2.2 — Dictionnaire des sciences philosophiques. 2. éd. (Franck, Adolphe.) Paris, 1875.

Phil 9558.25 — Dictionnaire du snobisme. (Jullian, T.) Paris, 1958.

Phil 6990.22 — Dictionnaire historique des miracles. (Romagne, M. l'abbe de.) Paris, 1824.

Phil 106.1.13 — Dictionnaire philosophique. (Volataire, Francois Marie Arouet de.) Paris, 1961.

Htn Phil 106.1.3* — Dictionnaire philosophique. (Voltaire, Francois Marie Arouet de.) London, 1765.

Htn Phil 106.1.2* — Dictionnaire philosophique. (Voltaire, Francois Marie Arouet de.) Londres, 1765.

Htn Phil 106.1* — Dictionnaire philosophique. (Voltaire, Francois Marie Arouet de.) n.p., 1765.

Phil 106.1.4 — Dictionnaire philosophique. (Voltaire, Francois Marie Arouet de.) Paris, 1816. 14v.

Phil 106.1.5 — Dictionnaire philosophique. (Voltaire, Francois Marie Arouet de.) Paris, 1935-36. 2v.

Phil 106.1.10 — Dictionnaire philosophique. (Voltaire, Francois Marie Arouet de.) Paris, 1954.

Phil 106.1.30 — Dictionnaire philosophique. (Voltaire, Francois Marie Arouet de.) Paris, 1967.

Phil 106.1.12 — Dictionnaire philosophique. 6. ed. (Voltaire, Francois Marie Arouet de.) Londres, 1767. 2v.

Phil 8593.7 — Dictionnaire philosophique de la religion. (Nonnotte, Claude.) n.p., 1772. 4v.

Phil 7084.4.20 — Dictionnaire psychanalytique des rêves. (Micheloud, Pierrette.) Paris, 1957.

Phil 623.45 — Dictionnaire rationaliste. Paris, 1964.

NEDL Phil 8897.67 — Didactics. (Walsh, Robert.) Philadelphia, 1836. 2v.

Phil 400.32 — Dide, Maurice. Les idealistes passionnés. Paris, 1913.

Phil 5243.31 — Dide, Maurice. Introduction à l'étude de la psychogénèse. Paris, 1926.

Phil 5243.31.5 — Dide, Maurice. Introduction à l'étude de la psychogénèse. Thèse. Paris, 1925. 2 pam.

Phil 2530.19 — Diderot, Denis. Dederot's early philosophical works. Chicago, 1916.

Htn Phil 2530.35* — Diderot, Denis. Lettre sur les aveugles. Londres, 1749.

Htn Phil 2530.40* — Diderot, Denis. Lettre sur les sourds et muets. n.p., 1751.

Phil 2530.15 — Diderot, Denis. Oeuvres philosophiques. Bruxelles, 1829. 6v.

Phil 2530.15.5 — Diderot, Denis. Oeuvres philosophiques. Paris, 1956.

Htn Phil 2530.30* — Diderot, Denis. Pensées philosophiques. La Haye, 1746.

Phil 2530.20 — Diderot, Denis. Selected philosophical writings. Cambridge, Eng., 1953.

Phil 2530.80.5 — Diderot: sur Terence. (Dieckmann, Herbert.) n.p., 1958?

Phil 8120.8 — Diderot à Valéry. (Traz, Georges de.) Paris, 1926.

Phil 2530.84 — Diderot als Kunstphilosophie. Inaug.-Diss. (Leo, Werner.) Erlangen, 1918.

Phil 2520.239 — Diderot and Descartes. (Vartanian, A.) Princeton, 1953.

Phil 2530.80.10 — Diderot's conception of genius. (Dieckmann, Herbert.) n.p., 1941?

Phil 2530.88 — Diderots Naturphilosophie. (Lerel, A.C.) Wien, 1950.

Phil 2530.88.2 — Diderots Naturphilosophie. (Lerel, A.C.) Wien, 1950.

Phil 2530.82 — Diderots Weltanschauung. (Roretz, Karl.) Wien, 1914.

Phil 2050.99 — Didier, J. Hume. Paris, 1913.

Phil 2115.101 — Didier, J. John Locke. Paris, 1911.

Phil 1870.99 Didier, Jean. Berkeley. Paris, 1911.
Phil 3552.280 Die Entwickelung der leibnizschen Monadenlehre bis zum Jahre 1695. Inaug. Diss. (Wendt, Emil.) Berlin, 1885.
Phil 200.8 Die Gemeinschaft der Einsamen. (Zimmermann, K.) Jena, 1919.
Phil 4012.4 Die Hegel a Croce e da Jellinek a Chiovenda. (Miranda, L.) Bari, 1921.
Phil 331.4 Die idee zum ursprung des gedankens. (Aars, Kristian B.) Kristiania, 1911.
Phil 9075.27 Die Lehre vom Gewissen in den Systemen des ethischen Idealismus. (Friedmann, J.) Budapest, 1904.
Phil 3480.115 Die mundi sensibilis at que intelligibilis forma. (Kant, Immanuel.) Hamburg, 1958.
Phil 3640.91 Die pädogogischen Gedanken...jungen Nietzsche. (Weber, Ernst.) Leipzig, 1907.
Phil 8601.13A Die politischen religionen. (Voegelin, Eric.) Stockholm, 1939.
Phil 6536.10 Die progressive myoklonus-epilepsie. (Lundborg, Herman B.) Upsala, 1903.
Phil 2055.1.82 Die Psychologie Henry Home's. Inaug.-Diss. (Joseph, M.) Halle, 1911.
Phil 5251.76 Die Rätsel der Seele: Tiefenpsychologie und Anthroposophie. 2. Aufl. (Lauer, Hans Erhard.) Freiburg, 1964.
Phil 3805.166 Diebow, Paul. Die Pädagogik Schleiermachers im Lichte seiner und unserer Zeit. Halle, 1894.
Phil 3552.299 Dieckhoff, A.W. Leibnitz Stellung zur Offenbarung. Rostock, 1888.
Phil 2530.80A Dieckmann, Herbert. Cinq leçons sur Diderot. Genève, 1959.
Phil 2530.80.5 Dieckmann, Herbert. Diderot: sur Terence. n.p., 1958?
Phil 2530.80.10 Dieckmann, Herbert. Diderot's conception of genius. n.p., 1941?
Phil 7060.66 Diederich, Benno. Von Gespenstergeschichten. Leipzig, 1903.
Phil 3640.386 Diefke, Max. Was Muss man von Nietzsche Wissen? Berlin, 1903.
Phil 8610.829.5 The diegesis. (Taylor, Robert.) Boston, 1832.
Phil 8610.829.15 The diegesis. (Taylor, Robert.) Boston, 1873.
Phil 8610.829.10 The diegesis. 3. ed. (Taylor, Robert.) London, 1845.
Phil 178.82 Diéguez, Manuel de. Science et nescience. Paris, 1970.
Phil 5213.3 Diehl, Frank. An historical and critical study of radical behaviorism. Baltimore, 1934.
Phil 5401.53.2 Diel, Paul. La peur et l'angoisse, phénomène central de la vie et de son évolution. 2e éd. Paris, 1968.
Phil 3940.1.90 Diels, Hermann. Gedächtnisrede auf Eduard Zeller. Berlin, 1908.
Phil 1108.8 Diels, Hermann. Kleine Schriften zur Geschichte der antiken Philosophie. Hildesheim, 1969.
Phil 3640.500 Diem, Gudrun. Das Wesen der Kunst im Denken Nietzsches. Schorndorf, 1953.
Phil 88.10 Diemer, Alwin. Philosophie. Frankfurt, 1958.
Phil 6313.25 Dienelt, Karl. Von Freud zu Frankel. Wien, 1967.
Phil 5535.60 Dienes, Zoltan Paul. The effects of structural relations on transfer. London, 1970.
Phil 5520.451 Dienes, Zoltau Paul. Thinking in structures. London, 1965.
Phil 3940.2.40 Dienst an der Welt. (Ziegler, L.) Darmstadt, 1925.
Phil 2880.1.55 Der Dienst desGeist-Menschen. (Saint-Martin, L.C.) Münster, 1858.
Phil 6115.11.14 Ein Dienst zur Nacht ist unser Leben. (Feuchtersleben, E.F.V.) Graz, 1958.
Phil 7084.6 Diepgen, Paul. Traum und Traumdeutung als medizinisch-naturwissenschaftliches Problem im Mittelalter. Berlin, 1912.
Phil 6313.22 Dieren, E. van. Professor Freud. Baarn, 1932.
Phil 1133.17 Diès, Auguste. Le cycle mystique. Paris, 1909.
Phil 3120.26.30 Diesseits und Jenseits. (Brod, Max.) Winterthur, 1947. 2v.
Phil 178.50 Dieterich, K. Grundzüge der Metaphysik. Freiburg im Breisgau, 1885.
Phil 3485.2 Dieterich, K. Kant und Newton. Tübingen, 1876.
Phil 3485.2.5 Dieterich, K. Kant und Rousseau. Tübingen, 1878.
Phil 510.134 Dieterich, K. Philosophie und Naturwissenschaft. Tübingen, 1875.
Phil 1020.2 Dieterici, F. Die Philosophie der Araber im X. Jahrhunderts. v.1-2,4-6,9,12-13. Leipzig, 1876-1895. 10v.
Phil 6115.11.17 The dietetics of the soul. (Feuchtersleben, E.F.V.) London, 1873.
Phil 6115.11.15 The dietetics of the soul. (Feuchtersleben, E.F.V.) N.Y., 1858.
Phil 178.14 Dietrich, K. Protest Gegen die moderne Wissenschaft. Hamburg, 1887.
Phil 7069.56.15 Dietz, Paul A. Parapsychologische woordentolk. Den Haag, 1956.
Phil 7082.118 Dietz, Paul Antoine. Mensch en droom. Leiden, 1935.
Phil 334.7 Dietzgen, J. The positive outcome of philosophy. Chicago, 1906.
Phil 3195.3.31 Dietzgen, Joseph. Das Acquisit der Philosophie und Briefe. Stuttgart, 1903.
Phil 3195.3.10 Dietzgen, Joseph. Ausgewählte Schriften. 1. Aufl. Berlin, 1954.
Phil 3195.3.6 Dietzgen, Joseph. Josef Dietzgens kleinere Philosophie. Stuttgart, 1903.
Phil 3195.3.80 Dietzgen, Joseph. Joseph Dietzgens Philosophie. München, 1910.
Phil 3195.3 Dietzgen, Joseph. Sämtliche Schriften. Wiesbaden, 1911. 3v.
Phil 3195.3.35 Dietzgen, Joseph. Schriften. Berlin, 1962.
Phil 3195.3.33 Dietzgen, Joseph. Das Wesen der menschlichen Kopfarbeit. Berlin, 1955.
Phil 8583.30 Dieu, la nature et la loi. (Desquiron de Saint Agnan, A.T.) Paris, 1814.
Phil 8661.5 Dieu, son existence et sa nature. (Garrigou-Lagrange, R.) Paris, 1914.
Phil 8667.7 Dieu. (Moisant, Xavier.) Paris, 1907.
Phil 8673.19 Dieu caché. (Steenberghen, Fernand van.) Louvain, 1961.
Phil 8660.3 Dieu dans la nature. (Flammarion, C.) Paris, 1867.
Phil 8660.3.7 Dieu dans la nature. 7. ed. (Flammarion, C.) Paris, 1871.
Phil 8661.25 Dieu dans le débat des hommes. (Gaboriau, Florent.) Paris, 1964.
Phil 8667.18 Dieu dans l'univers. Thèse. (Monod, Victor.) Paris, 1933.
Phil 2475.1.237 Le dieu de Bergson. (Rideau, Émile.) Paris, 1932.
Phil 2475.1.236 Le dieu de Bergson. Thèse. (Rideau, Émile.) Paris, 1932.
Phil 3552.468 Le Dieu de Leibniz. 1. éd. (Jalabert, Jacques.) Paris, 1960.
Phil 2880.8.102 Le dieu de Sartre. (Paissac, H.) Grenoble, 1950.
Phil 3827.6 Le Dieu de Spinoza. (Huan, G.) Arras, 1913.

Phil 8657.23 Dieu des athées: Marx, Sartre, Camus. (Coffy, Robert.) Lyon, 1965.
Phil 3494.68 Le Dieu des philosophes. (Moreau, Joseph.) Paris, 1969.
Phil 8597.62 Dieu religieux, dieu de la science. (Ruyer, Raymond.) Paris, 1970.
Phil 3425.572 Dieu est mort; étude sur Hegel. (Garaudy, Roger.) Paris, 1962.
Phil 9075.9 Dieu et la conscience. (Waddington, C.T.) Paris, 1870.
Phil 8666.9 Dieu et la création. (Lacour, J.B.) Paris, 1866.
Phil 2750.11.64 Dieu et la permission du mal. (Maritain, Jacques.) Paris, 1964.
Phil 8667.9 Dieu et l'agnosticisme contemporaine. 3. éd. (Michelet, Georges.) Paris, 1912.
Phil 400.39 Dieu et l'âme. (Coste, Adolphe.) Paris, 1880.
Phil 8706.4 Dieu et l'homme créateur. (Quevremont, Pierre.) Paris, 1965.
Phil 8692.11 Dieu et science. 2. éd. (Cyon, Élie de.) Paris, 1912.
Phil 8656.37 Dieu n'est pas mort. (Borne, Étienne.) Paris, 1959.
Phil 8673.21 Dieu ou rien? (Sertillanges, Antonio Gilbert.) Paris, 1965.
Phil 8658.26 Dieu pour l'homme d'aujourd'hui. (Duquesne, Jacques.) Paris, 1970.
Phil 8582.50 Les dieux. (Chartier, E.) Paris, 1934.
Phil 8707.32 Les Dieux et les rois, regards sur le pouvoir créateur. (Rueff, Jacques.) Paris, 1967.
Phil 9590.32 Les Dieux nous sont nées. (Sendy, Jean.) Paris, 1966-
Phil 8404.13 Diez, Max. Algemeine ästhetik. Leipzig, 1906.
Phil 3195.17.30 Diez, Max. Sprechen. Berlin, 1934.
Phil 8404.13.5 Diez, Max. Theorie des Gefühls zur Begrundung des Asthetik. Stuttgart, 1892.
Phil 4353.5 Diez y siete divagaciones. (Chavarri B., Misael.) Santiago de Chile, 1940. 2v.
Phil 5752.14 La difesa del libero arbitrio da Erasmo a Kant. 1. ed. (Capizzi, Antonio.) Firenze, 1963.
Phil 4260.112 Difesa dell'autorità della sacra scrittura contro Giambattista Vico. (Finetti, Giovanni F.) Bari, 1936.
Phil 4260.30 La difesa dell'umanesimo. (Vico, G.B.) Firenze, 1958.
Phil 274.4 Différence et répétition. Thèse. (Deleuze, Gilles.) Paris, 1968.
Phil 585.208 The difference of man and the difference it makes. (Adler, Mortimer Jerome.) N.Y., 1968.
Phil 5246.24 Les différentes manifestations. (Guérin, Jules.) Paris, 1899.
Phil 5240.35.2 Differential psychology. (Anastasi, Anne.) N.Y., 1949.
Phil 5240.35.3 Differential psychology. (Anastasi, Anne.) N.Y., 1956.
Phil 5240.35 Differential psychology. (Anastasi, Anne.) N.Y., 1937.
Phil 5627.10 The differentiation of the religious consciousness. (King, Irving.) N.Y., 1905.
Phil 5627.10.3 The differentiation of the religious consciousness. (King, Irving.) N.Y., 1905.
Phil 960.274 The differentiation theory of meaning in Indian logic. (Sharma, Dhirendra.) The Hague, 1969.
Phil 5856.5.2 Differentiell psykologi. (Ekman, Gösta.) Stockholm, 1966.
Phil 5258.35.3 Die differentielle Psychologie. (Stern, W.) Leipzig, 1921.
Phil 5258.35 Die differentielle Psychologie. (Stern, W.) Leipzig. 1911.
Phil 193.159A Les différents modes d'éxistence. (Souriau, Étienne.) Paris, 1943.
Htn Phil 3801.428* Differenz der Schelling'schen und Hegel'schen Philosophie. (Glaser, Johann K.) Leipzig, 1842.
Phil 3246.305 Die Differenz zwischen der Fichteschen und Hegelschen Systems in der Hegelschen Differenzschrift. (Girndt, Helmut.) Bonn, 1965.
Htn Phil 3801.449* Differenz des Fichte'schen und Schelling'schen Systems der Philosophie. (Hegel, Georg W.F.) Jena, 1801.
Phil 3425.40.55 Differenz des Fichte'schen und Schelling'schen Systems der Philosophie. (Hegel, Georg Wilhelm Friedrich.) Hamburg, 1962.
Phil 3425.621 Differenz und Versöhnung; eine Interpretation der Theologie G.W.F. Hegels nach seiner "Wissenschaft der Logik." 1. Aufl. (Koch, Traugott.) Gütersloh, 1967.
Phil 9347.11.2 Difficulties; an attempt to help. (Hicks, S.) London, 1922.
Phil 6315.17.30 Difficulties in the path of psychoanalysis. (Freud, Anna.) N.Y., 1969.
Phil 8660.7.2 The difficulties of infidelity. 2. ed. (Faber, G.S.) London, 1833.
Htn Phil 8628.3.5* Digby, K. Demonstratio immortalitatis animae. Francofurti, 1664.
Htn Phil 8628.3.8F* Digby, K. Demonstratio immortalitatis animae. Parisiis, 1651.
Htn Phil 8628.3.9F* Digby, K. Demonstratos immortalitatis animae rationalis. Paris, 1655.
Htn Phil 8628.3.2F* Digby, K. Two treatises...nature of bodies...nature of man's soul. Paris, 1644.
Htn Phil 8628.3.4* Digby, K. Two treatises. London, 1645. 2 pam.
Htn Phil 8628.3* Digby, K. Two treatises. London, 1658-57.
Htn Phil 1955.3.30* Digby, Kenelm. Of bodies and of man's soul. London, 1669.
Phil 5041.34 A digest of deductive logic for the use of students. (Barker, Johnson.) London, 1897.
Phil 2225.11 A digest of purposive values. (Pepper, Stephen Coburn.) Berkeley, 1947.
Phil 9163.3 Diggle, J.W. Home life. London, 1908.
Phil 5590.465 Diggory, James C. Self-evaluation. N.Y., 1966.
Phil 4195.36.5 La dignità dell'uomo. (Pico della Mirandola, Giovanni.) Matera, 1963.
Phil 4195.36.2 Dignità dell'uomo. 2. ed. (Pico della Mirandola, Giovanni.) Firenze, 1943.
Phil 4195.36 Dignità dell'uomo. 3. ed. (Pico della Mirandola, Giovanni.) Firenze, 1945.
Phil 365.47.17 La dignité humaine. (Lecomte du Noüy, Pierre.) N.Y., 1944.
Phil 365.47.18 La dignité humaine. (Lecomte du Noüy, Pierre.) N.Y., 1944.
Phil 1750.758 La dignité humaine et ses assises existentielles. (Marcel, Gabriel.) Paris, 1964.
Htn Phil 8876.36.4* The dignity of human nature. (Burgh, J.) Boston, 1794.
Htn Phil 8876.36.5* The dignity of human nature. (Burgh, J.) Hartford, 1802.
Phil 8876.36 The dignity of human nature. (Burgh, J.) London, 1754.
Phil 8876.36.3 The dignity of human nature. (Burgh, J.) London, 1767. 2v.
Phil 8876.36.6 The dignity of human nature. (Burgh, J.) N.Y., 1812.
Phil 1905.20A The dignity of man. (Baker, H.C.) Cambridge, 1947.
Phil 6313.17 Dignwall, E.J. Very peculiar people. London, 1950.
Phil 310.659.7 Dijalektička teorija značenja. 2. izd. (Marković, Mihajlo.) Beograd, 1971.

Phil 310.160 — Dijalektički i historijski materijalizam i odabrani tekstovi. (Vranicki, Predrag.) Zagred, 1958.

Phil 310.642 — Dijalektički i istoriski materijalizam. 2. Izd. (Ziherl, Boris.) Beograd, 1952.

VPhil 310.648 — Dijalektički materijalizam. 2. Izd. (Šešić, Bogdan.) Beograd, 1967.

Phil 310.255 — Dijalektički materijalizam. 4. vyd. (Kosanović, I.) Sarajevo, 1959.

Phil 310.788 — Dijalektika gradjanskog drustva. (Rodin, Davor.) Beograd, 1971.

Phil 310.655.5 — Dijalektika ljudskog sveta. (Zaječaranovič, Gligorije.) Novi Sad, 1969.

Phil 2070.89 — Dijk, I. van. Het pragmatisme van William James. Groningen, 1911.

Phil 5500.20 — Dijkhuis, J.H.M. Het beoordelen in de psychologie. Utrecht, 1960.

Phil 6327.28.85 — Dijkhuis, Johannes Josephus. De procestheorie van C.R. Rogers. Hilversum, 1964.

Phil 1750.166.135 — Dijkhuis, P. Polariteitsbesef als een der fundamenten van het humanisme. Assen, 1960.

Phil 9255.30 — Dikkers, S.J. Ironie als vorm van communicatie. Den Haag, 1969.

Phil 5759.1.2 — The dilemma of determinism. (James, W.) n.p. 1884.

Phil 8581.63 — The dilemma of religious knowledge. (Bennett, Charles A.) New Haven, 1931.

Phil 1750.164 — The dilemma of the liberated. (Munson, A.B.) N.Y., 1930.

Phil 5190.28.2 — Dilemmas. (Ryle, G.) Cambridge, Eng., 1962.

Phil 2840.55 — Les dilemmes de la métaphysique pure. (Renouvier, C.B.) Paris, 1901.

Phil 178.36 — Dilles, Ludwig. Wieg zur Metaphysik als exakten Wissenschaft. Stuttgart, 1903-06. 2v.

Phil 178.76 — Dilley, Frank B. Metaphysics and religious language. N.Y., 1964.

Phil 3552.107 — Dillmann, E. Eine neue Darstellung der leibnizischen Monadenlehre. Leipzig, 1891.

Phil 9070.150 — Dilman, Ilham. Sense and delusion. London, 1971.

Phil 4809.489.2 — Dílo. v.2- (Klíma, Ladislav.) Praha, 1948-

Phil 3195.6.101 — Dilthey, eine Einführung in seine Philosophie. (Bollnow, O.F.) Leipzig, 1936.

Phil 3195.6.150 — Dilthey; una filosofía de la vida. (Stefanovies, T.) Montevideo, 1961.

Phil 3900.1.81 — Dilthey, W. Zum Andenken an Friedrich Ueberweg. n.p., n.d.

Phil 3195.6.79.6 — Dilthey, Wilhelm. Biographisch-literarischer Grundriss der allgemeinen Geschichte der Philosophie. 6. Aufl. Trebnitz, 189-

Phil 3195.6.33 — Dilthey, Wilhelm. Briefwechsel zwischen Wilhelm Dilthey und den Grafen Paul York von Watenburg. Halle, 1923.

Phil 178.26 — Dilthey, Wilhelm. Einleitung in die Geisteswissenschaften. Leipzig, 1803.

Phil 3195.6.38 — Dilthey, Wilhelm. The essence of philosophy. Chapel Hill, 1954.

Phil 3195.6.30.5 — Dilthey, Wilhelm. Gesammelte Schriften. Stuttgart, 1957-12v.

Phil 3195.6.30 — Dilthey, Wilhelm. Gesammelte Schriften. v.1-9,11-12. Leipzig, 1923-36. 11v.

Phil 3195.6.30.10 — Dilthey, Wilhelm. Gesammelte Schriften. v.1-17. Stuttgart, 1962- 16v.

Phil 3195.6.40 — Dilthey, Wilhelm. Grundriss der allgemeinen Geschichte der Philosophie. Frankfurt, 1949.

Phil 178.26.5 — Dilthey, Wilhelm. Introduction à l'étude des sciences humaines (Einleitung in die Geisteswissenschaften). 1re éd. Paris, 1942.

Phil 3425.311 — Dilthey, Wilhelm. Die Jugendgeschichte Hegels. Berlin, 1905.

Phil 3195.6.75 — Dilthey, Wilhelm. Der junge Dilthey. Leipzig, 1933.

Phil 3195.6.76 — Dilthey, Wilhelm. Der junge Dilthey. 2. Aufl. Stuttgart, 1960.

Phil 3805.85 — Dilthey, Wilhelm. Leben Schleiermachers. Berlin, 1870.

Phil 3805.85.2 — Dilthey, Wilhelm. Leben Schleiermachers. 2. Aufl. Berlin, 1922.

Phil 3195.6.50 — Dilthey, Wilhelm. Meanings in history. London, 1961.

Phil 3195.6.35 — Dilthey, Wilhelm. Die Philosophie des Lebens. Frankfurt, 1946.

Phil 3195.6.45 — Dilthey, Wilhelm. Philosophy of existence. N.Y., 1957.

Phil 3195.6.31 — Dilthey, Wilhelm. Von deutscher Dichtung und Musik. Leipzig, 1933.

Phil 3195.6.31.2 — Dilthey, Wilhelm. Von deutscher Dichtung und Musik. 2. Aufl. Stuttgart, 1957.

Phil 3195.6.80 — Pamphlet box. Dilthey, Wilhelm. German dissertations.

VPhil 3195.6.180 — Dilthey. (Kuderowicz, Zbigniew.) Warszawa, 1967.

Phil 3195.6.102 — Dilthey. 2. Aufl. (Bollnow, O.F.) Stuttgart, 1955.

Phil 3195.6.195 — Dilthey e il diritto naturale. (Calabrò, Gaetano.) Napoli, 1966.

Phil 3195.6.185 — Dilthey e la comprensione del mondo umano. (Marini, Giuliano.) Milano, 1965.

Phil 3195.6.140 — Dilthey o la lírica del historicismo. (Waesimann, A.) Tucumán, 1959.

Phil 3195.6.89 — Dilthey und das Problem der Metaphysik. (Degener, Alfons.) Bonn, 1933.

Phil 3195.6.157 — Dilthey ve Rickert'te manevi ilimlerin temellendirilmesi. (Birand, Kâmiran.) Ankara, 1954.

Phil 3195.6.107 — Diltheys Auffassung des griechischen Geistes. (Bork, A.) Berlin, 1944.

Phil 3120.4.31 — Dilucidationes philosophicae de Deo. 3. ed. (Bilfinger, G.B.) Tubingae, 1746.

Phil 8658.5 — Diman, J.L. The theistic argument as affected by recent theories. Boston, 1881.

Phil 8403.40 — La dimensión estetica del hombre. (Calderaro, José.) Buenos Aires, n.d.

Phil 8599.20.2 — The dimensional idea as an aid to religion. (Tyler, W.F.) London, 1907.

Phil 8599.20 — The dimensional idea as an aid to religion. (Tyler, W.F.) N.Y., 1910.

Phil 5249.29 — Dimensionen der Intelligenz. (Jaeger, Adolf Otto.) Göttingen, 1967.

Phil 5545.244 — Dimensionen des Gedächtnisses. (Katzenberger, Lothar Friedrich.) Wurzburg, 1964.

Phil 5274.16 — Dimensionen des Verhaltens. (Pawlik, Kurt.) Bern, 1968.

Phil 585.190 — Dimensionen menschlicher Wirklichkeit. (Burkhardt, Hans.) Schweinfurt, 1969.

Phil 5585.227 — Dimensiones de la percepcion. (Oñativia, O.V.) Tucuman, 1963.

Phil 8612.82 — Dimensioni antropologiche della morte. (Bordoni, Marcello.) Roma, 1969.

Phil 177.112 — Les dimensions de l'être et du temps. (Chaix-Reys, Jules.) Paris, 1953.

Phil 5242.50 — Dimensions of behaviour. (Carlsson, N.G.) Lund, 1949.

Phil 585.173 — The dimensions of human evolution. (Mukerjee, Radhakamal.) London, 1963.

Phil 6123.10 — Dimensions of mind. (New York (City). University. Institution of Philosophy.) N.Y., 1960.

Phil 5590.45 — Dimensions of personality. (Eysenck, Hans Jurgen.) London, 1948.

Phil 5500.30 — Dimensions of response consistency in paired comparisons. (Sadacca, Robert.) Princeton, 1962.

Phil 2905.1.525 — Dimensions of the future; the spirituality of Teilhard de Chardin. Washington, 1968.

Phil 735.245 — The dimensions of values. (Mukerjee, Radhakamal.) London, 1964.

Phil 2520.121 — Dimier, Louis. Descartes. Paris, 1917.

Phil 2520.121.5 — Dimier, Louis. La vie raisonnable de Descartes. Paris, 1929.

VPhil 8404.24 — Dimitrov, D.N. Životot i umetnosta. Skopje, 1967.

Phil 6113.10 — Dimmler, H. System der Psychologie. München, n.d.

Phil 5243.34.15 — Dimnet, E. L'art de penser. Paris, 1930.

Phil 5243.34.10 — Dimnet, E. The art of thinking. London, 1929.

Phil 5243.34.5A — Dimnet, E. The art of thinking. N.Y., 1929.

Phil 5243.34.9A — Dimnet, E. The art of thinking. N.Y., 1929.

Phil 5243.34.3 — Dimnet, E. The art of thinking. N.Y., 1929.

Phil 8878.51.8 — Dimnet, Ernest. What we live by. London, 1932.

Phil 8878.51.5 — Dimnet, Ernest. What we live by. N.Y., 1932.

Phil 8583.38 — Dimond, S.G. Heart and mind. London, 1945.

Phil 5627.99 — Dimond, S.G. The psychology of the Methodist revival. London, 1926.

Phil 8581.114 — Din ve Lâiklik. (Başgil, Ali Fuad.) Istanbul, 1962.

Phil 2475.1.224 — La dinamica dello spirito nella conoscenza: saggio...Bergson. (Perego, Luigi.) Bologna, 1925.

Phil 6675.5 — La dinamica molecolare. (Fusinieri, A. von.) Foligno, 1866.

Phil 8622.66 — Dinamismo e maturità della fede. (Barruffo, Antonio.) Roma, 1968.

Phil 8590.42 — Dinber tarihi. (Kahraman, Ahmet.) Istanbul, 1965.

Phil 181.4 — Les diners baron D'Holbach. (Genlis, S.F. de.) Paris, 1822.

Phil 197.69 — Das Ding. (Winderlich, R.) Karlsruhe, 1924.

Phil 3415.40 — Das Ding an sich. (Hartmann, Eduard von.) Berlin, 1871.

Phil 353.3 — Das Ding an Sich und das Naturgesetz der Seele. (Wyneken, Ernst.) Heidelberg, 1901.

Phil 5241.145.5.2 — De dingen. 2. druk. (Berg, Jan Hendrik van den.) Nijkerk, 1966.

Phil 284.3 — Dinger, H. Prinzip der Entwickelung. Jena, 1896.

Phil 3195.15.35 — Dingler, Hugo. Die Ergreifung des Wirklichen. München, 1955.

Phil 1703.6 — Dingler, Hugo. Geschichte der Naturphilosophie. Berlin, 1932.

Phil 3195.15.30 — Dingler, Hugo. Der Glaube an die Weltmaschine und seine Uberwindung. Stuttgart, 1932.

Phil 3625.3.87 — Dingler, Hugo. Die Grundgedanken der Machschen Philosophie. Leipzig, 1924.

Phil 178.37 — Dingler, Hugo. Die Grundlagen der Naturphilosophie. Leipzig, 1913.

Phil 8878.53 — Dingler, Hugo. Das Handeln im Sinne des Höchsten Zieles. (Absolute Ethik). München, 1935.

Phil 178.37.10 — Dingler, Hugo. Metaphysik als Wissenschaft vom Letzten. München, 1929.

Phil 5043.29 — Dingler, Hugo. Philosophie der Logik und Arithmetik. München, 1931.

Phil 178.37.15 — Dingler, Hugo. Das System. München, 1930.

Phil 178.37.5 — Dingler, Hugo. Der Zusammenbruch der Wissenschaft und der Primat derPhilosophie. München, 1926.

Phil 178.37.7 — Dingler, Hugo. Der Zusammenbruch der Wissenschaft und der Primat der Philosophie. 2e Aufl. München, 1931.

Phil 7069.30.6 — Dingwall, E.J. Ghosts and spirits in the ancient world. London, 1930.

Phil 4464.1.30 — Diniz, Almachio. Questões actuaes de philosophia e direito. Rio de Janeiro, 1909.

Phil 2270.185 — Di Nola, Mario. Il presupposto biologico e individualista della sociologia spenceriana. Colombo, 1965.

Phil 5043.20 — Dinwiddie, William. Essentials of logic. N.Y., 1914.

Phil 3819.60 — Dio. (Spinoza, Benedictus de.) Lanciano, 1911.

Phil 4080.8.40 — Dio e il male. (Conti, Augusto.) Prato, 1866.

Phil 4073.60 — Dio e la predestinazione. (Campanella, Tommaso.) Firenze, 1949-51. 2v.

Phil 8654.114 — Dio é morto? 4. ed. Milano, 1968.

Phil 8672.20 — Dio nella ricerca umana. 3. ed. (Ricciotti, G.) Roma, 1954.

Phil 8592.124 — Dio esiste, yo me la encontre. (Morra, Gianfranco.) Bologna, 1970.

Htn — Phil 4934.1.30* — Diogenes Laertius. De vita et moribus philosophorum. Basiliae, 1524.

Htn — Phil 4934.2.30* — Dionysius Areopagita. Theologia vivificans. Argêtine, 1502.

Phil 3640.191 — Dionysos. 2e Aufl. (Würzbach, F.) München, 1922.

Phil 8633.1.3 — Dionysos and immortality. (Wheeler, B.I.) Boston, 1898.

Phil 3640.765 — Dionysos of God. (Lannoy, Joris C.) Brugge, 1968.

Phil 3640.470 — Dionysus. (Manthey-Zorn, Otto.) Amherst, 1956.

Phil 177.90 — Dios, el universo y la libertad. (Chávez, E.A.) Barcelona, 1935.

Phil 4973.41 — Dios, espíritu y materia; esencia. 2. ed. (Lizarte Martínez, Angel.) Montevideo, 1944.

Phil 5627.107.30 — Dios existe, yo me la encontre. (Frossard, Amdre.) Madrid, 1969.

Phil 4352.1.79 — Dios Mendoza, J. de. Bibliografia balmesiana. Barcelona, 1961.

Phil 8406.7.5 — Diotima; die Idee des Schönen. (Fischer, Kuno.) Leipzig, 1928.

Phil 8406.7 — Diotima; die Idee des Schönen. (Fischer, Kuno.) Stuttgart, 1852.

Phil 7050.10 — Diotrephes. The "knockings"Exposed. N.Y., 1850. 3 pam.

Phil 334.1 — Dippe, A. Untersuchungen über die Bedeutung der Denkform. Jena, 1893.

Phil 284.5 — Dippe, Alfred. Naturphilosophie. München, 1907.

Phil 7068.97.42 — Dippel, Joseph. Der neuere Spiritismus in seinem Wesen dargelegt und nach seinem Werte geprüft. 2. Aufl. München, 1897.

Phil 2477.7.81 — Dippel, Joseph. Versuch einer systematischen Darstellung der Philosophie des C. Bovillus. Würzburg, 1865.

Phil 3640.258 — Dippel, P.G. Nietzsche und Wagner. Bern, 1934.

Phil 4960.215 — Las direcciones filosóficas de la cultura argentina. (Ingenieros, José.) Buenos Aires, 1963.

Phil 7069.08.10 — The direct phenomena of spirtualism. (Bennett, E.T.) London, 1908.

Phil 5247.29.20 — Directed thinking. (Humphrey, G.) N.Y., 1948.

Phil 5930.18.4 — The direction of desire. (Bligh, Stanley M.) London, 1910.

Phil 672.182 The direction of time. (Reichenbach, Hans.) Berkeley, 1956.
Phil 5520.431 Directions in psycholinguistics. (Rosenberg, Sheldon.) N.Y., 1965.
Phil 9341.11 Directions prudential, moral, religious. (Burgh, J.) London, 1750.
Phil 8847.10 The directive in history. (Wieman, H.N.) Boston, 1949.
Phil 8892.80 Directives and norms. (Ross, Alf.) London, 1968.
Phil 1523.12.15 Directives pour la confection d'une monographie. (Steenberghen, F.) Louvain, 1961.
Phil 130.12 Directory of American philosophers. Albuquerque. 2,1967+ 4v.
Phil 10.62 Directory of applied psychologists. (American Association for Applied Psychology.) Bloomington, Ind.
Phil 6980.598 Directory of psychiatric clinics in the United States. 1. ed. (National Committee for Mental Hygiene.) N.Y., 1932.
Phil 3497.26 La direzione coscienza-intenzione nella filosofia di Kant e Husserl. (Pantaleo, Pasquale.) Bari, 1967.
Phil 8876.49 Il diritto. 3. ed. (Bunge, E.O.) Torino, 1909.
Phil 3483.70 Diritto e stato nel pensiero di Emanuele Kant. (Bobbio, Norberto.) Torino, 1957.
Phil 4260.220 Diritto e umanità in G.B. Vico. (Candela, Mercurio.) Empoli, 1968.
Phil 5243.65 Dirks, Heinz. Psychologie. Gütersloh, 1960.
Phil 1145.52 Dirlmeier, Franz. Filos und Filia im vorhellenistischen Griechentum. Inaug. Diss. München, 1931.
Phil 2750.23.85 Dirven, Edouard. De la forme à l'acte...Joseph Maréchal. Paris, 1965.
Phil 5262.50 Disaster, a psychological essay. (Wolfenstein, M.) Glencoe, Ill., 1957.
Phil 7069.38.4 Discarnate influence. (Bozzano, E.) London, 1938.
Phil 6990.12.5 Le discernement du miracle. (Saintyves, P.) Paris, 1909.
Phil 3310.1.85 Dischinger, J.N.P. Die Günther'sche Philosophie. Schaffhausen, 1852.
Phil 530.10 Les disciples anglais de Jacob Boehme. (Hutin, Serge.) Paris, 1960.
Phil 9070.43 Disciplina y rebeldia. (Onis y Sanchez, F. de.) San José, Costa Rica, 1917.
Phil 4114.25.3 Disciplinarum metaphysicarum elementa. (Genovesi, Antonio.) Bassani, 1785. 5v.
Phil 2005.13 The discipline of the cave. (Findlay, John N.) London, 1966.
Phil 8598.83 The disciplines of liberty. (Sperry, Willard L.) New Haven, 1921.
Phil 8598.83.5A The disciplines of liberty. (Sperry, Willard L.) New Haven, 1923.
Phil 5249.30 Disclosing man to himself. (Jourard, Sidney Marshall.) Princeton, 1968.
Phil 299.2 Disclosures of the universal mysteries. (Silberstein, S.J.) N.Y., 1896.
Phil 177.82 Le discontinu dans la philosophie et dans les sciences exactes. (Calvet, Adolphe.) Paris, 1923.
Htn Phil 8892.40* Discori...in sette giornate. (Romei, A.) Verona, 1586.
Phil 4120.8.45 Discorsi, 1938-50. (Guzzo, Augusto.) Torino, 1951.
Phil 9177.3 Discorsi de...ne'quali si ragiona compiutamente. (Grimaldi Robbio, Pelegro de.) Genova, 1585.
Phil 8430.14 Discorsi di letteratura e d'arte. (Calcara, A.) Marcianise, 1961.
Phil 8586.17 Discorsi di religione. (Gentile, G.) Firenze, 1920.
Phil 8586.17.2 Discorsi di religione. 2. ed. (Gentile, G.) Firenze, 1924.
Phil 4120.4.31 Discorsi di religone. 3. ed. (Gentile, Giovanni.) Firenze, 1934.
Phil 13.16 Discorsi e prolusioni. Torino.
Htn Phil 8900.6* I discorsi mi quali si tratta della nobilità. (Zuccolo, G.) Venetia, 1575.
Phil 4210.137F Discorso...per Antonio Rosmini. (Pedrotti, Pietro.) Rovereto, 1908.
Phil 177.87.5 Discorso. (Cavour, G.B. di.) Torino, 1861.
Phil 2520.45.12 Il discorso del metodo. (Descartes, René.) Assisi, 1911.
Phil 2520.45.5 Il discorso del metodo. (Descartes, René.) Milano, 19- .
Phil 3552.51.15 Discorso di metafisica "Hortus conclusus". (Leibniz, Gottfried Wilhelm.) Napoli, 1934.
Phil 4170.7.50 Discorso proemiale letto li 10 nov. 1850. (Mamiani della Rovere, Terenzio.) Genova, 1850.
Phil 4260.107F Discorso recitato il di primo anniversario del plebiscito dell'Italia meridionale. (Ranieri, A.) Napoli, 1861.
Phil 2520.35.52 Discorso sul metodo. (Descartes, René.) Firenze, 1962.
Phil 2520.45.25 Discorso sul metodo. (Descartes, René.) Napoli, 1937.
Phil 2520.45.18 Il discorso sul metodo. (Descartes, René.) Torino, 1926.
Phil 2520.45 Discorso sul metodo e meditazioni. (Descartes, René.) Bari, 1912. 2v.
Phil 4110.12.30 Discorso sulla speranza. (Fancelli, M.) Messina, 1960.
Phil 8419.27 Discorso sull'arte. (Santangelo, P.E.) Milano, 1956.
X Cg Phil 3246.55.10 Discours a la nation allemande. (Fichte, Johann Gottlieb.) Paris, 1895.
Phil 5825.6.4 Discours de la connaissance des bestes. 4. éd. (Pardies, Ignace.) Paris, 1896.
Phil 2520.35.39 Discours de la méthode. (Descarter, René.) Paris, 1937.
Phil 2520.35.15 Discours de la méthode. (Descartes, René.) Cambridge, Eng., 1923.
Phil 2520.35.21 Discours de la méthode. (Descartes, René.) Evreux, 1927.
Phil 2520.35.14 Discours de la méthode. (Descartes, René.) Londres, 1913.
Phil 2520.35.16 Discours de la méthode. (Descartes, René.) Paris, 1925.
Phil 2520.35.17 Discours de la méthode. (Descartes, René.) Paris, 1926.
Phil 2520.35.19 Discours de la méthode. (Descartes, René.) Paris, 1927.
Phil 2520.35.26 Discours de la méthode. (Descartes, René.) Paris, 1932.
Phil 2520.35.25 Discours de la méthode. (Descartes, René.) Paris, 1932.
Phil 2520.35.45 Discours de la méthode. (Descartes, René.) Paris, 1950.
Phil 2520.35.40 Discours de la méthode. (Descartes, René.) Paris, 1951.
Phil 2520.35.48 Discours de la méthode. (Descartes, René.) Paris, 1961.
Phil 2520.35.37 Discours de la méthode. (Ouvrages de l'esprit). (Descartes, René.) Manchester, 1941.
Phil 2520.35.47 Discours de la méthode. 2. ed. (Descarter, René.) Manchester, 1961.
Phil 2520.35.9 Discours de la méthode pour bien conduire sa raison et chercher la vérité dans les sciences. (Descartes, René.) Strasbourg, n.d.
Htn Phil 2520.35.1* Discours de la méthode pour bien conduire sa raison et chercher la vérité dans les sciences. (Descartes, René.) Leyde, 1637.
Phil 2520.35.3 Discours de la méthode pour bien conduire sa raison et chercher la vérité dans les sciences. (Descartes, René.) Paris, 1668.
Htn Phil 2520.35.13* Discours de la méthode pour bien conduire sa raison et chercher la vérité dans les sciences. (Descartes, René.) Paris, 1668.
Htn Phil 2520.35.12* Discours de la méthode pour bien conduire sa raison et chercher la vérité dans les sciences. (Descartes, René.) Paris, 1668.
Phil 2520.35.6 Discours de la méthode pour bien conduire sa raison et chercher la vérité dans les sciences. (Descartes, René.) Paris, 1876.
Phil 2520.35.8 Discours de la méthode pour bien conduire sa raison et chercher la vérité dans les sciences. (Descartes, René.) Paris, 1886.
Phil 2520.35.4 Discours de la méthode pour bien conduire sa raison et chercher la vérité dans les sciences. (Descartes, René.) Paris, 1894.
Phil 803.4.15 Discours de la méthode pour bien étudier l'histoire de la philosophie. (Deussen, P.) Paris, n.d.
Phil 3552.51.10 Discours de métaphysique. (Leibniz, Gottfried Wilhelm.) Paris, 1929.
Phil 3552.51.12 Discours de métaphysique et Correspondance aves Arnauld. (Leibniz, Gottfried Wilhelm.) Paris, 1957.
Phil 2475.1.71 Discours de réception. (Bergson, Henri.) Paris, 1918.
Phil 7060.6.7 Discours des spectres, ou visions. (Le Loyer, P.) Paris, 1608.
Htn Phil 6990.36* Discours d'un miracle avenu en la Basse Normandie. (Morry, A. de.) Paris, 1598.
Phil 7060.6.3 Discours et histoires des spectres, visions et apparitions des spirits. (Le Loyer, P.) Paris, 1605.
Phil 5520.401 Le discours et le symbole. (Ortigues, E.) Paris, 1962.
Phil 352.6 Le discours et l'intuition. (Vialatoux, J.) Paris, 1930.
Htn Phil 2520.35.10* A discours of a method. (Descartes, René.) London, 1649.
Phil 176.98 Discours philosophiques. (Bouillier, D.R.) Amsterdam, 1759.
Phil 9230.30 Discours prononcé devant la cour royale d'Aix à l'audience solennelle de rentrée. (Borély, Joseph.) Aix, 1836.
Htn Phil 8610.713.10* Discours sur la liberté de penser. (Collins, Anthony.) Londres, 1714.
Phil 6930.7 Discours sur la mélancolie. (Boieldiev, M.J.A.) Paris, 1808.
Phil 2475.1.35 Discours sur la politesse. (Bergson, Henri.) Paris, 1945.
Phil 8876.99 Discours sur la vertu. 2e éd. (Bouffleis, Stanislas de.) Paris, 1800.
Htn Phil 2490.51* Discours sur l'ensemble du positivisme. (Comte, Auguste.) Paris, 1848.
Phil 2805.55 Discours sur les passions de l'amour. (Pascal, Blaise.) Paris, 1900.
Phil 2805.282 Discours sur les passions de l'amour de Pascal. (Ducas, A.) Alger, 1953.
Phil 2805.183 Discours sur les pensées de M. Pascal. (Filleau de la Chaise, J.) Paris, 1922.
Phil 2490.53A Discours sur l'esprit positif. (Comte, Auguste.) Paris, 1844.
Phil 1915.60.4 Discourse...attributes of God. (Clarke, Samuel.) London, 1706. 2 pam.
Phil 1915.60.5 Discourse...attributes of God. (Clarke, Samuel.) London, 1711. 2 pam.
Phil 1915.60 Discourse...attributes of God. (Clarke, Samuel.) London, 1719. 2 pam.
Phil 1915.60.2 Discourse...attributes of God. (Clarke, Samuel.) London, 1719.
Phil 1915.60.3 Discourse...attributes of God. (Clarke, Samuel.) London, 1728.
Phil 1915.60.7 Discourse...attributes of God. 6th ed. (Clarke, Samuel.) London, 1725. 2 pam.
Htn Phil 2115.153* A discourse...in answer to Mr. Lock. (Barbon, N.) London, 1696.
Htn Phil 8597.14* A discourse...reason in matters of religion. (Rust, G.) London, 1683.
Htn Phil 1870.72* A discourse addressed to magistrates and men in authority. (Berkeley, G.) Dublin, 1738.
Htn Phil 9359.7* A discourse against painting...of women. (Tuke, Thomas.) London, 1616.
Htn Phil 8670.4* A discourse concerning the existence of God. (Pelling, E.) London, 1696.
Htn Phil 186.30* A discourse concerning the nature of man. (Lowde, James.) London, 1694.
Phil 8712.05 A discourse delivered at...dedication of...the chapel. (Wayland, Francis.) Providence, 1835.
Htn Phil 9346.9* A discourse of auxiliary beauty. (Gauden, John.) n.p., 1656.
Htn Phil 8876.13* Discourse of civil life. (Bryskett, Lodowick.) London, 1606.
Phil 8610.713.5 A discourse of free-thinking. (Collins, Anthony.) Stuttgart, 1965.
Htn Phil 8610.713* A discourse of free thinking occasioned by the rise and growth of a sect call'd free-thinker. (Collins, Anthony.) London, 1713. 3 pam.
Phil 9220.3A A discourse of friendship. (Taylor, Jeremy.) Cedar Rapids, 1913.
Phil 8595.1.3 A discourse of matters pertaining to religion. (Parker, T.) Boston, 1842.
Phil 8595.1 A discourse of matters pertaining to religion. (Parker, T.) Boston, 1847.
Phil 8595.1.2 A discourse of matters pertaining to religion. (Parker, T.) Boston, 1856.
Phil 8595.1.4A A discourse of matters pertaining to religion. (Parker, T.) Boston, 1907.
Htn Phil 8581.19* A discourse of natural and revealed religion. (Barrington, J.S.) n.p., n.d.
Phil 8581.13 A discourse of natural theology. (Brougham, H.) Philadelphia, 1835.
Phil 2205.30.8 Discourse of natural theology. (Brougham and Vaux, Henry Brougham.) London, 1835.
Phil 8581.13.3 A discourse of natural theology. 4. ed. (Brougham, H.) London, 1835.
Phil 1850.89 Discourse of the Baconian philosophy. (Tyler, S.) Frederick City, 1844.
Phil 1850.89.2 Discourse of the Baconian philosophy. (Tyler, S.) Frederick City, 1846.
Phil 1850.89.3 Discourse of the Baconian philosophy. (Tyler, S.) N.Y., 1850.
Phil 1850.89.5 Discourse of the Baconian philosophy. 3rd ed. (Tyler, S.) Washington, 1877.
Htn Phil 1930.5.30* A discourse of the grounds and reasons of the Christian religion. (Collins, Anthony.) London, 1724-37.
Phil 1930.5.35 A discourse of the grounds and reasons of the Christian religion. (Collins, Anthony.) London, 1737. 2 pam.
Htn Phil 1930.5.37* A discourse of the grounds and reasons of the Christian religion. (Collins, Anthony.) London, 1737. 2 pam.
Htn Phil 1930.5.29* A discourse of the grounds and reasons of the Christian religion. v.1-2. (Collins, Anthony.) London, 1724.

Htn Phil 9220.3.5* A discourse of the nature...of friendship. (Taylor, Jeremy.) London, 1671. 2 pam.

Phil 9045.10 Discourse on Christian patriotism. (Carpenter, L.) London, 1838.

Phil 7082.146 A discourse on dreams and night-visions. (Simpson, David.) Macclesfield, 1791.

Phil 3552.51 Discourse on metaphysics. (Leibniz, Gottfried Wilhelm.) Chicago, 1927.

Phil 3552.51.8 Discourse on metaphysics. (Leibniz, Gottfried Wilhelm.) La Salle, 1962.

Phil 3552.51.7 Discourse on metaphysics. (Leibniz, Gottfried Wilhelm.) Manchester, 1953.

Phil 2520.37 Discourse on method. (Descartes, René.) Chicago, 1899.

Phil 2520.37.10 Discourse on method. (Descartes, René.) London, 1901.

Htn Phil 1930.2.30* A discourse on religion. (Channing, William E.) Boston, 1821.

Phil 6128.3 A discourse on the influence of diseases on the intellectual and moral powers. (Smith, J.M.) N.Y., 1848.

Phil 2520.38 Discourse on the method of rightly conducting the reason. (Descartes, René.) Edinburgh, 1850.

Phil 5927.1 A discourse on the social relations of man. (Howe, S.G.) Boston, 1837.

Phil 490.1 Discourse on the soul and instinct. N.Y., 1849.

Phil 8705.1.2 A discourse on the soul and the principle of instinct. (Paine, M.) N.Y., 1848. 4 pam.

Phil 8705.1 A discourse on the soul and the principle of instinct. (Paine, M.) N.Y., 1848. 4 pam.

Phil 8598.6.10 A discourse on the studies of the university. (Sedgwick, Adam.) N.Y., 1969.

Phil 8598.6 A discourse on the studies of the university of Cambridge. (Sedgwick, Adam.) Cambridge, 1850.

Phil 8598.6.2 A discourse on the studies of the university of Cambridge. 2. ed. (Sedgwick, Adam.) Cambridge, 1834.

Phil 8598.6.4 A discourse on the studies of the university of Cambridge. 3. ed. (Sedgwick, Adam.) Cambridge, 1834.

Phil 3450.19.85.5 Discourse on thinking. (Heidegger, Martin.) N.Y., 1966.

Phil 193.26 A discourse on truth. (Shute, R.) London, 1877.

Phil 8585.8 Discourses...natural religion and social virtue. (Foster, J.) London, 1749-52.

Htn Phil 9358.7* Discourses...useful for vain modish ladies and their gallants. (Shannon, F.) London, 1696.

X Cg Phil 8418.24.5 Discourses. (Reynolds, J.) London, 1842.

Phil 8418.24 Discourses. (Reynolds, J.) London, 1884.

Phil 8655.1.6 Discourses concerning...God. (Abernethy, J.) Aberdeen, 1778. 2v.

Phil 8655.1.3 Discourses concerning...God. (Abernethy, J.) Dublin, 1743. 2v.

Htn Phil 2280.4.30F* Discourses concerning government. (Sidney, Algernon.) London, 1698.

Phil 7054.74 Discourses from the spirit-world. (Wilson, R.P.) N.Y., 1855.

Phil 2805.101.25 The discourses of Cleander and Eudoxe. (Daniel, Gabriel.) London, 1704.

Phil 8598.26 Discourses on...subjects of natural and revealed religion. (Scot, David.) Edinburgh, 1825.

Phil 7054.160 Discourses through the mediumship of Mrs. C. Tappan. (Tappan, Cora L.V.) London, 1875.

Phil 5258.104 Discovering ourselves. (Strecker, Edward A.) N.Y., 1931.

Phil 5258.104.5 Discovering ourselves. 2d ed. (Strecker, Edward A.) N.Y., 1943.

Htn Phil 7060.73* Discovery concerning ghosts. 2d ed. (Cruikshank, G.) London, 1864.

Phil 6123.5.5 Discovery of a lost trail. (Newcomb, C.B.) Boston, 1900.

Phil 978.41 The discovery of discoveries. (Mason, E.L.) n.p., n.d.

Phil 8701.22 The discovery of God. (Lubac, H. de.) N.Y., 1960.

Phil 6158.35 The discovery of love; a psychedelic experience with LSD-25. (Bishop, Malden Grange.) N.Y., 1963.

Phil 5425.110 The discovery of talent. (Wolfle, Dael Lee.) Cambridge, 1969.

Phil 6906.10 The discovery of the unconscious. (Ellenberger, Henri F.) N.Y., 1970.

Phil 672.258.1 The discovery of time. (Toulmin, Stephen Edelston.) London, 1965.

Phil 672.258 The discovery of time. (Toulmin, Stephen Edelston.) N.Y., 1965.

Phil 5827.10 Discrimination limens of pattern and size in the goldfish, Carassius auratus. Thesis. (Rowley, Jean B.) Worcester, Mass., 1934.

Phil 5827.7 Discrimination of light of different wave-lengths by fish. (Reeves, Cora Daisy.) N.Y., 1919.

Phil 5585.252 The discrimination process and development. 1. ed. (Fellows, Brian S.) Oxford, 1968.

Phil 4363.3.85 Discurso de la verdad. (Lede, Luis Perez de Guzman y Sanjuan.) Bilboa, 1954.

Phil 4363.3.38 Discurso de la verdad dedicado á la Imperial Majestad de Dios. (Manara Vicentelo de Leca, M. de.) Zaragoza, 1967.

Phil 4363.3.35 Discurso de la verdad dedicado á la Imperial Majestad de Dios. (Manara Vincentelo de Leca, M. de.) Madrid, 1878.

Phil 5245.28F Discurso leido...2 de julio de 1898. (Farpon y Tuñón, José.) Manila, 1898.

Phil 4313.1 Discurso leído en la universidad central. (Menéndez y Pelayo, M.) Madrid, 1889.

Phil 8404.3 Discurso tecnico delle arti. (Dorfles, Gillo.) Pisa, 1952.

Phil 4340.15 Discursos leídos en las recepciones públicas de la Real Academia Española. Ser. 2. (Academia...Madrid. Academia Española, Madrid.) Madrid, 1945- 6v.

Phil 2520.127 Discussio perysatitica. (Vincentius, Joannes.) Tolosae, 1677.

Phil 3493.2 Discussion des Antinomies Kantiennes. (Lorquet, N.H.A.) Paris, 1841.

Phil 7054.61.5 A discussion of the facts of...ancient and modern spiritualism. (Brittan, Samuel B.) N.Y., 1853.

Phil 1535.3 Discussioni di filosofia razionale. (Buscarini, G.) Milano, 1857. 2v.

Phil 4210.245 Discussioni rosminiane. (Brancaforte, Antonio.) Catania, 1968.

Phil 8402.64 Discussioni sull'arte e sulla condizione dell'uomo. (Bianca, Giovanni A.) Messina, 1965.

Phil 2725.2.35 Discussions critiques, et pensées diverses sur la religion et la philosophie. (Lamennais, F.R. de.) Paris, 1841.

Phil 2725.2.35.5 Les discussions critiques. (Le Guillou, Louis.) Paris, 1967.

Phil 192.90 Discussions metaphysiques. (Roche, Jean.) Paris, 1950.

Phil 3925.16.235 Discussions of Wittgenstein. (Rhees, Rush.) London, 1970.

Phil 2035.30.7 Discussions on philosophy and literature, education. (Hamilton, William.) N.Y., 1858.

Phil 2035.30 Discussions on philosophy and literature. (Hamilton, William.) London, 1852.

Phil 2035.30.2 Discussions on philosophy and literature. (Hamilton, William.) N.Y., 1853.

Phil 2035.30.3 Discussions on philosophy and literature. (Hamilton, William.) N.Y., 1855.

Phil 2035.30.1 Discussions on philosophy and literature. 2nd ed. (Hamilton, William.) London, 1853.

Phil 8610.798.11 Discussions philosophiques sur l'athéisme. (Gradis, David.) Paris, 1803.

Phil 978.59.22 Discussions with Krishnamurti in Europe, 1965. (Krishnamurti, J.) London, 1966.

Phil 8583.5 Disdier, H. Conciliation rationnelle du droit et du devoir. Genève, 1859. 2v.

Phil 5402.36 Disease, pain and suffering. (Bakan, David.) Chicago, 1968.

Phil 5330.40 Diseases of attention and perception. 1st ed. (Meldman, Monte Jay.) Oxford, 1970.

Phil 5545.22.5 Diseases of memory. (Ribot, T.) N.Y., 1882.

Phil 5545.22.6 Diseases of memory. (Ribot, T.) N.Y., 1883.

Phil 6327.46.10 The diseases of personality. (Ribot, Théodule.) Chicago, 1891.

Phil 7040.2.5 Diseases of personality. Photoreproduction. (Ribot, T.) N.Y., 1887.

Phil 6327.46.14 The diseases of personality. 4th ed. (Ribot, Théodule.) Chicago, 1906.

Phil 6311.21 Diseases of the nervous system resulting from accident and injury. (Bailey, Pearce.) N.Y., 1906.

Phil 5767.1.12 The diseases of the will. (Ribot, T.) Chicago, 1894.

Phil 5767.1.10 The diseases of the will. 3. ed. (Ribot, T.) Chicago, 1903.

Phil 5875.62 Disegno e linguaggio el bambino. (Fonzi, Ada.) Torino, 1968.

Phil 5875.110.5 Il disegno nella psicopatologia dell'età evolutiva. (Tuvo, Fulvio.) Trieste, 1966.

Phil 802.13 Disegno storico della filosofia. (Caramella, S.) Messina, 1931.

Phil 7059.21 Disembodied spirits. (Whytt, James.) London, 1840.

Phil 7067.46.20 Disertazioni sopra le apparizioni de spiriti. (Calmet, Augustin.) Venezia. 1770.

Phil 8878.10.5 Disney, J. Essay upon execution of laws vs. immorality and prophaneness. London, 1708.

Phil 8878.10 Disney, J. A second essay...execution...laws against immorality. London, 1710.

Phil 5360.24 Displacement of concepts. (Schon, Donald A.) London, 1963.

Phil 353.34 Dispositional properties. (Weissman, David J.) Carbondale, 1965.

Phil 8735.50 Disput über das teleologische Denken. (Schmitz, Josef.) Mainz, 1960.

Phil 1100.7 Disputatia literaria. (Baumhauer, Theodor C.M.) Trajuti ad Rhinum, 1844. 4 pam.

Phil 5628.50.5 Disputatio brevis ad categorica de proba stigmata utrum scilicet ea licita sit, necne. (Jordanaeus, Johannes.) Coloniae Agrippinae, 1630.

Phil 4513.4.31 Disputatio gradualis de philosopho curioso. (Asp, Matthia.) Upsaliae, 1730.

Phil 7067.00 Disputatio iuridica inauguralis de iure spectrorum...Andreas Becker. (Stryk, Johann S.) Halae Magdeburgicae, n.d.

Phil 7067.00.5 Disputatio iuridica inauguralis de iure spectrorum...Andreas Becker. (Stryk, Johann S.) Jenae, 1745.

Phil 1195.3 Disputatio literaria. (Baumhauer, T.C.M.) Rhenum, 1844.

Phil 6967.8 Disputatio medica inauguralis de insania. (Revere, John.) Edinburgh, 1811.

Htn Phil 3552.50* Disputatio metaphysica. (Leibniz, Gottfried Wilhelm.) Lipsiae, 1663.

Phil 6124.2 Disputatio philosophica. (Orth, H.) Jenae, 1674.

Phil 8667.14 Disputatio philosophica de contemplatione mortis. (Micrandu, J.) Stockholmiae, 1684.

Phil 3004.4 Disputation: drei Bücher vom Deutschen. (Ehrenberg, Hans.) München, 1923-25. 3v.

Phil 4195.34 Disputationes adversus astralogiam divinatricem. (Pico della Mirandola, Giovanni.) Firenze, 1946-52. 2v.

Phil 8670.3 Disputationes de Deo. (Parker, S.) London, 1678.

Htn Phil 1535.13* Disputationes de universa philosophia. (Mendoza, P.H. de.) Lugduni, 1617.

Phil 176.101 Disputationes metaphysicae. Fasc.1-3. (Backer, S. de.) Paris, 1920-1923.

Htn Phil 186.54* Disputationum Camaldulensium. Bk. 4. (Landino, C.) Argentoraci, 1508.

Phil 185.98 Disputed questions in philosophy. (Keleher, James Francis.) N.Y., 1965.

Htn Phil 2520.182* Disquisitio metaphysica. (Gassendi, Pierre.) Amsterodami, 1644.

Phil 179.27 Disquisitio philosophica de contingentia rerum. (Ewast, John-Bart.) Aboae, 1735.

Htn Phil 8735.2* A disquisition...final causes of natural things. (Boyle, R.) London, 1688.

Phil 2218.30 Disquisitions relating to matter and spirit. (Priestley, Joseph.) Birmingham, 1778-82. 3v.

Phil 2218.29 Disquisitions relating to matter and spirit. 1st ed. (Priestley, Joseph.) London, 1777.

Phil 3507.7 Disquisitionum philosophiae Kantianae. v.1-2. (Zallinger, J.A.) Augustae Vindelicorum, 1799.

Phil 5850.200 Dissatisfied worker. (Fisher, V.E.) N.Y., 1931.

Phil 1855.30 Dissertaions on leading philosophical topics. (Bain, Alexander.) London, 1903.

Phil 6046.91 Dissertatio academica, de chiromantiae vanitate. (Schulty, Christoph.) Regiomonti, 1691?

Phil 4513.4.41 Dissertatio academica de caussis obscuritatis philosophorum. (Asp, Matthia.) Upsaliae, 1733.

Phil 4513.4.47 Dissertatio academica de syncretismo philosophico. (Asp, Matthia.) Upsaliae, 1737.

Phil 4513.4.33 Dissertatio academica potiores antiquorum. (Asp, Matthia.) Upsaliae, 1732.

Htn Phil 5821.11* Dissertatio de carentia sensus et cognitionis in brutis. (Legrand, A.) London, 1675.

Phil 4570.1.60 Dissertatio de harmonia religionis et moralitatis. (Grubbe, Samuel.) Upsaliae, 1810.

Phil 490.7 Dissertatio de materialismo. (Ploucquet, G.) Tubingae, 1751.

Phil 4515.45 Dissertatio de notionibus religionis. (Boström, C.J.) Upsala, 1841.

Phil 3120.14.90 Dissertatio de realismo rationali Bardilii. (Grubbe, Samuel.) Upsaliae, 1806.

Phil 5190.23 Dissertatio gradualis. (Alstrin, Eric.) Upsaliae, 1725.

Phil 4513.4.45 Dissertatio gradualis de usu philosophiae in convertendis gentilibus. (Asp, Matthia.) Upsaliae, 1737.

Phil 4513.4.35 Dissertatio gradualis de vera perfectionis idea. (Asp, Matthia.) Upsaliae, 1732.

Phil 8670.5 Dissertatio historico-philosophica de atheismo. (Philipps, J.T.) London, 1716.

Phil 1195.5 Dissertatio inauguralis de sophistis Graeciae. (Gunning, C.P.) Amstelodami, 1915.

Phil 7060.134 Dissertatio iuridica de non rescindendo contractu conductionis ob natura spectrorum. (Thomasius, C.) Halle, 1711.

Phil 7085.9 Dissertatio medica inauguralis de somnambulis. (Steffanius, J.J.) Basileae, 1701.

Phil 4630.3.37 Dissertatio metaphysica de novis...axiomatibus...Leibnitus et Volfius. (Rydelius, Anders.) Lundini, 1725.

Phil 4520.5.25 Dissertatio philosophica, de angustis rationis humanae limitibus. (Boethius, Daniel.) Upsaliae, 1774.

Phil 270.35 Dissertatio philosophica, de concursu caussaë primaë cum secundis. (Alstrin, Eric Praeses.) Upsaliae, 1732.

Phil 5415.8 Dissertatio philosophica, de sympathia. (Fremling, Mattahaus.) Lundae, 1789.

Phil 4630.3.44 Dissertatio philosophica, fidelem praeceptorem...privatum adumbrans. Diss. (Rydelius, Anders.) Lundini, 1726.

Phil 4630.3.42 Dissertatio philosophica, gradualis de tempore. Diss. (Rydelius, Anders.) Lundini, 1726.

Phil 8875.23 Dissertatio philosophica. (Alstrin, Eric.) Upsala, 1723.

Phil 8580.19 Dissertatio philosophica. (Alstrin, Erico.) Upsaliae, 1728.

Phil 8406.17 Dissertatio philosophica. (Fremling, M.) Lundae, 1789.

Phil 4582.6.40 Dissertatio philosophica. (Hermansson, J.) Upsaliae, 1736.

Phil 197.53 Dissertatio philosophica. (Wetterburg, Jacobue.) Lundae, 1789.

Phil 4520.5.32 Dissertatio philosophica de morali ordine in eventu rerum jure postulato. (Boethius, Daniel.) Upsaliae, 1790.

Phil 4520.5.30 Dissertatio philosophica de origine atque indole nimiae divitiarum aestimationis. (Boethius, Daniel.) Upsaliae, 1788.

Phil 5816.8 Dissertatio philosophica de principio actionum. (Geraud, Petrus J.) Trajecti ad Rhenum, 1724.

Phil 180.46 Dissertatio philosophica de ratione praecepta philosophiae theoreticae tradendi. Pt.1-3. (Fremling, Matthaus.) Lundae, 1783-1787.

Phil 3504.39 Dissertatio philosophica de similitudine. (Wilmans, C.A.) Halis Saxonum, 1797.

Phil 3499.24 Dissertatio philosophica de summo bono secundum decreta philosophiae criticae. (Roos, Andreas Praeses.) Lundae, 1799.

Phil 4630.3.46 Dissertatio philosophica de vera rationis humanae definitioné. Diss. (Rydelius, Anders.) Lund, 1727.

Phil 4630.3.35 Dissertatio philosophica mepi...seu de excessu subtilitatis in philosophicae. (Rydelius, Anders.) Lund, 1726.

Phil 806.10 Dissertatio stationes successivas philosophiae progredientis abumbrans. (Grulle, Samuel.) Upsaliae, 1809.

Phil 2045.121 A dissertation...according to the principles of Mr. Hobbes. London, 1706.

Phil 9230.3 A dissertation...gaming. (Hey, R.) Cambridge, 1784-85. 3 pam.

Phil 6115.1 A dissertation...passions...disorders of the body. (Falconer, W.) London, 1796.

Htn Phil 5754.1.101* A dissertation concerning liberty and necessity. (Edwards, Jonathan.) Worcester, 1797.

Phil 9390.2 Dissertation on oaths. (Lewis, E.) Philadelphia, 1838.

Phil 2266.35 A dissertation on the origin of languages. (Smith, Adam.) Tübingen, 1970.

Phil 177.110.5 La dissertation philosophique. (Cuvillier, Armand.) Paris, 1958-62. 2v.

Phil 5761.13 Dissertation sur la liberté de l'homme. (La Luzerne, C.G. de.) Langres, 1808.

Phil 260.9 Dissertation sur la philosophie atomistique. (Lafaist, M.) Paris, 1833.

Htn Phil 2115.80* A dissertation upon the tenth chapter of the fourth book of Mr. Locke's Essay concerning human understanding. (Carroll, William.) London, 1706.

Phil 8670.5.5 Dissertationes historicae quatuor. (Philipps, J.T.) London, 1735.

Phil 2520.171 Dissertationis academicae. (Alstrin, Eric.) Holmiae, 1727.

Phil 175.36 Dissertationis academicae. pt.1-2. (Alstrin, Eric.) Upsaliae, 1728.

Phil 2138.38.5 Dissertations and discussions. v.2-5. v.1 rejected 1972. (Mill, John S.) N.Y., 1873-75. 4v.

Htn Phil 1860.40* Dissertations moral and critical. (Beattie, James.) Dublin, 1783. 2v.

Phil 1860.40.2 Dissertations moral and critical. (Beattie, James.) London, 1783.

Phil 1860.10 Dissertations moral and critical. Works 1-3. (Beattie, James.) Philadelphia, 1809. 3v.

Phil 8581.13.5 Dissertations on the subjects of science. (Brougham, H.) London, 1839. 2v.

Phil 13.17 Dissertations philosophiques. Paris.

Phil 7067.46.5 Dissertations sur les apparitions. (Calmet, Augustin.) Paris, 1746.

Phil 2050.18 Dissertations sur les passions. (Hume, David.) Amsterdam, 1759.

Htn Phil 8664.3* Dissertations sur l'existence de Dieu. (Jaquelot, I.) La Haye, 1697.

Phil 7067.46.18 Dissertazioni sopra le apparizioni di spiriti. (Calmet, Augustin.) Venezia, 1756.

Phil 7039.4.1 The dissociation of a personality. (Prince, Morton.) N.Y., 1906.

Phil 7039.4.3 The dissociation of a personality. (Prince, Morton.) N.Y., 1910.

Phil 7039.4.6 The dissociation of a personality. (Prince, Morton.) N.Y., 1925.

Phil 7039.4.8 The dissociation of a personality. (Prince, Morton.) N.Y., 1957.

Phil 5325.20 La dissociazione psicologica. (Renda, A.) Torino, 1905.

Phil 365.31.5 La dissolution opposée a l'évolution dans les sciences physiques et morales. (Lalande, André.) Paris, 1899.

Phil 5545.90 Les dissolutions de la mémoire. (Delay, Jean Paul Louis.) Paris, 1942.

Phil 5058.22.9 Distinction and the criticism of beliefs. (Sidgwick, A.) London, 1892.

Phil 630.6 Distinction between mind and its objects. (Bosanquet, B.) Manchester, 1913.

Phil 1020.8.20 La distinction de l'essence...d'après Ibn Sina. (Goichon, A.M.) Paris, 1937.

Phil 1020.8.20.2 La distinction de l'essence...d'après Ibn Sina. Thèse. (Goichon, A.M.) Paris, 1937.

Phil 2750.11.48.15 Distinguer pour unir. (Maritain, Jacques.) Paris, 1932.

Phil 2750.11.48.20 Distinguer pour unir. 4. éd. (Maritain, Jacques.) Paris, 1946.

Phil 2750.11.48.5 Distinguish to unite. (Maritain, Jacques.) London, 1959.

Phil 2750.11.48 Distinguish to unite. (Maritain, Jacques.) N.Y., 1959.

Phil 5465.7 The distribution and functions of mental imagery. (Betts, G.H.) N.Y., 1909.

Phil 9550.24 Distributive justice; a constructive critique of the utilitarian theory of distribution. (Rescher, Nicholas.) Indianapolis, 1966.

Phil 1750.370 Dit Philosophie der Existenz von der Renaissance bis zur Gegenwart. (Knittermeyer, H.) Wien, 1952.

Phil 5243.8 Dittes, F. Lehrbuch der Psychology. Wien, 1873.

Phil 8878.30 Dittes, F. Über die sittliche Freiheit. Leipzig, 1860.

Phil 8878.30.2 Dittes, F. Über die sittliche Freiheit. 2e Aufl. Leipzig, 1892.

Phil 8404.10 Dittes, Friedrich. Das Ästhetische nach seinem eigenthümlichen Grundwesen. Leipzig, 1854.

Phil 178.42 Dittes, Friedrich. Gesammelte Schriften. Heft I. Leipzig, 1893.

Phil 5043.7 Dittes, Friedrich. Praktische Logik. Wien, 1873.

Phil 5643.67 Dittler, Rudolf. Stereoskopisches Sehen und Messen. Leipzig, 1919.

Phil 5520.12 Dittrich, O. Grundzüge der Sprachpsychologie. Halle, 1903- 2v.

Phil 575.81 Dittrich, O. Individualismus, Universalismus, Personalismus. Berlin, 1917.

Phil 5520.12.5 Dittrich, O. Die Probleme der Sprachpsychologie. Leipzig, 1913.

Phil 8828.3.5A Dittrich, Ottmar. Geschichte der Ethik. Leipzig, 1926-32. 4v.

Phil 8828.3 Dittrich, Ottmar. Systeme der moral. Bd. 1-3. Leipzig, 1923-26. 3v.

Phil 349.20.25 Ditz, Erwin. Der Begriff der Maschine bei Julius Schultz. Inaug. Diss. Leipzig, 1935.

Phil 6122.16.2 Diurnal course of efficiency. (Marsh, H.D.) N.Y., 1906.

Phil 6122.16 Diurnal course of efficiency. (Marsh, H.D.) N.Y., 1906.

Phil 585.35 Il divenire e l'uomo. v.1-3. 2. ed. (Cardone, Domenico Antonio.) Palmi, 1956-57.

Phil 5520.385 The diversity of meaning. (Cohen, Laurence Jonathan.) London, 1962.

Phil 5520.385.2 The diversity of meaning. 2. ed. (Cohen, Laurence Jonathan.) London, 1966.

Phil 6961.19.5 The divided self; a study. (Laing, Ronald David.) Chicago, 1960.

Phil 5627.33 Le divin. (Hébert, Marcel.) Paris, 1907.

Phil 4752.2.45 The divine and the human. (Berdiaev, Nikolai Aleksandrovich.) London, 1949.

Phil 8595.16.29 Divine authority of the Bible. (Thomson, Robert.) Boston, 1807.

Phil 8656.23 The divine character vindicated. (Ballou, Moses.) N.Y., 1854.

Htn Phil 2145.60* Divine dialogues. (More, Henry.) London, 1668. 2v.

Htn Phil 2145.61* Divine dialogues. (More, Henry.) London, 1713.

Phil 8685.13 The divine drama; the manifestation of God. (Pike, G.R.) N.Y., 1899.

Phil 8663.2 Divine immanence. (Illingworth, J.) London, 1868.

Phil 8587.19.10 The divine instinct recommended to men. (Huber, M.) London, 1781.

Phil 6114.5.16 The divine law of cure. (Evans, W.F.) Boston, 1881.

Phil 2905.1.15 The divine milieu. 1st ed. (Teilhard de Chardin, Pierre.) N.Y., 1960.

Htn Phil 8658.9* Divine oracles; the true antidote against deism and false Christianity. Providence, 1797.

Phil 8662.14 Divine pedigree of man. (Hudson, T.J.) Chicago, 1899.

Phil 8674.7 Divine personality. (Trap, William M.) Ann Arbor, 1925.

Phil 575.52.7 Divine personality and human life. (Webb, C.C.J.) London, 1920.

Phil 2045.134 The divine politics of Thomas Hobbes. (Hood, F.C.) Oxford, 1964.

Htn Phil 4938.1.30* The divine Pymander. (Hermes Trismegistus.) London, 1650.

Phil 190.36 Divine science. (Prather, Charles E.) Denver, Col., 1915.

Phil 7069.40.19 Divine science and metaphysics. (Hendrickson, R.J.) N.Y., 1940.

Phil 8586.14 La divine synthèse. (Guilbert, A.V.F.) Paris, 1875. 3v.

Phil 978.61.5 The divine vision. (Dhopeshwarkar, A.D.) London, 1928.

Phil 8692.3 The divine wisdom...nature, man and bible. (Coutts, John.) London, 1907.

Phil 8404.3.10 Il divinire delle arti. (Dorfles, Gillo.) Torino, 1959.

Phil 8520.33 La divinisation du chrétien d'après les pères grecs. (Gross, J.) Paris, 1938.

Phil 8878.42 The divinity of desire. (Del Mar, E.) N.Y., 1906.

Phil 19.17.10 Divus Thomas; commentarium de philosophie. Piacenza. 41,1938+ 21v.

Phil 19.17.5 Divus Thomas; Jahrbuch für Philosophie und spekulative Theologie. Wien. 1914-1953 23v.

Phil 3195.6.155 Diwald, Hellmut. Wilhelm Dilthey. Göttingen, 1963.

Phil 8818.18.7 Dix, A. Der Egoismus. Leipzig, 1899.

Htn Phil 6946.8420* Dix, D.L. Memorial to Legislative Assembly of Nova Scotia (concerning confinement of insane persons). Halifax? 1850.

Phil 5643.22 Dix, J.H. Treatise...nature, treatment, morbid sensibility...retina. Boston, 1849.

Phil 9010.17 Dix, M. The drift of the age. Springfield, 1888.

Phil 3120.8.155 Dix, Petrus Gerandus. De verhouting van de psycologie tot de wijsbegeerte in der leer van Brentano. n.p., 1966.

Phil 1700.4 Dix années de philosophie. (Arréat, Lucien.) Paris, 1901.

Phil 6945.11 Pamphlet vol. Dix D.L. Memorials on insane and feebleminded. 15 pam.

Phil 178.57 Dixon, E.T. The guidance of conduct. London, 1928.

Phil 6673.13 Dixon, Jacob. Hygienic clairvoyance. London, 1859.

Phil 5695.2 Dixon, Norman F. Subliminal perception. London, 1971.

Phil 178.64.4.7 Dixon, W.M. The human situation. Harmondsworth, 1958.

Phil 178.64.4 Dixon, W.M. The human situation. London, 1938.

Phil 178.64.4.5 Dixon, W.M. The human situation. London, 1954.

Phil 178.64 Dixon, W.M. The human situation. N.Y., 1937.

Phil 178.64.6 Dixon, W.M. Thoughts for the times. Glasgow, 1941.

Phil 178.64.5 Dixon, W.M. Thoughts for the times. N.Y., 1941.

Phil 102.3.5 Dizionario de scienze filosofiche. (Ranzoli, C.) Milano, 1952.

Phil 102.3.6 Dizionario de scienze filosofiche. 6. ed. (Ranzoli, C.) Milano, 1963.

Phil 85.15   Dizionario di filosofia. (Abbagnano, Nicola.) Torino, 1961.

Phil 88.5   Dizionario di filosofia. Milano, 1957.

Phil 102.3   Dizionario di scienze filosofiche. (Ranzoli, C.) Milano, 1905.

Phil 102.3.2   Dizionario di scienze filosofiche. 2a ed. (Ranzoli, C.) Milano, 1916.

Phil 102.3.3   Dizionario di scienze filosofiche. 3a ed. (Ranzoli, C.) Milano, 1926.

Phil 102.3.4   Dizionario di scienze filosofiche. 4. ed. (Ranzoli, C.) Milano, 1943.

Phil 96.5   Dizionario di termini filosofia. (Lamanna, E.P.) Firenze, 1951.

Phil 86.5   Dizionario filosofico. (Boccalaro, M.A.) Bologna, 1951.

Phil 97.7   Dizionario filosofico. (Miano, V.) Torino, 1963.

Phil 8420.26   Djure Daničiča lekcije iz estetike. (Tartalja, Ivo.) Beograd, 1968.

Phil 8980.329   Dmitrenko, A.P. Kommunisticheskaia moral' i voinskii dolg. Moskva, 1960.

Phil 6111.16.20   Dmitriev, V.D. Vydaiushchiisia russkii uchenyi V.M. Bekhterev. Cheboksary, 1960.

Phil 8404.18   Dmitrieva, N.A. Izobrazhenie i slovo. Moskva, 1962.

Phil 5722.71   Do inconsciente. (Martins, D.) Braga, 1964.

Phil 187.170   Do pytannia pro pryrodu filosofs'kykh kategorii. (Mel'nykov, V.M.) Kyïv, 1959.

Phil 9070.8   Do something about it! (Kern, J.H.) N.Y., 1940.

Phil 8632.11   Do the dead still live? (Heagle, David.) Philadelphia, 1920

Phil 8610.904   Do we believe? (Hedderwick, J.A.) London, 1904.

Phil 8599.31   Do we still need religion? (Taft, Charles Phelps.) N.Y., 1942.

Phil 9166.7   Do you know your daughter? (Grossman, J.S.) N.Y., 1944.

Phil 8693.11   Doane, George W. The word of God to be studied with his works. Burlington, 1839.

Phil 5243.50   Dobbelstein, Herman. Der normale Mensch im Urteil der Psychiatrie. Einsiedeln, 1955.

Phil 1145.37   Dobbs, A.E. Philosophy and popular morals in ancient Greece. Dublin, 1907.

Phil 5350.3   Dobler, u. Die Lebenswende als Reifungskrisis. München, 1961.

Phil 8622.84   Dobraczyński, Jan. W co wierze. Wyd. 1. Warszawa, 1970.

Phil 334.10   Dobriianov, Velichko S. Metodologicheskie problemy teoreticheskogo i istoricheskogo poznaniia. Moskva, 1968.

Phil 5520.86   Dobrogaev, S.M. Charl'z Darvin o proiskhozhdenii rechi. Leningrad, 1945.

Phil 5520.86.10   Dobrogaev, S.M. Rechevye refleksy. Moskva, 1947.

VPhil 2225.5.145   Dobrosielski, Marian. Filozoficzny pragmatyzm C.S. Peirce'a. Warszawa, 1967.

Phil 8980.330.5   Dobrovol'skii, Eugenii N. Osoboe mnenie. Moskva, 1967.

Phil 8885.48   Dobrowěda. (Klácel, František M.) Praha, 1847.

Phil 5520.615   Dociekania semantyczne. (Wierzbicka, Anna.) Wrocław, 1969.

Phil 5243.38   Dockeray, F.C. General psychology. N.Y., 1932.

Phil 6331.4.5   Le docteur Roger Vittoz et l'angoisse de l'homme moderne. (Vittoz, Roger.) Paris, 1965.

Phil 8692.7   Doctine of evolution in its relation to theism. (Carpenter, W.B.) London, 1882.

Phil 1504.2.2   Doctor, Max. Die Philosophie. v.2, pt.2. Münster, 1895.

Phil 6110.19   The doctor alone can't cure you. (Alexander, R.) Overton, 1943.

Phil 5627.257   The doctor and the soul. (Frankl, V.E.) N.Y., 1957.

Phil 175.20   Doctor Charles E.C.B. Appleton: his life and literary relics. (Appleton, J.H.) London, 1881.

Phil 6315.2.132   Doctor Freud. (Ludwig, Emil.) N.Y., 1947.

Phil 5247.13.28   El Doctor Huarte de San Juan y su examen de ingenios. (Iriarte, Mauricio de.) Madrid, 1940.

Phil 6312.5.10   The doctor looks at life and death. (Collins, J.) N.Y., 1931.

Phil 8592.6.15   Doctor Martineau's philosophy; a survey. (Upton, Charles B.) London, 1905.

Phil 6685.13   Doctor Mesmer. (Purtscher, Nora.) London, 1947.

Phil 6327.16   Doctors of the mind; the story of the psychiatry. (Ray, Marie B.) Boston, 1942.

Phil 6327.16.7   Doctors of the mind, what psychiatry can do. (Ray, Marie B.) Boston, 1946.

Phil 850.2.5   Doctrina antigua. (Burnett, T.) London, 1736. 3 pam.

Phil 2520.178   Doctrina Cartesiana de vero et falso explicata atque examinata. (Baumann, Julius.) Berolini, 1860?

Phil 3120.8.135   La doctrina de la intencionalidad en Franz Brentano. (Satue, A.A.) Barcelona, 1961.

Phil 4365.2.45   La doctrina de la sociedad en Ortega y Gasset. (Cepeda Calzada, Pablo.) Valladolid, 1968.

Phil 186.24   La doctrina de los siglos. (Lagos, C.E.) Santiago, 1910.

Phil 4967.10   Las doctrinas políticas de Raimundo de Farias Brito. (Elias de Tejada, Francisco.) Sevilla, 1953.

Phil 6322.28.5   Doctrinas psicoanaliticas. (Mira y López, E.) Buenos Aires, 1963.

Phil 960.249   Doctrine and argument in Indian philosophy. (Smart, Ninian.) London, 1964.

Phil 2520.116   La doctrine cartésienne de la liberté et la théologie. (Gilson, E.) Paris, 1913.

Phil 2725.35.105   Une doctrine de la présence spirituelle; la philosophie de Louis Lavelle. (Ainval, Christiane d'.) Louvain, 1967.

Phil 3246.40   Doctrine de la science...de la connaissance. (Fichte, Johann Gottlieb.) Paris, 1843.

Phil 6400.7   Doctrine de l'aphasie. (Bernheim, Hippolyte.) Paris, 1907.

Phil 2490.142.2   La doctrine de l'éducation universelle dans la philosophie d'Auguste Comte. (Arbousse-Bastide, Paul.) Paris, 1957. 2v.

Phil 2490.142   La doctrine de l'éducation universelle dans la philosophie d'Auguste Comte. v.1-2. (Arbouss-Bastide, Paul.) Paris, 1957.

Phil 3825.3   La doctrine de Spinoza. (Ferriere, E.) Paris, 1899.

Phil 3503.8   La doctrine du droit de Kant. (Vosters, J.) Bruxelles, 1920.

Phil 190.41   Doctrine du réel. (Pichard, P.) Paris, 1889.

Phil 3499.36   La doctrine Kantienne de l'objectivité, l'autonomie comme devoir et devenir. (Rousset, Bernard.) Paris, 1967.

Phil 9150.13   La doctrine morale de l'évolution. (Bruneteau, E.) Paris, 1911.

Phil 182.35.5   The doctrine of degrees in knowledge, truth, and reality. (Haldane, Richard B.) London, n.d.

Phil 3246.237   The doctrine of God in the philosophy of Fichte. (Stine, R.W.) Philadelphia, 1945.

Phil 6112.4.20   The doctrine of human automatism. (Carpenter, W.B.) London, 1875.

Phil 960.163.5   The doctrine of Maya. 2nd ed. (Ray Chaudhuri, A.K.) Calcutta, 1950.

Htn   Phil 2218.45*   The doctrine of philosophical necessity. (Priestley, Joseph.) London, 1777.

NEDL   Phil 5400.5   The doctrine of the passions. (Watts, I.) London, 1751.

Htn   Phil 5400.5.6*   The doctrine of the passions. (Watts, I.) Trenton, n.d.

Phil 270.6   The doctrine of the transcendent use of the principle of causality. (Foster, F.H.) Leipzig, 1882.

Phil 5762.7   Doctrine of the will. (Mahan, Asa.) N.Y., 1846.

Phil 5769.1.2   Doctrine of the will. (Tappan, H.P.) N.Y., 1840.

Phil 5769.1.5   Doctrine of the will. (Tappan, H.P.) N.Y., 1841.

Phil 2630.1.83   La doctrine sociale de Gratry. Thèse. (Pointud-Guillemot, B.) Paris, 1917.

Phil 1630.24   Doctrines et figures humanistes. (Callot, Emile.) Paris, 1963.

Phil 192.45   Doctrines et problèmes. (Roure, L.) Paris, 1900.

Phil 1750.210   Les doctrines existentialistes de Kierkegaard à J.P. Sartre. (Jolivet, Régis.) Paris, 1948.

Phil 8877.32   The doctrines of life. (Carpenter, T.E.) Boston, 1913.

Phil 3425.239   Les doctrines politiques des philosophes de l'Allemagne; Leibnitz, Kant, Fichte, Hegel. (Basch, Victor.) Paris, 1927.

Phil 600.38   Les doctrines positivistes en France. (Guthlin, A.) Paris, 1873.

Phil 1135.24   Doctrines religieuses. (Louis, M.) Paris, 1909.

Phil 5231.5   Documentation sur la psychologie française. v.1-6. (Voutsinas, Dimitri.) Paris, 1958- 5v.

Phil 4065.98.5   Documenti della vita di Giordano Bruno. (Spampanato, V.) Firenze, 1933.

Phil 2400.1   Documents...l'histoire...philosophie. (André, Y.M.) Caen, 1844-56. 2v.

Phil 5238.192   Documents of Gestalt psychology. (Henle, Mary.) Berkeley, 1961.

Phil 8953.9   Dodd, C.H. Gospel and law. Cambridge, Eng., 1951.

Phil 8633.1.35   Dodd, Charles H. The communion of saints. Cambridge, 1936.

Phil 8878.12   Doddridge, P. A course of lectures...pneumatology, ethics. London, 1794.

Phil 8583.15   Dodge, Ebenezer. Evidences of Christianity. Boston, 1872.

Phil 9343.7   Dodge, Grace H. A bundle of letters to busy girls. N.Y., 1887.

Phil 9343.7.6   Dodge, Grace H. Thoughts of busy girls. N.Y., 1892.

Phil 5243.37   Dodge, Raymond. Conditions and consequences of human variability. New Haven, 1931.

Phil 5243.37.10   Dodge, Raymond. The craving for superiority. New Haven, 1931.

Phil 5643.43   Dodge, Raymond. An experimental study of visual fixation. Lancaster, 1907.

Phil 5520.46   Dodge, Raymond. Die motorischen Wortvorstellungen. Halle, 1909.

Phil 5043.8   Dodgson, C.L. The game of logic. London, 1886.

Phil 5043.8.7   Dodgson, C.L. Symbolic logic. pt.1. 4th ed. London, 1897.

RRC   Phil 8980.330   Dodon, Larisa L. Kul'tura povedeniia sovetskogo molodogo cheloveka. Izd. 3. Leningrad, 1957.

Phil 6673.3.5   Dods, J.B. The philosophy of electrical psychology. N.Y., 1850.

Phil 6673.3.6   Dods, J.B. The philosophy of electrical psychology. N.Y., 1852.

Phil 6673.3   Dods, J.B. Six lectures on philosophy of mesmerism. Boston, 1843.

Phil 7054.92.5   Dods, John B. Spirit manifestations. N.Y., 1854.

Phil 8878.13.5   Dodsley, R. The duties of human life. West Killingly, Conn., 1858.

Phil 8878.13.8   Dodsley, R. Economia della vita umana. N.Y., 1825.

Phil 8878.13.4   Dodsley, R. The economy of human life. Chicago, 1827.

Phil 8878.13.3.25   Dodsley, R. The economy of human life. Chisnick, 1825.

Htn   Phil 8878.58*   Dodsley, R. The economy of human life. Exeter, 1788.

Htn   Phil 8878.13.2*   Dodsley, R. The economy of human life. Leominster, Mass., 1797.

Phil 8878.13.9   Dodsley, R. The economy of human life. London, 1751.

Phil 8878.13.3.10   Dodsley, R. The economy of human life. London, 1806.

Htn   Phil 8878.13.9.5*   Dodsley, R. The economy of human life. n.p., 1769.

Htn   Phil 8878.13.12*   Dodsley, R. The economy of human life. N.Y., 1793.

Htn   Phil 8878.13.7*   Dodsley, R. The economy of human life. Norwich, 1795.

Phil 8878.13.4.15   Dodsley, R. The economy of human life. Philadelphia, 1845.

Htn   Phil 8878.13.15*   Dodsley, R. The economy of human life. Salem, 1795.

Phil 8878.13.10   Dodsley, R. The economy of human life. pt. 1-2. London, 1795.

Phil 8878.13.3   Dodsley, R. The economy of human life. v.1-2. Manchester, 1801.

Htn   Phil 8878.13*   Dodsley, R. The economy of human life. v.1-2. Philadelphia, 1786.

Phil 2475.1.119   Dodson, G.R. Bergson and the modern spirit. Boston, 1913.

Phil 5585.330   Dodwell, P.C. Visual pattern recognition. N.Y., 1970.

Phil 5592.110   Doebeli, Peter. Beiträge zur Psychodiagnostik. Zürich, 1959.

Htn   Phil 5545.93*   Doeblin, Alfred. Gedächtnisstörungen bei der Korsakoffschen Psychose. Berlin, 1905.

Phil 178.75   Doeblin, Alfred. Unser Dasein. Olten, 1964.

Phil 8612.20.5   Döden; populär framställning. (Block, Oscar.) Stockholm, 1904. 2v.

Phil 8658.12.2   Doedes, J.I. Inleidung tot de leer van God. Utrecht, 1880.

Phil 8953.1   Döllinger, J.J.I. von. Geschichte der Moralstreitigheiten. v.1-2. Nordlingen, 1889.

Phil 3823.2   Dörffling, M. Die Ansichten Spinozas. Leipzig, 1873.

Phil 1135.94   Doerfler, Josef. Vom mythos zum logos. Freistadt, 1914.

Phil 1108.1   Döring, A. Geschichte der griechischen Philosophie. Leipzig, 1903. 2v.

Phil 5043.17   Döring, A. Grundlinien der Logik. Leipzig, 1912.

Phil 8878.26   Döring, A. Philosophische Güterlehre. Berlin, 1888.

Phil 3246.233.5   Döring, W.O. Fichte, der Mann und sein Werke. Lübeck, 1911.

Phil 3485.5   Döring, W.O. Das Lebenswerk Immanuel Kants. 4. Aufl. Lübeck, 1914.

Phil 3246.233   Döring, W.O. Der Mann der Tat; eine Fichtebiographie. Lübeck, 1926.

Phil 6906.15   Doerner, Klaus. Bürger und Irre. Frankfurt, 1969.

Phil 3485.22   Doerpinghaus, Wilhelm. Der Begriff der Gesellschaft bei Kant. Köln? 1959?

Phil 3850.18.155   Doerry, Gerd. Der Begriff des Wertpersontypus bis Scheler und Spranger. Berlin, 1958.

Phil 6132.19   Does Christ still heal? (Wilson, H.B.) N.Y., 1917.

Phil 9070.144   Does it matter? (Watts, Alan Wilson.) N.Y., 1970.

Phil 7054.13   Does spiritualism transcend natural law? (Stevenson, William G.) Poughkeepsie, 1880.

Phil 7069.20.30   Does telepathy explain spiritualism? (Bazter, Francis K.) N.Y., 1920.

Phil 8890.68   Does the end justify the means? (Pontara, Giuliano.) Stockholm, 1967.

Phil 5875.62.5   The dog exercising machine. (De Bono, Edward.) London, 1970.

Phil 6113.5   Dogiel, A.S. Der Bau der Spinalganglien des Menschen und der Säugetiere. Jena, 1908.

Phil 186.86   Dogma en existentie. (Leendertz, W.) Amsterdam, 1933.
Phil 6315.19.30   The dogma of Christ. 1. ed. (Fromm, Erich.) N.Y., 1963.
Phil 5627.102.10   Dogma und Zwangsidee eine psychoanalytische Studie zur Entwicklung der Religion. (Reik, Theodor.) Leipzig, 1927.

Phil 310.6.12   The dogmatic principles of Soviet philosophy. (Bodrenski, J.M.) Dordrecht, Holland, 1963.

Phil 8587.80   Dogmatische verkenningen. (Heering, Herman Johan.) 's-Gravenhage, 1968.

Phil 310.6.10   Die dogmatischen Grundlagen der sowjetischen Philosophie. (Bodrenski, J.M.) Dordrecht, Holland, 1959.

Phil 4514.1.35   Den dogmatiska rationismens strid mot den spekulativa filosofien. (Borelius, J.J.) Stockholm, 1857.

Phil 186.25   Dogmatism and evolution. (Laguna, T. de.) N.Y., 1910.
Phil 3010.4   Dogmatismus und Skepticismus. (Rannengiesser, P.) Elberfeld, 1877.

Phil 1135.131   Le dogme grec. (Bois, Henri.) Paris, 1893.
Phil 332.4   Die Dogmen der Erkenntnistheorie. (Bon, F.) Leipzig, 1902.

Phil 5330.19   Dohrn, H. Das Problem der Aufmerksamkeit. Schleswig, 1876.

Phil 3640.690   Doisy, M. Nietzsche, homme et surhomme. Bruxelles, 1946.
Phil 8628.1   Dokimion, oder praktischen Versuch über ein reales Verhältniss der Geister der Verstorbenen. (Dedekind, G.E.W.) Hannover, 1797.

Phil 70.3.63   Doklady. Communications. (International Congress of Psychology, 14th, Montreal, 1954.) Moskva. 1954

Phil 70.1.12.5   Doklady i vystuplemia. (International Congress of Philosophy, 12th, Venice, 1958.) Moskva. 1958

Phil 70.34   Doklady na soveshchanii po voprosam psikhologii 3-8 iiulia 1953 g. (Vsesoiuznoe Soveshchanie po Voprosam Psikhologii, 2nd, Moskva, 1953.) Moskva, 1954.

Phil 310.638   Doktor Petur Genov za marksistkata filosofiia i bolshevizma. (Andreev, Kosta.) Sofiia, 1964.

Phil 3425.586   Doktryna moralna młodego Hegla. (Kuderowicz, Z.) Warszawa, 1962.

Phil 3425.12.5A   Dokumente zu Hegels Entwicklung. (Hegel, Georg Wilhelm Friedrich.) Stuttgart, 1936.

Phil 3425.288   Dokumente zu Hegels Entwicklung. (Hoffmeister, J.) Stuttgart, 1936.

Phil 5190.10.10   Dolce, Danilo. Conversazioni contedine. Milano, 1966.
Htn   Phil 5545.79*   Dolce, Lodovico. Dialogo nel quale si ragiona del modo di accrescere e conservar la memoria. Venetia, 1586.

Phil 8735.35   Dolch, Heimo. Kausalität im Verständnis des Theologen und der Begründer neuzeitlicher Physik. Freiburg, 1954.

Phil 803.16   Dolci, Alfredo. Da talete all'esistenzialismo. Milano, 1958.

NEDL   Phil 9513.1   Dole, C.F. The citizen and the neighbor. Boston, 1884.
Phil 8658.7   Dole, C.F. From agnosticism to theism. Boston, n.d.
Phil 8633.1.9   Dole, C.F. The hope of immortality, our reasons. N.Y., 1906.

Phil 9120.5   Dole, C.F. The problem of duty. N.Y., n.d.
Phil 8583.9.10   Dole, Charles F. A religion for the new day. N.Y., 1920.
Phil 8583.9.5   Dole, Charles F. The smoke and the flame. Boston, 1892.
Phil 8583.9   Dole, Charles F. Theology of civilization. N.Y., 1899.
Phil 284.12   Dole, George Henry. The philosophy of creation. N.Y., 1906.

Phil 5243.20   Doll, Edgar Arnold. The growth of intelligence. Diss. Princeton, 1920.

Phil 5548.70   Dollard, John. Scoring human motives. New Haven, 1959.
Phil 5401.16.5   Dollard, John. Victory over fear. N.Y., 1942.
Phil 9590.19   Dollars only. (Bok, E.W.) N.Y., 1926.
Phil 178.6   Dollfus, C. De la nature humaine. Paris, 1868.
Phil 7069.67.80   Dollo, Corrado. Momenti e problemi dello spiritualismo. Padova, 1967.

Phil 4190.1.80   Dollo, Corrado. Il pensiero filosofico di Francesco Orestano. Padova, 1967.

Phil 7140.120   Dolonne, A. Self healing by autosuggestion. London, 1923.
Phil 5070.11   The domain of belief. (Coke, Henry J.) London, 1910.
Phil 8585.32   The domain of selfhood. (Feldman, R.V.) London, 1934.
Phil 8892.49   The domain of utilitarian ethics. (Roberts, G.L.) Philadelphia, 1903.

Phil 1504.3   Domański, B. Die Psychologie des Nemesius. v.3, pt.1. Münster, 1900.

Phil 178.20   Domecq, J.B. Études analytiques sur les auteurs philosophiques. Tours, n.d.

Phil 1750.800   Domenach, Jean Marie. Le retour de tragique, essai. Paris, 1967.

Phil 9179.10   The domestic circle. (Thomson, John.) Edinburgh, n.d.
Phil 6951.1   The domestic guide in cases of insanity. (Bakewell, T.) Newcastle, 1809.

Phil 8735.12   Domet de Vorges, E. Cause efficiente et cause finale. Paris, 1888.

Phil 5275.7   Domin, Georg. Psychologie, philosophie, Menschenbild. Halle, 1964.

Phil 1701.17.5   Dominant themes of modern philosophy. (Boas, George.) N.Y., 1957.

Phil 5170.12   Le dominateur el les possibles. 1. éd. (Schuhl, Pierre M.) Paris, 1960.

Phil 978.79   Dominguez Acosta, F. La exondida senda. Caracas, 1941.
Phil 365.24   Dominicis, S.F. de. La dottrina dell'evoluzione: I. Torino, 1878.

Phil 6125.17   Dominion and power. 2d ed. (Patterson, C.B.) N.Y., 1902.
Phil 8592.122.15   Dommanget, Maurice. Le curé Meslier, athée. Paris, 1965.
Phil 165.378   Dommeyer, Frederick C. Current philosophical issues; essays in honor of Curt John Ducasse. Springfield, Illinois, 1966.

Phil 6113.15   Domrich, O. Die psychischen Zustände. Jena, 1849.
Phil 9175.3   Domstic duties. (Parkes, W.) N.Y., 1829.
Phil 5520.716   Le don de la parole. (Seuphor, Michel.) Saint-Aguilin-de-Pacy, 1970.

Phil 186.61   Don Juan, Los milagros y otros ensayos. (Lafora, G.R.) Madrid, 1927.

Phil 6327.4.25   Die don Juan-Gestalt. (Rank, Otto.) Leipzig, 1924.
Phil 7055.108   Don Luis de Alderete y Soto. (Mathias, Julio.) Málaga, 1969.

Phil 4363.3.80   Don Miguel de Manara. (Latour, A. de.) Paris, 1857.
Phil 4363.3.105   Don Miguel Mañara. (Granero, Jesus María.) Sevilla, 1963.
Phil 4809.727.80   Don Quijote české filosofie, Emanuel Rádl 1873-1942. (Hromádka, Josef Lukl.) V New Yorku, 1943.

Phil 6125.27   Don Quijote und Sancho Pansa vom gegenwartigen Stand der Typenlehre. (Portman, Adolf.) Basel, 1957.
Phil 6952.18.25   The Don Quixote of psychiatry. (Robinson, Victor.) N.Y., 1919.

Phil 4370.10   Doña Oliva Sabuco de Nantes. (Torner, F.M.) Madrid, 1935.
Phil 1930.8.105   Donagan, Alan. The later philosophy of R.G. Collingwood. Oxford, 1962.

Phil 575.84   Donahue, G.H. Parenthood and civilization. Boston, 1931.
Phil 6113.2.3   Donaldson, H.H. The growth of the brain. London, 1897.
Phil 334.8.5   Donat, J. Critica. 9. ed. Monachü, 1945.
Phil 8953.6   Donat, J. Summa philosophiae christianae. v.7-8. Oeniponte, 1920-21.

Phil 8693.16   Donat, Josef. Die Freiheit der Wissenschaft. 3. Aufl. Innsbruck, 1925.

Phil 178.67   Donat, Josef. Ontologia. 9. ed. Oeniponte, 1940.
Phil 6673.9   Donati, Alberto. I misteri svelati dello ipnotismo. Roma, 1886.

Phil 4210.153.5   Donati, B. Antonio Rosmini. Modena, 1941.
Phil 4210.153   Donati, B. Rosmini e Gioia. Firenze, 1949.
Phil 4260.91   Donati, Benvenuto. Autografi e documenti vichiani inediti o dispersi. Bologna, 1921.

Phil 4260.91.5   Donati, Benvenuto. Nuovi studi sulla filosofia civile di G.B. Vico. Firenze, 1936.

Phil 5043.26   Donati, G. La logica. Forli, 1920.
Phil 178.55   Donati, G. La metafisica. Savignano, 1921.
Phil 8878.46   Donati, G. La morale. Forli, 1918.
Phil 5243.60   Donceel, Joseph. Philosophical psychology. 2d ed. N.Y., 1961.

Phil 5643.99   Donders, F.C. Rapport aangaande het onderzoek van het gezichtsvermongen. Utrecht, 1877. 2 pam.

Phil 1740.14   Dondeyne, Albert. Contemporary European thought and Christian faith. Pittsburgh, 1958.

Phil 2520.370   Doney, Willis. Descartes; a collection of critical essays. 1st ed. Notre Dame, 1968.
Htn   Phil 7075.6.3*   La donna nuda. 3. ed. (Orsi, Alberto.) Milano, 1912.
Phil 1803.15   Donnell, Franklin H. Aspects of contemporary American philosophy. Würzburg, 1965.

Phil 9290.6   Donohue, John W. Work and education. Chicago, 1959.
Phil 4515.92   Dons, Waldemar. Om Boström̈ianismen. Christiania, 1874.
Phil 6128.39   The Don't Worry movement. (Seward, T.F.) N.Y., 1898.
Phil 5625.75.80   Dontchef-Dezeuze, M. L'image et les réflexes conditionnels dans les travaux de Pavlov. Paris, 1914.

Phil 165.10   Donum lustrale. Noviomagi, 1949.
Phil 4260.210   Donzelli, Maria. Natura e humanitas nel Giovane Vico. Napoli, 1970.

Phil 8591.82   Doomsday Cult; a study of conversion proselytization, and maintenance of faith. (Lofland, John.) Englewood Cliffs, 1966.

Phil 7069.25.13   The door of death wide open. (Guyard, J.) Boston, 1925.
Phil 7069.63.5   The door to the future. (Stearn, J.) Garden City, 1963.
Phil 3120.32.30   Door wetenschap tot wijsheid. (Beth, Evert Willem.) Assen, 1964.

Phil 3425.609   Dooren, Willem van. Het tolaliteitsbegrip bij Hegel en zijn voorgangers. Assen, 1965.

Phil 3195.19.30   Dooyeweerd, H. Verkenningen in de wijsbegeerte. Amsterdam, 1962.

Phil 3195.19.35   Dooyeweerd, H. Vernieuwing en bezinning. 2. druk. Zutphen, 1963.

Phil 334.14   Dooyeweerd, Herman. A new critique of theoretical thought. Amsterdam, 1953-58. 4v.

Phil 2750.11.210   Dopo Maritain. (Barbiellini Amidei, Gaspare.) Torino, 1967.

Phil 3925.16.245   Dopo Wittgenstein. (Antiseri, Dario.) Roma, 1967.
Phil 5066.227   Dopp, J. Logiques construites par une methode de déduction naturelle. Louvain, 1962.

Phil 2855.3.81   Dopp, Joseph. Félix Ravaisson. Louvain, 1933.
Phil 5043.33.5   Dopp, Joseph. Formal logic. N.Y., 1960.
Phil 5043.33   Dopp, Joseph. Leçons de logique formelle. v.1-3. Louvain, 1949-50. 2v.

Phil 5043.33.10   Dopp, Joseph. Notions de logique formelle. Louvain, 1965.
Phil 672.131   La doppa maschera dell'universo. (Zini, Zino.) Milano, 1914.

Phil 7042.2   Das Doppel-Ich. (Dessoir, Max.) Leipzig, 1890.
Phil 7042.2.2   Das Doppel-Ich. 2e Aufl. (Dessoir, Max.) Leipzig, 1896.
Phil 184.37   Doppeldenken; Grundlagen einer neuen Weltanschauung. (Jaller, Arthur.) Berlin, 1926.

Phil 6327.4.35   Der Doppelgänger. (Rank, Otto.) Zürich, 1925.
Phil 270.20   Die Doppelnatur der Causalität. (Noiré, Ludwig.) Leipzig, 1875.

Phil 7150.75   Der Doppelselbstmord. (Ghysbrecht, Paul.) München, 1967.
Phil 5242.13.5   Der doppelte Standpunkt...Psychologie. (Calkins, M.W.) Leipzig, 1905.

Phil 3552.264   Die doppelte Wahrheit...Leibniz und Hurne. Diss. (Rosenfeld, J.) Bern, 1912.

Phil 5520.9.2   Das Doppelwesen der Menschlichen Stimme. (Sutro, Emil.) Berlin, 1902.

Phil 5520.9.9   Das Doppelwesen in die Religion der Vernunft. (Sutro, Emil.) Berlin, n.d.

Htn   Phil 6673.19*   Doppet, F.A. Traité théorique. Turin, 1784.
Phil 5643.45   Dor, Louis. La fatigue oculaire et le surmenage visuel. Paris, 1900.

Phil 6113.30   Doran, F.S.A. Mind, a social phenomenon. N.Y., 1953.
Phil 6313.10   Dorcus, Roy M. Textbook of abnormal psychology. Baltimore, 1934.

Phil 6313.10.2   Dorcus, Roy M. Textbook of abnormal psychology. 2d ed. Baltimore, 1944.

Phil 8599.15   The Doré lectures. (Troward, T.) N.Y., 1909.
Phil 8599.15.5   The Doré lectures. (Troward, T.) N.Y., 1919.
Phil 6313.9   Dorer, M. Historische Grundlagen der Psychoanalyse. Leipzig, 1932.

Phil 4195.82   Dorez, Léon. Pic de la Mirandole en France, 1485-1488. Paris, 1897.

Phil 8404.3.20   Dorfles, Gillo. Artificio e natura. Torino, 1968.
Phil 8404.3.5   Dorfles, Gillo. Le ascillazioni del gusto. Milano, 1958.
Phil 8092.28   Dorfles, Gillo. Comunicazione e struttura nell'analisi di alcumi linguaggi artistici. Milano, 1970.

Phil 8404.3   Dorfles, Gillo. Discorso tecnico delle arti. Pisa, 1952.
Phil 8404.3.10   Dorfles, Gillo. Il divinire delle arti. Torino, 1959.
Phil 8430.64   Dorfles, Gillo. L'estetica del mito. Milano, 1967.
Phil 8448.11   Dorfles, Gillo. Kitsch: an anthology of bad taste. London, 1969.

Phil 8404.3.15   Dorfles, Gillo. Simbolo. Torino, 1962.
Phil 5592.172   Das Dorfspiel. (Zuest, R.) Bern, 1965.
Phil 2150.22.100   Doria, Francisco Antônio. Marcuse, vida e obra. Rio de Janeiro, 1969.

Phil 3808.180   Doring, W.O. Schopenhauer. Zürich, 1919.
Phil 7039.10   The Doris case of multiple personality. (Prince, Walter Franklin.) York, Pa., 1915-16. 2v.

Phil 6113.4 — Dorland, W.A.N. The age of mental virility. N.Y., 1908.
Phil 6113.22 — Dorm, T. G. Heymans' psychischer Monismus. Tübingen, 1922.
Phil 6113.17 — Dorman, Marcus. From matter to mind. London, 1895.
Phil 978.49.845 — Dornach, Switzerland. Goetheanum. Goetheanum. Dornach, 1961.
Phil 978.49.800 — Dornach. Goetheanum. Goetheanum. Dornach, 193-?
Phil 88.1 — Dorner, A. Encyklopädie der Philosophie. Leipzig, 1910.
Phil 8583.11.5 — Dorner, A. Grundprobleme der Religionsphilosophie. Berlin, 1903.
Phil 8583.11 — Dorner, A. Grundriss der Religionsphilosophie. Leipzig, 1903.
Phil 8583.11.15 — Dorner, A. Pessimismus...Nietzsche und Naturalismus. Leipzig, 1911.
Phil 8878.38 — Dorner, August. Individuelle und sozial Ethik. Berlin, 1906.
Phil 334.5 — Dorner, August. Das menschliche Erkennen. Berlin, 1887.
Phil 8953.5 — Dorner, I.A. System of Christian ethics. N.Y., 1887.
Phil 8672.26 — Dorogami zemli. (Romanov, Aleksandr A.) Moskva, 1965.
Phil 5125.10 — Dorolle, M. Les problèmes de l'induction. Paris, 1926.
Phil 4803.334.85 — Doroshevich, Engel's Konstantinovich. Aniol Dovgird - myslitel' epokhi Prosveshcheniia. Minsk, 1967.
Phil 530.20.125 — Dorothea von Montau. (Firtel, Hilde.) Freiburg in der Schweiz, 1968.
Htn — Phil 9343.8* — Dorrington, T. The excellent woman described. London, 1692.
Phil 5243.40 — Dorsey, J.M. The foundations of human nature. N.Y., 1935.
Phil 5590.443 — Dorsey, John Morris. The growth of self-insight. Detroit, 1962.
Phil 6313.24 — Dorsey, John Morris. Illness or allness; conversations of a psychiatrist. Detroit, 1965.
Phil 2255.1.112 — Dorward, Alan. Bertrand Russell. London, 1951.
Phil 2630.2.133 — Dos filosofos contemporaneos; Guyau-Bergson. (Molina, Enrique.) Santiago de Chile, 1925.
Phil 8595.27 — Los dos grandes problemas de la humanidad. (Pontanilles, E.) N.Y., 1882.
Phil 4979.5.85 — Dos ideas sobre la filosofía en la Nueva España. (Hernández Luna, Juan.) México, 1959.
Phil 6158.25 — Dossier LSD. Paris, 1967.
Phil 8690.14 — Dostizheniia estestvoznaniia i religiia. (Akademiia Nauk SSSR. Institutii Filosofii.) Moskva, 1960.
Phil 8658.10 — Dotterer, R.H. The argument for a finitist theology. Diss. Lancaster, Pa., 1917.
Phil 5043.22 — Dotterer, Ray H. Beginners' logic. N.Y., 1924.
Phil 5043.22.5 — Dotterer, Ray H. Beginners' logic. N.Y., 1938.
Phil 178.59 — Dotterer, Ray H. Philosophy by ways of the sciences. N.Y., 1929.
Phil 178.59.5 — Dotterer, Ray H. Postulates and implications. N.Y., 1955.
Phil 3850.27.190 — Dottor Schweitzer e dintorni. (Spinosa, Antonio.) Roma, 1960.
Phil 5710.13 — La dottrina dei temperamenti nell'antichità e ai nostri giorni. (Alfonso, Nicolo R.) Roma, 1902.
Phil 4260.130 — La dottrina del diritto naturale in G.B. Vico. (Bellofiore, L.) Milan, 1954.
Phil 4210.220 — La dottrina del sentimento fondamentale nella filosofia di A. Rosmini. (Piemontese, Filippo.) Milano, 1966.
Phil 5400.68 — La dottrina del sentimento nella storia della filosofia. (Ambrosi, L.) Roma, 1894.
Phil 2475.1.450 — La dottrina della conoscenza in Enrico Bergson. (Cavagna, Giordano Bruno.) Napoli, 1965.
Phil 1540.20 — La dottrina della conoscenza secondo Aristotele e la scuola. pt.1. (Buonamici, G.) Pisa, 1930.
Phil 5545.69 — La dottrina della "memoria", tedesco. (Dandolo, Giovanni.) Padova, 1893.
Phil 5545.69.15 — La dottrina della memoria. (Dandolo, Giovanni.) Réggio nell'Emilia, 1891.
Phil 400.63 — Dottrina della realtá del mondo esterno. Parte prima. (Chiapelli, A.) Firenze, 1886.
Phil 2270.137 — La dottrina delle due etiche di H. Spencer, e la morale come scienza. (Juvalta, Erminio.) n.p., n.d.
Phil 365.24 — La dottrina dell'evoluzione: I. (Dominicis, S.F. de.) Torino, 1878.
Phil 365.26 — La dottrina dell'evoluzione e la fil. (Bertinaria, F.) Genova, 1876.
Phil 4215.1.110 — La dottrina di G.D. Romognosi intorno alla civiltà. (Alecci, Romolo.) Padova, 1966.
Phil 4065.85 — La dottrina di Giordano Bruno. (Schiattarella, R.) Palermo, 1888.
Phil 3808.252 — La dottrina di Schopenhauer. (Vecchiotti, Icilio.) Roma, 1969.
Phil 3493.29 — La dottrina Kantiana del diritto e dello stato. (Lumia, Giuseppe.) Milano, 1960.
Phil 3500.75 — La dottrina Kantiana dello schematismo transcendentale. (Salvucci, Pasquale.) Urbino, 1957.
Phil 4170.6.30 — La dottrina positiva delle idealità. (Marchesini, G.) Roma, 1913.
Phil 400.28.5 — La dottrina positiva delle idealità. (Marischini, G.) Roma, 1913.
Phil 4260.130.5 — La dottrina providenza in G.B. Vico. (Bellofiore, L.) Padova, 1962.
Phil 2270.126 — La dottrina Spenceriana dell'inconoscibile. (Ardigó, R.) Roma, 1899.
Phil 5590.270 — Le dottrine caratterologiche di Ernest Kretschmer e Gerarhd Pfahler. (Metelli, Fabio.) Padova, 1958.
Phil 4210.129 — Lo dottrine di Antonio Rosmini...ed altri esaminate da Giuseppe Petri. (Petri, Giuseppe.) Torino, 1878.
Phil 3837.14 — Le dottrine giuridiche...di Spinoza e Hobbes. (Ricco, Cesare.) Giovinazzo, 1884.
Phil 2045.110 — Le dottrine politiche dell'Hobbes e dello Spinoza. (Battelli, G.) Firenze, 1904.
Phil 3832.9 — Le dottrine politiche e religiose di B. Spinoza. (Meozzi, A.) Arezzo, 1915.
Phil 2805.111 — D'où irent l' "Ad tuum, Domine Jesu, de Pascal? (Jovy, Ernest.) Paris, 1916. 2 pam.
Phil 7150.11 — Douay, Edmond. Suicide, ou La mort volontaire. Paris, 1870.
Phil 6327.4.36 — The double: a psychoanalytic study. (Rank, Otto.) Chapel Hill, 1971.
Phil 8602.46 — The double faith theory in Clement, Saadia, Averroes and St. Thomas. (Wolfson, H.A.) Philadelphia, 1942.
Phil 5520.60 — La double fonction du langage. (Paulhan, F.) Paris, 1929.
Phil 8953.8.6 — La double nature de l'amour. (D'Arcy, Martin Cyrile.) Paris, 1948.
Phil 13.12 — Doubleday papers in psychology. Garden City, N.Y. 1-17 4v.
Phil 6134.4A — Doubt and certainty in science. (Young, J.Z.) Oxford, 1951.
Phil 8622.10 — Doubt and faith. (MacGregor, G.) London, 1951.

Phil 8655.13 — Doubt's boundless sea. (Allen, D.C.) Baltimore, 1964.
Phil 8610.891.5 — Doubts in dialogue. (Bradlaugh, Charles.) London, 1909.
Phil 8404.21 — Doucher, Hans. Künstlerisches und rationalisiertes Sehen. München, 1967.
Phil 4200.1.80 — Douglas, A.H. Philosophy and psychology of...Pomponazzi. Cambridge, 1910.
Phil 2138.83 — Douglas, C. John Stuart Mill. Edinburgh, 1895.
Phil 7150.64 — Douglas, Jack D. The social meanings of suicide. Princeton, 1967.
Phil 1750.580 — Douglas, Kenneth. A critical bibliography of existentialism (the Paris School). New Haven, 1950.
Phil 8881.4.9 — Douglas, M. The life of Professor C.F. Gellert. London, 1810. 3v.
Phil 9390.6 — Douglas, Robert. Observations on the nature of oaths. Edinburgh, 1783.
Phil 5402.28 — La douleur. (Sarano, Jacques.) Paris, 1965.
Phil 5402.13 — La douleur physique. (Castez, G.) Paris, 1905.
Phil 9163.2 — Doumer, P. Livre de mes fils. Paris, 1906.
Phil 9495.115 — Douráes Castro. O racionalismo atrevido do Snr. Frederico de Ancede. Porto, 1915.
Phil 1200.21 — Dourif, J. Du stoïcisme et du christianisme considérés dans leurs rapports. Thèse. Paris, 186-?
Phil 3640.418 — Dournes, P. Nietzsche vivant. n.p., 1948.
Phil 5070.8 — Le doute. (Sollier, P.) Paris, 1909.
Phil 600.34 — A doutrina positivista. (Senna Freitas, J.J. de.) Póvoa de Varzim, n.d.
Phil 5645.3 — Dove, H.W. Darstellung der Farbenlehre. Berlin, 1853.
Htn — Phil 8658.3* — Dove, J. Atheism defined and confuted. London, 1656.
Phil 8693.3 — Dove, J. A vindication of the divine authority. n.p., 1888.
Phil 5425.76A — Dovski, Lee van. Genie und Eros. Olten-Bern, 1949. 3v.
Phil 7069.45.30 — Dowden, Hester. The book of Johannes, by Peter Fripp. London, 1945.
Phil 7069.45.25 — Dowding, H.C.T. Lychgate. London, 1945.
Phil 7069.43.10 — Dowding, H.C.T. Many mansions. London, 1943.
Phil 3640.111 — Dowerg, R. Friedrich Nietzsches "Geburt der Tragödie". Leipzig, 1902.
Phil 2835.80 — Downame, G. Commentarii in P. Rami Dialecticam. Francofurti, 1610.
Phil 6060.15A — Downey, June E. Graphology and the psychology of handwriting. Baltimore, 1919.
Phil 5585.18 — Downey, June Etta. Control processes in modified hand-writing. Chicago? 1908?
Phil 2520.349 — The downfall of Cartesianism, 1673-1712. (Watson, Richard A.) The Hague, 1966.
Phil 5352.16 — Downs, A. The value of unchosen alternatives. Santa Monica, 1966.
Phil 5500.40 — Downs, Anthony. Bureaucratic structure and decision-making. Santa Monica, 1966.
Phil 9070.14 — Dowry, S.S. The thoughts of youth. N.Y., 1932.
Phil 7069.26.5 — Doyle, Arthur Conan. The history of spiritualism. N.Y., 1926. 2v.
Phil 7069.18.95 — Doyle, Arthur Conan. The new revelation. N.Y., 1918.
Phil 7069.18.95.6 — Doyle, Arthur Conan. The new revelation. 6th ed. London, 1918.
Phil 7069.24.5 — Doyle, Arthur Conan. Our second American adventure. Boston, 1924.
Phil 7069.27.50 — Doyle, Arthur Conan. Phineas speaks. London, 1927.
Htn — Phil 7069.29.20* — Doyle, Arthur Conan. The Roman Catholic church, a rejoinder (to Herbert Thurston). London, 1929.
Phil 7069.20.115 — Doyle, Arthur Conan. Verbatim report of a public debate on "The truth of spiritualism" between A.C. Dolye and Joseph McCabe. London, 1920.
Phil 7069.19.93 — Doyle, Arthur Conan. The vital message. London, 1919.
Phil 7069.19.92 — Doyle, Arthur Conan. The vital message. N.Y., 1919.
Phil 7054.175.10 — Doyle, Arthur Conan. The wanderings of a spiritualist. London, 1921.
Phil 7054.175.11 — Doyle, Arthur Conan. The wanderings of a spiritualist. N.Y., 1921.
Phil 7069.28.16 — Doyle, Arthur Conan. A word of warning. London, 1928.
Phil 7069.22.5 — Doyle, Arthur Connan. Our American adventure. N.Y., 1923.
Phil 3120.2.105 — Dr. Bolzano und seine Gegner. Sulzbach, 1839.
Phil 5545.177 — Dr. Ewald Hartenbach's Kunst. 15. Aufl. (Hartenbach, E.) Quedlinburg, 1882.
Phil 5247.13.27 — Dr. Juan Huarte de San Juan. (Iriarte, Mauricio de.) Münster, 1938.
Phil 3850.12.85 — Dr. Karl Volkmar Stoys Leben. (Fröhlich, Gustaf.) Dresden, 1885.
Phil 575.51.40 — Dr. Klages, Entwurf einer Charakterkunde. (Hermann, Oskar.) Leipzig, 1920.
Phil 165.374 — Dr. S. Radhakrishnan souvenir volume. Moradabad, 1964.
Phil 3850.27.170 — Dr. Schweitzer of Lambaréné. (Cousins, Norman.) N.Y., 1960.
Phil 3635.90 — Dr P.J. Möbius als Philosoph. Inaug. Diss. (Lorenz, Heinrich.) Wiesbaden, 1899.
Phil 5465.132 — Dracoulidès, N.N. Psychanalyse de l'artiste et de son oeuvre. Genève, 1952.
Phil 7055.251 — Drage, Charles. William King's profession. London, 1960.
Phil 8583.27 — Draghicesco, D. Vérité et révélation. Paris, 1934. 2v.
Phil 178.62 — Drago, P.C. La genesi del problema fenomenologico. Milano, 1933.
Phil 196.8.80 — Drago, Pietro C. La filosofia di Bernardino Varisco. Firenze, 1944.
Phil 3485.12 — Drago, Pietro C. La mistica kantiana. Messina, 1929.
Phil 3552.314 — Drago del Boca, S. Leibniz. Milano, 1946.
Phil 3640.475 — Drain, Henri. Nietzsche et Gide. Paris, 1932.
Phil 630.21A — Drake, Durant. Essays in critical realism. London, 1920.
Phil 178.61 — Drake, Durant. Invitation to philosophy. Boston, 1933.
Phil 5243.30 — Drake, Durant. Mind and its place in nature. N.Y., 1925.
Phil 8878.28.10 — Drake, Durant. The new morality. N.Y., 1928.
Phil 8878.28.2 — Drake, Durant. Problems of conduct. Boston, 1921.
Phil 8583.14 — Drake, Durant. Problems of religion. Boston, 1916.
Phil 6313.11 — Drake, R.M. Outline of abnormal psychology. N.Y., 1936.
Phil 8582.80 — Drama ateizacije. Religija, ateizam i odgoj. (Cimić, Esad.) Sarajevo, 1971.
Phil 7069.34.45 — Un drama del espacio. Año 1932. Dictado por el espiritu de Blasco Ibáñez. (Vilanova, María.) Barcelona, 1934.
Phil 1750.575 — El drama del hombre actual. (Alonso-Fueyo, Sabino.) Valencia, 1966.
Phil 8666.17.11 — The drama of atheist humanism. (Lubac, Henri de.) Cleveland, 1969.
Phil 7069.32.50 — The drama of life after death. (Lawton, George.) N.Y., 1932.
Phil 5627.35 — The drama of the spiritual life. (Sears, Annie L.) N.Y., 1915.

Phil 978.49.240 Drama und Dichtung im Bewusstseins-Umschwung der Neuzeit. (Steiner, R.) Dornach, 1956.

Phil 176.212 The dramatic universe. (Bennett, J.G.) London, 1956-61. 2v.

Phil 2725.2.105 Drame de conscience. (Bovard, René.) Paris, 1961.

Phil 8666.17.7 Le drame de l'humanisme athée. (Lubac, Henri de.) Paris, 1963.

Phil 8666.17.10 Le drame de l'humanisme athée. 3. éd. (Lubac, Henri de.) Paris, 1945.

Phil 8666.17.6 Le drame de l'humanisme athée. 6. éd. (Lubac, Henri de.) Paris, 1959.

Phil 1702.12 Il dramma della metafisica nell'età contemporanea. (Ciardo, Manlio.) Bologna, 1967.

Phil 5520.448 Drange, Theodore. Type crossings. The Hague, 1966.

Phil 8693.4.6 Draper, J.W. Los conflictos entre la ciencia y la religión. Madrid, 1876.

Phil 8693.4.5 Draper, J.W. Historia de los conflictos entre la religión y la ciencia. Madrid, 1876.

Phil 8693.4.3 Draper, J.W. History of the conflict between religion and science. N.Y., 1875.

Phil 8693.4.3.10 Draper, J.W. History of the conflict between religion and science. N.Y., 1897.

Phil 4520.8.32 Drauma-joi, sannar sagnir. (Bjarnason, Ágúst.) Reykjavík, 1915.

Phil 7082.46 Draumar. (Jónasson, Hermann.) Reykjavík, 1912.
Phil 7082.62 Draumur. (Bjarnason, Halldór.) Reykjavík, 1879.
Phil 7082.52 Draumur. (Jóhannsson, Jón.) Akureyri, 1882.
Phil 7082.45 Draumur. (Símonardottir, Helga.) Reykjavík, 1916.
Phil 7082.51 Draumur. (Thorleifsdóttir, Elízabet.) Reykjavík, 1892.
Phil 7082.51.1 Draumur. (Thorleifsdóttir, Elízabet.) Reykjavík, 1905.
Phil 7082.52.2 Draumur. 2. Utgáfa. (Jóhannsson, Jón.) Reykjavík, 1916.

X Cg Phil 7082.50 Draumur Friðiks Andréssonar. (Andrésson, Friðik.) Reykjavík, 1904. (Changed to XM 1329)

Phil 7082.54 Draumvitran Guðmundar Einarssonar. (Einarsson, Guðmundur.) n.p., 1913?

Phil 5627.134.85A Drawing-room conversion; Oxford Group movement. (Eester, Allen W.) Durham, 1950.

Phil 5043.25 Drbal, M. Propadeutische Logik. Wien, 1885.
Phil 5640.28 Drbal, M.A. Über Natur der Sinne. Linz, 1860.
Phil 1750.171 Dreadful freedom. (Grene, M.) Chicago, 1948.
Phil 6332.6 Dreads and besetting fears. (Williams, T.A.) Boston, 1923.

Phil 7084.4.5 Dream analysis: a practical handbook for psycho-analysts. (Sharpe, Ella Freeman.) London, 1937.

Phil 7082.21 The dream and human societies. (Grunebaum, Gustave Edmund von.) Berkeley, 1966.

Phil 4752.2.55 Dream and reality. (Berdiaev, Nikolai Aleksandrovich.) London, 1950.

Phil 6480.167 Dream dictionary. Cincinnati, 1919.
Phil 7084.28.5 The dream in primitive cultures. (Lincoln, Jackson Steward.) London, 1935.

Phil 7082.184 Dream interpretation, a new approach. (French, Thomas Morton.) N.Y., 1964.

Phil 2750.11.72 The dream of Descartes. (Maritain, Jacques.) N.Y., 1944.
Phil 7082.154 The dream problem. (Maeder, Alphonse.) N.Y., 1916.
Phil 7082.110 The dream problem. (Narayan, Ram.) Delhi, 1917?-22. 2v.

Phil 7082.186 Dream psychology. (Nicoll, Maurice.) London, 1917.
Phil 8637.11 The dream that comes true. (Milne, J. Napier.) London, 1919.

Phil 7082.94 The dream world. (Mégroz, Rodolphe Louis.) N.Y., 1939.
Phil 575.79 Dreamers and doers. (Hamilton, O.P.) London, 1931.
Phil 1930.10.10 A dreamer's journey. (Autobiography.) (Cohen, M.R.) Boston, 1949.

Phil 7082.142 Dreaming. (Malcolm, Norman.) London, 1959.
Phil 7082.142.5 Dreaming and experience. (Lewis, Hywel David.) London, 1968.

Phil 7082.42 Dreams; God's forgotten language. (Sanford, John A.) Philadelphia, 1968.

Phil 978.8.25 Dreams; what they are and how they are caused. 4th ed. (Leadbeater, C.W.) London, 1908.

Phil 2475.1.66.5 Dreams. (Bergson, Henri.) N.Y., 1914.
Phil 7082.98 Dreams. (Stiles, Percy Goldthwait.) Cambridge, 1927.
Phil 7082.84 Dreams. (Wood, Clement.) N.Y., 1931.
Phil 7084.14.8 Dreams: what they are and what they mean. 3d ed. (Wickwar, John William.) London, 1918.

Phil 7082.194 Dreams and dreaming. (Mackenzie, Norman Jan.) N.Y., 1965.
Phil 5893.6 Dreams and myths; a study in race psychology. (Abraham, Karl.) N.Y., 1913.

Phil 7082.64.5 Dreams and personality. (Pierce, Frederick.) N.Y., 1931.
Phil 7082.180 Dreams and personality dynamics. (De Martino, Manfred F.) Springfield, 1959.

Phil 7082.82.2 Dreams and premonitions. 2d ed. (Rogers, Louis William.) Chicago, 1923.

Phil 7084.28 Dreams and primitive culture. (Rivers, William Halse Rivers.) Manchester, 1917-18.

Phil 6480.265 Dreams and symbols. (Caligor, Leopold.) N.Y., 1969.
Phil 6331.1 Dreams and the unconscious; an introduction to the study of psycho-analysis. (Valentine, C.W.) London, 1921.
Phil 7084.34 Dreams and the uses of regression. (Lewin, Bertram David.) N.Y., 1958.

Phil 7082.72 Dreams and their meanings. (Hutchinson, Horace Gordon.) London, 1901.

Phil 8951.20 Dreams come true. (Brown, Charles R.) N.Y., 1944.
Phil 6315.2.62.15A Dreams in folklore. (Freud, Sigmund.) N.Y., 1958.

Phil 6112.40.12 Dreams in the life of prayer: the approach of Edgar Cayce. 1st ed. (Bro, Harmon Hartzell.) N.Y., 1970.

Phil 3480.53A Dreams of a spirit seer. (Kant, Immanuel.) London, 1900.
Phil 3003.5 Drechsler, Adolf. Charakteristik der philosophischen Systeme seit Kant. Dresden, 1863.

Phil 3246.250 Drechsler, J. Fichtes Lehre vom Bild. Stuttgart, 1955.
Phil 5545.179 Drees, V.J. The effects of practice on memory performance. Thesis. Washington, 1941.

Phil 2733.115 Drefus, Ginette. La volonté selon Malebranche. Paris, 1958.

Phil 5643.12.9 Die Drehbare Bilderscheibe. (Hoppe, J.F.) Leipzig, 1884.
Phil 5640.24 Dreher, E. Beiträge zu einer exacten Psycho-Physiologie. Halle, 1880.

Phil 178.34.5 Dreher, Eugen. Beiträge zu einer exacten Psycho-Physiologie. n.p., 1880-91. 4 pam.

Phil 8430.12 Dreher, Eugen. Die Kunst in ihrer Beziehung. Berlin, 1878.

Phil 478.3 Dreher, Eugen. Der Materialismus. Berlin, 1892.
Phil 178.34 Dreher, Eugen. Philosophische Abhandlungen. Berlin, 1903.
Phil 5262.31 Drei Abhandlungen zur Gestalttheorie. (Wertheimer, M.) Erlangen, 1925.

Phil 6315.2.75.8 Drei Abhandlungen zur Sexualtheorie. (Freud, Sigmund.) Leipzig, 1910.

Phil 6315.2.75.10 Drei Abhandlungen zur Sexualtheorie. 7. Aufl. (Freud, Sigmund.) Wien, 1946.

Phil 185.18 Drei akademische Reden. (Kaftan, Julius.) Tübingen, 1908.
Phil 6961.9.5 Drei Aufsätze aus dem Aprariegebut. (Liepmann, Hugo.) Berlin, 1908.

Phil 1870.45.21 Drei Dialoge zwischen Hylas und Philonous. (Berkeley, G.) Berlin, 1955.

Phil 1870.45.20 Drei Dialoge zwischen Hylas und Philonous. (Berkeley, G.) Leipzig, 1926.

Phil 8581.49 Drei ewige Lichter. (Bolliger, A.) Berlin, 1903.
Phil 6867.30 Drei Formen missglückten : Verstiegenheit, Verschrobenheit, Maineriertheit. (Binswanger, Ludwig.) Tübingen, 1956.

Phil 6976.30 Drei Formen missglückten Daseins: Verstiegenheit, Verschrobenheit, Manieriertheit. (Binswanger, Ludwig.) Tübingen, 1956.

Phil 7069.39.45 Drei Forträge über Philosophie und Parapsychologie. (Poortman, Johannes J.) Leiden, 1939.

Phil 3499.6.5 Die drei Fragen Kants. (Romundt, H.) Berlin, 1887.
Phil 3480.28.100A Die drei Kritiken. (Kant, Immanuel.) Leipzig, 1933.
Phil 3210.65A Drei Motive und Gründe des Glaubens. (Fechner, G.T.) Leipzig, 1863.

Phil 635.2 Die drei Potenzen der Relation. Inaug. Diss. (Leisegang, Dieter.) Frankfurt, 1969.

Phil 8422.16 Drei Schriften zum ästhetischen Formproblem. (Vischer, R.) Halle, 1927.

Phil 3425.589 Drei Studien zu Hegel. (Adorno, T.W.) Frankfurt, 1963.
Phil 349.14 Die drei Welten der Erkenntnistheorie. (Schultz, J.) Göttingen, 1907.

Phil 5421.25.35 Die Dreigestalt der Liebe. 1. Aufl. (Philipp, Wolfgang.) Konstanz, 1967.

Phil 5243.41.2 Dreikurs, Rudolf. Grundbegriffe der Individualpsychologie. Stuttgart, 1969.

Phil 5243.41.5 Dreikurs, Rudolf. An introduction to individual psychology. London, 1935.

Phil 1504.11.6 Dreiling, R. Der Konzeptualismus. v.11, pt.6. Münster, 1913.

Phil 5418.6 Dreitzel, Hans Peter. Die Einsamkeit als soziologisches Problem. Zurich, 1970.

Phil 165.324 Drennen, D. A modern introduction to metaphysics. N.Y., 1962.

Phil 8599.19.120 Drescher, H.G. Glaube und Vernuft bei Ernst Troeltsch. Marburg, 1957.

Phil 1750.166.225 Dresden, Samuel. Het humanistische denken. Italië-Frankrijk 1450-1600. Amsterdam, 1968.

Phil 2230.5A Dresser, A.G. The philosophy of P.P. Quimby. Boston, 1895.

Phil 5243.24.5 Dresser, H. Psychology in theory and application. N.Y., 1924.

Phil 178.12.18 Dresser, H.W. A book of secrets. N.Y., 1902.
Phil 178.12.47 Dresser, H.W. The Christ ideal. N.Y., 1901.
Phil 178.12.16 Dresser, H.W. Education and the philosophical ideal. N.Y., 1900.

Phil 8878.45 Dresser, H.W. Ethics in theory and application. N.Y., 1925.

Phil 178.12.60 Dresser, H.W. The greatest truth. N.Y., 1907.
Phil 178.12.35 Dresser, H.W. Handbook of the new thought. N.Y., 1917.
Phil 178.12.27A Dresser, H.W. Health and the inner life. N.Y., 1906.
Phil 803.7 Dresser, H.W. A history of ancient and medieval philosophy. N.Y., 1926.

Phil 1703.5 Dresser, H.W. A history of modern philosophy. N.Y., 1928.
Phil 178.12.42 Dresser, H.W. A history of the new thought movement. N.Y., 1919.

Phil 178.12.29 Dresser, H.W. Human efficiency. N.Y., 1912.
Phil 178.12.55 Dresser, H.W. The immanent God. Boston, 1895.
Phil 178.12.2 Dresser, H.W. In search of a soul. Boston, 1897.
Phil 178.12.17 Dresser, H.W. Living by the spirit. N.Y., 1901.
Phil 178.12.25 Dresser, H.W. Man and the divine order. N.Y., 1903.
Phil 178.12.33 Dresser, H.W. A message to the well. N.Y., 1910.
Phil 178.12.19 Dresser, H.W. Methods and problems of spiritual healing. N.Y., 1899.

Phil 178.12.49 Dresser, H.W. On the threshold of the spiritual world. N.Y., 1919.

Phil 178.12.5 Dresser, H.W. The perfect whole. Boston, 1896.
Phil 178.12.7 Dresser, H.W. The perfect whole. 3rd ed. Boston, 1898.
Phil 178.12.26 Dresser, H.W. Philosophy of the spirit. N.Y., 1908.
Phil 178.12.40 Dresser, H.W. A physician to the soul. N.Y., 1908.
Phil 178.12.8 Dresser, H.W. The power of silence. Boston, 1895.
Phil 178.12.11 Dresser, H.W. The power of silence. N.Y., 1901.
Phil 178.12.11.9 Dresser, H.W. The power of silence. 2nd ed. N.Y., 1909.
Phil 178.12.9.5 Dresser, H.W. The power of silence. 7th ed. Boston, 1898.
Phil 178.12.43 Dresser, H.W. The religion of the spirit in modern life. N.Y., 1914.

Phil 178.12.37 Dresser, H.W. The spirit of the new thought. N.Y., 1917.
Phil 178.12.39 Dresser, H.W. The victorious faith, moral ideals in war time. N.Y., 1917.

Phil 178.12.14 Dresser, H.W. Voices of freedom. N.Y., 1899.
Phil 178.12.12 Dresser, H.W. Voices of hope. Boston, 1898.
Phil 7069.20.120 Dresser, Horatio W. The open vision. N.Y., 1920.
Phil 5627.118 Dresser, Horatio W. Outlines of the psychology of religion. N.Y., 1929.

Phil 2230.95 Dresser, J.A. The true history of mental science. Boston, 1899.

Phil 6113.6 Dressler, J.G. Beneke oder die Seelenlehre als Naturwissenschaft. Bautzen, 1840.

Phil 178.10 Dressler, J.G. Grundlehren der Psychologie und Logik. Leipzig, 1872.

Phil 6113.6.5 Dressler, J.G. Ist Beneke Materialist? Berlin, 1862.
Phil 5043.9 Dressler, J.G. Praktisch Denklehre. Bautzen, 1852.
Phil 5243.22 Dressler, Max. Vorlesungen über Psychologie. Heidelberg, 1900.

Phil 178.49 Dressler, Max. Die Welt als Wille zum Selbst. Seidelberg, 1904.

Phil 803.8 Dressoir, M. Lehrbuch der Philosophie. Berlin, 1925. 2v.

Phil 334.12 Dretske, Fred I. Seeing and knowing. London, 1969.
Phil 5813.3 Drever, James. Instinct in man. Cambridge, Eng., 1917.
Htn Phil 8628.4.2* Drew, Samuel. An original essay on the immateriality and immortality of the human soul. 1st American ed. Baltimore, 1810.

Phil 8628.4 Drew, Samuel. An original essay on the immateriality and immortality of the human soul. London, 1819.

Phil 8595.15.65 Drew, Samuel. Remarks on the 1st part of book entitled "The age of reason." 2. ed. N.Y., 1831.

Phil 1750.163 Drewinc, H. VierGestalten aus den Zeitalter des Humanismus. Saint Gallen, 1946.

Phil 3003.1 Drews, A. Die deutsche Spekulation seit Kant. Berlin, 1893. 2v.
Phil 3415.89.2 Drews, A. Eduard von Hartmanns philosophische System. Heidelberg, 1906.
Phil 3415.89 Drews, A. Eduard von Hartmanns philosophisches System. Heidelberg, 1902.
Phil 178.70 Drews, A. Einführung in die Philosophie. Berlin, 1921.
Phil 3415.89.5 Drews, A. Das Lebens Werk Eduard von Hartmanns. Leipzig, n.d.
Phil 3485.4 Drews, A.C.H. Kants Naturphilosophie als Grundlage seines Systems. Berlin, 1894.
Phil 1703.2.15 Drews, Arthur. Die deutsche Philosophie der Gegenwart. Berlin, 1922.
Phil 178.18 Drews, Arthur. Das Ich als Grundproblem der Metaphysik. Freiburg, 1897.
Phil 3640.83 Drews, Arthur. Nietzsches Philosophie. Heidelberg, 1904.
Phil 1703.2.3 Drews, Arthur. Die Philosophie im ersten Drittel des 19. Jahrhunderts. Berlin, 1920.
Phil 1703.2 Drews, Arthur. Die Philosophie im ersten Drittel des 19. Jahrhunderts. Leipzig, 1912.
Phil 1703.2.10 Drews, Arthur. Die Philosophie im lekten Drittel des 19. Jahrhunderts. Berlin, 1921.
Phil 1703.2.5 Drews, Arthur. Die Philosophie im zweiten Drittel des 19. Jahrhunderts. Berlin, 1913.
Phil 1703.2.6 Drews, Arthur. Die Philosophie im zweiten Drittel des 19. Jahrhunderts. Berlin, 1922.
Phil 5722.80 Drews, Arthur. Psychologie des Unbewussten. Berlin, 1924.
Htn Phil 8878.15* Drexelius, H. Nicetas feu triumphata incontinentia. Colonia Agrippina, 1631.
Htn Phil 3850.10.30* Die drey ersten Vorlesungen über die Philosophie des Lebens. (Schlegel, Friedrich von.) Wien, 1827.
Htn Phil 193.10.3* Die drey ersten Vorlesungen über die Philosophie des Lebens. (Schlegel, Friedrich von.) Wien, 1827.
Phil 4195.81 Dreydorff, Georg. Das System des Johannes Pico. Warburg, 1858.
Phil 2805.89 Dreydorff, J.G. Pascal sein Leben und seine Kämpfe. Leipzig, 1870.
Phil 178.43 Dreyer, Friedrich. Studien zu Methodenlehre und Erkenntnisskritik. Leipzig, 1895-1903.
Phil 575.32 Dreyer, Hans. Personalismus und Realismus. Berlin, 1905.
Phil 1050.4.13 Dreyer, Kare. Die religiöse Gedankenwelt des Salomo ibn Gabirol. Inaug. Diss. Leipzig, 1928.
Phil 860.8 Dreyer, Oskar. Untersuchungen zum Begriff des Gottgeziemenden in der Antike. Hildesheim, 1970.
Phil 5627.134.90 Driberg, Tom. The mystery of moral re-armament. N.Y., 1964.
Phil 178.22.5 Driesch, H. Das Ganze und die Summe. Leipzig, 1921.
Phil 745.7 Driesch, H. Geschichte des Vitalismus. 2e Aufl. Leipzig, 1922.
Phil 745.6A Driesch, H. The history and theory of vitalism. London, 1914.
Phil 3195.10.30 Driesch, H. Lebenserinnerungen. Basel, 1951.
Phil 5043.18A Driesch, H. Die Logik als Aufgabe. Tübingen, 1913.
Phil 178.22.25 Driesch, H. Man and the universe. London, 1929.
Phil 178.22.20 Driesch, H. Der Mensch und die Welt. Leipzig, 1928.
Phil 178.22.7 Driesch, H. Metaphysik. Breslau, 1924.
Phil 178.22 Driesch, H. Ordnungslehre. Jena, 1912.
Phil 178.22.2 Driesch, H. Ordnungslehre. Jena, 1923.
Phil 178.22.30 Driesch, H. Philosophische Forschungswege. Leipzig, 1930.
Phil 178.22.35 Driesch, H. Philosophische Gegenwartsfragen. Leipzig, 1933.
Phil 178.22.9 Driesch, H. The possibility of metaphysics. London, 1924.
Phil 5753.8.2 Driesch, H. Das Problem der Freiheit. 2. Aufl. Darmstadt, 1920.
Phil 745.7.9A Driesch, H. The problem of individuality. London, 1914.
Phil 745.7.15 Driesch, H. Über der grundsätzliche Unmöglichkeit einer "Vereinigung" von universeller Teleologie und Mechanismus. Heidelberg, 1914.
Phil 745.6.7 Driesch, H. Il vitalismo. Milano, 1911. 2v.
Phil 5043.18.10 Driesch, H. Wessen und Denken. Leipzig, 1922.
Phil 178.22.4 Driesch, H. Wirklichkeitslehre. Leipzig, 1922.
Phil 178.22.4.5 Driesch, H. Wirklichkeitslehre. 3e Aufl. Leipzig, 1930.
Phil 5243.28.8 Driesch, Hans. Alltagsrätsel des Seelenlebens. Stuttgart, 1938.
Phil 5243.28 Driesch, Hans. The crisis in psychology. Princeton, 1925.
Phil 8878.47.5 Driesch, Hans. Ethical principles in theory and practice. N.Y., 1927.
Phil 5243.28.5 Driesch, Hans. Grundprobleme der Psychologie. Leipzig, 1926.
Phil 6113.19 Driesch, Hans. Leib und Seele. Leipzig, 1916.
Phil 6113.19.3 Driesch, Hans. Leib und Seele. 3. Aufl. Leipzig, 1923.
Phil 284.6.10 Driesch, Hans. Metaphysik der Natur. München, 1926.
Phil 6113.19.9 Driesch, Hans. Mind and body. N.Y., 1927.
Phil 284.6 Driesch, Hans. Naturbegriffe und natururteile. Leipzig, 1904.
Phil 7069.43.20 Driesch, Hans. Parapsychologie. Zürich, 1943.
Phil 7069.43.22 Driesch, Hans. Parapsychologie. 3. Aufl. Zürich, 1952.
Phil 7069.33.60 Driesch, Hans. Psychical research. London, 1933.
Phil 8878.47 Driesch, Hans. Die sittliche Tat. Leipzig, 1927.
Phil 478.4 Driesch, Hans. Die Überwindung des Materialismus. Zürich, 1935.
Phil 284.6.5 Driesch, Hans. Zwei Vorträge zur Naturphilosophie. Leipzig, 1910.
Phil 5043.35 Drieschner, Rudolf. Untersuchungen zur dialogischen Deutung der Logik. Diss. Hambirg, 1966.
Phil 3195.10.90 Driesch's Philosophie. (Heinichen, Otto.) Leipzig, 1924.
Phil 9010.17 The drift of the age. (Dix, M.) Springfield, 1888.
Phil 178.11 Drious, C.J. Cours de philosophie. Paris, 1883.
Phil 178.27 Driscoll, John T. Pragmatism and the problem of the idea. N.Y., 1915.
Phil 3007.8.5 Der dritte Humanismus. 3. Aufl. (Helbing, Lothar.) Berlin, 1935.
Phil 1707.18 Die dritte Kraft. (Heer, Friedrich.) Frankfurt, 1959.
Phil 70.3.3 Dritter internationaler Congress für Psychologie in München. (International Congress of Psychology, 3rd, Munich, 1896.) München. 1897
Phil 6903.5 Driver, Edwin D. The sociology and anthropology of mental illness, a reference guide. Amherst, 1965.
Phil 6321.30.5 Drives, affects, behavior. (Loewenstein, R.) N.Y., 1953.
Phil 5243.10 Drobisch, M.W. Empirische Psychologie. Leipzig, 1842.
Phil 5243.10.1 Drobisch, M.W. Empirische Psychologie. 2e Aufl. Hamburg, 1898.
Phil 5243.10.2 Drobisch, M.W. Erste Grundlehren der mathematischen Psychologie. Leipzig, 1850.
Phil 8583.6 Drobisch, M.W. Grundlehren der Religionsphilosophie. Leipzig, 1840.
Phil 3485.8 Drobisch, M.W. Kants Dinge an sich und sein Erfahrungsbegriff. Hamburg, 1885.
Phil 5753.2 Drobisch, M.W. Die moralische Statistik. Leipzig, 1867.
Phil 3428.156 Drobisch, M.W. Über die Fortbildung der Philosophie durch Herbart. Leipzig, 1876.
Phil 5043.10.4 Drobisch, Moritz Wilehlm. Neue Darstellung der Logik nach ihren einfaschsten Verhältnissen mit Rücksicht auf Mathematik und Naturwissenschaft. 4. Aufl. Leipzig, 1875.
Phil 5043.10.3 Drobisch, Moritz Wilhelm. Die moralische Statistik und die menschliche Willens Freihet. Leipzig, 1867.
Phil 5043.10 Drobisch, Moritz Wilhelm. Neue Darstellung der Logik. Leipzig, 1851.
NEDL Phil 8980.2 Drobnitskii, Oleg G. Kratkii slovar' po etike. Moskva, 1965.
Phil 8828.5 Drobnitskii, Oleg G. Kritika sovremennykh burzhuaznykh eticheskikh kontseptsii. Moskva, 1967.
Phil 735.264 Drobnitskii, Oleg G. Mir ozhivshikh predmetov. Moskva, 1967.
Phil 8980.3 Drobnitskii, Oleg G. Slovar po etike. Izd. 2. Moskva, 1970.
Phil 2725.40 Drochner, Karl Heinz. Darstellung einiger Grundzüge des literarischen Werks von Pierre de la Primaudaye. Berlin, 1960.
Phil 7082.114 Dröm och vaka. (Cavallin, Paul.) Stockholm, 1901.
Phil 4803.822.30 Droga do filozofii i inne rozprowy filozoficzne. Wyd. 1. v.1- (Tatarkiewicz, Władysław.) Warszawa, 1971-
Phil 2477.15.32 Le droit de rêver. 2. éd. (Bachelard, Gaston.) Paris, 1970.
Phil 9070.51 Les droits de l'esprit et les exigences sociales. (Rencontres Internationales.) Neuchâtel, 1951.
Phil 5243.16 Dromard, Gabriel. Les mensonges de la vie intérieure. 2e éd. Paris, 1914.
Phil 6953.8 Dromard, Gabriel. La mimique ches les aliénés. Paris, 1909.
Phil 5374.3 Drossbach, M. Genesis des Bewusstseins. Leipzig, 1860.
Phil 8628.5 Drossbach, M. Die Harmonie der Ergebnisse der Naturforschung. Leipzig, 1858.
Phil 9495.8 Drossbach, M. Objecte der sinnlichen Wahrnehmung. Halle, 1865.
Phil 178.35 Drossbach, M. Über die Verschiedenengrade. Berlin, 1873.
Phil 284.2 Drossbach, M. Über Kraft und Bewegung. Halle, 1879.
Phil 3485.20 Drossbach, P. Kant und die Gegenwärtige Naturwissenschaft. Berlin, 1943.
Phil 5643.51 Drott, Anton. Die Aussengrenzen des Gesichtsfeldes für weisse und farbige Objecte beim normalen Auge. Inaug. Diss. Breslau, 1894?
Phil 7069.32.13 Drouet, Bessie Clarke. Station Astral. N.Y., 1932.
Htn Phil 9495.38* Drouet de Maupertny, J. Le commerce dangereux entre les deux sexes. Bruxelles, 1715.
Phil 2805.204 Droulers, C. La cité de Pascal. Paris, 1928.
Phil 8583.21 Drown, E.S. Religion or God? Cambridge, 1927.
Phil 2805.82 Droz, E. Étude sur le scepticisme de Pascal. Paris, 1886.
Phil 9245.1 Droz, F.X.J. The art of being happy. Boston, 1832.
Phil 9245.1.5 Droz, F.X.J. The art of being happy. London, 18- ?
Phil 8878.43 Droz, J. De la philosophie morale. 2e éd. Paris, 1824.
Phil 5500.15 Drozdov, A.V. Voprosy klassifikatsii suzhdenii. Leningrad, 1956.
Phil 3450.11.290 Druce, H. Edmund Husserls System der phänomenologischen Psychologie. Berlin, 1963.
Phil 3504.20 Die Druckschriften Immanuel Kants. (Warda, Arthur.) Wiesbaden, 1919.
Phil 5460.12 A drug-taker's notes. (Ward, R.H.) London, 1957.
Phil 6155.14 Drugs and phantasy: the effects of LSD, psilocykin and Sernyl on college students. 1st ed. (Polland, John C.) Boston, 1965.
Phil 6324.6 Drugs in psychoanalysis and psychopathology. (C.ton, Mortimer.) N.Y., 1962.
Phil 7060.138 The drummer of Tedworth...story of that demon. London, 1716.
Phil 5923.1 Drummond, D. Objections to phrenology. Calcutta, 1829.
Phil 9590.21 Drummond, D.D. Today we think of our tomorrows. Richmond, Va., 1945.
Phil 8693.5.40 Drummond, H. Lowell lectures on the ascent of man. 13th ed. N.Y., 1906.
Phil 8693.5.10A Drummond, H. Natural law in the spiritual world. N.Y., 1885.
Phil 8693.5.11 Drummond, H. Natural law in the spiritual world. N.Y., 1887.
Phil 8693.5.14 Drummond, H. Natural law in the spiritual world. N.Y., 189-.
Phil 8693.5.3 Drummond, H. Natural law in the spiritual world. Philadelphia, 1892.
Phil 8693.5.2 Drummond, H. Natural law in the spiritual world. 17th ed. London, 1885.
Phil 8693.5.20 Drummond, H. Naturens lagar och andens verld. Stockholm, 1888.
Phil 178.7.5 Drummond, W. Academical questions. London, 1805.
Phil 178.7 Drummond, W. Academical questions. London, 1805.
Phil 5374.286 Drury, Michael. The inward sea. 1st ed. Garden City, 1972.
Phil 9343.11 Drury, Samuel S. Backbone; the development of character. N.Y., 1923.
Phil 3195.9.83 Druskowitz, H. Eugen Dühring. Heidelberg, 1889.
Phil 8583.12 Drustowitz, H. Moderne Versuche eines Religionsersatzes. Heidelberg, 1886.
Phil 6319.1.214 Dry, Avis Mary. The psychology of Jung. London, 1961.
Phil 5627.85 Dryden, S.H. Daisy Dryden. 3. ed. Boston, 1909.
Phil 3485.26 Dryer, D.P. Kant's solution for verification in metaphysics. London, 1966.
Phil 2475.1.241 Dryssen, Carl. Bergson und die deutsche Romantik. Marburg, 1922.
Phil 8402.47 Du beau. (Bray, Lucien.) Paris, 1902.
Phil 343.16.25 Du cheminement de la pensée. (Meyerson, Émile.) Paris, 1931. 3v.
Phil 8591.4.5 Du christianisme et de son origine democratique. pt.1-2. (Leroux, Pierre.) Boussac, 1848.
Phil 180.57 Du consentement à l'être. (Forest, Aimé.) Paris, 1936.
Phil 5425.63 Du crétin au génie. (Voronoff, Serge.) N.Y., 1941.
Phil 6854.8 Du darfst Leben. (Tetaz, Numa.) Zürich, 1970.
Phil 6961.1 Du délire chez les dégénérés. (Legrain, M.) Paris, 1886.
Phil 6957.14 Du délire des negations (Syndrome de Cotard) dans la paralysie générale. (Henry, Jules.) Paris, 1896.
Phil 5635.10 Du déterminisme psychologique. (Lippmann, F.) Strasbourg, 1909.
Phil 186.81.5 Du devenir logique et de l'affectivité. v.1-2. (Lupasco, Stéphane.) Paris, 1935-1936. 2v.
Phil 186.81 Du devenir logique et de l'affectivité. v.1-2. Thèse. (Lupasco, Stéphane.) Paris, 1935.
Phil 8586.6 Du doute. (Gréard, Mlle.) Paris, 1867.

Phil 2725.11.30   Du fondement de l'induction. (Lachelier, Jules.) Paris, 1871.

Phil 6953.4   Du fractionnement des opérations cérébrales. (Descourtis, G.) Paris, 1882.

Phil 6953.4.2   Du fractionnement des opérations cérébrales. (Descourtis, G.) Paris, 1882.

Phil 8886.10   Du gout ou de la passion du bien-être matériel. (Lombarès, M. de.) Montauban, 1860?

Phil 8890.19   Du gouvernement des moeurs. (Polier de St. Germain, A. de.) Lausanne, 1785.

Phil 8420.23   Du juste milieu; traité général de philosophie et d'art. (Tollemonde, G. de.) Paris, 1910.

Phil 2496.82   Du livre de M. Cousin. (Wallon, J.) Paris, 1854.
Phil 6682.7   Du magnétisme. (Morin, A.S.) Paris, 1860.
Phil 6685.9   Du magnétisme animal. (Puységur, Armand Marie Jacques de Chastenet.) Paris, 1807.

Phil 6669.1   Du magnetisme animal en France. (Bertrand, A.) Paris, 1826.

Phil 476.2.5   Du matérialisme. (Böhner, A.N.) Genève, 1861.
Phil 6990.30   Du merveilleux, des miracles et des pelerinages au point de vue medical. (Grellety, L.) Paris, 1876.

Phil 525.23.5   Du moyen de manifester la perfection. (Pedrick, Katharinn F.) Paris, 1921.

Phil 6319.1.190.5   Du mythe à la religion. (Hostie, Raymond.) Bruges, 1955.
Phil 8685.1   Du panthéisme. (Daniélo, J.) Paris, 1848.
Phil 8881.6.5   Du perfectionnement moral. (Gerando, J.M.) Paris, 1826. 2v.

Phil 5402.8   Du plaisir et de la douleur. (Bouillier, F.) Paris, 1865.
Phil 5402.8.3   Du plaisir et de la douleur. 3e ed. (Bouillier, F.) Paris, 1885.

Phil 2415.5.10   Du positivisme à l'idéalisme. (Parodi, Dominique.) Paris, 1930. 2v.

Phil 600.20   Du positivisme au mysticisme. 2e éd. (Pacheu, Jules.) Paris, 1906.

Phil 8897.17   Du principe de la morale. (Wiart, E.) Paris, 1862.
Phil 6111.4   Du principe vital. (Bouiller, F.) Paris, 1862.
Phil 5627.220   Du protestantisme au catholicisme. (Neeser, Maurice.) Paris, 1926.

Phil 2750.13.30   Du refus à l'invocation. 11. éd. (Marcel, Gabriel.) Paris, 1956.

Phil 5545.73   Du rôle de la mémoire dans nos conceptions. (Eichthal, Eugène d'.) Paris, 1920.

Phil 3425.281   Du role de l'idée de contradiction chez Hegel. Thèse. (Sfard, D.) Nancy, 1931.

Phil 2520.137   Du rôle de l'idée de l'instant dans la philosophie de Descartes. (Wahl, Jean.) Paris, 1920.

Phil 178.16   Du role des concepts. (Dumesni, G.) Paris, 1892.
Phil 8828.2   Du sage antique au citoyen moderne. Paris, 1921.
Phil 2610.105   Du scepticisme de Gassendi. (Berr, Henri.) Paris, 1960.
Phil 7080.30   Du sommeil au point de vue physiologique et psychologique. (Lemoine, Albert.) Paris, 1855.

Phil 6681.4   Du sommeil et des états analogues. (Liébeault, A.A.) Paris, 1866.

Phil 8685.21   Du spiritualisme et de la nature. (Bersot, E.) Paris, 1846.

Phil 1200.21   Du stoïcisme et du christianisme considérés dans leurs rapports. Thèse. (Dourif, J.) Paris, 186-?

Phil 5241.113   Du style d'idées. (Benda, Julien.) Paris, 1948.
Phil 7150.1   Du suicide. (Brierre de Boismont, A.J.F.) Paris, 1856.
Phil 7150.8   Du suicide. (La Rue, F.A.H.) Québec, 1859.
Phil 7150.16   Du suicide chez les enfants. Thèse. (Moreau, Jacques.) Paris, 1906.

Phil 7150.1.2   Du suicide et la folie suicide. 2. éd. (Brierre de Boismont, A.J.F.) Paris, 1865.

Phil 2605.8.30   Du temporel à l'intemporel. (Fouéré, René.) Paris, 1960. 2v.

Phil 2725.35.20   Du temps et de l'eternité. (Lavelle, Louis.) Paris, 1945.
Phil 672.230   Du temps physique au temps romanesque. (Guillaumaud, Jacques.) Paris, 1965.

Phil 705.18   Du transcendentalisme considéré essentiellement dans sa définition et ses origines françaises. (Girard, William.) Berkeley, 1916.

Phil 176.190   Du und die Philosophie. (Brates, Georg.) Berlin, 1955.
Phil 8403.8   Du vrai, du beau et du bien. (Cousin, Victor.) Paris, 1853.

Phil 8403.8.6   Du vrai, du beau et du bien. 18. éd. (Cousin, Victor.) Paris, 1873.

Phil 1135.200   Dualism and demonology. Thesis. (Skovgaard Jensen, Søren.) København, 1966.

Phil 196.12.5   Dualism and monism. (Veitch, John.) Edinburg, 1895.
Phil 315.8   Dualism or duality? (Buckham, J.W.) n.p., 1913.
Phil 315.10   Le dualisme chez Platon. (Pétrement, Simone.) Paris, 1947.

Phil 3492.14   Le dualisme de la raison humaine; ou, Le criticisme de E. Kant. (Kinker, Johannes.) Amsterdam, 1850-52. 2v.

Phil 315.3   Le dualisme logique. (Stefanescu, M.) Paris, 1915.
Phil 315.4   Dualismen i vor nyeste philosophie. (Brandes, Georg.) Kjobenhavn, 1866.

Phil 315.7   Il dualismo nella filosofia. (Nahile, Emilia.) Napoli, 1931.

Phil 315.5   Der Dualismus mi modernen Weltbild. 2. Aufl. (Vierkandt, A.) Berlin, 1923.

Phil 315.2   Dualismus oder Monismus. (Stein, L.) Berlin, 1909.
Phil 5627.266.10   The duality of human existence. (Bakan, David.) Chicago, 1966.

Phil 5520.9.3   Duality of thought and language. (Sutro, Emil.) N.Y., 1904.

Phil 5520.9   Duality of voice. (Sutro, Emil.) N.Y., 1899.
Phil 8695.5.5   Duas allocuçõs; a religiaõ, amparo do homen na vida. (Ferreira da Silva, A.J.) Porto, 1911.

Phil 8693.25   Dubarle, D. Humanisme scientifique et raison chrétienne. Paris, 1953.

Phil 6312.28   De dubbelganger. (Carp, Eugène Antoine Desiré Émile.) Utrecht, 1964.

Phil 1712.9   Il dubbio metodico e la storia della filosofia. (Mondolfo, R.) Padova, 1905.

Phil 3260.87   Dubislav, W. Die Fries'che Lehre von der Begründung. Dömitz, 1926.

Phil 5190.4.10   Dubislav, W. Über die Definition. 2. Aufl. Berlin, 1927.
Phil 5190.4.10.3   Dubislav, W. Über die Definition. 3. Aufl. Leipzig, 1931.
Phil 7150.53   Dublin, L.I. Suicide. N.Y., 1963.
Phil 1870.134   Dublin. University. Trinity College. Library. Catalogue of manuscripts. Dublin, 1953.

Phil 8878.39   Duboc, Julius. Grundriss einer Einheitlichen. Leipzig, 1892.

Phil 178.15   Duboc, K.J. Hundert jahre Zeitgeist in Deutschland. Leipzig, 1889.

Phil 178.15.5   Duboc, K.J. Jenseits vom Wirklichen. Dresden, 1896.

Phil 9410.1   Duboc, K.J. Der Optimismus als Weltanschauung. Bonn, 1881.

Phil 2270.92   Dubois, J. Spencer et le principe de la morale. Paris, 1899.

Phil 8878.24   DuBois, P. The culture of justice. N.Y., 1907.
Phil 8878.24.10   DuBois, P. L'éducation de soi-même. Paris, 1913.
Phil 8878.24.7   DuBois, P. The education of self. N.Y., 1911.
Phil 8878.24.5   DuBois, P. Self-control and how to secure it. N.Y., 1909.
Phil 6113.8.20   Dubois, Paul. De l'influence de l'esprit sur le corps. 9. éd. Berne, 1910.

Phil 6113.8.5   Dubois, Paul. The influence of the mind on the body. N.Y., 1906.

Phil 6953.12.5   Dubois, Paul. Psychic treatment of nervous disorders. N.Y., 1905.

Phil 6313.3   Dubois, Paul. Les psychonévroses et leur traitement moral. 3e éd. Paris, 1909.

Phil 5272.2   Du Bois, Philip Hunter. An introduction to psychological statistics. N.Y., 1965.

Phil 1828.4   Dubois, Pierre. Le problème de la connaissance d'autrui dans la philosophie anglaise contemporaine. Paris, 1969.

Phil 8828.6   Dubois, Pierre. Le problème moral dans la philosophie anglaise de 1900 à 1950. Thèse. Paris, 1967.

NEDL   Phil 2705.81   Du Bois-Reymond, E. La Mettrie. Berlin, 1875.
Phil 2705.81.2   Du Bois-Reymond, E. La Mettrie. Berlin, 1875.
Phil 334.2   Du Bois-Reymond, P. Über die Grundlagen der Erkenntnis in der exacten Wissenschaften. Tübingen, 1890.

Phil 6673.14   Dubor, G. de. The mysteries of hypnosis. N.Y., 1923.
Phil 8404.14.5   Dubos, J.B. Reflexions critiques sur la poésie et sur la peinture. 6. éd. Paris, 1755. 3v.

Phil 8404.14   Dubos, Jean B. Critical reflections on poetry. London, 1748. 3v.

Phil 585.141   Dubos, René Jules. The torch of life. N.Y., 1962.
Phil 5243.17   Dubot, T. Psychologie. Paris, 1897.
Phil 6060.56   Dubouchet, Jeanne. L'analogie des phenomenes physiques et psychiques et l'écriture. Bruxelles, 1960.

Phil 6060.56.5   Dubouchet, Jeanne. L'écriture des adolescentes, étude psycho-pédagogique. Paris, 1967.

Phil 5243.70   Dubouchet-Buffet, Jeanne. Essai de formalisation de la psychologie fondé sur l'analogie des phénomènes psychiques et des phénomènes physiques. Thèse. Paris, 1965.

Phil 178.21   Dubray, C.A. Introductory philosophy. N.Y., 1912.
Phil 5243.13   Dubray, C.A. The theory of psychical dispositions. Washington, 1905.

Phil 6113.34   Dubrovskii, David I. Psikhicheskie iavleniia i mozg. Moskva, 1971.

Phil 5080.2   Dubs, Arthur. Das Wesen des Begriffs und des Begreifens. Halle, 1911.

Phil 5043.27   Dubs, Homer. Rational induction. Chicago, 1930.
Phil 310.285   Dubská, Irena. K problematice strankosti a vědeckosti marksistsko-leninskaia filosofii. Praha, 1960.

Phil 178.51   Dubuc, Paul. Essai sur la méthode en métaphysique. Paris, 1887.

Phil 600.17   Dubuisson, A. Positivisme intégral. Paris, 1910.
Phil 2805.282   Ducas, A. Discours sur les passions de l'amour de Pascal. Alger, 1953.

Phil 6113.29   Ducasse, C.J. Nature, mind and death. La Salle, Ill., 1951.

Phil 178.65   Ducasse, C.J. Philosophy as a science. N.Y., 1941.
Phil 8404.8   Ducasse, C.J. Art, the critics and you. N.Y., 1944.
Phil 8404.8.5   Ducasse, Curt. The philosophy of art. Toronto, 1929.
Phil 270.26   Ducasse, Curt J. Causation and the types of necessity. Seattle, 1924.

Phil 270.26.5   Ducasse, Curt J. Truth, knowledge and causation. London, 1968.

Phil 2490.131   Ducassé, P. Essai sur les origines intuitives du positivisme. Thèse. Paris, 1939.

Phil 2490.130   Ducassé, P. Méthode et intuition chez Auguste Comte. Thèse. Paris, 1939.

Phil 2733.107   Ducassé, Pierre. Malebranche; sa vie, son oeuvre, avec un exposé de sa philosophie. 1e éd. Paris, 1942.

Phil 600.50   Ducassé, Pierre. La méthode positive et l'intuition comtienne. Paris, 1939.

Phil 5753.5   Duchatel, Edmond. Les miracles de la volonté. Paris, 1914.

Phil 7060.141   Duchâtel, Edmond. La vue à distance...des cas de psychomètrie. Paris, 1910.

Phil 5425.42   Duche, Émile. De la precocité intellectuelle. Paris, 1901.

Phil 334.16   Duchenko, Mykola V. Problema ob'iekta v marksysto'ko-lenins'kvi Seorii piznanoria. Kyiv, 1970.

Htn   Phil 6000.2*   Duchenne, Guillaume B. Mécanisme de la physionomie humaine. Paris, 1876.

Phil 7149.2   Duckworth, J. Herbert. Autosuggestion and its personal application. N.Y., 1922.

Phil 2403.4   Duclaux, A.M.F.R. The French ideal. N.Y., 1911.
Phil 2805.195.5   Duclaux, A.M.F.R. Portrait of Pascal. London, 1927.
Phil 4073.128   Ducros, Franc. Tommaso Campanella, poète. Paris, 1969.
Phil 3485.3   Ducros, L. Quando et quomodo Kantium humius. Burgigalae, 1883.

Phil 310.65   Dudel, S.P. Zakony materialisticheskoi dialektiki. Moskva, 1958.

Phil 310.662   Dudel', Savva P. Zakon edinstva i bor'by protivopolozhnostei. Moskva, 1967.

Phil 1153.7   Dudley, D.R. A history of cynicism from Diogenes to the 6th century A.D. London, 1937.

Phil 7069.32.15   Dudley, E.E. Fingerprint demonstrations. Boston, 1932.
Phil 6113.9   Dudley, L. Egyptian elements in the legend of the body and soul. Baltimore, 1911.

Phil 8430.11A   Dudley, Louise. The humanities. 1. ed. N.Y., 1940. 2v.

Phil 8430.11.2   Dudley, Louise. The humanities. 2. ed. N.Y., 1951.
Phil 7069.28.20   Dudley, O.F. The abomination in our midst. London, 1928.
Phil 9245.26   Dudoc, J. Die Lust als socialethisches Entwickelungsprincip. Leipzig, 1900.

Phil 4363.2.84   Dudon, P. Le quiétiste espanol. Paris, 1921.
Phil 283.18   Due contributi di filosofia scientifica. (Colmoyer, Ciro.) Roma, 1904.

Phil 4070.1.96   Due del 48 - Ernest Renan and Cristoforo Bonavino saggio critico filosofico. (Gotran, P.) Firenze, 1891.

Phil 4065.70   Due dialoghi sconosciuti e due dialoghi noti. (Bruno, Giordano.) Roma, 1957.

Htn   Phil 9560.25*   Due dialogi della vergogna. (Pocaterra, A.) Ferrara, 1592. 2v.

Phil 310.146   Due fazy kommunisticheskogo obshchestva i zakonomernosti pererastatelnogo sotsializma v kommunizm. (Teriaev, G.V.) Moskva, 1962.

Phil 4080.8.85   Due filosofi italiani. (Barzellotti, G.) Roma, 1908.

Author and Title Listing

Phil 1750.166.153 Due saggi sull'umanesimo. (Spongano, Raffaele.) Firenze, 1964.

Phil 3195.9.75 Dühring, E. Cursus der Philosophie als streng wissenschaftlicher Weltanschauung und Lebensgestaltung. Leipzig, 1875.

Phil 803.2 Dühring, E. Kritische Geschichte der Philosophie. 2d Aufl. Berlin, 1873.

Phil 803.2.3 Dühring, E. Kritische Geschichte der Philosophie. 3e Aufl. Leipzig, 1878.

Phil 3195.9.77 Dühring, E. Sache, Leben, und Feinde. 2. Aufl. Leipzig, 1903.

Phil 8583.7.5 Dühring, E.K. Der Ersatz der Religion. Karlsruhe, 1883.

Phil 5043.11 Dühring, E.K. Logik und Wissenschaftstheorie. Leipzig, 1878.

Phil 5043.11.5 Dühring, E.K. Natürliche Dialektik. Berlin, 1865.

Phil 8583.7 Dühring, E.K. Der Werth des Lebens. Leipzig, 1881.

Phil 8583.7.3 Dühring, E.K. Der Werth des Lebens. 6. Aufl. Leipzig, 1902.

Phil 803.2.4 Duehring, Eugen. His Gesammtcursus der Philosophie. Leipzig, 1894-95. 3v.

Phil 3485.13 Dünnhaupt, Rudolf. Sittlichkeit, Staat und Recht bei Kant. Berlin, 1927.

Phil 2240.87 Dür, Seweryn. Reid a Kant. Opole, 1963.

Phil 9320.7 Duerckheim-Montmartin, Karlfried. Der Alltag als Übung vom Weg zur Verwandlung. 2. Aufl. Bern, 1966.

Phil 705.66 Dürckheim-Montmartin, Karlfried. Uberweltliches Leben in der Welt. Weilheim, 1968.

Phil 3640.174 Düringer, Adelbert. Nietzsche's Philosophie. 2. Aufl. Leipzig, 1906.

Phil 3640.245 Düringer, Adelbert. Nietzsches Philosophie und das neutige Christentum. Leipzig, 1907.

Phil 3808.118 Dueros, Louis. Schopenhauer. Thèse. Paris, 1883.

Phil 3425.332 Dürr, Agnes. Zum Problem der hegelschen Dialectik. Berlin, 1938.

Phil 5330.10 Dürr, E. Die Lehre von der Aufmerksamkeit. Leipzig, 1907.

Phil 334.4 Dürr, Ernst. Erkenntnis-Theorie. Leipzig, 1910.

Phil 8878.37.5 Dürr, Ernst. Grundzüge der Ethik von Dr. E. Dürr. Heidelberg, 1909.

Phil 630.20 Dürr, Ernst. Grundzüge einer realistischen Weltanschauung. Leipzig, 1907.

Phil 8878.37 Dürr, Ernst. Das Gute und das Sittliche. Heidelberg, 1911.

Phil 5066.56 Dürr, K. Lehrbuch der Logistik. Basel, 1954.

Phil 334.6 Dürr, Karl. Wesen und Geschichte der Erkenntnistheorie. Zürich, 1924.

Phil 5590.75 Dürr, Otto. Probleme der Gesinnungsbildung. Heidelberg, 1950.

Phil 5590.528 Duesberg, Hans. Person und Gemeinschaft. Bonn, 1970.

Phil 13.1.5 Duesseldorfer philosophische Bausteine. Düsseldorf. 1,1968+

Phil 193.245 Düsuncenin Tarihteki evrimi. (Suner, Soffet.) Istanbul, 1967.

Phil 3823.3 Duff, R.A. Spinoza's political and ethical philosophy. Glasgow, 1903.

Htn Phil 5425.1.5* Duff, W. Critical observations. London, 1770.

Phil 5425.1.3 Duff, W. An essay on original genius. Gainesville, Fla., 1964.

Htn Phil 5425.1* Duff, W. Essay on original genius. London, 1767.

Phil 6990.7 Duffel, O.L.V. van. Ofte van Goeden Will. Antwerpen, 1717.

Phil 5243.43 Duflo, J. Esquisse d'une énergétique mentale. Paris, 1936.

Phil 3475.3.95 Dufrenne, M. Karl Jaspers et la philosophie de l'existence. Paris, 1947.

Phil 8404.4.5 Dufrenne, Michel. Esthétique et philosophie. Paris, 1967.

Phil 8404.4 Dufrenne, Michel. Phénoménologie de l'expérience esthétique. Paris, 1953.

Phil 178.77 Dufrenne, Mikel. Jalons. La Haye, 1966.

Phil 2555.9.30 Dufrenne, Mikel. La notion d'a priori. 1. éd. Paris, 1959.

Phil 2555.9.31A Dufrenne, Mikel. The notion of the a priori. Evanston, Ill., 1966.

Phil 8878.40 Dugard, Marie. La culture morale. 8e éd. Paris, 1919.

Phil 8583.23 Dugard, Marie. Sur les frontières de la foi. Paris, 1928.

Phil 1145.51 Dugas, L. L'amité antique d'après les moeurs populaires. Thèse. Paris, 1894.

Phil 8878.34 Dugas, L. Cours de morale thérique et pratique. v.1-2. Paris, 1905-06.

Phil 5465.10 Dugas, L. L'imagination. Paris, 1903.

Phil 5545.65.10 Dugas, L. Les maladies de la mémoire et de l'imagination. Paris, 1931.

Phil 5545.65 Dugas, L. La mémoire et l'oubli. Paris, 1917.

Phil 2855.2.97 Dugas, L. La philosophie Théodule Ribot. Paris, 1924.

Phil 5520.48 Dugas, L. Le psittacisme et la pensée symbolique. Paris, 1896.

Phil 5525.24 Dugas, L. Psychologie du rire. Paris, 1902.

Phil 5401.3.5 Dugas, L. Les timides dans la littérature et l'art. Paris, 1925.

Phil 5401.3 Dugas, L. La timidité. Paris, 1898.

Phil 6805.2 Dugas, Laurent. La dépersonnalisation. Paris, 1911.

Phil 5627.241 Duguid, Julian. I am persuaded. N.Y., 1941.

Phil 5043.15.2 Duhamel, J.M.C. Des méthodes dans les sciences de raisonnement. pt.1. Paris, 1865.

Phil 5043.15 Duhamel, J.M.C. Des méthodes dans les sciences de raisonnement. v.1-5. Paris, 1865-73. 3v.

Phil 284.4.12 Duhem, P. The aim and structure of physical theory. N.Y., 1962.

Phil 284.4.10 Duhem, P. The aim and structure of physical theory. Princeton, 1954.

Phil 284.4.2 Duhem, P. La theorie physique, son objet, sa structure. 2. éd. Paris, 1914.

Phil 284.4 Duhem, P. La theorie physique. Paris, 1906.

Phil 284.4.7 Duhem, P. Ziel und Struktur der physikalischen Theorien. Leipzig, 1908.

Phil 3450.19.415 Duintjer, Otto D. De vraag naar her transcendentale. Leiden, 1966.

Phil 735.220 Dujoune, L. Teoría de los valoçes y filosofía de la historia. Buenos Aires, 1959.

Phil 3120.30.175 Dujoune, León. Martin Buber. Buenos Aires, 1966[1965]

Phil 4080.3.530 Dujovne, León. El pensamiento histórico de Benedetto Croce. Buenos Aires, 1968.

Phil 3823.11 Dujovne, Leon. Spinoza. Buenos Aires, 1941-45. 4v.

Phil 5886.20 Duke University. Center for the Study of Aging and Human Development. Normal aging: reports from the Duke longitudinal study, 1955-1969. Durham, N.C., 1970.

Phil 43.2 Duke University psychological monographs. Durham, N.C. 1-3,1931-1934

Phil 1050.4.5 Dukes, L. Salomo ben Gabirol. Hannover, 1860.

Phil 665.72 Dukh i real'nost'. (Berdiaev, N.A.) Paris, 1941-.

Phil 9513.14 Dukh vremeni. (Sheremetev, Vl.Vl.) Shankai, 1937.

Phil 7069.06.15 Dularfull fyrirbrigðid (Kvaran, E.H.) Reykjavik, 1906.

Phil 9575.10 Du Lassage, Henri. A moral e o capitalismo. Pôrto, 19-

Phil 3425.435 Dulckeit, Gerhard. Die Idee Gottes im Geiste der Philosophie Hegels. München, 1947.

Phil 4225.8.50 Dull'attualismo. (Sciacca, Michele Federico.) Milano, 1961.

Phil 4195.87 Dulles, A. Princeps concordiae: Pico della Mirandola. Cambridge, 1941.

Phil 2125.77 Dulles, J.H. McCosh bibliography. Princeton, 1895.

Phil 6113.21 Dulley, William. Body, soul and spirit. London, 1923.

Phil 4640.2.30 Dulmaetti og dultrú. (Fórólfsson, S.) Reykjavík, 1922.

Phil 7082.48 Dulraenar smásögur. (Jónsson, Brynjólfur.) Bessastadir, 1907.

Phil 7082.46.5 Dulrímir. (Jónasson, Hermann.) Reykjavík, 1914.

Phil 7069.15.60 Dulsýnir. (Sigfússon, S.) Reykjavik, 1915.

Phil 8658.27 Duluman, Evgraf K. Ideiia boga. Moskva, 1970.

Phil 4803.434.30 Dumania nad najwyzszemi zagadnieniami człowieka. (Gołuchowski, Józef.) Wilno, 1861. 2v.

Phil 7069.23.6 Dumanjó, L. Daniel. Habana, 1923.

Phil 1703.3 Du Marchie van Voorlhnipen, H. Nagelaten Geschriften. Arheim, 1886. 2v.

Phil 6980.241 Dumas, A.G. A psychiatric primer for the veteran's family and friends. Minneapolis, 1945.

Phil 5592.30 DuMas, F.M. Manifest structure analysis. Missoula, Montana, 1955.

Phil 2490.110 Dumas, G. Psychologie de deux messies positivistes Saint-Simon et Auguste Comte. Paris, 1905.

Phil 2490.111 Dumas, G. Quid Auguste Comte de suae altatis psychologis senserit. Lutetiae, 1900.

Phil 5525.5 Dumas, G. La sourire. Paris, 1906.

Phil 5403.6 Dumas, G. La tristesse et la joie. Paris, 1900.

Phil 5400.109 Dumas, G. La vie affective. 1. éd. Paris, 1948.

Phil 5243.29.10 Dumas, George. Nouveau traité de psychologie. v.1-8. Paris, 1930-36. 7v.

Phil 5243.29 Dumas, George. Traité de psychologie. Paris, 1923. 2v.

Phil 6625.2 Dumas, Georges. Les états intellectuels dans la mélancolie. Paris, 1895.

Phil 5627.169 Dumas, Georges. Le surnaturel et les dieux d'après les maladies mentales. Paris, 1946.

Phil 5655.1 Duméril, A.H.A. Des odeurs. Paris, 1843.

Phil 8583.41 Duméry, Henry. Critique et religion. Paris, 1957.

Phil 8583.41.5 Duméry, Henry. Phénoménologie et religion. 1. éd. Paris, 1958.

Phil 8658.17.3 Duméry, Henry. The problem of God in philosophy of religion. Evanston, Ill., 1964.

Phil 8658.17 Duméry, Henry. Le problème de Dieu en philosophie de la religion. Bruges, 1957.

Phil 8658.17.10 Duméry, Henry. Raison et religion dans la philosophie de l'actin. Paris, 1963.

Phil 1703.16 Duméry, Henry. Regards sur la philosophie contemporaine. Tournai, 1957.

Phil 8622.20 Duméry, Henry. La tentation de faire du bien. Paris, 1957.

Phil 178.16 Dumesni, G. Du role des concepts. Paris, 1892.

Phil 178.16.5 Dumesni, G. La sophistique contemporaine. Paris, 1912.

Phil 8628.6 Dumesnil, A. L'immortalite. Paris, 1861.

Phil 8878.48 Dumesnil, L.A.L. Examen politique, philosophique et moral. Caen, 1805.

Phil 5241.184.80 Dummer, Ethel Sturges. Mary Everest Boole; a pioneer student of the unconscious. n.p., 19- ?

Phil 8878.29 Dumont, Arsène. La morale basée sur la démogr. phie. Paris, 1901.

Phil 1190.25 Dumont, Jean-Paul. Les sceptiques grecs. Paris, 1966.

Phil 5525.26 Dumont, L. Des causes du rire. Paris, 1862.

Phil 5402.1 Dumont, L. Théorie scientifique de la sensibilité. Paris, 1875.

Phil 5402.1.3 Dumont, L. Vergnügen und Schmerz. Leipzig, 1876.

Htn Phil 5043.12* DuMoulin, Pierre. Elementa logica. Breamae, 1622.

Phil 3823.7 Dumrath, O.H. Spinoza. Stockholm, 1908.

Phil 5243.23.5 Dumville, B. The fundamentals of psychology. London, 1921.

Phil 5243.23.7 Dumville, B. The fundamentals of psychology. 2d ed. London, 1924.

Phil 8740.4 Dun, Angus. Not by bread alone. 2. ed. N.Y., 1942.

Phil 672.3.5 Dunan, C. Essai sur les formes a priori. Paris, 1884.

Phil 672.3 Dunan, C. Théorie psychologique de l'espace. Paris, 1895.

Phil 178.19.5 Dunan, Charles. Les deux idéalismes. Paris, 1911.

Phil 178.19 Dunan, Charles. Essais de philosophie générale. 5th ed. Paris, 1902.

Phil 5400.95 Dunbar, H.F. Emotions and bodily changes. N.Y., 1938.

Phil 5400.95.5 Dunbar, H.F. Psychosomatic diagnosis. N.Y., 1943.

Phil 3485.21 Duncan, A.R.C. Practical reason and morality. London, 1957.

Phil 2270.96 Duncan, D. Life and letters of Herbert Spencer. N.Y., 1908. 2v.

Phil 8583.8.2 Duncan, H. Sacred philosophy. v.3. Boston, 1839?

Phil 8583.8 Duncan, H. Sacred philosophy of the Seasons. Boston, 1839. 2v.

Htn Phil 178.33* Duncan, R. Prometheus (les grandes crucifics). Paris, 1919.

Phil 7069.45.50 Duncan, V.H.M. The trial of Mrs. Duncan. London, 1945.

Phil 478.1 Duncan, W.S. Conscious matter. London, 1881.

Phil 5043.13.7 Duncan, William. The elements of logick. Albany, 1811.

Phil 5043.13.2 Duncan, William. The elements of logick. Edinburgh, 1776.

Phil 5043.13 Duncan, William. The elements of logick. London, 1764.

Phil 5043.13.4 Duncan, William. The elements of logick. N.Y., 1802.

Phil 5043.13.3 Duncan, William. The elements of logick. Philadelphia, 1792.

Phil 1900.95 Duncan-Jones, A. Butler's moral philosophy. Harmondsworth, 1952.

Phil 310.105 Duncher, Hermann. Einführungen in den Marxismus. Berlin, 1959. 2v.

Phil 5243.68.2 Duncker, Karl. Zur Psychologie des Produktiven Denkens. 2e Neudruck. Berlin, 1966.

Phil 5421.25.70 D'une malédiction. (Worms, Jeannine.) Paris, 1963.

Phil 8886.78 D'une morale de l'amour à une sociologie de la raison. (Lamouche, André.) Paris, 1963. 2v.

Phil 1955.9.30 Dunham, B. Giant in chains. 1st ed. Boston, 1953.

Phil 803.17 Dunham, B. Heroes and heretics. 1st ed. N.Y., 1964.

Phil 3485.14 Dunham, B. A study in Kant's aesthetics. Diss. Lancaster, Pa., 1934.

Phil 8404.22 Dunham, Barrows. The artist in society. N.Y., 1960.

Phil 6953.20 Dunham, Henry Warren. Community and schizophrenia. Detroit, 1965.

Phil 3823.9 Dunham, J.H. Freedom and purpose; an interpretation of the psychology of Spinoza. Princeton, N.J., 1916.

Phil 8583.40 Dunham, J.H. The religion of philosophers. Philadelphia, 1947.

Phil 8878.49 Dunham, James. Principles of ethics. N.Y., 1929.

Phil 3823.5 Dunin-Borkowski, Stanislaus von. Der Junge de Spinoza. Münster, 1910.

Phil 3823.5.5 Dunin-Borkowski, Stanislaus von. Spinoza aus den Tagen Spinozas. Münster, 1933. 3v.

Phil 2340.10.190 Dunkel, Harold Baker. Whitehead on education. Columbus, 1965.

Phil 8583.19 Dunkmann, D.K. Religionsphilosophie. Gütersloh, 1917.

Phil 5243.15.20 Dunlap, K. Concerning fluctuating and inaudible sounds. n.p., 1908-1916. 15 pam.

Phil 5243.15.7 Dunlap, K. Elements of psychology. St. Louis, 1936.

Phil 5243.15.5 Dunlap, K. The elements of scientific psychology. St. Louis, 1922.

Phil 6313.5 Dunlap, K. Mysticism, Freudianism and scientific psychology. St. Louis, 1920. 2v.

Phil 5243.15.9 Dunlap, K. Old and new viewpoints in psychology. St. Louis, 1925.

Phil 6953.15 Dunlap, K. Research in methods of adjustment. Berkeley, 1941.

Phil 5243.15 Dunlap, K. A system of psychology. N.Y., 1912.

Phil 5435.10.5 Dunlap, Knight. Habits, their making and unmaking. N.Y., 1945.

Phil 6113.11 Dunlap, Knight. An outline of psychobiology. Baltimore, 1914.

Phil 6113.11.2 Dunlap, Knight. An outline of psychobiology. 2d ed. Baltimore, 1917.

Phil 5850.176 Dunlap, Knight. Personal adjustment. 1. ed. N.Y., 1946.

Phil 8583.39 Dunlap, Knight. Religion. N.Y., 1946.

Phil 5238.70 Dunlap and Associates, Stanford, Conn. Mathematical models of human behavior. Stanford, 1955.

Phil 9558.23 Dunn, Ellen Catherine. The concept of ingratitude in renaissance English moral philosophy. These. Washington, D.C., 1946.

Phil 5620.12 Dunn, Miriam Frances. The psychology of reasoning. Diss. n.p., 1926.

Phil 672.136.7 Dunne, John W. An experiment with time. London, 1952.

Phil 672.136A Dunne, John W. An experiment with time. N.Y., 1927.

Phil 672.136.5 Dunne, John W. An experiment with time. 3rd ed. N.Y., 1949.

Phil 672.136.10 Dunne, John W. An experiment with time. 4th ed. N.Y., 1938.

Phil 672.136.30 Dunne, John W. Intrusions? London, 1955.

Phil 672.136.17 Dunne, John W. The new immortality. London, 1938.

Phil 672.136.25 Dunne, John W. Nothing dies. London, 1940.

Phil 672.136.15 Dunne, John W. The serial universe. N.Y., 1938.

Phil 3823.12 Dunner, J. Baruch Spinoza and western democracy. N.Y., 1955.

Phil 8953.15 Dunphy, William. The new morality. N.Y., 1967.

Phil 7054.45.55 Dunraven, W.T.W.-Q. Experiences in spiritualism with D.D. Home. Glasgow, 1924.

Phil 5627.70 Dupain, J.M. Etude clinique sur le délire religieux. Thèse. Paris, 1888.

Phil 6673.10 Dupau, Jean A. Lettres physiologiques...sur le magnétisme. Paris, 1826.

Phil 8878.62 Dupleix, Scipion. L'ethique, ou Philosophie morale. Paris, 1610.

Phil 7069.66.20 Du Plessis, Izak David. Poltergeists of the south. Cape Town, 1966.

Phil 8828.8 Du Plessis, Pieter Gert Wessel. Opskorting van die etiese? Thesis. Potchefstroom, 1965.

Phil 8092.11 Duplessis, V. Surrealism. N.Y., 1963.

Phil 2725.2.87 Du Plessis de Grenédan, L. Examen des Paroles d'un croyant et du Livre du peuple. Rennes, 1840.

Phil 178.13 Dupont, A.H.H. Ontologie. Louvain, 1875.

Phil 178.41 Dupont, Paul. Les problèmes de la philosophie et leur enchainement scientifique. Paris, 1920.

Phil 284.14 Dupont de Nemours, P.S. Philosophie de l'univers. Paris, 1792.

Phil 6673.4.11 Du Potet, J. de S. Cours de magnétisme animal. Paris, 1834.

Phil 6673.4.10 Du Potet, J. de S. Cours de magnétisme en sept leçons. Paris, 1840.

Phil 6673.4.22 Du Potet, J. de S. Essai sur l'enseignement philosophique du magnétisme. Paris, 1845.

Phil 6673.4.15 Du Potet, J. de S. Exposé des expériences sur le magnétisme. Paris, 1821.

Phil 6673.4.19 Du Potet, J. de S. An introduction to the study of animal magnetism. London, 1838.

Phil 6673.4.21 Du Potet, J. de S. Le magnétisme opposé a la médecine. Paris, 1840.

Phil 6673.4.5 Du Potet, J. de S. Manuel de l'étudiant magnétiseur. 3e éd. Paris, 1854.

Phil 6673.4.7 Du Potet, J. de S. Manuel de l'étudiant magnétiseur. 5e éd. Paris, 1887.

Phil 6673.4.3 Du Potet, J. de S. Traité complet de magnétisme animal. 5e éd. Paris, 1894.

Phil 6673.4.17 Du Potet, J. de S. L'université de Montpellier et le magnétisme animal. Beziers, 1836.

Phil 5753.11 Duprat, G.L. L'éducation de la volonté et des facultés logiques. Paris, 1920.

Phil 6953.9 Duprat, G.L. L'instabilité mentale. Paris, 1898.

Phil 8878.22.2 Duprat, G.L. La morale. Théorie psycho-sociologique d'une conduite rationnelle. 2. ed. Paris, 1912.

Phil 8878.22 Duprat, G.L. Morals: a treatise on the psycho-sociological bases of ethics. London, 1903.

Phil 6313.12 Dupré, E. Pathologie de l'imagination et de l'émotivité. Paris, 1925.

Phil 1195.11 Dupréel, E. Les sophistes. Neuchâtel, 1949.

Phil 5075.2 Dupréel, Eugène. Essai sur les catégories. Bruxelles, 1906.

Phil 2555.11.71 Dupréel, Eugène. Similitude et dépassement. Paris, 1968.

Phil 8878.50 Dupréel, Eugène. Traité de morale. Bruxelles, 1932. 2v.

Phil 8878.50.1 Dupréel, Eugène. Traité de morale. Bruxelles, 1967. 2v.

Phil 665.8A DuPrel, C. Die Entdeckung der Seele durch die Geheimwissenschaften. v.1-2. Leipzig, 1894-95.

Phil 665.8.2 DuPrel, C. Die Entdeckung der Seele durch die Geheimwissenschaften. 2e Aufl. Leipzig, 1910. 2v.

Phil 7060.34 Du Prel, C.F. Die monistische Seelenlehre. Leipzig, 1888.

Phil 525.1 Du Prel, C.F. Die Philosophie der Mystik. Leipzig, 1885.

Phil 6673.15 Du Prel, Carl. Experimentalpsychologie und Experimentalmetaphysik. Leipzig, 1891.

Phil 7068.92.55 Du Prel, K.L.A.F.M.A. Das Rätsel des Menschen. Leipzig, 1892.

Phil 525.1.2 Du Prel, Karl. Die Philosophie der Mystik. 2e Aufl. Leipzig, 1910.

Phil 525.2 Du Prel, Karl. Philosophy of mysticism. London, 1889. 2v.

Phil 5780.10 Dupuis, Léon. Les aboulies sociales, le scrupule, la timidité, la susceptibilité, l'autoritarisme. Paris, 1940.

Phil 9343.10 Dupuy, La Chapelle. Instruction d'un père a sa fille. 3e éd. Paris, 1731.

Phil 9343.10.5 Dupuy, La Chapelle. Instruction d'un père a sa fille. 3e éd. Paris, 1750.

Phil 3850.18.150 Dupuy, Maurice. La philosophie de la religion. Paris, 1959.

Phil 3850.18.151 Dupuy, Maurice. La philosophie de la religion chez Max Scheler. Paris, 1959.

Phil 3850.18.153 Dupuy, Maurice. La philosophie de Max Scheler. Paris, 1959. 2v.

Phil 3850.18.152 Dupuy, Maurice. La philosophie de Max Scheler. 1. éd. Paris, 1959. 2v.

Phil 7080.2 Dupuy, P. Étude psycho-physiologique. Bordeaux, 1879.

Phil 2490.91 Dupuy, P. Le positivisme. Paris, 1911.

Phil 6953.5 Dupuy, Paul. De l'automatisme psychologique. Bordeaux, 1894.

Phil 8878.33 Dupuy, Paul. Les fondements de la morale. Paris, 1900.

Phil 8828.1 Dupuy, Paul. La question morale à la fin du XIXe siècle. Paris, 1897.

Phil 9558.27 DuPuy de Clinchamps, Philippe. Le snobisme. Paris, 1964.

Phil 8658.26 Duquesne, Jacques. Dieu pour l'homme d'aujourd'hui. Paris, 1970.

Phil 178.45 Durand, Eugène. Cours de philosophie. Paris, 1909-21. 2v.

Phil 5465.105 Durand, G. Les structures anthropologiques de l'imaginaire. Grenoble, 1960.

Phil 5465.105.2 Durand, G. Les structures anthropologiques de l'imaginaire. 2. éd. Paris, 1963.

Phil 6673.6 Durand, J.P. Cours théorique et C. de Braidisme. Paris, 1860.

Phil 6313.2 Durand, J.P. Le merveilleux scientifique. Paris, 1894.

Phil 8878.20 Durand, J.P. Nouvelles recherches sur l'esthetique et la morale. Paris, 1900.

Phil 178.39 Durand, J.P. Variétés philosophiques. 2e éd. Paris, 1900.

Phil 5403.14 Durand, Leo. The psychology of happiness. Blackstone, 1968.

Phil 7069.59.45 Durand, M. Technique et panthéon des mediums viêtnamiens. Paris, 1959.

Phil 5243.12 Durand, M.J.P. Essais de physiologie philosophique. Paris, 1866.

Phil 6113.1 Durand, P.J. Electro-dynamisme vital. Paris, 1855.

Phil 8878.16 Durand Desormeaux, F. Etudes philosophiques. Paris, 1884. 2v.

Phil 178.8 Durand Désormeaux, Fernand. Réflexions et pensées. Paris, 1884.

Phil 672.148.5 Durand-Doat, J. Essai sur l'étendue. Paris, 1928.

Phil 672.148 Durand-Doat, J. Essai sur l'étendue. Thèse. Paris, 1928.

Phil 178.56 Durand-Doat, J. Le sens de la métaphysique. Paris, 1928.

Phil 178.56.2 Durand-Doat, J. Le sens de la métaphysique. Thèse. Paris, 1928.

Phil 672.236 Durandeaux, Jacques. L'éternité dans la vie quotidienne. Paris, 1964.

Phil 8658.24 Durandeaux, Jacques. Question vivante a un Dieu mort. Paris, 1967.

Phil 6673.5 Durant, C.F. Exposition, or A new theory animal magnetism. N.Y., 1837.

Phil 9530.15 Durant, E.E. How to make your mark in life. Boston, 1917.

Phil 803.6.25 Durant, W. The story of philosophy. Cambridge, 1927.

Phil 803.6.5A Durant, W. The story of philosophy. N.Y., 1926.

Phil 803.6.18 Durant, W. The story of philosophy. N.Y., 1933.

Phil 803.6.19 Durant, W. The story of philosophy. N.Y., 1954.

Phil 1955.4.87 Durant, Will. Transition. N.Y., 1927.

Phil 5425.50 Durant, William. Adventures in genius. N.Y., 1931.

Phil 178.30.7 Durant, William. The mansions of philosophy. Garden City, 1941.

Phil 178.30.5 Durant, William. The mansions of philosophy. N.Y., 1929.

Phil 178.30.10 Durant, William. On the meaning of life. N.Y., 1932.

Phil 178.30 Durant, William. Philosophy and social problem. N.Y., 1917.

Phil 3485.16 Durante, Gaetano. Gli epigoni di Kant. Firenze, 1943.

Phil 2475.1.39.10 Duration and simultaneity. (Bergson, Henri.) Indianapolis, 1965.

Phil 8626.25 The duration of mind. (Barnes, C.T.) Salt Lake City, 1955.

Phil 978.49.715 Durch den Geist zur Wirklichkeits-Erkenntnis der Menschenrätsel. (Steiner, R.) Dornach, 1965- 6v.

Phil 3195.18.30 Durch die Tore der neuen Zeit. (Dessauer, Friedrich.) Göttingen, 1961.

Phil 3450.19.480 Durchblicke: Martin Heidegger zum 80. Geburtstag. Frankfurt, 1970.

Phil 3552.231 Durdik, Josef. Leibnitz und Newton. Halle, 1869.

Phil 8404.16 Durdík, Jcsef. Vseobecna aesthetika. Praha, 1875.

Phil 7103.4 Dureau, Alexis. Histoire de la médicine et des sciences occultes. Paris, 1869.

Phil 5643.73 La durée des sensations visuelles élémentaires. (Janet, P.) Paris, 1904.

Phil 2475.1.39 Durée et simultanéité. 2e éd. (Bergson, Henri.) Paris, 1923.

Phil 2475.1.39.5 Durée et sumultanéité à propos de la théorie d'Einstein. (Bergson, Henri.) Paris, 1922.

Htn Phil 2555.3.30* DuRefuge, E. Aulicus inculpatus. Amsterdam, 1644.

Phil 5592.160 Dureman, I. Psykometriska och experimentalpsykologiska metoder för klinisk tillämpning. Stockholm, 1959.

Phil 5643.96 Duret, René. Les aspects de l'image visuelle. Paris, 1936.

Phil 5585.54.7 Duret, René. Les facteurs pratiques de la croyance dans la perception. Paris, 1929?

Phil 5585.54.5 Duret, René. Les facteurs pratiques de la croyance dans la perception. Thèse. Paris, 1929.

Phil 5585.54.2 Duret, René. L'objet de la perception. Thèse. Paris, 1929.

Phil 5585.54 Duret, René. L'objet de la perception. Thèse. Paris, 1929.

Phil 284.1 Durfee, J.H. The Panidèa. Boston, 1846.

Phil 6400.38 Durieu, Colette. La rééducation des aphasiques. Bruxelles, 1969.

Phil 8583.18.2 Durkheim, É. Les formes élémentaires de la vie religieuse. 2. éd. Paris, 1925.

Phil 8583.18.5 Durkheim, É. Les formes élémentaires de la vie religieuse. 5e éd. Paris, 1968.

Phil 178.71 Durkheim, E. Pragmatisme et socilologie. Paris, 1955.
Phil 7150.27.20 Durkheim, E. Suicide; a study in sociology. Glencoe, 1962.
Phil 7150.27.5 Durkheim, E. La suicide. Paris, 1930.
Phil 7150.27.15 Durkheim, E. Le suicide. Paris, 1960.
Phil 2280.5.108 Duron, J. La pensée de George Santayana. Paris, 1950.
Phil 2280.5.108.2 Duron, J. La pensée de George Santayana. Thèse. Paris, 1950.
Phil 8878.32 DuRoussaux, L. Ethique; traité de philosophie morale. Bruxelles, 1907.
Phil 2905.1.245 Duroux, P.E. La prévie, la réconciliation de la science et la foi. Lyon, 1961.
Phil 7060.149 Duroy de Bruignac, A. Satan et la magie de nos jours. Paris, 1864.
Phil 6155.2 Durr, R.A. Poetic vision and the psychedelic experience. 1st ed. Syracuse, 1970.
Phil 6673.16 Durville, H. Magnétisme personnel ou psychique. Paris, 1905.
Phil 6673.16.5 Durville, H. The theory and practice of human magnetism. Chicago, 1900.
Phil 8878.17 Dusch, J.J. Moralische Briefe. Leipzig, 1772. 2v.
Phil 8878.17.5 Dusch, J.J. Moralische Briefe. v.2. Wien, 1771.
Phil 4756.1.41 Dusha cheloveka. Izd.2. (Frank, Semen L.) Paris, 1964.
Phil 4756.1.40 Dusha chelovieka. (Frank, Semen L.) Moskva, 1917.
Phil 3425.726 Duso, Giuseppe. Hegel interprete di Platone. Padova, 1969.
Phil 8622.78 Duss-von Werdt, Josef. Theologie aus Glaubenserfahrung. Zürich, 1969.
Phil 2905.1.485 Dussault, Gabriel. Panthéisme, action, oméga chez Teilhard de Chardin. Bruges, 1967.
Phil 5400.28 Dussauze, H. Les règles esthétiques et les lois du sentiment. Montauban, 1911.
Phil 2490.113 Dussauze, W. Essai sur la religion d'apres A. Comte. Thèse. Saint-Amand, 1901.
Phil 3003.9 Dussort, H. L'ecole de Marboug. Paris, 1963.
Phil 807.26 Düşünce tarihi. (Hançerlioğlu, Orhan.) Istanbul, 1970.
Phil 665.90 Dusza ludzka, jej istnienie i natura. (Pastuszka, J.) Lublin, 1947.
Phil 140.58 Pamphlet vol. Dutch addresses on psychology. 3 pam.
Phil 178.9.3 Dutens, Louis. Origine des découvertes. 3e éd. Louvain, 1796.
Phil 178.9.4 Dutens, Louis. Origine des découvertes. 4e éd. Paris, 1812.
Phil 178.9 Dutens, Louis. Recherches. v.1-2. Paris, 1766.
Phil 178.9.2 Dutens, Louis. Recherches. 2. éd. Paris, 1776. 2v.
Phil 8878.13.5 The duties of human life. (Dodsley, R.) West Killingly, Conn., 1858.
Phil 9342.12.5 The duties of women. (Cobbe, F.P.) Boston, 1881.
Phil 9342.1 Duties of young men. (Chapin, E.H.) Boston, 1846.
NEDL Phil 9342.1.5 Duties of young men. (Chapin, E.H.) Boston, 1848.
Phil 9342.1.10 Duties of young women. (Chapin, E.H.) Boston, 1850.
Phil 2885.82 Dutoit, E. Die Theorie des Milieu. Bern, 1899.
Phil 8583.31 Dutoit-Mombrini, P. La science du Christ et de l'homme. n.p., 1810. 3v.
Phil 1750.510 Dutt, K. Guru. Existentialism. Basavagundi, 1953.
Phil 1750.510.2 Dutt, K. Guru. Existentialism. Basavagundi, 1954.
Phil 5585.2 Duttenhofer. Die acht Sinne des Menschen. Nördlingen, 1858.
Phil 8595.16.3 Dutton, Thomas. A vindication of the age of reason, by Thomas Paine. London, 1795.
Phil 9120.2 Duty. (Seelye, J.H.) Boston, 1891.
Phil 9120.4.5 Duty. (Smiles, S.) Chicago, 1890.
Phil 9120.4.3 Duty. (Smiles, S.) London, 1880.
Phil 9120.4 Duty. (Smiles, S.) N.Y., 1881.
Phil 8886.9 Duty and faith. (Lloyd, J.) Manchester, 1884.
Phil 9120.161.10 Duty and ignorance of fact. (Prichard, H.A.) London, 1932.
Phil 9120.161 Duty and interest. (Prichard, H.A.) Oxford, 1928.
Phil 8847.12 Duty and utility. (Wedar, S.) Lund, 1952.
Phil 8887.37 Duty of altruism. (McConnell, R.M.) N.Y., 1910.
Phil 9341.1 Duty of American women to their country. (Beecher, C.E.) N.Y., 1845.
Phil 9245.9.50 Duty of happiness. (Avebury, John Lubbock.) Philadelphia, 1896.
Phil 5043.14 Duval-Jouve, J. Traité de logique. Paris, 1855.
Phil 803.9 Duvall, T.G. Great thinkers; the quest of life for its meaning. N.Y., 1937.
Phil 3640.171 Duverger, A. Friedrich Nietzsche een levensbeeld. Amsterdam, 1913.
Phil 5535.32 Duygusal anlam sistemlesi. (Toğrol, Beğlan.) Istanbul, 1967.
Phil 3195.20.30 Duynstee, Willem Jacob A.J. Verspreide opstellen. Roermond, 1963.
Phil 8581.54.5 Dva grada. (Bulgakov, C.) Moskva, 1911.
Phil 8980.456 Dva svity, dvi morali. (Hott, V.S.) Kyiv, 1959.
Phil 3489.31 Dva základní problémy Kantova kriticismu. (Hoppe, V.) Brno, 1932.
Phil 8980.787.25 Dvadtsatyi vek i moral'nye tsennosti chelovechestva. (Shishkin, Aleksandr F.) Moskva, 1968.
Phil 8980.712 Dve morali; moral' religioznaia i moral' kommunisticheskaia. (Prokof'ev, V.I.) Moskva, 1961.
Phil 4829.344.20 Dvornikovic, Vladimir. Barba ideja. Beograd, 1937.
Phil 5753.12 Dwelshauvers, G. L'exercice de la volonté. Paris, 1935.
Phil 5722.8 Dwelshauvers, G. L'inconscient. Paris, 1916.
Phil 5722.8.5 Dwelshauvers, G. Les mécanismes subconscients. Paris, 1925.
Phil 400.73 Dwelshauvers, G. Les méthodes de l'idéalisme scientifique. Paris, 1892. 2 pam.
Phil 5374.47 Dwelshauvers, G. Psychologie de l'apperception. Bruxelles, 1890.
Phil 5243.14.9 Dwelshauvers, George. L'étude de la pensée. Paris, 1934.
Phil 5243.14 Dwelshauvers, George. La synthèse mentale. Paris, 1908.
Phil 5213.2 Dwelshauvers, Georges. La psychologie française contemporaine. Paris, 1920.
Phil 8693.6 Dwight, T. Thoughts of a catholic anatomist. London, 1911.
Phil 384.10 Dworkin, Gerald. Determinism, free will, and moral responsibility. Englewood Cliffs, 1970.
Htn Phil 9560.17* Dyalogo de patientia. (Baldacchini, F.) Perosia, 1525.
Phil 4803.879.95 Dybiec, Julian. Michał wiszniewski. Wrocław, 1970.
Phil 7060.42 Dyer, T.F.T. The ghost world. London, 1893.
Phil 6113.27 Dyer, V.A. You can have it, personality. Long Beach, 1937.
Phil 8878.52 Dyer, W.A. The richer life. Garden City, 1911.
Phil 5400.85 Dyett, E.G. Une étude des émotions au moyen des tests. Thèse. Paris, 1932.
Phil 575.274 The dying self. 1st ed. (Fair, Charles M.) Middletown, Conn., 1969.

Htn Phil 9075.14.5* Dyke, J. Good conscience. 5. ed. London, 1632. 2 pam.
Phil 2250.92 Dykhuizen, George. The conception of God in the philosophy of Josiah Royce. Chicago, 1936.
Phil 8878.18 Dymond, J. Essays...principles of morality. London, 1867.
Phil 8878.18.4 Dymond, J. Essays...principles of morality. N.Y., 1834.
Phil 8878.18.2 Dymond, J. Essays...principles of morality. N.Y., 1844.
Phil 8878.18.5 Dymond, J. Essays...principles of morality. Philadelphia, 1896.
Phil 8967.15.5 The dynamic element in the church. (Rahner, Karl.) Freiburg, 1964.
Phil 6968.28 Dynamic era of court psychiatry, 1914-44. (Sharp, A.A.) Chicago, 1944.
Phil 346.3 The dynamic foundation of knowledge. (Philip, A.) London, 1913.
Phil 400.10 Dynamic idealism. (Lloyd, A.H.) Chicago, 1898.
Phil 9346.8 The dynamic of manhood. (Gulick, L.H.) N.Y., 1917.
Phil 6980.33 Dynamic psychiatry. (Alexander, F.) Chicago, 1952.
Phil 5242.67 Dynamic psychology. (Cruchon, Georges E.) N.Y., 1965.
Phil 5252.50 Dynamic psychology. (Moore, T.V.) Philadelphia, 1924.
Phil 5252.50.2 Dynamic psychology. 2d ed. (Moore, T.V.) Philadelphia, 1926.
Phil 5627.268.10 A dynamic psychology of religion. (Pruyser, Paul W.) N.Y., 1968.
Phil 8583.36 Dynamic religion, a personal experience. N.Y., 193-.
Phil 5251.41A A dynamic theory of personality. (Lewin, Kurt.) N.Y., 1935.
Phil 293.18 Dynamic universe. (McKaye, James.) N.Y., 1931.
Phil 5250.15.16 Dynamics in psychology. (Köhler, Wolfgang.) N.Y., 1940.
Phil 5548.108.5 The dynamics of action. (Atkinson, John W.) N.Y., 1970.
Phil 5421.20.100 The dynamics of aggression. (Megargee, Edwin I.) N.Y., 1970.
Phil 9400.20 The dynamics of aging. 1st ed. (Smith, E.S.) N.Y., 1956.
Phil 5421.10.5 The dynamics of anxiety and hysteria. (Eysenck, H.J.) London, 1957.
Phil 8421.4 Dynamics of art. (Ushenko, A.P.) Indiana, 1953.
Phil 5258.136A The dynamics of human adjustment. (Symonds, P.M.) N.Y., 1946.
Phil 5850.250.10 The dynamics of interviewing. (Kahn, Robert L.) N.Y., 1958.
Phil 5850.253.10 The dynamics of personal efficiency. 1. ed. (Laird, Donald A.) N.Y., 1961.
Phil 5590.522 The dynamics of personality. (Wolberg, Lewis Robert.) N.Y., 1970.
Phil 5625.108 Dynamics of response. (Notterman, Joseph M.) N.Y., 1965.
Phil 600.39 Die Dynamik der Geschichte nach der Geschichtsphilosophie des Positivismus. (Troeltsch, E.) Berlin, 1919. 101v.
Phil 9558.41 Dynamik der Pseudologie. (Van der Schaar, P.J.) München, 1964.
Phil 5465.75 Die Dynamik des schoepferischen Akts. (Weinberg, J.R.) Göttingen, 1954.
Phil 5592.184 La dynamique de l'examen psychologique. (Guillaumin, Jean.) Paris, 1965.
Phil 5520.437 La dynamique de l'expression et de la communication. (Guilhot, Jean.) Paris, 1962.
Phil 3552.304 Dynamique et métaphysique Leibniziennes. (Gueroult, M.) Paris, 1934.
Phil 5252.21 La dynamis et les trois ames. (Milliet, J.P.) Paris, 1908.
Phil 8967.15 Das Dynamische in der Kirche. (Rahner, Karl.) Freiburg, 1958.
Phil 6322.33 Dynamische Tiefenspsychologie. (Mayer, Felix.) Bern, 1953.
Phil 5250.15.17 Dynamische Zusammenhänge in der Psychologie. (Köhler, Wolfgang.) Bern, 1958.
Phil 3910.130 Dynamism in the cosmology of Christian Wolf. 1st ed. (Burns, John V.) N.Y., 1966.
Phil 190.39 Le dynamisme absolu. (Poirson, Charles.) Lyon, 1898.
Phil 8950.12 Le dynamisme de la morale chrétienne. (Anciaux, Paul.) Gembloux, 1968-69.
Phil 5241.75.80 Le dynamisme des structures inconscientes dans la psychologie d'Albert Burloud. (La Garanderie, Antoine de.) Louvain, 1969.
Phil 1108.4 Dynnik, M.A. Ocherk istorii filosofii klassicheskoi Gretsii. Moskva, 1936.
Phil 1210.10 Dyroff, A. Der Peripatos über das Greisenalter. Paderborn, 1939.
Phil 8953.4 Dyroff, A. Religion und Moral. Berlin, 1925.
Phil 8404.20 Dyroff, Adolf. Asthetik des tätigen Geistes. Bonn, 1948.
Phil 5243.18.4 Dyroff, Adolf. Einführung in die Psychologie. 4e Aufl. Leipzig, 1919.
Phil 178.40.5 Dyroff, Adolf. Einleitung in die Philosophie. Bonn, 1948.
Phil 1200.37 Dyroff, Adolf. Die Ethik der alten Stoa. Berlin, 1897.
Phil 8658.14 Dyroff, Adolf. Probleme der Gotteserkenntnis. Münster, 1928.
Phil 4210.106 Dyroff, Adolf. Rosmini. Mainz, 1906.
Phil 178.40 Dyroff, Adolf. Über den Existenzialbegriff. Freiburg im Breisgau, 1902.
Phil 3549.2.105 Dyserinck, Hugo. Graf Hermann Keyserling und Frankereich. Bonn, 1970.
Phil 8980.346.5 Dzhafarli, Teimuraz M. Besedy o kommunisticheskoi morali. Moskva, 1970.
Phil 8980.346 Dzhafarli, Teimuraz M. Byt' chelovekom na zemle. Moskva, 1968.
Phil 8828.10 Dzhafarli, Teimuraz M. Iz istorii domarksistskoi eticheskoi mysli. Tbilisi, 1970.
Phil 8404.26 Dzhibladze, Georgii N. Iskustvo i deistoitel'nost'. Tbilisi, 1971.
Phil 270.141 Dzhioev, Otar. Priroda istoricheskoi neobkhodimosti. Tbilisi, 1967.
Phil 4065.174 Dzhordano Bruno. (Gorfunkel', Aleksandr K.) Moskva, 1965.
Phil 4065.186 Dzhordano Bruno i genesis klassicheskoi nauki. (Kuznetsov, Boris G.) Moskva, 1970.
Phil 1870.182 Dzhordzh Berkli. (Bykhovskii, Bernard E.) Moskva, 1970.
Phil 4803.810.30 Dzieje filozoficznej myśli polskiej w okresie porozbiorowym. (Strzeszewski, Maurycy.) Kraków, 1912.
Phil 818.3 Dzieje filozofu w zarysie. (Straszewski, M.) Krakowie, 1894.
Phil 4803.799.2 Dzieła. v.1-7. (Sniadecki, Jan.) Warszawa, 1837-39. 3v.
Htn Phil 665.50* E., T. Vindiciae mentis. London, 1702.
Phil 3640.192 E. Gundolf und Kurt Heldebrandt, Nietzsche als Richter unsrer Zeit. (Gundolf, E.) Breslau, 1923.
Phil 200.2.15 E. Zellers kleine Schriften, unter Mitwirking. (Zeller, E.) Berlin, 1910. 3v.
Phil 1905.14.79 Pamphlet box. E.G. Boring.
Phil 7162.266 E.S.P.; a scientific evaluation. (Hansel, C.E.M.) N.Y., 1966.

Author and Title Listing

	Phil 7162.265	E.S.P.; beyond time and distance. (Lethbridge, Thomas C.) London, 1965.
	Phil 5066.195.5	E.W. Beth Memorial Colloquium, Institut Henri Poincaré, 1964. Logic and foundations of science. Dordrecht, 1968.
	Phil 3890.2.85	E.W. von Tschirnhaus. (Winter, Eduard.) Berlin, 1960.
Htn	Phil 2045.103*	Eachard, John. Some opinions of Mr. Hobbs. London, 1673.
	Phil 2255.1.155	Eames, Elizabeth Ramsden. Bertrand Russell's theory of knowledge. London, 1969.
	Phil 7069.20.10	The ear of Dionysius. (Balfour, Gerald W.) N.Y., 1920.
Htn	Phil 3824.3*	Earbery, Matthias. Deism examin'd and confuted in...Tractatus Theologico Politicus. London, 1697.
	Phil 6954.1	Earle, P. The curability of insanity. Philadelphia, 1887.
	Phil 6945.1	Earle, P. History description...Bloomingdale. N.Y., 1848-67. 21 pam.
	Phil 6954.1.5	Earle, P. A visit to thirteen asylums...insane, Europe. Philadelphia, 1841.
	Phil 335.8	Earle, William A. Objectivity. N.Y., 1955.
	Phil 303.13	The earliest cosmologies. (Warren, W.F.) N.Y., 1909.
	Phil 850.26	Earliest intellectual man's idea of the cosmos. (Marcer, S.A.B.) London, 1957.
	Phil 8968.5	Early Christian ethics in the West. (Scullard, H.H.) London, 1907.
	Phil 2490.155	Early essays on social philosophy. (Comte, Auguste.) London, 1911.
	Phil 8610.918	Early free thinking societies in America. (Riley, Isaac W.) N.Y., 1918.
	Phil 3001.22	Early German philosophy: Kant and his predecessors. (Beck, Lewis White.) Cambridge, 1969.
	Phil 1133.1.12A	Early Greek philosophers. 4th ed. (Burnet, John.) London, 1952.
	Phil 1106.3.9	Early Greek philosophy. (Benn, A.W.) London, 1908.
	Phil 1106.3.10	Early Greek philosophy. (Benn, A.W.) N.Y., n.d.
	Phil 1106.3.11	Early Greek philosophy. (Benn, A.W.) N.Y., 1909?
X Cg	Phil 1133.1.2	Early Greek philosophy. (Burnet, John.) London, 1892.
	Phil 1135.225	Early Greek philosophy and the Orient. (West, M.L.) Oxford, 1971.
	Phil 5535.44	Early learning in man and animal. (Sluckin, Wladyslaw.) London, 1970.
	Phil 7106.4	Early magnetism in its higher relations to humanity. (South, Thomas.) London, 1846.
	Phil 1506.14	Early medieval philosophy. (Burch, G.B.) N.Y., 1951.
	Phil 1133.28	The early philosophers of Greece. (McClure, Matthew T.) N.Y., 1935.
	Phil 1182.20	Early Pythagorean politics and theory. (Minar, Edwin L.) Baltimore, 1942.
	Phil 1870.136.5	The early reception of Berkeley's immaterialism, 1710-1733. (Bracken, Harry M.) The Hague, 1965.
	Phil 1870.136	The early reception of Berkeley's immaterialism. (Bracken, Harry M.) The Hague, 1959.
	Phil 3425.63	Early theological writings. (Hegel, Georg Wilhelm Friedrich.) Chicago, 1948.
	Phil 1955.6.55	The early works, 1882-1898. v.2,4. (Dewey, John.) Carbondale, 1967- 2v.
	Phil 2266.50	The early writings of Adam Smith. (Smith, Adam.) N.Y., 1967.
	Phil 3450.19.74.1	Earth and gods. (Vycinas, V.) The Hague, 1961.
	Phil 8581.93	Earth is enough. (Brownell, B.) N.Y., 1933.
	Phil 8704.2.5	The earth spaks to Bryan. (Osborn, H.F.) N.Y., 1925.
	Phil 7069.21.35	The earthen vessel. (Glenconner, Pamela.) London, 1921.
	Phil 585.186	Earthling and Hellene; a psychological mechanism of evolution and its effect on the human race. (Rendel, David.) Wimbledon, 1963.
	Phil 7069.60.10	East, John. Man the immortal. London, 1960.
	Phil 8597.38.10	East and West in religion. (Radhakrishnan, S.) London, 1933.
	Phil 978.49.100	The East in the light of the West. (Steiner, R.) London, 1922.
	Phil 489.3	The East-West conflict. (Eisenberg, Rafael.) N.Y., 1967.
	Phil 70.88	East-West Philosopher Conference. Philosophy and culture. 1. ed. Honolulu, 1962.
	Phil 930.70	East-West Philosophers Conference. The Chinese mind. Honolulu, 1967.
	Phil 960.265	East-west philosophers' conference. The Indian mind; essentials of Indian philosophy and culture. Honolulu, 1967.
	Phil 935.13	East-West Philosophers' Conference. The Japanese mind. Honolulu, 1967.
	Phil 575.272	East-West studies on the problem of the self. (Conference on Comparative Philosophy and Culture.) The Hague, 1968.
	Phil 8598.138.1	Easten wisdom and Western thought. (Saher, Purvezji Jamshedji.) London, 1969.
	Phil 960.256	Eastern lights; a brief account of some phases of life, thought and mysticism in India. (Sircar, Mahendranath.) Calcutta, 1935.
	Phil 9346.15	Eastern religions in the electric age. (Garabedian, John H.) N.Y., 1969.
	Phil 5525.20.15	Eastman, Max. Enjoyment of laughter. N.Y., 1936.
	Phil 5525.20A	Eastman, Max. The sense of humor. N.Y., 1921.
	Phil 5525.20.5	Eastman, Max. The sense of humor. N.Y., 1922.
	Phil 8879.29	Easton, L.D. Ethics. Dubuque, Iowa, 1955.
	Phil 3425.630	Easton, Loyd David. Hegel's first American followers. Athens, 1966.
	Phil 2805.218A	Eastwood, D.M. The revival of Pascal. Oxford, 1936.
	Phil 6329.1.8	Easy lessons in psychoanalysis. (Tridon, André.) N.Y., 1921.
	Phil 5062.7	Easy lessons on reasoning. (Smart, B.H.) Boston, 1857.
	Phil 3120.24.80	Eat oer it libben fan Prof. Dr. Tj. de Boer, 1866-1942. (Zee, Teartse van der.) Ljouwert, 1965.
	Phil 7069.40.12	Eaton, A.K. A message to a troubled world. Clarmont, Calif., 1940.
	Phil 900.13	Eaton, Gai. The richest vein. London, 1949.
	Phil 735.94	Eaton, Howard O. The Austrian theory of value. Norman, 1930.
	Phil 1900.82	Eaton, J.R.T. Bishop Butler and his critics. Oxford, 1877.
	Phil 335.2	Eaton, R.M. Symbolism and truth. Cambridge, 1925.
	Phil 5044.6	Eaton, Ralph M. General logic. N.Y., 1931.
	Phil 5465.56	L'eau et les rêves. (Bachelard, G.) Paris, 1942.
	Phil 2475.1.490	Ebacher, Roger. La philosophie dans la cité technique. Québec, 1968.
	Phil 8602.11.8	Ebauche de la religion naturelle...avec un supplément. (Wollaston, W.) La Haye, 1756. 3v.
	Phil 86.4	Ebauche d'un glossaire du langage philosophique. (Brothier, L.) Paris, 1863.
	Phil 6314.6	Ebaugh, Franklin Gessford. Psychiatry in medical education. N.Y., 1942.
	Phil 7140.12	Ebbard, R.J. How to acquire and strengthen will-power. London, 1905.
	Phil 6114.9	Ebbecke, Ulrich. Die kortikalen Erregungen. Leipzig, 1919.
	Phil 5244.7	Ebbinghaus, H. Abriss der Psychologie. Leipzig, 1908.
	Phil 5244.7.4	Ebbinghaus, H. Abriss der Psychologie. 6e Aufl. Leipzig, 1919.
	Phil 5244.7.15	Ebbinghaus, H. Grundzüge der Psychologie. Leipzig, 1911. 2v.
	Phil 5545.5.7A	Ebbinghaus, H. Memory. N.Y., 1913.
	Phil 5545.5.9	Ebbinghaus, H. Memory. N.Y., 1964.
	Phil 5244.7.9	Ebbinghaus, H. Précis de psychologie. Paris, 1910.
	Phil 5244.7.5	Ebbinghaus, H. Psychology, an elementary text-book. Boston, 1908.
	Phil 5545.5	Ebbinghaus, H. Über das Gedächtnis. Leipzig, 1885.
	Phil 3415.108	Ebbinghaus, Hermann. Über die hartmannsche Philosophie des Unbewussten. Düsseldorf, 1873.
	Phil 400.27	Ebbinghaus, J. Relativer und absoluter Idealismus. Leipzig, 1910.
	Phil 3790.11.90	Ebeling, C.D. Memoriae J.A.H. Reimari. Hamburgi, 1815.
	Phil 5244.1	Eberhard, J.A. Allgemeine Theorie des Denkens und Empfindens. Berlin, 1776.
	Phil 3552.233	Eberhard, J.A. Charakteristik des Leibnitz. Leipzig, n.d.
	Phil 850.8	Eberhard, J.A. Der Geist des Urchristenthums. Halle, 1807-08. 3v.
	Phil 8879.21	Eberhard, J.A. Sittenlehre der Vernunft. Berlin, 1786.
	Phil 3246.192	Eberhard, J.A. Über den Gott des Herrn Professor Fichte. Halle, 1799.
	Phil 8405.4	Eberhard, Johann. Handbuch der Ästhetik. Halle, 1803-04.
	Phil 3486.18.2	Eberhard, John. Philosophisches Archiv. Bruxelles, 1968. 2v.
	Phil 930.36F	Eberhard, Wolfram. Beiträge zur Kosmologischen Spekulation der Chinesen der Han - Zert. Inaug. Diss. Berlin, 1933.
	Phil 930.36.5	Eberhard, Wolfram. Guilt and sin in traditional China. Berkeley, 1967.
	Phil 8584.9	Eberhardt, Paul. Von der Möglichkeit und der Notwendigkeit der reinen Religion. Gotha, 1916.
	Phil 630.64	Eberle, Rolf A. Nominalistic systems. Dordrecht, 1970.
	Phil 9575.7	Ebersberg, Luise. Der Mensch und das Geld. Wien, 1826.
	Phil 5214.4	Ebert, Manfred. Die Bedeutung der Philosophie für die Entwicklung der Psychologie zur Einzelwissenschaft. Inaug. Diss. München, 1966.
	Phil 6114.18	Ebertin, B. Gehirn und Seele. Aalen, 1961.
	Phil 3200.15	Eberz, Otfried. Sophia und Logos oder die Philosophie der Wiederherstellung. München, 1967.
	Phil 3004.8	Ebinghaus, J. Gesammelte Aufsätze, Verträge und Reden. Hildesheim, 1968.
	Phil 3200.16.30	Ebner, Felix. Moe obrashchenie. 2. izd. Moskva, 1903.
	Phil 3200.14.5	Ebner, Ferdinand. Gesammelte Werke. 2. Aufl. Wien, 1952.
	Phil 3200.14	Ebner, Ferdinand. Notizen, Tagebücher, Lebenserinnerungen. v.1-2,3. München, 1963. 2v.
	Phil 1504.19.4	Ebner, J. Die Erkenntnislehre Richards von St. Viktor. v.19, pt.4-6. Münster, 1917.
	Phil 7069.67.75	Ebon, Martin. Beyond space and time. N.Y., 1967.
	Phil 7069.70	Ebon, Martin. Test your E.S.P. N.Y., 1970.
	Phil 3415.103	Ebrard, A. Eduard von Hartmann's Philosophie des Unbewussten. Gütersloh, 1876.
	Phil 3808.147	Ebstein, W. Arthur Schopenhauer seine wirklichen und vermeintlichen Krankheiten. Stuttgart, 1907.
	Phil 8879.24	Eby, L.S. The quest for moral law. N.Y., 1944.
	Phil 3640.77.15	Ecce homo. (Nietzsche, Friedrich.) Leipzig, 1908.
	Phil 3640.77.15.5	Ecce homo. (Nietzsche, Friedrich.) Leipzig, 1931.
	Phil 2880.1.60	Ecce homo. (Saint-Martin, L.C.) Lyon, 1959.
	Phil 8885.2	Eccentricity. (Kendall, J.) London, 1859.
	Phil 6114.15.5	Eccles, J.C. Facing reality; philosophical adventures by a brain scientist. London, 1970.
	Phil 6114.15	Eccles, J.C. The neurophysiological basis of mind. Oxford, 1953.
	Phil 6114.15.3	Eccles, J.C. The neurophysiological basis of mind. Oxford, 1960.
	Phil 1750.166.285	Echandia, Dario. Humanismo y tecnica. Bogota, 1969.
	Phil 7054.182	Une échappée sur l'infini. (Grimard, Edouard.) Paris, 1899.
	Phil 4355.5	Echarri, Jaime. Philosophia entis sensibilis. Romae, 1959.
	Phil 3450.19.315	Echauri, Raúl. El ser en la filosofía de Heidegger. Rosario, 1964.
	Phil 585.380	Les échelles d'âge dans la philosophie. Thèse. (Philibert, Michel André Jean.) Paris, 1968.
	Phil 8612.38	Echeverria, José. Réflexions métaphysiques sur la mort et la problème du sujet. Paris, 1957.
	Phil 978.7.15	Echoes from the Orient. 3rd ed. (Judge, W.Z.) Point Loma, Calif., 1921.
	Phil 8602.38	Echoes of larger life. (Welby-Gregory, Victoria.) London, 1929.
	Phil 3486.16	Eck, Samuel. Aus den grossen Tagen der deutschen Philosophie. Tübingen, 1901.
	Phil 179.14F	Eck, Samuel. Gedanke und Persönlichkeit. Giessen, 1914.
	Phil 3805.102	Eck, Samuel. Über die Herkunft des Individualitäts - Gedankens bei Schleiermacher. Giessen, 1908.
	Phil 974.8	Eckartshausen et la théosophie chrétienne. Thèse. (Faivre, Antoine.) Paris, 1969.
	Phil 6360.8	Eckensberger, Diethind. Sozialisationsbedingungen der öffentlichen Erziehung. 1. Aufl. Frankfurt am Main, 1971.
	Phil 5270.28	Eckensberger, Lutz H. Methodenprobleme der kulturvergleichenden Psychologie. Saarbrücken, 1970.
	Phil 6114.2	Ecker, A. Cerebral convolutions of man. N.Y., 1873.
	Phil 3640.98.15	Eckertz, Erich. Nietzsche als Künstler. München, 1910.
	Phil 665.66	Eckhardt, K.E. Irdische Unsterblichkeit. Weimar, 1937.
	Phil 3120.10.81	Eckstein, Ernst. Der Begriff des Daseins bei Julius Bergmann. Inaug. Diss. Erlangen, 1902.
	Phil 1109.2	Eckstein, F. Abriss der griechischen Philosophie. Frankfurt, 1955.
	Phil 3475.2.90	Eckstein, W. Wilhelm Jerusalem; sein Leben und Werken. Wien, 1935.
	Phil 5761.1	Eclaircissemens...difficultez...liberté. (La Placette, J.) Amsterdam, 1709.
Htn	Phil 8894.8.6*	Eclaircissement sur les moeurs. (Toussaint, F.V.) Amsterdam, 1762.
	Phil 8876.26	Eclectic moral philosophy. (Boyd, J.R.) N.Y., 1846.
	Phil 4440.2	Eclécticos portugueses del siglo XVIII y algunas de sus. (Carmen Rovira, María del.) Mexico, 1958.
	Phil 4025.1	L'eclettisma francese e la cultura filosofica meridionale. 1. ed. (Zerella, F.) Roma, 1953.
	Phil 6956.12	The eclipse of a mind. (Graves, Alonzo.) N.Y., 1942.
	Phil 8597.11.4	The eclipse of faith. 8. ed. (Rogers, H.) Boston, 1863.
	Phil 3120.30.73	Eclipse of God. (Buber, Martin.) N.Y., 1957.
	Phil 3450.28	Eclipse of reason. (Horkheimer, Max.) N.Y., 1947.
	Phil 5325.27	L'éclosion des pensées. (Lévêque, R.) Paris, 1938.

Phil 5325.156   L'éclosion des pensées. Thèse. (Lévêque, R.) Strasbourg, 1938.
Phil 8405.12   Eco, Umberto. La definizione dell'arte. Milano, 1968.
Phil 5520.565   Eco, Umberto. La strutture assente. Milano, 1968.
Phil 2725.35.80   Ecole, Jean. La metaphysique de l'être dans la philosophie de Louis Lavelle. Louvain, 1957.
Phil 2477.6.125   École, Jean. La metaphysique de l'être dans la philosophie de Maurice Blondel. Louvains, 1959.
Phil 1210.2   L'école d'Athènes. (Riambourg, Jean B.C.) Paris, 1829.
Phil 3003.9   L'ecole de Marboug. (Dussort, H.) Paris, 1963.
Phil 1210.5   École de Mégare. (Henne, Désiré.) Paris, 1843.
Phil 8890.30   Ecole des Hautes Études Sociales. Morale religieuse et morale laïque. Paris, 1914.
Phil 5465.58   L'école des muses. (Gilson, E.) Paris, 1951.
Phil 9245.7   L'école du bonheur. (Sigaud de la Fond, J.R.) Paris, 1785.
Phil 6322.47   L'école freudienne devant la musique. (Michel, André.) Paris, 1965.
Phil 530.15.30   L'école mystique de Lyon, 1776-1847. (Buche, Joseph.) Paris, 1935.
Phil 9342.16   L'écolier chrétien. (Callet, P.) Lyon, 1776.
Phil 5440.34   Ecological psychology. (Barker, Roger Garlock.) Stanford, Calif., 1968.
Phil 8878.13.8   Economia della vita umana. (Dodsley, R.) N.Y., 1825.
Phil 4080.3.325   Economia ed etica nello svolgimento. (Bruno, Antonino.) Siracusa, 1958.
Phil 8620.15   The economic basis of the problem of evil. (Carver, T.N.) Cambridge, 1908.
Phil 8890.45   Economic causes of moral progress. (Patten, Simon N.) Philadelphia, 1892.
Phil 8960.9   The economic order and religion. (Knight, F.H.) N.Y., 1945.
Phil 8887.39   Economics as the basis of living ethics. (Murdoch, J.G.) Troy, 1913.
Phil 6955.20   Economics of mental illness. (Fein, Rashi.) N.Y., 1958.
Phil 5545.48   Economy and training of memory. (Watt, H.J.) N.Y., 1911.
Phil 8878.13.4   The economy of human life. (Dodsley, R.) Chicago, 1827.
Phil 8878.13.3.25   The economy of human life. (Dodsley, R.) Chisnick, 1825.
Htn   Phil 8878.58*   The economy of human life. (Dodsley, R.) Exeter, 1788.
Htn   Phil 8878.13.2*   The economy of human life. (Dodsley, R.) Leominster, Mass., 1797.
Phil 8878.13.9   The economy of human life. (Dodsley, R.) London, 1751.
Phil 8878.13.3.10   The economy of human life. (Dodsley, R.) London, 1806.
Htn   Phil 8878.13.9.5*   The economy of human life. (Dodsley, R.) n.p., 1769.
Htn   Phil 8878.13.12*   The economy of human life. (Dodsley, R.) N.Y., 1793.
Htn   Phil 8878.13.7*   The economy of human life. (Dodsley, R.) Norwich, 1795.
Phil 8878.13.4.15   The economy of human life. (Dodsley, R.) Philadelphia, 1845.
Htn   Phil 8878.13.15*   The economy of human life. (Dodsley, R.) Salem, 1795.
Phil 8878.13.10   The economy of human life. pt. 1-2. (Dodsley, R.) London, 1795.
Phil 8878.13.3   The economy of human life. v.1-2. (Dodsley, R.) Manchester, 1801.
Htn   Phil 8878.13*   The economy of human life. v.1-2. (Dodsley, R.) Philadelphia, 1786.
Phil 2825.35   Écrits...textes réunis par Jacques Debouzy. (Politzer, Georges.) Paris, 1969. 2v.
Phil 6321.51   Écrits. (Lacan, Jacques.) Paris, 1966.
Phil 2490.59   Écrits de jeunesse, 1816-1828. Suivis du Mémoire sur la cosmogonie de Laplace, 1835. (Comte, Auguste.) Paris, 1970.
Phil 2905.1.350   Écrits du temps de la guerre, 1916-1919. (Teilhard de Chardin, Pierre.) Paris, 1965.
Phil 2475.1.78   Écrits et paroles. (Bergson, Henri.) Paris, 1957. 3v.
Phil 5066.282   Écrits logiques. (Herbrand, Jacques.) Paris, 1968.
Htn   Phil 3800.33.2*   Écrits philosophiques. (Schelling, F.W.J. von.) Paris, 1847.
Phil 3800.33   Écrits philosophiques. (Schelling, F.W.J. von.) Paris, 1847.
Phil 2477.11.30   Écrits philosphiques. 1. éd. (Brunschvicg, Léon.) Paris, 1951- 3v.
Phil 3480.80.75   Ecrits politiques. (Kant, Immanuel.) Paris, 1917.
Phil 3450.19.490   Les écrits politiques de Heidegger. (Palmier, Jean Michel.) Paris, 1968.
Phil 2805.380   Écrits sur Pascal. Paris, 1959.
Phil 6060.56.5   L'écriture des adolescentes, étude psycho-pédagogique. (Dubouchet, Jeanne.) Paris, 1967.
Phil 6060.1.4   L'ecriture et le caractère. 6e ed. (Crepieux-Jamin, J.) Paris, 189-?
Phil 6060.28   L'écriture et le subsconsient. (Menard, Pierre.) Paris, 1931.
Phil 3808.75.5   Écrivains et style. (Schopenhauer, Arthur.) Paris, 1905.
Phil 525.264.1   Ecstasy; a study of some secular and religious experiences. (Laski, Marghanita.) N.Y., 1968.
Phil 5628.10.15   Ecstasy or religious trance. (Arbman, Ernst.) Stockholm, 1963-70. 3v.
Phil 7069.24.21   L'ectoplasmie et la clairvoyance. (Geley, Gustave.) Paris, 1924.
Phil 4351.1.25   Las edades del hombre. (Amoroso Lima, A.) Buenos Aires, 1943.
Phil 672.128   Eddington, A.S. Raum, Zeit und Schwere. Braunschweig, 1923.
Phil 8694.4A   Eddington, Arthur. Science and the unseen world. N.Y., 1929.
Phil 8694.4.5   Eddington, Arthur. Science and the unseen world. N.Y., 1930.
Phil 293.6   Die eddische Kosmogonie. (Meyer, E.H.) Freiburg, 1891.
Phil 9344.1   Eddy, A.D. Addresses on duties of youth. N.Y., 1836.
Phil 8405.6   Eddy, Arthur. Delight, the soul of art. Philadelphia, 1902.
Phil 8584.1   Eddy, J. Thoughts on religion and morality. Providence, R.I., 1891.
Phil 8954.3   Eddy, S. Maker of men. N.Y., 1941.
Phil 6945.6   Eddy, T. Hints for introducing an improved mode of treating the insane in the asylum. N.Y., 1815.
Phil 8879.26   Edel, A. Ethical judgement. Glencoe, 1955.
Phil 8879.34   Edel, A. Method in ethical theory. London, 1963.
Phil 165.165   Edel, Reiner F. Ein Weiser lebt upter uns. Marburg, 1958.
Phil 3200.17   Edelmann, Johann Christian. Sämtliche Schriften in Einzelausgaben. Stuttgart, 1970. 5v.
Phil 575.127   Der Edelmensch und seine Werte. 2e Aufl. (Verweyen, J.M.) München, 1922.
Phil 1109.5   Edelstein, Ludwig. The idea of progress in classical antiquity. Baltimore, 1967.
Phil 1200.62   Edelstein, Ludwig. The meaning of stoicism. Cambridge, 1966.
Phil 5590.444   Edelweiss, Malomar Lund. Personalisation. Wien, 1964.

Phil 8879.22   Edfeldt, H. Om begreppet sedlighet. Upsala, 1877.
Phil 8584.8   Edfeldt, Hans. Filosofisk religionslära. Uppsala, 1903.
Phil 4515.83.10   Edfeldt, Hans. Granskning af kandidaten Waldemar. Upsala, 1875.
Phil 179.23   Edfeldt, Hans. Hvilken verldsförklaring uppfyller fordringarna för möjlighrtin of menniskans praktiska lif? Uppsala, 1868.
Phil 3486.12   Edfeldt, Hans. Kants lära om det moraliskt onda. Upsala, 1878.
Phil 4515.83   Edfeldt, Hans. Om Boströms ideelära. Uppsala, 1884.
Phil 8879.19   Edfeldt, Hans. Om de etiska grundbegreppen. Upsala, 1894.
Phil 7159.152   Edgar Cayce, mystery man of miracles. (Millard, Joseph.) N.Y., 1956.
Phil 6112.40.5   Edgar Cayce, the sleeping prophet. (Stearn, Jess.) Garden City, 1967.
Phil 6112.40.10   Edgar Cayce on dreams. (Bro, Harmon Hartzell.) N.Y., 1968.
Phil 7069.69.10   Edgar Cayce on E.S.P. 1st ed. (Agee, Doris.) N.Y., 1969.
Phil 7072.15   Edgar Cayce on reincarnation. (Langley, Noel.) N.Y., 1968.
Phil 7069.69.25   The Edgar Cayce reader. (Cayce, Edgar.) N.Y., 1969.
Phil 8879.23   Edgell, B. Ethical problems. London, 1929.
Phil 5244.19   Edgell, B. Mental life. London, 1926.
Phil 5545.156   Edgell, Beatrice. Theories of memory. Oxford, 1924.
Phil 2490.54   Edger, Henry. The positivist calendar. Long Island, N.Y., 1856.
Phil 978.23.3   Edger, L. The elements of theosophy. London, 1907.
Phil 6674.7.15   Edgerley, W.J. Cultivation of personal magnetism. 11. ed. Meriden, Conn., 1923.
Phil 6674.7   Edgerley, W.J. Lessons in the mechanics of personal magnetism. Washington, D.C., 1888.
Phil 7069.07.35   Edgerly, Webster. Book of the Psychic Society. Washington, 1907.
Phil 6750.267   Edgerton, Robert B. The look of competence; stigma in the lives of the mentally retarded. Berkeley, 1967.
Phil 8663.3.87   Edgett, G.W. The mistakes of R.G. Ingersoll on nature and God. Boston, 1881.
Phil 8879.18   Edgeworth, F.Y. New and old methods of ethics. Oxford, 1877.
Phil 5620.35   Edgley, Roy. Reason in theory and practice. London, 1969.
Phil 1695.31   Edie, James M. An invitation to phenomenology. Chicago, 1965.
Phil 4710.144   Edie, James M. Russian philosophy. 1. ed. Chicago, 1965. 3v.
Phil 5520.462   Edinburgh. University. Faculty of Social Sciences. Research Board. Conference on Psycholinguistics, 1966. Psycholinguistics papers. Edinburgh, 1966.
Phil 194.21.2   The Edinburgh lectures on mental science. (Troward, Thomas.) N.Y., 1915.
Phil 194.21.3   The Edinburgh lectures on mental science. 3d. ed. (Troward, Thomas.) London, 1908.
Phil 14.19   The Edinburgh psychological review. Edinburgh.
Phil 5814.3   Edinger, Ludwig. Über Tierpsychologie. Leipzig, 1909.
Phil 310.552   Edinstvo dialektiki, logiki i teorii poznaniia. (Kedrov, B.M.) Moskva, 1963.
Phil 3808.85   Edita und Inedita Schopenhaueriana. (Grisebach, E.R.) Leipzig, 1888.
Phil 2520.192   Une édition nouvelle du discours de la méthode de Descartes. (Picard, Émile.) Paris, 1934.
Phil 5421.35.10   Edmaier, Alois. Horizonte der Hoffnung. Regensburg, 1968.
Phil 1740.18   Edmaier, Alois. Die Philosophie der Gegenwart. Aschaffenburg, 1970.
Phil 3425.205   Edman, Alfred. Hegels lära om konstformerna. Helsingfors, 1856.
Phil 1980.4.11   Edman, Irwin. Candle in the dark. N.Y., 1939.
Phil 179.24.5   Edman, Irwin. The contemporary and his soul. N.Y., 1931.
Phil 1980.4.7   Edman, Irwin. Four ways of philosophy. N.Y., 1937.
Phil 165.27   Edman, Irwin. Landmarks for beginners in philosophy. N.Y., 1948?
Phil 1980.4A   Edman, Irwin. Philosophers holiday. N.Y., 1938.
Phil 1980.4.15   Edman, Irwin. Philosopher's quest. N.Y., 1947.
Phil 179.24.2   Edman, Irwin. Richard Kane looks at life. Boston, 1926.
Phil 179.24   Edman, Irwin. Richard Kane looks at life. Boston, 1926.
Phil 1980.4.20A   Edman, Irwin. Under whatever sky. N.Y., 1951.
Phil 1980.4.25   Edman, Irwin. The uses of philosophy. N.Y., 1955.
Phil 2630.5.90   Edmond Goblot, 1858-1935. (Kergomard, Jean.) Paris, 1937.
Phil 7054.52   Edmonds, J.W. Spiritualism. N.Y., 1855. 2v.
Phil 7054.52.4   Edmonds, J.W. Spiritualism. 4th ed. N.Y., 1853.
Phil 3450.11.210   Edmund Husserl, 1859-1959. La Haye, 1959.
Phil 3450.11.125A   Edmund Husserl. 2d ed. (Osborn, A.) Cambridge, 1949.
Phil 3450.11.122   Edmund Husserl zum Gednachtnis. (Landgrabe, Ludwig.) Prag, 1938.
Phil 3450.11.250   Edmund Husserls ethische Untersuchungen. (Roth, Alois.) Den Haag, 1960.
Phil 3450.11.260   Edmund Husserls Lehre von den sekundären Qualitäten. (Witschel, Guenter.) Bonn, 1961.
Phil 3450.11.380   Edmund Husserl's phenomenological psychology. (Kockelmans, Joseph John.) Pittsburgh, 1967.
Phil 3450.11.101   Edmund Husserl's phenomenology. (Welch, E.P.) Los Angeles, 1939.
Phil 3450.11.290   Edmund Husserls System der phänomenologischen Psychologie. (Druce, H.) Berlin, 1963.
Phil 3450.11.320   Edmund Husserls Theorie. (Claesges, Ulrich.) Köln, 1962.
Phil 3450.11.322   Edmund Husserls Theorie der Raumkonstitution. (Claesges, Ulrich.) Den Haag, 1964.
Phil 3450.11.315   Edmund Husserl's theory of meaning. (Mohanty, J.N.) The Hague, 1964.
Phil 3486.3   Edmunds, J. Kant's ethics: the Clavis to an index. Louisville, n.d.
Phil 978.49.860   Edmunds, L.F. Rudolf Steiner education. London, 1962.
Phil 7069.66.35   Edmunds, Simeon. Spiritualism: a critical survey. London, 1966.
Phil 2725.30   Edouard LeRoy et son fauteuil. (Daniel-Rops, Henry.) Paris, 1956.
Phil 5545.27   Edridge-Green, F.W. Memory and its cultivation. N.Y., 1897.
Phil 6314.4   Edson, D.O. Getting what we want. N.Y., 1921.
Phil 9245.134   Eduaimonie en het wezen der ethiek. (Boelen, Bernard J.) Leuven, 1949.
Phil 3415.93   Eduard von Hartmann, von Otto Braun. (Braun, Otto.) Stuttgart, 1909.
Phil 3415.96   Eduard von Hartmann. (Heymons, C.) Berlin, 1882.
Phil 3415.90.5   Eduard von Hartmann. (Kappstein, Theodor.) Gotha, 1907.
Phil 3415.109   Eduard von Hartmann. (Schnehen, W. von.) Stuttgart, 1929.
Phil 3425.247.5   Eduard von Hartmanns Kritik der dialektischen Methode Hegels. (Purpus, Wilhelm.) Ansbach, 1911.
Phil 3415.110   Eduard von Hartmanns Metaphysik und Religionsphilosophie. (Huber, Max.) Winterthur, 1954.

Phil 3415.103   Eduard von Hartmann's Philosophie des Unbewussten. (Ebrard, A.) Gütersloh, 1876.

Phil 3415.89.2   Eduard von Hartmanns philosophische System. (Drews, A.) Heidelberg, 1906.

Phil 3415.89   Eduard von Hartmanns philosophisches System. (Drews, A.) Heidelberg, 1902.

Phil 3415.99   Eduard von Hartmanns Religionsphilosophie des Unbewuszten. (Steffes, J.P.) Mergentheim, 1921?

Phil 5238.3   Education and psychology. (Colorado. College. Publication.) Colorado Springs. 1,1919

Phil 5925.2   Education and self-improvement. (Fowler, O.S.) N.Y., 1843-45. 7 pam.

Phil 2150.16.40   Education and the good life. (Mayer, Frederick.) Washington, 1957.

Phil 178.12.16   Education and the philosophical ideal. (Dresser, H.W.) N.Y., 1900.

Phil 978.59.55   Education and the significance of life. (Krishnamurti, J.) N.Y., 1953.

Phil 9075.19   L'éducation de la conscience. (Gillet, Marie S.) Paris, 1913.

Phil 5765.2   L'éducation de la volonté. (Payot, Jules.) Paris, 1900.
Phil 5765.2.3   L'éducation de la volonté. (Payot, Jules.) Paris, 1912.
Phil 5765.2.4   L'éducation de la volonté. (Payot, Jules.) Paris, 1941.

Phil 5753.11   L'éducation de la volonté et des facultés logiques. (Duprat, G.L.) Paris, 1920.

Phil 5753.7.2   L'éducation de l'effort psychologie-physiologie. 2. éd. (Demeny, Georges.) Paris, 1916.

Phil 5409.8   L'éducation de l'espérance. (Union des Religieuses Enseignantes.) Paris, 1959?

Phil 8878.24.10   L'éducation de soi-même. (DuBois, P.) Paris, 1913.
Phil 5400.56   L'éducation des sentiments. (Thomas, Félix.) Paris, 1899.
Phil 6113.33   Education for positive mental health. (Davis, James Allen.) Chicago, 1965.

Phil 2055.12.30   Education for privacy. (Hoor, Marten ten.) n.p., 1960.
Phil 978.74.45   Education in the new age. 1st ed. (Bailey, A.A. (Mrs.).) N.Y., 1954.

Phil 8886.23.5   L'éducation morale rationnelle. (Leclère, A.) Paris, 1909.

Phil 1865.175   The education of Jeremy Bentham. (Everett, Charles W.) N.Y., 1931.

Phil 2750.11.61   The education of man. (Maritain, Jacques.) Garden City, 1962.

Phil 8878.24.7   The education of self. (DuBois, P.) N.Y., 1911.
Phil 5400.96   The education of the emotions. (Phillips, M.) London, 1937.

Phil 5765.2.9   The education of the will. (Payot, Jules.) N.Y., 1909.
Phil 5765.2.9.5   The education of the will. (Payot, Jules.) N.Y., 1910.
Phil 5760.7   Education of the will in the light of modern research. Diss. (Kuntz, Leo F.) Washington, D.C., 1927.

Phil 5242.27   L'éducation psychologique à propos de la grande guerre. (Choisnard, P.) Paris, 1920.

Phil 5761.9   L'éducation rationelle de la volonté. 10e éd. (Lévy, Paul Emile.) Paris, 1917.

Phil 1750.160   The educational principles of American humanism. Diss. (Fondy, John T.) Washington, D.C., 1945.

Phil 2020.82   Educational theory...T.H. Green. (Leland, A.P.) N.Y., 1911.

Phil 370.2   Educazione ed esistenza. (Musu, Aldo M.) Padova, 1967.
Phil 4210.200   L'educazione religiosa nella pedagogia di A. Rosmini. (Colonna, Salvatore.) Lecce, 1963.

Phil 5627.93   Edward, Kenneth. Religious experience; its nature and truth. Edinburgh, 1926.

Phil 3415.81   Edward von Hartmann's Religion der Zukunft. (Hernan, C.F.) Leipzig, 1875.

Phil 5592.70   Edwards, A.L. The social desirability variable in personality assessment and research. N.Y., 1957.

Phil 8405.10   Edwards, A.T. The things which are seen. London, 1947.
Phil 5244.25.2   Edwards, Allen L. Statistical analysis. N.Y., 1958.
Phil 5244.25   Edwards, Allen L. Statistical analysis for students in psychology and education. N.Y., 1946.

Phil 5244.25.5   Edwards, Allen L. Statistical methods for the behavioral sciences. N.Y., 1964.

Phil 5272.20   Edwards, Allen Louis. Experimental design in psychological research. N.Y., 1951.

Phil 5272.20.3   Edwards, Allen Louis. Experimental design in psychological research. 3d ed. N.Y., 1968.

Phil 8584.10   Edwards, D.M. The philosophy of religion. N.Y., 1924.
Phil 8725.10   Edwards, David Lawrence. Religion and change. London, 1969.

Phil 7069.45.20   Edwards, H.J. The science of spirit healing. London, 1945.

Phil 7069.41.4   Edwards, Harry. The mediumship of Jack Webber. N.Y., 1941.

Phil 6114.23   Edwards, Henry James. The evidence for spirit healing. London, 1953.

Phil 8659.2   Edwards, John. A demonstration of the existence and providence of God. London, 1696.

Htn   Phil 1980.1.30*   Edwards, Jonathan. A careful...enquiry. Boston, 1754.
Htn   Phil 5754.1.6*   Edwards, Jonathan. A careful and strict enquiry...freedom of will. Albany, 1804.

Phil 5754.1.4   Edwards, Jonathan. A careful and strict enquiry...freedom of will. Glasgow, 1790.

Phil 5754.1.12   Edwards, Jonathan. Careful and strict enquiry into the modern...freedom. N.Y., 1828.

Htn   Phil 5754.1.10*   Edwards, Jonathan. Careful and strict enquiry into the modern...freedom of will. Boston, 1754.

Phil 5754.1.8   Edwards, Jonathan. Careful and strict enquiry into the modern...freedom of will. Boston, 1762.

Phil 5754.1.2   Edwards, Jonathan. A carefull and strict enquiry...freedom of will. 3. ed. London, 1768.

Htn   Phil 5754.1.101*   Edwards, Jonathan. A dissertation concerning liberty and necessity. Worcester, 1797.

Phil 5754.1.18   Pamphlet box. Edwards, Jonathan. Freedom of the will.
Phil 3120.30.210   Edwards, Paul. Buber and Buberism. Lawrence, 1971.
Phil 8879.28   Edwards, Paul. The logic of moral discourse. Glencoe, Ill., 1955.

Phil 165.105   Edwards, Paul. A modern introduction to philosophy. Glencoe, Illinois, 1957.

Phil 165.105.2   Edwards, Paul. A modern introduction to philosophy. N.Y., 1965.

Phil 440.8   Edwards, Rem Blanchard. Freedom, responsibiblity and obligation. The Hague, 1969.

Phil 5722.32.10   The EEG. (Simon, C.W.) Santa Monica, 1955.
Phil 972.17   Eek, Sven. Damodar and the pioneers of the theosophical movement. Adyar, 1965.

Phil 182.13.5   Eenige gedagten. (Helmont, F.M. van.) Amsterdam, 1690.

Phil 1145.53   Eernstman, J.P.A. Oikeios, etairos, epitedeios, filos; bejdtrage tot de kennis van de terminologie. Groningen, 1932.

Phil 5627.134.85A   Eester, Allen W. Drawing-room conversion; Oxford Group movement. Durham, 1950.

Phil 5647.5   The effect of adaptation on the temperature difference linien. Thesis. (Cowan, Edwina Abbott.) Princeton, N.J. 1914.

Phil 5817.10   Effect of age on habit formation in the albino rat. (Hubbert, Helen B.) Baltimore, 1915.

Phil 5244.21   The effect of distraction on reaction time. (Evans, John E.) N.Y., 1916.

Phil 5810.8   The effect of habit interference upon performance in maze learning. (Alm, O.W.) Worcester, 1931.

Phil 5247.46   The effect of incentives on accuracy of discrimination measured on the Galton bar. Thesis. (Hamilton, Hughbert C.) N.Y., 1929.

Phil 5645.30   The effect of intensity of light...eye and size...on the visibility curve. Diss. (Sloan, Louise L.) n.p., 1926?

Phil 5825.4   The effect of length of blind alleys on maze learning. (Peterson, Joseph.) N.Y., 1917.

Phil 5585.57   The effect of practice on the visual perception of form. (Seward, John P.) N.Y., 1931.

Phil 5819.4   The effect of segregation on the sex behavior of the white rat as measured by the abstraction method. (Jenkins, Marion.) Worcester, Mass., 1928.

Phil 5585.37   The effect of varied instructions on the perception of distance in terms of arm-movement. (Garrison, W.A.) Ithaca, 1924.

Phil 5249.6.15   Effective thinking. (Jastrow, J.) N.Y., 1931.
Phil 5400.72   The effects of emotional stimuli on the gastro-intestinal tone. (Brunswick, D.) Baltimore, 1924.

Phil 6120.23   Effects of induced stress on learning and performance. (Klier, Sol.) n.p., 1962.

Phil 5247.50   The effects of noise upon certain psychological and physical processes. Thesis. (Harmon, F.L.) N.Y., 1933.

Phil 5545.179   The effects of practice on memory performance. Thesis. (Drees, V.J.) Washington, 1941.

Phil 5548.107   Effects of praise and blame. (Johannesson, Ingvar.) Stockholm, 1967.

Phil 5535.60   The effects of structural relations on transfer. (Dienes, Zoltan Paul.) London, 1970.

Phil 5440.19   Effets nocifs du croisement des races sur la formation du caractère. Thèse. (Sériot, Pauline.) Paris, 1918.

Phil 3640.235.10   L'effondrement de Nietzsche. 4e éd. Photoreproduction. (Podach, Erich F.) Paris, 1931.

Phil 2730.102   L'effort chez Maine de Biran et Bergson. Thèse. (Thibaud, Marguerite.) Grenoble, 1939.

Phil 5649.23   Effort volontaire et chronaxie. Thèse. (Covaciu-Ulmeanu.) Paris, 1936.

Phil 5044.10   Efiroso, S.A. Ot Gegelia k Dzhennago. Moskva, 1960.
Phil 4004.2   Efirov, Svetozar A. Ital'ianskaia burzhuaznaia filosofiia XX veka. Moskva, 1968.

Phil 1050.20   Efros, Israel I. The problem of space in Jewish mediaeval philosophy. N.Y., 1917.

Phil 179.31   Egaña, Juan. Tractatus de re logica. Santiago, 1827.
Phil 1133.55   Egeiskaia predfilosofiia. (Chanyshev, Arsenii N.) Moskva, 1970.

Phil 8879.36   Egemen, Bedi Ziya. Terkiye ilminin problemlen. Ankara, 1965.

Phil 5465.171   Egen, Horst. Kinderzeichnungen und Umwelt. Bonn, 1967.
Phil 575.276   Egenskab og faellesskab. (Maal006, Erik.) København, 1969.

Phil 1540.45   Egentin, Richard. Gottesfreundschaft. Augsburg, 1928.
Phil 8050.50   Egger, Alais. Vorschule der Asthetik. Wien, 1872.
Phil 5643.9   Egger, V. L'oeil et l'oreille. Paris, 1886.
Phil 5520.1   Egger, V. La parole intérieure. Paris, 1881.
Phil 3925.16.305   Egidi, Rosaria. Studi di logica e filosofia della scienza. Roma, 1971.

Phil 5244.36   Egidius, Henry. Förstå människor. Lund, 1971.
Phil 9220.9   Eglinger, Ruth. Der Begriff der Freundschaft in der Philosophie. Inaug. Diss. Basel, 1916.

Phil 1730.8   L'église et les philosophes au dix-huitième siècle. (Lanfrey, Pierre.) Paris, 1855.

Phil 1730.8.3   L'église et les philosophes au dix-huitième siècle. (Lanfrey, Pierre.) Paris, 1879.

Phil 6998.2   Ego, hunger, and aggression; the beginning of Gestalt therapy. (Perls, Frederick S.) N.Y., 1969.

Phil 6334.10A   Ego and instinct; the psychoanalytic view of human nature. (Yankelovich, Daniel.) N.Y., 1970.

Phil 6321.58   The ego and its defenses. (Laughlin, Henry Prather.) N.Y., 1970.

Phil 193.64   The ego and its place in the world. (Shaw, C.G.) N.Y., 1913.

Phil 6980.210   Ego and milieu. (Cumming, John.) N.Y., 1962.
Phil 183.1   The ego and physical force. (Isbyam, I.C.) London, 1925.
Phil 6315.2.37.3   The ego and the id. (Freud, Sigmund.) London, 1950.
Phil 6315.2.37.4   The ego and the id. (Freud, Sigmund.) London, 1957.
Phil 6315.2.37.1   The ego and the id. (Freud, Sigmund.) N.Y., 1961.
Phil 6315.2.37.6   The ego and the id. (Freud, Sigmund.) N.Y., 1962.
Phil 6315.17.12   The ego and the mechanisms of defence. (Freud, Anna.) London, 1954.

Phil 6315.17.10   The ego and the mechanisms of defence. (Freud, Anna.) N.Y., 1950.

Phil 5258.136.5A   The ego and the self. (Symonds, P.M.) N.Y., 1951.
Phil 183.1.5   The ego and the spiritual truth. (Isbyam, I.C.) London, 1926.

Phil 5590.440   Ego in evolution. (Menaker, Esther.) N.Y., 1965.
Phil 6315.18.10   Ego psychology and the psychoses. (Federn, Paul.) N.Y., 1955.

Phil 7082.12   Ego synthesis in dreams. (Jones, Richard Matthew.) Cambridge, 1962.

Phil 8602.20   Egoism. (Wallis, Louis.) Chicago, 1905.
Phil 8875.18   Egoismo y altruismo. (Antieh, José.) Barcelona, 1906.
Phil 8878.18.7   Der Egoismus. (Dix, A.) Leipzig, 1899.
Phil 8885.24   Egoismus und Altruismus als Grundlage des Sittlichen. (Kutna, G.) Berlin, 1903.

Phil 8890.63   Egoizm. (Petrov, Erik F.) Moskva, 1969.
Phil 8645.75   Egorov, A.G. O reaktsionnoi sushchnosti. Moskva, 1961.
Phil 3018.7.7   Egotism in German philosophy. (Santayana, G.) N.Y., 1940.
Phil 3018.7A   Egotism in German philosophy. Photoreproduction. (Santayana, G.) London, 1916?

Phil 6314.5   Egyedi, H. Die Irrtümer der Psychoanalyse. Wien, 1933.
Phil 850.13   L'Égypte et les présocratiques. (Faure, J.A.) Paris, 1923.

Phil 8633.1.14   The Egyptian conception of immortality. (Reisner, George A.) Boston, 1912.

Phil 6113.9 — Egyptian elements in the legend of the body and soul. (Dudley, L.) Baltimore, 1911.

Phil 703.3 — Ehbinghaus, Julius. Traditionsfeindschaft und Traditionsgebundenheit. Frankfurt, 1969.

Phil 1750.115.185 — Ebel, Gerhard. Untersuchungen zu einer realistischen Grundlegung der phänomenologischen Wesensschau. München, 1965.

Phil 9495.164.5 — Ehemoral und Jansenismus. (Klomps, H.) Köln, 1964.

Phil 3585.10.97 — Ehlen, Nikolaus. Die ErkenntnisDer Aussenwelt nach Theodor Lipps. Inaug. Diss. Münster, 1914.

Phil 310.270 — Ehlen, Peter. Der Acheismus im dialektischen Materialismus. München, 1961.

Phil 2404.3 — Ehrard, J. L'idée de nature en France. Paris, 1963. 2v.

Phil 335.4 — Ehrat, P. Die Bedeutung der Logik. Zittau, 1896.

Phil 9560.60 — Ehre, Prestige, Gewissen. (Korff, Wilhelm.) Köln, 1966.

Phil 9344.8 — Ehrenberg, F. Der Charakter und die Bestimmung des Mannes. Leipzig, 1808.

Phil 8879.14 — Ehrenberg, F. Reden uber wichtige Gegenstande. Leipzig, 1804.

Phil 2805.288 — Ehrenberg, H. In der Schule Pascals. Heidelberg, 1954.

Phil 3004.4 — Ehrenberg, Hans. Disputation: drei Bücher vom Deutschen. München, 1923-25. 3v.

Phil 5244.13 — Ehrenberg, Hans. Kritik der Psychologie als Wissenschaft. Tübingen, 1910.

Phil 3004.3 — Ehrenberg, Hans. Die Parteiung der Philosophie. Leipzig, 1911.

Phil 8879.12 — Ehrenfels, C. System der Werttheorie. Leipzig, 1897.

Phil 285.5 — Ehrenfels, C.F. Cosmogony. N.Y., 1948.

Phil 285.1 — Ehrenfils, C. Kosmogonie. Jena, 1916.

Phil 3890.2.80 — Ehrenfried Walther von Tschirnhaus. (Verweyen, J.) Bonn, 1905.

Phil 5244.24 — Ehrenstein, Walter. Einführung in die Ganzheitspsychologie. Leipzig, 1934.

Phil 5244.24.5 — Ehrenstein, Walter. Probleme des höheren Seelenlebens. München, 1965.

Phil 6980.254 — Ehrenwald, Jan. From medicine man to Freud. N.Y., 1956.

Phil 7069.55.15 — Ehrenwald, Jan. New dimensions of deep analysis. N.Y., 1955.

Phil 7069.47.20 — Ehrenwald, Jan. Telepathy and medical psychology. London, 1947.

Phil 5465.168 — Ehrenzweig, Anton. The hidden order of art; a study in the psychology of artistic imagination. Berkeley, 1967.

Phil 5585.130 — Ehrenzweig, Anton. The psycho-analysis of artistic vision and hearing. London, 1953.

Phil 5585.130.2 — Ehrenzweig, Anton. The psycho-analysis of artistic vision and hearing. 2d ed. N.Y., 1965.

Phil 3850.27.60 — Ehrfurcht vor dens Leben. Bern, 1954?

Phil 285.8 — Ehrhardt, Arnold. The begining. N.Y., 1968.

Phil 5238.150 — Ehrhardt, H. Psychiatrie und Gesellschaft. Bern, 1958.

Phil 804.10 — Ehrhardt, Walter E. Philosophiegeschichte und geschichtlicher Septizismus. Bern, 1967.

Phil 1050.26 — Ehrich, J. Das Problem der Theodizes in der jüdischen Religionsphilosophie des Mittelalters. Inaug. Diss. Breslau, 1913.

Phil 1828.12 — Ehrle, Franz. Gesammelte Aufsätze zur englischen Scholastik. Roma, 1970.

Phil 5520.610 — Ehrlich, Stéphane. Les mécanismes du comportement verbal. Paris, 1968.

Phil 3486.10.5 — Ehrlich, W. Der Freiheitsbegriff bei Kant und Schopenhauer. Berlin, 1920.

Phil 5044.7 — Ehrlich, W. Intentionalität und Sinn. Halle, 1934.

Phil 3486.10 — Ehrlich, W. Kant und Husserl. Halle, 1923.

Phil 3200.8.5 — Ehrlich, W. Kulturgeschichtliche Autobiographie. Tübingen, 1961.

Phil 3200.8 — Ehrlich, W. Metaphysik. Tübingen, 1955.

Phil 3200.8.15 — Ehrlich, W. Metaphysik im erkenntniskritischen Grundriss. Halle, 1924.

Phil 3200.8.20 — Ehrlich, W. Ontologie des Bewusstseins. Zürich, 1940.

Phil 3200.8.10 — Ehrlich, W. System der Philosophie. Bad Ragaz, 1966.

Phil 8405.2.5 — Ehrlich, Walter. Asthetik. Chur, 1947.

Phil 8405.2 — Ehrlich, Walter. Aphorismen zur Philosophie der Kunst. Tübingen, 1962.

Phil 8879.30 — Ehrlich, Walter. Ethik. Tübingen, 1956.

Phil 735.210 — Ehrlich, Walter. Hauptprobleme der Wertphilosophie. Tübingen, 1959.

Phil 804.15 — Ehrlich, Walter. Philosophie der Geschichte der Philosophie. Bad Ragaz, 1965.

Phil 585.30 — Ehrlich, Walter. Philosophische Anthropologie. Tübingen, 1957.

Phil 575.76 — Ehrlich, Walter. Stufen der Personalität. Halle, 1930.

Phil 335.3 — Ehrlich, Walter. Das unpersonale Erlebnis. Halle, 1927.

Phil 335.3.10 — Ehrlich, Walter. Das Verstehen. Zürich, 1939.

Phil 5421.20.105 — Eibl-Eibesfeld, Irenäus. Liebe und Hass. München, 1970.

Phil 179.5 — Eichbaum-Lange, W. Was heisst Philosophie? Leipzig, 1902.

Phil 5244.11 — Eichberg, T. Psychologische Probleme. Stuttgart, 1907.

Phil 8879.38 — Eichhorn, Wolfgang. Wie ist Ethik als Wissenschaft möglich? Berlin, 1965.

Phil 3808.146 — Eichler, Oskar. Die Wurzeln des Frauenhasses bei Arthur Schopenhauer. Bonn, 1926.

Phil 5814.6 — Eichler, Walter. Über die Erregbarkeitsmessung. Inaug. Diss. München, 1929.

Phil 5545.73 — Eichthal, Eugène d'. Du rôle de la mémoire dans nos conceptions. Paris, 1920.

Phil 3450.29.90 — Eid, Volker. Die Kunst in christlicher Daseinsverantwortung nach Theodor Haecker. Thesis. Würzburg, 1968.

Phil 9390.12 — Eid und Frieden. (Bauernfeind, O.) Stuttgart, 1956.

Phil 6314.9 — Eidelberg, L. Take off your mask. N.Y., 1948.

Phil 5465.27.4 — Eidetic imagery and typological methods of investigation. (Jaensch, Erich.) London, 1930.

Phil 5465.27.2 — Die Eidetik und typologische Forschungsmethode in ihrer Bedeutung für die Jugendpsychologie. 2e Aufl. (Jaensch, Erich.) Leipzig, 1927.

Phil 14.17 — Eidos. Cordoba. 1,1969+

Phil 3791.31 — Eiehl, Alois. Über wissenschaftliche und nichtwissenschaftliche Philosophie. Freiburg, 1883.

Phil 8820.5 — Eifler, Günter. Ritterliches Tugendsystem. Darmstadt, 1970.

Phil 510.20.5 — Die Eigenart der Natur und der Eigensinn des Monismus. (Volkmann, Paul.) Leipzig, 1910.

Phil 5244.9.15 — Die Eigenart des Geistigen. (Erismann, T.) Leipzig, n.d.

Phil 8881.52 — Eigene Betrachtungen über die allgemeinsten Grundsätze der Sittenlehre. (Garve, Christian.) Bresslau, 1798.

Phil 3910.76 — Eigene Lebensbeschreibung. (Wolff, Christian von.) Leipzig, 1841.

Phil 396.12.2 — Das Eigene und das Fremde. Neue Beiträge zum sozialist. Humanismus. 2. Aufl. (Kurella, Alfred.) Berlin, 1970.

Phil 5627.102.5 — Der eigene und der fremde Gott; zur Psychoanalyse der religiösen Entwicklung. (Reik, Theodor.) Leipzig, 1923.

Phil 9120.160 — Eigengesetz oder Pflichtgebot? (Hofmann, Paul.) Berlin, 1920.

Phil 3425.70.50 — Eigenhändige Raudhemerkungen zu seiner Rechtsphilosophie. (Hegel, Georg Wilhelm Friedrich.) Leipzig, 1930.

Phil 5240.21 — Die Eigenkraft der Materie. (Adumkiewicz, A.) Wien, 1906.

Phil 53.3F — Eight annual meeting (typed announcements). (National Committee for Mental Hygiene.) n.p., 1916.

Phil 4010.2 — Eight philosophers of the Italian Renaissance. (Kristeller, P.O.) Stanford, 1964.

Phil 5627.134.40 — The eight points of the Oxford Group. (Benson, C.I.) Melbourne, 1936.

Phil 5017.6.5 — Eighteenth-century British logic and rhetoric. (Howell, W.S.) Princeton, 1971.

Phil 2421.10 — Eighteenth-century optimism. (Vereker, Charles.) Liverpool, 1967.

Phil 3246.32.5 — Eimige Vorlesungen über die Bestimmung des Gelehrten. (Fichte, Johann Gottlieb.) Jena, 1954.

Phil 665.27 — Ein neuer Weg zur Erforschung der Seele. (Hirt, Walter.) München, 1917.

Phil 7069.24.10 — Einar Níelsen, mídíll. Reykjavik, 1924.

Phil 7082.54 — Einarsson, Guðhundur. Draumvitran Guðhundar Einarssonar. n.p., 1913?

Phil 3494.70.2 — Die Einbildungskraft bei Kant. 2. Aufl. (Mörchen, Hermann.) Tübingen, 1970.

Phil 3549.10.80 — Die Einbildungskraft bei Rudolf Kassner. (Wieser, T.) Zürich, 1949.

Phil 3805.265 — Die eine Kirche und das zweifache Recht. Thesis. (Daur, Martin.) München, 1970.

Phil 8876.118.2 — Einfache Sittlichkeit. 2. Aufl. (Bollnow, Otto Friedrich.) Göttingen, 1957.

Phil 175.24 — Einfälle und Betrachtungen. (Auerbach, Mathias.) Dresden, 1904.

Phil 504.4 — Einflüsse der Naturwissenschaften auf unser Weltbild. (Sansgruber, Kurt.) Brigenz, 1962.

Phil 3025.1 — Einfluss der englischen Philosophen...deutschen Philosophen. (Zart, G.) Berlin, 1881.

Phil 3491.7 — Der Einfluss der Kantischen Psychologie auf die Pädagogik als Wissenschaft. (Jahn, Max.) Leipzig, 1885.

Phil 200.4 — Einfluss der Philosophie auf das Leben. (Zenetti, Jacob.) München, 1829.

Phil 1527.5 — Der Einfluss der protestantischen Schulphilosophie auf die orthodox-lutherische Dogmatik. (Weber, Hans Emil.) Darmstadt, 1969.

Phil 2885.86 — Der Einfluss Hegels auf die Bildung der Gedankenwelt Hippolyte Taines. (Engel, Otto.) Stuttgart, 1920.

Phil 2725.35.95 — Der Einfluss Kants auf die Erkenntnismetaphysik. (Rothkopf, Wolfgang.) München, 1960.

Phil 4065.160 — Der Einfluss Plotins auf Giordano Brunos Degli eroici furori. (Saraw, Julie.) Borna-Leipzig, 1916.

Phil 3805.184 — Der Einfluss Schellings auf die Entwicklung von Schleiermachers System. (Süskind, H.) Tübingen, 1909.

Phil 2262.87 — Der Einfluss Shaftesburys auf Herder. Diss. (Hatch, Irvin C.) Berlin? 1901?

Phil 5548.135 — Der Einfluss von Erfolgs- und Misserfolgsmotivierung auf das Behalten eigener Leistungen. Inaug. Diss. (Reiss, Gretel.) Münster? 1968?

Phil 5415.9 — Die Einfühlung. (Prandtl, A.) Leipzig, 1910.

Phil 8879.13 — Einführung...Philosophie des Geisteslebens. (Eucken, R.C.) Leipzig, 1908.

Phil 197.48 — Einführung in das moderne philosophische Denken. (Weinhandl, F.) Gotha-Stuttgart, 1924.

Phil 181.89 — Einführung in das Philosophieren. (Glockner, Hermann.) Berlin, 1944.

Phil 176.117 — Einführung in das philosophische Denken für Anfanger und Alleinlernende. (Bruhn, Wilhelm.) Leipzig, 1923.

Phil 5520.90 — Einführung in dei Sprachpsychologie. (Kainz, Friedrich.) Wien, 1946.

Phil 4825.1 — Einführung in den Jugoslawischen Marxismus-Leninismus; Organisation und Bibliographie. (Vrtăcĭã, Ludvík.) Dordrecht, 1963.

Phil 583.2 — Einführung in der Phänomenologie. (Reyer, Wilhelm.) Leipzig, 1926.

Phil 8080.3 — Einführung in die Ästhetik der Gegenwart. (Meumann, Ernst.) Leipzig, 1908.

Phil 5520.730 — Einführung in die allgemeine Semantik. (Stichl, Ulrich.) Bern, 1970.

Phil 5262.32 — Einführung in die Entwicklungspsychologie. (Werner, Heinz.) Leipzig, 1926.

Phil 5262.32.5 — Einführung in die Entwicklungspsychologie. 3. Aufl. (Werner, Heinz.) München, 1953.

Phil 5262.32.6 — Einführung in die Entwicklungspsychologie. 4. Aufl. (Werner, Heinz.) München, 1953.

Phil 335.1.2A — Einführung in die Erkenntnis-Theorie. 2. Aufl. (Eisler, Rudolf.) Leipzig, 1925.

Phil 352.9 — Einführung in die Erkenntnislehre. (Varga, A. von.) München, 1953.

Phil 337.7 — Einführung in die Erkenntnistheorie. (Glondys, Viktor.) Wien, 1923.

Phil 343.7 — Einführung in die Erkenntnistheorie. (Messer, August.) Leipzig, 1912.

Phil 349.7 — Einführung in die Erkenntnistheorie. (Störring, G.) Leipzig, 1909.

Phil 8885.41 — Einführung in die Ethik. 2. Aufl. (Kaelin, Bernard.) Sarnen, 1954.

Phil 8882.34 — Einführung in die Ethik auf Grundlage der Erfahrung. (Heymans, Gerardus.) Leipzig, 1922.

Phil 5241.31 — Einführung in die experimentelle Psychologie. (Bramshausen, N.) Leipzig, 1915.

Phil 5244.24 — Einführung in die Ganzheitspsychologie. (Ehrenstein, Walter.) Leipzig, 1934.

Phil 1706.5 — Einführung in die Geschichte der neueren Philosophie des Auslandes. (Guttler, C.) München, 1922.

Phil 1706.5.10 — Einführung in die Geschichte der Philosophie seit Hegel. (Güttler, C.) München, 1921.

Phil 6967.16 — Einführung in die Grundprobleme der Neurose. (Ringel, Erwin.) Wien, 1959.

Phil 185.75 — Einführung in die Logik, Ontologie, Kosmologie, Psychologie. 5. Aufl. (Kaelin, Bernard.) Sarnen, 1957.

Phil 5052.45 — Einführung in die Logik. (Menne, Albert.) Bern, 1966.

Phil 5041.61 — Einführung in die Logistik. (Becker, O.) Meisenheim, 1951.

Phil 5066.247 — Einführung in die Mathematische Logik: klassische Prädikatenlogik. (Hermes, Hans.) Stuttgart, 1963.

Phil 2475.1.57 — Einführung in die Metaphysik. (Bergson, Henri.) Jena, 1909.

Phil 182.93.10   Einführung in die Metaphysik. (Heidegger, M.) Tübingen, 1953.

Phil 182.93.10.2   Einführung in die Metaphysik. (Heidegger, M.) Tübingen, 1958.

Phil 182.37   Einführung in die Metaphysik. (Heymans, G.) Leipzig, 1905.

Phil 182.37.2   Einführung in die Metaphysik. 2. Aufl. (Heymans, G.) Leipzig, 1911.

Phil 5627.66   Einführung in die moderne Religionspsychologie. (Wunderle, G.) Kempten, 1923.

Phil 8897.47.5   Einführung in die Moral- und Rechtsphilosophie. (Weigelin, Ernst.) Leipzig, 1827.

Phil 3489.23   Einführung in die neukantische Philosophie. (Herrmann, Karl.) Halle, 1927.

Phil 3450.11.220   Einführung in die Phänomenologie Edmund Husserls. (Szilasi, Wilhelm.) Tübingen, 1959.

Phil 176.107   Einführung in die Philosophie. (Becher, Erich.) München, 1926.

Phil 178.70   Einführung in die Philosophie. (Drews, A.) Berlin, 1921.

Phil 3475.3.52   Einführung in die Philosophie. (Jaspers, Karl.) Zürich, 1958.

Phil 185.65   Einführung in die Philosophie. (Kraft, Viktor.) Wien, 1950.

Phil 186.67.5   Einführung in die Philosophie. (Leisegang, H.) Berlin, 1951.

Phil 188.18   Einführung in die Philosophie. (Nohl, H.) Frankfurt, 1935.

Phil 190.38   Einführung in die Philosophie. (Prandtl, Antonin.) Leipzig, 1922.

Phil 192.43   Einführung in die Philosophie. (Ruge, Arnold.) Leipzig, 1914.

Phil 193.119   Einführung in die Philosophie. (Schnass, F.) Osterwieck, 1928.

Phil 179.40   Einführung in die Philosophie. Greifswald, 1964. 2v.

Phil 176.107.5   Einführung in die Philosophie. 2. Aufl. (Becher, Erich.) Berlin, 1949.

Phil 182.94.20   Einführung in die Philosophie. 3. Aufl. (Hartmann, N.) Osnabrück, 1954.

Phil 186.67.8   Einführung in die Philosophie. 3. Aufl. (Leisegang, H.) Berlin, 1956.

Phil 192.37.3   Einführung in die Philosophie. 3e Aufl. (Richter, Raoul.) Leipzig, 1913.

Phil 192.37   Einführung in die Philosophie. 4e Aufl. (Richter, Raoul.) Leipzig, 1919.

Phil 188.18.5   Einführung in die Philosophie. 5. Aufl. (Nohl, H.) Frankfurt, 1953.

Phil 346.2   Einführung in die Philosophie der reinen Erfahrung. v.1-2. (Petzoldt, J.) Leipzig, 1900.

Phil 3903.3.95   Einführung in die Philosophie des Als Ob. (Fliess, B.) Bielefeld, 1922.

Phil 2520.160   Einführung in die Philosophie Descartes. (Aster, E. von.) München, 1921.

Phil 193.78   Einführung in die Philosophie vom Stand...Kritizismus. (Sternberg, Kurt.) Leipzig, 1919.

Phil 5241.64   Einführung in die Probleme der allgemeinen Psychologie. (Binswanger, L.) Berlin, 1922.

Phil 6315.2.270   Einführung in die Psychanalyse Sigmund Freuds. (Bally, Gustav.) Hamburg, 1961.

Phil 5241.53   Einführung in die Psychologie. (Brunswig, A.) München, 1921.

Phil 5255.8   Einführung in die Psychologie. (Pfänder, A.) Leipzig, 1904.

Phil 5260.6   Einführung in die Psychologie. (Ude, Johnson.) Graz, 1916.

Phil 3915.48   Einführung in die Psychologie. (Wundt, Wilhelm.) Leipzig, 1911.

Phil 165.448   Einführung in die Psychologie. Frankfurt, 1969.

Phil 5240.17.2   Einführung in die Psychologie. 2. Aufl. (Aster, Ernst von.) Leipzig, 1919.

Phil 5252.36.2   Einführung in die Psychologie. 2. Aufl. (Meerkatz.) Halle, 1919.

Phil 5255.8.2   Einführung in die Psychologie. 2. Aufl. (Pfänder, A.) Leipzig, 1920.

Phil 5257.58.5   Einführung in die Psychologie. 2. Aufl. (Rohracher, Hubert.) Wien, 1947.

Phil 5243.18.4   Einführung in die Psychologie. 4e Aufl. (Dyroff, Adolf.) Leipzig, 1919.

Phil 5257.58.6   Einführung in die Psychologie. 6. Aufl. (Rohracher, Hubert.) Wien, 1958.

Phil 6060.12.16   Einführung in die Psychologie der Handschrift. 2. Aufl. (Klages, Ludwig.) Heidelberg, 1928.

Phil 5252.120   Einführung in die Psychologie und die psychologischen Richtungen der Gegenwart. 2. Aufl. (Messer, August.) Leipzig, 1931.

Phil 8595.20   Einführung in die Religions-Psychologie. (Pariser, E.) Halle, 1914.

Phil 5520.325.1   Einführung in die Semantik. (Schaff, Adam.) Frankfurt, 1969.

Phil 5247.22.20   Einführung in die spezielle Psychologie. (Heymans, G.) Leipzig, 1932.

Phil 5066.8.5   Einführung in die symbolische Logik. (Carnap, Rudolf.) Wien, 1954.

Phil 5820.2   Einführung in die Tierpsychologie auf experimenteller und ethnologischer Grundlage. (Kafka, Gustav.) Leipzig, 1914.

Phil 1704.2   Einführung in eine wissenschaftliche Philosophie. (Eleutheropulos, A.) Leipzig, 1906.

Phil 3246.207   Einführung in Fichtes Reden an die deutsche Nation. 2. Aufl. (Schwarz, H.) Langensalza, 1925.

Phil 3640.203   Einführung in Friedrich Nietzsches Zarathustradichtung. (Kappstein, T.) Bielefeld, 1925.

Phil 3425.108.10   Einführung in Hegels Religionsphilosophie. (Lasson, G.) Leipzig, 1930.

Phil 179.3.106   Einführung in Rudolf Euckens Lebens- und Weltanschauung. (Heussner, A.) Göttingen, 1921.

Phil 193.111   Einführung in System und Geschichte der Philosophie. (Schmieder, J.) Leipzig, 1921.

Phil 3915.160   Einführung in Wilhelm Wundt's Philosophie und Psychologie. (Heussner, A.) Göttingen, 1920.

Phil 310.105   Einführungen in den Marxismus. (Duncker, Hermann.) Berlin, 1959. 2v.

Phil 5627.71   Einfürung in die Religionspsychologie. (Oesterreich, T.K.) Berlin, 1917.

Phil 5590.40   Einfurung in die Charakterkunde. (Becker, Josef.) Nurnberg, 1947.

Phil 9035.59.5   Einfurung in die Charakterkunde auf individualpsychologischer Grundlage. 2. Aufl. (Künkel, Fritz.) Leipzig, 1929.

Phil 9035.59.7   Einfurung in die Charakterkunde auf individualpsychologischer Grundlage. 8. Aufl. (Künkel, Fritz.) Leipzig, 1939.

Phil 818.24.10   Einfurung in die Geschichte der Philosophie. (Schilling, Kurt.) Heidelberg, 1949.

Phil 342.7   Einfurung in die Grundprobleme der Erkenntnistheorie. (Leser, Hermann.) Leipzig, 1911.

Phil 180.47   Einfurung in die Philosophie. (Falkenfeld, H.) Berlin, 1926.

Phil 6960.5.12   Einfurung in die psychiatrische Klenik. (Kraepelin, E.) Leipzig, 1905.

Phil 6960.5.11   Einfurung in die psychiatrische Klenik dreissez Vorlesungen. (Kraepelin, E.) Leipzig, 1901.

Phil 5066.8.6   Einfurung in die symbolische Logik mit besonderer Berucksichtigung. (Carnap, Rudolf.) Wien, 1960.

Phil 8592.23   Einfurung in ein System...Religions. (Mehlis, Goerg.) Tübingen, 1917.

Phil 6634.5   Einge especten vom vrij en dwangmatig herhalen. (Kuijper, Siem.) Hilversum, 1963.

Phil 3085.7.30   Eingriffe. (Adorno, Theodor W.) Frankfurt, 1963.

Phil 510.13.5   Einheit der Erkenntnis und Einheit des Seins. (Lipsius, Friedrich R.) Leipzig, 1913.

Phil 3246.202   Die Einheit der Fichteschen Philosophie. (Gurwitsch, G.) Berlin, 1922.

Phil 5640.27   Die Einheit der Sinne grundlinien einer Ästhesiologie. (Plessner, H.) Bonn, 1923.

Phil 332.18   Die Einheit des Erkenntnisproblems. (Boldt, Karl.) Leipzig, 1937.

Phil 179.3   Die Einheit des Geisteslebens. (Eucken, R.) Leipzig, 1888.

Phil 179.3.2   Die Einheit des Geisteslebens. 2. Aufl. (Eucken, R.) Berlin, 1925.

Phil 8877.50.5   Die Einheit des sittlichen Bewusstseins der Menschheit. (Cathrein, Victor.) Freiburg, 1914. 3v.

Phil 4065.182   Einheit und Vielheit in Denken und Sprache Giordano Brunos. (Huber, Karl.) Winterthur, 1965.

Phil 337.15   Die Einheit unseres Wirklichkeitsbildes und die Grenzen der Einzelwissenschaftes. (Grassi, E.) Bern, 1951.

Phil 5374.10   Einheiten und Relationen. (Lipps, Theodor.) Leipzig, 1902.

Phil 5253.10   Einheitswissenschaft und Psychologie. (Neurath, Otto.) Wien, 1933.

Phil 804.6   Einhorn, D. Begründung der Geschichte der Philosophie als Wissenschaft. Wien, 1919.

Phil 179.15   Einhorn, David. Der Kampf um einen Gegenstand der Philosophie. Wien, 1916.

Phil 5357.2   Einige allgemeinere Fragen der Psychologie und Biologie des Denkens. (Jaensch, E.R.) Leipzig, 1920.

Phil 3425.89   Einige Bemerkungen über den Standpankt, Welchen die deutsche Philosophie durch Hegel erreicht hat. (Keil, Oswald T.) Leipzig, 1828.

Phil 3500.56   Einige Bemerkungen über Kants philosophische Religionslehre. (Schulze, Gottlob E.) Kiel, 1795.

Phil 3246.206   Einige Fragen, veranlasst Durch. (Belthusen, J.C.) Helmstädt, 1799.

Phil 181.39.5   Einige Hauptprobleme der Metaphysik. (Geyser, Joseph.) Freiburg, 1923.

Phil 3210.61   Einige Ideen zur Schöpfungs- und Entwickelungsgeschichte der Organismen. (Fechner, G.T.) Leipzig, 1873.

Phil 8418.43   Einige philosophische und informationstheoretische Aspekte der moralisch-ästhetischen Verhaltensdetermination der Persönlichkeit. Diss. (Rochlitz, Manfred.) Leipzig? 1967?

Phil 930.7.55   Einige Verbesserungen zu Forke's Geschichte der chinesischen Philosophie. (Zach, E. von.) Batavia, 1939.

VPhil 1153.20   A einikusok. (Sebestyén, Károly.) Budapest, 1902.

Phil 806.20   Einleiteug in das Verständriss der Weltgeschichte. (Gladisch, August.) Posen, 1844.

Phil 5821.4   Einleitung...Gehirnphysiologie...Psychologie. (Loeb, J.) Leipzig, 1899.

Phil 186.13   Einleitung in das Studium der Philosophie. (Lindner, G.A.) Wien, 1866.

Phil 197.9.13A   Einleitung in der Philosophie. (Windelband, W.) Tübingen, 1914.

Phil 197.9.14A   Einleitung in der Philosophie. 2. Aufl. (Windelband, W.) Tübingen, 1920.

Phil 8407.10.5   Einleitung in die Ästhetik. (Groos, Karl.) Giessen, 1892.

Phil 3425.69   Einleitung in die Ästhetik. (Hegel, Georg Wilhelm Friedrich.) München, 1967.

Phil 5041.24   Einleitung in die allgemeine Logik und die Kritik der reinen Vernunft. (Buhle, J.G.) Göttingen, 1795.

Phil 187.156   Einleitung in die allgemeine Metaphysik. (Martin, Gottfried.) Köln, 1957.

Phil 5643.19   Einleitung in die Dioptrik des Auges. (Wüllner, F.H.A.) Leipzig, 1866.

Phil 1807.1   Einleitung in die englische Philosophie. (Höffding, H.) Leipzig, 1889.

Phil 8893.51   Einleitung in die Ethik. (Stange, Karl.) Leipzig, 1901.

Phil 178.26   Einleitung in die Geisteswissenschaften. (Dilthey, Wilhelm.) Leipzig, 1803.

Phil 192.72.5   Einleitung in die Geistwissenschaften. 2e Aufl. (Rothacker, E.) Tübingen, 1930.

Phil 1705.4.9   Einleitung in die Geschichte der neueren Philosophie. (Fischer, K.) Heidelberg, 1908.

Phil 1119.1   Einleitung in die Geschichte der Philosophie. (Otten, Alois.) Paderborn, 1895.

Phil 3425.70.75A   Einleitung in die Geschichte der Philosophie. 3. Aufl. (Hegel, Georg Wilhelm Friedrich.) Hamburg, 1959.

Phil 182.61   Einleitung in die Kategorienlehre. (Herpe, Hans.) Leipzig, 1921.

Phil 8890.40   Einleitung in die Moral. (Pörschke, K.L.) Libau, 1797.

Phil 8893.41   Einleitung in die Moralwissenschaft. (Simmel, G.) Berlin, 1892-93. 2v.

Phil 3425.273   Einleitung in die öffentlichen Vorlesungen über die Bedeutung der hegelschen Philosophie in der christlichen Theologie. (Marheineke, Philipp.) Berlin, 1842.

Phil 3425.73.4   Einleitung in die Phänomenologie des Geistes. (Hegel, Georg Wilhelm Friedrich.) Frankfurt, 1964.

Phil 176.160.5   Einleitung in die Philosophie. (Bense, Max.) München, 1941.

Phil 177.29   Einleitung in die Philosophie. (Cornelius, H.) Leipzig, 1903.

Phil 178.17.15   Einleitung in die Philosophie. (Dessoir, Max.) Stuttgart, 1936.

Phil 178.40.5   Einleitung in die Philosophie. (Dyroff, Adolf.) Bonn, 1948.

Phil 179.20   Einleitung in die Philosophie. (Endres, J.A.) Kempten, 1920.

Phil 180.12 — Einleitung in die Philosophie. (Frohschammer, J.) München, 1858.

Phil 184.12 — Einleitung in die Philosophie. (Jerusalem, W.) Wien, 1899.

Phil 184.12.2 — Einleitung in die Philosophie. (Jerusalem, W.) Wien, 1903.

Phil 184.12.3 — Einleitung in die Philosophie. (Jerusalem, W.) Wien, 1923.

Phil 185.47 — Einleitung in die Philosophie. (Kremer, Josef.) Graz, 1931.

Phil 185.12.7 — Einleitung in die Philosophie. (Külpe, O.) Leipzig, 1895.

Phil 186.60.15 — Einleitung in die Philosophie. (Litt, Theodor.) Leipzig, 1933.

Phil 187.69 — Einleitung in die Philosophie. (Muller, Aloys.) Berlin, 1925.

Phil 190.3.2 — Einleitung in die Philosophie. (Paulsen, F.) Berlin, 1892.

Phil 193.85 — Einleitung in die Philosophie. (Schütz, Ludwig.) Paderborn, 1879.

Phil 193.41 — Die Einleitung in die Philosophie. (Strümpell, L.) Leipzig, 1886.

Phil 3915.35 — Einleitung in die Philosophie. (Wundt, Wilhelm.) Leipzig, 1902.

Phil 178.17.17 — Einleitung in die Philosophie. 2. Aufl. (Dessoir, Max.) Stuttgart, 1946.

Phil 177.29.2 — Einleitung in die Philosophie. 2e Aufl. (Cornelius, H.) Leipzig, 1919.

Phil 190.3.3 — Einleitung in die Philosophie. 3e Aufl. (Paulsen, F.) Berlin, 1895.

Phil 185.12.4 — Einleitung in die Philosophie. 4. Aufl. (Külpe, O.) Leipzig, 1907.

Phil 185.12.5 — Einleitung in die Philosophie. 5. Aufl. (Külpe, O.) Leipzig, 1910.

Phil 185.12.8 — Einleitung in die Philosophie. 6. Aufl. (Külpe, O.) Leipzig, 1913.

Phil 5253.1 — Einleitung in die Psychologie. (Natorp, P.) Freiburg, 1888.

Phil 5258.58 — Einleitung in die Psychologie. (Stadler, August.) Leipzig, 1918.

Phil 5258.45 — Einleitung in die Psychologie als Wissenschaft. (Spitta, Heinrich.) Freiburg, 1886.

Phil 8586.16 — Einleitung in die Religionsphilosophie über die verschiedenen Standpunkt und Methoden zur Enforchung des Wesens der Religion. (Gese, Paul.) Göttingen, 1918.

Phil 6110.11 — Einleitung in die Seelenlehre. (Abel, J.F.) Stuttgart, 1786.

Phil 5240.25 — Einleitung in die Seelenlehre. (Abel, Jacob Friedrich von.) Stuttgart, 1786. 2 pam.

Phil 193.114 — Einleitung in die speculative Philosophie. (Schütz, C.G.) Lemgo, 1776.

Phil 293.8.75 — Einleitung in eine kritische Ausgabe von B. de Maillets Telliamed. (Neubert, Fritz.) Berlin, 1920.

Phil 3425.229.10 — Einleitung in Hegel's philosophische Abhandlungen. (Michelet, C.L.) Berlin, 1832.

Phil 179.29 — Einleitung in Natur und Geschichte. (Eschenmayer, C.H. von.) Erlangen, 1806.

Phil 510.9.10 — Einleitung und Begründung einer monistischen Erkenntnis-Theorie. (Noiré, Ludwig.) Mainz, 1877.

Phil 510.9.11 — Einleitung und Begründung einer monistischen Erkenntnis-Theorie. 2e Ausg. (Noiré, Ludwig.) Mainz, 1884.

Htn — Phil 3800.170* — Einleitung zu seinem Entwurf eines Systems der Naturphilosophie. (Schelling, F.W.J. von.) Jena, 1799.

Htn — Phil 3800.170.5* — Einleitung zu seinem Entwurf eines Systems der Naturphilosophie. (Schelling, F.W.J. von.) Jena, 1799. 2 pam.

Phil 3800.170.10 — Einleitung zu seinem Entwurf eines Systems der Naturphilosophie. (Schelling, F.W.J. von.) Leipzig, 1911.

Phil 210.70.1 — Einleitung zu richtigen Auslegung vernünftiger Reden und Schriften. (Chladenius, Johann Martin.) Düsseldorf, 1969.

Phil 3890.8.30.1 — Einleitung zur Sittenlehre. (Thomasius, Christian.) Hildesheim, 1968.

Phil 5059.24.2 — Einleitung zur Vernunftlehre. (Thomasius, Christian.) Hildesheim, 1968.

Phil 1850.128 — Einordnung, Wesen und Aufgaben...des Francis Bacon. (Minkowski, Helmut.) Leyde, 1933.

Phil 3640.88.7 — Der einsame Nietzsche. (Förster-Nietzsche, E.) München, 1915.

Phil 3120.30.90 — Einsame Zinesprache; Martin Buber und das Christentum. (Balthasar, Hans von.) Köln, 1958.

Phil 9515.3.99 — Die Einsamkeit. (Milch, W.) Frauenfeld, 1937.

Phil 5418.6 — Die Einsamkeit als soziologisches Problem. (Dreitzel, Hans Peter.) Zurich, 1970.

Phil 5418.2 — Einsamkeit in medizinisch-psychologischer, theologischer und soziologischer Sicht. (Stuttgarter Gemeinschaft "Arzt und Seelsorger".) Stuttgart, 1967.

Phil 8402.25.3 — Einschränkung des schonen Künste auf einen einzigen Grundsatz. 3. Aufl. (Batteux, Charles.) Leipzig, 1770.

Phil 165.339 — Einsichten. (Oehler, K.) Frankfurt a.M., 1962.

Phil 3200.12 — Einsiedel, August von. Ideen. Berlin, 1957.

Phil 8584.15A — Einstein, Albert. Cosmic religion. N.Y., 1931.

Phil 5590.474 — Einstellung als Determination individuellen Verhaltens. Habilitationsschrift. (Roth, Erwin.) Göttingen, 1967.

Phil 5790.2.25 — Einstellungen zum Tod und ihre soziale Bedingtheit. (Hahn, Alois.) Stuttgart, 1968.

Phil 185.95 — Einübung ins philosophische Denken. (Keilbach, Wilhelm.) München, 1960.

Phil 4120.4.84 — Der Einzelne und der Staat nachtreibung Giovanni Gentile. (Aebischer, Max.) Schweiz, 1954.

Phil 9050.5.5 — Der Einzelne und die Gesellschaft. (Thorsch, Berthold.) Dresden, 1940.

Phil 3480.21.3 — Der einzig mögliche Beweis vom Daseyn Gottes. (Kant, Immanuel.) Königsberg, 1770.

Htn — Phil 3480.21* — Der einzig mögliche Beweisgrund. (Kant, Immanuel.) Königsberg, 1763. 4 pam.

Phil 3480.21.5 — Der einzig mögliche Beweisgrund zu einer Demonstration des Daseyns Gottes. (Kant, Immanuel.) Königsberg, 1794.

Phil 3480.21.22 — Der einzig mögliche Beweisgrund zu einer Demonstration des Daseyns Gottes. 2. Aufl. (Kant, Immanuel.) Leipzig, 1902.

Phil 3480.21.23 — Der einzig mögliche Beweisgrund zu einer Demonstration des Daseyns Gottes. 3. Aufl. (Kant, Immanuel.) Leipzig, 1911.

Phil 5465.126 — Eiseley, Loren. The mind as nature. 1. ed. N.Y., 1962.

Phil 1850.159 — Eiseley, Loren Corey. Francis Bacon and the modern dilemma. Lincoln, 1962.

Phil 489.3 — Eisenberg, Rafael. The East-West conflict. N.Y., 1967.

Phil 7055.338 — Eisenbud, Jule. The world of Ted Serios. N.Y., 1967.

Phil 2070.161 — Eisendrath, Craig Ralph. The unifying moment; the psychological philosophy of William James and Alfred North Whitehead. Cambridge, 1971.

Phil 5244.8 — Eisenmeier, J. Die Psychologie und ihre Zentralestellung in der Philosophie. Halle, 1914.

Phil 3585.1.105 — Eisenring, Max F.E. Johann Heinrich Lambert und die wissenschaftliche Philosophie der Gegenwart. Zürich, 1942.

Phil 5520.70.5 — Eisenson, J. The psychology of communication. N.Y., 1963.

Phil 5520.70 — Eisenson, J. Psychology of speech. N.Y., 1938.

Phil 6420.42 — Eisenson, John. Stuttering; a symposium. N.Y., 1958.

Phil 8954.5 — Eisenstadt, Shmuel Noah. The Protestant ethic and modernization. N.Y., 1968.

Phil 5520.560 — Eisler, Frieda Goldman. Psycholinguistics: experiments in spontaneous speech. London, 1968.

Phil 8879.16.2 — Eisler, Julius. Lehrbuch der allgemeinen Ethik. 2e Aufl. Wien, 1912.

Phil 6114.4.5 — Eisler, R. Geist und Körper. Göttingen, 1911.

Phil 89.1.5 — Eisler, R. Handwörterbuch der Philosophie. Berlin, 1913.

Phil 89.1.7 — Eisler, R. Handwörterbuch der Philosophie. 2. Aufl. Berlin, 1922.

Phil 179.7 — Eisler, R. Kritische Einführung in die Philosophie. Berlin, 1905.

Phil 6114.4 — Eisler, R. Leib und Seele. Leipzig, 1906.

Phil 89.1.15 — Eisler, R. Philosophen - Lexikon. Berlin, 1912.

Phil 735.2A — Eisler, R. Studien zur Werttheorie. Leipzig, 1902.

Phil 89.1 — Eisler, R. Wörterbuch der Philosophie Begriffe und aus Drücke. Berlin, 1899.

Phil 89.1.4 — Eisler, R. Wörterbuch der Philosophie Begriffe und aus Drücke. 4. Aufl. Berlin, 1927-29. 3v.

Phil 335.1.5 — Eisler, Rudolf. Das Bewusstsein der Aussenwelt. Leipzig, 1901.

Phil 335.1.2A — Eisler, Rudolf. Einführung in die Erkenntnis-Theorie. 2. Aufl. Leipzig, 1925.

Phil 510.142 — Eisler, Rudolf. Geschichte des Monismus. Leipzig, 1910.

Phil 3486.14 — Eisler, Rudolf. Kant-Lexikon. Berlin, 1930.

Phil 3640.122.5 — Eisler, Rudolf. Nietzsche's Erkenntnistheorie und Metaphysik. Leipzig, 1902.

Phil 5244.12.3 — Eisler, Rudolf. Psychologie im Umriss. 3e Aufl. Leipzig, 1903.

Phil 3486.14.10 — Eisler, Rudolf. Die Weiterbildung der Kant'schen Prioritätslehre bis zur Gegenwart. Inaug. Diss. Leipzig, 1895.

Phil 89.1.8 — Eisler, Rudolf. Wörterbuch der philosophischen Begriffe. 4. Aufl. Berlin, 1927-30. 3v.

Phil 8735.8 — Eisler, Rudolf. Der Zweck; seine Bedeutung für Natur und Geist. Berlin, 1914.

Phil 6315.2.383 — Eissler, Kurt Robert. Sigmund Freud und die Wiener Universität. Bern, 1966.

Phil 6329.22.5 — Eissler, Kurt Robert. Talent and genius. N.Y., 1971.

Phil 9558.10.15 — Eitelkeit und Schamgefühl. (Grau, Kurt J.) Leipzig, 1928.

Phil 179.11 — Eitle, Johannes. Grundriss der Philosophie. Freiburg, 1892.

Phil 181.80.10 — Ejercicios espirituales. (Garcia Morente, Manuel.) Madrid, 1961.

Phil 2880.8.94 — Ekecrate; dialogue sur l'existentialisme. (Dauphin, E.J.) Montpellier, 1947.

Phil 179.25 — Ekelund, V. Attiskt. Stockholm, 1919.

Phil 9035.31 — Ekenhans, Theodor. Charakterbildung. Leipzig, 1908.

Phil 4757.2.120 — Ekkev, Martin H. Gurdjieff, de mens en zijn werk. Amsterdam, 1968.

Phil 3850.18.106 — Eklund, H. Evangelisches und Katholisches in Max Schelers Ethik. Inaug. Diss. Uppsala, 1932.

Phil 3850.18.105 — Eklund, H. Evangelisches und Katholisches in Max Schelers Ethik. Inaug. Diss. Uppsala, 1932.

Phil 4655.1.81 — Eklund, J.A. Pontus Wikner. Stockholm, 1903.

Phil 8610.964 — Ekmalian, A. Agnostitsizm i problema znaniia i very v burzhuaznoi filosofii. Erevan, 1964.

Phil 5856.5.2 — Ekman, Gösta. Differentiell psykologi. Stockholm, 1966.

Phil 6340.197 — Ekman, Karl. Nietzsches estetik. Helsingfors, 1920.

Phil 5627.134.105 — Ekman, Nils Gösta. Experiment med Gud. Stockholm, 1971.

Phil 8050.81 — Ekman, Rolf. Estetikens historia från sjuttonhundratalets början till och med Goethe. Lund, 1963.

Phil 8405.8 — Ekman, Rolf. Estetiska problem. Lund, 1954.

Phil 8405.8.2 — Ekman, Rolf. Estetiska problem. 2. uppl. Lund, 1960.

Phil 8405.8.5 — Ekman, Rolf. Problems and theories in modern aesthetics. Lund, 1960.

Phil 5260.10 — Eksperimental'nye osnovy psikhologii ustanovki. (Uznadze, Dmitrii N.) Tbilisi, 1961.

Phil 7076.18 — Die Ekstase. (Beck, Paul.) Bad Sachsa, 1906.

Phil 7076.16 — Die Ekstase in ihrer kulturellen Bedeutung. (Achelis, Thomas.) Berlin, 1902.

Phil 7076.14 — Die Ekstasen des Menschen. (Mantegazza, Paolo.) Jena, 1888.

Phil 5628.10.5.1 — Ekstatische Konfessionen. (Buber, Martin.) Leipzig, 1921.

Phil 281.7 — Ektropismen in ny teori om livets bevarande i varldsprocessen. (Auerbach, Felix.) Stockholm, 1913.

Phil 1750.784 — Ekzistsializm i naunchnoe poznanie. (Solov'ev, Erikh I.) Moskva, 1966.

Phil 4752.2.43 — Ekzistentsial'naia dialektika bozhestvennogo i chelovecheskogo. (Berdiaev, Nikolai Aleksandrovich.) Parizh, 1952.

Phil 8403.36 — El arte desde su esencia. (Camón, Aznar J.) Zaragoza, 1940.

Phil 11.13 — El buen deseo. Matanzas. 1-2,1884-1886

Phil 5252.45 — El materialismo psicofisico. (Masci, Filippo.) Napoli, 1901.

Phil 4265.4.10 — El metodo della filosofia. (Vailati, G.) Bari, 1957.

Phil 6315.2.120 — El psicoanalisis de Freud. (Castellano, Filemón.) Buenos Aires, 1941.

Phil 6314.3.2 — Elam, C. A physician's problems. Boston, 1869.

Phil 6314.3 — Elam, C. A physician's problems. London, 1869.

Phil 335.5 — Elbert, J.W. Etude sur la phénoménologie. Thèse. Nancy, 1930.

Phil 3824.1 — Elbogen, Ismar. Der Tractatus de Intellectus emendatione. Breslau, 1894.

Phil 3824.1.5 — Elbogen, Ismar. Der Tractatus de Intellectus emendatione. Diss. Breslau, 1898.

Phil 8694.2 — Elder, William. Ideas from nature. Philadelphia, 1898.

Phil 5244.20 — Elder, William. Studies in psychology. London, 1927.

Phil 2075.6.90A — The elder Henry James. (Warren, Austin.) N.Y., 1934.

Phil 179.44 — Elders, Fons. Filosofie als science-fiction. Amsterdam, 1968.

Phil 1155.10 — Gli eleati. (Albertelli, P.) Bari, 1939.

Phil 6980.575.5 — Electrical and drug treatment in psychiatry. (Paterson, A.S.) Amsterdam, 1963.

Phil 6685.12 — Electricité animale. (Petetin, J.H.D.) Paris, 1808.

Htn — Phil 6671.10* — Electro-biological phenomena. (Braid, James.) Edinburgh, 1851.

Phil 6113.1   Electro-dynamisme vital. (Durand, P.J.) Paris, 1855.
Htn   Phil 8582.16*   An elegant and learned discourse...light of nature. (Culverwel, N.) London, 1652.
Phil 3480.67.65   Eleinenta metaphysica juris doctrinae. (Kant, Immanuel.) Amstelaedami, 1799.
Phil 2275.80   Élémens de la philosophie de l'esprit humain. (Stewart, D.) Genève, 1808. 3v.
Phil 2523.30   Élémens d'idéologie. (Destutt de Tracy, A.L.C.) Paris, 1817-18. 4v.
Phil 2523.32   Élémens d'idéologie. (Destutt de Tracy, A.L.C.) Paris, 1825-27. 5v.
Phil 2045.61.30   Elemens philosophiques du bon citoyen. (Hobbes, Thomas.) Paris, 1651.
Phil 299.14   Das Element der Wirklichkeit und die Welt der Erfahrung. (Sapper, Karl.) München, 1924.
Phil 2515.4.99   L'élément historique dans...Cournot. (Lévêque, R.) Paris, 1938.
Phil 2515.4.100   L'élément historique dans la connaissance humaine d'après Cournot. Thèse. (Lévêque, R.) Strasbourg, 1938.
Htn   Phil 5043.12*   Elementa logica. (DuMoulin, Pierre.) Breamae, 1622.
Phil 4114.25   Elementa metaphysicae mathematicum in morem adornata. 2a ed. (Genovesi, Antonio.) Neapoli, 1751-56. 4v.
Phil 1535.18.4   Elementa philosophia. (Gredt, Joseph.) Barcinone, 1961. 2v.
Phil 176.11   Elementa philosophiae. (Baumeister, F.C.) Leipzig, 1755.
Phil 1535.18   Elementa philosophiae Aristotelico-Thomisticae. (Gredt, Joseph.) Romae, 1899.
Phil 181.90.5   Elementa philosophiae Aristotelico-Thomisticae. 7. ed. v.2. (Gredt, Joseph.) Friburgi, 1937.
Phil 1535.18.3   Elementa philosophiae Aristotelico-Thomisticae. 12. ed. (Gredt, Joseph.) Barcinone, 1958.
Phil 176.103   Elementa philosophiae instrumentalis. (Buddeus, J.F.) Halae Saxonum, 1724-25.
Phil 176.103.3   Elementa philosophiae instrumentalis. v.1-2. (Buddeus, J.F.) Halae-Saxonum, 1719-20.
Phil 176.103.5   Elementa philosophiae instrumentalis. v.1-2. (Buddeus, J.F.) Halae Saxonum, 1724-25.
Phil 176.103.10   Elementa philosophiae practicae. (Buddeus, J.F.) Halaeo Magdeburgical, 1724.
Phil 182.103.5   Elementa philosophiae rationalis et moralis. (Heineccius, J.G.) Amstelodami, 1733.
Phil 5050.15   Elementa philosophiae rationalis seu logicae. (Knutzen, M.) Regiomonti, 1747.
Phil 1535.36.12   Elementa philosophiae scholasticae. 11. and 12. ed. (Reinstadler, S.) Friburgi, 1923. 2v.
Phil 1535.36.13   Elementa philosophiae scholasticae. 13. ed. (Reinstadler, S.) Friburgi , 1929. 2v.
Htn   Phil 184.8.3*   Elementa philosophica. (Johnson, Samuel.) Philadelphia, 1752.
Htn   Phil 184.8*   Elementa philosophica. v.1-2. (Johnson, Samuel.) Philadelphia, 1752.
Htn   Phil 2045.60.25*   Elementa philosophica de cive. (Hobbes, Thomas.) Amsterdam, 1647.
Htn   Phil 2045.61*   Elementa philosophica de cive. (Hobbes, Thomas.) Amsterdam, 1657.
Htn   Phil 2045.61.5*   Elementa philosophica de cive. (Hobbes, Thomas.) Amsterdam, 1669.
Phil 2045.61.10   Elementa philosophica de cive. (Hobbes, Thomas.) Amsterdam, 1742.
Phil 2045.61.9   Elementa philosophica de cive. (Hobbes, Thomas.) n.p., 16- .
Phil 6980.45   Elementär barrpsykiatri. (Annell, A.L.) Stockholm, 1958.
Phil 5535.52   Elementare Lernprinzipien; Darstellung und Modifikation von Postulaten der Hull'schen Theorie. (Wendeler, Jürgen.) Weinheim, 1967.
Phil 5050.25   Elementare Logik. (Kutschera, Franz von.) Wien, 1967.
Phil 189.32   An elementary Christian metaphysics. (Owens, Joseph.) Milwaukee, 1963.
Phil 1535.26   Elementary course of Christian philosophy. (Brothers of the Christian Schools.) N.Y., 1893.
Phil 8877.86   An elementary ethics. (Castell, Alhurey.) Englewood Cliffs, 1955.
Phil 5258.34.4   Elementary experiments in psychology. (Seashore, C.E.) N.Y., 1909.
Phil 5245.42   Elementary general psychology. (Fernberger, Samuel W.) N.Y., 1937.
Phil 5059.13   An elementary handbook of logic. (Tookey, J.J.) N.Y., 1918.
Phil 5049.4.4.5   Elementary lessons in logic. (Jevons, W.S.) London, 1870.
Phil 5049.4.4.7   Elementary lessons in logic. (Jevons, W.S.) London, 1871.
Phil 5049.4.2.5   Elementary lessons in logic. (Jevons, W.S.) London, 1888.
Phil 5066.231   Elementary logic. (Mates, Benson.) N.Y., 1965.
Phil 5066.11.10A   Elementary logic. (Quine, Willard van Orman.) Boston, 1941.
Phil 5066.11.12   Elementary logic. (Quine, Willard van Orman.) Cambridge, 1966.
Phil 5066.11.11   Elementary logic. (Quine, Willard van Orman.) N.Y., 1965.
Phil 5057.11   An elementary logic. (Russell, J.E.) N.Y., 1906.
Phil 5058.22.5   Elementary logic. (Sidgwick, A.) Cambridge, 1914.
Phil 5059.14   Elementary logic. (Taylor, William J.) N.Y., 1909.
Phil 5062.32   An elementary logic. (Walcott, G.D.) N.Y., 1931.
Phil 8877.21.2   Elementary moral lessons. (Cowdery, M.F.) Philadelphia, 1856.
Phil 8877.21   Elementary moral lessons. (Cowdery, M.F.) Sandusky, 1855.
Phil 5062.34   Elementary philosophy. (Willcox, J.M.) Philadelphia, 1875.
Phil 5246.36   Elementary psychology. (Gates, Arthur I.) N.Y., 1925.
Phil 5247.18   Elementary psychology. (Harvey, N.A.) Chicago, 1914.
Phil 5250.5   Elementary psychology. (Kellogg, A.M.) N.Y., 1894.
Phil 5255.30   An elementary psychology. (Phillips, D.E.) Boston, 1927.
Phil 5258.95   Elementary psychology. (Shastri, Prabhu D.) Calcutta, 1928.
Phil 6325.12   An elementary psychology of the abnormal. 1. ed. (Pillsbury, Walter B.) N.Y., 1932.
Phil 8893.16.5   Elementary sketches of moral philosophy. (Smith, Sydney.) N.Y., 1850.
Phil 978.51   Elementary theosophy. 2d ed. (Rogers, L.W.) Chicago, 1923.
Phil 978.51.3   Elementary theosophy. 3rd ed. (Rogers, L.W.) Chicago, 1929.
Phil 5060.2   Elementary treatise on logic. (Ufford, H.G.) N.Y., 1823.
Phil 5062.11   Elementary treatise on logic. (Wilson, W.D.) N.Y., 1856.
Phil 8735.4   Elemente der empirischen Teleologie. (Cossmann, P.N.) Stuttgart, 1899.
Phil 178.5.2   Die Elemente der Metaphysik. (Deussen, P.) Aachen, 1877.
Phil 178.5   Elemente der Metaphysik. 2. Aufl. (Deussen, P.) Leipzig, 1890.

Phil 178.5.3   Die Elemente der Metaphysik. 6e Aufl. (Deussen, P.) Leipzig, 1919.
Phil 5066.60   Elemente der neuen Logik. (Juhos, B. van.) Frankfurt, 1954.
Phil 176.10.5   Elemente der Philosophie. (Baumann, Julius J.) Leipzig, 1891.
Phil 182.1.8   Elemente der Philosophie. (Hagemann, G.) Freiburg, 1911-1922. 3v.
Phil 192.26   Elemente der Philosophie. (Rausch, Alfred.) Halle, 1909.
Phil 182.1   Elemente der Philosophie. v.1-3. (Hagemann, G.) Münster, 1870.
Phil 192.26.3   Elemente der Philosophie. 3. Aufl. (Rausch, Alfred.) Halle, 1914.
Phil 193.165   Elemente der Philosophie und der Mathematik. (Speiser, A.) Basel, 1952.
Phil 5241.5   Die Elemente der Psychologie. (Ballauff, L.) Cöthen, 1877.
Phil 5257.24   Die Elemente der Psychologie. 3. Aufl. (Raaf, H. de.) Langensalza, 1908.
Phil 5500.2   Elemente der Psychologie des Urteils. (Schrader, E.) Leipzig, 1905.
Phil 3210.47   Elemente der Psychophysik. v.1-2. (Fechner, G.T.) Leipzig, 1860.
Phil 5585.23   Die Elemente der Reinen Wahrnehmung. (Braude, M.) Lemberg, 1899.
Phil 258.10   Elemente der Sprachkritik; eine Alternative zum Dogmatismus und Skeptizismus in der analytischen Philosophie. 1. Aufl. (Lorenz, Kuno.) Frankfurt am Main, 1970.
Phil 705.6   Elemente der transzendentalen Logik. (Barthel, E.) Strassburg, 1913.
Phil 3915.59.3   Elemente der Völkerpsychologie. 2. Aufl. (Wundt, Wilhelm.) Leipzig, 1913.
Phil 5757.8   Elemente einer philosophischen Freiheitslehre. (Hebler, Karl.) Berlin, 1887.
Phil 8586.25   Elemente zu einer religionsphilosophie auf Phänomenonologischer Grundlage. (Grundler, O.) Kempten, 1922.
Phil 8896.4.3   Elementi di etica. 3. ed. (Vidari, Giovanni.) Milano, 1911.
Phil 8896.4.4   Elementi di etica. 4. ed. (Vidari, Giovanni.) Milano, 1917.
Phil 8896.4.5   Elementi di etica. 5. ed. (Vidari, Giovanni.) Milano, 1923.
Phil 4112.30.2   Elementi di filosofia. (Galluppi, Pasquale.) Bologna, 1837. 3v.
Phil 181.10.5   Elementi di filosofia. (Gioja, M.) Milano, 1818. 2v.
Phil 181.10   Elementi di filosofia. (Gioja, M. E.) Lugano, 1834.
Phil 1535.5   Elementi di filosofia. (Liberatore, M.) Livorno, 1852.
Phil 187.8   Elementi di filosofia. (Mancino, S.) Palermo, 1846. 2v.
Phil 1535.10   Elementi di filosofia. (Pestalozza, A.) Milano, 1857. 2v.
Phil 4112.30   Elementi di filosofia. v.1-2. (Galluppi, Pasquale.) Firenze, 1834.
Phil 4112.30.5   Elementi di filosofia. v.1-6. 3. ed. (Galluppi, Pasquale.) Napoli, 1834-37. 3v.
Phil 4112.30.6   Elementi di filosofia. v.2. (Galluppi, Pasquale.) Roma, 1963-
Phil 8657.17   Elementi di filosofia. v.2. 4. ed. (Corte, P.A.) Torino, 1862.
Phil 4120.1.30   Elementi di filosofia ad uso de'Giovanetti. (Gioja, Melchiorre.) Milano, 1822. 2v.
Phil 4120.1.31   Elementi di filosofia ad uso de'Giovanetti. v.1-2. (Gioja, Melchiorre.) Milano, 1838.
Phil 4110.3.80   Gli elementi di filosofia del professore Francesco Fiorentino. (Marino, L.) Napoli, 1878.
Phil 175.31   Elementi di filosofia fondamentale. (Aquisto, B. d'.) Palermo, 1857.
Phil 187.72   Elementi di filosofia per le scuole secondarie. (Masci, Filippo.) Napoli, 1899-1904. 2v.
Phil 5053.7.4   Elementi di logica. (Nicoli, P.) Milano, 1912.
Phil 5055.10   Elementi di logica guiridica. (Piola, Giuseppe.) Roma, 1894.
Phil 8896.10   Elementi di morale e cenni di economia politica. 8. ed. (Vecchia, Paolo.) Torino, 1917?
Phil 5241.43   Elementi di psicologia sperimentale positiva. (Benigni, Edvige.) Torino, 1900.
Phil 4265.1.40   Elementi di una filosofia della potenzialità. (Vivante, Leone.) Firenze, 1953.
Phil 2523.31   Elementi d'ideologia. (Destutt de Tracy, A.L.C.) Milano, 1817-19. 10v.
Phil 5261.7   Elementi scientifici di psicologia e logica. 3-4. ed. pt.1-2. (Valdarnini, Angelo.) Torino, 1915.
Phil 4114.23   Elementorum artis logico criticae. (Genovesi, Antonio.) n.p., 1766.
Phil 4114.23.10   Elementorum artis logico criticae. (Genovesi, Antonio.) Neapoli, 1778.
Phil 8894.5.5   Elementos de ética ó filosofía moral. (Tiberghien, G.) Madrid, 1873.
Phil 8878.31   Elementos de filosofia. (Dalmau y Gratacós, F.) Barcelona, 1911.
Phil 181.128   Elementos de filosofia. 2. ed. (Garcia Bacca, J.D.) Caracas, 1961.
Phil 4965.2   Elementos de filosofía moderna. (Diaz de Gamarra y Dávalos, J.B.) México, 1963.
Phil 196.6   Elementos de ideolojia. (Varas, J. Miguel y Marin.) Santiago de Chile, 1830.
Phil 187.34   Elementos de la filosofia del espiritu humano. (Marin, V.) Santiago, 1834.
Phil 187.34.5   Elementos de la filosofia del espiritu humano. 3d ed. (Marin, V.) Santiago, 1872.
Phil 5057.28   Elementos de lógica. (Reajifo, F.M.) Bogota, 1930.
Phil 5052.20   Elementos de lógica. 2a ed. (Mendive, José.) Valladolid, 1887.
Phil 6119.8   Elementos de neurobiología. (Jakob, C.) Buenos Aires, 1923.
Phil 193.89   Elementos de philosophia. 3a ed. (Sinibaldi, T.) Coimbra, 1906. 2v.
Phil 5259.5.25   Elementos de psicología. (Titchener, E.B.) Paris, 1913.
Phil 8414.12   Elementos filosóficos de la literatura. (Nunez de Arenas, I.) Madrid, 1858.
Phil 5251.17   Elementry laboratory course in psychology. (Lanfeld, H.S.) Boston, 1916.
Phil 3831.7   Les éléments cartésiens. (Léon, Albert.) Paris, 1907.
Phil 5251.70   Éléments d'anthropologie. (Lacroze, René.) Paris, 1966.
Phil 6060.36   Éléments de graphologie pratique. (Trillat, Raymond.) Paris, 1944.
Phil 8584.17   Éléments de la philosophie du ciel. Paris, 1806.

Phil 6060.1.15 — Les éléments de l'écriture descanailles. (Crepieux-Jamin, J.) Paris, 1923.
Phil 5051.6.5 — Eléments de logique formelle. (Luquet, G.H.) Paris, 1909.
Phil 8894.15 — Eléments de morale théoretique et pratique appliquée a la pédagogie. 2. éd. (Thouverez, Émile.) Paris, 1911.
Phil 8894.5 — Éléments de morale universelle. (Tiberghien, G.) Bruxelles, 1879.
Phil 175.11 — Éléments de philosophie. (Aulard, A.) Paris, 1869.
Phil 177.45 — Éléments de philosophie. (Charles, Émile.) Paris, 1884-85. 2v.
Phil 177.68.20 — Éléments de philosophie. (Chartier, Émile.) Paris, 1949.
Phil 2605.4.31 — Éléments de philosophie. (Fonsegrive, George L.) Paris, 1891-1892. 2v.
Phil 181.2.5 — Éléments de philosophie. (Gatien-Arnoult, A.) Toulouse, 1864.
Phil 2750.11.59 — Éléments de philosophie. (Maritain, Jacques.) Paris, 1921-23. 2v.
Phil 176.35 — Éléments de philosophie chretienne. (Bunot, Albert Louis.) Paris, 1869.
Phil 2668.65 — Éléments de philosophie scientifique. (Janet, Paul A.R.) Paris, 1890.
Phil 197.47 — Éléments de philosophie scientifique et...morale. (Worms, René.) Paris, 1891.
Phil 5242.20 — Éléments de psychologie. (Cardols, Joseph.) Namur, 1890.
Phil 5258.98 — Éléments de psychologie. (Surbled, Georges.) Paris, 1894.
Phil 5258.98.2 — Éléments de psychologie. 2e éd. (Surbled, Georges.) Paris, 1894.
Phil 5241.48 — Éléments de psychologie humaine. (Biervliet, Jules Jean van.) Gand, 1895.
Phil 5245.6 — Éléments de psychologie mathematique. (Filachou, J.É.) Montpelier, 1877.
Phil 3915.46 — Éléments de psychologie physiologique. (Wundt, Wilhelm.) Paris, 1886. 2v.
Phil 5070.20 — Elements des Glaubens. Inaug. Diss. (Wagner, Hans.) München, 193-.
Phil 8877.18 — Éléments d'instruction morale et civique. (Compayré, J.G.) Paris, 1882.
Phil 2905.1.330 — Éléments du bâti scientifique Teilhardien. (Barral, Louis Marie.) Monaco, 1964.
Phil 9035.26.2 — Les éléments du caractère. 2e éd. (Malapert, P.) Paris, 1906.
Phil 5055.29.20 — Éléments d'une théorie de l'argumentation. (Perelman, Chaim.) Bruxelles, 1968.
Phil 5242.21 — Elements in thought and emotion. (Campion, George G.) London, 1923.
Phil 3480.67.60 — Éléments métaphysique de la doctrine du droit. (Kant, Immanuel.) Paris, 1853.
Phil 5500.16 — Elements of a theory of human problem solving. (Newell, Allen.) Santa Monica, 1957.
Phil 190.78 — Elements of analytic philosophy. (Pap, Arthur.) N.Y., 1949.
Phil 5258.97.5 — Elements of analytical psychology. 5th. ed. (Stephen, Henry.) Calcutta, 1922.
Phil 9035.8.2 — The elements of character. (Ware, M.G. Chandler.) Boston, 1854.
Phil 187.27.9 — Elements of constructive philosophy. (Mackenzie, J.S.) London, 1917.
Phil 5045.2 — The elements of deductive logic. (Fowler, Thomas.) Oxford, 1867.
Phil 5050.17 — The elements of deductive logic. 4th ed. (Kyle, William M.) Brisbane, 1957.
Phil 6128.10 — Elements of electrobiology. (Smee, Alfred.) London, 1849.
Phil 332.15 — Elements of epistemology. (Barron, J.T.) N.Y., 1931.
Phil 8889.4 — Elements of ethical science. (Ogden, John.) Bismarck, N.D., 1891.
Phil 8878.21 — Elements of ethics. (Davis, Noals K.) Boston, 1900.
Phil 8882.25 — The elements of ethics. (Hyslop, J.H.) N.Y., 1895.
Phil 8962.9 — The elements of ethics. (Miltner, C.C.) N.Y., 1931.
Phil 8887.25.6 — The elements of ethics. (Muirhead, J.H.) London, 1910.
Phil 8887.25 — The elements of ethics. (Muirhead, J.H.) N.Y., 1892.
Phil 5251.32 — Elements of experimental psychology. (La Vaissière, J. de.) St. Louis, 1926.
Phil 3915.59 — Elements of folk psychology. (Wundt, Wilhelm.) London, 1916.
Phil 5047.47 — The elements of formal logic. (Hughes, G.E.) N.Y., 1965.
Phil 192.13 — Elements of general philosophy. (Robertson, G.C.) London, 1896.
Phil 1105.6 — The elements of Greek philosophy from Thales to Aristotle. (Appleton, R.B.) London, 1922.
Phil 6051.11 — Elements of hand-reading. (Phanos (pseud.).) London, 1903.
Phil 5262.20.5 — Elements of human psychology. (Warren, H.C.) Boston, 1922.
Phil 5262.20.7 — Elements of human psychology. (Warren, H.C.) Boston, 1930.
Phil 6691.1 — Elements of hypnotism. (Vincent, R.H.) London, 1893.
Phil 960.146 — The elements of Indian logic. 2d ed. (Astreya, B.L.) Benares, 1934.
Phil 5043.2.5 — Elements of inductive logic. (Davis, N.K.) N.Y., 1895.
Phil 5258.12 — Elements of intellectual philosophy. (Scott, R.E.) Edinburgh 1805.
Phil 5260.1 — Elements of intellectual philosophy. (Upham, T.C.) Portland, 1827.
Phil 5262.4 — Elements of intellectual philosophy. (Wayland, F.) Boston, 1854.
Phil 5262.4.9 — Elements of intellectual philosophy. (Wayland, F.) N.Y., 1865.
Phil 5262.6 — Elements of intellectual philosophy. (Winslow, H.) Boston, 1850.
Phil 5262.6.3 — Elements of intellectual philosophy. (Winslow, H.) Boston, 1856.
Phil 5255.5.9 — The elements of intellectual science. (Porter, Noah.) N.Y., 1872.
Phil 5040.21.5 — The elements of logic. (Abbott, F.K.) London, 1947.
Phil 4352.1.50 — Elements of logic. (Balmes, Jaime.) N.Y., 1880.
Phil 5041.91 — The elements of logic. (Barker, Stephen Francis.) N.Y., 1965.
Phil 5041.8 — Elements of logic. (Barron, William.) N.Y., 1856.
Phil 5042.30 — Elements of logic. (Churchman, C.W.) Phildelphia, 1940.
Phil 5042.4 — Elements of logic. (Coppée, Henry.) Philadelphia, 1858.
Phil 5042.4.2 — Elements of logic. (Coppée, Henry.) Philadelphia, 1860.
Phil 5043.3 — Elements of logic. (Day, Henry N.) N.Y., 1867.
Phil 5047.9 — Elements of logic. (Hyslop, J.H.) N.Y., 1892.
Phil 5051.24A — The elements of logic. (Latta, Robert.) London, 1929.
Phil 5058.10 — The elements of logic. (Shedden, T.) London, 1864.
Phil 5059.2 — Elements of logic. (Tappan, H.P.) N.Y., 1844.
Phil 5059.10 — The elements of logic. (True, C.K.) Boston, 1840.
Phil 5062.6.7.5 — Elements of logic. (Whately, Richard.) Boston, 1852.

Phil 5062.6.8.5 — Elements of logic. (Whately, Richard.) Boston, 1859.
Phil 5062.6 — Elements of logic. (Whately, Richard.) London, 1829.
Phil 5062.6.5 — Elements of logic. (Whately, Richard.) London, 1840.
Phil 5062.6.6 — Elements of logic. (Whately, Richard.) London, 1844.
Phil 5062.6.2 — Elements of logic. (Whately, Richard.) N.Y., 1832.
Phil 5062.6.3.5 — Elements of logic. (Whately, Richard.) N.Y., 1836.
Phil 5049.12.9 — Elements of logic as a science of propositions. (Jones, E.E.C.) Edinburgh, 1890.
Phil 5043.13.7 — The elements of logick. (Duncan, William.) Albany, 1811.
Phil 5043.13.2 — The elements of logick. (Duncan, William.) Edinburgh, 1776.
Phil 5043.13 — The elements of logick. (Duncan, William.) London, 1764.
Phil 5043.13.4 — The elements of logick. (Duncan, William.) N.Y., 1802.
Phil 5043.13.3 — The elements of logick. (Duncan, William.) Philadelphia, 1792.
Phil 5047.3.2 — Elements of logick. (Hedge, Levi.) Boston, 1818.
Phil 5047.3.5 — Elements of logick. (Hedge, Levi.) Boston, 1823.
Phil 5047.3.7 — Elements of logick. (Hedge, Levi.) Boston, 1835.
Phil 5047.3.12 — Elements of logick. (Hedge, Levi.) N.Y., 1841.
Phil 5066.268 — Elements of mathematical logic. (Kreisel, Georg.) Amsterdam, 1967.
Phil 5066.226 — Elements of mathematical logic. (Novikov, P.S.) Edinburgh, 1964.
Phil 5066.42 — The elements of mathematical logic. 1st ed. (Rosenbloom, P.C.) N.Y., 1950.
Phil 5051.28.5 — Elements of mathematical logic. 2nd ed. (Lukasiewicz, Jan.) Oxford, 1964.
Phil 8890.8 — Elements of mental and moral science. (Payne, G.) London, 1828.
Phil 5260.1.5 — Elements of mental philosophy. (Upham, T.C.) N.Y., 1841.
Phil 5260.1.8 — Elements of mental philosophy. (Upham, T.C.) N.Y., 1857.
Phil 5260.1.9 — Elements of mental philosophy. (Upham, T.C.) N.Y., 1859.
Phil 5260.1.2 — Elements of mental philosophy. (Upham, T.C.) Portland, 1831. 2v.
Phil 5260.1.4 — Elements of mental philosophy. 3. ed. (Upham, T.C.) Portland, 1839. 2v.
NEDL Phil 178.5.5 — Elements of metaphysics. (Deussen, P.) London, 1894. (Changed to KD 25702)
Htn Phil 194.11* — Elements of metaphysics. (Taylor, A.E.) London, 1903.
Phil 5241.22 — The elements of mind. (Brooks, H.J.) London, 1902.
Phil 8875.2 — Elements of moral philosophy. (Adams, J.) Cambridge, 1837.
Phil 8878.8 — Elements of moral philosophy. (Dewar, D.) London, 1826. 2v.
Phil 8890.4 — Elements of moral philosophy. (Parkhurst, J.L.) Boston, 1832.
Phil 8897.19 — Elements of moral philosophy. (Winslow, H.) N.Y., 1856.
Phil 8880.10 — The elements of moral philosophy. v.1-3. (Fordyce, D.) London, 1758.
Phil 8893.55.2 — The elements of moral philosophy. 2. ed. (Seu, Mohit C.) London, 1913.
Phil 1860.60 — Elements of moral science. (Beattie, James.) Philadelphia, 1792-94. 2v.
Phil 8890.20.1 — Elements of moral science. (Porter, N.) N.Y., 1885.
Phil 8890.20 — Elements of moral science. (Porter, N.) N.Y., 1885.
Phil 8897.6 — Elements of moral science. (Wayland, F.) Boston, 1835.
Phil 8897.6.3 — The elements of moral science. (Wayland, F.) Boston, 1838.
Phil 8897.6.5 — The elements of moral science. (Wayland, F.) Boston, 1859.
Phil 8897.6.7 — The elements of moral science. (Wayland, F.) Boston, 1872.
Phil 8897.6.15 — The elements of moral science. (Wayland, F.) Cambridge, Mass., 1963.
Phil 8897.6.2 — The elements of moral science. (Wayland, F.) N.Y., 1835.
Phil 8897.6.20 — The elements of moral science. (Wayland, F.) Rangoon, 1885.
Phil 8897.6.10 — The elements of moral science. Abridged. (Wayland, F.) Boston, 1848.
Phil 1860.60.5 — Elements of moral science. v.1-2. (Beattie, James.) Baltimore, 1813.
Phil 1860.10.3 — Elements of moral science. Works 7-9. (Beattie, James.) Philadelphia, 1809. 3v.
Phil 8893.96 — Elements of morality. (Saltzmann, C.G.) Baltimore, 1811.
Phil 8897.14.1 — Elements of morality. (Whewell, W.) N.Y., 185-? 2v.
Phil 8897.14.2 — Elements of morality. (Whewell, W.) N.Y., 1854. 2v.
NEDL Phil 8897.14.5 — Elements of morality. 4th ed. (Whewell, W.) Cambridge, 1864.
Phil 8884.21 — Elements of morals. (Janet, Paul.) N.Y., 1884.
Phil 8887.44 — The elements of morals. 2. ed. (Mitra, Ambika C.) Calcutta, 1914.
Phil 6124.6 — Elements of neurophysiology. (Ochs, Sidney.) N.Y., 1965.
Phil 6962.3 — Elements of pathology of human mind. (Mayo, T.) London, 1838.
Htn Phil 2045.62* — Elements of philosophy. (Hobbes, Thomas.) London, 1656.
Phil 185.68 — Elements of philosophy. (Kattsoff, L.O.) N.Y., 1953.
Phil 5047.5 — Elements of philosophy comprising logic, ontology or general metaphysics. (Hill, Walter H.) Baltimore, 1884.
Phil 5922.4.25 — Elements of phrenology. (Combe, George.) Philadelphia, 1826.
Phil 5925.5 — Elements of phrenology. (Forman, J.G.) Cincinnati, 1844.
Phil 5251.1.15.3 — Elements of physiological psychology. (Ladd, G.T.) London, 1889.
Phil 5251.1.15 — Elements of physiological psychology. (Ladd, G.T.) N.Y., 1887.
NEDL Phil 5251.1.15.8 — Elements of physiological psychology. (Ladd, G.T.) N.Y., 1896.
Phil 5251.1.18 — Elements of physiological psychology. (Ladd, G.T.) N.Y., 1911.
Phil 5251.1.22 — Elements of physiology, psychology. (Ladd, G.T.) N.Y., 1911.
Phil 6311.5 — The elements of practical psychoanalysis. (Bousfield, Paul.) London, 1920.
Phil 5241.3.15 — Elements of psychology. (Baldwin, J.M.) N.Y., 1893.
Phil 3100.55 — The elements of psychology. (Beneke, F.E.) London, 1871.
Phil 2496.50.5 — Elements of psychology. (Cousin, Victor.) Hartford, 1834.
Phil 2496.50 — Elements of psychology. (Cousin, Victor.) N.Y., 1838.
Phil 2496.50.4 — Elements of psychology. (Cousin, Victor.) N.Y., 1855.
X Cg 2496.50.3 — Elements of psychology. (Cousin, Victor.) N.Y., 1856.
Phil 5243.27 — Elements of psychology. (Davis, N.K.) N.Y., 1892.
Phil 5243.3 — Elements of psychology. (Day, H.N.) N.Y., 1876.
Phil 5243.15.7 — Elements of psychology. (Dunlap, K.) St. Louis, 1936.
Phil 5247.57 — Elements of psychology. (Hill, D.J.) N.Y., 1888.
Phil 5250.45.2 — Elements of psychology. (Krech, David.) N.Y., 1965.
Phil 5252.86 — The elements of psychology. (Major, David R.) Columbus, 1913.
Phil 5252.17 — Elements of psychology. (Mellone, Sydney Herbert.) Edinburgh, 1907.

Phil 5257.7   Elements of psychology. (Robertson, G.C.) London, 1896.
Phil 5259.7.5   The elements of psychology. (Thorndike, E.L.) N.Y., 1905.
Phil 5252.9   Elements of psychology. pt. 1. Photoreproduction. (Morell, J.D.) London, 1853.
Phil 5241.86.5   Elements of psychology. 2. ed. (Barrett, J.F.) Milwaukee, 1931.
Phil 5259.7.6   The elements of psychology. 2d ed. (Thorndike, E.L.) N.Y., 1905.
Phil 2496.50.2   Elements of psychology. 3e éd. (Cousin, Victor.) N.Y., 1842.
Phil 5243.15.5   The elements of scientific psychology. (Dunlap, K.) St. Louis, 1922.
Phil 5066.26   Elements of symbolic logic. (Reichenbach, H.) N.Y., 1947.
Phil 3504.5   Elements of the critical philosophy...Kant. (Willich, A.F.M.) London, 1798.
Phil 2275.34   Elements of the philosophy of the human mind. (Stewart, D.) Boston, 1814-27. 3v.
Phil 2275.50   Elements of the philosophy of the human mind. (Stewart, D.) Boston, 1854.
Phil 2275.50.2   Elements of the philosophy of the human mind. (Stewart, D.) Boston, 1855.
Phil 2275.37   Elements of the philosophy of the human mind. (Stewart, D.) Boston, 1866.
Phil 2275.33   Elements of the philosophy of the human mind. (Stewart, D.) Brattleborough, 1808.
Phil 2275.33.2   Elements of the philosophy of the human mind. (Stewart, D.) Brattleborough, 1813.
Phil 2275.35   Elements of the philosophy of the human mind. (Stewart, D.) Cambridge, 1829. 2v.
Phil 2275.30   Elements of the philosophy of the human mind. (Stewart, D.) London, 1792.
Phil 2275.31.5   Elements of the philosophy of the human mind. (Stewart, D.) London, 1802.
Phil 2275.36   Elements of the philosophy of the human mind. (Stewart, D.) London, 1843.
Htn   Phil 2275.34.6*   Elements of the philosophy of the human mind. (Stewart, D.) N.Y., 1818. 2v.
Phil 2275.34.5   Elements of the philosophy of the human mind. (Stewart, D.) N.Y., 1818. 2v.
Phil 2275.31   Elements of the philosophy of the human mind. (Stewart, D.) Philadelphia, 1793.
Phil 2275.34.15   Elements of the philosophy of the human mind. v.1-2. (Stewart, D.) Albany, 1822.
Phil 2275.34.11   Elements of the philosophy of the human mind. v.1-2. (Stewart, D.) Boston, 1821.
Phil 2275.35.2   Elements of the philosophy of the human mind. v.1-2. (Stewart, D.) Cambridge, 1829.
Phil 2275.32   Elements of the philosophy of the human mind. v.2. (Stewart, D.) Boston, 1814.
Phil 176.16   Elements of the philosophy of the mind. (Belsham, T.) London, 1801.
Phil 5249.4   Elements of the psychology of cognition. (Jardine, R.) London, 1874.
Phil 8876.33   Elements of the science of ethics. (Bruce, J.) London, 1786.
Phil 8599.11   Elements of the science of religion. (Tiele, C.P.) Edinburgh, 1897-99. 2v.
Phil 978.23.3   The elements of theosophy. (Edger, L.) London, 1907.
Phil 104.1   Elements of thought. (Taylor, I.) London, 1843.
Phil 104.1.5   Elements of thought. (Taylor, I.) London, 1863.
Phil 104.1.9   Elements of thought. 2nd American ed. (Taylor, I.) N.Y., 1851.
Phil 8888.13   Éléments pour une éthique. 1st ed. (Nabert, Jean.) Paris, 1943.
Phil 8880.24   Les elements sociologiques de la morale. (Fouillée, Alfred.) Paris, 1905.
Phil 185.49   Elementy. (Kotarbiński, Tadeusz.) Lwów, 1929.
Phil 5051.28   Elementy logiki matematycznej. (Lukasiewicz, Jan.) Warszawa, 1929.
Phil 5066.308   Elementy matematicheskoi logiki i teorii mnozhestva. (Penzov, Inrii E.) Saratov, 1968.
Phil 5585.67   Elementy mysli. (Sechenov, I.M.) Moskva, 1943.
Phil 185.49.2   Elementy teorii poznania. Wyd. 2. (Kotarbiński, Tadeusz.) Wrocław, 1961.
Phil 310.736   Das Elend der kritischen Theorie. Theodor W. Adorno, Herbert Marcuse, Jürgen Habermas. (Rohrmoser, Günter.) Freiburg, 1970.
Phil 8665.18.1   Das Elend des Christentums. (Kahl, Joachim.) Reinbek bei Hamburg, 1969.
Phil 8879.17   Eleutheropoulos, A. Die Sittlichkeit und der philosophische Sittlichkeitswahn. Berlin, 1899.
Phil 8405.5   Eleutheropoulos, Abroleäs. Das Schöne. Berlin, 1905.
Phil 1704.2   Eleutheropulos, A. Einführung in eine wissenschaftliche Philosophie. Leipzig, 1906.
Phil 285.3   Eleutheropulos, A. Die exakten Grundlagen der Naturphilosophie. Stuttgart, 1926.
Phil 3450.7.81   Eleutheropulos, A. Max Heinze. Leipzig, 1909.
Phil 179.26   Eleutheropulos, A. Philosophie: allgemeine Weltanschauung. Zürich, 1911.
Phil 1109.1   Eleutheropulos, A. Philosophie und der Lebensauffassung der Griechtens. Berlin, 1900-01. 2v.
Phil 1109.1.5   Eleutheropulos, A. Die Philosophie und der sozialen Züstande (materielle und ideele Entwicklung) des Greichentums. 3e Aufl. Zürich, 1915.
Phil 1704.2.5   Eleutheropulos, A. Die Philosophie und die Lebensauffassung der germanisch-romanischen Völker. Berlin, 1901.
Phil 7054.106.5   Eleven days at Moravia. (Hazard, T.R.) Boston, 1872.
Phil 8584.22   Eley, A.S. God's own image. Luton, 1963.
Phil 3450.11.275   Eley, Lathan. Die Krise des a priori in der Transzendentalen. Den Haag, 1762.
Phil 5069.4   Eley, Lothar. Metakritik der formalen Logik. Den Haag, 1969.
Phil 3235.138   Élez, Iovo. Problema bytiia i myshleniia v filosofii Liudirga Feienbakha. Moskva, 1971.
Phil 3565.112   Elgström, Albin. Hermann Lotzes uppfattning af människans valfrihet. Lund, 1892.
Phil 285.6.2   Eliade, Mircea. Cosmos and history. N.Y., 1970.
Phil 285.6.5   Eliade, Mircea. Kosmos und Geschichte. Hamburg, 1966[1953]
Phil 285.6   Eliade, Mircea. The myth of the eternal return. N.Y., 1954.
Phil 285.6.1   Eliade, Mircea. Le mythe de l'eternel retour. Paris, 1969.
Phil 4967.10   Elias de Tejada, Francisco. Las doctrinas políticas de Raimundo de Farias Brito. Sevilla, 1953.
Phil 335.6   Elie, H. Le complexe significabile. Paris, 1936.
Phil 335.6.2   Elie, H. Le complexe significabile. Thèse. Paris, 1936.

Phil 2655.3   Élie Halévy. (Paris. École Libre des Sciences Politiques.) Paris, 1937.
Phil 9575.2   Eliot, C.W. Great riches. N.Y., 1906.
Phil 8879.2.3   Eliot, C.W. The happy life. N.Y., 1896.
Phil 8879.2.5   Eliot, C.W. The happy life. N.Y., 1896.
Phil 8879.2.9   Eliot, C.W. The happy life. N.Y., 1896.
Phil 8879.2A   Eliot, C.W. The happy life. N.Y., 1896-97.
Phil 8879.2.12   Eliot, C.W. The happy life. N.Y., 1905.
Phil 8584.7   Eliot, C.W. The religion of the future. Berlin, 1909.
Phil 8584.7.5   Eliot, C.W. The religion of the future. Boston, 1935.
Phil 9490.8   Eliot, C.W. The training for an effective life. Boston, 1915.
Phil 1885.94.2   Eliot, T.S. Knowledge and experience in the philosophy of F.H. Bradley. London, 1964.
Phil 1885.94   Eliot, T.S. Knowledge and experience in the philosophy of F.H. Bradley. N.Y., 1964.
Phil 9344.2   Eliot, W.G. Lectures to young men. St. Louis, 1852.
Phil 9344.2.3   Eliot, W.G. Lectures to young men. 6th ed. Boston, 1856.
Phil 9344.2.5   Eliot, W.G. Lectures to young women. Boston, 1860.
Htn   Phil 8659.3*   Elis, C. The folly of atheism. London, 1692.
Phil 5853.12   Elite and specialized interviewing. (Dexter, Lewis Anthony.) Evanston, 1970.
Phil 3640.585   Elitebildung durch agonale Auslese. (Troenle, Ludwig.) Wien, 1958.
Phil 7069.61.15   Elizabethan episode. (Roberts, D.O.) London, 1961.
Phil 8879.35.5   Elken, Rober. Ethik naturwissenschaftlich Fundiert und Kirche. Kassel, 1968.
Phil 8879.35   Elken, Robert. Konsequenzen der Naturwissenschaft. Kassel, 1963.
Phil 5238.238   El'kin, David G. Konspekt lektsii po psikhologii. v.3. Odessa, 1966.
Phil 2050.95   Elkin, W.B. Hume. Ithaca, 1904.
Phil 5865.5.40   Elkind, David. Children and adolescents. N.Y., 1970.
Phil 525.46   Elkinton, J. The light of mysticism. Philadelphia, 1907.
Phil 8735.11   Elkus, S.A. The concept of control. N.Y., 1907.
Phil 1750.420   Ell, Johannes. Der Existenzialismus in seinem Wesen und Werden. Bonn, 1955.
Phil 5244.18   Ellefsen, Olaf. Om moralens oprindelse. Kristiania, 1893.
Phil 5545.183   Ellenberger, F. Le mystère de la mémoire. Genève, 1947.
Phil 6906.10   Ellenberger, Henri F. The discovery of the unconscious. N.Y., 1970.
Phil 3640.198.15   Ellermann, H. Nietzsche und Klages. Inaug. Diss. Hamburg, 1933.
Phil 2138.148   Ellery, J.B. John Stuart Mill. N.Y., 1964.
Phil 6980.259   Ellery, R.S. Psychiatric aspects of modern warfare. Melbourne, 1945.
Phil 6954.7   Ellery, Reginald S. Schizophrenia, the Cinderella of psychiatry. Sidney, 1941.
Phil 6954.7.5   Ellery, Reginald S. Schizophrenia, the Cinderella of psychiatry. Sydney, 1944.
Phil 5642.19   Ellinger, A. Über Doppelempfindung. Diss. Stuttgart, 1889.
Phil 9558.3   Ellinger, G. Verhältniss der offentlichen Meinung zu Wahrheit und Lüge. Berlin, 1884.
Phil 4941.9   To Ellinikon ethnos ke i sighxroni epoxi. (Kriezes, T.A.) Athena, 1958.
Phil 8659.7   Elliot, George. God is spirit, God is love. London, 1895.
Phil 9035.70   Elliot, H.S.R. Human character. London, 1922.
Phil 2270.120   Elliot, Hugh S.R. Herbert Spencer. London, 1917.
Phil 8954.4   Elliot, W.H. As I was saying. London, 1944?
Phil 8954.4.5   Elliot, W.H. Bring me my bow. London, 1946.
Phil 2475.1.415   Elliots, Hugh Samuel Roger. Modern science and the illusions of Professor Bergson. London, 1912.
Phil 6674.5   Elliotson, John. The Harveian oration. London, 1846.
Phil 1750.151   Elliott, George R. Humanism and imagination. Chapel Hill, 1938.
Phil 5640.14   Elliott, John. Philosophical observations on the senses. London, 1780.
Phil 8629.3   Elliott, W.H. Rendezvous; the life that some call death. London, 1942.
Phil 6114.16   Ellis, Albert. How to line with a neurotic. N.Y., 1957.
Phil 2255.10.80   Ellis, Albert. Is objectivism a religion? N.Y., 1968.
Phil 705.42   Ellis, Charles Mayo. An essay on transcendentalism, 1842. Gainesville, 1954.
Htn   Phil 9344.7*   Ellis, Clement. The gentile sinner. Oxford, 1660.
Phil 7150.59   Ellis, E.R. Traitor within: our suicide problem. 1st ed. Garden City, N.Y., 1961.
Phil 2055.2.81   Ellis, Edith M. James Hinton. London, 1918.
Phil 5924.1   Ellis, G.W. Synopsis of phrenology. Boston, 1844.
Phil 1980.3.95A   Ellis, H. My life; autobiography of Havelock Ellis. Boston, 1939.
Phil 5425.18.5A   Ellis, H. A study of British genius. Boston, 1926.
Phil 5425.18   Ellis, H. Study of British genius. London, 1904.
Phil 179.17   Ellis, Havelock. The dance of life. Boston, 1923.
Phil 179.17.5   Ellis, Havelock. The dance of life. Boston, 1926.
Phil 179.17.15   Ellis, Havelock. The dance of life. Boston, 1929.
Phil 179.17.4   Ellis, Havelock. The dance of life. N.Y., 1923.
Phil 179.17.20   Ellis, Havelock. The dance of life. N.Y., 1929.
Phil 179.17.18   Ellis, Havelock. The dance of life. N.Y., 1929.
Phil 9495.29   Ellis, Havelock. Essays in war-time. 1st series. Boston, 1917.
Phil 9495.29.10   Ellis, Havelock. The philosophy of conflict. 2nd series. Boston, 1919.
Phil 9495.29.5   Ellis, Havelock. The philosophy of conflict. 2nd series. London, 1919.
Phil 7082.160   Ellis, Havelock. The world of dreams. Boston, 1911.
Phil 1980.3.79   Pamphlet box. Ellis, Havelock.
Phil 8584.2   Ellis, J. The knowledge of divine things from revelation. London, 1743.
Phil 8584.2.2   Ellis, J. The knowledge of divine things from revelation. London, 1747.
Phil 8584.2.3   Ellis, J. The knowledge of divine things from revelation. London, 1771.
Phil 9344.6   Ellis, John. Deterioration of the Puritan stock. N.Y., 1884.
Phil 8610.882   Ellis, John. Skepticism and divine relation. N.Y., 1882.
Phil 9164.1   Ellis, S. Stickney. The wives of England. N.Y., 1843.
Phil 9164.1.2   Ellis, S. Stickney. The wives of England. N.Y., 1843.
Phil 8879.4   Ellis, S.S. At our best. Boston, 1873.
Phil 9344.3   Ellis, S.S. Daughters of England. N.Y., 1843.
Phil 8879.3.5   Ellis, S.S. Guide to social happiness. v.1-2. N.Y., 1844-47.
Phil 9344.3.5   Ellis, S.S. Mothers of England. N.Y., 1844. 7 pam.
Phil 9344.3.7   Ellis, S.S. The woman of England. N.Y., 1843.
Phil 8879.3.2   Ellis, S.S. The women of England. v.1-2. Philadelphia, 1839.
Phil 8879.3   Ellis, S.S. The women of England. v.1-4. N.Y., 1843.
Phil 665.67   Ellis, W. The idea of the soul. London, 1940.

Phil 5725.1 — Ellis, W. Outlines of the history and formation of...understanding. London, 1847.

Phil 9070.17 — Ellis, William J. Studies of man. London, 1874.

Phil 5244.22 — Ellis, Willis D. Gestalt psychology and meaning. Berkeley, 1930.

Phil 5244.22.5 — Ellis, Willis D. A source book of Gestalt. London, 1950.

Phil 3585.9.81 — Ellissen, O.A. Friedrich Albert Lange. Leipzig, 1891.

Phil 3585.9.80 — Ellissen, O.A. Friedrich Albert Lange. Leipzig, 1894.

Phil 6114.14 — Ellsworth, P. Health and power. Holyoke, Mass., 1915.

Phil 8954.10 — Ellul, Jacques. Violence. N.Y., 1969.

Phil 8584.6 — Ellwood, C.A. The reconstruction of religion. N.Y., 1922.

Phil 804.1 — Elmendorf, J.J. Outlines of lectures on history of philosophy. N.Y., 1876.

Phil 5335.4 — Elms, Alan C. Role playing, reward, and attitude change. N.Y., 1969.

Phil 2750.20.10 — Eloge de la philosophie. (Merleau-Ponty, Maurice.) Paris, 1953.

Phil 2750.20.11 — Eloge de la philosophie. (Merleau-Ponty, Maurice.) Paris, 1962.

Phil 2750.8.91 — Éloge de M. Moreau de Maupertuis. (Tressan, Louis Elisabeth de la Vergne.) Nancy, 17- .

Htn Phil 2520.172* — Eloge de René Descartes. (Thomas, A.L.) Paris, 1765. 2 pam.

Htn Phil 2404.1* — Eloges de trois philosophes. London, 1753.

Phil 193.164 — Elogia della sapienza. (Sadoleto, J.) Napoli, 1950.

Phil 196.29.3 — Elogio de la vigilia. (Vassallo, Angel.) Buenos Aires, 1939.

Phil 4210.126 — Elogio di Antonio Rosmini letto l'11 giugno 1863 all'Accademia degli Eutelet. (Brogialdi, Adolfo.) Firenze, 1863.

Phil 8643.3.10 — Elpizon, oder Über meine Fortdauer im Tode. 3. Aufl. (Sintenis, F.) Köln, 1811. 6v.

Phil 179.32 — Elrick, C.F. Tertium quid; ratiocination. St. Louis, 1934.

Phil 585.402 — Els mots i els homes. 1. ed. (Ferrater Mora, Jose.) Barcelona, 1970.

Phil 5244.14 — Elsas, Adolf. Über die Psychophysik. Marburg, 1886.

Phil 5258.7.80 — Elschenbroich, Adalbert. Romantische Sehnsucht und Kosmogonie. Tübingen, 1971.

Phil 1170.7 — Elsee, Charles. Neoplatonism in relation to Christianity; an essay. Cambridge, 1908.

Phil 179.13 — Elsenhans, T. Die Aufgabe einer Psychologie der Deutung als Vorarbeit für die Geisteswissenschaften. Giessen, 1904.

Phil 3260.83 — Elsenhans, Theodor. Fries und Kant. v.1-2. Giessen, 1906.

Phil 3486.11 — Elsenhans, Theodor. Kants Rassentheorie und ihre bleibende Bedeutung. Leipzig, 1904.

Phil 5244.10.6 — Elsenhans, Theodor. Lehrbuch der Psychologie. Tübingen, 1920.

Phil 5244.10.9 — Elsenhans, Theodor. Lehrbuch der Psychologie. 3e Aufl. Tübingen, 1937-1938.

Phil 5244.10 — Elsenhans, Theodor. Psychologie und Logik. 5e Aufl. Berlin, 1920.

Phil 5244.10.10 — Elsenhans, Theodor. Selbstbeobachtung und Experiment in der Psychologie. Freiburg, 1897.

Phil 5244.6 — Elsenhaus, T. Psychologie und Logik. Leipzig, 1898.

Phil 89.5.3 — Elseviers filosofische en psychologische encyclopedie. 3. Druk. Amsterdam, 1966.

Phil 3486.6 — Elsmann, W. Begriff des höchsten Gutes bei Kant und Schleiermacher. Leipzig, 1887.

Phil 9344.10 — Elson, F.S. Quiet hints to ministers' wives. Boston, 1934.

Phil 5871.72 — Eltern, Kind und Neurose. 2. Aufl. (Richter, Horst Eberhard.) Stuttgart, 1967.

Phil 8400.18 — Elton, William. Aesthetics and language. Oxford, 1954.

Phil 6115.11.20 — Eltz-Hoffmann, L. Feuchtersleben. Salzburg, 1956.

Phil 6121.60 — The elusive mind; based on the first series of the Gifford lectures. (Lewis, Hywel David.) London, 1969.

Phil 3450.11.470 — Elveton, R.O. The phenomenology of Husserl. Chicago, 1970.

Phil 8584.14 — Elving, S. Five books of Joses, a catechism of rational religion. Newllano, La., 1930.

Phil 2340.10.102 — Ely, Stephen Lee. The religious availability of Whitehead's God. Madison, 1942.

Phil 4803.360.30 — Elzenberg, Henryk. Kłopot z istnieniem. Kraków, 1963.

Phil 4803.360.20 — Elzenberg, Henryk. Proby kontaktu; eseje i studia krytyczme. Kraków, 1966.

Phil 7069.08.50 — Die Emanation der psychophysischen Energie. (Kotik, N.) Wiesbaden, 1908.

Htn Phil 6115.18.5* — Emancipation. (Fletcher, Horace.) Chicago, 1895.

Phil 6128.17F — Emannuel Swedenborg's investigations in natural science and the basis for his statements concerning the functions of the brain. (Ramström, M.) Uppsala, 1910.

Phil 3484.10 — Emanuele Kant. v.1,3. (Cantoni, Carlo.) Milano, 1879-84. 2v.

Phil 3484.10.2 — Emanuele Kant. 2. ed. (Cantoni, Carlo.) Milano, 1907.

Phil 5203.20 — Emanuilova, E. Suvremenna materialisticheska psikhologiia. Sofiia, 1959.

Phil 8597.64 — Emanzipation und Freiheit. (Rohrmoser, Günter.) München, 1970.

Phil 5257.56 — Az emberi elme. (Ranschburg, Pál.) Budapest, 1923. 2v.

Phil 6131.10 — The embodied mind. (Vesey, Godfrey Norman A.) London, 1965.

Phil 285.4 — Embry, J. The Namic philosophy. N.Y., 1951.

Phil 6834.4 — Emde Boas, Coenrad van. Essays in erotiek. Amsterdam, 1969.

Phil 176.122.10 — The emergence of life. (Burke, J.B.) London, 1931.

Phil 187.29.15A — The emergence of novelty. (Morgan, C.L.) London, 1933.

Phil 2050.265 — The emergence of philosophy of religion. (Collins, James Daniel.) New Haven, 1967.

Phil 181.118 — The emergence of the modern mind. (Gruber, F.C.) Philadelphia, 1958.

Phil 2150.9 — Emergent evolution...the philosophy of C. Lloyd Morgan. (Ralston, H.J.) Boston, 1933.

Phil 365.12 — Emergent evolution. (Morgan, Conwy L.) London, 1923.

Phil 4260.87.5 — Emerico Amari in seinern Verhaltmiss zu G.B. Vico. (Werner, K.) Wien, 1880.

Phil 6314.1 — Emerson, L.E. Nervousness; its causes, treatment and prevention. Boston, 1918.

Htn Phil 1980.2.35* — Emerson, R.W. Essays. London, 1841.

Htn Phil 1980.2.30* — Emerson, R.W. Nature. Boston, 1836.

Phil 199.3 — Emerson and beyond. (Yerington, William.) Columbus, Ohio, 1929.

Phil 4210.185 — Emery, Cuthbert Joseph. Rosmini on human rights. London, 1957.

Phil 4210.185.5 — Emery, Cuthbert Joseph. The Rosminians. London, 1960.

Phil 3552.251 — Emery, J.A. Esprit de Leibnitz. Lyon, 1772. 2v.

Phil 3552.251.5 — Emery, J.A. Pensées de Leibnitz sur la religion. Paris, 1803. 2v.

Phil 8694.3 — Emery, J.A. Quelques lettres au physicien G.L. Le Sage. Paris, 1916.

Phil 2404.4 — Emery, Leon. De Montaigne à Teilhard de Chardin via Pascal et Rousseau. Lyon, 1965.

Phil 3425.248 — Emge, C.A. Hegels Logik und die Gegenwart. Karlsruhe, 1927.

Phil 8584.13 — Emge, Carl A. Der philosophische Gehalt der religiösen Dogmatik. München, 1929.

Phil 3808.220 — Emge, Carl August. Gedachtnisschrift für Arthur Schopenhauer zur 150. Wiederkehr seines Geburtstages. Berlin, 1938.

Phil 165.300 — Emge, Carl August. Kreise um Schopenhauer. Wiesbaden, 1962.

Phil 3585.30.5 — Emil Lask in der Auseinander-Setzung mit Heinrich Rickert. (Sommerhäuser, Hanspeter.) Berlin, 1965.

Phil 2477.1.140 — Émile Boutroux et la pensée religieuse. (Baillot, A.) Paris, 1957.

Phil 7140.116.50 — Emile Coué, the man and his work. (Macnaghten, H.) N.Y., 1922.

Phil 7140.116.80 — Émile Coué: sa méthode, son esprit, son influence. Paris, 1928.

Phil 7140.116.51 — Emile Coué and his life-work. (Baudouin, C.) N.Y., 1923.

Phil 2750.10.110 — Emile Meyerson. (Marcucci, Silvestro.) Torino, 1962.

Phil 530.55.7 — Emilie, Sister. Une âme mystique au temps présent. v.1-2. Louvain, 1926-27.

Phil 2477.1.130 — Emilio Boutroux y la filosofía universitaria en Francia. (Ingenieros, José.) Buenos Aires, 1923.

Htn Phil 4931.3.80* — Emlekkönyv Alexander Bernat hatvanadík születése napjára. (Dénes, Lajos.) Budapest, 1910.

Phil 8658.11 — Emma Livingston, infidel's daughter. (Dayton, A.C.) Nashville, Tenn., 1861.

Phil 2750.22.95 — Emmanuel Mounier, sa vie, son oeuvre, avec un exposé de sa philosophie. (Conilh, Jean.) Paris, 1966.

Phil 2750.22.90 — Emmanuel Mounier. (Guissard, L.) Paris, 1962.

Phil 2750.22.80 — Emmanuel Mounier. (Moix, Candide.) Paris, 1960.

Phil 6116.20 — The emmanuel movement, 1906-1929. (Greene, John G.) n.p., 1934.

Phil 6125.11 — The Emmanuel movement in a New England town. (Powell, Hyman R.) N.Y., 1909.

Phil 3501.14 — Emmanuele Kant. (Troilo, E.) Roma, 1924.

Phil 9530.33 — Emmel, Paul W. Experience, or A post-graduate course in life. Philadelphia, 1931.

Phil 179.19 — Emmelin, Axel. Enhets- och mangfaldsproblemet inom metfysiken. Lund, 1905.

Phil 585.15 — Emmet, D.M. Function. London, 1958.

Phil 179.33.5 — Emmet, D.M. The nature of metaphysical thinking. London, 1945.

Phil 179.33 — Emmet, D.M. Philosophy and faith. London, 1936.

Phil 2340.10.90A — Emmet, Dorothy M. Whitehead's philosophy of organism. London, 1932.

Phil 8879.40 — Emmet, Dorothy Mary. Rules, roles, and relations. N.Y., 1966.

Phil 5044.9 — Emmet, Eric Revell. Thinking clearly. N.Y., 1962.

Phil 6954.2.5 — Emminghaus, H. Allgemeine Psychopathologie. Leipzig, 1878.

Phil 6954.2 — Emminghaus, H. Die psychischen Störungen. Tübingen, 1887.

Phil 7054.120 — Emmons, S.B. The spirit land. Philadelphia, 1857.

Phil 5400.169 — Emoções e felicidade. (Vieira, Manuel.) Lisboa, 1964.

Phil 5400.155 — Emotion. (Hillman, J.) London, 1960.

Phil 5400.114 — L'émotion. 1. éd. (Forti, E.) Paris, 1952.

Phil 5400.167 — Emotion::bodily change, an enduring problem in psychology. (Canolland, D.K.) Princeton, 1962.

Phil 5400.55 — Emotion and endocrine activities. (Rikimaru, J.) n.p., 1924.

Phil 6969.6 — Emotion and insanity. (Thalbitzer, S.) London, 1926.

Phil 5400.145 — Emotion and personality. (Arnold, Magda B.) N.Y., 1960. 2v.

Phil 5400.101 — Emotion in man and animal. (Young, Paul T.) N.Y., 1943.

Phil 2880.8.150 — Emotion in thought of Sartre. (Fell, Joseph P.) N.Y., 1965.

Phil 5403.1.3 — The emotion of joy. (Dearborn, Gran N.) N.Y., 1899.

Phil 5252.84 — Emotional factors in learning. (Murphy, L.B.) N.Y., 1945.

Phil 5252.84.2 — Emotional factors in learning. (Murphy, L.B.) N.Y., 1946.

Phil 5590.420 — Emotional maturity. (Saul, Leon J.) Philadelphia, 1947.

Phil 6314.7.4 — Emotional problems of living. (English, Oliver Spurgeon.) N.Y., 1945.

Phil 6314.7.5 — Emotional problems of living. (English, Oliver Spurgeon.) N.Y., 1955.

Phil 5592.198 — Emotionalität und Wahrnehmung. (Hauss, Kurt.) Göttingen, 1970.

Phil 5400.185 — The emotions, morality and the brain. (Monakow, Constantin.) Washington, 1925.

Phil 2880.8.46 — The emotions, outline of a theory. (Sartre, Jean Paul.) N.Y., 1948.

Phil 5400.50.20A — The emotions. (Lange, C.G.) Baltimore, 1922.

Phil 2125.55 — The emotions. (McCosh, James.) N.Y., 1880.

Phil 5400.95 — Emotions and bodily changes. (Dunbar, H.F.) N.Y., 1938.

Phil 5400.160 — Emotions and emotional disorders. (Gellhorn, Ernest.) N.Y., 1963.

Phil 5400.100 — Emotions and memory. (Rapaport, David.) Baltimore, 1942.

Phil 5400.106 — Emotions and reason. (McGill, V.J.) Springfield, 1954.

Phil 5241.2.10 — The emotions and the will. (Bain, A.) London, 1865.

Phil 5241.2.13 — The emotions and the will. (Bain, A.) N.Y., 1886.

Phil 5241.2.10.15 — The emotions and the will. 3. ed. (Bain, A.) N.Y., 1875.

Phil 5400.38 — Les émotions chez les sujets en état d'hypnotisme. (Luys, Jules.) Paris, 1887.

Phil 5873.2 — Les émotions et la personnalité de l'enfant. Thèse. (Malrieu, Philippe.) Paris, 1952.

Phil 5873.2.2 — Les émotions et la personnalité de l'enfant. 2. éd. (Malrieu, Philippe.) Paris, 1967.

Phil 5241.2.15 — Le émotions et la volonté. 3e éd. (Bain, A.) Paris, 1885.

Phil 5400.27 — Les émotions et les états organiques. (Chabrier.) Paris, 1911.

Phil 5400.79 — Emotions of men. (Lund, Frederick H.) N.Y., 1930.

Phil 5400.79.5 — Emotions of men. (Lund, Frederick H.) N.Y., 1930.

Phil 5400.66 — Emotions of normal people. (Marston, W.M.) London, 1928.

Phil 735.165 — Emotive propositions. (Halldén, Sören.) Stockholm, 1954.

Phil 5400.62 — Le emozioni e la vita del subcosciente. (Ferrari, G.C.) Bologna, 1921.

Phil 2885.85 — Empart, L. L'empirisme et le naturalisme contemporain. Paris, 1870.

Phil 5415.11 — Empathies et connaissance d'autrui. (Maucorps, P.H.) Paris, 1960.

Phil 5421.15.5 — Empathy, its nature and uses. (Katz, R.L.) N.Y., 1963.

Phil 3120.22 — Empedokles, oder das Sakrament des freien Todes. (Blüher, Hans.) n.p., 1918.

Phil 5585.7   Empfinden und Denken. (Rau, A.) Giessen, 1896.
Phil 510.17   Empfindung und Bewusstsein. (Carneri, Bartolomäus von.) Bonn, 1893.
Phil 510.17.5   Empfindung und Bewusstsein. 2e Aufl. (Carneri, Bartolomäus von.) Stuttgart, 1906.
Phil 5252.28.5   Empfindung und Denken. (Messer, A.) Leipzig, 1908.
Phil 5585.56   Die Empfindungszeit. (Fröhlich, F.W.) Jena, 1929.
Phil 9560.10   The empire of silence. (Courtenay, Charles.) N.Y., 1916.
Phil 8656.27   The empirical argument for God in late British thought. (Bertocci, Peter Anthony.) Cambridge, 1938.
Phil 5255.54   Empirical foundations of psychology. (Pronko, N.H.) N.Y., 1952.
Phil 5247.9.4   Empirical psychology. (Hickok, L.P.) Boston, 1882.
Phil 5247.9.7   Empirical psychology. 2. ed. (Hickok, L.P.) N.Y., 1854.
Phil 9035.57   The empirical study of character. Diss. (McDonough, M.R.) Washington, 1929.
Phil 5627.139   An empirical study of the development of religious thinking in boys from twelve to sixteen years old. (Nagle, Urban.) Washington, 1934.
Phil 8887.123   Empiricism and ethics. (Monro, David Hector.) Cambridge, Eng., 1967.
Phil 2240.84   Empiricism and intuitionism in Reid's common sense philosophy. (Jones, O.McK.) Princeton, 1927.
Phil 331.2.21   L'empiriocriticismo. (Avenarius, R.) Roma, 1909.
Phil 510.155   Empiriomonizm. v.1-3. (Malenovskii, A.A.) S'ankt Peterburg, 1905-06.
Phil 5627.13   De empirische godsdienstpsychologie. (Geelkerken, J.G.) Amsterdam, 1909.
Phil 3415.91   Der empirische Pessimismus. (Weckesser, A.) Bonn, 1885.
Phil 5243.10   Empirische Psychologie. (Drobisch, M.W.) Leipzig, 1842.
Phil 5258.82   Empirische Psychologie. (Schmid, C.C.E.) Jena, 1791.
Phil 5258.50.5   Empirische Psychologie. (Schuchter, Josef.) Brixen, 1897.
Phil 5243.10.1   Empirische Psychologie. 2e Aufl. (Drobisch, M.W.) Hamburg, 1898.
Phil 4650.1.70   Den empiriska naturuppfattningen. 2. ed. (Vannérus, Allen.) Stockholm, 1913.
Phil 2885.85   L'empirisme et le naturalisme contemporain. (Empart, L.) Paris, 1870.
Phil 5068.98   L'empirisme logique. (Vax, Louis.) Paris, 1970.
Phil 4260.215   L'empirismo nella gnoseologia di Giambattista Vico. (Iannizzotto, Matteo.) Padova, 1968.
Phil 2070.113   L'empirismo radicale di William James. (Cugini, U.) Genova, 1925.
Phil 2050.84   Empirismus und Skepsis...Hume's. (Pfleiderer, E.) Berlin, 1874.
Phil 2050.181   Die empiristische Geschichtsauffassung Humes. (Goldstein, J.) Leipzig, 1903.
Phil 3525.30   Emporleitende Theil der Philosophie. (Krause, K.C.F.) Prag, 1869.
Phil 6060.82   Empreintes. (Bresard, Suzanne.) Neuchâtel, 1968.
Phil 6980.106   The empty fortress. (Bettelheim, Bruno.) N.Y., 1967.
Phil 75.54   Emunds, Heinz. Zugange zur Philosophie. Köln, 1959.
Phil 8430.57   En avant la zizique...et par ici les gros sous. (Vian, Boris.) Paris, 1966.
Phil 8960.10   En bog om religion og moral. (Kalmeyer, P.) København, 1956.
Phil 2905.1.530   En Chine avec Teilhard. (Rivière, Claude.) Paris, 1968.
Phil 3450.11.98.5   En découvrant l'existence avec Husserl et Heidegger. (Levinas, Emmanuel.) Paris, 1949.
Phil 3450.11.98.6   En découvrant l'existence avec Husserl et Heidegger. (Levinas, Emmanuel.) Paris, 1967.
Phil 1955.6.180   En el centenario de John Dewey. (Nassif, F.R.) La Plata, 1961.
Phil 5246.75   En el món del invidents. (Gómez Ibars, J.) Barcelona, 1963.
Phil 4357.5   En el reino de las sombras; Maria de la Luz. (Gastelum, B.J.) Mexico, 1937.
Phil 3640.82   En lesant Nietzsche. (Faguet, E.) Paris, 1904.
Phil 2805.432   En lisant Pascal. (Chinard, Gilbert.) Lille, 1948.
Phil 812.41.2   En los origenes de la filosofia. 2. ed. (Mondolfo, Rodolfo.) Buenos Aires, 1960.
Phil 2805.188   En prière avec Pascal. (Bremond, H.) Paris, 1923.
Phil 181.41   En pro y en contra. (González Serrano, U.) Madrid, 1894.
Phil 190.63   En quête d'un philosophie. (Parodi, D.) Paris, 1935.
Phil 190.63.7   En quête d'une philosophie; la conduite humaine et les valeurs idéales. (Parodi, D.) Paris, 1939.
Phil 2445.4.20   En souvenir de Michel Alexandre. (Alexandre, M.) Paris, 1956.
Phil 4352.1.101   En torno a Balmes. (Briones Ortún, Juan.) Bilboa, 1933.
Phil 4960.805   En torno a la filosofia en Chile, 1594-1810. (Hanisch Espíndola, Walter.) Santiago, 1963.
Phil 2905.1.645   En torno a Teilhard. (Grupo Español de Trabajo Teilhard de Chardin.) Madrid, 1969.
Phil 4987.89.85   En torno a Zubiri. (Marquinez Argote, Germán.) Madrid, 1965.
Htn   Phil 6045.60*   Enarratio pulcherrima principiorum chyromantiae. (Tricasso, Patricio.) Noribergae, 1560.
Phil 8879.20   Enberg, L.M. Moralfilosofiens elementer. Stockholm, 1831.
Phil 978.45   Encausse, G. La réincarnation. Paris, 1912.
Phil 6116.11F   L'encephale; structure et description inconographique du cerveau. (Gavoy, E.A.) Paris, 1886. 2v.
Phil 14.1   L'encéphale. Paris. 1-9 8v.
NEDL   Phil 14.1.8   L'encéphale. Paris. 1906-1929
Phil 7069.30.28   The enchanted boundary;...psychical phenomena 1820-1930. (Prince, Walter Franklin.) Boston, 1930.
Phil 8891.1.2   Enchiridion. (Quarles, F.) London, 1856.
Phil 8891.1   Enchiridion. 1658. Reprint. (Quarles, F.) London, 1568.
Htn   Phil 2145.48.5*   Enchiridion ethicum. (More, Henry.) Amstelodami, 1679.
Htn   Phil 2145.49.5*   Enchiridion ethicum. (More, Henry.) Amstelodami, 1695.
Htn   Phil 2145.49*   Enchiridion ethicum. (More, Henry.) Amstelodami, 1695.
Phil 2145.50   Enchiridion ethicum. (More, Henry.) London, 1711.
Phil 2145.55A   Enchiridion ethicum. (More, Henry.) N.Y., 1930.
Htn   Phil 2145.40*   Enchiridion metaphysicum. (More, Henry.) London, 1671.
Phil 3425.48.2   Enciclopedia delle scienze filosofiche. 2. ed. v.1-3. (Hegel, Georg Wilhelm Friedrich.) Bari, 1923. 2v.
Phil 89.6   Enciclopedia filosofica. Venezia, 1957-58. 4v.
Phil 3552.84   Encke, J.F. Rede...G.W. Leibnitz. Berlin, 1842.
Phil 8584.16   Enckendorff, M.L. Kindschaft zur Welt. Jena, 1927.
Phil 9164.2   Encontro Latino Americano, 3d, Rio de Janeiro, 1963. Tercero encontro Latino-Americano. Rio de Janeiro, 1963.
Phil 6985.10   Encounter; a weekend with intimate strangers. (Mann, John Harvey.) N.Y., 1970.
Phil 585.65   Encounter. (Kwant, Remy C.) Pittsburgh, 1960.
Phil 8703.5   The encounter of man and nature; the spiritual crisis of modern man. (Nasr, Segyed Hossein.) London, 1968.
Phil 1750.350   Encounter with nothingness. (Kuhn, H.) London, 1951.
Phil 5252.69.20   Encounter with reality. (Murphy, Gardner.) Boston, 1968.

Phil 4352.1.107   Encrucijada. (Sagarra y de Castellarnau, Fernando.) Barcelona, 1957.
Phil 7054.1   The encyclopaedia of death and life in the spirit world. (Francis, John R.) Chicago, 1985-1900. 3v.
Phil 7069.33.56   Encyclopaedia of psychic science. (Fodor, Nandor.) London, 1933?
Phil 7069.33.57   Encyclopaedia of psychic science. (Fodor, Nandor.) New Hyde Park, N.Y., 1966.
Htn   Phil 3425.43*   Encyclopädie der philosophischen Wissenschaften. (Hegel, Georg Wilhelm Friedrich.) Heidelberg, 1817.
Phil 3425.44   Encyclopädie der philosophischen Wissenschaften. (Hegel, Georg Wilhelm Friedrich.) Heidelberg, 1827.
Phil 3425.45   Encyclopädie der philosophischen Wissenschaften. (Hegel, Georg Wilhelm Friedrich.) Heidelberg, 1830.
Phil 3425.45.20   Encyclopädie der philosophischen Wissenschaften. (Hegel, Georg Wilhelm Friedrich.) Leiden, 1906.
Phil 3425.46   Encyclopädie der philosophischen Wissenschaften. 2. Aufl. (Hegel, Georg Wilhelm Friedrich.) Leipzig, 1920.
Phil 3425.45.4   Encyclopädie der philosophischen Wissenschaften. 4. Aufl. (Hegel, Georg Wilhelm Friedrich.) Berlin, 1845.
Phil 5062.18.3   Encyclopädie der philosophischen Wissenschaften in Verbindung mit W. Windelband. Pt.1. Logik. Photoreproduction. (Ruge, Arnold.) Tübingen, 1912.
Phil 89.4   Encyclopaedisch handbook van het moderne denken. Arnhem, 1931. 2v.
Phil 182.96   Encyclopädische Einleitung in das Studium der Philosophie. (Heydenreich, K.H.) Leipzig, 1703.
Phil 3808.111   Encyclopädisches Register...Schopenhauer. (Wagner, G.F.) Karlsruhe, 1909.
Phil 97.2   Encyclopädisches Wörterbuch der Philosophie. (Mellin, G.S.A.) Leipzig, 1797. 6v.
Phil 3625.1.153   Encyclopaidia Judaica. Moses Mendelssohn zur 200 jahrigen Wiederkehr seines Gehertstages. Berlin, 1929.
Phil 6325.25   Encyclopedia of aberrations. (Podolsky, Edward.) N.Y., 1953.
Phil 960.280   The encyclopedia of Indian philosophies. 1st ed. Delhi, 1970.
Phil 5204.14   The encyclopedia of mental health. N.Y., 1963. 6v.
Phil 6060.70   Encyclopedia of the written word. (Roman, Klara Goldzieher.) N.Y., 1968.
Phil 8892.52   Encyclopédie morale. (Rivarol, E.F. de.) Paris, 1803.
Phil 88.1   Encyklopädie der Philosophie. (Dorner, A.) Leipzig, 1910.
Phil 192.12.7   Encyklopädie der philosophischen Wissenschaften. (Ritter, Heinrich.) Göttingen, 1862-1864. 3v.
Phil 3850.13.31   Encyklopaedie der philosophischen Wissenschaften. (Schulze, G.E.) Göttingen, 1823.
Phil 3850.13.32   Encyklopaedie der philosophischen Wissenschaften. (Schulze, G.E.) Göttingen, 1824.
Phil 181.12   Encyklopädische Einleitung in die Philosophie. (Gockel, C.F.) Karlsruhe, 1855.
Phil 7150.58   The end of hope. (Kobler, Arthur.) N.Y., 1964.
Phil 4359.1.81   Endara, Julio. José Ingenieros y el porvenir de la filosofía. 2a ed. Buenos Aires, 192-.
Phil 9560.40   Ende und Anfang der Humanität. (Baden, H.J.) Gütersloh, 1955.
Phil 6682.9   Endemoniada de Santiago. (Marin, Carmen.) Valparaiso, 1857.
Phil 3808.80.2   Das Endergebniss der Arthur Schopenhauer Philosophie. (Asher, D.) Leipzig, 1885.
Phil 1504.17.2   Endes, J.A. Forschungen zur Geschichte der frümittelalterlichen Philosophie. v.17, pt.2-3. Münster, 1915.
Phil 8633.1.7   The endless life. (Crothers, S.M.) Boston, 1905.
Phil 3801.669.2   Die endlich offenbar Gewordene positive Philosophie der Offenbarung. (Paulus, H.E.G.) Darmstadt, 1843.
Htn   Phil 3801.669*   Die endlich offenbar Gewordene positive Philosophie der Offenbarung. (Paulus, H.E.G.) Darmstadt, 1843.
Phil 410.75   Das Endliche und das Unendliche. (Isenkrahe, Caspar.) Münster, 1915.
Phil 3819.43   Das Endliche und Unendliche. (Spinoza, Benedictus de.) Wiesbaden, 1947.
Phil 6675.9   Les endormeurs. (Fonvielle, W. de.) Paris, n.d.
Phil 2280.5.155   Endovitskii, V.D. Kritika filosofii amerikanskogo kriticheskogo realizma. Moskva, 1968.
Phil 3640.294   Endres, Hans. Rasse, Ehe, Zucht und Züchtung bei Nietzsche und Heute. Heidelberg, 1938.
Phil 179.20   Endres, J.A. Einleitung in die Philosophie. Kempten, 1920.
Phil 1509.5   Endres, J.A. Geschichte der mittelalterlichen Philosophie. 2. Aufl. Kemplin, 1911.
Phil 1504.8.3   Endres, J.A. Petrus Damiani. v.8, pt.3. Münster, 1910.
Phil 585.171   Endres, Josef. Man, as the ontological mean. N.Y., 1965.
Phil 8879.31   Endres, Josef. Menschliche Grundhaltungen. Salzubrg, 1958.
Phil 3195.2.120   Endres, Joseph A. Martin Deutinger. Mainz, 1906.
Phil 165.422   L'endurance de la pensée; pour saluer Jean Beaufret. Paris, 1968.
Phil 189.21.3   The enduring guest. (Overstreet, H.A.) N.Y., 1931.
Phil 2280.5.140   The enduring impact of G. Santayana. (Lamont, C.) N.Y., 1964.
Phil 165.50   The enduring questions. (Rader, M.M.) N.Y., 1956.
Phil 299.9   Energetische Weltanschauung? (Schnehen, W.) Leipzig, 1908.
Phil 2905.1.415   L'énergie dans la cosmogenèse de Pierre Teilhard de Chardin. (Decoux, René.) Cran-Annecy, 1964?
Phil 2475.1.45   L'énergie spirituelle. 5. éd. (Bergson, Henri.) Paris, 1920.
Phil 1750.425   L'énergie spirituelle et la destinée humaine. (Bertrand, Jean.) Nice, 1956.
Phil 6117.27   Energie und seelische Rechtkräfte. (Herz, H.) Leipzig, 1909.
Phil 5249.2.45   Energies of men. (James, William.) N.Y., 1917.
Phil 5249.2.48   Energies of men. (James, William.) N.Y., 1926.
Phil 5252.18.25   The energies of men. (McDougall, William.) N.Y., 1933.
Phil 14.31   Energy and character; the journal of bio-energetic research. Abbotsbury, Eng. 1,1971+
Phil 192.54   The energy concept. (Rohrbaugh, L.G.) Iowa City?, 1922.
Phil 310.768.2   Enerstvedt, Regi Th. Dialektikk o samfunnsvitenskap. 2. oppl. Oslo, 1970.
Phil 6980.263.5   Energie aliénée. Paris, 1967.
Phil 8430.89   L'enfance de l'art. (Kofman, Sarah.) Paris, 1970.
Phil 5871.20   L'enfant arriéré et sa mère. (Mannoni, Maud.) Paris, 1964.
Phil 8629.1   Enfantin, B.P. La vie éternelle. Paris, 1861.
Phil 6750.267.5   Les enfants de nulle part. (Maire, Luce.) Paris, 1967.
Phil 2648.54   L'enfer detruit. (Holbach, Paul Henri T.) Londres, 1769.
Phil 804.2.2   Enfield, W. History of philosophy. Dublin, 1792. 2v.
Phil 804.2.4   Enfield, W. History of philosophy. London, n.d. 2v.

Phil 804.2 — Enfield, W. History of philosophy. London, 1791. 2v.

Phil 804.2.3 — Enfield, W. History of philosophy. London, 1819. 2v.

Phil 804.2.5 — Enfield, W. History of philosophy. London, 1837.

Phil 8878.61 — The enforcement of morals. (Devlin, Patrick.) London, 1965.

Phil 6328.13 — Enführung in die Psychoanalyse. (Schultz-Hencke, Harald.) Jena, 1927.

Phil 3640.820 — Engadine; organe de la Société Nietzsche. Paris. 1,1969+

Phil 5374.35 — Die Enge des Bewusstseins. (Mager, Alois.) Stuttgart, 1920.

Phil 5374.185 — Die Enge des Bewusstseins. (Port, Kurt.) Esslingen, 1955.

Phil 179.1 — Engel, G.E. System der metaphysischen Grundbegriffe. Berlin, 1852.

Phil 2885.86 — Engel, Otto. Der Einfluss Hegels auf die Bildung der Gedankenwelt Hippolyte Taines. Stuttgart, 1920.

Phil 5520.632 — Engel, S. Morris. Language and illumination. The Hague, 1969.

Phil 179.42 — Engel, S. Morris. The problem of tragedy. Frederiction, N.B., 1960.

Phil 3246.228 — Engelbrecht, H.C. Johann Gottlieb Fichte. N.Y., 1933.

Phil 8829.3 — Engelhardt, Paulus. Sein und Ethos. Mainz, 1963.

Phil 610.2 — Engelhardt, Paulus. Zur Theorie der Praxis. Mainz, 1970.

Phil 1750.95 — Engelhardt, Wolf von. Der Mensch in der technischen Welt. Köln, 1957.

Phil 1807.1.5 — Den engelke philosophie i vortid. (Höffding, H.) Kjøbenhavn, 1874.

Phil 1504.4.4 — Engelkemper, W. Die religions-philosophische Lehre. v.4., pt.4. Münster, 1903.

Phil 3925.16.135 — Engelmann, Paul. Letters from Ludwig Wittgenstein with a memoir. Oxford, 1967.

Phil 3925.16.295 — Engelmann, Paul. Ludwig Wittgenstein: Briefe und Begegnungen. Wien, 1970.

Phil 3235.81.20 — Engels, Friedrich. Liudvig Feierbakh. 2. izd. Geneva, 1905.

Phil 3235.81.5 — Engels, Friedrich. Ludwig Feuerbach. Chicago, 1903.

Phil 3235.81.35 — Engels, Friedrich. Ludwig Feuerbach. Chicago, 1906.

Phil 3235.81.12 — Engels, Friedrich. Ludwig Feuerbach. Wien, 1927.

Phil 3235.81.30 — Engels, Friedrich. Ludwig Feuerbach. 3. Aufl. Berlin, 1952.

Phil 3235.81.25 — Engels, Friedrich. Ludwig Feuerbach and the end of classical German philosophy. Moscow, 1949.

Phil 3235.81.27 — Engels, Friedrich. Ludwig Feuerbach and the end of classical German philosophy. Moscow, 1950.

Phil 3235.81.15 — Engels, Friedrich. Ludwig Feuerbach and the outcome of classical German philosophy. N.Y., 1935.

Phil 3235.81.17 — Engels, Friedrich. Ludwig Feuerbach and the outcome of classical German philosophy. N.Y., 1941.

Phil 3235.81.24 — Engels, Friedrich. Ludwig Feuerbach et la fin de la philosophie classique allemande. Paris, 1945.

Phil 3235.81.8 — Engels, Friedrich. Ludwig Feuerbach und der Ausgang der klassischen deutschen Philosophie. 5. Aufl. Stuttgart, 1910.

Phil 3235.81.9 — Engels, Friedrich. Ludwig Feuerbach und der Ausgang der klassischen deutschen Philosophie. 6. Aufl. Stuttgart, 1919.

Phil 5592.40 — Engels, Helma. Der Scenotest. Münster, 1957.

Phil 3790.1.95 — Engert, Joseph. Herman S. Reimarus als Metaphysiker. Inaug. Diss. Paderborn, 1908.

Phil 3450.4.80 — Engstrom, Sigfrid. Studier till Wilhelm Hermanns etik. Uppsala, 1920.

Phil 3486.13 — England, Frederick E. Kant's conception of God. London, 1929.

Phil 8829.1 — England, G. An enquiry into the morals of the ancients. London, 1735.

Phil 1812.6.5 — England und die deutsche Philosophie. (Metz, Rudolf.) Stuttgart, 1941.

Phil 179.6 — Engle, J.S. Analytic interest psychology. Baltimore, 1904.

Phil 3552.128 — Engler, Otto. Darstellung und Kritik des leibnitzischen Optimismus. Inaug.-Diss. Jena, 1883.

Phil 92.2 — Englisch-Deutsch für Psychologen. (Hamilton, James A.) Frankfurt, 1931.

Phil 1801.3 — Die englische aufklärungs Philosophie. (Brockdorff, C.) München, 1924.

Phil 1822.2 — Englische Philosophie. (Wentscher, E.) Leipzig, 1924.

Phil 8629.2 — English, C.D. The philosophy of a future state. Philadelphia, 1885.

Phil 89.3.10 — English, Horace B. A student's dictionary of psychological terms. 3rd ed. Yellow Springs, Ohio, 1929.

Phil 6314.7 — English, Oliver Spurgeon. Common neuroses of children and adults. N.Y., 1937.

Phil 6314.7.4 — English, Oliver Spurgeon. Emotional problems of living. N.Y., 1945.

Phil 6314.7.5 — English, Oliver Spurgeon. Emotional problems of living. N.Y., 1955.

Phil 9380.9 — English, Raymond. The pursuit of purpose. London, 1947.

Phil 5244.23 — English, V.P. Human mind and its physical machine...human body. San Diego, 1937.

Phil 1817.5.3 — English and American philosophy since 1800. (Rogers, A.K.) N.Y., 1923.

Phil 7054.9 — English and parental versions of Bible...in the light of modern spiritualism. (Giles, A.E.) Boston, 1897.

Phil 8669.1.5 — English deism. (Orr, John.) Grand Rapids, 1934.

Phil 9150.7 — English evolutionary ethics. (Read, M.S.) N.Y., 1902.

Phil 5425.2.8 — English men of science. (Galton, F.) London, 1874.

Phil 5425.2.9 — English men of science. (Galton, F.) N.Y., 1875.

Phil 165.345 — The English mind. (Davies, H.S.) Cambridge, Eng., 1964.

Phil 8865.342.5 — The English moralists. (Willey, Basil.) London, 1964.

Phil 530.11.15.5 — The English mystical tradition. (Knowles, David.) London, 1961.

Phil 530.11.6 — The English mystics. (Bullett, G.W.) London, 1950.

Phil 530.11.15 — The English mystics. (Knowles, David.) London, 1927.

Phil 1815.5 — The English philosophers. (Paul, L.A.) London, 1953.

Phil 1818.3.5 — English philosophers and schools of philosophy. (Seth, J.) London, 1925.

Phil 1822.7 — English philosophy since 1900. (Warnock, G.J.) London, 1958.

Phil 5227.1.10 — English psychology. (Ribot, T.) London, 1873.

Phil 5227.1.5 — English psychology. (Ribot, T.) London, 1892.

Phil 530.11.20 — The English religious heritage. (Pepler, Conrad.) Saint Louis, 1958.

Phil 8110.8 — English taste in landscape. (Ogden, Henry.) Washington, 1955.

Phil 1818.4 — English thought for English thinkers. (Stock, Saint George.) London, 1912.

Phil 1818.2.10A — The English Utilitarians. (Stephen, Leslie.) London, 1950. 3v.

Phil 1818.2.6 — The English Utilitarians. (Stephen, Leslie.) n.p., n.d.

Phil 1818.2.5 — The English Utilitarians. v.2. (Stephen, Leslie.) London, 1900.

Phil 9550.16.5 — The English utilitarians. 2. ed. (Plamenatz, J.P.) Oxford, 1958.

NEDL Phil 2045.11 — English works. v.1-7,9-11. (Hobbes, Thomas.) London, 1839-45. 10v.

Phil 2045.14.2 — The English works of Thomas Hobbes of Malmesburg. (Hobbes, Thomas.) Aalen, 1966. 11v.

Phil 2045.14 — The English works of Thomas Hobbes of Malmesbury. (Hobbes, Thomas.) Aalen, 1962. 11v.

Phil 8879.33 — Engst, Jaroslav. Nekotorye problemy nauchnoi etiki. Moskva, 1960.

Phil 179.19 — Enhets- och mangfaldsproblemet inom metfysiken. (Emmelin, Axel.) Lund, 1905.

Phil 4369.5 — El enigma de la realidad. (Sondereguér, Pedro.) Buenos Aires, 1941.

Phil 7072.5 — The enigma of out-of-body travel. (Smith, Susy.) N.Y., 1965.

Phil 8643.32 — The enigma of the hereafter. (Siwek, Paul.) N.Y., 1952.

Phil 7069.67.5 — The enigma of the poltergeist. (Bayless, Raymond.) West Nyack, 1967.

Phil 8881.20.2 — Enigmas of life. (Greg, W.R.) Boston, 1873.

Phil 8881.20 — Enigmas of life. (Greg, W.R.) London, 1883.

Phil 7069.06.11 — Enigmas of psychical research. (Hyslop, James Hervey.) Boston, 1906.

Phil 8877.27 — Enigmas of the spiritual life. (Craufurd, A.H.) London, 1888.

Phil 8411.16 — L'énigme du beau. (Kornfeld, M.) Paris, 1942.

Phil 193.21.25 — L'enigme du monde. (Abauzit, Frank.) Paris, 1922.

Phil 3552.123.5 — Une énigme historique, le "vinculum substantialie" d'après Leibniz. 1. éd. (Blondel, Maurice.) Paris, 1930.

Phil 510.1.10 — Les énigmes de l'univers. (Haeckel, Ernst.) Paris, 1903.

Phil 818.20.5 — Gli enigmi della filosofia. (Steiner, R.) Milano, 1935.

Phil 3640.850 — L'enjeu des signes; lecture de Nietzsche. (Rey, Jean Michel.) Paris, 1971.

Phil 5525.20.15 — Enjoyment of laughter. (Eastman, Max.) N.Y., 1936.

Phil 575.74 — The enlargement of personality. (Denison, J.H.) N.Y., 1930.

Phil 5261.3.12 — Enleitung in die Psychologie der Gegenwart. (Villa, G.) Leipzig, 1902.

Phil 806.39 — The enlightenment, an interpretation. 1st ed. (Gay, Peter.) N.Y., 1966-69. 2v.

Phil 1730.16 — The enlightenment. (Lively, Jack.) London, 1966.

Phil 6674.1 — Ennemoser, J. Der Magnetismus in Verhältnisse zur Natur und Religion. Stuttgart, 1842.

Phil 6114.8 — Ennemoser, Joseph. Historisch-psychologische Untersuchungen...den Ursprung. 2. Aufl. Stuttgart, 1851.

Phil 735.99 — Ennismore, R.G. The values of life. London, 1931.

Phil 5407.5.2 — L'ennui; étude psychologique. (Tardieu, E.) Paris, 1903.

Phil 179.12 — Eno, Henry Lane. Activism. Princeton, N.J., 1920.

Phil 6980.263 — Enoch, M. David. Some uncommon psychiatric syndromes. Bristol, 1967.

Phil 4080.12.45 — L'enquête quotidienne. (Castelli, Enrico.) Paris, 1959.

Phil 2050.41.25 — Enquiries concerning the human understanding and concerning the principles of morals. 2nd ed. (Hume, David.) Oxford, 1927.

Phil 9346.3.2 — Enquiry...duties of the female sex. (Gisborne, T.) London, 1798.

Phil 2050.41 — An enquiry...human understanding. (Hume, David.) Chicago, 1904.

Phil 2050.41.5A — An enquiry...human understanding. (Hume, David.) Chicago, 1907.

Phil 2050.40 — An enquiry...human understanding. (Hume, David.) Oxford, 1894.

Phil 8877.22 — An enquiry...original of moral virtue. (Campbell, A.) London, 1734.

Phil 14.10 — Enquiry. London. 1-3,1948-1950 2v.

Htn NEDL Phil 9245.4* — An enquiry after happiness. (Lucas, R.) London, 1704.

Phil 9245.4.2 — An enquiry after happiness. (Lucas, R.) London, 1717. 2v.

Phil 9245.4.3 — An enquiry after happiness. (Lucas, R.) London, 1753. 2v.

Phil 9245.4.4 — An enquiry after happiness. pt.1. (Lucas, R.) Edinburgh, 1754.

Phil 9245.4.5 — An enquiry after happiness. v.1-2. (Lucas, R.) London, 1764.

Htn Phil 2050.69.2* — An enquiry concerning...morals. (Hume, David.) London, 1751.

Phil 2050.41.30 — An enquiry concerning human understanding. (Hume, David.) Chicago, 1906.

Htn Phil 2030.3.30* — An enquiry concerning political justice. (Godwin, William.) London, 1793. 2v.

Phil 8887.14 — An enquiry into...moral obligation. (Metcalf, D.) Boston, 1860.

Phil 8843.15 — An enquiry into goodness. (Sparshott, F.E.) Chicago, 1958.

Phil 8886.45.15 — An enquiry into moral nations. (Laird, John.) London, 1935.

Htn Phil 665.1.2* — An enquiry into nature of human soul. (Baxter, A.) London, 1745. 2v.

Phil 6327.17.15 — An enquiry into prognosis in the neuroses. (Ross, Thomas Arthur.) Cambridge, Eng., 1936.

Phil 8800.8 — An enquiry into the duties of men. (Gisborne, T.) London, 1794.

Phil 8881.11 — An enquiry into the duties of men. (Gisborne, T.) London, 1800. 2v.

Phil 8881.11.2 — An enquiry into the duties of men. (Gisborne, T.) London, 1824. 2v.

Phil 8829.1 — An enquiry into the morals of the ancients. (England, G.) London, 1735.

Phil 2128.60 — Enquiry into the origin of honour. (Mandeville, B.) London, 1732.

Htn Phil 2128.60.2* — Enquiry into the origin of honour. v.1-2. (Mandeville, B.) London, 1725-32.

Phil 9420.3 — Enquiry into the origin of the human appetites and affections. Lincoln, 1747.

Phil 2128.81 — An enquiry whether a general practice of virtue tends to the wealth or poverty...of a people. (Bluet.) London, 1725.

Phil 8897.76 — L'enracinement. 3. éd. (Weil, Simone.) Paris, 1949.

Phil 623.19 — Enriques, F. Scienza e razionalismo. Bologna, n.d.

Phil 5014.1.20 — Enriques, Federigo. L'évolution de la logique. Paris, 1926.

Phil 5014.1.30 — Enriques, Federigo. The historic development of logic. N.Y., 1929.

Phil 5014.1 — Enriques, Federigo. Per la storia della logica. Bologna, 1922.

Phil 5014.1.5 — Enriques, Federigo. Zur Geschichte der Logik. Leipzig, 1927.

Phil 310.774 — Ensaio critico sôbre os fundamentos da filosofia dialética. (Andrade, Almir de.) Rio de Janeiro, 1971.

Phil 4369.2.82 — Ensaio sobre a vida e a obra do filósofo Francisco Sanchez. (Cruz Costa, João.) São Paulo, 1942.

Phil 4466.4.30 — Ensaios de filosofia para a história. (Ferreira, A.) Coimbra, 1962.

Phil 1702.10 — Ensaios filosóficos. (Cannabrava, Euryalo.) Rio de Janeiro, 1957.

Phil 3500.52.5 — Ensayo de una clara exposición del contenido de la critica de la razón pura. (Schultz, John.) Cordoba, 1942.

Phil 5525.40 — Ensayo preliminar sobre lo cómico. (Victoria, Marcos.) Buenos Aires, 1941.

Phil 9590.28 — Ensayo sobre el destino. (Masferrer, A.) San Salvador, 1963.

Phil 4080.3.425 — Ensayo sobre el pensamiento de Benedetto Croce. (Marone, Gherardo.) Buenos Aires, 1946.

Phil 5258.68.30 — Ensayo sobre la teoria. (Garcia de Onrubia, Luis Felipe.) Buenos Aires, 1949.

Phil 336.6 — Ensayo sobre la teoría del conocimiento. (Franceschi, A.) La Plata, 1925.

Phil 8597.48 — Ensayo sobre tolerancia religiosa. 2. ed. (Rocafuerte, Vicente.) México, 1831.

Phil 181.80.5 — Ensayos. (Garcia Morente, Manuel.) Madrid, 1945.

Phil 4366.79.30 — Ensayos. (Pascual Ferrández, Antonio.) Barcelona, 1961. 20v.

Phil 2255.1.125 — Ensayos beligerantes: Bertrand Russell, James Joyce. (Bonifacino, V.) Montevideo, 1960.

Phil 4972.5.10 — Ensayos críticos. (Korn, Alejandro.) Buenos Aires, 193-.

Phil 4363.7.10 — Ensayos de convivencia. (Marias Aguilera, Julián.) Buenos Aires, 1955.

Phil 4363.4.30 — Ensayos de crítica filosófica. (Menéndez y Pelayo, M.) Madrid, 1918.

Phil 175.41 — Ensayos de filosofía prática. (Alessio, Roberto de.) Montevideo, 19- .

Phil 4363.7.33 — Ensayos de teoria. 3. ed. (Marias Aguilera, Julián.) Madrid, 1966.

Phil 4351.5 — Ensayos filosoficos. (Astrada, Carlos.) Bahia Blanca, 1925.

Phil 165.350 — Ensayos filosóficos. Buenos Aires, 1963.

Phil 6322.25 — Ensayos freudianos. (Marin, J.) Santiago de Chile, 1938.

Phil 801.35.10 — Ensayos liminares. (Bueno, Miquel.) México, 1962.

Phil 680.55 — Ensayos sobre el estructuralismo. (Francovich, Guillermo.) La Paz, Bolivia, 1970.

Phil 825.5 — Ensayos sobre filosofia en la historia. (Zea, Leopoldo.) Mexico, 1948.

Phil 4357.2.30 — Ensayos y cartas. (Giner de los Rios, Francisco.) Mexico, 1965.

Phil 14.16 — Ensayos y estudios. Bonn. 1-17 8v.

Phil 8879.5 — Ensor, G. The principles of morality. London, 1801.

Phil 5425.7.3 — Entartung. 2. Aufl. (Nordau, M.) Berlin, 1893. 2v.

Phil 5425.4.15 — Entartung und Genie. (Lombroso, C.) Leipzig, 1894.

Phil 6310.1.30 — Entdeckung der Seele. (Adler, Gerhard.) Zürich, 1934.

Phil 5251.31 — Die Entdeckung der Seele. (Lungwitz, H.) Leipzig, 1925.

Phil 665.8A — Die Entdeckung der Seele durch die Geheimwissenschaften. v.1-2. (DuPrel, C.) Leipzig, 1894-95.

Phil 665.8.2 — Die Entdeckung der Seele durch die Geheimwissenschaften. 2e Aufl. (DuPrel, C.) Leipzig, 1910. 2v.

Htn Phil 3801.749.10* — Entdeckungen über des Entdeckungen unserer neuesten Philosophen. (Paulus, H.E.G.) Bremen, 1835.

Phil 3195.10.99 — Der entelechiebegriff bei Aristoteles und Driesch. Inaug. Diss. (Burchard, H.) Quakenbrück, 1928.

Phil 6322.38 — Entfaltung des Psychoanalyse. (Mitscherlich, A.) Stuttgart, 1956.

Phil 3425.750 — Entfremdung. (Mueller, Friedrich.) Berlin, 1970.

Phil 1750.768 — Die Entfremdung als historische Kategorie. (Oizerman, Teodor Il'ich.) Berlin, 1965.

Htn Phil 283.8* — Enthosiasmo, de'misterii e maravigliose cause della compositione del mondo. (Camilla, G.) Vinegia, 1564.

Phil 7068.89.3 — Enthüllung des Spukes von Resau. 3. Aufl. (Müller, Egbert.) Berlin, 1889.

Htn Phil 3801.923* — Die Enthullte Geheimlehre des Herren von Schelling. Schaffhausen, 1844.

Htn Phil 2725.3* — An entire body of philosophy. (LeGrand, A.) London, 1694.

Phil 3120.15.33 — Der entlarvte Mensch. (Brunner, Constantin.) Haag, 1951.

Phil 4363.2.40 — Entrambasaguas y Pena, J. de. Miguel de Molinos, siglo XVII. Madrid, 1935?

Phil 672.210 — Entre el tiempo y la eternidad. (Restrepo, F.) Bogotá, 1960.

Phil 5917.168 — Entre la ciencia y la magia. 1. ed. (Carnicer, Ramón.) Barcelona, 1969.

Phil 8088.3 — Entre le classicisme et le romantisme. (Folkierski, W.) Cracovie, 1925.

Phil 4987.60.61 — Entre robles y tilos. (Zunino Dubois, J.C.) La Plata, 1962.

Phil 2520.54 — Entretien avec Burman. (Descartes, René.) Paris, 1937.

Phil 2805.74 — Entretien avec de Saci sur Épictète et Montaigne. (Pascal, Blaise.) Paris, 1875.

Phil 2805.74.10 — Entretien avec M. de Saci. 2. éd. (Pascal, Blaise.) Aix, 1946.

Phil 2805.74.20 — L'entretien de Pascal et Sacy. (Pascal, Blaise.) Paris, 1960.

Phil 2733.60 — Entretien d'un philosophe chrétien. (Malebranche, Nicolas.) Paris, 1708.

Phil 2733.60.5 — Entretien d'un philosophe chrétien et d'un philosophe chinois. (Malebranche, Nicolas.) Paris, 1936.

Phil 2733.60.7 — Entretien d'un philosophe chrétien et d'un philosophe chinois. Thèse. (Malebranche, Nicolas.) Marseille, 1936.

Phil 5253.13 — L'entretien psychologique. (Nahoum, Charles.) Paris, 1968.

Phil 2475.1.222.15 — Entretiens avec Bergson. (Chevalier, Jacques.) Paris, 1959.

Phil 1706.1.32 — Entretiens avec ceux d'hier et d'aujourd'hui. 2e éd. (Gaultier, Jules de.) Paris, 1912.

Phil 2805.101.15 — Entretiens de Cléandre et d'Eudoxe sur les lettres au provincial. 10. éd. (Daniel, Gabriel.) Pierre Marteau, 1968.

Phil 2750.19.115 — Entretiens Paul Ricoeur, Gabriel Marcel. (Ricoeur, Paul.) Paris, 1968.

Phil 70.45.5 — Entretiens philosophiques de Varsovie. (International Institute of Philosophy.) Wrocław, 1958.

Phil 14.18 — Entretiens psychiatriques. Paris. 1,1952+ 13v.

Phil 2520.161.10 — Entretiens sur Descartes. (Koyré, A.) N.Y., 1944.

Phil 585.414 — Entretiens sur la destinée humaine. (Morichon, René.) Limoges, 1970.

Phil 9450.66 — Entretiens sur la justice contemporaire. (Hamelin, Jacques.) Paris, 1970.

Phil 2733.36.4 — Entretiens sur la métaphysique. (Malebranche, Nicolas.) Paris, 1721. 2v.

Phil 2733.36 — Entretiens sur la métaphysique. (Malebranche, Nicolas.) Paris, 1871.

Phil 2733.36.5 — Entretiens sur la métaphysique. v.1-2. (Malebranche, Nicolas.) Paris, 1922.

Htn Phil 2605.2.30* — Entretiens sur la pluralité des mondes. (Fontenelle, B.) Paris, 1766.

Phil 181.131 — Entretiens sur le bon usage de la liberté. (Grenier, J.) Paris, 1948.

Phil 6674.6 — Entretiens sur le magnétisme animal. Paris, 1823.

Phil 672.256 — Entretiens sur le temps, sous la direction de Jeanne Hersch et René Poirier. Paris, 1967.

Phil 70.99 — Entretiens sur les notions de genése et de structure. (Gandillac, Maurice Patronnier de.) Paris, 1965.

Htn Phil 8701.9.5* — Entretiens sur les sciences dans lesquels on apprend comment l'on doit étudier les sciences. (Lamy, Bernard.) Bruxelles, 1684.

Phil 8701.9.7 — Entretiens sur les sciences dans lesquels on apprend comment l'on doit étudier les sciences. 3. éd. (Lamy, Bernard.) Lyon, 1706.

Phil 8701.9 — Entretiens sur les sciences dans lesquels on apprend comment l'on doit étudier les sciences. (Lamy, Bernard.) Lyon, 1724.

Phil 8701.9.9 — Entretiens sur les sciences dans lesquels on apprend comment l'on doit étudier les sciences. (Lamy, Bernard.) Paris, 1966.

Phil 5374.24.5 — Entricklungsgeschichte des Bewusstseins. (Legahn, August F.) Leipzig, 1914.

Phil 3010.9 — Die Entscheidung. (Kvochow, Christian C. von.) Stuttgart, 1958.

Phil 8956.24 — Entscheidung gegen das Gesetz. (Guenthöe, Anselm.) Freiburg, 1969.

Phil 665.27.5 — Die Entschleierung der Seele: eine neue Theorie. (Hirt, Walter.) Berlin, 1923.

Phil 3428.83 — Der Entschluss im dem Herbarts Metaphysik. (Turic, G.) Langensalza, 1892.

Phil 5643.49 — Die Entslehung der Gesichtswahrnehmung. (Ueberhorst, Karl.) Göttingen, 1876.

Phil 346.8 — Entstehen von Empfindung und bewisstsein. (Porten, Max von der.) Leipzig, 1910.

Phil 9035.55 — Entstehung der Charakters. (Wahle, Richard.) München, 1928.

Phil 3487.13 — Die Entstehung der Kantischen Ästhetik. Diss. (Falkenheim, H.) Berlin, 1890.

Phil 299.1 — Die Entstehung der physischen...Welt. (Schlesinger, J.) Wien, 1882.

Phil 5585.45 — Die Entstehung der Raumvorstellung. (Sachs, H.) Breslau, 1897.

Phil 7082.28 — Entstehung der Träume. (Weygandt, Wilhelm.) Leipzig, 1893.

Phil 5811.10.10 — Die Entstehung des Denkvermögens. (Bohn, Georges.) Leipzig, 1911?

Phil 5425.39 — Die Entstehung des Geniebegriffes. (Zilsel, Edgar.) Tübingen, 1926.

Phil 9075.16 — Die Entstehung des Gewissens. (Rée, Paul.) Berlin, 1885.

Phil 5374.34 — Entstehung des Selbstbewusstseins. (Czolbe, Heinrich.) Leipzig, 1856.

Phil 3428.85 — Entstehung und Bedeutung; Herbarts. (Ballauff, F.) Aurich, 1898.

Phil 5765.8 — Entstehung und Entwicklung der Kontingentismus. (Pelikán, F.) Berlin, 1915.

Phil 2905.1.140 — Entstehung und Zukunft des Menschen. (Kopp, Josef Vital.) Luzern, 1961.

Phil 9590.4 — Entufhrön. (Bonnard, L.C.) Paris, 1933.

Phil 600.54 — Entwertung der Kausalität. (Heyde, Johannes Erich.) Zürich, 1957.

Phil 813.2.5 — Die Entwickelung der abendländischen Philosophie Critik der reinen Vernunft. (Noire, L.) Mainz, 1883.

Phil 3805.90 — Entwickelung der Ethik Schleiermachers. (Bachmann, F.) Leipzig, 1892.

Phil 3552.101 — Die Entwickelung der leibnizischen Metaphysik. (Hahn, R.) Halle, 1899.

Phil 5585.20 — Entwickelung der Raumvorstellung. (Siegel, Carl.) Leipzig, 1899.

Phil 3415.104 — Die Entwickelung der religiösen...nach Eduard von Hartmann. (Lasson, A.) Halle, 1883.

Phil 270.15 — Entwickelung des Casualproblems. (Koenig, E.) Leipzig, 1888.

Phil 1135.135 — Entwickelung des Gottesbegriffes. (Rechenberg, C.M.) Leipzig, 1872.

Htn Phil 3801.570.10* — Entwickelungsgeschichte der neuesten deutschen Philosophie...Schelling. (Michelet, Carl L.) Berlin, 1843.

Phil 3012.1.5 — Entwickelungsgeschichte der neuesten deutschen Philosophie. (Michelet, C.L.) Berlin, 1843.

Phil 7052.6 — Die Entwickelungsgeschichte des Spiritismus. (Kiesewetter, Karl.) Leipzig, 1893.

Phil 978.49.840 — Entwicklung, Vererbung und Abstammungs. (Poppelbaum, H.) Dornach, 1961.

Phil 1540.75 — Die Entwicklung der Grandenlehre in der Hochscholastik. v.2. (Auer, J.) Freiburg, 1951.

Phil 1135.85 — Die Entwicklung der Grossen Erkenntnistheorie. (Freytag, W.) Hale, 1905.

Phil 3425.210 — Die Entwicklung der Hegelschen Sozialphilosophie. (Bülow, F.) Leipzig, 1920.

Phil 3565.127 — Die Entwicklung der Lotzeschen Psychologie. (Baerwald, Leo.) Berlin, 1905.

Phil 1500.1 — Die Entwicklung der mittelalterlicher Psychologie. (Werner, K.) Wien, 1876.

Phil 8969.16 — Die Entwicklung der Moraltheologie zur eigenständigen Disziplin. (Theiner, Johann.) Regensburg, 1970.

Phil 9560.9 — Die Entwicklung der Moraltugenden. (Tschubrovitz, P.) Leipzig, 1911.

Phil 672.153 — Die Entwicklung der Raumtheorien im 2. Hälfte des 17. Jahrhunderts. Inaug.-Diss. (Sander, Franz.) Halle, 1931.

Phil 745.8 — Die Entwicklung der vitalistischen Naturphilosophie im 20. Jahrhundert. Inaug. Diss. (Rudy, Hirsch.) Charlottenburg, 1927.

Phil 490.5 — Die Entwicklung der Welt auf atomistischer Grundlage. (Pfaff, A.B.I.F.) Heidelberg, 1883.

Phil 3491.18 — Die Entwicklung des Begriffs des Schönen bei Kant, unter besonderer Berücksichtigung des Begriffs verworrenen Erkenntnis. (Juchem, Hans Georg.) Bonn, 1970.

Phil 6315.19.10 — Die Entwicklung des Christusdogmas. (Fromm, Erich.) Wien, 1931.

Phil 5761.14.10   Die Entwicklung des experimentellen Willenspsychologie. (Lewin, Kurt.) Leipzig, 1929.

Phil 5875.125   Die Entwicklung des kindlichen Fragens. (Rieder, Oskar.) München, 1968.

Phil 6131.3.5   Die Entwicklung des menschlichen Geistes. (Verworn, M.) Jena, 1910.

Phil 8599.19.105   Die Entwicklung des philosophischen Gottesbegriffs bei Ernst Troeltsch. Inaug. Diss. (Wieneke, Friedrich.) Berlin, 1929.

Phil 3483.20   Die Entwicklung des Seelenbegriffes bei Kant. Inaug. Diss. (Brahn, Max.) Leipzig, 18- ?

Phil 5875.140   Entwicklung des sozialen Wertbewusstseins; eine empirische Untersuchung des sittlichen Beuresstseins bei Kindern und Jugendlichen. Thesis. (Mueller, Rudolf.) Weinheim, 1968.

Phil 2494.83   Entwicklung und Fortschritt nach Condorcet und A. Comte. Diss. (Krynska, S.) Bern, 1908.

Phil 8877.62   Entwicklung und Glückseligkeit. (Carneri, B.) Stuttgart, 1886.

Phil 3415.107   Entwicklung und Kritik der Erkenntnistheorie Eduard von Hartmanns. (Pohorilles, N.E.) Wien, 1911.

Phil 9035.67   Die Entwicklung zur sittlichen Persönlichkeit. (Neumann, Johannes.) Gütersloh, 1931.

Phil 1718.17   Der Entwicklungsgang der neueren Speculation. (Schaarschmidt, C.) Bonn, 1857.

Phil 811.22   Der Entwicklungsgang des philosophischen Denkens. (Lindner, Herbert.) Berlin, 1966.

Phil 4610.9.80   Entwicklungsgang und grundprobleme der philosophie Rasmus Nielsens. Inaug. Diss. (Asmussen, E.) Flensburg, 1911.

Phil 3425.123   Entwicklungsgeschichte der Hegel'schen Logik. (Schmid, Aloys.) Regensburg, 1858.

Phil 3497.14   Die Entwicklungsgeschichte der vorkritischen Raumphilosophie Kants. (Poppovich, N.M.) Wien, 1925.

Phil 5425.28   Die Entwicklungsgeschichte des Talentes und Genies. (Reibmayr, Albert.) München, 1908. 2v.

Phil 296.3   Entwicklungsgeschichte des Welt...Organismen. (Pivány, J.A.) Plauen, 1877.

Phil 6060.88   Entwicklungshemmungen und Graphologie. Thesis. (Stern, Martin.) Zürich, 1958.

Phil 510.141   Entwicklungstheorie und Monismus. (Wasmann, Erich.) Innsbruck, 1910.

Phil 978.49.735   Entwürfe, Fragmente und Paralipomenn zu den vier Mysteriendramen: Die Pforte der Einwiehung. (Steiner, R.) Dornach, 1969.

Phil 5058.18   Entwurf der Logik. (Strümpell, L.) Mitau, 1846.

Phil 8411.11   Entwurf einer Asthetik der Natur und Kunst. (Kirstein, Anton.) Paderborn, 1896.

Phil 2494.36   Entwurf einer historischen Darstellung. (Condorcet, M.J.A.N.) Frankfurt a.M., 1963.

Phil 8882.52   Entwurf eines geschlossenen Systems der ethischen Formen. (Hlucka, J.F.) Wien, 1924.

Phil 3528.60.1   Entwurf eines neuen Organon's der Philosophie. Meissen, 1801. (Krug, Wilhelm Traugott.) Bruxelles, 1969.

Phil 193.11   Entwurf eines Systems der Philosophie. v.1-3. (Schmid, F.X.) Wien, 1863-1868. 2v.

Phil 3805.37   Entwurf eines Systems der Sittenlehre. (Schleiermacher, Friedrich.) Berlin, 1835.

Phil 5244.5   Entwurf zu einer physiologischen Erklärung der psychischen Erscheinungen. (Exner, S.) Leipzig, 1894.

Phil 6328.10.20   Entwurf zu einer Psychiatrie auf psychoanalyischer Grundlage. (Schilder, Paul.) Leipzig, 1925.

Phil 6114.12   Entwurf zu einer psychologischen Erklärung der psychischen Erscheinungen. (Exner, Sigmund.) Leipzig, 1894.

Phil 6315.2.131   Der entzauberte Freud. 9. Aufl. (Ludwig, Emil.) Zürich, 1946.

Phil 5413.10   L'envie. (Raiga, Eugène.) Paris, 1932.

Phil 5413.16.5   Envy; a theory of social behaviour. (Schoeck, Helmut.) London, 1969.

Phil 5413.20   Envy and gratitude. (Klein, Melanie.) London, 1957.

Phil 3850.18.113   Enzelmensch Familie und Staat in der Philosophie Max Schelers. Inaug. Diss. (Bachus, A.) Düsseldorf, 1936.

Phil 3425.46.6   Enzyklopädie der philosophischen Wissenschaften. 6. Aufl. (Hegel, Georg Wilhelm Friedrich.) Hamburg, 1959.

Phil 8622.55   Epäilyksistä uskoon. (TüliIä, Osmo.) Helsinki, 1963.

Phil 575.240   L'épanouissement de la personnalité humaine par la conformité au Christ. (Bui-Kim-Duong, J.B.) Fribourg/Suisse, 1967.

Phil 8879.11   Ephemeriden der Menschkeit. v.1-4,5-8,9-12. Basel, 1777. 3v.

Phil 3425.243   Ephraim, F. Untersuchungen über den Freiheitsbegriff Hegels in seinen Jugendarbeiten. Berlin, 1928.

Phil 5545.39   Ephrussi, P. Experimentalle Beiträge...vom Gedächtnis. Leipzig, 1904.

Phil 1158.6   Epicureanism. (Wallace, W.) London, 1880.

Phil 1158.7   L'epicureismo e l'atomismo. (Ferri, Luigi.) Firenze, 1871.

Phil 4006.1   L'epicureismo italiano. (Gabotto, F.) Piemonte, 1889.

Phil 1158.35   L'epicureismo nella letteratura latina nel I secolo a.c. (Giuffrida, Pasquale.) Torino, 1940. 2v.

Phil 9550.13   L'épicurisme, l'ascétisme et la morale utilitaire. (Keim, Albert.) Paris, 1924.

Phil 1158.37   L'épicurisme. (Brun, Jean.) Paris, 1959.

Phil 6955.6   L'epidemia di istero-demonopatie. (Franzolini, F.) Reggio, 1879.

Phil 6965.20   Epidemiology and mental illness. (Plunkett, Richard.) N.Y., 1960.

Phil 3485.16   Gli epigoni di Kant. (Durante, Gaetano.) Firenze, 1943.

Phil 4845.227.34   Epikaira kai anepikaira. (Papanoutsos, Euangelos.) Athena, 1962.

Phil 8413.20   Epikur; Physiologie des Schönen. (Mantegazza, P.) Jena, 1891.

Phil 3780.36   Epilegomena...Wissenschaft der logischen Idee. (Rosenkranz, Karl.) Königsberg, 1862.

Phil 3270.11.35   Epilegomena. (Friedmann, H.) München, 1954.

Phil 6536.7   Die Epilepsie im Kindesalter mit besonderer Berücksichtigung erzieherischer, unterrichtlicher und forensischer Fragen. (Vogt, Heinrich.) Berlin, 1910.

Phil 6536.14   Epilepsy, a functional mental illness. (Rows, R.G.) N.Y., 1926.

Phil 6536.11   Epilepsy and cerebral localization. 1st ed. (Penfield, W.) Springfield, 1941.

Phil 6535.7   The epileptic and crippled child and adult. Photoreproduction. (Charity Organization Society, London.) London, 1893.

Phil 4073.32A   Epilogo magno (fisiologia italiana). (Campanella, Tommaso.) Roma, 1939.

Phil 3494.41   Épisodes Kantiens en Suisse et en France sous le Directoire. (Munteano, B.) Paris, 1935.

Phil 6990.3   Les épisodes miraculeux de Lourdes. (Lasserre, H.) Paris, 1884.

Phil 6322.70   Episodic behavioral disorders. (Monroe, Russell R.) Cambridge, 1970.

Phil 332.28   Épistémalogie et logique depuis Kant jusqu'a nos jours. 1. éd. (Bayer, R.) Paris, 1954.

Phil 14.15   Episteme; anuario de filosofía. Caracas. 1,1957+ 4v.

Phil 14.12   Episteme. Buenos Aires. 1947-1951

Phil 14.15.3   Episteme. Biblioteca filosofica. Caracas. 1

Phil 9530.5.5   Hé epistémé tou kalou richardou. (Franklin, B.) Paris, 1823.

Phil 510.149   Epistemological pluralism. (Chang, T.S.) Shanghai? 1932?

Phil 349.39.5   Épistémologie. 2e éd. (Steenberghen, Fernand van.) Louvain, 1947.

Phil 349.39.6   Épistémologie. 3e éd. (Steenberghen, Fernand van.) Louvain, 1956.

Phil 349.39.4   Épistémologie. 4e éd. (Steenberghen, Fernand van.) Paris, 1965.

Phil 330.18   L'épistémologie positive et la critique. (Mourelos, G.) Paris, 1962.

Phil 330.18.2   L'épistémologie positive et la critique meyersonienne. Thèse. (Mourelos, G.) Paris, 1962.

Phil 348.17   L'épistémologie thomiste. (Riet, G. van.) Louvain, 1946.

Phil 349.80   Epistemology; new essays in the theory of knowledge. (Stroll, Avrum.) N.Y., 1967.

Phil 330.2   Pamphlet vol. Epistemology. 6 pam.

Phil 330.4   Pamphlet vol. Epistemology. 5 pam.

Phil 333.7.2   Epistemology. (Coffey, Peter.) Gloucester, Mass., 1958. 2v.

Phil 330.6   Pamphlet vol. Epistemology. German diss. 5 pam.

Phil 330.5   Pamphlet vol. Epistemology. German diss. 1901-1931. 14 pam.

Phil 330.1   Pamphlet vol. Epistemology and logic. 16 pam.

Phil 2150.18.105.5   The epistemology of G.E. Moore. (Klemke, E.D.) Evanston, 1969.

Htn   Phil 3110.23*   Epistles. (Böhme, J.) London, 1649-50.

Phil 8962.3   Epistles of Saint John. (Maurice, F.D.) London, 1867.

Htn   Phil 2520.77*   Epistola...ad celeberrimum virum D. Gisbertum Voetium. (Descartes, René.) Amsterodami, 1643.

Phil 2115.70.15   Epistola su la tolleranza. (Locke, J.) Lanciano, 1920. 2v.

Phil 2520.13.16   Epistolae, Pars prima-tertia. (Descartes, René.) Amsterdam, 1682-83. 3v.

Phil 2520.75   Epistolae. (Descartes, René.) Amstelodami, 1682-83.

Phil 2520.75.2   Epistolae. (Descartes, René.) Francofurti ad Moenum, 1692.

Htn   Phil 2520.75.3*   Epistolae. v.1-2. (Descartes, René.) Amstelodami, 1668.

Phil 2520.75.15   Epistolae. v.1-2. (Descartes, René.) Amstelodami, 1714.

Htn   Phil 2520.75.5*   Epistolae. v.1-2. (Descartes, René.) Londini, 1668.

Htn   Phil 3552.74*   Epistolae ad diversos. Cum annotationibus suis primum divulgavit christian. (Leibniz, Gottfried Wilhelm.) Lipsiae, 1734-42. 4v.

Phil 4115.75   Epistolario. (Gioberti, V.) Firenze, 1927-37. 11v.

Phil 4210.75   Epistolario. pt.1, v.1-2. (Rosmini-Serbati, Antonio.) Torino, 1857. 2v.

Phil 4080.3.23   Epistolario. v.2. (Croce, Benedetto.) Napoli, 1967.

Phil 4196.30   Le epistole de imitatione di G. Pico. (Pico, G.F.) Firenze, 1954.

Phil 5404.1   L'epithymologie. (Urban, J.) Paris, 1939.

Phil 5938.3   An epitome of phrenology. (Shurtleff, N.R.) Boston, 1835.

Phil 7054.71   Epitome of spirit-intercourse. (Cridge, A.) Boston, 1854.

Phil 807.6   An epitome of the history of philosophy. (Henry, C.S.) N.Y., 1856. 2v.

Phil 2270.35   Epitome of the synthetic philosophy. (Spencer, Herbert.) N.Y., 1889.

Phil 2270.35.2   Epitome of the synthetic philosophy. (Spencer, Herbert.) N.Y., 1895.

Phil 4803.454.72   Épitre secrète à son altesse le Prince Louis-Napoléon sur les destinées de la France. (Hoene-Wroński, Józef Maria.) Metz, 1851.

Phil 8701.17   The epoch of creation. (Lord, Eleazar.) N.Y., 1851.

Phil 3801.566   Die Epochen der Schellingschen Philosophie von 1795 bis 1802. (Metzger, Wilhelm.) Heidelberg, 1911.

Phil 176.26.10   Die Epochen der Vernunft nach der Idee einer Apoditik. (Bouterwek, Friedrich.) Bruxelles, 1968.

Phil 801.31   Epochen der Vorzüglichsten philosophischen Begriffe. (Bardili, C.G.) Halle, 1788. 2 pam.

Phil 5910.2   Epps, J. Horae phrenologicae. London, 1829-1836. 6 pam.

Phil 5924.2.2   Epps, John. Internal evidences of Christianity deduced from phrenology. Boston, 1837.

Phil 5924.2   Epps, John. Internal evidences of Christianity deduced from phrenology. 2. ed. London, 1836.

Phil 3488.50   L'équivoque ontologique de la pensée Kantienne. (Granel, Gérard.) Paris, 1970.

Phil 1721.2   Er jeg nig? Traek of Jeg'ets psykologi. (Rudolph, Rigmor.) København, 1960.

Phil 525.131   L'era nuova del pensiero. (Vignoli, Tito.) Milano, 1885.

Phil 672.190   Eranos-Jahorbuch. Man and transformation. N.Y., 1964.

Phil 179.38A   Eranos-Jahrbuch. Man and time. N.Y., 1957.

Phil 14.13   Eranos-Jahrbuck. Spirit and nature. N.Y., 1954.

Phil 14.13.5   Eranos Jahrbuck. Zürich. 1,1933+ 33v.

Phil 14.11   Eranos Jahrbuck. Index. Zürich. 1,1933+ 2v.

Phil 8879.6.5   Eranus. Kaunas. 2,1931

Htn   Phil 3200.1.30*   Erasmus, D. Civilitas morum. Goslariae, 1733.

Phil 8879.6.6   Erasmus, D. Colloquia. Lugdunum Batavorum, 1636.

Htn   Phil 8879.6.2*   Erasmus, D. De civilitate morum. Rostochi, 1632.

Phil 8879.6A   Erasmus, D. Lingua, sive, de linguae. Basileae, 1547.

Erasmus, D. Lingua, sive, de linguae. Lugdunum Batavorum, 1641.

Htn   Phil 3200.1.35*   Erasmus, D. Stultitiae laus. Basiliae, 1676.

Phil 6954.5A   Erb, Wilhelm. Handbuch der Krankheiten des Nervensystems. 2e Aufl. Leipzig, 1876-78. 2v.

Phil 8448.15   Erbauliches, Belehrendes, wie auch Vergnügliches kitsch Lexion. (Richter, G.) Gütersloh, 1970.

Phil 179.16   Erberg, K. Tsel tvorchestva. Moskva, 1913.

Phil 6332.24   Die erbliche Lese- rechtssch Reiheschwäche. (Weinschenk, Curt.) Bern, 1962.

Phil 5404.4.5   Die Erblichkeit. (Ribot, T.) Paris, 1897.

Phil 5440.4.3   Die Erblichkeit. v.1-4. (Ribot, T.) Leipzig, 1876.

Phil 4080.10.85   Ercole, P. d'. Notizia degli scritti e del pensiere filosofico di Pietro Ceretti. Torino, 1866.

Phil 4080.10.80   Ercole, P. d'. Il saggio di panlogica ovvero l'enciclopedia filosofica. Torino, 1911.

Phil 8659.4   Ercole, P. d'. Il teismo filosofico cristiano. pt.1. Torino, 1884.

Phil 4115.107   Ercole, Pasquale d'. Commemorazione della personalità e del pensiero filosofico. Torino, 1901.

Phil 3425.624   Erdei, László. Der Anfang der Erkenntnis. Kritische Analyse des ersten Kapitels der Hegelschen Logik. Budapest, 1964.

Phil 978.49.572   Erdensterben und Weltenleben und anthroposophisdie Lebensgaben. 2. Aufl. (Steiner, R.) Dornach, 1967.

Phil 978.49.670   Erdenwissen und Himmelserkenntnis. (Steiner, R.) Dornach, 1966.

Phil 3480.30.6.5   Erdmann, B. Beiträge zur Geschichte...Anhang zur. 5. Aufl. Berlin, 1900.

Phil 5244.15   Erdmann, B. Grundzüge der Reproduktions Psychologie. Berlin, 1920.

Phil 3486.1.10   Erdmann, B. Historische Untersuchungen über Kants Prolegomena. Halle, 1904.

Phil 3486.1.5   Erdmann, B. Kant's Kriticismus. Leipzig, 1878. 3 pam.

Phil 5044.1A   Erdmann, B. Logik. Halle, 1892.
Phil 5044.1.2   Erdmann, B. Logik. 2e Aufl. Halle, 1907.
Phil 5044.1.3   Erdmann, B. Logik. 3e Aufl. Berlin, 1923.
Phil 3549.5.90   Erdmann, B. Martin Knutzen und seine Zeit. Leipzig, 1876.
Phil 3486.1   Erdmann, B. Reflexionen Kants zur kritischen Philosophie. Leipzig, 1882-84. 2v.

Phil 5044.1.6   Erdmann, B. Umrisse zur Psychologie des Denkens. 2e Aufl. Tübingen, 1908.

Phil 6114.11.10   Erdmann, B. Wissenschaftliche Hypothesen über Leib und Seele. Köln, 1907.

Phil 6114.6   Erdmann, B. Wissenschaftliche Hypothesen über Leib und Seele. Köln, 1908.

Phil 5465.18   Erdmann, Benno. Die Funktionen der Phantasie im wissenschaftlichen Denken. Berlin, 1913.

Phil 510.124   Erdmann, Benno. Über den modernen Monismus. Berlin, 1914.
Phil 270.21   Erdmann, Benno. Über Inhalt und Geltung des Kausalgesetzes. Halle, 1905.

Phil 804.3.25   Pamphlet box. Erdmann, Benno. History of philosophy.
Phil 5545.78   Erdmann, E.J.E.T. Vom Vergessen. Berlin, 1869.
Phil 179.22.15   Erdmann, J.E. Ernste Spiele. 3. Aufl. Berlin, 1875.
Phil 179.22.5   Erdmann, J.E. Filosofiska miniaturer. Stockholm, 1873.
Phil 804.3   Erdmann, J.E. Grundriss der Geschichte der Philosophie. Berlin, 1869-70. 2v.

Phil 804.3.3A   Erdmann, J.E. Grundriss der Geschichte der Philosophie. 3e Aufl. Berlin, 1878. 2v.

Phil 804.3.4   Erdmann, J.E. Grundriss der Geschichte der Philosophie. 4. Aufl. Berlin, 1896. 2v.

Phil 5044.5.4   Erdmann, J.E. Grundriss der Logik und Metaphysik. Halle, 1864.

Phil 5044.5.2   Erdmann, J.E. Grundriss der Logik und Metaphysik. 2e Aufl. Halle, 1843.

Phil 5244.2.8   Erdmann, J.E. Grundriss der Psychologie. 4. Aufl. Leipzig, 1862.

Phil 5244.2.9   Erdmann, J.E. Grundriss der Psychologie. 5e Aufl. Leipzig, 1873.

Phil 804.3.5   Erdmann, J.E. History of philosophy. London, 1890. 3v.

Phil 804.3.7   Erdmann, J.E. History of philosophy. v.1, 2d ed.; v.2, 3d ed. London, 1890-92. 2v.

Phil 804.3.6   Erdmann, J.E. History of philosophy. v.1, 2d ed.; v.2-3, 3d ed. London, 1891-92. 3v.

X Cg   Phil 804.3.7   Erdmann, J.E. History of philosophy. 2d ed. v.3. London, 1891.

Phil 6114.11   Erdmann, J.E. Leib und Seele nach ihrem Begriff und ihrem Verhältniss zur Einander. Halle, 1837.
Phil 285.2   Erdmann, J.E. Natur oder Schöpfung? Leipzig, 1840.
Phil 5044.5.10   Erdmann, J.E. Outlines of logic and metaphysics. 4th rev. ed. London, 1896.

Phil 3004.5   Erdmann, J.E. Preussen und die Philosophie. Halle, 1954.
Phil 5244.2   Erdmann, J.E. Psychologische Briefe. Leipzig, 1856.
Phil 5244.2.10   Erdmann, J.E. Psychologische Briefe. 3e Aufl. Leipzig, 1863.

Phil 5244.2.12   Erdmann, J.E. Psychologische Briefe. 5e Aufl. Leipzig, 1875.

Phil 3200.7   Erdmann, J.E. Über den Naturalismus. Halle, 1854.
Phil 5435.6   Erdmann, J.E. Über Gewohnheiten und Angewohnheiten. Berlin, 1858.

Phil 179.22   Erdmann, J.E. Vermischte Aufsätze. Leipzig, 1846.
Phil 1704.1   Erdmann, J.E. Versuch...Geschichte der neuern Philosophie. Riga, 1834-53. 6v.

Phil 1704.1.5   Erdmann, J.E. Versuch...Geschichte der neuern Philosophie. Faksimile. Stuttgart, 1932-33. 10v.

Phil 179.22.10   Erdmann, J.E. Wir leben Nicht auf der Erde. Berlin, 1852-71. 5 pam.

Phil 3246.98   Erdmann, Johann E. Fichte, der Mann der Wissenschaft und des Katheders. Halle, 1862.

Phil 3801.367   Erdmann, Johann E. Über Schelling. Halle, 1857.
Htn   Phil 3801.367.2*   Erdmann, Johann E. Über Schelling. Halle, 1857.
Phil 3425.455   Erdmann, Johann Eduard. Abhandlung über Leib und Seele. Leiden, 1902.

Phil 5390.2.2   Erdmann, Johann Eduard. Über Dummheit. Berlin, 1866.
Phil 1730.6   Erdmann, Karl. Die theologische und philosophische Aufklärung des achtszehuten und neunzehuten Jahrhunderts. Leipzig, 1849.

Phil 5520.7   Erdmann, Karl O. Die Bedeutung des Wortes. Leipzig, 1900.
Phil 5520.7.2   Erdmann, Karl O. Die Bedeutung des Wortes. 2. Aufl. Leipzig, 1910.

Phil 9590.32.5   L'ére du cerveau. (Sendy, Jean.) Paris, 1970.
Phil 4019.10   L'eredità del neo-idealismo italiana. (Tozzi, Antonio.) Firenze, 1953.

Phil 9150.4.9   L'eredità organica e la formazione delle idealità morale. (Pagnone, Annibale.) Torino, 1904.

Phil 6328.15   Eredmények a magyar kiaérleti gyógypedagógiai és orvosi psychologia. (Schnell, János.) Budapest, 1929.

Phil 8430.38   Das Ereignis es Schönen. (Nebel, G.) Stuttgart, 1953.
Phil 978.49.470   Das Ereignis der Christuserscheinung in der ätherischen Welt. (Steiner, R.) Dornach, 1965.

Phil 3120.30.39.5   Ereignisse und Begegnungen. (Buber, Martin.) Berlin, 193-?

Phil 3120.30.39   Ereignisse und Begegnungen. (Buber, Martin.) Leipzig, 1920.

Phil 8430.48   Eremeev, Arkadii F. Vek nauki i iskusstvo. Moskva, 1965.
Phil 600.64   Erfahrung, Begründing und Reflexion. 1. Aufl. (Schnaedelbach, Herbert.) Frankfurt, 1971.

Phil 8613.31   Die Erfahrung des Todes. (Landsberg, P.L.) Luzern, 1937.
Phil 352.1   Erfahrung und Denken. (Volkelt, J.) Hamburg, 1886.
Phil 352.1.2   Erfahrung und Denken. Aufl. 2. (Volkelt, J.) Leipzig, 1924.

Phil 3450.11.114   Erfahrung und Urteil. (Husserl, Edmund.) Prag, 1939.
Phil 3100.52   Erfahrungsseelenlehre als Grundlage alles Wissens in ihren Hauptzügen Dargestellt. (Beneke, F.E.) Berlin, 1820.

Phil 14.8   Erfahung und Denker, Schriften zur Forderung der Beziehungen zwischen Philosophie und Einzelwissenschaften. Berlin. 1-32 13v.

Phil 5440.35   De erfelijkheid in de oudere Grieksche wetenschap. (Geurts, P.M.M.) Nijmegen, 1941.

Phil 9530.55   Erfolg und Gesellschaft. (Lamprecht, H.) München, 1964.
Phil 3549.8.95   Erforscher und Künder des Lebens. (Klages, Ludwig.) Linz, 1947.

Phil 8587.33.3   Die Erforschung der Gefühle und moralischen Begriffe. 3. Aufl. (Hoppe, J.I.) Regensburg, 1876.

Phil 5251.9   Die Erforschung der physiologische Naturgesetze. (Lichthorn, C.) Breslau, 1875.

Phil 2733.30.20   Erforschung der Wahrheit. (Malebranche, Nicolas.) München, 1914.

Phil 3246.17.5   Erganzungsband. (Fichte, Johann Gottlieb.) Leipzig, 1934.
Phil 5210.8.5   Ergebnisse der sowjetischen Psychologie. (Akademiia Pedagogicheskikh Nauk RSFSR, Moscow. Institut Psikhologii.) Berlin, 1967.

Phil 978.49.330   Ergebrisse der Geistesforschung. (Steiner, R.) Dornach, 1960.

Phil 3195.15.35   Die Ergreifung des Wirklichen. (Dingler, Hugo.) München, 1955.

Phil 5044.4   Erhard, A. Handbuch der Logik. München, 1839.
Phil 5814.4   Erhard, H. Hypnose bei Tieren. Giessen, 1924.
Phil 179.2   Erhard, F. Metaphysik. Leipzig, 1894.
Phil 5125.5   Erhardt, F. Der Satz von Grunde als Prinzip der Schliessens. Halle, 1891.

Phil 3486.2.9   Erhardt, Franz. Bleibendes und Vergängliches in der Philosophie Kants. Leipzig, 1926.

Phil 3486.2.7   Erhardt, Franz. Die Grundgedanken der Kritik der reinen Vernunft. Leipzig, 1924.

Phil 3486.2   Erhardt, Franz. Kritik der Kantischen Antinomienlehre. Cöthen, 1888.

Phil 3824.2   Erhardt, Franz. Die Philosophie des Spinoza. Leipzig, 1908.

Phil 6114.10   Erhardt, Franz. Die Wechselwirkung zwischen Leib und Seele. Leipzig, 1897.

Phil 3824.2.5   Erhardt, Franz. Die Weltanschauung Spinozas. Stuttgart, 1928.

Phil 8735.13   Erhart, Franz. Mechanismus und Teleologie. Leipzig, 1890.
Phil 3120.17.90   Erich Becher als Vertreter des Eudämonismus. Diss. (Thöne, Fritz.) Giessen, 1933.

Phil 5593.45   Erickson, Mary R. Large scale Rorschach techniques. 1. ed. Springfield, Ill., 1945.

Phil 583.6   Erickson, Stephen A. Language and being: an analytic phenomenology. New Haven, 1970.

Phil 978.49.915   Ericsson-Skopnik, Brigitte. Nachweis der Zitate zu Rudolf Steiner Die Rätsel der Philosophie im ihrer Geschichte als Umriss Dargestellt. Dornach, 1969.

Phil 5244.34   Erik H. Erikson; the growth of his work. 1st ed. (Coles, Robert.) Boston, 1970.

Phil 5374.225   Eriksen, Charles. Behavior and awareness. Durham, 1962.
Phil 672.125   Eriksen, R. Consciousness, life and the fourth dimension. London, 1923.

Phil 7054.188   Eriksen, R. Sjaelens gaade. Kristiania, 1893.
Phil 5244.17   Eriksen, R. Taenkningens psychologiske utviklingsbetingelser. Kristiania, 1915.

Phil 179.21   Eriksen, Richard. Tidens kurs. Kristiania, 1912.
Phil 6314.12.5A   Erikson, Eric H. Identity; youth and crisis. 1st ed. N.Y., 1868.

Phil 6314.12   Erikson, Eric H. Insight and responsibility. N.Y., 1964.
Phil 8448.25   Eriksson, Olle. Estetisk upplevelse. Stockholm, 1970.
Phil 4580.79   Erindringer. (Høffding, Harald.) København, 1928.
Phil 6319.1.32   Erinneringen. (Jung, C.G.) Zürich, 1962.
Phil 5545.193   Erinnerung und Gedächtnis. (Nohl, Johanna.) Langensalza, 1932.

Phil 974.3.119   Erinnerungen. v.1-2. (Steiner, M.) Dornach, 1949.
Phil 3160.9.95   Erinnerungen an Carl Gustav Carus. (Kloppe, Wolfgang.) Berlin, 1969.

Phil 3808.225   Erinnerungen an das Schopenhauers Schöne Aussicht. (Franz-Schneider, Lucia.) Frankfurt, 1959.

Phil 3210.66   Erinnerungen an die letzten Tage der Odlehre und ihre Urhebers. (Fechner, G.T.) Leipzig, 1876.

Phil 3640.169   Erinnerungen an Friedrich Nietzsche. (Deussen, Paul.) Leipzig, 1901.

Phil 3195.4.81   Erinnerungen an Karl Daub. (Rosenkranz, Karl.) Berlin, 1837.

Phil 974.3.123   Erinnerungen an Rudolf Steiner. (Muecke, Johanna.) Basel, 1955.

Phil 6315.2.226   Erinnerungen an Sigmund Freud. (Binswanger, Ludwig.) Bern, 1956.

Phil 3940.1.85   Erinnerungen eines Neunzigjährigen. (Zeller, Eduard.) Stuttgart, 1908.

Phil 5850.188   Erismann, T. Angewandte Psychologie. Berlin, 1916.
Phil 720.41   Erismann, T. Denken und Sein. v.1. Wien, 1950.
Phil 5244.9.15   Erismann, T. Die Eigenart des Geistigen. Leipzig, n.d.
Phil 5244.9.5   Erismann, T. Psychologie. Berlin, 1920.
Phil 8879.27   Erismann, T. Sein und Wollen. Wien, 1953.
Phil 5244.9.23   Erismann, Theodor. Allgemeine Psychologie. 3. Aufl. Berlin, 1962-1965. 4v.

Phil 4630.1.35   Eristiska blad. (Ribbing, Sigurd.) Upsala, 1852.
Phil 2150.22.145   E'rivoluzionaria la dottrina di Marcuse? (Ulle, Dieter.) Torino, 1969.

Phil 8893.140   Erkendelse og lidenskab. (Simonsen, Andreas.) København, 1966.

Phil 341.16.5   Erkendelseslaeren og naturvidenskabens grundbegreber. (Kruse, F.V.) København, 1960.

Phil 3850.32.10   Erkenne dich Selbst. (Spann, Othmar.) Jena, 1935.
Phil 3850.32.10.2   Erkenne dich Selbst. 2. Aufl. (Spann, Othmar.) Graz, 1968.

Phil 735.8   Das Erkennen und die Werturteile. (Lüdemann, H.) Leipzig, 1910.

Phil 179.3.32.5   Erkennen und Leben. (Eucken, R.) Berlin, 1923.
Phil 179.3.32   Erkennen und Leben. (Eucken, R.) Leipzig, 1912.
Phil 5047.12.9   Erkennen und Schliessen. (Hamilton, E.J.) N.Y., 1912.
Phil 197.31   Erkennen und Sein, Losung des Problems. (Widemann, P.H.) Karlsruhe, 1885.

Phil 5046.22.10   Erkennen und Zeit. (Grebe, Wilhelm.) München, 1931.
Phil 332.12   Erkenntnis, Wissenschaft, Philosophie. (Baumgarten, Arthur.) Tübingen, 1927.

Phil 10.27.8   Erkenntnis; zugleich Annalen de Philosophie. Leipzig. 1-9,1925-1929 7v.

Phil 10.27.3   Erkenntnis; zugleich Annalen de Philosophie. Leipzig. 1-10 8v.

Phil 2050.240   Erkenntnis. (Schaefer, Alfred.) Berlin, 1960?
Phil 3585.10.97   Die ErkenntnisDer Aussenwelt nach Theodor Lipps. Inaug. Diss. (Ehlen, Nikolaus.) Münster, 1914.

Phil 3120.66.30   Erkenntnis der Existenz. (Barth, Heinrich.) Basel, 1965.

Phil 978.49.460 — Die Erkenntnis der Seele und des Geistes. (Steiner, R.) Dornach, 1965.

Phil 400.64 — Die Erkenntnis der Wirklichkeiten. (Beggerow, H.) Halle, 1927.

Phil 338.13 — Erkenntnis Probleme und Erkenntnistheorie. (Höfler, Alois.) Leipzig, n.d.

Phil 2070.86 — Die erkenntnis-theoretischen Grundlagen von William James "The Varieties of Religious Experience." (Paetz, W.) Eilenburg, 1907.

Phil 334.4 — Erkenntnis-Theorie. (Dürr, Ernst.) Leipzig, 1910.

Phil 337.11 — Erkenntnis und Glaube. (Grisebach, E.) Halle an der Saale, 1923.

Phil 338.44 — Erkenntnis und Interesse. (Habermas, Jürgen.) Frankfurt am Main, 1968.

Phil 343.4 — Erkenntnis und Irrtum. (Mach, E.) Leipzig, 1905.

Phil 343.4.3 — Erkenntnis und Irrtum. 2. Aufl. (Mach, E.) Leipzig, 1906.

Phil 186.60 — Erkenntnis und Leben. (Litt, Theodor.) Leipzig, 1923.

Phil 165.225 — Erkenntnis und Verantwortung. (Derbolav, Josef.) Düsseldorf, 1960.

Phil 735.276 — Erkenntnis und Wert. (Europaeisches Forum, Alpbach, Austria, 1946.) Salzburg, 1946.

Phil 341.16.10 — Erkenntnis und Wertung; das Grundproblem. (Kruse, F.V.) Berlin, 1960.

Phil 343.60 — Erkenntnis und Wirklichkeit. (Mercier, André.) Bern, 1968.

Phil 332.18.5 — Die Erkenntnisbeziehung. (Boldt, Karl.) Tübingen, 1937.

Phil 5060.3.5 — Erkenntniskritische Logik. (Uphues, G.) Halle, 1909.

Phil 5260.5 — Erkenntniskritische Psychologie. (Uphues, G.) Halle, 1909.

Phil 343.19 — Erkenntniskritische Weltanschauung. (Meisner, E.) Leipzig, 1936.

Phil 341.32 — Erkenntnislehre. (Kraft, Victor.) Wien, 1960.

Phil 349.36 — Erkenntnislehre. Bd. I-II. (Stumpf, Karl.) Leipzig, 1939-1940.

Phil 1504.2 — Die Erkenntnislehre. v.2, pt.1. (Baumgartner, M.) Münster, 1895.

Phil 1504.10.3 — Die Erkenntnislehre Anselms von Canterbury. (Fischer, J.) Münster, 1911.

Phil 1523.8 — Die Erkenntnislehre bei Beginn der Scholastik. (Schneider, Artur.) Fulda, 1921.

Phil 3260.86 — Die Erkenntnislehre bei Fries. Inaug. Diss. (Mechler, W.) Berlin, 1911.

Phil 400.21.5 — Die Erkenntnislehre des modernen Idealismus. (Willems, C.) Trier, 1906.

Phil 1504.19.4 — Die Erkenntnislehre Richards von St. Viktor. v.19, pt.4-6. (Ebner, J.) Münster, 1917.

Phil 3850.30.90 — Erkenntnislehre und Metaphysik Jakob Seuglers, 1799-1878. Inaug. Diss. (Fassbender, Johann.) Bonn, 1937.

Phil 2730.87 — Die Erkenntnislehre von Maine de Biran. (Baumgarten, Franz.) Krakau, 1911.

Phil 835.4 — Das Erkenntnisproblem; ein historischkritischer Versuch. (Thomas, Viktor.) Stuttgart, 1921.

Phil 341.9 — Das Erkenntnisproblem...kritische Lösung. (Kern, Berthold.) Berlin, 1911.

Phil 333.5 — Das Erkenntnisproblem in der Philosophie. (Cassirer, Ernst.) Berlin, 1906-57. 4v.

Phil 333.5.3 — Das Erkenntnisproblem in der Philosophie. 2. Aufl. (Cassirer, Ernst.) Berlin, 1911. 2v.

Phil 3425.115 — Das Erkenntnisproblem in Hegels Philosophie. (Phalén, A.) Upsala, 1912.

Phil 349.2 — Erkenntnisslehre. (Sengler, J.) Heidelberg, 1858.

Phil 3483.30 — Die Erkenntnisslehre des Aristoteles und Kant's. (Biese, Reinhold.) Berlin, 1877.

Phil 5058.7 — Erkenntnisstheoretische Logik. (Schuppe, W.) Bonn, 1878.

Phil 3552.99 — Die Erkenntnisstheorien bei Leibniz und Kant. (Volz, L.) Rostock, 1895.

Phil 8587.35 — Die erkenntnistheoretische Begründung der Religion. (Heinzelmann, G.) Basel, 1915.

Phil 352.3 — Erkenntnistheoretische Grundzüge der Naturwissenschaften. (Volkmann, P.) Leipzig, 1896.

Phil 352.3.5 — Erkenntnistheoretische Grundzüge der Naturwissenschaften. (Volkmann, P.) Leipzig, 1910.

Phil 3640.79.15 — Erkenntnistheoretische Schriften. (Nietzsche, Friedrich.) Frankfurt, 1968.

Phil 337.8 — Erkenntnistheoretische Studien auf antipsychologistischer Grundlage. (Gurland-Eljaschoff, E.) Bern, 1910.

Phil 14.20 — Der erkenntnistheoretische Subjektivismus. München. 1,1962+ 2v.

Phil 331.33.10 — Erkenntnistheoretische und methodologische Probleme der Wissenschaft. (Akademiia Nauk SSSR. Institut Filosofii.) Berlin, 1966.

Phil 341.15 — Erkenntnistheoretische Untersuchaungen. (Koch, Julius L.) Göppingen, 1918.

Phil 3195.6.91 — Die erkenntnistheoretischen Grundgedanken Wilhelm Diltheys. (Cüppers, Clemens.) Leipzig, 1933.

Phil 3195.6.92 — Die erkenntnistheoretischen Grundgedanken Wilhelm Diltheys. Inaug. Diss. (Cüppers, Clemens.) Leipzig, 1933.

Phil 3790.4.82 — Die erkenntnistheoretischen Grundlagen in Rickerts Lehre von der Transzendenz. Inaug. Diss. (Schneider, Max.) Dresden, 1918.

Phil 356.1.5 — Erkenntnistheorie...Grundlage. (Ziehen, T.) Jena, 1913.

Phil 835.6 — Erkenntnistheorie. (Kuntze, Friedrich.) München, 1927.

Phil 353.12 — Erkenntnistheorie. (Weinberg, Siegfried.) Berlin, 1930.

Phil 341.3 — Erkenntnistheorie der Naturforschung. (Kleinseter, H.) Leipzig, 1905.

Phil 310.80 — Die Erkenntnistheorie des dialektischen Materialismus. (Vries, Joseph de.) München, 1958.

Phil 3585.8.83 — Erkenntnistheorie des Ernst Laas. Inaug. Diss. (Gjurits, D.) Leipzig, 1902.

Phil 974.3.132 — Die Erkenntnistheorie Rudolf Steiners. (Kallert, Bernhard.) Stuttgart, 1960.

Phil 338.17.5 — Erkenntnistheorie und Lebensauffassung. (Höffding, H.) Leipzig, 1926.

Phil 960.39 — Erkenntnistheorie und Logik. (Shcherbatskii, F.I.) München, 1924.

Phil 341.5 — Erkenntnistheorie und Naturwissenschaft. (Külpe, O.) Leipzig, 1910.

Phil 3310.2.80 — Die Erkenntnistheorie von Carl Göring. Inaug. Diss. (Ganewa, R.) Heidelberg, 1910.

Phil 3890.6.80 — Die Erkenntnistheorie von Tetens. (Störring, Gustav.) Leipzig, 1901.

Phil 185.54 — Der Erkenntnistrieb als Lebens und Todesprinzip. (Klatzkin, Jakob.) Zürich, 1935.

Phil 353.11 — Erkjendelsens problem. (Wilkens, Claudius.) København, 1875.

Phil 8591.21 — Erkjendelses-teortisk religionsfilosofi. (Landmark, J.D.) Købenahvn, 1908.

Phil 5258.86 — Erklären und Verstehen in der Psychologie. (Schweizer, Walter.) Bern, 1924.

Phil 8423.23 — Das Erklären von Kunstwerken. (Woelfflin, H.) Köln, 1940.

Phil 5649.8.5 — Die Erklärung der Bewegungsempfindungen. Inaug. Diss. (Schäfer, Karl.) Jena, 1889.

Phil 5045.8.20 — Erklaerung der Logik. (Feder, J.G.H.) Wien, 1793-94. 3v.

Phil 7060.18 — Erklärung der Sinnestäuschungen. (Hoppe, J.F.) Würzburg, 1888.

Phil 7060.33 — Die Erklärung des Gedankenlesens. (Preyer, W.) Leipzig, 1886.

Phil 6420.4 — Erklärung des Stotterns, dessèn Heilung und Verhütung. (Greenbaum, Ferdinand.) Leipzig, 1897.

Phil 3246.223 — Erklärung über Fichte's Appellation. (Schaumann, J.C.G.) Giessen, 1799.

Phil 3488.18.5 — Erklärung und Vertheidigung von Kant's Kritik der reinen Vernueft wider die "sogenannten" Erläuterungen des J.H.v. Kirchmann. (Grapengiesser, C.) Jena, 1871.

Phil 4815.223.35 — Az erkölcsi világ. (Bodnár, Zsigmond.) Budapest, 1896.

Phil 3483.1 — Erläuternder Auszug. (Beck, J.S.) Riga, 1793-96. 3v.

Htn Phil 3801.763* — Erläuterung einiger Hauptpunkt der Philosophie. (Salat, Jakob.) Landshut, 1812.

Phil 3500.14 — Erläuterungen...Kant Critik der reinen Vernunft. (Schulze, J.) Frankfurt, 1791.

Phil 3500.14.2 — Erläuterungen...Kant Critik der reinen Vernunft. (Schulze, J.) Königsberg, 1784.

Phil 5240.25.5 — Erläuterungen wichtiger Gegenstände aus der philosophischen und christlichen Moral. (Abel, Jacob Friedrich von.) Tübingen, 1790.

Phil 3830.1.5 — Erläuterungen zu Benedict von Spinoza's Ethik. (Kirchmann, J.H. von.) Berlin, 1869.

Phil 3425.91.19 — Erläuterungen zu Hegel's Encyklopädie der philosophischen Wissenschaften. (Rosenkranz, K.) Leipzig, 1920.

Phil 3428.91 — Erläuterungen zu Herbarts Ethik. (Felsh.) Langensalza, 1899.

Phil 2115.121 — Erläuterungen zu John Locke's Versuch über den menschlichen Verstand. Abt II. (Kirchmann, J.H.) Berlin, 1874.

Phil 3492.1.5 — Erläuterungen zu Kant's kleinern Schriften. (Kirchmann, J.) Berlin, 1873.

Phil 3492.1 — Erläuterungen zu Kant's Kritik. (Kirchmann, J.) Berlin, 1869-73. 7 pam.

Phil 3483.14 — Erläuterungen zu Kant's Kritik der reinen Vernunft. (Bilharz, Altons.) Wiesbaden, 1884.

Phil 3640.162 — Erläuterungen zu Nietzsches Zarathustra. (Messer, August.) Stuttgart, 1922.

Phil 3415.36 — Erläuterungen zur Metaphysik der Bewussten. (Hartmann, Eduard von.) Berlin, 1874.

Phil 197.1.5 — Erläuterungen zur Organon der menschlichen Erkenntniss. (Wagner, J.) Ulm, 1854.

Phil 3830.1 — Erlauterungen zu Benedict von Spinoza's. (Kirchmann, J.H. von.) Berlin, 1870-72. 5 pam.

Phil 4803.462.45 — Erlebnis, Kunstwerk und Wert. (Ingarden, Roman.) Tübingen, 1969.

Phil 4580.37.5 — Erlebnis und Deutung; eine vergleichende Studie zur Religionspsychologie. (Høffding, Harald.) Stuttgart, 1923.

Phil 5425.60 — Das Erlebnis und die Leistung. Inaug. Diss. (Holste, Maria.) Düsseldorf, 1936.

Phil 293.24 — Erlebnis und Wirklichkeit. (Mally, E.) Leipzig, 1935.

Phil 5227.4 — Erlebnis und Wissen. (Ruin, Hans.) Helsingfors, 1921.

Phil 978.49.905 — Erlebte Pädagogik. (Grosse, Rudolf.) Dornach, 1968.

Phil 3915.77.50 — Erlebtes und Erkanntes. (Wundt, Wilhelm.) Stuttgart, 1920.

Phil 3915.78 — Erlebtes und Erkanntes. 2. Aufl. (Wundt, Wilhelm.) Stuttgart, 1921.

Phil 4620.1.5 — Erlendar Greiner. (Péturss, Helgi.) Reykjavík, 1955.

Phil 8590.25 — Der Erlösungs- und Heilsgedanke von freisinnig protestantischen Standpunkt. (Koppelmann, W.) Bonn, 1925.

Phil 7068.92.65 — Ermacora, G.B. I fatti spiritici e le ipotesi affrettate. Padova, 1892.

Phil 7060.44 — Ermacora, G.B. La telepatia. Padova, 1898.

Phil 3552.23.10 — Ermahnung anu die Deutschen. (Leibniz, Gottfried Wilhelm.) Darmstadt, 1967.

Phil 3565.88 — Ermanno Lotze e la sua filosofia. (Ambrosi, L.) Milano, 1912.

Phil 5047.4 — Ermhneia logica...burgersdicianae. (Heereboord, Adriano.) Cantabridgiae, 1663.

Phil 5047.4.5 — Ermhneia logica...burgersdicianae. (Heereboord, Adriano.) London, 1676.

Phil 1704.1.10 — Ermolenko, D.V. Kritika sovremennoi burzruaznoi filosofii. Moskva, 1959.

Phil 1804.5 — Ermolenko, Dimitrii V. Sovremennaia burzhuaznaia filosofiia SShA. Moskva, 1965.

Phil 6128.82 — Die Ermüdung; Symptome, Theorien, Messversache. (Schmidtke, Heinz.) Bern, 1965.

Phil 6122.7.4 — Die Ermüdung. (Mosso, A.) Leipzig, 1892.

Phil 4115.84 — Ern, V.F. Filosofiia dzhoberti. Moskva, 1916.

Phil 4755.1 — Ern, Vladimir F. Bor'ba za Logos. Moskva, 1911.

Phil 3425.82 — Erner, F. Die Psychologie der Hegelschen Schule. Leipzig, 1842-44. 2v.

Phil 2775.1.80 — Ernest Naville, sa vie et sa pensée. (Naville, E.) Genève, 1913-17. 2v.

Phil 2880.5.90 — Ernest Seillière. (Boudeau, J.M.L.) Paris, 1925.

Phil 978.49.285 — Die Erneuerung der pädagogisch-didaktischen Kunst. (Steiner, R.) Dornach, 1958.

Phil 8968.11 — Die Erneuerung des Abendlandes. (Schwellenbach, R.) Berlin, 1922.

Phil 3425.110 — Die Erneuerung des Hegelianismus. (Windelband, W.) Heidelberg, 1910.

Phil 3525.35 — Erneute Vernunftkritik. (Krause, K.C.F.) Prag, 1868.

Phil 5871.10 — Erni, Margrit. Das Vaterbild den Tocher. Diss. n.p., 1965.

Phil 3552.249 — Ernst, Charles. Die Tierseele in der leibnizschen Philosophie. Wiesbaden, 1918.

Phil 5421.5 — Ernst, F. Vom Heimweh. Zürich, 1949.

Phil 3486.7 — Ernst, W. Der Zweckbegriff bei Kant. Halle, 1909.

Phil 3625.3.80 — Ernst als Philosoph, Physiker und Psycholog, eine Monographie. (Henning, Hans.) Leipzig, 1915.

Phil 3120.55.85 — Ernst Bloch zu ehren. (Unseld, Siegfried.) Frankfurt, 1965.

Phil 176.69.80 — Ernst Blochs Revision des Marxismus. (Konferenz über Fragen der Blochschen Philosophie. Berlin, 1957.)

Phil 176.69.80.5 — Ernst Blochs Revision des Marxismus. (Leipzig. Universität.) Berlin, 1957.

Phil 3160.12.80 — Ernst Cassirer. (Rein, Mercedes.) Montevideo, 1959.

Phil 510.1.45 — Ernst Gekkel' pered sudom logiki. (Shiltov., A.) Khar'kov, 1907.

Phil 510.1.37   Ernst Haeckel. v.1-2. (Franz, Victor.) Jena, 1944.
Phil 510.1.25   Ernst Haeckel im Kampf gegen die christliche Weltanschauung. (Wobbermin, Georg.) Leipzig, 1906.
Phil 978.49.885   Ernst Haeckel und Rudolf Steiner. (Ballmer, Karl.) Besazio, 1965.
Phil 510.1.21   Ernst Haeckels Welträtsel oder der Neomaterialismus. (Menzi, Theodor.) Zürich, 1901.
Phil 3625.3.100   Ernst Mach. (Heller, K.) Wien, 1964.
Phil 3625.3.94   Ernst Mach. (Mises, R.) 's-Gravenhage, 1938.
Phil 3625.3.89   Ernst Mach: Gedächtnisrede. (Wlassak, R.) Leipzig, 1917.
Phil 5635.5.11   Ernst Mach's Philosophie. (Hell, B.) Stuttgart, 1907.
Phil 3625.3.105   Ernst Machs Überwindung des mechanischen Materialismus. (Adler, Friedrich.) Wien, 1918.
Phil 3745.1.80   Ernst Platner als Moralphilosophe. (Bergemann, P.) Halle, 1891.
Phil 3745.1.153   Ernst Platner und die Kunstphilosophie. (Bergmann, Ernst.) Leipzig, 1913.
Phil 8599.19.109   Ernst Troeltsch. (Köhler, Walther.) Tübingen, 1941.
Phil 3890.10.120   Ernst Troeltsch o el drama del historicismo. (Waismann, A.) Cordoba, 1955.
Phil 3890.10.100   Ernst Troeltschs historische Weltanschauung. (Brachmann, W.) Halle, 1940.
Phil 179.22.15   Ernste Spiele. 3. Aufl. (Erdmann, J.E.) Berlin, 1875.
Phil 8635.7   Ernster Blick. (Kast, J.) Würzburg, 1818.
Phil 3485.15   Ernstes und Heiteres über Kant. (Dahl, J.) Cottbus, 1933.
Phil 3018.25   Ernte deutscher Humanitat. 2. Aufl. (Siebecke, H.) Bad Nauheim, 1952.
Phil 7068.95.15   Erny, Alfred. Le psychisme expérimental. Paris, 1895.
Htn   Phil 9342.15*   Erö-paideia, or The institution of a young noble man. (Cleland, James.) Oxford, 1607.
Phil 4815.368.30   Erösdi, Mihály. Kritikus objectiv metaphysîka. Budapest, 1885.
Phil 9245.33.10   Erövringen av lyckan. (Payot, Jules.) Stockholm, 1923.
X Cg   Phil 7075.144   Erogeneity and libido. (Fliess, Robert.) N.Y., 1957.
Phil 4065.60.30   Eroici furori, Ubersetzt von L. Kuhlenbeck. (Bruno, Giordano.) Leipzig, 1898.
Phil 4170.12.10   Eroicità ed ereticalità della filosofia. (Mei, Flavio.) Milano, 1968.
Phil 6315.2.310.5   Eros and civilization; a philosophical inquiry into Freud. (Marcuse, Herbert.) Boston, 1966.
Phil 6315.32   Eros and civilization. (Marcuse, Herbert.) Boston, 1955.
Phil 6315.2.310.3   Eros and civilization. (Marcuse, Herbert.) N.Y., 1962.
Phil 176.132   Eros and Psyche. (Branford, B.) London, 1934.
Phil 1170.18   Eros and Psyche. (Rist, John M.) Toronto, 1964.
Phil 9495.160.15   Eros at bay; the illusion of modern love. (Koehn-Behrens, Charlotte.) London, 1962.
Phil 6315.2.310.10   Eros et civilization. (Marcuse, Herbert.) Paris, 1963.
Phil 2150.22.150   Eros i rewolucja. Wyd. 1. (Szewczyk, Jan.) Warszawa, 1971.
Htn   Phil 5052.31*   Erotemata dialectices. (Melanchthon, Philipp.) Lipsiae, 1559. 2 pam.
Phil 9340.12   Die Erotik. (Andreas-Salomé, Lou.) Frankfurt, 1910.
Phil 5627.39   Erotogenesis of religion. (Schroeder, Theodore.) N.Y., 1916.
Phil 5627.40   Erotogenesis of religion. (Schroeder, Theodore.) St. Louis, 1913.
Phil 5635.26   Erregung secundärer Empfindungen im Gebiete der Sinnesorgane. Inaug. Diss. (Deichmann, Ludwig.) Greifswald, 1889.
Phil 3018.7.9   L'erreur de la philosophie allemande. (Santayana, G.) Paris, 1917.
Phil 7069.30.8.15   L'erreur spirite. (Guénon, R.) Paris, 1930.
Phil 2725.2.73   Les erreurs. (Lamennais, F.R. de.) Bruxelles, n.d.
Phil 3450.19.100   Erro, C.A. Dialogo existencial. Buenos Aires, 1937.
Phil 6132.8   Errors of mind healing. (Willman, R.) St. Joseph, 1909.
Phil 8583.7.5   Der Ersatz der Religion. (Dühring, E.K.) Karlsruhe, 1883.
Phil 7068.36   Eine Erscheinung aus dem Nachtgebiete der Natur. (Kerner, J.) Stuttgart, 1826.
Phil 3497.30   Erscheinung bei Kant. Habilitationsschrift. (Prauss, Gerold.) Berlin, 1971.
Phil 5585.9.5   Die Erscheinung der Dinge. (Heman, Karl F.) Leipzig, 1881.
Phil 6320.7   Erscheinungsformen der Seele. (Kohnstamm, O.) München, 1927.
Phil 8419.14   Erschopfte Kunst oder Kunstformalismus? (Shishkov, G.) Schlehdorf, 1952.
Phil 396.20   Die erschreckende Zivilisation. (Salzburger Humanismusgespräch.) Wien, 1970.
Phil 3501.10   Die erste Antinomie Kants und der Pantheismus. (Toll, C.H.) Berlin, 1910.
Phil 3425.24   Erste Druckschriften. (Hegel, Georg Wilhelm Friedrich.) Leipzig, 1928.
Phil 3480.50.18   Erste Einleitung in die Kritik der Urteilskraft. (Kant, Immanuel.) Leipzig, 1927.
Phil 3480.50.18.3   Erste Einleitung in die Kritik der Urteilskraft. (Kant, Immanuel.) Stuttgart, 1965.
Phil 3480.50.18.4   Erste Einleitung in die Kritik der Urteilskraft. 2. Aufl. (Kant, Immanuel.) Hamburg, 1970.
Phil 181.26.3   Erste Gründe. 3. Aufl. v.1-2. (Gottsched, J.C.) Leipzig, 1739.
Phil 181.26.7   Erste Grunde der Weltweisheit. 7. Aufl. (Gottsched, J.C.) Leipzig, 1762. 2v.
Phil 181.26.5   Erste Grunder der Weltweisheit. (Gottsched, J.C.) Leipzig, 1749. 2v.
Phil 5243.10.2   Erste Grundlehren der mathematischen Psychologie. (Drobisch, M.W.) Leipzig, 1850.
Phil 5058.42   Erste Grundlinien der Logik oder Verstandeslehre. (Snell, F.W.D.) Gieosen, 1828.
Phil 3246.79.20   Erste und zweite Einleitung in die Wissenschaftslehre und Versuch einer neuen Darstellung der Wissenschaftslehre. (Fichte, Johann Gottlieb.) Hamburg, 1954.
Htn   Phil 3800.380*A   Erste Vorlesung in Berlin, 15 nov. 1841. (Schelling, F.W.J. von.) Stuttgart, 1841.
Phil 3246.44.10.5   Erste Wissenschaftslehre ven 1804. (Fichte, Johann Gottlieb.) Stuttgart, 1964.
Phil 5875.64   Erstellung eines Projektiven Verfahrens zur psychologischen Untersuchung nichtsprechender und hochgradig sprechbehinderten Kinder. (Muehling, Ursel.) Köln, 1968.
Htn   Phil 3800.160*A   Erster Entwurf eines Systems der Naturphilosophie. (Schelling, F.W.J. von.) Jena, 1799.
Phil 5520.636   Ertel, Suitbert. Psychophonetik; Untersuchungen über Lautsymbolik und Motivation. Göttingen, 1969.
Phil 804.8   Ertsei, D. Philosophia historiaja. Debreczen, 1825.
Phil 332.9   Ervaringswijsbegeerte. (Betz, H.J.) 's-Gravenhage, 1881.
Phil 3808.47   Das Erwacher aus dem Leben- Fraum. (Schopenhauer, Arthur.) Pfullingen, 1961.

Phil 3850.6.79   Der Erwerb aus...Leben: eine Selbstbiographie. (Schubert, G.H.) Erlangen, 1854-56. 3v.
Phil 8419.43   Erwin; vier Gespräche über das Schöne une die Kunst. (Solger, K.W.F.) Berlin, 1815. 2v.
Phil 8419.43.2   Erwin. (Solger, K.W.F.) München, 1971.
Phil 8584.21   Eryshev, A.A. Religiia, vrag ravnopraviia i druzhby narodov. Kiev, 1962.
Phil 6315.55   Erzieherliebe als Heilmittel. (Frost, M.) Bern, 1920.
Phil 974.3.145   Erziehung aus Menschenerkenntnis. (Hartmann, Georg.) Dornach, 1961.
Phil 974.3.147   Erziehung aus Menschenerkenntnis: von pädagogischen Impuls der Anthroposophie Rudolf Steiners. 2. Aufl. (Hartmann, Georg.) Dornach, 1969.
Phil 6328.2.28   Erziehung derEltern. (Stekel, Wilhelm.) Wien, 1934.
Phil 5765.2.5   Die Erziehung des Willens. (Payot, Jules.) Leipzig, 1901.
Phil 3475.3.180   Erziehung und Selbstsein. (Tollhoetter, Bernhard.) Rätingen, 1966.
Phil 978.49.679   Erziehungskunst; Methodisch-Didaktisches. 4. Aufl. (Steiner, R.) Dornach, 1966. 2v.
Phil 978.93   Es Ist an der Zeit. (Kuhn, Hans.) Nürnberg, 1965.
Phil 4210.124   Esame critico delle XL proposizioni rosminiane condaunate dalla S.R.U. inquisizione. (Morando, G.) Milano, 1905.
Phil 3425.237.5   Esame dell'Hegelianismo. (Allievo, G.) Torino, 1897.
Phil 5525.50   Esar, Evan. The humor of humor. London, 1954.
Phil 4462.1.30   Esboços e fragmentos. (Bevilaqua, Clovis.) Rio de Janeiro, 1899.
Phil 4960.605.20   Esbozo de una história de las ideas en el Brasil. (Cruz Costa, João.) México, 1957.
Phil 210.50   Esbroeck, Michel van. Herméneutique. Paris, 1968.
Phil 181.69.10   L'escalado des siécles. (Gorce, M.M.) Saint-Imier, 1967.
Phil 5871.60   Escalona, Sibylle Korsch. The roots of individuality. Chicago, 1968.
Phil 6315.19.20   Escape from authority. (Schaar, John H.) N.Y., 1961.
Phil 6315.19   Escape from freedom. (Fromm, Erich.) N.Y., 1941.
Phil 5590.455.6   Escape from loneliness. (Tournier, Paul.) Philadelphia, 1962.
Phil 4073.70   Escatologia. (Campanella, Tommaso.) Roma, 1969.
Phil 3001.7   Eschatologie en Historie. (Slotemaker de Bruine, N.A.C.) Wageningen, 1925.
Phil 8629.4   Eschatologie et cosmologie. Bruxelles, 1969.
Phil 8627.3.10   Eschatology. (Charles, R.H.) N.Y., 1963.
Phil 3425.272   Eschenmayer, C.A. Die Hegel'sche Religions-Philosophie. Tübingen, 1834.
Phil 3200.6   Eschenmayer, C.A. Die Philosophie. Erlangen, 1803.
Phil 8584.3   Eschenmayer, C.A. Religionsphilosophie. v.1-3. Tübingen, 1818-24. 2v.
Phil 6674.2   Eschenmayer, C.A. Versuch der scheinbare Magie der thierischen Magnetismus. Stuttgart, 1816.
Phil 5244.3   Eschenmayer, C.A.A. Psychologie. Stuttgart, 1817.
Phil 8879.7   Eschenmayer, C.A.A. System der Moralphilosophie. Stuttgart, 1818.
Phil 179.29   Eschenmayer, C.H. von. Einleitung in Natur und Geschichte. Erlangen, 1806.
Phil 6114.13   Eschricht, D.F. Om de uvilkaarlige livsyttringers forhold til de vilkaarlige. Kjøbenhavn, 1845.
Phil 8430.49   Esci. (Stardelov, Georgi.) Skopje, 1958.
Phil 574.8   Escobar, Edmundo. Francisco Larroyo y su personalismo crítico. 1. ed. México, 1970.
Phil 186.92   Escolas filosoficas. (Lins, I.M.de B.) Rio, 1939.
Phil 2475.1.460   Escritores doutrinados. (Ribeiro, Alvaro.) Lisboa, 1965.
Phil 2520.206   Escritos en honor de Descartes. (La Plata. Universidad Nacional.) La Plata, 1938.
Phil 4967.35   Escritos filosóficos. (Franceschi, Alfredo.) La Plata, 1968.
Phil 4973.5.6   Escritos filosóficos. (Lombardo Toledano, Vicente.) México, 1937.
Phil 5643.91   Escudo apologetico, physico, optico occidental. (Botelho de Oliveyra, B.) Lisboa, 1720.
Phil 4313.5   La escuela de Madrid. (Marias Aguilera, Julian.) Buenos Aires, 1959.
Phil 8146.2   La escuela estetica catalana contemporanea. (Querolgavaldá, M.) Madrid, 1953.
Phil 8581.45.15   Escursioni spirituali. (Buonaiuti, Ernesto.) Roma, 1921.
Phil 6674.4   Esdaile, James. Mesmerism in India. Hartford, 1847.
Phil 3483.92   Esegesi e letture kantiane. (Banfi, Antonio.) Urbino, 1969. 2v.
VPhil 2725.2.120   Eseję o dialogach wewnętrznych: Diderot, Lamennais. (Litwin, Jakub.) Warszawa, 1967.
Phil 5401.49   La esencia del valor. (Mexico (City). Universidad Nacional. Facultad de Filosofía y Letras.) México, 1964.
Phil 4960.205   Esencialismo. 1. ed. (Copelli y Marroni, Francisco.) Buenos Aires, 1957.
Phil 8406.16   La eseneia humana de las formos. (Ferrant, Angel.) Santander, 1952.
Phil 4120.1.45   Esercizio logico sugli errori d'ideologia. (Gioja, Melchiorre.) Milano, 1824.
Phil 3235.122   Esin, Ivan M. Die materialistishe Philosophie Ludwig Feuerbachs. 1. Aufl. Berlin, 1956.
Phil 8877.76   Esiste una morale? (Colesanti, Giulio.) Catania, 1937.
Phil 3450.19.440   Esistenza de essere in Heidegger. (Manno, Ambrogio Giacomo.) Napoli, 1967.
Phil 8673.9   Esistenza di Dio. (Sacchi, Gaetano.) Roma, 1919.
Phil 1750.378   Esistenza e coesistenza. (Galamini, L.) Milano, 1953.
Phil 2880.8.260   Esistenza e corporeità in Sartre. (Papone, Annagrazia.) Firenze, 1969.
Phil 194.19.35   L'esistenza e l'anima. (Tarozzi, Giuseppe.) Bari, 1930.
Phil 1750.340.8   Esistenza e persona. 3. ed. (Pareyson, Luigi.) Torino, 1966.
Phil 4110.15.80   Esistenza e realtà nella fenomenologia di Vito Fazio-Allmayer. (Fazio-Allmayer, Bruna.) Bologna, 1968.
Phil 3450.11.355   Esistenza e storia negli inediti di Husserl. (Piana, G.) Milano, 1965.
Phil 2750.20.125   Esistenza e struttura. (Bonomi, Andrea.) Milano, 1967.
Phil 1750.470   L'esistenzialismo. (Campbell, Robert.) Napoli, 1955.
Phil 1750.560   L'esistenzialismo. (Chiodi, Pietro.) Torino, 1957.
Phil 1750.285   Esistenzialismo. (Jaspers, Karl.) Roma, 1946.
Phil 1750.535   Esistenzialismo. (Oggioni, Emilio.) Bologna, 1956.
Phil 1750.368   Esistenzialismo. (Prini, P.) Roma, 1952.
Phil 4215.8.32   L'esistenzialismo. 1. ed. (Ruggiero, Guido de.) Bari, 1943.
Phil 1750.357   Esistenzialismo ateo ed esistenzialismo teistro. (Stefanini, L.) Padova, 1952.
Phil 1750.371   Esistenzialismo cristiano. (Archivio di Filosofia.) Padova, 1949.
Phil 3450.19.108   L'esistenzialismo di Heidegger. (Chiodi, Pietro.) Torino, 1947.

Phil 3450.19.108.3   L'esistenzialismo di Heidegger. 3e ed. (Chiodi, Pietro.) Torino, 1965.

Phil 1750.560.10   Esistenzialismo e fenomenologia. (Chiodi, Pietro.) Milano, 1963.

Phil 4018.8   Esistenzialismo e filosofia italiana. (Santucci, Antonio.) Bologna, 1959.

Phil 1750.480   Esistenzialismo e storicismo. 1. ed. (Paci, Enzo.) Milano, 1950.

Phil 1750.270   Esistenzialismo positivo; due saggi. 1. ed. (Abbagnano, Nicola.) Torino, 1948.

Phil 1750.450   L'esistenzialismo positivo di Nicola Abbagnano. (Giannini, G.) Brescia, 1956.

Phil 1750.372.5   Esistenzialismo teologico. (Castelli, Enrico.) Roma, 1966.

Phil 181.55   L'esistere quale oggetto di scienza e di storia. Parte 1a. (Greca, Carlo.) Girgenti, 1925.

Phil 3460.96   L'esito teologico della filosofia del linguaggio di Jacobi. (Olivetti, Marco M.) Padova, 1970.

Phil 9070.35   Eskartshausen, K. von. Klugheit vereind mit Tugend. Brünn, 1791.

Phil 3004.6   Esliu, Emilio. De la vida a la existencia en la filosofía contemporanea. La Plata, 1964.

NEDL Phil 14.4   The esoteric. Boston. 1-13 12v.
Phil 978.9.8   Esoteric Buddhism. (Sinnett, A.P.) Boston, 1885.
Phil 978.9.8.5   Esoteric Buddhism. 3d ed. (Sinnett, A.P.) Boston, 1886.
Phil 978.9.3   Esoteric Buddhism. 3rd ed. (Sinnett, A.P.) London, 1884.
Phil 978.9.7   Esoteric Buddhism. 5th ed. (Sinnett, A.P.) London, 1885.
Phil 978.9.9   Esoteric Buddhism. 6th ed. (Sinnett, A.P.) Boston, 1896.
Phil 978.6.25   Esoteric christianity. (Besant, Annie.) N.Y., 1902.
Phil 6114.5   Esoteric Christianity and mental therepeutics. (Evans, W.F.) Boston, n.d.

Phil 7069.64.5   ESP: a personal memoir. 1. ed. (Heywood, R.) N.Y., 1964.
Phil 5585.105   ESP and personality patterns. (Schmeidler, G.) New Haven, 1958.
Phil 7162.267.1   ESP and you. 1st ed. (Holzer, Hans W.) N.Y., 1968.
Phil 7162.267.5   ESP in life and lab. (Rhine, Louisa E.) N.Y., 1967.
Phil 7010.7   The ESP reader. (Knight, David C.) N.Y., 1969.
Phil 3483.43   L'espace et les temps chez Leibnizet chez Kant. (Biéma, Émile van.) Paris, 1908.

Phil 5465.170   L'espace figuratif et les structures de la personnalité, une épreuve clinique originale. (Le Men, Jean.) Paris, 1966. 2v.

Phil 672.214   L'espace humain. (Matoré, Georges.) Paris, 1962.
Phil 8080.12   Espacio y tiempo en el arte actual. (Hurtado, L.) Buenos Aires, 1941.

Phil 4376.2   España, sueño y verdad. (Zambrano, Maria.) Barcelona, 1965.

Phil 5252.46   Espèces et variétés d'intelligences. Thèse. (Mentré, F.) Paris, 1920.

Phil 5252.46.5   Espèces et variétés d'intelligences. Thèse. (Mentré, F.) Paris, 1920.

Phil 1504.3.5   Espenberger, J.N. Die Philosophie des Petrus Lombardus. v.3, pt.5. Münster, 1901.

Phil 6114.17   Espenschied, Richard. Der Leistungs kräftige Mensch. Hamburg, 1957.

Phil 5214.2   Esper, E.A. A history of psychology. Philadelphia, 1964.
Phil 5421.10.15   La espera y la esperanza. (Lain Entralgo, Pedro.) Madrid, 1957.

Phil 5421.10.16   La espera y la esperanza. 2. ed. (Lain Entralgo, Pedro.) Madrid, 1958.

Phil 2725.2.130   L'espérance et l'itinéraire de la certitude chez Lamennais. (Schmid, Beat.) Berne, 1970.

Phil 337.26   L'esperienza come oggettivazione. (Giovanni, Biagio de.) Napoli, 1962.

Phil 9513.25   L'esperienza e la prassi. (Carbonara, Cleto.) Napoli, 1964.

Phil 348.19   L'esperienza e la sua possibilita. (Rizzi, Erminio.) Padova, 1958.

Phil 186.80   L'esperienza e l'uomo. (Lombardi, F.) Firenze, 1935.
Phil 4005.12   Esperienza e metafisica. (Faggiotto, Pietro.) Padova, 1959.

Phil 181.145   Esperienza e metafisica nella filosofia moderna. (Garulli, Enrico.) Urbino, 1963.

Phil 8430.28   L'esperienza estetica e la vita del fanciullo. (Riverso, M.) Napoli, 1958.

Phil 8595.57   L'esperienza religiosa. (Paggiaro, Luigi.) Padova, 1964.
Phil 5627.267.15   Esperienza religiosa e coscienza religiosa e coscienza filosofica. (Banfi, Antonio.) Urbino, 1967.

Phil 1718.44   Esperienze del pensiero moderno. (Semerari, Giuseppe.) Urbino, 1969.

Phil 175.26.9   L'esperimento nella scienza. (Aliotta, Antonio.) Napoli, 1936.

Phil 5160.6   Espersen, Jon. Logik og argumenter. København, 1969.
Phil 2520.154   Espinas, Alfred. Etudes sur l'histoire de la philosophie de l'action. Paris, 1925. 2v.

Phil 4004.1   Espinas, Alfred. La philosophie expérimentale en Italie. Paris, 1880.

Phil 5814.2   Espinas, Alfred. Die Thierischen Gesellschaften; eine vergleichend- psychologische Untersuchung. 2. Aufl. Braunschweig, 1879.

Phil 8584.19   Espinosa, G. La mascarada cristiana. Santiago de Chile, 1940.

Phil 3824.4   Espinosa, G. Un pretendido interprete suramericano de Spinoza. Caracas, 1943.

Phil 3850.18.125   El espiritu y la vida en la filosofía de Max Scheler. (Gongora Perea, C.) Lima, 1943.

Phil 1020.7.3   La espiritualidad de Algozel y su sentido cristiano. (Asin Palacios, M.) Madrid, 1935-41.

Phil 530.40.55   Espiritualidad española. (Sainz Rodriguez, P.) Madrid, 1961.

Phil 530.70.12   Espiritualidad rusa por San Serafin de Sarov. Madrid, 1965.

Phil 4961.805.5   Espiritualismo y positivismo en el Uruguay. (Ardao, Arturo.) México, 1950.

Phil 4210.155   Esposito, G. Il sistema filosofico di Antonio Rosmini. 2a ed. Milano, 1933.

Phil 3915.162   Esposizione analitica del sistema di filosofia di Guglielmo Wundt. (Benzoni, R.) Palermo, 1890.

Phil 3800.195.5   Esposizione del mio sistema filosofico. (Schelling, F.W.J. von.) Bari, 1923.

Phil 4210.86   Esposizione del principio filosofico di Rosmini. (Ferre, Pietro Maria.) Verona, 1859.

Phil 4210.38   Esposizione del sistema morale dell'autore e compendio di etica. (Rosmini-Serbati, Antonio.) Mozara, 1952.

Phil 4210.80   Esposizione ragionata della filosofia. (Calza, G.) Intra, 1878-79. 2v.

Phil 4210.93.10   Esposizione sul sistema filosofico del nuovo saggio. (Tommaseo, N.) Torino, 1840?

Phil 1750.366   L'espressionismo. (Rognoni, L.) Torino, 1953.
Phil 181.45.19   L'esprit, acte pur. (Gentile, Giovanni.) Paris, 1925.
Phil 5242.36   L'esprit de contradiction. (Chavigny, P.) Paris, 1927.
Phil 9166.5   L'esprit de famille étude morale. (Godimus, Z.J.) Paris, 1870.

Phil 1511.3.11   L'esprit de la philosophie. (Gilson, Étienne.) Paris, 1948.

Phil 1511.3.10   L'esprit de la philosophie médiévale. (Gilson, Étienne.) Paris, 1932. 2v.

Phil 1511.3.12   L'esprit de la philosophie médiévale. 2e éd. (Gilson, Étienne.) Paris, 1944.

Phil 1507.1   Esprit de la philosophie scolastique. (Cupély.) Paris, 1867.

Phil 3552.251   Esprit de Leibnitz. (Emery, J.A.) Lyon, 1772. 2v.
Phil 8405.9   L'esprit des beaux-arts. v.1-2. (Estève, Pierre.) Paris, 1753.

Phil 5829.3.4   L'esprit des bêtes; zoologie passionnelle. (Toussenel, A.) Paris, 1884.

Phil 5829.3.2   L'esprit des bêtes; zoologie passionnelle. 2. éd. (Toussenel, A.) Paris, 1855.

Phil 6111.1.20   L'esprit et le corps. 3. ed. (Bain, A.) Paris, 1878.
Phil 187.116   L'esprit et le réel dans les limites du nombre et de la grandeur. (Maugé, F.) Paris, 1937.

Phil 187.116.4   L'esprit et le réel perçu. (Maugé, F.) Paris, 1937.
Phil 1850.122   Esprit et méthode de Bacon en philosophie. (Patru, G.A.) Paris, 1854.

Phil 5241.9.5   L'esprit humain et ses facultés. (Bautain, L.E.M.) Paris, 1859. 2v.

Phil 2805.228   L'esprit humain selon Pascal. (Benzécri, E.) Paris, 1939.
Phil 191.1.5   L'esprit nouveau. (Quinet, Edgar.) Paris, 1875.
Phil 191.1   L'esprit nouveau. 4. éd. (Quinet, Edgar.) Paris, 1875.
Phil 3003.4   L'esprit philosophique de l'Allemagne et la pensée française. (Delbos, Victor.) Paris, 1915.

Phil 930.58   L'ésprit synthétique de la Chine. (Liou, Kia-hway.) Paris, 1961.

Phil 7069.11.19   Esprits et médiums. (Flournoy, Théodore.) Genève, 1911.
Phil 5255.2.6   Esprits logiques et esprits faux. (Paulhan, F.) Paris, 1914.

Phil 5754.2   Espy, J.P. The human will. Cincinnati, 1860.
Phil 6990.48   Esquípulas. 1. ed. (García Aceituno, José Luis.) Jalapa, 1940.

Phil 6990.48.2   Esquípulas. 2. ed. (García Aceituno, José Luis.) Guatemala? 1954.

Phil 6954.3.5   Esquirol, Etienne. Des maladies mentales. v.1,2 and atlas. Paris, 1838. 3v.

Phil 6954.3   Esquirol, Etienne. Mental maladies. Philadelphia, 1845.
Phil 6954.3.10   Esquirol, Etienne. Von den Geisteskrankheiten. Bern, 1968.

Phil 286.5   Esquise d'une interprétation du monde. (Fouillée, Alfred.) Paris, 1913.

Phil 6672.2   Esquisse de la nature humaine. (Chardel, C.) Paris, 1826.
Phil 5210.11   Esquisse de la psychologie française. (Anzieu, Didier.) Paris, 1962?

Phil 8894.5.10   Esquisse de philosophie morale. (Tiberghien, G.) Bruxelles, 1854.

Phil 192.64   Esquisse d'un essai sur les facultés humaines. (Revel, Camille.) Lyons, 1927.

Phil 5251.19   Esquisse d'un système de psychologie rationnelle. (Lubac, Emile.) Paris, 1903.

Phil 5640.41   Esquisse d'un système des qualités sensibles. (Nogué, Jean.) Paris, 1943.

Phil 2494.31   Esquisse d'un tableau historique. (Condorcet, M.J.A.N.) n.p., 1795.

Phil 2494.30   Esquisse d'un tableau historique. (Condorcet, M.J.A.N.) Paris, 1798.

Htn   Phil 2494.31.5*   Esquisse d'un tableau historique. (Condorcet, N.J.A.N.) Paris, 1795.

Phil 2494.32   Esquisse d'un tableau historique. 2e éd. (Condorcet, M.J.A.N.) Paris, 1866.

Phil 2494.35   Esquisse d'un tableau historique des progrès de l'esprit humain. (Condorcet, M.J.A.N.) Paris, 1933.

Phil 2494.37   Esquisse d'un tableau historique des progrès de l'esprit humain. (Condorcet, M.J.A.N.) Paris, 1966.

Phil 2840.30   Esquisse d'une classification systématique. (Renouvier, C.B.) Paris, 1885-86. 2v.

Phil 978.49.95   Esquisse d'une cosmogonie psychologique, d'après des conférences faites à Paris en 1906. (Steiner, R.) Paris, 1928.

Phil 5545.2.6   Esquisse d'une éducation de la mémoire. 2. éd. (Biervliet, J.J. von.) Gand, 19- .

Phil 5243.43   Esquisse d'une énergétique mentale. (Duflo, J.) Paris, 1936.

Phil 5015.1   Esquisse d'une histoire de la logique. (Franck, A.) Paris, 1838.

Phil 960.31   Esquisse d'une histoire de la philosophie indienne. Thèse. (Masson-Oursel, Paul.) Paris, 1923.

Phil 960.31.2   Esquisse d'une histoire de la philosophie indienne. Thèse. (Masson-Oursel, Paul.) Paris, 1923.

Phil 8881.26   Esquisse d'une morale. (Guyau, M.) Paris, 1896.
Phil 184.18   Esquisse d'une philosophie. (Joussain, A.) Paris, 1912.
Phil 2725.2.30   Esquisse d'une philosophie. (Lamennais, F.R. de.) Paris, 1840-1846. 4v.

Phil 2605.7.31   Esquisse d'une philosophie concrète. 1. ed. (Fauré-Fremiet, P.) Paris, 1954.

Phil 5756.11   Esquisse d'une philosophie de la dignité humaine. (Gille, Paul.) Paris, 1924.

Phil 8598.24.2   Esquisse d'une philosophie de la religion. (Sabatier, Auguste.) Paris, 1897.

Phil 8598.24.3   Esquisse d'une philosophie de la religion d'après la psychologie et l'histoire. 10. éd. (Sabatier, Auguste.) Paris, 1937.

Phil 192.69   Esquisse d'une philosophie de structure. (Ruyer, R.) Paris, 1930.

Phil 192.69.2   Esquisse d'une philosophie de structure. Thèse. (Ruyer, R.) Paris, 1930.

Phil 2855.5.31   Esquisse d'une philosophie synthésiste. (Richard, C.) Paris, 1875.

Phil 8402.30   Esquisse d'une philsophie de l'art. (Bruyne, Edgar.) Bruxelles, 1930.

Phil 2840.99.20   Esquisse d'une théorie de la connaissance. (Verneaux, Roger.) Paris, 1954.

Phil 2880.8.44   Esquisse d'une théorie des émotions. (Sartre, Jean Paul.) Paris, 1939.

Phil 2880.8.45   Esquisse d'une théorie des émotions. (Sartre, Jean Paul.) Paris, 1963.

Phil 1750.188   Esquisse pour une histoire de l'existentialisme. (Wahl, Jean André.) Paris, 1949.

Phil 193.31.15   Esquisses de philosophie critique. (Spir, A. von.) Paris, 1887.

Phil 193.31.16   Esquisses de philosophie critique. (Spir, A. von.) Paris, 1930.

Phil 8877.7   Essai...bases...développmens de la moralité. (Charma, A.) Paris, 1834.

Phil 1020.1   Essai...Écoles philosophiques chez les Arabes. (Schmölders, A.) Paris, 1882.

Phil 2465.30   Essai analytique sur les facultés de l'âme. (Bonnet, Charles.) Copenhagen, 1760.

Phil 2465.30.5   Essai analytique sur les facultés de l'âme. v.1-2. 3e éd. (Bonnet, Charles.) Copenhagen, 1775.

Phil 600.7.79   Essai critique sur la philosophie positive. (Pellarin, Charles.) Paris, 1864.

Phil 342.10   Essai critique sur le droit d'affirmer. (Leclère, Albert.) Paris, 1901.

Phil 3483.6   Essai critique sur L'esthétique de Kant. (Basch, V.) Paris, 1896.

Phil 3483.6.2   Essai critique sur L'esthétique de Kant. 2. éd. (Basch, V.) Paris, 1904.

Phil 260.5   Essai critique sur l'hypothèse des Atoms. (Hannequin, A.) Paris, 1895.

Phil 284.8   Essai critique sur l'hytemorphisme. (Descoqus, P.) Paris, 1924.

Phil 4752.2.63   Essai d'autobiographie spirituelle. (Berdiaev, Nikolai Aleksandrovich.) Paris, 1958.

Phil 2730.84   Essai de biographie historique...Maine de Biran. (LaValette, Monbrun A. de.) Paris, 1914.

Phil 9035.15   Essai de classification naturelle des caracteres. (Ribery, C.) Paris, 1902.

Phil 5243.70   Essai de formalisation de la psychologie fondé sur l'analoge des phénomènes psychiques et des phénomènes physiques. Thèse. (Dubouchet-Buffet, Jeanne.) Paris, 1965.

Phil 5059.6   Essai de logique objective. (Tissot, C.J.) Paris, 1868.
Phil 5043.4   Essai de logique scientifique. (Delbœuf, J.) Liége, 1865.

Phil 176.138.20   Essai de metaphysique eschatologique. (Berdiaev, Nikolai A.) Paris, 1946.

Phil 181.53   Essai de métaphysique materialiste. (Guyon, René.) Paris, 1924.

Phil 8887.70   Essai de morale et de politique. (Molé, L.M.) Paris, 1791.

Phil 5243.4   Essai de philosophie analytique. (Delaperche, H.) Paris, 1872.

Phil 802.8.10   Essai de philosophie classique. (Carbonel, Pierre.) Paris, 1876.

Phil 365.22   Essai de philosophie évolutive. (Marichal, H.) Bruxelles, 1891.

Phil 5041.18   Essai de philosophie française. (Bouttier, M.Z.) Paris, 1844.

Phil 331.10   Essai de philosophie génèrale. 1. ed. (Anglès D'Auriac.) Paris, 1954. 2v.

Phil 181.47   Essai de philosophie générale élémentaire. (Guillou, Henri.) Paris, 1921.

Phil 2750.8.35   Essai de philosophie morale. (Maupertuis, P.L.M. de.) Berlin, 1749.

Phil 2750.8.37   Essai de philosophie morale. (Maupertuis, P.L.M. de.) Londres, 1750.

Phil 184.20   Essai de philosophie pour tous. (Jacquinet, M.) Paris, 1888.

Phil 8673.1   Essai de philosophie religieuse. (Saisset, É.E.) Paris, 1859.

Phil 190.35   Essai de philosophie scientifique. (Perriollat, Charles.) Paris, 1883.

Phil 5257.23   Essai de psychologie; sur le cerveau. (Riche, A.) Paris, 1881.

Phil 5242.3   Essai de psychologie. (Chardel, C.) Paris, 1838.
Phil 5245.10   Essai de psychologie. (Fournié, E.) Paris, 1877.
Phil 5242.43   Essai de psychologie critique sur la nature première. Thèse. (Clergué, G.) Paris, 1930.

Phil 5257.6.5   Essai de psychologie général. 10. éd. (Richet, Charles.) Paris, 1919.

Phil 2730.45   Essai de restitution de l'écrit...L'apperception immédiate. Thèse. (Maine de Biran, Pierre.) Paris, 1908.

Htn   Phil 3552.60*   Essai de Theodicée. (Leibniz, Gottfried Wilhelm.) Amsterdam, 1710. 3 pam.

Phil 6321.8   Essai descriptif sur les troubles psychopathiques avec lucidités d'esprit. (Lanterières, André.) Paris, 1885.

Phil 5655.3F   Essai d'olfactique physiologique. (Heyninx, Albert.) Bruxelles, 1919.

Phil 176.111.25   Essai d'un discours cohérent sur les rapports de Dieu et du monde. (Benda, Julien.) Paris, 1931.

Phil 4080.34   Essai d'un parallèle entre les forces physiques et les forces morales. (Carena, Giacinto.) Turin, 1817.

Phil 2725.2.77   Essai d'un système de philosophie catholique. (Lamennais, F.R. de.) Rennes, 1954.

Phil 193.40   Essai d'un ultimum organum. (Strada, G.J. de.) Paris, 1865. 2v.

Phil 8581.115   Essai d'une critique de la foi. (Bellet, Maurice.) Paris, 1968.

Phil 585.310   Essai d'une détermination esthétique de l'humain. Thèse. (Nabhani, Koribaa.) Alger, 1964.

Phil 850.45   Essai d'une histoire raisonnée de la philosophie païenne. (Koje've, Alexandre.) Paris, 1968.

Phil 5051.6   Essai d'une logique systematique et simplifiée. (Luquet, G.H.) Lille, 1913.

Phil 9120.165   Essai d'une nouvelle explication utilitariste du sentiment d'obligation. (Hopmann, W.) Genève, 1941.

Phil 181.156   Essai d'une philosophie du style. (Granger, Gilles Gaston.) Paris, 1968.

Phil 2725.30.30   Essai d'une philosophie première. (LeRoy, Edouard.) Paris, 1956- 2v.

Phil 720.15   Essai d'une théorie scientifique du concept de vérité. Thèse. (Ramousse, Gatien.) Saint-Amand, 1909.

Phil 1540.18   Essai historique sur les rapports entre la philosophie et la foi. Thèse. (Heitz, T.) Paris, 1909.

Phil 8880.21   Essai l'obligation morale. (Fulliquet, G.) Paris, 1898.
Phil 7140.125   Essai médico-psychologique sur l'autosuggestion. (Lestchinski, A.) Neuchâtel, 1924.

Phil 2115.48.2   Essai philosophique concernant l'entendement humaine. (Locke, J.) Amsterdam, 1700.

Phil 2115.48.7   Essai philosophique concernant l'entendement humaine. (Locke, J.) Amsterdam, 1735.

Phil 2115.48.12   Essai philosophique concernant l'entendement humaine. (Locke, J.) Amsterdam, 1755.

Phil 2115.48.5   Essai philosophique concernant l'entendement humaine. (Locke, J.) La Haye, 1714.

Phil 2115.48.10   Essai philosophique concernant l'entendement humaine. Abrégé. (Locke, J.) Genève, 1741.

Phil 2115.48.15   Essai philosophique concernant l'entendement humaine. Abrégé. (Locke, J.) Upsal, 1792.

Phil 2115.48.11   Essai philosophique concernant l'entendement humaine. 4e éd. (Locke, J.) Amsterdam, 1742.

Phil 2115.48.14   Essai philosophique concernant l'entendement humaine. 5e éd. (Locke, J.) Paris, 1799? 4v.

Phil 5811.2   Essai philosophique sur l'âme des bêtes. (Boullier, D.R.) Amsterdam, 1728.

Phil 5811.2.2   Essai philosophique sur l'âme des bêtes. (Boullier, D.R.) Amsterdam, 1737. 2v.

Phil 3480.56.20   Essai pour introduire en philosophie le concept de grandeur négative. (Kant, Immanuel.) Paris, 1949.

Phil 8401.14.5   Essai su le beau. (André Yves.) Paris, 1924.
Phil 2475.1.233   Essai sur la bergsonisme. (Jolivet, Régis.) Lyon, 1931.
Phil 735.123   Essai sur la compréhension des valeurs. Thèse. (Polin, Raymond.) Paris, 1945.

Phil 5041.42   Essai sur la connaissance approchée. Thèse. (Bachelard, G.) Paris, 1927.

Phil 8674.13   Essai sur la connaissance de Dieu. (Tresmoutant, Claude.) Paris, 1959.

Phil 8418.8.5   Essai sur la création artistique. (Rusu, Liviu.) Paris, 1935.

Phil 8418.8   Essai sur la création artistique comme révélation du sens de l'existence. (Rusu, Liviu.) Paris, 1935.

Phil 1123.9   Essai sur la formation de la pensée grecque. (Schuhl, Pierre Maxime.) Paris, 1934.

Phil 1123.9.10   Essai sur la formation de la pensée grecque. 2. ed. (Schuhl, Pierre Maxime.) Paris, 1949.

Htn   Phil 5761.20*   Essai sur la liberté de produire ses sentimens. (Luzac, E.) n.p., 1749.

Phil 5759.4   Essai sur la liberté morale. (Joyau, Emmanuel.) Paris, 1888.

Phil 2730.83   Essai sur la métaphysique...de Maine de Biran. (Favre, Charles.) Antibes, 1889.

Htn   Phil 2855.3.30*   Essai sur la métaphysique. (Ravaisson-Mollien, Felix.) Paris, 1846.

Phil 1850.94   Essai sur la méthode de Bacon. (Biechy, A.) Toulon, 1855.
Phil 2520.126   Essai sur la méthode de Descartes. Thèse. (Charpentier, T.V.) Paris, 1869.

Phil 178.51   Essai sur la méthode en métaphysique. (Dubuc, Paul.) Paris, 1887.

Phil 2705.80   Essai sur La Mettrie. (Paquet, H.R.R.) Paris, 1873.
Phil 2520.196   Essai sur la morale de Descartes. (Mesnard, Pierre.) Paris, 1936.

Phil 2520.196.5   Essai sur la morale de Descartes. Thèse. (Mesnard, Pierre.) Paris, 1936.

Phil 2733.110   Essai sur la mystique de Malebranche. (Cuvillier, A.) Paris, 1954.

Phil 8417.3   Essai sur la nature, le but et les moyens de l'imitation dans les beaux-arts. (Quatremère de Quincy, Antoine C.) Paris, 1823.

Phil 1930.5.25   Essai sur la nature de l'âme humaine. (Collins, Anthony.) Londres, 1769.

Phil 176.150   Essai sur la nature et la portee d'l'attitude metaphysique. (Benzecri, E.) Alcan, 1939.

Phil 8620.6.5   Essai sur la nécessité du mal. (Jenyns, Soame.) Paris, 1791.

Phil 5241.67   Essai sur la pensée. Thèse. (Badareu, D.) Paris, 1924.
Phil 2490.102   Essai sur la pensée religieuse d'Auguste Comte. (Boyer de Sainte-Suzanne, Raymond de.) Paris, 1923.

Phil 5590.60   Essai sur la personnalité. 1. éd. (Deschoux, M.) Paris, 1949.

Phil 575.89   Essai sur la personne. (Lemarié, O.) Paris, 1936.
Phil 2630.1.81   Essai sur la philosophie de Gratry. Thèse. (Pointud-Guillemot, B.) Paris, 1917.

Phil 1135.13   Essai sur la poésie philosophique en Grèce. (Breton, G.) Paris, 1882.

Phil 2050.232   Essai sur la politique de Hume. (Vlachos, Georges.) Athènes, 1955.

Phil 2805.176   Essai sur la psychologie de Blaise Pascal. (Maire, Albert.) Paris, 1922.

Phil 6053.10   Essai sur la psychologie de la main. (Vaschide, Nicolas.) Paris, 1909.

Phil 2490.113   Essai sur la religion d'apres A. Comte. Thèse. (Dussauze, W.) Saint-Amand, 1901.

Phil 5841.4   Essai sur la révolution sexuelle. (Guérin, Daniel.) Paris, 1969.

Phil 175.6.6   Essai sur la science. (Ancillon, F.) Paris, 1830.
Phil 5058.51   Essai sur la signification de la logique. (Serrus, Charles.) Paris, 1939.

Phil 6990.55   Essai sur la spiritualité de Bernadette. (Rairer, A.) Nevers, 1958.

Phil 6689.6.15   Essai sur la théorie du somnambulisme magnétique. (Tardy de Montravel, A.A.) Londres, 1787.

Phil 8418.14   Essai sur la valeur expressive de l'art. (Rogger, K.) Dijon, 1929.

Phil 2880.1.80   Essai sur la vie et la doctrine de St. Martin. (Caro, E.M.) Paris, 1852.

Phil 5360.12   Essai sur l'abstraction. (Bouisson, R.) Gap, 1942.
Phil 5374.158   Essai sur l'activité primitive du moi. (Nogué, J.) Paris, 1936.

Phil 5374.158.5   Essai sur l'activité primitive du moi. Thèse. (Nogué, J.) Paris, 1936.

Phil 3010.6   Essai sur l'anti-progressisme et ses origines dans la philosophie allemande moderne. Thèse. (Kauffmann, H.L.) Paris, 1936.

Phil 5325.7   Essai sur l'association. (Sollier, Paul.) Paris, 1907.
Phil 2520.123   Essai sur l'atomisme...la philosophie cartesienne. (Prost, Joseph.) Paris, 1907.

Phil 8407.9   Essai sur le beau, ou Éléments de philosophie esthétique. (Gioberti, V.) Bruxelles, 1843.

Phil 8401.14   Essai sur le beau. (André, Yves,) Amsterdam, 1760.
Phil 8416.32   Essai sur le beau. (Pirenne, H.E.) Paris, 1924.
Phil 9245.34   Essai sur le bonheur. (Beausobre, Louis de.) Berlin, 1758.

Phil 8407.16   Essai sur le développement du sentiment esthétique. (Grzegorzewska, M.) Paris, 1916.

Phil 8407.16.2   Essai sur le développement du sentiment esthétique. (Grzegorzewska, M.) Paris, 1916.

Phil 8419.44   Essai sur le génie dans l'art. (Séailles, G.) Paris, 1883.

Phil 8401.20   Essai sur le jugement. (Adam, Charles.) Paris, 1885.
Phil 5755.6   Essai sur le libre arbitre. (Fonsegrive, G.) Paris, 1887.

Call Number	Entry
Phil 3808.68	Essai sur le Libre Arbitre. (Schopenhauer, Arthur.) Paris, 1877.
Phil 3808.68.5	Essai sur le Libre Arbitre. 13. éd. (Schopenhauer, Arthur.) Paris, 1925.
Phil 525.45.5	Essai sur le mysticisme spéculatif. (Delacroix, H.) Paris, 1900.
Phil 8685.6	Essai sur le panthéisme. (Maret, H.L.C.) Paris, 1841.
Phil 8406.10	Essai sur le principe et les lois de la critique d'art. (Fontaine, André.) Paris, 1903.
Phil 348.15	Essai sur le problème le plus général, action et logique. Thèse. (Riveline, M.) Paris, 1939.
Phil 2475.1.405	Essai sur les problèmes. (Trevisan, A.) Fribourg, 1963.
Phil 3500.25	Essai sur le rapport entre le dualisme. (Stefanescu, M.) Paris, 1915.
Phil 8412.17	Essai sur le sentiment esthétique. (Lesparre, A. de G.) Paris, 1921.
Phil 5722.4.5	Essai sur le subconscient dans les oeuvres. (Chabaneix, P.) Bordeaux, 1897.
Phil 1200.29	Essai sur le système philosophique des stoïciens. (Ogereau, F.) Paris, 1885.
Phil 6673.4.22	Essai sur l'enseignement philosophique du magnétisme. (Du Potet, J. de S.) Paris, 1845.
Phil 5246.3	Essai sur les bases ontologiques...l'homme. (Garreau, P.) Paris, 1846.
Phil 5075.2	Essai sur les catégories. (Dupréel, Eugène.) Bruxelles, 1906.
Phil 8886.54	Essai sur les conditions du progrès moral. (Lenglart, Marcel.) Paris, 1934.
Phil 5090.7	Essai sur les conditions et les limites. 3e éd. (Milhaud, G.) Paris, 1912.
Phil 2475.1.40.6	Essai sur les données immédiates de la conscience. (Bergson, Henri.) Genève, 1945.
Phil 2475.1.40	Essai sur les données immédiates de la consciènce. (Bergson, Henri.) Paris, 1889.
Phil 2475.1.40.10	Essai sur les données immédiates de la conscience. (Bergson, Henri.) Paris, 1961.
X Cg Phil 5374.8	Essai sur les données immédiates de la conscience. 2. éd. (Bergson, H.) Paris, 1898.
NEDL Phil 5374.8.5	Essai sur les données immédiates de la conscience. 2. èd. (Bergson, H.) Paris, 1898.
Phil 2475.1.40.2	Essai sur les données immédiates de la consciènce. 9. éd. (Bergson, Henri.) Paris, 1911.
Phil 2475.1.40.4	Essai sur les données immédiates de la conscience. 43. éd. (Bergson, Henri.) Paris, 1944.
Phil 181.162	Essai sur les éléments de la philosophie. (Gley, Gérard.) Paris, 1817.
Phil 8887.49	Essai sur les éléments et l'évolution. (Mauxion, Marcel.) Paris, 1904.
Phil 338.5	Essai sur les elements principaux de la représentation. (Hamelin, O.) Paris, 1907.
Phil 338.5.2	Essai sur les elements principaux de la représentation. 2. ed. (Hamelin, O.) Paris, 1925.
Phil 177.22.5A	Essai sur les fondations de nos connaissances. (Cournot, A.A.) Paris, 1851. 2v.
Phil 525.91	Essai sur les fondements de la connaissance mystique. (Récéjac, Edonard.) Paris, 1897.
Phil 672.3.5	Essai sur les formes a priori. (Dunan, C.) Paris, 1884.
Phil 2115.133	Essai sur les idées religieuses de Locke. Thèse. (Milhac, F.) Genève, 1886.
Phil 672.141	Essai sur les limites de l'espace et du temps. (Jakubisiak, Augustin.) Paris, 1927.
Phil 2490.131	Essai sur les origines intuitives du positivisme. Thèse. (Ducassé, P.) Paris, 1939.
Phil 1050.9	Essai sur les origines se la philosophie. (Bois, Henri.) Paris, 1890.
Phil 5400.18.15	Essai sur les passions. (Ribot, T.) Paris, 1907.
Phil 5400.18.19	Essai sur les passions. 4. éd. (Ribot, T.) Paris, 1917.
Htn Phil 2648.40*	Essai sur les préjugés. (Holbach, Paul Henri T.) Amsterdam, 1770.
Phil 2648.41.2	Essai sur les préjugés. (Holbach, Paul Henri T.) Paris, 1795.
Phil 2648.41	Essai sur les préjugés. v.1-2. (Holbach, Paul Henri T.) Paris, 1800.
Phil 5242.42	Essai sur les principes d'une psychologie évolutive. (Chircoulesco, J.) Bucarest, 1929.
Phil 8125.10	Essai sur les tendances critiques. (Bite-Palevitch.) Paris, 1925.
Phil 5066.36.10	Essai sur les transformations des óperations logiques. 1. ed. (Piaget, Jean.) Paris, 1952.
Phil 1706.15	Essai sur l'esprit d'orthodoxie. (Grenier, Jean.) Paris, 1967.
Phil 2520.92	Essai sur l'esthétique de Descartes. (Krantz, É.) Paris, 1882.
Phil 3565.84	Essai sur l'esthétique de Lotze. (Matagrin, A.) Paris, 1901.
Phil 672.148.5	Essai sur l'étendue. (Durand-Doat, J.) Paris, 1928.
Phil 672.148	Essai sur l'étendue. Thèse. (Durand-Doat, J.) Paris, 1928.
Phil 5500.1	Essai sur l'évolution psychologique du jugement. (Ruyssen, T.) Nimes, 1904.
Phil 6155.18	Essai sur l'expérience hallucinogène. Paris, 1969.
Phil 2403.1	Essai sur l'histoire...philosophie en France. (Damiron, J.P.) Paris, 1846. 2v.
Phil 2403.1.10	Essai sur l'histoire...philosophie en France au dix-neuvième siècle. (Damiron, J.P.) Paris, 1828. 2v.
Phil 2403.1.11	Essai sur l'histoire...philosophie en France au XIXe siècle. (Damiron, J.P.) Paris, 1834. 2v.
Phil 4005.1	Essai sur l'histoire de la philosophie en Italie. (Ferri, L.) Paris, 1869. 2v.
Phil 400.124	Essai sur l'idéalisme moderne. (Meynier, Philippe.) Paris, 1957.
Phil 2520.161.5	Essai sur l'idée de Dieu...chez Descartes. (Koyré, A.) Paris, 1922.
Phil 2475.1.420	Essai sur l'idée de pureté chez Bergson. (Darkaoui, Assad Arabi.) Damas, 1963.
Phil 5465.5	Essai sur l'imagination créatrice. (Ribot, T.) Paris, 1900.
Phil 5465.5.4	Essai sur l'imagination créatrice. 4. éd. (Ribot, T.) Paris, 1914.
Phil 5465.5.3	Essai sur l'imagination créatrice. 6. éd. (Ribot, T.) Paris, 1921.
Phil 8643.20.3	Essai sur l'immortalité au point de vue du naturalisme évolutionniste. 3. éd. (Sabatier, Armand.) Paris, 1911.
Phil 2725.2.57	Essai sur l'indifférence en matière de religion. (Lamennais, F.R. de.) Paris, 1819-20. 2v.
Phil 2725.2.59	Essai sur l'indifférence en matière de religion. (Lamennais, F.R. de.) Paris, 1828. 5v.
Phil 2725.2.61	Essai sur l'indifférence en matière de religion. (Lamennais, F.R. de.) Paris, 1843. 4v.
Phil 8587.34.5	Essai sur l'objet religieux. Thèse. (Hauter, Charles.) Strasbourg, 1928.
Phil 186.63	Essai sur l'organisation du monde physique et moral. (Le Fébure, L.F.H.) Commercy, 1806.
Phil 2493.40.10	Essai sur l'origine des connaissances humaines. (Condillac, Étienne Bonnot.) Paris, 1798.
Phil 2493.40	Essai sur l'origine des connaissances humaines. v.1-2. (Condillac, Étienne Bonnot.) Amsterdam, 1788.
Phil 2493.40.3	Essai sur l'origine des connaissances humnaines. (Condillac, Étienne Bonnot.) Paris, 1924.
Phil 8591.22	Essai sur l'origine des cults. (La Belle, Alfred.) Paris, 1880.
Phil 2520.125	Essai sur l'origine des idées...sur le carthésianisme. (Ventura da Raulica, G.) Paris, 1853.
Phil 5247.13.19	Essai sur l'ouvrage. (Huarte de San Juan, J.) Paris, 1855.
Phil 728.5	Essai sur un. Thèse. (Singevin, Charles.) Paris, 1969.
Phil 672.154	Essai sur quelques caractères des notions d'espace et de temps. Thèse. (Poirier, René.) Paris, 1931.
Phil 819.2	Essai théorique et historique. (Tiberghien, G.) Bruxelles, 1844.
Phil 187.113	Essais. (Meyerson, E.) Paris, 1936.
Htn Phil 2750.5.30*	Les essais. (Montaigne, Michel de.) Lyon, 1595.
Phil 8620.38	Essais. Le don des langues. (Homo (pseud.).) Paris, 1931.
Phil 1718.11	Essais critiques sur les idées philosophiques contemporaines. (Steinilber, E.) Paris, 1912.
Phil 810.4	Essais de critique et d'histoire de philosophie. (Karppe, S.) Paris, 1902.
Phil 2840.40	Essais de critique générale. (Renouvier, C.B.) Paris, 1854-64. 4v.
Phil 2840.42	Essais de critique générale. (Renouvier, C.B.) Paris, 1912. 2v.
Phil 2840.41	Essais de critique générale. Premier essai. (Renouvier, C.B.) Paris, 1912. 2v.
Phil 2840.40.2	Essais de critique générale. v.1 pt.1-3; v.2, pt.1-3. (Renouvier, C.B.) Paris, 1875. 6v.
Phil 180.8.3	Essais de critique philosophique. (Franck, A.) Paris, 1885.
Phil 5062.1	Essais de logique. (Waddington, C.) Paris, 1857.
Phil 2270.40.30	Essais de morale, de science et d'esthétique. 5e éd. (Spencer, Herbert.) Paris, 1904.
Phil 8890.16	Essais de morale. (Placette, J.) Amsterdam, 1716-32 6v.
Phil 8880.56	Essais de morale prospective. (Fourastié, Jean.) Paris, 1967.
Phil 175.6.2	Essais de philosophie. (Ancillon, F.) Paris, 1832. 4v.
Phil 175.6	Essais de philosophie. (Ancillon, F.) Paris, 1832. 4v.
Phil 192.8	Essais de philosophie. (Remusat, C. de.) Paris, 1842. 2v.
Phil 196.1.5	Essais de philosophie critique. (Vacherot, E.) Paris, 1864.
Phil 176.21.5	Essais de philosophie et de morale. (Bersot, P.E.) Paris, 1864. 2v.
Phil 178.19	Essais de philosophie générale. 5th ed. (Dunan, Charles.) Paris, 1902.
Phil 3425.95.8	Essais de philosophie hégélienne. (Véra, A.) Paris, 1864.
Phil 8896.12	Essais de philosophie morale et de moral e religieuse. (Vinet, Alexandre.) Paris, 1837.
Phil 193.124	Essais de philosophie synthetique. (Sagcret, Emile.) Paris, 1928.
Phil 5243.12	Essais de physiologie philosophique. (Durand, M.J.P.) Paris, 1866.
Phil 6315.2.29	Essais de psychanalyse. (Freud, Sigmund.) Paris, 1948.
Phil 3552.61	Essais de Theodicée. (Leibniz, Gottfried Wilhelm.) Paris, 1720.
Phil 3552.60.10	Essais de Theodicée. (Leibniz, Gottfried Wilhelm.) Paris, 1962.
Phil 3552.60.5	Essais de Theodicée sur la bonté de Dieu. (Leibniz, Gottfried Wilhelm.) Amsterdam, 1720.
Phil 176.133	Essais d'esthétique, de philosophie et de littérature. (Basch, Victor.) Paris, 1934.
Phil 3850.1.45	Essais d'histoire religieuse et mélanges littéraires. (Strauss, D.F.) Paris, 1872.
Phil 2940.3.20	Essais et conférences. (Weil, Éric.) Paris, 1970. 2v.
Phil 3450.19.70.5	Essais et conférences. 2e éd. (Heidegger, Martin.) Paris, 1958.
Phil 187.28.11	Essais optimistes. (Mechnikov, I.I.) Paris, 1907.
Phil 2275.60.10	Essais philosophique sur les systèmes de Locke, Berkeley. (Stewart, D.) Paris, 1828.
Phil 176.23	Essais philosophiques. (Blein, A.) Paris, 1843.
Phil 2477.5.30	Essais philosophiques. (Boberil, Roger.) Rennes, 1910. 2 pam.
Htn Phil 2050.43*	Essais philosophiques sur l'entendement humain. (Hume, David.) Amsterdam, 1758. 2v.
Phil 2675.5	Essais philosophiques sur l'homme. (Jakob, L.H. von.) Saint-Pétersbourg, 1822.
Phil 2520.140.3	Essais sur Descartes. (Gouhier, Henri.) Paris, 1937.
Phil 2520.140.5	Essais sur Descartes. 2. éd. (Gouhier, Henri.) Paris, 1949.
Phil 336.5	Essais sur la connaissance. 2. ed. (Fonsegrive, G.) n.p., n.d. 2v.
Phil 8402.8.20	Essais sur la méthode en esthétique. (Bayer, Raymond.) Paris, 1953.
Phil 8612.30	Essais sur la mort. (Feier, I.) Bucarest, 1939.
NEDL Phil 960.2	Essais sur la philosophie des Hindous. (Colebrooke, H.T.) Paris, 1833.
Phil 8598.2	Essais sur la philosophie et la religion. (Saisset, É.) Paris, 1845.
Phil 5700.2	Essais sur la symbolique. (Rosolato, Guy.) Paris, 1969.
Phil 9420.5	Essais sur les passions et sur leurs caracteres. v.2. La Haye, 1748.
Phil 1520.2.5	Essais sur l'histoire générale et comparée des theologies et des philosophies médiévales. (Picavet, F.) Paris, 1913.
Phil 2905.1.220	Essais sur Teilhard de Chardin. (Russo, F.) Paris, 1962.
Htn Phil 283.9*	L'essamerone. (Cattani da Diacceto, F.) Florenza, 1563.
Phil 8876.18	An essay...good and evil. (Blakey, R.) Edinburgh, 1831.
Phil 8627.12	An essay...man's ultimate destination. (Carmichael, A.) Dublin, 1830.
X Cg Phil 8877.10	An essay...nature. Foundation. Moral virtue. (Clap, T.) New Haven, 1765.
NEDL Phil 5041.7	Essay...new analytic. Logical forms. (Baynes, T.S.) Edinburgh, 1850.

Author and Title Listing

	Phil 3499.4	Essay...unsolved ethical questions in Kant's. (Rowland, D.) London, 1871.
	Phil 665.64	The essay: let us think it over. 12th ed. (St. Cyr, E.) Chicago, 1936.
	Phil 2115.36.30	Essay concerning human understanding. (Locke, J.) Cambridge, 1931.
Htn	Phil 2115.36.31*	Essay concerning human understanding. (Locke, J.) Cambridge, 1931.
	Phil 2115.47.5	Essay concerning human understanding. (Locke, J.) Chicago, 1917.
	Phil 2115.36.31.12	Essay concerning human understanding. (Locke, J.) Chicago, 1956.
	Phil 2115.32.5	Essay concerning human understanding. (Locke, J.) Edinburgh, 1798. 3v.
	Phil 2115.30.3	Essay concerning human understanding. (Locke, J.) London, 1716. 2v.
	Phil 2115.30	Essay concerning human understanding. (Locke, J.) London, 1726. 2v.
	Phil 2115.30.2	Essay concerning human understanding. (Locke, J.) London, 1748. 2v.
	Phil 2115.31	Essay concerning human understanding. (Locke, J.) London, 1753. 2v.
	Phil 2115.32	Essay concerning human understanding. (Locke, J.) London, 1791. 2v.
	Phil 2115.34.15	Essay concerning human understanding. (Locke, J.) London, 1823. 3v.
	Phil 2115.35.25	Essay concerning human understanding. (Locke, J.) London, 1870.
	Phil 2115.36.31.10	Essay concerning human understanding. (Locke, J.) London, 1947.
	Phil 2115.36	Essay concerning human understanding. (Locke, J.) Oxford, 1894. 3v.
	Phil 2115.36.25A	Essay concerning human understanding. (Locke, J.) Oxford, 1924.
	Phil 2115.35.15	Essay concerning human understanding. (Locke, J.) Philadelphia, 1849.
	Phil 2115.35.19A	Essay concerning human understanding. (Locke, J.) Philadelphia, 185-?
	Phil 2115.35.17	Essay concerning human understanding. (Locke, J.) Philadelphia, 185-?
	Phil 2115.36.35	Essay concerning human understanding. An early draft. (Locke, J.) Oxford, 1936.
Htn	Phil 2115.36.33*	Essay concerning human understanding. Editor's ms. for edition of 1931. n.p., n.d.
Htn	Phil 2115.36.32*	Essay concerning human understanding. Photostat copy of Locke's original ms. (Locke, J.) n.p., n.d.
	Phil 2115.34.2	Essay concerning human understanding. v.1,3: 1st American ed. (Locke, J.) Boston, 1803-06. 3v.
	Phil 2115.32.3A	Essay concerning human understanding. v.1-2,3. (Locke, J.) London, 1795. 2v.
	Phil 2115.35	Essay concerning human understanding. v.1-2. (Locke, J.) N.Y., 1824.
	Phil 2115.33	Essay concerning human understanding. v.1-3. (Locke, J.) Edinburgh, 1801.
	Phil 2115.31.5	Essay concerning human understanding. v.2. (Locke, J.) Edinburgh, 1765.
	Phil 2115.30.4	Essay concerning human understanding. v.2. (Locke, J.) London, 1735.
NEDL	Phil 2115.34.5	Essay concerning human understanding. v.2. 2nd American ed. (Locke, J.) Boston, 1813.
	Phil 2115.34	Essay concerning human understanding. 1st American ed. (Locke, J.) Boston, 1803. 3v.
Htn	Phil 2115.34.3*	Essay concerning human understanding. 2nd American ed. (Locke, J.) Brattleboro, Vt., 1806. 3v.
Htn	Phil 2115*	Essay concerning human understanding. 2nd American ed. (Locke, J.) Brattleboro, Vt., 1806. 3v.
	Phil 2115.34.9	Essay concerning human understanding. 24th ed. (Locke, J.) London, 1817.
	Phil 2115.35.5	Essay concerning human understanding. 25th ed. (Locke, J.) London, 1825.
Htn	Phil 2115.2.1F*	An essay concerning humane understanding. (Locke, J.) London, 1690.
Htn	Phil 2115.2.2*	An essay concerning humane understanding. (Locke, J.) London, 1690.
Htn	Phil 2115.2.3F*	An essay concerning humane understanding. 2nd ed. (Locke, J.) London, 1694.
Htn	Phil 2115.2.2*A	An essay concerning humane understanding. 2nd ed. (Locke, J.) London, 1694.
Htn	Phil 2115.2.5F*	An essay concerning humane understanding. 3rd ed. (Locke, J.) London, 1695.
Htn	Phil 2115.2.7F*	An essay concerning humane understanding. 4th ed. (Locke, J.) London, 1700.
Htn	Phil 2115.2.9F*	An essay concerning humane understanding. 5th ed. (Locke, J.) London, 1706.
Htn	Phil 7150.17*	An essay concerning self-murther. (Adams, John.) London, 1700.
	Phil 2115.60.2	Essay for the understanding of St. Paul's epistles. (Locke, J.) Boston, 1820.
Htn	Phil 2115.60*	Essay for the understanding of St. Paul's epistles. (Locke, J.) Boston, 1820.
	Phil 5090.3.2	An essay in aid of a Grammar of assent. (Newman, J.H.) London, 1901.
	Phil 5066.44	An essay in modal logic. (Wright, G.H. van.) Amsterdam, 1951.
	Phil 187.57	An essay in practical philosophy: relations of wisdom and purpose. (McCarty, R.J.) Kansas City, Mo., 1922.
Htn	Phil 9358.5*	An essay of drapery. (Scott, William.) London, 1635.
	Phil 1200.61	An essay of the unity of Stoic philosophy. (Christensen, J.) Copenhagen, 1962.
	Phil 2115.151	An essay on...Mr. Locke. (Massie, J.) London, 1750.
	Phil 7060.77	Essay on apparitions. (Alderson, J.) London, 1823.
	Phil 260.13	Essay on atomism. 1st ed. (Whyte, Laucelot Law.) Middletown, Conn., 1961.
	Phil 1850.113.3	Essay on Bacon. (Macaulay, Thomas Babington.) Oxford, 19-
	Phil 5425.23	Essay on capacity and genius. (Hancock, Thomas.) London, 1817.
	Phil 2750.11.43	An essay on Christian philosophy. (Maritain, Jacques.) N.Y., 1955.
	Phil 293.9	An essay on creation. (McEwen, J.W.) Philadelphia, 1900.
	Phil 8403.20	An essay on critical appreciation. (Church, Ralph.) London, 1938.
	Phil 900.9	An essay on Eastern philosophy. (Motora, Y.) Leipzig, 1905.
	Phil 5425.17.5	An essay on genius, 1774. (Gerard, Alexander.) München, 1966.
	Phil 5425.17	An essay on genius. (Gerard, Alexander.) London, 1774.
X Cg	Phil 5425.17	An essay on genius. (Gerard, Alexander.) London, 1774.
	Phil 5817.1	Essay on instinct. (Hancock, T.) London, 1824.
NEDL	Phil 8877.12	An essay on intuitive morals. (Cobbe, F.P.) London, 1855-57. 2v.
	Phil 8877.12.2	An essay on intuitive morals. pt.1. (Cobbe, F.P.) Boston, 1859.
	Phil 5525.4	An essay on laughter. (Sully, J.) London, 1902.
	Phil 2150.22.35	An essay on liberation. (Marcuse, Herbert.) Boston, 1969.
	Phil 333.5.15	An essay on man. (Cassirer, Ernst.) New Haven, 1944.
	Phil 333.5.17	An essay on man. (Cassirer, Ernst.) New Haven, 1948.
	Phil 333.5.18	An essay on man. (Cassirer, Ernst.) New Haven, 1962.
	Phil 182.116	An essay on mankind. (Hirschfeld, G.) N.Y., 1957.
	Phil 177.85.2	An essay on metaphysics. (Collingwood, R.G.) Oxford, 1940.
	Phil 2050.24	Essay on miracles. (Hume, David.) London, 1882. 5 pam.
Htn	Phil 5754.1.22*	Essay on moral agency...remarks on Dana's Examination. (West, Samuel.) New Haven, 1772.
Htn	Phil 5754.1.23*	Essay on moral agency...remarks on Dana's Examination. (West, Samuel.) Salem, 1794.
	Phil 2340.13.30	An essay on morals. (Wylie, Philip.) N.Y., 1947.
	Phil 2050.204	An essay on Mr. Hume's essay on miracles. (Adams, William.) London, 1752.
	Phil 197.23.15	An essay on nature. (Woodbridge, F.J.E.) N.Y., 1940.
	Phil 2053.60.3A	Essay on nature and conduct of passions. (Hutcheson, F.) Glasgow, 1769.
	Phil 2053.60	Essay on nature and conduct of passions. (Hutcheson, F.) London, 1728.
Htn	Phil 2053.60.2*	Essay on nature and conduct of passions. (Hutcheson, F.) London, 1728. 2 pam.
Htn	Phil 182.23*	Essay on origin of man. (Hope, T.) London, 1831. 3v.
	Phil 5425.1.3	An essay on original genius. (Duff, W.) Gainesville, Fla., 1964.
Htn	Phil 5425.1*	Essay on original genius. (Duff, W.) London, 1767.
	Phil 2115.157	An essay on personal identity, in 2 parts. London, 1769.
	Phil 575.7	Essay on personality as a philosophical principle. (Richmond, W.) London, 1900.
	Phil 177.85	An essay on philosophical method. (Collingwood, R.G.) Oxford, 1933.
	Phil 5752.4	Essay on philosophical necessity. (Crombie, A.) London, 1893.
	Phil 2266.30.5	Essay on philosophical subjects. (Smith, Adam.) Basil, 1799.
	Phil 186.22	Essay on positive theology or a new system of philosophy. (Lorensen, C.) Waterbury, 1899.
	Phil 9560.1.5	Essay on prudence, by a lover of peace. n.p., 1839.
	Phil 8673.1.5	Essay on religious philosophy. (Saisset, E.E.) Edinburgh, 1863. 2v.
	Phil 8413.18	An essay on some subjects connected with taste. (MacKenzie, G.S.B.) Edinburgh, 1817.
	Phil 6123.1.5	Essay on superstition. (Newnham, W.) London, 1830.
	Phil 8400.20	An essay on taste. (Gerard, Alex.) London, 1759.
	Phil 8407.2	An essay on taste (1759). Facsimile. (Gerard, Alexander.) Gainesville, Fla., 1963.
	Phil 8599.30	Essay on the application of abstract reasoning to the Christian doctrines. 1. American ed. (Taylor, I.) Boston, 1832.
	Phil 4115.55	Essay on the beautiful. (Gioberti, V.) London, 1871.
	Phil 1020.36	Essay on the brotherhood of purity. (Lane-Poole, Stanley.) Lahore, 1954.
	Phil 5465.5.5	Essay on the creative imagination. (Ribot, T.) Chicago, 1906.
	Phil 960.121	An essay on the doctrine of the unreality of the world in the Advaita. (Dandoy, G.) Calcutta, 1919.
NEDL	Phil 8656.4	An essay on the existence...supreme creator. (Brown, W.L.) Aberdeen, 1816. 2v.
	Phil 9166.2	An essay on the filial duties. (Gibson, W.S.) London, 1848.
	Phil 342.11.5	Essay on the foundation of cognition. (Lambek, C.) Copenhagen, 1935.
	Phil 177.22.10	An essay on the foundations of our knowledge. (Cournot, A.A.) N.Y., 1956.
	Phil 5813.1	An essay on the future life of brute creatures. v.1-2. (Dean, R.) London, 1768.
Htn	Phil 7060.64*	Essay on the history...of apparitions. (Defoe, D.) London, 1727.
	Phil 8582.21	An essay on the immateriality and immortality of the soul. (Caulfield.) London, 1778.
	Phil 8880.12.25	An essay on the improvement of time. (Foster, John.) N.Y., 1866.
	Phil 9455.5	An essay on the influence of authority in matters of opinion. (Lewis, G.C.) London, 1894.
	Phil 5135.2	An essay on the influence of authority opinion. (Lewis, G.C.) London, 1849.
	Phil 2520.209	An essay on the metaphysics of Descartes. (Versfeld, M.) London, 1940.
	Phil 8876.32	An essay on the natural equality of men. (Brown, W.L.) London, 1794.
	Phil 8417.3.5	An essay on the nature, the end, and the means of imitation in the fine arts. (Quatremère de Quincy, Antoine C.) London, 1837.
	Phil 1860.50.2	Essay on the nature and immutability of truth. (Beattie, James.) Dublin, 1773.
Htn	Phil 1860.50*	Essay on the nature and immutability of truth. (Beattie, James.) Edinburgh, 1770.
	Phil 1860.50.5	Essay on the nature and immutability of truth. (Beattie, James.) Edinburgh, 1777.
	Phil 1860.50.6	Essay on the nature and immutability of truth. (Beattie, James.) Edinburgh, 1805.
	Phil 1860.50.3	Essay on the nature and immutability of truth. (Beattie, James.) London, 1773.
	Phil 1860.50.4	Essay on the nature and immutability of truth. (Beattie, James.) London, 1774.
	Phil 1860.50.13	Essay on the nature and immutability of truth. (Beattie, James.) London, 1823.
	Phil 1860.50.7	Essay on the nature and immutability of truth. (Beattie, James.) Philadelphia, 1809.
	Phil 8892.11	An essay on the nature and obligations of virtue. (Rutherforth, T.) Cambridge, 1744.
Htn	Phil 2100.1.30.2*	An essay on the origin of evil. (King, William.) London, 1732. 2v.
	Phil 8620.7.2	An essay on the origin of evil. (King, William.) London, 1758. 2v.
	Phil 8620.7.3	An essay on the origin of evil. (King, William.) London, 1781.
Htn	Phil 2100.1.30*	An essay on the origin of evil. 1st ed. and additions. (King, William.) London, 1731. 2v.

	Call No.	Title
Htn	Phil 2493.40.5*	An essay on the origin of human knowledge. (Contillac, Étienne Bonnot.) London, 1756.
	Phil 5374.4	Essay on the philosophy of self-consciousness. (Fitzgerald, P.F.) London, 1882.
	Phil 6116.23	Essay on the principles of mental hygiene. (Gorton, D.A.) Philadelphia, 1873.
	Phil 1900.89	Essay on the sceptical tendency of Butler's "analogy". (Hennell, Sara S.) London, 1859.
	Phil 5655.2	Essay on the senses of smell and taste. (Folsom, N.) Boston, 1863.
	Phil 705.42	An essay on transcendentalism, 1842. (Ellis, Charles Mayo.) Gainesville, 1954.
	Phil 705.1	Essay on transcendentalism. Boston, 1842.
Htn	Phil 9390.1.2*	Essay on truths of importance. (Herport, B.) London, 1768.
Htn	Phil 9390.1*	Essay on truths of importance. (Herport, B.) London, 1768.
	Phil 5041.13	Essay towards...system of logic. (Blakey, Robert.) London, 1834.
	Phil 1870.60.1.2	Essay towards a new theory. (Berkeley, G.) Dublin, 1709.
Htn	Phil 1870.60*	Essay towards a new theory of vision. (Berkeley, G.) Dublin, 1709.
Htn	Phil 1870.60.1*	Essay towards a new theory of vision. 2d ed. (Berkeley, G.) Dublin, 1709.
	Phil 7060.15	Essay towards a theory of apparitions. (Ferriar, J.) London, 1813.
	Phil 5054.1	An essay towards the improvement of reason. (Oldfield, J.) London, 1707.
Htn	Phil 2175.2.55*	An essay towards the theory of the ideal or intelligible world. pt.1-2. (Norris, John.) London, 1701-04. 2v.
	Phil 188.5.2	Essay towards the theory of the world. (Norris, J.) London, 1701-1704. 2v.
Htn	Phil 2175.2.40*	An essay towards the theory of the world. (Norris, John.) London, 1701. 2v.
	Phil 8878.10.5	Essay upon execution of laws vs. immorality and prophaneness. (Disney, J.) London, 1708.
	Phil 9230.12.5	An essay upon gaming. (Collier, Jeremy.) Edinburgh, 1885.
Htn	Phil 9230.12*	An essay upon gaming. (Collier, Jeremy.) London, 1713. (Transferred to Houghton Library 14/1/72)
Htn	Phil 1905.9.9*	An essay upon reason. (Burthogge, R.) London, 1694. 3 pam.
Htn	Phil 2115.107*	An essay upon reason and the nature of spirits. (Burthogge, Richard.) London, 1694-1755. 3 pam.
	Phil 4600.1.35	Essayer. (Landquist, John.) Stockholm, 1913.
Htn	Phil 1850.39*	The essayes or counsels. (Bacon, Francis.) London, 1625.
Htn	Phil 2750.5.35*	Essayes or Morall, politike, and militarie discourses. 3d ed. (Montaigne, Michel de.) London, 1632.
	Phil 8885.7	Essays, moral and literary. (Knox, V.) London, 1808. 3v.
	Phil 8880.44.5	Essays, moral and philosophical. (Forbes, Alexander.) London, 1734.
	Phil 2266.30.10	Essays; philosophical and literary. (Smith, Adam.) London, 1880?
	Phil 270.13	Essays...doctrine of causation. (Shepherd, M.) London, 1827.
	Phil 5135.1	Essays...opinions. (Bailey, S.) London, 1826.
	Phil 5135.1.3	Essays...opinions. (Bailey, S.) London, 1831.
	Phil 181.11.2	Essays...philosophy and religion. (Glanvill, J.) London, 1676.
Htn	Phil 181.11*	Essays...philosophy and religion. (Glanvill, J.) London, 1676.
	Phil 8878.18	Essays...principles of morality. (Dymond, J.) London, 1867.
	Phil 8878.18.4	Essays...principles of morality. (Dymond, J.) N.Y., 1834.
	Phil 8878.18.2	Essays...principles of morality. (Dymond, J.) N.Y., 1844.
	Phil 8878.18.5	Essays...principles of morality. (Dymond, J.) Philadelphia, 1896.
	Phil 176.66	Essays. (Burton, Asa.) Portland, 1824.
Htn	Phil 1980.2.35*	Essays. (Emerson, R.W.) London, 1841.
	Phil 3450.29.10	Essays. (Haecker, Theodor.) Munchen, 1958.
	Phil 187.11.2	Essays. (Martineau, J.) Boston, 1866. 2v.
	Phil 187.11	Essays. (Martineau, J.) Boston, 1866-1868. 2v.
	Phil 187.11.9	Essays. (Martineau, J.) N.Y., 1875. 2v.
	Phil 192.37.5	Essays. (Richter, Raoul.) Leipzig, 1913.
	Phil 2266.30	Essays. (Smith, Adam.) London, 1795.
	Phil 2270.40	Essays. (Spencer, Herbert.) London, 1858.
	Phil 2270.40.2	Essays. (Spencer, Herbert.) N.Y., 1865.
	Phil 2270.40.3.5	Essays. (Spencer, Herbert.) N.Y., 1868.
	Phil 2270.40.3	Essays. (Spencer, Herbert.) N.Y., 1871.
	Phil 2270.40.4	Essays. (Spencer, Herbert.) N.Y., 1874.
	Phil 2270.40.5	Essays. (Spencer, Herbert.) N.Y., 1891. 3v.
	Phil 2270.40.8	Essays. (Spencer, Herbert.) N.Y., 1896. 3v.
	Phil 3915.76.3	Essays. (Wundt, Wilhelm.) Leipzig, 1885.
	Phil 3915.76	Essays. (Wundt, Wilhelm.) Leipzig, 1906.
	Phil 2050.36	Essays: literary, moral, and political. (Hume, David.) London, 1880.
	Phil 2050.36.5	Essays: moral, political and literary. (Hume, David.) London, 1882. 2v.
	Phil 2050.37.5	Essays: moral, political and literary. (Hume, David.) London, 1903.
	Phil 2050.37.10	Essays: moral, political and literary. (Hume, David.) London, 1963.
	Phil 2050.37	Essays: moral, political and literary. (Hume, David.) N.Y., 1898. 2v.
X Cg	Phil 2270.39	Essays. v.1. (Spencer, Herbert.) N.Y., 1868.
	Phil 2270.39	Essays. v.2,3. (Spencer, Herbert.) London, 1868. 2v.
Htn	Phil 2050.15*	Essays. v.3-4. (Hume, David.) London, 1748-53. 2v.
	Phil 1860.10.2	Essays. Works 4-6. (Beattie, James.) Philadelphia, 1809. 3v.
	Phil 1850.40.4	Essays. 2nd ed. (Bacon, Francis.) London, 1857.
	Phil 1850.40	Essays. 3rd ed. (Bacon, Francis.) London, 1857.
	Phil 1850.40.2	Essays. 3rd ed. (Bacon, Francis.) London, 1858.
	Phil 8951.4.5	Essays and addresses. (Barbour, G.F.) Edinburgh, 1949.
	Phil 176.56.2A	Essays and addresses. (Bosanquet, B.) London, 1891.
	Phil 600.31.9	Essays and addresses. (Bridges, J.H.) London, 1907.
	Phil 978.6.13	Essays and addresses. v.2-4. (Besant, Annie.) London, 1912-13. 3v.
	Phil 8587.32	Essays and addresses on the philosophy of religion. (Hügel, Friedrich von.) London, 1921.
	Phil 8587.32.5	Essays and addresses on the philosophy of religion. (Hügel, Friedrich von.) London, 1926.
	Phil 3808.61.5	Essays and aphorisms. (Schopenhauer, Arthur.) Harmondsworth, Eng., 1970.
	Phil 197.19	Essays and notices: philosophical and psychological. (Whittaker, T.) London, 1895.
	Phil 2050.32	Essays and treatises. (Hume, David.) Edinburgh, 1793. 2v.
	Phil 2050.35	Essays and treatises. (Hume, David.) Edinburgh, 1804. 2v.
	Phil 2050.1	Essays and treatises. (Hume, David.) London, 1758.
	Phil 2050.2	Essays and treatises. (Hume, David.) London, 1768. 2v.
	Phil 2050.33	Essays and treatises. v.1-2,3-4. (Hume, David.) Basel, 1793. 2v.
Htn	Phil 3480.25.15*	Essays and treatises on moral, political and various philosophical subjects. (Kant, Immanuel.) London, 1798-99. 2v.
Htn	Phil 2050.31*	Essays and treatises on several subjects. (Hume, David.) London, 1760. 4v.
	Phil 2050.34.60	Essays and treatises on several subjects. (Hume, David.) London, 1764. 2v.
	Phil 2050.34	Essays and treatises on several subjects. (Hume, David.) n.p., n.d.
	Phil 4825.14	Essays aus der südslawischen Philosophie. (Zeremski, Sava D.) Novisad, 1939.
	Phil 3808.61	Essays from the Parerga and Paralipomena. (Schopenhauer, Arthur.) London, 1951?
	Phil 193.57A	Essays I-XXX. (Searle, A.) Cambridge, 1910.
	Phil 2880.8.35	Essays in aesthetics. (Sartre, Jean Paul.) N.Y., 1963.
	Phil 184.38	Essays in ancient and modern philosophy. (Joseph, H.W.B.) Oxford, 1935.
	Phil 1105.14	Essays in ancient Greek philosophy. (Anton, John Peter.) Albany, 1971.
	Phil 6319.2.5.5	Essays in applied psycho-analysis. (Jones, Ernest.) London, 1951.
	Phil 6319.2.5.7	Essays in applied psycho-analysis. (Jones, Ernest.) N.Y., 1964. 2v.
	Phil 630.19.2	Essays in common sense philosophy. (Joad, Cyril Edwin.) N.Y., 1920.
	Phil 5080.7	Essays in conceptual analysis. (Flew, A.) London, 1956.
	Phil 630.21A	Essays in critical realism. (Drake, Durant.) London, 1920.
	Phil 2075.7.30	Essays in criticism. (Jordan, Elijah.) Chicago, 1952.
	Phil 165.17	Essays in East-West philosophy. (Moore, C.A.) Honolulu, 1951.
	Phil 6834.4	Essays in erotiek. (Emde Boas, Coenrad van.) Amsterdam, 1969.
	Phil 8893.8.15	Essays in ethics and religion with other papers. (Seth, J.) Edinburgh, 1926.
	Phil 5043.16.5	Essays in experimental logic. (Dewey, J.) Chicago, 1916.
	Phil 1955.6.45	Essays in experimental logic. (Dewey, John.) N.Y., 1953.
	Phil 8610.923	Essays in freethinking. Series 1. (Cohen, Chapman.) London, 1923.
	Phil 8610.927.20	Essays in freethinking. 2. series. (Cohen, Chapman.) London, 1927.
	Phil 1122.20	Essays in Greek philosophy. (Robinson, Richard.) Oxford, 1969.
	Phil 165.442	Essays in honor of Carl G. Hempel. Dordrecht, 1970.
	Phil 1955.6.91	Essays in honor of John Dewey...seventeenth birthday. N.Y., 1929.
	Phil 6310.16	Essays in individual psychology. (Adler, Kurt.) N.Y., 1959.
	Phil 1050.7.9	Essays in Jewish philosophy. (Neumark, D.) Vienna, 1929.
	Phil 165.458	Essays in metaphysics, by members of the philosophy department, the Pennsylvania State University. University Park, 1970.
	Phil 3450.19.78	Essays in metaphysics. (Heidegger, Martin.) N.Y., 1960.
	Phil 190.76	Essays in modern scholasticism in honor of John F. McCormick. (Pegis, Anton C.) Westminster, Md., 1944.
	Phil 8887.77.5	Essays in moral philosophy. (Melden, A.I.) Seattle, 1958.
	Phil 8887.77	Essays in moral philosophy. (Melden, A.I.) Seattle, 1958.
	Phil 165.344	Essays in ontology. Iowa City, 1963.
	Phil 1750.780	Essays in phenomenology. (Natanson, Maurice Alexander.) The Hague, 1966.
	Phil 165.432	Essays in philosophical analysis. (Rescher, Nicholas.) Pittsburg, 1969.
	Phil 193.23	Essays in philosophical criticism. (Seth Pringle-Pattison, A.) London, 1883.
	Phil 185.7	Essays in philosophy. (Knight, W.) Boston, 1890.
	Phil 1830.50	Essays in philosophy. (Pennsylvania. State University. Philosophy Department.) University Park, Penn., 1962.
	Phil 197.45	Essays in philosophy. (Ward, James.) Cambridge, Eng., 1927.
	Phil 2255.6	Essays in philosophy and other pieces. (Ritchie, Arthur D.) London, 1948.
	Phil 193.123	Essays in philosophy by 17 Ph.D.'s of University of Chicago. (Smith, Thomas V.) Chicago, 1929.
	Phil 165.330	Essays in philosophy presented to Dr. T.M.P. Mahadevan. Madras, 1962.
	Phil 2070.27A	Essays in pragmatism. (James, William.) N.Y., 1948.
Htn	Phil 7068.99*	Essays in psychical research. (Spoer, Adela Goodrich-Freer.) London, 1899.
	Phil 7068.99.20	Essays in psychical research. 2. ed. (Spoer, Adela Goodrich-Freer.) London, 1899.
	Phil 165.18	Essays in psychology. Uppsala, 1951.
	Phil 5625.75.40	Essays in psychology and psychiatry. (Pavlov, Ivan P.) N.Y., 1962.
	Phil 6972.14.25	Essays in psychopathology. (White, William Alanson.) N.Y., 1925.
	Phil 184.3.10A	Essays in radical empiricism. (James, W.) N.Y., 1912.
	Phil 184.3.12	Essays in radical empiricism. (James, W.) N.Y., 1943.
	Phil 2340.10.96A	Essays in science and philosophy. (Whitehead, Alfred North.) N.Y., 1947.
	Phil 2340.10.96.2	Essays in science and philosophy. (Whitehead, Alfred North.) N.Y., 1948.
	Phil 7150.38.5	Essays in self-destruction. (Shneidman, Edwin S.) N.Y., 1967.
	Phil 2255.1.48	Essays in skepticism. (Russell, Bertrand Russell.) N.Y., 1962.
	Phil 811.11A	Essays in the history of ideas. (Lovejoy, Arthur O.) Baltimore, 1948.
	Phil 490.4.7	Essays in the history of materialism. (Plekhanov, G.V.) London, 1934.
	Phil 2225.5.20	Essays in the philosophy of science. (Peirce, C.S.) N.Y., 1957.
	Phil 9495.29	Essays in war-time. 1st series. (Ellis, Havelock.) Boston, 1917.
Htn	Phil 2050.34.50*	Essays moral and political. (Hume, David.) Edinburgh, 1741.
Htn	Phil 2050.34.55*	Essays moral and political. 2nd ed. (Hume, David.) Edinburgh, 1742.
	Phil 8709.15.5	Essays of an atheist. (Teller, Woolsey.) N.Y., 1945.
	Phil 3808.44	The essays of Arthur Schopenhauer. (Schopenhauer, Arthur.) N.Y., n.d.

Phil 6945.7 Essays on asylums for persons of unsound mind. v.1-2. (Galt, J.M.) Richmond, 1850-53.

Phil 2255.1.165 Essays on Bertrand Russell. (Klemke, E.D.) Urbana, Illinois, 1970.

Phil 5850.247.5 Essays on contemporary events. (Jung, Carl G.) London, 1947.

Phil 9035.14 Essays on decision of character. (Foster, John.) Burlington, 1830.

Phil 2270.40.35A Essays on education and kindred subjects. (Spencer, Herbert.) London, 1910.

Phil 6317.26.9 Essays on ego psychology. (Hartmann, Heinz.) London, 1964.

Phil 6317.26.10 Essays on ego psychology. (Hartmann, Heinz.) N.Y., 1964.
Phil 184.3.45 Essays on faith and morals. (James, W.) N.Y., 1943.
Phil 8610.873 Essays on freethinking and plain-speaking. (Stephen, Leslie.) London, 1873.

Phil 3270.12.105 Essays on Frege. (Klemke, E.D.) Urbana, 1968.
Phil 978.49.140 Essays on human science. (Spring, H.P.) Winter Park, 1943.

Phil 6327.9 Essays on hypochondriacal and other nervous affections. (Reid, J.) Philadelphia, 1817.

Phil 2266.30.50A Essays on I. Moral sentiment; II. Astronomical inquiries. (Smith, Adam.) London, 1869.

Phil 575.170 Essays on individuality. (Morley, Felix.) Philadelphia, 1958.

Phil 5754.1.31 Essays on liberty and necessity. (West, Samuel.) Boston, 1793.

Phil 5754.1.33 Essays on liberty and necessity. (West, Samuel.) New Bedford, 1795.

Phil 177.1.5 Essays on literature and philosophy. (Caird, Edward.) Glasgow, 1892. 2v.

Phil 177.1 Essays on literature and philosophy. (Caird, Edward.) N.Y., 1892. 2v.

Phil 5520.100 Essays on logic and language. (Flew, A.G.N.) Oxford, 1951.

Phil 5135.1.5 Essays on opinions and truth. (Bailey, S.) Boston, 1854.
Phil 210.76 Essays on philosophical method. (Hare, Richard Mervyn.) London, 1971.

Phil 140.65 Pamphlet vol. Essays on philosophy (Russian). 4 pam.
Phil 5922.4.5 Essays on phrenology. (Combe, George.) Philadelphia, 1822.

Phil 6021.2.4 Essays on physiognomy. (Lavater, Johann Caspar.) London, n.d.

Phil 6021.2 Essays on physiognomy. (Lavater, Johann Caspar.) London, 1789. 3v.

Htn Phil 6021.2.1F* Essays on physiognomy. (Lavater, Johann Caspar.) London, 1789-98. 5v.

Phil 6021.2.2 Essays on physiognomy. (Lavater, Johann Caspar.) London, 1797. 3v.

Phil 6021.2.3 Essays on physiognomy. (Lavater, Johann Caspar.) London, 1840.

Htn Phil 6021.2.5* Essays on physiognomy. 1st American ed. (Lavater, Johann Caspar.) Boston, 179-?

Phil 6021.2.12 Essays on physiognomy. 17th ed. (Lavater, Johann Caspar.) London, 18- .

Phil 2450.82 Essays on Pierre Bayle and religious controversy. (Rex, Walter.) The Hague, 1965.

Phil 2138.54 Essays on politics and culture. (Mill, John S.) Garden City, 1962.

Phil 8876.38 Essays on subjects of important enquiry. (Browne, I.H.) London, 1822.

Phil 2050.64 Essays on suicide. (Hume, David.) London, 1789.
Htn Phil 2240.33* Essays on the active powers of man. (Reid, Thomas.) Edinburgh, 1788.

Phil 2240.88 Essays on the active powers of the human mind. (Reid, Thomas.) Cambridge, Mass., 1969.

Phil 2240.25 Essays on the active powers of the human mind. (Reid, Thomas.) London, 1843.

Phil 525.5.5 Essays on the bases of mystic knowledge. (Récéjac, Edouard.) London, 1899.

Htn Phil 2262.79.1* Essays on the characteristics. (Brown, J.) London, 1751.
Phil 2262.79.2 Essays on the characteristics. (Brown, J.) London, 1752.
Phil 2262.79 Essays on the characteristics. 2d ed. (Brown, J.) London, 1751.

Phil 8598.106 Essays on the evolution of religion. (Spalding, K.J.) Oxford, 1954.

Phil 5135.1.4 Essays on the formation and publication of opinions. (Bailey, S.) London, 1837.

Phil 2240.49 Essays on the intellectual and active powers of man. v.3. (Reid, Thomas.) Dublin, 1790.

Phil 2240.60 Essays on the intellectual powers of man. (Reid, Thomas.) Cambridge, 1850.

Phil 2240.60.31 Essays on the intellectual powers of man. (Reid, Thomas.) Cambridge, 1969.

Phil 2240.59 Essays on the intellectual powers of man. (Reid, Thomas.) Dublin, 1786. 2v.

Htn Phil 2240.58* Essays on the intellectual powers of man. (Reid, Thomas.) Edinburgh, 1785.

Phil 2240.60.30 Essays on the intellectual powers of man. (Reid, Thomas.) London, 1941.

Phil 2240.60.3 Essays on the intellectual powers of man. 3rd ed. (Reid, Thomas.) Cambridge, 1852.

Htn Phil 2240.60.4* Essays on the intellectual powers of man. 4th ed. (Reid, Thomas.) Cambridge, 1853.

Phil 2240.60.6A Essays on the intellectual powers of man. 6th ed. (Reid, Thomas.) Boston, 1855.

Phil 2115.72 Essays on the law of nature. (Locke, J.) Oxford, 1954.
Phil 182.95 Essays on the logic of being. (Haserot, F.S.) N.Y., 1932.
Phil 6128.11.15 Essays on the natural origin of the mind. (Strong, C.A.) London, 1930.

Phil 8401.2.3 Essays on the nature and principles of taste. (Alison, Archibald.) Boston, 1812. 2v.

Phil 8401.2 Essays on the nature and principles of taste. (Alison, Archibald.) Edinburgh, 1790.

Phil 8401.2.5 Essays on the nature and principles of taste. (Alison, Archibald.) Hartford, 1821.

Phil 8401.2.2 Essays on the nature and principles of taste. 2. ed. (Alison, Archibald.) Edinburgh, 1811.

Phil 8401.2.4 Essays on the nature and principles of taste. 4th ed. (Alison, Archibald.) Edinburgh, 1815. 2v.

Phil 8677.1 Essays on the philosophy of theism. (Ward, W.G.) London, 1884. 2v.

Phil 2240.50 Essays on the powers of the human mind. (Reid, Thomas.) Edinburgh, 1803. 3v.

Phil 8882.6 Essays on the principles of human action. (Hazlitt, W.) London, n.d.

Htn Phil 2055.1.30* Essays on the principles of morality. (Home, Henry.) Edinburgh, 1751.

Phil 176.4A Essays on the pursuit of truth. (Bailey, S.) London, 1829.

Phil 176.4.3 Essays on the pursuit of truth. (Bailey, S.) London, 1831.

Phil 960.2.5 Essays on the religion and philosophy of the Hindus. (Colebrooke, H.T.) London, 1858.

Phil 8674.4 Essays on the wisdom of God. (Tyerman, D.) London, 1818.
Phil 1885.35 Essays on truth and reality. (Bradley, Francis H.) Oxford, 1914.

Phil 7054.72 Essays on various subjects. N.Y., 1861.
Phil 3925.16.96 Essays on Wittgenstein's Tractatus. (Copi, Irving Marmer.) London, 1966.

Htn Phil 1850.29.10* Essays or counsels, civil and moral...and discourse of the wisdom of the ancients. (Bacon, Francis.) London, 1701.

Htn Phil 1850.29* Essays or counsels, civil and moral...where unto is added the wisdom of the ancients. (Bacon, Francis.) London, 1673.

Phil 2070.108A Essays philosophical and psychological in honor of William James. N.Y., 1908.

Htn Phil 1850.27.10* Essays politiques et moraux. (Bacon, Francis.) Paris, 1621.

Phil 8887.7.2 Essays to do good. (Mather, C.) Dover, 1826.
Phil 8887.7.4 Essays to do good. (Mather, C.) London, 1816.
Phil 346.3.5 Essays towards a theory of knowledge. (Philip, A.) London, 1915.

Phil 5520.325.7 Essays über die Philosophie der Sprache. (Schaff, Adam.) Frankfurt, 1968.

Phil 8887.59.10 Essays upon several moral subjects. (Mackenzie, G.) London, 1713.

Phil 8877.15 Essays upon several moral subjects. v.1-4. (Collier, Jeremy.) London, 1702-09. 3v.

Phil 8877.15.2 Essays upon several moral subjects. 5th ed. pt. 1-2. (Collier, Jeremy.) London, 1703.

Phil 8877.15.4 Essays upon several moral subjects. 7th ed. pt. 1-2. (Collier, Jeremy.) London, 1732.

Phil 8697.5 Essays upon some controverted questions. (Huxley, T.H.) N.Y., 1892.

Phil 8697.5.3 Essays upon some controverted questions. (Huxley, T.H.) N.Y., 1893.

Phil 5627.27.15 Essays zur Religionspsychologie. (Runze, George.) Berlin, 1913.

Phil 8581.9 Esse and posse. (Braithwaite, H.T.) London, 1872.
Phil 3805.84 Esselborn, F.W. Die philosophischen Voraussetzingen von Schleiermachers Determinismus. Ludwigshafen, 1897.

Phil 5204.8.2 Essen, Jac van. Beschrijvend en verklarend woordenboek der psychologie. 2. Druk. Haarlem, 1953.

Phil 3425.34.35 Essence. (Hegel, Georg Wilhelm Friedrich.) n.p., n.d.
Phil 9450.14 The essence and the ethics of politics. (Cook, Silas A.) N.Y., 1915.

Phil 2655.7.30 L'essence de la manifestation. (Henry, Michel.) Paris, 1963. 2v.

Phil 3450.11.285 L'essence de la société selon Husserl. (Toulemont, Rene) Paris, 1962.

Phil 2477.17.30 Essence et existence. (Breton, Stanislas.) Paris, 1962.
Phil 4803.462.80 Essence et existence. (Tymieniecka, Anna Teresa.) Paris, 1957.

Phil 197.72.10 Essence et phénomènes. (Wohl, J.A.) Paris, 1958.
Phil 4080.3.36 The essence of aesthetic. (Croce, Benedetto.) London, 1921.

Phil 3235.72 The essence of Christianity. (Feuerbach, Ludwig.) N.Y., 1855.

Phil 3235.72.7 The essence of Christianity. (Feuerbach, Ludwig.) N.Y., 1957.

X Cg Phil 3235.72.5 The essence of Christianity. 2nd ed. (Feuerbach, Ludwig.) London, 1881.

Phil 7069.39.52 Essence of life in psychic phenomena. (Salminen, I.) Brooklyn, 1938.

Phil 3195.6.38 The essence of philosophy. (Dilthey, Wilhelm.) Chapel Hill, 1954.

Phil 3450.19.54 The essence of reasons. (Heidegger, Martin.) Evanston, 1969.

Phil 8581.37 Essence of religion. (Bowne, Borden P.) Boston, 1910.
Phil 3235.73 The essence of religion. (Feuerbach, Ludwig.) N.Y., 1873.
Phil 9530.44 The essence of success. (Platt, C.) London, 19- ?
Phil 187.121 The essence of the matter. (Moore, E.C.) Berkeley, 1940.
Phil 175.65 A essência da matéria e o sentido da vida. (Almeida, Fernando Pinho de.) Coimbra, 1967.

Phil 8893.34 The essential life. (Stanton, S.B.) N.Y., 1908.
Phil 525.33 The essential mysticism. (Cobb, Stanwood.) Boston, 1918.
Phil 6962.21 The essential psychoses and their fundamental syndromes. (Moore, T.V.) Baltimore, 1933.

Phil 2120.13.5 Essential society; an ontological reconstruction. (Laszlo, Ervin.) The Hague, 1963.

Phil 2280.5.79 The essential wisdom of George Santayana. (Munson, T.N.) N.Y., 1962.

Phil 2150.16.30 Essentialism. (Mayer, Frederick.) London, 1950.
Phil 5850.196 Essentials in interviewing. (Fenlason, Anne.) N.Y., 1962.
Phil 5620.22 Essentials in problem solving. (Kogan, Zuce.) Chicago, 1951.

Phil 8599.23 Essentials in the development of religion. (Turner, J.E.) London, 1934.

Phil 8418.6 The essentials of aesthetics in music. (Raymond, G.L.) N.Y., 1911.

Phil 8418.6.3 The essentials of aesthetics in music. 3.ed. (Raymond, G.L.) N.Y., 1921.

Phil 9035.24 The essentials of character. (Sisson, E.O.) N.Y., 1915.
Phil 8598.84 The essentials of Christianity. (Sheldon, Henry Clay.) N.Y., 1922.

Phil 960.41 The essentials of Eastern philosophy. (Shastri, P.D.) N.Y., 1928.

Phil 960.137.10 The essentials of Indian philosophy. (Hiriyanna, M.) London, 1949.

Phil 5041.16.5 The essentials of logic. (Bosanquet, B.) London, 1895.
Phil 5041.16.9 The essentials of logic. (Bosanquet, B.) London, 1914.
Phil 5042.2 The essentials of logic. (Collard, John.) London, 1796.
Phil 5043.20 Essentials of logic. (Dinwiddie, William.) N.Y., 1914.
Phil 5058.27 Essentials of logic. (Sellars, R.W.) Boston, 1917.
Phil 5058.27.5 The essentials of logic. (Sellars, R.W.) Boston, 1925.
Phil 5058.27.7 The essentials of logic. (Sellars, R.W.) Boston, 1945.
Phil 5062.22.9 Essentials of logic. (Wolf, Abraham.) London, 1926.
Phil 6122.21 Essentials of mental healing. (Marston, L.M.) Boston, 1887.

Phil 5241.28 Essentials of mental measurement. (Brown, W.) Cambridge, 1911.

Phil 5241.28.2A Essentials of mental measurement. 2. ed. (Brown, W.) Cambridge, Eng., 1921.

Phil 5241.28.3 Essentials of mental measurement. 3. ed. (Brown, W.) Cambridge, Eng., 1925.

Phil 5241.28.4 Essentials of mental measurement. 4. ed. (Brown, W.) Cambridge, Eng., 1940.

Phil 493.6.15 The essentials of modern materialism. (Seely, Charles Sherlock.) N.Y., 1969.

Phil 525.7.7 The essentials of mysticism and other essays. (Underhill, Evelyn.) London, 1920.

Phil 184.4 The essentials of philosophy. (Jamieson, G.) Edinburgh, 1859.

Phil 193.66 Essentials of philosophy. (Sellars, Roy Wood.) N.Y., 1917.

Phil 5241.38 Essentials of psychology. (Buell, C.S.) Boston, 1898.

Phil 5255.7.5 The essentials of psychology. (Pillsbury, W.B.) N.Y., 1915.

Phil 5255.7.8 The essentials of psychology. (Pillsbury, W.B.) N.Y., 1925.

Phil 5257.31 Essentials of psychology. (Radha-Krishnan, S.) London, 1912.

Phil 8615.5.10 The essentials of spirituality. (Adler, Felix.) N.Y., 1905.

Phil 8662.19 The essentials of theism. (Hawkins, D.J.) London, 1949.

Phil 8585.37 L'essentiel. (Ferrière, A.) Lausanne, 1952.

Phil 400.102 Essenza ed esistenza, idealità e realtà. (Bianca, Giovanni.) Catania, 1946.

Phil 179.30 Esser, Gerard. Metaphysica generalis in usum scholarum. Techny, Ill., 1933.

Phil 1170.22 Esser, Hans Peter. Untersuchungen zu Gebet und Gottesverehrung der Neuplatoniker. Köln, 1967.

Phil 179.35 Esser, Pieter H. Levensaspecten. Zutphen, 1946.

Phil 5244.4 Esser, W. Psychologie. Münster, 1854.

Phil 5044.2 Esser, Wilhelm. System der Logik. Münster, 1830.

Phil 3120.30.120 Essere e alterità in Martin Buber. (Babolin, Albino.) Padova, 1965.

Phil 8582.34 L'essere e il problema religioso. (Carabellese, P.) Bari, 1914.

Phil 8650.1 Essere e non essere. (Zucca, A.) Roma, 1920.

Phil 1750.290 Essere gli altri. 1. ed. (Vedaldi, A.) Torino, 1948.

Phil 4210.225 L'essere iniziale nell'ontologia di Rosmini. (Ottonello, Pier Paolo.) Milano, 1967.

Phil 4070.5.30 L'essere nella spontaneità creativa e nella riflessione razionale. (Boni, Guido.) Roma, 1953.

Phil 5044.12 Essler, Wilhelm Karl. Induktive Logik. Habilitationsschrift. Freiburg, 1970.

Phil 335.11 Essler, Wilhelm Karl. Wissenschaftstheorie. v.2. Freiburg, 1971.

Phil 4946.2 Estable, C. Psicología de la vocación. Montevideo, 1942.

Phil 6674.8 Estabrooks, G.H. Hypnotism. N.Y., 1943.

Phil 6114.20 Estabrooks, George Hoben. The future of the human mind. 1st ed. N.Y., 1961.

Phil 7069.47.40 Estabrooks, George Hoben. Spiritism. 1. ed. N.Y., 1947.

Phil 5402.3 Le estase umane. (Mantegazza, P.) Milano, 1887. 2v.

Phil 600.22 Estasén y Cortada, P. El positivismo. Barcelona, 1877.

Phil 5535.46 Estes, William Kaye. Learning theory and mental development. N.Y., 1970.

Phil 8890.49 Estestvennyi nravstvennyi zakon. (Popov I.V.) Sergiev., 1897.

Phil 8505.8.5 Estestvoznanie i religiia. (Butinova, M.S.) Moskva, 1957.

Phil 8420.14.5 Estetica; teoria generale dell'attività artistica. (Tilgher, A.) Roma, 1931.

Phil 8416.12 Estética. (Pareyson, Luigi.) Torino, 1954.

Phil 8422.10 Estética. 2. ed. (Vascoucelos, J.) México, 1936.

Phil 4080.3.31.10 Estetica come scienza dell'espressione e linguista generale. 10. ed. (Croce, Benedetto.) Bari, 1958.

Phil 4080.3.31 Estetica come scienza dell'espressione e linguistica generale. (Croce, Benedetto.) Milano, 1902.

Phil 4080.3.31.3 Estetica come scienza dell'espressione e linguistica generale. 3a ed. (Croce, Benedetto.) Bari, 1908.

Phil 4080.3.31.4 Estetica come scienza dell'espressione e linguistica generale. 4a ed. (Croce, Benedetto.) Bari, 1912.

Phil 8080.16 A estética contemporânea. 3. ed. (Meumann, Ernst.) Coimbia, 1930.

Phil 4963.2.5 Estética da crítica. (Cannabrava, Euryalo.) Rio de Janeiro, 1963.

Phil 8088.2 L'estetica dall'illuminismo. (Alfieri, V.) Milano, 1957.

Phil 3494.16.5 La estética de Kant. Thesis. (Morente, M.G.) Madrid, 1912.

Phil 8110.14 L'estetica del gusto nel settecento inglesa. 1. ed. (Formigari, Lia.) Firenze, 1962.

Phil 8430.64 L'estetica del mito. (Dorfles, Gillo.) Milano, 1967.

Phil 8092.8 Estetica del novecientos. (Zum Felde, A.) Buenos Aires, 1928?

Phil 8082.2 L'estetica del rinascimento e del Barocco. (Rocio, Montano.) Napoli, 1962.

Phil 8419.61 Estetica della forma. (Santinello, Giovanni.) Padova, 1962.

Phil 8110.9 L'estetica dell'empirismo inglese. (Anceschi, L.) Bologna, 1959.

Phil 1750.415 L'estetica dell'esistenzialismo. (Borrello, Oreste.) Messina, 1956.

Phil 400.117 L'estetica dell'idealismo tedesco. (Pareyson, L.) Torino, 1956.

Phil 3801.168 Estetica dell'identita. (Assunto, Rosario.) Urbino, 1962.

Phil 8430.76 L'estetica dell'oggettivo. (Tagliaferri, Aldo.) Milano, 1968.

Phil 4080.3.143 L'estetica di Benedetto Croce. (Colorni, E.) Milano, 1932.

Phil 4080.3.85 L'estetica di Benedetto Croce. (Masnovo, Omero.) Parma, 1914.

Phil 4080.3.230 L'estetica di Benedetto Croce. (Sainati, V.) Firenze, 1953.

Phil 4260.27 L'estetica di G.B. Vico allraverso la scienza nuova e gli scritti minari. (Vico, G.B.) Napoli, 1926.

Phil 3425.465 L'estetica di Hegel. (Vecchi, Giovanni.) Milano, 1956.

Phil 3425.354 L'estetica di Hegel e i suoi presupposti teoretici. (Puglisi, F.) Padova, 1953.

Phil 4225.15.80 L'estetica di M. Spirito. (Barrello, O.) Lugano, 1958.

Phil 3801.674 L'estetica di Schelling. (Pereyson, Luigi.) Torino, 1964.

Phil 4115.86.5 L'estetica di Vincenzo Gioberti. (Piccoli, Valentino.) Milano, 1921.

Phil 8140.7 L'estetica dopo Croce. (Pesce, Domenico.) Firenze, 1962.

Phil 8407.26 L'estetica e i suoi problemi. (Galli, E.) Napoli, 1936.

Phil 8407.27 L'estetica e i suoi problemi. (Guardo, V.) Siracusa, 1955.

Phil 8416.8 L'estetica e i suoi problemi. (Pareyson, Luigi.) Milano, 1961.

Phil 4115.87 L'estetica e la critica letteraria in V. Gioberti. (Sgroi, Carmelo.) Firenze, 1921.

Phil 4070.7.85 L'estetica filosofica di Antonio Banfi. (Carbonare, Cleto.) Napoli, 1966.

Phil 8418.7 Estética general. (Rogerio Sanchez, J.) Madrid, 1907.

Phil 8110.13 La estética inglesa del siglo XVIII. (Mirabent, F.) Barcelona, 1927.

Phil 8140.10 L'estetica italiana dopo Croce. (Plebe, Armando.) Padova, 1968.

Phil 8140.6 L'estetica italiana nella prima metà del secolo XX. (Giraldi, Giovanni.) Pisa, 1963.

Phil 8416.33 Estetica lezioni sur bello. 2. ed. (Pilo, Mario.) Milano, 1921.

Phil 3450.19.135 L'estetica nel pensiero di Heidegger. (Oberti, Elisa.) Milano, 1955.

Phil 8407.46 Estética operatoria en sus tres direcciones. (Guerrero, Luis Juan.) Buenos Aires, 1956-67. 3v.

Phil 5627.215.10 L'estetica pia. (Moretti-Costanzi, Teodorice.) Bologna, 1966.

Phil 8406.26 Estetica problematica. (Fanizza, Franco.) Manduria, 1963.

Phil 8403.19 L'estetica sperimentale. (Coen, Augusto.) Roma, 1920.

Phil 8415.9.5 Estetica teoria dell'oggetto artistico come presenz evidenziata. (Oberti, Elisa.) Milano, 1962.

Phil 4080.3.335 L'esteticca di Benedetto Croce nella storia del pensiero e della letteratura. (Tanga, Igino.) Roma, 1959.

Phil 8171.5.5 Esticheskaia mysl' narodov Zakavkaz'ia. (Apresian, Grant Z.) Moskva, 1968.

Phil 8402.26 Esticheskaia sushchnost' iskusstva. (Burov, A.I.) Moskva, 1956.

VPhil 8430.58 Esticheski paraleli. (Iastrebova, Netaliia A.) Sofiia, 1968.

Phil 8416.44 Esticheskii studii. (Pasi, Isak.) Sofiia, 1970.

Phil 4769.4.10 Esticheskie fragmenti. Pts.1-3. (Shpet, Gustav.) Peterburg, 1923.

Phil 8403.12 Esticheskie otnosheniia iskusstva k deistvitel'nosti. (Chernyshevskii, N.G.) Moskva, 1945.

Phil 8407.1 Esticheskii ideal. (Gromov, Evgenii S.) Moskva, 1961.

Phil 8413.37 Esticheskii ideal. (Murian, Vasim M.) Moskva, 1966.

Phil 8411.23 Estichkeskoe chuvstvo i iskusstvo. (Kublanov, B.G.) L'vov, 1956.

Phil 8430.74 Estichkeskoe chuvstvo i proizvedenie iskusstva. (Iuldashev, Lekal G.) Moskva, 1969.

Phil 8411.39 Estichkeskoe i etichekskoe v zhizni i v iskusstve. (Kuncheva, L.I.) Moskva, 1968.

Phil 8416.38 Estichkeskoe i khudozhestvennoe. (Pospelov, Gennadii N.) Moskva, 1965.

Phil 8411.37 Estichkeskoe mnogoobrazie iskusstva sotsialisticheskogo realizma. (Kucherenko, Georgii A.) Moskva, 1966.

Phil 8092.30 Estichkeskoe nasledie V.I. Lenina i problemy iskusstva. Moskva, 1971.

Phil 8400.37 Estichkeskoe sbornik statei. (Razumnyi, V.A.) Moskva, 1964.

Phil 8430.72 Estichkeskoe soznanie iskusstvo i religiia. (Iakovlev, Eugenii G.) Moskva, 1969.

Phil 8419.19.5 Estichkeskoe v deistvitel'nosti i v iskusstve. Moskva, 1959.

Phil 8418.42 Estichkeskoe vospitanie. (Razummyi, Vladimir A.) Moskva, 1969.

Phil 4080.28 Esteticità della dialettica nella vita dello spirito. (Ciardo, Manlio.) Pisa, 1965.

Phil 8419.50.5 Estetické vněmáné. (Šindelář, Dušan.) Praha, 1961.

Phil 585.397 Estetično, umenie a človek. (Váross, Marian.) Bratislava, 1969.

Phil 8412.8.10 Estetiikhan peruskysymyksia. (Laurila, K.S.) Porvoo, 1919.

Phil 8402.39 Estetik. (Brunius, Teddy.) Stockholm, 1961.

Phil 8030.6 Estetika; bibliografiia, 1956-60. (Apresian, Z.G.) Moskva, 1963.

Phil 8401.31.5 Estetika. (Astakhov, I.B.) Moskva, 1971.

Phil 4753.2.40 Estetika. (Chernyshevskii, N.G.) Moskva, 1958.

Phil 8400.48 Estetika. Moskva, 1966.

Phil 8005.5 Estetika. Praha. 2,1965+ 6v.

Phil 8400.47 Estetika: kategorii i iskusstvo. (Akademiia Nauk SSSR. Institut Filosofii.) Moskva, 1965.

Phil 4080.3.490 Estetika Benedetto Kroche. (Topuridze, Elena I.) Tbilisi, 1967.

Phil 8400.65 Estetika i chelovek. Moskva, 1967.

Phil 8050.86 Estetika i iskusstvo. (Trofimov, Pavel S.) Moskva, 1966.

Phil 8430.83 Estetika i proizvodstvo. Moskva, 1969.

Phil 8400.44 Estetika i sovremennost'. (Astakhov, Ivan B.) Moskva, 1965.

Phil 8402.60 Estetika i sovremennost'. (Belik, Aleksandr P.) Moskva, 1963.

Phil 8402.60.2 Estetika i sovremennost'. Izd. 2. (Belik, Aleksandr P.) Moskva, 1967.

Phil 8005.10 Estetika i zhizn! Moskva. 1,1971+

Phil 8420.25 Estetika marksizma-leninizma. (Trofimov, Pavel S.) Moskva, 1964.

Phil 8401.41 Estetika na modernoto izkustvo. (Avramov, Dimitur.) Sofiia, 1969.

Phil 8092.19 Estetika nových uměni. Vyd. 1. (Klivar, Miroslav.) Praha, 1970.

Phil 8400.56 Estetika segodnia. Moskva, 1968- 2v.

Phil 8050.81 Estetikens historia från sjuttonhundratalets början till och med Goethe. (Ekman, Rolf.) Lund, 1963.

Phil 8005.9 Estetiku, v zhizn'. Sverdlovsk. 2,1967+

Phil 8092.31 Estetischeski idei V.I. Lenina i sovremennost'. Kalinin, 1970.

Phil 8448.25 Estetisk upplevelse. (Eriksson, Olle.) Stockholm, 1970.

Phil 8405.8 Estetiska problem. (Ekman, Rolf.) Lund, 1954.

Phil 8405.8.2 Estetiska problem. 2. uppl. (Ekman, Rolf.) Lund, 1960.

Phil 8430.77 Estetychna tsinnist' tekhniky. (Sikors'kyi, Qurii D.) Kyïv, 1970.

Phil 8419.63 Estetychnyi ideal myttsia. (Shudria, Kateyna P.) Kyïv, 1967.

Phil 4803.522.5 Estetyka czyli umnictwo piękne. v.1-2. (Libelt, Karol.) Petersburg, 1854. 3v.

Phil 8405.9 Estève, Pierre. L'esprit des beaux-arts. v.1-2. Paris, 1753.

Phil 5203.9 Estey, H.G. A bibliography on psychology. Gardner, 1926.

Phil 5585.245 Esthetic perception of villagers in Northeast Thailand, a pilot study. (Business Research Limited, Bangkok.) Bangkok? 1965.

Phil 8400.1.1 Pamphlet vol. Esthetics. 5 pam.

Phil 8400.1 Pamphlet vol. Esthetics. 4 pam.

Phil 8400.1.4 Pamphlet vol. Esthetics. 4 pam.

Phil 8400.1.3 Pamphlet vol. Esthetics. 5 pam.

Phil 8400.1.2 Pamphlet vol. Esthetics. 5 pam.

Phil 8407.15 Esthetics. (Gordon, Kate.) N.Y., 1922.

Phil 5649.9 The esthetics of motion. (Browne, George H.) New Ulm, 1917.

Phil 8070.2.10   The esthetics of the Middle Ages. (Bruyne, Edgar de.) N.Y., 1969.
Phil 8403.27   Esthétique. (Challaye, F.) Paris, 1929.
Phil 8430.9   Esthétique. (Coculesco, P.) Paris, 1953.
Phil 8407.8   Esthétique. (Guastalla, Pierre.) Paris, 1925.
Phil 8412.30   Esthétique. (Lamouche, A.) Paris, 1961.
Phil 8412.38   Esthétique. (L'Andelyn, Charles de.) Neuchâtel, 1964.
Phil 8408.23   L'esthétique. 3. éd. (Huisman, Denis.) Paris, 1959.
Phil 8417.3.15   L'esthétique classique chez Quatremère. (Schneider, René.) Paris, 1910.
Phil 8092.10   L'esthétique contemporaine. (Morpurgo Taghabue, G.) Milan, 1960.
Phil 4080.3.147   L'esthétique de Benedetto Croce. (Lameere, Jean.) Paris, 1936.
Phil 2750.11.130   L'esthétique de Jacques Maritain. (Simonson, V.L.) Copenhagen, 1956.
Phil 8402.8.15   L'esthétique de la grâce. (Bayer, Raymond.) Paris, 1933. 2v.
Phil 8402.8.10   L'esthétique de la grâce. (Bayer, Raymond.) Paris, 1933. 2v.
Phil 5645.19   L'esthétique de la lumière. (Souriau, Paul.) Paris, 1913.
Phil 3450.19.275   Esthétique de Martin Heidegger. (Sadzik, J.) Paris, 1963.
Phil 3801.426   L'esthétique de Schelling d'après la philosophie de l'art. Thèse. (Gibelin, Jean.) Clermont-Ferrand, 1934.
Phil 3808.114.5   L'esthetique de Schopenhauer. (Fauconnet, A.) Paris, 1913.
Phil 3808.246   L'esthetique de Schopenhauer. (Rosset, Clément.) Paris, 1969.
Phil 2905.1.320   L'esthétique de Teilhard. (Périgord, Monique.) Paris, 1965.
Phil 8407.11   Esthétique des proportions dans la nature et dans les arts. (Ghyka, M.C.) Paris, 1927.
Phil 5649.8   L'esthétique du mouvement. (Souriau, Paul.) Paris, 1889.
Phil 8402.20   Esthétique et critique. (Bernard, Charles.) Paris, 1946.
Phil 8407.8.5   L'esthetique et l'art. (Guastalla, Pierre.) Paris, 1928.
Phil 8404.4.5   Esthétique et philosophie. (Dufrenne, Michel.) Paris, 1967.
Phil 8120.7   L'esthétique française contemporaine. (Feldman, V.) Paris, 1936.
Phil 8092.20   L'esthétique marxiste. (Arvon, Henri.) Paris, 1970.
Phil 8092.6   L'esthétique mondiale au XXe siècle. (Bayer, R.) Paris, 1961.
Phil 2750.22.100   L'esthétique personnaliste d'Emmanuel Mounier. (Charpentreau, Jacques.) Paris, 1966.
Phil 2490.125   L'esthétique positiviste. (Cherfils, C.) Paris, 1909.
Phil 3500.59   L'esthétique transcendantale et la science moderne. (Serrus, C.) Paris, 1930.
Phil 9145.8   Estienne, Antoine Minim. A charitable remonstrance. Edinburgh, 1887.
Phil 5243.2   An estimate of the human mind. (Davies, J.) London, 1828. 2v.
Phil 8876.30   An estimate of the manners and principles of the times. v.1-2. (Brown, John.) London, 1758.
Htn   Phil 8876.30.5*   An estimate of the manners and principles of the times. 2nd ed. (Brown, John.) London, 1757.
Htn   Phil 8584.4*   An estimate of the profit and loss of religion. Edinburgh, 1753.
Phil 5272.5   Estimating true-score distributions in psychological testing. (Lord, Frederick M.) Princeton, 1967.
Phil 1704.4   Estiú, Emilio. Del arte a la historia en la filosofía moderna. La Plata, 1962?
Phil 8879.8   Estlin, J.P. Familiar lectures on moral philosophy. London, 1818. 2v.
Phil 6674.3.5   Estlin, John B. An address...medical profession of Bristol and Bath. London, 1843.
Phil 6674.3   Estlin, John B. Remarks on mesmerism in 1845. London, 1845.
Phil 8595.16.9   Estlin, John P. Evidences of revealed religion. Bristol, 1796?
Phil 1200.28   El estoicismo. Tesis. (Boza Masvidal, A.A.) Habana, 1922.
Phil 6990.3.35   Estrade, J.B. Les apparitions de Lourdes. Tours, 1899.
Phil 6962.38   Estrangement and relationship. (Macnab, Francis A.) Bloomington, 1966.
Phil 4979.15.30   La estructura de la historia de la filosofía y otros ensayos. (Romero, Francisco.) Buenos Aires, 1967.
Phil 4330.15   Estudi sobre la filosofia a Catalunya en el siglo XVIII. (Clascar, Federico.) Barcelona, 1918.
Phil 8050.80   Estudios de estética. (Ramos, S.) México, 1963.
NEDL   Phil 42.5   Estudios de filosofía. (Córdoba, Argentina (City). Universidad Nacional. Centro de Estudios de Filosofía y Humanidades.) Córdoba.
Phil 825.10   Estudios de filosofía antigua y moderna. (Zucchi, Hernan.) Tucumán, 1956[1957]
Phil 1710.16   Estudios de filosofía contemporánea. 1st ed. (Korn, Alejandro.) Buenos Aires, 1963.
Phil 1711.15   Estudios de filosofía moderna. 1. ed. (Láscaris Comneno, Constantino.) San Salvador, 1966.
Phil 165.115   Estudios de historia de la filosofía. Tucumán, 1957. 2v.
Phil 4959.245   Estudios de historia de la filosofía en México. 1. ed. (México (City). Universidad Nacional. Consejo Técnico de Humanidades.) México, 1963.
Phil 193.48   Estudios de la filosofía. (Sanchez, C.L.) Buenos Aires, 1894.
Phil 192.104   Estudios de metafisica. (Roig Gironella, J.) Barcelona, 1959.
Phil 6980.460   Estudios de psicología dinámica. (Matte Blanco, Ignacio.) Santiago de Chile, 1955.
Phil 5245.81   Estudios de psicologia y de estetica. (Fingerman, G.) Buenos Aires, 1926.
Phil 4363.8   Estudios estéticos. (Mirabeut Vilaplana, Francisco.) Barcelona, 1957. 2v.
Phil 5241.44   Estudios filosóficos. (Bunge, Carlos O.) Buenos Aires, 1919.
Phil 186.75   Estudios filosóficos. (Lumbreras, Pedro.) Madrid, 1930.
Phil 4987.89.20   Estudios filosóficos. (Zubiri, Xavier.) Madrid, 1963.
Phil 4303.7   Estudios filosóficos. v.1-2. (Carreras y Artau, J.) Barcelona, 1966-1968.
Phil 4974.5   Estudios filosóficos. v.12. (Massera, José P.) Montevideo, 1954.
Phil 181.9   Estudios filosoficos y religiosos. (Giner, F.) Madrid, 1876.
Phil 331.27   Estudios gnoseológicos. (Alejandro, J.M.) Barcelona, 1961.
Phil 4351.2.5   Estudios literarios y filosóficos. (Arias, Alejandro C.) Montevideo, 1941.
Phil 5465.110   Estudios psicoanalíticos sobre la actividad creadora. 1. ed. (Greenacre, P.) México, 1960.

Phil 5246.22   Estudios psicológicos. (Gonzalez Serrano, U.) Madrid, 1892.
Phil 4972.5.80   Estudios sobre Alejandro Korn. (La Plata. Universidad Nacional.) La Plata, 1963.
Phil 4303.1.5   Estudios sobre médicos-filosófos españoles del siglo XIX. (Carreras y Artau, T.) Barcelona, 1952.
Phil 8599.3   Estudios sobre religion. (Tiberghien, G.) Madrid, 1873.
Phil 176.220   Estudos de filosofia. (Brito, Antonio J.) Lisboa, 1962.
Phil 192.99   Estudos gerais. (Ribeiro, Alvaro.) Lisboa, 1961.
Phil 196.13   Estudos philosóphicos. (Vaz, F.M.) Porto, 1897. 2v.
NEDL   Phil 1750.45   Az ész troufasztása. (Lukács, G.) Budapest, 1954.
VPhil 8050.92   Az esztétika alapvet elvei. (Kelecsényi, János.) Budapest, 1913.
Phil 8005.7   Esztetikai fuzetek. Budapest. 1,1934
Phil 8005.8   Esztetikai szemle. Budapest. 1-9,1935-1943 3v.
Phil 3246.219   Et was über Herrn Professor Fichte. Hamburg, 1799.
Phil 5041.85   Les étapes de la logique. 4. éd. (Boll, Marcel.) Paris, 1957.
Phil 400.90   Les étapes de la philosophie idéaliste. (Gardeil, H.D.) Paris, 1935.
Phil 6615.6   État mental des hystériques. (Janet, Pierre.) Paris, 1893-94. 2v.
Phil 1712.3   L'état présent de la philosophie. (Merten, O.) Namur, 1907.
Phil 6327.2   Les états dépresifs...chez les militaires. Thèse. (Raynier, Julien.) Paris, 1915.
Phil 6625.2   Les états intellectuels dans la mélancolie. (Dumas, Georges.) Paris, 1895.
Phil 181.71   Les états multiples de l'etre. (Guénon, R.) Paris, 1932.
Phil 5520.75.5A   ETC., a Review of General Semantics. Language, meaning and maturity. 1. ed. N.Y., 1954.
Phil 5520.245   ETC., a Review of General Semantics. Our language and our world. 1. ed. N.Y., 1959.
Phil 5460.9   Etchart, Carlos R. La ilusion. Buenos Aires, 1912.
Phil 7060.135   Etchart, Carlos R. Psychologie énergétique. Paris, 1914.
Phil 1750.166.100   Etcheverry, A. Le conflit actuel des humanismes. Paris, 1955.
Phil 1750.166.101   Etcheverry, A. Le conflit actuel des humanismes. Roma, 1964.
Phil 400.89   Etcheverry, A. L'idéalisme français contemporain. Paris, 1934.
Phil 400.89.9   Etcheverry, A. Vers l'immanence intégrale. Thèse. Paris, 1934.
Phil 335.9   Etcheverry, Auguste. L'homme dans le monde. Paris, 1963.
Phil 2520.190   Etendue et conscience. Thèse. (Marcel, Victor.) Nancy, 1932.
Phil 2733.106   Etendue et psychologie chez Malebranche. (Guéroult, Martial.) Paris, 1939.
Phil 5259.6.15   Pamphlet box Tetens, J.N.
Phil 177.35.30   Eternitá storicità della filosofia. (Croce, Benedetto.) Rieti, 1903.
Htn   Phil 1925.55*   Eternal and immutable morality. (Cudworth, R.) London, 1731.
Phil 9035.18   Eternal building, or The making of manhood. (Lemmon, G.J.) N.Y., 1899.
Phil 8637.7   The eternal life. (Münsterberg, S.) Boston, 1905.
Phil 801.29.5   The eternal magnet, a history of philosophy. (Behn, Siegfried.) N.Y., 1929.
Phil 8588.2   The eternal values. (Inge, W.R.) London, 1933.
Phil 735.90.5   The eternal values. (Münsterberg, H.) Boston, 1909.
Phil 2905.1.180.7   L'éternel féminin, étude sur un texte du père Teilhard de Chardin. (Lubac, Henri de.) Paris, 1968.
Phil 672.236   L'éternité dans la vie quotidienne. (Durandeaux, Jacques.) Paris, 1964.
Phil 510.137.5   L'éternité des esprits. (Aliotta, A.) Paris, 1924.
NEDL   Phil 300.1   Eternity of the universe. (Toulmin, G.H.) Philadelphia, 1830.
Phil 6676.3   Etherology and the phreno-philosophy. (Grimes, J.S.) Boston, 1850.
Phil 3819.31.9   Ethic demonstrated in geometrical order. (Spinoza, Benedictus de.) London, 1927.
Phil 3819.31.6   Ethic demonstrated in geometrical order. (Spinoza, Benedictus de.) N.Y., 1894.
Phil 3120.8.96   Die Ethic Franz Brentanos. (Margolius, Hans.) Leipzig, 1929.
Phil 3492.9   Die Ethic Kants. (Koppelmann, W.) Berlin, 1907.
Phil 8610.888   The ethic of freethought. (Pearson, Karl.) London, 1888.
Phil 8610.888.3A   The ethic of freethought. 2. ed. (Pearson, Karl.) London, 1901.
Phil 8876.61   The ethic of nature and its practical bearings. (Balsillie, David.) Edinburgh, 1889.
Phil 3819.36.33   Ethica, ordine geometrico demonstrata. (Spinoza, Benedictus de.) Hagae, 1914.
Phil 8888.11   Ethica. (Nivard, M.) Paris, 1928.
Phil 3819.33.10   Ethica. (Spinoza, Benedictus de.) Amsterdam, 19-.
VPhil 3819.36.60   Ethica. (Spinoza, Benedictus de.) München, 1919.
Phil 3819.36   Ethica. (Spinoza, Benedictus de.) 's Gravenhage, 1895.
Phil 8893.25   Ethica. (Stinson, J.H.) N.Y., 1860.
Phil 8894.20   Ethica. (Trojano, Paolo R.) Napoli, 1897.
Phil 8886.5.5   Ethica: or The ethics of reason. (Laurie, S.S.) London, 1885.
Phil 8877.25   Ethica aristotelica. (Crell, J.) Selenoburgi, n.d.
Phil 8960.2   Ethica catholica. (Kachnik, Josef.) Olomucii, 1910-12. 3v.
Phil 8892.74   Ethica et jus naturae in usum auditorum. (Roys, F.X.) Viennae, 1755.
Phil 3819.36.5   Ethica op meelkundige wijze uiteengezet. 3. druk. (Spinoza, Benedictus de.) Amsterdam, 1923.
Phil 3819.36.31   Ethica ordine geometrico demonstrata. (Spinoza, Benedictus de.) Hagae, 1905.
Phil 8950.3   Ethica theologiae ministra. (Alstrin, Eric.) Upsaliae, 1725.
Phil 8615.6.9   Ethical addresses. (New York Society for Ethical Culture.) Philadelphia. 2v.
Phil 8877.68.10   Ethical and political thinking. (Carritt, Edgar F.) Oxford, 1947.
Phil 400.45   The ethical and religious philosophy of idealism. (Mukerji, N.C.) Allahabad, 1922.
Phil 1900.86   Ethical and religious theories of Bishop Butler. (Taylor, W.E.) Toronto, 1903.
Phil 9150.33   The ethical animal. (Waddington, C.H.) London, 1960.
Phil 8656.12   Ethical approach to theism. (Barbour, G.F.) Edinburgh, 1913.
Phil 9150.10   Ethical aspects of evolution. (Benett, W.) Oxford, 1908.
Phil 194.35   The ethical basis of reality. (Thomas, E.E.) London, 1927.

Phil 8615.2.7 Ethical culture; its threefold attitude. (Sheldon, Walter L.) St. Louis, Mo? 188-?
Phil 9450.8 Ethical democracy. (Coit, S.) London, 1900.
Phil 8893.137 The ethical dimension. (Shirk, Evelyn Urban.) N.Y., 1965.
Phil 1900.70 Ethical discourses. (Butler, Joseph.) Philadelphia, 1855.
Phil 3838.4 The ethical doctrine of Spinoza. (Santayana, G.) Cambridge, 1886.
Phil 8882.19 An ethical essay. (Holyoke, E.A.) Salem, 1830.
Phil 8877.39 The ethical ideal of renunciation. Thesis. (Culp, C.J.) N.Y., 1914.
Phil 14.25F Ethical impact. N.Y. 1966-1967//
Phil 2475.1.139 Ethical implications of Bergson's philosophy. (Sait, Una B.) N.Y., 1914.
Phil 9150.3 The ethical import of Darwinism. (Schurman, J.G.) N.Y., 1887.
Phil 9150.3.2 The ethical import of Darwinism. (Schurman, J.G.) N.Y., 1888.
Phil 8879.26 Ethical judgement. (Edel, A.) Glencoe, 1955.
Phil 8885.56 Ethical knowledge. (Kupperman, Joel J.) London, 1970.
Phil 8615.01 Pamphlet box. Ethical movement.
Phil 8615.2 An ethical movement. (Sheldon, Walter L.) N.Y., 1896.
Phil 8834.4 The ethical movement in England, 1902. (Judge, M.H.) London, 1902.
Phil 8615.12 The ethical movement in Great Britain. (Spiller, G.) London, 1934.
Phil 3850.27.210 The ethical mysticism of Albert Schweitzer. (Clark, Henry.) Boston, 1962.
Phil 8615.6.5 Ethical pamphlets. (New York Society for Ethical Culture.) N.Y.
Phil 8865.636.5 Ethical philosophies of India. (Sharma, Ishwar Chandra.) London, 1965.
Phil 8900.5 Ethical philosophy and civilization. (Zinninger, E.D.) Los Angeles, 1935.
Phil 8615.5.15 An ethical philosophy of life. (Adler, Felix.) N.Y., 1918.
Phil 1915.81 Ethical philosophy of Samuel Clarke. (Le Rossignol, J.E.) Leipzig, 1892.
Phil 8893.11.18 The ethical philosophy of Sidgwick. Photoreproduction. (Hayward, F.H.) London, 1901.
Phil 8885.5 The ethical principle. (Kies, M.) Ann Arbor, 1892.
Phil 8878.47.5 Ethical principles in theory and practice. (Driesch, Hans.) N.Y., 1927.
Phil 8877.41 The ethical problem. (Carus, Paul.) Chicago, 1890.
Phil 8877.42 The ethical problem. 3rd ed. (Carus, Paul.) Chicago, 1910.
Phil 8879.23 Ethical problems. (Edgell, B.) London, 1929.
Phil 8877.14 Ethical questions. (Cogan, T.) London, 1817.
Phil 8505.20 The ethical record. London. 55,1950+ 8v.
Phil 14.3 Ethical record. N.Y.
Phil 14.2 Ethical record. Philadelphia. 1-3 2v.
Phil 8897.28.15 Ethical relativity. (Westermarck, E.) N.Y., 1932.
Phil 8615.20 Ethical religion. (Muzzey, David S.) N.Y., 1943.
Phil 8615.1 Ethical religion. (Salter, W.M.) Boston, 1889.
Phil 8615.1.3 Ethical religion. (Salter, W.M.) London, 1905.
Phil 2270.128 Ethical review. No. 4, Dec. 1906. Herbert Spencer memorial number. London, 1906.
Phil 9245.17 Ethical significances of pleasure. (Wright, W.K.) Chicago, 1906.
Phil 8875.28 Ethical standards and professional conduct. (American Academy of Political and Social Science, Philadelphia.) Philadelphia, 1955.
Htn Phil 1885.30* Ethical studies. (Bradley, Francis H.) London, 1876.
Phil 8876.27.12 Ethical studies. (Bradley, Francis Herbert.) N.Y., 1951.
Phil 8876.27.15 Ethical studies. 2nd ed. (Bradley, Francis Herbert.) London, 1969.
Phil 8876.27.7 Ethical studies. 2nd ed. (Bradley, Francis Herbert.) Oxford, 1927.
Phil 8876.27.16A Ethical studies. 2nd ed. (Bradley, Francis Herbert.) Oxford, 1967.
Phil 8878.36 An ethical system based on the laws of nature. (Deshumbert, Marius.) Chicago, 1917.
Phil 2266.83 The ethical system of Adam Smith. Thesis. (Muir, Ethel.) Halifax, N.S., 1898.
Phil 8870.15.2 Ethical theories. 2nd ed. (Melden, A.I.) N.Y., 1955.
Phil 8876.115 Ethical theory. (Barbour, R.R.P.) Adelaide, 1933.
Phil 8876.125 Ethical theory. (Brandt, Richard.) Englewood Cliffs, N.J., 1959.
Phil 8843.17 Ethical theory. (Swabey, W.C.) N.Y., 1961.
Phil 8886.86.5 The ethical theory of Clarence Irving Lewis. (Saydah, J. Roger.) Athens, Ohio, 1969.
Phil 3425.124 The ethical theory of Hegel. (Reyburn, Hugh A.) Oxford, 1921.
Phil 9420.2.9 An ethical treatise...passions. (Cogan, T.) Bath, 1807-10. 2v.
Phil 8882.70 Ethical value. (Hourani, G.F.) London, 1956.
Phil 8892.84 Ethical values in the age of science. (Roubiczek, Paul.) Cambridge, Eng., 1969.
Phil 8897.15 Ethices compendium. (Whitby, D.) London, 1713.
Phil 3499.29 De ethick en het probleem van het booze. Proef. (Rasker, A.J.) Assen, 1935.
Htn Phil 8893.4* Ethicorum. (Sculteti, A.) Argentinae, 1614.
Phil 8892.51 Ethicorum liber. v.1-2. (Rigerus, Johannes.) n.p., 16- ?
Phil 8886.34 Ethics, an exposition of principles. (Lynch, Arthur.) London, 1922.
Phil 8876.94 Ethics; an introduction to the philosophy of moral values. (Barrett, C.L.) N.Y., 1933.
Phil 3819.32 Ethics, demonstrated after the methods of geometers. (Spinoza, Benedictus de.) N.Y., 1888.
Phil 8882.42 Ethics, general and special. (Hill, Owen.) London, 1921.
Phil 8882.11 Ethics, or Moral philosophy. (Hill, W.H.) Baltimore, 1884.
Phil 8835.2.5 Ethics; origin and development. (Kropotkin, Petr Alekseevich.) N.Y., 1924.
Phil 8835.2.6 Ethics; origin and development. (Kropotkin, Petr Alekseevich.) N.Y., 1968.
Phil 8805 Pamphlet box. Ethics.
Phil 8805.1.2 Pamphlet vol. Ethics. 7 pam.
Phil 8805.4 Pamphlet box. Ethics.
Phil 8805.1 Pamphlet vol. Ethics. 12 pam.
Phil 9150.01 Pamphlet box. Ethics.
Phil 8887.18.9 Pamphlet vol. Ethics. 4 pam.
Phil 8876.119 Ethics. (Baylis, C.A.) N.Y., 1958.
Phil 8951.27 Ethics. (Bourke, V.J.) N.Y., 1959.
Phil 8878.11.9A Ethics. (Dewey, John.) N.Y., 1908.
Phil 8878.11.20A Ethics. (Dewey, John.) N.Y., 1932.
Phil 8878.11.12 Ethics. (Dewey and Tufts.) N.Y., 1929.
Phil 8879.29 Ethics. (Easton, L.D.) Dubuque, Iowa, 1955.
Phil 8879.32 Ethics. (Ewing, Alfred.) London, 1960.
Phil 8880.52 Ethics. (Frankena, W.) Englewood, 1963.
Phil 8831.10 Ethics. (Garnett, Arthur.) N.Y., 1960.
Phil 8882.50.5 Ethics. (Hartmann, N.) London, 1932. 3v.
Phil 8870.17 Ethics. (Johnson, Oliver A.) N.Y., 1958.
Phil 8887.21.7 Ethics. (Moore, George Edward.) N.Y., 1912.
Phil 8887.21.10 Ethics. (Moore, George Edward.) N.Y., 1965.
Phil 8888.15 Ethics. (Nowell-Smith, P.H.) Melbourne, 1954.
Phil 8889.5 Ethics. (Oesterle, J.A.) Englewood Cliffs, N.J., 1957.
Phil 8890.52 Ethics. (Pepper, Stephen Coburn.) N.Y., 1960.
Phil 8892.13.5 Ethics. (Rashdall, Hastings.) London, 1913.
Phil 8892.9 Ethics. (Ryland, F.) London, 1893.
Phil 8893.10.15 Ethics. (Sharp, F.C.) N.Y., 1928.
Phil 3819.35.25A Ethics. (Spinoza, Benedictus de.) N.Y., 1949.
Phil 8870.18 Ethics. (Thomson, Judith J.) N.Y., 1968.
Phil 8894.32 Ethics. (Tsanoff, Radoslov A.) N.Y., 1947.
Phil 8894.32.5 Ethics. (Tsanoff, Radoslov A.) N.Y., 1955.
Phil 8847.3 Ethics. (Ward, Stephen.) London, 1924.
Phil 8876.160 Ethics: an introduction to moral philosophy. (Banner, William Augustus.) N.Y., 1968.
Phil 9070.01 Pamphlet box. Ethics. Conduct of life.
Phil 8805.2 Pamphlet vol. Ethics. German dissertations, 1908-1921. 11 pam.
Phil 8805.5 Pamphlet box. Ethics. German dissertations.
Phil 9495.01 Pamphlet vol. Ethics. Sexual.
Phil 8887.138 Ethics: theory and practice. (McGann, Thomas F.) Chicago, 1971.
Phil 9560.01 Pamphlet box. Ethics. Virtues.
Phil 8881.61.5 Ethics. 4th ed. (Glenn, Paul J.) St. Louis, Mo., 1934.
Phil 8805.3 Pamphlet vol. Ethics. 1876-1910. 9 pam.
Phil 8878.11.8 Ethics [lecture]. (Dewey, John.) N.Y., 1908.
Phil 3819.35.26 Ethics and De intellectus emendatione. (Spinoza, Benedictus de.) London, 1922.
Phil 3819.45.7A Ethics and "De intellectus emendatione". (Spinoza, Benedictus de.) London, 1930.
Phil 8893.102 Ethics and language. (Stevenson, Charles Leslie.) New Haven, 1944.
Phil 8893.102.2 Ethics and language. (Stevenson, Charles Leslie.) New Haven, 1946.
Phil 8893.102.5 Ethics and language. (Stevenson, Charles Leslie.) New Haven, 1948.
Phil 8879.13.10 Ethics and modern thought. (Eucken, R.C.) N.Y., 1913.
Phil 8886.29 Ethics and moral science. (Lévy-Bruhl, L.) London, 1905.
Phil 8892.25.15 Ethics and moral tolerance. (Rogers, A.K.) N.Y., 1934.
Phil 8892.24 Ethics and natural law. (Raymond, George L.) N.Y., 1920.
Phil 8892.24.5 Ethics and natural law. 2. ed. (Raymond, George L.) N.Y., 1920.
Phil 8886.61.5 Ethics and policy decisions. (Leys, W.A.R.) N.Y., 1952.
Phil 8893.139 Ethics and progress. (Selsam, Howard.) N.Y., 1965.
Phil 8615.3 Ethics and religion. (Society of Ethical Propagandists.) London, 1900.
Phil 8887.121 Ethics and science. (Margenau, H.) Princeton, 1964.
Phil 8886.61 Ethics and social policy. (Leys, W.A.R.) N.Y., 1941.
Phil 8870.28 Ethics and society. (De George, Richard T.) Garden City, 1966.
Phil 8887.57 Ethics and some modern world problems. (McDougall, William.) N.Y., 1924.
Phil 8615.17 Ethics and the belief in a God. (Sheldon, Walter L.) St. Louis, 1892.
Phil 9171.8 Ethics and the family. (Lofthouse, William F.) London, 1912.
Phil 8965.2.5 Ethics and the Garger neighborhood, 1914. (Mabie, H.W.) Philadelphia, 1914.
Phil 1905.22A Ethics and the history of philosophy. (Broad, C.D.) London, 1952.
Phil 8892.75 Ethics and the human community. (Rader, M.M.) N.Y., 1964.
Phil 8885.19.7 Ethics and the materialist conception of history. (Kautsky, Karl.) Chicago, 1906.
Phil 8885.19.8 Ethics and the materialist conception of history. (Kautsky, Karl.) Chicago, 1907.
Phil 8885.19.5 Ethics and the materialist conception of history. (Kautsky, Karl.) Chicago, 1918.
Phil 8887.100 Ethics and the moral life. (Mayo, Bernard.) London, 1958.
Phil 8615.20.10 Ethics as a religion. (Muzzey, David S.) N.Y., 1951.
Phil 8615.20.12 Ethics as a religion. (Muzzey, David S.) N.Y., 1967.
Phil 8881.28 Ethics civil and political. (Gorton, D.A.) N.Y., 1902.
Phil 8887.34 Ethics descriptive and explanatory. (Mezes, S.E.) N.Y., 1901.
Phil 9339.01 Pamphlet box. Ethics for men and women.
Phil 8894.26 Ethics for today. (Titus, H.H.) Boston, 1936.
Phil 8879.10.8 Ethics for young people. (Everett, C.C.) Boston, 1891.
Phil 9344.9 Ethics for young people. (Everett, C.C.) Boston, 1893.
Phil 8877.82 Ethics in a business society. 1st ed. (Childs, M.W.) N.Y., 1954.
Phil 8961.17 Ethics in a Christian context. 1. ed. (Lehmann, P.L.) N.Y., 1963.
Phil 9450.18 Ethics in public administration. (Oppler, A.C.) Cambridge, 1942.
Phil 8878.45 Ethics in theory and application. (Dresser, H.W.) N.Y., 1925.
Phil 8882.66.5 Ethics in theory and practice. (Hill, Thomas E.) N.Y., 1956.
Phil 8876.108 The ethics of ambiguity. (Beauvoir, Simone de.) N.Y., 1949.
Phil 8877.75.5 The ethics of belief. (Clifford, William K.) London, 1947.
Phil 1900.100 Ethics of Butler and the philosophy of action in Bhogavadgita according to Madhusudana Sarasvati. (Sharma, Sukhde.) Varanasi, 1961.
Phil 8870.26 The ethics of change; a symposium. Toronto, 1969.
Phil 9045.14 Ethics of citizenship. (MacCunn, John.) Glasgow, 1894.
Phil 8885.39 The ethics of civilization. (Kamiat, A.H.) Washington, 1954.
Phil 9540.8 The ethics of compromise and the art of containment. (Smith, Thomas Vernor.) Boston, 1956.
Phil 9450.6 Ethics of democracy. (Post, Louis F.) N.Y., 1903.
Phil 5774.1 The ethics of freedom. (Young, G.P.) Toronto, 1911.
Phil 3425.65A The ethics of Hegel. (Hegel, Georg Wilhelm Friedrich.) Boston, 1893.
Phil 8881.47 The ethics of Hercules. (Givler, R.C.) N.Y., 1924.
Phil 8865.660 The ethics of Japan. (Suyematsu, Kencho.) Washington, 1907.
Phil 2138.55 The ethics of John Stuart Mill. (Mill, John S.) Edinburgh, 1897.
Phil 2020.140 The ethics of obedience; a study of the philosophy of T.H. Green. (Mukhopadhyay, Amal Kumar.) Calcutta, 1967.
Phil 600.23 The ethics of positivism. (Barzellotti, G.) N.Y., 1878.

Phil 6328.62.5	The ethics of psychoanalysis; the theory and method of autonomous psychotherapy. (Szasz, Thomas Stephen.) N.Y., 1965.
Phil 9150.9.3	The ethics of revolution. (Bixby, James T.) Boston, 1900.
Phil 9495.164	The ethics of sex. 1st ed. (Thielicke, H.) N.Y., 1964.
Phil 9530.9	Ethics of success. (Thayer, W.M.) Boston, 1893.
Phil 8865.342	The ethics of the Cambridge Platonists. (Austin, Eugene M.) Philadelphia, 1935.
Phil 2406.1	Ethics of the great French rationalists. (Gorham, Charles.) London, 1900.
Phil 8837.10	The ethics of the Hindus. (Maitra, Sushil Kumar.) Calcutta, 1925.
Phil 8666.8	Ethics of theism. (Leitch, A.) Edinburgh, 1868.
Phil 2045.20	The ethics of Thomas Hobbes, by E.H. Sneath. Photoreproduction. (Hobbes, Thomas.) Boston, 1898.
Phil 9575.01	Pamphlet box. Ethics of wealth.
Phil 2070.150	The ethics of William James. (Brennan, Bernard P.) N.Y., 1961.
Phil 2340.5.80	The ethics of William Wollaston. Diss. (Thompson, C.G.) Boston, 1922.
Phil 8847.15	Ethics since 1900. (Warnock, Mary.) London, 1960.
Phil 8847.15.2	Ethics since 1900. 2nd ed. (Warnock, Mary.) London, 1966.
Phil 8882.95	Ethiek der voorlopigheid. (Haering, Herman Johan.) Nijkerk, 1969.
Phil 8876.72	Ethiek of natuurlijke zedenleer. (Beysens, J.T.) Leiden, 1913.
Phil 2490.138	De ethiek van Auguste Comte. (Darp, Jan van.) Utrecht, 1910.
Phil 8910.2	Ethik; ein Repetitorium. (Behn, Siegfried.) Bonn, 1948.
Phil 8885.21.2	Ethik; Katechismus der Sittenlehre. 2e Aufl. (Kirchner, F.) Leipzig, 1898.
Phil 3280.55	Ethik, oder über die Kardinaltugenden. (Geulincx, A.) Hamburg, 1948.
Phil 8875.21	Ethik. (Achelis, J.) Leipzig, 1910.
Phil 8879.30	Ethik. (Ehrlich, Walter.) Tübingen, 1956.
Phil 8881.40	Ethik. (Gottschick, Johannes.) Tübingen, 1907.
Phil 8882.36	Ethik. (Harms, F.) Leipzig, 1889.
Phil 8882.50	Ethik. (Hartmann, N.) Berlin, 1926.
Phil 8882.41	Ethik. (Herrmann, W.) Tübingen, 1901.
Phil 8882.71	Ethik. (Hessen, J.) Leiden, 1954.
Phil 8882.16	Ethik. (Höffding, H.) Leipzig, 1888.
Phil 8882.37	Ethik. (Hoffmann, A.) Freiburg, 1897.
Phil 8885.27	Ethik. (Kirckner, F.) Leipzig, 1881.
Phil 8885.18.5	Ethik. (Koröman, Kristian.) Leipzig, 1904.
Phil 8886.43	Ethik. (Liebert, Arthur.) Berlin, 1924.
Phil 8887.53	Ethik. (Messer, A.) Leipzig, 1918.
Phil 8887.53.4	Ethik. (Messer, A.) Leipzig, 1925.
Phil 8887.75.10	Ethik. (Messner, J.) Innsbruck, 1955.
Phil 8890.38	Ethik. (Pfordten, O.) Berlin, 1919.
Phil 8893.39.10	Ethik. (Schwarz, Hermann.) Breslau, 1925.
Phil 8893.9	Ethik. (Seydel, R.) Leipzig, 1874.
Phil 3819.30.5	Ethik. (Spinoza, Benedictus de.) Berlin, 1868. 2 pam.
Phil 3819.30	Die Ethik. (Spinoza, Benedictus de.) Leipzig, 1875.
Phil 3819.30.25	Die Ethik. (Spinoza, Benedictus de.) Leipzig, 1910.
Phil 8897.30	Ethik. (Wentscher, M.) Leipzig, 1902.
Phil 8897.32.5	Ethik. (Wittman, M.) München, 1923.
Phil 3915.65.5	Ethik. (Wundt, Wilhelm.) London, 1897-1901. 3v.
Phil 3915.65	Ethik. (Wundt, Wilhelm.) Stuttgart, 1886.
Phil 8875.21.5	Ethik. 2nd ed. (Achelis, J.) Leipzig, 1900.
Phil 8882.50.7	Ethik. 3. Aufl. (Hartmann, N.) Berlin, 1949.
Phil 8969.18.3	Ethik. 3. Aufl. (Trillhaas, Wolfgang.) Berlin, 1970.
Phil 3915.65.10	Ethik. 4. Aufl. (Wundt, Wilhelm.) Stuttgart, 1912. 3v.
Phil 8882.41.5	Ethik. 5e Aufl. (Herrmann, W.) Tübingen, 1921.
Phil 3819.30.30	Ethik. 7. Aufl. (Spinoza, Benedictus de.) Leipzig, 192-?
Phil 3819.30.35	Ethik. 10. Aufl. (Spinoza, Benedictus de.) Leipzig, 1922.
Phil 8884.17.3	Ethik als Grundwissenschaft. (Jahn, Max.) Leipzig, 1905.
Phil 8884.17.10	Ethik als Grundwissenschaft. 4. Aufl. (Jahn, Max.) Leipzig, 1925. 2v.
Phil 8881.34	Ethik als Kritik der Weltgeschichte. (Görland, Albert.) Leipzig, 1914.
Phil 8876.75	Ethik als Kulturphilosophie. (Bergemann, Paul.) Leipzig, 1904.
Phil 8846.1	Die Ethik als Wissenschaft. (Voltz, H.) Strassburg, 1886.
Phil 8892.39	Ethik als Wissenschaft. 3. Aufl. (Rehmke, J.) Greifswald, 1925.
Phil 8835.3	Ethik als Wissenschaft ein methodologischer Versuch. (Keller, M.) Zürich, 1925.
Phil 8961.2	Die Ethik Calvins. (Lobstein, P.) Strassburg, 1877.
Phil 2050.211	Die Ethik David Hume's in ihrer geschichtlichen Stellung. (Gizycki, G. von.) Breslau, 1878.
Phil 3819.31	Ethik demonstrated in geometrical order. (Spinoza, Benedictus de.) London, 1883.
Phil 1145.18	Die Ethik der alten Griechen. (Schmidt, L.) Berlin, 1882.
Phil 1200.37	Die Ethik der alten Stoa. (Dyroff, Adolf.) Berlin, 1897.
Phil 8893.69	Ethik der Dekadenz. (Schulze, K.E.) Leipzig, 1925.
Phil 1145.87	Ethik der Griechen. (Schwartz, E.) Stuttgart, 1951.
Phil 1145.76	Die Ethik der Griechen und Römer. (Ziegler, T.) Bonn, 1886.
Phil 8828.4	Ethik des Mittelalters. (Dempf, Alois.) München, 1927.
Phil 2610.115	Die Ethik des Peter Gassendi. Inaug.-Diss. (Pfeiffer, Adalbert.) Borna, 1908.
Phil 400.4.15	Die Ethik des Positivismus nach Ernst Laas. Inaug. Diss. (Salamonowiez, L.) Dortmund, 1935.
Phil 9550.9	Der Ethik des Utilitarismus. Inaug. Diss. (Kaler, Emil.) Hamburg, 1885.
Phil 2055.1.81	Die Ethik Henry Homes. Inaug. Diss. (Norden, Joseph.) Halle, 1895.
Phil 3245.85	Die Ethik Immanuel Hermann Fichtes. Inaug. Diss. (Beckedorf, H.) Hannover, 1912.
Phil 9513.7	Ethik in der Schauweise der Wissenschaften. (Wiese, Leopold von.) Bern, 1947.
Phil 9513.7.2	Ethik in der Schauweise der Wissenschaften. 2. Aufl. (Wiese, Leopold von.) Bern, 1960.
Phil 8893.70	Ethik in entwickelnder Darstellung. (Sallwürk, E v.) Langensalza, 1920.
Phil 8886.91	Ethik in ihrer Grundlage aus Prinzipien entfaltet. (Lauth, Reinhard.) Stuttgart, 1969.
Phil 8967.4	Die Ethik jesu. (Rau, Albrecht.) Giessen, 1899.
Phil 3500.33.6A	Die Ethik Kants zur Einführung in die Kritik der praktischen Vernunft. (Stange, Carl.) Leipzig, 1920.
Phil 3552.117	Die Ethik Leibnizens. (Gesche, Paul.) Halle, 1891.
Phil 3819.30.55	Die Ethik nach geometrischer Methode dargestellt. (Spinoza, Benedictus de.) Hamburg, 1976.
Phil 8879.35.5	Ethik naturwissenschaftlich Fundiert und Kirche. (Elken, Rober.) Kassel, 1968.
Phil 3819.30.29	Ethik nebst Briefen Welche sich auf die Gegenstände der Ethik. Bd.1. (Spinoza, Benedictus de.) Berlin, 1812.
Phil 8893.127.5	Ethik ohme Moral. (Shvartsman, Klara Aronovna.) Berlin, 1967.
Phil 2805.94	Die Ethik Pascal. (Köster, Adolph.) Tübingen, 1907.
Phil 2805.94.3	Die Ethik Pascal. Inaug.-Diss. (Köster, Adolph.) Tübingen, 1908.
Phil 3805.210	Die Ethik Schleiermachers. (Jorgensen, Paul.) München, 1959.
Phil 2262.88	Die Ethik Shaftesburys. Diss. (Schonfeld, V.) Budapest, 1920.
Phil 3830.6	Die Ethik Spinozas über Gott und Geist. (Kellermann, B.) Berlin, 1922.
Phil 3827.1	Die Ethik Spinozas und die Philosophie Descartes. (Hann, F.G.) Innsbruck, 1875.
Phil 8430.31	Ethik und Asthetik. (Kunzle, Magnus.) Freiburg, 1910.
Phil 8691.30	Ethik und Atomzeitalter. (Boveri, Walter.) Zürich, 1958.
Phil 8877.64	Ethik und Hyperethik. (Coudenhove-Kalergi, R.N.) Leipzig, 1923.
Phil 8885.19.9	Ethik und materialistische Geschichtsauffassung. (Kautsky, Karl.) Stuttgart, 1906.
Phil 8885.19	Ethik und materialistische Geschichtsauffassung. (Kautsky, Karl.) Stuttgart, 1919.
Phil 8834.2.10	Ethik und Moralpädagogik. (Jodl, Friedrich.) Stuttgart, 1913.
Phil 3310.5.34	Ethik und Naturrecht. (Gutberlet, C.) Münster, 1883.
Phil 8905.10	Ethik und Politik. (Utz, Arthur Fridolin.) Stuttgart, 1970.
Phil 8881.43	Ethik und Religion. (Gutberlet, C.) Münster, 1892.
Phil 8890.44	Az ethikai megismerés természete. (Pauler, Ákós.) Budapest, 1904.
Phil 4845.227.38	Hē ēthikē syneidēsē kai tā problēmatā tes. (Papanoutsos, Euangelos.) Athena, 1962.
Phil 1145.18.1	Hé éthiké tón archaión Hellénón. (Schmidt, L.) Athenas, 1901.
Phil 8878.62	L'ethique, ou Philosophie morale. (Dupleix, Scipion.) Paris, 1610.
Phil 8878.32	Ethique; traité de philosophie morale. (DuRoussaux, L.) Bruxelles, 1907.
Phil 3819.33	Éthique. (Spinoza, Benedictus de.) Paris, 1907.
Phil 3819.33.5	Éthique. (Spinoza, Benedictus de.) Paris, 1908.
Phil 3819.33.3	Éthique. (Spinoza, Benedictus de.) Paris, 1908.
Phil 3819.33.20	Éthique. (Spinoza, Benedictus de.) Paris, 1961.
Phil 8892.4.10	L'éthique. Le bien et le mal. (Roberty, E. de.) Paris, 1896.
Phil 8892.4.5	L'éthique. Les fondements de l'éthique. 2. ed. (Roberty, E. de.) Paris, 1899.
Phil 8962.30	Éthique catholique et éthique protestante. (Mehl, Roger.) Neuchâtel, 1970.
Phil 4065.95	L'éthique de Giordano Bruno. (Charbonnel, J.R.) Paris, 1919.
Phil 3819.33.15	Éthique démontrée suivant l'ordre géométrique et divisée en cinq parties. v.1-2. (Spinoza, Benedictus de.) Paris, 1953.
Phil 1905.10.95	Ethique et idéalisme. (LeChevalier, C.) Paris, 1963.
Phil 4065.43	L'éthique et le deuxième dialogue du spaccio. (Bruno, Giordano.) Paris, 1919.
Phil 8894.6	Éthique ou science des moeurs. (Tissot, Joseph.) Paris, 1840.
Phil 8685.20	Ethisch pantheisme. (Hugenholtz, P.H.) Amsterdam, 1903.
Phil 3425.258.10	Die ethisch-politische Persönlichkeit des Philosophen. (Glockner, Hermann.) Tübingen, 1922.
Phil 8615.25	Ethisch-socialwissenschaftliche Vortragskurse. Bern. 1,1897
Phil 8897.50.2	Die ethische Aufgabe des Menschen. (Weiss, Berthold.) Berlin, 1893.
Phil 8892.29.7	Ethische fragmenten. 7. druk. (Ritter, P.H.) Haarlem, 1924.
Phil 3492.50	Ethische Grundfragen...Ethikvorselung Kants. (Küpenberg, Max.) Innsbruck, 1925.
Phil 8893.53	Ethische Grundfragen. (Störring, Gustav.) Leipzig, 1906.
Phil 8888.6.25	Ethische Methodenlehre. (Nelson, Leonard.) Leipzig, 1915.
Phil 8885.31	Ethische Präludien. (Kronenberg, Moritz.) München, 1905.
Phil 3415.69	Ethische Studien. (Hartmann, Eduard von.) Leipzig, 1898.
Phil 8897.53	Ethische stundien. (Wijnaendts Francken, C.J.) Haarlem, 1903.
Phil 3246.292	Die ethische Teleologie in Fichtes System als Grundlage seiner Geschichtsphilosophie. (Hammacher, Vlans.) Hadien, 1958.
Phil 8893.62	Ethische und philosophische Betrachtungen auf empirischer Grundlage. (Schwalb, Carl J.) Zürich, 1897.
Phil 8591.60	Ethische und religiöse Grundfragen im Denken der Gegenwart. (Leese, Kurt.) Stuttgart, 1956.
Phil 8870.25	Ethische verkenningen. Nijkerk, 1961. 10v.
Phil 8886.15	Die ethischen Grundfragen. (Lipps, T.) Hamburg, 1899.
Phil 8886.15.6	Die ethischen Grundfragen. 2e Aufl. (Lipps, T.) Hamburg, 1905.
Phil 8888.1.6	Die ethischen Ideen als die Waltenden Mächte. (Nahlowsky, J.W.) Langensalza, 1904.
Phil 3120.8.92	Die ethischen Theorien Franz Brentanos. (Hartlich, C.) Wurzburg, 1939.
Phil 8888.6.27	Ethischer Realismus. (Nelson, Leonard.) Leipzig, 1921.
Phil 8882.32.5	Ethisches Wissen und ethisches Handeln. (Hensel, P.) Freiburg, 1889.
Phil 3502.3	Die ethnologischen und anthropogeographischen...bei I. Kant und J.R. Forster. (Küpenberg, L.) Leipzig, 1886.
Phil 2648.58	Éthocratie. (Holbach, Paul Henri T.) Amsterdam, 1776.
Phil 14.7	The ethological journal. London.
Phil 1145.94	Ethos. (Riondato, E.) Padova, 1961.
Phil 5772.12	Ethos contra Logos. (Weidenbach, Oswald.) München, 1948.
Phil 2530.90	Ethos des Künstlers und Ethos der Kunst. (Heitmann, K.) Münster, 1964.
Phil 3450.11.336	L'ethos di Husserl. (Sancipriano, Mario.) Torino, 1967.
Phil 8885.45	Ethos und Ethik. (Kron, Helmut.) Frankfurt, 1960.
Phil 8892.79	Ethos und Naturrecht. (Rašovský, Adolf.) Wien, 1964.
Phil 3819.36.35	Etica...testo latino. (Spinoza, Benedictus de.) Bari, 1915.
Phil 8876.110	Ética. (Barboza, E.) Lima, 1936.
Phil 8881.35	Ética. (González y Martinez de Pinillos.) Madrid, 1911.
Phil 8886.73	Etica. (López Aranguren, José Luis.) Madrid, 1958.
Phil 8890.37	Etica. (Petrone, Igino.) Milano, 1918.
Phil 3819.36.70	Etica. (Spinoza, Benedictus de.) Madrid, 1940.
Phil 3819.36.30	L'etica. (Spinoza, Benedictus de.) Milano, 1913.
Phil 3819.36.20	L'etica. (Spinoza, Benedictus de.) Milano, 1914.
Phil 3819.36.40	Etica. (Spinoza, Benedictus de.) Milano, 1939.
Phil 8881.70	Etica: etica empirica; etica de bienes; etica formal; etica valorativa. (García Máynez, E.) México, 1944.
Phil 3819.36.25	Etica. Pt.1-2. (Spinoza, Benedictus de.) Firenze, 1924.
Phil 8886.73.2	Etica. 2. ed. (López Aranguren, José Luis.) Madrid, 1959.
Phil 8896.19	Etica. 2. ed. (Vasconcelos, J.) Mexico, 1939.

Phil 8980.866 — Etica comunista. (Vagovič, Stefano.) Roma, 1959.
Phil 8980.866.5 — L'etica comunista. (Vagovič, Stefano.) Roma, 1966.
Phil 8968.15.80 — La etica de situación y T. Steinbüchel. (Alcalá, M.) Barcelona, 1963.
Phil 600.14 — L'etica del positivismo. (Jodl, F.) Messina, 1909.
Phil 2053.90 — L'etica del senso morale in Francis Hutcheson. (Vigone, L.) Milano, 1954.
Phil 3825.6 — L'etica di B. Spinoza. (Ferrari, G.M.) Napoli, 1902.
Phil 1955.6.170 — L'etica di John Dewey. (Bansola, Adriano.) Milano, 1960.
Phil 2262.95 — L'etica di Lord Shaftesbury. (Zani, Lucio.) Milano, 1954.
Phil 2805.445 — L'etica di Pascal; corso di filiosfia morale dell'anno accademico 1965-1966. (Pareyson, Luigi.) Torino, 1966.
Phil 3835.6 — L'etica di Spinoza. (Pulcini, C.) Genova, 1914.
Phil 4060.9.30 — Etica e biografia. (Amendala, G.) Milano, 1953.
Phil 4080.3.456 — Etica e politica. (Bausola, Adriano.) Milano, 1966.
Phil 4080.3.25 — Etica e politica. (Croce, Benedetto.) Bari, 1931.
Phil 4080.3.28 — Etica e politica. 3. ed. (Croce, Benedetto.) Bari, 1945.
Phil 3808.235 — Etica e politica nel pensiero di Schopenhauer. (Mei, Flavio.) Milano, 1966.
Phil 2270.104 — L'etica evoluzionista...di Herbert Spencer. (Salvadori, Guglielmo.) Torino, 1903.
Phil 8875.26 — La ética formal. (Astrada, C.) La Plata, 1938.
Phil 8870.27 — Ética inspirado o exterminio. (Hume, Rolando.) Santa Fe, Argentina, 1960.
Phil 9450.59 — Etica politica. (Chiavacci, Enrico.) Roma, 1964.
Phil 8881.62 — Etica rinnovata su basi scientifiche. Pte.I. (Govi, Mario.) Firenze, 1935.
Phil 1200.43 — L'etica stoica da Zenone a Crisippo. (Mancini, Guido.) Padova, 1940.
Phil 8886.48 — Etica umana. (Longo, P.) Torino, 1924.
Phil 9495.27 — Ética y estética de los sexos. (Cansinos Assens, Rafael.) Madrid, 1920.
Phil 8892.59 — Etica y jurisprudencia. (Rodriguez, G.H.) Mexico, 1947.
Phil 9450.56 — Etica y política. (López Aranguren, J.L.) Madrid, 1963.
Phil 8865.534 — Eticheskaia mysl' v Azerbaidzhane. (Geiushev, Ziiaddin B.) Baku, 1968.
Phil 8905.28 — Eticheskoe i esteticheskoe. Leningrad, 1971.
Phil 3830.13 — Eticheskoe mirosezaresanie Spinozy. (Kechek'ian, Stepan F.) Moskva, 1914.
Phil 8827.10 — Eticità e cultura. 1. ed. (Ciarletta, Nicola.) Milano, 1960.
Phil 8980.498.25 — Etičko-humanisticki problemi socijalizma. (Krešić, Ljubinka.) Beograd, 1964.
Phil 2630.8.80 — Étienne Gilson. Paris, 1949.
Phil 165.145 — An Etienne Gilson tribute presented by his North American students. (O'Neil, Charles J.) Milwaukee, 1959.
Phil 2920.1.80 — Étienne Vacherot. (Ollé-Laprune, L.) Paris, 1898.
Phil 8956.6 — Etik. (Geismar, E.) København, 1926.
Phil 8882.16.3 — Etik. (Höffding, H.) København, 1913.
Phil 8882.16.5 — Etik. 5te udg. (Höffding, H.) København, 1926.
Phil 8885.18 — Etik I. (Kroman, Krist.) København, 1904.
Phil 8877.63 — Etik og sociologi. (Cohn, Georg.) Kjøbenhavn, 1913.
Phil 8893.127 — Etika...bez morali. (Shvartsman, Klara Aronovna.) Moskva, 1964.
Phil 8980.707 — Etika. (Popelová, J.) Praha, 1962.
Phil 8893.130 — Etika. (Selivanov, F.A.) Tomsk, 1961.
Phil 8888.17 — Etika. 2. izd. (Nedeljković, Dušan.) Beograd, 1969.
Phil 3246.236 — Etika Fikhte. (Vysheslavtsev, B.) Moskva, 1914.
Phil 3425.614 — Etika Gegelia i Krizis sovremennoi burzhuaznoi etiki. (Kissel, M.A.) Leningrad, 1966.
VPhil 8885.49 — Etika i ploboda. (Kangrga, Milan.) Zagreb, 1966.
Phil 8896.15 — Etika preobrazhennago erosa. (Vysheslavtsev, V.) Paris, 1931.
Phil 9150.21 — Etiken og evolutionslaeren. (Hanssen, Andreas.) København, 1915.
Phil 8882.35 — Etikens begrundelse. (Hansen, Søren.) København, 1903.
Phil 4635.2.33 — Etikens teoretiske grundlag. (Starke, C.N.) Kjøbenhavn, 1889.
Phil 8882.45 — Etikkens grundlag. (Hansen, Osvald.) Kobenhavn, 1916.
Phil 6949.366 — The etiology of neuroses. (Society of Medical Psycho-Analysts.) Palo Alto, Calif., 1966.
Phil 6959.10 — The etiology of schizophrenia. (Jackson, Donald.) N.Y., 1960.
Phil 3819.33.25 — L'étique. (Spinoza, Benedictus de.) Paris, 1930. 2v.
Phil 8897.52 — Etisk vurdering. (Wilkens, C.) København, 1916.
Phil 4650.1.69 — Etiska tankegångar. (Vannérus, Allen.) Stockholm, 1922.
Phil 8892.29.15 — Etiske fragmenter. (Ritter, P.H.) København, 1896.
Phil 4580.65 — Etiske undersøgelser. (Høffding, Harald.) København, 1891.
Phil 187.28.22 — Etiudy o prirode cheloveka. Izd. 2. (Mechnikov, I.I.) Moskva, 1905.
Phil 187.28.15 — Etiudy optimizma. (Mechnikov, I.I.) Moskva, 1907.
Htn   Phil 3585.4.33* — Etliche schöne Predigten. (Luther, Martin.) n.p., 1533.
Phil 8980.208 — Eto kasaetsia usekh. (Bezuglov, A.A.) Moskva, 1956.
Phil 8980.416 — Eto ukrashaet cheloveka. (Galdiaev, P.K.) Moskva, 1962.
Phil 5649.46 — Les étopes de l'intelligence sensori-motrice. (Lézine, Iréne.) Paris, 1969.
Phil 8592.122.20 — L'étrange figure du curé Meslier, 1664-1729. (Marchal, Jean.) Charleville, 1957.
Phil 6990.50 — L'étrange histoire des convulsionnaires de Saint-Medard. (Mousset, Albert.) Paris, 1953.
Phil 187.93.5 — Être et avoir. (Marcel, Gabriel.) Paris, 1935.
Phil 2920.2.30 — Être et individualite. (Vallin, Georges.) Paris, 1959.
Phil 8582.78 — L'être et la conscience morale. (Corvez, Maurice.) Louvain, 1968.
Phil 2630.10 — L'être et la pensée. (Gerard, Jacques.) Paris, 1954.
Phil 720.88 — Être et langage; essai sur la recherche de l'objectivité. (Lane, Gilles.) Paris, 1970.
Phil 2880.8.55 — L'être et le néant. (Sartre, Jean Paul.) Paris, 1943[1946].
Phil 2725.35.100 — L'être et le réel selon Louis Lavelle. (Levert, Paul.) Paris, 1960.
Phil 525.245 — L'être et le silence. (Choisy, Maryse.) Genève, 1965.
Phil 176.129.5 — L'être et les êtres. (Blondel, Maurice.) Paris, 1935.
Phil 176.129.6 — L'être et les êtres. (Blondel, Maurice.) Paris, 1963.
Phil 2750.25 — L'être et l'esprit. (Marc, André.) Paris, 1958.
Phil 2630.8.30 — L'être et l'essence. (Gilson, Étienne.) Paris, 1948.
Phil 2630.8.32 — L'être et l'essence. (Gilson, Étienne.) Paris, 1962.
Phil 3450.19.360 — Être et liberté. (Guilead, Reuben.) Louvain, 1965.
Phil 2905.1.95 — L'être humain selon Teilhard de Chardin. (Chauchard, Paul.) Paris, 1959.
Phil 3450.18.155 — L'être spirituel recherches sur la philosophie de N. Hartmann. (Breton, S.) Lyon, 1962.
Phil 5374.148.2 — L'être subconscient. (Geley, Gustave.) Paris, 1899.
Phil 5374.148 — L'être subconscient. 4e éd. (Geley, Gustave.) Paris, 1919.

Phil 8735.16 — Étrillard, E. Études philosophiques sur les causes premières et les causes finales. Paris, 1900.
Phil 179.10 — Ettinger-Reichmann, Regina. Die Immanenzphilosophie. Göttingen, 1916.
Phil 804.7 — Ettlinger, M. Philosophisches Lesebuch. München, 1925.
Phil 3195.2.125 — Ettlinger, Max. Die Asthetik Martin Deutingers. Kempten, 1925.
Phil 5814.5 — Ettlinger, Max. Beiträge zur Lehre von der Tierseele und ihrer Entwicklung. Münster, 1925.
Phil 3004.2 — Ettlinger, Max. Geschichte der Philosophie von der Romantik bis zur Gegenwart. München, 1924.
Phil 179.18 — Ettlinger, Max. Philosophische Fragen der Gegenwart. Kempten, 1911.
Phil 8707.18 — Étude biologique. (Regard, G.) Lausanne, 1937.
Phil 6955.5 — Étude clinique de la folie. (Foville, A.) Paris, 1871.
Phil 6682.1 — Étude clinique et expérimentale sur l'hypnotisme. (Magnin, P.) Paris, 1884.
Phil 6968.1 — Étude clinique sur la folie héréditaire. (Saury, H.) Paris, 1886.
Phil 5627.70 — Étude clinique sur le délire religieux. Thèse. (Dupain, J.M.) Paris, 1888.
Phil 860.6 — Étude comparative de la psychologie d'Aristote, d'Avicenne et de St.Thomas d'Aquin. (Ushida, Noriko.) Tokyo, 1968.
Phil 930.9.5 — Étude comparative sur les philosophies de Lao Tseu, Khong Tseu, Mo Tseu. Thèse. (Hoang, Tsen-Yue.) Lyon, 1925.
Phil 575.147.80 — Étude critique de la notion d'engagement chez E. Mounier. (Zaza, N.) Genève, 1955.
Phil 490.3 — Étude critique du matérialisme et du spiritualisme. (Pictet, Raoul.) Genève, 1897.
Phil 6952.23.10 — Étude critique et clinique de la doctrine des localisations motrices. (Charcot, J.M.) Paris, 1883.
Phil 2270.140 — Étude critique sur la sociologie de Herbert Spencer. (Diaconide, Elias.) Paris, 1938.
Phil 3808.129 — Étude critique système philosophique de Schopenhauer. (Millioud, Maurice.) Lausanne, 1893.
Phil 5243.14.9 — L'étude de la pensée. (Dwelshauvers, George.) Paris, 1934.
Phil 5627.109 — Étude de psychologie religieuse sur...la prière. Thèse. (Chansou, J.) Toulouse, 1927. 2 pam.
Phil 5400.85 — Une étude des émotions au moyen des tests. Thèse. (Dyett, E.G.) Paris, 1932.
Phil 6990.24 — Étude des manifestations surnaturelles au XIX siècle. (Daurelle.) Rome, 1878.
Phil 5241.95 — Une étude du préjugé au moyen des tests. Thèse. (Bone, H.) Paris, 1934.
Phil 3504.46 — Étude du role de l'imagination dans la conaissance chez Kant. Thèse. (Wolff, E.M.) Carcassonne, 1943.
Phil 5241.54 — L'étude expérimentale de l'intelligence. Photoreproduction. (Binet, Alfred.) Paris, 1922.
Phil 4080.1.80 — Étude historique...Cesare Cremonini. (Mabilleau, L.) Paris, 1881.
Phil 2138.112 — Étude historique et critique de la théorie de la perception extérieure chez John Stuart Mill. Thèse. (Wisniewski, J.) Paris, 1925.
Phil 8668.3 — Étude laique de la notion de Dieu. (Norlin, C.) Paris, 1906.
Phil 6671.22.5 — Étude magnétisme animal sous le point de vue d'une exacte pratique. 2. éd. (Baragnon, Petrus.) Paris, 1853.
Phil 5247.20 — Étude préparatoire à la détermination experimentale de diverses individuel intellects. (Hamelinck, M.) Gand, 1915.
Phil 7080.2 — Étude psycho-physiologique. (Dupuy, P.) Bordeaux, 1879.
Phil 6324.2 — Étude psychoanalytique. Le complex d'Oedipe. (Odier, Charles.) Genève, 1925.
Phil 5627.67 — Étude psychologique des plus anciens reveils religieux aux Etats-Unis. Thèse. (Kaltenbaach, J.) Genève, 1905.
Phil 5627.68 — Étude psychologique sur la prière d'après deux enquêtes américaines. Thèse. (Léo, A.) Cahors, 1905.
Phil 5243.5.10 — Étude psychophysique. (Delboeuf, J.R.L.) Belgium, 1873.
Phil 5253.14 — Étude quantitative sur l'évolution des opérations inteslectuelles. (Nassefat, Mortega.) Neuchâtel, 1963.
Phil 6673.7 — Étude scientifique sur le somnambulisme. (Despine, P.) Paris, 1880.
Phil 2805.91.3 — Étude sur Alexandre Vinet critique de Pascal. (Nazelle, R.J.) Alençon, 1901.
Phil 2520.164 — Étude sur Descartes. (Chartier, A.) Paris, 1928.
Phil 1850.111 — Étude sur François Bacon. (Barthélemy-Sainte-Hilaire, Jules.) Paris, 1890.
Phil 5640.26 — Étude sur la connaissance sensible des objets extérieurs. (Lemaire, J.) Liege, 1921.
Phil 4363.2.82 — Étude sur la doctrine de Molinos. Thèse. (Reynier, Frédéric.) Strasbourg, 1856.
Phil 1020.8.15 — Étude sur la métaphysique d'Avicenne. (Saliba, D.) Paris, 1926.
Phil 1020.8.16 — Étude sur la métaphysique d'Avicenne. Thèse. (Saliba, D.) Paris, 1926.
Phil 672.26 — Étude sur la notion d'espace d'après Descartes. Thèse. (Luguet, Henry.) Paris, 1875.
Phil 335.5 — Étude sur la phénoménologie. Thèse. (Elbert, J.W.) Nancy, 1930.
Phil 2725.8.82 — Étude sur la philosophie de Laromiguiere. (Lame, D.) Guéret, 1864.
Phil 2405.1 — Étude sur la philosophie en France au XIXe siècle. (Ferraz, Marin.) Paris, 1877.
Phil 1750.14 — Étude sur la sophistique contemporaine. (Gratry, A.J.A.) Paris, 1851.
Phil 5325.13 — Étude sur l'association des idées. (Mervoyer, P.M.) Paris, 1864.
Phil 2805.82 — Étude sur le scepticisme de Pascal. (Droz, E.) Paris, 1886.
Phil 6681.4.15 — Étude sur le zoomagnétisme. (Liébeault, A.A.) Paris, 1883.
Phil 6750.6 — Étude sur les tics. (Noir, J.) Paris, 1893.
Phil 672.18 — Étude sur l'espace et le temps. (Lechalas, G.) Paris, 1910.
Phil 5545.72 — Étude sur l'illusion de fausse reconnaissance. (Leroy, Eugène J.) Paris, 1898.
Phil 2733.81 — Étude sur Malebranche. (Blampignon, Emile Antoine.) Paris, 1862.
Phil 2651.81 — Etude sur Pierre Daniel Huet. (Flottes, J.B.M.) Montpellier, 1857.
Phil 6619.12 — Étude sur quelques paralysies d'origine psychique. (Grafé, A.) Bruxelles, 1889.
Phil 1870.92 — Étude sur vie et les oeuvres philosophiques de G. Berkeley. (Penjon, A.) Paris, 1878.
Phil 2477.15.35 — Études. (Bachelard, Gaston.) Paris, 1970.
Phil 178.20 — Études analytiques sur les auteurs philosophiques. (Domecq, J.B.) Tours, n.d.

Phil 2475.1.282 Études Bergsoniennes, hommage à Henri Bergson (1859-1941). Paris, 1942.

Phil 2475.1.301 Les études bergsoniennes. Paris. 1-8 7v.

Phil 6619.4.2 Études cliniques sur la grande hystérie ou hystéro-épilepsie. 2. ed. (Richer, Paul.) Paris, 1885.

Phil 6955.1.5 Études cliniques sur les maladies mentales et nerveuses. (Falret, J.P.) Paris, 1890.

Phil 5241.14 Études de l'homme. (Bonstetten, C.V. de.) Genève, 1821. 2v.

Phil 8878.41 Études de l'homme moral. (Dessaignes, J.P.) Paris, 1882. 3v.

Phil 8892.18 Études de morale. (Rauh, F.) Paris, 1911.

Phil 8961.16 Etudes de morale histoire et doctrine. (Lottin, O.) Gembloux, 1961.

Phil 8876.44 Études de morale positive. (Belot, G.) Paris, 1907.

Phil 8876.44.2 Études de morale positive. 2e éd. (Belot, G.) Paris, 1921. 2v.

Phil 176.54A Etudes de philosophie ancienne et de philosophie moderne. (Brochard, V.) Paris, 1912.

Phil 1106.16 Etudes de philosophie antique. (Bréhier, Émile.) Paris, 1955.

Phil 1122.5 Etudes de philosophie grecque. (Rodier, Georges.) Paris, 1926.

Phil 1511.3 Études de philosophie médiévale. (Gilson, Étienne.) Strasbourg, 1921.

Phil 1701.23.5 Études de philosophie moderne. (Bréhier, Émile.) Paris, 1965.

Phil 8876.10 Études de philosophie morale. (Baudrillart, H.) Paris, 1858. 2v.

Phil 8897.39 Études de philosophie morale. (Werner, Charles.) Genève, 1917.

Phil 1133.24 Etudes de philosophie presocratique. (Frenkian, A.M.) Cernăuti, 1933. 2v.

Phil 6316.1 Études de psychologie. (Gley, E.) Paris, 1903.

Phil 5252.25 Études de psychologie. Louvain, 1912.

Phil 5819.7 Etudes de psychologie animale. (Janssens, E.) Paris, 1939.

Phil 14.14 Études d'epistemologie genetique. Paris. 1,1957+ 15v.

Phil 8413.42 Études d'esthétique. (Michelés, Panagiótés Andreau.) Paris, 1967.

Phil 8070.2 Études d'esthétique médiévale. (Bruyne, Edgar de.) Brugge, 1946. 3v.

Phil 185.96 Etudes d'histoire de la pensée philosophique. (Koyré, Alexandre.) Paris, 1961.

Phil 801.10 Études d'histoire de la philosophie. (Boutroux, E.) Paris, 1908.

Phil 182.45.5 Études d'histoire des sciences. (Hannequin, A.) Paris, 1908. 2v.

Phil 525.45 Études d'histoire et de psychologie du mysticisme. (Delacroix, H.) Paris, 1908.

Phil 1520.6 Études d'histoire littéraire sur la scolastique médiévale. (Pelzer, Auguste.) Louvain, 1964.

Phil 2520.94 Études du Cartésianisme. (Mazure, P.A.) Paris, 1828.

Phil 177.5 Etudes élémentaires de philosophie. (Cardaillac, M.) Paris, 1830. 2v.

Phil 8412.7 Études esthétiques. (Lechalas, G.) Paris, 1902.

Phil 2725.2.83 Études et notice biographique. (Lamennais, F.R. de.) Paris, 1835.

Phil 7069.24.28 Études et réflexions d'un psychiste. (James, William.) Paris, 1924.

Phil 5827.9 Études expérimentales sur l'exitabilité de l'écorce cérébrale du chien. Thèse. (Rizzolo, Attilio.) Paris, 1928.

Phil 5241.21 Études familières de psychologie et de morale. (Bouillier, F.C.) Paris, 1884.

Phil 3425.430A Études Hegeliennes. (Grégoire, Franz.) Louvain, 1958.

Phil 2805.247A Etudes historiques et critiques sur la philosophie de Pascal. v.1-3. (Baudin, Émile.) Neuchâtel, 1946-47. 4v.

Phil 2401.4 Études littéraires: essais sur les philosophes. (Bondi, P.) Florence, 1918.

Phil 2805.355 Études médico-psychologiques sur Pascal. (Scholtens, M.) Haarlem, 1958.

Phil 8583.2 Études morales et religieuses. (Davesiès de Pontès, L.) Paris, 1869.

Phil 1350.6 Etudes morales sur l'antiquité. (Martha, Constant.) Paris, 1883.

Phil 1350.6.3 Etudes morales sur l'antiquité. (Martha, Constant.) Paris, 1896.

Phil 8827.3 Études morales sur le temps présent. (Caro, E.M.) Paris, 1855.

Phil 8827.3.2 Études morales sur le temps présent. (Caro, E.M.) Paris, 1869.

Phil 3640.361 Études nietzschéennes. Aix-en-Provence.

Phil 900.8 Études orientales. (Franck, Adolphe.) Paris, 1861.

Phil 2805.111.15 Études pascaliennes. (Jovy, Ernest.) Paris, 1927-36. 9v.

Phil 5815.1 Études philosophiques...animaux. (Fée, A.L.A.) Strasburg, 1853.

Phil 8878.16 Etudes philosophiques. (Durand Desormeaux, F.) Paris, 1884. 2v.

Phil 1535.17 Études philosophiques. (Farges, A.) Paris, 1893-1902. 8v.

Phil 187.7 Études philosophiques. (Mallet, C.A.) Paris, 1844. 2v.

Phil 14.6 Les études philosophiques. Marseille. 1,1926+ 25v.

Phil 14.28 Etudes philosophiques et littéraires. Rabat. 1-4,1967-1969//?

Phil 8735.16 Études philosophiques sur les causes premières et les causes finales. (Etrillard, E.) Paris, 1900.

Phil 5258.15 Études psychologiques. (Setchénov, J.) Paris, 1884.

Phil 3823.10 Études Spinozistes. (Darbon, A.D.) Paris, 1946.

Phil 2805.91.2 Études sur Blaise Pascal. (Vinet, A.) Lausanne, 1936.

Phil 2805.91.1 Études sur Blaise Pascal. (Vinet, A.) Paris, 1848.

Phil 2805.91 Études sur Blaise Pascal. (Vinet, A.) Paris, 1856.

Phil 2520.420 Etudes sur Descartes, Spinoza, Hildesheim. (Guéroult, Marital.) N.Y., 1970.

Phil 2520.194 Études sur Descartes. (Laberthonnière, L.) Paris, 1935. 2v.

Phil 2520.351 Études sur Descartes. (Rozsnyai, Ervin.) Budapest, 1964.

Phil 2520.199 Études sur Descartes. Paris, 1937.

Phil 3425.304 Études sur Hegel. (Revue de Métaphysique et de Morale.) Paris, 1931.

Phil 5525.3 Études sur le comique. Le rire. (Courdaveaux, V.) Paris, 1875.

Phil 187.28.2 Études sur la nature humaine. (Mechnikov, I.I.) Paris, 1903.

Phil 187.28 Études sur la nature humaine. 2. ed. (Mechnikov, I.I.) Paris, 1903.

Phil 187.28.3 Études sur la nature humaine. 5. ed. (Mechnikov, I.I.) Paris, 1917.

Phil 1522.2 Études sur la philosophie...moyen âge. (Rousselot, X.) Paris, 1840-42. 3v.

Phil 8664.4 Études sur la problème de Dieu dans la philosophie contemporaine. (Jolivet, R.) Lyon, 1932.

Phil 525.37.5 Études sur la psychologie des mystiques. v.1-2. (Maréchal, J.) Bruges, 1924-37.

Phil 3552.340 Études sur la signification historique de la philosophie de Leibniz. Thèse. (Brunner, F.) Paris, 1950[1951]

Phil 1135.15 Études sur la Théodicée de Platon. (Simon, J.) Paris, 1840.

Phil 8644.10 Études sur la théorie de l'avenir. (Turlot, F.C.) Paris, 1810. 2v.

Phil 365.1 Études sur la théorie de l'evolution. (Carrau, V.M.J.L.) Paris, 1879.

Phil 3831.16 Études sur la théorie démocratique. (Lacharrière, R.) Paris, 1963.

Phil 8592.122.10 Études sur le curé Meslier. (Société des Études Robespierristes.) Paris, 1966.

Phil 477.1 Études sur le matérialisme. (Cahagnet, A.) Argenteuil, 1869.

Phil 2520.116.15 Études sur le rôle de la pensée médiévale dans la formation du système cartésien. (Gilson, E.) Paris, 1930.

Phil 2520.116.15.5 Études sur le rôle de la pensée médiévale dans la formation du système cartésien. (Gilson, E.) Paris, 1951.

Phil 2725.11.31 Études sur le syllogisme. (Lachelier, Jules.) Paris, 1907.

Phil 806.8 Études sur les auteurs philosophiques: réponses aux questions. 3e éd. (Gasc-Desfosses, E.) Paris, 1909.

Phil 6969.4 Études sur les délires d'évolution démentielle précoce. Thèse. (Thuillier-Landry, L.) Paris, 1916.

Phil 5817.8 Études sur les facultés mentales des animaux. (Houzeau, Jean C.) Mons, 1872. 2v.

Phil 6952.9 Études sur les maladies cérébrales et mentales. (Cotard, J.) Paris, 1891.

Phil 8840.1.8 Études sur les moralistes français. 8e éd. (Prévost-Paradol, L.A.) Paris, 1895.

Phil 293.17 Études sur les origines. (Marin de Carranrais, E. de.) Paris, 1876.

Phil 800.3 Études sur les principaux philosophes. (Adams, C.) Paris, 1903.

Phil 5460.10.2 Études sur l'hallucination. Thèse. (Faure, Henri.) Paris, 1930. 2v.

Phil 4710.2 Études sur l'histoire de la pensée philosophique en Russie. (Koyré, A.) Paris, 1950.

Phil 2520.154 Études sur l'histoire de la philosophie de l'action. (Espinas, Alfred.) Paris, 1925. 2v.

Phil 193.9.13 Études sur l'humanisme. (Schiller, F.C.S.) Paris, 1909.

Phil 450.4 Etudes sur l'imagination de la vie. (Mansuy, Michel.) Paris, 1970.

Phil 3425.390 Études sur Marx et Hegel. (Hyppolite, Jean.) Paris, 1955.

Phil 3425.390.2 Etudes sur Marx et Hegel. 2. éd. (Hyppolite, Jean.) Paris, 1965.

Phil 2805.80.7 Études sur Pascal. (Cousin, Victor.) Paris, 1876.

Phil 2805.180 Études sur Pascal. Paris, 1923.

Phil 2805.217 Etudes sur Pascal de l'automatisme a la foi. (Desgrippes, George.) Paris, 19- .

Phil 8876.44.5 Études sur philosophie morale au XIXeme siècle. (Belot, G.) Paris, 1904.

Phil 2070.35.15 Études Théologiques et Religieuses. Cinquantenaire de la psychologie religieuse de William James. Montpellier, 1953.

Phil 3501.3 Etwas über den Werth der kritischen Philosophie. (Troitzsch, J.G.) Leipzig, 1780-1800. 3 pam.

Phil 5756.9 Etwas vom Begriff des Willens in der neueren Psychologie. (Gaede, Udo.) Berlin, 1911.

Phil 8961.15 Etyczna kultura starożytnego Rzymu. (Łapicki, B.) Łódź, 1958.

Phil 14.24 Etyka. Warzawa. 1,1966+ 3v.

Phil 14.27 Etyka i estetyka. Kyïv. 1,1965+ 3v.

Phil 2115.220 Euchner, Walter. Naturrecht und Politik bei John Locke. Frankfurt am Main, 1969.

Phil 179.3.15 Eucken, R. Colleted essays. London, 1914.

Phil 179.3 Eucken, R. Die Einheit des Geisteslebens. Leipzig, 1888.

Phil 179.3.2 Eucken, R. Die Einheit des Geisteslebens. 2. Aufl. Berlin, 1925.

Phil 179.3.32.5 Eucken, R. Erkennen und Leben. Berlin, 1923.

Phil 179.3.32 Eucken, R. Erkennen und Leben. Leipzig, 1912.

Phil 179.3.8 Eucken, R. Fundamental concepts of modern philosophical thought. N.Y., 1880.

Phil 179.3.28.5 Eucken, R. Geistesprobleme und Lebensfragen. Leipzig, 1918.

Phil 179.3.28.2 Eucken, R. Geistesprobleme und Lebensfragen. 2e Aufl. Leipzig, n.d.

Phil 179.3.5 Eucken, R. Geistige Strömungen derGegenwart. Leipzig, 1904.

Phil 179.3.6 Eucken, R. Geistige Strömungen der Gegenwart. 4e Aufl. Leipzig, 1909.

Phil 179.3.50 Eucken, R. Die geistigen Forderungen der Gegenwart. 3e Aufl. Berlin, 1918.

Phil 179.3.17 Eucken, R. Geistigen Lebensinhalt. Leipzig, 1896.

Phil 179.3.13 Eucken, R. Gesammelte Aufsätze zur Philosophie. Leipzig, 1903.

Phil 89.2 Eucken, R. Geschichte der philosophischen Terminologie. Leipzig, 1879.

Phil 179.3.60 Eucken, R. Geschichte und Kritik der grund Begriffe der Gegenwart. v.1-2. Leipzig, 1878.

Phil 179.3.31 Eucken, R. Die Grundbegriffe der Gegenwart. 2. Aufl. Leipzig, 1893.

Phil 179.3.67 Eucken, R. Der Kampf um die Religion in der Gegenwart. 1. und 2. Aufl. Langensalza, 1922.

Phil 179.3.19 Eucken, R. Der Kampf um einen Geistigen Lebensinhalt. Leipzig, 1918.

Phil 179.3.41 Eucken, R. Knowledge and life. N.Y., 1914.

Phil 179.3.75 Eucken, R. Lebenserinnerungen. Leipzig, 1921.

Phil 179.3.75.25 Eucken, R. Lebenserinnerungen. Stockholm, 1921.

Phil 179.3.21 Eucken, R. The life of the spirit. London, 1909.

Phil 179.3.29 Eucken, R. Life's basis and life's ideal. London, 1911.

Phil 179.3.7.4 Eucken, R. Main currents of modern thought. London, 1912.

Phil 179.3.27.15 Eucken, R. The meaning and value of life. London, 1909.

Phil 179.3.65 Eucken, R. Mensch und Welt. 3e Aufl. Leipzig, 1923.

Phil 179.3.70 Eucken, R. Moral und Lebensanschauung. 2. Aufl. Leipzig, 1917.

Phil 179.3.55 — Eucken, R. Naturalism or idealism? Photoreproduction. Cambridge, 1912.

Phil 179.03 — Eucken, R. Prolegomena...Einheit des Geisteslebens. Leipzig, 1885.

Phil 179.3.52 — Eucken, R. Prologomena und Epilog zu einer Philosophie des Geisteslebens. Berlin, 1922.

Phil 179.3.35 — Eucken, R. Religion and life. N.Y., 1912.

Phil 179.3.20 — Eucken, R. Rudolf Eucken; ein Geistesbild. Berlin, 1927?

Phil 179.3.76 — Eucken, R. Rudolf Eucken, his life, work and travels. London, 1921.

Phil 179.3.25 — Eucken, R. Der Sinn und Wert des Lebens. Leipzig, 1910.

Phil 179.3.27 — Eucken, R. Sinn und Wert des Lebens. 3rd ed. Leipzig, 1913.

Phil 179.3.27.3 — Eucken, R. Der Sinn und Wert des Lebens. 6. Aufl. Leipzig, 1918.

Phil 179.3.61 — Eucken, R. The spiritual outlook of Europe today. London, 1922.

Phil 8694.1 — Eucken, R. Wissenschaft und Religion. München, 1906.

Phil 179.3.45 — Eucken, R. Zur Sammlung der Geistert. Leipzig, 1914.

Phil 8879.13 — Eucken, R.C. Einführung...Philosophie des Geisteslebens. Leipzig, 1908.

Phil 8879.13.10 — Eucken, R.C. Ethics and modern thought. N.Y., 1913.

Phil 8879.13.5 — Eucken, R.C. Present-day ethics. London, 1913.

Phil 3004.1.2 — Eucken, Rudolf. Beiträge zur Einführung im die Geschichte der Philosophie. 2. Aufl. Leipzig, 1906.

Phil 8584.5.5 — Eucken, Rudolf. Christianity and the new idealism. London, 1909.

Phil 8829.2.9 — Eucken, Rudolf. Grundlinien einer neuen Lebensanschauung. Leipzig, 1907.

Phil 8829.2.10 — Eucken, Rudolf. Grundlinien einer neuen Lebensanschauung. 2e Aufl. Leipzig, 1913.

Phil 8584.5.16 — Eucken, Rudolf. Hauptprobleme der Religionsphilosophie der Gegenwart. Berlin, 1912.

Phil 8829.2 — Eucken, Rudolf. Die Lebensanschauungen der grossen Denker. Leipzig, 1890.

Phil 8829.2.2 — Eucken, Rudolf. Die Lebensanschauungen der grossen Denker. Leipzig, 1897.

Phil 8829.2.5 — Eucken, Rudolf. Die Lebensanschauungen der grossen Denker. Leipzig, 1905.

Phil 8829.2.7 — Eucken, Rudolf. Die Lebensanschauungen der grossen Denker. 12. Aufl. Leipzig, 1918.

Phil 8829.2.8 — Eucken, Rudolf. Der Lebensanschauungen der grossen Denker. 13e und 14e Aufl. Berlin, 1919.

Phil 8829.2.8.2 — Eucken, Rudolf. Die Lebensanschauungen der grossen Denker. 20. Aufl. Berlin, 1950.

Phil 8829.2.12 — Eucken, Rudolf. The problem of human life. N.Y., 1909.

Phil 8829.2.20 — Eucken, Rudolf. The problem of human life. N.Y., 1924.

Phil 8584.5.7 — Eucken, Rudolf. Der religiöse Wahrheitsbegriff in der Philosophie Rudolf Euckens. Göttingen, 1910.

Phil 400.34 — Eucken, Rudolf. Die Träger des deutschen Idealismus. Berlin, 1915.

Phil 3004.1.10 — Eucken, Rudolf. Die Träger des deutschen Idealismus. Berlin, 1916.

Phil 8584.5.3 — Eucken, Rudolf. The truth of religion. N.Y., 1911.

Phil 8584.5.14 — Eucken, Rudolf. Der Wahrheitsgehalt der Religion. Leipzig, 1901.

Phil 8584.5.15 — Eucken, Rudolf. Der Wahrheitsgehalt der Religion. Leipzig, 1901.

Phil 8584.5.15.4 — Eucken, Rudolf. Der Wahrheitsgehalt der Religion. 4. Aufl. Berlin, 1927.

Phil 8584.5 — Eucken, Rudolf. Das Wesen der Religion, philosophisch Betrachtet. Leipzig, 1901.

Phil 3525.87 — Eucken, Rudolf. Zur Erinnerung an K.C.F. Krause. Leipzig, 1881.

Phil 179.3.80 — Pamphlet box. Eucken, Rudolf.

Phil 193.243 — Euclides en Panini. (Staal, J.F.) Amsterdam, 1963.

Phil 1145.77 — Der Eudämonismus in der griechischen Philosophie. (Heinze, Max.) Leipzig, 1883.

Phil 9245.8 — Eudämonismus und Egoismus. (Pfleiderer, E.) Leipzig, 1880.

Phil 3195.9.83 — Eugen Dühring. (Druskowitz, H.) Heidelberg, 1889.

Phil 3195.9.81 — Eugen Dühring als Religionsphilosoph. Inaug. Diss. (Lau, Hamann.) Lübeck, 1907.

Phil 4365.1.82 — Eugeni d'Ors. (Capdevila, José Maria.) Barcino, 1965.

Phil 6940.5 — Eugenics Society, London. Family council law in Europe. London, 1930.

Phil 2520.172.5 — Eulogy of Descartes. (Thomas, A.L.) Cheltenham, 1826.

Htn · Phil 2120.3.30* — Euphues and his England. (Lyly, John.) London, 1588.

Phil 978.49.115 — Eurhythmy as visible song. (Steiner, R.) London, 1932.

Phil 978.49.120 — Eurhythmy as visible speech. (Steiner, R.) London, 1931.

Phil 810.14 — Eurooppalaisen ihmisen maailmansatsomus. (Ketoren, Oliva.) Helsingissa, 1961.

Phil 1721.5 — Europa in de spiegel. (Vloemans, Antoon.) Den Haag, 1957.

Phil 3552.127 — Der europäische Freiheitskampf. (Kiefl, Franz X.) Mainz, 1913.

Phil 192.67.10 — Der europäische Mensch. (Rintelen, Fritz J. von.) Wien, 1957.

Phil 806.17 — Die europäische Philosophie. (Glockuer, H.) Stuttgart, 1958.

Phil 1701.20 — Europäische Philosophie der Gegenwart. (Bochénski, J.M.) Bern, 1947.

Phil 1701.20.5 — Europäische Philosophie der Gegenwart. 2. Aufl. (Bochénski, J.M.) München, 1951.

Phil 632.5 — Europaeisches Forum, Alpach, Austria, 1948. Gesetz und Wirklichkeit. Innsbruck, 1949.

Phil 735.276 — Europaeisches Forum, Alpbach, Austria, 1946. Erkenntnis und Wert. Salzburg, 1946.

Phil 402.4 — De europäiske ideers historie. 2. opl. (Lund, Erik.) Gyldendal, 1963.

Phil 3640.286 — Europas Selbsbesinnung durch Nietzsche. (Kroekel, F.) München, 1929.

Phil 1710.13 — European philosophy today. (Kline, George.) Chicago, 1965.

Phil 535.20 — Het Europese nihilisme. (Graaff, Frank de.) Amsterdam, 1956.

Phil 978.49.117 — Eurythmie als sichtbarer Gesang. 1. Aufl. (Steiner, R.) Dornach, 1956.

Phil 7069.09.3 — Eusapia Palladino and her phenomena. (Carrington, Hereward.) N.Y., 1909.

Phil 179.9 — Eusebietti, Pietro. Corso elementare di filosofia. Milano, 1912. 3v.

Phil 525.109 — Eustace, C.J. An infinity of questions. London, 1946.

Phil 8584.18 — Eustace, C.J. Mind and the mystery. N.Y., 1937.

Htn · Phil 1535.4.4* — Eustachius a S. Paulo. Summa philosophiae quadripartita. Cantabrigiae, 1640.

Htn · Phil 1535.4.5* — Eustachius a S. Paulo. Summa philosophiae quadripartita. Cantabrigiae, 1640.

Htn · Phil 1535.4* — Eustachius a S. Paulo. Summa philosophiae quadripartita. Cantabrigiae, 1698.

Phil 8637.2 — Euthanasie. (Meister, J.H.) Paris, 1809.

Phil 6520.14 — Eva von Buttler die Messaline und Muckerin...Mysterien des Pietismus. (Christiany, L.) Stuttgart, 1870.

Phil 5062.29 — The evaluation of logic. (Williams, Henry H.) Chapel Hill, 1925.

Phil 5590.514 — The evaluation of personal constructs. (Bannister, Donald.) London, 1968.

Phil 8615.13 — An evaluation of the philosophy and pedagogy of ethical culture. Diss. (Bacon, S.F.) Washington, 1933.

Phil 7054.37.25 — El evangelio segun el espiritismo. (Rivail, H.L.D.) Barcelona, 1875.

Phil 8964.5 — Evangelische Ethik. (Oyen, Hendrik van.) Basel, 1952. 2v.

Phil 3850.18.106 — Evangelisches und Katholisches in Max Schelers Ethik. Inaug. Diss. (Eklund, H.) Uppsala, 1932.

Phil 3850.18.105 — Evangelisches und Katholisches in Max Schelers Ethik. Inaug. Diss. (Eklund, H.) Uppsala, 1932.

Phil 8894.4 — Das Evangelium der Wahrheit und Freiheit. (Thomassen, J.H.) Leipzig, 1871.

Phil 575.280 — Evans, Cedric Oliver. The subject of consciousness. London, 1970.

Phil 5044.8 — Evans, D.L. Logic, theoretical and applied. Garden City, 1937.

Phil 630.30.5 — Evans, Daniel L. New realism and old reality. Princeton, 1928.

Phil 630.30 — Evans, Daniel L. The status of values in new realism. Columbus, 1923.

Phil 2725.4.85 — Evans, David O. Pierre Leroux and his philosophy in relation to literature. n.p., 1929.

Phil 2725.4.89 — Evans, David O. Le socialisme romantique. Paris, 1948.

Phil 5814.1 — Evans, E.P. Evolutional ethics and animal psychology. N.Y., 1898.

Phil 2750.11.153 — Evans, J.W. Jacques Maritain. N.Y., 1963.

Phil 6314.10 — Evans, Jean. Three men. 1st ed. N.Y., 1954.

Phil 8430.66 — Evans, Joan. Taste and temperament. London, 1939.

Phil 5244.21 — Evans, John E. The effect of distraction on reaction time. N.Y., 1916.

Phil 325.14 — Evans, John Llewelyn. The foundations of empiricism. Cardiff, 1965.

Phil 8659.5 — Evans, Joseph. Theistic monism. London, 1928.

Phil 5871.116 — Evans, Judith L. Children in Africa: a review of psychological research. N.Y., 1970.

Phil 5645.58 — Evans, Ralph. Introduction to color. N.Y., 1961.

Phil 6319.1.230 — Evans, Richard Isadore. Conversation with Carl Jung and reactions from Ernest Jones. Princeton, 1964.

Phil 6315.19.45 — Evans, Richard Isadore. Dialogue with Erich Fromm. 1. ed. N.Y., 1966.

Phil 5240.70 — Evans, Richard Isadore. Gordon Allport. 1. ed. N.Y., 1970[1971]

Phil 8584.11.2 — Evans, Robert C.T. Man. What? Whence? Whither? 2. ed. Chatham, 1923.

Phil 6114.5.16 — Evans, W.F. The divine law of cure. Boston, 1881.

Phil 6114.5 — Evans, W.F. Esoteric Christianity and mental therepeutics. Boston, n.d.

Phil 6114.5.12 — Evans, W.F. A mental-cure illustrated influence of the mind on the body. Boston, 1884.

Phil 6114.5.4 — Evans, W.F. Mental medicine. 6. ed. Boston, 1881.

Phil 6114.5.7 — Evans, W.F. Mental medicine. 15th ed. Boston, 1885.

Phil 6114.5.8 — Evans, W.F. Soul and body. Boston, 1876.

Phil 5545.7 — Evans, W.L. Memory training. N.Y., 1889.

Phil 5252.88 — Evans, W.V. Belief and art. Chicago, 1939.

Phil 676.2 — L'eveil de l'intelligence. (Mourad, Youssef.) Paris, 1939.

Phil 410.3 — L'éveil spirituel, accomplissement personnel par la pensée créatrice. (Rohrbach, Marc Adrien.) Paris, 1969.

Phil 3486.4 — Evellin, F. Infini et quantité. Paris, 1880.

Evellin, F. La raison pure...essai sur la philosophie Kantienne. Paris, 1907.

Phil 9495.168.20 — Evely, Louis. Lovers in marriage. N.Y., 1968.

Phil 8584.12 — Evelyn, John. The history of religion. London, 1850. 2v.

Htn · Phil 9515.5* — Evelyn, John. Publick employment and active life prefered. London, 1667.

Htn · Phil 9344.5* — Evening amusement for the ladies. Boston, 1796.

Phil 645.3 — Evenings with skeptics. (Owen, J.) N.Y., 1881. 2v.

Phil 6954.4 — Evensen, Hans. Dementia praecox. Kristiania, 1904.

Phil 7054.110 — The eventful nights of August 20th. (Ewer, F.C.) N.Y., 1855.

Phil 8879.10.8 — Everett, C.C. Ethics for young people. Boston, 1891.

Phil 9344.9 — Everett, C.C. Ethics for young people. Boston, 1893.

Phil 3246.81 — Everett, C.C. Fichte's Science of knowledge. Chicago, 1884.

Phil 179.34 — Everett, C.C. Immortality. Boston, 1902.

Phil 5627.5 — Everett, C.C. The psychological elements of religious faith. N.Y., 1902.

Phil 5044.3.4 — Everett, C.C. The science of thought. Boston, 1882.

Phil 5044.3.5 — Everett, C.C. The science of thought. Rev. ed. Boston, 1890.

Phil 8879.10.5 — Everett, C.C. Theism and the Christian faith. N.Y., 1909.

Phil 8879.10 — Everett, C.C. The ultimate facts of ethics. Boston, 1887.

Phil 1865.175 — Everett, Charles W. The education of Jeremy Bentham. N.Y., 1931.

Phil 1865.198 — Everett, Charles Warren. Jeremy Bentham. London, 1966.

Phil 8954.2 — Everett, E.L. Impossible things and other essays. Philadelphia, 1932.

Phil 7054.112 — Everett, J. A book for skeptics being communications from angels. Columbus, 1853.

Phil 8879.25 — Everett, M.S. Ideals of life. N.Y., 1954.

Phil 8879.15 — Everett, W.G. Moral values. N.Y., 1918.

Phil 8642.4 — Everlasting punishment and modern speculation. (Reid, William.) Edinburgh, 1874.

Phil 8430.5 — Eversople, Finley. Christian faith and the contemporary arts. N.Y., 1962.

Phil 8877.6 — Every day life and every day morals. (Chaney, G.L.) Boston, 1885.

Phil 6122.35 — Every man a king. (Marden, Orison S.) N.Y., 1906.

Phil 9530.39.5 — Every man a winner. (Popplestone, C.E.) N.Y., 1936.

Phil 6980.157 — Everyday psychiatry. (Campbell, John D.) Philadelphia, 1945.

Phil 8691.25.2 — Everyman and the infinite. (Beckett, Lucile C.) London, n.d.

Phil 5425.67 — Everyman's genius. (Austin, Mary Hunter.) Indianapolis, 1925.

Phil 8877.77 — Everyman's monitor. (Coltman, J.) Philadelphia, 1815.

Phil 5240.41 — Everyman's psychology. 1. ed. (Adams, John.) Garden City, 1929.

Phil 8890.27   Everything bought with a price, or Moral commerce. Salem, 1820.

Phil 5090.01   Pamphlet box. Evidence.

Phil 325.10   Evidence and inference. (Hayden Colloquium on Scientific Concept and Method, M.I.T.) Chicago, 1960.

Phil 5068.60   Evidence and meaning: studies in analytic philosophy. (Fogelin, Robert J.) London, 1967.

Phil 7069.13.20   The evidence for communication with the dead. (Hude, Fru Anna.) London, 1913.

Phil 8632.18   The evidence for immortality. (Halsey, Don Peters.) N.Y., 1932.

Phil 6114.23   The evidence for spirit healing. (Edwards, Henry James.) London, 1953.

Phil 7060.91.5   The evidence for the supernatural. (Tuckett, I.L.) London, 1911.

Htn   Phil 2150.3.30*   Evidence from Scripture...the second coming of Christ. (Miller, William.) Troy, 1838.

Phil 8702.22   The evidence of God in an expanding universe. (Monsma, John C.) N.Y., 1958.

Phil 7069.39.50   Evidence of identity. (Richmond, K.) London, 1939.

Phil 5640.36   The evidence of our senses. (Wolters, A.W.P.) London, 1933.

Phil 7069.38.50   Evidence of purpose. (Richmond, Z.) London, 1939.

Phil 8626.4   The evidence of reason in proof of the immortality of the soul. (Baxter, A.) London, 1779.

Phil 8416.39   Évidences. (Pimienta, Gustave.) Paris, 1965.

Phil 8583.15   Evidences of Christianity. (Dodge, Ebenezer.) Boston, 1872.

Phil 7069.43.15   Evidences of immortality. (Wade, A.M.) N.Y., 1943.

Phil 8595.16.9   Evidences of revealed religion. (Estlin, John P.) Bristol, 1796?

Phil 177.19   Evidenza, amore e fede. (Conti, Augusto.) Florence, 1858. 2v.

Phil 8668.7   L'evidenza di Dio nella filosofia del secolo XIII. (Noto, Antonio di.) Padova, 1958.

Phil 3480.80.79   Den evigi fred. (Kant, Immanuel.) Fagershand, 1889.

Phil 8620.4   Evil and evolution. London, 1896.

Phil 3850.5.94   Evocation. (Claparède-Spir, H.) Genève, 1944.

Phil 4963.5   A evolução do pensamento de Pereira Barreta. (Barros, Roque Spencer Maciel de.) São Paulo, 1967.

Phil 4371.10   La evolución de la filosofía en España. (Montseny y Carret, Juan.) Barcelona 1968.

Phil 4371.5   La evolución de la filosofía en España. v.1-2. (Montseny y Carret, Juan.) Barcelona, 1934.

Phil 525.256.2   La evolución mística en el desenvolvimiento y vitalidad de la Iglesia. 2. ed. (González Arintero, Juan.) Madrid, 1968.

Phil 365.9   L'evoluisme. (Auvard, Alfred.) Paris, 1914.

Phil 8662.26   De evolutie van het godsdienstig bewustzijn. (Hidding, Klaas Albert Hendrik.) Utrecht, 1965.

Phil 8610.900   Evolution; an exposition of Christian dogmas and pagan myths. (Cooley, P.J.) N.Y., 1900.

Phil 8693.12.5   Evolution, and its bearing on religions. (Dadson, Arthur J.) London, 1901.

Phil 365.66   Evolution; Fortschrittsglaube und Heilserwartung. Ein Tagungsbericht. (Stuttgarter Gemeinschaft "Arzt und Seelsorger.") Stuttgart, 1970.

Phil 2905.1.115.5   Evolution; the theory of Teilhard de Chardin. (Delfgaauw, B.M.I.) London, 1969.

Phil 365.02   Pamphlet vol. Evolution. 2 pam.

Phil 365.01   Pamphlet box. Evolution.

Phil 365.42   Evolution. (Jevons, Frank B.) London, 1900.

Phil 8712.4.5   Evolution. (Woodrow, J.) Columbia, S.C., 1884.

Phil 365.34.5   Evolution. 2. ed. (Ghose, Aurobinclo.) Calcutta, 1923.

Phil 8701.11   Evolution and Christian faith. (Lane, H.H.) Princeton, 1923.

Phil 8696.16   Evolution and Christianity. (Gibbs, Jessie W.) Memphis, 1930.

Phil 9150.1.2   Evolution and effort. (Kelly, E.) N.Y., 1895.

Phil 9150.1.5   Evolution and effort. 2. ed. (Kelly, E.) N.Y., 1900.

NEDL   Phil 9150.5   Evolution and ethics. (Huxley, T.H.) London, 1893.

Phil 9150.31   Evolution and ethics. (Keith, Arthur.) N.Y., 1947.

Phil 5350.7   The evolution and growth of human behavior . 2d ed. (Munn, Norman Leslie.) Boston, 1965.

Phil 5251.67   Evolution and modification of behavior. (Lorenz, Konrad Zacharias.) Chicago, 1965.

Phil 9430.32   Evolution and optimism. (Stein, Ludwig.) N.Y., 1926.

Phil 187.177   Evolution and philosophy. (Melsen, Andreas Gerardus Maria van.) Pittsburgh, 1965.

Phil 365.35   Evolution and redemption. (Newsholme, H.P.) London, 1933.

Phil 8693.12   Evolution and religion. (Dadson, Arthur J.) London, 1893.

Phil 365.33   Evolution and religion. (O'Brien, J.A.) N.Y., 1932.

Phil 8704.2   Evolution and religion. (Osborn, H.F.) N.Y., 1923.

Phil 8708.1   Evolution and religion. (Savage, M.J.) Philadelphia, 1886.

Phil 8709.12   Evolution and religion. (Trumbull, William.) N.Y., 1907.

X Cg   Phil 8691.2   Evolution and religion. pt.1. (Beecher, H.W.) N.Y., 1885.

Phil 8672.14   Evolution and the Christian concept of God. (Raven, Charles E.) London, 1936.

Phil 365.50A   Evolution and the founders of pragmatism. (Wiener, P.P.) Cambridge, 1949.

Phil 365.32   Evolution and theology. (Messenger, E.C.) N.Y., 1932.

Phil 7054.157.5   L'évolution animique. (Delanne, Gabriel.) Paris, 1897.

Phil 978.66   Evolution as outlined in the Archaic Eastern records. (Crump, Basil.) Peking, 1930.

Phil 2475.1.50.10   L'évolution créatrice. (Bergson, Henri.) Genève, 1945.

Phil 2475.1.50   L'évolution créatrice. 4. éd. (Bergson, Henri.) Paris, 1908.

Phil 2475.1.50.2A   L'évolution créatrice. 5. éd. (Bergson, Henri.) Paris, 1909.

Phil 2475.1.50.4   L'évolution créatrice. 9. éd. (Bergson, Henri.) Paris, 1912.

Phil 2475.1.50.6   L'évolution créatrice. 10. éd. (Bergson, Henri.) Paris, 1912.

Phil 2475.1.50.8   L'évolution créatrice. 52. éd. (Bergson, Henri.) Paris, 1940.

Phil 850.19   L'évolution de la doctriné du pneuma. (Verbeke, G.) Paris, 1945.

Phil 5014.1.20   L'évolution de la logique. (Enriques, Federigo.) Paris, 1926.

Phil 5545.170   L'évolution de la mémoire. (Janet, Pierre.) Paris, 1928.

Phil 5545.44   L'évolution de la mémoire. (Peiron, Henri.) Paris, 1910.

Phil 8886.8.2   L'évolution de la morale. (Letourneau, C.) Paris, 1887.

Phil 8886.8   L'évolution de la morale. (Letourneau, C.) Paris, 1894.

Phil 672.160   L'évolution de la notion du temps. (Zawirski, Zygmunt.) Cracovie, 1936.

Phil 5520.665   Evolution der Sprache und Vernunft. (Hoepp, Gerhard.) Berlin, 1970.

Phil 5261.8.5   L'évolution des facultés conscientes. Thèse. (Varendonck, J.) Gand, 1921.

Phil 348.3   L'évolution des idées générales. (Ribot, T.) Paris, 1897.

Phil 348.3.4   L'évolution des idées générales. 4. éd. (Ribot, T.) Paris, 1915.

Phil 8842.9   L'évolution des moeurs. (Richard, Gaston.) Paris, 1925.

Phil 978.124   Evolution durch Inkarnation und Metamorphose. (Lorenzen, Iwer Thor.) Hamburg, 1969.

Phil 3246.217   L'évolution et la structure de la doctrine de la science chez Fichte. (Guerault, Martèal.) Paris, 1930. 2v.

Phil 3246.217.2   L'évolution et la structure de la doctrine de la science chez Fichte. Thèse. (Guerault, Martèal.) Strasbourg, 1930. 2 pam.

Phil 365.49   L'évolution humaine. (Przyluski, Jean.) Paris, 1942.

Phil 8702.3   Evolution illuminating the Bible. (Mackenzie, A.) London, 1891.

Phil 8702.13   Evolution in science and religion. (Millikan, R.A.) New Haven, 1927.

Phil 2905.1.460   Evolution in the afterlife. 1st ed. (Guerini, Edmund W.) N.Y., 1967.

Phil 6115.23.5   The evolution of an idea. 2d ed. (Frany, Shepherd I.) Los Angeles, 1929.

Phil 5817.9.5   Evolution of animal intelligence. (Holmes, S.J.) N.Y., 1911.

Phil 5374.9   The evolution of consciousness. (Hall, L.) London, 1901.

Phil 5374.30   The evolution of consciousness. (Tilby, A Wyatt.) London, 1922.

Phil 310.652A   The evolution of dialectical materialism. (Jordan, Zbigniew A.) London, 1967.

Phil 8843.11   Evolution of ethics...in great religions. (Sneath, E.H.) New Haven, 1927.

Phil 8610.907   The evolution of faith; an essay. (Hunt, E.J.) London, 1907.

Phil 348.3.5   Evolution of general ideas. (Ribot, T.) Chicago, 1899.

Phil 1145.75   Evolution of Greek moral education. (Lavell, C.F.) Kingston, 1911.

Phil 9245.52   The evolution of happiness. (Andrus, C.J.) Boston, 1936.

Phil 5247.65   The evolution of human nature. (Herrick, C.J.) Austin, 1956.

Phil 194.17.5   Evolution of idea; a thesis. (Taft, Oren B.) Chicago, 1926.

Phil 8637.6.5   The evolution of immortality. (McConnell, S.D.) N.Y., 1902.

Phil 8643.4   The evolution of immortality. (Stockwell, C.T.) Chicago, 1887.

Phil 815.3   The evolution of knowledge. (Perrin, R. St. J.) N.Y., 1905.

Phil 349.17   The evolution of knowledge. (Shann, George.) London, 1922.

Phil 978.6.20   Evolution of life and form. 2nd ed. (Besant, Annie.) London, 1900.

Phil 8702.4   The evolution of man and Christianity. (MacQueary, H.) N.Y., 1890.

Phil 1515.3   The evolution of medieval thought. (Knowles, David.) Baltimore, 1962.

Phil 5822.6   The evolution of mind. (McCabe, Joseph.) London, 1910.

Phil 5222.4.5   The evolution of modern psychology. (Müller-Freienfelds, R.) New Haven, 1935.

Phil 8847.2   The evolution of morality. (Wake, Charles S.) London, 1878. 2v.

Phil 8581.31   The evolution of religions. (Bierer, E.) N.Y., 1906.

Phil 8661.14   The evolution of the conception of God. (Greene, K.C.) Boston, 1934.

Phil 5261.8.8   The evolution of the concious faculties. (Varendonck, J.) N.Y., 1923.

Phil 8674.6   Evolution of the God and Christ ideas. (Tuttle, Hudson.) Berlin, 1906.

Phil 8655.4   Evolution of the idea of God. (Allen, G.) N.Y., 1897.

Phil 665.68   The evolution of the soul. (Sadler, W.S.) Chicago? 1941.

Phil 7060.28.10   The evolution of the soul and other essays. (Hudson, T J.) Chicago, 1904.

Phil 8707.8   The evolution of the world; or, Science from a religious point of view. (Rawson, F.L.) Garden City, 1909.

Phil 1135.20.5   The evolution of theology in the Greek philosophers. (Caird, Edward.) Glasgow, 1923.

Phil 185.43   The evolution of truth and other essays. (Knox,H.V.) London, 1930.

Phil 9150.27   Evolution og moral. (Jensen, J.V.) Kjøbenhavn, 1925.

Phil 8696.11   Evolution or Christianity, God or Darwin? (Goldsmith, W.M.) St. Louis, 1924.

Phil 8649.1.2   Evolution proving immortality. (Yeiser, J.O.) Omaha, 1917.

Phil 575.83   L'évolution psychologique de la personnalité. (Janet, Pierre.) Paris, 1929.

Phil 8580.7   L'évolution religieuse contemporaine chez les anglais, les américains, et les hindous. (Goblet d'Alviella, E.) Paris, 1884.

Phil 8598.139   Evolution technique et théologies. (Serrand, A.Z.) Paris, 1965.

Phil 8598.138.5   Evolution und Gottesidee. (Saher, Purvezji Jamshedji.) Ratigen, 1965.

Phil 2905.1.250   Evolution und Schöffung. (Hengstenberg, H.E.) München, 1963.

Phil 365.15   L'évolution universelle. (Petronievics, B.) Paris, 1921.

Phil 365.30   Evolution versus involution. (Derr, Ezra Z.) N.Y., 1885.

Phil 5814.1   Evolutional ethics and animal psychology. (Evans, E.P.) N.Y., 1898.

Phil 1750.166.90   Evolutionary humanism. (Huxley, J.S.) Melbourne, 1954.

Phil 193.66.5   Evolutionary naturalism. (Sellars, Roy Wood.) Chicago, 1922.

Phil 5258.199   An evolutionary psychologist. (Schroeder, Theodore.) Berkeley Heights, N.J., 1965.

Phil 1815.3   Evolutionary thought in America. (Persons, S.) New Haven, 1950.

Phil 8827.6   Evolutionism and idealism in ethics. Thesis. (Cohn, Frederick.) Omaha, Nebr., 1909.

Phil 336.1   L'évolutionnisme des idées-forces. (Fouillée, A.) Paris, 1890.

Phil 336.1.4   L'évolutionnisme des idées-forces. (Fouillée, A.) Paris, 1906.

Phil 2270.103   L'évolutionnisme en morale. (Halleux, Jean.) Paris, 1901.

Phil 2270.72   L'evoluzione del pensiero. (Spencer, Herbert.) Milano, 1909. 2v.

Phil 365.13   L'evoluzione e i suoi limiti. (Calderoni, G.) Roma, 1907.

Phil 2270.76   L'evoluzione morale. (Spencer, Herbert.) Milano, 1909.

Phil 1135.75   L'evoluzione presocratica. (Montagni, G.R.) Castello, 1912.

Phil 5421.25.45 — Evory, John J. The man and the woman; psychology of human love. N.Y., 1968.

Phil 5790.15 — Evrim, Selmin. Psikoloji açisindan şahsiyette bir buud olarak içedönüküluk-Dişadönüklük. Istanbul, 1967.

Phil 5058.110 — Evristicheskie printsipy i logicheskie ischisleniia. (Serebriannikov, Oleg F.) Moskva, 1970.

Phil 5068.71 — Evristika-nauka o tvorcheskom myshlenii. (Pushkin, Veniamin N.) Moskva, 1967.

Phil 5710.7 — Ewald, G. Temperament und Charakter. Berlin, 1924.

Phil 8694.5 — Ewald, Günter. Naturgestez und Schöpfung. Wuppertal, 1966.

Phil 3486.15 — Ewald, J.L. Über die Kantische Philosophie. Berlin, 1790.

Phil 179.8 — Ewald, O. Gründe und Abgründe. v.1-2. Berlin, 1909.

Phil 3486.5 — Ewald, O. Kants kritischer Idealismus. Berlin, 1908.

Phil 3640.84 — Ewald, Oscar. Nietzsches Lehre. Berlin, 1903.

Phil 2404.2 — Ewald, Oskar. Die französische Aufklärungsphilosophie. München, 1924.

Phil 175.12.9 — Ewald, Oskar. Richard Avenarius. Berlin, 1905.

Phil 5640.25 — Ewald Hering ein Gedenkwort der Psychophysik. (Hillebrand, F.) Berlin, 1918.

Phil 179.27 — Ewast, John-Bart. Disquisitio philosophica de contingentia rerum. Aboae, 1735.

Phil 5850.191.5 — Ewer, B.C. Applied psychology. N.Y., 1925.

Phil 7054.110 — Ewer, F.C. The eventful nights of August 20th. N.Y., 1855.

Phil 5465.178 — Ewert, Otto Maximilian. Phantasie und Intelligenz bei Jugendlichen. Weinheim, 1967.

Phil 978.49.400 — Das Ewige in der Menschenseele. (Steiner, R.) Dornach, 1962.

Phil 9070.103 — Die ewigen Grundlagen des Lebens. (Il'in, Ivan A.) Zürich, 1943.

Phil 8643.25.4 — Ewiges Leben. (Seeberg, R.) Leipzig, 1920.

Phil 8598.120 — Ewiges-Vergängliches. (Schulz-Angern, Karl Friedrich.) Berlin, 1958.

Phil 510.1.23 — Ewigkeit. (Haeckel, Ernst.) Berlin, 1915.

Phil 1540.90 — Die Ewigkeit der Welt. (Behler, Ernst.) München, 1965.

Phil 3007.9 — Die Ewigkeitswerte der deutschen Philosophie. (Hessen, Johannes.) Hamburg, 1943.

Phil 179.36 — Ewing, A.C. The fundamental questions of philosophy. N.Y., 1951.

Phil 335.7A — Ewing, A.C. Reason and intuition. London, 1941.

Phil 8879.32 — Ewing, Alfred. Ethics. London, 1960.

Phil 9240.6 — Ewing, Alfred C. The definition of good. N.Y., 1947.

Phil 400.88 — Ewing, Alfred C. Idealism. London, 1934.

Phil 400.88.3 — Ewing, Alfred C. Idealism. 3. ed. London, 1961.

Phil 400.88.5 — Ewing, Alfred C. The idealist tradition. Glencoe, Illinois, 1957.

Phil 9240.6.5 — Ewing, Alfred C. Second thoughts in moral philosophy. London, 1959.

Phil 179.36.3 — Ewing, Alfred Cyril. The fundamental questions of philosophy. N.Y., 1962.

Phil 3486.9 — Ewing, Alfred Cyril. Kant's treatment of causality. London, 1924.

Phil 1980.6 — Ewing, Alfred Cyril. Non-linguistic philosophy. London, 1968.

Phil 3486.9.6A — Ewing, Alfred Cyril. A short commentary on Kant's Critique of pure reason. Chicago, 1970.

Phil 365.52 — Ewing, Upton Clary. Thresholds of existence. N.Y., 1956.

Phil 5047.1 — Exact philosophy. (Halle, H.F.) London, 1848.

Phil 6990.8.5 — An exact relation of the wonderful cure of Mary Maillard. (Maillard, Mary.) London, 1730.

Phil 8599.18 — Exact science of Christianity. (Thompson, L. Buckland.) Garden City, N.Y., 1916.

Phil 5066.190 — Exacte logica. (Freudenthal, Hans.) Haarlem, 1961.

Phil 5066.190.2 — Exacte logica. 2. druk. (Freudenthal, Hans.) Haarlem, 1967.

Phil 3494.19.25 — Die exakte Aufdeckung des Fundaments der Sittlichkeit und Religion...Kant. (Marcus, Ernst.) Leipzig, 1899.

Phil 1135.163 — Das Exakte denken der Griechen. (Reidemeister, Kurt.) Hamburg, 1949.

Phil 5850.231 — Exakte Persönlichkeitsforschung. (Huth, Albert.) Leipzig, 1930.

Phil 285.3 — Die exakten Grundlagen der Naturphilosophie. (Eleutheropulos, A.) Stuttgart, 1926.

Phil 5592.80 — L'examen clinique en psychologie. (Rey, André.) Paris, 1958.

Phil 5627.145 — Examen critique, physique et théologique des convulsions. (Bonnaire, L. de.) n.p., 1733.

Phil 5243.5 — Examen critique de la loi psychophysique. (Delboeuf, J.R.L.) Paris, 1883.

Phil 3018.3 — Examen critique de la philosophie allemande. (Steininger, F.) Trèves, 1841.

Phil 4115.90 — Examen critique de la philosophie de Gioberti. (Bonnetty, A.) Paris, 1847-49. 2 pam.

Phil 3801.876.30 — Examen critique de la philosophie religieuse se Schelling. Thèse. (Weber, Alfred.) Strasbourg, 1860.

Phil 5247.13.18 — Examen de ingenios. (Huarte de San Juan, J.) Gainesville, 1959.

Htn Phil 5247.13.7* — Examen de ingenios. (Huarte de San Juan, J.) London, 1594.

Htn Phil 5247.13.9* — Examen de ingenios. (Huarte de San Juan, J.) London, 1604.

Phil 5247.13.17 — Examen de ingenios. (Huarte de San Juan, J.) London, 1698.

Htn Phil 5247.13* — Examen de ingenios para las sciencias. (Huarte de San Juan, J.) Antwerp? 1603.

Phil 5247.13.3 — Examen de ingenios para las sciencias. (Huarte de San Juan, J.) Barcelona, 1917.

Phil 5247.13.4 — Examen de ingenios para las sciencias. (Huarte de San Juan, J.) Madrid, 1930. 2v.

Phil 3500.42 — Examen de la doctrine de Kant. (Sarchi, Charles.) Paris, 1872.

Phil 1850.86 — Examen de la philosophie de Bacon. (Maestre, J. de.) Paris, 1836. 2v.

Phil 5925.1 — Examen de la phrenologie. (Flourens, M.J.) Paris, 1842.

Phil 5247.13.26 — Examen de l'examen des esprits. (Guibelet, J.) Paris, 1631.

Phil 575.16 — Examen del concepto de identidad. (Mouchet, E.) Buenos Aires, 1910.

Phil 480.5 — Exámen del materialismo moderno. (Fabié, Antonio M.) Madrid, 1875.

Phil 5247.13.13 — Examen des esprits et naiz aux sciences. (Huarte de San Juan, J.) Rouen, 1607.

Phil 5247.13.15 — L'examen des esprits pour les sciences. (Huarte de San Juan, J.) Paris, 1661.

Phil 2725.2.87 — Examen des Paroles d'un croyant et du Livre du peuple. (Du Plessis de Grenédan, L.) Rennes, 1840.

Htn Phil 8582.30* — Examen des prophéties qui servient de fondement de la religion chrétienne. (Collins, Anthony.) Londres, 1768.

Phil 476.1 — Examen du matérialisme. (Bergier, N.S.) Paris, 1771. 2v.

Phil 1180.5F — Examen du Pyrrhonisme. (Crousaz, J.P.) La Haye, 1733.

Phil 192.17 — Examen d'un ouvrage intitulé. (Rozaven, J.L.) Avignon, 1831.

Htn Phil 2648.60* — Examen impartial des principales religions. (Holbach, Paul Henri T.) n.p., n.d.

Phil 8581.2.10 — Examen in der allernatürlichsten Religion. (Basedow, J.B.) Leipzig, 1784.

Phil 3492.17 — Examen philosophique des Considérations sur le sentiment du sublime et du beau. (Kératry, A.H. de.) Paris, 1823.

Phil 8878.48 — Examen politique, philosophique et moral. (Dumesnil, L.A.L.) Caen, 1805.

Phil 5817.6 — Examen psychologique des animaux. (Hachet-Souplet, P.) Paris, 1900.

Htn Phil 1135.26F* — Examen vanitatis doctrinae gentium et veritatis Christianae disciplinae. (Picodella Mirandola, G.F.) Mirandulae, 1520.

Htn Phil 5754.1.19* — Examination...Edward's...freedom of will. (Dana, J.) Boston, 1770.

Htn Phil 5754.1.20* — Examination...Edward's...freedom of will. (Dana, J.) New Haven, 1773.

Phil 2035.80.6 — Examination...Hamilton's philosophy. (Mill, J.S.) Boston, 1865. 2v.

Phil 2035.80.2.10 — Examination...Hamilton's philosophy. (Mill, J.S.) Boston, 1868. 2v.

Phil 2035.80A — Examination...Hamilton's philosophy. (Mill, J.S.) London, 1865.

Phil 2035.80.2 — Examination...Hamilton's philosophy. 3rd ed. (Mill, J.S.) London, 1867.

Phil 2035.80.2.5 — Examination...Hamilton's philosophy. 3rd ed. (Mill, J.S.) London, 1867.

Phil 2035.80.8 — Examination...Hamilton's philosophy. 6th ed. (Mill, J.S.) London, 1889.

Htn Phil 2225.3.35* — Examination of...passages in the New Testament. (Paine, Thomas.) N.Y., n.d.

Phil 8712.4 — An examination of certain recent assaults on physical science. (Woodrow, J.) Columbia, S.C., 1873-74.

Phil 2150.11 — An examination of critical monism. (Melzer, J.H.) Ashland, 1937.

Htn Phil 8700.2* — Examination of Dr. Burnett's theory of the earth. (Keill, J.) Oxford, 1698.

Phil 8700.2.2 — Examination of Dr. Burnett's theory of the earth. (Keill, J.) Oxford, 1734. 2 pam.

Phil 2218.40 — An examination of Dr. Reid's Inquiry. 2d. ed. (Priestley, Joseph.) London, 1775.

Phil 270.1 — Examination of Gillespie's "First Cause". (Barrett, T.S.) London, 1869.

Phil 2138.30A — An examination of Hamilton's philosophy. (Mill, John S.) Boston, 1865. 2v.

Htn Phil 2138.30.2* — An examination of Hamilton's philosophy. (Mill, John S.) London, 1865.

Phil 2270.82 — Examination of Herbert Spencer's theory of the will. (Ground, W.D.) London, 1883.

Phil 600.47 — An examination of logical positivism. (Weinberg, J.R.) London, 1936.

Phil 2150.7.99 — Examination of McTaggart's philosophy. (Broad, Charles D.) Cambridge, Eng., 1933. 3v.

Htn Phil 5247.13.5* — The examination of men's wits. (Huarte de San Juan, J.) London, 1596.

Phil 2138.85 — An examination of Mr. J.S. Mill's philosophy. (McCosh, James.) London, 1866.

NEDL Phil 2138.85.2 — An examination of Mr. J.S. Mill's philosophy. (McCosh, James.) N.Y., 1866.

Phil 5938.2.2 — An examination of phrenology. (Sewall, T.) Boston, 1839.

Phil 5938.2 — An examination of phrenology. (Sewall, T.) Washington, 1837.

Phil 5249.2.85 — Examination of Prof. W. James' psychology. (Shargha, I.K.) London, 1909.

Phil 2475.1.109A — Examination of Professor Bergson's philosophy. (Balsillie, D.) London, 1912.

Phil 8595.16.7 — An examination of the age or reason. 2. ed. (Wakefield, Gilbert.) London, 1794.

Phil 2138.117 — An examination of the deductive logic of John S.Mill. (Jackson, Reginald.) London, 1941.

Phil 5241.4 — An examination of the human mind. (Ballantyne, J.) Edinburgh, 1828.

Phil 2270.141.5 — An examination of the philosophy of the unknowable as expounded by Herbert Spencer. (Lacy, William M.) Philaldelphia, 1883.

Phil 2270.141 — Examination of the philosophy of the unknowable as expounded by Herbert Spencer. (Lacy, William M.) Philadelphia, 1912.

Phil 8894.33 — An examination of the place of reason in ethics. (Toulmin, S.) Cambridge, England, 1950.

Htn Phil 2045.104* — An examination of the political part of Mr. Hobbs his Leviathan. (Lawson, George.) London, 1657.

Phil 2035.89 — Examination of the principles of the Scoto-Oxonian philosophy. (Bolton, M.P.W.) London, 1869.

Phil 8700.2.6 — Examination of the reflections on the theory of the earth. (Keill, J.) Oxford, 1699.

Phil 9550.2 — An examination of the utilitarian philosophy. (Grote, J.) Cambridge, 1870.

Phil 2070.119 — An examination of William James's philosophy. (Turner, J.E.) Oxford, 1919.

Phil 8880.18.10 — The examined life. (Fite, Warner.) Bloomington, Ind., 1957.

Phil 165.55 — The examined life. (Organ, F.W.) Boston, 1956.

Htn Phil 2520.65* — Excellent compendium of musik. (Descartes, R.) London, 1653.

Phil 8877.4 — Excellent contemplations divine and moral. (Capel, A.) London, 1683.

Htn Phil 9343.8* — The excellent woman described. (Dorrington, T.) London, 1692.

Phil 6962.7 — Les excentriques. (Moreau, P.) Paris, 1894.

Phil 8592.114 — Excercicios espirituales de las excelencias, provecho y necesidad. (Molina, Antonio de.) Barcelona, 1702.

Phil 2150.17.94A — Excerpts from civilization - the perilous adventure. (Mayo, Elton.) Cambridge, Mass. 19- .

Phil 365.4 — Excursions of an evolutionist. (Fiske, J.) Boston, 1884.

Phil 181.17 — The exegesis of life. (Greppo, C.) N.Y., 1889.

X Cg Phil 1850.59.10 — Exemplum tractatus de justitia universalis. (Bacon, Francis.) Metz, 1806. (Changed to XM 1503)

Phil 5753.12 — L'exercice de la volonté. (Dwelshauvers, G.) Paris, 1935.

Phil 5066.105 — Exercises in introductory symbolic logic. (Miller, J.W.) Montreal? 1955.

Author and Title Listing

Phil 5062.22 — Exercises in logic and scientific method. (Wolf, Abraham.) London, 1919.

Phil 5047.39 — Exercises in reasoning, with an outline of logic. (Holmes, R.W.) N.Y., 1940.

Htn Phil 1200.2* — Exercitatio de stoica mundi exustione. (Thomasius, J.) Leipzig, 1676.

Phil 6957.13 — Exercitationes duae...histerica. 2. ed. (Highmore, N.) Amstelodami, 1660.

Phil 8690.5 — Exercitium academicum. (Alstrin, Eric.) Upsaliae, 1727.

Phil 4513.4.37 — Exercitium academicum de philosophia parabolica. (Asp, Matthia.) Upsaliae, 1733.

Phil 365.27 — L'exigence idéaliste et le fait de l'évolution. (LeRoy, Édouard.) Paris, 1927.

Phil 2855.10.30 — Les exigences de la vie de l'esprit. (Revertin, Henri.) Neuchâtel, 1966.

Phil 8581.95.10 — Exigences philosophiques du christianisme. 1. éd. (Blondel, Maurice.) Paris, 1950.

Phil 2880.8.205 — Existance et realité polémique avec certaines thèses fondamentales dé "L'être et le néant" de Sartre. (Tordai, Záder.) Budapest, 1967.

Phil 4957.65 — Existe una filosofía de nuestra América? 1. ed. (Salazar, Bondy Augusto.) México, 1968[1969]

Phil 3475.3.245 — Existence, existenz, and transcendence. (Schrag, Oswald O.) Pittsburgh, 1971.

Phil 2115.6 — Existence, meaning, and reality in Locke's essay. (Moore, A.W.) Chicago, 1903.

Phil 310.746 — Existence, realita, masérie. Vyd. 1. (Fajkus, Brětislaw.) Praha, 1968.

Phil 5238.85 — Existence. (May, Rollo.) N.Y., 1958.

Phil 1750.190 — L'existence. Paris, 1945.

Phil 8632.10 — Existence after death implied by science. (Hunt, Jasper B.) London, 1910.

Phil 8667.22.10 — Existence and analogy. (Mascall, E.L.) London, 1949.

Phil 3450.19.15.1 — Existence and being. (Heidegger, Martin.) Chicago, 1970.

Phil 1750.665 — Existence and freedom. (Schrag, C.O.) Evanston, Ill., 1961.

Phil 1711.10 — Existence and inquiry, a study of thought in the modern world. (Lee, Ótis.) Chicago, 1949.

Phil 5421.25.20 — Existence and love. (Sadler, William Alan.) N.Y., 1969.

Phil 2750.11.40 — Existence and the existent. (Maritain, Jacques.) N.Y., 1948.

Phil 1750.738 — Existence and the world of freedom. (Wild, John.) Englewood, 1963.

Phil 1750.610 — Existence and therapy. (Sonnemann, Ulrich.) N.Y., 1954.

Phil 2055.7.90 — Existence as dialectical tension. (Luther, A.R.) The Hague, 1968[1969]

Phil 8599.48 — Existence chrétienne et philosophie. (Toinet, Paul.) Paris, 1965.

Phil 184.19.18 — L'existence d'après Karl Jaspers. (Tonquédec, J. de.) Paris, 1945.

Phil 8668.2 — L'existence de Dieu. (Nieuwentijt, B.) Paris, 1725.

Phil 1750.280 — Existence et existentialismes. (Lepp, Ignoce.) Paris, 1947.

Phil 165.338 — Existence et nature. (Congrès des Sociétés de Philosophie de Langue Française, 11th, Montpellier, 1961.) Paris, 1962.

Phil 9120.180 — Existence et obligation. (Henriot, Jacques.) Paris, 1967.

Phil 1722.12 — Existence et signification. (Waelkens, Alphonse de.) Louvain, 1958.

Phil 2477.6.130 — Existence et vérité. (Cartier, Albert.) Paris, 1955.

Phil 705.33 — Existence humaine et transeendance. (Wahl, J.) Neuchâtel, 1944.

Phil 9240.14 — L'existence malheureuse. (Grenier, Jean.) Paris, 1957.

Phil 8667.15 — The existence of God. (McCabe, J.) London, 1913.

Phil 6111.64 — The existence of mind. (Beloff, John.) London, 1962.

Phil 181.88 — L'existence temporelle. (Guitton, Jean.) Paris, 1949.

Phil 177.37.5 — La existencia como economía como desinterés y como caridad. (Caso, Antonio.) México, 1919.

Phil 2750.19.90 — L'existencialisme de M. Gabriel Marcel. (Rainho, Antonio Angelo Leite.) Lisbonne, 1955.

Phil 1750.512.3 — El existencialismo, filosofía de nuestro tiempo. 3. ed. (Amoroso Lima, Alceu.) Buenos Aires, 1951.

Phil 194.54 — Existencialismo; pensamiento oriental y psicoanalisis. (Tanasescu, Horia.) México, 1957.

Phil 1750.695 — Existencialismo. (Martins, Diamantino.) Braga, 1955.

Phil 1750.749 — Existencialismo y crisis de la filosofía. 2. ed. (Astrada, C.) Buenos Aires, 1963.

Phil 1750.335* — Existencialismo y existencialistas. (Alonso-Fueyo, S.) Valencia, 1949.

Phil 2880.8.100 — El existencialismo y la libertad readoro. 1. ed. (Fatone, V.) Buenos Aires, 1948.

Phil 2880.8.100.2 — El existencialismo y la libertad readoro. 2. ed. (Fatone, V.) Buenos Aires, 1949.

Phil 1750.494 — Existencialismo y moral. (Virasoro, Rafael.) Argentina, 1957.

VPhil 1750.816 — Existencializmus a fenomenológia. Bratislava, 1967.

Phil 1750.787 — L'existense délivrée de l'existentialisme. (Wintrebert, Paul Marie Joseph.) Paris, 1965.

Phil 2750.19.39 — The existential background of human dignity. (Marcel, Gabriel.) Cambridge, 1963.

Phil 6332.32 — The existential core of psychoanalysis. (Weisman, A.D.) Boston, 1965.

Phil 6131.7 — Existential foundations and psychology. (Van Kaam, Adrian.) Pittsburgh, 1966.

Phil 5282.5 — Existential humanistic psychology. Belmont, Calif., 1971.

Phil 5062.22.5 — The existential import of categorical predication. (Wolf, Abraham.) Cambridge, 1905.

Phil 2305.5.30 — Existential metaphysics. (Thalheimer, Alvin.) N.Y., 1960.

Phil 3585.20.5 — Existential phenomenology. (Luijpen, Wilhelmus Antonius Maria.) Pittsburgh, 1960.

Phil 1750.172 — Existential philosophers. (Schrader, George Alfred.) N.Y., 1967.

Phil 14.22 — Existential psychiatry. Chicago. 1,1966+

Phil 2880.8.60 — Existential psychoanalysis. (Sartre, Jean Paul.) N.Y., 1953.

Phil 6312.20.5 — Existential psychology. (Caruso, Igor A.) N.Y., 1964.

Phil 5238.88.2 — Existential psychology. 2d ed. (May, Rollo.) N.Y., 1969.

Phil 1750.798 — Existential thinking. (Boelen, Bernard Jacques Marie.) Pittsburgh, 1968.

Phil 1750.518 — Existential thought and fictional technique; Kierkegaard, Sartre, Beckett. (Kern, Edith G.) New Haven, 1970.

Phil 1750.753 — Existentialism; for and against. (Roubiczek, P.) Cambridge, 1964.

Phil 1750.510 — Existentialism. (Dutt, K. Guru.) Basavagundi, 1953.

Phil 1750.510.2 — Existentialism. (Dutt, K. Guru.) Basavagundi, 1954.

Phil 1750.220 — Existentialism. (Foulquié, Paul.) London, 1948.

Phil 1750.183 — Existentialism. (Harper, Ralph.) Cambridge, 1948.

Phil 1750.183.2 — Existentialism. (Harper, Ralph.) Cambridge, 1949.

Phil 4215.8.30 — Existentialism. (Ruggiero, Guido de.) London, 1946.

Phil 1750.825 — Existentialism. (Sanborn, Patricia F.) N.Y., 1968.

Phil 2880.8.42A — Existentialism. (Sartre, Jean Paul.) N.Y., 1947.

Phil 1750.552.25 — Existentialism. (Warnock, Mary.) London, 1970.

Phil 1750.505 — Existentialism. London, 1953. 2 pam.

Phil 4215.8.34 — Existentialism: disintegration of man's soul. (Ruggiero, Guido de.) N.Y., 1948.

Phil 1750.263.5 — Existentialism and Christian thought. (Troisfontaines, R.) London, 1950.

Phil 2880.8.65 — Existentialism and human emotions. (Sartre, Jean Paul.) N.Y., 1957.

Phil 3475.3.70 — Existentialism and humanism. (Jaspers, Karl.) N.Y., 1952.

Phil 2880.8.41.2 — Existentialism and humanism. (Sartre, Jean Paul.) London, 1960.

Phil 2880.8.41.3 — Existentialism and humanism. (Sartre, Jean Paul.) London, 1965.

Phil 1750.245 — Existentialism and literature in action. (Berger, G.) Buffalo, 1948.

Phil 6980.34 — Existentialism and psychiatry. (Allers, Rudolf.) Springfield, 1961.

Phil 1750.475 — Existentialism and religious belief. (Roberts, D.C.) N.Y., 1959.

Phil 8587.74 — Existentialism and religious liberalism. (Hayward, John.) Boston, 1962.

Phil 1750.365 — Existentialism and the modern predicament. (Heinemann, Fritz.) London, 1953.

Phil 1750.365.7 — Existentialism and the modern predicament. (Heinemann, Fritz.) N.Y., 1958.

Phil 1750.365.5 — Existentialism and the modern predicament. 2nd ed. (Heinemann, Fritz.) London, 1954.

Phil 1750.82 — Existentialism and Thomism. (Mihalich, J.C.) N.Y., 1960.

Phil 1750.715 — Existentialism as philosophy. (Molina, Fernando.) N.Y., 1962.

Phil 1750.455 — Existentialism from Dostoevsky to Sartre. (Kaufmann, W.A.) N.Y., 1956.

Phil 1750.364 — Existentialism from within. (Allen, E.L.) London, 1953.

Phil 1750.777 — Existentialism versus Marxism. (Novak, George Edward.) N.Y., 1966.

Phil 1750.169 — Het existentialisme. (Beerling, Reimer.) 's Gravenhage, 1947.

Phil 1750.181 — L'existentialisme. (Lefebvre, Henri.) Paris, 1946.

Phil 1750.173 — L'existentialisme. (Pesch, Edgar.) Paris, 1946.

Phil 1750.200 — L'existentialisme. Paris, 1948.

Phil 1750.440 — Existentialisme. 2. druk. (Redeker, Hans.) Amsterdam 1956.

Phil 1750.220.5 — L'existentialisme. 9e éd. (Foulquié, Paul.) Paris, 1955.

Phil 1750.220.12 — L'existentialisme. 12e éd. (Foulquié, Paul.) Paris, 1963.

Phil 1750.220.13 — L'existentialisme. 13e éd. (Foulquié, Paul.) Paris, 1964.

Phil 2880.8.40A — L'existentialisme est un humanisme. 5. ed. (Sartre, Jean Paul.) Paris, 1946.

Phil 1750.175 — Existentialisme et acte d'être. (Pruche, B.) Paris, 1947.

Phil 1750.240 — L'existentialisme et la sagesse des nations. (Beauvoir, S. de.) Paris, 1948.

Phil 1750.263 — Existentialisme et pensée chrétienne. 2e éd. (Troisfontaines, R.) Louvain, 1948.

Phil 1750.275 — L'existentialisme n'est pas un humanisme. (Kanapa, J.) Paris, 1947.

Phil 1750.405.5 — Existentialisme ou Marxisme. 2e éd. (Lukacs, G.S.) Paris, 1961.

Phil 1750.372 — Existentialisme théologique. (Castelli, Enrico.) Paris, 1948.

Phil 1750.372.2 — Existentialisme théologique. 2e éd. (Castelli, Enrico.) Paris, 1966.

Phil 1750.552.20 — Existentialismen. (Stenström, Thure.) Stockholm, 1966.

Phil 1750.305 — Der Existentialismus. (Hartwig, T.) Wien, 1948.

Phil 1750.405 — Existentialismus oder Marxismus? (Lukacs, G.S.) Berlin, 1951.

Phil 1750.445 — Existentialismus und Pädagogik. (Prohaska, L.) Freiburg, 1955.

Phil 585.285 — Existentialismus und Sozialismus. (Metzger, Arnold.) Pfullingen, 1968.

Phil 2880.8.138 — An existentialist aesthetic. (Kaelin, Eugene.) Madison, 1962.

Phil 197.92 — Existentialist essays. (Wainwright, Donald S.) N.Y., 1965.

Phil 2880.8.220 — Existentialist ethics. (Warnock, Mary.) London, 1967.

Phil 1750.790 — An existentialist ethics. 1st ed. (Barnes, Hazel Estella.) N.Y., 1967.

Phil 1750.230 — Existentialist philosophies. (Mounier, Emman.) London, 1948.

Phil 193.256 — The existentialist prolegomena. (Sontag, Frederick.) Chicago, 1969.

Phil 1750.360A — The existentialist revolt. (Reinhardt, Kurt Frank.) Milwaukee, 1952.

Phil 1750.360.2 — The existentialist revolt. 2nd ed. (Reinhardt, Kurt Frank.) N.Y., 1960.

Phil 1750.733 — Existentialist thinkers and thought. (Patha, Frederick.) N.Y., 1962.

Phil 1750.410 — Existentialist thought. (Grimsley, Ronald.) Cardiff, 1955.

Phil 1750.410.2 — Existentialist thought. 2nd ed. (Grimsley, Ronald.) Cardiff, 1969.

Phil 2880.8.86 — L'existentialiste est-il un philosophe? (Lefevre, Luc J.) Paris, 1946. 2v.

Phil 1750.788 — Les existentialistes et la politique. (Burnier, Michel Antoine.) Paris, 1966.

Phil 1750.355A — The existentialists. (Collins, J.D.) Chicago, 1952.

Phil 3585.20 — Existentiële fenomenologie. (Luijpen, Wilhelmus Antonius Maria.) Utrecht, 1959.

Phil 1750.595 — Existentiële zin en onzin. (Bos, Julius G.) Den Haag, 1960.

Phil 1750.315 — L'existentiel, philosophies et littératures de l'existence. (Deledalle, G.) Paris, 1949.

Phil 3475.3.110 — Existentiele metaphysica. (Springer, J.L.) Assen, 1951.

Phil 1750.630 — Existenz im Nichts. (Leist, Fritz.) München, 1961.

Phil 3790.30 — Existenz in dieser Zeit. (Richtscheid, Hans.) München, 1965.

Phil 3450.19.95.5 — Existenz und Offenbarung. (Pfeiffer, Johannes S.) Berlin, 1966.

Phil 1750.520 — Existenz und Transzendenz in der gegenwärtegen Philosophie. (Muehlethaler, Jakob.) Basel, 1958.

Phil 1750.420 — Der Existenzialismus in seinem Wesen und Werden. (Ell, Johannes.) Bonn, 1955.

Phil 1750.265 — Existenzialismus und christliche Ethos. (Steinbüchel, T.) Heidelberg, 1948.

Phil 1750.356 — Existenzialphilosophie und katholische Theologie. (Möller, J.) Baden-Baden, 1952.

Phil 3450.19.95   Existenzphilosophie; eine Einführung in Heidegger und Jaspers. (Pfeiffer, Johannes S.) Leipzig, 1933.
Phil 1750.177   Existenzphilosophie. (Hessen, J.) Essen, 1947.
Phil 1750.177.1   Existenzphilosophie. (Hessen, Johannes.) Basel, 1948.
Phil 184.19.20   Existenzphilosophie. (Jaspers, K.) Berlin, 1938.
Phil 1750.750   Existenzphilosophie. (Mueller-Schwefe, Hans Rudolf.) Zürich, 1961.
Phil 1750.325   Die Existenzphilosophie. 1e Aufl. (Reding, M.) Düsseldorf, 1949.
Phil 3475.3.71   Existenzphilosophie. 2. Aufl. (Jaspers, Karl.) Berlin, 1950.
Phil 1750.750.2   Existenzphilosophie. 2. Aufl. (Mueller-Schwefe, Hans Rudolf.) Göttingen, 1969.
Phil 1750.179   Existenzphilosophie. 2e Aufl. (Bollnow, O.F.) Stuttgart, 1942?
Phil 1750.351.2   Existenzphilosophie. 2e Aufl. (Gabriel, Leo.) Wien, 1968.
Phil 1750.179.5A   Existenzphilosophie. 3. Aufl. (Bollnow, O.F.) Stuttgart, 1949.
Phil 3450.19.95.3   Existenzphilosophie. 3e Aufl. (Pfeiffer, Johannes S.) Hamburg, 1952.
Phil 1750.179.20   Existenzphilosophie. 4e Aufl. (Bollnow, O.F.) Stuttgart, 1955.
Phil 1750.352   Existenzphilosophie im geistigen Leben der Gegenwart. (Müller, Max.) Heidelberg, 1949.
Phil 1750.352.3   Existenzphilosophie im geistigen Leben der Gegenwart. 3e Aufl. (Müller, Max.) Heidelberg, 1964.
Phil 1750.365.15   Existenzphilosophie Lebendig oder Tat? 2e Aufl. (Heinemann, Fritz.) Stuttgart, 1954.
Phil 3450.19.97   Die Existenzphilosophie Martin Heideggers. (Fischer, Alois.) Leipzig, 1935.
Phil 1750.351   Existenzphilosophie von Kierkegaard bis Sartre. (Gabriel, Leo.) Wien, 1951.
Phil 978.49.383   Exkurse in das Gebiet des Markus-Evangeliums. (Steiner, R.) Dornach, 1963.
Phil 9495.163   Exner, Adam. The amplexus reservatus seen in the history of Catholic doctrine on the use of marriage. Ottawa, 1963.
Phil 5593.69   Exner, John E. The Rorschach system. N.Y., 1969.
Phil 9495.28   Exner, M.J. The physician's answer. N.Y., 1913.
Phil 9495.28.5   Exner, M.J. Problems and principles of sex education. N.Y., 1915.
Phil 5244.5   Exner, S. Entwurf zu einer physiologischen Erklärung der psychischen Erscheinungen. Leipzig, 1894.
Phil 6114.12   Exner, Sigmund. Entwurf zu einer psychologischen Erklärung der psychischen Erscheinungen. Leipzig, 1894.
Phil 6114.12.5   Exner, Sigmund. Untersuchungen über die Localisation der Functionen. Wien, 1881.
Phil 6946.38   Exodus from pandemonium; human abuse and a reformation of public policy. (Blatt, Burton.) Boston, 1970.
Phil 978.79   La exondida senda. (Dominguez Acosta, F.) Caracas, 1941.
Phil 2200.10   The expansion of awareness. (Osborn, Arthur W.) Reigate, 1955.
Phil 8626.16   Expecto, an essay towards a biology of the world to come. (Bennett, F.S.M.) Chester, 1926.
Phil 6319.18   Experience, affect and behavior: psychoanalytic explorations of Adelaide McFadyne Johnson. (Johnson, Adelaide McFadyne.) Chicago, 1969.
Phil 165.280   Experience, existence and good. (Lieb, Irwin C.) Carbondale, 1961.
Phil 186.158   Experience, mind, and value. (Lemos, Ramon M.) Leiden, 1969.
Phil 9530.33   Experience, or A post-graduate course in life. (Emmel, Paul W.) Philadelphia, 1931.
Phil 8581.79   Experience, reason and faith. (Bewkes, E.G.) N.Y., 1940.
Phil 331.12   L'expérience. (Alquié, Ferdinand.) Paris, 1957.
Phil 165.125   Expérience - connaissance. (Grateloup, León.) Paris, 1957.
Phil 349.65   Experience and being. (Schrag, Calvin Orville.) Evanston, Ill., 1969.
Phil 5545.254.4   Experience and capacity; proceedings. (International Interdisciplinary Conference on Learning, Remembering and Forgetting.) N.Y., 1968.
Phil 2340.10.180   Experience and conceptual activity. (Burgers, Johannes Martinus.) Cambridge, Mass., 1965.
Phil 3850.16.115   Experience and culture; the philosophy of G. Simmel. (Weingartner, R.H.) Middletown, 1962.
Phil 189.23   Experience and its modes. (Oakeshott, Michael.) Cambridge,Eng., 1933.
Phil 3499.34   Experience and its systematization; studies in Kant. (Rotenstreich, Nathan.) The Hague, 1965.
Phil 178.38.5A   Experience and nature. (Dewey, John.) Chicago, 1925.
Phil 178.38.7A   Experience and nature. (Dewey, John.) Chicago, 1926.
Phil 348.13   Experience and prediction. (Reichenbach, Hans.) Chicago, 1938.
Phil 2280.17.80   Experience and reflection. (Singer, Edgar.) Philadelphia, 1959.
Phil 2225.10   Experience and substance. (Parker, D.H.) Ann Arbor, 1941.
Phil 346.22   Experience and the analytic. (Pasck, Alan.) Chicago, 1958.
Phil 1955.6.115   Experience and valuation. Thesis. (Wolstein, B.) N.Y., 1949.
Phil 2730.96   L'expérience de l'effort et de la grace chez Maine de Biran. (LeRoy, Georges.) Paris, 1937.
Phil 2730.96.5   L'expérience de l'effort et de la grace chez Maine de Biran. Thèse. (LeRoy, Georges.) Paris, 1937.
Phil 5400.190   L'expérience émotionnelle de l'espace. Thèse. (Kaufmann, Pierre.) Paris, 1967.
Phil 8430.19   L'expérience esthétique et l'idéal chrétien. (Loisel, A.) Paris, 1909.
Phil 525.241   L'expérience intérieure. 4. éd. (Bataille, Georges.) Paris, 1954.
Phil 5763.3.5   L'expérience intérieure de la liberté. (Nabert, Jean.) Paris, 1924.
Phil 5763.3   L'expérience intérieure de la liberté. Thèse. (Nabert, Jean.) Paris, 1923.
Phil 2940.2.30   L'expérience métaphysique. (Wahl, Jean André.) Paris, 1965.
Phil 525.236   L'expérience mystique. (Gobry, Ivan.) Paris, 1964.
Phil 5627.58   L'expérience mystique et l'activité subconsciente. (Pacheu, Jules.) Paris, 1911.
Phil 6316.22   The experience of anxiety. (Goldstein, M.) N.Y., 1963.
Phil 5627.126   Une expérience religieuse. (Fourrier, Maurice.) Paris, 1931.
Phil 5627.6.7   L'expérience religieuse. (James, William.) Paris, 1906.
Phil 5627.6.6   L'expérience religieuse. 2. éd. (James, William.) Paris, 1908.
Phil 5627.269   L'expérience religieuse fondamentale. (Rabut, Olivier A.) Paris, 1969.

Phil 5520.18.5   An experienced study in the psychology of reading. Theses. (Schmidt, William A.) Chicago, 1917.
Phil 5585.24   Expériences collectives sur le...confrontation. (Claparède, E.) Genève, 1906.
Phil 6980.112.50   Experiences in groups. (Bion, Wilfrid R.) London, 1961.
Phil 7054.45.55   Experiences in spiritualism with D.D. Home. (Dunraven, W.T.W.-Q.) Glasgow, 1924.
Phil 6956.6   The experiences of an asylum patient. (Grant-Smith, Rachel.) London, 1922.
Phil 530.40.60   La experiencia de Dios en los místicos españoles. (Gallegos Rocafull, J.M.) México, 1945.
Phil 165.275   Experiencia de la vida. Madrid, 1960.
Phil 4370.5   La experiencia humana. (Tagle, A.) Buenos Aires, 1938.
Phil 4353.10   Experiencia profunda del ser. (Cencillo, J.L.) Madrid, 1959.
Phil 176.60   La experiencia y la especulación. (Bruner, J.J.) Santiago de Chile, 1886.
Phil 5246.74   Experiencing and the creation of meaning. (Gendlin, Eugene.) N.Y., 1962.
Phil 5593.66   Experiential foundations of Rorschach's test. (Schachtel, Ernest G.) N.Y., 1966.
Phil 5627.261.10   L'experienza della prehiera. (Brezzi, Paolo.) Firenze, 1961.
Phil 5722.35   Experiment in depth. (Martin, P.W.) London, 1955.
Phil 2055.7.15A   Experiment in education. (Hocking, William E.) Chicago, 1954.
Phil 8880.47.10   An experiment in leisure. (Field, Joanna.) London, 1937.
Phil 5643.84   An experiment in linear space perception. (Maxfield, F.N.) Princeton, 1913.
Phil 6962.32   An experiment in mental patient rehabilitation. (Meyer, Henry F.) N.Y., 1959.
Phil 5246.56   An experiment in the development of critical thinking. Thesis. (Glaser, E.M.) N.Y., 1941.
Phil 6980.668   An experiment in the psychiatric treatment of promiscuous girls. (San Francisco, Department of Public Health.) San Francisco, 1945.
Phil 5627.134.105   Experiment med Gud. (Ekman, Nils Gösta.) Stockholm, 1971.
Phil 672.136.7   An experiment with time. (Dunne, John W.) London, 1952.
Phil 672.136A   An experiment with time. (Dunne, John W.) N.Y., 1927.
Phil 672.136.5   An experiment with time. 3rd ed. (Dunne, John W.) N.Y., 1949.
Phil 672.136.10   An experiment with time. 4th ed. (Dunne, John W.) N.Y., 1938.
Phil 5648.1   Experimenta de variarum cutis. (Kammler, A.) Vratislav, 1858.
Phil 5545.59   An experimental...study of human learning. (Perrin, F.A.C.) Princeton, 1914.
Phil 6121.28   Experimental analysis of instinctive behavior. (Lashley, K.S.) Lancaster, Pa., 1938.
Phil 6111.9   Experimental and clinical researches. (Brown-Séquard, C.E.) Richmond, 1855.
Phil 6959.7   Experimental catatonia, a general reaction form of the central nervous system. (Jong, Herman H. de.) Baltimore, 1945.
Phil 5272.20   Experimental design in psychological research. (Edwards, Allen Louis.) N.Y., 1951.
Phil 5272.20.3   Experimental design in psychological research. 3d ed. (Edwards, Allen Louis.) N.Y., 1968.
Phil 5594.158   Experimental design in psychology and the medical sciences. (Maxwell, A.E.) London, 1958.
Phil 5241.165   Experimental foundations of clinical psychology. (Bachrach, Arthur.) N.Y., 1962.
Phil 5261.17.25   Experimental foundations of general psychology. (Valentine, Willard Lee.) N.Y., 1938.
Phil 5261.17.26   Experimental foundations of general psychology. (Valentine, Willard Lee.) N.Y., 1946.
Phil 6681.16.5   Experimental hypnosis. (Le Cron, L.M.) N.Y., 1954.
Phil 5645.35   An experimental investigation of brightness constancy. (MacLeod, R.B.) N.Y., 1932.
Phil 5520.445   The experimental investigation of meaning. (Creelman, Marjorico Broer.) N.Y., 1966.
Phil 7054.63.4   Experimental investigation of the spirit manifestations. (Hare, Robert.) N.Y., 1856.
Phil 5243.36.12   An experimental manual in psychology. (Dashiell, J.F.) Boston, 1931.
Phil 14.9   Experimental metaphysics. London. 1-2,1945-1947+
Phil 5270.4   Experimental methods and instrumentation in psychology. (Sidowski, Joseph B.) N.Y., 1966.
Phil 1980.5   Experimental philosophy asserted and defended against some late attempts to undermine it. London, 1740.
Phil 7084.18   The experimental production of dreams during hypnosis. (Klein, David Ballin.) Austin, 1930.
Phil 5255.28   Experimental psychology; loose leaf laboratory manual. (Poffenberger, A.T.) Chicago, 1926.
Phil 5255.28.2   Experimental psychology; loose leaf laboratory manual. (Poffenberger, A.T.) N.Y., 1925?
Phil 5242.30   Experimental psychology. (Collins, Mary.) London, 1926.
Phil 5243.74   Experimental psychology. (D'Amato, Michael Richard.) N.Y., 1970.
Phil 5238.35   Experimental psychology. (Farrell, B.A.) N.Y., 1955.
Phil 5238.196.1   Experimental psychology. (Fraisse, Paul.) N.Y., 1968.
Phil 5251.34.15   Experimental psychology. (Lindworsky, J.) London, 1931.
Phil 5625.75.20   Experimental psychology. (Pavlov, Ivan P.) N.Y., 1957.
Phil 5258.29.5   Experimental psychology. (Stratton, G.M.) N.Y., 1914.
Phil 5262.9.35   Experimental psychology. (Woodworth, R.S.) N.Y., 1938.
Phil 5262.9.40   Experimental psychology. (Woodworth, R.S.) N.Y., 1950.
Phil 5262.9.43   Experimental psychology. (Woodworth, R.S.) N.Y., 1954.
VPhil 5205.45   Experimental psychology. (Woodworth, R.S.) N.Y., 1965.
VPhil 5205.41   Pamphlet box. Experimental psychology. Dissertations.
VPhil 5205.44   Pamphlet vol. Experimental psychology. Dissertations. (A-F). 7 pam.
VPhil 5205.42   Pamphlet vol. Experimental psychology. Dissertations. (L-Z). 8 pam.
VPhil 5205.43   Pamphlet vol. Experimental psychology. German dissertations. (G-J). 6 pam.
Phil 5259.5.9   Pamphlet vol. Experimental psychology. German dissertations. (K). 8 pam.
Phil 5259.5.9.5   Experimental psychology. v.1-2; v.2, pt.1. (Titchener, E.B.) n.p., 1901-27. 5v.
Phil 5240.58.2   Experimental psychology. v.1-2. (Titchener, E.B.) N.Y., 1927. 4v.
Phil 5241.54.5   Experimental psychology. 2. ed. (Andreas, Burton G.) N.Y., 1972.
Phil 5640.142   The experimental psychology of Alfred Binet; selected papers. (Binet, Alfred.) N.Y., 1969.
The experimental psychology sensory behavior. (Corso, John F.) N.Y., 1967.

Phil 14.21   Experimental Psychology Society. Monograph. Cambridge. 1,1961+ 3v.

Phil 7069.47.15   The experimental situation in psychical research. (Soal, Samuel G.) London, 1947.

Phil 5252.91   Experimental studies in psychodynamics. (MacKinnon, D.W.) Cambridge, 1948. 2v.

Phil 14.5   Experimental studies in psychology and pedagogy. Boston. 1-7,1902-1917 6v.

Phil 5545.74   Experimental studies in recall and recognition. (Achilles, E.M.) N.Y., 1920.

Phil 5810.5   Experimental studies of adaptive behavior in cats. Diss. (Adams, Donald K.) Baltimore, 1929.

Phil 5645.44   Experimental studies of colour and non-colour attitudes in school children and adults. (Lindberg, Bengt J.) Copenhagen, 1938.

Phil 5710.10   An experimental study of...temperaments. Diss. (Baxter, M.F.) Ithaca, N.Y., 1927.

Phil 6956.10   An experimental study of dermentia preacox. (Gotewood, Lee C.) Lancaster, 1909.

Phil 5409.6   Experimental study of expectation. (Pyle, W.H.) n.p., 1909.

Phil 6134.2   Experimental study of fatique. (Yoakum, C.S.) Chicago, 1909.

Phil 5262.26   An experimental study of hunger in its relation to activity. (Wada, Tomi.) N.Y., 1922.

Phil 6694.2   An experimental study of mental and physical functions in the normal and hypnotic states. Thesis. (Young, Paul C.) n.p., 1923.

Phil 6694.2.5   An experimental study of mental and physical functions in the normal and hypnotic states. (Young, Paul C.) Ithaca, 1925.

Phil 5635.20   An experimental study of sensation. (Holt, Edwin B.) Cambridge, Mass., 1903.

Phil 5520.34   An experimental study of silent thinking. (Clark, Ruth S.) N.Y., 1922.

Phil 5241.96   An experimental study of some of the conditions of mental activity. (Bergström, J.A.) Worcester, 1894.

Phil 6420.14   An experimental study of stuttering. Thesis. (Fletcher, John Madison.) Worcester, 1914.

Phil 5762.13   An experimental study of the factors and types of voluntary choice. (Martin, Alfred H.) N.Y., 1922.

Phil 5593.41   An experimental study of the rehability of the Rorschach psychodiagnostic technique. (Fosberg, I.A.) N.Y., 1941.

Phil 5643.43   An experimental study of visual fixation. (Dodge, Raymond.) Lancaster, 1907.

Phil 7069.38.5A   Experimental telepathy. (Warcollur, R.) Boston, 1939.

Phil 5545.39   Experimentalle Beiträge...vom Gedächtnis. (Ephrussi, P.) Leipzig, 1904.

Phil 5545.40   Experimentalle Beiträge zur Lehre vom Gedächtnis. (Pohlmann, A.) Berlin, 1906.

Phil 6673.15   Experimentalpsychologie und Experimentalmetaphysik. (Du Prel, Carl.) Leipzig, 1891.

Phil 7069.24.44   Experimente der Fernbewegung. (Schrenck von Notzing, Albert.) Stuttgart, 1924.

Phil 7069.24.12   Experimente mit Raphael Schermann. (Fischer, Oskar.) Berlin, 1924.

Phil 6120.8.25   De experimenteele psychologie en Kretschmer's constitutietypen. (Braat, J.P.) Amsterdam, 1934.

Phil 5421.15.30   Een experimentele methode om de juistheid van interpersonale perceptie zuiver te bepalen. Proefschrift. (Bezembinder, Thomas G.G.) Groningen, 1961.

Phil 5262.8   Experimentelle...Theorie des Denkens. (Watt, H.J.) Leipzig, 1904.

Phil 5374.162   Die experimentelle analyse der Bewusstseinsphänomenma. (Wirth, Wilhelm.) Brauschweig, 1908.

Phil 5520.74   Experimentelle Beiträge zur Analyse des Verhältnisses von Laut und Sinn. (Müller, H.) Berlin, 1935.

Phil 6116.13F   Experimentelle Beiträge zur Lehre von der Blut-Circulation in der Schädel-Rückgratshöhle. (Grashey, H.) München, 1892.

Phil 5585.16   Experimentelle Beiträge zur Psychologie...des Zeitsinns. (Katz, David.) Leipzig, 1906.

Phil 5643.121   Experimentelle Beiträge zur Theorie des binokularen Einfach- und Tefensehens. (Koenig, E.) Meisenheim, 1962.

Phil 6060.18.15   Experimentelle Graphologie. (Saudek, R.) Berlin, 1929.

Phil 5590.245   Experimentelle Persönlichkeitsanalyse nach dem Murray-Test. 1. Aufl. (Stern, Erich.) Zürich, 1952.

Phil 5640.42   Experimentelle Psychologie in Demonstrationen. (Brunswik, Egon.) Wien, 1935.

Phil 6680.2   Eine experimentelle Studie. (Krafft-Ebing, R. von.) Stuttgart, 1888.

Phil 7060.126   Experimentelle Studien. (Richet, C.) Stuttgart, 1891.

Phil 5725.4   Experimentelle und kritische Beiträge zur Psychologie des Verstehens. Inaug. Diss. (Reichner, H.) Leipzig, 1927.

Phil 5645.65   Experimentelle Untersuchüngen den Eindruckscharakter von Einzelfarben. (Schoenborn-Buchheim, Elisabeth.) Freiburg, 1963?

Phil 5325.18   Experimentelle Untersuchung der Bewusstseinsvorgänge. (Hintermann, H.) Zürich, 1916.

Phil 5643.133   Experimentelle Untersuchung über die anschauliche Grösse. Inaug. Diss. (Weber, Renate.) Tübingen? 1963?

Phil 5400.42.5   Experimentelle Untersuchungen. (Koch, Bernhard.) Leipzig, 1913.

Phil 5645.40   Experimentelle Untersuchungen. (Olsson, G.F.) Stockholm, 1938.

Phil 5767.4   Experimentelle Untersuchungen. (Rieger, Conrad.) Jena, 1885.

Phil 5520.594   Experimentelle Untersuchungen über den Zusammenhang von Sprachgestalt und Bedeutung. (Siddiqi, J.A.) Meisenheim, 1969.

Phil 5585.62   Experimentelle Untersuchungen über die Struktur des Wahrnehmungsraumens. (Akishige, Yoshiharu.) Fukuoka, 1937.

Phil 5058.30.10   Experimentelle Untersuchungen über Einfache schlussprozesse. (Störring, Gustav.) Leipzig, 1908.

Phil 5649.28   Experimentelle Untersuchungen von Bewegungsstilen. Inaug. Diss. (Berning, A.) Bonn, 1960.

Phil 5251.41.85   Die experimentelle Willenspsychologie Kurt Lewin. (Schwermer, Josef.) Meisenheim, 1966.

Phil 5722.6   Ein experimenteller Beitrag zur Erforschung. (Martin, L.) Leipzig, 1915.

Phil 7140.113   Experimenten omtrent suggestibilteit bij senuw- en zielszieken. (Meijer, A.F.) Amsterdam, 1919.

Phil 5279.10   Experimenter effects in behavioral research. (Rosenthal, Robert.) N.Y., 1966.

Phil 5270.32   The experimenter's dilemma. (Jung, John.) N.Y., 1971.

Phil 5258.101   Experiments in general psychology. (Scheidemann, Norma Valentine.) Chicago, 1929.

Phil 5650.38   Experiments in hearing. (Békésy, Georg von.) N.Y., 1960.

Phil 8887.78   Experiments in living. (MacBeath, A.) London, 1952.

Phil 5590.45.5   Experiments in personality. (Eysenck, Hans Jurgen.) London, 1960. 2v.

Phil 5190.45   Experiments in persuasion. (Rosnow, Ralph L.) N.Y., 1967.

Phil 7069.17.25   Experiments in psychical research at Leland Stanford Jr. University. (Coover, John Edgar.) n.p. 1917.

Phil 51.2   Experiments in psychical research at Stanford Junior University. (Coover, J.E.) Stanford, 1917.

Phil 7069.19.60   Experiments in psychical science. (Crawford, William J.) N.Y., 1919.

Phil 5245.27.5   Experiments in psychology. (Foster, William S.) N.Y., 1923.

Phil 5245.27   Experiments in psychology. (Foster, William S.) N.Y., 1923.

Phil 5645.10   Experiments on tne aesthetics of light and colour. (Baker, Emma S.) Toronto, 1903.

Phil 6060.18.10   Experiments with handwriting. (Saudek, R.) London, 1928.

Phil 7054.115.5   Explanation and history of the mysterious communion with spirits. 2. ed. (Capron, Eliab W.) Auburn, N.Y., 1850.

Phil 194.60   Explanation and meaning. (Taylor, Daniel Malcolm.) Cambridge, Eng., 1970.

Phil 2750.10.99   Explanation and reality in the philosophy of Emile Meyerson. (Kelley, T.R.) Princeton, 1937.

Phil 270.148   Explanation and understanding. (Wright Georg Henrik van.) Ithaca, N.Y., 1971.

Phil 5270.26   Explanation in the behavioral sciences. (Borger, Robert.) Cambridge, Eng., 1970.

Phil 5259.56   The explanation of behavior. (Taylor, Charles.) London, 1964.

Phil 5258.185   The explanation of human behavior. (Smith, Frederick Viggers.) London, 1951.

Phil 196.5.7   Explanation of Van Nostrand's theory of the mental constitution. (Wake, C.S.) Chicago, 1892.

Phil 3821.16   Explicatío spinozismi. Diss. (Boumann, L.) Berlin, 1828.

Phil 7068.53.5   Explication des tables parlantes. 1st ed. (Goupy, Louis.) Paris, 1860.

Phil 281.6.5   Explication universelle. (Ayais, H.) Paris, 1826. 2v.

Phil 181.20   Exploratio philosophica. (Grote, J.) Cambridge, 1865.

Phil 5599.85   L'exploration de la mentalité des noirs, le Congo T.A.T. (Ombredane, André.) Paris, 1969.

Phil 5649.2   L'exploration physiologique...du sens musculaire. (Gourgeon, J.) Paris, 1901.

Phil 192.77   Explorations. (Robertson, J.M.) London, 1923.

Phil 8893.104   Explorations in altruistic love and behavior. (Sorokin, Pitirim Aleksandrovich.) Boston, 1950.

Phil 8893.104.3   Explorations in altruistic love and behavior. (Sorokin, Pitirim Aleksandrovich.) N.Y., 1970.

Phil 5520.175   Explorations in awareness. (Bois, Joseph S.) N.Y., 1957.

Phil 5325.35   Explorations in cognitive dissonance. (Brehm, Jack W.) N.Y., 1962.

Phil 5465.158   Explorations in creativity. 1. ed. (Mooney, Ron Lawler.) N.Y., 1967.

Phil 575.95   Explorations in personality. (Harvard University. Harvard Psychological Clinic.) N.Y., 1938.

Phil 5421.30.5   Explorations in the psychology of stress and anxiety. (Rourke, Byron P.) Don Mills, Ontario, 1969.

Phil 5585.165   Explorations in transactional psychology. (Kilpatrick, F.P.) N.Y., 1961.

Phil 7112.5   Explorations of a hypnotist. (Bernstien, Abraham Emmanuel.) London, 1959.

Phil 7069.70.5   Explore your psychic world. (Worrall, Ambrose A.) N.Y., 1970.

Phil 5242.60   Exploring behavior. 1. ed. (Candland, D.K.) N.Y., 1961.

Phil 6316.8   Exploring the unconscious. (Groddeck, Georg.) London, 1933.

Phil 7069.59.50   Exploring the unseen world. 1. ed. (Steinour, Harold Heiges.) N.Y., 1959.

Phil 5262.42   Exploring your mind with the psychologists. (Wiggam, Albert E.) Indianapolis, 1928.

Phil 1870.98   Exposé critique de la philosophie de Berkeley. (Joussain, André.) Paris, 1921.

Phil 1870.98.3   Exposé critique de la philosophie de Berkeley. Thèse. (Joussain, André.) Paris, 1920.

Phil 6688.27   Exposé de différentes cures. (Société Harmonique des Amis-Reunis de Strasbourg.) Strasbourg, 1786.

Phil 6673.4.15   Exposé des expériences sur le magnétisme. (Du Potet, J. de S.) Paris, 1821.

Phil 190.116   Exposé d'un nouveau système philosophique. (Pezzani, André.) Paris, 1847.

Phil 7060.130   Expose of Newburyport excentricities. (Davis, H.P.) n.p., 1873.

Phil 6682.19   Exposé par ordre alphabétique des cures. (Mialle, S.) Paris, 1826. 2v.

Phil 75.58   Exposición del libro americano. (Inter-American Congress of Philosophy.) Buenos Aires, 1959?

Phil 575.105   Exposición y crítica del personalismo espiritualista de nuestro tiempo. (Larroyo, Francisco.) México, 1941.

Htn   Phil 5000.1*   Expositio super artem veterem Porphyrii et Aristotelis. Pts.1,2. Manuscripts. (Burley, Walter.) n.p., 1442?

Phil 6673.5   Exposition, or A new theory animal magnetism. (Durant, C.F.) N.Y., 1837.

Phil 6677.18   Exposition critique du système et de la doctrine mystique des magnétistes. (Hénin de Cuvillers, E.T.) Paris, 1822.

Phil 176.24   Exposition de la philosophie. (Blignières, C.) Paris, 1857.

Phil 7054.96   An exposition of modern spiritualism. (Post, S.) N.Y., 1861.

Phil 1915.63.2   An exposition of the church catechism. 2d ed. (Clarke, Samuel.) London, 1730.

Phil 1915.63.6   An exposition of the church catechism. 6th ed. (Clarke, Samuel.) London, 1756.

Phil 7054.105   An exposition of views...spirit manifestations. (Ballou, Adin.) Boston, 1852.

Phil 7054.105.2   An exposition of views...spirit manifestations. 2. ed. (Ballou, Adin.) Boston, 1853.

Phil 8876.31   An exposition of vulgar and common errors. (Brown, T. Redivivus.) Philadelphia, 1846.

Phil 6687.7   Exposition physiologique des phénomènes du magnétisme animal. (Roullier, A.) Paris, 1817.

Phil 3552.68   Exposition sur la religion. (Leibniz, Gottfried Wilhelm.) Paris, 1819.

Phil 290.3   Expository history of the cosmos. (Joffe, Isaac L.) N.Y., 1927.

Phil 8419.41   L'expression dans les beaux-arts. (Sully Prudhomme, R.F.A.) Paris, 1883.

Phil 8412.6.5   L'expression de la vie dans l'art. (Lalo, Charles.) Paris, 1933.

Phil 8420.28 — The expression of emotion in the visual arts: a philosophical inquiry. (Tilghman, Benjamin R.) The Hague, 1970.

Phil 575.115 — The expression of personality. (Wolff, W.) N.Y., 1943.

Phil 5400.165 — Expression of the emotions in man. (Symposium on Expression.) N.Y., 1963.

X Cg Phil 5400.18.50 — The expression of the emotions in man and animals. (Darwin, Charles.) London, 1872.

Phil 5400.19 — The expression of the emotions in man and animals. (Darwin, Charles.) N.Y., 1873.

Phil 5400.19.3.5 — The expression of the emotions in man and animals. (Darwin, Charles.) N.Y., 1894.

Phil 5400.19.3.10 — The expression of the emotions in man and animals. (Darwin, Charles.) N.Y., 1896.

Phil 5400.19.7 — The expression of the emotions in man and animals. (Darwin, Charles.) N.Y., 1897.

Phil 5400.19.4 — The expression of the emotions in man and animals. (Darwin, Charles.) N.Y., 1899.

Phil 5465.166 — Expression picturale et psychopathologie. (Wiart, Claude.) Paris, 1967.

Phil 6325.1.16 — Expressionism in art. (Pfister, Oskar.) N.Y., 1923.

Phil 4065.45.5 — The expulsion of the triumphant beast. (Bruno, Giordano.) New Brunswick, 1964.

Phil 7076.12 — Extase. (Bertrand, Alexandre Jacques François.) Paris, 1826.

Phil 5628.10 — L'extase et la personalité. Thèse. (Vernier, André.) Montauban, 1901.

Phil 7076.20.5 — Une extatique. (Janet, Pierre.) Paris, 1901.

Phil 5068.75 — Extension and comprehension in logic. (Frisch, Joseph C.) N.Y., 1969.

Phil 7052.8 — L'extériorisation de la motricité. (Rochas d'Aiglun, Albert de.) Paris, 1896.

Phil 6687.6.2 — L'extériorisation de la sensibilité. 2e éd. (Rochas d'Aiglun, A.) Paris, 1895.

Phil 6687.6 — L'extériorisation de la sensibilité. 6e éd. (Rochas, d'Aiglun, A.) Paris, 1909.

Phil 9035.100 — Les extériorises. (Taulemonde, Jean.) Lyon, 1958[1959]

Phil 7162.261.1 — The extra-sensory mind. (Walker, Kenneth M.) N.Y., 1965.

Phil 7069.34.25A — Extra-sensory perception. (Rhine, Joseph B.) Boston, 1934.

Phil 7069.34.25.2A — Extra-sensory perception. (Rhine, Joseph B.) Boston, 1935.

Phil 7069.34.26 — Extra-sensory perception. (Rhine, Joseph B.) Boston, 1964.

Phil 7160.5 — Extra-sensory perception. (Schmeidler, Gertrude R.) N.Y., 1969.

Phil 7069.40.6A — Extra-sensory perception after 60 years. N.Y., 1940.

Htn Phil 665.6* — The extraction of man's soul. (Woolnor, H.) London, 1655.

Phil 8740.2 — Extracts concerning the importance of religion and public worship. (Goodale, E.) Hallowell, 1820.

Phil 978.22 — Extracts from the Vâhan. (Corbett, S.) London, 1904.

Phil 7054.88 — Extracts from unpublished volumes. (Pierce, A.P.) Boston, 1868.

Htn Phil 1870.65.9* — Extrait des recherches sur les vertus de l'eau de goudron. (Berkeley, G.) Amsterdam, 1749.

Phil 180.19.9 — Extraits des grands philosophes. 6e éd. (Fouillée, Alfred.) Paris, 1917.

Phil 8844.1 — Extraits des moralistes. (Thamin, R.) Paris, 1897.

Phil 7082.30 — Extraordinary and well-authenticated dreams. (Grant, Alexander Henley.) London, 18- ?

Phil 5585.220 — Ey, Henri. La conscience. Paris, 1963.

Phil 6954.6 — Ey, Henri. Hallucinations et délire. Paris, 1934.

Phil 5722.74 — Ey, Henri. L'inconscient, 6e Colloque de Bonneval [1960] sous la direction de Henri Ey. Paris, 1966.

Phil 2805.475 — Eydoux, Emmanuel. Dialogue avec Blaise Pascal. Théâtre. Basel, 1968.

Phil 5643.126 — Eye and brain. (Gregory, Richard Langton.) N.Y., 1966.

Phil 5643.109 — Eyeless sight, a study of extra-retinal vision and the paroptic sense. (Romains, Jules.) N.Y., 1924.

Phil 672.22 — Eyfferth, Max. Der Begriff der Zeit. Berlin, 1870.

Phil 672.22.5 — Eyfferth, Max. Über die Zeit; philosophische Untersuchung. Berlin, 1871.

Phil 510.154 — Eyken, A. Reality and monads. Apeldoorn, 1950.

Phil 3808.155 — Eymer, Karl. Arthur Schopenhauer. n.p., 1915.

Phil 9145.6 — Eyre, L.L. Fashionable society. Philadelphia, 1889.

Phil 5421.10.5 — Eysenck, H.J. The dynamics of anxiety and hysteria. London, 1958.

Phil 5244.30 — Eysenck, H.J. Sense and nonsense in psychology. Harmondsworth, Middlesex, 1957.

Phil 6314.11 — Eysenck, Hans J. Behaviour therapy and the neuroses. Oxford, 1960.

Phil 6314.11.10 — Eysenck, Hans J. The causes and cures of neurosis. London, 1965.

Phil 6314.11.5 — Eysenck, Hans J. Handbook of abnormal psychology. N.Y., 1961.

Phil 5590.45.20 — Eysenck, Hans Jürgen. Readings in extraversion-introversion. London, 1970-

Phil 5590.45.15 — Eysenck, Hans Jurgen. The biological basis of personality. Springfield, 1967.

Phil 5590.45 — Eysenck, Hans Jurgen. Dimensions of personality. London, 1948.

Phil 5590.45.5 — Eysenck, Hans Jurgen. Experiments in personality. London, 1960. 2v.

Phil 5585.110 — Eysenck, Hans Jurgen. Perceptual processes and mental illness. N.Y., 1957.

Phil 5592.196 — Eysenck, Hans Jurgen. Personality structure and measurement. London, 1969.

Phil 5590.45.10 — Eysenck, Hans Jurgen. The structure of human personality. London, 1953.

Phil 5590.45.13 — Eysenck, Hans Jurgen. The structure of human personality. 3. ed. London, 1970.

Phil 8505.8 — Ezhegodnik. (Leningrad. Muzei Istorii Religii i Ateizma.) Moskva. 1,1957+ 6v.

Phil 705.31 — Ezilasi, Wilhelm. Wissenschaft als Philosophie. Zürich, 1945.

Phil 3640.94 — F. Nietzsche, R. Wagner e la tragedie Greca. (Tosi, T.) Firenze, 1905.

Phil 3640.188 — F. Nietzsche. (Fischer, E.L.) Regensburg, 1906.

Phil 3640.185 — F. Nietzsche. (Reiner, Julius.) Stuttgart, 1916.

Phil 3640.181 — F. Nietzsche e L. Tolstoi. (Petrone, Igino.) Napoli, 1902.

Phil 3890.1.115 — F.A. Trendelenburg. (Rosensbock, G.G.) Carbondale, 1964.

Phil 2280.7.85 — F.C.S. Schiller and the dimensions of pragmatism. (Winetrout, Kenneth.) Columbus, 1967.

Phil 4582.7.90 — F.G. Howitz, 1789-1826. (Thomsen, O.) København, 1924.

Phil 1885.90 — F.H. Bradley. (Lofthouse, W.F.) London, 1949. 2v.

Phil 1885.93 — F.H. Bradley. (Wollheim, Richard.) Harmondsworth, 1960[1959]

Phil 1885.93.2 — F.H. Bradley. 2d ed. (Wollheim, Richard.) Harmondsworth, 1969.

Phil 3460.81 — F.H. Jacobi im Verhaltniss zu seinen Zeitgenossen. (Deyks, F.) Frankfurt, 1848.

Phil 3460.80 — F.H. Jacobis Seben, Dichten und Denken. (Zirngiebl, E.) Wien, 1867.

Htn Phil 3801.197* — F.W.J. von Schelling. (Beckers, Hubert.) München, 1855.

Htn Phil 3801.469* — F.W.J. von Schelling. (Jung, Alexander.) Leipzig, 1864.

Phil 3801.470.2 — F.W.J. von Schelling. (Kapp, Christian.) Leipzig, 1843.

Htn Phil 3801.470* — F.W.J. von Schelling. (Kapp, Christian.) Leipzig, 1843.

Phil 3800.10 — F.W.J. von Schelling: Bibliographie. (Jost, J.) Bonn, 1927.

Phil 180.27 — Fabbricotti, Carlo A. Appunti critici di filosofia contemporanea. Firenze, 1910.

Phil 2138.110 — Fabbricotti, Carlo A. Positivismo? John Stuart Mill. Firenze, 1910.

Phil 8660.6 — Faber, F.W. The creator and the creature. London, 1889.

Phil 8660.7.2 — Faber, G.S. The difficulties of infidelity. 2. ed. London, 1833.

Phil 3310.17.80 — Faber, Heije. Het christelijk humanisme. Assen, 1963.

Phil 3005.10 — Faber, W. Wijsgeren in Nederland. Nijkerk, 1954.

Phil 3960.20 — Faber, W. Wijsgerin in Nederland. Nijkork, 1954.

Phil 4110.10.30 — Fabi, Bruno. Il tutto e il nulla. 1. ed. Milano, 1952.

Phil 3850.16.89 — Fabian, W. Kritik der Lebensphilosophie Georg Simmels. Breslau, 1926.

Phil 480.5 — Fabié, Antonio M. Exámen del materialismo moderno. Madrid, 1875.

Phil 8667.21 — La fable de Christ dévoilée. (Maréchal, P.S.) Paris, 1794.

Htn Phil 2128.50* — La fable des abeilles. (Mandeville, B.) London, 1750. 2v.

Htn Phil 2305.1.35* — The fable of Cupid and Psyche. (Taylor, Thomas.) London, 1795.

Htn Phil 2128.33.12* — Fable of the bees. (Mandeville, B.) Edinburgh, 1755. 2v.

Htn Phil 2128.27* — Fable of the bees. (Mandeville, B.) London, 1714.

Htn Phil 2128.28* — Fable of the bees. (Mandeville, B.) London, 1723.

Phil 2128.30 — Fable of the bees. (Mandeville, B.) London, 1725.

Phil 2128.31 — Fable of the bees. (Mandeville, B.) London, 1728-29. 2v.

Phil 2128.32 — Fable of the bees. (Mandeville, B.) London, 1729-32. 2v.

Phil 2128.43 — Fable of the bees. (Mandeville, B.) London, 1934.

Phil 2128.45 — Fable of the bees. (Mandeville, B.) N.Y., 1962.

Phil 2128.41A — Fable of the bees. (Mandeville, B.) Oxford, 1924. 2v.

Phil 2128.33.5 — Fable of the bees. Pt.II. (Mandeville, B.) London, 1730.

Phil 2128.29 — Fable of the bees. 3rd ed. (Mandeville, B.) London, 1724.

Phil 180.1 — Fabre, J. Cours de philosophie. Paris, 1870.

Phil 850.11 — Fabre, Joseph. La pensée antique (de Moise à Marcaurèle). Paris, 1902.

Phil 1705.6 — Fabre, Joseph. La pensée moderne. Paris, 1908.

Phil 1705.6.1 — Fabre, Joseph. La pensée moderne [de Luther à Leibniz]. Genève, 1970.

Phil 5245.1 — Fabre d'Envieu, J. Cours de philosophie. Paris, 1863-1866. 2v.

Phil 7082.168 — The fabric of dreams. (Craig, Katherine Taylor.) N.Y., 1918.

Phil 815.15 — Fabro, C. Storia della filosofia. Roma, 1954.

Phil 8660.21 — Fabro, Conelio. Introduzione all'ateismo moderno. Roma, 1964.

Phil 1750.525 — Fabro, Cornelio. Dall'essere all'esistente. Brescia, 1957.

Phil 4110.9.30 — Fabro, Cornelio. Problemi dell'esistenzialismo. Roma, 1945.

Phil 5520.712 — Faccani, Remo. I sistemi di segni e lo strutturalismo sovietico. Milano, 1969.

Phil 6021.10 — La faccia e l'anima. (Lima Fulza, G.) Milano, 1875.

Phil 2805.225 — Face à l'épreuve avec Pascal. (Desbruyères, P.) Lyon, 1944.

Phil 2905.1.230 — Face au prophétisme de Teilhard de Chardin. Bruxelles, 1963.

Phil 3832.17 — The face of Benedictus Spinoza. (Millner, Simond.) N.Y., 1946.

Phil 5400.208 — The face of emotion. (Izard, Carroll E.) N.Y., 1971.

Phil 8708.30 — Face to face with Darwinism. (Simonsson, Tord.) Lund, 1958.

Phil 90.5 — Fachwörterbuch der Philosophie. Zürich, 1945.

Phil 6114.15.5 — Facing reality; philosophical adventures by a brain scientist. (Eccles, J.C.) London, 1970.

Phil 3415.83 — Das Facit aus Eduard von Hartmann's Philosophie des Unbewussten. (Knauer, G.) Berlin, 1873.

Phil 3425.650 — Fackenheim, Emil L. The religious dimension in Hegel's thought. Bloomington, Ind., 1968[1967]

Phil 7082.2 — Façons d'endormi, façons d'éveillé. (Michaux, Henri.) Paris, 1969.

Phil 2030.6A — Fact, fiction and forecast. (Goodman, Nelson.) Cambridge, 1955.

Phil 2030.6.2 — Fact, fiction and forecast. 2d ed. (Goodman, Nelson.) Indianapolis, 1965.

Phil 194.36.10 — Fact: the romance of mind. (Taylor, H.O.) N.Y., 1932.

Phil 70.105.5 — Fact and existence; proceedings of the University of Western Ontario philosophy colloquium, 1966. (University of Western Ontario. Philosophy Colloquium.) Toronto, 1969. 2v.

Phil 70.105 — Fact and existence; proceedings of the University of Western Ontario philosophy colloquium, 1966. (University of Western Ontario. Philosophy Colloquium.) Oxford, 1969.

NEDL Phil 5249.6 — Fact and fable in psychology. (Jastrow, J.) Boston, 1901.

Phil 2255.1.73 — Fact and fiction. (Russell, Bertrand Russell.) London, 1961.

Phil 9400.17 — Fact book on aging. (United States. Federal Security Agency. Committee on Aging and Geriatrics.) Washington, D.C., 1952.

Phil 5585.54.7 — Les facteurs pratiques de la croyance dans la perception. (Duret, René.) Paris, 1929?

Phil 5585.54.5 — Les facteurs pratiques de la croyance dans la perception. Thèse. (Duret, René.) Paris, 1929.

Phil 5645.14 — Factor...sensitivity of retina to color. (Rand, G.) Princeton, 1913.

Phil 8893.87 — Factores morales. (Sibecas, S.) Habana, 1926.

Phil 5240.45 — Factorial analysis for non-mathematicians. (Adcock, C.J.) Carlton, 1954.

Phil 5585.68 — A factorial study of perception. (Thurstone, L.L.) Chicago, 1944.

Phil 5240.49 — Factors in mental evolution. (Adrian, E.D.A.) Oxford, 1960.

Phil 5643.74 Factors involved in the reduction of post-rotation nystagmus time. (Holsopple, J.Q.) Baltimore, 1924.

Phil 5242.39 Factors of human psychology. (Cole, Lawrence W.) Boulder, 1926.

Phil 5242.39.4 Factors of human psychology. (Cole, Lawrence W.) Boulder, 1930[1935]

Phil 5274.8 The factors of the mind. (Burt, Cyril.) London, 1940.

Phil 6945.50 Factors related to length of mental hospital stay. (Krause, Elliott Arthur.) Boston, 1966?

Phil 181.25 Factos do espirito humano. (Gonçalvez de Magalhães, J.G.) Rio de Janeiro, 1865.

Phil 28.7 Facts; a monthly magazine devoted to mental and spiritual phenomena. Boston. 1-6,1882-1887 4v.

Phil 2150.18.100 Facts, values and ethics. (Olthuis, James H.) Assen, 1968.

Phil 5070.32 Facts, words, and beliefs. (Sprigge, Timothy Lauro Squire.) N.Y., 1970.

Phil 170.5 Facts about Hegel and other essays. (Holland, F.M.) Boston, 1880-81.

Phil 2270.41 Facts and comments. (Spencer, Herbert.) N.Y., 1902.
Phil 2270.41.5 Facts and comments. (Spencer, Herbert.) N.Y., 1902.
Phil 2270.41.6 Facts and comments. (Spencer, Herbert.) N.Y., 1902.
Phil 8595.14 Facts and fancies. (Piercy, B.H.) London, 1913.
Phil 7052.10.2 Facts and fantasies, a sequel to Sights and sounds. (Spicer, Henry.) London, 1853.

Phil 6317.20 Facts and theories of psychoanalysis. (Hendrick, Ives.) N.Y., 1934.

Phil 6317.20.5A Facts and theories of psychoanalysis. 2d ed. (Hendrick, Ives.) N.Y., 1944.

Phil 6317.20.8 Facts and theories of psychoanalysis. 3rd ed. (Hendrick, Ives.) N.Y., 1958.

Phil 8893.102.15 Facts and values. (Stevenson, Charles Leslie.) New Haven, 1963.

Phil 6689.2 Facts in mesmerism. (Townehend, C.H.) Boston, 1841.
Phil 6689.2.2 Facts in mesmerism. (Townehend, C.H.) N.Y., 1841.
Phil 2270.81 Facts of consciousness and philosophy of Spencer. (Greene, W.B.) Boston, 1871.

Phil 8610.902 Facts worth knowing. (Brooklyn Philosophical Association.) N.Y., 1902.

Phil 5812.4 Les facultés mentales des animaux. (Foveau de Courmelles, F.V.) Paris, 1890.

Phil 186.95.5 Fadiman, Clifton. I believe. London, 1940.
Phil 186.95 Fadiman, Clifton. I believe. N.Y., 1939.
Phil 7069.05.15 Fads or facts. (Rayon, M.) Chicago, 1905.
Phil 510.20 Fähigkeiten der Naturwissenschaften und Monismus der Gegenwart. (Volkmann, Paul.) Leipzig, 1909.
Phil 3487.10 Färber, Max. Die Kantische Freiheitslehre. Berlin, 1921.
Phil 8880.49 Fagathey, Austin. Right and reason. St. Louis, 1953.
Phil 8880.49.2 Fagathey, Austin. Right and reason. 2nd ed. St. Louis, 1959.

Phil 8612.72 Fagerberg, Holsten. Om rätten att dö. Stockholm, 1967.
Phil 6321.51.15 Fages, Jean Baptiste. Comprendre Jacques Lacan. Toulouse, 1971.

Phil 5245.13 Faggi, A. Principi di psicologia moderna. Palermo, 1895.
Phil 270.38 Faggiotto, A. La causa trinitaria unica sostanza del cosmo. Padova, 1929.

Phil 8585.55 Faggiotto, Agostino. La religione nell'esperienza umana. Padova, 1967.

Phil 4005.12 Faggiotto, Pietro. Esperienza e metafisica. Padova, 1959.
Phil 180.88.5 Faggiotto, Pietro. Il problema della metafisica nel pensiero moderno. Padova, 1969-

Phil 180.88 Faggiotto, Pietro. Saggio sulla struttura della metafisica. Padova, 1965.

Phil 3640.82 Faguet, E. En lesant Nietzsche. Paris, 1904.
Phil 805.4 Faguet, E. Initiation philosophique. Paris, 1912.
Phil 180.23 Faguet, Emile. Initiation in philosophy. N.Y., 1914.
Phil 180.23.2 Faguet, Émile. Initiation philosophique. Paris, 1913.
Phil 8880.27 Faguet, Émile. Les préjugés nécessaires. Paris, 1911.
Phil 6675.1A Fahnestock, W.B. Statu volism. Chicago, 1871.
Phil 5590.471 Fahrenberg, Jochen. Psychophysiologische Persönlichkeitsforschung. Göttingen, 1967.

Phil 3425.295 Fahrenhorst, E. Geist und Freiheit im System Hegels. Leipzig, 1934.

Phil 5755.11 Fahrion, Karl. Das Problem der Willensfreiheit. Heidelburg, 1904.

Phil 3808.150 Fahsel, H. Die Überwindung des Pessimismus. Freiburg, 1927.

Phil 8582.28 La faillité des religions. (Claraz, Jules.) Paris, 1912.
Phil 3640.155 La faillite du surhomme et la physologie de Nietzsche. (De Villers, Sireyx.) Paris, 1920.

Phil 6332.30 The failure of psychoanalysis. (Wells, Harry K.) N.Y., 1963.

Phil 6115.33 Fair, Charles. The physical foundations of the psyche. Middletown, 1963.

Phil 575.274 Fair, Charles M. The dying self. 1st ed. Middletown, Conn., 1969.

Phil 7060.145 Fair and fatal warnings. London, 1800?
Phil 8585.1.5 Fairbairn, A.M. The philosophy of the Christian religion. London, 1905.

Phil 8585.1 Fairbairn, A.M. Studies...philosophy of religion and history. London, 1877.

Phil 8585.1.2 Fairbairn, A.M. Studies...philosophy of religion and history. 4. ed. N.Y., 1876.

Phil 8880.23 Fairbairn, R.B. Of the doctrine of morality in its relation to grace of redemption. N.Y., 1887.

Phil 9070.26 Fairbanks, Douglas. Youth points the way. N.Y., 1924.
Phil 2020.80.2A Fairbrother, W.H. Philosophy of Thomas Hill Green. 2nd ed. London, 1900.

Phil 6115.22 Fairburn, W.A. Mentality and freedom. N.Y., 1917.
Phil 8880.43.5 Fairchild, J.H. Moral philosophy. Oberlin, Ohio, 1869.
Phil 7054.65 Fairfield, F.G. Ten years with spiritual mediums. N.Y., 1875.

Phil 2805.81 Fait inédit de la vie de Pascal. (Collet, F.) Paris, 1848.

Phil 187.131 Le fait métaphysique. (Masson-Oursel, Paul.) Paris, 1941.
Phil 8701.2.4 Faith, the life of science. (Lewis, Tayler.) Albany, 1838.

Phil 8587.70 Faith. (Hutchison, J.A.) N.Y., 1956.
Phil 5070.6 Faith. (Inge, William R.) London, 1909.
Phil 8582.27 Faith and experience. 2. ed. (Chandler, Arthur.) London, 1912.

Phil 6111.53.2 Faith and health. 2. ed. (Brown, Charles R.) N.Y., 1910.
Phil 5070.6.5 Faith and its psychology. (Inge, William R.) N.Y., 1910.
Phil 8701.4.13 Faith and knowledge, April, 1902. (Lodge, Oliver Joseph.) London, 19-

Phil 8709.6 The faith and modern thought. (Temple, William.) London, 1913.

Phil 8575.5 Faith and philosophy; philosophical studies in religion and ethics. (Plantinga, Alvin.) Grand Rapids, 1964.

Phil 9513.30 Faith and politics. (Niebuhr, Reinhold.) N.Y., 1968.
Phil 8585.6.5 Faith and rationalism. (Fisher, G.P.) N.Y., 1879.
Phil 8585.6.6 Faith and rationalism. (Fisher, G.P.) N.Y., 1885.
Phil 8582.26.5 Faith and reason. (Collingwood, Robin George.) Chicago, 1968.

Phil 8586.10.25 Faith and reason in religion. (Galloway, G.) London, 1927.

Phil 8590.18.20 Faith and success. (King, Basil.) Garden City, 1928.
Phil 8905.5 Faith and technology; being the inaugural lecture of the Luton Industrial College. (Coulson, Charles Alfred.) London, 1969.

Phil 5627.264.10 Faith and the philosophers. (Hick, John.) N.Y., 1964.
Phil 8585.20.80 The faith and the war; a series of essays. (Foakes-Jackson, F.J.) London, 1915.

Phil 8580.9 Faith built on reason. (Abbot, F.L.) Boston, 1902.
Phil 6990.68 Faith healing; God or fraud? (Bishop, George Victor.) Los Angeles, 1967.

Phil 6311.29 Faith-healing. (Buckley, James M.) N.Y., 1900.
Phil 8637.13 Faith in a future life. (Martin, A.W.) N.Y., 1916.
Phil 8597.23.5 Faith in an age of fact. (Reisner, Edward H.) N.Y., 1937.
Phil 8656.5 Faith in God. (Buchanan, J.) London, 1857. 2v.
Phil 8660.26 Faith in the face of doubt. N.Y., 1968.
Phil 8602.19 Faith justified by progress. (Wright, H.W.) N.Y., 1916.
Phil 1930.10.30 The faith of a liberal. Selected essays. (Cohen Morris, R.) N.Y., 1946.

Phil 8599.22 Faith of a moralist. (Taylor, Alfred E.) London, 1930. 2v.

Phil 8602.26 The faith of all sensible people. (Wilson, D.A.) London, 1919.

Phil 8610.902.5 The faith of an agnostic. 2. ed. (Greenwood, Granville George.) London, 1919.

Phil 2405.4 The faith of reason. (Frankel, Charles.) N.Y., 1948.
Phil 2905.1.180.6 The faith of Teilhard de Chardin. (Lubac, Henri de.) London, 1965.

Phil 8610.897 Faith or fact. (Taber, H.M.) N.Y., 1897.
Phil 8589.12 A faith that enquires. (Jones, Henry.) N.Y., 1922.
Phil 8602.40 The faith that has come to me. (Widney, J.P.) Los Angeles, 1932.

Phil 6116.22 The faith that overcomes the world. (Gibson, Van R.) N.Y., 1926.

Phil 1050.24 Faithful rebels; a study in Jewish speculative thought. (Levine, I.) London, 1936.

Phil 8877.11 The faithful steward. (Clark, S.D.) Boston, 1853.
Phil 974.3.108 The faithful thinker. (Harwood, A.C.) London, 1961.
Phil 6315.50 Faithfull, Theodore. The mystery of the androgyne. London, 1938.

Phil 6990.43 Faiths that healed. (Major, R.H.) N.Y., 1940.
Phil 2270.41.9 Faits et commentaires. 2e éd. (Spencer, Herbert.) Paris, 1904.

Phil 974.8 Faivre, Antoine. Eckartshausen et la théosophie chrétienne. Thèse. Paris, 1969.

Phil 310.746 Fajkus, Brětislaw. Existence, realita, masérie. Vyd. 1. Praha, 1968.

Phil 1020.4.36 Fakhry, Majid. A history of Islamic philosophy. N.Y., 1970.

Phil 1020.4.7 Fakhry, Majid. Islamic occasionalism and its critique by Averroës and Aquinas. Paris, 1861.

Phil 1020.4.35 Fakhry, Majid. Islamic occasionalism and its critique by Averroës and Aquinas. London, 1958.

Phil 1020.4.8 Fakhry, Majid. Islamic occasionalism and its critique by Averros and Aquinas. Paris, 1869.

Phil 7069.26.60 Fakirs, fumistes et Cie. (Heuzé, P.) Paris, 1926.
Phil 3487.28 Falaturi, Abdal-Jawad. Zur Interpretation der Kantischen Ethik im Lichte der Achtung. Inaug. Diss. Bonn, 1965.

Phil 3487.2 Falckenberg, R. Gedächtnisrede auf Kant. Erlangen, 1904.
Phil 1705.1 Falckenberg, R. Geschichte der neueren Philosophie. Leipzig, 1886.

Phil 1705.1.2 Falckenberg, R. Geschichte der neueren Philosophie. 2e Aufl. Leipzig, 1892.

Phil 1705.1.3 Falckenberg, R. Geschichte der neueren Philosophie. 8e Aufl. Berlin, 1921.

Phil 1705.1.4 Falckenberg, R. Geschichte der neueren Philosophie. 9. Aufl. Berlin, 1927.

Phil 3565.113 Falckenberg, R. Hermann Lotze. Stuttgart, 1901.
Phil 1705.1.5 Falckenberg, R. History of modern philosophy. N.Y., 1893.
Phil 1705.1.7 Falckenberg, R. History of modern philosophy. N.Y., 1897.
Phil 3005.3.10 Falckenberg, Richard. La filosofía alemana desde Kant. Madrid, 1906.

Phil 3005.3.3 Falckenberg, Richard. Hilfslrich zur Geschichte der Philosophie seit Kant. 3e Aufl. Leipzig, 1917.

Phil 3005.3.7 Falckenberg, Richard. Über die gegenwärtige Lage der deutschen Philosophie. Leipzig, 1890.

Phil 4260.185 Falco, Enrico de. La biografia di G.B. Vico. Roma, 1968.
Phil 5815.4 Falco, Francesco. I fatti psichici della vita animale. Lucca, 1880.

Phil 8880.45 Falco, Francesco. L'ordine ed i fatti morali. Alessandria, 1874.

Phil 180.42 Falco, Francesco. L'uomo:saggio popolare. Piacenza, 1870.
Phil 7068.98.20 Falcomer, M.T. Contributo di fatti pella soluzione del problema di psicologia. Selessandria, 1898.

Phil 8633.1.30 Falconer, Robert A. The idea of immortality. Cambridge, 1930.

Phil 6115.1 Falconer, W. A dissertation...passions...disorders of the body. London, 1796.

Phil 9035.48 Falconnet de la Bellonie. La psycantropie ou nouvelle théorie de l'homme. v.1-3. Avignon, 1748.

Phil 2805.223 Falcucci, C. Le problème de la vérité chez Pascal. Thèse. Toulouse, 1939.

Phil 5245.46 Fales, Walter. Wisdom and responsibility. Princeton, 1946.

Phil 5245.17 Falinski, E. Cahiers de psychologie rationnelle. v.1-4. Paris, 1926.

Phil 665.36 Falke, R. Gibt es eine Seelenwanderung? Halle, 1904.
Phil 3270.1.81 Falken, H.N. Kuno Fischer und der litterarhistorische Methode. Berlin, 1892.

Phil 180.47 Falkenfeld, H. Einfuhrung in die Philosophie. Berlin, 1926.

Phil 3487.32 Falkenfeld, Hellmuth. Was ist uns Kant? Weimar, 1924.
Phil 165.15 Falkenhahn, W. Veritati. München, 1943.
Phil 3487.13 Falkenheim, H. Die Entstehung der Kantischen Ästhetik. Diss. Berlin, 1890.

Phil 2515.10.16 The fall into time. (Cioran, Émile M.) Chicago, 1970.
Phil 3640.195 Der "Fall" Nietzsche. (Schlaf, Johannes.) Leipzig, 1907.
Phil 3640.409 Der Fall Nietzsche. (Schlechta, Karl.) München, 1958.
Phil 3640.409.2 Der Fall Nietzsche. (Schlechta, Karl.) München, 1959.

Phil 6311.9 — Ein Fall von doppeltem Bewusstsein. Inaug. Diss. (Bohn, W.) Breslau, 1923.

Phil 3640.11.4 — Der Fall Wagner; und die Geburt der Trajödie. (Nietzsche, Friedrich.) Leipzig, 1888.

Phil 3640.52 — Der Fall Wagner. (Nietzsche, Friedrich.) Frankfurt, 1946.

Phil 3640.52.5 — Der Fall Wagner. (Nietzsche, Friedrich.) Leipzig, 1931.

Phil 5100.8 — Fallacies. (Hamblin, Charles Leonard.) London, 1970.

Phil 5100.2A — Fallacies. (Sidgwick, A.) N.Y., 1884.

Phil 5757.16 — The fallacies of fatalism. (Hooper, Charles E.) London, 1930.

Phil 7060.90 — Fallacy of ghosts, dreams and omens. (Ollier, Charles.) London, 1848.

Phil 3002.2 — The fallacy of the German state philosophy. (Crile, G.W.) Garden City, 1918.

Phil 1158.30 — Fallat, Jean. Le plaisir et la mort dans la philosophie d'Epicure. Paris, 1951.

Phil 672.32 — Fallen angels. London, 1894.

Phil 8406.24 — Fallico, A.B. Art and existentialism. Englewood Cliffs, 1962.

Phil 400.136 — Un fallito tentativo di riforma dello hegelismo. (Ciardo, Manlio.) Bari, 1948.

Phil 8880.70 — Fallot, Jean. Pouvoir et morale. Thèse. Saverne, 1967.

Phil 3270.17.50 — Falm, Leopold. De bezinning. Amsterdam, 1968.

Phil 5245.48 — Falorni, M.L. Lo studio psicologica dell'intelligenza e della matricità. Firenze, 1952.

Phil 6955.1 — Falret, J.P. Des maladies mentales. Paris, 1864.

Phil 6955.1.5 — Falret, J.P. Études cliniques sur les maladies mentales et nerveuses. Paris, 1890.

Phil 3480.87 — Die falsche Spitzfindigkeit der vier syllogistischen Figuren. (Kant, Immanuel.) Frankfurt, 1797.

Phil 8712.12 — Die falsche Wissenschaft. (Wessenberg, J.G. von.) Stuttgart, 1844.

Phil 8622.76 — Falsification and belief. (McKinnon, Alastair.) The Hague, 1970.

Phil 4710.90 — Fal'sifkatsiia istorii russkoi politicheskoi mysli v sovremennoi reaktsionnoi burzhuaznoi literature. (Pokrovskii, S.A.) Moskva, 1957.

Phil 4215.10.30 — La fame. 2. ed. (Raya, Gino.) Roma, 1963.

Phil 6750.235 — Familial feeblemindedness. (Town, C.H.) Buffalo, 1939.

Phil 176.5.13 — Familiar belief and transcendent reason. (Balfour, A.J.) London, n.d.

Phil 5262.3 — Familiar forensic view of man and law. (Warden, R.B.) Columbus, 1860.

Phil 6328.19.5 — Familiar forms of nervous disease. 2d ed. (Starr, Moses A.) N.Y., 1891.

Phil 8897.1.5 — Familiar introduction to the knowledge of ourselves. (Walker, S.) London, 1761.

Phil 8879.8 — Familiar lectures on moral philosophy. (Estlin, J.P.) London, 1818. 2v.

Phil 5925.7 — Familiar lessons on phrenology. v.2. (Fowler, L. (Mrs.).) N.Y., 1847.

Phil 2115.75 — Familiar letters. (Locke, J.) London, 1742.

Phil 2115.75.2 — Familiar letters. (Locke, J.) London, 1742.

Phil 2115.75.3 — Familiar letters. (Locke, J.) London, 1830.

Phil 7054.95 — Familiar spirits and spiritual manifestations. (Pond, E.) Boston, 1852.

Phil 9347.6 — Familiar talks to boys. (Hall, John.) N.Y., n.d.

Phil 6955.2 — Familiar views of lunacy and lunatic life. London, 1850.

Phil 9161.10 — Familielivets etik. (Broendum, L.C.) København, 1963.

Phil 9166.4 — La famille. (Gasparin, A.E.) Paris, 1867. 2v.

Phil 5440.7 — La famille névropathique. (Féré, C.) Paris, 1898.

Phil 9167.2 — The family, a religious institution. (Hopkins, E.) Troy, N.Y., 1840.

Phil 6962.34 — Family and class dynamics in mental illness. (Myers, Jerome K.) N.Y., 1959.

Phil 9165.1 — The family book. N.Y., 1835.

Phil 5259.55 — Family constellation. (Toman, Walter.) N.Y., 1961.

Phil 5259.55.2 — Family constellation. 2d ed. (Toman, Walter.) N.Y., 1969.

Phil 6940.5 — Family council law in Europe. (Eugenics Society, London.) London, 1930.

Phil 7060.92.60 — Family ghosts and ghostly phenomena. 1st ed. (O'Donnell, Elliot.) N.Y., 1934.

Phil 9169.1.1 — The family monitor. (James, J.A.) Boston, 1829.

Phil 9169.1.2 — The family monitor. (James, J.A.) Boston, 1833.

Phil 9169.1 — The family monitor. (James, J.A.) Concord, N.H., 1829.

Phil 7069.29.70 — Famous curses. (O'Donnell, Elliot.) London, 1929.

Phil 9200.1.5 — Fanaticism. (Taylor, Isaac.) London, 1833.

Phil 9200.1.10 — Fanaticism. (Taylor, Isaac.) London, 1853.

Phil 9200.1 — Fanaticism. (Taylor, Isaac.) N.Y., 1834.

Phil 9200.3 — Fanaticismus. (Rudin, Josef.) Olten, 1965.

Phil 9590.13 — Fanatismo y misticismo. (Menendez Samara, A.) México, 1940.

Phil 4110.12.30 — Fancelli, M. Discorso sulla speranza. Messina, 1960.

Phil 8406.22 — Fanciulli, G. La coscienza estetica. Torino, 1906.

Phil 3487.26 — Fang, Joong. Das Antinomenproblem im Entstehungsgang der Transzendentalphilosophie. Münster, 1957.

Phil 3487.27 — Fang, Joong. Kant - Interpretationen. Münster, 1967-

Phil 8406.26 — Fanizza, Franco. Estetica problematica. Manduria, 1963.

Phil 2225.5.170 — Fann, K.T. Peirce's theory of abduction. The Hague, 1970.

Phil 1845.16.5 — Fann, K.T. Symposium on J.L. Austin. London, 1969.

Phil 3925.16.210 — Fann, K.T. Wittgenstein's conception of philosophy. Oxford, 1969.

Phil 4080.3.185 — Fano, Giorgio. La filosofia del Croce. 1a ed. Milano, 1946.

Phil 5068.88 — Fano, Giorgio. Neopositivismo, analisi del linguaggio e cibernetica. Torino, 1968.

Phil 5465.9 — La fantasia. (Biuso, C.) Catania, 1903.

Phil 5465.14 — La fantasia. (Giachetti, Apriano.) Torino, 1912.

Phil 6321.5.10 — Fantasia of the unconscious. (Lawrence, David Herbert.) N.Y., 1930.

Phil 6321.5.8.2 — Fantasia of the unconscious and Psychoanalysis and the unconscious. (Lawrence, David Herbert.) London, 1971.

Phil 5465.24 — Fantasien. (Hammer, Bertil.) Uppsala, 1916.

Phil 3120.8.100 — Fanz Brentanos Ringen um eine neue Gottessicht. (Winter, E.) Brünn, 1941.

Phil 8830.4 — Faquet, Émile. La démission de la morale. Paris, 1910.

VPhil 1750.115 — Faragó, László. A harmadik humanismus és a harmadik birodalom. Budapest, 1935.

Phil 5645.48 — Die Farbe als psychologisches Untersuchungsmittel. (Lüscher, Max.) St. Gallen, 1949.

Phil 5592.20 — Die Farbe in des Persönlichkeitsdiagnostik. (Furrer, Walter.) Basel, 1953.

Phil 5645.41 — Farbe und Dasein. (Steinfels, W.) Jena, 1926.

Phil 5645.34 — Farben und Farben-Empfindung. (Weidlich, Karl.) Stettin, 1930.

Phil 5645.34.3 — Farben und Farben-Empfindung. (Weidlich, Karl.) Stettin, 1933.

Phil 5642.18 — Das Farbenhören und der synäthetische Faktor der Wahrnehmung. (Argelander, A.) Jena, 1927.

Phil 5645.20 — Die Farbenlehre. v.1-2,4. (Ostwald, Wilhelm.) Leipzig, 1918-22. 3v.

Phil 5645.20.2 — Die Farbenlehre. 2. Aufl. (Ostwald, Wilhelm.) Leipzig, 1921.

Phil 5645.18 — Der Farbensinn und seine Störungen. (Geuter, Peter.) Leipzig, 1914.

Phil 5592.25 — Der Farbenspiegel. (Frieling, H.) Göttingen, 1955.

Phil 5755.15.1 — Farber, Leslie H. The ways of the will. N.Y., 1966.

Phil 180.44A — Farber, M. Phenomenology as a method and as a philosophical discipline. n.p., 1928.

Phil 2405.5.5 — Farber, Marvin. L'activité philosophique contemporaine en France. 1. éd. Paris, 1950. 2v.

Phil 3450.11.117 — Farber, Marvin. The aims of phenomenology; the motives, methods, and impact of Husserl's thought. 1st ed. N.Y., 1966.

Phil 3450.11.118A — Farber, Marvin. The foundation of phenomenology; Edmund Husserl. Cambridge, 1943.

Phil 3450.11.118.3 — Farber, Marvin. The foundation of phenomenology. 3d ed. n.p., 1967[1943]

Phil 1750.96 — Farber, Marvin. Naturalism and subjectivism. Springfield, Ill., 1959.

Phil 2405.5.2 — Farber, Marvin. Philosophic thought in France and the United States. 2. ed. Albany, 1968.

Phil 3450.11.115A — Farber, Marvin. Philosophical essays in memory of Edmund Husserl. Cambridge, 1940.

Phil 7150.70 — Farber, Maurice. Theory of suicide. N.Y., 1968.

Phil 5238.191 — Farberow, N.L. Taboo topics. N.Y., 1963.

Phil 5215.4 — Farbstein, Wolf. Romantische Einflüsse in der Geschichte der Psychologie. Zürich, 1953.

Phil 510.146 — Die Farce des Jahrhunderts oder Des monisten Glück und Ende. (Friedrich, Gustav.) Leipzig, 1913.

Phil 6115.2.2 — Farges, A. Le cerveau, l'âme et les facultés. Paris, 1890.

Phil 1535.17 — Farges, A. Études philosophiques. Paris, 1893-1902. 8v.

Phil 525.81 — Farges, Albert. Les phénomènes mystiques distingués de leurs contrefaçons humaines et diaboliques. Paris, 1920.

X Cg Phil 2475.1.145 — Farges, Albert. Philosophie de M. Bergson. 2e ed. Paris, 1914.

Phil 8695.8 — Fargues, Paul. Transformisme et christianisme. Paris, 1909.

Phil 286.7 — Faria Gersão Ventura, Augusta. A maquina do mundo. Porto, 1944.

Phil 4967.20 — Farias Brito, Raymundo de. A base physica do espirito. Rio de Janeiro, 1912.

Phil 4967.20.10 — Farias Brito, Raymundo de. Finalidade do mundo. 2. ed. Rio de Janeiro, 1957. 3v.

Phil 4967.20.15 — Farias Brito, Raymundo de. Ineditos e dispersos, notas e variaçoes sôbre assuntos diversos. São Paulo, 1966.

Phil 4967.20.5 — Farias Brito, Raymundo de. O mundo interior. Rio de Janeiro, 1951.

Phil 4967.20.20 — Farias Brito, Raymundo de. Trechos escolhidos. Rio de Janeiro, 1967.

Phil 4352.2 — Farias Brito. (Rabello, Sylvio.) Rio de Janeiro, 1941.

Phil 4352.2.2 — Farias Brito. (Rabello, Sylvio.) Rio de Janeiro, 1967.

Phil 4967.20.80 — Farias Brito e a filosofia do espirito. (Nogueira, A.) Rio de Janeiro, 1962.

Phil 4352.2.5 — Farias Brito on uma adventura do esprito. (Cruz Costa, Joao.) Sao Paulo, 1942.

Phil 2905.1.465 — Faricy, Robert L. Teilhard de Chardin's theology of the Christian in the world. N.Y., 1967.

Phil 8406.25 — Fariña Nuñez, Eloy.Conceptos estéticos mitos guaraníes. Buenos Aires, 1926.

Phil 5190.37 — Faris, John A. Truth-functional logic. London, 1962.

Phil 180.2.35 — Farkas, S. Filozófiai értekezések. Aiud-Nagyenyed, 1938.

Phil 8630.1 — Farlin, J.W. A primer on the origin of knowledge. Saratoga Springs, 1835.

Phil 8660.14 — Farmer, H.H. The world and God. London, 1935.

Phil 7068.86.10F — Farmer, John S. Twixt two worlds. London, 1886.

Phil 8660.10 — Farnell, Lewis R. The attributes of God. Oxford, 1925.

Phil 8406.12 — Farnell, Lewis R. Hedonism and art. London, 1928.

Phil 8406.30 — Farner, Konrad. Der Aufstand der Abstrakt-Konkreten. Neuwied, 1970.

Phil 7054.3 — Farnese, A. A wanderer in the spirit lands. Chicago, 1901.

Phil 5245.25 — Farnsworth, B.B. Practical psychology for men and women. N.Y., 1923.

Phil 978.29.10 — Farnsworth, E.C. The deeper mysteries. Portland, Maine, 1921.

Phil 978.29.15 — Farnsworth, E.C. Glimpses of inner truth. Portland, 1923.

Phil 978.29.5 — Farnsworth, E.C. The heart of things. Portland, Maine, 1914.

Phil 8080.10 — Farnsworth, E.C. The ideales and tendencies of modern art. Portland, 1917.

Phil 978.29 — Farnsworth, E.C. Special teachings from the arcane science. Portland, Maine, 1913.

Phil 5245.28F — Farpon y Tuñón, José. Discurso leido...2 de julio de 1898. Manila, 1898.

Phil 8880.19 — Farr, Lorin G. Ideal and real; the students calendar. Portland, Maine, 1904.

Htn Phil 6115.12* — Farr, Samuel. A philosophical enquiry into the nature, origin, and extent of animal motion. London, 1771.

Phil 8695.10 — Farrar, Adam Storey. Science in theology: sermons. Philadelphia, 1860.

Phil 6951.5.10 — Farrar, C.B. The autopathography of C.W. Beers. n.p., 1908.

Phil 6951.5.12 — Farrar, C.B. Twenty-five years of mental hygiene; a tribute to C.W. Beers. n.p., 1933.

Phil 9345.9 — Farrar, Eliza W. The young lady's friend. Boston, 1837.

Phil 9342.3A — Farrar, Eliza W.R. Young lady's friend. Boston, 1836.

Phil 8630.13.5 — Farrar, F.W. Future retribution. N.Y., 1885.

Phil 8630.13 — Farrar, F.W. Mercy and judgment. London, 1881.

Phil 1350.9.2 — Farrar, F.W. Seekers after God. London, 1868.

Phil 1350.9.5 — Farrar, F.W. Seekers after God. London, 1891.

Phil 1350.9 — Farrar, F.W. Seekers after God. Philadelphia, 1868.

Phil 585.222 — Farré, Luis. Antropología filosófica. Madrid, 1968.

Phil 4960.225 — Farré, Luis. Cincuenta años de filosofia en Argentina. Buenos Aires, 1958.

Phil 1705.12 — Farré, Luis. Unamuno, William James y Kirkegaard y otros ensayos. Buenos Aires, 1967.

Phil 193.49.80 — Farré, Luis. Vida y pensamiento de Jorge Santayana. Madrid, 1953.

Phil 3640.376 — Farré, R. De l'influence de Nietzsche sur la pensée politique allemande. Thèse. Baden-Baden, 1947.

Phil 5238.35 — Farrell, B.A. Experimental psychology. N.Y., 1955.

Author and Title Listing

	Phil 5755.14A	Farrer, A.M. The freedom of the will. London, 1958.
	Phil 5755.14.2	Farrer, A.M. The freedom of the will. 2. ed. London, 1963.
	Phil 9240.22	Farrer, Austin. Love almighty and ills unlimited. 1st ed. Garden City, N.Y., 1961.
	Phil 2266.80.3	Farrer, J.A. Adam Smith. London, 1881.
	Phil 2266.80	Farrer, J.A. Adam Smith. N.Y., 1881.
	Phil 1850.141	Farrington, B. Francis Bacon. N.Y., 1949.
	Phil 1020.30	Farrukh, O.A. The Arab genius in science and philosophy. 2d ed. Washington, 1954.
	Phil 8631.12	The farther shore; an anthology...on the immortality of the soul. (Griffin, N.E.) Boston, 1934.
	Phil 8955.14	al Faruqi, Ismàil Ragi A. Christian ethics: a historical and systematic analysis of its dominant ideas. Montreal, 1967.
	Phil 5645.24	Farvernes elementaere aestetik. (Lehmann, A.) Kjøbenhavn, 1884.
	Phil 6683.1	Fascination. (Newman, J.B.) N.Y., 1847.
	Phil 180.61	La fase attuale della filosofia. Messina, 1936.
	Phil 180.92	Fasel, Georg K. Metaphysik. Duisburg, 1969.
	Phil 8840.2	Fashion and philosophy. (Paton, H.J.) Oxford, 1937.
	Phil 9145.6	Fashionable society. (Eyre, L.L.) Philadelphia, 1889.
	Phil 8406.21	Fasola, Giusta Nicco. L'arte nella vita dell'uomo. Pisa, 1956.
	Phil 8050.52	Fasola, Guista Nicco. Della critica. Firenze, 1947.
	Phil 3850.30.90	Fassbender, Johann. Erkenntnislehre und Metaphysik Jakob Seuglers, 1799-1878. Inaug. Diss. Bonn, 1937.
	Phil 5755.20.2	Fassbender, Martin. Wollen; eine königliche Kunst. 2. und 3. Aufl. Freiburg, 1916.
	Phil 8955.3	Fassler, A. A new gospel. N.Y., 1908.
	Phil 5250.24	Fassliche Darstellung der Erfahrungsseelenlehre. (Kiesewetter, J.G.C.) Wien, 1817.
	Phil 6122.12	Fat and blood. (Mitchell, S.W.) Philadelphia, 1884.
	Phil 310.60	Fataliev, K.M. Dialekticheskii materializm i voprosy estestvoznaniia. Moskva, 1958.
	Phil 310.60.5	Fataliev, K.M. Marksistko-leninskaia filosofii i estestroznaniia. Moskva, 1960.
	Phil 5757.14.2	Fatalism or freedom. (Herrick, C.J.) N.Y., 1926.
	Phil 1190.20	Fatalisme et liberté dans l'antique grecque. (Amand de Merdito, Emmanuel.) Louvain, 1945.
	Phil 5752.12	Fate, logic, and time. (Cahn, Steven.) New Haven, 1967.
	Phil 8707.10	Fate and freedom. (Russell, H.N.) New Haven, 1927.
	Phil 6049.31.2	Fate in the making; revelations of lifetime. (Hamon, Louis.) N.Y., 1931.
	Phil 9035.35	Fate mastered, destiny fulfilled. (Colville, N.J.) London, 1903.
	Phil 165.230	The fate of man. (Brinton, Crane.) N.Y., 1961.
	Phil 5768.13	Fated or free? (Slosson, P.W.) Boston, 1914.
	Phil 4796.96.21	Fath 'Ali-Akhund-zada. Izbrannye filosfskie proizvedeniia. Moskva, 1962.
	Phil 4796.96.20	Fath 'Ali-Akhund-zada. Izbrannye filosofskie proizvedeniia. Baku, 1953.
	Phil 5871.108	Father, child, and sex role. (Biller, Henry B.) Lexington, 1971.
	Phil 2733.6.2	Father Malebranche, his treatise...Search after truth. 2d ed. (Malebranche, Nicolas.) London, 1700.
	Phil 4983.5.95	Father Varela. (McCadden, Joseph James.) N.Y., 1969.
	Phil 9345.10	A father's advice to his son. London, n.d.
	Phil 9345.1	Fathers gift to his son. N.Y., 1821.
	Phil 9175.2	A father's instructions to his children. (Percival, T.) Dublin, 1790.
X Cg	Phil 9346.6.3	A father's legacy to his daughters. (Gregory, John.) Albany, 1821.
	Phil 9346.6	A father's legacy to his daughters. (Gregory, John.) London, 1822.
Htn	Phil 9346.6.5*	A father's legacy to his daughters. (Gregory, John.) N.Y., 1775.
Htn	Phil 9346.6.2*	A father's legacy to his daughters. (Gregory, John.) Philadelphia, 1781.
	Phil 1112.2	The fathers of Greek philosophy. (Hampden, R.D.) Edinburgh, 1862.
	Phil 6118.2	La fatigue. (Ioteyko, Josefa.) Paris, 1920.
	Phil 6111.61.1	Fatigue and impairment in man. 1. ed. (Bartley, Samuel Howard.) N.Y., 1947.
	Phil 6122.7	La fatigue intellectuelle et physique. (Mosso, A.) Paris, 1894.
	Phil 5643.45	La fatigue oculaire et le surmenage visuel. (Dor, Louis.) Paris, 1900.
	Phil 6122.7.3.5	Fatique. (Mosso, A.) N.Y., 1904.
	Phil 2880.8.100	Fatone, V. El existencialismo y la libertad readoro. 1. ed. Buenos Aires, 1948.
	Phil 2880.8.100.2	Fatone, V. El existencialismo y la libertad readoro. 2. ed. Buenos Aires, 1949.
	Phil 8585.47	Fatone, Vicente. Temas de mistica y religion. Bahía Blance, 1963.
	Phil 5815.4	I fatti psichici della vita animale. (Falco, Francesco.) Lucca, 1880.
	Phil 5241.45	I fatti psichici elementari. (Baratono, Adelchi.) Torino, 1900.
	Phil 7068.92.65	I fatti spiritici e le ipotesi affrettate. (Ermacora, G.B.) Padova, 1892.
	Phil 802.5	I fattori della evoluzione filosofica. (Cesca, Giovanni.) Padova, 1892.
	Phil 3808.114.5	Fauconnet, A. L'esthetique de Schopenhauer. Paris, 1913.
	Phil 8585.13	Fauenstädt, C.M.J. Briefe über natürliche Religion. Leipzig, 1858.
	Phil 180.24	Faug, Balthasar. Les vraies bases de la philosophie. 3e éd. Paris, 1887.
	Phil 2805.113F	Faugère, Armand P. Défense de Blaise Pascal. Paris, 1868.
	Phil 5421.6	Faulkner, Edwin Jerome. Man's quest for security; a symposium. Lincoln, 1966.
	Phil 5460.14.10	Faure, Henri. Les appartenances du délirant. Paris, 1965.
	Phil 5460.10.2	Faure, Henri. Études sur l'hallucination. Thèse. Paris, 1930. 2v.
	Phil 5460.10.5	Faure, Henri. Les hallucinations. Paris, 1936.
	Phil 5460.14	Faure, Henri. Hallucinations et réalité. Paris, 1964.
	Phil 5460.14.5	Faure, Henri. Les objets dans la folie. Paris, 1965. 2v.
	Phil 850.13	Faure, J.A. L'Egypte et les présocratiques. Paris, 1923.
	Phil 2605.7.31	Fauré-Fremiet, P. Esquisse d'une philosophie concrète. 1. ed. Paris, 1954.
	Phil 5245.37	Fauré-Fremiet, P. Pensée et re-création. Paris, 1934.
	Phil 5520.82	Fauré-Frémiet, P. La recréation du réel et l'équivoque. Paris, 1940.
	Phil 960.210	Fausset, H.I. Anson. The flame and the light. London, 1958.
	Phil 960.212	Fausset, H.I. Anson. The flame and the light. N.Y., 1969[1958]
	Phil 525.246	Fausset, Hugh I'Anson. The lost dimension. London, 1966.
	Phil 3790.4.88	Faust, August. Heinrich Rickert und seine Stellung innerhalb der eutschen Philosophie der Gegenwart. Tübingen, 1927.
	Phil 3246.230	Faust, August. Johann Gottlieb Fichte. Breslau, 1938.
	Phil 180.49	Faust, August. Der Möglichkeitsgedanke. Heidelberg, 1931-1932. 2v.
	Phil 8900.9	Faust i fiziki. (Zdotusskii, Igor P.) Moskva, 1968.
	Phil 2905.1.85	Faut-il brûler Teilhard de Chardin? (Teldy-Naim, Robert.) Paris, 1959.
	Phil 5545.8	Fauth, F. Das Gedächtnis. Gütersloh, 1888.
	Phil 5545.10.9	Fauvel-Gourand, F. First fundamental basis of phreno-mnemotechnic principles. N.Y., 1844.
	Phil 5545.10.10	Fauvel-Gourand, F. Phreno-mnemotechny. n.p., 1844.
	Phil 5545.10	Fauvel-Gourand, F. Phreno-mnemotechny. v.1-2. N.Y., 1844.
	Phil 5545.10.5	Fauvel-Gourand, F. Phreno-mnemotechny dictionary. pt.1. N.Y., 1844.
	Phil 5585.222	Fauville, A. Perception tachistoscopique et communication. Louvain, 1963.
	Phil 2730.83	Favre, Charles. Essai sur la métaphysique...de Maine de Biran. Antibes, 1889.
	Phil 1200.6	Favre, Jules. La morale des stoiciens. Paris, 1888.
	Phil 4540.10	Favrhold, David. Filosofi og samfund. København, 1968.
	Phil 3925.16.105	Favrholdt, D. An interpretation and critique of Wittgenstein's Tractatus. Copenhagen, 1964.
	Phil 6629.2	Fawcett, Benjamin. Über Melankolie. Leipzig, 1785.
	Phil 180.2.9	Fawcett, E.D. The individual and reality. London, 1909.
	Phil 180.2	Fawcett, E.D. The riddle of the universe. London, 1893.
	Phil 180.2.5	Fawcett, E.D. World as imagination. Series 1-2. London, 1916-1921. 2v.
	Phil 180.2.15	Fawcett, E.D. The Zermatt dialogues. London, 1931.
	Phil 5215.3	Fay, J.W. American psychology. New Brunswick, N.J., 1939.
	Phil 5520.442	Fay, Warren H. Temporal sequence in the perception of speed. The Hague, 1966.
	Phil 400.62	Faye, Eugène de. Idéalisme et réalisme. Paris, 1920.
	Phil 286.1	Faye, H.A.E. L'origine du monde. Paris, 1884.
	Phil 4110.15.80	Fazio-Allmayer, Bruna. Esistenza e realtà nella fenomenologia di Vito Fazio-Allmayer. Bologna, 1968.
	Phil 8050.91	Fazio-Allmayer, Bruna. Richerche di estetica e il guidizio stoico. Bologna, 1968.
	Phil 3487.29	Fazio-Allmayer, Bruna. L'uomo nella storia in Kant. Bologna, 1968.
	Phil 3425.125	Fazio-Allmayer, C. La teoria della libertà nella filosofia di Hegel. Messina, 1920.
	Phil 180.30	Fazio-Allmayer, V. Materia e sensazione. Milano, 1913.
	Phil 8430.15	Fazio-Allmayer, V. Moralità dell'arte. Firenze, 1953.
	Phil 1850.124	Fazio-Allmayer, V. Saggio su Francesco Bacone. Palermo, 1928.
	Phil 3425.530	Fazio Allmayer, Vito. Ricerche hegeliane. Firenze, 1959.
	Phil 2880.8.305	Fé, Franco. Sartre e il comunismo. Firenze, 1970.
	Phil 9070.13	Fe y valor. (Pereira Alves, A.) El Paso, 1937?
	Phil 5401.01	Pamphlet box. Fear.
X Cg	Phil 5401.1.10	Fear. (Mosso, A.) London, 1896.
	Phil 5401.13.10	Fear. (Oliver, John R.) N.Y., 1931.
	Phil 7069.20.340	Fear not the crossing. (Williams, Gail.) N.Y., 1920.
	Phil 6819.6	The fear of being a woman; a theory of maternal destructiveness. (Rheingold, Joseph Cyrus.) N.Y., 1964.
	Phil 5478.14	Fear of failure. (Birney, Robert Charles.) N.Y., 1969.
	Phil 6315.19.5	The fear of freedom. (Schaar, John H.) London, 1942.
	Phil 5625.83	Fearing, F. Reflex action. Baltimore, 1930.
	Phil 5245.2	Fearn, J. First lines of the human mind. London, 1820.
	Phil 5245.2.2	Fearn, J. A manual of the physiology of mind. London, 1829.
	Phil 5643.40	Fearn, John. Rational of the cause of cerebral vision. London, 1830? 4 pam.
	Phil 9590.22.3	Fearon, Arthur D. How to think. San Francisco, 1944.
	Phil 5401.60	Fears and phobias. (Marks, Issac M.) N.Y., 1969.
	Phil 8585.50	Feaver, J. Clayton. Religion in philosophical and cultural perspective. Princeton, 1967.
	Phil 6955.17	Feber, G.H.A. Beschouwingen over Psychopathenstrafrecht. Zwolle, 1932.
	Phil 2750.11.100A	Fecher, C.A. The philosophy of Jacques Maritain. Westminster, 1953.
	Phil 3210.35	Fechner, G.T. Atomenlehre. Leipzig, 1864.
	Phil 3210.25	Fechner, G.T. Ausgewählte Schriften. Berlin, 1907.
	Phil 3210.67	Fechner, G.T. Das Büchlein vom Leben nach dem Tode. Dresden, 1836.
	Phil 3210.67.2	Fechner, G.T. Das Büchlein vom Leben nach dem Tode. 3. Aufl. Hamburg, 1887.
	Phil 3210.67.3	Fechner, G.T. Das Büchlein vom Leben nach dem Tode. 6. Aufl. Hamburg, 1906.
	Phil 3210.67.4	Fechner, G.T. Das Büchlein vom Leben nach dem Tode. 8. Aufl. Leipzig, 1922.
	Phil 3210.65A	Fechner, G.T. Drei Motive und Gründe des Glaubens. Leipzig, 1863.
	Phil 3210.61	Fechner, G.T. Einige Ideen zur Schöpfungs- und Entwickelungsgeschichte der Organismen. Leipzig, 1873.
	Phil 3210.47	Fechner, G.T. Elemente der Psychophysik. v.1-2. Leipzig, 1860.
	Phil 3210.66	Fechner, G.T. Erinnerungen an die letzten Tage der Odlehre und ihre Urhebers. Leipzig, 1876.
	Phil 3210.49	Fechner, G.T. In Sachen der Psychophysik. Leipzig, 1877.
	Phil 3210.26.5	Fechner, G.T. Kleine Schriften. 2. Aufl. Leipzig, 1913.
	Phil 3210.26	Fechner, G.T. Kleine Schriften von Dr. Mises (pseud.). Leipzig, 1875.
	Phil 3210.69	Fechner, G.T. Kollektivmasslehre. Leipzig, 1897.
	Phil 3210.67.5	Fechner, G.T. Little book of life after death. Boston, 1912.
	Phil 3210.58	Fechner, G.T. Der Mensch im Kosmos. Berlin, 1949.
	Phil 3210.59	Fechner, G.T. Nanna. Hamburg, 1908.
	Phil 3210.67.9	Fechner, G.T. On life after death. Chicago, 1914.
	Phil 3210.67.10	Fechner, G.T. On life after death. Chicago, 1945.
	Phil 3210.67.12	Fechner, G.T. On life after death. N.Y., 1943.
	Phil 3210.77	Fechner, G.T. Religion of a scientist. N.Y., 1946.
	Phil 3210.51	Fechner, G.T. Revision der Hauptpunkte der Psychophysik. Leipzig, 1882.
	Phil 3210.30A	Fechner, G.T. Tagesansicht gegenüber der Nachtansicht. Leipzig, 1879.
	Phil 3210.30.5	Fechner, G.T. Tagesansicht gegenüber der Nachtansicht. 3. Aufl. Leipzig, 1919.
	Phil 3210.42	Fechner, G.T. Über das höchste Gut. Leipzig, 1846.
	Phil 3210.53	Fechner, G.T. Über die Frage des Weber'schen Gesetzes. Leipzig, 1884.
	Phil 3210.70	Fechner, G.T. Über die Methode der richtigen und falschen Fälle. Leipzig, 1884.
	Phil 3210.34	Fechner, G.T. Über die physikalische und philosophische Atomenlehre. Leipzig, 1855.
	Phil 3210.45	Fechner, G.T. Über die Seelenfrage. Leipzig, 1861.

Phil 3210.45.10 Fechner, G.T. Über die Seelenfrage. 2. Aufl. Hamburg, 1907.
Phil 3210.63 Fechner, G.T. Vorschule der Aesthetik. v.1-2. Leipzig, 1876.
Phil 3210.75 Fechner, G.T. Wissenschaftliche Briefe. Hamburg, 1890.
Phil 3210.40 Fechner, G.T. Zend-Avesta. Hamburg, 1906.
Phil 6955.10 Fechner, Gustav. In Sachen der Psychophysik. Leipzig, 1877.
Phil 3270.16.31 Fechner, O. Das System der ontischen Kategorien. Hildesheim, 1961.
Phil 5045.13 Fechner, Oskar. Das Verhältnis der Kategorienlehre zur formalen Logik. Rostock, 1927.
Phil 3210.87 Fechner als Naturphilosoph und Christ. (Dennert, E.) Gütersloh, 1902.
Phil 3565.89.5 Fechner und Lotze. (Wentscher, M.) München, 1925.
Phil 3210.83 Fechner's Metaphysik. (Liebe, R.) Greifswald, 1903.
Phil 3210.83.2 Fechner's Metaphysik. (Liebe, R.) Leipzig, 1903.
Phil 3120.11.82 Fechter, Paul. Die Grundlagen der Realdialektik. Inaug. Diss. München, 1906.
Phil 2115.118 Fechtner, Eduard. John Locke, ein Bild aus den geistigen Kämpfen Englands. Stuttgart, 1898.
Phil 7150.32 Fedden, Henry R. Suicide, a social and historical study. London, 1938.
Phil 8622.80 Fede e mondo moderno. Roma, 1969.
Phil 8622.88 Fede e verità nel Cristianesimo contemporaneo. (Scoppio, Domenico.) Bari, 1968.
Phil 8520.9 La fede nel soprannaturale. (Anzoletti, Luisa.) Milano, 1894.
Phil 8401.2.10 Fedeles, Constantin. Versuch über Alison's Ästhetik, Darstellung und Kritik. München, 1911.
Phil 4080.3.500 Fedeltà a Croce. (Mattioli, Raffaele.) Milano, 1966.
Phil 3487.7 Feder, Ernst. Von G.E. Schulze zu A. Schopenhauer. Diss. Aarau, 1901.
Phil 5045.8.20 Feder, J.G.H. Erklaerung der Logik. Wien, 1793-94. 3v.
Phil 3270.5.79 Feder, J.G.H. G.J.H. Feder's Lebens Natur und Grundsätze. Leipzig, 1825.
Phil 5045.8.14 Feder, J.G.H. Institutiones logical et metaphysicae. 4a ed. Gottingae, 1797.
Phil 8880.40 Feder, J.G.H. Lehrbuch der praktischen Philosophie. Göttingen, 1770.
Phil 5045.8 Feder, J.G.H. Logik und Metaphysik. Göttingen, 1769.
Phil 5045.8.5 Feder, J.G.H. Logik und Metaphysik. Wien, 1779.
Phil 180.50 Feder, J.G.H. Philosophische Bibliotek. v.1-4. Göttingen, 1788-1791. 2v.
Phil 3487.6 Feder, J.G.H. Ueber Raum und Caussalitat. Göttingen, 1787.
Phil 3246.241 Fédéralisme et raison d'état dans la pensée internationale de Fichte. (Vlachos, G.) Paris, 1948.
Phil 3246.241.5 Fédéralisme et raison d'état dans la pensée internationale de Fichte. Thèse. (Vlachos, G.) Paris, 1948.
Phil 15.65 Fédération française de la libre pensée. Bulletin mensuel de correspondance des groupes et adhérents fédérés. Paris. 1890-1893
Phil 2477.6.103 Federici Ajeoldi, G. Interpretazione del problema dell'essere in M. Blondel. Firenze, 1936.
Phil 3640.293 Federico Nietzsche. (Beonio-Brocchieri, V.) Roma, 1926.
Phil 3640.123 Federico Nietzsche. (Zoccoli, Ettore G.) Modena, 1898.
Phil 3640.62 Federico Nietzsche. 3. ed. (Nietzsche, Friedrich.) Milano, 1944.
Phil 3640.289 Federico Nietzsche y el anarquismo intelectual. (Sanz y Escartin, Eduardo.) Madrid, 1898.
Phil 7069.68.35 Federmann, Reinhard. Botschaft aus dem Jenseits. Tübingen, 1968.
Phil 8406.9 Federn, Karl. Das aesthetische Problem. Hannover, 1928.
Phil 6315.18.10 Federn, Paul. Ego psychology and the psychoses. N.Y., 1955.
Phil 6315.18.5 Federn, Paul. Ich-psychologie und die Psychosen. Bern, 1956.
Phil 6315.18 Federn, Paul. Das psychoanalytische Volksbuch. Bern, 1939.
Phil 6315.18.4 Federn, Paul. Das psychoanalytische Volksbuch. 5. Aufl. Bern, 1957.
Phil 4110.8.30 Fedi, Remo. Il bene e la libertà. Milano, 1944.
Phil 8980.386 Fedorenko, I.H. Kommunisticheskaia nravntvennost'. Kiev, 1958.
Phil 8980.386.5 Fedorenko, I.H. Osnovy marksistsko-leninskoi etiki. Kiev, 1958.
Phil 4756.2.30 Fedorov, N.F. Filosofiia obshchago dela. Izd.2. Kharbin, 1928-
Phil 4756.2.30.5 Fedorov, N.F. Filosofiia obshchago dela. v.2. Vernyi, 1913-
Phil 8585.45 Fedorov, N.I. U tserkovnoi ogrady. Buenos Aires, 1955.
Phil 310.10 Fedoseev, P.N. Usloviia materialicheskoi zhizni obshchestva. Moskva, 1954.
Phil 310.618 Fedoseev, Petr. Dialektika sovremennoi epokhi. Moskva, 1966.
Phil 6980.286 Fedotov, D.D. Ocherki po istorii otechestvennoi psikhiatrii, ytoria polovina XVIII. Moskva, 1957.
Phil 5815.1 Fée, A.L.A. Etudes philosophiques...animaux. Strasburg, 1853.
Phil 6750.11 Feeble minded, guide to study. (Sherlock, E.B.) London, 1911.
Phil 6750.13 Feeble-minded citizens in Pennsylvania. (Key, Wilhelmine E.) Philadelphia, 1915.
Phil 6750.15 Feeble-mindedness and insanity. (National Conference of Charities and Corrections.) Chicago, 1916?
Phil 5535.40 Feedback and human behavior. (Annett, John.) Baltimore, 1969.
Phil 5400.93.1 Feeling and emotion. (Gardiner, Harry Norman.) Westport, 1970.
Phil 338.36 Feeling and expression. (Hampshire, S.) London, 1961.
Phil 8412.40 Feeling and form; a theory of art developed from philosophy in a new key. (Langer, Susanne Katherina Knauth.) N.Y., 1953.
Phil 5400.57 Feeling experience and its modalities. (Phelan, G.B.) London, 1925.
Phil 5300.2A The feeling of effort. (James, W.) Boston, 1880.
Phil 5421.10 The feeling of superiority and anxiety-superior. (Remits, Ernest L.) Ottawa, 1955.
Phil 5258.19.5 Feeling psychologically treated. (Snider, D.J.) St.Louis, 1905.
NEDL Phil 5400.52 Feelings and emotions. (Feleky, A.) N.Y., 1922.
Phil 5400.65A Feelings and emotions. (Regmart, Martin L.) Worcester, Mass., 1928.
Phil 5400.30 The feelings of man. (Harvey, N.A.) Baltimore, 1914.
Phil 7069.26.90 Feerhow, F. Die menschliche Aura und ihre experimentelle Erforschung. 2.-3. Aufl. Leipzig, 1926.

Phil 3120.40.82 Feestbundel aangeboden aan Dr. J.D. Bierens de Haan. Assen, 1936.
Phil 5850.385.30 Fehlerbehandlung und Fehlerbewertung. (Weimer, H.) Leipzig, 1926.
Phil 8406.19 Feibleman, J. Aesthetics. N.Y., 1949.
Phil 180.77 Feibleman, James. Foundations of empiricism. The Hague, 1962.
Phil 180.75 Feibleman, James. Inside the great mirror. The Hague, 1958.
Phil 2225.5.100 Feibleman, James. An introduction to Peirce's philosophy. 1st ed. N.Y., 1946.
Phil 8880.55 Feibleman, James. Moral strategy. The Hague, 1967.
Phil 480.10 Feibleman, James. The new materialism. The Hague, 1970.
Phil 180.76 Feibleman, James. Ontology. Baltimore, 1951.
Phil 2005.9.32 Feibleman, James. Philosophers lead sheltered lives. London, 1952.
Phil 8695.11 Feibleman, James. The pious scientist. N.Y., 1958.
Phil 1170.15 Feibleman, James. Religious Platonism. London, 1959.
Phil 2005.9.30 Feibleman, James. The revival of realism. Chapel Hill, 1946.
Phil 2005.9.20 Feibleman, James. The two story world. 1st ed. N.Y., 1966.
Phil 2005.9.34 Feibleman, James. The way of a man. N.Y., 1969.
Phil 3450.19.255 Feick, Hildegard. Index zu Heideggers Sein und Zeit. Tübingen, 1961.
Phil 3450.19.1.2 Feick, Hildegard. Index zu Heideggers "Sein und Zeit". 2e Aufl. Tübingen, 1968.
Phil 8612.30 Feier, I. Essais sur la mort. Bucarest, 1939.
Phil 8520.55 Feiereis, Konrad. Die Umprägung der natürlichen Theologie in Religionsphilosophie. Leipzig, 1965.
Phil 8500.12 Feigel, F.K. Die französische Neokriticismus. Tübingen, 1913.
Phil 165.402 Feigl, Herbert. Readings in philosophical analysis. N.Y., 1949.
Phil 4466.5.30 Feijó, Diogo Antonio. Cadernos de filosofia. São Paulo, 1967.
Phil 665.42.5 Feilberg, Ludvig. Nutids själavård; om största utbytet av själens gåvor. Stockholm, 1917.
Phil 665.42 Feilberg, Ludvig. Om ligeløb og Kredsning i Sjaelelivet. Kjøbenhavn, 1896.
Phil 4540.5 Feilberg, Ludvig. Samlede skrifter. 3. udg. København, 1949- 2v.
Phil 7069.63.10 Feilding, Everard. Sittings with Eussapia Palladino and other studies. New Hyde Park, 1963.
Phil 6955.20 Fein, Rashi. Economics of mental illness. N.Y., 1958.
Phil 5545.9 Feinaigle, G. von. New art of memory. London, 1812.
Phil 8585.48 Feiner, Johannes. Mysterium salutis. Einsiedeln, 1965. 4v.
Phil 6121.26 Der Feinere bau des Nervensystems im Lichte neuester Forschungen. (Lenhossék, Mihaly.) Berlin, 1893.
Phil 190.110 Feiten, waarden, gebeurtenissen. Een deiktische ontologie. (Peursen, Cornetis A. van.) Hilversum, 1965[1966].
Phil 3475.3.80 Feith, R.C. Psychologismus und Transzendentalismus bei K. Jaspers. Bern, 1945.
Phil 8587.78 Fel sefe söligü. (Hançerlioğlu, Orhan.) Istanbul, 1967.
Phil 4812.196.80 Felber, Stanislav. Ján Bayer, slovenský baconista XVII storočia. Bratislava, 1953.
Phil 5245.19.5 Feldegg, F. Beiträge zur Philosophie des Gefühls. Leipzig, 1900.
Phil 5245.19 Feldegg, F. Das Gefühl als Fundament der Weltordnung. Wien, 1890.
Phil 6115.30 Feldenkrais, M. Body and mature behavior. N.Y., 1949.
Phil 3549.2.80 Feldkeller, P. Graf Keyserlings Erkenntnisweg zum Übersinnlichen. Darmstadt, 1922.
Phil 5245.49 Feldkeller, P. Das unpersönliche Denken. Berlin, 1949.
Phil 180.43 Feldkeller, Paul. Verständigung als philosophisches Problem. Erfurt, 1928.
Phil 8585.32 Feldman, R.V. The domain of selfhood. London, 1934.
Phil 5520.260 Feldman, Sandor S. Mannerisms of speech and gestures in everyday life. N.Y., 1959.
Phil 8120.7 Feldman, V. L'esthétique française contemporaine. Paris, 1936.
Phil 1955.6.95 Feldman, W.T. The philosophy of John Dewey. Baltimore, 1934.
Phil 1955.6.96 Feldman, W.T. The philosophy of John Dewey. Baltimore, 1934.
Phil 180.37 Feldmann, J. Schule der Philosophie. Paderborn, 1925.
Phil 5590.542 Fel'dshtein, David I. Psikhologicheskie problemy formirovaniia nravstvennykh kachestv lichnosti v podrostkovom vozraste. Dushanbe, 1969.
Phil 3450.19.50 Der Feldweg. (Heidegger, Martin.) Frankfurt, 1953.
NEDL Phil 5400.52 Feleky, A. Feelings and emotions. N.Y., 1922.
Phil 4803.522.20 Feleton polityczno-literacki. (Libelt, Karol.) Poznań, 1846.
Phil 525.175 Felice, Philippe de. Foules en délire. Paris, 1947.
Phil 4070.6.80 Felice Battaglia. (Marchello, G.) Torino, 1953.
Phil 9400.4A The felicities of sixty. (Lionberger, I.H.) Boston, 1922.
Phil 4352.1.150 Feliu Egidio, Vicente. Sistematizacion del pensamiento de Balmes en orden a la filosofia de la historia. Madrid, 1952.
Phil 6946.1.20 Felix, Robert Hanna. Mental illness; progress and prospects. N.Y., 1967.
Phil 2855.3.81 Félix Ravaisson. (Dopp, Joseph.) Louvain, 1933.
Phil 6128.66 Felix Schottlaender zum Gedächtnis. (Stuttgart. Institut für Psychotherapie und Tiefenpsychologie.) Stuttgart, 1959.
Phil 180.51 Felkin, F.W. A wordbook of metaphysics. London, 1932.
Phil 2880.8.150 Fell, Joseph P. Emotion in thought of Sartre. N.Y., 1965.
Phil 5750.001 Fellin, J. Die Willensfreiheit; zur Bibliographie. Graz, 1928.
Phil 8599.19.95 Fellner, Karl. Das überweltliche Gut und die innerweltlichen Güter. Diss. Leipzig, 1927.
Phil 8585.3 Fellowes, R. The religion of the universe. London, 1836.
Phil 8585.3.2 Fellowes, R. The religion of the universe. London, 1836.
Phil 5585.252 Fellows, Brian S. The discrimination process and development. 1. ed. Oxford, 1968.
Phil 5545.38.26 Fellows, G.S. "Loisette" exposed. N.Y., n.d.
Phil 2750.19.110 The fellowship of being; an essay on the concept of person in the philosophy of Gabriel Marcel. (O'Malley, John B.) The Hague, 1966.
Phil 384.20 Fellowship of Religious Humanists. Freedom of choice. Yellow Springs, Ohio, 1970.
Phil 7069.20.100 The fellowship of the picture. (Dearmer, Nancy K.) N.Y., 1920.
Htn Phil 2005.4.30F* Felltham, Owen. Resolves: Divine, moral, political. London, 1677.
Phil 978.49.855 Fels, Alice. Studien zur Einführung in die Mysteriendramen Rudolf Steiners. 2. Aufl. Dornach, 1961.

Phil 3120.2.95   Fels, Heinrich. Bernard Bolzano. Leipzig, 1929.
Phil 5245.29   Felsch. Die Hauptpunkte der Psychologie. Cöthen, 1904.
Phil 15.13   Felsefe arkivi. Istanbul. 1+ 3v.
Phil 195.13   Felsejeye gini. (Ulken, Hilmi Zuja.) Ankara, 1957. 2 pam.
Phil 8870.11   Felseneer, Jean. Morale de savants d'Hippocrate à Einstein. Bruxelles, 1946.
Phil 3428.91   Felsh. Erläuterungen zu Herbarts Ethik. Langensalza, 1899.
Phil 8880.1.15   Feltham, O. The beauties of Owen Felltham. N.Y., 1803.
Phil 8880.1.4   Feltham, O. Resolves. Cambridge, 1832.
Htn Phil 8880.1*   Feltham, O. Resolves. London, 1636.
Htn Phil 8880.1.12*   Feltham, O. Resolves. London, 1670.
Phil 8880.1.2   Feltham, O. Resolves. London, 1806.
Phil 8880.1.3   Feltham, O. Resolves. London, 1840.
Htn Phil 8880.1.3.2*   Feltham, O. Resolves. London, 1840.
Phil 8880.1.7   Feltham, O. Resolves. London, 1904.
Htn Phil 8880.1.8*   Feltham, O. Resolves. 2nd ed. London, 1628. 2 pam.
Htn Phil 8880.1.9*   Feltham, O. Resolves. 3rd ed. London, 1628.
Htn Phil 8880.1.10*   Feltham, O. Resolves. 4th ed. London, 1631.
Htn Phil 8880.1.11*   Feltham, O. Resolves. 5th ed. London, 1634.
Htn Phil 8800.6*   Feltham, Owen. Resolves. London, 1661.
Htn Phil 8800.6.2*   Feltham, Owen. Resolves. London, 1677.
Htn Phil 8800.6.5*   Feltham, Owen. Resolves. London, 1696.
Phil 8406.11   Feltkamp, W.C. Zien en verstaan. Amsterdam, 1946.
Phil 9345.2   Female aegis. London, 1798.
Phil 4073.120.5   Femiano, Salvatore Beniamino. La metafisica di Tommaso Campanella. Milano, 1968.
Phil 4073.120   Femiano, Salvatore Beniamino. Lo spiritualismo di Tommasco Campanella. Napoli, 1965. 2v.
Phil 6317.22.25   Feminine psychology. (Horney, Karen.) N.Y., 1967.
Phil 2475.1.257   Fénart, Michel. Les assertions bergsoniennes. Paris, 1936.
Phil 6315.16.8   Fenichel, Otto. Collected papers. N.Y., 1953-54. 2v.
Phil 6980.289.5   Fenichel, Otto. Perversionen, Psychosen, Charakterstörungen. Darmstadt, 1967.
Phil 6980.289   Fenichel, Otto. Problemas de ténica psicoanalitica. México, 1960.
Phil 6315.16.10   Fenichel, Otto. The psychoanalytic theory of neurosis. N.Y., 1945.
Phil 5850.196   Fenlason, Anne. Essentials in interviewing. N.Y., 1962.
Phil 5246.50   I fenomeni psichici. (Grassi-Bertazzi, G.B.) Catania, 1898.
Phil 325.3   Fenomenismo. (Sacheli, C.A.) Genova, 1925.
Phil 3625.3.84   Fenomenismo e relativismo nel pensiero di E. Mach. (Moschetti, L.) Genova, 1923.
Phil 1750.115.165   La fenomenologia. 1. ed. (Sini, Carlo.) Milano, 1965.
Phil 4200.9.30   La fenomenologia contemporanea e il problema dell'uomo. (Pucci, Raffaele.) Napoli, 1963.
Phil 3450.11.280   A fenomenologia de Husserl como fundamento. (Fragata, Júlio.) Braga, 1959.
Phil 192.110   Fenomenologia de la accion del hombre. (Rubert Condan, José Marin.) Madrid, 1961.
Phil 735.282   Fenomenologia del valore. (Preti, Giulio.) Milano, 1942.
Phil 3450.11.101.50   La fenomenologia di Husserl. (Pedroli, Guido.) Torino, 1958.
Phil 3450.11.435   La fenomenologia di Husserl e il pensiero contemporaneo. (Oggioni, Emilio.) Bologna, 1963.
Phil 1750.115.20   Fenomenologia e sociologia. (Archivio di Filosofia.) Padova, 1951.
Phil 583.18   Fenomenologie a problém intersubjektivity. 1. Vyd. (Mokrejš, Antonín.) Praha, 1969.
Phil 3585.20.10   Fenomenologie en atheisme. (Luijpen, Wilhelmus Antonius Maria.) Utrecht, 1963.
Phil 1750.690   Fenomenologie en emperische Menskunde. (Strasser, S.) Arnhem, 1962.
Phil 3585.20.22   Fenomenologie en metafysica. (Luijpen, Wilhelmus Antonius Maria.) Utrecht, 1966.
Phil 1750.115.55   De fenomenologie is een humorisme. (Luijpen, Wilhelmus Antonius Maria.) Amsterdam, 1961.
Phil 3585.20.30   Fenomenologie van het natuurrecht door W. Luijpen. (Luijpen, Wilhelmus Antonius Maria.) Utrecht, 1969.
Phil 2750.20.80   De fenomenologie van Merleau-Ponty. (Kwant, Remigius Cornelius.) Utrecht, 1962.
Phil 1750.115.75   Fenomenologiia i estetika. (Nikolov, Elit I.) Sofiia, 1965.
VPhil 3450.11.490   Fenomenologija analiza in kritika filosofije Edmunda Husserla. (Logar, Cene.) Ljubljana, 1970.
Phil 9220.18   Fentener van Vlissingen, Johannes. Een psychologische theorie van de vriendschap. Proefschrift. Arnhem, 1966.
Phil 4080.3.458   Feo, Italo de. Benedetto Croce e il suo mondo. Torino, 1966.
Phil 9070.112   Feofanov, Iurii V. Lichnoe dostoianie i lichnoe destoinstvo. Moskva, 1966.
Phil 9150.32   Ferabino, Aldo. Storia dell'uomo avantie dopo Cristo. Assisi, 1957.
Phil 6315.60   Ferdinand, Theodore N. Typologies of delinquency. N.Y., 1966.
Phil 5440.7   Féré, C. La famille névropathique. Paris, 1898.
Phil 6675.2   Féré, C. La médecine d'imagination. Paris, 1886.
Phil 5635.7   Féré, C. Sensation et mouvement. Paris, 1900.
Phil 9450.5   Ferencz II Rakoczi, Prince of Transylvania. Testament politique et moral. La Haye, 1751.
Phil 6315.1.16   Ferenczi, Sandor. Bausteine zur Psychoanalyse. Leipzig, 1927-39. 4v.
Phil 6315.1   Ferenczi, Sandor. Contributions to psycho-analysis. Boston, 1916.
Phil 6315.1.17   Ferenczi, Sandor. The development of psychoanalysis. N.Y., 1925.
Phil 6315.1.15   Ferenczi, Sandor. Final contributions to the problems and methods of psychoanalysis. London, 1955.
Phil 6315.1.18A   Ferenczi, Sandor. First contributions to psychoanalysis. London, 1952.
Phil 6315.1.13   Ferenczi, Sandor. Further contributions to the theory and technique of psycho-analysis. N.Y., 1927.
Phil 6315.1.20   Ferenczi, Sandor. Populäre vorträge über Psychoanalyse. Leipzig, 1922.
Phil 6315.1.5   Ferenczi, Sandor. Psycho-analysis and the war neurosis. Photoreproduction. London, 1921.
Phil 6315.1.10   Ferenczi, Sandor. Sex in psychoanalysis. N.Y., 1950.
Phil 6315.1.7   Ferenczi, Sandor. Versuch einer Genitaltheorie. Leipzig, 1924.
Phil 5585.246   Ferenczi, Victor. La perception de l'espace projectif. (Étude réalisée auprès des travailleurs africains analphabètes en France. Montréal, 1966.
Htn Phil 9345.6*   Fergurson, F. The young man. Nashua, N.H., 1848.

Phil 8800.7   Ferguson, A. Principles of moral and political science. Edinburgh, 1792. 2v.
Phil 8880.3   Ferguson, Adam. Grundsätze der Moralphilosophie. Leipzig, 1772.
Phil 8880.3.5   Ferguson, Adam. Institutes of moral philosophy. Edinburgh, 1769.
Phil 8585.18   Ferguson, G. The religion of democracy. N.Y., 1900.
Phil 7054.66   Ferguson, J.B. A record of communications from the spirit-spheres. Nashville, 1854.
Phil 180.63A   Ferm, V. First adventures in philosophy. N.Y., 1936.
Phil 805.10   Ferm, V. A history of philosophical systems. N.Y., 1950.
Phil 5627.149   Ferm, V. Religion in transition. London, 1937.
Phil 3090.42   Fermenta cognitionis. pt. 1-6. (Baader, Franz von.) Berlin, 1822-25. 5v.
Phil 4983.1.30   Fermentario. (Vaz Ferreira, Carlos.) Buenos Aires, 1940.
Phil 4983.1.32   Fermentario. (Vaz Ferreira, Carlos.) Montevideo, 1953.
Phil 5465.216   Fernald, Mabel Ruth. The diagnosis of mental imagery. Thesis. Princeton, N.J., 1912.
Phil 5440.17   Fernald, W.M. View at the foundatiuons...of character. Boston, 1865.
Phil 8880.60   Fernand-Laurent, Camille J. Morale et tyrannies. Paris, 1967.
Phil 8585.24   Fernandes de Santanna, Manuel. Apologetica. Lisboa, 1901.
Phil 9245.116   Fernández, Julio F. Proyecciónes espirituales del sufrimiento radiografia del dolor. San Salvador, 1964.
Phil 6315.56   Fernandez, M. The horizons of the mind. N.Y., 1964.
Phil 575.66   Fernandez, R. De la personnalité. Paris, 1928.
Phil 480.6   Fernandez de Santanna, M. O materialismo em face da sciencia. Lisboa, 1899. 2v.
Phil 4351.4.80   Fernández Largo, Jacinto. Introduccion al estudio del filósofo rancio. Madrid, 1959.
Phil 672.208   Fernández Suárez, Alvaro. El tiempo y el "hay". Madrid, 1955.
Phil 3525.95   Fernandez Valbuena, Ramiro. Se opone El Krausismo a la fé católica? Badajoz, 1882[1883]
Phil 4356.1.80   Fernando de Córdoba. (Ronilla y San Martin, A.) Madrid, 1911.
Phil 5245.42   Fernberger, Samuel W. Elementary general psychology. N.Y., 1937.
Phil 5635.24   Fernberger, Samuel W. Relation of methods of just perceptible differences and constant stimuli. n.p., 1912.
X Cg Phil 7075.152   Ferne Lände, fremde Sitten. 1. Aufl. (Luvandowski, Herbert.) Stuttgart, 1958.
Phil 5755.12   Fernkorn, C.M. Willensfreiheit und Verantwortlichkeit. Greifswald, 1927.
Phil 6400.11   Ferrand, Auguste. Le langage, la parole et les aphasies. Paris, 1894.
Phil 8406.16   Ferrant, Angel. La eseneia humana de las formos. Santander, 1952.
Phil 5045.4   Ferrari, Ambrogio. Introduzione alla logica. Alessandria, 1895.
Phil 4110.5.28   Ferrari, G. Filosofia della rivoluzione. v.1-2. Londra, 1851.
Phil 4110.5.30   Ferrari, G. Filosofia della rivoluzione. v.1-2. 2. ed. Milano, 1873.
Phil 4110.5.33   Ferrari, G. Filosofia della rivoluzione. 2. ed. Milano, 1923.
Phil 4260.81.10   Ferrari, G. Il genio di Vico. Lanciano, 1922.
Phil 4260.81   Ferrari, G. La mente di Giambattista Vico. Milano, 1837.
Phil 4260.81.5   Ferrari, G. Vico et l'Italie. Paris, 1839.
Phil 5400.62   Ferrari, G.C. Le emozioni e la vita del subcosciente. Bologna, 1911.
Phil 5245.22   Ferrari, G.C. Psychological papers. Reggio, 1896-1900.
Phil 6115.25   Ferrari, G.C. Ricerche ergografiche nella donna. Reggio Emilia, 1898.
Phil 4110.3.89   Ferrari, G.M. Commemorazione di Francesco Fiorentino. Roma, 1891.
Phil 3825.6   Ferrari, G.M. L'etica di B. Spinoza. Napoli, 1902.
Phil 4080.11.80F   Ferrari, G.M. Giovanni Caroli e la sua dottrina filosofica. Modena, 1926.
Phil 4260.99   Ferrari, G.M. Il Leibnitz gindicato da G.B. Vico. n.p., n.d.
Phil 8880.39   Ferrari, G.M. Il problema etico. Rome, 1902.
Phil 4215.1.80.5   Ferrari, Giuseppe. La mente di G.D. Romagnosi. Milano, 1913.
Phil 4215.1.80   Ferrari, Giuseppe. La mente di G.D. Romagnosi. Prato, 1839.
Phil 180.29   Ferrari, Giuseppe M. Scritti varj. v.1-3. Roma, 1899-1927. 3v.
Phil 2115.122   Ferrari, M. Locke e il sensismo francese. Modena, 1900.
Phil 4065.114   Ferrari, Sante. G. Bruno, F. Fiorentino, T. Mamiani. Mantova, 1887.
Phil 480.1   Ferraris, C.F. Il materialismo storico. Palermo, 1897.
Phil 8880.54   Ferraro, L. Dell'egoismo. Novara, 1963.
Phil 805.13.5.2   Ferrater, Mora José. El hombre en la encrucijada. 2. ed. Buenos Aires, 1965.
Phil 8612.56   Ferrater Mora, José. Being and death. Berkeley, Calif., 1965.
Phil 90.4   Ferrater Mora, José. Diccionario de filosofía. México, 1941.
Phil 90.4.10   Ferrater Mora, José. Diccionario de filosofía. 2. ed. México, 1944.
Phil 90.4.15   Ferrater Mora, José. Diccionario de filosofía. 3. ed. Buenos Aires, 1951.
Phil 90.4.16   Ferrater Mora, José. Diccionario de filosofía. 4. ed. Buenos Aires, 1958.
Phil 90.4.17   Ferrater Mora, José. Diccionario de filosofía. 5. ed. Buenos Aires, 1965.
Phil 585.402   Ferrater Mora, José. Els mots i els homes. 1. ed. Barcelona, 1970.
Phil 1740.12   Ferrater Mora, José. La filosofía actual. Madrid, 1969.
Phil 5066.110   Ferrater Mora, José. Lógica matemática. México, 1955.
Phil 805.13   Ferrater Mora, José. Man at the crossroads. Boston, 1957.
Phil 4356.3   Ferrater Mora, José. Obras selectas. Madrid, 1967. 2v.
Phil 8612.56.5   Ferrater Mora, José. El ser la muerte. Madrid, 1962.
Phil 4356.3.5   Ferrater Mora, José. El ser y el sentido. Madrid, 1967.
Phil 4356.3.10   Ferrater Mora, José. Variaciones sobre el espíritu. Buenos Aires, 1945.
Phil 9120.1   Ferraz, M. Philosophie du devoir. Paris, 1869.
Phil 2405.1   Ferraz, Marin. Etude sur la philosophie en France au XIXe siècle. Paris, 1877.
Phil 2405.2.5   Ferraz, Marin. Histoire de la philosophie pendant la révolution (1789-1804). Paris, 1889.
Phil 2405.2.3   Ferraz, Marin. Spiritualisme et libéralisme. 2e éd. Paris, 1887.
Phil 2405.2.2   Ferraz, Marin. Traditionalisme et ultramontanisme. 2e éd. Paris, 1880.

Phil 4210.115   Ferré, Pietro M. Degli universali secondo la teoria rosminiana. Casale, 1880-86. 11v.

Phil 4210.86   Ferre, Pietro Maria. Esposizione del principo filosofico di Rosmini. Verona, 1859.

Phil 5643.92   Ferree, C.E. Studies in physiological optics, Dec. 1928-Oct. 1934. Baltimore, 1934. 2v.

Phil 4466.4.30   Ferreira, A. Ensaios de filosofia para a história. Coimbra, 1962.

Phil 8695.5.3   Ferreira da Silva, A.J. A cultura das sciencias e os ensinamentos da igreja. Porto, 1908.

Phil 8695.5.5   Ferreira da Silva, A.J. Duas allocuçōs; a religiaō, amparo do homen na vida. Porto, 1911.

Phil 8695.5   Ferreira da Silva, A.J. O ideal religioso e a cultura scientifica. Porto, 1908.

Phil 5520.4   Ferrero, G. Les lois psychologiques du symbolisme. Paris, 1895.

Phil 1350.14   Ferrero, L. Storia del pitagorismo nel mondo romano. Torino, 1955.

Phil 3801.386   Ferri, Ettore de. La filosofia dell'identità di F. Schelling. Torino, 1925.

Phil 4005.1   Ferri, L. Essai sur l'histoire de la philosophie en Italie. Paris, 1869. 2v.

Phil 5325.2.5   Ferri, L. La psicologia dell'associazione dall'Hobbes. Roma, 1894.

Phil 4200.1.5F   Ferri, L. La psicologia di Pietro Pomponazzi. Roma, 1876.

Phil 5325.2   Ferri, L. La psychologie de l'association. Paris, 1883.

Phil 4110.5.95F   Ferri, Luigi. Cenno su Giuseppe Ferrari e le sul dottrine. Roma, 1877.

Phil 180.25F   Ferri, Luigi. Della idea del vero e...dell'essere. Roma, 1887.

Phil 1158.7   Ferri, Luigi. L'epicureismo e l'atomismo. Firenze, 1871.

Phil 4110.4.79   Pamphlet box. Ferri, Luigi.

Phil 7140.131   Ferri, N.A. The behavior of health. Boston, 1937.

Phil 4110.4.90F   Ferri commemorazione prof. Luigi. Roma, 1885.

Phil 7060.15   Ferriar, J. Essay towards a theory of apparitions. London, 1813.

Phil 6115.3   Ferrier, D. The Croonian lectures on cerebral localisation. London, 1890.

Phil 6115.3.5   Ferrier, D. The functions of the brain. N.Y., 1876.

Phil 6115.3.6   Ferrier, D. The functions of the brain. 2d ed. London, 1886.

Phil 1990.30   Ferrier, J.F. Institutes of metaphysic. Edinburgh, 1854.

Phil 1990.30.2   Ferrier, J.F. Institutes of metaphysic. 2nd ed. Edinburgh, 1856.

Phil 1110.1.5   Ferrier, J.F. Lectures on Greek philosophy. v.2. Edinburgh, 1866.

Phil 1110.1.6   Ferrier, J.F. Lectures on Greek philosophy. 2nd ed. Edinburgh, 1875.

Phil 1990.10A   Ferrier, J.F. Philosophical works. Edinburgh, 1875. 3v.

Phil 1990.10.5   Ferrier, J.F. Philosophical works. v.2. Edinburgh, 1881.

Phil 1110.1.7   Ferrier, J.F. Philosophical works. v.2. Edinburgh, 1888.

Phil 1990.79   Pamphlet box. Ferrier, James Frederick.

Phil 1750.515   Ferrier, Jean Louis. L'homme dans le monde. Neuchâtel, 1957.

Phil 978.50   Ferrier, John T. Life's mysteries unveiled. London, 1923.

Phil 1990.80   Ferrier James Frederick. (Haldane, E.S.) London, n.d.

Phil 8585.37   Ferrière, A. L'essentiel. Lausanne, 1952.

Phil 5245.75   Ferrière, A. L'orthogenèse lumaine. Neuchâtel, 1959.

Phil 6115.4   Ferrière, E. L'âme est la fonction du cerveau. Paris, 1883. 2v.

Phil 3825.1   Ferrière, E. La doctrine de Spinoza. Paris, 1899.

Phil 8735.21   Ferrière, Émile. La cause première d'après les données experimentales. Paris, 1897.

Phil 8585.4   Ferrières, C.E. Le théisme. 2. éd. v.1-2. Paris, 1790.

Phil 8880.2   Ferris, S. Mental perceptions. London, 1807.

Phil 180.41   Ferro, A.A. Concetto della filosofia. Savona, 1902.

Phil 3246.209   Ferro, A.A. La filosofia di G.A. Fichte. Savona, 1906.

Phil 180.41.10   Ferro, A.A. Scritti filosofici. Milano, 1932.

Phil 3903.1.91   Ferro, A.A. La teoria della conoscenza in G. Volkelt. Aosta, 1903.

Phil 180.54   Fersen, Alessandro. L'universo come guioco. Modena, 1936.

Phil 5625.114   Ferster, Charles B. Behavior principles. N.Y., 1968.

Phil 5625.97   Ferster, Charles B. Schedules of reinforcement. N.Y., 1957.

Phil 848.6   Fertig, Hermann. Die Auflösung der klassischen Substanzkonzeption und ein Versuch Rehabilitierung. Inaug. Diss. München, 1965.

Phil 6060.54   Fervers, Hans. Wie man Menschen beurteilt. Neuwied, 1959.

Phil 3850.27.122   Feschotte, Jacques. Albert Schweitzer. Paris, 1952.

Phil 3850.27.122.4   Feschotte, Jacques. Albert Schweitzer. 4. éd. Paris, 1958.

Phil 5421.20.125   Feshbach, Seymour. Television and aggression. 1. ed. San Francisco, 1971.

Phil 2730.97   Fessard, G. La méthode de réflexion chez Maine de Biran. Paris, 1938.

Phil 5400.51   Festa, Alfonso. Introduzione alla filosofia dell'affetto. Piacenza, 1829.

Phil 185.18.50   Festgabe für Julius Kaftan zu seinem 70. Geburtstage, 30 Sept. 1918. Tübingen, 1920.

Phil 5500.31   Festinger, L. Conflict, decision and dissonance. Stanford, 1964.

Phil 5325.30A   Festinger, Leon. A theory of cognitive dissonance. Evanston, Ill., 1957.

Phil 3160.6.81   Festner, Carl. Christian August Crusius als Metaphysiker. Halle, 1892.

Phil 3246.200   Festrede zur Saecularfeier Fichtes. (Lott, F.C.) Wien, 1862.

Phil 165.40   Festschrift. (Gropp, R.O.) Berlin, 1955.

Phil 3450.11.95   Festschrift Edmund Husserl. Halle an der Saale, 1929.

Phil 5238.240   Festschrift for B.F. Skinner. N.Y., 1970.

Phil 5238.130   Festschrift for Gardner Murphy. (Peatman, J.G.) N.Y., 1960.

Phil 3791.124   Festschrift für Alois Riehl. Halle, 1914.

Phil 165.408   Festschrift für Joseph Klien zum 70. Geburtstag. Göttingen, 1967.

Phil 165.334   Festschrift für Karl Joël zum 70. Geburtstage (27 März 1934). Basel, 1934.

NEDL Phil 3450.16.90   Festschrift für Paul Hensel Erlangen. Greiz, 1923.

Phil 3665.1.80   Festschrift für Paul Natorp zum siebzigsten Geburtstage. Berlin, 1924.

Phil 3195.10.100   Festschrift Hans Driesch zum 60. Geburtstag. v.1-2. Leipzig, 1927.

Phil 3903.1.81   Festschrift Johannes Volkelt zum 70. Geburtstage. München, 1918.

Phil 4762.1.95   Festschrift N.O. Losskij zum 60. Geburtstage. Bonn, 1934.

Phil 4513.5.90   Festskrift til Anathon Aall på 70. årsdagen hans, 15 Aug. 1837. Oslo, 1937.

Phil 4582.1.83   Festskrift till ägnad Axel Herrlin den 30 mars 1935. Lund, 1935.

Phil 4582.4.88   Festskrift tillägnad Axel Hägerström den 6 september 1928. Upsala, 1928.

Phil 4520.9.90   Festskrift tillägnad E.O. Burman. Upsala, 1910.

Phil 4600.2.90   Festskrift tillägnad Hans Larsson. Stockholm, 1927.

Phil 4610.7.90   Festskrift tillägnad Vitalis Norström. Göteborg, 1916.

Phil 5627.176   Festugière, André M.J. La sainteté. 1. éd. Paris, 1942.

X Cg Phil 7075.131   Der Fetischismus dargestellt für Ärzte und Kriminalogen. (Stekel, William.) Berlin, 1923.

Phil 3425.736   Fetscher, Iring. Hegels Lehre von Menschen. Stuttgart, 1970.

Phil 180.36   Fetzer, K.A. Philosophische Leitbegriffe. Tübingen, 1884.

Phil 5245.4   Feuchtersleben, E. von. Principles of medical psychology. London, 1847.

Phil 6115.11.14   Feuchtersleben, E.F.V. Ein Dienst zur Nacht ist unser Leben. Graz, 1958.

Phil 6115.11.17   Feuchtersleben, E.F.V. The dietetics of the soul. London, 1873.

Phil 6115.11.15   Feuchtersleben, E.F.V. The dietetics of the soul. N.Y., 1858.

Phil 6115.11.19   Feuchtersleben, E.F.V. Health and suggestion: the dietetics of the mind. N.Y., 1910.

Phil 6115.11.8   Feuchtersleben, E.F.V. Hygiene de l'âme. Paris, 1860.

Phil 6115.11.12   Feuchtersleben, E.F.V. Lehrbuch der ärtlichen Seelenkunde. Wien, 1845.

Phil 6115.11.2   Feuchtersleben, E.F.V. Zur Diätetik der Seele. Hamburg, 1880.

Phil 6115.11   Feuchtersleben, E.F.V. Zur Diätetik der Seele. Wien, 1867.

Phil 6115.11.6   Feuchtersleben, E.F.V. Zur Diätetik der Seele. 2. Aufl. Halle, 1893.

Phil 6115.11.4   Feuchtersleben, E.F.V. Zur Diätetik der Seele. 9. Aufl. Wien, 1852.

Phil 6115.11.20   Feuchtersleben. (Eltz-Hoffmann, L.) Salzburg, 1956.

Phil 6115.19   Feuchtwanger, E. Die Funktionen des Stirnhirns. Berlin, 1923.

Phil 6315.38   Feuer, L.S. Psychoanalysis and ethics. Springfield, 1955.

Phil 2225.5.95   Feuer, L.S. Review: Collected papers of Charles Sanders Peirce. v.6. Scientific metaphysics. Bruges, 1932.

Phil 3825.10   Feuer, L.S. Spinoza and The use of liberalism. Boston, 1958.

Phil 3235.77   Feuerbach, Ludwig. Ausgewahlte Briefe von und an L. Feuerbach. v.1-2. Leipzig, 1904.

Phil 3235.28   Feuerbach, Ludwig. Aussprüche aus seinen Werken. Leipzig, 1879.

Phil 3235.76   Feuerbach, Ludwig. Briefwechsel zwischen L. Feuerbach und C. Kapp, 1832-1848. Leipzig, 1876.

Phil 3235.72   Feuerbach, Ludwig. The essence of Christianity. N.Y., 1855.

Phil 3235.72.7   Feuerbach, Ludwig. The essence of Christianity. N.Y., 1957.

X Cg Phil 3235.72.5   Feuerbach, Ludwig. The essence of Christianity. 2nd ed. London, 1881.

Phil 3235.73   Feuerbach, Ludwig. The essence of religion. N.Y., 1873.

Phil 3235.11   Feuerbach, Ludwig. Gesammelte Werke. v.2-4,6-9. Berlin, 1967- 8v.

Phil 3235.25.5   Feuerbach, Ludwig. Grundsätze der Philosophie der Zukunft. Frankfurt, 1967.

Phil 3235.25   Feuerbach, Ludwig. Grundsätze der Philosophie der Zukunft. Zürich, 1843.

Phil 3235.126.5   Feuerbach, Ludwig. Istoriia filosofii. Moskva, 1967. 3v.

Phil 3235.78   Feuerbach, Ludwig. Kleine philosophische Schriften. Leipzig, 1950.

Phil 3235.15   Feuerbach, Ludwig. Ludwig Feuerbachs sämmtliche Werke. Stuttgart, 1903-11. 10v.

Phil 3235.20   Feuerbach, Ludwig. Manifestes philosophiques; textes choisis. Paris, 1960.

Phil 3235.60   Feuerbach, Ludwig. Philosophie der Zukunft. Stuttgart, 1922.

Phil 3235.75   Feuerbach, Ludwig. Philosophische Charakterentwicklung. v.1-2. Leipzig, 1874.

Phil 3235.50   Feuerbach, Ludwig. Qu'est-ce que la religion. Paris, 1850.

Phil 3235.10   Feuerbach, Ludwig. Sämmtliche Werke. Leipzig, 1846-90. 10v.

Phil 3235.74   Feuerbach, Ludwig. Sämmtliche Werke. v.1-13. Stuttgart, 1964. 12v.

Phil 3235.126   Feuerbach, Ludwig. Sockrinemia. Moskva, 1923.

Phil 3235.52   Feuerbach, Ludwig. Über Philosophie und Christenthum. Mannheim, 1839.

Phil 3235.55   Feuerbach, Ludwig. Vorlesungen über das Wesen der Religion nebst Zusätzen und Anmerkungen. Stuttgart, 1908.

Phil 3235.55.5   Feuerbach, Ludwig. Das Wesen der Religion. Leipzig, 1908.

Phil 3235.45.2   Feuerbach, Ludwig. Das Wesen des Christenthums. Leipzig, 1841.

Phil 3235.45.6   Feuerbach, Ludwig. Das Wesen des Christenthums. Leipzig, 1909.

Phil 3235.45   Feuerbach, Ludwig. Das Wesen des Christenthums. Stuttgart, 1903.

Phil 2045.102   Feuerbach, P.J.A. Anti-Hobbes. Erfurt, 1798.

Phil 3270.4.79   Feuerbach, P.J.A. Biographischer Nachlass. v.1-2. Leipzig, 1853.

Phil 3270.4.30   Feuerbach, P.J.A. Über Philosophie und Empirie in ihrem Verhältnisse zur positiven Rechtswissenschaft. Landshut, 1804.

Phil 1705.2   Feuerbach. Geschichte der neueren Philosophie. Ansbach, 1833-37. 2v.

Phil 3235.136   Feuerbach et la théologie de la sécularisation. (Xhauflaire, Marcel.) Paris, 1970.

Phil 3235.117   Feuerbach und die Religion. (Schilling, Werner.) München, 1957.

Phil 2450.81   Feuerback, L.A. Pierre Bayle. Ansbach, 1838.

Phil 2450.81.2   Feuerback, L.A. Pierre Bayle. 2. Aufl. Leipzig, 1848.

Phil 8830.1   Feuerlein, E. Die philosophische Sittenlehre. v.1-2. Tübingen, 1857-59.

Phil 3450.18.130   Feuerstein, R. Die Modallehre Nicolai Hartmanns. Köln? 1957.

Phil 3270.14.30   Feuling, Daniel. Hauptfragen der Metaphysik. 2. Aufl. Heidelberg, 1949.

Phil 504.2   Février, Paulette. Déterminisme et indéterminisme. 1. éd. Paris, 1955.

Phil 197.62   A few texts. Wise to the wise. (Wade, Joseph M.) Boston, 1892.

Phil 8620.23	A few words about the devil. (Bradlaugh, Charles.) N.Y., 1874.	
Phil 282.2	Few words on evolution and creation. (Boase, H.S.) London, 1882.	
Phil 9341.17	A few words to girls at school. (Beale, Dorothea.) n.p., 18- .	
Phil 165.376	Feyerabend, Paul. Mind, matter, and method. Minneapolis, 1966.	
Phil 6675.10	Feyrer, E.C. Practical psychology. Springfield, Mass., 1913.	
Phil 5045.12	Feys, R. Le raisonnement entermes de faite dans la logique russellienne. Louvain, 1928.	
Phil 5066.286	Feys, Robert. Dictionary of symbols of mathematical logic. Amsterdam, 1969.	
Phil 5066.24	Feys, Robert. Logistiek geformaliseerde logica. Antwerpen, 1944.	
Phil 5066.24.5	Feys, Robert. Modal logics. Louvain, 1965.	
Phil 5015.3	Feys, Robert. De onturkkeling van het logisch denken. Antwerpen, 1949.	
Phil 180.52	Fialko, N.M. Passivity and rationalization. N.Y., 1935.	
Phil 180.52.5	Fialko, N.M. Passivnost'. Paris, 1927.	
Phil 5755.4	Fiamingo, G. Individual determinism and social science. Philadelphia, 1896.	
Phil 4110.14.30	Fichera, G. Crisi e valori, ed altri saggi. Padova, 1958.	
Phil 400.134	Fichera, Giuseppe. La tematico religiosa nell idealismo attuale. Catania, 1969.	
Phil 7054.36	Fichet, I.H. von. Der neuere Spiritualismus; sein Werth. Leipzig, 1878.	
Phil 3246.350	Ficht; Sein und Reflexion. (Janke, Wolfgang.) Berlin, 1970.	
Phil 3246.173	Fichte, der Erzieher zum Deutschtum. (Bergmann, Ernst.) Leipzig, 1915.	
Phil 3246.211	Fichte, der Held unter der deutschen Denkern. (Stahr, Adolf.) Berlin, 1862.	
Phil 3246.98	Fichte, der Mann der Wissenschaft und des Katheders. (Erdmann, Johann E.) Halle, 1862.	
Phil 3246.233.5	Fichte, der Mann und sein Werke. (Döring, W.O.) Lübeck, 1925.	
Phil 3246.270	Fichte; ein Lebensbild. (Koestlin, Karl.) Tübingen, 1862.	
Phil 3246.330	Fichte, Feierbach, Marx. (Mader, Johann Karl.) Wien, 1968.	
Htn Phil 3801.391*	Fichte, I.H. Über die Bedingungen eines spekulativen Theismus. Elberfeld, 1835.	
Phil 3245.35	Fichte, Immanuel Hermann. Anthropologie: von der menschlichen Seele. Leipzig, 1860.	
Phil 3245.70.5	Fichte, Immanuel Hermann. Contributions to mental philosophy. London, 1860.	
Phil 3245.75	Fichte, Immanuel Hermann. Grundsätze für die Philosophie der Zukunft. Stuttgart, 1847.	
Phil 3245.30	Fichte, Immanuel Hermann. Grundzüge zur System der Philosophie. Heidelberg, 1833-46. 4v.	
Phil 3245.50.2	Fichte, Immanuel Hermann. Die Idee der Persönlichkeit. Elberfeld, 1834.	
Phil 3245.50	Fichte, Immanuel Hermann. Die Idee der Persönlichkeit. Leipzig, 1855.	
Phil 3246.82.2	Fichte, Immanuel Hermann. Johann Gottlieb Fichte's Leben und Ritter. Leipzig, 1862. 2v.	
Phil 3246.82	Fichte, Immanuel Hermann. Johann Gottlieb Fichte's Leben und Ritter. Sulzbach, 1830-31. 2v.	
Phil 3245.70	Fichte, Immanuel Hermann. Psychologie. Leipzig, 1864-73. 2v.	
Phil 3245.55	Fichte, Immanuel Hermann. Religion und Philosophie. Heidelberg, 1834.	
Phil 3245.32	Fichte, Immanuel Hermann. Sätze zur Vorschule der Theologie. Stuttgart, 1826.	
Phil 3245.43	Fichte, Immanuel Hermann. Die Seelenfortdauer und die Weltstellung des Menschen. Leipzig, 1867.	
Phil 3245.60	Fichte, Immanuel Hermann. Die speculative Theologie der Allgemeine Religionslehre. Heidelberg, 1846.	
Phil 3245.65	Fichte, Immanuel Hermann. System der Ethik. Leipzig, 1850-51. 2v.	
Phil 3245.45	Fichte, Immanuel Hermann. Die theistische Weltansicht. Leipzig, 1873.	
Phil 3245.40	Fichte, Immanuel Hermann. Über Gegen satz Wendepunkt und Zeit. Heidelberg, 1832.	
Phil 3245.20	Fichte, Immanuel Hermann. Vernuschte Schriften zur Philosophie, Theologie und Ethik. Leipzig, 1869. 2v.	
Phil 3245.25	Fichte, Immanuel Hermann. Zeitschrift für Philosophie und speculative Theologie. Bonn, 1937-56. 8v.	
Phil 3245.33	Fichte, Immanuel Hermann. Zur Seelenfrage. Leipzig, 1859.	
Phil 3245.79	Pamphlet box. Fichte, Immanuel Hermann. Philosophy. German and Dutch.	
Phil 3246.78.5	Fichte, Johann Gottlieb. Achtundvierzig Briefe. Leipzig, 1862.	
Phil 3246.55.12	Fichte, Johann Gottlieb. Addresses in the German nation. Photoreproduction. Chicago, 1923.	
Htn Phil 3246.49.2*	Fichte, Johann Gottlieb. Die Anweisung zum seeligen Leben. Berlin, 1806.	
Phil 3246.49A	Fichte, Johann Gottlieb. Die Anweisung zum seeligen Leben. Berlin, 1828.	
Phil 3246.49.5	Fichte, Johann Gottlieb. Die Anweisung zum seeligen Leben. Hamburg, 1954.	
Phil 3246.71.20A	Fichte, Johann Gottlieb. Appellation an das Publikum über...atheistischen. Jena, 1799.	
Phil 3246.35	Fichte, Johann Gottlieb. Die Bestimmung der Menschen. Berlin, 1825.	
Phil 3246.34.2	Fichte, Johann Gottlieb. Die Bestimmung der Menschen. Frankfurt, 1800.	
Htn Phil 3246.34*	Fichte, Johann Gottlieb. Die Bestimmung des Menschen. Berlin, 1800.	
Phil 3246.35.3A	Fichte, Johann Gottlieb. Die Bestimmung des Menschen. Leipzig, 1879.	
Phil 3246.35.8	Fichte, Johann Gottlieb. Die Bestimmung des Menschen. Leipzig, 1944.	
Phil 3246.35.10	Fichte, Johann Gottlieb. Die Bestimmung des Menschen. Stuttgart, 1966.	
Phil 3246.35.7	Fichte, Johann Gottlieb. Die Bestimmung des Menschen. 2. Aufl. Berlin, 1801.	
Phil 3246.35.8.5	Fichte, Johann Gottlieb. Die Bestimmung des Menschen. 2. Aufl. Leipzig, 1944.	
Phil 3246.78	Fichte, Johann Gottlieb. Briefe, Ausgewahlt und Herausgegeben von E. Bergmann. Leipzig, 1919.	
Phil 3246.78.9A	Fichte, Johann Gottlieb. Briefwechsel. Leipzig, 1925. 2v.	
Phil 3246.44.5	Fichte, Johann Gottlieb. Darstellung der Wissenschaftslehre aus dem Jahre 1801, 1804. v.1-2. Leipzig, 1922.	

Phil 3246.35.9	Fichte, Johann Gottlieb. Destination de l'homme. Paris, 1832.	
Phil 3246.35.5	Fichte, Johann Gottlieb. Destination of man. London, 1846.	
X Cg Phil 3246.55.10	Fichte, Johann Gottlieb. Discours a la nation allemande. Paris, 1895.	
Phil 3246.40	Fichte, Johann Gottlieb. Doctrine de la science...de la connaissance. Paris, 1843.	
Phil 3246.32.5	Fichte, Johann Gottlieb. Eimige Vorlesungen über die Bestimmung des Gelehrten. Jena, 1954.	
Phil 3246.17.5	Fichte, Johann Gottlieb. Erganzungsband. Leipzig, 1934.	
Phil 3246.79.20	Fichte, Johann Gottlieb. Erste und zweite Einleitung in die Wissenschaftslehre und Versuch einer neuen Darstellung der Wissenschaftslehre. Hamburg, 1954.	
Phil 3246.44.10.5	Fichte, Johann Gottlieb. Erste Wissenschaftslehre ven 1804. Stuttgart, 1969.	
Phil 3246.79.60	Fichte, Johann Gottlieb. Fichte für Heute. Bremen, 1944?	
Phil 3246.79.65	Fichte, Johann Gottlieb. Fichte Schriften zur Gesellschaftsphilosophie. v.1-2. Jena, 1928-29.	
Phil 3246.79.15A	Fichte, Johann Gottlieb. Fichtes Freiheitslehre. 1. Aufl. Düsseldorf, 1956.	
Phil 3246.50.9	Fichte, Johann Gottlieb. Första inledningen till vetenshapsläran. Stockholm, 1914.	
Phil 3246.18.4	Fichte, Johann Gottlieb. Gesamtausgabe der Bauerischen Akademie der Wissenschaften. Stuttgart, 1962. 9v.	
Htn Phil 3246.75*	Fichte, Johann Gottlieb. Der geschlossne Handelsstaat. Tübingen, 1800.	
Phil 3246.45.6	Fichte, Johann Gottlieb. Grundlage der gesammten Wissenschaftslehre. Hamburg, 1956.	
Phil 3246.45	Fichte, Johann Gottlieb. Grundlage der gesammten Wissenschaftslehre. Tübingen, 1802.	
Htn Phil 3246.38*	Fichte, Johann Gottlieb. Grundlage des Naturrechts nach Prinzipien der Wissenschaftslehre. Jena, 1796.	
Phil 3246.77.2	Fichte, Johann Gottlieb. Grundlage des Naturrechts nach Prinzipien der Wissenschaftslehre. 2. Aufl. Hamburg, 1967.	
Htn Phil 3246.45.8*	Fichte, Johann Gottlieb. Grundriss des Eigenthümlichen der Wissenschaftslehre. Jena, 1795.	
Phil 3246.45.20	Fichte, Johann Gottlieb. Grundriss des Eigenthümlichen der Wissenschaftslehre in Rücksicht. Leipzig, 194-.	
Htn Phil 3246.47*	Fichte, Johann Gottlieb. Die Grundzüge des gegenwartigen Zeitalters. Berlin, 1806.	
Phil 3246.47.26	Fichte, Johann Gottlieb. Die Grundzüge des gegenwartigen Zeitalters. Hamburg, 1956.	
Phil 3246.47.25	Fichte, Johann Gottlieb. Die Grundzüge des gegenwartigen Zeitalters. 2. Aufl. Leipzig, 1922.	
Htn Phil 3246.21*	Fichte, Johann Gottlieb. Das Herausgeber die philosophischen Journals. Jena, 1799-1815. 4 pam.	
Phil 3246.36	Fichte, Johann Gottlieb. Ideen über Gott und Unsterblichkeit. Leipzig, 1914.	
Phil 3246.54	Fichte, Johann Gottlieb Fichte über den Begriff des wahrhaften Kraiges. Leipzig, 1914.	
Phil 3246.35.12	Fichte, Johann Gottlieb. Männeskans bestammelse. Stockholm, 1923.	
Phil 3246.50	Fichte, Johann Gottlieb. Méthode...a la vie bienheureuse. Paris, 1845.	
Phil 3246.19	Fichte, Johann Gottlieb. Nachgelassene Schriften. Bd.2. Berlin, 1937.	
Phil 3246.15	Fichte, Johann Gottlieb. Nachgelassene Werke. Bonn, 1934-35. 3v.	
Phil 3246.18.3.5	Fichte, Johann Gottlieb. Nachgelassene Werke. Bonn, 1962. 3v.	
Phil 3246.18.3	Fichte, Johann Gottlieb. Nachgelassene Werke. Leipzig, 1924. 3v.	
Phil 3246.53	Fichte, Johann Gottlieb. Nature of the scholar. London, 1845.	
Phil 3246.53.2	Fichte, Johann Gottlieb. Nature of the scholar. 2nd ed. London, 1848.	
Phil 3246.76	Fichte, Johann Gottlieb. Neue Fichte-funde, aus der Heimat und Schweiz. Gotha, 1919.	
Phil 3246.58	Fichte, Johann Gottlieb. New exposition of the science of knowledge. Saint Louis, 1869.	
Phil 3246.66	Fichte, Johann Gottlieb. Philosophie der Maurerei. Leipzig, 1923.	
Phil 3246.71	Fichte, Johann Gottlieb. Die philosophischen Schriften zum Atheismusstreit. Leipzig, 1910.	
Phil 3246.66.5	Fichte, Johann Gottlieb. Philosophy of masonry. Seattle, 1945.	
Phil 3246.25.5	Fichte, Johann Gottlieb. Popular works. London, 1873.	
Phil 3246.26	Fichte, Johann Gottlieb. Popular works. London, 1889. 2v.	
Phil 3246.28	Fichte, Johann Gottlieb. Predigten. Leipzig, 1918.	
Phil 3246.59	Fichte, Johann Gottlieb. Rechtslehre vorgetragen von Ostern bis Michaelis 1812. Leipzig, 1920.	
Htn Phil 3246.55.2*	Fichte, Johann Gottlieb. Reden an die deutsche Nation. Berlin, 1808.	
Phil 3246.55.5	Fichte, Johann Gottlieb. Reden an die deutsche Nation. Leipzig, n.d.	
Phil 3246.55	Fichte, Johann Gottlieb. Reden an die deutsche Nation. Leipzig, 1824.	
Phil 3246.55.3	Fichte, Johann Gottlieb. Reden an die deutsche Nation. Leipzig, 1872.	
Phil 3246.55.6A	Fichte, Johann Gottlieb. Reden an die deutsche Nation. Leipzig, 1909.	
Phil 3246.55.7	Fichte, Johann Gottlieb. Reden an die deutsche Nation. Leipzig, 1944.	
Phil 3246.74	Fichte, Johann Gottlieb. Rufe an die deutsche Nation. Berlin, 1943.	
Phil 3246.10	Fichte, Johann Gottlieb. Sämmtliche Werke. Berlin, 1845-46. 8v.	
Phil 3246.11	Fichte, Johann Gottlieb. Sämmtliche Werke. Berlin, 1845-46. 11v.	
Phil 3246.18	Fichte, Johann Gottlieb. Sämmtliche Werke. Leipzig, 1924. 8v.	
Phil 3246.72.5	Fichte, Johann Gottlieb. Science of ethics...based on Science of knowledge. London, 1897.	
X Cg Phil 3246.58.2	Fichte, Johann Gottlieb. Science of knowledge. Philadelphia, 1868.	
X Cg Phil 3246.60	Fichte, Johann Gottlieb. Science of rights. London, 1889.	
Phil 3246.60.5	Fichte, Johann Gottlieb. Science of rights. Philadelphia, 1869.	
X Cg Phil 3246.60.5	Fichte, Johann Gottlieb. Science of rights. Philadelphia, 1869.	
Htn Phil 3246.77*	Fichte, Johann Gottlieb. Staatslehre. Berlin, 1820.	
Htn Phil 3246.72*	Fichte, Johann Gottlieb. Das System der Sittenlehre. Jena, 1798.	
Phil 3246.72.2	Fichte, Johann Gottlieb. Das System der Sittenlehre nach Prinzipien der Wissenschaftslehre. Neuausgabe, 1963.	

Phil 3246.72.3 — Fichte, Johann Gottlieb. Das System der Sittenlehre nach Prinzipien der Wissenschaftslehre, 1798. 2. Aufl. Hamburg, 1969.

Phil 3246.79.25 — Fichte, Johann Gottlieb. Tat und Freiheit, ein Fichtebuch. 3. Aufl. Hamburg, 1922.

Phil 3246.18.5 — Fichte, Johann Gottlieb. Eine Teilsammlung mit der Einfuhrung. Stuttgart, 1935.

Htn Phil 3246.65* — Fichte, Johann Gottlieb. Die Thatsachen des Bewusstseyns. Stuttgart, 1817.

Phil 3246.46 — Fichte, Johann Gottlieb. La theorie de la science expose de 1804. Thèse. Paris, 1967.

Htn Phil 3246.44* — Fichte, Johann Gottlieb. Über den Begriff der Wissenschaftslehre. Weimar, 1794.

Phil 3246.53.10 — Fichte, Johann Gottlieb. Über den Gelehrten. Berlin, 1956.

Phil 3246.73 — Fichte, Johann Gottlieb. Über den Unterschied des Geistes und des Buchstabens in der Philosophie. Leipzig, 1924.

Htn Phil 3246.20* — Fichte, Johann Gottlieb. Über der Begriff der Wissenschaftslehre. Jena, 1798-1822. 4 pam.

Phil 3246.53.5 — Fichte, Johann Gottlieb. Über die Bestimmung des Gelehrten. Berlin, 1812.

Phil 3246.79.10 — Fichte, Johann Gottlieb. Über die Einzig mögliche Störung der akademischen Freiheit. Heidelberg, 1905.

Htn Phil 3246.30* — Fichte, Johann Gottlieb. Versuch einer Critik aller Offenbarung. Königsberg, 1792.

Htn Phil 3246.30.5* — Fichte, Johann Gottlieb. Versuch einer Critik aller Offenbarung. Königsberg, 1793.

Phil 3246.68.3 — Fichte, Johann Gottlieb. Vocation of man. Chicago, 1906.
Phil 3246.68 — Fichte, Johann Gottlieb. Vocation of man. London, 1848.
Phil 3246.68.15 — Fichte, Johann Gottlieb. The vocation of man. N.Y., 1956.
Phil 3246.50.5 — Fichte, Johann Gottlieb. The way toward the blessed life. London, 1849.

Phil 3246.17 — Fichte, Johann Gottlieb. Werke. Leipzig, 1911. 6v.
Phil 3246.44.10 — Fichte, Johann Gottlieb. Wissenschaftslehre 1804. Frankfurt, 1966.

Phil 3246.86.5 — Fichte, seine Ethik...Problem des Individualismus. (Raich, Maria.) Tübingen, 1905.

Phil 3246.86 — Fichte, seine Ethik...Problem des Individualismus. Thesis. (Raich, Maria.) Tübingen, 1905.

Phil 1705.3.5 — Fichte, T.H. Beiträge zur Charakteristik der neueren Philosophie. Sulzbach, 1805.

Phil 1705.3 — Fichte, T.H. Beiträge zur Charakteristik der neueren Philosophie. Sulzbach, 1841.

Phil 3005.2 — Fichte, T.H. Fragen und Bedenken. Leipzig, 1876.
Phil 3246.80 — Fichte. (Adamson, R.) Philadelphia, 1881.
Phil 3246.80.3 — Fichte. (Adamson, R.) Philadelphia, 1892.
Phil 3246.208 — Fichte. (Heimsoeth, H.) München, 1923.
Phil 3246.180 — Fichte. (Maggiore, G.) Castello, 1921.
Phil 3246.179 — Fichte. (Messer, August.) Leipzig, 1920.
Phil 3246.255 — Fichte. (Pareyson, L.) Torino, 1950.
Phil 3246.214 — Fichte als politischen Denker. (Wallner, Nico.) Halle, 1926.

Phil 3246.170 — Fichte als religiöser Denker. (Gogarten, F.) Jena, 1914.
Phil 3246.243 — Fichte e la filosofia. (Massalo, A.) Firenze, 1948.
X Cg Phil 3246.92.5 — Fichte et son temps. (Léon, Xavier.) Paris, 1922-24. 2v.

Phil 3246.212.5 — Fichte-Forschungen. (Wundt, Max.) Stuttgart, 1929.
Phil 3246.79.60 — Fichte für Heute. (Fichte, Johann Gottlieb.) Bremen, 1944?

Phil 3246.79.50 — Eine Fichte-Sammlung. (Meyer, Friedrich.) Leipzig, 1921.
Phil 3246.201 — Die Fichte-Schelling'sche Wissenschaftslehre. (Kerler, D.H.) Ulm, 1917.

Phil 3246.79.65 — Fichte Schriften zur Gesellschaftsphilosophie. v.1-2. (Fichte, Johann Gottlieb.) Jena, 1928-29.

Phil 3246.215 — Fichte über das Volk. (Mayer, Otto.) Leipzig, 1913.
Phil 3246.178 — Fichte über den Krieg. (Moog, Willy.) Darmstadt, 1917.
Phil 3246.173.10 — Fichte und Carl Christian Erhard Schmid. (Bergmann, Ernst.) Leipzig, 1926?

Phil 3246.242 — Fichte und das Christentum. (Heekman, H.) Wurzburg, 1939.
Phil 3246.185 — Fichte und der demokratischen Gedanke. (Leibholz, G.) Freiburg, 1921.

Phil 3246.275 — Fichte und der deutsche Staatsgedanke. (Bauch, Bruno.) Beyer, 1925.

Phil 3246.173.5 — Fichte und der Nationalsozialismus. (Bergmann, Ernst.) Breslau, 1933.

Phil 3246.195 — Fichte und deutschlande Not. Berlin, 1919.
Phil 3246.213 — Fichte und die Gedankenwelt der Sturm und Drang. (Gelpcke, E.) Leipzig, 1928.

Phil 3246.90 — Fichte und Erigena. (Wotschke, Theodor.) Halle, 1896.
Phil 3246.204.2 — Fichte und unsere Zeit. 2. Aufl. (Bauch, Bruno.) Erfurt, 1921.

Phil 3246.176 — Fichte und Wir. (Schwarz, Hermann.) Osterwieck, 1917.
Phil 3246.169 — Fichtes filosofi i förhallande till Kants kriticism. (Hidvall, Karl Z.K.) Uppsala, 1914.

Phil 3246.79.15A — Fichtes Freiheitslehre. 1. Aufl. (Fichte, Johann Gottlieb.) Düsseldorf, 1956.

Phil 3246.245 — Fichtes Geist mitten unter uns. (Stiner, Rudolf.) Dornach, 1933.

Phil 3246.172 — Fichtes Idealismus und die Geschichte. (Lask, Emil.) Tübingen, 1914.

Phil 3246.190 — Fichte's Idee des deutschen Staates. (Nindelband, N.) Tübingen, 1921.

Phil 3246.93.5 — Fichtes Leben. (Medicus, Fritz.) Leipzig, 1914.
Phil 3246.250 — Fichtes Lehre vom Bild. (Drechsler, J.) Stuttgart, 1955.
Phil 3246.253 — Fichtes Reden an die deutsche Nation. (Froelich, Franz.) Berlin, 1907.

Phil 3246.91 — Fichtes Reden an die deutsche Nation. (Janson, F.) Berlin, 1911.

Phil 3246.234 — Fichtes Reden an die deutsche Nation. (Schmidt, Erich.) Berlin, 1908.

Phil 3246.174 — Fichtes Religionsphilosophie. (Hirsch, Emanuel.) Göttingen, 1914.

Phil 3246.258 — Fichtes Religionsphilosophie. (Ritzel, W.W.) Stuttgart, 1956.

Phil 3246.81 — Fichte's Science of knowledge. (Everett, C.C.) Chicago, 1884.

Phil 3246.202.5 — Fichtes System der konkreten Ethik. (Gurwitsch, G.) Tübingen, 1924.

Phil 3246.96.5 — Fichte's und Schelling's neueste Lehren von Gott und die Welt. (Fries, Jakob F.) Heidelberg, 1807.

Htn Phil 3801.407.5* — Fichte's und Schelling's neueste Lehren von Gott und die Welt. (Fries, Jakob F.) Heidelberg, 1807.

Htn Phil 3800.715* — Fichtes und Schellings philosophischer Briefwechsel. Stuttgart, 1856.

Phil 3246.83 — Fichtes und Schopenhauer's Lehre von Willen. (Schwabe, G.) Jena, 1887.

Htn Phil 4110.1.30F* — Ficino, Marsilio. Opera. Basileae, 1576. 2v.
Phil 3270.2.31 — Fick, Adolf. Die Welt als Vorstellung. Würzburg, 1870.

Htn Phil 3801.392* — Fick, Georg Karl. Vergleichende Darstellung der philosophen Systeme von Kant, Fichte, Schelling. Heilbronn, 1825.

Phil 8880.4 — Fiddes, R. A general treatise of morality. London, 1724.
Phil 525.16.13 — Fides et ratio; the book which introduced Jacob Boehme to William Law. (Hobhouse, S.H.) n.p., 1936.

Phil 8402.42.5 — Fiebig, Ernst. Bobriks Asthetik; Beiträge zur Lehre des ästhetischen Formalismus. Bonn, 1930.

Phil 3528.80 — Fiedler, A. Die staatswissenschaftlichen Anschauungen und die politische-publizistische Tätigkeit des Nachkantianers Wilhelm Traugott Krug. Inaug. Diss. Dresden, 1933.

Phil 735.120 — Fiedler, K. Die Stufen der Erkenntnis. München, 1929.
Phil 8406.28 — Fiedler, Konrad. Schriften zur Kunst. München, 1971. 2v.

Phil 180.5 — Field, G. Outlines of analogical philosophy. London, 1839. 2v.

Phil 8880.36 — Field, G.C. Moral theory. An introduction to ethics. London, 1922.
Phil 5245.34 — Field, G.C. Prejudice and impartiality. London, 1932.
Phil 180.28.5 — Field, G.C. Studies in philosophy. Bristol, 1935.
Phil 8880.47.10 — Field, Joanna. An experiment in leisure. London, 1937.
Phil 1750.70.5 — The field of consciousness. (Gurwitsch, Aron.) Pittsburgh, 1964.

Phil 5643.34 — The field of distinct vision. (Ruediger, W.C.) n.p., 1907.

Phil 8890.23.7A — The field of ethics. (Palmer, G.H.) Boston, 1901.
Phil 8890.23.9 — Field of ethics. (Palmer, G.H.) Boston, 1902.
Phil 575.91.5 — The field of personality. (Allport, G.W.) n.p., n.d.
Phil 186.28 — The field of philosophy. (Leighton, J.A.) Columbus, Ohio, 1918.

Phil 186.28.5 — The field of philosophy. 4.ed. (Leighton, J.A.) N.Y., 1930.

Phil 5241.59 — The field of psychology. (Bentley, I.M.) N.Y., 1924.
Phil 5251.41.25 — Field theory in social science. 1st ed. (Lewin, Kurt.) N.Y., 1951.

Phil 5520.215 — The field theory of meaning. (Ushenko, A.P.) Ann Arbor, 1958.

Phil 6315.13 — Fielding, W.J. The caveman within us. N.Y., 1922.
Phil 8585.19 — Fielding-Hall, H. The hearts of men. N.Y., 1901.
Phil 8585.19.3 — Fielding-Hall, H. The hearts of men. 3rd ed. London, 1904.

Phil 8585.19.5 — Fielding-Hall, H. The world soul. N.Y., 1913.
Phil 5850.111 — Fields of applied psychology. (Anastasi, A.) N.Y., 1964.
Phil 5246.47.8 — Fields of psychology. (Guilford, Joy Paul.) N.Y., 1940.
Phil 5247.48.2 — Fields of psychology. (Higginson, G.) N.Y., 1932.
Phil 5258.143 — Fields of psychology. (Seashore, R.H.) N.Y., 1942.
Phil 9520.3 — Fierens-Gevaert, H. La tristesse contemporaine. Paris, 1899.

Phil 705.46 — Fieschi, Andrea. Saggio sul trascendente e sul trascendentale. Padova, 1958.

Phil 1900.69 — Fifteen sermons. (Butler, Joseph.) London, 1836.
Phil 1900.60.4 — Fifteen sermons and six sermons. 4th ed. (Butler, Joseph.) London, 1749.

Phil 1900.60.5 — Fifteen sermons and six sermons. 5th ed. (Butler, Joseph.) London, n.d.

Phil 1900.60.2.6 — Fifteen sermons and six sermons. 6th ed. (Butler, Joseph.) London, 1792.

Phil 1900.60 — Fifteen sermons preached at the Rolls Chapel. (Butler, Joseph.) London, 1726.

Phil 9590.1 — The fifth dimension. (Alder, V.S.) London, 1940.
Phil 6980.350.25 — The fifth profession. 1st ed. (Henry, William Earl.) San Francisco, 1971.

Phil 8615.16 — Fiftieth anniversary of the Ethical movement. N.Y., 1926.
Phil 6321.40 — The fifty minute hour. (Lindner, R.M.) N.Y., 1955.
Phil 9400.5 — Fifty years and beyond. (Lathrop, S.G.) Chicago, 1881.
Phil 7069.27.60 — Fifty years in psychic research. (Snipes, Joseph F.) Boston, 1927.

Phil 4891.10.2 — Fifty years of Chinese philosophy, 1898-1848. (Brière, O.) N.Y., 1965.

Phil 4891.10 — Fifty years of Chinese philosophy, 1898-1950. (Brière, O.) London, 1956.

Phil 8610.929.15 — Fifty years of freethought. v.1. pt.1-2. (MacDonald, G.E.) N.Y., 1929-31. 2v.

Phil 8406.15 — Figari, Pedro. Art, esthétique, idéal. Paris, 1920.
Phil 8585.23.5 — Figgis, J.N. Civilisation at the cross roads. N.Y., 1912.
Phil 3640.115 — Figgis, J.N. The will to freedom. N.Y., 1917.
Phil 6315.30 — Fight against fears. (Freeman, L.) N.Y., 1951.
Phil 8610.917.10 — A fight for right. (Secular Society, Ltd.) London, 1917.
Phil 9495.120 — Fighting venereal diseases. (United States. Public Health Service.) Washington, 1920.

Phil 2475.1.266 — Figueroa, E.L. Bergson, exposición de sus ideas fundamentales. La Plata, 1930.

Phil 8630.6.4 — Figuier, L. Le lendemain de la mort. 4e éd. Paris, 1872.
Phil 4210.122F — La figura di Antonio Rosmini. (Fogazzaro, A.) Milano, 1897.

Phil 5643.180 — Figurale Nachwirkungen auf Kinästhetischen Gebiet bei Lageveränderung von Objekt und tastender Hand. (Schmidt, Udo.) Frankfurt, 1970.

Phil 1630.21 — Figure e idee della filosofia del Rinascimento. (Mondolfo, R.) Firenze, 1963.

Phil 819.8 — Figure e studii de storia della filosofia. (Troilo, E.) Roma, 1918.

Phil 5585.300 — The figure-ground phenomenon in experimental and phenomenological psychology. Thesis. (Bowman, Jan C.) Stockholm, 1968.

Phil 1195.12 — Figures di sofisti in Platon. (Antonelli, M.) Torino, 1948.

Phil 178.32 — Figures et doctrines des philosophes. 4e éd. (Delbos, Victor.) Paris, 1918.

Phil 818.22 — Figures i perspectives de la história del pensamiento. (Serra Hunter, J.) Barcelona, 1935.

Phil 8403.41 — Figures of speech or figures of thought. (Coomaraswamy, A.K.) London, 1946.

Phil 2050.200 — Fikcionalism novověké filosofie zvláště u Humea a Kanta. (Pelikán, Ferdinand.) Praha, 1928.

Phil 5245.6 — Filachou, J.E. Eléments de psychologie mathematique. Montpelier, 1877.

Phil 6955.16 — Filho, Roch. Psychiatria e hygiene mental. Maceló, 1936.
Phil 165.390 — Filia. Wijsgerige opstellen in vriendschap aangeboden aan Prof. Dr. J.H. Robbers. (Braun, Cornelis Gerardus Franciscus.) Nijmegen, 1966.

Phil 5068.44 — Filiasi Carcano, Paolo. La metodologia nel rinnovarsi del pensiero. Napoli, 1957.

VPhil 585.167.5 — Filipec, Jindřich. Člověk a moderní doba. Praha, 1966.
Phil 5015.2 — Filipor, R.P. Logic and dialecta in the Soviet Union. N.Y., 1952.

VPhil 1705.13 — Filipović, Vladimir. Novija filozofija Zapada i odabrani telestovi. Zagreb, 1968.

Phil 4110.6.30   Filippi, Liutprando. Realtà e idealità. Napoli, 1937.
Phil 4170.11.80   Filippo Maxi e il suo neocriticismo. (Pietrangeli, Alfonso.) Padova, 1962.
Phil 3850.18.180   Filippone, Vincenzo. Società e cultura nel pensiero di Max Scheler. Milano, 1964. 2v.
Phil 5015.4   Filkorn, V. Pre-dialectical logic. Bratislava, 1963.
Phil 2805.183   Filleau de la Chaise, J. Discours sur les pensées de M. Pascal. Paris, 1922.
Phil 960.284   Filliozat, Jean. Les philosophies de l'Inde. Paris, 1970.
Phil 5815.8   Filloux, Jean Claude. Le psychisme animal. Paris, 1959.
Phil 5815.8.3   Filloux, Jean Claude. Psychologie des animaux. 3. éd. Paris, 1960.
Htn   Phil 2005.5.30*   Filmer, Robert. Patriarcha. London, 1680.
Phil 1955.6.235   Filograsso, Nando. Meditazioni deweyane. Urbino, 1968.
Phil 8980.392   Filonovich, Pavel G. O kommunisticheskoi morali. Moskva, 1963.
Phil 1145.52   Filos und Filia im vorhellenistischen Griechentum. Inaug. Diss. (Dirlmeier, Franz.) München, 1931.
Phil 4513.1.35   Filosfi och vetenskap. (Ahlberg, A.) Stockholm, 1919.
Phil 2475.1.385   Filosfiia Anri Bergsona. (Chanyshev, A.N.) Moskva, 1960.
Phil 2255.1.114   Filosfiia Bertrana Rassela. (Narskii, I.S.) Moskva, 1962.
Phil 4513.1.31   Filosfiska essayer. (Ahlberg, A.) Stockholm, 1918.
Phil 5374.282   Filosifiia soznaniia. (Tugarinov, Vasilii P.) Moskva, 1971.
Phil 3552.488   Filosof i istnienie. Wyd. 1. (Cichowicz, Stanislaw.) Warszawa, 1970.
Phil 850.12   Filosofi antichi. (Tilgher, A.) Todi, 1921.
Phil 4070.7.35   Filosofi contemporanei. v.1-2. (Banfi, Antonio.) Milano, 1961.
Phil 1717.8.15   Filosofi del novecento. (Ruggiero, G. de.) Bari, 1934.
Phil 1717.8.20   Filosofi del novecento. 3e ed. (Ruggiero, G. de.) Bari, 1946.
Phil 1718.6   Filosofi del tempo nostro. (Sarlo, Francesco de.) Firenze, 1916.
Phil 645.65   Filosofi della scepsi. (Cariddi, Walter.) Lecce, 1968.
Phil 1630.23   I filosofi e le macchine, 1400-1700. (Rossi, P.) Milano, 1962.
Phil 1735.10   Filosofi e moralisti del novecento. (Tilgher, Adriano.) Roma, 1932.
Phil 1750.560.20   Filosofi esistenzialisti. (Mancini, Italo.) Urbino, 1964.
Phil 4001.3   I filosofi italiani dal XVIII al XIX secolo. (Braschi, C.) Milano, 1916.
Phil 4006.5.33   Filosofi italiani del quattro cento. (Garin, Eugenio.) Firenze, 1942.
Phil 4006.9.30   Filosofi italiani d'oggi et altri scritti. (Galli, Gallo.) Torino, 1958.
Phil 4513.1.38   Filosofi och dikt. (Ahlberg, A.) Stockholm, 1924.
Phil 4582.1.30   Filosofi och facksetenskap. (Herrlin, Axel.) Lund, 1905.
Phil 8597.34   Filosofi och religion. (Romberg, P.A.) Karlskrona, 1881.
Phil 183.3   Filosofi og filosofer. (Ipsen, J.J.) København, 1923.
Phil 4540.10   Filosofi og samfund. (Favrhold, David.) København, 1968.
Phil 4710.4   Filosofi Russi: saggio di storia della filosofia. (Jakovenko, B.) Firenze, 1925.
Phil 186.103   Filosofi vecchi e nuovi. (Luporini, C.) Firenze, 1947.
Phil 15.9   Filosofia, per joy d'amor. Torino. 1-2,1945-1947
Phil 15.17   Filosofia; revista do Centro de Estudos Escolásticos. Lisboa. 3,1956+ 8v.
Phil 15.12   Filosofia, revista trimestrale. Torino. 1,1950+ 24v.
Phil 194.31A   Filosofia, vita e modernita. (Troilo, Erminis.) Roma, 1906.
Phil 4012.6   Filosofia. (Miceli di Serradileo, R.) Verona, 1937.
Phil 28.20   Filosofia. (São Paulo (City). Universidade. Faculdade de Filosofia, Ciencias e Letras.) São Paulo.
Phil 8585.40   Filosofia. Palmi, 1956.
Phil 4006.5.40   La filosofia. v.1-2. (Garin, Eugenio.) Milano, 1947.
Phil 4313.5.10   Filosofia actual, y Existencialismo en España. (Marias Aguilera, Julian.) Madrid, 1955.
Phil 1740.12   La filosofia actual. (Ferrater Mora, José.) Madrid, 1969.
Phil 3005.3.10   La filosofia alemana desde Kant. (Falckenberg, Richard.) Madrid, 1906.
Phil 75.38   Filosofia alemana traducida al español. (Brugger, Ilse.) Buenos Aires, 1942.
Phil 75.38.5   Filosofia alemana traducida al español. Supplement. Pt.1. (Brugger, Ilse.) Buenos Aires, 1942.
Phil 4957.5   La filosofia americana, su razón y su sinrazón de ser. (Larroyo, Francisco.) Mexico, 1958.
Phil 4957.810   La filosofia americana como filosofia sin más. 1. ed. (Zea, Leopoldo.) México, 1969.
Phil 1830.40   La filosofia americana contemporanea. (Rigobello, Armando.) Torino, 1960.
Phil 1828.8   La filosofia analitica in Inghilterra. (Riverso, Emanuele.) Roma, 1969.
Phil 850.29   La filosofia antica. (Bogliolo, Luigi.) Torino, 1955.
Phil 1020.32.10   La filosofia arabe. (Cruz Hernández, Miguel.) Madrid, 1963.
Phil 4960.260   Filosofia argentina; los ideólogos. (Varela Dominguez de Ghioldi, Delfina.) Buenos Aires, 1938.
Phil 4260.152   Filosofia argentina: Vico en los escritos de Sarmiento. (Varela Domínguez de Ghiolai, Delfina.) Buenos Aires, 1950.
Phil 4195.83   La filosofia cabbalistica di Giovanni Pico. (Massetani, D.G.) Empoli, 1897.
Phil 181.125   La filosofia come sapere storico. (Garin, Eugenio.) Bari, 1959.
Phil 4959.230.10   La filosofia como compromiso, y otros ensayos. 1. ed. (Zea, Leopoldo.) México, 1952.
Phil 1701.18   Filosofia contemporana a istorici. (Bagdasar, N.) Bucureşti, 1930.
Phil 1706.12   Filosofia contemporanea. (Gaos, José.) Caracas, 1962.
Phil 1717.8   La filosofia contemporanea. (Ruggiero, G. de.) Bari, 1912.
Phil 1715.7   La filosofia contemporanea. 1. ed. (Paci, Enzo.) Milano, 1957.
Phil 1717.8.2   La filosofia contemporanea. 2a ed. (Ruggiero, G. de.) Bari, 1920. 2v.
Phil 1717.8.3   La filosofia contemporanea. 3a ed. (Ruggiero, G. de.) Bari, 1929. 2v.
Phil 4960.625.15   A filosofia contemporânea em São Paulo nos seus textos. (Vita, Luís Washington.) São Paulo, 1969.
Phil 4368.2.33   Filosofia contemporanea estudios y notas. (Romero, Francisco.) Buenos Aires, 1941.
Phil 4368.2.35   Filosofia contemporanea estudios y notas. 2. ed. (Romero, Francisco.) Buenos Aires, 1944.
Phil 4960.630   La filosofia contemporanea in Brasile. (Acerboni, Lidia.) Milano, 1968.
Phil 4005.2   La filosofia contemporanea in Italia. (Fiorentino, F.) Napoli, 1876.

Phil 4005.11   La filosofia contemporanea in Italia. 1. ed. Roma, 1958. 2v.
Phil 4005.5   La filosofia contemporanea in Italia dal 1870 al 1920. Napoli, 1928.
Phil 1830.45   La filosofia contemporanea in U.S.A. (Società Filosofica Romana.) Roma, 1958.
Phil 194.26   Filosofia critica. 1a ed. (Turró, R.) Madrid, 1919.
Phil 8422.3   Filosofia da arte; ensaio. (Vieira de Almeida, F.) Coimbra, 1942.
Phil 4960.640   A filosofia da escola do Recife. (Paim, Antônio.) Rio de Janeiro, 1966.
Phil 4473.78.30   Filosofia da plenitude. (Martins, Diamantino.) Braga, 1966.
Phil 3428.161   La filosofia de G.F. Herbart. (Poggi, Alfredo.) Genova, 1932.
Phil 2475.1.267   La filosofia de Henri Bergson. (García Morente, M.) Madrid, 1917.
Phil 3450.11.113   La filosofia de Husserl. (Xirau, J.) Buenos Aires, 1941.
Phil 3494.16   La filosofia de Kant. (Morente, M.G.) Madrid, 1917.
Phil 585.105   Filosofia de la existencia y antropologia filosófica. 1. ed. (Virasoro, M.A.) Bahía Blanca, 1960.
Phil 181.104   Filosofia de la filosofia e historia de la filosofia. (Gaos, José.) México, 1947.
Phil 3480.94   Filosofia de la historia. (Kant, Immanuel.) México, 1941.
Phil 575.136   Filosofia de la persona y otros ensayos de filosofia. (Romero, F.A.) Buenos Aires, 1944.
Phil 8599.37   Filosofia de la religion. (Todoli, José.) Madrid, 1955.
Phil 5250.15.80   La filosofia de las ciencias de Wolfgang Köhler. (Franquiz Ventura, José A.) México, 1941.
Phil 2475.1.200   La filosofia de lo inexpresable. (Zulen, P.S.) Lima, 1920.
Phil 4983.41   La filosofia de lo mexicano. (Villegas, Abelardo.) México, 1960.
Phil 735.119   La filosofia de los valores. (Larroyo, F.) México, 1936.
Phil 3450.19.96   La filosofia de Martin Heidegger. (Waelhens, A. de.) Madrid, 1945.
Phil 3450.19.140   La filosofia de Ser y tiempo de M. Heidegger. (Sepich, Juan R.) Buenos Aires, 1954.
Phil 4476.2.30   A filosofia de Silvestre Penheiro Ferreira. (Cardoso Rangel de Souza Coelho, Maria Luiza.) Braga, 1958.
Phil 1020.23.5   La filosofia degli arabi nel suo fiore. v.1-2. (Quadri, G.) Firenze, 1939.
Phil 1740.10   La filosofia degli ultimi cinquanti anni. (Banfi, Antonio.) Milano, 1957.
Phil 1130.2.17   La filosofia dei Greci nel suo sviluppo storico. (Zeller, Eduard.) Firenze, 193-. 2v.
Phil 8401.26   Filosofia del arte. (Alvarez, Villar A.) Madrid, 1962.
Phil 4080.3.185   La filosofia del Croce. 1a ed. (Fano, Giorgio.) Milano, 1946.
Phil 177.105.10   Filosofia del dialogo. (Calogero, G.) Milano, 1962.
Phil 4210.21   Filosofia del diritto. (Rosmini-Serbati, Antonio.) Napoli, 1856. 2v.
Phil 4215.1.85   La filosofia del diritto di G.D. Romagnosi. (Caboara, L.) Citta, 1930.
Phil 4080.3.200   La filosofia del espíritu. (Derisi, Octavio N.) Madrid, 1947.
Phil 3488.30   Filosofia del estado en Kant. (González Vicén, J.) Laguna, 1952.
Phil 4372.1.140   Filosofia del humanismo de Juan Luis Vives. (Montegú, Bernardo.) Madrid, 1961.
Phil 2630.1.85   La filosofia del Padre Gratry. 2. ed. (Marias Aguilera, J.) Buenos Aires, 1941.
Phil 3450.11.79.5   La filosofia del profondo in Husserl e in Zamboni. (Giulietti, Giovanni.) Treviso, 1965.
Phil 190.103   Filosofia del saber. (Palacios, L.E.) Madrid, 1962.
Phil 848.2   La filosofia dell' espirenza e la fondazione dell' umanesims. 2. restampa. (Carbonare, Cleto.) Napoli, 1961.
Phil 5238.165   Filosofia della alienazione e analisi esistenziale. (Archivio di Filosofia.) Padova, 1961.
Phil 2250.51   La filosofia della fedeltà. (Royce, Josiah.) Bari, 1911.
Phil 70.75.3   La filosofia della natura nel medioevo. (Congrès International de Philosophie Médiévale, 3rd, Passo della Mendola (Trento), 1964.) Milano. 1966
Phil 486.8   Filosofia della prassi e filosofia dello spirito. (Lovecchio, Antonino.) Palmi, 1928.
Phil 8877.34.5   Filosofia della pratica; economia ed etica. 2a ed. (Croce, Benedetto.) Bari, 1915.
Phil 8877.34.6   Filosofia della pratica; economia ed etica. 6. ed. (Croce, Benedetto.) Bari, 1950.
Phil 8877.34.4   Filosofia della pratica; economica ed etica. (Croce, Benedetto.) Bari, 1909.
Phil 8595.33   La filosofia della religione e il problema della vita. (Padovani, U.A.) Milano, 1937.
Phil 3493.46   La filosofia della religione in Kant. (Lamacchio, Ada.) Mandeiria, 1969-
Phil 4110.5.28   Filosofia della rivoluzione. v.1-2. (Ferrari, G.) Londra, 1851.
Phil 4110.5.30   Filosofia della rivoluzione. v.1-2. 2. ed. (Ferrari, G.) Milano, 1873.
Phil 4110.5.33   La filosofia della rivoluzione. 2. ed. (Ferrari, G.) Milano, 1923.
Phil 15.4   La filosofia della scuoli italiane, revista bimestrale. Firenze. 1-16,1870-1885 16v.
Phil 802.20   La filosofia della storia della filosofia. Milano, 1954.
Phil 4005.6   La filosofia della storia nei pensatori italiani. (Fontana, B.) Imola, 1873.
Phil 2750.11.195   La filosofia della storia nel pensiero politico di Jacques Maritain. (Forni, Guglielmo.) Bologna, 1965.
Phil 176.172   Filosofia della vita. (Bedetti, A.) Cremons, 1952.
Phil 4080.12.30   Filosofia della vita. (Castelli, Enrico.) Roma, 1924.
Phil 177.46.5   La filosofia della vita. (Cesca, Giovanni.) Messina, 1903.
Phil 4112.50   Filosofia della volonta. (Galluppi, Pasquale.) Napoli, 1832-40. 4v.
Phil 4210.87   La filosofia dell'abate Antonio Rosmini esaminata. 4a ed. (Avogadro della Motta, Emiliano.) Napoli, 1877.
Phil 3270.12.100   La filosofia dell'aritmetica di Gottlob Frege. (Trinchero, Mario.) Giappichelli, 1967.
Phil 4070.7.45   Filosofia dell'arte; scelta. (Banfi, Antonio.) Roma, 1962.
Phil 8400.4   Filosofia dell'arte. (Archivio di Filosofia.) Roma, 1953.
Phil 8403.29   La filosofia dell'arte. (Cartalano, F.) Torino, 1875.
Phil 8407.6.5   La filosofia dell'arte. (Gentile, G.) Milano, 1931.
Phil 8420.19   Filosofia dell'arte. (Testa, Aldo.) Bologna, 1959.
Phil 8416.16   Filosofia dell'arte. 2. ed. (Petruzzellis, N.) Mazara, 1952.
Phil 8416.16.2   Filosofia dell'arte. 3. ed. (Petruzzellis, N.) Napoli, 1964.

Phil 802.19	Filosofia dell'arte e filosofia come totalità. (Ciardo, M.) Bari, 1953.
Phil 8407.6	La filosofia dell'arte in compendio, ad uso delle scuole. (Gentile, G.) Firenze, 1934.
Phil 4215.3.45	La filosofia dell'assurdo. (Rensi, Giuseppe.) Milano, 1937.
Phil 4215.3.33	La filosofia dell'autorita. (Rensi, Giuseppe.) Palermo, 1920.
Phil 177.46	La filosofia dell'azione. (Cesca, Giovanni.) Milano, 1907.
Phil 8894.27	Filosofia delle morali. (Tilgher, A.) Roma, 1937.
Phil 5520.29	La filosofia delle parole. 3. ed. (Garlanda, Federico.) Roma, 1905?
Phil 4001.4.5	La filosofia delle scuole italiane. (Bonavino, C.) Capolago, 1852.
Phil 4001.4.6	La filosofia delle scuole italiane. 2. ed. (Bonavino, C.) Firenze, 1863.
Phil 4080.32	La filosofia dell'esperienza di Cleto Carbonara. (Martano, Giuseppe.) Napoli, 1965.
Phil 848.2.3	La filosofia dell'espirenza e la fondazione dell Umanesimo. 3. ed. (Carbonare, Cleto.) Napoli, 1969.
Phil 5520.675	Filosofia dell'espressione. (Colli, Giorgio.) Milano, 1969.
Phil 3801.386	La filosofia dell'identità di F. Schelling. (Ferri, Ettore de.) Torino, 1925.
Phil 176.51.29	La filosofia dell'intuizione. (Bergson, H.) Lanciano, 1922.
Phil 2340.10.140	La filosofia dell'organismo di A.N. Whitehead. (Orsi, Concetta.) Napoli, 1955.
Phil 194.13.25	La filosofia dell'umanesimo di P.R. Trojano, 1863-1909. (Venturini, M.) Torino, 1919.
Phil 585.183	La filosofia dell'uomo di M.T. Antonelli. Roma, 1963.
Phil 1845.11.10	La filosofia di Alfred Jules Ayer. (Gozzelino, Giorgio M.) Zürich, 1964.
Phil 4210.81.4	La filosofia di Antonio R-S. Pt. 1. (Nardi, P. de.) Bellinzona, 1881.
Phil 4210.132	La filosofia di Antonio Rosmini. (Pederzolli, G.) Rovereto, 1887.
Phil 3808.198	La filosofia di Arturo Schopenhauer. (Stefano Escher di, Anna.) Padova, 1958.
Phil 4080.8.87	La filosofia di Augusto Conti. (Lantrua, A.) Padova, 1955.
Phil 4080.8.80	La filosofia di Augusto Conti. (Romano, Pietro.) Genova, 1895.
Phil 4265.6.90	La filosofia di B. Varisco. (Librizzi, C.) Catania, 1936.
Phil 4080.3.195	La filosofia di Benedetto Croce. (Lombardi, A.) Roma, 1946.
Phil 4080.3.122	La filosofia di Benedetto Croce. 2a ed. (Chiocchetti, E.) Milano, 1920.
Phil 4080.3.123	La filosofia di Benedetto Croce. 3a ed. (Chiocchetti, E.) Milano, 1924.
Phil 4080.3.281	La filosofia di Benedetto Croce e la crisi della società italiana. (Abbate, Michele.) Torino, 1966.
Phil 4080.3.280	La filosofia di Benedetto Croce e la crisi della società italiano. (Abbate, Michele.) Torino, 1955.
Phil 4265.6.95	La filosofia di Bernardino Varisco. (Calogero, G.) Messina, 1950.
Phil 196.8.80	La filosofia di Bernardino Varisco. (Drago, Pietro C.) Firenze, 1944.
Phil 2520.186.10	La filosofia di Descartes. (Olgiati, Francesco.) Milano, 1937.
Phil 2477.1.136	La filosofia di Emile Boutroux. (Liguori-Barbieri, E.) Pisa, 1926.
Phil 2475.1.149	La filosofia di Enrico Bergson. (Olgiati, Francesco.) Torino, 1914.
Phil 4365.1.15	La filosofia di Eugenio d'Ors. (Aranguren, José.) Milano, 1953.
Phil 4060.8.83	La filosofia di Francesco Acri. (Paggiaro, L.) Padova, 1953.
Phil 2115.29	La filosofia di G. Locke. (Locke, J.) Firenze, 1920-21. 2v.
Phil 3246.209	La filosofia di G.A. Fichte. (Ferro, A.A.) Savona, 1906.
Phil 4260.119	La filosofia di G.B. Vico e l'età barocca. (Giusso, Lorenzo.) Roma, 1943.
Phil 3425.420	La filosofia di G.G.F. Hegel. (Banfi, Antonio.) Milano, 1956.
Phil 4260.108	La filosofia di Giambattista Vico. (Chiocchetti, E.) Milano, 1935.
Phil 4260.85.2	La filosofia di Giambattista Vico. 2a ed. (Croce, B.) Bari, 1922.
Phil 4115.91.2	La filosofia di Gioberti. (Spaventa, B.) Napoli, 1870.
Phil 4115.91	La filosofia di Gioberti. v.1. (Spaventa, B.) Napoli, 1863.
Phil 4065.140	La filosofia di Giordano Bruno. (Badaloni, Nicola.) Firenze, 1955.
Phil 4065.115	La filosofia di Giordano Bruno. (Soliani, B.) Firenze, 1930.
Phil 4065.91	La filosofia di Giordano Bruno. (Troilo, Erminio.) Torino, 1904.
Phil 4065.122	La filosofia di Giordano Bruno nei suoi motivi plotiniani. (Saracista, M.) Firenze, 1935.
Phil 1870.97	La filosofia di Giorgio Berkeley. (Levi, Adolfo.) Torino, 1922.
Phil 4120.4.81	La filosofia di Giovanni Gentile. (Chiocchetti, E.) Milano, 1922.
Phil 3915.159	La filosofia di Guglielmo Wundt. (Prever, G.) Cuorgné, 1904.
Phil 2725.11.85	La filosofia di Jules Lachelier. (Agosti, Vittorio.) Torino, 1952.
Phil 4110.1.80	La filosofia di Marsilio Ficino. (Saitta, Giuseppe.) Messina, 1923.
Phil 4112.87	La filosofia di Pasquale Galluppi. (Giuli, G. de.) Palermo, 1935.
Phil 4112.89	La filosofia di Pasquale Galluppi. (Napoli, G. di.) Padova, 1947.
Phil 4195.85	La filosofia di Pico della Mirandola. (Semprini, G.) Milano, 1936.
Phil 3808.107.5	La filosofia di Schopenhauer. (Melli, Giuseppe.) Firenze, 1905.
Phil 2045.112	La filosofia di Thommaso Hobbes. (Levi, Adolfo.) Milano, 1929.
Phil 2240.85	La filosofia di Tomaso Reid. (Sciacca, M.F.) Napoli, 1938.
Phil 2240.85.3	La filosofia di Tommaso Reid. 3a ed. (Sciacca, M.F.) Milano, 1963.
Phil 2340.10.215	La filosofia di Whitehead e i problemi del tempo e della struttura. (Paci, Enzo.) Milano, 1965.

Phil 2070.144	La filosofia di William James. (Riconda, G.) Torino, 1962.
Phil 4225.8.58	Filosofia e antifilosofia. (Sciacca, Michele Federico.) Milano, 1968.
Phil 8582.46	Filosofia e apologetica. (Castelli, Enrico.) Roma, 1929.
Phil 177.58	Filosofia e buddhismo. (Costa, Alessandro.) Torino, 1913.
Phil 177.62.5	Filosofia e diritto. v.1-4. (Cicala, F.B.) Città di Castello, 1924.
Phil 800.18	Filosofia e filologia. (Alfieri, Vittorio Enzo.) Napoli, 1967.
Phil 801.33.5	La filosofia e il suo passato. (Bréhier, É.) Napoli, 1965.
Phil 600.2	Filosofia e la ricerca positiva. (Angiuli, A.) Napoli, 1869.
Phil 4060.5.30	La filosofia e la scuola. (Angiulli, A.) Napoli, 1888.
Phil 4070.7.10	La filosofia e la vita spirituale. (Banfi, Antonio.) Roma, 1967.
Phil 5520.443	Filosofia e linguaggio. (Pittau, Massimo.) Pisa, 1962.
Phil 5520.116	Filosofia e linguaggio. Padova, 1950.
Phil 1750.842	La filosofia e l'unità della cultura. (Pucci, Raffaele.) Napoli, 1970.
Phil 186.154	Filosofia e metafisica. (Lugarini, Leo.) Urbino, 1964.
Phil 4225.8.46	Filosofia e metafisica. v.1-2. 2. ed. (Sciacca, Michele Federico.) Milano, 1962.
Phil 8890.56	Filosofia e morale. (Padovani, U.A.) Padova, 1960.
Phil 2403.9	Filosofia e politica nel Settecento francese. (Diaz, F.) Torino, 1962.
Phil 4479.1.30	Filosofia e politica no destino de Portugal. (Sylvan, F.) Lisboa, 1963.
Phil 1714.4	Filosofia e psicologia nel pensiero postromantico. (Oggioni, Emilio.) Bologna, 1955.
Phil 6980.93	Filosofia e psiquiatria. (Barahona Fernandes, Henrique João de.) Coimbra, 1966.
Phil 4210.154	Filosofia e religione in Antonio Rosmini. (Rovea, G.) Domodossola, 1951.
Phil 4080.17.5	Filosofia e religione in un metafisico laico. 1. ed. (Nobile Ventura, O.M.) Milano, 1951.
Phil 165.65	Filosofia e simbolismo. (Archivio di Filosofia.) Roma, 1956.
Phil 812.42	Filosofia e storia della filosofia, 1933-1959. (Mazzantini, Carlo.) Torino, 1960.
Phil 4080.3.455	Filosofia e storia nel pensiero crociano. (Bausola, Adriano.) Milano, 1965.
Phil 4080.3.65	Filosofia e storiografia. (Croce, Benedetto.) Bari, 1949.
Phil 4080.30	Filosofia e verità; saggi e note. (Cristaldi, Giuseppe.) Milano, 1965.
Phil 15.35	Filosofia e vita. Rome. 3,1962+ 7v.
Phil 15.35.2	Filosofia e vita. Indici generali. Roma. 1960+
Phil 2150.18.80	Filosofia ed etica scientifica. (Campanale, D.) Bari, 1962.
Phil 4352.1.45	Filosofia elemental. (Balmes, Jaime.) Madrid, 1935.
Phil 177.19.5	Filosofia elementare. (Conti, Augusto.) Firenze, 1913.
Phil 4960.650	Filosofia em São Paulo. (Reale, Miguel.) São Paulo, 1962.
Phil 4960.245	La filosofía en Argentina actual. (Caturelli, Alberto.) Córdoba, 1963.
Phil 4960.405	La filosofía en Bolivía. (Francovich, Guillermo.) Buenos Aires, 1945.
Phil 4960.635	La filosofía en el Brasil. (Gómez Robledo, Antonio.) México, 1946.
Phil 4961.605	La filosofía en el Perú. (Salazar Bondy, Augusto.) Wáshington, 1955.
Phil 2255.1.20	La filosofía en el siglo XX y otros ensayos. (Russell, Bertrand Russell.) Montevideo, 1962.
Phil 4961.805.10	La filosofía en el Uruguay en el siglo XX. (Ardao, Arturo.) México, 1956.
Phil 4960.235	La filosofía en la Argentina. (Torchia Estrada, Juan Carlos.) Washington, 1961.
Phil 4959.235	La filosofía en la historía política de México. 1. ed. (Villegas, Abelardo.) México, 1966.
Phil 4959.230.5	La filosofía en México. v.1-2. (Zea, Leopoldo.) Mexico, 1955.
Phil 3705.3.90	La filosofía energetica. (Rolla, A.) Torino, 1907.
Phil 2880.8.120	La filosofía existenziale di Jean Paul Sartre. (Palumbo, Giovanni.) Palermo, 1953.
Phil 4322.1	La filosofía española. (Vidart, Louis.) Madrid, 1866.
Phil 4312.8	Filosofía española contemporánea; temas y autores. (Lopez Quintas, Alfonso.) Madrid, 1970.
Phil 4372.1.120	La filosofía española de Luis Vives. (Puigdollers Oliver, Mariano.) Barcelona, 1940.
Phil 4301.2	Filosofía española en America, 1936-1966. (Abellán, José Luis.) Madrid, 1967.
Phil 4319.3	Filosofía española y portuguesa de 1500 a 1650. (Spain.) Madrid, 1948.
Phil 3482.9	La filosofía etico-giuridica de Kant a Spencer. Pt.I. (Aguanno, G. d'.) Palermo, 1895.
Phil 3823.14	La filosofía etico-politica di Spinoza. (Deregilris, Arturo.) Torino, 1963.
Phil 1735.12	La filosofía Europea nel secolo decimonono. (Rava, Adolfo.) Padova, 1932.
Phil 1535.1.10	La filosofía fondamentale. v.1-2. (Balmes, Giacomo.) Napoli, 1851.
Phil 2421.7	La filosofía francese contemporanea. 1a ed. (Valentini, Francesco.) Milano, 1958.
Phil 2402.5	La filosofía francese e italiana del settecento. 3a ed. v.1-2. (Capone Braga, A.) Padova, 1947.
Phil 1535.1.5	Filosofía fundamental. (Balmès, Jaime.) Paris, 18- . 2v.
Phil 4352.1.40	Filosofía fundamental. 2. ed. (Balmes, Jaime.) Barcelona, 1848. 4v.
Phil 1107.7	La filosofía greca. (Carbonara, Cleto.) Napoli, 1951. 2v.
Phil 1117.5	La filosofía greca. (Melli, G.) Firenze, 1922.
Phil 1107.7.2	La filosofía greca: Aristotele. 2. ed. (Carbonara, Cleto.) Napoli, 1967.
Phil 1107.7.3	La filosofía greca. Platone. 2. ed. (Carbonara, Cleto.) Napoli, 1969.
Phil 1701.16	Filosofía in margine. (Baratono, Adelchi.) Milano, 1930.
Phil 4018.2	La filosofía italiana. (Spaventa, Bertrando.) Bari, 1908.
Phil 4018.2.5	La filosofía italiana. 3. ed. (Spaventa, Bertrando.) Bari, 1926.
Phil 4012.6.10	La filosofía italiana actual. (Miceli di Serradileo, R.) Buenos Aires, 1940.
Phil 4006.2.30	La filosofía italiana contemporanea. (Gentile, G.) Firenze, 1941.
Phil 193.121	Filosofía italiana e umanesimo. (Saitta, G.) Venezia, 1928.
Phil 4005.10	La filosofía italiana fra Ottocento e Novecento. Torino, 1954.

Phil 4011.4   La filosofia italiana negli ultimi cento anni. (Lombardi, Franco.) Asti, 1958?

Phil 186.46   Filosofia izobreteniia. (Lapshin', I.) Praga, 1924. 2v.

Phil 4957.20   La filosofía latinoamericana contemporanea. (Sánchez Reulet, Aníbal.) Washington, 1949.

Phil 1505.5   La filosofia medievale. (Abbagmano, N.) Bari, 1963.

Phil 4961.126.5   Filosofía mexicana. 1. ed. (Ibarguengoitía, Antonio.) Mexico, 1967.

Phil 4959.215   Filosofía mexicana de nuestros días. (Gaos, José.) México, 1954.

Phil 1721.7.5   Filosofía moderna y contemporanea. (Vélez Correa, Jaime.) Madrid, 1965.

Phil 1750.24   Filosofía moderna y filosofía tomista. (Derisi, Octavio N.) Buenos Aires, 1941.

Phil 8893.58   Filosofia morale. (Seta, Ugo della.) Roma, 1917-19. 2v.

Phil 8894.20.10   La filosofia morale. (Trojano, Paolo R.) Torino, 1902.

Phil 8880.30   Filosofia morale. 3a ed. (Friso, Luigi.) Milano, 1913.

Phil 4210.190   La filosofia morale di Antonio Rosmini. 3a ed. (Sciacca, M.F.) Milano, 1958.

Phil 3503.15   La filosofia morale di Emanuele Kant. (Verondini, Enrico.) Bologna, 1966.

Phil 3494.36   La filosofia morale di Emmanuel Kant. (Marchi, Vittore.) Roma, 1931.

Phil 2733.121   La filosofia morale di Malebranche. (Verga, Leonardo.) Milano, 1964.

Phil 8894.23   Filosofia morale e nozioni affini. (Tarrozzi, G.) Bologna, 1911.

Phil 5247.13.80   La filosofia natural de Huarte de San Juan. (Dantin Gallego, J.) Madrid, 1952.

Phil 4080.40.5   La filosofia nella storia civile del mondo. (Cardone, Domenico Antonio.) Roma, 1966.

Phil 4960.605.10   A filosofía no Brasil. (Cruz Costa, João.) Pôrto Alegre, 1945.

Phil 4225.8.32   La filosofia oggi. 3. ed. (Sciacca, Michele Federico.) Milano, 1958. 2v.

Phil 4012.7   La filosofia politica de Italia en el siglo XIX. (Mondolfo, Rodolfo.) Buenos Aires, 1942.

Phil 4215.1.86   La filosofia politica di Romagnosi. (Caboara, L.) Roma, 1936.

Phil 3801.272   La filosofia politica di Schelling. (Cesa, Claudio.) Bari, 1969.

Phil 4073.86   La filosofia politica di Tommaso Campanella. (Treves, Paulo.) Bari, 1930.

Phil 4961.805   Filosofía pre-universitaria en el Uruguay. (Ardao, Arturo.) Montevideo, 1945.

Phil 4002.5   La filosofia scolastica in Italia nell'ora presente. (Contri, Siro.) Bologna, 1931.

Phil 4810.2   Filosofia slovenského osvietenstva. Vyd. 1. (Muenz, Teodor.) Bratislava, 1961.

Phil 585.224   Filosofia social. (Silva, Antonio da.) Évora, 1966.

Phil 4080.3.139   La filosofia teoretica di Benedetto Croce. (Pardo, Ferruccio.) Napoli, 1928.

Phil 3494.61   La filosofia trascendentale. (Mathieu, V.) Torino, 1958.

Phil 4080.5.31   Filosofia universale. (Corleo, Simone.) Palermo, 1860-63. 2v.

Phil 510.156   Filosofia universitária. (Carvalho, Rubens di Souza.) Rio de Janeiro, 1964.

Phil 181.9.5   Filosofía y arte. (Giner, H.) Madrid, 1878.

Phil 1717.16   Filosofía y razón. (Roig Gironella, J.) Madrid, 1948.

Phil 4809.894.1   Filosofické spisy. (Zahradmk, Vincenc.) Praha, 1907-18. 3v.

Phil 4809.393   Filosofické studie. (Fischer, Josef L.) Praha, 1968.

Phil 15.16   Filosófický časopis. Praha. 4,1956+ 20v.

Phil 310.606   Filosofie a politika. (Samek, Antonín.) Praha, 1963.

Phil 310.796.2   Filosofie a současnost. 2. vyd. (Cvekl, Jiří.) Praha, 1969.

Phil 179.44   Filosofie als science-fiction. (Elders, Fons.) Amsterdam, 1968.

Phil 346.13   Filosofie der Wetenschappen. (Pos, Hendrik J.) Arnhem, 1940.

Phil 5520.481   Filosofie jazyku. (Horálek, Karel.) Praha, 1967.

Phil 1710.3.5   Filosofie posledních let před válkou. 2. vyd. (Krejčí, F.) Praha, 1930.

Phil 4807.4   Filosofie v dějinách českého národa. Vyd. 1. (Konference o dějinách české filosofie, Liblice, 1958.) Praha, 1958.

Phil 310.621   Filosofie v neklidné době. (Nový, Lubomír.) Praha, 1965.

Phil 4502.2   Filosofien i Danmark i dit 18. og 19. aarhundrede. (Hansen, Oscar.) København, 1897.

Phil 4500.2   Filosofien i Norden. (Aall, Anathon.) Kristiania, 1919.

Phil 4500.4.5   Filosofien i Norden efter 1900. (Holm, Søren.) København, 1967.

Phil 4500.4   Filosofien i Norden før 1900. (Holm, Søren.) København, 1967.

Phil 4508.5   Filosofien i Sverige. (Höffding, Harald.) Stockholm, 1879.

Phil 4600.2.48   Filosofien och politiken. (Larsson, Hans.) Stockholm, 1915.

Phil 822.7   Filosofiens historia efter Pontus Wikner's kollegium. (Wikner, Pontus.) Rock Island, Ill., 1896.

Phil 802.9   Filosofiens historia i sammandrag. (Claeson, Gustaf.) n.p., n.d.

Phil 822.3   Filosofiens historia i sammandrag. (Wägner, S.) Lund, 1914.

Phil 800.5   Filosofiens historie. (Aall, Anothon.) Oslo, 1929.

Phil 1718.9.5   Filosofiens historie. (Schjelderup, Harald K.) Oslo, 1925.

Phil 181.49   Filosofiens historiska hufvudformer. (Geijer, Reinhold.) Uppsala, 1916.

Phil 184.34   Filosofiens og apdragelsene grundproblemer. (Jørgensen, J.) København, 1928.

Phil 4635.4.31   Filosofiens uppgift. (Schéele, Frans von.) Upsala, 1899.

Phil 3850.20.84   Filosofies opooedkundige sketse. (Smits, J.P.) Amsterdam, 1929.

Phil 1801.10   Filosofiia amerikanskogo prosveshcheniia. (Baskin, M.P.) Moskva, 1955.

Phil 8980.801   Filosofiia bor'by. (Sokolov, Andrei V.) Moskva, 1909.

Phil 2050.250   Filosofiia D. Iuma. (Mikhalenko, Iu.P.) Moskva, 1962.

Phil 2050.268   Filosofiia Davida Iuma. (Narskii, Igor' S.) Moskva, 1967.

Phil 4115.84   Filosofiia dzhoberti. (Ern, V.F.) Moskva, 1916.

Phil 3425.238   Filosofiia Gegelia. (Il'in, Ivan A.) Moskva, 1918.

Phil 3425.500   Filosofiia Gegelia. (Ovsiannikov, M.F.) Moskva, 1959.

Phil 310.625   Filosofiia i marksizm. (Deborin, Abram M.) Moskva, 1926.

Phil 310.720   Filosofiia i nauchnyi kommunizm. Moskva, 1968.

Phil 310.320   Filosofiia i politika. (Deborin, A.M.) Moskva, 1961.

Phil 4873.5   Filosofiia i sotsiologiia v Pakistane. (Stepovniants, Marietta Tigranovna.) Moskva, 1967.

Phil 70.100.15   Filosofiia i sovnemennost'. Moskva, 1971.

Phil 310.310   Filosofiia i sovremennost'. (Mitin, M.B.) Moskva, 1960.

Phil 4756.1.29   Filosofiia i zhizn', etiudy i nabroski po filosofii kul'tury. (Frank, Semen L.) Sankt Peterburg, 1910.

Phil 801.37   Filosofiia i zhizn'. (Baskin, M.P.) Moskva, 1961.

Phil 8656.35   Filosofiia imeni. (Bulgakov, S.N.) Parizh, 1953.

Phil 3235.120   Filosofiia Ludviga Feierbakha. (Baskin, M.P.) Moskva, 1957.

Phil 310.530   Filosofiia marksizma i neopozitivizma. Moskva, 1963.

Phil 5520.726   Filosofiia na lingvistikata sreshchu lingvisticheskata filosofiia. (Spasov, Dobrin I.) Sofiia, 1970.

Phil 4710.50   Filosofiia na Ukraïni. Vyd. 2. (Chizhevskii, O.) Praga, 1928.

Phil 3450.18.90   Filosofiia Nikolaia Gartmana. (Gornshtein, T.N.) Leningrad, 1969.

Phil 4756.2.30   Filosofiia obshchago dela. Izd.2. (Fedorov, N.F.) Kharbin, 1928-

Phil 4756.2.30.5   Filosofiia obshchago dela. v.2. (Fedorov, N.F.) Vernyi, 1913-

Phil 1750.730   Filosofiia otohaianiia i strakha. (Chalin, M.L.) Moskva, 1962.

Phil 4800.16   Filosofiia pol'skogo Prosveshcheniia. (Osipova, Elena Vladimirovna.) Moskva, 1961.

Phil 5068.50   Filosofiia reopozitivizma i semantiki. (Mshvenieradze, V.V.) Moskva, 1961.

Phil 3838.30   Filosofiia Spinozy i sovremennost'. (Sokolov, V.V.) Moskva, 1964.

Phil 8581.69.3   Filosofiia svobodnogo dukha. v.1-2. (Berdiaev, N.A.) Parizh, 1927.

Phil 4710.16   Filosofiia v Rossii; materialy. (Bobrov, E.A.) Kazan, 1899.

Phil 2855.7.35   Filosofiia Zh. B. Robine, ocherk iz istorii frantsuzskogo materializma XVIII v. (Sitkovskii, E.) Moskva, 1936.

Phil 4752.1.32   Filosofiia zhivogo opyta. (Malinovskii, Aleksandr A.) Moskva, 1920.

Phil 4065.50.15   Filosofiiata na Dzhordano Bruno. (Boyanov, Slavi.) Sofiia, 1969.

Phil 98.3.2   Filosofiký sborník pro sannonsy neboli autigorgias. 2. vyd. (Neff, Vladimir.) Praha, 1970.

Phil 197.85   Filosofins historia. (Wedberg, Anders.) Stockholm, 1958. 3v.

Phil 91.5   Filosofisch lexicon. (Grooten, J.) Antwerpen, 1958.

Phil 4570.1.30   Filosofisk rätts- och samhälls-lära. (Grubbe, Samuel.) Upsala, 1839.

Phil 8584.8   Filosofisk religionslära. (Edfeldt, Hans.) Uppsala, 1903.

Phil 8875.19   Filosofisk sedelära. v.1-4. (Åberg, L.H.) Uppsala, 1893-94.

Phil 4605.74.31   Filosofiska dis Kussioner. (Marc-Wogan, Konrad.) Stockholm, 1967.

Phil 4600.1.31   Filosofiska essayer. (Landquist, John.) Stockholm, 1906.

Phil 4575.25   Filosofiska föreläsningar, 1806-1812. (Höijer, B.C.H.) Lund, 1931.

Phil 4630.5.2   Filosofiska föreläsningar. (Rydberg, V.) Stockholm, 1900-01. 4v.

Phil 4508.4   Den filosofiska forskningen i Sverige. (Nyblaseus, Axel.) Lund, 1873-97. 3v.

Phil 4635.7.9   Filosofiska fragment. v.1-2. (Stjernhjelm, Georg.) Stockholm, 1924.

Phil 175.34   De filosofiska grundproblemen. (Ahlberg, Alf.) Stockholm, 1922.

Phil 4650.1.51   Filosofiska konturer. (Vannérus, Allen.) Göteborg, 1902.

Phil 179.22.5   Filosofiska miniaturer. (Erdmann, J.E.) Stockholm, 1873.

Phil 5520.754.2   Filosofiska och språkvetenskapliga grundfrågor inom betydelseläran. 2. uppl. (Regnell, Hans.) Stockholm, 1971.

Phil 8701.24   Filosofiska och teologiska essayer. (Lindroth, Hjalmer.) Stockholm, 1965.

Phil 4570.1.5   Filosofiska skrifter i Urval. v.1-5. (Grubbe, Samuel.) Lund, 1876. 7v.

Phil 4635.4.33   Filosofiska studier. Första samlingen. (Schéele, Frans von.) Stockholm, 1899.

Phil 184.34.5   Filosofiske forelassninger son indledning tilvidenskabelige studier. (Jørgensen, J.) København, 1926.

Phil 807.5   Filosofiske problemer. (Hoffding, H.) København, 1902.

Phil 807.24.7   Filosofiske problemer og filosofiske argumentationer. 2. Opl. (Hartnack, Justus.) København, 1970.

Phil 3450.19.390   Dei filosofiske vilkår for sanning. (Skirbekk, Gunnar.) Oslo, 1966.

Phil 15.8A   Filosofiskie zapiski. Moskva. 1-6,1946-1953 6v.

Phil 807.24   Filosofisns historie. (Hartnack, Justus.) København, 1969.

Phil 4353.12   Un filosofo catalan, Antonio Comellas y Cluet. (Gomez Izquierdo, A.) Madrid, 1907.

Phil 1715.10   El filósofo en la sociedad actual. (Pinilla, Antonio.) Lima, 1959.

Phil 3195.10.117   El filósofo Hans Driesch. (Coviello, A.) Tucumán, 1942.

Phil 4960.655   Filósofos brasileños. (Francovich, Guillermo.) Buenos Aires, 1943.

Phil 4959.240   Filósofos mexicanos del siglo XVI. (Robles, Oswaldo.) Mexico, 1950.

Phil 1695.48   Los filósofos modernos en la independencia latino-americana. 1. ed. (Cardiel Reyes, Raul.) México, 1964.

Phil 4450.6   Filósofos portugueses do séc. XVIII. v.1-3. (Andrade, A.A. de.) Lisboa, 1957-

Phil 8877.37   Filósofos y doctrinas morales. (Caso, Antonio.) Mexico, 1915.

Phil 176.240   Filósofos y filosofias. (Betancur, Cayetano.) Bogota, 1969.

Phil 2402.6   Filósofos y moralistas franceses. (Caso, A.) México, 1943.

Phil 4368.2.60   Filósofos y problemas. 2. ed. (Romero, Francisco.) Buenos Aires, 1957.

Phil 15.50   Filosofs'ka dumka. Kyïv. 1970+

Phil 15.14   Filosofska misül. Sofiiá. 1,1945+ 26v.

Phil 90.6   Filosofskaia entsiklopediia. Moskva, 1960-70. 5v.

Phil 960.244   Filosofskaia mysl' nezavisimoi Indii. (Litman, Aleksei D.) Moskva, 1966.

Phil 4791.8   Filosofskaia mysl' v Gruzii v pervoi chetverti XX veka. (Sheroziia, Apollon Epifonovich.) Tbilisi, 1963.

Phil 4710.75   Filosofskaia nauka v SSSR za 25 let. (Mitin, M.B.) Moskva, 1943.

Phil 15.25   Filosofski pregled. Sofiia. 1-4,1929-1942 18v.

Phil 4757.5   Filosofskie i obshchestvenno-politicheskie vozzreniia Afanasiia Gassieva. (Tsallaev, Khariton K.) Ordzhonikidze, 1966.

Phil 4720.6   Filosofskie idei russkogo prosveshcheniia. (Kamenskii, Zakhar A.) Moskva, 1971.

Phil 165.427   Filosofskie nauki. Stavropol', 1967.
Phil 4769.8.21   Filosofskie ocherki. (Strakhov, N.N.) Sankt
     Peterbrug, 1895.
Phil 4772.10.5   Filosofskie ocherki. (Vvedenskii, A.I.) Praga, 1924.
Phil 8655.19   Filosofskie problemy ateizma. (Akademiia Nauk SSSR.
     Institut Filosofii.) Moskva, 1965.
Phil 8600.6   Filosofskie problemy Kritiki religii. (Ugrinovich,
     Dimitrii M.) Moskva, 1965.
Phil 5066.170   Filosofskie problemy mnogoznachnoi logiki. (Zinov'ev,
     Aleksandr A.) Moskva, 1960.
Phil 8598.125.5   Filosofskie problemy proiskhozhdeniia religii. (Sukhov,
     Andrei D.) Moskva, 1967.
Phil 5545.228   Filosofskie problemy teorii pamiati. (Rogovin, Mikhail S.)
     Moskva, 1966.
Phil 15.20   Filosofskie voprosy estestvoznaniia. Moskva. 1-3   3v.
Phil 6110.26   Filosofskie voprosy fiziologii vysshei nervnoi
     deiatel'nosti. (Akademiia Nauk SSSR. Institut Filosofii.)
     Moskva, 1963.
Phil 15.55   Filosofskie voprosy logicheskogo analiza nauchnogo znaniia.
     Erevan. 1,1969+   2v.
Phil 5253.21   Filosofskie voprosy modelirovaniia psikhiki. (Novik, Il'ia
     B.) Moskva, 1969.
Phil 310.485   Filosofskie voprosy sovremennogo ucheniia o dvizhenii v
     prirode. (Leningrad. Universitet.) Leningrad, 1962.
Phil 5040.26   Filosofskie voprosy sovremennoi formal'noi logiki.
     (Akademiia Nauk SSSR. Institut Filosofii.) Moskva, 1962.
Phil 4770.5   Filosofskie vzgliady I.R. Tarkhnishvili. (Avaliani, S.Sh.)
     Tbilisi, 1957.
Phil 102.8   Filosofskii slovar'. (Radlov, Ernest L.) Sankt
     Peterburg, 1904.
Phil 102.5.7   Filosofskii slovar'. (Rozental, Mark Moiseevich.)
     Moskva, 1963.
Phil 102.8.2   Filosofskii slovar'. Izd. 2. (Radlov, Ernest L.)
     Moskva, 1913.
Phil 102.5.8   Filosofskii slovar'. Izd. 2. (Rozental, Mark Moiseevich.)
     Moskva, 1963.
Phil 4762.2.30   Filosofskiia kharakteristiki i rechi. (Lopatin, Lev M.)
     Moskva, 1911.
Phil 185.53   Filosofskitě printsipi na prirodata. (Khristov, M.)
     Sofia, 1935.
Phil 310.1.5   Filosofsko-sotsiologicheskaia literatura marksizma za
     1917-1927. (Rozanov, Iakov S.) Moskva, 1928.
Phil 5590.475.5   Filosofsko-sotsiologicheskie problemy seorii lichnosti.
     Photoreproduction. Moskva, 1969. 2v.
Phil 672.195   Filosofskoe znachenie prostranstvenno-vremennykh
     predstavlenii v fizike. (Sviderskii, V.I.)
     Leningrad, 1956.
Phil 930.62   Filosofy drevnego kitaia. (Kuo, Mo-jo.) Moskva, 1961.
Phil 310.629   Filová, Elena. Materializmus proti holizmu.
     Bratislava, 1963.
Phil 4826.2   Filozofi. Novi Sad, 1966.
Phil 310.445.15   Filozofia człowieka. 3. Wyd. (Schaff, Adam.)
     Warszawa, 1965.
Phil 4803.472.20   Filozofia ekonomii materialnej ludzkiego społeczństwa.
     (Kamieński, Henryk.) Warszawa, 1959.
Phil 4803.522.15   Filozofia i krytyka. Wyd. 2. v.1-6. (Libelt, Karol.)
     Poznań, 1874-75. 3v.
Phil 4710.125   Filozofia i myśl społeczna rosyjska, 1825-1861. (Walicki,
     Andrzej.) Warzawa, 1961.
Phil 4110.11.35   Filozofia i seoria piękna Marsilia Ficina. Wyd. 1.
     (Kuczyńska, Alicja.) Warszawa, 1970.
Phil 1718.40   A filozófia is közügy! Tanulmányok. (Sándor, Pál.)
     Budapest, 1968.
Phil 182.1.81   A filozófia kis tükre. 2. kiad. (Halasy-Nagy, J.)
     Budapest, 193-?
Phil 310.755   Filozofia marksislowska. Wyd. 1. Warszawa, 1970.
VPhil 2280.5.150   Filozofia moralna Santayany. Wyd. 1. (Szmyd, Jan.)
     Warszawa, 1968.
Phil 4803.313.20   Filozofia na rozdrozu. Wyd. 1. (Czezowski, Tadeusz.)
     Warszawa, 1965.
Phil 850.31   Filozofia okresu sosarstwa rzymekiego. (Legowiiz, J.)
     Warszawa, 1962.
Phil 4800.26   Filozofia polska. Warszawa, 1967.
Phil 600.59   Filozofia pozytywistyczna. (Kolakowski, Leszek.)
     Warszawa, 1966.
Phil 4803.241.90   Filozofia pracy Stanisława Brzozowskiego. Wyd. 1.
     (Trzebuchowski, Pavel.) Warszawa, 1971.
Phil 281.14   Filozofia przyrody. (Amczyk, S.) Lublin, 1963.
Phil 4803.108.25   Filozofia społeczna. (Abramowski, Edward.)
     Warszawa, 1965.
Phil 2045.155   Filozofia strachu i nadziei. Wyd. 1. (Wudel, Witold.)
     Warszawa, 1971.
Phil 4810.4   Filozofia v boji o dnešok. Vyd. 1. (Uher, Ján.)
     Bratislava, 1961.
Phil 4013.7   Filozofia włoskiego odrodzenia. (Nowicki, Andrzej.)
     Warszawa, 1967.
Phil 9070.109   Filozofia życia. Wyd. 1. (Kuczyński, Janusz.)
     Warszawa, 1965.
Phil 310.25   Filozófiai elöadasok es tanulmányok. (Fogarasi, Bela.)
     Budapest, 1952.
Phil 180.2.35   Filozófiai értekezések. (Farkas, S.)
     Aiud-Nagyenyed, 1938.
Phil 15.18   Filozófiai évkönyv. Budapest. 1,1952
Phil 102.5.10   Filozoficky slovnik. (Rozental, Mark Moiseevich.)
     Bratislava, 1965.
VPhil 2225.5.145   Filozoficzny pragmatyzm C.S. Peirce'a. (Dobrosielski,
     Marian.) Warszawa, 1967.
Phil 310.445.5   Filozofiia człowiekas. 2. Wyd. (Schaff, Adam.)
     Warszawa, 1962.
Phil 15.30   Filozofija. Beograd. 1,1957+   9v.
VPhil 2255.1.140   Filozofija Bertranda Russella: strasno traženje izvesnosti.
     (Knjazeva-Adamović, Svetlana.) Zagreb, 1966.
Phil 4829.160.80   Filozofija Djue Arnolda. (Despot, Branko.) Zagreb, 1970.
Phil 8581.113   Filozofija i kršćanstvo. (Bošnjak, Branko.) Zagreb, 1966.
Phil 4803.282.80   Filozofija Augusta Hr. Cieszkowskiego w świetle zasad
     filozofji. (Kowalski, Kazimierz Józef.) Poznań, 1929.
Phil 75.72   Filozofski tokovi na Slovenskem. (Verbinc, Franc.)
     Ljubljana, 1966.
Phil 75.72.5   Filozofski tokovi na Slovenskem. (Verbinc, Franc.)
     Ljubljana, 1970.
Phil 3640.119.10   Filser, Benno. Die Ästhetik Nietzsches. Passau, 1917.
Phil 2475.1.299.5   La fin d'une parade philosophique, le Bergsonisme.
     (Politzer, Georges.) Paris, 1967.
Phil 8735.1   Final causes. (Call, W.M.W.) London, 1891.
Phil 2668.50.4   Final causes. 2d ed. (Janet, Paul A.R.) N.Y., 1883.
Phil 2668.50.5   Final causes. 3d ed. (Janet, Paul A.R.) N.Y., 1884.
Phil 6315.1.15   Final contributions to the problems and methods of
     psychoanalysis. (Ferenczi, Sandor.) London, 1955.

Phil 7039.12   The final face of Eve. (Lancaster, Evelyn.) N.Y., 1958.
Phil 5590.460   Final integration in the adult personality. (Arasteh, A.
     Reza.) Leiden, 1965.
Phil 193.25.3   The final philosophy. (Shields, C.W.) N.Y., 1877.
Phil 9230.13   Final report. (Great Britain. Commission on Lotteries and
     Betting, 1932-33.) London, 1933.
Phil 4967.20.10   Finalidade do mundo. 2. ed. (Farias Brito, Raymundo de.)
     Rio de Janeiro, 1957. 3v.
Phil 3450.18.175   Finalität. (Moeslang, Alois.) Freiburg, 1964.
Phil 8842.10   La finalité morale. (Rohmer, J.) Paris, 1939.
Phil 8842.10.5   La finalité morale chez les théologiens de Saint Augustin
     à Duns Scot. Thèse. (Rohmer, J.) Paris, 1938.
Phil 2475.1.261   Le finalité morale dans le Bergsonisme. (Rolland, E.)
     Paris, 1937.
Phil 2520.231   Finance, J. de. Cogito cartésien et réflexion thomiste.
     Thèse. Paris, 1946[1945].
Phil 2605.12.30   Finance, Joseph de. Connaissance de l'être, traité
     d'ontologie. Paris, 1966.
Phil 8880.63   Finance, Joseph de. Grundlegung der Ethik.
     Freiburg, 1968.
Phil 5190.65   Finazzo, Giancarlo. Sulla dialettica dell'apriori.
     Roma, 1966.
Phil 3450.19.320   Finazzo, Giancarlo. L'umo e il mondo nella filosofia di M.
     Heidegger. Roma, 1963.
Phil 1850.106   Finch, A. Elley. On the inductive philosophy.
     London, 1872.
Phil 5090.1   Finch, A.E. The pursuit of truth. London, 1873.
Phil 2805.224   Finch, D. La critique philosophique de Pascal au XVIIIe
     siècle. Diss. Philadelphia, 1940.
Phil 3925.16.290   Finch, Henry Leroy. Wittgenstein - the early philosophy.
     N.Y., 1971.
Phil 5520.10   Finck, F.N. Die Aufgabe und Gliederung der
     Sprachwissenschaft. Halle, 1905.
Phil 180.40   Finckh, T. Lehrbuch der philosophischen Propädeutik.
     Heidelberg, 1909.
Phil 9070.7   Find your own frontier. (Bartlett, A.C.) Boston, 1940.
Phil 5465.194   Das Finden als Moment des Schöpferischen. (Braeuer,
     Gottfried.) Tübingen, 1966.
Phil 2138.152   Findikoğlu, Z.F. Stuart Mill ve Türkiyedeki tesirleri.
     Istanbul, 1963.
Phil 5850.385.70   Finding your way in life. (Weston, Sidney A.) N.Y., 1942.
Phil 6980.292   Findl, Fritz. Die psychiatriochen Theorien Rudolf Arndt's.
     München, 1960.
Phil 7069.31.7   Findlay, J.A. A landmaerum annars heims. Reykjavik, 1934?
Phil 180.86   Findlay, J.N. Language, mind and value. London, 1963.
Phil 3625.11.85   Findlay, J.N. Meinong's theory of objects. London, 1933.
Phil 3625.11.86   Findlay, J.N. Meinong's theory of objects and values. 2.
     ed. Oxford, 1963.
Phil 2005.13   Findlay, John N. The discipline of the cave.
     London, 1966.
Phil 165.386   Findlay, John N. Studies in philosophy: British Academy
     lectures. London, 1966.
Phil 2005.14   Findlay, John N. The transcendence of the cave.
     London, 1967.
Phil 252.5   Findlay, John Niemayer. Ascent to the absolute:
     metaphysical papers and lectures. London, 1970.
Phil 3425.460   Findlay, John Niemayer. Hegel. London, 1958.
Phil 8880.50   Findlay, John Niemayer. Values and intentions.
     London, 1961.
Phil 735.280   Findlay, Niemayer. Axiological ethics. London, 1970.
Phil 8630.15   Findlay, Stephen. Immortal longings. London, 1961.
Phil 181.62   Fine art of living. (Goldberg, Isaac.) Boston, 1930.
Phil 8892.45   Il fine dell'uomo. (Rignano, E.) Bologna, 1928.
Phil 4260.112   Finetti, Giovanni F. Difesa dell'autorità della sacra
     scrittura contro Giambattista Vico. Bari, 1936.
Phil 9470.14   Fingarette, Herbert. On responsibility. N.Y., 1967.
Phil 5590.272   Fingarette, Herbert. Self-deception. London, 1969.
Phil 3005.9   Finger, Otto. Von der Materialität der Seele.
     Berlin, 1961.
Phil 5245.81   Fingerman, G. Estudios de psicologia y de estetica.
     Buenos Aires, 1926.
Phil 7069.32.15   Fingerprint demonstrations. (Dudley, E.E.) Boston, 1932.
Phil 310.558   Fingert, B.A. Kratkii uchebnik istoricheskogo
     materializma. Leningrad, 1930.
Phil 6315.54   Fingrette, H. The self in transformation. N.Y., 1963.
Phil 6115.29   Fink, David H. Release from nervous tension. N.Y., 1943.
Phil 336.16   Fink, Eugen. Alles und Nichts. Den Haag, 1959.
Phil 8612.78   Fink, Eugen. Metaphysik und Tod. Stuttgart, 1969.
Phil 3640.785   Fink, Eugen. Nietzsches Philosophie. 2e Aufl. Köln, 1968.
Phil 180.70.5   Fink, Eugen. Oase des Glücks. Freiburg, 1957.
Phil 3640.704   Fink, Eugen. La philosophie de Nietzsche. Paris, 1965.
Phil 180.70.10   Fink, Eugen. Sein. Den Haag, 1968.
Phil 1750.115.70   Fink, Eugen. Studien zur Phänomenologie, 1930-1939. Den
     Haag, 1966.
Phil 180.70   Fink, Eugen. Zur ontologischen Frühgeschichte von Raum,
     Zeit, Bewegung. Den Haag, 1957.
Phil 8880.68   Fink, Hans. Moralbegrundelse og logik. København, 1970.
Phil 5245.65   Finkelstein, Ben A. Psychologische skizzen.
     Amsterdam, 1957.
Phil 180.58   Finlayson Elliot, Clarence. Intuicion del ser.
     Santiago, 1938.
Phil 180.53   Finley, John H. The mystery of the mind's desire.
     N.Y., 1936.
Phil 1110.4   Finley, John Huston. Four stages of Greek thought.
     Stanford, 1966.
Phil 5245.26   Finnbogason, G. L'intelligence sympathetique.
     Paris, 1913.
Phil 7069.16.17   Finnbogason, Gudmundur. Pörfin á vinnuvísindum.
     Reykjavik, 1916.
Phil 5245.39   Finner, P.F. An introduction to experimental psychology.
     N.Y., 1935.
Phil 9245.21   Finot, Jean. Progrès et bonheur. Paris, 1914. 2v.
Phil 5627.32   Finot, Jean. Saints, inités et possédés modernes.
     Paris, 1918.
Phil 4170.6.40   Le finzioni dell'anima. (Marchesini, G.) Bari, 1905.
Phil 1750.161   Fiolle, Jean. La crise de l'humanisme. Paris, 1937.
Phil 310.808   Fiorani, Eleonora. Friedrich Engels e il materialismo
     dialettico. Milano, 1971.
Phil 9560.14.10   Fiore di Virtù. The Florentine Fior di virtù of 1491.
     Philadelphia, 1953.
Phil 9560.14.5   Fiore di virtù. Firenze, 1856.
Phil 9560.14.20   Fiore di virtù dans la litterature roamaine. (Cartojan,
     N.) n.p., n.d.
Phil 9560.14   Fiore di virtù historiato. Vinegia, 1545.
Phil 9560.14.18   Fiore di virtù in literature românesca. (Cartojan, N.)
     Bucarsti, 1928.
Phil 4235.9.80   Fiorensoli, Dario. Il pensiero filosofico di Guiseppe
     Tarozzi. Padova, 1964.

Phil 805.6.3   Fiorentino, F. Compendio di storia della filosofia. vol. 1-2, pt.1. Firenze, 1921-22. 2v.

Phil 4120.6.90   Fiorentino, F. Della vita e delle opere di Vincenzo de Grazia. Napoli, 1877.

Phil 4005.2   Fiorentino, F. La filosofia contemporanea in Italia. Napoli, 1876.

Phil 4200.1.6   Fiorentino, F. Luigi Ferri: la psicologia di Pietro Pomponazzi. Napoli, 1877.

Phil 805.6.2   Fiorentino, F. Manuele di storia della filosofia. Torino, 1921. 2v.

Phil 4065.119   Fiorentino, F. Il panteismo di Giordano Bruno. Napoli, 1861.

Phil 4200.1.82   Fiorentino, F. Pietro Pomponazzi. Firenze, 1868.
Phil 4005.2.5   Fiorentino, F. Scritti varii di letteratura, filosofia e critica. Napoli, 1876.

Phil 4235.1.82   Fiorentino, Francesco. Bernardino Telesio ossia studi storici su l'idea della natura nel risorgimento italiano. Firenze, 1872-74. 2v.

Phil 336.14   Fireman, Peter. Perceptualistic theory of knowledge. N.Y., 1954.

Phil 336.10   Fireman, Peter. Sound thinking. N.Y., 1947.
Phil 9172.3   The fireside: an aid to parents. (Muzzey, A.B.) Boston, 1854.

Phil 8581.91.10   A firm faith for today. 1. ed. (Bosley, Harold A.) N.Y., 1950.

Phil 1140.8   Firniani, S. Le idee psicologiche in Grecia nel periodo presofistico e l'esposizione critica di Aristotele. Napoli, 1904.

Phil 4073.97   Firpo, Luigi. Bibliografia degli scritti di Tommaso Campanella. Torino, 1940.

Phil 4073.113   Firpo, Luigi. L'iconografia di Tommaso Campanella. Firenze, 1964.

Phil 4065.145   Firpo, Luigi. Il processo di Giordano Bruno. Napoli, 1949.

Phil 4073.97.5   Firpo, Luigi. Ricerche Campanelliane. Firenze, 1947.
Phil 4200.6.80   Firrito, Giovanni. Ontologia e assiologia critica nel pensiero di Nicola Petruzzellis. Napoli, 1967.

Phil 180.63A   First adventures in philosophy. (Ferm, V.) N.Y., 1936.
Phil 6420.38   First aide for stutterers. (Heltman, Harry J.) Boston, 1943.

Phil 2125.30   First and fundamental truths. (McCosh, James.) N.Y., 1889.

Phil 978.59.35   The first and last freedom. (Krishnamurti, J.) London, 1954.

Phil 197.16.4   First and last things. (Wells, H.G.) London, 1918.
Phil 197.16   First and last things. (Wells, H.G.) N.Y., 1908.
Phil 5058.28.5   A first book in logic. (Smith, Henry B.) N.Y., 1922.
Phil 187.26.5   A first book in metaphysics. (Marvin, W.T.) N.Y., 1912.
Phil 5242.13.9   A first book in psychology. (Calkins, M.W.) N.Y., 1910.
Phil 5242.13.10   A first book in psychology. 2. ed. (Calkins, M.W.) N.Y., 1911.

Phil 5242.13.12   A first book in psychology. 4. ed. (Calkins, M.W.) N.Y., 1914.

Phil 8677.4   The first cause. (Whish, J.C.) London, 1855.
Phil 8696.9   First chapter of Genesis as the rock foundation for science and religion. (Gridley, Albert L.) Boston, 1913.

Phil 6315.1.18A   First contributions to psychoanalysis. (Ferenczi, Sandor.) London, 1952.

Phil 192.29A   A first course in philosophy. (Russell, J.E.) N.Y., 1913.
Phil 8585.5   The first day in heaven. London, 1820.
Phil 184.26.30   A first encounter with philosophy. (Joad, C.E.M.) London, 1952.

Phil 978.6.90   The first five lives of Annie Besant. (Nethercot, A.H.) Chicago, 1960.

Phil 5592.135   The first five minutes. (Pittenger, R.E.) Ithaca, 1960.
Phil 5545.10.9   First fundamental basis of phreno-mnemotechnic principles. (Fauvel-Gourand, F.) N.Y., 1844.

Phil 3585.20.6   A first introduction to existential phenomenology. (Luijpen, Wilhelmus Antonius Maria.) Pittsburgh, 1969.

Phil 3450.11.395   A first introduction to Husserl's phenomenology. (Kockelmans, Joseph John.) Pittsburgh, 1967.

Phil 3480.52.20   First introduction to the Critique of judgment. (Kant, Immanuel.) Indianapolis, 1965.

Phil 5242.30.7   A first laboratory guide in psychology. (Collins, Mary.) London, 1926.

Phil 5242.30.5   A first laboratory guide in psychology. (Collins, Mary.) London, 1926.

Phil 5062.26   First lessons in logic. (Waite, Dorothy J.) London, 1923.
Phil 5245.2   First lines of the human mind. (Fearn, J.) London, 1820.
Phil 5066.228   First-order functional calculus. (Keene, G.B.) London, 1964.

Phil 6980.573   First Pan-African psychiatric conference. (Pan-African Psychiatric Conference, 1st, Abeokuta, 1961.) Ibadan, 1962?

Phil 2270.45   First principles. (Spencer, Herbert.) London, 1862.
Phil 2270.45.2   First principles. (Spencer, Herbert.) London, 1862.
Htn   Phil 2270.45.1*   First principles. (Spencer, Herbert.) London, 1862.
Htn   Phil 2270.45.2.5*   First principles. (Spencer, Herbert.) London, 1862.
Phil 2270.30   First principles. (Spencer, Herbert.) London, 1870.
Phil 2270.45.7   First principles. (Spencer, Herbert.) N.Y., n.d.
Phil 2270.45.3   First principles. (Spencer, Herbert.) N.Y., 1864.
Phil 2270.45.3.10   First principles. (Spencer, Herbert.) N.Y., 1865.
Phil 2270.45.3.15   First principles. (Spencer, Herbert.) N.Y., 1866.
Phil 2270.45.4   First principles. (Spencer, Herbert.) N.Y., 1873.
Phil 2270.45.4.7   First principles. (Spencer, Herbert.) N.Y., 188-?
Phil 2270.45.17   First principles. (Spencer, Herbert.) N.Y., 188-.
Phil 2270.45.4.10   First principles. (Spencer, Herbert.) N.Y., 188-?
Phil 2270.45.5   First principles. (Spencer, Herbert.) N.Y., 1886.
Phil 2270.45.15   First principles. (Spencer, Herbert.) N.Y., 1892.
Phil 2270.45.25   First principles. (Spencer, Herbert.) N.Y., 1894.
Phil 2270.45.27   First principles. (Spencer, Herbert.) N.Y., 1896.
Phil 2270.45.9   First principles. (Spencer, Herbert.) N.Y., 1900.
Phil 2270.45.30   First principles. (Spencer, Herbert.) N.Y., 1958.
Phil 2270.45.14   First principles. 4th ed. (Spencer, Herbert.) N.Y., 1885.
Phil 8877.5.2   First principles of ethics. (Champlin, J.T.) N.Y., n.d.
Phil 8672.1   First principles of faith. (Randles, M.) London, 1884.
Phil 8876.17   First principles of moral science. (Birks, T.R.) London, 1873.

Phil 978.61.10   First principles of theosophy. 3d ed. (Dhopeshwarkar, A.D.) Adyar, Madras, 1923.

Phil 193.4   First steps in philosophy. (Salter, W.M.) Chicago, 1892.
Phil 176.34.5   First truths. (Buffier, Claude.) London, 1780.
Phil 530.20.125   Firtel, Hilde. Dorothea von Montau. Freiburg in der Schweiz, 1968.

Phil 7069.31.8   Firth, Violet M. Spiritualism in the light of occult science. London, 1931.

Phil 5585.215   Fisandt, Kai von. Havaitsemisen maailma. Helsinki, 1962.

Phil 3450.11.124   Fisch, Isidor. Husserl's Internationalitäts und Urteilslehre. Inaug. Diss. Basel, 1942.

Phil 1805.5   Fisch, M.H. Classic American philosophers. N.Y., 1951.
Phil 5365.4   Fisch, Rudolf. Konfliktmtivation und Examen. Meisenheim am Glan, 1970.

Phil 5245.80   Fischel, Werner. Struktur und Dynamik. Bern, 1962.
Phil 5815.10.2   Fischel, Werner. Vom Leben zum Erleben. 2. Aufl. München, 1967.

Phil 3450.19.97   Fischer, Alois. Die Existenzphilosophie Martin Heideggers. Leipzig, 1935.

Phil 336.12   Fischer, Anton. Die philosophischen Grundlagen der wissenschaftlichen Erkenntnis. Wien, 1947.

Phil 336.12.2   Fischer, Anton. Die philosophischen Grundlagen der wissenschaftlichen Erkenntnis. 2. Aufl. Wien, 1967.

Phil 180.62   Fischer, E. Zum Geisteskampf der Gegenwart. Basel, 1941.
Phil 5755.2A   Fischer, E.K.B. Über die menschliche Freiheit. Heidelberg, 1888.

Phil 3640.188   Fischer, E.L. F. Nietzsche. Regensburg, 1906.
Phil 6675.8   Fischer, E.L. Der sogenante Lebensmagnetismus oder Hypnotismus. Mainz, 1883.

Phil 5245.20   Fischer, E.L. Theorie der Gesichtswahrnehmung. Mainz, 1891.

Phil 2270.88   Fischer, E.L. Über den Gesetz der Entwicklung. Würzburg, 1875.

Phil 9345.8   Fischer, E.L.C. Heart and soul culture. Philadelphia, 1912.

Phil 180.31   Fischer, Engelbert Lorenz. Das Grundproblem der Metaphysik. Mainz, 1894.

Phil 8620.31   Fischer, Engelbert Lorenz. Das Problem des Übels und die Theodicee. Mainz, 1883.

Phil 336.4   Fischer, Englebert Lorenz. Die Grundfragen der Erkenntnistheorie. Mainz, 1887.

Phil 8050.56   Fischer, Ernest. Von der Notwendigkeit der Kunst. Dresden, 1959.

Phil 8092.13.5   Fischer, Ernst. Art against ideology. London, 1969.
Phil 8092.13.10   Fischer, Ernst. Auf den Spuren der Wirklichkeit. Reinbek, 1968.

Phil 440.4   Fischer, Ernst. Freiheit und Persönlichkeit. Wien, 1947.
Phil 8092.13   Fischer, Ernst. Kunst und Koexistenz. Reinbek, 1966.
Phil 3246.260   Fischer, F. Wohin, gehen wir? Langensalza, 1931.
Phil 5045.1   Fischer, Friedrich. Lehrbuch der Logik. Stuttgart, 1838.
Phil 400.1   Fischer, Friedrich. Über den Begriff der Philosophie. Tübingen, 1830.

Phil 6015.2   Fischer, G.H. Ausdruck und Persönlichkeit. Leipzig, 1934.
Phil 3425.249   Fischer, Hugo. Hegels Methode in ihrer ideengeschichtlichen Notwendigkeit. Habilitationsschrift. München, 1928.

Phil 3640.236   Fischer, Hugo. Nietzsche apostata, oder die Philosophie des Argernisses. Erfurt, 1931.

Phil 1504.10.3   Fischer, J. Die Erkenntnislehre Anselms von Canterbury. Münster, 1911.

Phil 8612.36   Fischer, J.A. Studien zum Todesgedanken in der Alten Kirche. München, 1954.

Phil 5374.26   Fischer, J.C. Das Bewusstsein. Leipzig, 1874.
Phil 5755.1.3   Fischer, J.C. Die Freiheit des menschlichen Willens und die Einheit der Naturgesetze. 2. Aufl. Leipzig, 1871.

Phil 3415.80   Fischer, J.C. Hartmann's Philosophie des Unbewussten. Leipzig, 1872.

Phil 5755.1   Fischer, J.C. Über die Freiheit des menschlichen Willens und die Einheit der Naturgesetze. Leipzig, 1858.

Phil 4809.393   Fischer, Josef L. Filosofické studie. Praha, 1968.
Phil 1850.82.10   Fischer, K, Franz Bacon von Verulam. Leipzig, 1856.
Phil 1705.4.9   Fischer, K. Einleitung in die Geschichte der neueren Philosophie. Heidelberg, 1908.

Phil 1850.82   Fischer, K. Frances Bacon of Verulam. London, 1857.
Phil 1850.82.5   Fischer, K. Francis Bacon und seine Nachfolger. 2e Aufl. Leipzig, 1875.

Phil 1705.4   Fischer, K. Geschichte der neueren Philosophie. v.1-6. Mannheim, 1854-77. 7v.

Phil 1705.4.4   Fischer, K. Geschichte der neueren Philosophie. v.1-8. Heidelberg, 1889-1901. 10v.

Phil 1705.4.2   Fischer, K. Geschichte der neueren Philosophie. v.1-9. München, 1875-93. 10v.

Phil 1705.4.3   Fischer, K. Geschichte der neueren Philosophie. v.2-10. Heidelberg, 1898-1904. 7v.

Phil 1705.4.50   Fischer, K. Geschichte der neueren Philosophie im Urteil der Jahrzehnte 1852-1924. Heidelberg, 1925.

Phil 1705.4.6   Fischer, K. History of modern philosophy. N.Y., 1887.
Phil 1705.4.8   Fischer, K. Kort inledning till nyare filosofia historia. Stockholm, 1866.

Phil 180.6   Fischer, K.P. Grundzüge des Systems der Philosophie. Frankfurt, 1848-1855. 3v.

Phil 180.6.2   Fischer, K.P. Grundzüge des Systems der Philosophie. v.2,3. Erlangen, 1850-1855. 2v.

Phil 8660.9   Fischer, K.P. Die Idee der Gottheit. Stuttgart, 1839.
Phil 480.4   Fischer, K.P. Die Unwahrheit des Sensualismus und Materialismus. Erlangen, 1853.

Phil 180.6.7   Fischer, K.P. Die Wissenschaft der Metaphysik im Grundrisse. Stuttgart, 1834.

Phil 3090.82   Fischer, K.P. Zur hundertjährigen Geburtsfeier Franz von Baaders. Erlangen, 1865.

Phil 3270.1.31   Fischer, Kuno. Die Apologie meiner Lehre. Mannheim, 1854.
Phil 3825.7.2A   Fischer, Kuno. Baruch Spinoza's Leben und Charakter. Heidelberg, 1946.

Phil 3825.7   Fischer, Kuno. Baruch Spinoza's Leben und Charakter. Mannheim, 1865.

Phil 3487.1.5   Fischer, Kuno. Commentary on Kant's Critick of pure reason. London, 1866.

Phil 2520.119.15.5   Fischer, Kuno. Descartes' Leben, Werke und Lehre. 5e Aufl. Heidelberg, 1912.

Phil 8406.7.5   Fischer, Kuno. Diotima; die Idee des Schönen. Leipzig, 1928.

Phil 8406.7   Fischer, Kuno. Diotima; die Idee des Schönen. Stuttgart, 1852.

Phil 3246.199.5   Fischer, Kuno. Geschichte der neuern Philosophie. Heidelberg, 1869.

Phil 3487.1.4   Fischer, Kuno. Geschichte der neuern Philosophie. 2. Aufl. Bd.3,4. Heidelberg, 1869. 2v.

Phil 3425.118   Fischer, Kuno. Hegels Leben, Werke und Lehre. v.1-2. Heidelberg, 1901.

Phil 3487.1.15   Fischer, Kuno. Die hundertjährige Gedächtnissfeier der Kantischen Kritik der reinen Vernunft. 2. Aufl. Heidelberg, 1892.

Phil 3270.1.32   Fischer, Kuno. Das Interdict meiner Vorlesungen. Mannhein, 1854.

Phil 3246.199   Fischer, Kuno. Johann Gottlieb Fichte. Stuttgart, 1862.

Phil 3487.1.8 Fischer, Kuno. Kant's leben und die Grundlagen seiner Lehre. Heidelberg, 1906.
Phil 3487.1 Fischer, Kuno. Kritik der Kantischen Philosophie. München, 1883.
Phil 3487.1.2 Fischer, Kuno. Kritik der Kantischen Philosophie. 2. Aufl. Heidelberg, 1892.
Phil 5045.6.3 Fischer, Kuno. Philosophische Schriften. System der Logik und Metaphysik. 3e Aufl. Heidelberg, 1909.
Phil 5045.6.2 Fischer, Kuno. System der Logik und Metaphysik oder Wissenschaftslehre. 2e Aufl. Heidelberg, 1865.
Phil 3850.1.95 Fischer, Kuno. Über David Friedrich Strauss. Heidelberg, 1908.
Phil 336.7.5 Fischer, L. The structure of thought. London, 1930.
Phil 180.33 Fischer, Ludwig. Grundriss des Systems der Philosophie als Bestimmungslehre. Wiesbaden, 1890.
Phil 180.33.10 Fischer, Ludwig. Das Vollwirkliche und das Als-ob. Berlin, 1921.
Phil 180.33.5 Fischer, Ludwig. Wirklichkeit, Wahrheit und Wissen. Berlin, 1919.
Phil 3805.87 Fischer, M. Schleiermachers. Berlin, 1899.
Phil 7069.24.12 Fischer, Oskar. Experimente mit Raphael Schermann. Berlin, 1924.
Phil 6315.28 Fischer, S. Principles of general psychopathology. N.Y., 1950.
Phil 3640.97 Fischer, W. Nietzsches Bild. München, 1911.
Phil 5421.10.45 Fischer, William Frank. Theories of anxiety. N.Y., 1970.
Phil 3450.4.90 Fischer-Appelt, Peter. Metaphysik im Horizent der Theologie Wilhelm Herrmanns. München, 1965.
Phil 180.56 Fischer-Mampoteng, F.C. Menschsein als Aufgabe. Heidelberg, 1928.
Phil 5045.9 Fischhaber, G.C.F. Lehrbuch der Logik. Stuttgart, 1818.
Phil 5045.15 Fischl, J. Logik; ein Lehrbuch. 2. Aufl. Graz, 1952[1946].
Phil 805.11 Fischl, Johann. Geschichte der Philosophie. Graz, 1948-53. 5v.
Phil 4809.393.330 Fišer, zbyněk. Útěcha z ontologie. Vyd. 1. Praha, 1967.
Phil 7069.12.10 Fish, Eben. Voices from the open door. Cleveland, 1912.
Phil 7080.44 Fish, Luther S. Knowledge exchanged; phenomenon of sleep. Cheveland, 1920.
Phil 6315.20 Fishbein, M. Why men fail. N.Y., 1928.
Phil 8585.6.5 Fisher, G.P. Faith and rationalism. N.Y., 1879.
Phil 8585.6.6 Fisher, G.P. Faith and rationalism. N.Y., 1885.
Phil 8585.6 Fisher, G.P. The grounds of theistic and Christian belief. N.Y., 1883.
Phil 8585.6.3 Fisher, G.P. The grounds of theistic and Christian belief. N.Y., 1885.
Phil 5585.312 Fisher, Gerald H. The frameworks for perceptual localization. Newcastle-upon-Tyne, 1968.
Phil 5245.44 Fisher, R.A. The psychology of desire. Saskatoon, 1930.
Phil 5360.8 Fisher, S.C. The process of generalizing abstraction. Thesis. Princeton, N.J., 1916.
Phil 6115.32.5 Fisher, Seymour. Body experience in fantasy and behavior. N.Y., 1970.
Phil 6115.32 Fisher, Seymour. Body image and personality. Princeton, N.J., 1958.
Phil 6955.3 Fisher, T.W. Plain talk about insanity. Boston, 1872.
Phil 5850.200 Fisher, V.E. Dissatisfied worker. N.Y., 1931.
Phil 6315.14 Fisher, Vivian E. An introduction to abnormal psychology. N.Y., 1929.
Phil 6980.293 Fisher, Vivian Ezra. The meaning and practice of psychotherapy. N.Y., 1950.
Phil 6115.5 Fisher, W.S. Observations on mental phenomena. Philadelphia, 1851.
Phil 5627.108 Fishers of men. (Clark, Glenn.) Boston, 1928.
Phil 8660.16 Fishler, Max. What the great philosophers thought about God. Los Angeles, 1958.
Phil 296.15 Fisica e metafisica. (Pavese, Roberto.) Padova, 1964[1965]
Phil 6121.13 Fisiologia dei centri nervosi encefalici. (Lussana, F.) Padova, 1871. 2v.
Phil 5402.3.5 Fisiologia del dolore. (Mantegazza, P.) Firenze, 1880.
Phil 6125.12.3 La fisiologia del sistema nervoso. (Panizza, M.) Roma, 1897.
Phil 5411.5.4 Fisiologia dell'odio. 4a ed. (Mantegazza, P.) Milano, 1889.
Phil 5645.23 Fisiologia e psicologia del colore. (Sergi, Giuseppe.) Milano, 1881.
Htn Phil 5245.7* Fiske, J. The composition of mind. N.Y., 1872. 3 pam.
Phil 8630.3 Fiske, J. The destiny of man. Boston, 1884.
Phil 365.4 Fiske, J. Excursions of an evolutionist. Boston, 1884.
Phil 8660.2.7 Fiske, J. The idea of God. Boston, 1891.
Phil 8633.1.5 Fiske, J. Life everlasting. Boston, 1900.
Phil 8630.3.6A Fiske, J. Life everlasting. Boston, 1901.
Phil 286.2.3 Fiske, J. Outlines of cosmic philosophy. Boston, 1874. 2v.
Htn Phil 286.2*A Fiske, J. Outlines of cosmic philosophy. Boston, 1875. 2v.
Phil 286.2.9 Fiske, J. Outlines of cosmic philosophy. Boston, 1902. 4v.
Phil 286.2.15 Fiske, J. Outlines of cosmic philosophy. Boston, 1916. 4v.
Phil 286.2.2 Fiske, J. Outlines of cosmic philosophy. London, 1874. 2v.
Phil 286.2.5 Fiske, J. Outlines of cosmic philosophy. 11. ed. Boston, 1890. 2v.
Phil 8585.17.5 Fiske, J. Studies in religion. Boston, 1902.
Phil 8585.17 Fiske, J. Through nature to God. Boston, 1899.
Phil 180.16 Fiske, J. The unseen world and other essays. Boston, 1876.
Phil 2005.1.80 Pamphlet box. Fiske, J.
Phil 8880.5 Fiske, N. The moral monitor. v.2. Worcester, Mass., 1801.
Phil 2115.175 Fislosofiia Dzhona Lokka. (Narshii, I.S.) Moskva, 1960.
Phil 6025.4.9 Fisonomia dell'huomo. (Porta, G.B.) Venetia, 1652.
Phil 6023.1 La fisonomia nell'arte e nella scienza. (Nicefaro, A.) Firenze, 1952.
Phil 180.55 Fiszer, E. Unité et intelligibilité. Paris, 1936.
Phil 180.55.5 Fiszer, E. Unité et intelligibilité. Thèse. Paris, 1936.
Phil 5066.46 Fitch, F.B. Symbolic logic. N.Y., 1952.
Phil 6115.20 Fitch, Michael H. The physical basis of mind and morals. Chicago, 1914.
Phil 9050.9 Fitch, R.E. A certain blind man. N.Y., 1944.
Phil 8880.18.9 Fite, Warner. An adventure in moral philosophy. London, 1926.
Phil 8880.18.10 Fite, Warner. The examined life. Bloomington, Ind., 1957.
Phil 8880.18.2 Fite, Warner. An introductory study of ethics. N.Y., 1906.
Phil 5374.48 Fite, Warner. The living mind. N.Y., 1930.
Phil 8880.18.5 Fite, Warner. Moral philosophy. N.Y., 1925.
Phil 7068.98.30 Fitler, C.H. New thoughts. Philadelphia, 1898.
Htn Phil 2225.7.32* Fitzgerald, John J. The new education; three papers. Boston, 1887.
Phil 2225.5.135 Fitzgerald, John J. Peirce's theory of signs as foundation for pragmatism. The Hague, 1966.
Phil 5374.4 Fitzgerald, P.F. Essay on the philosophy of self-consciousness. London, 1882.
Phil 8880.6 Fitzgerald, P.F. The rational, or scientific ideal of morality. London, 1897.
Phil 8610.890 Fitzgerald, P.F. (Mrs.). A protest against agnosticism. London, 1890.
Phil 5160.1 Fitzgerald, Penelope F. A treatise...sufficient reason. London, 1887.
Phil 8660.13 Fitzpatrick, M.S. Mind and the universal frame. Dublin, 1935.
Phil 5247.78 The five ages of man. (Heard, G.) N.Y., 1964[1963]
Phil 5650.43 Five articles on the perception of sound, 1938-1940. (Schouteu, Jan F.) Eindhoven, 1960.
Phil 8584.14 Five books of Joses, a catechism of rational religion. (Elving, S.) Newllano, La., 1930.
Phil 5500.50 The five-day course in thinking. (De Bono, Edward.) N.Y., 1967.
Phil 8581.48 Five discourses on positive religion. (Bridges, J.H.) London, 1882.
Phil 5640.4 Five gateways of knowledge. (Wilson, G.) Philadelphia, 1857.
Phil 5640.4.7 The five gateways of knowledge. 7th ed. (Wilson, G.) London, 1881.
Phil 575.10.10 The five great philosophies of life. (Hyde, W. De W.) N.Y., 1932.
Phil 2150.22.42 Five lectures. (Marcuse, Herbert.) Boston, 1970.
Phil 5242.29 Five lectures on the problem of mind. (Cunningham, G.W.) Austin, 1925.
Phil 9358.12 Five lessons for young men. (Southwick, Solomon.) Albany, 1837.
Htn Phil 2725.6.31* Five letters concerning the inspiration of the Holy Scriptures. (LeClerc, Jean.) London, 1690.
Phil 197.8.5 Five questions in psychology and metaphysics. (Wilson, W.D.) N.Y., 1877.
Phil 8876.96 The five redeemers. (Barnett, M.J.) Boston, 1890.
Phil 5640.2 Five senses of man. (Bernstein, J.) N.Y., 1876.
Phil 5640.2.4 Five senses of man. (Bernstein, J.) N.Y., 1890.
Phil 1900.62 Five sermons preached at the Rolls Chapel. (Butler, Joseph.) N.Y., 1950.
Phil 8876.88 Five types of ethical theory. (Broad, C.D.) London, 1930.
Phil 8876.88.5 Five types of ethical theory. (Broad, C.D.) London, 1951.
Phil 5640.17 The five windows of the soul. (Aitken, E.H.) London, 1913.
Phil 6312.10 Five-year report. (Chicago. Institute for Psychoanalysis.) Chicago, 1937. 2v.
Phil 978.10 Five years of theosophy. London, 1885.
Phil 5650.36 Fiziologicheskaia akustika. (Akademiia Nauk SSSR. Biblioteka.) Moskva, 1960.
Phil 5220.6 Fiziologicheskaia shkola I.P. Pavlova. (Kvasov, Dmitrii G.) Leningrad, 1967.
Phil 5815.5 Fjeld, Harriett A. The limits of learning ability in rhesus monkeys. Thesis. Worcester, Mass., 1934.
Phil 8050.54 Flaccus, L.W. Artists and thinkers. N.Y., 1916.
Phil 8406.20 Flaccus, L.W. The spirit and substance of art. N.Y., 1926.
Phil 8406.20.5 Flaccus, L.W. The spirit and substance of art. N.Y., 1931.
Phil 8406.20.8 Flaccus, L.W. The spirit and substance of art. N.Y., 1941.
Phil 8406.20.9 Flaccus, L.W. The spirit and substance of art. N.Y., 1947.
Phil 5045.17 Flach, W. Negation und Andersheit. München, 1959.
Phil 336.17 Flach, W. Zur Prinzipienlehre der Auschauung. Hamburg, 1963.
Phil 8893.12.15 Flaig, Josef. Christoph Sigwarts Beiträge zu Grundlegung und Aufbau der Ethik. Stuttgart, 1912.
Phil 9400.11 Flake, A. Life at eighty as I see it. Nashville, 1944.
Phil 8880.41 Flake, Otto. Die moralische Idee. München, 1921.
Phil 3270.10.31 Flake, Otto. Das neuantike Weltbild. Darmstadt, 1922.
Phil 3640.334 Flake, Otto. Nietzsche. 2e Aufl. Baden-Baden, 1947.
Phil 1750.734 Flam, L. De onverzoenlijken. St. Niklaas, 1959.
Phil 3425.619 Flam, Leopold. De bewustwording; beschouwingen bij de fenomenologie van de geest van Hegel. Bruxelles, 1966.
Phil 180.72.5 Flam, Leopold. Le crépuscule des dieux et l'avenir de l'homme. Paris, 1966.
Phil 3270.17.30 Flam, Leopold. Denken en existeren. Amsterdam, 1964.
VPhil 5015.5 Flam, Leopold. De geschiedenis van de dialektiek. St. Niklaas, 1964.
VPhil 8660.22 Flam, Leopold. Geschiedenis van het atheisme. 1. uitg. Brussel, 1964. 4v.
Phil 3270.17.40 Flam, Leopold. Gestalten van de Westerse subjectiriteit. Amsterdam, 1965.
Phil 805.15 Flam, Leopold. L'homme et la conscience tragique. Bruxelles, 1964.
Phil 1750.65 Flam, Leopold. De krisis van de burgerlijke moraal. Antwerpen, 1956.
Phil 3640.450 Flam, Leopold. Nietzsche. Bussum, 1955.
Phil 1750.540 Flam, Leopold. Ontbinding en protest. Antwerpen, 1959.
Phil 1706.11 Flam, Leopold. La philosophie au tournant de notre temps. Bruxelles, 1961.
Phil 3270.17.35 Flam, Leopold. Proeven over het tragisch bewiestzijn en de geschiedenis. Antwerpen, 1963.
Phil 180.72 Flam, Leopold. Profielen. Antwerpen, 1957.
Phil 805.14 Flam, Leopold. Verleden en toehomst van de filosofie. Amsterdam, 1962.
Phil 3640.452 Flam, Leopold. Wie was Nietzsche? Antwerpen, 1960.
Phil 310.701 Flam, Léopold. Wording en ontbinding van de filosofie. Amsterdam, 1969.
Phil 3270.17.45 Flam, Leopold. Zelfvervreemding en zelfzijn. Amsterdam, 1966.
Phil 960.210 The flame and the light. (Fausset, H.I. Anson.) London, 1958.
Phil 960.212 The flame and the light. (Fausset, H.I. Anson.) N.Y., 1969[1958]
Phil 8660.3 Flammarion, C. Dieu dans la nature. Paris, 1867.
Phil 8660.3.7 Flammarion, C. Dieu dans la nature. 7. ed. Paris, 1871.
Phil 7069.07.17 Flammarion, C. Les forces naturelles inconnues. Paris, 1907.
Phil 7069.21.31 Flammarion, C. Imod døden. Kjøbenhavn, 1921.
Phil 7060.67.5 Flammarion, C. L'inconnu et les problèmes psychiques. Paris, 1900.
Phil 7069.00.28 Flammarion, C. L'inconnu, The unknown. N.Y., 1900.

Phil 7069.07.18 Flammarion, C. Mysterious psychic forces. Boston, 1907.
Phil 8630.4 Flammarion, C. Récits de l'infini. Paris, 1873.
Phil 8630.4.5 Flammarion, C. Stories of infinity. Boston, 1873.
Phil 7069.21.30 Flammarion, Camille. Death and its mystery. pt.1,3. N.Y., 1921-23. 2v.
Phil 7069.24.15 Flammarion, Camille. Haunted houses. London, 1924.
Phil 7069.24.15.2 Flammarion, Camille. Haunted houses. N.Y., 1924.
Phil 7069.20.130 Flammarion, Camille. La mort et son mystère. Paris, 1920-1921. 2v.
Phil 5465.56.42 La flamme d'une chandelle. 2. éd. (Bachelard, G.) Paris, 1962.
Phil 7054.27 Flashes of light from the spirit land. (Putnam, A.) Boston, 1892.
Phil 185.52.10 The flashlights of truth. (King, Mrs. E.D.) Los Angeles, 1918.
Phil 3487.14 Flatt, Johann F. Briefe über den moralischen Erkenntnisgrund der Religion überhaupt. Tübingen, 1789.
Phil 6115.6.7 Flechsig, P. Gehirn und Seele. 2e Ausg. Leipzig, 1896.
Phil 6115.6.9 Flechsig, P. Die Leitungsbahnen im Gehirn und Rückenmark. Leipzig, 1876.
Phil 6115.6.5 Flechsig, P. Localisation der geistigen Vorgänge. Leipzig, 1896.
Phil 6115.6.12 Flechsig, P. Meine myelogenetische Hirnlehre. Berlin, 1927.
Phil 6115.6 Flechsig, P. Plan des menschlichen Gehirns. Leipzig, 1883.
Phil 3425.289 Flechtheim, O.K. Hegels Strafrechtstheorie. Brünn, 1936.
Phil 180.60 Flechtner, H.J. Freiheit und Bindung. Berlin, 1935.
Phil 1510.10 Fleckenskein, J.O. Scholastik, Barock exakte Wissenschaften. Einsiedeln, 1949.
Phil 3552.319 Fleckenstein, Joachim O. Gottfried Wilhelm Leibniz. München, 1908.
Phil 5525.9 Fleet, F.R. Theory of wit and humor. London, 1890.
Phil 6976.20 Flegel, Horst. Schizophasie in linguistischer Deutung. Berlin, 1965.
Phil 310.784 Fleischer, Helmut. Marxismus und Geschichte. Frankfurt, 1969.
Phil 3450.18.115F Fleischer, Helmut. Nicolai Hartmanns Ontologie des idealen Seins. Thesis. Erlangen? 1954.
Phil 3270.4.80 Fleischmann, M. Anselm von Feuerbach der Jurist, als Philosoph. Inaug. Diss. München, 1906.
Phil 3425.656 Fleishmann, Eugène. La science universelle ou la logique de Hegel. Paris, 1968.
Htn Phil 8880.7* Fleming, C. A scale of first principles. London, 1755.
Phil 8880.8 Fleming, W. A manual of moral philosophy. London, 1867.
Phil 8880.8.2 Fleming, W. A manual of moral philosophy. London, 1870.
Phil 90.1.3 Fleming, William. Vocabulary of philosophy. London, 1857.
Phil 90.1 Fleming, William. Vocabulary of philosophy. London, 1858.
Phil 90.1.4 Fleming, William. Vocabulary of philosophy. 4th ed. N.Y., 1887.
Phil 8125.4 Flemming, Willi. Der Wandel des deutschen Naturgefühls. Halle, 1931.
Phil 480.2 Flentje, L. Das Leben und die todte Natur. Cassel, 1866.
Phil 5520.102 Flesch, R.F. The art of clear thinking. 1. ed. N.Y., 1951.
Phil 6115.17 Fletcher, E.A. Law of rhythmic breath. N.Y., 1908.
Phil 2805.280 Fletcher, F.T.H. Pascal and the mystical tradition. Oxford, 1954.
Htn Phil 6115.18.5* Fletcher, Horace. Emancipation. Chicago, 1895.
Phil 9245.24 Fletcher, Horace. Happiness. N.Y., 1898.
Phil 9245.24.3 Fletcher, Horace. Happiness as found in forethought minus fearthought. Chicago, 1897.
Phil 6115.18.6.5 Fletcher, Horace. Menticulture, or The ABC of true living. Chicago, 1897.
Phil 6115.18.7.5 Fletcher, Horace. Menticulture. Chicago, 1898.
Phil 6115.18.7 Fletcher, Horace. Menticulture. Chicago, 1898.
Phil 6115.18.9 Fletcher, Horace. The new menticulture. London, 1905.
Phil 6115.18.10 Fletcher, Horace. The new menticulture. N.Y., 1903.
Phil 6115.18 Fletcher, Horace. Optimism; a real remedy. Chicago, 1908.
Phil 5925.4 Fletcher, J. The mirror of nature...science of phrenology. Boston, 1838.
Phil 5925.4.2 Pamphlet box. Fletcher, J. The mirror of nature.
Phil 6420.14 Fletcher, John Madison. An experimental study of stuttering. Thesis. Worcester, 1914.
Phil 6420.14.5 Fletcher, John Madison. The problem of stuttering. N.Y., 1928.
Phil 8955.8 Fletcher, Joseph Francis. Situation ethics. Philadelphia, 1966.
Phil 805.3 Fletcher, O.O. Introduction to philosophy. N.Y., 1913.
Phil 5401.15 Fletcher, P. Life without fear. N.Y., 1939.
Phil 2490.180 Fletcher, Ronald. Auguste Comte and the making of sociology: delivered on November 4, 1965 at the London School of Economics. London, 1966.
Phil 5838.257 Fletcher, Ronald. Instinct in man in the light of recent work in comparative psychology. N.Y., 1957.
Phil 8880.26 Fleuriau, A. de. L'activité réfléchie. Paris, 1911.
Phil 6115.13.6 Fleury, D.M. de. Introduction à la médicine de l'esprit. 6. éd. Paris, 1900.
Phil 6115.13 Fleury, D.M. de. Medicine and the mind. London, 1900.
Phil 6955.13 Fleury, M. de. Les grands symptômes neurasthéniques. Paris, 1901.
Phil 6955.13.10 Fleury, M. de. Manuel pour l'étude des maladies du système nerveaux. Paris, 1904.
Phil 5080.7 Flew, A. Essays in conceptual analysis. London, 1956.
Phil 2050.242 Flew, A. Hume's philosophy of belief. London, 1961.
Phil 5520.100 Flew, A.G.N. Essays on logic and language. Oxford, 1951.
Phil 5520.100.10 Flew, A.G.N. Logic and language. 2. ser. Oxford, 1953.
Phil 665.95 Flew, Antony. Body, mind and death. N.Y., 1964.
Phil 8660.23 Flew, Antony. God and philosophy. 1st American ed. N.Y., 1966.
Phil 180.39 Flewelling, R. Creative personality. N.Y., 1926.
Phil 176.27.8 Flewelling, R.T. Personalism and the problems of philosophy. N.Y., 1915.
Phil 2475.1.201 Flewelling, Ralph. Bergson and personal realism. N.Y., 1920.
Phil 3903.3.95 Fliess, B. Einführung in die Philosophie des Als Ob. Bielefeld, 1922.
Phil 6315.24 Fliess, R. The psycho-analytic reader. London, 1950.
X Cg Phil 7075.144 Fliess, Robert. Erogeneity and libido. N.Y., 1957.
Phil 7084.2 Fliess, Robert. The revival of interest in the dream. N.Y., 1953.
Phil 8670.17.2 The flight from God. (Picard, Max.) London, 1951.
Phil 186.74 The flight from reason. (Lunn, A.H.M.) N.Y., 1931.
Phil 5841.26 The flight from woman. (Stern, Karl.) N.Y., 1965.
Phil 3808.132 Flink, Carl G. Schopenhauers Seelenwanderungslehre. Berlin, 1906.
Phil 8660.4.5 Flint, R. Anti-theistic theories. (Baird lectures for 1877). Edinburgh, 1879.
Phil 8660.4 Flint, R. Theism. (Baird lectures for 1876). Edinburgh, 1877.
Phil 8660.4.4 Flint, R. Theism (Baird lectures for 1876). 10. ed. London, 1902.
Phil 4260.82 Flint, R. Vico. Philadelphia, 1884.
Phil 8610.903 Flint, Robert. Agnosticism. Edinburgh, 1903.
Phil 180.20 Flint, Robert. Philosophy as scientia scientarum. N.Y., 1904.
Phil 9075.84 Flither, Andreas. Wirklichkeit und Mass des Menschen. München, 1967.
Phil 3450.14.80 Flitner, Willy. August Ludwig Hülsen und der Bund der freien Männer. Naumberg, 1913.
Phil 5245.8 Flögel, C.F. Geschichte des menschlichen Verstandes. Breslau, 1776.
Phil 3450.19.435 Floestad, Guttorm. Heidegger. En innføring i hans filosofi. Oslo, 1968.
Phil 4080.3.132 Flora, F. Croce. Milano, 1927.
Phil 2475.1.208.5 Flore de G'nose, Laggrond, Pellis et Bergson. (Nicolardot, F.) Paris, 1924.
Phil 75.30 Florence. Biblioteca Filosofica. Catalogo della Biblioteca filosofica. Text and supplement. Firenze, 1910.
Phil 9560.14.10 The Florentine Fior di virtù of 1491. (Fiore di Virtù.) Philadelphia, 1953.
Phil 8647.5 Florenzi Waddington, M. Della immortalita dell'anima. Firenzi, 1868.
Phil 4110.2.31 Florenzi Waddington, Marianna. Saggi di psicologia e di logica. Firenze, 1864.
Phil 4110.2.35 Florenzi Waddington, Marianna. Saggio sulla filosofia dello spirito. Firenze, 1867.
Phil 4976.5.80 Flores Caballero, Luis. Humanismo y revolución en América Latina; bosquejo de interpretación del pensamiento materialista de Antenor Orrego. Lima, 1968.
Phil 2475.1.139.5 Florian, M. Der Begriff der Zeit bei Henri Bergson. Greifswald, 1914.
Phil 5585.305 Florida studies in the helping professions. (Combs, Arthur Wright.) Gainesville, 1969.
Phil 2515.4.101 Floss, S.W. An outline of the philosophy of Antoine-Augustin Cournot. Philadelphia, 1941.
Phil 2651.81 Flottes, J.B.M. Etude sur Pierre Daniel Huet. Montpellier, 1857.
Phil 2725.2.69 Flottes, J.B.M. M. l'abbé F. de Lamennais réfuté. Paris, 1825.
Phil 5722.76 Flottes, Pierre. L'histoire et l'inconscient humain. Genève, 1965.
Phil 5925.1.5 Flourens, M.J. De la phrénologie et des études vraies sur la cerveau. Paris, 1863.
Phil 5925.1 Flourens, M.J. Examen de la phrenologie. Paris, 1842.
Phil 180.14 Flourens, P. Fontenelle. Paris, 1847-1851. 5 pam.
Phil 5245.23 Flourens, Pierre. De la raison du genié et...folie. Paris, 1861.
Phil 5245.23.5 Flourens, Pierre. De la vie et de l'intelligence. 2. éd. Paris, 1858.
Phil 5815.2 Flourens, Pierre. De l'instinct et de l'intelligence des animaux. 4e éd. Paris, 1861.
Phil 5815.2.5.2 Flourens, Pierre. Psychologie comparée. 2e éd. Paris, 1864.
Phil 6315.11 Flournoy, Henri. La psychanalyse, les médecins et le public. Neuchâtel, 1924.
Phil 7060.80.9 Flournoy, J. Des Indes à la planète Mars. Paris, 1900.
Phil 5642.11 Flournoy, T. Des phénomènes de synopsie. Paris, 1893.
Phil 5627.73 Flournoy, T. Le génie religieux. Neuchâtel, 1904.
Phil 180.7 Flournoy, T. Métaphysique et psychologie. Genève, 1890.
Phil 180.7.2 Flournoy, T. Métaphysique et psychologie. 2. éd. Genève, 1919.
Phil 5249.2.28A Flournoy, T. La philosophie de William James. St. Blaise, 1911.
Phil 2070.84.5 Flournoy, T. Die Philosophie von William James. Tübingen, 1930.
Phil 2070.84A Flournoy, T. Philosophy of William James. N.Y., 1917.
Phil 7069.21.33 Flournoy, Theodor. Spiritismus und experimental-psychologie. Leipzig, 1921.
Phil 7069.11.19 Flournoy, Théodore. Esprits et médiums. Genève, 1911.
Phil 7069.00.30 Flournoy, Théodore. From India to the planet Mars. N.Y., 1900.
Phil 7069.11.20 Flournoy, Theodore. Spiritism and psychology. N.Y., 1911.
Phil 5245.31 Flower, J.C. Psychology simplified. London, 1928.
Phil 5627.65.5 Flower, John C. An approach to the psychology of religion. London, 1927.
Phil 5627.65 Flower, John C. Psychological studies of religious questions. London, 1924.
Phil 7069.33.52 Flower-life in ethic. (Wells, Helen B.) N.Y., 1933. 2 pam.
Phil 530.20.32A The flowering of mysticism. (Jones, R.M.) N.Y., 1939.
Phil 8610.941 Floyd, W. Christianity cross-examined. N.Y., 1941.
Phil 8585.30 Floyd, William. Our gods on trial. N.Y., 1931.
Phil 8670.17 Die Flucht vor Gott. 2. Aufl. (Picard, Max.) Erlenbach, 1935.
Phil 5330.20 The fluctuation of attention. (Hylan, J.P.) N.Y., 1898.
Htn Phil 170.2* Fludd, Robert. Mosaicall philosophy. London, 1659.
Htn Phil 170.2.5F* Fludd, Robert. Philosophia moysaica. Goudae, 1638.
Phil 3805.186 Flückiger, Felix. Philosophie und Theologie bei Schleiermacher. Basel, 1947?
Phil 510.125.4 Flügel, D. Monismus und Theologie. 4e Aufl. Gotha, 1914.
Phil 180.18.5 Flügel, D. Die Probleme der Philosophie und ihre Lösungen historisch-critisch Dargestellt. 2.Aufl. Cöthen, 1888.
Phil 180.18 Flügel, D. Die Probleme der Philosophie und ihre Losungen. Cöthen, 1906.
Phil 6315.15 Flügel, G.C. Men and their motives. London, 1934.
Phil 5215.2.10 Flügel, J.C. A hundred years of psychology, 1833-1933. London, 1964.
Phil 5215.2.12 Flügel, J.C. A hundred years of psychology, 1833-1933. N.Y., 1964.
Phil 5215.2.5 Flügel, J.C. A hundred years of psychology, 1833-1933. 2nd ed. London, 1951.
Phil 5245.45.6 Flügel, John Carl. Man, morals and society. Harmondsworth, 1962.
Phil 5245.45.2 Flügel, John Carl. Man, morals and society. London, 1945.
Phil 5245.45.5 Flügel, John Carl. Man, morals and society. N.Y., 1955.
Phil 900.2 Fluegel, M. Philosophy, qabbala and vedánta. Baltimore, 1902.
Phil 665.56 Flügel, O. Die Seelenfrage. Cöthen, 1878.
Phil 8585.26 Flügel, O. Zur philosophie der Christentums. Langensalza, 1899.
Phil 3428.89 Flügel, Otto. Die Bedeutung der Metaphysik Herbarts. Langensalza, 1902.
Phil 8880.29 Flügel, Otto. Das Ich und die sittlichen Ideen im Leben. 5e Aufl. Langensalza, 1912.

Phil 8880.29.5 — Flügel, Otto. Das Ich und die sittlichen Ideen im Leben der Völker. Langensalza, 1885.

Phil 3428.89.5 — Flügel, Otto. Der philosophie J.F. Herbart. Leipzig, 1905.

Phil 3195.1.81 — Flügel, Otto. Religionsphilosophie der Schule Herbarts, Drobisch und Hartenstein. Langensalza, 1905.

Phil 5815.3 — Fluegel, Otto. Das Seelenleben der Tiere. 3e Aufl. Langensalza, 1897.

Phil 8660.12 — Flügel, Otto. Das Wunder und die Erkennbarkeit Gottes. Langensalza, 1869.

Phil 3487.18 — Flügge, C.W. Versuch einer historisch-kritischen Darstellung. Hannover, 1796-98. 2v.

Phil 3425.362 — Flügge, J. Die sittlichen Grundlagen des Denkens. Hamburg, 1953.

Phil 5400.120 — Flugel, J.C. Studies in feeling and desire. London, 1955.

Phil 7069.06.5 — Flugrit gegn andatrúnni. Reykjavik, 1906.

Phil 43.1 — Flugschriften. (Deutscher Monistenbund.) Brackwede. 3-30,1906-1914 16v.

Phil 7069.22.12 — Der Fluidalkörper des Menschen...okkulten Erscheinungen. (Hein, Rudolf.) Leipzig, 1922.

Phil 6687.1.15 — Le fluide des magnétiseurs. (Reichenback, C.) Paris, 1891.

Phil 2496.88 — Flumen historicum: Victor Cousin's aesthetic and its sources. (Will, Frederic.) Chapel Hill, 1965.

Phil 1812.15 — Fly and the fly-bottle. 1. ed. (Mehta, Ved P.) Boston, 1962.

Phil 8955.4 — Flynn, V.S. The norm of morality. Diss. Washington, 1928.

Phil 8585.20.80 — Foakes-Jackson, F.J. The faith and the war; a series of essays. London, 1915.

Phil 5627.268 — Fobry, Joseph B. The pursuit of meaning. Boston, 1968.

Phil 4080.3.420 — Focher, Ferruccio. Profilo dell'opera di Benedetto Croce. Cremona, 1963.

Htn — Phil 3425.574 — Focht, I. Mogućnost, nužnost, slučajnost, stvarnost. Sarajevo, 1961.

Phil 5245.40 — Focht, Mildred. What is Gestalt-theory. Diss. N.Y., 1935.

Phil 5252.18.54 — Fochtman, V.A. Das Lieb-Seele-Problem bei George Trumbull Ladd und William McDougall. Inaug. Diss. München, 1928.

Phil 8406.18.5 — Focillon, Henri. Vie des formes. 3. ed. Paris, 1947.

Phil 8406.18 — Focillon, Henri. Vita delle forme, di Henri Focillon. Padova, 1945.

Phil 75.31 — Fock, G. Philosophie. Leipzig, 1936.

Phil 5850.271 — The focused interview. (Merton, R.K.) Glencoe, Ill., 1956.

Phil 5520.420 — Fodor, J.A. The structure of language. Englewood Cliffs, N.J., 1964.

Phil 5245.86 — Fodor, Jerry A. Psychological explanation. N.Y., 1968.

Phil 7069.64.20 — Fodor, Nandor. Between two worlds. West Nyack, 1966.

Phil 7069.33.56 — Fodor, Nandor. Encyclopaedia of psychic science. London, 1933?

Phil 7069.33.57 — Fodor, Nandor. Encyclopaedia of psychic science. New Hyde Park, N.Y., 1966.

Phil 3790.8.82 — Föhållandet mellan moral och religion...den Ritschelska skolan. (Rosén, Hugo.) Lund, 1919.

Phil 3195.6.170 — Foejo, W. Introducción a Dilthey. Xalapa, 1962.

Phil 5755.16 — Földesi, Tamás. The problem of free will. Budapest, 1966.

Phil 5871.118 — Förälder i 70-talet. Stockholm, 1971.

Phil 1133.44 — Före Sokrates. (Regnéll, Hans.) Stockholm, 1969.

Phil 4515.40 — Föreläsningar i etiken. (Boström, C.J.) Upsala, 1897.

Phil 4515.35 — Föreläsningar i religionsfilosofi. (Boström, C.J.) Stockholm, 1885.

Phil 70.36 — Förhandlingar. (Nortisk Psykologmøte.) 1947-1956 4v.

Phil 4630.3.31 — Förnufts-öfningar. (Rydelius, Anders.) Linköping, 1737.

Phil 5870.35 — Förskolealderns psykologi. (Bruun, Ulla-Britta.) Göteborg, 1968.

Phil 3833.5 — Försök till en framställning, af Spinozismens nufvidsatser. (Norinder, A.V.) Upsala, 1851.

Phil 4515.91.5 — Försök till en lärobok i allmän samhällslära. (Åberg, L.H.) Upsala, 1879.

Phil 8630.14 — Foerst-Crato, Ilse. Ausblicke ins Paradies. München, 1958.

Phil 3246.50.9 — Första inledningen till vetenshapsläran. (Fichte, Johann Gottlieb.) Stockholm, 1914.

Phil 5244.36 — Förstå människor. (Egidius, Henry.) Lund, 1971.

Phil 9165.3.6 — Foerster, F.W. Lebensführung. Berlin, 1922.

Phil 9165.3 — Foerster, F.W. Lebenskunde, ein Buch für Knaben und Mädchen. Berlin, 1907.

Phil 9495.14.2 — Foerster, F.W. Marriage and the sex problem. London, 1911.

Phil 9495.14 — Foerster, F.W. Marriage and the sex problem. N.Y., n.d.

Phil 8630.11 — Foerster Lecture. On immortality of the soul. N.Y. 1933+

Phil 3640.88.7 — Förster-Nietzsche, E. Der einsame Nietzsche. München, 1915.

Phil 3640.88.15 — Förster-Nietzsche, E. Friedrich Nietzsche and die Frauen seiner Zeit. München, 1935.

Phil 3640.88.3 — Förster-Nietzsche, E. Der junge Nietzsche. Leipzig, 1912.

Phil 3640.88 — Förster-Nietzsche, E. Das Leben Friedrich Nietzsche's. Leipzig, 1895. 2v.

Phil 3640.88.5 — Förster-Nietzsche, E. Life of Nietzsche. N.Y., 1912-15. 2v.

Phil 3640.88.10 — Förster-Nietzsche, E. The Nietzsche-Wagner correspondence. N.Y., 1921.

Phil 3640.88.9 — Förster-Nietzsche, E. Wagner und Nietzsche zur zeit Freundschaft. München, 1915.

Phil 3640.88.6 — Förster-Nietzsche, E. The young Nietzsche. London, 1912.

Phil 3552.53 — Den förutbestämda harmonien. (Leibniz, Gottfried Wilhelm.) Stockholm, 1927.

Phil 2045.144 — Foester, Winfried. Thomas Hobbes und der Puritanismus. Berlin, 1969.

Phil 2520.155 — Fog, B.J. Cartesius. Kjøbenhavn, 1856.

Phil 5080.4 — A fogalom problémája a teozta logikaban. (Pauler, Ákos.) Budapest, 1915.

Phil 310.25 — Fogarasi, Bela. Filozófiai elöadasok es tanulmányok. Budapest, 1952.

Phil 5045.16 — Fogarasi, Béla. Logik. Berlin, 1956.

Phil 5045.16.2 — Fogarasi, Béla. Logika. 2. kiadás. Budapest, 1953.

Phil 4210.122F — Fogazzaro, A. La figura di Antonio Rosmini. Milano, 1897.

Phil 5068.60 — Fogelin, Robert J. Evidence and meaning: studies in analytic philosophy. London, 1967.

Phil 6420.26 — Fogerty, Elsie. Stammering. N.Y., 1930.

Phil 8586.57 — Foi au Christ et dialogues du Chrétien. (Goedt, Michel de.) Bruges, 1967.

Phil 3425.778 — La foi chez Hegel. (Léonard, Andre.) Paris, 1970.

Phil 8672.19 — La foi des athées. (Kostenne, P.) Paris, 1953.

Phil 5627.174 — La foi des éclairés. (Witwicki, Władisław.) Paris, 1939.

Phil 8707.36 — La foi d'un mal-eroyant ou mentalité scientifique et vie de foi. (Roqueplo, Philippe.) Paris, 1969.

Phil 2905.1.630 — Foi en l'homme; l'apologétique de Teilhard de Chardin. (Jarque i Jutglar, Joan E.) Paris, 1969.

Phil 8505.9 — Foi et technique. (Pax Romana, International Catholic Movement for Intellectual and Cultural Affairs.) Paris, 1960.

Phil 3475.3.165 — La foi philosophique chez Jaspers et Saint Thomas d'Aquin. (Welte, Bernard.) Bruges, 1958.

Phil 6112.5.5 — La foi qui guérit. (Charcot, J.M.) Paris, 1897.

Phil 2805.255 — La foi selon Pascal. v.1-2. Thèse. (Russier, Jeanne.) Paris, 1949.

Phil 6675.3 — Foissac, P. Rapports...sur magnétisme animal. Paris, 1833.

Phil 270.54 — Foissac, Pierre. La chance ou la destinée. Paris, 1876.

Phil 11.9.5 — Folge der Beihefte. Erfurt. 3-13,1920-1924+ 4v.

Phil 15.1 — Folia neuro-biologica. Leipzig. 1-12 11v.

Htn — Phil 7075.10* — La folie erotique. (Ball, B.) Paris, 1888.

Phil 6955.22 — Folie et déraison. (Foucault, Michel.) Paris, 1961.

Phil 5421.20.5 — Folkard, M.S. A sociological contribution to the understanding of aggression and its treatment. Coulsdon, 1961.

Phil 8088.3 — Folkierski, W. Entre le classicisme et le romantisme. Cracovie, 1925.

Phil 4372.1.145 — El folklore en las obras de Luis Vives. (Gayano, Lluch Rafael.) Valencia, 1941.

Phil 9150.19 — Folkmar, D. L'anthropologie philosophique. Thèse. Paris, 1899.

Phil 5938.7.10 — Follen, Charles. Funeral oration. Boston, 1832.

Phil 5938.7.5 — Follen, Charles. Funeral oration. v.1-3. Boston, 1832-1840.

Phil 7069.19.163 — The follies and frauds of spiritualism. (Mann, Walter.) London, 1919.

Phil 9345.12 — Folliet, Joseph. Adam et Eve. Lyon, 1965.

Htn — Phil 8659.3* — The folly of atheism. (Elis, C.) London, 1692.

Phil 6955.9 — Folsom, C.F. Abstract of the statutes of the United States, and of the several territories relating to the custody of the insane. Philadelphia, 1884.

Phil 6955.4 — Folsom, C.F. Four introductory lectures on insanity. Cambridge, 1875-80. 4 pam.

Phil 6955.4.5 — Folsom, C.F. Mental disease. n.p., 1886.

Phil 6115.7 — Folsom, C.F. The relation of our public schools to the disorders of the nervous system. Boston, 1886.

Phil 5655.2 — Folsom, N. Essay on the senses of smell and taste. Boston, 1863.

Phil 5245.30 — Foltz, Otto. Grundriss der Psychologie für Lehrer- und Lehrerinen-Bildungs-Anstalten. Osterwiech-Harz, 1910.

Phil 3450.19.99 — Folwart, H. Kant, Husserl, Heidegger. Breslau, 1936.

Phil 310.556 — Fomina, V.A. Aktual'nye problemy istoricheskogo materializma. Moskva, 1963.

Phil 8878.59 — La fonchion morale. (Delvolvé, J.) Paris, 1951.

Phil 5545.36 — La fonction de la mémoire. (Paulhan, F.) Paris, 1904.

Phil 5465.38.5 — La fonction de l'imagination. (Lacroze, René.) Paris, 1938.

Phil 5465.38 — La fonction de l'imagination. (Lacroze, René.) Paris, 1938.

Phil 8893.65 — La fonction pratique de la finalité. (Sourian, M.) Paris, 1925.

Phil 8893.65.2 — La fonction pratique de la finalité. Thèse. (Sourian, M.) Paris, 1925.

Phil 9495.131 — La fonction sexuelle au point de vue de l'éthique et de l'hygiène sociales. (Sicard de Plauzales, J.) Paris, 1908.

Phil 6116.5.85 — Les fonctions du cerveau, doctrines de F. Goltz. (Soury, Jules.) Paris, 1886.

Phil 5252.166 — Les fonctions psychologiques et les oeuvres. Thèse. (Meyerson, Ignace.) Paris, 1948.

Phil 5242.26 — Les fonctions supérieures du système nerveux. (Cros, A.) Paris, 1874.

Phil 5053.4 — Fondamenti del calcolo logico. (Nagy, Albino.) Napoli, 1890.

Phil 8400.12 — I fondamenti del giudizio estetico. (Arata, Rodolfo.) Bologna, 1960.

Phil 1119.5 — I fondamenti della filosofia classica. 2. ed. (Olgiati, F.) Milano, 1953.

Phil 5520.495 — I fondamenti della filosofia del linguaggio. (Bacchin, Giovanni Romano.) Assisi, 1965.

Phil 4120.4.35 — I fondamenti della filosofia del oiritto. 3. ed. (Gentile, Giovanni.) Firenze, 1937.

Phil 3450.11.375 — Fondamenti della logica di Husserl. (Voltaggio, Franco.) Milano, 1965.

Phil 5241.45.5 — Fondamenti di psicologia sperimentale. (Baratono, Adelchi.) Torino, 1906.

Phil 8593.22 — Fondamenti di scienza delle religioni. 1. ed. (Nilsson, M.P.) Firenze, 1950.

Phil 8422.13 — Fondamenti di una filosofia dell'espressione. (Volpe, G. della.) Bologna, 1936.

Phil 2475.1.465 — I fondamenti logico-metafisici del bergsonismo e altri scritti. (Colletti, Giovanni.) Padova, 1963.

Phil 575.150 — I fondamenti metafisici "dignitas hominis". (Massa, Eugenio.) Torino, 1954.

Phil 4769.1.108 — I fondamenti spirituali della vita. (Solove'ev, V.S.) Bologna, 1922.

Phil 400.27.9 — Il fondamento dell' idealismo etico. (Morselli, Emilio.) Livorno, 1911.

Phil 4080.38 — Fondamento e problemi della metafisica. (Campanale, Domenico.) Bari, 1968-

Phil 3493.13.5 — Il fondamento morale...secondo Kant. (Lamanna, E.P.) Firenze, 1949.

Phil 1705.10 — Fondane, B. La conscience malheureuse. Paris, 1936.

Phil 336.8 — Fondard, L. De la forme a l'idée. Marseille, 1937.

Phil 2490.160 — Les fondateurs de la sociologie. (Gurvitch, Georges.) Paris, 1957.

Phil 8870.42 — La fondazione del giudizio morale. Padova, 1968.

Phil 3450.11.440 — Fondazione della logica in Husserl. (Bosio, Franco.) Milano, 1966.

Phil 3480.66.49 — Fondazione della metafisica dei costumi. (Kant, Immanuel.) Torino, 1923.

Phil 3480.66.50 — Fondazione della metafisica dei costumi. (Kant, Immanuel.) Torino, 1925?

Phil 5046.21 — Fondazione della metodalogia. (Govi, Mario.) Torino, 1929.

Phil 3503.30 — Fondazione e modalita in Kant. (Veca, Salvatore.) Milano, 1969.

Phil 8735.40.5 — Fondazione Giorgio Cini, Venice. Centro de Cultura e Civiltà. Causalità e finalità. Firenze, 1959.

Phil 8735.40 — Fondazione Giorgio Cini, Venice. Centro de Cultura e Civiltà. Il valore del fine nel mondo. Firenze, 1955.

Phil 4120.4.95 — Fondazione Giovanni Gentile per gli Studi Filosofici. Giovanni Gentile. Firenze, 1948-51. 13v.

	Phil 7150.48	Fondazione Piero Varenna, Milan. Assistenza medico sociale ai tenfati suicide. Milano, 1959.
	Phil 3808.69.3	Le fondement de la morale. 3. éd. (Schopenhauer, Arthur.) Paris, 1888.
	Phil 3808.69.8	Le fondement de la morale. 11. éd. (Schopenhauer, Arthur.) Paris, 1925.
	Phil 187.84	Le fondement de la philosophie. (Maar, Jean.) Paris, 1925.
	Phil 5829.8	Le fondement physiologique des instincts des systèmes nutritif. Thèse. (Thorlakson, B.C.) Paris, 1926.
	Phil 8884.11	Le fondement psychologique de la morale. (Joussain, A.) Paris, 1909.
	Phil 6121.24	Les fondements biologiques de la psychologie. (Lhermitte, J.) Paris, 1925.
	Phil 5066.1	Les fondements de la logique symbolique. v.1-2. (Greenwood, T.) Paris, 1938.
	Phil 3480.65.15	Fondements de la métaphysique des moeurs. 2. éd. (Kant, Immanuel.) Paris, 1907?
	Phil 8878.33	Les fondements de la morale. (Dupuy, Paul.) Paris, 1900.
	Phil 8581.68.15	Les fondements intellectuels de la foi chrétienne. (Broglie, Paul.) Paris, 1905.
	Phil 5255.72	Les fondements théoriques et méthodologiques de la psychologie. (Paulus, Jean.) Bruxelles, 1965.
	Phil 2750.11.110	Les fondements thornistes du personnalisme de Maritain. (Croteau, Jacques.) Ottawa, 1955.
	Phil 1750.160	Fondy, John T. The educational principles of American humanism. Diss. Washington, D.C., 1945.
	Phil 2405.3	Fonsegrive, G. De Taine à Régny. L'évolution des idées. Paris, 1917.
	Phil 5755.6	Fonsegrive, G. Essai sur le libre arbitre. Paris, 1887.
	Phil 336.5	Fonsegrive, G. Essais sur la connaissance. 2. ed. n.p., n.d. 2v.
	Phil 270.18	Fonsegrive, G.L. La causalité efficiente. Thèse. Paris, 1891.
	Phil 1850.98	Fonsegrive, G.L. François Bacon. Paris, 1893.
	Phil 8880.25	Fonsegrive, George. Morale et societé. 4e ed. Paris, 1908.
	Phil 2605.4.31	Fonsegrive, George L. Éléments de philosophie. Paris, 1891-1892. 2v.
	Phil 2800.1.87	Fonsegrive, Georges. Léon Ollé-Laprune, l'homme et le penseur. Paris, 1912.
	Phil 8406.10	Fontaine, André. Essai sur le principe et les lois de la critique d'art. Paris, 1903.
	Phil 2605.10.30	Fontan, Pierre. L'intention réaliste. Paris, 1965.
	Phil 4005.6	Fontana, B. La filosofia della storia nei pensatori italiani. Imola, 1873.
	Phil 4060.2.85	Fontanesi, Giuseppina. Il problema dell'amore nell'opera di Leone Ebreo. Venezia, 1934.
	Phil 7060.152	Fontenay, G. de. La photographie et l'étude des phénomènes psychiques. Paris, 1912.
	Phil 7068.98.10	Fontenay, Guillaume de. A propos d'Eusapia Paladino. Paris, 1898.
Htn	Phil 2605.2.30*	Fontenelle, B. Entretiens sur la pluralité des mondes. Paris, 1766.
	Phil 180.14	Fontenelle. (Flourens, P.) Paris, 1847-1851. 5 pam.
	Phil 4967.32	Fontes, Gloria Marly Duarte. Alexandre Rodrigues Ferreira: aspectos de sua vida e obra. Manaus, 1966.
	Phil 4210.123F	Le fonti del sistema filosofico di Antonio Rosmini. (Lilla, V.) Milano, 1897.
	Phil 4260.85.5	Le fonti della gnoseologia Vichiana. (Croce, B.) Napoli, 1912.
	Phil 6675.9	Fonvielle, W. de. Les endormeurs. Paris, n.d.
	Phil 5875.62	Fonzi, Ada. Disegno e linguaggio el bambino. Torino, 1968.
	Phil 5627.134.25	Foot, Stephen. Life began yesterday. N.Y., 1935.
	Phil 8620.17	The foot-prints of Satan. (Read, H.) N.Y., 1874.
	Phil 8610.888.10	Foote, G.W. The Bible handbook of freethinkers and inquiring Christians. London, 1900.
	Phil 7060.27.3	Footfalls on the boundary of another world. (Owen, R.D.) Philadelphia, 1865.
	Phil 5057.19	Footnotes to formal logic. (Rieber, Charles H.) Berkeley, 1918.
	Phil 7068.59.10	Footsteps of spirits. London, 1859.
	Phil 5535.4	Foppa, Klaus. Lernen, Gedächtnis, Verhalten. Köln, 1965.
	Phil 9220.7	For friendship's sake. (Bacon, Francis.) N.Y., 1900.
	Phil 8882.60	For my children. (Hires, H.) N.Y., 1943.
	Phil 165.173	For Roman Ingarden. 's Gravenhage, 1959.
	Phil 5627.134.4	For sinners only. (Russell, Arthur J.) N.Y., 1932.
	Phil 6420.32	For stutterers. (Blanton, Smiley.) N.Y., 1936.
	Phil 5790.10	For the love of money. (Knight, James Allen.) Philadelphia, 1968.
	Phil 2255.10.34	For the new intellectual; the philosophy of Ayn Rand. (Rand, Ayn.) N.Y., 1961.
	Phil 9450.40	For what purpose? (Speer, James.) Washington, 1960.
	Phil 3504.15	Forberg und Kant. (Wesselsky, Anton.) Leipzig, 1913.
	Phil 8880.44.5	Forbes, Alexander. Essays, moral and philosophical. London, 1734.
	Phil 9245.2	Forbes, J. Of happiness in its relations to work and knowledge. London, 1850.
	Phil 9490.6	Forbes, W.C. Letter to an undergraduate. n.p., 1904.
	Phil 5070.10	Forbes, Waldo. Cycles of personal belief. Boston, 1917.
	Phil 6959.1.29	La force et la faiblesse psychologiques. (Janet, Pierre.) Paris, 1932.
	Phil 476.3.3	Force et matière. (Büchner, L.) Paris, 1863.
	Phil 6128.15.3	The force of mind. (Schofield, A.T.) N.Y., 1903.
	Phil 9560.13	Force of right purpose. (Robbins, C.) Boston, 1859.
	Phil 7069.07.17	Les forces naturelles inconnues. (Flammarion, C.) Paris, 1907.
	Phil 6687.6.9	Les forces non définies. (Rochas d'Aiglun, A. de.) Paris, 1887.
	Phil 5245.32.5	Ford, Adelbert. Group experiments in elementary psychology. N.Y., 1932.
	Phil 7069.58.10	Ford, Arthur. Nothing so strange. 1. ed. N.Y., 1958.
	Phil 5245.18	Ford, Corydon. The synthesis of mind. n.p., 1883-1893.
	Phil 8955.5	Ford, J.C. Contemporary moral theology. Westminster, Md., 1958-63. 2v.
	Phil 5593.46	Ford, Mary E.N. The application of the Rorschach test to young children. Minneapolis, 1946.
	Phil 7054.18	Ford, S.L. Interwoven. Letters from a son to his mother. Boston, 1905.
	Phil 5238.244	Forderungen an die Psychologie. (Hardesty, Francis P.) Bern, 1965.
	Phil 6319.1.188	Fordham, F. An introduction to Jung's psychology. London, 1953.
	Phil 6319.1.205	Fordham, M.S.M. Contact with Jung. London, 1963.
	Phil 6315.46	Fordham, M.S.M. New developments in analytical psychology. London, 1957.
	Phil 6319.1.204	Fordham, M.S.M. The objective psyche. London, 1958.
	Phil 5870.50	Fordham, Michael Scott Montague. Children as individuals. London, 1969.
	Phil 8880.10	Fordyce, D. The elements of moral philosophy. v.1-3. London, 1758.
	Phil 6115.21.3	Forel, A. Gehirn und Seele. 4. Aufl. Bonn, 1894.
	Phil 6115.21.4	Forel, A. Gehirn und Seele. 5. und 6. Aufl. Bonn, 1899.
	Phil 6115.21.5	Forel, A. Gehirn und Seele. 12. Aufl. Leipzig, 1914.
	Phil 6115.21	Forel, A. Hygiene of nerves and mind in health and disease. London, 1907.
	Phil 6675.6	Forel, A. Hypnotism and cerebral activity. Worcester, 1899.
	Phil 6675.6.5	Forel, A. Hypnotism or suggestion and psychotherapy. N.Y., 1907.
	Phil 6675.6.7	Forel, A. Der Hypnotismus. 2. Aufl. Stuttgart, 1891.
	Phil 6315.6	Forel, Auguste. L'activité psychique. Genève, 1919.
	Phil 9495.43	Forel, Auguste. Sexuelle Ethik. München, 1908.
	Phil 6315.12	Forel, O.L. La psychologie des névroses. Genève, 1925.
	Phil 180.57	Forest, Aimé. Du consentement à l'être. Paris, 1936.
	Phil 180.78	Forest, Aimé. Orientazioni metafisiche. Milano, 1960.
	Phil 7069.34.35	Foretold; stories of modern second-sight. (Streamline (pseud.).) Stirling 1934.
	VPhil 9590.30	Forever into the past and future. (De Condé, Minerva E.) Boston, 196-.
	Phil 2050.212	The forgotten Hume, le bon David. (Mossner, E.C.) N.Y., 1943.
	Phil 7082.174A	The forgotten language. (Fromm, Erich.) N.Y., 1951.
	Phil 8612.26	The forgotten purpose. (Baghdigian, B.K.) Kansas City, 1934.
	Phil 5585.240	Forgus, Ronald H. Perception. N.Y., 1966.
	Phil 480.3	Forichon, L. Le matérialisme et la phrénologie. Paris, 1840.
	Phil 930.7.5	Forke, A. Geschichte der alten chinesischen Philosophie. Hamburg, 1927.
	Phil 930.7.8	Forke, A. Geschichte der mittelalterlichen chinesischen Philosophie. Hamburg, 1934.
	Phil 930.7.10	Forke, A. Geschichte der neueren chinesischen Philosophie. Hamburg, 1938.
	Phil 930.7	Forke, A. The world conception of the Chinese. London, 1925.
	Phil 5645.70	Form, farve og emotioner. (Rattleff, Anker.) København, 1958.
	Phil 8419.8	Form als Schicksa. 2. Aufl. (Scheffler, K.) Erlenbach, 1943.
	Phil 5170.9	Form and content in logic. (Wright, G.H.) Cambridge, 1949.
	Phil 8407.37	Form and function; remarks on art. (Greenough, H.) Berkeley, 1947.
	Phil 5374.31	Die Form der Bewusstheit. (Nasgaard, S.) München, 1923.
	Phil 5046.22	Die Form des Erkennens. (Grebe, Wilhelm.) München, 1929.
	Phil 5645.55	Form kolarisme. (Brandt, Frithiof.) København, 1958.
	Phil 5545.70	The form of the learning curves for memory. Private ed. (Kjerstad, C.L.) Chicago, 191-?
	Phil 5246.27.5	Die Form und die Bewegungsgesetze des Geistes. (Glogau, Gustav.) Breslau, 1880. 2 pam.
	Phil 8422.11	Form und Gehalt in der Ästhetik. (Vogt, T.) Wien, 1865.
	Phil 3496.5	Form und Geist. (Odebrecht, Rudolf.) Berlin, 1930.
	Phil 337.2	Form und Materie des Erkennens. (Gross, Felix.) Leipzig, 1910.
	Phil 70.50	La forma. (Semana Española de Filosofía, 4th, Madrid, 1957.) Madrid, 1959.
	Phil 1540.72	La forma Aristotelica in una "Quaestio" medievale. (Cilento, V.) Napoli, 1961.
	Phil 4961.45.3	La formación de la mentalidad mexicana. (Romanell, P.) México, 1954.
	Phil 4959.225	La formación de la mentalidad mexicana. 1. ed. (Romanell, Patrick.) México, 1954.
	Phil 8406.4.5	Formaggio, Dino. L'arte come comunicazione. Milano, 1953.
	Phil 8406.4	Formaggio, Dino. L'idea di artisticita. Milano, 1962.
	Phil 5190.75	A formal analysis of conditionals. (Barker, John A.) Carbondale, 1969.
	Phil 3504.45	The formal and material elements of Kant's ethics. (Washington, W.M.) N.Y., 1898.
	Phil 5047.11.25	Formal and transcendental logic. (Husserl, Edmund.) The Hague, 1969.
	Phil 5545.58	Formal discipline...experimental psychology. Thesis. (Coover, J.E.) Princeton, 1916.
	Phil 5041.55	Formal logic. (Bennett, A.A.) N.Y., 1939.
Htn	Phil 1955.2.30*	Formal logic. (De Morgan, Augustus.) London, 1847.
	Phil 5043.5	Formal logic. (DeMorgan, Augustus.) London, 1847.
	Phil 5043.33.5	Formal logic. (Dopp, Joseph.) N.Y., 1960.
	Phil 5055.25A	Formal logic. (Prior, Arthur N.) Oxford, 1955.
	Phil 5058.24	Formal logic. (Schiller, F.C.S.) London, 1912.
	Phil 5049.22	Formal logic: its scope and limits. (Jeffrey, Richard C.) N.Y., 1967.
	Phil 5055.25.2	Formal logic. 2nd ed. (Prior, Arthur N.) Oxford, 1962.
	Phil 5043.5.3	Formal logic (1847). (DeMorgan, Augustus.) London, 1926.
	Phil 5066.195	Formal methods. (Beth, Evert W.) Dordrecht, 1962.
	Phil 5500.55	Formal representation of human judgment. (Symposium on Cognition, 3rd, Carnegie Institute of Technology, 1967.) N.Y., 1968.
	Phil 5066.232	Formal systems and recursive functions. (Logic Colloquiam, 8th, Oxford, 1963.) Amsterdam, 1965.
	Phil 5011.6	Formale Logik. (Bochénski, I.M.) Freiburg, 1956.
	Phil 5051.46.4	Formale Logik. 4. Aufl. (Lorenzen, Paul.) Berlin, 1970.
	Phil 3500.39	Die formale Logik Kant's in ihren Beziehungen zur Transcendentalen. (Steckelmacher, M.) Breslau, 1879.
	Phil 5047.11.10	Formale und transzendentale Logik. (Husserl, Edmund.) Halle, 1929.
	Phil 5066.130	Le formalisme logic-mathématique et le problème du non-sens. (Crahay, Franz.) Paris, 1957.
	Phil 4215.3.31	Formalismo e amoralismo giuridico. (Rensi, Giuseppe.) Verona, 1914.
	Phil 8893.86.5	Der formalismus in der Ethik und die materiale Wertethik. 2. Aufl. (Scheler, Max.) Halle, 1921.
	Phil 5066.225.5	Formal'naia logika i metodologiia nauki. (Akademiia Nauk SSSR. Institut Filosofii.) Moskva, 1964.
	Phil 5925.5	Forman, J.G. Elements of phrenology. Cincinnati, 1844.
	Phil 5535.58	La formation continue des adultes. 1. ed. (Goguelin, Pierre.) Paris, 1970.
	Phil 4260.120	La formation de la pensée philosophique de G.B. Vico. (Chaix-Ruy, Jules.) Gap, 1943.
	Phil 332.19	La formation de l'esprit scientifique. Photoreproduction. (Bachelard, Gaston.) Paris, 1938.
	Phil 3503.6	La formation de l'influence Kantienne en France. (Vallois, M.) Paris, 1925?
	Phil 3503.6.5	La formation de l'influence Kantienne en France. Thèse. (Vallois, M.) Paris, 1924.

Phil 5435.14 La formation des habitudes. (Guillaume, Paul.) Paris, 1968.

Phil 5625.90 La formation du concept de reflexe aux XVII et XVIII siècles. (Canguilhem, G.) Paris, 1955.

Phil 1807.2 La formation du radicalisme philosophique. (Halévy, E.) Paris, 1901-04. 3v.

Phil 3450.11.345 The formation of Husserl's concept of constitution. (Sokolowski, Robert.) The Hague, 1964.

Phil 5242.17 The formation of opinion. (Clark, William.) Cambridge, 1888?

Phil 1930.8.110 The formative years of R.G. Collingwood. (Johnston, William Murray.) The Hague, 1967[1968]

Phil 3450.11.87 La formazione del pensiero di Husserl e il problema della costituzione della natura materiale e della natura animale. (Paci, Enzo.) Milano, 1967.

Phil 2750.11.225 La formazione del pensiero di J. Maritain. (Pavan, Antonio.) Padova, 1967.

Phil 3778.96 La formazione della filosofia di K.L. Reinhold, 1784-1794. (Pupi, Angelo.) Milano, 1966.

Phil 4115.88 La formazione della filosofia giobertiana. (Caramella, S.) Genova, 1926.

Phil 8430.81 La forme et l'intelligible. (Klein, Robert.) Paris, 1970.

Phil 5058.36 Formel logik, grundlag for forelaesninger. 2. udg. (Starcke, Carl N.) Kjøbenhavn, 1922.

Phil 5047.23 Formel logik, til brug ved forelaesninger. 6. udgave. (Høffding, Harald.) København, 1913.

Phil 5041.41 Formel logik. (Brandt, F.) København, 1927.

Phil 4580.31 Formel logik. (Køffding, Harald.) København, 1884.

Phil 5041.41.5 Formel logik til brug ved filosofikum. 3e udg. (Brandt, F.) København, 1930.

Phil 5047.24 Formella logiken baserad på identitetsprincipen. (Hjelmérus, Alfred.) Lund, 1889.

Phil 5365.2 Formen der Reaktion auf Konflikte. Diss. (Nesswetha, Wilhelm.) Bonn, 1964.

Phil 349.24 Die Formen des Wissens und die Bildung. (Scheler, Max.) Bonn, 1925.

Phil 5592.100 Formen und Ausprägung der seelischen Nachreifung. (Wallis, Ingeborg.) Berlin, 1959.

Phil 5648.20 Die Formenwelt des Tastsinnes. (Révész, Géza.) Haag, 1938. 2v.

Phil 2475.1.305 Les formes du mouvement chez Bergson. (Marietti, A.) Le Puy, 1953.

Phil 8583.18.2 Les formes élémentaires de la vie religieuse. 2. éd. (Durkheim, E.) Paris, 1925.

Phil 8583.18.5 Les formes élémentaires de la vie religieuse. 5e éd. (Durkheim, E.) Paris, 1968.

Phil 343.25 Formes structurées et modes productifs. (Mouloud, N.) Paris, 195-?

Htn Phil 805.1.3* Formey, J.H.S. A concise history of philosophy. London, 1766.

Phil 805.1.5 Formey, J.H.S. A concise history of philosophy and philosophers. Glasgow, 1767.

Phil 805.1.9 Formey, J.H.S. Histoire abrégée de la philosophie. Amsterdam, 1760.

Htn Phil 805.1* Formey, J.H.S. History of philosophy. London, 1766.

Phil 8110.14 Formigari, Lia. L'estetica del gusto nel settecento inglesa. 1. ed. Firenze, 1962.

Phil 325.20 Formigari, Lia. Linguistica ed empirismo nel Seicento inglese. Bari, 1970.

Phil 310.460 Formirovanie filosofii marksizma. (Oizerman, T.I.) Moskva, 1962.

Phil 8980.403 Formirovanie moral'nogo oblika sovetskogo rabochego. Moskva, 1961.

Phil 5850.138.5 Formirovanie poniatiia o drugom cheloveke kak lichnosti. (Bodalev, Aleksei A.) Leningrad, 1970.

Phil 5643.178 Formirovanie zritel'nogo obraza. (Zinchenko, Vladimir P.) Moskva, 1969.

Phil 5066.242.5 Formirovanre matematicheskoi logiki. (Stiazhkin, Nikolai Ivanovich.) Moskva, 1967.

Phil 9550.18 Forms and limits of utilitarianism. (Lyons, David.) Oxford, 1965.

Phil 8893.104.5 Forms and techniques of altruistic and spiritual growth. (Sorokin, Pitirim Aleksandrovich.) Boston, 1954.

Phil 8893.104.6 Forms and techniques of altruistic and spiritual growth. Boston, 1954. (Sorokin, Pitirim Aleksandrovich.) N.Y., 1971.

Phil 8418.20 The forms of things unknown. (Read, Herbert.) London, 1960.

Phil 735.125 The forms of value. (Hilliard, A.L.) N.Y., 1950.

Phil 960.13 La formule bouddhique des douze causes. (Oltramare, P.) Geneve, 1909.

Phil 8980.248 Formuvannia komunistychnoi idei nosti osoby. (Burdiva, Alla I.) Kyïv, 1970.

Phil 343.56 Formy i soderzhanie mephleniia. (Mamardashvili, M.K.) Moskva, 1968.

Phil 310.511 Formy myshleniia. (Akademiia Nauk SSSR. Institut Filosofii.) Moskva, 1962.

Phil 310.330 Formy obshchestvennogo soznaniia. (Gak, G.M.) Moskva, 1960.

Phil 310.110 Formy obshchestvennogo soznaniia. (Kelle, V.Z.) Moskva, 1959.

Phil 4260.111 Fornaca, Remo. Il pensiero educativo di Giambattista Vico. Torino, 1957.

Phil 5414.50 Fornari, Franco. Psicanalisi della situazione atomica. Milano, 1970.

Phil 7069.64.15 Fornell, Earl W. The unhappy medium. Austin, 1964.

Phil 2490.104 Fornelli, N. L'opera di Augusto Comte, in occasione del primo centenario della sua nascita. Milano, 1898.

Phil 8585.33 Fornerod, A. Religion et théologie. Lausanne, 1932.

Phil 2750.11.195 Forni, Guglielmo. La filosofia della storia nel pensiero politico di Jacques Maritain. Bologna, 1965.

Phil 1750.115.135 Forni, Guglielmo. Il sogno finito. Bologna, 1967.

Phil 4640.2.30 Fórólfsson, S. Dulmaetti og dultrú. Reykjavík, 1922.

Phil 990.23 Foroughi, A.H. Systeme de philosophie dynamo synthetique. Paris, 1940. 2v.

Phil 990.20 Foroughir, A.H. Civilisation et synthèse. Paris, 1936.

Phil 8880.58 Forrest, John K. Reality or preachment; the moral crisis of our time. Boston, 1967.

Htn Phil 9345.4* Forrester, J. Polite philosopher. London, 1758.

Phil 3825.5 Forsberg, N.A. Jemförande betraktelse af Spinozas och Malebranches metafysiska principier. Upsala, 1864.

Phil 6400.21 Forsboom, Bernhard. Das Buch Emanuel. München, 1957.

Htn Phil 3625.1.89* Das forschen Nach licht und recht. Berlin, 1782.

Phil 193.31.9 Forschung nach der Gewissheit. Leipzig, 1869.

Phil 1123.11 Forschungen. (Schmekel, A.) Berlin, 1938.

Phil 1504.17.5 Forschungen über die lateinischen Aristoteles. v.17, pt.5-6. (Grabmann, M.) Münster, 1916.

Phil 1170.24 Forschungen zum Neuplatonismus. (Theiler, Willy.) Berlin, 1966.

Phil 1118.2 Forschungen zur Geschichte der Erkenntnissproblems im Alterthum. (Natorp, Paul.) Berlin, 1884.

Phil 1504.17.2 Forschungen zur Geschichte der frümittelalterlichen Philosophie. v.17, pt.2-3. (Endes, J.A.) Münster, 1915.

Phil 15.60 Forschungen zur Logik und zur Grundlegen der exakten Wissenschaften. Reprinted 1970. Leipzig. N.F. 1-8,1937-1943//

Phil 15.6 Forschungen zur Philosophie und ihrer Geschichte. Halle. 1-16 9v.

Phil 189.33 Forståelsesformer. Et filosofisk bidrag. (Østerberg, Dag.) Oslo, 1966.

Phil 7054.173.10 Forster, David. The vital choice, Endor or Calvary. London, 1919.

Phil 8408.37 Förstudier till en konstfilosofi på psykologisk grundval. (Hirn, Yrjö.) Helsingfors, 1896.

Phil 5627.143 Forsyth, D. Psychology and religion. London, 1935.

Phil 9165.5 Forsyth, P.T. Marriage, its ethic and religion. London, 1912.

Phil 8585.20 Forsyth, P.T. Principle of authority in relation to certainty. London, 1912.

Phil 8880.11 Forsyth, R. The principles of moral science. Edinburgh, 1805.

Phil 5755.9 Forti, E. La décision; essai d'analyse psychologique. Thèse. Paris, 1926.

Phil 5400.114 Forti, E. L'émotion. 1. éd. Paris, 1952.

Phil 1540.36 Fortin, E.L. Christianisme et culture phillosophique au cinquième siècle. Paris, 1959.

Phil 9345.7 Fortin, P. Testament, ou Conseils fideles d'un bon pere. Leide, 1653.

Phil 5245.9 Fortlage, A.R.K. Acht psychologische Vorträge. Jena, 1869.

Phil 5245.9.10 Fortlage, A.R.K. Beiträge zur Psychologie. Leipzig, 1875.

Phil 5245.9.5 Fortlage, A.R.K. System der Psychologie. Leipzig, 1855. 2v.

Phil 5245.9.15 Fortlage, A.R.K. Vier psychologische Vorträge. Jena, 1874.

Phil 1135.17 Fortlage, C. Ueber die Denkweise der altesten Philosophen. München, 1829.

Phil 3005.1 Fortlage, K. Genetische Geschichte der Philosophie seit Kent. Leipzig, 1852.

X Cg Phil 180.21 Fortlage, Karl. Sechs philosophische Vorträge. 2. Ausg. Jena, 1872.

Phil 5627.264.25 Fortmann, Henricus Martinus Maria. Als zienda onzienlijke. v.1-3. Hilversum, 1964- 4v.

Phil 2490.174 Fortschritt und Gegenrevolution. Die Gesellschaftslehre Comtes in ihrer sozialen Funktion. (Massing, Otwin.) Stuttgart, 1966.

Phil 15.40 Fortschritte der Psychoanalyse. Göttingen. 1-3 2v.

Phil 15.3 Fortschritte der Psychologie und ihrer Anwendungen. 1-4 4v.

Phil 5228.3 Die Fortschritte der Völkerpsychologie. (Sganzini, Carlo.) Bern, 1913.

Phil 3665.5.30 Fortschritte und Rückschritte der Philosophie. (Nelson, Leonard.) Frankfurt, 1962.

Phil 7082.38.5 Fortschritte und Technik der Traumdeutung. (Stekel, Wilhelm.) Wien, 1935.

Phil 3805.195 Der fortschrittliche Gehalt der Pädagogik Schleiermachers. (Schuffenhauer, Heinz.) Berlin, 1956.

Phil 2270.116 La fortuna di Herbert Spencer in Italia. (Ranzoli, C.) Verona, 1904.

Phil 4110.13.30 Fortunato da Brescia. Philosophia sensuum mechanica methodice tractata atque ad usus academicos accommodata. Venetiis, 1756.

Phil 5752.9 Fortune and fate from Democritus to St. Thomas Aquinas. (Cioffari, Vincenzo.) N.Y., 1935.

Phil 9070.25 A fortune to share. (Young, Vashni.) Indianapolis, 1931.

Phil 5938.10.5 Forty years in phrenology. (Sizer, Nelson.) N.Y., 1891.

Phil 7069.36.5 Forty years of psychic research; a plain narrative of fact. (Garland, Hamlin.) N.Y., 1936.

Phil 15.7 Forum philosophicum. 1930-1931

Phil 5593.41 Fosberg, I.A. An experimental study of the rehability of the Rorschach psychodiagnostic technique. N.Y., 1941.

Phil 6015.1.5 Fosbroke, Gerald Eltac. Character qualities outlined and related. N.Y., 1923.

Phil 6015.1 Fosbroke, Gerald Eltac. Character reading through analysis of the features. N.Y., 1914.

Phil 8630.9.10 Fosdick, H.E. The assurance of immortality. N.Y., 1916.

Phil 8630.9 Fosdick, H.E. Spiritual values and eternal life. Cambridge, 1927.

Phil 8585.27A Fosdick, Harry E. Adventurous religion and other essays. 1st ed. N.Y., 1926.

Phil 7080.3 Fosgate, B. Sleep. N.Y., 1850.

Phil 8612.62 Foss, Martin. Death, sacrifice, and tragedy. Lincoln, 1966.

Phil 805.9 Foss, Martin. The idea of perfection in the western world. Princeton, 1946.

Phil 180.64 Foss, Martin. Symbol and metaphor in human experience. Princeton, N.J., 1949.

Phil 2030.5.5 Fossils and presences. (Guérard, A.L.) Standord, Calif., 1957.

Phil 9165.4.2 Foster, F. Thoughts on the times. London, 1779.

Phil 270.6 Foster, F.H. The doctrine of the transcendent use of the principle of causality. Leipzig, 1882.

Phil 3640.231A Foster, George B. Friedrich Nietzsche. N.Y., 1931.

Phil 5400.99 Foster, George S. Our hunches; the effect of emotions on our lives and habits. N.Y., 1942.

Htn Phil 9345.5* Foster, H. (Webster). Boarding school. Boston, 1829.

Phil 8585.8 Foster, J. Discourses...natural religion and social virtue. London, 1749-52.

Phil 9165.2 Foster, J. The married state. Hartford, 18- .

Phil 9035.14.5 Foster, John. Decision of character. N.Y., 19-

Phil 8880.12.25 Foster, John. An essay on the improvement of time. N.Y., 1866.

Phil 9035.14 Foster, John. Essays on decision of character. Burlington, 1830.

Phil 5039.18 Foster, Marguerite H. Probability, confirmation, and simplicity; readings in the philosophy of inductive logic. N.Y., 1966.

Phil 3425.261 Foster, Michael B. Die Geschichte als Schicksal des Geistes in der hegelschenPhilosophie. Tübingen, 1929.

Phil 5627.78 Foster, R.S. Philosophy of Christian experience. 3d series. N.Y., 1890.

Phil 9495.22 Foster, W.T. The social emergency. Boston, 1914.

Phil 5245.27 Foster, William S. Experiments in psychology. N.Y., 1923.

Phil 5245.27.5 Foster, William S. Experiments in psychology. N.Y., 1923.

Phil 6952.27 Foster home care for mental patients. (Crutcher, H.B.) N.Y., 1944.
Phil 5190.43 Fotheringham, Wallace C. Perspectives on persuasion. Boston, 1966.
Phil 8955.10 Fotion, Nicholas G. Moral situation. Yellow Springs, 1968.
Phil 5245.15.5 Foucault, Marcel. Cours de psychologie. Paris, 1926.
Phil 7082.120 Foucault, Marcel. De somniis observationes et cogitationes. Thesis. Paris, 1901.
Phil 5648.4.5 Foucault, Marcel. L'illusion paradoxale et le seuil de Weber. Montpelier, 1910.
Phil 5245.15.10 Foucault, Marcel. Premières leçons de psychologie expérimentale a l'usage des candidats au baccalauréat. Paris, 1930.
Phil 5245.15 Foucault, Marcel. La psychophysique. Paris, 1901.
Phil 6955.22 Foucault, Michel. Folie et déraison. Paris, 1961.
Phil 6955.23 Foucault, Michel. Madness and civilization. N.Y., 1965.
Phil 2840.88 Foucher, Louis. La jeunesse de Renouvier et sa première philosophie. Paris, 1927.
Phil 2840.88.2 Foucher, Louis. La jeunesse de Renouvier et sa première philosophie. Thèse. Paris, 1927. 2 pam.
Phil 2405.10 Foucher, Louis. La philosopie catholique en France au XIX siècle avant la renaissance Thomiste et dans son rapporrt avecelle. Paris, 1955.
Htn Phil 2733.32* Foucher, Simon. Critique de la recherche de la verité. Paris, 1675.
Phil 2520.102 Foucher de Careil, A. Descartes, la princesse Elizabeth et la reine Christine. Paris, 1879.
Phil 2520.102.2 Foucher de Careil, A. Descartes, la princesse Elizabeth et la reine Christine. Paris, 1909.
Phil 2520.102.5 Foucher de Careil, A. Descartes et la princesse palatine. Paris, 1862.
Phil 3552.86.15 Foucher de Careil, Alexandre. Leibniz, Descartes et Spinoza. Paris, 1862.
Phil 3552.86.5 Foucher de Careil, Alexandre. Leibniz et les deux sophies. Paris, 1876.
Phil 3552.86.10 Foucher de Careil, Alexandre. Leibniz et Pierre-le-Grand. Paris, 1874.
Phil 3552.86 Foucher de Careil, Alexandre. Leibniz la philosophie juive et la cabale. Paris, 1861.
Phil 3425.83 Foucher de Careil, L.A. Hegel et Schopenhauer. Paris, 1862.
Phil 2605.6.31 Foucou, L. Les preliminaires de la philosophie. Paris, 1879.
Phil 2605.8.30 Fouéré, René. Du temporel à l'intemporel. Paris, 1960. 2v.
Phil 978.59.100 Fouéré, René. Krishnamurti. 2d ed. Bombay, 1954.
Phil 5045.18 Fougeyrollas, Pierre. Contradiction et totalité. Paris, 1964.
Phil 180.80 Fougeyrollas, Pierre. La philosophie en question. Paris, 1960.
Phil 6315.2.470 Fougeyrollas, Pierre. La révolution freudienne. Paris, 1970.
Phil 8830.3 Fouillée, A. Critique; systèmes de morale contemporaine. Paris, 1883.
Phil 2520.89 Fouillée, A. Descartes. Paris, 1893.
Phil 336.1 Fouillée, A. L'évolutionnisme des idées-forces. Paris, 1890.
Phil 336.1.4 Fouillée, A. L'évolutionnisme des idées-forces. Paris, 1906.
Phil 5755.3 Fouillée, A. La liberté et le déterminisme. Paris, 1872.
Phil 5755.3.2 Fouilleé, A. La liberté et le déterminisme. 2. éd. Paris, 1884.
Phil 8881.26.21 Fouillée, A. La morale, l'art...d'après Guyau. Paris, 1909.
Phil 336.1.6 Fouillée, A. Morale des idées-forces. Paris, 1908.
Phil 336.1.7 Fouillée, A. Morale des idées-forces. 2. ed. Paris, 1908.
Phil 400.28 Fouilleé, A. Le mouvement idéaliste et la réaction contre la science positive. 3. ed. Paris, 1913.
Phil 336.1.5 Fouillée, A. La psychologie des idées-forces. Paris, 1893. 2v.
Phil 9035.10 Fouillée, A. Tempérament et caractère. Paris, 1895.
Phil 180.19.5 Fouillée, Alfred. L'avenir de la metaphysique fondée sur l'experience. Paris, 1889.
Phil 8880.24 Fouillée, Alfred. Les elements sociologiques de la morale. Paris, 1905.
Phil 286.5 Fouillée, Alfred. Esquisse d'une interprétation du monde. Paris, 1913.
Phil 180.19.9 Fouillée, Alfred. Extraits des grands philosophes. 6e éd. Paris, 1917.
Phil 805.5.4 Fouillée, Alfred. Histoire de la philosophie. 14e éd. Paris, 1919.
Phil 3487.3.3 Fouillée, Alfred. Le moralisme de Kant et l'amoralisme contemporain. Paris, 1921.
Phil 3487.3.2 Fouillée, Alfred. Le moralisme de Kant et l'amoralisme contemporain. 2. éd. Paris, 1905.
Phil 180.19 Fouillée, Alfred. La pensée. 2e éd. Paris, 1911.
Phil 2605.1.79 Pamphlet box. Fouillée, Alfred.
Phil 3640.117.5 Fouillée, Alfred E. Nietzsche et l'immoralisme. Paris, 1902.
Phil 3640.117 Fouillée, Alfred E. Nietzsche et l'immoralisme. 3e éd. Paris, 1913.
Phil 6990.3.9 Les foules de Lourdes. 21. éd. (Huysmans, J.K.) Paris, 1906.
Phil 525.175 Foules en délire. (Felice, Philippe de.) Paris, 1947.
Phil 7080.54 Foulkes, David. The psychology of sleep. N.Y., 1966.
Phil 180.68.15 Foulquié, Paul. Cours de philosophie. Paris, 1961.
Phil 90.8 Foulquié, Paul. Dictionnaire de la langue philosophique. Paris, 1962.
Phil 1750.220 Foulquié, Paul. Existentialism. London, 1948.
Phil 1750.220.5 Foulquié, Paul. L'existentialisme. 9e éd. Paris, 1955.
Phil 1750.220.12 Foulquié, Paul. L'existentialisme. 12e éd. Paris, 1963.
Phil 1750.220.13 Foulquié, Paul. L'existentialisme. 13e éd. Paris, 1964.
Phil 180.68.5 Foulquié, Paul. Nouveau précis de philosophie a l'usage des candidats au baccalauréat. Paris, 1955. 3v.
Phil 180.68 Foulquié, Paul. Précis de philosophie. 2. ed. v.2-3. Paris, 1955.
Phil 5215.5 Foulquié, Paul. La psychologie contemporaine. Paris, 1951.
Phil 180.68.10 Foulquié, Paul. Quelques conseils pour la dissertation. 3. ed. Paris, 1956.
Phil 45.10 Foundation for Research on the Nature of Man. FRNM bulletin. Durham, N.C. 1,1965+
Phil 341.16 The foundation of human thought. (Kruse, F.V.) London, 1949.
Phil 2750.11.147 The foundation of Jacques Maritain's political philosophy. (Jung, Hava Yol.) Gainesville, Florida, 1960.
Phil 3450.18.110 A foundation of ontology. (Samuel, O.) N.Y., 1953.

Phil 3450.11.118A The foundation of phenomenology; Edmund Husserl. (Farber, Marvin.) Cambridge, 1943.
Phil 3450.11.118.3 The foundation of phenomenology. 3d ed. (Farber, Marvin.) n.p., 1967[1943]
Phil 5240.33 Foundations and sketch plan of a conational psychology. (Alexander, S.) Cambridge, Eng., 1911.
Phil 5590.6 Foundations for a science of personality. (Angyal, Andras.) N.Y., 1941.
Phil 6962.20 Foundations of abnormal psychology. (Moss, Fred August.) N.Y., 1932.
Phil 8415.5A The foundations of aesthetics. (Ogden, C.K.) London, 1922. 2v.
Phil 5270.1 Foundations of behavioral research. (Kerlinger, Frederick, N.) N.Y., 1965.
Phil 176.5.8 Foundations of belief. (Balfour, A.J.) London, 1901.
Phil 176.5.5 Foundations of belief. (Balfour, A.J.) N.Y., 1895.
Phil 9035.21 The foundations of character. (Shand, A.F.) London, 1914.
Phil 9035.21.2 The foundations of character. (Shand, A.F.) London, 1920.
Phil 5625.110 Foundations of conditioning and learning. (Kimble, Gregory A.) N.Y., 1967.
Phil 5068.6 Foundations of empirical knowledge. (Ayer, A.J.) London, 1940.
Phil 325.14 The foundations of empiricism. (Evans, John Llewelyn.) Cardiff, 1965.
Phil 180.77 Foundations of empiricism. (Feibleman, James.) The Hague, 1962.
Phil 8887.9 The foundations of ethics. (Maude, J.E.) N.Y., 1887.
Phil 8707.20 Foundations of ethics. (Ross, W.D.) Oxford, 1939.
Phil 5252.63A The foundations of experimental psychology. (Murchison, C.A.) Worcester, 1929.
Phil 5274.23 The foundations of factor analysis. (Mulaik, Stanley A.) N.Y., 1971.
Phil 5058.28.17 Foundations of formal logic. (Smith, Henry B.) Philadelphia, 1922.
Phil 5243.40 The foundations of human nature. (Dorsey, J.M.) N.Y., 1935.
Phil 5125.23 Foundations of inductive logic. (Harrod, R.F.) London, 1956.
Phil 5066.261.5 The foundations of intuitionistic mathematics. (Kleene, Stephen Cole.) Amsterdam, 1965.
Phil 342.26 The foundations of knowledge. (Landesman, Charles.) Englewood Cliffs, 1970.
Phil 345.1 Foundations of knowledge. (Ormond, A.T.) London, 1900.
Phil 4845.227.32.3 The foundations of knowledge. (Papanoutsos, Euangelos.) Albany, 1968.
Phil 5066.75 Foundations of logic and math. 1. ed. (Zeisler, E.B.) Chicago, 1955- 3v.
Phil 5066.122 Foundations of mathematical logic. (Curry, Haskell Brooks.) N.Y., 1963.
Phil 6111.45 Foundations of mental health. (Bianchi, L.) N.Y., 1930.
Phil 182.132 The foundations of metaphysics in science. (Harris, Errol E.) London, 1965.
Phil 8882.88 The foundations of morality. (Hazlitt, H.) Princeton, N.J., 1964.
Phil 8886.30 The foundations of morality. (Leathes, Stanley.) London, 1882.
Phil 6952.24.15 Foundations of neuropsychiatry. 2. ed. (Cobb, Stanley.) Baltimore, 1941.
Phil 575.47 The foundations of personality. (Myerson, Abraham.) Boston, 1921.
Phil 5590.18 The foundations of personality. (Myerson, Abraham.) Boston, 1926.
Phil 6972.14.20 Foundations of psychiatry. (White, William Alanson.) N.Y., 1921.
Phil 5270.2 Foundations of psychological research. (Kurtz, Kenneth Hassett.) Boston, 1965.
Phil 5241.112 Foundations of psychology. (Boring, E.G.) N.Y., 1948.
Phil 5252.43 The foundations of psychology. (Moore, J.S.) Princeton, 1921.
Phil 5252.43.5 The foundations of psychology. 2d ed. (Moore, J.S.) Princeton, 1933.
Phil 6323.18 Foundations of psychopathology. (Nemiah, J.C.) N.Y., 1961.
Phil 8581.17 Foundations of religion in the mind and heart of man. (Byles, J.B.) London, 1875.
Phil 8602.9 The foundations of religious belief. (Wilson, W.D.) N.Y., 1883.
Phil 4973.7 Foundations of social determinism. (Lins, Mario.) Rio de Janeiro, 1959.
Phil 7069.20.310 The foundations of spiritualism. (Smith, Walter W.) N.Y., 1920.
Phil 3480.67.85 Foundations of the metaphysics of morals. (Kant, Immanuel.) Chicago, 1950.
Phil 735.102 Foundations of the philosophy of value. (Osborne, Harold.) Cambridge, 1933.
Phil 3925.16.195 The foundations of Wittgenstein's late philosophy. (Specht, Ernst Konrad.) Manchester, 1969.
Phil 3007.5.5 Founders of modern psychology. (Hall, G.S.) N.Y., 1912.
Phil 3007.5.10 Founders of modern psychology. (Hall, G.S.) N.Y., 1924.
Phil 7069.68.5 The founders of psychical research. (Gauld, Alan.) London, 1968.
Phil 7054.6.35 The fountain. 1st ed. (Davis, A.J.) Boston, 1870.
Phil 8965.13.15 The four cardinal virtues. (Pieper, Josef.) N.Y., 1965.
Htn Phil 2050.30* Four dissertations. (Hume, David.) London, 1757.
Phil 8587.71 Four existentialist theologians. (Herberg, Will.) Garden City, N.Y., 1958.
Phil 8610.894.5 Four hundred years of freethought. (Putnam, S.P.) N.Y., 1894.
Phil 6955.4 Four introductory lectures on insanity. (Folsom, C.F.) Cambridge, 1875-80. 4 pam.
Phil 8587.27.3 Four key-words of religion. 2. ed. (Huntington, William R.) N.Y., 1899.
Phil 8610.929.25 Four lectures on freethought and life. (Cohen, Chapman.) London, 1929.
Phil 5520.508 Four-letter word games. (Hartogs, Renatas.) N.Y., 1967.
Phil 9358.18 Four lives. (Swan, John N.) Boston, 1935.
Phil 9420.12 The four loves. (Lewis, C.S.) London, 1960.
Phil 1713.4.2 Four modern philosophers. (Naess, Arne.) Chicago, 1968.
Phil 8826.2.5 Four phases of morals; Socrates, Aristotle, Christianity, Utilitarianism. 2nd ed. (Blackie, J.S.) Edinburgh, 1874.
Phil 8826.2 Four phases of morals. (Blackie, J.S.) Edinburgh, 1871.
Phil 176.157 Four philosophies. (Butler, J.) N.Y., 1951.
Phil 1707.14 Four prophets of our destiny. (Hubben, William.) N.Y., 1952.
Phil 1110.4 Four stages of Greek thought. (Finley, John Huston.) Stanford, 1966.

Phil 1135.161 Four views of time in ancient philosophy. (Callahan, John F.) Cambridge, 1948.
Phil 1980.4.7 Four ways of philosophy. (Edman, Irwin.) N.Y., 1937.
Phil 8880.56 Fourastié, Jean. Essais de morale prospective. Paris, 1967.
Phil 6990.3.15 Fourcade, M. l'abbé. L'apparition...grotté de Lourdes en 1858. Tarbes, 1862.
Htn Phil 2605.3.30* Fourier, C. Le nouveau monde. Paris, 1829.
Phil 5400.86.5 Fourier, C. The passions of the human soul. London, 1851. 2v.
Phil 5245.10 Fournié, É. Essai de psychologie. Paris, 1877.
Phil 5627.126 Fourrier, Maurice. Une expérience religieuse. Paris, 1931.
Phil 672.15.5 The fourth dimension. (Hinton, Charles H.) London, 1904.
Phil 4771.3A The fourth way. 1st American ed. (Uspenskii, P.D.) N.Y., 1957.
Phil 281.5 Fourviéro, Savié de. La creacioun dou mounde. Avignoun, 1891. 2v.
Phil 6750.5 Fous et Bouffons. (Moreau, P.) Paris, 1888.
Phil 6962.22 Les fous satisfaits. (Mondain, Paul.) Paris, 1933.
Phil 5812.4 Foveau de Courmelles, F.V. Les facultés mentales des animaux. Paris, 1890.
Phil 6675.7 Foveau de Courmelles, F.V. L'hypnotisme. Paris, 1890.
Phil 6955.5 Foville, A. Étude clinique de la folie. Paris, 1871.
Phil 6115.24 Foville, A. Traite complet de l'anatomie, de la physiologie et de la pathologie du système nerveux. Pt.1. Paris, 1844.
Phil 8585.9 Fowle, T.W. A new analogy. London, 1881.
Phil 8695.2 Fowle, T.W. The reconciliation of religion and science. London, 1873.
Phil 5385.6 Fowler, Harry. Curiosity and exploratory behavior. N.Y., 1965.
Phil 1850.83A Fowler, J. Bacon. N.Y., 1881.
Phil 5925.6 Fowler, J.A. A manual of mental science for teachers and students. London, 1897.
Phil 7054.111.2 Fowler, J.H. New Testament "miracles". 2. ed. Boston, 1856.
Phil 7054.111.5 Fowler, J.H. New Testament "miracles". 2. ed. Boston, 1859.
Phil 5925.7 Fowler, L. (Mrs.). Familiar lessons on phrenology. v.2. N.Y., 1847.
Phil 5925.3.6 Fowler, L.N. The principles of phrenology and physiology. N.Y., 1842.
Phil 9530.12 Fowler, M.C. The boy! How to help him succeed. Boston, 1902.
Phil 9010.18 Fowler, Montague. The morality of social pleasures. London, 1910.
Phil 5545.28 Fowler, O.G. Fowler on memory, phrenology...cultivation of memory. N.Y., 1842.
Phil 5925.2 Fowler, O.S. Education and self-improvement. N.Y., 1843-45. 7 pam.
Phil 5925.3.4 Fowler, O.S. The illustrated self-instructor in phrenology. N.Y., n.d.
Phil 5925.3.1 Fowler, O.S. The illustrated self-instructor in phrenology. N.Y., 1853.
Phil 5925.3 Fowler, O.S. The illustrated self-instructor in phrenology. N.Y., 1855.
Phil 5925.3.3 Fowler, O.S. The illustrated self-instructor in phrenology. N.Y., 1859.
Phil 5925.2.13 Fowler, O.S. Life: its science, laws...improvement. Boston, 1871.
Phil 9495.17 Fowler, O.S. Love and parentage. N.Y., 1855.
Phil 9165.6.5 Fowler, O.S. Love and parentage. 40th ed. N.Y., 1869.
Phil 5925.3.20 Fowler, O.S. Matrimony. Philadelphia, 1841.
Phil 5925.3.11 Fowler, O.S. Phrenology proved. N.Y., 1838.
Phil 5925.3.10 Fowler, O.S. Phrenology proved. N.Y., 1839.
Phil 5925.2.2 Fowler, O.S. Physiology, animal and mental. N.Y., 1853. 3 pam.
Phil 9495.18.5 Fowler, O.S. The physiology of marriage. Boston, 1860.
Phil 5925.2.5 Fowler, O.S. Practical phrenology. N.Y., 1844. 2 pam.
Phil 9495.17.15 Fowler, O.S. Private lectures on perfect men, women and children. N.Y., 1880.
Phil 5925.2.16 Fowler, O.S. Religion: natural and revealed. 3. ed. N.Y., 1844.
Phil 5925.2.16.10 Fowler, O.S. Religion: natural and revealed. 10. ed. N.Y., 1848.
Phil 8880.13 Fowler, O.S. Self culture and perfection of character. N.Y., 1856.
Phil 5925.2.18 Fowler, O.S. Self-culture and the perfection of character. N.Y., 1868.
Phil 5925.3.25 Fowler, O.S. Sexual science; including manhood, womanhood and their mutual interrelations. Philadelphia, 1870.
Phil 5925.3.15 Fowler, O.S. Sexuality restored. Boston, 1870.
Phil 5925.2.3 Pamphlet box. Fowler, O.S. Minor writings.
Phil 2115.90.4 Fowler, T. Life of Locke. N.Y., n.d.
Phil 2115.90 Fowler, T. Locke. London, 1880.
Phil 2115.90.3 Fowler, T. Locke. N.Y., 1880?
Phil 2115.90.7 Fowler, T. Locke. N.Y., 1899.
Phil 8880.14 Fowler, T. The principles of moral. v.1-2. Oxford, 1886-87.
Phil 2262.81A Fowler, T. Shaftesbury and Hutcheson. London, 1882.
Phil 2262.81.5A Fowler, T. Shaftesbury and Hutcheson. N.Y., 1883.
Phil 5045.2 Fowler, Thomas. The elements of deductive logic. Oxford, 1867.
Phil 5045.2.6 Fowler, Thomas. Inductive logic. Oxford, 1883.
Phil 5045.2.5 Fowler, Thomas. Inductive logic. Oxofrd, 1876.
Phil 5045.2.15 Fowler, Thomas. Logic, deductive and inductive. Oxford, 1904-05.
Phil 8880.38 Fowler, Thomas. Progressive morality; an essay in ethics. London, 1884.
Phil 5545.28 Fowler on memory, phrenology...cultivation of memory. (Fowler, O.G.) N.Y., 1842.
Phil 8585.10.2 Fownes, G. Chemistry as exemplifying the wisdom and beneficence of God. London, 1849.
Phil 8585.10 Fownes, G. Chemistry as exemplifying the wisdom and beneficence of God. N.Y., 1844.
Phil 8660.15 Fox, Adam. God is an artist. London, 1957.
Phil 6675.13 Fox, Alfred J. Mind "magic". N.Y., 1937.
Phil 5245.33 Fox, Charles. Mind and its body. London, 1931.
Phil 6615.10 Fox, Charles Daniel. Psychopathology of hysteria. Boston, 1913.
Phil 6955.14 Fox, E.L. Pahological anatomy of nervous centres. London, 1874.
Phil 8955.1 Fox, J.J. Religion and morality. N.Y., 1899.
Phil 8585.11 Fox, W.J. On the religious ideas. London, 1849.
Phil 8612.22 Fox, W.J. Reports of lectures delivered at the chapel So. Place, Finsburg. Nos. 9,10,12. London, 1838.
Phil 9045.18 Fox, William J. Reports of lecture on morality. London, 1836.
Phil 9045.18.5 Fox, William J. Reports of lectures delivered. London, 1838.
Phil 7069.32.40 Fox - Taylor automatic writing, 1869-1892. (Taylor, Sarah E.L.) Minneapolis, 1932.
Phil 7069.32.45 Fox - Taylor automatic writing, 1969-1892. (Taylor, Sarah E.L.) Boston, 1936.
Phil 180.82 Foxe, Arthur N. The common sense from Heraclitus to Pierce. N.Y., 1962.
Phil 9166.6 Le foyer, scènes de la vie de famille aux États Unis. (Girault, A.) Paris, 1875.
Phil 4362.1.80 Fr. Luis de León y la filosofia espanole. (Gutierrez, P.F.M.) Madrid, 1885.
Phil 3640.545 Fr. Nitsshe. (Rogachev, B.) Parizh, 1909.
Phil 4605.2.31 Fra før Kant. (Menzinger, A.) København, 1918.
Phil 8414.9 Fra kaos til form. (Nadiani, A.) Oslo, 1949.
Phil 807.12 Fra Plato til Bergson. (Helms, Poul F.) København, 1919.
Phil 4073.82 Fra Tommaso Campanella: la sua congiura. (Amabile, L.) Napoli, 1882-. 3v.
Phil 4065.129 Fraccari, G. G. Bruno. 1. ed. Milano, 1951.
Phil 3270.15.31 Frackenheim, Emil L. Metaphysics and historicity. Milwaukee, 1961.
Phil 199.1 The fractional family. (Young, A.) N.Y., 1864.
Phil 5815.6 Fraenkel, G.S. The orientation of animals. Oxford, Eng., 1940.
Phil 3260.152.5 Fraenkel, Georg. Die kritische Rechtsphilosophie bei Fries. Göttingen, 1912.
Phil 5545.163 Fränkl, Ernst. Über Vorstellungs-Elemente und Aufmerksamkeit. Augsburg, 1905.
Phil 3450.19.335 Fraga, Gustavo de. Sobre Heidegger. Coimbra, 1965.
Phil 3450.11.280 Fragata, Júlio. A fenomenologia de Husserl como fundamento. Braga, 1959.
Phil 3450.11.270 Fragata, Júlio. Problemas da fenomenologia de Husserl. Braga, 1962.
Phil 3120.30.51 Die Frage an den Einzelnen. (Buber, Martin.) Berlin, 1936.
Phil 8589.21 Die Frage der Entmychologisierung. (Jaspers, Karl.) München, 1954.
Phil 6315.2.47 Die Frage der Laienanalyse. (Freud, Sigmund.) Wien, 1926.
Phil 8598.56 Die Frage der Wahrheit der christlichen Religion. (Störring, G.) Leipzig, 1920.
Phil 3489.27.15 Die Frage nach dem Ding. (Heidegger, Martin.) Tübingen, 1962.
Phil 585.185 Die Frage nach dem Menschen. (Rombach, Heinrich.) Freiburg, 1966.
Phil 8597.33 Die Frage nach dem Wesen der Religion. (Reischle, Max.) Freiburg, 1889.
Phil 352.5.2 Die Frage nach den Grenzen der Erkenntnis. 2. Aufl. (Verworm, Max.) Jena, 1917.
Phil 8586.36.10 Die Frage nach Gott. (Gogarten, Friedrich.) Tübingen, 1968.
Phil 8893.84 Fragen der Ethik. (Schlick, Moritz.) Wien, 1930.
Phil 31.5.5 Fragen der Philosophie ein Materialbeitrag...im Spiegel der Zeitschrift "Voprosy Filosofii", 1947-1956. (Goerdt, Wilhelm.) Köln, 1960.
Phil 8708.40 Fragen der Physik an die Theologie. 1. Aufl. (Schiffers, Norbert.) Düsseldorf, 1968.
Phil 185.69 Fragen und Aufgaben der Ontologie. (Krings, H.) Tübingen, 1954.
Phil 3005.2 Fragen und Bedenken. (Fichte, T.H.) Leipzig, 1876.
Phil 4600.4.32 Fragment och miniatyrer. 2. uppl. (Lidforss, Bengt.) Malmö, 1912.
Phil 6327.12.40 Fragment of a great confession. (Reik, Theodor.) N.Y., 1949.
Htn Phil 1865.29* A fragment on government. (Bentham, Jeremy.) London, 1776.
Phil 8837.1.15 A fragment on Mackintosh. (Mill, James.) London, 1835.
Phil 8837.1.16 A fragment on Mackintosh. (Mill, James.) London, 1870.
Phil 187.47 A fragment on the human mind. (Merz, John T.) Edinburgh, 1919.
Phil 182.32 Fragmentary papers on science. (Holland, Henry.) London, 1875.
Phil 3494.39 Fragmente aus Kants Leben. (Mortzfeldt, J.C.) Königsberg, 1802.
Phil 3665.9.30 Fragmente keines Vorsokratikers. (Neuhaeusler, Anton Otto.) München, 1968.
Phil 193.59.25A Fragmente und Aufsätze. (Simmel, G.) München, 1923.
Phil 8877.34.9 Fragmente zur Ethik; Übersetzt von J. Schlosser. (Croce, Benedetto.) Zürich, 1922.
Phil 3552.405.5 Fragmente zur Logik. (Leibniz, G.W.) Berlin, 1960.
Phil 2035.60 Fragments de philosophie. (Hamilton, William.) Paris, 1840.
Phil 2520.86 Fragments de philosophie Cartésienne. (Cousin, V.) Paris, 1845.
Phil 2496.32 Fragments de philosophie moderne. (Cousin, Victor.) Paris, 1856.
Phil 600.7.5 Fragments de philosophie positive et de sociologie. (Littré, Émile.) Paris, 1876.
Phil 184.40 Fragments de vie intérieure. (Josipovici, J.) Aix-en-Provence, 1937.
Phil 293.12 Fragments du "Schema d'une nouvelle philosophie de l'univers". (Merezhkovskii, K.S.) Genève, 1920.
Phil 176.45 Fragments in philosophy and science. (Baldwin, J.M.) N.Y., 1902.
Phil 6315.2.152 Fragments of an analysis with Freud. (Wortis, J.) N.Y., 1954.
Phil 978.21 Fragments of occult truth. no. 1-8. n.p., 1881.
Phil 187.54 Fragments of philosophy: Democracy. (Motion, George.) Nelson, B.C., 1920.
Phil 8877.28 Fragments of the elements and principles of the life of man. (Curbipet.) Bombay, 1904.
Phil 7069.21.40 Fragments of truth. (Ingalese, Richard.) N.Y., 1921.
Phil 8881.19 Fragments on ethical subjects. (Grote, G.) London, 1876.
Phil 177.87 Fragments philosophiques. (Cavour, G.B. de.) Turin, 1841.
Phil 2496.30 Fragments philosophiques. (Cousin, Victor.) Paris, 1838. 2v.
Phil 1107.1 Fragments philosophiques. (Cousin, Victor.) Paris, 1840.
Phil 2805.24 Fragments philosophiques. (Pascal, Blaise.) Paris, 1875.
Phil 2805.25 Fragments philosophiques. (Pascal, Blaise.) Paris, 1876.
Phil 2855.1.31 Les fragments philosophiques. (Royer-Tollard.) Paris, 1913.
Phil 2733.78 Fragments philosophiques inédits et correspondance. Thèse. (Vidgrain, Joseph.) Caen, 1923.
Phil 2750.19.42 Fragments philosophiques 1909-1914. (Marcel, Gabriel.) Louvain, 1962.
Phil 3640.72 Fragments sur l'énergie et la puissance. (Nietzsche, Friedrich.) Paris, 1957.

Phil 165.171 Fragmenty filozoficzne, seria trzecia. Warszawa, 1967.
Phil 3805.170 Frahne, A. Der Begriff der Eigentümlichkeit oder Individualität bei Schleiermacher. Halle, 1884.
Phil 5238.196.1 Fraisse, Paul. Experimental psychology. N.Y., 1968.
Phil 5245.50 Fraisse, Paul. Manuel pratique de psychologie expérimentale. 1. éd. Paris, 1956.
Phil 5585.140 Fraisse, Paul. Psychologie du temps. 1. éd. Paris, 1957.
Phil 5585.140.2 Fraisse, Paul. Psychologie du temps. 2. éd. Paris, 1967.
Phil 5585.140.3 Fraisse, Paul. The psychology of time. N.Y., 1963.
Phil 5585.140.5 Fraisse, Paul. Les structures rythmiques. Thèse. Bruxelles, 1956.
Phil 5238.196 Fraisse, Paul. Traité de psychologie expérimentale. Paris, 1963. 9v.
Phil 4815.558.85 Fraknói, Vilmos. Martinovics élete. Budapest, 1921.
Phil 4815.558.80 Fraknói, Vilmos. Martinovicsnak istentagadó elveket hirdető, imént fölfedezett francia munkája. Budapest, 1920.
Phil 1830.25 The frame of order. (Winny, James.) London, 1957.
Phil 5876.22 Frames of mind. (Hudson, Liam.) London, 1968.
Phil 5585.312 The frameworks for perceptual localization. (Fisher, Gerald H.) Newcastle-upon-Tyne, 1968.
Phil 7069.34.15 Framhaldslif og nútímaþekking. (Jónsson, J.) Reykjavik, 1934.
Phil 8877.34.8 Frammenti di etica. (Croce, Benedetto.) Bari, 1922.
Phil 3808.60.40 Frammenti di storia della filosofia. (Schopenhauer, Arthur.) Milano, 1926?
Phil 4515.97 Framställning af Boströmska filosofien. (Kalling, P.) Örebro, 1868.
Phil 8050.41 Framställning af de förnämsta esthetiska systemerna. (Ljunggren, G.) Lund, 1856. 2v.
Phil 298.3 Framställning af teorierna om det kosmiska före Sölger och Hegel. (Rindell, E.) Helsingfors, 1885.
Phil 3850.9.92 Framställning och kritik af J.S. Mills, Lotzes och Sigwarts...i logiken. (Pira, Karl.) Stockholm, 1897.
Phil 2490.54.20 Framställning öfver den positive anden. (Comte, Auguste.) Stockholm 1875.
Phil 8586.8.10 Framtidens irreligion. (Guyau, M.J.) Stockholm, 1907.
Phil 800.20 Fran antikens och medeltidens tankevärd. (Ahlberg, A.) Stockholm, 1966.
Phil 805.20 Franca, Leonel. Noções de história da filosofia. Rio de Janeiro, 1967.
Phil 15.11 France. Centre d'Études et Recherches Psycho-Techniques. Bulletin. 5,1956+ 9v.
Phil 1750.166.50 France. Centre National de la Recherche Scientifique. Pensée humaniste et tradition chrêtienne aux XVe et XVIe siècle. Paris, 1950.
Phil 6675.12 France. Commissaires Chargée de l'Examen du Magnétisme Animal. Rapport des commissaires chargée par le roi de l'examen du magnétisme animal. Paris, 1784.
Phil 530.15.15 La France mystique. v.1-2. 3e ed. (Jacob, A.A.) Amsterdam, 1860.
Phil 3825.8.5 Francès, Madeleine. Spinoza. Paris, 1937.
Phil 3825.8 Francès, Madeleine. Spinoza dans les pays Néerlandais. Paris, 1937.
Phil 5585.223 Francès, R. Quelques aspects du développement perceptif. Paris, 1962.
Phil 8430.60 Frances, Robert. Psychologie de l'esthétique. Paris, 1968.
Phil 1850.82 Frances Bacon of Verulam. (Fischer, K.) London, 1857.
Phil 336.6 Franceschi, A. Ensayo sobre la teoría del conocimiento. La Plata, 1925.
Phil 4967.35 Franceschi, Alfredo. Escritos filosóficos. La Plata, 1968.
Phil 3549.2.99 Franceschi, G.J. Keyserling. 2. ed. Buenos Aires, 1929.
Phil 978.59.90 Franceschi, G.J. El Señor Krishnamurti. Buenos Aires, 1935.
Phil 4060.8.30 Francesco Arri e il suo spiritualismo. (Calderaro, Francesco.) Roma, 1941.
Phil 1850.147.5 Francesco Bacone, dalla magia alla scienza. (Rossi, Paolo.) Bari, 1957.
Phil 4369.2.90 Francesco Sanchez. (Miccolis, Salvatore.) Bari, 1965.
Phil 4225.66.80 Francesco Storella. (Antonaci, Antonio.) Galatina, 1966.
Phil 623.2 Franchi, A. Il razionalismo del Popolo. Losanna, 1861.
Phil 1705.8 Franchi, Ausonio. Letture su la storia della filosofia moderna. Milano, 1863. 2v.
Phil 4080.3.235 Franchini, R. Note biografiche di Benedetto Croce. Torino, 1953.
Phil 4080.3.460 Franchini, Raffaello. Croce interprete di Hegel e altri saggi filosofici. Napoli, 1964.
Phil 180.84.5 Franchini, Raffaello. La logica della filosofia. Napoli, 1967.
Phil 180.84 Franchini, Raffaello. L'oggetto della filosofia. Napoli, 1962.
Phil 848.4 Franchini, Raffaello. Le origini della dialettica. Napoli, 1961.
Phil 848.4.2 Franchini, Raffaello. Le origini della dialettica. 2. ed. Napoli, 1965.
Phil 4080.3.461 Franchini, Raffaello. La teoria della storia di Benedetto Croce. Napoli, 1966.
Phil 2555.12.30 Franchir le Rubicon. (Dartan, Jacques.) Paris, 1968.
Phil 7054.1 Francis, John R. The encyclopaedia of death and life in the spirit world. Chicago, 1985-1900. 3v.
Phil 2805.365 Francis, Raymond. Les pensées de Pascal en France de 1842 à 1942. Paris, 1959.
Phil 1850.127 Francis Bacon; a biography. (Sturt, Mary.) London, 1932.
Phil 1850.135 Francis Bacon, a map of days. (Gundry, W.G.C.) London, 1946.
NEDL Phil 1850.101 Francis Bacon, a sketch of his life. (Steeves, G.W.) London, 1910.
Phil 1850.80A Francis Bacon. (Abbott, E.A.) London, 1885.
Phil 1850.140 Francis Bacon. (Anderson, Fulton H.) Los Angeles, 1962.
Phil 1850.141 Francis Bacon. (Farrington, B.) N.Y., 1949.
Phil 1850.112 Francis Bacon. (Heussler, Hans.) Breslau, 1889.
Phil 1850.145A Francis Bacon. (Jameson, T.H.) N.Y., 1954.
Phil 1850.84.2 Francis Bacon. (Lovejoy, B.G.) London, 1888.
Phil 1850.153 Francis Bacon. (Patrick, J.M.) London, 1961.
Phil 1850.133 Francis Bacon. (Skemp, A.R.) London, 1912.
Phil 1850.120 Francis Bacon. (Taylor, Alfred.) London, 1926?
Phil 1850.16.15 Francis Bacon. The great instauration. (Bacon, Francis.) Garden City, 1962.
Phil 1850.158 Francis Bacon. 1st ed. (Bowen, Catherine.) Boston, 1963.
Phil 1850.159 Francis Bacon and the modern dilemma. (Eiseley, Loren Corey.) Lincoln, 1962.
Phil 1850.162 Francis Bacon on the nature of man. (Wallace, Karl Richards.) Urbana, 1967.
Phil 1850.82.5 Francis Bacon und seine Nachfolger. 2e Aufl. (Fischer, K.) Leipzig, 1875.

Phil 1850.102 Francis Bacon und seine Quellen. (Wolff, E.) Berlin, 1910. 2v.
Phil 1850.147.10 Francis Bacon from magic to science. (Rossi, Paolo.) London, 1968.
Phil 1850.157 Francis Bacon's intellectual milieu. (Whitaker, Virgil Keeble.) Los Angeles, 1962.
Phil 1885.81 Francis Herbert Bradley, 1846-1924. London, n.d.
Phil 2053.80 Francis Hutcheson, his life, teaching and position in the history of philosophy. (Scott, William Robert.) Cambridge, 1900.
Phil 2053.80.2 Francis Hutcheson, his life, teaching and position in the history of philosophy. (Scott, William Robert.) N.Y., 1966.
Phil 2053.92 Francis Hutcheson and contemporary ethical theory. (Blackstone, William T.) Athens, Ga., 1965.
Phil 7060.47 Francisci, Erasmus. Der höllischen Proteus...Erscheinder Gespenster. Nürnberg, 1695.
Phil 1850.95 Francisci Baconi de re litteraria judicia. (Jacquinet, P.) Paris, 1863.
Htn Phil 1850.1.11F* Francisci Baconi operum moralium. (Bacon, Francis.) Londini, 1638. 2 pam.
Phil 4829.867.80 Francisci Veber theoria de persona; internum drama philosofi sloveni. (Zečevič, Seraphinus.) Montréal, 1954.
Phil 4372.3.85 Francisco de Valles, el Divino. (Ortega, Euselio.) Madrid, 1914.
Phil 574.8 Francisco Larroyo y su personalismo crítico. 1. ed. (Escobar, Edmundo.) México, 1970.
Phil 4368.2.90 Francisco Romero, 1891: vija y obra. (Rodríguez Acala, Hugo.) N.Y., 1964.
Phil 4368.2.80 Francisco Romero on problems of philosophy. (Harris, Marjorie.) N.Y., 1960.
Phil 4200.2.01 Franciskus Patricijus. (Premec, Vladimir.) Beograd, 1968.
Phil 2477.10.90 Francisque Bouillier. (Latreille, C.) Paris, 1907.
Phil 5090.5 Franck, A. De la certitude. Paris, 1847.
Phil 5015.1 Franck, A. Esquisse d'une histoire de la logique. Paris, 1838.
Phil 180.8.3 Franck, A. Essais de critique philosophique. Paris, 1885.
Phil 8880.42 Franck, A. Menniskans sedliga lif. Stockholm, 1870.
Phil 180.8 Franck, A. Moralistes et philosophes. Paris, 1872.
Phil 180.8.5 Franck, A. Nouveaux essais de critique philosophique. Paris, 1890.
Phil 1705.5 Franck, A. Philosophes modernes. Paris, 1879.
Phil 8585.12 Franck, A. Philosophie et religion. Paris, 1869.
Phil 2880.1.81 Franck, A. La philosophie mystique...Saint-Martin. Paris, 1866.
Phil 90.2.3 Franck, Adolphe. Diccionaire des sciences philosophiques. 2e éd. Paris, 1875.
Phil 90.2 Franck, Adolphe. Dictionnaire des sciences philosophiques. Paris, 1844. 6v.
Phil 90.2.2 Franck, Adolphe. Dictionnaire des sciences philosophiques. 2. éd. Paris, 1875.
Phil 900.8 Franck, Adolphe. Études orientales. Paris, 1861.
Phil 8630.10 Franck, K. Wie wird's sein? Halle, 1901.
Phil 480.7 Franck, Otto. Der Weg zur Wirklichkeit. Leipzig, 1928.
Phil 3487.30 Francke, Georg Samuel. Über die Eigenschaft der Analysis und der analytischen Methode in der Philosophie. Bruxelles, 1968.
Phil 3808.152 Francken, C.J. Wijnaendts. Arthur Schopenhauer, een levensbeeld. Haarlem, 1905.
Phil 7068.86.11 Franco, P.G. Die Geister der Finsterniss. Ausburg, 1886.
Phil 2905.1.205 Francoeur, Robert. The world of Teilhard. Baltimore, 1961.
Phil 5245.14 François, A. Leçons élémentaires de psychologie. Paris, 1897.
Phil 180.26 François Adolphe. Les grands problèmes. Paris, 1895.
Phil 1850.25.5 François Bacon. (Bacon, Francis.) Paris, 1926.
Phil 1850.98 François Bacon. (Fonsegrive, G.L.) Paris, 1893.
Phil 1850.149 François Bacon. (Haukart, Robert.) Paris, 1957.
Phil 1850.107 François Bacon. (Lemaire, Paul.) Paris, 1913.
Phil 6115.8 François-Franck, C. Leçons sur les fonctions motrices du cerveau et sur l'épilepsie cérébrale. Paris, 1887.
Phil 3450.2.80 François Hemsterhuis, le Socrate hollandais. (Boulan, Emile.) Groningue, 1924.
Phil 2655.1.80 François Hemsterhuis. (Grucker, E.) Paris, 1866.
Phil 2150.22.105 François Perroux interroge Herbert Marcuse qui répond. (Perroux, François.) Paris, 1969.
Phil 4967.5.5 Francovich, Guillermo. El cinismo. Puebla, 1963.
Phil 680.55 Francovich, Guillermo. Ensayos sobre el estructuralismo. La Paz, Bolivia, 1970.
Phil 4960.405 Francovich, Guillermo. La filosofía en Bolivia. Buenos Aires, 1945.
Phil 4960.655 Francovich, Guillermo. Filósofos brasileños. Buenos Aires, 1943.
Phil 4967.5 Francovich, Guillermo. Hijos de la roca. México, 1954.
Phil 4967.5.10 Francovich, Guillermo. Supay; diálogos. Sucre, 1939.
Phil 3270.13.21 Frank, Erich. Knowledge. Chicago, 1955.
Phil 8585.35A Frank, Erich. Philosophical understanding and religious truth. 1st ed. London, 1945.
Phil 8955.2 Frank, F.H.R. System du christliche Sittlichkeit. Erlangen, 1884-87. 2v.
Phil 9070.136 Frank, Hannelore. Auf der Suche nach dem eigenen Ich. Stuttgart, 1969.
Phil 8630.7.9 Frank, Henry. The challenge of the war. Boston, 1919.
Phil 8630.7 Frank, Henry. Modern light on immortality. 2. ed. Boston, 1909.
Phil 8630.7.5 Frank, Henry. Psychic phenomena; science and immortality. 2. ed. Boston, 1916.
Phil 165.336 Frank, J. Horizons of a philosopher. Leiden, 1963.
Phil 6315.52 Frank, J.D. Persuasion and healing. London, 1961.
Phil 2005.8.79 Pamphlet box. Frank, Jerome D.
Phil 5068.8 Frank, P. Between physics and philosophy. Cambridge, 1941.
Phil 270.39.5 Frank, P. Le principe de causalité et ses limites. Paris, 1937.
Phil 3120.2.87 Frank, P. Die philosophischen Problem in Dr. Bolzano's "Erbauungsreden". Inaug. Diss. Pritzwalk, 1926.
Phil 270.39 Frank, Philipp. Das Kausalgesetz und seine Grenzen. Wien, 1932.
Phil 286.8 Frank, S.L. Smysl zhizni. Paris, 1925.
Phil 4756.1.45 Frank, Semen L. La connaissance et l'être. Paris, 1935.
Phil 4756.1.41 Frank, Semen L. Dusha cheloveka. Izd.2. Paris, 1964.
Phil 4756.1.40 Frank, Semen L. Dusha chelovieka. Moskva, 1917.
Phil 4756.1.29 Frank, Semen L. Filosofiia i zhizn', etiudy i nabroski po filosofii kul'tury. Sankt Peterburg, 1910.
Phil 4756.1.45.5 Frank, Semen L. God with us; three meditations. London, 1946.

Phil 4710.143 Frank, Semen L. Iz istorii russkoi filosofskoi mysli kontsa XIX i nachala XX v. Washington, 1965.
Phil 4756.1.35 Frank, Semen L. Krushenie kumirov. Berlin, 1924.
Phil 4756.1.47.1 Frank, Semen L. Nepostizhimoe. München, 1971.
Phil 4756.1.43 Frank, Semen L. Reality and man. London, 1965.
Phil 4756.1.42 Frank, Semen L. Real'nost' i chelovek; metafizika chelovecheskogo bytiia. Parizh, 1956.
Phil 4756.1.48 Frank, Semen L. Religiia i nauka. Posev, 1959.
Phil 4710.158 Frank, Semen L. Die russische Weltanschauung. 1. Aufl. Darmstadt, 1967.
Phil 4756.1.46 Frank, Semen L. S nami Bog; tri razmyshleniia. Paris, 1964.
Phil 4756.1.37 Frank, Semen L. Svet vo t'me; opyt khristianskoi etikhi i sotsial'noi filosofii. Parizh, 1949
Phil 4756.1.30 Frank, Semen L. Vvedenie v filosofiiu. Berlin, 1923.
Phil 4756.1.33 Frank, Semen L. Zhivoe znanie. Berlin, 1923.
Phil 585.20 Frank, W.D. The rediscovery of man. N.Y., 1958.
Phil 5627.134.34 Frank Buchman. London, 1958.
Phil 5627.134.77 Frank Buchman's secret. (Howard, Peter.) Garden City, N.Y., 1962.
Phil 5850.205 Frankard, Paul. Analyse critique de la notion de validité. Louvain, 1958.
Phil 3428.92 Franke, Friedrich. J.F. Herbart; Grundzüge seiner Lehre. Leipzig, 1909.
Phil 5400.192 Franke, Joachim. Ausdruck und Konvention. Habilitationsschrift. Göttingen, 1967.
Phil 665.75A Frankel, Charles. The case for modern man. 1st ed. N.Y., 1956.
Phil 2405.4 Frankel, Charles. The faith of reason. N.Y., 1948.
Phil 1830.30 Frankel, Charles. The golden age of American philosophy. N.Y., 1960.
Phil 2005.12 Frankel, Charles. The love of anxiety, and other essays. 1st ed. N.Y., 1945.
Phil 8585.31 Franken, J.C. Kritische Philosophie und Dialektischen Theologie. Proefschrift. Amsterdam, 1932.
Phil 8880.52 Frankena, W. Ethics. Englewood, 1963.
Phil 7180.2 Frankenau, Rasmus. Tildragelser under ahnelser. Kjøbenhavn, 1804.
Phil 6980.305 Frankenstein, C. Persönlichkeitswandel. München, 1964.
Phil 6315.66 Frankenstein, Carl. Die Ausserlichkeit des Lebensstils. Amsterdam, 1959.
Phil 2520.410 Frankfurt, Harry G. Demons, dreamers, and madmen. Indianapolis, 1970.
Phil 3808.234 Frankfurt am Main. Stadt- und Universitätsbibliothek. Arthur Schopenhauer. Frankfurt, 1960.
Phil 3487.25 Frankfurt Universität. Kant und die Wissenchaften. Frankfurt, 1955.
Phil 1750.359 Frankl, V.C. Logos und Existenz. Wien, 1951.
Phil 5627.257 Frankl, V.E. The doctor and the soul. N.Y., 1957.
Phil 8695.3 Frankland, F.W. Thoughts on ultimate problems. 4. ed. London, 1911.
Htn Phil 2005.7.25* Pamphlet box. Frankland, F.W. Collection of pamphlets, formerly property of William James.
Phil 180.11 Pamphlet box. Frankland's miscellaneous philosophical writings.
Phil 9530.5.5 Franklin, B. Hē epistēme tou kalou richardou. Paris, 1823.
NEDL Phil 8880.15 Franklin, B. Saggi di morale. v.1-2. Volterre, 1834.
Phil 9530.5.2 Franklin, B. The way to wealth. N.Y., 1848.
Htn Phil 9530.5* Franklin, B. The way to wealth. Paris, 1795.
Phil 9150.12 Franklin, C.K. What nature is. Boston, 1911.
Phil 5645.32.2 Franklin, Christine L. Colour and colour theories. London, 1929.
Phil 8669.2 Franklin, Maria. Observations on the chronology of scripture. N.Y., 1795.
Phil 5755.18 Franklin, Richard Langdon. Freewill and determinism: a study of rival conceptions of man. London, 1968.
Phil 5250.15.80 Franquiz Ventura, José A. La filosofia de las ciencias de Wolfgang Köhler. México, 1941.
Phil 1915.83 Fránquiz Ventura, José Antonio. Borden Parker Browne's treatment of the problem of change and identity. Rio Piedras, 1942.
Phil 3450.2.85 Frans Hemsterhuis, een philosofenleven. (Brummel, L.) Haarlem, 1925.
Phil 2422.2 Fransche moralisten. (Wijnaendts Francken, C.J.) Haarlem, 1904.
Phil 310.300 Frantsev, I.P. Istoricheskii materializm i sotsial'naia filosofiia sovremennoi burzhazii. Moskva, 1960.
Phil 2410.1 Frantsuzskaia burzhuaznaia filosofiia dvadtsatogo veka. (Kuznetsov, Vitalii N.) Moskva, 1970.
Phil 3801.406 Frantz, Constantin. Schelling's positive Philosophie. Pt.1-3. Cöthen, 1879-80.
Phil 6115.23.5 Frany, Shepherd I. The evolution of an idea. 2d ed. Los Angeles, 1929.
Phil 6115.23 Frany, Shepherd I. On the functions of the cerebrum. N.Y., 1907.
Phil 3005.7 Franz, Erich. Deutsche Klassik und Reformation. Halle, 1937.
Phil 6955.11 Franz, S.I. Handbook of mental examining methods. 2. ed. N.Y., 1919.
Phil 5245.35 Franz, S.I. Psychology. 1. ed. N.Y., 1933.
Phil 5643.25.2 Franz, Shepherd I. After images. N.Y., 1899.
X Cg Phil 6315.13 Franz, Shepherd I. Collected papers. n.p., 1911-13.
Phil 510.1.37 Franz, Victor. Ernst Haeckel. v.1-2. Jena, 1944.
Phil 6682.3.85 Franz Anton Mesmer, Reinhold Schneider. (Look, Maria van.) Freiburg, 1969.
Phil 6682.3.80 Franz Anton Mesmer. (Jensen, Ann.) N.Y., 1967.
Phil 6689.10 Franz Anton Mesmer. (Tischner, Rudolf.) München, 1928.
Phil 6676.10 Franz Anton Mesmer. Photoreproduction. (Goldsmith, M.) London, 1934.
Phil 3090.85 Franz Baaders Jugendgeschichte...von Baaders. (Lieb, Fritz.) München, 1926.
Phil 1850.82.10 Franz Bacon von Verulam. (Fischer, K,) Leipzig, 1856.
Phil 3120.8.81 Franz Brentano. (Kraus, Oskar.) München, 1919.
Phil 3120.8.89 Franz Brentano als Religionsphilosophie. (Skrbensky, L.H.) Zürich, 1937.
Phil 3120.8.126 Franz Brentano as wysgeer. (Taljaard, J.A.L.) Franeker, 1955.
Phil 3120.8.130 Franz Brentano und die Scholastik. (Windischer, Johannes.) Innsbruck, 1936.
Phil 3120.8.150 Franz Brentano's analysis of truth. (Srzednicki, Jan.) The Hague, 1965.
Phil 3120.8.85 Franz Brentanos Kantkritik. Inaug. Diss. (Hoppenstedt, W. von.) Kiel, 1933.
Phil 3120.8.110 Franz Brentanos Lehre von den Gemütsbewegungen. (Mueller, Richard.) Brünn, 1943.
Phil 3120.8.82 Franz Brentanos Stellung zur Phänomenologie und Gegenstandstheorie. (Kraus, Oskar.) Leipzig, 1924.

Phil 3450.2.87 Franz Hemsterhuis, seine Philosophie und ihr Einfluss auf dei deutschen Romantiker. (Paritzky, J.E.) Berlin, 1926.
Phil 3640.90.5 Franz Overbeck und Friedrich Nietzsche. (Bernoulli, Carl A.) Jena, 1908. 2v.
Phil 3808.225 Franz-Schneider, Lucia. Erinnerungen an das Schopenhauers Schöne Aussicht. Frankfurt, 1959.
Phil 3090.89 Franz von Baader. (Siegl, Josef.) München, 1957.
Phil 3090.87 Franz von Baader et le romantisme mystique. Thesis. (Susini, Eugene.) Paris, 1942. 2v.
Phil 3090.87.5 Franz von Baader et le romantisme mystique. v.2-3. (Susini, Eugene.) Paris, 1942. 2v.
Phil 3090.80.5 Franz von Baader in seinem Verhällnitz zu Hegel und Schelling. (Hoffmann, F.) Leipzig, 1850.
Phil 3090.84 Franz von Baader und die Möglichkeit unbedingter pädagogischer Zielsetzung. (Reber, M.) Nürnburg, 1925.
Phil 3090.83 Franz von Baader und die philosophische Romantik. (Baumgardt, D.) Halle, 1927.
Phil 3090.90 Franz von Baaders philosophischer Gedanke der Schöpfung. (Hemmerle, Klaus.) Freiburg, 1963.
Phil 5247.13.33 Franzbach, Martin. Lessings Huarte-Übersetzung, 1752. Hamburg, 1965.
Phil 8880.32 Franze, Paul. Das höchste Gut. Berlin, 1912.
Phil 8880.31 Franze, Paul. Idealistische Sittenlehre. Leipzig, 1909.
Phil 3310.7.90 Franzelin, B. Die neueste Lehre Geysers über des Kausali-Tatspriuzip. Innsbruck, 1924.
Phil 3120.2.101 Franzis, Emerich. Bernard Bolzano. Münster, 1933.
Phil 2655.1.82 Franziskus Hemsterhuis und der deutsche Irrationalismus. (Bulle, F.) Jena, 1911.
Phil 2404.2 Die französische Aufklärungsphilosophie. (Ewald, Oskar.) München, 1924.
Phil 3489.44 Französische Kantinterpreten im 20. Jahrhundert. (Heinz, Rudolf.) Bonn, 1966.
Phil 8500.12 Die französische Neokriticismus. (Feigel, F.K.) Tübingen, 1913.
Phil 2421.1 Französische Philosophie. (Vorländer, Karl.) Breslau, 1923.
Phil 2422.5.5 Französische Philosophie. 1e Aufl. (Wahl, Jean A.) Säkingen, 1948.
Phil 2412.5 Die französische Philosophie der Gegenwart. (Müller, Max.) Karlsruhe, 1926.
Phil 2428.20 Der französische Strukturalismus. (Schiwy, Günther.) Reinbek, 1969.
Phil 6955.6 Franzolini, F. L'epidemia di istero-demonopatie. Reggio, 1879.
Phil 1750.560.15 Franzosischer Existentialismus. (Bollnow, Otto Friedrich.) Stuttgart, 1965.
Phil 5520.66 La frase infantil monopalábrica y la intelligencia. (Pita, Enrique B.) Buenos Aires, 1935.
Phil 2005.2.81 Fraser, A.C. Biographica philosophica. 2d ed. Edinburgh 1905.
Phil 2115.92 Fraser, A.C. Locke. Edinburgh, 1890.
Phil 2115.92.2A Fraser, A.C. Locke. Philadelphia, 1890.
Phil 8660.5.2 Fraser, A.C. Philosophy of theism. N.Y., 1895.
Phil 8660.5 Fraser, A.C. Philosophy of theism. 2. ed. Edinburgh, 1899.
Phil 8660.5.3 Fraser, A.C. Philosophy of theism. 2. series. N.Y., 1896.
Phil 180.9 Fraser, A.C. Rational philosophy. Edinburgh, 1858.
Phil 2240.81 Fraser, A.C. Thomas Reid. London, 1898.
Phil 2005.2.80 Pamphlet box. Fraser, A.C.
NEDL Phil 1870.84.1 Fraser, Alexander Campbell. Berkeley. Edinburgh, 1881.
Phil 1870.84 Fraser, Alexander Campbell. Berkeley. Philadelphia, 1881.
Phil 1870.84.2.3 Fraser, Alexander Campbell. Berkeley. Philadelphia, 1899.
Phil 1870.84.3 Fraser, Alexander Campbell. Life and letters of George Berkeley. Oxford, 1871.
Phil 5245.55 Fraser, John Munro. Psychology. N.Y., 1956.
Phil 672.231 Fraser, Julius Thomas. The voices of time. N.Y., 1966.
Phil 7080.38 Fraser-Harris, D.F. Morpheus, or The future of sleep. London, 1928.
Phil 3910.126 Frauendienst, W. Christian Wolff als Staatsdenker. Berlin, 1927.
Phil 476.3.50 Frauenstadt, J. Der Materialismus. Leipzig, 1856.
Phil 3808.82 Frauenstädt, C.M.J. Briefe über des Schopenhauerische Philosophie. Leipzig, 1854.
Phil 3808.82.5 Frauenstädt, C.M.J. Neue Brief über Schopenhauerische Philosophie. Leipzig, 1876.
Phil 3808.83 Frauenstädt, C.M.J. Schopenhauer-Lexikon. Leipzig, 1871. 2v.
Htn Phil 3808.83.1* Frauenstädt, C.M.J. Schopenhauer-Lexikon. Leipzig, 1871. 2v.
Phil 8406.5 Frauenstädt, J. Aesthetische Fragen. Dessau, 1853.
Phil 3487.16 Frauenstädt, J. Immanuel Kant. Leipzig, 1872.
Htn Phil 3801.405* Frauenstädt, J. Schelling's Vorlesungen in Berlin. Berlin, 1842.
Phil 3801.405.5 Frauenstädt, J. Schelling's Vorlesungen in Berlin. Berlin, 1842.
Phil 8880.33 Frauenstädt, Julius. Das sittliche Leben. Leipzig, 1866.
Phil 8585.13.15 Frauestädt, C.M.J. Blicke in die intellectuelle, physische und moralische Welt. Leipzig, 1869.
Phil 8585.13.10 Frauestädt, C.M.J. Studien und Kritiken zur Theologie und Philosophie. Berlin, 1840.
Phil 5045.19.2 Fraunce, Abraham. The lawyer's logic, 1588. Menston, Eng., 1969.
Phil 5045.19.5 Fraunce, Abraham. The shepherd's logic. Menston, 1969.
Phil 960.169 Frauwallner, E. Geschichte der indischen Philosophie. Salzburg, 1953. 2v.
Phil 4065.88.12 Fray Giordano Bruno y su tiempo. 2a ed. (Paris Zezin, Luis.) Madrid, 1886.
Phil 8630.5A Frazer, J.G. Belief in immortality. London, 1913-24. 3v.
Phil 7060.62 Frazer, John. Deuteroskopia; or, A brief discourse concerning the second sight. Edinburgh, 1820
Phil 5400.7 Frédault, F. Les passions. Paris, n.d.
Phil 3640.85 Frederic Nietzsche. (Albert, H.) Paris, 1903.
Phil 15.45 Frederic W.H. Mayers memorial lecture. London. 16,1966+
Phil 3487.9 Frederichs, F. Ueber Kant's Princip der Ethik. Berlin, 1875.
Phil 8587.32.109 Frederico von Hügel. (Zari, A.) Pinerolo, 1935.
Phil 6836.2 Frederics, Diana. Diana; a strange autobiography. N.Y., 1939.
Phil 5592.75 Frederiksen, Norman Oliver. Response set as a measure of personality. Princeton, 1958.
Phil 2520.305 Frédérix, Pierre. Monsieur Réné Descartes en son temps. Paris, 1959.
Phil 5520.408 Fredriksson, G. Det politiska språket. 2. uppl. Uppsala, 1963.
Phil 5762.24 Free action. (Melden, Abraham Irving.) London, 1964.
Htn Phil 8620.6* A free inquiry into the nature and origin of evil. (Jenyns, Soame.) London, 1761.

Phil 192.28.21A — A free man's worship. 2d ed. (Russell, B.) Portland, 1927.

Phil 8595.37 — Free religion. (Persons, Stow.) New Haven, 1947.

X Cg — Phil 8585.14 — Free Religious Association. Freedom and fellowship. Boston, 1875.

Phil 8505.2 — The Free Religious Association. (Potter, W.J.) Boston, 1892.

Phil 9513.9 — Free society and moral crisis. (Angell, Robert Cooley.) Ann Arbor, 1958.

Phil 8610.888.12 — Pamphlet vol. Free thought. 14 pam.

Phil 15.2 — Free thought magazine. Chicago. 1899-1919 3v.

Phil 8610.854.2 — Free thoughts concerning religion. 2. ed. (Davis, A.J.) Boston, 1854.

Phil 665.2 — Free thoughts concerning souls. (Colliber, S.) London, 1734.

Htn — Phil 2128.65* — Free thoughts on religion. (Mandeville, B.) London, 1720.

Phil 5811.8.5 — Free thoughts upon the brute-creation: wherein Father Bougeant's Philosophical amusement is examined. (Hildrop, John.) London, 1751.

Phil 190.32 — Free will and destiny. (Pitt, St. George Lane-Fox.) London, 1920.

Phil 5751.20 — Free will and determinism. (Berofsky, Bernard.) N.Y., 1966.

Phil 5762.22 — Free will and determinism. (Munn, Allan M.) Toronto, 1960.

Phil 5768.18 — Free will and determinism. (Solly, J.R.) London, 1922.

Phil 5767.2.3A — Free will and four English philosophers. (Rickaby, Joseph.) London, 1906.

Phil 5757.5 — Free will and human responsibility. (Horne, H.H.) N.Y., 1912.

Phil 5753.13 — The free will controversy. (Davidson, M.) London, 1942.

Phil 3450.43F — Freed, Louis Franklin. R.F.A. Hoernle. Johannesburg, 1965.

Phil 1870.88 — Freedman, L.A. Substanz und Causalitat bei Berkeley. Strassburg, 1902.

Phil 6834.20 — Freedman, Mark. Homosexuality and psychological functioning. Belmont, Calif., 1971.

Phil 384.5 — Freedom, determinism, indeterminism. (Spakovski, Anatol.) The Hague, 1963.

Phil 8958.3 — Freedom, love and truth. (Inge, W.R.) Boston, 1939?

Phil 440.8 — Freedom, responsibiblity and obligation. (Edwards, Rem Blanchard.) The Hague, 1969.

Phil 1955.6.20 — Freedom and culture. (Dewey, John.) N.Y., 1939.

Phil 5761.25 — Freedom and determinism. (Lehrer, Keith.) N.Y., 1966.

Phil 1830.10 — Freedom and experience. (Hook, Sidney.) Ithaca, 1947.

X Cg — Phil 8585.14 — Freedom and fellowship. (Free Religious Association.) Boston, 1875.

Phil 8876.60 — Freedom and liberty. (Benett, William.) London, 1920.

Phil 5767.11.10 — Freedom and nature. (Ricoeur, Paul.) Evanston, Ill., 1966.

Phil 3823.9 — Freedom and purpose; an interpretation of the psychology of Spinoza. (Dunham, J.H.) Princeton, N.J., 1916.

Phil 1930.10.80 — Freedom and reason. (Baron, S.W.) Glencoe, Ill., 1951.

Phil 8882.68.5 — Freedom and reason. (Hare, Richard Mervyn.) Oxford, 1963.

Phil 8401.34.5 — Freedom and the artist. (Apresian, Zorii Grantovich.) Moscow, 1968.

Phil 2070.164 — Freedom and the moral life. (Roth, John K.) Philadelphia, 1969.

Phil 8581.69A — Freedom and the spirit. (Berdyaev, N.A.) N.Y., 1935.

Phil 5765.11 — Freedom and the will. (Pears, D.F.) London, 1966.

Phil 5768.3 — Freedom as an ethical postulate. (Seth, J.) Edinburgh, 1891.

Phil 978.59.50 — Freedom from the known. 1st ed. (Krishnamurti, J.) N.Y., 1969.

Phil 4752.2.105 — Freedom in God...on Berdyaev. (Allen, E.) London, 1950. 4 pam.

Phil 2750.11.67 — Freedom in the modern world. (Maritain, Jacques.) London, 1935.

Phil 384.20 — Freedom of choice. (Fellowship of Religious Humanists.) Yellow Springs, Ohio, 1970.

Phil 5768.22 — Freedom of choice. (Simon, Yves.) N.Y., 1969.

Phil 5761.24.1 — Freedom of choice affirmed. (Lamont, Corliss.) Boston, 1969.

Phil 5761.24 — Freedom of choise affirmed. (Lamont, Corliss.) N.Y., 1967.

Phil 645.37 — The freedom of doubt. (Preyre, A.E.) London, 1953.

Phil 6112.2.9 — Freedom of life. (Call, A.P.) Boston, 1905.

Phil 5752.10 — The freedom of man. (Compton, Arthur H.) New Haven, 1935.

Phil 5757.1.4 — Freedom of mind in willing. (Hazard, R.G.) Boston, 1889.

Phil 5757.1.2 — Freedom of mind in willing. (Hazard, R.G.) N.Y., 1865.

Phil 5620.32 — The freedom of reason. (Kolenda, K.) San Antonio, 1964.

Phil 5757.18 — Freedom of the individual. (Hampshire, Stuart.) N.Y., 1965.

Phil 5755.14A — The freedom of the will. (Farrer, A.M.) London, 1958.

Phil 384.25 — The freedom of the will. (Lucas, John Randolph.) Oxford, 1970.

Phil 5772.1 — Freedom of the will. (Whedon, D.D.) N.Y., 1864.

Phil 5755.14.2 — The freedom of the will. 2. ed. (Farrer, A.M.) London, 1963.

Phil 5754.1.27 — Freedom of the will vindicated. (Stewart, J.G.) Glasgow, 1876.

Phil 5761.17.5 — Freedom of will. (Lossky, N.O.) London, 1932.

Phil 5535.34 — Freedom to learn. (Rogers, Carl Ransom.) Columbus, Ohio, 1969.

Phil 978.49.200 — Freeman, Arnold. Who was Rudolf Steiner? Sheffield, 1944.

Phil 8610.926 — Freeman, C.R.B. Towards the answer. Derbyshire, 1926.

Phil 1705.11 — Freeman, David. Recent studies in philosophy and theology. Philadelphia, 1962.

Phil 5245.43 — Freeman, E. Principles of general psychology. N.Y., 1939.

Phil 6315.64 — Freeman, Erika. Insights: conversations with Theodor Reik. Englewood Cliffs, 1971.

Phil 2225.5.97 — Freeman, Eugene. The categories of Charles Peirce. Diss. Chicago, 193-.

Phil 6115.26 — Freeman, G.L.V. Introduction to physiological psychology. N.Y., 1934.

Phil 1133.26 — Freeman, Kathleen. The pre-Socratic philosophers. Cambridge, Mass., 1946[1947]

Phil 1133.26.2 — Freeman, Kathleen. The pre-Socratic philosophers. Oxford, 1946.

Phil 2130.80 — Freeman, Kenneth D. The role of reason in religion: a study of Henry Mansel. The Hague, 1969.

Phil 6315.30 — Freeman, L. Fight against fears. N.Y., 1951.

Phil 6955.18 — Freeman, Thomas. Chronic schizophrenia. London, 1958.

Phil 6996.5 — Freeman, Walter. Psychosurgery. Springfield, 1942.

Phil 1980.3.102 — Freeman-Ishill, Rose. Havelock Ellis. Berkeley Heights, N.J., 1959.

NEDL — Phil 15.5F — Freethinker. London. 10-48,1890-1928

Phil 15.5.10 — Freethinker of America. Bulletin. N.Y. 1,1937+ 5v.

Phil 8610.877.15 — The freethinker's catechism. (Monteil, Edgar.) N.Y., 19-?

Phil 8610.877.17 — The freethinker's catechism. (Monteil, Edgar.) N.Y., 19-?

Phil 623.17 — Freethinkers of the nineteenth century. (Courtney, J.E.) London, 1920.

Htn — Phil 2300.40* — Freewill, foreknowledge. v.1-2. (Tucker, Abraham.) London, 1763.

Phil 5755.18 — Freewill and determinism: a study of rival conceptions of man. (Franklin, Richard Langdon.) London, 1968.

Phil 5752.6 — The freewill problem. (Carr, Herbert W.) London, 1928.

Phil 3270.12.40 — Frege, Gottlob. Funktion, Begriff, Bedeutung. Göttingen, 1962.

Phil 3270.12.50 — Frege, Gottlob. Kleine Schriften. Hildesheim, 1967.

Phil 3270.12.45 — Frege, Gottlob. Logische Untersuchungen. Göttingen, 1966.

Phil 3270.12.37 — Frege, Gottlob. Translations from the philosophical writings. 2nd ed. Oxford, 1966.

Phil 3270.12.33 — Frege, Gottlob. Translations from the philosophical writings of Gottlob Frege. Oxford, 1952.

Phil 3270.12.35 — Frege, Gottlob. Translations from the philosophical writings of Gottlob Frege. Oxford, 1960.

Phil 5066.259.5 — Frege and Gödel; two fundamental texts in mathematical logic. (Van Heijenoort, Jean.) Cambridge, 1970.

Phil 3270.12.90 — Frege's logical theory. (Sternfeld, Robert.) Carbondale, 1966.

Phil 2415.3.25 — Frégier, J.C. Portalis, philosophes-chrétien. Paris, 1861.

Phil 7016.2 — Frei, Gebhard. Probleme der Parapsychologie. München, 1969.

Phil 19.17.8 — Freiburger Zeitschrift für Philosophie und Theologie. Freiburg. 1,1954+ 13v.

Phil 19.17.9 — Freiburger Zeitschrift für Philosophie und Theologie. Ökumenische Beihefte. Freiburg. 1,1968+

Phil 8610.853 — Die Freidenker in der Religion. pt.3. (Noack, L.) Bern, 1853-55.

Phil 8430.92 — Freidizm i burzhuaznoe iskusstvo. (Afasizhev, Marat Nurbievich.) Moskva, 1971.

Phil 9540.9 — Freie Akademie Nüremberg. Toleranz eine Grundforderung geschtlicher Existenz. Nürnberg, 1960.

Phil 181.40 — Der freie Mensch. (Gleichen-Russwurm, A. von.) Berlin, 1918.

Phil 476.3.53 — Die freie Naturbetrachtung. (Strohecker, J.R.) Augsburg, 1869.

Phil 8402.42 — Freie vorträge über Ästhetik. (Bobrik, Eduard.) Zürich, 1834.

Phil 5759.2 — Der freie Wille, eine Entwicklung in Gesprächen. (Joël, Karl.) München, 1908.

Phil 5768.2 — Der freie Wille. (Scholten, J.H.) Berlin, 1874.

Phil 5767.10.5 — Freiheit, Wollen und Aktivität. (Reiner, Hans.) Leipzig, 1927.

Phil 2138.40.14 — Die Freiheit. (Mill, John S.) Leipzig, 1928.

Phil 2138.40.16 — Die Freiheit (On Liberty) Übers. 3. Aufl. (Mill, John S.) Darmstadt, 1970.

Phil 176.221 — Freiheit als Problem der Wissenschaft. (Berlin. Freie Universität.) Berlin, 1962.

Phil 5767.12 — Die Freiheit der Willensbildung. (Ramm, T.) Stuttgart, 1960.

Phil 8693.16 — Die Freiheit der Wissenschaft. 3. Aufl. (Donat, Josef.) Innsbruck, 1925.

Phil 5760.12 — Die Freiheit des körpergebundenen Willens. (Kircher, Veronica.) Freiburg, 1957.

Phil 5764.1 — Die Freiheit des Menschen. (Otto, F.W.) Gütersloh, 1872.

Phil 5759.5 — Die Freiheit des menschlichen Willens. (Jäkel, Josef.) Wien, 1906.

Phil 5755.1.3 — Die Freiheit des menschlichen Willens und die Einheit der Naturgesetze. 2. Aufl. (Fischer, J.C.) Leipzig, 1871.

Phil 5768.17 — Die Freiheit des Willens als Grundlage der Sittlichkeit. (Schwartzkopff, P.) Leipzig, 1885.

Phil 5762.16 — Die Freiheit des Willens und ihre Grenzen. (Medicus, Fritz.) Tübingen, 1926.

Phil 2880.2.90 — Freiheit in Wirtschaft, Staat und Religion: die Philosophie der Gesellschaft von Charles Secrétan. (Lehner, Felix.) Zürich, 1967.

Phil 440.12 — Freiheit ist anders. (Schuette, Hermann Günther.) München, 1970.

Phil 180.60 — Freiheit und Bindung. (Flechtner, H.J.) Berlin, 1935.

Phil 9240.15 — Die Freiheit und das Gute. (Siewerth, Gustav.) Freiburg, 1959.

Phil 3549.11.5 — Freiheit und Gnade. (Kroner, Richard.) Tübingen, 1969.

Phil 5755.7 — Freiheit und Notwendigkeit als elemente einer einheitlichen Weltanschauung. (Froehlich, Joseph Anselm.) Leipzig, 1908.

Phil 310.714 — Freiheit und Notwendigkeit in der Geschichte; zur Kritik des historischen Materialismus. (Piroschkow, Vera.) München, 1970.

Phil 440.4 — Freiheit und Persönlichkeit. (Fischer, Ernst.) Wien, 1947.

Phil 2880.8.156 — Freiheit und Person. (Hana, Ghanem Georges.) München, 1965.

Phil 182.124 — Freiheit und Seinsordnung. (Hengstenberg, Hans Edward.) Stuttgart, 1961.

Phil 8620.47 — Freiheit und Tod. (Metzger, A.) Tübingen, 1955.

Phil 3801.768 — Freiheit und Wirklichkeit. (Sandkuehler, Hans-Jörg.) Frankfurt, 1968.

Phil 3805.173 — Freiheit und Wirklichkeit. (Ungern-Sternberg, Arthur Freiherr von.) Gotha, 1931.

Phil 181.50.10 — Freiheit und Zucht. (Grisebach, E.) Zurich, 1936.

Phil 5258.205 — Freiheit und Zwang im Schicksal des Einzelnen. (Szondi, Lipot.) Bern, 1968.

Phil 3499.9 — Freiheit Unstirblichkeit und Gott. (Ruisch, Arnold.) Leipzig, 1913.

Phil 3486.10.5 — Der Freiheitsbegriff bei Kant und Schopenhauer. (Ehrlich, W.) Berlin, 1920.

Phil 3835.7 — Der Freiheitsbegriff in der Lehre Spinozas. (Palmodo, Kurt.) Weiden, 1920.

Phil 3246.229 — Freiheitsides und Rechtsbegriff in der Philosophie von Johann Gottlieb Fichte. (Oestereich, H.) Jena, 1935.

Phil 3495.7 — Die Freiheitslehre bei Kant. (Neumark, David.) Hamburg, 1896.

Phil 3280.88 — Das Freiheitsproblem in der Metaphysik und Ethik bei Arnold Geulincx. Inaug. Diss. (Hausmann, P.) Stuttgart, 1934.

Phil 5772.10 — Die Freihert des menschlichen Willens. (Wiesner, Johann.) Wien, 1909.

Phil 6315.2.400 — Freijo Balsebre, Enrique. El problema religioso en la historia de la psicologia médica contemporánea. Vitoria, 1966.

Phil 3100.84 — Freimuth, F.W. Die wichtigsten Grundlehren und Vorzüge der Psychologie Dr. Beneke's. Bautzen, 1845.

Phil 3002.3   Freiheit und Form. 2e Aufl. (Cassirer, Ernst.) Berlin, 1918.

Phil 1510.5   Fremantle, A.J. The age of belief. Boston, 1955.
Phil 525.249   Fremantle, Anne Jackson. The Protestant mystics. 1st ed. Boston, 1964.

Phil 8735.15   Die fremddienliche Zweckmässigkeit der Pflanzgallen und dieHypothese eines überindividuellen Seelischen. (Becher, Erich.) Leipzig, 1917.

Phil 176.33.10   Fremdes und Eignes. (Büchner, L.) Leipzig, 1890.
Phil 6978.5.5   Fremdes unter uns. (Fryes, F.B.M.) Meppel, 1968.
Phil 8406.17   Fremling, M. Dissertatio philosophica. Lundae, 1789.
Phil 5415.8   Fremling, Matthaus. Dissertatio philosophica, de sympathia. Lundae, 1789.
Phil 180.46   Fremling, Matthaus. Dissertatio philosophica de ratione praecepta philosophiae theoreticae tradendi. Pt.1-3. Lundae, 1783-1787.

Phil 8695.6   Frémont, G. Que l'orgueil de l'esprit est le grand écueil de la foi. Paris, 1900.

Phil 2905.1.400   Frenaud, Georges. Pensée philosophique et religieuse du père Teilhard de Chardin. Le Chesnay, 1965.

Phil 7150.22   Frenay, A.D. The suicide problem in the United States. Diss. Boston, 1927.

Phil 5245.47   French, T.M. The integration of behavior. Chicago, 1952-58. 3v.

Phil 7082.184   French, Thomas Morton. Dream interpretation, a new approach. N.Y., 1964.

Phil 6060.22   French, William L. The psychology of handwriting. N.Y., 1922.

Htn   Phil 8886.21*   The French Academie. (La Primaudaye, P. de.) London, 1586.

Phil 2428.5   French existentialism; a Christian critique. (Kingston, Frederick Temple.) Toronto, 1961.

Phil 2418.7   French free-thought from Gassendi to Voltaire. (Spink, John Stephenson.) London, 1960.

Phil 2403.4   The French ideal. (Duclaux, A.M.F.R.) N.Y., 1911.
Phil 8865.372   French moralists; the theory of the passions, 1585-1649. (Levi, Anthony.) Oxford, 1964.

Phil 705.48   French philosophers and New England transcendentalism. (Leighton, Walter Leatherbee.) Charlottesville, 1908.

Phil 2401.2   French philosophies of the romantic period. (Boas, George.) Baltimore, 1925.

Phil 1133.24   Frenkian, A.M. Etudes de philosophie presocratique. Cernăuti, 1933. 2v.

Phil 645.39   Frenkian, Aram M. Scepticismul grec şi filosofia indiană. Bucuresti, 1957.

Phil 3552.270   Frenzel, Bernhard. Der Associationsbegriff bei Leibniz. Leipzig, 1898.

Phil 3640.735   Frenzel, Ivo. Friedrich Nietzsche; an illustrated biography. N.Y., 1967.

Phil 3640.736   Frenzel, Ivo. Friedrich Nietzsche in Selbstzeugnissen und Bilddokumenten. Reinbek, 1968.

Phil 5100.5   Frequent fallacies. (Moore, William H.) Boston, 1931.
Phil 1750.166.140   Frerichs, J.G. Waarde van de mens en menselijke waardigheid. Zaandam, 1960.

Phil 2475.1.455   Fressin, Augustin. La perception chez Bergson et chez Merleau-Ponty. Paris, 1967.

Phil 5045.7.5   Fretag, Bruno baron von. Irrational oder Rational? Berlin, 1935.

Phil 6992.4   Frétigny, Roger. L'imagerie mentale; introduction à l'onirothérapie. Genève, 1968.

Phil 6315.2.425   Freud, a man obsessed. (Kushner, Martin D.) Philadelphia, 1967.

Phil 6315.17.30   Freud, Anna. Difficulties in the path of psychoanalysis. N.Y., 1969.

Phil 6315.17.12   Freud, Anna. The ego and the mechanisms of defence. London, 1954.

Phil 6315.17.10   Freud, Anna. The ego and the mechanisms of defence. N.Y., 1950.

Phil 6315.17.16   Freud, Anna. Indications for child analysis, and other papers, 1945-56. London, 1969.

Phil 6315.17.8   Freud, Anna. Psychoanalysis for teachers and parents. Boston, 1960.

Phil 6980.308   Freud, Anna. The pyscho-analytical treatment of children. London, 1946.

Phil 5870.75   Freud, Anna. Research at the Hampstead Child-Therapy Clinic and other papers, 1956-1965. London, 1970.

Phil 6315.17.14   Freud, Anna. Writings of Anna Freud. v.2,4-6. N.Y., 1967. 4v.

Phil 6315.2.420   Freud; enfant de son siècle. (Brandell, Gunnar.) Paris, 1967.

Phil 6315.2.215   Freud, Freudismo y las verdades sociales [a las cieñanos de su nacimiento, 6 de mayo, 1856-1956]. (Relgis, Eugen.) Montevideo, 1956.

Phil 6315.2.134   Freud, his life and his mind. (Pruner, Helen W.) N.Y., 1947.

Phil 6315.2.210   Freud, Martin. Glory reflected. London, 1957.
Phil 6315.2.127A   Freud, master and friend. (Sacho, H.) Cambridge, Mass., 1944.

Phil 6315.2.390   Freud; political and social thought. 1. ed. (Roazen, Paul.) N.Y., 1968.

Htn   Phil 6400.3*   Freud, S. Zur Auffassung der Aphasien. Leipzig, 1891.
Phil 6315.2.8.40A   Freud, Sigmund. Aus den Anfänger der Psychoanalyse. London, 1950.

Htn   Phil 6315.2.74*   Freud, Sigmund. Aus der Geschichte einer infantilen Neurose. Leipzig, 1924.

Phil 6315.2.79   Freud, Sigmund. An autobiographical study. London, 1935.
Phil 6315.2.79.5   Freud, Sigmund. An autobiographical study. 2d ed. London, 1946.

Phil 6315.2.53   Freud, Sigmund. The basic writings of Sigmund Freud. N.Y., 1938. 3v.

Phil 6315.2.70   Freud, Sigmund. Beyond the pleasure principle. N.Y., 1924.

Phil 6315.2.59.10   Freud, Sigmund. Beyond the pleasure principle. N.Y., 1950.

Phil 6315.2.79.30   Freud, Sigmund. Brautbriefe. Frankfurt, 1968.
Phil 6315.2.66   Freud, Sigmund. Briefe 1873-1939. Frankfurt, 1960.
Phil 6315.2.66.10   Freud, Sigmund. Briefe 1873-1939. 2. Aufl. Frankfurt, 1968.

Phil 6315.2.69   Freud, Sigmund. Briefe 1907-1926. Sigmund Freud and Karl Abraham. Frankfurt, 1965.

Phil 6315.2.66.5   Freud, Sigmund. Briefe 1909-39. Frankfurt, 1963.
Phil 6315.2.26   Freud, Sigmund. Briefwechsel. Frankfurt, 1968.
Phil 6315.2.9   Freud, Sigmund. Cinq leçons sur la psychoanalyse. Paris, 1923.

Phil 6315.2.113.2   Freud, Sigmund. Civilisation. London, 1953.
Phil 6315.2.51   Freud, Sigmund. Civilization and its discontents. N.Y., 1930.

Phil 6315.2.51.5A   Freud, Sigmund. Civilization and its discontents. N.Y., 1962.
Phil 6315.2.8.30A   Freud, Sigmund. Collected papers. London, 1949. 5v.
Phil 6315.2.34   Freud, Sigmund. Collected papers. London, 1957-69. 4v.
Phil 6315.2.35   Freud, Sigmund. Collected papers. N.Y., 1924-5.
Phil 6315.2.8.31   Freud, Sigmund. Collected papers. N.Y., 1959. 5v.
Phil 6315.2.350   Freud, Sigmund. The collected papers of Sigmund Freud. (Studies in parapsychology, v.10). N.Y., 1963.
Phil 6315.2.62.10   Freud, Sigmund. Délire et rêves dans la "gradiva" de Jenson. 8. éd. Paris, 1949.
Phil 6315.2.62.7   Freud, Sigmund. Delusion and dream, and other essays. Boston, 1968.
Phil 6315.2.62.5   Freud, Sigmund. Delusion and dream. N.Y., 1917.
Phil 6315.2.78   Freud, Sigmund. Dictionary of psychoanalysis. N.Y., 1950.
Phil 6315.2.62.15A   Freud, Sigmund. Dreams in folklore. N.Y., 1958.
Phil 6315.2.75.8   Freud, Sigmund. Drei Abhandlungen zur Sexualtheorie. Leipzig, 1910.
Phil 6315.2.75.10   Freud, Sigmund. Drei Abhandlungen zur Sexualtheorie. 7. Aufl. Wien, 1946.
Phil 6315.2.37.3   Freud, Sigmund. The ego and the id. London, 1950.
Phil 6315.2.37.4   Freud, Sigmund. The ego and the id. London, 1957.
Phil 6315.2.37.1   Freud, Sigmund. The ego and the id. N.Y., 1961.
Phil 6315.2.37.6   Freud, Sigmund. The ego and the id. N.Y., 1962.
Phil 6315.2.29   Freud, Sigmund. Essais de psychanalyse. Paris, 1948.
Phil 6315.2.47   Freud, Sigmund. Die Frage der Laienanalyse. Wien, 1926.
Phil 8585.28A   Freud, Sigmund. The future of an illusion. London, 1928.
Phil 8585.28.2   Freud, Sigmund. The future of an illusion. London, 1949.
Phil 8585.28.3   Freud, Sigmund. The future of an illusion. London, 1928.
Phil 6315.2.5.6A   Freud, Sigmund. A general introduction to psycho-analysis. Garden City, 1938.
Phil 6315.2.5.5   Freud, Sigmund. A general introduction to psycho-analysis. N.Y., 1935.
Phil 6315.2.5.7   Freud, Sigmund. A general introduction to psycho-analysis. N.Y., 1937.
Phil 6315.2.36   Freud, Sigmund. A general selection from the works of Sigmund Freud. London, 1937.
Phil 6315.2.38   Freud, Sigmund. A general selection from the works of Sigmund Freud. N.Y., 1957.
Phil 6315.2.2   Freud, Sigmund. Gesammelte Schriften. Leipzig, 1924-34. 12v.
Phil 6315.2   Freud, Sigmund. Gesammelte Werke. v. 1-14,16-18. London, 1940-46. 16v.
Phil 6315.2.68   Freud, Sigmund. Group psychology and the analysis of the ego. N.Y., 192-?
Phil 6315.2.68.5A   Freud, Sigmund. Group psychology and the analysis of the ego. N.Y., 1967.
Htn   Phil 6315.2.60*   Freud, Sigmund. Hemmung, Symptom und Angst. Leipzig, 1926.
Phil 6315.2.3.5   Freud, Sigmund. History of the psychoanalytic movement. N.Y., 1917.
Phil 6315.2.37.5   Freud, Sigmund. Das Ich und das Es. Leipzig, 1923.
Phil 6315.2.42.5A   Freud, Sigmund. Inhibitions, symptoms and anxiety. London, 1961.
X Cg   Phil 6480.23.6   Freud, Sigmund. The interpretation of dreams. London, 1932.
Phil 7082.8.20   Freud, Sigmund. The interpretation of dreams. London, 1954.
Phil 6480.23.18   Freud, Sigmund. The interpretation of dreams. N.Y., 1950.
X Cg   Phil 6480.23.5   Freud, Sigmund. The interpretation of dreams. 4th ed. London, 1915. 2v.
Phil 6315.2.6   Freud, Sigmund. Introductory lecture on psycho-analysis. London, 1922.
Phil 6315.2.59.3   Freud, Sigmund. Jenseits des Lustprinzips. 3. Aufl. Leipzig, 1923.
Phil 5525.6.10   Freud, Sigmund. Jokes and their relation to the unconscious. London, 1960.
Phil 6315.2.67   Freud, Sigmund. Letters. 1st ed. N.Y., 1960.
Phil 6315.2.26.6   Freud, Sigmund. The letters of Sigmund Freud and Arnold Zweig. London, 1970.
Phil 6315.2.26.5   Freud, Sigmund. The letters of Sigmund Freud and Arnold Zweig. N.Y., 1970.
Phil 6315.2.52   Freud, Sigmund. The living thoughts of Freud. N.Y., 1941.
Phil 6315.2.73   Freud, Sigmund. Ma vie et la psychanalyse. 23. éd. Paris, 1949.
Phil 6315.2.44   Freud, Sigmund. Massenpsychologie und Ich-Analyse. Leipzig, 1921.
Htn   Phil 5380.77*   Freud, Sigmund. Massenpsychologie und Ich-Analyse. Leipzig, 1921.
Phil 6315.2.79.10   Freud, Sigmund. Moïse et la monothéisme. 8 éd. Paris, 1948.
Phil 6315.2.22   Freud, Sigmund. New introductory lectures on psycho-analysis. N.Y., 1958.
Phil 6315.2.79.15   Freud, Sigmund. On aphasia. London, 1953.
Phil 6315.2.21   Freud, Sigmund. On creativity and the unconscious. N.Y., 1958.
Phil 6480.23.13   Freud, Sigmund. On dreams. London, 1924.
Phil 7082.8.5   Freud, Sigmund. On dreams. N.Y., 1952.
Phil 6315.2.56   Freud, Sigmund. On the history of the psychoanalytic movement. N.Y., 1966.
Phil 6315.2.20.15   Freud, Sigmund. On war, sex and neurosis. N.Y., 1947.
Phil 6315.2.12   Freud, Sigmund. The origin and development of psychoanalysis. Chicago, 1955.
Phil 6315.2.79.20A   Freud, Sigmund. The origins of psycho-analysis. 1st ed. N.Y., 1954.
Phil 6315.2.8.20   Freud, Sigmund. An outline of psychoanalysis. 1st. ed. N.Y., 1949.
Phil 6315.2.8   Freud, Sigmund. Over psychoanalyse. Leiden, 1912.
Phil 6315.2.43A   Freud, Sigmund. The problem of anxiety. N.Y., 1936.
Phil 6315.2.46A   Freud, Sigmund. The problem of lay analysis. N.Y., 1927.
Phil 6315.2.79.25   Freud, Sigmund. Psychanalyse. 2. éd. Paris, 1965.
Phil 6315.2.28   Freud, Sigmund. A psycho-analytic dialogue. London, 1965.
Phil 6315.2.57   Freud, Sigmund. Psychoanalysis and faith. London, 1963.
Phil 6315.2.57.1   Freud, Sigmund. Psychoanalysis and faith. N.Y., 1964.
Phil 6315.2.33   Freud, Sigmund. Psychopathology of everyday life. London, 1914.
Phil 6315.2.33.5   Freud, Sigmund. Psychopathology of everyday life. London, 1917.
Phil 6315.2.33.6   Freud, Sigmund. Psychopathology of everyday life. N.Y., 1917.
Phil 6315.2.33.8   Freud, Sigmund. The psychopathology of everyday life. N.Y., 1966.
Phil 6315.2.46.10   Freud, Sigmund. The question of lay analysis. 1. ed. N.Y., 1950.
Phil 6315.2.25   Freud, Sigmund. Reflections on war and death. N.Y., 1918.

Phil 6315.2.20.7 — Freud, Sigmund. Sammlung kleiner Schriften. 3. Aufl. 1e, 2e Folge. Leipzig, 1920-21. 2v.

Htn — Phil 6315.2.20* — Freud, Sigmund. Sammlung kleiner Schriften zur Neurosenlehre. 2e, 4e, 5e Folge. Leipzig, 1909-22. 3v.

Phil 6315.2.20.5 — Freud, Sigmund. Sammlung kleiner Schriften zur Neurosenlehre aus den Jahren 1893-1906. 2. Aufl. 1e, 2e Folge. Leipzig, 1911-21. 2v.

Phil 6315.2.58 — Freud, Sigmund. Schriften aus dem Nachlass 1892-1938. London, 1941.

Phil 6315.2.72 — Freud, Sigmund. Selbstdarstellung. London, 1946.

Phil 6315.2.72.5 — Freud, Sigmund. Selbstdarstellung. 2. Aufl. Wien, 1936.

X Cg — Phil 6315.2.19 — Freud, Sigmund. Selected papers on hysteria and other psychoneuroses. N.Y., 1912.

Phil 6315.2.3.10A — Freud, Sigmund. The standard edition of the complete psychological works. v.1-20,22-23. London, 1953-64. 22v.

Phil 6315.2.18 — Freud, Sigmund. Studien zur Psychoanalyse der Neurosen aus den Jahren 1913-25. Wien, 1926.

Phil 6315.2.40 — Freud, Sigmund. Studienausgabe. v.1,4,6,8,10. Frankfurt, 1969. 6v.

Phil 6315.2.45 — Freud, Sigmund. The psychologie collective et analyse du moi. Paris, 1924.

Phil 6315.2.75.14 — Freud, Sigmund. Three contributions to the theory of sex. 4th ed. N.Y., 1948.

Phil 6315.2.75.17 — Freud, Sigmund. Three essays on the theory of sexuality. London, 1962.

Phil 6315.2.75.15 — Freud, Sigmund. Three essays on the theory of sexuality. 1st English ed. London, 1949.

Phil 7082.8.14 — Freud, Sigmund. Die Traumdeutung. 4. Aufl. Leipzig, 1914.

Htn — Phil 6480.23* — Freud, Sigmund. Die Traumdeutung. Leipzig, 1909.

Phil 6315.2.75.12 — Freud, Sigmund. Trois essais sur la théorie de la sexualité. 51. éd. Paris, 1949.

Phil 6315.2.75.11 — Freud, Sigmund. Trois essais sur la théorie de le sexualité. 23e éd. Paris, 1925.

Phil 7082.8.2 — Freud, Sigmund. Über den Traum. 2. Aufl. Wiesbaden, 1911.

Htn — Phil 6480.23.7* — Freud, Sigmund. Über den Traumdeutung. Wiesbaden, 1901.

Htn — Phil 6315.2.4.5* — Freud, Sigmund. Über Psychoanalyse. Leipzig, 1910.

Phil 6315.2.6.10 — Freud, Sigmund. Über Psychoanalyse. 2e Aufl. Leipzig, 1912.

Phil 6315.2.4A — Freud, Sigmund. Über Psychoanalyse. 5e Aufl. Leipzig, 1920.

Phil 6315.2.6.5 — Freud, Sigmund. Über Psychoanalyse. 6e Aufl. Leipzig, 1922.

Phil 6315.2.7 — Freud, Sigmund. Über Psychoanalyse. 7e Aufl. Leipzig, 1924.

Phil 6315.2.7.5 — Freud, Sigmund. Über Psychoanalyse. 9e Aufl. Wien, 1946.

Htn — Phil 6315.2.64.1* — Freud, Sigmund. Das Unbehagen in der Kultur. Wien, 1930.

Phil 6315.2.64 — Freud, Sigmund. Das Unbehagen in der Kultur. Wien, 1931.

Phil 6315.2.14 — Freud, Sigmund. Die Unbewusste. Frankfurt, 1960.

Phil 6315.2.65 — Freud, Sigmund. Vier psychoanalytische Krankengeschichten. Wien, 1932.

Phil 6315.2.9.10 — Freud, Sigmund. Vorlesungen zur Einführung. 2. Aufl. Leipzig, 1918.

Phil 6315.2.10.10 — Freud, Sigmund. Vorlesungen zur Einführung in die Psychoanalyse. Berlin, 1933.

Phil 6315.2.10A — Freud, Sigmund. Vorlesungen zur Einführung in die Psychoanalyse. 2. Aufl. Leipzig, 1922.

Phil 6315.2.10.5A — Freud, Sigmund. Vorlesungen zur Einführung in die Psychoanalyse. 4. Aufl. Leipzig, 1922.

Phil 5525.6.5A — Freud, Sigmund. Wit and its relation to the unconscious. N.Y., 1916.

Htn — Phil 5525.6* — Freud, Sigmund. Der Witz und seine Beziehung zum Unbewussten. Leipzig, 1905.

Phil 5525.6.3 — Freud, Sigmund. Der Witz und seine Beziehung zum Unbewussten. 2. Aufl. Leipzig, 1912.

Htn — Phil 6315.2.76* — Freud, Sigmund. Zeitgemässes über Krieg und Tod. Leipzig, 1924.

Htn — Phil 6315.2.61* — Freud, Sigmund. Die Zukunft einer Illusion. Wien, 1927.

Phil 6315.2.80 — Pamphlet box. Freud, Sigmund.

Phil 6315.2.240 — Freud; the mind of the moralist. (Rieff, Philip.) N.Y., 1959.

Phil 6315.2.116 — Freud, un gran explorador del alma. (Seguin, C.A.) Buenos Aires, 1940.

Phil 6313.16 — Freud. (Dempsey, P.J.R.) Cork, 1956.

Phil 6315.2.245 — Freud. (Loewenstein, Rudolph Maurice.) N.Y., 1951.

Phil 6315.2.465 — Freud. 1st American ed. (Mannoni, O.) N.Y., 1971.

Phil 6315.2.160 — Freud. 1st ed. (Schoenwald, R.L.) N.Y., 1956.

Phil 6315.2.146.5 — Freud - 1956. (Zilboorg, G.) N.Y., 1956.

Phil 6315.2.103 — Freud als ethnoloog. Proefschrift. (Schelts van Kloosterhuis, E.) Amsterdam, 1933.

Phil 6315.2.115.5 — Freud als Kulturkritiker. Mit einem Briefe S. Freuds. (Reik, Theodor.) Wien, 1930.

Phil 6315.2.375 — Freud and America. (Ruitenbeek, Hendrik Marinus.) N.Y., 1966.

Phil 6315.44 — Freud and contemporary culture. (New York. Academy of Medicine.) N.Y., 1957.

Phil 6315.2.405 — Freud and his early circle; the struggles of psychoanalysis. (Brome, Vincent.) London, 1967.

Phil 6315.2.88.3 — Freud and his time. (Wittels, Fritz.) N.Y., 1931.

Phil 6315.2.88 — Freud and his time. (Wittels, Fritz.) N.Y., 1931.

Phil 6315.2.444 — Freud and philosophy. (Ricoeur, P.) New Haven, 1970.

Phil 6315.2.340 — Freud and political thought. 1st. ed. (Johnston, Thomas E.) N.Y., 1965.

Phil 6315.2.175 — Freud and religious belief. (Philp, Howard Littleton.) London, 1956.

Phil 6315.2.157A — Freud and the crisis of our culture. (Trilling, L.) Boston, 1955.

Phil 6315.2.285 — Freud and the post-Freudians. (Brown, J.A.C.) Baltimore, 1961.

Phil 6315.2.220A — Freud and the 20th century. (Nelson, B.N.) N.Y., 1958.

Phil 6315.2.82.10 — Freud dans la société d'après guerre. (Hesnard, Angelo.) Genève, 1946.

Phil 6325.32 — Freud et la morale. (Plé, Albert.) Paris, 1969.

Phil 6317.22.85 — Freud et la psychanalyse américaine Karen Horney. (Brés, Yvon.) Paris, 1970.

Phil 6315.2.435 — Freud et la religion. (Plé, Albert.) Paris, 1968?

Phil 6315.2.205 — Freud in der Gegenwart. Frankfurt, 1957.

Phil 6315.2.142 — Freud or Jung. (Glover, E.) London, 1950.

Phil 6315.2.141A — Freud or Jung. (Glover, E.) N.Y., 1950.

Phil 6327.22 — Freud und Adler. (Rühle, Alice G.) Dresden, 1924.

Phil 9420.4 — Freud und Leid des Menschengeschlechte. (Schneider, G.H.) Stuttgart, 1883.

Phil 75.3 — Freude, C.G.A. Wegweiser. Ebersbach, 1858. 2v.

Phil 8880.46 — Freudenberg, G. Grenzen der Ethik. Leipzig, 1927.

Phil 805.7 — Freudenberg, G. Die philosophiegeschichtliche Wahrheit. Inaug. Diss. Berlin, 1921.

Phil 5066.190 — Freudenthal, Hans. Exacte logica. Haarlem, 1961.

Phil 5066.190.2 — Freudenthal, Hans. Exacte logica. 2. druk. Haarlem, 1967.

Phil 5066.253 — Freudenthal, Hans. The language of logic. Amsterdam, 1966.

Phil 3825.4 — Freudenthal, J. Spinoza, sein Leben und seine Lehre. Stuttgart, 1904.

Phil 3825.4.2 — Freudenthal, J. Spinoza: Leben und Lehre. 2. Aufl. v.1-2. Heidelberg, 1927.

Phil 3487.17 — Freudenthal, Jacob. Immanuel Kant. Breslau, 1904.

Phil 3625.1.121 — Freudenthal, M. Zum zweihundertjährigen Geburtstag Moses Mendelssohns; vier Abhandlungen. Berlin, 1929.

Phil 6327.21.90 — The Freudian left: Wilhelm Reich, Geza Roheim, Albert Marcuse. 1st ed. (Robinson, Paul Arnold.) N.Y., 1969.

Phil 5755.5.2 — The Freudian wish and its place in ethics. (Holt, E.B.) N.Y., 1915.

Phil 5755.5 — The Freudian wish and its place in ethics. (Holt, E.B.) N.Y., 1915.

Phil 6315.2.185 — Freudiana. (Roback, A.A.) Cambridge, Mass., 1957.

Phil 6315.2.107 — Freudiana. (Roback, A.A.) n.p., n.d. 3 pam.

Phil 6315.2.91 — Le freudisme; exposé et critique. (Laumonier, J.) Paris, 1925.

Phil 6315.2.280 — Freud's concept of repression and defense, its theoretical and observational language. (Madison, P.) Minneapolis, 1961.

Phil 6315.2.124 — Freud's contribution to psychiatry. (Brill, A.A.) N.Y., 1944.

Phil 6315.2.90.2 — Freud's Neurosenlehre. 2. Aufl. (Hitschmann, Eduard.) Leipzig, 1913.

Phil 6315.2.415 — Freuds psykoanalys, presentation och kritik. (Marc-Wogan, Konrad.) Stockholm, 1967.

Phil 6315.2.90.5 — Freud's theories of the neuroses. (Hitschmann, Eduard.) N.Y., 1913.

Phil 6315.2.90.6 — Freud's theories of the neuroses. (Hitschmann, Eduard.) N.Y., 1913.

Phil 6315.2.99 — Freuds tragischer Komplex. 2e Aufl. (Maylan, Charles E.) München, 1929.

Phil 180.48 — Freund, Ludwig. Am Ende der Philosophie. München, 1930.

Phil 180.48.10 — Freund, Ludwig. Philosophie: ein unlösbares Problem. München, 1933.

Phil 9450.27 — Freund, Ludwig. Politik und Ethik. Frankfurt, 1955.

Phil 9450.27.2 — Freund, Ludwig. Politik und Ethik. 2. Aufl. Gütersloh, 1961.

Phil 9220.15 — Die Freundschaft. (Brelting, Rudolf.) Düsseldorf, 1956.

Phil 9220.10.9 — Freundschaft. (Gleichen-Russwurm, Alexander von.) Stuttgart, 1918?

Phil 1145.50 — Der Freundschafts begriff der Alten. (Curtius, E.) Göttingen, 1863.

Phil 575.20 — Frew, D.I. Cosmic inquiry pertaining to origin and development of individuality. Salt Lake City, 1907.

Phil 8050.53 — Frey, Dagobert. Grundlegung zu einer vergleichenden Kunstwissenschaft. Innsbruck, 1949.

Phil 8406.13 — Frey, Dagobert. Kunstwissenschaftliche Grundfragen. Wien, 1946.

Phil 5400.43 — Frey, Max von. Die Gefühle und ihr Verhältnis zu den Empfindungen. Leipzig, 1894.

Phil 5045.11 — Frey, T. Die Theorie der diskursiven Erkenntnis. Dorpat, 1929.

Phil 5238.206 — Frey-Wehrlin, Caspar J. Spectrum Psychologiae, ein Freundesgabe. Zürich, 1965.

Phil 8610.759 — Freydenker-Lexicon. (Trinius, Johann Anton.) Leipzig, 1759.

Phil 8610.759.5F — Freydenker-Lexicon. (Trinius, Johann Anton.) Torino, 1966.

Phil 8880.37.3 — Freyer, Hans. Antäus. Jena, 1922.

Phil 9450.55 — Freyer, Hans. Pallas Athene. Jena, 1935.

Phil 180.38.10 — Freyer, Hans. Prometheus: Ideen zur Philosophie der Kultur. Jena, 1923.

Phil 180.38 — Freyer, Hans. Theorie des objektiven Geistes. Leipzig, 1923.

Phil 180.38.5 — Freyer, Hans. Theorie des objektiven Geistes. 3. Aufl. Leipzig, 1934.

Phil 1705.7 — Freyer, Johannes. Geschichte der Geschichte der Philosophie. Leipzig, 1912.

Phil 5045.3 — Freyer, Paul. Beispiele zur Logik. Berlin, 1889.

Phil 5751.1.5 — Die Freyheit des menschlichen Willens. (Bockshammer, G.F.) Stuttgart, 1821.

Phil 5335.8 — Freyhold, Michaela von. Autoritarismus und politische Apathie. Frankfurt, 1971.

Phil 3246.340 — Freymüthige Gedanken über Fichte's Appellation gegen die Anklage des Atheismus und deren Veranlassung. (Ludwig, Karl Friedrich Ernst.) Bruxelles, 1968.

Phil 8430.43 — Freyre, G. Arte, ciêncis e trópico. São Paulo, 1962.

Phil 5045.7.3 — Freytag, Bruno baron von. Logik. Stuttgart, 1955-67. 2v.

Phil 1135.85 — Freytag, W. Die Entwicklung der Grossen Erkenntnistheorie. Hale, 1905.

Phil 5045.7 — Freytag, Willy. Der Realismus und Dastransscendenzproblem. Halle, 1902.

Phil 180.35 — Freytag, Willy. Über den Begriff der Philosophie. Halle, 1904.

Phil 3487.8 — Freytag, Willy. Über den Kantischen Idealismus. Leipzig, 1894.

Phil 8406.23 — Friche, V.M. Problemy iskusstvovedeniia: sbornik statei. Moskva, 1930.

Phil 3850.18.108 — Frick, Paul. Der weltanschauliche Hintergrund der materialen Wertethik Max Schelers. Diss. Stuttgart, 1933.

Phil 3487.11 — Fricker, K.V. Zu Kants Rechtsphilosophie. Lipsiae, 1885.

Phil 3640.640 — Fridrikh Nitsche. (Slobodskoi, I.) Sankt Peterburg, 1905.

Phil 8880.66 — Fried, Charles. An anatomy of values; problems of personal and social choice. Cambridge, 1970.

Phil 5867.35 — Fried, Edrita. Active/passive: the crucial psychological dimension. N.Y., 1970.

Phil 5465.145 — Fried, Edrita. Artistic productivity and mental health. Springfield, Ill., 1964.

Phil 3270.3.95 — Fried, Günther. Phantasie Wahrheit und Erkenntnis. Inaug. Diss. Tübingen, 1929.

Phil 180.89 — Friedberg, Felix. Thoughts about life. N.Y., 1954.

Phil 8601.15 — Friede. (Vogeler, H.) Bremen, 1922.

Phil 6315.58 — Friedemann, Adolf. Die Begegnung mit dem kranken Menschen. Bern, 1966.

Phil 3800.12 — Friederich Wilhelm Joseph von Schelling. (Schneeberger, G.) Bern, 1954.

Phil 180.66 — Friederichs, K. Die Selbstgestaltung des Lebendigen. München, 1955.

Phil 3640.193 — Friedrch Nietzsche und die klassische Philologie. Photoreproduction. (Howard, E.) Gotha, 1920.

Phil 6315.4 — Friedländer, A. Der Morphinismus, Kokainismus, Alkoholismus und Saturnismus. Jena, 1913.

Phil 5215.1 — Friedländer, A.A. Die neuzeitliche psychologische Strömungen. Lubeck, 1926.

Phil 7069.30.7   Friedländer, A.A. Telepathie und Hellsehen. Stuttgart, 1930.

Phil 5421.10.3   Friedlaender, Julius. Der Pessimismus im Lichte einer höheren Weltauffassung. Berlin, 1893.

Phil 8050.34   Friedlaender, L. Über die Entstehung und Entwicklung des Gefühls für das Romantische in der Natur. Leipzig, 1873.

Phil 1135.23   Friedländer, M. Griechische Philosophie im alten Testament. Berlin, 1904.

Phil 8406.14   Friedländer, Max J. On art and connoisseurship. London, 1942.

Phil 8406.14.5   Friedländer, Max J. Von Kunst und Kennerschaft. Zürich, 1946.

Phil 3640.112   Friedlaender, S. Friedrich Nietzsche, intellektuale Biographie. Leipzig, 1911.

Phil 5045.5   Friedlaender, S. Logik, die Lehre von Denken. Berlin, 191-?

Phil 180.34   Friedlaender, S. Schöpferische Indifferenz. München, 1918.

Phil 9495.12   Friedlander, B. Die liebe Platons. Berlin, 1909.

Phil 9530.48   Friedländer, Max. Wie Rationalisiert man sein Leben. Zürich, 1943?

Phil 3808.159   Friedlander, Salomo. Schopenhauer, seine Persönlichkeit in seinen Werken. Bd.II. Stuttgart, 1907.

Phil 3120.30.80   Friedman, M.S. Martin Buber. Chicago, 1955.

Phil 585.187   Friedman, Maurice Stanley. To deny our nothingness. N.Y., 1967.

Phil 165.375   Friedman, Maurice Stanley. The worlds of existentialism. N.Y., 1964.

Phil 5245.82   Friedman, Neil. The social nature of psychological research. N.Y., 1967.

Phil 3552.312   Friedmann, G. Leibniz et Spinoza. Paris, 1946.
Phil 3552.312.2   Friedmann, G. Leibniz et Spinoza. Paris, 1962.

Phil 8905.30   Friedmann, Georges. La puissance et la sagesse. Paris, 1971.

Phil 3270.11.35   Friedmann, H. Epilegomena. München, 1954.
Phil 3270.11.31   Friedmann, H. Sinnvolle Odyssee. München, 1950.
Phil 400.61   Friedmann, H. Die Welt der Formen. Berlin, 1925.
Phil 400.61.5   Friedmann, H. Die Welt der Formen. 2e Aufl. München, 1930.

Phil 3270.11   Friedmann, H. Wissenschaft und Symbol. München, 1949.
Phil 9075.27   Friedmann, J. Die Lehre vom Gewissen in den Systemen des ethischen Idealismus. Budapest, 1904.

Phil 6955.12   Friedmann, M. Uber den Wahn. v.1-2. Wiesbaden, 1894.
Phil 5413.5   Friedmann, Max. Uber die Psychologie der Eifersucht. Wiesbaden, 1911.

Phil 3160.7.85   Friedmann, P. Darstellung und Kritik der naturalistischen Weltanschauung H. Czolbes. Inaug. Diss. Berlin, 1905.

Phil 6955.8   Friedreich, H.B. Historisch-kritische Darstellung der Theorien über das Wesen und den Sitz der psychischen Krankheiten. Leipzig, 1836.

Phil 5245.16.3   Friedreich, J.B. System der gerichtlichen Psychologie. 3e Aufl. Regensburg, 1852.

Phil 5045.10   Friedrich, E.F. Beiträge zur Förderung der Logik. Leipzig, 1864.

Phil 510.146   Friedrich, Gustav. Die Farce des Jahrhunderts oder Des monisten Glück und Ende. Leipzig, 1913.

Phil 3460.98   Friedrich, Heinrich Jacobi. Philosoph und Literat der Goethezeit. Frankfurt, 1971.

Phil 3100.127   Friedrich, J. Friedrich Edward Beneke. Wiesbaden, 1898.
Phil 3270.3.88   Friedrich, J. Jakob Frohschammer. Fürth, 1896.
Phil 3640.172   Friedrich, Nietzsche, zijn leven en zijn werk. (Proost, K.F.) Uitgave, 1920.

Phil 3890.1.84   Friedrich Adolf Trendelenburg. (Weiss, Antonia R.) Kallmünz, 1960.

Phil 3585.9.81   Friedrich Albert Lange. (Ellissen, O.A.) Leipzig, 1891.
Phil 3585.9.80   Friedrich Albert Lange. (Ellissen, O.A.) Leipzig, 1894.
Phil 3120.6.85   Friedrich Bouterwek. Inaug. Diss. (Struck, Gustav.) Rostock, 1919.

Phil 3805.82   Friedrich Daniel Ernst Schleiermacher. (Theil.) Berlin, 1835.

Phil 5500.24   Friedrich-Ebert-Stiftung. Überwindung von Vorurteilen. 2. Aufl. Hannover, 1960.

Phil 3100.127   Friedrich Edward Beneke. (Friedrich, J.) Wiesbaden, 1898.
Phil 3100.125   Friedrich Edward Beneke. (Löwenberg, Adolf.) Berlin, 1901.

Phil 3100.80   Friedrich Edward Benekes Leben. (Granzow, O.) Bern, 1899.
Phil 310.808   Friedrich Engels e il materialismo dialettico. (Fiorani, Eleonora.) Milano, 1971.

Phil 3460.91   Friedrich Heinrich Jacobi. (Hebeisen, A.) Bern, 1960.
Phil 3460.87   Friedrich Heinrich Jacobi. (Schlichtegroll, A.H.F.) München, 1819.

Phil 3460.86A   Friedrich Heinrich Jacobi. (Schmid, F.A.) Heidelberg, 1908.

Phil 3475.1.80   Friedrich Jodl - eine Studie. (Börner, W.) Stuttgart, 1911.

Phil 3475.1.81   Friedrich Jodl sein Leben und Wirken. (Jodl, Margarete.) Stuttgart, 1920.

Phil 8125.34   Friedrich Justus Riedel. (Wilhelm, Richard.) Heidelberg, 1933.

Phil 3640.735   Friedrich Nietzsche; an illustrated biography. (Frenzel, Ivo.) N.Y., 1967.

Phil 3640.291.5   Friedrich Nietzsche, der Prophet der schenkenden Tugend. 2e Aufl. (Ackerknecht, E.) Stettin, 1926.

Phil 3640.675   Friedrich Nietzsche, ein Kampfer gegen seine Zeit. (Steiner, Rudolf.) Dornach, 1963.

Phil 3640.112   Friedrich Nietzsche, intellektuale Biographie. (Friedlaender, S.) Leipzig, 1911.

Phil 3640.404   Friedrich Nietzsche. (Blunck, R.) München, 1953.
Phil 3640.107.5   Friedrich Nietzsche. (Brandes, G.) London, 1914.
Phil 3640.107   Friedrich Nietzsche. (Brandes, G.) N.Y., 1909.
Phil 3640.292   Friedrich Nietzsche. (Copleston, F.) London, 1942.
Phil 3640.231A   Friedrich Nietzsche. (Foster, George B.) N.Y., 1931.
Phil 3640.80   Friedrich Nietzsche. (Gallwitz, H.) Dresden, 1898.
Phil 3640.227   Friedrich Nietzsche. (Hirsch, Moriz.) Stuttgart, 1924.
Phil 3640.338A   Friedrich Nietzsche. (Hofmiller, Josef.) Hamburg, 1947.
Phil 3640.125   Friedrich Nietzsche. (Hollitscher, Jakob.) Wein, 1904.
Phil 3640.87   Friedrich Nietzsche. (Kalthoff, A.) Berlin, 1900.
Phil 3640.161   Friedrich Nietzsche. (Kohler, F.P.) Leipzig, 1921.
Phil 3640.242   Friedrich Nietzsche. (Kretzer, Eugen.) Leipzig, 1895.
Phil 3640.363   Friedrich Nietzsche. (Landry, H.) Berlin, 1931.
Phil 3640.420   Friedrich Nietzsche. (Lauscher, A.) Essen, 1909.
Phil 3640.701   Friedrich Nietzsche. (Leider, Kurt.) Lübeck, 1963.
Phil 3640.106.4   Friedrich Nietzsche. (Lichtenberger, H.) Dresden, 1900.
Phil 3640.495   Friedrich Nietzsche. (Liebmann, K.) München, 1943.
Phil 3640.515   Friedrich Nietzsche. (Mehring, Franz.) Berlin, 1957.
Phil 3640.218.2   Friedrich Nietzsche. (Mügge, M.A.) London, 1908.
Phil 3640.218   Friedrich Nietzsche. (Mügge, M.A.) London, 1912.
Phil 3640.218.5   Friedrich Nietzsche. (Mügge, M.A.) N.Y., 1915?

Phil 3640.194   Friedrich Nietzsche. (Norström, Vitalis.) Stockholm, 1901.
Phil 3640.100A   Friedrich Nietzsche. (Orage, A.R.) Chicago, 1911.
Phil 3640.745   Friedrich Nietzsche. (Puetz, Heinz Peter.) Stuttgart, 1967.
Phil 3640.248   Friedrich Nietzsche. (Schrempf, Christof.) Göttingen, 1922.
Phil 3640.697   Friedrich Nietzsche. (Sørensen, V.) København, 1963.
Phil 3640.175   Friedrich Nietzsche. (Weigand, Wilhelm.) München, 1893.
Phil 3640.82.15   Friedrich Nietzsche. (Willy, Rudolf.) Zürich, 1904.
Phil 3640.455A   Friedrich Nietzsche. (Wolff, H.M.) Bern, 1956.
Phil 3640.173   Friedrich Nietzsche. (Wÿck, B.H.C.K.) Baarn, 1920.
Phil 3640.370   Friedrich Nietzsche. (Zahn, L.) Düsseldorf, 1950.
Phil 3640.89   Friedrich Nietzsche. (Ziegler, Theobald.) Berlin, 1900.
Phil 3640.214   Friedrich Nietzsche: ein Kämpfer gegen seiner Zeit. (Steiner, Rudolf.) Weimar, 1895.
Phil 3640.214.2   Friedrich Nietzsche: ein Kämpfer gegen seiner Zeit. 2e Aufl. (Steiner, Rudolf.) Dornich, 1926.
Phil 3640.80.5   Friedrich Nietzsche. Ein Lebensbild. (Gallwitz, H.) Dresden, 1898.
Phil 3640.106.5   Friedrich Nietzsche. 2e Aufl. (Lichtenberger, H.) Dresden, 1900.
Phil 3640.93.2   Friedrich Nietzsche. 3. Aufl. (Richter, R.) Leipzig, 1917.
Phil 3640.218.4   Friedrich Nietzsche. 4th ed. (Mügge, M.A.) London, 1914.
Phil 3640.118.6   Friedrich Nietzsche. 6e Aufl. (Riehl, Alois.) Stuttgart, 1920.
Phil 3640.118.7   Friedrich Nietzsche. 7e Aufl. (Riehl, Alois.) Stuttgart, 1920.
Phil 3640.185.10   Friedrich Nietzsche. 8. Aufl. (Reiner, Julius.) Berlin, 191-.
Phil 3640.285   Friedrich Nietzsche - der Deutsche! (Kniggendorf, W.) Erfurt, 1938.
Phil 3640.402   Friedrich Nietzsche als Naturphilosoph. (Mittasch, A.) Stuttgart, 1952.
Phil 3640.88.15   Friedrich Nietzsche und die Frauen seiner Zeit. (Förster-Nietzsche, E.) München, 1935.
Phil 3640.103   Friedrich Nietzsche and his new gospel. (Hamblen, E.S.) Boston, 1911.
Phil 3640.425   Friedrich Nietzsche der erkstatische Nihilist. (Obenauer, K.J.) Jena, 1924.
Phil 3640.118A   Friedrich Nietzsche der Künstler und der Denker. (Riehl, Alois.) Stuttgart, 1897.
Phil 3640.118.2   Friedrich Nietzsche der Künstler und der Denker. 2e Aufl. (Riehl, Alois.) Stuttgart, 1898.
Phil 3640.171   Friedrich Nietzsche een levensbeeld. (Duverger, A.) Amsterdam, 1913.
Phil 3640.278   Friedrich Nietzsche im Dritten Reich. (Scheuffler, G.) Erfurt, 1933.
Phil 3640.207   Friedrich Nietzsche in seinen Werken. (Andreas-Salomé, L.) Dresden, 1924?
Phil 3640.736   Friedrich Nietzsche in Selbstzeugnissen und Bilddokumenten. (Frenzel, Ivo.) Reinbek, 1968.
Phil 3640.224   Friedrich Nietzsche und das Christentum drei Vorträge. (Schian, Martin.) Görlitz, 1902.
Phil 3640.301   Friedrich Nietzsche und das Dritte Reich. (Gawronsky, Dimitry.) Bern, 1935.
Phil 3640.270.90   Friedrich Nietzsche und das Erkenntnisproblem. (Ritteleyer, F.) Leipzig, 1903.
Phil 3640.694   Friedrich Nietzsche und der französische Geist. (Wilhelm, J.) Hamburg, 1939.
Phil 3640.201   Friedrich Nietzsche und der heutige Christentum. (Odenwald, T.) Giessen, 1926.
Phil 3640.90.12A   Friedrich Nietzsche und der moderne Mensch. 2. ^ufl. (Gutersohn, U.) St. Gallen, 1945.
Phil 3640.156   Friedrich Nietzsche und der Zusammenbruch der Kultur. (Muckle, Friedrich.) München, 1921.
Phil 3640.200.15   Friedrich Nietzsche und die deutsche Zukunft. (Oehler, Richard.) Leipzig, 1935.
Phil 3640.279   Friedrich Nietzsche und die Juden. (Lonsbach, R.M.) Stockholm, 1939.
Phil 3640.372   Friedrich Nietzsche und die Religion. (Pfeie, H.) Regensburg, 1948.
Phil 3640.271   Friedrich Nietzsche und die Religion. (Rittelmeyer, F.) Ulm, 1904.
Phil 3640.200.9   Friedrich Nietzsche und die Vorsokratiker. (Oehler, Richard.) Leipzig, 1904.
Phil 3640.223   Friedrich Nietzsche und Friedrich Naumann als Politiker. (Biedenkapp, Georg.) Göttingen, 1901.
Phil 3640.235.20   Friedrich Nietzsche und Lou Salomé. (Podach, Erich F.) Zürich, 1938.
Phil 3640.190.5   Friedrich Nietzsche und Richard Wagner. (Bélart, Hans.) Berlin, 1907.
Phil 3640.314   Friedrich Nietzsche und seine Herrenmoral. (Kronenberg, M.) München, 1901.
Phil 3640.99   Friedrich Nietzsche und seine philosophischen Irrwege. (Türck, Hermann.) München, 1894.
Phil 3640.76.5   Friedrich Nietzsches Briefe an Mutter und Schwester. (Nietzscher, Friedrich.) Leipzig, 1909. 2v.
Phil 3640.190   Friedrich Nietzsches Ethik. (Bélart, Hans.) Leipzig, 1901.
Phil 3640.190.20   Friedrich Nietzsches Freundschafts-Tragödie mit Richard Wagner und Cosime Wagner-Liszt. (Bélart, Hans.) Dresden, 1912.
Phil 3640.111   Friedrich Nietzsches "Geburt der Tragödie". (Dowerg, R.) Leipzig, 1902.
Phil 3640.205   Friedrich Nietzsches Kulturphilosophie und Umwertungslehre. (Bubnoff, N. von.) Leipzig, 1924.
Phil 3640.190.11   Friedrich Nietzsches Leben. 2. Aufl. (Bélart, Hans.) Berlin, 1910?
Phil 3640.128.2   Friedrich Nietzsches Meinung über Staaten und Kriege. 2e Aufl. (Brahn, Max.) Leipzig, 1915.
Phil 3640.202   Friedrich Nietzsches Morallehre. (Kräutlein, Jonathan.) Leipzig, 1926.
Phil 3640.297   Friedrich Nietzsches Randglassen zu Bizets Carmen. (Daffner, H.) Regenburg, 1938.
Phil 3640.300   Friedrich Nietzsches Weltanschauung und ihre Gefahren. (Stein, Ludwig.) Berlin, 1893.
Phil 3640.235.25   Friedrich Nietzsches Werke des Zusammenbruchs. (Podach, Erich F.) Heidelberg, 1961.
Phil 3745.5.90   Friedrich Paulsen, sein Leben und sein Werk. (Speck, Johannes.) Langensalza, 1926.
Phil 3850.10.80   Friedrich Schlegels Philosophie Anschauungen in ihrer Entwicklung und systematischen Ausgestaltung. (Serch, Paul.) Berlin, 1905.
Phil 3805.176   Friedrich Schleiermacher, ein Lebens- und Charakterbild. (Schenkel, D.) Elberfeld, 1868.

Phil 3805.228 Friedrich Schleiermacher. (Redeker, Martin.) Berlin, 1968.

Phil 3805.20 Friedrich Schleiermacher. (Schleiermacher, Friedrich.) Langensalza, 1912.

Phil 3805.224 Friedrich Schleiermacher: the evolution of a nationalist. (Dawson, Jerry F.) Austin, 1966.

Phil 3805.223 Friedrich Schleiermachers Begründung der Pädagogik als Wissenschaft. (Suenkel, Wolfgang.) Düsseldorf, 1964.

Phil 3805.165 Friedrich Schleiermachers Psychologie. Inaug. Diss. (Geyer, Otto.) Leipzig, 1895.

Phil 3552.126 Friedrich Spie and the théodicée of Leibniz. (Lieder, F.W.C.) Urbana, 1912.

Phil 8422.7.30 Friedrich T. Vischer und das Problem der nachhegelschen Asthetik. (Oelmueller, W) Stuttgart, 1959.

Phil 3900.1.82 Friedrich Ueberweg. (Lange, F.A.) Berlin, 1871.

Phil 8587.32.117 Friedrich von Hügel. (Steinmann, J.) Paris, 1962.

Htn   Phil 3801.685*A Friedrich Wilhelm Joseph Schelling. (Pfleiderer, Otto.) Stuttgart, 1875.

Phil 3801.768.10 Friedrich Wilhelm Joseph Schelling. (Sandkuehler, Hans-Jörg.) Stuttgart, 1970.

Phil 3801.516 Friedrich Wilhelm Joseph von Schelling. (Lendi-Wolff, Christian.) Bad Ragaz, 1954.

Phil 3005.5 Friedrichs, A. Klassische Philosophie und Wirtschaftswissenschaft. Gotha, 1913.

Phil 3825.9 Friedrichs, Max. Der Substanzbegriff Spinozas neu und gegen die herrschenden Ansichten zu Gunsten des Philosophen erläutert. Inaug. Diss. Greifswald, 1894.

Phil 7140.124 Friedrichs, T. Zur Psychologie der Hypnose und der Suggestion. Stuttgart, 1922.

Phil 5592.25 Frieling, H. Der Farbenspiegel. Göttingen, 1955.

Phil 9345.11 Friend, N.E. (Mrs.). Love and you. N.Y., 1933.

Phil 8585.29 Friend, Nellie E. God and you. N.Y., 1929.

Phil 9343.5 Friendly advice to industrious persons. 4th ed. (Davis, William.) London, 1817.

Phil 9162.7 Friendly counsel for girls. (Cox, S.) N.Y., 1868.

Phil 8633.4 The friendly disputants. (Irvine, M.C.) London, 1859.

Phil 8877.47 The friendly life. (Cope, Henry F.) N.Y., 1909.

Phil 9145.5 Friends for Pennsylvania, New Jersey and Delaware. Address on some growing evils of the day. Philadelphia, 1882.

Phil 3850.27.240 Friends of Albert Schweitzer. A tribute on the ninetieth birthday of Albert Schweitzer. Boston, 1964.

Phil 530.20.75 Friends of God. (Seesholtz, A.G.) N.Y., 1934.

Phil 9220.8 Friendship; Cicero, Bacon, Emerson. Chicago, 1890.

Phil 5421.25 Friendship, love, and values. (Nesbitt, Michael.) Princeton, 1959.

Phil 9220.6 Friendship: two essays by Cicero and Emerson. N.Y., n.d.

Phil 8892.6 Friendship in death. (Rowe, E.S.) London, 1733-34.

Htn   Phil 8892.6.3* Friendship in death. (Rowe, E.S.) N.Y., 1795.

Htn   Phil 8892.6.5* Friendship in death. (Rowe, E.S.) New Haven, 1802.

Htn   Phil 8892.6.2* Friendship in death. (Rowe, E.S.) Philadelphia, 1805.

Phil 9220.11 Friendship the master-passion. (Trumbull, H.C.) Philadelphia, 1894.

Phil 1980.3.94 Friendship's odyssey. (Delisle, Françoise Roussel.) London, 1946.

Phil 8585.36 Fries, Heinrich. Die Katholische religions philosophie der Gegenwart. Heidelberg, 1949.

Phil 3260.40 Fries, J.F Lehren der Liebe des Glaubens. Heidelberg, 1823.

Phil 805.2.5 Fries, J.F. Beträge zur Geschichte der Philosophie. Heidelberg, 1819.

Phil 805.2 Fries, J.F. Die Geschichte der Philosophie. Halle, 1837-40. 2v.

Phil 3260.33A Fries, J.F. Handbuch der praktischen Philosophie oder der philosophischen Zwecklehre. Heidelberg, 1818-32. 2v.

Phil 3260.60 Fries, J.F. Handbuch der psychischen Anthropologie. Jena, 1837.

Phil 3260.39 Fries, J.F. Die mathematische Naturphilosophie. Heidelberg, 1822.

Phil 3260.49 Fries, J.F. System der Logik. Heidelberg, 1811.

Phil 3260.50 Fries, J.F. System der Logik. Heidelberg, 1837.

Phil 3260.50.5 Fries, J.F. System der Logik. 3e Aufl. Leipzig, 1914.

Phil 3260.30 Fries, J.F. System der Metaphysik. Heidelberg, 1824.

Phil 3260.31 Fries, J.F. System der Philosophie als evidente Wissenschaft. Leipzig, 1804.

Phil 3260.32 Fries, J.F. Wissen, Glaube und Ahndung. Jena, 1805.

Phil 3246.96.5 Fries, Jakob F. Fichte's und Schelling's neueste Lehren von Gott und die Welt. Heidelberg, 1807.

Htn   Phil 3801.407.5* Fries, Jakob F. Fichte's und Schelling's neueste Lehren von Gott und die Welt. Heidelberg, 1807.

Htn   Phil 3801.407* Fries, Jakob F. Reinhold, Fichte und Schelling. Leipzig, 1803.

Phil 3246.191.5 Fries, Jakob F. Reinhold, Fichte und Schelling. Leipzig, 1803.

Htn   Phil 3801.407.10* Fries, Jakob F. Von deutscher Philosophie...ein Votum für F.H. Jacobi gegen...Schelling. Heidelberg, 1812.

Phil 3260.35.2 Fries, Jakob Friedrich. Neue oder anthropologische Kritik der Vernunft. 2. Aufl. Berlin, 1935. 3v.

Phil 3260.152 Fries' Lehre von Ahndung in Asthetik. (Weiss, Georg.) Göttingen, 1912.

Phil 3260.83 Fries und Kant. v.1-2. (Elsenhans, Theodor.) Giessen, 1906.

Phil 3260.87 Die Fries'che Lehre von der Begründung. (Dubislav, W.) Dömitz, 1926.

X Cg   Phil 9495.141 Frigidity in women. (Hitschmann, E.) Washington, 1936.

Phil 3801.406.20 Frigo, Gianfranco. Matematismo e spinozismo nel primo Schelling. Padova, 1968.

Phil 5768.10.30 Frihedens filosofi. (Steiner, Rudolf.) København, 1924.

Phil 5400.130 Frijda, N.H. De betekenis van de gelaatsexpressie. Amsterdam, 1956.

Phil 5400.130.5 Frijda, N.H. Gelaat en karakter. Haarlem, 1958.

Phil 665.55 Fringe, J.W. Life everlasting and psychic evolution. London, 1919.

Phil 2070.133 The fringe of William James's psychology, the basis of logic. (McGilvary, Evander B.) n.p., 1911.

Phil 3850.18.190 Frings, Manfred S. Max Scheler. Pittsburgh, 1965.

Phil 575.286 Frings, Manfred S. Person und Dasein. Zur Frage der Ontologie des Wertseins. Den Haag, 1969.

Phil 6315.3.2 Frink, H.W. Morbid fears and compulsions, their psychology. London, 1921.

Phil 6315.3 Frink, H.W. Morbid fears and compulsions, their psychology. N.Y., 1918.

Phil 8880.28 Frins, Victor. De actibus humanis. Friburgi Brisgoviae, 1897-1911.

Phil 8610.713.40 La friponnerie laïque des pretendus esprits forts d'Angleterre. (Bentley, Richard.) Amsterdam, 1738.

Phil 5068.75 Frisch, Joseph C. Extension and comprehension in logic. N.Y., 1969.

Phil 3005.12 Frischeisen-Köhler, M. Geistige Werte. Berlin, 1915.

Phil 180.22 Frischeisen-Köhler, M. Moderne Philosophie. Stuttgart, 1907.

Phil 3850.16.95 Frischeisen-Köhler, Max. Georg Simmel. Berlin, 1919.

Phil 336.3 Frischeisen-Köhler, Max. Wissenschaft und Wirklichkeit. Leipzig, 1912.

Phil 187.23.7 Frischkopf, B. Die Psychologie der neuen Löwener-Schule. Luzern, 1908.

Phil 8880.30 Friso, Luigi. Filosofia morale. 3a ed. Milano, 1913.

Phil 2005.6.31 Friswell, J.H. Hä och der i verlden. Stockholm, 1870.

Phil 4065.92.3 Frith, I. Life of Giordano Bruno. Boston, 1887.

Phil 4065.92 Frith, I. Life of Giordano Bruno. London, 1887.

Phil 6115.34 Fritsch, Vilma. La gauche et la droite. Paris, 1967.

Phil 7054.19 Fritz, (pseud.). Where are the dead? or Spiritualism explained. Manchester, 1873.

Phil 2255.1.115 Fritz, C.A. Bertrand Russell's construction of the external world. London, 1952.

Phil 3450.19.116 Fritz, E. Die Seinsfrage bei Martin Heidegger. Stuttgart, 1950.

Phil 1182.15 Fritz, K. Pythagorean politics in southern Italy. N.Y., 1940.

Phil 1135.160 Fritz, K. von. Philosophie und sprachlicher Ausdruck. N.Y., 1938.

Phil 3625.12.80 Fritz Mauthners Kritik der Sprache. (Krieg, Max.) München, 1914.

Phil 180.45 Fritzsche, A.R. Vorschule der Philosophie. Leipzig, 1906.

Phil 3160.3.81 Fritzsche, R.A. Hermann Cohen. Berlin, 1922.

Phil 45.10 FRNM bulletin. (Foundation for Research on the Nature of Man.) Durham, N.C. 1,1965+

Phil 8955.6 Frodl, Ferdinand. Gesellschaftslehre. Wien, 1936.

Phil 525.130 Froebe-Kapteyn, Olga. Mensch und Wandlung. Zürich, 1955.

Phil 5649.15 Froeberg, Sven. Relation between magnitude of stimulus and the time of reaction. Diss. N.Y., 1907.

Phil 5245.21.7 Fröbes, Joseph. Cursus brevior psychologiae speculativae in usum scholarum. Parisiis, 1933.

Phil 5245.21 Fröbes, Joseph. Lehrbuch der experimentellen Psychologie. Freiburg, 1917. 2v.

Phil 5245.21.2A Fröbes, Joseph. Lehrbuch der experimentellen Psychologie. 2. und 3. Aufl. Freiburg, 1922-1923. 2v.

Phil 9513.12 Fröhlich, C.W. Über den Menschen und seine Verhältnisse. Berlin, 1960.

Phil 5585.56 Fröhlich, F.W. Die Empfindungszeit. Jena, 1929.

Phil 3487.15 Fröhlich, G. Immanuel Kant. Langensalza, 1890.

Phil 3850.12.85 Fröhlich, Gustaf. Dr. Karl Volkmar Stoys Leben. Dresden, 1885.

Phil 8695.4 Froehlich, J. Das Gesetz von der Erhaltung der Kraft und der Geist des Christentums. Leipzig, 1903.

Phil 5755.7 Froehlich, Joseph Anselm. Freiheit und Notwendigkeit als elemente einer einheitlichen Weltanschauung. Leipzig, 1908.

Phil 5755.8 Froehlich, Joseph Anselm. Der Wille zu höheren Einheit. Heidelberg, 1905.

Phil 3640.33 Die fröhliche Wissenschaft. (Nietzsche, Friedrich.) Leipzig, 1887.

Phil 3640.33.5 Die fröhliche Wissenschaft. (Nietzsche, Friedrich.) München, 1959.

Phil 3640.17.5 Die fröhliche Wissenschaft. (Nietzsche, Friedrich.) Stuttgart, 1956.

Phil 3246.253 Froelich, Franz. Fichtes Reden an die deutsche Nation. Berlin, 1907.

Phil 5520.49 Fröschels, E. Psychologie der Sprache. Leipzig, 1925.

Phil 5755.10 Fröschels, E. Wille und Vernunft. Leipzig, 1925.

Phil 6420.18 Froeschels, Emil. Das Stottern: assoziative Aphasie. Leipzig, 1925.

Phil 978.58 Frohnmeyer, L.J. Die theosophische Bewegung. Stuttgart, 1920.

Phil 180.12 Frohschammer, J. Einleitung in die Philosophie. München, 1858.

Phil 510.22 Frohschammer, J. Monaden und Weltphantasie. München, 1879.

Phil 8585.15 Frohschammer, J. Das neue Wissen und der neue Glaube. Leipzig, 1873.

Phil 5245.12 Frohschammer, J. Die Phantasie als Grundprincip des Weltprocesses. München, 1877.

Phil 180.12.10 Frohschammer, J. Die Philosophie als Idealwissenschaft und System. München, 1884.

Phil 180.12.5 Frohschammer, J. System der Philosophie im Umriss. München, 1892.

Phil 180.12.15 Frohschammer, J. Über das Mysterium magnum des Daseins. Leipzig, 1891.

Phil 286.6 Frohschammer, J. Über die Aufgabe der Naturphilosophie. München, 1861.

Phil 3487.4 Frohschammer, J. Ueber die Bedeutung der Einbildungskraft. München, 1879.

Phil 8695.9 Frohschammer, J. Über die Freiheit der Wissenschaft. München, 1861.

Phil 8660.8.5 Frohschammers Stellung zum Theismus. (Wüchner, J.G.) Paderborn, 1911.

Phil 6315.2.475 Froidizmat i preodoliavaneto mu v Bulgariia. (Stoev, Stoiu G.) Sofiia, 1969.

Phil 5625.75.85 Frolov, I.P. I.P. Pavlovs i ego uchenie ob uslovnykh refleksakh. Moskva, 1936.

Phil 5625.75.95 Frolov, I.P. Ivan Petrovich Pavlov. 2. izd. Moskva, 1953.

Phil 5625.75.87 Frolov, I.P. Pavlov and his school. London, 1937.

Phil 8735.55 Frolov, I.T. O prichinnosti i tselesoobraznosti v zhivoi prirode. Moskva, 1961.

Phil 5245.70 From, Franz. Menneshe kundskab. København, 1959. 2v.

Phil 5585.315.5 From, Franz. Perception of other people. N.Y., 1971.

Phil 5066.11.20 From a logical point of view. (Quine, Willard van Orman.) Cambridge, Mass., 1953.

Phil 5066.11.21 From a logical point of view. 2nd ed. (Quine, Willard van Orman.) N.Y., 1963.

Phil 7069.24.24 From agnosticism to belief. (Hill, J.A.) London, 1924.

Phil 8658.7 From agnosticism to theism. (Dole, C.F.) Boston, n.d.

Phil 5270.10 From anxiety to method in the behavioral sciences. (Devereux, George.) The Hague, 1968.

Phil 978.78 From atom to kosmos. (Plummer, L.G.) Point Loma, 1940.

Phil 2417.4A From beast-machine to man-machine. (Rosenfield, Leonora D.C.) N.Y., 1941.

Phil 2417.4.5 From beast-machine to man-machine. (Rosenfield, Leonora D.C.) N.Y., 1968.

Phil 9540.2 From bigotry to brotherhood. (Wise, J.W.) N.Y., 1953?

Phil 3625.5.45 From critical to speculative idealism. (Atlas, S.) The Hague, 1964.

Phil 165.1 From Descartes to Kant. (Smith, T.V.) Chicago, 1940.

Phil 575.10 From Epicurus to Christ...study in...personality. (Hyde, W. De W.) N.Y., 1904.

Phil 5066.259 From Frege to Gödel; a source book in mathematical logic, 1879-1931. (Van Heijenoort, Jean.) Cambridge, 1967.
Phil 3011.8.2 From Hegel to Nietzsche: the revolution in nineteenth century thought. 1st ed. (Loewith, Karl.) N.Y., 1964.
Phil 7069.00.30 From India to the planet Mars. (Flournoy, Théodore.) N.Y., 1900.
Phil 525.84 From intellect to intuition. (Bailey, A.A.) N.Y., 1932.
Phil 1821.5 From John Stuart Mill to William James. (Vogt, P.B.) Washington, 1914.
Phil 1706.1.10 From Kant to Nietzsche. (Gaultier, Jules de.) London, 1961.
Phil 974.3.15 From Luther to Steiner. (Steiner, Rudolf.) London, 1923.
Phil 6113.17 From matter to mind. (Dorman, Marcus.) London, 1895.
Phil 7054.81.19 From matter to spirit. (De Morgan, Sophia Elisabeth.) London, 1863.
Phil 6980.254 From medicine man to Freud. (Ehrenwald, Jan.) N.Y., 1956.
Phil 6685.7.5 From Mesmer to Christian Science. (Podmore, F.) N.Y., 1964.
Phil 8878.57 From morality to religion. (Burgh, W.G. de.) London, 1938.
Phil 8598.16 From old to new. (Statham, F.) London, 1872.
Phil 2750.20.110 From phenomenology to metaphysics. (Kwant, Remigius Cornelius.) Pittsburgh, 1966.
Phil 1170.11.3 From Platonism to Neoplatomism. 3rd ed. (Merlan, Philip.) The Hague, 1969.
Phil 1170.11 From Platonism to Neoplatonism. (Merlan, Philip.) The Hague, 1953.
Phil 1170.11.2 From Platonism to Neoplatonism. 2nd ed. (Merlan, Philip.) The Hague, 1960.
Phil 1506.7 From Plotinus to St. Thomas Aquinas. (Brade, W.R.V.) London, 1926.
Phil 8875.17 From poverty to power. (Allen, James.) N.Y., 1907.
Phil 1817.20 From Puritanism to Platonism in seventeenth century England. (Roberts, James Deotis.) The Hague, 1968.
Phil 8582.20 From religion to philosophy. (Cornford, F.M.) London, 1912.
Phil 1133.30 From religion to philosophy. (Cornford, F.M.) N.Y., 1957.
Phil 8598.86 From science to God. 1. ed. (Schmidt, K.) N.Y., 1944.
Phil 2905.1.177 From science to theology. (Crespy, Georges.) Nashville, 1968.
Phil 1750.455.12 From Shakespeare to existentialism. (Kaufmann, W.A.) Freeport, N.Y., 1971.
Phil 1750.455.11 From Shakespeare to existentialism. (Kaufmann, W.A.) Garden City, 1960.
Phil 8581.23 From talk to text. (Ballard, A.) N.Y., 1904.
Phil 291.7 From the closed world to the infinite universe. (Koyré, Alexandre.) Baltimore, 1957.
Phil 860.4 From the many to the one: a study of personality and views of human nature in the context of ancient Greek society, values and beliefs. (Adkins, Arthur William Hope.) London, 1970.
Phil 8655.11 From the stone age to Christianity. (Albright, W.F.) Baltimore, 1940.
Phil 5374.151 From the unconcious to the conscious. (Geney, Gustave.) N.Y., 1921.
Phil 5374.150 From the unconscious to the conscious. (Geley, Gustave.) Glasgow, 1920.
Phil 6315.2.115A From thirty years with Freud. (Reik, Theodor.) N.Y., 1940.
Phil 8593.4 From whence, what, where? (Nichols, J.R.) Boston, 1882.
Phil 6115.9 Fromentel, Henry de. Les synalgies et les synesthésies. Paris, 1888.
Phil 3487.5 Fromm, E. Das Kantbildnis der grafen Keyserling. n.p., n.d.
Phil 6315.19.30 Fromm, Erich. The dogma of Christ. 1. ed. N.Y., 1963.
Phil 6315.19.10 Fromm, Erich. Die Entwicklung des Christusdogmas. Wien, 1931.
Phil 6315.19 Fromm, Erich. Escape from freedom. N.Y., 1941.
Phil 7082.174A Fromm, Erich. The forgotten language. N.Y., 1951.
Phil 6315.19.41 Fromm, Erich. The heart of man. 1st ed. N.Y., 1968.
Phil 8880.48A Fromm, Erich. Man for himself. N.Y., 1947.
Phil 6315.19.16 Fromm, Erich. Psychoanalysis and religion. New Haven, 1971.
Phil 6315.2.235A Fromm, Erich. Sigmund Freud's mission. 1st ed. N.Y., 1959.
Phil 1695.29 Fromm, Erich. Socialist humanism. 1st ed. Garden City, N.Y., 1965.
Phil 6315.26A Fromm-Reichmann, F. Principles of intensive psychotherapy. Chicago, 1950.
Phil 6980.309 Fromm-Reichmann, Frieda. Progress in psychotherapy. N.Y., 1956.
Phil 6980.309.5 Fromm-Reichmann, Frieda. Psychoanalysis and psychotherapy. Chicago, 1959.
Phil 3808.84 Frommann, H. Arthur Schopenhauer. Jena, 1872.
Phil 5245.84 Fromme, Allan. Our troubled selves. N.Y., 1967.
Phil 5627.215 Die Frommigkeit der Gegenwart. (Gruehn, W.) Münster, 1956.
Phil 5024.1 Fromsy sosydojiokuluna göre mokhyinmensei. (Öner, Nécoti.) Ankara, 1965.
Phil 8418.13 Frondes agrestes. (Ruskin, J.) N.Y., 1875.
Phil 575.151A Frondizi, R. The nature of the self. New Haven, 1953.
Phil 735.242 Frondizi, R. What is value? La Salle, 1963.
Phil 8980.572.10 Front dushi. (Mikhalevich, Aleksandr Vl.) Kiev, 1970.
Phil 630.62 Fronteras de lo real. (Sosa López, Emilio.) Córdoba, Argentina, 1965.
Phil 8887.80 Les frontières de la morale et de la religion. Thèse. (MacGregor, G.) Paris, 1952.
Phil 5374.265 Frontières de l'homme. (Kalmar, Jacques M.) Neuchâtel, 1968.
Phil 6127.28 Frontiers in physiological psychology. (Russel, Roger.) N.Y., 1966.
Phil 5252.151 Frontiers of psychology. (Mann, J.H.) N.Y., 1963.
Phil 5252.18.37 The frontiers of psychology. (McDougall, William.) N.Y., 1934.
Phil 7069.62 Frontiers of revelation. (Banks, Frances.) London, 1962.
Phil 7069.68.25 Frontiers of the unknown: the insights of psychical research. (MacKenzie, Andrew.) London, 1968.
Phil 8660.25 Frontistès, Mario. Il est un Dieu. Padova, 1964.
Phil 336.11.5 Froschels, Emil. The human race, a study in the nature of knowledge. N.Y., 1947.
Phil 336.11 Froschels, Emil. The human race. N.Y., 1947.
Phil 5627.107.30 Frossard, Amdre. Díos existe, yo me la encontre. Madrid, 1969.
Phil 5627.180.5 Frost, Bede. The art of mental prayer. London, 1935.
Phil 6315.55 Frost, M. Erzieherliebe als Heilmittel. Bern, 1920.
Phil 1850.121 Frost, Walter. Bacon und die Naturphilosophie. München, 1927.
Phil 3487.12 Frost, Walter. Der Begriff der Urteilskraft bei Kant. Halle, 1906.
Phil 3425.256 Frost, Walter. Hegels Ästhetik. München, 1928.
Phil 180.32 Frost, Walter. Naturphilosophie. v.1. Leipzig, 1910.
Phil 3808.135 Frost, Walter. Schopenhauer als erbe Kants in der philosophischen Seelenanalyse. Bonn, 1918.
Phil 7072.2 Frost flowers on the windows. (Alberg, Albert.) Chicago, 1899.
Phil 6955.15 Frostig, Jakób. Das schizophrene Denken. Leipzig, 1929.
Phil 8406.8 Frothingham, A.L. The philosophy of art. Princeton, 1894.
Phil 8585.22 Frothingham, E.L. Christian philosophy. Baltimore, 1888-1890. 2v.
Phil 180.10A Frothingham, Ephraim L. Philosophy as absolute science. Boston, 1864.
Phil 8585.16 Frothingham, O.B. The religion of humanity. N.Y., 1873.
Phil 705.3.7A Frothingham, Octavius Brooks. Transcendentalism in New England, a history. Gloucester, Mass., 1965.
Phil 705.3.5 Frothingham, Octavius Brooks. Transcendentalism in New England. Boston, 1903.
NEDL Phil 705.3 Frothingham, Octavius Brooks. Transcendentalism in New England. N.Y., 1876.
Phil 7069.29.105 Frú Piper og Ensk-Vestraena Salarransóknarfjelagid (Sage, Michel.) Reykjavik, 1929.
Phil 8880.53 Fruchon, Pierre. Création ou consentement. Paris, 1963.
Phil 8890.10.5 Früchte der Einsamkeit. (Penn, W.) Friedensthal, 1803.
Phil 1730.18 Frühaufklärung; der Kampf Gegen den Konfessionalismus in Mittel- und Osteuropa und die deutsch-slawische Begegnung. (Winter, Eduard.) Berlin, 1966.
Phil 1112.12 Frühe griechische Denker. (Hildebrandt, Kurt.) Bonn, 1968.
Phil 3480.19.10 Frühere nocht nicht Gesammelte Kleine Schriften. (Kant, Immanuel.) Lintz, 1795.
Phil 3480.28.38 Frühschriften. (Kant, Immanuel.) Berlin, 1961. 2v.
Phil 5755.13 Fruit, John P. Determinism from Hobbes to Hume. Inaug. Diss. Leipzig, 1895.
Phil 53.5 Fruition of an eden...in honor of the fiftieth anniversary of the New York Psychoanalytics Society. (Wangh, Martin.) N.Y., 1962.
Phil 974.3.118 Fruits of anthroposophy. (Kaufmann, G.) London, 1922.
Phil 8890.10 Fruits of solitude, in reflections and maxims. (Penn, W.) N.Y., 1813.
Phil 6320.19 La frustration. (Kramer, Charles.) Neuchâtel, 1959.
Phil 5478.5 Frustration and aggression. New Haven, 1943.
Phil 5478.5.6 Frustration and aggression. New Haven, 1947.
Phil 510.128 Frutiger, P. Volonté er conscience. Genève, 1920.
Phil 5520.30.5 Fruttchey, Frank. Voice, speech, thinking. 2. ed. Detroit, Mich., 1920.
Phil 8880.16.2 Fry, Caroline. The listner. Philadelphia, 1832. 2v.
Phil 8880.16 Fry, Caroline. The listner. Philadelphia, 1833. 2v.
Phil 8880.16.5 Fry, Caroline. A word to women. Philadelphia, 1840.
Phil 8406.6F Fry, R.E. Transformations; critical and speculative essays on art. N.Y., 1927.
Phil 5525.61 Fry, W.F. Sweet madness. Palo Alto, 1963.
Phil 3640.645 Fryderyk Nietzsche. (Brzozowski, S.L.) Stanisławów, 1907.
Phil 3640.705 Fryderyk Nietzsche. (Gillner, Helmut.) Warszawa, 1965.
Phil 3640.625 Fryderyk Nietzsche w piśmiennictwie polskim lat 1890-1914. (Weiss, Tomasz.) Wrocław, 1961.
Phil 5045.14A Frye, A.M. Rational belief. N.Y., 1941.
Phil 9490.20 Frye, Northrop. The morality of scholarship. Ithaca, 1967.
Phil 5245.41 Fryer, D. An outline of general psychology. N.Y., 1936.
Phil 6978.5.5 Fryes, F.B.M. Fremdes unter uns. Meppel, 1968.
Phil 4260.118.5.2 Fubini, Mario. Stile e umanità di Giambattista Vico. 2. ed. Milano, 1965.
Phil 4260.118 Fubini, Mario. Stile i umanità di Giambattista Vico. Bari, 1946.
Phil 2496.86 Fuchs, C.E. Die Philosophie Victor Cousins. Berlin, 1847.
Phil 8955.7 Fuchs, Emil. Christliche und marxistische Ethik. Leipzig, 1958. 2v.
Phil 8880.34 Fuchs, Emil. Gut und Böse. Tübingen, 1906.
Phil 3805.88 Fuchs, Emil. Schleiermachers Religionsbegriff und religiöse Stellung zur Zeit der ersten Ausgabe der Reden, 1799-1806. Inaug. Diss. Giessen, 1900.
Phil 3246.171 Fuchs, Emil. Vom Werden dreier Denker. Tübingen, 1914.
Phil 3805.260 Fuchs, Emil. Von Schleiermacher zu Marx. Berlin, 1969.
Phil 8955.13.5 Fuchs, Josef. Moral und Moraltheologie nach dem Konzil. Freiburg, 1969.
Phil 8955.13 Fuchs, Josef. Le renouveau de la théologie morale selon Vatican II. Paris, 1968.
Phil 9495.159.2 Fuchs, Josef Jesuit. De castitate et ordine sexuali. 2nd ed. Roma, 1960.
Phil 5548.10 Fuchs, R. Gewissheit. Meisenheim am Glan, 1954.
Phil 6315.9.2 Fuchs, R.F. Phisiologische Praktikum für Mediziner. 2. Aufl. Wiesbaden, 1912.
Phil 8612.76 Fuchs, Werner. Todesbilder in der modernen Gesellschaft. Frankfurt, 1969.
Phil 177.44 Führende Denker. (Cohn, Jonas.) Leipzig, 1907.
Phil 3791.40 Führende Denker und Forscher. (Riehl, Alois.) Leipzig, n.d.
Phil 805.25 Fuelleborn, Georg Gustav. Beträge zur Geschichte der Philosophie. pt.1-12. Bruxelles, 1968. 5v.
Phil 7150.51 Fuellkrug, Gerhard. Der Selbstmord. Schwerin, 1919.
Phil 5640.13 Die fünf Sinne. (George, L.) Berlin, 1846.
Phil 5640.2.3 Die fünf Sinne des Menschen. (Bernstein, J.) Leipzig, 1875.
Phil 3640.16 Fünf Vorreden in fünf ungeschriebenen Büchern. (Nietzsche, Friedrich.) Berlin, 1943.
Phil 1050.4.17 La fuente de la vída. (Solomon Ibn-Gabirol.) Madrid, 1901.
Phil 4961.140 Fuentes de la filosofía latinoamericana. (Pan American Union.) Washington, 1967.
Phil 3487.20 Fuentes Mares, J. Kant y la evolución de la conciencia socio-política moderna. México, 1946.
Phil 4961.615 Fuentes para la historía de la filosofía en el Perú. (Mejia Valera, Manuel.) Lima, 1963.
Phil 5241.55.21 Fürst, Joseph. Grundriss der empirischen Psychologie und Logik. 21e Aufl. Stuttgart, 1928.
Phil 6990.21.5 Fürst Alexander von Hohenlohe-Schillings. Inaug. Diss. (Sebastian, L.) Kempten, 1918.
Phil 8660.20 Fuerstenberg, E. Der Selbstwiderspruch des philosophischen Atheismus. Regensburg, 1960.
Phil 8406.2 Fuerstenberg, Hans. Les sources de la création artistique. Monaco, 1962.
Phil 5075.6 Fuerstengerg, Hans. Dialectique du XX siècle. Paris, 1956.
Phil 8883.3.7 Las fuerzas morales. Obra póstuma. (Ingenieros, José.) Buenos Aires, 1926.
Phil 2250.55 Fugitive essays. (Royce, Josiah.) Cambridge, 1920.

Author and Title Listing

Phil 5627.150 — Fuglsang-Damgaard, H. Religionspsykologi. København, 1933.
Phil 6319.3 — Fugues et vagabondage. (Joffroy, A.) Paris, 1909.
Phil 3801.410 — Fuhrmans, H. Schelling's Philosophie der Weltalter. Düsseldorf, 1954.
Phil 5500.36 — Fulcher, Gordon Scott. Common sense decision-making. Evanston, Ill., 1965.
X Cg Phil 6694.3 — Full, concise instructions in mesmerism. 3. ed. (Younger, D.) London, 1887.
Phil 1915.82.2 — A full account of the late proceedings in convocation relating to Dr. Clarke's writings about the Trinity. London, 1714.
Phil 9245.119 — Full happiness. (Naguib, Mohammad.) Cairo, n.d.
Phil 5245.38 — Fuller, B. The tyranny of the mind. London, 1935.
Phil 805.8 — Fuller, B.A.G. A history of philosophy. N.Y., 1938.
Phil 1133.20A — Fuller, Benjamin A.G. History of Greek philosophy. N.Y., 1923. 3v.
Phil 7069.16.20 — Fuller, George A. Wisdom of the ages. 2. ed. Boston, 1916.
Phil 5545.29 — Fuller, H.H. The art of memory. St. Paul, Minn., 1898.
Phil 8880.20 — Fuller, J. Introductio ad prudentiam, or Directions. London, 1731.
Phil 8880.20.10 — Fuller, J. Introductio ad prudentiam, or Directions. London, 1787. 2v.
Phil 8880.20.5 — Fuller, J. Introductio ad prudentiam, or Directions. pt.2. London, 1727.
Phil 8880.17.2 — Fuller, T. The holy state and the profane state. London, 1840.
Phil 8880.17 — Fuller, T. The holy state and the profane state. London, 1840.
Phil 978.12 — Fullerton, Alex. The Wilkesbarre letters on theosophy. N.Y., n.d.
Phil 410.5 — Fullerton, G.S. Conception of the infinite. Philadelphia, 1887.
Phil 8880.35 — Fullerton, G.S. Handbook of ethical theory. N.Y., 1922.
Phil 180.17.5 — Fullerton, G.S. An introduction to philosophy. N.Y., 1906.
Phil 180.17.12 — Fullerton, G.S. An introduction to philosophy. N.Y., 1921.
Phil 3825.2 — Fullerton, G.S. On Spinozistic immortality. Philadelphia, 1899.
Phil 5649.13 — Fullerton, G.S. On the perception of small differences. Philadelphia, 1892.
Phil 180.17.2 — Fullerton, G.S. A system of metaphysics. N.Y., 1914.
Phil 286.4 — Fullerton, G.S. The world we live in. N.Y., 1912.
Phil 8880.21 — Fulliquet, G. Essai l'obligation morale. Paris, 1898.
Phil 5402.7 — Fulliquet, G. Le problème de la souffrance. Genève, 1909.
Phil 3832.12 — Fullkomlighetsbegreppet i Spinozas filosofi. Diss. (Meurling, H.) Uppsala, 1928.
Phil 6115.10 — Fullom, S.W. The human mind. v.1-2. London, 1858.
Phil 7069.29.40 — Fullwood, A.M. The song of Sano Tarot. N.Y., 1929.
Phil 6115.27 — Fulton, J.F. Physiology of the nervous system. London, 1938.
Phil 6115.27.5 — Fulton, J.F. Physiology of the nervous system. London, 1939.
VPhil 6115.27.7 — Fulton, J.F. Physiology of the nervous system. 2. ed. London, 1943.
Phil 6115.27.15 — Fulton, J.F. Physiology of the nervous system. 3. ed. N.Y., 1949.
Phil 8612.55 — Fulton, Robert Lester. Death and identity. N.Y., 1965.
Phil 8695.7 — Fulton, William. Nature and God. Edinburgh, 1927.
Phil 3246.290 — Funche, Eduard. Neues zu den politischen Anschauungen des Jungen Fichte. Hildesheim, 1915.
Phil 477.8 — La función espiritual. (Cía y Alvarez, J.M.) Madrid, 1944.
Phil 343.31 — La función social de los saberes liberales. (Millán Puellas, A.) Madrid, 1961.
Phil 180.13 — Funck-Brentano, T. Les sciences humaines: la philosophie. Paris, 1868.
Phil 1750.15 — Funck-Brentano, T. Les sophistes grecs...et contemporains. Paris, 1879.
Phil 672.4A — Funcke, D. Grundlagen der Raumwissenschaft. Hannover, 1875.
Phil 8887.41.5 — Function, feeling, and conduct. (Meakin, F.) N.Y., 1910.
Phil 585.15 — Function. (Emmet, D.M.) London, 1958.
Phil 5040.14 — The function and forms of thought. (Avey, A.E.) N.Y., 1927.
Phil 8957.3 — The function of Christian ethics. (Holt, A.E.) Chicago, 1904.
Phil 5831.3 — The function of the vibrissae in the behavior of the white rat. (Vincent, S.B.) Chicago, 1912.
Phil 6322.4 — Functional nerve disease. (Miller, Hugh C.) London, 1920.
Phil 6312.4 — Functional nervous disorders. (Core, D.E.) Bristol, 1922.
Phil 6120.16 — Functional neuroanatomy. (Krieg, Wendell J.S.) Philadelphia, 1942.
Phil 6121.6 — Die Functions-Localisation die Grosshirnrinde. (Luciani, L.) Leipzig, 1886.
Phil 6115.3.5 — The functions of the brain. (Ferrier, D.) N.Y., 1876.
Phil 6115.3.6 — The functions of the brain. 2d ed. (Ferrier, D.) London, 1886.
Phil 3640.204 — Fundament und Einheit in Friedrich Nietzsches Philosophie. (Kalina, P.E.) Leipzig, 1898.
Phil 8890.13 — Fundamenta jurisprudentae naturalis. (Pestel, F.G.) Lugdunum Batavorum, 1777.
Phil 6311.1.5 — Fundamental conceptions of psychoanalysis. (Brill, A.A.) N.Y., 1921.
Phil 179.3.8 — Fundamental concepts of modern philosophical thought. (Eucken, R.) N.Y., 1880.
Phil 184.23 — Fundamental ends of life. (Jones, R.M.) N.Y., 1924.
Phil 7069.27.40 — The fundamental facts of spiritualism. (Holms, A.C.) London, 1927.
Phil 5241.117 — Fundamental fundamentals. (Brill, Albert.) N.Y., 1955.
Phil 8582.1.5 — The fundamental ideas of Christianity. (Caird, J.) Glasgow, 1899. 2v.
Phil 176.96 — Fundamental-Philosophie. (Biunde, F.X.) Trier, 1838.
Phil 177.10 — Fundamental Philosophie. (Chalybäur, H.M.) Kiel, 1861.
Phil 4352.1.99 — Die Fundamental-Philosophie des Jaime Balmes. Inaug. Diss. (Hermkes, Maria.) Krefeld, 1919.
Phil 5374.220 — Fundamental physical theory and the concept of consciousness. (Greidanus, J.H.) Oxford, 1961.
Phil 3246.87.2 — Fundamental principle of Fichte's philosophy. (Talbot, E.B.) N.Y., 1906.
Phil 3246.87 — Fundamental principle of Fichte's philosophy. Diss. (Talbot, E.B.) N.Y., 1906.
Phil 3480.65.40 — Fundamental principles of the metaphysics of ethics. (Kant, Immanuel.) London, 1907.
Phil 177.8 — Fundamental problems. (Carus, Paul.) Chicago, 1889.

Phil 177.8.3 — Fundamental problems. 2nd ed. (Carus, Paul.) Chicago, 1891.
Phil 186.23 — The fundamental problems of metaphysics. (Lindsay, J.) Edinburgh 1910.
Phil 179.36 — The fundamental questions of philosophy. (Ewing, A.C.) N.Y., 1951.
Phil 179.36.3 — The fundamental questions of philosophy. (Ewing, Alfred Cyril.) N.Y., 1962.
Phil 5246.47.10A — Fundamental statistics in psychology and education. (Guilford, Joy Paul.) N.Y., 1942.
Phil 5246.47.12 — Fundamental statistics in psychology and education. 4. ed. (Guilford, Joy Paul.) N.Y., 1965.
Phil 188.12.80 — Fundamentalanalyse und Regionalanalyse. (Brelage, Manfred.) Köln, 1957.
Phil 3090.81 — Die Fundamentalbegriffe von Franz von Baader's Ethik. (Hamberger, Julius.) Stuttgart, 1858.
Phil 8589.16 — Fundamentalism versus modernism. (Johnson, J.W.) N.Y., 1925.
Phil 3528.40 — Fundamentalphilosophie. (Krug, Wilhelm Traugott.) Leipzig, 1827.
Phil 3528.40.5 — Fundamentalphilosophie. 2. Aufl. (Krug, Wilhelm Traugott.) Züllichan, 1819.
Phil 192.51 — Fundamentals. (Rattray, R.F.) Leicester, 1925.
Phil 8960.3 — Fundamentals of Christianity. (Kent, Charles F.) Philadelphia, 1925.
Phil 8895.3 — Fundamentals of ethics. (Urban, W.M.) N.Y., 1930.
Phil 5243.36.10 — Fundamentals of general psychology. (Dashiell, J.F.) Boston, 1937.
Phil 960.165.5 — The fundamentals of Hinduism. (Chatterjee, S.) Calcutta, 1950.
Phil 5259.19.9 — The fundamentals of human motivation. (Troland, L.T.) N.Y., 1928.
Phil 5042.24 — The fundamentals of logic. (Chapman, Frank M.) N.Y., 1933.
Phil 8597.39 — Fundamentals of modern religion. (Rattray, R.F.) London, 1932.
Phil 5243.36 — Fundamentals of objective psychology. (Dashiell, J.F.) Boston, 1928.
Phil 181.64 — Fundamentals of philosophy. (Gamertsfelder, Walter Sylvester.) N.Y., 1930.
Phil 6328.29 — Fundamentals of psychiatry. (Strecker, E.A.) London, 1944.
Phil 5243.23.5 — The fundamentals of psychology. (Dumville, B.) London, 1921.
Phil 5246.72 — Fundamentals of psychology. (Geldard, F.A.) N.Y., 1962.
Phil 5255.7 — Fundamentals of psychology. (Pillsbury, W.B.) N.Y., 1916.
Phil 5243.23.7 — The fundamentals of psychology. 2d ed. (Dumville, B.) London, 1924.
Phil 5066.32 — Fundamentals of symbolic logic. (Ambrose, Alice.) N.Y., 1948.
Phil 978.68 — Fundamentals of the esoteric philosophy. (Purucker, G. de.) Philadelphia, 1932.
Phil 341.11 — Fundamente der Erkenntnistheorie und ursssenschaftslehre. (Kauffmann, Max.) Leipzig, 1890.
Phil 5590.355 — Fundamente der Persönlichkeitspsychologie. (Waszhewitz, B.) München, 1960.
Phil 8892.72 — Fundamento constitutivo de la moral. (Rubert y Candau, José M.) Madrid, 1956.
Phil 281.11 — Fundamentum Weltanschauung. (Alt, Theodor.) Mannheim, 1920.
Phil 5938.7.10 — Funeral oration. (Follen, Charles.) Boston, 1832.
Phil 5938.7.5 — Funeral oration. v.1-3. (Follen, Charles.) Boston, 1832-1840.
Phil 930.29.5 — Fung, Yu-lan. A history of Chinese philosophy. Peiping, 1937.
Phil 930.29.8 — Fung, Yu-lan. A history of Chinese philosophy. Princeton, 1953. 2v.
Phil 930.29.10 — Fung, Yu-lan. The spirit of Chinese philosophy. London, 1941.
Phil 9150.11 — Funk, I.K. The next step in evolution. N.Y., 1902.
Phil 7069.07.21 — Funk, Isaac K. The psychic riddle. N.Y., 1907.
Phil 7060.54 — Funk, Isaac Kaufmann. The widow's mite and other psychic phenoma. N.Y., 1904.
Phil 1760.15A — Funke, Gerhard. Die Aufklärung, in ausgewählten Texten Dargestellt. Stuttgart, 1963.
Phil 2730.104 — Funke, Gerhard. Maine der Biran. Bonn, 1947.
Phil 1750.115.100 — Funke, Gerhard. Phänomenologie- Metaphysik oder Methode? Bonn, 1966.
Phil 1750.500 — Funke, Gerhard. Zur transzendentalen Phänomenologie. Bonn, 1957.
NEDL Phil 5520.15.7 — Funke, O. Innere Sprachform. Reichenberg, 1924.
Phil 6115.31 — Funkenstein, D.H. Mastery of stress. Cambridge, Mass., 1957.
Phil 3925.4.80 — Funker, F. Über Wirblichkeit und Logik; eine kritische Darlegung der Lehre Richard Wahles. Cernauti, 1924.
Phil 3270.12.40 — Funktion, Begriff, Bedeutung. (Frege, Gottlob.) Göttingen, 1962.
Phil 3270.12.80 — Funktion und Gegenstand. (Bartelett, J.M.) München, 1961.
Phil 6111.16 — Die Funktionen der Nervencentra. (Bechterew, W. von.) Jena, 1908. 3v.
Phil 5465.18 — Die Funktionen der Phantasie im wissenschaftlichen Denken. (Erdmann, Benno.) Berlin, 1913.
Phil 6115.19 — Die Funktionen des Stirnhirns. (Feuchtwanger, E.) Berlin, 1923.
Phil 5821.6 — Die Funktionen des zentralen Nervensystems. (Lewandowsky, M.) Jena, 1907.
Phil 1750.765 — Funzione delle scienze e significato dell'uomo. (Paci, Enzo.) Milano, 1963.
Phil 1845.16 — Furberg, M. Locutionary and illocutionary acts. Göteborg, 1963.
Phil 5401.1.12 — Die Furcht. (Mosso, A.) Leipzig, 1889.
Phil 8955.11 — Furfey, Paul Hanly. The morality gap. N.Y., 1968.
Phil 8955.9 — Furger, Franz. Gewissen und Klugheit in der katholischen Moraltheologie der letzten Jahrzehnte. Luzern, 1965.
Phil 1133.52 — Furley, David J. Studies in presocratic philosophy. London, 1970-
Phil 1158.38 — Furley, David J. Two studies in the Greek atomists. Princeton, N.J., 1967.
Phil 5465.120 — Furlong, E.J. Imagination. London, 1961.
Phil 5545.184 — Furlong, E.J. A study in memory. London, 1951.
Phil 4960.230 — Fúrlong Cárdiff, Guillermo. Nacimiento y desarollo de la filosofía en el Rio de la Plata, 1536-1810. Buenos Aires, 1952.
Phil 310.762 — Furman, Aleksei E. Istoricheskii materializon. Moskva, 1970.
Phil 310.705 — Furman, Aleksei E. Materialisticheskaia dialektika. Moskva, 1969.
Phil 8585.25 — Furman, R.T. What a man told his son. N.Y., 1924.

Phil 5592.20   Furrer, Walter. Die Farbe in des Persönlichkeitsdiagnostik. Basel, 1953.

Phil 336.2   Furry, W.D. The aesthetic experience. Its nature in epistemology. Baltimore, 1908.

Phil 5545.180   Furst, Bruno. How to remember. N.Y., 1944.

Phil 3640.290   Furstenthal, Achim. Maske und Scham bei Nietzsche. Diss. Basel, 1940.

Phil 5245.60   Furtado, Diogo. Vultos e problemas. Coimbra, 1957.

Phil 5865.5.25   Furth, Hans G. Piaget and knowledge. Englewood Cliffs, 1969.

Phil 5650.45   Furth, Hans G. Thinking without language. N.Y., 1966.

Phil 7054.15   Further communications from the world of spirits. (Mayer, John (Mrs.)) N.Y., 1861.

Phil 6315.1.13   Further contributions to the theory and technique of psycho-analysis. (Ferenczi, Sandor.) N.Y., 1927.

Phil 7069.23.21   A further criticism of the psychical claims concerning Glastonbury Abbey. (Wilkins, H.J.) Bristol, 1923.

Phil 6947.1.5   Further report. (Great Britain. Commissioners in Lunacy.) London, 1862.

Phil 2055.15.30   Further speculations. (Hulme, Thomas E.) Minnesota, 1955.

Phil 5822.7   A further study of the delayed reaction in the albino rat. (McAllister, W.G.) Baltimore, 1932.

Phil 90.3   Furtmair, M. Philosophisches Real-Lexikon. Augsburg, 1853.

Phil 6315.5   Furtmüller, Carl. Psychoanalyse und ethik. München, 1912.

Phil 3425.364   Fusch, Carl-Ludwig. Der Bildungsbegriff des Jungen Hegel. Weinheim, 1953.

Phil 4115.105   Fusco, Maria. Vincenzo Gioberti, critico letterario. Catania, 1940.

Phil 6675.5   Fusinieri, A. von. La dinamica molecolare. Foligno, 1866.

Phil 6980.712.10   The fusion of psychiatry and social science. (Sullivan, Harry Stack.) N.Y., 1964.

Phil 2250.113   Fuss, Peter Lawrence. The moral philosophy of Josiah Royce. Cambridge, 1965.

Phil 8624.105   The future as the presence of shared hope. N.Y., 1968.

Phil 8624.5   Pamphlet box. Future life.

Phil 8643.29   The future life. 1. ed. (Spencer, Frederick A.M.) London, 1935.

Phil 7054.5   The future life as described...by spirits. 4th ed. (Sweet, Elizabeth.) Boston, 1873.

Phil 7054.173   The future life in the light of modern inguiry. (McComb, Samuel.) N.Y., 1919.

Phil 8630.12   The future life of the good. Boston, 1839.

Phil 8585.28A   The future of an illusion. (Freud, Sigmund.) London, 1928.

Phil 8585.28.2   The future of an illusion. (Freud, Sigmund.) London, 1949.

Phil 8585.28.3   The future of an illusion. (Freud, Sigmund.) N.Y., 1928.

Phil 8658.25   The future of belief; theism in a world come of age. (Dewart, Leslie.) N.Y., 1966.

Phil 2905.1.50   The future of man. (Teilhard de Chardin, Pierre.) London, 1964.

Phil 8972.12   Future of man. (Warner, F.E.) London, 1944.

Phil 2905.1.48   The future of man. 1st American ed. (Teilhard de Chardin, Pierre.) N.Y., 1964.

Phil 3475.3.77   The future of mankind. (Jaspers, Karl.) Chicago, 1961.

Phil 2255.1.77   The future of science. (Russell, Bertrand Russell.) N.Y., 1959.

Phil 6114.20   The future of the human mind. 1st ed. (Estabrooks, George Hoben.) N.Y., 1961.

Phil 8630.13.5   Future retribution. (Farrar, F.W.) N.Y., 1885.

Phil 182.115   Fyra dygder. (Hedenjus, I.) Stockholm, 1955.

Phil 4513.3.33   Fyra föreläsningar. (Aberg, L.N.) Uppsala, 1891.

Phil 5252.140   Fysiologický základ logického myšlení. (Menert, Evžen.) Praha, 1960.

Phil 8881.1   G., W.A. The contrast: duty and pleasure, right and wrong. London, 1890.

Phil 4060.3.35   G. Allievo...per essere aggregato...Universita di Torino. (Allievo.) Torino, 1858.

Phil 4065.114   G. Bruno, F. Fiorentino, T. Mamiani. (Ferrari, Sante.) Mantova, 1887.

Phil 4065.129   G. Bruno. 1. ed. (Fraccari, G.) Milano, 1951.

Phil 6113.22   G. Heymans' psychischer Monismus. (Dorm, T.) Tübingen, 1922.

Phil 8610.940.5   G. Hovah explains. (Richberg, Donald.) Washington, 1940.

Phil 8599.25   G. Teichmüllers Philosophie des Christentums von E. Tennmann. (Teichmüller, Gustav.) Tartu, 1931.

Phil 4260.80   G.B. Vico. (Cantoni, C.) Torino, 1867.

Phil 4260.145   G.B. Vico. (Jacobelli Isoldi, Angela Maria.) Bologna, 1960.

Phil 4260.105   G.B. Vico. (Tommaseo, Niccolo.) Torino, 1930.

Phil 4260.100   G.B. Vico: volume commemorativo. (Gemelli, A.) Milano, 1926.

Phil 4260.83.2   G.B. Vico als Geschichtsphilosoph. (Klemm, Otto.) Leipzig, 1906.

Phil 4260.83   G.B. Vico als Geschichtsphilosoph. Inaug. Diss. (Klemm, Otto.) Leipzig, 1906.

Phil 4215.1.105   G.D. Romagnosi. (Credali, A.) Modena, 1935.

Phil 4215.1.01   G.D. Romagnosi. (Cusani Confalonieri, L.G.) Carate Brianza, 1928.

Phil 4215.1.103   G.D. Romagnosi. (Mistrali, Dario.) Borgo San Donnino, 1907.

Phil 3837.1   G.E. Lessing's Stellung zur Philosophie des Spinoza. (Rehorn, K.W.A.) Frankfurt, 1877.

Phil 2150.18.110   G.E. Moore; essays in retrospect. (Ambrose, Alice.) London, 1970.

Phil 187.59.85   G.E. Moore. (White, Alan R.) Oxford, 1958.

Phil 2150.18.115   G.E. Moore e la filosofia analitica inglese. (Granese, Alberto.) Firenze, 1970.

Phil 2150.18.90   G.E. Moore on the naturalistic fallacy. (Lewy, C.) London, 1964.

Phil 2150.18.85   G.E. Moore's analyses of beauty. (Brunius, Teddy.) Uppsala, 1964[1965].

Phil 2150.15.90   G.H. Mead, sociologue et philosophe. 1. ed. (Victoroff, David.) Paris, 1953.

Phil 3270.5.79   G.J.H. Feder's Lebens Natur und Grundsätze. (Feder, J.G.H.) Leipzig, 1825.

Phil 5041.43   G.J.P.J. Bolland's colleges uitgegeven door Ester vas Hunes. (Bolland, G.J.P.J.) Haarlem, 1923.

Phil 3552.471   G.W. Leibnits i russkaia kul'tura. (Chuchmarev, Vladimir I.) Moskva, 1968.

Phil 3552.110.5   G.W. Leibniz. (Bodemann, E.) Hannover, 1876.

Phil 3552.344   G.W. Leibniz. (Corsano, A.) Napoli, 1952.

Phil 3552.298   G.W. Leigniz und die China Mission. (Merkel, Franz R.) Leipzig, 1920.

Phil 3235.81.29   Gabaraev, S.S. Materializm Feierbakha. Tbilisi, 1955.

Phil 2520.430   Gabaude, Jean Marc. Liberté et raison. v. 1- Toulouse, 1970-

Phil 8881.60   Gabelli, Aristide. L'uomo e le scienze morali. Torino, 1920.

Phil 978.49.900   Gabert, Erich. Die Weltgeschichte und das Menschen-Ish. Stuttgart, 1967.

Phil 5246.21   Gabius, P. Denkökonomie und Energieprinzip. Berlin, 1913.

Phil 3488.34   Gablentz, Otto Heinrich von der. Kants politische Philosophie und die Weltpolitik unserer Tage. Berlin, 1956.

Phil 181.1.15   Gabler, G.A. De verae philosophiae erga religionem Christianam pietate. Berolini, 1836.

Phil 3425.84   Gabler, G.A. Die hegelsche Philosophie. Berlin, 1843.

Phil 3425.84.10   Gabler, G.A. Kritik des Bewusstseins. Leiden, 1901.

Phil 181.1   Gabler, G.A. Lehrbuch der philosophischen Propädeutik. Erlangen, 1827.

Phil 181.1.2   Gabler, G.A. Lehrbuch der philosophischen Propädeutik. Erlangen, 1827.

Phil 1695.23   Gaboriau, F. Novelle initiation philosophique. Tournai, 1962. 6v.

Phil 8661.25   Gaboriau, Florent. Dieu dans le débat des hommes. Paris, 1964.

Phil 8612.65   Gaboriau, Florent. Interview sur la mort avec Karl Rabner. Paris, 1967.

Phil 4006.1   Gabotto, F. L'epicureismo italiano. Piemonte, 1889.

Phil 8956.18   Gaboury, Placide. Un monde ambigu. Montréal, 1968.

Phil 1750.351.2   Gabriel, Leo. Existenzphilosophie. 2e Aufl. Wien, 1968.

Phil 1750.351   Gabriel, Leo. Existenzphilosophie von Kierkegaard bis Sartre. Wien, 1951.

Phil 5046.25.5   Gabriel, Leo. Integrale Logik. Wien, 1965.

Phil 5046.25   Gabriel, Leo. Logik der Weltanschauung. 1. Aufl. Graz, 1949.

Phil 806.15   Gabriel, Leo. Vom Brahma zur Existenz. 2. Aufl. Wien, 1954.

Phil 585.205   Gabriel, Mesmin. Le mal de la culture. Port-au-Prince, 1962.

Phil 8586.22   Gabriel, R.H. Christianity and modern thought. New Haven, 1924.

Phil 2750.19.100   Gabriel Marcel. (Cain, Seymour.) London, 1963.

Phil 2750.19.95   Gabriel Marcel. (Peccorini Letona, Francisco.) Barcelona, 1959.

Phil 2750.13.85   Gabriel Marcel et Karl Jaspers. (Ricoeur, Paul.) Paris, 1948.

Phil 2750.19.130   Gabriel Marcel et le théisme existentiel. (Widmer, Charles.) Paris, 1971.

Phil 310.540   Gabriel'ian, G.G. Marksistskaia logika kak dialektika i teoriia poznaniia. Erevan, 1963.

Phil 1075.6   Gabriel'ian, Genri. Ocherk istorii armianskoi mysli. Erevan, 1962.

VPhil 337.29   Gabryl, Franciszek. Noetyka. Vyd. 2. Lublin, 1931.

Phil 16.8   La gaceta filosófica de los Neokantianos de Mexico.

Phil 8407.40   Gacher, Dmitrii I. Studii, statii, pisma i spomeni. Sofiia, 1964.

Phil 3310.18   Gadamer, H.G. Kleine Schriften. Tübingen, 1967. 3v.

Phil 1133.47   Gadamer, Hans G. Um die Begriffswelt der Vorsokratiker. Darmstadt, 1968.

Phil 165.440   Gadamer, Hans Georg. Philosophisches Lesebuch. Frankfurt a.M., 1965- 3v.

Phil 210.30   Gadamer, Hans Georg. Le problème de la conscience historique. Louvain, 1963.

Phil 210.31   Gadamer, Hans Georg. Wahrheit und Methode. Tübingen, 1960.

Phil 6316.6   Gadelius, Bror. Det mänskliga själslivet i belysning av sinnessjukläkarens erfarenhet. Stockholm, 1921-24. 4v.

Phil 8407.17   Gadmann, E. Subjekt und Objekt des ästischen Aktes. Halle, 1904.

Phil 3640.686   Gaède, E. Nietzsche et Valéry. Paris, 1962.

Phil 5756.9   Gaede, Udo. Etwas vom Begriff des Willens in der neueren Psychologie. Berlin, 1911.

Phil 5592.202   Gaestrin, Jan Emanuel. Den svårfångade intelligensen. 2. uppl. Stockholm, 1968.

Phil 5870.10   Gästrin, Jan Emanuel. Teoretisk barnpsykologi. Stockholm, 1966.

Phil 337.12   Gätschenberger, R. Zeichen, die Fundamente des Wissens. Stuttgart, 1932.

Phil 7069.02.5   Gaffield, E.C. A celestial message. Boston, 1902.

Phil 7069.00.32   Gaffield, E.C. A series of meditations on the ethical and physical relation of spirit to the human organism. Syracuse,.N.Y., 1900.

Phil 3235.134   Gagen, Michael von. Ludwig Feuerbach. München, 1970.

Phil 8696.12   Gager, C.S. The relation between science and theology. Chicago, 1925.

Phil 5246.82   Gagey, Jacques. Analyse spectacle de la psychologie. Paris, 1970.

Phil 2477.15.115   Gagey, Jacques. Gaston Bachelard; ou, La conversion à l'imaginaire. Paris, 1969.

Phil 9495.168.25   Gagey, Roland. La révolution sexuelle. Paris, 1968.

Phil 6840.2   Gagey, Roland. La volupté dans la souffrance. Paris, 1970?

Phil 2725.19.95   Gagnebin, S. La philosophie de l'institutio. St.-Blaise, 1912.

Phil 2880.8.235   Gahamanyi, Célestin. La conception de la liberté chez Jean-Paul Sartre et chez Maurice Merleau-Ponty. Fribourg? 1967.

Phil 181.120   Gaigneron, le. Le secret de l'être. Paris, 1955.

Htn   Phil 9346.12*   Gailhard, J. The compleat gentleman. Savoy, 1678.

Phil 337.3   Gaillard, Gaston. De l'étude des phénomènes du point de vue de leur probleme particular. Paris, 1903.

Phil 4752.2.190   Gaith, Jérome. Nicolas Berdiaeff. Beyrouth, 1968.

Phil 310.330   Gak, G.M. Formy obshchestvennogo soznaniia. Moskva, 1960.

Phil 310.275   Gak, G.M. Uchenie ob obshchestvennom soznanii v svete teorii poznaniia. Moskva, 1960.

Phil 3890.1.110   Gál, Keleman. Trendelenburg Bölcseleti rendszere tekintettie. Kolozsvárt, 1895.

Phil 4710.130   Galaktionov, A.A. Istoriia russkoi filosofii. Moskva, 1961.

Phil 4710.168   Galaktionov, Anatolii A. Russkaia filosofiia XI-XIX vekov. Leningrad, 1970.

Phil 1750.378   Galamini, L. Esistenza e coesistenza. Milano, 1953.

Phil 4260.93   Galasso, Antonio. Del criterio della verita nella scienza e nella storia secondo G.B. Vico. Milano, 1877.

Phil 4080.3.300   Galati, Vito Giuseppe. Colloqui con Benedetto Croce. Brescia, 1952.

Phil 8980.416   Galdiaev, P.K. Eto ukrashaet cheloveka. Moskva, 1962.

Phil 5246.28   Gale, Harlow. Psychological studies. Minneapolis, 1900.

Phil 672.242   Gale, Richard. The language of time. London, 1968.

Htn   Phil 181.32*   Gale, Theophilus. Philosophia generalis in duas partes disterminata. London, 1676.

Phil 2250.85 Galgano, Maria. Il pensiero filosofico e morale di Josiah Royce. Roma, 1921.

Phil 623.46 Galifret, Yves. Le crépuscule des magiciens. 2. éd. Paris, 1965.

Htn Phil 4120.7.30* Galilei, Galileo. Dialogo. Fiorenza, 1632.

Phil 8407.38 Galileo as a critic of the arts. (Panofsky, E.) The Hague, 1954.

Phil 5465.65 Galimberti, A. L'imaginazione. Torino, 1954.

Phil 5585.218 Galindez, J. El papel del cuerpo en la percepción. Tucuman, 1963.

Phil 5440.12 Galippe, V. L'hérédité des stigmates de dégénérescence. Paris, 1905.

Phil 8586.56 Galitskaia, I.A. Mysli o religii. Moskva, 1962.

Phil 481.1 Galitzine, E. De l'analyse de la force. v.1-3. Paris, 1845. 2v.

Phil 5480.1 Gall, F.J. Des dispositions innées de l'âme. Paris, 1811.

Phil 5926.1.6 Gall, F.J. On the functions of the brain. Boston, 1835. 6v.

Phil 8673.6.7 Gallagher, Denis Maria. Pringle-Pattison's idea of God. Washington, D.C., 1933.

Phil 2750.11.152 Gallagher, Donald. The achievement of Jacques and Raïssa Maritain. 1st ed. N.Y., 1962.

Phil 337.24 Gallagher, K.T. The philosophy of knowledge. N.Y., 1964.

Phil 8400.35 Gallatin, A.E. Of art: Plato to Picasso. N.Y., 1945.

Phil 8586.9 Gallaudet, T.H. The class-book of natural theology. 2nd ed. Hartford, 1837.

Phil 9575.9 Gallegas Rocafull, J.M. Un aspecto del orden cristiano. México, 1943.

Phil 530.40.60 Gallegos Rocafull, J.M. La experiencia de Dios en los místicos españoles. México, 1945.

Phil 4959.220 Gallegos Rocafull, José Manuel. El pensamiento mexicano en los siglos XVI y XVII. México, 1951.

Phil 4070.1.85 Galletti, B. Critica dell'Ultima critica di Cristoforo Bonavino. Palermo, 1889.

Phil 1111.13 Galli, Dario. Il pensiero greco. Padova, 1954.

Phil 806.25 Galli, Dario. Sensei e soluzzi della filosofia europea. Bologna, 1959.

Phil 4210.180 Galli, Dario. Studi rosminiani. Padova, 1957.

Phil 8881.48 Galli, E. Alle radici della morale. Milano, 1919.

Phil 8407.26 Galli, E. L'estetica e i suoi problemi. Napoli, 1936.

Phil 181.51 Galli, Ettore. Alle soglie della metafisica. Milano, 1922.

Phil 5374.37 Galli, Ettore. Nel domonio dell' "io". Milano, 1919.

Phil 5246.33.5 Galli, Ettore. Nel mondo dello spirito. Milano, 1919.

Phil 5246.33 Galli, Ettore. Nel mondo dello spirito. Milano, 1920.

Phil 1111.14 Galli, Gallo. Corso di storia della filosofia; I sofisti. Socrate, Alcuni dialoghi platonici. Torino, 1954.

Phil 4006.9.30 Galli, Gallo. Filosofi italiani d'oggi et altri scritti. Torino, 1958.

Phil 4210.127 Galli, Gallo. Kant e Rosmini. Città de Castello, 1914.

Phil 3488.3 Galli, Gallo. Kant e Rosmini. Citta di Castello, 1914.

Phil 181.57.10 Galli, Gallo. Lineamenti di filosofia. Bologna, 1935.

Phil 4120.9.30 Galli, Gallo. Linee fondamentali d'une filosofia dello spirito. Torino, 1961.

Phil 181.57.5 Galli, Gallo. Saggio sulla dialettica della realta spirituale. Milano, 1933.

Phil 181.57 Galli, Gallo. Spirito e realta. Milano, 1927.

Phil 2520.221 Galli, Gallo. Studi cartesiani. Torino, 1943.

Phil 2840.95 Galli, Gallo. Studi storico-critici sulla filosofia di C. Renouvier. v.1-2. Gubbio, 1933-35.

Phil 181.57.15 Galli, Gallo. Tri studi di filosofia. Torino, 1956.

Phil 4120.9.35 Galli, Gallo. L'uomo nell'assoluto. Torino, 1965.

Phil 5590.480 Galli, Norberto. La caratterologia di G. Heymans e di R. LeSenne. Zürich, 1965.

Phil 3826.15 Gallicet Calvetti, Carla. Spinoza. Milano, 1968.

Phil 2225.5.93 Gallie, W.B. Peirce and pragmatism. Harmondsworth, 1952.

Phil 5545.68 Gallinger, A. Zur Grundlegung einer Lehre von der Erinnerung. Halle, 1914.

Phil 7059.18 Gallion, D.A. Know thyself, o man! Keokuk, Iowa, 1865.

Phil 2880.8.225 Gallo, Blas Raúl. Jean Paul Sartre y el marxismo. Buenos Aires, 1966.

Phil 4120.9.82 Gallo Galli. 2. ed. Torino, 1968.

Phil 3488.7.23 Gallovich, J. Kant criticismusa az Isten létéröl. Inaug. Diss. Eger, 1887.

Phil 8586.10.25 Galloway, G. Faith and reason in religion. London, 1927.

Phil 8586.10.17 Galloway, G. The philosophy of religion. N.Y., 1927.

Phil 8586.10.5 Galloway, G. Principles of religious development. London, 1909.

Phil 8586.10.9 Galloway, G. Religion and modern thought. Edinburgh, 1922.

Phil 8586.10 Galloway, G. Studies in the philosophy of religion. Edinburgh, 1904.

Phil 9495.139 Galloway, T.W. Sex and life. N.Y., 1920.

Phil 9455.20 Gallup, G.H. A guide to public opinion polls. Princeton, 1944.

Phil 4112.55.3 Galluppi, Pasquale. Considerazioni filosofiche sull'idealismo transcendentale. 3a ed. Torino, 1857.

Phil 4112.30.2 Galluppi, Pasquale. Elementi di filosofia. Bologna, 1837. 3v.

Phil 4112.30 Galluppi, Pasquale. Elementi di filosofia. v.1-2. Firenze, 1834.

Phil 4112.30.5 Galluppi, Pasquale. Elementi di filosofia. v.1-6. 3. ed. Napoli, 1834-37. 3v.

Phil 4112.30.6 Galluppi, Pasquale. Elementi di filosofia. v.2. Roma, 1963-

Phil 4112.50 Galluppi, Pasquale. Filosofia della volonta. Napofi, 1832-40. 4v.

Phil 4112.31 Galluppi, Pasquale. Introduzione allo studio della filosofia. Milano, 1832.

Phil 4112.40 Galluppi, Pasquale. Lettere filosofiche. Firenze, 1833.

Phil 4112.39.5 Galluppi, Pasquale. Lettere filosofiche. Firenze, 1842.

Htn Phil 4112.39* Galluppi, Pasquale. Lettere filosofiche. Messina, 1827.

Phil 4112.40.2 Galluppi, Pasquale. Lettere filosofiche. Napoli, 1838.

Phil 4112.40.6 Galluppi, Pasquale. Lettere filosofiche. 2a ed. Firenze, 1925.

Phil 4112.40.7 Galluppi, Pasquale. Lettere filosofiche e lezioni di logica e metafisica. Torino, 1925?

Phil 4112.41 Galluppi, Pasquale. Lettres philosophiques. Paris, 1844.

Phil 4112.45 Galluppi, Pasquale. Lezioni di logica e metafisica. v.1-4. Milano, 1845-46. 2v.

Phil 4112.75 Galluppi, Pasquale. Una memoria. Padova, 1957.

Phil 4112.35 Galluppi, Pasquale. Saggio filosofico. v.1-6. 1a ed. Milano, 1846-47. 3v.

Phil 4112.60 Galluppi, Pasquale. Sull'analisi e la sintesi. Firenze, 1935.

Phil 4112.79 Pamphlet vol. Galluppi, Pasquale. 4 pam.

Phil 4112.88 Il Galluppi. (Auria, Renata d'.) Roma, 1942.

Phil 4112.84 Galluppi e Kant nella dottrina morale. (Campari, A.) Conegliano, 1907.

Phil 4112.82 Galluppi e la filosofia italiana. (Pagano, V.) Napoli, 1897.

Phil 3640.80 Gallwitz, H. Friedrich Nietzsche. Dresden, 1898.

Phil 3640.80.5 Gallwitz, H. Friedrich Nietzsche. Ein Lebensbild. Dresden, 1898.

Phil 8956.5 Gallwitz, Hans. Das Problem der Ethik...Gegenwart. Göttingen, 1891.

Phil 585.110 Gal'perin, S.I. Kritika teorii biologizatsii cheloveka. Leningrad, 1960.

Phil 6945.7 Galt, J.M. Essays on asylums for persons of unsound mind. v.1-2. Richmond, 1850-53.

Phil 5246.45 Galt, William. Phyloanalysis. London, 1933.

Phil 5425.2.8 Galton, F. English men of science. London, 1874.

Phil 5425.2.9 Galton, F. English men of science. N.Y., 1875.

Phil 5425.2A Galton, F. Hereditary genius. London, 1869.

Phil 5425.2.6 Galton, F. Hereditary genius. London, 1925.

Phil 5425.2.5 Galton, F. Hereditary genius. N.Y., 1891.

Phil 5425.2.2 Galton, F. Hereditary genius. 2. ed. London, 1892.

Phil 5246.1.10 Galton, F. Inquiries into human faculty and its development. London, 1907.

Phil 5246.1.9 Galton, F. Inquiries into the human faculty. London, 1928.

Phil 5246.1.2A Galton, F. Inquiries into the human faculty. N.Y., 1883.

Phil 5425.2.18 Galton, F. Memories of my life. London, 1908.

Phil 5425.2.20 Galton, F. Memories of my life. N.Y., 1909.

Phil 5425.2.13 Galton, F. Noteworthy families (Modern science). London, 1906.

Phil 5440.3 Galton, F. Record of family faculties. London, 1884.

Phil 5400.82 Galvanic skin reflex and the measurement of emotions. (Wang, Ging Hsi.) Canton, China, 1930?

Phil 4210.161 Gambaro, Angiolo. Antonio Rosmini nella cultura del sus tempo. Torino, 1955?

Phil 5090.2 Gambier, J.E. Introduction...moral evidence. v.1-2. London, 1808-1818.

Phil 5545.166 Gamble, E.A.M. A study in memorising various materials by the reconstruction method. Lancaster, Pa., 1909.

Phil 9230.15 Gambling, should it be legalized? (Peterson, V.W.) Chicago, Ill., 1945.

Phil 600.26 Gamboa, Ignacio. El positivismo filosófico. Mérida, 1899.

Phil 806.30 Gambra Ciudad, R. Historia sencilla de la filosofia. Madrid, 1961.

Phil 623.48 Gambra Ciudad, Rafael. El silencio de Dios. Madrid, 1968.

Phil 6128.47.7 The game of life and how to play it. 7th ed. (Shinn, F.S. (Mrs.).) N.Y., 1927.

Phil 5043.8 The game of logic. (Dodgson, C.L.) London, 1886.

Phil 5242.16 The game of mind. (Campbell, P.A.) N.Y., 1913.

Phil 1885.87 Gamertsfelder, W.S. Thought, existence and reality as viewed by F.H. Bradley and B. Bosanquet. Columbus, 1920.

Phil 181.64 Gamertsfelder, Walter Sylvester. Fundamentals of philosophy. N.Y., 1930.

Phil 6980.685 Games analysts play. (Shepard, Martin.) N.Y., 1970.

Phil 600.37 Den gamla tiden inför den nya. (Nyström, Anton.) Stockholm, 1875.

Phil 5421.20.90 Gamm, Hans-Jochen. Aggression und Friedensfähigkeit in Deutschland. München, 1968.

Phil 8598.49 Gammal och my religiositet. (Segerstedt, T.K.) Stockholm, 1915.

Phil 3890.9.90 Gamper, J. Paul Vital Ignoz Troxlers Leben und Philosophie. Diss. Bern, 1907.

Phil 7009.210 Gandee, Lee R. Strange experience; the autobiography of a hexenmeister. Englewood Cliffs, 1971.

Phil 960.14.5 Gandhi, V.R. Speeches and writings of the Karma philosophy. Bombay, 1913.

Phil 70.99 Gandillac, Maurice Patronnier de. Entretiens sur les notions de genése et de structure. Paris, 1965.

Phil 4080.3.350 Gandolfo, Antonio. Benedetto Croce, critico dei contemporanei. Padova, 1968.

Phil 978.120 Ganesha. (Leevwen, A.J.H. van.) Amsterdam, 1969.

Phil 3310.2.80 Ganewa, R. Die Erkenntnistheorie von Carl Göring. Inaug. Diss. Heidelberg, 1910.

Phil 3246.303 Der Gang des Denkens in der Philosophie Johann Gottlieb Fichtes. (Brueggen, Michael.) München, 1964.

Phil 1707.13 Der Gang des Geistes. (Heiss, R.) Bern, 1948.

Phil 5649.18 Gang und Charakter. (Bogen, H.) Leipzig, 1931.

Phil 5058.80 Gangheitliche Logik. v.1-2. (Spann, Othmar.) Salzburg, 1957.

Phil 5068.67 Ganguli, Hermanta Kumar. Philosophy of logical construction. 1st ed. Calcutta, 1963.

Htn Phil 2520.148* Ganguli, S. Descartes. Bombay, 1900.

Phil 3925.16.190 Ganguly, Sachindranath. Wittgenstein's Tractatus, a preliminary. Santiniketan, 1968.

Phil 5374.159 Ganne De Beaucoudrey, E. Perception et courant de conscience. Thèse. Paris, 1936.

Phil 8615.11 Gannett, W.C. The religion of the "ethical culture societies." Chicago, 1885.

Phil 181.160 Gans, Abraham. Pathologie en therapie der filosofie. Wassenaar, 1968.

Phil 3826.6 Gans, M.E. Spinozismus. Wien, 1907.

Phil 181.42 Gans, Max E. Zur Psychologie der Begriffsmetaphysik. Wien, 1914.

Phil 9150.30 Gantz, K.F. The beginnings of Darwinian ethics: 1859-1871. Chicago, 1939.

Phil 3552.125 Ganz, Hans. Das Unbewusste bei Leibniz...Theorien. Zürich, 1917.

Phil 6310.1.91 Ganz, M. Adlers psykologi. Stockholm, 1939.

Phil 6310.1.90 Ganz, M. La psychologie d'Alfred Adler. Neuchâtel, 1935.

Phil 197.26 Das Ganze der Philosophie und ihr Ende. (Wahle, R.) Wien, 1896.

Phil 178.22.5 Das Ganze und die Summe. (Driesch, H.) Leipzig, 1921.

Phil 165.12 Die Ganzheit in Philosophie und Wissenschaft. (Heinrich, Walter.) Wien, 1950.

Phil 185.51 Ganzheit und Form. (Krueger, F.) Berlin, 1932.

Phil 730.34 Ganzheit und Gemeinschaft. (Pichler, Hans.) Wiesbaden, 1967.

Phil 5058.82 Ganzheitliche Logik. 2. Aufl. (Spann, Othmar.) Graz, 1971.

Phil 5258.192 Ganzheitspsychologie::Grundlagen. (Sander, F.) München, 1962.

Phil 5262.49 Ganzheitspsychologie und Strukturtheorie. (Wellek, A.) Bern, 1955.

Phil 5286.7 Ganzheitspsychologie und Strukturtheorie. 2. Aufl. (Wellek, Albert.) Berlin, 1969. 4v.

Phil 3549.8.115 Ganzoni, Werner. Die neue Schau der Seele. Wien, 1957.

Phil 3160.12.85 Gaona, Francisco. Das Raumproblem in Cassirers Philosophie der Mythologie. Tübingen, 1965.

Phil 2733.87 Gaonach, J.M. La théorie des idées dans la philosophie de Malebranche. Brest, 1908.

Phil 3450.11.240 Gaos, J. Introducción a la fenomenología. México, 1960.

Phil 1111.7 Gaos, José. Antologia filosofica; la filosofia griega. México, 1940.

Phil 3488.40 Gaos, José. Las críticas de Kant. Caracas, 1962.

Phil 181.132 Gaos, José. De la filosofia. Mexico, 1962.

Phil 1706.12 Gaos, José. Filosofia contemporanea. Caracas, 1962.

Phil 181.104 Gaos, José. Filosofia de la filosofia e historia de la filosofia. México, 1947.

Phil 4959.215 Gaos, José. Filosofía mexicana de nuestros días. México, 1954.

Phil 1750.776 Gaos, José. Museo de filósofos. 1. ed. México, 1960.

Phil 4957.10 Gaos, José. Pensamiento de lengua española. México, 1945.

Phil 4307.1 Gaos, José. Pensamiento español. México, 1945.

Phil 3625.7.90 Gaquoin, Karl. Die transcendentale Harmonie bei Ernst Marcus. Wiesbaden, 1907.

Phil 9346.15 Garabedian, John H. Eastern religions in the electric age. N.Y., 1969.

Phil 8696.27 Garadzha, Vikton I. Neotomizm. Razum. Nauka. Moskva, 1969.

Phil 5246.77 Garan, D.G. The paradox of pleasure and relativity. N.Y., 1963.

Phil 5246.77.5 Garan, D.G. Relativity for psychology. N.Y., 1968.

Phil 8980.417 Garaudy, R. Qu'est-ce que la morale marxiste. Paris, 1963.

Phil 337.16 Garaudy, R. La théorie matérialiste de la connaissance. 1. ed. Paris, 1953.

Phil 3425.572 Garaudy, Roger. Dieu est mort; étude sur Hegel. Paris, 1962.

Phil 310.643.1 Garaudy, Roger. Marxism in the twentieth century. London, 1970.

Phil 310.643 Garaudy, Roger. Marxisme du XXe siècle. Paris, 1966.

Phil 337.16.5 Garaudy, Roger. Die materialistische Erkenntnistheorie. Berlin, 1960.

Phil 2406.3 Garaudy, Roger. Perspectives de l'homme. 2e éd. Paris, 1960.

Phil 2880.8.142 Garaudy, Roger. Questions à Jean Paul Sartre. Paris, 1960.

Phil 3425.612 Garauly, Roger. Le problème Hégélien. Paris, 196-.

Phil 5627.25 Garban, Louis. Deviations morbides du sentiment religieux. Paris, 1911.

Phil 960.4 Garbe, R. Die Samkhya - Philosophie. Leipzig, 1894.

Phil 960.4.5 Garbe, Richard. The philosophy of ancient India. Chicago, 1897.

Phil 3488.16 Garbeis, F.W. Das Problem des Bewusstseins in der Philosophie Kants. Wien, 1924.

Phil 5046.24 Garciá, David. Introducció a la logística. Barcelona, 1934. 2v.

Phil 9590.3 García, E.A. Negación de la nueva verdad. Buenos Aires, 1929.

Phil 9070.36 Garcia, Garia. Modelando el porvenir. Lima, 1944.

Phil 6990.48 García Aceituno, José Luis. Esquípulas. 1. ed. Jalapa, 1940.

Phil 6990.48.2 García Aceituno, José Luis. Esquípulas. 2. ed. Guatemala? 1954.

Phil 4961.65 García Bacca, J.D. Antología del pensamiento filosófico en Colombia. Bogotá, 1955.

Phil 181.128 Garcia Bacca, J.D. Elementos de filosofia. 2. ed. Caracas, 1961.

Phil 4357.3.32 Garcia Bacca, J.D. Inoitacion a filosofar. v.1-2. Mexico, 1940-42.

Phil 181.128.5 Garcia Bacca, J.D. Introduccion literaria a la filosofia. 2. ed. Caracas, 1964.

Phil 181.128.10 Garcia Bacca, J.D. Metafisica natural estabilizada y problematica. Mexico, 1963.

Phil 1111.5 Garcia Bacca, J.D. Sobre estetica griega. Mexico, 1943.

Phil 287.6 Garcia Bacca, Juan D. Tipos historicos del filosofar físico. Tucuman, 1941.

Phil 4961.915 García Bacca, Juan David. Antología del pensamiento filosófico venezolano. Caracas, 1954.

Phil 3450.19.215 Garcia Bacca, Juan David. Comentarios a la esencia de la poesia de Heidegger. Caracas, 1956.

Phil 806.37 García Bacca, Juan David. Siete modelos de filosofar. Venezuela, 1941.

Phil 3640.296 Garcia Barcena, R. Responso heroico. La Habana, 1943.

Phil 181.135 Garcia Calderon, Francisco. Ideologías. Paris, 1918.

Phil 4352.1.120 Garcia de Los Santos, B. Vida de Balmes. Madrid, 1848.

Phil 5258.68.30 Garcia de Onrubia, Luis Felipe. Ensayo sobre la teoria. Buenos Aires, 1949.

Phil 4357.10 García Lahiguera, Fernando. La libertad. Valencia, 1961.

Phil 720.65 García López, Jesús. El valor de la verdad y otros estudios. Madrid, 1965.

Phil 8881.70 García Máynez, E. Etica: etica empirica; etica de bienes; etica formal; etica valorativa. México, 1944.

Phil 2475.1.267 García Morente, M. La filosofia de Henri Bergson. Madrid, 1917.

Phil 181.80.10 Garcia Morente, Manuel. Ejercicios espirituales. Madrid, 1961.

Phil 181.80.5 Garcia Morente, Manuel. Ensayos. Madrid, 1945.

Phil 181.80 Garcia Morente, Manuel. Lecciones preliminares de filosofia. Tucuman, 1938.

Phil 8407.42 Garcia Prado, Carlos. Teorías estéticas. Madrid, 1962.

Phil 181.3 Garcia Tuduri, Mercedes. Introducción a la filosofía. 4. ed. Habana, 1962.

Phil 5046.32 Garcia Tuduri, R. Lógica. 7. ed. Habana, 1959.

Phil 6316.9 Gard, W.L. Some neurological and psychological aspects of shock. Thesis. n.p., 1908.

Phil 9420.8 Gardair, J. Philosophie de Saint Thomas. Les passions et la volonté. Paris, 1892.

Phil 9560.12 Gardair, J. Philosophie de Saint Thomas. Les passions et la volonté. Paris, 1901.

Phil 337.6 Gardair, M.J. Philosophie de Saint Thomas. La connaissance. Paris, 1895.

Phil 665.52 Gardeil, A. La structure de l'âme et l'expérience mystique. Paris, 1927. 2v.

Phil 400.90 Gardeil, H.D. Les étapes de la philosophie idéaliste. Paris, 1935.

Phil 5046.5 Garden, F. An outline of logic or the use of teachers and students. 2nd ed. London, 1871.

Phil 5756.14 Gardet, Louis. La mesure de notre liberté. Tunis, 1946.

Phil 1020.28 Gardet, Louis. La pensée religieus d'Avicenne. Paris, 1951.

Phil 525.165 Gardet, Louis. Thèmes et textes mystiques. Paris, 1958.

Phil 8696.3 Gardiner, F. Occasional papers. Middletown, Conn., 1881. 3 pam.

Phil 5400.93.1 Gardiner, Harry Norman. Feeling and emotion. Westport, 1970.

Phil 4073.95 Gardner, E.G. Tommaso Campanella and his poetry. Oxford, 1923.

Phil 5195.2 Gardner, Martin. Logic machines and diagrams. N.Y., 1958.

Phil 8520.22 Gardner, P. The growth of Christianity. London, 1907.

Phil 8586.32 Gardner, P. Modernity and the churches. London, 1909.

Phil 7054.45.50 Gardy, Louis. Le médium D.D. Home. Genève, 189-.

Phil 4210.84 Garelli, V. Antonio Rosmini. Torino, 1861.

Phil 8881.46 Garello, Luigi. Levjathan; ricerche sulla natura morale dell'uomo. Torino, 1910.

Phil 3808.233 Garewicz, Jan. Rozdroza pesymizmu. Wyd. 1. Wroctaw, 1965.

Phil 3808.250 Garewicz, Jan. Schopenhauer. Wyd. 1. Warszawa, 1970.

Phil 181.35 Garfein-Garski, Stan. Ein neuer Versuch über das Wesen der Philosophie. Heidelberg, 1909.

Phil 6316.20 Garfield, Sol. Introductory clinical psychology. N.Y., 1961.

Phil 3925.16.170 Gargani, Aldo Giorgio. Linguaggio di esperienza in Ludwig Wittgenstein. Firenze, 1966.

Phil 8407.28 Gargiulo, A. Scritti di estetica. Firenze, 1952.

Phil 4006.6.30 Garilli, G. La crisi dell'immanentismo. Palermo, 1953.

Htn Phil 9030.5.5* Garimberto, G. Della fortuna libri sei. Vinetia, 1550.

Phil 1511.6 Garin, E. Dal medioeno al rinascimento. Firenze, 1950.

Phil 1750.625 Garin, Eugenio. Bilancio della fenomenologia. Padova, 1960.

Phil 4006.5.55 Garin, Eugenio. Cronache di filosofia italiana, 1900-1943. Bari, 1966.

Phil 4006.5.45 Garin, Eugenio. Cronache di filosofia italiana. Bari, 1955.

Phil 4006.5.50 Garin, Eugenio. Cronache di filosofia italiana. 2. ed. Bari, 1959.

Phil 1730.34 Garin, Eugenio. Dal rinascimento all'illuminismo. Studi e ricerche. Pisa, 1970.

Phil 4006.5.33 Garin, Eugenio. Filosofi italiani del quattro cento. Firenze, 1942.

Phil 4006.5.40 Garin, Eugenio. La filosofia. v.1-2. Milano, 1947.

Phil 181.125 Garin, Eugenio. La filosofia come sapere storico. Bari, 1959.

Phil 4195.86 Garin, Eugenio. Giovanni Pico della Mirandola. Firenze, 1937.

Phil 4195.88 Garin, Eugenio. Giovanni Pico della Mirandola. Parma? 1963.

Phil 4006.5.38 Garin, Eugenio. Italian humanism. Oxford, 1965.

Phil 4006.5.35 Garin, Eugenio. Der italienische Humanismus. Bern, 1947.

Phil 4006.5.60 Garin, Eugenio. Storia della filosofia italiana. Torino, 1966. 3v.

Phil 1540.50A Garin, Eugenio. Studi sul platonismo medievale. Firenze, 1958.

Phil 4006.5.37 Garin, Eugenio. L'umanesemio italiano. Bari, 1952.

Phil 1540.21 Garin, Pierre. La théorie de l'idée suivant l'école thomiste. Thèse. Bruges, 1932.

Phil 2520.189 Garin, Pierre. Thèses cartésiennes et thèses thomistes. Thèse. Bruges, 193-.

Phil 4210.159 Garioni Bertolatti, G. Antonio Rosmini. Torino, 1957.

Phil 7069.36.5 Garland, Hamlin. Forty years of psychic research; a plain narrative of fact. N.Y., 1936.

Phil 7069.08.20 Garland, Hamlin. The shadow world. N.Y., 1908.

Phil 5520.29 Garlanda, Fedérico. La filosofia delle parole. 3. ed. Roma, 1905?

Phil 7084.4 Garma, Angel. Psicoanálisis de los sueños. Buenos Aires, 1940.

Phil 5590.456 Garmonicheskii chelovek. (Akademiia Nauk SSSR. Institut Filosofii.) Moskva, 1965.

Phil 5246.76A Garner, W.R. Uncertainty and structure as psychological concepts. N.Y., 1962.

Phil 8586.47 Garnett, A.C. A realistic philosophy of religion. Chicago, 1942.

Phil 8831.10 Garnett, Arthur. Ethics. N.Y., 1960.

Phil 5816.9 Garnett, Arthur C. Instinct and personality. London, 1928.

Phil 5246.42 Garnett, Arthur C. The mind in action. London, 1931.

Phil 5246.42.5 Garnett, Arthur C. The mind in action. N.Y., 1932.

Phil 735.111 Garnett, Arthur C. Reality and value. New Haven, 1937.

Phil 5585.231 Garnett, Arthur Campbell. The perceptual process. London, 1965.

Phil 8881.69 Garnett, C.B. Wisdom in conduct. N.Y., 1940.

Phil 3488.42 Garnett, Christopher Broune. The Kantian philosophy of space. Port Washington, N.Y., 1965.

Phil 2240.80 Garnier, A. Critique de la philosophie de Thomas Reid. Paris, 1840.

Phil 1145.8 Garnier, A. De la morale dans l'Antiquité. Paris, 1865.

Phil 5246.2 Garnier, A. La psychologie et la phrénologie comparées. Paris, 1839.

Phil 5246.2.10 Garnier, A. Traite des facultés de l'âme. Paris, 1865. 3v.

Phil 6956.7 Garnier, P.E. Des idées de grandeur dans le délire des persécutions. Paris, 1878.

Phil 3640.712 Garnier, Paul-Louis. Réflexions sur Nietzsche. Paris, 1902.

Phil 2750.11.220 Garofalo, Gaetano. Jacques Maritain. Saggio critico. Bari, 1969.

Phil 410.78 Garofalo, Lydia. Il problema dell'infinito dal rinascimento a Kant. Napoli 1931.

Phil 4080.3.390 Garosci, A. Il pensiero politico di Benedetto Croce. Torino, 1962.

Phil 5816.12 Garratt, G. Marvels and mysteries of instinct. 3rd ed. London, 1862.

Phil 5246.3 Garreau, P. Essai sur les bases ontologiques...l'homme. Paris, 1949.

Phil 5850.211 Garrett, A.M. Interviewing, its principles and methods. N.Y., 1942.

Phil 7069.49 Garrett, Eileen Jeanette Lyttle. Adventures in the supernormal. N.Y., 1949.

Phil 7069.43 Garrett, Eileen Jeanette Lyttle. Awareness. N.Y., 1943.

Phil 7055.211 Garrett, Eileen Jeanette Lyttle. Many voices; the autobiography of a medium. N.Y., 1968.

Phil 7069.39.19 Garrett, Eileen Jeanette Lyttle. My life as a search for the meaning of mediumship. London, 1939.

Phil 7069.50 Garrett, Eileen Jeanette Lyttle. The sense and nonsense of prophecy. N.Y., 1950.

Phil 7069.41.7 Garrett, Eileen Jeanette Lyttle. Telepathy in search of a lost faculty. N.Y., 1941.

Phil 5246.29.6 Garrett, Henry E. General psychology. 2. ed. N.Y., 1961.

Phil 5216.2 Garrett, Henry E. Great experiments in psychology. N.Y., 1930.

Phil 5216.2.5 Garrett, Henry E. Great experiments in psychology. N.Y., 1941.

Phil 5246.29.5 Garrett, Henry E. Psychology. N.Y., 1950.

Phil 5246.29 Garrett, Henry E. A study of the relation of accuracy to speed. N.Y., 1922.

Phil 6676.9 Garrett, Thomas L. Hypnotism. N.Y., 1934.
Phil 8661.5 Garrigou-Lagrange, R. Dieu, son existence et sa nature. Paris, 1914.
Phil 8661.5.5 Garrigou-Lagrange, R. God, His existence and His nature. St. Louis, 1934-36. 2v.
Phil 8735.19 Garrigou-Lagrange, Reginaldo. Le réalisme du principe de finalité. Paris, 1932.
Phil 5585.37 Garrison, W.A. The effect of varied instructions on the perception of distance in terms of arm-movement. Ithaca, 1924.
Phil 8881.24 Garrison, W.P. Parables for school and home. N.Y., 1897.
Phil 2805.470 Garrone, Gabriel Marie. Ce que croyait Pascal. Tours, 1969.
Phil 3488.22 Gartelmann, Henri. Sturz der Metaphysik als Wissenschaft. Berlin, 1893.
Phil 5651.77 Garten, S. Die Bedeutung unserer Sinne für die Orientierung in Luftraume. Leipzig, 1917.
Phil 181.145 Garulli, Enrico. Esperienza e metafisica nella filosofia moderna. Urbino, 1963.
Phil 3450.19.505 Garulli, Enrico. Problemi dell'Ur-Heidegger. Urbino, 1969.
Phil 3826.14 Garulli, Enrico. Saggi su Spinoza. Urbino, 1958.
Phil 1135.153 Garve, C. Legendorum philosophorum veterum praecepta nonnulla et exemplum. Leipzig, 1770.
Phil 8881.52 Garve, Christian. Eigene Betrachtungen über die allgemeinsten Grundsätze der Sittenlehre. Bresslau, 1798.
Phil 8831.3 Garve, Christian. Übersicht der vornehmsten Principien der Sittenlehre. Breslau, 1798.
Phil 7080.50 Garvey, Chester R. Activity of young children during sleep. Minneapolis, 1939.
Phil 5246.44 Garvey, M.A. A manual of human culture. London, 1866.
Phil 8881.75 Garvin, Lucius. A modern introduction to ethics. Boston, 1953.
Phil 806.8 Gasc-Desfosses, E. Études sur les auteurs philosophiques: réponses aux questions. 3e éd. Paris, 1909.
Phil 806.12 Gasiorowski, W. Historja filozofji. Sandomierz, 1928.
Phil 8696.18 Gaskell, A. (Mrs.). Whence? Whither? Why? N.Y., 1939.
Phil 5520.2 Gaskell, J. Sense and sound. Philadelphia, 1854.
Phil 5246.49 Gaskell, John. New elements from old subjects presented as the basis for a science of mind. Philadelphia, 1874.
Phil 6116.17 Gaskell, Walter H. The involuntary nervous system. London, 1916.
Phil 5238.195 Gaskill, H.S. Counterpoint. N.Y., 1963.
Phil 510.1.50 Gasman, Daniel. The scientific origins of National Socialism: Social Darwinism in Ernst Haeckel and the German Monist League. London, 1971.
Phil 9245.3 Gasparin, A.E. Le bonheur. Paris, 1874.
Phil 9075.3.5 Gasparin, A.E. La conscience. 3. éd. Paris, 1873.
Phil 9166.4 Gasparin, A.E. La famille. Paris, 1867. 2v.
Phil 9166.4.5 Gasparin, A.E. Le mariage au point de vue chrétien. 2. éd. Paris, 1844.
Phil 7054.164 Gasparin, Agénov. Science vs. modern spiritualism. N.Y., 1857. 2v.
Phil 9520.1 Gasparin, V.B. Human sadness. London, 1864.
Phil 3826.1 Gaspary, A. Spinoza und Hobbes. Berlin, 1873.
Phil 8956.1A Gass, F.W.H.J. Geschichte der christlichen Ethik. Berlin, 1881-87. 2v.
Phil 9430.30 Gass, W. Optimismus und Pessimismus. Berlin, 1876.
Phil 3850.16.105 Gassen, Kurt. Zuch des Dankes an G. Simmel. Berlin, 1958.
Phil 2610.7 Gassendi, P. Abregé de la philosophie de Gassendi. 2e ed. v.1-7. Lyon, 1684. 6v.
Htn Phil 2610.7.5* Gassendi, P. Abregé de la philosophie de Mr. Gassendi. Paris, 1675.
NEDL Phil 2610.15 Gassendi, P. Institutio logica, et Philosophiae Epicuri syntagma. London, 1668.
Phil 2610.1 Gassendi, P. Opera omnia. Florentiae, 1727. 6v.
Htn Phil 2610.35* Gassendi, P. Three discourses of happiness, virtue and liberty. London, 1699.
Htn Phil 2520.182* Gassendi, Pierre. Disquisitio metaphysica. Amsterodami, 1644.
Phil 1750.166.160 Gastão, Manuel M. Humanismos e suas diversas interpretações. Lisboa, 1963.
Phil 8881.51 Gasté, Maurice de. Réalités imaginatives. Paris, 1911.
Phil 4357.5 Gastelum, B.J. En el reino de las sombras; Maria de la Luz. Mexico, 1937.
Phil 181.58 Gastelum, B.J. Inteligencia y simbolo. Madrid, 1927.
Phil 4357.2.79 Pamphlet box. Gastelum, B.J.
Phil 9035.28 Gaston, William. An address delivered before the American Whig and Cliosophic Societies. 2d ed. Princeton, 1835.
Phil 2477.15.115 Gaston Bachelard; ou, La conversion à l'imaginaire. (Gagey, Jacques.) Paris, 1969.
Phil 2477.15.85 Gaston Bachelard. (Dagognet, François.) Paris, 1965.
Phil 2477.15.95 Gaston Bachelard et les élements. (Mansuy, Michel.) Paris, 1969.
Phil 8586.1 Gastrell, F. The certainty and necessity of religion. London, 1697.
Phil 8586.1.2 Gastrell, F. The certainty and necessity of religion. London, 1703.
Phil 8595.4.113 Gastrow, Paul. Pfleiderer als Relionsphilosophie. Berlin, 1913.
Phil 9230.6 Gataker, T. Antithesis de sorte. Lugdunum Batavorum, 1659-60. 3 pam.
Htn Phil 9230.4.5* Gataker, T. Of the nature and use of lots. London, 1619.
Htn Phil 9230.4* Gataker, T. Of the nature and use of lots. London, 1627.
Phil 8414.15.2 The gate of appreciation. (Noyes, Carleton E.) Boston, Mass., 1907.
Phil 7069.20.40 The gate of remembrance. 3. ed. (Bond, Frederick B.) Boston, 1920.
Phil 7069.20.42 The gate of remembrance. 4th ed. (Bond, Frederick B.) N.Y., 1921.
Phil 8407.39 Gatecki, L. Problematyka estetiki. Kraków, 1962.
Phil 5246.36 Gates, Arthur I. Elementary psychology. N.Y., 1925.
Phil 5246.30 Gates, G.S. Individual differences as affected by practice. N.Y., 1922.
Phil 7082.20 Gates of horn and ivory. (Hill, Brian.) N.Y., 1968.
Phil 978.49.25 The gates of knowledge. (Steiner, R.) Chicago, Ill., 1922.
Phil 6480.194 The gates of the dream. (Roheim, Geza.) N.Y., 1952.
Phil 5640.16 The gateways of knowledge. (Dell, J.A.) Cambridge, 1912.
Phil 365.57 Gatewood, Willard B. Preachers, pedagogues, and politicians. Chapel Hill, 1966.
Phil 181.2.5 Gatien-Arnoult, A. Eléments de philosophie. Toulouse, 1864.
Phil 181.2 Gatien-Arnoult, A. Programe d'un cours de philosophie. Paris, 1835.
Phil 5046.6.1 Gatry, A.J.A. Logic. LaSalle, Ill., 1944.
Phil 5046.6.2 Gatry, A.J.A. Philosophie. Logique. Paris, 1855. 2v.

Phil 5876.30 Gattegno, Caleb. The adolescent and his will. N.Y., 1971.
Phil 181.78 Gattell, B.B. The light of the mind. Philadelphia, 1938.
Phil 585.240 Gattgno, Caleb. Conscience de le conscience. Neuchâtel, 1967.
Phil 181.68 Gatti, Stanislao. Scritti varii di filosofia e letteratura. Napoli, 1861. 2v.
Phil 3488.47 Gattulo, Mario. Categoria e oggetto in Kant. 1. ed. Firenze, 1968.
Phil 6115.34 La gauche et la droite. (Fritsch, Vilma.) Paris, 1967.
Phil 6117.52 Les gauchers. (Hécaen, Henry.) Paris, 1963.
Phil 5592.105 Gauchet, F. La caracterologie d'Heymans. Paris, 1959.
Phil 8050.51 Gauckler, T.G. Le beau et son histoire. Paris, 1873.
Htn Phil 9346.9* Gauden, John. A discourse of auxiliary beauty. n.p., 1656.
Phil 5853.4 Gauguelin, François. Savoir communiquer. Paris, 1970.
Phil 1504.12 Gaul, L. Alberts des Grossen Verhältnis zu Palto. v.12, pt.1. Münster, n.d.
Phil 7069.68.5 Gauld, Alan. The founders of psychical research. London, 1968.
Phil 5246.37 Gault, Robert H. Outline of general psychology. N.Y., 1925.
Phil 8696.15 Gaulter, A. The riddle of nature. London, 1929.
Phil 3640.167.5 Gaultier, J. de. Nietzsche. Paris, 1926.
Phil 3640.167.2 Gaultier, J. de. Nietzsche et la réforme philosophique. 2. éd. Paris, 1904.
Phil 400.55 Gaultier, J. de. Les raisons de l'idéalisme. 2e éd. Paris, 1906.
Phil 1706.1.25 Gaultier, Jules de. Bovarysm. N.Y., 1970.
Phil 1706.1.23 Gaultier, Jules de. Le Bovarysme. 3. éd. Photoreproduction. Paris, 1902.
Phil 1706.1 Gaultier, Jules de. De Kant à Nietzsche. Paris, 1900.
Phil 1706.1.6 Gaultier, Jules de. De Kant à Nietzsche. 6e éd. Paris, 19- .
Phil 8881.37 Gaultier, Jules de. La dépendance de la morale et l'indépendance des moeurs. Paris, 1907.
Phil 1706.1.32 Gaultier, Jules de. Entretiens avec ceux d'hier et d'aujourd'hui. 2e éd. Paris, 1912.
Phil 1706.1.10 Gaultier, Jules de. From Kant to Nietzsche. London, 1961.
Phil 1706.1.13 Gaultier, Jules de. La philosophie officielle et la philosophie. Paris, 1922.
Phil 1706.1.43 Gaultier, Jules de. La sensibilité métaphysique. 3e éd. Paris, 1924.
Phil 1706.1.35 Gaultier, Jules de. La vie mystique de la nature. Paris, 1924.
Phil 1706.2 Gaultier, P. La pensée contemporaine. Paris, 1911.
Phil 8881.42.3 Gaultier, Paul. L'ideal moderne. Paris, 1911.
Phil 8881.42.15 Gaultier, Paul. La leçon des moeurs contemporaines. 2e éd. Paris, 1930.
Phil 8881.42.9 Gaultier, Paul. Les moeurs du temps. 3e éd. Paris, 1928.
Phil 8407.14.4 Gaultier, Paul. Le sens de l'art. 4. éd. Paris, 1911.
Phil 8407.14.10 Gaultier, Paul. The meaning of art. Philadelphia, 1914.
Phil 2605.1.83 Gaune de Beaucourdey, E. La psychologie et la métaphysique des idéesforces chez Alfred Fouillée. Thèse. Paris, 1936.
Phil 2270.85.5 Gaupp, Otto. Herbert Spencer. Stuttgart, 1897.
Phil 2270.85.2 Gaupp, Otto. Herbert Spencer. Stuttgart, 1900.
Phil 7140.110 Gaupp, Robert. Wahn und Irrtum im Leben der Völker. Tübingen, 1916.
Phil 1706.8 Gause, Hermann. Über die Problematik der neueren Philosophie. Inaug. Diss. Basel, 1928.
Phil 8881.68 Gaussault, Abbe. Le portrait d'un honneste homme. 2e éd. Paris, 1694.
Phil 6676.2 Gauthier, A. Histoire du somnambulisme. Paris, 1842. 2v.
Phil 5620.29 Gauthier, Daniel Peter. Practical reasoning. Oxford, 1963.
Phil 5620.29.2 Gauthier, Daniel Peter. Practical reasoning. Oxford, 1966.
Phil 2045.146 Gauthier, David Peter. The logic of Leviathan; the moral and political theory of Thomas Hobbes. Oxford, 1969.
Phil 1020.9.3 Gauthier, L. Introduction à l'étude de la philosophie musulmane. Paris, 1923.
Phil 1020.9 Gauthier, L. La philosophie Musulmane. Paris, 1900.
Phil 1020.12 Gauthier, L. La théorie d'Ibn Rochd. Paris, 1909.
Phil 4195.105 Gautier-Vignal, L. Pic de la Mirandole, 1463-94. Paris, 1937.
Phil 6116.11F Gavoy, E.A. L'encephale; structure et description inconographique du cerveau. Paris, 1886. 2v.
Phil 4803.497.480 Gawecki, Bolesław J. Władysław Mieczysław Kozłowski, 1858-1935. Wrocław, 1961.
Phil 4803.454.79.5 Gawecki, Bolesław J. Wroński i o Wrońskim; katalog. Warszawa, 1958.
Phil 16.10 Gawein; tydschrift van de psychologische kring aan de Vijneegen Universiteit. Vijneegen, 2,1953+ 10v.
Phil 3640.301 Gawronsky, Dimitry. Friedrich Nietzsche und das Dritte Reich. Bern, 1935.
Phil 9560.7.5 Gay, Antoine. L'honneur, sa place dans la morale. Paris, 1913.
Phil 5816.7 Gay, Henri. Observations sur les instincts de l'homme et l'intelligence des animaux. Paris, 1878.
Phil 9480.1 Gay, M.F.S. Physiologie du ridicule. Bruxelles, 1833.
Phil 2406.4A Gay, P. The party of humanity. 1st ed. N.Y., 1963.
Phil 806.39.5 Gay, Peter. The bridge of criticism. 1st ed. N.Y., 1970.
Phil 8661.23 Gay, Peter. Deism, an anthology. Princeton, 1968.
Phil 806.39 Gay, Peter. The enlightenment, an interpretation. 1st ed. N.Y., 1966-69. 2v.
Phil 974.4.35 Gay, S.E. The life works of Mrs. Besant. London, 1913?
Phil 7068.83.6 Gay, Susan E. John William Fletcher, clairvoyant. London, 1883.
Phil 3640.4 La gaya ciencia. (Nietzsche, Friedrich.) Valencia, 1910?
Phil 4372.1.145 Gayano, Lluch Rafael. El folklore en las obras de Luis Vives. Valencia, 1941.
Phil 8030.4 Gayley, Charles. A guide to the literature of aesthetics. Berkeley, 1890.
Phil 7040.43 Gaylin, Willard. The meaning of despair. N.Y., 1968.
Phil 1020.7.5 Gazali. Photoreproduction. (Carra de Vaux, Le Bon.) Paris, 1902.
Phil 2805.102 Gazier, A. Les derniers jours de Blaise Pascal. Paris, 1911.
Phil 5360.13 Geach, P.T. Mental acts. N.Y., 1957.
Phil 5046.36 Geach, Peter. Reference and generality. Ithaca, N.Y., 1962.
Phil 5016.4 Geach, Peter Thomas. A history of the corruptions of logic: an inaugural lecture. Leeds, 1968.
Phil 5627.132.3 Das Gebet. 5. Aufl. (Heiler, Friedrich.) München, 1923.
Phil 8586.21 Gebete eines Weisen. Thal Ehrenbreitstein, 1786.
Phil 5627.129 Gebetsstimmung und Gebet. (Bolley, Alphons.) Düsseldorf, 1930.

Phil 6956.18   Gebhard, Erwin. Psychiatrie in unserer Zeit. Göttingen, 1969.

Phil 3808.156   Gebhardt, Carl. Schopenhauer-Bilder, Grundlagen einer Ikonographie. Frankfurt, 1913.

Phil 3819.75   Gebhardt, Carl. Spinoza, Lebensbeschreibung und Gespräche. Leipzig, 1914.

Phil 3826.11   Gebhardt, Carl. Spinoza; vier Reden. Heidelberg, 1927.

Phil 8696.24   Gebrochenes Weltbild. 1. Aufl. (Gilch, Gerhard.) Stuttgart, 1966.

Phil 6980.319   Gebsattel, V.E.F. von. Imago Hominis. Schweinfurt, 1964.

Phil 365.68   Gebser, Hans. Der unsichtbare Ursprung. Evolution als Nachvollzug. Olten, 1970.

Phil 8412.29   Die Geburt der Aphrodite. (Lion, Ferdinand.) Heidelberg, 1955.

Phil 974.3.115   Die Geburt der Geisteswissenschaft. (Wachsmuth, G.) Dornach, 1941.

Phil 1133.45   Die Geburt der Philosophie. (Nebel, Gerhard.) Stuttgart, 1967.

Phil 3640.58.5   Die Geburt der Tragödie aus dem Geiste der Musik. (Nietzsche, Friedrich.) Leipzig, 1931.

Phil 6125.8   Gedachten over geest. (Polak, A.J.) n.p., 1894.

Phil 3808.220   Gedachtnisschrift für Arthur Schopenhauer zur 150. Wiederkehr seines Geburtstages. (Emge, Carl August.) Berlin, 1938.

Phil 5545.8   Das Gedächtnis. (Fauth, F.) Gütersloh, 1888.

Phil 5545.182   Das Gedächtnis. (Lasson, Adolf.) Berlin, 1894.

Phil 5545.63   Das Gedächtnis. (Offner, Max.) Berlin, 1909.

Phil 5545.63.5   Das Gedächtnis. (Offner, Max.) Berlin, 1913.

Phil 5545.41   Das Gedächtnis. (Ziehen, T.) Berlin, 1908.

Phil 5545.63.2   Das Gedächtnis. 2. Aufl. (Offner, Max.) Berlin, 1911.

Phil 5545.85   Gedächtnis-Ausbildung. (Gloy, Hans.) Berlin, 1913.

Phil 5545.244.1   Gedächtnis oder Gedächtnisse? (Katzenberger, Lothar Friedrich.) München, 1967.

Phil 5545.164   Das Gedächtnis und seine Erziehung. (Brunswig, Alfred.) Berlin, 1926.

Phil 3940.1.90   Gedächtnisrede auf Eduard Zeller. (Diels, Hermann.) Berlin, 1908.

Phil 3487.2   Gedächtnisrede auf Kant. (Falckenberg, R.) Erlangen, 1904.

Phil 3200.3.81   Gedächtnisschrift auf Johann August Eberhard. (Nicolai, Friedrich.) Berlin, 1810.

Phil 3832.18   Gedächtnissrede auf Benedict von Spinoza. (Marbach, G.O.) Halle, 1831.

Htn Phil 3801.234*   Gedächtnissrede auf Friedrich Wilhelm Joseph von Schelling. (Brandis, Christian A.) Berlin, 1856.

Htn Phil 5545.93*   Gedächtnisstörungen bei der Korsakoffschen Psychose. (Doeblin, Alfred.) Berlin, 1905.

Phil 3625.8.38   Gedancken von der Ehre. (Meier, Georg Friedrich.) Halle, 1746.

Phil 16.4   Der Gedanke. Berlin. 1-8,1860-1873 2v.

Phil 4752.2.135   Der Gedanke der ewigen Schoepfung. (Klamroth, E.) Hamburg, 1963.

Phil 400.31.10   Der Gedanke des Ideal-Reichs in der idealistischen Philosophie von Kant bis Hegel. (Sydow, Eckhart von.) Leipzig, 1914.

Phil 735.19   Gedanke und Erlebnis; Umriss einer Philosophie des Wertes. (Mutius, Gerhard von.) Darmstadt, 1922.

Phil 179.14F   Gedanke und Persönlichkeit. (Eck, Samuel.) Giessen, 1914.

Phil 2805.44   Gedanken. (Pascal, Blaise.) Leipzig, 1881.

Phil 8423.16.15   Gedanken über die Nachahmung der griechischen Werke in der Malerei und Bildhauerkunst. (Winckelmann, Johann Joachim.) Stuttgart, 1969.

Htn Phil 3585.1.50*   Gedanken über die schönen und soliden Wissenschaften. (Strnadt, A.) Dresden, 1794.

Phil 8735.10   Gedanken über die Teleologie in der Natur. (Baerenbach, Friedrich von.) Berlin, 1878.

Phil 9362.15.5   Gedanken über Geschlechtsprobleme. (Weininger, Otto.) Berlin, 1922.

Phil 343.9   Gedanken über Grundprobleme der Erkenntnistheorie. (Merton, Adolf.) München, 1916.

Phil 3808.75.10   Gedanken über Schriftstellerei und ahnliche Gegenslande. (Schopenhauer, Arthur.) Dortmund, 1943.

Phil 184.12.8   Gedanken und Denker. (Jerusalem, W.) Wien, 1905.

Phil 184.12.10   Gedanken und Denker. 2. Aufl. (Jerusalem, W.) Wien, 1925.

Phil 186.12.5   Gedanken und Thatsachen. (Liebmann, O.) Strassburg, 1882-1899. 2v.

Phil 3625.8.41   Gedanken vom philosophischen Predigen. (Meier, Georg Friedrich.) Halle, 1762.

Phil 3480.34.5   Gedanken von der wahren Schätzung des lebendigen Kräfte...Mechäniker. (Kant, Immanuel.) Amsterdam, 1968.

Htn Phil 3480.34*   Gedanken von der wahren Schätzung des lebendigen Kräfte. (Kant, Immanuel.) Königsberg, 1746.

Phil 3625.8.30   Gedanken von Scherzen. (Meier, Georg Friedrich.) Halle, 1754.

Phil 5258.74.5   Gedanken zur Daseinsgestaltung. (Spranger, Eduard.) München, 1954.

Phil 299.21   Gedanken zur Naturphilosophie. (Schilder, Paul.) Wien, 1928.

Phil 3501.18   Gedanken zur Prüfung von Kants...der Sitten, Leipzig, 1789. (Tilling, Christian Gottfried.) Bruxelles, 1968.

Phil 5247.86   Gedankengänge in Psychologie. (Hector, Heinz.) Paderborn, 1965.

Phil 3500.33.4   Der Gedankengang der Kritik der reinen Vernunft. (Stange, Carl.) Leipzig, 1920.

Phil 5241.130   Das Gedankenleben und seine Beherrschung. (Boehme, Edwin.) Cöln, 1959.

Phil 7069.18.159   Gedankenlesen und Hellsehen. (Werner-Hagen.) Berlin, 1918.

Phil 6615.16   Gedankenmacht und Hysterie. (Schleich, Carl Ludwig.) Berlin, 1922.

Phil 181.61   Geddes, Patrick. The world without and the world within. Bournville, 1905.

Phil 2520.240   Gedenkfeier anlässlich des drei hundertjährigen Todestagen des Philosophen René Descartes. (Berlin. Freie Universität.) Berlin, 1950.

Phil 3800.67   Gedichte. (Schelling, F.W.J. von.) Jena, 1917.

Phil 3800.61A   Gedichte und poetische Übersetzungen. (Schelling, F.W.J. von.) Leipzig, 1913.

Phil 3640.25.10   Gedichte und Sprüche. (Nietzsche, Friedrich.) Leipzig, 1901.

Phil 3640.25   Gedichte und Sprüche. (Nietzsche, Friedrich.) Leipzig, 1908.

Phil 3640.25.7   Gedichte und Sprüche. (Nietzsche, Friedrich.) Leipzig, 1916.

Phil 3640.12.10   Gedichts. (Nietzsche, Friedrich.) Leipzig, 1923.

Phil 3492.34.15   Gedrängter Auszug aus Kants Kritik der reinen Vernunft. (Kieswetter, J.G.K.C.) Berlin, 1795.

Phil 6980.668.10   Gedragstherapie in het bijzonder de methode van wedenkerige remming. (Santer-Weststrate, Henrietta Cornelia.) Assen, 1964.

Phil 8407.50   Geel, Jacobus. Onderzoek en phantasie. Leiden, 1838.

Phil 5627.13   Geelkerken, J.G. De empirische godsdienstpsychologie. Amsterdam, 1909.

Phil 5500.33   Geer, J.P. van de. A psychological study of problem solving. Amsterdam, 1957.

Phil 5279.25.2   Geer, Johannes Petrus van de. De mening van de psycholoog. 2. druk. Haarlem, 1968.

Phil 9495.170.5   Geets, Claude. Psychanalyse et morale sexuelle. Paris, 1970.

Phil 6311.56   Der gefährdete Mensch. (Bodamer, Joachim.) Freiburg, 1968.

Phil 3808.248   Das gefesselte Engagement; zur Ideologie der Kontemplativen Asthetik Schopenhauer. (Bahr, Hans Dieter.) Bonn, 1970.

Phil 1190.18   Geffers, A. De arcesilae successoribus disputatio. Göttingen, 1845.

Phil 291.1   Das Gefüge der Welt. (Keyserling, H.) München, 1906.

Phil 5400.80   Das Gefühl. (Wreschner, Arthur.) Leipzig, 1931.

Phil 5400.75   Das Gefühl. (Ziegler, T.) Stuttgart, 1893.

Phil 5400.75.5   Das Gefühl. 5e Aufl. (Ziegler, T.) Berlin, 1912.

Phil 5245.19   Das Gefühl als Fundament der Weltordnung. (Feldegg, F.) Wien, 1890.

Phil 5635.38   Gefühl und Affekt. Inaug. Diss. (Steige, R.) Breslau? 1937.

Phil 5400.60   Gefühl und Erkennen. (Szymanski, J.S.) Berlin, 1926.

Phil 5250.13.80   Gefühl und Ganzheit. (Odebrecht, Rudolf.) Berlin, 1929.

Phil 8415.3   Gefühl und schöpferische Gestaltung. (Odebrecht, R.) Berlin, 1929.

Phil 5400.157   Gefühl und Strebung. (Grossart, Friedrich.) München, 1961.

Phil 5400.43   Die Gefühle und ihr Verhältnis zu den Empfindungen. (Frey, Max von.) Leipzig, 1894.

Phil 5400.13   Das Gefühlsleben. (Nahlowsky, J.W.) Leipzig, 1884.

Phil 5400.9   Die Gefühlslehre...von Kant bis auf unsere Zeit. (Bobtschew, N.) Leipzig, 1888.

Phil 5400.61   Die Gefühlslehre in der neuesten französischen Psychologie. (Savescu, Michael.) Leipzig, 1900.

Phil 5400.74   Das Gefühlsproblem. (Lagerborg, R.) Leipzig, 1905.

Phil 177.44.5   Gefühlston und Sättigung der Farben. (Cohn, Jonas.) n.p., 1899-1915. 16 pam.

Phil 5253.9   Die Gefühlswerte. (Noltenius, F.) Leipzig, 1927.

Phil 3425.774   Gegel'. (Gulyga, Arsenii V.) Moskva, 1970.

Phil 3425.303   Gegel' v Rossii. (Chyzhevs'kyi, Dmytro.) Parizh, 1939.

Phil 325.5   Gegen den Empirismus. (Meurer, W.) Leipzig, 1925.

Phil 1715.14   Gegen den Strom. (Pfeiffer, Johannes.) Itzehoe, 1964.

Phil 8598.43   Gegen den Strom. (Schrempf, C.) Stuttgart, 1922. 5v.

Phil 6332.5   Gegen Psycho-Analyse. (Wolfram, E.) Leipzig, 1918.

Phil 3905.90   Gegen Weininger. (Sturm, Bruno.) Wien, 1912.

Phil 978.49.510   Gegensätze in der Menschheitsentwickelung; 11 Vorträge. (Steiner, R.) Dornach, 1967.

Phil 1750.10   Der Gegensatz...der neueren Philosophie. (Hermann, C.) Leipzig, 1877.

Phil 181.83   Der Gegensatz. (Guardini, R.) Mainz, 1925.

Phil 3549.8.100   Der Gegensatz vom Seele und Geist bei Ludwig Klages. (Benduk, Hugo.) Werli, 1935.

Phil 3310.19.80   Die Gegensatzphilosophie Romano Guardinis in ihren Grundlagen und Folgerungen. (Wucherer-Huldenfeld, Karl.) Wien, 1968.

Phil 1050.4.9   Die gegenseitigen Beziehungen. (Seyerlen, R.) Jena, 1899.

Phil 192.21   Der Gegenstand der Erkenntniss. (Rickert, H.) Freiburg, 1892.

Phil 192.21.2   Der Gegenstand der Erkenntniss. (Rickert, H.) Tübingen, 1904.

Phil 192.21.3   Der Gegenstand der Erkenntniss. 3. Aufl. (Rickert, H.) Tübingen, 1915.

Phil 192.21.3.6   Der Gegenstand der Erkenntniss. 6. Aufl. (Rickert, H.) Tübingen, 1928.

Phil 348.9   Der Gegenstand der Erkenntnistheorie. 4. und 5. Aufl. (Rickert, H.) Tübingen, 1921.

Phil 5247.30   Der Gegenstand der Psychologie. (Häberlin, Paul.) Berlin, 1921.

Phil 5050.16   Gegenstand und Umgreifendes. (Knauss, G.) Basel, 1954.

Phil 193.151   Gegenstands und verhältnislehre. (Schjoth, Emil.) Oslo, 1938.

Phil 5047.32.10   Gegenstandslogik und Denklogik Vorschlag zu einer Neugestaltung der Logik. 2. Aufl. (Honecker, M.) Berlin, 1928.

Phil 5052.38   Gegenstandstheoretische Grundlagen der Logik und Logistik. (Mally, Ernst.) Leipzig, 1912.

Phil 190.19   Die gegenwärtige Aufgabe der Philosophie. (Prantl, Karl.) München, 1852. 8 pam.

Phil 8957.13.10   Die Gegenwärtige Heilsstunde. (Haering, Bernhard.) Freiburg, 1964.

Phil 181.50.5   Gegenwart. (Grisebach, E.) Halle, 1928.

Phil 3425.625   Gegenwart Christi in der Gesellschaft; eine Studie zu Hegels Dialektik. (Marsch, Wolf Dieter.) München, 1965.

Phil 165.175   Die Gegenwart der Griechen im neueren Denken. (Henrich, Dieter.) Tübingen, 1960.

Phil 192.115   Die Gegenwart der Philosophie. (Rombach, Heinrich.) Freiburg, 1962.

Phil 3006.1   Gegenwart und Philosophie in Deutschland. (Gruppe, O.F.) Berlin, 1855.

Phil 6319.1.73   Gegenwart und Zukunft. (Jung, C.G.) Zürich, 1957.

Phil 978.49.880   Gegenwartsaufgaben der Menschheit. (Steffen, Albert.) Schweiz, 1966.

Phil 182.83   Die Gegenwartslinie, Wesen und Grenzen des Determinismus. (Heidrich, E.) Görlitz, 1925.

Phil 8587.36   Gegenwartsphilosophie und christliche Religion. (Hegenwald, H.) Leipzig, 1913.

Phil 1511.1.5   Der Gegenwartswert der geschichtlichen Erforschung der mittelalterlichen Philosophie. (Grabmann, M.) Wien, 1913.

Phil 8881.3   Géhant, J.B.V. Science du bien et du mal. Paris, 1848. 2v.

Phil 6111.34   Geheime Seelenkräfte. (Brandler-Pracht, Karl.) Berlin, 1921.

Phil 353.23   Das Geheimnis der Gegensätze. (Wemme, G.) Krailling, 1960.

Phil 8416.14   Das Geheimnis der Kunst. (Perls, Hugo.) Zürich, 1959.

Phil 978.49.740   Das Geheimnis der Trinität. (Steiner, R.) Dornach, 1970.

Phil 3850.48   Das Geheimnis des ewigen Lebens und des jüngsten Tages. (Sydow, W.) Berlin, 1960?

Phil 3705.5   Das Geheimnis des Lebens. (Hauck, W.A.) Heidelberg, 1947.

Phil 978.49.540   Das Geheimnis des Todes; Wesen und Bedeutung Mitteleuropas und die europäischen Volksgeister. (Steiner, R.) Dornach, 1967.

Phil 3425.117   Das Geheimniss der hegelschen Dialektik. (Schmitt, E.H.) Halle, 1888.

Phil 187.86.10   Geheimnisse der Seele. (Müller-Freienfels, R.) München, 1927.

Phil 974.3.110   Geheimwissenschaft. (Apel, Max.) Charlettenburg, 1922.

Phil 6121.7.12   Das Gehirn. (Luys, J.) Leipzig, 1877.

Phil 6111.10.3   Das Gehirn als Organ des Geistes. (Bastian, H.C.) Leipzig, 1882.

Phil 5643.23   Gehirn und Auge. (Mauthner, L.) Wiesbaden, 1881.

Phil 6132.22   Gehirn und Bewusstsein. (Wahle, R.) Wien, 1884.

Phil 6125.1   Gehirn und Geist. (Piderit, T.) Leipzig, 1868.

Phil 6111.19   Gehirn und Seele. (Becher, E.) Heidelberg, 1911.

Phil 6114.18   Gehirn und Seele. (Ebertin, B.) Aalen, 1961.

Phil 5258.60   Gehirn und Seele. (Schultz, Paul.) Leipzig, 1906.

Phil 6115.6.7   Gehirn und Seele. 2e Ausg. (Flechsig, P.) Leipzig, 1896.

Phil 6115.21.3   Gehirn und Seele. 4. Aufl. (Forel, A.) Bonn, 1894.

Phil 6115.21.4   Gehirn und Seele. 5. und 6. Aufl. (Forel, A.) Bonn, 1899.

Phil 6115.21.5   Gehirn und Seele. 12. Aufl. (Forel, A.) Leipzig, 1914.

Phil 6962.13   Gehirnpathologie. 2. Aufl. (Monakow, Constantin von.) Wien, 1905. 2v.

Phil 3006.8   Gehl, W. Der germanische Schicksalsglaube. Berlin, 1939.

Phil 400.96   Gehlen, A. Idealismus und Existentialphilosophie. Leipzig, 1933.

Phil 5756.13   Gehlen, A. Theorie der Willensfreiheit. Berlin, 1933.

Phil 181.77   Gehlen, A. Wirklicher und unwirklicher Geist. Leipzig, 1931.

Phil 3246.240   Gehlen, Arnold. Deutschtum und Christentum bei Fichte. Berlin, 1935.

Phil 8881.82   Gehlen, Arnold. Moral und Hypemoral. Frankfurt, 1969.

Phil 3310.15   Gehlen, Arnold. Theorie der Willensfeiheit und frühe philosophische Schriften. Neuvied, 1965.

Phil 3195.10.95   Gehlen, Arnold. Zur Theorie der Setzung und des setzungshaften Wissens bei Driesch. Inaug. Diss. Leipzig, 1927.

Phil 3195.10.105   Gehlen, Arnold. Zur Theorie der Setzung und des setzungshaften Wissens bei Driesch. Leipzig, 1927.

Phil 8050.90   Gehrig, Hans. Wesen und Bestand ästhetischer Bildung in Geschichte und Begenwart. Zürich, 1964.

Phil 8586.31   Gehring, Albert. The religion of thirty great thinkers. Boston, 1925.

Phil 8881.36   Gehring, Albert. Shadows and realities. Cleveland, 1912.

Phil 6116.18   Gehring, J.G. The hope of the variant. N.Y., 1923.

Phil 191.2   Geht es aufwärts? (Quensel, H.) Cöln, 1904.

Phil 6116.10   Gehuchten, Arthur van. Anatomie du système nerveux de l'homme. Louvain, 1900. 2v.

Phil 181.102   Geiger, G.R. Philosophy and the social order. Boston, 1947.

Phil 1955.6.140   Geiger, George R. John Dewey in perspective. N.Y., 1958.

Phil 8881.65   Geiger, George R. Towards an objective ethics. Yellow Springs, 1938.

Phil 181.37.2   Geiger, Joseph R. Some religious implications of pragmatism. Chicago, 1919.

Phil 7150.2   Geiger, K.A. Der Selbstmord. Augsburg, 1888.

Phil 2630.12   Geiger, Louis Bertrand. Philosophie et spiritualité. Paris, 1963. 2v.

Phil 7060.10.80   Geiger, M. Aufklärung und Erweckung. Zürich, 1963.

Phil 181.75   Geiger, M. Die Wirklichkeit der Wissenschaften und die Metaphysik. Bonn, 1930.

Phil 8407.23   Geiger, M. Zugänge zur Ästhetik. Leipzig, 1928.

Phil 5246.38   Geiger, Moritz. Methodologische und experimentelle Beiträge zur Quantitätslehre. Leipzig, 1907.

Phil 3552.132   Geijer, K.R. Huru förhäller sig Leibniz' metafysik. Upsala, 1876.

Phil 3425.206   Geijer, R. Hegelianism och positivism. Lund, 1883.

Phil 4570.3.81   Geijer, R. Humanistika sektionen contra den sakkunniga nämden. Lund, 1887.

Phil 4570.3.31   Geijer, R. Samvetet. Stockholm, 1905.

Phil 181.49   Geijer, Reinhold. Filosofiens historiska hufvudformer. Uppsala, 1916.

Phil 3565.111   Geijer, Reinhold. Hermann Lotzes tankar om tid och timlighet i kritisk belysning. Lund, 1886.

Phil 4600.4.80   Geijerstam, G.L. af. Sä minns Bengt Lidforss. Stockholm, 1945.

Phil 6312.15   Geikie Cobb, W.J. Spiritual healing. London, 1914.

Phil 2115.89A   Geil, Georg. Über die Abhängigkeit Locke's von Descartes. Strassburg, 188-.

Phil 8956.6   Geismar, E. Etik. København, 1926.

Phil 75.4   Geissler, C.A. Bibliographisches Handbuch der philosophischer Literatur. Leipzig, 1850.

Phil 410.7   Geissler, Kurt. Die Grundsätze und das Wesen des Unendlichen in der Mathematik und Philosophie. Leipzig, 1902.

Phil 181.43   Geissler, Kurt. Das System der Seinsgebiete als Grundlage einer umfassenden Philosophie. Leipzig, 1919.

Phil 5330.12   Geissler, L.R. The measurement of attention. n.p., 1909.

Phil 2555.10.81   Geissler, Rolf. Boureau-Deslandes, ein Materialist der Frühaufklärung. 1. Aufl. Berlin, 1967.

Phil 5350.5.5   Geist, Harold. The psychological aspects of the aging process with sociological implications. St. Louis, 1968.

Phil 341.42   Der Geist als Materie in Gehirnphysiologie und Kausalitätstheorie. (Kraus, Hermann.) Nurnberg, 1963.

NEDL Phil 185.44   Der Geist als Widersacher der Seele. v.1-3. (Klages, Ludwig.) Leipzig, 1929-1932. 4v.

NEDL Phil 185.44.2   Der Geist als Widersacher der Seele. v.1-3. Gesantverzeichnis. (Klages, Ludwig.) Leipzig, 1933. 4v.

Phil 185.44.5   Der Geist als Widersacher der Seele. 3. Aufl. (Klages, L.) München, 1954. 2v.

Htn   Phil 3801.875*   Der Geist der allerneuesten Philosophie der Herren Schelling, Hegel. v.1-2. (Weiller, K. von.) München, 1803-05.

Phil 8594.10   Der Geist der Antike und die christliche Welt. (Otto, Walter F.) Bonn, 1923.

Phil 3503.3   Geist der kritischen Philosophie. (Venturini, Karl.) Altona, 1796-97. 2v.

Phil 3801.806   Der Geist der Liebe und das Schicksal. (Staiger, Emil.) Frauenfeld, 1935.

Phil 1718.2   Der Geist der neueren Philosophie. (Schellwien, R.) Leipzig, 1895.

Phil 176.69   Geist der Utopie. (Bloch, Ernst.) München, 1918.

Phil 3425.66   Der Geist des Christentums und sein Schicksal. (Hegel, Georg Wilhelm Friedrich.) Gütersloh, 1970.

Phil 3552.28   Geist des Herrn von Leibniz. (Leibniz, Gottfried Wilhelm.) Wittenburg, 1775. 2v.

Phil 850.8   Der Geist des Urchristenthums. (Eberhard, J.A.) Halle, 1807-08. 3v.

Phil 1735.8   Der Geist des XIX. Jahrhunderts. (Bergmann, Ernst.) Breslau, 1922.

Phil 1735.8.2   Der Geist des XIX. Jahrhunderts. 2. Aufl. (Bergmann, Ernst.) Breslau, 1927.

Phil 189.4.10   Der Geist in der Natur. (Oersted, H.C.) München, 1850-1851. 2v.

Phil 193.153   Geist oder Stoff? (Schmick, J.H.) Leipzig, 1889.

Phil 3425.342   Der Geist und das Absolute. (Möller, Joseph.) Paderborn, 1951.

Phil 1135.235   Der Geist und das Eine. Inaug. Diss. (Hager, Fritz-Peter.) Bern, 1970.

Phil 5247.30.5   Der Geist und die Triebe: eine Elementarpsychologie. (Häberlin, Paul.) Basel, 1924.

Phil 341.7   Geist und Freiheit. (Köhler, Watther.) Tübingen, 1914.

Phil 3425.295   Geist und Freiheit im System Hegels. (Fahrenhorst, E.) Leipzig, 1934.

Phil 6111.13   Geist und Körper, Seele und Leib. (Busse, L.) Leipzig, 1903.

Phil 6111.13.2   Geist und Körper, Seele und Leib. 2. Aufl. (Busse, L.) Leipzig, 1913.

Phil 6114.4.5   Geist und Körper. (Eisler, R.) Göttingen, 1911.

Phil 6129.3.3   Geist und Körper. (Tuke, D.H.) Jena, 1888.

Phil 6111.1.9   Geist und Körper. 2. Aufl. (Bain, A.) Leipzig, 1881.

Phil 3640.384   Geist und Leben. (Landmann, M.) Bonn, 1951.

Phil 1135.172   Geist und Lust. (Lieberg, Godo.) Tübingen, 1959.

Phil 331.6   Geist und Materie. (Apel, Paul.) Berlin, 1905. 2v.

Phil 6128.59.5   Geist und Materie. (Schroedinger, Erwin.) Braunschweig, 1959.

Phil 3310.10   Geist und Sache. (Grebe, W.) Frankfurt, 1934.

Phil 3255.80   Geist und Schrift bei Sebastian Franck. (Hegler, Alfred.) Freiburg, 1892.

Phil 3549.8.130   Geist und Seele. (Lewin, James.) Berlin, 1931.

Phil 6122.28   Geist und Seele. (Marschik, S.) Leipzig, 1906.

Phil 5249.32   Geist und Seele im technischen Zeitalter. (Jaeger, Marc A.) Zürich, 1968.

Phil 3850.31   Geist und Sein. (Schmalenbach, H.) Basel, 1939.

Phil 978.49.370   Geist und Stoff, Leben und Tod. (Steiner, R.) Dornach, 1961.

Phil 186.35.15   Geist und Welt der Dialektik. (Liebert, Arthur.) Berlin, 1929.

Phil 3790.16.30   Geist und Wirklichkeit. (Reidemeister, Kurt.) Berlin, 1953.

Phil 7068.86.11   Die Geister der Finsterniss. (Franco, P.G.) Ausburg, 1886.

Phil 7069.58   Geistererscheinungen und Vorzeichen. (Jaffe, Aniela.) Zürich, 1958.

Phil 3415.68   Die Geisterhypothese des Spiritismus und seine Phantome. (Hartmann, Eduard von.) Leipzig, n.d.

Phil 7069.25.4   Geisterkenntnis. (Danmar, William.) Leipzig, 1925.

Phil 5203.18   Geistes und naturwissenschaftliche Abhandlungen der Mitglieder des Wiener Arbeitskreises. (Baatz, Walter.) Wien, 1957.

Phil 8602.44   Das Geisteserbe der Gegenwart und die Theologie. (Weber, H.E.) Leipzig, 1925.

Phil 5828.4   Die Geisteskräfte der Menschen. (Strumpell, L.) Leipzig, 1878.

Phil 6958.4   Geisteskrankheiten. (Ilberg, Georg.) Leipzig, 1907.

Phil 6958.4.2   Geisteskrankheiten. 2. Aufl. (Ilberg, Georg.) Leipzig, 1918.

Phil 665.14   Geistesleben und Descendenzlehre. (ipper, P.) Naumburg, 1885.

Phil 179.3.28.5   Geistesprobleme und Lebensfragen. (Eucken, R.) Leipzig, 1918.

Phil 179.3.28.2   Geistesprobleme und Lebensfragen. 2e Aufl. (Eucken, R.) Leipzig, n.d.

Phil 1707.6.5   Die Geistesstromungen der Gegenwart.%Hessen, Johannes.) Freiburg, 1937.

Phil 978.49.530   Geisteswissenschaft als Erkenntuis der Grundimpulse sozialer Gestaltung. (Steiner, R.) Dornach, 1967.

Phil 978.49.305   Geisteswissenschaft als Lebensgut. (Steiner, R.) Dornach, 1959.

Phil 978.49.230   Geisteswissenschaft und die Lebensforderungen der Gegenwart. pt.1-8. (Steiner, R.) Dornach, 1950. 2v.

Phil 199.5   Geisteswissenschaft und Willensgesetz. (Yura, T.) Berlin, 1931.

Phil 978.49.625   Geisteswissenschaftliche Grundlage zum Gedeihen der Landwirtschaft; landwirtschaftlicher Kursus. 4. Aufl. (Steiner, R.) Dornach, 1963.

Phil 3850.42   Die geistige Arbeit. (Speiser, Andreas.) Basel, 1955.

Phil 5827.1.28   Die geistige Entwicklung im Tierreich. (Romanes, G.J.) Leipzig, 1885.

Phil 978.49.30   Die geistige Führung des Menschen und der Menschheit. (Steiner, R.) Dornach, 1925.

Phil 6125.19   Das geistige Heilverfahren. (Pieper, Gustav.) Magdeburg, 1929.

Phil 1711.1   Die geistige Krisis der Gegenwart. (Liebert, A.) Berlin, 1923.

Phil 5250.84   Das geistige Leben der Person in den persönlichkeitspsychologischen Schichttheorien. Inaug. Diss. (Knapp, Franz.) Heidelberg? 1967?

Phil 179.3.5   Geistige Strömungen derGegenwart. (Eucken, R.) Leipzig, 1916.

Phil 179.3.6   Geistige Strömungen der Gegenwart. 4e Aufl. (Eucken, R.) Leipzig, 1909.

Phil 16.9   Geistige Überlieferung. Berlin. 1-2,1940-1942 2v.

Phil 978.49.655   Geistige und soziale Wandlungen in der Menschheitsentwickelung; achtzehn Vorträge. (Steiner, R.) Dornach, 1966.

Phil 5440.20   Geistige Veranlagung und Vererbung. (Sommer, Georg.) Leipzig, 1916.

Phil 978.49.535   Die geistige Vereinigung der Menschheit durch den Christus-Impuls. 1. Aufl. (Steiner, R.) Dornach, 1968.

Phil 525.258   Geistige Versenkung. (Bodmershof, Wilhelm.) Zürich, 1965.

Phil 193.156   Geistige Wandlung. (Schubart, W.) Luzern, 1940.

Phil 3005.12   Geistige Werte. (Frischeisen-Köhler, M.) Berlin, 1915.

Phil 978.49.420   Geistige Wirkenskräfte. (Steiner, R.) Dornach, 1964.

Phil 5252.26.10   Die geistige Wirklichkeit. (Meyer, Semi.) Stuttgart, 1925.

Phil 179.3.50   Die geistigen Forderungen der Gegenwart. 3e Aufl. (Eucken, R.) Berlin, 1918.

Phil 1801.4   Die geistigen Grundlagen des amerikanischen Gemeinwesens. (Baumgarten, E.) Frankfurt, 1936-8. 2v.

Phil 179.3.17   Geistigen Lebensinhalt. (Eucken, R.) Leipzig, 1896.

Phil 530.20.50   Das geistige Leben. 7. Aufl. (Denifle, H.) Graz, 1920.

Phil 665.88   Die Geistseele des Menschen. (Conrad-Martius, H.) München, 1960.

Phil 8865.534   Geiushev, Ziiaddin B. Eticheskaia mysl' v Azerbaidzhane. Baku, 1968.

Phil 5627.87.2   Die Gekreuzigte. 2. Aufl. (Scherr, J.) Leipzig, 1874.

Phil 5400.134 Gelaat, gebaar en klankexpressie. (Ginneken, J. van.) Leiden, 1919.
Phil 5400.130.5 Gelaat en karakter. (Frijda, N.H.) Haarlem, 1958.
Phil 3450.19.85.2 Gelassenheit. 2e Aufl. (Heidegger, Martin.) Pfullingen, 1960.
Phil 5590.315 Gelbmann, Frederich J. Authoritarianism and temperament. Washington, 1958.
Phil 3826.12 Gelbraus, Samuel. Die Metaphysik der Ethik Spinozas im Quellenlichte der Kabbalah. Wien, 1917.
Phil 5246.72 Geldard, F.A. Fundamentals of psychology. N.Y., 1962.
Phil 5640.50 Geldard, Frank A. The human senses. N.Y., 1962.
Phil 1607.10 Gelder, Herman Arend Enno van. The two reformations in the 16th century. The Hague, 1961.
Phil 130.14 Geldsetzer, L. Philosophengalerie. Düsseldorf, 1967.
Phil 7067.46.15 Gelehrte Verhandlung der Materi von Erscheinungen der Geisteren. 3. Aufl. (Calmet, Augustin.) Augspurg. 1751.
Phil 7067.46.16 Gelehrte Verhandlung der Materi von Erscheinungen der Geisteren. 3. Aufl. (Calmet, Augustin.) Augspurg. 1757.
Phil 7069.24.22 Geley, Gustave. Clairvoyance and materialisation, a record of experiments. London, 1927.
Phil 5374.149 Geley, Gustave. De l'inconscient au conscient. Paris, 1919.
Phil 7069.24.21 Geley, Gustave. L'ectoplasmie et la clairvoyance. Paris, 1924.
Phil 5374.148.2 Geley, Gustave. L'être subconscient. Paris, 1899.
Phil 5374.148 Geley, Gustave. L'être subconscient. 4e éd. Paris, 1919.
Phil 5374.150 Geley, Gustave. From the unconscious to the conscious. Glasgow, 1920.
Phil 5246.86 Gelinas, Robert P. The teenager and psychology. 1. ed. N.Y., 1971.
Phil 9528.3.5A Gellert, C.F. Instructions from a father to his son. Boston, 1823.
Phil 8881.4 Gellert, C.F. Leçons de morale. Utrecht, 1772. 2v.
Htn Phil 8881.4.5* Gellert, C.F. Moralische Vorlesungen. v. 1-3. Leipzig, 1770.
Phil 5400.160 Gellhorn, Ernest. Emotions and emotional disorders. N.Y., 1963.
Phil 5625.86.5 Gellhorn, Ernst. Autonomic imbalance and the hypothalamus. Minneapolis, 1957.
Phil 5625.86 Gellhorn, Ernst. Autonomic regulations. N.Y., 1943.
Phil 181.133 Gellner, Ernest. Thought and change. Chicago, 1965.
Phil 5068.42 Gellner, Ernest. Words and things. London, 1959.
Phil 8696.23 Geloof en natuurwetenschap; studies over de verhouding van christelijk geloof en moderne natuurwetenschap. 's-Gravenhage, 1965-67. 2v.
Phil 185.97 Geloof en wetenschap. (Kalsbeek, L.) Baarn, 1962.
Phil 3246.213 Gelpcke, E. Fichte und die Gedankenwelt der Sturm und Drang. Leipzig, 1928.
Phil 345.3 Die Geltungsgrundlagen metaphysischer Urteile. (Overhuber, H.E.) München, 1928.
Phil 3450.19.10.5 Gelven, Michael. A commentary on Heidegger's Being and time. N.Y., 1970.
Phil 525.16.5 Gem, S. Harvey. The mysticism of William Law. London, 1914.
Phil 5425.102 Gemant, Andrew. The nature of the genius. Springfield, Ill., 1961.
Phil 5057.6 Gemeinfassliche Darstellung der Denklehre. (Rion, J.) Reutlingen, 1844.
Phil 3483.41 Gemeinfassliche Darstellung der Kantischen Lehren über Sittlichkeit, Freyheit, Gottheit und Unsterblichkeit. v.1-2. (Bernhardi, A.B.) Freyberg, 1796-97.
Phil 3246.96 Gemeinfassliche Darstellung des Fichteschen Systems and der daraus. (Schad, Johann B.) Erfurt, 1800-02. 3v.
Phil 6328.25 Gemeinsame Tagträume. (Sachs, Hanns.) Leipzig, 1924.
Phil 5249.12 Die gemeinsame Wurzel der Kunst, Moral und Wissenschaft. (Jäger, Hermann.) Berlin, 1909.
Phil 193.195 Gemeinschaft des Gustes. Wien, 1957.
Phil 175.5 Gemeinverständliche Weisheitslehre. (Amersin, F.) Triest, 1881.
Phil 4260.100 Gemelli, A. G.B. Vico: volume commemorativo. Milano, 1926.
Phil 3488.15 Gemelli, A. Immanuel Kant, 1724-1924. Milano, 1924.
Phil 4006.4 Gemelli, A. Il mio contributo alla filosofia neoscolastica. Milano, 1926.
Phil 6319.1.195 Gemelli, A. Psicologia e religione nella concezione analitica di C.G. Jung. Milano, 1955.
Phil 5246.25.10 Gemelli, Agostino. Introducione alla psicologia. Milano, 1947.
Phil 5246.25.5 Gemelli, Agostino. Nuovo orizzonti della psicologia sperimentale. 2. ed. Milano, 1923.
Phil 5246.25.3 Gemelli, Agostino. Psicologia e biologia. 3. ed. Firenze, 1913.
Phil 8696.10 Gemelli, Agostino. Religione e scienza. Milano, 1920.
Phil 8696.10.5 Gemelli, Agostino. Scienza ed apologetica. Milano, 1920.
Phil 4260.92 Gemmingen, Otto. Vico, Hamann und Herder. Inaug. Diss. Borna, 1918.
Phil 8408.26 Gems of wisdom from the writings of A.R. Howell. (Howell, A.R.) Sussex, 1958.
Phil 5400.122 Das Gemüt. (Strasser, S.) Antwerpen, 1956.
Phil 5400.73 Das Gemüth. 2e Aufl. (Jungmann, J.) Freiburg, 1885.
Phil 9035.33 Gemüth und Charakter sechs Vorträge. (Wolff, Hermann.) Leipzig, 1882.
Phil 5400.50.6 Die Gemüthsbewegungen. 2e Aufl. (Lange, C.G.) Würzburg, 1910.
Phil 6967.22 The Genain quadruplets. (Rosenthal, David.) N.Y., 1963.
Phil 3425.215 Genberg, P. Belysning och granskning af Hegelska philosophiens. Lund, 1846.
Phil 4570.2.6 Genberg, P. Valda skrifter. v.1-2. Stockholm, 1878.
Phil 8881.54 Genberg, Paul. De principio philosophiae moralis. Diss. Lundae, 1846.
Phil 5246.74 Gendlin, Eugene. Experiencing and the creation of meaning. N.Y., 1962.
Phil 735.270 Genealogia e scienza dei valori. (Solimini, Maria.) Manduria, 1968.
Phil 2475.1.510 Une généalogie du spiritualisme français. (Janicaud, Dominique.) La Haye, 1969.
Phil 3640.34 The genealogy of morals. (Nietzsche, Friedrich.) N.Y., 1918.
Phil 181.60 Gener, Pompeyo. Inducciones, ensayos de filosofia y de critica. Barcelona, 1901.
Phil 5241.128 General experimental psychology. (Baker, Lawrence.) N.Y., 1960.
Phil 5241.103 General experimental psychology. (Bills, A.G.) N.Y., 1934.
Phil 5819.6 General factors in transfer of training in the white rat. (Jackson, T.A.) Worcester, 1932.
Phil 8897.58 General introduction to ethics. (Wright, William K.) N.Y., 1929.
Phil 6315.2.5.6A A general introduction to psycho-analysis. (Freud, Sigmund.) Garden City, 1938.
Phil 6315.2.5.5 A general introduction to psycho-analysis. (Freud, Sigmund.) N.Y., 1935.
Phil 6315.2.5.7 A general introduction to psycho-analysis. (Freud, Sigmund.) N.Y., 1937.
Phil 5246.31.5 General introduction to psychology. (Griffith, C.R.) N.Y., 1924.
Phil 5246.31.2 General introduction to psychology. (Griffith, C.R.) N.Y., 1928.
Phil 3552.35 General investigations concerning the analysis of concepts and truths. (Leibniz, Gottfried Wilhelm.) Athens, 1968.
Phil 5044.6 General logic. (Eaton, Ralph M.) N.Y., 1931.
Phil 5241.30.15 General principles of human reflexology. (Bekhterev, V.) London, 1933.
Phil 5252.23.5 The general problems of psychology. (MacDougall, R.) N.Y., 1922.
Phil 5241.99 General psychology. (Brennan, R.E.) N.Y., 1932.
Phil 5242.46 General psychology. (Cattell, R.B.) Cambridge, Mass., 1941.
Phil 5243.38 General psychology. (Dockeray, F.C.) N.Y., 1932.
Phil 5247.19.2 General psychology. (Hunter, W.S.) Chicago, 1919.
Phil 5247.19.7 General psychology. (Hunter, W.S.) Chicago, 1927.
Phil 5252.69A General psychology. (Murphy, Gardner.) N.Y., 1933.
Phil 5258.66.2 General psychology. (Smith, Stevenson.) N.Y., 1927.
Phil 5258.116 General psychology. (Sprott, W.J.H.) London, 1937.
Phil 5261.15.10 General psychology. (Vaughan, W.F.) Garden City, 1936.
Phil 5261.15.25 General psychology. 1st ed. (Vaughan, W.F.) N.Y., 1939.
Phil 5246.29.6 General psychology. 2. ed. (Garrett, Henry E.) N.Y., 1961.
Phil 5257.44 General psychology for college students. (Rexroad, Carl N.) N.Y., 1929.
Phil 5246.41 General psychology for professional students. (Gilliland, A.R.) Boston, 1930.
Phil 5258.35.20 General psychology from the personalistic standpoint. (Stern, W.) N.Y., 1938.
Phil 6959.4.18 General psychopathology. (Jaspers, K.) Chicago, 1967.
Phil 6959.4.17 General psychopathology. (Jaspers, K.) Manchester, 1963.
Phil 5041.54 A general scheme for natural systems. (Biser, I.) Philadelphia, 1938.
Phil 6315.2.36 A general selection from the works of Sigmund Freud. (Freud, Sigmund.) London, 1937.
Phil 6315.2.38 A general selection from the works of Sigmund Freud. (Freud, Sigmund.) N.Y., 1957.
Phil 5520.05 Pamphlet box. General semantics.
Phil 5520.466 General semantics. pt.1. (Clauss, Karl.) Berlin, 1966. 2v.
Phil 5520.255 General semantics. 1. ed. (Longebaugh, T.) N.Y., 1957.
Phil 5520.105 General semantics bulletin. Lakeville, Conn. 1-13
Phil 16.6 General semantics monographs. Chicago.
Phil 5520.96.15 General semantics seminar, 1937. 2. ed. (Korzybski, Alfred.) Lakeville, Conn., 1964.
NEDL Phil 8685.9 General sketch...history of pantheism. (Plumptre, C.E.) London, 1881. 2v.
Phil 7069.28.45 A general survey of psychical phenomena. (Lambert, Helen C.S.) N.Y., 1928.
Phil 5150.1 General theory of notational relativity. (Sheffer, H.M.) Cambridge, 1921.
Phil 735.20.12 General theory of value. (Perry, Ralph Barton.) Cambridge, Mass., 1954.
Phil 735.20.5A General theory of value. (Perry, Ralph Barton.) N.Y., 1926.
Phil 8880.4 A general treatise of morality. (Fiddes, R.) London, 1724.
Phil 2490.51.15 A general view of positivism. (Comte, Auguste.) N.Y., 1957.
X Cg Phil 2490.51.7 A general view of positivism. 2d ed. (Comte, Auguste.) London, 1880.
Phil 2275.65 A general view of the progress of...philosophy. (Stewart, D.) Boston, 1822.
Phil 8837.1.2 A general view of the progress of ethical philosophy. (Mackintosh, James.) Philadelphia, 1832.
Phil 8837.1.3 A general view of the progress of ethical philosophy. (Mackintosh, James.) Philadelphia, 1834.
Phil 8837.1.4 A general view of the progress of ethical philosophy. (Mackintosh, James.) Edinburgh, 1837.
Phil 8893.115A Generalization in ethics. 1. ed. (Singer, M.G.) N.Y., 1961.
Phil 8700.18 Genes. (Klotz, John William.) Saint Louis, 1959.
Phil 3450.19.525 A gênese da ontologia fundamental de Martin Heidegger. (MacDowell, João Augusto A. Amazonas.) São Paulo, 1970.
Phil 1135.85.16 La genèse de la sensation...chez Protagoras, Platon et Aristote. Thèse. (Salzi, Pierre.) Paris, 1934.
Phil 1135.85.15 La genèse de la sensation...chez Protagoras. (Salzi, Pierre.) Paris, 1934.
Phil 2477.6.165 Genèse de l'action; Blondel, 1882-1893. (Saint-Jean, Raymond.) Bruges, 1965.
Phil 672.24 La genèse de l'idée de temps. 2e éd. (Guyau, M.J.) Paris, 1902.
Phil 3450.11.135 La genèse de l'intentionalité dans la philosophie de Husserl. (Lauer, Quentin.) Paris, 1954.
Phil 5817.6.9 La genèse des instincts. (Hachet-Souplet, P.) Paris, 1912.
Phil 6990.31 La genèse des miracles. (Regnault, Félix.) Paris, 1910.
Phil 2905.1.35 Genèse d'une pensée. (Teilhard de Chardin, Pierre.) Paris, 1961.
Phil 3425.319.5A Genèse et structure de la phénoménologie de l'esprit de Hegel. (Hyppolite, Jean.) Paris, 1946.
Phil 3425.319 Genèse et structure de la phénoménologie de l'esprit de Hegel. Thèse. (Hyppolite, Jean.) Paris, 1946.
Phil 8705.3 Geneses and modern science. (Perce, W.R.) N.Y., 1897.
Phil 3484.24 La genesi del criticismo kantiano. v.1-2. (Campo, M.) Varese, 1953-
Phil 178.62 La genesi del problema fenomenologico. (Drago, P.C.) Milano, 1933.
Phil 4225.8.90 Genesi e sviluppo del rosminianesimo nel pensiero di Michele F. Sciacca. (Pignoloni, Emilio.) Milano, 1964. 2v.
Phil 7054.37.33 El génesis, los milagros. (Rivail, H.L.D.) Barcelona, 1871.
Phil 7054.37.35 El génesis. (Rivail, H.L.D.) San Martin de Provensals, 1887.
Phil 6111.29 The genesis and evolution of the individual soul. (Bevan, J.O.) London, 1909.
Phil 8692.4 Genesis and geology. (Crofton, D.) Boston, 1857.
Phil 8696.20A Genesis and geology. (Gillispie, C.C.) Cambridge, Mass., 1951.
Phil 8696.20.5 Genesis and geology. (Gillispie, C.C.) Cambridge, 1969.

Phil 5374.3   Genesis des Bewusstseins. (Drossbach, M.) Leipzig, 1860.
Phil 8430.34   The genesis of art form. (Raymond, G.L.) N.Y., 1893.
Phil 8430.22   The genesis of art form. (Raymond, G.L.) N.Y., 1893.
Phil 5625.116 The genesis of the classical conditioned response. 1. ed.
                 (Martin, Irene.) Oxford, 1969.
Phil 8696.4   Genesis of the earth and of man. 2. ed. (Poole, R.S.)
                 London, 1860.
Phil 1715.11   The genesis of twentieth century philosophy. 1. ed.
                 (Prosch, H.) Garden City, N.Y., 1964.
Phil 5865.5.20 Genetic epistomology. (Piaget, Jean.) N.Y., 1970.
Phil 6328.48   A genetic field theory of ego formation. (Spitz, René.)
                 N.Y., 1959.
Phil 6118.5   Genetic neurology. (International Conference on the
                 Development of the Nervous System.) Chicago, 1950.
Phil 182.16   Genetic philosophy. (Hill, D.J.) N.Y., 1893.
Phil 5250.3.6 Genetic psychology. (Kirkpatrick, E.A.) N.Y., 1925.
Phil 16.3   Genetic psychology monographs. Worcester. 1,1920+ 56v.
Phil 5041.29.2 Genetic theory of reality. (Baldwin, J.M.) N.Y., 1915.
Phil 6960.10   Genetics of schizophrenia. (Kallmann, F.J.) N.Y., 1938.
Phil 3005.1   Genetische Geschichte der Philosophie seit Kant.
                 (Fortlage, K.) Leipzig, 1852.
Phil 3450.11.505 Genetische Phänomenologie und Reduktion. (Aguirre,
                 Antonio.) Den Haag, 1970.
Phil 186.50   Das genetische Prinzip. (Ludowici, A.) München, 1913.
Phil 5865.10   Genetische Psychologie, systematischen historisch.
                 v.1,7,9,12. (Kriekemans, Albert.) Tielt, 1965- 4v.
Phil 310.45   Genevès, F. L'imposture scientifique du matérialisme
                 historique allemand. Bordeaux, 1957.
Phil 5374.151 Geney, Gustave. From the unconcious to the conscious.
                 N.Y., 1921.
Phil 3640.196 Det geniala vansinnet. (Bjerre, Poul.) Göteborg, 1903.
Phil 5425.15   Der geniale Mensch. (Türck, H.) Berlin, 1899.
Phil 5425.15.10 Der geniale Mensch. 8. Aufl. (Türck, H.) Berlin, 1917.
Phil 5425.15.15 Der geniale Mensch. 10. Aufl. (Türck, H.) Berlin, 1920?
Phil 5425.47.3 Geniale Menschen. 5. Aufl. (Kretschmer, Ernst.)
                 Berlin, 1958.
Phil 8956.8.15 Genicot, Edouard. Casus conscientiae propositi ac soluti.
                 6. ed. Louvain, 1928.
Phil 5425.44.4 Genie, Irrsinn und Ruhm. (Lange, Wilhelm.) München, 1967.
Phil 5425.44.3 Genie, Irrsinn und Ruhm. 3. Aufl. (Lange, Wilhelm.)
                 München, 1942.
Phil 5425.44.25 Genie, Irrsinn und Ruhm. 4. Aufl. (Lange, Wilhelm.)
                 München, 1956.
Phil 5425.35A Das Genie. (Brentano, F.) Leipzig, 1892.
Phil 1817.3.5.5 Le génie américain. (Riley, I.W.) Paris, 1921.
Phil 2050.19   Le génie de M. Hume. (Hume, David.) London, 1770.
Phil 2805.192 Le génie de Pascal. (Brunschvicg, L.) Paris, 1924.
Phil 2805.404 Génie de Pascal. (Guitton, J.) Paris, 1962.
Phil 8583.22   Le génie des religions. (Descamps, E.) Paris, 1923.
Phil 2422.6   Le génie et la folie au dix-huitième siècle. (Willard,
                 Nedd.) Paris, 1963.
Phil 5425.44   Genie-Irrsinn und Ruhm. (Lange, Wilhelm.) München, 1928.
Phil 5425.44.5 Das Genie-Problem; eine Einführung. (Lange, Wilhelm.)
                 München, 1931.
Phil 5425.44.10 Das Genie-Problem. 3. Aufl. (Lange, Wilhelm.)
                 München, 1941.
Phil 5627.73   Le génie religieux. (Flournoy, T.) Neuchâtel, 1904.
Phil 5425.5.6 Genie und Entartung. 2. Aufl. (Hirsch, William.)
                 Berlin, 1894.
Phil 5425.76A Genie und Eros. (Dovski, Lee van.) Olten-Bern, 1949.
                 3v.
Phil 5425.72   Genie und Talent. (Müller, Willy.) München, 1940.
Phil 5425.9   Genie und Wahnsinn. (Radestock, P.) Breslau, 1884.
Phil 575.56   Die Geniereligion. (Zilsel, Edgar.) Wien, 1918.
Phil 5425.44.23 Genies als Problem. 2. Aufl. (Lange, Wilhelm.)
                 München, 1941.
Phil 5425.40   El genio; ensayo sobre su génesis. (Palcos, Alberto.)
                 Buenos Aires, 1920.
Phil 5425.16   Il genio. (Bovio, G.) Milano, 1900.
Phil 5425.34.3 Il genio. 3. ed. (Padovan, A.) Milano, 1923.
Phil 200.7   Il genio dell'uomo. 2a ed. (Zarcone, O.) Palermo, 1850.
Phil 4260.81.10 Il genio di Vico. (Ferrari, G.) Lanciano, 1922.
Phil 4215.3.38 Il genio etico, ed altri saggi. (Rensi, Giuseppe.)
                 Bari, 1912.
Phil 5425.10   Genius, fame and the comparison of races. (Cooley, C.H.)
                 Philadelphia, 1897.
Phil 5425.61   Genius. (Palmer, William J.) Los Angeles, 1937.
Phil 5425.46   Genius: some revaluations. (Jacobson, A.C.) N.Y., 1926.
Phil 5425.51   Genius and creative intelligence. (Hirsch, N.D.M.)
                 Cambridge, 1931.
Phil 5425.5   Genius and degeneration. (Hirsch, William.) N.Y., 1896.
Phil 5425.43   Genius and disaster. (Marks, Jeannette.) London, 1928.
Phil 5425.92   Genius and epilepsy. (Bryant, J.E.) Concord, Mass., 1953.
Phil 5425.6   Genius and insanity. (Macdonald, A.) Lewes, 1892.
Phil 3450.38   Genius der Menscheit. (Hoffmann, Gustov.)
                 Delmenhorst, 1959.
Phil 5425.90   Genius in the making. (Carroll, H.A.) N.Y., 1940.
Phil 5425.107 Genius und Wahn. (Venzmer, Gerhard.) Stuttgart, 1964.
Phil 8586.43   Genlis, S.F. La religion considérée comme l'unique base du
                 bonheur et de la véritable philosophie. Orleans, 1787.
Phil 8586.43.5 Genlis, S.F. La religion considérée comme l'unique base du
                 bonheur et de la véritable philosophie. Maestricht, 1787.
Phil 181.4   Genlis, S.F. de. Les diners baron D'Holbach. Paris, 1822.
Phil 4803.454.80 Gennadii, Sitkii. Zakon tvoreniia. Buenos Aires, 1956.
Phil 720.85   Gennaro, Guiseppe de. Saggio sui rapporti fra ubertà e
                 causalità. Padova, 1958.
Phil 184.27   Gennem modsabninger. (Jacobsen, O.T.) København, 1905.
Phil 2407.5   Gennembrudsmaend i nyere fransk filosofi. (Hansen, V.)
                 København, 1952.
Phil 18.21   Genootschap voor zuivore Rede. (De idee; orgaan van het
                 Bolliano.) Utrecht. 1-19,1923-1941 18v.
Phil 4114.20   Genovesi, Antonio. Autobiografia, lettere a altri scritti.
                 Milano, 1963.
Phil 4114.45   Genovesi, Antonio. Della diceosina o sia della filosofia
                 sul religione. Napoli, n.d. 3v.
Phil 4114.31   Genovesi, Antonio. Delle scienze metafisiche.
                 Napoli, 1791.
Phil 4114.30   Genovesi, Antonio. Delle scienze metafisiche.
                 Venezia, 1782.
Phil 4114.32   Genovesi, Antonio. Denoihnsion stoixeia, metafisikis.
                 Vienna, 1806.
Phil 4114.25.3 Genovesi, Antonio. Disciplinarum metaphysicarum elementa.
                 Bassani, 1785. 5v.
Phil 4114.25   Genovesi, Antonio. Elementa metaphysicae mathematicum in
                 morem adornata. 2a ed. Neapoli, 1751-56. 4v.
Phil 4114.23   Genovesi, Antonio. Elementorum artis logico criticae.
                 n.p., 1766.
Phil 4114.23.10 Genovesi, Antonio. Elementorum artis logico criticae.
                 Neapoli, 1778.
Phil 4114.75   Genovesi, Antonio. Lettere familiari. Venezia, 1844.
                 2v.
Phil 4114.50   Genovesi, Antonio. Lettere filosofiche. Napoli, 1785.
Phil 4114.40   Genovesi, Antonio. La logica. Napoli, 1790.
Phil 4114.47   Genovesi, Antonio. Meditazioni filosofiche sulla religione
                 e sulla morale. Bassano, 1783.
Phil 4114.71   Genovesi, Antonio. Opuscoli e lettere familiari.
                 Venezia, 1827.
Phil 5525.42   Les genres du risible. (Aubouin, Elie.) Marseille, 1948.
Phil 5525.42.2 Les genres du risible. Thèse. (Aubouin, Elie.)
                 Marseille, 1948.
Phil 8831.6   Gent, W. Der sittliche Mensch. Meisenheim, 1950.
Phil 5400.22   Gent, W. Volumpulscurven bei Gefühlen und Affecten.
                 Leipzig, 1903.
Phil 575.148   Gent, Werner. Person und Psychotherapie. Göttingen, 1951.
Phil 672.151   Gent, Werner. Die Philosophie des Raumes und der Zeit.
                 Bonn, 1926.
Phil 672.151.2 Gent, Werner. Die Philosophie des Raumes und der Zeit. 2.
                 Aufl. v.1-2. Hildesheim, 1962.
Phil 672.151.10 Gent, Werner. Das Problem der Zeit. Hildesheim, 1965.
Phil 8661.22   Gent, Werner. Untersuchungen zum Problem des Atheismus.
                 Hildesheim, 1964.
Phil 193.49.41 The genteel tradition; nine essays. (Santayana, G.)
                 Cambridge, 1967.
Phil 193.49.40A The genteel tradition at bay. (Santayana, G.) N.Y., 1931.
Phil 1818.7   The genteel tradition in American philosophy...public
                 address...1911. (Santayana, George.) Berkeley, 1911.
Phil 8400.24A Genteno, A. The intent of the artist. Princeton, 1941.
Phil 2805.197 Gentile, F. Pascal: saggio d'interpretazione storica.
                 Bari, 1927.
Phil 4235.1.85 Gentile, G. Bernardino Telesio. Bari, 1911.
Phil 4006.2.7 Gentile, G. Dal Genovesi al Galuppi. Napoli, 1903.
Phil 8586.17   Gentile, G. Discorsi di religione. Firenze, 1920.
Phil 8586.17.2 Gentile, G. Discorsi di religione. 2. ed. Firenze, 1924.
Phil 8407.6.5 Gentile, G. La filosofia dell'arte. Milano, 1931.
Phil 8407.6   Gentile, G. La filosofia dell'arte in compendio, ad uso
                 delle scuole. Firenze, 1934.
Phil 4006.2.30 Gentile, G. La filosofia italiana contemporanea.
                 Firenze, 1941.
Phil 4065.102.2 Gentile, G. Giordana Bruno i el pensiero del rinascimento.
                 2a ed. Firenze, 1925.
Phil 4065.102 Gentile, G. Giordano Bruno i el pensiero de rinascimento.
                 Firenze, 1920.
Phil 4065.102.8 Gentile, G. Giordano Bruno nella storia della cultura.
                 Milano, 1907.
Phil 4006.2.20 Gentile, G. Memorie italiane e problemi della filosofia e
                 della vita. Firenze, 1936.
Phil 4006.2.5A Gentile, G. Le origini della filosofia contemporanea in
                 Italia. v. 1-3. Messina, 1917-21. 4v.
Phil 4006.2.18 Gentile, G. Il pensiero italiano del rinascimento. 3. ed.
                 Firenze, 1940.
Phil 4006.2.15 Gentile, G. Il pensiero italiano del secolo XIX.
                 Milano, 1928.
Phil 8407.6.10 Gentile, G. Philosophie der Kunst. Berlin, 1934.
Phil 4006.2   Gentile, G. I problemi della scolastica e il pensiero
                 italiano. Bari, 1913.
Phil 4006.2.2 Gentile, G. I problemi della scolastica e il pensiero
                 italiano. 2a ed. Bari, 1923.
Phil 3425.209 Gentile, G. La riforma della dialettica Hegeliana.
                 Messina, 1913.
Phil 3425.209.5 Gentile, G. La riforma della dialettica Hegeliana. 2a ed.
                 Messina, 1923.
Phil 4115.99   Gentile, G. Rosmini e Gioberti. Pisa, 1898.
Phil 4210.117 Gentile, G. Rosmini e Gioberti. Pisa, 1898.
Phil 4210.117.2 Gentile, G. Rosmini e Gioberti. 2. ed. Firenze, 1955.
Phil 5046.11   Gentile, G. Sistema di logica come teoria del conscere.
                 Pisa, 1917.
Phil 4006.2.8 Gentile, G. Storia della filosofia italiani dal Genovesi
                 al Galuppi. 2a ed. Milano, 1930. 2v.
Phil 4006.2.9 Gentile, G. Studi sul rinascimento. Firenze, 1923.
Phil 4006.2.10 Gentile, G. Studi sul rinascimento. 2a ed. Firenze, 1936.
Phil 1350.7   Gentile, G. Studi sullo stoicismo romano. Trani, 1904.
Phil 4225.1.95 Gentile, Giovanni. Bertrando Spaventa. Firenze, 1920.
Phil 4120.4.125 Gentile, Giovanni. Il concetto moderno della scienza e il
                 problema universitario. Roma, 1921.
Phil 4120.4.31 Gentile, Giovanni. Discorsi di religone. 3. ed.
                 Firenze, 1934.
Phil 181.45.19 Gentile, Giovanni. L'esprit, acte pur. Paris, 1925.
Phil 4120.4.35 Gentile, Giovanni. I fondamenti della filosofia del
                 oiritto. 3. ed. Firenze, 1937.
Phil 4120.4.55 Gentile, Giovanni. Genile. Roma, 1966.
Phil 4120.4.45 Gentile, Giovanni. Introduzione alla filosofia.
                 Milano, 1933.
Phil 4120.4.90 Gentile, Giovanni. Introduzione alla filosofia. 2. ed.
                 Firenze, 1952.
Phil 4120.4.11 Gentile, Giovanni. Opere. v. 1-28,30-38,42.
                 Firenze, 1942. 36v.
Phil 4120.4.126 Gentile, Giovanni. La religione: il modernismo e i
                 rapporti tra religione e filosofia. Firenze, 1965.
Phil 181.45   Gentile, Giovanni. Saggi critici. Ser. I. Napoli, 1921.
Phil 181.45.30 Gentile, Giovanni. Scritti vari. Lanciano, 1920-1926.
                 5v.
Phil 4260.94.5 Gentile, Giovanni. Studi vichiani. Firenze, 1927.
Phil 4260.94   Gentile, Giovanni. Studi vichiani. Messina, 1915.
Phil 181.45.9 Gentile, Giovanni. Teoria generale dello spirito come atto
                 puro. 2a ed. Pisa, 1918.
Phil 181.45.11 Gentile, Giovanni. Teoria generale dello spirito come atto
                 puro. 3a ed. Bari, 1920.
Phil 181.45.15 Gentile, Giovanni. Teoria generale dello spirito come atto
                 puro. 6a ed. Firenze, 1944.
Phil 181.45.5 Gentile, Giovanni. The theory of mind as pure act.
                 London, 1922.
Phil 1135.158 Gentile, M. La metafisica presofistica. Padova, 1939.
Phil 181.164.2 Gentile, Marino. Come si pone il problema meta fisico. 2.
                 ed. Padova, 1965.
Phil 8831.7   Gentile, Marino. I grandi moralisti. Torino, 1955.
Phil 8586.30   Gentile, P. Sommario d'un filosofia della religione.
                 Bari, 1923.
Phil 4120.4.55 Gentile. (Gentile, Giovanni.) Roma, 1966.
Phil 4120.4.87 Gentile. (Romanelli, P.) N.Y., 1938.
Phil 4120.4.83 Gentile e Croce. (Sarlo, F. de.) Firenze, 1925.
Htn 9344.7*   The gentile sinner. (Ellis, Clement.) Oxford, 1660.
Htn 9355.10* Le gentilhomme. (Pasquier, N.) Paris, 1611. 3 pam.
Phil 525.71   Gentilini, B. De la mística. Santiago de Chile, 1926.
Phil 2880.8.112 Gentiloni Silverj, F. Jean Paul Sartre contro la speranza.
                 Roma, 1952.

Phil 4215.4.80 — Gentiluomo, D. L'ontognoseologia di Cesare Ranzoli. Padova, 1951.

Phil 4060.4.80 — Gentiluomo, Domenico. Il relativismo sperimentale di Antonio Aliotta nel suo svolgimento storico. Roma, 1955.

Phil 9346.13 — The gentleman and lady of pleasure's amusement. London, 1759.

Phil 9343.2.2 — Gentleman instructed. (Darell, W.) London, 1707. 2v.
Phil 9343.2 — Gentleman instructed. (Darell, W.) London, 1723.
Phil 8878.19 — The gentleman instructed. (Darell, W.) London, 1738.
Phil 8961.19 — Der Gentleman und der Christ. (Lorenz, Willy.) Wien, 1967.

Htn Phil 1845.1.25* — The gentleman's calling. (Allestree, Richard.) London, 1660.

Phil 9346.7 — The gentleman's library. 2d ed. London, 1722.
Htn Phil 9362.12* — The gentleman's monitor. (Waterhoues, E.) London, 1665.
Phil 5816.5.3 — Gentry, Thomas G. Intelligence in plants and animals. N.Y., 1900.

Phil 5816.5 — Gentry, Thomas G. Life and immortality. Philadelphia, 1897.

Phil 8631.8 — Genung, John F. The life indeed. Boston, 1921.
Phil 5640.9 — Genzmer, A.O.H. Untersuchungen über die Sinneswahrnehmungen des neugeborenen Menschen. Halle, n.d.

Phil 5640.9.2 — Genzmer, A.O.H. Untersuchungen über die Sinneswahrnehmungen des neugeborenen Menschen. Halle, 1882.

Phil 8701.1 — Geognosy, or The facts and principles of geology against theories. (Lord, D.N.) N.Y., 1855.

Phil 8656.6.5 — Geologie und Mineralogie. (Buckland, W.) Neufchatel, 1838-39. 2v.

Phil 8702.1 — Geology and geologists. (Macbriar, R.M.) London, 1843.
Phil 8656.6 — Geology and mineralogy...natural theology. (Buckland, W.) London, 1837. 2v.

Phil 8656.6.2 — Geology and mineralogy...natural theology. (Buckland, W.) Philadelphia, 1841. 2v.

Phil 8709.7 — Geology as an interpreter of scripture. (Thomson, S.H.) Cincinnati, 1858.

Phil 2520.13.12 — Geometria. 3a ed. (Descartes, René.) Amsterdam, 1683. 2v.

Phil 2493.100 — The geometric spirit; the Abbe de Condillac and the French Enlightenment. (Knight, Isabel F.) New Haven, 1968.

Phil 7069.39.55 — Geometric telepathy. (Thompson, L.S.) Los Angeles, 1939.
Phil 8587.16.2 — Geometry and faith. (Hill, T.) Boston, 1882.
Phil 8587.16 — Geometry and faith. (Hill, T.) N.Y., 1849.
Phil 6117.10.3 — Die geopsychischen Erscheinungen. (Hellpach, W.) Leipzig, 1911.

Phil 6117.10.5 — Die geopsychischen Erscheinungen. 2. Aufl. (Hellpach, W.) Leipzig, 1917.

Phil 3625.14.90 — Georg Elias Müller. (Turner, William D.) Cambridge, 1928.
Phil 3195.8.80 — Georg Friedrich Daumer. Inaug. Diss. (Birkenbihl, M.) Aschaffenburg, 1905.

Phil 3625.8.95 — Georg Friedrich Meier als mitbegründer der deutschen Athetik unter Benutzung ungedruckter Quellen. (Bergmann, E.) Leipzig, 1910.

Phil 3625.8.25 — Georg Friedrich Meiers Metaphysik. v.1-4. (Meier, Georg Friedrich.) Halle, 1755-59. 3v.

Phil 3850.16.21 — Georg Simmel, 1858-1918. (Simmel, Georg.) Columbus, 1959.
Phil 3850.16.118 — Georg Simmel. (Coser, Lewis A.) Englewood, 1965.
Phil 3850.16.95 — Georg Simmel. (Frischeisen-Köhler, Max.) Berlin, 1919.
Phil 3850.16.81 — Georg Simmels Bedeutung für die Geistesgeschichte. (Adler, Max.) Wien, 1919.

Phil 3450.17.92 — Georg von Hertlings Gesellschaftlslehre. Inaug. Diss. (Urbanowski, J.) Battrop, 1936.

Phil 3425.91.10 — Georg Wilhelm F. Hegel's Leben. (Rosenkranz, K.) Berlin, 1844.

Phil 3425.280 — Georg Wilhelm Freidrich Hegel. (Siegel, Carl.) Graz, 1931.

Phil 3425.595.7 — Georg Wilhelm Freidrich Hegel in Nürnberg 1808-1816. (Beyer, W.R.) Nürnberg, 1966.

Phil 5520.638 — George, Frank Honywill. Models of thinking. London, 1970.
Htn Phil 2030.2.30* — George, Henry. Progress and poverty. San Francisco, 1879.
Phil 8586.13 — George, J.F.L. Mythus und Sage. Berlin, 1837.
Phil 5640.13 — George, L. Die fünf Sinne. Berlin, 1846.
Phil 5046.1 — George, L. Die Logik als Wissenschaftslehre Dargestellt. Berlin, 1868.

Phil 3425.85 — George, L. Princip und Methode der Philosophie. Berlin, 1842.

Phil 3310.3.31 — George, L. System der Metaphysik. Berlin, 1844.
Phil 365.60 — George, Nicolas. D'Einstein à Teilhard. Paris, 1964.
Phil 5246.4 — George, S. Lehrbuch der Psychologie. Berlin, 1854.
Phil 1870.160 — George Berkeley, a reappraisal. (Ritchie, Arthur David.) Manchester, 1967.

Phil 1870.123.5 — George Berkeley. (Bender, Frans.) Baarn, 1966.
Phil 1870.140 — George Berkeley. (Jessop, T.E.) London, 1959.
Phil 1870.138 — George Berkeley. (Leroy, André Louis.) Paris, 1959.
Phil 1870.117A — George Berkeley. (Wild, John.) Cambridge, 1936.
Phil 1870.132 — George Berkeley and the proofs for the existence of God. (Sillem, E.A.) London, 1957.

Phil 1870.122 — George Berkeley in Apulia. (Brayton, Alice.) Boston, 1946.

Phil 1870.122.5 — George Berkeley in Newport. (Brayton, Alice.) Newport, R.I., 1954.

Phil 1870.101 — George Berkeley Leben und Lehre. (Metz, Rudolf.) Stuttgart, 1925.

Phil 1870.114 — George Berkeley und die englische Literatur. (Oertel, Hans.) Halle, 1934.

Phil 1870.123 — George Berkeley's philosophy re-examined. (Bender, Frans.) Amsterdam, 1946.

Phil 2042.5 — George Dawes Hicks. (DeBurgh, William George.) London, 1944.

Phil 2150.15.80 — George Herbert Mead. (Lee, G.C.) N.Y., 1945.
Phil 2150.15.30 — George Herbert Mead. (Mead, George Herbert.) N.Y., 1968.
Phil 2225.7.90A — George Herbert Palmer, 1842-1933; memorial addressses. Cambridge, 1935.

Phil 182.100 — George Holmes Howison, philosopher and teacher. (Howison, G.H.) Berkeley, 1934.

Phil 8662.5.25 — George Jacob Holyoake and modern atheism. (Collet, S.D.) London, 1855.

Phil 2280.5.101 — George Santayana; an American philosopher in exile. (Clemens, C.) Webster Groves, 1937.

Phil 2280.5.102 — George Santayana. (Howgate, G.W.) Philadelphia, 1938.
Phil 2280.5.90 — George Santayana. pt.1-2. (Larrabee, H.A.) n.p., 1931.
Phil 2280.5.102.2 — George Santayana. Thesis. (Howgate, G.W.) Philadelphia, 1938.

Phil 2280.5.97 — George Santayana's theory of knowledge. Diss. (Hoor, M.) n.p., 1923.

Phil 2150.1.85 — George Sylvester Morris; his philosophical career and theistic idealism. (Jones, Marc Edmund.) Philadelphia, 1948.

Phil 5251.1.30 — George Trumbull Ladd: pioneer American psychologist. (Mills, Eugene S.) Cleveland, 1969.
Phil 2490.89 — Georges, A. Le système psychologique d'Auguste Comte. Lyon, 1908.
Phil 2477.20.80 — Georges Bastide, philosophe de la valeur. (Pradines, Marie Thérèse.) Toulouse, 1970.
Phil 5520.460 — The Georgetown bibliography of studies contributing to the psycholinguistics of language learning. (Walters, Theodore W.) Washington, 1965.
Phil 16.13 — Georgia psychologist; official publication of Georgia Psychological Association. Atlanta. 20,1967+
Phil 3425.568 — Georgiav, F.I. Protivopolozhnost' Marksistskogo i Gegelevskogo ucheniia o sozhanii. Moskva, 1961.
Phil 310.240 — Georgiev, F.I. Kategorii materialisticheskoi dialektiki. Moskva, 1960.
Phil 310.745 — Georgiev, Filipp I. Problema protivorechiia. Moskva, 1969.
Phil 5046.44 — Georgius, Trapezuntius. De re dialectica libellus. Frankfurt, 1966.
Phil 850.17 — Georgov, Ivan. Istoriia na filosofiiata. Sofiia, 1926.
Phil 2750.20.150 — Geraets, Théodore F. Vers une nouvelle philosophie transcendantale. La Haye, 1971.
Phil 8881.6.5 — Gerando, J.M. Du perfectionnement moral. Paris, 1826. 2v.
Phil 8881.6 — Gerando, J.M. Self-education. Boston, 1830.
Phil 8881.6.2 — Gerando, J.M. Self-education. 2nd ed. Boston, 1832.
Phil 8881.6.4 — Gerando, J.M. Self-education. 3rd ed. Boston, 1860.
Phil 5246.5 — Gerando, J.M. de. Des signes et de l'art de penser. Paris, 1800. 4v.
Phil 806.1 — Gerando, J.M. de. Histoire comparée des systèmes de philosophie. Paris, 1822-23. 4v.
Phil 8400.20 — Gerard, Alex. An essay on taste. London, 1759.
Phil 5425.17.5 — Gerard, Alexander. An essay on genius, 1774. München, 1966.
Phil 5425.17 — Gerard, Alexander. An essay on genius. London, 1774.
X Cg Phil 5425.17 — Gerard, Alexander. An essay on genius. London, 1774.
Phil 8407.2 — Gerard, Alexander. An essay on taste (1759). Facsimile. Gainesville, Fla., 1963.
Phil 1870.106 — Gerard, J. De idealismi aprud Berkeleium. Sancti Clodoaldi, 1874.
Phil 6316.3 — Gérard, J. La grande névrose. Paris, 1889.
Phil 2730.92 — Gérard, J. La philosophie de Maine de Biran. Paris, 1876.
Phil 2630.10 — Gerard, Jacques. L'être et la pensée. Paris, 1954.
Phil 178.46.80 — Gerard, Jacques. La metaphysique de Paul Decoster. Paris, 1945.
Phil 8586.12 — Gérard, Philippe Louis. Le Comte de Valmont ou les égaremens de la raison. Paris, 1775.
Phil 5246.15 — Gerard-Varet, G. L'ignorance et l'irréflexion. Paris, 1899.
Phil 2270.112 — Geraskoff, Michael. Die sittliche Erziehung nach Herbert Spencer. Zürich, 1912.
Phil 5816.8 — Geraud, Petrus J. Dissertatio philosophica de principio actionum. Trajecti ad Rhenum, 1724.
Phil 181.5 — Gerber, G. Das Ich. Berlin, 1893.
Phil 2270.180 — Gerbert Spencer. Idei svoboda i prava. (Gol'denveizer, A.S.) Sankt Peterburg, 1904.
Phil 3640.400 — Gerbes, Hans E. Zum 50. Todestag Friedrich Nietzsches. n.p., 195-.
Phil 2733.95 — Gerdil, G.S. Défense du sentiment du P. Malebranche. Turin, 1748.
Phil 2115.113 — Gerdil, G.S. L'immatérialité de l'âme...contre Locke. Turin, 1747.
Phil 575.288 — Gergen, Kenneth J. The concept of self. N.Y., 1971.
Phil 3488.11 — Gerhard, Carl. Kant's Lehre von der Freiheit. Heidelberg, 1885.
Phil 3640.251 — Gerhard, H.F. Die künstlerischen Mittel der Darstellung in Nietzsches "Zarathustra". Berlin, 1896.
Phil 5425.29.3 — Gerhardi, Karl A. Das Wesen des Genies. Jauer, 1908.
Phil 181.6 — Gerhart, E.V. An introduction to study of philosophy. Philadelphia, 1858.
Phil 6313.1 — Gerichtliche psychopathologie. (Delbrück, A.) Leipzig, 1897.
Phil 8881.31 — Gerkrath, E. Grundlinien der Ethik. Charlottenburg, 1912.
Phil 8881.49 — Gerlach, G.W. De differentia, quae inter Plotini et Schellingii doctrinam de numine summo intercedit. Thesis.
Htn Phil 3801.419* — Viterbegae, 1811.
Phil 5046.17 — Gerlach, G.W. Grundriss der Logik. 2e Aufl. Halle, 1822.
Phil 8881.49 — Gerlach, G.W. Grundriss der philosophischen Lugendlehre. Halle, 1829.
Phil 1145.80 — Gerlach, Julius. Haner hagados. Inaug. Diss. Munchen, 1932.
Phil 3488.8 — Gerland, G. Immanuel Kant, seine geographischen und anthropologischen Arbeiten. Berlin, 1906.
Phil 5628.55 — Gerlich, Fritz. Die Stigmatisierte Therese Neumann von Konnersreuth. München, 1929. 2v.
Phil 7069.65.5 — Gerloff, Hans. The crisis in parapsychology. Tittmoning, 1965.
Phil 7069.65.6 — Gerloff, Hans. The crisis in parapsychology. 2. supplement. Tittmoning, 1966.
Phil 7069.65.7 — Gerloff, Hans. The crisis in parapsychologia. 3. supplement. Bayerisch Gmain, 1967.
Phil 6990.3.112 — Gerloff, Hans. Die Heilungen von Lourdes im Lichte der Parapsychologie. Büdingen-Gettenbach, 1959.
Phil 3481.17 — Pamphlet vol. German and Dutch philosophy - Kant - Biography and criticism. 5 pam.
Phil 3481.20 — Pamphlet box. German and Dutch philosophy - Kant - Biography and criticism.
Phil 3481.7 — Pamphlet vol. German and Dutch philosophy - Kant - Biography and criticism. 19 pam.
Phil 3481.12 — Pamphlet vol. German and Dutch philosophy - Kant - Biography and criticism. 22 pam.
Phil 3481.15 — Pamphlet vol. German and Dutch philosophy - Kant - Biography and criticism. 15 pam.
Phil 3481.6 — Pamphlet vol. German and Dutch philosophy - Kant - Biography and criticism. 17 pam.
Phil 3481.3 — Pamphlet vol. German and Dutch philosophy - Kant - Biography and criticism. 24 pam.
Phil 3481.1 — Pamphlet vol. German and Dutch philosophy - Kant - Biography and criticism. 39 pam.
Phil 3481.5 — Pamphlet vol. German and Dutch philosophy - Kant - Biography and criticism. 9 pam.
Phil 3481.9 — Pamphlet vol. German and Dutch philosophy - Kant - Biography and criticism. 11 pam.
Phil 3481.2 — Pamphlet vol. German and Dutch philosophy - Kant - Biography and criticism. 17 pam.
Phil 3481.10 — Pamphlet vol. German and Dutch philosophy - Kant - Biography and criticism. 5 pam.

Phil 3481.4   Pamphlet vol. German and Dutch philosophy - Kant - Biography and criticism. 11 pam.

Phil 3481.11   Pamphlet vol. German and Dutch philosophy - Kant - Biography and criticism. German dissertations. 17 pam.

Phil 3481.16   Pamphlet vol. German and Dutch philosophy - Kant - Biography and criticism. German dissertations. 15 pam.

Phil 3481.19   Pamphlet box. German and Dutch philosophy - Kant - Biography and criticism. German dissertations.

Phil 3481.18   Pamphlet vol. German and Dutch philosophy - Kant - Biography and criticism. German dissertations. 14 pam.

Phil 3481.13   Pamphlet vol. German and Dutch philosophy - Kant - Biography and criticism. German dissertations. 17 pam.

Phil 3481.14   Pamphlet vol. German and Dutch philosophy - Kant - Biography and criticism. German dissertations. 19 pam.

Phil 3481.8   Pamphlet vol. German and Dutch philosophy - Kant - Biography and criticism. German dissertations. 16 pam.

Phil 102.4   German-English dictionary of psychological terms. (Ruckmick, C.A.) Iowa City, 1928.

Phil 8125.04   Pamphlet vol. German esthetics. German. A-K. 6 pam.
Phil 8125.02   Pamphlet vol. German esthetics. German. L-W. 6 pam.
Phil 3450.19.28   German existentialism. (Heidegger, Martin.) N.Y., 1965.
Phil 3482.2.5   German Kantian bibliography. v.1-3. (Adickes, E.) Boston, 1896[1893]

Phil 2998.14   Pamphlet vol. German philosophers. A-H. German dissertations. 10 pam.

Phil 2998.15   Pamphlet vol. German philosophers. L-W. German dissertations. 9 pam.

Phil 3003.3A   German philosophy and politics. (Dewey, John.) N.Y., 1915.

Phil 3003.3.5   German philosophy and politics. (Dewey, John.) N.Y., 1942.

Phil 3012.2   German philosophy in relation to the war. (Muirhead, J.H.) London, 1917.

Phil 5227.2.5   German psychology of to-day. (Ribot, T.) N.Y., 1886.
Phil 5227.2.6   German psychology of to-day. (Ribot, T.) N.Y., 1899.
Phil 623.10.5   German rationalism. (Hagenbach, K.R.) Edinburgh, 1865.
Phil 3006.8   Der germanische Schichsalsglaube. (Gehl, W.) Berlin, 1939.

Phil 3640.24   Germans, Jews and France. (Nietzsche, Friedrich.) Newark, 1935.

Phil 6125.29   Germany. Heer Inspection des Personalprüfwesens. Menschen Formen. Berlin, 1941.

Phil 3450.11.155   Germenes de idealismo en las investigaciones logicas de Husserl. (Casaubon, Juan A.) Buenos Aires? 1956?

Phil 181.59   Germer, Hugo. Schönheit, Güte, Zweck. 1. Teil: Kant und Schopenhauer. Berlin, 1908.

Phil 165.347   Gerner-Beuerle, M. Schäpferisches Leben. München, 1964.
Phil 5246.78   Gernhammer, Vilhelm. And og sjael; symboler og symbolik. v.1-2. Silkeborg, 1968.

Phil 3488.41   Gerresheim, E. Die Bedeutung des Terminus transzendental in Immanuel Kants Kritik der reinen Vernunft. Inaug. Diss. Köln, 1962.

Phil 3450.22   Gerritsen, T.J.C. La philosophie de Heymass. Paris, 1938.
Phil 3450.22.1   Gerritsen, T.J.C. La philosophie de Heymass. Paris, 1938.

Phil 7072.6   Gerry, Elbridge T. The number "spirit" photograph case. N.Y., 1869.

Phil 3488.43   Gersch, Walter. Der transzendentale Existenzbeweis in Kants Kritischer Metaphysik der ausserbewussten Wirklichkeit. Würzburg, 1938.

Phil 4757.1.30   Gershenzon, M.O. Kliuch very. Peterburg, 1922.
Phil 4757.1.35   Gershenzon, M.O. Troistvennyi obraz sovershenstva. Moskva, 1918.

Phil 4710.145   Gershenzon, Mikhail O. Istoriia molodoi Rossii. Moskva, 1923.

VPhil 5590.558   Gerstmann, Stanisław. Osobowość. Wyd. 1. Warszawa, 1970.
Phil 3488.21   Gertanner, Christoph. Ueber das Kantische Prinzip für die Naturgeschichte. Göttingen, 1796.

Phil 5655.5   Der Geruch. (Henning, H.) Leipzig, 1916.
Phil 181.7   Géruzez, E. Cours de philosophie. Paris, 1840.
Phil 181.38   Gesammelte Abhandlungen. (Güttler, Karl.) München, 1918.
Phil 343.5.19   Gesammelte Abhandlungen. (Meinong, A.) Leipzig, 1913. 2v.

Phil 5643.29   Gesammelte Abhandlungen der physiologischen Optik. (Konig, Arthur.) Leipzig, 1903.

Phil 184.52   Gesammelte Abhandlungen zur Frage des Seins. (Janssen, O.) München, 1963.

Phil 3004.8   Gesammelte Aufsätze, Verträge und Reden. (Ebhinghaus, J.) Hildesheim, 1968.

Phil 3120.22.5   Gesammelte Aufsätze. (Blüher, Hans.) Jena, 1919.
Phil 5593.10   Gesammelte Aufsätze. (Rorschach, Hermann.) Bern, 1965.
Phil 3808.143   Gesammelte Aufsätze über Schopenhauer. (Herrig, Hans.) Leipzig, 1894.

Phil 6972.2.5   Gesammelte Aufsätze und kritische Riferate. (Wernicke, C.) Berlin, 1893.

Phil 1828.12   Gesammelte Aufsätze zur englischen Scholastik. (Ehrle, Franz.) Roma, 1970.

Phil 978.49.152   Gesammelte Aufsätze zur Kultur- und Zeitgeschichte, 1887-1901. (Steiner, R.) Dornach, 1966.

Phil 179.3.13   Gesammelte Aufsätze zur Philosophie. (Eucken, R.) Leipzig, 1903.

Phil 57.5   Gesammelte Dissertations. (Rostock. Universitat.) Rostock.

Phil 182.37.10   Gesammelte kleinere Schriften. (Heymans, G.) Den Haag, 1927. 3v.

Phil 3415.38   Gesammelte philosophische Abhandlungen Philosophie Unbewussten. (Hartmann, Eduard von.) Berlin, 1872.

Phil 3790.9.20   Gesammelte philosophische Aufsätze. (Rehmke, J.) Erfurt, 1928.

Phil 4080.3.10   Gesammelte philosophische Schriften in deutscher Übertragung. v.1 (no.1-4), v.2 (no. 1-3). (Croce, Benedetto.) Tübingen, 1927-1930. 7v.

Phil 3195.6.30.5   Gesammelte Schriften. (Dilthey, Wilhelm.) Stuttgart, 1957- 12v.

Phil 6315.2.2   Gesammelte Schriften. (Freud, Sigmund.) Leipzig, 1924-34. 12v.

Phil 3310.8.21   Gesammelte Schriften. (Glockner, Hermann.) Berlin, 1963-66.

Phil 3528.10   Gesammelte Schriften. (Krug, Wilhelm Traugott.) Braunschweig, 1830-45. 12v.

Phil 3585.30   Gesammelte Schriften. (Lask, Emil.) Tübingen, 1923. 3v.

Phil 187.68   Gesammelte Schriften. (Marty, Anton.) Halle, 1916-1918. 2v.

Phil 3625.1.10   Gesammelte Schriften. (Mendelssohn, Moses.) Leipzig, 1843-45. 8v.

Phil 189.4   Gesammelte Schriften. (Oersted, H.C.) Leipzig, 1850-1851. 6v.

Phil 978.49.895   Gesammelte Schriften. (Steiner, Marie von Sivers.) Dornach, 1967.

Phil 3480.14.4   Gesammelte Schriften. Allgemeiner Kantindex. (Kant, Immanuel.) Bonn, 1966. 3v.

Phil 3480.14.5   Gesammelte Schriften. Bd.X-XII. (Kant, Immanuel.) Berlin, 1922. 3v.

Phil 3310.1.3   Gesammelte Schriften. Bd.1-9. (Günther, Anton.) Wien, 1882. 9v.

Phil 178.42   Gesammelte Schriften. Heft I. (Dittes, Friedrich.) Leipzig, 1893.

Phil 3480.14.2.2   Gesammelte Schriften. Personenindex. Nachträge. (Kant, Immanuel.) Bonn, 1966.

Phil 3480.14.2   Gesammelte Schriften. Personenindex. v.A-L. (Kant, Immanuel.) Bonn, 1964- 6v.

Phil 3480.14.1   Gesammelte Schriften. Personenindex. v.1-23. (Kant, Immanuel.) Bonn, 1962-

Phil 3625.1.15A   Gesammelte Schriften. v.1-3,7,11,16. (Mendelssohn, Moses.) Berlin, 1929-32. 6v.

Phil 3850.46.1   Gesammelte Schriften. v.1-3,8. (Spranger, Eduard.) Tübingen, 1969- 4v.

Phil 3665.5.2   Gesammelte Schriften. v.1-8. (Nelson, Leonard.) Hamburg, 1970. 7v.

Phil 3195.6.30   Gesammelte Schriften. v.1-9,11-12. (Dilthey, Wilhelm.) Leipzig, 1923-36. 11v.

Phil 3195.6.30.10   Gesammelte Schriften. v.1-17. (Dilthey, Wilhelm.) Stuttgart, 1962- 16v.

Phil 3480.14   Gesammelte Schriften. v.1-24,28. (Kant, Immanuel.) Berlin, 1900-36. 27v.

Phil 3085.7.1   Gesammelte Schriften. 1. Aufl. (Adorno, Theodor W.) Frankfurt, 1971.

Phil 3120.2.3   Gesammelte Schriften. 2. Ausg. (Bolzano, Bernard.) Wien, 1882.

Phil 3585.14.10   Gesammelte Schriften in zehn Bäuden. (Lessing, Theodor.) Prag, 1935.

Phil 3415.48   Gesammelte Studien und Aufsätze. (Hartmann, Eduard von.) Berlin, 1876.

Phil 4065.15   Gesammelte Werke. (Bruno, Giordano.) Leipzig, 1904-09. 6v.

Phil 3450.11.30   Gesammelte Werke. (Husserl, Edmund.) Haag, 1950-52. 12v.

Phil 3625.5.2   Gesammelte Werke. (Maimon, Salomon.) Hildesheim, 1965. 6v.

Phil 3640.10.15   Gesammelte Werke. (Nietzsche, Friedrich.) München, 1929-29. 23v.

Phil 3850.44.3   Gesammelte Werke. (Schrempf, Christof.) Stuttgart, 1930-40.

Phil 3022.4.5   Gesammelte Werke. (Wust, Peter.) Münster, 1963. 10v.

Phil 6315.2   Gesammelte Werke. v. 1-14,16-18. (Freud, Sigmund.) London, 1940-46. 16v.

Phil 2138.2   Gesammelte Werke. v.1-3, 4-6, 7-9, 10-12. (Mill, John S.) Leipzig, 1869-80. 4v.

Phil 3160.4.3   Gesammelte Werke. v.1-14. (Carriere, M.) Leipzig, 1886-94. 12v.

Phil 3235.11   Gesammelte Werke. v.2-4,6-9. (Feuerbach, Ludwig.) Berlin, 1967- 8v.

Phil 3425.13A   Gesammelte Werke. v.4,7. (Hegel, Georg Wilhelm Friedrich.) Hamburg, 1968. 2v.

Phil 3200.14.5   Gesammelte Werke. 2. Aufl. (Ebner, Ferdinand.) Wien, 1952.

Phil 6116.12   Gesammelte Abhandlungen. v.1-2. (Goldscheider, A.) Leipzig, 1898.

Phil 3910.10   Gesammlete kleine Philosophie Schrifften. (Wolff, Christian von.) Magdeburg, 1736-40. 6v.

Phil 3910.12   Gesammelte Werke. (Wolff, Christian von.) Hildesheim, 1962- 22v.

Phil 3120.55.20   Gesamtausgabe. (Bloch, Ernst.) Frankfurt, 1961. 15v.
Phil 3625.11   Gesamtausgabe. Herausgeber: Rudolf Haller und R. Kindinger. (Meinong, Alexius.) Graz, 1968- 3v.

Phil 3246.18.4   Gesamtausgabe der Bauerischen Akademie der Wissenschaften. (Fichte, Johann Gottlieb.) Stuttgart, 1962. 9v.

Phil 197.28   Die Gesamterfahrung vom Gesichtspunkt des Primörmonismus. (Willy, Rudolf.) Zürich, 1908.

Phil 801.16   Gesamtgeschichte der Philosophie. 2. Aufl. (Baumann, J.) Gotha, 1903.

Phil 5203.25   Gesamtverzeichnis der deutschsparchigen psychologischen Literatur der Jahre 1942 bis 1960. (Wellek, Albert.) Göttingen, 1965.

Phil 3552.117   Gesche, Paul. Die Ethik Leibnizens. Halle, 1891.
Phil 8610.870   Geschichiedenis van het scepticisme der zeventiende eeuw in de voornaamste europeesche staten. 1e aflevering. (Was, H.) Utrecht, 1870.

Phil 3012.1   Geschichte...Philosophie in Deutschland. (Michelet, C.L.) Berlin, 1837-38. 2v.

Phil 3425.261   Die Geschichte als Schicksal des Geistes in der hegelschen Philosophie. (Foster, Michael B.) Tübingen, 1929.

Phil 260.1   Geschichte de Atomistik. (Sasswitz, K.) Hamburg, 1890. 2v.

Phil 801.32   Die Geschichte der abendländischen Philosophie eine Geschichte des geistigen Fortschritts der Menscheit. (Baumgarten, A.) Genève, 1945.

Phil 8050.30   Geschichte der Asthetik. (Utitz, Emil.) Berlin, 1932.
Phil 8050.5   Geschichte der Asthetik. Köln, 1962.
Phil 8062.4   Die Geschichte der Asthetik im Altertum. (Walter, Julius.) Leipzig, 1893.

Phil 8125.38   Geschichte der Aesthetik in Deutschland. (Lotze, H.) München, 1868.

Phil 8125.24   Geschichte der Aesthetik in Deutschland. (Lotze, Hermann.) München. 1848.

Phil 8050.36   Geschichte der Asthetik und Kunstphilosophie. (Bergmann, E.) Leipzig, 1914.

Phil 930.7.5   Geschichte der alten chinesischen Philosophie. (Forke, A.) Hamburg, 1927.

Phil 1106.10   Geschichte der alten Philosophie. (Bertling, Oskar.) Leipzig, 1907.

Phil 1117.6   Geschichte der alten Philosophie. (Meyer, Hans.) München, 1925.

Phil 1127.2.9   Geschichte der alten Philosophie. (Windelband, W.) Nördlingen, 1888.

Phil 1105.7   Geschichte der antiken Philosophie. (Aster, E.) Berlin, 1920.

Phil 1114.1   Geschichte der antiken Philosophie. (Joël, Karl.) Tübingen, 1921.

Phil 3015.3   Geschichte der aristotelischen Philosophie in protestantischen Deutschland. (Petersen, Peter.) Leipzig, 1921.

Phil 811.24   Geschichte der Aufklärung und des Atheismus. (Ley, Hermann.) Berlin, 1966- 3v.

Phil 210.74 — Die Geschichte der axiomatischen Methode im 16. und Beginnenden 17. Jahrhundert. (Schueling, Hermann.) Hildesheim, 1969.

Phil 930.27 — Geschichte der chinesischen Philosophie. (Zenker, E.V.) Reichenberg, 1926-27. 2v.

Phil 8956.1A — Geschichte der christlichen Ethik. (Gass, F.W.H.J.) Berlin, 1881-87. 2v.

Phil 8961.3 — Geschichte der christlichen Ethik. (Luthardt, C.E.) Leipzig, 1888-93. 2v.

Phil 8968.2 — Geschichte der christlichen Moral. (Stäudlin, C.F.) Göttingen, 1808.

Phil 1511.3.19 — Die Geschichte der christlichen Philosophie. (Gilson, Étienne.) Paderborn, 1937.

Phil 8520.3 — Geschichte der christlichen Religionsphilosophie seit der Reformation. (Pünjer, G.C.B.) Braunschweig, 1880-83. 2v.

Phil 8951.1 — Geschichte der christlichen Sitte. (Bestmann, H.J.) Nödling, 1880-85. 2v.

Phil 1350.10 — Geschichte der Denk- und Glaubensfreiheit. (Schmidt, W.A.) Berlin, 1847.

Phil 810.17 — Geschichte der Denkstile. (Keyserling, Arnold.) Wien, 1968.

Phil 400.23 — Geschichte der deutschen Idealismus. (Kronenberg, M.) München, 1909. 2v.

Phil 530.20.25 — Geschichte der deutschen Mystik im Mittelalter. (Preger, Wilhelm.) Leipzig, 1874-1893. 3v.

Phil 3018.6 — Geschichte der deutschen Naturphilosophie. (Siegel, C.) Leipzig, 1913.

Phil 3025.2 — Geschichte der deutschen Philosophie. (Zeller, Eduard.) München, 1873.

Phil 3011.1 — Geschichte der deutschen Philosophie - Kant. (Lotze, R.H.) Leipzig, 1882.

Phil 3025.2.2 — Geschichte der deutschen Philosophie seit Liebniz. 2. Aufl. (Zeller, Eduard.) München, 1875.

Phil 1800.1 — Geschichte der englischen Philosophie. (Aster, E.) Bielefeld, 1927.

Phil 338.20 — Geschichte der Erkenntnistheorie. (Hönigswald, R.) Berlin, 1933.

Phil 8828.3.5A — Geschichte der Ethik. (Dittrich, Ottmar.) Leipzig, 1926-32. 4v.

Phil 8835.1 — Geschichte der Ethik. (Köstlin, K.R.) Tübingen, 1887.

Phil 8847.5 — Geschichte der Ethik. (Wentscher, Max.) Berlin, 1931.

Phil 8850.1 — Geschichte der Ethik. (Ziegler, T.) Bonn, 1881-86. 2v.

Phil 8834.2 — Geschichte der Ethik. v.1-2. (Jodl, Friedrich.) Stuttgart, 1882-1889.

Phil 8831.14 — Geschichte der Ethik. v.2. Gütersloh, 1967.

Phil 8834.2.5 — Geschichte der Ethik. 4. Aufl. (Jodl, Friedrich.) Stuttgart, 1923-30. 3v.

Phil 1705.7 — Geschichte der Geschichte der Philosophie. (Freyer, Johannes.) Leipzig, 1912.

Phil 1504.6.3 — Geschichte der Gottesbewise. v.6, pt.3. (Grunwald, G.) Münster, 1907.

Phil 1145.41 — Geschichte der griechischen Ethik. (Wendt, M.) Leipzig, 1908. 2v.

Phil 1108.1 — Geschichte der griechischen Philosophie. (Döring, A.) Leipzig, 1903. 2v.

Phil 1123.2 — Geschichte der griechischen Philosophie. (Schwegler, A.) Tübingen, 1859.

Phil 1123.6 — Die Geschichte der griechischen Philosophie zur Übersicht. pts.1-2. (Strümpell, L.) Leipzig, 1854-61.

Phil 960.169 — Geschichte der indischen Philosophie. (Frauwallner, E.) Salzburg, 1953. 2v.

Phil 960.170 — Geschichte der indischen Philosophie. (Ruben, Walter.) Berlin, 1954.

Phil 4007.10 — Geschichte der italienischen Philosophie von den Anfängen des 19. Jahrhunderts bis zur Gegenwart. (Hoellhuber, Ivo.) München, 1969.

Phil 1122.2.10 — Geschichte der jonischen Philosophie. (Ritter, Heinrich.) Berlin, 1821.

Phil 1050.7 — Geschichte der jüdischen Philosophie der Mittelalters. (Neumark, D.) Berlin, 1907. 3v.

Phil 5325.3 — Geschichte der Lehre...Association der Ideen. (Hissmann, M.) Göttingen, 1777.

Phil 1133.10 — Geschichte der Lehre von den Keimkräften von der Stoa bis zum Ausgang der Patristik. (Meyer, Hans.) Bonn, 1914.

Phil 5025.1 — Geschichte der Logik. (Prantl, Carl von.) Leipzig, 1855-70. 3v.

Phil 5028.2 — Geschichte der Logik. (Scholz, Heinrich.) Berlin, 1931.

Phil 5025.1.2 — Geschichte der Logik. v.2. (Prantl, Carl von.) Leipzig, 1885.

Phil 5025.1.1 — Geschichte der Logik. v.2. 2e Aufl. (Prantl, Carl von.) Leipzig, 1855-1885.

X Cg Phil 5025.1 — Geschichte der Logik. v.4. (Prantl, Carl von.) Leipzig, 1855-70.

Phil 5025.1.4 — Geschichte der Logik im Abendlande. v.1-4. (Prantl, Carl von.) Berlin, 1957. 3v.

Phil 5025.1.3 — Geschichte der Logik im Abendlande. v.1-4. (Prantl, Carl von.) Graz, 1955. 3v.

Phil 978.49.705 — Die Geschichte der Menschheit und die Weltanschauungen der Kulturvölker. (Steiner, R.) Dornach, 1968.

Phil 822.9 — Geschichte der Metaphysik. (Wundt, Max.) Berlin, 1931.

Phil 282.4.5 — Geschichte der Meynungen...Grundursachen. (Batteux, C.) Leipzig, 1773.

Phil 930.7.8 — Geschichte der mittelalterlichen chinesischen Philosophie. (Forke, A.) Hamburg, 1934.

Phil 1527.1.8 — Geschichte der mittelalterlichen Philosophie. (Wulf, M. de.) Tübingen, 1913.

Phil 1509.5 — Geschichte der mittelalterlichen Philosophie. 2. Aufl. (Endres, J.A.) Kemplin, 1911.

Phil 8953.1 — Geschichte der Moralstreitigheiten. v.1-2. (Döllinger, J.J.I. von.) Nordlingen, 1889.

Phil 3011.3 — Geschichte der nachkantischen Philosophie. (Lehmann, G.) Berlin, 1931.

Phil 1718.3 — Geschichte der Naturphilosophie, Bacon. pt.1-2. (Schaller, J.) Leipzig, 1841-6.

Phil 1703.6 — Geschichte der Naturphilosophie. (Dingler, Hugo.) Berlin, 1932.

Phil 930.7.10 — Geschichte der neueren chinesischen Philosophie. (Forke, A.) Hamburg, 1938.

Phil 3018.5 — Geschichte der neueren deutschen Philosophie. (Seibert, C.) Gottingen, 1898.

Phil 3022.1 — Die Geschichte der neueren deutschen Philosophie. v.1-3. (Weber, T.) Münster, 1873.

Phil 3018.5.3 — Geschichte der neueren deutschen Philosophie. 2e Aufl. (Seibert, C.) Gottingen, 1905.

Phil 5213.1 — Geschichte der neueren deutschen Psychologie. (Dessoir, M.) Berlin, 1897.

Phil 331.5.10 — Geschichte der neueren Erkenntnistheorie. (Aster, Ernst von.) Berlin, 1921.

Phil 1701.3 — Geschichte der neueren Philosophie. (Buhle, J.G.) Göttlieb, 1800-1804. 6v.

Phil 1705.1 — Geschichte der neueren Philosophie. (Falckenberg, R.) Leipzig, 1886.

Phil 1705.2 — Geschichte der neueren Philosophie. (Feuerbach.) Ansbach, 1833-37. 2v.

Phil 1718.1 — Geschichte der neueren Philosophie. (Stöckl, A.) Mainz, 1883. 2v.

Phil 1722.2A — Die Geschichte der neueren Philosophie. (Windelband, W.) Leipzig, 1878-80. 2v.

Phil 1705.4 — Geschichte der neueren Philosophie. v.1-6. (Fischer, K.) Mannheim, 1854-77. 7v.

Phil 1705.4.4 — Geschichte der neueren Philosophie. v.1-8. (Fischer, K.) Heidelberg, 1889-1901. 10v.

Phil 1705.4.2 — Geschichte der neueren Philosophie. v.1-9. (Fischer, K.) München, 1875-99. 10v.

Phil 1705.4.3 — Geschichte der neueren Philosophie. v.2-10. (Fischer, K.) Heidelberg, 1898-1904. 7v.

Phil 1705.1.2 — Geschichte der neueren Philosophie. 2e Aufl. (Falckenberg, R.) Leipzig, 1892.

Phil 1705.1.3 — Geschichte der neueren Philosophie. 8e Aufl. (Falckenberg, R.) Berlin, 1921.

Phil 1705.1.4 — Geschichte der neueren Philosophie. 9. Aufl. (Falckenberg, R.) Berlin, 1927.

Phil 1705.4.50 — Geschichte der neueren Philosophie im Urteil der Jahrzehnte 1852-1924. (Fischer, K.) Heidelberg, 1924.

Phil 3246.199.5 — Geschichte der neuern Philosophie. (Fischer, Kuno.) Heidelberg, 1869.

Phil 3487.1.4 — Geschichte der neuern Philosophie. 2. Aufl. Bd.3,4. (Fischer, Kuno.) Heidelberg, 1869. 2v.

Phil 7069.24.18 — Geschichte der okkultischen (metapsychischen) Forschung von der Antike bis zur Gegenwart. Pfullingen, 1922.

Phil 800.10.10 — Geschichte der Philosophie. (Akademiia Nauk SSSR.) Berlin, 1959- 6v.

Phil 801.1 — Geschichte der Philosophie. (Bauer, W.) Halle, 1863.
Phil 801.15 — Geschichte der Philosophie. (Bergmann, J.) Berlin, 1892-93. 2v.

Phil 801.13 — Die Geschichte der Philosophie. (Brockdorff, C. von.) Hildesheim, 1906.

Phil 801.13.2 — Die Geschichte der Philosophie. (Brockdorff, C. von.) Osterwieck, 1908.

Phil 805.11 — Geschichte der Philosophie. (Fischl, Johann.) Graz, 1948-53. 5v.

Phil 805.2 — Die Geschichte der Philosophie. (Fries, J.F.) Halle, 1837-40. 2v.

Phil 806.5 — Geschichte der Philosophie. (Grätz, H. von.) Langensalza, 1861.

Phil 807.14 — Geschichte der Philosophie. (Hermann, C.) Leipzig, 1867.
Phil 807.18 — Geschichte der Philosophie. (Hirschberger, Johannes.) Freiburg, 1949-51. 2v.

Phil 1707.1A — Geschichte der Philosophie. (Höffding, H.) Leipzig, 1895. 2v.

Phil 810.1.9 — Geschichte der Philosophie. (Kirchner, F.) Leipzig, 1911.
Phil 812.43 — Geschichte der Philosophie. (Mayr, Franz Karl.) Kevelaer, 1966.

Phil 1712.5 — Geschichte der Philosophie. (Messer, A.) Leipzig, 1913.
Phil 813.3 — Geschichte der Philosophie. (Noack, L.) Weimar, 1853.
Phil 815.1 — Die Geschichte der Philosophie. (Poetter, F.C.) Elberfeld, 1874.

Phil 817.1 — Geschichte der Philosophie. (Reinhold, C.E.G.) Jena, 1845. 2v.

Phil 817.2 — Geschichte der Philosophie. (Ritter, A.H.) Hamburg, 1829-45. 12v.

Phil 817.16 — Geschichte der Philosophie. (Rothenbücher, A.) Berlin, 1904.

Phil 818.24A — Geschichte der Philosophie. (Schilling, Kurt.) München, 1943-44. 2v.

Phil 818.24.5 — Geschichte der Philosophie. (Schilling, Kurt.) München, 1951. 2v.

Phil 818.1 — Geschichte der Philosophie. (Schwegler, F.C.A.) Stuttgart, 1870.

Phil 818.1.3.3 — Geschichte der Philosophie. (Schwegler, F.C.A.) Stuttgart, 1882.

Phil 821.1.3 — Geschichte der Philosophie. (Vorländer, K.) Leipzig, 1911. 2v.

Phil 821.1.15 — Geschichte der Philosophie. (Vorländer, K.) Leipzig, 1964. 4v.

Phil 822.2A — Geschichte der Philosophie. (Windelband, W.) Freiburg, 1892.

Phil 806.9 — Geschichte der Philosophie. Leipzig, 1925.
Phil 810.2 — Geschichte der Philosophie. v.1-2. (Kinkel, W.) Giessen, 1906.

Phil 821.1 — Geschichte der Philosophie. v.1-2. (Vorländer, K.) Leipzig, 1903.

Phil 818.8 — Geschichte der Philosophie. v.1-3. (Sigwart, H.C.W.) Stuttgart, 1844.

Phil 817.2.1 — Geschichte der Philosophie. v.1-4. (Ritter, A.H.) Hamburg, 1929-53.

Phil 819.1 — Geschichte der Philosophie. v.1-11. (Tennemann, W.G.) Leipzig, 1798-1819. 12v.

Phil 3483.8 — Geschichte der Philosophie. v.5. (Bauch, Bruno.) Leipzig, 1911.

Phil 807.10 — Geschichte der Philosophie. 2. Aufl. (Hamma, Mattheas.) Münster, 1908.

Phil 806.16 — Geschichte der Philosophie. 2. Aufl. v.1-4,6,8-11. Berlin, 1954. 6v.

Phil 817.2.4 — Geschichte der Philosophie. 2e Aufl. (Ritter, A.H.) Hamburg, 1836-53. 12v.

Phil 807.18.5 — Geschichte der Philosophie. 5. Aufl. (Hirschberger, Johannes.) Freiburg, 1961-60. 2v.

Phil 821.1.6 — Geschichte der Philosophie. 6. Aufl. (Vorländer, K.) Leipzig, 1921.

Phil 821.1.7 — Geschichte der Philosophie. 7. Aufl. (Vorländer, K.) Leipzig, 1927. 2v.

Phil 818.1.3 — Geschichte der Philosophie. 8e Aufl. (Schwegler, F.C.A.) Stuttgart, 1873.

Phil 821.1.9 — Geschichte der Philosophie. 9. Aufl. (Vorländer, K.) Hamburg, 1949-55. 2v.

Phil 818.1.4 — Geschichte der Philosophie. 13. Aufl. (Schwegler, F.C.A.) Stuttgart, 1885.

Phil 800.14.14 — Geschichte der Philosophie. 14. Aufl. (Aster, Ernst von.) Stuttgart, 1963.

Phil 818.1.4.5 — Geschichte der Philosophie. 14. Aufl. (Schwegler, F.C.A.) Stuttgart, 1887.

Phil 351.1.5 — Geschichte der Philosophie als Erkenntniskritik. (Uphues, G.K.) Halle, 1909.

Phil 1115.2   Geschichte der Philosophie alter Zeit. (Krug, W.T.)
               Leipzig, 1827.
Phil 1523.1   Geschichte der Philosophie der Mittelalters. (Stöckl, A.)
               Mainz, 1864-6. 3v.
Phil 1619.2   Geschichte der Philosophie der Renaissance. (Schultze,
               Fritz.) Jena, 1874.
Phil 1050.3   Geschichte der Philosophie des Judenthums. (Spiegler,
               J.S.) Leipzig, 1890.
Phil 4308.1   Geschichte der Philosophie im spanischen Kulturbereich.
               (Höllhuber, I.) München, 1967.
Phil 811.5   Geschichte der Philosophie im Umriss. (Loewenthal, E.)
               Berlin, 1896.
Phil 812.6   Geschichte der Philosophie in Atlertum und Mittelalter.
               (Messer, August.) Leipzig, 1919.
Phil 802.7   Geschichte der Philosophie in gemeinverständlicher
               Darstellung. (Cunz, T.) Marburg, 1911.
Phil 812.5   Geschichte der Philosophie in übersichtlcher Darstellung.
               v.1-3. (Mannheimer, A.) Frankfurt, 1903-08.
Phil 1710.1   Geschichte der Philosophie mit besonderer Berücksichtung
               der Neuzeit. (Knauer, V.) Wien, 1876.
Phil 1710.1.2 Geschichte der Philosophie mit besonderer Berücksichtung
               der Neuzeit. 2e Aufl. (Knauer, V.) Wien, 1882.
Phil 801.16.5 Geschichte der Philosophie nach Ideengehalt und Beweisen.
               (Baumann, J.) Gotha, 1890.
Phil 3006.3.2 Geschichte der Philosophie seit Kant. 2. Aufl. (Gramzow,
               Otto.) Charlottenburg, 1919-28. 2v.
Phil 3018.18   Geschichte der Philosophie unserer Zeit. (Schod, J.B.)
               Jena, 1800.
Phil 1712.5.2 Geschichte der Philosophie vom Beginn der Neuzeit zum Ende
               des 18. Jahrhunderts. (Messer, A.) Leipzig, 1912.
Phil 1712.5.4 Geschichte der Philosophie vom Beginn der Neuzeit zum Ende
               des 18. Jahrhunderts. (Messer, A.) Leipzig, 1920.
Phil 1712.5.4.10 Geschichte der Philosophie vom Beginn der Neuzeit zum Ende
               des 18. Jahrhunderts. 6e und 7e Aufl. (Messer, A.)
               Leipzig, 1923.
Phil 3004.2   Geschichte der Philosophie von der Romantik bis zur
               Gegenwart. (Ettlinger, Max.) München, 1924.
Phil 850.15   Geschichte der Philosophie von ihren Uranfängen. (Hanus,
               G.J.) Olmütz, 1850.
Phil 1115.3   Geschichte der Philosophie von Sokrates bis Aristoteles.
               (Kinkel, Walter.) Berlin, 1922.
Phil 812.7   Geschichte der Philosophie von Thales. (Michelis, F.)
               Braumsberg, 1865.
Phil 1133.46   Die Geschichte der Philosophie vor Sokrates. (Broecker,
               Walter.) Frankfurt, 1965.
Phil 812.8   Geschichte der Philosophie zum Gebrauche. (Mener, J.B.)
               Bonn, 1882.
Phil 1718.9.10 Geschichte der philosophischen Ideen von der Renaissance
               bis zur Gegenwart. (Schjelderup, Harald K.) Berlin, 1929.
Phil 8846.2   Geschichte der philosophischen Moral. (Vorländer, F.)
               Marburg, 1855.
Phil 89.2   Geschichte der philosophischen Terminologie. (Eucken, R.)
               Leipzig, 1879.
Phil 5212.1   Geschichte der Psychologie. (Carus, F.A.) Leipzig, 1808.
Phil 5220.1   Geschichte der Psychologie. (Klemm, O.) Leipzig, 1911.
Phil 5228.1   Geschichte der Psychologie. (Siebeck, H.) Gotha, 1880-84.
Phil 5228.1.2 Geschichte der psychologie. v.1-2. (Siebeck, H.)
               Amsterdam, 1961.
Phil 5217.8.2 Geschichte der Psychologie. 2. Aufl. (Hehlmann, Wilhelm.)
               Stuttgart, 1967.
Phil 5230.1   Die Geschichte der Psychologie und der Psychiatrik in
               Spanien. (Ullersperger, J.B.) Würzburg, 1871.
Phil 525.76   Geschichte der quietistischen Mystik in der katholischen
               Kirche. (Heppe, Heinrich.) Berlin, 1875.
Phil 1750.11   Geschichte der Romantik...philosophische Geschichte.
               (Schmidt, H.J.) Leipzig, 1850. 2v.
Phil 1511.1A   Geschichte der scholastischen Methode. (Grabmann, M.)
               Freiburg, 1909. 2v.
Phil 1515.1   Geschichte der scholastischen Philosophie. (Kaulich, W.)
               Prag, 1863.
Phil 665.37   Die Geschichte der Seele. (Reich, E.) Minden, 1884.
Phil 5258.7.5 Die Geschichte der Seele. (Schubert, G.H. von.)
               Stuttgart, 1833.
Phil 5258.7.6 Die Geschichte der Seele. (Schubert, G.H. von.)
               Stuttgart, 1850. 2v.
Phil 819.3   Die Geschichte der spekulativen Philosophie. (Tiedemann, D.)
               Marburg, 1791-97. 6v.
Phil 5520.670 Die Geschichte der Sprachphilosophie von der Antike bis zur
               Gegenwart. (Coseriu, Eugenio.) Stuttgart, 1969.
Phil 8060.2   Geschichte der Theorie der Kunst. v.1-2. (Müller, Eduard.)
               Breslau, 1834-37.
Phil 9220.1   Geschichte der Vorst...Freundschaft. (Staudlin, C.F.)
               Hannover, 1826.
Phil 3625.5.60 Geschichte des eigenen Lebens. (Atlas, S.) Berlin, 1935.
Phil 8520.4A   Geschichte des Englischen Deismus. (Lechler, G.V.)
               Stuttgart, 1881.
Phil 1190.7   Die Geschichte des griechischen Skeptizismus.
               (Goedeckemyer, A.) Leipzig, 1905.
Phil 4710.60   Geschichte des Hegelianismus in Russland. (Jakovenko,
               B.U.) Prag, 1938.
Phil 978.49.210 Geschichte des Hypnotismus und des Somnambulismus.
               (Steiner, R.) Basel, 1941.
Phil 400.11   Geschichte des Idealismus. (Willmann, O.)
               Braunschweig, 1894-1897. 3v.
Phil 270.41   Geschichte des Kausalproblems in der neueren Philosophie.
               (Wentscher, E.S.) Leipzig, 1921.
Phil 486.1   Geschichte des Materialismus. (Lange, F.A.)
               Iserlohn, 1873-75. 2v.
Phil 486.1.6A Geschichte des Materialismus. 3e Aufl. (Lange, F.A.)
               Iserlohn, 1876-77. 2v.
Phil 5245.8   Geschichte des menschlichen Verstandes. (Flögel, C.F.)
               Breslau, 1776.
Phil 510.142   Geschichte des Monismus. (Eisler, Rudolf.) Leipzig, 1910.
Phil 623.12   Geschichte des Naturalismus. (Staudlin, C.F.)
               Göttingen, 1800.
Phil 665.23   Geschichte des Seelenbegriffes. (Révész, Béla.)
               Stuttgart, 1917.
Phil 7068.98.5 Geschichte des Spiritismus. (Baudidi Vesme, C.)
               Leipzig, 1898-1900.
Phil 978.49.215 Die Geschichte des Spiritismus. (Steiner, R.)
               Basel, 1941.
Phil 410.10   Geschichte des Unendlichkeitsproblems im abendländischen
               Denken bis Kant. (Cohn, Jonas.) Leipzig, 1896.
Phil 1117.3   Geschichte des Ursprungs. (Meiners, C.) Lemzo, 1781-82.
Phil 745.7   Geschichte des Vitalismus. 2e Aufl. (Driesch, H.)
               Leipzig, 1922.
Phil 900.3   Geschichte und abendländischen Philosophie. (Roth, E.)
               Mannheim, 1846.

Phil 3890.10.110 Geschichte und Begriff. (Schaaf, J.J.) Tübingen, 1946.
Phil 8599.26   Geschichte und Existenz. (Thielicke, H.) Gütersloh, 1935.
Phil 645.6   Geschichte und Geist des Skepticismus. (Stäudlin, C.F.)
                  Leipzig, 1794.
Phil 3018.21   Geschichte und Geschichtlichkeit in der deutschen
                  Philosophie der Gegenwart. Inaug. Diss. (Schroeter, R.)
                  Kölm am Rhein, 1937.
Phil 8418.18   Geschichte und Gesetze des Ästhetischen. (Redeker, Horst.)
                  Berlin, 1970.
Phil 807.13   Geschichte und Grundfragen der Metaphysik. (Hamma, M.)
                  Freiburg, 1876.
Phil 179.3.60   Geschichte und Kritik der grund Begriffe der Gegenwart.
                  v.1-2. (Eucken, R.) Leipzig, 1878.
Phil 645.16   Geschichte und Kritik des ethischen Skepticismus.
                  (Kreibig, J.K.) Wien, 1896.
Phil 525.12   Geschichte und Kritik des Mysticismus. (Heinroth, J.C.A.)
                  Leipzig, 1830.
Phil 645.32   Geschichte und Kritik des Skepticismus und Irrationalismus.
                  (Tafel, J.F.I.) Tübingen, 1834.
Phil 3450.11.416 Geschichte und Lebenswelt. (Janssen, Paul.) Den
                  Haag, 1970.
Phil 3450.11.415 Geschichte und Lebenswelt. Inaug. Diss. (Janssen, Paul.)
                  Köln, 1964.
Phil 850.3   Geschichte unserer abendländischen Philosophie. (Röth, E.)
                  Mannheim, 1862. 2v.
Phil 1150.5   Geschichtliche Darstellung der jüdisch-alexandrinischen
                  Religions-Philosophie. (Dähne, A.F.) Halle, 1834.
                  2v.
Phil 672.6   Die geschichtliche Entwickelung des Bewegungsbegriffes.
                  (Lange, C.C.L.) Leipzig, 1886.
Phil 978.49.160   Geschichtliche Notwendigkeit und Freiheit. (Steiner, R.)
                  Dornach, 1939.
Phil 978.49.162   Geschichtliche Notwendigkeit und Freiheit. 2. Aufl.
                  (Steiner, R.) Dornach, 1966.
Phil 822.6.5   Geschichtlicher Überblick über die Entwicklung der
                  Philosophie bis zu ihrer letzten Phase. (Wahle, R.)
                  Wien, 1895.
Phil 3195.6.145   Die Geschichtlichkeit als Wesensverfassung des Menschen.
                  (Grzesik, Juergen.) Bonn, 1961.
Phil 4752.2.170   Geschichtlichkeit und Mystik im Denken Nikolaj Berdjaews.
                  (Meusel, Joachim.) Berlin? 1962?
Phil 8583.28.15   Die Geschichts- und Kulturphilosophie Christopher Dawson.
                  (Schlagberger, Frans Xavier.) München, 1965?
Phil 2050.199   Die Geschichtsauffassung David Hume's im Rahmen seines
                  philosophischen Systems. Inaug. Diss. (Wegrich, Arno.)
                  Köln, 1926.
Phil 2496.87   Die Geschichtslehre Victor Cousins. (Cornelius, Alfred.)
                  Genève, 1958.
Phil 2490.126   Die Geschichtsphilosophie Auguste Comtes. (Mehlis, G.)
                  Leipzig, 1909.
Phil 2490.121   Die Geschichtsphilosophie Auguste Comtes. Inaug.-Diss.
                  (Marcuse, A.) Stuttgart, 1932.
Phil 3565.125   Geschichtsphilosophie bei Lotze. Diss. (Schröder, Arthur.)
                  Leipzig, 1896.
Phil 810.6   Geschichtsphilosophie der Philosophiegeschichte. (Kafka,
                  G.) Berlin, 1933.
Phil 3425.231   Die Geschichtsphilosophie Hegels. (Leese, Kurt.)
                  Berlin, 1922.
Phil 3425.232.5   Die Geschichtsphilosophie Hegels und der Hegelianer bis auf
                  Marx und Hartman. (Barth, Paul.) Darmstadt, 1967.
Phil 3425.232   Die Geschichtsphilosophie Hegels und der Hegelianer bis auf
                  Marx und Hartman. 2. Aufl. Photoreproduction. (Barth,
                  Paul.) Leipzig, 1925.
Phil 3245.86.2   Die Geschichtsphilosophie Immanuel Hermann Fichtes.
                  (Najdanović, D.) Berlin, 1940.
Phil 3245.86   Die Geschichtsphilosophie Immanuel Hermann Fichtes.
                  (Najdanović, D.) Berlin, 1940.
Phil 3801.522   Geschichtsphilosophie Schellings, 1792-1809. Inaug. Diss.
                  (Lisco, Heinrich.) Jena, 1884.
Phil 4769.1.99   Die Geschichtsphilosophie Wladimir Solowjews.
                  (Kaschewnikoff, A.) Bonn, 1930.
Phil 3160.3.91   Das Geschichtsproblem in der Philosophie Hermann Cohen.
                  (Kaplan, Simon.) Berlin, 1930.
Phil 5011.7   Geschiedenis der logica. (Beth, Evert Willem.) Den
                  Haag, 1948.
Phil 809.3   Geschiedenis der wijsbegeerte. (Jansen, W.)
                  Zutphen, 1919-21. 2v.
Phil 5593.66.20   Geschiedenis en perspectieven van de Rorschach.
                  Proefschrift. (Riemsdijk, Jan van.) Utrecht, 1966.
Phil 8050.58   Geschiedenis van de aesthetica. (Bruyne, E. de.)
                  Antwerpen, 1951. 5v.
VPhil 5015.5   De geschiedenis van de dialektiek. (Flam, Leopold.) St.
                  Niklaas, 1964.
Phil 3960.16.5   De geschiedenis van de wijsbegeerte in Nederland tot het einde
                  der negentiende eeuw. (Sassen, Ferdinand.)
                  Amsterdam, 1959.
Phil 1718.20   Geschiedenis van de wijshegeerte der negentiende eeuw.
                  (Sassen, F.) Antwerpen, 1934.
Phil 8832.2   Geschiedenis van de zedenlier. (Hoekstra, S.)
                  Amsterdam, 1896. 2v.
VPhil 8660.22   Geschiedenis van het atheisme. 1. uitg. (Flam, Leopold.)
                  Brussel, 1964. 4v.
Phil 1750.115.120 De geschiedenis van het fenomenologisch denken. (Bakker,
                  Reinout.) Antwerp, 1964.
Phil 3963.4   Geschiedenis van het humanisme in Nederland. (Constandse,
                  Anton Levien.) Den Haag, 1967.
Phil 3905.30.10   Geschlecht und Charakter. (Weininger, Otto.)
                  Berlin, 1932.
Phil 3905.30   Geschlecht und Charakter. (Weininger, Otto.) Wien, 1903.
Phil 3905.30.3   Geschlecht und Charakter. 3. Aufl. (Weininger, Otto.)
                  Wien, 1904.
Phil 5841.16   Die Geschlechtsleben in der Völkerpsychologie. (Stoll,
                  Otto.) Leipzig, 1908.
Htn Phil 3246.75* Der geschlossne Handelsstaat. (Fichte, Johann Gottlieb.)
                  Tübingen, 1800.
Phil 8411.25   Geschmackslehre oder Ästhetik. (Krug, W.T.) Wien, 1818.
                  2v.
Phil 6965.24   Geschonden feeld. (Plokker, J.H.) 's-Gravenhage, 1962.
Phil 5871.15   Geschwisterkonstellation und psychische Fehlentwicklung.
                  (Dechêne, Hans C.) München, 1967.
Phil 8586.16   Gese, Paul. Einleitung in die Religionsphilosophie über
                  die verschiedenen Standpunkt und Methoden zur Enforchung
                  des Wesens der Religion. Göttingen, 1918.
Phil 5413.13   Gesell, Arnold L. Jealousy. Diss. Worcester, 1906.
Phil 6332.20   Gesellschaft, Kultur und psychische Störung. (Wyrsch, J.)
                  Stuttgart, 1960.
Phil 5046.26   Gesellschaft für Deutsch-Ravjetische Freundschaft. Über
                  formale Logik und Dialektik. Berlin, 1954.

Phil 5816.6 — Gesellschaft für Tierpsychologie. Die Seele des Tieres. Berlin, 1916.

Phil 9495.167.10 — Die Gesellschaft und das Böse. (Plack, Arno.) München, 1967.

Phil 6980.321 — Gesellschaft zur Orderung Tiefenpsychologischer und Psychotherapeutischer Forschung und Weiterbildung in München. Möglichkeiten moderner Psychotherapien. Göttingen, 1967.

Phil 3090.24.5 — Gesellschaftslehre. (Baader, Franz von.) München, 1957.

Phil 8955.6 — Gesellschaftslehre. (Frodl, Ferdinand.) Wien, 1936.

Phil 1200.5 — Die Gesellschaftslehre der Stoiker. (Haake, A.) Berlin, 1887.

Phil 3850.29.20 — Gesemmelte Aufsätze, 1926-1936. (Schlich, M.) Wien, 1938.

Phil 270.11 — Das Gesets der Causalität in der Natur. (Schellwein, R.) Berlin, 1876.

Phil 3850.29.30 — Gesetz, Kausalität und Wahrscheinlichkeit. (Schlick, M.) Wien, 1948[1938]

Phil 8890.61 — Das Gesetz. Der Morgen der Menschheit. (Pohl, Hermann Paul Albert.) Berlin, 1966.

Phil 8957.13.5 — Das Gesetz Christi. 4. Aufl. (Haering, Bernhard.) Freiburg, 1957.

Phil 291.6 — Das Gesetz deines Lebens. (Künkel, H.) Jena, 1933.

Phil 5768.6 — Das Gesetz der Freiheit. Ein Beiträg zur Reinigung der Volksreligion. (Salzbrunner, B.) Nürnberg, 1869.

Phil 8419.15 — Das Gesetz der Schönheit. (Schulze-Soelde, W.) Darmstadt, 1925.

Phil 270.40 — Das Gesetz der Ursache. (Geyser, Joseph.) München, 1933.

Phil 8887.58 — Das Gesetz der Vernunft und die ethischen Strömungen der Gegenwart. (Marcus, E.) Herford, 1907.

Phil 4720.9 — Gesetz und Determination in der Sowjetphilosophie. (Rapp, Friedrich.) Dordrecht, 1968.

Phil 3552.326 — Gesetz und Freiheit. (Matzat, H.L.) Köln, 1948.

Phil 632.5 — Gesetz und Wirklichkeit. (Europaeisches Forum, Alpach, Austria, 1948.) Innsbruck, 1949.

Phil 8705.12 — Gesetz von der Erhaltung der Energie und der christliche Glaube. (Pollach, Friedrich.) Fulda, 1913.

Phil 8695.4 — Das Gesetz von der Erhaltung der Kraft und der Geist des Christentums. (Froehlich, J.) Leipzig, 1903.

Phil 672.12 — Die Gesetze der menschlichen Herzens. (Krause, A.) Lahr, 1876.

Phil 5643.97 — Gesetze des Sehens. (Metzger, W.) Frankfurt, 1936.

Phil 8605.1 — Die gesetze Göttes. (Zweifel, H.) München, 1876.

Phil 338.6.2 — Gesetze und Elemente des wissenschaftlichen Denkens. (Heymans, G.) Leipzig, 1894.

Phil 338.6 — Gesetze und Elemente des wissenschaftlichen Denkens. (Heymans, G.) Leipzig, 1905.

Phil 338.6.3 — Die Gesetze und Elemente des wissenschaftlichen Denkens. v.1-2. (Heymans, G.) Leiden, 1890-94.

Phil 8677.11.10 — Gesetze und Mysterien der Liebe. 1. Aufl. (Weill, Alexandre.) Berlin, 1895.

Phil 5058.108 — Die Gesetze unseres Denkens. (Strombach, Werner.) München, 1970.

Phil 291.18 — Der Gesetzesbegriff in der Philosophie und den Einzelwissenschaften. (Kroeber, Günter.) Berlin, 1968.

Phil 5643.163 — Gesetzlichkeit bei stroboskopischen Alternattivbewegungen. (Hoeth, Friedrich.) Frankfurt, 1966.

Phil 6017.3 — Gesicht und Charakter. 2. Aufl. (Herland, Leo.) Zürich, 1956.

Phil 177.101 — Das Gesicht unserer Zeit. (Christiansen, Broder.) München, 1931.

Phil 5643.56 — Die Gesichts-Empfindungen und ihre Analyse. (Kries, Johannes von.) Leipzig, 1882.

Phil 6020.2.3 — Der Gesichtsausdruck des Menschen. 3. und 4. Aufl. (Krukenberg, H.) Stuttgart, 1923.

Phil 6035.1 — Gesichtsausdruck und Wertraum. Inaug. Diss. (Zirwes, Ernst.) Würzburg, 1935.

Phil 5252.30.5 — Die Gesichtspunkte und der Tatsachen der psychophysischen Methodik. (Müller, G.E.) Wiesbaden, 1904.

Phil 7067.29 — Das Gespenst auf dem Klapperfeld. Frankfurt, 1729.

Phil 7060.256 — Gespenster und Spuk. (Kummerich, M.) Ludwigshafenam Bodensee, 1921.

Phil 7054.35 — Der Gespensterglaube der Gegenwart. (Henke, O.) Mülheim, 1881.

Phil 7060.37 — Gespenstersagen. (Rauschink, Gottfried Peter.) Rudolstadt, 1817.

Phil 6325.10.5 — Gespräch über Psychoanalyse zwischen Frau, Dichter und Arzt. (Prinzhorn, Hans.) Heidelberg, 1927.

Phil 3850.32.24 — Gespräch über Unsterblichkeit; Betrachtungen zweier Krieger im Felde. (Spann, Othmar.) Graz, 1965.

Phil 9500.5 — Gespräche am Krankenbett. (Lindenberg, Wladimir.) München, 1959.

Phil 3120.30.125 — Gespräche mit Martin Buber. (Kraft, Werner.) München, 1966.

Phil 3428.61 — Gespräche über das Böse. (Herbart, J.F.) Königsberg, 1817.

Htn   Phil 2050.68.10* — Gespräche über natürliche Religion. (Hume, David.) Leipzig, 1781.

Phil 6980.573.5 — Gesprengte Fesseln der Psychose. (Pankow, Gisela.) München, 1968.

Phil 181.72 — Gessen, S.I. Weltanschauung Ideologie. Praha, 1934.

Phil 4870.18 — Gessler, Clara. Westlicher Wissensdrang-Indische Weisheit. Zürich, 1970.

Phil 6676.1 — Gessman, G. Magnetismus und Hypnotismus. Wien, 1887.

Phil 6048.89.7 — Gessmann, G.W. Katechismus der Handelskunst. Berlin, 1921.

Phil 6048.97.4 — Gessmann, G.W. Katechismus der Handflächenkunde. 4. Aufl. Berlin, 1922.

Phil 6060.17.3 — Gessmann, G.W. Katechismus der Handschriften-Deutung. 3. Aufl. Berlin, 1922.

Phil 5926.2.2 — Gessmann, G.W. Katechismus der Kopfformkunde. 2. Aufl. Berlin, 1921.

Phil 1540.19 — Gessner, Jakob. Die Abstraktionslehre in der Scholastik bis Thomas von Aquin. Inaug.-Diss. Tulda, 1930.

Phil 8597.45 — Gestalt eines christlichen Humanismus. (Rüssel, H.W.) Amsterdam, 1940.

Phil 5247.53 — Gestalt psychology. (Hartmann, G.W.) N.Y., 1936.

Phil 5250.15.11 — Gestalt psychology. (Köhler, Wolfgang.) N.Y., 1929.

Phil 5250.15.15 — Gestalt psychology. (Köhler, Wolfgang.) N.Y., 1929.

Phil 5250.15.15.10

Phil 5250.15.15.5 — Gestalt psychology. (Köhler, Wolfgang.) N.Y., 1947.

Phil 5244.22 — Gestalt psychology. (Köhler, Wolfgang.) N.Y., 1947.

Gestalt psychology and meaning. (Ellis, Willis D.) Berkeley, 1930.

Phil 5262.31.15 — Gestalt theory. (Wertheimer, M.) N.Y., 1944.

Phil 5255.33.10 — The gestalt theory and the problem of configuration. (Petermann, B.) London, 1932.

Phil 6998.2.11 — Gestalt therapy. (Perls, Frederick S.) N.Y., 1969.

Phil 5767.6 — Gestalt und Gesetz. (Riezler, Kurt.) München, 1924.

Phil 165.430 — Gestalt und Wirklichkeit. Berlin, 1967.

Phil 5262.48.20 — Gestalt und Zeit. 2. Aufl. (Weizäcker, Viktor.) Göttingen, 1960.

Phil 5262.40 — Die Gestaltanalyse. (Weinhandl, F.) Erfurt, 1927.

Phil 3640.235.15 — Gestalten um Nietzsche. (Podach, Erich F.) Weimar, 1932.

Phil 3925.11.30 — Gestalten und Gedanken. 4. Aufl. (Wust, Peter.) München, 1950.

Phil 3270.17.40 — Gestalten van de Westerse subjectiriteit. (Flam, Leopold.) Amsterdam, 1965.

Phil 5238.145 — Gestalthaftes Sehen...zum hundertjahrigen Geburtstag von Christian von Ehrenfels. (Weinhandl, Ferdinand.) Darmstadt, 1960.

Phil 5262.48.5 — Der Gestaltkreis. 3. Aufl. (Weizäcker, Viktor.) Stuttgart, 1947.

Phil 5241.70.5 — Das Gestaltprinzip im Leben des Menschen und der Tiere. (Bühler, Karl.) Bern, 1960.

Phil 5252.65 — Das Gestaltproblem. (Mathaei, Rupprecht.) München, 1929.

Phil 5286.15 — Das Gestaltproblem in der Psychologie im Lichte analytischer Besimmung. (Petermann, Bruno.) Leipzig, 1931.

Phil 5286.10 — Gestaltpsychologie. (Katz, David.) Basel, 1944.

Phil 5286.10.2 — Gestaltpsychologie. 2. Aufl. (Katz, David.) Basel, 1948.

Phil 5286.10.4 — Gestaltpsychologie. 4. Aufl. (Katz, David.) Basel, 1969.

Phil 6319.1.69 — Gestaltungen des Unbewussten. (Jung, C.G.) Zürich, 1950.

Phil 200.6.3 — Gestaltwandel der Götter. 3. Aufl. (Ziegler, L.) Darmstadt, 1922. 2v.

Phil 6060.45 — Gestaltwandel und Gestaltzerfall. (Sievers, A.) Bonn, 1962.

Phil 5649.30 — Les gestes et la personnalité. (Bergès, Jean.) Paris, 1967.

Phil 978.49.440 — Gesteswissenschaftliche Behandlung. (Steiner, R.) Dornach, 1964.

Phil 4363.3.110 — Gestoso y Pérez, José. Valdes y Mañara. Sevilla, 1890.

Phil 2905.1.280 — Il gesuita proibito. (Vigorelli, G.) Milano, 1963.

Phil 978.49.778 — Die gesunde Entwickelung des Leiblich-Physischen als Grundlage der freien Entfaltung des Seelison-Geistigen. 3. Aufl. (Steiner, R.) Dornach, 1969.

Phil 2648.35.9 — Der gesunde Menschenverstand. 2e Aufl. (Holbach, Paul Henri T.) Baltimore, 1856.

Phil 2648.35.11 — Der gesunde Menschenverstand. 2e Aufl. (Holbach, Paul Henri T.) Baltimore, 1860.

Phil 2115.117 — Getschmann, W. Die Pädagogik des John Locke. Köthen, 1881.

Phil 5850.326.9 — Getting more out of life. (Roback, A.A.) n.p., 1937.

Phil 5420.5.5 — Getting rid of self-consciousness. (Roback, A.A.) n.p., 1934.

Phil 8892.50 — Getting the most out of life. (Rines, George E.) Boston, 1935.

Phil 6314.4 — Getting what we want. (Edson, D.O.) N.Y., 1921.

Phil 6049.65 — Gettings, Fred. The book of the hand. London, 1965.

Phil 9530.65 — Getty, Jay Paul. The golden age. N.Y., 1968.

Htn   Phil 2520.166* — Geulincx, A. Annotata majora in principia philosophiae R. Des Cartes. Dordraci, 1691.

Phil 3280.60 — Geulincx, A. Arnold Geulincx collegium oratorium i. e. nova methodus omnis generis orationes. Amsterdam, 1968.

Phil 3280.31 — Geulincx, A. De virtute et primis ejuis proprietatiilus. Pretoria, 1961.

Phil 3280.55 — Geulincx, A. Ethik, oder über die Kardinaltugenden. Hamburg, 1948.

Phil 3280.50 — Geulincx, A. Gnôthi Seauton, sive ethica. Amsterdam, 1709.

Phil 3280.10 — Geulincx, A. Opera philosophica. Hagae, 1891. 3v.

Phil 3280.30 — Geulincx, A. Van de Hooft-Deuchden. Antwerp, 1895.

Phil 3280.82 — Geulincx' ethisches System. (Göpfert, E.) Breslau, 1883.

Phil 5440.35 — Geurts, P.M.M. De erfelijkheid in de oudere Grieksche wetenschap. Nijmegen, 1941.

Phil 5645.18 — Geuter, Peter. Der Farbensinn und seine Störungen. Leipzig, 1936.

Phil 9075.82 — Geweten en vrijheid. Utrecht, 1968.

Phil 9075.77 — Gewetens groei en gewetens functie. (Mönks, Franz.) Nijmegen, 1967.

Phil 9075.28 — Das Gewissen, Erscheinungsformen und Theorie. (Stoker, H.G.) Bonn, 1925.

Phil 9075.38 — Das Gewissen. (Kabisch, R.) Göttingen, 1906.

Phil 9075.23 — Das Gewissen. (Schmidt, W.) Leipzig, 1889.

Phil 5374.255 — Das Gewissen als Problem. (Petrilowitsch, Nikolaus.) Darmstadt, 1966.

Phil 6315.2.330 — Das Gewissen bei Freud und Jung. (Spengler, Ernst.) Zürich, 1964.

Phil 9075.94 — Das Gewissen des Kindes. 2. Aufl. (Scholl, Robert.) Stuttgart, 1970.

Phil 3640.460 — Das Gewissen in der Philosophie Nietzsches. (Sonns, Stefan.) Winterthur, 1955.

Phil 8955.9 — Gewissen und Klugheit in der katholischen Moraltheologie der letzten Jahrzehnte. (Furger, Franz.) Luzern, 1965.

Phil 5414.45 — Gewissen und Schuld. (Benda, Clemens Ernst.) Stuttgart, 1970.

Phil 5548.10 — Gewissheit. (Fuchs, R.) Meisenheim am Glan, 1954.

Phil 1200.32 — Gewissheit und Wahrheit; der Streit zwischen Stoa und akademischen Skepsis. (Hartmann, H.) Halle (Saale), 1927.

Phil 352.1.15 — Gewissheit und Wahrheit. (Volkelt, J.) München, 1918.

Phil 2630.9 — Gex, Maurice. Variétés philosophiques. Lausanne, 1948.

Phil 1504.7.2 — Geyer, B. Sententiae divinitatis. Ein Sentanzenbuch der gilbertschen Schule. v.7, pt.2-3. Münster, 1909.

Phil 974.3.60 — Geyer, C.K.L. Rudolf Steiner und die Religion. München, n.d.

Phil 181.33 — Geyer, D.L. Pragmatic theory of truth as developed by Peirce, James and Dewey. n.p., 1914?

Phil 3310.20 — Geyer, H.F. Philosophisches Tagebuch. Freiburg, 1969. 3v.

Phil 5246.62 — Geyer, Horst. Über die Dummheit. Göttingen, 1954.

Phil 3805.165 — Geyer, Otto. Friedrich Schleiermachers Psychologie. Inaug. Diss. Leipzig, 1895.

Phil 600.44 — Geymonat, L. Il problema della conoscenza nel positivismo. Torino, 1931.

Phil 287.7 — Geymonat, Ludovico. La nuova filosofia della natura in Germania. Torino, 1934.

Phil 806.18 — Geymonat, Ludoviro. Storia del pensiero filosofico. Milano, 1955-55.

Phil 5046.16.5 — Geyser, J. Auf dem Kampffelde der Logik. Freiburg, 1926.

Phil 5046.16 — Geyser, J. Grundlagen der Logik und Erkenntnislehre. Munster, 1909.

Phil 5246.14 — Geyser, J. Grundlegung der empirischen Psychologie. Bonn, 1902.

Phil 5246.14.5 — Geyser, J. Lehrbuch der allgemeinen Psychologie. 2. Aufl. Munster, 1912.

Phil 5246.14.10 — Geyser, J. Die Seele, ihr Verhältnis zum Bewusstsein. Leipzig, 1914.

Phil 181.39 Geyser, Joseph. Allgemeine Philosophie...der Natur. Münster, 1915.

Phil 181.39.5 Geyser, Joseph. Einige Hauptprobleme der Metaphysik. Freiburg, 1923.

Phil 270.40 Geyser, Joseph. Das Gesetz der Ursache. München, 1933.

Phil 8669.3.25 Geyser, Joseph. Intellekt oder Gemüt? Eine philosophische Studie über Rudolf Ottos Buch "Das Heilige". Freiburg, 1922.

Phil 3850.18.81 Geyser, Joseph. Max Schelers Phänomenologie der Religion. Freiburg, 1924.

Phil 8520.19 Geyser, Joseph. Das philosophische Gottesproblem in seinen wichtigsten Auffassungen. Bonn, 1899.

Phil 8407.33 Ghelli, Nino. Problematica dell'arte. Roma, 1958.

Phil 287.12 Ghirardi, Olsen A. Cosmología y ciencia ficcion. Córdoba, Argentina, 1970.

Phil 5465.192.1 Ghiselin, Brewster. The creative process; a symposium. N.Y., 1955.

Phil 4060.1.95 Ghisleri, Arcangelo. Nel LXX compleanno di Roberto Ardigò. Cremona, 1898.

Phil 365.34.5 Ghose, Aurobinclo. Evolution. 2. ed. Calcutta, 1923.
Phil 4872.109.2 Ghose, Aurobindo. The life divine. N.Y., 1949.
Phil 4872.109.3 Ghose, Aurobindo. The life divine. 3rd ed. N.Y., 1965.
Phil 8586.28 Ghose, J.C. The positive religion. Calcutta, n.d.
Phil 525.254 Ghose, Sisirkumar. Mystics and society; a point of view. N.Y., 1968.

Phil 5250.80 The ghost in the machine. (Koestler, Arthur.) London, 1967.

Phil 7060.49 Ghost stories. Philadelphia 1854.
Phil 7060.42 The ghost world. (Dyer, T.F.T.) London, 1893.
Phil 7060.151.20 The ghost world. (Wickwar, J.W.) London, 1919.
Phil 7054.123.5 Ghostland. (Britten, Emma H.) Boston, 1876.
Phil 7060.92.9 Ghostly phenomena. (O'Donnell, Elliot.) London, n.d.
Phil 8663.3.34 The ghosts, and other lectures. (Ingersoll, Robert G.) Peoria, Ill., 1878.

Phil 7069.70.15 The ghosts about us. (Burke, Clara Baker.) Philadelphia, 1969.

Phil 7069.54 Ghosts and poltergeists. (Thurston, Herbert.) Chicago, 1954.

Phil 7069.30.6 Ghosts and spirits in the ancient world. (Dingwall, E.J.) London, 1930.

Phil 7060.151 Ghosts I have seen. (Tweedale, V.C.) N.Y., 1919.
Phil 7069.27.19 Ghosts in the Great War. (Daily News, London.) London, 1927.

Phil 7060.92.57 Ghosts of London. (O'Donnell, Elliot.) London, 1932.
Phil 7069.68.10 Ghosts of the Golden West. (Holzer, Hans W.) Indianapolis, 1968.

Phil 7069.11.49 The ghosts of Versailles. (Iremonger, L.) London, 1957.
Phil 7069.57.10 Ghosts vivisected. (Stirling, A.M.W.P.) London, 1957.
Phil 7069.51.5 Ghosts with a purpose. (O'Donnell, Elliot.) London, 1951.
Phil 8407.11 Ghyka, M.C. Esthétique des proportions dans la nature et dans les arts. Paris, 1927.

Phil 1182.30 Ghyks, M.C. Le nombre d'or. v.1-2. Paris, 1952.
Phil 7150.75 Ghysbrecht, Paul. Der Doppelselbstmord. München, 1967.
Phil 8631.14 Ghyvelde, F. de. Le ciel, séjour des élus. Montréal, 1912.

Phil 8050.82 Giacchelti, Vincenzo. Il giardino della mala biscia. Firenze, 1965.

Phil 5465.14 Giachetti, Apriano. La fantasia. Torino, 1912.
Phil 4285.1.90 Giacomo Zabarella il filosofo Pietro Pompanazzi. (Ragnisco, P.) Roma, 1886-87.

Phil 2190.15 Giacon, C. Guglielmo di Occam. Milano, 1941. 2v.
Phil 270.63 Giacon, Carlo. La causalità nel razionalismo moderno. Milano, 1954.

Phil 181.134 Giacon, Carlo. Interiorita e metafisica. Bologna, 1964.
Phil 4210.191 Giacon, Carlo. L'oggettivita in Antonio Rosmini. Milano, 1960.

Phil 165.454 Giacon, Carlo. Saggi e ricerche su Alessandro di Afrodisia, Avicenna, Miceli, Brentano, Jaspers, Ingarden, Carr. Padova, 1970.

Phil 4260.146 Giambattista Vico, primo scopritore della scienza estetica. (Croce, B.) Napoli, 1901.
Phil 4260.135 Giambattista Vico. (Columbu, Mario.) Trani, 1957.
Phil 4260.110.5 Giambattista Vico. (Corsano, Antonio.) Bari, 1956.
Phil 4260.90 Giambattista Vico. (Longo, Michele.) Torino, 1921.
Phil 4260.160 Giambattista Vico. (Tagliacozzo, Giorgio.) Baltimore, 1969.

Phil 4260.87 Giambattista Vico als Philosophie und Gelehrterforscher. (Werner, K.) Wien, 1881.

Phil 4260.200 Giambattista Vico nel terzo centenario della nascita. Napoli, 1971.

Phil 4260.85.25 Giambattista Vico nella critica di Benedetto Croce. (Scrocca, A.) Napoli, 1919.

Phil 4260.106 Giambattista Vico und das Problem der Bildung. Inaug. Diss. (Löhde, Hermann.) Erlangen, 1932.

Phil 8881.57.5 Giambioni, Bono. Della miseria dell'uomo. Firenze, 1836.
Phil 8881.57 Giambioni, Bono. Della miseria dell'uomo. Milano, 1847.
Phil 4215.1.91 Gian Domenico Roamgnosi filosofo e giureconsulto. Pt.2. (Aguanno, Giuseppe d'.) Parma, 1906.

Phil 4065.88 Giancola, Francesco. Giordano Bruno. Roma, 1885.
Phil 4196.80 Gianfrancesco Pico della Mirandola, 1469-1533. (Schmitt, Charles B.) The Hague, 1967.

Phil 1750.450 Giannini, G. L'esistenzialismo positivo di Nicola Abbagnano. Brescia, 1956.

Phil 8661.40 Giannini, Giorgio. L'ateismo nella filosofia italiana contemporanea. Roma, 1969.

Phil 181.130 Giannini, Giorgio. I presupposti della trascendenza. Milano, 1959.

Phil 1135.77 Giannini, Giorgio. Il problema antropologico. Roma, 1965.
Phil 705.52 Giannini, Giorgio. La tematica della trascendenza. Roma, 1964.

Phil 4225.8.110 Giannuzzi, Eugenio. L'uomo e il suo destino. Cosenza, 1968.

Phil 1955.9.30 Giant in chains. 1st ed. (Dunham, B.) Boston, 1953.
Phil 1133.40 The giants of pre-sophistic Greek philosophy. (Cleve, Felix M.) The Hague, 1965.

Phil 1133.40.2 The giants of pre-sophistic Greek philosophy. 2nd ed. (Cleve, Felix M.) The Hague, 1969. 2v.

Phil 4260.08 Gianturco, Elio. A selective bibliography of Vico scholarship, 1948-68. Firenze, 1968.

Phil 8050.82 Il giardino della mala biscia. (Giacchelti, Vincenzo.) Firenze, 1965.

Phil 4369.2.84 Giarratano, C. Il pensiero di Francesco Sanchez. Napoli, 1903.

Phil 2050.244 Giarrizzo, G. David Hume politico e storico. Torino, 1962.

Phil 2885.88 Gibaudan, R. Les idées sociales de Taine. Paris, 1928.
Phil 5246.70 Gibb, Andrew. In search of sanity. N.Y., 1942.

Phil 6676.4 Gibbes, R.W. Lecture on the magnetism of the human body. Columbia, 1843.

Phil 5922.4.50 Gibbon, C. The life of George Combe. London, 1878. 2v.

Phil 665.33 Gibbons, J. Theories of the transmigration of souls. London, 1907.

Phil 6116.24PF Gibbs, F.A. Atlas of electroencephalography. Cambridge, Mass., 1941.

Phil 7150.55 Gibbs, J.P. Status integration and suicide. Eugene, Oreg., 1964.

Phil 8696.16 Gibbs, Jessie W. Evolution and Christianity. Memphis, 1930.

Phil 3801.426 Gibelin, Jean. L'esthétique de Schelling d'après la philosophie de l'art. Thèse. Clermont-Ferrand, 1934.

Phil 7068.99.33 Gibier, P. Psychism; analysis of things existing. 3. ed. N.Y., 1899.

Phil 7054.39 Gibier, P. Le spiritisme. Paris, 1887.
Phil 181.8 Gibon, A.E. Cours de philosophie. Paris, 1842. 2v.
Phil 2520.179 Gibson, A.B. The philosophy of Descartes. London, 1932.
Phil 5246.58 Gibson, A.B. Thinkers at work. London, 1946.
Phil 8586.62 Gibson, Alexander Boyce. Theism and empiricism. London, 1970.

Phil 5585.295 Gibson, Eleanor Jack. Principles of perceptual learning and development. N.Y., 1969.

Phil 8610.881.20 Gibson, Ellen E. The godly women of the Bible. N.Y., 1881.

Phil 5585.70 Gibson, J. The perception of the visual world. Boston, 1950.

Phil 2115.111.15A Gibson, James. John Locke. London, 1933.
Phil 5585.243 Gibson, James Jerome. The senses considered as perceptual systems. Boston, 1966.

Phil 8881.50 Gibson, R.W. The morality of nature. N.Y., 1923.
Phil 8696.1 Gibson, S.T. Religion and science. London, 1875.
Phil 6116.22 Gibson, Van R. The faith that overcomes the world. N.Y., 1926.

Phil 8881.29 Gibson, W.R.B. A philosophical introduction to ethics. London, 1904.

Phil 5046.8 Gibson, W.R.B. The problem of logic. London, 1908.
Phil 179.3.82 Gibson, W.R.B. Rudolf Eucken's philosophy of life. London, 1907.

Phil 9166.2 Gibson, W.S. An essay on the filial duties. London, 1848.
Phil 665.36 Gibt es eine Seelenwanderung? (Falke, R.) Halle, 1904.
Phil 5753.16 Gibt es einen freien Willen? (Danner, Manfred.) Hamburg, 1967.

Phil 7069.56.5 Gibt es Geister? Bern, 1956.
Phil 8422.2 Gibt es Kunstgesetze. (Volbehr, Theodor.) Esslingen, 1906.

Phil 5722.2 Gibtesunbewusste und vererbte Vorstellungen? (Schuster, P.R.) Leipzig, 1879.

Phil 6315.2.265 Gicklhorn, Josef. Sigmund Freuds akademische Laufbahn im. Wien, 1960.

Phil 1200.34 Gidionsen, W. De es quad stoici naturae comienienter vivendum esse, principium ponunt. Lipsiae, 1852.

Phil 3925.16.225 Giegel, Hans Joachim. Die Logik der seelischen Ereignisse. Thesis. Frankfurt, 1969.

Phil 3270.4.82 Gielhammer, L. Die politischen Grundlagen. Berlin, 1928.
Phil 287.2 Giera, Jules. Les deux creations. Paris, 1872.
Phil 530.20.100 Gieraths, Gundolf Maria. Reichtum des Lebens. Düsseldorf, 1956.

Phil 7069.24.42 Giese, F. Die Lehre von den Gedankenwellen. 2.-3. Aufl. Leipzig, 1924.

Phil 5850.214.10 Giese, Fritz. Arbeits- und Berufspsychologie. Halle, 1928.

Phil 5374.42 Giése, Fritz. Das ausserpersönliche Unbewusste. Braunschweig, 1924.

Phil 3640.318 Giese, Fritz. Nietzsche...die Erfüllung. Tübingen, 1934.
Phil 5850.214.15 Giese, Fritz. Psychoanalytische Psychotechnik. Leipzig, 1924.

Phil 5246.23 Giese, Fritz. Psychologische Beiträge. Langensalza, 1916-
Phil 5204.6.2 Giese, Fritz. Psychologische Wörterbuch. Tübingen, 1950.
Phil 91.4 Giese, Fritz. Psychologisches Wörterbuch. Leipzig, 1921.
Phil 5246.23.9 Giese, Fritz. Psychotechnisches Praktikum. Halle, 1923.
Phil 5850.214 Giese, Fritz. Theorie der Psychotechnik: Grundzüge der praktischen Psychologie. Braunschweig, 1925.

Phil 3425.226 Giese, G. Hegels Staatsidee und der Begriff der Staatserziehung. Halle, 1926.

Phil 7082.132 Giessler, Carl Max. Aus den Tiefen des Traumlebens. Halle-Saale, 1890.

Phil 8696.28 Giesswein, Sándor. Vilagegyetem es a lélek világa. Budapest, 1913.

Phil 8407.32 Giesz, L. Phänomenologie des Kitsches. Heidelberg, 1960.
Phil 3640.359 Giesz, Ludwig. Nietzsche. Stuttgart, 1950.
Phil 8448.11.7 Giesz, Ludwig. Phanomenologie des Kitsches. 2. Aufl. München, 1971.

Htn Phil 181.24* Gifford, A. Lectures. Frankfurt, n.d.
Phil 6420.36.1 Gifford, Mabel F. Correcting nervous speech disorders. N.Y., 1940.

Phil 6420.36.5 Gifford, Mabel F. How to overcome stammering. N.Y., 1940.
Phil 7054.45 The gift of D.D. Home. (Home, Daniel Dunglas (Mrs.).) London, 1890.

Phil 6132.42 The gift of healing. 1st ed. (Worrall, Ambrose A.) N.Y., 1965.

Phil 8643.12 The gift of immortality. (Slattery, C.L.) Boston, 1916.
Phil 8643.16 The gift of immortality. (Stanley, T.P.) Collingswood, 1969.

Phil 7159.173 A gift of prophecy: the phenomenal Jeane Dixon. (Montgomery, Ruth S.) N.Y., 1965.

Phil 2115.170 Giganti, Maria A. John Locke e i limiti della scienza. Padova, 1957.

Phil 181.112 Gignoux, Victor. Cours de philosophie. v.3. Paris, 1950.
Phil 1111.9.5 Gigon, Olof. Grundprobleme der antiken Philosophie. Bern, 1959.

Phil 1111.9 Gigon, Olof. Der Ursprung der griechischen Philosophie von Hesiod bis Parmenides. Berlin, 1945.

Phil 4307.4 Gil Cremades, Juan José. El reformismo español; Krausismo. Barcelona, 1969.

Phil 3640.272 Gil Salguero, L. Persona y destino. Buenos Aires, 1934.
Phil 5216.1 Gilardin, Alphonse. Considérations sur les divers systèmes de psychologie. Paris, 1883.

Phil 5046.3 Gilbart, J.W. Logic for the million. London, 1860.
Phil 5046.3.5 Gilbart, J.W. Logic for the million. 5th ed. London, 1857.

Phil 5592.179 Gilberstadt, Harold. A handbook for clinical and actuarial MMPI interpretation. Philadelphia, 1965.

Phil 8881.71 Gilbert, Headley B. Temptation. Dallas, Texas, 1949.
Phil 8407.25 Gilbert, K. Aesthetic studies: architecture and poetry. Durham, 1952.

Phil 2477.6.81 Gilbert, K. Maurice Blondel's philosophy of action. Chapel Hill, 1924.

Phil 8092.7 Gilbert, Katherine Everett. Studies in recent aesthetic. Chapel Hill, 1927.

Phil 8631.4 Gilbert, L. Side-lights on immortality. London, 1903.

Phil 8050.78 Gilbert, Mesk. A history of aesthetics. N.Y., 1939.

Phil 1607.5A Gilbert, Neal. Renaissance concepts of method. N.Y., 1960.

Phil 1135.25 Gilbert, O. Griechische Religionsphilosophie. Leipzig, 1911.

Phil 181.106 Gilby, Thomas. Phoenix and turtle. London, 1950.

Phil 8696.24 Gilch, Gerhard. Gebrochemes Weltbild. 1. Aufl. Stuttgart, 1966.

Htn Phil 8661.13* Gildon, Charles. The deist's manual. London, 1705.

Phil 1515.2.5 Gilen, Leonhard. Kleutgen und die Theorie des Erkenntnisbildes. Meisenheim, 1956.

Phil 8881.7 Giles, A.E. Moral pathology. London, 1895.

Phil 7054.9 Giles. A.E. English and parental versions of Bible...in the light of modern spiritualism. Boston, 1897.

Phil 4756.5.30 Giliarov-Platonov, N.P. Sbornik sochinenii. v.1-2. Moskva, 1899-1900.

Phil 4756.5.31 Giliarov-Platonov, N.P. Voprosy very i tserkvi. Moskva, 1905.

Phil 8696.26 Gilkey, Langdon Brown. Religion and the scientific future; reflections on myth, science, and theology. 1. ed. N.Y., 1970.

Phil 5627.24 Gill, E.H.K. Psychological aspects of Christian experience. Boston, 1915.

Phil 8586.41 Gill, Eric. The necessity of belief. London, 1936.

Phil 181.46 Gille, E. Cours de philosophie. Paris, 1876.

Phil 5756.11 Gille, Paul. Esquisse d'une philosophie de la dignité humaine. Paris, 1924.

Phil 8956.10 Gilleman, Gérard. The primacy of charity in moral theology. Westminster, 1959.

Phil 8620.52 Gillen, Louis Bertrand. La théorie des oppositions et la théologie du péché, au XIIIe siècle. Paris, 1937.

Phil 5867.20 Gilles, Brigitte. Untersuchungen zur Periodik im Spielverhalten 6-10 jähriger Kinder. Bonn, 1965.

Phil 8661.8.30 Gillespie, W.H. The necessary existence of God. Edinburgh, 1843.

Phil 2494.81 Gillet, M. L'Utopie de Condorcet. Paris, 1883.

Phil 9075.19 Gillet, Marie S. L'éducation de la conscience. Paris, 1913.

Phil 8520.31 Gillett, C.R. The McAlpin collection of British history and theology. N.Y., 1924.

Phil 8586.49 Gillett, H.T. The spiritual basis of democracy. Oxford, 1952.

Phil 5590.574 Gilligan, Sonja Carl. The heterosexuals are coming; the fusion strategy. N.Y., 1971.

Phil 5246.41 Gilliland, A.R. General psychology for professional students. Boston, 1930.

Phil 5246.41.4 Gilliland, A.R. Psychology of individual differences. N.Y., 1939.

Phil 1955.6.25 Gillio-Tos, M.T. Il pensiero di Giovanni Dewey. Napoli, 1938.

Phil 8881.8 Gilliot, A. Physiologie du sentiment. Paris, 1848. 2v.

Phil 8696.20A Gillispie, C.C. Genesis and geology. Cambridge, Mass., 1951.

Phil 8696.20.5 Gillispie, C.C. Genesis and geology. Cambridge, 1969.

Phil 3640.705 Gillner, Helmut. Fryderyk Nietzsche. Warszawa, 1965.

Phil 2475.1.99 Gillouin, R. Henri Bergson. Paris, 1910.

Phil 2475.1.106 Gillouin, R. La philosophie de M. Henri Bergson. Paris, 1911.

Phil 2475.1.105 Gillouin, R. La philosophie de M. Henri Bergson. Paris, 1911.

Phil 5402.2 Gilman, B.T. Syllabus of...lectures on the psychology of pain. Worcester, Mass., 1893.

Phil 5525.29 Gilman, Bradley. A clinic on the comic. Nice, 1926.

Phil 8881.10 Gilman, N.P. Conduct as a fine art. Boston, 1891.

Phil 2055.7.80A Gilman, R.C. The bibliography of William E. Hocking. Waterville, Me., 1951.

Phil 5246.80 Gilmer, Beverly von Haller. Psychology. N.Y., 1970.

Phil 5046.9.5 Gilmore, J.H. Outlines of logic. N.Y., 1888.

Phil 5046.9 Gilmore, J.H. Outlines of logic. Rochester, 1876.

Phil 8434.2.15 Gilpin, W. Observations on forest scenery. Edinburgh, 1834.

Htn Phil 8434.2* Gilpin, W. Remarks on forest scenery, and other woodland views. London, 1791. 2v.

Phil 8434.2.10 Gilpin, W. Remarks on forest scenery, and other woodland views. 3. ed. London, 1808. 2v.

Htn Phil 8434.2.5* Gilpin, W. Three essays: on picturesque beauty. London, 1792.

Phil 8881.9 Gilson, B. Manuel de philosophie morale. Louvain, 1883.

Phil 181.73.5 Gilson, E. Being and some philosophers. Toronto, 1949.

Phil 181.73.7 Gilson, E. Being and some philosophers. 2. ed. Toronto, 1952.

Phil 181.73 Gilson, E. Christianisme et philosophie. Paris, 1936.

Phil 2520.116.10 Gilson, E. Descartes et la métaphysique scolastique. Bruxelles, 1924.

Phil 2520.116 Gilson, E. La doctrine cartésienne de la liberté et la théologie. Paris, 1913.

Phil 5465.58 Gilson, E. L'école des muses. Paris, 1951.

Phil 2520.116.15 Gilson, E. Études sur le rôle de la pensée médiévale dans la formation du système cartésien. Paris, 1930.

Phil 2520.116.15.5 Gilson, E. Études sur le rôle de la pensée médiévale dans la formation du système cartésien. Paris, 1951.

Phil 2520.117 Gilson, E. Index scolastico-cartésien. Paris, 1912.

Phil 2520.116.5 Gilson, E. La liberté chez Descartes et la théologie. Paris, 1913.

Phil 181.74.5 Gilson, E. Metaphysics in modern times. Chicago, 1940.

Phil 181.73.10 Gilson, E. Le philosophe et la théologie. Paris, 1960.

Phil 181.73.15 Gilson, E. The philosopher and theology. N.Y., 1962.

Phil 8407.41.5 Gilson, Étienne. The arts of the beautiful. N.Y., 1965.

Phil 1020.8.19 Gilson, Étienne. Avicenne et le point de départ de Duns Scot. Paris, 1927.

Phil 2630.8.35 Gilson, Étienne. Breakdown of morals and Christian education. n.p., 1952?

Phil 1511.3.11 Gilson, Étienne. L'esprit de la philosophie. Paris, 1948.

Phil 1511.3.10 Gilson, Étienne. L'esprit de la philosophie médiévale. Paris, 1932. 2v.

Phil 1511.3.12 Gilson, Étienne. L'esprit de la philosophie médiévale. 2e éd. Paris, 1944.

Phil 2630.8.30 Gilson, Étienne. L'être et l'essence. Paris, 1948.

Phil 2630.8.32 Gilson, Étienne. L'être et l'essence. Paris, 1962.

Phil 1511.3 Gilson, Étienne. Études de philosophie médiévale. Strasbourg, 1921.

Phil 1511.3.19 Gilson, Étienne. Die Geschichte der christlichen Philosophie. Paderborn, 1937.

Phil 2630.8.21 Gilson, Étienne. A Gilson reader. Garden City, 1957.

Phil 8586.45 Gilson, Étienne. God and philosophy. New Haven, 1941.

Phil 1511.3.13.15 Gilson, Étienne. History of Christian philosophy in the Middle Ages. London, 1955.

Phil 1511.3.13.10A Gilson, Étienne. History of Christian philosophy in the Middle Ages. N.Y., 1955.

Phil 1511.3.17 Gilson, Étienne. Introduction à la philosophie chrétienne. Paris, 1960.

Phil 2630.8.38 Gilson, Étienne. Introduction aux arts du beau. Paris, 1963.

Phil 5520.605 Gilson, Étienne. Linguistique et philosophie. Paris, 1969.

Phil 8407.41 Gilson, Étienne. Matiéres et formes. Paris, 1964.

Phil 1511.3.23 Gilson, Étienne. Medieval universalism and its present value. N.Y., 1937.

Phil 1511.3.5 Gilson, Étienne. La philosophie au moyen âge. v.2. Paris, 1922.

Phil 1511.3.7 Gilson, Étienne. La philosophie au moyen âge. 2e éd. Paris, 1944.

Phil 630.43 Gilson, Étienne. Le réalisme méthodique. Paris, 1936?

Phil 630.43.7 Gilson, Étienne. Réalisme thomiste. Paris, 1939.

Phil 1511.3.22 Gilson, Étienne. Reason and revelation in the Middle Ages. N.Y., 1959.

Phil 1511.3.15 Gilson, Étienne. Les sources gréco-arabes de l'augustinisme avicennisant. Paris, 1930.

Phil 1511.3.13.5A Gilson, Étienne. The spirit of mediaeval philosophy. N.Y., 1940.

Phil 8740.10 Gilson, Étienne. Théologie et histoire de la spiritualité. Paris, 1943.

Phil 8586.45.5 Gilson, Étienne. Les tribulations de Sophie. Paris, 1967.

Phil 806.13.1 Gilson, Étienne. The unity of philosophical experience. N.Y., 1937.

Phil 806.13.2 Gilson, Étienne. The unity of philosophical experience. N.Y., 1946.

Phil 3120.8.115 Gilson, Lucie. Méthode et métaphysique selon Franz Brentano. Paris, 1955.

Phil 3120.8.120 Gilson, Lucie. La psychologie descriptive selon Franz Brentano. Paris, 1955.

Phil 2630.8.21 A Gilson reader. (Gilson, Étienne.) Garden City, 1957.

Phil 665.77 Gindl, I. Seele und Geist. Wien, 1955.

Phil 181.9 Giner, F. Estudios filosoficos y religiosos. Madrid, 1876.

Phil 181.9.5 Giner, F. Filosofía y arte. Madrid, 1878.

Phil 4357.2.30 Giner de los Rios, Francisco. Ensayos y cartas. Mexico, 1965.

Phil 5246.6 Giner de los Rios, Francisco. Lecciones sumarias de psicología. Midrid, 1877.

Phil 4357.2.3 Giner de los Rios, Francisco. Obras completas. v.1-19. Madrid, 1916-27. 15v.

Phil 4357.2.31 Giner de los Rios, Francisco. El pensamiento vivo de Giner de los Rios. Buenos Aires, 1949.

Phil 1806.2 Ginestier, Paul. La pensée anglo-saxonne depuis 1900. 1e éd. Paris, 1956.

Phil 8708.29 Ginger, Ray. Six days or forever? Boston, 1958.

Phil 2477.19.82 Ginisty, Bernard. Conversion spirituelle et engagement prospectif, essai pour une lecture de Gaston Berger. Paris, 1966.

Phil 5400.134 Ginneken, J. van. Gelaat, gebaar en klankexpressie. Leiden, 1919.

Phil 5520.14 Ginneken, J. van. Principes de linguistic psychologique. Paris, 1907.

Phil 6998.4.5 Ginott, Haim G. Group psychotherapy with children. N.Y., 1961.

Phil 8831.5 Ginsberg, M. Moral progress; being the Frazer lecture delivered within the University of Glasgow on 18th April 1944. Glasgow, 1944.

Phil 8881.73 Ginsberg, Morris. Reason and experience in ethics. London, 1956.

Phil 6980.326 Ginsburg, S.W. A psychiatrist's views on social issues. N.Y., 1963.

Phil 9530.56 Ginzberg, Eli. Talent and performance. N.Y., 1964.

Phil 3808.149 Giobbe e Schopenhauer. (Allievo, G.) Torino, 1912.

Phil 4115.31 Gioberti, V. Cours de philosophie, 1841-1842. Milano, 1947.

Phil 8407.9.5 Gioberti, V. Del bello. 2. ed. Firenze, 1845.

Phil 4115.30 Gioberti, V. Del buono, del bello. Firenze, 1850.

Phil 4115.30.2 Gioberti, V. Del buono, del bello. Firenze., 1853.

Phil 4115.30.5 Gioberti, V. Del buono. Napoli, 1848.

Phil 4115.51 Gioberti, V. Della filosofia della rivelazione. Torino, 1856.

Phil 4115.40 Gioberti, V. Della protologia. Torino, 1857-58. 2v.

Phil 4115.75 Gioberti, V. Epistolario. Firenze, 1927-37. 11v.

Phil 8407.9 Gioberti, V. Essai sur le beau, ou Eléments de philosophie esthétique. Bruxelles, 1843.

Phil 4115.55 Gioberti, V. Essay on the beautiful. London, 1871.

Phil 4115.65 Gioberti, V. Grundzüge eines Systems der Ethik. Mainz, 1848.

Phil 4115.35 Gioberti, V. Introduction à l'étude de la philosophie. Moulins, 1845-47. 4v.

Phil 4115.36 Gioberti, V. Introduction à l'étude de la philosophie. Paris, 1847. 3v.

Phil 4115.34.6 Gioberti, V. Introduzione allo studio della filosofia. Firenze, 1926.

Phil 4115.34 Gioberti, V. Introduzione allo studio della filosofia. Milano, 1850. 2v.

Phil 4115.33 Gioberti, V. Introduzione allo studio della filosofia. v.1-2. Brusselle, 1840. 3v.

Phil 4115.33.10 Gioberti, V. Introduzione allo studio della filosofia. v.1-4. Napoli, 1846-47.

Phil 4115.33.5 Gioberti, V. Introduzione allo studio della filosofia. 2a ed. v.1-4. Capolago, 1845-46. 2v.

Phil 4115.24 Gioberti, V. L'Italia, la chiesa e la civiltà universale. Torino, 1926.

Phil 4115.98 Gioberti, V. Una lettera inedita a Taparelli d'Azeglio. Roma, 1923.

Phil 2725.2.95 Gioberti, V. Lettera intorno alle dottrine filosofiche e politiche del sig. di Lamennais. Lucca, 1845. 2 pam.

Phil 2725.2.95.2 Gioberti, V. Lettera intorno alle dottrine filosofiche e religiose del sig. di Lamennais. Milano, 1971.

Phil 4115.76 Gioberti, V. Lettere inedite di V. Gioberti e P. Galluppi. Roma, 1920.

Phil 4115.53 Gioberti, V. Meditazioni filosofiche inedite. Firenze, 1909.

Phil 4115.25 Gioberti, V. Nuova protologia brani scelti da tutte le sue opere. Bari, 1912. 2v.

Phil 4115.14   Gioberti, V. Opere. v. 1-16. Napoli, 1845- 7v.
Phil 4115.12   Gioberti, V. Opere edite ed inedite. v. 1-7, 13. Brusselle, 1843-44. 6v.
Phil 4115.23   Gioberti, V. Pagine scelte, edite ed inedite. Torino, 1922.
Phil 4115.27   Gioberti, V. Pensieri. Torino, 1859-60. 2v.
Phil 4115.60   Gioberti, V. Il pensiero civile. Torino, 1901.
Phil 4115.81   Gioberti, V. Primo centenario di V. Gioberti. Torino, 1901. 2 pam.
Phil 4115.40.5   Gioberti, V. Protologia; estratti. Torino, 1924.
Phil 4115.96   Gioberti, V. Réponse à un article. Bruxelles, 1844.
Phil 4115.20   Gioberti, V. Scritti scelti. Torino, 1954.
Phil 4115.28   Gioberti, V. Studi filologici. Torino, 1867.
Phil 4115.50   Gioberti, V. Teorica del sovranaturale. Capolago, 1850. 2v.
Phil 4115.50.5   Gioberti, V. Teorica del sovranaturale. Venezia, 1850.
Phil 4115.42   Gioberti, V. La teorica delle mente umana. Milano, 1910.
Phil 4210.92   Gioberti, Vincenzo. Degli errori filosofici di Antonio Rosmini. Napoli, 1845.
Phil 4210.92.2   Gioberti, Vincenzo. Degli errori filosofici di Antonio Rosmini. 2a ed. Capolago, 1846. 3v.
Phil 4210.92.15   Gioberti, Vincenzo. Risposta agli attachi di G. di Cavour. Torino, 1848.
Phil 4115.89   Gioberti. (Palhories, F.) Paris, 1929.
Phil 4115.79   Gioberti. (Guide bibliografiche). (Bruers, A.) Roma, 1924.
Phil 4115.94   Gioberti e il problema religioso del risorgimento. (Rinaldi, A.) Firenze, 1929.
Phil 4115.92   Gioberti e la filosofia nuova italiana. (Luciani, P.) Napoli, 1866-72. 3v.
Phil 4115.82.5   Gioberti e Zarelli. Pisa, 1851.
Phil 181.10.5   Gioja, M. Elementi di filosofia. Milano, 1818. 2v.
Phil 181.10   Gioja, M. E. Elementi di filosofia. Lugano, 1834.
Phil 4120.1.50   Gioja, Melchiorre. La causa di Dio e degli uomini difesa dagl'insulti degli empj e dalle pretensioni dei fanatici. Lugano, 1834.
Phil 4120.1.35   Gioja, Melchiorre. Del merito e delle ricompenae. Torino, 1853. 2v.
Phil 4120.1.32F   Gioja, Melchiorre. Del merito e delle ricompense; trattato storico e filosofico. v. 1-2. 2. ed. Lugano, 1830.
Phil 4120.1.33   Gioja, Melchiorre. Del merito e delle ricompense. Lugano, 1839. 2v.
Phil 4120.1.30   Gioja, Melchiorre. Elementi di filosofia ad uso de'Giovanetti. Milano, 1822. 2v.
Phil 4120.1.31   Gioja, Melchiorre. Elementi di filosofia ad uso de'Giovanetti. v.1-2. Milano, 1838.
Phil 4120.1.45   Gioja, Melchiorre. Esercizio logico sugli errori d'ideologia. Milano, 1824.
Phil 4120.1.40   Gioja, Melchiorre. Ideologia. Milano, 1822-23. 2v.
Phil 4120.1.10   Gioja, Melchiorre. Opere minori. Lugano, 1832-37. 17v.
Phil 4120.1.8   Gioja, Melchiorre. Opere principali. Lugano, 1838-40. 16v.
Phil 4120.1.80   Pamphlet vol. Gioja, Melchiorre. 4 pam.
Phil 181.158   Giorda, Renato. Psicologia dell'avere. Roma, 1968.
Phil 4065.102.2   Giordana Bruno i el pensiero del rinascimento. 2a ed. (Gentile, G.) Firenze, 1925.
Phil 575.141   Giordani, Roberto. Dalla dialettica alla apodittica. Roma, 1946.
Phil 4065.84   Giordano Bruno, Gedanken über seine Lehre. (Stein, H. von.) Leipzig, 1900.
Phil 4065.101   Giordano Bruno, his life, thought and martyrdom. (Boulting, William.) London, 1916.
Phil 4065.107.10   Giordano Bruno, ou L'univers infinj comme fondement de la philosophie moderne. (Namer, Émile.) Paris, 1966.
Phil 4065.135   Giordano Bruno. (Baldi, E.) Firenze, 1955.
Phil 4065.101.2   Giordano Bruno. (Boulting, William.) London, 1914.
Phil 4065.124   Giordano Bruno. (Brandt, C.) Buenos Aires, 1940.
Phil 4065.94A   Giordano Bruno. (Brinton, D.G.) Philadelphia, 1890.
Phil 4065.128   Giordano Bruno. (Cicuttini, L.) Milano, 1950.
Phil 4065.88   Giordano Bruno. (Giancola, Francesco.) Roma, 1885.
Phil 4065.118.5   Giordano Bruno. (Guzzo, Augusto.) Torino, 1960.
Phil 4065.103   Giordano Bruno. (Labriola, Arturo.) Roma, 1924?
Phil 4065.100   Giordano Bruno. (Levi, David.) Torino, 1887.
Phil 4065.86   Giordano Bruno. (Louis, G.) Berlin, 1900.
Phil 4065.87   Giordano Bruno. (McIntyre, J.S.) London, 1903.
Phil 4065.83   Giordano Bruno. (Morselli, E.) Torino, 1888.
Phil 4065.110   Giordano Bruno. (Olschki, L.) Bari, 1927.
Phil 4065.89   Giordano Bruno. (Riehl, A.) Edinburgh, 1905.
Phil 4065.89.20   Giordano Bruno. (Riehl, A.) Leipzig, 1889.
Phil 4065.123   Giordano Bruno. (Schwartz, M.) Erfurt, 1939.
Phil 4065.127   Giordano Bruno. (Singer, D. (Waley).) N.Y., 1950.
Phil 4065.178   Giordano Bruno. (Szemere, Samu.) Budapest, 1917.
Phil 4065.96   Giordano Bruno. (Tocco, Felice.) Firenze, 1886.
Phil 4065.91.5   Giordano Bruno. (Troilo, Erminio.) Roma, 1918.
Phil 4065.173   Giordano Bruno. (Yates, F.A.) London, 1964.
Phil 4065.109   Giordano Bruno: la vita e l'uomo. (Mariano, R.) Roma, 1881.
Phil 4065.27   Giordano-Bruno. 2. ed. (Bruno, Giordano.) Milano, 1944.
Phil 4065.89.5   Giordano-Bruno. 2e, Aufl. (Riehl, A.) Leipzig, 1900.
Phil 4065.25   Giordano-Bruno-Buch. (Bruno, Giordano.) Bad Oldesloe, 1927.
Phil 4065.82   Giordano Bruno da Nola. (Berti, D.) Torino, 1889.
Phil 4065.176   Giordano Bruno e i suoi tempi. (Previti, Luigi.) Prato, 1887.
Phil 4065.116   Giordano Bruno e il Vaticano. (Battaglini, F.) Roma, 1889.
Phil 4065.112   Giordano Bruno e le sue opere. (Cotugno, R.) Trani, 1907.
Phil 4065.102   Giordano Bruno i el pensiero de rinascimento. (Gentile, G.) Firenze, 1920.
Phil 4065.102.8   Giordano Bruno nella storia della cultura. (Gentile, G.) Milano, 1907.
Phil 4065.165   Giordano Bruno tra l'umanesimo e lo stoicismo. (Ciardo, Manlio.) Bologna, 1960.
Phil 4065.81   Giordano Bruno und Nicolaus von Cusa. (Clemens, F.J.) Bonn, 1847.
Phil 4065.113   Giordano Bruno und seine Weltanschauung. (Reiner, Julius.) Berlin, 19-?
Phil 4065.50.4   Giordano Bruno von der Ursache dem Prinzip und dem Einen. 4e aufl. (Bruno, Giordano.) Leipzig, 1923.
Phil 4065.105.15   Giordano Bruno's Lehre vom Kleinsten als die Quelle der prastabilierten Harmonie des Leibnitz. 2. Aufl. (Brunnhofer, H.) Leipzig, 1899.
Phil 4065.104   Giordano Brunos metafysik. (Wickström, V.H.) Lund, 1883.
Phil 4065.97   Giordano Bruno's Philosophie in den Hauptbegriffen Materie und Form. (Wilde, Georg.) Breslau, 1901.
Phil 4065.105   Giordano Bruno's Weltanschauung. (Brunnhofer, H.) Leipzig, 1882.

Phil 4080.3.340   Giordano-Orsini, Gian Napoleon. Benedetto Croce. Carbondale, 1961.
Phil 4215.2.86   Giordano-Zocchi, V. Tommaso Rossi. Napoli, 1866.
Phil 4215.1.97   Giorgi, A. de. Biografia di G.D. Romagnosi e catalogo delle sue opere. Parma, 1874.
Phil 8407.48   Giorgi, Rubina. Simbolo e schema. Padova, 1968.
Phil 3640.250   Giorgianni, E. Nietzsche. Roma, 1931.
Phil 5068.26   Giorgianni, Virgilio. Neopositivismo e scienza de diritto. Roma, 1956.
Phil 3488.28   Giorgiantonio, M. Kant e la critica del nostro tiempo. Napoli, 1953.
Htn   Phil 250.2*   Giorgio, F. De harmonia mundi totius. Venice, 1525.
Phil 1870.105   Giorgio Berkeley. (Papini, G.) Milano, 1908.
Phil 16.1   Giornale critico della filosofia italiana. Messina. 1920+ 43v.
Phil 16.7   Giornale di metafisica; revista bimestrale di filosofica. 1,1946+ 25v.
Phil 16.12   Giornale italiano per la ricerca psichica. Milano. 1,1963+
Phil 4215.3.90   Giornata Rensiana, Genova. Giuseppe Rensi. Milano, 1967.
Phil 4080.17.20   Giornate di Studi Carabellesiani, Bologna, 1960. Giornate di studi carabellesiani. Genoa, 1964.
Phil 4080.17.20   Giornate di studi carabellesiani. (Giornate di Studi Carabellesiani, Bologna, 1960.) Genoa, 1964.
Phil 4260.102.10   Giovambattista Vico. Il suo secolo e le sue opere. Pt.1. (Cotugno, R.) Trani, 1890.
Phil 4080.3.375   Il Giovane Croce e il Marxismo. (Agazzi, E.) Torino, 1962.
Phil 1955.6.230   Il Giovane Dewey. 1. ed. (Granese, Alberto.) Firenze, 1966.
Phil 4210.76   Giovane età e primi studi di Antonio Rosmini-Serbati. (Rosmini-Serbati, Antonio.) Italia, 1860.
Phil 3235.127   Il giovane Feuerbach. (Cesa, C.) Bari, 1963.
Phil 4120.4.135   Il giovane Gentile e Marx. (Signorato, Alberto.) Milano, 1966.
Phil 4210.72   Il giovane Rosmini. (Rosmini-Serbati, Antonio.) Urbino, 1963.
Phil 337.26   Giovanni, Biagio de. L'esperienza come oggettivazione. Napoli, 1962.
Phil 4006.3.15   Giovanni, V. Della filosofia moderna in Sicilia libri due. Palermo, 1868.
Phil 4006.3   Giovanni, V. Storia della filosofia in Sicilia. Palermo, 1873. 2v.
Htn   Phil 4006.3.10*   Giovanni, V. Sullo stato attuale...filosofici in Sicilia. Palermo, 1854.
Phil 4006.3.12   Giovanni, V. Sullo stato attuale...filosofici in Sicilia. Palermo, 1854.
Phil 8586.29   Giovanni, V. di. Critica religiosa e filosofia lettere e saggi. Palermo, 1897. 2v.
Phil 4060.6.90   Giovanni, V. di. D'acquisto e la filosofia della creazione in Sicilia. Firenze, 1868.
Phil 4195.80   Giovanni, V. di. Giovanni Pico. Palermo, 1894.
Phil 4170.8.90   Giovanni, V. di. Il Miceli ovvero dell'ente uno e reale. Palermo, 1864.
Phil 181.48   Giovanni, V. di. Prelezioni di filosofia. Palermo, 1877.
Phil 4120.3.30   Giovanni, V. di. Principii di filosofia prima. Palermo, 1863. 2v.
Phil 181.48.5   Giovanni, V. di. Principii di filosofia prima. Palermo, 1878. 3v.
Phil 4170.9.90   Giovanni, V. di. Salvatore Mancino e l'ecletticismo in Sicilia. Palermo, 1867.
Phil 4120.3.32   Giovanni, V. di. Sofismi e buon senso, serati campestri. 2. ed. Palermo, 1873.
Phil 4065.103.5   Giovanni Bovio e Giordano Bruno. (Labriola, Arturo.) Napoli, 1911.
Phil 4080.11.80F   Giovanni Caroli e la sua dottrina filosofica. (Ferrari, G.M.) Modena, 1926.
Phil 4120.4.95   Giovanni Gentile. (Fondazione Giovanni Gentile per gli Studi Filosofici.) Firenze, 1948-51. 13v.
Phil 4120.4.50   Giovanni Gentile. (Piglianu, A.) Sassari, 1953.
Phil 4120.4.130   Giovanni Gentile. (Spirito, Ugo.) Firenze, 1969.
Phil 4120.4.105   Giovanni Gentile. (Vettori, V.) Firenze, 1954.
Phil 4120.4.100   Giovanni Gentile a la sua scuola. (Andreola, A.) Milano, 1951.
Phil 4120.4.140   Giovanni Gentile on the existence of God. (Smith, William Aloysius.) Louvain, 1970.
Phil 2115.135   Giovanni Locke. (Tarantino, G.) Milano, 1886.
Phil 4195.80   Giovanni Pico. (Giovanni, V. di.) Palermo, 1894.
Phil 4195.86   Giovanni Pico della Mirandola. (Garin, Eugenio.) Firenze, 1937.
Phil 4195.88   Giovanni Pico della Mirandola. (Garin, Eugenio.) Parma? 1963.
Phil 4195.100   Giovanni Pico della Mirandola. (Monnerjahn, E.) Wiesbaden, 1960.
Phil 4195.107   Giovanni Pico della Mirandola. (Napoli, Giovanni di.) Roma, 1965.
Phil 4195.84   Giovanni Pico della Mirandola. (Semprini, G.) Todi, 1921.
Phil 4195.40   Giovanni Pico della Mirandola: his life. (Rigg, J.M.) London, 1890.
Phil 2138.89.5   Giovanni Stuart Mill e l'utilitarismo. (Zuccante, G.) Firenze, 1922.
Phil 2138.122   Giovanni Stuart Mill e l'utilitarismo inglese. (Casellato, S.) Padova, 1951.
Phil 9343.14   Gioventu atea? (Dentico, Salvatore.) Palermo, 1967.
Phil 4260.124   La giovinezza di Giambattista Vico. 2. ed. (Nicolini, F.) Bari, 1932.
Phil 8140.6   Giraldi, Giovanni. L'estetica italiana nella prima metà del secolo XX. Pisa, 1963.
Phil 5246.35   Giran, Paul. Les origines de la pensée. Paris, 1923.
Phil 8631.10   Girard, Victor. La transmigration des âmes. Paris, 1888.
Phil 705.18   Girard, William. Du transcendentalisme considéré essentiellement dans sa définition et ses origines françaises. Berkeley, 1916.
Phil 8661.35.5   Girardi, Giulio. Credenti e non credenti per un mondo nuovo. Firenze, 1969.
Phil 8661.35   Girardi, Giulio. Dialogue et révolution. Paris, 1969.
Phil 2805.90.5   Giraud, V. Blaise Pascal études d'histoire morale. Paris, 1910.
Phil 2805.90   Giraud, V. Pascal l'homme, l'oeuvre, l'influence. Fribourg, 1898.
Phil 2805.90.3   Giraud, V. Pascal l'homme, l'oeuvre, l'influence. Paris, 1905.
Phil 2805.90.15   Giraud, V. Soeurs de grands hommes: J. Pascal. Paris, 1926.
Phil 2805.90.9   Giraud, V. La vie héroïque de Blaise Pascal. 15. éd. Paris, 1943.
Phil 2725.2.99   Giraud, Victor. La vie tragique de Lamennais. Paris, 1933.

Phil 8631.6 Giraudet, Jules. Y a-t-il une vie future? Paris, 1864.
Phil 9166.6 Girault, A. Le foyer, scènes de la vie de famille aux Etats Unis. Paris, 1875.
Phil 4070.10.30 Girdamo Balduino. (Papuli, Giovanni.) Manduzia, 1967.
Phil 8696.25 Giret, André. L'astronomie et le sentiment religieux. Paris, 1965.
Phil 5627.94 Girgensohn, K. Der seelische Aufbau des religiösen Erlebens. Leipzig, 1921.
Phil 5627.94.5 Girgensohn, K. Der seelische Aufbau des religiösen Erlebens. 2. Aufl. Gütersloh, 1930.
Phil 8586.18 Girgensohn, Karl. Die religion. Leipzig, 1903.
Phil 8881.53 Girini Corio, Gioseffo. L'antropologie. n.p., 1761. 2v.
Phil 9362.13 The girl wanted. (Waterman, Nixon.) Chicago, 1910.
Phil 9352.14 Girls: faults and ideals. (Miller, James R.) N.Y., 1892.
Phil 9355.8 Girls and women. (Paine, Harriet E.) Boston, 1890.
Phil 3246.305 Girndt, Helmut. Die Differenz des Fichtesche und Hegelschen Systems in der Hegelschen Differenzschrift. Bonn, 1965.
Phil 4688.110.30 Girnius, Juozas. Idealas ir laikas. Chicago, 1966.
Phil 4688.110.32 Girnius, Juozas. Laisve ir būtist. Brooklyn, 1953.
Phil 4688.110.36 Girnius, Juozas. Tauta ir tautine ištikimybé. Chicago, 1961.
Phil 4688.110.34 Girnius, Juozas. Žmogus de Dievo. Chicago? 1964.
Phil 4075.84 Girolamo Cardano e il suo tempo. (Bellini, Angelo.) Milano, 1947.
Phil 8661.33 Gironella, José María. Cien españoles y Dios. 3. ed. Barcelona, 1969.
Phil 9346.2 Girot. Le moraliste de la jeunesse. London, 1801.
Phil 9346.3.2 Gisborne, T. Enquiry...duties of the female sex. London, 1798.
Phil 8800.8 Gisborne, T. An enquiry into the duties of men. London, 1794.
Phil 8881.11 Gisborne, T. An enquiry into the duties of men. London, 1800. 2v.
Phil 8881.11.2 Gisborne, T. An enquiry into the duties of men. London, 1824. 2v.
Phil 8881.11.6 Gisborne, T. The principles of moral philosophy. London, 1790.
Phil 8586.3 Gisborne, T. The testimony of natural theology to Christianity. London, 1818.
Phil 3488.10 Gisevius, H. Kant's view on Raum und Zeit. Hannover, 1890.
Phil 6116.8 Giss, A.J. Die menschliche Geistestätigkeit in der Weltentwicklung. Leipzig, 1910.
Phil 817.17 The gist of philosophy. (Reitmeister, L.A.) N.Y., 1936.
Phil 7054.46 The gist of spiritualism. 3. ed. (Chase, W.) Boston, 1867.
Phil 7068.65.4 The gist of spiritualism. 4th ed. (Chase, Warren.) Boston, 1865.
Phil 3850.27.205 Gittleman, D. Albert Schweitzer. n.p., 1959.
Phil 1158.35 Giuffrida, Pasquale. L'epicureismo nella letteratura latina nel I secolo a.c. Torino, 1940. 2v.
Phil 4112.87 Giuli, G. de. La filosofia di Pasquale Galluppi. Palermo, 1935.
Phil 2520.181 Giuli, Guido de. Cartesio. Firenze, 1933.
Phil 181.67 Giuliani, G. Intorno al principio...della filosofia civile. Napoli, 1862.
Phil 400.57 Giuliano, B. Il valore dell'ideali. Torino, 1916.
Phil 3450.11.79.5 Giulietti, Giovanni. La filosofia del profondo in Husserl e in Zamboni. Treviso, 1965.
Phil 4265.1.80 Giulio Cesare Vanini e il suo tempi. (Palumbo, R.) Napoli, 1878.
Phil 2520.158 Giunchi, O. L'individualismo nel Cartesio e nel Rousseau. Novara, 1918.
Phil 4110.5.90 Giuseppe Ferrari. (Cantoni, Carlo.) Milano, 1878.
Phil 4110.5.80 Giuseppe Ferrari. L'evoluzione del suo pensiero (1838-1860). (Rota Ghibandi, Silvia.) Firenze, 1969.
Phil 4215.3.80 Giuseppe Rensi. (Buonaiui, E.) Roma, 1945.
Phil 4215.3.90 Giuseppe Rensi. (Giornata Rensiana, Genova.) Milano, 1967.
Phil 2475.1.430 Giusso, Lorenzo. Bergson. Milano, 1949.
Phil 4260.119 Giusso, Lorenzo. La filosofia di G.B. Vico e l'età barocca. Roma, 1943.
Phil 4065.150 Giusso, Lorenzo. Scienza e filosofia in Giordano Bruno. Napoli, 1955.
Phil 4006.8.30 Giusso, Lorenzo. La tradizione ermetica nella filosofia italiana. Roma, 1955?
Phil 2050.260 Giustizia e bene comune in David Hume. (Castignone, Silvana.) Milano, 1964.
Phil 8886.40 La giustizia e la morale. (Laudatio, Giorgio.) Trani, 1902.
Phil 8877.73 Give yourself a new deal. (Clarke, F. (Mrs.).) Boston, 1933.
Phil 8881.47 Givler, R.C. The ethics of Hercules. N.Y., 1924.
Phil 5246.17 Givler, Robert C. The conscious cross-section. Seattle, 1915.
Phil 5246.17.7 Givler, Robert C. Psychology; the science of human behavior. N.Y., 1922.
Phil 8881.12A Gizycki, G. Grundzüge der Moral. Leipzig, 1883.
Phil 8881.12.10 Gizycki, G. Moralphilosophie. Leipzig, n.d.
Phil 8881.12.5 Gizycki, G. Students manual of ethical philosophy. London, 1889.
Phil 2050.211 Gizycki, G. von. Die Ethik David Hume's in ihrer geschichtlichen Stellung. Breslau, 1878.
Phil 3488.9 Gizycki, G. von. Kant und Schopenhauer. Leipzig, 1888.
Phil 2262.82 Gizycki, G. von. Die Philosophie Shaftesbury's. Leipzig, 1876.
Phil 365.29 Gizycki, G. von. Philosophische Consequenzen der Lamarck-Darwin. Leipzig, 1876.
Phil 9346.11 Gizycki, Paul von. Vom Baume der Erkenntnis. Berlin, 1897.
Phil 6760.5 Gjedde, Georg. Bogen om Jesper. København, 1971.
Phil 5440.27 Gjellerup, Karl. Arvelighed og moral. Kjøbenhavn, 1881.
Phil 5756.8 Gjerdsjø, O. Determinismen og dens konsekvenser. Kristiania, 1907.
Phil 3585.8.83 Gjurits, D. Erkenntnistheorie des Ernst Laas. Inaug. Diss. Leipzig, 1902.
Phil 8881.25 Gladden, W. Plain thoughts on the art of living. Boston, 1868.
Phil 8956.2 Gladden, Washington. Ruling ideas of the present age. Boston, 1895.
Phil 806.20 Gladisch, August. Einleiteug in das Verständniss der Weltgeschichte. Posen, 1844.
Phil 1900.84 Gladstone, W.E. Studies subsidiary to works of...Butler. Oxford, 1896.
Phil 481.2 Glagolev, B. Materializm v svete sovremennoi nauki. Frankfurt, 1946.

Phil 310.370.5 A glance at historical materialism. (Podosetnik, V.M.) Moscow, 1965.
Phil 181.14 A glance at philosophy. (Goodrich, Samuel G.) Boston, 1845.
Phil 735.150.2 Glansdorff, Maxime. Les déterminants de la théorie générale de la valeur et ses applications en esthétique, en religion, en morale, en économie et en politique. 2e éd. Bruxelles, 1966.
Phil 735.150 Glansdorff, Maxime. Théorie générale de la valeur et ses applications en esthétique et en économie. Bruxelles, 1954.
Phil 181.11.2 Glanvill, J. Essays...philosophy and religion. London, 1676.
Htn Phil 181.11* Glanvill, J. Essays...philosophy and religion. London, 1676.
Phil 645.2.5 Glanvill, J. Scepsis scientifica: or, Confest ignorance, the way to science. London, 1885.
Phil 665.13 Glanvill, Joseph. A letter on praeexistence to Richard Baxter. Osceola, 1890.
Htn Phil 665.12* Glanvill, Joseph. Lux orientalis. London, 1662.
Htn Phil 8696.13* Glanvill, Joseph. Philosophia pia. London, 1671.
Htn Phil 2030.1.30* Glanvill, Joseph. Scepsis scientifica. London, 1665.
Htn Phil 665.12.2* Glanvill, Joseph. Two choice and useful treatises: Lux orientalis and A discourse of truth, by Dr. Rust. London, 1682.
Htn Phil 337.4* Glanvill, Joseph. The vanity of dogmatizing. London, 1661. 2 pam.
Phil 337.4.5 Glanvill, Joseph. The vanity of dogmatizing. N.Y., 1931.
Phil 337.4.6 Glanvill, Joseph. The vanity of dogmatizing. Facsimile reprints of the London editions of 1661, 1665 and 1676. Brighton, 1970.
Phil 7069.36.7 Glardon, R. Le spiritisme en face de l'historie. Lausanne, 1936.
Phil 3475.3.130 Das Glasein in der "Philosophie" von K. Jaspers. (Räber, T.) Bern, 1955.
Phil 3488.32 Glasenapp, H. von. Kant und die Religionen des Ostens. Kitzmingen, 1954.
Phil 960.161 Glasenapp, H. von. Die philosophie der Inder. Stuttgart, 1949.
Phil 5246.56 Glaser, E.M. An experiment in the development of critical thinking. Thesis. N.Y., 1941.
Phil 5590.451 Glaser, Eric Michael. The psysiological basis of habituation. London, 1966.
Phil 2733.97 Glaser, J.C. Vergleichung der Philosophie des Malebranche und Spinoza. Berlin, 1846.
Htn Phil 3801.428* Glaser, Johann K. Differenz der Schelling'schen und Hegel'schen Philosophie. Leipzig, 1842.
Phil 9495.149 Glasgow, M. Problems of sex. Boston, 1949.
Phil 7054.114 Glass, C.E. Advance thought. London, 1876.
Htn Phil 9166.3.5* Glasse, S. Advice from a lady of quality to her children. Boston, 1796.
Htn Phil 9166.3* Glasse, S. Advice from a lady of quality to her children. 3. ed. Newbury Port, 1778. 2v.
Phil 6980.328 Glasser, William. Mental health or mental illness? N.Y., 1960.
Phil 6980.328.5 Glasser, William. Reality therapy, a new approach to psychiatry. N.Y., 1965.
Phil 7069.23.7 The Glastonbury scripts. Glastonbury. 1-9
Phil 8622.56 Der Glaube - was ist das? (Buhr, H.) Pfullingen, 1963.
Phil 3195.15.30 Der Glaube an die Weltmaschine und seine Überwindung. (Dingler, Hugo.) Stuttgart, 1932.
Phil 8951.24.5 Der Glaube bei Emil Brunner. (Valken, L.) Freiburg, 1947.
Phil 3120.30.89 Der Glaube Martin Bubers. (Goldstein, Walter Benjamin.) Jerusalem, 1966.
Phil 8661.21 Glaube oder Unglaube. (Goldstein, Walter Benjamin.) Jerusalem, 1964.
Phil 3475.3.160 Glaube und Freiheit. (Lohff, Wenzel.) Gütersloh, 1957.
Phil 8586.36.60 Glaube und Geschichte. Festschrift für Friedrich Gogarten. (Runte, H.) Giessen, 1948.
Phil 8586.36.50 Glaube und Geschichte bei Friedrich Gogarten und Wilhelm Hermann. Inaug. Diss. (Schräter, Fritz.) Kothenanhalt, 1932?
Phil 3110.55.30 Glaube und Tat. (Böhme, J.) Berlin, 1957.
Phil 8622.40 Glaube und Unglaube. (Heer, Friedrich.) München, 1959.
Phil 8622.45 Glaube und Unglaube. Zürich, 1959.
Phil 8599.19.120 Glaube und Vernuft bei Ernst Troeltsch. (Drescher, H.G.) Marburg, 1957.
Phil 8586.36.5 Glaube und Wirklichkeit. (Gogarten, Friedrich.) Jena, 1928.
Phil 3565.122 Glaube und Wissen bei Lotze. (Thieme, K.) Leipzig, 1888.
Phil 8622.82.2 Glaube und Zukunft. 2. Aufl. (Ratzinger, Joseph.) München, 1971.
Phil 8691.20 Glauben und Wissen. (Bruhn, Wilhelm.) Leipzig, 1921.
Phil 3425.30 Glauben und Wissen. (Hegel, Georg Wilhelm Friedrich.) Hamburg, 1962.
Phil 3895.30 Glauben und Wissen. (Ulrici, H.) Leipzig, 1858.
Phil 8587.28.5 Glauben und Wissen. 2. Aufl. (Hoppe, Edmund.) Gütersloh, 1922.
Phil 3625.15.87 Glauben und Wissen. 3. Aufl. (Messer, A.) München, 1924.
Phil 3120.30.205 Der Glaubensbegriff Martin Bubers. 1. Aufl. (Wachinger, Lorenz.) München, 1970.
Phil 2805.178 Das Glaubensproblem bei Pascal. (Laros, M.) Düsseldorf, 1918.
Phil 8622.57 Das Glaubensproblem in der Religionsphilosophie. (Lutzenberger, H.) München? 1962.
Phil 5520.680 Glaubwürdigkeit im Sprachgebrauch. 1. Aufl. (Goessmann, Wilhelm.) München, 1970.
Phil 1880.30 Gleanings from a literary life 1830-80. (Bowen, F.) N.Y., 1880.
Phil 7054.68 Gleason, S.W. The spirit home: a closet companion. Boston, 1852.
Phil 3925.16.220 Glebe Møller, Jens. Wittgenstein or religionen. København, 1969.
Phil 8980.428 Glebova, Tamara G. Pis'ma k tebe. Moskva, 1965.
Phil 8881.27 Gleed, J.W. Real life. n.p., 1899.
Phil 806.7 Gleich, S. von. Von Thales bis Steiner. Stuttgart, 1920.
Phil 978.90 Gleich, Sigismund. Die Wahrheit als Gesamtanfang aller Weltansichten. Stuttgart, 1957.
Phil 8407.18.5 Gleichen-Russwurm, A. Die Schönheit. Stuttgart, 1916?
Phil 8407.18 Gleichen-Russwurm, A. Sieg der Freude. Stuttgart, 1913.
Phil 181.40 Gleichen-Russwurm, A. von. Der freie Mensch. Berlin, 1918.
Phil 181.40.5 Gleichen-Russwurm, A. von. Philosophische Profile. Stuttgart, 1922.
Phil 9220.10.9 Gleichen-Russwurm, Alexander von. Freundschaft. Stuttgart, 1918?
Phil 187.50 Die Gleichförmigkeit in der Welt. (Marbe, Karl.) München, 1916-1919. 2v.

Phil 9495.21   Das gleichgeschlechtliche Leben der Naturvölker. (Karsch-Haach, F.) München, 1911.

Phil 5651.2   Gleichgewicht und Otolithenorgan. (Verworn, M.) Bonn, 1891.

Phil 3428.96.4   Gleichmann, A. Über Herbarts Lehre von der Stufen des Unterrichts. 4. Aufl. Langensalza, 1904.

Phil 8430.16   Gleizes, A. Vers une conscience plastique; la forme et l'histoire. Paris, 1932.

Phil 6116.1   Glen, J. Theory of the influence exerted by the mind over the body. London, 1855.

Phil 7069.21.35   Glenconner, Pamela. The earthen vessel. London, 1921.

Phil 7072.6.5   Glendinning, Andrew. The veil lifted; modern developments of spirit photography. London, 1894.

Phil 8881.61.5   Glenn, Paul J. Ethics. 4th ed. St. Louis, Mo., 1934.

Phil 1722.13   Główne zagadnienia i kierunki filozofii. v.1-2. 2. Wyd. (Warsaw. Univerystet.) Warszawa, 1960.

Phil 6316.1   Gley, E. Études de psychologie. Paris, 1903.

Phil 181.162   Gley, Gérard. Essai sur les éléments de la philosophie. Paris, 1817.

Phil 310.225.5   Glezerman, G.E. The laws of social development. Moscow, 196-?

Phil 310.225   Glezerman, G.E. Ozakonakh obskchestvennogo razvitiia. Moskva, 1960.

Phil 4225.8.48   Gliarieti contro la verticale. (Sciacca, Michele Federico.) Milano, 1969.

Phil 5838.269   Glickman, Stephen E. The neurological basis of motivation. N.Y., 1969.

Phil 5850.219   Glidewell, John C. Choice points. Cambridge, Mass., 1970.

Phil 978.29.15   Glimpses of inner truth. (Farnsworth, E.C.) Portland, 1923.

Phil 8640.11   Glimpses of the future life. (Ponton, M.) London, 1873.

Phil 7069.11.50   Glimpses of the next state (the education of an agnostic). (Moore, William U.) London, 1911.

Phil 7060.86   Glimpses of the supernatural. (Lee, F.G.) London, 1875.

Phil 6112.19.5   Glints of wisdom. (Colville, W.W.J.) N.Y., 1910.

Phil 3200.5.90   Glockner, H. Johann Eduard Erdmann. Stuttgart, 1932.

Phil 165.14   Glockner, H. Philosophisches lesebuch. Stuttgart, 1949-50. 2v.

Phil 3310.8   Glockner, Hermann. Das Abenteuer des Geistes. Stuttgart, 1938.

Phil 3310.8.30   Glockner, Hermann. Bilderbuch meiner Jugend; Erinnerungen. Bonn, 1970. 2v.

Phil 181.89   Glockner, Hermann. Einführung in das Philosophieren. Berlin, 1944.

Phil 3425.258.10   Glockner, Hermann. Die ethisch-politische Persönlichkeit des Philosophen. Tübingen, 1922.

Phil 3310.8.21   Glockner, Hermann. Gesammelte Schriften. Berlin, 1963-66.

Phil 3425.258   Glockner, Hermann. Hegel. Stuttgart, 1929.

Phil 3425.336   Glockner, Hermann. Hegel und seine Philosophie. Heidelberg, 1931.

Phil 806.17   Glockuer, H. Die europäische Philosophie. Stuttgart, 1958.

Phil 3552.93.5   Glöckner, G. Der Gottesbegriff bei Leibniz. Langensalza, 1888.

Phil 5465.16   Glogan, Gustav. Die Phantasie. Halle, 1884.

Phil 5246.27.5   Glogau, Gustav. Die Form und die Bewegungsgesetze des Geistes. Breslau, 1880. 2 pam.

Phil 5246.27   Glogau, Gustav. Grundriss der Psychologie. Breslau, 1884.

Phil 337.7   Glondys, Viktor. Einführung in die Erkenntnistheorie. Wien, 1923.

Phil 9070.15   The glorious game. (Robert, B.R.) N.Y., 1929.

Phil 8581.73   The glory of God. (Ballou, Robert O.) N.Y., 1938.

Phil 8890.23   The glory of the imperfect. (Palmer, G.H.) Boston, 1891.

Phil 8890.23.5   The glory of the imperfect. (Palmer, G.H.) Boston, 1915.

Phil 8890.23.3   The glory of the imperfect. (Palmer, G.H.) N.Y., 1898.

Phil 6315.2.210   Glory reflected. (Freud, Martin.) London, 1957.

Phil 6304.2   Glossaire de psychiatrie. (Moor, Lise.) Paris, 1966.

Phil 978.47   Glossaire raisonné de la théosophie du qnosticisme et de l'ésotérisme. (Darlès, Jean.) Paris, 1910.

Phil 18.7.10   Glossary for the use of translators of psycho-analytical works. (International journal of Psycho-analysis. Supplement.) London.

Phil 1511.4   Glossner, M. Das Objektivität-Prinzip der aristotelisch-scholastischen Philosophie. Regensburg, 1880.

Phil 5628.5.5   The glossolalia phenomenon. 1st ed. (Horton, Wade H.) Cleveland, 1966.

Phil 6315.2.142   Glover, E. Freud or Jung. London, 1950.

Phil 6315.2.141A   Glover, E. Freud or Jung. N.Y., 1950.

Phil 9380.2A   Glover, E. The psychology of fear and courage. Harmondsworth, Eng., 1940.

Phil 6316.12.15   Glover, Edward. The birth of the ego; a nuclear hypothesis. N.Y., 1968.

Phil 6316.12   Glover, Edward. An investigation of the technique of psycho-analysis. Baltimore, 1940.

Phil 6316.12.20   Glover, Edward. Psycho-analysis; a handbook for medical practitioners and students of comparitive psychology. 2d ed. London, 1949.

Phil 6316.12.10   Glover, Edward. Selected papers on psycho-analysis. London, 1956- 2v.

Phil 6316.12.5   Glover, Edward. The technique of psycho-analysis. London, 1955.

Phil 5756.16   Glover, Jonathan. Responsibility. London, 1970.

Phil 5246.18   Glover, William. Know your own mind...book of practical psychology. Cambridge, 1915.

Phil 5040.19   Główne zasady metodologji nauk i logiki. (Adjukiewicz, Kazimierz.) Warszawa, 1928.

Phil 5545.85   Gloy, Hans. Gedächtnis-Ausbildung. Berlin, 1913.

Phil 8882.12   Glück. (Hilty, K.) Frauenfeld, 1894.

Phil 8882.12.3   Glück. (Hilty, K.) Frauenfeld, 1900.

Phil 9590.29   Glück. (Sanders, Willy.) Köln, 1965.

Phil 3745.14.5   Glück und Kontemplation. 1. Aufl. (Pieper, Josef.) München, 1957.

Phil 9245.15   Glück und Sittlichkeit. (Schwarz, H.) Halle, 1902.

Phil 5520.22   Gmelin, J.G. Zur Psychologie der Aussage. Hannover, 1909.

Phil 5046.7   Gneisse, K. Deduction und Induction. Strassburg, 1899.

Phil 3488.12   Gneisse, Karl. Das sittliche Handeln nach Kants Ethik. Colmar, 1895.

Phil 349.61   Gnoselogicheskii analiz em kosti znaniia. (Sukhotin, Anatoli K.) Tomsk, 1968.

Phil 4210.57   Gnoseologia. (Rosmini-Serbati, Antonio.) Messina, 1953.

Phil 8411.23.5   Gnoseologicheskaia priroda literatury i iskusstva. (Kulvanov, B.G.) L'vov, 1958.

Phil 400.123   Gnoseologicheskie korni idealizma. (Cherkasin, P.P.) Moskva, 1961.

Phil 337.37   Gnoseologicheskie problemy formalizatsii. Minsk, 1969.

Phil 331.35   Gnoseologicheskie problemy teorii znakov. (Abrahamian, Lev.) Erevan, 1965.

Phil 5520.286   Gnoseologicheskie voprosy semiotiki. (Reznikov, Lazar' O.) Leningrad, 1964.

Phil 4710.79   Gnoseologicheskoe soderzhanie logicheskikh form i metodov. (Moskalenko, F.Ia.) Kiev, 1960.

Phil 1810.5   Gnoseologiia sovremennaia pragmatizma. (Kursanov, G.A.) Moskva, 1958.

Phil 165.8   Das gnoseologische Problem. (Ballauff, T.) Göttingen, 1949.

Phil 4845.227.32.2   Gnosiologia. 2. ed. (Papanoutsos, Euangelos.) Athena, 1962.

Phil 185.49.5   Gnosiology; the scientific approach to the theory of knowledge. 1. English ed. (Kotarbiński, Tadeusz.) Oxford, 1966.

Phil 8598.110.5   Gnosis. (Schuon, Frithjof.) London, 1959.

Phil 3110.190   Die Gnosis Jakob Böhmes. (Weiss, Victor.) Zürich, 1955.

Phil 3280.50   Gnôthi Seauton, sive ethica. (Geulincx, A.) Amsterdam, 1709.

Phil 6328.10.30   Goals and desires of man, a psychological survey of life. (Schilder, Paul.) N.Y., 1942.

Phil 5270.12   Gobar, Ash. Philosophic foundations of genetic psychology and Gestalt psychology. The Hague, 1969.

Phil 5643.7   Goblet, H.F. A theory of sight, or How we see. London, 1869.

Phil 8580.7.15   Goblet d'Alviella, E. The contemporary evolution of religious thought in England. London, 1885.

Phil 8580.7   Goblet d'Alviella, E. L'évolution religieuse contemporaine chez les anglais, les américains, et les hindous. Paris, 1884.

Phil 8661.1   Goblet D'Alviella, E. Lectures on the origin and growth of the conception of God. London, 1892.

Phil 735.86   Goblot, E. La logique des jugements de valeur. Paris, 1927.

Phil 91.3   Goblot, E. Le vocabulaire philosophique. Paris, 1901.

Phil 5046.12.4   Goblot, Edmond. Traité de logique. Paris, 1922.

Phil 525.236   Gobry, Ivan. L'expérience mystique. Paris, 1964.

Phil 8881.77   Gobry, Ivan. Le modèle en morale. Paris, 1962.

Phil 8881.74   Gobry, Ivan. Les niveause de la vie morale. 1. éd. Paris, 1956.

Phil 181.12   Gockel, C.F. Encyklopädische Einleitung in die Philosophie. Karlsruhe, 1855.

Phil 5046.4   Gockel, C.F. Propädentische Logik und Hodegetik. Karlsruhe, 1839.

Phil 6016.1.5   Goclenius, R. Besonderephysiognomische und chromantische Anmerkungen. Hamburg, 1692.

Phil 6016.1   Goclenius, R. Physiognomica et chiromantica specialia. Marpurgi Cattorum, 1621.

Phil 5046.46   Goclenius, Rudolph. Problemata logica. v.1-5. Frankfurt, 1967.

Phil 8667.23   God, being an introduction to the science of metabiology. (Murry, John M.) London, 1929.

Phil 8661.5.5   God, His existence and His nature. (Garrigou-Lagrange, R.) St. Louis, 1934-36. 2v.

Phil 3819.38   God, man, and human welfare. (Spinoza, Benedictus de.) Chicago, 1909.

Phil 8582.62   God, man and the absolute. (Cleobury, F.H.) London, 1947?

Phil 8581.69.5   God, man and the church. (Berdiaev, N.A.) London, 1937.

Phil 8656.15   God; revelation by Christianity and astronomical science. (Brewster, F.C.) Newport, 1922.

Phil 1135.205   God, time, being; studies in the transcendental tradition in Greek philosophy. Thesis. (Whittaker, John.) Bergen, 1970.

Phil 8666.1   God. (Lacordaire, P.J.B.H.D.) London, 1870.

Phil 8666.12   God. (Lattey, Cuthbert.) London, 1931.

Phil 282.12.10   God and creation. (Boodin, J.E.) N.Y., 1934. 2v.

Phil 8620.44   God and evil. (Joad, C.E.M.) London, 1943.

Phil 8620.53   God and evil. (Pike, Nelson.) Englewood Cliffs, 1764.

Phil 8692.15   God and evolution. (Cohen, Chapman.) London, 1925.

Phil 8670.15   God and human progress. (Parkes, J.W.) Harmondsworth, Eng., 1944.

Phil 8673.11   God and intelligence in modern philosophy. (Sheen, F.J.) London, 1925.

Phil 8598.73   God and man. (Shumaker, E.E.) N.Y., 1909.

Phil 8580.21.5   God and man's destiny. 1. ed. (Alexander, H.B.) N.Y., 1936.

Phil 8677.9.80   God and Mr. Wells. (Archer, William.) N.Y., 1917.

Phil 8656.17   God and my neighbor. (Blatchford, R.) Chicago, 1919.

Phil 8656.17.5   God and my neighbor. (Blatchford, R.) London, 1904.

Phil 193.128.10   God and nature. (Stout, G.F.) Cambridge, Eng., 1952.

Phil 8670.21.5   God and other minds. (Plantinga, Alvin.) Ithaca, 1967.

Phil 575.52   God and personality. (Webb, C.C.J.) Aberdeen, 1919.

Phil 8586.45   God and philosophy. (Gilson, Étienne.) New Haven, 1941.

Phil 8660.23   God and philosophy. 1st American ed. (Flew, Antony.) N.Y., 1966.

Phil 818.29   God and polarity; a synthesis of philosophies. (Sheldon, W.H.) New Haven, 1954.

Phil 8661.17   God and progress. (Gururmurti, D.) Madras, 1945.

Phil 8709.26   God and rationality. (Torrance, Thomas Forsyth.) London, 1971.

Phil 8610.894   God and sin in the appetites. (Hartmann, J.) N.Y., 1894.

Phil 1845.3.110A   God and space time. (Stiernotte, A.P.N.F.) N.Y., 1954.

Phil 289.1   God and the astronomers. (Inge, W.R.) London, 1933.

Phil 175.40   Goal and the cosmic order. (Anderson, C.A.F.) N.Y., 1939.

Phil 8581.83   God and the new knowledge. (Brown, Oswald E.) Nashville, 1926.

Phil 8670.22   God and timelessness. (Pike, Nelson craft.) N.Y., 1970.

Phil 8735.52   God and world order. (Ward, L.R.) Saint Louis, 1961.

Phil 8585.29   God and you. (Friend, Nellie E.) N.Y., 1929.

Phil 672.228   God beyond time. (Reyner, John Hereward.) London, 1965.

VPhil 7069.68   God bless U, daughter. (Swanson, Mildred Burris.) Independance, 1968.

Phil 5627.134.70   God does guide us. (Sangster, W.E.) N.Y., 1934.

Phil 3805.252   God en wereld. (Oranje, Leendert.) Kampen, 1968.

Phil 5627.63   The God-experience. (Mudge, E.L.) Cincinnati, 1923.

Phil 8667.17   God in Christian experience. (Matthews, W.R.) N.Y., 193-?

Phil 1135.136   God in Greek philosophy. (Hack, R.K.) Princeton, 1931.

Phil 8655.6   God in his world. (Alden, H.M.) N.Y., 1890.

Phil 8661.11   God in idea and experience. (Griffths, Rees.) Edinburgh, 1931.

Phil 8657.21   God in modern philosophy. (Collins, J.D.) Chicago, 1959.

Phil 3801.434A   God in the philosophy of Schelling. Diss. (Gray-Smith, R.) Philadelphia, 1933.

Phil 8660.15   God is an artist. (Fox, Adam.) London, 1957.

Phil 8659.7   God is spirit, God is love. (Elliot, George.) London, 1895.

Phil 8662.4   God manifest. (Hiller, T.O.P.) London, 1858.

Phil 8662.18   The God of reason. (Heydon, J.K.) N.Y., 1942.

Phil 8707.13   The God of science. (Reuterdahl, A.) Minneapolis, 1928.

Phil 8692.19 God of the scientists. (Chauvin, Rémy.) Baltimore, 1960.
Phil 8655.3 God or no God. (Anderson, J.H.) Osceola, Neb., 1889.
Phil 8677.9.5 God the invisible king. (Wells, H.G.) London, 1917.
Phil 8677.9 God the invisible king. (Wells, H.G.) N.Y., 1917.
Htn Phil 8656.11* God the known and God the unknown. (Butler, Samuel.) London, 1909.
Phil 8662.15 God transcendent. (Heim, Karl.) London, 1935.
Phil 8602.78 The God we seek. (Weiss, P.) Carbondale, 1964.
Phil 8673.15 The God who speaks. (Streeter, B.H.) N.Y., 1936.
Phil 4756.1.45.5 God with us; three meditations. (Frank, Semen L.) London, 1946.
Phil 8707.17 God without thunder. (Ransom, J.C.) N.Y., 1930.
Phil 7069.22.10 Godard, André. Le surnaturel contemporain. Paris, 1922.
Phil 3640.283 Goday, V. Bersanelli. Humanidad. Buenos Aires, 1940.
Phil 8881.58 Goddard, H.C. Morale. N.Y., 1918.
Phil 705.5.5A Goddard, H.C. Studies in New England transcendentalism. N.Y., 1908.
Phil 705.5 Goddard, H.C. Studies in New England transcendentalism. Thesis. N.Y., 1908.
Phil 5246.20.5 Goddard, H.H. Human efficiency and levels of intelligence. Princeton, 1920.
Phil 5246.20 Goddard, H.H. Psychology of the normal and subnormal. N.Y., 1919.
Phil 5628.10.10 De goddelijke waanzin. (Baumann, Evert Dirk.) Assen, 1932.
Phil 6619.14 Godefroy, Jan C.L. Onderzoekingen over de aandachtsbepaling bij gezonden en zielszieken. Groningen, 1915?
Phil 3826.2 Godfernaux, A. De Spinoza. Paris, 1894.
Phil 5246.7 Godfernaux, A. Le sentiment et la pensée. Paris, 1894.
Phil 5246.7.3 Godfernaux, A. Le sentiment et la pensée. 3. éd. Paris, 1907.
Phil 8661.12.5 Godfrey, W.S. Theism found wanting. London, 1920.
Phil 9166.5 Godimus, Z.J. L'esprit de famille étude morale. Paris, 1870.
Htn Phil 9162.1* A godlie forme of household government. (Carr, Roger.) London, 16- ?
Phil 181.28 Godlover, H.B. Science of minds. n.p., n.d.
Htn Phil 9162.1.5* A godly forme of household government. (Carr, Roger.) London, 1621.
Phil 8610.881.20 The godly women of the Bible. (Gibson, Ellen E.) N.Y., 1881.
Phil 6332.9.15 Gods, devils, and men. (Whitehead, George.) London, 1928.
Phil 8709.18.5 God's amazing world. (Tóth, T.) N.Y., 1935.
Phil 5867.30 Gods and games; toward a theology of play. (Miller, David LeRoy.) N.Y., 1970.
Phil 978.16.13 The gods await. (Tingley, K.A. (Mrs.).) Point Loma, California, 1926.
Phil 8662.10 God's breath in man. (Harris, T.L.) Santa Rosa, 1891.
Phil 5251.51 God's failure or man's folly? (Lundholm, H.) Cambridge, 1949.
Phil 8602.30.3 God's image in man. (Wood, Henry.) Boston, 1892.
Phil 8584.22 God's own image. (Eley, A.S.) Luton, Eng., 1963.
Phil 7069.20.240 God's smile. (Magnussen, Julius.) N.Y., 1920.
Phil 7069.18.97 God's world. Chicago, 1918.
Phil 3821.20 Het Godsbegrip bij Spinoza. (Brakell Buys, W.R. de V. van.) Utrecht, 193-?
Phil 8594.2.5 De godsdienst. (Opzoomer, C.W.) Amsterdam, 1864.
Phil 8661.2.3 Godwin, B. Lectures on the atheistic controversy. Boston, 1835.
Phil 8661.2 Godwin, B. Lectures on the atheistic controversy. London, 1834.
Phil 8881.38 Godwin, John H. Active principles, or Elements of moral science. London, 1885.
Phil 8881.13A Godwin, W. Thoughts on man. London, 1831.
Htn Phil 2030.3.30* Godwin, William. An enquiry concerning political justice. London, 1793. 2v.
Phil 2050.91 Goebel, H. Das Philosophie in Humes Geschichte von England. Marburg, 1897.
Phil 1133.18 Goebel, Karl. Die vorsokratische Philosophie. Bonn, 1910.
Phil 3805.99 Goebel, Louis. Herder und Schleiermachers Reden. Gotha, 1904.
Phil 1190.7 Goedeckmeyer, A. Die Geschichte des griechischen Skeptizismus. Leipzig, 1905.
Phil 8831.2 Goedewaagen, T. Die logische rechtvaadiging der zedelijkheid bij Fichte, Schelling en Hegel. Proefschrift. Amsterdam, 1923.
Phil 3640.275 Goedewaagen, T. Nietzsche. 's-Gravenhage, 1933.
Phil 181.63.5 Goedewaagen, T. Het spectrum der philosophie in de 20e eeuw. Leiden, 1933.
Phil 181.63 Goedewaagen, T. Summa contra metaphysicos. Utrecht, 1931.
Phil 8586.57 Goedt, Michel de. Foi au Christ et dialogues du Chrétien. Bruges, 1967.
Phil 6116.30 Goër de Herve, Jacques de. Mécanisme et intelligence. Paris, 1969.
Phil 672.174 Goeje, C.H. de. Space, time and life; and, What is time? v.1-2. Leiden, 1949.
Phil 5016.1 Göldel, R.W. Die Lehre von der Identität in der deutschen Logik-Wissenschaft seit Lotze. Inaug. Diss. Leipzig, 1935.
Phil 8407.13 Göller, Adolf. Das ästhetische Gefühl. Stuttgart, 1905.
Phil 672.268 Goelz, Walter. Dasein und Raum. Habilitationsschrift. Tübingen, 1970.
Phil 3280.82 Göpfert, E. Geulincx' ethisches System. Breslau, 1883.
Phil 3140.81 Göpfert. Claubergstudien. Meiningen, 1898.
Phil 8956.9 Göransson, N.J. Utkast till en undersökning af religionen. Sköfde, 1899.
Phil 31.5.5 Goerdt, Wilhelm. Fragen der Philosophie ein Materialbeitrag...im Spiegel der Zeitschrift "Voprosy Filosofii", 1947-1956. Köln, 1960.
Phil 4710.152 Goerdt, Wilhelm. Die Sowjetphilosophie. Basel, 1967.
Phil 181.13 Göring, C. System der kritischen Philosophie. Leipzig, 1874. 2v.
Phil 5756.7 Göring, Carl. Über die Menschlichefreiheit. Leipzig, 1876.
Phil 5640.21 Goering, W. Raum und Stoff. Berlin, 1876.
Phil 3488.14 Görland, A. Aristoteles und Kant bezüglich der idee der theoretischen Erkenntnis. Giessen, 1909.
Phil 177.28.2 Görland, A. Index zu Hermann Cohens Logik...Erkenntnis. Berlin, 1906.
Phil 8407.19 Görland, Albert. Ästhetik; kritische Philosophie des Stils. Hamburg, 1937.
Phil 8881.34 Görland, Albert. Ethik als Kritik der Weltgeschichte. Leipzig, 1914.
Phil 5115.6 Görland, Albert. Die Hypothese. Göttingen, 1911.
Phil 8881.34.5 Görland, Albert. Neubegründung der Ethik aus ihrem Verhältnis zu den besonderen Gemeinschaftswissenschaften. Berlin, 1918.
Phil 310.612 Goerlich, J. Zur Problematik der materialistische Dialektischen. Berlin, 1965.
Phil 310.734 Goerlich, Johann Wolfgang. Semantik und dialektischer Materialismus; Darstellung und Analyse der modernen marxistisch-leninistischen Wissenschaftstheorie in der DDR. Berlin, 1969.
Phil 6316.15.5 Goerres, Albert. An den Grenzen der Psychoanalyse. München, 1968.
Phil 6316.15 Goerres, Albert. The methods and experience of psychoanalysis. London, 1962.
Phil 2905.1.675 Goerres, Ida F.C. Teilhard de Chardin als Christ und als Mensch. Wiesbaden, 1971.
Phil 5850.221.10 Goersdorf, Kurt. Arbeitsfreude - Leistungsanstrengungen. München, 1958.
Phil 5046.18 Goesch, H. Über die kritische Logik. Berlin, 1904.
Phil 8586.24 Goeschel, C.F. Beiträge zur Spekulativen philosophie. Berlin, 1838.
Phil 8631.1.5 Göschel, C.F. Der Mensch nach Leib, Seele und Geist. Leipzig, 1856.
Phil 8631.1 Göschel, C.F. Von den Beweisen für die Unsterblichkeit der Menschlichen Seele. Berlin, 1835.
Phil 3425.87 Goeschel, K.F. Hegel und seine Zeit. Berlin, 1832.
Phil 3488.20.5 Goess, G.F.D. Systematische Darstellung der Kantischen Vernunftkritik zum gebrauch akademischer Vorlesungen. Nürnberg, 1794.
Phil 3488.20 Goess, G.F.D. Ueber die Critik der reinen Vernunft. Erlangen, 1793.
Phil 3488.36 Goessl, Max. Untersuchungen zum Verhältnis von Recht und Sittlichkeit. München, 1941.
Phil 5520.680 Goessmann, Wilhelm. Glaubwürdigkeit im Sprachgebrauch. 1. Aufl. München, 1970.
Phil 5645.4.8 Goethe, J.W. von. Theory of colours. London, 1840.
Htn Phil 5645.4.2* Goethe, J.W. von. Zur Farbenlehre. Tübingen, 1810. 2v.
X Cg Phil 5645.4 Goethe, J.W. von. Zur Farbenlehre. Tübingen, 1810. 3v.
Phil 5645.4.25 Goethe, Schopenhauer und die Farbenlehre. (Ostwald, Wilhelm.) Leipzig, 1918.
Phil 974.3.117 Goethe in unserer Zeit. (Wachsmuth, G.) Dornach, 1949.
Phil 978.49.198 Der Goetheanismus ein Umwandlungsimpuls und Auferstehungsgedanke: Menschenwissenschaft und Sozialwissenschaft. (Steiner, R.) Dornach, 1967.
Phil 978.49.845 Goetheanum. (Dornach, Switzerland. Goetheanum.) Dornach, 1961.
Phil 978.49.800 Goetheanum. (Dornach. Goetheanum.) Dornach, 193-?
Phil 978.49.335 Der goetheanumgedanke Insnitten der Kulturkresis der Gegenwart. (Steiner, R.) Dornach, 1961.
Phil 978.49.195 Goethes Geistesart in unseren Schicksalsschweren tagen und die deutsche Kultur. (Steiner, R.) Dornach, 1930.
Phil 5645.4.27 Goethes Relativitätstheorie der Farbe. (Barthel, Ernst.) Bonn, 1923.
Phil 1750.166.10 Goethescher Geist und zwanzigstes Jahrhundert. (Boucher, Maurice.) Mainz, 1947.
Phil 2255.1.113 Götlind, E. Bertrand Russell's theories of causation. Inaug. Diss. Uppsala, 1952.
Phil 3850.27.255 Götting, Gerald. Albert Schweitzer- Pionier der Menschlichkeit. Berlin, 1970.
Phil 8893.47.2 Göttliche Weltordnung und religionslose Sittlichkeit. (Schneider, Wilhelm.) Paderborn, 1909.
Phil 1050.4.20 Der göttliche Wille (Logosbegriff) bei Gabirol. (Bieler, Majer.) Breslau, 1933.
Htn Phil 3801.431* Goetz, Johann K. Anti-Sextus, oder über der absolute Erkenntniss von Schelling. Heidelberg, 1807.
Phil 3801.431.2 Goetz, Johann K. Anti-Sextus, oder über der absolute Erkenntniss von Schelling. Heidelberg, 1807.
Phil 3640.357 Götz, K.A. Nietzsche als Ausnahme. Freiburg, 1949.
Phil 3640.32 Götzen-Dämmerung. (Nietzsche, Friedrich.) Leipzig, 1889.
Phil 3640.17.8 Götzendämmerung. (Nietzsche, Friedrich.) Stuttgart, 1954. 2v.
Phil 978.18.3 Goffield, E.C. The past revealed. Boston, 1905.
Phil 8407.29 Goffin, Peter (pseud.). The realm of art. London, 1946.
Phil 6946.1.15 Goffman, E. Asylums. Garden City, 1961.
Phil 6946.1.16 Goffman, Erving. Asylums: essays on the social situation of mental patients and other inmates. Chicago, 1970.
Phil 3246.170 Gogarten, F. Fichte als religiöser Denker. Jena, 1914.
Phil 8586.36.10 Gogarten, Friedrich. Die Frage nach Gott. Tübingen, 1968.
Phil 8586.36.5 Gogarten, Friedrich. Glaube und Wirklichkeit. Jena, 1928.
Phil 8586.36 Gogarten, Friedrich. Ich Glaube an den dreieinigen Gott. Jena, 1926.
Phil 9450.20 Gogartin, F. Politische Ethik. Jena, 1932.
Phil 5535.58 Goguelin, Pierre. La formation continue des adultes. 1. ed. Paris, 1970.
Phil 1020.8.20 Goichon, A.M. La distinction de l'essence...d'aprés Ibn Sina. Paris, 1937.
Phil 1020.8.20.2 Goichon, A.M. La distinction de l'essence...d'aprés Ibn Sina. Thèse. Paris, 1937.
Phil 1020.8.21 Goichon, A.M. Lexique de la langue...d'Ibn Sina. Paris, 1938.
Phil 1020.8.23 Goichon, A.M. La philosophie d'Avicenne et son influence in Europe médiévale. Paris, 1944.
Phil 337.23 Goidukov, I.G. Rot' praktiki v protsesse poznaniia. Moskva, 1964.
Phil 5046.38 Gokieli, Levan P. Logika. v.1- Tbilisi, 1965. 2v.
Phil 6140.2 Golann, Stuart E. Coordinate index reference guide to community mental health. N.Y., 1969.
Phil 672.246 Gold, Thomas. The nature of time. Ithaca, 1967.
Phil 8882.18.2 Gold foil. 5th ed. (Holland, J.G.) N.Y., 1859.
Phil 1980.3.98 Goldberg, I. Havelock Ellis; a biographical and critical survey. N.Y., 1926.
Phil 181.62 Goldberg, Isaac. Fine art of living. Boston, 1930.
Phil 623.43 Gol'dberg, N.M. Svobodomyslie i ateizm v SShA, XVII-XIX vv. Leningrad, 1965.
Phil 6319.1.196 Goldbrunner, Josef. Individuation. London, 1955.
Phil 6319.1.196.3 Goldbrunner, Josef. Individuation. 3. Aufl. Freiburg, 1966.
Phil 5627.266 Goldbrunner, Josef. Realisation; Anthropologie in Seelsorge und Erziehung. Greiburg, 1966.
Phil 9530.65 The golden age. (Getty, Jay Paul.) N.Y., 1968.
Phil 1830.30 The golden age of American philosophy. (Frankel, Charles.) N.Y., 1960.
VPhil 978.114 The golden hoard. (Merchant, Francis.) Houston, 1959.
Phil 7054.26 Golden light angel's visits to my farm in Florida. N.Y., 1892.
Phil 5627.60.10 The golden sequence. 2. ed. (Underhill, E.) London, 1932.
Phil 4363.2.37 Golden thoughts from the spiritual guide. (Molinos, M. de.) N.Y., 1883.
Phil 9162.3 The golden wedding ring...marriage. (Clowes, John.) Boston, 1832.

Author and Title Listing

Phil 193.36.5   Das goldene ABC der Philosophie. (Steudel, A.) Berlin, 1891.

Phil 7084.36   Das goldene ägyptisch-arabische Traumbuch. (Abu Schirin.) Heidenheim, 1960.

Phil 8407.43   Gol'dentrikht, Semen S. O prirode esteticheskogo tvorchestva. Moskva, 1966.

Phil 2270.180   Gol'denveizer, A.S. Gerbert Spencer. Idei svoboda i prava. Sankt Peterburg, 1904.

Phil 6956.16   Goldfarb, W. Childhood schizophrenia. Cambridge, 1961.

Phil 3488.6   Goldfriedrich, J.A. Kants Asthetik. Leipzig, 1895.

Phil 5246.84   Goldman, Alvin I. A theory of human action. Englewood Cliffs, N.J., 1970.

Phil 1050.25   Goldman, S. The Jew and the universe. N.Y., 1936.

Phil 3488.26.5   Goldmann, L. La communauté humaine et l'univers chez Kant. Paris, 1948.

Phil 3488.26.1   Goldmann, L. Immanuel Kant. London, 1971.

Phil 3488.26   Goldmann, L. Mensch, Gemeinschaft und Welt in der Philosophie Immanuel Kants. Zürich, 1945.

Phil 1730.24   Goldmann, Lucien. Der christliche Bürger und die Aufklärung. Neuwied, 1968.

Phil 310.155.1   Goldmann, Lucien. Dialektische Untersuchungen. Neuwied, 1966.

Phil 181.136.5   Goldmann, Lucien. The human sciences and philosophy. London, 1969.

Phil 310.155   Goldmann, Lucien. Recherches dialectiques. 2. éd. Paris, 1959.

Phil 181.136   Goldmann, Lucien. Sciences humaines et philosophie. Paris, 1966.

Phil 2805.450   Goldmann, Lucien. Weltflucht und Politik. Neuwied, 1967.

Phil 9070.16   Goldmann, R.L. The good fight. N.Y., 1935.

Phil 3200.10   Goldmund, M. Die Philosophie Franz Erhardts. Leipzig, 1937.

Phil 672.139   Goldsbrough, G.F. Recent discussions on "Time". London, 1927.

Phil 5756.3   Goldscheid, R. Grundlinien zu einer Kritik der Willenskraft. Wien, 1905.

Phil 8881.41   Goldscheid, Rudolf. Zur Ethik des Gesamtwellens. Leipzig, 1902.

Phil 6316.2   Goldscheider, A. Die Bedeutung der Reize für Pathologie und Therapie. Leipzig, 1898.

Phil 6116.12   Goldscheider, A. Gesammette Abhandlungen. v.1-2. Leipzig, 1898.

Phil 9430.26   Goldschmidt, Kurt Walter. Der Wert des Lebens. Berlin, 1908.

Phil 3488.4.10   Goldschmidt, L. Kant Kritik oder Kantstudium? Gotha, 1896.

Phil 3488.4.15   Goldschmidt, L. Kant über Freiheit. Gotha, 1904.

Phil 3488.4.25   Goldschmidt, L. Kant und Haeckel. Gotha, 1906.

Phil 3488.4.5   Goldschmidt, L. Kant und Helmholtz. Hamburg, 1898.

Phil 3488.4.20   Goldschmidt, L. Kant's "Privatmeinungen" über das Jenseits. Gotha, 1905.

Phil 3488.4.30   Goldschmidt, L. Weder Kant noch Goethe. Gotha, 1920.

Phil 3488.4   Goldschmidt, L. Zur Wiedererweckung Kantischer Lehre. Gotha, 1910.

Phil 1200.55   Goldschmidt, V.E. Le système stoïcien et l'idée de temps. Paris, 1953.

Phil 337.10   Goldschmidt, W. Der Linguismus und die Erkenntnistheorie der Verweisungen. Zürich, 1936.

Phil 6676.10   Goldsmith, M. Franz Anton Mesmer. Photoreproduction. London, 1934.

Phil 2045.139   Goldsmith, M.M. Hobbes's science of politics. N.Y., 1966.

Phil 8696.11   Goldsmith, W.M. Evolution or Christianity, God or Darwin? St. Louis, 1924.

Phil 3925.5.80   Goldstandt, H. Weissenborns Stellung zum Theismus. Inaug. Diss. Würzburg, 1917.

Phil 2050.181   Goldstein, J. Die empiristische Geschichtsauffassung Humes. Leipzig, 1903.

Phil 1706.3   Goldstein, J. Wandlungen in der Philosophie der Gegenwerk. Leipzig, 1911.

Phil 5246.52A   Goldstein, K. Human nature. Cambridge, 1940.

Phil 5246.53   Goldstein, K. Human nature in the light of psychopathology. Cambridge, Mass., 1947.

Phil 6400.20.2   Goldstein, Kurt. Language and language disturbances. N.Y., 1948.

Phil 6400.17   Goldstein, Kurt. The problem of the meaning of words based upon observation of aphasic patients. Worcester, 1936.

Phil 3625.1.111   Goldstein, L. Die Bedeuterung Moses Mendelssohn. Inaug. Diss. Konigsberg, 1897.

Phil 3625.1.113   Goldstein, L. Moses Mendelssohn. Konigsberg, 1904.

Phil 6316.22   Goldstein, M. The experience of anxiety. N.Y., 1963.

NEDL Phil 735.83   Goldstein, M. Der Wert des Zwecklosen. Dresden, 1920.

Phil 3160.3.100   Goldstein, Walter. Hermann Cohen. Jerusalem, 1963.

Phil 2880.8.175   Goldstein, Walter. Jean Paul Sartre und Martin Buber. Jerusalem, 1965.

Phil 3120.30.87   Goldstein, Walter Benjamin. Die Botschaft Martin Bubers. Jerusalem, 1952-56. 3v.

Phil 3120.30.89   Goldstein, Walter Benjamin. Der Glaube Martin Bubers. Jerusalem, 1969.

Phil 8661.21   Goldstein, Walter Benjamin. Glaube oder Unglaube. Jerusalem, 1964.

Phil 3120.30.88   Goldstein, Walter Benjamin. Martin Buber. Jerusalem, 1967.

X Cg   Phil 6116.2   Golgi, C. Sulla fina anatomia degli organi centrali. Napoli, 1886.

Phil 3425.744   Golosov, Viktor F. Ratsional'noe i misticheskoe v gegelevskoi teorii iavliaiushchegosia dukha. Krasnoiarsk, 1969.

Phil 310.7.10   Golovakha, I.P. Marksistskaia filosofiia v poznavalmosti mira. Kiev, 1955.

Phil 8980.432   Golovan, I.P. Po dolgu grazhdanina. Moskva, 1962.

Phil 337.38   Golovanov, Viacheslav N. Zakony v sisteme naukhnogo znaniia. Moskva, 1970.

Phil 9070.39   Golpes en cantera reflexiva. (Zúñiga, Pallais M.) San José, 1931.

Phil 9430.29   Golther, L. von. Der moderne Pessimismus. Leipzig, 1878.

Phil 585.154   Goltz, B. Hinter den Feigenblättern. Berlin, 1862-64.

Phil 6116.5   Goltz, F.L. Über die Verrichtungen. Bonn, 1881.

Phil 4757.3.25   Golubinskii, F.A. Premudrost' i blagost' Bozhiia v sud'bakh mira i cheloveka; o konechnych prichinakh. 4. izd. Sankt Peterburg, 1894.

Phil 4803.434.30   Gołuchowski, Józef. Dumania nad najwyzszemi zagadnieniami człowieka. Wilno, 1861. 2v.

Phil 8661.6   Gomer, A. de. Journée solitaire de l'homme sensible. Paris, 1800.

Phil 8881.45   Gomer, A. de. L'obligation morale raisonnée. Paris, 1913.

Phil 8612.29   Gómez de la Serna, R. Los muertos, las muertas y otras fantasmagarias. Madrid, 1935.

Phil 5246.75   Gómez Ibars, J. En el món de invidents. Barcelona, 1963.

Phil 4353.12   Gomez Izquierdo, A. Un filosofo catalan, Antonio Comellas y Cluet. Madrid, 1907.

Phil 1735.6   Gómez Izquierdo, Alberto. Historia de la filosofía del siglo XIX. Zaragoza, 1903.

Phil 4960.635   Gómez Robledo, Antonio. La filosofía en el Brasil. México, 1946.

Phil 4372.1.82   Gomis, J.B. Criterio social de Luis Vives. Madrid, 1946.

Phil 9245.30   Gomperz, H. Kritik des Hedonismus. Stuttgart, 1898.

Phil 1145.32   Gomperz, H. Die Lebensauffassung der griechischen Philosophen. Jena, 1904.

Phil 3310.14   Gomperz, H. Philosophical studies. Boston, 1953.

Phil 5246.40   Gomperz, H. Über Sinn und Sinngebilde. Tübingen, 1929.

Phil 960.44   Gomperz, Heinrich. Die indische Theosophie. Jena, 1925.

Phil 5756.4   Gomperz, Heinrich. Das Problem der Willensfreiheit. Jena, 1907.

Phil 8881.44   Gomperz, Heinrich. Über den Begriff des sittlichen Ideals. Bern, 1902.

Phil 287.3   Gomperz, Heinrich. Weltanschauungslehre. Jena, 1905-08. 2v.

Phil 1111.1.11   Gomperz, T. Greek thinkers; a history of ancient philosophy. London, 1905-13. 4v.

Phil 1111.1.9   Gomperz, T. Greek thinkers and history of ancient philosophy. v.4. London, 1901.

Phil 1111.1   Gomperz, T. Griechische Denker. Leipzig, 1893. 3v.

Phil 1111.1.5   Gomperz, T. Griechische Denker. Leipzig, 1903-09. 3v.

Phil 1111.1.7   Gomperz, T. Griechische Denker. 4. Aufl. Berlin, 1922-31. 3v.

Phil 2138.93   Gomperz, T. John Stuart Mill. Wien, 1889.

Phil 9220.13   Gonçalves Viana, M. Psicolgia da Amizade. Porto, 1943.

Phil 9400.26   Gonçalves Viana, Mário. Psicologia da maturidade e da velhice. Porto, 196-.

Phil 5411.8   Gonçalves Viana, Mário. Psicologia do ódio. Porto, 196-.

Phil 181.25.5   Gonçalvez de Magalhães, J.G. Commentarios e pensamentos. Rio de Janeiro, 1880.

Phil 181.25   Gonçalvez de Magalhães, J.G. Factos do espirito humano. Rio de Janeiro, 1865.

Phil 365.55   Gondge, Thomas A. The ascent of life. Toronto, 1961.

Phil 337.13   Gondin, W.R. Prefaces to inquiry; a study in the origins and relevance of modern theories of knowledge. N.Y., 1941.

Phil 5875.115   Gondolatsch, Karl Heinz. Untersuchung der Sympathieäbhängigkeit von Aussageleiustungen bei Kindern und Jugendlichen. Köln, 1958.

Phil 5254.4   Gondslkodastan az eggetemesitö (inductiv) s lehoźo (deductiv) módazer alapján. (Oreg, J.) Nagy Köros, 1877.

Phil 7069.19.100   Gone west, by a soldier doctor. (Grove, Harriet McC.) N.Y., 1919.

Phil 4073.126   Gonfunkel', Aleksandrkh. Tommaso Kampanella. Moskva, 1969.

Phil 3850.18.125   Gongora Perea, C. El espiritu y la vida en la filosofía de Max Scheler. Lima, 1943.

Phil 2520.342   Gonhier, Henri. La pensée métaphysique de Descartes. Paris, 1962.

Phil 2733.130   Gonnell, Desmond. The vision in God; Malebranche's scholastic sources. Louvain, 1967.

Phil 672.220   Gonseth, F. Le problème du temps. Neuchâtel, 1964.

Phil 70.90   Gonseth, Ferdinand. La metaphysique et l'ouverture. Paris, 1960.

Phil 5722.45   Gonseth, J.P. Théâtre de veille et théâtre de songe. Neuchâtel, 1950.

Phil 6316.11A   Gontard, G.V. In defense of love; a protest against "soul surgery" N.Y., 1940.

Phil 806.4   Gonzalez, Z. Histoire de la philosophie. Paris, 1890-91. 4v.

Phil 806.38   Gonzalez Alvarez, Angel. Manual de historia de la filosofía. 3. ed. Madrid, 1964.

Phil 8661.18   Gonzalez Alvarez, Angel. El tema de Dios en la filosofía existencial. Madrid, 1945.

Phil 525.256.2   González Arintero, Juan. La evolución mística en el desenvolvimiento y vitalidad de la Iglesia. 2. ed. Madrid, 1968.

Phil 760.2   González Asenjo, Florencio. El todo y las partes; estudios de ontología formal. Madrid, 1962.

Phil 1750.726   Gonzalez Casanova, Pablo. El misoneismo y la modernidad cristiana en el siglo XVIII. México, 1948.

Phil 806.36   González Cominero, N. Historia philosophiae. v.1. Romae, 1960. 2v.

Phil 310.631   González Duran, Guillermo. La dialéctica comunista a la luz de la ciencia. La Paz, 1965.

Phil 181.41   González Serrano, U. En pro y en contra. Madrid, 1894.

Phil 5246.22   Gonzalez Serrano, U. Estudios psicológicos. Madrid, 1892.

Phil 5248.2.25   González Velez, J. Resumen sintético y brevisémo del sistema de psicología. Habana, 192-.

Phil 3488.30   González Vicén, J. La filosofía del estado en Kant. Laguna, 1952.

Phil 806.4.2   Gonzalez y Diaz Turíon, Ceferino. Historia de la filosofía. Madrid, 1886. 4v.

Phil 8881.35   González y Martinez de Pinillos. Ética. Madrid, 1911.

Phil 181.122   Gonzalo Cosar, M. Introducción a la filosofía. Madrid, 196-.

Phil 2045.119A   Gooch, G.P. Hobbes; annual lecture on a master mind. London, 1939.

Phil 181.82   Gooch, L.C. Instinct vs. reason; the problem of man. Yazoo City, Miss., 1938.

Phil 8893.147   Good, freewill and God. (Sen Gupta, Santosh Chandra.) Calcutta, 1963.

Phil 8877.95   Good, God and man; an outline of the philosophy of self-ism. (Creasey, John.) London, 1967.

Phil 5046.40   Good, Thomas. A brief English tract of logick, 1677. Facsimile. Leeds, 1967.

Phil 3120.30.75   Good and evil. (Buber, Martin.) N.Y., 1953.

Phil 9240.5   The good and the clever. (Lindsay, A.D.) Cambridge, 1945.

Phil 9070.57   Good behavior. (Nicolson, Harold Georg.) London, 1955.

Phil 9070.50.5   Good behavior; being a study of certain types of activity. (Nicolson, Harold Georg.) Garden City, 1956.

Phil 2255.1.76   The good citizen's alphabet. (Russell, Bertrand Russell.) London, 1953.

Phil 9045.5   Good citizenship. (Cleveland, E.) Philadelphia, 1908.

Htn   Phil 9075.14.5*   Good conscience. 5. ed. (Dyke, J.) London, 1632. 2 pam.

Phil 9070.16   The good fight. (Goldmann, R.L.) N.Y., 1935.

Phil 8591.50   Good gorilla. (Lunn, Arnold.) London, 1944.

Phil 9402.40   The good in existential metaphysics. (Salmon, E.G.) Milwaukee, 1953.

Phil 8884.24   A good life. (Jordan, E.) Chicago, 1949.

Phil 8897.23.3   A good life. (Wright, T.) Boston, 1837.

Phil 8877.44.5   The good man and the good. (Calkins, Mary W.) N.Y., 1928.

Phil 8881.15.5   Good morals and gentle manners. (Gow, A.M.) N.Y., 1873.

	Phil 2648.35	Good sense; or natural ideas. (Holbach, Paul Henri T.) N.Y., 1831.
	Phil 8882.31.5	Good talking a fine art. (Huntington, F.D.) Syracuse, 1892.
	Phil 8882.31	Good talking and good manners. (Huntington, F.D.) Syracuse, 1887.
	Phil 9166.1	A good wife God's gift. Boston, 1796.
	Phil 8890.42	The good will. (Paton, H.J.) London, 1927.
	Phil 8610.902.15	Good without God. (Adams, R.C.) N.Y., 1902.
	Phil 8740.2	Goodale, E. Extracts concerning the importance of religion and public worship. Hallowell, 1820.
	Phil 5246.46	Goodenough, Florence L. Developmental psychology. N.Y., 1934.
	Phil 5246.46.5	Goodenough, Florence L. Developmental psychology. 2. ed. N.Y., 1945.
	Phil 8956.4	Gooding, W.M. A philosophy of the moral nature of man. Newark, 1877.
	Phil 2030.6A	Goodman, Nelson. Fact, fiction and forecast. Cambridge, 1955.
	Phil 2030.6.2	Goodman, Nelson. Fact, fiction and forecast. 2d ed. Indianapolis, 1965.
	Phil 2030.6.5A	Goodman, Nelson. Languages of art. Indianapolis, 1968.
	Phil 2030.6.10	Goodman, Nelson. Problems and projects. Indianapolis, 1972.
	Phil 1750.115.3A	Goodman, Nelson. The structure of appearance. Cambridge, 1951.
	Phil 1750.115.2	Goodman, Nelson. The structure of appearance. Indianapolis, 1966.
	Phil 8881.59	Goodman, R.M. The philosophy of life. Marietta, Ga., 1863.
	Phil 181.14	Goodrich, Samuel G. A glance at philosophy. Boston, 1845.
	Phil 7060.43.5	Goodrich-Freer, A. The alleged haunting of B-- house. London, 1899.
	Phil 5066.125	Goodstein, R.L. Mathematical logic. Leicester, 1957.
	Phil 5500.13	Goodwill and ill will. (Sharp, F.C.) Chicago, 1950.
	Phil 8696.8	Goodwin, H. Walks in the regions of science and faith. London, 1883.
Htn	Phil 6480.26*	Goodwin, P. The mystery of dreames. London, 1658.
	Phil 7069.10.3	Gook, Arthur. Andatrúin. Akureyri, 1914.
	Phil 7069.18.98	Gook, Arthur. Andatrúin afhjúpud Akureyri, 1918.
	Phil 960.260	Gopinatha, Kaviraja. Aspects of Indian thought. Burdwan, 1966.
	Phil 6316.25	Goraber, Gustav Hans. Die Not des Lebens und ihre Überwindung. Bern, 1966.
	Phil 8407.35.5	Goranov, Krusto. Istoricheskiias zhivos na izkustvoto. Sofiia, 1970.
	Phil 8407.35	Goranov, Krusto. Sudurzhanie i forma v izkustvoto. Sofiia, 1958.
	Phil 181.69.10	Gorce, M.M. L'escalade des siécles. Saint-Imier, 1967.
	Phil 181.69	Gorce, M.M. Premiers principes de philosophie. Paris, 1933.
	Phil 1511.5	Gorce, M.M. Science moderne et philosophie médiévale. Paris, 1938.
	Phil 181.69.5	Gorce, M.M. Traité de philosophie. Paris, 1938.
	Phil 5545.222	Gorczyński, S. Sztuka pamietania. Warszawa, 1963.
	Phil 5850.221.20	Gorden, Raymond L. Interviewing: strategy, techniques, and tactics. Homewood, Ill., 1969.
	Phil 5500.12	Gordin, Jakob. Untersuchungen zur Theorie des unendlichen Urteils. Berlin, 1929.
	Phil 9450.50	Gordis, R. Politics and ethics. Santa Barbara, Calif., 1961.
	Phil 3826.3	Gordon, A. Spinoza's Psychologie der Affekte mit Rücksicht auf Descartes. Breslau, 1874.
	Phil 5627.107.25	Gordon, Albert. The nature of conversion. Boston, 1967.
	Phil 8633.1	Gordon, G.A. Immortality and the new theodicy. Boston, 1896.
	Phil 8631.3	Gordon, G.A. The witness to immortality. Boston, 1900.
	Phil 9230.8	Gordon, G.W. A lecture before Boston young men's societies on the subject of lotteries. Boston, 1833.
	Phil 5590.429	Gordon, J.E. Personality and behavior. N.Y., 1963.
	Phil 8881.63	Gordon, John. A new estimate of manners and principles. pt.1-2. Cambridge, Eng., 1760.
	Phil 8407.15	Gordon, Kate. Esthetics. N.Y., 1922.
	Phil 5465.52A	Gordon, Kate. Studies in the theory of imagination. Los Angeles, 1941.
	Phil 6316.7	Gordon, R.G. The neurotic personality. London, 1927.
	Phil 575.58	Gordon, R.G. Personality. London, 1926.
	Phil 575.58.3	Gordon, R.G. Personality. N.Y., 1928.
	Phil 8696.19	Gordon, Ronald G. The philosophy of a scientist. London, 1947.
	Phil 8586.2	Gordon, T. A new method of demonstrating...the four fundamental points of religion. London, 1756.
	Phil 7054.142	Gordon, William R. A three-fold test of modern spiritualism. N.Y., 1856.
	Phil 5240.70	Gordon Allport. 1. ed. (Evans, Richard Isadore.) N.Y., 1970[1971]
	Phil 5246.12.12	Gordy, J.P. New psychology. N.Y., 1902.
	Phil 8831.4	Gore, Charles. Philosophy of the good life. London, 1930.
	Phil 5465.44	Gore, W.C. The imagination in Spinoza and Hume. Chicago, 1902.
	Phil 3488.13	Goretti, Cesare. Il carattere formale della filosofia giuridica Kantiana. Milano, 1922.
	Phil 4065.174	Gorfunkel', Aleksandr K. Dzhordano Bruno. Moskva, 1965.
	Phil 8610.919.20	Gorham, C.T. A plain man's plea for rationalism. London, 1919.
	Phil 9075.34	Gorham, C.T. Why we do right. London, 1924.
	Phil 2406.1	Gorham, Charles. Ethics of the great French rationalists. London, 1900.
	Phil 8436.5	Gori, Gino. Il grottesco nell'arte e nella letteratura. Roma, 1926.
	Phil 8050.55	Gori, Gino. Studi di estetica dell'irrazionale. Milano, 1921.
	Phil 1135.40	Goring, C. Über den Begriff der Ursache in der griechischen Philosophie. Leipzig, 1874.
	Phil 3195.15.83	Gorn, Erhard. Die Philosophie Hugo Dinglers. Dusseldorf, 1960.
	Phil 8407.34	Gornfel'd, A.G. Puti tvorchestva. Peterburg, 1922.
	Phil 3450.18.90	Gornshtein, T.N. Filosofiia Nikolaia Gartmana. Leningrad, 1969.
	Phil 6990.3.95	Gorod chudes svoimi i chuzhimi glazami. (Stolarek, Z.) Moskva, 1961.
	Phil 8881.33	Gorodenskii, N. Nravstvennoe soznanie cheloviechestva. Sergiev, 1903.
	Phil 181.140.2	Gorovitz, Samuel. Philosophical analysis. N.Y., 1967.
	Phil 525.42	Gorres, J. Die christliche Mystik. Bd.1-2,3,4[1],4[2]. Regensburg, 1836-42.
	Phil 5374.245.10	Gorsen, Peter. Zur Phänomenologie des Bewusstseinsstroms. Bonn, 1966.
	Phil 5046.27	Gorskii, D.D. Logika. Moskva, 1956.
	Phil 5360.14	Gorskii, D.P. Vopsosy abstraktsii i obrazovanie poniatiia. Moskva, 1961.
	Phil 5046.48.2	Gortari, Eli de. Introducción a la lógica dialéctica. 2. ed. México, 1959.
	Phil 1050.18	Gortein, H. Der Optimismus und Pessimismus in der jüdischen Religionsphilosophie. Berlin, 1890.
	Phil 6116.23	Gorton, D.A. Essay on the principles of mental hygiene. Philadelphia, 1873.
	Phil 8881.28	Gorton, D.A. Ethics civil and political. N.Y., 1902.
	Phil 6116.15	Gorton, D.A. The monism of man. N.Y., 1893.
	Phil 9245.138	Gosling, Justin Cyril Bertrand. Pleasure and desire: the case for hedonism reviewed. Oxford, 1969.
	Phil 8953.9	Gospel and law. (Dodd, C.H.) Cambridge, Eng., 1951.
	Phil 8971.1	The gospel for a world of sin. (Van Dyke, Henry.) N.Y., 1899.
	Phil 7054.168	The gospel of nature. (Sherman, M.L.) Chicago, 1877.
	Phil 3640.106A	The gospel of superman. (Lichtenberger, H.) N.Y., 1912.
	Phil 3640.106.2	The gospel of superman. (Lichtenberger, H.) N.Y., 1926.
	Phil 8643.19	The gospel of the hereafter. (Smyth, John P.) N.Y., 1910.
	Phil 8643.19.10	The gospel of the hereafter. (Smyth, John P.) N.Y., 1930.
	Phil 8952.6	The gospel of work. (Cunningham, W.) Cambridge, 1902.
	Phil 5535.6	Goss, Albert E. Paired-associates learning; the role of meaningfulness, similarity. N.Y., 1965.
	Phil 5246.88	Gosselin, Albert. L'homme en ce monde et le sens de la vie. Paris, 1970.
	Phil 2905.1.565	Gosztonyi, Alexander. Der Mensch und die Evolution; Teilhard de Chardins philosophische Anthropologie. München, 1968.
	Phil 6116.16F	Gotch, Francis. On the mammalian nervous system. London, 1891.
	Phil 6956.10	Gotewood, Lee C. An experimental study of dermentia preacox. Lancaster, 1909.
	Phil 3552.490	Gotfrid Vil'gel'm Leibnits, 1646-1716. (Pogrebyskii, Iosif B.) Moskva, 1971.
	Phil 3640.800	Goth, Joachim. Nietzsche und die Rhetorik. Tübingen, 1970.
	Phil 3585.10.80	Gothot, Heinrich. Die Grundbestimmungen über die Psychologie des Gefühls bei Theodor Lipps. Mülheim-Ruhr, 1921.
	Phil 4070.1.96	Gotran, P. Due il 48 - Ernest Renan e Cristoforo Bonavino saggio critico filosofico. Firenze, 1891.
	Phil 8430.32	Gotshalk, D.W. Art and the social order. Chicago, 1947.
	Phil 9240.32	Gotshalk, D.W. Patterns of good and evil. Urbana, 1963.
	Phil 181.74	Gotshalk, D.W. Structure and reality. N.Y., 1937.
	Phil 2030.7.5	Gotshalk, Dilman Walter. Human aims in modern perspective. Yellow Springs, Ohio, 1966.
	Phil 2030.7	Gotshalk, Dilman Walter. The promise of modern life. Yellow Springs, Ohio, 1958.
	Phil 585.235	Gott, Mensch und Welt in der Metaphysik von Descartes bis zu Nietzsche. (Loewith, Karl.) Göttingen, 1967.
	Phil 8598.144	Gott: Fehlanzeige? (Standinger, Hugo.) Tries, 1968.
	Phil 193.177	Der Gott der neuzeitlichen Metaphysik. (Schulz, Walter.) Pfullingen, 1957.
	Phil 8587.54	"Gott haben." (Hanse, H.) Berlin, 1939.
	Phil 8673.16	Gott in der Geschichte. (Schütz, A.) Salzburg, 1936.
	Phil 8586.36.70	Gott in Jesus; der Ansatz der Christologie Friedrich Gogartens. (Weth, Rudolf.) München, 1968.
	Phil 3640.681	Gott ist tot. (Biser, Eugen.) München, 1962.
	Phil 8698.15	Gott sprach-es-ward. (Schueppe, Otto.) Bern, 1970.
	Phil 3801.450.5	Gott und das Denken nach Schellings Spätphilosophie. (Hemmerle, Klaus.) Freiburg, 1968.
	Phil 3895.35	Gott und der Mensch. Bd.1. (Ulrici, H.) Leipzig, 1873.
	Phil 3895.35.2	Gott und der Mensch. 2. Aufl. Bd.1-2. (Ulrici, H.) Leipzig, 1874. 2v.
	Phil 3895.40	Gott und die Natur. (Ulrici, H.) Leipzig, 1862.
	Phil 3895.40.2	Gott und die Natur. (Ulrici, H.) Leipzig, 1875.
	Phil 3895.40.5	Gott und die Natur. 2. Aufl. (Ulrici, H.) Leipzig, 1866.
	Phil 8672.8	Gott und die Seele. Inaug. Diss. (Reinhard, J.) Erlangen, 1908.
	Phil 1112.8	Gott und Seele bin Lichte der griechischen Philosophie. (Huonder, Quirin.) München, 1954.
	Phil 8666.15	Gott und Teufel im 20. Jahrhundert. 4. Aufl. (Lederer, Julius.) Berlin, 1910?
	Phil 8665.27	Gott und Welt in der klassischen Metaphysik. (Kromer, Klaus.) Stuttgart, 1969.
	Phil 8657.9	Gott und Wissenschaft. v.1-2. (Cyon, E. von.) Leipzig, 1912.
	Phil 1135.210	Gottähnlichkeit, Vergöttlichung und Erhöhung zu seligem Leben. (Roloff, Dietrich.) Berlin, 1970.
	Phil 3425.720	Gottes Tod und Hegels Auferstehung. (Reidinger, Otto.) Berlin, 1969.
	Phil 3552.93.5	Der Gottesbegriff bei Leibniz. (Glöckner, G.) Langensalza, 1888.
	Phil 8665.30	Der Gottesbegriff der spekulativen Theologie. (Kruger, Klaus.) Berlin, 1970.
	Phil 3270.7.80	Der Gottesbegriff Franks. Inaug. Diss. (Römer, Alfred.) Halle, 1912.
	Phil 8673.4	Die Gottesbeweise. (Staab, K.) Paderborn, 1909.
	Phil 3415.90	Die Gottesbeweise Eduard von Hartmanns. (Paulus, H.) Würzburg, 1907.
	Phil 3425.682	Das Gottesbild des Jungen Hegel. Thesis. (Guereñu, Ernesto de.) Freiburg, 1969.
	Phil 3120.30.35	Gottesfinsterrns. (Buber, Martin.) Zürich, 1953.
	Phil 1540.45	Gottesfreundschaft. (Egentin, Richard.) Augsburg, 1928.
	Phil 8643.9	Der Gottesgedanke in der Geschichte der Philosophie. (Schwarz, H.) Heidelberg, 1913.
	Phil 8598.81	Die Gottesidee der Offenbarung. (Steckelmacher, M.) Mannheim, 1890.
	Phil 8677.12.2	Die Gottesidee in religiöser und spekulativer Richtung. (Walter von Walthoffen, Hippolyt.) Wien, 1904.
	Phil 4580.117	Das Gottesproblem bei Harald Høffding. Inaug. Diss. (Hürtgen, Robert.) Bonn, 1928.
	Phil 3552.125.9	Gottfried Wilhelm Leibniz. Gestorben 1716. (Wundt, Wilhelm.) Stuttgart, 1916.
	Phil 3552.244	Gottfried Wilhelm Leibniz als Deutscher. (Dafert, F.W.) Wien, 1883.
	Phil 3552.31	Gottfried Wilhelm Leibniz; Gott, Geist, Güte. (Leibniz, Gottfried Wilhelm.) Gütersloh, 1947.
	Phil 3552.472	Gottfried Wilhelm Leibniz; philosopher and politician in the service of a universal culture. (Vennelusch, Joachim.) Bad Godesberg, 1966.
	Phil 3552.319	Gottfried Wilhelm Leibniz. (Fleckenstein, Joachim O.) München, 1908.
	Phil 3552.318	Gottfried Wilhelm Leibniz. (Hamburger Akademische Rundschau.) Hamburg, 1946.
	Phil 3552.94.9	Gottfried Wilhelm Leibniz. (Kirchner, Friedrich.) Cöthen, 1876.

Phil 3552.470 Gottfried Wilhelm Leibniz. (Morawietz, Kurt.) Hannover, 1962.
Phil 3552.296 Gottfried Wilhelm Leibniz. (Pfleiderer, Edmund.) Leipzig, 1870.
Phil 3552.330 Gottfried Wilhelm Leibniz. (Stieler, Georg.) Paderborn, 1950.
Phil 3552.242.5 Gottfried Wilhelm Leibniz als Sprachforscher und Etynologie. v.1-2. (Neff, L.) Heidelburg, 1870-71.
Phil 3552.87 Gottfried Willhelm Freiherr von Leibnitz. (Guhrauer, G.E.) Breslau, 1842. 2v.
Phil 3120.2.82 Gotthardt, J. Das Wahrheits Problem. Inaug. Diss. Trier, 1918.
Phil 3120.2.84 Gotthardt. J. Bolzano Lehre vom "Satz an Sich". Berlin, 1909.
Phil 3850.6.75 Gotthilf Heinrich Schubert in seinen Briefen. (Schubert, G.H.) Stuttgart, 1918.
Phil 3850.3.81 Gotthilf Samuel Steinbart, 1738-1809. Inaug. Diss. (Alberty, Gerhard.) Gotha, 1930.
Phil 3850.3.80 Gotthilf Samuel Steinbart. (Hildenbrand, R.) Herne, n.d.
Phil 8655.15 Die Gottlosenbewegung der Gegenwart. 1. und 2. Aufl. (Algermissen Konrad.) Hannover, 1933.
Phil 3549.10.30 Der Gottmensch. (Kassner, Rudolf.) Leipzig, 1938.
Phil 2255.1.128 Gottschalk, Herbert. Bertrand Russell: a life. London, 1965.
Phil 3475.3.200 Gottschalk, Herbert. Karl Jaspers. Berlin, 1966.
Phil 6316.30 Gottschalk, Louis. The measurement of psychological states through the content analysis of verbal behavior. Berkeley, 1969.
Phil 181.26.3 Gottsched, J.C. Erste Gründe. 3. Aufl. v.1-2. Leipzig, 1762.
Phil 181.26.7 Gottsched, J.C. Erste Grunde der Weltweisheit. 7. Aufl. Leipzig, 1762. 2v.
Phil 181.26.5 Gottsched, J.C. Erste Grunder der Weltweisheit. Leipzig, 1749. 2v.
Phil 3910.83 Gottsched, J.C. Historische Lobschrift des Herrn C. von Wolf. Halle, 1755.
Phil 8881.40 Gottschick, Johannes. Ethik. Tübingen, 1907.
Phil 8407.22 Goudal, Jean. Volontés de l'art moderne. Paris, 1927.
Phil 5850.221.15 Goude, G. On fundamental measurement in psychology. Stockholm, 1962.
Phil 5648.14 Goudge, Mabel E. A qualitative and quantitative study of Weber's illusion. Thesis. Worcester, Mass., 1918.
Phil 2225.5.102 Goudge, T.A. The thought of C.S. Peirce. Toronto, 1950.
Phil 535.40 Goudsblom, Johan. Nihilisme en cultuur. Amsterdam, 1960.
Phil 7068.63.35 Gougenot des Mousseaux, H.R. Les médiateurs et les moyens de la magie. Paris, 1863.
Phil 5592.180 Gough, Harrison Gould. The adjective checklist manual. Palo Alto, 1965.
Phil 2115.159 Gough, J.W. John Locke's political philosophy. Oxford, 1950.
Phil 2475.1.400 Gouhier, Henri. Bergson et le Christ des évangiles. Paris, 1961.
Phil 2805.430 Gouhier, Henri. Blaise Pascal. Paris, 1966.
Phil 2730.100 Gouhier, Henri. Les conversions de Maine de Biran. Paris, 1947.
Phil 2520.140.3 Gouhier, Henri. Essais sur Descartes. Paris, 1937.
Phil 2520.140.5 Gouhier, Henri. Essais sur Descartes. 2. éd. Paris, 1949.
Phil 2490.123 Gouhier, Henri. La jeunesse d'Auguste Comte et la formation du positivisme. Paris, 1933-36. 3v.
Phil 2733.94.10 Gouhier, Henri. Malebranche. Paris, 1929.
Phil 2477.19.80 Gouhier, Henri. Notice sur la vie et les travaux de Gaston Berger, 1896-1960. Paris, 1962.
Phil 2733.94.6 Gouhier, Henri. La philosophie de Malebranche. Paris, 1948.
Phil 2733.94 Gouhier, Henri. La philosophie de Malebranche et son expérience religieuse. Paris, 1926.
Phil 2733.94.5 Gouhier, Henri. La philosophie de Malebranche et son expérience religieuse. Thèse. Paris, 1926. 2 pam.
Phil 2520.140.8 Gouhier, Henri. Les premières pensées de Descartes. Paris, 1958.
Phil 2733.94.7 Gouhier, Henri. La vocation de Malebranche. Paris, 1926.
Phil 3488.7 Goujon, H. Kant et Kantistes. Lille, 1901.
Phil 181.81 Gould, G.M. The infinite presence. N.Y., 1910.
Phil 6116.6 Gould, G.M. Righthandedness and lefthandedness. Philadelphia, 1908.
Phil 5643.52A Gould, George M. Biographic clinics. Philadelphia, 1903-05. 6v.
Phil 8586.4 Gould, George M. The meaning and method of life. N.Y., 1893.
Phil 8586.23 Gould, Gerald. The helping hand. London, 1922.
Phil 7068.53.5 Goupy, Louis. Explication des tables parlantes. 1st ed. Paris, 1860.
Phil 181.27 Gourd, J.J. Le phénomène; esquisse de philosophie génèrale. Paris, 1888.
Phil 8586.11 Gourd, J.J. Philosophie de la religion. Paris, 1911.
Phil 5649.2 Gourgeon, J. L'exploration physiologique...du sens musculaire. Paris, 1901.
Phil 1730.4 Gourju, Pierre. La philosophie du dix-huitième siècle dévoilée par elle-même. Paris, 1816. 2v.
Phil 181.34 Gourmont, Rémy de. Promenades philosophiques. 3rd series. Paris, 1913. 3v.
Phil 5653.7 Le goût. (Marchand, L.) Paris, 1903.
Phil 8892.55 Le gouvernement de soi. (Roche, J.) Paris, 1938.
Phil 8972.3 Government of the thoughts. (Walker, James.) Boston, 1899.
Htn Phil 8881.14.2* Government of the thoughts. Longon, 1700.
Htn Phil 8881.14* Government of the tongue. Oxford, 1675.
Phil 8881.62 Govi, Mario. Etica rinnovata su basi scientifiche. Pte.I. Firenze, 1935.
Phil 5046.21 Govi, Mario. Fondazione della metodalogia. Torino, 1929.
Phil 181.70 Govi, Mario. Preludi filosofici e politici. Milano, 1935.
Phil 4467.2.30 Govies, Pinharanda. Peregrinação do absoluto. Lisboa, 1965.
Phil 530.105.5 Govindācārya, Alkondavilli. A metaphysique of mysticism. Mysore, 1923.
Phil 8881.15.5 Gow, A.M. Good morals and gentle manners. N.Y., 1873.
Phil 6956.1 Gowers, W.R. Lectures on the diagnosis of disease of the brain. London, 1885.
Phil 1845.11.10 Gozzelino, Giorgio M. La filosofia di Alfred Jules Ayer. Zürich, 1964.
Phil 3085.10.81 Graaf, Bob de. Petrus Apherdianus, ludimagister ca. 1510-1580. Nieuwkoop, 1968.
Phil 8831.8 Graaf, Johannes de. De bezinning over goed en kwaad in de geschiedenis of het menselijk denken. Utrecht, 1957- 3v.
Phil 8980.435 Graaf, Johannes de. Moraal, marxisme en ethiek in de sowietunie. Hilversum, 1967.

Phil 3450.19.114 Graaff, F. de. Het schuldprableem ein de existentiephilosophie van Martin Heidegger. 's Gravenhage, 1951.
Phil 535.20 Graaff, Frank de. Het Europese nihilisme. Amsterdam, 1956.
Phil 270.137 Grabbé, Geneviéve. Les conditions d'une perception de la causalité. Paris, 1967.
Phil 6980.335 Graber, Gustav. Seelenspiegel des Kindes. Zürich, 1946.
Phil 5246.65 Graber, Gustav Hans. Psychologie des Mannes. Bern, 1957.
Phil 5871.112.2 Graber, Gustav Hans. Ursprung, Einheit und Zwiespalt der Seele. München, 1970.
Phil 3450.18.160 Grabes, H. Der Begriff des a priori in Nicolai Hartmanns Erkenntismetaphysik und Ontologie. Köln, 1962.
Phil 7069.16.25 Grabinski, B. Neuere mystik. Hildesheim, 1916.
Phil 7069.22.11 Grabinski, B. Spuk und Geistererscheinungen oder was sonst? 2. Aufl. Hildesheim, 1922.
Phil 1504.17.5 Grabmann, M. Forschungen über die lateinischen Aristoteles. v.17, pt.5-6. Münster, 1916.
Phil 1511.1.5 Grabmann, M. Der Gegenwartswert der geschichtlichen Erforschung der mittelalterichen Philosophie. Wien, 1913.
Phil 1511.1A Grabmann, M. Geschichte der scholastischen Methode. Freiburg, 1909. 2v.
Phil 530.20.55 Grabmann, M. Die Kulturwerte der deutschen Mystik des Mittelalters. Augsburg, 1923.
Phil 1020.4.20 Grabmann, M. Der lateinische Awerroismus des 13 Jahrhunderts. München, 1931.
Phil 1511.1.15 Grabmann, M. Mittelalterliches Geistesleben. München, 1926-36. 3v.
Phil 1511.1.10 Grabmann, M. Die Philosophie des Mittelalters. Berlin, 1921.
Phil 1540.79 Grabmann, Martin. Interpretazioni medievale del voûsnointinós. Padova, 1965.
Phil 3488.19 Grabowsky, N. Kants Grundirrtümer in seiner Kritik der reinen Vernunft, und die Reformation des geistigen Innenlebens der Menschheit. Leipzig, 1907.
Phil 3850.27.119 Grabs, R. Albert Schweitzer. Berlin, 1948.
Phil 3850.27.106 Grabs, R. Albert Schweitzer. Berlin, 1949.
Phil 3850.27.106.10
Phil 3483.2 Grabs, R. Sinngeburg des Lebens. Hamburg, 1950. Die Grabstätte Immanuel Kants. (Bessel-Hagen, F.) Königsberg, 1880.
Phil 3488.24 Gračanin, G. La personnalité morale d'après Kant. Thèse. Paris, 1929.
Phil 2733.104 La grace et la liberté dans Malebranche. (Labbas, Lucien.) Paris, 1931.
Phil 2733.104.15 La grace et la liberté dans Malebranche. Thèse. (Labbas, Lucien.) Paris, 1931. 2 pam.
Phil 4351.6.80 La gracia divina en el correlativismo. (Delgado Varela, José M.) Madrid, 1961.
Htn Phil 6021.2.80* Gradation de la tête de grenouille jusqu'au profil d'Appollon, d'après les idées du sa célèbre Lavater. Paris, 17- ?
Phil 978.72 Graded lessons in theosophy. (Ljungström, O.) Lund, 1935.
Phil 8643.8 Grades of life. Letters on immortality. (Sopote, M.) Oxford, 1909.
Phil 8610.798.11 Gradis, David. Discussions philosophiques sur l'athéisme. Paris, 1803.
Phil 8610.798.10 Gradis, David. Réponse à divers contradicteurs sur la coéternelle existence de la matière. Paris, 1798-99.
Phil 8980.162 Gradiva za pouk temeljev socialistične morale. (Artač, Marija.) Ljubljana, 1969.
Phil 450.6 Gradman, Hans. Menschsein ohne Illusionen. München, 1970.
Phil 3805.181 Graeber, Martin. Die Sakramentstheorie Schleiermachers und ihre Weiterbildung innerhalb der kritischen Theologie des 19. Jahrhunderts. Inaug. Diss. Wuppertal, 1937.
Phil 8740.8 Graef, Hilda C. The light and the rainbow. London, 1959.
Phil 5628.55.15 Graef, Hilda Charlotte. The case of Therese Neumann. Cork, 1950.
Phil 525.160 Graef, Hilda Charlotte. Der siebenfarbige Bogen auf den Spuren der grossen Mystiker. Frankfurt, 1959.
Phil 525.240 Graef, Hilda Charlotte. The story of mysticism. 1st ed. Garden City, N.Y., 1965.
Phil 4600.2.50 Gränsen mellan sensation och emotion. 2e uppl. (Larsson, Hans.) Lund, 1911.
Phil 5816.4 Graeser, Kurt. Die Vorstellungen der Tiere. Berlin, 1906.
Phil 1112.6 Den graeske naturfilosofi indtil sofisterne. (Helms, Poul.) København, 1926.
Phil 5203.3 Grässe, J.G.T. Bibliotheca psychologica. Leipzig, 1848.
Phil 7140.126 Graeter, Karl. Menschenleiden als Lebensgeheimnis...Autosuggestion. Kandern, 1926.
Phil 806.5 Grätz, H. von. Geschichte der Philosophie. Langensalza, 1861.
Phil 7082.192 Graevenitz, Jutta von. Bedeutung und Deutung des Traumes in der Psychotherapie. Darmstadt, 1968.
Phil 8586.33 Graf, A. Per una fede. Milano, 1906.
Phil 1504.14 Graf, G. Des Theodor Abû Kurra Traktat. v.14, pt.1. Münster, n.d.
NEDL Phil 177.32 Graf August Cieszkowski's "Philosophie der Tat". (Zoltowski, A.) Posen, 1904.
Phil 3549.2.94 Graf Edward von Keyserling und seinepisches Werk. Inaug. Diss. (Shilpnagel, U.) Rostock, 1929.
Phil 3549.2.96 Graf Hermann Keyserling. (Hupfeld, R.) Bonn, 1922.
Phil 3549.2.105 Graf Hermann Keyserling und Frankereich. (Dyserinck, Hugo.) Bonn, 1970.
Phil 3549.2.70 Graf Hermann Kyserling. (Keyserling, Hermann.) Innsbruck, 1948.
Phil 3549.2.80 Graf Keyserlings Erkenntnisweg zum Übersinnlichen. (Feldkeller, P.) Darmstadt, 1922.
Phil 6619.12 Grafé, A. Étude sur quelques paralysies d'origine psychique. Bruxelles, 1889.
Phil 126.5 Gráficos de historia de la filosofia. (Quiles, Ismael.) Buenos Aires, 1940.
Phil 6060.3 Grafologia. (Lombroso, C.) Milano, 1895.
Phil 735.235 Graham, Angus C. The problem of value. London, 1961.
Phil 8586.15 Graham, Bothwell. Philosophy of Christianity. Columbia, 1917.
Phil 8661.15 Graham, Bothwell. The self-evolution of God and His creation of nature. Greenville, S.C., 1923.
Phil 181.31 Graham, C. The true philosophy of mind. Louisville, 1869.
Htn Phil 2045.90* Graham, C.M. Loose remarks on certain positions to be found in Mr. Hobbes's Philosophical rudiments of government and society. 2nd ed. London, 1769.
Phil 6307.332 Graham, Thomas F. Medieval minds; mental health in the Middle Ages. London, 1967.
Phil 8586.5 Graham, W. The creed of science, religious, moral and social. London, 1881.
Phil 400.2 Graham, W. Idealism. London, 1872.

Phil 2905.1.545 Le grain de sénevé. De la science à la religion avec Teilhard de Chardin. (Tanner, Henri.) Saint-Maurice, 1967.
Phil 8580.15 Das Gralsreich als Streiter wider den Untergang des Abendlandes. (Abbetmeyer, Theo.) Heilbronn, 1926.
Phil 3488.44 Gram, Moltke S. Kant: disputed questions. Chicago, 1967.
Phil 4260.149 Grambattista Vico al cospetto del secolo XIX. (Marini, Cesare.) Napoli, 1852.
Phil 5520.744 La grammaire logique. (Brisset, Jean Pierre.) Paris, 1970.
Phil 5520.20 Grammar and thinking. (Sheffield, A.D.) N.Y., 1912.
Phil 5090.3A Grammar of assent. (Newman, J.H.) N.Y., 1870.
Phil 8610.921 A grammar of freethought. (Cohen, Chapman.) London, 1921.
Phil 735.230 A grammar of human values. (Mezing, Otto O.) Pittsburgh, 1961.
Phil 197.37 The grammar of life. (Wrench, G.T.) London, 1908.
Phil 5520.80 A grammar of motives. (Burke, Kenneth.) N.Y., 1945.
Phil 6048.99.5 The grammar of palmistry. (St. Hill, K.) Philadelphia, 19- .
Htn Phil 5049.1* Grammatica rationis sive institutiones logicos. (Jack, Gilbert.) Oxonii, 1675.
Phil 5643.101 Gramont, A. Problèmes de la vision. Paris, 1939.
Phil 4080.3.205 Gramsci, Antonio. Il materialismo storico e la filosofia di Benedetto Croce. 2. ed. Torino, 1949.
Phil 3006.3.2 Gramzow, Otto. Geschichte der Philosophie seit Kant. 2. Aufl. Charlottenburg, 1919-28. 2v.
Phil 187.73F Una gran revolucion, ó La razon del hombre juzgada por sí misma. (Madiedo, M.M.) Caracas, 1876.
Phil 16.15 Granada, Spain (City). Universidad. Cátedra Francisco Suárez. Anales. Granada. 9,1969+
Phil 181.65 Granberry, John C. Students' prolegomena to philosophy. Ann Arbor, 1931.
Phil 8062.3 Grand, Y. Recherche des principes d'une philosophie des arts, dits d'imitation chez Platon, Aristote et Plotin. Lausanne, 1952.
Phil 4467.1.30 A grand concepcão de Deus. (Guimarães, M.) Rio, 1940.
Htn Phil 477.4* Grand essay. (Coward, W.) London, 1704.
Htn Phil 8635.1* The grand question debated. (Kenrick, W.) Dublin, 1751. 2 pam.
Phil 1865.181 The grand social enterprise; a study of Jeremy Bentham in his relation to liberal nationalism. (Kayser, E.L.) N.Y., 1932.
Phil 165.28 Grande antologia filosofica. (Padovani, U.A.) Milano, 1954. 16v.
Phil 4769.1.81 La grande controverse et la politique chrétienne. (Solov'ev, V.S.) Paris, 1953.
Phil 2905.1.285 La grande illusion de Teilhard de Chardin. (Vernet, M.) Paris, 1964.
Phil 6316.3 La grande névrose. (Gérard, J.) Paris, 1889.
Phil 6312.13 As grandes crises do homen ensaio de psicopatologia individual e colectiva. (Cebola, Luiz.) Lisboa, 1945.
Phil 801.35 Las grandes direcciones de la filosofia. (Bueno, Miguel.) México, 1957.
Phil 4319.1 Los grandes escolásticos espanoles de los siglos XVI y XVII. (Solana, Marcial.) Madrid, 1928.
Phil 5243.42 Les grandes formes de la vie mentale. (Delacroix, Henri.) Paris, 1934.
Phil 4260.95 Les grandes lignes de la philosophie historique et juridique de Vico. (Cochery, M.) Paris, 1923.
Phil 8587.1.5 Les grandes questions. (Hannotin, E.) Paris, 1867.
Phil 600.41 Les grandes types de l'humanité. (Laffitte, P.) Paris, 1875-76. 2v.
Phil 4365.1.10 Grandeza y servidumbre de la intelegencia. (Ors y Rovira, E. d'.) Madrid, 1919.
Phil 4080.3.395 Grandi, M. Benedetto Croce e il seicento. Milano, 1962.
Phil 802.10 I grandi filosofi e i grandi sistemi filosofici. (Cosentini, F.) Torino, 1925.
Phil 3500.80 Grandi interpreti di Kant. (Salvucci, Pasquale.) Urbino, 1958.
Phil 8831.7 I grandi moralisti. (Gentile, Marino.) Torino, 1955.
Phil 5620.10 Grandjean, F. La raison et la vue. Paris, 1920.
Phil 525.190 Grandjean, Louis E. Alt anden gang. København, 1960.
Phil 2475.1.175 Grandjian, Frank. Une révolution dans la philosophie. 2e ed. Genève, 1916.
Phil 6990.3.42 Grandmaison de Bruno, F. Twenty cures at Lourdes. St. Louis, 1912.
Phil 190.60.5 De grandparadox. (Poortman, J.J.) Assen, 1961.
Phil 1750.166 Les grands appels de l'homme contemporain. Paris, 1946.
Phil 1750.166.185 Les grands appels de l'humanisme contemporain, christianisme, marxisme. (Niel, André.) Paris, 1966.
Phil 1706.9 Les grands courants de la pensée contemporaine. (Grevillot, J.M.) Paris, 1948.
Phil 1718.29.5 Les grands courants de la pensée modiale contemporaine. v.1-3. (Sciacca, Michele Federico.) Milan, 1958- 6v.
Phil 1122.8 Les grands couvants de la pensée antique. (Rivaud, Albert.) Paris, 1929.
Phil 1718.28 Les grands maîtres de l'humanisme européen. (Spenlé, J.E.) Paris, 1952.
Phil 530.20.53 Les grands mystiques allemands du XIVe siècle. (Hornstein, X. de.) Lucerne, 1922.
Phil 5425.49 Grands Névropathes. (Cabanés, Auguste.) Paris, 1930-31. 3v.
Phil 3808.112 Les grands philosophes; Schopenhauer. (Ruyssen, T.) Paris, 1911.
Phil 2490.25 Les grands philosophes...choix de textes. (Hubert, René.) Paris, 1927.
Phil 3480.26 Les grands philosophes. (Kant, Immanuel.) Paris, 1909.
Phil 180.26 Les grands problèmes. (François Adolphe.) Paris, 1895.
Phil 6955.13 Les grands symptômes neurasthéniques. (Fleury, M. de.) Paris, 1901.
Phil 8586.19 Grane, Georg. Selbstbwusstsein und Willensfreiheit. Berlin, 1904.
Phil 3488.50 Granel, Gérard. L'équivoque ontologique de la pensée Kantienne. Paris, 1970.
Phil 3450.11.455 Granel, Gérard. Le sens du temps et de la perception chez E. Husserl. Paris, 1968.
Phil 9035.110 Granell Mañiz, Manuel. La recindad humana. Madrid, 1969.
Phil 1750.166.15 Granell Muñiz, M. El humanismo como responsabilidad. Madrid, 1959.
Phil 4961.910 Granell Muñiz, Manuel. Del pensar venezolano. Caracas, 1967.
Phil 5627.260.5 Graneris, Giuseppe. La vita della religion e nella storia delle religioni. Torino, 1960.
Phil 4363.3.105 Granero, Jesus Maria. Don Miguel Mañara. Sevilla, 1963.
Phil 2150.18.115 Granese, Alberto. G.E. Moore e la filosofia analitica inglese. Firenze, 1970.
Phil 1955.6.230 Granese, Alberto. Il Giovane Dewey. 1. ed. Firenze, 1966.
Phil 5246.8 Granger, F.S. Psychology. London, 1891.
Phil 5160.5.2 Granger, Giles. La raison. 2. éd. Paris, 1958.
Phil 181.156 Granger, Gilles Gaston. Essai d'une philosophie du style. Paris, 1968.
Phil 2494.87 Granger, Gilles Gaston. La mathématique sociale du marquis de Condorcet. 1. éd. Paris, 1956.
Phil 337.22 Granger, Gilles Gaston. Pensée formelle et sciences de l'homme. Paris, 1960.
Phil 440.10 Grani svobody. (Pavidovich, Vsevolod E.) Moskva, 1969.
Phil 6400.18 Granich, L. Aphasia: a guide to retraining. N.Y., 1947.
Phil 3640.715 Granier, Jean. Le problème de la vérité dans la philosophie de Nietzsche. Paris, 1966.
Phil 4515.83.10 Granskning af kandidaten Waldemar. (Edfeldt, Hans.) Upsala, 1875.
Phil 4655.1.80.2 Granskning af P. Wikners kritik. (Åberg, L.H.) Stockholm, 1882.
Phil 7082.30 Grant, Alexander Henley. Extraordinary and well-authenticated dreams. London, 18- ?
Phil 7082.30.5 Grant, Alexander Henley. The literature and curiosities of dreams. London, 1865. 2v.
Phil 8610.853.10 Grant, B. Christianity and secularism. London, 1853.
Phil 900.11 Grant, Francis. Oriental philosophy. N.Y., 1936.
Phil 1806.5 Grant, George. Philosophy in the mass age. N.Y., 1960.
Phil 7069.30.8 Grant, Isabel. Conversations with the other world. London, 1930.
Phil 8586.39 Grant, Malcolm. A new argument for God. London, 1934.
Phil 7054.171 Grant, Miles. Spiritualism unveiled. Boston, 1866.
Phil 5643.100 Grant, V.W. Psychological optics. Chicago, 1938.
Phil 5425.108 Grant, Vernon W. Great abnormals; the pathological genius of Kafka, Van Gogh, Strindenberg and Poe. N.Y., 1968.
Phil 6956.6 Grant-Smith, Rachel. The experiences of an asylum patient. London, 1922.
Phil 287.5 Grant Watson, E.L. Man and his universe. London, 1940.
Phil 6116.3.5 Granville, J.M. Common mind troubles. Salem, 1879.
Phil 6116.3 Granville, J.M. The secret of a clear head. Salem, 1879.
NEDL Phil 5545.11 Granville, J.M. Secret of a good memory. Boston, 1887.
Phil 5545.11.5 Granville, J.M. Secret of a good memory. n.p., 1906.
Phil 7080.4 Granville, J.M. Sleep and sleeplessness. Boston, 1881.
Phil 3100.80 Granzow, O. Friedrich Edward Benekes Leben. Bern, 1899.
Phil 3260.81 Grape, Johannes. Die Prinzipien der Ethik bei Fries. Dessau, 1903.
Phil 3488.18.5 Grapengiesser, C. Erklärung und Vertheidigung von Kant's Kritik der reinen Vernueft wider die "sogenannten" Erläuterungen des J.H.v. Kirchmann. Jena, 1871.
Phil 3488.18 Grapengiesser, C. Kants Lehre von Raum und Zeit, Kuno Fischer und Adolf Trendelenburg. Jena, 1870.
Phil 5330.21.5 La graphique psychométrique de l'attention. (Patrizi, M.L.) Turin, 1895.
Phil 6060.34 Graphologia. v.1-2,3-4. Bern, 1945. 2v.
Phil 6060.12.25 Graphologie. 4. Aufl. (Klages, Ludwig.) Heidelberg, 1949.
Htn Phil 6060.1.10* La graphologie en exemples. (Crepieux-Jamin, J.) Paris, 1899.
Phil 6060.80 Graphologie in Vorlesungen. (Pophal, Rudolf.) Stuttgart, 1965- 3v.
Phil 6060.84 Die graphologische Intelligenzdiagnose. (Schneevoigt, Ihno.) Bonn, 1968.
Phil 6965.26 Graphologische Untersuchungen an den Handelschriften von Schizophren-Paranoiden und Epileptikern. Abhandlung. (Poljak, Leo.) Tübingen, 1957.
Phil 6060.12.20 Graphologisches lesebuch. (Klages, Ludwig.) Bonn, 1930.
Phil 6060.46 Graphology. (Rand, H.A.) Cambridge, Mass., 1947.
Phil 6060.15A Graphology and the psychology of handwriting. (Downey, June E.) Baltimore, 1919.
Phil 5520.37.5 La graphomanie. (Lourié, Ossip.) Paris, 1920.
Phil 2825.5 Grappe, André. La pensée de Maurice Pradines. Paris, 1938.
Phil 6116.13F Grashey, H. Experimentelle Beiträge zur Lehre von der Blut-Circulation in der Schädel-Rückgratshöhle. München, 1892.
Phil 9245.10 Grasset, B. Sur le plaisir. Paris, 1954.
Phil 6676.6 Grásset, J. L'hypnotisme et la suggestion. 4. éd. Paris, 1916.
Phil 7060.69 Grasset, J. L'occultisme: hier et aujourd'hui. Montpelier, 1908.
Phil 7069.04.35 Grasset, J. Le spiritisme devant la science. Montpellier, 1904.
Phil 2490.99 Grasset, Joseph. Un demifou de génie. Montpelier, 1911.
Phil 6956.5.2 Grasset, Joseph. Demifous et demiresponsables. 2. éd. Paris, 1908.
Phil 6116.9.5 Grasset, Joseph. Introduction physiologique à l'étude de la philosophie. Paris, 1908.
Phil 5651.6 Grasset, Joseph. Les maladies de l'orientation et de l'equilibre. Paris, 1901.
Phil 6956.11 Grasset, Joseph. Le psychisme inférieur. 2. éd. Paris, 1913.
Phil 6956.5.5 Grasset, Joseph. The semi-insane and semi-responsible. N.Y., 1907.
Phil 337.15 Grassi, E. Die Einheit unseres Wirklichkeitsbildes und die Grenzen der Einzelwissenschaftes. Bern, 1951.
Phil 1750.29 Grassi, E. Von Ursprung und Grenzen der Geistewissenschaften und Naturwissenschaften. Bern, 1950.
Phil 3552.111.9 Grassi-Bertazzi, G. L'inconscio nella filosofia di Leibnitz. Catania, 1903.
Phil 5246.50 Grassi-Bertazzi, G.B. I fenomeni psichici. Catania, 1898.
Phil 5046.19 Grassmann, R. Die Logik. Stettin, 1900.
Phil 181.36 Grassmann, R. Das Weltleben oder die Metaphysik. Stettin, 1881.
Phil 5545.12 Gratacap, A. Théorie de la mémoire. Montpellier, 1866.
Phil 165.125 Grateloup, León. Expérience - connaissance. Paris, 1957.
Phil 5401.10 Gratia, L.E. Le "trac" et la timidité. 2e éd. Paris, 1926.
Phil 3493.14 Die Gratistätte Immanuel Kants auf Grund authentischer Quellen dargestellt. (Lomber, Wilhelm.) Königsberg, 1924.
Phil 8661.9.2 Gratry, A. De la connaissance de Dieu. 2. éd. Paris, 1854. 2v.
Phil 8661.9 Gratry, A. De la connaissance de Dieu. 9. éd. Paris, 1918. 2v.
Phil 9346.5.5 Gratry, A.J. Les sources. 16. éd. Paris, 1921.
Phil 5246.9 Gratry, A.J.A. De la connaissance de l'âme. Paris, 1857. 2v.
Phil 1750.14 Gratry, A.J.A. Étude sur la sophistique contemporaine. Paris, 1851.
Phil 5046.6 Gratry, A.J.A. Logique. Paris, 1868. 2v.
Phil 8881.16 Gratry, A.J.A. La morale et la loi de l'histoire. Paris, 1871. 2v.
Phil 1750.14.10 Gratry, A.J.A. Les sophistes et la critique. Paris, 1864.
Phil 2630.1.25 Gratry, a cura di Angelica Marrucchi. (Gratry, Auguste.) Milano, 1923.

Phil 2630.1.25   Gratry, Auguste. Gratry, a cura di Angelica Marrucchi. Milano, 1923.

Phil 2630.1.35   Gratry, Auguste. Méditations inédites. Paris, 1926.
Phil 2630.1.79   Gratry, Auguste. Souvenirs de ma jeunesse. 5e ed. Paris, 1897.

Phil 2630.1.20   Gratry, Auguste. Studien. Regensburg, 1858-1859. 3v.
Phil 9346.5   Gratry, A.J. Les sources. v.1-2. Paris, 1862-69.
Phil 2630.1.84   Gratrys Theorie der religiosen Erkenntnis. (Braun, Ludwig L.) Strassburg, 1914.
Phil 1750.130   Grattan, Clinton H. The critique of humanism; a symposium. N.Y., 1930.

Phil 1750.130.5A   Grattan, Clinton H. The critique of humanism. N.Y., 1930.
Phil 6316.13   Gratton, Henri. Psychoanalyses d'hier et d'aujourd'hui comme thérapeutiques. Paris, 1955.

Phil 6049.09   Gratz, Thomas Donelson. Palmistry made easy. Philadelphia, 1909.

Phil 3640.530   Grau, Gerd Günther. Christlicher Glaube und intellektuelle Redlichkeit. Frankfurt, 1958.

Phil 9558.10.15   Grau, Kurt J. Eitelkeit und Schamgefühl. Leipzig, 1928.
Phil 5046.20   Grau, Kurt J. Grundriss der Logik. Leipzig, 1918.
Phil 5722.20   Grau, Kurt Joachim. Bewusstsein, Unbewusstes, Unterbewusstes. München, 1922.

Phil 5585.224   Grauman, C.F. Grundlagen einer Phänomenologie und Psychologie der Perspektivität. Berlin, 1960.
Phil 5520.438   Graumann, Carl F. Denken. Köln, 1965.
Phil 6830.6.4   Die Grausamkeit mit besonder Bezugnahme auf sexuelle Factoren. 4. Aufl. (Rau, Hans.) Berlin, 1921.

Phil 5520.586   Grava, Arnolds. A structural inquiry into the symbolic representation of ideas. The Hague, 1969.

Phil 287.4   Grave, F. Das Chaos als objektive Weltregion. Berlin, 1924.

Phil 1806.10   Grave, Selwyn A. The Scottish philosophy of common sense. Oxford, 1960.

Phil 6956.12   Graves, Alonzo. The eclipse of a mind. N.Y., 1942.
Phil 2835.82   Graves, F.P. Peter Ramus and educational reforms of the 16th century. N.Y., 1912.

X Cg   Phil 8631.11   Graves, Hiram A. Attractions of heaven. Boston, 1846?
Phil 7082.72.5   Graves, Robert. The meaning of dreams. London, 1924.
Phil 181.29   Gravesande, G.J. Introductio ad philosophiam. Leidae, 1736.

Phil 7069.15.28   Gravies, L.C. The natural order of spirit. Boston, 1915.
Phil 9346.10A   Gray, Arthur Herbert. Men, women and God. N.Y., 1922.
Phil 8696.7   Gray, Asa. Natural science and religion. N.Y., 1880.
Phil 2905.1.595   Gray, Donald P. The one and the many. N.Y., 1969.
Phil 3425.307A   Gray, J.G. Hegel's Hellenic ideal. N.Y., 1941.
Phil 7069.20.140   Gray, James M. Spiritism and the fallen angels in the light of the Old and New Testaments. N.Y., 1920.

Phil 5625.75.100   Gray, Jeffrey Alan. Pavlov's typology. N.Y., 1964.
Phil 5850.221   Gray, John S. Psychology in use. N.Y., 1941.
Phil 7082.136   Gray, Robert. The theory of dreams: in which an inquiry is made into the powers and faculties of the human mind. v.1-2. London, 1808.

Phil 3801.434A   Gray-Smith, R. God in the philosophy of Schelling. Diss. Philadelphia, 1933.

Phil 9558.7   Grayson, P.W. Vice unmasked; an essay. N.Y., 1830.
Phil 181.15   Grazia, V. de. Saggio...della scienza umana. Napoli, 1839.

Phil 5090.4   Gréard, Mlle. La certitude philosophique. Paris, 1883.
Phil 8586.6   Gréard, Mlle. Du doute. Paris, 1867.
Phil 5425.108   Great abnormals; the pathological genius of Kafka, Van Gogh, Strindenberg and Poe. (Grant, Vernon W.) N.Y., 1968.

Phil 6957.12   The great abnormals. (Hyslop, T.B.) London, 1925.
Phil 7060.139.5   The great Amherst mystery. 10th ed. (Hubbell, Walter.) N.Y., 1916

Phil 8703.2.5   The great amphibium; four lectures. (Needham, Joseph.) London, 1931.

Phil 1750.126.3   The great betrayal. (Benda, Julien.) London, 1928.
Phil 7069.19.20   The great beyond and its inhabitants. (Boyce, Adam.) London, 1919.

Phil 8882.26   Great books as life teachers. (Hillis, N.D.) Edinburgh, 1900.

Phil 9230.13   Great Britain. Commission on Lotteries and Betting, 1932-33. Final report. London, 1933.

Phil 9230.13.5F   Great Britain. Commission on Lotteries and Betting, 1932-33. Minutes of evidence...first 24 days, Thursday, 30 June, 1932-Thursday, 23 February, 1933. Pt.1-24. London, 1932-33.

Phil 6947.1.5   Great Britain. Commissioners in Lunacy. Further report. London, 1847.

Phil 292.8A   The great chain of being. (Lovejoy, A.O.) Cambridge, Mass., 1936.

Phil 292.8.5   The great chain of being. (Lovejoy, A.O.) Cambridge, Mass., 1957.

Phil 292.8.6   The great chain of being. (Lovejoy, A.O.) Cambridge, Mass., 1965.

Phil 293.21   The great design. (Mason, F.B. (Mrs.).) N.Y., 1935.
Phil 7054.82   Great discussion of modern spritualism. (Grimes, J.S.) Boston, 1860.

Phil 8591.44.15A   The great divorce. (Lewis, Clive Staples.) N.Y., 1946.
Phil 8591.8   The great enigma. (Lilly, W.S.) N.Y., 1892.
Phil 5254.3.5   The great enterprise. 1st. ed. (Overstreet, H. Allen.) N.Y., 1952.

Phil 5216.2   Great experiments in psychology. (Garrett, Henry E.) N.Y., 1930.

Phil 5216.2.5   Great experiments in psychology. (Garrett, Henry E.) N.Y., 1941.

Phil 9575.3   Great fortunes: The winning, the using. (Jenks, J.W.) N.Y., 1906.

Phil 530.20.90   The great German mystics. (Clark, J.M.) Oxford, 1949.
Phil 7054.6.9   The great harmonia. 4th ed. (Davis, A.J.) Boston, 1870. 5v.

Phil 8663.3.83   The great Ingersoll controversy. Photoreproduction. N.Y., 189-?

Phil 6317.33   Great men. (Hitschmann, E.) N.Y., 1956.
Phil 9530.19   Great men being the substance of a lecture. Calcutta, 1868.

Phil 8708.29.10   The great monkey trial. 1. ed. (De Camp, Lyon Sprague.) Garden City, 1968.

Phil 8636.4   The great morning. (Lathbury, C.) Minneapolis, 1911.
Phil 2115.148   The great Mr. Locke, America's philosopher, 1783-1861. (Curti, M.) n.p., 19- .

Phil 130.5   The great philosophers. (Tomlin, E.W.F.) London, 1949?
Phil 184.19.35   The great philosophers. 1. American ed. (Jaspers, K.) N.Y., 1962. 2v.

Phil 809.4   Great philosophies of the world. (Joad, C.E.M.) N.Y., 1933.

Phil 7069.28.40   The great problem and the evidence. (Johnson, G.L.) London, 1928.

Phil 196.8   The great problems. (Varisco, B.) London, 1914.
Phil 7069.02.17   The great psychological crime. 11th ed. (Richardson, J.E.) Chicago, 1912.

Phil 5232.10   The great psychologists. (Watson, Robert Irving.) Philadelphia, 1963.

Phil 5232.10.2   The great psychologists from Aristotle to Freud. 2. ed. (Watson, Robert Irving.) Philadelphia, 1968.

Phil 197.66   The great quest. (Woods, A.) n.p., n.d.
Phil 9575.2   Great riches. (Eliot, C.W.) N.Y., 1906.
Phil 1524.1   The great schoolmen of the Middle Ages. (Townsend, W.J.) London, 1881.

Phil 7054.127   The great secret, and its unfoldment in occultism. 2. ed. (Davies, Charles M.) London, 1896.

Phil 803.9   Great thinkers; the quest of life for its meaning. (Duvall, T.G.) N.Y., 1937.

Phil 812.21   Great visions of philosophy. (Mantague, W.) La Salle, Ill., 1950.

Phil 7069.06.35   The great work. 12. ed. (Richardson, J.E.) Chicago, 1911.
Phil 8894.17.20   The greatest thing ever known. (Trine, Ralph W.) N.Y., 1898.

Phil 178.12.60   The greatest truth. (Dresser, H.W.) N.Y., 1907.
Phil 821.1.20   Greatness and philosophy. (Vycinas, Vincent.) The Hague, 1966.

Phil 665.20   The greatness of the human soul. (Kirk, Edward N.) Boston, 1844.

Phil 3310.10   Grebe, W. Geist und Sache. Frankfurt, 1934.
Phil 5046.22.10   Grebe, Wilhelm. Erkennen und Zeit. München, 1931.
Phil 5046.22   Grebe, Wilhelm. Die Form des Erkennens. München, 1929.
Phil 181.55   Greca, Carlo. L'esistere quale oggetto di scienza e di storia. Parte 1a. Girgenti, 1925.

Phil 806.14   Greca, Carlo. Storia della filosofia. Palermo, 1951.
Phil 806.14.2   Greca, Carlo. Storia della filosofia. 2. ed. Firenze, 1956.

Phil 260.14   Grécki atomisti a epikuros. (Okál, M.) Bratislava, 1953.
Phil 1535.18.5   Gredt, Joseph. Die aristotelisch-thomistische Philosophie. Freiburg, 1935. 2v.

Phil 1535.18.4   Gredt, Joseph. Elementa philosophia. Barcinone, 1961. 2v.

Phil 1535.18   Gredt, Joseph. Elementa philosophiae Aristotelico-Thomisticae. Romae, 1899.

Phil 181.90.5   Gredt, Joseph. Elementa philosophiae Aristotelico-Thomisticae. 7. ed. v.2. Friburgi, 1937.

Phil 1535.18.3   Gredt, Joseph. Elementa philosophiae Aristotelico-Thomisticae. 12. ed. Barcinone, 1958.

Phil 8620.24   Gree, Peter. The problem of evil. London, 1920.
Phil 600.25   Greef, Guillaume. Problémes de philosophie positive. Paris, 1900.

Phil 5477.16   Greeff, Etienne de. L'homme et son juge. Paris, 1962.
Phil 8062.2   Greek aesthetic theory...in...Plato and Aristotle. (Warry, John Gibson.) London, 1962.

Phil 1158.25.2   The Greek atomists and Epicurus. (Bailey, Cyril.) N.Y., 1964.

Phil 1158.25A   The Greek atomists and Epicurus. (Bailey, Cyril.) Oxford, 1928.

Phil 1153.15   The Greek cynics. (Sayre, Farrand.) Baltimore, 1948.
Phil 1145.74   Greek ethical thought. (Oakeley, Hilda D.) London, 1925.
Phil 8600.4   The Greek gospel; an interpretation of the coming faith. (Usher, E.P.) Grafton, Mass., 1909.

Phil 1020.44   Greek into Arabic. (Walzer, Richard.) Cambridge, 1962. 2v.

Phil 1020.44.2   Greek into Arabic. (Walzer, Richard.) Oxford, 1962.
Phil 1145.35   Greek morality in relation to institutions. (Jones, W.H.S.) London, 1906.

Phil 1106.3   The Greek philosophers. (Benn, A.W.) London, 1882. 2v.

Phil 1106.3.2A   The Greek philosophers. (Benn, A.W.) London, 1914.
Phil 1111.12   The Greek philosophers from Thales to Aristotle. (Guthrie, William.) N.Y., 1950.

Phil 1120.4   Greek philosophical terms; a historical lexicon. (Peters, Francis E.) N.Y., 1967.

Phil 1111.12.5   Greek philosophy. (Guthrie, William.) Cambridge, Eng., 1953.

Phil 1124.3   Greek philosophy. (Taylor, M.E.J.) London, 1924.
Phil 1126.2   Greek philosophy. (Vogel, C.) Leiden, 1950. 3v.
Phil 1100.1   Pamphlet vol. Greek philosophy. German. 8 pam.
Phil 1100.2   Pamphlet vol. Greek philosophy. German dissertations. 16 pam.

Phil 1100.3   Pamphlet box. Greek philosophy. German dissertations. 7 pam.

Phil 1106.8   Greek philosophy. pt. 1. (Burnet, J.) London, 1914.
Phil 1106.8.4   Greek philosophy. pt.1. (Burnet, J.) London, 1928.
Phil 1133.23   Greek philosophy before Plato. (Scoon, Robert.) Princeton, 1928.

Phil 1190.9   The Greek sceptics. (Patrick, Mary M.) N.Y., 1929.
Phil 1190.4   Greek sceptics from Pyrrho to Sextus. (Maccoll, N.) London, 1869.

Phil 1190.30   Greek skepticism; a study in epistemology. (Stough, Charlotte L.) Berkeley, 1969.

Phil 1195.21   Greek sophists in the Roman empire. (Bowersock, Glen Warren.) Oxford, 1969.

Phil 1140.5   Greek theorie of elementary cognition. (Beare, J.G.) Oxford, 1906.

Phil 1111.1.11   Greek thinkers; a history of ancient philosophy. (Gomperz, T.) London, 1905-13. 4v.

Phil 1111.1.9   Greek thinkers and history of ancient philosophy. v.4. (Gomperz, T.) London, 1901.

Phil 1122.6.5   Greek thought. (Robin, Léon.) N.Y., 1928.
Phil 1850.137.5   Green, Adwin W. Sir Francis Bacon. N.Y., 1966.
Phil 1850.137   Green, Adwin W. Sir Francis Bacon. Syracuse, N.Y., 1948.
Phil 9070.121   Green, Celia Elizabeth. The human evasion. London, 1969.
Phil 5585.250   Green, David Marvin. Signal detection theory and psychophysics. N.Y., 1966.

Phil 5535.38   Green, Edward J. An annotated bibliography of visual discrimination learning. N.Y., 1969.

Phil 7054.138   Green, Frances H. Biography of Mrs. Semantha Mettler. N.Y., 1853.

Phil 5246.32.5   Green, G.H. The mind in action. London, 1923.
Phil 7084.16   Green, George Henry. The terror-dream. London, 1927.
Phil 7069.21.37   Green, H.L. Think on these things. Pasadena, 1921.
Phil 181.16   Green, Joseph Henry. Spiritual philosophy. London, 1865.
Phil 9230.14   Green, Peter. Betting and gambling. London, 1927.
Phil 8407.30   Green, Peter. The problem of art; a text book of aesthetics. London, 1937.

Phil 8956.7   Green, Peter. The problem of right conduct. London, 1931.
Phil 6956.15   Green, Sidney L. A manual of first aid for mental health. N.Y., 1955.

	Phil 2020.30A	Green, T.H. Prolegomena to ethics. Oxford, 1883.
	Phil 2020.30.2A	Green, T.H. Prolegomena to ethics. 2d ed. Oxford, 1884.
	Phil 2020.30.3A	Green, T.H. Prolegomena to ethics. 3d ed. Oxford, 1890.
	Phil 2020.30.4	Green, T.H. Prolegomena to ethics. 4th ed. Oxford, 1899.
	Phil 2020.30.5	Green, T.H. Prolegomena to ethics. 5th ed. Oxford, 1924.
	Phil 2020.30.15	Green, T.H. Prolegomena to ethics. 5th ed. Oxford, 1929.
Htn	Phil 2020.32*	Green, T.H. The witness of God and faith. London, 1886.
	Phil 2020.10	Green, T.H. Works. v.1,3. London, 1886-88. 2v.
X Cg	Phil 2020.15A	Green, T.H. Works of Thomas H. Green. London, 1906. 3v.
	Phil 5465.110	Greenacre, P. Estudios psicoanalíticos sobre la actividad creadora. 1. ed. México, 1960.
	Phil 5590.115A	Greenacre, P. Trauma, growth and personality. London, 1953.
	Phil 6625.10	Greenacre, Phyllis. Affective disorders. N.Y., 1961.
	Phil 6420.4	Greenbaum, Ferdinand. Erklärung des Stotterns, dessèn Heilung und Verhütung. Leipzig, 1897.
	Phil 6980.335.20	Greenberg, Ira A. Psychodrama and audience attitude change. Beverly Hills, 1968.
	Phil 4065.126	Greenberg, S. The infinite in Giordano Bruno. N.Y., 1950.
	Phil 9070.20	Greenbie, M.L.B. The art of living in wartime. N.Y., 1943.
	Phil 9590.12	Greene, Alice. The philosophy of silence. N.Y., 1940.
	Phil 7069.11.30	Greene, Anvernetta (pseud.). Psychisms through Anvernetta Greene. Newark, 1911.
	Phil 8696.21	Greene, J.C. Darwin and the modern world view. Baton Rouge, 1961.
	Phil 6420.28	Greene, James S. I was a stutterer; stories from life. N.Y., 1932.
	Phil 6116.20	Greene, John G. The emmanuel movement, 1906-1929. n.p., 1934.
	Phil 8661.14	Greene, K.C. The evolution of the conception of God. Boston, 1934.
	Phil 2880.8.132	Greene, Norman. Jean Paul Sartre. Ann Arbor, 1960.
	Phil 2270.81	Greene, W.B. Facts of consciousness and philosophy of Spencer. Boston, 1871.
Htn	Phil 705.26*	Greene, William B. Transcendentalism. West Brookfield, 1849.
	Phil 6316.23	Greenfield, Norman S. Psychoanalysis and current biological thought. Madison, 1965.
	Phil 8407.37	Greenough, H. Form and function; remarks on art. Berkeley, 1947.
	Phil 2030.1.80	Greenslet, F. Joseph Glanvill. N.Y., 1900.
	Phil 6316.27	Greenson, Ralph R. The technique and practice of psychoanalysis. London, 1967.
	Phil 972.15	Greenwalt, E.A. The Point Loma community in California, 1897-1942. Berkeley, 1955.
	Phil 5046.34	Greenwood, David. The nature of science. N.Y., 1959.
	Phil 5520.195	Greenwood, David. Truth and meaning. N.Y., 1957.
	Phil 8610.902.5	Greenwood, Granville George. The faith of an agnostic. 2. ed. London, 1919.
	Phil 5640.38	Greenwood, Major. Physiology of the special senses. London, 1910.
	Phil 5066.1	Greenwood, T. Les fondements de la logique symbolique. v.1-2. Paris, 1938.
	Phil 8956.22	Greet, Kenneth. The art of moral judgement. London, 1970.
	Phil 337.17	Greeve, T.M. Moral aesthetic and religious insight. New Brunswick, N.J., 1957.
	Phil 8610.883	Greg, Percy. Without God. London, 1883.
	Phil 8881.20.2	Greg, W.R. Enigmas of life. Boston, 1873.
	Phil 8881.20	Greg, W.R. Enigmas of life. London, 1883.
	Phil 8586.37	Greg, William R. The creed of Christendom. London, 1851.
	Phil 8586.37.10	Greg, William R. The creed of Christendom. 5th ed. London, 1877. 2v.
	Phil 6676.5	Gregary, William. Letters to a candid inquirer on animal magnetism. London, 1851.
	Phil 5246.51	Gregg, F.M. Psychology of a growing personality. Lincoln, 1938.
	Phil 8586.50	Gregg, R.B. Self-transcendence. London, 1956.
NEDL	Phil 181.150	Gregg, Richard B. What's it all about and what am I? N.Y., 1968.
	Phil 181.150.5	Gregg, Richard B. What's it all about and what am I? 1. Indian ed. Ahmedabad, 1967.
	Phil 8661.19	Grégoire, A. Immanence et transcendance. Bruxelles, 1939.
	Phil 2128.85	Grégoire, F. Bernard de Mandeville et la "Fable des Abeilles". Thèse. Nancy, 1947.
	Phil 337.18	Gregoire, F. La nature du psychique. 1. ed. Paris, 1957.
	Phil 8831.12	Grégoire, François. Leo grandes doctrines morales. Paris, 1958.
	Phil 3425.734	Grégoire, Franz. L'attitude Hégélienne devant l'existence. Louvain, 1953.
	Phil 3425.430A	Grégoire, Franz. Études Hegeliennes. Louvain, 1958.
	Phil 1750.390	Gregoire, Franz. Questions concernant l'existentialisme. 2. ed. Louvain, 1955.
	Phil 310.611	Gregor, A. James. A survey of Marxism. N.Y., 1965.
	Phil 6316.4	Gregor, Adalbert. Leitfaden der experimentellen Psychopathologie. Berlin, 1910.
	Phil 3488.39	Gregor, Mary J. Laws of freedom. N.Y., 1963.
	Phil 5046.10	Gregory, D.S. Practical logic. Philadelphia, 1881.
	Phil 8956.3	Gregory, Daniel. Christian ethics. Philadelphia, 1875.
	Phil 5816.1.2	Gregory, J. A comparative view...man...animal world. London, 1765.
	Phil 5816.1	Gregory, J. A comparative view...man...animal world. London, 1766.
	Phil 5525.23A	Gregory, J.C. The nature of laughter. London, 1924.
X Cg	Phil 9346.6.3	Gregory, John. A father's legacy to his daughters. Albany, 1821.
	Phil 9346.6	Gregory, John. A father's legacy to his daughters. London, 1822.
Htn	Phil 9346.6.5*	Gregory, John. A father's legacy to his daughters. N.Y., 1775.
Htn	Phil 9346.6.2*	Gregory, John. A father's legacy to his daughters. Philadelphia, 1781.
	Phil 8696.17	Gregory, R.A. Religion in science and civilization. London, 1940.
	Phil 2115.124	Gregory, Raymond. A study of Locke's theory of knowledge. Wilmington, Ohio, 1919.
	Phil 2115.124.5	Gregory, Raymond. A study of Locke's theory of knowledge. Thesis. Wilmington, Ohio, 1919.
	Phil 5643.126	Gregory, Richard Langton. Eye and brain. N.Y., 1966.
	Phil 1540.55	Gregory, Tullio. Platonismo medievale. Roma, 1958.
	Phil 2610.110	Gregory, Tullio. Scetticismo ed empirismo. Bari, 1961.
	Phil 5374.220	Greidanus, J.H. Fundamental physical theory and the concept of consciousness. Oxford, 1961.
	Phil 2050.196	Greig, John Y.T. David Hume. London, 1931.
	Phil 530.20.15	Greith, Carl. Die deutsche Mystik. Freiburg, 1861.
	Phil 1116.3	Den grekiska filosofien. (Larsson, Hans.) Stockholm, 1921.
	Phil 6990.30	Grellety, L. Du merveilleux, des miracles et des pelerinages au point de vue medical. Paris, 1876.
	Phil 1750.171	Grene, M. Dreadful freedom. Chicago, 1948.
	Phil 337.27	Grene, Marjorie. The knower and the known. N.Y., 1966.
	Phil 3450.19.150	Grene, Marjorie. Martin Heidegger. London, 1957.
	Phil 1111.2	Grenet, P.B. Histoire de la philosophie ancienne. Paris, 1960.
	Phil 2905.1.165	Grenet, Paul. Teilhard de Chardin. Paris, 1961.
	Phil 8631.13	Grenfell, W.T. On immortality. Boston, 1912.
	Phil 9070.31	Grenfell, W.T. The prize of life. N.Y., 1914.
	Phil 181.108	Grenier, H. Thomistic philosophy. Charlotte-town, Canada, 1950. 4v.
	Phil 181.131.5	Grenier, J. Conversations on the good uses of freedom. 1. American ed. Cambridge, 1967.
	Phil 181.131	Grenier, J. Entretiens sur le bon usage de la liberté. Paris, 1948.
	Phil 8407.44.5	Grenier, Jean. L'art et ses problèmes. Lausanne, 1970.
	Phil 735.121	Grenier, Jean. Le choix. Paris, 1941.
	Phil 1706.15	Grenier, Jean. Essai sur l'esprit d'orthodoxie. Paris, 1967.
	Phil 9240.14	Grenier, Jean. L'existence malheureuse. Paris, 1957.
	Phil 8080.18	Grenier, Jean. L'imitation et les principes de l'esthétique classique. Paris, 1963.
	Phil 2725.13.90	Grenier, Jean. La philosophie de Jules Lequier. Paris, 1936.
	Phil 2725.13.91	Grenier, Jean. La philosophie de Jules Lequier. Thèse. Paris, 1936.
	Phil 8407.44	Grenier, Jean. Vicissitudes de l'esthétique et révolutions du gout. Paris, 1966.
	Phil 8586.38	Grensted, L.W. Philosophical implications of Christianity. Oxford, 1930.
	Phil 5627.192	Grensted, L.W. The psychology of religion. N.Y., 1952.
Htn	Phil 2115.96*	Grenville. Oxford and Locke. London, 1829.
	Phil 8411.10	Die Grenzen der Ästhetik. (Keussler, G. von.) Leipzig, 1902.
	Phil 348.26	Grenzen der Erkenntnis. (Reinisch, Leonhard.) Freiburg, 1969.
	Phil 8880.46	Grenzen der Ethik. (Freudenberg, G.) Leipzig, 1927.
	Phil 8401.8	Die Grenzen der Kunst und die Buntfarbigkeit der Antike. (Alt, Theodor.) Berlin, 1886.
	Phil 978.49.759	Grenzen der Naturerkenntnis. 4. Aufl. (Steiner, R.) Dornach, 1969.
	Phil 194.7	Grenzen der Philosophie. (Tobias, W.) Berlin, 1875.
	Phil 6025.9.10	Die Grenzen der Physiognomik; mit 30 Bildtafeln. (Picard, Max.) Erlenbach, 1937.
	Phil 510.1.24	Grenzen der Religion und Naturwissenschaft. (Hansen, Adolf.) Giessen, 1908.
	Phil 575.110	Grenzen der Seele. (Lucka, E.) Berlin, 1916.
	Phil 1730.22	Grenzen liberaler Aufklärung bei Kant und Anderen. (Denker, Rolf.) Stuttgart, 1968.
	Phil 333.4.5	Die Grenzen und der Ursprung der menschlichen Erkenntniss. (Czolbe, H.) Jena, 1865.
	Phil 16.2	Grenzfragen der Nerven und Seelenlebens. Wiesbaden. 1-130 20v.
	Phil 8708.42.5	Grenzfragen zwischen Naturwissenschaft und Glaube. (Spülbeck, Otto.) München, 1970.
	Phil 8520.60	Grenzwege. (Krieger, Evelina.) Freiburg, 1968.
	Phil 6117.10	Die Grenzwissenschaften der Psychologie. (Hellpach, W.) Leipzig, 1902.
	Phil 181.17	Greppo, C. The exegesis of life. N.Y., 1889.
	Phil 8586.7	Gresley, W. Thoughts on religion and philosophy. London, 1875.
	Phil 8407.12	Greswell, R. On education in the principles of art. Oxford, 1844.
	Phil 1706.9	Grevillot, J.M. Les grands courants de la pensée contemporaine. Paris, 1948.
Htn	Phil 8500.1*	Grew, N. Cosmologia sacra. London, 1701.
	Phil 5545.13.2	Grey, R. Memoria technica. Dublin, 1796.
	Phil 5545.13	Grey, R. Memoria technica. London, 1730.
	Phil 5545.13.3	Grey, R. Memoria technica. London, 1806.
	Phil 7060.111.15	The grey ghost book. (Middleton, Jessie A.) London, 1915.
	Phil 1865.81	Greyvenstein, J.H.J.A. Het sociale utilisme van Bentham. Utrecht, 1911.
	Phil 8881.78	Grice, Geoffry R. The grounds of moral judgement. Cambridge, 1967.
	Phil 8696.9	Gridley, Albert L. First chapter of Genesis as the rock foundation for science and religion. Boston, 1913.
	Phil 7054.69	Gridley, J.A. Astounding facts from the spirit world. South Hampton, 1854.
	Phil 1124.2	Griechenlands erste Philosophen. (Tiedemann, D.) Leipzig, 1780.
	Phil 1111.1	Griechische Denker. (Gomperz, T.) Leipzig, 1893. 3v.
	Phil 1111.1.5	Griechische Denker. (Gomperz, T.) Leipzig, 1903-09. 3v.
	Phil 1111.1.7	Griechische Denker. 4. Aufl. (Gomperz, T.) Berlin, 1922-31. 3v.
	Phil 8587.65.10	Griechische oder biblische Theologie. (Hessen, Johannes.) München, 1962.
	Phil 1107.3	Die griechische Philosophie. (Capelle, Wilhelm.) Berlin, 1922-34. 3v.
	Phil 1135.23	Griechische Philosophie im alten Testament. (Friedländer, M.) Berlin, 1904.
	Phil 1135.23.9	Griechische Philosophie und altes Testament. (Heinisch, Paul.) Münster, 1913-14. 2v.
	Phil 1112.7.5	Die griechische Philosophie von Thales bis Platon. (Hoffmann, Ernst.) Heidelberg, 1951.
	Phil 1112.7	Die griechische Philosophie von Thales bis Platon. (Hoffmann, Ernst.) Leipzig, 1921.
	Phil 1116.4	Griechische Philosophie von Thales bis Platon. (Leisegang, H.) Breslau, 1922.
	Phil 1135.52	Griechische Philosophinnen. (Poestion, J.C.) Bremen, 1882.
	Phil 1135.25	Griechische Religionsphilosophie. (Gilbert, O.) Leipzig, 1911.
	Phil 1127.3	Griechische Weltanschauung. (Wundt, Max.) Leipzig, 1910.
	Phil 3915.66.2	Griechische Weltanschauung. 2. Aufl. (Wundt, Wilhelm.) Leipzig, 1917.
	Phil 1118.3	Griechische Weltanschauung in ihrer Bedeutung für die Gegenwart. (Nestle, W.) Stuttgart, 1946.
	Phil 1195.17	Grieder, H. Die Bedeutung der Sophistik. Basel, 1962.
	Phil 5403.10	Griefs and discontents. (Rochlin, Gregory.) London, 1965.
	Phil 5400.172	Griefs and discontents. 1. ed. (Rochlin, Gregory.) Boston, 1965.
	Phil 4635.9.30	Grieg, Harald V. Torgny Segershedt. Oslo, 1945.
	Phil 5525.22	Grieg, J.Y.J. The psychology of laughter and comedy. London, 1923.
	Phil 6956.2.5	Griesinger, W. Mental pathology and therapeutics. London, 1867.

Phil 6956.2   Griesinger, W. Die Pathologie und Therapie der psychischen Krankheiten. Braunschweig, 1871.

Htn Phil 6956.2.2*   Griesinger, W. Die Pathologie und Therapie der psychischen Krankheiten. Stuttgart, 1867.

Phil 5627.266.15   Griesl, Gottfried. Pastoralpsychologische Studien. Innsbruck, 1966.

Phil 3640.184   Griesser, Luitpold. Nietzsche und Wagner. Wien, 1923.

Phil 2050.243   Grieve, C.M. The man of (almost) independent mind. Edinburgh, 1962.

Phil 3925.16.100   Griffin, J.P. Wittgenstein's logical atomism. Oxford, 1964.

Phil 8631.12   Griffin, N.E. The farther shore; an anthology...on the immortality of the soul. Boston, 1934.

Phil 5648.9   Griffing, H. On sensations from pressure and impact. N.Y., 1895.

Phil 5246.31.5   Griffith, C.R. General introduction to psychology. N.Y., 1924.

Phil 5246.31.2   Griffith, C.R. General introduction to psychology. N.Y., 1928.

Phil 5816.10   Griffith, C.R. An historical survey of vestibular equilibration. Urbana, 1922.

Phil 5850.222   Griffith, C.R. An introduction to applied psychology. N.Y., 1936.

Phil 5246.31.10   Griffith, C.R. Principles of systematic psychology. Urbana, 1943.

Phil 8586.48   Griffith, G.O. Interpreters of man. London, 1943.

Phil 181.18   Griffith, J. Behind the veil. London, 1876.

Phil 5246.39   Griffith, Percy. A synthetic psychology. London, 1927.

Phil 337.35   Griffiths, A. Phillips. Knowledge and belief. London, 1967.

Phil 2855.8.80   Griffiths, David Albert. Jean Reynaud, encyclopédiste de l'époque romantique d'après sa correspondance inédite. Paris, 1965.

Phil 5465.26   Griffitts, Charles H. Individual differences in imagery. Diss. n.p., 1919?

Phil 8661.11   Griffths, Rees. God in idea and experience. Edinburgh, 1931.

Phil 8407.24   Griggs, Edward. The philosophy of art. N.Y., 1913.

Phil 8881.55   Griggs, Edward H. The use of the margin. N.Y., 1907.

Phil 8610.914   Griggs, H.S. The book of truth. Brooklyn, 1914.

Phil 3488.38   Grigor'ian, B.T. Neokantianstvo. Moskva, 1962.

Phil 1020.40   Grigorian, S.N. Iz istorii filosofii Srednei Azii i Irana VII-XII vv. Moskva, 1960.

Phil 1020.41   Grigorian, S.N. Izbrannye proizredenii myshtelei stran Blizhnego Srednego Vostoka. Moskva, 1961.

Phil 1135.167   Grilli, A. Il problema della vita contemplativa nel mondo greco-romano. 1. ed. Milano, 1953.

Phil 4073.104.10   Grillo, F. Questioni Campanelliane. Cosenza, 1961.

Phil 4073.104.2   Grillo, F. A supplement to the critical bibliography. N.Y., 1957. 2v.

Phil 4073.104   Grillo, F. Tommaso Campanella in America. N.Y., 1954.

Phil 8586.60   Grillo, Friedrich. Aphoristische Darstellung der Religion. Bruxelles, 1968.

Phil 365.62   Grillo, Ugo. Ultimo umanesimo. Bari, 1966.

Phil 4260.133   Grimaldi, A.A. The universal humanity of Giambattista Vico. N.Y., 1958.

Phil 9177.3   Grimaldi Robbio, Pelegro de. Discorsi de...ne'quali si ragiona compiutamente. Genova, 1585.

Phil 9245.38   Grimanelli, P. La morale positive et le bonheur. Paris, 1924.

Phil 7054.182   Grimard, Edouard. Une échappée sur l'infini. Paris, 1899.

Phil 6676.3   Grimes, J.S. Etherology and the phreno-philosophy. Boston, 1850.

Phil 7054.82   Grimes, J.S. Great discussion of modern spritualism. Boston, 1860.

Phil 6116.4   Grimes, J.S. The mysteries of human nature. Boston, 1860.

Phil 6116.14   Grimké, S.S. Personified unthinkables, an argument against physical causation. Ann Arbor, 1884.

Phil 2520.142   Grimm, E. Descartes' Lehre von den angeborenen Ideen. Inaug.-Diss. Jena, 1873.

Phil 337.1   Grimm, E. Zur Geschichte der Erkenntnis Problems. Leipzig, n.d.

Phil 8586.27   Grimm, E. Die zwei Wege im religiösen Denken. Göttingen, 1922.

Phil 3640.212   Grimm, Eduard. Das Problem Friedrich Nietzsches. Berlin, 1899.

Phil 3280.84   Grimm, Eduard. Arnold Geulincx' Erkenntnisstheorie und Occasionalismus. Jena, 1875.

Phil 1750.410   Grimsley, Ronald. Existentialist thought. Cardiff, 1955.

Phil 1750.410.2   Grimsley, Ronald. Existentialist thought. 2nd ed. Cardiff, 1960.

Phil 2050.107   Grimthorpe, E.B. A review of Hume and Huxley on miracles. London, 1883.

Phil 2880.2.85   Grin, Edmond. Les origines et l'évolution de la pensée de Charles Secrétan. Lausanne, 1930.

Phil 5865.2   Grinder, Robert Eugene. A history of genetic psychology. N.Y., 1967.

Phil 5816.11   Grindley, G.C. The intelligence of animals. London, 1937.

Phil 9495.68   Grindon, Leopold Hartley. The sexuality of nature. Boston, 1868.

Phil 6945.18   Grines, J.M. Institutional care of mental patients in the United States. Chicago, 1934.

Phil 5238.38A   Grinker, R.R. Toward a unified theory of human behavior. 1. ed. N.Y., 1956.

Phil 6956.13   Grinker, Roy. War neuroses in North Africa. N.Y., 1943.

Phil 6980.336.5   Grinker, Roy R. Men under stress. Philadelphia, 1945.

Phil 6327.11.10   Grinstein, A. The index of psychoanalytic writings. N.Y., 1956-60. 10v.

Phil 7082.10   Grinstein, Alexander. On Sigmund Freud's dreams. Detroit, 1968.

Htn Phil 6016.2*   Grisaldi, Paolo. Guidicio di fisionomia. Trevigi, 1620.

Phil 337.11   Grisebach, E. Erkenntnis und Glaube. Halle an der Saale, 1923.

Phil 181.50.10   Grisebach, E. Freiheit und Zucht. Zurich, 1936.

Phil 181.50.5   Grisebach, E. Gegenwart. Halle, 1928.

Phil 337.11.5   Grisebach, E. Probleme der wirklichen Bildung. München, 1923.

Phil 181.50   Grisebach, E. Wahrheit und Wirklichkeiten. Halle, 1919.

Phil 3808.85   Grisebach, E.R. Edita und Inedita Schopenhaueriana. Leipzig, 1888.

Phil 720.35   Grisebach, Eberhard. Was ist Wahrheit in Wirklichkeit? Bern, 1941.

Phil 3808.107.10   Grisebach, Eduard. Schopenhauer. Berlin, 1905.

Phil 2805.107   Griselle, E. Pascal et les Pascalins d'après des documents contemporains. Fribourg, 1908.

Phil 8661.20   Grison, M. Théologie naturelle, ou théodicée. Paris, 1959.

Phil 960.142   Griswold, Hervey De Witt. Brahman: a study in the history of Indian philosophy. N.Y., 1900.

Phil 310.703   Gritsenko, Ivan I. Istoricheskoe i logicheskoe v marksistskoi filosofii. Rostov-na-Donn, 1969.

Phil 8407.4   Griveau, Maurice. Histoire esthétique de la nature. Paris, 1927-30. 3v.

Phil 8407.7   Griveau, Maurice. La sphère de beauté, lois d'évolution. Paris, 1901.

Phil 5046.42   Grize, Jean Blaise. Logique et connaissance. Genève, 1965.

VPhil 3640.766   Grlić, Danko. Ko je Niče. Beograd, 1969.

Phil 181.152   Grlić, Danko. Zašto. Zagreb, 1968.

Phil 5465.184   Groch, Judith. The right to create. 1. ed. Boston, 1970.

Phil 4080.36   Grocholl, Wolfgang. Der Mensch in seinem ursprünglichen Sein nach der Lehre Landulfs von Neapel. München, 1969.

Phil 8661.7   Groddeck, G. Hin zu Gottnatur. 2. Aufl. Leipzig, 1909.

Phil 6316.8.15   Groddeck, Georg. Au fond de l'homme cela. Paris, 1963.

Phil 6316.8.8   Groddeck, Georg. Das Buch vom Es; psychoanalytische Briefe an eine Freuden. 3. Aufl. Leipzig, 1934.

Phil 6316.8.12   Groddeck, Georg. Das Buch vom Es. Wiesbaden, 1961.

Phil 6316.8   Groddeck, Georg. Exploring the unconscious. London, 1933.

Phil 6316.8.13   Groddeck, Georg. The look of the it. N.Y., 1961.

Phil 5520.58   Groddeck, Georg. Der Mensch als Symbol. Wien, 1933.

Phil 6316.8.20   Groddeck, Georg. Psychoanalytische Schriften zur Literatur und Kunst. Wiesbaden, 1964.

Phil 6316.8.10   Groddeck, Georg. Psychoanalytische Schriften zur Psychosomatik. Wiesbaden, 1966.

Phil 5520.424   Grodziński, Eugeniusz. Znaczenie słowa w języku naturalnym. Warszawa, 1964.

Phil 2520.118   Gröber, D. Descartes; Methode des richtigen Vernunftgebrauches 1637. Strassburg, 1914.

Phil 8586.40   Gröbner, Wolfgang. Der Weg Aufwärts. Wien, 1935.

Phil 5875.100   De groei van het geweten. (Andriessen, H.) Zeist, 1965.

Phil 3805.250   Groell, Johannes. Rezeptivität und Spontaneität. Inaug. Diss. Münster? 1966?

Phil 3808.141   Groener, M. Schopenhauer und die Juden. München, 1920.

Phil 3450.10.80   Groenewegen, H.J. Paulus van Hermert, als godgeleerde en als wijsgeer. Proefschrift. Amsterdam, 1889.

Phil 3006.6   Groethuysen, B. Introduction a la pensée philosophique allemande depuis Nietzsche. Paris, 1926.

Phil 585.422   Groethuysen, Bernhard. Antropoligia filosofica. Napoli, 1969.

Phil 585.421   Groethuysen, Bernhard. Philosophische Anthprologie. München, 1931.

Phil 978.98   Grohmann, Gerbert. Die Pflanze als Lichtsinnesorgan der Erde. Stuttgart, 1962.

Htn Phil 3801.435*   Grohmann, J.C.A. De recentissimae philosophiae vanitate. Vitebergae, 1809.

Phil 3488.48   Grohmann, Johann Christian August. Dem Andenken Kants. Berlin 1804. Bruxelles, 1969.

Phil 8586.35   Grohmann, W. Lutherische Metaphysik. Leipzig, 1904.

Phil 3625.16.90   Grohrock, R. Der Kampf der Wesenskultur gegen die Bewusstseinskultur bei Johannes Müller. Inaug. Diss. Speyer, 1937.

Phil 6315.2.360   Grollman, Earl Alan. Judaism in Sigmund Freud's world. N.Y., 1965.

Phil 8407.1   Gromov, Evgenii S. Esteticheskii ideal. Moskva, 1961.

Phil 8407.1.5   Gromov, Evgenii S. Khudozhestvennoe tvorchestvo. Moskva, 1970.

Phil 3006.4   Gronau, Gotthard. Die Philosophie der Gegenwart. Langensalza, 1920-22. 2v.

Phil 3745.20   Gronden en Grenzen. (Peprzak, Adrien T.B.) Haarlem, 1966.

Phil 3665.4.30   Gronden van zekerheid of Die regte betooguyse der wiskundigen. (Nieuwenlijt, B.) Amsterdam, 1728.

Phil 5850.171   Grondvormen van menselijke relaties. (Defares, Peter Bernard.) Assen, 1963.

Phil 6990.3.60   Groneman, William. Bernadette Soubirous. Leuven, 1933.

Phil 1111.6   Groningen, B.A. In the grip of the past. Leiden, 1953.

Phil 3801.437   Groos, Friedrich. Die Schellingische Gottes- und s freiheits - Lehre. Tübingen, 1819.

Phil 400.65   Groos, H. Der deutsche Idealismus und das Christentum. München, 1927.

Phil 5756.12   Groos, Helmut. Die Konsequenzen und Inkonsequenzen des Determinismus. München, 1931.

Phil 5816.3.5   Groos, K. Die Spiele der Menschen. Jena, 1899.

Phil 5816.3   Groos, K. Die Spiele der Thiere. Jena, 1896.

Phil 8407.10   Groos, Karl. Der ästhetische Genuss. Giessen, 1902.

Phil 181.52   Groos, Karl. Der Aufbau der Systeme. Leipzig, 1924.

Phil 8407.10.10   Groos, Karl. Beiträge zur Asthetik. Tübingen, 1924.

Phil 8407.10.5   Groos, Karl. Einleitung in die Asthetik. Giessen, 1892.

Phil 735.104   Groos, Karl. Zur Psychologie und Metaphysik des Wert-Erlebens. Berlin, 1932.

Phil 8881.66   Groos, R. Wertethik oder religiöse Sittlichkeit? München, 1933.

Phil 1750.123   Groot, J.V. de. Denkers van onzen tijd. Uitgevers, 1918.

Phil 91.5   Grooten, J. Filosofisch lexicon. Antwerpen, 1958.

Phil 165.40   Gropp, R.O. Festschrift. Berlin, 1955.

Phil 310.405   Gropp, R.O. Was ist der dialektische Materialismus? München, 1960.

Phil 310.50   Gropp, Rugard Otto. Der dialektische Materialismus. Leipzig, 1958.

Phil 3006.10   Gropp, Rugard Otto. Von Cusanus bis Marx. Leipzig, 1965.

Phil 310.50.5   Gropp, Rugard Otto. Zu Fragen der Geschichte der Philosophie und des dialektischen Materialismus. Berlin, 1959.

Phil 4060.1.98   Groppali, A. Nel settantesimo anniversario di Roberto Ardigò. Torino, 1898.

Htn Phil 8881.67*   Gros, J.D. Natural principles of rectitude. N.Y., 1795.

Phil 1706.10   Grose. Grote filosofieën en de huidige mens. Amsterdam, 1959.

Phil 258.15   Gross, Barry R. Analytic philosophy; an historical introduction. N.Y., 1970.

Phil 337.2   Gross, Felix. Form und Materie des Erkennens. Leipzig, 1910.

Phil 3488.5   Gross, Felix. Kant und Wir. Heidelberg, 1913.

Phil 8520.33   Gross, J. La divinisation du chrétien d'après les pères grecs. Paris, 1938.

Phil 8631.2   Gross, J.B. The belief in immortality. Philadelphia, 1882.

Phil 8881.18   Gross, J.B. What makes us unhappy? Philadelphia, 1882.

Phil 5592.170   Gross, Martin L. The brain watchers. N.Y., 1962.

Phil 6956.4   Gross, Otto. Über psychopatische Minderwertigkuten. Wien, 1909.

Phil 5046.15   Gross, Peter. Vorschule der Logik. Berlin, 1890.

Phil 5400.157   Grossart, Friedrich. Gefühl und Strebung. München, 1961.

Phil 2270.125   Grosse, Ernst. Herbert Spencer's Lehre von dem Unerkennbaren. Leipzig, 1890.

Phil 8407.21   Grosse, Ernst. Kunstwissenschaftliche Studien. Tübingen, 1900.

Phil 978.49.905   Grosse, Rudolf. Erlebte Pädagogik. Dornach, 1968.

Phil 6049.67   Das grosse Buch der Hand. (Mangoldt, Ursula von.) Weilheim, 1967.

Phil 806.3   Grosse Denker. Leipzig, n.d. 2v.

Phil 1750.41   Die grosse Kontroverse. (Herzberg, Günther.) Meisenheim, 1953.

Phil 5425.24   Grosse Männer. (Ostwald, W.) Leipzig, 1909.

Phil 481.4   Grosse Materialisten. (Gurst, Guenter.) Leipzig, 1965.

Phil 178.63   Der grosse Universende. (Dallago, Carl.) Innsbruck, 1924.

Phil 1750.132.10   Grosselin, O. The intuitive voluntarism of Irving Babbitt. Latrohe, Pa., 1951.

Phil 1750.740   Die grossen Dialektiker des 19. Jahrhunderts. (Heiss, R.) Köln, 1963.

Phil 1819.1   Die grossen englischen Philosophen, Locke, Berkeley, Hume. (Thormeyer, Paul.) Leipzig, 1915.

Phil 184.19.30   Die grossen Philosophen. (Jaspers, K.) München, 1957.

Phil 9495.169.10   Die grossen Tabus. (Speicher, Günter.) Düsseldorf, 1969.

Phil 296.8.3   Die grossen Welträtsel. (Pesch, Tilmann.) Freiburg, 1907. 2v.

Phil 5046.37   Grosser, S. Pharus intellectus, sive logica. Lipsiae, 1703.

Phil 1850.28   Grosskanzlers von England moralische, politische und ökonomische Versuche. (Bacon, Francis.) Breslau, 1762.

Phil 6316.8.30   Grossman, Carl M. The wild analyst. N.Y., 1965.

Phil 9166.7   Grossman, J.S. Do you know your daughter? N.Y., 1944.

Phil 2636.82.3   Grossman, Mordecai. The philosophy of Helvetius. N.Y., 1926.

Phil 2636.82   Grossman, Mordecai. Philosophy of Helvetius. Thesis. N.Y., 1926.

Phil 9530.60.2   Grossmann, Gustav. Meine Daktor-Dissertation...die Revolution der Begabten. 2. Aufl. München, 1964.

Phil 6676.7   Grossmann, J. Die Bedeutung der hypnotischen Suggestion als Heilmittel. Berlin, 1894.

Phil 8881.32   Grossmann, L. The real life. N.Y., 1914.

Phil 3270.12.110   Grossmann, Reinhardt S. Reflections on Frege's philosophy. Evanston, 1969.

Phil 337.25   Grossmann, Reinhardt Siegbert. The structure of mind. Madison, 1965.

Phil 8696.2   Grote, A.R. The new infidelity. N.Y., 1881.

Phil 5046.23   Grote, Albert. Über die Funktion der Copula. Leipzig, 1935.

Phil 8881.19   Grote, G. Fragments on ethical subjects. London, 1876.

Phil 2030.4   Grote, George. Analysis of the influence of natural religion on the temporal happiness of mankind. London, 1822.

Phil 2035.80.20A   Grote, George. Review of the work of Mr. John Stuart Mill. London, 1868.

Phil 9550.2   Grote, J. An examination of the utilitarian philosophy. Cambridge, 1870.

Phil 181.20   Grote, J. Exploratio philosophica. Cambridge, 1865.

Phil 8881.17   Grote, J. The moral ideals. Cambridge, 1876.

Phil 3552.119.5   Grote, Ludwig. Leibniz und seine Zeit. Hannover, 1869.

Phil 1706.10   Grote filosofieën en de huidige mens. (Grose.) Amsterdam, 1959.

Phil 3903.5.35   Het grote gebeuren. (Verhoeven, Cornelius W.M.) Utrecht, 1966.

Phil 5640.34   Grotenfelt, A. Das Webersche Gesetz und die psychische Relativität. Helsingfors, 1888.

Phil 8080.11   Das Groteske, seine Gestaltung in Malerei und Dichtung. (Kayser, Wolfgang.) Oldenburg, 1957.

Phil 8125.36   Das Groteske in der Ästhetik seit Kant. (Krudewig, B.) Bergisch, 1934.

Phil 8080.11.1   Das Groteske in Malerei und Dichtung. (Kayser, Wolfgang.) Reinbek, 1960.

Phil 8050.65.5   The grotesque in art and literature. (Kayser, W.) Bloomington, 1963.

Phil 5875.170   Grotloh-Amberg, Heidi. Beeinflussung des Verhaltens durch den Schuleintritt. Bern, 1971.

Phil 8436.5   Il grottesco nell'arte e nella letteratura. (Gori, Gino.) Roma, 1926.

Phil 530.50.5   Groult, Pierre. Les mystiques des Pays-Bas. Louvain, 1927.

Phil 2270.82   Ground, W.D. Examination of Herbert Spencer's theory of the will. London, 1883.

Phil 193.64.9   The ground and goal of human life. (Shaw, C.G.) N.Y., 1919.

Phil 5125.19.5A   The ground of induction. (Williams, Donald C.) N.Y., 1963.

Phil 8881.78   The grounds of moral judgement. (Grice, Geoffry R.) Cambridge, 1967.

Htn   Phil 294.4.2F*   Grounds of natural philosophy. 2. ed. (Newcastle, M.L.C.) London, 1668.

Phil 8585.6   The grounds of theistic and Christian belief. (Fisher, G.P.) N.Y., 1883.

Phil 8585.6.3   The grounds of theistic and Christian belief. (Fisher, G.P.) N.Y., 1885.

Phil 5062.17.8   Groundwork of logic. (Welton, James.) London, 1921.

Phil 5258.27.5   Groundwork of psychology. (Stout, G.F.) N.Y., 1903.

Phil 5258.27.6   Groundwork of psychology. 2d ed. (Stout, G.F.) London, 1927.

Phil 343.2   The groundwork of science. (Mivart, G.) N.Y., 1898.

Phil 8591.55   Groundwork of the philosophy of religion. (Lee, Atkinson.) London, 1946.

Phil 5245.32.5   Group experiments in elementary psychology. (Ford, Adelbert.) N.Y., 1932.

Phil 70.65   Group for the Advancement of Psychiatry. Symposium. N.Y. 1-7 2v.

Phil 5252.18.8   The group mind. (McDougall, William.) Cambridge, 1920.

Phil 5252.18.8.3   The group mind. (McDougall, William.) N.Y., 1920.

Phil 5252.18.8.2   The group mind. 2d ed. (McDougall, William.) N.Y., 1920.

Phil 6315.2.68   Group psychology and the analysis of the ego. (Freud, Sigmund.) N.Y., 192-?

Phil 6315.2.68.5A   Group psychology and the analysis of the ego. (Freud, Sigmund.) N.Y., 1967.

Phil 6320.15   Group psychotherapy; theory and practice. (Klapman, J.W.) N.Y., 1946.

Phil 6985.20A   Group psychotherapy. (Powdermaker, Florence.) Cambridge, 1953.

Phil 6985.5   Group psychotherapy. (Sigrell, B.) Stockholm, 1968.

Phil 16.11   Group psychotherapy of Southern California. Annual report. Los Angeles. 1-2,1953-1955

Phil 6998.4.5   Group psychotherapy with children. (Ginott, Haim G.) N.Y., 1961.

Phil 8602.18   Group theories of religion and the individual. (Webb, C.C.J.) London, 1916.

Phil 6980.367A   Group therapy. (Johnson, James A.) N.Y., 1963.

Phil 900.6   Grousset, René. Histoire de la philosophie orientale; Inde, Chine, Japan. Paris, 1923.

Phil 960.135   Grousset, René. Les philosophies indiennes, les systèmes. v.1-2. Paris, 1931.

Phil 8881.21   Grove, H. A system of moral philosophy. London, 1749.

Phil 8881.21.4   Grove, H. A system of moral philosophy. London, 1755. 2v.

Phil 7069.19.100   Grove, Harriet McC. Gone west, by a soldier doctor. N.Y., 1919.

Phil 6116.21.5   Groves, E.R. Introduction to mental hygiene. N.Y., 1930.

Phil 6116.21   Groves, E.R. Readings in mental hygiene. N.Y., 1936.

Phil 5246.48   Groves, Ernest R. Understanding yourself, the mental hygiene of personality. N.Y., 1935.

Phil 6128.46.7   Growing into life. (Seabury, David.) N.Y., 1928.

Phil 5548.20   The growth and structure of motives. (Olds, James.) Glencoe, Ill., 1956.

Phil 8520.22   The growth of Christianity. (Gardner, P.) London, 1907.

Phil 1885.83   The growth of F.H. Bradley's logic. (Kagey, Rudolf.) N.Y., 1931.

Phil 5243.20   The growth of intelligence. Diss. (Doll, Edgar Arnold.) Princeton, 1920.

Phil 1701.5   The growth of modern philosophy. (Burns, C. Delisle.) London, 1909.

Phil 1807.2.15   The growth of philosophic radicalism. (Halévy, E.) London, 1949.

Phil 1807.2.20   The growth of philosophic radicalism. (Halévy, E.) London, 1952.

Phil 5520.53.2   The growth of reason. (Lorimer, F.) N.Y., 1929.

Phil 5590.443   The growth of self-insight. (Dorsey, John Morris.) Detroit, 1962.

Phil 6113.2.3   The growth of the brain. (Donaldson, H.H.) London, 1897.

Phil 5240.32   The growth of the mind. (Armstrong-Jones, K.) Edinburgh, 1929?

Phil 186.49.5   Growth of the mind in relation to culture. (Lambek, C.) Copenhagen, 1936.

Phil 978.9.18   The growth of the soul. 2nd ed. (Sinnett, A.P.) London, 1905.

Phil 8583.37   The growth of the spiritual life. (Dent, Phyllis.) London, 1944.

Phil 3488.27   Groyeff, F. Deutung und Darstellung der theoretischen Philosophie Kants. Hamburg, 1951.

Phil 4822.2   Grozev, Groziu. Istoriia na bŭlgarskata filosofiia. Sofiia, 1957- 2v.

Phil 8401.36   Groznoto. (Angelov, Valentin.) Sofiia, 1964.

Phil 3552.346.2   Grua, Gaston. Jurisprudence universelle et théodicée selon Leibniz. Thèse. Paris, 1953.

Phil 3552.346.5   Grua, Gaston. La justice humaine selon Leibniz. Thèse. Paris, 1956.

Phil 4829.491.80   Grubačić, Kosta. Božidar Knežević. Sarajevo, 1962.

Phil 2520.173   Grubbe, S. De philosophia Cartesii observationes. Diss. Upsaliae, 1807.

Phil 3801.436   Grubbe, Samuel. Animadversiones in constructionem materiae Schellingianam. Pt.1-4. Upsaliae, 1818.

Phil 4570.1.20   Grubbe, Samuel. Bidrag till utredandet af samhällslärans grundbegrepp. 1. delen. Upsala, 1826.

Phil 4570.1.60   Grubbe, Samuel. Dissertatio de harmonia religionis et moralitatis. Upsaliae, 1810.

Phil 3120.14.90   Grubbe, Samuel. Dissertatio de realismo rationali Bardilii. Upsaliae, 1806.

Phil 4570.1.30   Grubbe, Samuel. Filosofisk rätts- och samhälls-lära. Upsala, 1839.

Phil 4570.1.5   Grubbe, Samuel. Filosofiska skrifter i Urval. v.1-5. Lund, 1876. 7v.

Phil 181.118   Gruber, F.C. The emergence of the modern mind. Philadelphia, 1958.

Phil 5046.13   Gruber, F.X. Philosophie des Denkens. Bern, 1842.

Phil 735.200   Gruber, Frederick C. Aspects of value. Philadelphia, 1959.

Phil 5465.124   Gruber, Howard E. Contemporary approaches to creative thinking. N.Y., 1962.

Phil 3552.362   Gruber, J.D. Commercii epistolici Leibnitiani. Hanoverae, 1745. 2v.

Phil 7069.25.15   Gruber, K. Parapsychologische Erkenntnisse. München, 1925.

Phil 2655.1.80   Grucker, E. François Hemsterhuis. Paris, 1866.

Phil 8125.22   Grucker, Emile. Histoire des doctrines litteraires. Paris, 1883.

Phil 8407.5   Grudin, Louis. A primer of aesthetics. N.Y., 1930.

Phil 5627.215   Gruehn, W. Die Frommigkeit der Gegenwart. Münster, 1956.

Phil 630.26   Grün, Karl. Die Philosophie in der Gegenwart. Leipzig, 1876.

Phil 672.219   Gruenbaum, A. Philosophical problems of space and time. 1st ed. N.Y., 1963.

Phil 181.56   Grünbaum, A.A. Herrschen und Leiben als Grundmotive der philosophische Weltanschauungen. Bonn, 1925.

Phil 5066.320   Grünberg, Teo. Sembolik mantik. Istanbul, 1968.

Phil 179.8   Gründe und Abgründe. v.1-2. (Ewald, O.) Berlin, 1909.

Phil 8956.26.2   Gruendel, Johannes. Wandelbares und Unwandelbares in der Moraltheologie. 2. Aufl. Düsseldorf, 1971.

Phil 3935.1.80   Gruender, Karl Fried. Zur Philosophie des Grafen Paul Vorck von Wartenburg. Göttingen, 1970.

Phil 3425.385   Gründlinien einer geisteswissenschaftlichen Pädagogik bei G.W.F. Hegel. (Nicolin, F.) Bonn, 1955.

Phil 1504.7.6   Grünfeld, A. Die Lehre vom göttlichen Willen. v.7, pt.6. Münster, 1909.

Phil 3120.30.140   Grünfeld, Werner. Der begegnungscharakter der Wirklichkeit...Martin Bubers. Ratingen, 1965.

Phil 181.66.5   Gruenhut, Ladislaus. Metafizikai világnézet. Baja? 1934.

Phil 181.66   Grünhut, Ladislaus. Das Wesen und der Wert des Seins. Leipzig, 1931.

Phil 585.85F   Grünsteidl, Edmund. Der Mensch zwischen Atom und Universum. Wien, 1958?

Phil 3640.795   Gruenter, Karlfried. Der Streit um Nietzsches "Geburt der Tragödie". Hildersheim, 1969.

Phil 6319.1.200   Gruesen, J.J. The philosophical implication of C.G. Jung's individuation process. Washington, 1956.

Phil 3640.159.5   Grützmacher, R.H. Nietzsche. Leipzig, 1921.

Phil 3640.159.15   Grützmacher, R.H. Nietzsche und wir Christen. Berlin, 1910.

Phil 5246.60   Gruhle, H.W. Verstehen und Einfühlen. Berlin, 1953.

Phil 5246.60.5   Gruhle, H.W. Verstehende Psychologie. 2. Aufl. Stuttgart, 1956.

Phil 3425.696   Grujić, P.M. Hegel und Sowjetphilosophie der Gegenwart. Bern, 1969.

Phil 806.10   Grulle, Samuel. Dissertatio stationes successivas philosophiae progredientis abumbrans. Upsaliae, 1809.

Phil 8892.48   Der Grund der sittlichen Bindung und das sittlich Gute. (Reiner, Hans.) Halle, 1932.

Phil 1133.37   Grund und Gegenwart als Frageziel der frühgriechischen Philosophie. (Breden, Heribert.) Den Haag, 1962.

Phil 292.2   Die Grundbegriffe...Kösmogonien. (Lukas, F.) Leipzig, 1893.

Phil 349.13.2   Die Grundbegriffe der Erkenntnis. (Stadler, A.) Leipzig, 1913.

Phil 349.13   Grundbegriffe der Erkenntnis. (Stadler, A.) Leipzig, 1918.

Phil 8882.49   Die Grundbegriffe der ethischen Wissenschaften. (Hartenstein, G.) Leipzig, 1844.

Phil 179.3.31   Die Grundbegriffe der Gegenwart. 2. Aufl. (Eucken, R.) Leipzig, 1893.

Phil 5243.41.2   Grundbegriffe der Individualpsychologie. (Dreikurs, Rudolf.) Stuttgart, 1969.

Phil 98.2   Grundbegriffe der philosophischen Sprache. (Neuhaeusler, Anton Otto.) München, 1963.

Phil 5247.64   Grundbegriffe der Seelenkunde. (Huber, Kurt.) Ettal, 1955.

Phil 6332.55   Grundbegriffe der Tiefenpsychologie. (Wiesenhuetter, Eckhart.) Darmstadt, 1969.

Phil 8885.6   Die Grundbegriffe des Rechts und der Moral. (Kirchmann, J.H. von.) Berlin, 1873.

Phil 1122.9.5   Grundbegriffe griechischer Wissenschaftslehre. 2. Aufl. (Rüfner, Vinzenz.) Bamberg, 1947.

Phil 3585.10.80   Die Grundbestimmungen über die Psychologie des Gefühls bei Theodor Lipps. (Gothot, Heinrich.) Mülheim-Ruhr, 1921.

Phil 182.27   Grunddragen. (Hvalgrens, E.) Göteborg, 1879.

Phil 4630.2.38   Grunddragen af den filosofiska imputationsläran. (Rein, T.) Helsingfors, 1863.

Phil 801.22   Grunddragen af filosofiens historia. (Bensow, Oscar.) Stockholm, 1916. 2v.

Phil 3425.222   Grunddragen af Hegels filosofi och ästetik. (Norelius, G.) Norrköping, 1893.

Phil 1112.4   Grunddragen af philosophiens historia. 1a afd. (Hammarsköld, L.) Stockholm, 1825.

Phil 818.15   Grunddragen of filosofiens historia. (Schwegler, A.) Örebro, 1856.

Phil 5401.47   Grundformen der Angst und die Antinomien des Lebens. (Riemann, Fritz.) München, 1961.

Phil 3120.27.32   Grundformen und Erkenntnis menschlichen Daseins. 2. Aufl. (Binswanger, L.) Zürich, 1953.

Phil 5358.2   Grundformen und theoretische Perspektiven psychologischer Kompensation. (Seifert, Karl Heinz.) Meisenheim, 1969.

Phil 349.4   Die Grundfrage der Erkenntnisstheorie. (Steiner, R.) n.p., 1891.

Phil 8876.56   Die Grundfrage der Ethik. (Becher, Erich.) Köln, 1908.

Phil 8581.92   Die Grundfrage der Religion. (Baumann, J.) Stuttgart, 1895.

Phil 8413.14   Grundfragen der Ästhetik. (Medicus, Fritz.) Jena, 1917.

Phil 336.4   Die Grundfragen der Erkenntnistheorie. (Fischer, Englebert Lorenz.) Mainz, 1887.

Phil 8897.32   Die Grundfragen der Ethik. (Wittman, M.) Kempten, 1909.

Phil 210.72   Grundfragen der Hermeneutik. (Coreth, Emerich.) Freiburg, 1969.

Phil 810.10   Grundfragen der Philosophie. (Krueger, Gerhard.) Frankfurt, 1958.

Phil 8893.53.10   Grundfragen der philosophischen Ethik. (Störring, Gustav.) Meisenheim, 1967.

Phil 5643.82   Grundfragen der psychophysiologischen Optik. (Stöhr, Adolf.) Leipzig, 1904.

Phil 5520.57   Grundfragen der Sprachphysiognomik. (Werner, Heinz.) Leipzig, 1932.

Phil 193.68   Grundfragen der Weltanschauung. 2e Aufl. (Schwarz, H.) Leipzig, 1912.

Phil 181.154   Grundfragen der Wissenschaften und ihre Wurzeln in der Metaphysik. Salzburg, 1967.

Phil 193.167   Grundfragen des menschlichen Seins. (Steinberg, W.) München, 1953.

Phil 3842.7   Der Grundganke der Ethik des Spinoza. (Wrzecionko, R.) Wien, 1894.

Phil 3486.2.7   Die Grundgedanken der Kritik der reinen Vernunft. (Erhardt, Franz.) Leipzig, 1924.

Phil 3625.3.87   Die Grundgedanken der Machschen Philosophie. (Dingler, Hugo.) Leipzig, 1924.

Phil 7054.131   Die Grundgedanken des Spiritismus und die Kritik derselben. (Schultze, F.) Leipzig, 1883.

Phil 6957.10   Grundgedanken zur Wissenschaftslehre der Psychopathologie. (Hellpach, W.) Leipzig, 1906.

Phil 490.6   Das Grundgesetz alles neuro-psychologischen Lebens. (Pikler, G.) Leipzig, 1900.

Phil 5762.15   Grundgesetze des Sollens. (Mally, Ernst.) Graz, 1926.

Phil 5053.7   Grundideernes logik. (Nielsen, R.) Kjøbenhavn, 1864-66. 2v.

Phil 978.49.665   Die Grundimpulse des weltgeschichtlichen Werdens der Menschheit. 2. Aufl. (Steiner, R.) Dornach, 1965.

Phil 8967.20   Grundintention und sittliches Tun. (Reiners, Hermann.) Freiburg, 1966.

Phil 182.6.5   Grundiss der Philosophie. Abt. 1. (Hartsen, F.A.) Nordhausen, 1875.

Phil 735.145   Die Grundkategorien des Lebendigen. (Müller, A.) Meisenheim, 1954.

Phil 5042.45   Grundkurs der Logik. (Czech, Albert.) Bonn, 1970.

Phil 8893.95.5   Die Grundlage der Ethik. (Schrempf, C.) Stuttgart, 1936.

Phil 3246.45.6   Grundlage der gesammten Wissenschaftslehre. (Fichte, Johann Gottlieb.) Hamburg, 1956.

Phil 3246.45   Grundlage der gesammten Wissenschaftslehre. (Fichte, Johann Gottlieb.) Tübingen, 1802.

Phil 4803.846.30   Grundlage der universellen Philosophie. (Trentowski, Bronisław F.) Karlsruhe, 1837.

Phil 3246.315   Die Grundlage der Wissenschaftslehre in ihrem Umrisse. (Schumann, Karl.) Den Haag, 1968[1969]

Htn   Phil 3246.38*   Grundlage des Naturrechts nach Prinzipien der Wissenschaftslehre. (Fichte, Johann Gottlieb.) Jena, 1796.

Phil 3246.77.2   Grundlage des Naturrechts nach Prinzipien der Wissenschaftslehre. 2. Aufl. (Fichte, Johann Gottlieb.) Hamburg, 1967.

Phil 8411.13   Grundlagen der Asthetik. (Külpe, O.) Leipzig, 1921.

Phil 5257.68   Grundlagen der allgemeinen Psychologie. (Rubinshtein, Sergei A.) Berlin, 1958.

Phil 575.51.4   Die Grundlagen der Charakterkunde. 4e Aufl. (Klages, Ludwig.) Leipzig, 1926.

Phil 575.51.9   Die Grundlagen der Charakterkunde. 5e Aufl. (Klages, Ludwig.) Jena, 1937.

Phil 575.51.8   Die Grundlagen der Charakterkunde. 7e und 8e Aufl. (Klages, Ludwig.) Leipzig, 1936.

Phil 575.51.12   Die Grundlagen der Charakterkunde. 11e Aufl. (Klages, Ludwig.) Bonn, 1951.

Phil 5247.37.2   Die Grundlagen der Denkpsychologie. 2. Aufl. (Hönigswald, R.) Leipzig, 1925.

Phil 8965.12   Die Grundlagen der evangelischen Ethik. (Piper, Otto.) Gütersloh, 1928.

Phil 3497.9   Die Grundlagen der Kantschen Philosophie. (Porten, M. von der.) Leipzig, 1914.

Phil 9495.168.15   Grundlagen der Katholischen Sexualethik. (Müller, Michael.) Regensburg, 1968.

Phil 8980.787.5   Die Grundlagen der kommunistischen Moral. (Shishkin, Aleksandr F.) Berlin, 1958.

Phil 5060.3.10   Grundlagen der Logik. (Uphues, Karl.) Breslau, 1883.

Phil 5046.16   Grundlagen der Logik und Erkenntnislehre. (Geyser, J.) Munster, 1909.

Htn   Phil 332.4.9*   Die Grundlagen der Logik und Mathematik. (Bon, F.) n.p., 193-. 2v.

Phil 310.6.15   Grundlagen der marxistischen Philosophie. (Akadamiia Nauk SSSR. Institut Filosofii.) Berlin, 1960.

Phil 178.37   Die Grundlagen der Naturphilosophie. (Dingler, Hugo.) Leipzig, 1913.

Phil 306.4   Grundlagen der Naturphilosophie. (Ziehen, T.) Leipzig, 1922.

Phil 3450.33.13   Grundlagen der Ontologie Nicolai Hartmanns. (Caspar, Caspar Toni.) Tübingen, 1955.

Phil 190.48   Grundlagen der Philosophie. (Pauler, A. von.) Berlin, 1925.

Phil 6317.26   Die Grundlagen der Psychoanalyse. (Hartmann, Heinz.) Leipzig, 1927.

Phil 5265.1.9   Die Grundlagen der Psychologie. v.1-2. (Ziehen, Theodor.) Leipzig, 1915.

Phil 5251.3   Die Grundlagen der Psychophysik. (Langer, P.) Jena, 1876.

Phil 6020.4   Die Grundlagen der Psysiognomik. (Kassner, Rudolf.) Leipzig, 1922.

Phil 672.4A   Grundlagen der Raumwissenschaft. (Funcke, D.) Hannover, 1875.

Phil 3120.11.82   Die Grundlagen der Realdialektik. Inaug. Diss. (Fechter, Paul.) München, 1906.

Phil 5585.29   Die Grundlagen der Wahrnehmungslehre. (Linke, Paul F.) München, 1918.

Phil 5585.29.2   Die Grundlagen der Wahrnehmungslehre. 2. Aufl. (Linke, Paul F.) München, 1928.

Phil 2045.114   Die Grundlagen des ethisch-politischen Systems von Hobbes. (Łubieński, Z.) München, 1932.

Phil 5810.4   Die Grundlagen des Gedächtnisses, der Vererbung und der Instinkte. (Alsberg, M.) München, 1906.

Phil 299.11   Die Grundlagen des Weltsystems. (Scheffler, Hermann.) Braunschweig, 1898.

Phil 410.2   Grundlagen einer allgemeinen Monnichfaltigkeitslehre. (Cantor, Georg.) Leipzig, 1883.

Phil 349.1   Grundlagen einer Erkenntnisstheorie. (Schubert-Soldern, R. von.) Leipzig, 1884.

Phil 5585.224   Grundlagen einer Phänomenologie und Psychologie der Perspektivität. (Grauman, C.F.) Berlin, 1960.

Phil 735.114   Die Grundlagen einer wissenschaftlichen Wertlehre. (Kraft, V.) Wien, 1937.

Phil 735.114.5   Die Grundlagen einer wissenschaftlichen Wertlehre. 2. Aufl. (Kraft, V.) Wien, 1951.

Phil 282.7.19   Grundlagen und Grenzen des Naturerkennens. (Becher, Erich.) München, 1928.

Phil 8893.42   Grundlagen zu einer Ethik. (Schubert-Soldern, R. von.) Leipzig, 1887.

Phil 4520.5.20   Grundlaggning till metaphysiken för seder. (Kant, Immanuel.) Upsala, 1797.

Phil 176.10.11   Die grundlegenden Thatsachen. 2e Aufl. (Baumann, Julius J.) Stuttgart, 1902.

Phil 5246.14   Grundlegung der empirischen Psychologie. (Geyser, J.) Bonn, 1902.

Phil 344.3   Grundlegung der Erkenntnistheorie. (Nink, Caspar.) Frankfurt am Main, 1930.

Phil 8892.39.5   Grundlegung der Ethic als Wissenschaft. (Rehmke, J.) Leipzig, 1925.

Phil 8877.62.12   Grundlegung der Ethik. (Carneri, B.) Stuttgart, 19- .

Phil 8880.63   Grundlegung der Ethik. (Finance, Joseph de.) Freiburg, 1968.

Phil 8882.108   Grundlegung der Ethik. (Hengstenberg, Hans Eduard.) Stuttgart, 1969.

Phil 176.1   Grundlegung der kritischen Philosophie. (Bärenbach, F.) Leipzig, 1879.

Phil 5041.47.7   Grundlegung der Logik. Ausgewählte Paragraphen aus der Wissenschaftslehre. (Balzano, Bernard.) Hamburg, 1963.

Phil 3428.81   Die Grundlegung der mathematische Psychologie. (Lange, F.A.) Duisburg, 1865.

Phil 3500.94   Die Grundlegung der Menschenwürde bei I. Kant. (Santeler, J.) Innsbruck, 1962.

Phil 3120.45.45   Grundlegung der Philosophie. (Brandenstein, Béla.) Halle, 1926[1970] 6v.

Phil 5057.21   Grundlegung der philosophischen Wissenschaften und Elemente der Logik. (Richter, A.) Halle, 1888.

Phil 5262.2   Grundlegung der Psychologie. (Waitz, T.) Hamburg, 1846.

Phil 5053.6   Grundlegung der reinen Logik. (Neudecker, G.) Würzburg, 1882.

Phil 510.25   Grundlegung der Wertlehre. (Heyde, Erich.) Leipzig, 1916.

Phil 6020.3.5   Grundlegung der Wissenschaft von Ausdruck. (Klages, L.) Leipzig, 1936.

Phil 342.3   Die Grundlegung des Intuitivismus. (Losskii, N.) Halle, 1908.

Phil 351.2   Grundlegung des Systems aller möglichen Erfahrung. (Ulrich, Georg.) Berlin, 1876.

Phil 8415.3.5   Grundlegung einer ästhetischen Werttheorie. (Odebrecht, R.) Berlin, 1927-

Phil 8895.2   Grundlegung für eine moderne praktisch-ethische Lebensanschauung. (Unold, J.) Leipzig, 1896.

Phil 8876.112   Grundlegung und Anfban der Ethik. (Brentano, F.) Bern, 1952.

Phil 8050.53   Grundlegung zu einer vergleichenden Kunstwissenschaft. (Frey, Dagobert.) Innsbruck, 1949.

Phil 8876.76   Die Grundlegung zur einer Wissenschaft der Ethik. (Braileanu, T.) Wien, 1919.

Phil 8887.69   Grundlegung zur Ethik. (Margolius, Hans.) Berlin, 1936.

Phil 3480.20   Grundlegung zur Metaphysik. (Kant, Immanuel.) Riga, 1792-98. 3 pam.

Phil 3480.65.12   Grundlegung zur Metaphysik der Sitten. (Kant, Immanuel.) Gotha, 1930.

Phil 3480.64.10   Grundlegung zur Metaphysik der Sitten. (Kant, Immanuel.) Grätz, 1796. 2 pam.

Phil 3480.65.8   Grundlegung zur Metaphysik der Sitten. (Kant, Immanuel.) Leipzig, 1904.

Phil 3480.65.7   Grundlegung zur Metaphysik der Sitten. (Kant, Immanuel.) Leipzig, 1906.

Phil 3480.65.10 Grundlegung zur Metaphysik der Sitten. (Kant, Immanuel.) München, 1925.
Htn Phil 3480.64* Grundlegung zur Metaphysik der Sitten. (Kant, Immanuel.) Riga, 1785.
Phil 3480.65A Grundlegung zur Metaphysik der Sitten. (Kant, Immanuel.) Riga, 1797.
Phil 3480.65.13 Grundlegung zur Metaphysik der Sitten. (Kant, Immanuel.) Stuttgart, 1967.
Phil 3480.65.5 Grundlegung zur Metaphysik der Sitten. v.1-2. (Kant, Immanuel.) Königsberg, 1803.
Htn Phil 3480.64.5* Grundlegung zur Metaphysik der Sitten. 2. Aufl. (Kant, Immanuel.) Riga, 1786.
Phil 3480.64.7 Grundlegung zur Metaphysik der Sitten. 4. Aufl. (Kant, Immanuel.) Frankfurt, 1794. 2 pam.
Phil 3480.65.6 Grundlegung zur Metaphysik der Sitten. 5. Aufl. (Kant, Immanuel.) Leipzig, 1920.
Phil 3100.42 Grundlegung zur Physik der Sitten. (Beneke, F.E.) Berlin, 1822.
Phil 3499.6.20 Grundlegung zur Reform der Philosophie. (Romundt, H.) Berlin, 1885.
Phil 5047.14 Grundlehren der Logik und Psychologie. (Höfler, Alois.) Leipzig, 1906.
Htn Phil 3801.934* Die Grundlehren der neu- Schelling'schen und der Hegel'schen Philosophie. Reutlingen, 1847.
Phil 3801.934.2 Die Grundlehren der neu- Schelling'schen und der Hegel'schen Philosophie. Reutlingen, 1847.
Phil 1115.1 Grundlehren der Philosophie. (Kühnemann, E.) Berlin, 1899.
Phil 5251.23 Die Grundlehren der Psychologie. (Losskii, N.O.) Leipzig, 1904.
Phil 5247.23.4 Grundlehren der Psychologie. 4. Aufl. (Höfler, Alois.) Wien, 1908.
Phil 5247.23.7 Grundlehren der Psychologie. 7. Aufl. (Höfler, Alois.) Wien, 1919.
Phil 5241.5.3 Die Grundlehren der Psychologie und ihre Anwendung auf die Lehre. (Ballauf, L.) Cöthen, 1890.
Phil 178.10 Grundlehren der Psychologie und Logik. (Dressler, J.G.) Leipzig, 1872.
Phil 8583.6 Grundlehren der Religionsphilosophie. (Drobisch, M.W.) Leipzig, 1840.
Phil 8586.25 Grundler, O. Elemente zu einer religionsphilosophie auf Phänomenonologischer Grundlage. Kempten, 1922.
Phil 197.5 Grundlinien de Philosophie. (Werner, K.) Regensburg, 1855.
Phil 8881.31 Grundlinien der Ethik. (Gerkrath, E.) Charlottenburg, 1912.
Phil 5635.5.7 Grundlinien der Lehre vom den Bewegungsempfindungen. (Mach, Ernst.) Leipzig, 1875.
Phil 5043.17 Grundlinien der Logik. (Döring, A.) Leipzig, 1912.
Phil 5058.32 Grundlinien der Logik in schematischer Darstellung. (Schultze, Fritz.) Leipzig, 1902.
Phil 8893.83.10 Grundlinien der Moralphilosophie. (Salat, Jakob.) München, 1827.
Phil 182.53 Grundlinien der Philosophie als Aufgabe. (Hoffner, Paul.) Mainz, 1881. 2v.
Phil 5047.26 Grundlinien der Philosophie der Logik. (Hinrichs, H.F.W.) Halle, 1826. 2 pam.
Htn Phil 3425.70.1* Grundlinien der Philosophie des Rechts. (Hegel, Georg Wilhelm Friedrich.) Berlin, 1821.
Phil 3425.70.15 Grundlinien der Philosophie des Rechts. (Hegel, Georg Wilhelm Friedrich.) Leiden, 1902.
Phil 3425.70.5 Grundlinien der Philosophie des Rechts. (Hegel, Georg Wilhelm Friedrich.) Leipzig, 1911.
Phil 3425.70.9 Grundlinien der Philosophie des Rechts. 2. Aufl. (Hegel, Georg Wilhelm Friedrich.) Leipzig, 1921.
Phil 3425.70.10 Grundlinien der Philosophie des Rechts. 3. Aufl. (Hegel, Georg Wilhelm Friedrich.) Leipzig, 1930.
Phil 3425.70.18 Grundlinien der Philosophie des Rechts. 4. Aufl. (Hegel, Georg Wilhelm Friedrich.) Hamburg, 1955.
Phil 3425.70.19 Grundlinien der Philosophie des Rechts. 4. Aufl. (Hegel, Georg Wilhelm Friedrich.) Berlin, 1956.
Phil 2045.83 Grundlinien der Philosophie von T. Hobbes. (Brandt, G.) Kiel, 1895.
Phil 6317.16 Grundlinien der Psychoanalyse. (Hoeberlin, Carl.) München, 1925.
Phil 5262.11 Grundlinien der Psychologie. (Witasek, S.) Leipzig, 1908.
Phil 3805.255 Grundlinien der Theologie Schleiermachers. (Stalder, Robert.) Wiesbaden, 1969.
Phil 3100.60 Grundlinien des natürlichen System der praktischen Philosophie. (Beneke, F.E.) Berlin, 1837-41. 2v.
Phil 6117.1 Grundlinien einer allgemeinen Psychophysiologie. (Herzen, A.) Leipzig, 1889.
Phil 4065.90 Grundlinien einer Ethik bei Giordano Bruno. (Hartung, E.B.) Leipzig, 1878.
Phil 8829.2.9 Grundlinien einer neuen Lebensanschauung. (Eucken, Rudolf.) Leipzig, 1907.
Phil 8829.2.10 Grundlinien einer neuen Lebensanschauung. 2e Aufl. (Eucken, Rudolf.) Leipzig, 1913.
Phil 5261.13 Grundlinien einer organischen Wissenschafte der menschlichen Seele. (Vorländer, F.) Berlin, 1841.
Phil 6615.8 Grundlinien einer Psychologie der Hysterie. (Hellpach, Willy.) Leipzig, 1904.
Phil 332.1 Grundlinien einer Theorie des Bewusstseins. (Bergmann, J.) Berlin, 1870.
Phil 3805.35 Grundlinien eines Kritik...Sittenlehre. (Schleiermacher, Friedrich.) Berlin, 1803.
Phil 4515.34 Grundlinien eines philosophischen Systems. (Boström, C.J.) Leipzig, 1923.
Phil 1719.6 Grundlinien eines realistischen Systems der Philosophie. (Thyssen, Johannes.) Bonn, 1966. 2v.
Phil 400.47 Grundlinien idealer Weltanschauung. (Seidenberger, J.B.) Braunschweig, 1902.
Phil 5756.3 Grundlinien zu einer Kritik der Willenskraft. (Goldscheid, R.) Wien, 1905.
Phil 5220.3 Grundlinien zur Aristotelisch-Thomistischen Psychologie. (Knauer, V.) Wien, 1885.
Phil 4630.1.31 Grundlinier till anthropololgien. 4. uppl. (Ribbing, Sigurd.) Upsala, 1870.
Phil 817.12 Grundlinier till philosophiens historia. (Ribbing, Sigurd.) Upsala, 1864.
Phil 4515.31 Grundlinier till philosophiska civil- och criminalrätten. (Boström, C.J.) Stockholm, 1903.
Phil 4515.31.3 Grundlinier till philosophiska civil- och criminalrätten. (Boström, C.J.) Upsala, 1883.
Phil 4515.32.5 Grundlinier till philosophiska statslärans propaedeutik. (Boström, C.J.) Upsala? 1859?
Phil 4515.32.2 Grundlinier till philosophiska statslärans propaedeutik. 2. uppl. (Boström, C.J.) Upsala, 1884.

Phil 4515.32.3 Grundlinier till philosophiska statslärans propaedeutik. 3. uppl. (Boström, C.J.) Stockholm, 1901.
Phil 9410.6.2 Der grundlose Optimismus. (Landesmann, H.) Dresden, 1897.
Phil 3895.45 Das Grundprincip der Philosophie. (Ulrici, H.) Leipzig, 1845-46. 2v.
Phil 3501.8 Die Grundprinzipien der Kantischen Moralphilosophie. (Thon, O.) Berlin, 1895.
Phil 3425.296 Die Grundprinzipien der Religionsphilosophie Hegels und der Theologie Schleiermachers. (Schultz, Werner.) Berlin, 1937.
Phil 338.2 Das Grundproblem der Erkenntnissth. (Hartmann, E. von.) Leipzig, 1889.
Phil 8876.68 Das Grundproblem der Ethik. (Bohlin, F.) Uppsala, 1923.
Phil 3425.284 Das Grundproblem der hegelschen Philosophie. (Steinbüchel, T.) Bonn, 1933.
Phil 180.31 Das Grundproblem der Metaphysik. (Fischer, Engelbert Lorenz.) Mainz, 1894.
Phil 3483.11 Das Grundproblem Kants. (Brunswig, A.) Leipzig, 1914.
Phil 8419.3 Grundprobleme der Ästhetik. (Sturmfels, W.) München, 1963.
Phil 1111.9.5 Grundprobleme der antiken Philosophie. (Gigon, Olof.) Bern, 1959.
Phil 333.2 Grundprobleme der Erkenntniss. (Caspari, O.) Berlin, 1876-79. 2v.
Phil 3838.5 Die Grundprobleme der Ethik Spinoza's. (Scheidemantel, H.) Leipzig, 1898.
Phil 3483.18.5 Grundprobleme der Kritik der reinen Vernunft. (Buchenau, A.) Leipzig, 1914.
Phil 176.99 Die Grundprobleme der Metaphysik. (Bayrhoffer, K.T.) Marburg, 1835.
Phil 192.21.20 Grundprobleme der Philosophie. (Rickert, H.) Tübingen, 1934.
Phil 193.110 Grundprobleme der Philosophie. (Siegel, Carl.) Wien, 1925.
Phil 193.67A Grundprobleme der Philosophie. (Stern, Paul.) Berlin, 1903.
Phil 5243.28.5 Grundprobleme der Psychologie. (Driesch, Hans.) Leipzig, 1926.
Phil 8583.11.5 Grundprobleme der Religionsphilosophie. (Dorner, A.) Berlin, 1903.
Phil 176.158.5 Die Grundragen der Philosophie. 4. Aufl. (Brunner, August.) Freiburg, 1956.
Phil 5252.51 Grundrids af psykologi og paedogogik. 2. utg. (Mortensen, M.) København, 1901.
Phil 8419.37 Grundriss der Ästhetik. (Stoeckl, A.) Mainz, 1871.
Phil 3195.6.40 Grundriss der allgemeinen Geschichte der Philosophie. (Dilthey, Wilhelm.) Frankfurt, 1949.
Phil 974.3.85 Grundriss der Anthroposophie in engem Anschluss an die Schriften Dr. Rudolf Steiners. (Tröger, Walter.) Breslau, 1921.
Phil 3483.1.15 Grundriss der critischen Philosophie. (Beck, J.S.) Halle, 1796.
Phil 5241.55.10 Grundriss der empirischen Psychologie und Logik. 7. Aufl. (Beck, Joseph.) Stuttgart, 1887.
Phil 5241.55.21 Grundriss der empirischen Psychologie und Logik. 21e Aufl. (Fürst, Joseph.) Stuttgart, 1928.
Phil 6119.3 Grundriss der Erfahrungs-Seelenlehre. (Jakob, L.H.) Halle, 1791.
Phil 349.10.5A Grundriss der Erkenntnistheorie und Logik. (Schuppe, W.) Berlin, 1894.
Phil 349.10 Grundriss der Erkenntnistheorie und Logik. 2. Aufl. (Schuppe, W.) Berlin, 1910.
Phil 5041.5 Grundriss der ersten Logik. (Bardili, C.G.) Stuttgart, 1800.
Phil 8875.15 Grundriss der Ethik. 2e Aufl. (Allihn, Friedrich H.) Langensalza, 1898.
Phil 1130.3 Grundriss der Geschichte der griechischen Philosophie. (Zeller, Eduard.) Leipzig, 1883.
Phil 1130.6.9 Grundriss der Geschichte der griechischen Philosophie. (Zeller, Eduard.) Leipzig, 1911.
Phil 1130.3.8 Grundriss der Geschichte der griechischen Philosophie. 8th ed. (Zeller, Eduard.) Leipzig, 1907.
Phil 1130.3.9 Grundriss der Geschichte der griechischen Philosophie. 9th ed. (Zeller, Eduard.) Leipzig, 1909.
Phil 1130.3.13 Grundriss der Geschichte der griechischen Philosophie. 13e Aufl. (Zeller, Eduard.) Leipzig, 1928.
Phil 804.3 Grundriss der Geschichte der Philosophie. (Erdmann, J.E.) Berlin, 1869-70. 2v.
Phil 817.7 Grundriss der Geschichte der Philosophie. (Rehmke, J.) Berlin, 1896.
Phil 817.7.5 Grundriss der Geschichte der Philosophie. (Rehmke, J.) Bonn, 1959.
Phil 819.1.3 Grundriss der Geschichte der Philosophie. (Tennemann, W.G.) Leipzig, 1820.
Phil 820.1.7.7 Grundriss der Geschichte der Philosophie. (Ueberweg, F.) Basel, 1960.
Phil 820.1.1 Grundriss der Geschichte der Philosophie. (Ueberweg, F.) Berlin, 1894. 3v.
Phil 820.1.3 Grundriss der Geschichte der Philosophie. (Ueberweg, F.) Berlin, 1894-97. 5v.
Phil 820.1.2 Grundriss der Geschichte der Philosophie. v 1-2,3. 7. Aufl. (Ueberweg, F.) Berlin, 1886-88. 2v.
Phil 820.1.4 Grundriss der Geschichte der Philosophie. v.1-2,4. 9. Aufl. (Ueberweg, F.) Berlin, 1902. 3v.
Phil 820.1.6 Grundriss der Geschichte der Philosophie. v.1-2. 6. ed. (Ueberweg, F.) Berlin, 1880-1914.
Phil 820.01 Grundriss der Geschichte der Philosophie. v.1-3. (Ueberweg, F.) Berlin, 1863.
Phil 820.1 Grundriss der Geschichte der Philosophie. v.1-3. (Ueberweg, F.) Berlin, 1868-71. 2v.
Phil 820.1.6.5 Grundriss der Geschichte der Philosophie. v.2. 10. ed. (Ueberweg, F.) Berlin, 1915.
Phil 820.1.7 Grundriss der Geschichte der Philosophie. v.2-4. 11. Aufl. (Ueberweg, F.) Berlin, 1914-28. 3v.
Phil 804.3.3A Grundriss der Geschichte der Philosophie. 3e Aufl. (Erdmann, J.E.) Berlin, 1878. 2v.
Phil 820.01.3 Grundriss der Geschichte der Philosophie. 3rd ed. (Ueberweg, F.) Berlin, 1867.
Phil 804.3.4 Grundriss der Geschichte der Philosophie. 4. Aufl. (Erdmann, J.E.) Berlin, 1896. 2v.
Phil 817.7.7 Grundriss der Geschichte der Philosophie. 5. Aufl. (Rehmke, J.) Frankfurt, 1965.
Phil 819.1.5 Grundriss der Geschichte der Philosophie. 5. Aufl. (Tennemann, W.G.) Leipzig, 1829.
Phil 820.1.2.5 Grundriss der Geschichte der Philosophie. 5. Aufl. (Ueberweg, F.) Berlin, 1880.
Phil 820.1.5 Grundriss der Geschichte der Philosophie. 10. ed. (Ueberweg, F.) Berlin, 1906. 4v.

Phil 820.1.7.5A Grundriss der Geschichte der Philosophie. 12. Aufl. (Ueberweg, F.) Berlin, 1926-51. 5v.
Phil 6060.90 Grundriss der Graphologie. (Wieser, Roda.) München, 1969.
Phil 3525.60 Grundriss der historischen Logik. (Krause, K.C.F.) Jena, 1803.
Phil 5041.21.10 Grundriss der Logik. (Braniss, C.J.) Breslau, 1830.
Phil 5046.20 Grundriss der Logik. (Grau, Kurt J.) Leipzig, 1918.
Phil 5047.29 Grundriss der Logik. (Hillebrand, J.) Heidelberg, 1820.
Phil 5058.18.5 Grundriss der Logik. (Strümpell, L.) Leipzig, 1881.
Phil 5059.19 Grundriss der Logik. (Tieftrunk, J.H.) Halle, 1801.
Phil 5046.17 Grundriss der Logik. 2e Aufl. (Gerlach, G.W.) Halle, 1822.
Phil 5044.5.4 Grundriss der Logik und Metaphysik. (Erdmann, J.E.) Halle, 1864.
Phil 5059.16 Grundriss der Logik und Metaphysik. (Thiele, G.) Halle, 1878.
Phil 5044.5.2 Grundriss der Logik und Metaphysik. 2e Aufl. (Erdmann, J.E.) Halle, 1843.
Phil 5058.100 Grundriss der Logik und Übersicht über die Griechische Philosophie für die prima der Gymnasien. (Schulze, Ernst.) Leipzig, 1886.
Phil 187.65.5 Grundriss der Metaphysik. (Merten, J.) Trier, 1848.
Phil 179.11 Grundriss der Philosophie. (Eitle, Johannes.) Freiburg, 1892.
Phil 182.73 Grundriss der Philosophie. (Hermann, E.) Lahr, 1906.
Phil 185.22.6 Grundriss der Philosophie. 2e Aufl. (Koch, J.L.A.) Göppingen, 1885.
Phil 3450.6.80 Grundriss der Philosophie nach Friedrich Harms. (Zimmer, Friedrich.) Tübingen, 1902.
Phil 3805.36.5 Grundriss der philosophischen Ethik. (Schleiermacher, Friedrich.) Berlin, 1841.
Phil 3805.36 Grundriss der philosophischen Ethik. (Schleiermacher, Friedrich.) Leipzig, 1911.
Phil 8881.49 Grundriss der philosophischen Lugendlehre. (Gerlach, G.W.) Halle, 1829.
Phil 3850.13.25 Grundriss der philosophischen Wissenschaften und Zerbst. (Schulze, G.E.) Wittenberg, 1788-90. 2v.
Phil 6972.2.10 Grundriss der Psychiatrie in klinischen Vorlesungen. v.1-2. (Wernicke, C.) Leipzig, 1894.
Phil 5241.61 Grundriss der Psychologie. (Baumgartner, M.) Dillingen, 1906.
Phil 5246.27 Grundriss der Psychologie. (Glogau, Gustav.) Breslau, 1884.
Phil 5250.2.5 Grundriss der Psychologie. (Külpe, Oswald.) Leipzig, 1893.
Phil 5252.83 Grundriss der Psychologie. (Marf, Gustav.) Bern, 1943.
Phil 5258.22 Grundriss der Psychologie. (Strümpell, L.) Leipzig, 1884.
Phil 5262.24 Grundriss der Psychologie. (Wollny, F.) Leipzig, 1887.
Phil 5244.2.8 Grundriss der Psychologie. 4. Aufl. (Erdmann, J.E.) Leipzig, 1862.
Phil 5244.2.9 Grundriss der Psychologie. 5e Aufl. (Erdmann, J.E.) Leipzig, 1873.
Phil 5251.12 Grundriss der Psychologie für Juristen. (Lipmann, O.) Leipzig, 1908.
Phil 5245.30 Grundriss der Psychologie für Lehrer- und Lehrerinen-Bildungs-Anstalten. (Foltz, Otto.) Österwiech-Harz, 1910.
Phil 6121.10 Grundriss der psychophysik. (Lipps, G.F.) Leipzig, 1909.
Phil 8583.11 Grundriss der Religionsphilosophie. (Dorner, A.) Leipzig, 1903.
Phil 5627.194 Grundriss der Religionspsychologie. (Hellpach, Willy.) Stuttgart, 1951.
Phil 5248.1 Grundriss der Seelenheilkunde. (Ideler, K.W.) Berlin, 1835-38. 2v.
Phil 5257.26.2 Grundriss der Seelenlehre. 2. Aufl. (Rüegg, H.R.) Bern, 1864.
Htn Phil 3246.45.8* Grundriss des Eigenthümlichen der Wissenschaftslehre. (Fichte, Johann Gottlieb.) Jena, 1795.
Phil 3246.45.20 Grundriss des Eigenthümlichen der Wissenschaftslehre in Rücksicht. (Fichte, Johann Gottlieb.) Leipzig, 194-.
Phil 3915.47.7 Grundriss des Psychologie. (Wundt, Wilhelm.) Leipzig, 1896.
Phil 3915.47.4 Grundriss des Psychologie. 2. Aufl. (Wundt, Wilhelm.) Leipzig, 1897.
Phil 3915.47.10 Grundriss des Psychologie. 4. Aufl. (Wundt, Wilhelm.) Leipzig, 1901.
Phil 3915.47.5 Grundriss des Psychologie. 7. Aufl. (Wundt, Wilhelm.) Leipzig, 1905.
Phil 3915.47.9 Grundriss des Psychologie. 9. Aufl. (Wundt, Wilhelm.) Leipzig, 1909.
Phil 298.10 Grundriss des Seins. (Reinl, Kurt.) München, 1958.
Phil 180.33 Grundriss des Systems der Philosophie als Bestimmungslehre. (Fischer, Ludwig.) Wiesbaden, 1890.
Phil 8408.31 Grundriss einer allgemeinen Ästhetik. (Hermann, C.) Leipzig, 1857.
Phil 5050.5.4 Grundriss einer allgemeinen Logik. (Kiesewetter, J.G.C.C.) Berlin, 1796-1802. 2v.
Phil 5050.5 Grundriss einer allgemeinen Logik. (Kiesewetter, J.G.C.C.) Leipzig, 1824-25. 2v.
Phil 5050.5.2 Grundriss einer allgemeinen Logik. 2. Aufl. (Kiesewetter, J.G.C.C.) Berlin, 1795-96. 2v.
Phil 8878.39 Grundriss einer Einheitlichen. (Duboc, Julius.) Leipzig, 1892.
Phil 801.7 Grundriss einer Geschichte de Philosophie. (Buschings, A.F.) Berlin, 1772-4. 2v.
Phil 2725.2.31 Grundriss einer Philosophie. v.1-3. (Lamennais, F.R. de.) Paris, 1841. 3v.
Phil 9070.53 Grundriss einer praktischen Philosophie. (Holzamer, Karl.) Frankfurt am Main, 1951.
Phil 5050.5.6 Grundriss einer reinen allgemeinen Logik nach kantischen Grundsaetzen. (Kiesewetter, J.G.C.C.) Berlin, 1791.
Phil 189.9.5 Grundriss einer Seinswissenschaft. v.1-2. (Opitz, H.G.) Leipzig, 1897-1899.
Phil 8050.49 Grundriss eines Systems. (Baer, Hans.) Strassburg, 1913.
Phil 5242.24 Grundritz der Psychologie. 2. Aufl. (Crüger, J.) Leipzig, 1902.
Phil 5066.185 Grundüge der mathematischen Logik. (Scholz, H.) Berlin, 1961.
Phil 3850.13.55 Grundsätze der allgemeinen Logik. (Schulze, G.E.) Göttingen, 1831.
Phil 2205.40.30 Grundsätze der Moral und Politik. (Paley, W.) Leipzig, 1787. 2v.
Phil 8587.14.10 Grundsätze der moralischen Gotteslehre. (Heydenreichs, K.H.) Leipzig, 1792.
Phil 8880.3 Grundsätze der Moralphilosophie. (Ferguson, Adam.) Leipzig, 1772.
Phil 3235.25.5 Grundsätze der Philosophie der Zukunft. (Feuerbach, Ludwig.) Frankfurt, 1967.

Phil 3235.25 Grundsätze der Philosophie der Zukunft. (Feuerbach, Ludwig.) Zürich, 1843.
Phil 3500.10.15 Die Grundsätze der reinen Erkenntnisstheorie in der Kantischen Philosophie. (Stadler, A.) Leipzig, 1876.
Phil 3850.70 Grundsätze der reinen Philosophie. (Selle, Christian Gottlieb.) Bruxelles, 1969.
Phil 3245.75 Grundsätze für die Philosophie der Zukunft. (Fichte, Immanuel Hermann.) Stuttgart, 1847.
Phil 410.7 Die Grundsätze und das Wesen des Unendlichen in der Mathematik und Philosophie. (Geissler, Kurt.) Leipzig, 1902.
Phil 3491.1 Die grundsätzliche Unanehmbarkeit. (Jonquière, Georg.) Bern, 1917.
Phil 978.49.785.3 Die Grundsteinlegung der Allgemeinen Anthroposophischen Gesellschaft. 3. Aufl. (Steiner, R.) Dornach, 1969.
Phil 5051.15 Grundtankernes system. v.1-3. (Lyng, Georg V.) Christiania, 1882-1887.
Phil 4582.5.30 Grundtraek af metafysik. (Halvorson, G.) Kristiania, 1891.
Phil 3565.58 Grundtraek af religionsfilosofien. (Lotze, Hermann.) København, 1886.
Phil 5250.12.15 Grundtraek af sjaelelaeren. 6. udg. (Kroman, Kristian.) København, 1920.
Phil 5250.12.17 Grundtraek af sjaelelaeren. 7. udg. (Kroman, Kristian.) København, 1928.
Phil 3110.192 Die Grundvorstellungen Jacob Böhme. (Solms-Rödelheim, Günther.) München, 1960.
Phil 3552.67.30 Grundwahrheiten der Philosophie. (Leibniz, Gottfried Wilhelm.) Frankfurt, 1962.
Phil 8423.12 Grundwissenschaftliche Unterlage der Kunstwissenschaft. (Wieckberg, W.) Charlottenburg, 1922.
Phil 348.2 Grundzüge...Erkenntnisslehre. (Reinhold, C.E.) Schleswig, 1822.
Phil 8412.19.5 Grundzüge der Asthetik; Diktate aus den Vorlesungen. 2. Aufl. (Lotze, Hermann.) Leipzig, 1888.
Phil 3120.8.50 Grundzüge der Asthetik. (Brentano, Franz.) Bern, 1959.
Phil 5645.22 Grundzüge der ästhetischen Farbenlehre. (Utitz, Emil.) Stuttgart, 1908.
Phil 8423.4 Grundzüge der allgemeinen Ästhetik. (Witasek, Stephan.) Leipzig, 1904.
Phil 5130.6 Grundzüge der Aussagenlogik. (Czayka, Lothar.) München, 1971.
Phil 193.13 Grundzüge der Einleitung in die Philosophie. (Schmid, L.) Giessen, 1860.
Phil 8876.98 Grundzüge der Ethik. (Bauch, Bruno.) Stuttgart, 1935.
Phil 8893.39.5 Grundzüge der Ethik. (Schwarz, Hermann.) Leipzig, 1896.
Phil 8897.35 Grundzüge der Ethik. (Wentscher, E.) Leipzig, 1913.
Phil 8893.3 Grundzüge der Ethik und Rechtsphilosophie. (Schuppe, W.) Breslau, 1881.
Phil 8878.37.5 Grundzüge der Ethik von Dr. E. Dürr. (Dürr, Ernst.) Heidelberg, 1909.
Phil 5252.34 Grundzüge der forensischen Psychologie. (Marbe, K.) München, 1913.
Phil 5047.2 Grundzüge der Logik. (Hartsen, F.A.) Berlin, 1873.
Phil 5051.30 Grundzüge der Logik. (Lipps, T.) Hamburg, 1893.
Phil 3565.65 Grundzüge der Logik. (Lotze, Hermann.) Leipzig, 1883.
Phil 3565.65.5 Grundzüge der Logik und Encyklopädie der Philosophie. 3e Aufl. (Lotze, Hermann.) Leipzig, 1891.
Phil 1535.27.2 Grundzüge der Logik und Noëtik. (Huber, Sebastian.) Paderborn, 1906.
Phil 3493.19 Die Grundzüge der materialen Ethik Kants. (Laupichler, Max.) Berlin, 1931.
Phil 178.50 Grundzüge der Metaphysik. (Dieterich, K.) Freiburg im Breisgau, 1885.
Phil 3565.45.5A Grundzüge der Metaphysik. (Lotze, Hermann.) Leipzig, 1883.
Phil 3850.19.30 Die Grundzüge der Metaphysik. (Suabedissen, D.T.A.) Marburg, 1836.
Phil 3925.3.31 Grundzüge der Metaphysik. (Weisse, Christian Hermann.) Hamburg, 1835.
Phil 3565.45.12 Grundzüge der Metaphysik. 2. Aufl. (Lotze, Hermann.) Leipzig, 1887.
Phil 296.9 Die Grundzüge der monistischen und dualistischen Weltanschauung. (Portig, Gustav.) Stuttgart, 1904.
Phil 8881.12A Grundzüge der Moral. (Gizycki, G.) Leipzig, 1883.
Phil 3565.60 Grundzüge der Naturphilosophie. (Lotze, Hermann.) Leipzig, 1882.
Phil 3565.60.2 Grundzüge der Naturphilosophie. 2. Aufl. (Lotze, Hermann.) Leipzig, 1889.
Phil 2880.8.140 Grundzüge der Ontologie Sartres in ihrem Verhältnis zu Hegels Logik. (Hartmann, Klaus.) Berlin, 1963.
Phil 2045.65 Grundzüge der Philosophie. v.1-3. (Hobbes, Thomas.) Leipzig, 1915-18.
Phil 193.37.5 Grundzüge der philosophie. 2e Aufl. v.1-2. (Stöckl, Albert.) Mainz, 1910.
Phil 193.34 Grundzüge der philosophischen Naturwissenschaft. (Steffens, H.) Berlin, 1806.
Phil 3850.19.50 Die Grundzüge der philosophischen Tugend- und Rechtslehre. (Suabedissen, D.T.A.) Marburg, 1839.
Phil 3915.45 Grundzüge der physiologischen Psychologie. (Wundt, Wilhelm.) Leipzig, 1874.
Phil 3915.45.3 Grundzüge der physiologischen Psychologie. (Wundt, Wilhelm.) Leipzig, 1887- .
Phil 3915.45.2 Grundzüge der physiologischen Psychologie. v.1-2. (Wundt, Wilhelm.) Leipzig, 1880.
Phil 3915.45.4 Grundzüge der physiologischen Psychologie. 4. Aufl. (Wundt, Wilhelm.) Leipzig, 1893. 2v.
Phil 3915.45.5 Grundzüge der physiologischen Psychologie. 5. Aufl. (Wundt, Wilhelm.) Leipzig, 1902. 3v.
Phil 3915.45.6 Grundzüge der physiologischen Psychologie. 6. Aufl. (Wundt, Wilhelm.) Leipzig, 1910. 3v.
Phil 3565.35.2 Grundzüge der praktischen Philosophie. (Lotze, Hermann.) Leipzig, 1882.
Phil 3565.35 Grundzüge der praktischen Philosophie. 3. Aufl. (Lotze, Hermann.) Leipzig, 1899.
Phil 5244.7.15 Grundzüge der Psychologie. (Ebbinghaus, H.) Leipzig, 1911. 2v.
Phil 5247.4 Grundzüge der Psychologie. (Hartsen, F.A.) Berlin, 1874.
Phil 3565.69 Grundzüge der Psychologie. (Lotze, Hermann.) Leipzig, 1881.
Phil 5252.12.9A Grundzüge der Psychologie. (Münsterberg, H.) Leipzig, 1900.
Phil 5252.12.10 Grundzüge der Psychologie. 2. Aufl. (Münsterberg, H.) Leipzig, 1918.
Phil 5250.14 Grundzüge der Psychologie und Logik. 2. Aufl. (Königbauer, J.) Regensburg, 1893.
Phil 5251.20 Grundzüge der Psychophysiologie. (Lehmann, Alfred.) Leipzig, 1912.

Phil 5850.278	Grundzüge der Psychotechnik. (Münsterberg, H.) Leipzig, 1914.
Phil 8602.23	Grundzüge der Religionsphilosophie. (Wunderle, Georg.) Paderborn, 1918.
Phil 3565.72	Grundzüge der Religionsphilosophie. 2e Aufl. (Lotze, Hermann.) Leipzig, 1884.
Phil 8599.11.5	Grundzüge der Religionswissenschaft. (Tiele, C.P.) Tübingen, 1904.
Phil 5244.15	Grundzüge der Reproduktions Psychologie. (Erdmann, B.) Berlin, 1920.
Phil 8897.45	Grundzüge der Sittenlehre. (Witte, J.H.) Bonn, 1882.
Phil 187.85	Grundzüge der speculativen Kritik. (Mehring, G.) Heilbronn, 1844.
Phil 5520.12	Grundzüge der Sprachpsychologie. (Dittrich, O.) Halle, 1903- 2v.
Phil 5066.70	Grundzüge der theorelischen Logik. 2. Aufl. (Hilbert, D.) Berlin, 1949.
Phil 5047.33A	Grundzüge der theoretischen Logik. (Hilbert, David.) Berlin, 1928.
Phil 5047.33.5	Grundzüge der theoretischen Logik. 2e Aufl. (Hilbert, David.) Berlin, 1938.
Phil 8876.39.5	Grundzüge der wissenschaftlichen und technischen Ethik. (Bon, Fred.) Leipzig, 1896.
Htn Phil 3246.47*	Die Grundzüge des gegenwartigen Zeitalters. (Fichte, Johann Gottlieb.) Berlin, 1806.
Phil 3246.47.26	Die Grundzüge des gegenwartigen Zeitalters. (Fichte, Johann Gottlieb.) Hamburg, 1956.
Phil 3246.47.25	Die Grundzüge des gegenwartigen Zeitalters. 2. Aufl. (Fichte, Johann Gottlieb.) Leipzig, 1922.
Phil 3640.775	Grundzüge des Nietzsche-Verständnisses in der Deutung seiner Philosophie. (Ries, Wiebrecht.) Maulburg, 1967?
Phil 180.6	Grundzüge des Systems der Philosophie. (Fischer, K.P.) Frankfurt, 1848-1855. 3v.
Phil 180.6.2	Grundzüge des Systems der Philosophie. v.2,3. (Fischer, K.P.) Erlangen, 1850-1855. 2v.
Phil 3808.232	Grundzüge einer Asthetik nach Schopenhauer. (Klee, Hermann.) Berlin, 1875.
Phil 8962.22.5	Grundzüge einer christlichen Ethik. (Marck, Wilhelm Henricus Marie van der.) Düsseldorf, 1967.
Phil 8890.36	Grundzüge einer Ethik. (Pichler, Hans.) Graz, 1919.
Phil 333.4	Grundzüge einer extensionalen Erkenntnisstheorie. (Czolbe, H.) Plauen, 1875.
Phil 6327.4.13	Grundzüge einer genetischen Psychologie. v.1-2. (Rank, Otto.) Wien, 1927-28.
Phil 3018.24	Grundzüge einer Geschichte der artdeutschen Philosophie. (Schwarz, Hermann.) Berlin, 1937.
Phil 5228.2	Grundzüge einer Geschichte der deutschen Psychologie. (Sommer, R.) Würzburg, 1892.
Phil 5252.38.5	Grundzüge einer Lebenspsychologie. (Müller-Freienfels, R.) Leipzig, 1924-25. 2v.
Phil 8412.9	Grundzüge einer Lehre vom Schönen. (Landmann, E.) Basel, 1940.
Phil 338.11	Grundzüge einer Metaphysik der Erkenntnis. (Hartmann, N.) Berlin, 1921.
Phil 3425.291	Grundzüge einer neuen Theorie des Denkens in Hegels Logik. (Günther, G.) Leipzig, 1933.
Phil 735.85	Grundzüge einer personalistischen Werttheorie. (Wilken, F.) Jena, 1924.
Phil 630.20	Grundzüge einer realistischen Weltanschauung. (Dürr, Ernst.) Leipzig, 1907.
Phil 5649.38	Grundzüge einer tensor-algebraischen Psycho-Dynamik. v.1-2. (Zweig, Adam.) Zürich, 1965.
Phil 4115.65	Grundzüge eines Systems der Ethik. (Gioberti, V.) Mainz, 1848.
Htn Phil 3801.876*	Grundzüge und Kritik der Philosophien Kant's, Fichte's und Schelling's. 2. Aufl. (Wendell, Johann A.) Coburg, 1824.
Phil 3504.47	Grundzüge und Kritik der Philosophien Kant's. (Wendel, J.A.) Coburg, 1810.
Phil 5643.11.9	Grundzüge zur Lehre vom Lichtsinne. (Hering, E.) Leipzig, 1920.
Phil 3245.30	Grundzüge zur System der Philosophie. (Fichte, Immanuel Hermann.) Heidelberg, 1833-46. 4v.
Phil 8412.19	Grundzuge der Asthetik. 3. Aufl. (Lotze, Hermann.) Leipzig, 1906.
Phil 3821.4	Grundzuge der Erkenntnisztheorie Spinozas. (Busolt, Georg.) Berlin, 1875.
Phil 6319.7	Grundzuge einer Physiologie und Klinik der psychophysischen Persönlichkeit. (Jaensch, W.) Berlin, 1926.
Phil 176.19	Grundzuge zur Wissenschaft. (Berger, J.E.) Altona, 1817. 4v.
Phil 7082.21	Grunebaum, Gustave Edmund von. The dream and human societies. Berkeley, 1966.
Phil 3246.263 Phil 8419.43.80	Gruner, C.G. Ein paare Worte zur Belehrung. Jena, 1799.
Phil 3475.3.120	Grunert, B. Solgers Lehre vom Schönen in ihrem Verhältnis zur Kunstlehre. Marburg, 1960.
Phil 7069.20.145	Grunert, P.L. Objektive Norm. Inaug. Diss. Bonn, 1953.
Phil 818.32.5	Grunewald, F. Physikalisch-mediumistische Untersuchungen. Pfullingen, 1920.
	Grunfragen der Philosophie in Horizont der Seinsdifferenz. (Siewerth, G.) Düsseldorf, 1963.
Phil 337.5.5 Phil 337.5	Grung, Frants. Aandslaenker. Kjøbenhavn, 1886.
	Grung, Frants. Das Problem der Gewissheit. Heidelberg, 1886.
Phil 600.42	Grunicke, Lucia. Der Begriff der Tatsache in der positivistischen Philosophie des 19. Jahrhunderts. Halle, 1930.
Phil 3110.185	Grunsky, H.A. Jacob Böhme. Stuttgart, 1956.
Phil 3110.95	Grunsky, H.A. Jakob Böhme als Schöpfer einer germanischen Philosophie des Willens. Hamburg, 1940.
Phil 1504.6.3	Grunwald, G. Geschichte der Gottesbewise. v.6, pt.3. Münster, 1907.
Phil 3826.4	Grunwald, Max. Spinoza in Deutschland. Gekrönte Preisschrift. Berlin, 1897.
Phil 3450.11.90	Grunwaldt, H.H. Ueber die Phänomenologie Husserl. Berlin, 1927.
Phil 3425.244	Grupe, Walter. Mundts und Kühnes Verhältnis zu Hegel und seinen Gegnern. Halle, 1928.
Phil 2905.1.645	Grupo Español de Trabajo Teilhard de Chardin. En torno a Teilhard. Madrid, 1969.
Phil 181.19	Gruppe, O.F. Antäus. Berlin, 1831.
Phil 3006.1	Gruppe, O.F. Gegenwart und Philosophie in Deutschland. Berlin, 1855.
Phil 1135.28	Gruppe, O.F. Die kosmischen Systeme der Griechen. Berlin, 1851.
Phil 1735.2	Gruppe, Otto F. Wendepunkt der Philosophie im neunzehnten Jahrhundert. Berlin, 1834.
Phil 16.14	Gruppenpsychotherapie und Gruppendynamik. Göttingen. 1,1968+ 3v.

Phil 3246.220	Grusber, J.G. Eine Stimme aus dem Publikum über Gottes Sein und Wesen. Leipzig, 1799.
Phil 310.340	Grushin, B.H. Ocherki logiki istoricheskogo issledovaniia. Moskva, 1961.
Phil 181.21 Phil 181.21.10	Gruyer, L.A. Méditations critiques. Paris, 1847.
	Gruyer, L.A. Observations sur le dieu-monde de M. Vacherot et de M. Tiberghien. Paris, 1860.
Phil 181.21.5	Gruyer, L.A. Opuscules philosophiques. Bruxelles, 1851.
Phil 5246.10	Gruyer. L.A. Les causes...phénomènes de l'âme. Paris, 1844.
Phil 4803.435.30 Phil 8407.16.2	Grzegorczyk, Andrzej. Schemaly i człowiek. Kraków, 1963.
	Grzegorzewska, M. Essai sur le développement du sentiment esthétique. Paris, 1916.
Phil 8407.16	Grzegorzewska, M. Essai sur le développement du sentiment esthétique. Paris, 1916.
Phil 3195.6.145	Grzesik, Juergen. Die Geschichtlichkeit als Wesensverfassung des Menschen. Bonn, 1961.
Phil 3826.9	Grzymisch, S. Spinoza's Lehren von der Ewigkeit und Unsterblichkeit. Breslau, 1898.
Phil 3665.1.79	Gschwind, H. Die philosophischen Grundlagen von Natorps Sozialpadagogik. Leipzig, 1920.
Phil 5590.516	Gschwind, Martin. Die Wertfunktion des Menschen. Mainz, 1969.
Phil 181.23	Gualberto, G. Raccolta di opuscoli filosofici. Pisa, 1766. 3v.
Phil 7054.51.5 Phil 2805.220	Guardian spirits. (Werner, H.) N.Y., 1847.
	Guardini, R. Christliches Bewusstsein...Pascal. Leipzig, 1935.
Phil 181.83 Phil 8631.15 Phil 9166.8	Guardini, R. Der Gegensatz. Mainz, 1925.
	Guardini, R. The last things. London, 1954.
	Guardini, R. Neue Jugend und katholischer Geist. Mainz, 1929.
Phil 8586.54	Guardini, Romano. Religion und Offenbarung. Würzburg, 1958.
Phil 8407.27 Phil 8407.8 Phil 8407.8.5 Phil 4120.2.30	Guardo, V. L'estetica e i suoi problemi. Siracusa, 1955.
	Guastalla, Pierre. Esthétique. Paris, 1925.
	Guastalla, Pierre. L'esthetique et l'art. Paris, 1928.
	Guastalla, Cosmo. Le ragioni del fenomenismo. v. 1-3. Palermo, 1921-23. 2v.
Phil 6315.2.195	Guatemala (city). Universidad Nacional. Primer centenario del racimiento. Guatemala, 1956.
Phil 5216.5	Gučas, Alfonsas. Psichologijos raidci Lietuvoje. Vilnius, 1968.
Phil 3425.338	Guccione Monroy, Nino. Hegel ed il problema della moralità. Trapani, 1951.
Phil 4655.1.48	"Gud är kärleken." 2. uppl. (Wikner, Pontus.) Stockholm, 1895.
Phil 7068.70.33	Güldinstubbe, J. von. Positive Pneumatologie. 2. Aufl. Bern, n.d.
Phil 8408.13 Phil 181.71.5	Die Gültigkeit der Kunst. (Hirsch, W.) Köln, 1957.
	Guénon, R. Autorité spirituelle et pouvoir temporel. Paris, 1929.
Phil 7069.30.8.15 Phil 181.71 Phil 181.71.10 Phil 971.5.5	Guénon, R. L'erreur spirite. Paris, 1930.
	Guénon, R. Les états multiples de l'etre. Paris, 1932.
	Guénon, R. La métaphysique orientale. 2. ed. Paris, 1945.
	Guénon, R. Le theosophise; histoire d'une pseudo-religion. 2. ed. Paris, 1929.
Phil 2630.7.32	Guénon, René. La règne de la quantité et les signes des temps. 4. ed. Paris, 1950.
Phil 2630.7.30	Guénon, René. The reign of quantity and the signs of the times. London, 1953.
Phil 2630.7.39	Guénon, René. Symboles fondament aux de la science sacrée. Paris, 1962.
Phil 3006.5	Günther, A. Die Juste-Milieus in der deutschen Philosophie. Wien, 1838.
Phil 8685.19 Phil 3310.1.3	Günther, A. Thomas a Scrupulis. Wien, 1835.
	Günther, Anton. Gesammelte Schriften. Bd.1-9. Wien, 1882. 9v.
Phil 3310.1.30	Günther, Anton. Januskӧpfe zur Philosophie und Theologie. Wien, 1834.
Phil 5756.5 Phil 337.9	Günther, Carl. Die Willensfreiheit. Berlin, 1909.
	Günther, E. Die ontologischen Grundlagen der neueren Erkenntnislehre. Halle, 1933.
Phil 3425.291	Günther, G. Grundzüge einer neuen Theorie des Denkens in Hegels Logik. Leipzig, 1933.
Phil 5046.30	Guenther, Gotthard. Idee und Grundriss einer nicht-aristotalischen Logik. Hamburg, 1959.
Phil 2020.135	Günther, Oskar. Das Verhältnis der Ethik T.H. Greens zu Derjenigen Kants. Inaug. Diss. Dresden, 1915.
Phil 3310.1.127 Phil 3310.1.85	Günther und Blemens. (Knoodt, Peter.) Wien, 1853-54.
	Die Günther'sche Philosophie. (Dischinger, J.N.P.) Schaffhausen, 1852.
Phil 8956.24	Guenthӧe, Anselm. Entscheidung gegen das Gesetz. Freiburg, 1969.
Phil 1735.4 Phil 5816.2	Guepin, Anec. Philosophie du XIXe siècle. Paris, 1854.
	Guer, S.A. Histoire critique de l'âme des bêtes. v.1-2. Amsterdam, 1749.
Phil 2030.5A Phil 2030.5.5	Guérard, A.L. Battle in the sea. Cambridge, 1954.
	Guérard, A.L. Fossils and presences. Standord, Calif., 1957.
Phil 8661.45	Guérard des Lauriers, Michel L. La preuve de Dieu et les cinq voies. Roma, 1966.
Phil 3246.217.2	Guerault, Martèal. L'evolution et la structure de la doctrine de la science chez Fichte. Thèse. Strasbourg, 1930. 2 pam.
Phil 3246.217	Guerault, Martèal. L'evolution et la structure de la doctrine de la science chez Fichte. Paris, 1930. 2v.
Phil 3425.682	Guereñu, Ernesto de. Das Gottesbild des Jungen Hegel. Thesis. Freiburg, 1969.
Phil 5841.4	Guérin, Daniel. Essai sur la révolution sexuelle. Paris, 1969.
Phil 5246.24	Guérin, Jules. Les différentes manifestations. Paris, 1899.
Phil 1135.155	Guérin, Pièrre. L'idée de justice dans la conception de l'univers les premiers philosophes grecs. Paris, 1934.
Phil 1135.155.5	Guérin, Pièrre. L'idée de justice dans la conception de l'univers les premiers philosophes grecs. Thèse. Strasbourg, 1934.
Phil 8586.55.5	Guerin, Pierre. Pensée constructive et réalités spirituelle. Paris, 1934.
Phil 8586.55	Guerin, Pierre. Vérité et religion; essai le problème. Paris, 1934.
Phil 2905.1.460	Guerini, Edmund W. Evolution in the afterlife. 1st ed. N.Y., 1967.
Phil 1535.31	Guerinois, J.C. Clypeus philosophiae Thomisticae. Venetiis, 1729. 7v.
Phil 6990.21.10	Pamphlet vol. Guerisons du P. de Hohenlohe. 4 pam.

Phil 3552.304   Gueroult, M. Dynamique et métaphysique Leibniziennes. Paris, 1934.

Phil 3625.5.93   Gueroult, M. La philosophie transcendantale de Salomon Maimon. Paris, 1929.

Phil 3625.5.94   Gueroult, M. La philosophie transcendantale de Salomon Maimon. Thèse. Paris, 1929.

Phil 2520.420   Guéroult, Marital. Etudes sur Descartes, Spinoza, Hildesheim. N.Y., 1970.

Phil 1870.130   Guéroult, Martial. Berkeley. Paris, 1956.

Phil 2520.242   Gueroult, Martial. Descartes, selon l'ordre des raisons. Paris, 1953. 2v.

Phil 2733.106   Guéroult, Martial. Etendue et psychologie chez Malebranche. Paris, 1939.

Phil 2733.106.5   Guéroult, Martial. Malebranche. Paris, 1955. 3v.

Phil 2520.242.5   Gueroult, Martial. Nouvelles réflexions sur la preuve ontologique de Descartes. Paris, 1955.

Phil 4007.5   Guerra, Augusto. Il mondo della sicurezza; Ardigo, Labriola, Croce. Firenze, 1963.

Phil 175.26   La guerra eterna e il dramma dell'esistenza. (Aliotta, Antonio.) Napoli, 1917.

Phil 175.26.2   La guerra eterna e il dramma dell'esistenza. 2a ed. (Aliotta, Antonio.) Napoli, 1920.

Phil 5246.54   Guerrero, L.J. Psicología. 4. ed. Buenos Aires, 1943.

Phil 8125.2   Guerrero, Luis. Panorama de la estética clásica-romántica alemana. La Plata, 1934.

Phil 8407.46   Guerrero, Luis Juan. Estética operatoria en sus tres direcciones. Buenos Aires, 1956-67. 3v.

Phil 3552.415   Guerrier, V.I. Leibnits i ego vek. Sankt Peterburg, 1868.

Phil 5425.54.5   Guerster, Eugen. Macht und Geheimnis der Dummheit. Zürich, 1967.

Phil 8598.12.15   Guesses at the riddle of existence. (Smith, Goldwin.) N.Y., 1897.

Phil 9560.38   The guest of honour. (Barrett, E.B.) Dublin, 1954.

Phil 1706.5.10   Güttler, C. Einführung in die Geschichte der Philosophie seit Hegel. München, 1921.

Phil 5246.34   Güttler, C. Psychologie und Philosophie. München, 1896.

Phil 8586.26   Güttler, C. Wissen und Glauben. 2e Aufl. München, 1904.

Phil 181.38   Güttler, Karl. Gesammelte Abhandlungen. München, 1918.

Phil 3808.207   Guetzlaff, Victor. Schopenhauer ueber die Thiere und den Tierschutz. Berlin, 1879.

Phil 1828.10   Guffey, George Robert. Traherne and the seventeenth-century English platonists, 1900-1966. London, 1969.

Phil 3552.315   Guggenberger, Alois. Leibniz. Stuttgart, 1947.

Phil 182.94.82   Guggenberger, Alois. Der Menschengeist und das Sein. Krailling vor München, 1942.

Phil 8407.31   Guggenheimer, R.H. Creative vision in artist and audience. N.Y., 1950.

Phil 8407.31.5   Guggenheimer, R.H. Sight and insight, a prediction of new perceptions in art. N.Y., 1945.

Phil 817.8.20   Guggiero, Guido de. Storia della filosofia. v.1 (pt. 1-2), v.2 (pt. 1-3), v.3-10. Bari, 1918. 13v.

Phil 181.85   Guglielmini, H. Temas existenciales. Buenos Aires, 1939.

Phil 2190.15   Guglielmo di Occam. (Giacon, C.) Milano, 1941. 2v.

Phil 5058.7.18   Guglielmo Schuppe e la filosofia dell'immanerza. (Pelazza, Amelio.) Milano, 1914.

Phil 5190.50   Guha Mozumdar, Roby. Possibilism. Calcutta, 1966.

Phil 3552.87   Guhrauer, G.E. Gottfried Willhelm Freiherr von Leibnitz. Breslau, 1842. 2v.

Phil 337.14   Guia, Michele. Storia delle science ed epistemologia. Torino, 1945.

Phil 4363.2.5   Guia espiritual. (Molinos, M. de.) Barcelona, 1906.

Phil 5247.13.26   Guibelet, J. Examen de l'examen des esprits. Paris, 1631.

Phil 178.57   The guidance of conduct. (Dixon, E.T.) London, 1928.

Phil 5203.12   Guide de l'étudiant en psychologie. (Carron, René.) Paris, 1953.

Phil 9245.63   Le guide du bonheur. 2. éd. (Delessert, Benjamin Guron.) Paris, 1840.

Phil 8420.24   A guide to aesthetics. (Torossian, A.) Stanford, 1937.

Phil 9290.9   A guide to civilized loafing. (Overstreet, Harry A.) N.Y., 1934.

Phil 6048.95   A guide to palmistry. (Henderson, Eliza Easter.) Boston, 1895.

Phil 97.5   Guide to philosophical terminology. (Melzer, J.H.) Ashland, Ohio, 1938.

Phil 184.26.15   Guide to philosophy. (Joad, C.E.M.) London, 1936.

Phil 184.26.18   Guide to philosophy. (Joad, C.E.M.) N.Y., 1956.

Phil 9455.20   A guide to public opinion polls. (Gallup, G.H.) Princeton, 1944.

Phil 5865.5.16   A guide to reading Piaget. (Brearley, Molly.) N.Y., 1967.

Phil 75.35   A guide to readings in philosophy. (Hope, R.) Ann Arbor, 1939.

Phil 8879.3.5   Guide to social happiness. v.1-4. (Ellis, S.S.) N.Y., 1844-47.

Phil 8030.4   A guide to the literature of aesthetics. (Gayley, Charles.) Berkeley, 1890.

Phil 9450.16   Guide to the philosophy of morals and politics. (Joad, C.E.M.) N.Y., 1938.

Phil 1955.6.250   Guide to the works of John Dewey. Carbondale, 1970.

Phil 978.13   A guide to theosophy. (Tukarama Tatya.) Bombay, 1887.

Phil 5059.17   A guide to thinking; a beginner's book in logic. (Templin, Olin.) Garden City, N.Y., 1927.

Phil 5042.40   Guides to straight thinking. 1st ed. (Chase, Stuart.) N.Y., 1956.

Phil 6676.8   Guidi, Franc. Il magnetismo animale. Milano, 1860.

Phil 1535.22   Guidi, P.L. Principia philosophica. v.1-2. Florentiae, 1913-14.

Htn   Phil 6016.2*   Guidicio di fisionomia. (Grisaldi, Paolo.) Trevigi, 1620.

Phil 6310.6   Guiding human misfits. (Adler, Alexandra.) N.Y., 1938.

Phil 6310.6.2   Guiding human misfits. (Adler, Alexandra.) N.Y., 1939.

Phil 8401.33   Guidizio estetico critica e censura. (Assunto, Rosario.) Firenze, 1963.

Phil 8586.14   Guilbert, A.V.F. La divine synthèse. Paris, 1875. 3v.

Phil 8661.3   Guilbert, A.V.F. Monde et Dieu. Paris, 1879.

Phil 8610.875.10   Guild, E.E. The pro and con of supernatural religion...together with a sketch of the life of the author. N.Y., 1876.

Phil 3450.19.360   Guilead, Reuben. Etre et liberté. Louvain, 1965.

Phil 5590.265   Guilford, J.P. Personality. N.Y., 1959.

Phil 5246.47.8   Guilford, J.P. Fields of psychology. N.Y., 1940.

Phil 5246.47.10A   Guilford, Joy Paul. Fundamental statistics in psychology and education. N.Y., 1942.

Phil 5246.47.12   Guilford, Joy Paul. Fundamental statistics in psychology and education. 4. ed. N.Y., 1965.

Phil 5246.47   Guilford, Joy Paul. Laboratory studies in psychology. N.Y., 1934.

Phil 5246.47.15   Guilford, Joy Paul. The nature of human intelligence. N.Y., 1967.

Phil 5246.47.6   Guilford, Joy Paul. Psychometric methods. N.Y., 1954.

Phil 5246.47.5A   Guilford, Joy Paul. Psychometric methods. 1. ed. N.Y., 1936.

Phil 5520.437   Guilhot, Jean. La dynamique de l'expression et de la communication. Paris, 1962.

Phil 337.28   Guilhot, Jean. Introduction à la psychiatrie de la connaissance. Paris, 1966.

Phil 8661.28.2   Guilhot, Jean. La psychiatrie morale et le problème de Dieu. Paris, 1967.

Phil 8661.28   Guilhot, Jean. La psychiatrie morale et le problème de Dieu. Thesis. La Haye, 1967.

Phil 806.35   Giuliano, Balbino. Il cammino del pensiero. Firenze, 1962.

Phil 6952.23.80   Guillain, Georges. J.M. Charcot, 1825-1893. N.Y., 1959.

Phil 6116.25   Guillain, Georges. Travaux neurologiques de guerre. Paris, 1920.

Phil 7050.11   Guillard, J.-C.A. Table qui douse et table qui répond. Paris, 1853. 3 pam.

Phil 672.230   Guillaumaud, Jacques. Du temps physique au temps romanesque. Paris, 1965.

Phil 5635.4   Guillaume, J.A.M. Nouveau traité des sensations. Paris, 1876. 2v.

Phil 5816.13   Guillaume, P. La psychologie animale. Paris, 1940.

Phil 5435.14   Guillaume, Paul. La formation des habitudes. Paris, 1968.

Phil 5246.43.10   Guillaume, Paul. Manuel de psychologie. Paris, 1944.

Phil 5246.43   Guillaume, Paul. Psychologie. Paris, 1931.

Phil 5246.43.5   Guillaume, Paul. La psychologie de la forme. Paris, 1937.

Phil 5592.184   Guillaumin, Jean. La dynamique de l'examen psychologique. Paris, 1965.

Phil 806.2   Guillon, M.N.S. Histoire générale de la philosophie. Paris, 1835. 4v.

Phil 181.47   Guillou, Henri. Essai de philosophie générale élémentaire. Paris, 1921.

Phil 8407.20   Guillou, R. L'art invincible. Paris, 1948.

Phil 8881.22   Guilly, E.P. La nature et la morale. Paris, 1884.

Phil 5414.35   Guilt. (McKenzie, John.) London, 1962.

Phil 5414.30   Guilt and grace. (Tournier, Paul.) London, 1962.

Phil 930.36.5   Guilt and sin in traditional China. (Eberhard, Wolfram.) Berkeley, 1967.

Phil 4467.1.30   Guimarães, M. A grand concepção de Deus. Rio, 1940.

Phil 6956.8   Guimares, A. De hygiene mental e sua importancia em mosso meio. San Paulo, 1926.

Phil 6615.2   Guinon, Georges. Les agents provocateurs de l'hystérie. Paris, 1889.

Phil 8612.74   Guiomar, Michel. Principes d'une esthétique de la mort. Paris, 1967.

Phil 5520.180   Guiraud, P. La sémantique. 1. éd. Paris, 1955.

Phil 8586.52   Guirdham, A. Christ and Freud. London, 1959.

Phil 5246.68   Guirdham, Arthur. Man: divine or social. London, 1960.

Phil 8586.44   Guisan, René. Reliquiae. Lausanne, 1535.

Phil 6956.3   Guislain, J. Leçons orales phrénopathies. Paris, 1880. 2v.

Phil 2750.22.90   Guissard, L. Emmanuel Mounier. Paris, 1962.

Phil 3640.310   Guisso, Lorenzo. Nietzsche. Milano, 1942.

Phil 2805.404   Guitton, J. Génie de Pascal. Paris, 1962.

Phil 2630.11.5   Guitton, Jean. Apprendre à vivre et à penser. Paris, 1957.

Phil 2630.11.25   Guitton, Jean. Le clair et l'obscur. Paris, 1962.

Phil 287.10   Guitton, Jean. De la signification du cosmos. Paris, 1966.

Phil 2630.11.20   Guitton, Jean. Dialogue avec les précurseurs. Aubier, 1962.

Phil 181.88   Guitton, Jean. L'existence temporelle. Paris, 1949.

Phil 2630.11.12   Guitton, Jean. The Guitton journals, 1952-1955. London, 1963.

Phil 2630.11.40   Guitton, Jean. Histoire et destinée. Paris, 1970.

Phil 2630.11   Guitton, Jean. Invitation a la pensée et à la vie. Paris, 1956.

Phil 2630.11.10   Guitton, Jean. Journal. Paris, 1959. 2v.

Phil 181.87   Guitton, Jean. Justification du temps. Paris, 1941.

Phil 2630.11.8   Guitton, Jean. Make your mind work for you. N.Y., 1958.

Phil 181.87.5   Guitton, Jean. Man in time. Notre Dame, Ind., 1966.

Phil 2630.11.15   Guitton, Jean. Une mère dans sa vallée. Paris, 1961.

Phil 2630.11.30   Guitton, Jean. Oeuvres complètes. v.1-2. Paris, 1966.

Phil 2805.270   Guitton, Jean. Pascal et Leibniz. Paris, 1951.

Phil 2630.11.2   Guitton, Jean. La pensée moderne et le catholicisme. v.6,7,9,10. Aix, 1936. 5v.

Phil 8956.12   Guitton, Jean. Rapport de Jean Guitton sur les prix de vertu. Paris, 1964.

Phil 2475.1.380   Guitton, Jean. La vocation de Bergson. Paris, 1960.

Phil 2630.11.12   The Guitton journals, 1952-1955. (Guitton, Jean.) London, 1963.

Phil 2406.6   Guittoy, Jean. Regards sur la pensée française, 1870-1940. Paris, 1968.

Phil 8881.23.15   Guizot, F.P.G. Méditations et études morales. Paris, 1864.

Phil 8586.34.5   Guizot, F.P.G. Méditations sur la religion chrétienne. Paris, 1866-1868. 3v.

Phil 8586.34.3   Guizot, F.P.G. Méditations sur l'essence de la religion. Paris, 1866.

Phil 8586.34.2   Guizot, F.P.G. Méditations sur l'essence de la religion chrétienne. 1e série. Paris, 1864.

Phil 8586.34   Guizot, F.P.G. Méditations sur l'essence de la religion chrétienne. 1e série. Paris, 1864.

Phil 7069.25.14   Gulat-Wellenburg, W.K.H. Der physikalische Mediumismus. Berlin, 1925.

Phil 7140.121.5   Gulat-Wellenburg. Das Wunder der Autosuggestion. Kempten im Allgäu, 1925.

Phil 3310.12   Gulden, P.H. Albert Görlands systematische Philosophie. Assen, 1943.

Phil 3425.520   Gulian, C.I. Metoda si sistem la Hegel. Bucuresti, 1957. 2v.

Phil 4816.8   Gulian, C.I. Peredovye rumynskie mysliteli XVIII-XIXVV. Moskva, 1961.

Phil 9346.8   Gulick, L.H. The dynamic of manhood. N.Y., 1917.

Phil 6116.7   Gulick, L.H. Mind and work. N.Y., 1908.

Phil 5272.8   Gulliksen, Harold. Mathematical solutions for psychological problems. n.p., 1958.

Phil 5357.3   Gulliksen, Harold. Reliability for the law of comparative judgment. n.p., 1957. 2 pam.

Phil 8696.6   Gulliver, John P. Christianity and science. Andover, 1880.

Phil 195.6   Gulmer, Karl. Von der Sache der Philosophie. Freiburg, 1959.

Phil 3006.9.5   Gulyga, A.V. Der deutsche Materialismus am Ausgang des 18. Jahrhunderts. Berlin, 1966.

Phil 3006.9 — Gulyga, A.V. Iz istorii nemetskogo materializma. Moskva, 1962.
Phil 3425.774 — Gulyga, Arsenii V. Gegel'. Moskva, 1970.
Phil 1750.166.155 — Gumanizm; opyt filosofskoetich i potsial issled problemy. (Petrosian, M.J.) Moskva, 1964.
Phil 9245.59 — Gumpert, M. The anatomy of happiness. N.Y., 1951.
Phil 75.5 — Gumposh, V.P. Die philosophische Literatur der Deutschen. Regensburg, 1851.
Phil 5425.86 — Gun, W.T.J. Studies in hereditary ability. London, 1928.
Phil 1135.41 — Gundel, Wilhelm. Beiträge zur...Ananke und Heimarmene. Giessen, 1914.
Phil 1504.4.2 — Gundissalinus de divisione philosophiae. v.4, pt.2-3. (Baur, L.) Münster, n.d. 2v.
Phil 3640.192 — Gundolf, E. E. Gundolf und Kurt Heldebrandt, Nietzsche als Richter unsrer Zeit. Breslau, 1923.
Phil 1850.135 — Gundry, W.G.C. Francis Bacon, a map of days. London, 1946.
Phil 9560.64 — Güneş batidan doğmustur. (Kuş, Nuri.) Kütahya, 1970.
Phil 287.1 — Gunkel, H. Schöpfung und Chaos. Göttingen, 1895.
Phil 3826.7 — Gunn, J.A. Benedict Spinoza. Melbourne, 1925.
Phil 2406.2 — Gunn, J.A. Modern French philosophy. London, 1922.
Phil 2406.2.2 — Gunn, J.A. Modern French philosophy. N.Y., 1922.
Phil 672.145 — Gunn, J.A. The problem of time. London, 1929.
Phil 5203.6 — Gunn, John A. Psyche and Minerva. Melbourne, 1930.
Phil 2475.1.202 — Gunn, John Alex. Bergson and his philosophy. London, 1920.
Phil 1511.3.14 — Gunn, W.W. A modern social philosophy. Cutting, 1937.
Phil 1195.5 — Gunning, C.P. Dissertatio inauguralis de sophistis Graeciae. Amstelodami, 1915.
Phil 3826.5 — Gunning, J.H. Spinoza en de idee der personlijkleid. 2. druk. Baarn, 1919.
Phil 310.605 — Guntau, Martin. Naturforschung und Weltbild. Berlin, 1964.
Phil 2475.1.500 — Gunter, Pete Addison Y. Bergson and the evolution of physics. 1st ed. Knoxville, 1969.
Phil 8586.42 — Gunther, G. Christliche Metaphysik und das Schicksal des modernen Bewusstseins. Leipzig, 1937.
Phil 181.110 — Gunther, H.R.G. Personlichkeit und Geschichte. Augsburg, 1947.
Phil 6316.14 — Guntrip, H.J.S. Personality structure and human interaction. London, 1961.
Phil 6316.14.5 — Guntrip, H.J.S. Personality structure and human interaction. N.Y., 1961.
Phil 6316.14.10 — Guntrip, Henry James Samuel. Psychoanalytic theory, therapy, and the self. N.Y., 1971.
Phil 6956.17 — Guntrip, Henry James Samuel. Schizoid phenomena, object relations and the self. London, 1968.
Phil 8092.5 — Gunzenhaeuser, R. Asthetisches Mass und Ästhetische Information. Hamburg, 1962.
Phil 7054.81.15 — Guppy, Samuel. Mary Jane; or spiritualism chemically explained. London, 1863.
Phil 8881.80 — Gupta, Rajender Kumas. Studien zur Ethik. Bonn, 1967.
Phil 5850.226 — Gürdev, Dinó. Strukturen analiz na obshtestvenoto Sŭznanie. Sofiia, 1970.
Phil 4757.2.120 — Gurdjieff, de mens en zijn werk. (Ekkev, Martin H.) Amsterdam, 1968.
Phil 4757.2.30A — Gurdjieff, Georges Ivanovitch. All and everything. v.1-2. 1st ed. N.Y., 1950. 2v.
Phil 4757.2.32 — Gurdjieff, Georges Ivanovitch. The herald of coming good. Chicago, 1966.
Phil 4757.2.115 — Gurdjieff remembered. (Peters, Arthur A.) London, 1965.
Phil 8696.22 — Gurev, Grigorii. Velikii konflikt. Moskva, 1965.
Phil 5400.44 — Gurewitsch, Aron. Zur Geschichte des Achtungsbegriffes und zur Theorie der sittlichen Gefühle. Inaug. Diss. Würzburg, 1897.
Phil 6116.28 — Gurin, Gerald. Americans view their mental health. N.Y., 1960.
Phil 337.8 — Gurland-Eljaschoff, E. Erkenntnistheoretische Studien auf antipsychologistischer Grundlage. Bern, 1910.
Htn Phil 5246.16.2* — Gurley, R.R. Skeleton project of a science of psychology. n.p., n.d.
Htn Phil 5246.16* — Gurley, R.R. Skeleton project of a science of psychology. n.p., n.d.
Phil 7068.92.35 — Gurney, Edmund. Les hallucinations télépathiques. 2. ed. Paris, 1892.
Phil 7068.86.20A — Gurney, Edmund. Phantasms of the living. London, 1886. 2v.
Phil 7069.18.100 — Gurney, Edmund. Phantasms of the living. London, 1918.
Phil 5435.11 — Gurney, Joseph J. Thoughts on habit and discipline. Philadelphia, 1877.
Phil 181.44 — Gurnhill, James. Christian philosophy discussed under the topics of absolute values. London, 1921.
Phil 181.44.5 — Gurnhill, James. Interpretation of the spiritual philosophy. London, 1920.
Phil 1750.550 — Gurr, John E. The principle of sufficient reason in some scholastic systems. Milwaukee, 1959.
Phil 481.4 — Gurst, Guenter. Grosse Materialisten. Leipzig, 1965.
Phil 8661.17 — Gururmurti, D. God and progress. Madras, 1945.
Phil 310.582 — Gurvich, S.S. Voprosy dialektich materializma; k lektsiiam. Kiev, 1964.
Phil 3006.7.5 — Gurvitch, G. Les tendances actuelles de la philosophie allemande. Paris, 1949.
Phil 3006.7 — Gurvitch, G. Les tendances actuelles de la philosophie allemande. Photoreproduction. Paris, 1930.
Phil 5016.2 — Gurvitch, Georges. Dialectique et sociologie. Paris, 1962.
Phil 2490.160 — Gurvitch, Georges. Les fondateurs de la sociologie. Paris, 1957.
Phil 8881.64 — Gurvitch, Georges. Morale théorique et science des moeurs. Paris, 1937.
Phil 8881.64.2 — Gurvitch, Georges. Morale théorique et science des moeurs. 2. éd. Paris, 1948.
Phil 1750.70.5 — Gurwitsch, Aron. The field of consciousness. Pittsburgh, 1964.
Phil 1750.773 — Gurwitsch, Aron. Studies in phenomenology and psychology. Evanston, 1966.
Phil 1750.70 — Gurwitsch, Aron. Théorie du champ de la conscience. Paris, 1957.
Phil 3246.202 — Gurwitsch, G. Die Einheit der Fichteschen Philosophie. Berlin, 1922.
Phil 3246.202.5 — Gurwitsch, G. Fichtes System der konkreten Ethik. Tübingen, 1924.
Phil 8092.16 — Gus, Mikhail S. Modernizm bez maski. Moskva, 1966.
Phil 5374.63 — Gusdorf, G. La découverte de soi. Thèse. 1. éd. Paris, 1948.
Phil 181.114 — Gusdorf, G. Mythe et métaphysique. Paris, 1953.
Phil 181.114.5 — Gusdorf, G. Traité de métaphysique. Paris, 1956.
Phil 5520.110 — Gusdorf, George. La parole. 1. éd. Paris, 1955.

Phil 5520.110.5 — Gusdorf, George. Speaking (La parole). Evanston, Ill., 1965.
Phil 8881.72A — Gusdorf, Georges. Traité de l'existence morale. Paris, 1949.
Phil 8881.72.5 — Gusdorf, Georges. La vertu de force. 1. éd. Paris, 1957.
Phil 4795.2.2 — Guseinov, Geidar. Iz istorii obshechestvennoi i filosofskoi mysli v Azerbaidzhane. Izd. 2. Baku, 1958.
Phil 2750.1.79 — Gusgens, J. Die Naturphilosophie des Joannes...Magnenus. Bonn, 1910.
Phil 193.69.8 — Gustav Engel...Klangfarbe. (Stumpf, K.) n.p., 1888-1915. 23 pam.
Phil 3210.28 — Gustav Theodor Fechner. (Lasswitz, K.) Stuttgart, 1902.
Phil 3210.81.2 — Gustav Theodor Fechner. (Lasswitz, Kurd.) Stuttgart, 1896.
Phil 3210.81 — Gustav Theodor Fechner. (Lasswitz, Kurd.) Stuttgart, 1910.
Phil 3210.82 — Gustav Theodor Fechner. (Wundt, W.) Leipzig, 1901.
Phil 2905.3.80 — Gustave Thibon, témoin de la lumière. (Chabanis, Christian.) Paris, 1967.
Phil 3450.36 — Gustige Kämpf der Zeit im Spiegel und Lebens. (Hessen, Johannes.) Nürnberg, 1959.
Phil 5046.14 — Gustrin, E.F. Nägra anmarkningar angående den formella logiken. Lund, 1876.
Phil 8875.14 — Gut und Böse. (Aars, K.B.R.) Christiania, 1907.
Phil 8880.34 — Gut und Böse. (Fuchs, Emil.) Tübingen, 1906.
Phil 8892.76.5 — Gut und Böse. (Reiner, Hans.) Freiburg, 1965.
Phil 5627.95.15 — Gut und Böse im Glauben der Völker. (Mensching, Gustav.) Leipzig, 1941.
Phil 5627.95.17 — Gut und Böse im Glauben des Völker. 2. Aufl. (Mensching, Gustav.) Stuttgart, 1950.
Phil 3310.5.34 — Gutberlet, C. Ethik und Naturrecht. Münster, 1883.
Phil 8881.43 — Gutberlet, C. Ethik und Religion. Münster, 1892.
Phil 3310.5.33 — Gutberlet, C. Logik und Erkenntnisstheorie. Münster, 1882.
Phil 510.23 — Gutberlet, C. Der mechanische Monismus. Paderborn, 1893.
Phil 3310.5.31 — Gutberlet, C. Die Metaphysik. Münster, 1880.
Phil 3310.5.35 — Gutberlet, C. Naturphilosophie. Münster, 1885.
Phil 3310.5.32 — Gutberlet, C. Die Psychologie. Münster, 1881.
Phil 5246.19 — Gutberlet, C. Die Psychologie. 2. Aufl. Münster, 1890.
Phil 5246.19.10 — Gutberlet, C. Psychophysik. Mainz, 1905.
Phil 3310.5.30 — Gutberlet, C. Die Theodicee. Münster, 1878.
Phil 5756.6.2 — Gutberlet, C. Die Willensfreiheit und ihre Gegner. 2. Aufl. Fulda, 1907.
Phil 672.28 — Gutberlet, Constantin. Die neue Raumtheorie. Mainz, 1882.
Phil 8882.48 — Das Gute. (Häberlin, Paul.) Basel, 1926.
Phil 8878.37 — Das Gute und das Sittliche. (Dürr, Ernst.) Heidelberg, 1911.
Phil 3640.90.12A — Gutersohn, U. Friedrich Nietzsche und der moderne Mensch. 2. Aufl. St. Gallen, 1945.
Phil 7082.16 — Gutheil, Emil Arthur. The handbook of dream analysis. N.Y., 1951.
Phil 600.38 — Guthlin, A. Les doctrines positivistes en France. Paris, 1873.
Phil 6316.10 — Guthrie, E.R. The psychology of human conflict. N.Y., 1938.
Phil 181.76.5 — Guthrie, H. Introduction au problème de l'histoire de la philosophie. Paris, 1937.
Phil 181.76 — Guthrie, H. Introduction au problème de l'histoire de la philosophie. Thèse. Paris, 1937.
Phil 5756.1 — Guthrie, M. Causational and free will. London, 1877.
Phil 2270.84.5A — Guthrie, M. On Mr. Spencer's data of ethics. London, 1884.
Phil 2270.84 — Guthrie, M. On Mr. Spencer's formula of evolution. London, 1878.
Phil 2270.84.8 — Guthrie, M. On Mr. Spencer's unification of knowledge. London, 1882.
Phil 1111.12 — Guthrie, William. The Greek philosophers from Thales to Aristotle. N.Y., 1950.
Phil 1111.12.5 — Guthrie, William. Greek philosophy. Cambridge, Eng., 1953.
Phil 1111.12.10 — Guthrie, William. A history of Greek philosophy. Cambridge, 1962. 3v.
Phil 4372.1.87 — Gutiérrez, Alberto. El pensamiento filosófico de Juan Luis Vives. Buenos Aires, 1940.
Phil 8661.30 — Gutiérrez, Antonio José. La providencia y España. San Sebastián, 1941.
Phil 525.6 — Gutiérrez, Marcelino. El misticismo ortodoxo en sus relaciones con la filosofia. Valladolid, 1886.
Phil 4362.1.80 — Gutierrez, P.F.M. Fr. Luis de León y la filosofia espanole. Madrid, 1885.
Phil 181.79 — Gutkind, Eric. The absolute collective. London, 1937.
Phil 181.79.5 — Gutkind, Eric. The body of God. N.Y., 1969.
Phil 5046.50 — Guttenplan, Samuel D. Logic: a comprehensive introduction. N.Y., 1971.
Phil 3625.1.87 — Guttenstein, B. M. Mendelssohn's Verdienste und die Bildung seines Volkes. Heidelberg, 1829.
Phil 1706.5 — Guttler, C. Einführung in die Geschichte der neueren Philosophie des Auslandes. München, 1922.
Phil 1050.4 — Guttmann, J. Die philosophie der Soloman ibn Gabirol. Göttingen, 1889.
Phil 1050.21 — Guttmann, J. Die Philosophie des Judentums. München, 1933.
Phil 1504.10.4 — Guttmann, J. Die philosophischen Lehren. v.10, pt.4. Münster, 1911.
Phil 1955.6.130 — Gutzke, M.G. John Dewey's thought and its implications for Christian education. N.Y., 1956.
Phil 2515.8.80 — Guy, Alain. Métaphysique et intuition; le message de Jacques Chevalier. Paris, 1940.
Phil 4307.2 — Guy, Alain. Les philosophes espagnols d'hier et d'aujourd'hui. Toulouse, 1956. 2v.
Phil 2005.10.80 — Guy Cromwell Field. (Allan, Donald James.) London, 1956.
Phil 7069.25.13 — Guyard, J. The door of death wide open. Boston, 1925.
Phil 2605.1.80 — Guyau, Augustin. La philosophie...d'Alfred Fouillée. Paris, 1913.
Phil 2630.2.10 — Guyau, J.M. Philosophische Werke. Leipzig, 1912-1914. 6v.
Phil 2630.2.35 — Guyau, J.M. Sittlichkeit ohne Pflicht. Leipzig, 1909.
Phil 8881.26 — Guyau, M. Esquisse d'une morale. Paris, 1896.
Phil 1158.5 — Guyau, M. La morale d'Epicure. Paris, 1878.
Phil 8407.3 — Guyau, M. Les problèmes de l'esthétique comtemporaine. Paris, 1884.
Phil 8881.26.5 — Guyau, M. A sketch of morality. London, 1898.
Phil 8586.8.10 — Guyau, M.J. Framtidens irreligion. Stockholm, 1907.
Phil 672.24 — Guyau, M.J. La genèse de l'idée de temps. 2e éd. Paris, 1902.
Phil 8586.8.3 — Guyau, M.J. L'irréligion de l'avenir. 18. éd. Paris, 1912.
Phil 8586.8.15 — Guyau, M.J. Die irreligion der Zukunft. Leipzig, 192-?

Phil 8831.1 Guyau, M.J. La morale anglaise contemporaine. Paris, 1878.
Phil 8586.8.5 Guyau, M.J. The non-religion of the future. London, 1897.
Phil 2630.2.129 Guyaus estetik. (Nilsson, A.) Lund, 1909.
Phil 6990.3.88 Guynot, Ernest. Sainte Bernadette. Paris, 1959.
Phil 9558.20 Guyon, René. La cruauté. Paris, 1927.
Phil 181.53 Guyon, René. Essai de métaphysique materialiste. Paris, 1924.
Phil 8696.5 Guyot, Arnold. Creation. N.Y., 1884.
Phil 1135.165 Guyot, Henri. L'infinite divine depuis Philon le Juif jusqu'à Platin. Paris, 1906.
Phil 8881.39 Guyot, Yves. La morale: la moralé théologique. Paris, 1883.
Phil 4080.3.250 Guzzo, A. Croce e Gentile. Lugano, 1953.
Phil 4006.7.30A Guzzo, A. Gli hegeliani d'Italia. Torino, 1953.
Phil 4065.118 Guzzo, Augusto. I dialoghi del Bruno. Torino, 1932.
Phil 4120.8.45 Guzzo, Augusto. Discorsi, 1938-50. Torino, 1951.
Phil 4065.118.5 Guzzo, Augusto. Giordano Bruno. Torino, 1960.
Phil 181.84 Guzzo, Augusto. Idealisti ed empiristi; saggi. Firenze, 1935.
Phil 3488.17 Guzzo, Augusto. Kant precritico. Torino, 1924.
Phil 4120.8.35 Guzzo, Augusto. La moralitá. Torino, 1950.
Phil 4120.8.40 Guzzo, Augusto. Parerga. Torino, 1956.
Phil 3826.8 Guzzo, Augusto. Il pensiero di B. Spinoza. Firenze, 1924.
Phil 3826.8.2 Guzzo, Augusto. Il pensiero di B. Spinoza. 2. ed. Torino, 1964.
Phil 4120.8.30 Guzzo, Augusto. La scienza. Torino, 1955.
Phil 400.67 Guzzo, Augusto. Verità e realtà: apologia dell'idealismo. Torino, 1925.
Phil 3450.19.510 Guzzoni, Giorgio. Considerazioni intorno alla prima sezione de Sein und Zeit. Urbino, 1969.
Phil 3425.590 Guzzoni, Ute. Werden zu Sich. Freiburg, 1963.
Phil 3808.86 Gwinner, W. Arthur Schopenhauer. Leipzig, 1862.
Phil 3808.86.3 Gwinner, W. Arthur Schopenhauer. Leipzig, 1922.
Phil 3808.86.15 Gwinner, W. Denkrede auf Arthur Schopenhauer. Leipzig, 1888.
Phil 3808.86.10 Gwinner, W. Schopenhauer und seine Freunde. Leipzig, 1863.
Phil 3808.86.5 Gwinner, W. Schopenhauer's Leben. Leipzig, 1878.
Phil 3808.86.7 Gwinner, W. Schopenhauer's Leben. Leipzig, 1910.
Phil 8593.12 Gyldene ord ur mensklighetens allmänna religion. 2. uppl. (Nyström, A.) Stockholm, 1880.
Phil 8961.21 Den gylne regel og andre humanistiske moralnormer. (Langfeldt, Gabriel.) Oslo, 1966.
Phil 1925.85 Gysi, Lydia. Platonism and Cartesianism. Bern, 1962.
Phil 2885.83 H. Taine. (Margerie, Amédée de.) Paris, 1894.
Phil 2885.100 H. Taine. (Salomon, Michel.) Paris, 1908.
Phil 974.2.7 H.P. Blavatsky, a great betrayal. (Cleather, A.L. (Mrs.).) Calcutta, 1922.
Phil 974.2.5 H.P. Blavatsky, her life and work for humanity. (Cleather, A.L. (Mrs.).) Calcutta, 1922.
Phil 974.2.65 H.P. Blavatsky, Tibet and Tulka. (Borborka, Geoffrey A.) Madras, 1966.
Phil 974.1 Pamphlet box. H.P. Blavatsky.
Phil 978.5.810 H.P. Blavatsky and the theosophical movement. (Ryan, C.J.) Point Loma, Calif., 1937.
Phil 974.2.9 H.P. Blavatsky as I knew her. (Cleather, A.L. (Mrs.).) Calcutta, 1923.
Phil 974.2.10 H.P. Blavatsky as I knew her. (Cleather, A.L. (Mrs.).) N.Y., 1923. 3 pam.
Phil 974.2.35 H.P.B. in memory of Helena Petrovna Blavatsky. London, 1931.
Phil 3415.106.8 Haacke, Hermann. Neuere Stimmen der Kritik über Eduard von Hartmanns Werke. Leipzig 1898.
Phil 3415.106.9 Haacke, Hermann. Stimmen der Kritik über Eduard von Hartmanns Werke. Leipzig, 1904.
Phil 182.57 Haacke, Wilhelm. Vom Strome des Seins. Leipzig, 1905.
Phil 1750.98 Haag, Karl Hanz. Kritik der neueren Ontologie. Stuttgart, 1960.
Phil 1750.100 Haag, Karl Hanz. Kritik der neueren Ontololgie. Stuttgart, 1960.
Phil 1707.29 Haag, Karl Heinz. Die Lehre vom Sein in der modernen Philosophie. Frankfurt, 1963.
Phil 3425.654 Haag, Karl Heinz. Philosophischer Idealismus. Frankfurt, 1967.
Phil 6980.346 Haakanson, Kaj. Psykisk sjukdom: illusioner och realiteter; en teoretisk studie. Uppsala, 1968.
Phil 1200.5 Haake, A. Die Gesellschaftslehre der Stoiker. Berlin, 1887.
Phil 3007.14 Haan, A.A.M. de. Het wijsgerig onderwijs aan het gymnasium illustre. Harderwijk, 1960.
Phil 6117.40 Haanel, C.F. The master key. St. Louis, 1919.
Phil 1750.17 Haas, A. Über der Einfluss der Epicureischen...Philosophie des 16 und 17 Jahrhunderts. Berlin, 1896.
Phil 1190.10 Haas, Leander. De philosophorum scepticorum successionibus. Inaug. Diss. Wurciburgi, 1875.
Phil 2225.5.110 Haas, W.P. The conception of law. Fribourg, 1964.
Phil 5247.28 Haas, Wilhelm. Die psychische Dingwelt. Bonn, 1921.
Phil 1750.40 Haas, William S. The destiny of the mind. N.Y., 1956.
Phil 8411.43.80 Haase, Rudolf. Hans Kayser. Basel, 1968.
Phil 5325.46 Håseth, Kjell Johan. Norske ord-assosiasjonsnormer. Oslo, 1968.
Phil 1750.560.25 Habachi, René. Une philosophie pour notre temps. Beirut? 1961.
Phil 1750.560.35 Habachi, René. Vers une pensée méditerranéenne. v.1-4. Beyrouth, 1956- 2v.
Phil 8882.59 Habas, R.A. Morals for moderns. N.Y., 1939.
Phil 4513.2.35 Haben die naturgesetze Wirklichkeit? (Aars, K.B.R.) Christiania, 1907.
Phil 288.10 Haber, Francis. The age of the world. Baltimore, 1959.
Phil 5643.150 Haber, Ralph Norman. Contemporary theory and research in visual perception. N.Y., 1968.
Phil 5548.106 Haber, Ralph Norman. Current research in motivation. N.Y., 1966.
Phil 6677.5 Haberman, J.V. Hypnosis. N.Y., 1910.
Phil 3801.445.50 Habermas, J. Das Absolute und die Geschichte. Bonn, 1954.
Phil 338.44 Habermas, Jürgen. Erkenntnis und Interesse. Frankfurt am Main, 1968.
Phil 338.44.1 Habermas, Jürgen. Knowledge and interests. Boston, 1971.
Phil 3030.8 Habermas, Jürgen. Philosophisch-politische Profile. 7. Aufl. Frankurt, 1971.
Phil 807.15 Habert, O. Le primat de l'intelligence dans l'histoire de la pensée. Paris, 1926.
Phil 8697.25 Habgood, J.S. Religion and science. London, 1964.
Phil 8697.25.2 Habgood, J.S. Truths in tension. 1. ed. N.Y., 1965.
Phil 5435.8A Habit. (James, William.) N.Y., 1890.
Phil 5435.8.3A Habit. (James, William.) N.Y., 1914.
Phil 5822.1.10A Habit and instinct. (Morgan, C.L.) London, 1896.

Phil 5252.13 Habit and intelligence. (Murphy, J.J.) London, 1869. 2v.
Phil 5252.13.2 Habit and intelligence. 2d. ed. (Murphy, J.J.) London, 1879.
Phil 5435.7 Habit interference in sorting cards. (Brown, Warner.) Berkeley, 1914.
Phil 5435.10.5 Habits, their making and unmaking. (Dunlap, Knight.) N.Y., 1945.
Phil 9560.57 Habits and virtues. (Klubertanz, George Peter.) N.Y., 1965.
Phil 5435.9 L'habitude, essai de métaphysique scientifique. (Chevalier, J.) Paris, 1929.
Phil 5435.5 Habitude ou train? (Nicolardot, F.) Paris, 1922.
Phil 1535.1.40 Habla Balmes. (Balmes, Jaime.) Barcelona, 1958.
Phil 8663.6 Hablar de Dios. (Illanes, José L.) Madrid, 1970.
Phil 3801.445 Habluetzel, Rudolf. Dialektik und Einbildungskraft. Basel, 1954.
Phil 5817.6.5 Hachet-Souplet, P. De l'animal à l'enfant. Paris, 1913.
Phil 5817.6 Hachet-Souplet, P. Examen psychologique des animaux. Paris, 1900.
Phil 5817.6.9 Hachet-Souplet, P. La genèse des instincts. Paris, 1912.
Phil 1750.166.190 Hacia un humanismo americano. (Orrego, Antenor.) Lima, 1966.
Phil 4979.5.30 Hacia un nuevo humanismo. 1. ed. (Ramos, Samuel.) México, 1940.
Phil 4987.53.30 Hacia un saber sobre el alma. (Zambrano, María.) Buenos Aires, 1950.
Phil 8883.3.2 Hacia una moral sin dogmas. 2a ed. (Ingenieros, José.) Buenos Aires, 1919.
Phil 7069.29.45 Hack, Gwendolyn Kelley. Modern psychic mysteries. London, 1929.
Phil 1135.136 Hack, R.K. God in Greek philosophy. Princeton, 1931.
Phil 3790.8.85 Hack, Valentin. Die Auffassung vom Wesen der Religion bei A. Ritschl. Diss. Leipzig, 1911.
Phil 9347.10 Hackley, E.A. (Mrs.). The colored girl beautiful. Kansas City, 1916.
Phil 930.30.10 Hackmann, H. Chinesche wijsgeeren. Amsterdam, 1930. 2v.
Phil 930.30 Hackmann, H. Chinesische Philosophie. München, 1927.
Phil 3489.28 Hacks, Jakob. Über Kant's synthetische Urteile a priori. Pt.1-4. Kattowitz, 1895-99.
Phil 5066.258 Hackstaff, L.H. Systems of formal logic. Dordrecht, 1966.
Phil 5400.180 HAD. (Carstens, Erik.) Kóbenhavn, 1967.
Phil 1707.20 Hadas, Mases. Humanism: the Greek ideal. 1. ed. N.Y., 1960.
Phil 1750.166.200 Hadas, Moses. The living tradition. N.Y., 1967.
Phil 5757.12.6 Haddock, F.C. Power of will. 55th ed. Meriden, 1915.
Phil 6677.11.2 Haddock, J.W. Somnolism and psycheism. 2d ed. London, 1851.
Phil 6317.2.10 Hadfield, J.A. Psychologi och moral. 2a uppl. Stockholm, 1924.
Phil 5247.51 Hadfield, J.A. Psychology and modern problems. London, 1935.
Phil 6317.2 Hadfield, J.A. Psychology and morals. London, 1923.
Phil 6317.2.7 Hadfield, J.A. Psychology and morals. N.Y., 1928.
Phil 6317.2.8 Hadfield, J.A. Psychology and morals. 8th ed. London, 1930.
Phil 6117.33 Hadfield, J.A. The psychology of power. N.Y., 1923.
Phil 6117.33.5 Hadfield, J.A. The psychology of power. N.Y., 1924.
Phil 1707.3 Hadley, A.T. Some influences in modern philosophic thought. New Haven, 1913.
Phil 9450.7 Hadley, A.T. Standards of public morality. N.Y., 1907.
Phil 5247.68 Hadley, John M. Clinical and counseling psychology. 1. ed. N.Y., 1958.
Phil 8408.41 Hadživasilev, Mito. Odraz, izraz. Skopje, 1958.
Phil 2005.6.31 Hä och der i verlden. (Friswell, J.H.) Stockholm, 1870.
Phil 5068.24 Haeberli, Hans. Der Begriff der Wissenschaft im logischen Positivismus. Bern, 1955.
Phil 8620.50 Häberlin, P. Das Böse. Bern, 1960.
Phil 2270.98 Häberlin, P. Herbert Spencer's Grundlagen der Philosophie. Leipzig, 1908.
Phil 8408.16 Häberlin, Paul. Allgemeine Ästhetik. Basel, 1929.
Phil 182.43.5 Häberlin, Paul. Anthropologie philosophique. Paris, 1943.
Phil 9035.42 Häberlin, Paul. Der Charakter. Basel, 1925.
Phil 5247.30 Häberlin, Paul. Der Gegenstand der Psychologie. Berlin, 1921.
Phil 5247.30.5 Häberlin, Paul. Der Geist und die Triebe: eine Elementarpsychologie. Basel, 1924.
Phil 8882.48 Häberlin, Paul. Das Gute. Basel, 1926.
Phil 288.8 Häberlin, Paul. Leben und Lebensform. Basel, 1957.
Phil 6117.38 Häberlin, Paul. Leib und Seele. Bern, 1927.
Phil 585.345 Haeberlin, Paul. Der Mensch, eine philosophische Anthropologie. Zürich, 1969.
Phil 182.43.10 Häberlin, Paul. Naturphilosophische Betrachtungen. Zurich, 1939-1940. 2v.
Phil 182.43.15 Häberlin, Paul. Philosophin perennis. Berlin, 1952.
Phil 5520.31 Häberlin, Paul. Symbol in der Psychologie. Bern, 1916.
Phil 182.43 Häberlin, Paul. Wissenschaft und Philosophie. Basel, 1910. 2v.
Phil 510.1.10 Haeckel, Ernst. Les énigmes de l'univers. Paris, 1903.
Phil 510.1.23 Haeckel, Ernst. Ewigkeit. Berlin, 1915.
Phil 510.1.16 Haeckel, Ernst. Haeckel und Allmers. Bremen, 1941.
Phil 510.1.1.5 Haeckel, Ernst. Monism. London, 1894.
Phil 510.1.1.7 Haeckel, Ernst. Monism. London, 1895.
Phil 510.1.1 Haeckel, Ernst. Der Monismus als Band zwischen Religion und Wissenschaft. Bonn, 1893.
Phil 510.1.7.5 Haeckel, Ernst. The riddle of the universe. London, 1925.
Phil 510.1.6A Haeckel, Ernst. The riddle of the universe. N.Y., 1900.
Phil 510.1.7.10 Haeckel, Ernst. The substance of the riddle of the universe. N.Y., 1927.
Phil 8610.905 Haeckel, Ernst. A universal monistic alliance. Los Angeles, 1905.
Phil 510.1.4 Haeckel, Ernst. Världsgåtorna. Stockholm, 1905.
Phil 510.1.3 Haeckel, Ernst. Die Welträthsel. Bonn, 1903.
Phil 510.1.2.5 Haeckel, Ernst. Die Welträthsel. Stuttgart, 1899.
Phil 510.1.3.5 Haeckel, Ernst. Die Welträthsel. Stuttgart, 1903.
Phil 510.1.2.4 Haeckel, Ernst. Die Welträthsel. 6e Aufl. Bonn, 1901.
Phil 510.1.2 Haeckel, Ernst. Die Welträthsel. 7e Aufl. Bonn, 1901.
Phil 510.1.2.6 Haeckel, Ernst. Die Welträtsel; gemeinverständliche Studien über monistische Philosophie. Berlin, 1961.
Phil 510.1.8 Haeckel, Ernst. Die wereldraadselen. Baarn, 1913.
Phil 510.1.15 Haeckel, Ernst. The wonders of life. N.Y., 1905.
Phil 510.1.16 Haeckel und Allmers. (Haeckel, Ernst.) Bremen, 1941.
Phil 510.1.17 Haeckel's critics answered. (McCabe, Joseph.) London, 1903.
Phil 510.1.18 Haeckel's critics answered. (McCabe, Joseph.) London, 1910.
Phil 510.1.20 Haeckel's monism false. (Ballard, Frank.) London, 1905.

Phil 510.1.14 — Häckels Welträthsel nach ihren starken und schwachen Seiten. (Baumann, J.) Leipzig, 1900.

Phil 8587.51.5 — Haecker, T. Der Christ und die Geschichte. Leipzig, 1935.

Phil 8587.51 — Haecker, T. Christentum und Kultur. München, 1927.

Phil 5400.112 — Haecker, T. Metaphysik des Fühlens. 4. Aufl. München, 1950.

Phil 8587.51.10 — Haecker, T. Opuscula. Olten, 1949.

Phil 8408.11 — Haecker, T. Schönheit; ein Versuch. Leipzig, 1936.

Phil 8408.10 — Haecker, T. Schönheit; ein Versuch. 3. Aufl. München, 1953.

Phil 3450.29.10 — Haecker, Theodor. Essays. Munchen, 1958.

Phil 3450.29 — Haecker, Theodor. Journal in the night. London, 1950.

Phil 3450.29.20 — Haecker, Theodor. Satire und Polemik. München, 1961.

Phil 3450.29.73 — Haecker, Theodor. Tag- und Nachtbücher, 1939-1945. 3e Aufl. München, 1959.

Phil 3450.29.70 — Haecker, Theodor. Tag- und Nachtbücher. München, 1947.

Phil 3450.29.75 — Haecker, Theodor. Vergil. Schönheit Metaphysik des Fühlens. München, 1967.

Phil 3450.29.7 — Haecker, Theodor. Was ist der Mensch? München, 1965.

Phil 3450.29.5 — Haecker, Theodor. Was ist der Mensch? 2e Aufl. Leipzig, 1934.

Phil 1750.363 — Haefliger, O. Wider den Existentialismus. Bern, 1949.

Phil 8587.66 — Hägerström, A.A.T. Religionsfilosofi. Stockholm, 1949.

Phil 4582.4.45 — Hägerström, Axel. Inquiries into the nature of law and morals. Stockholm, 1953.

Phil 3489.11 — Hägerström, Axel. Kants Ethik...dargestellt. Upsala, 1902.

Phil 4582.4.35 — Hägerström, Axel. Om den moraliska känslan och driften sasom förnuftiga. Upsala, 1895.

Phil 4582.4.33 — Hägerström, Axel. Om moraliska föreställningars sanning. Stockholm, 1911.

Phil 8587.76 — Haegerstroem, Axel. Philosophy and religion. London, 1964.

Phil 4582.4.46 — Hägerström, Axel. Ratten och Viljan. Lund, 1961.

Phil 4582.4.49 — Hägerström, Axel. Socialfilosofiska uppsatser. Stockholm, 1966.

Phil 4582.4.40 — Hägerström, Axel. De socialistiska idéernas historia. Stockholm, 1946.

Phil 4582.4.38 — Hägerström, Axel. Stat och rätt. Upsala, 1904.

Phil 4582.4.31 — Hägerström, Axel. Undersökning af den empiristiska etikens möjlighet. Upsala, 1895.

Phil 4582.4.90 — Hägerströmstudier. (Vannérus, Allen.) Stockholm, 1930.

Phil 3450.41 — Haekstra, Sytze. Oratio de summae veritatis cognoscendae ratione atque via. Amstelodami, 1857.

Phil 6049.57 — Hände als Symbol und Gestalt. 7. Aufl. (Jursch, Hanna.) Stuttgart, 1957.

Phil 720.67 — Haensel, Carl. Über den Irrtum. Heidelberg, 1965.

Phil 1707.17 — Haensel, Ludwig. Begegnungen und Auseinandersetzungen mit Denkern und Dichtern der Neuzeit. Wien, 1957.

Phil 5190.22 — Hänssler, Ernst H. Zur Theorie der Analogie und des sogenannten Analogieschlusses. Diss. Stuttgart, 1927.

Phil 5520.112 — Haerber, W.L. A scientific foundation of philosophy. Los Angeles, 1952.

Phil 5520.112.1 — Haerber, W.L. A scientific foundation of philosophy. Los Angeles, 1960.

Phil 574.6 — Haering, Bernhard. The Christian existentialist. N.Y., 1968.

Phil 8957.13.10 — Haering, Bernhard. Die Gegenwärtige Heilsstunde. Freiburg, 1964.

Phil 8957.13.5 — Haering, Bernhard. Das Gesetz Christi. 4. Aufl. Freiburg, 1957.

Phil 8957.13 — Haering, Bernhard. Macht und Ohnmacht der Religion. Salzburg, 1956.

Phil 8957.13.20 — Haering, Bernhard. Morality is for persons. N.Y., 1971.

Phil 574.6.5 — Haering, Bernhard. Personalismus in Philosophie und Theologie. München, 1968.

Phil 8957.13.15 — Haering, Bernhard. Toward a Christian moral theology. Notre Dame, 1966.

Phil 8882.95 — Haering, Herman Johan. Ethiek der voorlopigheid. Nijkerk, 1969.

Phil 482.4 — Haering, T.L. Die Materialisierung des Geistes. Tübingen, 1919.

Phil 575.61 — Haering, T.L. Über Individualität in Natur- und Geisteswelt. Leipzig, 1926.

Phil 3425.254 — Haering, Theodor L. Hegel, sein Wollen und sein Werke. Leipzig, 1929-1938. 2v.

Phil 3007.10.5 — Haering, Theodor Lorenz. Das deutsche in der deutschen Philosophie. 2. Aufl. Stuttgart, 1942.

Phil 3007.10 — Haering, Theodor Lorenz. Die deutsche und die europäische Philosophie. Stuttgart, 1943.

Phil 338.45 — Haering, Theodor Lorenz. Philosophie des Verstehens. Tübingen, 1963.

Phil 5850.227.14 — Haernqvist, Kjell. Tillämpad psykologi. 4. uppl. Stockholm, 1966.

Phil 3640.280 — Härtle, H. Nietzsche und der Nationalsozialismus. 2e Aufl. München, 1939.

Phil 182.102 — Haesaert, J. Introduction a la philosophie expérimentale. Gand, 1920.

Phil 5411.10 — Haesler, Alfred A. Leben mit dem Hass. Reinbeck, 1969.

Phil 978.49.850 — Haeusler, Friedrich. Weltenville und Menschenziele in der Geschichte. Dornach, 1961.

Phil 8408.20 — Haezrahi, P. The contemplative activity; a study in aesthetics. N.Y., 1956.

Phil 8882.85 — Haezrahi, P. The price of morality. London, 1961.

Phil 7054.136 — Hafed, prince of Persia. London, 1876.

Phil 848.8 — Pamphlet vol. Haffner, Paul. Der Materialismus. 2 pam.

Phil 7150.80 — Haffter, Carl. Selbstmordversuche bei Kindern und Jugendlichen. Basel, 1966.

Phil 3850.18.100 — Hafkesbrink, H. Das Problem des religiösen Gegenstandes bei Max Scheler. Diss. Gütersloh, 1930.

Phil 3850.27.111 — Hagedorn, Hermann. Prophet in the wilderness. N.Y., 1947.

Phil 9035.51 — Hagemann, C.L.A. Was ist Charakter und wie Kann er durch die Erziehung gebildet? Dorpat, 1881.

Phil 182.1.8 — Hagemann, G. Elemente der Philosophie. Freiburg, 1911-1922. 3v.

Phil 182.1 — Hagemann, G. Elemente der Philosophie. v.1-3. Münster, 1870.

Phil 182.1.10 — Hagemann, G. Logik und Nötik. 9e und 10e Aufl. Freiburg, 1915.

Phil 3425.706 — Hagen, Eduard von. Abstraktion und Konkretion bei Hegel und Kierkegaard. Bonn, 1969.

Phil 623.10.5 — Hagenbach, K.R. German rationalism. Edinburgh, 1865.

Phil 1135.235 — Hager, Fritz-Peter. Der Geist und das Eine. Inaug. Diss. Bern, 1970.

Phil 310.165 — Hager, Kurt. Der dialektische Materialismus die theoretische Grundlage der Politik der SED. 3. Aufl. Berlin, 1959.

Phil 3549.8.120 — Hager, Wilhelm. Ludwig Klages im Memoriam. München, 1957.

Phil 3255.89 — Haggenmacher, O. Über Sebastian Francks Erstlingsschrift. Zürich, 1892.

Phil 978.122 — Hagmann, Diego. Antwort auf Lebensrätsel. Zürich, 1968.

Phil 2520.250 — Hagmann, Moritz. Descartes. Winterthur, 1955.

Phil 2520.250.2 — Hagmann, Moritz. Descartes in der Auffassung durch die Historiker der Philosophie. Winterthur, 1955.

Phil 6957.35 — Hagnell, Olle. A prospective study of the incidences of mental disorder. Stockholm, 1966.

Phil 5790.2.25 — Hahn, Alois. Einstellungen zum Tod und ihre soziale Bedingtheit. Stuttgart, 1968.

Phil 3565.118 — Hahn, Gustav. Der Allbeseelungsgedanke bei Lotze. Stuttgart, 1925.

Phil 338.21 — Hahn, Hans. Logik, Mathematik und Naturerkennen. Wien, 1933.

Phil 974.3.130 — Hahn, Herbert. Rudolf Steiner wie ich ihn Sah und Erlebte. Stuttgart, 1961.

Phil 3425.698 — Hahn, Manfred. Bürgerlicher Optimismus im Niedergang. München, 1969.

Phil 288.4 — Hahn, Otto. Die Philosophie des Bewussten. Tubingen, 1887.

Phil 3552.101 — Hahn, R. Die Entwickelung der leibnizischen Metaphysik. Halle, 1899.

Phil 1504.5.2 — Hahn S. Thomas Bradwardinus. v.5, pt.2. Münster, 1905.

Phil 338.16 — Haig, J. Philosophy, or The science of truth. London, 1861.

Phil 5520.24 — Haig, James. Symbolism or mind matter; language as elements of thinking. Edinburgh, 1869.

Phil 8622.50 — Hailsham, Quinten McG. The need for faith in a scientifc age. Glasgow, 1961.

Phil 5411.7 — La haine. Thèse. (Mathis, René.) Nancy, 1927.

Phil 3640.228 — Haiser, Franz. Im Anfang war der Streit. München, 1921.

Phil 5545.176 — Hajdu, H. Das mnemotechnische Schrifttum. Wien, 1936.

Phil 182.1.81 — Halasy-Nagy, J. A filozófia kis tükre. 2. kiad. Budapest, 193-?

Phil 8685.4.5 — Die Halb-Kantianer und der Pantheismus (veranlasst durch Jäsche's Pantheismus). (Pitter, A.H.) Berlin, 1827.

Phil 6317.13 — Halberg, F. Om det abnorme. København, 1907.

Phil 7150.26 — Halbwachs, M. Les causes du suicide. Paris, 1930.

Phil 5545.158 — Halbwachs, Maurice. Les cadres sociaux de la mémoire. Paris, 1925.

Phil 3552.122 — Halbwachs, Maurice. Leibniz. Paris, 1907.

Phil 3552.122.5 — Halbwachs, Maurice. Leibniz. Paris, 1929.

Phil 5545.158.5 — Halbwachs, Maurice. La mémoire collective. 1. éd. Paris, 1950.

Phil 2520.109A — Haldane, E.S. Descartes, his life and times. London, 1905.

Phil 1990.80 — Haldane, E.S. Ferrier James Frederick. London, n.d.

Phil 8882.55 — Haldane, J.B.S. Science and ethics. London, 1928.

Phil 182.111 — Haldane, J.S. Materialism. London, 1932.

Phil 182.101.7 — Haldane, J.S. The philosophy of a biologist. Oxford, 1935.

Phil 182.101.5A — Haldane, J.S. The philosophy of a biologist. Oxford, 1935.

Phil 182.101 — Haldane, J.S. The sciences and philosophy. London, 1928.

Phil 182.101.10 — Haldane, John Burdon Sanderson. Science and life. London, 1968.

Phil 338.10.5 — Haldane, R.B. The philosophy of humanism. New Haven, 1922.

Phil 338.10.4 — Haldane, R.B. Le regne de la relativité. Paris, 1922.

Phil 338.10 — Haldane, R.B. The reign of relativity. New Haven, 1921.

Phil 338.10.2 — Haldane, R.B. The reign of relativity. 2. ed. London, 1921.

Phil 182.35.5 — Haldane, Richard B. The doctrine of degrees in knowledge, truth, and reality. London, n.d.

Phil 182.35.10 — Haldane, Richard B. Human experience; a study of its structure. London, 1929.

Phil 182.35.9 — Haldane, Richard B. Human experience; a study of its structure. N.Y., 1926.

Phil 182.35.2 — Haldane, Richard B. The pathway to reality. London, 1905.

Phil 182.35.3 — Haldane, Richard B. The pathway to reality. London, 1926.

Phil 1807.3 — Haldar, H. Neo-Hegelianism. London, 1927.

Phil 7069.20.150 — Haldeman, Isaac M. Can the dead communicate with the living? N.Y., 1920.

Phil 8408.38 — Halder, A. Kunst und Kult. Freiburg, 1964.

Phil 9167.1 — Hale, M. A letter of advice to his grandchildren. Boston, 1817.

Phil 3640.96 — Halévy, D. Life of Friedrich Nietzsche. N.Y., 1911.

Phil 3640.96.5A — Halévy, D. Nietzsche. Paris, 1944.

Phil 1807.2 — Halévy, E. La formation du radicalisme philosophique. Paris, 1901-04. 3v.

Phil 1807.2.15 — Halévy, E. The growth of philosophic radicalism. London, 1949.

Phil 1807.2.20 — Halévy, E. The growth of philosophic radicalism. London, 1952.

Phil 6980.347 — Haley, Jay. The power tactics of Jesus Christ and other essays. N.Y., 1969.

Phil 7069.35.10 — Haley, P.S. Modern loaves and fishes. San Francisco, 1935.

Phil 5722.1 — Half-hour Recreations. Half-hour recreations in popular science. no.6. Boston, 1871.

Phil 5722.1 — Half-hour recreations in popular science. no.6. (Half-hour Recreations.) Boston, 1871.

Phil 8685.5 — Half truths and the truth. (Manning, J.M.) Boston, 1872.

Phil 7069.26.10 — Halford, J. The voice. London, 1926.

Phil 7069.36.20 — Halifax, Charles L.W. Lord Halifax's ghost book. 3. ed. London, 1936.

Phil 9167.3.9F — Halifax, G.S. The lady's new-years gift, or Advice to a daughter. Kensington, 1927.

NEDL Phil 8882.1 — Hall, A. A manual of morals. Andover, 1848.

Phil 8882.1.2 — Hall, A. A manual of morals. Boston, 1850.

Phil 8882.29 — Hall, B. Life and love and peace. N.Y., 1909.

Phil 6315.2.450 — Hall, Calvin S. A primer of Freudian psychology. London, 1956.

Phil 5590.215 — Hall, Calvin S. Theories of personality. N.Y., 1957.

Phil 5590.215.2 — Hall, Calvin S. Theories of personality. N.Y., 1965.

Phil 5590.215.2.2 — Hall, Calvin S. Theories of personality. 2. ed. N.Y., 1965.

Phil 6480.213 — Hall, Calvin Springer. The content analysis of dreams. N.Y., 1966.

Phil 7082.72.20 — Hall, Calvin Springer. The meaning of dreams. N.Y., 1953.

Phil 8632.7 — Hall, Charles A. They do not die. London, 1918.

Phil 6677.9 — Hall, Charles R. Mesmerism. 1st American ed. N.Y., 1845.

Phil 2055.16.30 — Hall, E.W. Categorical analysis. Chapel Hill, 1964.

Phil 182.117 — Hall, E.W. Philosophical systems. Chicago, 1960.

Phil 5585.237 — Hall, Edward Twitchell. The hidden dimension. 1. ed. Garden City, N.Y., 1966.

Phil 735.130A — Hall, Everett W. What is value? London, 1952.

Phil 8697.6   Hall, F.J. Recent work of angelican theologians. Chicago, 1912.

Phil 8882.39   Hall, G. Stanley. Morale. N.Y., 1920.

Phil 3007.5   Hall, G.S. Aspects of German culture. Boston, 1881.

Phil 5645.7   Hall, G.S. Color-perception. n.p., 1878.

Phil 3007.5.5   Hall, G.S. Founders of modern psychology. N.Y., 1912.

Phil 3007.5.10   Hall, G.S. Founders of modern psychology. N.Y., 1924.

Phil 5401.2   Hall, G.S. Study of fears. Worcester, 1897.

Phil 8632.16   Hall, G.S. Thanataphobia and immortality. n.p., 1915.

Phil 6117.32   Hall, H.J. The untroubled mind. Boston, 1915.

Phil 9347.6   Hall, John. Familiar talks to boys. N.Y., n.d.

Phil 5374.9   Hall, L. The evolution of consciousness. London, 1901.

Phil 8610.801.5   Hall, Robert. Modern infidelity considered. Philadelphia, 1853.

Phil 7054.64   Hall, S.C. The use of spiritualism? Glasgow, 1876.

Phil 9347.8   Hall, S.S. Bliss of marriage; or How to get a rich wife. New Orleans, 1858.

Phil 6677.7   Hall, Spencer T. Mesmeric experiences. London, 1845.

Phil 7054.40   Hall, T.B. Modern spiritualism; or Opening way. Boston, 1883.

Phil 7068.99.40   Hall, T.B. The purity and destiny of modern spiritualism. Boston, 1899.

Phil 7054.40.5   Hall, T.B. Three articles on modern spiritualism. Boston, 1863.

Phil 8957.4   Hall, T.C. History of ethics...Christianity. N.Y., 1910.

Phil 7069.62.5   Hall, Trevor. The spiritualists; story of F. Cook and Wm. Crookes. London, 1962.

Phil 7069.65.30   Hall, Trevor H. New light on old ghosts. London, 1965.

X Cg   Phil 9495.11   Hall, W.S. Biological, physiological and sociological reproduction, also sexual hygiene. 14. ed. Chicago, 1913.

Phil 8832.5   Hall-Quest, A.L. It's not our fault. N.Y., 1929.

Phil 6957.1   Hallaran, W.G. Practical observations, causes, cure insanity. Cork, 1818.

Phil 9070.120   Halldén, Söken. Handbok för Tveksamma. Solna, 1968

Phil 735.165   Halldén, Sören. Emotive propositions. Stockholm, 1954.

Phil 5066.115   Halldén, Sören. On the logic of 'better'. Lund, 1957.

Phil 8612.67   Halldén, Sören. Universum, döden och den logiska analysen. Lund, 1967.

Phil 5047.1   Halle, H.F. Exact philosophy. London, 1848.

Phil 182.128   Halle, L.J. Men and nations. Princeton, 1962.

Phil 9530.50   Halle, L.J. On facing the world. N.Y., 1950.

Phil 5247.1.2   Halleck, R.P. Psychology and psychic culture. N.Y., 1895.

Phil 6117.36   Hallervorden, E. Arbeit und Wille. pt.1-2. Würzburg, 1897.

Phil 3925.16.130   Hallett, Garth. Wittgenstein's definition of meaning as use. N.Y., 1967.

Phil 672.150   Hallett, H.F. Alternitas; a Spinozistic study. Oxford, 1930.

Phil 3827.12   Hallett, H.F. Benedict de Spinoza. London, 1957.

Phil 3827.12.5   Hallett, H.F. Creation, emanation and salvation, a Spinozistic study. The Hague, 1962.

Phil 182.63   Hallett, T.G.P. That life is the origin and purpose of the universe. London, 1916.

Phil 2270.103   Halleux, Jean. L'évolutionnisme en morale. Paris, 1901.

Phil 600.45   Halleux, Jean. Les principes du positivisme contemporain. Paris, 19- ?

Phil 6317.30   Halliday, James. Psychosocial medicine. N.Y., 1948.

Phil 2730.108   Hallie, P.P. Maine de Biran, reformer. Cambridge, 1959.

Phil 9558.50   Hallie, Phillip Paul. The paradox of cruelty. 1. ed. Middletown, Conn., 1969.

Phil 182.54   Hallier, Ernst. Die Weltanschauung des Naturforschers. Jena, 1875.

Phil 9167.3   Hallifax, de M. Airs d'un père à sa fille. London, 1757.

Phil 8587.58   Hallimond, J.G. The miracle of answered prayers. N.Y., 1916.

Phil 6317.6.10   Hallingworth, H.L. Abnormal psychology. N.Y., 1930.

Phil 6317.6   Hallingworth, H.L. The psychology of functional neuroses. N.Y., 1920.

Phil 3900.1.83   Hallmer, Lars. Om Friedrich Ueberwegs "System der logik". Lund, 1877.

Phil 8587.40   Hallock, C. Luminous bodies here and hereafter (the shining ones). N.Y., 1906.

Phil 5460.10   L'hallucination. (Quercy, Pierre.) Paris, 1930. 2v.

Phil 5460.15   Hallucinations. (APA-AAAS Symposium on Hallucinations.) N.Y., 1962.

Phil 5460.10.5   Les hallucinations. (Faure, Henri.) Paris, 1936.

Phil 7060.14.9   Hallucinations. 1st American ed. (Brierre de Boismont, A.) Philadelphia, 1853.

Phil 5460.6   Hallucinations and illusions. (Parish, E.) London, 1897.

Phil 6954.6   Hallucinations et délire. (Ey, Henri.) Paris, 1934.

Phil 5460.14   Hallucinations et réalité. (Faure, Henri.) Paris, 1964.

Phil 7068.92.35   Les hallucinations télépathiques. 2. ed. (Gurney, Edmund.) Paris, 1892.

Phil 7068.99.4   Les hallucinations volontaires. (Dheur, P.) Paris, 1899.

Phil 6155.12   Hallucinogenic drug research; impact on science and society. Beloit, Wis., 1970.

Phil 6155.16   Hallucinogenic drugs: a perspective with special reference to peyote and cannabis. (McGlothlin, William Herschel.) Santa Monica, 1964.

Phil 5238.105   Halmos, Paul. Readings in general psychology. London, 1959.

Phil 8632.18   Halsey, Don Peters. The evidence for immortality. N.Y., 1932.

Phil 5590.295   Halsman, Phillipe. Jump book. N.Y., 1959.

Phil 6117.46   Halstood, W.C. Brain and intelligence. Chicago, 1947.

Phil 5374.18   Halt, E.B. The concepts of consciousness. London, 1914.

Phil 338.38   Halt, Everett W. Our knowledge of fact and value. Chapel Hill, 1961.

Phil 6947.1940   Een halve eeuw. (Venray, Netherlands. Psychiatrisch Ziekenhuis Sint Anna.) Venray, 1961?

Phil 6947.1854   Een halve eeuw arbeid op psychiatrisch-neurologischgen, terrein 1910-1960. (Amsterdam. Valerius-Kliniek.) Wagenin, 1960.

Phil 4582.5.30   Halvorson, G. Grundtraek af metafysik. Kristiania, 1891.

Phil 3552.484   Halz, Hans Heinz. Herr und Knecht bei Leibniz und Hegel. Berlin, 1968.

Phil 8408.24   Hamann, J.G. Scritti e frammenti di estetica. Roma, 1938.

Phil 5425.59   Hamann, Otto. Biologie deutscher Dichter und Denker. Zürich, 1923.

Phil 8408.33   Hamann, R. Ästhetik. 2. Aufl. Leipzig, 1919.

Phil 3425.12.3   Hamann. (Hegel, Georg Wilhelm Friedrich.) Stuttgart, 1902.

Phil 3504.19   Hamann und Kant. (Weber, Heinrich.) München, 1904.

Phil 3090.81.5   Hamberger, Julius. Die Cardinalpunkte der F. Baader'schen Philosophie. Stuttgart, 1855.

Phil 3090.81   Hamberger, Julius. Die Fundamentalbegriffe von Franz von Baader's Ethik. Stuttgart, 1858.

Phil 3640.103   Hamblen, E.S. Friedrich Nietzsche and his new gospel. Boston, 1911.

Phil 5100.8   Hamblin, Charles Leonard. Fallacies. London, 1970.

Phil 3160.12.10   Hamburg, C.H. Symbol and reality. The Hague, 1956.

Phil 8587.45   Hamburger, Leo. Die Religion in ihrer dogmatischen und ihrer reinen Form. München, 1930.

Phil 5585.43   Hamburger, R. Neue Theorie der Wahrnehmung und des Denkens. Berlin, 1927.

Phil 3552.318   Hamburger Akademische Rundschau. Gottfried Wilhelm Leibniz. Hamburg, 1946.

Phil 5625.80   Hamel, I.A. A study and analysis of the conditioned reflex. Diss. Washington, 1918.

Phil 9450.66   Hamelin, Jacques. Entretiens sur la justice contemporaine. Paris, 1970.

Phil 338.5   Hamelin, O. Essai sur les elements principaux de la représentation. Paris, 1907.

Phil 338.5.2   Hamelin, O. Essai sur les elements principaux de la représentation. 2. ed. Paris, 1925.

Phil 2520.111   Hamelin, O. Le système de Descartes. Paris, 1911.

Phil 2520.111.2   Hamelin, O. Le système de Descartes. 2e éd. Paris, 1921.

Phil 2840.98   Hamelin, Octave. Le système de Renouvier. Paris, 1927.

Phil 5247.20   Hamelinck, M. Étude préparatoire à la détermination experimental de diverses individuel intellects. Gand, 1915.

Phil 9245.13   Hamerton, P.G. The quest of happiness. Boston, 1897.

Phil 6957.18   Hamilton, A.M. Recollections of an alienist. N.Y., 1916.

Phil 525.20   Hamilton, C.H. A psychological interpretation of mysticism. Diss. Chicago, 1916.

Phil 5247.2   Hamilton, D.H. Autology...mental science. Boston, 1873.

Phil 8882.2A   Hamilton, E. A series of popular essays. Boston, 1817. 2v.

Phil 5047.12.9   Hamilton, E.J. Erkennen und Schlieszen. N.Y., 1912.

Phil 5247.3   Hamilton, E.J. The human mund. N.Y., 1883.

Phil 5047.12   Hamilton, E.J. The modalist, or The laws of rational conviction. Boston, 1891.

Phil 8882.27   Hamilton, E.J. The moral law - theory and practice of duty. N.Y., 1902.

Phil 5247.3.9   Hamilton, E.J. The perceptionalist. N.Y., 1891.

Phil 5247.3.7   Hamilton, E.J. The perceptionalist. N.Y., 1912.

Phil 5047.12.3   Hamilton, E.J. Perzeptionalismus und Modalismus. N.Y., 1911.

Phil 5585.17   Hamilton, F.M. The perceptual factors in reading. N.Y., 1907.

Phil 2475.1.204   Hamilton, George R. Bergson and future philosophy. London, 1921.

Phil 6317.15   Hamilton, Gilbert V. An introduction to objective psychopathology. St. Louis, 1925.

Phil 5817.11   Hamilton, Gilbert V. A study of perseverance reactions. N.Y., 1916.

Phil 8662.1   Hamilton, Hugh. An attempt to prove the existance...of the supreme unoriginated being. London, 1785.

Phil 5247.46   Hamilton, Hughbert C. The effect of incentives on accuracy of discrimination measured on the Galton bar. Thesis. N.Y., 1929.

Phil 92.2   Hamilton, James A. Englisch-Deutsch für Psychologen. Frankfurt, 1931.

Phil 6990.5   Hamilton, M. Incubation....Pagan...Christian Churches. London, 1906.

Phil 575.79   Hamilton, O.P. Dreamers and doers. London, 1931.

Phil 7069.42.5   Hamilton, T. Glen. Intention and survival. Toronto, 1942.

Phil 2035.30.7   Hamilton, William. Discussions on philosophy and literature, education. N.Y., 1858.

Phil 2035.30   Hamilton, William. Discussions on philosophy and literature. London, 1852.

Phil 2035.30.2   Hamilton, William. Discussions on philosophy and literature. N.Y., 1853.

Phil 2035.30.3   Hamilton, William. Discussions on philosophy and literature. N.Y., 1855.

Phil 2035.30.1   Hamilton, William. Discussions on philosophy and literature. 2nd ed. London, 1853.

Phil 2035.60   Hamilton, William. Fragments de philosophie. Paris, 1840.

Phil 2035.40   Hamilton, William. Lectures on metaphysics and logic. Boston, 1859-60. 2v.

Phil 2035.40.5   Hamilton, William. Lectures on metaphysics and logic. Boston, 1860.

Phil 2035.40.3   Hamilton, William. Lectures on metaphysics and logic. Edinburgh, 1859. 4v.

Phil 2035.40.10   Hamilton, William. Lectures on metaphysics and logic. N.Y., 1880.

Phil 2035.51   Hamilton, William. Metaphysics. Cambridge, 1861.

Phil 2035.51.9   Hamilton, William. Metaphysics. Cambridge, 1864.

Phil 2035.51.15   Hamilton, William. The metaphysics of Sir William Hamilton. Boston, 1872.

Phil 2035.51.19   Hamilton, William. The metaphysics of Sir William Hamilton. Boston, 1877[1861]

Phil 2035.20   Hamilton, William. Philosophy. N.Y., 1853.

Phil 2035.65   Hamilton, William. Philosophy. N.Y., 1855.

Phil 2035.79   Pamphlet box. Hamilton, William.

Phil 8882.40   Hamilton, William E. Studies in moral science. Chicago, 1916.

Phil 2035.88   Hamilton. (Veitch, J.) Philadelphia, 1882.

Phil 8697.8   Hamlin, G.S. Human nature. N.Y., 1917.

Phil 5585.242   Hamlyn, David Walter. The psychology of perception. London, 1957.

Phil 5585.180   Hamlyn, David Walter. Sensation and perception. N.Y., 1961.

Phil 3195.13.90   Hamm, Anton. Die Philosophie Hugo Delffs als Begründung eine theistischen Idealrealismus im Sinne christlicher Weltanschauung. Inaug. Diss. Bottrop, 1934.

Phil 807.13   Hamma, M. Geschichte und Grundfragen der Metaphysik. Freiburg, 1876.

Phil 807.10   Hamma, Mattheas. Geschichte der Philosophie. 2. Aufl. Münster, 1908.

Phil 3425.191   Hammacher, Emil. Die Bedeutung der Philosophie Hegels. Leipzig, 1911.

Phil 182.140   Hammacher, Klaus. Kritik und Leben. v.2. München, 1969.

Phil 3246.292   Hammacher, Vlans. Die ethische Teleologie in Fichtes System als Grundlage seiner Geschichtsphilosophie. Hadien, 1958.

Phil 182.87   Hammarsköld, L. Strödda afhandlingar öfver ämnen inom philosophiens gebiet. Mariefred, 1827.

Phil 4508.2   Hammarsköld, Lorenzo. Historiska antickningar rörande fortgängen och utvecklingen af det philosophiska studium i Sverige. Stockholm, 1821.

Phil 1112.4   Hammarsköld, L. Grunddragen af philosophiens historia. 1a afd. Stockholm, 1825.

Phil 5465.24   Hammer, Bertil. Fantasien. Uppsala, 1916.

Phil 6677.20 — Hammerschlag, Heinz F. Hypnotism and crime. Hollywood, Calif., 1957.

Phil 3120.30.92 — Hammerstein, Franz von. Das Messiasproblem bei Martin Buber. Stuttgart, 1958.

Phil 1707.9 — Hammond, A.L. Anti-intellectualism in present philosophy. Diss. Baltimore, 1926.

Phil 182.122 — Hammond, A.L. Proprieties and vagaries. Baltimore, 1961.

Phil 7054.62.2 — Hammond, Charles. Light from the spirit world. N.Y., 1852.

Phil 7054.62.5 — Hammond, Charles. Philosophy of the spirit world. N.Y., 1853.

Phil 7054.62 — Hammond, Charles. Pilgrimage of Thos. Paine. N.Y., 1852.

Phil 3120.65.30 — Hammond, Kenneth R. The psychology of Egon Brunswik. N.Y., 1966.

Phil 5922.6.8 — Hammond, L.M. (Mrs.). Trials and triumphs of an orphan girl; biography. Cortland, N.Y., 1859.

Phil 8408.14 — Hammond, Robert. Lineamenti d'estetica fondati sul problema gnoseologico. Aleppo, 1926.

Phil 8030.5 — Hammond, W.A. A bibliography of aesthetics and of the philosophy of the fine arts from 1900-1932. N.Y., 1934.

Phil 6957.2 — Hammond, W.A. Cerebral hyperaemia. N.Y., 1878.

Phil 6317.1 — Hammond, W.A. On certain conditions of nervous derangement. N.Y., 1881.

Phil 6317.1.2 — Hammond, W.A. On certain conditions of nervous derangement. 3d ed. N.Y., 1883.

Phil 7080.5.5 — Hammond, W.A. On wakefulness. Philadelphia, 1866.

NEDL Phil 7080.5.2 — Hammond, W.A. Sleep and its derangements. Philadelphia, 1869.

Phil 6957.2.5 — Hammond, W.A. A treatise on insanity in its medical relations. N.Y., 1891.

Phil 6957.2.9 — Hammond, W.A. A treatise on the diseases of the nervous system. 6. ed. N.Y., 1876.

Phil 6957.5 — Hamon, A. La responsabilité. Lyon, 1897.

Phil 6048.94.5 — Hamon, Louis. Cheiro's language of the hand. N.Y., 1894.

Phil 6048.94.7 — Hamon, Louis. Cheiro's language of the hand. N.Y., 1895.

X Cg Phil 6048.94.9 — Hamon, Louis. Cheiro's language of the hand. 9th ed. N.Y., 1897.

Phil 6053.12 — Hamon, Louis. Cheiro's memoirs. Philadelphia, 1912.

Phil 6048.94.10 — Hamon, Louis. Comfort's palmistry guide by Cheiro (pseud.) palmist. Augusta, 1894.

Phil 6049.31.2 — Hamon, Louis. Fate in the making; revelations of lifetime. N.Y., 1931.

Phil 8882.3 — Hampden, R.D. A course of lectures...study, moral philosophy. London, 1835.

Phil 1112.2 — Hampden, R.D. The fathers of Greek philosophy. Edinburgh, 1862.

Phil 5047.48 — Hampel, Hans-Jürgen. Variabilität und Disziplinierung des Denkens. München, 1967.

Phil 3827.9 — Hamphire, S. Spinoza. Harmondsworth, 1951.

Phil 3827.9.3 — Hamphire, S. Spinoza. London, 1956.

Phil 338.36 — Hampshire, S. Feeling and expression. London, 1961.

Phil 5757.18 — Hampshire, Stuart. Freedom of the individual. N.Y., 1965.

Phil 3827.14 — Hampshire, Stuart. Spinoza and the idea of freedom. London, 1960.

Phil 2055.10.30 — Hampshire, Stuart. Thought and action. London, 1959.

Phil 17.13 — The Hampstead clinic psychoanalytic library. N.Y. 1,1969+ 3v.

Phil 5240.42.5 — Hamptaufgaben der sowjetischen psychologischen Wissenschaft. (Ananiew, B.G.) Berlin, 1952.

Phil 6117.34 — Han, S.J. The problem of mind and evil. n.p., 1922.

Phil 2880.8.156 — Hana, Ghanem Georges. Freiheit und Person. München, 1965.

Phil 1020.80 — Hanafi, Hasan. Les méthodes d'exegese. Le Caire, 1965.

Phil 8697.20 — Hanaghan, J. Society, evolution and revelation. Dublin, 1957.

Phil 182.77 — Hanan, F. A layman to his sons. London, 1924.

Phil 9245.142 — Hancerlioğlu, Orhan. Başlangicidan bugüne mutluluk düsüncesi. Istanbul, 1969.

Phil 5590.552 — Hançerlioğlu, Orhan. Başlangicindan bugüne erdem açisindan düşünce. Istanbul, 1966.

Phil 807.26 — Hançerlióğlu, Orhan. Düşünce tarihi. Istanbul, 1970.

Phil 8587.78 — Hançerlioğlu, Orhan. Fel sefe sölüğü. Istanbul, 1967.

Phil 5520.552 — Hançerlioğlu, Oshan. Başlan-gicindan bugüne erdem açisindan düşünce. 2. b. Istanbul, 1966.

Htn Phil 8662.2* — Hancock, J. Arguments to prove the being of God. London, 1707.

Phil 5817.1 — Hancock, T. Essay on instinct. London, 1824.

Phil 5425.23 — Hancock, Thomas. Essay on capacity and genius. London, 1817.

Phil 8697.10 — Hand, J.E. Ideals of science and faith. N.Y., 1904.

Phil 6051.3 — Hand-book of modern palmistry. (Metz, V. de.) N.Y., 1885?

Phil 5241.3 — Hand book of psychology. Senses and intellect. 1. ed. (Baldwin, J.M.) N.Y., 1889.

Phil 6049.33 — The hand of man. (Jaquin, Noel.) London, 1933.

Phil 9070.120 — Handbok för Tveksamma. (Halldén, Söken.) Solna, 1968

Phil 5050.20F — Handbok i logik. (Kauger, F.) Stockholm, 1959.

Phil 801.2 — Handbook...history of philosophy. (Box, E.B.) London, 1886.

Phil 801.2.5 — Handbook...history of philosophy. (Box, E.B.) London, 1908.

Phil 5592.179 — A handbook for clinical and actuarial MMPI interpretation. (Gilberstadt, Harold.) Philadelphia, 1965.

Phil 5241.92.15 — Handbook in psychology, to accompany Boring's Psychology. (Wedell, C.H.) N.Y., 1936.

Phil 6314.11.5 — Handbook of abnormal psychology. (Eysenck, Hans J.) N.Y., 1961.

Phil 5886.15 — Handbook of aging and the individual. (Birren, James Emmett.) Chicago, 1960.

Phil 8962.5 — A handbook of Christian ethics. (Murray, J.C.) Edinburgh, 1908.

Phil 5548.104 — Handbook of consumer motivations. (Dichter, E.) N.Y., 1964.

Phil 5238.226 — Handbook of contemporary Soviet psychology. (Cole, Michael.) N.Y., 1969.

Phil 7082.16 — The handbook of dream analysis. (Gutheil, Emil Arthur.) N.Y., 1951.

Phil 5241.100 — Handbook of elementary psychology. (Billings, E.G.) N.Y., 1939.

Phil 8880.35 — Handbook of ethical theory. (Fullerton, G.S.) N.Y., 1922.

Phil 5238.18 — Handbook of experimental psychology. (Stevens, S.S.) N.Y., 1951.

Phil 5252.63.10 — Handbook of general experimental psychology. (Murchison, C.A.) Worcester, 1934.

Phil 5255.7.15 — Handbook of general psychology. (Pillsbury, W.B.) N.Y., 1942.

Phil 801.12 — Handbook of history and development of philosophy. (Bevan, J.O.) London, 1916.

Phil 5850.341.5 — Handbook of industrial psychology. (Smith, May.) N.Y., 1944.

Phil 6132.20 — Handbook of instructions for healing and helping others. (Winbigler, C.F.) Los Angeles, 1918.

Phil 5041.80 — A handbook of logic. (Brennan, Joseph Gerard.) N.Y., 1957.

Phil 5052.41 — Handbook of logic. (Morell, J.D.) London, 1866.

Phil 5041.80.2 — A handbook of logic. 2nd ed. (Brennan, Joseph Gerard.) N.Y., 1961.

Phil 5251.60.10 — Handbook of mathematical psychology. (Luce, Robert D.) N.Y., 1963. 2v.

Phil 5262.62 — Handbook of measurement and assessment in behavioral sciences. (Whitla, Dean.) Reading, 1968.

Phil 6955.11 — Handbook of mental examining methods. 2. ed. (Franz, S.I.) N.Y., 1919.

Phil 6048.83.2 — Handbook of modern palmistry. 2. ed. (Metz, V. de.) N.Y., 1883.

Phil 8877.1.2 — Handbook of moral philosophy. (Calderwood, H.) London, 1872.

Phil 8877.1 — Handbook of moral philosophy. (Calderwood, H.) London, 1884.

Phil 8877.1.5 — Handbook of moral philosophy. (Calderwood, H.) London, 1895.

Phil 8877.1.3 — Handbook of moral philosophy. 6th ed. (Calderwood, H.) London, 1879.

Phil 5590.498 — Handbook of personality theory and research. (Borgatta, Edgar.) Chicago, 1968.

Phil 102.5.1 — Handbook of philosophy. (Rozental, Mark Moiseevich.) N.Y., 1949.

Phil 5203.37 — Handbook of psychological literature. (Loattit, Chauncey McKinley.) Bloomington, Ind., 1932.

Phil 5241.3.2 — Handbook of psychology...feeling and will. (Baldwin, J.M.) N.Y., 1891.

Phil 5252.14 — Handbook of psychology. (Murray, J.C.) Boston, 1888.

Phil 5241.3.3 — Handbook of psychology. Senses and intellect. (Baldwin, J.M.) N.Y., 1890.

Phil 6951.9 — Handbook of psychology and mental disease. 4. ed. (Burr, Colonel Bell.) Philadelphia, 1915.

Phil 5237.512 — Handbook of Soviet psychology. (Slobin, Dan Isaac.) White Plains, N.Y., 1966.

NEDL Phil 818.1.7 — Handbook of the history of philosophy. (Schwegler, F.C.A.) Edinburgh, 1867.

Phil 818.5A — Handbook of the history of philosophy. (Stöckl, A.) N.Y., 1911.

Phil 818.1.8 — Handbook of the history of philosophy. 2d ed. (Schwegler, F.C.A.) Edinburgh, 1868.

Phil 818.1.12 — Handbook of the history of philosophy. 5th ed. (Schwegler, F.C.A.) N.Y., 1873.

Phil 818.1.16 — Handbook of the history of philosophy. 9th ed. (Schwegler, F.C.A.) Edinburgh, 1884.

Phil 178.12.35 — Handbook of the new thought. (Dresser, H.W.) N.Y., 1917.

Phil 7069.64.27 — A handbook on the occult. (Hunt, Douglas.) London, 1967.

Phil 6400.33.5 — Handbook speech pathology. (Travis, Lee E.) N.Y., 1957.

Phil 3485.18 — A handbook to Kant's Critique of pure reason. (Das, Ras-Vihari.) Bombay, 1949.

Phil 8405.4 — Handbuch der Ästhetik. (Eberhard, Johann.) Halle, 1803-04.

Phil 17.7 — Handbuch der biologischen Arbeitsmethoden. Abteilung VI. Berlin. 1920-1935+ 8v.

Phil 8957.14 — Handbuch der christlichen Moral. (Hoermann, Karl.) Innsbruck, 1958.

Phil 8972.1 — Handbuch der christlichen Sittenlehre. (Wuttke, K.F.A.) Leipzig, 1874-75. 2v.

Phil 8897.33 — Handbuch der Ethik. (Wolff, H.) Leipzig, n.d.

Phil 6968.4 — Handbuch der Geisteskrankheiten. (Schüle, H.) Leipzig, 1880.

Phil 1106.4 — Handbuch der Geschichte der griechisch-römischen Philosophie. (Brandes, C.A.) Berlin, 1835-60. 5v.

Phil 75.65 — Handbuch der Geschichte der Philosophie. v.2, pt.1. (Totok, Wilhelm.) Frankfurt, 1964. 2v.

Phil 8957.11 — Handbuch der katholische Sittenlehre. v.1-5. Düsseldorf, 1938. 7v.

Phil 75.8 — Handbuch der klassischen philosophischen Literatur. (Schaller, Karl A.) Halle, 1816.

Phil 6328.36 — Handbuch der klinischen Psychologie. v.1-2. (Stern, Erich.) Zürich, 1954. 3v.

Phil 6954.5A — Handbuch der Krankheiten des Nervensystems. 2e Aufl. (Erb, Wilhelm.) Leipzig, 1876-78. 2v.

Phil 75.79 — Handbuch der Literatur der Geschichte der Philosophie. (Ortloff, Johann Andreas.) Düsseldorf, 1968.

Phil 5051.23.7 — Handbuch der Logik, Übersetzung von W. Sesemann. (Losskiĭ, N.O.) Leipzig, 1927.

Phil 5044.4 — Handbuch der Logik. (Erhard, A.) München, 1839.

Phil 8876.11.5 — Handbuch der Moral. (Baumann, Julius.) Leipzig, 1879.

Phil 9045.2 — Handbuch der Moral für den Bürgerstand. (Bahrdt, C.F.) Halle, 1790.

Phil 185.10 — Handbuch der Philosophie. (Krug, W.T.) Leipzig, 1828.

Phil 17.6 — Handbuch der Philosophie. München. 1-4 4v.

Phil 185.10.2 — Handbuch der Philosophie und der philosophischen Literatur. v.1-2. (Krug, Wilhelm Traugott.) Düsseldorf, 1969.

Phil 5640.32 — Handbuch der Physiologie der niederen Sinne. (Skramlik, E. von.) Leipzig, 1926.

Phil 5640.35 — Handbuch der Physiologie des Menschen. v.3. Braunschweig, 1905.

Phil 5640.35.5 — Handbuch der Physiologie des Menschen. v.3-4. Braunschweig, 1904-09. 3v.

Phil 5643.8.5 — Handbuch der physiologischen Optik. (Helmholtz, H.) Hamburg, 1896.

Phil 3260.33A — Handbuch der praktischen Philosophie oder der philosophischen Zwecklehre. (Fries, J.F.) Heidelberg, 1818-32. 2v.

Phil 3260.60 — Handbuch der psychischen Anthropologie. (Fries, J.F.) Jena, 1837.

Phil 5241.70 — Handbuch der Psychologie. (Bühler, Karl.) Jena, 1922.

Phil 5250.37.10 — Handbuch der Psychologie. (Katz, David.) Basel, 1951.

Phil 5250.37.11 — Handbuch der Psychologie. (Katz, David.) Basel, 1960.

Phil 5250.20 — Handbuch der Psychologie. (Kaulich, W.) Graz, 1870. 3 pam.

Phil 7150.62 — Handbuch der Selbstmordverhütung. (Thomas, Klaus.) Stuttgart, 1964.

Phil 193.28 — Handbuch der theoretischen Philosophie. (Sigwart, H.C.W.) Tübingen, 1820.

Phil 5820.2.5 — Handbuch der vergleichenden Psychologie. (Kafka, Gustav.) München, 1922. 3v.

Phil 185.10.15 — Handbuch i philosophien. (Krug, W.T.) Stockholm, 1831.

Phil 5058.11 — Handbuch zu Vorlesungen über Logik. (Sigwart, H.C.W.) Tübingen, 1835.

Phil 6132.31 — Handedness, right and left. (Wile, Ira S.) Boston, 1934.

Phil 8878.53 — Das Handeln im Sinne des Höchsten Zieles. (Absolute Ethik.) (Dingler, Hugo.) München, 1935.

Phil 97.12   Handlexikon der Philosophie. (Metzke, Erwin.) Heidelberg, 1948.

Phil 1955.6.150   Handlin, Oscar. John Dewey's challenge to education. N.Y., 1959.

Phil 4595.1.31   Handling og iaggttagelse. (Krebs, C.) København, 1913.

Phil 6053.6   Hands of celebrities. (St. Hill, Katharine.) Westminster, 1889?

Phil 6322.65   The hands of the living god. (Milner, Marion Blackett.) London, 1969.

Phil 6060.5   Handschrift und Charakter. (Schneidemühl, Georg.) Leipzig, 1911.

Phil 6060.12.5   Handschrift und Charakter. 2e Aufl. (Klages, Ludwig.) Leipzig, 1920.

Phil 6060.12.10   Handschrift und Charakter. 3. und 4. Aufl. (Klages, Ludwig.) Leipzig, 1921.

Phil 6060.12.5.20   Handschrift und Charakter. 23. Aufl. (Klages, Ludwig.) Bonn, 1949.

Phil 6060.5.2   Die Handschriftenbeurteilung. 2e Aufl. (Schneidemühl, Georg.) Leipzig, 1918.

Phil 6060.57.2   Handschriftendeutung auf tiefenpsychologischen Grundlage. 2. Aufl. (Teillard, Ania.) Bern, 1963.

Phil 4710.1   Handschriftliche...Philosophie in Russland. (Bezobrazova, M.) Leipzig, 1892.

Phil 3808.23.5   Der handschriftliche Nachlass. v.1-3,5. (Schopenhauer, Arthur.) Frankfurt, 1966. 4v.

Phil 3640.435   Der handschriftliche Nachlass Friedrich Nietzsches. (Mette, H.J.) Leipzig, 1932.

Phil 3525.20.2   Handschriftlicher Nachlass; Anthropologie. (Krause, K.C.F.) Göttingen, 1848.

Phil 3525.20   Handschriftlicher Nachlass; Logik. (Krause, K.C.F.) Göttingen, 1836.

Phil 3525.20.4   Handschriftlicher Nachlass; Rechtsphilosophie. (Krause, K.C.F.) Leipzig, 1874.

Phil 3525.20.3   Handschriftlicher Nachlass; Religionsphilosophie. (Krause, K.C.F.) Dresden, 1834-43. 2v.

Phil 3808.23   Handschriftlicher Nachlass. (Schopenhauer, Arthur.) Leipzig, 1895.

Phil 6311.10.15   Handwörterbuch der medizinischen Psychologie. (Birnbaum, Karl.) Leipzig, 1930.

Phil 89.1.5   Handwörterbuch der Philosophie. (Eisler, R.) Berlin, 1913.

Phil 89.1.7   Handwörterbuch der Philosophie. 2. Aufl. (Eisler, R.) Berlin, 1922.

Phil 6328.21   Handwörterbuch der Psychoanalyse. (Sterba, Richard.) Wien, 1936-31

Phil 6060.32   Handwriting analysis. (Lewinson, T.S.) N.Y., 1942.
Phil 6060.40.5   Handwriting analysis. (Sonnemann, Ulrich.) N.Y., 1953.
Phil 6060.40.10   Handwriting analysis as a psychodiagnostic tool. (Sonnemann, Ulrich.) N.Y., 1964.

Phil 735.266   Handy, Rollo. Value theory and the behavioral sciences. Springfield, Ill., 1969.

Phil 8882.38   Handyside, John. The historical method in ethics and other essays. Liverpool, 1920.

Phil 1145.80   Haner hagados. Inaug. Diss. (Gerlach, Julius.) Munchen, 1932.

Phil 6957.19   Hanes, E.L. The minds and nerves of soldiers. Pasadena, Calif., 1941.

Phil 6957.20   Hanfmann, E. Conceptual thinking in schizophrenia. N.Y., 1942.

Phil 9513.18   Hanis, Robert T. Social ethics. Philadelphia, 1962.
Phil 3585.8.85   Hanisch, Rudolf. Der Positivismus von Ernst Laas. Inaug. Diss. Halle, 1902.

Phil 4960.805   Hanisch Espíndola, Walter. En torno a la filosofía en Chile, 1594-1810. Santiago, 1963.

Phil 3110.171   Hankamer, P. Jakob Böhme, Gestalt und Gestaltung. Bonn, 1924.

Phil 7069.63   Hankey, M. James Hewat McKenzie, pioneer of psychical research. Londnon, 1963.

Phil 5425.41   Hankin, Ernest H. Common sense and its cultivation. London, 1926.

Phil 3827.1   Hann, F.G. Die Ethik Spinozas und die Philosophie Descartes. Innsbruck, 1875.

Phil 2475.1.395   Hanna, T. The Bergsonian heritage. N.Y., 1962.
Phil 1750.655   Hanna, Thomas. The lyrical existentialists. 1 ed. N.Y., 1962.

Phil 5247.36   Hannahs, E.H. Lessons in psychology. Albany, 1908.
Phil 8080.17   Hannay, Howard. Roger Fry and other essays. London, 1937.
Phil 260.5   Hannequin, A. Essai critique sur l'hypothèse des Atoms. Paris, 1895.

Phil 182.45.5   Hannequin, A. Études d'histoire des sciences. Paris, 1908. 2v.

Phil 3552.252   Hannequin, A. Quae fuerit prior Leibnitii philosophia. Thesis. Paris, 1895.

Phil 8587.1.5   Hannotin, E. Les grandes questions. Paris, 1867.
Phil 8587.1   Hannotin, E. Nouvelle théologie philosophique. Paris, 1846. 2v.

Phil 6117.19   Hannover, A. Recherches microscopiques sur le système nerveux. Copenhagne, 1844.

Phil 6952.26   Hanover Bank, New York. The mental hygiene movement from the philanthropic standpoint. N.Y., 1939.

Phil 6049.62   Hans, Gebärde und Charakter. (Kiener, Franz.) München, 1962.

Phil 3160.5.81   Hans Cornelius Erkenntnistheorie im Verhältnis zu der Kants. Diss. (Saal, Ernst.) Giessen, 1919.

Phil 3195.10.120   Hans Driesch. (Wenzl, Aloys.) Basel, 1951.
Phil 8411.43.80   Hans Kayser. (Haase, Rudolf.) Basel, 1968.
Phil 4600.2.80   Hans Larsson. (Nyman, Alf.) Stockholm, 1945.
Phil 3903.3.80   Hans Vaihinger en de als-ob-philosophie. (Smit, H.W.V.D.V.) Baarn, 1925.

Phil 8587.54   Hanse, H. "Gott haben." Berlin, 1939.
Phil 7162.266   Hansel, C.E.M. E.S.P.; a scientific evaluation. N.Y., 1966.

Phil 510.1.24   Hansen, Adolf. Grenzen der Religion und Naturwissenschaft. Giessen, 1908.

Phil 5757.10   Hansen, H.C. Om begrebet frihed en filosofisk afhandling. Kristiania, 1896.

Phil 8882.43   Hansen, Hans C. Moral, religion og videnskab. Kjøbenhavn, 1890.

Phil 182.71   Hansen, O. Opdragelseslaere. Kjobenhavn, 1898.
Phil 4502.2   Hansen, Oscar. Filosofien i Danmark i dit 18. og 19. aarhundrede. København, 1897.

Phil 3489.12   Hansen, Oscar. Undersøgelser verdrørende grundlaget for Kants erkendelsesteori. København, 1892.

Phil 8882.45   Hansen, Osvald. Etikkens grundlag. København, 1916.
Phil 8882.35   Hansen, Søren. Etikens begrundelse. København, 1903.
Phil 2407.5   Hansen, V. Gennembrudsmaend i nyere fransk filosofi. København, 1952.

Phil 4580.116   Hansen, V. Harald Høffding som religionsfilosof. København, 1923.

Phil 2070.92.5   Hansen, V. William James og det religiøse. København, 1936.

Phil 2070.92   Hansen, V. William James og hans breve. Stockholm, 1922.
Phil 2840.93.5   Hansen, Valdemar. Charles Renouvier; hans liv og hans tanker. København, 1962.

Phil 2840.93   Hansen, Valdemar. Charles Renouvier og frihedsproblemet. København, 1928.

Phil 4595.4.30   Hansen, Valdemar. K. Kroman. København, 1955.
Phil 8430.68   Hanslick, Eduard. Vom Musikalisch-Schönen. 16. Aufl. Wiesbaden, 1966.

Phil 165.24   Hanslmeier, J. Natur, Geist, Geschichte. München, 1950.
Phil 5247.21   Hanspaul, F. Die Seelentheorie und die Gesetze. 2. Aufl. Berlin, 1901.

Phil 9150.21   Hanssen, Andreas. Etiken og evolutionslaeren. København, 1915.

Phil 3450.18.145   Hanthack, K. Nicolai Hartmann und das Ende der Ontologie. Berlin, 1962.

Phil 850.15   Hanus, G.J. Geschichte der Philosophie von ihren Uranfängen. Olmütz, 1850.

Phil 6990.3.106   The happening at Lourdes. (Neame, Alan.) London, 1968.
Phil 9245.24   Happiness. (Fletcher, Horace.) N.Y., 1898.
Phil 8882.12.5   Happiness. (Hilty, K.) N.Y., 1903.
Htn   Phil 9245.37*   Happiness. (Phelps, William L.) N.Y., 1927.
Phil 9245.37.2   Happiness. (Phelps, William L.) N.Y., 1927.
Phil 9245.24.3   Happiness as found in forethought minus fearthought. (Fletcher, Horace.) Chicago, 1897.

Phil 9070.85   Happiness for you now. 2d ed. (Way, Joseph.) Adyar, 1959.
Phil 9550.8   The happiness of nations. (Mackaye, J.) N.Y., 1915.
Phil 525.230   Happold, F.C. Mysticism. Baltimore, 1967.
Phil 2401.2.10   The happy beast in French thought of the 17th century. (Boas, George.) Baltimore, 1933.

Phil 9167.5   The happy family. (Hodges, George.) N.Y., 1906.
Phil 525.101.10   The happy issue. (Allen, Warner.) London, 1948.
Phil 8879.2.5   The happy life. (Eliot, C.W.) N.Y., 1896.
Phil 8879.2.9   The happy life. (Eliot, C.W.) N.Y., 1896.
Phil 8879.2.3   The happy life. (Eliot, C.W.) N.Y., 1896.
Phil 8879.2A   The happy life. (Eliot, C.W.) N.Y., 1896-97.
Phil 8879.2.12   The happy life. (Eliot, C.W.) N.Y., 1905.
Phil 9245.40   A happy life. (Steele, Mary D.) Dayton, Ohio, 1895.
Phil 7055.156   A happy medium: the life of Caroline Randolph Chapman. (Weldon, Warren.) Englewood Cliffs, 1970.

Phil 3425.252   Har Hegel öfvervunnit dualismen? (Sahlin, C. Yngve.) Upsala, 1851.

Phil 4580.113   Harald Høffding, als Religionsphilosoph. (Schott, Georg.) München, 1913.

Phil 4580.81.5   Harald Høffding. (Rindom, E.) Kjøbenhavn, 1918.
Phil 4580.113.3   Harald Høffding als Religionsphilosoph. Inaug. Diss. (Schott, Georg.) München, 1913.

Phil 4580.120   Harald Høffding en zijne beteekenis voor godsdienstwipbegeerte en zedeleer. (Horreüs de Hass, G.) Huister Heide, 1930.

Phil 4580.119   Harald Høffding in memoriam. København, 1932.
Phil 4580.116   Harald Høffding som religionsfilosof. (Hansen, V.) København, 1923.

X Cg   Phil 4777.433   Harassek, S. Józef Gołuchowski. Kraków, 1924.
Phil 4800.6   Harassek, Stefan. Kant w Polsce przed rokiem 1830. Kraków, 1916.

Phil 5402.9   Harbin, R.M. Paradoxical pain. Boston, 1916.
Phil 9450.3   Harcourt, W.G.G.V.V. The morality of public men. London, 1852.

Phil 9450.3.2   Harcourt, W.G.G.V.V. The morality of public men. 2. ed. London, 1853.

Phil 8632.17   Hardenberg, H. Wir sollen nicht sterben. Darmstadt, 1920.
Phil 5238.244   Hardesty, Francis P. Forderungen an die Psychologie. Bern, 1965.

Phil 9500.10.5   Hárdi, István. Psychologie am Krankenbett. Budapest, 1968.

Phil 182.112   Hardie, C.D. Background to modern thought. London, 1947.
Phil 8957.15   Harding, A.L. Religion, morality, and law. Dallas, 1956.
Phil 6317.31   Harding, M.E. Psychic energy, its source and goal. N.Y., 1947.

Phil 6317.31.2   Harding, M.E. Psychic energy. 2. ed. N.Y., 1963.
Phil 6317.42   Harding, Mary Esther. The "I" and the "not-I"; a study in the development of consciousness. N.Y., 1965.

Phil 5465.36   Harding, R.E.M. Towards a law of creative thought. London, 1906.

Phil 5627.98   Hardman, Oscar. Psychology and the church. London, 1925.
Phil 8697.9   Hardwick, J.C. Religion and science. London, 1920.
Phil 8610.884.20   Hardwick, H.J. Popular faith unveiled. n.p., 1884?
Phil 2725.35.110   Hardy, Gilbert G. La vocation de la liberté chez Louis Lavelle. Paris, 1968.

Phil 7069.19.110   Hardy, Thomas J. Spiritism in the light of the faith. London, 1919.

Phil 974.2.40   Hare, H.E. Who wrote the Mahatma letters? London, 1936.
Phil 8882.68.10   Hare, Richard Mervyn. Descriptivism. London, 1965?
Phil 210.76   Hare, Richard Mervyn. Essays on philosophical method. London, 1971.

Phil 8882.68.5   Hare, Richard Mervyn. Freedom and reason. Oxford, 1963.
Phil 8882.68   Hare, Richard Mervyn. The language of morals. Oxford, 1952.

Phil 5190.88   Hare, Richard Mervyn. Practical inferences. London, 1971.
Phil 7054.63.4   Hare, Robert. Experimental investigation of the spirit manifestations. N.Y., 1856.

Phil 5247.32   Harford, C.F. Mind as a force. London, 1924.
Phil 6049.01.5   Hargett, Joseph Bryant. New discoveries in palmistry. N.Y., 1901.

Phil 5590.190   Haring, D.G. Personal character and cultural milieu. N.Y., 1949.

Phil 9450.68   Haring, Philip S. Political morality; a general theory of politics. Cambridge, Mass., 1970.

Phil 8697.2   Hark, J.M. The unity of truth in Christianity and evolution. N.Y., 1888.

Phil 8832.7   Harkness, G.E. The sources of western culture. London, 1955.

Phil 8587.44   Harkness, George E. Conflicts in religious thought. N.Y., 1929.

Phil 8587.44.15   Harkness, George E. The recovery of ideals. N.Y., 1937.
Phil 8587.44.10   Harkness, George E. Religious living. N.Y., 1937.
Phil 8587.44.5   Harkness, George E. The resources of religion. N.Y., 1936.

Phil 8957.2   Harless, G.C.A. System of Christian ethics. Edinburgh, 1868.

Phil 3110.89   Harless, G.C.A. von. Jakob Böhme und die Alchymisten. Berlin, 1870.

Phil 7069.61.30   Harlow, Samuel R. A life after death. 1. ed. Garden City, 1961.

Phil 630.37 — Harlow, V.E. Bibliography and genetic study of American realism. Oklahoma City, 1931.

VPhil 1750.115 — A harmadik humanizmus és a harmadik birodalom. (Faragó, László.) Budapest, 1935.

Phil 5247.50 — Harmon, F.L. The effects of noise upon certain psychological and physical processes. Thesis. N.Y., 1933.

Phil 5274.12 — Harmon, Harry Horace. Some observations on factor analysis. Santa Monica, 1955.

Phil 3552.82 — Harmonia...praestabilita...Leibnitii. (Bilfingeri, G.B.) Tubingae, 1741.

Phil 8702.14 — Harmonia entre a sciencia a fé. v.2. (Mir, Miguel.) Coimbra, 1892.

Phil 7054.6.55 — The harmonial man. (Davis, A.J.) Boston, 1853.

Phil 270.100 — De harmonie der dingen. (Baumann, Evert D.) Leiden, 1933.

Phil 8628.5 — Die Harmonie der Ergebnisse der Naturforschung. (Drossbach, M.) Leipzig, 1885.

Phil 585.226 — L'harmonie vitale; à temps nouveau, philosophie nouvelle. (Silvestre, Georges.) Paris, 1964.

Phil 186.79.5 — Les harmonies de l'être exprimées par les nombres. v.1-2. (Lacuria, P.F.G.) Paris, 1899.

Phil 8430.25 — Harmonism and conscious evolution. (Walston, C.) London, 1922.

Phil 190.27.5 — L'harmonisme. (Prat, Louis.) Paris, 1927.

Phil 9347.14 — The harmonium. Chicago, 1881.

Phil 8692.3.9 — The harmony and unity of the kingdom of God. (Coutts, John.) London, 1922.

Phil 5938.1 — The harmony of phrenology with scripture. (Scott, W.) Edinburgh, 1837.

Phil 6980.348.50 — Harms, Ernest. Origins of modern psychiatry. Springfield, 1967.

Phil 5627.162 — Harms, Ernst. Psychologie und Psychiatrie der Conversion. Leiden, 1939.

Phil 182.4.3 — Harms, F. Abhandlungen zur systematischen Philosophie. Berlin, 1868.

Phil 3007.1 — Harms, F. Der Anthropologismus. Leipzig, 1845.

Phil 8882.36 — Harms, F. Ethik. Leipzig, 1889.

Phil 3246.95 — Harms, F. Johann Gottlieb Fichte. Kiel, 1862.

Phil 182.4.10 — Harms, F. Metaphilosophie. Leipzig, 1895.

Phil 807.4 — Harms, F. Die Philosophie in ihrer Geschichte. Berlin, 1878-81. 2v.

Phil 3007.1.5 — Harms, F. Die Philosophie seit Kant. Berlin, 1876.

Phil 3007.1.7 — Harms, F. Die Philosophie seit Kant. Berlin, 1879.

Phil 182.4 — Harms, F. Prolegomena zur Philosophie. Braunschweig, 1852.

Phil 5247.25 — Harms, F. Psychologie. Leipzig, 1897.

Phil 3425.278 — Harms, F. Zur Erinnerungen an Georg W.F. Hegel. Berlin, 1871.

Phil 5047.19 — Harms, Friedrick. Logik. Leipzig, 1886.

Phil 8587.26.3 — Harnack, Adolf. Das Wesen des Christentums. Leipzig, 1903.

Phil 8587.26 — Harnack, Adolf. Das Wesen des Christentums. 4. Aufl. Leipzig, 1901.

Phil 8587.26.12 — Harnack, Adolf. What is Christianity? London, 1901.

Phil 8587.26.16 — Harnack, Adolf. What is Christianity? 2. ed. N.Y., 1903.

Phil 8587.26.13 — Harnack, Adolf. What is Christianity? 2. ed. N.Y., 1904.

Phil 3489.30 — Harnack, Adolf von. Immanuel Kant, 1724-1924. Berlin, 1924.

Phil 8125.20 — Harnack, Otto. Die klassische Ästhetik der Deutschen. Leipzig, 1892.

Phil 8587.26.80 — Harnack's Wesen des Christentums und die religiösen Strömmungen der Gegenwart. (Rolffs, Ernst.) Leipzig, 1902.

Phil 7060.93 — Harper, C.G. Haunted houses. London, 1907.

Phil 7069.27.45 — Harper, C.G. Haunted houses. 3. ed. London, 1927.

Phil 1750.183 — Harper, Ralph. Existentialism. Cambridge, 1948.

Phil 1750.183.2 — Harper, Ralph. Existentialism. Cambridge, 1949.

Phil 9245.130 — Harper, Ralph. The path of darkness. Cleveland, 1968.

Phil 5238.203 — Harper, Robert J.C. The cognitive processes. Englewood Cliffs, N.J., 1964.

Phil 1512.2 — Harper, Thomas. Metaphysics of the school. London, 1879. 3v.

Phil 8587.50 — Harper, W.A. Personal religious beliefs. Boston, 1937.

Phil 3160.2.85 — Harpf, Adolf. Darwin in der Ethik. Leoben, 1901.

Phil 6677.17 — Harraden, L.A. Complete illustrated course of twenty lessons in magnetic healing. n.p., 1899.

Phil 3850.1.86 — Harraeus, K. David Friedrich Strauss. Leipzig, n.d.

Phil 8408.45 — Harries, Karsten. The meaning of modern art. Evanston, 1968.

Phil 182.39 — Harriman, F. Philosophy of common sense. N.Y., 1907.

Phil 5247.61 — Harriman, P.L. Twentieth century psychology. N.Y., 1946.

Htn Phil 2055.4.30F* — Harrington, James. The oceana of James Harrington. Dublin, 1737.

Phil 6317.25 — Harrington, M. Biological approach to the problem of abnormal behavior. Lancaster, Pa., 1938.

Phil 5247.77 — Harris, Chester. Problems in measuring change. Madison, 1963.

Phil 6117.14 — Harris, D.F. Nerves. London, 1913.

Phil 5238.125 — Harris, Dale B. The concept of development. Minneapolis, 1957.

Phil 338.26 — Harris, E.E. Nature, mind of modern science. London, 1954.

Phil 338.39 — Harris, E.E. Objectivity and reason. Johannesburg, 1955.

Phil 9347.13 — Harris, Erdman. Twenty-one. N.Y., 1931.

Phil 182.132 — Harris, Errol E. The foundations of metaphysics in science. London, 1965.

Phil 8697.21 — Harris, Errol E. Revelation through reason. New Haven, 1958.

Phil 8882.4 — Harris, G. Moral evolution. Boston, 1896.

Phil 2055.6 — Harris, G. A philosophical treatise. London, 1876. 2v.

Phil 5440.16 — Harris, George. Christ's teaching concerning heredity. n.p., 1887.

Phil 4120.4.89 — Harris, Henry S. The social philosophy of Giovanni Gentile. Urbana, 1960.

Phil 5871.30 — Harris, Irving D. The promised seed; a comparative study of eminent first and later sons. N.Y., 1964.

Phil 974.2.70 — Harris, Iverson L. Mme. Blatavsky defended. San Diego, 1971.

Phil 8632.14 — Harris, J. Immortality. London, 1927.

Phil 7060.48 — Harris, J. Inferences from haunted houses. London, 1901.

Phil 8587.2.5 — Harris, J. Man primeval. Boston, 1849.

Phil 182.30 — Harris, J. Philosophical arrangements. London, 1775.

Phil 8587.2.2 — Harris, J. The pre-Adamite earth. Boston, 1849.

Phil 8587.2.3 — Harris, J. The pre-Adamite earth. Boston, 1850.

Phil 9245.12 — Harris, J. Three treatises. London, 1744.

Htn Phil 9245.12.2* — Harris, J. Three treatises. London, 1765.

Phil 9245.12.2 — Harris, J. Three treatises. London, 1765.

Phil 9245.12.3 — Harris, J. Three treatises. London, 1772.

Phil 8632.6 — Harris, J.C. The inevitable future. 4. ed. Sydney, 1917.

Phil 3489.8 — Harris, John, of Montreal. Review of Kant's Critique of pure reason. Supplement to Theology and science of goverment. Montreal, 1874.

Phil 2490.105 — Harris, M.S. The positive philosophy of Auguste Comte. Thesis. Hartford, 1923.

Phil 4368.2.80 — Harris, Marjorie. Francisco Romero on problems of philosophy. N.Y., 1960.

Phil 8662.3 — Harris, S. The philosophical basis of Theism. N.Y., 1883.

Phil 8662.10 — Harris, T.L. God's breath in man. Santa Rosa, 1891.

Phil 6317.54 — Harris, Thomas Anthony. I'm OK, you are OK: a practical guide to transactional analysis. N.Y., 1969.

Phil 1807.7 — Harris, Victor I. All coherence gone. Chicago, 1949.

Phil 1900.93 — Harris, W.G. Teleology in the philosophy of Joseph Butler and Abraham Tucker. Thesis. Philadelphia, 1941.

Phil 182.5.5 — Harris, W.T. A collection of philosophical and psychological essays; extracts from periodicals. n.p., n.d.

Phil 3425.86 — Harris, W.T. Hegel's logic. Chicago, 1890.

Phil 3425.86.5 — Harris, W.T. Hegel's logic. 2d ed. Chicago, 1895.

Phil 182.5 — Harris, W.T. Introduction to the study of philosophy. N.Y., 1889.

Phil 182.5.9 — Harris, W.T. Philosophy in outline. N.Y., 1883.

Phil 8697.16 — Harrison, A.J. The ascent of faith. N.Y., 1894.

Phil 600.11 — Harrison, F. The creed of a layman. London, 1907.

Phil 600.11.2 — Harrison, F. The creed of a layman. N.Y. 1907.

Phil 2270.95 — Harrison, F. The Herbert Spencer lecture. Oxford, 1905.

Phil 2270.85 — Harrison, F. Nature and reality of religion. A controversy. N.Y., 1885.

Phil 182.39.5 — Harrison, F. The philosophy of common sense. London, 1907.

Phil 8632.9 — Harrison, Frederic. A modern symposium. Detroit, 1878.

Phil 6957.6 — Harrison, G.L. Legislation on insanity. Philadelphia, 1884.

Phil 8882.115 — Harrison, Jonathan. Our knowledge of right and wrong. London, 1971.

Phil 5125.23 — Harrod, R.F. Foundations of inductive logic. London, 1956.

Phil 5590.110 — Harrower, M.R. Appraising personality. 1. ed. N.Y., 1952.

Phil 5247.54 — Harrower, M.R. The psychologist at work. London, 1937.

Phil 165.355 — Harry Austryn Wolfson. (American Academy for Jewish Research.) Jerusalem, 1965.

Phil 6957.7.5 — Hart, Bernard. The modern treatment of mental disorders. Manchester, 1918.

Phil 6957.7 — Hart, Bernard. The psychology of insanity. Cambridge, 1914.

Phil 6957.7.3 — Hart, Bernard. The psychology of insanity. Cambridge, 1921.

Phil 6957.7.4 — Hart, Bernard. The psychology of insanity. Cambridge, 1925.

Phil 6957.7.4.10 — Hart, Bernard. The psychology of insanity. Cambridge, 1962.

Phil 6957.7.4.7 — Hart, Bernard. The psychology of insanity. 4. ed. N.Y., 1937.

Phil 6317.17.5 — Hart, Bernard. Psychopathology; its development and place in medicine. Cambridge, 1939.

Phil 6317.17.2 — Hart, Bernard. Psychopathology. N.Y., 1927.

Phil 1512.10 — Hart, C.A. Aspects of the new scholastic philosophy. N.Y., 1932.

Phil 5217.1 — Hart, Charles A. The Thomistic concept of mental faculty. Diss. Washington, 1930.

Phil 6677.1 — Hart, E. Hypnotism, mesmerism. N.Y., 1893.

Phil 6677.1.5 — Hart, E. Hypnotism, mesmerism and the new witchcraft. London, 1896.

Phil 1865.190 — Hart, H.L.A. Bentham. London, 1962?

Phil 9490.7.2 — Hart, J.S. Mistakes of educated men. Philadelphia, 1862.

Phil 182.80 — Hart, Joseph K. Inside experience. N.Y., 1927.

Phil 182.81 — Hart, Julius. Die neue Welterkenntnis. Leipzig, 1902.

Phil 8408.8 — Hart, Julius. Revolution der Ästhetik als Einleitung zu einer Revolution der Wissenschaft. Berlin, 1909.

Phil 8610.889.10 — Hart, William. The candle from under the bushel. N.Y., 1889.

Htn Phil 9560.22* — Hartcliffe, John. A treatise of moral and intellectual virtues. London, 1691.

Phil 7106.6 — Harte, Richard. Hypnotism and the doctors. London, 1903.

Phil 5545.177 — Hartenbach, E. Dr. Ewald Hartenbach's Kunst. 15. Aufl. Quedlinburg, 1882.

Phil 6957.15 — Hartenberg, P. La névrose d'angoisse. Paris, 1902.

Phil 6017.1.2 — Hartenberg, Paul. Physionomie et caractère. Paris, 1911.

Phil 3805.174 — Hartenstein, G. De ethice a Schleiermachero propositae fundamento. Pt.1-2. Lipsiae, 1837.

Phil 3552.250 — Hartenstein, G. De materiae apud Leibnitium notione et ad monadas relatione. Lipsiae, 1846.

Phil 8882.49 — Hartenstein, G. Die Grundbegriffe der ethischen Wissenschaften. Leipzig, 1844.

Phil 182.41.5 — Hartenstein, G. Historisch-philosophische Abhandlungen. Leipzig, 1870.

Phil 2115.5 — Hartenstein, G. Locke's Lehre. Leipzig, 1861.

Phil 182.41 — Hartenstein, G. Probleme und Grundlehren der allgemeinen Metaphysik. Leipzig, 1836.

Phil 3428.160 — Hartenstein, G. Über die neuesten Darstellungen und Beurtheilungen der Herbart'schen Philosophie. Leipzig, 1838.

Phil 8408.25 — Hartford, H. Has God been insulted here? Chicago, 1952.

Phil 5047.46 — Hartkopf, Werner. Die Strukturformen der Probleme. Berlin, 1958.

Phil 338.27 — Hartland-Swann, John. An analysis of knowing. London, 1958.

Phil 5627.266.30 — Hartler, Josef. Religiös roll och Kristusliv. Lund, 1966.

Htn Phil 2038.30* — Hartley, D. Observations on man. London, 1749. 2v.

Phil 2038.31 — Hartley, D. Observations on man. London, 1791. 3v.

Phil 2038.32 — Hartley, D. Observations on man. London, 1801. 3v.

Phil 2038.33 — Hartley, D. Observations on man. London, 1810.

Phil 2038.34 — Hartley, D. Observations on man. v.1-2. Gainesville, Fla., 1966.

Phil 2038.50 — Hartley, D. Theory of the human mind. London, 1775.

Phil 5247.67 — Hartley, Eugene Leonard. Outside readings in psychology. N.Y., 1950.

Phil 2038.80 — Hartley and James Mill. (Bower, G.S.) London, 1881.

Phil 2038.80.5 — Hartley and James Mill. (Bower, G.S.) N.Y., 1881.

Phil 2038.81 — Hartley und Priestley. Photoreproduction. (Schoenlank, B.) Halle, 1901.

Phil 3120.8.92 — Hartlich, C. Die ethischen Theorien Franz Brentanos. Wurzburg, 1939.

Phil 8408.7 — Hartman, H.G. Aesthetics: a critical theory of art. Columbus, 1919.

Phil 735.262 — Hartman, Robert S. The structure of value; foundations of scientific axiology. Carbondale, 1967.

Phil 5047.37 Hartman, S.J. A textbook of logic. N.Y., 1936.
Phil 182.85 Hartmann, Alma. Zwischen Dichtung und Philosophie. Berlin, 1912.
Phil 400.75 Hartmann, Alma von. Zurück zum Idealismus. Berlin, 1902.
Phil 3415.87 Hartman, Dühring und Lange. (Vaihinger, H.) Faerlohn, 1876.
Phil 5247.17 Hartmann, E. Die moderne Psychologie. Leipzig, 1901.
Phil 3425.247 Hartmann, E. v. Ueber die dialektische Methode. Berlin, 1868.
Phil 338.2 Hartmann, E. von. Das Grundproblem der Erkenntnissth. Leipzig, 1889.
Phil 3549.1.85 Hartmann, E. von. J.H. von Kirchmanns erkentnisstheoretischer Realismus. Berlin, 1875.
Phil 65.2 Hartmann, E.V. Phänomenologie des sittlechen Bewusstens. 3 Aufl. Berlin, 1924.
Phil 3415.15 Hartmann, Eduard von. Ausgewählte Werke. Leipzig, 1888. 12v.
Phil 3415.50 Hartmann, Eduard von. Le Darwinisme. Paris, 1877.
Phil 3415.61.3 Hartmann, Eduard von. Die des Christenthums. 3. Aufl. Leipzig, 1888.
Phil 3415.40 Hartmann, Eduard von. Das Ding an sich. Berlin, 1871.
Phil 3415.36 Hartmann, Eduard von. Erläuterungen zur Metaphysik der Bewussten. Berlin, 1874.
Phil 3415.69 Hartmann, Eduard von. Ethische Studien. Leipzig, 1898.
Phil 3415.68 Hartmann, Eduard von. Die Geisterhypothese des Spiritismus und seine Phantome. Leipzig, n.d.
Phil 3415.38 Hartmann, Eduard von. Gesammelte philosophische Abhandlungen Philosophie Unbewussten. Berlin, 1872.
Phil 3415.48 Hartmann, Eduard von. Gesammelte Studien und Aufsätze. Berlin, 1876.
Phil 3415.57.2 Hartmann, Eduard von. Kategorienlehre. 2. Aufl. v.1-3. Leipzig, 1923.
Phil 3415.55 Hartmann, Eduard von. Kritische Grundlegung der trancedentalen Realismus. Berlin, 1875.
Phil 3415.72 Hartmann, Eduard von. Kritische Wanderungen durch die Philosophie der Gegenwart. Leipzig, 1889.
Phil 3415.19 Hartmann, Eduard von. Lichtstrahlen aus Eduard von Hartmann's sämmtlichen Werken. Berlin, 1881.
Phil 3415.71 Hartmann, Eduard von. Moderne Probleme. Leipzig, 1886.
Phil 3415.71.2 Hartmann, Eduard von. Moderne Probleme. 2. Aufl. Leipzig, 1888.
Phil 3415.42 Hartmann, Eduard von. Neukantianismus, Schopenhauerianismus. Berlin, 1877.
Phil 3415.65 Hartmann, Eduard von. Phänomenologie des sittlichen Bewussten. 1879.
Phil 3415.65.2 Hartmann, Eduard von. Phänomenologie des sittlichen Bewusstseins. 3. Aufl. Berlin, 1924.
Phil 3415.31 Hartmann, Eduard von. Philosophie de L'inconscient. Paris, 1877. 2v.
Phil 3415.73.5 Hartmann, Eduard von. Philosophie des Schonen. 2. Aufl. Berlin, 1924.
Phil 3415.30.1 Hartmann, Eduard von. Philosophie des Unbewussten. Berlin, 1869.
Phil 3415.30.15 Hartmann, Eduard von. Philosophie des Unbewussten. 2. Aufl. Leipzig, 1923. 3v.
Phil 3415.30.1.2 Hartmann, Eduard von. Philosophie des Unbewussten. 4. Aufl. Berlin, 1872.
Phil 3415.30 Hartmann, Eduard von. Philosophie des Unbewussten. 5. Aufl. Berlin, 1873.
Phil 3415.30.3 Hartmann, Eduard von. Philosophie des Unbewussten. 6. Aufl. Berlin, 1874.
Phil 3415.30.2 Hartmann, Eduard von. Philosophie des Unbewussten. 8. Aufl. Berlin, 1878. 2v.
Phil 3415.30.9 Hartmann, Eduard von. Philosophie des Unbewussten. 9. Aufl. Berlin, 1882.
Phil 3415.43 Hartmann, Eduard von. Philosophische Fragen. Leipzig, 1885.
Phil 3415.32.15 Hartmann, Eduard von. Philosophy of the unconcious. N.Y., 1931.
Phil 3415.32.16 Hartmann, Eduard von. Philosophy of the unconcious. N.Y., 1931.
Phil 3415.32.8 Hartmann, Eduard von. Philosophy of the unconcious. 2nd ed. London, 1893. 2v.
Phil 3415.32.2 Hartmann, Eduard von. Philosophy of the unconscious. London, 1884. 3v.
Phil 3415.32 Hartmann, Eduard von. Philosophy of the unconscious. London, 1884. 3v.
Phil 3415.74 Hartmann, Eduard von. Das Problem des Lebens. 2. Aufl. Berlin, 1925.
Phil 3415.62.2 Hartmann, Eduard von. La religion de L'Avenir. Paris, 1876.
Phil 3415.62 Hartmann, Eduard von. La religion de L'Avenir. Paris, 1877.
Phil 3415.60 Hartmann, Eduard von. Die Religion des Geistes. Berlin, 1882.
Phil 3415.63 Hartmann, Eduard von. The religion of the future. London, 1886.
Phil 3415.67 Hartmann, Eduard von. Religious metaphysics. N.Y., 1883.
Phil 3415.61 Hartmann, Eduard von. Die Selbstzersetzung des Christenthums. 2. Aufl. Berlin, 1874.
Phil 3415.45 Hartmann, Eduard von. The sexes compared and other essays. London, 1895.
Phil 3415.70 Hartmann, Eduard von. System der Philosophie im Grundriss. Bad Sachsa, 1907-09. 8v.
Phil 3415.35 Hartmann, Eduard von. Das Umbewusste...Physiologie. Berlin, 1872.
Phil 3415.35.2 Hartmann, Eduard von. Das Umbewusste...Physiologie. 2. Aufl. Berlin, 1877.
Phil 3415.39 Hartmann, Eduard von. Verldsprocessens väsen eller det omedvetnas filosofi. Stockholm, 1877-78.
Phil 3415.66 Hartmann, Eduard von. Zur Geschichte und Begründung des Pessimismus. Berlin, 1880.
Phil 3415.79 Pamphlet box. Hartmann, Eduard von. Philosophy. German and Dutch.
Phil 978.92 Hartmann, F. Ausgewählte theasophische Werke. Calw-Wimberg, Württ, 1959.
Phil 182.44.5 Hartmann, F. The life of Jehoshua, the prophet of Nazareth. Boston, 1889.
Phil 182.44 Hartmann, F. The life of Jehoshua, the prophet of Nazarette. London, 1909.
Phil 5651.3 Hartmann, F. Die Orientierung; die Physiologie. Leipzig, 1902.
Phil 5247.53 Hartmann, G.W. Gestalt psychology. N.Y., 1936.
Phil 974.3.145 Hartmann, Georg. Erziehung aus Menschenerkenntnis. Dornach, 1961.
Phil 974.3.147 Hartmann, Georg. Erziehung aus Menschenerkenntnis: von pädagogischen Impuls der Anthroposophie Rudolf Steiners. 2. Aufl. Dornach, 1969.

Phil 5247.3.300 Hartmann, George W. A collection of miscellaneous papers. n.p., n.d.
Phil 1200.32 Hartmann, H. Gewissheit und Wahrheit; der Streit zwischen Stoa und akademischer Skepsis. Halle (Saale), 1927.
Phil 3640.465 Hartmann, H. Nietzsche, critique d'art. Manosque, 1955.
Phil 1707.11 Hartmann, Hans. Denkendes Europa; ein Gang durch die Philosophie der Gegenwart. Berlin, 1936.
Phil 6317.26.9 Hartmann, Heinz. Essays on ego psychology. London, 1964.
Phil 6317.26.10 Hartmann, Heinz. Essays on ego psychology. N.Y., 1964.
Phil 6317.26 Hartmann, Heinz. Die Grundlagen der Psychoanalyse. Leipzig, 1927.
Phil 6980.348 Hartmann, Heinz. La psicología del yo y el problema de la adaptación. México, 1961.
Phil 6980.348.10 Hartmann, Heinz. Psychoanalysis and moral values. N.Y., 1960.
Phil 8610.894 Hartmann, J. God and sin in the appetites. N.Y., 1894.
Phil 3565.81 Hartmann, K.R.E. Lotze's Philosophie. Leipzig, 1888.
Htn Phil 3801.446* Hartmann, K.R.E. von. Schelling's positive Philosophie. Berlin, 1869.
Phil 3801.446.2 Hartmann, K.R.E. von. Schelling's positive Philosophie. Berlin, 1869.
Phil 7060.103 Hartmann, K.R.E. von. Der Spiritismus. Leipzig, 1885.
Phil 2880.8.140 Hartmann, Klaus. Grundzüge der Ontologie Sartres in ihrem Verhältnis zu Hegels Logik. Berlin, 1963.
Phil 165.328 Hartmann, Klaus. Lebendiger Realismus. Bonn, 1962.
Phil 2880.8.160 Hartmann, Klaus. Sartres Sozialphilosophie. Berlin, 1966.
Phil 288.6 Hartmann, L. Sind Naturgesetze Veränderlich? Halle, 1926.
Phil 8408.18 Hartmann, N. Asthetik. Berlin, 1953.
Phil 182.94.19 Hartmann, N. Der Aufbau der realen Welt. 2. Aufl. Meisenheim, 1949.
Phil 182.94.20 Hartmann, N. Einführung in die Philosophie. 3. Aufl. Osnabrück, 1954.
Phil 8882.50.5 Hartmann, N. Ethics. London, 1932. 3v.
Phil 8882.50 Hartmann, N. Ethik. Berlin, 1926.
Phil 8882.50.7 Hartmann, N. Ethik. 3. Aufl. Berlin, 1949.
Phil 338.11 Hartmann, N. Grundzüge einer Metaphysik der Erkenntnis. Berlin, 1921.
Phil 3450.18.80 Hartmann, N. Kleinere Schriften. Berlin, 1955. 3v.
Phil 182.94.16 Hartmann, N. Möglichkeit und Wirklichkeit. Berlin, 1938.
Phil 182.94.18 Hartmann, N. Neue Wege der Ontologie. Stuttgart, 194-.
Phil 182.94.17 Hartmann, N. Philosophie der Natur. Berlin, 1950.
Phil 3007.7.2A Hartmann, N. Die Philosophie des deutschen Idealismus. 2. Aufl. Berlin, 1960.
Phil 3450.33.10 Hartmann, N. Philosophische Gespräche. Göttingen, 1954.
Phil 182.94.10 Hartmann, N. Das Problem des Geistigen Seins. Berlin, 1933.
Phil 182.94.10.5 Hartmann, N. Das Problem des geistigen Seins. 2. Aufl. Berlin, 1949.
Phil 182.94.12 Hartmann, N. Teleologisches Denken. Berlin, 1951.
Phil 182.94 Hartmann, N. Zum Problem der Realitätsgegebenheit. Berlin, 1931.
Phil 182.94.15 Hartmann, N. Zur Grundlegung der Ontologie. Berlin, 1935.
Phil 3450.18.79 Pamphlet box. Hartmann, N.
Phil 182.94.18.3 Hartmann, Nicolai. Neue Wege der Ontologie. 3.Aufl. Stuttgart, 1949.
Phil 585.350 Hartmann, Otto Julius. Der Kampf um den Menschen in Natur, Mythos und Geschichte. Freiburg, 1969.
Phil 3270.4.84 Hartmann, Richard. P.J.A. Feuerbachs politische. Berlin, 1961.
Phil 3850.18.142 Hartmann, Wilfried. Max Scheler; Bibliographie. Stuttgart, 1963.
Phil 3850.18.140 Hartmann, Wilfried. Die Philosophie Max Schelers in ihren Beziehungen zu Eduard von Hartmann. Düsseldorf, 1956.
Phil 3415.98 Hartmann's inductive Philosophie im Chassidismus. (Marcus, A.) Wien, 1888.
Phil 3415.80 Hartmann's Philosophie des Unbewussten. (Fischer, J.C.) Leipzig, 1872.
Phil 630.58 Hartnach, Justice. Den ydre verdens eksistens. København, 1964.
Phil 325.7 Hartnack, J. Analysis of the problem of perception in British empiricism. Thesis. Copenhagen, 1950.
Phil 182.131 Hartnack, J. Philosophical problems. Copenhagen, 1962.
Phil 807.24.7 Hartnack, Justus. Filosofiske problemer og filosofiske argumentationer. 2. Opl. København, 1970.
Phil 807.24 Hartnack, Justus. Filosofins historie. København, 1969.
Phil 3489.45 Hartnack, Justus. Kant's theory of knowledge. N.Y., 1967.
Phil 5047.49 Hartnack, Justus. Logik. Klassik og moderne. København, 1968.
Phil 3925.16.93 Hartnack, Justus. Wittgenstein and modern philosophy. Garden City, 1965.
Phil 3925.16.92 Hartnack, Justus. Wittgenstein und die Moderne Philosophie. Stuttgart, 1962.
Phil 5520.508 Hartogs, Renatas. Four-letter word games. N.Y., 1967.
Phil 182.6.5 Hartsen, F.A. Grundiss der Philosophie. Abt. 1. Nordhausen, 1875.
Phil 5047.2 Hartsen, F.A. Grundzüge der Logik. Berlin, 1873.
Phil 5247.4 Hartsen, F.A. Grundzüge der Psychologie. Berlin, 1874.
Phil 182.6.10 Hartsen, F.A. Die Philosophie als Wissenschaft. Heidelberg, 1876.
Phil 5247.4.5 Hartsen, F.A. Princepes de psychologie. Paris, 1872.
Phil 5047.2.5 Hartsen, F.A. Principes de logique exposés d'après une méthode nouvelle. Paris, 1872.
Phil 182.6 Hartsen, F.A. Principes de philosophie. Paris, 1877.
Phil 5247.4.10 Hartsen, F.A. Untersuchungen über Psychologie. Leipzig, 1869.
Phil 9430.15 Hartsen, F.A. von. Die Moral des Pessimismus. Leipzig, n.d.
Phil 9430.15.5 Hartsen, F.A. von. Die Moral des Pessimismus. Nordhausen, 1874.
Phil 1750.145 Hartshore, Charles. Beyond humanism. Chicago, 1937.
Phil 9035.75 Hartshore, H. Studies in deceit. 1928.
Phil 9035.77 Hartshore, H. Studies in the organization of character. N.Y., 1930.
Phil 5635.35 Hartshore, C. The philosophy and psychology of sensation. Chicago, 1934.
Phil 2225.5.90 Hartshorne, Charles. Continuity, the form of forms in Charles Peirce. n.p., 1929.
Phil 2055.9.40 Hartshorne, Charles. Creative synthesis and philosophic method. London, 1970.
Phil 2055.9.35 Hartshorne, Charles. The logic of perfection. LaSalle, Ill., 1962.
Phil 8662.17 Hartshorne, Charles. Man's vision of God, and the logic of theism. Chicago, 1941.
Phil 2055.9.30 Hartshorne, Charles. Reality as social process. Glencoe, Ill., 1953.
Phil 4065.90 Hartung, E.B. Grundlinien einer Ethik bei Giordano Bruno. Leipzig, 1878.
Phil 288.5 Hartung, G. Philosophie und Naturwissenschaft. n.p., n.d.

Phil 585.181 — Hartung, Henri. Unité de l'homme. Paris, 1963.
Phil 288.7 — Hartung, J.F. Die physikalische Energie und die Brücke. Obersalzbrunn, 1928.
X Cg   Phil 7075.139 — Hartwell, S.W. A citizen's handbook of sexual abnormalities and the mental hygiene approach to their prevention. Washington, 1951.
Phil 1750.305 — Hartwig, T. Der Existentialismus. Wien, 1948.
Phil 4668.121.80 — Harva, Uno. Die Philosophie von G.I. Hartman. Turku, 1935.
Phil 5203.11.15 — The Harvard list of books in psychology. (Harvard University.) Cambridge, 1949.
Phil 5203.11.20 — The Harvard list of books in psychology. (Harvard University.) Cambridge, 1955.
Phil 5203.11.24 — The Harvard list of books in psychology. Compiled and annotated by the psychologists in Harvard University. 4th ed. (Harvard University.) Cambridge, 1971.
Phil 5203.11.22A — The Harvard list of books in psychology. 3. ed. (Harvard University.) Cambridge, 1964.
Phil 47.1.9 — Harvard Medical School. Department of Neurology. Contributions from Massachusetts General Hospital. Boston. 1,1906
Phil 17.8 — Harvard psychological studies. Lancaster, Pa. 1-5,1903-1922 5v.
Phil 5203.11.15 — Harvard University. The Harvard list of books in psychology. Cambridge, 1949.
Phil 5203.11.20 — Harvard University. The Harvard list of books in psychology. Cambridge, 1955.
Phil 5203.11.24 — Harvard University. The Harvard list of books in psychology. Compiled and annotated by the psychologists in Harvard University. 4th ed. Cambridge, 1971.
Phil 5203.11.22A — Harvard University. The Harvard list of books in psychology. 3. ed. Cambridge, 1964.
Phil 5047.40 — Harvard University. Department of Philosophy. Logic cases for philosophy, 1919-1920. Cambridge, Mass., 1920.
Phil 5203.11.10 — Harvard University. Department of Psychology. Books in psychology. v.1-2. Cambridge, 1938.
Phil 9380.7 — Harvard University. Department of Psychology. Worksheets on morale. Cambridge, 1943.
Phil 575.95 — Harvard University. Harvard Psychological Clinic. Explorations in personality. N.Y., 1938.
Phil 5650.30 — Harvard University. Psycho-Acoustic Laboratory. A bibliography in audition. v.1-2. Cambridge, 1950.
Phil 5650.25 — Harvard University. Psycho-Acoustic Laboratory. Bibliography on hearing. Cambridge, 1955.
Phil 5203.11 — Harvard University. Psychology Library. Selected reference list. Cambridge, 1936.
Phil 6674.5 — The Harveian oration. (Elliotson, John.) London, 1846.
Phil 5247.18 — Harvey, N.A. Elementary psychology. Chicago, 1914.
Phil 5400.30 — Harvey, N.A. The feelings of man. Baltimore, 1914.
Phil 5548.102 — Harvey, O.J. Motivation and social interaction. N.Y., 1963.
Phil 974.3.108 — Harwood, A.C. The faithful thinker. London, 1961.
Phil 5850.235 — Harwood, Sumner. How to work with people. Cambridge, 1940.
Phil 8408.25 — Has God been insulted here? (Hartford, H.) Chicago, 1952.
Phil 2255.1.68 — Has man a future? (Russell, Bertrand Russell.) London, 1961.
Phil 8692.14 — Has science discovered God? (Cotton, Edward.) N.Y., 1931.
Phil 5241.46 — Has the psychological laboratory proved helpful. (Billia, Lorenzo M.) Chicago, 1909.
Phil 630.34 — Hasan, S.Z. Realism: an attempt to trace its origin. Cambridge, 1928.
Phil 9030.3 — Le hasard. (Revel, Camille.) Paris, 1905.
Phil 270.55 — Hasard et contingence. (Segond, J.L.P.) Paris, 1938.
Phil 270.60 — Hasard et probabilités. (Coculeseo, P.) Paris, 1949.
Phil 270.57 — Le hasard sa loi et ses conséquences dans les sciences et en philosophie. (Revel, Camille.) Paris, 1905.
Phil 3246.235 — Hase, K. von. Jenaisches Fichte - Büchlein. Leipzig, 1856.
Phil 3255.85 — Hase, Karl A. Sebastian Frank von Wörd der Schwarmgeist. Leipzig, 1869.
Phil 5535.62 — Haseloff, Otto Walter. Psychologie des Lernens: Methoden, Ergebnisse, Anwendungen. Berlin, 1970.
Phil 9075.24 — Hasenclever, K.H. Die Berührung und Verwerthung der Gewissens. Karleruhe, 1877.
Phil 5643.81 — Hasenclever, R. Die Raumvorstellung aus der Gesichtssinne. Berlin, 1842.
Phil 3850.14.30 — Hasenfuss, Josef. Herman Schell als existentieller Denker und Theologie. 1. Aufl. Würzburg, 1951.
Phil 182.95 — Haserot, F.S. Essays on the logic of being. N.Y., 1932.
Phil 3850.18.200 — Haskamp, Reinhold J. Spekulativer und Phänomenologischer. Freiburg, 1966.
Phil 6957.8 — Haskell, E. The trial of Ebenezer Haskell in lunacy. Philadelphia, 1869.
Phil 5247.5 — Haslam, J. Sound mind. London, 1819.
Phil 4803.497.30 — Hasło dobrej roboty. Wyd. 1. (Kotarbiński, Tadeusz.) Warszawa, 1968.
Phil 8408.36.2 — Haspers, John. Meaning and truth in the art. Hamden, Connecticut, 1946.
Phil 8408.36 — Haspers, John. Meaning and truth in the arts. Chapel Hill, 1947.
Phil 3790.7.81 — Hasse, Heinrich. Die Philosophie Raoul Richters. Leipzig, 1914.
Phil 2050.175 — Hasse, Heinrich. Das Problem der Gültigkeit. Leipzig, 1919.
Phil 3640.177 — Hasse, Heinrich. Das Problem des Sokrates. Leipzig, 1918.
Phil 3808.114.15 — Hasse, Heinrich. Schopenhauer. München, 1926.
Phil 3808.114.10 — Hasse, Heinrich. Schopenhauer Erkenntnislehre. Leipzig, 1913.
Phil 3808.114.12 — Hasse, Heinrich. Schopenhauers Religionsphilosophie und ihre Bedeutung für die Gegenwart. Frankfurt, 1924.
Phil 3489.26 — Hasse, J.G. Lezte aeusserungen Kant's von einem seiner Tischgenossen. Königsberg, 1804.
Phil 807.9.2 — Hasse, Karl P. Von Plotin zu Goethe. Jena, 1912.
Phil 807.9 — Hasse, Karl P. Von Plotin zu Goethe. Leipzig, 1909.
Phil 525.15.15 — Hasse, Karl P. Das Wesen der Persönlichkeit. Meerane, 1913.
Phil 9075.30 — Hassel, H. De conscientia theses morales. Diss. Aboae, 1738.
Htn   Phil 9347.16* — Hassen, Martin. De noncommutándo sexus habitu. Vitembergae, 1714.
Phil 182.7 — Hassler, K.D. Paragraphen für den Unterricht in der Philosophie. Ulm, 1832.
Phil 182.7.2 — Hassler, K.D. Paragraphen für den Unterricht in der Philosophie. 2. Aufl. Ulm, 1852.
Htn   Phil 3801.447* — Hast, Johann. Andeutungen über Glauben und Wissen. Münster, 1842.

Phil 974.2.50 — Hastings, B. (Mrs.). Defence of Madame Blavatsky. Worthing, 1937. 2v.
Phil 282.16 — Hat wereldraadsel. (Bolland, G.J.P.J.) Leiden, 1896.
Phil 672.234 — Hatano, Seiichi. Time and eternity. Tokyo? 1963.
Phil 7054.86 — Hatch, Cora L.V. Two lectures on the present crisis. N.Y., 1860.
Phil 182.47 — Hatch, D.P. Scientific occultism. Los Angeles, 1905.
Phil 8587.41 — Hatch, D.P. The twentieth century Christ. Boston, 1906.
Phil 2262.87 — Hatch, Irvin C. Der Einfluss Shaftesburys auf Herder. Diss. Berlin? 1901?
Phil 735.256 — Hatcher, Harlan Henthorne. The persistent quest for values: what are we seeking? Columbia, 1966.
Phil 6117.44 — Hathaway, S.R. Physiological psychology. N.Y., 1942.
Phil 5465.142 — Hatterer, Lawrence J. The artist in society. N.Y., 1965.
Phil 5640.136.10 — Hatwell, Yvette. Privation sensorielle et intelligence. Paris, 1966.
Phil 2805.106 — Hatzfeld, A. Pascal. Paris, 1901.
Phil 3120.8.87 — Hauber, V. Wahrheit und Evidenz bei Franz Brentano. Inaug. Diss. Stuttgart, 1936.
Phil 8050.57.5 — Hauch, J.C. Aesthetiske afhandlinger og recensioner. Kjøbenhavn,1869. 1861.
Phil 8050.57 — Hauch, J.C. Afhandlinger og aesthetiske betragtninger. Kjøbenhavn, 1855.
Phil 8050.57.10 — Hauch, J.C. Afhandlinger og aesthetiske betragtninger. Kjøbenhavn, 1869.
Phil 3489.7 — Hauck, P. Urteile und Kategorien; eine Studie zu Kants Logik. Strassburg, 1903.
Phil 3705.5 — Hauck, W.A. Das Geheimnis des Lebens. Heidelburg, 1947.
Phil 92.3 — Hauer, E. Philosophen Lexikon. Lief. 1-6. Berlin, 1937.
Phil 3665.5.90 — Hauer, Eugen. Person und Handlung in der Ethik Leonard Nelsons. Inaug. Diss. Bonn, 1928.
Phil 974.3.95 — Hauer, J.W. Werden und Wesen der Anthroposophie. Stuttgart, 1923.
Phil 3640.325 — Hauff, R. von. Nietzsches Stellung zur christlichen Demut. Inaug. Diss. Tübingen, 1939.
Phil 3808.106 — Hauff, W. Die Überwindung des Schopenhauerschen Pessimismus durch F. Nietzsche. Halle, 1904.
Phil 3100.83 — Hauffe, G. Professor Dr. Eduard Beneckes Psychologie als Naturwissenschaft. Borna, n.d.
Phil 1850.149 — Haukart, Robert. François Bacon. Paris, 1957.
Phil 7069.40.16 — Haunted England. (Hole, C.) London, 1940.
Phil 7060.92.25 — Haunted highways and byways. (O'Donnell, Elliot.) London, 1914.
Phil 7060.38.2 — Haunted homes. (Ingram, J.H.) London, 1884.
Phil 7060.38 — Haunted homes. (Ingram, J.H.) London, 1884.
NEDL Phil 7060.38.15 — The haunted homes and family traditions of Great Britain. (Ingram, J.H.) London, 1912.
Phil 7060.38.3 — The haunted homes and family traditions of Great Britain. 3. ed. (Ingram, J.H.) London, 1886.
NEDL Phil 7060.38.5 — The haunted homes and family traditions of Great Britain. 5. ed. (Ingram, J.H.) London, 1901.
Phil 7060.38.9 — The haunted homes and family traditions of Great Britain. 5th ed. (Ingram, J.H.) London, 1901.
Phil 7069.24.15 — Haunted houses. (Flammarion, Camille.) London, 1924.
Phil 7069.24.15.2 — Haunted houses. (Flammarion, Camille.) N.Y., 1924.
Phil 7060.93 — Haunted houses. (Harper, C.G.) London, 1907.
Phil 7069.27.45 — Haunted houses. 3. ed. (Harper, C.G.) London, 1927.
Phil 7060.92.15 — Haunted houses of London. (O'Donnell, Elliot.) London, 1909.
Phil 7069.51 — Haunted people. 1. ed. (Carrington, H.) N.Y., 1951.
Phil 7060.92.35 — Haunted places in England. (O'Donnell, Elliot.) London, 1919.
Phil 7069.57.5 — Haunted waters. (O'Donnell, Elliot.) London, 1957.
Phil 7069.36.13 — The haunting of Cashen's Gap. (Price, Harry.) London, 1936.
Phil 3489.33 — Haupt-Momente der kritischen Philosophie. (Herbart, J.F.) Münster, 1883.
Phil 349.42 — Die haupt Probleme der Erkenntnistheorie. (Schneider, Friedrich.) München, 1959.
Phil 810.3 — Die haupt Probleme der Philosophie. (Knauer, Vincenz.) Wien, 1892.
Phil 5257.33 — Die Hauptergebnisse der modernen Psychologie. (Ruttmann, W.J.) Leipzig, 1914.
Phil 1508.2 — Die Hauptform mittelalterlicher Weltanschanung. (Dempf, Alois.) München, 1925.
Phil 8886.3 — Hauptfragen der Ethik. (Landmann, R.) Leipzig, 1874.
Phil 3270.14.30 — Hauptfragen der Metaphysik. 2. Aufl. (Feuling, Daniel.) Heidelberg, 1949.
Phil 187.65 — Die Hauptfragen der Metaphysik in Verbindung mit der Speculation. (Merten, J.) Trier, 1840.
Phil 5400.15 — Die Hauptgesetze des menschlichen Gefühlslebens. (Lehmann, A.) Leipzig, 1892.
Phil 5400.15.2 — Die Hauptgesetze des menschlichen Gefühlslebens. 2. Aufl. (Lehmann, A.) Leipzig, 1914.
Phil 5062.2 — Die Hauptlehren der Logic. (Waitz, F.H.W.) Erfurt, 1840.
Phil 1718.9 — Hauptlinien der Entwicklung der Philosophie von mitte des 19. Jahrhunderts bis zur Gegenwart. (Schjelderup, Harald K.) n.p., n.d.
Phil 182.66 — Hauptmann, C. Die Metaphysik in der modernen Physiologie. Jena, 1894.
Phil 8882.32 — Hauptprobleme der Ethik. 2e aufl. (Hensel, P.) Leipzig, 1913.
Phil 193.59.2.3A — Hauptprobleme der Philosophie. (Simmel, G.) Leipzig, 1910.
Phil 193.59.2A — Hauptprobleme der Philosophie. (Simmel, G.) Leipzig, 1911.
Phil 193.59.3 — Hauptprobleme der Philosophie. 7. Aufl. (Simmel, G.) Berlin, 1950.
Phil 178.44.10 — Die Hauptprobleme der Philosophie und Religion. (Delff, Heinrich K.H.) Leipzig, 1886.
Phil 8584.5.16 — Hauptprobleme der Religionsphilosophie der Gegenwart. (Eucken, Rudolf.) Berlin, 1912.
Phil 735.106 — Hauptprobleme der Wertphilosophie. (Cohn, Aron.) Wien, 1934.
Phil 735.210 — Hauptprobleme der Wertphilosophie. (Ehrlich, Walter.) Tübingen, 1959.
Phil 3428.97 — Die Hauptpuncte der Herbartschen Metaphysik. (Strümpell.) Braunschweig, 1840.
Htn Phil 3801.450* — Hauptpuncte der Metaphysik. (Herbart, Johann F.) Göttingen, 1808.
Phil 2050.85 — Die Hauptpunkte der Humeschen Erkenntnislehre. (Petzholtz, E.) Berlin, 1880.
Phil 185.50 — Die Hauptpunkte der Metaphysik. (Kirchner, F.) Cöthen, 1880.
Phil 5245.29 — Die Hauptpunkte der Psychologie. (Felsch.) Cöthen, 1904.
Phil 5222.4 — Die Hauptrichtungen der gegenwärtigen Psychologie. (Müller-Freienfelds, R.) Leipzig, 1929.

Author and Title Listing

Phil 3428.95.2 — Die Hauptsächlichstein der Herbartschen Psychologie. 2. Aufl. (Ostermann, W.) Oldenburg, 1894.

Phil 3625.1.125 — Die Hauptschriften zum pantheismus Streit. (Scholz, Heinrich.) Berlin, 1916.

Phil 3552.24 — Hauptschriften zur Grundelung der Philosophie. (Leibniz, Gottfried Wilhelm.) Leipzig, 1904-06. 2v.

Phil 3552.24.5.3 — Hauptschriften zur Grundelung der Philosophie. 3. Aufl. (Leibniz, Gottfried Wilhelm.) Hamburg, 1966. 2v.

Phil 2520.21.5 — Hauptschriften zur Grundlegung seiner Philosophie. (Descartes, René.) Heidelberg, 1930.

Phil 1718.25 — Hauptströmungen der Gegenwartphilosophie. (Stegmüller, W.) Wien, 1952.

Phil 1718.25.2 — Hauptströmungen der Gegenwartphilosophie. 2. Aufl. (Stegmüller, W.) Stuttgart, 1960.

Phil 1740.16.4 — Hauptströmungen der Gegenwartsphilosophie. 4. Aufl. (Stegmüller, Wolfgang.) Stuttgart, 1969.

Phil 3552.57A — Die Hauptwerke. 3. Aufl. (Leibniz, Gottfried Wilhelm.) Stuttgart, 1949.

Phil 1512.1 — Haureau, B. De la philosophie scolastique. Paris, 1850. 2v.

Phil 1512.1.2 — Haureau, B. Histoire de la philosophie scolastique. Paris, 1872-80. 3v.

Phil 7060.95 — Hauréau, M.B. Mémoire sur les récits d'apparitions. Paris, 1875.

Phil 338.22 — Hausdorff, Felix. Das Chaos im kosmischer Auslese. Leipzig, 1898.

Phil 9450.62 — Hauser, Richard. Was des Kaisers ist. 1. Aufl. Frankfurt, 1968.

Phil 5878.5 — Hauser, Stuart T. Black and white identity formation: studies in the psychosocial development of lower socioeconomic class adolescent boys. N.Y., 1971.

Phil 3489.1 — Hausius, K.G. Materialen zur Geschichte der critischen Philosophie. Leipzig, 1793. 2v.

Phil 5066.270 — Hausman, Alan. Carnap and Goodman: two formalists. Iowa City, 1967.

Phil 3280.88 — Hausmann, P. Das Freiheitsproblem in der Metaphysik und Ethik bei Arnold Geulincx. Inaug. Diss. Würzburg, 1934.

Phil 5592.198 — Hauss, Kurt. Emotionalität und Wahrnehmung. Göttingen, 1970.

Phil 5247.33 — Hautefeuille, F. d'. Le privilege de l'intelligence. Paris, 1923.

Phil 8587.34.5 — Hauter, Charles. Essai sur l'objet religieux. Thèse. Strasbourg, 1928.

Phil 8587.34.2 — Hauter, Charles. Religion et réalité. Thèse. Strasbourg, 1922.

Phil 5585.215 — Havaitsemisen maailma. (Fisandt, Kai von.) Helsinki, 1962.

Phil 2280.1.95 — Havard, William C. Henry Sidgwick and later utilitarian political philosophy. Gainesville, 1959.

Phil 5761.3 — Have you a strong will? (Leland, C.G.) London, 1899.
Phil 5761.3.2 — Have you a strong will? (Leland, C.G.) London, 1902.
Phil 5761.3.3 — Have you a strong will? (Leland, C.G.) London, 1903.
Phil 5761.3.10 — Have you a strong will? (Leland, C.G.) N.Y., 1919.
Phil 5465.163 — Havelka, Jaroslav. The nature of the creative process in art. The Hague, 1968.

Phil 1980.3.98 — Havelock Ellis; a biographical and critical survey. (Goldberg, I.) N.Y., 1926.

Phil 1980.3.92 — Havelock Ellis, in appreciation. Berkeley Heights, N.J., 1929.

Phil 1980.3.90 — Havelock Ellis, philosopher of love. (Peterson, Houston.) Boston, 1928.

Phil 1980.3.100 — Havelock Ellis. (Calde-Marshall, A.) London, 1959.
Phil 1980.3.102 — Havelock Ellis. (Freeman-Ishill, Rose.) Berkeley Heights, N.J., 1959.

Phil 182.126 — Havemann, Hans. Der polare Mensch. Hannover, 1923.
Phil 7068.90.10 — Haven, Gilbert. Heavenly messenger. Washington, 1890.
Phil 807.1 — Haven, J. A history of philosophy. N.Y., 1876.
Phil 5247.6.1 — Haven, J. Mental philosophy. Boston, 1872.
Phil 8882.5.2 — Haven, J. Moral philosophy. Boston, 1874.
Phil 3640.183 — Havenstein, M. Nietzsche als Erzieher. Berlin, 1922.
Phil 3489.34 — Havet, Jacques. Kant et le problème du temps. Paris, 1946.

Phil 8408.39 — Havryliuk, P.J. Spetsyfichni osoblynosti zmistu i formy v mystetstvi. Kyïv, 1963.

Phil 8408.52 — Havryliuk, Pedro I. Problema estetychnoko i teoriia upravlinnia. Kyïv, 1970.

Phil 9347.1 — Hawes, J. Lectures to young men. Boston, 1856.
Phil 9347.1.2 — Hawes, J. Lectures to young men. Hartford, 1832.
Phil 5203.10 — Hawes, M. What to read on psychology. Chicago, 1942.
Phil 630.25 — Hawes, R.P. The logic of contemporary English realism. Thesis. N.Y., 1923.

Phil 8662.19 — Hawkins, D.J. The essentials of theism. London, 1949.
Phil 182.105 — Hawkins, D.J.B. Approach to philosophy. London, 1938.
Phil 182.105.5 — Hawkins, D.J.B. Being and becoming. N.Y.,1954.
Phil 270.45 — Hawkins, D.J.B. Causality and implication. London, 1937.
Phil 338.24 — Hawkins, D.J.B. The criticism of experience. London, 1945.

Phil 1707.16 — Hawkins, D.J.B. Crucial problems of modern philosophy. London, 1957.

Phil 1707.16.5 — Hawkins, D.J.B. Crucial problems of modern philosophy. Notre Dame, 1962.

Phil 1512.12 — Hawkins, D.J.B. A sketch of mediaeval philosophy. London, 1946.

Phil 8882.73 — Hawkins, Denis J.B. Man and morals. London, 1960.
Phil 8408.3 — Hawkins, Denis John B. The concepts of aesthetics. London, 1942.

Phil 3925.16.88 — Hawkins, Dennis John Bernard. Wittgenstein and the cult of language. London, 1957.

Phil 288.20 — Hawley, Don. The nature of things. N.Y., 1959.
Phil 8610.903.10 — Hawley, J.S. Tradition versus truth. N.Y., 1903.
Phil 5047.41 — Hawley, Thomas de R. Infallible logic. Lansing, 1896.
Phil 5590.175 — Hawthorn, H.B. Sociology of personality functioning. Sioux City, Iowa, 1955.

Phil 8430.17 — Hay, D.R. The science of beauty, as developed in nature. Edinburgh, 1856.

Phil 2805.399 — Hay, Malcolm. The prejudices of Pascal. London, 1962.
Phil 5520.75 — Hayakawa, S.I. Language in action. N.Y., 1941.
Phil 5520.75.2 — Hayakawa, S.I. Language in action. N.Y., 1941.
Phil 5520.75.10 — Hayakawa, S.I. Symbol, status. 1. ed. N.Y., 1963.
Phil 5520.432 — Hayden, Donald E. Classics in semantics. N.Y., 1965.
Phil 8697.15 — Hayden, W.B. Science and revelation. Boston, 1852.
Phil 7054.102.2 — Hayden, William B. On the phenomena of modern spiritualism. 2. ed. Boston, 1855. 2 pam.

Phil 325.10 — Hayden Colloquium on Scientific Concept and Method, M.I.T. Evidence and inference. Chicago, 1960.

Phil 70.89 — Hayden Colloquium on Scientific Concept and Method, M.I.T. Parts and wholes. N.Y., 1963.

Phil 270.131 — Hayden Colloquium on Scientific Method and Concept. Massachusetts Institute of Technology. Cause and effect. N.Y., 1965.

Phil 5247.63 — Hayek, F.A. von. Individualism: true and false. Dublin, 1946.

Phil 2138.121.1 — Hayek, Friedrich Augustus von. John Stuart Mill and Harriet Taylor; their correspondence and subsequent marriage. London, 1951.

Phil 2138.121 — Hayek, Friedrich Augustus von. John Stuart Mill and Harriet Taylor; their friendship and subsequent marriage. London, 1951.

Phil 2477.6.108 — Hayen, A. Bibliographie blondelienne. Bruxelles, 1953.
Phil 5648.12 — Hayes, M.H.S. A study of cutaneous after-sensations. Chicago, 1912.

Phil 5400.24 — Hayes, Samuel P. Study of the affective qualities. n.p., 1906.

Phil 3808.148 — Haym, R. Arthur Schopenhauer. Berlin, 1864.
Phil 3425.88A — Haym, Rudolf. Hegel und seine Zeit. Berlin, 1857. — X Cg
Phil 3425.88.2 — Haym, Rudolf. Hegel und seine Zeit. 2. Aufl. Leipzig, 1927.

Phil 3801.448.5 — Hayner, Paul Collins. Reason and existence; Schelling's philosophy of history. Leiden, 1967.

Phil 8632.19 — Haynes, E.S.P. The belief in personal immortality. N.Y., 1913.

Phil 7069.28.12 — Haynes, Frederick H. The book of spiritual wisdom by "Cuno". London, 1928.

Phil 7069.61.40 — Haynes, Renée. The hidden springs. London, 1961.
Phil 5247.76 — Hays, W. Statistics for psychologists. N.Y., 1963.
Phil 5850.227 — Hayward, C.N. Re-creating human nature. N.Y., 1914.
Phil 5247.31.5 — Hayward, C.W. What is psychology? N.Y., 1923.
Phil 8893.11.18 — Hayward, F.H. The ethical philosophy of Sidgwick. Photoreproduction. London, 1901.

Phil 5425.57 — Hayward, F.H. Professionalism and originality. Chicago, 1917.

Phil 182.34 — Hayward, J.K. A rebuttal of spiritism. N.Y., 1903.
Phil 8587.74 — Hayward, John. Existentialism and religious liberalism. Boston, 1962.

Phil 8419.70 — Hazard, form, and value. (Slattery, Mary Francis.) Detroit, 1971.

Phil 1750.31 — Hazard, P. Die Herrschaft der Vernunft. Hamburg, 1949.
Phil 5817.2 — Hazard, R.G. Animals, not automata. N.Y., 1875.
Phil 270.7.10 — Hazard, R.G. Causation and freedom in willing. Boston, 1889.

Phil 5757.1.4 — Hazard, R.G. Freedom of mind in willing. Boston, 1889.
Phil 5757.1.2 — Hazard, R.G. Freedom of mind in willing. N.Y., 1865.
Phil 270.7 — Hazard, R.G. Man a creative first cause. Boston, 1883.
Phil 270.7.2 — Hazard, R.G. Man a creative first cause. Boston, 1883.
Phil 270.7.3* — Hazard, R.G. Man a creative first cause. Boston, 1883. — Htn
Phil 5757.1.6 — Hazard, R.G. Two letters on causation and freedom. Boston, 1869.

Phil 5757.1.7 — Hazard, R.G. Zwei Briefe über Verursachung und Freiheit im Wollen Gerichtet. N.Y., 1875.

Phil 182.48 — Pamphlet vol. Hazard, Rowland G. 7 pam.
Phil 7054.106.5 — Hazard, T.R. Eleven days at Moravia. Boston, 1872.
Phil 7054.106 — Hazard, T.R. Mediums and mediumship. Boston, 1872.
Phil 7054.106.2 — Hazard, T.R. Mediums and mediumship. Boston, 1873.
Phil 5585.35 — Hazelhoff, F.F. De waarnemingstijd. Proefschrift. Groningen, 1923.

Phil 8882.88 — Hazlitt, H. The foundations of morality. Princeton, N.J., 1964.

Phil 8882.6 — Hazlitt, W. Essays on the principles of human action. London, n.d.

Phil 5421.25.15 — Hazo, Robert G. The idea of love. N.Y., 1967.
Phil 8677.19 — He came down from heaven. (Williams, Charles.) London, 1938.

Phil 9530.25 — He can who thinks he can. (Marden, Orison S.) N.Y., 1908.
Phil 8667.22 — He who is; a study in traditional theism. (Mascall, E.L.) London, 1943.

Phil 630.39 — Heacock, Roger. Der monistische Realismus im amerikanischen Denken. Inaug. Diss. Berlin? 1933.

Phil 6400.14 — Head, Henry. Aphasia and kindred disorders of speech. Cambridge, Eng., 1926. 2v.

Phil 6117.30 — Head, Henry. Studies in neurology. London, 1920. 2v.
Phil 5645.5 — Head, J.F. Color blindness. Boston, 1881.
Phil 8632.20 — Head, Joseph. Reincarnation. N.Y., 1961.
Phil 8620.44.5 — Headlam, A.C. Why I am satisfied; an open letter to Prof. C.E.M. Joad. Oxford, 1944.

Phil 182.62.15 — The headquarters of reality. (Holmes, Edmond.) London, 1933.

Phil 9230.25 — Heads, I win; tails, you lose. (Olmsted, Charlotte.) N.Y., 1962.

Phil 5938.10 — Heads and faces. (Sizer, N.) N.Y., 1890. — NEDL
Phil 8632.11 — Heagle, David. Do the dead still live? Philadelphia, 1920
Phil 6980.644 — Heal the hurt child. (Riese, Hertha.) Chicago, 1962.
Phil 6113.23 — Healing currents from the battery of life. 2. ed. (De Voe, W.) Chicago, 1905.

Phil 7054.54.5 — The healing of the nations. 2. ed. (Linton, Charles.) N.Y., 1855.

Phil 7054.54.7 — The healing of the nations. 2. series. (Linton, Charles.) Philadelphia, 1864.

Phil 7069.27.23 — Healing through spirit agency. (Saunders, R.H.) London, 1927.

Phil 6128.44 — Health; its recovery and maintanance, by Abduhl Latif. (Saunders, R.H.) London, 1928.

Phil 6114.14 — Health and power. (Ellsworth, P.) Holyoke, Mass., 1915.
Phil 6115.11.19 — Health and suggestion: the dietetics of the mind. (Feuchtersleben, E.F.V.) N.Y., 1910.

Phil 178.12.27A — Health and the inner life. (Dresser, H.W.) N.Y., 1906.
Phil 9347.2.25 — Health and wealth. (Hubbard, E.) East Aurora, 1908.
Phil 6127.19 — The health of the mind. (Rees, John R.) Cambridge, Eng., 1929.

Phil 6128.38.2 — Health through self-control in thinking, breathing, eating. (Spinney, W.A.) Boston, 1907.

Phil 6317.18.10 — Healy, William. Personality information and action. N.Y., 1938.

Phil 6317.18.2 — Healy, William. The structure and meaning of psychoanalysis as related to personality and behavior. N.Y., 1953.

Phil 5247.78 — Heard, G. The five ages of man. N.Y., 1964[1963]
Phil 365.46 — Heard, G. Pain, sex and time. N.Y., 1939.
Phil 8882.58 — Heard, G. The third morality. London, 1937.
Phil 8832.6 — Heard, Gerald. Morals since 1900. London, 1950.
Phil 5627.132.10 — Heard, Gerald. A preface to prayer. 1. ed. N.Y., 1944.
Phil 8587.47.5 — Heard, Gerald. The recollection. Palo Alto, 1944.
Phil 8587.47 — Heard, Gerald. Social substance of religion. London, 1931.

Phil 5650.24 — Hearing; its psychology and physiology. (Stevens, Stanley S.) N.Y., 1938.

Author and Title Listing

Phil 5650.13 Hearing. (Ogden, Robert M.) N.Y., 1924.
Phil 5650.20 Hearing in man and animals. (Beatty, R.T.) London, 1932.
Phil 5650.5 The hearing of primitive peoples. (Bruner, A.G.) N.Y., 1908.
Phil 5217.7 Hearnshaw, L.S. A short history of British psychology, 1840-1940. London, 1964.
Phil 7069.55.20 The heart aflame. (Saint-Clair, Simone.) London, 1955.
Phil 8583.38 Heart and mind. (Dimond, S.G.) London, 1945.
Phil 9345.8 Heart and soul culture. (Fischer, E.L.C.) Philadelphia, 1912.
Phil 5627.137.5 Heart and spirit. (Johnsen, T.) Oslo, 1934.
Phil 6315.19.41 The heart of man. 1st ed. (Fromm, Erich.) N.Y., 1968.
Phil 2805.112.15 The heart of Pascal. (Stewart, Hugh F.) Cambridge, 1945.
Phil 978.29.5 The heart of things. (Farnsworth, E.C.) Portland, Maine, 1914.
Phil 9174.1 The hearth-stone. (Osgood, S.) N.Y., 1854.
NEDL Phil 9174.1.3 The hearth-stone. (Osgood, S.) N.Y., 1854.
Phil 9174.1.2 The hearth-stone. (Osgood, S.) N.Y., 1876.
Phil 8585.19 The hearts of men. (Fielding-Hall, H.) N.Y., 1901.
Phil 8585.19.3 The hearts of men. 3rd ed. (Fielding-Hall, H.) London, 1904.
Phil 5247.43 Heath, Archie E. How we behave. London, 1927.
Phil 575.45 Heath, Arthur G. The moral and social significance of the conception of personality. Oxford, 1921.
Phil 5590.21A Heath, C.W. What people are. Cambridge, Mass., 1945.
Phil 672.158 Heath, L.R. The concept of time. Photoreproduction. Chicago, 1936.
Phil 5402.27 Heath, R.G. The role of pleasure in behavior. N.Y., 1964.
Phil 8402.52.5 The heaven of invention. (Boas, George.) Baltimore, 1962.
Phil 3235.115 Heaven wasn't his destination; the philosophy of Ludwig Feuerbach. (Chamberlain, W.B.) London, 1941.
Phil 5627.41 Heavenly bridegrooms...erotogenetic...religion. N.Y., 1918.
Phil 1750.152.10 The heavenly city of the eighteenth-century philosophers. (Becker, Carl Lotus.) New Haven, 1968.
Phil 8668.1.5 The heavenly father. (Naville, E.) Boston, 1867.
Phil 7068.90.10 Heavenly messenger. (Haven, Gilbert.) Washington, 1890.
Phil 8693.17 The heavens and faith. (Davidson, M.) London, 1936.
Phil 5247.15 Hebberd, S.S. An introduction...science of thought. Madison, 1892.
Phil 3460.91 Hebeisen, A. Friedrich Heinrich Jacobi. Bern, 1960.
Phil 978.59.95 Heber, Lilly. Krishnamurti and the world crisis. London, 1935.
Phil 182.40 Hébert, M. Le pragmatisme. Paris, 1908.
Phil 5627.33 Hébert, Marcel. Le divin. Paris, 1907.
Phil 182.58 Hebler, Carl. Philosophische Aufsätze. Leipzig, 1869.
Phil 3827.10 Hebler, Carl. Spinoza's Lehre vom Verhältniss der Substanz zu ihren Bestimmtheiten Dargestellt. Bern, 1850.
Phil 5757.8 Hebler, Karl. Elemente einer philosophischen Freiheitslehre. Berlin, 1887.
Phil 6315.2.385 The Hebrew Moses; an answer to Sigmund Freud. (Weiss-Rosmarin, Trude.) N.Y., 1939.
Phil 1050.23 The Hebrew philosophical genius. (Macdonald, D.B.) Princeton, 1936.
Phil 8593.2 Hebrew Theism, common basis of Judaism, Christianity and Mohammedism. (Newman, F.W.) London, 1874.
Phil 6117.52 Hécaen, Henry. Les gauchers. Paris, 1963.
Phil 5247.33.2 Hecke, Gustav. Psychologie. 2. Aufl. Braunschweig, 1919.
Phil 3640.213 Heckel, K. Nietzsche: sein Leben und seine Lehre. Leipzig, 1922.
Phil 3640.213.5 Heckel, K. Nietzsche: sein Leben und seine Lehre. Leipzig, 1922.
Phil 5525.17 Hecker, Ewald. Die Physiologie und Psychologie des Lachens. Berlin, 1873.
Phil 8587.5 Hecker, I.T. Aspirations of nature. N.Y., 1857.
Phil 5927.2 Hecker, J. Scientific basis of education demonstrated. N.Y., 1867.
Phil 3808.87.5 Hecker, M.F. Metaphysik und Asketik. Bonn, 1896.
Phil 3808.87 Hecker, M.F. Schopenhauer. Köln, 1897.
Phil 5548.103.5 Heckhausen, H. The anatomy of achievement motivation. N.Y., 1967.
Phil 5548.103 Heckhausen, H. Hoffnung und Furcht in der Leistungsmotivation. Meisenheim, 1963.
Phil 5594.154 Hector, H. Der 7-Quadrate-Test. Paderborn, 1954.
Phil 5247.86 Hector, Heinz. Gedankengänge in Psychologie. Paderborn, 1965.
Phil 8610.904 Hedderwick, J.A. Do we believe? London, 1904.
Phil 3120.21.5 Heden en verleden. (Beerling, Reinier Franciscus.) Arnhem, 1962.
Phil 4620.2.90 Hedenius, I. Adolf Phalén in memoriam. Uppsala, 1937.
Phil 182.115 Hedenius, I. Fyra dygder. Stockholm, 1955.
Phil 8882.90.5 Hedenius, Ingemar. Den omoraliska anständigheten. Stockholm, 1969.
Phil 1870.118 Hedenius, Ingemar. Sensationalism and theology in Berkeley's philosophy. Inaug. Diss. Uppsala, 1936.
Phil 8882.90 Hedenius, Ingemar. Sjn studier i praktish filosof. Uppsala, 1968.
Phil 8587.72 Hedenius, Ingemar. Tor och roetande. Stockholm, 1949.
Phil 7082.58 Hedenius, Per. Om drömmen. Stockholm, 1880.
Phil 182.8 Hedge, F.H. Atheism in philosophy. Berlin, 1884.
Phil 8587.6 Hedge, F.H. Reason in religion. Boston, 1865.
Phil 8587.6.5 Hedge, F.H. Ways of the spirit. Boston, 1877.
Phil 5047.3.2 Hedge, Levi. Elements of logick. Boston, 1818.
Phil 5047.3.5 Hedge, Levi. Elements of logick. Boston, 1823.
Phil 5047.3.7 Hedge, Levi. Elements of logick. Boston, 1835.
Phil 5047.3.12 Hedge, Levi. Elements of logick. N.Y., 1841.
Phil 8406.12 Hedonism and art. (Farnell, Lewis R.) London, 1928.
Phil 9245.14 Hedonistic theories. (Watson, J.) Glasgow, 1895.
Phil 8882.47 Heegaard, P.C.V. Indledning til den rationelle ethik. Kjøbenhavn, 1866.
Phil 8587.38 Heegaard, P.S.V. Om intolerance, isaer i henseende til religios overbevisning. Kjobenhavn, 1878.
Phil 182.70 Heegaard, S. Om opdragelse. 4e Opl. v.1-2. Kjøbenhavn, 1893.
Phil 3246.242 Heekman, H. Fichte und das Christentum. Wurzburg, 1939.
Phil 8662.20 Heer, Freidrich. Alle Moglichkeit liegt bei uns. Nürnberg, 1958.
Phil 1707.18 Heer, Friedrich. Die dritte Kraft. Frankfurt, 1959.
Phil 8622.40 Heer, Friedrich. Glaube und Unglaube. München, 1959.
Phil 9200.2.5 Heer, Friedrich. Sieben Kapitel aus der Geschichte des Schreckens. Zürich, 1957.
Htn Phil 3450.3.30* Heereboord, Adriani. Meletemata philosophica. Amsterdam, 1680.
Phil 5047.4 Heereboord, Adriano. Ermhneia logica...burgersdicianae. Cantabridgiae, 1663.
Phil 5047.4.5 Heereboord, Adriano. Ermhneia logica...burgersdicianae. London, 1676.
Htn Phil 182.10.3* Heereboort, A. Meletemata philosophica. Amsterdam, 1665.
Phil 182.10A Heereboort, A. Meletemata philosophica. Amsterdam, 1680.
Phil 8587.53 Heering, H.J. De religienze toekomstverwachting. Amsterdam, 1937.
Phil 8587.80 Heering, Herman Johan. Dogmatische verkenningen. 's-Gravenhage, 1968.
Phil 288.3 Heermance, E.L. Chaos or cosmos? N.Y., 1922.
Phil 6400.35 Heese, Gerhard. Sprachpflege kurs für Schwerhörige und Ertaubte. Berlin, 1963.
Phil 2115.112A Hefelbower, S.G. The relation of John Locke to English deism. Chicago, 1918.
Phil 3425.300.5 Hefte zu Hegels Dialektik. (Lenin, V.I.) München, 1969.
Phil 3640.682 Heftrich, Eckhard. Nietzsches Philosophie. Frankfurt, 1962.
Phil 3425.229.15 Hegel, der unwiderlegte Weltphilosoph. (Michelet, C.L.) Leipzig, 1870.
Phil 1707.4A Hegel, E.W.F. Vorlesungen und der Geschichte der Philosophie. Berlin, 1840. 3v.
Phil 3425.321.10 Hegel; eine Vergegenwäitigung. (Kojève, Alexandre.) Stuttgart, 1958.
Phil 3425.611 Hegel, G.W. Propédeutique philosophique. Génève, 1964.
Phil 807.2.25 Hegel, G.W.F. Hegels Geschichte der Philosophie. München, 1923.
Phil 807.2 Hegel, G.W.F. Lectures on history of philosophy. London, 1892-96. 3v.
Phil 807.2.20 Hegel, G.W.F. Vorlesungen über die Geschichte der Philosophie. Leiden, 1908.
Phil 807.2.27 Hegel, G.W.F. Vorlesungen über die Geschichte der Philosophie. Leipzig, 1938.
Htn Phil 3801.449* Hegel, Georg W.F. Differenz des Fichte'schen und Schelling'schen Systems der Philosophie. Jena, 1801.
Phil 3425.62 Hegel, Georg Wilhelm Friedrich. Die absolute Religion. Leipzig, 1929.
Phil 3425.56.10 Hegel, Georg Wilhelm Friedrich. Ästhetik. Berlin, 1955.
Phil 3425.28.5 Hegel, Georg Wilhelm Friedrich. Berliner Schriften. Hamburg, 1956.
Phil 3425.14 Hegel, Georg Wilhelm Friedrich. Briefe von und an Hegel. Hamburg, 1952-53. 4v.
Phil 3425.56 Hegel, Georg Wilhelm Friedrich. Cours d'esthétique. Paris, 1840-43. 2v.
Phil 3425.40.55 Hegel, Georg Wilhelm Friedrich. Differenz des Fichte'schen und Schelling'schen Systems der Philosophie. Hamburg, 1962.
Phil 3425.12.5A Hegel, Georg Wilhelm Friedrich. Dokumente zu Hegels Entwicklung. Stuttgart, 1936.
Phil 3425.63 Hegel, Georg Wilhelm Friedrich. Early theological writings. Chicago, 1948.
Phil 3425.70.50 Hegel, Georg Wilhelm Friedrich. Eigenhändige Raudhemerkungen zu seiner Rechtsphilosophie. Leipzig, 1930.
Phil 3425.69 Hegel, Georg Wilhelm Friedrich. Einleitung in die Asthetik. München, 1967.
Phil 3425.70.75A Hegel, Georg Wilhelm Friedrich. Einleitung in die Geschichte der Philosophie. 3. Aufl. Hamburg, 1959.
Phil 3425.73.4 Hegel, Georg Wilhelm Friedrich. Einleitung in die Phänomenologie des Geistes. Frankfurt, 1964.
Phil 3425.48.2 Hegel, Georg Wilhelm Friedrich. Enciclopedia delle scienze filosofiche. 2. ed. v.1-3. Bari, 1923. 2v.
Htn Phil 3425.43* Hegel, Georg Wilhelm Friedrich. Encyclopädie der philosophischen Wissenschaften. Heidelberg, 1817.
Phil 3425.44 Hegel, Georg Wilhelm Friedrich. Encyclopädie der philosophischen Wissenschaften. Heidelberg, 1827.
Phil 3425.45 Hegel, Georg Wilhelm Friedrich. Encyclopädie der philosophischen Wissenschaften. Heidelberg, 1830.
Phil 3425.45.20 Hegel, Georg Wilhelm Friedrich. Encyclopädie der philosophischen Wissenschaften. Leiden, 1906.
Phil 3425.45.4 Hegel, Georg Wilhelm Friedrich. Encyclopädie der philosophischen Wissenschaften. 4. Aufl. Berlin, 1845.
Phil 3425.46 Hegel, Georg Wilhelm Friedrich. Encyclopädie der philosophischen Wissenschaften. 2. Aufl. Leipzig, 1920.
Phil 3425.46.6 Hegel, Georg Wilhelm Friedrich. Enzyklopädie der philosophischen Wissenschaften. 6. Aufl. Hamburg, 1959.
Phil 3425.24 Hegel, Georg Wilhelm Friedrich. Erste Druckschriften. Leipzig, 1928.
Phil 3425.34.35 Hegel, Georg Wilhelm Friedrich. Essence. n.p., n.d.
Phil 3425.65A Hegel, Georg Wilhelm Friedrich. The ethics of Hegel. Boston, 1893.
Phil 3425.66 Hegel, Georg Wilhelm Friedrich. Der Geist des Christentums und sein Schicksal. Gütersloh, 1970.
Phil 3425.13A Hegel, Georg Wilhelm Friedrich. Gesammelte Werke. v.4,7. Hamburg, 1968. 2v.
Phil 3425.30 Hegel, Georg Wilhelm Friedrich. Glauben und Wissen. Hamburg, 1962.
Htn Phil 3425.70.1* Hegel, Georg Wilhelm Friedrich. Grundlinien der Philosophie des Rechts. Berlin, 1821.
Phil 3425.70.15 Hegel, Georg Wilhelm Friedrich. Grundlinien der Philosophie des Rechts. Leiden, 1902.
Phil 3425.70.5 Hegel, Georg Wilhelm Friedrich. Grundlinien der Philosophie des Rechts. Leipzig, 1911.
Phil 3425.70.9 Hegel, Georg Wilhelm Friedrich. Grundlinien der Philosophie des Rechts. 2. Aufl. Leipzig, 1921.
Phil 3425.70.10 Hegel, Georg Wilhelm Friedrich. Grundlinien der Philosophie des Rechts. 3. Aufl. Leipzig, 1930.
Phil 3425.70.18 Hegel, Georg Wilhelm Friedrich. Grundlinien der Philosophie des Rechts. 4. Aufl. Hamburg, 1955.
Phil 3425.70.19 Hegel, Georg Wilhelm Friedrich. Grundlinien der Philosophie des Rechts. 4. Aufl. Berlin, 1956.
Phil 3425.12.3 Hegel, Georg Wilhelm Friedrich. Hamann. Stuttgart, 1930.
Phil 3425.20.5 Hegel, Georg Wilhelm Friedrich. Hegel; highlights, an annotated selection. N.Y., 1968.
Phil 3425.38 Hegel, Georg Wilhelm Friedrich. Hegel; Volk, Staat. Stuttgart, 1942.
Phil 3425.28.12 Hegel, Georg Wilhelm Friedrich. Hegel. Frankfurt, 1955.
Phil 3425.28.10 Hegel, Georg Wilhelm Friedrich. Hegel. Frankfurt, 1957.
Phil 3425.75.5 Hegel, Georg Wilhelm Friedrich. Hegel Brevier. Zürich, 1951.
Phil 3425.76.50 Hegel, Georg Wilhelm Friedrich. Hegel on tragedy. 1st ed. Garden City, N.Y., 1962.
Phil 3425.37 Hegel, Georg Wilhelm Friedrich. Hegel's doctrine of reflection. N.Y., 1881.
Phil 3425.77 Hegel, Georg Wilhelm Friedrich. Hegels erstes System. Heidelberg, 1915.
Phil 3425.77.2 Hegel, Georg Wilhelm Friedrich. Hegels erstes System. Heidelberg, 1918.
Phil 3425.74.5 Hegel, Georg Wilhelm Friedrich. Hegel's first principle. Saint Louis, 1869.
Phil 3425.39.2 Hegel, Georg Wilhelm Friedrich. Hegel's logic of world and idea. Oxford, 1929.

Phil 3425.23   Hegel, Georg Wilhelm Friedrich. Hegels Philosophie. Berlin, 1917.

Phil 3425.74   Hegel, Georg Wilhelm Friedrich. Hegels philosophiska propädentik. Helsingfors, 1845.

Phil 3425.50   Hegel, Georg Wilhelm Friedrich. Hegel's philosophy of mind. Oxford, 1894.

Phil 3425.46.12   Hegel, Georg Wilhelm Friedrich. Hegel's philosophy of nature. London, 1970.

Phil 3425.46.10   Hegel, Georg Wilhelm Friedrich. Hegel's philosophy of nature. Oxford, 1970.

Phil 3425.29.20   Hegel, Georg Wilhelm Friedrich. Hegel's political writings. Oxford, 1964.

Phil 3425.60.55   Hegel, Georg Wilhelm Friedrich. Hegels Religionsphilosophie in gekürzter Form. Jena, 1905.

Phil 3425.34.28   Hegel, Georg Wilhelm Friedrich. Hegel's Science of logic. N.Y., 1969.

Phil 3425.56.20   Hegel, Georg Wilhelm Friedrich. The introduction to Hegel's Philosophy of fine art. London, 1886.

Phil 3425.56.5   Hegel, Georg Wilhelm Friedrich. The introduction to Hegel's Philosophy of fine art. London, 1905.

Phil 3425.33   Hegel, Georg Wilhelm Friedrich. Jenenser Logik Metaphysik und Naturphilosophie. Leipzig, 1923.

Phil 3425.33.10   Hegel, Georg Wilhelm Friedrich. Jenenser Realphilosophie. Leipzig, 1931-32. 2v.

Phil 3425.64   Hegel, Georg Wilhelm Friedrich. Das junge Hegel in Stuttgart. Marbach, 1970?

Phil 3425.60.3   Hegel, Georg Wilhelm Friedrich. Leçons sur la philosophie de la religion. pt.1-5. Paris, 1954-59. 3v.

Phil 3425.40.25   Hegel, Georg Wilhelm Friedrich. Leçons sur la philosophie de l'histoire. Paris, 1937.

Phil 3425.60.5   Hegel, Georg Wilhelm Friedrich. Lectures on the philosophy of religion. London, 1895. 3v.

Phil 3425.60.6   Hegel, Georg Wilhelm Friedrich. Lectures on the philosophy of religion. N.Y., 1962. 3v.

Phil 3425.32   Hegel, Georg Wilhelm Friedrich. Logic. Oxford, 1874.

Phil 3425.32.2   Hegel, Georg Wilhelm Friedrich. Logic. 2nd ed. Oxford, 1892.

Phil 3425.31   Hegel, Georg Wilhelm Friedrich. Logique. v.1-2. Paris, 1859.

Phil 3425.35   Hegel, Georg Wilhelm Friedrich. Logique subjective. Paris, 1854.

Phil 3425.60.17   Hegel, Georg Wilhelm Friedrich. Die Naturreligion. Leipzig, 1927.

Phil 3425.75   Hegel, Georg Wilhelm Friedrich. Neue Briefe...und Verwandtes. Leipzig, 1912.

Phil 3425.42   Hegel, Georg Wilhelm Friedrich. Nürnberger Schriften. Leipzig, 1938.

Phil 3425.72.90   Hegel, Georg Wilhelm Friedrich. Phänomenologie des Geistes. Leipzig, 1907.

Phil 3425.73   Hegel, Georg Wilhelm Friedrich. Phänomenologie des Geistes. Leipzig, 1907.

Phil 3425.73.2.5   Hegel, Georg Wilhelm Friedrich. Phänomenologie des Geistes. Leipzig, 1937. 2v.

Phil 3425.73.2   Hegel, Georg Wilhelm Friedrich. Phänomenologie des Geistes. 2. Aufl. Berlin, 1841.

Phil 3425.73.1   Hegel, Georg Wilhelm Friedrich. Phänomenologie des Geistes. 2. Aufl. Leipzig, 1921.

Phil 3425.73.2.10   Hegel, Georg Wilhelm Friedrich. Phänomenologie des Geistes. 6. Aufl. Hamburg, 1952.

Phil 3425.73.20   Hegel, Georg Wilhelm Friedrich. La phénoménologie de l'esprit. Paris, 1939-41. 2v.

Phil 3425.73.5   Hegel, Georg Wilhelm Friedrich. The phenomenology of mind. London, 1910.

Phil 3425.73.8A   Hegel, Georg Wilhelm Friedrich. The phenomenology of mind. 2nd ed. London, 1955.

Phil 3425.73.9   Hegel, Georg Wilhelm Friedrich. The phenomenology of mind. 2nd ed. London, 1961.

Phil 3425.73.10A   Hegel, Georg Wilhelm Friedrich. The phenomenology of mind. 2nd ed. London, 1966.

Phil 3425.60   Hegel, Georg Wilhelm Friedrich. Philosophie de la religion. Paris, 1876-78. 2v.

Phil 3425.22   Hegel, Georg Wilhelm Friedrich. Philosophie in wörtlichen Auszügen. Berlin, 1843.

Phil 3425.56.15   Hegel, Georg Wilhelm Friedrich. The philosophy of art. Edinburgh, 1886.

Phil 3425.56.25   Hegel, Georg Wilhelm Friedrich. The philosophy of art. N.Y., 1879.

Phil 3425.56.30   Hegel, Georg Wilhelm Friedrich. The philosophy of fine art. London, 1920. 4v.

Phil 3425.20   Hegel, Georg Wilhelm Friedrich. The philosophy of Hegel. N.Y., 1953.

Phil 3425.40.5.6   Hegel, Georg Wilhelm Friedrich. The philosophy of history. N.Y., 1900.

Phil 3425.40.5.9A   Hegel, Georg Wilhelm Friedrich. The philosophy of history. N.Y., 1944.

Phil 3425.40.5.10A   Hegel, Georg Wilhelm Friedrich. The philosophy of history. N.Y., 1956.

Phil 3425.71   Hegel, Georg Wilhelm Friedrich. Philosophy of right. London, 1896.

Phil 3425.71.11   Hegel, Georg Wilhelm Friedrich. Philosophy of right. Oxford, 1967.

Phil 3425.15   Hegel, Georg Wilhelm Friedrich. Politische Schriften. Frankfurt am Main, 1966.

Phil 3425.25   Hegel, Georg Wilhelm Friedrich. Populäre Gedanken aus seinen Werker. Berlin, 1873.

Phil 3425.40.50   Hegel, Georg Wilhelm Friedrich. Premières publications. Thèse. Paris, 1952.

Phil 3425.74.2   Hegel, Georg Wilhelm Friedrich. Propédiutique philosophique. Paris, 1963.

Phil 3425.40.30   Hegel, Georg Wilhelm Friedrich. Reason in history. N.Y., 1953.

Phil 3425.60.19   Hegel, Georg Wilhelm Friedrich. Die Religionen der geistigen Individualität. Leipzig, 1927.

Phil 3425.12   Hegel, Georg Wilhelm Friedrich. Sämtliche Werke. Stuttgart, 1927-40. 29v.

Phil 3425.19   Hegel, Georg Wilhelm Friedrich. Schriften zur Gesellschaftsphilosophie. Jena, 1923.

Phil 3425.41   Hegel, Georg Wilhelm Friedrich. Schriften zur Politik und Rechtsphilosophie. Leipzig, 1913.

Phil 3425.34.31A   Hegel, Georg Wilhelm Friedrich. Science of logic. London, 1951. 2v.

Phil 3425.34.29   Hegel, Georg Wilhelm Friedrich. Science of logic. London, 1961. 2v.

Phil 3425.34.30   Hegel, Georg Wilhelm Friedrich. Science of logic. N.Y., 1929.

Phil 3425.28   Hegel, Georg Wilhelm Friedrich. Selections. N.Y., 1929.

Phil 3425.76   Hegel, Georg Wilhelm Friedrich. Der Staat. Leipzig, 1924.

Phil 3425.52   Hegel, Georg Wilhelm Friedrich. Studienausgabe. Ausgewählt. Frankfurt, 1968. 3v.

Phil 3425.36   Hegel, Georg Wilhelm Friedrich. The subjective logic of Hegel. London, 1855.

Phil 3425.68.5   Hegel, Georg Wilhelm Friedrich. System der Sittlichkeit. Osterwiech, 1893.

Phil 3425.72   Hegel, Georg Wilhelm Friedrich. System der Wissenschaft. Bamberg, 1807.

Phil 3425.61   Hegel, Georg Wilhelm Friedrich. Theologische Judendschriften. Tübingen, 1907.

Phil 3425.71.5   Hegel, Georg Wilhelm Friedrich. Theory of right, duties, and religion. Ann Arbor, 1892.

Phil 3425.55   Hegel, Georg Wilhelm Friedrich. Die Verfassung des deutschen Reichs. Stuttgart, 1935.

Phil 3425.40.10   Hegel, Georg Wilhelm Friedrich. Die Vernunft in der Geschichte. Hamburg, 1955.

Phil 3425.60.20   Hegel, Georg Wilhelm Friedrich. Vorlesungen über die Beweise vom Dasein Gottes. Leipzig, 1930.

Phil 3425.40.6   Hegel, Georg Wilhelm Friedrich. Vorlesungen über die Philosophie der Geschichte. Leipzig, 1907.

Phil 3425.60.10   Hegel, Georg Wilhelm Friedrich. Vorlesungen über die Philosophie der Religion. Berlin, 1840. 2v.

Phil 3425.60.15   Hegel, Georg Wilhelm Friedrich. Vorlesungen über die Philosophie der Religion. Leiden, 1901. 2v.

Phil 3425.60.16   Hegel, Georg Wilhelm Friedrich. Vorlesungen über die Philosophie der Religion. Leipzig, 1944-

Phil 3425.60.12   Hegel, Georg Wilhelm Friedrich. Vorlesungen über die Philosophie der Religion. Hamburg, 1966. 2v.

X Cg   Phil 3425.40.7   Hegel, Georg Wilhelm Friedrich. Vorlesungen über die Philosophie der Weltgeschichte. v.2-5. Leipzig, 1920. 4v.

Phil 3425.40.11   Hegel, Georg Wilhelm Friedrich. Vorlesungen über die Philosophie der Weltgeschichte. Leipzig, 1944. 4v.

X Cg   Phil 3425.8   Hegel, Georg Wilhelm Friedrich. Werke. Berlin, 1832-45. 14v.

Phil 3425.10   Hegel, Georg Wilhelm Friedrich. Werke. Berlin, 1832-87. 19v.

Phil 3425.9   Hegel, Georg Wilhelm Friedrich. Werke. Berlin, 1835-45. 20v.

Phil 3425.11   Hegel, Georg Wilhelm Friedrich. Werke. Leipzig, 1909.

Phil 3425.13.5   Hegel, Georg Wilhelm Friedrich. Werke. v.1-2,4-20. Frankfurt, 1969- 21v.

Phil 3425.27A   Hegel, Georg Wilhelm Friedrich. The wisdom of religion of a German philosopher. London, 1897.

Phil 3425.29.12   Hegel, Georg Wilhelm Friedrich. Wissenschaft der Logik. Göttingen, 1966-

Phil 3425.34   Hegel, Georg Wilhelm Friedrich. Wissenschaft der Logik. Leipzig, 1923. 2v.

Phil 3425.29.10   Hegel, Georg Wilhelm Friedrich. Wissenschaft der Logik. Leipzig, 1948.

Htn   Phil 3425.29*   Hegel, Georg Wilhelm Friedrich. Wissenschaft der Logik. Nürnberg, 1912. 3v.

Phil 510.1.19   Hegel, Haeckel, Kossuth und das zwölfte Gebot. (Chwolson, O.D.) Braunschweig, 1906.

Phil 3425.108.5   Hegel; handschriftliche Zusätze zu seiner Rechtsphilosophie. (Lasson, G.) Leipzig, 1914. 3v.

Phil 3425.20.5   Hegel; highlights, an annotated selection. (Hegel, Georg Wilhelm Friedrich.) N.Y., 1968.

Phil 3425.570   Hegel, oder die Entwicklung. (Seeberger, W.) Stuttgart, 1961.

Phil 3425.628   Hegel; philosophe de l'histoire vivante. Thèse. (Hondt, Jacques d'.) Paris, 1966.

Phil 3425.114   Hegel; sa vie et ses oeuvres. (Roques, P.) Paris, 1912.

Phil 3425.254   Hegel, sein Wollen und sein Werke. (Haering, Theodor L.) Leipzig, 1929-1938. 2v.

Phil 3425.91.35   Hegel; Sendschreiben an...Carl Friedrich Bachmann. (Rosenkranz, K.) Königsberg, 1843.

Phil 3425.38   Hegel; Volk, Staat. (Hegel, Georg Wilhelm Friedrich.) Stuttgart, 1942.

Phil 3425.108A   Hegel...Gedankenwelt in Auszügen aus seine Werken. (Lasson, G.) Stuggart, 1906.

Phil 3425.108   Hegel...Gedankenwelt in Auszügen aus seine Werken. Stuttgart, 1906.

Phil 3425.112   Hegel. (Archambault, P.) Paris, n.d.

Phil 3425.253   Hegel. (Brunswig, Alfred.) München, 1922.

X Cg   Phil 3425.80.3A   Hegel. (Caird, Edward.) Edinburgh, 1883.

Phil 3425.80.7   Hegel. (Caird, Edward.) Edinburgh, 1891.

Phil 3425.212   Hegel. (Caird, Edward.) Milano, 191-

X Cg   Phil 3425.80   Hegel. (Caird, Edward.) Philadelphia, 1883.

NEDL   Phil 3425.80.5   Hegel. (Caird, Edward.) Philadelphia, 1896.

Phil 3425.662   Hegel. (Chatelet, François.) Paris, 1968.

Phil 3425.400   Hegel. (Cresson, André.) Paris, 1955.

Phil 3425.460   Hegel. (Findlay, John Niemayer.) London, 1958.

Phil 3425.258   Hegel. (Glockner, Hermann.) Stuttgart, 1929.

Phil 3425.28.12   Hegel. (Hegel, Georg Wilhelm Friedrich.) Frankfurt, 1955.

Phil 3425.28.10   Hegel. (Hegel, Georg Wilhelm Friedrich.) Frankfurt, 1957.

Phil 3425.724   Hegel. (Heintel, Peter.) Göttingen, 1970.

Phil 3425.235   Hegel. (Köstlin, K.R.) Tübingen, 1870.

Phil 3425.346   Hegel. (Litt, Theodor.) Heidelberg, 1953.

Phil 3425.470   Hegel. (Meulen, Jan van der.) Hamburg, 1958.

Phil 3425.525   Hegel. (Mueller, Gustav E.) Bern, 1959.

Phil 3425.344   Hegel. (Sehring, L.) Berlin, 1908.

Phil 3425.126   Hegel. (Thomsen, A.) København, 1905.

VPhil 3425.620   Hegel. wyd. 2. (Kroński, Tadeusz.) Warszawa, 1966.

Phil 3425.608   Hegel. 1st ed. (Kaufmann, W.A.) Garden City, N.Y., 1965.

Phil 3425.758   Hegel à Francfort; ou Judaisme, christianisme, hégelianisme. (Bourgeois, Bernard.) Paris, 1970.

Phil 3425.91.13A   Hegel als deutscher Nationalphilosoph. (Rosenkranz, K.) Leipzig, 1870.

Phil 3425.104A   Hegel and Hegelianism. (Mackintosh, R.) Edinburgh, 1903.

Phil 3425.742   Hegel and the philosophy of religion; the Wofford Symposium. (Wofford Symposium on Hegel and the Philosophy of Religion, Wofford College, 1968.) The Hague, 1970.

Phil 3425.91.15   Hegel as national philosopher of Germany. (Rosenkranz, K.) St.Louis, 1874.

Phil 3425.303.5   Hegel bei den Slaven. 2. Aufl. (Chyzhevs'kyi, Dmytro.) Darmstadt, 1961.

Phil 3425.303.2   Hegel bei den Slaven 2. Aufl. (Chyzhevs'kyi, Dmytro.) Bad Homburg, 1961.

Phil 3425.595.2   Hegel-Bilder; Kritik der Hegel-Deutungen. 2. Aufl. (Beyer, W.R.) Berlin, 1967.

Phil 3425.595   Hegel-Bilder. (Beyer, W.R.) Berlin, 1964.

Phil 3425.75.5   Hegel Brevier. (Hegel, Georg Wilhelm Friedrich.) Zürich, 1951.

Phil 3425.700   Hegel Deutung der Sprache. (Bodanmer, Theodor.) Hamburg, 1969.

Phil 3425.708   Hegel e il problema della filosofia come storia. (Sabetti, Alfredo.) Napoli, 1967.

Phil 3425.640   Hegel e la metafisica classica. (Chiereghin, Franco.) Padova, 1966.

Phil 3425.760   Hegel e Marx nella polemica del diritto pubblico. (Carbonara, Cleto.) Napoli, 1967.

Phil 3425.338   Hegel ed il problema della moralità. (Guccione Monroy, Nino.) Trapani, 1951.

Phil 3425.660   Hegel en son temps, Berlin, 1818-1831. (Hondt, Jacques d'.) Paris, 1968.

Phil 3425.770   Hegel et la pensée moderne. 1. éd. (Hondt, Jacques d'.) Paris, 1970.

Phil 3425.90   Hegel et la philosophie allemande. (Ott, A.) Paris, 1844.
Phil 3425.603.1   Hegel et la religion. (Chapelle, A.) Paris, 1964. 2v.
Phil 3425.603   Hegel et la religion. (Chapelle, A.) Paris, 1964.
Phil 3425.603.2   Hegel et la religion. Annexes. (Chapelle, A.) Nanur, 1967.

Phil 3425.340.1   Hegel et l'état. (Weil, Eric.) Paris, 1950.
Phil 3425.340   Hegel et l'état. Thèse. (Weil, Eric.) Paris, 1950.
Phil 3425.587   Hegel et l'hégélianisme. (Serreau, R.) Paris, 1962.
Phil 3425.83   Hegel et Schopenhauer. (Foucher de Careil, L.A.) Paris, 1862.

Phil 3425.475   Hegel Ethik aus dem Geist der Religion. (Schmandt, Jürgen.) Bonn, 1957.

Phil 3425.14.5   Hegel in Berichten seines Zeitgenossen companion von to Briefe von und an Hegel. (Nicolin, Günther.) Hamburg, 1970.

Phil 3425.228   L'Hegel in Italia. (Lucia, V. de.) Vasto, 1888.
Phil 3425.562   Hegel in Nürnberg. (Schmidt, G.) Tübingen, 1960.
Phil 3425.726   Hegel interprete di Platone. (Duso, Giuseppe.) Padova, 1969.

Phil 3425.582   Hegel Jahrbuch. München. 1961+ 3v.
Phil 3425.358   Hegel nel centenario. (Milan. Universita Cattolica del Sacro Cuare.) Milano, 1932.

Phil 3425.119   Hegel och Boströms rättsfilosofiska grundtankar. (Åberg, Lawrence H.) Upsala, 1885.

Phil 3425.566   Hegel on art. (Kaminsky, Jack.) N.Y., 1969.
Phil 3425.76.50   Hegel on tragedy. 1st ed. (Hegel, Georg Wilhelm Friedrich.) Garden City, N.Y., 1962.

Phil 3011.4   Die Hegel-Renaissance in der deutschen Philosophie. (Levy, H.) Charlottenburg, 1927.

Phil 3425.255   Hegel romantico e mistico (1793-1800). (Volpe, Galvano di.) Firenze, 1929.

Phil 3425.652   Hegel secret, recherches sur les sources cachées de la pensée de Hegel. (Hondt, Jacques d'.) Paris, 1968.

Phil 3425.553   Hegel-Studien; Beiheft. Bonn. 3-6 3v.
Phil 3425.552   Hegel-Studien. Bonn. 1-5 4v.
Phil 3425.580   A Hegel symposium. (Travis, Don Carlos.) Austin, 1962.
Phil 3425.299   Hegel über Offenbarung. (Müller, G.R.) München, 1939.
Phil 3425.440   Hegel und Blondel. (Henrici, Peter.) Pullach, 1958.
Phil 3425.617   Hegel und das Ende der Geschichte. (Maurer, R.K.) Stuttgart, 1965.

Phil 3425.229   Hegel und der Empirismus. (Michelet, C.L.) Berlin, 1873.
Phil 3425.545   Hegel und der Marxismus über den Widerspruch. (Stiehler, Gottfried.) Berlin, 1960.

Phil 3425.220.5   Hegel und der nationale Machtstaatsgedanke in Deutschland. (Heller, Hermann.) Aalen, 1963.
Phil 3425.220   Hegel und der nationale Machtstaatsgedanke in Deutschland. (Heller, Hermann.) Leipzig, 1921.

Phil 3425.241   Hegel und der Staat. v.1-2. (Rosenzweig, Franz.) Aalen, 1962.

Phil 3425.442   Hegel und die Analogia Entis. (Heintel, Erich.) Bonn, 1958.

Phil 3425.766   Hegel und die Folgen. 1. Aufl. (Kaltenbrunner, Gerd Klaus.) Freiburg, 1970.

Phil 3425.320   Hegel und die Franzosen. (Knoop, Bernhard.) Stuttgart, 1941.

Phil 3425.01   Hegel und die Hegelianer; eine Bibliothek. (Hellersberg firm, booksellers. Berlin.) Charlottenburg, 1927?

Phil 3425.262   Hegel und die hegelsche Schule. (Moog, Willy.) München, 1930.

Phil 3425.318   Hegel und die Idee der Volksordnung. (Schmidt, Werner.) Leipzig, 1944.

Phil 3425.268   Hegel und die logische Frage der Philosophie in der Gegenwart. (Hermann, Conrad.) Leipzig, 1878.

Phil 3425.324   Hegel und Kierkegaard. (Bense, Max.) Köln, 1948.
Phil 3425.207   Hegel und Plotin. (Jong, K.H.E. de.) Leiden, 1916.
Phil 3425.276   Hegel und sein Werk. (Steinhart, C.) Naumburg, 1841.
Phil 3425.336   Hegel und seine Philosophie. (Glockner, Hermann.) Heidelberg, 1931.

Phil 3425.87   Hegel und seine Zeit. (Goeschel, K.F.) Berlin, 1832.
Phil 3425.88A   Hegel und seine Zeit. (Haym, Rudolf.) Berlin, 1857.
X Cg Phil 3425.88.2   Hegel und seine Zeit. 2. Aufl. (Haym, Rudolf.) Leipzig, 1927.

Phil 3425.696   Hegel und Sowjetphilosophie der Gegenwart. (Grujié, P.M.) Bern, 1969.

Phil 3425.450   Hegel y la estatica. (Piérola, R.A.) Tucumán, 1956.
Phil 3425.635   Gli Hegeliani di Napoli. (Oldrini, Guido.) Milano, 1964.
Phil 4006.7.30A   Gli hegeliani d'Italia. (Guzzo, A.) Torino, 1953.
Phil 3425.277   Hegelianism and human personality. (Hirä-Läl, H.) Calcutta, 1910.

Phil 3425.92A   Hegelianism and personality. (Seth, A.) Edinburgh, 1887.
Phil 3425.92.2   Hegelianism and personality. 2d ed. (Seth, A.) Edinburgh, 1893.

Phil 3425.206   Hegelianism och positivism. (Geijer, R.) Lund, 1883.
Phil 3425.626   Hegelianisme et christianisme. (Rondet, Henri.) Paris, 1965.

Phil 3425.95.12   L'hégélianisme et la philosophie. (Véra, A.) Paris, 1861.
Phil 3425.237   L'Hegelianismo, la scienza e la vita. (Allievo, G.) Milano, 1868.

Phil 4225.1.100   L'hegelismo di Bertrando Spaventa. (Bortot, Renato.) Firenze, 1968.

Phil 3425.693   Hegelova estetika, Marksovi osnovi estetike i današnje estetičke perspektive. (Nedeljković, Dušan.) Beograd, 1971.

Phil 3425.577.2   Hegel's aesthetics; a critical exposition. (Kedney, J.S.) Chicago, 1885.

Phil 3425.577   Hegel's aesthetics; a critical exposition. 2nd ed. (Kedney, J.S.) Chicago, 1892.

Phil 3425.256   Hegels Ästhetik. (Frost, Walter.) München, 1928.
Phil 3425.279   Hegels Ansicht über die Apriorität von Zeit und Raum und die kantischen Kategorien. (Rackwitz, Max.) Halle, 1891.

Phil 3425.780   Hegels Auffassung des Mythos in seinen Frühschriften. (Rebstock, Hans Otto.) Freiburg, 1971.

Phil 3425.738   Hegels Begriff der Dialektik und das Prinzip des Idealismus. (Becker, Werner.) Stuttgart, 1969.

Phil 3425.385.2   Hegels Bildungstheorie. (Nicolin, F.) Bonn, 1955.
Phil 3425.195   Hegel's charlatanism exposed. (Kelly, Michael.) London, 1911.

Phil 3425.73.20.10   Hegel's concept of experience. 1st ed. (Heidegger, Martin.) N.Y., 1970.

Phil 3425.20.10   Hegel's concept of experience. 1st ed. (Heidegger, Martin.) N.Y., 1970.

Phil 3425.704   Hegel's critique of Aristotle's philosophy of mind. (Weiss, Frederich Gustav.) The Hague, 1969.

Phil 3425.375   Hegels dialektische Ontologie und die thomistische Analektik. (Lakebrink, Bernhard.) Köln, 1955.

Phil 3425.39   Hegel's doctrine of formal logic. (Macran, H.S.) Oxford, 1912.

Phil 3425.37   Hegel's doctrine of reflection. (Hegel, Georg Wilhelm Friedrich.) N.Y., 1881.

Phil 3425.348   Hegel's educational ideas. (Bryant, W. McK.) N.Y., 1896.
Phil 3425.116   Hegel's educational theory and practice. Photoreproduction. (Mackenzie, Millicent Hughes.) London, 1909.

Phil 3425.128   Hegels Einfluss auf die Religionsphilosophie in Deutschland. (Aschkenasy, R.) Berlin, 1907.

Phil 3425.78A   Hegel's Entwürfe zur Enzyklopädie und Propadentik. (Lowenberg, Jacob.) Leipzig, 1912.

Phil 3425.77   Hegels erstes System. (Hegel, Georg Wilhelm Friedrich.) Heidelberg, 1915.
Phil 3425.77.2   Hegels erstes System. (Hegel, Georg Wilhelm Friedrich.) Heidelberg, 1918.

Phil 3425.218   Hegel's ethical teaching. (Chang, W.S.) Shanghai, 1925.
Phil 3425.768   Hegels Fichtekritik und die Wissenschaftslehre von 1804. (Siep, Ludwig.) Freiburg, 1970.

Phil 3425.630   Hegel's first American followers. (Easton, Loyd David.) Athens, 1966.

Phil 3425.74.5   Hegel's first principle. (Hegel, Georg Wilhelm Friedrich.) Saint Louis, 1869.

Phil 3425.710   Hegels Geisteskrankheit. (Treher, Wolfgang.) Emmendin, 1969.

Phil 807.2.25   Hegels Geschichte der Philosophie. (Hegel, G.W.F.) München, 1923.

Phil 3425.490   Hegels Gottesbeweis. (Albrecht, Wolfgang.) Berlin, 1958.
Phil 3425.307A   Hegel's Hellenic ideal. (Gray, J.G.) N.Y., 1941.
Phil 3425.410   Hegels Kritik der Romantik. (Poeggeler, Otto.) Bonn, 1956.

Phil 3504.37   Hegels Kritik Kants. (Wyneken, G.A.) Greifswald, 1898.
Phil 3504.37.5   Hegels Kritik Kants. Inaug. Diss. (Wyneken, G.A.) Greifswald, 1898.

Phil 3425.205   Hegels lära om konstformerna. (Edman, Alfred.) Helsingfors, 1856.

Phil 3425.118   Hegels Leben, Werke und Lehre. v.1-2. (Fischer, Kuno.) Heidelberg, 1901.

Phil 3425.554   Hegels Lehre über Staat und Recht und seine Strafrechtstheorie. (Piontkovskii, A.A.) Berlin, 1960.

Phil 3425.772   Hegels Lehre vom absoluten Geist als theologisch-politischer Traktat. (Theunissen, Michael.) Berlin, 1970.

Phil 3425.236   Hegels Lehre vom Widerspruch. (Bullinger, A.) Dillingen, 1884.

Phil 3425.294   Hegels Lehre von der Religion und Kunst von dem Standpuncte des Glaubens ausbeurtheilt. Leipzig, 1842.

Phil 3425.360   Hegels Lehre von Gott. (Schmidt, E.) Gütersloh, 1952.
Phil 3425.736   Hegels Lehre von Menschen. (Fetscher, Iring.) Stuttgart, 1970.

Phil 3425.86   Hegel's logic. (Harris, W.T.) Chicago, 1890.
Phil 3425.105A   Hegel's logic. (Hibben, J.G.) N.Y., 1902.
Phil 3425.86.5   Hegel's logic. 2d ed. (Harris, W.T.) Chicago, 1895.
Phil 3425.39.2   Hegel's logic of world and idea. (Hegel, Georg Wilhelm Friedrich.) Oxford, 1929.

Phil 3425.330   Hegels Logik. (Wundt, M.) Köln, 1949.
Phil 3425.248   Hegels Logik und die Gegenwart. (Emge, C.A.) Karlsruhe, 1927.

Phil 3425.249   Hegels Methode in ihrer ideengeschichtlichen Notwendigkeit. Habilitationsschrift. (Fischer, Hugo.) München, 1928.
Phil 3425.91.22   Hegel's Naturphilosophie. (Rosenkranz, K.) Berlin, 1902.
Phil 3425.694   Hegels "objektive Logik" eine Einführung. (Rademaker, Hans.) Bonn, 1969.

Phil 3425.97   Hegels Offenbarungsbegriff. (Werner, J.) Leipzig, 1887.
Phil 3425.292   Hegels Ontologie und die Grundlegung einer Theorie der Geschichtlichkeit. (Marcuse, H.) Frankfurt, 1932.

Phil 3425.192   Hegel's phaenomenologie I-II, proeve van tekstverklaring. Proefschrift. (Bruijn, J.C.) Amsterdam, 1923.

Phil 3425.78.10   Hegel's phenomenology. (Lowenberg, Jacob.) La Salle, Ill., 1965.

Phil 3425.23   Hegels Philosophie. (Hegel, Georg Wilhelm Friedrich.) Berlin, 1917.

Phil 3425.298   Hegels philosophische Entwicklung. (Schwarz, Justus.) Frankfurt, 1938.

Phil 3425.74   Hegels philosophiska propädentik. (Hegel, Georg Wilhelm Friedrich.) Helsingfors, 1845.

Phil 3425.50   Hegel's philosophy of mind. (Hegel, Georg Wilhelm Friedrich.) Oxford, 1894.

Phil 3425.46.12   Hegel's philosophy of nature. (Hegel, Georg Wilhelm Friedrich.) London, 1970.
Phil 3425.46.10   Hegel's philosophy of nature. (Hegel, Georg Wilhelm Friedrich.) Oxford, 1970.

Phil 3425.102A   Hegel's philosophy of the state. (Morris, G.S.) Chicago, 1887.

Phil 3425.752   Hegel's political philosophy. 1st ed. (Kaufmann, Walter Arnold.) N.Y., 1970.

Phil 3425.29.20   Hegel's political writings. (Hegel, Georg Wilhelm Friedrich.) Oxford, 1964.

Phil 3425.305   Hegels rättsfilosofi. (Burman, E.O.) Uppsala, 1939.
Phil 3425.180   Hegels Religionsphilosophie. (Richert, Hans.) Bromberg, 1900.

Phil 3425.60.55   Hegels Religionsphilosophie in gekürzter Form. (Hegel, Georg Wilhelm Friedrich.) Jena, 1905.

Phil 3425.34.28   Hegel's Science of logic. (Hegel, Georg Wilhelm Friedrich.) N.Y., 1969.

Phil 3425.246   Hegels Shakespeare-Interpretation. (Salditt, Maria.) Berlin, 1927.

Phil 3425.121   Hegels Socialphilosophie. (Mayer-Moreau, K.) Tubingen, 1910.

Phil 3425.599   Hegels spekulative Deutung der Infinitesimalrechnung. (Rehm, Margarete.) Köln, 1963.

Phil 3425.245   Hegels Staatsidee. (Lowenstein, Julius.) Berlin, 1927.
Phil 3425.226   Hegels Staatsidee und der Begriff der Staatserziehung. (Giese, G.) Halle, 1926.

Phil 3425.286   Hegels Staatsphilosophie. (Trott zu Solz, A. v.) Göttingen, 1932.

Phil 3425.289   Hegels Strafrechtstheorie. (Flechtheim, O.K.) Brünn, 1936.

Phil 3425.271   Hegels Theorie des objektiven Geistes. (Wenke, Hans.) Halle, 1927.

Phil 3425.260   Hegels Wissenschaft von der Wirklichkeit und ihre Quellen. (Schelling-Wollny, Kurt.) München, 1929.

Phil 3425.250   Hegels Zurechnungslehre und der Begriff der objektiven Zurechnung. (Larenz, Karl.) Leipzig, 1927.

Phil 3425.275   Die Hegel'sche Geschichtsanschauung. (Springer, Anton T.H.) Tübingen, 1848.

Phil 3050.6   Die Hegelsche Linke; Texte aus den Werken. (Loewith, Karl.) Stuttgart, 1962.

Phil 3425.600   Die Hegelsche Logik als Selbsterfassung der Persönlichkeit. (Redlich, A.) Brinkum, 1964.

Phil 3425.84   Die hegelsche Philosophie. (Gabler, G.A.) Berlin, 1843.

Phil 3425.598   Die Hegelsche Rechte. (Luebbe, Hermann.) Stuttgart, 1962.

Phil 3425.272   Die Hegel'sche Religions-Philosophie. (Eschenmayer, C.A.) Tübingen, 1834.

Phil 3425.240   Die hegelsche und rosenkranzsche Logik. (Lassalle, F.) Leipzig, 1927.

Phil 3425.203   Hegelska philosophien. (Afzelius, F.G.) Upsala, 1843.

Phil 3425.200   Det hegelska systemet och den spekulativa ethiken. (Borelius, J.J.) Lund, 1853.

Phil 8587.36   Hegenwald, H. Gegenwartsphilosophie und christliche Religion. Leipzig, 1913.

Phil 6117.9   Héger, P. La mission de la physiologie expérimentale. Bruxelles, 1899.

Phil 6750.269   Heggland, Ruth. Ti år med Erik; en mors beretning om sin hjerneskadede sønn. Oslo, 1969.

Phil 530.20.20   Hegler, A. Beiträge zur Geschichte der Mystik in der Reformationszeit. Berlin, 1906.

Phil 3489.3   Hegler, A. Die Psychologie in Kant's Ethik. Freiburg, 1891.

Phil 3255.80   Hegler, Alfred. Geist und Schrift bei Sebastian Franck. Freiburg, 1892.

Phil 3255.80.5   Hegler, Alfred. Sebastian Francks lateinische Paraphrase der deutschen Theologie und seine hollandische erhaltenen Traktate. Tübingen, 1901.

Phil 7069.35.65   Hegy, Reginald. A witness through the centuries. N.Y., 1935.

Phil 5217.8.2   Hehlmann, Wilhelm. Geschichte der Psychologie. 2. Aufl. Stuttgart, 1967.

Phil 8587.12   Hehn, Johannes. Wege zum Monotheismus. Würzburg, 1913.

Phil 5757.15   Heiberg, J.L. Om den menneskelige Frihed. Kiel, 1824.

Phil 8587.39   Heiberg, J.L. Religion og moral. 2. oplag. Kjobenhavn, 1911.

Phil 5217.5   Heidbreder, Edna. Seven psychologies. N.Y., 1961.

Phil 3450.19.325   Heidegger, being and truth. (Versényi, Laszlo.) New Haven, 1965.

Phil 3450.19.520   Heidegger, Kant and time. (Sherover, Charles M.) Bloomington, 1971.

Phil 182.93.10   Heidegger, M. Einführung in die Metaphysik. Tübingen, 1953.

Phil 182.93.10.2   Heidegger, M. Einführung in die Metaphysik. Tübingen, 1958.

Phil 182.93.13   Heidegger, M. Introduction à la métaphysique. Paris, 1958.

Phil 182.93.12   Heidegger, M. An introduction to metaphysics. New Haven, 1959.

Phil 3640.620   Heidegger, M. Nietzsche. Pfullingen, 1961. 2v.

Phil 182.93.8   Heidegger, M. Qu'est-ce que la métaphysique? Paris, 1937.

Phil 182.93.5   Heidegger, M. Was ist Metaphysik? Bonn, 1931.

Phil 3450.19.40A   Heidegger, Martin. Aus der Erfahrung des Denkens. Pfullingen, 1954.

Phil 3450.19.32   Heidegger, Martin. Being and time. London, 1962.

Phil 3450.19.85.5   Heidegger, Martin. Discourse on thinking. N.Y., 1966.

Phil 3450.19.70.5   Heidegger, Martin. Essais et conférences. 2e éd. Paris, 1958.

Phil 3450.19.78   Heidegger, Martin. Essays in metaphysics. N.Y., 1960.

Phil 3450.19.54   Heidegger, Martin. The essence of reasons. Evanston, 1969.

Phil 3450.19.15.1   Heidegger, Martin. Existence and being. Chicago, 1970.

Phil 3450.19.50   Heidegger, Martin. Der Feldweg. Frankfurt, 1953.

Phil 3489.27.15   Heidegger, Martin. Die Frage nach dem Ding. Tübingen, 1962.

Phil 3450.19.85.2   Heidegger, Martin. Gelassenheit. 2e Aufl. Pfullingen, 1960.

Phil 3450.19.28   Heidegger, Martin. German existentialism. N.Y., 1965.

Phil 3425.20.10   Heidegger, Martin. Hegel's concept of experience. 1st ed. N.Y., 1970.

Phil 3425.73.20.10   Heidegger, Martin. Hegel's concept of experience. 1st ed. N.Y., 1970.

Phil 3450.19.20   Heidegger, Martin. Holzwege. Frankfurt, 1950.

Phil 3450.19.23A   Heidegger, Martin. Holzwege. 3e Aufl. Frankfurt, 1957.

Phil 3450.19.77   Heidegger, Martin. Identität und Differenz. 2e Aufl. Pfullingen, 1957.

Phil 3450.19.77.5   Heidegger, Martin. Identity and difference. 1st ed. N.Y., 1969.

Phil 3489.27.10   Heidegger, Martin. Kant and the problem of metaphysics. Bloomington, 1962.

Phil 3489.27   Heidegger, Martin. Kant und das Problem der Metaphysik. Bonn, 1929.

Phil 3489.27.2   Heidegger, Martin. Kant und das Problem der Metaphysik. 2. Aufl. Frankfurt, 1951.

Phil 1750.166.30.5   Heidegger, Martin. Lettre sur l'humanisme. Paris, 1957.

Phil 3450.19.38   Heidegger, Martin. Martin Heidegger. Frankfurt, 1969.

Phil 3450.19.110   Heidegger, Martin. Martin Heideggers Einfluss auf die Wissenschaften aus Anlass seines Sechzig sun Geburtstages verfasst Carlos Astrada. Bern, 1949.

Phil 3450.19.76   Heidegger, Martin. Phänomenologie und Theologie. Frankfurt, 1970.

Phil 3450.19.64   Heidegger, Martin. Poetry, language, thought. 1. ed. N.Y., 1971.

Phil 3450.19.73   Heidegger, Martin. The question of being. N.Y., 1958.

Phil 3450.19.75   Heidegger, Martin. Der Satz vom Grund. Pfullingen, 1957.

Phil 3450.19.30   Heidegger, Martin. Sein und Zeit. 7e Aufl. Tübingen, 1953.

Phil 3450.19.30.10   Heidegger, Martin. Sein und Zeit. 10e Aufl. Tübingen, 1963.

Phil 3450.19.82   Heidegger, Martin. Die Technik und die Kehre. Pfullingen, 1962.

Phil 1750.166.30   Heidegger, Martin. Über den Humanismus. Frankfurt, 1949.

Phil 3450.19.57   Heidegger, Martin. Unterwegs zur Sprache. Pfullingen, 1959.

Phil 3450.19.63   Heidegger, Martin. Der Ursprung des Kunstwerkes. Stuttgart, 1960.

Phil 3450.19.59.1   Heidegger, Martin. Vom Wesen der Wahrheit. Frankfurt, 1949.

Phil 3450.19.60   Heidegger, Martin. Vom Wesen der Wahrheit. 3e Aufl. Frankfurt, 1954.

Phil 3450.19.55A   Heidegger, Martin. Vom Wesen des Grundes. 4e Aufl. Frankfurt, 1955.

Phil 3450.19.70   Heidegger, Martin. Vorträge und Anpätze. Pfullingen, 1954.

Phil 3450.19.35A   Heidegger, Martin. Was heisst Denken? Tübingen, 1954.

Phil 3450.19.65   Heidegger, Martin. Was ist das - die Philosophie? Pfullingen, 1956.

Phil 3450.19.67   Heidegger, Martin. Was ist das- die Philosophie? 2. Aufl. Pfullingen, 1960.

Phil 3450.19.25   Heidegger, Martin. Was ist Metaphysik? Bonn, 1929.

Phil 3450.19.10   Heidegger, Martin. Was ist Metaphysik? 4e Aufl. Frankfort, 1943.

Phil 3450.19.10.2   Heidegger, Martin. Was ist Metaphysik? 7e Aufl. Frankfort, 1955.

Phil 3450.19.74   Heidegger, Martin. Wegmarken. Frankfurt, 1967.

Phil 3489.27.20   Heidegger, Martin. What is a thing? Chicago, 1968.

Phil 3450.19.36   Heidegger, Martin. What is called thinking? N.Y., 1968.

Phil 3450.19.65.2   Heidegger, Martin. What is philosophy? N.Y., 1958.

Phil 3450.19.58   Heidegger, Martin. Zur Sache des Denkens. Tübingen, 1969.

Phil 3450.19.45   Heidegger, Martin. Zur Seinsfrage. Frankfurt, 1956.

Phil 3450.19.460   Heidegger; Perspektiven zur Deutung seines Werks. (Poeggeler, Otto.) Köln, 1970.

Phil 3450.19.330   Heidegger. (Ijsseling, Samuel.) Antwerpen, 1964.

Phil 3450.19.118A   Heidegger. (Lowith, Carl.) Frankfurt, 1953.

Phil 3450.19.530   Heidegger. (Regina, Umberto.) Milano, 1970-

Phil 3450.19.350   Heidegger. (Trotignon, Pierre.) Paris, 1965.

Phil 3450.19.106   Heidegger. (Vanni Rovighi, S.) Brescia, 1945.

Phil 3450.19.435   Heidegger. En innføring i hans filosofi. (Floestad, Guttorm.) Oslo, 1968.

Phil 3450.19.280   Heidegger: through phenomenology. (Richardson, W.J.) The Hague, 1963.

Phil 3450.19.500   Heidegger and the path of thinking. Pittsburgh, 1970.

Phil 3450.19.430   Heidegger and the quest for truth. Chicago, 1968.

Phil 3450.19.455   Heidegger-Bibliographie. (Sass, Hans-Martin.) Meisenheim am Glan, 1968.

Phil 3450.19.235   Heidegger e il problema Kantiano. (Padellaro De Angelis, Rosa.) Torino, 1960.

Phil 3450.19.370   Heidegger e la filosofia. (Manno, Mario.) Roma, 1962.

Phil 3450.19.410   Heidegger e la filosofia di valori. (Battaglia, Felice.) Bologna, 1967.

Phil 3485.34   Heidegger et Kant. (Declève, Henri.) La Haye, 1970.

Phil 3450.19.120   Heidegger und die Dichtting. (Buddeberg, Else R.) Stuttgart, 1953.

Phil 3450.19.242   Heidegger und die Theologie. (Noller, Gerhard.) München, 1967.

Phil 3450.19.230   Heidegger und die Tradition. (Marx, Werner.) Stuttgart, 1961.

Phil 3450.19.125   Heidegger und Hegel. (Meulen, J.A. van der.) Groningen, 1953.

Phil 3450.19.94A   Heidegger und Jaspers. (Brecht, F.J.) Wuppertal, 1948.

Phil 3450.19.2   Heideggeriana. Milano. 1,1967+

Phil 3450.19.540   Heidegger's metahistory of philosophy: amor fati, being and truth. (Magnus, Bernd.) The Hague, 1970.

Phil 3450.19.285   Heidegger's philosophy. (King, M.) N.Y., 1964.

Phil 3450.19.375   Heideggers Sprachdenken. (Bock, Irmgard.) München, 1964.

Phil 17.4   Heidelberger Abhandlungen zur Philosophie und ihrer Geschichte. Tübingen. 1-32,1924-1945 31v.

Phil 3850.18.170   Heidemann, I. Untersuchungen zur Kantkritik Max Schelers. Köln? 1955.

Phil 5867.10   Heidemann, Ingeborg. Der Begriff des Spieles und das ästhetische Weltbild in der Philisophie der Gegenwart [play]. Berlin, 1968.

Phil 6677.2   Heidenhain, R.P.H. Animal magnetism. London, 1880.

Phil 8581.43.2   Heidentum, Christentum, Judentum. (Brod, M.) München, 1921. 2v.

Phil 8581.43   Heidentum, Christentum, Judentum. (Brod, M.) München, 1922. 2v.

Phil 5850.228.20   Heider, Fritz. The psychology of interpersonal relations. N.Y., 1958.

Phil 5850.228.20.5   Heider, Fritz. The psychology of interpersonal relations. N.Y., 1967.

Phil 2038.82   Heider, Maria. Studien über David Hartley. Inaug. Diss. Bergisch Gladbach, 1913.

Htn   Phil 182.29*   Heidfeld, J. Octavum renata. Herbornae Nassoviorum, 1621.

Htn   Phil 182.29.15*   Heidfeld, J. Quintum renata. Herbornae Nassoviorum, 1608.

Phil 182.29.10   Heidfeld, J. Sphinx philosophica. Herbornae Nassoviorum, 1600.

Phil 182.83   Heidrich, E. Die Gegenwartslinie, Wesen und Grenzen des Determinismus. Görlitz, 1925.

Phil 2475.1.335   Heidsieck, F. Henri Bergson et la notion d'espace. Paris, 1957.

Phil 8432.2   Heidsieck, F. L'inspiration. 1. éd. Paris, 1961.

Phil 5402.24   Heidsieck, François. Plaisir et tempérance. Paris, 1962.

Phil 6310.1.40   Heilen und Bilden. (Adler, A.) München, 1914.

Phil 6310.1.39   Heilen und Bilden. (Adler, A.) München, 1922.

Phil 6310.14   Das heilende Wort. (Allwohn, Adolf.) Göttingen, 1958.

Phil 5627.132.3   Heiler, Friedrich. Das Gebet. 5. Aufl. München, 1923.

Phil 5627.132.5   Heiler, Friedrich. Prayer. London, 1932.

Phil 5627.132.7   Heiler, Friedrich. Prayer. N.Y., 1958.

Phil 8632.21   Heiler, Friedrich. Unsterblichkeitsglaube und Jenseitshoffnung in der Geschichte der Religionen. München, 1950.

Phil 182.78   Heiler, Josef. Das Absolute. München, 1921.

Phil 978.49.483   Heileurythmie; acht Vorträge. 3. Aufl. (Steiner, R.) Dornach, 1966.

Phil 978.49.760   Heilfaktoren für den sozialen Organismus. 1. Aufl. (Steiner, R.) Dornach, 1969.

Phil 5635.30   Heilig, G. Die sinnlichen Gefühle des Menschen. Jena, 1919.

Phil 5627.95   Die heilige Schweigen. (Mensching, Gustav.) Giessen, 1926.

Phil 5627.95.5   Das heilige Wort. (Mensching, Gustav.) Bonn, 1937.

Phil 5247.40   Heilmann, K. Psychologie und Logik. 15. Aufl. Berlin, 1913.

Phil 5047.31   Heilner, R. System der Logik. Leipzig, 1897.

Phil 978.49.578   Heilpädagogischer Kursus. 3. Aufl. (Steiner, R.) Dornach, 1965.

Phil 6329.14   Heilung aus der Begegnung. (Trüb, Hans.) Stuttgart, 1951.

Phil 6335.10   Die heilung durch den Geist; Mesmer, Mary Baker, Eddy, Freud. (Zweig, S.) Wien, 1936.

Phil 6322.5   Heilung und Entwicklung im Seelenleben. (Maeder, Alphonse.) Zürich, 1918.

Phil 6990.3.112   Die Heilungen von Lourdes im Lichte der Parapsychologie. (Gerloff, Hans.) Büdingen-Gettenbach, 1959.

Phil 6980.717 Heilwege der Tiefenpsychologie. (Szondi, Lipot.) Bern, 1956.
Phil 270.22 Heim, Gustav. Ursache und Bedingung. Leipzig, 1913.
Phil 8662.15 Heim, Karl. God transcendent. London, 1935.
Phil 338.4 Heim, Karl. Psychologismus oder Antipsychologismus. Berlin, 1902.
Phil 8697.18 Heim, Karl. The transformation of the scientific world view. N.Y., 1953.
Phil 338.4.5 Heim, Karl. Das Weltbild der Zukunst. Berlin, 1904.
Phil 960.136.5 Heimann, B. Indian and Western philosophy. London, 1937.
Phil 960.136 Heimann, B. Studien zur Eigenart indischen Denkens. Tübingen, 1930.
Phil 3425.223 Heimann, B. System und Methode in Hegels Philosophie. Leipzig, 1927.
Phil 8408.15 Heimann, B. Über den Geschmack. Berlin, 1924.
Phil 665.104 Heimann, Hans. Die Seele-Grenzbegriff der Naturwissenschaft und Theologie. Bern, 1966.
Phil 8525.5 Heimbeck, Raeburne Seeley. Theology and meaning: a critique of metatheological scepticism. Stanford, 1969.
Phil 5645.57 Heimendahl, E. Licht und Farbe. Berlin, 1961.
Phil 288.22 Heimendahl, Eckart. Dialog des Abendlandes. München, 1966.
Phil 8598.134 Heimkehr Gottes in seine Wirklichkeit. (Schoell, F.) Erbstetten, 1962.
Phil 5841.24 Heimler, Adolf. Reifung und Geschlecht. München, 1966.
Phil 3246.208 Heimsoeth, H. Fichte. München, 1923.
Phil 1707.8.6 Heimsoeth, H. Metaphysik der Neuzeit. München, 1967.
Phil 3160.6.85 Heimsoeth, H. Metaphysik und Kritik bei Christian August Crusius. Berlin, 1926.
Phil 2520.113 Heimsoeth, H. Die Methode der Erkenntnis bei Descartes. Giessen, 1912.
Phil 3450.18.105 Heimsoeth, H. Nicolai Hartmann, der Denker und sein Werk. Göttingen, 1952.
Phil 1707.8 Heimsoeth, H. Die sechs grossen Themen der abendländischen Metaphysik. Berlin, 1922.
Phil 1707.8.3 Heimsoeth, H. Die sechs grossen Themen der abendländischen Metaphysik. 3e Aufl. Stuttgart, 1954?
Phil 3489.43 Heimsoeth, Heinz. Transzendentale Dialektik. Ein Kommentar zu Kants Kritik der reinen Vernunft. Berlin, 1966- 4v.
Phil 5421.5.5 Das Heimweh. Thesis. (Ramming-Thoen, Fortunata.) Zürich, 1958.
Phil 665.28 Hein, Joseph. Aktualität oder Substantialität der Seele? Inaug. Diss. Paderborn, 1916.
Phil 6400.25 Hein, Leopold. Speech and voice. London, 1942.
Phil 7069.22.12 Hein, Rudolf. Der Fluidalkörper des Menschen...okkulten Erscheinungen. Leipzig, 1922.
Phil 3007.2.5 Heine, H. Religion and philosophy in Germany. Boston, 1959.
Phil 3007.2 Heine, H. Religion and philosophy in Germany. London, 1882.
Phil 7069.60.15 Heine, Hilda G. The vital sense. London, 1960.
Phil 182.103.5 Heineccius, J.G. Elementa philosophiae rationalis et moralis. Amstelodami, 1733.
Phil 182.107 Heinemann, F. Odysseus oder die Zukunft der Philosophie. Stockholm, 1939.
Phil 2050.217 Heinemann, Fritz. David Hume. Paris, 1940.
Phil 1750.365 Heinemann, Fritz. Existentialism and the modern predicament. London, 1953.
Phil 1750.365.7 Heinemann, Fritz. Existentialism and the modern predicament. N.Y., 1958.
Phil 1750.365.5 Heinemann, Fritz. Existentialism and the modern predicament. 2nd ed. London, 1954.
Phil 1750.365.15 Heinemann, Fritz. Existenzphilosophie Lebendig oder Tat? 2e Aufl. Stuttgart, 1954.
Phil 1750.365.10 Heinemann, Fritz. Jenseits des Existentialismus. Zürich, 1957.
Phil 807.16 Heinemann, Fritz. Die Lehre von der Zweckbestimmung der Menschen. Breslau, 1926.
Phil 1707.10 Heinemann, Fritz. Neue Wege der Philosophie, Geist, Leben, Existenz. Leipzig, 1929.
Phil 807.16.5 Heinemann, Fritz. Die Philosophie im XX Jahrhundert. Stuttgart, 1959.
Phil 8957.20 Heinen, Wilhelm. Liebe als sittliche Grundkraft und ihre Fehlformen. 3. Aufl. Basel, 1968.
Phil 3195.10.90 Heinichen, Otto. Driesch's Philosophie. Leipzig, 1924.
Phil 1145.85 Heinimann, Felix. Nomos und physis. Basel, 1945.
Phil 1135.23.9 Heinisch, Paul. Griechische Philosophie und altes Testament. Münster, 1913-14. 2v.
Phil 5360.2 Heinrich, E. Untersuchungen zur Lehre vom Begriff. Inaug. Diss. Göttingen, 1910.
Phil 5330.6.2 Heinrich, W. Die moderne psysiologische Psychologie...Aufmerksamkeit. Leipzig, 1895.
Phil 5330.6 Heinrich, W. Die moderne psysiologische Psychologie...Aufmerksamkeit. Zürich, 1899.
Phil 3801.448 Heinrich, W. Schellings Lehre von den Letzten Dingen. Salzburg, 1955.
Phil 807.17.2 Heinrich, W. Zarys historii filozofii średniowiecznej. Warszawa, 1963.
Phil 807.17 Heinrich, W. Zarys historji filozofji. Warszawa, 1925-30.
Phil 5247.62 Heinrich, W. Zur Prinzipienfrage der Psychologie. Zürich, 1899.
Phil 165.12 Heinrich, Walter. Die Ganzheit in Philosophie und Wissenschaft. Wien, 1950.
Phil 5762.14 Heinrich Hertz - für die Willensfreiheit? (Manno, R.) Leipzig, 1900.
Phil 3790.4.85 Heinrich Rickert und der philosophische transzendenta subjektivismus. Inaug. Diss. (Beck, Friedrich.) Erlangen, 1925.
Phil 3790.4.88 Heinrich Rickert und seine Stellung innerhalb der eutschen Philosophie der Gegenwart. (Faust, August.) Tübingen, 1927.
Phil 3850.47 Heinrich Scholz. (Seifert, Hans.) Münster, 1958.
Phil 3850.20.80 Heinrich Steffens. Diss. (Bruck, Reinhard.) Borna, 1906.
Phil 6317.14 Heinroth, D.F.C.A. Lehrbuch der Storungen des Seelenlehre. v.1-2. Leipzig, 1818.
Phil 482.1 Heinroth, J.C. Über die Hypothese der Materie. Leipzig, 1828.
Phil 525.12 Heinroth, J.C.A. Geschichte und Kritik des Mysticismus. Leipzig, 1830.
Phil 9558.1 Heinroth, J.C.A. Die Lüge. Leipzig, 1834.
Phil 5247.39 Heinroth, J.C.A. Die Psychologie als Selbsterkenntnisslehre. Leipzig, 1827.
NEDL Phil 8882.7 Heinroth, J.C.A. Der Schlüssel zu Himmel und Hölle. Leipzig, 1839.
Phil 182.9 Heinroths, J. Pisteodicee. Leipzig, 1829.
Phil 8587.68 Heins, Karl. Die Wandlung im naturwissenschaftlicher Weltbild. 2. Aufl. Hamburg, 1951.
Phil 5627.110 Heinsius, Wilhelm. Krisen katholischer Frömmigkeit. Berlin, 1925.
Phil 3640.284 Heintel, E. Nietzsches "System" in seinen Grundbegriffen. Leipzig, 1939.
Phil 3450.46 Heintel, Erich. Die beiden Labyrinthe der Philosophie. Wien, 1968.
Phil 3425.442 Heintel, Erich. Hegel und die Analogia Entis. Bonn, 1958.
Phil 3425.724 Heintel, Peter. Hegel. Göttingen, 1970.
Phil 3489.44 Heinz, Rudolf. Französische Kantinterpreten im 20. Jahrhundert. Bonn, 1966.
Phil 17.12 Heinz Werner lecture series. Worcester, Mass. 1,1966
Phil 3640.330 Heinze, Kurt. Verbrechen und Strafe bei Friedrich Nietzsche. Berlin, 1939.
Phil 1135.80 Heinze, M. Die Lehre vom Logos. Oldenburg, 1872.
Phil 1145.77 Heinze, Max. Der Eudämonismus in der griechischen Philosophie. Leipzig, 1883.
Phil 3450.7.80 Heinze, Max. Philosophische Abhandlungen. Berlin, 1906.
Phil 3489.10 Heinze, Max. Vorlesungen Kants über Metaphysik aus drei Semestern. Leipzig, 1894.
Phil 5757.11 Heinzel, G. Versuch einer Lösung des Willensproblems. Inaug. Diss. Breslau, n.d.
Phil 3915.150 Heinzelmann, G. Der Begriff der Seele und die Idei der Unsterblichkeit. Tübingen, 1910.
Phil 8587.35 Heinzelmann, G. Die erkenntnistheoretische Begründung der Religion. Basel, 1915.
Phil 6315.2.370 Heirs to Freud. (Ruitenbeek, Hendrik Marinus.) N.Y., 1966.
Phil 3007.16 Heise, Wolfgang. Aufbruch in die Illusion. 1. Aufl. Berlin, 1964.
Phil 5374.38 Heisler, N. Ein Ausflug in das Gebiet des Bewusstseins. Basel, 1892.
Phil 1707.13 Heiss, R. Der Gang des Geistes. Bern, 1948.
Phil 1750.740 Heiss, R. Die grossen Dialektiker des 19. Jahrhunderts. Köln, 1963.
Phil 6317.34 Heiss, Robert. Allgemeine, Tiefenpsychologie. Bern, 1956.
Phil 6317.34.5 Heiss, Robert. Allgemeine Tiefenpsychologie. Bern, 1964.
Phil 9035.72 Heiss, Robert. Die Lehre vom Charakter. Berlin, 1936.
Phil 5047.35 Heiss, Robert. Logik des Widerspruchs. Berlin, 1932.
Phil 5047.35.5 Heiss, Robert. Wesen und Formen der Dialektik. Köln, 1952.
Phil 3790.24 Heitere Erinnerungen. (Rothacker, E.) Frankfurt, 1963.
Phil 2530.90 Heitmann, K. Ethos des Künstlers und Ethos der Kunst. Münster, 1962.
Phil 1540.18 Heitz, T. Essai historique sur les rapports entre la philosophie et la foi. Thèse. Paris, 1909.
Phil 1750.25 Heitzman, M. Mikolaj Hill. Studjum z historji filozofji atomistycznej. Krakow, 192-?
Phil 6400.23 Hekaen, Henry. Pathologie du langage. Paris, 1965.
Phil 6317.4 Hélat, C. Névroses et possessions diaboliques. 2. éd. Paris, 1898.
Phil 3090.91 Helberger-Frobenius, Sebastian. Macht und Gewalt in der Philosophie Franz von Baaders. Bonn, 1969.
Phil 3007.8.5 Helbing, Lothar. Der dritte Humanismus. 3. Aufl. Berlin, 1935.
Phil 6980.350 Held, Fritz. Jugendpsychiatrische Studien. Berlin, 1966.
Phil 3450.11.310 Held, Klaus. Lebendige Gegenwart. Köln, 1963.
Phil 3450.11.311 Held, Klaus. Lebendige Gegenwart. Thesis. Den Haag, 1966.
Phil 8832.8 Held, Virginia. The bewildered age. N.Y., 1962.
Phil 974.2.15 Helena Petrovna Blavatsky. (Tingley, K.A. (Mrs.).) Point Loma, Calif., 1921.
Phil 525.41 Helfferich, A. Die christliche Mystik. Gotha, 1842. 2v.
Phil 182.11.10 Helfferich, A. Die Metaphysik als Grundwissenschaft. Hamburg, 1846.
Phil 182.11 Helfferich, A. Der Organismus der Wissenschaft. Leipzig, 1856.
Phil 3827.5 Helfferich, A. Spinoza und Leibniz. Hamburg, 1846.
Phil 8685.22 Helios. (Masferrer, A.) San Salvador, 1963.
Phil 5850.228 Helke, J.W. Korrelation oder Wertigkeit? Inaug. Diss. Leipzig, 1935.
Phil 5635.5.11 Hell, B. Ernst Mach's Philosophie. Stuttgart, 1907.
Phil 801.27.5 Hellas. (Bjarnason, Á.) Reykjavik, 1910.
Phil 4520.8.34 Hellas. (Bjarnason, Ágúst.) Reykjavík, 1910.
Phil 7069.22.14 Hellberg, E. Telepathie. Prien, 1922.
Phil 3790.30.5 Helle Nächte; drei Stücke Existenzphilosophie. (Richtscheid, Hans.) München, 1968.
Phil 7054.24 Helleberg, C.C. A book written by the spirits of the so-called dead. Cincinnati, 1883.
Phil 9035.90 Hellek, A. Die Polarität im Aufbau des Charakters. Bern, 1950.
Phil 182.12 Hellenbach, L.B. Eine Philosophie des gesunden Menschenverstandes. Wien, 1876.
Phil 182.12.6 Hellenbach, L.B. Die Vorurtheile des gemeinen Verstandes. Wien, 1880.
Phil 3640.241 Hellenbrecht, H. Das Problem der freien Rhythmen mit Bezug auf Nietzsche. Berlin, 1931.
Phil 3640.265 Hellenbrecht, H. Das Problem der freien Rhythmen mit Bezug auf Nietzsche. Inaug. Diss. Bern, 1931.
Phil 1135.130 The Hellenic origins of Christian asceticism. (Swain, Joseph W.) N.Y., 1916.
Phil 1117.12 Hellenika. (Menzel, Adolf.) Baden, 1938.
Phil 1170.17 Hellēnikē philosophia kai christianikon dogma. (Koytsogiannopoyloy, D.I.) Athens, 1960.
Phil 3801.807 Das hellenisch-deutsche Weltbild. (Stefansky, Georg.) Bonn, 1925.
Phil 1133.22 Hellenistic philosophies (From the death of Socrates to A.D. 451). (More, Paul E.) Princeton, 1923.
Phil 1116.4.5 Hellenistische Philosophie von Aristoteles bis Plotin. (Leisegang, H.) Breslau, 1923.
Phil 3640.699 Heller, E. Nietzsche. Frankfurt am Main, 1964.
Phil 9400.18 Heller, Edward. Spiegel des Altes. Affoltern, 1956.
Phil 3425.220.5 Heller, Hermann. Hegel und der nationale Machtstaatsgedanke in Deutschland. Aalen, 1963.
Phil 3425.220 Heller, Hermann. Hegel und der nationale Machtstaatsgedanke in Deutschland. Leipzig, 1921.
Phil 3489.19 Heller, Josef. Kants Persönlichkeit und Leben. Berlin, 1924.
Phil 3850.22.90 Heller, Joseph E. Solgers Philosophie der ironischen Dialektik. Berlin, 1928.
Phil 3850.22.90.2 Heller, Joseph E. Solgers Philosophie der ironischen Dialektik. Diss. Berlin, 1928.
Phil 3625.3.100 Heller, K. Ernst Mach. Wien, 1964.
Phil 8408.17 Heller, R. Das Wesen der Schönheit. Wein, 1936.
Phil 8408.28 Heller-Heinzelmann, R. L'immaginazione e la vita estetica. Firenze, 1933.
Phil 3425.01 Hellersberg firm, booksellers. Berlin. Hegel und die Hegelianer; eine Bibliothek. Charlottenburg, 1927?
Phil 182.84 Hellmund, H. Das Wesen der Welt. Zürich, 1927.

Phil 5421.10.40   Hellner, Hans. Über die Angst. Stuttgart, 1969.
Phil 2655.5.30   Hello, E. L'homme. Paris, 1872.
Phil 6117.10.3   Hellpach, W. Die geopsychischen Erscheinungen. Leipzig, 1911.
Phil 6117.10.5   Hellpach, W. Die geopsychischen Erscheinungen. 2. Aufl. Leipzig, 1917.
Phil 6117.10   Hellpach, W. Die Grenzwissenschaften der Psychologie. Leipzig, 1902.
Phil 6957.10   Hellpach, W. Grundgedanken zur Wissenschaftslehre der Psychopathologie. Leipzig, 1906.
Phil 6957.10.5   Hellpach, W. Die Hysterie und die moderne Schule. n.p., 1905-1913. 11 pam.
Phil 5627.160   Hellpach, W. Übersicht der Religionspsychologie. Leipzig, 1939.
Phil 5247.75   Hellpach, W. Das Wellengesetz unseres Lebens. Hamburg, 1941.
Phil 6615.8   Hellpach, Willy. Grundlinien einer Psychologie der Hysterie. Leipzig, 1904.
Phil 5627.194   Hellpach, Willy. Grundriss der Religionspsychologie. Stuttgart, 1951.
Phil 3450.26.10   Hellpach, Willy. Universitas litterarum. Stuttgart, 1948.
Phil 3450.26   Hellpach, Willy. Zwischen Wittenberg und Rom. Berlin, 1931.
Phil 7068.72.20   Hellsehen des Unbewussten. (Hoppe, I.) Freiburg., 1872.
Phil 4515.82   Hellström, Carl. Om viljefrihetsläran i Boströms definitiva filosofi. Uppsala, 1919.
Phil 7069.26.9   Hellwig, A. Okkultismus und Wissenschaft. Stuttgart, 1926.
Phil 5500.41   Helmer, Olaf. A use of sumulation for the study of future values. Santa Monica, 1966.
Phil 8587.8   Helmersen, A. von. Die Religion. Graz, 1875.
Phil 5643.8.5   Helmholtz, H. Handbuch der physiologischen Optik. Hamburg, 1896.
Htn   Phil 5643.8.10   Helmholtz, H. Optique physiologique. Paris, 1867.
Htn   Phil 5643.8*   Helmholtz, H. Physiologischen Optik. v.1 and Atlas. Leipzig, 1867. 2v.
Phil 338.12   Helmholtz, H. Schriften zur Erkenntnistheorie. Berlin, 1921.
Phil 5643.8.12   Helmholtz, H. Treatise on physiological optics. Rochester, N.Y., 1924-25. 3v.
Phil 5585.3.5A   Helmholtz, Hermann van. Helmholtz on perception; its physiology and development. N.Y., 1968.
Phil 5585.3   Helmholtz, Hermann van. Thatsachen in der Wahrnehmung. Berlin, 1879.
Phil 5585.3.5A   Helmholtz on perception; its physiology and development. (Helmholtz, Hermann van.) N.Y., 1968.
Phil 182.13.5   Helmont, F.M. van. Eenige gedagten. Amsterdam, 1690.
Htn   Phil 182.13*   Helmont, F.M. van. Macrocosm and microcosm. London, 1685.
Phil 5865.5.30   Helmore, Geoffrey Anthony. Piaget: a practical consideration. 1st ed. N.Y., 1969.
Phil 1112.6   Helms, Poul. Den graeske naturfilosofi indtil sofisterne. København, 1926.
Phil 807.12   Helms, Poul F. Fra Plato til Bergson. København, 1919.
Phil 6677.12.5   Hélot, C. L'hypnotisme franc et l'hypnotisme vrai. Paris, 1909.
Phil 6128.46.12   Help yourself to happiness. (Seabury, David.) N.Y., 1937.
Phil 187.17.9   The helpful science. (Mivart, St. G.) N.Y., 1895.
Phil 5853.14   Helping and human relations. (Carkhuff, Robert R.) N.Y., 1969. 2v.
Phil 8586.23   The helping hand. (Gould, Gerald.) London, 1922.
Phil 7069.67   Helping yourself with E.S.P. (Manning, A.G.) West Nyack, 1967.
Phil 194.1   Helps to understanding of nature. (Taylor, B.S.) Albion, 1894.
Phil 5722.50   Helsdingen, R.J. van. Beelden uit het onbewuste. Arnhem, 1957.
Phil 6319.1.221   Helsdingen, R.J. van. Jung. Den Haag, 1964.
Phil 5247.38   Helson, Harry. The psychology of Gestalt. Urbana, 1926.
Phil 6420.38   Heltman, Harry J. First aide for stutterers. Boston, 1943.
Phil 8636.10   Helvedes strategi. (Lindhardt, P.G.) n.p., 1958.
Phil 2636.91   Helvetius; a study in persecution. (Smith, David Warner.) Oxford, 1965.
Phil 2636.25.5   Helvétius, C.A. De l'esprit, de l'homme. 4e éd. Paris, 1909.
Phil 2636.41   Helvétius, C.A. De l'esprit, or Essays on the mind. London, 1759.
Phil 2636.41.2   Helvétius, C.A. De l'esprit, or Essays on the mind. 2. ed. London, 1810.
Htn   Phil 2636.40*   Helvétius, C.A. De l'esprit. Amsterdam, 1758.
Htn   Phil 2636.40.1*   Helvétius, C.A. De l'esprit. Paris, 1759.
Phil 2636.40.6   Helvétius, C.A. De l'esprit. Paris, 1843.
Phil 2636.25.6   Helvétius, C.A. De l'esprit. Paris, 1959.
Phil 2636.40.2   Helvétius, C.A. De l'esprit. v.1-4. Paris, 1793. 2v.
Htn   Phil 2636.32*   Helvétius, C.A. De l'homme. London, 1773. 2v.
Phil 2636.34   Helvétius, C.A. De l'homme. Paris, 1773.
Phil 2636.10   Helvétius, C.A. Oeuvres complètes. London, 1777. 2v.
Phil 2636.12   Helvétius, C.A. Oeuvres complètes. Paris, 1793. 5v.
Phil 2636.12.2   Helvétius, C.A. Oeuvres complètes. Paris, 1793-97. 10v.
Htn   Phil 2636.10.7*   Helvétius, C.A. Oeuvres complètes. v.1-2. London, 1781.
Phil 2636.11   Helvétius, C.A. Oeuvres complètes. v.3-7. Deuxponts, 1784. 5v.
Phil 2636.31.2   Helvétius, C.A. A treatise on man. London, 1810. 2v.
Phil 2636.31   Helvétius, C.A. A treatise on man. London, 1877. 2v.
Phil 2636.44   Helvétius, C.A. Le vrai sens du système de la nature. Londres, 1774.
Phil 2636.79   Pamphlet box. Helvétius, C.A.
Phil 2636.90   Helvétius. (Cumming, Ian.) London, 1955.
Phil 2636.81   Helvétius. (Séverac, J.B.) Paris, n.d.
Phil 2636.80   Helvétius sa vie et son oeuvre. (Keim, A.) Paris, 1907.
Phil 2477.3.31   Les Helviennes. 5. éd. (Barruel, Augustine.) Paris, 1812. 4v.
Phil 2477.3.33   Les Helviennes. 7e éd. (Barruel, Augustine.) Paris, 1830. 4v.
Phil 2636.88   Helvitius, ein streitbarer Atheist das 18. Jahrhunderts. (Momdzhian, Khashik.) Berlin, 1959.
Phil 9035.78.5   Helwig, Paul. Charakterologie. 2. Aufl. Stuttgart, 1951.
Phil 9035.78   Helwig, Paul. Charakterologie. Leipzig, 1936.
Phil 5421.25.10   Helwig, Paul. Liebe und Feindschaft. München, 1964.
Phil 6117.41   Helwig, Paul. Seele als Ausserung. Leipzig, 1936.
Phil 5757.2   Heman, C.F. Zur Geschichte der Lehre von der Freiheit des menschlichen Willens. Leipzig, 1887.

Phil 5585.9.5   Heman, Karl F. Die Erscheinung der Dinge. Leipzig, 1881.
Phil 6420.22   A hemato-respiratory study of 101 consecutive cases of stammering. Thesis. (Trumper, Max.) Philadelphia, 1928.
Phil 5817.12   Hement, Felix. De l'instinct et de l'intelligence. Paris, 1880.
Phil 2905.1.575   Hemkben, Johannes. Pierre Teilhard de Chardin in Selbstzeugnissen und Bilddokumenten. Reinbek, 1966.
Phil 8592.106   The hemlock and the cross. (MacGregor, Geddes.) Philadelphia, 1963.
Phil 4600.2.37   Hemmabyarna världsbetrakleser i femton kapitel. (Larsson, Hans.) Stockholm, 1916.
Phil 3090.90   Hemmerle, Klaus. Franz von Baaders philosophischer Gedanke der Schöpfung. Freiburg, 1963.
Phil 3801.450.5   Hemmerle, Klaus. Gott und das Denken nach Schellings Spätphilosophie. Freiburg, 1968.
Phil 8882.100   Hemming, James. Individual morality. London, 1969.
Htn   Phil 6315.2.60*   Hemmung, Symptom und Angst. (Freud, Sigmund.) Leipzig, 1926.
Phil 8887.50.10   Hemmungen des Lebens. (Müller, Johannes.) München, 193-?
Phil 8887.50.11   Hemmungen des Lebens. (Müller, Johannes.) München, 1956.
Phil 5247.52   Hempel, Carl G. Der Typus Begriff im Lichte der neuen Logik. Leiden, 1936.
Phil 5817.13   Hempelmann, F. Tierpsychologie vom Standpunkte des Biologen. Leipzig, 1926.
Htn   Phil 8587.9*   Hemsterhuis, F. Aristée ou de la divinité. Paris, 1778-79. 2 pam.
Phil 3450.12.100   Hemsterhuis, F. Lettre sur l'homme et ses rapports. New Haven, 1964.
Phil 182.14   Hemsterhuis, F. Oeuvres philosophiques. Paris, 1792. 2v.
Phil 182.14.1   Hemsterhuis, F. Oeuvres philosophiques. Paris, 1809. 2v.
Phil 182.14.2   Hemsterhuis, F. Oeuvres philosophiques. v.3. Leuwarde, 1850.
Phil 182.14.10   Hemsterhuis, F. Philosophische Schriften. Karlsruhe, 1912. 2v.
Phil 182.14.5   Hemsterhuis, F. Vermischte philosophische Schriften. Leipzig, 1782. 3v.
Phil 3450.2.79   Pamphlet box. Hemsterhuis, F.
Phil 7054.150   Henck, E.C. Spirit voices. Philadelphia, 1853.
Phil 3195.2.90   Henckmann, Wolfhart. Das Wesen der Kunst in der$Ästhetik Martin Deutingers. München, 1966.
Phil 3489.36   Hendel, C.W. The philosophy of Kant and our modern world. N.Y., 1957.
Phil 2050.176A   Hendel, C.W. Studies in the philosophy of David Hume. Princeton, 1925.
Phil 1955.6.155   Hendel, Charles W. John Dewey and the experimental spirit in philosophy. N.Y., 1959.
Phil 8882.28   Henderson, C.H. The children of good fortune. N.Y., 1905.
Phil 6317.24   Henderson, D.K. Psychopathic states. N.Y., 1939.
Phil 6957.17.20   Henderson, D.K. A text-book of psychiatry for students and practitioners. Oxford, 1947.
Phil 6957.17.5   Henderson, D.K. A text-book of psychiatry for students and practitioners. 2. ed. London, 1930.
Phil 6957.17.7   Henderson, D.K. A text-book of psychiatry for students and practitioners. 3. ed. London, 1933.
Phil 5545.35   Henderson, E.N. A study of memory. n.p., n.d.
Phil 6048.95   Henderson, Eliza Easter. A guide to palmistry. Boston, 1895.
Phil 4843.4   Henderson, George Patrick. The revival of Greek thought, 1620-1830. Albany, 1970.
Phil 6317.50   Henderson, Joseph. Thresholds of initiation. 1. ed. Middletown, 1967.
Phil 8735.6A   Henderson, L.J. The order of nature. Cambridge, 1917.
Phil 8735.6.5A   Henderson, L.J. The order of nature. Cambridge, 1925.
Phil 7150.57   Hendin, H. Suicide and Scandinavia. N.Y., 1964.
Phil 7150.98   Hendin, Herbert. Black suicide. N.Y., 1969.
Phil 6317.45   Hendin, Herbert. Psychoanalysis and social research; the psychoanalytic study of the non-patient. Garden City, 1965.
Phil 6317.20.15   Hendrick, Ives. The birth of instinct. Freeport, 1961.
Phil 6317.20   Hendrick, Ives. Facts and theories of psychoanalysis. N.Y., 1934.
Phil 6317.20.5A   Hendrick, Ives. Facts and theories of psychoanalysis. 2d ed. N.Y., 1944.
Phil 6317.20.8   Hendrick, Ives. Facts and theories of psychoanalysis. 3rd ed. N.Y., 1958.
Phil 7069.40.19   Hendrickson, R.J. Divine science and metaphysics. N.Y., 1940.
Phil 1750.110   Hengslenberg, Hans Eduard. Philosophische Anthropologie. Stuttgart, 1957.
Phil 705.37   Hengstenberg, H.E. Autonomismus und Transzendenzphilosophie. Heidelberg, 1950.
Phil 2905.1.250   Hengstenberg, H.E. Evolution und Schöffung. München, 1963.
Phil 8697.19   Hengstenberg, Hans E. Sein und Ursprünglichkeit. München, 1958.
Phil 8882.108   Hengstenberg, Hans Eduard. Grundlegung der Ethik. Stuttgart, 1969.
Phil 182.124   Hengstenberg, Hans Edward. Freiheit und Seinsordnung. Stuttgart, 1961.
Phil 6677.18   Hénin de Cuvillers, E.T. Exposition critique du système et de la doctrine mystique des magnétistes. Paris, 1822.
Phil 3260.85   Henke, E.L.T. Jakob Friedrich Fries. Leipzig, 1867.
Phil 5627.37   Henke, Frederick G. A study in the psychology of ritualism. Diss. Chicago, 1910.
Phil 7054.35   Henke, O. Der Gespensterglaube der Gegenwart. Mülheim, 1881.
Phil 182.65   Henkel, Fred. Creative psychics, the art of regeneration. Los Angeles, 1917.
Phil 5247.7   Henle, F.G.J. Anthropologische Vorträge. Braunschweig, 1876-80.
Phil 5238.192   Henle, Mary. Documents of Gestalt psychology. Berkeley, 1961.
Phil 5066.38A   Henle, Paul. Structure, method, and meaning. N.Y., 1951.
Phil 182.113   Henle, R.J. Method in metaphysics. Milwaukee, 1951.
Phil 5757.6   Henle, Rudolf. Vorstellungs- und Willentheorie. Leipzig, 1910.
Phil 5640.11   Henmon, V.A.C. Time of perception as a measure of differences in sensations. N.Y., 1906.
Phil 5635.22   Henmon, V.A.C. The time of perception as a measure of differences in sensations. N.Y., 1906.
Phil 1210.5   Henne, Désiré. École de Mégare. Paris, 1843.
Phil 3640.211   Henne am Rhyn, O. Anti-Zarathustra. Altenburg, 1899.
Phil 3640.211.5   Henne am Rhyn, O. Anti-Zarathustra. 2e Aufl. Altenburg, 1901?
Phil 8587.10.15   Hennell, S.S. Christianity and infidelity. London, 1857.
Phil 8587.10.5   Hennell, S.S. Comparativism. London, 1869.

Phil 8587.10 Hennell, S.S. Present religion. v.1-2. London, 1865-87. 3v.
Phil 8587.10.10 Hennell, S.S. Thoughts in aid of faith. London, 1860.
Phil 1900.89 Hennell, Sara S. Essay on the sceptical tendency of Butler's "analogy". London, 1859.
Phil 5645.36 Henneman, R.H. A photometric study of the perception of object color. N.Y., 1935.
Phil 288.12 Hennemann, Gerhard. Naturphilosophie in 19. Jahrhundert. Freiburg, 1959.
Phil 8697.23 Hennemann, Gerhard. Philosophie, Religion, moderne Naturwissenschaft. Witten, 1955.
Phil 720.94 Hennemann, Gerhard. Zum Problem der Voraussetzungslosigkeit und Objektivtät in der Wissenschaft. Photoreproduction. Bonn, 1947.
Phil 3195.6.95 Hennig, J. Lebensbegriff und Lebenskategorie. Inaug. Diss. Aachen, 1934.
Phil 3120.1.125 Hennig, M. A.E. Biedermanns Theorie...religiöse Erkenntnis. Leipzig, 1902.
Phil 7069.06.7 Hennig, R. Die moderne Spuk- und Geisterglaube. Hamburg, 1906.
Phil 7069.05.35 Hennig, R. Wunder und Wissenschaft. Hamburg, 1905.
Phil 5330.22 Henning, H. Die Aufmerksamkeit. Berlin, 1925.
Phil 5655.5.2 Henning, H. Der Geruch. 2e Aufl. Leipzig, 1924.
Phil 5655.5 Henning, H. Der Geruch. Leipzig, 1916.
Phil 3625.3.80 Henning, Hans. Ernst als Philosoph, Physiker und Psycholog, eine Monographie. Leipzig, 1915.
Phil 5247.44 Henning, Hans. Psychologie der Gegenwart. Berlin, 1925.
Phil 7082.116 Henning, Hans. Der Traum. Wiesbaden, 1914.
Phil 7080.14 Hennings, Justus Christian. Von den Träumen und Nachtwandlern. Weimar, 1784.
Phil 8882.87 Henningsen, N. Moral-hvad er det? København, 1962.
Phil 8662.6 Henri, P.E. Religion d'amour ou Dieu existe. Marseille, 1910.
Phil 5648.7 Henri, V. Raumwahrnehmungen des Tastsinnes. Berlin, 1898.
Phil 5648.7.2 Henri, V. Raumwahrnehmungen des Tastsinnes. Berlin, 1898.
Phil 2475.1.132 Henri Bergson, an account of his life. (Ruhe, A.) London, 1914.
Phil 2475.1.365 Henri Bergson; exposition. (Bibliothèque Nationale, Paris.) Paris, 1959.
Phil 2475.1.90 Henri Bergson; the philosophy of change. (Carr, H.W.) London, 1911.
Phil 2475.1.185.5 Henri Bergson; the philosophy of change. (Carr, Herbert W.) London, 1919.
Phil 2475.1.440 Henri Bergson. (Barlow, Michel.) Paris, 1966.
Phil 2475.1.222.5A Henri Bergson. (Chevalier, Jacques.) N.Y., 1928.
Phil 2475.1.222.10 Henri Bergson. (Chevalier, Jacques.) Paris, 1928.
Phil 2475.1.99 Henri Bergson. (Gillouin, R.) Paris, 1910.
Phil 2475.1.263.5 Henri Bergson. (Jankélévitch, V.) Paris, 1959.
Phil 2475.1.304 Henri Bergson. (Jurévics, Pauls.) Freiburg, 1949.
Phil 2475.1.355 Henri Bergson. (Pflug, Günther.) Berlin, 1959.
Phil 2475.1.133 Henri Bergson. (Ruhe, A.) Stockholm, 1914.
Phil 2475.1.292 Henri Bergson. (Valery, Paul.) Paris, 1945.
Phil 2475.1.225 Henri Bergson. (Wilm, E.C.) N.Y., 1914.
Phil 2475.1.269 Henri Bergson. Essais et témoignages inédits recueilles. (Béguin, Albert.) Neuchâtel, 1941.
Phil 2475.1.335 Henri Bergson et la notion d'espace. (Heidsieck, F.) Paris, 1957.
Phil 2475.1.272 Henri Bergson et le catholicisme. (Sertillanges, A.G.) Paris, 1941.
Phil 2475.1.320 Henri Bergson et les lettres françaises. (Arbour, Romeo.) Paris, 1955.
Phil 2475.1.196 Henri Bergson und das Problem des Verhältnisses zwischen Leib und Seele. (Kerler, Dietrich H.) Ulm, 1917.
Phil 2475.1.247 Henri Bergson und meine Ideen. (Kann, Albert.) Wien, 1935.
Phil 2475.1.212 Henri Bergson's filosofi i omrids. (Jorgensen, J.) København, 1917.
Phil 2475.1.216 Henri Bergsons intuitionsfilosofi. (Jacobbson, M.) Lund, 1911.
Phil 2475.1.213 Henri Bergsons Philosophie der Persönlichkeit. (Schrecker, P.) München, 1912.
Phil 2880.8.92 Henri-Hoyen, E. Sartre contre l'homme. Genève, 1947.
Phil 8423.20 Henri Wölfflin; sa théorie, ses prédécesseurs. (Levy, Hanna.) Rottweil, 1936.
Phil 3489.38 Henrich, Adolf. Kant's Deduktion der reinen Verstandesbegriffe. Emmerich, 1885.
Phil 165.175 Henrich, Dieter. Die Gegenwart der Griechen im neueren Denken. Tübingen, 1960.
Phil 8662.24 Henrich, Dieter. Der ontologische Gottesbeweis. Tübingen, 1960.
Phil 165.175.5 Henrich, Dieter. Subjektivität und Metaphysik. Frankfurt, 1966.
Phil 3850.27.105 Henrich, R. They thought he was mad; Albert Schweitzer. N.Y., 1940.
Phil 210.10 Henrichs, Norbert. Bibliographie der Hermeneutik und ihrer Anwendungs Gereiche seit Schleiermacher. Düsseldorf, 1968.
Phil 3425.440 Henrici, Peter. Hegel und Blondel. Pullach, 1958.
Htn Phil 3085.1.35* Henrici Cornelii Agrippae. (Agrippa von Nettesheim, H.C.) Coloniae, 1575.
Phil 193.34.5 Henrik Steffens indledning til föreläsninger in Kobenhavn 1803. (Steffens, H.) Kobenhavn, 1905.
Phil 9120.180 Henriot, Jacques. Existence et obligation. Paris, 1967.
Phil 807.6 Henry, C.S. An epitome of the history of philosophy. N.Y., 1856. 2v.
Phil 5545.67 Henry, Charles. Mémoire et habitude. Paris, 1911.
Phil 5635.11 Henry, Charles. Sensation et énergie. Paris, 1911.
Phil 9010.23 Henry, Charlton. An inquiry into the consistency of popular amusements. Charleston, S.C., 1825.
Phil 6957.14 Henry, Jules. Du délire des negations (Syndrome de Cotard) dans la paralysie générale. Paris, 1896.
Phil 6117.13 Henry, M. Charles. Psycho-biologie et energétique. Paris, 1909.
Phil 2655.7.30 Henry, Michel. L'essence de la manifestation. Paris, 1963. 2v.
Phil 2730.113 Henry, Michel. Philosophie et phénoménologie du corps. Paris, 1965.
Phil 7054.128 Henry, T.S. "Spookland", a record of research. Chicago, 1902.
Phil 5465.85 Henry, W.E. The analysis of fantasy. N.Y., 1956.
Phil 6980.350.25 Henry, William Earl. The fifth profession. 1st ed. San Francisco, 1971.
Phil 5350.2.8A Henry Bergson: philosophy of change. (Carr, H.W.) London, 1911.
Phil 192.3 Henry Holbeach. (Rands, W.B.) London, 1865. 2v.
Phil 192.3.2 Henry Holbeach. (Rands, W.B.) London, 1866. 2v.
Phil 8589.5.45 Henry James. (Hoover, Dwight W.) Grand Rapids, 1969.

Phil 2145.80 Henry More. Essai sur les doctrines théosophiques chez les platoniciens de Cambridge. (Hutin, Serge.) Hildesheim, 1966.
Phil 2280.1.80 Henry Sidgwick. (Sidgwick, A.) London, 1906.
Phil 2280.1.95 Henry Sidgwick and later utilitarian political philosophy. (Havard, William C.) Gainesville, 1959.
Phil 5247.72 Henrysson, Sten. Applicability of factor analysis in the behavioral science. Stockholm, 1957.
Phil 2050.177 Henschen, W.A. Bidrag till kännedomen af David Humes filosofiska betydelse. Upsala, 1863.
Phil 8882.32.5 Hensel, P. Ethisches Wissen und ethisches Handeln. Freiburg, 1889.
Phil 8882.32 Hensel, P. Hauptprobleme der Ethik. 2e aufl. Leipzig, 1913.
Phil 9575.4 Hensel, W.U. Wealth and worth. South Bethlehem, Pa., 1907.
Phil 5817.3 Henslow, G. Mind in man and animals. London, 1853-81. 2 pam.
Phil 8587.11 Henslow, G. Proofs of the truth of spiritualism. London, 1919.
Phil 7069.19.120 Henslow, G. The theory of evolution of living things. London, 1873.
Phil 5627.134 Henslow, George. The proofs of the truths of spiritualism. 2. ed. London, 1919.
Phil 8957.10 Henson, H.H. The Oxford group movement. N.Y., 1933.
Phil 182.18.5 Henson, Herbert H. Christian morality; natural, developing, final. Oxford, 1936.
Phil 182.18.8 Henton, J. The art of thinking. London, 1879.
Phil 8832.1 Henton, J. Philosophy and religion. London, 1881.
Phil 6060.11 Hentsch, Alice Adele. De la littérature didactique du Moyen Age. Photoreproduction. Halle, 1903.
Phil 3195.3.82 Henze, A. Die Chirogrammatonamtie. Leipzig, 1862.
Phil 5850.228.15 Hepner, Adolf. Josef Dietzgens philosophische Lehren. Stuttgart, 1916.
Phil 5047.42 Hepner, Harry W. Psychology applied to life and work. N.Y., 1942.
Phil 8957.8 Hepp, M.H. Thinking things through. N.Y., 1956.
Phil 525.76 Heppe, H. Christliche Sittenlehre. Elberfeld, 1882.
Phil 9347.7 Heppe, Heinrich. Geschichte der quietistischen Mystik in der katholischen Kirche. Berlin, 1875.
Phil 4757.2.32 Hepworth, G. Rocks and shoals. Boston, 1870.
Phil 9560.26 The herald of coming good. (Gurdjieff, Georges Ivanovitch.) Chicago, 1966.
Phil 3489.29 Herault de Séchelles, M.J. Théorie de l'ambition. Paris, 1802.
Phil 70.93 Herausfoderung an Professor Kant in Königsberg. (Heynig, J.G.) Leipzig, 1798.
Phil 1750.380 Die Herausforderung. (Darmtaedter, Gespräch.) München, 1963.
Phil 2045.165 Die Herausforderung des Existenzialismus. (Spoerri, Theophil F.) Hamburg, 1954.
Die Herausforderung des Verfassungsstaates; Hobbes und englische Juristen. (Kriele, Martin.) Neuwied, 1970.
Htn Phil 3246.21* Das Herausgeber die philosophischen Journals. (Fichte, Johann Gottlieb.) Jena, 1799-1815. 4 pam.
Phil 3428.35 Herbart, J.F. Allgemeine Metaphysik. Königsberg, 1828-29. 2v.
Phil 3428.34 Herbart, J.F. Allgemeine Pädagogik. Göttingen, 1806.
Phil 3428.36 Herbart, J.F. Allgemeine practische Philosophie. Göttingen, 1808.
Phil 3428.36.5 Herbart, J.F. Allgemeine praktische Philosophie. 3. Ausg. Hamburg, 1891.
Phil 3428.40 Herbart, J.F. De attentionis. Regiomonti, 1822.
Phil 3428.66 Herbart, J.F. Der principio logico exclusi medii. Gottingae, 1833.
Phil 3428.61 Herbart, J.F. Gespräche über das Böse. Königsberg, 1817.
Phil 3489.33 Herbart, J.F. Haupt-Momente der kritischen Philosophie. Münster, 1883.
Phil 3489.32 Herbart, J.F. Immanuel Kants Gedächtnissfeyer zu Königsberg am 22stem April 1812. Königsberg, 1811.
Phil 3428.31 Herbart, J.F. Introduzione alla filosofia. 2. ed. Bari, 1927.
Phil 3428.15 Herbart, J.F. Kleinere philosophische Schriften und Abhandlungen. Leipzig, 1842-43. 3v.
Phil 3428.37 Herbart, J.F. Kurze Encyklopädie der Philosophie. Halle, 1841.
Phil 3428.30 Herbart, J.F. Lehrbuch zur Einleitung in die Philosophie. Königsberg, 1837.
Phil 3428.30.5 Herbart, J.F. Lehrbuch zur Einleitung in die Philosophie. 2. Aufl. Königsberg, 1821.
Phil 3428.30.55 Herbart, J.F. Lehrbuch zur Einleitung in die philosophie. 4. Aufl. Leipzig, 1912.
Phil 3428.44 Herbart, J.F. Lehrbuch zur Psychologie. Hamburg, 1900.
Phil 3428.43 Herbart, J.F. Lehrbuch zur Psychologie. Königsberg, 1816.
Phil 3428.43.5 Herbart, J.F. Lehrbuch zur Psychologie. 3. Aufl. Leipzig, 1887.
Phil 3428.47 Herbart, J.F. Psychologie als Wissenschaft. Königsberg, 1824. 2v.
Phil 3428.67 Herbart, J.F. Psychologische Untersuchungen. Göttingen, 1839-40.
Phil 3428.10 Herbart, J.F. Sämmtliche Werke. Leipzig, 1850-52. 12v.
Phil 3428.11 Herbart, J.F. Sämmtliche Werke. v.1-19. Langensalza, 1887-1912. 14v.
Phil 3428.45 Herbart, J.F. Text-book in psychology. N.Y., 1891.
Phil 3428.65 Herbart, J.F. Über meiner Streit met der Modephilosophie. Königsberg, 1814.
Phil 3428.63 Herbart, J.F. Über philosophisches Studium. Leipzig, 1873.
Htn Phil 3801.450* Herbart, Johann F. Hauptpuncte der Metaphysik. Göttingen, 1808.
Phil 3428.82 Herbart, Spinoza, Kant. (Thomas, K.) Langensalza, 1875.
Phil 3428.164 Herbart Bibliographie, 1842-1963. (Schmitz, Josef Nikolaus.) Weinheim, 1964.
Phil 3428.86 Herbarts Asthetik. (Ziechner, A.) n.p., n.d.
Phil 3428.162 Herbarts Bedeutung für die Psychologie. (Hintz, R.) Berlin, 1900.
Phil 3428.94 Herbarts' metafyzica, psychologie en ethiek. (Raaf, H. de.) Groningen, 1904.
Phil 3428.87 Herbarts Metaphysik. (Moosherr, T.) Basel, 1898.
Phil 3428.90F Herbarts praktische Philosophie. (Trendelenburg, A.) Berlin, 1856.
Phil 3428.163 Herbarts Stellung zum Eudämonismus. (Regler, Walter.) Leipzig, 1900.
Phil 5374.28 Herbart'sch und Bergmann'sche Problem des Bewusstseins. Inaug. Diss. (Richter, Rudolf.) Greifswald, 1883?
Phil 8587.71 Herberg, Will. Four existentialist theologians. Garden City, N.Y., 1958.

Htn Phil 2040.31* Herbert, E. De causis errorum. London, 1645.
Phil 2040.35.2 Herbert, E. De religione gentilium. Amsterdam, 1700.
Phil 2040.30.15 Herbert, E. De veritate. Bristol, 1937.
Htn Phil 2040.30.3* Herbert, E. De veritate. London, 1633.
Htn Phil 2040.30.2* Herbert, E. De veritate. London, 1633.
Htn Phil 2040.30* Herbert, E. De veritate. Paris, 1624.
Phil 6317.11.9 Herbert, S. The unconscious in life and art. London, 1932.
Phil 6317.11 Herbert, S. The unconscious mind. London, 1923.
Phil 630.2 Herbert, T.M. Realistic assumptions of modern science. London, 1879.
Phil 2040.80 Herbert di Cherbury e la scuola di Cambridge. (Carlini, Armando.) Roma, 1917.
Phil 2150.22.135 Herbert Marcuse: and exposition and a polemic. (MacIntyre, Alasdair C.) N.Y., 1970.
Phil 2150.22.120 Herbert Marcuse ou la Quête d'un univers trans-prométhéen. (Nicolas, André.) Paris, 1969.
Phil 2150.22.115 Herbert Marcuses dritter Weg. (Steigerwald, Robert Reinhold.) Köln, 1969.
Phil 2270.94A Herbert Spencer; an estimate and review. (Royce, Josiah.) N.Y., 1904.
Phil 2270.190 Herbert Spencer; the evolution of a sociologist. (Peel, John David Yeadon.) London, 1971.
Phil 2270.118.10 Herbert Spencer; Zürcher Rathaus-Vortrag gehalten am 6. dezember 1906. (Stadler, August.) Zürich, 1907.
Phil 2270.120 Herbert Spencer. (Elliot, Hugh S.R.) London, 1917.
Phil 2270.85.5 Herbert Spencer. (Gaupp, Otto.) Stuttgart, 1897.
Phil 2270.85.2 Herbert Spencer. (Gaupp, Otto.) Stuttgart, 1900.
Phil 2270.93.16A Herbert Spencer. (Hudson, William Henry.) London, 1916.
Phil 2270.100 Herbert Spencer. (Parisot, E.) Paris, n.d.
Phil 2270.127A Herbert Spencer. (Thomson, J.A.) London, 1906.
Phil 2270.130 Herbert Spencer. (Thouverez, Émile.) Paris, 1913.
Phil 2270.118.2 Herbert Spencer. Spencers Ethik. (Stadler, August.) Leipzig, 1913.
Phil 2270.118 Herbert Spencer. Spencers Ethik. (Stadler, August.) Leipzig, 1913.
Phil 2270.151 Herbert Spencer betrayed. (Tillet, A.W.) London, 1939.
Phil 2270.95 The Herbert Spencer lecture. (Harrison, F.) Oxford, 1905.
Phil 2270.135 Herbert Spencer och utvecklingsfilosofien. (Bager-Sjögren, J.) Lund, 1893.
Phil 2270.87 Herbert Spencer on American nervousness. (Beard, G.M.) N.Y., 1883.
Phil 2270.86 Herbert Spencer on the Americans and the Americans on Spencer. N.Y., 1883.
Phil 2270.97 Herbert Spencer y sus doctrinas sociológicas. (Quesada, E.) Buenos Aires, 1907.
Phil 2270.165 Herbert Spencers Einführung in die Soziologie. (Wiese, Leopold von.) Köln, 1960.
Phil 2270.98 Herbert Spencer's Grundlagen der Philosophie. (Häberlin, P.) Leipzig, 1908.
Phil 2270.125 Herbert Spencer's Lehre von dem Unerkennbaren. (Grosse, Ernst.) Leipzig, 1890.
Phil 2270.133 Herbert Spencer's Prinzipien der Ethik. (Jaeger, Max.) Hamburg, 1922.
Phil 2270.139 Herbert Spencer's sociology. (Rumney, J.) London, 1934.
Phil 2270.89 Herbert Spencer's System der Philosophie. (Michelet, C.L.) Halle, 1882.
Phil 5374.16 Herbertz, R. Bewusstsein und Unbewusstes. Köln, n.d.
Phil 672.130 Herbertz, R. Die Philosophie des Raumes. Stuttgart, 1912.
Phil 75.19 Herbertz, R. Die philosophische Literatur. Stuttgart, 1912.
Phil 1135.115 Herbertz, R. Das Wahreitsproblem in der griechischen Philosophie. Berlin, 1913.
Phil 182.50 Herbertz, Richard. Philosophie und Einzelwissenschaften. Bern, 1913.
Phil 182.50.5 Herbertz, Richard. Das philosophische Urerlebnis. Bern, 1921.
Phil 5047.20 Herbertz, Richard. Prolegomena zu einer realistischen Logik. Halle, 1916.
Phil 4769.1.89 Herbigny, Michel d'. Un Neuman Russe: Vladimir Soloviev (1853-1900). 2. ed. Paris, 1911.
Phil 7069.19.130 Herbine, Charlotte G. The meeting of the spheres. N.Y., 1919.
Phil 5066.282 Herbrand, Jacques. Écrits logiques. Paris, 1968.
Phil 8612.15 Herder, Novalis und Kleist. (Unger, Rudolf.) Frankfurt, 1922.
Phil 3499.13 Herder Gegen Kant. (Rätze, J.G.) Leipzig, 1800.
Phil 3805.99 Herder und Schleiermachers Reden. (Goebel, Louis.) Gotha, 1904.
Phil 3552.365 Herders Auseinadersetzung mit der Philosophie Leibnitzens. Diss. (Blumenthal, Erwin.) Hamburg, 1934.
Phil 3450.27.80 Herders humaniteitsphilosophie. (Smits, Everard J.F.) Assen, 1939.
Phil 8640.13 The hereafter in Jewish and Christian thought. (Pilcher, C.V.) London, 1940.
Phil 5425.2A Hereditary genius. (Galton, F.) London, 1869.
Phil 5425.2.6 Hereditary genius. (Galton, F.) London, 1925.
Phil 5425.2.5 Hereditary genius. (Galton, F.) N.Y., 1891.
Phil 5425.2.2 Hereditary genius. 2. ed. (Galton, F.) London, 1892.
Phil 5440.8 Hereditary traits. (Proctor, R.A.) N.Y., 1882.
Phil 5440.5 L'hérédité. (Sanson, A.) Paris, 1893.
Phil 6953.11 L'hérédité dans les maladies du système nerveux. (Dejerine, J.) Paris, 1886.
Phil 5440.12 L'hérédité et les stigmates de dégénérescence. (Galippe, V.) Paris, 1905.
Phil 5440.4.9 L'hérédité psychologique. 2. éd. (Ribot, T.) Paris, 1882.
Phil 5440.4.2 Heredity. (Ribot, T.) N.Y., 1891.
Phil 5440.6 Heredity. (Thompson, E. Rowell.) Boston, 1882.
Phil 5440.1 Heredity and Christian problems. (Bradford, A.H.) N.Y., 1895.
Phil 5440.32.5 Heredity and environment. (Schwesinger, G.) N.Y., 1933.
Phil 5440.33 Heredity in mental traits. 1. ed. (Sen Gupta, N.) London, 1941.
Phil 575.71 L'hérédo; essai sur le drame intérieur. (Daudet, Léon A.) Paris, 1916.
Phil 5421.25.40 The heresy of self-love. (Zweig, Paul.) N.Y., 1968.
Phil 5643.11 Hering, E. Beiträge zur Physiologie. v.1-5. Leipzig, 1861-
Phil 5643.11.9 Hering, E. Grundzüge zur Lehre vom Lichtsinne. Leipzig, 1920.
Phil 5643.11.10 Hering, E. Outline of a theory of the light sense. Cambridge, 1964.
Phil 5643.11.5 Hering, E. Zur Lehre vom Lichtsinne. Wien, 1878.
Phil 5247.26 Hering, Ewald. Die Deutungen des psychophysischen Gesetzes. Tübingen, 1909.
Phil 5545.37.5 Hering, Ewald. On memory and specific energies of the nervous system. 2. ed. Chicago, 1897.

Phil 5545.37.10 Hering, Ewald. On memory and the specific energies of the nervous system. 4. ed. Chicago, 1905.
Phil 5545.37 Hering, Ewald. Über das Gedächtnis. Leipzig, 1905.
Phil 6117.23 Hering, Ewald. Zur Theorie der Nerventhätigkeit. Leipzig, 1899.
Phil 8587.42 Hering, Jean. Phénoméologie et philosophie religieuse. Thèse. Strasbourg, 1925.
Phil 8592.64 Heritage and destiny. (Mackay, J.A.) N.Y., 1943.
Phil 6328.60 L'héritage de Freud. (Saada, Denise.) Paris, 1966.
Phil 705.39 L'héritage Kantien et la révolution copernicienne. (Vuillemin, Jules.) Paris, 1954.
Phil 3504.43 The heritage of Kant. (Whitney, G.T.) Princeton, 1939.
Phil 182.118 Herk, Konrad. Das leuchten des dunckels. Antwerpen, 1960.
Phil 6017.3 Herland, Leo. Gesicht und Charakter. 2. Aufl. Zürich, 1956.
Htn Phil 8882.7.25* Herle, Charles. Wisdomes tripos. London, 1655.
Htn Phil 8882.8* Herle, Charles. Wisdom's tripos. London, 1670.
Phil 5238.190 Herlrich, E. Der Mens als Persönlichkeit und Problem. München, 1963.
Phil 585.408 Hermach, Yiří. Uskutěcnění současného ǒovǒka. 1. vyd. Praha, 1969.
Phil 525.30.2 Herman, E. The meaning and value of mysticism. 2nd ed. London, 1916.
Phil 3790.1.95 Herman S. Reimarus als Metaphysiker. Inaug. Diss. (Engert, Joseph.) Paderborn, 1908.
Phil 3790.1.100 Herman S. Reimarus und seine Schitzschrift für die vernünftigen Verehrer Gottes. (Strauss, D.F.) Leipzig, 1862.
Phil 3850.14.30 Herman Schell als existentieller Denker und Theologie. 1. Aufl. (Hasenfuss, Josef.) Würzburg, 1951.
Phil 5643.8.30 Herman von Helmholtz und der Akkommodationstheorie. (Tscherning, M.) Leipzig, 1910.
Phil 182.46 Hermance, W.E. Unorthodox conception of being. N.Y., 1912.
Phil 8050.46 Hermann, C. Die Ästhetik in ihrer Geschichte und als wissenschaftliches System. Leipzig, 1876.
Phil 1750.10 Hermann, C. Der Gegensatz...der neueren Philosophie. Leipzig, 1877.
Phil 807.14 Hermann, C. Geschichte der Philosophie. Leipzig, 1867.
Phil 8408.31 Hermann, C. Grundriss einer allgemeinen Asthetik. Leipzig, 1857.
Phil 3195.11.90 Hermann, C. Max Dessoir Mensch und Werk. Stuttgart, 1929.
Phil 3425.268 Hermann, Conrad. Hegel und die logische Frage der Philosophie in der Gegenwart. Leipzig, 1878.
Phil 182.73 Hermann, E. Grundriss der Philosophie. Lahr, 1906.
Phil 338.23 Hermann, G. Die Bedeutung der modernen Physik für die Theorie der Erkenntnis. Leipzig, 1937.
Phil 3489.40 Hermann, Horst. Das Problem der objektiven Realität bei Kant. Mainz, 1961.
Phil 6317.27 Hermann, Imre. Psychoanalyse und Logik. Leipzig, 1924.
Phil 3489.48 Hermann, István. Kant teleológiája. Budapest, 1968.
Phil 6315.2.85 Hermann, István. Sigmund Freud. Budapest, 1964.
Phil 575.51.40 Hermann, Oskar. Dr. Klages, Entwurf einer Charakterkunde. Leipzig, 1920.
Phil 8080.20 Hermann, Rolf-Dieter. Künstler und Interpret; zur Modernen Asthetik. Bern, 1967.
Phil 3160.3.81 Hermann Cohen. (Fritzsche, R.A.) Berlin, 1922.
Phil 3160.3.100 Hermann Cohen. (Goldstein, Walter.) Jerusalem, 1963.
Phil 3160.3.83 Hermann Cohen. (Kinkel, N.) Stuttgart, 1924.
Phil 3160.3.82 Hermann Cohen. (Natorp, Paul.) Marburg, 1918.
Phil 3160.3.95 Hermann Cohen und Martin Buber. (Levin-Goldschmidt, Hermann.) Genève, 1946.
Phil 3160.3.98 Hermann Cohen's philosophy of Judaism. (Melher, Jehuda.) N.Y., 1968.
Phil 3565.80 Hermann Lotze. (Caspari, O.) Breslau, 1883.
Phil 3565.113 Hermann Lotze. (Falckenberg, R.) Stuttgart, 1901.
Phil 3565.89 Hermann Lotze. (Wentscher, M.) Heidelberg, 1913.
Phil 3565.80.5 Hermann Lotze. 2. Aufl. (Caspari, O.) Breslau, 1895.
Phil 3565.115 Hermann Lotze über das Unbewusste. (Otto, Clemens.) Labes, 1900.
Phil 3565.130 Hermann Lotzes Bedeutung für das Problem der Beziehung. (An, Ho-Sang.) Bonn, 1967.
Phil 3565.111 Hermann Lotzes tankar om tid och timlighet i kritisk belysning. (Geijer, Reinhold.) Lund, 1886.
Phil 3565.112 Hermann Lotzes uppfattning af människans valfrihet. (Elgström, Albin.) Lund, 1892.
Phil 3790.1.97 Hermann S. Reimarus als Metaphysiker. Inaug. Diss. (Büttner, Wilhelm.) Paderborn, 1909.
Phil 8957.7 Hermanns, W. Uber den Begriffs der Mässigung. Inaug. Diss. Aachen, 1918.
Phil 8587.67 Hermans, F. Histoire doctrinale de l'humanisme chrétien. Tournai, 1948. 4v.
Phil 8581.110 Hermans, Francis. L'humanisme religieux de l'abbé Henri Bremond, 1865-1933. Paris, 1965.
Phil 3925.16.175.2 Hermans, Willem Frederich. Wittgenstein in de mode en karze mier niet. 2. druk. Amsterdam, 1967.
Phil 8957.22 Hermanson, Robert Fredrik. Oikeus ja uskonnolliset totuudet. Porvoossa, 1921.
Phil 4582.6.40 Hermansson, J. Dissertatio philosophica. Upsaliae, 1736.
Phil 4582.6.30 Hermansson, J. Quaestio philosophica an philosophus passit errare? Upsaliae, 1728.
Phil 4582.6.35 Hermansson, J. Speciminis academici. Upsaliae, 1733.
Phil 5047.16 Hermant, Paul. Les principales théories de la logique contemporaine. Paris, 1909.
Phil 8413.12 Hermara, a study in compatative aesthetics. (McAlpen, Colin.) London, 1915.
Phil 1870.128 Hermathena. Homage to George Berkeley. Dublin, 1953.
Phil 210.5 Hermeneutics; interpretation theory in Schlelermacher, Dilthey, Heidegger, and Gadamer. (Palmer, Richard E.) Evanston, 1969.
Phil 210.78 Hermeneutik als Weg heutiger Wissenschaft. Salzburg, 1971.
Phil 210.68 Hermeneutik und Dialektik. Aufsätze. Hans-Georg Gadamer zum 70. Geburtstag. Tübingen, 1970. 2v.
Phil 210.50 Herméneutique. (Esbroeck, Michel van.) Paris, 1968.
Phil 8440.5 Hermeren, Göran. Representation and meaning in the visual arts. Lund, 1969.
Phil 5066.5 Hermes, H. Semiotik; eine Theorie der Zeichengestalten als Grundlage für Untersuchungen von formalisierten Sprachen. Leipzig, 1938.
Phil 5066.247 Hermes, Hans. Einführung in die Mathematische Logik: klassische Prädikatenlogik. Stuttgart, 1963.
Phil 17.9 L'Hermes. Paris. 1-4,1826-1829 2v.
Htn Phil 4938.1.30* Hermes Trismegistus. The divine Pymander. London, 1650.
Phil 187.32.90 The hermit philosopher of Liendo. (Stephens, I.K.) Dallas, 1951.
Phil 4352.1.99 Hermkes, Maria. Die Fundamental-Philosophie des Jaime Balmes. Inaug. Diss. Krefeld, 1919.

Phil 3415.81   Hernan, C.F. Edward von Hartmann's Religion der Zukunft. Leipzig, 1875.

Phil 4979.5.85   Hernández Luna, Juan. Dos ideas sobre la filosofía en la Nueva España. México, 1959.

Phil 4979.5.80   Hernández Luna, Juan. Samuel Ramos. México, 1956.

Phil 6317.48   Hernfeld, Fred Farau. La psychologie des profondeurs, des origines à nos jours. Paris, 1960.

Phil 5238.204   Hernnstein, Richard J. A source book in history of psychology. Cambridge, 1965.

Phil 2880.4.80   Hérnon, Camille. La philosophie de M. Sully Prudhomme. Paris, 1907.

Phil 194.16.10   The Herodian me. (Thayer, H.D.) Atlantic City, 1930.

Phil 7069.35.15   Herodius (pseud.). Show me the way; spirit counsels for right living. Boston, 1935.

Phil 803.17   Heroes and heretics. 1st ed. (Dunham, B.) N.Y., 1964.

Phil 4065.60   The heroic enthusiasts. pt.1-2. (Bruno, Giordano.) London, 1887-1889. 2v.

Phil 9350.3.15   Heroines in obscurity. (Keddie, H.) London, 1871.

Phil 4065.75   Heroische Leidenschaften und individuelles Leben. (Bruno, Giordano.) Hamburg, 1957.

Phil 9560.28   Heron, Grace. What word will you choose? Chicago, 1932.

Phil 6048.85.1   Heron-Allen, Edward. A manual of cheirosophy. 10th ed. London, 1885.

Phil 1123.13   Le heros, le sage et l'événement dans l'humanisme grec. (Schaerer, René.) Paris, 1964.

Phil 182.61   Herpe, Hans. Einleitung in die Kategorienlehre. Leipzig, 1921.

Phil 182.61.10   Herpe, Hans. Idee und Existenz. Hamburg, 1935.

Htn   Phil 9390.1*   Herport, B. Essay on truths of importance. London, 1768.

Htn   Phil 9390.1.2*   Herport, B. Essay on truths of importance. London, 1768.

Phil 3552.484   Herr und Knecht bei Leibniz und Hegel. (Halz, Hans Heinz.) Berlin, 1968.

Phil 2880.8.230   Herra, Rafael Angel. Sartre y los prolegómenos a la antropología. Ciudad Universitaria, 1968.

Phil 5247.13.29   Herrero Pouas, Antolin. Juan Huarte de San Juan. Madrid, 1941.

Phil 5817.15.3   Herrick, C. Judson. Brains of rats and men. Chicago, 1930.

Phil 5325.28   Herrick, C.J. Awareness. Philadelphia, 1939.

Phil 5247.65   Herrick, C.J. The evolution of human nature. Austin, 1956.

Phil 5757.14.2   Herrick, C.J. Fatalism or freedom. N.Y., 1926.

Phil 6117.20   Herrick, C.J. An introduction to neurology. Philadelphia, 1916.

Phil 6117.43   Herrick, C.J. Introduction to neurology. Philadelphia, 1918.

Phil 6117.20.5   Herrick, C.J. An introduction to neurology. 3. ed. Philadelphia, 1924.

Phil 6117.20.10   Herrick, C.J. An introduction to neurology. 5th ed. Philadelphia, 1934.

Phil 5247.45.2   Herrick, C.J. The thinking machine. 2. ed. Chicago, 1929.

Phil 3808.143   Herrig, Hans. Gesammelte Aufsätze über Schopenhauer. Leipzig, 1894.

Phil 182.90   Herrigel, E. Die metaphysische Form. Tübingen, 1929.

Phil 5520.646   Herriot, Peter. An introduction to the psychology of language. London, 1970.

Phil 4582.1.30   Herrlin, Axel. Filosofi och facksetenskap. Lund, 1905.

Phil 5545.159   Herrlin, Axel. Minuet. Stockholm, 1917.

Phil 6317.12   Herrlin, Axel. Själslifvets underjordiska verld. Malmo, 1901.

Phil 5425.31   Herrlin, Axel. Snille och sjalssjukdom. Lund, 1903.

Phil 3484.9   Herrmann, C.G. Kant und Hemsterhuis in Rüksicht ihrer definitionen der Schönheit. Erfurt, 1791.

Phil 3270.18.1   Herrmann, Friedrich Wilhelm von. Bibliographie Eugen Fink. Den Haag, 1970.

Phil 3450.11.500   Herrmann, Friedrich-Wilhelm von. Husserl und die Meditationen des Descartes. Frankfurt, 1971.

Phil 3245.84   Herrmann, H.A. Die Philosophie Immanuel Hermann Fichtes. Berlin, 1928.

Phil 3850.18.88   Herrmann, J. Die Prinzipien der formalen Gesetzes Ethik Kants und der materialen Wertethik Schelers. Diss. Breslau, 1928.

Phil 3489.23   Herrmann, Karl. Einführung in die neukantische Philosophie. Halle, 1927.

Phil 3552.385   Herrmann, Karl. Das Staatsdenken bei Leibniz. Bonn, 1958.

Phil 8587.13.90   Herrmann, R. Christentum und Geschichte bei W. Herrmann. Leipzig, 1914.

Phil 5590.534   Herrmann, T. Lehrbuch der empirischen Persönlichkeitsforschung. Göttingen, 1969.

Phil 3195.6.01   Herrmann, Ulrich. Bibliographie Wilhelm Dilthey. Berlin, 1969.

Phil 3195.6.210   Herrmann, Ulrich. Die Pädagogik Wilhelm Diltheys. Göttingen, 1971.

Phil 8882.41   Herrmann, W. Ethik. Tübingen, 1901.

Phil 8882.41.5   Herrmann, W. Ethik. 5e Aufl. Tübingen, 1921.

Phil 8587.13   Herrmann, W. Die Religion. Halle, 1879.

Phil 5867.40   Herron, R.E. Child's play. N.Y., 1971.

Phil 1750.31   Die Herrschaft der Vernunft. (Hazard, P.) Hamburg, 1949.

Phil 3017.9   Die Herrschaft der Zahl. (Reichmann, Eberhard.) Stuttgart, 1968.

Phil 181.56   Herrschen und Leiben als Grundmotive der philosophische Weltanschauungen. (Grünbaum, A.A.) Bonn, 1925.

Phil 182.104   Hersch, J. L'illusion philosophique. Paris, 1936.

Phil 182.104.2   Hersch, J. L'illusion philosophique. Paris, 1964.

Phil 9347.3   Hersey, H.E. To girls. A budget of letters. Boston, 1901.

Phil 575.101   Hertel, François. Pour un ordre personnaliste. Montréal, 1942.

Phil 1504.14.5   Hertling, G. von. Albertus Magnus, Beiträge zu seiner Würdigung. 2. Aufl. v.14, pt.5-6. Münster, 1914.

Phil 2115.94   Hertling, G. von. John Locke und die Schule von Cambridge. Freiburg, 1892. 2v.

Phil 1707.7   Hertling, G.F. von. Historische Beiträge zur Philosophie. München, 1914.

Phil 7150.10   Hertog, Mattheus M. De zedelijke waardeering den zelfmoord. 's Gravenhage, 1913.

Phil 3808.88   Hertslet, M.L. Schopenhauers-Register. Leipzig, 1890.

Phil 5247.41   Hertz, Paul. Über das Denken...Auschauung. Berlin, 1923.

Phil 3120.50.30   Hertz-Eichenrode, Dieter. Der jünghegelianer Bruno Bauer im Vormärz. Berlin, 1959.

Phil 5876.10.5   Hertzman-Ericson, Merit. Svåra unga år. Stockholm, 1967.

Phil 8587.43   Hervey, Jacob. Ausserlesene Briefe über verschiedne Gegenstände aus der Sittenlehre und Religion. Hamburg, 1762.

Htn   Phil 6669.4*   Hervier, C. Lettre sur la découverte du magnetisme. Pekin, 1784.

Phil 6315.2.460   Herwig, Hedda Juliane. Therapie der Menscheit. München, 1969.

Phil 6117.27   Herz, H. Energie und seelische Rechtkräfte. Leipzig, 1909.

Phil 3805.178   Herz, Henriette de Lemos. Schleiermacher und seine Lieben. Magdeburg, 1910.

Phil 182.97   Herz, M. Betrachtungen aus der Spekulativen Weltweisheit. Königsberg, 1771.

Phil 6957.16   Herz, M. Versuch über den Schwindel. Berlin, 1786.

Phil 8408.34   Herz, Marcus. Versuch über den Geschmach und die ursachen seiner Verschiednheit. Leipzig, 1776.

Phil 182.79.5   Herzberg, Alex. The psychology of philosophers. London, 1929.

Phil 182.79A   Herzberg, Alex. Zur Psychologie der Philosophie und der Philosophen. Leipzig, 1926.

Phil 6980.351.5   Herzberg, Alexander. Active psychotherapy. N.Y., 1946.

Phil 1707.26   Herzberg, G. Der Zeitgeist. Meisenheim, 1960.

Phil 1750.41   Herzberg, Günther. Die grosse Kontroverse. Meisenheim, 1953.

Phil 510.143   Herzberg, L. Die philosophischen Hauptströmungen im Monistenbund. Inaug. Diss. Leipzig, 1928.

Phil 6117.1.5   Herzen, A. Les conditions physiques de la conscience. Genève, 1886.

Phil 6117.1   Herzen, A. Grundlinien einer allgemeinen Psychophysiologie. Leipzig, 1889.

Phil 3850.18.95   Herzfeld, Hans. Begriff und Theorie vom Geist bei Max Scheler. Diss. Leipzig, 1930.

Phil 8408.32   Herzog, J.A. Was ist Asthetisch? Leipzig, 1900.

Phil 3850.22.95   Herzog, Reinhart. Die Bewahrung der Vernunft. Inaug. Diss. München, 1953.

Phil 585.182   Heschel, Abraham Joshua. Who is man? Stanford, Calif., 1965.

Phil 3450.34   Heske, Franz. Organik. Berlin, 1954.

Phil 6315.2.82   Hesmard, Angelo. La psychanalyse; theorie sexuelle de Freud. Paris, 1924.

Phil 5722.11   Hesnard, A. L'inconscient. Paris, 1923.

Phil 5374.41   Hesnard, A. La relativité de la conscience de soi. Paris, 1924.

Phil 6315.2.82.15   Hesnard, Angelo. De Freud à Lacan. Paris, 1970.

Phil 6315.2.82.10   Hesnard, Angelo. Freud dans la société d'après guerre. Genève, 1946.

Phil 8882.69   Hesnard, Angelo. Morale sans péché. Paris, 1954.

Phil 6315.2.455   Hesnard, Angelo. L'oeuvre de Freud et son importance pour le monde moderne. Paris, 1960.

Phil 2515.5.91   Hess, G. Alain (Emile Chartier) in der Reihe der französischen Moralisten. Berlin, 1932.

Phil 2515.5.90   Hess, G. Alain (Emile Chartier) in der Reihe der französischen Moralisten. Inaug.-Diss. Berlin, 1931.

Phil 3640.695   Hess, K. Von Nietzsche zu Pannwitz. Lagnau, 1963.

Phil 1504.19.2   Hessen, J. Die Begründung der Erkenntnis. v.19, pt.2-3. Münster, 1916.

Phil 8882.71   Hessen, J. Ethik. Leiden, 1954.

Phil 1750.177   Hessen, J. Existenzphilosophie. Essen, 1947.

Phil 3415.105   Hessen, J. Die Kategorienlehre Eduard von Hartmanns. Leipzig, 1924.

Phil 3850.18.130   Hessen, J. Max Scheler. Essen, 1948.

Phil 8520.21.2   Hessen, J. Die Religionsphilosophie des Neukantianismus. 2. Aufl. Freiburg, 1924.

Phil 3007.9   Hessen, Johannes. Die Ewigkeitswerte der deutschen Philosophie. Hamburg, 1943.

Phil 1750.177.1   Hessen, Johannes. Existenzphilosophie. Basel, 1948.

Phil 1707.6.5   Hessen, Johannes. Die Geistesstromungen der Gegenwart. Freiburg, 1937.

Phil 3450.36   Hessen, Johannes. Griechische oder biblische Theologie. München, 1962.

Phil 3450.30.5   Hessen, Johannes. Gustige Kämpf der Zeit im Spiegel und Lebens. Nürnberg, 1959.

Phil 3450.30   Hessen, Johannes. Im Ringen um eine zeitnahe Philosophie. Nürnberg, 1959.

Phil 3450.30.10   Hessen, Johannes. Lehrbuch der Philosophie. München, 1947-50. 3v.

Phil 1740.6   Hessen, Johannes. Lehrbuch der Philosophie. 2e Aufl. v.3. München, 1950-

Phil 1707.6   Hessen, Johannes. Die Philosophie des 20. Jahrhunderts. Rottenburg, 1951.

Phil 8587.65.3   Hessen, Johannes. Die philosophischen Stromungen der Gegenwart. München, 1923.

Phil 8587.65   Hessen, Johannes. Platonismus und Prophetismus. 2. Aufl. München, 1955.

Phil 8587.65.5   Hessen, Johannes. Religionsphilosophie. v.1-2. Essen, 1948.

Phil 182.146   Hessen, Johannes. Religionsphilosophie. 2. Aufl. v.1-2. München, 1955.

Phil 1512.7   Hessen, John. Von der Aufgabe der Philosophie und dem Wesen des Philosophen; zwei Vorlesungen. Heidelberg, 1947.

Phil 482.3   Hessen, John. Patristische und scholastische Philosophie. Breslau, 1922.

Phil 270.34   Hessen, Robert. Die Philosophie der Kraft. Stuttgart, 1913.

Phil 3450.24.10   Hessen, S. Individuelle Kausalität. Berlin, 1909.

Phil 3450.24   Hessing, Jacob. Logica als leer van zuivere rede. Deel. 1. Bussum, 1941.

Phil 3827.8.5   Hessing, Jacob. Das Selbsthewusstwerden des Geistes. Stuttgart, 1936.

Phil 3827.8   Hessing, Siegfried. Spinoza dreihundert Jahre Ewigkeit. Den Haag, 1962.

Phil 6060.12.55   Hessing, Siegfried ed. Spinoza-Festschrift. Heidelberg, 1933.

Phil 3549.8.45   Hestia, 1960-61...Ludwig Klages. (Schuerer, Wilhelm.) Bonn, 1960.

Phil 4472.89.30   Hestia. Bonn. 1963+

Phil 5590.574   Heterodoxia. (Lourencao, Eduardo.) Coimbra, 1967. 2v.

Phil 7069.52   The heterosexuals are coming; the fusion strategy. (Gilligan, Sonja Carl.) N.Y., 1971.

Phil 7069.40.4   Hettinger, John. Telepathy and spiritualism. N.Y., 1952.

Phil 5870.25   Hettinger, John. The ultra-perceptive faculty. London, 1940.

Phil 1540.14   Hetzer, Hildegard. Zur Psychologie des Kindes. Darmstadt, 1967.

Phil 270.27   Heuel, Meinolf. Die Lehre vom Human Naturale bei Thomas Aquin, Bonaventura und Duns Scotus. Inaug. Diss. Koblenz, 1927.

Phil 5757.13   Heuer, W. Warum Fragen die menschen Warum? Heidelberg, 1921.

Phil 7074.5   Heuer, Wilhelm. Kausalität und Willensfreiheit. Heidelberg, 1924.

Phil 900.4   L'heure des révélations; le livre des temps. (Laval.) Montpellier, 1969.

Heurnius, O. Barbaricae philosophiae. Lugdunum Batavorum, 1600.

Phil 182.15 Heusde, P.W. Die Socratic Schule. v.1-2. Erlangen, 1838.
Phil 3450.13.32 Heusde, P.W. De Socratische school of Wijsgeerte. Utrecht, 1834. 2v.
Phil 3450.16.10 Heusel, Paul. Kleine Schriften und Vorhäge. Tübingen, 1930.
Phil 978.118 Heuser, Annie. Bewisstseinsfragen des Erziehers. Dornach, 1966.
Phil 4070.8.80 Heuser, H. Ludwig Buzorinis. München, 1961.
Phil 3246.218 Heusinger, J.H.G. Über das idealistisch-atheistische System des Professor Fichte in Jena. Dresden, 1799.
Phil 1850.112 Heussler, Hans. Francis Bacon. Breslau, 1889.
Phil 3801.451 Heussler, Hans. Schellings Entwicklungslehre dargestellt. Frankfurt, 1882.
Phil 179.3.106 Heussner, A. Einführung in Rudolf Euckens Lebens- und Weltanschauung. Göttingen, 1921.
Phil 3915.160 Heussner, A. Einführung in Wilhelm Wundt's Philosophie und Psychologie. Göttingen, 1920.
Phil 3489.25 Heussner, A. Hilfs-Büchlein für Kant-Leser. v.1-2. Göttingen, 1921-22.
Phil 3489.25.3 Heussner, A. Kleines Kant-Wörterbuch. Göttingen, 1925.
Phil 3007.3 Heussner, Alfred. Die philosophischen Weltanschauungen. 5. Aufl. Göttingen, 1919.
Phil 281.8 Das heutige Weltbild. (Adler, Arthur.) Brieg, 1922.
Phil 7069.26.60 Heuzé, P. Fakirs, fumistes et Cie. Paris, 1926.
Phil 7069.26.50 Heuzé P. Où en est la métapsychique. Paris, 1926.
Phil 1707.12 Hevigel, H. Das neue Denken. Berlin, 1928.
Phil 9347.15 Hewett, M.E.G. High school lectures. London, 1889.
Phil 7054.79 Hewitt, S.C. Messages from the superior state. Boston, 1853.
Phil 9230.3 Hey, R. A dissertation...gaming. Cambridge, 1784-85. 3 pam.
Phil 9230.3.7 Hey, R. Three dissertations on...gaming. Cambridge, 1812.
Phil 7069.44 Heyday of a wizard. 1. ed. (Burton, Jean.) N.Y., 1944.
Phil 7052.20 The heyday of spiritualism. (Brown, Slater.) N.Y., 1970.
Phil 510.25 Heyde, Erich. Grundlegung der Wertlehre. Leipzig, 1916.
Phil 182.120 Heyde, Johannes. Wege zur Klarheit. Berlin, 1960.
Phil 400.60 Heyde, Johannes E. Realismus oder Idealismus. Leipzig, 1924.
Phil 735.84 Heyde, Johannes E. Wert. Erfurt, 1926.
Phil 600.54 Heyde, Johannes Erich. Entwertung der Kausalität. Zürich, 1957.
Phil 3489.4 Heydenreich, C.H. Originalität über die kritische Philosophie. Leipzig, 1793.
Phil 182.96 Heydenreich, K.H. Encyclopädische Einleitung in das Studium der Philosophie. Leipzig, 1703.
Phil 9167.6 Heydenreich, K.H. Vesta; kleine Schriften zur Philosophie des Lebens. v.1-5. Leizpig, 1798-1803. 4v.
Phil 8587.14 Heydenreichs, K.H. Betrachtungen über die Religion. v.1-2. Leipzig, 1904.
Phil 8587.14.3 Heydenreichs, K.H. Beträchtungen über die Philosophie. Leipzig, 1790-91. 2 pam.
Phil 8587.14.10 Heydenreichs, K.H. Grundsätze der moralischen Gotteslehre. Leipzig, 1792.
Phil 338.15 Heyder, Carl. Die Lehre von den Ideen. Frankfurt am Main, 1874.
Phil 8662.18 Heydon, J.K. The God of reason. N.Y., 1942.
Phil 3120.11.85 Heydorn, H.J. Julius Bahnsen. Göttingen, 1952.
Phil 6317.21.104 Heyer, Gustav R. Der Organism der Seele. 4. Aufl. München, 1959.
Phil 6317.21.5 Heyer, Gustav R. The organism of the mind. N.Y., 1934.
Phil 8408.4 Heyl, Bernard. New bearings in esthetics and art criticism. New Haven, 1957.
Phil 8620.24.5 Heyl, Paul R. The mystery of evil. Chicago, 1920.
Phil 182.37 Heymans, G. Einführung in die Metaphysik. Leipzig, 1905.
Phil 182.37.2 Heymans, G. Einführung in die Metaphysik. 2. Aufl. Leipzig, 1911.
Phil 5247.22.20 Heymans, G. Einführung in die spezielle Psychologie. Leipzig, 1932.
Phil 182.37.10 Heymans, G. Gesammelte kleinere Schriften. Den Haag, 1927. 3v.
Phil 338.6.2 Heymans, G. Gesetze und Elemente des wissenschaftlichen Denkens. Leipzig, 1894.
Phil 338.6 Heymans, G. Gesetze und Elemente des wissenschaftlichen Denkens. Leipzig, 1905.
Phil 338.6.3 Heymans, G. Die Gesetze und Elemente des wissenschaftlichen Denkens. v.1-2. Leiden, 1890-94.
Phil 5247.22 Heymans, G. Das Künftige Jahrhundert der Psychologie. Leipzig, 1911.
Phil 5247.22.5 Heymans, G. Quantitative Untersuchungen über der öptische Paradoxon. n.p., 1896-1913. 13 pam.
Phil 8882.34 Heymans, Gerardus. Einführung in die Ethik auf Grundlage der Erfahrung. Leipzig, 1914.
Phil 3415.96 Heymons, C. Eduard von Hartmann. Berlin, 1882.
Phil 3489.29.10 Heynig, J.G. Berichtigung der Urtheile des Publikums über Kant und seine Philosophie. Cölln, 1797.
Phil 3489.29 Heynig, J.G. Herausfoderung an Professor Kant in Königsberg. Leipzig, 1798.
Phil 338.25 Heynig, J.G. Plato und Aristoteles. Amberg, 1804.
Phil 5655.3F Heyninx, Albert. Essai d'olfactique physiologique. Bruxelles, 1919.
Phil 3489.21 Heyse, Hans. Der Begriff der Ganzheit und die Kantische Philosophie. München, 1927.
Phil 9560.68 Heyst, Jacques. Hypothèse de la vérité. Versailles, 1960.
Phil 7069.64.5 Heywood, R. ESP: a personal memoir. 1. ed. N.Y., 1964.
Phil 7069.59.5 Heywood, Rosalind. The sixth sense. London, 1959.
Phil 182.28.5 Hibben, J.G. A defence of prejudice. N.Y., 1911.
Phil 3425.105A Hibben, J.G. Hegel's logic. N.Y., 1902.
Phil 5047.8 Hibben, J.G. Inductive logic. N.Y., 1896.
Phil 5047.8.8 Hibben, J.G. Logic, deductive and inductive. N.Y., 1910[1905].
Phil 3425.105.15 Hibben, J.G. La logica di Hegel. Torino, 1910.
Phil 1707.2A Hibben, J.G. Philosophy of the enlightenment. N.Y., 1910.
Phil 182.28 Hibben, J.G. The problems of philosophy. N.Y., 1898.
Phil 182.28.2 Hibben, J.G. The problems of philosophy. N.Y., 1899.
Phil 182.28.3 Hibben, J.G. The problems of philosophy. N.Y., 1908.
Phil 7060.17 Hibbert, S. Sketches of the philosophy of apparitions. Edinburgh, 1824.
Phil 7060.17.2 Hibbert, S. Sketches of the philosophy of apparitions. London, 1825.
Phil 17.1 The Hibbert journal. London. 1,1902+ 73v.
X Cg Phil 17.1 The Hibbert journal. London. 8
Phil 8832.4A Hibino, Yutaka. Nippon shindo ron; or, The national ideals of the Japanese people. Cambridge, Eng., 1928.
Phil 5627.264.10 Hick, John. Faith and the philosophers. N.Y., 1964.
Phil 5247.9.4 Hickok, L.P. Empirical psychology. Boston, 1882.
Phil 5247.9.7 Hickok, L.P. Empirical psychology. N.Y., 1854.
Phil 5247.9 Hickok, L.P. Rational psychology. Auburn, 1849.
Phil 5247.9.5 Hickok, L.P. Rational psychology. N.Y., 1876.

Phil 8882.9.5 Hickok, L.P. A system of moral science. Boston, 1880.
Phil 8882.9 Hickok, L.P. A system of moral science. Schenectady, 1853.
Phil 8882.9.3 Hickok, L.P. A system of moral science. 3rd ed. N.Y., 1873.
Phil 288.1.25 Pamphlet box. Hickok, Laurens. Perseus. Rational cosmology.
Phil 288.1 Hickok, S.P. Rational cosmology. N.Y., 1958.
Phil 288.1.8 Hickok, S.P. Review of rational cosmology. n.p., 18- ?
Phil 7069.18.110 Hicks, Betsey B. The bugle. N.Y., 1918.
Phil 3489.17 Hicks, G.D. Die Begriffe Phänomenon und Noumenon. Leipzig, 1897.
Phil 1870.112 Hicks, G.D. Berkeley. London, 1932.
Phil 630.46 Hicks, G.D. Critical realism. London, 1938.
Phil 8662.16 Hicks, G.D. The philosophical bases of theism. London, 1937.
Phil 8520.1 Hicks, L.E. A critique of design-arguments. N.Y., 1883.
Phil 1200.76 Hicks, Robert Drew. Stoic and Epicurean. N.Y., 1962.
Phil 9347.11.2 Hicks, S. Difficulties; an attempt to help. London, 1922.
Phil 585.179 Hidalgo, Alberto. El universo está cerca. Buenos Aires, 1945.
Phil 7069.61.10 Hidden channels of the mind. (Rhine, Louisa E.) N.Y., 1961.
Phil 5585.237 The hidden dimension. 1. ed. (Hall, Edward Twitchell.) Garden City, N.Y., 1966.
Phil 8673.23 Hidden God; how do we know that God exists? (Steenberghen, Fernand van.) Saint Louis, 1966.
Phil 8893.34.10 The hidden happiness. (Stanton, S.B.) N.Y., 1917.
Phil 5465.168 The hidden order of art; a study in the psychology of artistic imagination. (Ehrenzweig, Anton.) Berkeley, 1967.
Phil 7069.30.45 The hidden path. (Wells, Helen.) Floral Park, N.Y., 1930. 4 pam.
Phil 7069.30.46F The hidden path. v.2. (Wells, Helen B.) N.Y., 1934.
Phil 5258.180.5 The hidden remnant. (Sykes, G.) London, 1962.
Phil 5258.180 The hidden remnant. 1. ed. (Sykes, G.) N.Y., 1962.
Phil 7069.61.40 The hidden springs. (Haynes, Renée.) London, 1961.
Phil 978.32.5 The hidden way across the threshold. (Street, J.C.) Boston, 1887.
Phil 8662.26 Hidding, Klaas Albert Hendrik. De evolutie van het godsdienstig bewustzijn. Utrecht, 1965.
Phil 3246.169 Hidvall, Karl Z.K. Fichtes filosofi i förhallande till Kants kriticism. Uppsala, 1914.
Phil 974.3.150 Hiebel, Friedrich. Rudolf Steiner im Geistesgang des Abendlandes. Bern, 1965.
Phil 5590.572.4 Hiebsch, Hans. Sozialpsychologische Grundlagen der Persönlichrechtsformung. 4. Aufl. Berlin, 1969.
Phil 3246.160 Hielscher, H. Das Denksystem Fichtes. Berlin, 1913.
Phil 3831.9.3 La hiérarchie dans l'univers chez Spinoza. Thèse. (Lasbax, Émile.) Paris, 1919.
Phil 3585.14.20 Hieronimus, E. Theodor Lessing. Hannover, 1964.
Phil 4075.78 Hieronymi Cardani mediolanensis. (Cardano, Girolamo.) Amstelaedami, 1654.
Phil 3450.15.80 Hieronymus Hirnhaim. (Barach, C.S.) Wien, 1864.
Phil 3450.15.90 Hieronymus Hiruhaim: zum deutschen Geist im Barock Böhmens. (Klitzner, Julius.) Prag, 1943.
Phil 17.10 The hierophant. N.Y. 1-12,1842-1843
Phil 5590.450 Hiese, Manfred. Übertragungsphänomene bei verwahrlosten männlichen Jugendlichen. Erlangen, 1965.
Phil 9347.12 Higford, William. Institutions: or Advice to his grandson. London, 1818.
Phil 75.70 Higgins, Charles L. The bibliography of philosophy. Ann Arbor, 1965.
Phil 5247.48.2 Higginson, G. Fields of psychology. N.Y., 1932.
Phil 5247.48.5 Higginson, G. Psychology. N.Y., 1936.
Phil 8587.15.6 Higginson, T.W. L'affinité des religions. Paris, n.d.
Htn Phil 8587.15.5* Higginson, T.W. L'affinité des religions. Paris, n.d.
Phil 8587.15 Higginson, T.W. The sympathy of religions. Boston, 1876.
Phil 8587.15.2 Higginson, T.W. The sympathy of religions. Chicago, 1893.
Phil 3925.16.145 High, Dallas. Language, persons, and belief studies in Wittgenstein's Philosophical investigations. N.Y., 1967.
Phil 8697.26 High, Dallas M. New essays on religious language. N.Y., 1969.
Htn Phil 3110.36.2* High and deep searching out. (Böhme, J.) London, 1656.
Phil 3110.36.5 High and deep searching out. (Böhme, J.) London, 1909.
Phil 5374.234.30 High priest. (Leary, Timothy Francis.) N.Y., 1968.
Phil 9347.15 High school lectures. (Hewett, M.E.G.) London, 1889.
Phil 7054.8 Higher aspects of spiritualism. (Moses, William S.) London, 1880.
Phil 5374.50.15 The higher consciouness. (Saunders, H.S.) Toronto, 1924.
Phil 6121.45.2 Higher cortical functions in man. (Luria, Aleksandr Romanovich.) N.Y., 1966.
Phil 184.41 The higher foolishness. (Jordan, David S.) Indianapolis, 1927.
Phil 185.52.5 The higher metaphysics. (King, Mrs. E.D.) Los Angeles, 1918.
NEDL Phil 8591.3 The higher ministry of nature. (Leifchild, J.R.) London, 1872.
Phil 5465.214 The higher powers of man. Thesis. (Smith, Frederick Madison.) Lamoni, Ia., 1918.
Phil 2100.3.30 The higher realism. (Kemble, Duston.) Cincinnati, 1903.
Phil 6117.49 Highet, G. Man's unconquerable mind. N.Y., 1954.
Phil 7069.08.24 Highland second-sight. (Macrae, Norman.) Dingwall, 1908?
Phil 6957.13 Highmore, N. Exercitationes duae...histerica. 2. ed. Amstelodami, 1660.
Phil 5757.9 Hight, G.A. The unity of will. London, 1906.
Phil 6121.34 La higiene mental en México. (Lechuga, Z.G.) México, 1937.
Phil 1750.552.10 Hijmans, Benjamin Lodwijk. Classics and the philosophy of existence. Winnipeg, 1965.
Phil 4967.5 Hijos de la roca. (Francovich, Guillermo.) México, 1954.
Phil 182.144 Hilmi, Selhattin. 100 soruda felsefe el kilabi. Istanbul, 1970.
Phil 5757.7 Hilber, H. (pseud.). Über Willenseinheit bei Arbeitsgehmeinschaft. Leipzig, 1914.
Phil 5066.70 Hilbert, D. Grundzüge der theorelischen Logik. 2. Aufl. Berlin, 1949.
Phil 5047.33A Hilbert, David. Grundzüge der theoretischen Logik. Berlin, 1928.
Phil 5047.33.5 Hilbert, David. Grundzüge der theoretischen Logik. 2e Aufl. Berlin, 1938.
Phil 5047.33.10 Hilbert, David. Principles of mathematical logic. N.Y., 1950.
Phil 5757.17 Hilbert, Gerhard. Moderne Willensziele. Leipzig, 1911.
Phil 8408.6.5 Hildebrand, A. Das Problem der Form in der Bildendenkunst. 6. Aufl. Strassburg, 1908.
Phil 8408.6 Hildebrand, A. The problem of form in painting and sculpture. N.Y., 1907.

Author and Title Listing

Phil 8587.82 Hildebrand, Alice M. (Jourdain) von. Introduction to a philosophy of religion. Chicago, 1971.

Phil 3450.33.2 Hildebrand, Christa. Die Wertethik bei Dietrick von Hildebrand. Düsseldorf, 1959.

Phil 8957.12 Hildebrand, D. von. Christian ethics. N.Y., 1953.

Phil 3450.33.5 Hildebrand, D. von. Die Menschkeit am Scheideweg. Regensburg, 1955.

Phil 3450.33.7 Hildebrand, D. von. Metaphysik der Gemeinscheaft. Regensburg, 1955.

Phil 3450.33 Hildebrand, D. von. The new tower of Babel. N.Y., 1953.

Phil 8957.12.5 Hildebrand, D. von. Sittliche Grundhaltungen. Mainz, 1954.

Phil 8957.12.10 Hildebrand, D. von. Transformation in Christ. Baltimore, 1960.

Phil 8957.12.7 Hildebrand, D. von. True morality and its counterfeits. N.Y., 1955.

Phil 9495.127.6 Hildebrand, Dietrich von. In defence of purity. Chicago, 1920.

Phil 9495.127.5 Hildebrand, Dietrich von. Reinheit und Jungfräulichkeit. Köln, 1927.

Phil 3640.165 Hildebrandt, K. Nietzsches Weltkampf mit Sokrates und Plato. Dresden, 1922.

Phil 182.129 Hildebrandt, K. Ein Weg zur Philosophie. Bonn, 1962.

Phil 1112.12 Hildebrandt, Kurt. Frühe griechische Denker. Bonn, 1968.

Phil 3552.338 Hildebrandt, Kurt. Leibniz und das Reich der Gnade. Haag, 1953.

Phil 5205.34 Hildebrant, R. Zur Kritik der Psychologie. Marburg, 1946. 4 pam.

Phil 3850.3.80 Hildenbrand, R. Gotthilf Samuel Steinbart. Herne, n.d.

Phil 8882.10.15 Hildreth, R. Letter. Boston, 1844.

Phil 8882.10 Hildreth, R. Theory of morals. Boston, 1844.

Phil 5811.8.5 Hildrop, John. Free thoughts upon the brute-creation: wherein Father Bougeant's Philosophical amusement is examined. London, 1751.

Phil 3489.25 Hilfs-Büchlein für Kant-Leser. v.1-2. (Heussner, A.) Göttingen, 1921-22.

Phil 3005.3.3 Hilfslrich zur Geschichte der Philosophie seit Kant. 3e Aufl. (Falckenberg, Richard.) Leipzig, 1917.

Phil 6317.35 Hilgard, E.R. Psychoanalysis as science. N.Y., 1956.

Phil 5247.66.3 Hilgard, Ernest R. Introduction to psychology. 3. ed. N.Y., 1962.

Phil 5535.10.3 Hilgard, Ernest Ropiequet. Theories of learning. 3. ed. N.Y., 1966.

Phil 7118.10 Hilgard, Josephine Rohrs. Personality and hypnosis. Chicago, 1970.

Phil 6677.10 Hilgu, Wilhelm. Die Hypnose und die Suggestion. Jena, 1909.

Phil 6117.4 Hill, A. The plan of the central nervous system. Chicago, 1885.

Phil 7082.20 Hill, Brian. Gates of horn and ivory. N.Y., 1968.

Phil 5247.57 Hill, D.J. Elements of psychology. N.Y., 1888.

Phil 182.16 Hill, D.J. Genetic philosophy. N.Y., 1893.

Phil 8662.8 Hill, J. Thoughts concerning God and nature. London, 1755.

Phil 7054.132 Hill, J. Arthu. Spiritualism. N.Y., 1919.

Phil 7069.24.24 Hill, J.A. From agnosticism to belief. London, 1924.

Phil 9347.9 Hill, James L. The worst boys in town. Boston, 1919.

Phil 7069.11.40 Hill, John A. New evidences in psychical research. London, 1911.

Phil 7069.20.162 Hill, John A. Psychical miscellanea. London, 1919.

Phil 7069.20.160 Hill, John A. Psychical miscellanea. N.Y., 1920.

Phil 7069.18.112 Hill, John Arthur. Man is a spirit. N.Y. 1918.

Phil 7069.17.26 Hill, John Arthur. Psychical investigations. N.Y., 1917.

Phil 6117.18 Hill, Leonard. Physiology and pathology of cerebral circulation. London, 1896.

Phil 8697.14 Hill, Mabel. Wise men worship. 1. ed. N.Y., 1931.

Phil 8882.42 Hill, Owen. Ethics, general and special. London, 1921.

Phil 5247.27 Hill, Owen Aloysuis. Psychology and natural theology. N.Y., 1921.

Phil 6957.3 Hill, R.G. Lunacy: Its past and its present. London, 1870.

Phil 9010.27 Hill, Richard. An address to persons of fashion. Baltimore, 1807.

Phil 9010.27.2 Hill, Richard. An address to persons of fashions. 6th ed. Shrewsbury, 1771.

Phil 8587.16.2 Hill, T. Geometry and faith. Boston, 1882.

Phil 8587.16 Hill, T. Geometry and faith. N.Y., 1849.

Phil 338.34 Hill, T.E. Contemporary theories of knowledge. N.Y., 1961.

Phil 8957.5 Hill, Thomas. The hydrostatic paradox in morals. Portland, 1880.

Phil 8957.5.5 Hill, Thomas. The postulates of revelation and of ethics. Boston, 1895.

Phil 8882.66A Hill, Thomas E. Contemporary ethical theories. N.Y., 1950.

Phil 8882.66.5 Hill, Thomas E. Ethics in theory and practice. N.Y., 1956.

Phil 8882.11 Hill, W.H. Ethics, or Moral philosophy. Baltimore, 1884.

Phil 5047.5 Hill, Walter H. Elements of philosophy comprising logic, ontology or general metaphysics. Baltimore, 1884.

Phil 9375.4 Hillard, G.S. Dangers and duties of the merchantile profession. Boston, 1850.

Phil 5640.25 Hillebrand, F. Ewald Hering ein Gedenkwort der Psychophysik. Berlin, 1918.

Phil 5170.6 Hillebrand, F. Die neuen theorien der Kategorischen Schlüsse. Wien, 1891.

Phil 5115.8 Hillebrand, F. Zur Lehre von der Hypothesenbildung. Wien, 1896.

Phil 5643.176 Hillebrand, Franz. Lehre von den Gesichtsempfindungen auf Grund hinterlassener Aufzeichnungen. Wien, 1929.

Phil 5047.29 Hillebrand, J. Grundriss der Logik. Heidelberg, 1820.

Phil 182.17.15 Hillebrand, J. Lehrbuch der theoretischen Philosophie. Mainz, 1826.

Phil 182.17.10 Hillebrand, J. Der Organismus der philosophischen Idee. Dresden, 1842.

Phil 182.17 Hillebrand, J. Philosophie des Geistes. Heidelberg, 1835-1836. 2v.

Phil 182.17.20 Hillebrand, J. Universal-philosophische Prolegomena. Mainz, 1830.

Phil 8408.9 Hillebrand, K. Zwölf Briefe eines ästhetischen Ketzer's. 2. Aufl. Berlin, 1874.

Phil 2490.114 Hillemand, C. La vie et l'oeuvre de A.C. et de Pierre Laffitte. Paris, 1908.

Phil 3450.25 Hiller, Kurt. Der Aufbruch zum Paradies; Sätze. München, 1922.

Phil 3450.25.10 Hiller, Kurt. Die Weisheit der Langenweile. Leipzig, 1913.

Phil 8662.4 Hiller, T.O.P. God manifest. London, 1858.

Phil 735.125 Hilliard, A.L. The forms of value. N.Y., 1950.

Phil 8882.26 Hillis, N.D. Great books as life teachers. Edinburgh, 1900.

Phil 8882.26.9 Hillis, N.D. A man's value to society. Edinburgh, 1901.

Phil 9245.16.2 Hillis, N.D. Quest of happiness. N.Y., 1902.

Phil 8882.26.5 Hillis, N.D. Right living as a fine art. N.Y., 1899.

Phil 5400.155 Hillman, J. Emotion. London, 1960.

Phil 8662.22 Hills, Ernest. Philosophie et athéisme. Paris, 1923.

Phil 5592.130 Hills, J.R. The influence of instructions of repeated measurement on personality inventory scores. Princeton, 1959.

Phil 5069.8 Hilpinen, Risto. Deontic logic: introductory and systematic readings. Dordrecht, 1971.

Phil 7060.56 Hilscher, M.P.C. Nachricht von einem gewissen Monche in Dresden. Dresden, 1729.

Phil 5238.189 Hiltmann, H. Dialektik und Dynamik der Person. Köln, 1963.

Phil 5401.46 Hiltner, S. Constructive aspects of anxiety. N.Y., 1963.

Phil 5066.235 Hilton, Alice Mary. Logic, computing machines, and automation. Cleveland, 1964.

Phil 8882.12 Hilty, K. Glück. Frauenfeld, 1894.

Phil 8882.12.3 Hilty, K. Glück. Frauenfeld, 1900.

Phil 8882.12.5 Hilty, K. Happiness. N.Y., 1903.

Phil 8882.12.9 Hilty, K. Steps of life, further essays on happiness. N.Y., 1907.

Phil 1865.179 Himes, N.E. Jeremy Bentham and the genesis of English Neo-Malthusianism. London, 1936.

Phil 8701.3 Himmelsbild und Weltanschauung. (Troels Lund, Troels Frederik.) Leipzig, 1900.

Phil 8701.3.4 Himmelsbild und Weltanschauung. 4. Aufl. (Troels Lund, Troels Frederik.) Leipzig, 1913.

Phil 8701.3.6 Himmelsbild und Weltanschauung. 5. Aufl. (Troels Lund, Troels Frederik.) Leipzig, 1929.

Phil 3120.30.62 Hin Weise. (Buber, Martin.) Zürich, 1953.

Phil 8661.7 Hin zu Gottnatur. 2. Aufl. (Groddeck, G.) Leipzig, 1909.

Phil 3801.233 Hinauf zum Idealismus! Schelling-Studien. (Braun, Otto.) Leipzig, 1908.

Phil 7069.30.9 Hinchliffe, Emilie. The return of Captain W.G.R. Hinchliffe. London, 1930.

Phil 8887.50.12 Hindrances of life. (Müller, Johannes.) N.Y., 1909.

Phil 9045.6 The hindrances to good citizenship. (Bryce, J.) New Haven, 1909.

Phil 9045.6.2 The hindrances to good citizenship. (Bryce, J.) New Haven, 1909[1919]

Phil 5047.6 Hinds, Samuel. Introduction to logic. Oxford, 1827.

Phil 525.210 Hindu and Muslim mysticism. (Zaehner, R.C.) London, 1960.

Phil 8837.8 Hindu ethics. (McKenzie, John.) London, 1922.

Phil 960.9.5 Hindu logic as preserved in China and Japan. (Sugivra, Sadajiro.) Philadelphia, 1900.

Phil 530.105 Hindu mysticism. (Dasgupta, S.N.) Chicago, 1927.

Phil 3425.730 Hingebung und Begriff. (Wolff, Kurt Heinrich.) Neuwied, 1968.

Phil 6317.7 Hingley, R.H. Psycho-analysis. London, 1921.

Phil 5817.16 Hingston, R.W.G. Problems of instinct and intelligence. London, 1928.

Phil 6317.10 Hinkle, Beatrice. The re-creating of the individual. N.Y., 1923.

Phil 400.21 Hinman, E.L. The physics of idealism. Lincoln, 1906.

Phil 8592.43 Hinrichs, B. Die religionsphilosophischen Elemente in J. David Michaelis' Dogmatik. Diss. Göttingen, 1911.

Phil 5047.26 Hinrichs, H.F.W. Grundlinien der Philosophie der Logik. Halle, 1826. 2 pam.

Phil 5204.20 Hinsée, Leland Earl. Psychiatric dictionary, with encyclopedic treatment of modern terms. N.Y., 1940.

Phil 5643.44 Hinshelwood, J. Letter, word, and mind blindness. London, 1900.

Phil 5400.105 Hinsie, L.E. The person in the body. N.Y., 1945.

Phil 6957.28 Hinsie, Leland. The treatment of schizophrenia. Baltimore, 1930.

Phil 3480.32.65.2 Hinske, Norbert. Kant-Seitenkondordanz. Darmstadt, 1970.

Phil 3489.47 Hinske, Norbert. Kants Begriff des Transzendentalen. Pt.1. Stuttgart, 1970.

Phil 585.154 Hinter den Feigenblättern. (Goltz, B.) Berlin, 1862-64.

Phil 5325.18 Hintermann, H. Experimentelle Untersuchung der Bewusstseinsvorgänge. Zürich, 1916.

Phil 338.40 Hintikka, K.J.J. Knowledge and belief. Ithaca, 1962.

Phil 5039.20 Hintikka, Kaarlo Jaakko J. Aspects of inductive logic. Amsterdam, 1966.

Phil 5066.314 Hintikka, Kaarlo Jaakko Johani. Models for modalities. Dordrecht, Holland, 1969.

Phil 5520.648 Hintikka, Kaarlo Jaakko Juhani. Information and inference. Dordrecht, 1970.

Phil 4668.123.30 Hintikka, Kaarlo Jaakko Juhani. Tieto on valtaa ja muita aatehistoriallisia esseitä. Porvoo, 1969.

Phil 182.33.2 Hinton, C.H. Scientific romances. London, 1886.

Phil 182.33 Hinton, C.H. Scientific romances. Nos. 1-5,7-8. London, 1884-1888. 7v.

Phil 672.15.5 Hinton, Charles H. The fourth dimension. London, 1904.

Phil 672.15.10 Hinton, Charles H. A language of space. London, 1906.

Phil 672.15 Hinton, Charles H. A new era of thought. London, 1888.

Phil 672.15.7 Hinton, Charles H. The recognition of the fourth dimension. Washington, 1902.

Phil 182.18 Hinton, J. Man and his dwelling place. N.Y., 1859.

NEDL Phil 2055.2.80 Hinton, James. Life and letters. London, 1885.

Phil 9520.2.2 Hinton, James. The mystery of pain. Boston, 1886.

Phil 9520.2.3 Hinton, James. The mystery of pain. London, 1866.

Phil 9520.2.1 Hinton, James. The mystery of pain. London, 1879.

Phil 9520.2.5 Hinton, James. The mystery of pain. N.Y., 1914.

Phil 2055.2.20 Hinton, James. Selections from manuscripts. London, 1870. 4v.

Phil 9359.4 Hints addressed to the young men of the United States. 2d ed. (Todd, J.) Northampton, 1845.

Phil 7069.18.80 Hints and observations for those investigating the phenomena of spiritualism. (Crawford, William J.) N.Y., 1918.

Phil 9245.6 Hints for an essay on the pursuit of happiness. (Oliver, B.L.) Chicago, 1818.

Phil 6945.6 Hints for introducing an improved mode of treating the insane in the asylum. (Eddy, T.) N.Y., 1815.

Phil 9179.4 Hints for the household. Photoreproduction. (Thayer, W.M.) Boston, 1853.

Phil 978.20 Hints on esoteric theosophy. no. 1-2. Calcutta, 1882.

Phil 6111.40 Hints on metaphysics. (Butts, Bryan J.) Boston, 1885.

Phil 9495.20.2 Hints to young men. (Ware, J.) Boston, 1879.

Phil 9375.1 Hints to young trademen. Boston, 1838.

Phil 3428.162 Hintz, R. Herbarts Bedeutung für die Psychologie. Berlin, 1900.

Phil 4802.6 Hinz, Henryk. Polska mysl filosoficzna. Warszawa, 1964.

Author and Title Listing

Phil 6692.5 — Hipnotisms teatral. (Wolff, C.) Barcelona, 19- .

Phil 8110.11 — Hipple, W.J. The beautiful, the sublime, and the picturesque in eighteenth-century British aesthetic theory. Carbondale, 1957.

Phil 5590.5 — Hippocrate avait raison. (Periot, M.) Marseille, 1941.

Phil 2885.80 — Hippolito Taine. (Barzellotti, G.) Roma, 1895.

Phil 2885.90 — Hippolyte Taines Theorie. (Schmidt, O.A.) Halle, 1936.

Phil 3425.277 — Hirā-Lāl, H. Hegelianism and human personality. Calcutta, 1910.

Phil 8882.60 — Hires, H. For my children. N.Y., 1943.

Phil 5635.17.5 — Hiriartborde, Edmond. Les aptitudes rythmiques. Paris, 1968.

Phil 8408.19 — Hiriyanna, M. Art experience. Mysore, 1954.

Phil 960.137.10 — Hiriyanna, M. The essentials of Indian philosophy. London, 1949.

Phil 960.137.20 — Hiriyanna, M. Indian philosophical studies. Mysore, 1957.

Phil 960.137.25 — Hiriyanna, M. The mission of philosophy. Mysore, 1960.

Phil 960.137 — Hiriyanna, M. Outlines of Indian philosophy. London, 1932.

Phil 960.137.15 — Hiriyanna, M. Popular essays in Indian philosophy. Mysore, 1952.

Phil 960.137.5 — Hiriyanna, M. The quest after perfection. Madras, 1941.

Phil 960.137.8 — Hiriyanna, M. The quest after perfection. Mysore, 1952.

Phil 8632.12 — Hirn, G.A. La vie future et la science moderne. Colmar, 1890.

Phil 8408.37 — Hirn, Yrjö. Förstudier till en konstfilosofi på psykologisk grundval. Helsingfors, 1896.

Phil 6111.21 — Das Hirngewicht des Menschen. (Bischoff, T.L.W. von.) Bonn, 1880.

Phil 3450.15.85 — Hirnhaim, H. De typho generis humani. Prague, 1676.

Phil 3450.18.95 — Hirning, H. Nicolai Hartmanns Lehre. Tübingen, 1937.

Phil 3246.197 — Hirsch, E. Christentum und Geschichte in Fichtes Philosophie. Tübingen, 1920.

Phil 3246.174 — Hirsch, Emanuel. Fichtes Religionsphilosophie. Göttingen, 1914.

Phil 3805.235 — Hirsch, Emanuel. Schleiermachers Christusglaube drei Studien. 1. Aufl. Gütasloh, 1968.

Phil 8882.110 — Hirsch, Maximilian. Das Problem der Vernunftherrschaft. Leipzig, 1922.

Phil 3640.227 — Hirsch, Moriz. Friedrich Nietzsche. Stuttgart, 1924.

Phil 5425.51 — Hirsch, N.D.M. Genius and creative intelligence. Cambridge, 1931.

Phil 3489.24 — Hirsch, Richard. Kant-Bibliothek. Wien, 1929.

Phil 8408.13 — Hirsch, W. Die Gültigkeit der Kunst. Köln, 1957.

Phil 8408.21 — Hirsch, W. Substanz und Thema in der Kunst. Amsterdam, 1961.

Phil 5425.5.6 — Hirsch, William. Genie und Entartung. 2. Aufl. Berlin, 1894.

Phil 5425.5 — Hirsch, William. Genius and degeneration. N.Y., 1896.

Phil 3450.39.30 — Hirsch, Wolfgang. Die Normen des Seins. Amsterdam, 1959?

Phil 210.60 — Hirsch, Wolfgang. Über die Grundlagen einer universalen Methode der Philosophie. Bad Homburg, 1969.

Phil 5525.63 — Hirsch, Wolfgang. Worüber lachen wir? Heidelberg, 1963.

Phil 807.18 — Hirschberger, Johannes. Geschichte der Philosophie. Freiburg, 1949-51. 2v.

Phil 807.18.5 — Hirschberger, Johannes. Geschichte der Philosophie. 5. Aufl. Freiburg, 1961-60. 2v.

Phil 182.116 — Hirschfeld, G. An essay on mankind. N.Y., 1957.

Phil 3640.237 — Hirschhorn, S. Vom Sinn des Tragischen bei Nietzsche. Freiburg, 1930.

Phil 8587.62 — Hirschmann, Eva. Phänomenologie der Religion. Proefschrift. Würzburg, 1940.

Phil 5650.42 — Hirsh, Ira Jean. The measurement of hearing. N.Y., 1952.

Phil 8957.9 — Hirst, E.W. Jesus and the moralists. London, 1935.

Phil 8882.33 — Hirst, E.W. Self and neighbor. London, 1919.

Phil 8957.9.5 — Hirst, E.W. Studies in Christian love. London, 1944.

Phil 338.28 — Hirst, R.J. The problems of perception. London, 1959.

Phil 5593.62 — Hirt, Michael. Rorschach science; readings in theory and method. N.Y., 1962.

Phil 665.27 — Hirt, Walter. Ein neuer Weg zur Erforschung der Seele. München, 1917.

Phil 665.27.5 — Hirt, Walter. Die Entschleierung der Seele: eine neue Theorie. Berlin, 1923.

Phil 8408.5 — Hirth, Georg. Aufgaben der Kunstphysiologie. München, 1891.

Phil 6117.24 — Hirth, George. Lokalisations-Psychologie. Die Lokalisationstheorie. 2. Aufl. München, 1895.

Phil 1145.66 — Hirzel, R. Was die Wahrheit war für die Griechen. Jena, 1905.

Phil 803.2.4 — His Gesammtcursus der Philosophie. (Duehring, Eugen.) Leipzig, 1894-95. 2v.

Phil 1821.15 — Hisotire des idées en Grande-Bretagne. (Vitoux, Pierre.) Paris, 1969.

Phil 3827.2 — Hissbach, K. Ist ein Durch...Spinoza und Leibniz Vorchanden? Weimar, 1889.

Phil 5325.3 — Hissmann, M. Geschichte der Lehre...Association der Ideen. Göttingen, 1777.

Phil 6619.8.5 — Histeria y sugestión 5. ed. (Ingenieros, José.) Buenos Aires, 1919.

Phil 1520.2 — Histoire...des philosophies médiévales. (Picavet, F.) Paris, 1905.

Phil 3838.1 — Histoire...ouvrages de B. de Spinoza. (Saintes, A.) Paris, 1842.

Phil 805.1.9 — Histoire abrégée de la philosophie. (Formey, J.H.S.) Amsterdam, 1760.

Phil 806.1 — Histoire comparée des systèmes de philosophie. (Gerando, J.M. de.) Paris, 1822-23. 4v.

Phil 4265.1.81 — Histoire critique de Jules César Vanini. (Baudouin, A.) Toulouse, n.d.

Phil 803.1 — Histoire critique de la philosophie. (Deslandes, A.F.B.) London, 1742. 3v.

Phil 5816.2 — Histoire critique de l'âme des bêtes. v.1-2. (Guer, S.A.) Amsterdam, 1749.

Phil 1150.3 — Histoire critique de l'ecole d'Alexandrie. (Vacherot, E.) Paris, 1846-51. 3v.

Phil 1750.9 — Histoire critique des doctrines religieuses et philosophiques. (Barthoemiss, C.) Paris, 1855. 2v.

Phil 6673.2.3 — Histoire critique du magnétisme animal. (Deleuze, J.P.F.) Paris, 1813. 2v.

Phil 6673.2 — Histoire critique du magnétisme animal. (Deleuze, J.P.F.) Paris, 1819. 2v.

Phil 623.7 — Histoire critique du rationalisme en Allemagne. (Saintes, A.) Paris, 1841.

Phil 2520.95 — Histoire de Descartes avant 1637. (Millet, J.) Paris, 1867.

Phil 5028.3 — Histoire de la dialectique. (Sándor, Pál.) Paris, 1947.

Phil 6950.6 — Histoire de la folie. (Cassinelli, B.) Paris, 1939.

Phil 8610.959 — Histoire de la libre-pensée. (Bayet, Albert.) Paris, 1959.

Htn Phil 2725.16.30* — Histoire de la littérature anglaise. (Legouis, Émile.) Paris, 1924.

Phil 8712.3.15 — Histoire de la lutte entre la science et la théologie. (White, Andrew Dickson.) Paris, 1899.

Phil 7103.4 — Histoire de la médicine et des sciences occultes. (Dureau, Alexis.) Paris, 1869.

Phil 8837.2 — Histoire de la morale. (Martin, L.A.) Paris, 1859.

Phil 802.22 — Histoire de la pensée. v.1-3. (Chevalier, Jacques.) Paris, 1955- 2v.

Phil 165.395 — L'histoire de la philosophie; ses problèmes, ses méthodes. Paris, 1964.

Phil 801.21 — Histoire de la philosophie. (Bréhier, É.) Paris, 1926. 9v.

Phil 801.21.6 — Histoire de la philosophie. (Bréhier, É.) Paris, 1963. 3v.

Phil 801.21.6.1 — Histoire de la philosophie. (Bréhier, É.) Paris, 1969.

Phil 802.6.5 — Histoire de la philosophie. (Conti, Augusto.) Paris, n.d. 2v.

Phil 806.4 — Histoire de la philosophie. (Gonzalez, Z.) Paris, 1890-91. 4v.

Phil 809.2.10 — Histoire de la philosophie. (Janet, P.) Paris, 1921.

Phil 812.2 — Histoire de la philosophie. (Matter, J.) Paris, 1854.

Phil 817.21 — Histoire de la philosophie. (Rivaud, Albert.) Paris, 1948- 3v.

Phil 817.5 — Histoire de la philosophie. (Robert, A.A.) Québec, 1912.

Phil 818.36 — Histoire de la philosophie. (Steenberghen, Ferdinand van.) Louvain, 1964.

Phil 819.4 — Histoire de la philosophie. (Tissot, C.J.) Paris, 1840.

Phil 819.10 — Histoire de la philosophie. (Truc, Gonzague.) Paris, 1950.

Phil 809.2.15 — Histoire de la philosophie. Supplement. (Janet, P.) Paris, 1929.

Phil 817.21.2 — Histoire de la philosophie. 2. ed. (Rivaud, Albert.) Paris, 1960.

Phil 821.3 — Histoire de la philosophie. 3e éd. (Vallet, P.) Paris, 1886.

Phil 805.5.4 — Histoire de la philosophie. 14e éd. (Fouillée, Alfred.) Paris, 1919.

Phil 3001.1 — Histoire de la philosophie allemande. (Barchou, A.T.H.) Paris, 1836. 2v.

Phil 3001.5 — Histoire de la philosophie allemande. (Bréhier, Émile.) Paris, 1921.

Phil 3022.2 — Histoire de la philosophie allemande. (Willm, J.) Paris, 1846-49. 4v.

Phil 3001.5.3 — Histoire de la philosophie allemande. 3. ed. (Bréhier, Emile.) Paris, 1954.

Phil 1803.10 — Histoire de la philosophie américaine. 1e éd. (Deledalle, G.) Paris, 1954.

Phil 1111.2 — Histoire de la philosophie ancienne. (Grenet, P.B.) Paris, 1960.

Phil 1116.1 — Histoire de la philosophie ancienne. (Laforet, N.J.) Bruxelles, 1866. 2v.

Phil 1122.2 — Histoire de la philosophie ancienne. (Ritter, Heinrich.) Paris, 1835-36. 4v.

Phil 818.14 — Histoire de la philosophie ancienne. (Sortais, G.) Paris, 1912.

Phil 260.2A — Histoire de la philosophie atomistique. (Mabilleau, S.) Paris, 1895.

Phil 2520.83.5 — Histoire de la philosophie Cartésienne. (Bouillier, F.) Paris, 1854. 2v.

Phil 2520.83.6 — Histoire de la philosophie Cartésienne. (Bouillier, F.) Paris, 1868. 2v.

Phil 1522.1.5 — Histoire de la philosophie chretienne. (Ritter, A.H.) Paris, 1843-4. 2v.

Phil 802.8.2 — Histoire de la philosophie depuis les temps les plus reculés jusqu'à nos jours. 2e éd. (Carbonel, Pierre.) Avignon, 1882.

Phil 1817.1 — Histoire de la philosophie en Angleterre. (Rémusat, C.F.) Paris, 1875. 2v.

Phil 2422.1 — Histoire de la philosophie en Belgique. (Wulf, M. de.) Bruxelles, 1910.

Phil 815.32 — Histoire de la philosophie et metaphysique. (Paris. Institut Catholique. Faculte de Philosophie.) Paris, 1955.

Phil 822.1 — Histoire de la philosophie européenne. (Weber, A.) Paris, 1872.

Phil 822.1.2 — Histoire de la philosophie européenne. (Weber, A.) Paris, 1886.

Phil 822.1.4 — Histoire de la philosophie européenne. (Weber, A.) Paris, 1957. 3v.

Phil 1722.11 — Histoire de la philosophie européenne. (Weber, Alfred.) Paris, 1957.

Phil 822.1.3 — Histoire de la philosophie européenne. 9e éd. (Weber, A.) Paris, 1925.

Phil 1117.4 — Histoire de la philosophie ionienne. (Mallet, Charles.) Paris, 1842.

Phil 1020.48 — Histoire de la philosophie islamique. (Corbin, H.) Paris, 1964.

Phil 1527.1 — Histoire de la philosophie médiévale. (Wulf, M. de.) Louvain, 1900.

Phil 1527.1.6.25 — Histoire de la philosophie médiévale. v.1-2. (Rand, E.K.) Cambridge, Mass., 1934.

Phil 1527.1.6 — Histoire de la philosophie médiévale. 4e éd. (Wulf, M. de.) Louvain, 1912.

Phil 1527.1.6.5 — Histoire de la philosophie médiévale. 5e éd. (Wulf, M. de.) Louvain, 1924-25. 2v.

Phil 1527.1.6.7A — Histoire de la philosophie médiévale. 6e éd. (Wulf, M. de.) Louvain, 1934-47. 3v.

Phil 1701.3.5 — Histoire de la philosophie moderne. (Buhle, J.G.) Paris, 1816. 6v.

Phil 1715.1 — Histoire de la philosophie moderne. (Papillen, Fernand.) Paris, 1876. 2v.

Phil 1717.2 — Histoire de la philosophie moderne. (Ritter, A.H.) Paris, 1861. 3v.

Phil 1721.6 — Histoire de la philosophie moderne. (Verneaux, Roger.) Paris, 1958.

Phil 1707.1.12 — Histoire de la philosophie moderne. 2e éd. (Höffding, H.) Paris, 1908. 2v.

Phil 8834.1 — Histoire de la philosophie morale. (Janet, P.) Paris, 1858. 2v.

Phil 817.30 — Histoire de la philosophie occidentale. (Revel, Jean François.) Paris, 1968-

Phil 900.6 — Histoire de la philosophie orientale; Inde, Chine, Japan. (Grousset, René.) Paris, 1923.

Phil 850.1 — Histoire de la philosophie payenne. (Levesque de Bruiquy, J.) La Haye, 1724.

Phil 2405.2.5 — Histoire de la philosophie pendant la révolution (1789-1804). (Ferraz, Marin.) Paris, 1889.

Phil 1512.1.2 — Histoire de la philosophie scolastique. (Haureau, B.) Paris, 1872-80. 3v.

Phil 5222.8 — Histoire de la psychologie. (Müller, T.L.) Paris, 1960.

Phil 5257.64 — Histoire de la psychologie. (Reuchlin, Maurice.) Paris, 1957.

Phil 1140.1 — Histoire de la Psychologie des Grecs. (Chaignet, A.E.) Paris, 1887-93. 5v.

Phil 5627.86 — Histoire de la vie et de la conversion de Guillaume Köllner. (Köllner, G.) Genève, 1823.

Phil 3500.1 — Histoire de la vie et de la philosophie de Kant. (Saintes, A.) Paris, 1844.

Phil 2477.2.80 — Histoire de la vie et des ouvrages de Bordas-Demoulin. (Huet, François.) Paris, 1861.

Phil 1150.2 — Histoire de l'ecole d'Alexandrie. (Simon, J.) Paris, 1845. 2v.

Phil 1210.6 — Histojre de l'école de Mégare et des écoles d'Élis et d'Erétrie. (Mallet, Charles.) Paris, 1845.

Phil 8050.24 — Histoire de l'esthétique. (Buyer, Raymond.) Paris, 1961.

Phil 8120.6A — Histoire de l'esthétique française, 1700-1900. (Mustoxidi, T.M.) Paris, 1920.

Phil 1117.3.5 — Histoire de l'origine...der sciences dans la Grèce. (Meiners, C.) Paris, 1799. 5v.

Phil 282.4 — Histoire des causes premières. (Batteux, C.) Paris, 1769.

Phil 6128.21 — Histoire des doctrines...les fonctions du cerveau. (Soury, Jules.) Paris, 1891.

Phil 8125.22 — Histoire des doctrines litteraires. (Grucker, Emile.) Paris, 1883.

Phil 4003.1 — Histoire des doctrines philosophiques dans l'Italie. (Debrit, M.) Paris, 1859.

Phil 2403.8 — Histoire des idées en France. 2e éd. (Daval, Roger.) Paris, 1956.

Phil 960.140 — L'histoire des idées theosophiques dans l'Inde. (Oltramare, Paul.) Paris, 1906-23. 2v.

Phil 6990.4 — Histoire des miracules et des convulsionnaires de Saint-Médard. (Mathieu, P.F.) Paris, 1864.

Phil 2805.249.10 — Histoire des Pensées de Pascal. (Lafuma, Louis.) Paris, 1954.

Phil 811.4 — Histoire des progrès de l'esprit humain dans les sciences et dans les arts que en dépendent. (Savérien, A.) Paris, 1777.

NEDL Phil 2402.1 — Histoire des révolutions de la philosophie. (Caraman, V.A.C.) Paris, 1845-48. 3v.

Phil 5425.13 — Histoire des sciences et des savants. (Candolle, A. de.) Genève, 1885.

Phil 1145.5 — Histoire des theories...dans l'Antiquité. (Denis, J.) Paris, 1856. 2v.

Phil 1145.6 — Histoire des theories...dans l'Antiquité. (Denis, J.) Paris, 1879. 2v.

Phil 8587.67 — Histoire doctrinale de l'humanisme chrétien. (Hermans, F.) Tournai, 1948. 4v.

Phil 8685.12 — Histoire du panthéisme populaire. (Jundt, A.) Strasbourg, 1875.

Phil 5525.65 — Histoire du rure à travers le monde. (Nohain, Jean.) Paris, 1965.

Phil 8412.4 — Histoire du sentiment de la nature. (Laprade, Victor de.) Paris, 1882.

Phil 6676.2 — Histoire du somnambulisme. (Gauthier, A.) Paris, 1842. 2v.

Phil 1522.5.5 — Histoire d'une faillite philosophique: la scolastique. (Rougier, Louis.) Paris, 1966.

Phil 193.205 — L'histoire el la vie. (Shul'gyn, O.) Paris, 1957.

Phil 8407.4 — Histoire esthétique de la nature. (Griveau, Maurice.) Paris, 1927-30. 3v.

Phil 2630.11.40 — Histoire et destinée. (Guitton, Jean.) Paris, 1970.

Phil 5722.76 — L'histoire et l'inconscient humain. (Flottes, Pierre.) Genève, 1965.

Phil 1750.760 — Histoire et mystère. (Lacroix, Jean.) Tournai, 1962.

Phil 188.6 — Histoire et philosophie. (Nourrison, J.F.) Paris, 1860.

Phil 6687.12 — Histoire et philosophie du magnétisme. (Rouxel.) Paris, 1895. 2v.

Phil 8598.69 — Histoire et philosophie religieuse. (Saint René-Taillandier, R.G.E.) Paris, 1859.

Phil 7076.10 — Histoire et rénovation de l'automatismé spirituel. (Isou, Isidore.) Paris, 1967.

Phil 2840.60 — Histoire et solution des problèmes métaphysiques. (Renouvier, C.) Paris, 1901.

Phil 806.2 — Histoire générale de la philosophie. (Guillon, M.N.S.) Paris, 1835. 4v.

Phil 802.2.5 — Histoire générale de la philosophie. 8e éd. (Cousin, V.) Paris, 1867.

Phil 802.2.5.11 — Histoire générale de la philosophie. 11e éd. (Cousin, V.) Paris, 1884.

Htn Phil 1850.75.5* — Histoire naturelle. (Bacon, Francis.) Paris, 1631.

Phil 5831.6.5 — Histoire naturelle de la connaissance chez le singe inférieur; le concret. (Verlaine, Louis.) Paris, 1935-36. 3v.

Htn Phil 2705.40* — Histoire naturelle de l'ame. (La Mettrie, Julien Offray de.) La Haye, 1745.

Phil 3001.4 — Histoire philosophique de l'academie de Prusse. (Bartholmiss, C.J.W.) Paris, 1850. 2v.

Phil 5247.14 — Histoire philosophique de l'homme. Londres, 1766.

Phil 801.14 — Histoire populaire de la philosophie. (Brothier, Léon.) Paris, 1861.

Phil 801.14.3 — Histoire populaire de la philosophie. 3. ed. (Brothier, Léon.) Paris, 1907.

Htn Phil 6677.8* — Histoire véritable du magnétisme animal. La Haye, 1785.

Phil 8670.5.10 — Historia atheismi. (Philipps, J.T.) Altdorfi Noricorum, 1713. 3 pam.

Phil 801.5.2 — Historia critica philosophiae. (Brucker, J.) Lipsiae, 1867. 6v.

Phil 801.5.3 — Historia critica philosophiae. (Brucker, J.) Lipsiae, 1867. 6v.

Phil 801.5 — Historia critica philosophiae. (Brucker J.) Lipsiae, 1742-67. 6v.

Phil 281.10 — Historia da creaçao do mundo conforme as ideas de Moizes. (Alvarea de Queiroz, M.) Porto, 1762.

Phil 8228.2 — História das idéias estéticas no Brasil. (Tobias, José Antônio.) São Paulo, 1967.

Phil 4960.640.5 — História das idéias filosóficas no Brasil. (Paim, Antônio.) São Paulo, 1967.

Phil 818.23 — História de filosofia; ou Pensamento filosófico através dos séculos. (Serrano, J.) Rio de Janeiro, 1944.

Phil 806.4.2 — Historia de la filosofia. (Gonzalez y Diaz Turíon, Ceferino.) Madrid, 1886. 4v.

Phil 4363.7.25 — Historia de la filosofía. 19. ed. (Marías Aguilera, Julián.) Madrid, 1966.

Phil 1735.6 — Historia de la filosofía del siglo XIX. (Gómez Izquierdo, Alberto.) Zaragoza, 1903.

Phil 4313.2 — Historia de la filosofía en España hasta el siglo XX. (Mendez Bejarano, M.) Madrid, 192-.

Phil 4957.45 — Historia de la filosofía en Latinoamérica. (Kempff Mercado, Manfredo.) Santiago de Chile, 1958.

Phil 4302.4 — Historia de la filosofía española. (Bonilla y San Martin, A.) Madrid, 1908.

Phil 4302.4.5 — Historia de la filosofía española. (Bonilla y San Martin, A.) Madrid, 1911.

Phil 1020.32 — Historia de la filosofía española. (Cruz Hernández, Miguel.) Madrid, 1957. 2v.

Phil 4319.1.5 — Historia de la filosofía española. (Solana, Marcial.) Madrid, 1940-41. 3v.

Phil 1721.7 — Historia de la filosofía moderna y contemporánea. (Vélez Correa, Jaime.) Bogotá, 1959.

Phil 817.6 — Historia de la filosofía y terminología filosofica. 2. ed. (Reyes Ruiz, Jesús Maria.) Granada, 1910.

Phil 4957.25 — História de las doctrinas filosóficas en Latinoamérica. 1. ed. (Larrayo, Francisco.) México, 1968.

NEDL Phil 8145.2 — Historia de las ideas. (Menendez y Pelayo.) Madrid, 1890.

Phil 4959.5 — Historia de las ideas en Centroamérica. (Lascaris Comneno, Constantino.) San José de Costa Rica, 1970.

Phil 4961.605.5 — História de las ideas en el Perú contemporáneo. (Salazar Bondy, Augusto.) Lima, 1965.

Phil 8693.4.5 — Historia de los conflictos entre la religion y la ciencia. (Draper, J.W.) Madrid, 1876.

Phil 821.5 — Historia del pensamiento filosofico. (Varsencelos, Jóse.) Mexico, 1937.

Htn Phil 8893.66* — La historia dell'huomo. (Sensi, Lodovico.) Perugia, 1577.

Phil 600.58 — História do positivismo no Brasil. (Lins, Ivan Monteiro de Barros.) São Paulo, 1964.

Htn Phil 2045.75* — Historia ecclesiastica. (Hobbes, Thomas.) Augustae, 1688.

Phil 8050.26 — Historia estetyki. (Tatarkiewicz, Wladyslaw.) Wrocław, 1960. 2v.

Phil 4800.18 — Historia filozofii polskiej. (Wasik, Wiktor.) Warszawa, 1958-66. 2v.

Htn Phil 1850.73* — Historia naturalis. (Bacon, Francois.) Londini, 1622.

Htn Phil 1850.75* — Historia naturalis et experimentalis de ventis. (Bacon, Francis.) Amstelodami, 1662. 3 pam.

Htn Phil 1850.74* — Historia naturalis et experimentalis de ventis. (Bacon, Francis.) Lugdunum Batavorum, 1638.

Phil 1123.3.4 — Historia philosophiae. (Stanley, T.) Lipsiae, 1711.

Phil 1123.3.5 — Historia philosophiae. (Stanley, T.) Lipsiae, 1743.

Phil 806.36 — Historia philosophiae. v.1. (Gonzalez Cominero, N.) Romae, 1960. 2v.

Phil 1122.3.17 — Historia philosophiae graecae. (Ritter, Heinrich.) Gotha, 1898.

Phil 1122.3.25 — Historia philosophiae graecae. 9th ed. (Ritter, Heinrich.) Gotha, 1913.

Phil 1122.3.27 — Historia philosophiae graecae. 10 ed. (Ritter, Heinrich.) Gotha, 1934.

Phil 1122.3.9 — Historia philosophiae graecae et romanae. (Ritter, Heinrich.) Gotha, 1864.

Phil 1122.3.11 — Historia philosophiae graecae et romanae. 5. ed. (Ritter, Heinrich.) Gotha, 1875.

Phil 1122.3.12 — Historia philosophiae graecae et romanae. 6. ed. (Ritter, Heinrich.) Gotha, 1878.

Phil 1122.3.13 — Historia philosophiae graecae et romanae. 7.ed. (Ritter, Heinrich.) Gotha, 1888.

Phil 1122.3.5 — Historia philosophiae graeco-romanae. (Ritter, Heinrich.) Gotha, 1857.

Phil 1122.3 — Historia philosophiae graeco-romanae. (Ritter, Heinrich.) Hamburg, 1838.

Phil 332.10 — Historia philosophica doctrinae de ideis. (Brucker, Jacob.) Augustae Vindelicorum, 1723.

VPhil 5225.11 — Historia psychologii. (Pasluszha, Yózet.) Lublin, 1971.

Phil 806.30 — Historia sencilla de la filosofía. (Gambra Ciudad, R.) Madrid, 1961.

Phil 8050.44 — Historia tòn aisthètikòn theòriòn. (Kampanès, Aristos.) Athèna, 1936.

Htn Phil 1850.65* — Historia vitae et mortis. (Bacon, Francis.) Amstelodami, 1663.

Htn Phil 1850.63* — Historia vitae et mortis. (Bacon, Francis.) Lugdunum Batavorum, 1636.

Htn Phil 1850.64* — Historia vitae et mortis. (Bacon, Francis.) Lugdunum Batavorum, 1637.

Phil 4964.10 — História y filosofía. (Chaves, Osvaldo.) Buenos Aires, 1958.

Phil 807.3 — Historiae philosophicae. (Hornius, G.) Lugdunum Batavorum, 1755.

Phil 3910.77.10 — Historiam doctrinae recentius controversae de mundo optimo. (Baumeister, F.C.) Lipsiae, 1741.

Phil 8657.6 — Historic aspects...being attributes of God. (Cazenove, J.G.) London, 1886.

Phil 7069.36.15 — Historic British ghosts. (Sergeant, P.W.) London, 1936.

Phil 5014.1.30 — The historic development of logic. (Enriques, Federigo.) N.Y., 1929.

Phil 7060.68 — Historic ghosts and ghost hunters. (Bruce, Henry Addington Bayley.) N.Y., 1908.

Htn Phil 2295.27* — Historical account of life. (Toland, John.) London, 1718-22. 3 pam.

Phil 1712.1 — Historical and critical...philosophy, XIX century. (Morell, J.D.) London, 1846. 2v.

Phil 1712.1.2 — Historical and critical...philosophy, XIX century. (Morell, J.D.) N.Y., 1848.

Phil 1712.1.6 — Historical and critical...philosophy, XIX century. (Morell, J.D.) N.Y., 1856.

Phil 672.156 — An historical and critical examination of English space and time theories. Thesis. (Baker, John Tull.) Bronxville, N.Y., 1930.

Phil 5213.3 — An historical and critical study of radical behaviorism. (Diehl, Frank.) Baltimore, 1934.

Phil 5221.8 — The historical development of British psychiatry. (Leigh, D.) Oxford, 1961.

Phil 3002.1.6 — Historical development of speculative philosophy. (Chalybäus, H.) Edinburgh, 1854.

Phil 623.11 — An historical enquiry into the probable causes of the rationalist character lately predominant in the theology of Germany. (Pusey, E.B.) London, 1828.

Phil 5400.1 — Historical illustrations of the origin and progress of the passions. (Burgess, S.W.) London, 1825. 2v.

Phil 801.11 — An historical interpretation of philosophy. (Bascom, John.) N.Y., 1893.

Phil 8837.6 — Historical introduction to ethics. (Moore, T.V.) N.Y., 1915.

Phil 812.18 — An historical introduction to modern philosophy. (Miller, Hugh.) N.Y., 1947.

Phil 5222.3 Historical introduction to modern psychology. (Murphy, Gardner.) N.Y., 1929.

Phil 5222.3.5A Historical introduction to modern psychology. (Murphy, Gardner.) N.Y., 1949.

Phil 5222.3.5.2 An historical introduction to modern psychology. 2. ed. (Murphy, Gardner.) N.Y., 1930.

Phil 815.25 An historical introduction to philosophical thinking. (Perelman, C.) N.Y., 1965.

Phil 310.555.3 Historical materialism. (Chesnokov, Dimitrii I.) Moscow, 1969.

Phil 310.2.5 Historical materialism. (Cornforth, M.C.) N.Y., 1954.

Phil 310.325 Historical materialism. (Witt-Hansen, J.) Copenhagen, 1960.

Phil 310.696.2 Historical materialism: basic problems. Moscow, 1968.

Phil 1915.80 Historical memoires of...Dr. S. Clarke. (Whiston, W.) London, 1730.

Phil 8882.38 The historical method in ethics and other essays. (Handyside, John.) Liverpool, 1920.

Phil 6972.17 Historical notes on psychiatry. Photoreproduction. (Whitwell, James Richard.) Philadelphia, 1937.

Phil 2421.2 Historical pessimism in the French enlightenment. (Vyverberg, H.S.) Cambridge, 1958.

Phil 5232.12 Historical roots of contemporary psychology. (Wolman, Benjamin B.) N.Y., 1968.

Phil 8598.131 Historical selections in the philosophy of religion. (Smart, Ninian.) London, 1962.

Phil 5011.1 Historical sketch of logic. (Blakey, R.) London, 1851.

Phil 801.10.5 Historical studies in philosophy. (Boutroux, E.) London, 1912.

Phil 3002.1.7 Historical survey of speculative philosophy. (Chalybäus, H.) Andover, 1854.

Phil 3002.1.5 Historical survey of speculative philosophy. (Chalybäus, H.) London, 1854.

Phil 5816.10 An historical survey of vestibular equilibration. (Griffith, C.R.) Urbana, 1922.

Phil 4260.125 The historical theory of Giambattista Vico. (Berry, Thomas.) Washington, 1949.

Phil 310.641 Historický materialismus. Praha, 1965.

Phil 6671.18 Historie académique du magnétisme animal. (Burdin, C.) Paris, 1841.

Phil 803.1.5 Historie critique de la philosophie. (Deslandes, A.F.B.) Amsterdam, 1756. 4v.

Phil 6671.4.9 Historie de l'hypnotisme expérimental. (Bérillon, E.) Paris, 1902.

Phil 801.9 Historie des sciences de l'organisation. (Blainville, H. de.) Paris, 1845. 3v.

Phil 3002.1 Historie entwickelischen der speculativen Philosophie. (Chalybäus, H.) Leipzig, 1860.

Phil 310.15 Historie Materialismus und europäisches Geschichtsdenken. 1. Aufl. (Landesverband Nordshein-West-Tälischer Geschichte.) Düsseldorf, 1954.

Htn Phil 1850.64.5* Historie of life and death. (Bacon, Francis.) London, 1638.

Htn Phil 1850.57* The historie of the raigne of...Henry VII. (Bacon, Francis.) London, 1622.

Phil 1711.2 Les historiens de l'esprit humain. (Lenoir, R.) Paris, 1926.

Phil 8893.60 Historisch-kritische Darstellung der pathologischen Moralprincipien. (Stein, F.J.) Wien, 1871.

Phil 6955.8 Historisch-kritische Darstellung der Theorien über das Wesen und den Sitz der psychischen Krankheiten. (Friedreich, J.B.) Leipzig, 1836.

Htn Phil 3801.197.16* Historisch-kritische Erläuterungen zu Schelling's Abhandlungen über die Quelle der ewigen Wahrheiten. (Beckers, Hubert.) München, 1858.

Phil 182.41.5 Historisch-philosophische Abhandlungen. (Hartenstein, G.) Leipzig, 1870.

Phil 6114.8 Historisch-psychologische Untersuchungen...den Ursprung. 2. Aufl. (Ennemoser, Joseph.) Stuttgart, 1851.

Phil 5232.2 Historisch-psychologischer Tractat. (Wollny, F.) Leipzig, 1892.

Phil 1707.7 Historische Beiträge zur Philosophie. (Hertling, G.F. von.) München, 1914.

Phil 3890.1.30 Historische Beiträge zur Philosophie. (Trendelenburg, A.) Berlin, 1846-67. 3v.

Phil 310.730 Das historische Gesetz; zur Kritik der materialistischen Geschichtsauffassung von Jakob Hollitscher. (Hollitscher, Jakob J.) Dresden, 1901.

Phil 6313.9 Historische Grundlagen der Psychoanalyse. (Dorer, M.) Leipzig, 1932.

Phil 3501.11 Das Historische in Kants Religionsphilosophie. (Troeltsch, E.) Berlin, 1904.

Phil 3910.83 Historische Lobschrift des Herrn C. von Wolf. (Gottsched, J.C.) Halle, 1755.

NEDL Phil 497.7 Der historische Materialismus. (Woltmann, L.) Düsseldorf, 1900.

Phil 3486.1.10 Historische Untersuchungen über Kants Prolegomena. (Erdmann, B.) Halle, 1904.

Phil 2880.8.185 Historische Vernunft und direkte Aktion. (Zehm, Günter Albrecht.) Stuttgart, 1964.

Phil 3890.10.90 Die historische Wahrheit bei Ernst Troeltsch. Diss. (Liehrich, H.) Giessen, 1937.

Phil 3494.12 Die historischen Voraussetzungen,...der Kantischen Lehre. (Monzel, Alois.) Bonn, 1912.

Phil 1170.9 Historisk framställning och granskning utaf hufvudpunkterna i Plotini theoretiska philosophi. Thesis. (Hultkrantz, C.A.) Stockholm, 1851.

Phil 3552.284 Historisk öfversigt af den på monadlären grundade metafysikens utveckling. (Sjöberg, Gustaf M.) Upsala, 1868.

Phil 3246.188 Historisk öfversigt af Fichtes naturrält och Babergs outik deraf. (Widmark, Elof.) Upsala, 1854.

Phil 4508.2 Historiska anteckningar rörande fortgängen och utvecklingen af det philosophiska studium i Sverige. (Hammarsköld, Lorenzo.) Stockholm, 1821.

Phil 4635.6.30 Det historiska sammanhanget mellan Humes skepticism och Kants kriticism. (Sjöholm, L.A.) Upsala, 1869.

Phil 8599.19.20 Der Historismus und seine Uberwindung; fünf Vorträge. (Troeltsch, Ernst.) Berlin, 1924.

Phil 819.9 Historja filozofji. (Tatarkiewiaz, W.) Lwów, 1931. 2v.

Phil 806.12 Historja filozofji. (Gasiorowski, W.) Sandomierz, 1928.

Phil 812.12 Historja filozofji. (Myślicki, Ignacy.) Warszawa, 1930.

Phil 1735.16 History, man, and reason; a study in nineteenth-century thought. (Mandelbaum, Maurice H.) Baltimore, 1971.

Phil 5241.92.20 History, psychology and science. (Boring, E.G.) N.Y., 1963.

Phil 672.226 History, time and deity. (Brandon, Samuel George Frederick.) Manchester, 1965.

Phil 960.11 History...mediaeval school of Indian logic. (Vidyabhusana, Satis Chandra.) Calcutta, 1909.

Phil 6118.1 The history and power of mind. (Ingalese, R.) N.Y., 1903.

Phil 6118.1.3 The history and power of mind. 8th ed. (Ingalese, R.) N.Y., 1905.

Phil 6311.2.2 The history and practice of psychanalysis. (Bjerre, P.) Boston, 1920.

Phil 343.20 History and science. (Miller, H.) Berkeley, 1939.

Phil 745.6A The history and theory of vitalism. (Driesch, H.) London, 1914.

Phil 8837.5 History as past ethics. (Myers, P.V.) Boston, 1913.

Phil 6945.1 History description...Bloomingdale. (Earle, P.) N.Y., 1848-67. 21 pam.

Phil 8703.2.15 History is on our side. (Needham, Joseph.) London, 1946.

Htn Phil 1850.64.7* History naturall and experimentall, of life and death. (Bacon, Francis.) London, 1638.

Phil 7052.7.5 The history of a strange case. (Abbott, D.P.) Chicago, 1908.

Phil 8050.38 A history of aesthetic. (Bosanquet, B.) London, 1892.

Phil 8050.38.5 A history of aesthetic. (Bosanquet, B.) London, 1922.

Phil 8050.78 A history of aesthetics. (Gilbert, Mesk.) N.Y., 1939.

Phil 8050.95 History of aesthetics. (Tatarkiewicz, Wladyslaw.) The Hague, 1970.

Phil 1818.8 A history of American philosophy. (Schneider, H.W.) N.Y., 1946.

Phil 1818.8.2 A history of American philosophy. 2nd ed. (Schneider, H.W.) N.Y., 1963.

Phil 5227.6 History of American psychology. (Roback, A.A.) N.Y., 1951.

Phil 5227.6.2 History of American psychology. (Roback, A.A.) N.Y., 1964.

Phil 803.7 A history of ancient and medieval philosophy. (Dresser, H.W.) N.Y., 1926.

Phil 812.20 A history of ancient and medieval philosophy. (Mayer, F.) N.Y., 1950.

Phil 1106.3.15 History of ancient philosophy. (Benn, A.W.) London, 1912.

Phil 850.32 A history of ancient philosophy. (Brady, Ignatius.) Milwaukee, 1959.

Phil 1122.2.5 History of ancient philosophy. (Ritter, Heinrich.) Oxford, 1838-46. 4v.

Phil 1122.2.6 History of ancient philosophy. (Ritter, Heinrich.) Oxford, 1838-46. 4v.

Phil 1127.2 History of ancient philosophy. (Windelband, W.) N.Y., 1899.

Phil 1127.2.5 History of ancient philosophy. (Windelband, W.) N.Y., 1901.

Phil 1127.2.7 History of ancient philosophy. (Windelband, W.) N.Y., 1956.

Phil 1119.6 A history of ancient Western philosophy. (Owens, Joseph.) N.Y., 1959.

Phil 930.29.5 A history of Chinese philosophy. (Fung, Yu-lan.) Peiping, 1937.

Phil 930.29.8 A history of Chinese philosophy. (Fung, Yu-lan.) Princeton, 1953. 2v.

Phil 1511.3.13.15 History of Christian philosophy in the Middle Ages. (Gilson, Étienne.) London, 1955.

Phil 1511.3.13.10A History of Christian philosophy in the Middle Ages. (Gilson, Etienne.) N.Y., 1955.

Phil 1153.7 A history of cynicism from Diogenes to the 6th century A.D. (Dudley, D.R.) London, 1937.

Phil 7082.166A A history of dreams. (Ratcliff, Arthur James John.) Boston, 1923.

Phil 1135.5 A history of eclecticism in Greek philosophy. (Zeller, Eduard.) London, 1883.

Phil 1130.9 History of eclecticism in Greek philosophy. (Zeller, Eduard.) London, 1883.

Phil 1818.5 A history of English philosophy. (Sorley, William R.) Cambridge, Eng., 1920.

Phil 1818.5.5 A history of English philosophy. (Sorley, William R.) N.Y., 1920.

Phil 623.9 The history of English rationalism in the nineteenth century. (Benn, A.W.) London, 1906. 2v.

Phil 623.9.5 The history of English rationalism in the nineteenth century. (Benn, A.W.) N.Y., 1962. 2v.

Phil 1818.2.8 History of English thought in the eighteenth century. v.2. (Stephen, Leslie.) London, 1927.

Phil 1818.2.7.5 History of English thought in the eighteenth century. v.2. 3rd ed. (Stephen, Leslie.) N.Y., 1902.

Phil 1818.2.4 History of English thought in the eighteenth century. 3rd ed. (Stephen, Leslie.) N.Y., 1949. 2v.

Phil 1818.2.15 History of English thought in the 18th century. (Stephen, Leslie.) N.Y., 1962. 2v.

Phil 1818.2 History of English thought in XVIIIth century. (Stephen, Leslie.) N.Y., 1876. 2v.

Phil 1818.2.3 History of English thought in XVIIIth century. 3rd ed. (Stephen, Leslie.) London, 1902.

Phil 9550.5 A history of English utilitarianism. (Albee, Ernest.) London, 1902.

Phil 9550.5.2 A history of English utilitarianism. (Albee, Ernest.) London, 1957.

Phil 8957.4 History of ethics...Christianity. (Hall, T.C.) N.Y., 1910.

Phil 8826.8 History of ethics. (Bourke, Vernon Joseph.) Garden City, 1968.

Phil 8836.2 History of European morals. (Lecky, W.E.H.) London, 1869. 2v.

Phil 8836.2.11 History of European morals. (Lecky, W.E.H.) N.Y., 1913. 2v.

Phil 8836.2.13 History of European morals. (Lecky, W.E.H.) N.Y., 1926.

Phil 8836.2.5 History of European morals. v.1. (Lecky, W.E.H.) N.Y., 1876.

Phil 8836.2.6 History of European morals. 3. ed. (Lecky, W.E.H.) N.Y., 1897. 2v.

Phil 812.4 The history of European philosophy. (Marvin, W.T.) N.Y., 1917.

Phil 1712.2 History of European thought, 19th century. (Merz, J.T.) Edinburgh, 1896-1914. 4v.

Phil 1712.2.4 History of European thought, 19th century. (Merz, J.T.) Edinburgh, 1904. 2v.

Phil 1712.2.3A History of European thought, 19th century. v.1-3. (Merz, J.T.) Edinburgh, 1907-1912. 3v.

Phil 1712.2.5 A history of European thought in the nineteenth century. (Merz, J.T.) Edinburgh, 1912-27. 4v.

Phil 1712.2.6 A history of European thought in the nineteenth century. (Merz, J.T.) N.Y., 1965. 4v.

Phil 5211.4A	A history of experimental psychology. (Boring, E.G.) N.Y., 1929.
Phil 5211.4.5	A history of experimental psychology. 2. ed. (Boring, E.G.) N.Y., 1950.
Phil 5211.4.7A	A history of experimental psychology. 2. ed. (Boring, Edwin Garrigues.) N.Y., 1957.
Phil 5011.6.6	A history of formal logic. (Bochénski, I.M.) Notre Dame, Ind., 1961.
Phil 8610.913A	A history of freedom of thought. (Bury, J.B.) N.Y., 1913.
Phil 8610.913.5A	A history of freedom of thought. 2. ed. (Bury, J.B.) London, 1952.
Phil 8610.929	A history of freethought in the nineteenth century. (Robertson, J.M.) London, 1929.
Phil 8610.929.5	A history of freethought in the nineteenth century. (Robertson, J.M.) N.Y., 1930. 2v.
Phil 8610.929.9	A history of freethought in the nineteenth century. 4. ed. (Robertson, J.M.) London, 1936. 2v.
Phil 5865.2	A history of genetic psychology. (Grinder, Robert Eugene.) N.Y., 1967.
Phil 1112.1	History of Greek and Roman philosophy. London, 1853.
Phil 1133.20A	History of Greek philosophy. (Fuller, Benjamin A.G.) N.Y., 1923. 3v.
Phil 1111.12.10	A history of Greek philosophy. (Guthrie, William.) Cambridge, 1962. 3v.
Phil 1130.4A	History of Greek philosophy. (Zeller, Eduard.) London, 1881. 2v.
Phil 4960.605.5	A history of ideas in Brazil. (Cruz Costa, João.) Berkeley, 1964.
Phil 960.215	History of Indian epistemology. 2d ed. (Prasad, Jwala.) Delhi, 1958.
Phil 960.11.5	A history of Indian logic. (Vidyabhusana, Satis Chandra.) Calcutta, 1921.
Phil 960.28.2	A history of Indian philosophy. (Dasgupta, Surendra Nath.) Cambridge, 1963.
Phil 960.190A	History of Indian philosophy. (Umesha, Mishra.) Allahabad, 1957.
Phil 960.28	A history of Indian philosophy. v. 2-5. (Daqupta, S.) Cambridge, Eng., 1922-49. 4v.
Phil 960.43	History of Indian philosophy. v.2,7. (Belvalkar, S.K.) Poona, 1927-33. 2v.
Phil 802.3	History of intellectual development. v.1,3. (Crozier, F.B.) London, 1897. 2v.
Phil 1020.4.36	A history of Islamic philosophy. (Fakhry, Majid.) N.Y., 1970.
Phil 9347.4	The history of man. 3d ed. Dublin, 1791.
NEDL Phil 486.1.5.3	History of materialism. (Lange, F.A.) Boston, 1879-81. 3v.
Phil 486.1.5	History of materialism. (Lange, F.A.) London, 1877. 3v.
Phil 486.1.5.7A	History of materialism and criticism of its importance. v.1-3. 3rd ed. (Lange, F.A.) London, 1925.
Phil 486.1.5.9	History of materialism and criticism of its present importance. Photoreproduction. (Lange, F.A.) Boston, 1880-81. 3v.
NEDL Phil 486.1.5.8	The history of materialism and criticism of its present importance. v.1-3. 3rd ed. (Lange, F.A.) N.Y., 1925.
Phil 5066.242.1	History of mathematical logic from Leibniz to Peano. (Stiazhkin, Nikolai Ivanovich.) Cambridge, Mass., 1969.
Phil 1527.1.5.20	History of mediaeval philosophy. (Wulf, M. de.) N.Y., 1952.
Phil 6695.1	A history of medical psychology. (Zilboorg, G.) N.Y., 1941.
Phil 1050.10	History of medieval Jewish philosophy. (Husik, I.) N.Y., 1916.
Phil 1527.1.5.9	History of medieval philosophy. (Wulf, M. de.) London, 1926. 2v.
Phil 1527.1.5A	History of medieval philosophy. 3. ed. (Wulf, M. de.) London, 1909.
Phil 1702.11	A history of modern European philosophy. (Collins, James Daniel.) Milwaukee, 1961.
Phil 1701.6	History of modern philosophy. (Benn, A.W.) London, 1912.
Phil 1701.6.25	History of modern philosophy. (Benn, A.W.) London, 1930.
Phil 1701.4	History of modern philosophy. (Burt, Bery C.) Chicago, 1892. 2v.
Phil 1703.5	A history of modern philosophy. (Dresser, H.W.) N.Y., 1928.
Phil 1705.1.5	History of modern philosophy. (Falckenberg, R.) N.Y., 1893.
Phil 1705.1.7	History of modern philosophy. (Falckenberg, R.) N.Y., 1897.
Phil 1705.4.6	History of modern philosophy. (Fischer, K.) N.Y., 1887.
X Cg Phil 1707.1.5	History of modern philosophy. (Höffding, H.) London, 1900.
Phil 1707.1.6.5	A history of modern philosophy. (Höffding, H.) London, 1920. 2v.
Phil 1712.17A	A history of modern philosophy. (Mayer, Frederick.) N.Y., 1951.
Phil 1722.8	A history of modern philosophy. (Wright, W.K.) N.Y., 1941.
Phil 1707.1.6	History of modern philosophy. v.2. (Höffding, H.) London, 1908.
Phil 1707.1.6.10	A history of modern philosophy. v.2. (Höffding, H.) London, 1924.
Phil 2411.2	History of modern philosophy in France. (Levy-Bruhl, L.) London, 1899.
Phil 5228.18	A history of modern psychology. (Schultz, Duane P.) N.Y., 1969.
Phil 1812.9	History of modern thought, the English, Irish and Scotch schools. (Mahony, M.J.) N.Y., 1933.
Phil 8847.1	History of moral philosophy in England. (Whewell, W.) London, 1852.
Phil 8826.3	History of moral science. (Blakey, R.) Edinburgh, 1836. 2v.
Phil 1020.46	A history of Muslim philosophy. (Sharif, M.M.) Wiesbaden, 1963. 2v.
Phil 8626.23	History of opinions on the scriptural doctrine of retribution. (Beecher, E.) N.Y., 1878.
Phil 1822.6	A history of philosophical ideas in America. (Werkmeister, W.H.) N.Y., 1949.
Phil 805.10	A history of philosophical systems. (Ferm, V.) N.Y., 1950.
Phil 802.15.5	A history of philosophy. (Copleston, F.) Westminster, 1960. 8v.
Phil 804.2.2	History of philosophy. (Enfield, W.) Dublin, 1792. 2v.
Phil 804.2.4	History of philosophy. (Enfield, W.) London, n.d. 2v.
Phil 804.2	History of philosophy. (Enfield, W.) London, 1791. 2v.

Phil 804.2.3	History of philosophy. (Enfield, W.) London, 1819. 2v.
Phil 804.2.5	History of philosophy. (Enfield, W.) London, 1837.
Phil 804.3.5	History of philosophy. (Erdmann, J.E.) London, 1890. 3v.
Htn Phil 805.1*	History of philosophy. (Formey, J.H.S.) London, 1766.
Phil 805.8	A history of philosophy. (Fuller, B.A.G.) N.Y., 1938.
Phil 807.1	A history of philosophy. (Haven, J.) N.Y., 1876.
Phil 807.8	History of philosophy. (Hunter, T.) N.Y., 1900.
Phil 812.22	A history of philosophy. (Martin, S.G.) N.Y., 1947.
Phil 812.30	A history of philosophy. (Mascia, Carmin.) Paterson, N.J., 1957.
Phil 817.22	History of philosophy. (Radhakrishnan, S.) London, 1952. 2v.
Htn Phil 1123.3*	A history of philosophy. (Stanley, T.) London, 1687.
Phil 1123.3.3	History of philosophy. (Stanley, T.) London, 1701.
Phil 819.7.2A	A history of philosophy. (Thilly, F.) N.Y., 1914.
Phil 819.7.5	A history of philosophy. (Thilly, F.) N.Y., 1955.
Phil 819.5.2	History of philosophy. (Turner, W.) Boston, 1903.
Phil 819.5.7	History of philosophy. (Turner, W.) Boston, 1929.
Phil 820.1.14	History of philosophy. (Ueberweg, F.) London, 1874-75. 2v.
Phil 820.1.8A	History of philosophy. (Ueberweg, F.) N.Y., 1872-4. 2v.
Phil 820.1.10	History of philosophy. (Ueberweg, F.) N.Y., 1874. 2v.
Phil 1722.3	A history of philosophy. (Webb, C.C.J.) London, 1915.
Phil 822.12	A history of philosophy. (Webb, Clement C.J.) N.Y., 1915.
Phil 822.1.5	History of philosophy. (Weber, A.) N.Y., 1896.
Phil 822.1.12	History of philosophy. (Weber, A.) N.Y., 1909.
Phil 822.1.14	History of philosophy. (Weber, A.) N.Y., 1912.
Phil 822.1.15A	History of philosophy. (Weber, A.) N.Y., 1925.
Phil 807.20	A history of philosophy. N.Y., 1962. 4v.
Phil 804.3.7	History of philosophy. v.1, 2d ed.; v.2, 3d ed. (Erdmann, J.E.) London, 1890-92. 2v.
Phil 804.3.6	History of philosophy. v.1, 2d ed.; v.2-3, 3d ed. (Erdmann, J.E.) London, 1891-92. 3v.
Phil 802.15	A history of philosophy. v.1,4-8. (Copleston, F.) London, 1946-50. 6v.
Phil 801.21.5A	The history of philosophy. v.1-3,5-7. (Bréhier, É.) Chicago, 1963. 7v.
Phil 1123.3.1	History of philosophy. v.1-3. (Stanley, T.) London, 1656-60. 2v.
Htn Phil 1123.3.2*	A history of philosophy. v.1-3. (Stanley, T.) London, 1656-60. 2v.
Phil 822.2.11	History of philosophy. 2. ed. (Windelband, W.) N.Y., 1901.
X Cg Phil 804.3.7	History of philosophy. 2d ed. v.3. (Erdmann, J.E.) London, 1891.
Phil 819.7.7	A history of philosophy. 3. ed. (Thilly, F.) N.Y., 1957.
Phil 811.3.3	History of philosophy. 3d ed. (Lewes, G.H.) London, 1867. 2v.
Phil 818.1.5	History of philosophy in epitome. (Schwegler, F.C.A.) N.Y., 1856.
Phil 818.1.6.5	History of philosophy in epitome. (Schwegler, F.C.A.) N.Y., 1864.
Phil 1020.3.6	The history of philosophy in Islam. (Boer, T.J. de.) London, 1961.
Phil 960.40.4	A history of pre-Buddhistic Indian philosophy. (Barua, B.M.) Calcutta, 1921.
Phil 960.40.5	A history of pre-Buddhistic Indian philosophy. (Barua, B.M.) Delhi, 1970.
Phil 6311.2	The history of psychanalysis. (Bjerre, P.) Boston, 1919.
Phil 6980.133	The history of psychiatry. (Alexander, Franz G.) N.Y., 1966.
Phil 6906.5	A history of psychiatry. (Schneck, Jerome M.) Springfield, Ill., 1960.
Phil 6324.4	A history of psychoanalysis in America. (Oberndorf, Clarence.) N.Y., 1953.
Phil 5211.2A	History of psychology. (Baldwin, J.M.) N.Y., 1913. 2v.
Phil 5211.6	History of psychology. (Brennan, R.E.) N.Y., 1945.
Phil 5211.1	History of psychology. (Brett, G.S.) London, 1912-21. 3v.
Phil 5211.1.5	History of psychology. (Brett, G.S.) London, 1953.
Phil 5214.2	A history of psychology. (Esper, E.A.) Philadelphia, 1964.
Phil 5220.1.5	A history of psychology. (Klemm, O.) N.Y., 1914.
Phil 5225.1A	The history of psychology. (Pillsbury, W.B.) N.Y., 1929.
Phil 5238.224	History of psychology. (Sahakian, William S.) Itasca, Ill., 1968.
Phil 5227.6.10	History of psychology and psychiatry. (Roback, A.A.) N.Y., 1961.
Phil 5222.5A	A history of psychology in autobiography. (Murchinson, C.A.) Worcester, 1930-36. 4v.
Phil 623.8.5	History of rationalism. (Hurst, J.J.) London, 1867.
Phil 623.8.3	History of rationalism. (Hurst, J.J.) N.Y., 1865.
Phil 8584.12	The history of religion. (Evelyn, John.) London, 1850. 2v.
Phil 4710.35A	History of Russian philosophy. (Losskii, N.O.) N.Y., 1951.
Phil 4710.85.5	A history of Russian philosophy. (Zen'kovskii, V.V.) N.Y., 1953. 2v.
Phil 645.50.5	The history of scepticism. (Popkin, Richard H.) Assen, 1964.
Phil 645.50	The history of scepticism from Erasmus to Descartes. (Popkin, Richard H.) Assen, 1960.
Phil 645.50.7	The history of scepticism from Erasmus to Descartes. (Popkin, Richard H.) N.Y., 1964.
Phil 5220.7	A history of scientific psychology. (Klein, David Ballin.) N.Y., 1970.
Phil 7069.26.5	The history of spiritualism. (Doyle, Arthur Conan.) N.Y., 1926. 2v.
Phil 7150.54	The history of suicide in India. 1st ed. (Thakur, Upendra.) Delhi, 1963.
Phil 8050.28	The history of taste. (Chambers, Frank.) N.Y., 1932.
Phil 5325.17	A history of the association psychology. (Warren, Howard C.) N.Y., 1921.
Phil 5325.17.2	A history of the association psychology. Diss. (Warren, Howard C.) Baltimore, 1921.
Phil 7054.103	History of the Chicago artesian well. (Shufeldt, G.A., Jr.) Chicago, 1867. 2 pam.
Phil 8520.32	History of the Christian philosophy of religion. (Pünjer, G.C.B.) Edinburgh, 1887.
Phil 8693.4.3	History of the conflict between religion and science. (Draper, J.W.) N.Y., 1875.
Phil 8693.4.3.10	History of the conflict between religion and science. (Draper, J.W.) N.Y., 1897.

	Phil 5016.4	A history of the corruptions of logic: an inaugural lecture. (Geach, Peter Thomas.) Leeds, 1968.
	Phil 4897.15	A history of the development of Japanese thought from 592 to 1868. v.1-2. (Nakamura, Hajime.) Tokyo, 1967.
	Phil 8620.13A	History of the devil and idea of evil. (Carus, D.P.) Chicago, 1900.
	Phil 7059.10	History of the earth's formation. (Walrath, M.E.) N.Y., 1868.
	Phil 296.4	The history of the heavens. (Pluche, N.A.) London, 1740. 2v.
	Phil 178.12.42	A history of the new thought movement. (Dresser, H.W.) N.Y., 1919.
	Phil 7059.9	History of the origin of all things. (Arnold, L.M.) n.p., 1852.
NEDL	Phil 801.3	History of the philosophy of the mind. (Blakey, R.) London, 1848. 4v.
	Phil 801.3.2	History of the philosophy of the mind. (Blakey, R.) London, 1850. 4v.
	Phil 294.1	History of the prehistoric ages. (Nason, L.H.) Chicago, 1880.
	Phil 809.2	History of the problems of philosophy. (Janet, P.) London, 1902. 2v.
	Phil 6315.2.3.5	History of the psychoanalytic movement. (Freud, Sigmund.) N.Y., 1917.
	Phil 7054.73	A history of the recent developments in spiritual manifestations. Philadelphia, 1851.
	Phil 623.1.5	History of the rise and influence of the spirit of rationalism in Europe. (Lecky, W.E.H.) London, 1865. 2v.
	Phil 623.1A	History of the rise and influence of the spirit of rationalism in Europe. (Lecky, W.E.H.) N.Y., 1866. 2v.
	Phil 623.1.7	History of the rise and influence of the spirit of rationalism in Europe. (Lecky, W.E.H.) N.Y., 1968. 2v.
	Phil 623.1.20	History of the rise and influence of the spirit of rationalism in Europe. v.1-2. (Lecky, W.E.H.) London, 1910.
	Phil 6990.2	History of the robe of Jesus Christ. (Marx, J.) Philadelphia, 1845.
	Phil 1524.4	History of the schoolmen. (Thomas, Elliott C.) London, 1941.
	Phil 7054.93	History of the strange sounds or rappings. (Dewey, D.M.) Rochester, 1850.
	Phil 7052.9	The history of the supernatural. (Howitt, William.) Philadelphia, 1863. 2v.
	Phil 8712.3.5	History of the warfare of science with theology in Christendem. (White, Andrew Dickson.) N.Y., 1896. 2v.
NEDL	Phil 8712.3.9	History of the warfare of science with theology in Christendem. (White, Andrew Dickson.) N.Y., 1901. 2v.
	Phil 8712.3.10	History of the warfare of science with theology in Christendem. (White, Andrew Dickson.) N.Y., 1910. 2v.
	Phil 8712.3.11	History of the warfare of science with theology in Christendem. (White, Andrew Dickson.) N.Y., 1920. 2v.
	Phil 8712.3.12	A history of the warfare of science with theology in Christendem. (White, Andrew Dickson.) N.Y., 1965.
	Phil 800.13.2	A history of western European philosophy. 2d ed. (Aleksandrov, G.F.) New Haven, 1949.
	Phil 809.5	A history of Western philosophy. (Jones, W.T.) N.Y., 1952.
	Phil 817.19.5	History of Western philosophy. (Russell, B.R.) London, 1947.
	Phil 817.19A	A history of Western philosophy. (Russell, B.R.) N.Y., 1945.
	Phil 809.5.2	A history of Western philosophy. 2d ed. (Jones, W.T.) N.Y., 1969. 4v.
	Phil 4800.2.2	Historya logiki jako teoryi pozuania w Polsce. Wyd. 2. (Struve, Henryk.) Warszawa, 1911.
	Phil 75.6	Hiszmann, M. Anleitung der Literatur der Philosophie. Göttingen, 1778.
	VPhil 182.136	Hit és haladás; mult és jövö tarsadalmi kifejlés fokozatos hitnyilvánulasaként fogvaföl. Torda, 1908.
	Phil 8697.4	Hitchcock, C.H. The relations of geology to theology. Andover, 1867.
	Phil 5409.5	Hitchcock, C.M. The psychology of expectation. N.Y., 1903.
	Phil 8587.17	Hitchcock, E. The religion of geology...connected sciences. Boston, 1851.
	Phil 8587.17.5	Hitchcock, E. Religious truth. Boston, 1857.
X Cg	Phil 9495.141	Hitschmann, E. Frigidity in women. Washington, 1936.
	Phil 6317.33	Hitschmann, E. Great men. N.Y., 1956.
	Phil 6315.2.90.2	Hitschmann, Eduard. Freud's Neurosenlehre. 2. Aufl. Leipzig, 1913.
	Phil 6315.2.90.6	Hitschmann, Eduard. Freud's theories of the neuroses. N.Y., 1913.
	Phil 6315.2.90.5	Hitschmann, Eduard. Freud's theories of the neuroses. N.Y., 1913.
	Phil 8685.3	Hittell, J.S. A plea for pantheism. N.Y., 1857.
	Phil 6957.11	Hitzig, E. Über den Quärulantenwahnsinn. Leipzig, 1895.
	Phil 6117.35	Hitzig, E. Untersuchungen über das Gehirn. Berlin, 1874.
Htn	Phil 8882.13*	The hive. Worcester, Mass., 1795.
Htn	Phil 8882.13.2*	The hive. Worcester, Mass., 1796.
	Phil 5780.15.15	Hjärntvätt. (Waechter, Michael.) Stockholm, 1965.
	Phil 4610.12.80	Hjalmar Neiglick. (Mustelin, Olof.) Helsingfors, 1966.
	Phil 5047.24.5	Hjelmérus, Alfred. Den aristoteliska logiken jämförd med modern logik. Umea, 1918.
	Phil 5047.24	Hjelmérus, Alfred. Formella logiken baserad på identitetsprincipen. Lund, 1889.
	Phil 5047.36	Hlučka, F. Das Problem der Logik als Entwicklung des Prinzips der Heterothese. Leipzig, 1939.
	Phil 8882.52	Hlucka, J.F. Entwurf eines geschlossenen Systems der ethischen Formen. Wien, 1924.
	Phil 5047.17	Hoag, C.G. The logic of argument. Haverford, 1909.
	Phil 930.9.5	Hoang, Tsen-Yue. Etude comparative sur les philosophies de Lao Tseu, Khong Tseu, Mo Tseu. Thèse. Lyon, 1925.
	Phil 3489.14	Hoar, Robert. Der angebliche Mysticismus Kants. Brugg, 1895.
	Phil 5110.1	Hoaxes. (MacDougall, C.D.) N.Y., 1940.
	Phil 2045.119A	Hobbes; annual lecture on a master mind. (Gooch, G.P.) London, 1939.
	Phil 2045.02	Hobbes, Thomas. A bibliography by H. MacDonald and M. Hargreaves. London, 1952.
	Phil 2045.61.35	Hobbes, Thomas. De cive; or, The citizen. N.Y., 1949.
Htn	Phil 2045.70*	Hobbes, Thomas. Decameron physiologicum. London, 1678.
	Phil 2045.61.30	Hobbes, Thomas. Elemens philosophiques du bon citoyen. Paris, 1651.
Htn	Phil 2045.60.25*	Hobbes, Thomas. Elementa philosophica de cive. Amsterdam, 1647.
Htn	Phil 2045.61*	Hobbes, Thomas. Elementa philosophica de cive. Amsterdam, 1657.
Htn	Phil 2045.61.5*	Hobbes, Thomas. Elementa philosophica de cive. Amsterdam, 1669.
	Phil 2045.61.10	Hobbes, Thomas. Elementa philosophica de cive. Amsterdam, 1742.
	Phil 2045.61.9	Hobbes, Thomas. Elementa philosophica de cive. n.p., 16- .
Htn	Phil 2045.62*	Hobbes, Thomas. Elements of philosophy. London, 1656.
NEDL	Phil 2045.11	Hobbes, Thomas. English works. v.1-7,9-11. London, 1839-45. 10v.
	Phil 2045.14.2	Hobbes, Thomas. The English works of Thomas Hobbes of Malmesburg. Aalen, 1966. 11v.
	Phil 2045.14	Hobbes, Thomas. The English works of Thomas Hobbes of Malmesbury. Aalen, 1962. 11v.
	Phil 2045.20	Hobbes, Thomas. The ethics of Thomas Hobbes, by E.H. Sneath. Photoreproduction. Boston, 1898.
	Phil 2045.65	Hobbes, Thomas. Grundzüge der Philosophie. v.1-3. Leipzig, 1915-18.
Htn	Phil 2045.75*	Hobbes, Thomas. Historia ecclesiastica. Augustae, 1688.
Htn	Phil 2045.59*	Hobbes, Thomas. Human nature. London, 1650.
Htn	Phil 2045.77F*	Hobbes, Thomas. Last sayings. London, 1680.
	Phil 2045.53	Hobbes, Thomas. Leviatano. Bari, 1911-12. 2v.
	Phil 2045.53.10	Hobbes, Thomas. Il leviatano. Messina, 1930.
Htn	Phil 2045.47.5*	Hobbes, Thomas. Leviathan, sive de materia civitatis. London, 1678.
	Phil 2045.49.5	Hobbes, Thomas. Leviathan. Amstelodami, 1670.
	Phil 2045.49	Hobbes, Thomas. Leviathan. Amsterdam, 1667.
	Phil 2045.52.5	Hobbes, Thomas. Leviathan. Cambridge, 1935.
Htn	Phil 2045.48*	Hobbes, Thomas. Leviathan. London, 1651.
Htn	Phil 2045.48.5F*	Hobbes, Thomas. Leviathan. London, 1651.
	Phil 2045.51.9	Hobbes, Thomas. Leviathan. London, 1894.
	Phil 2045.52.15	Hobbes, Thomas. Leviathan. London, 1940.
	Phil 2045.52.25	Hobbes, Thomas. Leviathan. London, 1947.
NEDL	Phil 2045.50.2	Hobbes, Thomas. Leviathan. Oxford, 1881.
	Phil 2045.50.9	Hobbes, Thomas. Leviathan. Oxford, 1909.
	Phil 2045.52.20	Hobbes, Thomas. Leviathan. Oxford, 1946.
	Phil 2045.52.27	Hobbes, Thomas. Leviathan. Oxford, 1957.
	Phil 2045.52.28	Hobbes, Thomas. Leviathan. Oxford, 1967.
	Phil 2045.54	Hobbes, Thomas. Leviathan. Paris, 1921.
	Phil 2045.54.5	Hobbes, Thomas. Leviathan. Part I. Chicago, 1949.
	Phil 2045.51.3A	Hobbes, Thomas. Leviathan. 3rd ed. London, 1887.
Htn	Phil 2045.78.5F*	Hobbes, Thomas. Life. London, 1680.
	Phil 2045.55	Hobbes, Thomas. Metaphysical system. Chicago, 1910.
	Phil 2045.27A	Hobbes, Thomas. The metaphysical system of Hobbes. Chicago, 1905.
	Phil 2045.1	Hobbes, Thomas. Moral and political works. London, 1750.
Htn	Phil 2045.64*	Hobbes, Thomas. Mr. Hobbes considered in his loyalty, religion, reputation and manners. London, 1662.
	Phil 2045.67	Hobbes, Thomas. Naturrecht und allgemeines Staatsrecht in den Anfangsgründen. Berlin, 1926.
	Phil 2045.15	Hobbes, Thomas. Oeuvres philosophiques et politiques. Neufchatel, 1787. 2v.
Htn	Phil 2045.63*	Hobbes, Thomas. Of libertie and necessity. London, 1654.
	Phil 2045.10.5	Hobbes, Thomas. Opera philosophica. Aalen, 1961. 5v.
Htn	Phil 2045.3*	Hobbes, Thomas. Opera philosophica. Amstelodami, 1668. 2v.
	Phil 2045.12	Hobbes, Thomas. Opera philosophica. London, 1839-45. 5v.
	Phil 2045.10	Hobbes, Thomas. Opera philosophica. London, 1839-45. 5v.
Htn	Phil 2045.60*	Hobbes, Thomas. Philosophical rudiments concerning goverment and society. London, 1651.
	Phil 2045.25	Hobbes, Thomas. Philosophy of Hobbes in extracts and notes from his philosophy. Minneapolis, 1903.
	Phil 2045.58	Hobbes, Thomas. Quadratura circuli. n.p., 1669.
	Phil 2045.26	Hobbes, Thomas. Selections. N.Y., 1930.
Htn	Phil 2045.31*	Hobbes, Thomas. Tracts. London, 1678-82. 2 pam.
Htn	Phil 2045.31.5*	Hobbes, Thomas. Tracts. London, 1681.
Htn	Phil 2045.32*	Hobbes, Thomas. Tracts. London, 1682-84. 2 pam.
Htn	Phil 2045.30*	Hobbes, Thomas. Vita. Carolopoli, 1680-8-? 4 pam.
Htn	Phil 2045.30.2*	Hobbes, Thomas. Vita. Carolopoli, 1681.
Htn	Phil 2045.4*	Hobbes, Thomas. Works in Latin. Amsterdam, 1668-70.
	Phil 2045.116.5	Pamphlet box. Hobbes, Thomas.
	Phil 2045.136	Hobbes. (Brown, Keith C.) Cambridge, 1965.
	Phil 2045.115	Hobbes. (Laird, John.) London, 1934.
	Phil 2045.128	Hobbes. (Peters, Richard.) Harmondsworth, 1956.
NEDL	Phil 2045.81	Hobbes. (Roberstson, G.C.) Philadelphia, 1886.
	Phil 2045.81.4	Hobbes. (Robertson, George Croan.) St. Clair Shores, Michigan, 1970.
	Phil 2045.86	Hobbes. (Stephen, Leslie.) London, 1904.
	Phil 2045.86.2	Hobbes. (Stephen, Leslie.) London, 1904.
	Phil 2045.100	Hobbes im Lichte seiner didaktischen und pädagogischen Bedeutung. (Brockdorff, Cay von.) Kiel, 1919.
	Phil 2045.85	Hobbes Leben und Lehre. (Tönnies, F.) Stuttgart, 1896.
	Phil 2045.135	Hobbes' system of ideas; a study in the political significance of philosophical theories. (Watkins, J.W.N.) London, 1965.
	Phil 2045.99	Hobbes und die Staatsphilosophie. (Hönigswald, R.) München, 1924.
	Phil 2045.139	Hobbes's science of politics. (Goldsmith, M.M.) N.Y., 1966.
Htn	Phil 2045.97*	Hobbius Heauton-timorumenos. (Wallis, John.) Oxford, 1662.
	Phil 3450.19.101	Hoberg, C.A. Das Dasein des Menschen. Zeuleuroda, 1937.
	Phil 3450.19.102	Hoberg, C.A. Das Dasein des Menschen. Inaug. Diss. Zeuleuroda, 1937.
	Phil 4110.1.85	Hobert, Werner. Metaphysik des Marsilius Ficinus. Inaug. Diss. Koblenz, 1930.
	Phil 365.25	Hobhouse, L.T. Development and purpose. London, 1913.
	Phil 365.25.2	Hobhouse, L.T. Development and purpose. London, 1927.
	Phil 5817.5	Hobhouse, L.T. Mind in evolution. London, 1901.
	Phil 5817.5.2	Hobhouse, L.T. Mind in evolution. London, 1915.
	Phil 5817.5.5	Hobhouse, L.T. Mind in evolution. 3d ed. London, 1926.
	Phil 8882.30	Hobhouse, L.T. Morals in evolution. London, 1908. 2v.
	Phil 8832.3.5	Hobhouse, L.T. Morals in evolution. 5th ed. London, 1925.
	Phil 8882.30.10	Hobhouse, L.T. The rational good. London, 1947.
	Phil 338.1	Hobhouse, L.T. Theory of knowledge. London, 1896.
	Phil 2055.5.95	Hobhouse, Leonard Trelawney. Sociology and philosophy. Cambridge, 1966.
	Phil 525.16.13	Hobhouse, S.H. Fides et ratio; the book which introduced Jacob Boehme to William Law. n.p., 1936.

Phil 6314.8 — Hobman, J.B. David Eder; memoirs of a modern pioneer. London, 1945.
Phil 2055.5.90 — Hobson, John A. L.T. Hobhouse; his life and work. London, 1931.
Phil 623.44 — Hobson, John Atkinson. Rationalism and humanism. London, 1933.
Phil 6957.9 — Hoch, August. Benign stupors. N.Y., 1921.
Phil 5585.229 — Hochberg, Julian E. Perception. Englewood Cliffs, N.J., 1964.
Phil 3489.18 — Hochdorf, Max. Das Kantbuch. Berlin, 1924.
Phil 3450.21 — Hoche, A. Jahresringe. München, 1937.
Phil 7082.70 — Hoche, Alfred. Das Träumende ich. Jena, 1927.
Phil 3808.154 — Hochfeld, Sophus. Das künstlerische in der Aprache Schopenhauers. Leipzig, 1912.
Phil 8882.56 — Hochfelder, J. The supreme law of the future man. 2nd ed. N.Y., 1909.
Phil 3450.44 — Hochgesang, Michael. Mythos und Logik im 20. Jahrhundert. München, 1965.
Phil 6319.1.260 — Hochheimer, Wolfgang. The psychotherapy of C.G. Jung. N.Y., 1969.
Phil 1512.9 — Hochsteller, E. Die subjektiven GrundlagenDer scholastischen Ethik. Halle, 1915.
Phil 5425.45 — Hock, Alfred. Die methodische Entwicklung der Talente und des Genies. Leipzig, 1920.
NEDL Phil 2520.90 — Hock, C.F. Cartesius und seine Gegner. Wien, 1835.
Phil 9035.27 — Hocking, W.E. Human nature and its remaking. New Haven, 1918.
Phil 9035.27.5 — Hocking, W.E. Human nature and its remaking. New Haven, 1923.
Phil 9035.27.12 — Hocking, W.E. Human nature and its remaking. New Haven, 1932.
Phil 8587.37 — Hocking, W.E. Illicit naturalizing of religion. Chicago, 1923.
Phil 8662.7 — Hocking, W.E. The meaning of God in human experience. New Haven, Conn., 1912.
Phil 8662.7.6A — Hocking, W.E. The meaning of God in human experience. New Haven, Conn., 1924.
Phil 8662.7.5 — Hocking, W.E. The meaning of God in human experience. New Haven, 1923.
Phil 8633.1.36.5 — Hocking, W.E. The meaning of immortality in human experience. N.Y., 1957.
Phil 8697.17 — Hocking, W.E. Science and the idea of God. Chapel Hill, 1944.
Phil 5247.42A — Hocking, W.E. The self: its body and freedom. New Haven, 1928.
Phil 8633.1.36 — Hocking, W.E. Thoughts on death and life. N.Y., 1937.
Phil 182.88A — Hocking, W.E. Types of philosophy. N.Y., 1929.
Phil 182.88.7A — Hocking, W.E. Types of philosophy. N.Y., 1939.
Phil 182.88.3 — Hocking, W.E. Types of philosophy. 3d ed. N.Y., 1959.
Phil 2055.7.15A — Hocking, William E. Experiment in education. Chicago, 1954.
Phil 3489.22 — Hocking, William E. Immanuel Kant and international policies. Washington, D.C., 1924.
Phil 1807.4 — Hocking, William E. Lectures on recent trends in American philosophy. Claremont, 1941.
Phil 338.8 — Hocking, William E. Papers on logic and epistemology. v.1-6. N.Y., 1905.
Phil 735.7 — Hocking, William E. Papers on the theory of value. Lancaster, Pa., 1908. 2 pam.
Phil 2055.7.10 — Hocking, William E. Varieties of educational experience. Madison, N.H., 1952. 2v.
Phil 2055.7.5 — Hocking, William E. What man can make of man. N.Y., 1942.
Phil 8957.6 — Hocking, William J. Modern problems and Christian ethics. London, 1898.
Phil 3640.176 — Hocks, Erich. Das Verhältnis der Erkenntnis zur Unendlichkeit der Welt bei Nietzsche. Leipzig, 1914.
Phil 338.3 — Hodder, A. The adversaries of the sceptic. London, 1901.
Htn Phil 8632.13* — Hoddesdon, H. A treatise, concerning the death and resurrection of our bodies. London, 1606.
Phil 3120.30.200 — Hodes, Aubrey. Martin Buber; an intimate portrait. N.Y., 1971.
Phil 5627.127 — Hodge, Alexander. Prayer and its psychology. Thesis. London, 1931.
Phil 9245.48 — Hodge, George. The pursuit of happiness. N.Y., 1906.
Phil 5421.25.30 — Hodge, Marshall B. Your fear of love. Garden City, 1967.
Phil 630.3 — Hodge, W.H. Intuitive perception, presented by a new philosophy of natural realism. Lancaster, 1903.
Phil 9167.5 — Hodges, George. The happy family. N.Y., 1906.
Phil 8587.69 — Hodges, H.A. Languages, standpoints, attitudes. London, 1953.
Phil 3195.6.94.5 — Hodges, Herbert A. The philosophy of Wilhelm Dilthey. London, 1952.
Phil 3195.6.94 — Hodges, Herbert A. Wilhelm Dilthey. London, 1944.
Phil 9550.22 — Hodgson, D.H. Consequences of utilitarianism. Oxford, 1967.
Phil 8697.7 — Hodgson, Leonard. Theology in an age of science. Oxford, 1944.
Phil 182.19.11 — Hodgson, S.H. Metaphysic of experience. London, 1898. 4v.
Phil 182.19 — Hodgson, S.H. Philosophy and experience. London, 1885.
Phil 182.19.5 — Hodgson, S.H. Philosophy of reflection. London, 1878. 2v.
Phil 182.19.13 — Hodgson, S.H. The relation of philosophy to science, physical and psychological. London, 1884.
Phil 338.7 — Hodgson, S.H. Some cardinal points in knowledge. London, n.d.
Phil 8882.14 — Hodgson, S.H. The theory of practice. London, 1870. 2v.
Phil 182.19.8 — Hodgson, S.H. Time and space. A metaphysical essay. London, 1865.
Phil 807.11 — Hodgson, Shadworth H. Philosophy in relation to its history. London, 1880.
Phil 6677.14 — Hodson, Geoffrey. The science of seership. Philadelphia, 1930.
Phil 6317.16 — Hoeberlin, Carl. Grundlinien der Psychoanalyse. München, 1925.
Phil 185.29 — Die höchste Aufgabe der Philosophie. (Kühne, B.) Einsiedeln, 1880.
Phil 8880.32 — Das höchste Gut. (Franze, Paul.) Berlin, 1912.
Phil 196.14 — Die höchsten FragenBeleuchtet von den grössten Denkern der Neuzeit. (Vogel, August.) Berlin, 1896-
Phil 5628.50.25 — Höcht, Johannes Maria. Träger der Wundmale Christi. Wiesbaden, 1951-52. 2v.
Phil 182.99 — Höcksmann, F.X. Der Weg zum Sinn des Seins. Wien, 1933.
Phil 4803.454.1 — Hoëné Wronski. (Hoene-Wroński, Józef Maria.) Paris, 1970.
Phil 8882.15 — Hoefer, F. L'homme devant ses oeuvres. Paris, 1872.
Phil 3195.6.115 — Hoefer, Josef. Vom Leben zur Wahrheit. Freiburg, 1936.
Phil 1707.1.19A — Höffding, H. A brief history of modern philosophy. N.Y., 1912.
Phil 1707.1.25 — Höffding, H. Compendio di storia della filosofia moderna. Torino, 1923.
Phil 338.17.9 — Höffding, H. Les conceptions de la vie. Paris, 1928.
Phil 1807.1 — Höffding, H. Einleitung in die englische Philosophie. Leipzig, 1889.
Phil 1807.1.5 — Höffding, H. Den engelke philosophie i vortid. Kjøbenhavn, 1874.
Phil 338.17.5 — Höffding, H. Erkenntnistheorie und Lebensauffassung. Leipzig, 1926.
Phil 8882.16 — Höffding, H. Ethik. Leipzig, 1888.
Phil 8882.16.3 — Höffding, H. Etik. København, 1913.
Phil 8882.16.5 — Höffding, H. Etik. 5te udg. København, 1926.
Phil 1707.1A — Höffding, H. Geschichte der Philosophie. Leipzig, 1895. 2v.
Phil 1707.1.12 — Höffding, H. Histoire de la philosophie moderne. 2e éd. Paris, 1908. 2v.
X Cg Phil 1707.1.5 — Höffding, H. History of modern philosophy. London, 1900.
Phil 1707.1.6.5 — Höffding, H. A history of modern philosophy. London, 1920. 2v.
Phil 1707.1.6 — Höffding, H. History of modern philosophy. v.2. London, 1908.
Phil 1707.1.6.10 — Höffding, H. A history of modern philosophy. v.2. London, 1924.
Phil 3489.16 — Höffding, H. Kontinuiteten i Kants filosofiske udviklingsgang. Kjøbenhavn, 1893.
Phil 1707.1.15 — Höffding, H. Lehrbuch der Geschichte der neueren Philosophie. Leipzig, 1907.
Phil 182.36.17 — Höffding, H. Den menneskelige tanke. Kjobenhavn, 1910.
Phil 182.36.15 — Höffding, H. Der menschliche Gedanke. Leipzig, 1911.
Phil 1707.1.13 — Höffding, H. Modern philosophers. London, 1915.
Phil 1707.1.9 — Höffding, H. Moderne Philosophen. Leipzig, 1905.
Phil 5247.10.6 — Höffding, H. Outlines of psychology. London, 1892.
Phil 5247.10.8 — Höffding, H. Outlines of psychology. London, 1904.
Phil 5247.10.15 — Höffding, H. Pensée humaine. Paris, 1911.
Phil 1707.1.11 — Höffding, H. Philosophes contemporains. Paris, 1908.
Phil 3007.6 — Höffding, H. Philosophien i Tydskland efter Hegel. Kjøbenhavn, 1872.
Phil 182.36 — Höffding, H. Philosophische Probleme. Leipzig, 1903.
Phil 8632.2 — Höffding, H. The philosophy of religion. London, 1906.
Phil 182.36.6 — Höffding, H. The problems of philosophy. N.Y., 1905.
Phil 182.36.5 — Höffding, H. The problems of philosophy. N.Y., 1905.
Phil 182.36.7 — Höffding, H. The problems of philosophy. N.Y., 1906.
Phil 5247.10.13 — Höffding, H. Psychologie in Umrissen auf Grundläge der Erfahrung. Leipzig, 1887.
Phil 5247.10.14 — Höffding, H. Psychologie in Umrissen auf Grundläge der Erfahrung. Leipzig, 1893.
Phil 5247.10.3 — Höffding, H. Psykologi i omrids paa grundlag af erfaring. 3. ed. København, 1892.
Phil 5247.10.4 — Höffding, H. Psykologi i omrids paa grundlag af erfaring. 9. ed. København, 1920.
Phil 5247.10.19 — Höffding, H. Psykologiske undersogeler. Kjøbenhavn, 1889.
Phil 338.17 — Höffding, H. Der Relationsbegriff. Leipzig, 1922.
Phil 3827.3.7 — Høffding, H. Spinozas ethica, analyse og karakteristik. Heidelberg, 1924.
Phil 3827.3.5 — Høffding, H. Spinozas ethica, analyse og karakteristik. København, 1918.
Phil 3827.3 — Høffding, H. Spinozas liv og laere. København, 1877.
Phil 1707.1.8 — Höffding, H. Storia della filosofia moderna. Torino, 1913. 2v.
Phil 4580.66 — Høffding, Harald. Der Begriff der Analogie. Leipzig, 1924.
Phil 4580.66.10 — Høffding, Harald. Le concept d'analogie. Paris, 1931.
Phil 4580.20 — Høffding, Harald. Correspondence entre H. Høffding et G. Meyerson. Copenhague, 1939.
Phil 4580.30 — Høffding, Harald. Danske filosofer. København, 1909.
Phil 4580.79 — Høffding, Harald. Erindringer. København, 1928.
Phil 4580.37.5 — Høffding, Harald. Erlebnis und Deutung; eine vergleichende Studie zur Religionspsychologie. Stuttgart, 1923.
Phil 4580.65 — Høffding, Harald. Etiske undersøgelser. København, 1891.
Phil 4508.5 — Høffding, Harald. Filosofien i Sverige. Stockholm, 1879.
Phil 5047.23 — Høffding, Harald. Formel logik, til brug ved forelaesningar. 6. udgave. København, 1909.
Phil 4580.35.7 — Høffding, Harald. Kort oversigt over den nyere filosofis historie. 7e ed. Kjøbenhavn, 1919.
Phil 4580.35.9 — Høffding, Harald. Kort oversigt over den nyere filosofis historie. 9e ed. Kjøbenhavn, 1905.
Phil 4580.15 — Høffding, Harald. Mindre arbejder. Räkke 1-2. København, 1899-1905.
Phil 4580.62 — Høffding, Harald. Morale essai sur les principes théoriques. Paris, 1903.
Phil 4580.36 — Høffding, Harald. Den nyere filosofis historie. København, 1894-95. 2v.
Phil 4580.36.3 — Høffding, Harald. Den nyere filosofis historie. v.1-10. Kjøbenhavn, 1921-22. 2v.
Phil 4580.37 — Høffding, Harald. O plevelse og tydning religionsfilosofiske studier. Kjøbenhavn, 1918.
Phil 4580.64 — Høffding, Harald. Om grundlaget for den humane ethik. Kjøbenhavn, 1876.
Phil 4580.33.5 — Høffding, Harald. Personlighetsprincipen i filosofin. Stockholm, 1911.
Phil 2475.1.169 — Höffding, Harald. Philosophie de Bergson. Paris, 1916.
Phil 5047.23.5 — Høffding, Harald. Det psykologiske grundlag for logiske domme. København, 1899.
Phil 4580.38.15 — Høffding, Harald. Regionsphilosophie. Leipzig, 1901.
Phil 4580.51 — Høffding, Harald. La relativité philosophique. Paris, 1924.
Phil 4580.67 — Høffding, Harald. Religiøse tanketyper. København, 1927.
Phil 4580.38.20 — Høffding, Harald. Religionsfilosofi. 3e ed. København, 1924.
Phil 4580.63 — Høffding, Harald. Den store humor. Kjøbenhavn, 1916.
Phil 4580.50 — Høffding, Harald. Der totalitätsbegriff. Leipzig, 1917.
Phil 4580.40 — Høffding, Harald. Totalitet som kategori en erkendelsesteoretisk undersøgelse. København, 1917.
Phil 4580.32 — Høffding, Harald. Ved aarhundredeskiftet. København, 1901.
Phil 8855.4 — Höffe, Otfried. Praktische Philosophie. München, 1971.
Phil 5520.498 — Hoeffe, Wilhelm Laziar. Sprachlicher Ausdrucksgehalt und akustische Struktur. Ratingen bei Düsseldorf, 1960.
Phil 338.13 — Höfler, Alois. Erkenntnis Probleme und Erkenntnistheorie. Leipzig, n.d.
Phil 5047.14 — Höfler, Alois. Grundlehren der Logik und Psychologie. Leipzig, 1906.
Phil 5247.23.4 — Höfler, Alois. Grundlehren der Psychologie. 4. Aufl. Wien, 1908.
Phil 5247.23.7 — Höfler, Alois. Grundlehren der Psychologie. 7. Aufl. Wien, 1919.

Phil 5247.23.15   Höfler, Alois. Hundert psychologische Schulversuche. 4. Aufl. Leipzig, 1918.
Phil 5047.14.10   Höfler, Alois. Logik. 2e Aufl. Wien, 1922.
Phil 5047.14.5   Höfler, Alois. Philosophische Propädeutik. Prag, 1890.
Phil 5247.23.8   Höfler, Alois. Physiologische oder experimentelle Psychologie am Gymnasium? Wien, 1898.
Phil 5247.23.20   Höfler, Alois. Psychologie. 2e Aufl. Wien, 1930.
Phil 5247.23.25   Höfler, Alois. Zur Propädeutik-Frage. Wien, 1884.
Phil 165.210   Höfling, Helmut. Beiträge zer Philosphie und Wissenschaft. München, 1960.
Phil 179.3.105   Höhlmann, Hans. Rudolf Euckens Theologie. Berlin, 1903.
Phil 4575.25   Höijer, B.C.H. Filosofiska föreläsningar, 1806-1812. Lund, 1931.
Phil 4575.10   Höijer, B.C.H. Samlade skrifter. Stockholm, 1825-27. 5v.
Phil 1153.10   Höistad, R. Cynic hero and cynic king. Uppsala, 1948.
Phil 5247.70   Hoejgaard, Mogens. Mennesker og andre dyr. København, 1959.
Phil 8832.2   Hoekstra, S. Geschiedenis van de zedenlier. Amsterdam, 1896. 2v.
Phil 8882.44   Hoekstra, S. Zedenleer. Amsterdam, 1894. 3v.
Phil 3489.5   Hölder, Alfred. Darstellung der Kantischen Erkenntnisstheorie. Tübingen, 1873.
Phil 4308.1   Höllhuber, I. Geschichte der Philosophie im spanischen Kulturbereich. München, 1967.
Phil 4007.10   Hoellhuber, Ivo. Geschichte der italienischen Philosophie von den Anfängen des 19. Jahrhunderts biz zur Gegenwart. München, 1969.
Phil 672.235   Hoelling, Joachim. Ontologische Beiträge zum Raum-Zeit-Problem. Freiburg? 1965.
Phil 7060.47   Der höllischen Proteus...Erscheinder Gespenster. (Francisci, Erasmus.) Nürnberg, 1695.
Phil 5645.28   Höllner, Hans. Die Störungen des Farbensinnes ihre klinische Bedeutung und ihre Diagnose. Berlin, 1912.
Phil 1112.10   Hoelscher, Vvo. Anfanchisches Fragen; Studien zur Frühen griechischen Philosophie. Göttingen, 1968.
Phil 402.14   Hoelzle, Erwin. Idee und Ideologie. Bern, 1969.
Phil 1707.24   Hoenderdaal, G.J. De mens in tweeotrijd. Arnhem, 1956.
Phil 182.69F   Hoëné Wronski, J.M. Prospectus de la philosophie absolue et son développement. Paris, 1878.
Phil 4803.454.66   Hoene-Wroński, Józef Maria. Adresse aux nations slaves sur les destinées du monde. Paris, 1847.
Phil 4803.454.70   Hoene-Wroński, Józef Maria. Caméralistique; économie politique et finances. Paris, 1884.
Phil 4803.454.40   Hoene-Wroński, Józef Maria. Le destin de la France, de l'Allemagne, et de la Russie, comme prolégomènes du messianisme. Paris, 1842.
Phil 4803.454.72   Hoene-Wroński, Józef Maria. Épitre secrète à son altesse le Prince Louis-Napoléon sur les destinées de la France. Metz, 1851.
Phil 4803.454.1   Hoene-Wroński, Józef Maria. Hoëné Wronski. Paris, 1970.
Phil 4803.454.60   Hoene-Wroński, Józef Maria. Kodeks prawodawstwa społecznego absolutnego. Warszawa, 1923.
Phil 4803.454.32   Hoene-Wroński, Józef Maria. Lit do papiezy o maglacej potrzebie obechej spełnienia religli. Warszawa, 1928.
Phil 4803.454.30   Hoene-Wroński, Józef Maria. Messianisme; ou Réforme absolue du savoir humain. Paris, 1847. 3v.
Phil 4803.454.35   Hoene-Wroński, Józef Maria. Messianisme; philosophie absolue. Paris, 1876.
Phil 4803.454.50   Hoene-Wroński, Józef Maria. Messianisme, union finale de la philosophie et de la religion. Paris, 1831.
Phil 4803.454.55   Hoene-Wroński, Józef Maria. Metapolityke. Warszawa, 1923.
Phil 4803.454.65F   Hoene-Wroński, Józef Maria. Nomothétique messianique. Paris, 1881.
Phil 4803.454.74F   Hoene-Wroński, Józef Maria. Odezwa do narodóv slawianskich wzgledem przeznaczeń świata. Paryz, 1848.
Phil 4803.454.5   Hoene-Wroński, Józef Maria. L'oeuvre philosophique de Hoené Wronski. Paris, 1933-36. 2v.
Phil 4803.454.51   Hoene-Wroński, Józef Maria. Prodrom mesjanizmu albo filozofji absolutnej. Lwów, 1921.
Phil 4803.454.41   Hoene-Wroński, Józef Maria. Prolegomena do mesjanizmu. Lwów, 1922-25. 3v.
Phil 4803.454.45   Hoene-Wroński, Józef Maria. Propédeutigue messianique. v.2. Paris, 1875.
Phil 4803.454.46   Hoene-Wroński, Józef Maria. Propedeutyka mesjaniczna. v.2. Warszawa, 1925.
Phil 4803.454.61   Hoene-Wroński, Józef Maria. Reforma absolutna przeto ostateczna wiedzy ludzkiej. Paryz, 1891.
Phil 4803.454.21   Hoene-Wroński, Józef Maria. Sept manuscrits inédits, écrits de 1803 à 1806. Paris, 1879.
Phil 4803.454.22F   Pamphlet vol. Hoene-Wroński, Józef Maria. Miscellaneous writings. 9 pam.
Phil 4803.454.23   Pamphlet vol. Hoene-Wroński, Józef Maria. Miscellaneous writings. 3 pam.
Phil 4803.454.20   Pamphlet vol. Hoene-Wroński, Józef Maria. Miscellaneous writings. 4 pam.
Phil 4803.454.85   Hoene-Wroński. (Zieleńczyk, Adam.) Warszawa, 1930-?
Phil 4803.454.100   Hoene-Wroński i jego udział w rozwinięciu ostatecznem wiedzy ludzkiej. (Bukaty, Antoni.) Paryz, 1844.
Phil 288.15   Hoenen, Peter. Cosmologia. 5. ed. Romae, 1956.
Phil 288.15.5   Hoenen, Peter. The philosophical nature of physical bodies. West Baden Springs, Ind., 1955.
Phil 288.15.10   Hoenen, Peter. The philosophy of inorganic compounds. West Baden Springs, Ind., 1960.
Phil 288.15.2   Hoenen, Peter. Quaestiones noeticae de extensione corporea. Romae, 1955.
Phil 5047.34   Hönigswald, R. Beiträge zur Erkenntnistheorie uhd Methodenlehre. Leipzig, 1906.
Phil 4007.1   Hönigswald, R. Denker der italienischen Renaissance; Gestalten und Probleme. Basel, 1938.
Phil 338.20   Hönigswald, R. Geschichte der Erkenntnistheorie. Berlin, 1933.
Phil 5247.37.2   Hönigswald, R. Die Grundlagen der Denkpsychologie. 2. Aufl. Leipzig, 1925.
Phil 2045.99   Hönigswald, R. Hobbes und die Staatsphilosophie. München, 1924.
Phil 1707.5   Hönigswald, R. Die Philosophie von der Renaissance bis Kant. Berlin, 1923.
Phil 1750.118   Hönigswald, R. Philosophische Motive im neuzeitlichen Humanismus. Breslau, 1918.
Phil 5247.37.10   Hönigswald, R. Vom Problem des Rhythmus. Leipzig, 1926.
Phil 3625.3.83   Hönigswald, R. Zur Kritik der Machschen Philosophie. Berlin, 1903.
Phil 288.17   Hoenigswald, Richard. Schriften aus dem Nachlass. Stuttgart, 1957- 8v.
Phil 645.23   Hönigswald, Richard. Die Skepsis in Philosophie und Wissenschaft. Göttingen, 1914.

Phil 1112.3   Hönigwald, R. Die Philosophie des Altertums. München, 1917.
Phil 5520.665   Hoepp, Gerhard. Evolution der Sprache und Vernunft. Berlin, 1970.
Phil 6049.40   Hördin min og höndin jn. (Sigurðsson, J.S.) Reykjavík, 1940.
Phil 338.48   Hoeres, Walter. Kritik der transzendentalphilosophischen Erkenntnistheorie. Stuttgart, 1969.
Phil 5650.1   Höring, Adolf. Versuche über das Unterscheidungsvermögen des Hörsinnes für Zeitgrössen. Inaug. Diss. Tübingen, 1864.
Phil 5520.492   Hoermann, Hans. Psychologie der Sprache. Berlin, 1967.
Phil 5520.492.2   Hoermann, Hans. Psychologie der Sprache. Berlin, 1970.
Phil 8957.14   Hoermann, Karl. Handbuch der christlichen Moral. Innsbruck, 1958.
Phil 8815.5   Hoermann, Karl. Lexikon der christlichen Moral. Innsbruck, 1969.
Phil 400.52   Hoernlé, R.F.A. Idealism as a philosophical doctrine. London, 1924.
Phil 400.52.5   Hoernlé, R.F.A. Idealism as a philosophy. N.Y., 1927.
Phil 182.49.5   Hoernlé, R.F.A. Matter, life, mind and God. London, 1923.
Phil 182.49   Hoernlé, R.F.A. Studies in contemporary metaphysics. N.Y., 1920.
Phil 182.49.10.2   Hoernlé, R.F.A. Studies in philosophy. Cambridge, Mass., 1952.
Phil 182.49.10   Hoernlé, R.F.A. Studies in philosophy. London, 1952.
Phil 288.24   Hoerz, Herbert. Naturphilosophie von der Spekulation zur Wissenschaft. Berlin, 1969.
Phil 5643.163   Hoeth, Friedrich. Gesetzlichkeit bei stroboskopischen Alternativbewegungen. Frankfurt, 1966.
Phil 1750.115.155   Hoeven, Johannes van der. Kritische ondervraging van de fenomenologische rede. Amsterdam, 1963.
Phil 2520.330   Hoeven, Pieter van der. Metafysica en fysica bij Descartes. Gorinchem, 1961.
Phil 5477.14   Hövmann, H. Konflikt und Entscheidung. Göttingen, 1960.
Phil 3455.3.80   Hof, Ulrich im. Isaak Iselin. Basel, 1947. 2v.
Phil 3455.3.85   Hof, Ulrich im. Isaak Iselin und die Spätaufklärung. Bern, 1967.
Phil 6317.36   Hoff, Hans. Die Zeit und ihre Neurose.ien, 1956.
Phil 5047.7   Hoffbauer, J.C. Unfangsgrunde der Logik. Halle, 1810.
Phil 8882.102   Hoffbauer, Johann C. Untersuchungen über die wichtigsten Gegenstände. Dortmund, 1799-
Phil 5068.90   Hoffbauer, Johann Christoph. Versuch über die sicherste und leichteste Anwendung der Analysis in den philosophischen Wissenschaften (Leipzig). Bruxelles, 1968.
Phil 807.5   Hoffding, H. Filosofiske problemer. København, 1902.
Phil 5525.18   Hoffding, Harald. Humor als Lebensgefühl. Leipzig, 1918.
Phil 3120.55.82   Hoffen worauf? (Marsch, Wolf.) Hamburg, 1963.
Phil 6980.354   Hoffer, Abram. Niacin therapy in psychiatry. Springfield, Ill., 1962.
Phil 7150.25   Hoffman, F.L. Suicide problems. Newark, 1927.
Phil 5047.10   Hoffman, F.S. Sphere of science. N.Y., 1898.
Phil 7060.122   Hoffman, Frank S. Psychology and common life. N.Y., 1912.
Phil 9390.14   Hoffman, H.B. Loyalty by oath. Wallingford, 1957.
Phil 338.47   Hoffman, Robert. Language, minds, and knowledge. N.Y., 1970.
Phil 5817.4   Hoffman, S. Thier-Psychologie. Stuttgart, 1881.
Phil 8882.37   Hoffmann, A. Ethik. Freiburg, 1897.
Phil 3489.6   Hoffmann, A. Immanuel Kant. Halle, 1902.
Phil 2520.108.5   Hoffmann, A. René Descartes. Stuttgart, 1905.
Phil 2520.108.6   Hoffmann, A. René Descartes. 2. Aufl. Stuttgart, 1923.
Phil 5374.14.9   Hoffmann, Alfred. Vom Bewusstsein. Leipzig, 1907.
Phil 3270.1.84   Hoffmann, E. Kuno Fischer: Rede...seine 100. Geburtstages. Heidelberg, 1924.
Phil 3890.1.105   Hoffmann, Edmund. Die Psychologie Friedrich Adolf Trendelenburgs. Inaug. Diss. Greifswald, 1892?
Phil 1112.7.5   Hoffmann, Ernst. Die griechische Philosophie von Thales bis Platon. Heidelberg, 1951.
Phil 1112.7   Hoffmann, Ernst. Die griechische Philosophie von Thales bis Platon. Leipzig, 1921.
Phil 3090.80   Hoffmann, F. Biographie Franz von Baader's. Leipzig, 1857.
Phil 3090.80.5   Hoffmann, F. Franz von Baader in seinem Verhällnitz zu Hegel und Schelling. Leipzig, 1850.
Phil 1135.21   Hoffmann, F. Über die Gottes Idee des Anagoras. Wurzbrug, 1860.
Phil 3090.80.15   Hoffmann, F. Vorhalle zur speculativen Lehre F. Baader's. Aschaffenburg, 1836.
Phil 3090.80.10   Hoffmann, F. Zur Würdigung des Vorurthelie über der Lehre Baaders. Leipzig, 1855.
Phil 182.52   Hoffmann, Franz. Philosophische Schriften. v.1-2,4. Erlangen, 1868-1877. 3v.
Phil 3450.38   Hoffmann, Gustov. Genius der Menscheit. Delmenhorst, 1959.
Phil 9035.47.5   Hoffmann, H. Charakter und Umwelt. Berlin, 1928.
Phil 9035.47   Hoffmann, H. Das Problem des Charakteraufbaus. Berlin, 1926.
Phil 8697.11   Hoffmann, J.G. Kurtze Fragen von den natürlichen Dingen. Halle, 1757.
Phil 974.3.105   Hoffmann, K. Die Anthroposophie Rudolf Steiners und die moderne Geisleswissenschaft. Diss. Giessen, 1928.
Phil 182.20   Hoffmann, K. Philosophische Propädeutik. Passan, 1872.
Phil 8615.10   Hoffmann, P. La religion basée sur la morale. 2. éd. Bruxelles, 1901.
Phil 75.23   Hoffmans, Jean. La philosophie et les philosophes. Bruxelles, 1920.
Phil 3425.288   Hoffmeister, J. Dokumente zu Hegels Entwicklung. Stuttgart, 1936.
Phil 92.4   Hoffmeister, J. Wörterbuch der philosophischen Begriffe. Hamburg, 1955.
Phil 182.53   Hoffner, Paul. Grundlinien der Philosophie als Aufgabe. Mainz, 1881. 2v.
Phil 972.16   Hoffnung in Wichts. (Schwarz, W.) München, 1961.
Phil 5548.103   Hoffnung und Furcht in der Leistungsmotivation. (Heckhausen, H.) Meisenheim, 1963.
Phil 3475.3.195   Hoffnung und Sorge. (Jaspers, Karl.) München, 1965.
Phil 5252.39.2   Die Hoffnungslosigkeit allen Psychologie. (Mobius, P.) Halle, 1907.
Phil 3489.42   Hofman, Franz. Kants erst Antinomie in ihrer Stellung als Indirekter. Mainz? 1961.
Phil 182.21   Hofmann, A.W. Inaugural address. Boston, 1883.
Phil 6117.50   Hofmann, H. Religion and mental health. N.Y., 1961.
Phil 182.91   Hofmann, P. Metaphysik oder verstehende Sinnwissenschaft? Berlin, 1929.
Phil 182.91.5   Hofmann, P. Sinn und Geschichte. München, 1937.
Phil 5374.23   Hofmann, Paul. Die antithetische Struktur des Bewusstseins. Berlin, 1914.

Phil 1807.6   Holmes, E.C. Social philosophy and the social mind. N.Y., 1942.

Phil 1807.5A   Holmes, E.C. Social philosophy and the social mind. Thesis. N.Y., 1942.

Phil 6117.45.5   Holmes, E.S. This thing called life. N.Y., 1948.

Phil 182.62.15   Holmes, Edmond. The headquarters of reality. London, 1933.

Phil 182.62.10   Holmes, Edmond. Philosophy without metaphysics. London, 1930.

Phil 182.62   Holmes, Edmond. What is philosophy? London, 1905.

Phil 6117.45   Holmes, Ernest R. New thought terms and their meanings. N.Y., 1942.

Phil 6117.22   Holmes, F.L. The law of mind in action. N.Y., 1919.

Phil 8632.5   Holmes, John H. Is death the end? N.Y., 1915.

Phil 400.3   Holmes, N. Realistic idealism in philosophy itself. Boston, 1888. 2v.

Htn   Phil 6117.5*A   Holmes, O.W. Mechanism in thought and morals. Boston, 1871.

Phil 6117.5.7   Holmes, O.W. Mechanism in thought and morals. Boston, 1879.

Phil 6117.5.6   Holmes, O.W. Mechanism in thought and morals. Boston, 1882.

Phil 5047.39   Holmes, R.W. Exercises in reasoning, with an outline of logic. N.Y., 1940.

Phil 5047.38   Holmes, R.W. The rhyme of reason; a guide to accurate and mature thinking. N.Y., 1939.

Phil 4120.4.85   Holmes, Roger W. The idealism of Giovanni Gentile. N.Y., 1937.

Phil 5817.9.5   Holmes, S.J. Evolution of animal intelligence. N.Y., 1911.

Phil 7054.190   Holmes, W.H.G. Memories of the supernatural in east and west. London,, 1941.

Phil 7069.27.40   Holms, A.C. The fundamental facts of spiritualism. London, 1927.

Phil 3808.212   Holn, Søren. Schopenhauer ethik. Kjøbenhavn, 1932.

Phil 6677.16   Holsbéel, H. von. Lettres sur le magnétisme animal. Bruxelles, 1863.

Phil 5643.74   Holsopple, J.Q. Factors involved in the reduction of post-rotation nystagmus time. Baltimore, 1924.

Phil 3489.52   Holst, Johann Ludolf. Uber das Fundament der gesammten Philosophie des Herrn Kant. Halle, 1791. Bruxelles, 1968.

Phil 5425.60   Holste, Maria. Das Erlebnis und die Leistung. Inaug. Diss. Düsseldorf, 1936.

Phil 3805.164   Holstein, Günther. Die Staatsphilosophie Schleiermachers. Bonn, 1923.

Phil 1145.10   Holstein, R. Bedeutung des 7 Jahrhunderts. Stettin, 1903.

Phil 8957.3   Holt, A.E. The function of Christian ethics. Chicago, 1904.

Phil 5755.5.2   Holt, E.B. The Freudian wish and its place in ethics. N.Y., 1915.

Phil 5755.5   Holt, E.B. The Freudian wish and its place in ethics. N.Y., 1915.

Phil 630.5.5A   Holt, E.B. The new realism. N.Y., 1912.
Phil 630.5.7   Holt, E.B. The new realism. N.Y., 1922.
Phil 630.5.10   Holt, E.B. The new realism. N.Y., 1925.

Phil 5247.47A   Holt, Edwin B. Animal drive and the learning process. N.Y., 1931.

Phil 5635.20   Holt, Edwin B. An experimental study of sensation. Cambridge, Mass., 1903.

Phil 7060.100   Holt, H. On the cosmic relations. Boston, 1914. 2v.

Phil 7069.19.140   Holt, Henry. The cosmic relations and immortality. Boston, 1919. 2v.

Phil 7069.15.30   Holt, Henry. On the cosmic relations. Boston, 1915. 2v.

Phil 5841.6   Holter, Harriet. Sex roles and social structure. Oslo, 1970.

Phil 8677.14   The holy and the living God. (Willink, M.D.R.) London, 1931.

Phil 8880.17   The holy state and the profane state. (Fuller, T.) London, 1840.

Phil 8880.17.2   The holy state and the profane state. (Fuller, T.) London, 1840.

Phil 8582.29   Holy writ and modern thought. (Coxe, A. Cleveland.) N.Y., 1892.

Phil 2205.84.5   Holyoake, G.J. Paley's natural theology refuted in his own words. London, 1851.

Phil 8610.890.30   Holyoake, G.J. What would follow on the effacement of Christianity. Buffalo, 1890.

Phil 8662.5.9   Holyoake, George Jacob. The last trial for atheism in England. 5. ed. London, 1878.

Phil 8662.5.5   Holyoake, George Jacob. The report of the four nights' public discussion...on the truth of Christianity. London, 1850.

Phil 8662.5   Holyoake, George Jacob. Secularism, scepticism and atheism. London, 1870.

Phil 8662.5.10   Holyoake, George Jacob. Why do the clergy avoid discussion. London, 1852.

Phil 8882.19   Holyoke, E.A. An ethical essay. Salem, 1830.
Phil 2880.8.110   Holz, H.H. Jean Paul Sartre. Meisenheim, 1951.
Phil 3552.380   Holz, Hans H. Leibniz. Stuttgart, 1958.
Phil 2150.22.85   Holz, Hans Heinz. Utopie und Anarchismus; zur Kritik der kritischen Theorie H. Marcuses. Köln, 1968.

Phil 705.64   Holz, Harald. Transzendentalphilosophie und Metaphysik. Mainz, 1966.

Phil 9070.53   Holzamer, Karl. Grundriss einer praktischen Philosophie. Frankfurt am Main, 1951.

Phil 7162.267.1   Holzer, Hans W. ESP and you. 1st ed. N.Y., 1968.
Phil 7069.68.10   Holzer, Hans W. Ghosts of the Golden West. Indianapolis, 1968.

Phil 7069.68.30   Holzer, Hans W. The lively ghosts of Ireland. London, 1968.

Phil 7069.68.20   Holzer, Hans W. Psychic investigator. 1st ed. N.Y., 1968.
Phil 7055.310.25   Holzer, Hans W. The psychic world of Bishop Pike. N.Y., 1970.

Phil 7069.69   Holzer, Hans W. Window to the past. Garden City, 1969.
Phil 3489.50   Holzhey, Helmut. Kants Erfahrungsbegriff. Basel, 1970.
Phil 5400.140   Holzkamp, Klaus. Ausdrucksverstehen im Erlebnisaspekt. Inaug. Diss. Berlin, 1956.

Phil 5247.80   Holzkamp, Klaus. Theorie und Experiment in der Psychologie. Berlin, 1964.

Phil 338.42   Holzkamp, Klaus. Wissenschaft als Handlung. Berlin, 1968.
Phil 5247.69   Holzner, Burket. Amerikanische und deutsche Psychologie. Würzburg, 1958?

Phil 5850.230.100   Holzschuher, L. von. Praktische Psychologie. 2. Aufl. Seebruck am Chiemsee, 1955.

Phil 3450.19.20   Holzwege. (Heidegger, Martin.) Frankfurt, 1950.
Phil 3450.19.23A   Holzwege. 3e Aufl. (Heidegger, Martin.) Frankfurt, 1957.
Phil 6117.45.50   Homaday, William H.D. The inner light. N.Y., 1964.

Phil 1870.128   Homage to George Berkeley. (Hermathena.) Dublin, 1953.
Phil 5627.270   Homans, Peter. Theology after Freud; an interpretive inquiry. Indianapolis, 1970.

Phil 4362.10   El hombre, ser indigente: el pensamiento antropológico de Pedro Lain Entralgo. (Soler Puigoriol, Pedro.) Madrid, 1966.

Phil 177.95   El hombre. (Carrasquilla R., Humberto.) Medellin, 1934.
Phil 1750.680   El hombre. (Civera, Marin.) México, 1956.
Phil 585.162   El hombre como síntesis del universo. 1. ed. (Román, Julián.) Rosario, 1965.

Phil 805.13.5.2   El hombre en la encrucijada. 2. ed. (Ferrater, Mora José.) Buenos Aires, 1965.

Phil 9070.80   El hombre en vilo. (Corts Grau, José.) Madrid, 1958.
Phil 9035.29.3   El hombre mediocre. 3d ed. (Ingegnieros, José.) Buenos Aires, 1917.

Phil 476.3.11   El hombre segum la ciencia. (Büchner, L.) Barcelona, 1869.

Phil 4980.1.30   Hombres y engranajes. (Sabato, Ernesto R.) Buenos Aires, 1951.

Phil 7052.5   Home, D.D. Lights and shadows of spiritualism. London, 1878.

Phil 7054.45.9   Home, Daniel Douglas. Incidents in my life. N.Y., 1863.
Phil 7054.45.11   Home, Daniel Douglas. Incidents in my life. London, 1863.
Phil 7054.45.14   Home, Daniel Douglas. Incidents in my life. 5th ed. N.Y., 1864.

Phil 7054.45.5   Home, Daniel Dunglas (Mrs.). D.D. Home, his life and mission. London, 1888.

Phil 7054.45   Home, Daniel Dunglas (Mrs.). The gift of D.D. Home. London, 1890.

Phil 8882.20   Home, H. Introduction to the art of thinking. Edinburgh, 1764.

Htn   Phil 2055.1.30*   Home, Henry. Essays on the principles of morality. Edinburgh, 1751.

Phil 9178.5   Home, the basis of the state. (Seymour, A.) Boston, 1869.
Phil 9163.3   Home life. (Diggle, J.W.) London, 1908.
Phil 9182.3   Home life: what it is, and what it needs. (Ware, J.F.W.) Boston, 1864.

Phil 2270.160   Home life with Herbert Spencer. (Two (pseud.).) Bristol, 1906.

Phil 6420.30   A home study course in the correction of stuttering and stammering. (Wolfe, Paul J.) n.p., 1932.

Phil 8692.3.7   Homely thoughts on the city of God and way to find it. (Coutts, John.) London, 1921.

Phil 8897.27   The homely virtues. (Watson, John.) N.Y., 1902.
Phil 585.198   O homem contemporâneo. (Melo, Roneu de.) Lisboa, 1965.
Phil 9240.30   O homem em face da dor. (Veloso, Agostinho.) Lisboa, 1961.

Phil 2475.1.251   Homenaje a Bergson. (Córdoba, Argentina. Universidad Nacional. Instituto de Filosofía.) Córdoba, 1936.

Phil 2475.1.270   Homenaje a Bergson. (Mexico City. Universidad Nacional. Facultad de Filosofía y Estudios Superiores. Centro de Estudios Filosóficos.) México, 1941.

Phil 3640.304   Homenaje a Friedrich Nietzsche en el primer centenario de su nacimiento. (Blanco, Julio E.) Baranquilla, 1944.

Phil 4987.89.80   Homenaje a Xavier Zubiri. Madrid, 1953.
Phil 4987.89.90   Homenaje a Xavier Zubiri. Madrid, 1970. 2v.
Phil 4363.3.101   Homenaje al venerable siervo de dios, Don Miguel. Sevilla, 1925.

Phil 2490.171   Homenajes: Augusto Comte. 1. ed. (Mendieta y Núñez, L.) México, 1961.

Phil 2055.1.35   Homes, Henry. Versuche über die ersten Gründe der Sittlichkeit. Braunschweig, 1768.

Phil 3850.27.130   Hommage a Albert Schweitzer. Paris, 1955.
Phil 165.100   Hommage á Gaston Bachelard. Paris, 1957.
Phil 5238.182   Hommage à Georges Henyer. Paris, 1961.
Phil 2750.17.90   Hommage à Henri Mieville. Lausanne, 1948.
Phil 165.462   Hommage à Jean Hyppolite. 1. ed. Paris, 1971.
Phil 2477.6.105   Hommage à Maurice Blondel. Paris, 1946.
Phil 1527.1.50   Hommage à Monsieur le Professeur Maurice de Wulf. Louvain, 1934.

Phil 6315.2.250   Hommage à Sigmund Freud. (Revue Francaise de Psychanalyse.) Paris, 1956.

Phil 487.5   L'homme, esprit ou matière?. (Mayer, Charles L.) Paris, 1949.

Phil 165.23   L'homme, le monde. Grenoble, 1948.
Phil 8896.22   L'homme, maître de sa destinée. (Vernet, Maurice.) Paris, 1956.

Phil 8599.40   Homme, qui suis-je? (Le Trocquer, René.) Paris, 1957.
Phil 2655.5.30   L'homme. (Hello, E.) Paris, 1872.
Phil 585.404   L'homme à la recherche de son humanité. (Légaut, Marcel.) Paris, 1971.

Phil 1123.13.10   L'homme antique et la structure du monde interieur d'Homère à Socrate. (Schaerer, René.) Paris, 1958.

Phil 8587.73   L'homme au regard de la foi. Paris, 1959.
Phil 194.15   L'homme dan sa triple vie. (Tounissoux, M. L'Abbé.) Paris, n.d.

Phil 335.9   L'homme dans le monde. (Etcheverry, Auguste.) Paris, 1963.

Phil 1750.515   L'homme dans le monde. (Ferrier, Jean Louis.) Neuchâtel, 1957.

Phil 2520.216   L'homme de Descartes. (Mattei, André.) Paris, 1940.
Phil 2880.1.42   L'homme de désir. (Saint-Martin, L.C.) Londres, 1808.
Htn   Phil 2880.1.40*   L'homme de désir. (Saint-Martin, L.C.) Lyon, 1790.
Phil 5425.4.5   L'homme de génie. (Lombroso, C.) Paris, 1889.
Htn   Phil 2520.34.10*   L'homme de René Descartes et la formation du Foetus. (Descartes, René.) Paris, 1677.

Phil 2880.8.106   L'homme de Sartre. (Prucke, B.) Grenoble, 1949.
Phil 1123.13.5   L'homme devant ses choix dans la tradition grecque. (Schaerer, René.) Louvain, 1965.

Phil 8882.15   L'homme devant ses oeuvres. (Hoefer, F.) Paris, 1872.
Phil 6111.36   L'homme droit et l'homme gauche. (Biervliet, J.J.) Gand, 1901.

Phil 735.18.5   L'homme du ressentiment. (Scheler, Max.) Paris, 1933.
Phil 5246.88   L'homme en ce monde et le sens de la vie. (Gosselin, Albert.) Paris, 1970.

Phil 525.252   L'homme et la connaissance. Paris, 1965.
Phil 805.15   L'homme et la conscience tragique. (Flam, Leopold.) Bruxelles, 1964.

Phil 8735.5   L'homme et la création. 2. éd. (Desdouits, M.) Paris, 1846.

Phil 6978.10   L'homme et la douleur. (Bricout, Jacques.) Paris, 1969.
Phil 8612.45.2   L'homme et la mort. (Morin, Edgar.) Paris, 1951.
Phil 8612.45   L'homme et la mort dans l'histoire. (Marin, Edgar.) Paris, 1951.

Phil 5819.2   L'homme et l'animal. (Joly, H.) Paris, 1877.
Phil 6121.38   L'homme et le complexe normal. (La Rivière, A.) Paris, 1961.

Phil 5627.151   L'homme et le péché. Paris, 1938.

Phil 672.165   L'homme et le temps. Photoreproduction. (Burgelin, Pierre.) Paris, 1945.

Phil 5811.3   L'homme et les animaux. (Bourbon del Monte, J.B.F.) Paris, 1877.

Phil 5257.6   L'homme et l'intelligence. (Richet, Charles.) Paris, 1884.

Phil 2805.50   L'homme et l'oeuvre. (Pascal, Blaise.) Paris, 1956.

Phil 194.47   L'homme et sa raison. (Thévenaz, P.) Neuchâtel, 1956. 2v.

Phil 5421.10.35   L'homme et son angoisse. (Barraud, Jean.) Paris, 1969.

Phil 70.75.1   L'homme et son destin, d'après les penseurs du moyen âge. (Congrès International de Philosophie Médiévale, 1st, Louvain and Brussels, 1958.) Louvain. 1960

Phil 585.176   L'homme et son destin. (Jeuscher, Ernest.) Paris, 1961.

Phil 5477.16   L'homme et son juge. (Greeff, Etienne de.) Paris, 1962.

Phil 5627.266.20   L'homme et son lieu. Psychologie et foi. (Tournier, Paul.) Neuchâtel, 1966.

Phil 8612.52.5   L'homme et son ultime option, Mysterium mortis. (Boros, Ladislaus.) Paris, 1966.

Htn   Phil 2520.34*   L'homme et un traitte de la formation du Foetus. (Descartes, René.) Paris, 1664.

Phil 2750.32.30   L'homme face à son destin. (Mayer, Charles Leopold.) Paris, 1964.

Htn   Phil 192.60.5   L'homme impuissant. (Richet, Charles.) Paris, 1927.

Htn   Phil 2705.30*   L'homme machin. v.1-2. (La Mettrie, Julien Offray de.) Leyde, 1748.

Phil 2705.35   L'homme machine, suivi de l'Art de jouir. (La Mettrie, Julien Offray de.) Paris, 1921.

Phil 2705.35.6   L'homme machine. (La Mettrie, Julien Offray de.) Paris, 1966.

Phil 2705.35.5A   L'homme machine. (La Mettrie, Julien Offray de.) Princeton, 1960.

Phil 184.47   L'homme métaphysique. (Jolivet, Régis.) Paris, 1958.

Phil 585.188.2   L'homme microscopique. 2e éd. (Auger, Pierre.) Paris, 1966.

Phil 8876.102   L'homme moral, ou Règles de conduite prises dans sa propre nature. (Briel, C.) Sens, 179-

Phil 585.157   L'homme normal. (Chauchard, P.) Paris, 1963.

Htn   Phil 2705.85*   L'homme plus que machine. (Luface, Elie.) Londres, 1748.

Phil 2750.19.26   L'homme problematique. (Marcel, Gabriel.) Paris, 1955.

Phil 2750.24.30   L'homme quelconque. (Menetrier, Jacques.) Paris, 1959.

Phil 9240.10.5   L'homme révolté. 94. éd. (Camus, Albert.) Paris, 1952.

Phil 2880.8.96   L'homme Sartre. (Bligbeder, Marc.) Paris? 1947.

Phil 476.3.6   L'homme selon la science. (Büchner, L.) Paris, 1870.

Phil 585.125   L'homme social. (Aolliet, Joseph.) Paris, 1942.

Phil 5390.6   L'homme stupide. (Richet, Charles.) Paris, 1919.

Phil 3475.3.235   Hommel, Claus Uwe. Chiffer und Dogma. Zürich, 1968.

Phil 1750.367.5   Hommes, Jakob. Dialektik und Politik. 1e Aufl. Köln, 1968.

Phil 3007.12   Hommes, Jakob. Krise der Freiheit. Regensburg, 1958.

Phil 310.18   Hommes, Jakob. Der technische Eros. Freiburg, 1955.

Phil 1750.367   Hommes, Jakob. Zwiespältiges Dosein. Freiburg, 1953.

Phil 2750.19.25   Les hommes contre l'humain. (Marcel, Gabriel.) Paris, 1951.

Phil 1750.166.85   Hommes et machines. (Laloup, Jean.) Tournai, 1953.

Phil 8663.3.93   Homo (pseud.). Analogy, or The theology of nature. New Haven, 1885.

Phil 8620.38   Homo (pseud.). Essais. Le don des langues. Paris, 1931.

Phil 195.9   Homo Abyssus. (Ulrich, Ferdinand.) Johannes, 1961.

Phil 9075.71   Homo duplex. (Hylkema, G.W.) Haarlem, 1963.

Phil 5259.42   Homo faber. (Tyrrell, G.N.M.) London, 1952.

Phil 5275.10   Homo informationicus, réflexions sur l'homme et l'informatique. (Pelikán, Pavel.) Nancy, 1967.

Phil 5259.38   Homo sapiens. 2. Aufl. (Thirring, H.) Wien, 1948.

Phil 9470.6   Homo sapiens socialis, principles of the philosophy of responsibility. (Jordan, Rudolf.) Johannesburg, 1944.

Phil 187.8.5   Homo viator. (Marcel, Gabriel.) London, 1951.

Phil 187.8.7   Homo viator. (Marcel, Gabriel.) Paris, 1952.

Phil 6834.10   Homosexual liberation; a personal view. (Murphy, John.) N.Y., 1971.

Phil 6834.1   Homosexuality; a bibliography of literature published since 1959 and available in New Zealand. (Millett, Antony P.U.) Wellington, 1967.

Phil 6834.15   Homosexuality: a selective bibliography of over 3000 items. (Parker, William.) Metuchen, N.J., 1971.

Phil 6834.20   Homosexuality and psychological functioning. (Freedman, Mark.) Belmont, Calif., 1971.

Phil 5242.56.5   Homs psychologicus. (Schein-Coen.) London, 1970.

Phil 8170.7   Honcharenko, M.V. Mystetstvo i estetichne vychovannia. Kyïv, 1963.

Phil 3425.628   Hondt, Jacques d'. Hegel; philosophe de l'histoire vivante. Thèse. Paris, 1966.

Phil 3425.660   Hondt, Jacques d'. Hegel en son temps, Berlin, 1818-1831. Paris, 1968.

Phil 3425.770   Hondt, Jacques d'. Hegel et la pensée moderne. 1. éd. Paris, 1970.

Phil 3425.652   Hondt, Jacques d'. Hegel secret, recherches sur les sources cachées de la pensée de Hegel. Paris, 1968.

Phil 1870.110   Hone, J.M. Bishop Berkeley. London, 1931.

Phil 338.19   Honecker, M. Das Denken. Berlin, 1925.

Phil 5047.32.10   Honecker, M. Gegenstandslogik und Denklogik Vorschlag zu einer Neugestaltung der Logik. 2. Aufl. Berlin, 1928.

Phil 5047.32   Honecker, M. Logik: eine Systematik der logischen Probleme. Berlin, 1927.

Phil 8594.13.10   Honest religion. (Oman, John.) Cambridge, Eng., 1941.

Phil 8610.967.5   Honest to man. (Ratnathicam, Daniel S.) Colombo, 1967.

Phil 9560.7.5   L'honneur, sa place dans la morale. (Gay, Antoine.) Paris, 1913.

Phil 9560.7   L'honneur sentiment et principle moral. (Terraillon, E.) Paris, 1912.

Phil 5645.42   Honoré, Paul. Color light and vision. Detroit, 1938.

Phil 6677.19   Hont, A.E. La lumière sur le magnétisme. Neuchâtel, 1880.

Phil 5047.30   Honthem, J. Der logische Algorithmus. Berlin, 1895.

Phil 9347.5   Hood, E.P. Self formation. 3d ed. London, 1878.

Phil 2045.134   Hood, F.C. The divine politics of Thomas Hobbes. Oxford, 1964.

Phil 8662.9   Hood, John. The beauty of God. Baltimore, 1908.

Phil 1701.15   Hoofdfiguren der geschiedenis van het urjsgeerig denden. 2e druk. (Bierens de Haan, J.) Haarlem, 1927.

Phil 5241.39   Hoofdlijnen eener psychologie met metafysischen grondslag. (Bierens de Haan, P.) Amsterdam, 1898.

Phil 9400.35   Hoofdproblemen der volwassenheid. (Wijngaarden, H.M.) Utrecht, 1950.

Phil 8951.14   Hoofdstukken uit de bijzondere ethiek. v.1-5. (Beysens, J.T.) Bussum, 1917-19-.

Phil 2475.1.211   Hoogveld, J.E.H.J. "De nieuwe wijsbegeerte." Een studie over Henri Bergson. Utrecht, 1915.

Phil 5247.59   Hook, A. The human mind. London, 1940.

Phil 1830.11   Hook, Sidney. American philosophers at work. N.Y., 1956.

Phil 70.40   Hook, Sidney. Determinism and freedom in the age of modern science. N.Y., 1958.

Phil 1830.10   Hook, Sidney. Freedom and experience. Ithaca, 1947.

Phil 1955.6.103A   Hook, Sidney. John Dewey. N.Y., 1939.

Phil 1955.6.104   Hook, Sidney. John Dewey. N.Y., 1950.

Phil 182.82   Hook, Sidney. The metaphysics of pragmatism. Chicago, 1927.

Phil 6317.38   Hook, Sidney. Psychoanalysis. N.Y., 1959.

Phil 2055.13.30   Hook, Sidney. The quest for being. N.Y., 1961.

Phil 2055.13.35   Hook, Sidney. Religion in a free society. Lincoln, 1967.

Phil 6317.9.5   Hoop, J.H. van der. Bewusstseinstypen und ihre Beziehung zur Psychopathologie. Bern, 1937.

Phil 6317.9A   Hoop, J.H. van der. Character and the unconscious. London, 1923.

Phil 6317.9.10   Hoop, J.H. van der. Conscious orientation. London, 1939.

Phil 5047.13   Hooper, C.E. The anatomy of knowledge. London, 1906.

Phil 182.56.2   Hooper, Charles. Common sense and the rudiments of philosophy. 2d ed. London, 1920.

Phil 5757.16   Hooper, Charles E. The fallacies of fatalism. London, 1930.

Phil 2280.5.97   Hoor, M. George Santayana's theory of knowledge. Diss. n.p., 1923.

Phil 2055.12.30   Hoor, Marten ten. Education for privacy. n.p., 1960.

Phil 8589.5.45   Hoover, Dwight W. Henry James. Grand Rapids, 1969.

Phil 2835.86   Hooykaas, Reijer. Humanisme, science et réforme. Leyde, 1958.

Phil 75.35   Hope, R. A guide to readings in philosophy. Ann Arbor, 1939.

Htn   Phil 182.23*   Hope, T. Essay on origin of man. London, 1831. 3v.

Phil 5590.26.5   Hope for man. (Liebman, Joshua Loth.) N.Y., 1966.

Phil 8626.18   The hope of a world to come underlying Judaism and Christianity. (Bavan, Edwyn R.) London, 1930.

Phil 8633.1.9   The hope of immortality, our reasons. (Dole, C.F.) N.Y., 1906.

Phil 8627.2.2   The hope of the human race. (Cobbe, F.P.) London, 1874.

Phil 8627.2   The hope of the human race. (Cobbe, F.P.) London, 1880.

Phil 6116.18   The hope of the variant. (Gehring, J.G.) N.Y., 1923.

Phil 9362.1   Hopes and helps for the young. (Weaver, G.S.) N.Y., 1855.

Phil 8408.54   Hopf, Andreas. Die Struktur des östhetischen Urteils. München, 1968.

Phil 1135.150   Hopgner, T. Orient und griechische Philosophie. Leipzig, 1925.

Phil 9167.2   Hopkins, E. The family, a religious institution. Troy, N.Y., 1840.

Phil 8882.21.3   Hopkins, M. The connexion between taste and morals. Boston, 1841.

Phil 8882.21.2   Hopkins, M. The connexion between taste and morals. Boston, 1841.

Phil 8882.21   Hopkins, M. The connexion between taste and morals. Boston, 1842.

Phil 8882.21.15   Hopkins, M. The law of love and love as a law. N.Y., 1885.

Phil 8882.21.12   Hopkins, M. The law of love and love as a law. 3rd ed. N.Y., 1871.

Phil 8882.21.5.3   Hopkins, M. Lectures on moral science. Boston, 1865.

Phil 5247.11.7   Hopkins, M. An outline of man; or, The body and mind in one system. N.Y., 1889.

Phil 5247.11.3   Hopkins, M. An outline study of man. N.Y., 1883.

Phil 6317.23   Hopkins, P. The psychology of social movements. London, 1938.

Phil 5627.262.5   Hopkins, Pryns. The social psychology of religious experience. N.Y., 1962.

Phil 9070.38   Hopkinson, A.W. Pastor's psychology. London, 1944.

Phil 9120.165   Hopmann, W. Essai d'une nouvelle explication utilitariste du sentiment d'obligation. Genève, 1941.

Phil 8587.28.5   Hoppe, Edmund. Glauben und Wissen. 2. Aufl. Gütersloh, 1922.

Phil 8587.28   Hoppe, Edmund. Natur und Offenbarung. 2. Aufl. Hannover, 1904.

Phil 4372.1.80   Hoppe, G. Psychologie des Juan Luis Vives. Berlin, 1901.

Phil 7068.72.20   Hoppe, I. Hellsehen des Unbewussten. Freiburg., 1872.

Phil 5643.12.9   Hoppe, J.F. Die Drehbare Bilderscheibe. Leipzig, 1884.

Phil 7060.18   Hoppe, J.F. Erklärung der Sinnestäuschungen. Würzburg, 1888.

NEDL   Phil 5643.12.5   Hoppe, J.F. Psychologish-physiologische Optik. Leipzig, 1881.

Phil 5643.12   Hoppe, J.F. Die Schein-Bewegungen. Würzburg, 1879.

Phil 8587.33.3   Hoppe, J.I. Die Erforschung der Gefühle und moralischen Begriffe. 3. Aufl. Regensburg, 1876.

Phil 338.14   Hoppe, J.I. Die persönliche Denkthätigkeit. Würzburg, 1880.

Phil 5047.22   Hoppe, James. Die kleine Logik. Paderborn, 1869.

Phil 325.1   Hoppe, R. Zulänglichkeit des Empirismus...Philosophie. Berlin, 1852.

Phil 3489.31   Hoppe, V. Dva základní problémy Kantova kriticismu. Brno, 1932.

Phil 3120.8.85   Hoppenstedt, W. von. Franz Brentanos Kantkritik. Inaug. Diss. Kiel, 1933.

Phil 1850.96.3   Hoppus, J. An account of Lord Bacons Novum Organon Scientiarum. London, 1827. 3 pam.

Phil 1850.96.2   Hoppus, J. An account of Lord Bacons Novum Organon Scientiarum. London, 1827. 3 pam.

Phil 1850.96   Hoppus, J. An account of Lord Bacon's Novum Organon Scientiarum. London, 1827-28.

Phil 5910.2   Horae phrenologicae. (Epps, J.) London, 1829-1836. 6 pam.

Phil 5520.481   Horálek, Karel. Filosofie jazyku. Praha, 1967.

Phil 310.610   Horbach, U.I. O vidakh protivorechii. Minsk, 1964.

Phil 8408.42   Hordiienko, Anatolii. Mystetstvo, diisnist' i svoboda khudozhn'oï tvorchosti. Kyïv, 1966.

Phil 182.51   Horion, Charles. Testament philosophique...essai de synthése revolutioniste. Bruxelles, 1909.

Phil 5585.185   L'horizon des esprits. (Moreau, J.) Paris, 1960.

Phil 176.88.10   The horizon of experience. (Burne, C.D.) N.Y., 1934.

Phil 8657.34   Horizons de l'athéisme. (Cottier, Georges.) Paris, 1969.

Phil 165.336   Horizons of a philosopher. (Frank, J.) Leiden, 1963.

Phil 6315.56   The horizons of the mind. (Fernandez, M.) N.Y., 1964.

Phil 333.13   The horizons of thought. (Conger, George P.) Princeton, 1933.

Phil 5421.35.10   Horizonte der Hoffnung. (Edmaier, Alois.) Regensburg, 1968.

Phil 3450.28.10   Horkheimer, Max. Dialektik der Aufklärung. Amsterdam, 1947.

Phil 3450.28   Horkheimer, Max. Eclipse of reason. N.Y., 1947.

Phil 3450.28.15   Horkheimer, Max. Kritische Theorie. Frankfurt, 1968. 2v.

Phil 3450.28.20   Horkheimer, Max. Die Sehnsucht nach dem ganz Anderen. Hamburg, 1970.

Phil 5832.16   De hormische psychologie van den mensch. (Wimersama Greidanus, H.T. van.) Leiden, 1946.

Phil 3425.692   Horn, András. Kunst und Freiheit. Den Haag, 1969.

Phil 182.98.5   Horn, E. Der Begriff des Begriffes. München, 1932.

Phil 182.98   Horn, E. Der Begriff des Begriffes. Inaug. Diss. München, 1931.

Phil 8882.46   Horn, E.F.B. Mennesket og moralen. Malling, 1877.

Phil 8587.33   Horn, E.F.B. Tolv forebaesninger over tro og taenkning. Kristiania, 1896.

Phil 3800.725   Horn, F. Schelling und Swedenborg. Zürich, 1954.

Phil 3475.3.190   Horn, H. Philosophischer und christlicher Glaube. Essen, 1961.

Phil 5047.44   Horn, Heinz. Widerspiegelung und Begriff. Berlin, 1958.

Phil 7054.144   Horn, Henry J. Strange visitors. N.Y., 1869.

Phil 900.5   Horn, J. Uber die biblische Gnosis. Hannover, 1805.

Phil 3827.4   Horn, J.F. Spinoza's Staatslehre. Dessau, 1851.

Phil 182.134   Horn, Joachim Christian. Monade und Begriff. Der Weg von Leibniz zu Hegel. Wien, 1965.

Phil 6117.37   Horn, Paul. Über nervöse Erkrankungen nach Eisenbahnunfällen. Bonn, 1913.

Phil 5757.5   Horne, H.H. Free will and human responsibility. N.Y., 1912.

Phil 8882.51   Horne, H.H. Jesus as a philosopher, and other radio talks. N.Y., 1927.

Phil 3640.124   Horneffer, Auguste. Nietzsche als Moralist und Schriftsteller. Jena, 1906.

Phil 8587.31   Horneffer, Ernst. Das klassische Ideal. 2-3. Aufl. Leipzig, 1909.

Phil 8587.30   Horneffer, Ernst. Die künftige Religion. Leipzig, 1909.

Phil 3640.121.5   Horneffer, Ernst. Nietzsche-Vorträge. Leipzig, 1920.

Phil 3640.121.15   Horneffer, Ernst. Vorträge über Nietzsche. Berlin, 1903.

Phil 3640.121.10   Horneffer, Ernst. Vorträge über Nietzsche. Berlin, 1906.

Phil 3246.205   Horneffer, Martha. Die Identitätslehre Fichtes in den Jahren 1801-1806. Leipzig, 1925.

Phil 6317.22.25   Horney, Karen. Feminine psychology. N.Y., 1967.

Phil 6317.22A   Horney, Karen. The neurotic personality of our time. N.Y., 1937.

Phil 6317.22.5A   Horney, Karen. New ways in psychoanalysis. N.Y., 1939.

Phil 6317.22.20   Horney, Karen. Our inner conflict. N.Y., 1945.

Phil 6317.22.10A   Horney, Karen. Self-analysis. N.Y., 1942.

Phil 807.3   Hornius, G. Historiae philosophicae. Lugdunum Batavorum, 1755.

Phil 530.20.53   Hornstein, X. de. Les grands mystiques allemands du XIVe siècle. Lucerne, 1922.

Phil 4803.846.80   Horodyski, Władysław. Bronisław Trentowski (1808-1869). Kraków, 1913.

Phil 1750.166.270   Horosz, William. The promise and peril of human purpose. Saint Louis, 1970.

Phil 2636.85   Horowitz, I.L. Claude Helvetius. N.Y., 1954.

Phil 4065.130A   Horowitz, I.L. The Renaissance philosophy of Giordano Bruno. N.Y., 1952.

Phil 5465.182.5   Horowitz, Mardi Jon. Image formation and cognition. N.Y., 1970.

Phil 8633.1.23   Horr, George E. The Christian faith and eternal life. Cambridge, 1923.

Phil 4580.120   Horreüs de Hass, G. Harald Høffding en zijne beteekenis voor godsdienstwipbegeerte en zedeleer. Huister Heide, 1930.

Phil 5876.25.3   Horrocks, John Edwin. The psychology of adolescence; behavior and development. 3rd ed. Boston, 1969.

Phil 182.138   Hors'kyï, Vilen S. Sotsial'ne seredovishche ta istoriko-filosofs'kyi protses. Kyïv, 1969.

Phil 6117.8A   Horsley, V. The brain and spinal cord. London, 1892.

Phil 5592.194   Horst, Paul. Personality; measurement of dimensions. 1. ed. San Francisco, 1968.

Phil 7069.40.14   Hort, Gertrude M. Three famous occultists: Dr. John Dee. Photoreproducton. Philadelphia, 1940.

Phil 1504.5.3   Horten, M. Buch der Ringsteine Alfārābis. v.5, pt.3. Münster, 1906.

Phil 1020.18.5   Horten, M. Die Philosophie des Islam. München, 1923.

Phil 1020.18.10   Horten, M. Die spekulative und positive Theologie des Islam. Hildesheim, 1967.

Phil 990.26   Horten, Max. Die philosophischen Ansichten von Razi und Tusi. Bonn, 1910.

Phil 2477.9.81   Horton, W.M. The philosophy of the Abbé Bantain. N.Y., 1926.

Phil 5628.5.5   Horton, Wade H. The glossolalia phenomenon. 1st ed. Cleveland, 1966.

Phil 8520.34.3   Horton, Walter M. Contemporary continental theology. 2. ed. N.Y., 1938.

Phil 8520.34   Horton, Walter M. Contemporary English theology; an American interpretation. N.Y., 1936.

Phil 8662.13   Horton, Walter M. Theism and the modern mood. N.Y., 1930.

Phil 5247.12   Horwicz, A. Psychologische Analysen. v.1-2. Halle, 1872-78. 3v.

Phil 8882.53   Horwicz, Adolf. Moralische Briefe. Magdebourg, 1878.

Phil 6957.22   Hoskins, Roy G. The biology of schizophrenia. 1. ed. N.Y., 1946.

Phil 8882.80   Hospers, John. Human conduct. N.Y., 1961.

Phil 182.114.7   Hospers, John. An introduction to philosophical analysis. Englewood Cliffs, 1967.

Phil 182.114   Hospers, John. An introduction to philosophical analysis. London, 1956.

Phil 9070.11   Hostel, G. Out of the wilderness. N.Y., 1940.

Phil 6319.1.190   Hostie, Raymond. Analytische Psychologie en Godsdienst. Utrecht, 1954.

Phil 6319.1.190.5   Hostie, Raymond. Du mythe à la religion. Bruges, 1955.

Phil 5412.10   The hostile mind. (Saul, Leon Joseph.) N.Y., 1956.

Phil 8408.30   Hostinsky, Otakar. O umění. Praha, 1956.

Phil 8408.30.10   Hostinský, Otakar. Otakara Hostinského esthetika. Praha, 1921.

Phil 5520.430   Hotopf, W.H.N. Language, thought and comprehension. London, 1965.

Phil 8980.456   Hott, V.S. Dva svity, dvi morali. Kyiv, 1959.

Phil 3640.575   Hotter, Karl. Das Bildungsproblem in der Philosophie Nietzsches. München, 1958.

Phil 930.54   Hou, Wai-lu. A short history of Chinese philosophy. Peking, 1959.

Phil 2880.8.145   Houbart, Jacques. Un père déuaturé. Paris, 1964.

Phil 5039.2   Houde, Roland. Readings in logic. Dubuque, 1958.

Phil 7069.24.25   Houdini, Harry. A magician among the spirits. N.Y., 1924.

Phil 8587.49   Houf, Horace T. What religion is and does. N.Y., 1935.

Phil 8587.56   Hough, Lynn Harold. Whither Christianity. N.Y., 1929.

Phil 5251.22   Houptbegriffe der Psychologie. (Leuchtenberger, G.) Berlin, 1896.

Phil 8882.70   Hourani, G.F. Ethical value. London, 1956.

Phil 525.9   Hours with the mystics. (Vaughan, R.A.) London, 1856. 2v.

Phil 525.9.2   Hours with the mystics. 2nd ed. (Vaughan, R.A.) London, 1860. 2v.

Phil 5047.15   Hourticq, R. Leçons de logique et de morale. Paris, 19-?

Phil 8663.3.45   The house of death. (Ingersoll, Robert G.) London, 1897.

Phil 6315.2.101A   The house that Freud built. (Jastrow, Joseph.) N.Y., 1932.

Phil 5625.87   Householder, A.S. Some notes for simple Pavlovian learning. Santa Monica, 1951.

Phil 8610.929.35   Housman, L. The religious advance toward rationalism, delivered at Conway Hall on Sept. 25, 1929. London, 1929.

Phil 270.8   Houten, S. van. Causalitäs-Gesetz in der Socialwissen. Harlem, 1888.

Phil 5817.8   Houzeau, Jean C. Études sur les facultés mentales des animaux. Mons, 1872. 2v.

Phil 974.3.70   Hovels, Karl. Beiträge zur Kritik der anthroposophischen Welt- und Lebensanschauung. Inaug. Diss. Rheinland, 1926.

Phil 2805.435   Hoven, Pieter van der. Blaise Pascal. Baarn, 1964.

Phil 8957.1   Hovey, A. Pascal. Boston, 1875.

Phil 7054.2   How and why I became a spiritualist. 4th ed. (Danskin, W.A.) Baltimore, 1869.

Phil 5827.8   How animals find their way about. (Rabaud, E.) Leipzig, 1928.

Phil 8582.59   How can I bear suffering? (Christlieb, M.L.) London, 1944.

Phil 7069.29.90   How do the dead communicate. (Spiritual and Ethical Society, New York.) n.p., 1929.

Phil 7069.23.8   How I know that the dead do live. Boston, 1923.

Phil 3925.18.30   How I see philosophy. (Waismann, Friedrich.) N.Y., 1968.

Phil 343.34   How language makes us know. (Mesthene, Emmanuel G.) The Hague, 1964.

Phil 6127.24   How never to be tired, or Two lifetimes in one. (Ray, Marie B. Lyons.) Indianapolis, Ind., 1944.

Phil 7069.40.17   The "how" of divine revelation. (Wood, E.C.) Camden, N.J., 1940.

Phil 192.40.10   How philosophy uses its past. (Randall, J.H.) N.Y., 1963.

Phil 8602.1   How religion arises. (Ward, D.J.H.) Boston, 1888.

Phil 5058.28.21   How the mind falls into error. (Smith, Henry B.) N.Y., 1923.

Phil 7140.12   How to acquire and strengthen will-power. (Ebbard, R.J.) London, 1905.

Phil 9353.1   How to be a lady. (Newcomb, H.) Boston, 1850.

Phil 9173.1   How to be a man: a book for boys. (Newcomb, H.) Boston, 1850.

Phil 9070.6   How to be happy though human. (Wolfe, W.B.) N.Y., 1931.

Phil 9070.30   How to develop your will-power. (Major, Clare Tree.) N.Y., 1920.

Phil 175.52.5   How to do things with words. (Austin, John L.) Cambridge, 1962.

Phil 9070.59   How to find happiness and keep it. 1st ed. (Ashley Montagu, M.F.) Garden City, 1942.

Phil 9530.1   How to get rich. (Butler, B.F.) Boston, 1888.

Phil 9530.40   How to improve your human relations, by straight thinking. (Reilly, William J.) N.Y., 1942.

Phil 3819.39.10   How to improve your mind. (Spinoza, Benedictus de.) N.Y., 1956.

Phil 5850.135.15   How to interview. (Bertine, Eleanor.) N.Y., 1931.

Phil 5850.135.20   How to interview. 2. ed. (Bertine, Eleanor.) N.Y., 1934.

Phil 5850.135.30   How to interview. 3. ed. (Bingham, Walter van Dyke.) N.Y., 1941.

Phil 6114.16   How to line with a neurotic. (Ellis, Albert.) N.Y., 1957.

Phil 9070.138   How to live in the present tense. (Kemelman, Haim.) South Brunswick, 1970.

Phil 8876.55   How to live on 24 hours a day. (Bennett, Arnold.) N.Y., 1910.

Phil 6112.2.11   How to live quietly. (Call, A.P.) Boston, 1914.

Phil 9035.19   How to make a rational fight for character. (King, Henry C.) N.Y., 1911.

Phil 9035.84.10   How to make a rational fight for character. (King, Henry C.) N.Y., 1916.

Phil 525.23   How to make perfection appear. (Pedrick, Katharine F.) Boston, 1919.

Phil 8876.55.7   How to make the best of life. (Bennett, Arnold.) N.Y., 1923.

Phil 9530.15   How to make your mark in life. (Durant, E.E.) Boston, 1917.

Phil 8887.3   How to observe. Morals and manners. (Martineau, H.) London, 1838.

Phil 8887.3.3   How to observe. Morals and manners. (Martineau, H.) N.Y., 1838.

Phil 8887.3.2   How to observe. Morals and manners. (Martineau, H.) N.Y., 1838.

Phil 6128.32   How to obtain happiness and health. (Snyder, John Jacob.) Chicago, 1905.

Phil 194.12   How to obtain our own. (True, H.B.) N.Y., 1909.

Phil 6420.36.5   How to overcome stammering. (Gifford, Mabel F.) N.Y., 1940.

Phil 8876.106   How to overcome your 7 deadly enemies. (Barrett, J.W.) N.Y., 1939.

Phil 7140.116.7   How to practice suggestion and autosuggestion. (Coué, Émile.) N.Y., 1923.

NEDL Phil 5929.2.5   How to read character. N.Y., 1870.

Phil 6122.63   How to relax. (Miller, W.H.) N.Y., 1944.

Phil 5545.180   How to remember. (Furst, Bruno.) N.Y., 1944.

Phil 5545.56   How to remember without memory systems or with them. (Miles, E.H.) London, 1901.

Phil 8876.83   How to sleep on a windy night. (Bentley, Joseph.) Philadelphia, 1928.

Phil 7069.18.140   How to speak with the dead. (Sciens, (pseud.).) N.Y., 1918.

Phil 5545.14   How to strengthen the memory. (Holbrook, M.S.) N.Y., n.d.

Phil 5545.14.2   How to strengthen the memory. (Holbrook, M.S.) N.Y., 1886.

Phil 9035.3   How to study character. (Hyde, T.A.) N.Y., 1884.

Phil 9530.35   How to succeed in life. (Kleiser, Grenville.) N.Y., 1934.

Phil 5520.109   How to talk with people. (Lee, I.J.) N.Y., 1952.

Phil 5938.10.10   How to teach according to temperament and mental development. (Sizer, Nelson.) N.Y., 1877.

Phil 9590.22.3   How to think. (Fearon, Arthur D.) San Francisco, 1944.

Phil 5465.54   How to think creatively. (Hutchinson, E.D.) N.Y., 1949.

Phil 5059.20.5   How to think straight. (Thouless, R.H.) N.Y., 1939.

Phil 5059.20.10   How to think straight. (Thouless, R.H.) N.Y., 1941.

Phil 801.20   How to understand philosophy. (Baker, A.E.) N.Y., 1926.

Phil 9530.2   How to win fortune. (Carnegie, A.) N.Y., 1890.

Phil 9530.38.15   How to win friends and influence people. (Carnegie, Dale.) N.Y., 1937.

Phil 9530.38.28   How to win friends and influence people. 28th ed. (Carnegie, Dale.) N.Y., 1937.

Phil 5850.235   How to work with people. (Harwood, Sumner.) Cambridge, 1940.

Phil 6128.46   How to worry successfully. (Seabury, David.) Boston, 1936.

Phil 5247.43   How we behave. (Heath, Archie E.) London, 1927.

Phil 978.61   How we remember our past lives. (Jinarājadāsa, C.) Chicago, 1923.

Phil 8628.8   How you live when you die. (Desmond, Shaw.) London, 1942.

Phil 1112.5   Howald, E. Die Anfänge der europäischen Philosophie. München, 1925.

Phil 400.31   Howaleivsky, M. Über die Antinomienlehre als Begründung des transzendentalen idealismus. Inaug. Diss. Göttingen, 1914.

Phil 5170.8   Howard, D.T. Analytical syllogistics. Evanston, 1946.

Phil 3640.193   Howard, E. Friedirch Nietzsche und die klassische Philologie. Photoreproduction. Gotha, 1920.

Htn   Phil 2520.131*   Howard, E. Remarks on...new philosophy of Descartes. London, 1701.

Phil 5627.134.54   Howard, Peter. Design for dedication. Chicago, 1964.

Phil 5627.134.77   Howard, Peter. Frank Buchman's secret. Garden City, N.Y., 1962.

Phil 5627.134.75   Howard, Peter. Ideas have legs. London, 1945.

Phil 5627.134.76   Howard, Peter. Ideas have legs. N.Y., 1946.

Phil 5627.134.55   Howard, Peter. Innocent men. London, 1941.
Phil 5627.134.55.5

Phil 5627.134.56   Howard, Peter. Innocent men. London, 1941.

Phil 5627.134.56.5   Howard, Peter. The world rebuilt...Frank Buchman. London, 1951.

Phil 8419.26.5   Howard, Peter. The world rebuilt. N.Y., 1952.

Phil 8050.67   Howard, W.G. Reiz ist Schönheit in Bewegung; a Rettung of Joseph Spence. n.p., 1909.

Phil 6677.13   Howard, W.G. Ut pictura poesis; a historical investigation. Cambridge, 1909.

Phil 6317.19.5   Howard, W.L. Hypnotism as a therapeutic agent. Baltimore, 1893.

Phil 6317.19   Howden, R.A. The man in the street and the new psychology. London, 1935.

Phil 8882.57   Howden, R.A. The mind in conflict. London, 1931.

Phil 6317.29   Howe, E.G. Morality and reality. London, 1934.

Phil 6317.28   Howe, Eric Graham. Invisible anatomy. London, 1944.

Phil 8697.28   Howe, Eric Graham. The triumphant spirit. London, 1943.

Phil 9455.8   Howe, Günter. Die Christenheit im Atomzeitalter. Stuttgart, 1970.

   Howe, M.A. de Wolfe. Public opinion,...an oration...Connecticut Beta of Phi Beta Kappa Society, July 28, 1852. Hartford, 1852.

Phil 6750.3.7   Howe, S.G. Causes and prevention of idiocy. Boston, 1874.

Phil 5927.1   Howe, S.G. A discourse on the social relations of man. Boston, 1837.

Phil 6750.3   Howe, S.G. Report to the legislature. Boston, 1847.

Phil 6750.3.5   Howe, S.G. Report to the legistature of Massachusetts upon idiocy. Boston, 1848.

Phil 8408.26   Howell, A.R. Gems of wisdom from the writings of A.R. Howell. Sussex, 1958.

Phil 5017.6.5   Howell, W.S. Eighteenth-century British logic and rhetoric. Princeton, 1971.

Phil 5017.6   Howell, W.S. Logic and rhetoric in England. N.Y., 1961.

Phil 5017.5   Howell, W.S. Logic and rhetoric in England. Princeton, 1956.

Phil 6985.30   Howells, John Gwilym. Theory and practice of family psychiatry. N.Y., 1971.

Phil 182.108   Howells, T.H. Hunger for wholiness. Denver, 1940.

Phil 8408.35   Howes, E.D. (Mrs.). The psychology of beauty. Boston, 1905.

Phil 2280.5.102   Howgate, G.W. George Santayana. Philadelphia, 1938.

Phil 2280.5.102.2   Howgate, G.W. George Santayana. Thesis. Philadelphia, 1938.

Phil 182.100   Howison, G.H. George Holmes Howison, philosopher and teacher. Berkeley, 1934.

Phil 2050.81   Howison, G.H. Hume and Kant. San Francisco, 1884. 2 pam.

Phil 400.12   Howison, G.H. Limits of evolution. N.Y., 1901.

Phil 400.12.3   Howison, G.H. Limits of evolution. 2nd ed. N.Y., 1905.

Phil 7052.9   Howitt, William. The history of the supernatural. Philadelphia, 1863. 2v.

Phil 2050.194   Howitz, Franz G. Determinismen eller Hume imod Kant. Kjøbenhavn, 1824.

Phil 5627.56.7   Howley, John. Psychology and mystical experience. London, 1920.

Phil 3808.236   Hoyack, Louis. Schopenhauer, waarheid en dwaling. Deventer, 1968.

Phil 3827.16   Hoyack, Louis. Spinoza als uitgangspant. Deventer, 1965.

Phil 482.6   Hoyle, Fred. Man and materialism. 1st ed. N.Y., 1956.

Phil 288.21   Hoyle, Fred. Man in the universe. N.Y., 1966.

Phil 5217.6   Hoyos, C.G. Denkschrift zur Lage der Psychologie. Wiesbaden, 1964.

Phil 8602.28   Hrad är sanning? (Wimmer, Richard.) Stockholm, 1894.

Phil 4809.727.80   Hromádka, Josef Lukl. Don Quijote české filosofie, Emanuel Rádl, 1873-1942. V New Yorku, 1943.

Phil 5853.2   Hruschka, Erna. Versuch einer theoretischen Grundlegung des Beratungsprozesses. Habilitationsschrift. Meisenheim am Glan, 1969.

Phil 310.588   Hrušovský, I. Tri iniciatívy v dejinách filozofie. Bratislava, 1959.

Phil 310.440   Hrušovský, I. Z minulosti a sučasnosti filozofi. Bratislava, 1961.

Phil 4812.457.20   Hrušovský, Igor. Kapitoly z téorie vedy. Bratislava, 1968.

Phil 182.142   Hrušovský, Igor. Probleme der Philosophie. Bratislava, 1970.

Phil 4812.457.35   Hrušovský, Igor. Problémy, portréty, retrospektívy. Vyd. 1. Bratislava, 1965.

Phil 4812.457.31   Hrušovský, Igor. Strukturation und Apperzeption des Konkreten. Bratislava, 1966.

Phil 310.410   Hrzal, L. Predmet a metoda historického materializmu. Praha, 1961.

Phil 930.28A   Hu, Suh. Development of logical method in China. Shanghai, 1922.

Phil 9390.8   Huad en falsk eed alvorlig oc forfaerlig betyde effter som den hellige scrifft udviser. n.p., 1605.

Phil 3827.6   Huan, G. Le Dieu de Spinoza. Arras, 1913.

Phil 3640.119   Huan, Gabriel. La philosophie de Frédéric Nietzsche. Paris, 1917.

Phil 1905.10.80.5   Huang, Chia-cheng. De l'humanisme à l'absolutisme. Paris, 1954.

Phil 1905.10.80.2   Huang, Chia-cheng. Le néo-hegelianisme en Angleterre. Paris, 1954.

Phil 1905.10.80   Huang, Chia-cheng. Le néo-hegelianisme en Angleterre. Paris, 1954.

Phil 9513.35   Huant, Ernest. Masses, morale et machines. Paris, 1967.

Htn   Phil 5247.13.22*   Huarte de San Juan, J. Anacrise, ou Parfait jugement et examen. Lyon, 1580.

Phil 5247.13.19   Huarte de San Juan, J. Essai sur l'ouvrage. Paris, 1855.

Phil 5247.13.18   Huarte de San Juan, J. Examen de ingenios. Gainesville, 1959.

Htn   Phil 5247.13.7*   Huarte de San Juan, J. Examen de ingenios. London, 1594.

Htn   Phil 5247.13.9*   Huarte de San Juan, J. Examen de ingenios. London, 1604.

Phil 5247.13.17   Huarte de San Juan, J. Examen de ingenios. London, 1698.

Htn   Phil 5247.13*   Huarte de San Juan, J. Examen de ingenios para las sciencias. Antwerp? 1603.

Phil 5247.13.3   Huarte de San Juan, J. Examen de ingenios para las sciencias. Barcelona, 1917.

Phil 5247.13.4   Huarte de San Juan, J. Examen de ingenios para las sciencias. Madrid, 1930. 2v.

Phil 5247.13.13   Huarte de San Juan, J. Examen des esprits et naiz aux sciences. Rouen, 1607.

Phil 5247.13.15   Huarte de San Juan, J. L'examen des esprits pour les sciences. Paris, 1661.

Htn   Phil 5247.13.5*   Huarte de San Juan, J. The examination of men's wits. London, 1596.

Phil 5247.13.21   Huarte de San Juan, J. Prüfung der Köpfe zu den Wissenschaften. Zerbst, 1752.

Phil 9347.2.25   Hubbard, E. Health and wealth. East Aurora, 1908.

Phil 1150.10   Hubbard, E. Hypatia. N.Y., 1908.

Phil 9347.2.3   Hubbard, E. A message to Garcia. East Aurora, 1899.

Phil 9347.2.13   Hubbard, E. A message to Garcia. n.p., 192-.

Phil 9347.2   Hubbard, E. A message to Garcia. N.Y., 1900.

Htn   Phil 9347.2.5*   Hubbard, E. A message to Garcia. N.Y., 1906.

Phil 21.6   Hubbard, Elbert. Little journeys to the homes of great philosophers. East Aurora, n.d.

Phil 7068.96.30   Hubbard, H.S. Beyond. Boston, 1896.

Phil 6317.32.2   Hubbard, L. Ron. Dianetics. Johannesburg, 1958.

Phil 6317.32   Hubbard, L. Ron. Dianetics. N.Y., 1950.

Phil 6317.32.5   Hubbard, L. Ron. Scientology. London, 1956.

Phil 182.60   Hubbe-Schleiden, Wilhelm. Das Dasein als Lust, Leid, und Liebe. Braunschweig, 1891.

Phil 8662.25   Hubbeling, H.G. Is the Christian God-conception philosophically inferior? Assen, 1963.

Phil 3827.15.5   Hubbeling, H.G. Spinoza. Baarn, 1966.

Phil 3827.15   Hubbeling, H.G. Spinoza's methodology. Assen, 1964.

Phil 3925.16.125   Hubbeling, Hubertus Gerinus. Inleiding tot het denken van Wittgenstein. Assen, 1965.

Phil 7060.139.5   Hubbell, Walter. The great Amherst mystery. 10th ed. N.Y., 1916.

Phil 1707.14   Hubben, William. Four prophets of our destiny. N.Y., 1952.

Phil 5817.10   Hubbert, Helen B. Effect of age on habit formation in the albino rat. Baltimore, 1915.

Phil 338.43   Hubenko, Volodymer I. Znannia i peretvorennia diistnosti. Kyiv, 1968.

Phil 310.661   Huber, Eduard. Um eine "dialektische Logik". München, 1966.

Phil 165.185   Huber, Gerhard. Philosophie und deristliche Existenz. Basel, 1960.

Phil 7069.59.20   Huber, Guido. Übersinnliche Gaben. 1. Aufl. Zürich, 1959.

Phil 182.72   Huber, J. Kleine Schriften. Leipzig, 1871.

Phil 5545.15   Huber, J.N. Psychological Studien. München, 1878.

Phil 9430.4   Huber, J.W. Der Pessimismus. München, 1876.

Phil 8632.25   Huber, Johannes. Die Idee der Unsterblichkeit. München, 1864.

Phil 5757.4   Huber, Johannes. Über die Willensfreiheit. München, 1858.

Phil 4065.182   Huber, Karl. Einheit und Vielheit in Denken und Sprache Giordano Brunos. Winterthur, 1965.

Phil 8408.27   Huber, Kurt. Asthetik. Ettal, 1954.

Phil 5247.64   Huber, Kurt. Grundbegriffe der Seelenkunde. Ettal, 1955.

Phil 3552.332   Huber, Kurt. Leibniz. München, 1951.

Phil 8587.19.10   Huber, M. The divine instinct recommended to men. London, 1781.

Phil 8587.19   Huber, M. The world unmasked. London, 1736.

Phil 182.24   Huber, M. World unmasked. London, 1736.

Phil 182.24.2   Huber, M. World unmasked. London, 1786.

Phil 3415.110   Huber, Max. Eduard von Hartmanns Metaphysik und Religionsphilosophie. Winterthur, 1954.

Phil 9530.66   Huber, Richard M. The American idea of success. 1st ed. N.Y., 1971.

Phil 1535.27.2   Huber, Sebastian. Grundzüge der Logik und Noëtik. Paderborn, 1906.

Phil 2805.268   Hubert, M.L., Sister. Pascal's unfinished Apology. New Haven, 1952.

Phil 9050.3   Hubert, P.G. Liberty and a living. 2nd ed. N.Y., 1904.

Phil 2648.90   Hubert, René. D'Holbach et ses amis. Paris, 1928.

Phil 2490.25   Hubert, René. Les grands philosophes...choix de textes. Paris, 1927.

Phil 338.18   Hubert, René. Le sens du réel. Paris, 1925.

Phil 9558.10.5   Hubris. (Payne, Robert.) N.Y., 1960.

Phil 130.6.5   Hubscher, Arthur. Denker unserer Zeit. München, 1956-57. 2v.

Phil 130.6   Hubscher, Arthur. Philosophen der Gegenwart. München, 1949.

Phil 3450.19.425   Huch, Kurt Jürgen. Philosophiegeschichtliche Voraussetzungen der Heideggerschen Ontologie. Frankfurt, 1967.

Phil 3489.15   Huch, Lilly. Der Begriff Wissenschaft im Kantischen Sinne. Berlin, 1917.

Phil 182.106.5   Huch, Ricarda. Vom Wesen des Menschen; Natur und Geist. 3. Aufl. Prein, 1922.

Phil 6117.12   Huckel, O. Mental medicine. N.Y., 1909.

Phil 9075.11   Huckel, O. Modern study of conscience. Philadelphia, 1907.

Phil 7069.13.20   Hude, Fru Anna. The evidence for communication with the dead. London, 1913.

Phil 8905.25   Hudon, Louis-Nazaire. Le corps humain dans la pensée de Dieu. Alma, 1967.

Phil 974.2.44   Hudson, Irene B. Who wrote the Mahatma letters? Answered. Victoria, 1936.

Phil 9590.6   Hudson, J.W. The old faiths perish. N.Y., 1939.

Phil 182.55   Hudson, Jay W. The truths we live by. N.Y., 1921.

Phil 5876.22   Hudson, Liam. Frames of mind. London, 1968.

Phil 8662.14   Hudson, T.J. Divine pedigree of man. Chicago, 1899.

Phil 6117.42   Hudson, T.J. The law of mental medicine. Chicago, 1903.

Phil 7060.28   Hudson, T.J. Law of psychic phenomena. Chicago, 1893.

Phil 8632.1.12   Hudson, T.J. A scientific demonstration...future life. 12th ed. Chicago, 1922.

Phil 7060.28.10   Hudson, T J. The evolution of the soul and other essays. Chicago, 1904.

Phil 7068.96.7.9   Hudson, Thomson J. The law of psychic phenomena. 30. ed. Chicago, 1905.

Phil 8882.105   Hudson, William Donald. The is-ought question. London, 1969.

Phil 2215.85   Hudson, William Donald. Reason and right: a critical examination of Richard Price's philosophy. London, 1970.

Phil 2270.93.16A   Hudson, William Henry. Herbert Spencer. London, 1916.
Phil 2270.92.90   Hudson, William Henry. An introduction to the philosophy of Herbert Spencer. N.Y., 1894.

Phil 2270.93   Hudson, William Henry. An introduction to the philosophy of Herbert Spencer. 2nd ed. N.Y., 1900.

Phil 3450.19.200   Huebener, Wolfgang. Untersuchungen zur Denhart Martin Heideggers. Berlin, 1960.

Phil 1750.369   Huebner, F.M. Umgang mit Gätterbilden. Frankfurt, 1950.
Phil 3808.169   Hübscher, Arthur. Arthur Schopenhauer. Leipzig, 1938.
Phil 3808.169.10   Hübscher, Arthur. Leben mit Schopenhauer. Frankfurt, 1966.

Phil 3808.169.5   Hübscher, Arthur. Schopenhauer. Stuttgart, 1952.
Phil 3808.242   Hübscher, Arthur. Schopenhauer-Bildnisse. Frankfurt, 1968.

Phil 1707.28   Huebscher, Arthur. Van Hegel zu Heidegger. Stuttgart, 1961.

Phil 8587.32.112   Hügel, Friedrich. Baron von Hügel, man of God. London, 1947.

Phil 8587.32   Hügel, Friedrich von. Essays and addresses on the philosophy of religion. London, 1921.

Phil 8587.32.5   Hügel, Friedrich von. Essays and addresses on the philosophy of religion. London, 1926.

Phil 8587.32.25   Hügel, Friedrich von. Reading from Friedrich von Hügel. London, 1928.

Phil 8587.32.85   Hügel, Friedrich von. Selected letters 1896-1924. London, 1928.

Phil 8587.32.87   Hügel, Friedrich von. Some letters. London, 1925.
Phil 3850.18.84   Hügelmann, H. Max Schelers Persönlichkeitsidee. Diss. Leipzig, 1927.

Phil 3450.19.165   Hühnerfeld, Paul. In Sachen Heidegger. Hamburg, 1959.
Phil 3450.11.330   Huelsmann, H. Zur Theorie der Sprache bei E. Husserl. München, 1964.

Phil 3450.18.135   Hülsmann, Heinz. Die Methode in der Philosophie Nicolai Hartmanns. 1e Aufl. Düsseldorf, 1959.

Phil 6990.17   Huelster, A. Miracles in the light, science and history. Chicago, 19- .

Phil 8957.18   Huemmeler, Hans. Jugend an der Maschine. Freiburg, 1932.
Phil 3850.50   Huenermann, Peter. Trinitorische Anthropologie bei Franz Anton Staudenmaiet. Freiburg, 1962.

Phil 4580.117   Hürtgen, Robert. Das Gottesproblem bei Harald Høffding. Inaug. Diss. Bonn, 1928.

Phil 2651.82   Huet, évêque d'Avranches. (Bartholmess, B.J.W.) Paris, 1850.

Phil 1750.6   Huet, F. La révolution philosophique. Paris, 1871.
Phil 182.25   Huet, F. La science de l'esprit. Paris, 1864. 2v.
Phil 2477.2.80   Huet, François. Histoire de la vie et des ouvrages de Bordas-Demoulin. Paris, 1861.

Phil 2651.40   Huet, Pierre Daniel. Philosophical treatise concerning the weakness of human understanding. London, 1728.

Phil 2651.30   Huet, Pierre Daniel. Traité philosophique de la faiblesse. London, 1741.

Phil 2651.80   Huet. (DeGournay, M.F.A.) Caen, 1854.
Phil 978.49.50   Der Hüter der Schwelle, Seelenvorgänge in scenischen Bildern. (Steiner, R.) Berlin, 1922.

Htn   Phil 2520.91*   Huetii, P.D. Censura philosophiae Cartesianae. Paris, 1689.

Phil 2905.1.420   Hugedé, Norbert. Le cas Teilhard de Chardin. Paris, 1966.
Phil 8685.20   Hugenholtz, P.H. Ethisch pantheisme. Amsterdam, 1903.
Phil 5047.47   Hughes, G.E. The elements of formal logic. N.Y., 1965.
Phil 8882.22   Hughes, H. Principles, natural and supernatural morals. London, 1890-91. 2v.

Phil 1900.175   Hughes, Henry. A critical examination of Butler's analogy London, 1898.

Phil 6000.4   Hughes, Henry. Die Mimik des Menschen auf grundvoluntarischer Psychologie. Frankfurt, 1900.

Phil 5125.8   Hughes, Henry. The theory of inference. London, 1894.
Phil 1750.90.2   Hughes, Henry Stuart. Consciousness and society. N.Y., 1961.

Phil 5247.58   Hughes, P. Introduction to psychology. Bethlehem Pa., 1928.

Phil 8610.925   Hughes, R. Why I quit going to church. N.Y., 1925.
Phil 5757.3   Hughes, T. The human will. London, 1867.
Phil 9560.2   Hughes, T. True manliness. Boston, 1880?
Phil 8587.55   Hughes, T.H. Psychology and religious truth. London, 1942.

Phil 2605.9.80   Hugo, C.L. Refutation du système de Monsr. Faidy. Luxemburg, 1699.

Phil 3195.15.81   Hugo Dingler. (Krampf, W.) München, 1956.
Phil 3195.12.90   Hugo Dinglers philosophisches System. Inaug. Diss. (Scheele, Fritz.) Corbach, 1933.

Phil 2150.6.80   Hugo Münsterberg, his life and work. (Münsterberg, M.) N.Y., 1922.

Phil 1512.11   Hugon, Edward. Cursus philosophiae thomistica. 3. éd. v.1-6. Paris, 1928. 3v.

Phil 92.1   Hugon, Paul D. Our minds and our motives. N.Y., 1928.
Phil 182.74   Hugonin, F. Ontologie. Paris, 1856-1857. 2v.
Phil 7069.11.70   Hugsíminn. (Russel, Fox.) Reykjavik, 1911.
Phil 6117.11   Huguenin, G. Allgemeine Pathologie der Krankheiten des Nervensystems. Zürich, 1873.

Phil 182.59   Hugueny, Charles. Systéme de la nature. Nancy, 1890.
Phil 8662.12   Huhn, Friedrich. Der Beweis vom dasein Gottes. Berlin, 1927.

Phil 575.190   Huibregtse, Kornelis. Anthropologisch-historische benadering van het moderne subjectgevoel. Haarlem, 1950.

Phil 182.68   Huidobro, E. Programma analitico razonado de metafisica. Lima, 1923.

Phil 8408.23   Huisman, Denis. L'esthétique. 3. éd. Paris, 1959.
Phil 1135.60   Huit, C. Philosophie de la nature chez les anciens. Paris, 1901.

Phil 2515.18   Huit essais sur le mal. (Caraco, Albert.) Neuchâtel, 1963.

Phil 182.42   Huizinga, A.V.C.P. The American philosophic pragmatism. Boston, 1911.

Phil 6677.15   Hull, C.L. Hypnosis and suggestibility. N.Y., 1933.
Phil 5247.56   Hull, C.L. Mind, mechanism and adaptive behavior. Lancaster, 1937.

Phil 5247.56.5   Hull, C.L. Principles of behavior. N.Y., 1943.
Phil 7059.12.13   Hull, Moses. All about devils. Chicago, 1890.
Phil 7059.12.11   Hull, Moses. Jesus and the mediums. Chicago, 1890.
Phil 7059.12   Hull, Moses. The question settled. Boston, 1869.

Phil 7059.12.9   Hull, Moses. The spiritual Alps and how we ascend them. 5th ed. Chicago, 1895.

Phil 7059.12.5   Hull, Moses. Two in one...spiritualism of the Bible settled. Chicago, 1895.

Phil 7059.12.15   Hull, Moses. Which: spiritualism or Christianity? N.Y., 1873.

Phil 2055.15.30   Hulme, Thomas E. Further speculations. Minnesota, 1955.
Phil 2055.15.37   Hulme, Thomas E. Speculations; essays on humanism and the philosophy of art. London, 1965.

Phil 2055.15.34A   Hulme, Thomas E. Speculations; essays on humanism and the philosophy of art. N.Y., 1924.

Phil 2055.15.35   Hulme, Thomas E. Speculations. 2nd ed. London, 1958.
Phil 1750.166.95   Hulst, H.C von. Phänomenologie en natuurwetenschap. Utrecht, 1953.

Phil 1170.9   Hultkrantz, C.A. Historisk framställning och granskning utaf hufvudpunkterna i Plotini theoretiska philosophi. Thesis. Stockholm, 1851.

Phil 3640.35.5   Humain, trop humain. (Nietzsche, Friedrich.) Paris, 1899.
Phil 5258.68.10   Human ability. (Spearman, C.) London, 1950.
Phil 70.6   Human action: conceptual and empirical issues. N.Y., 1969.
Phil 8878.60   Human acts. (D'Arcy, E.) Oxford, 1963.
Phil 5421.20.40   Human aggression. 1. American ed. (Storr, Anthony.) N.Y., 1968.

Phil 2030.7.5   Human aims in modern perspective. (Gotshalk, Dilman Walter.) Yellow Springs, Ohio, 1966.

Phil 7059.8   The human aura. (Rebman, F.J.) Storm Lake, Iowa, 1912.
Phil 5247.19.25   Human behavior. (Hunter, W.S.) Chicago, 1928.
Phil 5255.46   Human behavior. (Paton, S.) N.Y., 1921.
Phil 6121.17   The human brain. (Lewis, W. Bevan.) London, 1882.
Phil 6121.45.5   Human brain and psychological processes. (Luria, Aleksandr Romanovich.) N.Y., 1966.

Phil 9035.70   Human character. (Elliot, H.S.R.) London, 1922.
Phil 8882.80   Human conduct. (Hospers, John.) N.Y., 1961.
Phil 5850.308   Human conduct. (Peters, C.C.) N.Y., 1918.
Phil 5251.33   Human conduct and the law. (Love, Mary C.) Menasha, 1925.
Phil 8877.31   Human confessions. (Crane, F.) Chicago, 1911.
Phil 6111.38   Human culture and cure. pt.3-4. (Babbitt, E.D.) Los Angeles, 1898.

Phil 187.118.10   Human desires and their fulfilment. (Monsarrat, K.W.) Liverpool, 1950.

Phil 8701.21   Human destiny. (Lecomte du Nouy, Pierre.) N.Y., 1947.
Phil 8647.9   Human destiny in the light of revelation. (Weir, J.F.) Boston, 1903.

Phil 178.12.29   Human efficiency. (Dresser, H.W.) N.Y., 1912.
Phil 5246.20.5   Human efficiency and levels of intelligence. (Goddard, H.H.) Princeton, 1920.

Phil 2905.1.18   Human energy. (Teilhard de Chardin, Pierre.) London, 1969.

Phil 2200.1   The human enterprise. (Otto, Max Carl.) N.Y., 1940.
Phil 9070.121   The human evasion. (Green, Celia Elizabeth.) London, 1969.

Phil 182.35.10   Human experience; a study of its structure. (Haldane, Richard B.) London, 1929.

Phil 182.35.9   Human experience; a study of its structure. (Haldane, Richard B.) N.Y., 1926.

Phil 7069.31.31   Human experiences. (Prince, Walter Franklin.) Boston, 1931.

Phil 6025.9.5   The human face. (Picard, Max.) London, 1931.
Phil 6028.1   Human faces. (Simms, J.) N.Y., 1887.
Htn   Phil 7054.124*   Human fads, foibles, fallacies. (Knaggs, Samuel T.) Sydney, 1898.

Phil 188.17   Human freedom and a plea for philosophy. (Nevin, J.W.) Mercersburg, 1850.

Phil 8602.60   Human freedom and social order. (Wild, John.) Darban, N.C., 1959.

Phil 6132.37   The human frontier. (Williams, Roger J.) N.Y., 1946.
Phil 5250.76   Human growth and the development of personality. 1. ed. (Kahn, Jack Harold.) N.Y., 1965.

Phil 6049.42.8A   The human hand. (Wolff, C.) N.Y., 1943.
Phil 8633.1.50   Human immortality. (James, William.) Boston, 1900.
Phil 8633.1.2A   Human immortality. Two supposed objections. (James, W.) Boston, 1897. 2v.

Phil 5360.20   Human information processing. (Schroder, Harold M.) N.Y., 1967.

Phil 5255.5.6   The human intellect. 4th ed. (Porter, Noah.) N.Y., 1887.
Phil 2255.1.45   Human knowledge; its scope and limits. (Russell, Bertrand Russell.) London, 1948.

Phil 349.6   Human knowledge. (Skrochowski, F.) Cnacow, 1893.
Phil 705.9   Human learning favorable to true religion. (Bradford, Alden.) Boston, 1841.

Phil 8897.12.5A   Human life; or Practical ethics. (Wette, W.M.L. de.) Boston, 1842. 2v.

Phil 8897.12.9   Human life; or Practical ethics. (Wette, W.M.L. de.) Boston, 1856. 2v.

Phil 8876.55.20   The human machine. (Bennett, Arnold.) London, 1920.
Phil 8876.55.13A   The human machine. (Bennett, Arnold.) N.Y., 1911.
Phil 5243.44.5   The human machine. (Deut, John Y.) N.Y., 1937.
Phil 6123.6   The human machine. (Nisbet, J.F.) London, 1899.
Phil 6683.2   Human magnetism. (Newman, W.) London, 1845.
Phil 6683.2.2   Human magnetism. (Newman, W.) N.Y., 1845.
Phil 177.99   Human meaning of science. (Compton, A.H.) Chapel Hill, 1940.

Phil 5247.59   The human mind. (Hook, A.) London, 1940.
Phil 5252.77   The human mind. (Mackenzie, M.) Philadelphia, 1941.
Phil 6322.19   The human mind. (Menninger, Karl Augustus.) N.Y., 1930.
Phil 6322.19.2   The human mind. (Menninger, Karl Augustus.) N.Y., 1930.
Phil 5252.130   The human mind. (Murphy, James G.) Belfast, 1873.
Phil 5258.202   The human mind. (Nobel Conference, 3d, Gustavus Adolphus College, 1967.) Amsterdam, 1967.

Phil 5258.25.11   Human mind. (Sully, J.) N.Y., 1892. 2v.
Phil 6115.10   The human mind. v.1-2. (Fullom, S.W.) London, 1858.
Phil 6322.19.5   The human mind. 2d ed. (Menninger, Karl Augustus.) N.Y., 1937.

Phil 6322.19.7   The human mind. 3d ed. (Menninger, Karl Augustus.) N.Y., 1945.

Phil 5244.23   Human mind and its physical machine...human body. (English, V.P.) San Diego, 1937.

Phil 6980.611   Human moods. (Prick, Joseph Jules Guillaume.) Assen, 1968.

Phil 5548.25   Human motivation. (Schreier, F.T.) Glencoe, Ill., 1957.
Phil 5548.130   Human motivation. (Vernon, Magdalen Dorothea.) London, 1969.

Phil 5255.32.5   Human motives. (Putnam, J.J.) Boston, 1921.
Phil 5247.3   The human mund. (Hamilton, E.J.) N.Y., 1883.
Phil 5258.102A   Human nature; a first book in psychology. (Schoen, M.) N.Y., 1930.

Phil 9240.3   Human nature, or The nature of evil. (Skinner, Clarence R.) Boston, 1939.

Author and Title Listing

	Phil 5241.89	Human nature. (Butler, J.R.) N.Y., 1933.
	Phil 5246.52A	Human nature. (Goldstein, K.) Cambridge, 1940.
	Phil 8697.8	Human nature. (Hamlin, G.S.) N.Y., 1917.
Htn	Phil 2045.59*	Human nature. (Hobbes, Thomas.) London, 1650.
NEDL	Phil 17.3	Human nature. London. 1-11,1807-1877 11v.
	Phil 9035.27	Human nature and its remaking. (Hocking, W.E.) New Haven, 1918.
	Phil 9035.27.5	Human nature and its remaking. (Hocking, W.E.) New Haven, 1923.
	Phil 9035.27.12	Human nature and its remaking. (Hocking, W.E.) New Haven, 1932.
	Phil 5259.7.22	Human nature and the social order. (Thorndike, E.L.) Cambridge, 1969.
	Phil 5259.7.20	Human nature and the social order. (Thorndike, E.L.) N.Y., 1940.
	Phil 2050.213	Human nature and utility in Hume's social philosophy. (Ross, William W.G.) Garden City, N.Y., 1942.
	Phil 2050.213.5	Human nature and utility in Hume's social philosophy. Thesis. (Ross, William G.) Garden City, N.Y., 1942.
	Phil 5259.7.3	The human nature club. (Thorndike, E.L.) N.Y., 1900.
	Phil 5259.7	The human nature club. (Thorndike, E.L.) N.Y., 1901.
	Phil 5246.53	Human nature in the light of psychopathology. (Goldstein, K.) Cambridge, Mass., 1947.
	Phil 6325.26	The human nature of science; researchers at work in psychiatry. (Perry, Stewart Edmond.) N.Y., 1966.
	Phil 1750.129.5	The human parrot and other essays. (Belgion, Montgomery.) London, 1931.
	Phil 5590.130	The human person. (Arnold, M.B.) N.Y., 1954.
	Phil 7069.07.25	Human personality. (Myers, F.W.H.) N.Y., 1907.
	Phil 7069.19.173	Human personality and its survival of bodily death. (Myers, Fred W.H.) London, 1919.
	Phil 7069.19.170	Human personality and its survival of bodily death. (Myers, Fred W.H.) London, 1919.
	Phil 7069.03.10	Human personality and its survival of bodily death. (Myers, Frederic William Henry.) N.Y., 1903. 2v.
	Phil 575.86	Human personality and the environment. (Campbell, C.M.) N.Y., 1934.
	Phil 1750.166.150	Human possibilities. (Kiley, W.) N.Y., 1963.
	Phil 5590.260A	Human potentialities. (Murphy, Gardner.) N.Y., 1958.
	Phil 187.118	Human powers and their relations. (Monsarrat, K.W.) Liverpool, 1938.
	Phil 575.268	The human predicament and dissolution and wholeness. (Morgan, George W.) Providence, 1968.
	Phil 5500.16.5	Human problem solving. (Newell, Allen.) Englewood Cliffs, 1972.
	Phil 9560.1	Human prudence. (De Britaine, W.) Dedham, 1806.
	Phil 5241.89.10	Human psychology. (Butler, J.R.) N.Y., 1936.
	Phil 5249.3.2	Human psychology. (Janes, Elijah.) N.Y., 1886.
	Phil 5249.3.5	Human psychology. (Janes, Elijah.) Oakland, 1884.
	Phil 5249.3	Human psychology. (Janes, Elijah.) Oakland, 1885.
	Phil 5262.20	Human psychology. (Warren, H.C.) Boston, 1919.
	Phil 336.11.5	The human race, a study in the nature of knowledge. (Froschels, Emil.) N.Y., 1947.
	Phil 336.11	The human race. (Froschels, Emil.) N.Y., 1947.
	Phil 9070.21.10	Human relations. (Landau, Rom.) London, 1948.
	Phil 5850.387.5	Human relations in interracial housing. (Wilner, D.M.) Minneapolis, 1955.
	Phil 5850.131	Human relationships. 1. ed. (Bertine, Eleanor.) N.Y., 1958.
	Phil 9520.1	Human sadness. (Gasparin, V.B.) London, 1864.
	Phil 181.136.5	The human sciences and philosophy. (Goldmann, Lucien.) London, 1969.
	Phil 5640.50	The human senses. (Geldard, Frank A.) N.Y., 1962.
	Phil 178.64.4.7	The human situation. (Dixon, W.M.) Harmondsworth, 1958.
	Phil 178.64.4	The human situation. (Dixon, W.M.) London, 1938.
	Phil 178.64.4.5	The human situation. (Dixon, W.M.) London, 1954.
	Phil 178.64	The human situation. (Dixon, W.M.) N.Y., 1937.
	Phil 8587.21.2	Human society: Graham lectures. (Huntington, F.D.) N.Y., 1860.
	Phil 8892.62	Human society in ethics and politics. (Russell, Bertrand Russell.) London, 1954.
	Phil 8892.62.5	Human society in ethics and politics. (Russell, Bertrand Russell.) N.Y., 1955.
	Phil 5520.16	Human speech; its physical basis. (MacNamara, N.C.) N.Y., 1909.
	Phil 5710.8.3	Human temperaments; studies in character. 3. ed. (Mercier, C.A.) London, 1923?
	Phil 1750.166.35.5	The human tradition. (Blackham, H.J.) Boston, 1953.
	Phil 1750.166.35.7	The human tradition. (Blackham, H.J.) Boston, 1954.
	Phil 2050.259	Human understanding: studies in the philosophy of David Hume. (Sesonske, Alexander.) Belmont, Calif., 1965.
	Phil 8893.57	Human value. (Sturt, Henry.) Cambridge, 1923.
	Phil 735.97	Human values. (Parker, DeWitt H.) N.Y., 1931.
	Phil 194.36.2	Human values and verities. (Taylor, H.O.) London, 1928.
	Phil 194.36	Human values and verities. (Taylor, H.O.) N.Y., 1928.
Htn	Phil 194.36.4*	Human values and verities. Pt.I. (Taylor, H.O.) N.Y., 1929.
	Phil 194.36.3	Human values and verities. Pt.I. (Taylor, H.O.) N.Y., 1929.
	Phil 5257.40	Human vibrations. (Richter, Conrad.) Harrisburg, 1925.
	Phil 5754.2	The human will. (Espy, J.P.) Cincinnati, 1860.
	Phil 5757.3	The human will. (Hughes, T.) London, 1867.
	Phil 8870.30	A humane society. (Rosenberg, Stuart E.) Toronto, 1962.
	Phil 5242.6	Humanics. (Collins, T.W.) N.Y., 1860.
	Phil 3640.283	Humanidad. (Goday, V. Bersanelli.) Buenos Aires, 1940.
	Phil 8595.28	Humanism; a new religion. (Potter, Charles F.) N.Y., 1930.
	Phil 8662.27	Humanism, atheism; principles and practice. Moscow, 1966?
	Phil 8662.30	Humanism, atheism; principles and practice. Moscow, 1968?
	Phil 8580.17.10	Humanism. (Ames, Edward S.) Chicago, 1931.
	Phil 1750.131	Humanism. (King, William Peter.) Nashville, 1931.
	Phil 4872.193.30	Humanism. (Mukerjea, Jyoti S.) Nagpur, 19- .
	Phil 8597.35	Humanism. (Reese, Curtis W.) Chicago, 1926.
	Phil 1750.162	Humanism. (Richards, P.S.) London, 1934.
	Phil 1707.20	Humanism: the Greek ideal. 1. ed. (Hadas, Mases.) N.Y., 1960.
	Phil 1750.151	Humanism and imagination. (Elliott, George R.) Chapel Hill, 1938.
	Phil 960.167	Humanism and Indian thought. (Chakravarti, A.) Madras, 1937.
	Phil 8889.7	Humanism and moral theory. (Osbert, Reuben.) London, 1959.
	Phil 1750.146	Humanism and naturalism. (Leander, F.) Göteborg, 1937.
	Phil 1817.8	Humanism and new world ideals. (Reiser, O.L.) Yellow Springs, Colorado, 1933.
	Phil 1750.166.240	Humanism and politics. (Levi, Albert William.) Bloomington, 1969.
	Phil 185.46	Humanism and science. (Keyser, Cassius Jackson.) N.Y., 1931.
	Phil 1750.166.20	Humanism as a philosophy. (Lamont, Corliss.) N.Y., 1949.
	Phil 1750.166.21	Humanism as a philosophy. 2nd ed. (Lamont, Corliss.) N.Y., 1949.
	Phil 8602.42	Humanism as a way of life. (Walker, Joseph.) N.Y., 1932.
	Phil 8592.72	Humanism as the next step. (Marain, L.) Boston, 1954.
	Phil 1750.166.105	Humanism in practice. (Roshwald, M.) London, 1955.
	Phil 1750.751	Humanism in the contemporary era. (Rotenstreich, N.) The Hague, 1963.
	Phil 1750.132A	Humanism of Irving Babbitt. Diss. (McMahon, Francis E.) Washington, D.C., 1931.
	Phil 193.9.5A	Humanism philosophical essays. (Schiller, F.C.S.) London, 1903.
	Phil 193.9.6	Humanism philosophical essays. 2. ed. (Schiller, F.C.S.) London, 1912.
	Phil 8580.24A	Humanism states its case. (Auer, J.A.C.F.) Boston, 1933.
	Phil 2835.86	Humanisme, science et réforme. (Hooykaas, Reijer.) Leyde, 1958.
	Phil 2963.5	L'Humanisme belge. État de la question, vecherches, perspectives. Anvers, 1966.
	Phil 2520.255.5	L'humanisme de Descartes. (Lefèvre, Roger.) Paris, 1957.
	Phil 1750.166.25	L'humanisme du 20e siècle. (Ulmann, Andre.) Paris, 1946.
	Phil 1750.153	L'humanisme en Alsace. (Association Guillaume Budé.) Paris, 1939.
	Phil 1750.166.230	Het humanisme en zijn historische achtergrond. (Vogel, Cornelia Johanna de.) Assen, 1968.
	Phil 1750.166.120	Humanisme et Renaissance. (Renaudet, Augustin.) Genève, 1958.
	Phil 1750.166.60	Humanisme et surhumanisme. (Rey, Gabriel.) Paris, 1951.
	Phil 2750.11.54	Humanisme intégral. (Maritain, Jacques.) Paris, 1936.
	Phil 8581.110	L'humanisme religieux de l'abbé Henri Bremond, 1865-1933. (Hermans, Francis.) Paris, 1965.
	Phil 8693.25	Humanisme scientifique et raison chrétienne. (Dubarle, D.) Paris, 1953.
	Phil 1712.23	El humanismo. (Mañero Mañero, Salvador.) Madrid, 1963.
	Phil 1750.166.255	El humanismo científico de los comunistas. (Millas, Orlando.) Santiago de Chile, 1968.
	Phil 1750.166.15	El humanismo como responsabilidad. (Granell Muñiz, M.) Madrid, 1959.
	Phil 1750.166.180	Humanismo y cruz. (Panikkar, Raimundo.) Madrid, 1963.
	Phil 396.14	Humanismo y revolución. (Miro Quesada, Francisco.) Lima, 1969.
	Phil 4976.5.80	Humanismo y revolución en América Latina; bosquejo de interpretación del pensamiento materialista de Antenor Orrego. (Flores Caballero, Luis.) Lima, 1968.
	Phil 1750.796	Humanismo y sociedad. 1. ed. (Tierno Galván, Enrique.) Barcelona, 1964.
	Phil 1750.166.285	Humanismo y tecnica. (Echandia, Dario.) Bogota, 1969.
	Phil 1750.166.160	Humanismos e suas diversas interpretações. (Gastão, Manuel M.) Lisboa, 1963.
	Phil 1750.166.210	Los humanismos y el hombre. (Corts Grau, José.) Madrid, 1967.
	Phil 193.9.15	Humanismus...pragmatische Philosophie. (Schiller, F.C.S.) Leipzig, 1911.
	Phil 396.18	Humanismus. (Oppermann, Hans.) Darmstadt, 1970.
	Phil 3015.5	Der Humanismus. (Prang, Helmut.) Bamburg, 1947.
	Phil 1710.10	Humanismus der Gegenwart. (Kaegi, Werner.) Zürich, 1959.
	Phil 1750.725	Humanismus heute. Berlin, 1961.
	Phil 1750.166.260	Humanismus ohne Gott. (Mueller-Schwefe, Hans Rudolf.) Stuttgart, 1967.
	Phil 8505.4	Humanist. American Humanist Association. Yellow Springs, Ohio. 10,1950+ 7v.
	Phil 1750.166.91	The humanist frame. (Huxley, J.S.) London, 1961.
	Phil 1750.166.92	The humanist frame. (Huxley, J.S.) N.Y., 1962.
	Phil 396.5	The humanist outlook. (Ayer, Alfred Jules.) London, 1968.
	Phil 8505.5	Humanist pamphlet. Yellow Springs, Ohio.
	Phil 8597.35.10	Humanist sermons. (Reese, Curtis W.) Chicago, 1927.
	Phil 8897.78	Humanistic ethics. (Williams, G.) N.Y., 1951.
	Phil 1750.555.6	Humanistic existentialism; the literature of possibility. (Barnes, Hazel Estella.) Lincoln, 1967.
	Phil 5057.23	Humanistic logic for the mind in action. (Reiser, Oliver L.) N.Y., 1930.
	Phil 2280.7.35	Humanistic pragmatism. (Schiller, F.C.S.) N.Y., 1966.
	Phil 5242.56	Humanistic psychology. (Cohen, John.) London, 1958.
	Phil 1750.166.225	Het humanistische denken. Italië-Frankrijk 1450-1600. (Dresden, Samuel.) Amsterdam, 1968.
	Phil 1630.40	Die humanistische Tradition in der Romania. (Buck, August.) Hamburg, 1968.
	Phil 4570.3.81	Humanistiska sektionen contra den sakkunniga nämden. (Geijer, R.) Lund, 1887.
	Phil 186.43	Die Humanität als Mysterium. (Lublinski, Samuel.) Jena, 1907.
	Phil 8597.50	Humanität und Idealismus. (Roetschi, R.) Bern, 1943.
	Phil 1750.166.110	El humanitarismo. (Relgis, Eugen.) Buenos Aires, 1956.
	Phil 1135.168	Humanitas. (Beckmann, F.) Münster, 1952.
	Phil 8598.96	Humanitas Christiana. (Sellmair, Josef.) München, 1950.
	Phil 8656.44	Humanité de Dieu. (Barbotin, Edmond.) Paris, 1970.
	Phil 2515.4.94	L'humanité de l'avenir, d'après Cournot. (Ruyer, R.) Paris, 1930.
	Phil 2515.4.95	L'humanité de l'avenir, d'après Cournot. Thèse secondaire. (Ruyer, R.) Paris, 1930.
	Phil 585.390	Humanité de l'homme. (Barbotin, Edmond.) Paris, 1970.
	Phil 8430.11A	The humanities. 1. ed. (Dudley, Louise.) N.Y., 1940. 2v.
	Phil 8430.11.2	The humanities. 2. ed. (Dudley, Louise.) N.Y., 1951.
	Phil 1750.166.65	Humanitus. (Przymara, E.) Nuinberg, 1952.
	Phil 8600.5	Humanity and deity. (Urban, W.M.) London, 1951.
	Phil 2225.2.35	The humanity of man. (Perry, R.B.) N.Y., 1956.
	Phil 5520.441	The humanity of words. (Sendel, Bess Selher.) Cleveland, 1958.
	Phil 8610.889.5	Humanity's gain from unbelief. (Bradlaugh, C.) London, 1889.
	Phil 8610.889.7	Humanity's gain from unbelief. (Bradlaugh, C.) London, 1929.
	VPhil 310.659	Humanizam i dijalektika. (Marković, Mihajlo.) Beograd, 1967.
	Phil 1750.766	Humanizam i socijalizam. (Bošnjak, Branko.) Zagreb, 1963.
	Phil 310.676	Humanizam Marksove dijalektike i dijalektike humanizma danas. (Nedeljković, Dušan.) Beograd, 1968.
	Phil 4803.896.235	Humanizm i poznanie. (Znaniecki, Florian.) Warszawa, 1912.
	Phil 3640.36	Humano, demasiado humano. (Nietzsche, Friedrich.) Valencia, 1909?
	Phil 2880.8.287	Humans being; the world of Jean-Paul Sartre. (McMahon, Joseph H.) Chicago, 1971.

Phil 3850.5.90 — Humanus. African Spir. Leipzig, 1892.
Phil 2250.110 — Humbach, K.T. Das Verhältnis von Einzelperson und Gemeinschaft nach Josiah Royce. Heidelberg, 1962.
Phil 2805.243 — Humbert, Pierre. Cet effrayant génie...l'oeuvre scientifique de Pascal. Paris, 1947.
Phil 807.19 — Humbert, Pierre. Philosophes et savantes. Paris, 1953.
Phil 75.86 — Humdert Jahre philosophische Bibliothek 1868-1968. (Richter, Richard.) Hamburg, 1968.
Phil 978.39 — Hume, A.C. No revelation infallible. Calcutta, 1883.
Phil 2050.59 — Hume, David. An abstract of a treatise of human nature, 1740. Cambridge, Eng., 1938.
Phil 2050.59.2 — Hume, David. An abstract of a treatise of human nature, 1740. Hamden, Conn., 1965.
Phil 2050.66 — Hume, David. Anfänge und Entwicklung der Religion. Leipzig, 1909.
Htn Phil 2050.78* — Hume, David. Concise and genuine account of dispute between Mr. Hume and Mr. Rousseau. London, 1766.
Phil 2050.72 — Hume, David. David Hume: philosophical historian. Indianapolis, 1965.
Phil 2050.68.15 — Hume, David. Dialoge über natürliche Religion. 3e Aufl. Leipzig, 1905.
Phil 2050.68 — Hume, David. Dialogues concerning natural religion. Edinburgh, 1907.
Phil 2050.68.3 — Hume, David. Dialogues concerning natural religion. N.Y., 1948.
Phil 2050.67A — Hume, David. Dialogues concerning natural religion. 2nd ed. London, 1779.
Phil 2050.67.10 — Hume, David. Dialogues sur la religion naturelle. Paris, 1964.
Phil 2050.18 — Hume, David. Dissertations sur les passions. Amsterdam, 1759.
Phil 2050.41.25 — Hume, David. Enquiries concerning the human understanding and concerning the principles of morals. 2nd ed. Oxford, 1927.
Phil 2050.41 — Hume, David. An enquiry...human understanding. Chicago, 1904.
Phil 2050.41.5A — Hume, David. An enquiry...human understanding. Chicago, 1907.
Phil 2050.40 — Hume, David. An enquiry...human understanding. Oxford, 1894.
Htn Phil 2050.69.2* — Hume, David. An enquiry concerning...morals. London, 1751.
Phil 2050.41.30 — Hume, David. An enquiry concerning human understanding. Chicago, 1956.
Htn Phil 2050.43* — Hume, David. Essais philosophiques sur l'entendement humain. Amsterdam, 1758. 2v.
Phil 2050.24 — Hume, David. Essay on miracles. London, 1882. 5 pam.
Phil 2050.36 — Hume, David. Essays: literary, moral, and political. London, 1880.
Phil 2050.36.5 — Hume, David. Essays: moral, political and literary. London, 1882. 2v.
Phil 2050.37.5 — Hume, David. Essays: moral, political and literary. London, 1903.
Phil 2050.37.10 — Hume, David. Essays: moral, political and literary. London, 1963.
Phil 2050.37 — Hume, David. Essays: moral, political and literary. N.Y., 1898. 2v.
Htn Phil 2050.15* — Hume, David. Essays. v.3-4. London, 1748-53. 2v.
Phil 2050.32 — Hume, David. Essays and treatises. Edinburgh, 1793. 2v.
Phil 2050.35 — Hume, David. Essays and treatises. Edinburgh, 1804. 2v.
Phil 2050.1 — Hume, David. Essays and treatises. London, 1758.
Phil 2050.2 — Hume, David. Essays and treatises. London, 1768. 2v.
Phil 2050.33 — Hume, David. Essays and treatises. v.1-2,3-4. Basel, 1793. 2v.
Htn Phil 2050.31* — Hume, David. Essays and treatises on several subjects. London, 1760. 4v.
Phil 2050.34.60 — Hume, David. Essays and treatises on several subjects. London, 1764. 2v.
Phil 2050.34 — Hume, David. Essays and treatises on several subjects. n.p., n.d.
Htn Phil 2050.34.50* — Hume, David. Essays moral and political. Edinburgh, 1741.
Htn Phil 2050.34.55* — Hume, David. Essays moral and political. 2nd ed. Edinburgh, 1742.
Phil 2050.64 — Hume, David. Essays on suicide. London, 1789.
Htn Phil 2050.30* — Hume, David. Four dissertations. London, 1757.
Phil 2050.19 — Hume, David. Le génie de M. Hume. London, 1770.
Htn Phil 2050.68.10* — Hume, David. Gespräche über natürliche Religion. Leipzig, 1781.
Phil 2050.68.7 — Hume, David. Hume's dialogues concerning natural religion. London, 1947.
Phil 2050.41.11A — Hume, David. An inquiry concerning human understanding. N.Y., 1955.
Phil 2050.39.5 — Hume, David. An inquiry concerning the principles of morals. N.Y., 1957.
Phil 2050.77.25 — Hume, David. A letter from a gentleman to his friend in Edinburgh (1745). Facsimile. Edinburgh, 1967.
Phil 2050.76 — Hume, David. Letters. Edinburgh, 1841.
Phil 2050.75 — Hume, David. Letters. Oxford, 1888.
Phil 2050.77.15 — Hume, David. Letters. Oxford, 1932. 2v.
Htn Phil 2050.82.2* — Hume, David. Life. London, 1777.
Htn Phil 2050.82.3* — Hume, David. Life. London, 1777. 5 pam.
Phil 2050.59.25 — Hume, David. Moral and political philosophy. N.Y., 1948.
Phil 2050.67.5 — Hume, David. The natural history of religion. Stanford, 1957.
Phil 2050.68.17 — Hume, David. Die Naturgeschichte der Religion. Frankfurt, 1911.
Phil 2050.77.20 — Hume, David. New letters. Oxford, 1954.
Phil 2050.20 — Hume, David. Oeuvres philosophiques choisies. Paris, 1912. 2v.
Phil 2050.20.5 — Hume, David. Oeuvres philosophiques choisies. Paris, 1930.
Phil 2050.37.20 — Hume, David. Pensées philosophiques, morales, critiques, littéraires et politiques. Londres, 1767.
Phil 2050.35.85 — Hume, David. Philosophical essays. 1st American ed. Philadelphia, 1817. 2v.
Htn Phil 2050.34.25* — Hume, David. Philosophical essays concerning human understanding. 2nd ed. London, 1750.
Htn Phil 2050.34.27* — Hume, David. Philosophical essays concerning human understanding. 2nd ed. London, 1751.
Phil 2050.10 — Hume, David. Philosophical works. Edinburgh, 1826. 4v.
Phil 2050.11A — Hume, David. Philosophical works. Edinburgh, 1854. 4v.
Phil 2050.71A — Hume, David. Philosophy of Hume. N.Y., 1893.
Htn Phil 2050.73* — Hume, David. Political discourses. Edinburgh, 1752.
Phil 2050.59.40 — Hume, David. Political essays. N.Y., 1953.

Phil 2050.3A — Hume, David. Private correspondence...1761-76. London, 1820.
Phil 2050.45 — Hume, David. Ricerche sull'intelletto umano e sui principii della morale. Bari, 1910.
Phil 2050.45.5 — Hume, David. Ricerche sull'intelletto umano e sui principii della morale. 2a ed. Bari, 1927.
Phil 2050.23 — Hume, David. Selections. N.Y., 1927.
Phil 2050.23.2 — Hume, David. Selections. N.Y., 1955.
Phil 2050.68.25 — Hume, David. Storia naturale della religione e saggio sul suicidio. Bari, 1928.
Phil 2050.59.30 — Hume, David. Theory of knowledge. Edinburgh, 1951.
Phil 2050.59.35 — Hume, David. Theory of politics. Edinburgh, 1951.
Phil 2050.60 — Hume, David. Traité de la nature humaine. Paris, 1878.
Phil 2050.60.28 — Hume, David. Traktat über die menschliche Natur. Hamburg, 1895-1906. 2v.
Phil 2050.60.30 — Hume, David. Traktat über die menschliche Natur. v.1-2. Leipzig, 1923.
Phil 2050.60.5 — Hume, David. Trattato della natura humana. Torino, 1924.
Phil 2050.59.4 — Hume, David. A treatise of human nature. Harmondsworth, 1969.
Phil 2050.59.3 — Hume, David. A treatise of human nature. Oxford, 1964.
Phil 2050.70 — Hume, David. Treatise of morals. Photoreproduction. Boston, 1893.
Phil 2050.51 — Hume, David. Treatise on human nature. London, 1874. 2v.
Phil 2050.53 — Hume, David. Treatise on human nature. Oxford, 1888.
Phil 2050.58 — Hume, David. Treatise on human nature. Oxford, 1928.
Phil 2050.52 — Hume, David. Treatise on human nature. v.2. London, 1878.
Phil 2050.60.25 — Hume, David. Über die menschliche Natur. Bd.2. Halle, 1791.
Htn Phil 2050.42.12* — Hume, David. Eine Untersuchung über den menschlichen Verstand. Jena, 1793.
Phil 2050.42 — Hume, David. Eine Untersuchung über den menschlichen Verstand. Leipzig, 1893.
Phil 2050.42.8 — Hume, David. Eine Untersuchung über den menschlichen Verstand. 8e Aufl. Leipzig, 1920.
Phil 2050.37.25 — Hume, David. Eine Untersuchung über die Principien der Moral. Wien, 1883.
Phil 2050.69.30 — Hume, David. Untersuchung über diePrinzipien der Moral. Leipzig, 1929.
Phil 2050.77A — Hume, David. Unveröffentlichte Briefe David Humes. Leipzig, 1929.
Phil 2050.78.5 — Hume, David. Writings on economics. Madison, 1955.
Phil 2050.178 — Hume, Kant e lo scetticismo filosofico. (Casazza, G.) Roma, 1913.
Phil 8735.57 — Hume, Newton, and the design argument. (Hurlbutt, Robert H.) Lincoln, 1965.
Phil 2050.216 — Hume, o Il genio dell'empirismo. (Volpe, Galvano della.) Firenze, 1939.
Phil 2050.238 — Hume, precursor of modern empiricism. (Zabeeh, F.) The Hague, 1960.
Phil 8870.27 — Hume, Rolando. Ética inspirado o exterminio. Santa Fe, Argentina, 1960.
Phil 2050.99 — Hume. (Didier, J.) Paris, 1913.
Phil 2050.95 — Hume. (Elkin, W.B.) Ithaca, 1904.
Phil 2050.87 — Hume. (Huxley, Thomas H.) London, 1879.
Phil 2050.87.8 — Hume. (Huxley, Thomas H.) London, 1909.
Phil 2050.87.5.7A — Hume. (Huxley, Thomas H.) N.Y., 19- ?
Phil 2050.87.4A — Hume. (Huxley, Thomas H.) N.Y., 1879.
Phil 2050.87.3 — Hume. (Huxley, Thomas H.) N.Y., 1879.
Phil 2050.87.5 — Hume. (Huxley, Thomas H.) N.Y., 189-?
Phil 2050.87.10 — Hume. (Huxley, Thomas H.) N.Y., 1894.
Phil 2050.88.15 — Hume. (Knight, William.) Edinburgh, 1905.
Phil 2050.88 — Hume. (Knight, William.) Philadelphia, 1886.
Phil 2050.257 — Hume. (Pra, Mario dal.) Milano, 1949.
Phil 2050.266 — Hume. 1st ed. (Chappell, Vere Claiborne.) Garden City, N.Y., 1966.
Phil 2050.81 — Hume and Kant. (Howison, G.H.) San Francisco, 1884. 2 pam.
Phil 2050.275 — Hume and present day problems; the symposia read at the joint session of the Aristotelian Society, the Scots Philosophical Club and the Mind Association at Edinburgh, July 7th-10th, 1939. N.Y., 1968.
Phil 2050.105 — Hume e il principio di causa. (Paoli, Alessandro.) Napoli, 1882.
Phil 2050.219 — Hume e l'illuminismo inglese. 2a ed. (Baratono, A.) Milano, 1944.
Phil 3493.42 — Hume und Kant. (Lauener, Henri.) Bern, 1969.
Phil 2050.202 — Hume und Kant über den Causalbegriff. Inaug. Diss. (Schultze, W.F.) Rostock, 1870.
Phil 2050.254 — Humes Bild vom Menschen. (Mall, Rom Adhar.) Köln, 1963.
Phil 2050.280 — Hume's concept of man. (Mall, Rom Adhar.) Bombay, 1967.
Phil 2050.68.7 — Hume's dialogues concerning natural religion. (Hume, David.) London, 1947.
Phil 2050.245 — Hume's doctrine of space. (Broad, C. D.) London, 1961.
Phil 2050.261 — Hume's first principles. (Anderson, Robert Fendel.) Lincoln, 1966.
Phil 2050.227.1 — Hume's intentions. (Passmore, John A.) N.Y., 1968.
Phil 2050.208 — Hume's philosophy in his principal work, a treatise of human nature, and in his essays. (Kruse, F.V.) London, 1939.
Phil 2050.242 — Hume's philosophy of belief. (Flew, A.) London, 1961.
Phil 2050.198 — Hume's philosophy of human nature. (Laird, John.) N.Y., 1932.
Phil 2050.100 — Hume's place in ethics. Diss. (Shearer, Edna Aston.) Bryn Mawr, 1915.
Phil 2050.236 — Humes Stellung in der englischen Philosophie. v.1-2. (Uhl, Josef.) Prag, 1890-91.
Phil 2050.278 — Hume's theory of imagination. (Wilbanks, Jan.) The Hague, 1968.
Phil 2050.206 — Hume's theory of knowledge. (Maund, Costance.) London, 1937.
Phil 2050.209 — Hume's theory of the external world. (Price, H.H.) Oxford, 1940.
Phil 2050.205 — Hume's theory of the understanding. (Church, R.W.) London, 1935.
Phil 2050.197 — Humes uppfattning av jagets identitet. (Tegen, Einar.) Uppsala, 1932.
Phil 2050.110 — Det Hume'ske problem. (Münster, O.) København, 1912.
Phil 5525.64.10 — Humor; en aesthetisk studie. (Holm, Søren.) København, 1964.
Phil 5525.18 — Humor als Lebensgefühl. (Hoffding, Harald.) Leipzig, 1918.
Phil 6980.132 — Humor in der Neurologie und Psychiatrie. (Bratz, Emil.) Berlin, 1930.
Phil 476.3.2.10 — Der Humor in Kraft und Stoff. (Büchner, L.) Darmstadt, 1856.
Phil 5525.50 — The humor of humor. (Esar, Evan.) London, 1954.

Phil 5525.30 | Der Humor und seine Begründung. (Victor, C.R.) Bremen, 1925.
Phil 5247.29.20 | Humphrey, G. Directed thinking. N.Y., 1948.
Phil 5247.29.15 | Humphrey, G. The nature of learning in its relation to the living system. London, 1933.
Phil 5247.29 | Humphrey, G. The story of man's mind. Boston, 1923.
Phil 5247.29.5 | Humphrey, G. The story of man's mind. N.Y., 1932.
Phil 8610.877.5 | Humphrey, G.H. Christianity and infidelity. N.Y., 1877.
Phil 978.83 | Humphrey, Christmas. Karma and rebirth. London, 1943.
Phil 7069.20.170 | Humphreys, Eliza Margaret J.G. The truth of spiritualism. Philadelphia, 1920.
Phil 182.110 | Humphreys, H.S. The cylindriad. Evansville, 1942.
Phil 2150.18.95 | Hund, William Byrne. The theory of goodness in the writings of George Edward Moore, 1873-1958. Notre Dame, Ind., 1964.
Phil 178.15 | Hundert jahre Zeitgeist in Deutschland. (Duboc, K.J.) Leipzig, 1889.
Phil 5247.23.15 | Hundert psychologische Schulversuche. 4. Aufl. (Höfler, Alois.) Leipzig, 1918.
Phil 3487.1.15 | Die hundertjährige Gedächtnissfeier der Kantischen Kritik der reinen Vernunft. 2. Aufl. (Fischer, Kuno.) Heidelberg, 1892.
Phil 1715.6.5 | A hundred years of philosophy. (Passmore, John Arthur.) London, 1962.
Phil 1715.6.7 | A hundred years of philosophy. 2nd ed. (Passmore, John Arthur.) London, 1966.
Phil 5215.2.10 | A hundred years of psychology, 1833-1933. (Flügel, J.C.) London, 1964.
Phil 5215.2.12 | A hundred years of psychology, 1833-1933. (Flügel, J.C.) N.Y., 1964.
Phil 5215.2.5 | A hundred years of psychology, 1833-1933. 2nd ed. (Flügel, J.C.) London, 1951.
Phil 197.17 | Hundredth century philosophy. (Wheeler, C.K.) Boston, 1906.
Phil 182.108 | Hunger for wholiness. (Howells, T.H.) Denver, 1940.
Phil 5247.49 | Hungerford, H. Bunkless psychology. Washington, 1933.
Phil 5871.90 | Hunt, David. Parents and children in history. N.Y., 1970.
Phil 7069.64.27 | Hunt, Douglas. A handbook on the occult. London, 1967.
Phil 8610.907 | Hunt, E.J. The evolution of faith; an essay. London, 1907.
Phil 5360.16.1 | Hunt, Earl Busby. Concept learning. N.Y., 1966.
Phil 9375.2 | Hunt, F. Worth and wealth. N.Y., 1857.
Phil 7069.31.10 | Hunt, H. Ernest. Spiritualism for the enquirer. London, 1931.
Phil 5247.74 | Hunt, J. Intelligence and experience. N.Y., 1961.
Phil 6957.4 | Hunt, J.H. Astounding disclosures. n.p., 1851.
Phil 8632.10 | Hunt, Jasper B. Existence after death implied by science. London, 1910.
Phil 7040.22A | Hunt, Joseph M. Personality and the behavior disorders. N.Y., 1944. 2v.
Phil 7075.154 | Hunt, Morton M. The natural history of love. N.Y., 1959.
Phil 5247.81 | Hunt, Morton M. The thinking animal. Boston, 1964.
Phil 5780.15 | Hunter, Edward. Brainwashing. N.Y., 1956.
Phil 5780.15.2 | Hunter, Edward. Brainwashing. N.Y., 1960.
Phil 5545.190 | Hunter, I.M.L. Memory. Harmondsworth, 1957.
Phil 6949.363 | Hunter, Richard A. Three hundred years of psychiatry, 1535-1860; a history presented in selected English texts. London, 1963.
Phil 807.8 | Hunter, T. History of philosophy. N.Y., 1900.
Phil 5817.7 | Hunter, W.S. The delayed reaction in animals and children. Cambridge, n.d.
Phil 5247.19.2 | Hunter, W.S. General psychology. Chicago, 1919.
Phil 5247.19.7 | Hunter, W.S. General psychology. Chicago, 1927.
Phil 5247.19.25 | Hunter, W.S. Human behavior. Chicago, 1928.
Phil 2045.132A | The hunting of Leviathan. (Mintz, Samuel.) Cambridge, 1962.
Phil 8882.31.5 | Huntington, F.D. Good talking a fine art. Syracuse, 1892.
Phil 8882.31 | Huntington, F.D. Good talking and good manners. Syracuse, 1887.
Phil 8587.21.2 | Huntington, F.D. Human society: Graham lectures. N.Y., 1860.
Phil 8587.24 | Huntington, H. Cué bono? or What shall it profit. London, 1912.
Phil 8587.27.3 | Huntington, William R. Four key-words of religion. 2. ed. N.Y., 1899.
Phil 2520.132 | Hunze, Max. Die Sittenlehre des Descartes. Leipzig, 1872.
Phil 8587.29 | Hunzinger, A.W. Das Christentum im Weltanschauungskampf. 3. Aufl. Leipzig, 1919.
Phil 8587.29.10 | Hunzinger, A.W. Hunzinger. Hamburg, 1921-22. 2v.
Phil 8587.29.10 | Hunzinger. (Hunzinger, A.W.) Hamburg, 1921-22. 2v.
Phil 1112.8 | Huonder, Quirin. Gott und Seele bin Lichte der griechischen Philosophie. München, 1954.
Phil 8277.2 | Huonder, Quirin. Das Unsterblichkeitsproblem in der abendländischenPhilosophie. Stuttgart, 1970.
Phil 3549.2.96 | Hupfeld, R. Graf Hermann Keyserling. Bonn, 1922.
Phil 5047.43 | Huppé, B.J. Logic and language. 1st ed. N.Y., 1956.
Phil 6945.25 | Hurd, Henry M. The institutional care of the insane in the United States and Canada. Baltimore, 1916-17. 4v.
Phil 8882.23 | Hurd, R. Moral and political dialogues. London, 1760.
Phil 482.5 | Huré, Jules. Les origines judéo-chrétiennes du matérialisme contemporain. Paris, 1928.
Phil 8735.57 | Hurlbutt, Robert H. Hume, Newton, and the design argument. Lincoln, 1965.
Phil 5640.127 | Hurst, A.F. The Croonian lectures. London, 1920.
Phil 623.8.5 | Hurst, J.J. History of rationalism. London, 1867.
Phil 623.8.3 | Hurst, J.J. History of rationalism. N.Y., 1865.
Phil 8080.12 | Hurtado, L. Espacio y tiempo en el arte actual. Buenos Aires, 1941.
Phil 182.133 | Hurtado, Manuel. The positive absolutes. Mexico, 1963.
Phil 3552.132 | Huru förhåller sig Leibnitz' metafysik. (Geijer, K.R.) Upsala, 1876.
Phil 9380.10 | Hurvich, L.M. Beginnings of a bibliography on psychological factors in morale. n.p., n.d.
Phil 5643.128 | Hurvich, Leo Maurice. The perception of brightness and darkness. Boston, 1966.
Htn Phil 4938.2.30* | Hus, J. Liber egregius de unitate ecclesiae. n.p., n.d.
Phil 5850.232 | Husband, R.W. Applied psychology. N.Y., 1934.
Phil 8612.28 | Husemann, F. Vom Bild und Sinn des Todes. Dresden, 1938.
Phil 8612.28.5 | Husemann, F. Vom Bild und Sinn des Todes. 2. Aufl. Stuttgart, 1954.
Phil 978.91 | Husemann, F. Wege und Irrwege in die geistige Welt. Stuttgart, 1962.
Phil 9070.126 | Husén, Torsten. Livsåskådning och religion. Stockholm, 1968.
Phil 5247.84.4 | Husén, Torsten. Psykologi. 4. uppl. Stockholm, 1966.
Phil 5238.248 | Husén, Torsten. Psykologisk bredvielläsning. v. 1-2. Stockholm, 1967.

Phil 1050.10 | Husik, I. History of medieval Jewish philosophy. N.Y., 1916.
Phil 1050.10.10 | Husik, I. Philosophial essays. Oxford, 1952.
Phil 1050.6 | Husik, Isaac. Judah Messer Leon's commentary on the Vitus logica. Leiden, 1906.
Phil 8408.48 | Hussain, Fakhir. Le jugement esthétique. Paris, 1968.
Phil 338.32 | Husser, Friedrich F. Zu einem Prinzip der Messung. Meisenhem am Glan, 1960.
Phil 3450.11.370 | Husserl; an analysis of his phenomenology. (Ricoeur, Paul.) Evanston, 1967.
Phil 3450.11.445 | Husserl, dalla logica alla fenomenologia. (Raggiunti, Renzo.) Firenze, 1967.
Phil 19.9 | Husserl, E. Jahrbuch für Philosophie und phänomenologische Forschung. Halle, 1913. 13v.
Phil 3450.11.60 | Husserl, Edmund. Briefe an roman ingarden. Den Haag, 1968.
Phil 3450.11.40A | Husserl, Edmund. Cartesian meditations. The Hague, 1960.
Phil 3450.40 | Husserl, Edmund. Cartesian meditations. The Hague, 1960.
Phil 3450.11.62 | Husserl, Edmund. The crisis of European sciences and transcendental phenomenology. Evanston, 1970.
Phil 3450.11.114 | Husserl, Edmund. Erfahrung und Urteil. Prag, 1939.
Phil 5047.11.25 | Husserl, Edmund. Formal and transcendental logic. The Hague, 1969.
Phil 5047.11.10 | Husserl, Edmund. Formale und transzendentale Logik. Halle, 1929.
Phil 3450.11.30 | Husserl, Edmund. Gesammelte Werke. Haag, 1950-52. 12v.
Phil 3450.11.50 | Husserl, Edmund. The idea of phenomenology. The Hague, 1964.
Phil 182.67.4 | Husserl, Edmund. Ideas: general introduction to pure phenomenology. London, 1931.
Phil 182.67.4.2 | Husserl, Edmund. Ideas: general introduction to pure phenomenology. London, 1952.
Phil 182.67 | Husserl, Edmund. Ideen zu einer reinen Phänomenologie und phänomenologischen Philosophie. Halle, 1913.
Phil 5047.11.4 | Husserl, Edmund. Logical investigations. 2nd ed. N.Y., 1970. 2v.
Phil 5047.11.15 | Husserl, Edmund. Logique formelle et logique transcendantale. Paris, 1957.
Phil 5047.11 | Husserl, Edmund. Logische Untersuchungen. Halle, 1900.
Phil 5047.11.3 | Husserl, Edmund. Logische Untersuchungen. v. 1-2, pt. 1-2. Tübingen, 1968[1913]. 3v.
Phil 5047.11.2 | Husserl, Edmund. Logische Untersuchungen. 2. Aufl. v. 1-2, pt. 1-2. Halle, 1913. 3v.
Phil 182.67.5 | Husserl, Edmund. Méditations cartésiennes. Paris, 1931.
Phil 3450.11.75 | Husserl, Edmund. The Paris lectures. The Hague, 1964.
Phil 3450.11.55 | Husserl, Edmund. Phenomenology and the crisis of philosophy. N.Y., 1965.
Phil 3450.11.35 | Husserl, Edmund. The phenomenology of internal time-consciousness. Bloomington, 1964.
Phil 3450.11.48 | Husserl, Edmund. Philosophie als strenge Wissenschaft. Frankfurt am Main, 1965.
Phil 3450.11.45 | Husserl, Edmund. La philosophie comme science rigoureuse. Thèse. Paris, 1954.
Phil 5047.11.20 | Husserl, Edmund. Recherches logiques. Paris, 1959. 3v.
Phil 3450.11.79 | Pamphlet box. Husserl, Edmund.
Phil 3450.11.425 | Husserl; ou, Le retour aux choses. (Christoff, Daniel.) Paris, 1966.
Phil 3450.11.350 | Husserl, sa vie, son oeuvre. (Keekell, Lothar.) Paris, 1964.
Phil 3450.11.340 | Husserl. (Robberechts, L.) Paris, 1964.
Phil 3450.11.202 | Husserl. (Wahle, Jean A.) Paris, 1961.
Phil 3450.11.200 | Husserl. Paris, 1959.
Phil 3450.11.200 | Husserl. v.1-2. (Wahle, Jean A.) Paris, 1958.
Phil 3450.11.480 | Husserl and phenomenology. (Pivčević, Edo.) London, 1970.
Phil 3450.11.215 | Husserl et la pensée moderne. (Colloque International de Phénoménologie.) La Haye, 1959.
Phil 3450.11.500 | Husserl und die Meditationen des Descartes. (Herrmann, Friedrich-Wilhelm von.) Frankfurt, 1971.
Phil 3492.75 | Husserl und Kant. (Kern, Iso.) Den Haag, 1964.
Phil 3450.11.124 | Husserl's Internationalitäts und Urteilslehre. Inaug. Diss. (Fisch, Isidor.) Basel, 1942.
Phil 3450.11.102 | Husserls Phänomenologie und Schuppes Logik. (Zocher, Rudolf.) München, 1932.
Phil 8434.4 | Hussey, C. The picturesque. London, 1927.
Phil 6677.3A | Husson, H.M. Report on the magnetical experiments. Boston, 1836.
Phil 2475.1.296 | Husson, León A. L'intellectualisme de Bergson. Paris, 1947.
Phil 2475.1.297 | Husson, León A. L'intellectualisme de Bergson. Thèse. Paris, 1947.
Phil 2053.60.3A | Hutcheson, F. Essay on nature and conduct of passions. Glasgow, 1769.
Phil 2053.60 | Hutcheson, F. Essay on nature and conduct of passions. London, 1728.
Htn Phil 2053.60.2* | Hutcheson, F. Essay on nature and conduct of passions. London, 1728. 2 pam.
Phil 2053.65 | Hutcheson, F. Illustrations on the moral sense. Cambridge, 1971.
Htn Phil 2053.50* | Hutcheson, F. Inquiry into...beauty and virtue. London, 1725.
Phil 2053.50.2 | Hutcheson, F. Inquiry into...beauty and virtue. London, 1726.
Htn Phil 2053.50.3* | Hutcheson, F. Inquiry into...beauty and virtue. London, 1729.
Phil 2053.50.4 | Hutcheson, F. Inquiry into...beauty and virtue. London, 1738.
Phil 2053.52 | Hutcheson, F. Metaphysicae synopsis. n.p., 1742.
Phil 2053.40 | Hutcheson, F. Philosophiae moralis. v.1-3. Glasgow, 1742.
Htn Phil 2053.70* | Hutcheson, F. Reflections upon laughter. Glasgow, 1750.
X Cg Phil 2053.41.2 | Hutcheson, F. A short introduction to moral philosophy. v.1,2-3. Glasgow, 1764. 2v.
Htn Phil 2053.41* | Hutcheson, F. A short introduction to moral philosophy. v.1-3. Glasgow, 1747.
Phil 182.26 | Hutcheson, F. Synopsis metaphysicae. Glasguae, 1756.
Phil 2053.30 | Hutcheson, F. System of moral philosophy. Glasgow, 1755. 2v.
Htn Phil 2053.30.1* | Hutcheson, F. System of moral philosophy. London, 1755. 2v.
Phil 288.2 | Hutchins, S. Theory of the universe. N.Y., 1868.
Phil 5465.54 | Hutchinson, E.D. How to think creatively. N.Y., 1949.
Phil 7082.72 | Hutchinson, Horace Gordon. Dreams and their meanings. London, 1901.
Phil 8587.57 | Hutchinson, Paul. The ordeal of western civilization. Boston, 1933.
Phil 8587.70 | Hutchison, J.A. Faith. N.Y., 1956.
Phil 5590.570.2 | Huth, Albert. Diagnose der Person. 2. Aufl. Bern, 1963.

Phil 5850.231   Huth, Albert. Exakte Persönlichkeitsforschung. Leipzig, 1930.

Phil 530.10   Hutin, Serge. Les disciples anglais de Jacob Boehme. Paris, 1960.

Phil 2145.80   Hutin, Serge. Henry More. Essai sur les doctrines théosophiques chez les platoniciens de Cambridge. Hildesheim, 1966.

Phil 1807.8   Hutin, Serge. La philosophie anglaise et américaine. Paris, 1958.

Phil 8586.36.80   Hutorität und Begegnung. (Nievergelt, Hans-Ulrich.) Zürich, 1963.

Phil 6117.48   Hutschnecker, A.A. The will to line. London, 1952.

Phil 338.41   Hutten, Ernest. The origins of science. London, 1962.

Phil 170.3   Hutton, James. Investigation of the principles of knowledge. Edinburgh, 1794. 3v.

NEDL Phil 8697.1   Hutton, R.H. Aspects of religious and scientific thought. London, 1899.

Phil 6834.6   Hutton, Robert. Of those alone. London, 1958.

Phil 182.109   Huxley, A. Unser Glaube. Stockholm, 1939.

Phil 8587.60.7   Huxley, Aldous. The perennial philosophy. N.Y., 1964.

Phil 8587.60   Huxley, Aldous. The perennial philosophy. 1. ed. N.Y., 1945.

Phil 8587.60.5   Huxley, Aldous. The perennial philosophy. 5. ed. N.Y., 1945.

Phil 1750.166.90   Huxley, J.S. Evolutionary humanism. Melbourne, 1954.

Phil 1750.166.91   Huxley, J.S. The humanist frame. London, 1961.

Phil 1750.166.92   Huxley, J.S. The humanist frame. N.Y., 1962.

Phil 8587.48   Huxley, J.S. Religion without revelation. N.Y., 1927.

Phil 8587.48.2   Huxley, J.S. Religion without revelation. N.Y., 1957.

Phil 8697.13   Huxley, Julian S. What dare I think? London, 1931.

Phil 8697.13.5   Huxley, Julian S. What dare I think? N.Y., 1931.

Phil 9070.107   Huxley, Laura. You are not the target. N.Y., 1965.

Phil 8697.5   Huxley, T.H. Essays upon some controverted questions. N.Y., 1892.

Phil 8697.5.3   Huxley, T.H. Essays upon some controverted questions. N.Y., 1893.

NEDL Phil 9150.5   Huxley, T.H. Evolution and ethics. London, 1893.

Phil 8697.5.15   Huxley, T.H. Science and Christian tradition; essays. N.Y., 1898.

Phil 8697.5.20   Huxley, T.H. Science and Christian tradition; essays. N.Y., 1913.

Phil 2050.87   Huxley, Thomas H. Hume. London, 1879.

Phil 2050.87.8   Huxley, Thomas H. Hume. London, 1909.

Phil 2050.87.5.7A   Huxley, Thomas H. Hume. N.Y., 19- ?

Phil 2050.87.3   Huxley, Thomas H. Hume. N.Y., 1879.

Phil 2050.87.4A   Huxley, Thomas H. Hume. N.Y., 1879.

Phil 2050.87.5   Huxley, Thomas H. Hume. N.Y., 189-?

Phil 2050.87.10   Huxley, Thomas H. Hume. N.Y., 1894.

Htn   Phil 2055.3.30*   Huxley, Thomas H. The Romanes lecture 1893. London, 1893.

Phil 8882.64   Huxley, Thomas H. Touchstone for ethics. 1st ed. N.Y., 1941.

Phil 8408.22   Huyghe, René. L'art et l'âme. Paris, 1960.

Phil 6990.3.9   Huysmans, J.K. Les foules de Lourdes. 21. éd. Paris, 1906.

Phil 4610.10.30   Hva er filosofi? (Naess, Arne.) Oslo, 1965.

Phil 182.130   Hva er metafysikk: Aristoteles, Bergson, Heidegger. Oslo, 1962.

Phil 4610.7.18   Hvad är sanning. (Norström, V.) Göteborg, 1899.

Phil 192.52   Hvad er kultur? (Rein, Doris.) Kristiania, 1916.

Phil 4610.7.35   Hvad vi behöfva. (Norström, V.) Stockholm, 1901.

Phil 4655.1.53   Hvad vi behöfva. (Wikner, Pontus.) Upsala, 1865.

Phil 8581.47   Hvad vi veta, hvad vi tro och hvad vi vilja. (Bergstedt, C.F.) Stockholm, 1878.

Phil 182.27   Hvalgrens, E. Grunddragen. Göteborg, 1879.

Phil 130.13   Hvem taenkte hvad; filosofiens hvem-hvad-hvor. (Thomsen, Henrik.) København, 1961.

Phil 7069.13.32   Hví slaer pú mig? v.1-2. (Nielsson, H.) Reykjavik, 1913.

Phil 179.23   Hvilken verldsförklaring uppfyller fordringarna för möjlighrtin af menniskans praktiska lif? (Edfeldt, Hans.) Uppsala, 1868.

Phil 4582.3.32   Hwasser, Israel. Mannens ynglingaålder. Upsala, 1856.

Phil 4582.3.31   Hwasser, Israel. Om vår tids ungdom. Upsala, 1842.

Phil 978.5.9.25   Hyat, T.P. A check list of some books and authors. Stanford, 1940.

Phil 8800.1   Hyde, E. The miscellaneous works. London, 1751.

Phil 8587.46   Hyde, Laurence. The prospects of humanism. London, 1931.

Phil 2055.8.35   Hyde, Lawrence. An introduction to organic philosophy. Reigate, 1955.

Phil 2055.8.30   Hyde, Lawrence. Isis and Osiris. London, 1946.

Phil 9035.3   Hyde, T.A. How to study character. N.Y., 1884.

Phil 8882.24.15   Hyde, W. De W. Are you human? N.Y., 1916.

Phil 8882.24.9   Hyde, W. De W. The cardinal virtues. N.Y., 1902.

Phil 575.10.10   Hyde, W. De W. The five great philosophies of life. N.Y., 1932.

Phil 575.10   Hyde, W. De W. From Epicurus to Christ...study in...personality. N.Y., 1904.

Phil 8882.24   Hyde, W. De W. Practical ethics. N.Y., 1892.

Phil 400.30.5   Hyde, W. De W. Practical idealism. N.Y., 1899.

Phil 8882.24.8   Hyde, W. De W. Self-measurement. N.Y., 1912.

Phil 9167.4   Hyde, William de W. The quest of the best. N.Y., 1913.

Phil 7069.17.20   Hydesville in history. (Cadwallader, Mary E.) Chicago, 1917.

Phil 8957.5   The hydrostatic paradox in morals. (Hill, Thomas.) Portland, 1880.

Phil 3850.27.140   Hygen, J.B. Albert Schweitzers Kulturkritik. Göttingen, 1955.

Phil 3850.27.141   Hygen, J.B. Albert Schweitzers tanker om kulturen. Oslo, 1954.

Phil 6115.11.8   Hygiene de l'âme. (Feuchtersleben, E.F.V.) Paris, 1860.

Phil 665.21   Hygiene del alma. n.p., n.d.

Phil 6112.25.6   Hygiene of mind. 6th ed. (Clouston, T.S.) London, 1912.

Phil 6115.21   Hygiene of nerves and mind in health and disease. (Forel, A.) London, 1907.

Phil 6117.3   Hygiene of the brain. (Holbrook, M.L.) N.Y., 1878.

Phil 6115.11.28   The hygiene of the soul; the memoir of a physician and philosopher. (Pollak, G.) N.Y., 1910.

Phil 6673.13   Hygienic clairvoyance. (Dixon, Jacob.) London, 1859.

Phil 5330.20   Hylan, J.P. The fluctuation of attention. N.Y., 1898.

Phil 5627.3A   Hylan, J.P. Public worship. Chicago, 1901.

Phil 5590.285   Hylander, Ernst. Vom Umgang mit sich Selbst. München, 1958.

Phil 1140.7   Hylē anthrōpinē. (Philippson, L.) Berolini, 1831.

Phil 9075.71   Hylkema, G.W. Homo duplex. Haarlem, 1963.

Phil 1512.14   Hyman, Arthur. Philosophy in the Middle Ages. N.Y., 1967.

Phil 5247.79   Hyman, R. The nature of psychological inquiry. Englewood Cliffs, N.J., 1964.

Phil 2905.1.42   Hymn of the universe. (Teilhard de Chardin, Pierre.) London, 1965.

Phil 2905.1.40   Hymne de l'univers. (Teilhard de Chardin, Pierre.) Paris, 1961.

Phil 8587.25   Hyndman, F.A. The time of transition. London, 1900.

Phil 1150.9   Hypatia, die Philosophin von Alexandria. (Wolf, S.) Vienna, 1879.

Phil 1150.10   Hypatia. (Hubbard, E.) N.Y., 1908.

Phil 1150.11A   Hypatia von Alexandria. (Meyer, W.A.) Heidelberg, 1886.

Phil 6670.2   Hypnos och suggestion. (Abrutz, Sydney.) Stockholm, 1925.

Phil 6681.3   Die Hypnose. (Lehmann, A.) Leipzig, 1890.

Phil 5814.4   Hypnose bei Tieren. (Erhard, H.) Giessen, 1924.

Phil 6677.10   Die Hypnose und die Suggestion. (Hilgu, Wilhelm.) Jena, 1909.

Phil 5822.5   Hypnose und Katalepsie bei Tieren. (Mangold, Ernst.) Jena, 1914.

Phil 6677.5   Hypnosis. (Haberman, J.V.) N.Y., 1910.

Phil 6672.16   Hypnosis. 1st ed. (Chertok, León.) Oxford, 1966.

Phil 6677.15   Hypnosis and suggestibility. (Hull, C.L.) N.Y., 1933.

Phil 6682.24   Hypnosis through the world. (Marcuse, F.L.) Springfield, Ill., 1964.

NEDL Phil 17.5   The hypnotic magazine. Chicago.

Phil 6686.1.5   Hypnotic therapeutics. (Quackenbos, J.D.) N.Y., 1908.

Phil 6680.2.3   Hypnotische Experimente. (Kraft-Ebing, R. von.) Stuttgart, 1893.

Phil 7113.5   Hypnotism; masterpiece of myths. (Clements, John.) Manchester, 1966.

Phil 6677.1   Hypnotism, mesmerism. (Hart, E.) N.Y., 1893.

Phil 6677.1.5   Hypnotism, mesmerism and the new witchcraft. (Hart, E.) London, 1896.

Phil 6671.25   Hypnotism. (Björnström, F.J.) N.Y., 1889.

Phil 6674.8   Hypnotism. (Estabrooks, G.H.) N.Y., 1943.

Phil 6676.9   Hypnotism. (Garrett, Thomas L.) N.Y., 1934.

Phil 6682.6.3   Hypnotism. (Moll, Albert.) London, 1892.

Phil 6682.6.9   Hypnotism. (Moll, Albert.) London, 1909?

Phil 6692.10   Hypnotism. (Weitzenhoffer, André M.) N.Y., 1953.

Phil 6671.15.6   Hypnotism: its history, practice, and theory. (Bramwell, J.M.) N.Y., 1956.

Phil 6682.6.15   Hypnotism. 2. ed. (Moll, Albert.) London, 1890.

Phil 6671.15.5   Hypnotism. 2nd ed. (Bramwell, J.M.) London, 1906.

Phil 6682.6.4   Hypnotism. 4th ed. (Moll, Albert.) London, 1898.

Phil 6675.6   Hypnotism and cerebral activity. (Forel, A.) Worcester, 1899.

Phil 6677.20   Hypnotism and crime. (Hammerschlag, Heinz F.) Hollywood, Calif., 1957.

Phil 6692.3   Hypnotism and its application to practical medecine. (Wetterstrand, O.G.) N.Y., 1899.

Phil 6681.6.5   Hypnotism and spiritism...travel. 2. ed. (Lapponi, Guiseppe.) N.Y., 1915.

Phil 6688.17   Hypnotism and suggestion. (Satow, Louis.) London, 1923.

Phil 6682.11   Hypnotism and suggestion in theraputics. (Mason, Rufus O.) N.Y., 1911.

Phil 6694.1   Hypnotism and telepathy. (Yeshilian, M.A.) N.Y., 1917.

Phil 7106.6   Hypnotism and the doctors. (Harte, Richard.) London, 1903.

Phil 6677.13   Hypnotism as a therapeutic agent. (Howard, W.L.) Baltimore, 1893.

Phil 6688.6   Hypnotism as it is. (Sage, X.L.) N.Y., 1897.

Phil 6688.6.2   Hypnotism as it is. (Sage, X.L.) Rochester, 1899.

Phil 6669.11   Hypnotism comes of age. 1st ed. (Wolfe, Bernard.) Indianapolis, 1948.

Phil 6681.15   Hypnotism in the treatment of disease. (Lloyd, B. Layton.) London, 1934.

Phil 6675.6.5   Hypnotism or suggestion and psychotherapy. (Forel, A.) N.Y., 1907.

Phil 6689.1   Hypnotisme, suggestion. (Tarkhanof, J.R.) Paris, 1891.

Phil 6671.5   Hypnotisme. (Bernheim, H.) Paris, 1891.

Phil 6675.7   L'hypnotisme. (Foveau de Courmelles, F.V.) Paris, 1890.

Phil 6682.17   L'hypnotisme. (Moreau, P.G.) Paris, 1891.

Phil 6671.5.3   Hypnotisme and suggestion. (Bernheim, H.) Paris, 1910.

Phil 6687.10   Hypnotisme et croyances anciennes. (Regnier, L.R.) Paris, 1891.

Phil 6678.1   L'hypnotisme et la stigmatisation. (Imbert-Gourbeyre, A.) Paris, 1899.

Phil 6676.6   L'hypnotisme et la suggestion. 4. éd. (Grásset, J.) Paris, 1916.

Phil 6671.4   Hypnotisme experimental. (Bérillon, E.) Paris, 1884.

Phil 6677.12.5   L'hypnotisme franc et l'hypnotisme vrai. (Hélot, C.) Paris, 1909.

Phil 6672.7   L'hypnotisme scientifique. (Crocq, Jean J.) Paris, 1896.

Phil 6682.18   O hypnotismo. 3. ed. (Medeiros e Albuquerque, J.J. de C. da C.) Rio de Janeiro, 1926.

Phil 6680.4   Hypnotismus, animismus. (Kaplan, Leo.) Leipzig, 1917.

Phil 6685.5   Der Hypnotismus. (Preyer, W.) Wien, 1890.

Phil 6687.3   Der Hypnotismus. (Rieger, C.) Jena, 1884.

Phil 6675.6.7   Der Hypnotismus. 2. Aufl. (Forel, A.) Stuttgart, 1891.

Phil 3915.43   Hypnotismus und Suggestion. (Wundt, Wilhelm.) Leipzig, 1892.

Phil 6689.7.3   Hypnotismus und Suggestion. 3e Aufl. (Trömner, Ernst.) Leipzig, 1919.

Phil 6332.13   Hypoanalysis. (Wolberg, Lewis R.) N.Y., 1945.

Phil 6110.17   The hypothalamus and central levels of autonomic function. (Association for Research in Nervous and Mental Diseases.) Baltimore, 1940.

Phil 5115.6   Die Hypothese. (Görland, Albert.) Göttingen, 1911.

Phil 9560.68   Hypothèse de la vérité. (Heyst, Jacques.) Versailles, 1960.

Phil 197.9.7   Die Hypothese des Unbewussten. (Windelband, W.) Heidelberg, 1914.

Phil 186.82   Hypothèse sur l'évolution physique et métaphysique de l'énergie. (Lambert, Henri.) Bruxelles, 1935.

Phil 293.15   Hypothesen über einige kosmologische und geologische Momente. (Mikos, J.) Leipzig, 1895.

Phil 5640.125.7   Hypothesenfreie Theorie der Gegenfarben. (Pikler, Gyula.) Leipzig, 1919.

Phil 194.17   Hypothesis for a ceptacle theory. (Taft, Oren B.) Chicago, 1900.

Phil 193.86   The hypothesis of the universality of life. (Shearon, William.) St. Louis, 1922.

Phil 5115.10   Hypothetical reasoning. (Rescher, Nicholas.) Amsterdam, 1964.

Phil 2655.6.30   Hyppolite, J. Leçon inaugurale faite le jeudi 19 déc. 1963. Nougent-le-Rotrou, 1964.

Phil 2750.27.30   Hyppolite, Jean. Sens et existence dans la philosophie de Maurice Merleau-Ponty. Oxford, 1963.

Phil 3425.390   Hyppolite, Jean. Études sur Marx et Hegel. Paris, 1955.

Phil 3425.390.2   Hyppolite, Jean. Études sur Marx et Hegel. 2. éd. Paris, 1965.

Phil 3425.319.5A   Hyppolite, Jean. Genèse et structure de la phénoménologie de l'esprit de Hegel. Paris, 1946.

Phil 3425.319   Hyppolite, Jean. Genèse et structure de la phénoménologie de l'esprit de Hegel. Thèse. Paris, 1946.
Phil 3425.319.15   Hyppolite, Jean. Introduction à la philosophie de l'historie de Hegel. Paris, 1948.
Phil 3425.319.10   Hyppolite, Jean. Logique et existence. 1. ed. Paris, 1953.
Phil 3425.390.5   Hyppolite, Jean. Studies on Marx and Hegel. N.Y., 1969.
Phil 7084.38   Hyppolite, Michelson Paul. La mentalité haitienne et le domaine du rêve. Port-au-Prince, 1965.
Phil 8882.25   Hyslop, J.H. The elements of ethics. N.Y., 1895.
Phil 5047.9   Hyslop, J.H. Elements of logic. N.Y., 1892.
Phil 8632.8.5   Hyslop, J.H. Life after death. N.Y., 1919.
Phil 5047.9.5   Hyslop, J.H. Logic and argument. N.Y., 1907.
Phil 182.38   Hyslop, J.H. Problems of philosophy. N.Y., 1905.
Phil 7069.19.147   Hyslop, James H. Contact with the other world. N.Y., 1919.
Phil 7069.06.10   Hyslop, James Hervey. Borderland of psychical research. 2. ed. Boston, 1906.
Phil 7069.06.11   Hyslop, James Hervey. Enigmas of psychical research. Boston, 1906.
Phil 7069.06.11.5   Hyslop, James Hervey. Problem der Seelenforschung. Stuttgart, 1909.
Phil 7069.08.22   Hyslop, James Hervey. Psychical research and the resurrection. Boston, 1908.
Phil 7069.05.10   Hyslop, James Hervey. Science and a future life. Boston, 1905.
Phil 7069.10.5   Hyslop, James Hervey. Science and a future life. 5. ed. Boston, 1910.
Phil 6957.12.7   Hyslop, T.B. The borderland, some of the problems of insanity. N.Y., 1925.
Phil 6957.12   Hyslop, T.B. The great abnormals. London, 1925.
Phil 6117.6   Hyslop, T.B. Mental physiology. Philadelphia, 1895.
Phil 6615.22   Hysteria; the history of a disease. (Veith, Ilza.) Chicago, 1965.
Phil 6615.12.5   Hysteria. (Kretschmer, Ernst.) N.Y., 1926.
Phil 6615.12.3   Hysterie, reflex und instikt. 3. Aufl. (Kretschmer, Ernst.) Leipzig, 1944.
Phil 6957.10.5   Die Hysterie und die moderne Schule. (Hellpach, W.) n.p., 1905-1913. 11 pam.
Phil 8882.75   Hytten, E. The concept of morality. Stockholm, 1959.
Phil 2050.111   I. Hume's psykologiska härledning av kausalitetsföreställningell. Hypotesen om det omedvetna i empirisk psykologi. (Phalén, Adolf.) Uppsala, 1914.
Phil 3495.8   I. Kant's Auferstehung aus dem Grabe. (Noack, L.) Leipzig, 1861.
Phil 3492.33   I. Kants Grundlegung zur Metaphysik der Sitten. (Kunhardt, H.) Lübeck, 1800.
Phil 5520.584   I.A. Richard's theory of literature. (Schiller, Jerome Paul.) New Haven, 1969.
Htn   Phil 4372.1.31*   I.L. Vivis Valentini, de disciplinis libri XII. (Vives, Juan Luis.) Batavorum Lugduni, 1636.
Phil 4769.6.83.5   I.M. Sechenov. (Rubinshtein, Sergei L.) Moskva, 1957.
Phil 5625.75.110   I.P. Pavlov v vospominaniiakh sovremennikov. Leningrad, 1967.
Phil 5625.75.85   I.P. Pavlovs i ego uchenie ob uslovnykh refleksakh. (Frolov, I.P.) Moskva, 1936.
Phil 5258.197   I.Q.: a Mensa analysis and history. (Serebriakoff, Victor.) London, 1966.
Phil 177.73   I am. (Constable, F.C.) London, 1928.
Phil 978.77.3   The "I am" discourses. 2d ed. (King, G.R.) Chicago, 1940.
Phil 8610.917   I am not afraid, are you? (Ricker, M.M.) East Aurora, N.Y., 1917.
Phil 5627.241   I am persuaded. (Duguid, Julian.) N.Y., 1941.
Phil 9530.38.50   I am winning friends. (Roback, A.A.) Cambridge, 1938.
Phil 6317.42   The "I" and the "not-I"; a study in the development of consciousness. (Harding, Mary Esther.) N.Y., 1965.
Phil 3120.30.44   I and thou. (Buber, Martin.) Edinburg, 1958.
Phil 3120.30.44.3   I and thou. (Buber, Martin.) N.Y., 1970.
Phil 3120.30.44.5   I and thou. 2. ed. (Buber, Martin.) N.Y., 1958.
Phil 186.95.5   I believe. (Fadiman, Clifton.) London, 1940.
Phil 186.95   I believe. (Fadiman, Clifton.) N.Y., 1939.
Phil 5850.157.5   I believe in life. (Cheatham, T.A.) Pinehurst, N.C., 1941.
Phil 9070.29   I dare you! Four fold development. 8. ed. (Danforth, William Henry.) St. Louis, Mo., 1938.
Phil 530.35.10   I det Høje. (Jørgensenn, J.) Kristiania, 1908.
Phil 8610.916   I don't know, do you? (Ricker, M.M.) East Aurora, N.Y., 1916.
Phil 7069.18.120   "I heard a voice." N.Y., 1918.
Phil 3425.200.5   I hvad afseende är Hegel Pantheist? (Borelius, J.J.) Upsala, 1851.
Phil 6968.24   I knew 3000 lunatics. (Small, Victor R.) N.Y., 1935.
Phil 9495.162.1   I loved a girl (including I loved a young man); young Africans speak. (Trobisch, Walter.) N.Y., 1965.
Phil 4655.1.72   I mensklighetens lifsfrågor. (Wikner, Pontus.) Stockholm, 1889. 2v.
Phil 5627.134.20   I was a pagan. (Kitchen, V.C.) N.Y., 1934.
Phil 6420.28   I was a stutterer; stories from life. (Greene, James S.) N.Y., 1932.
Phil 5627.108.25   I will lift up mine eyes. 9. ed. (Clark, Glenn.) N.Y., 1937.
Phil 575.142.10   Ia i mir ob"ektov. (Berdiaev, N.A.) Paris, 193-?
Phil 165.388   Iadir, C.A. The world of philosophy. Lahore, 1965.
Phil 183.6   Iadov, V.A. Ideologiia kak forma dukhovnoi deiatel'nosti obshchestva. London, 1961.
Phil 4135.1   Iaja, Donato. Saggi filosofici. Napoli, 1886.
Phil 310.677   Iakhot, Ovshii O. Ocherk marksistskoi filosofii. Moskva, 1968.
Phil 3425.287   Iakovenko, B.-V. Ein Beitrag zur Geschichte des Hegelianismus in Russland. Prag, 1934.
Phil 3425.287.5   Iakovenko, B.-V. Ein Beitrag zur Geschichte des Hegelianismus in Russland. Prag, 1934.
Phil 4805.10   Iakovenko, Boris V. La philosophie tchécoslovaque contemporaine. Prague, 1935.
Phil 8430.72   Iakovlev, Eugenii G. Esteticheskoe soznanie iskusstvo i religiia. Moskva, 1969.
Phil 5585.345   Iakttagelse och upplevelse. (Sandstroem, Carl Ivar.) Stockholm, 1969.
Phil 8980.459   Iakuba, Elena A. Pravoi nravstvennost'kak reguliatory obshchestvennykh otnoshenii pri sotsializme. Khav'kov, 1970.
Phil 339.5   Iakushevskii, I.T. Praktika i ee rol' v protsese poznaniia. Moskva, 1961.
Htn   Phil 4939.1.30*   Iamblichus. Iamblichus de mysteriis. Lugduni, 1570.
Htn   Phil 4939.1.30*   Iamblichus de mysteriis. (Iamblichus.) Lugduni, 1570.
Phil 4260.215   Iannizzotto, Matteo. L'empirismo nella gnoseologia di Giambattista Vico. Padova, 1968.

Phil 5218.5   Iaroshevskii, Mikhail G. Istoriia psikhologii. Moskva, 1966.
Phil 4769.6.84   Iaroshevskii, Mikhail G. Ivan Mikhailovich Sechenov 1825-1905. Leningrad, 1968.
Phil 5218.5.5   Iaroshevskii, Mikhail G. Psikhologiia v XX stoletii. Moskva, 1971.
Phil 8409.3   Iastrebova, Nataliia. Konflikti v estetichnogo. Sofiia, 1964.
VPhil 8430.58   Iastrebova, Netaliia A. Esteticheski paraleli. Sofiia, 1968.
Phil 1135.175   Iatrophilosophers of the Hellenic states. (Precope, J.) London, 1961.
Phil 4769.4.15   Iavlenie i smysl. (Shpet, Gustav.) Moskva, 1914.
Phil 5520.707   Iazyk, rech', rechevaia deiatel'nost'. (Leon'tev, Aleksei A.) Moskva, 1969.
Phil 5520.482   Iazyk i myshlenie. Moskva, 1967.
Phil 5520.708   Iazyk i poznanie mira. (Ismailov, B.) Tashkent, 1969.
Phil 4961.126.5   Ibarguengoitía, Antonio. Filosofía mexicana. 1. ed. Mexico, 1967.
Phil 8588.1   Ibarreta, R.H. La religion al alcance de todos. 5. ed. Madrid, 1884.
Phil 8588.1.5   Ibarreta, R.H. La religion al alcance de todos. 35. ed. Barcelona, 1912.
Phil 4957.60   The Ibero-American enlightenment. Urbana, 1971.
Phil 1020.8.12   Ibn Sina. Metaphysices compendium...Latinum...N. Carame. Roma, 1926.
Phil 1020.8.9   Ibn Sina. Die metaphysik Ayicennas. Halle, 1907-09.
Phil 1020.8.5   Pamphlet box. Ibn Sina.
Phil 4585.1.31   Ibsen, Sigurd. Menneskelig kvintessens. Kristiania, 1911.
Phil 3585.28.5   Ich, du, wir. 1. Aufl. (Lotz, Johannes Baptist.) Frankfurt, 1968.
Phil 175.10   Das Ich. (Asmus, P.) Halle, 1873.
Phil 6316.32   Das Ich. (Coeppert, Hans.) München, 1968.
Phil 181.5   Das Ich. (Gerber, G.) Berlin, 1893.
Phil 178.18   Das Ich als Grundproblem der Metaphysik. (Drews, Arthur.) Freiburg, 1897.
Phil 9240.36   Die Ich-du-Beziehung als Erfahrungsgrundlage der Ethik. (Brod, Viktor.) München, 1967.
Phil 8586.36   Ich Glaube an den dreieinigen Gott. (Gogarten, Friedrich.) Jena, 1926.
Phil 6315.18.5   Ich-psychologie und die Psychosen. (Federn, Paul.) Bern, 1956.
Phil 6315.2.37.5   Das Ich und das Es. (Freud, Sigmund.) Leipzig, 1923.
Phil 5258.85   Das ich und die Dämonen. (Schleich, Carl Ludwig.) Berlin, 1924.
Phil 8880.29   Das Ich und die sittlichen Ideen im Leben. 5e Aufl. (Flügel, Otto.) Langensalza, 1912.
Phil 8880.29.5   Das Ich und die sittlichen Ideen im Leben der Völker. (Flügel, Otto.) Langensalza, 1885.
Phil 4752.2.65   Das Ich und die Welt der Objekte. (Berdiaev, Nikolai Aleksandrovich.) Darmstadt, 195-?
Phil 3120.30.42   Ich und Du. (Buber, Martin.) Heidelberg, 1958.
Phil 3120.30.43.5   Ich und Du. (Buber, Martin.) Köln, 1966.
Phil 3120.30.43   Ich und Du. (Buber, Martin.) Leipzig, 1923.
Phil 6128.65   Das ich und seine Welt. (Schottlaender, Felix.) Stuttgart, 1959.
Phil 8418.20.5   Icon and idea. (Read, Herbert.) Harvard, 1955.
Phil 4073.113   L'iconografia di Tommaso Campanella. (Firpo, Luigi.) Firenze, 1964.
Htn   Phil 6100.13*   Iconographie photographique des centres nerveux. Texte et atlas. (Luys, J.) Paris, 1873. 2v.
Phil 6128.80   The id and the regulatory principles of mental functioning. (Schur, Max.) London, 1967.
Phil 5258.44.5   Idati della esperienza psichica. (Sarlo, Francesco de.) Firenze, 1903.
Phil 8597.40   Iddio, l'uomo e la religione. (Rogeri, G.) Revere, 1887.
Phil 1135.185   Idea, numero e anima. (Pesce, Domenico.) Padova, 1961.
Phil 8050.79   Idea. 2. Aufl. (Panofsky, E.) Berlin, 1960.
Phil 2045.94   Idea and essence in the philosophies of Hobbes and Spinoza. (Balz, Albert G.A.) N.Y., 1918.
Phil 8670.10   A idéa de Deus. (Pereira de Sampaio, José.) Porto, 1902.
Phil 3195.6.114   La idea de estructura psiquica in Dilthey. (Mayz Vallenilla, Ernesto.) Caracas, 1949.
Phil 4363.7.5   Idea de la metafísica. (Marias Aguilera, Julián.) Buenos Aires, 1954.
Phil 6046.55   L'idea del futuro rappresentato dalle linee della mano. (Azzi, G.) Lucca, 1655.
Phil 3500.95   L'idea della libertà. (Sciacca, Guiseppe M.) Palermo, 1963.
Phil 8406.4   L'idea di artisticita. (Formaggio, Dino.) Milano, 1962.
Phil 194.19.30   L'idea di esistenza e la pensabilità del reale trascendente. (Tarozzi, Giuseppe.) Bologna, 1927.
Phil 1135.34   L'idea di giustizia nel pensiero greco. (Caiazzo, D.) Roma, 1958.
Phil 3425.213   L'idea di Hegel. (Maturi, S.) Napoli, 1894.
Phil 176.128   Idea di una filosofia della vita. (Bertini, G.M.) Firenze, 1933.
Phil 8894.23.15   Idea di una scienza del bene. (Tarrozzi, G.) Firenze, 1901.
Phil 400.68   L'idea e il mondo. (Pavese, R.) Torino, 1925.
Phil 1718.23   Idea man of today. (Smith, V.E.) Milwaukee, 1950.
Phil 3480.33.10   The idea of a universal history on a cosmopolitical plan. (Kant, Immanuel.) Hanover, N.H., 1927.
Phil 1880.50   The idea of cause. (Bowen, F.) N.Y., 1879.
Phil 1880.50.2   The idea of cause. (Bowen, F.) N.Y., 1879.
Phil 315.12   The idea of conflict. (Singer, Kent.) Melbourne, 1949.
Phil 583.4   The idea of dialogal phenomenology. (Strasser, Stephan.) Pittsburgh, 1969.
Phil 440.2   The idea of freedom. (Adler, Mortimer J.) Garden City, N.Y., 1958-61. 2v.
Phil 8656.10   The idea of God...in the light of language. (Baynes, H.) London, 1895.
Phil 8660.2.7   The idea of God. (Fiske, J.) Boston, 1891.
Phil 8595.17   The idea of God. (Seth Prugle Pattison, A.) Aberdeen, 1917.
Phil 8601.16   Idea of God. (Varadachari, K.) Tirupati, 1950.
Phil 8673.6.2   The idea of God. 2. ed. (Pattison, A.) N.Y., 1920.
Phil 8656.31   The idea of God in British and American personal idealism. Thesis. (Baskfield, G.T.) Washington, 1933.
Phil 8672.9   The idea of God in relation to theology. (Read, E.A.) Chicago, 1900.
Phil 9245.120   The idea of happiness. (McGill, Vivian Jerauld.) N.Y., 1967.
Phil 8633.1.30   The idea of immortality. (Falconer, Robert A.) Cambridge, 1930.
Phil 8643.22   The idea of immortality. (Seth Pringle-Pattison, A.) Oxford, 1922.

Phil 8890.60 The idea of justice and the problem of argument. (Perelman, Chaim.) London, 1963.
Phil 5421.25.15 The idea of love. (Hazo, Robert G.) N.Y., 1967.
Phil 283.14.5 The idea of nature. (Collingwood, Robin George.) Oxford, 1964.
Phil 805.9 The idea of perfection in the western world. (Foss, Martin.) Princeton, 1946.
Phil 575.26 The idea of personality. Diss. (Moroney, Timothy.) Washington, 1919.
Phil 3450.11.50 The idea of phenomenology. (Husserl, Edmund.) The Hague, 1964.
Phil 1109.5 The idea of progress in classical antiquity. (Edelstein, Ludwig.) Baltimore, 1967.
Phil 1801.5 The idea of the absolute in modern British philosophy. Thesis. (Barron, J.T.) Washington, D.C., 1929.
Phil 8669.3.5 The idea of the holy. (Otto, Rudolf.) London, 1928.
Phil 665.67 The idea of the soul. (Ellis, W.) London, 1940.
Phil 735.92 The idea of value. (Laird, John.) Cambridge, Eng., 1929.
Htn Phil 3120.3.35* Idea philosophiae. (Burgeridicii, F.) Oxonii, 1667.
Htn Phil 8876.35* Idea philosophiae tum moralis. (Burgersdyck, F.) Oxoniae, 1631.
Phil 8876.35.3 Idea philosophiae tum moralis. 2a ed. (Burgersdyck, F.) Lugduni, 1629.
Phil 5465.95 Idea-tracking. (Armstrong, Frank A.) N.Y., 1960.
Phil 7054.178 Idea vera dello spiritismo. (Azzi, Gaetano.) Torino, 1895.
Phil 8880.19 Ideal and real; the students calendar. (Farr, Lorin G.) Portland, Maine, 1904.
Phil 6945.10 Ideal characters of officers of a hospital for the insane. (Ray, Isaac.) Philadelphia, 1873.
Phil 3525.55 Ideal de la humanidad para la vida. 2. ed. (Krause, K.C.F.) Madrid, 1871.
Phil 5590.23.2 Das Ideal der Persönlichkeit. 2. Aufl. (Sawicki, Franz.) Paderborn, 1922.
Phil 8418.12 L'idéal esthétique. (Roussel-Despierres, F.) Paris, 1904.
Phil 9357.6 L'ideal et la jeunesse. (Reclus, Elisée.) Bruxelles, 1894.
Phil 3492.20 Das Ideal im System der Kantischen Philosophie. (Kellermann, B.) Berlin, 1920.
Phil 2885.34.14 The ideal in art. (Taine, Hippolyte Adolphe.) N.Y., 1874.
Phil 8887.23 The ideal life. (Mosby, E.F.) Cincinnatti, Ohio, 1877.
Phil 8881.42.3 L'ideal moderne. (Gaultier, Paul.) Paris, 1911.
Phil 8886.24.9 L'idéal moral du matérialisme et la guerre. (Lanessan, J.I. de.) Paris, 1918.
Phil 8583.17 The ideal of Christian worship. (Delany, Selden P.) Milwaukee, 1909.
Phil 8695.5 O ideal religioso e a cultura scientifica. (Ferreira da Silva, A.J.) Porto, 1908.
Phil 6132.17.9 Ideal suggestion through mental photography. 9. ed. (Wood, Henry.) Boston, 1899.
Phil 4688.110.30 Idealas ir laikas. (Girnius, Juozas.) Chicago, 1966.
Phil 177.105.30 Ideale del dialogo o ideale della scienza? (Spirito, Ugo.) Roma, 1966.
Phil 187.114 Die Ideale der Humanität. (Masaryk, T.G.) Wien, 1902.
Phil 4260.41 L'ideale educativo. (Vico, G.B.) Napoli, 1954.
Phil 186.4 Ideale Fragen. (Lazarus, M.) Berlin, 1878.
Phil 193.118 Ideale Lebensziele. (Svoboda, A.V.) Leipzig, 1901. 2v.
Phil 400.14 Die Ideale und die Seele. (Kretschmer, E.) Leipzig, 1900.
Phil 8877.52 Ideale und Güter; Untersuchungen zur Ethik. (Class, Gustav.) Erlangen, 1886.
Phil 1106.9 Ideale und materielle Lebensauschauung. (Blass, F.) Kiel, 1889.
Phil 6961.22 Idealer og realiteter i et psykiatrisk sykehus. (Loechen, Yngvar.) Oslo, 1970.
Phil 8080.10 The ideales and tendencies of modern art. (Farnsworth, E.C.) Portland, 1917.
Phil 2070.65.4 Gli ideali della vita. 4a ed. (James, William.) Torino, 1916.
Phil 2070.65.5 Gli ideali della vita. 5a ed. (James, William.) Torino, 1921.
Phil 176.89 Idealism, possible and impossible. (Blundell, A.) London, 1911.
Phil 400.88 Idealism. (Ewing, Alfred C.) London, 1934.
Phil 400.2 Idealism. (Graham, W.) London, 1872.
Phil 400.44 Idealism. (Walker, W.) London, 1919.
Phil 400.88.3 Idealism. 3. ed. (Ewing, Alfred C.) London, 1961.
Phil 400.38 Idealism and the modern age. (Adams, George P.) New Haven, 1919.
Phil 8658.6 Idealism and theology. (D'Arcy, C.F.) London, 1899.
Phil 400.26 Idealism and theory of knowledge. (Caird, E.) London, 1903.
Phil 400.52 Idealism as a philosophical doctrine. (Hoernlé, R.F.A.) London, 1924.
Phil 400.52.5 Idealism as a philosophy. (Hoernlé, R.F.A.) N.Y., 1927.
Phil 400.25.2 Idealism as a practical creed. 2nd ed. (Jones, H.) Glasgow, 1910.
Phil 4655.3.33 Idealism och materialism. (Waerland, Are.) Uppsala, 1924.
Phil 4120.4.85 The idealism of Giovanni Gentile. (Holmes, Roger W.) N.Y., 1937.
Phil 176.85.13 L'idéalisme contemporain. (Brunschvicg, L.) Paris, 1905.
Phil 176.85.15 L'idéalisme contemporain. 2e éd. (Brunschvicg, L.) Paris, 1921.
Phil 2725.11.100 L'idéalisme de Lachelier. (Manchaussat, Gaston.) Paris, 1961.
Phil 2840.99.10 L'idéalisme de Renouvier. (Verneaux, Roger.) Paris, 1945.
Phil 2840.99.5 L'idéalisme de Renouvier. Thèse. (Verneaux, Roger.) Paris, 1943.
Phil 400.5 L'idéalisme en Angleterre. (Lyon, G.) Paris, 1888.
Phil 1815.8 L'idéalisme en Angleterre. (Pucelle, Jean.) Neuchâtel, 1955.
Phil 400.62 Idéalisme et réalisme. (Faye, Eugène de.) Paris, 1920.
Phil 400.89 L'idéalisme français contemporain. (Etcheverry, A.) Paris, 1934.
Phil 3493.20 L'idéalisme Kantien. Thèse. (Lachièze-Rey, P.) Paris, 1931.
Phil 3493.20.5 L'idéalisme Kantien. Thèse. 2. éd. (Lachièze-Rey, P.) Paris, 1950.
Phil 1870.90 Het idealisme van Berkeley. (Malan, D.F.) Utrecht, 1905.
Phil 400.70 L'idealismo. (Mignosi, Pietro.) Milano, 1927.
Phil 4120.4.82 L'idealismo attuale di Giovanni Gentile. (La Via, G.) Trani, 1925.
Phil 400.83 Idealismo cristiano. (Stefunini, L.) Padova, 1931?
Phil 4120.4.80 L'idealismo dell'atto e il problema delle categorie. (Volpe, Galvano della.) Bologna, 1924.
Phil 1870.107 L'idealismo di G. Berkeley. (Olgiati, F.) Milano, 1926.
Phil 2655.3.90 L'idealismo di O. Hamelin. (Carbonara, C.) Napoli, 1927?
Phil 400.104 Idealismo e filosofia. (La Via, Vincenzo.) Messina, 1942.

Phil 4215.9.80 L'idealismo e i suoi limiti nel pensiero di Antonio Renda. (Caracciolo, C.) Palermo, 1960.
Phil 400.53 L'idealismo e la filosofia. (Ranzoli, C.) n.p., n.d.
Phil 4060.1.40 L'idealismo e la scienza. (Ardigo, Roberto.) Roma, 1919.
Phil 400.100 Idealismo ed esistenzialismo. (Bartolomeis, F. de.) Napoli, 1944.
Phil 2630.6.80 Un idealismo estético; la filosofia de Jules de Gaultier. (Barrenechea, M.A.) Buenos Aires, 1921.
Phil 3246.91.9 L'idealismo etico di Fichte. (Perego, Luigi.) Modena, 1911.
Phil 3450.11.475 L'idealismo fenomenologico di Edmund Husserl. (Baratta, Giorgio.) Urbino, 1969.
Phil 400.92 Idealismo fenomenológico y metafísica existencial. (Astrada, Carlos.) Buenos Aires, 1936.
Phil 400.56 Idealismo filosofico e realismo politico. (Lugaro, E.) Bologna, 1920.
Phil 8592.44 L'idealismo indeterminista. (Masci, Filippo.) Napoli, 1898.
Phil 4080.17 L'idealismo italiano. (Carabellese, P.) Napoli, 1938.
Phil 400.77 L'idealismo italiano e i suoi critici. (Spirito, Ugo.) Firenze, 1930.
Phil 400.20.5 L'idealismo moderno. (Villa, Guido.) Torino, 1905. 2v.
Phil 3246.198 L'idealismo soggetivo di I.G. Fichte. (Cesca, G.) Padova, 1895.
Phil 18.14 Idealismus. Zürich. 1,1934
Phil 400.18 Idealismus. 3e Aufl. (Muff, Christian.) Halle, 1902.
Phil 400.18.5 Idealismus. 5e Aufl. (Muff, Christian.) Halle, 1911.
Phil 400.96 Idealismus und Existentialphilosophie. (Gehlen, A.) Leipzig, 1933.
Phil 400.59 Idealismus und Kultur. (Sternberg, K.) Berlin, 1923.
Phil 400.27.15 Idealismus und Realismus. (Kinkel, Walter.) Göttingen, 1911.
Phil 1818.6 Idealismus undRealismus in der englischen Philosophie der Gegenwart. (Salomaa, J.E.) Helsinki, 1929.
Phil 400.132 Der Idealismus von Kant bis Hegel. (Stiehler, Gottfried.) Berlin, 1970.
Phil 400.88.5 The idealist tradition. (Ewing, Alfred C.) Glencoe, Illinois, 1957.
Phil 8597.38 An idealist view of life. (Radhakrishnan, S.) N.Y., 1932.
Phil 400.32 Les idealistes passionnés. (Dide, Maurice.) Paris, 1913.
Phil 181.84 Idealisti ed empiristi; saggi. (Guzzo, Augusto.) Firenze, 1935.
Phil 400.86 The idealistic argument in recent British and American philosophy. (Cunningham, G.W.) N.Y., 1933.
Phil 400.5.5 Idealistic beginnings in England. (Turner, J.P.) n.p., 1910.
Phil 8591.35 The idealistic conception of religion. (Lion, Aline.) Oxford, 1932.
Phil 5052.34 Idealistic logic. (Morris, C.R.) London, 1933.
Phil 400.29.5 The idealistic reaction against science. (Aliotta, A.) London, 1914.
Phil 960.168.2A Idealistic thought of India. (Raju, P.T.) Cambridge, Mass., 1953.
Phil 960.168 Idealistic thought of India. (Raju, P.T.) London, 1953.
Phil 497.8 Das idealistische Argument in der Kritik des Materialismus. (Wartenberg, Mzcislaw.) Leipzig, 1904.
Phil 3890.16 Idealistische Briefe Marburg. (Tiedemann, Dieterich.) Bruxelles, 1969.
Phil 3425.613 Die idealistische Dialektik der Praxis bei Hegel. (Sobotka, Milan.) Praha, 1965.
Phil 8880.31 Idealistische Sittenlehre. (Franze, Paul.) Leipzig, 1909.
Phil 310.732 Idealistische und materialistische Dialektik; das Verhältnis von Herrschaft und Knechtschaft bei Hegel und Marx. (Becker, Werner.) Stuttgart, 1970.
Phil 400.4 Idealistische und Positivistische. (Laas, E.) Berlin, 1879-1884. 3v.
Phil 2415.4 Les idealogues. (Picavet, F.) Paris, 1891.
Phil 8893.101 Ideals and illusions. (Stebbing, L.S.) London, 1941.
Phil 8843.9 Ideals of conduct. (Stoops, J.D.) N.Y., 1926.
Phil 8843.13 The ideals of East and West. (Saunders, K.J.) Cambridge, Eng., 1934.
Phil 8843.13.2 The ideals of East and West. (Saunders, K.J.) N.Y., 1934.
Phil 187.114.5 The ideals of humanity and How to work. (Masaryk, T.G.) London, 1938.
Phil 8879.25 Ideals of life. (Everett, M.S.) N.Y., 1954.
Phil 8897.31 Ideals of life - symposium on the coming man. (Wood, W.) N.Y., 1892.
Phil 8697.10 Ideals of science and faith. (Hand, J.E.) N.Y., 1904.
Phil 187.114.10 Ideály humanitní. (Masaryk, T.G.) Praha, 1901.
Phil 4963.4 Idearío filosófico, 1953-1961. (Basave Fernandez del Valle, A.) Monterrey, 1961.
Phil 4352.1.155 Idearío político de Balmes. (Corts Grau, José.) Madrid, 1934.
Phil 182.67.4 Ideas: general introduction to pure phenomenology. (Husserl, Edmund.) London, 1931.
Phil 182.67.4.2 Ideas: general introduction to pure phenomenology. (Husserl, Edmund.) London, 1952.
Phil 5360.36 Ideas and concepts. (Weinberg, Julius Rudolph.) Milwaukee, 1970.
Phil 4352.1.82 Las ideas de Balmes. (Roure, Narciso.) Madrid, 1910.
Phil 8412.10.80 Las ideas estéticas de Lipps. (Remos, y Rubio, J.J.) Habana, 1925.
Phil 8694.2 Ideas from nature. (Elder, William.) Philadelphia, 1898.
Phil 3450.19.210 Las ideas gnoseologicas de Heidegger. (Sacristán Luzón, Manuel.) Barcelona, 1959.
Phil 5627.134.75 Ideas have legs. (Howard, Peter.) London, 1945.
Phil 5627.134.76 Ideas have legs. (Howard, Peter.) N.Y., 1946.
Phil 165.110 Ideas in context. (Satin, J.H.) Boston, 1958.
Phil 8709.2.50 Ideas in nature overlooked by Dr. Tyndall. (McCosh, James.) N.Y., 1875.
Phil 4961.918 Ideas sociales del positivismo en Venezuela. (Nuño, Alicia de.) Caracas, 1969.
Phil 4365.2.42 Ideas y creencias. (Ortega y Gasset, José.) Buenos Aires, 1940.
Phil 4368.2.40 Ideas y figuras. 2. ed. (Romero, Francisco.) Buenos Aires, 1958.
Phil 5261.4 Ideas y observaciones. (Vaz Ferreira, C.) Montevideo, 1905.
Phil 332.11 Die Idee. (Bauch, Bruno.) Leipzig, 1926.
Phil 4803.241.30 Idee. (Brzozowski, Stanisław L.) Lwów, 1910.
Phil 176.115.9 Idee - studies. 3e druk. (Bierens de Haan, J.D.) Amsterdam, 1920.
Phil 8876.51.5 L'idée de bien. (Bayet, Albert.) Paris, 1908.
Phil 1540.16 L'idée de chrétienté chez les scolastiques du XIIIe siècle. (Landry, Bernard.) Paris, 1929.
Phil 2725.44 L'idée de commencement. (Levert, Paule.) Paris, 1961.
Phil 8657.1 L'idée de Dieu. (Caro, E.M.) Paris, 1868.

Phil 2070.134.5   L'idée de Dieu chez William James. Thèse. (Cornesse, Marie.) Grenoble, 1933.

Phil 8656.13.3   L'idée de Dieu et l'esprit humain. 4. éd. (Balfour, A.J.B.) Paris, 1916.

Phil 8657.1.2   L'idée de Dieu et ses nouveaux critiques. (Caro, E.M.) Paris, 1864.

Phil 3823.18   L'idée d'expression dans la philosophie de Spinoza. Thèse. (Deleuze, Gilles.) Paris, 1968.

Phil 8735.17   L'idée de finalité. (Lesparre, A. de G.) Paris, 1916.

Phil 1135.155   L'idée de justice dans la conception de l'univers les premiers philosophes grecs. (Guérin, Pièrre.) Paris, 1934.

Phil 1135.155.5   L'idée de justice dans la conception de l'univers les premiers philosophes grecs. Thèse. (Guérin, Pièrre.) Strasbourg, 1934.

Phil 5761.19   L'idée de la liberté morale. (Leuridan, Charles.) Paris, 1936.

Phil 4363.7.6   Idée de la métaphysique. (Marias Aguilera, Julián.) Toulouse, 1969.

Phil 8612.25   L'idée de la mort et de l'eternité. (Marminia, A.) Paris, 1865.

Phil 2750.13.100   L'idée de la participation chez Gabriel Marcel. (Lê Thanh Tri.) Fribourg? 1959.

Phil 575.25   L'idée de la personnalité. Thèse. (Jeanmaire, Charles.) Toulouse, 1882.

Phil 3450.11.195   L'idée de la phénoménologie. (Muralt, André de.) Paris, 1958.

Phil 6327.14   L'idée de l'homme dans la neurologie contemporaine. (Reese, W.) Paris, 1938.

Phil 289.2   Idée de monde et philosophie de la nature. Paris, 1966.

Phil 2404.3   L'idée de nature en France. (Ehrard, J.) Paris, 1963. 2v.

Phil 270.50   L'idée de necessité. (Laporte, Jean.) Paris, 1941.

Phil 810.12   L'idée de preuve en imétaphysique. (Kasm, Badi.) Paris, 1959.

Phil 2840.90   L'idée de progrès dans la philosophie de Renouvier. (Mouy, P.) Paris, 1927.

Phil 2840.90.2   L'idée de progrès dans la philosophie de Renouvier. Thèse. (Mouy, P.) Paris, 1927.

Phil 600.19   L'idée de relation. (Rodrigues, Gustave.) Paris, 1904.

Phil 9470.2   L'idée de responsabilité. (Lévy-Bruhl, L.) Paris, 1884.

Phil 2733.104.10   L'idée de science dans Malebranche et son originalité. (Labbas, Lucien.) Paris, 1931.

Phil 2070.60   L'idée de vérité. (James, William.) Paris, 1913.

Phil 2475.1.495   L'idée de vie chez Bergson et la critique de la métaphysique. (Trotignon, Pierre.) Paris, 1968.

Phil 3845.3.5   L'idée de vie dans la philosophie de Spinoza. (Zac, Sylvain.) Paris, 1963.

Phil 184.11   Die Idee der Entwicklung. (Jacoby, L.) Berlin, 1874. 2v.

Phil 184.11.2   Die Idee der Entwicklung. (Jacoby, L.) Zürich, 1886.

Phil 3483.83   Die Idee der Freiheit in der Philosophie Kants. (Boeversen, F.) Heidelberg, 1962.

Phil 8660.9   Die Idee der Gottheit. (Fischer, K.P.) Stuttgart, 1839.

Phil 1135.70   Die Idee der Menschheit. (Müller, E.) Leipzig, 1877.

Phil 3245.50.2   Die Idee der Persönlichkeit. (Fichte, Immanuel Hermann.) Elberfeld, 1834.

Phil 3245.50   Die Idee der Persönlichkeit. (Fichte, Immanuel Hermann.) Leipzig, 1855.

Phil 575.11   Idee der Persönlichkeit bei den englischen Denken. (Jones, W.T.) Jena, 1906.

Phil 575.3   Die Idee der Person. (Oginski, T.) Breslau, 1853.

Phil 5627.95.10   Die Idee der Sünde. (Mensching, Gustav.) Leipzig, 1931.

Phil 3801.563   Die Idee der Transzendentalphilosophie. (Meier, F.) Winterthur, 1961.

Phil 8632.25   Die Idee der Unsterblichkeit. (Huber, Johannes.) München, 1864.

Phil 2750.20.85   De idee der zelfvervramding. (Roosfen, S.) Delft, 1963.

Phil 5421.20.85   Die Idee des Friedens und die menschliche Aggressivität. (Mitscherlich, Alexander.) Frankfurt, 1969.

Phil 365.7   L'idée d'evolution. (Richard, G.) Paris, 1903.

Phil 1955.6.220   L'idée d'expérience dans la philosophie de John Dewey. Thèse. (Debdalle, Gerald.) Paris, 1966.

Phil 4265.1.85   Idee di G.C. Vanini sull...evoluzione. (Cattaneo, G.) Milano, 1885.

Phil 2412.10.2   L'idée du bonheur dans la littérature et la pensée françaises. 2e éd. (Mauzi, Robert.) Paris, 1965.

Phil 176.68   L'idée du Phénomène. Thèse. (Boirac, Émile.) Paris, 1894.

Phil 4190.1.35   Idee econcetti. (Orestano, Francesco.) Milano, 1939.

Phil 6111.42   Idee einer neuen Hirnanatomie (1811). (Bell, Charles.) Leipzig, 1911.

Phil 176.53.15   Idee einer Spoditktik. (Bouterwek, F.) Halle, 1799. 2v.

Phil 630.40   L'idée et le réel. (Chevalier, Jacques.) Grenoble, 1932.

Phil 3640.85.5   Le idee fondamentali de F. Nietzsche. (Orestano, Francesco.) Palermo, 1903.

Phil 5251.11   Idée générales de psychologie. (Liguet, G.H.) Paris, 1906.

Phil 3425.435   Die Idee Gottes im Geiste der Philosophie Hegels. (Dulckeit, Gerhard.) München, 1947.

Phil 3497.6   L'idée ou Critique du Kantisme. (Piat, C.) Paris, n.d.

Phil 1140.8   Le idee psicologiche in Grecia nel periodo presofistico e l'esposizione critica di Aristotele. (Firniani, S.) Napoli, 1904.

Phil 5262.68   Idee und Denken. (Wulf, Berthold.) Stuttgart, 1964.

Phil 182.61.10   Idee und Existenz. (Herpe, Hans.) Hamburg, 1935.

Phil 801.30   Die Idee und Geschichte der Philosophie. (Bayrhoffer, K.T.) Marburg, 1838.

Phil 5046.30   Idee und Grundriss einer nicht-aristotelischen Logik. (Guenther, Gotthard.) Hamburg, 1959.

Phil 402.14   Idee und Ideologie. (Hoelzle, Erwin.) Bern, 1969.

Phil 2750.284.5   Idee und Perception. (Twardowski, K.) Wien, 1892.

Phil 3480.33   Idee zu einer allgemeinen Geschichte in weltbürgerlicher Absicht. (Kant, Immanuel.) Wiesbaden, 1914.

Phil 3120.21.10   Ideeën en idolen. (Beerling, Reinier Franciscus.) Arnhem, 1968.

Phil 3805.25   Ideen, Reflexionen und Betrachtungen aus Schleiermachers Werken. (Schleiermacher, Friedrich.) Berlin, 1854.

Phil 3200.12   Ideen. (Einsiedel, August von.) Berlin, 1957.

Phil 18.6   Ideen and Leben. Paderborn. 1-13 13v.

Phil 3426.36   Ideen über Gott und Unsterblichkeit. (Fichte, Johann Gottlieb.) Leipzig, 1914.

Phil 2150.22.40.2   Ideen zu einer kritischen Theorie der Gesellschaft. 2e Aufl. (Marcuse, Herbert.) Frankfurt, 1969.

Phil 3800.140.2   Ideen zu einer Philosophie der Natur. v.1-2. (Schelling, F.W.J. von.) Leipzig, 1797.

Htn Phil 3800.140*   Ideen zu einer Philosophie der Natur. v.1-2. (Schelling, F.W.J. von.) Leipzig, 1797.

Htn Phil 3800.140.5*A   Ideen zu einer Philosophie der Natur. 2e Aufl. (Schelling, F.W.J. von.) Landshut, 1803.

Phil 182.67   Ideen zu einer reinen Phänomenologie und phänomenologischen Philosophie. (Husserl, Edmund.) Halle, 1913.

Phil 177.36   Ideen zur Geschichte der Philosophie. (Carus, F.A.) Leipzig, 1809.

Phil 8402.10   Ideen zur Metaphysik des Schönen. (Bouterwek, F.) Leipzig, 1807.

Phil 8897.38   Ideen zur praktischen Philosophie. (Wallaschek, R.) Tübingen, 1886.

Phil 340.6   Die Ideenlehre. (Jordon, Bruno.) Leipzig, 1928.

Phil 4600.2.32   Ideer och makter. 2. uppl. (Larsson, Hans.) Lund, 1909.

Phil 177.68.10   Idées; Platon, Descartes, Hegel. (Chartier, Émile.) Paris, 1932.

Phil 3640.216   Les idées de Nietzsche sur la musique. (Lasserre, Pierre.) Paris, 1919?

Phil 8965.8   Idées directrices de la morale chrétienne. (Piat, Clodius.) Paris, 1917.

Phil 187.99.5   Idées et archetypes de Platon à Elie Cartan. (Muller, Maurice.) Neuchâtel, 1959.

Phil 4800.4   Les idées françaises dans la philosophie nationale et la poésie patriotique de la Bologne. (Kozłowski, Władysław M.) Grenoble, 1923.

Phil 8599.44.2   Les idées maîtresses de la métaphysique chrétienne. (Tresmontant, Claude.) Paris, 1962.

Phil 8842.1   Les idées morales du temps present. (Rod, É.) Paris, 1891.

Phil 2490.92   Les idées politiques d'Auguste Comte. (Chiappini, T.) Paris, 1913.

Phil 2885.88   Les idées sociales de Taine. (Gibaudan, R.) Paris, 1928.

Phil 365.56   Ideia razvitiia v burzhuaznoifilas, XIX i XV vekov. (Bogomolov, A.S.) Moskva, 1962.

Phil 8658.27   Ideiia boga. (Duluman, Evgraf K.) Moskva, 1970.

Phil 4883.2   Ideino-politicheskie techeniia v Kazakhstane Kontsa XIX-nachala XX veka. (Beisembiev, Kasym Beisembievich.) Alma-Ata, 1961.

Phil 4683.161.30   Idejas un isteniba; esejas. 2. izd. (Jurevičs, Pauls.) Stockholm, 1965.

Phil 6958.5   Ideler, K.W. Biographieen Geisteskranker. Berlin, 1841.

Phil 5248.1   Ideler, K.W. Grundriss der Seelenheilkunde. Berlin, 1835-38. 2v.

Phil 5627.18A   Ideler, K.W. Versuch einer Theorie des religiösen Wahnsinns. Halle, 1848-50. 2v.

Phil 6332.28   Identification and its familial determinants. (Winch, R.F.) Indianapolis, 1962.

Phil 4525.3.30   Identiska och syntetiska satser. (Cavallin, P.) Lund, 1894.

Phil 4080.13.30   Identità o contraddizione? (Caria, G.M. de.) Palermo, 1924.

Phil 3450.19.77   Identität und Differenz. 2e Aufl. (Heidegger, Martin.) Pfullingen, 1957.

Phil 3850.1.105   Identität und Immanenz; zur Genese der Theologie von David Friedrich Strauss, eine theologie- und philosophiegeschichtliche Studie. (Müller, Gotthold.) Zürich, 1968.

Phil 343.16.15   Identität und Wirklichkeit. (Meyerson, Émile.) Leipzig, 1930.

Phil 3246.205   Die Identitätslehre Fichtes in den Jahren 1801-1806. (Horneffer, Martha.) Leipzig, 1925.

NEDL Phil 343.16   Identité et réalité. (Meyerson, Émile.) Paris, 1908.

Phil 343.16.5   Identité et réalité. 2. éd. (Meyerson, Émile.) Paris, 1912.

Phil 343.16.11   Identité et réalité. 4. éd. (Meyerson, Émile.) Paris, 1932.

Phil 343.16.12   Identité et réalité. 5. éd. (Meyerson, Émile.) Paris, 1951.

Phil 6314.12.5A   Identity; youth and crisis. 1st ed. (Erikson, Eric H.) N.Y., 1868.

Phil 6105.233   Identity. Mental health and value systems. (Soddy, Kenneth.) London, 1961.

Phil 5401.38   Identity and anxiety. (Stein, Maurice R.) Glencoe, 1960.

Phil 5401.38.2   Identity and anxiety. (Stein, Maurice R.) Glencoe, 1962.

Phil 3450.19.77.5   Identity and difference. 1st ed. (Heidegger, Martin.) N.Y., 1969.

Phil 274.6   Identity and individuation. N.Y., 1971.

Phil 343.16.10   Identity and reality. (Meyerson, Émile.) London, 1930.

Phil 343.16.16   Identity and reality. (Meyerson, Émile.) N.Y., 1962.

Phil 274.2   Identity and spatio-temporal continuity. (Wiggins, David.) Oxford, 1967.

Phil 402.20   Ideoligija i politika. (Ratković, Radoslav.) Beograd, 1971.

Phil 4120.1.40   Ideologia. (Gioja, Melchiorre.) Milano, 1822-23. 2v.

Phil 4210.22.5   Ideologia (Nuovo saggio sull'origine delle idee). (Rosmini-Serbati, Antonio.) Torino, 1851-52. 3v.

Phil 310.700   L'ideología marxista. (Lojacono, Giorgio.) Roma, 1968. 3v.

Phil 4210.145   L'ideología rosminiana nei rapporti con la gnoseologia agostiniano-tomistica. (Ceriani, G.) Milano, 1937.

Phil 181.135   Ideologías. (Garcia Calderon, Francisco.) Paris, 1917.

Phil 960.253   Ideologicheskie techeniia sovremennoi Indii. (Komarov, N.) Moskva, 1965.

Phil 310.634   Ideologie, Wissenschatt, Philosophie. (Barion, Jakob.) Bonn, 1966.

Phil 402.2   Ideologies. (Corbett, Patrick.) N.Y., 1966.

Phil 930.76   Ideologiia i kul'tura Drevnego Kitaia. (Rubin, Vitalii A.) Moskva, 1970.

Phil 183.6   Ideologiia kak forma dukhovnoi deiatel'nosti obshchestva. (Iadov, V.A.) London, 1961.

Phil 1750.852   Ideologiia sovremennogo reformizma. Moskva, 1970.

Phil 6328.62   Ideology and insanity. (Szasz, Thomas Stephen.) Garden City, 1970.

Phil 1020.64.2   Ideology of the future. 2nd ed. (Rafi-ud-din, Muhammad.) Karachi, 1956.

Phil 2475.1.375   Ideové kořeny současného umění. (Černý, V.) Praha, 1929.

Phil 8958.1   Ideström, A. Kristendomen och det etiska behovet. Stockholm, 1918.

Phil 6750.7.10   Idiocy. (Seguin, E.) Albany, 1907.

Phil 6750.7   Idiocy and its treatment. (Seguin, E.) N.Y., 1866.

Phil 185.71   The idiom of contemporary thought. (Knox, Crawford.) London, 1958.

Phil 6750.9   L'idiotie. (Voisin, J.) Paris, 1893.

Phil 5590.492   Das Idividuum und seine Welt. (Thomae, Hans.) Göttingen, 1968.

Phil 2280.5.84   The idler and his works. (Santayana, George.) N.Y., 1957.

Phil 400.13.5   Idola theatri; a criticism of Oxford thought and thinkers. (Sturt, H.) London, 1906.

Phil 5251.66   Idolen van de psycholoog. (Linschoten, Johannes.) Utrecht, 1964.

Phil 4710.50.15   Ievdokymenko, V.I. Z istorii filosofs'koi dumky na Ukraini. Kyïv, 1965.

Phil 7060.104.9   If a man die shall he live again? (Wallace, A.R.) San Francisco, 1888.

Phil 9530.46   If you want to get ahead. (Sherman, Ray W.) Boston, 1934.

Phil 5548.83   Iff, Werner. La motivation à l'avancement professionnel. Paris, 1962.

Phil 8878.55   The if's and ought's of ethics. (DeBoer, Cecil.) Grand Rapids, Mich., 1936.

Phil 990.1.3   Igbal, S.M. The development of metaphysics in Persia. Lahore, 19- .

Phil 990.1.2   Igbal, S.M. The development of metaphysics in Persia. London, 1908.

Phil 6111.54   La igiene mentale ed it potenziamento della stirpe. (Bianchini, M.L.) Roma, 1937.

Phil 4809.447.90   Ignác Jan Hanuš. Vyd. 1. (Loužil, Jaromír.) Praha, 1971.

Phil 5590.385   Ignat'ev, E.I. Voprosy psikhologii lichnosti. Moskva, 1960.

Phil 5246.15   L'ignorance et l'irréflexion. (Gerard-Varet, G.) Paris, 1899.

Phil 2915.33   The ignorant philosopher. (Voltaire, F.M.A. de.) Glasgow, 1767.

Phil 2915.35   The ignorant philosopher. (Voltaire, F.M.A. de.) London, 1779.

Phil 2915.31   The ignorant philosopher. (Voltaire, F.M.A. de.) N.Y., 185-?

Phil 3890.9.95   Ignoz Paul Vital Troxler. (Spiess, Emil Jakob.) Bern, 1967.

Phil 7069.68.60   Igrejas reunidas, plano divino. 1. ed. (Daurado, Alzira Guanaes.) Rio de Juneiro, 1968.

Phil 585.150   Ihmisen probleemi. (Ahlman, Erik.) Helsinki, 1953.

Phil 525.65   Ihringer, Bernhard. Der Schuldbegriff bei den Mystikern der Reformationszeit. Bern, 1912.

Phil 4080.3.205   Il materialismo storico e la filosofia di Benedetto Croce. 2. ed. (Gramsci, Antonio.) Torino, 1949.

Phil 3450.19.330   Ijsseling, Samuel. Heidegger. Antwerpen, 1964.

Phil 1870.103   Ikbal Kishen, Shargha. A critical essay on Berkeley's theory of perception. Allababad, n.d.

Phil 8698.10   Ikeda, Daisaku. Science and religion. Tokyo, 1965.

Phil 8660.25   Il est un Dieu. (Frontistès, Mario.) Padova, 1964.

Phil 6958.4   Ilberg, Georg. Geisteskrankheiten. Leipzig, 1907.

Phil 6958.4.2   Ilberg, Georg. Geisteskrankheiten. 2. Aufl. Leipzig, 1918.

Phil 585.266   Il'enkov, Eval'd V. Ob idolakh i idealakh. Moskva, 1968.

Phil 339.10   Iliadi, A.N. Prakticheskaia priroda chelovecheskogo poznaniia. Moskva, 1962.

Phil 2475.1.300   Iliev, Alhanasso. Le Bergsonisme. Sofia, 193-?

Phil 4759.1.40   Il'in, I.A. Aksiomy religioznago opyta. Paris, 1953.

Phil 4759.1.35   Il'in, I.A. O soprotivlenii zlu siloiu. Berlin, 1925.

Phil 4759.1.45   Il'in, I.A. Poiushchee serdtse. Miunkhen, 1958.

Phil 4759.1.50   Il'in, I.A. Put' k ochevidnosti. Miunkhen, 1957.

Phil 4759.1.30   Il'in, I.A. Religioznyi smysl filosofii. Paris,, n.d.

Phil 9070.103   Il'in, Ivan A. Die ewigen Grundlagen des Lebens. Zürich, 1943.

Phil 3425.238   Il'in, Ivan A. Filosofiia Gegelia. Moskva, 1918.

Phil 3425.315   Il'in, Ivan A. Die Philosophie Hegels als kontemplative Gotteslehre. Bern, 1946.

Phil 9070.103.5   Il'in, Ivan A. Put' dukhovnago obnovleniia. Miunkhen, 1962.

Phil 850.40   Ilk cağ felsefesi torihi. (Birand, Kámiran.) Ankara, 1958.

Phil 8663.6   Illanes, José L. Hablar de Dios. Madrid, 1970.

Phil 3450.11.105   Illemann, U. Die Vor- phänomenologische philosophie Edmund Husserls. Inaug. Diss. n.p., 1932.

Phil 8587.37   Illicit naturalizing of religion. (Hocking, W.E.) Chicago, 1923.

Phil 8663.2   Illingworth, J. Divine immanence. London, 1868.

Phil 18.9   Illinois. University. Psychological laboratory. Studies from the psychological laboratory of University of Illinois. Lancaster, Pa. 1,1909

Phil 6313.24   Illness or allness; conversations of a psychiatrist. (Dorsey, John Morris.) Detroit, 1965.

Htn   Phil 3110.169*   The illuminate of Görlitz, or Jakob Böhme's (1575-1624) life and philosophy. (Vetterling, H.) Leipzig, 1923.

Phil 6122.39   Illumination; spiritual healing. (Mills, James P.) N.Y., 1970.

Phil 18.2   Illuminator. Boston. 1,1835

Phil 3484.23.5   L'illuminismo critico. (Casula, Mario.) Milano, 1967.

Phil 1195.9   L'illuminismo della sofistica greca. (Saitta, G.) Milano, 1938.

Phil 8592.112   Illuminismo e cristianesimo. (Magnino, B.) Brescia, 1960. 3v.

Phil 1730.26   L'illuminismo tedesco. (Merker, Nicolao.) Bari, 1968.

Phil 2417.5   Gli illuministi francesi. (Rossi, Pietro.) Torino, 1962.

Phil 5254.9   Illusion and anxiety. (Oraison, Mark.) N.Y., 1963.

Phil 5767.5   Die Illusion der Willensfreiheit. (Rée, Paul.) Berlin, 1885.

Phil 8636.8.5   The illusion of immortality. (Lamont, Corliss.) N.Y., 1935.

Phil 8636.8.7   The illusion of immortality. 2. ed. (Lamont, Corliss.) N.Y., 1950.

Phil 8636.8.10   The illusion of immortality. 3. ed. (Lamont, Corliss.) N.Y., 1959.

Phil 5648.4.5   L'illusion paradoxale et le seuil de Weber. (Foucault, Marcel.) Montpelier, 1910.

Phil 182.104   L'illusion philosophique. (Hersch, J.) Paris, 1936.

Phil 182.104.2   L'illusion philosophique. (Hersch, J.) Paris, 1964.

Phil 5460.1.5   Die Illusionen. (Sully, J.) Leipzig, 1884.

Phil 296.14   Der Illusionismus und die Rettung. (Panizza, O.) Leipzig, 1895.

Phil 5460.1.3   Illusions: a psychological study. (Sully, J.) N.Y., 1884.

Phil 5460.1.2   Illusions: a psychological study. pt.1-2. (Sully, J.) N.Y., 1884.

Phil 365.31.15   Les illusions évolutionnistes. (Lalande, André.) Paris, 1930.

Phil 25.21   The illustrated annual of phrenology, 1882. N.Y., 1875.

Phil 6051.15   Illustrated palmistry. (La Seer, E.J.) N.Y., 1904.

Phil 6673.8   The illustrated practical mesmerist. 6th ed. (Davey, William.) London, 1862?

Phil 5925.3.4   The illustrated self-instructor in phrenology. (Fowler, O.S.) N.Y., n.d.

Phil 5925.3.1   The illustrated self-instructor in phrenology. (Fowler, O.S.) N.Y., 1853.

Phil 5925.3   The illustrated self-instructor in phrenology. (Fowler, O.S.) N.Y., 1855.

Phil 5925.3.3   The illustrated self-instructor in phrenology. (Fowler, O.S.) N.Y., 1859.

Phil 6129.3   Illustration of the mind upon the body. (Tuke, D.H.) London, 1872.

Phil 6129.3.2   Illustration of the mind upon the body. 2d ed. (Tuke, D.H.) Philadelphia, 1884.

Phil 5051.7A   Illustrations of logic. (Lafleur, P.T.) Boston, 1899.

NEDL Phil 9558.13   Illustrations of lying, in all its branches. 2. ed. (Opie, Amelia A. (Mrs.).) Boston, 1826.

Phil 2205.32   Illustrations of Paley's natural theology. (Paxton, J.) Boston, 1827.

Htn   Phil 5922.2*   Illustrations of phrenology. (Calvert, G.H.) Baltimore, 1832.

Phil 600.31.5   Illustrations of positivism. (Bridges, J.H.) Chicago, 1915.

Phil 6100.14   Illustrations of the gross morbid anatomy of the brain in the insane. (Blackburn, I.W.) Washington, 1908.

Phil 9560.3   Illustrations of the law of kindness. (Montgomery, G.w.) Utica, 1841.

Phil 5057.20.7   Illustrations of the methods of reasoning. (Robinson, D.S.) N.Y., 1927.

Phil 5435.1   Illustrations of unconscious memory in disease. (Creighton, C.) London, 1886.

Phil 2270.65   Illustrations of universal progress. (Spencer, Herbert.) N.Y., 1864.

Phil 2053.65   Illustrations on the moral sense. (Hutcheson, F.) Cambridge, 1971.

Phil 4482.1.95   Um iluminista portugues do século XVIII; Luiz Antonio Verney. (Cabral de Moncada, L.) Coimbra, 1941.

Phil 5460.9   La ilusion. (Etchart, Carlos R.) Buenos Aires, 1912.

Phil 4363.14   Ilustración y reforma de la Iglesia. (Mestre, Antonio.) Valencia, 1968.

Phil 3640.228   Im Anfang war der Streit. (Haiser, Franz.) München, 1921.

Phil 3492.28   Im Anfang war die Tat: Versuch einer Orientierung in der Philosophie Kants. (Kutter, Hermann.) Basel, 1924.

Phil 176.33.15   Im Dienste der Wahrheit. (Büchner, L.) Giessen, 1900.

Phil 165.140   Im Dienste der Wahrheit. Bern, 1958.

Phil 3210.84   Im GeisteFechners. (Pastor, Willy.) Leipzig, 1901.

Phil 8602.28.5   Im Kampf um die Weltanschauung. 3. und 4. Aufl. (Wimmer, Richard.) Freiburg, 1888.

Phil 800.4   Im Kampf um unsere Stellung zu Welt und Leben. (Albrich, K.) Leipzig, 1924.

Phil 960.144   Im Kampfe mit der Zauberwelt des Hinduismus. (Väth, Alfons.) Berlin, 1928.

Phil 6317.54   I'm OK, you are OK: a practical guide to transactional analysis. (Harris, Thomas Anthony.) N.Y., 1969.

Phil 3450.30.5   Im neunen eine zeitnahe Philosophie. (Hessen, Johannes.) Nürnberg, 1959.

Phil 3925.11.40   Im Sinnkreis des Ewigen. 1. Aufl. (Wust, Peter.) Graz, 1954.

Phil 410.84   Im Spielfeld von Endlichkeit und Unendlichkeit. (Welte, Bernhard.) Frankfurt, 1967.

Phil 282.19   The image. (Boulding, K.E.) Ann Arbor, 1956.

Phil 6328.10.40   The image and appearance of the human body. (Schilder, Paul.) N.Y., 1950.

Phil 2805.465   L'image dans l'oeuvre de Pascal. (Le Guern, Michel.) Paris, 1969.

Phil 5875.15   L'image d'autrui chez l'enfant. (Lévy-Schoen, Ariane.) Paris, 1964.

Phil 6321.14   L'image de notre corps. (L'hermitte, J.J.) Paris, 1939.

Phil 5374.170   L'image dynamique. (Vincent, M.) Paris, 1955.

Phil 5625.75.80   L'image et les réflexes conditionnels dans les travaux de Pavlov. (Dontchef-Dezeuze, M.) Paris, 1914.

Phil 5465.148   L'image fascinante et le surréel. (Lefebve, Maurice Jean.) Paris, 1965.

Phil 5465.182.5   Image formation and cognition. (Horowitz, Mardi Jon.) N.Y., 1970.

Phil 5465.12   L'image mentale; évolution et dissolution. (Philippe, Jean.) Paris, 1903.

Phil 5465.150   L'image mentale chez l'enfant, étude sur le développement. (Piaget, Jean.) Paris, 1966.

Phil 5421.25.5   The image of love. (Benda, Clemen Ernst.) N.Y., 1961.

Phil 6992.4   L'imagerie mentale; introduction à l'onirothérapie. (Frétigny, Roger.) Genève, 1968.

Phil 2520.176   Images; Descartes et Pascal. (Petit, Henri.) Paris, 1930.

Phil 5465.149   Images, images, essais sur le rôle et les pouvoirs de l'imagination. (Caillois, Roger.) Paris, 1966.

Phil 5545.47   Les images. (Peillaube, E.) Paris, 1910.

Phil 1712.18   Images de l'homme. (Mehl, Roger.) Genève, 1953.

Phil 5465.46   Les images de Taine à Binet. Thèse complementaire. (Reeb, Eugène.) Nancy, 1938.

Phil 3120.30.74   Images of good and evil. (Buber, Martin.) London, 1952.

Phil 5421.35.5   Images of hope. (Lynch, William F.) Baltimore, 1965.

Phil 1712.18.2   Images of man. (Mehl, Roger.) Richmond, 1965.

Phil 5465.35.10   L'imaginaire. (Sartre, Jean P.) Paris, 1940.

Phil 5465.23   Imagination, mind's dominant power. (Leeming, B.C.) N.Y., 1926.

Phil 5465.35.5   L'imagination; psychologie. (Sartre, Jean P.) Paris, 1940.

Phil 5465.218   L'imagination, son importance, sa nature. (Thomas de Saint-Laurent, Raymond de.) Avignon, 1970.

Phil 5465.40   Imagination. (Cadman, S. Parkes.) N.Y., 1930.

Phil 5465.10   L'imagination. (Dugas, L.) Paris, 1903.

Phil 5465.120   Imagination. (Furlong, E.J.) London, 1961.

Phil 5465.35.15   Imagination. (Sartre, Jean P.) Ann Arbor, 1962[1960]

Phil 5465.35   L'imagination. (Sartre, Jean P.) Paris, 1936.

Phil 5465.19   L'imagination. 2. éd. (Joly, Henri.) Paris, 1883.

Phil 5465.42   Imagination and dramatic instinct. (Curry, S.S.) Boston, 1896.

Phil 5465.20   Imagination and fancy. (Strang, W.) London, 1913.

Phil 5465.34   Imagination and human nature. (Welch, Livingston.) London, 1935.

Phil 6980.661   Imagination and reality; psycho-analytical essays, 1951-1961. (Rycroft, Charles.) London, 1968.

Phil 8582.42   Imagination and religion. (Cadman, S.P.) N.Y., 1926.

Phil 5465.80   Imagination and thinking. (McKellar, Peter.) London, 1957.

Phil 2115.180   The imagination as a means of grace. (Tuveson, E.L.) Berkeley, 1960.

Phil 5465.17   L'imagination de l'artiste. (Sourian, Paul.) Paris, 1901.

Phil 2520.101   L'imagination et les Math Selon Descartes. (Boutroux, P.) Paris, 1900.

Phil 5465.44   The imagination in Spinoza and Hume. (Gore, W.C.) Chicago, 1902.

Phil 3900.2   The imagination of reason. (Unger, E.) London, 1952.

Phil 3450.11.495   L'imagination selon Husserl. (Saraiva, Maria Manuela.) La Haye, 1970.

Phil 5465.65   L'imaginazione. (Galimberti, A.) Torino, 1954.

Phil 187.83   L'imaginazione creatrice nella filosofia. (Marchesini, A.) Torino, 1905.

Phil 5465.138 — Imaginer et réaliser. (Schuhl, P.M.) Paris, 1963.
Phil 18.4 — Imago. Leipzig. 1-23 23v.
Phil 6980.319 — Imago Hominis. (Gebsattel, V.E.F. von.) Schweinfurt, 1964.
Phil 6678.1 — Imbert-Gourbeyre, A. L'hypnotisme et la stigmatisation. Paris, 1899.
Phil 5628.50.20 — Imbert-Gourbeyre, Antoine. La stigmatisation, l'extase divine, et les miracles de Lourdes. Clermont-Ferrand, 1894. 2v.
Phil 7069.59.30 — Imbert-Nergal, R. Les sciences occultes ne sont pas des sciences. Paris, 1959.
Phil 2905.1.615 — Imbrighi, Gastone. La paleogeografia in Teilhard de Chardin. L'Aguila, 1967.
Phil 6958.3 — Imianitoff, Mme. Contribution à l'étude du rôle des emotions. Thèse. Paris, 1917.
Phil 5467.01 — Pamphlet box. Imitation.
Phil 176.45.5 — Imitation. (Baldwin, J.M.) n.p., 1894-1904. 8 pam.
Phil 8080.18 — L'imitation et les principes de l'esthétique classique. (Grenier, Jean.) Paris, 1963.
Phil 5467.5 — Imitation in education. (Deahl, J.N.) N.Y., 1900.
Phil 5467.1 — Imitation or mimetic force. (Steel, R.) London, 1900.
Phil 5467.2 — L'imitazione; studio di psicologia. (Pistolesi, G.) Torino, 1910.
Phil 8610.925.30 — The immaculate deception. (Schott, Walter E.) Sausahto, Calif., 1925.
Phil 525.60 — The immaculate perception. (Parke, Jean.) N.Y., 1927.
Phil 8408.28 — L'immaginazione e la vita estetica. (Heller-Heinzelmann, R.) Firenze, 1933.
Phil 2477.6.80 — Immanence: essai critique sur le doctrine de M. Maurice Blondel. 2e éd. (Tonquedec, J. de.) Paris, 1913.
Phil 8658.13 — Immanence and incarnation. (Davenport, S.F.) Cambridge, 1925.
Phil 8661.19 — Immanence et transcendance. (Gregoire, A.) Bruxelles, 1939.
Phil 178.12.55 — The immanent God. (Dresser, H.W.) Boston, 1895.
Phil 705.19 — Immanenza e trascendenza. (Banfi, Antonio.) Alessandria, 1924.
Phil 8666.24.2 — Immanenza e trascendenza. 2. ed. (Librizzi, Carmelo.) Padova, 1966.
Phil 179.10 — Die Immanenzphilosophie. (Ettinger-Reichmann, Regina.) Göttingen, 1916.
Phil 8588.4 — Immanuel, ein Buch für Christum und Juden. Bruxelles, 1968.
Phil 3245.87 — Immanuel Hermann Fichte. (Rakate, Georg.) Leipzig, 1915.
Phil 3497.3.4.5 — Immanuel Kant; his life and doctrine. (Paulsen, Friedrich.) N.Y., 1963.
Phil 3488.8 — Immanuel Kant, seine geographischen und anthropologischen Arbeiten. (Gerland, G.) Berlin, 1906.
Phil 3488.15 — Immanuel Kant, 1724-1924. (Gemelli, A.) Milano, 1924.
Phil 3489.30 — Immanuel Kant, 1724-1924. (Harnack, Adolf von.) Berlin, 1924.
Phil 3482.5 — Immanuel Kant. (Apel, Max.) Berlin, 1904.
Phil 3483.8.8 — Immanuel Kant. (Bauch, Bruno.) Berlin, 1917.
Phil 3483.47 — Immanuel Kant. (Becher, Erich.) München, 1924.
Phil 3483.45 — Immanuel Kant. (Bouterwek, F.) Hamburg, 1805.
Phil 3484.6.5 — Immanuel Kant. (Chamberlain, H.S.) London, 1914. 2v.
Phil 3485.23 — Immanuel Kant. (Delekat, Friedrich.) Heidelberg, 1963.
Phil 3487.16 — Immanuel Kant. (Frauenstädt, J.) Leipzig, 1872.
Phil 3487.17 — Immanuel Kant. (Freudenthal, Jacob.) Breslau, 1904.
Phil 3487.15 — Immanuel Kant. (Fröhlich, G.) Langensalza, 1890.
Phil 3488.26.1 — Immanuel Kant. (Goldmann, L.) London, 1971.
Phil 3489.6 — Immanuel Kant. (Hoffmann, A.) Halle, 1902.
Phil 3491.4 — Immanuel Kant. (Jackmann, R.B.) Königsberg, 1804.
Phil 3492.21 — Immanuel Kant. (Königsberg. Universität.) Leipzig, 1924.
Phil 3492.4 — Immanuel Kant. (Kroeger, A.E.) New York, 1872.
Phil 3492.7 — Immanuel Kant. (Külpe, O.) Leipzig, 1907.
Phil 3492.76 — Immanuel Kant. (Kuypers, Karel.) Baarn, 1966.
Phil 3493.11 — Immanuel Kant. (Landtman.) Stockholm, 1922.
Phil 3494.45 — Immanuel Kant. (Martin, Gottfried.) Köln, 1951.
Phil 3495.9 — Immanuel Kant. (Northwestern University. Evanston, Illinois.) Chicago, 1925.
Phil 3497.3A — Immanuel Kant. (Paulsen, Friedrich.) Stuttgart, 1898.
Phil 3503.4.15 — Immanuel Kant. (Vorländer, K.) Leipzig, 1924. 2v.
Phil 3504.22.5 — Immanuel Kant. (Ward, James.) London, 1923.
Phil 3504.31 — Immanuel Kant. (Wasianski, E.A.C.) Upsala, 1810.
Phil 3504.23A — Immanuel Kant. (Wilm, E.C.) New Haven, 1925.
Phil 3499.1 — Immanuel Kant. Königsberg, 1882-87. 3 pam.
Phil 3492.30 — Immanuel Kant: der modernen Zeit. 2. Aufl. (Kolb, Victor.) Wien, 1919.
Phil 3484.6 — Immanuel Kant. Die Persönlichkeit...in das Werke. (Chamberlain, H.S.) München, 1905.
Phil 3484.6.3 — Immanuel Kant. Die Persönlichkeit...in das Werke. 3. Aufl. (Chamberlain, H.S.) München, 1916.
Phil 3484.6.4 — Immanuel Kant. Die Persönlichkeit...in das Werke. 4. Aufl. (Chamberlain, H.S.) München, 1921.
Phil 3483.40 — Immanuel Kant: sein Leben und sein Lehre. v.1-2. (Brückmann, R.) Königsberg, 1918-19.
Phil 3482.6.2 — Immanuel Kant. 2. Aufl. (Aster, Ernst.) Leipzig, 1918.
Phil 3483.8.9 — Immanuel Kant. 2. Aufl. (Bauch, Bruno.) Berlin, 1921.
Phil 3483.15 — Immanuel Kant. 2. Aufl. (Borowski, L.E.) Halle, 1907.
Phil 3485.23.2 — Immanuel Kant. 2. Aufl. (Delekat, Friedrich.) Heidelberg, 1966.
Phil 3483.8.3 — Immanuel Kant. 3. Aufl. (Bauch, Bruno.) Berlin, 1920.
Phil 3494.45.4 — Immanuel Kant. 4. Aufl. (Martin, Gottfried.) Berlin, 1969.
Phil 3497.3.5 — Immanuel Kant. 4. Aufl. (Paulsen, Friedrich.) Stuttgart, 1904.
Phil 3497.3.6 — Immanuel Kant. 6. Aufl. (Paulsen, Friedrich.) Stuttgart, 1920.
Phil 3500.54 — Immanuel Kant als Pädagoge. (Schwarz, W.) Langensalza, 1915.
Phil 3500.73 — Immanuel Kant als Philosoph und Soziologe. (Stemberger, R.) Wien, 1953.
Phil 3489.22 — Immanuel Kant and international policies. (Hocking, William E.) Washington, D.C., 1924.
Phil 3492.32.5 — Immanuel Kant Auffassung von der Bibel und seine Auslegung derselben. (Kügelgen, C.W. von.) Leipzig, 1896.
Phil 3504.38A — Immanuel Kant in England, 1793-1838. (Wellek, René.) Princeton, 1931.
Phil 3504.31.5 — Immanuel Kant in seinen letzten Lebensjahren. (Wasianski, E.A.C.) Königsberg, 1804.
Phil 3504.31.10 — Immanuel Kant in seinen letzten Lebensjahren. (Wasianski, E.A.C.) Zürich, 1925.
Phil 3480.67.95 — An Immanuel Kant reader. (Kant, Immanuel.) N.Y., 1960.
Phil 3493.9.5 — Immanuel Kant und Alexander von Humboldt. Inaug. Diss. (Lind, Paul von.) Erlangen, 1897.

Phil 3493.32 — Immanuel Kant und David Hume's, dialogues concerning natural religion. (Löwisch, Dieter-Jürgen.) Bonn, 1964.
Phil 3504.60 — Immanuel Kant und die Pädagogik. (Weisskopf, Traugott.) Zürich, 1970.
Phil 3503.4.25 — Immanuel Kant und sein Einfluss auf der deutsche Denken. 2. Aufl. (Vorländer, K.) Bielefeld, 1922.
Phil 3492.26 — Immanuel Kant und seine Bedeutung für die Naturforschung der Gegenwart. (Kries, J. von.) Berlin, 1924.
Phil 3504.18 — Immanuel Kant und seine Weltanschauung. (Windelband, W.) Heidelberg, 1904.
Phil 3492.2.5 — Immanuel Kant wider Kuno Fischer. (Krause, A.) Lahr, 1884.
Phil 3504.20.5 — Immanuel Kants Bücher. (Warda, Arthur.) Berlin, 1922.
Phil 3504.20.9 — Immanuel Kants Cetzte Ehrung. (Warda, Arthur.) Königsberg, 1924.
Phil 3503.5 — Immanuel Kant's Erkenntnisstheorie nach ihren Grundprincipien Analysirt. (Volkelt, Johannes.) Leipzig, 1879.
Phil 3483.24 — Immanuel Kants förhallande till den filosofiska teologien. (Bring, Gustaf.) Lund, 1876.
Phil 3489.32 — Immanuel Kants Gedächtnissfeyer zu Königsberg am 22stem April 1812. (Herbart, J.F.) Königsberg, 1811.
Phil 3493.23 — Immanuel Kants Geld-Theorie. (Lembke, B.) Danzig, 1933.
Phil 3480.50.30 — Immanuel Kant's Kritik der Urteilskraft. (Kant, Immanuel.) Berlin, 1869.
Phil 3500.36 — Immanuel Kants Leben. (Schmidt, H.) Halle, 1858.
Phil 3503.4 — Immanuel Kant's Leben. (Vorländer, K.) Leipzig, 1911.
Phil 3503.4.2 — Immanuel Kants Leben. 2. Aufl. (Vorländer, K.) Leipzig, 1921.
Phil 3494.13.5 — Immanuel Kants Leben und Philosophie. (Messer, A.) Stuttgart, 1924.
Phil 3500.114 — Immanuel Kants Lehre und ihre Auswirkungen. (Salem, Joseph.) Gelsenkirchen-Buer, 1969.
Phil 3493.14.5 — Immanuel Kants letzte Lebensjahre und Tod. (Lomber, Wilhelm.) Königsberg, 1923.
Phil 3483.32 — Immanuel Kants Philosophie der Geschichte. (Brotherus, K.R.) Helsingfors, 1905.
Phil 3480.57.10 — Immanuel Kant's Prolegomena zu einer jeden künftigen Metaphysik. 3. Aufl. (Kant, Immanuel.) Berlin, 1893. 3 pam.
Phil 2115.113 — L'immatérialité de l'âme...contre Locke. (Gerdil, G.S.) Turin, 1747.
Phil 2070.114 — The immediate apprehension of God according to William James and W.E. Hocking. (Leuba, J.H.) n.p., 1924?
Phil 5190.15 — Immediate experience and meditation. (Joachim, Harold.) Oxford, 1919.
NEDL Phil 2050.97 — Immediate perception as held by Reid and Hamilton. (Latimer, J.E.) Leipzig, 1880.
Phil 176.234 — L'immediato e la sua negazione. (Bacchin, Giovanni Romano.) Perugia, 1967.
Phil 8637.10 — The immortal hope. (Mellone, S.H.) Edinburgh, 1910.
Phil 8627.5 — Immortal life. (Curtis, L.Q.) N.Y., 1901.
Phil 8647.1 — The immortal life. (Weiss, J.) Boston, 1880.
Phil 8630.15 — Immortal longings. (Findlay, Stephen.) London, 1961.
Phil 8644.5 — The immortal manhood. 2. ed. (Teed, Cyrus R.) Estero, 1909.
Phil 8962.12 — The immortal soul in danger. (Masaryk, J.G.) London, 1941.
Phil 8626.1.10 — A immortalidade, a morte e a vida. (Baguenault de Puchesse, F.) Porto, 1903.
Phil 8642.7 — L'immortalità dell'anima nei maestri francescani del secolo XIII. (Rovighi, S.V.) Milano, 1936.
Phil 8626.1 — L'immortalité, la mort et la vie. (Baguenault de Puchesse, F.) Paris, 1868.
Phil 8628.6 — L'immortalite. (Dumesnil, A.) Paris, 1861.
Phil 8633.3 — Immortality; an essay. N.Y., 1917.
Phil 8627.8 — Immortality. (Clarke, W.N.) New Haven, 1920.
Phil 179.34 — Immortality. (Everett, C.C.) Boston, 1902.
Phil 8632.14 — Immortality. (Harris, J.) London, 1927.
Phil 8635.4.5 — Immortality. (Keyserling, Hermann.) London, 1938.
Phil 8642.3 — Immortality. (Rogers, C.F.) London, 1930?
Phil 8643.35 — Immortality. (Streeter, B.H.) London, 1925.
Phil 7069.37.45 — Immortality. (Taylor, William G.L.) Boston, 1937.
Phil 8643.39 — Immortality and resurrection. (Stendahl, Krister.) N.Y., 1965.
Phil 8633.1.33 — Immortality and the cosmic process. (Matthews, Shailer.) Cambridge, 1933.
Phil 8633.1.22 — Immortality and the modern mind. (Lake, Kirsopp.) Cambridge, 1922.
Phil 8633.1.22.3 — Immortality and the modern mind. (Lake, Kirsopp.) Cambridge, 1922.
Phil 8633.1 — Immortality and the new theodicy. (Gordon, G.A.) Boston, 1896.
Phil 8633.1.31 — Immortality and the present mood. (Bixler, Julius S.) Cambridge, 1931.
Phil 8649.1 — Immortality established through science. (Yeiser, J.O.) Omaha, n.d.
Phil 8626.13 — Immortality in post-Kantian idealism. (Brightman, E.S.) Cambridge, 1925.
Phil 8633.1.26 — Immortality of man. (Krüger, G.) Cambridge, 1927.
Htn Phil 8627.10* — The immortality of the human soul. (Charleton, W.) London, 1657.
Phil 8626.5 — The immortality of the soul. (Browne, I.H.) Cambridge, 1795.
Phil 7069.31.20 — The immortality of the soul. (Jacoby, Samuel A.) Los Angeles, 1931.
Phil 8636.05 — The immortality of the soul. (Lodge, Oliver Joseph.) Boston, 1908.
Htn Phil 2150.5.31* — The immortality of the soul. (More, Henry.) London, 1659.
Htn Phil 2145.70* — The immortality of the soul. (More, Henry.) London, 1659.
Phil 8637.20.5 — The immortality of the soul. 2d ed. (Mattison, H.) Philadelphia, 1866.
Phil 8643.3 — Immortality or annihilation? (Sintenis, F.) London, 1827.
Phil 8890.9.5 — The immutable right. (Peabody, A.P.) Boston, 1858.
Phil 7069.21.31 — Imod døden. (Flammarion, C.) Kjøbenhavn, 1921.
Phil 8582.11 — An impartial enquiry. v.1-2. (Colliber, S.) London, 1728-29.
Phil 175.9.5 — The impartial philosopher. (Argens, J.B.) London, 1749. 2v.
Phil 9245.47 — Impassioned day. (Powys, Llewelyn.) London, 1931.
Phil 6311.17 — The imperative conquest. (Bull, Titus.) N.Y., 1936.
Phil 9070.104F — Imperatives and ethics. (Bergstroem, L.) Stockholm, 1962.
Phil 5058.13.15 — Die Impersonalien. (Sigwart, H.C.W.) Freiburg, 1888.
Phil 5520.39 — Die Impersonalien in sprachpsychologischer, logischer und linguistischer Hinsicht. (Beck, Ernst H.F.) Leipzig, 1922.
Phil 5041.16.15 — Implication and linear inference. (Bosanquet, B.) London, 1920.

Phil 5125.40   The implications of induction. (Cohen, Laurence Jonathan.) London, 1970.

Phil 8592.90   The importance of being human. (Mascall, E.L.) N.Y., 1958.

Phil 9355.4   The importance of liberal tastes and good intellectual habits. (Potter, Horatio.) Troy, N.Y., 1837.

Phil 186.88   The importance of living. (Lin, Yu-t'ang.) N.Y., 1937.

Phil 9558.42   The importance of lying. (Ludwig, Arnold M.) Springfield, Ill, 1965.

Phil 1504.2.6   Die Impossibilia. v.2. pt.6. (Baeumker, C.) Münster, 1898.

Phil 8954.2   Impossible things and other essays. (Everett, E.L.) Philadelphia, 1932.

Phil 310.45   L'imposture scientifique du matérialisme historique allemand. (Genevès, F.) Bordeaux, 1957.

Phil 192.60.10   The impotence of man. (Richet, Charles.) Boston, 1929.

Phil 8423.17   Impressionismus und Expressionismus. (Werner, Alfred.) Leipzig, 1917.

Phil 5828.21   Imprinting and early learning. (Sluchin, Wladyslaw.) Chicago, 1965.

Phil 184.42   The imprisoned splendour. (Johnson, R.C.) London, 1953.

Phil 2138.155.1   The improvement of mankind; the social and political thought of John Stuart Mill. (Robson, John Mercel.) Toronto, 1968.

Phil 2138.155   The improvement of mankind; the social and political thought of John Stuart Mill. (Robson, John Mercel.) Toronto, 1968.

Phil 3819.39.5   Improvement of the understanding. (Spinoza, Benedictus de.) N.Y., 1901.

Phil 3819.39   Improvement of the understanding. (Spinoza, Benedictus de.) Washington, 1901.

Phil 5545.172   Improving the memory for faces and names. (Weinland, J.D.) Boston, 1934.

Phil 978.49.502   Die Impulisierung des weltgeschichtlichen Gescheheus durch geistige Mächte; sieben Vorträge. 2. Aufl. (Steiner, R.) Dornach, 1966.

Phil 5470.1   Pamphlet box. Impulse.

Phil 6328.2.10   Impulshandlungen. (Stekel, Wilhelm.) Berlin, 1922.

Phil 6976.35   In a darkness. 1. ed. (Wechsler, James Arthur.) N.Y., 1972.

Phil 8633.2   In after days; thoughts on the future life. N.Y., 1910.

Phil 3850.27.94   In Albert Schweitzer's realms. (Robock, A.A.) Cambridge, 1962.

Phil 6998.2.5   In and out the garbage pail. (Perls, Frederick S.) Lafayette, Calif., 1969.

Htn   Phil 4931.2.30F*   In Aristotelis meteorolicus libros commentaria. (Alexander, A.) n.p., 1527.

Phil 2070.138A   In commemoration of William James, 1842-1942. N.Y., 1942.

Phil 197.50   In de school ijer wysbegeerte. (Wielenga, B.) Amsterdam, 1924.

Phil 1930.14.30   In defence of philosophy against positivism and pragmatism. (Cornforth, Maurice Campbell.) London, 1950.

Phil 1930.14.31   In defence of philosophy against positivism and pragmatism. (Cornforth, Maurice Campbell.) N.Y., 1950.

Phil 9495.127.6   In defence of purity. (Hildebrand, Dietrich von.) Chicago, 1920.

Phil 2225.12   In defence of reason. (Paton, H.J.) London, 1951.

Phil 8877.94   In defense of free will. (Campbell, Charles Arthur.) London, 1967.

Phil 6316.11A   In defense of love; a protest against "soul surgery" (Gontard, G.V.) N.Y., 1940.

Phil 9245.50.10   In defense of sensuality. (Powys, J.C.) N.Y., 1930.

Phil 8591.43.5   In den Gegilden der Gottoffenbarung. (Ludendorff, Mathilde S.) Pähl, 1959.

Phil 2805.288   In der Schule Pascals. (Ehrenberg, H.) Heidelberg, 1954.

Htn   Phil 6012.9*   In disem Biechlin wurt erfunden von Cöplexion der Menschen. (Cocles, Bartolommeo della Rocca.) Strassburg, 1516.

Phil 9220.5.5   In friendship's name. (Streamer, Volney.) Chicago, 1891.

Phil 9220.5.6   In friendship's name. 10th ed. (Streamer, Volney.) N.Y., 1899.

Phil 9220.5.9   In friendship's name. 14th ed. (Streamer, Volney.) N.Y., 1904.

Phil 9220.5.11   In friendship's name. 16th ed. (Streamer, Volney.) N.Y., 1909.

Phil 4265.3.32   In inquiry into speculative and experimental science. (Vera, A.) London, 1856.

Phil 6951.6   In irritation and insanity. (Broussais, F.J.V.) Columbia, 1831.

Phil 193.134.5   In job's balances. (Shestov, L.) London, 1932.

Phil 4520.2.30   In jus natuarae recentiorum stricturae. Diss. (Biberg, N.F.) Upsaliae, 1818.

Htn   Phil 193.149*   In lode della filosofia. (Salicino, A.) Fiorenza, 1569.

Phil 960.255   In man's own image. 1. ed. (Roy, Ellen (Gottschalk).) Calcutta, 1948.

Phil 3120.22.25F   In medias res. (Blüher, Hans.) Jena, 1920.

Phil 4080.3.305   In memoria di Carlo Cantoni. (Cantoni, Carlo.) Pavia, 1908.

Phil 4110.3.95F   In memoria di Francesco Fiorentino. Catanzaro, 1889.

Phil 4110.2.81   In morte della M. sa Marianna Florenzi Waddington tributo di dolore. Perugia, 1870.

Phil 7069.50.10   In my mind's eye. 1. ed. (Marion, Frederick.) N.Y., 1950.

Phil 396.10   In our image and likeness; humanity and divinity in Italian humanist thought. (Trinkaus, Charles Edward.) London, 1970. 2v.

Htn   Phil 5041.11*   In P. Rami. (Beurhusius, F.) London, 1581.

Phil 2750.20.15   In praise of philosophy. (Merleau-Ponty, Maurice.) Evanston, 1963.

Phil 5867.25   In praise of play; toward a psychology of religion. (Neale, Robert Edward.) N.Y., 1969.

Phil 185.54.5   In praise of wisdom. (Klatzkin, Jakob.) N.Y., 1943.

Phil 8712.18   In pursuit of truth. (Wood, A.) London, 1927.

Phil 8887.91   In quest of a new ethics. (Mayer, Charles L.) Boston, 1954.

Phil 8886.62   In quest of morals. (Lanz, H.) Stanford, 1941.

Phil 7069.69.40   In quest of the unseen. 1st ed. (Laubscher, Barend Jacob Frederick.) N.Y., 1969.

Phil 8610.913.10   In quest of truth. (Stansbury, H.) London, 1917.

Phil 3210.49   In Sachen der Psychophysik. (Fechner, G.T.) Leipzig, 1877.

Phil 6955.10   In Sachen der Psychophysik. (Fechner, Gustav.) Leipzig, 1877.

Phil 3450.19.165   In Sachen Heidegger. (Hühnerfeld, Paul.) Hamburg, 1959.

Phil 3805.168   In Schleiermacherianam christianae fidei expositionem. Diss. (Petrelli, C.M.J.) Upsaliae, 1840.

Phil 8597.42   In search of a religion. (Robinson, D.F.) Chester, 1938.

Phil 178.12.2   In search of a soul. (Dresser, H.W.) Boston, 1897.

Phil 8663.4   In search of God and immortality. Boston, 1961.

Phil 1750.166.130   In search of humanity. (Cobban, Alfred.) London, 1960.

Phil 1750.166.132   In search of humanity. (Cobban, Alfred.) N.Y., 1960.

Phil 5250.39   In search of maturity. (Künkel, Fritz.) N.Y., 1944.

Phil 176.224   In search of philosophic understanding. (Burth, Edwin Arthur.) N.Y., 1966.

Phil 193.132.15   In search of reality. (Samuel, Herbert S.) Oxford, 1957.

Phil 5246.70   In search of sanity. (Gibb, Andrew.) N.Y., 1942.

Phil 6968.36   In search of sanity. (Stefan, Gregory.) New Hyde Park, 1966.

Phil 4771.1A   In search of the miraculous. 1. ed. (Uspenskii, P.D.) N.Y., 1949.

Phil 6117.31   In search of the soul and the mechanism of thought, emotion and conduct. (Hollander, Bernard.) London, 1920. 2v.

Phil 4225.8.44   In spirito e verità. 4. ed. (Sciacca, Michele Federico.) Milano, 1960.

Phil 7069.38.58   In the dawn beyond death. (Thomas, Charles D.) London, 1938?

Phil 7069.38.58.5   In the dawn beyond death. (Thomas, Charles D.) London, 194-.

Phil 8642.10   In the end, God. 1. ed. (Robinson, John Arthur Thomas.) N.Y., 1968.

Phil 177.79A   In the evening of my thought. (Clemenceau, G.) Boston, 1929. 2v.

Phil 2905.1.325   In the field with Teilhard de Chardin. (Barbour, George Brown.) N.Y., 1965.

Phil 1111.6   In the grip of the past. (Groningen, B.A.) Leiden, 1953.

Phil 1845.12   In the last analysis. (Armstrong, A.E.) N.Y., 1956.

Phil 8598.64   In the morningland. (Stuart-Glennie, John S.) London, 1873.

Phil 6112.31   In the name of common sense. (Chappell, M.N.) N.Y., 1938.

Phil 5850.279.17   In the realm of mind. (Myers, Charles S.) Cambridge, Eng., 1937.

X Cg   Phil 2070.129.10   In the spirit of William James. (Perry, R.B.) New Haven, 1938.

Phil 7059.11.2   In the world celestial. 2. ed. (Bland, T.A.) Chicago, 1902.

Phil 8894.17.3   In tune with the infinite. (Trine, Ralph W.) N.Y., 1897.

Phil 193.139   In tune with the universe. (Signpost (pseud.).) London, 1932.

Phil 1750.60   In und Gegen. (Przywara, Erich.) Nürnberg, 1955.

Phil 5780.2.5   The inaccuracy of movement. (Hollingworth, H.L.) N.Y., 1909.

Phil 5780.2   The inaccuracy of movement. (Hollingworth, H.L.) N.Y., 1909.

Phil 5590.436   L'inadaptation, phénomèn social. Paris, 1963.

Phil 8580.40   Inanç ve hareket bütünlüğü bakimindan din terbiyesi. (Armaner, Neda.) Istanbul, 1967.

Phil 182.21   Inaugural address. (Hofmann, A.W.) Boston, 1883.

Htn   Phil 2138.65*   Inaugural address to...University of St. Andrews. (Mill, John S.) London, 1867.

Phil 8893.27   Inaugural dissertation, moral philosophy. (Sturman, E.A.) London, 1871.

Phil 6951.10   An inaugural dissertation on insanity. Thesis. (Beck, Theodric R.) N.Y., 1811.

Phil 2840.87   Inauguration d'un buste de C. Renouvier le 4 mai 1911. (Montpellier. Université.) Montpellier, 1911.

Phil 4110.3.92   Inaugurazione del monumento a Francesco Fiorentino in Sambiase, 15 novembre 1908. (Chimirri, Bruno.) Catanzaro, 1908.

Phil 3425.647   Incardona, Nunzio. L'assunzione hegeliana. Palermo, 1965.

Phil 183.8   Incardona, Nunzio. Radicalità e filosofia. Palermo, 1968.

Phil 8674.11   The incarnate Lord. (Thornton, L.S.) London, 1928.

Phil 7082.22.5   L'incertitude qui vient des rêves. (Caillois, Roger.) Paris, 1956.

Phil 2475.1.306   Inchiesta sul Bergsonismo. (Cuisa, Niso.) Sassari, 1953.

Phil 7060.31   Inchiesta sulla trasmissione del pensiero. (Lombroso, C.) Torino., 1946.

Phil 808.3   Inciarte, Fernando. Die Reflexionsbestimmungen un dialektischen Denken. Köln, 1957.

Phil 7054.45.9   Incidents in my life. (Home, Daniel Douglas.) N.Y., 1863.

Phil 7054.45.11   Incidents in my life. (Home, Daniel Dunglas.) London, 1863.

Phil 7054.45.14   Incidents in my life. 5th ed. (Home, Daniel Dunglas.) N.Y., 1864.

NEDL   Phil 978.5.800   Incidents in the life of Madame Blavatsky. (Sinnett, A.P.) London, 1886.

Phil 5400.26   Les inclinations; leur role dans la psychologie des sentiments. (Revault d'Allonnes, G.) Paris, 1907.

Phil 293.25.5   L'incohérence universelle. 1. éd. (Matisse, G.) Paris, 1953.

Phil 7060.59   Incolorum alterius mundi phenoemena. (Bissel, J.) Dillingen, 1685.

Phil 190.55   L'inconditionnalité de la philosophie. (Philippe, Oscar.) Paris, 1932.

Phil 190.55.5   L'inconditionnalité de la philosophie. Thèse. (Philippe, Oscar.) Nancy, 1932.

Phil 3425.422   Inconfro con Hegel. (Banfi, Antonio.) Urbino, 1965.

Phil 7060.67.5   L'inconnu et les problèmes psychiques. (Flammarion, C.) Paris, 1900.

Phil 5722.74   L'inconscient, 6e Colloque de Bonneval [1960] sous la direction de Henri Ey. (Ey, Henri.) Paris, 1966.

Phil 5722.8   L'inconscient. (Dwelshauvers, G.) Paris, 1916.

Phil 5722.11   L'inconscient. (Hesnard, A.) Paris, 1923.

Phil 5875.145   L'inconscient et la psychologie de l'enfant. 1. éd. (Mauco, Georges.) Paris, 1970.

Phil 6672.6   L'inconscient étude sur l'hypnotisme. (Coste, P. Marie Léon.) Paris, 1889.

Phil 6315.2.275   Inconscient freudien et problèmes de liberté. (Vennes, Gaston.) Trois Rivières, 1960.

Phil 3552.111.9   L'inconscio nella filosofia di Leibnitz. (Grassi-Bertazzi, G.) Catania, 1903.

Phil 3500.116   Inconsequenzen, und auffallende Widersprüche in der Kantischen Philosophie, Dessau, 1792. (Schaeffer, Wilhelm Friedrich.) Bruxelles, 1969.

Phil 4060.1.30   An inconsistent preliminary objection against positivism. (Ardigo, Roberto.) Cambridge, 1910.

Phil 4210.157   Incontro Internazionale Rosminiano, Bolzana. La problematica politico-sociale nel pensiero di Antonio Rosmini. Roma, 1955.

Phil 5850.253   Increasing personal efficiency. (Laird, Donald A.) N.Y., 1925.

Phil 5850.253.5   Increasing personal efficiency. (Laird, Donald A.) N.Y., 1925.

Phil 6332.3   Increasing your mental efficiency. (Williams, Edward H.) N.Y., 1914.

Phil 6990.5   Incubation....Pagan...Christian Churches. (Hamilton, M.) London, 1906.

Phil 4525.1.31   Indad. (Christensen, S.) København, 1918.

Htn   Phil 6045.22.21*   Indagine, Joannes. The book of palmestry and physiognomy. London, 1683.

Htn   Phil 6045.22.35*   Indagine, Joannes. La chiromance et phisiognomie. Rouen, 1638.

Phil 6045.22.40   Indagine, Joannes. La chiromance et phisionomie. Paris, 1662?

Htn   Phil 6045.22.25*   Indagine, Joannes. Chiromance et physiognomonie. Lyon, 1549.

Phil 6045.22.9   Indagine, Joannes. Chiromantia. Argentorati, 1531.
Htn   Phil 6045.22.7*   Indagine, Joannes. Chiromantia. Paris, 1543.
Htn   Phil 6045.22.13*   Indagine, Joannes. Chiromantia. Paris, 1547.
Htn   Phil 6045.22.15*   Indagine, Joannes. Introductiones apostelesmaticae in physiognomiam. Argentorati, 1622.

Phil 6045.22.17   Indagine, Joannes. Introductiones apotelesmaticae in physiognomiam. Argentorati, 1630.

Phil 6045.22.19   Indagine, Joannes. Introductiones apotilesmaticae in physiognomiam. Argentorati, 1672.

Phil 1701.54   Indagini di storia della filosofia. (Bausola, Adriano.) Milano, 1969.

Phil 8411.18   Indecency and the seven arts, and other adventures of a pragmatist in aesthetics. (Kallen, H.M.) N.Y., 1930.

Phil 2120.8.30   The independent mind. (Lamont, Corliss.) N.Y., 1951.
Phil 8691.23   Independent young thinkers. (Boorman, W.R.) Boston, 1933.
Phil 2411.4   L'indeterminismo nella filosofia francese contemporanea. (Levi, Adolfo.) Firenze, 1904.

Phil 18.17   Index; revista ibero-americana. Buenos Aires. 3-4,1941-1945 5v.

Phil 3120.8.60F   Index. (Brentano, Franz.) Highland Park, Illinois, 1959.
NEDL   Phil 19.1.5   Index. (Journal of mental science.) London, n.d.
Phil 19.1.5   Index. (Journal of mental science.) London, 1879-1928.
NEDL   Phil 19.2.6   Index. (Journal of nervous and mental disease.) N.Y., 1914-1925.

Phil 18.7.5   Index. v.1-10. (International journal of psycho-analysis.) London, n.d.

Phil 17.1.5   Index. v.1-10. (The Hibbert journal.) Boston, 1902-1911.
Phil 6327.11.10   The index of psychoanalytic writings. (Grinstein, A.) N.Y., 1956-60. 10v.

Phil 75.25   Index philosphique. Paris. 1-2,1902-1903 2v.
Phil 6327.11   Index psychoanalyticus, 1893-1926. (Rickman, J.) London, 1928.

Phil 2520.117   Index scolastico-cartésien. (Gilson, E.) Paris, 1912.
Phil 3450.19.255   Index zu Heideggers Sein und Zeit. (Feick, Hildegard.) Tübingen, 1961.

Phil 3450.19.1.2   Index zu Heideggers "Sein und Zeit". 2e Aufl. (Feick, Hildegard.) Tübingen, 1968.

Phil 177.28.2   Index zu Hermann Cohens Logik...Erkenntnis. (Görland, A.) Berlin, 1906.

Phil 3925.16.215   Index zu Ludwig Wittgensteins "Tractatus logico-philosophicus" und Wittgenstein - Bibliographie. (Borgis, Ilona.) Frieburg, 1968.

Phil 48.14   Indian Academy of Philosophy. Journal. Calcutta. 1,1961+
Phil 960.136.5   Indian and Western philosophy. (Heimann, B.) London, 1937.

Phil 8633.1.34   Indian conceptions of immortality. (Clark, W.E.) Cambridge, 1934.

Phil 7069.21.57   Indian ghost stories. (Mukerji, S.) Allahabad, 1921.
Phil 400.87   Indian idealism. (Dasgupta, S.N.) Cambridge, Eng., 1933.
Phil 18.12   Indian journal of psychology. Calcutta. 1-33 9v.
Phil 960.265   The Indian mind; essentials of Indian philosophy and culture. (East-west philosophers' conference.) Honolulu, 1967.

Phil 70.8   Indian philosophical congress, 1st, Calcutta, 1925. Proceedings. Calcutta. 36,1927+ 4v.

Phil 70.8.5F   Indian Philosophical Congress. Silver jubilee commemoration volume. Madras, 1950. 2v.

Phil 18.5   The Indian philosophical review. Bombay. 2-4 2v.
Phil 960.137.20   Indian philosophical studies. (Hiriyanna, M.) Mysore, 1957.

Phil 960.128   Indian philosophy. (Radhakrishnan, S.) London, 1923. 2v.

Phil 960.175   Indian philosophy. (Sharma, C.) Banaras, 1952.
Phil 5228.6   Indian psychology; perception. (Sinha, Jadunath.) London, 1934.

Phil 5228.6.5   Indian psychology. (Sinha, Jadunath.) Calcutta, 1958.
Phil 960.148   Indian realism. (Sinha, Judunath.) London, 1938.
Phil 960.257   Indian thought; a critical survey. (Damodaran, K.) Bombay, 1967.

Phil 960.1   Indian thought. (Brockie, W.) Sunderland, 1876.
Phil 8610.911   Indiana Rationalist Association. The light of reason. Indianapolis, Ind., 1911.

Phil 18.24   Indianejournal of philosophy. 1-4,1959-1964// 3v.
Phil 6315.17.16   Indications for child analysis, and other papers, 1945-56. (Freud, Anna.) London, 1969.

Phil 8674.2   The indications of the creator. (Taylor, G.) N.Y., 1852.
Phil 58.2.25   An indictment of the present administration of the Society for Psychical Research. (Bradley, Herbert Dennis.) London, 1931.

Phil 960.152   Indienschau und Indiendeutung romantischer Philosophen. (Sommerfeld, S.) Zürich, 1943.

Phil 960.258   Indiiskaia filosofiia novogo vremeni. (Brodov, Vasilii V.) Moskva, 1967.

Phil 6350.2   Indikation zur analytischen Psychotherapie mit Hilfe des "Experimentellen Triebdiagnostik". (Buerli, Alois.) Bern, 1970.

Phil 8960.6   The indirect voluntary, or Voluntarium in causa. Diss. (Kramer, H.G.) Washington, 1935.

Phil 400.16   Der indische Idealismus. (Kassner, R.) München, 1903.
Phil 960.37   Indische Philosophie. (Strauss, Otto.) München, 1925.
Phil 960.155   Indische Psychologie. (Abegg, Emil.) Zürich, 1945.
Phil 960.44   Die indische Theosophie. (Gomperz, Heinrich.) Jena, 1925.
Phil 978.30   Die indische Theosophie. (Speyer, J.S.) Leipzig, 1914.
Phil 978.30.5   De indische Theosophie en hare beteekenis voor ons. (Speyer, J.S.) Leiden, 1910.

Phil 8598.138   Indische Weisheit und das Abendland. (Saher, Purvezji Jamshedji.) Meisenheim, 1965.

Phil 665.70   The indispensable soul. (Crawshaw, William H.) N.Y., 1931.

Phil 5590.510   Individ, persenlighet och medmänsklig miljö. (Aamark, Curt.) Stolkholm, 1969.

Phil 3832.22   Individu et communauté chez Spinoza. (Matheron, Alexandre.) Paris, 1969.

Phil 177.34   The individual. (Cooley, W.F.) N.Y., 1909.
Phil 8844.3   The individual and his relation to society. (Tufts, J.H.) N.Y., 1904.

Phil 5627.189   The individual and his religion. (Allport, Gordon W.) N.Y., 1950.

Phil 5627.189.3   The individual and his religion. (Allport, Gordon W.) N.Y., 1951.

Phil 180.2.9   The individual and reality. (Fawcett, E.D.) London, 1909.
Phil 5241.3.30A   The individual and society. (Baldwin, J.M.) Boston, 1911.
Phil 8894.13   The individual and society. Thesis. (Tomkins, D.B.) Somerville, N.J., 1915.

Phil 5590.432   The individual and the crowd. (Ruitenbeek, H.M.) N.Y., 1964.

Phil 8886.68   The individual and the social order. (Leighton, J.A.) N.Y., 1927.

Phil 5590.3   Individual ascendency. (Brill, A.) N.Y., 1938.
Phil 5352.5   Individual choice behavior. (Luce, Robert.) N.Y., 1959. 2v.

Phil 5755.4   Individual determinism and social science. (Fiamingo, G.) Philadelphia, 1896.

Phil 8876.45   Individual development of man. (Beary, H.R.) N.Y., 1909.
Phil 5246.30   Individual differences as affected by practice. (Gates, G.S.) N.Y., 1922.

Phil 5465.26   Individual differences in imagery. Diss. (Griffitts, Charles H.) n.p., 1919?

X Cg   Phil 2138.95   Individual liberty, legal, moral, and licentious. 2nd ed. (Vasey, George.) London, 1877.

Phil 8882.100   Individual morality. (Hemming, James.) London, 1969.
Phil 5262.35   Individual psychology. (Wexberg, Erwin.) N.Y., 1929.
Phil 3640.263   Individual psychology and Nietzsche. (Crookshank, F.G.) London, 1933.

X Cg   Phil 7075.130   Individual psychology and sexual difficulties. pt.1-2. London, 1932-34.

Phil 18.5.10   Individual psychology bulletin. Chicago. 4,1944+ 10v.
Phil 6310.1.27A   The individual psychology of Alfred Adler. 1st ed. (Adler, A.) N.Y., 1956.

Phil 6328.1   Den individual psykologiska frage ställningen inom psykistrien. (Sjobring, H.) Uppsala, 1913.

Phil 5247.63   Individualism: true and false. (Hayek, F.A. von.) Dublin, 1946.

Phil 2138.111   Individualism and individuality in the philosophy of John Stuart Mill. (Street, Charles L.) Milwaukee, 1926.

Phil 2750.22.125   Individualisme, collectivisme, personnalisme dans l'oeuvre d'Emmanuel Mounier. (Vu Duy Tu.) Bonn, 1962.

Phil 315.16   Individualisme contre autoritarisme. (Lavergne, Bernard.) Paris, 1959.

Phil 9035.98   Le individualisme radical fondé sur la caractérologie. (Wolff, Edgar Maurice.) Paris, 1955.

Phil 2520.158   L'individualismo nel Cartesio e nel Rousseau. (Giunchi, O.) Novara, 1918.

Phil 8846.3   L'individualismo nelle dottrine morali del secolo XIX. (Vidari, Giovanni.) Milano, 1909.

Phil 575.81   Individualismus, Universalismus, Personalismus. (Dittrich, O.) Berlin, 1917.

Phil 8847.4   Der Individualismus. (Winter, F.J.) Leipzig, 1880.
Phil 3915.82   Individualismus oder Evolutionismus? (Sommer, Hugo.) Berlin, 1887.

Phil 2045.133   Individualismus und Absolutismus. (Schnur, R.) Berlin, 1963.

Phil 978.49.910   Individualismus und offenbare Religion. (Lindenberg, Christoph.) Stuttgart, 1970.

Phil 18.11   Pamphlet box. Individualist pamphlets. London.
Phil 187.99   Individualité, causalité, indeterminisme. (Muller, Maurice.) Paris, 1932.

Phil 2520.230   L'individualité selon Descartes. (Lewis, G.) Paris, 1950.
Phil 2520.230.2   L'individualité selon Descartes. Thèse. (Lewis, G.) Paris, 1950.

Phil 4630.7.80   Individualitet och universalitet hos Waldemar Rudin. (Aaberg, Bengt.) Lund, 1968.

Phil 8633.1.8   Individuality and immortality. (Ostwald, W.) Boston, 1906.

Phil 575.87   Individuality in a collective world. (Morgan, B.S.) N.Y., 1935.

Phil 5402.35   Individuality in pain and suffering. (Petrie, Asenath.) Chicago, 1967.

Phil 5585.266   Individual'noe razvitie cheloveka i konstantnost' vospriiatiia. (Anan'ev, Boris G.) Moskva, 1968.

Phil 5590.538   Individual'nyi stil' deiatel'nosti v zavisimosti ot tipologicheskikh svoistv nervnoi sistemy. (Klimov, Evgenii A.) Kazan', 1969.

Phil 6310.1.99   Individualpsychologie. (Rattner, J.) München, 1963.
Phil 5262.35.5   Individualpsychologie. 2. Aufl. (Wexberg, Erwin.) Leipzig, 1928.

Phil 193.200   Individuals. (Strawson, P.F.) London, 1959.
Phil 6319.1.196   Individuation. (Goldbrunner, Josef.) London, 1955.
Phil 6319.1.196.3   Individuation. 3. Aufl. (Goldbrunner, Josef.) Freiburg, 1966.

Phil 408.2   L'individuation à la lumière des notions de forme et d'information. Thèse. (Simondon, Gilbert.) Paris, 1964.

Phil 3790.4.90   Das Individuelle als Gegenstand der Erkenntnis. (Miller-Rostoska, A.) Winterthur, 1955.

Phil 978.49.580   Individuelle Geistwesen und ihr Wirken in der Seele des Menschen. (Steiner, R.) Dornach, 1966.

Phil 3850.16.45   Das individuelle Gesetz. (Simmel, Georg.) Frankfurt, 1968.

Phil 270.34   Individuelle Kausalität. (Hessen, S.) Berlin, 1909.
Phil 5251.20.15   Den individuelle sjaelelige udrikling. (Lehmann, Alfred.) København, 1920.

Phil 8877.90   Individuelle und collektive Ethik. (Cysarz, Herbert.) Tübingen, 1958.

Phil 8878.38   Individuelle und sozial Ethik. (Dorner, August.) Berlin, 1906.

Phil 2905.1.555   L'individuo e il collettivo nella durata secondo Pierre Teilhard de Chardin. (Vidoni, Egidio.) Milano, 1966[1965].

Phil 8886.67   Das Individuum in der Rolle des Mitmenschen. (Löwith, K.) München, 1928.

Phil 190.75   Das Individuum und die Beertung menschlicher Existenzen. 2. Aufl. Photoreproduction. (Popper, J.) Dresden, 1920.

Phil 176.80.5   Individuum und Welt als Werk. (Burckhardt, Georg E.) München, 1920.

Phil 1603.2   The individual and the cosmos in Renaissance philosophy. (Cassier, E.) N.Y., 1963.

Phil 8882.47   Indledning til den rationale ethik. (Heegaard, P.C.V.) Kjøbenhavn, 1866.

Phil 348.4.80   Indledning til filosofi som grundvidenskab efter Johs. (Palmoe, E.) København, 1954.

Phil 186.49   Indledning til kulturens filosofi. (Lambek, C.) København, 1920.

Phil 181.60   Inducciones, ensayos de filosofía y de crítica. (Gener, Pompeyo.) Barcelona, 1901.

Phil 5125.38   Induction, acceptance and rational belief. (Swain, Marshall.) Dordrecht, 1970.

Phil 5125.2   L'induction. (Biéchy, A.) Paris, 1869.

Phil 5125.30   Induction: some current issues. 1st ed. (Wesleyan Conference on Induction.) Middleton, 1963.
Phil 5125.6   Induction and deduction. (Naden, Constance C.W.) London, 1890.
Phil 185.1   Inductions. (Keratry, A.H.) Paris, 1818.
Phil 185.1.2   Inductions. (Keratry, A.H.) Paris, 1841.
Phil 178.25   Inductive inquiries in physiology, ethics, and ethnology. (Dana, A.H.) N.Y., 1873.
Phil 5041.4   Inductive logic. (Ballantine, W.G.) Boston, 1896.
Phil 5045.2.6   Inductive logic. (Fowler, Thomas.) Oxford, 1883.
Phil 5045.2.5   Inductive logic. (Fowler, Thomas.) Oxofrd, 1876.
Phil 5047.8   Inductive logic. (Hibben, J.G.) N.Y., 1896.
Phil 2138.35.12   Die inductive Logik. (Mill, John S.) Braunschweig, 1849.
Phil 5066.180.5   Inductive probability. (Day, John P.) London, 1961.
Phil 5066.180   Inductive probability. (Day, John P.) N.Y., 1961.
Phil 5250.3   Inductive psychology. (Kirkpatrick, E.A.) N.Y., 1895.
Phil 5125.22   Inductive reasoning. (Bagchi, S.) Calcutta, 1953.
Phil 9513.16   An inductive study of standards of right. (Wilson, Matthew Hale.) Boston, 1916.
Phil 5044.12   Induktive Logik. Habilitationsschrift. (Essler, Wilhelm Karl.) Freiburg, 1970.
Phil 5042.60   Induktive Logik und Wahrscheinlichkeit. (Carnap, Rudolf.) Wien, 1959.
Phil 18.10   Industrial psychology. Hamilton. 2,1927
Phil 9400.14   Industrial Relations Research Association. The aged and society. Champaign, 1950.
Phil 5465.60   Industrial Research Institute, New York. The nature of creative thinking. N.Y., 1952?
Phil 9558.2   Industry and idleness. (Beecher, H.W.) Philadelphia, 1850.
Phil 9558.2.5   Industry and idleness. (Beecher, H.W.) Philadelphia, 1896.
Phil 5125.7   L'induzione. Pt.1-3. (Benzoni, Roberto.) Genova, 1894.
Phil 75.40   Ineditos de filosofia em Portgal. (Costa, M.G.) Porto, 1949.
Phil 4967.20.15   Ineditos e dispersos, notas e variaçoes sôbre assuntos diversos. (Farias Brito, Raymundo de.) São Paulo, 1966.
Phil 8419.38   La inevitabile illusione; rilievi modali dell'estetica. (Severgnini, D.) Torino, 1960.
Phil 1504.13.6   Das Inevitable des Honorius Augustodunensis. v.13, pt.6. (Baeumker, F.) Münster, 1914.
Phil 8632.6   The inevitable future. 4. ed. (Harris, J.C.) Sydney, 1917.
Htn   Phil 8591.11*   The infallibility of human judgement. (Lyons.) London, 1724.
Phil 5047.41   Infallible logic. (Hawley, Thomas de R.) Lansing, 1896.
Phil 5520.98   The infancy of speech and the speech of infancy. (Stein, Leopold.) London, 1949.
Phil 7060.48   Inferences from haunted houses. (Harris, J.) London, 1901.
Phil 8610.881.10   An infidel abroad. (Bennett, D.M.) N.Y., 1881.
Phil 8610.854.15   Infidelity. (Pearson, Thomas.) N.Y., 1854.
Phil 7054.113   The infidelity of the times. (Corning, W.H.) Boston, 1854.
Phil 8610.929.20   Infidels and heretics. (Darrow, C.) Boston, 1929.
Phil 2415.10   Les infiltrations germaniques dans la pensée française. (Pervicax (pseud.).) Paris, 1945.
Phil 410.3   Infini et quantité. (Evellin, F.) Paris, 1880.
Phil 1135.165   L'infinite divine depuis Philon le Juif jusqu'à Platin. (Guyot, Henri.) Paris, 1906.
Phil 4065.126   The infinite in Giordano Bruno. (Greenberg, S.) N.Y., 1950.
Phil 181.81   The infinite presence. (Gould, G.M.) N.Y., 1910.
Phil 4065.184   The infinite worlds of Giordano Bruno. (Paterson, Antoinette Mann.) Springfield, 1970.
NEDL   Phil 1135.154.5   El infinitio en el pensamiento de la antiguedad clasica. (Mondolfo, R.) Buenos Aires, 1952.
Phil 1135.154   L'infinito nel pensiero dei Greci. (Mondolfo, R.) Firenze, 1934.
Phil 1135.154.10   L'infinito nel pensiero dell'antichita classica. (Mondolfo, R.) Firenze, 1956.
Phil 410.81   Infinity. (Benardete, José A.) Oxford, 1964.
Phil 5374.49   Infinity and ego. (Ishyam, J.C.) London, 1930.
Phil 525.109   An infinity of questions. (Eustace, C.J.) London, 1946.
Phil 5425.82   The infirmities of genius. (Belt, W.R.) London, 1952.
Phil 7140.122   Influence; how to exert it. (Yoritomo-Tashi.) N.Y., 1916.
Phil 3808.151.2   Influence de la philosophie de Schopenhauer en France. Thèse. (Baillot, A.) Paris, 1927. 2 pam.
Phil 2730.35   Influence de l'habitude. (Maine de Biran, Pierre.) Paris, 1803.
Phil 2730.35.3   Influence de l'habitude sur la faculté de penser. 1e éd. (Maine de Biran, Pierre.) Paris, 1954.
Phil 2490.120   L'influence des femmes sur Auguste Comte. Thèse. (Varney, M.M.) Paris, 1931.
Phil 1195.19   L'influence des sophistes sur Aristote, Épicur, stoiciens et sceptiques. (Wiśniewski, Bohdan.) Wrocław, 1970.
Phil 1020.65   L'influence du stoicisme sur la pensée musulmane. (Jad'an, Fahme.) Beyrauth, 1968.
Phil 6119.4   Influence of bodily posture on mental activities. (Jones, E.E.) N.Y., 1907.
Phil 6117.25   The influence of caffein on mental and motor efficiency. (Hollingworth, H.L.) N.Y., 1912.
Phil 5643.134   The influence of culture on visual perception. (Segall, Marshall H.) Indianapolis, 1966.
Phil 1955.6.35   The influence of Darwin on philosophy. (Dewey, John.) N.Y., 1951.
Phil 2520.87   The influence of Descartes on metaphysical speculation in England. (Cunningham, William.) London, 1876.
Phil 5330.16   Influence of distractions on the formation of judgments in lifted weight experiments. (Mitchell, David.) Princeton, 1914.
Phil 6112.13   Influence of education and training in preventing diseases of nervous system. (Carter, R.B.) London, 1855.
Phil 2730.35.5   The influence of habit on the faculty of thinking. (Maine de Biran, Pierre.) Baltimore, 1929.
Phil 5249.14   Influence of incentive and punishment upon reaction-time. (Johanson, A.M.) N.Y., 1922.
Phil 5592.130   The influence of instructions of repeated measurement on personality inventory scores. (Hills, J.R.) Princeton, 1959.
Phil 1865.170   The influence of J. Bentham on English democratic development. (Lundin, Hilda G.) Iowa City, 1920.
Phil 6113.7   Influence of joy. (Dearborn, G.V.N.) Boston, 1916.
Phil 5520.28   The influence of language on thought. (Wilson, William D.) Albany, 1879.
Phil 5545.24   Influence of memory. (Thompson, L.) Boston, 1840.
Phil 8896.8   The influence of moral causes upon opinion. (Verplanck, G.C.) N.Y., 1834.

Phil 5630.3   The influence of rumour on human thought and action. (Chadwick, Thomas.) Manchester, 1932.
Phil 5640.15   Influence of stimulus...duration on reaction time. (Wells, G.R.) Princeton, 1913.
Phil 6113.8.5   The influence of the mind on the body. (Dubois, Paul.) N.Y., 1906.
Phil 5850.299.5   Influencing human behavior. (Overstreet, H.A.) N.Y., 1925.
Phil 5850.299   Influencing human behavior. (Overstreet, H.A.) N.Y., 1925.
Phil 4080.3.510   L'influenza culturale di Benedetto Croce. (Contini, Bian Franco.) Milano, 1967.
Phil 3425.560   L'influenza dello Spinozismo nella formazione. (Chiereghin, F.) Padova, 1961.
Phil 4960.270   Influenza italiana nella filosofia rioplatense. Firenze, 1969.
Phil 4080.3.93   Influssi del pensiero Kantiano vell Croce. (Romano Palazzo, F.) Bari, 1938.
Phil 6112.35   L'influx nerveux et la psychologie. (Chauchard, P.) Paris, 1969.
Phil 8693.13   Infor de stora varldsproblemen. (Dalin, C.O.) Stockholm, 1912.
Phil 4803.537.80   Information about Professor Wincenty Lutosławski for those who wish to organize his lectures. Wilno, 1930.
Phil 5066.243   Information and confirmation. (Toernelohm, Håkan.) Göteborg, 1964.
Phil 5535.26   Information and human learning. (Biggs, John Burville.) Melbourne, 1968.
Phil 5520.648   Information and inference. (Hintikka, Kaarlo Jaakko Juhani.) Dordrecht, 1970.
Phil 310.692.5   Information and reflection on some problems of cybernetics and how contemporary dialectical materialism copes with them. (Kirschenmann, Peter Paul.) Dordrecht, 1970.
Phil 8663.5   Information Catholiques Internationales. L'athéisme. Paris, 1963.
Phil 8430.3.5   Information theory and esthetic perception. (Moles, Abraham A.) Urbana, 1966.
Phil 5256.5   Information theory in psychology. (Quastler, H.) Glencoe, 1955.
Phil 5057.42   Les infortunes de la raison. (Regnier, André.) Paris, 1966.
Phil 6118.1   Ingalese, R. The history and power of mind. N.Y., 1903.
Phil 6118.1.3   Ingalese, R. The history and power of mind. 8th ed. N.Y., 1905.
Phil 7069.21.40   Ingalese, Richard. Fragments of truth. N.Y., 1921.
Phil 8409.2   Ingarden, R. Untersuchungen zur Ontologie der Kunst. Tübingen, 1962.
Phil 4803.462.45   Ingarden, Roman. Erlebnis, Kunstwerk und Wert. Tübingen, 1969.
Phil 4803.462.30   Ingarden, Roman. Issledovaniia po estetike. Moskva, 1962.
Phil 4803.462.21   Ingarden, Roman. O dziele literackim. Warszawa, 1960.
Phil 4803.462.40   Ingarden, Roman. Przezijni, dzieło, wartość. Kraków, 1966.
Phil 4803.462.50   Ingarden, Roman. Psycho-fizjologiuzna teorja poznania i jejkrytyka. Lwów, 1930.
Phil 4803.462.1   Ingarden, Roman. Spór o istnienie świata. Kraków, 1947-48. 2v.
Phil 4803.462.2   Ingarden, Roman. Spór o istnienie świata. Wyd. 2. Warszawa, 1960-61. 2v.
Phil 4803.462.35   Ingarden, Roman. Der Streit um die Existenz der Welt. v.1-2. Tübingen, 1964-65. 3v.
Phil 4803.462.5   Ingarden, Roman. Studia z estetyki. Warszawa, 1957-70. 3v.
Phil 4803.462.20   Ingarden, Roman. Szkice z filozofii literatury. Lódź, 1947.
Phil 4803.462.10   Ingarden, Roman. U podsław sevrii poznania. Wyd. 1. Warszawa, 1971.
Phil 339.1   Ingarden, Roman. Über die Stellung der Erkenntnistheorie im System der Philosophie. Halle an der Saale, 1926.
Phil 9470.16   Ingarden, Roman. Über die Verantwortung. Stuttgart, 1970.
Phil 4803.462.55   Ingarden, Roman. Vom Erkennen des literarischen Kunstwerks. Tübingen, 1968.
Phil 4803.462.60   Ingarden, Roman. Z badań nad folozofią współczesną. Warszawa, 1963.
Phil 8698.1   Inge, W.P. Science and ultimate truth. London, 1926.
Phil 8958.2   Inge, W.R. Christian ethics and modern problems. London, 1930.
Phil 8588.2   Inge, W.R. The eternal values. London, 1933.
Phil 8958.3   Inge, W.R. Freedom, love and truth. Boston, 1939?
Phil 289.1   Inge, W.R. God and the astronomers. London, 1933.
Phil 8588.2.5   Inge, W.R. Personal religion and the life of devotion. London, 1924.
Phil 5070.6   Inge, William R. Faith. London, 1909.
Phil 5070.6.5   Inge, William R. Faith and its psychology. N.Y., 1910.
Phil 530.11.5   Inge, William R. Studies of English mystics. London, 1907.
Phil 9035.29.3   Ingegneros, José. El hombre mediocre. 3d ed. Buenos Aires, 1917.
Phil 808.1   Ingegneros, José. Proposiciones relativas al porvenir de la filosofía. v.1-2. Buenos Aires, 1918.
Phil 5248.2   Ingenieros, J. Principios de psicología biológica. Madrid, 1913.
Phil 5248.2.5   Ingenieros, J. Prinzipien der biologischen Psychologie. Leipzig, 1922.
Phil 4970.1.20   Ingenieros, José. Antología; su pensamiento en sus mejores páginas. Buenos Aires, 1961.
Phil 4309.1   Ingenieros, José. La cultura filosófica en España. Madrid, 1916.
Phil 4960.215   Ingenieros, José. Las direcciones filosóficas de la cultura argentina. Buenos Aires, 1963.
Phil 2477.1.130   Ingenieros, José. Emilio Boutroux y la filosofía universitaria en Francia. Buenos Aires, 1923.
Phil 8883.3.7   Ingenieros, José. Las fuerzas morales. Obra póstuma. Buenos Aires, 1926.
Phil 8883.3.2   Ingenieros, José. Hacia una moral sin dogmas. 2a ed. Buenos Aires, 1919.
Phil 6619.8.5   Ingenieros, José. Histeria y sugestión 5. ed. Buenos Aires, 1919.
Phil 6619.10   Ingenieros, José. Le langage musical et ses troubles hystériques. Paris, 1907.
Phil 4970.1.11   Ingenieros, José. Obras completas. Buenos Aires, 1962. 8v.
Phil 6958.2   Ingenieros, José. Simulación de la locura. 8. ed. Buenos Aires, 1918.
Phil 4970.1.30   Ingenieros, José. La simulación en la lucha por la vida. Valencia, 191-?
Phil 4260.126   Ingens sylva. 1. ed. (Paci, Enzo.) Milano, 1949.
Phil 8663.3.32   Ingersol, Robert G. The Christian religion. n.p., 1851?

Phil 8663.3.33 Ingersoll, Robert G. The Christian religion. Manchester, 1882.
Phil 8663.3.40 Ingersoll, Robert G. The Christian religion. N.Y., 1882.
Phil 8663.3.12 Ingersoll, Robert G. Collection of Robert G. Ingersoll's famous speeches. N.Y., 1906.
Phil 8663.3.34 Ingersoll, Robert G. The ghosts, and other lectures. Peoria, Ill., 1878.
Phil 8663.3.45 Ingersoll, Robert G. The house of death. London, 1897.
Phil 8663.3.37 Ingersoll, Robert G. Ingersoll to the clergy. N.Y., 1897.
Phil 8663.3.2 Ingersoll, Robert G. Ingersollia. Chicago, 1899.
Phil 8663.3.75 Ingersoll, Robert G. Letters. N.Y., 1951.
Phil 8663.3.35 Ingersoll, Robert G. The limits of toleration. N.Y., 1889.
Htn Phil 8663.3.31* Ingersoll, Robert G. An oration on the Gods. Peoria, 1872.
Phil 8663.3.3 Ingersoll, Robert G. The works. N.Y., 1900-02. 12v.
Phil 8663.3.06 Pamphlet vol. Ingersoll, Robert G. 6 pam.
Phil 8663.3.80 Pamphlet box. Ingersoll, Robert G. Biography and Criticism.
Phil 8663.3.07 Pamphlet vol. Ingersoll, Robert G. 1884-1922. 25 pam.
Phil 8663.3.86.2 Ingersoll in Canada. 2. ed. (Pringle, Allen.) Toronto, 1880.
Phil 8663.3.95 Ingersoll the magnificent. (Lewis, Joseph.) N.Y., 1957.
Phil 8663.3.37 Ingersoll to the clergy. (Ingersoll, Robert G.) N.Y., 1897.
Phil 8663.3.2 Ingersollia. (Ingersoll, Robert G.) Chicago, 1899.
Phil 8663.3.88 Ingersoll's Christmas sermon delivered by Rev. L.A. Lambert. (Lambert, L.A.) Akron, 1898.
Phil 5048.1 Ingleby, C.M. Outlines of theoretical logic. Cambridge, 1856.
Phil 9450.58 Inglis, B. Private conscience - public mortality. London, n.d.
Phil 183.2 Ingraham, A. Swain school lectures. Chicago, 1903. 2v.
Phil 6118.4 Ingraham, F.D. Spina bifida and cranium bifidum. Boston, 1944.
Phil 7060.38 Ingram, J.H. Haunted homes. London, 1884.
Phil 7060.38.2 Ingram, J.H. Haunted homes. London, 1884.
NEDL Phil 7060.38.15 Ingram, J.H. The haunted homes and family traditions of Great Britain. London, 1912.
Phil 7060.38.3 Ingram, J.H. The haunted homes and family traditions of Great Britain. 3d. ed. London, 1886.
NEDL Phil 7060.38.5 Ingram, J.H. The haunted homes and family traditions of Great Britain. 5. ed. London, 1901.
Phil 7060.38.9 Ingram, J.H. The haunted homes and family traditions of Great Britain. 5th ed. London, 1901.
Phil 2490.95.5 Ingram, John K. Practical morals. London, 1904.
Phil 6319.1.65 Der Inhalt der Psychose. (Jung, C.G.) Leipzig, 1908.
Phil 6319.1.67 Der Inhalt der Psychose. 2. Aufl. (Jung, C.G.) Leipzig, 1914.
Phil 5477.12 Inhibition and choice. (Diamond, Solomon.) N.Y., 1963.
Phil 6315.2.42.5A Inhibitions, symptoms and anxiety. (Freud, Sigmund.) London, 1961.
Phil 8403.34 Iniciação estética. (Cochofel, J.J.) Lisboa, 1958.
Phil 5241.106 Iniciación en la psicologia. v.1-2. (Bernal del Riesgo, A.) La Habana, 1936.
Phil 193.238 Iniciación filosofia. (Salazar Bondy, Augusto.) Lima, 1964.
Phil 5052.48.2 Iniciación lógica. 2. ed. (Miro, Quesada Cantuarias.) Lima, 1969.
Phil 5053.2 Initia philosophiae logicae. (Nieuwenhuis, Jacobi.) Lugdunum Batavorum, 1831.
Phil 3095.52 Initia philosophiae practicae primae acroamatice. (Baumgarten, A.G.) Halae, 1760.
Phil 978.49.75 Das Initiaten-Bewusstsein. (Steiner, R.) Dornach, 1927.
Phil 978.49.76 Das Initiaten-Bewusstsein. (Steiner, R.) Freiburg, 1955.
Phil 978.49.77 Das Initiaten-Bewusstsein: die Wahren und die falschen Wege der geistigen Forschung. (Steiner, R.) Dornach, 1969.
Phil 978.74.20 Initiation, human and solar. 3d. ed. (Bailey, A.A. (Mrs.).) N.Y., 1926.
Phil 6122.65 Initiation à la connaissance de l'homme. (Mabille, P.) Paris, 1949.
Phil 186.6 Initiation à la philosophie. (Lemaire, C.) Paris, 1843. 2v.
Phil 178.69 Initiation à la philosophie. 1. éd. (Deschoux, M.) Paris, 1951.
Phil 1718.21 Initiation à la philosophie contemporaine. (Séronya, Henri.) Paris, 1933.
Phil 2905.1.275 Initiation à Teilhard de Chardin. (Madaule, J.) Paris, 1963.
Phil 187.145 Initiation and design, and other essays. (MacCallum, Reid.) Toronto, 1953.
Phil 978.49.36 Initiation and its results. (Steiner, R.) N.Y., 1909.
Phil 180.23 Initiation into philosophy. (Faguet, Emile.) N.Y., 1914.
Phil 805.4 Initiation philosophique. (Faguet, E.) Paris, 1912.
Phil 180.23.2 Initiation philosophique. (Faguet, Emile.) Paris, 1913.
Phil 978.49.445 Initiationswissenschaft und Sternenerkenntnis. (Steiner, R.) Dornach, 1964.
Phil 4080.3.365 Inizio e svolgimento della filosofia dello spirito di Benedetto Croce. (Albeggiani, Ferdinando.) Palermo, 1960?
Phil 735.272 Inledning i värdeteori. 2. uppl. (Moritz, Manfred.) Lund, 1968.
Phil 5240.24 Inledning til psychologien. (Aars, K.B.R.) Kristiania, 1898.
Phil 811.1.3 Inledning till det filosofiska tänkandet. (Landtman, G.) Helsingfors, 1920.
Phil 175.35 Inledning till philosphiens system. (Atterbom, P.D.A.) Upsala, 1835.
Phil 1717.5.9 Inleiding tot de hedendaagsche wijsbegeerte. (Riehl, Alois.) Zutphen, 1918.
Phil 177.140 Inleiding tot de metafysica. (Claeys, R.H.) Gent, 1968.
Phil 5265.2 Inleiding tot de psychologie. (Zwanenburg, S.) Utrecht, 1926.
Phil 3903.5.30 Inleiding tot de verwondering. (Verhoeven, Cornelius W.M.) Utrecht, 1967.
Phil 190.3.8.5 Inleiding tot de wijsbegeerte. (Paulsen, F.) Amsterdam, 1910.
Phil 197.52 Inleiding tot de wijsbegeerte. (Wynaendts Franchen, C.J.) Haarlem, 1905.
Phil 1126.3 Inleiding tot de wijsbegeerte van de Grieken en de Romeinen. (Vos, Harmen de.) Nijkerk, 1963.
Phil 3925.16.125 Inleiding tot het denken van Wittgenstein. (Hubbeling, Hubertus Gerinus.) Assen, 1965.
Phil 8658.12.2 Inleiding tot de leer van God. (Doedes, J.I.) Utrecht, 1880.
Phil 8642.9 La inmortalidad del alma a la luz de los filósofos. (Rey Altuna, Luis.) Madrid, 1959.
Phil 5477.01 Pamphlet box. Innate ideas.
Phil 575.90 Inner life of humanity. Pt.1. (Lochman, M.) n.p., 1936.

Phil 6117.45.50 The inner light. (Homaday, William H.D.) N.Y., 1964.
Phil 8581.82 The inner world...philosophy of Christianity. (Buckham, J.W.) N.Y., 1941.
Phil 6332.11.5 The inner world of choice. (Wickes, F.G.) N.Y., 1963.
Phil 6332.11 Inner world of man. (Wickes, F.G.) N.Y., 1938.
Phil 978.49.710 Der innere Aspekt des sozialen Rätsels. (Steiner, R.) Dornach, 1968.
NEDL Phil 5520.15.7 Innere Sprachform. (Funke, O.) Reichenberg, 1924.
Phil 5627.198 Die innere Welt. 2. Aufl. (Trillhaas, W.) München, 1955.
Phil 3500.92 Innerer Sinn und Erkenntnis in der Kantischen Philosophie. (Schulz, H.) Düsseldorf, 1962.
Phil 6400.1.3 Die innerliche Sprache und die verschiedenen Formen der Aphasie. (Ballet, G.) Leipzig, 1890.
Phil 3120.40.55 Innerlijk perspectief. (Bierens de Haan, J.D.) Assen, 1966.
Phil 8889.9F Innføring i moralfilosofi. (Ofstad, Harald.) Stockholm, 1964.
Phil 5627.134.55 Innocent men. (Howard, Peter.) London, 1941.
Phil 5627.134.55.5 Innocent men. (Howard, Peter.) London, 1941.
Phil 8634.7 Innseits; zur Verständigung über die Jenseitsfrage. (Jaeger, Paul.) Tübingen, 1917.
Phil 5812.8 The innumerable instincts of man. (Claremont, C.A.) London, 1940.
Phil 4357.3.32 Inoitacion a filosofar. v.1-2. (Garcia Bacca, J.D.) Mexico, 1940-42.
Phil 8598.12.5 Inquest of light. (Smith, Goldwin.) N.Y., 1906.
Phil 8581.34 L'inquiétude religieuse. 2nd series. (Bremond, Henri.) Paris, 1909. 2v.
Phil 8598.28 L'inquiétude religieuse du temps présent. (Stapfer, P.) Paris, 1912.
Phil 18.22 Inquire. Oslo. 1,1958+ 10v.
Phil 5240.1.3 Inquiries...intellectual powers. (Abercrombie, J.) Boston, 1835.
Phil 5240.1 Inquiries...intellectual powers. (Abercrombie, J.) Edinburgh, 1831.
Phil 5240.1.2 Inquiries...intellectual powers. (Abercrombie, J.) N.Y., 1832.
Phil 5240.1.4 Inquiries...intellectual powers. (Abercrombie, J.) N.Y., 1838.
Phil 5246.1.10 Inquiries into human faculty and its development. (Galton, F.) London, 1907.
Phil 5246.1.9 Inquiries into the human faculty. (Galton, F.) London, 1928.
Phil 5246.1.2A Inquiries into the human faculty. (Galton, F.) N.Y., 1883.
Phil 4582.4.45 Inquiries into the nature of law and morals. (Hägerström, Axel.) Stockholm, 1953.
Phil 6952.12 An inquiry...nature, origin, mental derangement. (Crichton, A.) London, 1798. 2v.
X Cg Phil 5753.4 An inquiry...power of the will. (Day, Jeremiah.) New Haven, 1838. 4v.
Phil 8602.3.2 An inquiry...religion. (Ware, H.) Cambridge, 1842. 2v.
Phil 8602.3 An inquiry...religion. (Ware, H.) Cambridge, 1842. 2v.
Phil 8890.11 An inquiry chiefly on principles of religion. (Penrose, John M.A.) London, 1820.
Phil 2050.41.11A An inquiry concerning human understanding. (Hume, David.) N.Y., 1955.
Phil 6952.7.5 An inquiry concerning the indications of insanity. (Conolly, John.) London, 1964.
Phil 2050.39.5 An inquiry concerning the principles of morals. (Hume, David.) N.Y., 1957.
Phil 6128.19 An inquiry how far the vital and animal actions of the more perfect animals can be accounted for independent of the brain. (Simson, T.) Edinburgh, 1752.
Htn Phil 2053.50* Inquiry into...beauty and virtue. (Hutcheson, F.) London, 1725.
Phil 2053.50.2 Inquiry into...beauty and virtue. (Hutcheson, F.) London, 1726.
Htn Phil 2053.50.3* Inquiry into...beauty and virtue. (Hutcheson, F.) London, 1729.
Phil 2053.50.4 Inquiry into...beauty and virtue. (Hutcheson, F.) London, 1738.
Phil 2280.18.5 Inquiry into being. (Sikora, Joseph John.) Chicago, 1965.
Phil 270.12 Inquiry into limits...nature of causation. (Scott, R.E.) Edinburgh, 1810.
Phil 5068.7.4 An inquiry into meaning and truth. (Russell, Bertrand Russell.) London, 1951.
Phil 5068.7.6 An inquiry into meaning and truth. (Russell, Bertrand Russell.) London, 1966.
Phil 1890.40.2 Inquiry into relation of cause and effect. (Brown, T.) Andover, 1822.
Phil 5933.1 An inquiry into the claims of phrenology, to rank among the sciences. (Noble, Daniel.) Manchester, 1837.
Phil 9010.23 An inquiry into the consistency of popular amusements. (Henry, Charlton.) Charleston, S.C., 1825.
Phil 5764.4 An inquiry into the freedom of decision. (Ofstad, H.) Oslo, 1961.
Phil 2240.30A An inquiry into the human mind. (Reid, Thomas.) Edinburgh, 1764.
Phil 2240.32 An inquiry into the human mind. (Reid, Thomas.) N.Y., 1824.
Phil 2240.30.2A An inquiry into the human mind. 2nd ed. (Reid, Thomas.) Edinburgh, 1765.
Phil 2240.31 An inquiry into the human mind. 4th ed. (Reid, Thomas.) London, 1785.
Phil 8892.8.2 An inquiry into the influence of physical causes upon the moral faculty. (Rush, Benjamin.) Philadelphia, 1839.
Htn Phil 2266.68* An inquiry into the nature and causes of the wealth of nations. (Smith, Adam.) London, 1776. 2v.
Phil 2266.70 An inquiry into the nature and causes of the wealth of nations. (Smith, Adam.) London, 1796. 3v.
Phil 6968.12.15 An inquiry into the nature of hallucination. (Sidis, Boris.) n.p., 1904-12. 10 pam.
Phil 9245.25 An inquiry into the principles of human happiness and human duty. (Ramsey, George.) London, 1843.
Phil 5242.12 An inquiry into the process of human experience. (Cyples, W.) London, 1880.
Phil 7069.34.5 Inquiry into the unknown. (Besterman, T.) London, 1934.
Phil 600.1 Inquiry into theories of history. v.1-10. (Adam, W.) London, 1862.
Phil 175.63 Insan ve insanötesi. (Arvasi, S. Ahmet.) Istanbul, 1970.
Phil 6961.3.2 The insane in foreign countries. (Letchworth, W.P.) N.Y., 1889.
Phil 6980.635.26 Insanity, art and culture. (Reitman, F.) N.Y., 1959.
Phil 6968.7 Insanity, its classification. (Spitzka, E.C.) N.Y., 1887.

Phil 6309.2 Insanity and idiocy in Massachusetts; report of the Commission on lunacy, 1855. (Massachusetts Commission on Lunacy.) Cambridge, 1971.

Phil 6959.2 Insanity and insane asylums. (Jarvis, E.) Louisville, Ky., 1841.

Phil 6951.3 Insanity and its treatment. (Blandford, G.F.) Edinburgh, 1892.

Phil 6969.5 Insanity in ancient and modern life. (Tuke, Daniel H.) London, 1878.

Phil 6960.1 The insanity of doubt. (Knapp, P.C.) Baltimore, 1890.

Phil 5425.3 Insanity of genius. (Nisbet, J.F.) London, 1891.

Phil 8843.20 Insanlar ve ahlâklar. (Sena, Cemil.) Istanbul, 1970.

Phil 5627.124.20 Inside Buchmanism. (Williamson, G.) London, 1954.

Phil 182.80 Inside experience. (Hart, Joseph K.) N.Y., 1927.

Phil 6980.141 Inside psychotherapy. (Bry, Adelaide.) N.Y., 1972.

Phil 6980.112 The inside story. 1. ed. (Bingham, J.) N.Y., 1953.

Phil 180.75 Inside the great mirror. (Feibleman, James.) The Hague, 1958.

Phil 7069.18.90 Insight. (Cushman, Emma Crow.) Boston, 1918.

Phil 342.18.2 Insight. (Lonergan, Bernard J.F.) N.Y., 1964.

Phil 6314.12 Insight and responsibility. (Erikson, Eric H.) N.Y., 1964.

Phil 6315.64 Insights: conversations with Theodor Reik. (Freeman, Erika.) Englewood Cliffs, 1971.

Phil 665.49 Insights and heresies. (Scofield, A.) Boston, 1913.

Phil 190.106.5 Insights and illusions of philosophy. Translation. 1st American ed. (Piaget, Jean.) N.Y., 1971.

Phil 18.33 Insikt och handling. Lund. 1,1955+

Phil 6952.10 Insistent and fixed ideas. (Cowles, E.) Baltimore, 1888.

Phil 7080.45 Insomnia, how to combat it. (Collins, Joseph.) N.Y., 1930.

Phil 7080.19 Insomnia: its causes and cure. (Sawyer, James.) Birmingham, 1904.

Phil 7080.39 Insomnia and its therapeutics. (MacFarlane, A.W.) N.Y., 1891.

Phil 7080.6 Insomnia and other disorders of sleep. (Lyman, H.M.) Chicago, 1885.

Phil 8432.2 L'inspiration. 1. éd. (Heidsieck, F.) Paris, 1961.

Phil 8707.11.2 Inspiration or evolution. 2. ed. (Riley, W.B.) Cleveland, 1926.

Phil 5627.134.80 Inspired children. 1. ed. (Jones, Olivin Mary.) N.Y., 1933.

Phil 9575.5 Inspired millionaires...America. (Lee, G.S.) Northampton, 1908.

Phil 6953.9 L'instabilité mentale. (Duprat, G.L.) Paris, 1898.

Phil 960.180 Instant et cause. (Silburn, Lilian.) Paris, 1955.

Phil 5465.130 Les instants privilégiés. (Maire, Gilbert.) Aubier, 1962.

Phil 5838.261 Instinct, an enduring problem in psychology. (Birney, Robert C.) Princeton, 1961.

Phil 5819.2.7 L'instinct; ses rapports. 2. éd. (Joly, H.) Paris, 1873.

Phil 5819.2.5 L'instinct. (Joly, H.) Paris, 1869.

Phil 5828.15 Instinct. (Shepherd, James.) Kirkcaldy, 1884.

Phil 5829.9 L'instinct: théories - réalité. (Thomas, Maurice.) Paris, 1929.

Phil 5812.1.2 Instinct. 2nd ed. (Chadbourne, P.A.) N.Y., 1872.

Phil 5812.1 Instinct. 2nd ed. (Chadbourne, P.A.) N.Y., 1883.

Phil 5822.1.25 Instinct and experience. (Morgan, C.L.) N.Y., 1912.

Phil 5822.10 Instinct and intelligence. (MacNamara, N.C.) London, 1915.

Phil 5813.5 Instinct and intuition. (Debblee, George B.) London, 1929.

Phil 5816.9 Instinct and personality. (Garnett, Arthur C.) London, 1928.

Phil 5819.1 Instinct and reason...science of education. (Jarrold, T.) London, 1736.

Phil 8592.17 Instinct and reason. (Marshall, H.K.) N.Y., 1898.

Phil 348.1 Instinct and reason. (Ramsay, G.) London, 1862.

Phil 6327.5A Instinct and the unconscious. (Rivers, W.H.R.) Cambridge, Eng., 1920.

Phil 6327.5.5 Instinct and the unconscious. 2. ed. (Rivers, W.H.R.) Cambridge, Eng., 1924.

Phil 5421.20.15 L'instinct combatif; problèmes de psychologie et d'éducation. 3. éd. (Bovet, Pierre.) Neuchâtel, 1961.

Phil 5838.256 L'instinct dans le comportement des animaux et de l'homme. Paris, 1956.

Phil 5590.532 Instinct en karakter proeve eener characterologie op instinct-psychologischen grondalag. Proefschrift. (Wimersma Greidanus, H.T.) Zeist, 1933.

Phil 6327.5.15 L'instinct et l'inconscient. (Rivers, W.H.R.) Paris, 1926.

Phil 5813.3 Instinct in man. (Drever, James.) Cambridge, Eng., 1917.

Phil 5838.257 Instinct in man in the light of recent work in comparative psychology. (Fletcher, Ronald.) N.Y., 1957.

Phil 5832.3.4 Instinct und Intelligenz im Thierreich. (Wasmann, E.) Freiburg, 1899.

Phil 181.82 Instinct vs. reason; the problem of man. (Gooch, L.C.) Yazoo City, Miss., 1938.

Phil 5828.19 Instinctive behavior. (Schiller, C.H.) N.Y., 1957.

Phil 5838.259 Les instincts. (Viaud, Gaston.) Paris, 1959.

Phil 5380.5.15 Instincts of the herd in peace and war. 3. ed. (Trotter, Wilfred.) N.Y., 1941.

Phil 585.406.2 Instinkt, Psyche, Geltung. 2. Aufl. (Claessens, Dieter.) Köln, 1970.

Phil 5252.18.60 Die Instinkt-Psychologie William McDougalls. (Becker, F.) Reichenberg, 1933.

Phil 5820.1 Instinkt und freier Wille. (Körner, F.) Leipzig, 1875.

Phil 5820.1.5 Instinkt und freier Wille. 2. Aufl. (Körner, F.) Leipzig, 1878.

Phil 5828.13 Instinkterna och det mänskliga känslolivet. (Söderhjelm, H.) Helsingfors, 1913.

Phil 1535.19 Institutionum philosophicarum cursus. v.2-3. Besancon, 1821. 2v.

Phil 176.37.10 Instituionum metaphysicarum libri II. (Burgerdijck, F.P.) n.p., 1647.

Phil 310.6 Institut Filosofii. Akadamiia Nauk SSSR. O dialicheskii materializme; sbornik statei. Moskva, 1952.

Phil 48.10 Institut Général Psychologique, Paris. Bulletin. Paris. 1-33,1900-1933 22v.

NEDL Phil 48.5 Institut Général Psychologique. Mémoires. Paris. 1-5+ 5v.

Phil 48.5.10 Institut Général Psychologique. Notes et documents concernant l'oeuvre, 1900-1921. Paris, 1921.

Phil 8870.12 Institute for Religious Studies, Jewish Theological Seminary of America. Conflict of loyalties. N.Y., 1952.

Phil 18.26 Institute of Applied Psychology. Review. N.Y. 1,1961+ 3v.

Phil 48.6F Pamphlet box. Institute of general semantics.

Phil 48.16 Institute of Psychophysical Research. Proceedings. Oxford. 1,1968+ 2v.

Phil 6980.362 Institute on Preventive Psychiatry, State University of Iowa. Proceedings. Iowa City. 1-4 2v.

Phil 5061.3 Institutes of logic. (Veitch, John.) Edinburgh, 1885.

Phil 1990.30 Institutes of metaphysic. (Ferrier, J.F.) Edinburgh, 1854.

Phil 1990.30.2 Institutes of metaphysic. 2nd ed. (Ferrier, J.F.) Edinburgh, 1856.

Phil 8880.3.5 Institutes of moral philosophy. (Ferguson, Adam.) Edinburgh, 1769.

Phil 2218.35 Institutes of natural and revealed religion. 2nd ed. (Priestley, Joseph.) Birmingham, 1782. 2v.

NEDL Phil 2610.15 Institutio logica, et Philosophiae Epicuri syntagma. (Gassendi, P.) London, 1668.

Phil 5062.3 Institutio logicae. (Wallis, J.) Oxonii, 1715.

Htn Phil 2725.3.35* Institutio philosophiae. (LeGrand, A.) London, 1678.

Htn Phil 2725.3.30* Institutio philosophiae. (LeGrand, A.) London, 1680.

Phil 9348.1 The institution of a gentleman. London, 1839.

Phil 6945.18 Institutional care of mental patients in the United States. (Grines, J.M.) Chicago, 1934.

Phil 6945.25 The institutional care of the insane in the United States and Canada. (Hurd, Henry M.) Baltimore, 1916-17. 4v.

Phil 9150.15 Institutional ethics. (Kies, Marietta.) Boston, 1894.

Phil 3310.15.20 Die Institutionenlehre Arnold Gehlens. (Jonas, Friedrich.) Tübingen, 1966.

Phil 5051.40 Institutiones dialecticae, vulgo summulae, ad primam partem philosophici cursus pertinentes. (Lossada, Luis de.) Salmanticae, 1721.

Phil 801.5.7 Institutiones historiae philosophicae. (Brucker, J.) Lipsiae, 1747.

Phil 5058.44 Institutiones logicae. (Storchenau, S.) Venetiis, 1819.

Phil 5062.9 Institutiones logicae. (Wijnperse, D. van de.) Groningae, 1767.

Phil 1535.9.5 Institutiones logicae et ontologicae quas secundum principia S. Thomae Aquinatis. (Pesch, T.) Friburgi, 1914.

Phil 5045.8.14 Institutiones logical et metaphysicae. 4a ed. (Feder, J.G.H.) Gottingae, 1797.

Phil 176.11.5 Institutiones metaphysicae. (Baumeister, F.C.) Wittebergae, 1775.

Phil 176.11.3 Institutiones metaphysicae. (Baumeister, F.C.) Wittenbergae, 1749.

Phil 197.7 Institutiones metaphysicae. (Wijnperse, D.) Lugdunum Batavorum, 1770.

Phil 178.52 Institutiones metaphysicae generalis; éléments d'ontologie. (Descoqs, Paul.) Paris, 1925.

Phil 1535.8 Institutiones philosophiae. (P.) Parisiis, 1868. 2v.

Phil 165.353 Institutiones philosophiae. Torino, 1961-63. 7v.

Phil 3910.77.15 Institutiones philosophiae naturalis. (Baumeister, F.C.) Olomueii, 1774.

Phil 1535.9 Institutiones philosophiae naturalis. (Pesch, T.) Friburgi, 1880.

Phil 3910.77.3 Institutiones philosophiae rationalis methodo Wolfii conscriptae. 5. ed. (Baumeister, F.C.) Vitembergae, 1741.

Phil 4080.24 Institutiones philosophicae. (Corsini, Edoardo.) Venetius, 1743.

Phil 194.20 Institutiones philosophicae. (Tongiorgi, Salvator.) Romae, 1861. 3v.

Phil 1535.24 Institutiones philosophicae. (Urráburu, J.J.) Vallistoleli, 1891-1908. 8v.

Phil 1535.5.15 Institutiones philosophicae. v.1-3. 10th ed. (Liberatore, M.) Romae, 1857.

Phil 8951.18 Institutiones theologiae moralis. (Buddeus, J.F.) Lipsiae, 1719.

Phil 8956.8 Institutiones theologiae moralis quas in Collegio Lovaniensi Societatis Jesu. 12. ed. (Cenicot, Edouard.) Louvain, 1931.

Phil 9347.12 Institutions: or Advice to his grandson. (Higford, William.) London, 1818.

Phil 3552.256 Institutions léibnitiennes. (Sigorgne, P.) Lyon, 1768.

Htn Phil 3120.3.30* Institutionum logicarum. (Burgeridicii, F.) Cantabrigiae, 1647. 2 pam.

Htn Phil 5041.25.2* Institutionum logicarum. (Burgersdijck, Franco.) Cantabrigiae, 1647-80. 3 pam.

Htn Phil 5041.25.3* Institutionum logicarum. (Burgersdijck, Franco.) Cantabrigiae, 1668-1670. 3 pam.

Htn Phil 5041.25* Institutionum logicarum. (Burgersdijck, Franco.) Lugdunum Batavorum, 1642-60. 2 pam.

Htn Phil 3120.3.31* Institutionum logicarum. Libri duo. (Burgeridicii, F.) Cantabrigiae, 1660.

Htn Phil 5041.25.4* Institutionum logicarum libri duo. (Burgersdijck, Franco.) Cantabrigiae, 1680. 3 pam.

X Cg Phil 176.37.5 Institutionum metaphyricarum libri II. (Burgersdijck, F.P.) Hagae Comitis, 1657.

Phil 176.37.6 Institutionum metaphyricarum libri II. (Burgersdijck, F.P.) Lugdunum Batavorum, 1642.

Phil 4352.1.115 Instituto de España. Centenario de Jaime Balmes. Madrid, 1947.

Phil 48.8 Instituto di Studi Filosofici, Rome. Testi e documenti. Firenze. 1,1949

Phil 75.42 Instituto di Studi Filosofici. Bibliografia filosofica italiana dal 1900 al 1950. Roma, 1950. 4v.

Phil 70.63 Instituto di Studi Filosofici. Pubblicazione. Milano. 1940-1952 9v.

Phil 9361.2 Instrucçam. (Valenca, Francisco P. de.) Lisboa, 1745. 3 pam.

Phil 9343.10 Instruction d'un père à sa fille. 3e éd. (Dupuy, La Chapelle.) Paris, 1731.

Phil 9343.10.5 Instruction d'un père à sa fille. 3e éd. (Dupuy, La Chapelle.) Paris, 1750.

Phil 8876.66 Instruction morale. 10e éd. (Broglie, Paul.) Paris, 18- .

Phil 6673.2.5 Instruction pratique sur le magnétisme animal. (Deleuze, J.P.F.) Paris, 1825.

Phil 9528.3.5A Instructions from a father to his son. (Gellert, C.F.) Boston, 1823.

Htn Phil 5055.19* L'instrumento de la filosofia. (Piccolomini, A.) Roma, 1561.

Phil 190.28 Insuffisance des philosophies de l'intuition. (Piat, Clodius.) Paris, 1908.

Phil 2750.11.54.5 Integral humanism. (Maritain, Jacques.) N.Y., 1968.

Phil 5046.25.5 Integrale Logik. (Gabriel, Leo.) Wien, 1965.

Phil 5485.6 Integral'nyi intelleks. (Sheinin, Iulian M.) Moskva, 1970.

Phil 186.142 The integrating mind. (Lynch, W.F.) N.Y., 1962.

Phil 6980.606.5 Integrating sociological and psychoanalytic concepts. (Pollak, Otto.) N.Y., 1956.

Phil 5245.47   The integration of behavior. (French, T.M.) Chicago, 1952-58. 3v.

Phil 6319.1.60   Integration of the personality. (Jung, C.G.) N.Y., 1939.

Phil 6128.13.8   The integrative action of the nervous system. (Sherrington, C.S.) Cambridge, Eng., 1948.

Phil 6128.13   The integrative action of the nervous system. (Sherrington, C.S.) N.Y., 1906.

Phil 6128.13.7A   The integrative action of the nervous system. (Sherrington, C.S.) New Haven, 1926.

Phil 6120.24   Integrative activity of the brain; an interdisciplinary approach. (Konorski, Jerzy.) Chicago, 1967.

Phil 6121.27   Integrative functions of the cerebral cortex. (Lashley, K.S.) Baltimore, 1933.

Phil 5252.64   Integrative psychology. (Marston, W.M.) London, 1931.

Phil 8401.29   L'integrazione estetica, studi e ricerche. (Assunto, Rosario.) Milano, 1959.

Phil 5585.41   Le integrazioni psichiche e la percezione. (Dandolo, G.) Padova, 1898.

Phil 5753.10   Le integrazioni psichiche e la volontà. (Dandolo, G.) Padova, 1900.

Phil 6980.709   The integrity of the personality. (Storr, Anthony.) N.Y., 1961.

Phil 181.58   Inteligencia y simbolo. (Gastelum, B.J.) Madrid, 1927.

Phil 186.15   Intellect, the emotions and moral nature. (Lyall, W.) Edinburgh, 1855.

Phil 5255.14   L'intellect actif. Thèse. (Piat, Clodius.) Paris, 1890.

Phil 2225.18   Intellect and hope; essays in the thought of Michael Polanyi. (Langford, Thomas A.) Durham, 1968.

Phil 1905.25   Intellectual calculus. (Ball, Frank N.) Ipswich, 1957.

Phil 2880.8.126   L'intellectual communiste. (Naville, Pierre.) Paris, 1956.

Phil 6111.75   The intellectual functions of the frontal lobes. (Brickner, Richard Max.) N.Y., 1936.

Phil 1718.38   An intellectual history of modern Europe. (Stromberg, Roland N.) N.Y., 1966.

Phil 186.64.10   Intellectual intuition and ideal being. (Losskii, N.O.) Praha, 1934.

Phil 1701.48   Intellectual movements in modern European history. (Baumer, Franklin Le van.) N.Y., 1965.

Phil 5262.6.10   Intellectual philosophy. 8th ed. (Winslow, H.) Boston, 1863.

Phil 8897.4   Intellectual pursuits. (Waters, R.) N.Y., 1892.

Phil 170.1   Intellectual symbolism. (Chase, P.E.) Philadelphia, 1863.

Phil 2115.87   Intellectualism of Locke. (Webb, T.E.) London, 1857.

Phil 2475.1.296   L'intellectualisme de Bergson. (Husson, León A.) Paris, 1947.

Phil 2475.1.297   L'intellectualisme de Bergson. Thèse. (Husson, León A.) Paris, 1947.

Phil 5242.25   L'intellectuel. (Cartault, A.) Paris, 1914.

Phil 5835.2   Die intellectuellen Eigenschaften der Pferde. (Zürn, Friedrich A.) Stuttgart, 1899.

Phil 8669.3.25   Intellekt oder Gemüt? Eine philosophische Studie über Rudolf Ottos Buch "Das Heilige". (Geyser, Joseph.) Freiburg, 1922.

Phil 1145.40   Der Intellektualismus in der griechischen Ethik. (Wendt, M.) Leipzig, 1907.

Phil 4600.2.52   Den intellektuella askadningens filosofi. (Larsson, Hans.) Stockholm, 1920.

Phil 4582.4.95   Den intellektuella spärren; trous svårigheter i belysning av Axel Hägerströms filosofi. (Klingberg, Wilhelm.) Stockholm, 1966.

Phil 8622.62   Intellektuelle Redlichkeit und christlicher Glaube. (Rahner, Karl.) Wien, 1966.

Phil 185.16.5   Die intellektuellen Funktionen. (Kreibig, J.C.) Wien, 1909.

Phil 7069.25.3   Die intellektuellen Phänomene. (Baerwald, R.) Berlin, 1925.

Phil 187.72.5   Intelletualismo e pragmatismo. (Masci, Filippo.) Napoli, 1911.

Phil 5242.37   Intelligence, and mental growth. (Claremont, C.A.) N.Y., 1928.

Phil 5465.204   Intelligence, creativity and cognitive style. (Shouksmith, George.) London, 1970.

Phil 5241.98   Intelligence, its manifestations and measurement. (Boynton, P.L.) N.Y., 1933.

Phil 5258.208   L'intelligence; mythes et réalités. (Salvat, Henri.) Paris, 1969.

Phil 5241.68   L'intelligence. (Bourdon, B.) Paris, 1926.

Phil 22.3.5   Intelligence. N.Y.

Phil 5257.16   L'intelligence. Thèse. (Rith, L.) Paris, 1912.

Phil 5262.70   Intelligence and ability. (Wiseman, Stephen.) Baltimore, 1967.

Phil 5871.45   Intelligence and cultural environment. (Vernon, Philip Ewart.) London, 1969.

Phil 5247.74   Intelligence and experience. (Hunt, J.) N.Y., 1961.

Phil 5241.111   Intelligence and fertility. (Burt, Cyril.) London, 1947.

Phil 5258.134   Intelligence and its deviations. (Sherman, Mandel.) N.Y., 1945.

Phil 5249.21.3   L'intelligence avant le langage. (Janet, Pierre.) Paris, 1936.

Phil 5828.18   L'intelligence des animaux. (Sire, Marcel.) Paris, 1954.

Phil 5827.3   L'intelligence des bêtes. (Rendu, V.) Paris, 1863.

Phil 5820.4.15   L'intelligence des singes supérieurs. (Köhler, Wolfgang.) Paris, 1927.

Phil 5823.2   Intelligence et instinct. (Nadaillac, J.F.A.) Paris, 1892.

Phil 346.5   L'intelligence et la vie. (Piat, Clodius.) Paris, 1915.

Phil 5592.85   L'intelligence et le caractère. (Maistriaux, Robert.) Paris, 1959.

Phil 6122.42   L'intelligence et le cerveau. (Matisse, Georges.) Paris, 1909.

Phil 5257.6.10   L'intelligence et l'homme. (Richet, Charles.) Paris, 1927.

Phil 196.19.5   Intelligence in expression. (Vivante, Leone.) London, 1925.

Phil 5816.5.3   Intelligence in plants and animals. (Gentry, Thomas G.) N.Y., 1900.

Phil 1955.6.22   Intelligence in the modern world. (Dewey, John.) N.Y., 1939.

Phil 5816.11   The intelligence of animals. (Grindley, G.C.) London, 1937.

Phil 5825.8   The intelligence of animals. (Pitt, Frances.) London, 1931.

Phil 6750.216   The intelligence of the feeble-minded. (Binet, Alfred.) Baltimore, 1916.

Phil 7069.34.60   The intelligence of the spaces. (Wells, Helen B.) N.Y., 1934.

Phil 5245.26   L'intelligence sympathetique. (Finnbogason, G.) Paris, 1913.

Phil 6127.18   Intelligent living. (Riggs, A.F.) Garden City, 1929.

Phil 5240.7   Die Intelligenz, eine Einführung in die Haupttatdachenfet. (Anschütz, Georg.) Harz, 1913.

Phil 5762.9   Intelligenz und Wille. 3. Aufl. (Meumann, Ernst.) Leipzig, 1920.

Phil 5762.9.4   Intelligenz und Wille. 4. Aufl. (Meumann, Ernst.) Leipzig, 1925.

Phil 5261.16   L'intelligenza. (Varvaro, P.) Palermo, 1927.

Phil 8416.19   L'intelligenza nell'arte. (Piemontese, F.) Milano, 1955.

Phil 5820.4.10   Intelligenzprüfungen an Menschenaffen. 2. Aufl. (Köhler, Wolfgang.) Berlin, 1921.

Phil 8088.4   Intelligible beauty in aesthetic thought. (Will, F.) Tübingen, 1958.

Phil 735.10.5   The intelligible world. (Urban, W.M.) London, 1929.

Phil 5520.413   Intension and decision. (Martin, R.M.) Englewood Cliffs, N.J., 1963.

Phil 6985.25   Intensive group psychotherapy. (Bach, George Robert.) N.Y., 1954.

Phil 8400.24A   The intent of the artist. (Genteno, A.) Princeton, 1941.

Phil 1845.14.2   Intention. (Anscombe, G.E.M.) Oxford, 1958.

Phil 418.10   Intention. (Anscombe, Gertrude Elizabeth Margaret.) Oxford, 1957.

Phil 7069.42.5   Intention and survival. (Hamilton, T. Glen.) Toronto, 1942.

Htn   Phil 2250.30*   The intention of the Prometheus Bound of Aeschylus. Thesis. (Royce, Josiah.) Berkeley, 1875.

Phil 196.30   L'intention philosophique. 1. ed. (Vialatoux, J.) Paris, 1932.

Phil 2605.10.30   L'intention réaliste. (Fontan, Pierre.) Paris, 1965.

Phil 4080.3.201   L'intention spéculative de Benedetto Croce. (Filosofia dello spirito). (Merlotti, Eric.) Neuchâtel, 1970.

Phil 5548.140   Intentional behavior; an approach to human motivation. (Ryan, Thomas Arthur.) N.Y., 1970.

Phil 6750.26   Intentionalität, Reaktivität und Schwachsinn. (Nöll, Heinrich.) Halle, 1926.

Phil 5044.7   Intentionalität und Sinn. (Ehrlich, W.) Halle, 1934.

Phil 70.102   Intentionality, minds, and pereception. (Wayne State University. Symposium in the Philosophy of Mind, 1962.) Detroit, 1967.

Phil 5068.102   Intenzionale e dialettica. (Moscato, Alberto.) Firenze, 1969.

Phil 4160.5.280   Intenzionalità e storia in Renato Lazzarini. (Modenato, Francesca.) Bologna, 1967.

Phil 70.16   Inter-American Congress of Philosophy, 1st, Port-au-Prince, 1944. Travaux du congrès international de philosophie. Port-au-Prince, 1947.

Phil 75.58   Inter-American Congress of Philosophy. Exposición del libro americano. Buenos Aires, 1959?

Phil 8592.6.8   Inter Amicos. (Martineau, James.) London, 1901.

Phil 70.104   Interamerican Congress of Philosophy, 7th, Laval University, 1967. Proceedings of the congress. Quebec, 1967-68. 2v.

Phil 70.16.5   Interamerican Congress of Psychology. Actas. 1,1953 2 pam.

Phil 5238.210   Interamerican Congress of Psychology. 3rd, Austin, Texas, 1955. Psychological approaches to intergroup and international understanding. Austin, 1956.

Phil 5238.210.6   Interamerican Congress of Psychology. 6th, Rio de Janeiro, 1959. Promovido pela Sociedade Interamericana de Psicologia com a cooperação de Associação Brasileira de Psicologia Aplicada. Rio de Janeiro, 1960.

Phil 5850.250.15   Interbehavioral psychology. (Kantor, J.R.) Bloomington, 1958.

Phil 6127.20   Intercortical systems. (Rosett, J.) N.Y., 1933.

Phil 3270.1.32   Das Interdict meiner Vorlesungen. (Fischer, Kuno.) Mannhein, 1854.

Phil 5465.90   Interdisciplinary Symposium on Creativity, Michigan State University of Agriculture. Creativity and its cultivation. N.Y., 1959.

Phil 5330.18   Das Interesse. 3e Aufl. (Ostermann, W.) Oldenburg, 1912.

Phil 4513.6.31   Interessen som normativ idé. (Aall, H.H.) Kristiania, 1913.

Phil 5325.8   Interference and adaptability. (Culler, A.J.) N.Y., 1912.

Phil 5780.8   The interference of will-impulses. (Roback, Abraham A.) Lancaster, Pa., 1918.

Phil 2880.13.100   An interior metaphysics. (Scheurer, Pierre.) Weston, Mass., 1966.

Phil 181.134   Interiorita e metafisica. (Giacon, Carlo.) Bologna, 1964.

Phil 4225.8.30   L'interiorità oggettiva. (Sciacca, Michele Federico.) Milano, 1958.

Phil 4225.7   L'interiorità teologica dello storicismo. (Severgnini, D.) Roma, 1940. 3v.

Phil 8622.25   Interiorité et vie spirituelle. Paris, 1954.

Htn   Phil 5440.11.2*   Intermarriage. (Walker, Alexander.) N.Y., 1839.

Phil 5440.11   Intermarriage. (Walker, Alexander.) N.Y., 1839.

Phil 5062.17   An intermediate logic. (Welton, James.) London, 1911.

Phil 5062.17.5   Intermediate logic. 4th ed. (Welton, James.) London, 1938.

Phil 6834.2   Intermediate types among primitive folk. (Carpenter, Edward.) N.Y., 1914.

Phil 5924.2.2   Internal evidences of Christianity deduced from phrenology. (Epps, John.) Boston, 1837.

Phil 5924.2   Internal evidences of Christianity deduced from phrenology. 2. ed. (Epps, John.) London, 1836.

Phil 5232.6   The internal senses in Latin, Arabic, and Hebrew philosophic texts. (Wolfson, H.A.) Cambridge, 1935.

Phil 48.12   International Association of Applied Psychology. Bulletin. Paris. 1,1952+ 3v.

Phil 6949.368   International Colloquium of Psychopathology of Expression, 4th, Washington, 1966. Psychiatry and art. Basel, 1968.

Phil 6118.6   International Conference on Student Mental Health. The student and mental health. London, 1959.

Phil 6118.5   International Conference on the Development of the Nervous System. Genetic neurology. Chicago, 1950.

Phil 70.4   International Congress for Analytical Psychology, 1st, Zurich, 1958. Current trends in analytical psychology. London, 1961.

Phil 70.83   International Congress of Applied Psychology, 14th, Copenhagen, 1961. Proceedings. Copenhagen, 1962. 5v.

Phil 70.83.16   International Congress of Applied Psychology, 16th, Amsterdam, 1968. Proceedings of the XVIth International Congress of Applied Psychology. Amsterdam, 1969.

Phil 70.5   International Congress of Arts and Sciences, St. Louis, 1904. Proceedings. Philosophy and mathematics. Washington, 1906.

Phil 6958.6 — International Congress of Charities, Corrections and Philanthrophy, Chicago, 1893. Commitment, detention care, and treatment of the insane. Baltimore, 1894.

Phil 70.1 — International Congress of Philosophy, 1st, Paris, 1900. Bibliothèque. Paris. 1900-1903

Phil 70.1.2 — International Congress of Philosophy, 2nd, Geneva, 1904. Rapports. Genève. 1905

Phil 70.1.3 — International Congress of Philosophy, 3rd, Heidelberg, 1908. Bericht über den III International Kongress. Heidelberg. 1909

Phil 70.1.3.2 — International Congress of Philosophy, 3rd, Heidelberg, 1908. Kurzer Gesamt-Bericht die Tätigkeit in der Sektionen und allgemeinen Sitzungen. Heidelberg. 1908

Phil 70.1.4 — International Congress of Philosophy, 4th, Bologna, 1911. Revue de metaphysique et de morale. Paris. 1911

Phil 70.1.5 — International Congress of Philosophy, 5th, Naples, 1924. Atti del v. congresso internazionale. Napoli. 1925

Phil 70.1.6 — International Congress of Philosophy, 6th, Cambridge, Mass., 1926. Proceedings. N.Y. 1927

Phil 70.1.7 — International Congress of Philosophy, 7th, Oxford, 1930. Proceedings. London. 1931

Phil 70.1.8 — International Congress of Philosophy, 8th, Prague, 1934. Actes du huitième congrés international de philosophie à Prague. Prague. 1936

Phil 70.1.10 — International Congress of Philosophy, 10th, Amsterdam, 1948. Proceedings. Amsterdam. 1949 2v.

Phil 70.1.11 — International Congress of Philosophy, 11th, Brussels, 1953. Proceedings. Amsterdam. 1953 4v.

Phil 70.1.12 — International Congress of Philosophy, 12th, Venice, 1958. Atti. Actes. Firenze. 1958-1961 12v.

Phil 70.1.12.5 — International Congress of Philosophy, 12th, Venice, 1958. Doklady i vystuplemia. Moskva. 1958

Phil 585.166 — International Congress of Philosophy, 13th, Mexico, 1963. Delegation from the USSR. Chelovek i epokha. Moskva, 1964.

VPhil 585.167 — International Congress of Philosophy, 13th, Mexico, 1963. Člověk, kto si? Bratislava, 1965.

Phil 70.100.5 — International Congress of Philosophy, 13th, México, 1963. Memorias del XIII congreso internacional de filosofía, México. México. 1-10 10v.

Phil 70.100 — International Congress of Philosophy, 13th, México, 1963. Symposia. 1. ed. México. 1963

Phil 70.1.14 — International Congress of Philosophy. Akten des XIV. Wien. 1968 6v.

Phil 70.120 — International Congress of Philosophy. Beiträge der bulgarischen Teilnehmer an dem XIV. Wien, 1968.

Phil 70.3.2 — International Congress of Psychology, 2nd, London, 1892. Proceedings at the 2d session. London. 1892

Phil 70.3.3 — International Congress of Psychology, 3rd, Munich, 1896. Dritter internationaler Congress für Psychologie in München. München. 1897

Phil 70.3.4 — International Congress of Psychology, 4th, Paris, 1900. Compte rendu des séances et texte des mémoires. Paris. 1901

Phil 70.3.6 — Pamphlet box. International congress of psychology, 4th, 1900.

Phil 70.3.10 — International Congress of Psychology, 5th, Rome, 1905. Atti del V Congresso internazionale di psicologia. Roma. 1905

Phil 70.3.15 — International Congress of Psychology, 6th, Geneva, 1909. Rapports et comptes rendus. Genève. 1910

Phil 70.3.25 — International Congress of Psychology, 8th, Groningen, 1926. Proceedings and papers. Groningen. 1827

Phil 70.3.30 — International Congress of Psychology, 9th, New Haven, 1929. Proceedings and papers. Princeton, N.J. 1930

Phil 70.3.35 — International Congress of Psychology, 10th, Copenhagen, 1932. Papers read to the Xth International Congress of Psychology at Copenhagen, 1932. The Hague. 1935

Phil 70.3.40 — International Congress of Psychology, 11th, Paris, 1937. Rapports et comptes rendus. Paris. 1938

Phil 70.3.45 — International Congress of Psychology, 12th, Edinburgh, 1948. Proceedings and papers. Edinburgh. 1950

Phil 70.3.50 — International Congress of Psychology, 13th, Stockholm, 1951. Proceedings and papers. Stockholm. 1952

Phil 70.3.63 — International Congress of Psychology, 14th, Montreal, 1954. Doklady. Communications. Moskva. 1954

Phil 70.3.60 — International Congress of Psychology, 14th, Montreal, 1954. Proceedings. Amsterdam. 1955

Phil 70.3.52 — International Congress of Psychology, 14th, Montreal, 1954. Proceedings. Actes. Amsterdam. 1955

Phil 70.3.55 — International Congress of Psychology, 15th, Brussels, 1957. Actes. Proceedings. Amsterdam. 1959

Phil 70.3.65 — International Congress of Psychology, 17th, Washington, 1963. Proceedings. Comptes rendus. Amsterdam. 1963

Phil 70.3.71 — International Congress of Psychology, 18th, Moscow, 1966. Symposium. Moskva. 1966 19v.

Phil 70.3.70 — International Congress of Psychology, 18th, Moscow, 1966. Tezisy soobshchenii. Abstracts of communications. Moskva. 1966 3v.

Phil 5585.311 — International Congress of Psychology, 18th, Moscow, 1966. Vospriiatie prostranstva i vremeni. Leningrad, 1969.

Phil 70.3.90 — International Congress of Psychology, 19th, London, 1969. Deviatnadtsatyi mezhdnnarodnyi psikhologicheskii Kongress, 27 iialia - 2 avgusta 1969 g., London, Angliia. Moskva, 1970.

Phil 70.3 — International Congress of Psychology. Congrès international de psychologie physiologique. Paris. 1890

Phil 5593.65 — International Congress of Rorschach and Projective Methods. Comptes rendus. Paris, 1967-68. 4v.

Phil 8400.36 — International Congress on Aesthetics, 1st, Berlin, 1913. Bericht. Stuttgart, 1913.

Phil 8400.36.2 — International Congress on Aesthetics, 2nd, Paris, 1937. Deuxième congrès international d'esthétique. Paris, 1937. 2v.

Phil 8400.36.3 — International Congress on Aesthetics, 3rd, Venice, 1956. Proceedings of the third international congress on aesthetics. v. 1-2. Torino, 1957.

Phil 8400.36.4 — International Congress on Aesthetics, 5th, Amsterdam, 1964. Actes du cinquième congrès international d'esthétique, Amsterdam, 1964. La Haye, 1969.

Phil 8505.6 — International Congress on Humanism and Ethical Culture. Proceedings. Utrecht.

Phil 70.2.15 — International Congress on Mental Hygiene. Program.

Phil 9495.23 — International Congress on School Hygiene, 4th, Buffalo, 1913. Report of sex education sessions. N.Y., 1913.

Phil 70.24 — International Council for Philosophy and Humanistic Studies. International council for philosophy and humanistic studies. Paris, 1949.

Phil 70.24 — International council for philosophy and humanistic studies. (International Council for Philosophy and Humanistic Studies.) Paris, 1949.

Phil 130.16 — International directory of philosophy and philosophers. Bowling Green, Ohio. 1,1965+

Phil 8505.7 — International Humanist and Ethical Union Regional Conference, Antwerp. Proceedings.

Phil 48.7 — International Institute for Psychical Research, Ltd. Bulletin. London.

Phil 70.86.10 — International Institute of Philosophy. Démonstration, vérification, justification. Liège, 1968.

Phil 70.45.5 — International Institute of Philosophy. Entretiens philosophiques de Varsovie. Wrocław, 1958.

Phil 70.17 — International Institute of Philosophy. Nature des problemes en philosophie. Paris, 1949.

Phil 70.86 — International Institute of Philosophy. Traditional cultural values. Mysore, 1959.

Phil 5545.254.2 — International Interdisciplinary Conference on Learning, Remembering and Forgetting. The organization of recall; proceedings. N.Y., 1967.

Phil 5545.254.4 — International Interdisciplinary Conference on Learning, Remembering and Forgetting. Experience and capacity; proceedings. N.Y., 1968.

Phil 5545.254.3 — International Interdisciplinary Conference on Learning, Remembering and Forgetting. Readiness to remember; proceedings of the third conference on learning, remembering, and forgetting. N.Y., 1969. 2v.

Phil 18.2.5 — International journal for philosophy of religion. Tallahasse, Fla. 1,1970+

Phil 18.1.5 — International journal of ethics. Seventy-five year index. Chicago, 1890. 2v.

Phil 18.1 — International journal of ethics. Philadelphia. 1+ 69v.

Phil 18.19 — International journal of group psychotherapy. N.Y. 1,1951+ 18v.

Phil 18.16 — International journal of individual psychology. Chicago. 1935-1937 9v.

Phil 18.23 — International journal of parapsychology. N.Y. 1959+ 5v.

Phil 18.18 — International journal of professional ethics. Zürich.

Phil 18.27 — International journal of psychiatry. N.Y. 1,1965+ 5v.

Phil 18.7.5 — International journal of psycho-analysis. Index. v.1-10. London, n.d.

Phil 18.7 — The international journal of psycho-analysis. London. 1,1920+ 44v.

Phil 18.7.10 — International journal of Psycho-analysis. Supplement. Glossary for the use of translators of psycho-analytical works. London.

Phil 18.28 — International journal of psychology. Paris. 1,1966+ 3v.

Phil 18.20 — International journal of social psychiatry. London. 1,1955+ 10v.

Phil 18.30 — International journal of symbology. Atlanta. 1,1969+

Phil 18.31 — International logic review. Bologna. 1,1970+

Phil 48.9 — International Metaphysical League. Convention proceedings. Boston.

Phil 3640.79.60 — International Nietzsche bibliography. (Reichert, Herbert William.) Chapel Hill, N.C., 1960.

Phil 3640.79.60.5 — International Nietzsche bibliography. (Reichert, Herbert William.) Chapel Hill, 1968.

Phil 18.15 — International Philosophical Library. Periodical publication. Prague. 1-4,1935-1940 4v.

Phil 18.25 — International philosophical quarterly. N.Y. 1,1961+ 10v.

Phil 9450.57 — International public morals. (Tri-ennial Congress of the International Union for the Protection of Public Morality, 3rd, London, 1961.) Rushden, 1961?

Phil 6313.23 — International resources in clinical psychology. (David, H.P.) N.Y., 1964.

Phil 18.13 — International Tagung für angewandte Psychopathologie. Referate und Vorträge. Berlin. 1931

Phil 18.3.10 — The international theosophist. Dublin. 1,1898

Phil 8400.50 — Internationale Hegelkongress, 5th, Salzburg, 1964. Bor'ba idei v estetike. Moskva, 1966.

Phil 3552.7 — Der Internationale Leibniz-Kongress in Hannover. (Internationaler Leibniz-Kongress.) Hannover, 1968.

Phil 2905.1.370 — Internationale Teilhard-Bibliographie. (Polgár, Ladislaus.) Freiburg, 1965.

Phil 6310.1.102 — Internationale Vereinegung für Individualpsychologie, Vienna. Alfred Adler zum Gedenken. Wien, 1957.

Phil 18.8.3 — Internationale Zeitschrift für individual Psychologie. Leipzig. 1-2 2v.

Phil 3552.7 — Internationaler Leibniz-Kongress. Der Internationale Leibniz-Kongress in Hannover. Hannover, 1968.

Phil 18.8.5 — Internationaler Psychoanalytischer Verlag. Almanach. Vienna. 1926-1936 11v.

Phil 3425.79.50 — Internationales Hegelbund. Veroeffentlichungen. Tübingen. 1,1931 2v.

Phil 18.3.5 — The internationlist. Dublin. 1897-1898

Phil 70.3.1 — Internatonal Congress of Psychology, 1st, Paris, 1889. Congress international de psychologie physiologique. Paris. 1889

Phil 6110.28 — Interoception and behaviour. (Adám, György.) Budapest, 1967.

Phil 18.32 — Interpersonal development; international journal for humanistic approaches to group psychotherapy, sensitivity training, and organizational development. Basel. 1,1970+

Phil 5590.220 — Interpersonal diagnosis of personality. (Leary, Timothy.) N.Y., 1957.

Phil 5850.254 — Interpersonal perception. (Lainz, Ronald David.) London, 1966.

Phil 6329.19 — Interpersonal psychoanalysis. (Thompson, Clara M.) N.Y., 1964.

Phil 6980.712 — The interpersonal theory of psychiatry. 1. ed. (Sullivan, Harry Stack.) N.Y., 1953. 4v.

Phil 187.149 — The interplay of opposites. (Mueller, G.E.) N.Y., 1956.

Phil 4210.190.5 — Interpretarioni rosminiane. (Sciacca, M.F.) Milano, 1958.

Phil 210.40 — Interpretation, theory and practice. Baltimore, 1969.

Phil 18.29 — Interpretation. Montréal. 1,1967+ 2v.

Phil 210.25 — Interpretation: the poetry of meaning. 1st ed. (Consultation on Hermeneutics.) N.Y., 1967.

Phil 3925.16.105 — An interpretation and critique of Wittgenstein's Tractatus. (Favrholdt, D.) Copenhagen, 1964.

Phil 5520.170 — Interpretation and preciseness. (Naess, Arne.) Oslo, 1953.

Phil 3500.24 — L'interprétation de la doctrine de Kant. (Stériad, A.) Paris, 1913.

Phil 1850.117.5 — L'interprétation de la nature dans le Valerius terminus. (Lalande, A.) Mâcon, 1901.

Phil 5520.145.15   Interpretation in teaching. (Richards, Ivor Armstrong.) N.Y., 1938.

Phil 8963.3   Interpretation of Chirstian ethics. (Niebuhr, R.) N.Y., 1935.

X Cg   Phil 6480.23.6   The interpretation of dreams. (Freud, Sigmund.) London, 1932.

Phil 7082.8.20   The interpretation of dreams. (Freud, Sigmund.) London, 1954.

Phil 6480.23.18   The interpretation of dreams. (Freud, Sigmund.) N.Y., 1950.

Phil 7082.38.6   The interpretation of dreams. (Stekel, Wilhelm.) N.Y., 1943. 2v.

X Cg   Phil 6480.23.5   The interpretation of dreams. 4th ed. (Freud, Sigmund.) London, 1915. 2v.

Phil 187.29   The interpretation of nature. (Morgan, C.L.) Bristol, 1905.

Phil 187.29.3   The interpretation of nature. (Morgan, C.L.) N.Y., 1906.

Phil 8708.2.7   The interpretation of nature. 2. ed. (Shaler, N.S.) Boston, 1893.

Phil 7069.55.2A   The interpretation of nature and the psyche. (Jung Institute, Zürich.) London, 1955.

Phil 7069.55   The interpretation of nature and the psyche. (Jung Institute, Zürich.) N.Y., 1955.

Phil 5592.190   The interpretation of psychological tests. (Allison, Joel.) N.Y., 1968.

Phil 8581.52.10   The interpretation of religion. (Baillie, John.) N.Y., 1928.

Phil 8602.15.9   The interpretation of religious experience. (Watson, J.) Glasgow, 1912. 2v.

Phil 6950.7.6   Interpretation of schizophrenia. (Arieti, S.) N.Y., 1955.

Phil 6950.7   Interpretation of schizophrenia. (Arieti, S.) N.Y., 1955.

Phil 181.44.5   Interpretation of the spiritual philosophy. (Gurnhill, James.) London, 1920.

Phil 2340.10.150   An interpretation of Whitehead's metaphysics. (Christian, William A.) New Haven, 1959.

Phil 5627.75   Interprétation psychologique des visions intellectuelles. (Leroy, E.B.) Paris, 1907.

Phil 5241.3.9   Interpretation sociale et morale des principes du développement mental. (Baldwin, J.M.) Paris, 1899.

Phil 1850.147   L'interpretazione baconiana delle janole antiche. (Rossi, Paolo.) Roma, 1953.

Phil 2477.6.103   Interpretazione del problema dell'essere in M. Blondel. (Federici Ajeoldi, G.) Firenze, 1936.

Phil 3425.328   Interpretazione di Hegel. (Negri, Enrico de.) Firenze, 1943.

Phil 3425.328.1   Interpretazione di Hegel. (Negri, Enrico de.) Firenze, 1969.

Phil 3801.781   Interpretazione di Schelling. (Semerari, Giuseppe.) Napoli, 1958.

Phil 3450.19.515   L'interpretazione heideggeriana dei presocratici. (De Cecchi Duso, Gianna.) Padova, 1970.

Phil 4080.3.265   Interpretazioni crociane. (Attisani, A.) Messina, 1953.

Phil 4080.3.470   Interpretazioni crociane di R. Assunto. (Convegno Crociano, Bari.) Bari, 1965.

Phil 1701.58   Interpretazioni della filosofia moderna. (Bonafede, Giulio.) Palermo, 1965.

Phil 1540.79   Interpretazioni medievale del voûsnointinós. (Grabmann, Martin.) Padova, 1965.

Phil 8586.48   Interpreters of man. (Griffith, G.O.) London, 1943.

Phil 4080.3.520   Interpreti do Croce. (Biscione, Michele.) Napoli, 1968.

Phil 5590.438   Interpreting personality theories. (Bischof, Ledford J.) N.Y., 1964.

Phil 6310.18   Les interréactions des facteurs religieux et psychologiques en hygiène mentale. Thèse. (Amidieu du Clos-Vinarie-Paule.) Québec, 1958.

Phil 6110.18   The interrelationship of mind and body. (Association for Research in Nervous and Mental Diseases.) Baltimore, 1939.

Phil 5520.50   Interrogative thought and the means of its expression. (Owen, E.T.) Madison, 1904.

Phil 8612.65   Interview sur la mort avec Karl Rabner. (Gaboriau, Florent.) Paris, 1967.

Phil 5850.211   Interviewing, its principles and methods. (Garrett, A.M.) N.Y., 1942.

Phil 5850.221.20   Interviewing: strategy, techniques, and tactics. (Gorden, Raymond L.) Homewood, Ill., 1969.

Phil 7054.18   Interwoven. Letters from a son to his mother. (Ford, S.L.) Boston, 1905.

Phil 5252.170   Intimate behaviour. (Morris, Desmond.) London, 1971.

Phil 8876.78   Intimations. (Barry, John D.) San Francisco, 1913.

Phil 8633.1.15   Intimations of immortality in the sonnets of Shakespeare. (Palmer, George H.) Boston, 1912.

Phil 181.67   Intorno al principio...della filosofia civile. (Giuliani, G.) Napoli, 1862.

Phil 284.10   Intorno al valore della scienza. (Dandolo, G.) Padova, 1908.

Phil 4080.3.155   Intorno alla concezione del diritto nel sistema di Benedetto Croce. (Ascoli, M.) Roma, 1925.

Phil 4080.3.70   Intorno alla dialettica. v.1-2. (Croce, Benedetto.) Bari, 1952.

Phil 4060.2.83   Intorno alla vita di Leone Ebreo. (Sonne, I.) Firenze, 1934.

Phil 4015.3   Intorno allo stato e ai bisogni attuali della filosofia teoretica in Italia. (Pennisi, S.) Firenze, 1862. 3v.

Phil 6112.24   Intra-cranial circulation and its relation to physiology of brain. (Cappie, James.) Edinburgh, 1890.

Phil 5240.55   The intrapsyic self. (Ariete, Silvano.) N.Y., 1967.

Phil 196.36.10   Introdução à filosofia. (Vita, Luis Washington.) São Paulo, 1964.

Phil 4303.1   Introduccio a la història del pensament filosofic a Catalunya. (Carreras y Artau, T.) Barcelona, 1931.

Phil 5046.24   Introducció a la logística. (Garciá, David.) Barcelona, 1934. 2v.

Phil 3195.6.170   Introducción a Dilthey. (Foejo, W.) Xalapa, 1962.

Phil 3450.11.240   Introducción a la fenomenología. (Gaos, J.) México, 1960.

Phil 181.122   Introducción a la filosofia. (Gonzalo Cosar, M.) Madrid, 1960.

Phil 181.3   Introducción a la filosofia. 4. ed. (Garcia Tuduri, Mercedes.) Habana, 1957.

Phil 3195.6.105   Introduccion a la filosofia de Dilthey. (Puccirelli, E.) Buenos Aires, 1944.

Phil 1750.675   Introducción a la filosofia esencialista. (Oromi, Miguel.) Madrid, 1961.

Phil 5046.48.2   Introducción a la lógica dialéctica. 2. ed. (Gortari, Eli de.) México, 1959.

Phil 5066.155   Introduccion a la logica simbolica. (Stahl, Gerold.) Santiago, Chile, 1956.

Phil 1540.38   Introducción a la psicología de los coñimbricenses. (Zilli, José B.) Bonn, 1961.

Phil 5241.85   Introducción a la psicología experimental. (Barbado, M.) Madrid, 1928.

Phil 8896.3.5   Introducción á la sabiduria. (Vives, Juan Luis.) Valencia, 1779.

Phil 4979.10.30   Introducción a una filosofía de la era atómica. (Rodríguez Delgado, Rafael.) Habana, 1950.

Phil 672.164   Introducción a una filosofía de lo temporal. (Pemartin, J.) Sevilla, 1937.

Phil 4962.10   Introducción a una metafisica de la contingencia. (Alvarez, González.) Cuenca, 1959.

Phil 4983.1.90   Introducción a Vaz Ferreira. (Ardao, Arturo.) Montevideo, 1961.

Phil 1750.495   Introducción al estudio de la fenomenologia de Husserl. (Virasoro, Rafael.) Rosario, 195-?

Phil 4351.4.80   Introduccion al estudio del filósofo rancio. (Fernández Largo, Jacinto.) Madrid, 1959.

Phil 2905.1.263   Introduccion al pensamiento de Teilhard de Chardin. 2. ed. (Tresmontant, Claude.) Madrid, 1960.

Phil 4961.905   Introducción al positivismo venezolano. (Beltrán Guerrero, Luis.) Caracas, 1956?

Phil 4317.5   La introducción de la filosofía moderna en España. 1. ed. (Quiroz-Martinez, Olga Victoria.) Mexico, 1949.

Phil 4959.210   La introducción de la filosofia moderna en México. (Navarro, Bernabé.) México, 1948.

Phil 181.128.5   Introduccion literaria a la filosofia. 2. ed. (Garcia Bacca, J.D.) Caracas, 1964.

Phil 1530.10   Una introducción moderna a la filosofía escolástica. (Zaragüeta Bengoechea, Juan.) Granada, 1946.

Phil 5246.25.10   Introducione alla psicologia. (Gemelli, Agostino.) Milano, 1947.

Phil 1050.1   Introductio ad historia philosophiae ebraeorum. (Buddeus, J.F.) Halae, 1702.

Phil 181.29   Introductio ad philosophiam. (Gravesande, G.J.) Leidae, 1736.

Phil 8880.20   Introductio ad prudentiam, or Directions. (Fuller, J.) London, 1731.

Phil 8880.20.10   Introductio ad prudentiam, or Directions. (Fuller, J.) London, 1787. 2v.

Phil 8880.20.5   Introductio ad prudentiam, or Directions. pt.2. (Fuller, J.) London, 1727.

Phil 5090.2   Introduction...moral evidence. v.1-2. (Gambier, J.E.) London, 1808-1818.

Phil 5070.1.2   Introduction...philosophy of primary beliefs. (Lowndes, R.) London, 1865.

Phil 5070.1   Introduction...philosophy of primary beliefs. (Lowndes, R.) London, 1865.

Phil 5247.15   An introduction...science of thought. (Hebberd, S.S.) Madison, 1892.

Phil 5241.12   An introduction...study...mind. (Bishop, D.) London, 1849.

Phil 5241.12.5   An introduction...study...mind. (Bishop, D.) London, 1857.

Phil 3425.321   Introduction à la lecture de Hegel. (Kojève, Alexandre.) Paris, 1947.

Phil 5041.78   Introduction à la logique contemporaine. (Blanché, Robert.) Paris, 1957.

Phil 6115.13.6   Introduction à la médicine de l'esprit. 6. éd. (Fleury, D.M. de.) Paris, 1900.

Phil 182.93.13   Introduction à la métaphysique. (Heidegger, M.) Paris, 1958.

Phil 2477.6.140   Introduction à la metaphysique de Maurice Blondel. (Tresmontant, C.) Paris, 1963.

Phil 7069.26.40   Introduction à la métapsychique humaine. (Sudre, R.) Paris, 1926.

Phil 2905.1.260   Introduction à la pensée de Teilhard de Chardin. (Tresmoutant, Claude.) Paris, 1962.

Phil 3006.6   Introduction à la pensée philosophie allemande depuis Nietzsche. (Groethuysen, B.) Paris, 1926.

Phil 2070.33   Introduction à la philosophie. (James, William.) Paris, 1914.

Phil 186.56   Introduction à la philosophie. (Le Senne, R.) Paris, 1925.

Phil 186.56.5   Introduction à la philosophie. (Le Senne, R.) Paris, 1939.

Phil 190.30   Introduction à la philosophie. (Petitot, H.) Paris, 1914.

Phil 194.5   Introduction à la philosophie. (Tiberghien, G.) Bruxelles, 1868.

Phil 192.85.3   Introduction à la philosophie. 4. ed. (Raeymaeker, Louis de.) Louvain, 1956.

Phil 1511.3.17   Introduction à la philosophie chrétienne. (Gilson, Étienne.) Paris, 1960.

Phil 3425.95   Introduction à la philosophie de Hegel. (Véra, A.) Paris, 1845-55. 3 pam.

Phil 3425.95.15   Introduction à la philosophie de Hegel. 2. éd. (Véra, A.) Paris, 1864.

Phil 8581.77A   Introduction à la philosophie de la prière. (Brémond, H.) Paris, 1929.

Phil 3425.319.15   Introduction à la philosophie de l'historie de Hegel. (Hyppolite, Jean.) Paris, 1948.

Phil 176.155   Introduction à la philosophie de l'individu. (Bouchet, Henri.) Paris, 1949.

Phil 182.102   Introduction à la philosophie expérimentale. (Haesaert, J.) Gand, 1920.

Phil 4080.3.275   Introduction à la philosophie politique de Benedetto Croce. (Comoth, René.) Liège, 1955.

Phil 337.28   Introduction à la psychiatrie de la connaissance. (Guilhot, Jean.) Paris, 1966.

Phil 5520.718   Introduction à la psycholinguistique. 1. éd. (Peterfalvi, Jean Michel.) Paris, 1970.

Phil 5251.25   Introduction à la psychologie. (Larguier des Bancels, Jean.) Paris, 1921.

Phil 5812.6   Introduction à la psychologie comparée. (Choisnard, Paul.) Paris, 1924.

Phil 5627.27.5   Introduction à la psychologie des convertis. (Mainage, T.) Paris, 1913.

Phil 5252.162   Introduction à la psychologie structurale. 2. ed. (Mucchielli, Roger.) Bruxelles, 1968.

Phil 270.3   Introduction à la recherche des causes premières. (Bertauld, P.A.) Paris, 1876.

Phil 6311.34   Introduction à la théorie des instincts. 1. éd. (Bonaparte, Marie.) Paris, 1951.

NEDL Phil 176.85.3   Introduction à la vie de l'esprit. 3e éd. (Brunschvicg, L.) Paris, 1920.

Phil 196.26.5   Introduction à la vie imparfaite. 1. ed. (Vialle, L.) Paris, 1947.

Phil 525.49   Introduction à la vie mystique. (Lejeune, Paul.) Paris, 1899.

Phil 7082.80   Introduction à l'analyse des rêves. (Baudouin, Charles.) Genève, 1945.

Phil 7082.80.1   Introduction à l'analyse des rêves. (Baudouin, Charles.) Paris, 1950.

Phil 346.17   Introduction à l'épistémologie génétique. 1. éd. (Piaget, Jean.) Paris, 1950. 3v.

Phil 8414.10   Introduction à l'esthétique. (Nédoncelle, M.) Paris, 1953.

Phil 4115.35   Introduction à l'étude de la philosophie. (Gioberti, V.) Moulins, 1845-47. 4v.

Phil 4115.36   Introduction à l'étude de la philosophie. (Gioberti, V.) Paris, 1847. 3v.

Phil 1020.9.3   Introduction à l'étude de la philosophie musulmane. (Gauthier, L.) Paris, 1923.

Phil 5243.31   Introduction à l'étude de la psychogénèse. (Dide, Maurice.) Paris, 1926.

Phil 5243.31.5   Introduction à l'étude de la psychogénèse. Thèse. (Dide, Maurice.) Paris, 1925. 2 pam.

Phil 813.4   Introduction à l'étude de l'histoire de la philosophie. (Nicolas, Michel.) Paris, 1849-50. 2v.

Phil 178.26.5   Introduction à l'étude des sciences humaines (Einleitung in die Geisteswissenschaften). 1re éd. (Dilthey, Wilhelm.) Paris, 1942.

Phil 6990.34.5   Introduction à l'étude du merveilleux et du miracle. 3. éd. (Touquédec, J. de.) Paris, 1923.

Phil 1522.4   Introduction à l'étude et à l'enseignement de la scolastique. (Richard, J.) Paris, 1913.

Phil 5525.60   Introduction à l'étude scientifique du rire. n.p., n.d.

Phil 8120.2   Introduction à l'histoire de l'esthétique. (Soreil, A.) Bruxelles, 1930.

Phil 8120.3   Introduction à l'histoire de l'esthétique française. (Soreil, A.) Bruxelles, 1955.

Phil 2725.35.65   Introduction à l'ontologie. 1. éd. (Lavelle, Louis.) Paris, 1947.

Phil 176.175   Introduction à tous les cours de philosophie. (Bounet, G.) Paris, 1952.

Phil 5865.5.10   Introduction à un examen philosophique de la psychologie de l'intelligence chez Jean Piaget. (Desbiens, Jean Paul.) Québec, 1968.

Phil 5635.15   Introduction à une étude du courant de chaleur. Thèse. (Desvaux, Antoine.) Paris, 1914.

Phil 4080.12.35   Introduction à une phenomenologie de notre epoque. (Castelli, Enrico.) Paris, 1949.

Phil 340.7   Introduction au problème de la connaissance. (Jacques, É.) Louvain, 1953.

Phil 181.76.5   Introduction au problème de l'histoire de la philosophie. (Guthrie, H.) Paris, 1937.

Phil 181.76   Introduction au problème de l'histoire de la philosophie. Thèse. (Guthrie, H.) Paris, 1937.

Phil 2515.6.5   Introduction au socialisme rationnel de Colins. (Rons, Ivo.) Neuchâtel, 1968.

Phil 2630.8.38   Introduction aux arts du beau. (Gilson, Étienne.) Paris, 1963.

Phil 1750.225   Introduction aux existentialismes. (Mounier, Emman.) Paris, 1947.

Phil 1540.94   Introduction aux mystiques rhéno-flamands. (Cognet, Louis.) Paris, 1968.

Phil 6322.21   Introduction biologique à l'étude de la neurologie et de la psychopathologie. (Monakow, Constantin von.) Paris, 1928.

Phil 5374.165   Introduction critique à une découverte de la pensée. (Nevratil, Michel.) Paris, 1954.

Phil 3838.10   Introduction critique aux oeuvres de Spinoza. (Saisset, Emile.) Paris, 1860.

Phil 295.4   Introduction du sens cosmique en philosophie. (Oliveira, I. de.) Paris, 1962.

Phil 176.112   Introduction générale à la philosophie. (Baudin, E.) Paris, 1927.

Phil 6116.9.5   Introduction physiologique à l'étude de la philosophie. (Grasset, Joseph.) Paris, 1908.

Phil 6122.57   An introduction to a Christian psycho-therapy. (Murray, J.A.C.) Edinburgh, 1938.

Phil 8587.82   Introduction to a philosophy of religion. (Hildebrand, Alice M. (Jourdain) von.) Chicago, 1971.

Phil 6328.10.21   Introduction to a psychoanalytic psychiatry. (Schilder, Paul.) N.Y., 1928.

Phil 6315.14   An introduction to abnormal psychology. (Fisher, Vivian E.) N.Y., 1929.

Phil 8403.13   An introduction to aesthetics. (Canitt, Edgar.) London, 1949.

Phil 850.21A   An introduction to ancient philosophy. (Armstrong, A.H.) London, 1947.

Phil 850.21.5   An introduction to ancient philosophy. 2d ed. (Armstrong, A.H.) London, 1949.

Phil 850.21.10   An introduction to ancient philosophy. 3d ed. (Armstrong, A.H.) London, 1957.

Phil 850.21.11   An introduction to ancient philosophy. 3d ed. (Armstrong, A.H.) Westminster, Md., 1959.

Phil 5822.8   An introduction to animal psychology. (Munn, Norman L.) Boston, 1933.

Phil 5850.222   An introduction to applied psychology. (Griffith, C.R.) N.Y., 1936.

Phil 4752.2.90   Introduction to Berdyaev. (Clarke, O.G.) London, 1950.

Phil 5645.58   Introduction to color. (Evans, Ralph M.) N.Y., 1961.

Phil 525.105   Introduction to comparative mysticism. (Marquette, Jacques de.) N.Y., 1949.

Phil 192.114   Introduction to comparative philosophy. (Raju, P.) Lincoln, 1962.

Phil 5822.1A   Introduction to comparative psychology. (Morgan, C.L.) London, 1884.

Phil 5822.1.3   Introduction to comparative psychology. (Morgan, C.L.) London, 1894.

Phil 3001.12   An introduction to contemporary German philosophy. (Brock, Werner.) Cambridge, 1935.

Phil 5062.37   An introduction to critical thinking. (Wérkmeister, W.H.) Lincoln, Neb., 1948.

NEDL Phil 1925.81   Introduction to Cudworth's treatise...with life. (Scott, William Robert.) London, 1891.

Phil 5051.32   An introduction to deductive logic. (Leblanc, H.) N.Y., 1955.

Phil 8884.13   An introduction to ethics, for training colleges. (Johnston, George A.) London, 1915.

Phil 2672.35   Introduction to ethics. (Jouffroy, Théodore S.) Boston, 1840. 2v.

Phil 2672.35.1   Introduction to ethics. (Jouffroy, Théodore S.) Boston, 1841. 2v.

Phil 2672.35.2   Introduction to ethics. (Jouffroy, Théodore S.) Boston, 1845. 2v.

Phil 2672.35.10   Introduction to ethics. (Jouffroy, Théodore S.) Boston, 1873. 2v.

Phil 8887.124   An introduction to ethics. (Mabbott, John David.) London, 1966.

Phil 8887.26   An introduction to ethics. (Murray, J.C.) Paisley, 1891.

Phil 8894.11.5   Introduction to ethics. (Thilly, F.) N.Y., 1913.

Phil 2672.35.3   Introduction to ethics. v.1-2. (Jouffroy, Théodore S.) Boston, 1858.

Phil 8886.72   An introduction to ethics. 3. ed. (Lillie, William.) London, 1957.

Phil 1750.710   An introduction to existentialism. (Olson, Robert.) N.Y., 1962.

Phil 5274.20   An introduction to experimental design in psychology. (Johnson, Homer H.) N.Y., 1971.

Phil 5245.39   An introduction to experimental psychology. (Finner, P.F.) N.Y., 1935.

Phil 5252.19.8   An introduction to experimental psychology. (Myers, C.S.) Cambridge, 1911.

Phil 4200.2.15   An introduction to Francesco Patrizi's Nova de universis philosophia. Thesis. (Brickman, Benjamin.) N.Y., 1941.

Phil 5049.12.5   An introduction to general logic. (Jones, E.E.C.) London, 1892.

Phil 187.156.5   An introduction to general metaphysics. (Martin, Gottfried.) London, 1961.

Phil 5254.1   An introduction to general psychology. (Ogden, R.M.) N.Y., 1914.

Phil 2020.86   Introduction to Green's moral philosophy. (Lamont, W.D.) London, 1934.

Phil 7140.140   An introduction to group therapy. (Slavson, S.R.) N.Y., 1943.

Phil 7140.140.6   An introduction to group therapy. (Slavson, S.R.) N.Y., 1954.

Phil 3425.302   Introduction to Hegel. (Mure, G.R.G.) Oxford, 1940.

Phil 3425.718   An introduction to Hegel's metaphysics. (Soll, Ivan.) Chicago, 1969.

Phil 3425.56.20   The introduction to Hegel's Philosophy of fine art. (Hegel, Georg Wilhelm Friedrich.) London, 1886.

Phil 3425.56.5   The introduction to Hegel's Philosophy of fine art. (Hegel, Georg Wilhelm Friedrich.) London, 1905.

Phil 1703.1   Introduction to History of modern philosophy. (Dewing, Arthur Stone.) Philadelphia, 1903.

Phil 960.132   Introduction to Indian philosophy. (Prasad, Jwala.) Allahabad, 1928.

Phil 960.165   An introduction to Indian philosophy. 4th ed. (Chatterjee, S.) Calcutta, 1950.

Phil 5243.41.5   An introduction to individual psychology. (Dreikurs, Rudolf.) London, 1935.

Phil 5850.341   An introduction to industrial psychology. (Smith, May.) London, 1943.

Phil 1020.47   An introduction to Islamic cosmological doctrines. (Naso, S.H.) Cambridge, 1964.

Phil 6319.1.188   An introduction to Jung's psychology. (Fordham, F.) London, 1953.

Phil 3504.14   An introduction to Kant's critical philosophy. (Whitney, G.J.) N.Y., 1914.

Phil 3504.44   Introduction to Kant's Critique of pure reason. (Weldon, Thomas D.) Oxford, 1945.

Phil 3484.12   An introduction to Kant's philosophy. (Clark, Norman.) London, 1925.

Phil 1717.11.15   An introduction to living philosophy. (Robinson, D.S.) N.Y., 1932.

Phil 5041.75   Introduction to logic. (Bachhuber, A.H.) N.Y., 1957.

Phil 5042.65   Introduction to logic. (Clark, Romane.) Princeton, N.J., 1962.

Phil 5047.6   Introduction to logic. (Hinds, Samuel.) Oxford, 1827.

Phil 5052.36   An introduction to logic. (Maritain, J.) London, 1937.

Phil 5052.8   An introduction to logic. (Monck, W.H.S.) Dublin, 1880.

Phil 5057.41   Introduction to logic. (Rescher, N.) N.Y., 1964.

Phil 5057.14   An introduction to logic. (Russell, L.J.) London, 1914.

Phil 5058.70.9   Introduction to logic. (Suppes, Patrick.) Princeton, N.J., 1966.

Phil 5058.70.10   Introduction to logic. (Suppes, Patrick.) Princeton, N.J., 1968.

Phil 3480.70.10A   Introduction to logic. Photoreproduction. (Kant, Immanuel.) London, 1885.

Phil 5049.9.5   An introduction to logic. 2nd rev. ed. (Joseph, Horace William Brindley.) Oxford, 1931.

Phil 5049.9.2.1   An introduction to logic. 2nd rev. ed. (Joseph, Horace William Brindley.) Oxford, 1967.

Phil 5042.25   Introduction to logic and scientific method. (Cohen, Morris R.) N.Y., 1934.

Phil 5042.25.2   Introduction to logic and scientific method. (Cohen, Morris R.) N.Y., 1936.

Phil 5058.60   Introduction to logic theory. (Strawson, P.F.) London, 1952.

Phil 5058.17   An introduction to logical science. (Spalding, W.) Edinburgh, 1857.

Phil 5041.95   An introduction to logick, 1773. (Bentham, Edward.) Menston, 1967.

Phil 5535.1   An introduction to mathematical learning theory. (Atkinson, Richard G.) N.Y., 1965.

Phil 5066.14.5A   Introduction to mathematical logic. (Church, Alonzo.) Princeton, 1956.

Phil 5066.288   An introduction to mathematical logic. (Robison, Gerson B.) Englewood Cliffs, 1969.

Phil 5272.10   Introduction to mathematical psychology. (Restle, Frank.) Reading, Mass., 1970.

Phil 6116.21.5   Introduction to mental hygiene. (Groves, E.R.) N.Y., 1930.

Phil 5252.9.5   Introduction to mental philosophy. (Morell, J.D.) London, 1862.

Phil 2475.1.56.2   An introduction to metaphysics. (Bergson, Henri.) London, 1913.

Phil 2475.1.56   An introduction to metaphysics. (Bergson, Henri.) N.Y., 1912.

Phil 182.93.12   An introduction to metaphysics. (Heidegger, M.) New Haven, 1959.

Phil 197.8   Introduction to metaphysics. (Wilson, W.D.) Ithaca, 1872.

Phil 5254.8   An introduction to method in psychology. 2d ed. (O'Neil, William Matthew.) Parkville, 1962.

Phil 1750.700   Introduction to modern existentialism. (Breisach, Ernst.) N.Y., 1962.

Phil 5051.12   An introduction to modern logic. (Lodge, Rupert C.) Minneapolis, 1920.

Phil 1702.7   An introduction to modern philosophy. (Castell, Alburey.) N.Y., 1943.

Phil 1709.2   Introduction to modern philosophy. (Joad, C.E.M.) London, 1924.

Phil 1750.166.175 — Introduction to modernity. (Mollenauer, Robert.) Austin, 1965.

Phil 5548.85.5 — An introduction to motivation. (Atkinson, John W.) Princeton, 1964.

Phil 6117.20 — An introduction to neurology. (Herrick, C.J.) Philadelphia, 1916.

Phil 6117.43 — Introduction to neurology. (Herrick, C.J.) Philadelphia, 1918.

Phil 6117.20.5 — An introduction to neurology. 3. ed. (Herrick, C.J.) Philadelphia, 1924.

Phil 6117.20.10 — An introduction to neurology. 5th ed. (Herrick, C.J.) Philadelphia, 1934.

Phil 6317.15 — An introduction to objective psychopathology. (Hamilton, Gilbert V.) St. Louis, 1925.

Phil 2255.10.32 — Introduction to objectivist epistemology. (Rand, Ayn.) N.Y., 1967.

Phil 2055.8.35 — An introduction to organic philosophy. (Hyde, Lawrence.) Reigate, 1955.

Phil 2225.5.100 — An introduction to Peirce's philosophy. 1st ed. (Feibleman, James.) N.Y., 1946.

Phil 5590.100 — An introduction to personality study. (Cattell, R.B.) London, 1950.

Phil 182.114.7 — An introduction to philosophical analysis. (Hospers, John.) Englewood Cliffs, 1967.

Phil 182.114 — An introduction to philosophical analysis. (Hospers, John.) London, 1956.

Phil 5227.10 — An introduction to philosophical psychology. (Reith, Herman.) Englewood Cliffs, N.J., 1956.

Phil 176.94 — An introduction to philosophy. (Brightman, E.S.) N.Y., 1925.

Phil 177.49 — An introduction to philosophy. (Cunningham, H.E.) Boston, 1920.

Phil 805.3 — Introduction to philosophy. (Fletcher, O.O.) N.Y., 1913.

Phil 180.17.5 — An introduction to philosophy. (Fullerton, G.S.) N.Y., 1906.

Phil 180.17.12 — An introduction to philosophy. (Fullerton, G.S.) N.Y., 1921.

Phil 184.12.5 — Introduction to philosophy. (Jerusalem, W.) N.Y., 1910.

Phil 184.12.7 — Introduction to philosophy. (Jerusalem, W.) N.Y., 1932.

Phil 185.12 — Introduction to philosophy. (Külpe, O.) London, 1897.

Phil 186.16 — Introduction to philosophy. (Ladd, G.T.) N.Y., 1890.

Phil 811.9 — Introduction to philosophy. (Lewis, John.) London, 1937.

Phil 187.60.7 — An introduction to philosophy. (Maritain, J.) London, 1937.

Phil 2750.11.52 — An introduction to philosophy. (Maritain, Jacques.) London, 1930.

Phil 190.56 — Introduction to philosophy. (Patrick, G.T.W.) Boston, 1924.

Phil 190.56.5 — Introduction to philosophy. (Patrick, G.T.W.) London, 1935.

Phil 192.85 — Introduction to philosophy. (Raeymaeker, Louis de.) N.Y., 1948.

Phil 192.96 — Introduction to philosophy. (Rosenberg, Max.) N.Y., 1955.

Phil 1717.12 — An introduction to philosophy. (Russell, Leonard.) London, 1929.

Phil 192.50 — An introduction to philosophy. (Ryan, J.H.) N.Y., 1924.

Phil 193.158 — An introduction to philosophy. (Sinclair, W.A.) London, 1944.

Phil 197.9.15 — Introduction to philosophy. (Windelband, W.) London, 1921.

Phil 190.3.7 — Introduction to philosophy. 2. American ed. (Paulsen, F.) N.Y., 1928.

Phil 190.3.7.5 — Introduction to philosophy. 2. American ed. (Paulsen, F.) N.Y., 1930.

Phil 193.179 — Introduction to philosophy. 2d. ed. (Sinha, Jadunath.) Calcutta, 1957.

Phil 165.7 — An introduction to philosophy through literature. (Baldwin, R.C.) N.Y., 1950.

Phil 6115.26 — Introduction to physiological psychology. (Freeman, G.L.V.) N.Y., 1934.

Phil 5265.1.6 — Introduction to physiological psychology. (Ziehen, Theodor.) London, 1895.

Phil 5265.1.5 — Introduction to physiological psychology. (Ziehen, Theodor.) n.p., 1892.

Phil 5548.75 — An introduction to psychoanalytic theory of motivation. (Toman, Walter.) N.Y., 1960.

Phil 5258.187 — Introduction to psychological research. (Scott, William.) N.Y., 1962.

Phil 5272.2 — An introduction to psychological statistics. (Du Bois, Philip Hunter.) N.Y., 1965.

Phil 5241.15 — Introduction to psychological theory. (Bowne, B.P.) N.Y., 1887.

Phil 5240.6.9 — An introduction to psychology. (Angell, J.R.) N.Y., 1918.

Phil 5241.52 — An introduction to psychology. (Brierley, S.S. (Mrs.).) London, 1921.

Phil 5242.13 — An introduction to psychology. (Calkins, M.W.) N.Y., 1901.

Phil 5247.58 — Introduction to psychology. (Hughes, P.) Bethlehem Pa., 1928.

Phil 5250.40 — An introduction to psychology. (Karn, H.W.) N.Y., 1955.

Phil 5252.67 — An introduction to psychology. (Morgan, John J.B.) N.Y., 1927.

Phil 5252.69.15 — An introduction to psychology. (Murphy, Gardner.) N.Y., 1951.

Phil 5252.14.5 — An introduction to psychology. (Murray, J.C.) Boston, 1904.

Phil 5257.38 — An introduction to psychology. (Reyburn, H.A.) Cape Town, 1924.

Phil 5258.34.13 — Introduction to psychology. (Seashore, C.E.) N.Y., 1923.

Phil 3915.49A — Introduction to psychology. (Wundt, Wilhelm.) London, 1912.

Phil 5264.2.2 — Introduction to psychology. (Yerkes, R.M.) N.Y., 19l1.

Phil 5247.66.3 — Introduction to psychology. 3. ed. (Hilgard, Ernest R.) N.Y., 1962.

Phil 5252.82.13 — Introduction to psychology. 3d ed. (Morgan, Clifford Thomas.) N.Y., 1966.

Phil 6980.721 — An introduction to psychotherapy. (Tarachow, S.) N.Y., 1963.

Phil 630.49 — Introduction to realistic philosophy. (Wild, John.) N.Y., 1948.

Phil 5042.15A — An introduction to reflective thinking. (Columbia Association in Philosophy.) Boston, 1923.

Phil 8592.105 — Introduction to religious philosophy. (MacGregor, Geddes.) London, 1960.

Phil 1527.1.10 — An introduction to scholastic philosophy. (Wulf, M. de.) N.Y., 1956.

Phil 6313.15 — Introduction to scientology. 2d ed. (De Mille, A.) Los Angeles, 1953.

Phil 5066.8 — Introduction to semantics. (Carnap, Rudolf.) Cambridge, 1942.

Phil 5520.325.2 — Introduction to semantics. (Schaff, Adam.) N.Y., 1962.

Phil 5066.8.2 — Introduction to semantics and formalization of logic. (Carnap, Rudolf.) Cambridge, 1959.

Phil 8887.51 — An introduction to social ethics. (Mecklin, John M.) N.Y., 1920.

Phil 5252.18.6 — An introduction to social psychology. (McDougall, William.) Boston, 1926.

Phil 5252.18.5.4 — An introduction to social psychology. 3d ed. (McDougall, William.) London, 1910.

Phil 5252.18.3 — An introduction to social psychology. 15th ed. (McDougall, William.) Boston, 1923.

Phil 5585.60 — An introduction to space perception. (Carr, H.A.) N.Y., 1935.

Phil 4265.3.30 — Introduction to speculative logic and philosophy. (Vera, A.) St. Louis, 1873.

Phil 3838.21 — An introduction to Spinoza's Ethic. (Shauki, Alexander.) London, 1938.

Phil 680.25 — Introduction to structuralism. (Lane, Michael.) N.Y., 1970.

Phil 1865.80 — Introduction to study of Bentham's works. (Burton, J.H.) Edinburgh, 1843.

Phil 5645.15 — Introduction to study of colour vision. (Parsons, J.H.) Cambridge, 1915.

Phil 181.6 — An introduction to study of philosophy. (Gerhart, E.V.) Philadelphia, 1858.

Phil 5066.58 — Introduction to symbolic logic. (Basson, A.H.) London, 1953.

Phil 5051.27A — An introduction to symbolic logic. (Langer, S.K. (Mrs.).) Boston, 1937.

Phil 5066.58.2 — Introduction to symbolic logic. 2nd ed. (Basson, A.H.) London, 1957.

Phil 5066.52.2 — An introduction to symbolic logic. 2nd ed. (Langer, S.K.K.) N.Y., 1953.

Phil 5066.8.10 — Introduction to symbolic logic and its applications. (Carnap, Rudolf.) N.Y., 1958.

Phil 187.26 — Introduction to systematic philosophy. (Marvin, W.T.) N.Y., 1903.

Phil 2905.1.130.5 — An introduction to Teilhard de Chardin. 1st American ed. (Wildiers, N.M.) N.Y., 1968.

Phil 9558.6 — An introduction to the art of lying. London, 1744.

Phil 8882.20 — Introduction to the art of thinking. (Home, H.) Edinburgh, 1764.

Phil 3494.6 — Introduction to the critical philosophy. (Monck, W.H.S.) Dublin, 1874.

Phil 5243.45 — Introduction to the fields of psychology. (Dexter, E.S.) N.Y., 1938.

Phil 802.2.8 — Introduction to the history of philosophy. (Cousin, V.) Boston, 1832.

Phil 5052.27 — An introduction to the logic of reflection. (McClure, M.T.) N.Y., 1925.

Phil 525.49.5 — An introduction to the mystical life. (Lejeune, Paul.) London, 1915.

Phil 1750.775 — Introduction to the new existentialism. (Wilson, Colin.) London, 1966.

Phil 2100.4.30 — An introduction to the philosophy of animate nature. (Koren, H.J.) St. Louis, 1955.

Phil 185.67.5 — Introduction to the philosophy of being. (Klubertanz, G.P.) N.Y., 1955.

Phil 2270.92.90 — An introduction to the philosophy of Herbert Spencer. (Hudson, William Henry.) N.Y., 1894.

Phil 2270.93 — An introduction to the philosophy of Herbert Spencer. 2nd ed. (Hudson, William Henry.) N.Y., 1900.

Phil 291.8.5 — An introduction to the philosophy of nature. (Koren, Henry.) Pittsburg, 1960.

Phil 8582.1.2 — An introduction to the philosophy of religion. (Caird, J.) N.Y., 1880.

Phil 8582.64 — An introduction to the philosophy of religion. (Caird, John.) N.Y., 1881.

Htn Phil 1865.49* — An introduction to the principles of morals and legislation. (Bentham, Jeremy.) London, 1789.

Phil 1865.51.10 — An introduction to the principles of morals and legislation. (Bentham, Jeremy.) Oxford, 1907.

Htn Phil 1865.50.1* — Introduction to the principles of morals and legislation. (Bentham, Jeremy.) London, 1823. 2v.

Phil 1865.51A — An introduction to the principles of morals and legislation. (Bentham, Jeremy.) N.Y., 1948.

Phil 1865.51.15 — An introduction to the principles of morals and legislation. (Bentham, Jeromy.) London, 1970.

Phil 1865.50 — Introduction to the principles of morals and legislation. v.1-2. (Bentham, Jeremy.) London, 1823.

Phil 6328.21.8 — Introduction to the psychoanalytic theory of the libido. 3d ed. (Sterba, Richard.) N.Y., 1968.

Phil 5520.646 — An introduction to the psychology of language. (Herriot, Peter.) London, 1970.

Phil 5627.59 — An introduction to the psychology of religion. (Thouless, Robert H.) N.Y., 1923.

Phil 5627.59.5 — An introduction to the psychology of religion. 2. ed. (Thouless, Robert H.) Cambridge, Eng., 1928.

Phil 3425.321.5 — Introduction to the reading of Hegel. (Kojève, Alexandre.) N.Y., 1969.

Phil 8886.25 — Introduction to the science of ethics. (Laguna, T. de.) N.Y., 1914.

Phil 8413.22 — Introduction to the study of aesthetics. (Moffat, J.C.) Cincinnati, 1856.

Phil 6673.4.19 — An introduction to the study of animal magnetism. (Du Potet, J. de S.) London, 1838.

Phil 960.172 — An introduction to the study of Hinduism. 2. ed. (Pal, B.C.) Calcutta, 1951.

Phil 3110.85.50 — An introduction to the study of Jacob Boehme's writings. (Penny. A.J.) N.Y., 1901.

Phil 176.113 — An introduction to the study of logic and metaphysics. (Barrett, Thomas S.) London, 1875.

Phil 182.5 — Introduction to the study of philosophy. (Harris, W.T.) N.Y., 1889.

Phil 187.56.9 — Introduction to the study of philosophy. (McTaggart, J.M.E.) Cambridge, Eng., 190-.

Phil 814.1 — An introduction to the study of philosophy. (Oldham, A.) Dublin, 1909.

Phil 193.42 — Introduction to the study of philosophy. (Stuckenberg, J.H.W.) N.Y., 1888.

Phil 184.8.5 — Introduction to the study of philosophy. 2. ed. (Johnson, Samuel.) London, 1743.

Phil 6132.43 — An introduction to the study of the mind. (White, William Alanson.) Washington, 1924.

Phil 5585.39A — An introduction to the theory of perception. (Parsons, John H.) Cambridge, 1927.

Phil 6320.11.80 Introduction to the work of M. Klein. (Segal, H.) N.Y., 1964.

Phil 7054.6.50 Introduction to the writings of Andrew J. Davis. (Davis, A.J.) Boston, 1930.

Phil 5249.22 An introduction to theory and practice of psychology. (Jones, Llewellyn W.) London, 1934.

Phil 3791.36 Introduction to theory of science and metaphysics. (Riehl, Alois.) London, 1894.

Phil 735.268 Introduction to value theory. (Rescher, Nicholas.) Englewood Cliffs, N.J., 1969.

Phil 802.23 An introduction to Western philosophy. (Coleburt, Russell.) N.Y., 1957.

Phil 2070.157 Introduction to William James. (Reck, Andrew J.) Bloomington, 1967.

Phil 3925.16.265 An introduction to Wittgenstein's Tractatus. (Anscombe, Gertrude Elizabeth Margaret.) London, 1959.

Htn Phil 6045.22.15* Introductiones apostelesmaticae in physiognomiam. (Indagine, Joannes.) Argentorati, 1622.

Phil 6045.22.17 Introductiones apotelesmaticae in physiognomiam. (Indagine, Joannes.) Argentorati, 1630.

Phil 6045.22.19 Introductiones apotilesmaticae in physiognomiam. (Indagine, Joannes.) Argentorati, 1672.

Phil 5520.750 Introductions à la sémiologie. (Mounin, Georges.) Paris, 1971.

Phil 176.126 Introductioon to philosophical analysis. (Burnham, James.) N.Y., 1932.

Phil 8896.13 An introductory address to the course of lectures before the young men's Association for MutualImprovement in the city of Albany. (Vermilye, T.E.) Albany, 1837.

Phil 6316.20 Introductory clinical psychology. (Garfield, Sol.) N.Y., 1961.

Phil 188.19 Introductory course in philosophy. (Nicholson, J.A.) N.Y., 1939.

Phil 187.33.5 Introductory course in philosophy. Syllabus. (Montague, W.P.) N.Y., 1920.

Phil 6315.2.6 Introductory lecture on psycho-analysis. (Freud, Sigmund.) London, 1922.

Phil 5262.5 Introductory lessons on mind. (Whately, R.) Boston, 1859.
Phil 5262.5.2 Introductory lessons on mind. (Whately, R.) London, 1859.
Phil 8897.13 Introductory lessons on morals. (Whately, R.) Cambridge, 1856.

Phil 8897.13.3 Introductory lessons on morals. (Whately, R.) Cambridge, 1860.

Phil 8897.13.5 Introductory lessons on morals. (Whately, R.) London, 1855.

Phil 5042.7 An introductory logic. (Creighton, J.E.) N.Y., 1898.
Phil 5042.7.2 An introductory logic. (Creighton, J.E.) N.Y., 1900.
Phil 5042.29 An introductory logic. (Creighton, J.E.) N.Y., 1938.
Phil 5042.7.3 An introductory logic. 3rd ed. (Creighton, J.E.) N.Y., 1909.

Phil 5042.29.5 An introductory logic. 4th ed. (Creighton, J.E.) N.Y., 1923.

Phil 5042.7.10 An introductory logic. 4th ed. (Creighton, J.E.) N.Y., 1927.

Phil 178.21 Introductory philosophy. (Dubray, C.A.) N.Y., 1912.
Phil 5242.62 Introductory psychology for students of education. (Conklin, Edmund Smith.) N.Y., 1939.

Phil 8880.18.2 An introductory study of ethics. (Fite, Warner.) N.Y., 1906.

Phil 5052.9.9 An introductory text-book of logic. 9th ed. (Mellone, S.H.) Edinburgh, 1917.

Phil 4260.140 Introduzione a G.B. Vico. (Badaloni, Nicola.) Milano, 1961.

Phil 2150.22.97 Introduzione a Marcuse. 2. ed. (Proto, Mario.) Manduria, 1968.

Phil 310.756 Introduzione a una dialettica dei complementari. (Conz, Gianni.) Padova, 1970.

Phil 5190.36 Introduzione ai problemi dell'assiomatica. (Agazzi, Evandro.) Milano, 1961.

Phil 630.60 Introduzione al realismo critico. (Ruvo, Vincenzo de.) Padova, 1964.

Phil 3494.44 Introduzione alla analitica Kantiaña. Serie 2. (Massolo, Arturo.) Firenze, 1946.

Phil 4170.18.30 Introduzione alla critica della scienza. (Magnini, Carlomagno.) Bologna, 1969.

Phil 1750.115.140 Introduzione alla fenomenologia come scienza. (Sini, Carlo.) Milano, 1965.

Phil 4120.4.45 Introduzione alla filosofia. (Gentile, Giovanni.) Milano, 1933.

Phil 4170.5.30 Introduzione alla filosofia. (Maturi, S.) Bari, 1913.
Phil 187.151 Introduzione alla filosofia. (Miceli di Serradileo, Riccardo.) Roma, 1957.

Phil 190.3.8 Introduzione alla filosofia. (Paulsen, F.) Milano, 1911.
Phil 4210.20 Introduzione alla filosofia. (Rosmini-Serbati, Antonio.) Casalle, 1850.

Phil 193.122 Introduzione alla filosofia. (Sarlo, F. de.) Milano, 1928.

Htn Phil 196.21* Introduzione alla filosofia. (Varvaro, Paolo.) Palermo, 1925.

Phil 4210.20.10 Introduzione alla filosofia. v.1-4. (Rosmini-Serbati, Antonio.) Torino, 1924-25. 2v.

Phil 4120.4.90 Introduzione alla filosofia. 2. ed. (Gentile, Giovanni.) Firenze, 1952.

Phil 3428.31 Introduzione alla filosofia. 2. ed. (Herbart, J.F.) Bari, 1927.

Phil 190.40.2 Introduzione alla filosofia. 2a ed. (Piccoli, V.) Milano, 1924.

Phil 1750.835 Introduzione alla filosofia come metocultura. (Penati, Giancarlo.) Milano, 1968.

Phil 2840.91 Introduzione alla filosofia del Renouvier. (Concato, E.) Marostica Vicenza, 1921.

Phil 2775.5.80 Introduzione alla filosofia dell' amore di Maurice Nédoncelle. (Valenziano, Crispino.) Roma, 1965.

Phil 5400.51 Introduzione alla filosofia dell'affetto. (Festa, Alfonso.) Piacenza, 1829.

Phil 4001.4 L'introduzione alla filosofia delle scuole italiane. (Bonavino, C.) Italia, 1852.

Phil 177.97 Introduzione alla filosofia e dottrina della practica. (Caramella, S.) Messina, 1936.

Phil 5251.2 Introduzione alla filosofia naturale di pensiero. (Lallebasque.) Lugano, 1824.

Phil 5045.4 Introduzione alla logica. (Ferrari, Ambrogio.) Alessandria, 1895.

Phil 5066.140 Introduzione alla logica simbolica. (Pasquinelli, Alberto.) Torino, 1957.

Phil 8400.26 Introduzione alla metafisica della poesia. (Pastore, A.) Padova, 1957. 2 pam.

Phil 5593.58.5 Introduzione alla psicodiagnosi di Rorschach. (Chiari, Silvano.) Firenze, 1958.

Phil 8892.32 Introduzione alla scepsi etica. (Rensi, Giuseppe.) Firenze, n.d.

Phil 5520.480.2 Introduzione alla semantica. 2. ed. (Mauro, Tullio de.) Bari, 1966.

Phil 1116.5 Introduzione alla storia della filosofia greca e appendice di testi tradotti. (Lasacco, Michele.) Bari, 1929.

Phil 177.62 Introduzione alla teoria dell'essere le relazioni ontotetiche. (Cicala, F.B.) Città di Castello, 1923.

Phil 4015.6 Introduzione all'aristotelismo padovano. (Poppi, Antonino.) Padova, 1970.

Phil 8660.21 Introduzione all'ateismo moderno. (Fabro, Conelio.) Roma, 1964.

Phil 9560.19 Introduzione alle virtù. (Rosini, G.) Firenze, 1810.
Phil 1750.270.5 Introduzione all'esistenzialismo. (Abbagnano, Nicola.) Torino, 1947.

Phil 1750.270.8 Introduzione all'esistenzialismo. 3. ed. (Abbagnano, Nicola.) Torino, 1948.

Phil 4080.3.120 Introduzione allo studio...B. Croce. (Castellano, G.) Bari, 1920.

Phil 4112.31 Introduzione allo studio della filosofia. (Galluppi, Pasquale.) Milano, 1832.

Phil 4115.34.6 Introduzione allo studio della filosofia. (Gioberti, V.) Firenze, 1926.

Phil 4115.34 Introduzione allo studio della filosofia. (Gioberti, V.) Milano, 1850. 2v.

Phil 4115.33 Introduzione allo studio della filosofia. v.1-2. (Gioberti, V.) Brusselle, 1840. 3v.

Phil 4115.33.10 Introduzione allo studio della filosofia. v.1-4. (Gioberti, V.) Napoli, 1846-47.

Phil 4115.33.5 Introduzione allo studio della filosofia. 2a ed. v.1-4. (Gioberti, V.) Capolago, 1845-46. 2v.

Phil 960.27 Introduzione allo studio della filosofia indiana. (Suali, Luigi.) Pavia, 1913.

Phil 4260.121 Introduzione allo studio di G.B. Vico. (Amerio, Franco.) Torino, 1947.

Phil 3503.10 Introduzione allo studio di Kant. (Vanni Rovighi, Sofia.) Como, 1945.

Phil 5252.45.5 Introduzione generale alla psicologia. (Masci, Filippo.) Milano, 1926.

Phil 8448.20 Introspection: the artist looks at himself. Tulsa, 1971.
Phil 672.136.30 Intrusions? (Dunne, John W.) London, 1955.
Phil 180.58 Intuicion del ser. (Finlayson Elliot, Clarence.) Santiago, 1938.

Phil 2125.81 De intuitieve philosophie van James McCosh. (Volbeda, S.) Grand Rapids, n.d.

Phil 342.3.10 L'intuition, la matière et la vie. (Losskii, N.) Paris, 1928.

Phil 5262.39A Intuition. (Wild, K.W.) Cambridge, Eng., 1938.
Phil 4600.2.45 Intuition. 3e uppl. (Larsson, Hans.) Stockholm, 1910.
Phil 4600.2.46 Intuition. 4e uppl. (Larsson, Hans.) Stockholm, 1920.
Phil 2475.1.89 L'intuition Bergsonienne. (Segoud, J.) Paris, 1913.
Phil 2750.11.160 L'intuition dans la philosophie de Jacques Maritain. (Sampaio, L.F.A.) Paris, 1963.

Phil 672.155 L'intuition de l'instant. (Bachelard, Gaston.) Paris, 1932.

Phil 672.239 L'intuition de l'instant. (Bachelard, Gaston.) Paris, 1966.

Phil 6969.7 L'intuition délirante. (Targowla, René.) Paris, 1931.
Phil 5258.64 Intuition et anitié. (Segond, J.) Paris, 1919.
Phil 5255.25.5 Intuition et réflexion. Thèse. (Paliard, Jacques.) Paris, 1925.

NEDL Phil 176.51.20 Intuition og rerdansanskueke oversat af Knud Terlov. (Bergson, H.) Kobenhavn, 1914.

Phil 420.4 Intuition und Begriff. (Rothacker, Erich.) Bonn, 1963.
Phil 2750.11.200 Intuition und Transzendenz. (Reiter, Josef.) München, 1967.

Phil 5252.115 Intuition versus intellect. (Maslow, Paul.) N.Y., 1957.
Phil 2475.1.198 Der Intuitionismus und seine Elemente bei Henri Bergson. (Meckauer, Walter.) Leipzig, 1917.

Phil 8876.24.5 Intuitions and summaries of thought. (Bovee, C.N.) Boston, 1862. 2v.

Phil 2125.52 Intuitions of the mind. (McCosh, James.) London, 1860.
Phil 2125.52.5 Intuitions of the mind. 3rd ed. (McCosh, James.) N.Y., 1874.

Phil 4600.2.44 Intuitionsproblemet. (Larsson, Hans.) Stockholm, 1912.
Phil 342.3.5 The intuitive basis of knowledge. (Losskii, N.) London, 1919.

Phil 630.3 Intuitive perception, presented by a new philosophy of natural realism. (Hodge, W.H.) Lancaster, 1903.

Phil 1750.132.10 The intuitive voluntarism of Irving Babbitt. (Grosselin, O.) Latrohe, Pa., 1951.

Phil 340.2 L'intuito nella conoscenza. (Jaja, Donato.) Napoli, 1894.
Phil 4080.3.129 L'intuizione di Benedetto Croce. (Zanacchi, G.) Palermo, 1925.

Phil 187.87 L'intuizione e la verità di fatto saggio; psicologico-metafisico. (Montalto, F.) Roma, 1924.

Phil 187.87.5 L'intuizione e la verità di fatto saggio; psicologico-metafisico. 2. ed. (Montalto, F.) Roma, 1930.

Phil 2270.136 Le intuizioni morali e l'eredità nello Spencer. (Pagnone, A.) Torino, 1897.

Phil 5380.90.5 The invasion from Mars. (Cantril, H.) Princeton, 1947.
Phil 6327.21.46 The invasion of compulsory sex-morality. (Reich, Wilhelm.) N.Y., 1971.

Phil 3837.4 Inventaire de livrés de B. Spinoza. (Rovijen, A.J.L. van.) La Haye, 1888.

Phil 5465.33 L'invention. (Bouthoul, G.) Paris, 1930.
Phil 5722.23.10 Invention and the unconscious. (Montmasson, J.M.) London, 1931.

Phil 8592.100 L'invention divine. (Martin-Deslias, N.) Paris, 1957.
Phil 5465.212 L'inventique. (Kaufmann, Arnold.) Paris, 1970.
Phil 5465.128 Inventivity. (Mueller, Robert E.) N.Y., 1963.
Phil 2515.3.32 L'invérifiable; les problèmes de la métaphysique. 2e éd. (Cresson, A.) Paris, 1920.

Phil 8893.105 Investigaciones sobre la estructura aporético-dialéctica. (Sambarino, Mario.) Montevideo, 1959-60.

Phil 5828.7 The investigation of mind in animals. (Smith, E.M.) Cambridge, 1915.

Phil 5828.7.2 The investigation of mind in animals. 2. ed. (Smith, E.M.) Cambridge, 1923.

Phil 5041.15.6 An investigation of the laws of thought. (Boole, George.) N.Y., 1951.

Phil 170.3 Investigation of the principles of knowledge. (Hutton, James.) Edinburgh, 1794. 3v.

Phil 6316.12 An investigation of the technique of psycho-analysis. (Glover, Edward.) Baltimore, 1940.

Phil 6317.29 Invisible anatomy. (Howe, Eric Graham.) London, 1944.

Phil 6310.10 The invisible curtain. (Anthony, Joseph.) N.Y., 1957.
Phil 978.8.30 Invisible helpers. (Leadbeater, C.W.) London, 1899.
Phil 8886.36 An invisible kingdom. (Lilly, William S.) London, 1919.
Phil 4600.7.30 Invita Minerva. (Lagerborg, Rolf.) Stockholm, 1918.
Phil 2630.11 Invitation a la pensée et à la vie. (Guitton, Jean.) Paris, 1956.
Phil 1695.31 An invitation to phenomenology. (Edie, James M.) Chicago, 1965.
Phil 178.61 Invitation to philosophy. (Drake, Durant.) Boston, 1933.
Phil 8581.52.20 Invitation to pilgrimage. (Baillie, John.) London, 1942.
Phil 6116.17 The involuntary nervous system. (Gaskell, Walter H.) London, 1916.
Phil 1905.27.30 The inward morning. (Bugbee, H.G.) State College, Pa., 1958.
Phil 525.238 The inward Odyssey. (Schnapper, Edith B.) London, 1965.
Phil 5374.286 The inward sea. 1st ed. (Drury, Michael.) Garden City, 1972.
Phil 3552.80 Inwiefern ist Leibniz in der Psychologie ein Vorgänger Herbarts. (Barchudarian, J.) Jena, 1889.
Phil 349.70 Io cogitante ed io problematico. (Sarti, Sergio.) Brescia, 1962.
Phil 8958.7 Ioann, Bishop of San Francisco. Beloe inochestvo. Berlin, 1932.
Phil 8958.6 Ioann, Bishop of San Francisco. Vremia very. N'iu-Iork, 1954.
Phil 4195.40.5 Ioannis Pici Mirandulae...vita. (Pico della Mirandola, Giovanni.) Modena, 1963.
Htn Phil 5412.3* Ioannis VVieri De ira morbo. (Wier, Johann.) Basileae, 1577.
Phil 2045.101 Iodice, A. Le teorie di Hobbes e Spinoza. Napoli, 1901.
Phil 4080.3.320 Iofrida, Vincenzo. La liberta come fondamento dello stato. Milano, 1959.
Phil 9220.4.3 Ioläus; anthology of friendship. 3d ed. (Carpenter, Edward.) London, 1915.
Phil 1133.49 Ionici; testimonianze e frammenti. Introduzione. 1. ed. (Maddalena, Antonio.) Firenze, 1963.
Phil 1133.41 Ioniiskaia filosofiia. (Mikhailova, Engelina N.) Moskva, 1966.
Phil 8958.9 Iorio, Tommaso Angelo. Theologia moralis. 5. ed. Neapoli, 1960-64. 3v.
Phil 3195.3.84 Iosif Ditsgen. (Volkova, V.V.) Moskva, 1961.
Phil 5402.6 Ioteyko, I. Psycho-physiologie de la douleur. Paris, 1909.
Phil 6118.2 Ioteyko, Josefa. La fatigue. Paris, 1920.
Phil 808.4 Iovchuk, Mikhail T. Kratkii ocherk istorii filosofii. 2e Izd. Moskva, 1969.
Phil 310.772 Iovchuk, Mikhail T. Leninism, filosofskie traditsii i sovremennost'. Moskva, 1970.
Phil 310.421 Iovchuk, Mikhail T. Problemy marksistsko-leninskoi filosofii. Moskva, 1965.
Phil 48.1.10 Iowa. University. Studies in character. Iowa City. 1-4,1927-1931 2v.
Phil 48.1 Iowa. University. Studies in psychology. Iowa City. 1-7,1897-1918 2v.
Phil 3640.750 Ipostesi su Nietzsche. (Vattimo, Gianni.) Torino, 1967.
Phil 5115.1.5 L'ipotesi nella filosofia di Ernesto Naville. (Varano, Francesco S.) Gubbio, 1931.
Phil 665.14 ipper, P. Geistesleben and Descendenzlehre. Naumburg, 1885.
Phil 183.3 Ipsen, J.J. Filosofi og filosofer. København, 1923.
Phil 4190.2.80 Ira finito e infinito; saggio sul pensiero di Carmelo Ottaviano. (Mazzarella, Pasquale.) Padova, 1961.
Phil 9070.48.5 Iranschähr, H.K. Der Meister und sein Jünger. Olten, 1948-1950. 2v.
Phil 5243.9 Irbal, M. Lehrbuch der empirischen Psychologie. Wien, 1885.
Phil 665.66 Irdische Unsterblichkeit. (Eckhardt, K.E.) Weimar, 1937.
Phil 6958.1 Ireland, W.W. The blot upon the brain. Edinburgh, 1885.
Phil 6958.1.3 Ireland, W.W. The blot upon the brain. N.Y., 1886.
Phil 6958.1.5 Ireland, W.W. Through the ivory gate. Edinburgh, 1889.
Phil 7069.11.49 Iremonger, L. The ghosts of Versailles. London, 1957.
Phil 2520.197 Iriarte, J. Kartesischer oder sanchezischer Zweifel? Inaug.-Diss. Bothrop, 1935.
Phil 4309.5 Iriarte, Joaquin S.J. Menendez Pelayo y la filosofia española. Madrid, 1947.
Phil 5247.13.28 Iriarte, Mauricio de. El Doctor Huarte de San Juan y su examen de ingenios. Madrid, 1940.
Phil 5247.13.27 Iriarte, Mauricio de. Dr. Juan Huarte de San Juan. Münster, 1938.
Phil 310.776 Iribadzhakov, Nikolai. Leninizum, filosofiia, ideologicheska borba. Sofiia, 1970.
Phil 7069.65.37 Irish ghost stories. (Byrne, Patrick.) Cork, 1968.
Phil 18.34 The Irish journal of psychology. Dublin. 1,1971+
Phil 18.3 The Irish theosophist. Dublin. 1-5,1892-1897 5v.
Phil 8698.5 Irkolin, N.E. Vera i znanie; o Boge, religii. Muinkhen, 1961.
Phil 8446.2 Ironia e verità. (Pagliaro, Antonino.) Milano, 1970.
Phil 2050.256 The ironic Hume. (Price, John Valdimir.) Austin, 1965.
Phil 9255.19 L'ironie. (Jankélévitch, Vladimir.) Paris, 1936.
Phil 9255.30 Ironie als vorm van communicatie. (Dikkers, S.J.) Den Haag, 1969.
Phil 9255.25 Ironie und Ironiker. Diss. (Staecker, Karlheinz.) Mainz? 1963.
Phil 8883.2 Irons, D. Study in psychology of ethics. Edinburgh, 1903.
Phil 8663.1 Irons, W.J. On the whole doctrine of final causes. London, 1836.
Phil 9425.5 Ironside, Henry A. The way of peace. N.Y., 1940.
Phil 6315.19.25 El irracionalismo en Erich Fromm. (Torres, M.) México, 1960.
Phil 6332.23 Irrational despair. (Wolstein, B.) N.Y., 1962.
Phil 1750.167.5 Irrational man. (Barrett, William.) Garden City, 1958.
Phil 5045.7.5 Irrational oder Rational? (Fretag, Bruno baron von.) Berlin, 1935.
Phil 623.22 Der irrationale Mensch. (Strich, Walter.) Berlin, 1928.
Phil 343.11 Irrationalismus. (Müller-Freienfels, R.) Leipzig, 1922.
Phil 3483.28.5 Das Irrationalitätsproblem in der Asthetik und Logik. 2. Aufl. (Baeumler, Alfred.) Darmstadt, 1967.
Phil 4215.3.35 L'irrazionale, il lavoro, l'amore. (Rensi, Giuseppe.) Milano, 1923.
Phil 193.258 Irrealidad e idealidad. 1. ed. (Salazar Bondy, Augusto.) Lima, 1965.
Phil 8586.8.3 L'irréligion de l'avenir. 18. éd. (Guyau, M.J.) Paris, 1912.
Phil 8586.8.15 Die irreligion der Zukunft. (Guyau, M.J.) Leipzig, 192-?
Phil 1107.2 Die Irrthümer der altclassischen Philosophie. (Caspari, Otto.) Heidelberg, 1868.
Phil 6314.5 Die Irrtümer der Psychoanalyse. (Egyedi, H.) Wien, 1933.

Phil 2880.1.35 Irrtümer und Wahrheit. (Saint-Martin, L.C.) Stuttgart, 1925. 2v.
Phil 349.37 Der Irrtum in der Philosophie. (Schwarz, Baldwin.) Münster, 1934.
Phil 3808.127 Irvine, David. Philosophy and Christianity; an introduction to the works of Schopenhauer. London, 1907.
Phil 1930.17.80 Irvine, E.F. A pioneer of the new psychology. Chatham, 1963.
Phil 8633.4 Irvine, M.C. The friendly disputants. London, 1859.
Phil 1750.135 Irving Babbitt. (MacCampbell, D.) n.p., 1935.
Phil 6950.5 Is anyone sane. (Abby, Carl.) Boston, 1935.
Phil 9075.13 Is conscience an emotion? (Rashdall, H.) Boston, 1914.
Phil 8632.5 Is death the end? (Holmes, John H.) N.Y., 1915.
Phil 8673.12 Is divine existence credible? (Smith, N.K.) London, 1931.
Phil 8633.1.12 Is immortality desirable? (Dickinson, G.L.) Boston, 1909.
Phil 9495.15.4 Is it D? A book for every man. (Storer, H.R.) Boston, 1867.
Phil 2070.30.5A Is life worth living? (James, William.) Philadelphia, 1895.
Htn Phil 2070.30* Is life worth living? (James, William.) Philadelphia, 1896.
Phil 8884.1A Is life worth living? (James, William.) Philadelphia, 1896.
Phil 8884.1.6 Is life worth living? (James, William.) Philadelphia, 1904.
Phil 8884.1.5 Is life worth living? (James, William.) Philadelphia, 1904.
Phil 8887.30 Is life worth living? (Mallock, W.H.) N.Y., 1879.
Phil 7140.6 Is man a free agent? (Loryea, J.H.) London, 1902.
Phil 2255.10.80 Is objectivism a religion? (Ellis, Albert.) N.Y., 1968.
Phil 8882.105 The is-ought question. (Hudson, William Donald.) London, 1969.
Phil 672.16 Is position in time or space absolute or relative? (Russell, B.) London, 1901.
Phil 196.40 Is reality meaningful? Static contradictions and dynamic resolutions between facts and value. (Van Nuys, Kevin.) N.Y., 1966.
Phil 8662.25 Is the Christian God-conception philosophically inferior? (Hubbeling, H.G.) Assen, 1963.
Phil 8626.11 Is the life of man eternal? (Blades, Franklin.) N.Y., 1911.
Phil 6128.33 Is the mind a coherer? (Sarjant, L.G.) London, 1912.
Phil 176.52 Is there anything new under the sun? (Bjorkman, E.) N.Y., 1911.
Phil 1050.22 Isaac Israeli on the internal senses. (Wolfson, Harry A.) N.Y., 1935.
Phil 3625.1.170 Isaacs, Abram Samuel. Step by step. Philadelphia, 1910.
Phil 5870.60 Isaacs, Susan (Fairhurst). The nursery years. N.Y., 1968.
Phil 6118.9 Isaacson, R.L. Basic readings in neuropsychology. N.Y., 1964.
Phil 5248.3 Isaacson, Robert Lee. Psychology, the science of behavior. N.Y., 1965.
Phil 3455.3.80 Isaak Iselin. (Hof, Ulrich im.) Basel, 1947. 2v.
Phil 3455.3.85 Isaak Iselin und die Spätaufklärung. (Hof, Ulrich im.) Bern, 1967.
Phil 8605.4 Isätalät-ordens (sanningssökarnes) vishetslära. (Zethraeus, A.G.) Stockholm, 1900.
Phil 7069.37 Isaiah as read by a clairvoyant. (Cole, M.A.) Boston, 1937.
Phil 183.1 Isbyam, I.C. The ego and physical force. London, 1925.
Phil 183.1.5 Isbyam, I.C. The ego and the spiritual truth. London, 1926.
Phil 8883.4 Isbyam, I.C. (pseud.). The self-seeker and his search. London, 1926.
Phil 9515.3.88 Ischer, R. J.G. Zimmermann's Leben und Werke. Bern, 1893.
Phil 3455.2 Isendoorn, Gisbert. Cursus logicus systematicus et agonisticus. Francofurti, 1666.
Phil 410.75 Isenkrahe, Caspar. Das Endliche und das Unendliche. Münster, 1915.
Phil 410.75.5 Isenkrahe, Caspar. Untersuchungen über das Endliche und das Unendliche. Bonn, 1920. 3v.
Phil 3455.1.01 Isenkrahe-Bibliographie. 3e Aufl. (Miller, Wilhelm A.) Berlin, 1927.
Phil 5645.46 Ishihara, S. The series of plates designed as tests for colour-blindness. 8. ed. Tokyo, 1939.
Phil 5374.49 Ishyam, J.C. Infinity and ego. London, 1930.
Phil 2055.8.30 Isis and Osiris. (Hyde, Lawrence.) London, 1946.
Phil 6672.4 Isis Revelata: an inquiry into animal magnetism. (Colquhoun, J.C.) London, 1836. 2v.
Phil 978.5.5 Isis unveiled. v.1-2. (Blavatsky, H.P.) Point Loma, California, 1919. 4v.
VPhil 8951.31 Iskanja. (Brumen, Vinko.) Buenos Aires, 1967.
Phil 4803.537.30 Iskierki warszawskie. (Lutosĺawski, Wincenty.) Warszawa, 1911.
NEDL Phil 186.73.20 Iskierki Warszawskie. Ser. 1. (Lutosĺawski, W.) Warszawa, 1911.
Phil 1718.46 Iskon i smisao. (Šarčević, Abdulah.) Sarajevo, 1971.
Phil 8404.23 Iskusstvo i elita. (Davydov, Iurii N.) Moskva, 1966.
Phil 8426.8 Iskusstvo i estetika. (Zis', Avner Ia.) Moskva, 1967.
Phil 8416.11 Iskusstvo i literatura. (Plekhanov, Georgii Valentinovich.) Moskva, 1948.
Phil 8420.5 Iskusstvo i moral'. (Tolstykh, V.) Moskva, 1962.
Phil 8411.38.5 Iskusstvo i my. (Kogan, Lev Naumovich.) Moskva, 1970.
Phil 8419.31 Iskusstvo i narod; sbornik. (Siunerberg, K.A.) Peterburg, 1922.
Phil 8400.51 Iskusstvo i narod. Moskva, 1966.
Phil 8416.11.15 Iskusstvo i obshchestvennaia zhizn'. (Plekhanov, Georgii Valentinovich.) Moskva, 1922.
Phil 8401.31 Iskusstvo i problema prekrasnogo. (Astakhov, I.B.) Moskva, 1963.
Phil 8430.47 Iskusstvo i sovremennost'. (Ladyhina, Aryadna B.) Minsk, 1964.
Phil 5465.210 Iskusstvo nak protsess. (Markov, Mark E.) Moskva, 1970.
Phil 8400.59 Iskusstvo revoliutsiei prizvannoe. Moskva, 1969.
Phil 8905.15 Iskusstvo uravstvennoe i bezuravstvennoe. Moskva, 1969.
Phil 8404.26 Iskustvo i deistoitel'nost'. (Dzhibladze, Georgii N.) Tbilisi, 1971.
Phil 1020.60.5 Islam duzancesi ve tarihteki yeri. (Ulken, H.Z.) Ankara, 1959.
Phil 1020.75 Islam felsefesi der'sleri. (Sunar, Cavit.) Ankara, 1967.
Phil 1020.60 Islam felsefesi kounyoklou ve teni. (Ulken, H.Z.) Ankara, 1967.
Phil 1020.70 Islâm felsefesinde Allah'in varliğinin delilleri. (Çubukçu, I.A.) Ankara, 1967.
Phil 1020.4.7 Islamic occasionalism and its critique by Averroës and Aquinas. (Fakhry, Majid.) Paris, 1861.
Phil 1020.4.35 Islamic occasionalism and its critique by Averroës and Aquinas. (Fakhry, Majid.) London, 1958.

Phil 1020.4.8 — Islamic occasionalism and its critique by Averros and Aquinas. (Fakhry, Majid.) Paris, 1869.

Phil 525.215 — Islamische Mystiker. (Andrae, Tor.) Stuttgart, 1960.

Phil 2490.32 — L'islamisme au point de vue social. (Comte, Auguste.) Paris, 1911.

Phil 8892.53 — The Isle of Good Intent. (Rainsford, F.B.) Boston, 1936.

Phil 5520.708 — Ismailov, B. Iazyk i poznanie mira. Tashkent, 1969.

Phil 8633.5 — Ismard, M. De l'immortalité de l'âme. Paris, 1802.

Phil 1730.10 — Az ismeret eredetének kérdése a XVII és XVIII szazad filozofiai küzdelmeiben Kantig. (Seredi, P. Lajos.) Eperjes, 1889.

Phil 1135.215 — Isnardi Parente, Margherita. Techne. 1. ed. Firenze, 1966.

Phil 183.4 — Isola, I.G. Il metodo secondo dialogo filosofico. Modena, 1871.

Phil 5640.138 — Isolation; clinical and experimental approaches. (Brownfeld, Charles A.) N.Y., 1965.

Phil 1135.181 — Isonomia. (Maw, Jürgen.) Berlin, 1964.

Phil 7076.10 — Isou, Isidore. Histoire et rénovation de l'automatismé spirituel. Paris, 1967.

Htn   Phil 8883.1* — Israel, L.S. d'. Talmudic maxims. Boston, 1848.

Phil 3120.30.78 — Israel and the world. 2. ed. (Buber, Martin.) N.Y., 1963.

Phil 6318.1 — Israeli, Nathan. Abnormal personality and time. Photoreproduction. N.Y., 1936.

Phil 6980.363.20 — Isserlin, Max. Psychotherapie. Berlin, 1926.

Phil 5066.326 — Issledovanie logicheskikh sistem. Moskva, 1970.

Phil 5258.198 — Issledovaniia myshleniia v sovetskoi psikhologii. (Shorokhova, Ekaterina V.) Moskva, 1966.

Phil 4803.462.30 — Issledovaniia po estetike. (Ingarden, Roman.) Moskva, 1962.

Phil 5255.76 — Issledovaniia po psikhologii ustanovki. (Prangishvili, Aleksandr S.) Tbilisi, 1967.

Phil 5585.74 — Issledovaniia po psikhologii vospriiatiia; sbornik. (Akademiia Nauk, SSSR. Institut Filosofii. Sektsiia Psikhologii.) Moskva, 1948.

Phil 5870.70 — Issues in child psychology. (Rogers, Dorothy.) Belmont, 1969.

Phil 5590.518 — Issues in personality theory. 1. ed. (Sanford, Nevitt.) San Francisco, 1970.

Phil 8691.33 — Issues in science and religion. (Barbour, Ian G.) Englewood Cliffs, N.J., 1966.

Phil 8636.8 — Issues of immortality. (Lamont, Corliss.) N.Y., 1932.

Phil 8705.15 — Issues of the age. (Pedder, Henry C.) N.Y., 1874.

Phil 6113.6.5 — Ist Beneke Materialist? (Dressler, J.G.) Berlin, 1862.

Phil 1870.89 — Ist Berkeley ein Freihändler? (Raffel, Friedrich.) Kiel, 1904.

Phil 186.98 — Ist das Leben sinnlose Schinderei? (Ludendorff, M.S.) München, 1935.

Phil 5811.12 — Ist das tier Unvernünftig? 31. Aufl. (Bauke, Leopold.) Stuttgart, 191-?

Phil 3495.2 — Ist der Begriff des Schönen bei Kant. (Nicolai, G.W.) Kiel, 1889.

Phil 2880.8.43 — Ist der Existentialismus ein Humanismus? (Sartre, Jean Paul.) Zürich, 1947.

Phil 6328.23 — Ist die aggressivität ein übel? (Sandström, T.) Stockholm, 1939.

Phil 6060.26 — Ist die Graphologie zuverlässig? (Bobertag, Otto.) Heidelberg, 1929.

Phil 672.138 — Ist die Welt vierdimensional? (Schultze, A.) Leipzig, 1922.

Phil 1504.5.4 — Ist duns scotus indeterminist? v.5, pt.4. (Minges, Parthenius.) Münster, 1905.

Phil 3827.2 — Ist ein Durch...Spinoza und Leibniz Vorchanden? (Hissbach, K.) Weimar, 1889.

Phil 188.9 — Ist metaphysikfreie Naturwissenschaft möglich? (Nelson, L.) Göttingen, 1908.

Phil 5250.13.5 — Ist Philosophie ohne Psychologie möglich? Eine Erwiderung. (Krueger, Felix.) München, 1896.

Phil 343.14 — Ist Wissenschaft überhaupt Möglich? (Meurer, W.) Leipzig, 1894.

Phil 6619.6 — Isterismo e sentimento. 19. ed. (Cattani, Giuseppe.) Milano, 1894.

Phil 310.614 — Istina v marksistskoi i domarksovoi filosofii. (Volovik, L.A.) Moskva, 1965.

Phil 5822.12 — Istinto e società animale. (Miatto, A.) Firenze, 195-?

Phil 808.2 — Istituto di Studi Filosofici, Rome. La philosophie de l'histoire de la philosophie. Roma, 1956.

Phil 75.42.5 — Istituto di Studi Filosofici. Bibliografia ragionata delle riviste filosofiche italiane dal 1900 al 1955. Roma, 1963.

Phil 70.60 — Istituto di Studi Filosofici Serione di Torino. La ricerca filodofica. Roma, 1941.

Phil 8887.5 — Istoria critica della vita civile. (Martinelli, V.) Napoli, 1764. 2v.

Phil 1715.5 — Istoria filosofiei moderne. Bucurestti, 1937.

Phil 4816.10 — Istoria gîradirii sociale şi filozofice în Romînia. (Academia Republicii Socialiste România, Bucharest. Institutul de Filozofie.) Bucureşti, 1964.

Phil 310.554 — Istoricheskii materializm; kurs lektsii. (Kelle, Vladislav Zh.) Moskva, 1962.

Phil 310.555 — Istoricheskii materializm. (Chesnokov, Dimitrii I.) Moskva, 1964.

Phil 310.170 — Istoricheskii materializm. (Karavaev, G.G.) Leningrad, 1959.

Phil 310.1.5.5 — Istoricheskii materializm. (Rozanov, Iakov S.) Kiev, 1925.

Phil 310.555.2 — Istoricheskii materializm. izd. 2. (Chesnokov, Dimitrii I.) Moskva, 1965.

Phil 310.9A — Istoricheskii materializm. Izd. 2. (Konstantinov, F.V.) Moskva, 1954.

Phil 310.300 — Istoricheskii materializm i sotsial'naia filosofiia sovremennoi burzhazii. (Frantsev, I.P.) Moskva, 1960.

Phil 310.762 — Istoricheskii materializon. (Furman, Aleksei E.) Moskva, 1970.

Phil 8407.35.5 — Istoricheskiias zhivos na izkustvoto. (Goranov, Krusto.) Sofiia, 1970.

VPhil 310.5.10 — Istoricheskiiat materializum. (Oshakov, Zhivko.) Sofiia, 1958.

Phil 310.5.12 — Istoricheskiiat materializu i sotsiologiiatu. 2. izd. (Oshakov, Zhivko.) Sofiia, 1970.

Phil 310.703 — Istoricheskoe i logicheskoe v marksistskoi filosofii. (Gritsenko, Ivan I.) Rostov-na-Donn, 1969.

Phil 8062.8 — Istoriia antichnoi estetiki. (Losev, Aleksei F.) Moskva, 1969.

Phil 1105.10 — Istoriia antichnoi filosofii. (Asmus, Valentin F.) Moskva, 1965.

Phil 1075.5 — Istoriia armians boi filosofii. (Chaloian, V.K.) Erevan, 1959.

Phil 8676.6 — Istoriia ateizma. 3. izd. (Voronitsyn, I.P.) Moskva, 1930.

Phil 930.52 — Istoriia drevnekitaiskoi ideologii. (Yang, Jung-kuo.) Moskva, 1957.

Phil 8412.39 — Istoriia esteticheskikh kategorii. (Losev, Aleksei F.) Moskva, 1965.

Phil 8050.20 — Istoriia estetiki. (Akademiia Khudozhestv SSSR. Institut Teorii i Istorii Iskusstva.) Moskva, 1962- 5v.

Phil 800.10 — Istoriia filosofii. (Akademiia Nauk SSSR. Institut Filosofii.) Moskva, 1940-1941. 2v.

Phil 800.10.5 — Istoriia filosofii. (Akademiia Nauk SSSR. Institut Filosofii.) Moskva, 1957. 7v.

Phil 3235.126.5 — Istoriia filosofii. (Feuerbach, Ludwig.) Moskva, 1967. 3v.

Phil 4710.172.3 — Istoriia filosofii narodov SSSR. Izd. 3. (Bogatov, Vitalii V.) Moskva, 1970.

Phil 4710.153 — Istoriia filosofiiata v SSSR. v.1- Moskva, 1968- 4v.

Phil 4791.2 — Istoriia gruzinskoi filosofii. (Nutsubidze, Shalva Isakovich.) Tbilisi, 1960.

Phil 310.671 — Istoriia i kommunizm. (Kim, Makvim P.) Moskva, 1968.

Phil 8670.20.5 — Istoriia i teo.iia ateizma. (Pantskhawa, I.D.) Moskva, 1962.

Phil 940.5 — Istoriia koreiskoi filosofii. (Chŏng, Chin-sŏk.) Moskva, 1966.

Phil 5022.5 — Istoriia logiki. (Makovel'skii, Aleksandr O.) Moskva, 1967.

Phil 5025.3 — Istoriia logiki novogo vremeni. (Popov, P.S.) Moskva, 1960.

Phil 4710.145 — Istoriia molodoi Rossii. (Gershenzon, Mikhail O.) Moskva, 1923.

Phil 4822.2 — Istoriia na bŭlgarskata filosofiia. (Grozev, Groziu.) Sofiia, 1957- 2v.

Phil 850.17 — Istoriia na filosofiiata. (Georgov, Ivan.) Sofiia, 1926.

Phil 4822.1 — Istoriia na filosofskata misul v Bulgariia. Sofiia, 1970-

Phil 8505.8.10 — Istoriia papstva i inkvizitsii. (Leningrad. Muzei Istorii Religii i Ateizma.) Moskva, 1959.

Phil 8655.18 — Istoriia pravoslaviia i russkogo ateizma. (Akademiia Nauk SSSR. Muzei Istorii Religii i Ateizma.) Leningrad, 1960.

Phil 5218.5 — Istoriia psikhologii. (Iaroshevskii, Mikhail G.) Moskva, 1966.

Phil 4710.130 — Istoriia russkoi filosofii. (Galaktionov, A.A.) Moskva, 1961.

Phil 4710.85 — Istoriia russkoi filosofii. (Zen'kovskii, V.V.) Paris, 1949. 2v.

Phil 5225.5 — Istoriia sovetskoi psikhologii. (Petrovskii, Artur V.) Moskva, 1967.

Phil 1526.3 — Istoriia srednevekovoi filosofii. (Vaintrob, M.) Riga, 1929.

Phil 8525.20 — Istoriia svobodo mysliia i ateizma v Evrope. (Sokolov, Nikolai P.) Moskva, 1966.

Phil 800.12 — Istoriia zapnoevropliskoi filosofii. Izd. 2. (Aleksandrov, G.F.) Moskva, 1946.

Phil 75.66 — Istoriia zarubezhnoi domarksistskoi filosofii, za 1917-1962 gody. (Akademiia Nauk SSSR. Fundamental'naia Biblioteka Obshchestvennykh Nauk.) Moskva, 1963.

Phil 1711.5 — Istoriko-filosofskie etiudy. (Luppal, I.K.) Moskva, 1935.

Phil 1735.14 — Istoriko-filosofskii sbornik. Moskva, 1969.

Phil 310.390 — Istoriko-filosofskoe vvedenie k kursu dialektiki i istoricheskogo materializma. (Makarov, Aleksei D.) Moskva, 1961.

Phil 310.390.2 — Istoriko-filosofskoe vvedenie k kursu marksistsko-leninskoi filosofii. 2. Izd. (Makarov, Aleksei D.) Moskva, 1967.

Phil 310.256 — Istoriski materijalizam. 3. izd. (Kosanović, I.) Sarajevo, 1960.

Phil 346.34 — Istorizm kak metod nauchnogo poznaniia. (Podhorytov, Gennadii A.) Leningrad, 1967.

Phil 4115.24 — L'Italia, la chiesa e la civiltà universale. (Gioberti, V.) Torino, 1926.

Phil 4015.4 — L'Italia filosofica contemporanea. (Pompa, Raffaele.) Salerno, 1875.

Phil 530.35.30 — Italia mistica. (Adriani, Maurilio.) Roma, 1968.

Phil 530.35.7 — L'Italia mistica. (Misciattelli, Piero.) Firenze, 1932.

Phil 4006.5.38 — Italian humanism. (Garin, Eugenio.) Oxford, 1965.

Phil 3998.1 — Pamphlet box. Italian philosophy.

Phil 3998 — Pamphlet box. Italian philosophy.

Phil 4004.2 — Ital'ianskaia burzhuaznaia filosofiia XX veka. (Efirov, Svetozar A.) Moskva, 1968.

Phil 70.1.12.10 — Ital'ianskaia vstrecha filosov; o XII Mezhdunarodnom filosofskom Kongresse. (Prudian, Georg.) Erevan, 1959.

Phil 4210.125 — Die italien Philosophie. (Werner, Karl.) Wien, 1884.

Phil 4006.5.35 — Der italienische Humanismus. (Garin, Eugenio.) Bern, 1947.

Phil 4022.1 — Die italienische Philosophie. v. 1-5. (Werner, K.) Wien, 1884-86. 2v.

Phil 2520.88.25 — Iter per mundum Cartesii. (Daniel, Gabriel.) Amesteledami, 1694.

Phil 2775.3.30 — L'itinéraire de la conscience. (Naulin, Paul.) Paris, 1963.

Phil 1750.126.10 — Itinéraire de Sirius a Jérusalem. (Bourquin, Constant.) Paris, 1931.

Phil 178.69.5 — Itinéraire philosophique. (Deschoux, M.) Paris, 1964-1971. 5v.

Phil 1712.20 — Itineraire philosophique. (Muller, Philippe.) Neuchâtel, 1956.

Phil 2477.6.87 — L'itinéraire philosophique de M. Blondel. (Lefévre, Frédéric.) Paris, 1928.

Phil 2725.25.95 — Itinerario al valore in R. Le Senne. (Magnani, Giovanni S.I.) Roma, 1971.

Phil 193.134.15 — L'itinerario filosofico di Leone Sestov. (Déchet, Ferruccio.) Milano, 1964.

Phil 9070.128 — It's a playboy world. (Banowsky, William Slater.) Old Tappan, 1969.

Phil 5850.148.5 — It's how you take it. (Caner, George C.) N.Y., 1946.

Phil 8832.5 — It's not our fault. (Hall-Quest, A.L.) N.Y., 1929.

Phil 9070.50 — It's up to you A way to a better life. (Ross, William.) N.Y., 1950.

Phil 9530.45.5 — It's your future. (Panzer, Martin.) N.Y., 1943.

Phil 5585.190 — Ittelson, William H. Perceptual changes in psychopathology. New Brunswick, N.J., 1961.

Phil 5585.190.5 — Ittelson, William H. Visual space perception. N.Y., 1960.

Phil 3805.91 — Iuäbicker, R. Uber Schleiermachers erkenntnisstheoretische Grundausicht. Berlin, 1871.

Phil 70.103 — Iubileinaia Nauchnaia Sessiia Vuzov Ural'skoi zony, Sverdlovsk. Materialy. Sverdlovsk, 1967?

Phil 6980.363.5 — Iudin, Tikhon I. Ocherki istorii otechestvennoi psikhiatrii. Moskva, 1951.

Phil 730.27 — Iugai, Geragim A. Dialektika chasti i tselogo. Alma-Ata, 1965.

Phil 8430.74 Iuldashev, Lekal G. Esteticheskoe chuvstvo i proizvedenie iskusstva. Moskva, 1969.

Phil 310.480 Iurova, I.L. Dialekticheskii materializm i chastnye nauki. Moskva, 1962.

Phil 310.750 Iurova, Inna L. Ob otnoshenii marksistski-leninskoi filosofii k estestrosnamiu. Moskva, 1970.

Phil 3552.247 Ivaldi, I.G. Il platonismo di Plotino, Sant'Agosinto, Cartesio, Leibniz. Napoli, n.d.

Phil 4769.6.84 Ivan Mikhailovich Sechenov 1825-1905. (Iaroshevskii, Mikhail G.) Leningrad, 1968.

Phil 5625.75.95 Ivan Petrovich Pavlov. 2. izd. (Frolov, I.P.) Moskva, 1953.

Phil 8171.300 Ivan'o Ivan V. Spetsyfika mystetstva. Kyïv, 1970.

Phil 3246.88 Ivanoff, C. Darstellung der Ethik Johann Gottlieb Fichtes. Leipzig, 1899.

Phil 3428.84 Ivanoff, T. Die abweichungen Steinthals von Herbart. Jena, 1893.

Phil 310.21 Ivanov, A.I. Vozniknoveniie marksizma, revoliutsionnyi perevorst v filosofii. Moskva, 1966.

Phil 8673.34 Ivanov, Ivan G. Rol' estestvornaniia v razvitii ateisticheskogo miroponimaniia. Moskva, 1969.

Phil 8409.4 Ivanov, Pavel L. O sushchnosti krasoty. Moskva, 1967.

Phil 8980.463 Ivanov, Vladimir G. Ocherki marksistsko-leninskoi etiki. Leningrad, 1963.

Phil 2520.105A Iverach, James. Descartes, Spinoza...new philosophy. N.Y., 1904.

Phil 2520.105.2 Iverach, James. Descartes, Spinoza and the new philosophy. Edinburgh, 1904.

Phil 5048.2 Iversen, H. To essays om vor erkendelse. Kjøbenhavn, 1918.

Phil 735.286 Ivin, Aleksandr A. Osnovaniia logiki otsenok. Moskva, 1970.

Phil 5066.175 Iwanicki, J. Dedukcja naturalna i logistyczna. Warszawa, 1949.

Phil 2750.12.90 Iwanicki, J. Morin et les démonstrations mathématiques de l'existence de Dieu. Paris, 1936.

Phil 3552.305.5 Iwanicki, Joseph. Leibniz et les démonstrations mathématiques de l'existence de Dieu. Thèse. Strasbourg, 1933.

Phil 3552.305 Iwanicki, Joseph. Leibniz et les démonstrations mathématiques de l'existence de Dieu. Strasbourg, 1933.

Phil 978.19 Iyer, S.S. Theosophical miscellanies. v.1-2. Calcutta, 1883.

Phil 310.395 Iyöväenluohan maailmankatsomus. (Lehév, Iwere.) Helsinki, 1959.

Phil 6681.6.3 Ipnotismo e spiritismo. 3. ed. (Lapponi, Guiseppe.) Roma, 1907.

Phil 8828.10 Iz istorii domarksistskoi eticheskoi mysli. (Dzhafarli, Teimuraz M.) Tbilisi, 1970.

Phil 8050.10 Iz istorii esteticheskoi mysli drevnosti i srednevekov'ia. (Akademiia Nauk SSSR. Institut Filosofii.) Moskva, 1961.

Phil 8050.15 Iz istorii esteticheskoi mysli novogo vremeni. (Akademiia Nauk SSSR. Institut Filosofii.) Moskva, 1959.

Phil 8843.16 Iz istorii eticheskikh uchenii. (Shishkin, A.F.) Moskva, 1959.

Phil 1020.40 Iz istorii filosofii Srednei Azii i Irana VII-XII vv. (Grigorian, S.N.) Moskva, 1960.

Phil 4780.4 Iz istorii filosofskoi i obshchestvenno-politicheskoi mysli Belorussii. (Akademiia nauk BSSR, Minsk. Instytut filosofii.) Minsk, 1962.

Phil 4710.160 Iz istorii filosofskoi i obshchestvenno-politicheskoi mysli narodov Dagestana v XIX v. (Abdullaev, Magomed A.) Moskva, 1968.

Phil 310.420 Iz istorii marksistsko-leninskoi filosofii posle vtoroi mirovoi voeny. Moskva, 1961.

Phil 3006.9 Iz nemetskogo materializma. (Gulyga, A.V.) Moskva, 1962.

Phil 4795.2.2 Iz obshechestvennoi i filosofskoi mysli v Azerbaidzhane. Izd. 2. (Guseinov, Geidar.) Baku, 1958.

Phil 1020.38 Iz istorii razvitiia...musli v uzbekistane. (Muminov, I.M.) Tashkent, 1957.

Phil 4710.7 Iz istorii russkoi filosofii, sbornik. (Moscow. Universitet. Filosofskii Fakul'tet.) Leningrad, 1949.

Phil 4710.7.5 Iz istorii russkoi filosofii, sbornik. (Moscow. Universitet. Filosofskii Fakul'tet.) Moskva, 1951.

Phil 4710.7.5.2 Iz istorii russkoi filosofii, sbornik. (Moscow. Universitet. Filosofskii Fakul'tet.) Moskva, 1952.

Phil 4710.7.7 Iz istorii russkoi filosofii, XVIII-XIX vv. (Moscow. Universitet. Filosofskii Fakul'tet.) Moskva, 1952.

Phil 4710.7.15 Iz istorii russkoi filosofii XIX-go-nachala XX-go veka. Moskva, 1969.

Phil 4710.143 Iz istorii russkoi filosofskoi mysli kontsa XIX i nachala XX v. (Frank, Semen L.) Washington, 1965.

Phil 5237.516.10 Iz istorii russkoi psikhologii. (Sokolov, Mikhail V.) Moskva, 1961.

Phil 8170.9 Iz istorii sovetskoi esteticheskoi mysli. Moskva, 1967.

Phil 1695.34 Iz istorii zarubezhno filosofii XIX-XX vehov. (Bogomdov, Aleksei S.) Moskva, 1967.

Phil 8181.2 Iz istoriiata na esteticheskata misul v Bulgariia. (Tsenkov, Boris.) Sofiia, 1964.

Phil 978.88 Iz rukopisei Anny Nikolaevny Shmidt. (Schmidt, A.N.) Moskva, 1916.

Phil 5400.208 Izard, Carroll E. The face of emotion. N.Y., 1971.

Phil 6990.3.100 Izard, Francis. The meaning of Lourdes. London, 1939.

Phil 8598.67.5 Izbra mye ateisticheskie proizve - deniia. (Skvortsov-Stepanov, I.I.) Moskva, 1959.

Phil 4809.486.20 Izbrani proizvedeniia. (Kiselimchev, Asen.) Sofiia, 1964.

Phil 4829.860.2 Izbrani spisi. (Ušeničnik, Aleš.) Ljubljana, 1939-41. 10v.

Phil 4796.96.21 Izbrannye filosfskie proizvedeniia. (Fath 'Ali Ahad-zda.) Moskva, 1962.

Phil 5585.67.5 Izbrannye filosofskie i psikhologicheskie proizvedeniia. (Sechenov, I.M.) Moskva, 1947.

Phil 4796.96.20 Izbrannye filosofskie proizvedeniia. (Fath 'Ali Ahad-zda.) Baku, 1953.

Phil 4751.4.25 Izbrannye filosofskie trudy. v.1- (Asmus, Valentin F.) Moskva, 1969- 2v.

Phil 4763.1.30 Izbrannye obshchestvenno-politicheskie sochineniia. (Malinovskii, V.F.) Moskva, 1958.

Phil 1020.41 Izbrannye proizredenii myshtelei'stran Blizhnego Srednego Vostoka. (Grigorian, S.N.) Moskva, 1961.

Phil 930.66 Izbrannye proizuedeniia progeniia kitaiskikh myslitelei novogo vremeni, 1840-1898. (Akademiia Nauk SSSR. Institut Filosofii.) Moskva, 1961.

Phil 4802.4 Izbrannye proizvedeniia progressivnykh pol'skikh myslitelei. (Moscow. Universitet. Filosofskii fakultet.) Moskva, 1956-58. 3v.

Phil 4710.7.10A Izbrannye proizvedeniia russkikh myslitelei vtoroi poloviny XVIII v. (Moscow. Universitet. Filosofskii Fakul'tet.) Leningrad, 1952. 2v.

Phil 5625.75.5 Izbrannye trudy. (Pavlov, Ivan P.) Moskva, 1950.

Phil 5059.21.6A Izbrannye trudy russkikh XIX v. (Tavanets, P.V.) Moskva, 1956.

VPhil 8400.49 Izkustvo i kritika. (Bakalov, Georgi.) Sofiia, 1906.

Phil 4824.676.30 Izkustvoiživot. (Pavlov, Todor Dimitrov.) Sofiia, 1953.

Phil 8980.572 Izmeniat'sia. (Mikhalevich, Aleksandr Vl.) Moskva, 1964.

Phil 8404.18 Izobrazhenie i slovo. (Dmitrieva, N.A.) Moskva, 1962.

Phil 8958.5 Izu Loiteque, Gofronia. Libertad. Venezuela, 1944.

Phil 5520.406 Izutsu, T. Language and magic. Tokyo, 1956.

Phil 11.37 Izvestiia. (Bulgarska Akademiiana naukite, Sofiia. Institut po Filosofiia.) Sofia. 1+ 14v.

Phil 978.59.120 J. Kishnamurti and awareness in action. (Dhopeshwarkar, A.D.) Bombay, 1967.

Phil 2115.134.5 J. Locke: sa vie et son oeuvre. (Marion, Henri.) Paris, 1878.

Phil 2115.134 J. Locke: sa vie et son oeuvre. 2e éd. (Marion, Henri.) Paris, 1893.

Phil 3120.1.80 J.A.E. Biedermann. (Maosherr, T.) Jena, 1893.

Phil 4260.116.5 J.B. Vico et l'illuminisme athée. (Chaix-Ruy, Jules.) Paris, 1968.

Phil 19.60 J.B.S.P.; journal of the British society for phenomenology. Manchester, England. 1,1970+

Phil 3428.92 J.F. Herbart; Grundzüge seiner Lehre. (Franke, Friedrich.) Leipzig, 1909.

Phil 3428.153 J.F. Herbart, sein Leben und seine Philosophie. (Kinkel, Walter.) Giessen, 1903.

Phil 9515.3.83 J.G. Zimmermann. (Bodemann, E.) Hannover, 1878.

Phil 9515.3.90 J.G. Zimmermann's "Einsamkeit". Inaug. Diss. (Melzer, Friso.) Breslau, 1930.

Phil 9515.3.88 J.G. Zimmermann's Leben und Werke. (Ischer, R.) Bern, 1893.

Phil 3270.5.80 J.G.H. Feders Erkenntnistheorie und Metaphysik. Inaug. Diss. (Pachaly, E.) Leipzig, 1906.

Phil 3549.1.85 J.H. von Kirchmanns erkenntnisstheoretischer Realismus. (Hartmann, E. von.) Berlin, 1875.

Phil 6952.23.80 J.M. Charcot, 1825-1893. (Guillain, Georges.) N.Y., 1959.

Phil 2138.175 J.S. Mill e la cultura filosofica britannica. (Restaino, Franco.) Firenze, 1968.

Phil 3790.20.10 Ja und Nein. (Rosenstock, Eugen.) Heidelberg, 1968.

Phil 3625.4.35 Ja zur Wirklichkeit. (Müller, J.) Weilheim, 1963.

Phil 5585.48 Jaager, Johan J. de. De physiologische tijd bij psychische processen. Proefschrift. Utrecht, 1865.

Phil 4073.102 Jacabelli Isaldi, A.M. Tomaso Campanella. Milano, 1953.

Phil 2805.265 Jaccard, L.F. Blaise Pascal. Neuchâtel, 1951.

Phil 5651.7 Jaccard, Pierre. Le sens de la direction et l'orientation lointaine chez l'homme. Paris, 1932.

Htn Phil 184.1.2* Jack, G. Primae philosophiae institutiones. Cantabrigia, 1649.

Htn Phil 184.1* Jack, G. Primae philosophiae institutiones. Lugdunum Batavorum, 1628.

Htn Phil 5049.1* Jack, Gilbert. Grammatica rationis sive institutiones logicos. Oxonii, 1675.

Phil 8664.1 Jack, R. Mathematical principles of theology. London, 1747.

Phil 3491.4 Jackmann, R.B. Immanuel Kant. Königsberg, 1804.

Phil 8589.14.5 Jacks, L.P. A living universe (Hibbert lectures, 1923). N.Y., 1924.

Phil 8589.14.12 Jacks, L.P. The revolt against mechanism. London, 1934.
Phil 8589.14.9 Jacks, L.P. The revolt against mechanism. N.Y., 1934.
Phil 9349.3 Jacks, William. Singles from life's gathering. Glasgow, 1902.

Phil 6119.12 Jackson, A.S. The answer is...your nerves. Madison, Wis., 1942.

Phil 8884.5 Jackson, A.W. Deafness and cheerfulness. Boston, 1901.
Phil 6959.10 Jackson, Donald. The etiology of schizophrenia. N.Y., 1960.

Phil 5545.60 Jackson, George. Jackson's new...system of mnemonics. London, 1816.

Phil 6119.1.5 Jackson, J.H. Observations on the localisation of movements in the cerebral hemispheres. n.p., n.d.

Phil 8884.12 Jackson, John. The sinfulness of little sins. 5th ed. London, 1851.

Phil 6319.5 Jackson, Josephine A. Outwitting our nerves. N.Y., 1921.
Phil 6119.11 Jackson, Josephine Agnes. Outwitting our nerves. N.Y., 1921.

Phil 6119.11.5 Jackson, Josephine Agnes. Outwitting our nerves. 2d ed. N.Y., 1932.

Phil 2138.117 Jackson, Reginald. An examination of the deductive logic of John S.Mill. London, 1941.

Phil 5819.6 Jackson, T.A. General factors in transfer of training in the white rat. Worcester, 1932.

Phil 8589.1 Jackson, W. The philosophy of natural theology. London, 1874.

Phil 5545.60 Jackson's new...system of mnemonics. (Jackson, George.) London, 1816.

Phil 6959.9 Jaco, E.G. The social epidemiology of mental disorders. N.Y., 1960.

Phil 530.15.15 Jacob, A.A. La France mystique. v.1-2. 3e ed. Amsterdam, 1860.

Phil 672.250 Jacob, André. Temps et langage. Paris, 1967.

Phil 6319.12 Jacob, Hans. Western psychotherapy and Hindu-Sādhanā. London, 1961.

Phil 2520.223 Jacob, S.M. Notes on Descartes' règles pour la direction de l'esprit. London, 1948.

Phil 340.3 Jacob, T. Allgemeiner Theil der Erkenntnislehre. Berlin, 1853.

Phil 184.25 Jacob, T. Aus der Lehre vom Ganzen. Berlin, 1855.
Phil 3110.165 Jacob Boehme, the Teutonic philosopher. (Swainson, W.P.) London, 1921.

Phil 3110.185 Jacob Böhme. (Grunsky, H.A.) Stuttgart, 1956.
Phil 3110.85.5 Jacob Boehme. (Martensen, Hans L.) Leipzig, 1882.
Phil 3110.85.10 Jacob Boehme. (Martensen, Hans L.) London, 1949.
Phil 3110.86 Jacob Boehme. (Penny, A.J.) London, 1912.
Phil 3110.85 Jacob Boehme. Photoreproduction. (Martensen, Hans L.) London, 1885.

Phil 3110.6 Jacob Boehme Society. Quarterly. 1-3,1952-1956 2v.
Phil 3085.2.85 Jacob Friedrich Abel als Philosophie. Inaug. Diss. (Aders, Fritz.) Berlin, 1893.

Phil 3260.80 Jacob Friedrich Fries. (Strasosky, H.) Hamburg, 1891.
Phil 2475.1.216 Jacobbson, M. Henri Bergsons intuitionsfilosofi. Lund, 1911.

Phil 4260.145 Jacobelli Isoldi, Angela Maria. G.B. Vico. Bologna, 1960.
Phil 672.264 Jacobelli Isoldi, Angela Maria. Tempo e significato. Roma, 1968.

Phil 3829.3.25 Jacobi, F.E. Jacobi's Spinoza Büchlein. München, 1912.

Phil 3829.3.10 Jacobi, F.E. Sulla dottrina dello Spinoza. Bari, 1914.
Phil 3829.3 Jacobi, F.E. Über die Lehre des Spinoza. Breslau, 1789.
Htn Phil 3829.3.20* Jacobi, F.E. Wider Mendelssohns Beschuldigung Betreffend die Briefe über die Lehre des Spinoza. Leipzig, 1786.
Phil 3460.75 Jacobi, F.H. Briefe an Friedrich Bouterwek. Göttingen, 1868.
Htn Phil 2050.189* Jacobi, F.H. David Hume über den Glauben. Breslau, 1787.
Htn Phil 3460.72* Jacobi, F.H. Jacobi an Fichte. Hamburg, 1799.
Phil 3460.70 Jacobi, F.H. Jacobis auserlesener Briefwechsel. Leipzig, 1825. 2v.
Phil 3460.20 Jacobi, F.H. Nachlass. Ungedruckte Briefe. Leipzig, 1869.
Phil 3460.21 Jacobi, F.H. Schriften. Berlin, 1926.
Phil 3460.30.2 Jacobi, F.H. Von den göttlichen Dingen und ihrer Offenbarung. Leipzig, 1822.
Phil 3460.10 Jacobi, F.H. Werke. Leipzig, 1812-25. 7v.
Phil 6319.1.181.2 Jacobi, Jolan. Complex, archetype. N.Y., 1959.
Phil 6319.1.181.3 Jacobi, Jolan. Complex, archtype. London, 1959.
Phil 6319.1.181 Jacobi, Jolan. Komplex. Zürich. 1957.
Phil 6319.1.182 Jacobi, Jolan. Die Psychologie von C.G. Jung. Zürich, 1945.
Phil 6319.1.183 Jacobi, Jolan. Die Psychologie von C.G. Jung. 4. Aufl. Zürich, 1959.
Phil 6319.1.180 Jacobi, Jolan. The psychology of C.G. Jung. London, 1942.
Phil 6319.1.183.6 Jacobi, Jolan. The psychology of C.G. Jung. New Haven, 1962.
Phil 6319.1.185 Jacobi, Jolan. The psychology of C.G. Jung. 5th ed. London, 1951.
Phil 6319.1.183.10 Jacobi, Jolan. Der Weg zur Individuation. Zürich, 1965.
Phil 6959.3.2 Jacobi, M.P. The prevention of insanity. Boston, 1880-82. 3 pam.
Phil 6959.3 Jacobi, M.P. The prevention of insanity. Boston, 1882.
Phil 6115.6.8 Jacobi, M.P. (Mrs.). Considerations on Flechsig's "Gehirn und Seele". N.Y., 1897.
Phil 3475.4 Jacobi, Maximilian. Naturleben und Geistesleben. Leipzig, 1851.
Htn Phil 3460.72* Jacobi an Fichte. (Jacobi, F.H.) Hamburg, 1799.
Phil 3460.94.5 Jacobi und Schelling. (Weischedel, Wilhelm.) Darmstadt, 1969.
Phil 3460.70 Jacobis auserlesener Briefwechsel. (Jacobi, F.H.) Leipzig, 1825. 2v.
Phil 3460.82 Jacobis Garten zu Pempelfort. (Schaumburg, E.) Aachen, 1873.
Phil 3829.3.25 Jacobi's Spinoza Büchlein. (Jacobi, F.E.) München, 1912.
Phil 6854.12 Jacobs, Jerry. Adolescent suicide. N.Y., 1971.
Phil 8615.21 Jacobs, Leo. Three types of practical ethical movements. N.Y., 1922.
Phil 3491.14 Jacobs, Wilhelm Gustav. Trieb als sittliches Phänomen. Bonn, 1967.
Phil 6319.13 Jacobsen, Edith. The self and the object world. London, 1965.
Phil 184.27 Jacobsen, O.T. Gennem modsabninger. København, 1905.
Phil 3890.7.81 Jacobskötter, A. Die Psychologie Dieterich Tiedemanns. Inaug. Diss. Erlangen, 1898.
Phil 5425.46 Jacobson, A.C. Genius: some revaluations. N.Y., 1926.
Phil 5630.10 Jacobson, David J. The affairs of Dame Rumor. N.Y., 1948.
Phil 6319.20 Jacobson, Edith. Psychotic conflict and reality. N.Y., 1967.
Phil 5400.175 Jacobson, Edmund. Biology of emotions:new understanding derived from biological multidisciplinary investigation. Springfield, 1967.
Phil 6119.10 Jacobson, Edmund. Progressive relaxation. Chicago, 1931.
Phil 7080.49.5 Jacobson, Edmund. You can sleep well. N.Y., 1938.
Phil 6119.10.5 Jacobson, Edmund. You must relax. N.Y., 1934.
Phil 340.4 Jacobson, J. Über die Beziehungen zwischen Kategorien und Urtheilsfarmen. Inaug. Diss. Königsberg, 1877.
Phil 3491.9 Jacobson, Julius. Ueber die Auffindung des Apriori. Berlin, 1876.
Phil 7020.2 Jacobson, Nils-Olof. Liv efter döden? Salna, 1971.
Phil 290.1 Jacobsson, M. Naturens lag. Stockholm, 1914.
Phil 8589.15 Jacobsson, M. Om förhållandet mellan religion och moral. Stockholm, 1917.
Phil 184.24 Jacobsson, M. Pragmatiska uppfostringsprinciper. Lund, 1912.
Phil 3552.278 Jacoby, Daniel. De Leibnitii studiis Aristotelicis. Berolini, 1867.
Phil 5049.26 Jacoby, G. Die Ansprüche der Logistiker. Stuttgart, 1962.
Phil 6119.5 Jacoby, G.W. Suggestion and psychotherapy. N.Y., 1912.
Phil 184.13.7 Jacoby, Günther. Allgemeine der Wirklichkeit. Halle, 1925.
Phil 2225.2.80 Jacoby, Günther. Die "neue Wirklichkeitslehre". Berlin, 1914?
Phil 184.13 Jacoby, Günther. Der Pragmatismus. Leipzig, 1909.
Phil 184.13.6 Pamphlet vol. Jacoby, Günther. Der Pragmatismus. 10 pam.
Phil 6060.30 Jacoby, Hans. Analysis of handwriting. London, 1939.
VPhil 6060.30.5 Jacoby, Hans. Self-knowledge through handwriting. London, 1941.
Phil 184.11 Jacoby, L. Die Idee der Entwicklung. Berlin, 1874. 2v.
Phil 184.11.2 Jacoby, L. Die Idee der Entwicklung. Zürich, 1886.
Phil 340.5 Jacoby, P.J. "Common sense" e Pistemology. Thesis. NOtre Dame, 1942.
Phil 7069.31.20 Jacoby, Samuel A. The immortality of the soul. Los Angeles, 1931.
Phil 7060.76 Jacolliot, Louis. Occult science in India. N.Y., 1908.
Phil 184.2 Jacques, A. Manuel de philosophie. Paris, 1855.
Phil 184.2.2 Jacques, A. Manuel de philosophie. Paris, 1857.
Phil 184.2.9 Jacques, A. Manuel de philosophie. 9. ed. Paris, 1883.
Phil 340.7 Jacques, E. Introduction au problème de la connaissance. Louvain, 1953.
Phil 2805.407 Jacques, E. Le troisième centenaire de la mort de la Blaise Pascal. Bruxelles, 1963.
Phil 8410.5 Jacques, G.H. A system of aesthetics. Dublin, 1921-
Phil 4352.1.85 Jacques Balmes, sa vie et ouvrages. (Blanche-Raffin, A. de.) Paris, 1849.
Phil 2750.11.153 Jacques Maritain. (Evans, J.W.) N.Y., 1963.
Phil 2750.11.90 Jacques Maritain. (Phelan, G.B.) N.Y., 1937.
Phil 2750.11.150 Jacques Maritain. (Viotto, Piero.) Brescia, 1957.
Phil 2750.11.142 Jacques Maritain. Paris, 1957.
Phil 2750.11.220 Jacques Maritain. Saggio critico. (Garofalo, Gaetano.) Bari, 1969.
Phil 2750.11.150.3 Jacques Maritain. 3. ed. (Viotto, Piero.) Brescia, 1965.
Phil 184.20 Jacquinet, M. Essai de philosophie pour tous. Paris, 1888.
Phil 1850.95 Jacquinet, P. Francisci Baconi de re litteraria judicia. Paris, 1863.

Phil 1020.65 Jad'an, Fahme. L'influence du stoicisme sur la pensée musulmane. Beyrauth, 1968.
Phil 3745.8.10 Jäckle, E. Rudolf Pannwitz. Hamburg, 1937.
Phil 5249.29 Jaeger, Adolf Otto. Dimensionen der Intelligenz. Göttingen, 1967.
Phil 6119.2 Jaeger, G. Die Neuralanalyse. Leipzig, 1881.
Phil 3801.464 Jäger, G. Schellings politische Anschauungen. Berlin, 1939.
Phil 9150.17 Jaeger, Gustav. Die Darwin'sche Theorie und ihre Stellung. Stuttgart, 1869.
Phil 5249.12 Jäger, Hermann. Die gemeinsame Wurzel der Kunst, Moral und Wissenschaft. Berlin, 1909.
Phil 5249.32 Jaeger, Marc A. Geist und Seele im technischen Zeitalter. Zürich, 1968.
Phil 5249.24 Jaeger, Marc A. Relativitätstheorie des Menschengeistes. Zürich, 1958.
Phil 2270.133 Jaeger, Max. Herbert Spencer's Prinzipien der Ethik. Hamburg, 1922.
Phil 8634.7 Jaeger, Paul. Innseits; zur Verständigung über die Jenseitsfrage. Tübingen, 1917.
Phil 1114.10 Jaeger, Werner W. Die Theologie der Frühen griechischen Denker. Stuttgart, 1953.
Phil 1114.5.2 Jaeger, Werner W. The theology of the early Greek philosophers. London, 1968.
Phil 1114.5 Jaeger, Werner W. The theology of the early Greek philosophers. Oxford, 1947.
Phil 680.5 Jaeggi, Urs. Ordnung und Chaos. Frankfurt, 1968.
Phil 3801.465.15 Jaehnig, Dieter. Schelling. v.2. Pfullingen, 1966.
Phil 5759.5 Jäkel, Josef. Die Freiheit des menschlichen Willens. Wien, 1906.
Phil 3552.272 Jaenicke, Kurt. Das Verhaltnis des Korperlichen zum Geistigen und die Entwicklung des Geistigen bei Leibniz. Cöthen, 1913.
Phil 5357.2 Jaensch, E.R. Einige allgemeiner Fragen der Psychologie und Biologie des Denkens. Leipzig, 1920.
Phil 5465.27.4 Jaensch, Erich. Eidetic imagery and typological methods of investigation. London, 1930.
Phil 5465.27.2 Jaensch, Erich. Die Eidetik und typologische Forschungsmethode in ihrer Bedeutung für die Jugendpsychologie. 2e Aufl. Leipzig, 1927.
Phil 5465.27.5 Jaensch, Erich. Die Streitfrage zwischen Assoziation. Berlin, 1927.
Phil 5249.19 Jaensch, Erich. Über Gestaltpsychologie und Gestalttheorie. Langensalza, 1929.
Phil 630.36 Jaensch, Erich. Vorfragen der Wirklichkeitsphilosophie. Leipzig, 1931.
Phil 6319.7 Jaensch, W. Grundzuge einer Physiologie und Klinik der psychophysischen Persönlichkeit. Berlin, 1926.
Phil 5643.13 Jaesche, E. Das räumliche Sehen. Stuttgart, 1879.
Phil 5374.52 Jaesche, E. Werden, Sein und Erscheinungsweise des Bewusstseins. Heidelberg, 1887.
Phil 8685.4 Jäsche, G.B. Der Pantheismus. Berlin, 1826-32. 3v.
Phil 7069.28.35 Jaeschke, Willy K. Die parapsychologischen Erscheinungen. 2. Aufl. Leipzig, 1928.
Phil 5585.40.2 Jeusch, Erich. Über den Aufbau der Wahrnehmungswelt. 2. Aufl. Leipzig, 1927-1931. 2v.
Phil 7069.58.2 Jaffe, Aniela. Apparitions and precognition. New Hyde Park, N.Y., 1963.
Phil 6319.1.270 Jaffé, Aniela. Aus Leben und Werkstatt von C.G. Jung. Zürich, 1968.
Phil 7069.58 Jaffe, Aniela. Geistererscheinungen und Vorzeichen. Zürich, 1958.
Phil 6319.1.236 Jaffé, Aniela. The myth of meaning in the work of C.G. Jung. London, 1970.
Phil 6319.1.235 Jaffé, Aniela. Der Mythus vom Sinn in Werk von C.G. Jung. Zürich, 1967.
Phil 672.152.5 Jaffé, George. Über Raum. Berlin, 1954.
Phil 672.152 Jaffé, George. Zwei Dialoge über Raum und Zeit. Leipzig, 1931.
Phil 290.5 Jaffe, Haym. Natural law as controlled but not determined by experiment. Thesis. Philadelphia, 1934.
Phil 2675.1.31 Jaffre, F.A. Cours de philosophie adapté au programme du baccalauréat ès lettres. Lyon, 1878.
Phil 3120.55.100 Jager, Alfred. Reich ohne Gott; zur Eschatologie Ernst Blochs. Zürich, 1969.
Phil 5258.85.5 Jaget och demonierna. (Schleich, Carl Ludwig.) Stockholm, 1925.
Phil 7120.2 Jagot, Paul Clément. Traité méthodique de magnétisme personnel. Paris, 1969.
Phil 6319.9 Jahn, Ernst. Machtwille und Minderwertigkeitsgefuhl. Berlin, 1931.
Phil 5627.170 Jahn, Ernst. Religion und Individualpsychologie. Wien, 1933.
Phil 2050.191 Jahn, Franz. David Humes Kausalitätstheorie. Inaug. Diss. Leipzig, 1895.
Phil 5525.7 Jahn, Franz. Das Problem des Komischen. Potsdam, 1904.
Phil 8409.465.30 Jahn, Jiljí. Pozmání a život. Praha, 1948.
Phil 8400.22 Jahn, Johannes. Die Kunstwissenschaft der Gegenwart in Selbstdarstellungen. Leipzig, 1924.
Phil 5249.1 Jahn, M. Psychologie als Grundwissenschaft der Pädagogik. Leipzig, 1883.
Phil 5249.1.2 Jahn, M. Psychologie als Grundwissenschaft der Pädagogik. Leipzig, 1897.
Phil 3491.7 Jahn, Max. Der Einfluss der Kantischen Psychologie auf die Pädagogik als Wissenschaft. Leipzig, 1885.
Phil 8884.17.3 Jahn, Max. Ethik als Grundwissenschaft. Leipzig, 1905.
Phil 8884.17.10 Jahn, Max. Ethik als Grundwissenschaft. 4. Aufl. Leipzig, 1925. 2v.
Phil 6119.14 Jahoda, Marie. Current concepts of positive mental health. N.Y., 1959.
Phil 50.5 Jahrbuch. (Keyserluig-Gesellschaft für freie Philosophie.) Düsseldorf. 2v.
Phil 28.23 Jahrbuch. (Schweizerische philosophische Gesellschaft.) Basel. 1,1941+ 28v.
Phil 28.32 Jahrbuch. (Studiengesellschaft für praktische Psychologie.) Lüneburg. 1953-1955 3v.
Phil 28.23.10 Jahrbuch. Beihefte. (Schweizerische philosophische Gesellschaft.) Basel. 1,1943+ 11v.
Phil 3808.124 Jahrbuch der...Gesellschaft. (Schopenhauer - Gesellschaft.) Kiel. 1912-1969+ 48v.
Phil 19.20 Jahrbuch der Charakterologie. Berlin. 1-6,1924-1929 5v.
Phil 19.36 Jahrbuch der Psychoanalyse; Beiträge zur Theorie und Praxis. Köhn. 1,1960+ 6v.
Phil 19.9 Jahrbuch für Philosophie und phänomenologische Forschung. (Husserl, E.) Halle, 1913. 13v.

Phil 19.17 — Jahrbuch für Philosophie und spekulative Theologie. Paderborn, 1887. 25v.

Phil 19.14 — Jahrbuch für psychoanalytische Forschungen. Leipzig. 6,1914+ 6v.

Phil 19.32 — Jahrbuch für Psychologie und Psychotherapie. Würzburg. 1,1952+ 18v.

Phil 19.10 — Jahrbücher der Philosophie. (Köhler, M.F.) Berlin, 1913. 3v.

Phil 19.25 — Jahrbücher für speculative Philosophie und die philosophische Bearbeitung der empirischen Wissenschaften. Darmstadt. 1846-1847 4v.

Phil 978.49.590 — Der Jahres kreislauf als Atmungsvorgang der Erde und die vier grossen Festeszeiten. (Steiner, R.) Dornach, 1966.

Phil 3450.21 — Jahresringe. (Hoche, A.) München, 1937.

Phil 1730.12 — Das Jahrhundert der Aufklärung. (Marck, Siegfried.) Leipzig, 1923.

Phil 6959.5 — Jahrmärker, M. Zur Frage der Dementia Praecox. Halle, 1903.

NEDL Phil 19.5 — Jahrsbericht...Neurologie und Psychiatrie. Berlin. 1-23 23v.

Phil 4352.1.145 — Jaime Balmes; estudio y antologia. (Sainz de Robles, Federico Carlos.) Madrid, 1964.

Phil 340.2 — Jaja, Donato. L'intuito nella conoscenza. Napoli, 1894.

Phil 6980.365 — Jakab, Irene. Zeichnungen und Gemälde der Geisteskranken. Budapest, 1956.

Phil 4802.1 — Jakiej filozofii Polacy potrzebują. Wyd. 1. Warszawa, 1970.

Phil 6119.8 — Jakob, C. Elementos de neurobiología. Buenos Aires, 1923.

Phil 8622.12 — Jakob, J. Der Konflikt. Basel, 1952.

Phil 6119.3 — Jakob, L.H. Grundriss der Erfahrungs-Seelenlehre. Halle, 1791.

Phil 8884.20 — Jakob, L.H. Philosophische sittenlehre. Halle, 1794.

Phil 8664.2 — Jakob, L.H. Über die Beweise für das Daseyn Gottes. Liebau, 1798.

Phil 2675.5 — Jakob, L.H. von. Essais philosophiques sur l'homme. Saint-Pétersbourg, 1822.

Htn Phil 3625.1.100* — Jakob, Ludwig H. Prüfung der Mendelssohnschen Morgenstunden oder aller spekulativen Beweise für das Daseyn. Leipzig, 1786.

Phil 3110.84.5 — Jakob Böhme, der deutsche Philosoph. (Peip, A.) Hamburg, 1862.

Phil 3110.172 — Jakob Böhme, der Görlitzer Mystiker. 2. Aufl. (Ludwig, Else.) Bad Smiedeberg, 1924.

Phil 3110.171 — Jakob Böhme, Gestalt und Gestaltung. (Hankamer, P.) Bonn, 1924.

Phil 3110.151 — Jakob Böhme. (Deussen, Paul.) Leipzig, 1911.

Phil 3110.155 — Jakob Boehme. (Kielholz, A.) Leipzig, 1919.

Htn Phil 3110.88* — Jakob Böhme. (Lamotte-Fouqué, Friedrich.) Greiz, 1831.

Phil 3110.178 — Jakob Böhme. (Sillig, J.F.) Perna, 1801.

Phil 3110.95 — Jakob Böhme als Schöpfer einer germanischen Philosophie des Willens. (Grunsky, H.A.) Hamburg, 1940.

Phil 3110.5 — Die Jakob Böhme-Ausgaben. (Buddecke, W.) Göttingen, 1937. 2v.

Phil 3110.84 — Jakob Böhme der deutsche Philosoph. (Peip, A.) Leipzig, 1860.

Phil 3110.89 — Jakob Böhme und die Alchymisten. (Harless, G.C.A. von.) Berlin, 1870.

Phil 3110.179 — Jakob Böhme und Gorlitz. (Jecht, Richard.) Gorlitz, 1924.

Phil 3110.176 — Jakob Böhme und Issac Newton. Inaug. Diss. (Popp, K.R.) Leipzig, 1935.

Htn Phil 3110.25*A — Jakob Böhme's theosophick philosophy. (Taylor, Edward.) London, 1691.

Phil 3260.88 — Jakob F. Fries' Lehre von der unmittelbaren Erkenntnis. (Kastil, Alfred.) Göttingen, 1912.

Phil 3260.85 — Jakob Friedrich Fries. (Henke, E.L.T.) Leipzig, 1867.

Phil 3270.3.88 — Jakob Frohschammer. (Friedrich, J.) Fürth, 1896.

Phil 3270.3.85 — Jakob Frohschammer. (Münz, Bernhard.) Breslau, 1894.

Phil 3705.1.80 — Jakob Hermann Abereit. Inaug. Diss. (Zehme, Berthold.) Lindau, 1920.

Phil 9558.8 — Jakobovits, J. Lüge im Urteil der neuesten deutschen Ethiker. Inaug. Diss. Paderborn, 1914.

Phil 4710.4 — Jakovenko, B. Filosofi Russi: saggio di storia della filosofia. Firenze, 1925.

Phil 4710.4.10 — Jakovenko, B. Ocherki russkoi filosofii. Berlin, 1922.

Phil 4710.60 — Jakovenko, B.U. Geschichte des Hegelianismus in Russland. Prag, 1938.

Phil 184.31 — Jakowenko, B. Vom Wesen des Pluralismus. Bonn, 1928.

Phil 5759.6 — Jakubisiak, A. La pensée et le libre arbitre. Paris, 1936.

Phil 672.141 — Jakubisiak, Augustin. Essai sur les limites de l'espace et du temps. Paris, 1927.

Phil 3552.468 — Jalabert, Jacques. Le Dieu de Leibniz. 1. éd. Paris, 1960.

Phil 184.37 — Jaller, Arthur. Doppeldenken; Grundlagen einer neuen Weltanschauung. Berlin, 1926.

Phil 178.77 — Jalons. (Dufrenne, Mikel.) La Haye, 1966.

Phil 6952.7.35 — James, E. A memoir of John Conolly. London, 1869?

Phil 8664.6 — James, E.O. The concept of deity. London, 1950.

Phil 8589.18 — James, E.O. Social functions of religion. Nashville, 1940.

Phil 830.5 — James, Edwin Oliver. Creation and cosmology. Leiden, 1969.

Phil 2020.81 — James, G.F. Thomas Hill Green und der Utilitarismus. Halle, 1894.

Phil 8589.5.20 — James, H. Christianity, the logic of creation. N.Y., 1857.

Phil 8589.5 — James, H. Lectures and miscellanies. Redfield, N.Y., 1852.

Phil 8589.5.5A — James, H. Literary remains. Boston, 1885.

Phil 8589.5.15 — James, H. Moralism and Christianity, or Man's experience and destiny, in three lectures. N.Y., 1850.

Phil 8620.5 — James, H. The nature of evil. N.Y., 1855.

Phil 8589.5.10A — James, H. Society, the redeemed form of man. Boston, 1879.

Phil 9169.1.1 — James, J.A. The family monitor. Boston, 1829.

Phil 9169.1.2 — James, J.A. The family monitor. Boston, 1833.

Phil 9169.1 — James, J.A. The family monitor. Concord, N.H., 1829.

Phil 9169.1.5 — James, J.A. The marriage ring. Boston, 1842?

Phil 9349.1 — James, J.A. Young man from home. N.Y., 1839.

Phil 6679.1 — James, John. Mesmerism, with hints for beginners. London, 1879.

Phil 184.3.35 — James, W. Collected essays and reviews. N.Y., 1920.

Phil 5759.1.2 — James, W. The dilemma of determinism. n.p. 1884.

Phil 184.3.10A — James, W. Essays in radical empiricism. N.Y., 1912.

Phil 184.3.12 — James, W. Essays in radical empiricism. N.Y., 1912.

Phil 184.3.45 — James, W. Essays on faith and morals. N.Y., 1943.

Phil 5300.2A — James, W. The feeling of effort. Boston, 1880.

Phil 8633.1.2A — James, W. Human immortality. Two supposed objections. Boston, 1897. 2v.

Phil 184.3.22.5A — James, W. The meaning of truth. N.Y., 1914.

Phil 184.3.30 — James, W. Memories and studies. London, 1911.

Phil 184.3.30.5 — James, W. Memories and studies. N.Y., 1912.

Phil 184.3.30.10 — James, W. Memories and studies. N.Y., 1968.

Phil 184.3.41 — James, W. On the vital reserves. N.Y., 1922.

Phil 184.3.24 — James, W. A pluralistic universe. London, 1909.

NEDL Phil 184.3.16.2 — James, W. A pluralistic universe. London, 1920.

Phil 184.3.15 — James, W. Pragmatism, a new name. London, 1909.

Phil 184.3.16 — James, W. Pragmatism, a new name. N.Y., 1907.

Phil 184.3.16.3 — James, W. Pragmatism, a new name. N.Y., 1908.

Phil 184.3.16.5 — James, W. Pragmatism, a new name. N.Y., 1922.

Phil 184.3.17 — James, W. Pragmatism, a new name. N.Y., 1928.

Phil 184.3.17.5 — James, W. Pragmatism. N.Y., 1943.

Phil 184.3.20 — James, W. Pragmatism. Stockholm, 1916.

Phil 184.3.19 — James, W. Le pragmatisme. Paris, 1911.

Phil 184.3.21 — James, W. Le pragmatisme. Paris, 1918.

Phil 184.3.34A — James, W. Der Pragmatismus. Leipzig, 1908.

Phil 184.3.34.5 — James, W. Selected papers on philosophy. London, 1927.

Phil 184.3.27A — James, W. Selected papers on philosophy. London, 1929.

Phil 184.3.28 — James, W. Some problems of philosophy. N.Y., 1911.

Phil 184.3.7.30 — James, W. Some problems of philosophy. N.Y., 1911.

Phil 184.3.7.15 — James, W. Viljan till tro och andra essayer. Stockholm, 1908.

Phil 184.3.6 — James, W. La volonté de croire. Paris, 1920.

Phil 184.3 — James, W. The will to believe. London, 1937.

— James, W. The will to believe and other essays. N.Y., 1897.

Phil 184.3.3.10 — James, W. The will to believe and other essays in popular philosophy. London, 1905.

Phil 184.3.3.15 — James, W. The will to believe and other essays in popular philosophy. London, 1912.

Phil 184.3.3.5A — James, W. The will to believe and other essays in popular philosophy. N.Y., 1898.

Phil 184.3.3.7 — James, W. The will to believe and other essays in popular philosophy. N.Y., 1899.

Phil 184.3.3 — James, W. The will to believe and other essays in popular philosophy. N.Y., 1899.

Phil 184.3.5 — James, W. The will to believe and other essays in popular philosophy. N.Y., 1927.

Phil 184.3.4.5 — James, W. The will to believe and other essays in popular philosophy. 1st ed. N.Y., 1923.

Phil 184.3.7.25 — James, W. Der Wille zum Glauben. Stuttgart, 1899.

Phil 2070.76.5A — James, William. As William James said: extracts from the published writings. N.Y., 1942.

Phil 2070.40 — James, William. Causeries pédagogiques. 4th ed. Lausanne, 1917.

Phil 5249.2.45 — James, William. Energies of men. N.Y., 1917.

Phil 5249.2.48 — James, William. Energies of men. N.Y., 1926.

Phil 2070.27A — James, William. Essays in pragmatism. N.Y., 1948.

Phil 7069.24.28 — James, William. Études et réflexions d'un psychiste. Paris, 1924.

Phil 5627.6.7 — James, William. L'expérience religieuse. Paris, 1906.

Phil 5627.6.6 — James, William. L'expérience religieuse. 2. éd. Paris, 1908.

Phil 5435.8A — James, William. Habit. N.Y., 1890.

Phil 5435.8.3A — James, William. Habit. N.Y., 1914.

Phil 8633.1.50 — James, William. Human immortality. Boston, 1900.

Phil 2070.65.4 — James, William. Gli ideali della vita. 4a ed. Torino, 1916.

Phil 2070.65.5 — James, William. Gli ideali della vita. 5a ed. Torino, 1921.

Phil 2070.60 — James, William. L'idée de vérité. Paris, 1913.

Phil 2070.33 — James, William. Introduction a la philosophie. Paris, 1914.

Htn Phil 2070.30.5A — James, William. Is life worth living? Philadelphia, 1895.

Phil 2070.30* — James, William. Is life worth living? Philadelphia, 1896.

Phil 8884.1A — James, William. Is life worth living? Philadelphia, 1896.

Phil 8884.1.5 — James, William. Is life worth living? Philadelphia, 1904.

Phil 8884.1.6 — James, William. Is life worth living? Philadelphia, 1904.

Phil 2070.75A — James, William. Letters. Boston, 1920. 2v.

Phil 2070.75.3A — James, William. The letters of William James. Boston, 1920. 2v.

Phil 2070.75.5 — James, William. The letters of William James. v.1-2. Boston, 1926.

Phil 2070.75.15 — James, William. The letters of William James and Théodore Flournoy. Madison, 1966.

Phil 8634.2.5 — James, William. Människans odödlighet. Stockholm, 1908.

Phil 2070.50 — James, William. Máttur manna. Reykjavík, 1925.

Phil 2070.28 — James, William. The meaning of truth. N.Y., 1914.

Phil 8634.2.7 — James, William. Menneskets udødelighed. Kjøbenhavn, 1918.

Phil 2070.34 — James, William. The moral philosophy of William James. N.Y., 1969.

Phil 5249.2.40 — James, William. Några livsideal samt de store männen och deres omgiming. Stockholm, 1917.

Phil 2070.31 — James, William. On some Hegelisms. London, 1882.

Phil 5249.2.38 — James, William. On some of life's ideals. N.Y., 1900.

Phil 2070.35 — James, William. Philosophie de l'expérience. Paris, 1917.

Phil 2070.25.5 — James, William. The philosophy of William James, selected from his chief works. N.Y., 194-.

Phil 2070.25.7 — James, William. The philosophy of William James, selected from his chief works. N.Y., 1953.

Phil 2070.27.5 — James, William. Pragmatism. Chicago, 1955.

Phil 2070.26 — James, William. Pragmatism. N.Y., 1925.

Phil 2070.27.10 — James, William. Pragmatism. N.Y., 1949.

Phil 5249.2.35 — James, William. Précis de psychologie. 3. éd. Paris, 1912.

Phil 2070.46.10 — James, William. Principî di psicologia (estratti). Torino, 1928.

Phil 5249.2.24 — James, William. Principii di psicologia. Milano, 1901.

Phil 5249.2.21 — James, William. Principios de psicología. Madrid, 1909. 2v.

Phil 5249.2.02 — James, William. The principles of psychology. London, 1891. 2v.

Htn Phil 5249.2* — James, William. Principles of psychology. N.Y., 1890. 2v.

Phil 5249.2A — James, William. Principles of psychology. N.Y., 1890. 2v.

Phil 5249.2.1 — James, William. Principles of psychology. N.Y., 1890. 2v.

Phil 5249.2.3 — James, William. Principles of psychology. N.Y., 1896. 2v.

NEDL Phil 5249.2.01 — James, William. Principles of psychology. N.Y., 1927. James, William. Principles of psychology. v.2. N.Y., 1890.

Phil 5249.2.2   James, William. Principles of psychology. v.2. N.Y., 1899.
Phil 5249.2.13   James, William. Psychologie. Leipzig, 1909.
Phil 2070.46.20A   James, William. Psychology. Cleveland, 1948.
Phil 5249.2.5.3   James, William. Psychology. N.Y., 1891.
Phil 5249.2.4A   James, William. Psychology. N.Y., 1892.
Phil 5249.2.11   James, William. Psychology. N.Y., 1893.
Phil 5249.2.6   James, William. Psychology. N.Y., 1900.
Phil 5249.2.6.10   James, William. Psychology. N.Y., 1907.
Phil 5249.2.13.5   James, William. Psychology. N.Y., 1909.
Phil 5249.2.5.5   James, William. Psychology. N.Y., 1923.
Phil 5249.2.5.10   James, William. Psychology. N.Y., 1961.
Phil 5249.2.16   James, William. Psykologi. Uppsala, 1925.
Phil 5627.6.8   James, William. Religiøs røynsle i sine ymse former. Øslo, 1920.
Phil 5627.6.10   James, William. Den religiösa erfarenheten. Stockholm, 1906.
Phil 5627.6.11   James, William. Den religiösa erfarenheten. Stockholm, 1923.
Phil 5627.6.12.25   James, William. Die religiöse Erfahrung. Leipzig, 1907.
Phil 5627.6.13   James, William. Die religiöse Erfahrung. Leipzig, 1914.
Phil 5627.6.12A   James, William. Religiøse erfaringer. København, 1906.
Phil 2070.35.10   James, William. Religiøse erfaringer en undersøgelse af den menneskelige natur. 3e udg. Nørregade, 1919.
Phil 7069.09.5A   James, William. Report on Mrs. Piper's Hodgson-control. n.p., 1909.
Phil 2070.55   James, William. Saggi pragmatisti. Lanciano, 1919.
Phil 2070.75.10   James, William. Selected letters. N.Y., 1961.
Phil 2070.07   James, William. The sense of dizziness in deaf-mutes. n.p., 1882-1911. 11 pam.
Phil 2070.51   James, William. Sentiment of rationality. Aberdeen, 18- .
Phil 2070.09   James, William. The sentiment of rationality. n.p., 1879-1907. 8 pam.
Phil 2070.51.5   James, William. Sentiment of rationality. N.Y., 1905.
Phil 5249.2.20   James, William. Sjalslifrets. Uppsala, 1898.
Phil 2070.49   James, William. La théorie de l'émotion. 5e éd. Paris, 1917.
Phil 5627.6.14   James, William. La varie forme della coscienza religiosa. n.p., n.d.
Phil 5627.6.3   James, William. Varieties of religious experience. London, 1915.
Phil 5627.6.5.16   James, William. Varieties of religious experience. London, 1960.
Htn   Phil 5627.6.2*   James, William. Varieties of religious experience. N.Y., 1902.
Phil 5627.6.2.5   James, William. Varieties of religious experience. N.Y., 1902.
Htn   Phil 5627.6.1*   James, William. Varieties of religious experience. N.Y., 1902.
Phil 5627.6.2.4   James, William. Varieties of religious experience. N.Y., 1902.
NEDL   Phil 5627.6.5   James, William. Varieties of religious experience. N.Y., 1903.
Phil 5627.6.5.10   James, William. Varieties of religious experience. N.Y., 1904.
Phil 5627.6.4A   James, William. Varieties of religious experience. N.Y., 1928.
Phil 5627.6.5.15   James, William. Varieties of religious experience. N.Y., 1936.
Phil 2070.54   James, William. William James. Harmondsworth, 1950.
Phil 2070.76   James, William. William James: extraits de sa correspondance. Paris, 1924.
Phil 2070.20   James, William. William James on psychical research. N.Y., 1960.
Phil 2070.76.11   James, William. A William James reader. Boston, 1972.
Phil 2070.23   James, William. The writings of William James; a comprehensive edition. N.Y., 1967.
Phil 2070.162   James e la crisi della coscienza contemporanea. 2. ed. (Roggerone, Giuseppe Agostino.) Milano, 1967.
Phil 7069.63   James Hewat McKenzie, pioneer of psychical research. (Hankey, M.) Londnon, 1963.
Phil 2055.2.81   James Hinton. (Ellis, Edith M.) London, 1918.
Phil 2280.15.80   James Hutchinson Stirling, his life and work. (Stirling, Amelia H.) London, 1912.
Phil 6325.28.1   James Jackson Putnam and psychoanalysis. (Putnam, James Jackson.) Cambridge, 1971.
Phil 8592.6.6   James Martineau and his Great Book. (Sunderland, J.T.) Toronto, 1905.
Phil 8887.4.18   James Martineaus Ethik...Kritik. Inaug. Diss. (Wilkinson, J.J.) Leipzig, 1898.
Phil 1930.13.30   James McKeen Cattell. (Cattell, James M.) Lancaster, Pa., 1947. 2v.
Phil 49.2   James Millikin University. Studies in linguistic psychology. Decatur, Ill.
Phil 2340.6.90   James Ward, 1843-1925. (Sorley, W.R.) London, 192-.
Phil 1850.145A   Jameson, T.H. Francis Bacon. N.Y., 1954.
Phil 270.9   Jamieson, G. Causality. London, 1872.
Phil 184.4   Jamieson, G. The essentials of philosophy. Edinburgh, 1859.
Phil 9349.5   Jamin, F. Conseils aux jeunes de France après la victoire. 2e éd. Paris, 1921.
Phil 2520.99   Jammes. Le sens commun de M. Gerbet. Paris, 1827.
Phil 4812.196.80   Ján Bayer, slovenský baconista XVII storočia. (Felber, Stanislav.) Bratislava, 1953.
Phil 4803.799.80   Jan Śniadecki, jego zycie i działalność naukowa. (Śwież awski, Leon.) Petersburg, 1898.
Phil 4803.799.90   Jan Śniadecki. (Chamcówna, Mirosława.) Kraków, 1963.
Phil 4803.799.85   Jan Śniadecki jako nauczyciel narodu. (Chrzanowski, Ignacy.) Kraków, 1930.
Phil 184.53   Jancke, Rudolf. Ursprung und Arten des realen Seins. Bern, 1963.
Phil 9255.15   Jancke, Rudolf. Das Wesen der Ironie. Leipzig, 1929.
Phil 5249.11   Jander, E. Leitfaden der Psychologie. Leipzig, 1908.
Phil 5525.58   Janentzky, C. Mystik und Rationalismus. München, 1922.
Phil 6021.2.87   Janentzky, C.J.C. Lavaters physiognomische Fragmente. Halle, 1916.
Phil 5249.3.2   Janes, Elijah. Human psychology. N.Y., 1886.
Phil 5249.3.5   Janes, Elijah. Human psychology. Oakland, 1884.
Phil 5249.3   Janes, Elijah. Human psychology. Oakland, 1885.
Phil 1850.92   Janet, P. Bacon Verulamius. Angers, 1889.
Phil 2409.1   Janet, P. La crise philosophique. Paris, 1865.
Phil 5643.73   Janet, P. La durée des senstaions visuelles élémentaires. Paris, 1904.
Phil 809.2.10   Janet, P. Histoire de la philosophie. Paris, 1921.
Phil 809.2.15   Janet, P. Histoire de la philosophie. Supplement. Paris, 1929.
Phil 8834.1   Janet, P. Histoire de la philosophie morale. Paris, 1858. 2v.

Phil 809.2   Janet, P. History of the problems of philosophy. London, 1902. 2v.
Phil 1750.4   Janet, P. Les maîtres de la pensée moderne. Paris, 1883.
Phil 3009.1   Janet, P. Le matérialisme contemporaine...Allem. Paris, 1864.
Phil 184.30   Janet, P. Philosophie; questions complémentaires. Paris, 1925.
Phil 184.30.5   Janet, P. Philosophie; questions complémentaires. 5e éd. Paris, 1936.
Phil 184.30.15   Janet, P. Philosophie. 8e éd. Paris, 1929.
Phil 2409.1.5   Janet, P. La philosophie française contemporaine. Paris, 1879.
Phil 8884.21   Janet, Paul. Elements of morals. N.Y., 1884.
Phil 2496.84   Janet, Paul. Victor Cousin et son oeuvre. Paris, 1885.
Phil 2668.50   Janet, Paul A.R. Les causes finales. Paris, 1876.
Phil 2668.45   Janet, Paul A.R. Le cerveau et la pensée. Paris, 1867.
Phil 2668.65   Janet, Paul A.R. Éléments de philosophie scientifique. Paris, 1890.
Phil 2668.50.4   Janet, Paul A.R. Final causes. 2d ed. N.Y., 1883.
Phil 2668.50.5   Janet, Paul A.R. Final causes. 3d ed. N.Y., 1894.
NEDL   Phil 2668.35.5   Janet, Paul A.R. The materialism of the present day. London, 1866.
Phil 2668.35   Janet, Paul A.R. Le matérialisme contemporain. Paris, 1875.
Phil 2668.55   Janet, Paul A.R. Petits éléments de morale. Paris, 1870.
Phil 2725.2.85   Janet, Paul A.R. La philosophie de Lamennais. Paris, 1890.
Phil 2668.60   Janet, Paul A.R. Philosophie du bonheur. Paris, 1864.
Phil 2668.70   Janet, Paul A.R. Principes de la métaphysique et de psychologie. Paris, 1897. 2v.
Phil 2668.40   Janet, Paul A.R. Les problèmes du XIXe siècle. 2e éd. Paris, 1873.
Phil 2668.55.5   Janet, Paul A.R. Theory of morals. N.Y., 1883.
Phil 2668.30   Janet, Paul A.R. Traité élémentaire de philosophie. Paris, 1880.
Phil 5545.173   Janet, Pierre. L'amnésie continue. Paris, 1893.
Phil 5400.91   Janet, Pierre. L'amour et la haine. Paris, 1932.
Phil 6959.1   Janet, Pierre. L'automatisme psychologique. Paris, 1889.
Phil 6959.1.3   Janet, Pierre. L'automatisme psychologique. 2. ed. Paris, 1894.
Phil 7076.20   Janet, Pierre. De l'angoisse à l'extase. Paris, 1926-28. 2v.
Phil 5249.21   Janet, Pierre. Les débuts de l'intelligence. Paris, 1935.
Phil 6615.6   Janet, Pierre. État mental des hystériques. Paris, 1893-94. 2v.
Phil 5545.170   Janet, Pierre. L'évolution de la mémoire. Paris, 1928.
Phil 575.83   Janet, Pierre. L'évolution psychologique de la personnalité. Paris, 1929.
Phil 7076.20.5   Janet, Pierre. Une extatique. Paris, 1901.
Phil 6959.1.29   Janet, Pierre. La force et la faiblesse psychologiques. Paris, 1932.
Phil 5249.21.3   Janet, Pierre. L'intelligence avant le langage. Paris, 1936.
Phil 6615.6.7   Janet, Pierre. The major symptoms of hysteria. 2. ed. N.Y., 1920.
Phil 6615.6.8   Janet, Pierre. The major symptoms of hysteria. 2. ed. N.Y., 1929.
Phil 6959.1.20   Janet, Pierre. La médecine psychologique. Paris, 1923.
Phil 6959.1.12   Janet, Pierre. Les médications psychologiques. Paris, 1919. 3v.
Phil 6959.1.5   Janet, Pierre. Les névroses. Paris, 1909.
  Janet, Pierre. Névroses et idées fixes. Paris, 1898. 2v.
Phil 6959.1.9A   Janet, Pierre. Les obsessions et la psychasthénie. Paris, 1903. 2v.
Phil 5249.21.5   Janet, Pierre. La pensée interieure et ses troubles. pts.1-6. Paris, 1927.
Phil 6959.1.25   Janet, Pierre. Principles of psychotherapy. N.Y., 1924.
Phil 6959.1.18   Janet, Pierre. Psychological healing. N.Y., 1925. 2v.
Phil 2475.1.510   Janicaud, Dominique. Une généalogie du spiritualisme français. La Haye, 1969.
Phil 6679.2   Janin de Combe Blanche, J. Reponse au discours. Genève, 1784.
Phil 6679.3   Janis, I.L. Are the cominform countries using hypnotic techniques to elicit confessions. Santa Monica, Calif., 1949.
Phil 5590.275   Janis, Irving L. Personality and persuasibility. New Haven, 1959.
Phil 3246.350   Janke, Wolfgang. Ficht; Sein und Reflexion. Berlin, 1970.
Phil 8589.25   Jankélévetch, V. Láusterité et la vie morale. Paris, 1956.
Phil 184.39   Jankélévitch, V. L'alternative. Paris, 1938.
Phil 2475.1.263   Jankélévitch, V. Bergson. Paris, 1931.
Phil 2475.1.263.5   Jankélévitch, V. Henri Bergson. Paris, 1959.
Phil 3801.465   Jankélévitch, V. L'odyssée de la conscience dans la dernière philosophie de Schelling. Thèse. Paris, 1932.
Phil 3801.465.5   Jankélévitch, V. L'odyssée de la conscience dans la dernière philosophie de Schelling. Paris, 1933.
Phil 184.39.5   Jankélévitch, V. Philosophie première. 1. ed. Paris, 1954.
Phil 8612.61   Jankélévitch, Valdimir. La mort. Paris, 1966.
Phil 5407.7   Jankélévitch, Vladimir. L'aventure, l'ennui, le sérieux. Paris, 1963.
Phil 9255.19   Jankélévitch, Vladimir. L'ironie. Paris, 1936.
Phil 2675.4   Jankélévitch, Vladimir. Le je-ne-sais-quoi et le presque-Dieu. 1. éd. Paris, 1957.
Phil 9075.35.5   Jankélévitch, Vladimir. La mauvaise conscience. Paris, 1933.
Phil 9075.74   Jankélévitch, Vladimir. La mauvaise conscience. Paris, 1966.
Phil 2675.4.30   Jankélévitch, Vladimir. Le pardon. Paris, 1967.
Phil 2675.4.5   Jankélévitch, Vladimir. Le pur et l'impur. Paris, 1960.
Phil 9075.35   Jankélévitch, Vladimir. Valeur et signification de la mauvais conscience. Thèse. Paris, 1933.
Phil 2675.4.10   Jankélévitch, Vladimir. Vladimir Jankélévitch, ou De l'Effectivité. Paris, 1969.
Phil 5520.422   Jánoska, G. Die sprachlichen Grundlagen der Philosophie. Graz, 1962.
Phil 6319.15   Janse de Jonge, Adriaan Leendert. Psychopathologie en mensbeschouwing. Kampen, 1968.
Phil 6060.74   Jansen, Abraham. Toetsing van grafologische uitspraken. Amsterdam, 1963.
Phil 3491.5   Jansen, B. Der Kritizismus Kants. München, 1925.
Phil 1750.150   Jansen, B. Die Pflege der Philosophie. Fulda, 1938.
Phil 3491.5.15   Jansen, B. La philosophie religieuse de Kant. Paris, 1934.

Phil 2805.286 Jansen, Paule. De Blaise Pascal à Henry Hammond. Paris, 1954.
Phil 809.3 Jansen, W. Geschiedenis der wijsbegeerte. Zutphen, 1919-21. 2v.
Phil 2805.210 Le jansénisme; Pascal et Port-Royal. (Chaix-Ruy, Jules.) Paris, 1930.
Phil 3491.16 Jansohn, Heinz. Kants Lehre von der Subjektivität. Bonn, 1969.
Phil 3246.91 Janson, F. Fichtes Reden an die deutsche Nation. Berlin, 1911.
Phil 184.28.5 Janssen, O. Dasein und Wirklichkeit. München, 1938.
Phil 184.52 Janssen, O. Gesammelte Abhandlungen zur Frage des Seins. München, 1963.
Phil 400.108 Janssen, O. Seinsordnung und Gehalt der Idealitäten. Meisenheim/Glan, 1950.
Phil 184.28 Janssen, O. Vorstudien zur Metaphysik. Halle, 1921. 2v.
Phil 3450.11.416 Janssen, Paul. Geschichte und Lebenswelt. Den Haag, 1970.
Phil 3450.11.415 Janssen, Paul. Geschichte und Lebenswelt. Inaug. Diss. Köln, 1964.
Phil 2840.80 Janssens, B. Le néo-criticisme de Charles Renouvier. Louvain, 1904.
Phil 5819.7 Janssens, E. Études de psychologie animale. Paris, 1939.
Phil 8884.7 Janssens, E. La morale de l'impératif catégorique et la morale du bonheur. Louvain, 1921.
Phil 2805.109 Janssens, Edgard. La philosophie et l'apologétique de Pascal. Louvain, 1906.
Phil 574.2 Janssens, Louis. Personalisme en democratisering. Brussel, 1957.
Phil 3310.1.30 Januskȫpfe zur Philosophie und Theologie. (Günther, Anton.) Wien, 1834.
Phil 935.13 The Japanese mind. (East-West Philosophers' Conference.) Honolulu, 1967.
Phil 935.11 Die japanische Philosophie. (Lüth, Paul.) Tübingen, 1944.
Phil 3780.91 Japtok, E. Karl Rosenkranz als Literaturkritiker. Freiburg, 1964.
Htn Phil 8664.3* Jaquelot, I. Dissertations sur l'existence de Dieu. La Haye, 1697.
Phil 5710.5.2 Jaques, D.H. The temperaments. N.Y., 1879.
Phil 6049.33 Jaquin, Noel. The hand of man. London, 1933.
Phil 6049.34 Jaquin, Noel. Our revealing hands. N.Y., 1934.
Phil 4961.116 Jaramillo Uribe, Jaime. El pensamiento colombiano en el siglo XIX. Bogotá, 1964.
Phil 5049.2 Jardine, George. Outlines. Philosophy. Education. Logic. Glasgow, 1818.
Phil 5249.4 Jardine, R. Elements of the psychology of cognition. London, 1874.
Phil 8410.2 Jarett, J.L. The quest for beauty. Englewood Cliffs, 1957.
Phil 3000.5 Jargon der Eigentlichkeit; zur deutschen Ideologie. (Adorno, Theodor W.) Frankfurt, 1967.
Phil 5819.5 Jarmer, Karl. Das Seelenleben der Fische. München, 1928.
Phil 1750.635.5 Jaroszewski, T.M. Renesans scholastyki. Warszawa, 1961.
Phil 310.445.25 Jaroszewski, Tadeusz M. Alienacja? Warszawa, 1965.
Phil 575.254 Jaroszewski, Tadeusz M. Osobowość i własność. Warszawa, 1965.
Phil 2905.1.1 Jarque i Jutglar, Joan E. Bibliographie générale des oeuvres et articles sur Pierre Teilhard de Chardin parus jusqu'à fin décembre 1969. Fribourg, 1970.
Phil 2905.1.630 Jarque i Jutglar, Joan E. Foi en l'homme; l'apologétique de Teilhard de Chardin. Paris, 1969.
Phil 5819.1 Jarrold, T. Instinct and reason...science of education. London, 1736.
Phil 6959.2 Jarvis, E. Insanity and insane asylums. Louisville, Ky., 1841.
Phil 4210.91 Jarvis, Stephen E. Rosmini, a Christian philosopher. 2. ed. Market Weighton, 1888.
Phil 7060.83 Jarvis, T.M. Accredited ghost stories. London, 1823.
Phil 5249.16 Jascalevich, A.A. Three conceptions of mind. N.Y., 1926.
Phil 3552.258 Jasinowski, B. Die analytische Urteilslehre Leibnizens. Diss. Wien, 1918.
Phil 809.6 Jasinowski, Bogumil. Saber y dialectia. Santiago, 1957.
Phil 5585.315 Jaspars, Joseph Maria Franciscus. On social perception. Leiden, 1966.
Phil 5325.37 Jaspars, Joseph Maria Franciscus. De vrienden van mijn vrienden. Leiden, 1967.
Phil 3552.273 Jasper, Joseph. Leibniz und die Scholastik. Inaug. Diss. Münster, 1898-99.
Phil 6959.4 Jaspers, K. Allgemeine Psychopathologie. Berlin, 1913.
Phil 184.19.20 Jaspers, K. Existenzphilosophie. Berlin, 1938.
Phil 6959.4.18 Jaspers, K. General psychopathology. Chicago, 1967.
Phil 6959.4.17 Jaspers, K. General psychopathology. Manchester, 1963.
Phil 184.19.35 Jaspers, K. The great philosophers. 1. American ed. N.Y., 1962. 2v.
Phil 184.19.30 Jaspers, K. Die grossen Philosophen. München, 1957.
Phil 6959.4.25 Jaspers, K. The nature of psychotherapy. Manchester, 1964.
Phil 184.19.10 Jaspers, K. Philosophie. Berlin, 1932. 3v.
Phil 184.19.25 Jaspers, K. Der philosophische Glaube. München, 1948.
Phil 184.19.11 Jaspers, K. Philosophy. v.1-. Translation. Chicago, 1969-71. 3v.
Phil 184.19 Jaspers, K. Psychologie der Weltanschauung. Berlin, 1919.
Phil 184.19.5A Jaspers, K. Psychologie der Weltanschauung. Berlin, 1925.
Phil 184.19.15 Jaspers, K. Vernunft und Existenz. Groningen, 1935.
Phil 809.10 Jaspers, Karl. Aneignung und Polemik. München, 1968.
Phil 3475.3.76 Jaspers, Karl. Die Atombombe und die Zükunft des Menschen. München, 1960.
Phil 3475.3.73 Jaspers, Karl. La bombe atomique et l'avenir de l'homme. Paris, 1958.
Phil 3475.3.57 Jaspers, Karl. Chiffren der Transzendenz. München, 1970.
Phil 2520.202 Jaspers, Karl. Descartes und die Philosophie. Berlin, 1937.
Phil 2520.202.5 Jaspers, Karl. Descartes und die Philosophie. 2. Aufl. Berlin, 1948.
Phil 3475.3.52 Jaspers, Karl. Einführung in die Philosophie. Zürich, 1958.
Phil 1750.285 Jaspers, Karl. L'esistenzialismo. Roma, 1946.
Phil 3475.3.70 Jaspers, Karl. Existentialism and humanism. N.Y., 1952.
Phil 3475.3.71 Jaspers, Karl. Existenzphilosophie. 2. Aufl. Berlin, 1950.
Phil 8589.21 Jaspers, Karl. Die Frage der Entmychologisierung. München, 1954.
Phil 3475.3.77 Jaspers, Karl. The future of mankind. Chicago, 1961.
Phil 3475.3.195 Jaspers, Karl. Hoffnung und Sorge. München, 1965.
Phil 3475.3.230 Jaspers, Karl. Kleine Schule des philosophischen Denkens. München, 1967.
Phil 3475.3.67 Jaspers, Karl. Lebensfragen der deutschen Politik. München, 1963.
Phil 8589.21.2 Jaspers, Karl. Myth and Christianity. N.Y., 1958.
Phil 3640.267 Jaspers, Karl. Nietzsche. Berlin, 1936.
Phil 3640.267.4 Jaspers, Karl. Nietzsche: an introduction to the understanding of his philosophical activity. Tucson, 1965.
Phil 3640.267.3 Jaspers, Karl. Nietzsche. 2e Aufl. Berlin, 1947.
Phil 3640.267.5 Jaspers, Karl. Nietzsche und das Christentum. Hameln, 1946.
Phil 3475.3.40 Jaspers, Karl. Die ontwort on Sigrid Undset. Konstang, 1947.
Phil 3475.3.47A Jaspers, Karl. The perennial scope of philosophy. N.Y., 1949.
Phil 3475.3.205 Jaspers, Karl. Philosophical faith and revelation. N.Y., 1967.
Phil 3475.3.66 Jaspers, Karl. Philosophie und Offenbarungsglaube. Hamburg, 1963.
Phil 3475.3.42 Jaspers, Karl. Philosophie und Welt. München, 1958.
Phil 3475.3.58 Jaspers, Karl. Philosophie und Wissenschaft. Zürich, 1949.
Phil 3475.3.225 Jaspers, Karl. Philosophische Aufsätze. Frankfurt, 1967.
Phil 3475.3.78 Jaspers, Karl. Der philosophische Glaube Angesichts der Offenbarung. München, 1962.
Phil 5049.20.5 Jaspers, Karl. Philosophische Logik. München, 1958.
Phil 3475.3.220 Jaspers, Karl. Provokationen; Gespräche und Interviews. München, 1969.
Phil 3475.3.62 Jaspers, Karl. Reason and anti-reason in our time. New Haven, 1952.
Phil 3475.3.61 Jaspers, Karl. Reason and anti-reason in our time. 1st British ed. London, 1952.
Phil 3475.3.56.1 Jaspers, Karl. Reason and existenz; five lectures. London, 1956.
Phil 3475.3.75 Jaspers, Karl. Rechenschaft und Ausbuik. München, 1951.
Phil 3801.465.10 Jaspers, Karl. Schelling. München, 1955.
Phil 3475.3.25 Jaspers, Karl. Schicksal und Wille. München, 1967.
Phil 3475.3.35 Jaspers, Karl. Die Schuldfrage. 2. Aufl. Zürich, 1946.
Phil 3475.3.20 Jaspers, Karl. Three essays. 1st ed. N.Y., 1964.
Phil 5049.20.3 Jaspers, Karl. Truth and symbol. N.Y., 1959.
Phil 5049.20.10 Jaspers, Karl. Über das tragische. München, 1952.
Phil 3475.3.55 Jaspers, Karl. Vernunft und Existenz. Bremen, 1949.
Phil 3475.3.55.5 Jaspers, Karl. Vernunft und Existenz. München, 1960.
Phil 3475.3.60 Jaspers, Karl. Vernunft und Windervernunft. München, 1950.
Phil 5049.20 Jaspers, Karl. Von der Wahrheit. München, 1947.
Phil 3475.3.74 Jaspers, Karl. Wahrheit, Freiheit und Friede. München, 1958.
Phil 3475.3.37 Jaspers, Karl. Wahrheit und Wissenschaft. München, 1960.
Phil 3475.3.65 Jaspers, Karl. Way of wisdom. New Haven, 1951.
Phil 3475.3.23 Jaspers, Karl. Werk und Wirkung. München, 1963.
Phil 3475.3.72 Jaspers, Karl. Wo stehen wir heute. Olten, 1961.
Phil 1718.26 Jaspers als Blickpunkt für neue Einsichten. (Sahm, August.) Worms am Rhein, 1952.
Phil 3475.3.215 Jaspers and Bultmenn. (Long, Eugene Thomas.) Durham, 1968.
Phil 960.150 Jast, Louis S. Reincarnation and karma. N.Y., 1944.
Phil 5249.6.25 Jastrow, J. The betrayal of intelligence. N.Y., 1938.
Phil 9035.16.5 Jastrow, J. Character and temperament. N.Y., 1915.
Phil 5249.6.15 Jastrow, J. Effective thinking. N.Y., 1931.
NEDL Phil 5249.6 Jastrow, J. Fact and fable in psychology. Boston, 1901.
Phil 5249.2.89 Jastrow, J. Notes in psychology. Madison, 1912.
Phil 5249.6.5 Jastrow, J. The psychology of conviction. Boston, 1918.
Phil 9035.16 Jastrow, J. The qualities of men. Boston, 1910.
Phil 5545.16 Jastrow, J. Statistical study of memory. N.Y., 1891.
Phil 5722.15 Jastrow, J. The subconscious. Boston, 1906.
Phil 5249.6.10 Jastrow, J. The time-relations of mental phenomena. n.p. 1890-1912. 10 pam.
Phil 5249.6.20 Jastrow, J. Wish and wisdom. N.Y., 1935.
Phil 6315.2.101A Jastrow, Joseph. The house that Freud built. N.Y., 1932.
Phil 5850.244 Jastrow, Joseph. Keeping mentally fit, a guide to everyday psychology. N.Y., 1928.
Phil 5850.244.5 Jastrow, Joseph. Keeping mentally fit. N.Y., 1928.
Phil 8430.30 Jaszi, Oszhai. Muveszet és erkölcs. Budapest, 1908.
Phil 340.1.2 Jaures, J. De la réalite du monde sensible. Paris, 1891.
Phil 340.1 Jaures, J. De la réalite du monde sensible. Paris, 1902.
Phil 184.6 Javary, L.A. La certitude. Paris, 1847.
Phil 8664.9 Javaux, J. Prouver Dieu? Paris, 1968.
Phil 310.565 Javůrek, Zdenck. Dialektika oleccného a zuláštního. Praha, 1962.
Phil 4803.497.90 Jawonski, Manek. Tadeusz Kotarbiński. Wyd. 1. Warszawa, 1971.
Phil 270.110 Jaworski, M. Arystolelesowska i tomistyczna teoria przyczyry sprawczej na tle pojęcia bytu. Lublin, 1958.
Phil 9169.2 Jay, W. Thoughts on marriage. Boston, 1833.
Phil 8419.65 Jazyk umění. (Šabouk, Sáva.) Praha, 1969.
Phil 5066.266 Jdel'son, A.V. Matematicheskaia teoriia logicheskogo vyvoda. Moskva, 1967.
Phil 2905.1.69 Je m'explique. (Teilhard de Chardin, Pierre.) Paris, 1966.
Phil 2675.4 Le je-ne-sais-quoi et le presque-Dieu. 1. éd. (Jankélévitch, Vladimir.) Paris, 1957.
Phil 5413.13 Jealousy. Diss. (Gesell, Arnold L.) Worcester, 1906.
Phil 2630.11.35 Jean Guitton, vu par Jacques André. Troyes, 1963.
Phil 2630.3.82 Jean-Jacques Gourd 1850-1909. (Trial, Louis.) Nimes, 1914.
Phil 2630.2.131 Jean-Marie Guyau. (Bjarnason, Águst.) Kobenhavn, 1911.
Phil 2630.2.127 Jean Marie Guyaus Religionsphilosophie. (Schumm, Felix.) Tübingen, 1913.
Phil 2775.6.80 Jean Nabert; ou, L'exigence absolue. (Levert, Paule.) Paris, 1971.
Phil 2880.8.80 Jean Paul Sartre; ou une littérature philosophique. (Campbell, Robert.) Paris, 1945.
Phil 2880.8.81 Jean Paul Sartre. (Campbell, Robert.) Paris, 1946.
Phil 2880.8.132 Jean Paul Sartre. (Greene, Norman.) Ann Arbor, 1960.
Phil 2880.8.110 Jean Paul Sartre. (Holz, H.H.) Meisenheim, 1951.
Phil 2880.8.190 Jean Paul Sartre. (Nauta, Lolle Wibe.) Door, 1966.
Phil 2880.8.162 Jean-Paul Sartre. (Niel, André.) Paris, 1966.
Phil 2880.8.282 Jean-Paul Sartre. (Richter, Liselotte.) N.Y., 1970.
Phil 2880.8.115 Jean Paul Sartre. (Streller, Justus.) N.Y., 1960.
Phil 2880.8.240 Jean Paul Sartre. (Struyker Boudier, C.E.M.) Tielt, 1967.
Phil 2880.8.216 Jean-Paul Sartre: his philosophy. (Lafarge, René.) Notre Dame, 1970.
Phil 2880.8.90 Jean-Paul Sartre. Photoreproduction. (Juin, Hubert.) Bruxelles, 1946.
Phil 2880.8.270 Jean-Paul Sartre: the philosopher as a literary critic. (Suhl, Benjamin.) N.Y., 1970.
Phil 2880.8.112 Jean Paul Sartre contro la speranza. (Gentiloni Silverj, F.) Roma, 1952.
Phil 2880.8.175 Jean Paul Sartre und Martin Buber. (Goldstein, Walter.) Jerusalem, 1965.

Phil 2880.8.225   Jean Paul Sartre y el marxismo. (Gallo, Blas Raúl.) Buenos Aires, 1966.

Phil 2880.8.290   Jean-Paul Sartres "Kritik der dialektischen Vernunft". (Schwarz, Theodor.) Berlin, 1967.

Phil 4195.90   Jean Pic de la Mirandole. (Condier, Pierre Marie.) Paris, 1957.

Phil 2515.22.20   Jean-Pierre de Crousaz et le conflit des idées au siècle des lumières. (LaHarpe, Jacqueline Ellen Violette de.) Genève, 1955.

Phil 2855.8.80   Jean Reynaud, encyclopéciste de l'époque romantique d'après sa correspondance inédite. (Griffiths, David Albert.) Paris, 1965.

Phil 184.45   Jeandidier, A. Le panpsychisme vital. Paris, 1954.
Phil 8589.11   Jeanette, Agnes. The seventh seal. Philadelphia, 1920.
Phil 575.25   Jeanmaire, Charles. L'idée de la personnalité. Thèse. Toulouse, 1882.

Phil 1514.2   Jeanneau, E. La philosophie médiévale. Paris, 1963.
Phil 1750.115.30A   Jeanson, F. La phénoménologie. Paris, 1951.
Phil 2880.8.98   Jeanson, Francis. Le problème moral et la pensée de Sartre. Paris, 1947.

Phil 2880.8.99   Jeanson, Francis. Le problème moral et la pensée de Sartre. Paris, 1965.

Phil 2675.3.30   Jeanson, Francis. La vraie vérité, alibi. Paris, 1954.
Phil 2880.8.195   Jeason, Francis. Textes de Jean Paul Sartre. Paris, 1966.
Phil 3110.179   Jecht, Richard. Jakob Böhme und Gorlitz. Gorlitz, 1924.
Phil 4803.537.45F   Jeden łatwy zywot. (Lutosławski, Wincenty.) Dzięgielów? 1932.

Phil 3830.7   Jednostka i mieskończoność. (Kołakowski, L.) Warszawa, 1958.

VPhil 2750.22.110   Jędrzejczak, Klara. Problemy rewolucji i socjalizmu we współczesnej katolickiej myśli filozoficznej. Poznań, 1967.

Phil 1900.98   Jeffner, Anders. Butler and Hume on religion. Stockholm, 1966.

Phil 5640.45   Jeffress, Lloyd A. Cerebral mechanisms in behavior. N.Y., 1951.

Phil 5249.26   Jeffrey, Melville. Beyond sense perception. 1. ed. Los Angeles, 1953.

Phil 5049.22   Jeffrey, Richard C. Formal logic: its scope and limits. N.Y., 1967.

Phil 585.25   Jeffreys, M.V.C. Mystery of man. London, 1957.
Phil 5645.6.10   Jeffries, B.J. Color blindness. Boston, 1878. 3 pam.
Phil 5645.6   Jeffries, B.J. Color blindness. Boston, 1879.
Phil 5645.6.15   Jeffries, B.J. Color-names, color-blindness. Boston, 1882.

Phil 5645.6.5   Jeffries, B.J. Report of the examination of school children for color blindness. Boston, 1880.

Phil 9075.17   Jeffs, Harry. Concerning conscience. London, 1912.
Phil 8580.32   Jeg er nemlig ikke religiøs. (Aggebo, Anker.) København, 1959.

Phil 1050.16   Jehuda Hallevi's philosophy in its principles. (Neumark, D.) Cinncinati, 1908.

Phil 5049.24   Jelenský, Simon. Logika. Praha, 1926.
Phil 8884.19   Jelgersma, D.G. De ontkenning der moraal. Amsterdam, 1896.

Phil 6319.6   Jelliffe, S.E. Psychoanalysis and the drama. N.Y., 1922.
Phil 3808.139   Jellinck, G. Die Weltanschauungen Leibnitz und Schopenhauer's ihre Gründe und ihre Berechtigung. Wien, 1872.

Phil 3552.88   Jellinek, G. Die Weltanschauungen Leibnitz' und Schopenhauer's, ihre Gründe und ihre Berechtigung. Wien, 1872.

Phil 290.2.3   Jellinek, K. Das Weltengeheimnis. Stuttgart, 1922.
Phil 974.3.109   Jellinek, Karl. Das Mysterium des Menschen. Zürich, 1960. 2v.

Phil 5655.10   Jellinek, Paul. Die psychologischen Grundlagen der Parfümerie. 2. Aufl. Heidelberg, 1965.

Phil 188.12.5   Jemand und ich. (Natorp, Paul.) Stuttgart, 1906.
Phil 3825.5   Jemförande betraktelse af Spinozas och Malebranches metafysiska principer. (Forsberg, N.A.) Upsala, 1864.

Phil 3001.10   Jena und die Philosophie des deutschen Idealismus. (Bauch, Bruno.) Jenä, 1922.

Phil 3246.235   Jenaisches Fichte - Büchlein. (Hase, K. von.) Leipzig, 1856.

Phil 3425.33   Jenenser Logik Metaphysik und Naturphilosophie. (Hegel, Georg Wilhelm Friedrich.) Leipzig, 1923.

Phil 3425.33.10   Jenenser Realphilosophie. (Hegel, Georg Wilhelm Friedrich.) Leipzig, 1931-32. 2v.

Phil 3491.6   Jenisch, D. Über Grundlugen und Werth der Entdeckungen des Herrn Professor Kant. Berlin, 1796.

Phil 8410.8   Jenkins, I. Art and the human enterprise. Cambridge, 1958.

Phil 5819.4   Jenkins, Marion. The effect of segregation on the sex behavior of the white rat as measured by the abstraction method. Worcester, Mass., 1928.

Phil 9575.3   Jenks, J.W. Great fortunes: The winning, the using. N.Y., 1906.

Phil 6049.42   Jennings, Alice May. Your hand tells all; a manual of simplified palmistry. N.Y., 1942.

Phil 5590.16   Jennings, Helen H. Leadership and isolation. N.Y., 1943.
Phil 720.61   Jenny, Guido. Auf der Suche nach Wahrheit. Zürich, 1961.
Phil 525.64   Der jenseitige Mensch. (Mattiesen, Emil.) Berlin, 1925.
Phil 1750.365.10   Jenseits des Existentialismus. (Heinemann, Fritz.) Zürich, 1957.

Phil 6315.2.59.3   Jenseits des Lustprinzips. 3. Aufl. (Freud, Sigmund.) Leipzig, 1923.

Phil 178.15.5   Jenseits vom Wirklichen. (Duboc, K.J.) Dresden, 1896.
Phil 3640.31.2   Jenseits von Gut und Böse. (Nietzsche, Friedrich.) Leipzig, 1886.

Phil 3640.54   Jenseits von Gut und Böse. (Nietzsche, Friedrich.) Leipzig, 193-.

Phil 3640.17.7   Jenseits von Gut und Böse. (Nietzsche, Friedrich.) Stuttgart, 1959.

Phil 8885.20   Jenseits von Optimismus und Pessimismus. (Kerler, Dietrich H.) Ulm, 1914.

Phil 575.137   Jenseits von Person und Sache. (Mutius, Gerhard von.) München, 1925.

Phil 6682.3.80   Jensen, Ann. Franz Anton Mesmer. N.Y., 1967.
Phil 3246.226   Jensen, F.C. Kann man Herrn Professor Fichte mit Recht beschuldigen. Kiel, 1799.

Phil 9150.27   Jensen, J.V. Evolution og moral. Kjøbenhavn, 1925.
Phil 6959.11   Jensen, Susanne. Ein Versuch zur quantitativen Analyse des gruppenpsychotherapeutischen Prozesses mit schizophrenen Patienten. Bonn, 1965.

Phil 3665.3.80   Jentgens, Gerhard. Der philosophische Entwicklungsgang des Johannes Neeb 1767-1843. Düsseldorf, 1922.

Phil 8620.6.5   Jenyns, Soame. Essai sur la nécessité du mal. Paris, 1791.

Htn Phil 8620.6*   Jenyns, Soame. A free inquiry into the nature and origin of evil. London, 1761.

Phil 5049.25   Jepson, R.W. Clear thinking. 4th ed. London, 1948.
Phil 1865.186   Jeremy Bentham; an odyssey of ideas. (Mack, Mary P.) London, 1962.

Phil 1865.183   Jeremy Bentham, bicentenary celebrations. (London. University. University College Library.) London, 1948.

Phil 1865.190.7   Jeremy Bentham. (Atkinson, Charles.) N.Y., 1969.
X Cg   Phil 1865.82   Jeremy Bentham. (Atkinson, Charles M.) London, 1905.
Phil 1865.198   Jeremy Bentham. (Everett, Charles Warren.) London, 1966.
Phil 1865.186.2   Jeremy Bentham. (Mack, Mary P.) N.Y., 1963.
Phil 1865.178   Jeremy Bentham (1748-1832). (Stocks, John L.) Manchester, 1933.

Phil 1865.179   Jeremy Bentham and the genesis of English Neo-Malthusianism. (Himes, N.E.) London, 1936.

Phil 1865.182   Jeremy Bentham and the law. (Keeton, G.W.) London, 1948.
Phil 1865.188   Jeremy Bentham and University College. (Burns, J.H.) London, 1962.

Phil 1865.176.5   Jeremy Bentham 1832-2032...Bentham centenary lecture...on June 6th, 1930. (Ogden, Charles K.) London, 1932.

Phil 5051.28.15   Jermen, Frane. Med logiko in filozofijo. Ljubljana, 1971.
Phil 8664.5   Jernegan, P.F. Man and his God. n.p., 1927.
Phil 4075.81   Jerome Cardan. (Waters, W.G.) London, 1898.
Phil 4075.80   Jerome Cardan. v.2. (Morley, H.) London, 1854.
Phil 2805.321   Jerphagnon, L. Le caractère de Pascal. Paris, 1962.
Phil 2805.320   Jerphagnon, L. Pascal et la souffrance. Paris, 1956.
Phil 5790.5   Jerphagnon, Lucien. De la banalité. Paris, 1965.
Phil 5645.39   Jerrentrup, F. Allgemein Orientierende experimental psychologische Untersuchungen über den zeitlichen Verlauf von Farbwandelspielen. Inaug. Diss. Bochum, 1936.

Phil 3625.1.58A   Jerusalem, and other Jewish writings. (Mendelssohn, Moses.) N.Y., 1969.

Phil 8589.2   Jerusalem, J.F.W. Betrachtungen über die vornehmsten Wahrheiten der Religion. 5. Aufl. Braunschweig, 1776-91. 3v.

Phil 8589.2.10   Jerusalem, J.F.W. Nachgelassene Schriften. Braunschweig, 1792-93. 2v.

Phil 184.12   Jerusalem, W. Einleitung in die Philosophie. Wien, 1899.
Phil 184.12.2   Jerusalem, W. Einleitung in die Philosophie. Wien, 1903.
Phil 184.12.3   Jerusalem, W. Einleitung in die Philosophie. Wien, 1923.
Phil 184.12.8   Jerusalem, W. Gedanken und Denker. Wien, 1905.
Phil 184.12.10   Jerusalem, W. Gedanken und Denker. 2. Aufl. Wien, 1925.
Phil 184.12.5   Jerusalem, W. Introduction to philosophy. N.Y., 1910.
Phil 184.12.7   Jerusalem, W. Introduction to philosophy. N.Y., 1932.
Phil 400.20   Jerusalem, W. Der kritische Idealismus und die reine Logik. Wien, 1905.

Phil 5249.8   Jerusalem, W. Lehrbuch der Psychologie. Wien, 1902.
Phil 5249.8.10   Jerusalem, W. Lehrbuch der Psychologie. 4. Aufl. Wien, 1907.

Phil 5500.3   Jerusalem, W. Die Urtheilsfunction. Wien, 1895.
Phil 3640.247   Jesinghaus, W. Nietzsche und Christus. Berlin, 1913.
Phil 3640.247.5   Jesinghaus, W. Nietzsches Stellung zu Weib. 3e Aufl. Leipzig, 1907.

Phil 5249.10   Jessen, Peter. Physiologie des menschlichen Denkens. Hannover, 1872.

Phil 5249.10.5   Jessen, Peter. Versuch einer wissenschaftlichen Begründung der Psychologie. Berlin, 1855.

Phil 8959.4   Jessof, T.E. Law and love. London, 1940.
Phil 2050.02   Jessop, T.E. A bibliography of David Hume. London, 1938.
Phil 1870.78   Jessop, T.E. A bibliography of George Berkeley. London, 1934.

Phil 1870.140   Jessop, T.E. George Berkeley. London, 1959.
Phil 2045.125   Jessop, T.E. Thomas Hobbes. London, 1960.
Phil 1809.4   Jesuit Philosophical Association of the Eastern States. Phases of American culture. Freeport, 1969.

Phil 8662.15.80   Jesus, our leader...Karl Heim. (Allen, E.) London, 1950.
Phil 8597.36.5   Jesus and the gospel of love. (Raven, Charles E.) London, 1931.

Phil 7059.12.11   Jesus and the mediums. (Hull, Moses.) Chicago, 1890.
Phil 8957.9   Jesus and the moralists. (Hirst, E.W.) London, 1935.
Phil 8882.51   Jesus as a philosopher, and other radio talks. (Horne, H.H.) N.Y., 1927.

Phil 8965.3   Jesus Christ and the Christian character. (Peabody, F.G.) N.Y., 1906.

Phil 7069.22.30   Jesus' teachings; by Shakespeare's spirit. N.Y., 1922.
Phil 8510.25   Jesus und die Religionsgeschichte. (Larsen, H. Martensen.) Freiburg, 1898. 3 pam.

Phil 3640.722   Jette, Celine. The philosophy of Nietzsche in the light of Thomistic principles. 1st ed. N.Y., 1967.

Phil 4720.2   Jeu, Bernard. La philosophie soviétique et l'Occident. Paris, 1969.

Phil 2445.6.30   Le jeu du monde. (Axelos, Kostas.) Paris, 1969.
Phil 6980.398.40   De jeudpsychiatriche diensten in Nederland. (Kraft, Thomas.) Utrecht, 1960.

Phil 8884.14   Jeudon, L. La morale de l'honneur. Paris, 1911.
Phil 3425.550   La jeune Hegel et la vision morale du monde. (Peperzak, Adrien.) La Haye, 1960.

Phil 9357.2   Le jeune homme. (Rozan, C.) Paris, 1878.
Phil 9161.5   La jeune mariée. (Brière, L. de la.) Paris, 1896.
Phil 9362.16.6   Jeunesse. 8e ed. (Wagner, C.) Paris, 1893.
Phil 2490.112   La jeunesse d'Auguste Comte et la formation du positivisme. (Gouhier, Henri.) Paris, 1933-36. 3v.

Phil 2840.88   La jeunesse de Renouvier et sa première philosophie. (Foucher, Louis.) Paris, 1927.

Phil 2840.88.2   La jeunesse de Renouvier et sa première philosophie. Thèse. (Foucher, Louis.) Paris, 1927. 2 pam.

Phil 585.176   Jeuscher, Ernest. L'homme et son destin. Paris, 1961.
Phil 575.19   Jevons, F.B. Personality. N.Y., 1913.
Phil 365.42   Jevons, Frank B. Evolution. London, 1900.
Phil 8589.7   Jevons, Frank B. Religion in evolution. London, 1906.
Phil 8884.2   Jevons, W. Systematic morality. v.1-2. London, 1827.
Phil 5049.4.4.5   Jevons, W.S. Elementary lessons in logic. London, 1870.
Phil 5049.4.4.7   Jevons, W.S. Elementary lessons in logic. London, 1871.
Phil 5049.4.2.5   Jevons, W.S. Elementary lessons in logic. London, 1888.
Phil 5049.3.4   Jevons, W.S. Logic (science primers). N.Y., 1880.
Phil 5049.3.6   Jevons, W.S. Logic (science primers). N.Y., 1884.
Phil 5049.3.7   Jevons, W.S. Logic (science primers). N.Y., 1885.
Phil 5049.9   Jevons, W.S. Logica. Milano, 1920.
Phil 5049.6   Jevons, W.S. The principles of science. London, 1874. 2v.

Phil 5049.6.6   Jevons, W.S. The principles of science. London, 1887.
Phil 5049.6.2.5   Jevons, W.S. The principles of science. N.Y., 1874.
Phil 5049.6.18   Jevons, W.S. The principles of science. N.Y., 1958.
Phil 5049.7   Jevons, W.S. Pure logic. London, 1864.
Phil 5049.8   Jevons, W.S. Pure logic and other minor works. London, 1890.

Phil 5049.5.2   Jevons, W.S. Studies in deductive logic. London, 1880.
Phil 5049.7.5   Jevons, W.S. The substitution of similars. London, 1869.

Phil 1050.25 The Jew and the universe. (Goldman, S.) N.Y., 1936.
Phil 6119.6 Jewett, F.G. Control of body and mind. Boston, 1908.
Phil 3120.30.105 A Jewish critique of the philosophy. (Berkovits, Eliezer.) N.Y., 1962.
Phil 4803.108.95 Jezierski, Romuald. Poglądy etyczne Edwarda Abramowskiego. Wyd. 1. Poznań, 1970.
Phil 7082.140 Ježower, Ignaz. Das Buch der Träume. Berlin, 1928.
Phil 5520.325.3 Język a poznanie. (Schaff, Adam.) Warszawa, 1964.
Phil 5066.223 Język i nauka. (Stonert, H.) Warszawa, 1964.
Phil 4803.130.35 Jezyk i poznanie. Wyd. 1. (Ajdukiewicz, Kazimierz.) Warszawa, 1960-
Phil 960.131 Jhā, Gangānātha. The philosophical discipline. Calcutta, 1928.
Phil 974.6 Pamphlet box. Jiddu Krishnamurti.
Phil 978.61 Jinarājadāsa, C. How we remember our past lives. Chicago, 1923.
Phil 974.4.20 Jinarajadasa, C. A short biography of Annie Besant. Adyar, Madras, 1932.
Phil 2520.260 Joachim, H.H. Descartes's Rules for the direction of the mind. London, 1957.
Phil 3829.1.7 Joachim, H.H. Spinoza's Tractus. Oxford, 1940.
Phil 3829.1.10 Joachim, H.H. A study of the Ethics of Spinoza. N.Y., 1964.
Phil 3829.1 Joachim, H.H. A study of the Ethics of Spinoza. Oxford, 1901.
Phil 5190.15 Joachim, Harold. Immediate experience and meditation. Oxford, 1919.
Phil 5049.19 Joachim, Harold H. Logical studies. Oxford, 1948.
Phil 720.74 Joachim, Harold Henry. The nature of truth. Ann Arbor, 1969.
Phil 270.59 Joachim, J. Das Problem der Gesetzlicheit. Hamburg, 1949- 2v.
Phil 184.26 Joad, C.E.M. After-dinner philosophy. London, 1926.
Phil 5068.12 Joad, C.E.M. A critique of logical positivism. London, 1950.
Phil 184.26.30 Joad, C.E.M. A first encounter with philosophy. London, 1952.
Phil 8620.44 Joad, C.E.M. God and evil. London, 1943.
Phil 809.4 Joad, C.E.M. Great philosophies of the world. N.Y., 1933.
Phil 184.26.15 Joad, C.E.M. Guide to philosophy. London, 1936.
Phil 184.26.18 Joad, C.E.M. Guide to philosophy. N.Y., 1956.
Phil 9450.16 Joad, C.E.M. Guide to the philosophy of morals and politics. N.Y., 1938.
Phil 1709.2 Joad, C.E.M. Introduction to modern philosophy. London, 1924.
Phil 184.26.5A Joad, C.E.M. Matter, life and value. London, 1929.
Phil 184.26.25 Joad, C.E.M. Philosophy. London, 1944.
Phil 184.26.20 Joad, C.E.M. Philosophy for our time. London, 1940.
Phil 184.26.9 Joad, C.E.M. Return to philosophy. London, 1935.
Phil 184.26.12 Joad, C.E.M. Return to philosophy. N.Y., 1936.
Phil 365.40 Joad, C.E.N. The meaning of life. London, 1928.
Phil 8884.18 Joad, Cyril E.M. Common-sense ethics. N.Y., 1921.
Phil 8589.17.10 Joad, Cyril E.M. Counter attack from the East. London, 1933.
Phil 8589.17.15A Joad, Cyril E.M. Counter attack from the East. 1. Indian ed. Bombay, 1951.
Phil 8589.17 Joad, Cyril E.M. Present and future of religion. London, 1930.
Phil 8699.5 Joad, Cyril E.M. The recovery of belief. London, 1952.
Phil 8884.18.6 Joad, Cyril E.M. Thrasymachus; or The future of morals. London, 1925.
Phil 8884.18.7 Joad, Cyril E.M. Thrasymachus. N.Y., 1926.
Phil 2075.5.30 Joad, Cyril E.W. Decadence. London, 1948.
Phil 2075.5.31 Joad, Cyril E.W. Decadence. N.Y., 1949.
Phil 630.19.7 Joad, Cyril Edwin. Common sense theology. London, 1922.
Phil 630.19.2 Joad, Cyril Edwin. Essays in common sense philosophy. N.Y., 1920.
Phil 4195.7F Joannes Pieus Mirandulanus Opera omnia. (Pico della Mirandola, Giovanni.) Torino, 1971.
Phil 5049.15.15 Joannes XXI, Pope. Petri hispani summulae logicales. Torino, 1947.
Phil 5049.15 Joannes XXI, Pope. Summulae logicales. Venetiis, 1597.
Phil 4360.2 Joannes XXI. Obras filosoficas. 2. ed. Barcelona, 1961.
Phil 1135.53 Joannides, A. Pragmateia peri tes par Athenagorai filosofikes geoses. Jena, 1883.
Phil 165.326 Joaquim de Carvalho no Brazil. Coimbra, 1958.
Phil 184.15.3 Jochnick, W. Menniskan. Stockholm, 1881. 5 pam.
Phil 5249.15 Jochnick, W. Mensklighetens vitigaste frågor. v.1-2. Stockholm, 1880-81.
Phil 184.15.5 Jochnick, W. Några grundlinjer fill filosofien. Stockholm, 1895.
Phil 184.16 Jodl, F. Aus der Werkstatt der Philosophie. Wien, 1911.
Phil 600.14 Jodl, F. L'etica del positivismo. Messina, 1909.
Phil 2050.83 Jodl, F. Leben und Philosophie David Hume's. Halle, 1872.
Phil 3235.110 Jodl, F. Ludwig Feuerbach. 2. Aufl. Photoreproduction. Stuttgart, 1921.
Phil 2045.88 Jodl, F. Studien...über Ursprung des Sittlichen; Hobbes. München, n.d.
NEDL Phil 184.16.5 Jodl, F. Vom Lebenswege. Stuttgart, 1916-1917. 2v.
Phil 8884.16 Jodl, Friedrich. Allgemeine Ethik. 1. und 2. Aufl. Stuttgart, 1918.
Phil 8834.2.10 Jodl, Friedrich. Ethik und Moralpädagogik. Stuttgart, 1913.
Phil 8834.2 Jodl, Friedrich. Geschichte der Ethik. v.1-2. Stuttgart, 1882-1889.
Phil 8834.2.5 Jodl, Friedrich. Geschichte der Ethik. 4. Aufl. Stuttgart, 1923-30. 2v.
Phil 5249.5 Jodl, Friedrich. Lehrbuch der Psychologie. Stuttgart, 1896.
Phil 5249.5.5 Jodl, Friedrich. Lehrbuch der Psychologie. 2. Aufl. v.1-2. Stuttgart, 1903.
Phil 8615.8.15 Jodl, Friedrich. Über das Wesen und die Aufgabe der ethischen Gesellschaft. 2. Aufl. Wien, 1903.
Phil 3475.1.81 Jodl, Margarete. Friedrich Jodl sein Leben und Wirken. Stuttgart, 1920.
Phil 1135.62 Joël, Kar. Der Ursprung der Naturphilosophie aus dem Geiste der Mystik. Basel, 1903.
Phil 5759.2 Joël, Karl. Der freie Wille, eine Entwicklung in Gesprächen. München, 1908.
Phil 1114.1 Joël, Karl. Geschichte der antiken Philosophie. Tübingen, 1921.
Phil 3640.94.5 Joël, Karl. Nietzsche und die Romantik. Jena, 1905.
Phil 3640.94.6 Joël, Karl. Nietzsche und die Romantik. 2. Aufl. Jena, 1923.
Phil 1709.1.2 Joël, Karl. Die philosophische Krisis derGegenewart. 2e Aufl. Leipzig, 1919.
Phil 1709.1 Joël, Karl. Die philosophische Krisis der Gegenwart. Leipzig, 1914.
Phil 525.39 Joël, Karl. Der Ursprung der Naturphilosophie aus dem Geiste der Mystik. Jena, 1906.
Phil 9065.4 Joehr, W.A. Der Kompromiss als Problem der Gesellschaft. Tübingen, 1958.
Phil 184.32 Joël, K. Philosophenwege. Berlin, 1901.
Phil 665.30 Joël, Karl. Seele und Welt. Jena, 1912.
Phil 809.1.2 Joel, M. Beiträge zur Geschichte der Philosophie. Breslau, 1885.
Phil 809.1 Joel, M. Beiträge zur Geschichte der Philosophie. Bd.1-2. Breslau, 1876.
Phil 3829.2 Joel, Manuel. Spinoza's theologisch-politischer Traktat. Breslau, 1870.
Phil 5620.15 Jönsson, A. Om den förnuftiga känslan. Lund, 1868.
Phil 5249.25 Joereskog, K.G. Statistical estimation in factor analysis. Stockholm, 1963.
Phil 1709.3 Jørgensen, J. Brudshjkher ar filosofiens historii. København, 1917.
Phil 184.34 Jørgensen, J. Filosofiens og apdragelsene grundproblemer. København, 1928.
Phil 184.34.5 Jørgensen, J. Filosofiske forelassninger son indledning tilvidenskabelige studier. København, 1926.
Phil 5066.20 Jørgensen, J. Traek af deduktionsteoriens Udvikling i den nyere Tid. København, 1937.
Phil 3665.1.85 Jørgensen, J.F. Paul Natorp som repraesentant for den kritiske idealisme. København, 1918.
Phil 9070.106 Jørgensen, T.G. Livsforståelse moralloven livets ophør. København, 1964.
Phil 530.35.10 Jørgensenn, J. I det Høje. Kristiania, 1908.
Phil 1620.5 Joffanin, Giuseppe. L'uomo antico nel pensiero del Rinascimento. Bologna, 1957.
Phil 290.3 Joffe, Isaac L. Expository history of the cosmos. N.Y., 1927.
Phil 5819.10 Joffe, J.M. Prenatal determinants of behaviour. 1. ed. Oxford, 1969.
Phil 8410.9 Joffe, Jeremiia I. Kul'tura i stil'. Leningrad, 1927.
Phil 6319.3 Joffroy, A. Fugues et vagabondage. Paris, 1909.
Phil 3270.3.90 Johann, F. Systematische und kritische Darstellung der Psychologie Jakob Frohschammers. Würzburg, 1899.
Phil 8612.80 Johann, Horst Theodor. Trauer und Trost. München, 1968.
Phil 2075.10 Johann, Robert O. Building the human. N.Y., 1968.
Phil 8664.7 Johann, Robert O. The pragmatic meaning of God. Milwaukee, 1966.
Phil 3200.5.90 Johann Eduard Erdmann. (Glockner, H.) Stuttgart, 1932.
Phil 3428.158 Johann Friedrich Herbart's philosophische Lehre von der Religion. (Schoel, A.) Dresden, 1884.
Phil 8419.39 Johann G. Sulzer; Personlichkeit und Kunstphilosophie. (Wili, Hans.) St. Gallen, 1945.
Phil 3246.310 Johann Gottlieb Fichte; Bibliographie. (Baumgartner, Hans Michael.) Stuttgart, 1968.
Phil 3246.93A Johann Gottlieb Fichte; Dreizehn Vorlesungen gehalten and der Universität Halle. (Medicus, Fritz.) Berlin, 1905.
Phil 3246.288 Johann Gottlieb Fichte; ein Vortrag zu Fichtes hundertjahrischen Geburtstag. Raiserslauterer, 1862.
Phil 3246.299 Johann Gottlieb Fichte, 1762-1962. (Berlin. Deutsche Staats Bibliothek.) Berlin, 1962.
Phil 3246.228 Johann Gottlieb Fichte. (Engelbrecht, H.C.) N.Y., 1933.
Phil 3246.230 Johann Gottlieb Fichte. (Faust, August.) Breslau, 1938.
Phil 3246.199 Johann Gottlieb Fichte. (Fischer, Kuno.) Stuttgart, 1862.
Phil 3246.95 Johann Gottlieb Fichte. (Harms, F.) Kiel, 1862.
Phil 3246.301 Johann Gottlieb Fichte. (Schulz, W.) Pfullingen, 1962.
Phil 3246.239 Johann Gottlieb Fichte. (Unruh, F.F. von.) Stuttgart, 1942.
Phil 3246.212 Johann Gottlieb Fichte. (Wundt, Max.) Stuttgart, 1927.
Phil 3246.173.2 Johann Gottlieb Fichte der Erzieher. 2. Aufl. (Bergmann, Ernst.) Leipzig, 1928.
Phil 3246.227 Johann Gottlieb Fichte im Verhältniss zu Kirche und Staat. (Lasson, Adolf.) Berlin, 1863.
Phil 3246.196 Johann Gottlieb Fichte nach seinen Briefen. (Spir, A.) Leipzig, 1879.
Phil 3246.203 Johann Gottlieb Fichte nach seinen Leben, Lehren und Wirken. (Noack, Ludwig.) Leipzig, 1862.
Phil 3246.54 Johann Gottlieb Fichte über den Begriff des wahrhaften Kraiges. (Fichte, Johann Gottlieb.) Leipzig, 1914.
Phil 3246.99 Johann Gottlieb Fichte und der neuere Socialismus. (Lindau, Hans.) Berlin, 1900.
Phil 3246.189 Johann Gottlieb Fichtes idealism. (Sahlin, Enar.) Upsala, 1888.
Phil 3246.82.2 Johann Gottlieb Fichte's Leben und Ritter. (Fichte, Immanuel Hermann.) Leipzig, 1862. 2v.
Phil 3246.82 Johann Gottlieb Fichte's Leben und Ritter. (Fichte, Immanuel Hermann.) Sulzbach, 1830-31. 2v.
Phil 3246.99.10 Johann Gottlieb Fichtes Lehren von Staat und Gesellschaft in ihrem Verhältnis zum neueren Sozialismus. (Lindau, Hans.) n.p., 1899.
Phil 3246.89 Johann Gottlieb Fichte's Religionsphilosophie. (Zimmer, F.) Berlin, 1878.
Phil 3585.1.90 Johann Heinrich Lambert; eine Darstellung seiner kosmologischen und philosophischen Leistungen. (Lepsius, J.) München, 1881.
Phil 3585.1.100F Johann Heinrich Lambert. (Loewenhaupt, Friedrich.) Mülhausen, 1943?
Phil 3585.1.105 Johann Heinrich Lambert und die wissenschaftliche Philosophie der Gegenwart. (Eisenring, Max F.E.) Zürich, 1942.
Phil 3585.1.85 Johann Heinrich Lamberts Konzeption einer Geometrie auf einer imaginären Kugel. (Peters, Wilhelm S.) Bonn, 1961.
Phil 3585.1.80 Johann Heinrich Lamberts Philosophie und seine Stellung zu Kant. Inaug. Diss. (Baensch, Otto.) Magdeburg, 1902.
Phil 3890.6.84 Johann Nicolaus Tetens. Inaug. Diss. (Uebele, Wilhelm.) Berlin, 1911.
Phil 3270.4.86 Johann Paul Anselm Feuerbach. (Kipper, Eberhard.) Köln, 1969.
Phil 8423.16 Johann Winckelmann, G. Ephraim Lessing klassische Schönheit. (Winckelmann, Johann Joachim.) Jena, 1906.
Phil 3140.80 Johannes Clauberg. (Müller, H.) Jena, 1891.
Phil 978.49.275 Das Johannes-Evangelium. 7. Aufl. (Steiner, R.) Dornach, 1955.
Phil 3450.5.80 Johannes Huber. (Zirngiebl, Eberhard.) Gotha, 1881.
Phil 3625.4.81 Johannes Müllers philosophische Anschauungen. Inaug. Diss. (Post, Karl.) Halle, 1905.
Phil 3790.9.80 Johannes Rehmke. (Rehmke, J.) Leipzig, 1921.
Phil 3903.1.95 Johannes Volkelts lära am det tragiska. (Ponnér, Jarl W.) Lund, 1956.
Phil 2675.6.80 Johannes von Jandun. (Schmugge, Ludwig.) Stuttgart, 1966.
Phil 5548.107 Johannesson, Ingvar. Effects of praise and blame. Stockholm, 1967.
Phil 7082.52 Jóhannsson, Jón. Draumur. Akureyri, 1882.
Phil 7082.52.2 Jóhannsson, Jón. Draumur. 2. Útgáfa. Reykjavík, 1916.

Phil 5585.155 — Johansen, Martin. Voluminalfigurale faenomener. København, 1959.

Phil 5249.14 — Johanson, A.M. Influence of incentive and punishment upon reaction-time. N.Y., 1922.

Phil 5049.17 — Johanson, Johan. Apharismi e logica transcendali quas praeside Samuel Grubbs. Upsaliae, 1815.

Phil 3491.2 — Johansson, J. Kants eticka asikt. Lund, 1902.

Phil 8430.62 — John, Erhard. Probleme der marxistisch-leninistischen Ästhetik. Halle, 1968.

Phil 5545.246 — John, Erwin Roy. Mechanisms of memory. N.Y., 1967.

Phil 1750.782 — John, Helen James. The Thomist spectrum. N.Y., 1966.

Phil 8581.18.8 — John Balguy, an English moralist of the 18th century. (Jones, H.D.) Leipzig, 1907.

Phil 1905.11.80 — John Bascom, prophet. (Robinson, Sanford.) N.Y., 1922.

Phil 1955.6.245 — John Dewey; a checklist of translations, 1900-1967. (Boyston, JoAnn.) Carbondale, 1969.

Phil 1955.6.112 — John Dewey; a Marxian critique. (Okun, Sid.) Chicago, 1942.

Phil 1955.6.92 — John Dewey, the man and his philosophy. Cambridge, 1930.

Phil 1955.6.210 — John Dewey. (Bernstein, Richard.) N.Y., 1966.

Phil 1955.6.160 — John Dewey. (Blewett, John.) N.Y., 1960.

Phil 1955.6.103A — John Dewey. (Hook, Sidney.) N.Y., 1939.

Phil 1955.6.104 — John Dewey. (Hook, Sidney.) N.Y., 1950.

Phil 1955.6.119 — John Dewey. (Nathanson, J.) N.Y., 1951.

Phil 1955.6.2 — John Dewey. (Thomas, Milton H.) Chicago, 1962.

Phil 1955.6.24 — John Dewey. 1st ed. (Dewey, John.) Indianapolis, 1955.

Phil 1955.6.200 — John Dewey and Arthur F. Bentley. (Dewey, John.) New Brunswick, 1964.

Phil 1955.6.155 — John Dewey and the experimental spirit in philosophy. (Hendel, Charles W.) N.Y., 1959.

Phil 1955.6.190 — John Dewey and the world view. (Lawson, D.E.) Carbondale, 1964.

Phil 1955.6.117 — John Dewey en sus noventa años. (Pan American Union. Division of Philosophy, Letters and Sciences.) Washington, 1949.

Phil 1955.6.140 — John Dewey in perspective. (Geiger, George R.) N.Y., 1958.

Phil 1955.6.150 — John Dewey's challenge to education. (Handlin, Oscar.) N.Y., 1959.

Phil 1955.6.215 — John Dewey's theory of inquiry and truth. (Nissen, Lowell.) The Hague, 1966.

Phil 1955.6.130 — John Dewey's thought and its implications for Christian education. (Gutzke, M.G.) N.Y., 1956.

Phil 8660.2.10 — John Fiske on the idea of God. (Shanahan, E.T.) Washington, 1897.

Phil 2030.8 — John Grote. (MacDonald, Lauchlin D.) The Hague, 1966.

Phil 2150.12.80 — John Henry Muirhead. (Ross, W.D.) London, 1940?

Phil 5090.3.80 — John Henry Newman. (Zeno, Father.) Leiden, 1957.

Phil 2115.118 — John Locke, ein Bild aus den geistigen Kämpfen Englands. (Fechtner, Eduard.) Stuttgart, 1898.

Phil 2115.143 — John Locke, en filosofis forberedelse og grunnleggelse (1632-1689). (Christophersen, H.O.) Oslo, 1932.

Phil 2115.144 — John Locke, 1632-1704. (Smith, N.K.) Manchester, 1933.

Phil 2115.149A — John Locke. (Aaron, Richard Ithamar.) London, 1937.

Phil 2115.168 — John Locke. (Cranston, M.W.) London, 1957.

Phil 2115.101 — John Locke. (Didier, J.) Paris, 1911.

Phil 2115.111.15A — John Locke. (Gibson, James.) London, 1933.

Phil 2115.155 — John Locke. (Schärer, E.) Leipzig, 1860.

Phil 2115.185 — John Locke. (Viano, Carlo A.) Torino, 1960.

Phil 2115.195 — John Locke. (Viano, Carlo A.) Torino, 1960.

Phil 2115.198 — John Locke. Il pensiero filosofico e pedagogico. (Bartolomeis, Francesco de.) Firenze, 1967.

Phil 2115.210 — John Locke: problems and perspectives. (Yolton, John W.) London, 1969.

Phil 2115.149.5 — John Locke. 2nd ed. (Aaron, R.I.) Oxford, 1955.

Phil 2115.149.3 — John Locke. 3rd ed. (Aaron, Richard Ithamar.) Oxford, 1971.

Phil 2115.147.2 — John Locke and English literature of the eighteenth century. (MacLean, K.) N.Y., 1962.

Phil 2115.147 — John Locke and English literature of the eighteenth century. (MacLean, K.) New Haven, 1936.

Phil 2115.163 — John Locke and the way of ideas. (Yolton, John W.) London, 1956.

Phil 2115.170 — John Locke e i limiti della scienza. (Giganti, Maria A.) Padova, 1957.

Phil 2115.94 — John Locke und die Schule von Cambridge. (Hertling, G. von.) Freiburg, 1892. 2v.

Phil 2115.159 — John Locke's political philosophy. (Gough, J.W.) Oxford, 1950.

Phil 2150.7.90 — John McTaggart Ellis McTaggart, 1866-1925. (Broad, Charles D.) London, 1928.

Phil 2150.7.95 — John McTaggart Ellis McTaggart. (Dickinson, G.L.) Cambridge, Eng., 1931.

Phil 3850.4.81 — John Michael Sailer's Lehre vom Menschen. Diss. (Wolf, L.) Giessen, 1937.

Phil 2138.79.12 — John Mill's boyhood visit to France. (Mill, John S.) Toronto, 1960.

Phil 2150.8.90 — John Stuart Mackenzie, 1860-1935. (Muirhead, J.H.) London, 1936?

Phil 2150.8.79 — John Stuart Mackenzie. (Mackenzie, J.S.) London, 1936.

Phil 2138.23 — John Stuart Mill; a selection of his works. (Mill, John S.) N.Y., 1966.

Phil 2138.81A — John Stuart Mill. (Bain, A.) London, 1882.

Phil 2138.81.5 — John Stuart Mill. (Bain, A.) N.Y., 1882.

Phil 2138.127 — John Stuart Mill. (Borchard, Ruth.) London, 1957.

Phil 2138.132 — John Stuart Mill. (Cranston, M.W.) London, 1958.

Phil 2138.83 — John Stuart Mill. (Douglas, C.) Edinburgh, 1895.

Phil 2138.148 — John Stuart Mill. (Ellery, J.B.) N.Y., 1964.

Phil 2138.93 — John Stuart Mill. (Gomperz, T.) Wien, 1889.

Phil 2138.90 — John Stuart Mill. (Lewels, Max.) Münster, 1902.

Phil 2138.165 — John Stuart Mill. (Ryan, Alan.) N.Y., 1970.

Phil 2138.86 — John Stuart Mill. (Spencer, H.) Boston, 1873.

Phil 2138.113 — John Stuart Mill. (The Examiner, London.) London, 1873.

Phil 2138.180 — John Stuart Mill: a critical study. (McCloskey, Henry John.) London, 1971.

Phil 2138.125 — John Stuart Mill and French thought. (Mueller, I.W.) Urbana, 1956.

Phil 2138.121.1 — John Stuart Mill and Harriet Taylor; their correspondence and subsequent marriage. (Hayek, Friedrich Augustus von.) London, 1951.

Phil 2138.121 — John Stuart Mill and Harriet Taylor; their friendship and subsequent marriage. (Hayek, Friedrich Augustus von.) London, 1951.

Phil 2138.145 — John Stuart Mill and the ends of life. (Berlin, Isaiah.) London, 1960?

Phil 2138.135 — John Stuart Mill and the Harriet Taylor myth. (Pappe, H.O.) Melbourne, 1960.

Phil 2138.120 — John Stuart Mill and the London and Westminster review. v.1-2. (Towers, C.M.D.) Boston, 1892.

Phil 2138.106 — John Stuart Mill's Theorie über den psychologischen Ursprung des Vulgärglaubens an die Aussenwelt. Inaug. Diss. (Störring, G.W.) Berlin, 1889.

Phil 2295.87 — John Toland als politischer Schriftsteller. Inaug. Diss. (Seeber, Anna.) Schramberg, 1933.

X Cg   Phil 2295.80 — John Toland und der Monismus der Gegenwart. (Berthold, G.) Heidelberg, 1876.

Phil 7068.83.6 — John William Fletcher, clairvoyant. (Gay, Susan E.) London, 1883.

Phil 5500.60 — Johnsen, Erik. Studies in multiobjective decision models. Lund, 1968.

Phil 5627.137.5 — Johnsen, T. Heart and spirit. Oslo, 1934.
Phil 2340.10.130.5

Phil 2340.10.130 — Johnson, A.H. Whitehead's philosophy of civilization. Boston, 1958.

— Johnson, A.H. Whitehead's theory of reality. Boston, 1952.

Phil 6319.18 — Johnson, Adelaide McFadyne. Experience, affect and behavior: psychoanalytic explorations of Adelaide McFadyne Johnson. Chicago, 1969.

Phil 5520.128 — Johnson, D.McE. The psychology of thought and judgment. N.Y., 1955.

Phil 184.36 — Johnson, E.V. Universal tradition. v.6. Alexandria, Va., 1932.

Phil 184.7 — Johnson, Edward. Nuces philosophicae, or The philosophy of things. London, 1842.

Phil 7060.35 — Johnson, F. The new psychic studies. N.Y., 1887.

Phil 9349.2 — Johnson, F. True womanhood. Cambridge, 1882.

Htn   Phil 8589.4* — Johnson, F.H. What is reality? Boston, 1891.

Phil 7069.28.40 — Johnson, G.L. The great problem and the evidence. London, 1928.

Phil 5274.20 — Johnson, Homer H. An introduction to experimental design in psychology. N.Y., 1971.

Phil 8589.16 — Johnson, J.W. Fundamentalism versus modernism. N.Y., 1925.

Phil 6980.367A — Johnson, James A. Group therapy. N.Y., 1963.

Phil 5545.32 — Johnson, L.D. Memoria technica. 3. ed. Boston, 1847.

Phil 8870.17 — Johnson, Oliver A. Ethics. N.Y., 1958.

Phil 9560.44 — Johnson, Oliver A. Rightness and goodness. The Hague, 1959.

Phil 8884.25 — Johnson, Oliver Adolph. Moral knowledge. Hague, 1966.

Phil 8884.25.5 — Johnson, Oliver Adolph. The moral life. London, 1969.

Phil 5853.6.5 — Johnson, Paul Emanuel. Person and counselor. Nashville, 1967.

Phil 184.42 — Johnson, R.C. The imprisoned splendour. London, 1953.

Phil 525.235 — Johnson, R.C. The light and the gate. London, 1964.

Phil 7069.56 — Johnson, R.C. Psychical research. N.Y., 1956.

Phil 8090.5 — Johnson, Robert Vincent. Aestheticism. London, 1969.

Phil 705.2 — Johnson, S. Transcendentalism. n.p., n.d.

Htn   Phil 184.8.3* — Johnson, Samuel. Elementa philosophica. Philadelphia, 1752.

Htn   Phil 184.8* — Johnson, Samuel. Elementa philosophica. v.1-2. Philadelphia, 1752.

Phil 184.8.5 — Johnson, Samuel. Introduction to the study of philosophy. 2. ed. London, 1743.

Phil 7060.109 — Johnson, Samuel. Spiritualism tested by science. New Haven, 1858.

Phil 5520.85 — Johnson, Wendel. People in guandaries. N.Y., 1946.

Phil 5049.16.1 — Johnson, William Ernest. Logic. N.Y., 1964. 3v.

Phil 5049.16A — Johnson, William Ernest. Logic. pt.1. Cambridge, Eng., 1921-24. 3v.

Phil 3640.342 — Johnsson, Milker. Nietzsche och tredje riket. Stockholm, 1943.

Phil 5238.60 — Johnston, D.K. Religion und wissenschaftliches Heilverfahren. Bahn, 1925. 7 pam.

Phil 5049.28 — Johnston, Frederick S. The logic of relationship. N.Y., 1968.

Phil 1870.100 — Johnston, G.A. The development of Berkeley's philosophy. London, 1923.

Phil 8884.13 — Johnston, George A. An introduction to ethics, for training colleges. London, 1915.

Phil 1830.2 — Johnston, George A. Selections from the Scottish philosophy of common sense. Chicago, 1915.

Phil 8634.4 — Johnston, R.F. Letters to a missionary. London, 1918.

Phil 6315.2.340 — Johnston, Thomas E. Freud and political thought. 1st. ed. N.Y., 1965.

Phil 1930.8.110 — Johnston, William Murray. The formative years of R.G. Collingwood. The Hague, 1967[1968]

Phil 184.49 — Johnstone, Henry Webb. Philosophy and argument. State College, Pa., 1959.

Phil 575.284 — Johnstone, Henry Webb. The problem of the self. University Park, 1970.

Phil 5049.14 — Johnstone, Lawrence. A short introduction to the study of logic. London, 1887.

Phil 5627.269.10 — Johoda, Gustav. The psychology of superstition. London, 1969.

Phil 8888.20 — Joie, souffrance et vie morale. (Nassent, Georges.) Paris, 1968.

Phil 5403.3 — La joie passive. (Mignard, M.) Paris, 1909.

Phil 6946.1.5 — Joint Commission on Mental Illness and Health. Action for mental health. N.Y., 1961.

Phil 7069.17.27 — Joire, Paul. Psychical and supernormal phenomena. N.Y., 1917.

Phil 6060.20 — Joire, Paul. Traité de graphologie scientifique. 2d ed. Paris, 1921.

Phil 5019.5 — Joja, A. Studii de logica. Bucuresti, 1960. 3v.

Phil 5525.6.10 — Jokes and their relation to the unconscious. (Freud, Sigmund.) London, 1960.

Phil 9450.17 — Joklík, F. Naše dějinné poslání; čaovas úvaha politicko-ethická. Praha, 1919?

Phil 5643.124 — Jolansky, Samuel. Optical illusion. N.Y., 1964.

Phil 585.220 — Jolif, Jean Y. Comprendre l'homme. Paris, 1967-

Phil 2725.19.90 — Jolivet, R. A la recherche de Dieu. Paris, 1931.

Phil 8664.4 — Jolivet, R. Études sur le problème de Dieu dans la philosophie contemporaine. Lyon, 1932.

Phil 2725.11.90 — Jolivet, Régis. De Rosmini à Lachelier. Paris, 1953.

Phil 1750.210 — Jolivet, Régis. Les doctrines existentialistes de Kierkegaard à J.P. Sartre. Paris, 1948.

Phil 2475.1.233 — Jolivet, Régis. Essai sur le bergsonisme. Lyon, 1931.

Phil 184.47 — Jolivet, Régis. L'homme métaphysique. Paris, 1958.

Phil 184.35 — Jolivet, Régis. La notion de substance. Paris, 1929.

Phil 184.35.5 — Jolivet, Régis. La notion de substance. Paris, 1929.

Phil 8612.34 — Jolivet, Régis. Le problème de la mort chez M. Heidegger et J.P. Sartre. Paris, 1950.

Phil 2880.8.155 — Jolivet, Régis. Sartre, ou La théologie de l'absurde. Paris, 1965.

Phil 2880.8.154 Jolivet, Régis. Sartre: the theology of the absurd. Westminster, 1967.
Phil 94.2 Jolivet, Régis. Vocabulaire de la philosophie. 4. ed. Lyon, 1957.
Phil 8959.3 Joly, C. Traité des restitutions des grands. Amsterdam, 1665.
Phil 184.9.5 Joly, H. Cours de philosophie. 7. ed. Paris, 1882.
Phil 5819.2 Joly, H. L'homme et l'animal. Paris, 1877.
Phil 5819.2.7 Joly, H. L'instinct; ses rapports. 2. éd. Paris, 1873.
Phil 5819.2.5 Joly, H. L'instinct. Paris, 1869.
Phil 2733.85 Joly, H. Malebranche. Paris, 1901.
Phil 184.9 Joly, H. Nouveau cours de philosophie. Paris, n.d.
Phil 5627.74.2 Joly, H. Psychologie des saints. 2. éd. Paris, 1897.
Phil 5465.19 Joly, Henri. L'imagination. 2. éd. Paris, 1883.
Phil 9349.4 Joly, Henri. Pour les jeunes. Paris, 1879.
Phil 5249.23.5 Joly, Henri. Psychologie des grands hommes. 2. éd. Paris, 1891.
Phil 3310.15.20 Jonas, Friedrich. Die Institutionenlehre Arnold Gehlens. Tübingen, 1966.
Phil 2075.8 Jonas, Hans. The phenomenon of life. 1st ed. N.Y., 1966.
Phil 7082.46 Jónasson, Hermann. Draumar. Reykjavík, 1912.
Phil 7082.46.5 Jónasson, Hermann. Dulrímir. Reykjavík, 1914.
Phil 340.8 Jonckheere, A. La lecture de l'expérience. Paris, 1958.
Phil 9035.30 Jones, A.J. Character in the making. London, 1913.
Phil 5049.11.2 Jones, A.L. Logic inductive and deductive. N.Y., 1909.
Phil 179.3.114 Jones, Abel John. Rudolf Eucken. London, 1913.
Phil 7069.10.10 Jones, Amanda T. A psychic autobiography. N.Y., 1910.
Phil 585.212.2 Jones, Arthur. Menschsein als Auftrag. 2. Aufl. Bern, 1967.
Phil 8589.10 Jones, David A. Philosophic thought and religion. London, 1919.
Phil 6119.4 Jones, E.E. Influence of bodily posture on mental activities. N.Y., 1907.
Phil 5049.12.9 Jones, E.E.C. Elements of logic as a science of propositions. Edinburgh, 1890.
Phil 5049.12.5 Jones, E.E.C. An introduction to general logic. London, 1892.
Phil 5049.12 Jones, E.E.C. A new law of thought and its logical bearings. Cambridge, 1911.
Phil 8589.19.8 Jones, E.S. The Christ of the Mount. N.Y., 1935.
Phil 5402.22.15 Jones, Eli Stanley. Christ and human suffering. N.Y., 1933.
Phil 6319.2.5.5 Jones, Ernest. Essays in applied psycho-analysis. London, 1951. 2v.
Phil 6319.2.5.7 Jones, Ernest. Essays in applied psycho-analysis. N.Y., 1964. 2v.
Phil 6315.2.151 Jones, Ernest. The life and work of Sigmund Freud. London, 1961.
Phil 6315.2.150A Jones, Ernest. The life and work of Sigmund Freud. 1st ed. N.Y., 1953. 3v.
Phil 6319.2.2 Jones, Ernest. Papers on psycho-analysis. London, 1918.
Phil 6319.2.6 Jones, Ernest. Papers on psycho-analysis. N.Y., 1913.
Phil 6319.2.1 Jones, Ernest. Papers on psycho-analysis. N.Y., 1919.
Phil 6319.2.4 Jones, Ernest. Papers on psycho-analysis. 4th ed. Baltimore, 1938.
Phil 6319.2.4.5 Jones, Ernest. Papers on psycho-analysis. 5th ed. Boston, 1961.
Phil 6319.2.4.6 Jones, Ernest. Papers on psycho-analysis. 5th ed. Boston, 1967.
Phil 6119.9 Jones, F. Wood. The matrix of the mind. Honolulu, 1928.
Phil 2075.4.30 Jones, G.V. Democracy and civilization. London, 1946.
Phil 400.25.2 Jones, H. Idealism as a practical creed. 2nd ed. Glasgow, 1910.
Phil 484.2 Jones, H.B. Croonian lectures on matter and force. London, 1868.
Phil 8581.18.8 Jones, H.D. John Balguy, an English moralist of the 18th century. Leipzig, 1907.
Phil 3491.20 Jones, Hardy E. Kant's principle of personality. Madison, 1971.
Phil 5249.27 Jones, Harold Ellis. Studies in human development. N.Y., 1966.
Phil 3565.82.5 Jones, Henry. A critical account of the philosophy of Lotze. Glasgow, 1895.
Phil 3565.82 Jones, Henry. A critical account of the philosophy of Lotze. N.Y., 1895.
Phil 8589.12 Jones, Henry. A faith that enquires. N.Y., 1922.
Phil 1930.6.125 Jones, Henry. The life and philosophy of Edward Caird. Glasgow, 1921.
Phil 8592.6.80 Jones, Henry. The philosophy of Martineau in relation to the idealism of the present day. London, 1905.
Phil 2035.82A Jones, J.H. Know the truth. Hamilton's theory. N.Y., 1865.
Phil 5415.5 Jones, J.W.L. Sociality and sympathy. N.Y., 1903.
Phil 8634.5 Jones, John Daniel. Our life beyond. Boston, 1914.
Phil 6959.6 Jones, Kathleen. Mental health and social policy. London, 1960.
Phil 5249.22 Jones, Llewellyn W. An introduction to theory and practice of psychology. London, 1934.
Phil 2150.1.85 Jones, Marc Edmund. George Sylvester Morris; his philosophical career and theistic idealism. Philadelphia, 1948.
Phil 6319.11 Jones, Maxwell. Social psychiatry. London, 1952.
Phil 2240.84 Jones, O.McK. Empiricism and intuitionism in Reid's common sense philosophy. Princeton, 1927.
Phil 5627.134.80 Jones, Olivin Mary. Inspired children. 1. ed. N.Y., 1933.
Phil 340.9 Jones, P. Chopin. The nature of knowledge. N.Y., 1964.
Phil 530.20.32A Jones, R.M. The flowering of mysticism. N.Y., 1939.
Phil 184.23 Jones, R.M. Fundamental ends of life. N.Y., 1924.
Phil 8589.13 Jones, R.M. Religious foundations. N.Y., 1923.
Phil 7082.12 Jones, Richard Matthew. Ego synthesis in dreams. Cambridge, 1962.
Phil 7082.12.5 Jones, Richard Matthew. The new psychology of dreaming. N.Y., 1970.
Phil 8699.1 Jones, Richard U. The scientifc eye of faith. Boston, 1935.
Phil 525.55.10 Jones, Rufus M. Some exponents of mystical religion. N.Y., 1930.
Phil 525.55 Jones, Rufus M. Studies in mystical religion. London, 1919.
Phil 5929.1 Jones, S. Practical phrenology. Boston, 1836.
Phil 9035.36 Jones, W. Tudor. The training of mind and will. London, 1920.
Phil 1145.35 Jones, W.H.S. Greek morality in relation to institutions. London, 1906.
Phil 5627.152 Jones, W.L. A psychological study of religious conversion. London, 1937.
Phil 3009.2 Jones, W.T. Contemporary thought of Germany. N.Y., 1931. 2v.

Phil 809.5 Jones, W.T. A history of Western philosophy. N.Y., 1952.
Phil 809.5.2 Jones, W.T. A history of Western philosophy. 2d ed. N.Y., 1969. 4v.
Phil 575.11 Jones, W.T. Idee der Persönlichkeit bei den englischen Denken. Jena, 1906.
Phil 3491.10 Jones, W.T. Morality and freedom in...Kant. London, 1940.
Phil 184.29 Jones, W.T. Nature, thought and personal experience. London, 1926.
Phil 6119.7 Jones, Wallace Franklin. A study of handedness. Vermillion, S.D., 1918.
Phil 5500.32 Jones, William. On decision-making in large organizations. Santa Monica, 1964.
Phil 8589.6 Jones, William T. Spiritual ascent of man. N.Y., 1917.
Phil 6959.7 Jong, Herman H. de. Experimental catatonia, a general reaction form of the central nervous system. Baltimore, 1945.
Phil 1200.42 Jong, K.H.E. De stoa; een wereld-philosophie. Amsterdam, 1937.
Phil 3425.207 Jong, K.H.E. de. Hegel und Plotin. Leiden, 1916.
Phil 3491.1 Jonquière, Georg. Die grundsätzliche Unanehmbarkeit. Bern, 1917.
Phil 7069.31.55 Jónsdóttir, J. Bréf frá Íngu. Winnipeg, 1931.
Phil 8959.6 Jonsen, Albert R. Responsibility in modern religious ethics. Washington, 1968.
Phil 75.7 Jonsius, Johannes. De scriptoribus historiae philosophicae. Jena, 1716.
Phil 3491.3 Jonson, Erik. Det kategoriska imperativet. Akademisk avhandling. Uppsala, 1924.
Phil 7082.48 Jónsson, Brynjólfur. Dulraenar smásögur. Bessastadir, 1907.
Phil 7069.06.13 Jónsson, G. Ur dularheimum. Reykjavik, 1906.
Phil 6128.17.5 Jonsson, Inge. Swedenborgs konespondenslära. Stockholm, 1969.
Phil 7069.34.15 Jónsson, J. Framhaldslif og nútímaþekking. Reykjavik, 1934.
Phil 5620.8 Jonsson, K.G. Undersökningar...problemräkningens förutsättningar och förlopp. Uppsala, 1919.
Phil 75.47 Joó, Tibor. Magyar nyelvü filozófiai kézúratók a Széchenyi Könyitárban. Budapest, 1940.
Phil 9230.1 Joostens, P. Alea, sive de curanda ludendi in pecuniam cupiditate. Amsterodami, 1642.
Phil 7069.45.65 Jordan, Alfred McKay, (Mrs.). Science from the unseen. N.Y., 1945.
Phil 9430.18 Jordan, D.S. The philosophy of despair. San Francisco, 1902.
Phil 184.41 Jordan, David S. The higher foolishness. Indianapolis, 1927.
Phil 8410.3 Jordan, E. The aesthetic object; an introduction to the philosophy of value. Bloomington, 1937.
Phil 8884.24 Jordan, E. The good life. Chicago, 1949.
Phil 2075.7.30 Jordan, Elijah. Essays in criticism. Chicago, 1952.
Phil 2075.7.35 Jordan, Elijah. Metaphysics. Evanston, Ill., 1956.
Phil 9035.4 Jordan, F. Character as seen in body and parentage. London, 1890.
Phil 8884.23 Jordan, Furneaux. Moral nerve and the error of literary verdicts. London, 1901.
Phil 5627.105 Jordan, G.J. A short psychology of religion. N.Y., 1927.
Phil 5549.17 Jordan, G.J. The story of psychology. London, 1926.
Phil 510.133 Jordan, H. Die Lebenserscheinungen. Leipzig, 1911.
Phil 2805.99 Jordan, H.R. Blaise Pascal. London, 1909.
Phil 5520.56 Jordan, Leo. Die Kunst des begrifflichen Denkens. München, 1926.
Phil 5520.56.10 Jordan, Leo. Schule der Abstraktion und der Dialektik. München, 1932.
Phil 2340.10.230 Jordan, Martin. New shapes of reality: aspects of A.N. Whitehead's philosophy. London, 1968.
Phil 5500.28 Jordan, Nehemiah. Decision-making under uncertainty and problem solving. Santa Monica, 1960.
Phil 5585.214 Jordan, Nehemiah. Perception. Santa Monica, 1961.
Phil 5249.31 Jordan, Nehemiah. Themes in speculative psychology. London, 1968.
Phil 5325.40F Jordan, Nehemiah. The theory of cognitive dissonance. Washington, 1964.
Phil 8589.30 Jordan, Placidus. Antwort auf Wort. München, 1969.
Phil 9470.6 Jordan, Rudolf. Homo sapiens socialis, principles of the philosophy of responsibility. Johannesburg, 1944.
Phil 4926.160.30 Jordan, Rudolf. The new perspective, an essay. Chicago, 1951.
Phil 1200.27.2 Jordan, T. The stoic moralists, and the Christians in the first two centuries. 2d ed. Dublin, 1884.
Phil 2138.91 Jordan, W. Program des königlichen Gymnasiums. Stuttgart, 1870.
Phil 8884.4.2 Jordan, W.G. Kingship of self-control individual problems. N.Y., 1899.
Phil 8884.4 Jordan, W.G. Kingship of self-control individual problems. N.Y., 1901.
Phil 8884.4.17 Jordan, W.G. The majesty of calmness. N.Y., 1900.
Phil 8884.4.13 Jordan, W.G. The power of purpose. N.Y., 1910.
Phil 8884.9 Jordan, W.G. The power of truth. N.Y., 1902.
Phil 8884.4.5 Jordan, W.G. Self-control, its kingship and majesty. N.Y., 1905.
Phil 310.652A Jordan, Zbigniew A. The evolution of dialectical materialism. London, 1967.
Phil 4800.20 Jordan, Zbigniew A. Philosophy and ideology. Dordrecht, 1963.
Phil 8410.6 Jordán de Urríes y Azara, José. Resumen de teoría general del arte. 1. ed. Madrid, 1933.
Phil 5628.50.5 Jordanaeus, Johannes. Disputatio brevis ad categorica de proba stigmata utrum scilicet ea licita sit, necne. Coloniae Agrippinae, 1630.
Phil 4065.80.5 Jordano Bruno. (Bartholmess, C.) Paris, 1846-47. 2v.
Phil 4065.80 Jordano Bruno. (Bartholmess, C.) Paris, 1846-47. 2v.
Phil 340.36 Jordon, Bruno. Die Ideenlehre. Leipzig, 1928.
Phil 2475.1.212 Jorgensen, J. Henri Bergson's filosofi i omrids. København, 1917.
Phil 3805.210 Jorgensen, Paul. Die Ethik Schleiermachers. München, 1959.
Phil 5049.18 Jorgenson, J. A treatise of formal logic. Copenhagen, 1931. 3v.
Phil 184.50 Jorn, A. Naturens orden; de divisione naturae. 2. Opl. København, 1962.
Phil 4964.5 José Augustin Caballero y las origines de la conciencia cubana. (Agramonte y Pichardo, R.) La Habana, 1952.
Phil 4359.1.83 José Ingenieros. (Bermann, G.) Buenos Aires, 1926.
Phil 4359.1.81 José Ingenieros y el porvenir de la filosofía. 2a ed. (Endara, Julio.) Buenos Aires, 192-.
Phil 3195.3.6 Josef Dietzgens kleinere Philosophie. (Dietzgen, Joseph.) Stuttgart, 1903.

Phil 3195.3.82	Josef Dietzgens philosophische Lehren. (Hepner, Adolf.) Stuttgart, 1916.
Phil 5440.18	Josefovici, U. Die psychische Vererbung. Leipzig, 1912.
Phil 1870.109A	Joseph, H.W.B. A comparison of Kant's idealism with that of Berkeley. London, 1929.
Phil 184.38	Joseph, H.W.B. Essays in ancient and modern philosophy. Oxford, 1935.
Phil 3552.320	Joseph, H.W.B. Lectures on the philosophy of Leibniz. Oxford, 1949.
Phil 8884.22	Joseph, H.W.B. Some problems of ethics. Oxford, 1931.
Phil 5049.9.5	Joseph, Horace William Brindley. An introduction to logic. 2nd rev. ed. Oxford, 1931.
Phil 5049.9.2.1	Joseph, Horace William Brindley. An introduction to logic. 2nd rev. ed. Oxford, 1967.
Phil 2055.1.82	Joseph, M. Die Psychologie Henry Home's. Inaug.-Diss. Halle, 1911.
Phil 1900.85	Joseph Butler als zedekundige. (Weeda, W.H.) Utrecht, 1899.
Phil 3195.3.80	Joseph Dietzgens Philosophie. (Dietzgen, Joseph.) München, 1910.
Phil 2030.1.85	Joseph Glanvill. (Cope, Jackson I.) St. Louis, 1956.
Phil 2030.1.80	Joseph Glanvill. (Greenslet, F.) N.Y., 1900.
Phil 2030.1.81	Joseph Glanvill and physical research in the seventeenth century. (Redgrove, H. Stanley.) London, 1921.
Phil 3450.20.10	Joseph Hillebraud. Diss. (Schreiher, H.W.) Giessen, 1937.
Phil 2218.86A	Joseph Priestley. (Thorpe, J.E.) London, 1906.
Phil 2218.89	Joseph Priestley and the problem of pantiscocracy. (Park, Mary Cathryne) Philadelphia, 1947.
Phil 2218.88	Joseph Priestley and the problem of pantiscocracy. Diss. (Park, Mary Cathryne.) Philadelphia, 1947.
Phil 5627.101	Josey, C.C. The psychology of religion. N.Y., 1927.
Phil 5819.3	Josey, Charles C. The role of instinct in social psychology. N.Y., 1921.
Phil 5819.3.5	Josey, Charles C. The social philosophy of instinct. N.Y., 1922.
Phil 2250.112	Josiah Royce. (Buranelli, V.) N.Y., 1964.
Phil 2250.91	Josiah Royce. (Norborg, Sven.) Oslo, 1934.
Phil 2250.90	Josiah Royce and Indian thought. (Leidecker, K.F.) N.Y., 1931.
Phil 2250.106	Josiah Royce's seminar, 1913-1914. (Costello, Harry.) New Brunswick, 1963.
Phil 2250.88.2	Josiah Royces Versuch einer Synthese von Pragmatismus und Objektivität. (Rothman, W.) Jena, 1926.
Phil 2250.88	Josiah Royces Versuch einer Synthese von Pragmatismus und Objektivität. Inaug. Diss. (Rothman, W.) Jena, 1926.
Phil 184.40	Josipovici, J. Fragments de vie intérieure. Aix-en-Provence, 1937.
Phil 9245.18	Joslyn, R. The philosophy of happiness. Elgin, n.d.
Phil 3160.3.87	Jospe, Alfred. Die Unterscheidung von Mythos und Religion hei Hermann Cohen. Inaug. Diss. Oppeln, 1932.
Phil 5759.3	Joss, Hermann. Der Wille. Bern, 1921.
Phil 3090.01	Jost, J. Bibliographie der Schriften Franz v. Baaders. Bonn, 1926.
Phil 3800.10	Jost, J. F.W.J. von Schelling: Bibliographie. Bonn, 1927.
Phil 8410.7.5	Jouffroy, T.S. Cours d'esthétique. 2. éd. Paris, 1863.
Phil 8410.7	Jouffroy, T.S. Cours d'esthétique suivi de la thèse de l'art. 1. éd. Paris, 1843.
Phil 2672.40	Jouffroy, Théodore S. Le cahier vert; comment les dogmes finissent. Lettres inédites. Paris, 1924.
Phil 2672.75	Jouffroy, Théodore S. Correspondance. Paris, 1901.
Phil 2672.31	Jouffroy, Théodore S. Cours de droit naturel. Paris, 1835. 3v.
Phil 2672.31.5	Jouffroy, Théodore S. Cours de droit naturel. 4. éd. v.2. Paris, 1866.
Phil 2672.35	Jouffroy, Théodore S. Introduction to ethics. Boston, 1840. 2v.
Phil 2672.35.1	Jouffroy, Théodore S. Introduction to ethics. Boston, 1841. 2v.
Phil 2672.35.2	Jouffroy, Théodore S. Introduction to ethics. Boston, 1845. 2v.
Phil 2672.35.10	Jouffroy, Théodore S. Introduction to ethics. Boston, 1873. 2v.
Phil 2672.35.3	Jouffroy, Théodore S. Introduction to ethics. v.1-2. Boston, 1858.
Phil 2672.29	Jouffroy, Théodore S. Mélanges philosophiques. Paris, 1833.
Phil 2672.30	Jouffroy, Théodore S. Mélanges philosophiques. Paris, 1838.
Phil 2672.30.5	Jouffroy, Théodore S. Mélanges philosophiques. 4e éd. v.1-2. Paris, 1866.
Phil 2672.36	Jouffroy, Théodore S. Moral philosophy. N.Y., 1862.
Phil 2672.30.2	Jouffroy, Théodore S. Nouveaux mélanges philosophiques. Paris, 1842.
Phil 2672.30.3	Jouffroy, Théodore S. Nouveaux mélanges philosophiques. 2e éd. Paris, 1861.
Phil 8725.20	Jouguelet, Pierre. Laïcité, liberté et vérité. Tournai, 1970.
Phil 2477.6.185	Jouhaud, Michel. Le problème de l'être et l'expérience morale chez Maurice Blondel. Paris, 1970.
Phil 184.10	Jouin, R.P.L. Compendium logicae et metaphysicae. N.Y., 1884.
Phil 5249.30	Jourard, Sidney Marshall. Disclosing man to himself. Princeton, 1968.
Phil 5590.235.2A	Jourard, Sidney Marshall. Personal adjustment. 2. ed. N.Y., 1963.
Phil 5590.568.1	Jourard, Sidney Marshall. The transparent self. N.Y., 1971.
Phil 184.14	Jourdain, Charles. Nociones de filosofía. Valparaiso, 1870.
Phil 184.21.9	Jourdain, Charles. Notions de philosophie. Paris, 1865.
Phil 184.21.15	Jourdain, Charles. Notions de philosophie. 15e ed. Paris, 1875.
Phil 410.8	Jourdain, E.F. On the theory of the infinite in modern thought. London, 1911.
Phil 192.28.28	Jourdain, P. The philosophy of Mr. B*rtr*nd R*ss*ll. London, 1918.
Phil 40.10	Journal. (American Psychoanalytic Association.) N.Y. 1,1953+ 21v.
Phil 8505.15	Journal. (American Scientific Affiliation.) Mankato. 1,1949+ 6v.
Phil 58.3.9	Journal. (American Society for Psychical Research.) N.Y. 1,1907+ 62v.
Phil 2630.11.10	Journal. (Guitton, Jean.) Paris, 1959. 2v.
Phil 48.14	Journal. (Indian Academy of Philosophy.) Calcutta. 1,1961+
Phil 2730.60.2	Journal. (Maine de Biran, Pierre.) Neuchâtel, 1954. 3v.
Phil 6327.4.60	Journal. (Otto Rank Association.) Doylestown. 1,1966+ 2v.
Phil 25.131	Journal. (Philosophical Association; Amravate.) Nagpur. 2v.
Phil 55.7	Journal. (Psychologists League, New York.) N.Y. 1-4,1937-1940 2v.
Phil 58.1	Journal. (Society for Psychical Research, London.) London. 1,1884+ 36v.
Phil 40.10.5	Journal. Monograph series. (American Psychoanalytic Association.) N.Y. 1,1958+ 4v.
Phil 19.51	Journal at creative behavior. Buffalo. 1,1967+
Phil 19.7	Journal de psychologie. Paris. 1+ 51v.
Phil 19.18	Journal du magnétisme. Paris. 1-20,1845-1861 20v.
Phil 6689.6	Journal du traitement magnétique. (Tardy de Montravel, A.A.) London, 1786. 2 pam.
Phil 6689.6.3	Journal du traitement magnétique. (Tardy de Montravel, A.A.) Strasbourg, 1787.
Phil 19.46	Journal for anthroposophy. N.Y. 1,1965+
Phil 19.48	Journal for philosophic understanding. Mercer Island, Washington. 1-2
Phil 19.55	The journal for the study of consciousness. Philadelphia. 1,1968+
Phil 19.22	Journal für Psychologie und Neurologie. 1-49 47v.
Phil 3450.29	Journal in the night. (Haecker, Theodor.) London, 1950.
Phil 2730.60	Journal intimé. 5e éd. (Maine de Biran, Pierre.) Paris, 1927-1931. 2v.
Phil 187.93	Journal métaphysique. (Marcel, Gabriel.) Paris, 1927.
Phil 19.13	The journal of abnormal psychology. Boston. 1,1906+ 65v.
Phil 6319.4	Journal of abnormal psychology. Boston. 1919?
Phil 8010.5	The journal of aesthetic education. Champaigne, Ill. 1,1966+ 5v.
Phil 8010.3	Journal of aesthetics and art criticism. N.Y. 6,1947+ 20v.
Phil 19.35	Journal of analytical psychology. London. 1,1955+ 7v.
Phil 19.53	Journal of applied behavior analysis. Lawrence, Kan. 1,1968+
Phil 19.12	Journal of applied psychology. Worcester. 1,1917+ 54v.
Phil 19.66	Journal of autism and childhood schizophrenia; devoted to all psychoses and severe disorders of behavior in childhood. Washington. 1,1971+
Phil 19.64	Journal of child development. Tokyo. 1,1965+
Phil 19.27	The journal of Christian philosophy. N.Y.
Phil 17.11	Journal of clinical and experimental hypnosis. N.Y. 1,1953+ 15v.
Phil 19.29	Journal of consulting psychology. Lancaster, Pa. 1,1937+ 25v.
Phil 19.59	Journal of cross-cultural psychology; international and interdisciplinary. Bellingham, Washington. 1,1970+
Phil 19.37	Journal of existential psychiatry. N.Y. 1-8,1960-1968// 8v.
Phil 19.16	Journal of experimental psychology. Princeton. 1,1916+ 76v.
Phil 19.45	Journal of experimental research in personality. N.Y. 1,1965+ 2v.
Phil 19.23	Journal of general psychology. Worcester. 1,1928+ 51v.
Phil 19.39	Journal of humanistic psychology. Palo Alto. 1,1961+ 5v.
Phil 19.62	Journal of Indian philosophy. Dordrecht. 1,1970+
Phil 19.42	Journal of mathematical psychology. N.Y. 1,1964+ 5v.
NEDL Phil 19.1.5	Journal of mental science. Index. London, n.d.
Phil 19.1.5	Journal of mental science. Index. London, 1879-1928.
Phil 6319.10	Journal of Mental Science. Recent progress in psychiatry. London. 1944
NEDL Phil 19.1	Journal of mental science. London. 2-75,1856-1929 45v.
Phil 19.1	Journal of mental science. London. 76,1930+ 43v.
Phil 19.47	Journal of modern subjectivism. Mercer Island, Washington. 59-71
NEDL Phil 19.2.6	Journal of nervous and mental disease. Index. N.Y., 1914-1925.
NEDL Phil 19.2	Journal of nervous and mental disease. Chicago. 1-70,1874-1829 70v.
Phil 19.2	Journal of nervous and mental disease. Chicago. 71-105,1930-1947 35v.
Phil 19.15	The journal of neurology and psychopathology. Bristol. 1+ 34v.
Phil 19.30	Journal of parapsychology. Durham, N.C. 1,1937+ 31v.
Phil 19.44	Journal of personality and social psychology. Ann Arbor, Mich. 1,1965+ 10v.
Phil 19.68	Journal of phenomenological psychology. Pittsburgh. 2,1971+
Phil 19.63	Journal of philosophical logic. Dordrecht. 1,1972+
Phil 19.21	Journal of philosophical studies. London. 1,1926+ 38v.
Phil 19.6.5	Journal of philosophy, psychology and scientifc methods. N.Y. 1-12,1904-1915 12v.
Phil 19.6	Journal of philosophy, psychology and scientific methods. N.Y. 1,1904+ 95v.
X Cg Phil 19.6	Journal of philosophy, psychology and scientific methods. N.Y. 9
Phil 19.6.10	Journal of philosophy, psychology and scientific methods. Fifty year index, 1904-53; and ten year supplement, 1954-63. N.Y., 1962-64. 2v.
Phil 19.3	Journal of practical metaphysics. Boston. 1-3
Phil 25.175	Journal of psychedelic drugs. San Francisco. 1,1967+
Phil 19.11.5	Journal of psycho-asthetics. Supplements. Fairbault, 1911.
Phil 19.11	Journal of psycho-asthetics. Fairbault. 1+ 49v.
Phil 19.34	Journal of psychological researches. Madras. 1,1957+ 3v.
Phil 19.23.15	The journal of psychology. Worcester, Mass. 1,1935+ 48v.
Phil 19.49	Journal of psychophysical research. Oxford. 1,1967+
Phil 10.15	Journal of religious psychology. Worcester. 1-7,1904-1915 7v.
Phil 19.24	The journal of social psychology. Worcester. 1,1930+ 56v.
Phil 19.33	Journal of social therapy. N.Y. 1,1957+ 11v.
Phil 19.4	Journal of speculative philosophy. St. Louis. 1-22,1867-1893 21v.
Phil 19.28	The journal of symbolic logic. Menasha, Wis. 1,1936+ 24v.
Phil 19.38	Journal of the dynamic sciences. Hollywood. 1,1961+
Phil 19.43	Journal of the history of philosophy. Berkeley. 2,1964+ 6v.
Phil 19.26	Journal of thought and philosophy in general. Ocean Park, Calif. 1-4
Phil 19.57	Journal of transpersonal psychology. Stanford, California. 1,1969+

Phil 19.50 Journal of value enquiry. The Hague. 1,1967+
Phil 19.40 Journal of verbal learning and verbal behavior. N.Y. 1,1962+ 6v.
Phil 1870.73.5 Le journal philosophique. Commonplace book. (Berkeley, G.) Paris, 1908.
Phil 8661.6 Journée solitaire de l'homme sensible. (Gomer, A. de.) Paris, 1800.
Phil 3552.480 Journées, Leibniz. Leibniz, 1646-1716, aspects de l'homme et de l'oeuvre. Paris, 1968.
Phil 2733.125 Journées Malebranche, Paris, 1965. Malebranche l'homme et l'oeuvre, 1638-1715. Paris, 1967.
Phil 8654.105 Journées Universitaires, 44th, Pau, France, 1967. Qui est notre Dieu? n.p., n.d.
Phil 8620.51 Journet, C. The meaning of evil. N.Y., 1963.
Phil 2805.256 Journet, C. Vérité de Pascal. St. Maurice, 1951.
Phil 8664.12 Journet, Charles. Connaissance et inconnaissance de Dieu. Paris, 1969.
Phil 9240.26 Journet, Charles. Le mal. Bruges? 1961.
Phil 1750.26 Journey through dread. (Ussher, A.) N.Y., 1955.
Phil 575.282 The journeying self; a study in philosophy and social role. (Natanson, Maurice Alexander.) Reading, Mass., 1970.
Phil 270.10 Journeyman (pseud.). Beneficence design in problem of evil...causation. N.Y., 1849.
Phil 184.18 Joussain, A. Esquisse d'une philosophie. Paris, 1912.
Phil 8884.11 Joussain, A. Le fondement psychologique de la morale. Paris, 1909.
Phil 5400.71 Joussain, A. Les passions humaines. Paris, 1928.
Phil 5249.20 Joussain, A. Les sentiments et l'intelligence. Paris, 1930.
Phil 1870.98 Joussain, André. Exposé critique de la philosophie de Berkeley. Paris, 1921.
Phil 1870.98.3 Joussain, André. Exposé critique de la philosophie de Berkeley. Thèse. Paris, 1920.
Phil 8589.9 Joussain, André. Romantisme et religion. Paris, 1910.
Phil 5374.190 Joussain, André. Les systèmes de la vie. Paris, 1958.
Phil 8520.80 Joussain, André. Temps présent et religion. Toulouse, 1967.
Phil 9430.28 Jouvin, Léon. Le pessimisme. Paris, 1892.
Phil 4710.65 Jovchuk, M.T. Osnovnye cherty russkoi klassicheskoi filosofii XIX v. Moskva, 1945.
Phil 2805.111 Jovy, Ernest. D'où irent l' "Ad tuum, Domine Jesu, de Pascal? Paris, 1916. 2 pam.
Phil 2805.111.15 Jovy, Ernest. Etudes pascaliennes. Paris, 1927-36. 9v.
Phil 530.15.25 Jovy, Ernest. Une mystique en pays Perthois au XVIIe siècle Marie Darizy de Verget. Vitry-Le-François, 1913.
Phil 2805.111.5 Jovy, Ernest. Pascal et Saint Ignace. Paris, 1923.
Phil 2805.111.10 Jovy, Ernest. Pascal n'a pa inventé le haquet, démonstration lexicographique. Paris, 1923.
Phil 49.6 Jowett papers, 1968-1969. Oxford, 1970.
Phil 3850.27.102 Joy, C.R. Music in the life of Albert Schweitzer. 1st ed. N.Y., 1951.
Phil 5403.12 Joy; expanding human awareness. (Schutz, William Carl.) N.Y., 1968.
Phil 5115.3 Joyau, E. De l'invention dans les arts. Paris, 1879.
Phil 5759.4 Joyau, Emmanuel. Essai sur la liberté morale. Paris, 1888.
Phil 2409.2 Joyau, Emmanuel. La philosophie en France pendant la révolution. Paris, 1893.
Phil 5049.10 Joyce, G.A. Principles of logic. London, 1908.
Phil 6990.15 Joyce, G.H. The question of miracles. St. Louis, 1914.
Phil 9245.56 The joyful heart. (Schauffler, Robert H.) Boston, 1914.
Phil 3640.77.25 The joyful wisdom. (Nietzsche, Friedrich.) London, n.d.
Phil 3640.77.27 Joyful wisdom. (Nietzsche, Friedrich.) N.Y., 1960.
Phil 9245.28 The joys of living. (Marden, Orison S.) N.Y., 1913.
X Cg Phil 4777.433 Józef Goluchowski. (Harassek, S.) Kraków, 1924.
Phil 4803.468.80 Józefa Joteyko. Wyd. 1. (Lipkowski, Otton.) Warszawa, 1968.
Phil 4260.148 Juan Batista Vico y el mundo histórico. 1. ed. (Uscatescu, George.) Madrid, 1956.
Phil 5247.13.29 Juan Huarte de San Juan. (Herrero Pouas, Antolin.) Madrid, 1941.
Phil 5247.13.25 Juan Huarte und der Psychognosis der Renaissance. Inaug. Diss. (Klein, Anton.) Bonn, 1913.
Phil 4372.1.135 Juan Luis Vives. (Noreña, Carlos G.) The Hague, 1970.
Phil 4372.1.93 Juan Luis Vives. 1. ed. (Ríos Sarmiento, Juan.) Madrid, 1940.
Phil 2750.18.80 Jubilé Albert Michotte. (Louvain. Université Catholique.) Louvain, 1947.
Phil 8969.2 Jubilee essays. (Tenney, E.P.) Boston, 1862.
Phil 3491.18 Juchem, Hans Georg. Die Entwicklung des Begriffs des Schönen bei Kant, unter besonderer Berücksichtigung des Begriffs verworrenen Erkenntnis. Bonn, 1970.
Phil 1050.6 Judah Messer Leon's commentary on the Vitus logica. (Husik, Isaac.) Leiden, 1906.
Phil 6980.516 Judaism and psychiatry. (Noveck, Simon.) N.Y., 1956.
Phil 6315.2.360 Judaism in Sigmund Freud's world. (Grollman, Earl Alan.) N.Y., 1965.
Phil 8620.3 Judas Ischariot. v.1-2. (Daub, C.) Heidelberg, 1816-18.
Phil 5249.7.5.3 Judd, C.H. Laboratory equipment for psychological experiments. N.Y., 1907.
Phil 5249.7.5.2 Judd, C.H. Laboratory manual of psychology. N.Y., 1907.
Phil 5249.7.2 Judd, C.H. Psychology. General introduction. Boston, 1917.
Phil 5249.7 Judd, C.H. Psychology. General introduction. N.Y., 1907.
Phil 5648.16 Judd, Charles H. Über Reumwahrnehmungen im Gebiet des Tastsinnes. Inaug. Diss. Leipzig, 1896.
Phil 2225.1.80 Judd, W.B. Noah Porters Erkenntnislehre. Jena, 1897.
Phil 8834.4 Judge, M.H. The ethical movement in England, 1902. London, 1902.
Phil 978.7.15 Judge, W.Z. Echoes from the Orient. 3rd ed. Point Loma, Calif., 1921.
Phil 978.7.5 Judge, W.Z. Letters that have helped me. N.Y., 1891.
Phil 978.7.9 Judge, W.Z. Letters that have helped me. 4th ed. N.Y., 1891.
Phil 978.7.3 Judge, W.Z. The ocean of theosophy. Point Loma, Calif., 1926[1923]
Phil 978.7.2 Judge, W.Z. The ocean of theosophy. 2nd ed. N.Y., 1893.
Phil 5500.01 Pamphlet box. Judgment.
Phil 5500.6 Judgment as belief. (Lewis, T.A.) Baltimore, 1910.
Phil 8583.28.5 The judgment of the nations. (Dawson, Christopher H.) N.Y., 1942.
Phil 5640.33 The judgment of very weak sensory stimuli. (Brown, Warner.) Berkeley, 1914.
Phil 193.72.5 The judicial office and other matters. (Slesser, Henry H.) London, 1943.
Phil 8655.2 Judicium de judiciis. (Ancillon, L.F.) Berolini, 1792.

Phil 7054.148 Judson, Abby A. The bridge between two worlds. Minneapolis, 1894.
Phil 7068.95.20 Judson, Abby A. Why she became a spiritualist. 3. ed. Cincinnati, 1895.
Phil 8664.10 Jüchen, Aurel von. Atheismus in West und Ost. 1. Aufl. Berlin, 1968.
Phil 7069.64 Juegenson, F. Rosterna från rymden. Stockholm, 1964.
Phil 400.51 Jünemann, F. Der philosophische Idealismus und das Grundproblem der Erkenntnistheorie. Neisse, 1913. 4v.
Phil 3491.8 Jünemann, Franz. Kantiana. Leipzig, 1909.
Phil 3120.50.30 Der jünghegelianer Bruno Bauer im Vormärz. (Hertz-Eichenrode, Dieter.) Berlin, 1959.
Phil 1750.143 Juganaru, P. L'apologie de la guerre dans la philosophie contemporaine. Thèse. Paris, 1913.
Phil 192.80.2 Le jugement d'existence. (Rabeau, G.) Paris, 1938.
Phil 192.80 Le jugement d'existence. (Rabeau, G.) Wetteren, 1937.
Phil 8408.48 Le jugement esthétique. (Hussain, Fakhir.) Paris, 1968.
Phil 3500.43 Le jugement réfléchissant dans la philosophie critique de Kant. (Souviau, M.) Paris, 1926.
Phil 3500.43.2 Le jugement réfléchissant dans la philosophie critique de Kant. Thèse. (Souviau, M.) Paris, 1926.
Phil 8582.4 Jugements d'un mourant sur la vie. (Caumont, G.) Paris, 1876.
Phil 8957.18 Jugend an der Maschine. (Huemmeler, Hans.) Freiburg, 1932.
Phil 3195.16.80 Jugendgeschichte Adolf Dyroffs. 2. Aufl. (Szylkarski, W.) Bonn, 1948.
Phil 3425.311 Die Jugendgeschichte Hegels. (Dilthey, Wilhelm.) Berlin, 1905.
Phil 6980.350 Jugendpsychiatrische Studien. (Held, Fritz.) Berlin, 1966.
Phil 3640.21 Jugendschriften. (Nietzsche, Friedrich.) München, 1923.
Phil 5203.27 Jugoslovenska psihološka bibliografija, period od 1952-1964 god. Beograd, 1964.
Phil 4635.5.81.3 Juhana Vilhelm Snellman. (Rein, T.) Helsingissä, 1928.
Phil 4630.2.80 Juhlajulkaisu omistettu Th. Reinille hänen täyttäessään 80 vuotta. Helsingissä, 1918.
Phil 5066.560 Juhos, B. van. Elemente der neuen Logik. Frankfurt, 1954.
Phil 2880.8.90 Juin, Hubert. Jean-Paul Sartre. Photoreproduction. Bruxelles, 1946.
Phil 2725.14.92 Jules Lagneau. (Canivez, André.) Paris, 1965. 2v.
Phil 2725.14.85 Jules Lagneau. (Union pour l'Action Morale, Paris.) Paris, n.d.
Phil 2725.13.98 Jules Lequier. (Tilliette, Xavier.) Paris, 1964.
Phil 2725.13.80 Jules Lequier e il problema della liberta. (Petterlini, Arnaldo.) Milano, 1969.
Phil 3491.12 Julia, Didier. La question de l'homne et la fondement de la philosophie. Aubier, 1964.
Phil 8410.4 Julianez Islas, L. El culto di lo bello. La Plata, 1929.
Phil 5520.654 Juliard, Pierre. Philosophies of language in eighteenth-century France. The Hague, 1970.
Phil 2805.315 Julien Eymard d'Angers. Pascal et ses précurseurs. Paris, 1954.
Phil 2705.82 Julien Offray de La Mettrie. (Poritzky, J.E.) Berlin, 1900.
Phil 5780.24 Julius, Fritz Hendrik. Tierkreis. v.1-2. Freiburg, 1964-
Phil 3120.11.85 Julius Bahnsen. (Heydorn, H.J.) Göttingen, 1952.
Phil 3120.11.80 Julius Bahnsen und die Hauptprobleme seiner charakterologie. (Thodoroff, C.) Erlangen, 1910.
Phil 3270.9.80 Julius Frauenstädt, sein Leben, seine Schriften und seine Philosophie. Inaug. Diss. v.8. (Berger, Hermann.) Rostock, 1911.
Phil 9558.25 Jullian, T. Dictionnaire du snobisme. Paris, 1958.
Phil 9349.6 Jumigny, de. Le père gouverneur de Son fils. Bourbes, 1780.
Phil 5590.295 Jump book. (Halsman, Phillipe.) N.Y., 1959.
Phil 1540.7.2 Jundt, A. Les amis de Dieu au quatorzième siècle. Thèse. Strasbourg, 1879.
Phil 8685.12 Jundt, A. Histoire du panthéisme populaire. Strasbourg, 1875.
Phil 530.20.30 Jundt, Auguste. Les amis de Dieu au quatorzième siècle. Paris, 1879.
Htn Phil 3801.469* Jung, Alexander. F.W.J. von Schelling. Leipzig, 1864.
Phil 6319.1.6 Jung, C.G. Analytical psychology. N.Y., 1916.
Phil 6319.1.255 Jung, C.G. Analytical psychology: its theory and practice. London, 1968.
Phil 6319.1.11 Jung, C.G. Analytische Psychologie und Erziehung. Heidelberg, 1926.
Phil 5627.190 Jung, C.G. Arin. Zürich, 1951.
Phil 6319.1.5.10 Jung, C.G. Basic writings. N.Y., 1959.
Phil 6319.1.47 Jung, C.G. Die Bedeutung des Vaters für das Schicksal des Einzelnen. 4. Aufl. Zürich, 1962.
Phil 6319.1.30 Jung, C.G. Bewusstes und Unbewusstes. Frankfurt, 1957.
Phil 6319.1.49 Jung, C.G. Die Beziehungen der Psychotherapie zur Seelsorge. Zürich, 1932.
Phil 5722.18 Jung, C.G. Die Beziehungen zwischen dem ich und dem Unbewussten. Darmstadt, 1928.
Phil 5722.18.5 Jung, C.G. Die Beziehungen zwischen dem ich und dem Unbewussten. Zürich, 1935.
Phil 6319.1.5A Jung, C.G. Collected papers on analytical psychology. London, 1916.
Phil 6319.1.5.5 Jung, C.G. Collected papers on analytical psychology. London, 1922.
Phil 6319.1.5.7A Jung, C.G. Collected works. v.1,3-5,7-9,11-17. N.Y., 1953-63. 14v.
Phil 6319.1.5.8 Jung, C.G. Collected works. v.1,3-17. London, 1953-63. 15v.
Phil 6319.1.5.6 Jung, C.G. Collected works. v.7. 2nd ed. N.Y., 1966 2v.
Phil 6319.1.16 Jung, C.G. Diagnostische Assoziationsstudien. v.1-2. Leipzig, 1915.
Phil 6319.1.32 Jung, C.G. Erinneringen. Zürich, 1962.
Phil 6319.1.73 Jung, C.G. Gegenwart und Zukunft. Zürich, 1957.
Phil 6319.1.69 Jung, C.G. Gestaltungen des Unbewussten. Zürich, 1950.
Phil 6319.1.65 Jung, C.G. Der Inhalt der Psychose. Leipzig, 1908.
Phil 6319.1.67 Jung, C.G. Der Inhalt der Psychose. 2. Aufl. Leipzig, 1914.
Phil 6319.1.60 Jung, C.G. Integration of the personality. N.Y., 1939.
Phil 6319.1.71A Jung, C.G. Man and his symbols. London, 1964.
Phil 6319.1.43 Jung, C.G. Modern man in search of a soul. N.Y., 1947.
Phil 6319.1.34 Jung, C.G. Neurosis, dreams, reflections. N.Y., 1963.
Phil 6319.1.5.9 Jung, C.G. Praxis der Psychotherapie. v.1,3-4,6-8,11,14-16. Zürich, 1958.
Phil 6319.1.68 Jung, C.G. Psyche and symbol. Garden City, 1958.
Phil 6319.1.10.5 Jung, C.G. Die Psychologie der Ubertragung. Zürich, 1946.
Phil 6319.1.72 Jung, C.G. Psychologische Abhandlungen. Leipzig, 1914.
Phil 6319.1.56 Jung, C.G. Psychology and religion. New Haven, 1955.
Phil 6319.1.9.5 Jung, C.G. Psychology of the unconscious. London, 1916.

Phil 6319.1.9A   Jung, C.G. Psychology of the unconscious. N.Y., 1916.
Phil 6319.1.74   Jung, C.G. Psychotherapeutische Zeitfragen. Leipzig, 1914.
Phil 6319.1.37   Jung, C.G. Seelenprobleme der Gegenwart. Zürich, 1932.
Phil 6319.1.15   Jung, C.G. Studies in word association. London, 1918.
Phil 6319.1.8.2   Jung, C.G. Symbole der Wandlung. Zürich, 1952.
Phil 6319.1   Jung, C.G. The theory of psychoanalysis. N.Y., 1915.
Phil 6319.1.13   Jung, C.G. Two essays on analytical psychology. London, 1928.
Phil 6319.1.14   Jung, C.G. Two essays on analytical psychology. N.Y., 1928.
Phil 6319.1.36   Jung, C.G. Uber die Psychologie des Unbewussten. 5. Aufl. Zürich, 1943.
Phil 5722.18.15   Jung, C.G. Über die Archetypen. Zürich, 1935.
Phil 6319.1.7   Jung, C.G. Über die Energetik der Seele und andere psychologische Abhandlungen. Zürich, 1928.
Phil 6959.8   Jung, C.G. Über die Psychologie der Dementia Praecox. Halle, 1907.
Phil 6319.1.36.2   Jung, C.G. Über die Psychologie des Unbewussten. 7 Aufl. Zürich, 1960.
Phil 6319.1.35   Jung, C.G. Das Unbewusste im normalen und kranken. Zürich, 1926.
Phil 6319.1.62.1   Jung, C.G. The undiscovered self. N.Y., 1958.
Phil 6319.1.70   Jung, C.G. Versuch einer Darstellung der psycho analytischen Theorie. Leipzig, 1913.
Phil 6319.1.76   Jung, C.G. Von den Wurzeln des Bewusstsens. Zürich, 1954.
Phil 6319.1.7.9   Jung, C.G. Wandlungen und Symbole der Libido. Leipzig, 1912.
Phil 6319.1.8   Jung, C.G. Wandlungen und Symbole der Libido. 2. Aufl. Leipzig, 1925.
Phil 6319.1.78   Jung, C.G. Welt der Psyche. Zürich, 1954.
Phil 6319.1.45   Jung, C.G. Wirklichkeit des Seele. Zürich, 1934.
Htn   Phil 6319.1.25*   Jung, C.G. Zur Psychologie und Pathologie sogenannter occulter Phänomene. Inaug. Diss. Leipzig, 1902.
Phil 6319.1.01   Pamphlet box. Jung, C.G. Psychology.
Phil 5850.247   Jung, Carl G. Aufsätze zur Zeitgeschichte. Zürich, 1946.
Phil 5249.13.30   Jung, Carl G. Bericht über das Berliner Seminar. Berlin, 1933.
Phil 5249.13.28   Jung, Carl G. C.G. Jung: psychological reflections. Princeton, 1970.
Phil 5249.13.20   Jung, Carl G. Contributions to analytical psychology. London, 1928.
Phil 5850.247.5   Jung, Carl G. Essays on contemporary events. London, 1947.
Phil 5249.13.15   Jung, Carl G. Psychological factors determining human behavior. Cambridge, 1937.
Phil 5249.13.27   Jung, Carl G. Psychological reflections. N.Y., 1953.
Phil 5249.13   Jung, Carl G. Psychological types. London, 1923.
Phil 5249.13.5   Jung, Carl G. Psychological types. n.p., 192-.
Phil 5249.13.25   Jung, Carl G. Psychologische Betrachtungen; eine Auslese aus den Schriften. Zürich, 1945.
Phil 5325.15.7   Jung, Carl G. Die psychologische Diagnose des Tatbestandes. Zurich, 1941.
Phil 5249.13.8   Jung, Carl G. Psychologische Typen. Zürich, 1921.
Phil 5249.13.7   Jung, Carl G. Psychologische Typen. Zürich, 1925.
Phil 5249.13.9   Jung, Carl G. Psychologische Typen. Zürich, 1930.
Phil 5249.13.10   Jung, Carl G. Psychologische Typen. Zürich, 1946.
Phil 5325.15   Jung, Carl G. Über das Verhalten der Reaktionszeit. Leipzig, 1915.
Phil 8589.20.3   Jung, Carl Gustav. Answer to Job. Cleveland, 1964.
Phil 8589.20   Jung, Carl Gustav. Antwort auf Hiob. Zürich, 1952.
Phil 1850.90   Jung, E. Causa finalis. Giessen, 1893.
Phil 184.22   Jung, E. Le principe constitutif de la nature organique. Paris, 1923.
Phil 5841.20.8   Jung, Emma. Animus and Anima. N.Y., 1957.
Phil 5841.20.5   Jung, Emma. Animus und Anima. Zürich, 1967.
Phil 2750.11.147   Jung, Hava Yol. The foundation of Jacques Maritain's political philosophy. Gainesville, Florida, 1960.
Phil 3903.2.125   Jung, Johannes. Karl Vogts Weltanschauung. Paderborn, 1915.
Phil 3903.2.126   Jung, Johannes. Karl Vogts Weltanschauung. Inaug. Diss. Paderborn, 1915.
Phil 5270.32   Jung, John. The experimenter's dilemma. N.Y., 1971.
Phil 6319.1.221   Jung. (Helsdingen, R.J. van.) Den Haag, 1964.
Phil 6319.1.208   Jung and analytical psychology. (Meier, Carl A.) Newton, Mass., 1959.
Phil 5627.259   Jung and St. Paul. (Cox, David.) N.Y., 1959.
Phil 6319.1.202   Jung and the problem of evil. (Philip, Howard Littleton.) London, 1958.
Phil 6319.1.80   Jung-Institut, Zürich, Studien zur analytischen Psychologie. Zürich, 1955. 2v.
Phil 49.4   Jung-Institut, Zürich. Studien. Zürich. 1,1949+ 18v.
Phil 7069.55.2A   Jung Institute, Zürich. The interpretation of nature and the psyche. London, 1955.
Phil 7069.55   Jung Institute, Zürich. The interpretation of nature and the psyche. N.Y., 1955.
Htn   Phil 7060.10.7*   Jung Stilling, J.H. Theorie der Geister-Kunde. Nürnberg, 1808 .
Phil 7060.10   Jung Stilling, J.H. Theory of pneumatology. London, 1834.
Phil 3823.5   Der Junge de Spinoza. (Dunin-Borkowski, Stanislaus von.) Münster, 1910.
Phil 3195.6.75   Der junge Dilthey. (Dilthey, Wilhelm.) Leipzig, 1933.
Phil 3195.6.76   Der junge Dilthey. 2. Aufl. (Dilthey, Wilhelm.) Stuttgart, 1960.
Phil 3425.322   Der junge Hegel. (Lukács, G.) Zürich, 1948.
Phil 3425.64   Das junge Hegel in Stuttgart. (Hegel, Georg Wilhelm Friedrich.) Marbach, 1970?
Phil 3492.24   Der Junge Kant. (Köster, Adolph.) Berlin, 1914.
Phil 3552.438   Der junge Leibniz das Keich und Europa. (Wiedeburg, P.H.) Wiesbaden, 1962. 3v.
Phil 3640.88.3   Der junge Nietzsche. (Förster-Nietzsche, E.) Leipzig, 1912.
Phil 3640.540   Der junge Nietzsche in den Jahren. (Schulze, Friedrich.) Leipzig, 1941.
Phil 3640.355   Jungen, F. Nietzsche. Frankfurt, 1949.
Phil 5258.105   The jungle of the mind. (Swift, Edgar J.) N.Y., 1931.
Phil 5400.73   Jungmann, J. Das Gemüth. 2e Aufl. Freiburg, 1885.
Phil 2520.129   Jungmann, Karl. René Descartes, eine Einführung. Leipzig, 1908.
Phil 2805.261   Jungo, Michel. Le vocabulaire de Pascal. Paris, 1950.
Phil 6319.1.240   Jung's contribution to our time. (Bertine, Eleanor.) N.Y., 1968.
Phil 6319.1.197   Jung's psychology and its social meaning. (Progoff, Ira.) London, 1953.
Phil 5477.10   Junker, Erika. Über unterschiedliches Behalten eigener Leistungen. Frankfurt, 1960.

Phil 270.51   Junkersfeld, M.J. The Aristotelian-Thomistic concept of chance. Indiana, 1945.
Phil 2475.1.304   Jurévičs, Pauls. Henri Bergson. Freiburg, 1949.
Phil 4683.161.30   Jurévičs, Pauls. Idejas un isteniba; esejas. 2. izd. Stockholm, 1965.
Phil 2475.1.228   Jurévičs, Pauls. Le problème de la connaissance dans la philosophie de Bergson. Paris, 1930.
Phil 3552.346.2   Jurisprudence universelle et théodicée selon Leibniz. Thèse. (Grua, Gaston.) Paris, 1953.
Phil 5640.132   Juritsch, M. Sinn und Geist. Freiburg, 1961.
Phil 6049.57   Jursch, Hanna. Hände als Symbol und Gestalt. 7. Aufl. Stuttgart, 1957.
Phil 735.110   Jury, G.S. Value and ethical objectivity. London, 1937.
Phil 6127.18.10   Just nerves. (Riggs, A.F.) Boston, 1922.
Htn   Phil 665.3.3*   Just scrutiny...modern notions of the soul. (Coward, William.) London, 1705?
Phil 978.62   Juste, Michael. The white brother; an occult autobiography. London, 192-?
Phil 8878.1   Le juste et l'utile. (Dameth, C.M.H.) Paris, 1859.
Phil 3006.5   Die Juste-Milieus in der deutschen Philosophie. (Günther, A.) Wien, 1838.
Phil 8877.91   La justice, l'homme et la liberté. (Casamayor, Louis.) Paris, 1964.
Phil 8965.13.10   Justice. (Pieper, Josef.) London, 1957.
Phil 8951.22   Justice and the law of love. (Braun, K.) London, 1950.
Phil 8951.21A   Justice and the social order. (Brunner, Heinrich E.) London, 1945.
Phil 165.130   La justice et la violence. (Derathé, Robert.) Paris, 1969.
Phil 8890.60.1   Justice et raison. (Perelman, Chaim.) Bruxelles, 1963.
Phil 3552.346.5   La justice humaine selon Leibniz. Thèse. (Grua, Gaston.) Paris, 1956.
Phil 181.87   Justification du temps. (Guitton, Jean.) Paris, 1941.
Phil 8893.45   The justification of the good. (Solov'ev, Vladimir.) N.Y., 1918.
Phil 3552.118   Justus-Georgius Schottelius i. Leibniz und Schottelius. (Schmarsow, A.) Strassburg, 1877.
Phil 484.4   Juul, Jensen. Uffe sjoel og legeme. København, 1970.
Phil 8959.8   Juva, Mikko. Tästa on kysymys. Söderström, 1965.
Phil 8884.15.5   Juvalta, E. Il metodo dell'economica pura nell'etica. Pavia, 1907.
Phil 8884.15.15   Juvalta, E. Prolegomeni a una morale distinta dalla metafisica. Pavia, 1901.
Phil 8884.15   Juvalta, E. Il vecchio e il nuovo problema della morale. Bologna, 1914.
Phil 2270.137   Juvalta, Erminio. La dottrina delle due etiche di H. Spencer, e la morale come scienza. n.p., n.d.
Phil 9170.1   K., J.P.A. Bildungslehre...zum ehelichen Glücke. Düsseldorf, 1807.
Phil 4595.4.30   K. Kroman. (Hansen, Valdemar.) København, 1955.
Phil 8419.7   K.W.F. Solger's Vorlesungen über Ästhetik. (Solger, K.W.F.) Leipzig, 1829.
Phil 5252.105   K issledovaniiu problem psikhologicheskoi voiny; sbornik statei. (Mertsalov, V.S.) Miunkhen, 1955.
Phil 310.285   K problematice stranickosti a vědeckosti marksistsko-leninskaia filosofii. (Dubská, Irena.) Praha, 1960.
Phil 5722.83   K probleme soznaniia i bessoznatel'nogo psikhicheskogo. v.1-. (Sheroziia, Apollon E.) Tbilisi, 1969.
Phil 850.50   K tekstologicheskomu analizn antichnoi filosofi. (Komarova, Vera Ia.) Leningrad, 1969.
Phil 5068.100   K voprosu o kritike sovremennogo angliiskogo pozitivizma. (Zaichenko, Georgii A.) Khar'kov, 1971.
Phil 8426.9   K základní otázce estetiky. (Zykmund, Václav.) Praha, 1957.
Phil 6960.9   Kaan, Hanns. Der neurasthenische Angstaffect bei Zwangsvorstellungen und der primordiale Grübelzwang. Wien, 1892.
Phil 7060.154   Kaarsberg, H.S. Om satanismen. København, 1896.
Phil 3640.187   Kaatz, Hugo. Die Weltanschauung Friedrich Nietzsches. Dresden, 1892.
X Cg   Phil 7075.140   Kabale und Liebe. (Linsert, Richard.) Berlin, 1931.
Phil 3842.12   The kabbalah and Spinoza's philosophy. (Waton, Harry.) N.Y., 1931-32. 2v.
Phil 9075.38   Kabisch, R. Das Gewissen. Göttingen, 1906.
Phil 3552.114.5A   Kabitz, Willy. Die Philosophie des Jungen Leibnitz. Heidelberg, 1909.
Phil 3246.94   Kabitz, Willy. Studien zur Entwicklungsgeschichte der Fichteschen Wissenschaftslehre. Berlin, 1902.
Phil 5066.284   Kac, Mark. Mathematics and logic. N.Y., 1968.
Phil 8960.2   Kachnik, Josef. Ethica catholica. Olomucii, 1910-12. 3v.
Phil 3492.65   Kaczmaeck, S. Początki Kantyzmu. Poznań, 1961.
Phil 4803.334.80   Kaczmarek, Stefan. Aniol Dowgird, filozof nieznany. Poznań, 1963.
Phil 4803.334.81   Kaczmarek, Stefan. Aniol Dowgird, filozof nieznany. Warszawa, 1965.
Phil 179.3.86   Kade, Richard. Rudolf Euckens noologische Methode. Leipzig, 1912.
Phil 5700.6   Kadinsky, David. Der Mythos der Maschine. Bern, 1969.
Phil 5330.32   Käellén, Elov. Uppmärksamhetsförloppens psykologi. Akademisk avhandling. Göttesburg, 1959.
Phil 1710.10   Kaegi, Werner. Humanismus der Gegenwart. Zürich, 1959.
Phil 8885.41   Kaelin, Bernard. Einführung in die Ethik. 2. Aufl. Sarnen, 1954.
Phil 185.75   Kaelin, Bernard. Einführung in die Logik, Ontologie, Kosmologie, Psychologie. 5. Aufl. Sarnen, 1957.
Phil 2880.8.138   Kaelin, Eugene. An existentialist aesthetic. Madison, 1962.
Phil 188.13   Kämpande intelligens. (Nyman, A.) Malmö, 1911.
Phil 3850.66   Kämpfende Wissenschaft. 2. Aufl. (Spann, Othmar.) Graz, 1969.
Phil 3640.182   Kämpfer, Hartfried. Zum Nietzsche-Verständnis. Celle, 1919.
Phil 185.33   Kaeppelin, E.R. El universo, Dios y el hombre, ó Creador, creacion y criaturas. Paris, 1864.
Phil 7069.66.45   Den kära okunnigheten, eller, Den fördolda kunskapen. (Vallberg, Viktor.) Stockholm, 1966.
Phil 9359.8   Kärlek och lycka af Elsa Törne, [Pseud.]. (Tenow, Elsa.) Stockholm, 1910.
Phil 810.6   Kafka, G. Geschichtsphilosophie der Philosophiegeschichte. Berlin, 1933.
Phil 1133.19.10   Kafka, Gustav. Der Ausklang der antiken Philosophie und das Erwachen einer neuen Zeit. n.p., n.d.
Phil 5820.2   Kafka, Gustav. Einführung in die Tierpsychologie auf experimenteller und ethnologischer Grundlage. Leipzig, 1914.

Phil 5820.2.5   Kafka, Gustav. Handbuch der vergleichenden Psychologie. München, 1922. 3v.

Phil 291.15   Kafka, Gustav. Naturgesetz, Freiheit und Wunder. Paderborn, 1940.

Phil 1133.19A   Kafka, Gustav. Die Vorsokratiker. München, 1921.

Phil 3492.5   Kaftan, J. Rede...Jubiläums...Königreichs Preussen 18 Januar 1901. Berlin, 1901.

Phil 8590.26.5   Kaftan, Julius. Das Christentum und die Philosophie. 3. Aufl. Leipzig, 1896.

Phil 3640.243   Kaftan, Julius. Das Christentum und Nietzsches Herremoral. Berlin, 1897.

Phil 185.18   Kaftan, Julius. Drei akademische Reden. Tübingen, 1908.

Phil 5250.72   Kagan, J. Birth to maturity. N.Y., 1962.

Phil 5465.155   Kagan, Jerome. Creativity and learning. Boston, 1967.

Phil 8400.41   Kagan, Moisei S. Lektsii po marksistsko-leninskoi estetike. Leningrad, 1963- 3v.

Phil 8400.41.2   Kagan, Moisei S. Lektsii po marksistsko-leninskoi estetike. Izd. 2. Leningrad, 1971.

Phil 4769.6.82   Kaganov, V. Mirovozzrenie I.M. Sechenova. Moskva, 1943.

Phil 5548.112   Kages, Wolfgang. Der menschliche Antrieb. Psychologie und Psychopathologie. Stuttgart, 1967.

Phil 1885.83   Kagey, Rudolf. The growth of F.H. Bradley's logic. N.Y., 1931.

Phil 2905.1.110   Kahane, E. Teilhard de Chardin. Paris, 1960.

Phil 8665.18.1   Kahl, Joachim. Das Elend des Christentums. Reinbek bei Hamburg, 1969.

Phil 5760.1   Kahl, W. Die Lehre von Primat des Willens. Strassburg, 1886.

Phil 185.58   Kahl-Furthmann, G. Das Problem des Nicht. Berlin, 1934.

Phil 2050.103   Kahle, C.M. De Davidis Humii philosophia. Inaug. Diss. Berolini, 1832?

Phil 8411.8   Kahlert, August. System der Ästhetik. Leipzig, 1846.

Phil 6112.40.15   Kahn, David E. My life with Edgar Cayce. 1. ed. Garden City, 1970.

Phil 6320.8   Kahn, Eugen. Psychopathic personalities. New Haven, 1931.

Phil 5250.76   Kahn, Jack Harold. Human growth and the development of personality. 1. ed. N.Y., 1965.

Phil 2520.124   Kahn, Lina. Metaphysics of the supernatural as illustrated by Descartes. N.Y., 1918.

Phil 5850.250.10   Kahn, Robert L. The dynamics of interviewing. N.Y., 1958.

Phil 6320.12   Kahn, S. Psychological and neurological definitions and the unconcious. Boston, 1940.

Phil 6680.7A   Kahn, S. Suggestion and hypnosis made practical. Boston, 1945.

Phil 6816.5   Kahn, Samuel. Make inferiorities and superiorities work for you. Ossining, N.Y., 1954.

Phil 5592.176.5   Kahn, Samuel. T.A.T. and understanding people. N.Y., 1966.

Phil 5250.38   Kahn, T.C. The Kahn test of symbol arrangement. n.p., 1949.

Phil 6960.15   Kahn, Theodore. Psychological techniques in diagnosis and evaluation. N.Y., 1960.

Phil 5250.38   The Kahn test of symbol arrangement. (Kahn, T.C.) n.p., 1949.

Phil 8411.32   Kahnweiler, D. Confessions esthétiques. Paris, 1963.

Phil 3801.472   Kahr-Wallerstein, C. Schellings Frauen: Caroline und Pauline. Bern, 1959.

Phil 8590.42   Kahraman, Ahmet. Dinbar tarihi. Istanbul, 1965.

Phil 3625.1.105   Kahut, Adolf. Moses Mendelssohn und seine Familie. Dresden, 1886.

Phil 5250.32.5   Kaila, Eino. Personlighetens psykologi. Helsingfors, 1935.

Phil 3830.11   Kaim, J.R. Die Philosophie Spinozas. München, 1921.

Phil 5250.23   Kaim, J.R. Psychologische Probleme in der Philosophie. München, 1921.

Phil 6328.40.5   Kain, Gestalten des Bösen. (Szondi, Lipot.) Bern, 1969.

Phil 600.49   Kainer, J. Seven lectures on the doctrine of positivism...May, June and July, 1879. London, 1880.

Phil 8411.20.5   Kainz, F. Vorlesungen über Ästhetik. Detroit, 1962.

Phil 8411.20   Kainz, F. Vorlesungen über Ästhetik. Wien, 1948.

Phil 5520.90   Kainz, Friedrich. Einführung in dei Sprachpsychologie. Wien, 1946.

Phil 185.36   Kaires, Theophilos. Philosophiká. Athens, 1910.

Phil 5643.14   Kaiser, H. Compendium der physiologische Optik. Wiesbaden, 1872.

Phil 3549.19   Kaiser, Josef. Summe der Filosofie. München, 1961.

Phil 291.5   Kaiser, Wilhelm. Kosmos und Menschenwesen im Spiegel der platonischen Körper. Basel, 1930.

Phil 310.90   Kajedra dialektiki i istoricheskogo materializme. (Konimunisticheskaia Partiia Sovetskogo Soiuza Vysshaia Partiinaia Shkola.) Moskva. 1-3,1958-1963+ 3v.

Phil 4769.1.115   Kak myslil Vladimir Solov'ev o voskresenie. (Piaskovskii, N.Ia.) Moskva, 1901.

Phil 5203.15   Kak nauka ob"iasniaet psikhologicheskoi deiatel'nosti cheloveka. (Moscow. Gosudarstvennaia Biblioteka SSSR. Imeni V.I. Lenina.) Moskva, 1954.

Phil 3450.11.365   Kakabadze, Zurab. Problema ekzistentsial'nogo kriziza i transtsendental'naia fenomenologiia Edmunda Gusserlia. Tbilisi, 1966.

Phil 585.396   Kakabadze, Zurab M. Chelovek kak filosofskaia problema. Tbilisi, 1970.

Phil 310.635   Kalandarishvili, Grigorii. Problema otrazheniia dvizheniia v logike poniatii. Tbilisi, 1966.

Phil 310.365   Kalatskii, V.P. Dialekticheskogo materializm. Moskva, 1961.

Phil 8092.26   Kalelin, Eugene Francis. Art and existence: a phemomenological aesthetics. Lewisburg, Pa. 1971.

Phil 9550.9   Kaler, Emil. Der Ethik des Utilitarismus. Inaug. Diss. Hamburg, 1884.

Phil 6980.372   Kalff, Dora M. Sandspiel. Zürich, 1966.

Phil 960.17.5   Kali the mother. (Noble, M.E.) London, 1900.

Phil 3492.10   Kalich, Karl. Cantii, Schellingii, Fichtii de filio divino sententiam. Diss. Lipsiae, 1870.

Phil 5525.43   Kalina, J. Bojové poslanie humoru a satiry. Bratislava, 1953.

Phil 3640.204   Kalina, P.E. Fundament und Einheit in Friedrich Nietzsches Philosophie. Leipzig, 1898.

Phil 575.253.5   Kalinin, Ananii I. Rol' truda v razvitii lichnosti v usloviiakh stroitelstva kommunizma. Cheboksary, 1969.

Phil 341.30   Kalinowski, J. Teoria poznania praktycznego. Lublin, 1960.

Phil 720.82   Kalinowski, Jerzy. Le problème de la vérité en morale et en droit. Thése. Lyon, 1967.

Phil 8885.54   Kalinowski, Jerzy. Querelle de la science normative, une contribution à la théorie de la science. Paris, 1969.

Phil 2280.5.95   Kallen, H.M. America and the life of reason. N.Y., 1921.

Phil 1810.2   Kallen, H.M. American philosophy today and tomorrow. N.Y., 1935.

Phil 8050.70   Kallen, H.M. Art and freedom; a historical and biographical interpretation. N.Y., 1942. 2v.

Phil 8411.18   Kallen, H.M. Indecency and the seven arts, and other adventures of a pragmatist in aesthetics. N.Y., 1930.

Phil 2070.81A   Kallen, H.M. William James and Henri Bergson. Chicago, 1914.

Phil 974.3.132   Kallert, Bernhard. Die Erkenntnistheorie Rudolf Steiners. Stuttgart, 1960.

Phil 5325.50   Kallich, Martin. The association of ideas and critical theory in eighteenth-century England. The Hague, 1970.

Phil 4515.97   Kalling, P. Framställning af Boströmska filosofien. Örebro, 1868.

Phil 4515.88   Kalling, P. Om kunskapen; studier. Upsala, 1875.

Phil 6960.10   Kallmann, F.J. Genetics of schizophrenia. N.Y., 1938.

Phil 6320.25   Kalmar, Jacques M. Anti-pensée et monde des conflits. Neuchâtel, 1967.

Phil 5374.265   Kalmar, Jacques M. Frontières de l'homme. Neuchâtel, 1968.

Phil 8960.10   Kalmeyer, P. En bog om religion og moral. København, 1956.

VPhil 2520.390   Kalocsai, Dezso. Descartes etikája. Budapest, 1964.

Phil 1145.96   Kalos Kai Agaltos. (Wankel, H.) Frankfurt, 1961.

Phil 8400.21   Kaloshen, F.I. Protiv revizionizma v estetike. Moskva, 1960.

Phil 8411.24   Kaloshin, F.I. Soderzhanie odforma v proizvedeniiakh iskusstva. Leningrad, 1953.

NEDL Phil 20.2   The Kalpaka; India's only psychic review. Tinnevelly.

Phil 185.97   Kalsbeek, L. Geloof en wetenschap. Baarn, 1962.

Phil 5627.67   Kaltenbaach, J. Étude psychologique des plus anciens reveils religieux aux Etats-Unis. Thèse. Genève, 1905.

Phil 3425.766   Kaltenbrunner, Gerd Klaus. Hegel und die Folgen. 1. Aufl. Freiburg, 1970.

Phil 3640.87   Kalthoff, A. Friedrich Nietzsche. Berlin, 1900.

Phil 1135.14   Kalthoff, A. Die Philosophie der Griechen. Berlin, 1901.

Phil 3640.87.7   Kalthoff, A. Zarathustra-Predigten. Jena, 1908.

Phil 5066.234   Kaluzhnin, Lev A. Chto takoe matematicheskala logika. Moskva, 1964.

Phil 3565.85   Kalweit, P.F.M. Die praktische Begründung des Gottesbegriffs bei Lotze. Jena, 1900.

Phil 1020.55   Kamali, Sabin Ahmad. Types of Islamic thought in criticism and reconstruction. Aligarh, 1963.

Phil 3235.132   Kamenka, Eugene. The philosophy of Ludwig Feuerbach. London, 1970.

Phil 4720.6   Kamenskii, Zakhar A. Filosofskie idei russkogo prosveshcheniia. Moskva, 1971.

Phil 5100.3   Kamiat, A.H. The critique of poor reason. N.Y., 1936.

Phil 8885.39   Kamiat, A.H. The ethics of civilization. Washington, 1954.

Phil 575.99   Kamiat, A.H. Social forces in personality stunting. Cambridge, 1933.

Phil 4803.472.20   Kamieński, Henryk. Filozofia ekonomii materialnej ludzkiego społecznstwa. Warszawa, 1959.

Phil 6320.13   Kaminski, Gerhard. Das Bild vom Ander. Berlin, 1959.

Phil 5284.2   Kaminski, Gerhard. Verhaltenstheorie und Verhaltensmodifikation. Stuttgart, 1970.

VPhil 185.108   Kamiński, Stanisław. Z teorii i metodologii metafizyki. Wyd. 1. Lublin, 1962.

Phil 3425.566   Kaminsky, Jack. Hegel on art. N.Y., 1969.

Phil 5520.582   Kaminsky, Jack. Language and ontology. Carbondale, 1969.

Phil 8590.44   Kamlah, Wilhelm. Der Ruf des Steuermanns. Stuttgart, 1954.

Phil 1750.845   Kamlah, Wilhelm. Utopie, Eschatologie, Geschichtsteleologie. Mannheim, 1969.

Phil 720.55   Kamlah, Wilhelm. Wissenschaft, Wahrheit, Existenz. Stuttgart, 1960.

Phil 3450.23   Kamm, P. Philosophie und Pädagogik Paul Häberlins in ehren Wandlungen. Diss. Zürch, 1958.

Phil 5545.76   Kammel, W. Uber die erste Einzelerinnerung. Leipzig, 1913.

Phil 5648.1   Kammler, A. Experimenta de variarum cutis. Vratislav, 1858.

Phil 4073.115   Kampanella. Izd. 3. (Shtekli, Al'fred E.) Moskva, 1966.

Phil 8642.1   Das Kampaner Thal. (Richter, J.P.F.) Erfurt, 1797.

Phil 8050.44   Kampanés, Aristos. Historia tōn aisthētikōn theōriōn. Athēna, 1936.

Phil 3625.16.90   Der Kampf der Wesenskultur gegen die Bewusstseinskultur bei Johannes Müller. Inaug. Diss. (Grohrock, R.) Speyer, 1937.

Phil 8826.6   Der Kampf um den Lebenssinn den Vorläufern der modernen Ethik. (Baumgardt, D.) Leipzig, 1933.

Phil 585.350   Der Kampf um den Menschen in Natur, Mythos und Geschichte. (Hartmann, Otto Julius.) Freiburg, 1969.

Phil 179.3.67   Der Kampf um die Religion in der Gegenwart. 1. und 2. Aufl. (Eucken, R.) Langensalza, 1922.

Phil 665.24   Der Kampf um die Seele. (Schmidt, Wilhelm.) Gütersloh, 1909.

Phil 179.15   Der Kampf um einen Gegenstand der Philosophie. (Einhorn, David.) Wien, 1916.

Phil 179.3.19   Der Kampf um einen Geistigen Lebensinhalt. (Eucken, R.) Leipzig, 1918.

Phil 8885.37   Der Kampf ums recht des Stärkeren und seine Entwickelung. (Katô, Hiroyuke.) Tokyô, 1893.

Phil 3415.84   Der Kampf um's Unbewusste. (Plümacher, O.) Berlin, 1881.

Phil 3415.84.2   Der Kampf um's Unbewusste. (Plümacher, O.) Leipzig, 1890.

Phil 7069.14.58   Die Kampf und die Materialisationsphänomene. (Schrenck von Notzing, Albert.) München, 1914.

Phil 193.65.5   Der Kampf zweier Weltanschauungen. (Spicker, Gideon.) Stuttgart, 1898.

Phil 193.78.5   Der Kampf zwischen Pragmatismus und Idealismus in Philosophie und Weltkrieg. (Sternberg, Kurt.) Berlin, 1917.

Phil 6324.8   Kampleksler ve insanlar. (Örgü, Halis.) Istanbul, 1969.

Phil 5520.512   Kamrath, Gerhard. Vernunft und Sprache. Heidelberg, 1964.

Htn Phil 3808.59*   Kan menneskets frie villie bevises ar dets selvebevidsthed. (Schopenhauer, Arthur.) Trodhjem, 1840.

Phil 4655.1.52   Kan philosophien bringa någon välsignelse at mensklighten? 2. uppl. (Wikner, Pontus.) Upsala, 1864.

Phil 341.44   Kanak, Fedvi M. Sub'ieks, ob'iekt i fizychne piznannia. Kyiv, 1970.

Phil 1750.275   Kanapa, J. L'existensialisme n'est pas un humanisme. Paris, 1947.

Phil 5850.250   Kandhi, S. The winning of wealth. Boston, 1932.

Phil 5460.5   Kandinsky, V. Kritische und klinische Betrachtungen im Gebiete der Sinnestäuschungen. Berlin, 1885.

Phil 8885.25   Kane, Robert. Worth lectures. London, 1920.

Phil 4899.162.30   Kaneko, Shōseki. Über das Wesen und den Ursprung des Menschen. Osaka, 1932.

Phil 8622.72 — Kanellopoulos, Panagiōtēs. Ascent to faith. 1st ed. N.Y., 1966.

Phil 6998.6 — Kanfer, Frederick H. Learning foundations of behavior therapy. N.Y., 1970.

VPhil 8885.49 — Kangrga, Milan. Etika i ploboda. Zagreb, 1966.

Phil 8885.49.5 — Kangrga, Milan. Razmisljanja o etici. Zagreb, 1970.

Phil 3552.334 — Kanitz, H.J. Das übergegensätzliche Gezeigt am Kontinuitätsprinzip bei Leibniz. Hamburg, 1951.

Phil 5722.60 — Kankeleit, Otto. Des Unbewusste als Keimstätte des Schöpferischen. München, 1959.

Phil 185.30 — Kann, A. Ein philosophischer Gedankengang. Wien, 19- .

Phil 2475.1.247 — Kann, Albert. Henri Bergson und meine Ideen. Wien, 1935.

Phil 3246.226 — Kann man Herrn Professor Fichte mit Recht beschuldigen. (Jensen, F.C.) Kiel, 1799.

Phil 3625.1.93 — Kanngiesser, G. Dje Stellung M. Mendelssohn's in der Geschichte der Asthitik. Frankfurt, 1868.

Phil 185.23 — Kanovitch, A. The will to beauty. N.Y., 1922.

Phil 185.23.2 — Kanovitch, A. The will to beauty. N.Y., 1923.

Phil 5765.9 — Kansalgesetz und Willensfreiheit. (Planck, Max.) Berlin, 1923.

Phil 8980.472 — Kánský, Jiří. Čo je zmyslom našho života? Bratislava, 1961.

Phil 8980.472.5 — Kánský, Jiří. Morálka dnes a zajtra. Bratislava, 1963.

Phil 3485.28 — Kant; a collection of critical essays. 1st ed. (Wolff, Robert.) Notre Dame, 1967.

Phil 349.3 — Kant, Hume und Berkeley. (Spicker, G.) Berlin, 1875.

Phil 3450.19.99 — Kant, Husserl, Heidegger. (Folwart, H.) Breslau, 1936.

Phil 3499.40 — Kant; il problema della conoscenza. (Romano, Vincenzo.) Napoli, 1965.

Phil 3480.69.2 — Kant, Immanuel. Allgemeine Naturgeschichte. Theorie des Himmels. Frankfurt, 1799.

Htn Phil 3480.69.1* — Kant, Immanuel. Allgemeine Naturgeschichte. Theorie des Himmels. Königsberg, 1755.

Phil 3480.69 — Kant, Immanuel. Allgemeine Naturgeschichte. Theorie des Himmels. Leipzig, 1890.

Phil 3480.69.3 — Kant, Immanuel. Allgemeine Naturgeschichte. Theorie des Himmels. Zeitz, 1798.

Phil 3480.69.4 — Kant, Immanuel. Allgemeine Naturgeschichte. Theorie des Himmels. 4. Aufl. Zeitz, 1808.

Phil 3480.69.6 — Kant, Immanuel. Allgemeine Naturgeschichte und Theorie des Himmels. Berlin, 1955.

Phil 3480.77 — Kant, Immanuel. En Andeskadares drömmar i ljusetay metafysikens drömmar. Lund, 1921. 10v.

Htn Phil 3480.19.7* — Kant, Immanuel. Anhang zu den Zerstreuten Aufsatzen. Frankfurt, 1794.

Phil 3480.40 — Kant, Immanuel. Anthropologie. Königsberg, 1820.

Phil 3480.40.4 — Kant, Immanuel. Anthropologie in pragmatischer Hinsicht. Leipzig, 1833.

Phil 3480.40.13 — Kant, Immanuel. Anthropologie in pragmatischer Hinsicht. Leipzig, 1899.

Phil 3480.40.5 — Kant, Immanuel. Anthropologie in pragmatischer Hinsicht. Paris, 1863.

Htn Phil 3480.40.2* — Kant, Immanuel. Anthropologie in pragmatischer Hinsicht. 2. Aufl. Königsberg, 1800.

Phil 3480.40.15 — Kant, Immanuel. Anthropologie in pragmatischer Hinsicht. 5. Aufl. Leipzig, 1912.

Phil 3480.40.16 — Kant, Immanuel. Anthropologie in pragmatischer Hinsicht. 6. Aufl. Leipzig, 1922.

Phil 3480.40.3 — Kant, Immanuel. Anthropologie in pragmatischer Hinsicht Abgefasst. Frankfurt, 1799.

Phil 3480.28.30 — Kant, Immanuel. Antologia Kantiana. Torino, 1925.

Htn Phil 3480.40.49* — Kant, Immanuel. Anweisung zur Menschen und Weltkenntniss. 4. Aufl. Leipzig, 1831.

Phil 3480.28.35 — Kant, Immanuel. Ausgewählt und Bearbeitet von L. Weis. Hamburg, 1906.

Phil 3480.126 — Kant, Immanuel. Ausgewählte Kleine Schriften. Hamburg, 1965.

Phil 3480.19.13 — Kant, Immanuel. Ausgewählte Kleine Schriften. Leipzig, 1919.

Phil 3480.80.80 — Kant, Immanuel. Avhandlingar om fred och rätt. Stockholm, 1915.

Htn Phil 3480.82.1* — Kant, Immanuel. Beobachtungen über das Gefühl des Schönen und Erhabenen. Königsberg, 1764.

Phil 3480.82.6 — Kant, Immanuel. Beobachtungen über das Gefühl des Schönen und Erhabenen. Berlin, 1910.

Phil 3480.82.4 — Kant, Immanuel. Beobachtungen über das Gefühl des Schönen und Erhabenen. Grätz, 1797.

Htn Phil 3480.82* — Kant, Immanuel. Beobachtungen über das Gefühl des Schönen und Erhabenen. Riga, 1771.

Phil 3480.92.5 — Kant, Immanuel. Briefe. Göttingen, 1970.

Phil 3480.90 — Kant, Immanuel. Briefwechsel. Leipzig, 1922.

Phil 3480.92 — Kant, Immanuel. Briefwechsel. Leipzig, 1924. 2v.

Phil 3480.91 — Kant, Immanuel. Briefwechsel. München, 1912. 3v.

Phil 3480.67.10 — Kant, Immanuel. Che cosa significa orientarsi nel pensare. Lanciano, 1930.

Phil 3480.86.25 — Kant, Immanuel. Le conflit des facultes en trois sections, 1798. Paris, 1935.

Phil 3480.64.50 — Kant, Immanuel. Constitutio principii metaphysicae morum zwantziger. Lipsiae, 1795.

Phil 3480.69.5 — Kant, Immanuel. Cosmogony. Glasgow, 1900.

Phil 3480.51.30 — Kant, Immanuel. Critica del giudizio. Bari, 1907.

Phil 3480.46.23 — Kant, Immanuel. Critica della ragion pratica. Bari, 1909.

Phil 3480.46.25 — Kant, Immanuel. Critica della ragion pratica. 3. ed. Bari, 1924.

Phil 3480.31.8 — Kant, Immanuel. Critica della raigon pura. v.1-2. Bari, 1910.

Phil 3480.31.9 — Kant, Immanuel. Critica della raigon pura. 2. ed. Bari, 1919-21. 2v.

Phil 3480.32.60 — Kant, Immanuel. Critica ratiunii pure. Bucuresti, 1930.

Phil 3480.32 — Kant, Immanuel. Critick of pure reason. London, 1838.

Phil 3480.44.3 — Kant, Immanuel. Critik der practischen Vernunft. Frankfurt, 1791.

Phil 3480.44.5 — Kant, Immanuel. Critik der practischen Vernunft. Frankfurt, 1795.

Phil 3480.44.8 — Kant, Immanuel. Critik der practischen Vernunft. Grätz, 1796.

Phil 3480.45.5 — Kant, Immanuel. Critik der practischen Vernunft. Leipzig, 1827.

Htn Phil 3480.44* — Kant, Immanuel. Critik der practischen Vernunft. Riga, 1788.

Htn Phil 3480.45* — Kant, Immanuel. Critik der practischen Vernunft. Riga, 1797.

Htn Phil 3480.45.3* — Kant, Immanuel. Critik der practischen Vernunft. 5. Aufl. Leipzig, 1818.

Phil 3480.30.17 — Kant, Immanuel. Critik der reinen Vernunft, 1781. 1. Aufl. Riga, 1905.

Htn Phil 3480.29* — Kant, Immanuel. Critik der reinen Vernunft. Riga, 1781.

Phil 3480.30.03 — Kant, Immanuel. Critik der reinen Vernunft. Neueste Aufl. Frankfurt, 1794.

Phil 3480.30.07 — Kant, Immanuel. Critik der reinen Vernunft. v.1-2,3-4. Grätz, 1795. 2v.

Phil 3480.29.4 — Kant, Immanuel. Critik der reinen Vernunft. 2. Aufl. Riga, 1787.

Htn Phil 3480.29.2* — Kant, Immanuel. Critik der reinen Vernunft. 2. Aufl. Riga, 1787.

Phil 3480.30.01 — Kant, Immanuel. Critik der reinen Vernunft. 3. Aufl. Frankfurt, 1791.

Htn Phil 3480.30* — Kant, Immanuel. Critik der reinen Vernunft. 3. Aufl. Riga, 1790.

Htn Phil 3480.30.02* — Kant, Immanuel. Critik der reinen Vernunft. 4. Aufl. Riga, 1794.

Phil 3480.30.05 — Kant, Immanuel. Critik der reinen Vernunft. 4. Aufl. Riga, 1794.

Phil 3480.30.1 — Kant, Immanuel. Critik der reinen Vernunft. 5. Aufl. Leipzig, 1799.

Phil 3480.30.2.10 — Kant, Immanuel. Critik der reinen Vernunft. 6. Aufl. Leipzig, 1818.

Phil 3480.30.2 — Kant, Immanuel. Critik der reinen Vernunft. 7. Aufl. Leipzig, 1828.

Htn Phil 3480.48* — Kant, Immanuel. Critik der Urtheilskraft. Berlin, 1790.

Phil 3480.48.2 — Kant, Immanuel. Critik der Urtheilskraft. Berlin, 1790. 2 pam.

Htn Phil 3480.50* — Kant, Immanuel. Critik der Urtheilskraft. Berlin, 1793.

Phil 3480.50.05 — Kant, Immanuel. Critik der Urtheilskraft. Frankfurt, 1794.

Phil 3480.50.1 — Kant, Immanuel. Critik der Urtheilskraft. Grätz, 1797. 2v.

Htn Phil 3480.50.2* — Kant, Immanuel. Critik der Urtheilskraft. Grätz, 1799.

Phil 3480.50.4 — Kant, Immanuel. Critik der Urtheilskraft. Hamburg, 1884.

Phil 3480.46 — Kant, Immanuel. Critique de la raison pratique. Paris, 1848.

Phil 3480.46.5 — Kant, Immanuel. Critique de la raison pratique. 2. éd. Paris, 1902.

Phil 3480.31.2 — Kant, Immanuel. Critique de la raison pure. Paris, 1869. 2v.

Phil 3480.31.20 — Kant, Immanuel. Critique de la raison pure. Paris, 1927.

Phil 3480.31.1 — Kant, Immanuel. Critique de la raison pure. 1. éd. Paris, 1835. 2v.

Phil 3480.31 — Kant, Immanuel. Critique de la raison pure. 2. éd. Paris, 1845. 2v.

Phil 3480.31.5 — Kant, Immanuel. Critique de la raison pure. 3. éd. Paris, 1864. 2v.

Phil 3480.51 — Kant, Immanuel. Critique du jugement. Paris, 1846. 2v.

Phil 3480.52.12 — Kant, Immanuel. The critique of judgement. Oxford, 1961.

Phil 3480.52.13A — Kant, Immanuel. The critique of judgement. Oxford, 1964.

Phil 3480.52.2 — Kant, Immanuel. Critique of judgement. 2d ed. London, 1914.

Phil 3480.52.10 — Kant, Immanuel. Critique of judgment. N.Y., 1951.

Phil 3480.47.15 — Kant, Immanuel. Critique of practical reason. Chicago, 1950.

Phil 3480.47.20 — Kant, Immanuel. Critique of practical reason. N.Y., 1956.

Phil 3480.47.7A — Kant, Immanuel. Critique of practical reason. 6th ed. London, 1959.

Phil 3480.32.9 — Kant, Immanuel. Critique of pure reason. Edinburgh, 1881.

Htn Phil 3480.32.3* — Kant, Immanuel. Critique of pure reason. London, 1855.

Phil 3480.32.2 — Kant, Immanuel. Critique of pure reason. London, 1855.

Phil 3480.32.5 — Kant, Immanuel. Critique of pure reason. London, 1869.

Phil 3480.32.6 — Kant, Immanuel. Critique of pure reason. London, 1878.

Phil 3480.32.8A — Kant, Immanuel. Critique of pure reason. London, 1881. 2v.

Htn Phil 3480.32.8.2* — Kant, Immanuel. Critique of pure reason. London, 1881. 2v.

Phil 3480.32.8.9 — Kant, Immanuel. Critique of pure reason. London, 1887.

Phil 3480.32.20 — Kant, Immanuel. Critique of pure reason. London, 1929.

Phil 3480.32.21 — Kant, Immanuel. Critique of pure reason. London, 1933.

Phil 3480.32.10 — Kant, Immanuel. Critique of pure reason. N.Y., 1882.

Phil 3480.32.7.5 — Kant, Immanuel. Critique of pure reason. N.y., 1900.

Phil 3480.32.26A — Kant, Immanuel. Critique of pure reason. N.Y., 1961.

Phil 3480.32.17 — Kant, Immanuel. Critique of pure reason. 2. ed. N.Y., 1927.

Phil 3480.52.9 — Kant, Immanuel. Critique of teleological judgment. Oxford, 1928.

Phil 3480.22 — Kant, Immanuel. Deines Lebens Sinn. Wien, 1951.

Phil 3480.22.2 — Kant, Immanuel. Deines Lebens Sinn. 2. Aufl. Wien, 1953.

Phil 3480.115 — Kant, Immanuel. Die mundi sensibilis at que intelligibilis forma. Hamburg, 1958.

Phil 3480.53A — Kant, Immanuel. Dreams of a spirit seer. London, 1900.

Phil 3480.28.100A — Kant, Immanuel. Die drei Kritiken. Leipzig, 1933.

Phil 3480.80.75 — Kant, Immanuel. Ecrits politiques. Paris, 1917.

Phil 3480.21.3 — Kant, Immanuel. Der einzig mögliche Beweis vom Daseyn Gottes. Königsberg, 1770.

Htn Phil 3480.21* — Kant, Immanuel. Der einzig mögliche Beweisgrund. Königsberg, 1763. 4 pam.

Phil 3480.21.5 — Kant, Immanuel. Der einzig mögliche Beweisgrund zu einer Demonstration des Daseyns Gottes. Königsberg, 1794.

Phil 3480.21.22 — Kant, Immanuel. Der einzig mögliche Beweisgrund zu einer Demonstration des Daseyns Gottes. 2. Aufl. Leipzig, 1902.

Phil 3480.21.23 — Kant, Immanuel. Der einzig mögliche Beweisgrund zu einer Demonstration des Daseyns Gottes. 3. Aufl. Leipzig, 1911.

Phil 3480.67.65 — Kant, Immanuel. Eleinenta metaphysica juris doctrinae. Amstelaedami, 1799.

Phil 3480.67.60 — Kant, Immanuel. Eléments métaphysique de la doctrine du droit. Paris, 1853.

Phil 3480.50.18 — Kant, Immanuel. Erste Einleitung in die Kritik der Urteilskraft. Leipzig, 1927.

Phil 3480.50.18.3 — Kant, Immanuel. Erste Einleitung in die Kritik der Urteilskraft. Stuttgart, 1965.

Phil 3480.50.18.4 — Kant, Immanuel. Erste Einleitung in die Kritik der Urteilskraft. 2. Aufl. Hamburg, 1970.

Phil 3480.56.20 — Kant, Immanuel. Essai pour introduire en philosophie le concept de grandeur négative. Paris, 1949.

Htn Phil 3480.25.15* — Kant, Immanuel. Essays and treatises on moral, political and various philosophical subjects. London, 1798-99. 2v.

Phil 3480.80.79 — Kant, Immanuel. Den evigi fred. Fagershand, 1889.

Phil 3480.87 — Kant, Immanuel. Die falsche Spitzfindigkeit der vier syllogistischen Figuren. Frankfurt, 1797.

Phil 3480.94 — Kant, Immanuel. Filosofía de la historia. México, 1941.

Phil 3480.52.20 — Kant, Immanuel. First introduction to the Critique of judgment. Indianapolis, 1965.

Phil 3480.66.49 — Kant, Immanuel. Fondazione della metafisica dei costumi. Torino, 1923.

Phil 3480.66.50 — Kant, Immanuel. Fondazione della metafisica dei costumi. Torino, 1925?

Author and Title Listing

Phil 3480.65.15 — Kant, Immanuel. Fondements de la métaphysique des moeurs. 2. éd. Paris, 1907?

Phil 3480.67.85 — Kant, Immanuel. Foundations of the metaphysics of morals. Chicago, 1950.

Phil 3480.19.10 — Kant, Immanuel. Frühere nocht nicht Gesammelte Kleine Schriften. Lintz, 1795.

Phil 3480.28.38 — Kant, Immanuel. Frühschriften. Berlin, 1961. 2v.

Phil 3480.65.40 — Kant, Immanuel. Fundamental principles of the metaphysics of ethics. London, 1907.

Phil 3480.34.5 — Kant, Immanuel. Gedanken von der wahren Schätzung des lebendigen Kräfte...Mechäniker. Amsterdam, 1968.

Htn Phil 3480.34* — Kant, Immanuel. Gedanken von der wahren Schätzung des lebendigen Kräfte. Königsberg, 1746.

Phil 3480.14.4 — Kant, Immanuel. Gesammelte Schriften. Allgemeiner Kantindex. Bonn, 1966. 3v.

Phil 3480.14.5 — Kant, Immanuel. Gesammelte Schriften. Bd.X-XII. Berlin, 1922. 3v.

Phil 3480.14.2.2 — Kant, Immanuel. Gesammelte Schriften. Personenindex. Nachträge. Bonn, 1966.

Phil 3480.14.2 — Kant, Immanuel. Gesammelte Schriften. Personenindex. v.A-L. Bonn, 1964- 6v.

Phil 3480.14.1 — Kant, Immanuel. Gesammelte Schriften. Personenindex. v.1-23. Bonn, 1962-

Phil 3480.14 — Kant, Immanuel. Gesammelte Schriften. v.1-24,28. Berlin, 1900-36. 27v.

Phil 3480.26 — Kant, Immanuel. Les grands philosophes. Paris, 1909.

Phil 4520.5.20 — Kant, Immanuel. Grundlaggning till metaphysiken för seder. Upsala, 1797.

Phil 3480.20 — Kant, Immanuel. Grundlegung zur Metaphysik. Riga, 1792-98. 3 pam.

Phil 3480.65.12 — Kant, Immanuel. Grundlegung zur Metaphysik der Sitten. Gotha, 1930.

Phil 3480.64.10 — Kant, Immanuel. Grundlegung zur Metaphysik der Sitten. Grätz, 1796. 2 pam.

Phil 3480.65.8 — Kant, Immanuel. Grundlegung zur Metaphysik der Sitten. Leipzig, 1904.

Phil 3480.65.7 — Kant, Immanuel. Grundlegung zur Metaphysik der Sitten. Leipzig, 1906.

Phil 3480.65.10 — Kant, Immanuel. Grundlegung zur Metaphysik der Sitten. München, 1925.

Htn Phil 3480.64* — Kant, Immanuel. Grundlegung zur Metaphysik der Sitten. Riga, 1785.

Phil 3480.65A — Kant, Immanuel. Grundlegung zur Metaphysik der Sitten. Riga, 1797.

Phil 3480.65.13 — Kant, Immanuel. Grundlegung zur Metaphysik der Sitten. Stuttgart, 1967.

Phil 3480.65.5 — Kant, Immanuel. Grundlegung zur Metaphysik der Sitten. v.1-2. Königsberg, 1803.

Htn Phil 3480.64.5* — Kant, Immanuel. Grundlegung zur Metaphysik der Sitten. 2. Aufl. Riga, 1786.

Phil 3480.64.7 — Kant, Immanuel. Grundlegung zur Metaphysik der Sitten. 4. Aufl. Frankfurt, 1794. 2 pam.

Phil 3480.65.6 — Kant, Immanuel. Grundlegung zur Metaphysik der Sitten. 5. Aufl. Leipzig, 1920.

Phil 3480.33.10 — Kant, Immanuel. The idea of a universal history on a cosmopolitical plan. Hanover, N.H., 1927.

Phil 3480.33 — Kant, Immanuel. Idee zu einer allgemeinen Geschichte in weltbürgerlicher Absicht. Wiesbaden, 1914.

Phil 3480.67.95 — Kant, Immanuel. An Immanuel Kant reader. N.Y., 1960.

Phil 3480.50.30 — Kant, Immanuel. Immanuel Kant's Kritik der Urteilskraft. Berlin, 1869.

Phil 3480.57.10 — Kant, Immanuel. Immanuel Kant's Prolegomena zu einer jeden künftigen Metaphysik. 3. Aufl. Berlin, 1893. 3 pam.

Phil 3480.70.10A — Kant, Immanuel. Introduction to logic. Photoreproduction. London, 1885.

Phil 3480.25.30 — Kant, Immanuel. Kant. Oxford, 1963.

Phil 3480.28.40 — Kant, Immanuel. Kant- Aussprüche. Leipzig, 1901.

Phil 3480.28.40.3 — Kant, Immanuel. Kant- Aussprüche. Leipzig, 1909.

Phil 3480.131.3 — Kant, Immanuel. Kant Laienbrevier. 3. Aufl. München, 1916.

Phil 3480.19.30 — Kant, Immanuel. Kantische Blumenlese. v.1-2. Zittau, 1813-

Phil 3480.32.50 — Kant, Immanuel. Kantova Kritika čistého rozmysla. Praha, 1930.

Phil 3480.93 — Kant, Immanuel. Kants Briefe ausgewählt. Leipzig, 1911.

Phil 3480.69.5.10 — Kant, Immanuel. Kant's cosmogony, as in his essay on The retardation of the rotation of the earth and his national history and theory of the heavens. N.Y., 1968.

Phil 3480.39 — Kant, Immanuel. Kant's inaugural dissertation and early writings on space. London, 1929.

Phil 3480.70.21 — Kant, Immanuel. Kant's introduction to logic and his essay on the mistaken subtilty of the four figures. N.Y., 1963.

Phil 3480.132 — Kant, Immanuel. Kant's political writings. Cambridge, 1970.

Phil 3480.28.4 — Kant, Immanuel. Kants Weltanschauung. Darmstadt, 1919.

Htn Phil 3480.19* — Kant, Immanuel. Kleine Schriften. Neuwied, 1793.

Phil 3480.18.12 — Kant, Immanuel. Kleinere philosophische Schriften. Leipzig, 1921.

Phil 3480.28.12 — Kant, Immanuel. Kleinere Schriften zur Ethik und Religionsphilosophie. Berlin, 1870.

Phil 3480.28 — Kant, Immanuel. Kleinere Schriften zur Geschichts- Philosophie Ethik und Politik. Leipzig, 1913.

Phil 3480.24.5 — Kant, Immanuel. Kleinere Schriften zur Logik und Metaphysik. Berlin, 1870.

Phil 3480.24.2 — Kant, Immanuel. Kleinere Schriften zur Logik und Metaphysik. v.1-4. 2. Aufl. Leipzig, 1905.

Phil 3480.28.15 — Kant, Immanuel. Kleinere Schriften zur Natur- Philosophie. v.1-2. Berlin, 1872-73.

Phil 3480.85.3 — Kant, Immanuel. De kracht van den wil in het beheerschen van ziekelijke aandoeningen. 3. druk. Leeuwarden, 1885.

Phil 3480.45.7 — Kant, Immanuel. Kritik der praktischen Vernunft. Berlin, 1869.

Phil 3480.30.3.2A — Kant, Immanuel. Kritik der praktischen Vernunft. Leipzig, 1878?

Phil 3480.45.10 — Kant, Immanuel. Kritik der praktischen Vernunft. 3. Aufl. Heidelberg, 1882. 2 pam.

Phil 3480.45.15 — Kant, Immanuel. Kritik der praktischen Vernunft. 7. Aufl. Leipzig, 1920.

Phil 3480.45.16 — Kant, Immanuel. Kritik der praktischen Vernunft. 9. Aufl. Leipzig, 1929.

Phil 3480.45.18 — Kant, Immanuel. Kritik der praktischen Vernunft als Prüfung der tätigen Vernunft. 3. Aufl. Lübeck, 1919.

Phil 3480.45.17 — Kant, Immanuel. Kritik der praktischen Vernunft als Prüfung der tätigen Vernunft. 3. Aufl. Lübeck, 1922.

Phil 3480.45.25 — Kant, Immanuel. Kritik der praktischen Vernun t nebst Grundlegung zur Metaphysik der Sitten. Leipzig, 1925.

Phil 3480.30.10 — Kant, Immanuel. Kritik der reinen Vernunft. Berlin, 1868-69.

Phil 3480.30.5A — Kant, Immanuel. Kritik der reinen Vernunft. Berlin, 1889.

Phil 3480.30.45 — Kant, Immanuel. Kritik der reinen Vernunft. Berlin, 1928.

Phil 3480.30.15 — Kant, Immanuel. Kritik der reinen Vernunft. Halle, 1899?

Phil 3480.30.5.5 — Kant, Immanuel. Kritik der reinen Vernunft. Hamburg, 1889.

Phil 3480.30.56 — Kant, Immanuel. Kritik der reinen Vernunft. Heldeberg, 1884.

Phil 3480.30.7 — Kant, Immanuel. Kritik der reinen Vernunft. Kiel, 1881.

Phil 3480.30.8 — Kant, Immanuel. Kritik der reinen Vernunft. Leipzig, 1853.

Phil 3480.30.9 — Kant, Immanuel. Kritik der reinen Vernunft. Leipzig, 1868.

Phil 3480.30.4 — Kant, Immanuel. Kritik der reinen Vernunft. Leipzig, 1878.

Phil 3480.30.20 — Kant, Immanuel. Kritik der reinen Vernunft. Leipzig, 1920.

Phil 3480.30.27 — Kant, Immanuel. Kritik der reinen Vernunft. Leipzig, 1925.

Phil 3480.30.29 — Kant, Immanuel. Kritik der reinen Vernunft. Leipzig, 1926.

Phil 3480.30.40 — Kant, Immanuel. Kritik der reinen Vernunft. Lübeck, 1926.

Phil 3480.30.35 — Kant, Immanuel. Kritik der reinen Vernunft. München, 1920.

Phil 3480.30.44 — Kant, Immanuel. Kritik der reinen Vernunft. Stuttgart, 1904.

Phil 3480.32.65 — Kant, Immanuel. Kritik der reinen Vernunft. Wiesbaden, 1956-64. 6v.

Phil 3480.30.3 — Kant, Immanuel. Kritik der reinen Vernunft. 2. Verb. Aufl. Leipzig, 1877.

Phil 3480.30.6 — Kant, Immanuel. Kritik der reinen Vernunft. 5. Aufl. Berlin, 1900.

Phil 3480.30.18 — Kant, Immanuel. Kritik der reinen Vernunft. 10. Aufl. Leipzig, 1913.

Phil 3480.30.25 — Kant, Immanuel. Kritik der reinen Vernunft. 12. Aufl. Leipzig, 1922.

Phil 3480.50.40 — Kant, Immanuel. Kritik der Ürtheilskraft für Uneingeweihte. Berlin, 1804.

Phil 3480.50.10A — Kant, Immanuel. Kritik der Urtheilskraft. Leipzig, 1878?

Phil 3480.50.22 — Kant, Immanuel. Kritik der Urtheilskraft. Stuttgart, 1925.

Phil 3480.50.13A — Kant, Immanuel. Kritik der Urtheilskraft. 3. Aufl. Leipzig, 1902.

Phil 3480.50.15 — Kant, Immanuel. Kritik der Urtheilskraft. 5. Aufl. Leipzig, 1922.

Phil 3480.52 — Kant, Immanuel. Kritik of judgment. London, 1892.

Phil 3480.60 — Kant, Immanuel. Leçons de metaphysique. Paris, 1843.

Phil 3480.67.75 — Kant, Immanuel. Lectures on logic. London, 1930.

Phil 3480.100 — Kant, Immanuel. Die letzten Gedanken. Hamburg, 1902.

Phil 3480.25.55 — Kant, Immanuel. The living thoughts of Kant. N.Y., 1940.

Phil 3480.35.5 — Kant, Immanuel. Lo disertatio de 1770, sobre la forma y los principios del mundo sensible y del inteligible. Madrid, 1961.

Htn Phil 3480.70* — Kant, Immanuel. Logik. Königsberg, 1800.

Phil 3480.70.1 — Kant, Immanuel. Logik. Königsberg, 1801.

Phil 3480.70.2 — Kant, Immanuel. Logik. Reutlingen, 1801.

Phil 3480.70.20 — Kant, Immanuel. Logik. 2. Aufl. Leipzig, 1876.

Phil 3480.70.3 — Kant, Immanuel. Logik. 3. Aufl. Leipzig, 1920.

Phil 3480.70.5 — Kant, Immanuel. Logique. Paris, 1840.

Phil 3480.70.6 — Kant, Immanuel. Logique. 2. éd. Paris, 1862.

Phil 3499.1.5 — Kant, Immanuel. Lose blätter aus Kants nach lass, Mitgetheit von Rudolf Reicke. Königsberg, 1889-98.

Phil 3480.27.5 — Kant, Immanuel. Lose Blätter aus Kants Nachloss. Königsberg, 1889-98.

Htn Phil 3480.40.50* — Kant, Immanuel. Menschenkunde oder philosophische Anthropologie. Leipzig, 1831.

Phil 3480.40.52 — Kant, Immanuel. Menschenkunde oder philosophische Anthropologie. Quedlunburg, 1838.

Phil 3480.62 — Kant, Immanuel. Metafisica de Kant. Madrid, 1877.

Phil 3480.66.51 — Kant, Immanuel. La metafisica dei costumi. v.1-2. Torino, 1923-25.

Htn Phil 3480.67.70* — Kant, Immanuel. The metaphysic of morals, divided into metaphisical elements of law and of ethics. v.1-2. London, 1799.

Htn Phil 3480.36* — Kant, Immanuel. Metaphysicae cum geometria junctae usus in philosophiam naturicam. Regiomonti, 1756.

Phil 3480.67.110 — Kant, Immanuel. The metaphysical elements of justice. Indianapolis, 1965.

Phil 3480.81.4.1 — Kant, Immanuel. Metaphysical foundations of natural science. Indianapolis, 1970.

Phil 3480.61 — Kant, Immanuel. Metaphysical works. London, 1836.

NEDL Phil 3480.66.3 — Kant, Immanuel. The metaphysics of ethics. 3. ed. Edinburgh, 1871.

Htn Phil 3480.63* — Kant, Immanuel. Die Metaphysik der Sitten. Königsberg, 1797.

Phil 3480.63.15 — Kant, Immanuel. Metaphysik der Sitten. Leipzig, 1870.

Htn Phil 3480.81* — Kant, Immanuel. Metaphysische Anfangsgründe der Jugendlehre. Königsberg, 1797.

Phil 3480.81.3 — Kant, Immanuel. Metaphysische Anfangsgründe der Jugendlehre. 2. Aufl. Königsberg, 1803.

Htn Phil 3480.81.2* — Kant, Immanuel. Metaphysische Anfangsgründe der Jugendlehre. 2. Aufl. Kreuznach, 1800.

Phil 3480.81.5 — Kant, Immanuel. Metaphysische Anfangsgründe der Jugendlehre. 2. Aufl. Kreuznach, 1800.

Phil 3480.81.4 — Kant, Immanuel. Metaphysische Anfangsgründe der Naturwesenschaft. Leipzig, 1914.

Phil 3480.55.12 — Kant, Immanuel. Metaphysische Anfangsgründe Naturwissenschaft. Frankfurt, 1794.

Phil 3480.55.15 — Kant, Immanuel. Metaphysische Anfangsgründe Naturwissenschaft. Grätz, 1796. 3 pam.

Phil 3480.55 — Kant, Immanuel. Metaphysische Anfangsgründe Naturwissenschaft. Leipzig, 1800.

Phil 3480.56A — Kant, Immanuel. Metaphysische Anfangsgründe Naturwissenschaft. Leipzig, 1900.

Htn Phil 3480.55.2* — Kant, Immanuel. Metaphysische Anfangsgründe Naturwissenschaft. Riga, 1786.

Phil 3480.55.4 — Kant, Immanuel. Metaphysische Anfangsgründe Naturwissenschaft. Riga, 1787.

Phil 3480.67.50.5 — Kant, Immanuel. Metaphysische Anfangsgrunde der Rechtslehre. Frankfurt, 1797.

Htn Phil 3480.67.50* — Kant, Immanuel. Metaphysische Anfangsgrunde der Rechtslehre. Königsberg, 1797.

Htn Phil 3480.67.51* — Kant, Immanuel. Metaphysische Anfangsgrunde der Rechtslehre. 2. Aufl. Königsberg, 1798.

Phil 3480.67.80A — Kant, Immanuel. The moral law, or Kant's Groundwork of the metaphysic of morals. London, 1947?

Phil 3480.67.100 — Kant, Immanuel. The moral law. London, 1961.

Phil 3480.67.90 — Kant, Immanuel. The moral law. N.Y., 1950.

Phil 3480.76 — Kant, Immanuel. Das nachgelassene Werk. Lahr, 1888.

Htn   Phil 3480.19.11*   Kant, Immanuel. Neue Kleine Schriften. Berlin? 1795.

Phil 3480.32.67   Kant, Immanuel. O pus Postumum. Berlin, 1936.

Phil 3480.82.8   Kant, Immanuel. Observations on the feeling of the beautifull and sublime. Berkeley, 1960.

Phil 3480.80.125   Kant, Immanuel. Az örök héke. Budapest, 1918.

Phil 3480.52.15   Kant, Immanuel. On philosophy in general. Calcutta, 1935.

Phil 3480.10   Kant, Immanuel. Opera ad philosophiam criticam. Leipzig, 1796-98. 4v.

Phil 3480.82.25   Kant, Immanuel. Opmerkingen over het gevoll van Schoone en Vorheveve. Sneck, 1919.

Phil 3480.25.40   Kant, Immanuel. Il pensiero filosofico di E.K. v.1-2. Firenze, 1926-25.

Phil 3480.80.15   Kant, Immanuel. Perpetual peace. Los Angeles, 1932.

Phil 3480.127   Kant, Immanuel. Philosophical correspondence. Chicago, 1967.

Phil 3480.17   Kant, Immanuel. Die philosophischen Hauptvorlesungen. München, 1924.

Phil 3480.25.10   Kant, Immanuel. The philosophy of Kant. Glasgow, 1927.

Phil 3480.25.50A   Kant, Immanuel. The philosophy of Kant. N.Y., 1949.

Phil 3480.25.5   Kant, Immanuel. The philosophy of Kant. 2d ed. Glasgow, 1923.

Phil 3480.25   Kant, Immanuel. Philosophy of Kant as contained in extracts. N.Y., 1888.

Phil 3480.25.2   Kant, Immanuel. Philosophy of Kant as contained in extracts. N.Y., 1891.

Phil 3480.67.105   Kant, Immanuel. The philosophy of law. Edinburgh, 1887.

Phil 3480.101.2   Kant, Immanuel. Physische Geographie. Leipzig, 1803-07. 2v.

Htn   Phil 3480.101*   Kant, Immanuel. Physische Geographie. v.1-2. Königsberg, 1802.

Htn   Phil 3480.78.5*   Kant, Immanuel. Politische Meinungen. n.p., 1794.

Htn   Phil 3480.78*   Kant, Immanuel. Politische Meinungen. n.p., 1796.

Phil 3480.19.25   Kant, Immanuel. Populäre Schriften. Berlin, 1911.

Phil 3480.65.20   Kant, Immanuel. Principes métaphysiques de la morale. Paris, 1837.

Phil 3480.65.23   Kant, Immanuel. Principes métaphysiques de la morale. 3. éd. Paris, 1854.

Phil 3480.67.55   Kant, Immanuel. Principes métaphysiques du droit. Paris, 1837.

Phil 3480.52.25   Kant, Immanuel. Principie di estetica. Bari, 1935.

Phil 3480.59   Kant, Immanuel. Prolegomena and metaphysical foundations. Photoreproduction. London, 1883.

Phil 3480.57.40   Kant, Immanuel. Prolegomena in Sprachlicher Bearbeitung, von Emil Kühn. Gotha, 1908.

Htn   Phil 3480.58*   Kant, Immanuel. Prolegomena to any future metaphysics. Chicago, 1902.

Phil 3480.58.5   Kant, Immanuel. Prolegomena to any future metaphysics. Chicago, 1926.

Phil 3480.58.22   Kant, Immanuel. Prolegomena to any future metaphysics. Manchester, Eng., 1953.

Phil 3480.58.10   Kant, Immanuel. Prolegomena to any future metaphysics. 3d ed. Chicago, 1912.

Phil 3480.57.7   Kant, Immanuel. Prolegomena zu einer jeden künftigen Metaphysik. Frankfurt, 1798.

Phil 3480.57.5   Kant, Immanuel. Prolegomena zu einer jeden künftigen Metaphysik. Grätz, 1795.

Htn   Phil 3480.57.2*   Kant, Immanuel. Prolegomena zu einer jeden künftigen Metaphysik. Riga, 1783. 2 pam.

Htn   Phil 3480.57.3*   Kant, Immanuel. Prolegomena zu einer jeden künftigen Metaphysik. Riga, 1783.

Phil 3480.57.13   Kant, Immanuel. Prolegomena zu einer jeden künftigen Metaphysik. 4. Aufl. Leipzig, 1905.

Phil 3480.57.14   Kant, Immanuel. Prolegomena zu einer jeden künftigen Metaphysik. 5. Aufl. Leipzig, 1913.

Phil 3480.57.15   Kant, Immanuel. Prolegomena zu einer jeden künftigen Metaphysik. 6. Aufl. Leipzig, 1920.

Phil 3480.57   Kant, Immanuel. Prolegomena zu künftigen Metaphysik. Frankfurt, 1794.

Phil 3480.58.40   Kant, Immanuel. Prolégomènes a toute métaphysique future. Paris, 1891.

Phil 3480.58.45   Kant, Immanuel. Prolégomènes a toute métaphysique future. Paris, 1930.

Phil 3480.58.60   Kant, Immanuel. Prolegomeni ad ogni metafisica futura. Torino, 1926.

Phil 3480.58.70   Kant, Immanuel. Prolehomena to kozhnoï maîbutn'oi metafisyky. L'Viv, 1930.

Phil 3480.67.20   Kant, Immanuel. Qu'est-ceque s'orienter dans la pensée. Paris, 1959.

Phil 3480.71.15   Kant, Immanuel. La religion dans les limites de la raison. Paris, 1913.

Htn   Phil 3480.71.2.6*   Kant, Immanuel. Die Religion innerhalb der Grenzen der blossen Vernunft. Frankfurt, 1793.

Htn   Phil 3480.71.2.5*   Kant, Immanuel. Die Religion innerhalb der Grenzen der blossen Vernunft. Frankfurt, 1793.

Phil 3480.71.2.7   Kant, Immanuel. Die Religion innerhalb der Grenzen der blossen Vernunft. Frankfurt, 1794.

Phil 3480.71.13   Kant, Immanuel. Die Religion innerhalb der Grenzen der blossen Vernunft. Hamburg, 1966.

Phil 3480.71.2   Kant, Immanuel. Die Religion innerhalb der Grenzen der blossen Vernunft. Königsberg, 1784.

Htn   Phil 3480.70.75*   Kant, Immanuel. Die Religion innerhalb der Grenzen der blossen Vernunft. Königsberg, 1793.

Phil 3480.71.10   Kant, Immanuel. Die Religion innerhalb der Grenzen der blossen Vernunft. 2. Aufl. Leipzig, 1875.

Phil 3480.71.4   Kant, Immanuel. Die Religion innerhalb der Grenzen der blossen Vernunft. 4. Aufl. Leipzig, 1919.

Phil 3480.71.12   Kant, Immanuel. Die Religion innerhalb der Grenzen der blossen Vernunft. 5. Aufl. Leipzig, 1937.

Phil 3480.71.5   Kant, Immanuel. Religion within the boundary of Pure reason. Edinburgh, 1838.

Phil 3480.71.7   Kant, Immanuel. Religion within the limits of reason alone. Chicago, 1934.

Phil 3480.71.8   Kant, Immanuel. Religion within the limits of reason alone. 2sd ed. La Salle, 1960.

Phil 3480.120   Kant, Immanuel. Réponse á Eberhard. Paris, 1959.

Phil 3480.19.12   Kant, Immanuel. Sämmtliche Kleine Schriften. Königsberg, 1797. 3v.

Phil 3480.12   Kant, Immanuel. Sämmtliche Werke. Leipzig, 1838-40. 12v.

Phil 3480.13A   Kant, Immanuel. Sämmtliche Werke. Leipzig, 1867-68. 8v.

Phil 3480.16   Kant, Immanuel. Sämtliche Werke. v.1-9 und Ergänzungsband. 10. Aufl. Leipzig, 1913. 10v.

Htn   Phil 3480.19.20*   Kant, Immanuel. Sammlung einiger bisher unbekannt gebliebener kleiner Schriften. Königsberg, 1800.

Phil 3480.28.17   Kant, Immanuel. Schriften zur Naturphilosophie. 3. Aufl. Leipzig, 1922. 3v.

Phil 3480.28.25   Kant, Immanuel. Scritti minori. Bari, 1923.

Phil 3480.130   Kant, Immanuel. Selected pre-critical writings and correspondence. Manchester, 1968.

Phil 3480.25.20A   Kant, Immanuel. Selections. N.Y., 1929.

Phil 3480.125   Kant, Immanuel. Sochineniia. Moskva, 1963. 6v.

Htn   Phil 3480.86.2*   Kant, Immanuel. Der streit der Facultaeten. Königsberg, 1798.

Htn   Phil 3480.86*   Kant, Immanuel. Der streit der Facultaeten. Königsberg, 1798.

Phil 3480.86.10   Kant, Immanuel. Der Streit der Fakultäten. Hamburg, 1959.

Phil 3480.86.5   Kant, Immanuel. Der Streit der Fakultäten. Leipzig, 1922.

Phil 3480.71.21   Kant, Immanuel. Theorie de Kant sur la religion dans limites. Paris, 1842.

Htn   Phil 3480.72.5*   Kant, Immanuel. Theorie der Reinmoralischen Religion. Elberfeld, 1798.

Htn   Phil 3480.72*   Kant, Immanuel. Theorie der Reinmoralischen Religion. Riga, 1796.

Phil 3480.26.10   Kant, Immanuel. Theorie und praxis. Leipzig, 1913.

Phil 3480.53.6   Kant, Immanuel. Traüme eines Geistersehers. Leipzig, 1880?

Htn   Phil 3480.53.5*   Kant, Immanuel. Traüme eines Geistersehers. Riga, 1766.

Phil 3480.18.16   Kant, Immanuel. Trois opuscules scientifiques. Mistral, 1914.

Htn   Phil 3480.70.80*   Kant, Immanuel. Ueber das radikale Böse in der menschlichen Natur. Pt. 1. n.p., 1792.

Phil 3480.75.30   Kant, Immanuel. Über den Gemeinspruch: Das mag in der Theorie richtig sein taugt. Frankfurt, 1968.

Htn   Phil 3480.75.25*   Kant, Immanuel. Über den Gemeinspruch: Das mag in Theorie richtig sein taugt, aber nicht für die Praxis. Berlin, 1793. 2 pam.

Phil 3480.75.20   Kant, Immanuel. Über den Gemeinspruch: Das mag in Theorie richtig sein taugt, aber nicht für die Praxis. Frankfurt, 1946.

Htn   Phil 3480.75*   Kant, Immanuel. Über des Ausgesetzte Preisfrage. Königsberg, 1803-04. 2 pam.

Htn   Phil 3480.89*   Kant, Immanuel. Über die Büchmacheren. Königsberg, 1798.

Phil 3480.22.5   Kant, Immanuel. Über die Form und die Prinzipien der Sinnen - und Geisteswelt. Hamburg, 1958.

Htn   Phil 3480.43*   Kant, Immanuel. Über eine Entdeckung, nach der alle neue Critik der reinen Vernunft. Königsberg, 1791-97. 2 pam.

Phil 3480.43.5   Kant, Immanuel. Über eine Entdeckung, nach der alle neue Critik der reinen Vernunft. Grätz, 1796. 2 pam.

Htn   Phil 3480.68*   Kant, Immanuel. Über moralische und politische Gegenstände. Frankfurt, 1795.

Htn   Phil 3480.74.5*   Kant, Immanuel. Über Pädogik. Königsberg, 1803.

Htn   Phil 3480.74.7*   Kant, Immanuel. Über Pädogik. Königsberg, 1803.

Phil 3480.74.15   Kant, Immanuel. Über Pädogik. Leipzig, 1924.

Phil 3480.74   Kant, Immanuel. Über Pädogik. 3. Aufl. Langensalza, 1901.

Htn   Phil 3480.42*   Kant, Immanuel. Untersuchung über die Deutlichkeit der Grundsätze der naturlichen Theologie und der Moral. Berlin, 1764. 2 pam.

Phil 3480.80.50   Kant, Immanuel. Vens la paix perpetuelle. 1. éd. Paris, 1958.

Htn   Phil 3480.54*   Kant, Immanuel. Verkündigung des nahen Abschlusses eines Traktats zum ewigen Frieden in der Philosophie. Ulm, 1798.

Phil 3480.18   Kant, Immanuel. Vermischte Schriften. Halle, 1799-1807. 4v.

Phil 3480.18.7   Kant, Immanuel. Vermischte Schriften. Leipzig, 1912.

Phil 3480.18.9   Kant, Immanuel. Vermischte Schriften. Leipzig, 1922.

Phil 3480.18.5   Kant, Immanuel. Vermischte Schriften und Briefwechsel. Berlin, 1873.

Htn   Phil 3480.84.3*   Kant, Immanuel. Versuch den Begriff der negativen Grössen in die Weltweisheit einzuführen. Königsberg, 1763.

Phil 3480.84   Kant, Immanuel. Versuch den Begriff der negativen Grössen in die Weltweisheit einzuführen. Grätz, 1797.

Phil 3480.88   Kant, Immanuel. Von dem ersten Grunde des Unterschiedes der Gegenden im Raume. Steglitz, 1768[1920]

Htn   Phil 3480.85.5*   Kant, Immanuel. Von der Macht des Gemüths durch den blossen Vorsatz seiner krankhaften Gefühle Meister zu seyn. Jena, 1798.

Phil 3480.85.6.10   Kant, Immanuel. Von der Macht des Gemüths durch den blossen Vorsatz seiner krankhaften Gefühle Meister zu seyn. Königsberg, 1798?

Htn   Phil 3480.85.6*   Kant, Immanuel. Von der Macht des Gemüths durch den blossen Vorsatz seiner krankhaften Gefühle Meister zu seyn. Jena, 1798.

Phil 3480.85.7   Kant, Immanuel. Von der Macht des Gemüths durch den blossen Vorsatz seiner krankhaften Gefühle Meister zu seyn. Frankfurt, 1800.

Phil 3480.85.6.15   Kant, Immanuel. Von der Macht des Gemüths durch den blossen Vorsatz seiner krankhaften Gefühle Meister zu seyn. Leipzig, 1824?

Phil 3480.85.9   Kant, Immanuel. Von der Macht des Gemüths durch den blossen Vorsatz seiner krankhaften Gefühle Meister zu seyn. 2. Aufl. Leipzig, 1824.

Phil 3480.85.10   Kant, Immanuel. Von der Macht des Gemüths durch den blossen Vorsatz seiner krankhaften Gefühle Meister zu seyn. 3. Aufl. Leipzig, 1836.

Phil 3480.85.11   Kant, Immanuel. Von der Macht des Gemüths durch den blossen Vorsatz seiner krankhaften Gefühle Meister zu seyn. 6. Aufl. Leipzig, 1852.

Phil 3480.85.20   Kant, Immanuel. Von der Macht des Gemüths durch den blossen Vorsatz seiner krankhaften Gefühle Meister zu seyn. Heidelberg, 1924.

Htn   Phil 3480.75.15*   Kant, Immanuel. Von der verschiedenen Racen der Menschen. Königsberg, 1775.

Phil 3480.97   Kant, Immanuel. Von der Würde des Menschen. Leipzig, 1944.

Phil 3480.41   Kant, Immanuel. Eine Vorlesung Kants über Ethik. Berlin, 1924.

Phil 3480.41.2   Kant, Immanuel. Eine Vorlesung Kants über Ethik. 2. Aufl. Berlin, 1925.

Phil 3480.41.10   Kant, Immanuel. Vorlesungen. Berlin, 1961.

Phil 3480.59.25   Kant, Immanuel. Vorlesungen Kants über Metaphysik aus drei Semestern. Leipzig, 1894.

Htn   Phil 3480.73.5*   Kant, Immanuel. Vorlesungen über der philosophische Religionslehre. Leipzig, 1794-1817. 2 pam.

Phil 3480.73   Kant, Immanuel. Vorlesungen über der philosophische Religionslehre. Leipzig, 1830.

Htn   Phil 3480.59.20*   Kant, Immanuel. Vorlesungen über die Metaphysik. Erfurt, 1821.

Phil 3480.59.21   Kant, Immanuel. Vorlesungen über die Metaphysik. 2. Aufl. Rosswein, 1924.

Htn   Phil 3480.19.15*   Kant, Immanuel. Vorzügliche Kleine Schriften und Aufsätze. Bd.1-2. Leipzig, 1833.

Phil 3480.19.16   Kant, Immanuel. Vorzügliche Kleine Schriften und Aufsätze. v.1-2. Quedlinburg, 1838.

Phil 3480.11   Kant, Immanuel. Werke. Leipzig, 1838-39. 10v.
Phil 3480.15   Kant, Immanuel. Werke. v.1-7,9,11. Berlin, 1912. 9v.
X Cg   Phil 3480.15   Kant, Immanuel. Werke. v.8,10. Berlin, 1912. 2v.
Phil 3480.16.25   Kant, Immanuel. Werke in acht Büchern. v.1-4,5-8. Berlin, 1921. 2v.
Phil 3480.105   Kant, Immanuel. Wörte Kants. Minden, 1911.
Phil 3480.83   Kant, Immanuel. Worin besteht der Fortschritt zum bessern im Menschengeschlecht? Wiesbaden, 1917.
Htn   Phil 3480.19.5*   Kant, Immanuel. Zerstreute Aufsätze. Frankfurt, 1793.
Phil 3480.79.10   Kant, Immanuel. Zum ewigen Frieden. Berlin, 1917.
Htn   Phil 3480.79.3*   Kant, Immanuel. Zum ewigen Frieden. Königsberg, 1795. 2 pam.
Htn   Phil 3480.79*   Kant, Immanuel. Zum ewigen Frieden. Königsberg, 1795.
Htn   Phil 3480.79.4*   Kant, Immanuel. Zum ewigen Frieden. Königsberg, 1796.
Phil 3480.79.7   Kant, Immanuel. Zum ewigen Frieden. Leipzig, 1881?
Phil 3480.79.12   Kant, Immanuel. Zum ewigen Frieden. 2. Aufl. Leipzig, 1919.
Phil 3480.24   Kant, Immanuel. Zur Logik und Metaphysik. 2. Aufl. Leipzig, 1921. 4v.
Phil 3480.110   Kant, Immanuel. Zwei Schriften über die Grundlegenden der Naturwissenschaften. Berlin, 1920.
Phil 3480.68.5   Kant, Immanuel. Zwo Abhandlungen über moralische Gegenstände. 2. Aufl. Königsberg, 1796.
Phil 3018.9   Kant, Lotze, and Ritschl. (Stählin, Leonhard.) Edinburgh, 1889.
Phil 3018.9.5   Kant, Lotze, and Ritschl. (Stählin, Leonhard.) Leipzig, 1888.
Phil 8885.34   Kant, Otto. Zur Biologie der Ethik. Wien, 1932.
Phil 3484.9.5   Kant; sa vie, son oeuvre, avec un exposé de sa philosophie. (Cresson, André.) Paris, 1941.
Phil 3484.9.10   Kant; sa vie, son oeuvre, avec un exposé de sa philosophie. 5. éd. (Cresson, André.) Paris, 1959.
Phil 3503.4.5   Kant, Schiller, Goethe. (Vorländer, K.) Leipzig, 1907.
Phil 5768.12   Kant, Schopenhauer, Ihering. (Schuch, Hermann.) München, 1907.
Phil 3500.49   Kant, Schopenhauer, Nietzsche und deren...Gemüt. (Sturm, A.) Langensalza, 1921.
Phil 3492.13   Kant; sein Leben und sein Lehre. 5. Aufl. (Kronenberg, M.) München, 1918.
Phil 3492.13.6   Kant; sein Leben und sein Lehre. 6. Aufl. (Kronenberg, M.) München, 1922.
Phil 3499.10.5   Kant, seine Anhänger und seine Gegner. (Reininger, Robert.) München, 1923.
Phil 3484.7   Kant. (Cantecor, G.) Paris, n.d.
Phil 3480.25.30   Kant. (Kant, Immanuel.) Oxford, 1963.
Phil 3492.45   Kant. (Kayser, Rudolf.) Wien, 1935.
Phil 3492.36   Kant. (Köhler, W.) Berlin, 1913.
Phil 3492.44   Kant. (Körner, Stephan.) Harmondsworth, 1955.
Phil 3492.44.5   Kant. (Koerner, Stephan.) Harmondsworth, 1960.
Phil 3492.13.3   Kant. (Kronenberg, M.) München, 1897.
Phil 3492.19   Kant. (Kühnemann, E.) München, 1923-24. 2v.
Phil 3493.13   Kant. (Lamanna, E.P.) Milano, 1926. 2v.
Phil 3493.21   Kant. (Lindsay, A.D.) London, 1934.
Phil 3497.3.7   Kant. (Paulsen, Friedrich.) Milano, 1914.
Phil 3499.5   Kant. (Ruyssen, T.) Paris, 1900.
Phil 3503.13   Kant. (Vitier, M.) La Habana, 1958.
Phil 3504.1   Kant. (Wallace, William.) Edinburgh, 1882.
Phil 3504.1.20   Kant. (Wallace, William.) Edinburgh, 1886.
Phil 3504.1.10   Kant. (Wallace, William.) Edinburgh, 1902.
Phil 3504.1.15   Kant. (Wallace, William.) Edinburgh, 1911.
Phil 3504.1.3   Kant. (Wallace, William.) Philadelphia, 1882.
Phil 3507.9.5   Kant. (Zwingmann, H.) Berlin, 1924.
Phil 3493.40   Kant. Ancora un episodio dell' allanza di religione e filosofia. (Lacorte, Carmelo.) Urbino, 1969.
Phil 3488.44   Kant: disputed questions. (Gram, Moltke S.) Chicago, 1967.
Phil 3504.28   Kant: Naturgesetze, Natur- und Gotteserkennen. (Weis, Ludwig.) Berlin, 1903.
Phil 3500.20.2   Kant: sechzehn Vorlesungen. (Simmel, G.) Leipzig, 1904.
Phil 3500.20   Kant: sechzehn Vorlesungen. (Simmel, G.) Leipzig, 1905.
Phil 3500.20.3   Kant: sechzehn Vorlesungen. 3. Aufl. (Simmel, G.) München, 1913.
Phil 3500.20.4   Kant: sechzehn Vorlesungen. 4. Aufl. (Simmel, G.) München, 1918.
Phil 3500.20.6   Kant: sechzehn Vorlesungen. 5. Aufl. (Simmel, G.) München, 1921.
Phil 3492.31   Kant: sein System als Theorie des Kulturbewusstseins. (Kynast, R.) München, 1928.
Phil 3494.72   Kant: the philosophy of right. (Murphy, Jeffrie G.) London, 1970.
Phil 3492.13.2   Kant. 2. Aufl. (Kronenberg, M.) München, 1904.
Phil 3492.13.5   Kant. 4. Aufl. (Kronenberg, M.) München, 1910.
Phil 3487.27   Kant - Interpretationen. (Fang, Joong.) Münster, 1967-
Phil 3482.2   Kant - Studien. (Adickes, E.) Kiel, 1895. 2v.
Phil 3480.28.40   Kant- Aussprüche. (Kant, Immanuel.) Leipzig, 1901.
Phil 3480.28.40.3   Kant- Aussprüche. (Kant, Immanuel.) Leipzig, 1909.
Phil 3500.10.5   Kant akademische Vorlesungen. (Stadler, A.) Leipzig, 1912.
Phil 3503.4.10   Kant als Deutscher. (Vorländer, K.) Darmstadt, 1919.
Phil 3504.32   Kant als Metaphysiker. (Wundt, Max.) Stuttgart, 1924.
Phil 3482.2.7   Kant als Naturforscher. (Adickes, E.) Berlin, 1924. 2v.
Phil 3499.14   Kant als Philosoph der Modernen. (Rickert, H.) Tübingen, 1924.
Phil 3503.5.10   Kant als Philosoph des Unbedingten. (Volkelt, Johannes.) Erfurt, 1924.
Phil 3483.16   Kant als Philosophie des Katholizismus. (Bund, Hugo.) Berlin, 1913.
Phil 3483.44   Kant als Politiker. (Borries, Kurt.) Leipzig, 1928.
Phil 3503.25   Kant als theoloog. (Vas, Harmen de.) Baarn, 1968.
Phil 3494.62   Kant and current philosophical issues. (Milmed, Bella Kussy.) N.Y., 1961.
Phil 3504.3A   Kant and his English critics. (Watson, J.) N.Y., 1881.
Phil 3504.7.15   Kant and his philosophical revolution. (Wenley, R.M.) Edinburgh, 1910.
Phil 3483.10A   Kant and Spencer. (Bowne, B.P.) Boston, 1912.
Phil 3484.5   Kant and Spencer. (Carus, Paul.) Chicago, 1899.
Phil 3489.27.10   Kant and the problem of metaphysics. (Heidegger, Martin.) Bloomington, 1962.
Phil 3489.24   Kant-Bibliothek. (Hirsch, Richard.) Wien, 1929.
Phil 3484.17F   Kant-Bildnisse. (Clasen, Karl H.) Königsberg, 1924.
Phil 3488.7.23   Kant criticismus az Isten létéröl. Inaug. Diss. (Gallovich, J.) Eger, 1887.
Phil 3497.3.9   Kant der Philosophie des Protestantismus. (Paulsen, Friedrich.) Berlin, 1899.
Phil 3488.28   Kant e la critica del nostro tiempo. (Giorgiantonio, M.) Napoli, 1953.
Phil 4210.127   Kant e Rosmini. (Galli, Gallo.) Città de Castello, 1914.

Phil 3488.3   Kant e Rosmini. (Galli, Gallo.) Citta di Castello, 1914.
Phil 3500.21.15   Kant et Aristote. 2. éd. (Sentroul, C.) Louvain, 1913.
Phil 3488.7   Kant et Kantistes. (Goujon, H.) Lille, 1901.
Phil 3493.52   Kant et la mort de la métaphysique. (Lebrun, Gérard.) Paris, 1970.
Phil 3497.13   Kant et la science moderne. (Pesch, T.) Paris, 1894.
Phil 3493.44.3   Kant et le Kantisme. 3. éd. (Lacroix, Jean.) Paris, 1969.
Phil 3489.34   Kant et le problème du temps. (Havet, Jacques.) Paris, 1946.
Phil 3504.24.2   Kant-Festschrift zu Kants 200. Geburtstag am April 1924. 2. Aufl. (Wieser, F.) Berlin, 1924.
Phil 3504.24   Kant-Festschrift zu Kants 200. Geburtstag am 22 April 1924. (Wieser, F.) Berlin, 1924.
Phil 3492.42.5   Kant for everyman. (Klinke, Willibald.) N.y., 1962.
Phil 3497.18   Kant Heute. (Przywara, Erich.) München, 1930.
Phil 3497.21   Kant i Kantianstvo. (Popov, Sergei I.) Moskva, 1961.
Phil 3640.345   Kant im Urteil Nietzsches. (Ackermann, O.) Tübingen, 1939.
Phil 3483.52   Kant Immanuel; halálának századik évfordulójára. (Bárány, Gerö.) Kolozsvár, 1904.
Phil 3504.21F   Kant in Italien. (Werner, Karl.) Wien, 1881.
Phil 3496.2   Kant in Österreich und Vincenz. (Ortner, F.) Klagenfurt, 1904.
Phil 3488.4.10   Kant Kritik oder Kantstudium? (Goldschmidt, L.) Gotha, 1901.
Phil 3480.131.3   Kant Laienbrevier. 3. Aufl. (Kant, Immanuel.) München, 1916.
Phil 3486.14   Kant-Lexikon. (Eisler, Rudolf.) Berlin, 1930.
Phil 3493.25   Kant nel realismo. (Leni di Spadafora, F.) Paris, 1953.
Phil 3494.24   Kant oder Laplace? (Meydenbauer, A.) Marburg, 1880.
Phil 3497.19.10   Kant on friendship. (Paton, Herbert J.) London, 1956.
Phil 3500.38   Kant on the moral life. (Scott, John W.) London, 1924.
Phil 3488.17   Kant precritico. (Guzzo, Augusto.) Torino, 1924.
Phil 3503.4.6   Kant-Schiller-Goethe. 2. Aufl. (Vorländer, K.) Leipzig, 1923.
Phil 3480.32.65.2   Kant-Seitenkondordanz. (Hinske, Norbert.) Darmstadt, 1970.
Phil 3481.50   Kant Studien; philosophische Studien. Berlin. 1-60,1904-1969+ 55v.
Phil 3481.50.5   Kant Studien. Ergänzungshefte. Berlin. 1-97,1915-1968+ 26v.
Phil 3483.85.5   Kant studies today. (Beck, Lewis White.) La Salle, 1969.
Phil 3489.44   Kant teleológiájá. (Hermann, István.) Budapest, 1968.
Phil 3488.4.15   Kant über Freiheit. (Goldschmidt, L.) Gotha, 1904.
Phil 3495.10   Kant über Krieg und Frieden. (Natorp, Paul.) Erlangen, 1924.
Phil 3483.94   Kant über Metaphysik und Erfahrung. (Broecker, Walter.) Frankfurt, 1970.
Phil 3499.28   Kant und Antikant. (Rüther, H.) Paderborn, 1921.
Phil 3500.21.5   Kant und Aristoteles. (Sentroul, C.) n.p., 1911.
Phil 3497.12   Kant und Bolzano. (Palágyi, Melchiar.) Halle, 1902.
Phil 3494.2   Kant und Crusius. (Marquardt, A.) Kiel, 1885.
Phil 3500.29   Kant und Darwin. (Schultze, F.) Jena, 1875.
Phil 3482.2.16   Kant und das Ding an sich. (Adickes, E.) Berlin, 1924.
Phil 3500.53   Kant und das freie Wort und Gerechtigkeit und...bei Kant. (Siehr, Carl.) Königsberg, 1927.
Phil 3501.22   Kant und das Problem der Analogie. (Takeda, Sueo.) Den Haag, 1969.
Phil 3489.27   Kant und das Problem der Metaphysik. (Heidegger, Martin.) Bonn, 1929.
Phil 3489.27.2   Kant und das Problem der Metaphysik. 2. Aufl. (Heidegger, Martin.) Frankfurt, 1951.
Phil 3503.4.30   Kant und der Sozialismus unter besonderer Verücksichtigung der neuesten theoretischen Bewegung innerhalb des Marxismus. (Vorländer, K.) Berlin, 1900.
Phil 3482.2.25   Kant und die als-ob-Philosophie. (Adickes, E.) Stuttgart, 1927.
Phil 3485.11   Kant und die catholische Wahrheit. (Deneffe, A.) Freiburg, 1922.
Phil 3494.31   Kant und die deutsche Aufgabe. (Meissinger, K.A.) Frankfurt, 1924.
Phil 3493.6   Kant und die Epigonen. (Liebmann, Otto.) Berlin, 1912.
Phil 3485.20   Kant und die Gegenwärtige Naturwissenschaft. (Drossbach, P.) Berlin, 1943.
Phil 3500.46   Kant und die Gottesbeweise. (Schreiber, C.) Dresden, 1921.
Phil 3495.10.10   Kant und die Marburger Schule. (Natorp, Paul.) Berlin, 1912.
Phil 3492.8   Kant und die Naturwissenschaft. (König, E.) Braunschweig, 1907.
Phil 3195.10.110   Kant und die Philosophie Drieschs. Inaug. Diss. (Zilberis, B.) Vilkaviskis, 1932.
Phil 3483.46   Kant und die philosophische Aufgabe unserer Zeit. (Beneke, F. Eduard.) Berlin, 1832.
Phil 3507.4.5   Kant und die positive Philosophie. (Zimmerman, R.) Wien, 1874.
Phil 3488.32   Kant und die Religionen des Ostens. (Glasenapp, H. von.) Kitzmingen, 1954.
Phil 3493.27   Kant und die Scholastik Heute. (Lotz, J.B.) Pullach, 1955.
Phil 3487.25   Kant und die Wissenschaften. (Frankfurt Universität.) Frankfurt, 1955.
Phil 3500.20.5   Kant und Goethe. (Simmel, G.) Berlin, 1906.
Phil 3488.4.25   Kant und Haeckel. (Goldschmidt, L.) Gotha, 1906.
Phil 3494.17   Kant und Hegel. (Marck, S.) Tübingen, 1917.
Phil 3488.4.5   Kant und Helmholtz. (Goldschmidt, L.) Hamburg, 1898.
Phil 3492.2A   Kant und Helmholtz. (Krause, A.) Lahr, 1878.
Phil 3489.9   Kant und Hemsterhuis in Rüksicht ihrer definitionen der Schönheit. (Herrmann, C.G.) Erfurt, 1791.
Phil 3501.2   Kant und Herbart. (Thomas, K.) Berlin, 1840-69. 2 pam.
Phil 3493.16   Kant und Herder als Deuter der Geistigen Welt. (Litt, Theodor.) Leipzig, 1930.
Phil 3493.16.5   Kant und Herder als Deuter der Geistigen Welt. 2. Aufl. (Litt, Theodor.) Heidelberg, 1949.
Phil 3486.10   Kant und Husserl. (Ehrlich, W.) Halle, 1923.
Phil 3504.12   Kant und kein Ende? 2. Aufl. (Wernieke, A.) Braunschweig, 1907.
Phil 3500.69   Kant und Königsberg. (Stavenhagen, F.) Gottingen, 1949.
Phil 3485.2   Kant und Newton. (Dieterich, K.) Tübingen, 1876.
Phil 3485.2.5   Kant und Rousseau. (Dieterich, K.) Tübingen, 1878.
Phil 3850.18.115   Kant und Scheler. Diss. (Alpheus, Karl.) Freiburg, 1936.
Phil 3492.15   Kant und Schiller. (Kesseler, Kurt.) Bunzlau, 1910.
Phil 3488.9   Kant und Schopenhauer. (Gizycki, G. von.) Leipzig, 1888.
Phil 3503.35.4   Kant und seine Lehre. Eine Einführung in die kritische Philosophie. 4. Aufl. (Valentiner, Theodor.) Stuttgart, 1969.
Phil 3494.5   Kant und seine Nachfolger. (Mirbt, E.S.) Jena, 1841.

Phil 3502.1   Kant und seine Vorgänger. (Uphues, G.K.) Berlin, 1906.

Phil 3488.5   Kant und Wir. (Gross, Felix.) Heidelberg, 1913.

Phil 3494.4   Kant vor und nach dem Jahre 1770. (Michelis, F.) Braunsberg, 1871.

Phil 4800.6   Kant w Polsce przed rokiem 1830. (Harassek, Stefan.) Kraków, 1916.

Phil 3487.20   Kant y la evolución de la conciencia socio-política moderna. (Fuentes Mares, J.) México, 1946.

Phil 3492.29   Kant zum Gedächtnis. (Kinkel, Walter.) Osterwieck, 1924.

Phil 3487.5   Das Kantbildnis der grafen Keyserling. (Fromm, E.) n.p., n.d.

Phil 3489.18   Das Kantbuch. (Hochdorf, Max.) Berlin, 1924.

Phil 50.1   Kantgesellschaft. Philosophische Vorträge. Berlin. 1-31,1912-1928 3v.

Phil 3552.316   Kanthack, K.H. Leibniz. Berlin, 1946.

Phil 3549.17   Kanthack, Katharina. Vom Sinn der Selbsterkenntnis. Berlin, 1958.

Phil 8677.7   Kantian and Lutheran elements in Ritschls' conception of God. (Walcott, G.D.) N.Y., 1904.

Phil 3500.8   Kantian ethics. (Schurman, J.G.) London, 1881.

Phil 3501.15   Kantian ethics. (Teale, A.E.) London, 1951.

Phil 3488.42   The Kantian philosophy of space. (Garnett, Christopher Broune.) Port Washington, N.Y., 1965.

Phil 3500.65A   Kantian studies. (Smith, A.H.) Oxford, 1947.

Phil 3494.53A   The Kantian thing-in-itself. (Miller, Oscar W.) N.Y., 1956.

Phil 3491.8   Kantiana. (Jünemann, Franz.) Leipzig, 1909.

Phil 3481.51F   Kantiana. Wiesbaden.

Phil 3496.1   Kantisch-Fries'sche Religionsphilosophie. (Otto, R.) Tübingen, 1909.

Phil 3503.4.3   Die Kantische Begründung der Moralprinzips. (Vorländer, K.) Solingen, 1889.

Phil 3480.19.30   Kantische Blumenlese. v.1-2. (Kant, Immanuel.) Zittau, 1813-

Phil 3487.10   Die Kantische Freiheitslehre. (Färber, Max.) Berlin, 1921.

Phil 3495.11   Die Kantische Lehre vom Schematismus der reinen Verstandesbegriffe. Diss. (Neide, P.S.) Halle, 1878.

Phil 3500.41   Die Kantische Philosophie und die Religion. (Schmalenbach, H.) Göttingen, 1926.

Phil 3501.12   Kantischen den Reformen oder Kategorien. (Tittel, Gottlof August.) Frankfurt, 1787.

Phil 3504.8.5   Kantischer Kriticismus Gegenüber unkritischen Dilettantismus. (Witte, J.H.) Bonn, 1885.

Phil 3497.17   Kantischer Kritizismus und englische Philosophie. (Pfleiderer, Edmund.) Halle, 1881.

Phil 3494.50   Kantisches Staatsdenken und der Preussische Staat. (Mueller, Johannes.) Kitzingen, 1954.

Phil 3497.13.6   Le kantisme et ses erreurs. (Pesch, T.) Paris, 1897.

Phil 3504.26   Kantlexikon. (Wegner, Gustav.) Berlin, 1893.

Phil 5850.250.15   Kantor, J.R. Interbehavioral psychology. Bloomington, 1958.

Phil 5250.17   Kantor, J.R. Principles of psychology. N.Y., 1924-26. 2v.

Phil 5250.17.2A   Kantor, J.R. Problems of physiological psychology. Bloomington, 1947.

Phil 5250.17.10   Kantor, J.R. Psychology and logic. Bloomington, 1945. 2v.

Phil 5220.5   Kantor, J.R. The scientific evolution of psychology. Chicago, 1963. 2v.

Phil 5250.17.5   Kantor, J.R. A survey of the science of psychology. Bloomington, 1933.

Phil 3480.32.50   Kantova Kritika čistého rozmysla. (Kant, Immanuel.) Praha, 1930.

Phil 3500.18   Kants, Schleiermacher's och Bostroms etiska. (Sahlin, C.Y.) Upsala, 1877.

Phil 3493.33   Kants aestetik. (Loegstrup, Kocud Ejler Christian.) København, 1965.

Phil 3488.6   Kants Ästhetik. (Goldfriedrich, J.A.) Leipzig, 1895.

Phil 3493.1   Kants Analogien der Erfahrung. (Laas, E.) Berlin, 1876.

Phil 3483.86   Kant's analytic. (Bennett, Jonathan Francis.) Cambridge, 1966.

Phil 3492.23   Kants ansicht von der Grundlage der Empfindung. (Kessler, A.) Darmstadt, 1903.

Phil 3482.2.12   Kants Ansichten über Geschichte und Bau der Erde. (Adickes, E.) Tübingen, 1911.

Phil 3494.23   Kants Ansichten über Krieg und Frieden. (Moog, Willy.) Leipzig, n.d.

Phil 3483.58   Kants Apriorismus. (Beier, Franz.) Pfullingen, 1933.

Phil 3499.7   Kants Auffassung des Verhaltnisses von Gläuben und Wissen. (Richter, Otto.) Lauban, 1905.

Phil 3499.12   Kants Bedeutung auf Grund der Entwicklungsgeschichte Seiner Philosophie. (Runze, Max.) Berlin, 1881.

Phil 3489.47   Kants Begriff des Transzendentalen. Pt.1. (Hinske, Norbert.) Stuttgart, 1970.

Phil 3482.2.100   Kant's Begründung der "Deutschen Philosophie". (Aebi, Magdalena.) Basel, 1947.

Phil 3484.2.25   Kant's Begrundung der Aesthetik. (Cohen, H.) Berlin, 1889.

Phil 3484.2.5A   Kant's Begrundung der Ethik. (Cohen, H.) Berlin, 1877.

Phil 3480.93   Kants Briefe ausgewählt. (Kant, Immanuel.) Leipzig, 1911.

Phil 3494.76   Kant's concept of geography and its relation to recent geographical thought. (May, Joseph Austin.) Toronto, 1970.

Phil 3494.74   Kant's concept of teleology. (McFarland, John D.) Edinburgh, 1970.

Phil 3486.13   Kant's conception of God. (England, Frederick E.) London, 1929.

Phil 3480.69.5.10   Kant's cosmogony, as in his essay on The retardation of the rotation of the earth and his national history and theory of the heavens. (Kant, Immanuel.) N.Y., 1968.

Phil 3494.1   Kant's critical philosophy. v.1,3. (Mahaffy, J.P.) London, 1872. 2v.

Phil 3494.8   Kant's Critique of pure reason. (Morris, G.S.) Chicago, 1882.

Phil 3493.7   Kants deduktion av kategorierna. 2. uppl. (Larsson, Hans.) Lund, 1914.

Phil 3489.38   Kant's Deduktion der reinen Verstandesbegriffe. (Henrich, Adolf.) Emmerich, 1885.

Phil 3485.8   Kants Dinge an sich und sein Erfahrungsbegriff. (Drobisch, M.W.) Hamburg, 1885.

Phil 3483.54   Kants Dissertation vom Jahre 1770 und ihre Beziehung zur Kritik der Reinen Vernunft. (Bodansky, Siegfried.) Friedele, 1911-13.

Phil 3495.15   Kant's doctrine of the "thing-in-itself". (Nakashima, R.) New Haven, 1889.

Phil 3484.2.8   Kant's Einfluss auf die deutsche Kultur. (Cohen, H.) Berlin, 1883.

Phil 3489.50   Kants Erfahrungsbegriff. (Holzhey, Helmut.) Basel, 1970.

Phil 3483.36   Kants erkenntnis-theoretischer Idealismus. (Böhringer, A.) Freiburg, 1888.

Phil 3504.25.5   Kant's Erkenntnislehre. (Willems, C.) Trier, 1919.

Phil 3482.5.7   Kants Erkenntnistheorie und seine Stellung zur Metaphysik. (Apel, Max.) Berlin, 1895.

Phil 3489.42   Kants erst Antinomie in ihrer Stellung als Indirekter. (Hofman, Franz.) Mainz? 1961.

Phil 3499.32   Kant's ethical theory. (Ross, H.D.) Oxford, 1954.

Phil 3497.2   Kant's ethics. (Porter, N.) Chicago, 1886.

Phil 3486.3   Kant's ethics: the Clavis to an index. (Edmunds, J.) Louisville, n.d.

Phil 3492.12.5   Kant's ethics and Schopenhauer's criticism. (Kelly, Michael.) London, 1910.

Phil 3489.11   Kants Ethik...dargestellt. (Hägerström, Axel.) Upsala, 1902.

Phil 3493.17   Kants Ethik. (Liebert, Arthur.) Berlin, 1931.

Phil 3494.13   Kant's Ethik. (Messer, A.) Leipzig, 1904.

Phil 3500.30   Kants Ethik. (Strecker, Reinhard.) Giessen, 1909.

Phil 3483.21   Kants Ethik bei den englischen Moralphilosophen des 19. Jahrhunderts. (Baake, Wilhelm.) Leipzig, 1911.

Phil 3507.12   Kants Ethik und das Problem der Einheit von Freiheit und Gesetz. Thesis. (Zwingelberg, Hans Willi.) Bonn, 1969.

Phil 3491.2   Kants eticka asikt. (Johansson, J.) Lund, 1902.

Phil 3484.18.5   Kant's first critique. (Cassirer, H.W.) London, 1954.

Phil 3507.3   Kants Gedanken über Krieg und Frieden. (Zickendraht, K.) Tübingen, 1922.

Phil 3504.40   Kants Gesellschaftslehre. (Weissfeld, M.) Bern, 1907.

Phil 3488.19   Kants Grundirrtümer in seiner Kritik der reinen Vernunft, und die Reformation des geistigen Innenlebens der Menschheit. (Grabowsky, N.) Leipzig, 1907.

Phil 3507.10   Kants Grundlehre. (Zocher, Rudolf.) Erlangen, 1959.

Phil 3480.39   Kant's inaugural dissertation and early writings on space. (Kant, Immanuel.) London, 1929.

Phil 3501.1   Kant's intellektuelle Anschauung. (Thiele, G.) Halle, 1876.

Phil 3480.70.21   Kant's introduction to logic and his essay on the mistaken subtilty of the four figures. (Kant, Immanuel.) N.Y., 1963.

Phil 3500.62   Kant's kategorischen Imperativ nach seiner Genesis und Bedeutung für die Wissenschaft. (Schramm, G.) Bamberg, 1873.

Phil 3503.5.5   Kant's kategorischer Imperativ. (Volkelt, Johannes.) Wien, 1875.

Phil 3500.44   Kants kennis der grieksche Philosophie. Thesis. (Samsom, A.) Alphen aan den Rijn, 1927.

Phil 3500.71   Kants Konzeption der Modalbegriffe. (Schneiberger, Guido.) Basel, 1952.

Phil 3486.1.5   Kant's Kriticismus. (Erdmann, B.) Leipzig, 1878. 3 pam.

Phil 3493.50   Kants Kritik af erkendelsen og refleksionen. (Loegstrup, Knud Ejler Christian.) København, 1970.

Phil 3492.22   Kants kritik af heibnizianismen. (Klinberg, A.G.) Upsala, 1869.

Phil 3494.21   Kants Kritik der reinen Vernunft. (Menzel, A.) Berlin, 1922.

Phil 3499.27   Kants Kritik der reinen Vernunft. (Rosikat, K.A.) Königsberg, 1901.

Phil 3499.6.13   Kants Kritik der reinen Vernunft Abgekürzt auf Grund ihrer Entstehungsgeschichte. (Romundt, H.) Gotha, 1905.

Phil 3494.29   Kant's Kritik der reinen Vernunft und Herder's Metakritik. Diss. (Michalsky, O.) Breslau, 1883.

NEDL Phil 3483.28   Kant's Kritik der Urteilskraft. (Baeumler, Alfred.) Halle, 1923.

Phil 3499.12.5   Kants Kritikan Humes Skepticismus. (Runze, Max.) Berlin, 1880.

Phil 3486.5   Kants kritische Idealismus. (Ewald, O.) Berlin, 1908.

Phil 3499.10.10   Kants kritischer Idealismus. (Reininger, Robert.) Leipzig, 1912.

Phil 3504.12.15   Kants kritischer Werdegang. (Wernicke, A.) Braunschweig, 1911.

Phil 3486.12   Kants om det moraliskt onda. (Edfeldt, Hans.) Upsala, 1878.

Phil 3487.1.8   Kant's leben und die Grundlagen seiner Lehre. (Fischer, Kuno.) Heidelberg, 1906.

Phil 3484.11   Kants Leben und Lehre. (Cassirer, Ernst.) Berlin, 1921.

Phil 3500.40   Kants Leben und Lehre. (Schöndorffer, O.) Leipzig, 1924.

Phil 3500.58   Kants Lebenswerk als Gabe und Aufgabe. (Schilling, Georg.) Detmold, 1924.

Phil 3499.19   Kant's Lehre vom den synthetischen Urtheilen...Mathematik. (Reichardt, W.) Leipzig, 1888.

Phil 3500.15   Kant's Lehre vom Genie. (Schlaff, O.) Göttingen, 1901.

Phil 3504.17   Kant's Lehre vom Gewissen. (Wohlrabe, Wilhelm.) Halle, 1888.

Phil 3500.26   Kants Lehre vom Glauben. (Sänger, E.A.) Leipzig, 1903.

Phil 3497.16   Kant's Lehre vom Idealen Christus. (Paul, Ludwig.) Kiel, 1869.

Phil 3500.32   Kant's Lehre vom Intelligiblencharakter. (Sornmerlath, Ernst.) Leipzig, 1917.

Phil 3483.18   Kants Lehre vom kategorischen Imperativ. (Buchenau, A.) Leipzig, 1913.

Phil 3483.18.2   Kants Lehre vom kategorischen Imperativ. 2. Aufl. (Buchenau, A.) Leipzig, 1923.

Phil 3500.51   Kant's Lehre vom radicalen Bösen. Diss. (Schultheis, P.) Leipzig, 1873.

Phil 3493.5   Kants Lehre vom Schematismus der reinen Verstandesbegriffe. Teil I. (Levy, Heinrich.) Halle, 1907.

Phil 3489.13   Kant's Lehre vom Schlusse. Inaug. Diss. (Hofmann, Paul.) Berlin, 1901.

Phil 3499.10   Kants Lehre vom Unneren sinn und seine Theorie der Erfahrung. (Reininger, Robert.) Wein, 1900.

Phil 3502.2   Kant's Lehre von dem Verhältnisse der Kategorien zu der Erfahrung. (Ueberhorst, C.) Göttingen, 1878.

Phil 3482.2.30   Kants Lehre von der doppelten Affektion unseres ich als Schlüssel zu seiner Erkenntnis Theorie. (Adickes, E.) Tübingen, 1929.

Phil 3494.18   Kants Lehre von der Entwicklung in Natur und Geschichte. (Menzer, Paul.) Berlin, 1911.

Phil 3488.11   Kant's Lehre von der Freiheit. (Gerhard, Carl.) Heidelberg, 1885.

Phil 3492.6   Kant's Lehre von der Sinnlichkeit. (Kuberka, F.) Halle, 1905.

Phil 3491.16   Kants Lehre von der Subjektivität. (Jansohn, Heinz.) Bonn, 1969.

Phil 3488.18   Kant's Lehre von Raum und Zeit, Kuno Fischer und Adolf Trendelenburg. (Grapengiesser, C.) Jena, 1870.

Phil 3488.10   Kant's Lehre von Raum und Zeit. (Gisevius, H.) Hannover, 1890.

Phil 3497.19   Kant's metaphysic of experience. (Paton, Herbert J.) London, 1936. 2v.

Phil 3494.45.5A   Kant's metaphysics and theory of science. (Martin, Gottfried.) Manchester, Eng., 1955.

Phil 3500.100   Kants Metaphysik der Natur. (Schäfer, Lothar.) Berlin, 1966.

Phil 3482.20   Kant's moral philosophy. (Acton, Harry Burrows.) London, 1970.

Phil 3504.58   Kant's moral religion. (Wood, Allen W.) Ithaca, 1970.

Phil 3504.52   Kant's moral theology. (Walsh, William Henry.) London, 1963.

Phil 3485.4   Kants Naturphilosophie als Grundlage seines Systems. (Drews, A.C.H.) Berlin, 1894.

Phil 3483.60   Kant's objectiver Idealismus. (Burckhardt, W.) Naumburg, 1898.

Phil 3489.19   Kants Persönlichkeit und Leben. (Heller, Josef.) Berlin, 1924.

Phil 3494.5.5   Kant's Philosophie. (Mirbt, E.S.) Jena, 1851.

Phil 3485.17   Kants Philosophie des Asthetischen. (Denckmann, G.) Heidelberg, 1947.

Phil 3499.6   Kants philosophische Religionslehre. (Romundt, H.) Gotha, 1902.

Phil 3492.12A   Kants philosophy as rectified by Schopenhauer. (Kelly, Michael.) London, 1909.

Phil 3504.30   Kant's philosophy of religion. (Webb, Clement C.J.) Oxford, 1926.

Phil 3494.48   Kants Platosuffassung. (Mollowilz, Gerhard.) Berlin, 1935.

Phil 3480.132   Kant's political writings. (Kant, Immanuel.) Cambridge, 1970.

Phil 3488.34   Kants politische Philosophie und die Weltpolitik unserer Tage. (Gablentz, Otto Heinrich von der.) Berlin, 1956.

Phil 3500.63   Kant's pre-critical ethics. (Schilpp, P.A.) Evanston, 1938.

Phil 3500.63.2   Kant's pre-critical ethics. 2d ed. (Schilpp, P.A.) Evanstown, 1960.

Phil 3491.20   Kant's principle of personality. (Jones, Hardy E.) Madison, 1971.

Phil 3488.4.20   Kant's "Privatmeinungen" über das Jenseits. (Goldschmidt, L.) Gotha, 1905.

Phil 3494.20   Kant's Psychologie. (Meyer, Jürgen B.) Berlin, 1870.

Phil 3486.11   Kants Rassentheorie und ihre bleibende Bedeutung. (Elsenhans, Theodor.) Leipzig, 1904.

Phil 3483.37   Kants religion. (Boette, Werner.) Langensalza, 1920.

Phil 3500.41.10   Kants Religion. (Schmalenbach, H.) Berlin, 1929.

Phil 3500.55   Kants Religion innerhalb der Grenzen der blossen Vernunft. (Schultz, Martin.) Königsberg, 1927.

Phil 3494.19.30   Kants Revolutionsprinzip (Kopernikanisches Prinzip). (Marcus, Ernst.) Herford, 1902.

Phil 3500.93   Kants Schrift. (Salmony, H.A.) Zürich, 1962.

Phil 3504.25   Kant's Sittenlehre. (Willems, C.) Trier, 1919.

Phil 3507.6   Kants Sittenlehre in gemeinverständlischer Darstellung. (Ziegeler, E.) Leipzig, 1919.

Phil 3485.26   Kant's solution for verification in metaphysics. (Dryer, D.P.) London, 1966.

Phil 3507.9   Kants Staatstheorie. (Zwingmann, H.) München, 19- ?

Phil 3500.48   Kants Stellung in der Geistesgeschichte. (Selz, Otto.) Mannheim, 1924.

Phil 3493.1.5   Kants Stellung in der Geschichte des Conflicts zwischen Glauben und Wissen. (Laas, E.) Berlin, 1882.

Phil 3482.2.35   Kants Systematik als Systembilden der Factor. (Adickes, E.) Berlin, 1887.

Phil 3497.8   Kant's Teleologie. (Pekelharing, C.) Gröningen, 1916.

Phil 3500.10   Kant's Teleologie. (Stadler, A.) Berlin, 1874.

Phil 3484.2   Kant's Theorie der Erfahrung. (Cohen, H.) Berlin, 1871.

Phil 3484.2.2   Kant's Theorie der Erfahrung. 2. Aufl. (Cohen, H.) Berlin, 1885.

Phil 3484.2.3   Kant's Theorie der Erfahrung. 3. Aufl. (Cohen, H.) Berlin, 1918.

Phil 3500.10.10   Kants Theorie der Materie. (Stadler, A.) Leipzig, 1883.

Phil 3497.23   Kants Theorie der Naturwissenschaft. (Plaass, Peter.) Göttingen, 1965.

Phil 3499.15   Kant's Theorie der reinmoralischen Religion. (Remer, G.L.) Rega, 1796.

Phil 3483.80   Kant's theory of knowledge. (Bird, G.) London, 1962.

Phil 3489.45   Kant's theory of knowledge. (Hartnack, Justus.) N.Y., 1967.

Phil 3497.5   Kant's theory of knowledge. (Prichard, H.) Oxford, 1909.

Phil 3504.53   Kant's theory of mental activity. (Wolff, Robert Paul.) Cambridge, 1963. 2v.

Phil 3500.108   Kant's transcendental logic. (Swing, Thomas K.) New Haven, 1969.

Phil 3482.3.5   Kant's transcendentale idealität des Raumes und der zeit. Pt.1-5. (Arnoldt, Emil.) Königsberg, 1870-72.

Phil 3482.8   Kant's transcendentale Logik. (Albert, Georg.) Wien, 1895.

Phil 3493.7.5   Kants transcendentala deduktion af kategorierna. (Larsson, Hans.) Lund, 1914.

Phil 3486.9   Kant's treatment of causality. (Ewing, Alfred Cyril.) London, 1924.

Phil 3492.70.2   Kants und Schillers Begründung der Ästhetik. (Kühnemann, Eugen.) Marburg, 1895.

Phil 3492.70   Kants und Schillers Begründung der Ästhetik. (Kühnemann, Eugen.) München, 1895.

Phil 3497.3.19   Kants Verhaltnis zur Metaphysik. (Paulsen, Friedrich.) Berlin, 1900.

Phil 3500.102   Kants Weg vom Krieg zum Frieden. (Saher, Hans.) München, 1968-

Phil 3480.28.4   Kants Weltanschanung. (Kant, Immanuel.) Darmstadt, 1919.

Phil 3492.18.5   Kant's Weltanschauung. (Kroner, Richard.) Chicago, 1956.

Phil 3492.18   Kants Weltanschauung. (Kroner, Richard.) Tübingen, 1914.

Phil 3494.19.5   Kants Weltgebäude. (Marcus, Ernst.) München, 1917.

Phil 3494.19.6   Kants Weltgebäude. 2. Aufl. (Marcus, Ernst.) München, 1920.

Phil 3483.13   Kants wipbegeerte, kortelijk verklaard. (Burger, D.) 's Gravenhage, 1881.

Phil 3492.39.5   Kants Wohnhaus. 2. Aufl. (Kuhrke, Walter.) Königsberg, 1924.

Phil 3504.6   Kants works und life. (Wirgman, T.) n.p., n.d.

Phil 3504.29   Kants Zeitlehre. (Wallenberg, G.) Berlin, 1896.

Phil 3500.90   Kants Zurechnungsidee und Freiheitsantinomie. (Stoikhammer, Morris.) Köln, 1961.

Phil 3494.7   Die Kant'sche Erkenntnislehre. (Montgomery, E.) München, 1871.

Phil 3850.27.250   Kantzenbach, Friedrich Wilhelm. Albert Schweitzer, Wirklichkeit und Legende. Göttingen, 1969.

Phil 3495.17   Kanův kriticismus a problém hodnoty. (Novák, Mirko.) V Bratislave, 1936.

Phil 1830.35   Kanvitz, Milton R. The American pragmatists. N.Y., 1960.

Phil 1750.799   Kanz, Heinrich. Der Sinn heutigen Philosophierens. Ratingen, 1967.

Phil 4756.2.31   Kapitalisticheskii stroi v izobrazhenii N.F. Fedorova. (Setniskii, N.A.) Kharbin, 1926. 2 pam.

Phil 4807.2   Kapitaly z dějin českého revolučního myšlení. Vyd. 1. (Bělka, František.) Havlíčkův Brod, 1960.

Phil 4810.6   Kapitoly z dějin slovenskej filozofie. (Várossová, Elena.) Bratislava, 1957.

Phil 4812.457.20   Kapitoly z téorie vedy. (Hrušovský, Igor.) Bratislava, 1968.

Phil 1710.12   Kaplan, A. The new world of philosophy. N.Y., 1961.

Phil 5238.120   Kaplan, Bernard. Perspectives in psychological theory. N.Y., 1960.

Phil 5590.437   Kaplan, Bert. Studying personality cross-culturally. N.Y., 1961.

Phil 575.230   Kaplan, Bert. Studying personality crossculturally. Evanston, Illinois, 1961.

Phil 5627.79   Kaplan, J.H. Psychology of prophecy. Philadelphia, 1908.

Phil 6680.4   Kaplan, Leo. Hypnotismus, animismus. Leipzig, 1917.

Phil 6320.2   Kaplan, Leo. Psychoanalytische Probleme. Leipzig, 1916.

Phil 3808.157   Kaplan, Leo. Schopenhauer und der Animismus. Leipzig, 1925.

Phil 8411.14   Kaplan, Leo. Versuch einer Psychologie der Kunst. Baden-Baden, 1930.

Phil 6320.14   Kaplan, Oscar J. Mental disorders in later life. Stanford, Calif., 1945.

Phil 3160.3.91   Kaplan, Simon. Das Geschichtsproblem in der Philosophie Hermann Cohen. Berlin, 1930.

Phil 5250.11   Kaploun, Albert. Psychologie générale. Lausanne, 1919.

Phil 3801.470.2   Kapp, Christian. F.W.J. von Schelling. Leipzig, 1843.

Htn   Phil 3801.470*   Kapp, Christian. F.W.J. von Schelling. Leipzig, 1843.

Htn   Phil 3801.471*   Kapp, Christian. Sendschreiben an den...von Schelling. n.p., 1830.

Htn   Phil 3801.471.10*   Kapp, Christian. Über den Ursprung der Menschen und Völker nach der mosaischen Genesis. Nürnberg, 1829.

Phil 291.10   Kapp, Reginald O. Towards a unified cosmology. London, 1960.

Phil 2240.82   Kappes, M. Der "common sense" als Princip der Gewissheit. München, 1890.

Phil 3640.203   Kappstein, T. Einführung in Friedrich Nietzsches Zarathustradichtung. Bielefeld, 1925.

Phil 179.3.84   Kappstein, T. Rudolf Eucken. Berlin, 1909.

Phil 3415.90.5   Kappstein, Theodor. Eduard von Hartmann. Gotha, 1907.

Phil 310.543   Kaprielian, Henri. Osnovy marksistskoi logiki. Erevan, 1968.

Phil 9035.54   Karakter. (Stipriaan Luiscius, J.M. van.) Haag, 1925.

Phil 9035.92   Karakterkundig woordenbock des Nederlands taal. (Vbbink, G.) Baarn, 1951.

Phil 3492.55   Karapetian, H.A. Kriticheskii analiz filosofii Kanta. Erevan, 1958.

Phil 310.170   Karavaev, G.G. Istoricheskii materializm. Leningrad, 1959.

Phil 9495.154   Kardiner, A. Sex and morality. 1st ed. Indianapolis, Ind., 1954.

Phil 5250.36A   Kardiner, Abram. The psychological frontiers of society. N.Y., 1945.

Phil 5653.8   Kare, M.R. Physiological and behavioral aspects of taste. Chicago, 1961.

X Cg   Phil 9495.124.2   Karezza, ethics of marriage. (Stockham, A.B. (Mrs.).) Chicago, 1898.

Phil 9495.124   Karezza, ethics of marriage. (Stockham, A.B. (Mrs.).) Chicago, 1903.

Phil 1200.25   Karg, F. Stoicos' Aëatheiae falso suspectos. Lipsiae, 1716.

Phil 260.16   Kargon, Robert. Atomism in England from Hariot to Newton. Oxford, 1966.

Phil 4595.3.31   Karitz, Anders. Philosophie und Spezialforschung. Lund, 1932.

Phil 3525.83   Karl C.F. Krause's Leben und Lehre. (Leonhardi, Hermann.) Leipzig, 1902.

Phil 3525.90   Karl Christian Friedrich Krause. (MacCauley, Clay.) Berkeley, Calif., 1925.

Phil 3525.92   Karl Christian Friedrich Krause. (Proksch, A.) Leipzig, 1880.

Phil 3525.84   Karl Christian Friedrich Krause als philosophischer Denker Gewürdigt. (Leonhardi, Hermann.) Leipzig, 1905.

Phil 8411.5   Karl Christian Friedrich Krause's Abriss der Asthetik oder der Philosophie des schönen Kunst. (Krause, K.C.F.) Göttingen, 1837.

Phil 3525.85   Karl Christian Friedrich Krause's Leben, Lehre und Bedeutung. (Martin, B.R.) Leipzig, 1885.

Phil 3745.6.95   Karl Christian Planck. (Planck, M.) Stuttgart, 1950.

Phil 3745.6.90   Karl Christian Plancks Anthropologie auf der Grundlage seiner Logik des reinen Denkens. Inaug. Diss. (Borne, G. von dem.) Winnendens, 1930.

Phil 3160.9.30   Karl Gustav Carus und Carl Fr. Ph. von Martins. (Carus, Karl Gustav.) Halle, 1939.

Phil 3475.3.200   Karl Jaspers. (Gottschalk, Herbert.) Berlin, 1966.

Phil 3475.3.150   Karl Jaspers. (Piper, R.C.) München, 1958.

Phil 3475.3.140   Karl Jaspers. (Schilpp, P.A.) Stuttgart, 1957.

Phil 3475.3.175   Karl Jaspers. (Tilliette, Xavier.) Paris, 1960.

Phil 3475.3.95   Karl Jaspers et la philosophie de l'existence. (Dufrenne, M.) Paris, 1947.

Phil 3475.3.210   Karl Jaspers in der Kritik. (Schneiders, Werner.) Bonn, 1965.

Phil 3475.3.250   Karl Jaspers in Selbstzeugnissen und Bilddokumenten. (Saner, Hans.) Reinbek, 1970.

Phil 3475.3.185F   Karl Jaspers in Übersetzungen. (Bentz, Hans Wille.) Frankfurt, 1961.

Phil 3475.3.85   Karl Jaspers und Heinrich Richert Existenzialismus und Wertphilosophie. (Ramming, G.) Bern, 1948.

Phil 3475.3.115   Karl Jaspers zum siebzigsten Geburtslag. Bern, 1953.

Phil 3778.92   Karl Leonard Reinholds Elementarphilosophie. (Klemmt, Alfred.) Hamburg, 1958.

Phil 3778.90   Karl Leonhard Reinholds Leben. (Reinhold, E.) Jena, 1825.

Phil 3780.91   Karl Rosenkranz als Literaturkritiker. (Japtok, E.) Freiburg, 1964.

Phil 3780.90   Karl Rosenkranz und Hegel. (Metzke, Erwin.) Leipzig, 1929.

Phil 3903.2.125   Karl Vogts Weltanschauung. (Jung, Johannes.) Paderborn, 1915.

Phil 3903.2.126   Karl Vogts Weltanschauung. Inaug. Diss. (Jung, Johannes.) Paderborn, 1915.

Phil 8665.20   Karliak, A.S. Ocherki po nauchnomu ateizmu. Minsk, 1961.

Phil 5190.85.2   Karlins, Marvin. Persuasion; how opinions and attitudes are changed. 2nd ed. N.Y., 1970.

Phil 978.6.64 Karma. (Theosophical manual IV). (Besant, Annie.) London, 1897.

Phil 978.83 Karma and rebirth. (Humphreys, Christmas.) London, 1943.

Phil 960.38 Karma and reincarnation in Hindu. Thesis. (Yevtić, Paul.) London, 1927.

Phil 5250.40 Karn, H.W. An introduction to psychology. N.Y., 1955.

Phil 1050.15.9 Karo, Jakob. Kritische Untersuchungen zu Levi hen Gersons (Ralbag) Widerlegung des Aristotelischen Zeitbegriffes. Inaug. Diss. Leipzig, 1935.

Phil 4803.522.80 Karol Libelt jako działacz polityczny i społeczny, ur. 1807 um. 1875. (Kosmowska, J.W.) Poznań, 1918.

Phil 5592.65A Karon, Bertram P. The Negro personality. N.Y., 1958.

Phil 5066.229 Karp, Carol R. Languages with expressions of infinite length. Amsterdam, 1964.

Phil 6327.4.80 Karpf, Jay B. The psychology and psychotherapy of Otto Rank. N.Y., 1953.

Phil 5643.72 Karplus, S. Beitrag zur Lehre von den Geschichtsempfindungen. Inaug. Diss. Berlin, 1902.

Phil 810.4 Karppe, S. Essais de critique et d'histoire de philosophie. Paris, 1902.

Phil 8665.23 Karpushin, Vladimir A. Populiarnye lektsii po ateizmu. 2. izd. Moskva, 1965.

Phil 575.296 Karquel, André. La tragédie cosmique de la conscience. Paris, 1970.

Phil 4761.2.30 Karsavin, L.P. O comnenii, nauke i vere. Berlin, 1925.
Phil 4761.2.35 Karsavin, L.P. O nachalakh. Berlin, 1925.
Phil 4761.2.40 Karsavin, L.P. Tserkov', lichnost' i gosudarstvo. Parizh, 1927.

Phil 9495.21 Karsch-Haack, F. Das gleichgeschlechtliche Leben der Naturvölker. München, 1911.

Phil 2520.197 Kartesischer oder sanchezischer Zweifel? Inaug.-Diss. (Iriarte, J.) Bothrop, 1935.

Phil 6960.12 Kasanin, J.S. Language and thought in schizophrenia. Berkeley, 1944.

Phil 3890.10.130 Kasch, W.F. Die Sozialphilosophie von Ernst Troeltsch. Tübingen, 1963.

Phil 8590.33 Kasch, Wilhelm. Atheistischer Humanismus und christliche Existenz in der Gegenwart. Tübingen, 1964.

Phil 4769.1.99 Kaschewnikoff, A. Die Geschichtsphilosophie Wladimir Solowjews. Bonn, 1930.

Phil 672.146 Kaschmieder, E. Zeitbezug und Sprache. Berlin, 1929.
Phil 3549.8.140 Kasdorff, Hans. Ludwig Klages Werk und Wirkung. Bonn, 1969.

Phil 810.12 Kasm, Badi. L'ideé de preuve en imétaphysique. Paris, 1959.

Phil 3801.474 Kasper, Walter. Das Absolute in der Geschichte. Mainz, 1965.

Phil 8411.36.2 Kassil', Lev A. "Delo vkusa". Izd. 2. Moskva, 1964.
Phil 3640.298 Kassler, K. Nietzsche und das Recht. München, 1941.
Phil 400.16 Kassner, R. Der indische Idealismus. München, 1903.
Phil 3549.10 Kassner, Rudolf. Buch der Erinnerung. Leipzig, 1938.
Phil 3549.10.2 Kassner, Rudolf. Buch der Erinnerung. 2. Aufl. Erlenbach, 1954.

Phil 3549.10.30 Kassner, Rudolf. Der Gottmensch. Leipzig, 1938.
Phil 6020.4 Kassner, Rudolf. Die Grundlagen der Psysiognomik. Leipzig, 1922.

Phil 3549.10.5 Kassner, Rudolf. Motive; essays. Berlin, 1906.
Phil 3549.10.45 Kassner, Rudolf. Das neunzehnte Jahrhundert; Ausdruck und Grösse. Erlenbach, 1947.

Phil 6020.4.5 Kassner, Rudolf. Physiognomik. München, 1932.
Phil 6020.4.6 Kassner, Rudolf. Physiognomik. Wiesbaden, 1951.
Phil 3549.10.35 Kassner, Rudolf. Transfiguration. Erlenbach, 1946.
Phil 3549.10.50 Kassner, Rudolf. Umgang der Jahre. Erlenbach, 1949.
Phil 3549.10.40 Kassner, Rudolf. Wandlung. Zürich, 1946.
Phil 3549.10.60 Kassner, Rudolf. Wer indische Gedanke. 2. Aufl. Leipzig, 1921.

Phil 3549.10.55 Kassner, Rudolf. Zahl und Gesichte. Wiesbaden, 1956.
Phil 291.4 Kassowitz, Max. Welt - Leben - Seele. Wien, 1908.
Phil 8635.7 Kast, J. Ernster Blick. Würzburg, 1818.
Phil 5250.31 Kastein, G.W. Eine Kritik der Ganzheitstheorien. Leiden, 1937.

Phil 5520.455 Kastein, Shulamith. The birth of language; the case history of a non-verbal child. Springfield, 1966.

Phil 341.10 Kastenholz, Joseph. Der Begriff des Dinges in der Philosophie der Gegenwart. Inaug. Diss. Bonn, 1916.

Phil 3120.8.98 Kastil, A. Die Philosophie Franz Brentanos. München, 1951.

Phil 3260.88 Kastil, Alfred. Jakob F. Fries' Lehre von der unmittelbaren Erkenntnis. Göttingen, 1912.

Phil 2520.153 Kastil, Alfred. Studien zur neueren Erkenntnistheorie. Halle, 1909.

Phil 3195.2.95 Kastner, Lorenz. Martin Deutinger's Leben und Schriften. München, 1875.

Phil 6327.15 Die Kastrationsangst des Weibes. (Rado, Sandor.) Wien, 1934.

Phil 4796.96.80 Kasumov, Mekhbaly Mamedovich. M.F. Akhundov i russkaia revoliutsionno-demokraticheskaia estetika. Baku, 1954.

Phil 4795.6 Kasumov, Mekhbaly Mamedovich. Ocherki po istorii peredovoi filosofskoi i obshchestvenno-politicheskoi mysli azerbaidzhanskogo naroda v XIX veke. Baku, 1959.

Phil 4803.454.79 Katalog dzieł i rekopisów Hoene-Wrońskiego. (Dickstein, Samuel.) Kraków, 1896.

Phil 8411.17 Katann, O. Asthetisch-literarische Arbeiten. Wien, 1918.
Phil 810.1 Katechismus der Geschichte der Philosophie. (Kirchner, F.) Leipzig, 1877.

Phil 6048.89.7 Katechismus der Handelskunst. (Gessmann, G.W.) Berlin, 1921.

Phil 6048.97.4 Katechismus der Handflächenkunde. 4. Aufl. (Gessmann, G.W.) Berlin, 1922.

Phil 6060.17.3 Katechismus der Handschriften-Deutung. 3. Aufl. (Gessmann, G.W.) Berlin, 1922.

Phil 5926.2.2 Katechismus der Kopfformkunde. 2. Aufl. (Gessmann, G.W.) Berlin, 1921.

Phil 5050.13 Katechismus der Logik. (Kirchner, F.) Leipzig, 1890.
Phil 8885.15 Ein Katechismus der moral und Politik für das deutsche Volk. 2e Aufl. Leipzig, 1891.

Phil 185.4 Katechismus der Philosophie. (Kirchmann, J.) Leipzig, 1881.

Phil 5250.10.5 Katechismus der Psychologie. (Kirchner, F.) Leipzig, 1883.

Phil 8597.24 Katechismus der Religionsphilosophie. (Runze, Georg.) Leipzig, 1901.

Phil 3160.15.5 Der kategoriale Ort des Seelischen in der Naturwirklichkeit. (Avé-Lallemant, E.) München, 1959.

Phil 9030.7 Kategorie nahodilého v dějinách filosofického myšlení. (Bartoš, Jaromír.) Praha, 1965.

Phil 310.3.8 Kategorien der materialistischen Dialektik. (Rozental', M.M.) Moskva, 1959.

Phil 5585.21 Die Kategorien der sinnlichen Perception. (Stiborius.) Leipzig, 1890.

Phil 192.68 Die Kategorien des Lebendigen. (Ranke, Karl E.) München, 1928.

Phil 5075.4 Kategorienlehre. (Brentano, F.) Leipzig, 1933.
Phil 5075.3 Kategorienlehre. (Spann, Othmar.) Jena, 1924.
Phil 3415.57.2 Kategorienlehre. 2. Aufl. v.1-3. (Hartmann, Eduard von.) Leipzig, 1923.

Phil 5075.3.3 Kategorienlehre. 3. Aufl. (Spann, Othmar.) Graz, 1969.
Phil 3415.105 Die Kategorienlehre Eduard von Hartmanns. (Hessen, J.) Leipzig, 1924.

Phil 310.748 Kategorii dialektiki i metodologiia sovremennoi nauki. Voronezh, 1970.

Phil 310.675 Kategorii kachestva i kolichestva. (Shliakhtenko, Sergei G.) Leningrad, 1968.

Phil 8980.616 Kategorii marksistsko-leninskoi etiki. (Kommunisticheskaia Partiia Sovetskogo Soiuza. Novosibirskaia Vysshaia Partiinaia Shkola.) Moskva, 1965.

Phil 8980.159 Kategorii marksistskoi etiki. (Arkhangel'skii, Leonid M.) Moskva, 1963.

Phil 310.3.5 Kategorii materialisti cheskoi dialektiki. (Rozental', M.M.) Moskva, 1956.

Phil 310.240 Kategorii materialisticheskoi dialektiki. (Georgiev, F.I.) Moskva, 1960.

Phil 310.786 Kategoriia dialektilei kak stupeni poznaniia. Moskva, 1971.

Phil 310.637 Kategoriia mery v marksistskoi dialektike. (Kuz'min, Vsevolod P.) Moskva, 1966.

Phil 8419.66 Kategoriia prekrasnogo i obshchestvennyi ideal. (Stolovich, Leonid N.) Moskva, 1969.

Phil 3483.25 Kategorilära enligt Kantiska principer. Akademisk afhandling. (Barkman, H.) Upsala, 1901.

Phil 3485.1 Der kategorische Imperativ. (Deussen, Paul.) Kiel, 1891.
Phil 3494.19.2 Der kategorische Imperativ. (Marcus, Ernst.) München, 1921.

Phil 3485.1.5 Der kategorische Imperativ. 2. Aufl. (Deussen, Paul.) Kiel, 1903.

Phil 3491.3 Det kategoriska imperativet. Akademisk avhandling. (Jonson, Erik.) Uppsala, 1924.

Phil 8980.759 Katehoriia dovir'ia v marksysts'kii etytsi. (Rutkovs'kyi, Borys O.) Kyiv, 1970.

Phil 7069.16.30 Kates, George W. The philosophy of spiritualism. Boston, 1916.

Phil 9070.56 Kates, J.W. The use of life. 1st ed. N.Y., 1953.
Phil 5238.180 Katholieke Centrale Vereniging voor Geestelijke Volksgezondheid. Serie geestelijke volksgezondheid. 20-42 6v.

Phil 8590.31 Die katholische Glaubenswelt. v.3. Freiburg, 1961.
Phil 8585.36 Die katholische religions philosophie der Gegenwart. (Fries, Heinrich.) Heidelberg, 1949.

Phil 8712.20 Katholische Weltanschauung und freie Wissenschaft. (Wahrmund, L.) München, 1908.

Phil 7069.33.46 Katie Fox, epochmaking medium. (Taylor, William G.L.) N.Y., 1933.

Phil 6327.24 Der Katillon. (Rohitsek, A.) Zürich, 1925.
Phil 735.115 Katkov, Georg. Untersuchungen zur Werttheorie und Theodizee. Brünn, 1937.

Phil 8885.37 Katô, Hiroyuke. Der Kampf ums recht des Stärkeren und seine Entwickelung. Tokyô, 1893.

Phil 5627.36 Kato, Katsuji. The psychology of oriental religious experience. Menaska, Wis., 1915.

Phil 5500.11 Katona, G. Psychologie der Relationserfassung und des Vergleichens. Leipzig, 1924.

Phil 5250.34.5 Katona, George. Organizing and memorizing. N.Y., 1949.
Phil 20.9 Katowice, Poland (city). Wyzsza Szkota Pedagogiczna. Sekcja Pedagogiczna. Prace psychologiczne. 1,1967+

Phil 525.262 Katsaros, Thomas. The Western mystical tradition. New Haven, 1969-

Phil 3195.6.99 Katsube, Kenzo. Wilhelm Diltheys Methode der Lebensphilosophie. Hiroschima, 1931.

Phil 9070.40 Katterhenry, E.A. Can you take it? St. Louis, Mo., 1944.
Phil 185.68 Kattsoff, L.O. Elements of philosophy. N.Y., 1953.
Phil 185.68.5 Kattsoff, L.O. Logic and the nature of reality. The Hague, 1956.

Phil 8885.47 Kattsoff, Louis Osgood. Making moral decisions. The Hague, 1965.

Phil 5645.33.5 Katz, David. Der Aufbau der Farbwelt. 2. Aufl. Leipzig, 1930.

Phil 5585.16 Katz, David. Experimentelle Beiträge zur Psychologie...des Zeitsinns. Leipzig, 1906.

Phil 5286.10 Katz, David. Gestaltpsychologie. Basel, 1944.
Phil 5286.10.2 Katz, David. Gestaltpsychologie. 2. Aufl. Basel, 1948.
Phil 5286.10.4 Katz, David. Gestaltpsychologie. 4. Aufl. Basel, 1969.
Phil 5250.37.10 Katz, David. Handbuch der Psychologie. Basel, 1951.
Phil 5250.37.11 Katz, David. Handbuch der Psychologie. Basel, 1960.
Phil 5250.37.6 Katz, David. Psychological atlas. N.Y., 1948.
Phil 5250.37.5 Katz, David. Psychologischer Atlas. Basel, 1945.
Phil 5250.37.20 Katz, David. Studien zur experimentellen Psychologie. Basel, 1953.

Phil 5520.447 Katz, Jerrold J. The philosophy of language. N.Y., 1966.
Phil 5125.29 Katz, Jerrold J. The problem of induction and its solution. Chicago, 1965.

Phil 5421.15.5 Katz, R.L. Empathy, its nature and uses. N.Y., 1963.
Phil 5545.233 Katzenberger, Lothar Friedrich. Auffassung und Gedächtnis. München, 1967.

Phil 5545.244 Katzenberger, Lothar Friedrich. Dimensionen des Gedächtnisses. Wurzburg, 1964.

Phil 5545.244.1 Katzenberger, Lothar Friedrich. Gedächtnis oder Gedächtnisse? München, 1967.

Phil 3492.16 Katzer, Ernst. Luther und Kant. Giessan, 1910.
Phil 8411.23.10 Kaublanov, B.G. Mystetstvo iak forma piznannia diisnosti. Kyiv, 1867.

Phil 3010.6 Kauffmann, H.L. Essai sur l'anti-progressisme et ses origines dans la philosophie allemande moderne. Thèse. Paris, 1934.

Phil 6680.5.2 Kauffmann, M. Suggestion und Hypnose. 2. Aufl. Berlin, 1923.

Phil 341.11 Kauffmann, Max. Fundamente der Erkenntnistheorie und urssenschaftslehre. Leipzig, 1890.

Phil 341.22 Kaufman, G.D. Relativism, knowledge and faith. Chicago, 1960.

Phil 5465.212 Kaufmann, Arnold. L'inventique. Paris, 1970.
Phil 8411.27 Kaufmann, F. Das Reich des Schönen. Stuttgart, 1960.
Phil 974.3.118 Kaufmann, G. Fruits of anthroposophy. London, 1922.
Phil 8635.3 Kaufmann, H. Die Unsterblichkeitsbeweise. Paderborn, 1912.

Phil 185.13 Kaufmann, P. The temple of truth. Cincinnati, 1858.

Phil 5400.190 Kaufmann, Pierre. L'expérience émotionnelle de l'espace. Thèse. Paris, 1967.

Phil 5251.41.90 Kaufmann, Pierre. Kurt Lewin, une théorie du change dans les sciences de l'homme. Paris, 1968.

Phil 1750.455 Kaufmann, W.A. Existentialism from Dostoevsky to Sartre. N.Y., 1956.

Phil 1750.455.12 Kaufmann, W.A. From Shakespeare to existentialism. Freeport, N.Y., 1971.

Phil 1750.455.11 Kaufmann, W.A. From Shakespeare to existentialism. Garden City, 1960.

Phil 3425.608 Kaufmann, W.A. Hegel. 1st ed. Garden City, N.Y., 1965.

Phil 1750.455.10 Kaufmann, W.A. The owl and the nightingale. London, 1959.

Phil 185.72 Kaufmann, Walter Arnold. Critique of religion and philosophy. 1. ed. N.Y., 1958.

Phil 3425.752 Kaufmann, Walter Arnold. Hegel's political philosophy. 1st ed. N.Y., 1970.

Phil 3640.368.3 Kaufmann, Walter Arnold. Nietzsche: philosopher, psychologist, antichrist. Cleveland, 1964.

Phil 3640.368.4 Kaufmann, Walter Arnold. Nietzsche: philosopher, psychologist, antichrist. 3. ed. Princeton, N.J., 1968.

Phil 978.75 Kauga, D.D. Where theosophy and science meet. Adyar, 1938.

Phil 5050.20F Kauger, F. Handbok i logik. Stockholm, 1959.

Phil 165.382 Kaulbach, Friedrich. Kritik und Metaphysik; Studien. Berlin, 1966.

Phil 210.65 Kaulbach, Friedrich. Philosophie der Beschreibung. Köln, 1968.

Phil 1515.1 Kaulich, W. Geschichte der scholastischen Philosophie. Prag, 1863.

Phil 5250.20 Kaulich, W. Handbuch der Psychologie. Graz, 1870. 3 pam.

Phil 8885.1 Kaulich, W. System der Ethik. Prag, 1877.

Phil 185.27 Kaulish, W. System der Metaphysik. Prag, 1874.

Phil 50.35 Kaunas. Universitetas. Teologijos-Filosofijos Fakultetas. Leidiniai. Kaunas. 8-18 2v.

Phil 6319.1.245 Kaune, Fritz Jürgen. Selbstverwirklichung. München, 1967.

Phil 810.5 Kaunitz, M.M. Philosophy for plain people. N.Y., 1926.

Phil 270.144 Der Kausalbegriff in Philosophie und Physik. (Titze, Hans.) Meisenheima, 1964.

Phil 270.28 Kausale und konditionale Weltanschauung. 2. aufl. (Verworn, Max.) Jena, 1918.

Phil 270.39 Das Kausalgesetz und seine Grenzen. (Frank, Philipp.) Wien, 1932.

Phil 270.46 Kausalität. (Skilvierwski, S.L.) Paderborn, 1930.

Phil 270.16 Kausalität Determinismus. (Petersen, J.) München, 1909.

Phil 8735.35 Kausalität im Verständnis des Theologen und der Begründer neuzeitlicher Physik. (Dolch, Heimo.) Freiburg, 1954.

Phil 270.29 Kausalität und Originalität. (Neef, Fritz.) Tübingen, 1918.

Phil 5757.13 Kausalität und Willensfreiheit. (Heuer, Wilhelm.) Heidelberg, 1924.

Phil 270.19 Der Kausalitätsbegriff. (Meyer-Pforzheim, C.W.) Hamburg, 1914.

Phil 1504.13.5 Das Kausalprinzip. v.13, pt.5. (Schulemann, G.) Münster, 1915.

Phil 270.17 Das Kausalproblem. (Lang, Albert.) Köln, 1904.

Phil 3565.123 Das Kausalproblem in Lotzes Philosophie. (Wentscher, E.) Halle, 1903.

Phil 365.43 Kausika, N. The new evolution, being a general solution of all modern life problems, based on truth. Nemmara, 1936.

Phil 3450.19.205 Kauthack, Katherina. Das Denken des Martin Heideggers. Berlin, 1959.

Phil 8885.19.7 Kautsky, Karl. Ethics and the materialist conception of history. Chicago, 1906.

Phil 8885.19.8 Kautsky, Karl. Ethics and the materialist conception of history. Chicago, 1907.

Phil 8885.19.5 Kautsky, Karl. Ethics and the materialist conception of history. Chicago, 1918.

Phil 8885.19.9 Kautsky, Karl. Ethik und materialistische Geschichtsauffassung. Stuttgart, 1906.

Phil 8885.19 Kautsky, Karl. Ethik und materialistische Geschichtsauffassung. Stuttgart, 1919.

Phil 1870.116 Kaveeshwar, G.W. The metaphysics of Berkeley critically examined in the light of modern philosophy. Mandleshwar, 1933.

Phil 8665.4 Kawaguchi, U. The bearing of the evolutionary theory on the conception of God. Thesis. Menasha, Wis., 1916.

Phil 5545.17 Kay, D. Memory. London, 1888.

Phil 5545.17.3 Kay, D. Memory. N.Y., 1888.

Phil 5875.70 Kay, William. Moral development: a psychological study of moral growth from childhood to adolescence. London, 1968.

Phil 1020.5 Kayser, C. Das Buch von der Erkenntniss der Wahrheit. Leizig, 1889.

Phil 1865.181 Kayser, E.L. The grand social enterprise; a study of Jeremy Bentham in his relation to liberal nationalism. N.Y., 1932.

Phil 8430.55.2 Kayser, Hans. Akróasis, die Lehre von der Harmonik der Welt. 2. Aufl. Basel, 1964.

Phil 3890.8.101 Kayser, R. Christian Thomasius und der Pietismus. Hamburg, 1900.

Phil 3492.45 Kayser, Rudolf. Kant. Wien, 1935.

Phil 3830.10 Kayser, Rudolf. Spinoza; Bildnis eines geistigen Helden. Wien, 1932.

Phil 3830.10.5 Kayser, Rudolf. Spinoza. N.Y., 1946.

Phil 8050.65.5 Kayser, W. The grotesque in art and literature. Bloomington, 1963.

Phil 8080.11 Kayser, Wolfgang. Das Groteske, seine Gestaltung in Malerei und Dichtung. Oldenburg, 1957.

Phil 8080.11.1 Kayser, Wolfgang. Das Groteske in Malerei und Dichtung. Reinbek, 1960.

Phil 3625.1.107 Kayserling, M. Moses Mendelssohn. Leipzig, 1862.

Phil 3625.1.195 Kayserling, Meyer. Moses Mendelssohn's philosophische und religiöse Grundsätze mit Hinblick auf Lessing. Leipzig, 1856.

Phil 8735.61 Kazakevich, Tat'iana A. Tselesoobraznost' i tsel' v obshchestvennom razvitii. Leningrad, 1969.

Phil 8590.32 Kazhdan, Al.P. Proiskhozhdenie khristianstva i ego sushchnost'. Moskva, 1962.

Phil 8171.200 Kazykhanova, Batish R. Rol' khudozhestvennogo naslediia v esteticheskom vospitanii. Alma-ata, 1967.

Phil 720.26 Kearney, C.M. Two neglected aspects of the truth situation. Thesis. Chicago, 1933.

Phil 5620.6 Keary, C.F. The pursuit of reason. Cambridge, 1910.

Phil 6750.265 Keblon, Lars. The structure of abilities at lower levels of intelligence. Stockholm, 1965.

Phil 3830.13 Kechek'ian, Stepan F. Eticheskoe mirosezaresanie Spinozy. Moskva, 1914.

Phil 310.375 Kechov, B.M. O povtoriaemosti v protsesse razoitiia. Moskva, n.d.

Phil 5050.2.5 Keckermann, B. Systema logicae. Coloniae, 1611. 2 pam.

Htn Phil 5050.2* Keckermann, B. Systema logicae minus. Hanoviae, 1606.

Phil 185.15 Keckermann, B. Systema physicum. Hanoviae, 1623.

Phil 5000.2 Keckermanni, B. Systema systematum. Hanoviae, 1613.

Phil 9350.3.15 Keddie, H. Heroines in obscurity. London, 1871.

Phil 9350.3.7 Keddie, H. Papers for thoughtful girls. Boston, 1864.

Phil 9350.3.8 Keddie, H. Sweet counsel. Boston, 1866.

Phil 3425.577.2 Kedney, J.S. Hegel's aesthetics; a critical exposition. Chicago, 1885.

Phil 3425.577 Kedney, J.S. Hegel's aesthetics; a critical exposition. 2nd ed. Chicago, 1892.

Phil 8885.9 Kedney, J.S. Problems in ethics. N.Y., 1900.

Phil 310.552 Kedrov, B.M. Edinstvo dialektiki, logiki i teorii poznaniia. Moskva, 1963.

Phil 260.17 Kedrov, Bonifatii M. Triaspekta atomistiki. Moskva, 1969. 3v.

Phil 8700.7 Keebler, R.S. The Tennessee evolution case. Memphis, 1925.

Phil 3450.11.350 Keekell, Lothar. Husserl, sa vie, son oeuvre. Paris, 1964.

Phil 8960.14 Keeling, Michael. Morals in free society. London, 1967.

Phil 5050.14 Keeling, S.V. Logic and reasoning. London, 1929.

Phil 3492.25 Keeling, S.V. La nature de l'expérience chez Kant et chez Bradley. Thèse. Montpellier, 1925.

Phil 2520.187 Keeling, Stanley V. Descartes. London, 1934.

Phil 2520.187.2 Keeling, Stanley V. Descartes. 2d ed. London, 1968.

Phil 5066.228 Keene, G.B. First-order functional calculus. London, 1964.

Phil 6060.19 Keene, John H. The mystery of handwriting. Boston, 1896.

Phil 6122.55 Keeping a sound mind. (Morgan, John J.B.) N.Y., 1934.

Phil 5850.244 Keeping mentally fit, a guide to everyday psychology. (Jastrow, Joseph.) N.Y., 1928.

Phil 5850.244.5 Keeping mentally fit. (Jastrow, Joseph.) N.Y., 1928.

Phil 1865.182 Keeton, G.W. Jeremy Bentham and the law. London, 1948.

Phil 187.32.85 Keeton, Morris. The philosophy of Edmund Montgomery. Dallas, 1950.

Phil 630.35 Keferstein, H. Die Realität der Aussenwelt in der Philosophie. Käthen, 1883.

Phil 3120.12.80 Kegel, Martin. Bruno Bauers Übergang von der hegelschen Rechten zum Radikalismus. Inaug. Diss. Leipzig, 1908.

Phil 5590.13.5 Kehl, R. Psicología da personalidade. 2. ed. Rio de Janeiro, 1941.

Phil 4972.22 Kehl, Renato. Bio-perspectivas. Rio de Janeiro, 1938.

Phil 341.8 Kehr, Theodor. Das Bewusstseinsproblem. Tübingen, 1916.

Phil 1504.7.4 Keicher, O. Raymundus Lullus. v.7, pt.4-5. Münster, 1909.

Phil 3425.89 Keil, Oswald T. Einige Bemerkungen über den Standpankt, Welchen die deutsche Philosophie durch Hegel erreicht hat. Leipzig, 1928.

Phil 5421.20.135 Keil, Siegfried. Aggression und Mitmenschlichkeit. Stuttgart, 1970.

Phil 8590.22 Keilbach, W. Die Problematik der Religionen. Paderborn, 1936.

Phil 185.95 Keilbach, Wilhelm. Einübung ins philosophische Denken. München, 1960.

Phil 5548.144 Keiler, Peter. Wollen und Wert. Berlin, 1970.

Htn Phil 8700.2* Keill, J. Examination of Dr. Burnett's theory of the earth. Oxford, 1698.

Phil 8700.2.2 Keill, J. Examination of Dr. Burnett's theory of the earth. Oxford, 1734. 2 pam.

Phil 8700.2.6 Keill, J. Examination of the reflections on the theory of the earth. Oxford, 1699.

Phil 6120.10 Keiller, William. Nerve tracts of the brain and cord. N.Y., 1927.

Phil 2636.80 Keim, A. Helvétius sa vie et son oeuvre. Paris, 1907.

Phil 9550.13 Keim, Albert. L'épicurisme, l'ascétisme et la morale utilitaire. Paris, 1924.

Phil 6121.6.5 Das Keinhirn. (Luciani, L.) Leipzig, 1893.

Phil 3640.113 Keiper, Wilhelm. Nietzsche, poeta. Buenos Aires, 1911.

Phil 3790.8.80 Keirstead, W.C. Metaphysical presuppositions of Ritschl. Chicago, 1905.

Phil 5250.86 Keiter, Friedrich. Verhaltensforschung im Rahmen der Wissenschaften vom Menschen. Göttingen, 1969.

Phil 9150.31 Keith, Arthur. Evolution and ethics. N.Y., 1947.

Phil 7069.48.5 Keith, C.C. Worlds beyond. Hastings, Neb., 1948.

Phil 7069.45.55 Keith, Cassius C. The dawn of a new day, a revelation. Kansas City, Mo., 1945.

Phil 1135.82 Kelber, Wilhelm. Die Logoslehre von Heraklit bis Origenes. Stuttgart, 1958.

VPhil 8050.92 Kelecsényi, János. Az esztétika alapvet elvei. Budapest, 1913.

Phil 185.98 Keleher, James Francis. Disputed questions in philosophy. N.Y., 1965.

Phil 310.110 Kelle, V.Z. Formy obshchestvennogo soznaniia. Moskva, 1959.

Phil 310.554 Kelle, Vladislav Zh. Istoricheskii materializm; kurs lektsii. Moskva, 1962.

Phil 310.554.2 Kelle, Vladislav Zh. Kurs istoricheskogo materializma. 2. Izd. Moskva, 1969.

Phil 8590.21 Keller, Aaron. Das Prinzip der Dialektik in der Theologie. Inaug. Diss. Erlangen-Bruck, 1934.

Phil 2475.1.152 Keller, Adolf. Eine Philosophie des Lebens. (H. Bergson). Jena, 1914.

Phil 2050.112 Keller, Anton. Das Causalitätsproblem bei Malebranche und Hume. Rastatt, 1899.

Phil 5520.439 Keller, Benjamin. Toward an informal and creative conference method. Santa Monica, 1965.

Phil 3120.19.90 Keller, E. Die Philosophie Bruno Bauchs, als Ausdruck germanischer Geisteshaltung. Stuttgart, 1935.

Phil 400.80 Keller, Erich. Das Problem des Irrationalen im wertphilosophischen Idealismus der Gegenwart. Berlin, 1931.

Phil 5250.55 Keller, F. Principles of psychology. N.Y., 1950.

Phil 5220.4 Keller, F.S. The definition of psychology. N.Y., 1937.

Phil 9410.2 Keller, Helen. Optimism. N.Y., 1903.

Phil 5620.2 Keller, J. Der Ursprung der Vernunft. Heidelberg, 1884.

Phil 8835.3 Keller, M. Ethik als Wissenschaft ein methodologischer Versuch. Zürich, 1925.

Phil 5760.10 Keller, W. Psychologie und Philosophie des Wollens. München, 1954.

Phil 3830.6 Kellerman, B. Die Ethik Spinozas über Gott und Geist. Berlin, 1922.

Phil 3492.20 Kellermann, B. Das Ideal im System der Kantischen Philosophie. Berlin, 1920.

Phil 2490.182   Kellermann, Paul. Kritik liner Soziologie der Ordnung: Organismus und System bei Comte, Spencer und Parsons. 1. Aufl. Freiburg, 1967.

Phil 8885.23   Kellerwessel, Josef. Beitrage zur Theorie der sittlichen Erkenntnis. Münster, 1919.

Phil 2475.1.315   Kelley, J.J. Bergson's mysticism. Thesis. Fribourg, 1954.

Phil 2750.10.99   Kelley, T.R. Explanation and reality in the philosophy of Emile Meyerson. Princeton, 1937.

Phil 400.97   Kellner, Eva. Mann und Frau im deutschen Idealismus. Inaug. Diss. Berlin, 1937.

Phil 5249.13.99   Kellner, Kurt. C.G. Jung's Philosophie auf der Grundlage seiner Tiefenpsychologie. Inaug. Diss. Düren, 1937.

Phil 5250.5   Kellogg, A.M. Elementary psychology. N.Y., 1894.

Phil 8589.5.40   Kellogg, J.A. Philosophy of Henry James. N.Y., 1883.

Phil 5440.26   Kellogg, V.L. Mind and heredity. Princeton, 1923.

Phil 5050.8   Kells, S.C. Typical methods of thinking. N.Y., 1910.

Phil 4972.6.30   Kelly, Celso. Valores do espirito; ensaios. Rio de Janeiro, 195-?

Phil 9150.1.2   Kelly, E. Evolution and effort. N.Y., 1895.

Phil 9150.1.5   Kelly, E. Evolution and effort. 2. ed. N.Y., 1900.

Phil 5279.25.5   Kelly, Everett Lowell. The prediction of performance in clinical psychology. N.Y., 1969.

Phil 3425.195   Kelly, Michael. Hegel's charlatanism exposed. London, 1911.

Phil 3492.12.5   Kelly, Michael. Kant's ethics and Schopenhauer's criticism. London, 1910.

Phil 3492.12A   Kelly, Michael. Kants philosophy as rectified by Schopenhauer. London, 1909.

Phil 5250.65   Kelly, William L. Die neuscholastische und die empirische Psychologie. Meisenheim, 1961.

Phil 6320.20   Kelman, Harold. New perspectives in psychoanalysis. N.Y., 1965.

Phil 8635.12   Kelsey, Denys. Many lifetimes. 1. ed. Garden City, N.Y., 1967.

Phil 8610.890.20   Kelso, John R. The real blasphemers. N.Y., 189-?

Phil 2100.3.30   Kemble, Duston. The higher realism. Cincinnati, 1903.

Phil 9070.138   Kemelman, Haim. How to live in the present tense. South Brunswick, 1970.

Phil 291.9   Kemeny, John G. A philosopher looks at science. Princeton, N.J., 1959.

Phil 7069.24.29   Kemmerich, M. Wunderbare Tatsachen aus dem Reich des Übersinnlichen. Kempten im Allgäu, 1924.

Phil 8885.46   Kemp, J. Reason, action and morality. London, 1964.

Phil 8590.3   Kemp, J.T. van der. Tentamen theologiae dunatscopicae. Lugdunum Batavorum, 1775.

Phil 185.90   Kemp, Peter. Person og tänkning. København, 1960.

Phil 3100.81   Kempen, Aloys. Benekes religions Philosophie im Zusammenhang seines Systems, seine Gottes- und Unsterblickkeitslehre. Münster, 1914.

Phil 6320.1   Kempf, E.J. The autonomic functions and the personality. N.Y., 1918.

Phil 6320.1.9   Kempf, E.J. Physiology of attitude. n.p., 1935.

Phil 6320.1.5   Kempf, E.J. Psychopathology. St. Louis, 1921.

Phil 5592.181   Kempf, H.E. Der Bild-Test. Inaug. Diss. Marburg, 1964?

Phil 735.254   Kempff Mercado, Manfredo. Cuando valen los valores? Maracaibo, 1965.

Phil 4957.45   Kempff Mercado, Manfredo. Historia de la filosofía en Latinoamérica. Santiago de Chile, 1958.

Phil 810.16   Kempski, Jürgen von. Brechungen. Reinbek, 1964.

Phil 5440.10   Kendall, H. The kinship of men. Boston, 1888.

Phil 8885.2   Kendall, J. Eccentricity. London, 1859.

Phil 5545.200   Kendall, Patricia L. Conflict and mood. Glencoe, Ill., 1954.

Phil 9362.4   Kendrick, William. Whole duty of woman. Walpole, 1797.

Phil 6120.6   Kenilworth, W.W. Le contrôle psychique. Paris, 1914.

Phil 6120.6.5   Kenilworth, W.W. Thoughts on things psychic. N.Y., 1911.

Phil 5425.80   Kenmare, D. Stolen fire. London, 1951.

Phil 5590.55   Kenmare, D. World invisible. London, 1949.

Phil 8960.8   Kenmare, D. (pseud.). The philosophy of love. London, 1942.

Phil 1810.4   Kennedy, Gail. Pragmatism and American culture. Boston, 1950.

Phil 5650.26   Kennedy, Helen. A study of children's hearing as it relates to reading. Thesis. n.p., 1942.

Phil 3640.101.5   Kennedy, J.M. Nietzsche. London, 1914.

Phil 3640.101   Kennedy, J.M. The quintessence of Nietzsche. London, 1909.

Phil 9220.14   Kennell, Earl. This is friendship. N.Y., 1949.

Phil 349.42.5   Kennen und Erkennen. 2. Aufl. (Schneider, Friedrich.) Bonn, 1967.

Phil 5655.4   Kenneth, J.H. Osmics; the science of smell. Edinburgh, 1922.

Phil 165.364   Kennick, William E. Metaphysics; readings and reappraisals. Englewood Cliffs, N.J., 1966.

Phil 346.11   Kennisleer contra materie-realisme. (Polak, L.) Amsterdam, 1912.

Phil 187.38   De kennisleer van het Anglo-Amerikanisch pragmatisme. (Muller, J.B.) 's-Gravenhage, 1913.

Phil 5400.159   Kenny, A. Action, emotion and will. London, 1963.

Phil 2520.375   Kenny, Anthony. Descartes; a study of his philosophy. N.Y., 1968.

Htn   Phil 8635.1*   Kenrick, W. The grand question debated. Dublin, 1751. 2 pam.

Phil 6120.22   Kent, Caron. Man's hidden resources. Melbourne, Arkansas, 1962?

Phil 8960.3   Kent, Charles F. Fundamentals of Christianity. Philadelphia, 1925.

Phil 8665.7   Kent, G. Det absolute gudshegreb. Kristiania, 1886.

Phil 585.120.10   Kentaurische Philosophie; Vorträge und Abhandlungen. (Wein, Hermann.) München, 1968.

Phil 6120.15   Kenyon, F. The myth of the mind. London, 1941.

Phil 8400.54.5   Keper, Gyorgy. The nature and art of motion. N.Y., 1965.

Phil 8400.54   Kepes, Gyorgy. Structure in art and in science. N.Y., 1965.

Phil 5525.1   Keppler, J.F. Kritische Untersuchungen. Cilli, 1792.

Phil 8590.24A   Keppler, P.W. von. Wahre und falsche Reform. Freiburg, 1903.

Phil 8620.35   Keppler, Paul. Das Problem des Leidens in der Moral. Freiburg im Breisgau, 1894.

Phil 9520.4.8   Keppler, Paul W. Das Problem des Leidens. 8. und 9. Aufl. Freiburg, 1919.

Phil 185.1   Keratry, A.H. Inductions. Paris, 1818.

Phil 185.1.2   Keratry, A.H. Inductions. Paris, 1841.

Phil 3492.17   Kératry, A.H. de. Examen philosophique des Considérations sur le sentiment du sublime et du beau. Paris, 1823.

Phil 1182.35   Kerenyi, K. Pythagoras und Orpheus. 3. Aufl. Zürich, 1950.

Phil 3092.1.5   Kerényi, Karoly. Bach ofen und die Zukunft des Humanismus. Zürich, 1945.

Phil 8590.34   Kerényi, Karoly. Umgang mit Göttlichem. Göttingen, 1955.

Phil 8590.34.2   Kerényi, Karoly. Umgang mit Göttlichem. 2. Aufl. Göttingen, 1961.

Phil 2630.5.90   Kergomard, Jean. Edmond Goblot, 1858-1935. Paris, 1937.

Phil 5627.268.5   Kerkelijkheid en persoonlijkheidskenmerken in twee Zuiderzeepolders. (Smolenaars, A.J.) Amsterdam, 1968.

Phil 1710.2   Kerler, D.H. Die auferstandene Metaphysik. Ulm, 1921.

Phil 3246.201   Kerler, D.H. Die Fichte-Schelling'sche Wissenschaftslehre. Ulm, 1917.

Phil 3850.18.82   Kerler, D.H. Max Scheler. Ulm, 1917.

Phil 3640.246   Kerler, D.H. Nietzsche und die Vergeltungsidee. Ulm, 1910.

Phil 343.5.50   Kerler, D.H. Über Annahmen; eine Streitschrift. Ulm, 1910.

Phil 185.34   Kerler, D.H. Weltwille und Wertwille. Leipzig, 1925.

Phil 2475.1.196   Kerler, Dietrich H. Henri Bergson und das Problem des Verhältnisses zwischen Leib und Seele. Ulm, 1917.

Phil 8885.20   Kerler, Dietrich H. Jenseits von Optimismus und Pessimismus. Ulm, 1914.

Phil 3246.177   Kerler, Dietrich H. Die Philosophie des Absoluten in der Fichteschen Wissenschaftslehre. Inaug. Diss. Ansbach, 1917.

Phil 5270.1   Kerlinger, Frederick, N. Foundations of behavioral research. N.Y., 1965.

Phil 5325.24   Kern, B. Assoziationspsychologie und Erkenntnis. Berlin, 1913.

Phil 341.9   Kern, Berthold. Das Erkenntnisproblem...kritische Lösung. Berlin, 1911.

Phil 291.3   Kern, Berthold. Weltanschauungen und Welterkenntnis. Berlin, 1911.

Phil 185.17   Kern, Berthold P. Das Problem des Lebens in kritischer Bearbeitung. Berlin, 1909.

Phil 1750.518   Kern, Edith G. Existential thought and fictional technique; Kierkegaard, Sartre, Beckett. New Haven, 1970.

Phil 575.145   Kern, Hans. Die Masken der Siecle. Leipzig, 194-.

Phil 3160.9.80   Kern, Hans. Die Philosophie des Carl Gustav Carus. Berlin, 1926.

Phil 3492.75   Kern, Iso. Husserl und Kant. Den Haag, 1964.

Phil 9070.8   Kern, J.H. Do something about it! N.Y., 1940.

Phil 7069.30.10   Kernahan, C. "Black objects". London, 1930.

Phil 8665.2   Kernahan, C. The lonely God. London, n.d.

Phil 7069.20.180   Kernahan, Coulson. Spiritualism. N.Y., 1920.

Phil 8835.6   Kerner, George. The revolution in ethical theory. N.Y., 1966.

Phil 7068.36   Kerner, J. Eine Erscheinung aus dem Nachtgebiete der Natur. Stuttgart, 1826.

Phil 6680.1.5   Kerner, J. The Seeress of Prevorst. N.Y., 1855.

Phil 6680.1.6   Kerner, J. Die Seherin von Prevorst. Leipzig, 18- .

Htn   Phil 6680.1*   Kerner, J. Die Seherin von Prevorst. Stuttgart, 1829. 2v.

Phil 6680.1.4.5   Kerner, J. Die Seherin von Prevorst. 2. Aufl. Stuttgart, 1892.

Phil 6680.1.4   Kerner, J. Die Seherin von Prevorst. 4. Aufl. Stuttgart, 1746.

Phil 341.1   Kerry, B. System einer Theorie der Grenzbegriffe. Leipzig, 1890.

Phil 179.3.90   Kesseler, K. Rudolf Euckens Bedeutung für das modern Christentum. Bunzlau, 1912.

Phil 179.3.91   Kesseler, K. Die Vertiefung der kantischen Religions-Philosophie. Bunzlau, 1908.

Phil 3492.15   Kesseler, Kurt. Kant und Schiller. Bunzlau, 1910.

Phil 8590.15   Kesseler, Kurt. Kritik der neukantischen religionsphilosophie der Gegenwart. Leipzig, 1920.

Phil 3492.15.5   Kesseler, Kurt. Die lösung der widersprüche des Dasiens. Bunzlau, 1909.

Phil 8590.15.5   Kesseler, Kurt. Religionsphilosophie. Leipzig, 1927.

Phil 3640.393   Kesselring, M. Nietzsche und sein Zarathustra in psychiatrischer Beleuchtung. Aehren Verlag, 1954.

Phil 3492.23   Kessler, A. Kants ansicht von der Grundlage der Empfindung. Darmstadt, 1903.

Phil 5635.25   Kessler, Jacob. Untersuchungen über den Temperatursinn. Inaug. Diss. Bonn, 1884.

Phil 179.3.81   Kessler, K. Rudolf Euckens Werk. Bunzlau, 1911.

Phil 185.2   Kessler, R. Praktische Philosophie. Leipzig, 1691.

Phil 1750.805   Ketcham, Charles Brown. The search for meaningful existence. N.Y., 1968.

Phil 810.14   Ketoren, Oliva. Eurooppalaisen ihmisen maailmansatsomus. Helsingissa, 1961.

Phil 2005.11   Kettler, David. The social and political thought of Adam Ferguson. Columbus, 1965.

Phil 8885.40   Kettner, F. Biosophy and spiritual democracy. N.Y., 1954.

Phil 3830.9   Kettner, F. Spinoza, the biosopher. N.Y., 1932.

Phil 8700.12   Kettner, F. The synthesis of science and religion. N.Y., 1939.

Phil 8411.10   Keussler, G. von. Die Grenzen der Ästhetik. Leipzig, 1902.

Phil 3808.137   Keutel, Otto. Über die Zweck Mässigkeit in der Natur bei Schopenhauer. Leipzig, 1897.

Phil 341.38   Kevorkian, Hamlet. Veroiatnoe i dostovernoe znanie. Erevan, 1965.

Phil 5250.19   Key, Ellen. Krinns-psykologi och krinnlig logik. Stockholm, 1896.

Phil 8590.16   Key, Ellen. Der Lebensglaube. Berlin, 1906.

Phil 8886.8.10   Key, Ellen. Moralens utveckling: fri bearbetning efter Letourneau. Stockholm, 1903.

Phil 6750.13   Key, Wilhelme E. Feeble-minded citizens in Pennsylvania. Philadelphia, 1915.

Phil 177.84.5   Key-notes for daily harmonies. (Clark, S.C.) Boston, 1898.

Phil 5047.27   A key to Holman and Irvine's questions on logic. (Holman, H.) London, n.d.

Phil 8637.19   A key to the secret vault. (Murphy, R.W.) San Francisco, 1890.

Phil 7069.35.50   Key to the spaces...dictated by A.P. Mathewson. (Wells, Helen B.) N.Y., 1935.

Phil 978.5.24   The key to theosophy. (Blavatsky, H.P.) London, 1889.

Phil 978.5.26   The key to theosophy. (Blavatsky, H.P.) Los Angeles, 1920.

Phil 978.5.25   The key to theosophy. 2nd American ed. (Blavatsky, H.P.) N.Y., 1896.

Phil 978.5.27   The key to theosophy. 4th ed. (Blavatsky, H.P.) Point Loma, Calif., 1923.

Phil 8887.22   A key to true happiness. (Morton, E.) Hudson, Ohio, 1854.

Phil 2340.10.185   A key to Whitehead's Process and realty. (Sherburne, Donald W.) N.Y., 1966.

Phil 6990.41 — Keyes, F.P.W. (Mrs.). The sublime shepherdess; the life of St. Bernadette of Lourdes. N.Y., 1940.

Phil 5050.3 — Keynes, J.N. Studies and exercises in formal logic. London, 1884.

Phil 5050.3.2 — Keynes, J.N. Studies and exercises in formal logic. 2nd ed. London, 1887.

Phil 5050.3.5 — Keynes, J.N. Studies and exercises in formal logic. 4th ed. London, 1928.

Phil 8700.1 — Keyser, C.J. Science and religion, rational and superrational. New Haven, 1914.

Phil 5250.22 — Keyser, C.J. Thinking about thinking. N.Y., 1926.

Phil 185.46 — Keyser, Cassius Jackson. Humanism and science. N.Y., 1931.

Phil 8665.3 — Keyser, L.S. A system of natural theism. Burlington, Ia., 1917.

Phil 8885.16 — Keyser, Leander S. A system of general ethics. Burlington, 1918.

Phil 810.17 — Keyserling, Arnold. Geschichte der Denkstile. Wien, 1968.

Phil 291.1 — Keyserling, H. Das Gefüge der Welt. München, 1906.

Phil 185.35 — Keyserling, H. Philosophie als Kunst. Darmstadt, 1920.

Phil 185.35.2 — Keyserling, H. Philosophie als Kunst. 2. Aufl. Darmstadt, 1922.

Phil 185.35.10 — Keyserling, H. The recovery of truth. N.Y., 1929.

Phil 3808.196 — Keyserling, H. Schopenhauer als Verbilder. Leipzig, 1910.

Phil 341.14.5 — Keyserling, H. Graf von. Creative understanding. N.Y., 1929.

Phil 341.14 — Keyserling, H. Graf von. Schöpferische Erkenntnis. Darmstadt, 1922.

Phil 3549.2.45 — Keyserling, Hermann. The art of life. London, 1937.

Phil 3549.2.60 — Keyserling, Hermann. Betractungen der Stille und Besinnlichkeit. Jena, 1942.

Phil 3549.2.47 — Keyserling, Hermann. Das Buch vom persönlichen Leben. Stuttgart, 1936.

Phil 3549.2.40 — Keyserling, Hermann. Das Buch vom Ursprung. Baden-Baden, 1947.

Phil 3549.2.70 — Keyserling, Hermann. Graf Hermann Kyserling. Innsbruck, 1948.

Phil 8635.4.5 — Keyserling, Hermann. Immortality. London, 1938.

Phil 3549.2.79.15 — Keyserling, Hermann. Kritik des Denkens. Innsbruck, 1948.

Phil 3549.2.35 — Keyserling, Hermann. Mensch und Erde in Darstellungen. Darmstadt, 1927.

Phil 3549.2.50 — Keyserling, Hermann. Menschen als Sinnbilder. Darmstadt, 1926.

Phil 3549.2.79.5 — Keyserling, Hermann. Die neuentstehende Welt. Darmstadt, 1926.

Phil 3549.2.79.10 — Keyserling, Hermann. Reise durch die Zeit. Innsbruck, 1948.

Phil 3549.2.75.7 — Keyserling, Hermann. Das Reisetagebuch eines Philosophen. Darmstadt, 1956. 3v.

Phil 3549.2.75.5 — Keyserling, Hermann. Das Reisetagebuch eines Philosophen. 7. Aufl. Darmstadt, 1923. 2v.

Phil 3549.2.30.2 — Keyserling, Hermann. South American meditations. 1st ed. N.Y., 1932.

Phil 3549.2.30 — Keyserling, Hermann. Südamerikanische Meditationen. Stuttgart, 1932.

Phil 3549.2.78 — Keyserling, Hermann. The travel diary of a philosopher. London, 1925. 2v.

Phil 3549.2.78.2 — Keyserling, Hermann. The travel diary of a philosopher. N.Y., 1925. 2v.

Phil 3549.2.78.5 — Keyserling, Hermann. The travel diary of a philosopher. N.Y., 1929.

Phil 8635.4 — Keyserling, Hermann. Unsterblichkeit. 2. Aufl. München, 1911.

Phil 3549.2.25 — Keyserling, Hermann. Der Weg zur Vollendung. Darmstadt. 1-20,1924-1932 2v.

Phil 3549.2.52 — Keyserling, Hermann. Wiedergeburt. Darmstadt, 1927.

Phil 3549.2.79.2 — Keyserling, Hermann. The world in the making. London, 1927.

Phil 3549.2.79 — Keyserling, Hermann. The world in the making. N.Y., 1927.

Phil 3549.2.99 — Keyserling. 2. ed. (Franceschi, G.J.) Buenos Aires, 1929.

Phil 185.3 — Keyserlingh, H. von. Menschen-Kenntnis oder Anthropologie. Berlin, 1827.

Phil 185.3.5 — Keyserlingh, H. von. Metaphysik. Heidelberg, 1818.

Phil 3246.221 — Keyserlingk, H.W.E. von. Vergleich zwischen Fichtens System. Königsberg, 1817.

Phil 50.5 — Keyserluig-Gesellschaft für freie Philosophie. Jahrbuch. Düsseldorf. 2v.

Phil 4756.6.50 — Kh.M. Fataliev. (Platonov, G.V.) Makhachkala, 1964.

Phil 720.59 — Khachaturian, Haig. The coherence theory of truth. Beirut, 1961.

Phil 5068.68 — Khachaturian, Haig. A critical study in method. The Hague, 1967.

Phil 5066.230 — Kharin, N.N. Matematicheskaia logika i teoriia mnozhestv. Moskva, 1963.

Phil 4710.11.5 — Khaskhachikh, F.I. Materie und Bewusstsein. 5. Aufl. Berlin, 1957.

Phil 4710.11 — Khaskhachikh, F.I. Materiia i soznanie. Moskva, 1951.

Phil 4710.80 — Khaskhachikh, F.I. O poznavaemosti mira. Moskva, 1946.

Phil 341.36 — Khaskhatrick, Fedor I. Voprosy teorii poznaniia dialekticheskogo materializma. Moskva, 1967.

Phil 4791.6 — Khidasheli, Shalva Vasil'evich. Osnovnye mirovozzrencheskie napravleniia v feodal'noi Gruzii. Tbilisi, 1962.

Phil 8980.481 — Khmara, V.V. Cheloveku nado verit. Moskva, 1960.

Phil 5435.13 — Khodzhava, Z.I. Problema navyka v psikhologii. Tbilisi, 1960.

Phil 310.726 — Khotiakova, Valentina Alekseevna. Chelovek i istoriia. Moskva, 1970.

Phil 310.315 — Khrestomatiia po marksistsko-leninskoi filosofii. Moskva, 1961. 3v.

Phil 8581.94 — Khristianstvo i aktivnaia uslovnost'. (Berdiaev, N.A.) Parizh, 194-.

Phil 4752.2.60 — Khristianstvo i antisimitizm. (Berdiaev, Nikolai Aleksandrovich.) Parizh, 1946.

Phil 4769.3 — Khristianstvo i kul'tura. (Spektorskii, E.) Sankt Peterburg, 1925.

Phil 8968.20 — Khristianstvo i pravstvennost'. (Sidorov, D.I.) Moskva, 1962.

Phil 185.53 — Khristov, M. Filosofskitĕ printsipi na prirodata. Sofia, 1935.

Phil 8170.4 — Khudozhestvennoe nasledie i esteticeskoe vospitanie. (Matsa, Ivan.) Moskva, 1959.

Phil 8407.1.5 — Khudozhestvennoe tvorchestvo. (Gromov, Evgenii S.) Moskva, 1970.

Phil 8411.38 — Khudozhestvennyi vkus. (Kogan, Lev Naumovich.) Moskva, 1966.

Phil 291.12 — Khudushin, Fedor S. Chelovck i priroda. Moskva, 1966.

Phil 5520.288 — Kibernetika, semiotika, lingvistika. (Martynov, Viktor V.) Minsk, 1966.

Phil 270.108 — Kibernetika i kategoriia prichinnosti. (Musabaeva, N.A.) Alma-Ata, 1965.

Phil 551.1 — Kichanova, Inga M. Desiat' ispovedi. Moskva, 1971.

Phil 5585.244 — Kidd, Aline Halstead. Perceptual development in children. N.Y., 1966.

Phil 8581.10.2 — Kidd, J. Bridgewater treatises [2]. On the adaptation of external nature to the physical condition of man. Philadelphia? 1836?

Phil 8885.4 — Kidd, J. Morality and religion. Edinburgh, 1895.

Phil 8590.2.2 — Kidd, J. On the adaption of external nature, physical condition, Man. Philadelphia, 1883.

X Cg Phil 8590.2 — Kidd, J. On the adaption of external nature, physical condition of man. London, 1852.

Phil 5050.4 — Kidd, R.B. A deliniation, primary principal reasoning. London, 1856.

Phil 7054.77F — Kidder, L. A spiritual communicating diagram. n.p., n.d.

Phil 7054.28 — Kiddle, H. Spiritual communications. Boston, 1879.

Phil 5643.115 — Kiefer, Theodor. Der visuelle Mensch. München, 1956.

Phil 3552.127 — Kiefl, Franz X. Der europäische Freiheitskampf. Mainz, 1913.

Phil 3552.127.5 — Kiefl, Franz X. Leibniz und die religiöse Wiedervereinigung Deutschlands. 2. Aufl. München, 1925.

Phil 3808.130 — Kiehl, Daniel. Naturlÿke historie van den Filistijn. 's Gravenhage, 1895.

Phil 5685.5 — Kielblock, A. The stage fright. Boston, 1891.

Phil 3110.155 — Kielholz, A. Jakob Boehme. Leipzig, 1919.

Phil 8030.8 — Kiell, Norman. Psychiatry and psychology in the visual arts and aesthetics. Madison, 1965.

Phil 6049.62 — Kiener, Franz. Hans, Gebärde und Charakter. München, 1962.

Phil 1135.174 — Kienle, W. Die Berichte über die Sukressionen der Philosophen. Berlin, 1961.

Phil 1750.810 — Kierkegaard, Nietzsche, Heidegeger. (DeFeo, Nicola Massimo.) Milano, 1964.

Phil 3640.261 — Kierkegaard und Nietzsche. (Löwith, Karl.) Frankfurt am Main, 1933.

Phil 2280.13.30 — Kierkegaardian philosophy in the faith of a scholar. (Swenson, D.) Philadelphia, 1949.

Phil 3450.19.130 — Kierkegaards und Heideggers Existenzanalyse und ihr Verhaltnis. 1-3. Aufl. (Logstrup, K.E.C.) Berlin, 1950.

Phil 8885.5 — Kies, M. The ethical principle. Ann Arbor, 1892.

Phil 9150.15 — Kies, Marietta. Institutional ethics. Boston, 1894.

Phil 6680.3 — Kiesewetter, C. Mesmer's Leben und Lehre. Leipzig, 1893.

Phil 5250.24 — Kiesewetter, J.G.C. Fassliche Darstellung der Erfahrungsseelenlehre. Wien, 1817.

Phil 8885.28 — Kiesewetter, J.G.C. Über den ersten Grundsatz der Moralphilosophie. Berlin, 1790-1791. 2v.

Phil 5050.5.3 — Kiesewetter, J.G.C.C. Compendium einer allgemeinen Logik. Berlin, 1796.

Phil 5050.5.4 — Kiesewetter, J.G.C.C. Grundriss einer allgemeinen Logik. Berlin, 1796-1802. 2v.

Phil 5050.5 — Kiesewetter, J.G.C.C. Grundriss einer allgemeinen Logik. Leipzig, 1824-25. 2v.

Phil 5050.5.2 — Kiesewetter, J.G.C.C. Grundriss einer allgemeinen Logik. 2. Aufl. Berlin, 1795-96. 2v.

Phil 5050.5.6 — Kiesewetter, J.G.C.C. Grundriss einer reinen allgemeinen Logik nach kantischen Grundsaetzen. Berlin, 1791.

Phil 5050.5.15 — Kiesewetter, J.G.C.C. Lärobok i logiken. Abo, 1806.

Phil 5050.5.5 — Kiesewetter, J.G.C.C. Logik zum Gebrauch für Schulen. Leipzig, 1832.

Phil 3492.34.4 — Kiesewetter, J.G.K.C. Darstellung der wichtigsten Wahrheiten der kritischen Philosophie. Berlin, 1824.

Phil 3492.34.15 — Kiesewetter, J.G.K.C. Gedrängter Auszug aus Kants Kritik der reinen Vernunft. Berlin, 1795.

Phil 3492.34.2 — Kiesewetter, J.G.K.C. Versuch einer...Darstellung der wichtigsten Wahrheiten der kritischen Philosophie. Berlin, 1803. 2v.

Phil 3492.34 — Kiesewetter, J.G.K.C. Versuch einer...Darstellung der wichtigsten Wahrheiten der neuern Philosophie. Berlin, 1795.

Phil 7052.6 — Kiesewetter, Karl. Die Entwickelungsgeschichte des Spiritismus. Leipzig, 1893.

Phil 5780.27 — Kiesler, Charles A. The psychology of commitment. N.Y., 1971.

RRC Phil 6980.383 — Kiev, Ari. Psychiatry in the Communist world. N.Y., 1968.

Phil 20.8 — Kiev. Universitet. Visnyk. Seriia filosofii. Kiev. 1,1967+

Phil 5593.51 — Kijm, J.M. De varianten bij de intentionaliteit bij de Rorschachtest. Nijmegen, 1951.

Phil 8980.485 — Kiknadze, Dmitrii A. Potrebnosti, povedenie, vospitanie. Moskva, 1968.

Phil 3801.485 — Kile, Frederick O. Die theologischen Grundlagen von Schellings Philosophie der Freiheit. Leiden, 1965.

Phil 1750.166.150 — Kiley, W. Human possibilities. N.Y., 1963.

Phil 1750.134 — Killeen, M.V. Man in the new humanism. Thesis. Washington, D.C., 1934.

Phil 5585.165 — Kilpatrick, F.P. Explorations in transactional psychology. N.Y., 1961.

Phil 310.671 — Kim, Makvim P. Istoriia i kommunizm. Moskva, 1968.

Phil 5625.110 — Kimble, Gregory A. Foundations of conditioning and learning. N.Y., 1967.

Phil 7084.8 — Kimmins, Charles William. Children's dreams. London, 1920.

Phil 5525.34 — Kimmins, G.W. The springs of laughter. London, 1928.

Phil 8885.42 — Kimpel, B.F. Principles of moral philosophy. N.Y., 1960.

Phil 8622.8 — Kimpel, B.F. Religious faith, language, and knowledge. N.Y., 1952.

Phil 8590.29 — Kimpel, B.F. The symbols of religious faith. N.Y., 1954.

Phil 5832.9.5 — Kinaesthetic and organic sensations. (Watson, John B.) Lancaster, 1907.

Phil 5870.55 — Das Kind in der Entwicklung. (Zulliger, Hans.) Bern, 1969.

Phil 5871.50 — Kind ohne Vater. (Landolf, Peter.) Bern, 1968.

VPhil 978.116 — Kinderkrankheinten im Lichte der Anthroposphie. (Wilmar, F.H.J.) Zeist, 1966.

Phil 5820.3 — Kindermann, H. Lola, or The thought and speech of animals. London, 1922.

Phil 5258.22.5 — Die kinderpsychologischen Bestrebungen L. Strümpells. (Unger, Rudolf.) Strassburg, 1912.

Phil 5465.171 — Kinderzeichnungen und Umwelt. (Egen, Horst.) Bonn, 1967.

Phil 8584.16 — Kindschaft zur Welt. (Enckendorff, M.L.) Jena, 1927.

Phil 20.10 — Kinesis. Carbondale, Ill. 1,1968+

Phil 7069.19.150 — King, Basil. The abolishing of death. N.Y., 1919.

Phil 8590.18.25 — King, Basil. Adventures in religion. Garden City, 1929.

Phil 8590.18.3 — King, Basil. The conquest of fear. Garden City, 1921.

Phil 8590.18.20 — King, Basil. Faith and success. Garden City, 1928.

Phil 5374.53   King, C. Daly. The psychology of consciousness. London, 1932.
Phil 6120.12   King, D.M. Nerves and personal power. N.Y., 1922.
Phil 8700.8   King, David. The principles of geology explained. N.Y., 1851.
Phil 978.77.6   King, G.R. Ascended master discourses. Chicago, 1937.
Phil 978.77.7   King, G.R. Ascended master light. Chicago, 1938.
Phil 978.77.3   King, G.R. The "I am" discourses. 2d ed. Chicago, 1940.
Phil 978.77.2   King, G.R. The magic presence. Chicago, 1935.
Phil 978.77.1   King, G.R. Unveiled mysteries. 2d ed. Chicago, 1935.
Phil 8620.7.8   King, Gulielmo. De origine mali. Dublinii, 1702.
Phil 9220.2.20 King, H.C. Laws of friendship human and devine. N.Y., 1919.
Phil 8885.10.5 King, H.C. National living. N.Y., 1912.
Phil 6960.13   King, H.E. Psychomotor aspects of mental disease. Cambridge, Mass., 1954.
Phil 9035.19   King, Henry C. How to make a rational fight for character. N.Y., 1911.
Phil 9035.84.10 King, Henry C. How to make a rational fight for character. N.Y., 1916.
Phil 8590.10.7 King, Henry C. Letters on the greatness and simplicity of the Christian faith. Boston, 1906.
Phil 8590.10.9 King, Henry C. Reconstruction in theology. N.Y., 1901.
Phil 8590.10   King, Henry C. Religion as life. N.Y., 1913.
Phil 8590.10.5 King, Henry C. Seeing life whole; a Christian philosophy of life. N.Y., 1923.
Phil 8590.10.15 King, Henry C. Seeming unreality of the spiritual life. N.Y., 1911.
Phil 8590.7   King, I. The development of religion. N.Y., 1910.
Phil 5627.10.3 King, Irving. The differentiation of the religious consciousness. N.Y., 1905.
Phil 5627.10   King, Irving. The differentiation of the religious consciousness. N.Y., 1905.
Phil 7069.20.190 King, John S. Dawn of the awakened mind. N.Y., 1920.
Phil 3450.19.285 King, M. Heidegger's philosophy. N.Y., 1964.
Phil 7054.109   King, M.M. The spiritual philosophy vs. diabolism. Boston, 1871.
Phil 7059.19   King, Maria M. Real life in the spirit land. 5. ed. Hammonton,N.J., 1892.
Phil 185.52.15 King, Mrs. E.D. Aum, the cosmic silence. Los Angeles, 1918. 2 pam.
Phil 185.52.10 King, Mrs. E.D. The flashlights of truth. Los Angeles, 1918.
Phil 185.52.5   King, Mrs. E.D. The higher metaphysics. Los Angeles, 1918.
Phil 185.52   King, Mrs. E.D. The lotus path. Los Angeles, 1917.
NEDL Phil 2115.93.10 King, Peter. The life and letters of John Locke. London, 1858.
Phil 2115.92.90 King, Peter. Life of John Locke. London, 1829.
Phil 2115.93A   King, Peter. Life of John Locke. London, 1830. 2v.
Phil 720.50   King, Peter D. The principle of truth. N.Y., 1960.
Phil 5238.194   King, R.A. Readings for an introduction to psychology. N.Y., 1961.
Phil 8656.14.25 King, Thomas S. A short review of Edward Beecher's work on the conflict of ages. 2. ed. Boston, 1854.
Phil 5250.26   King, W.P. Behaviourism; a symposium by Josiah Morse. London, 1930.
Htn Phil 2100.1.30.2* King, William. An essay on the origin of evil. London, 1732. 2v.
Phil 8620.7.2   King, William. An essay on the origin of evil. London, 1758. 2v.
Phil 8620.7.3   King, William. An essay on the origin of evil. London, 1781.
Htn Phil 2100.1.30* King, William. An essay on the origin of evil. 1st ed. and additions. London, 1731. 2v.
Phil 1750.131   King, William Peter. Humanism. Nashville, 1931.
Phil 6968.19   The kingdom of evils. (Souhard, E.E.) N.Y., 1922.
Phil 8657.12   The kingdom of God. (Candlish, J.S.) Edinburgh, 1884.
Phil 8673.5   The kingdom of God. (Schwab, L.H.) N.Y., 1897.
Phil 978.59.2   The kingdom of happiness. (Krishnamurti, J.) N.Y., 1930.
Phil 6964.4   The kingdom of the lost. (Ogden, J.A.H.) London, 1947.
Phil 189.25   The kingdoms of the spirit. (Oldfield, C.H.) London, 1924.
Phil 8647.6   The king's garden. (Woodruff, J.L.M.) N.Y., 1902.
X Cg Phil 978.44 Kingsford, Anna. The perfect way, or The finding of Christ. London, 1909.
Phil 7069.20.192 Kingsford, S.M. Psychical research for the plain man. London, 1920.
Phil 8884.4.2   Kingship of self-control individual problems. (Jordan, W.G.) N.Y., 1899.
Phil 8884.4   Kingship of self-control individual problems. (Jordan, W.G.) N.Y., 1901.
Phil 974.2.20   Kingsland, W. Was she a charlatan? London, 1927.
Phil 400.46   Kingsland, William. Scientific idealism. London, 1909.
Phil 1150.4   Kingsley, C. Alexandria and her schools. Cambridge, 1854.
Phil 365.44   Kingson, B. The moving tent. Wellington, 1936.
Phil 2428.5   Kingston, Frederick Temple. French existentialism; a Christian critique. Toronto, 1961.
Phil 2340.8.80 Kingston, Ontario. Queen's University. Faculty of Arts. Philosophical essays presented to John Watson. Kingston, 1922.
Phil 3160.3.83 Kinkel, N. Hermann Cohen. Stuttgart, 1924.
Phil 810.2.5   Kinkel, W. Allgemeine Geschichte der Philosophie. Osterwieck, 1920-27. 4v.
Phil 810.2   Kinkel, W. Geschichte der Philosophie. v.1-2. Giessen, 1906.
Phil 1115.3   Kinkel, Walter. Geschichte der Philosophie von Sokrates bis Aristoteles. Berlin, 1922.
Phil 400.27.15 Kinkel, Walter. Idealismus und Realismus. Göttingen, 1911.
Phil 3428.153   Kinkel, Walter. J.F. Herbart, sein Leben und seine Philosophie. Giessen, 1903.
Phil 3492.29   Kinkel, Walter. Kant zum Gedächtnis. Osterwieck, 1924.
Phil 185.21.2   Kinkel, Walter. Vom Sein und von der Seele. 2. Aufl. Giessen, 1914.
Phil 3492.14   Kinker, Johannes. Le dualisme de la raison humaine; ou, Le criticisme de E. Kant. Amsterdam, 1850-52. 2v.
Phil 9170.2   Kinney, A. The conquest of death. N.Y., 1893.
Phil 5590.449   Kinsella, Noël A. Toward a theory of personality development. Fredericton, N.B., 1966.
Phil 5841.12   Kinsey, a biography. (Christenson, Cornelia Vos.) Bloomington, 1971.
Phil 5440.10   The kinship of men. (Kendall, H.) Boston, 1888.
Phil 5535.42   Kintsch, Walter. Learning, memory, and conceptual processes. N.Y., 1970.
Phil 3270.4.86 Kipper, Eberhard. Johann Paul Anselm Feuerbach. Köln, 1969.

Phil 8581.10.7 Kirby, W. Bridgewater treatises [7]. On the power...God. Philadelphia, 1837.
Phil 9513.22   Kirche, Bekenntnis und Sozialethos. Genf, 1934.
Phil 5760.12   Kircher, Veronica. Die Freiheit des körpergebundenen Willens. Freiburg, 1957.
Phil 7069.21.43 Kirchhoff, P. Der moderne Okkultismus in Lichte des Experiments! Köln, 1921.
Phil 6020.5   Kirchhoff, Robert. Allgemeine Ausdruckslehre. Göttingen, 1957.
Phil 3492.1.5   Kirchmann, J. Erläuterungen zu Kant's kleinern Schriften. Berlin, 1873.
Phil 3492.1   Kirchmann, J. Erläuterungen zu Kant's Kritik. Berlin, 1869-73. 7 pam.
Phil 185.4   Kirchmann, J. Katechismus der Philosophie. Leipzig, 1881.
Phil 2115.121   Kirchmann, J.H. Erläuterungen zu John Locke's Versuch über den menschlichen Verstand. Abt II. Berlin, 1874.
Phil 8411.12   Kirchmann, J.H. von. Ästhetik auf realistischer Grundlage. Berlin, 1868. 2v.
Phil 3830.1.5   Kirchmann, J.H. von. Erläuterungen zu Benedict von Spinoza's Ethik. Berlin, 1869.
Phil 3830.1   Kirchmann, J.H. von. Erlauterungen zu Benedict von Spinoza's. Berlin, 1870-72. 5 pam.
Phil 8885.6   Kirchmann, J.H. von. Die Grundbegriffe des Rechts und der Moral. Berlin, 1873.
Phil 5250.1   Kirchmann, J.H. von. Die Lehre vom Wissen. Berlin, 1871.
Phil 3010.1   Kirchner, C.K. Die speculativen Systeme seit Kant. Leipzig, 1860.
Phil 8885.21.2 Kirchner, F. Ethik; Katechismus der Sittenlehre. 2e Aufl. Leipzig, 1898.
Phil 810.1.9   Kirchner, F. Geschichte der Philosophie. Leipzig, 1911.
Phil 185.50   Kirchner, F. Die Hauptpunkte der Metaphysik. Cöthen, 1880.
Phil 810.1   Kirchner, F. Katechismus der Geschichte der Philosophie. Leipzig, 1877.
Phil 5050.13   Kirchner, F. Katechismus der Logik. Leipzig, 1890.
Phil 5250.10.5 Kirchner, F. Katechismus der Psychologie. Leipzig, 1883.
Phil 5250.10   Kirchner, F. A student's manual of psychology. London, 1888.
Phil 3552.94.9 Kirchner, Friedrich. Gottfried Wilhelm Leibniz. Cöthen, 1876.
Phil 3552.120   Kirchner, Friedrich. Leibnitz's Stellung zur katholischen Kirche. Berlin, 1874.
Phil 3552.94.5 Kirchner, Friedrich. Leibniz's Psychologie. Cöthen, 1875.
Phil 95.1.5   Kirchner, Friedrich. Wörterbuch der philosophischen Begriffe. Leipzig, 1944.
Phil 95.1.3   Kirchner, Friedrich. Wörterbuch der philosophischen Grundbegriffe. Heidelberg, 1886.
Phil 95.1   Kirchner, Friedrich. Wörterbuch der philosophischen Grundbegriffe. Heidelberg, 1890.
Phil 8885.27   Kirckner, F. Ethik. Leipzig, 1881.
Phil 4769.1.90 Kireev, A.A. Slavianofil'stvo i natsionalizm; otvet k Solov'evy. Petrograd, 1890.
Phil 6960.8   Kirehhoff. Beziehungen das Dämonen- und Hexenwesens zur deutschen Irrenpflege. Berlin, 1888.
Phil 665.20   Kirk, Edward N. The greatness of the human soul. Boston, 1844.
Phil 1133.35A   Kirk, G.S. The presocratic philosophers. Cambridge, Eng., 1957.
Phil 1133.35.4 Kirk, G.S. The presocratic philosophers. Cambridge, Eng., 1962.
Phil 8635.2   Kirk, H.C. The possibility of not dying. N.Y., 1883.
Phil 8885.36   Kirk, K.E. Personal ethics. Oxford, 1934.
Phil 8960.4   Kirk, Kenneth E. Conscience and its problems. London, 1927.
Phil 6945.3   Kirkbride, T.S. On the construction, organization and general arrangements of hospitals for the insane. Philadelphia, 1854.
Phil 6945.20   Kirkbride, T.S. On the construction, organization and general arrangements of hospitals for the insane. 2. ed. Philadelphia, 1880.
Phil 7069.22.45 Kirken og den psykiske Forskning. (Nielsson, H.) København, 1922.
Phil 8885.35   Kirkham, S.D. Where dwells the soul serene. 3rd ed. San Francisco, 1907.
Phil 185.5   Kirkman, T.P. Philosophy without assumptions. London, 1876.
Phil 5250.3.6   Kirkpatrick, E.A. Genetic psychology. N.Y., 1925.
Phil 5250.3   Kirkpatrick, E.A. Inductive psychology. N.Y., 1895.
Phil 6120.13   Kirkpatrick, E.A. Mental hygiene for effective living. N.Y., 1934.
Phil 8885.11   Kirn, O. Sittliche Lebens anschauungen der Gegenwart. 2. Aufl. Leipzig, 1911.
Phil 8885.11.5 Kirn, O. Vårtids etiska Lifsåskådningar. Stockholm, 1909.
Phil 8960.1   Kirn, Otto. Zur Feier des Reformationsfestes. Leipzig, 1906.
Phil 310.692   Kirschenmann, Peter. Kybernetik, Information, Widerspiegelung. München, 1969.
Phil 310.692.5 Kirschenmann, Peter Paul. Information and reflection on some problems of cybernetics and how contemporary dialectical materialism copes with them. Dordrecht, 1970.
Phil 3850.27.155 Kirschner, Carol F. A selection of writings of and about Albert Schweitzer. Boston, 1958.
Phil 5211.3.2   Die Kirse der Psychologie. 2. Aufl. (Bühler, Karl.) Jena, 1929.
Phil 8411.11   Kirstein, Anton. Entwurf einer Ästhetik der Natur und Kunst. Paderborn, 1896.
Phil 185.6.5   Kirwan, R. Metaphysical essays. London, 1809.
Phil 185.6   Kirwan, R. Metaphysical essays. London, 1809.
Phil 8980.486   Kiselev, Askol'd A. V.I. Lenin i voprosy etiki. L'vov, 1969.
Phil 4809.486.20 Kiselimchev, Asen. Izbrani proizvedeniia. Sofiia, 1964.
Phil 5625.75.90 Kiselinchev, A. Die marxistisch-leninistische Widerspiegelungstheorie und die Lehre Pawlows. Berlin, 1957.
Phil 935.5   Kishinami, T. The development of philosophy in Japan. Princeton, 1915.
Phil 291.14   Kiss, Elek. A világ fejlődése az atom szemléletében. Kolozsvár, 1946.
Phil 5066.30   Kiss, Stephen A. Transformations on lattices and structures of logic. N.Y., 1947.
X Cg Phil 9182.2 A kiss for a blow. (Wright, H.C.) Boston, 1858. (Changed to XP 9413)
Phil 4843.8   Kissabou, Maria I. Hē philosophia en Helladi apo tēs Anastaseōs tou ethnous. Athena, 1951.
Phil 3425.614   Kissel, M.A. Etika Gegelia i Krizis sovremennoi burzhuaznoi etiki. Leningrad, 1966.
Phil 310.779   Kissel', Mikhail A. Uchenie o dialektike v burzhnarnoi filosofii XX veka. Leningrad, 1970.

Phil 3450.13.90 Kist, N.C. Memoriam Heusdii. Lugduni Batavorum, 1839.
Phil 960.18 Kitch, Ethel May. The origin of subjectivity in Hindu thought. Chicago, 1917.
Phil 5627.134.20 Kitchen, V.C. I was a pagan. N.Y., 1934.
Phil 2475.1.85 Kitchin, D.B. Bergson for beginners. London, 1913.
Phil 8448.11 Kitsch: an anthology of bad taste. (Dorfles, Gillo.) London, 1969.
Phil 1750.78 Kittaka, Rin'ichi. New method of philosophy: an introduction to radiciology. Tokyo, 1967.
Phil 8885.22 Kittel, Rudolf. Sittliche fragen. Stuttgart, 1885.
Phil 720.68 Kittinger, Kenneth C. A cranium shake-up and a new philosophy to alter the war spirit in man. Los Angeles, 1967.
Phil 8633.1.37 Kittredge, George L. The old Teutonic idea of the future life. Cambridge, 1937.
Phil 9350.2 Kittredge, H.C. Ten minute talks to boys. Concord, N.H., 1917.
Phil 3808.133 Kiy, Victor. Der Pessimismus und die Ethik Schopenhauers. Berlin, 1866.
Phil 4655.1.82.2 Kjellberg, Elis. Carl Pontus Wikner. Stockholm, 1902.
Phil 4655.1.82 Kjellberg, Elis. Carl Pontus Wikner. Upsala, 1888.
Phil 4655.1.83 Kjellberg, Elis. Mer om och af Pontus Wikner. Upsala, 1913.
Phil 5545.70 Kjerstad, C.L. The form of the learning curves for memory. Private ed. Chicago, 191-?
Phil 3830.8 Klaar, Alfred. Spinoza, sein Leben und seine Lehre. Berlin, 1926.
Phil 8885.48 Klácel, František M. Dobrowěda. Praha, 1847.
Phil 6020.3 Klages, L. Ausdrucksbewegung von Gestaltungskraft. Leipzig, 1923.
Phil 185.44.5 Klages, L. Der Geist als Widersacher der Seele. 3. Aufl. München, 1954. 2v.
Phil 6020.3.5 Klages, L. Grundlegung der Wissenschaft von Ausdruck. Leipzig, 1936.
Phil 5585.66 Klages, L. Vom Wesen des Rhythmus. Kampen auf Sylt, 1934.
Phil 6060.12.16 Klages, Ludwig. Einführung in die Psychologie der Handschrift. 2. Aufl. Heidelberg, 1928.
Phil 3549.8.95 Klages, Ludwig. Erforscher und Künder des Lebens. Linz, 1947.
NEDL Phil 185.44 Klages, Ludwig. Der Geist als Widersacher der Seele. v.1-3. Leipzig, 1929-1932. 4v.
NEDL Phil 185.44.2 Klages, Ludwig. Der Geist als Widersacher der Seele. v.1-3. Gesamtverzeichnis. Leipzig, 1933. 4v.
Phil 6060.12.25 Klages, Ludwig. Graphologie. 4. Aufl. Heidelberg, 1949.
Phil 6060.12.20 Klages, Ludwig. Graphologisches lesebuch. Bonn, 1930.
Phil 575.51.4 Klages, Ludwig. Die Grundlagen der Charakterkunde. 4e Aufl. Leipzig, 1926.
Phil 575.51.9 Klages, Ludwig. Die Grundlagen der Charakterkunde. 5e Aufl. Jena, 1937.
Phil 575.51.8 Klages, Ludwig. Die Grundlagen der Charakterkunde. 7e und 8e Aufl. Leipzig, 1936.
Phil 575.51.12 Klages, Ludwig. Die Grundlagen der Charakterkunde. 11e Aufl. Bonn, 1951.
Phil 6060.12.5 Klages, Ludwig. Handschrift und Charakter. 2e Aufl. Leipzig, 1920.
Phil 6060.12.10 Klages, Ludwig. Handschrift und Charakter. 3. und 4. Aufl. Leipzig, 1921.
Phil 6060.12.5.20 Klages, Ludwig. Handschrift und Charakter. 23. Aufl. Bonn, 1949.
Phil 3549.8.92 Klages, Ludwig. Mensch und Erde. München, 1920.
Phil 3549.8.35 Klages, Ludwig. Mensch und Erde. Stuttgart, 1956.
Phil 3549.8.90 Klages, Ludwig. Persönlichkeit. Potsdam, 1927.
Phil 575.51.20 Klages, Ludwig. Les principes de la caractérologie. Paris, 1930.
Phil 575.51 Klages, Ludwig. Prinzipien der Charakterologie. 3e Aufl. Leipzig, 1921.
Phil 6060.12 Klages, Ludwig. Die Probleme der Graphologie. Leipzig, 1910.
Phil 3640.198 Klages, Ludwig. Die psychologischen Errungenschaften Nietzsches. Leipzig, 1926.
Phil 3640.198.5 Klages, Ludwig. Die psychologischen Errungenschaften Nietzsches. 2e Aufl. Leipzig, 1930.
Phil 3549.8.30 Klages, Ludwig. Rhyghmen und Runen aus dem Nachlass. Leipzig, 1944.
Phil 3549.8.5 Klages, Ludwig. Sämmtliche Werke. Supplement. Bonn, 1966.
Phil 3549.8.2 Klages, Ludwig. Sämtliche Werke. v.1,2,6-8. Bonn, 1964. 5v.
Phil 575.51.15 Klages, Ludwig. The science of character. London, 1929.
Phil 3549.8.40 Klages, Ludwig. Vom Sinn des Lebens. Jena, 1943.
Phil 7082.176 Klages, Ludwig. Vom Traumbewusstsein. Hamburg, 1952.
Phil 5374.44.2 Klages, Ludwig. Vom Wesen des Bewusstseins. 2e Aufl. Leipzig, 1926.
Phil 5374.44.5 Klages, Ludwig. Vom Wesen des Bewusstseins. 4. Aufl. München, 1955.
Phil 575.51.30 Klages, Ludwig. Vorschule der Charakterkunde. 2e Aufl. Leipzig, 1937.
Phil 6060.12.30 Klages, Ludwig. Was die Graphologie nicht kann. Zürich, 1949.
Phil 3549.8.85 Klages, Ludwig. Die Wissenschaft am Scheidewege von Leben und Geist. Leipzig, 1932.
Phil 6060.50 Klages, Ludwig. Zur Ausdruckslehre und Charakterkunde. Heidelberg, 1927.
Phil 4752.2.135 Klamroth, E. Der Gedanke der ewigen Schoepfung. Hamburg, 1963.
Phil 3090.88 Klamroth, Erich. Die Weltanschauung Franz von Baaders in ihrem Gegensatz zu Kant. Berlin, 1965.
Phil 5593.54 Klapfer, Bruno. Developments in the Rorschach technique. Yonkers-on-Hudson, 1954. 2v.
Phil 6320.15 Klapman, J.W. Group psychotherapy; theory and practice. N.Y., 1946.
Phil 3905.92 Klaren, Georg. Otto Weininger, der Mensch, sein Werk und sein Leben. Wien, 1924.
Phil 5066.241 Klassenlogik und formale Einteilung der Wissenschaft. (Laserna, Mario.) Berlin, 1963?
Phil 5590.448.2 Klassifikatsiis lichnosti. 2. izd. (Lazurskii, Aleksandr F.) Moskva, 1923.
Phil 978.49.805 Klassik. (Lauer, H.E.) Basel, 1950.
Phil 130.3 Die Klassiker der Philosophie. (Brøsch, M.) Leipzig, 1884-85. 3v.
Phil 8583.34 Klassiker du religiösen Weltanschauung. Bd.1. (Dennert, E.) Hamburg, 1922.
Phil 8125.20 Die klassische Asthetik der Deutschen. (Harnack, Otto.) Leipzig, 1892.
Phil 8587.31 Das klassische Ideal. 2-3. Aufl. (Horneffer, Ernst.) Leipzig, 1909.
Phil 8080.13 Die klassische Kulturkritik und das Dilemma der Dekadenz. (Redeker, Horst.) Berlin, 1958.

Phil 1750.552.5 Klassische Metaphysik. (Lakebrink, Bernhard.) Freiburg, 1967.
Phil 3005.5 Klassische Philosophie und Wirtschaftswissenschaft. (Friedrichs, A.) Gotha, 1913.
Phil 6120.18 Klatt, F. Lebensmächte. Jena, 1939.
Phil 185.54 Klatzkin, Jakob. Der Erkenntnistrieb als Lebens und Todesprinzip. Zürich, 1935.
Phil 185.54.5 Klatzkin, Jakob. In praise of wisdom. N.Y., 1943.
Phil 5520.542 Klaus, Georg. Spezielle Erkenntnistheorie. 2. Aufl. Berlin, 1966.
Phil 9045.19 Klausen, Gottlieb E. Rede über den Gemeingeist. Altona, 1797.
Phil 5780.23 Klausner, Samuel Z. The quest for self-control. N.Y., 1965.
Phil 5790.40 Klebelsberg, Dieter von. Risikoverhalten als Persönlichkeitsmerkmal. Bern, 1969.
Phil 8960.20 Kleber, Karl-Heinz. De parvitate materiae in sexto. Regensburg, 1971.
Phil 3808.232 Klee, Hermann. Grundzüge einer Ästhetik nach Schopenhauer. Berlin, 1875.
Phil 5820.7 Klee, James Butt. Problems of selective behavior. Lincoln, 1951.
Phil 5066.261.5 Kleene, Stephen Cole. The foundations of intuitionistic mathematics. Amsterdam, 1965.
Phil 5066.261 Kleene, Stephen Cole. Mathematical logic. N.Y., 1967.
Phil 8885.26 Kleffler, Henri. Philosophie du sens commun. Paris, 1894-95. 3v.
Phil 6120.1 Klein, A. Die modernen Theorien über Verhältnis von Leib und Seele. Breslau, 1906.
Phil 5247.13.25 Klein, Anton. Juan Huarte und der Psychognosis der Renaissance. Inaug. Diss. Bonn, 1913.
Phil 5500.26 Klein, Burton Harold. The decision-making problem in development. Santa Monica, 1960.
Phil 6120.20 Klein, David B. Mental hygiene. N.Y., 1944.
Phil 7084.18 Klein, David Ballin. The experimental production of dreams during hypnosis. Austin, 1930.
Phil 5220.7 Klein, David Ballin. A history of scientific psychology. N.Y., 1970.
Phil 6140.20 Klein, Donald Charles. Community dynamics and mental health. N.Y., 1968.
Htn Phil 3801.488* Klein, Georg M. Betrachtungen über den gegenwartigen Zustand der Philosophie...Schellingsche Philosophie. Nürnberg, 1813.
Phil 3640.266 Klein, Johannes. Die Dichtung Nietzsches. München, 1936.
Phil 6320.11.19 Klein, M. Contributions to psycho-analysis, 1921-1945. London, 1968.
Phil 6320.11.17A Klein, M. Contributions to psycho-analysis. London, 1950.
Phil 6320.11 Klein, M. Love, hate and reparation. London, 1937.
Phil 6320.11.10 Klein, M. New directions in psycho-analysis. London, 1955.
Phil 6320.11.25 Klein, M. Our adult world. N.Y., 1963.
Phil 6320.11.5 Klein, M. Die Psychoanalyse des Kindes. Wien, 1932.
Phil 341.37 Klein, Martin. Der zerstückelte Gott. München, 1967.
Phil 5413.20 Klein, Melanie. Envy and gratitude. London, 1957.
Phil 8430.81 Klein, Robert. La forme et l'intelligible. Paris, 1970.
Phil 3640.520 Klein, Werner. Nietzsches Kampf gegen den göttlichen Zwang. Stuttgart, 1940.
Phil 5645.37 Kleine Beiträge zur Psychophysik der Farbenempfindungen. (Müller, G.E.) Leipzig, 1934.
Phil 3890.8.120 Kleine deutsche Schriften. (Thomasius, Christian.) Halle, 1894.
Phil 5047.22 Die kleine Logik. (Hoppe, James.) Paderborn, 1869.
Phil 349.35 Kleine Logik der Geisteswissenschaften. (Schmidt, Franz.) München, 1938.
Phil 197.15 Kleine Philosophie und politische Schriften. (Weber, H.B. von.) Stuttgart, 1839.
Phil 176.75 Kleine philosophische Schriften. (Barach, Carl S.) Wien, 1878.
Phil 3235.78 Kleine philosophische Schriften. (Feuerbach, Ludwig.) Leipzig, 1950.
Htn Phil 3625.1.35* Kleine philosophische Schriften. (Mendelssohn, Moses.) Berlin, 1789.
Phil 192.12.5 Kleine philosophische Schriften. v.1-3. (Ritter, Heinrich.) Kiel, 1839-1840.
Phil 8423.16.5 Kleine Schriften, Vorreden, Entwürfe. (Winckelmann, Johann Joachim.) Berlin, 1968.
Phil 3090.25 Kleine Schriften. (Baader, Franz von.) Würzburg, 1847.
Phil 3270.12.50 Kleine Schriften. (Frege, Gottlob.) Hildesheim, 1967.
Phil 3310.18 Kleine Schriften. (Gadamer, H.G.) Tübingen, 1967. 3v.
Phil 182.72 Kleine Schriften. (Huber, J.) Leipzig, 1871.
Htn Phil 3480.19* Kleine Schriften. (Kant, Immanuel.) Neuwied, 1793.
Phil 3565.10 Kleine Schriften. (Lotze, Hermann.) Leipzig, 1885-91. 4v.
Phil 193.27 Kleine Schriften. (Sigwart, Christoph von.) Freiburg, 1881. 2v.
Phil 3915.8 Kleine Schriften. (Wundt, Wilhelm.) Leipzig, 1910-11. 2v.
Phil 3210.26.5 Kleine Schriften. 2. Aufl. (Fechner, G.T.) Leipzig, 1913.
Phil 176.53 Kleine schriften philosophischen. Bd.1. (Bouterwek, F.) Göttingen, 1818.
Phil 3805.18 Kleine Schriften und Predigten. (Schleiermacher, Friedrich.) Berlin, 1969-70. 3v.
Phil 3450.16.10 Kleine Schriften und Vorhäge. (Heusel, Paul.) Tübingen, 1930.
Phil 3210.26 Kleine Schriften von Dr. Mises (pseud.) (Fechner, G.T.) Leipzig, 1875.
Phil 3925.3.50 Kleine Schriften zur Aesthetik und ästhetischen Kritik. (Weisse, Christian Hermann.) Leipzig, 1867.
Phil 3925.3.52 Kleine Schriften zur Asthetik und ästhetischen Kritik. (Weisse, Christian Hermann.) Hildesheim, 1966.
Phil 1108.8 Kleine Schriften zur Geschichte der antiken Philosophie. (Diels, Hermann.) Hildesheim, 1969.
Phil 1123.7.5 Kleine Schriften zur griechischen Philosophie. 2. Aufl. (Stenzel, Julius.) Darmstadt, 1957.
Phil 3552.21.5 Kleine Schriften zur Metaphysik. (Leibniz, Gottfried Wilhelm.) Frankfurt, 1965.
Phil 3475.3.230 Kleine Schule des philosophischen Denkens. (Jaspers, Karl.) München, 1965.
Phil 5241.180 Kleine Theorie des praktischen Denkens. (Berdelle, Philipp.) Mainz, 1969.
Phil 818.28 Kleine Weltgeschichte der Philosophie. 3. Aufl. (Staerig, H.J.) Stuttgart, 1953.
Phil 5590.390 Kleiner, Fritz. Das Problem der Persönlichkeit in der amerikanischen Psychologie. München, 1961.
Phil 3480.18.12 Kleinere philosophische Schriften. (Kant, Immanuel.) Leipzig, 1921.

Phil 3552.21 Kleinere philosophische Schriften. (Leibniz, Gottfried Wilhelm.) Jena, 1740.

Phil 3552.22 Kleinere philosophische Schriften. (Leibniz, Gottfried Wilhelm.) Leipzig, 1883.

Phil 189.8 Kleinere philosophische Schriften. (Olzelt-Newin, A.) Leipzig, 1903.

Phil 4829.803.20 Kleinere philosophische Schriften. (Spakovski, Anatol.) Velika Kikinda, 1938.

Phil 3428.15 Kleinere philosophische Schriften und Abhandlungen. (Herbart, J.F.) Leipzig, 1842-43. 3v.

Phil 3450.18.80 Kleinere Schriften. (Hartmann, N.) Berlin, 1955. 3v.

Phil 3480.28.12 Kleinere Schriften zur Ethik und Religionsphilosophie. (Kant, Immanuel.) Berlin, 1870.

Phil 3480.28 Kleinere Schriften zur Geschichts- Philosophie Ethik und Politik. (Kant, Immanuel.) Leipzig, 1913.

Phil 3480.24.5 Kleinere Schriften zur Logik und Metaphysik. (Kant, Immanuel.) Berlin, 1870.

Phil 3480.24.2 Kleinere Schriften zur Logik und Metaphysik. v.1-4. 2. Aufl. (Kant, Immanuel.) Leipzig, 1905.

Phil 3480.28.15 Kleinere Schriften zur Natur- Philosophie. v.1-2. (Kant, Immanuel.) Berlin, 1872-73.

Phil 3489.25.3 Kleines Kant-Wörterbich. (Heussner, A.) Göttingen, 1925.

Phil 5068.5 Kleines Lehrbuch des Positivismus. (Mises, R.E. von.) The Hague, 1939.

Phil 3745.14 Kleines Lesebuch von den Tugenden des menschlichen Herzens. 5. Aufl. (Pieper, Josef.) München, 1957.

Phil 130.7 Kleines Philosophenlexikon. (Decurtins, C.) Affoltern, 1952.

Phil 99.2 Kleines philosophiches Wörterbuch. (Odebrecht, Rudolf.) Berlin, 1909.

Phil 99.1 Kleines philosophisches Wörterbuch. (Odebrecht, Rudolf.) Berlin, 1908.

Phil 5204.24 Kleines psychologisches Lexicon. (Berka, M.) Wien, 1949.

Phil 85.10 Kleines Worterbuch der Philosophie. (Austeda, F.) Frankfurt, 1954.

Phil 5643.155 Kleinhans, Walter H. Stufen der ganzheitlichen Auffassung bei 2- bis 7 järigen Kindern. Thesis. Weinheim, 1966.

Phil 7060.45 Kleinpaul, R. Die Lebendigen und die Toten. Leipzig, 1898.

Phil 7060.45.5 Kleinpaul, R. Volkspsychologie, Berlin, 1914.

Phil 5250.28 Kleinpeter, H. Vorträge zur Einführung in die Psychologie. Leipzig, 1914.

Phil 341.6 Kleinpeter, Hans. Der Phänomenalismus. Leipzig, 1913.

Phil 341.3 Kleinseter, H. Erkenntnistheorie der Naturforschung. Leipzig, 1905.

Phil 9530.35 Kleiser, Grenville. How to succeed in life. N.Y., 1934.

Phil 2150.18.105.5 Klemke, E.D. The epistemology of G.E. Moore. Evanston, 1969.

Phil 2255.1.165 Klemke, E.D. Essays on Bertrand Russell. Urbana, Illinois, 1970.

Phil 3270.12.105 Klemke, E.D. Essays on Frege. Urbana, 1968.

Phil 2150.18.105 Klemke, E.D. Studies in the philosophy of G.E. Moore. Chicago, 1969.

Phil 3255.83 Klemm, Karl. Das Paradoxen als Ausdrucksform der spekulativen Mystik Sebastian Francks. Inaug-Diss. Leipzig, 1937.

Phil 5220.1 Klemm, O. Geschichte der Psychologie. Leipzig, 1911.

Phil 5220.1.5 Klemm, O. A history of psychology. N.Y., 1914.

Phil 4260.83.2 Klemm, Otto. G.B. Vico als Geschichtsphilosoph. Leipzig, 1906.

Phil 4260.83 Klemm, Otto. G.B. Vico als Geschichtsphilosoph. Inaug. Diss. Leipzig, 1906.

Phil 3778.92 Klemmt, Alfred. Karl Leonard Reinholds Elementarphilosophie. Hamburg, 1958.

Phil 5400.33 Klencke, P.F.H. Diätetik der Seele. 2e Aufl. Leipzig, 1873.

Phil 3915.148 Klenke, Friedrich. Der Mensch. Graz, 1908.

Phil 5360.30 Klerk, Lein Friedrich Wolfgang de. Probabilistic concept learning. Proefschrift. Leiden? 1968.

Phil 3492.38 Kleuker, Johann. De libertate morali ex ratione Kantiana. Osnabrugi, 1789.

Phil 8665.8 Kleutgen, J. Praeter introductionem continens partem primamque est De ipso deo. Ratisbonae, 1881.

Phil 1515.2 Kleutgen, R.P. La philosophie scolastique. Paris, 1868-70. 4v.

Phil 1515.2.5 Kleutgen und die Theorie des Erkenntnisbildes. (Gilen, Leonhard.) Meisenheim, 1956.

Phil 4752.2.120 Kleveta druzei. (Osipov, N.) Miunkhen, 1958.

Phil 4803.755.80 Kliauchenia, Aliaksandr S. Stefan Rudnianskii. Minsk, 1968.

Phil 5710.22 Klibansky, R. Saturn and melancholy. London, 1964.

Phil 185.57A Klibansky, Raymond. Philosophy and history. Oxford, 1936.

Phil 1710.7 Klibasky, Raymond. La philosophie au milieu du 20e siècle. Firenze, 1958. 4v.

Phil 6327.28.80 Klient-sentrert rådgivning og terapi...Carl R. Rogers' psykologi. (Braaten, Leif Johan.) Oslo, 1967.

Phil 6120.23 Klier, Sol. Effects of induced stress on learning and performance. n.p., 1962.

Phil 4809.489.2 Klíma, Ladislav. Dílo. v.2- Praha, 1948-

Phil 186.12.11 Die Klimax der Theorieen. (Liebmann, O.) Strassburg, 1884.

Phil 3235.130 Klimkeit, Hans-Joachim. Das Wunderverstaendnis Ludwig Feuerbaches in religionsphanomenologischer Sicht. Bonn, 1965.

Phil 5590.538 Klimov, Evgenii A. Individual'nyi stil' deiatel'nosti v zavisimosti ot tipologicheskikh svoistv nervnoi sistemy. Kazan', 1969.

Phil 3492.22 Klinberg, A.G. Kants kritik af heibnizianismen. Upsala, 1869.

Phil 3830.12 Kline, G.L. Spinoza in Soviet philosophy. London, 1952.

Phil 1710.13 Kline, George. European philosophy today. Chicago, 1965.

Phil 2340.10.175 Kline, George Louis. Alfred North Whitehead. Englewood Cliffs, 1963.

Phil 6671.27 Kline, M.V. A scientific report on the search for Bridey Murphy. N.Y., 1956.

Phil 4582.4.95 Klingberg, Wilhelm. Den intellektuella spärren; trous svårigheter i belysning av Axel Hägerströms filosofi. Stockholm, 1916.

Phil 5203.31 Klingelhofer, Edward L. A bibliography of psychological research and writings on Africa. Uppsala, 1967.

Phil 6310.2.8 Klinische Beitrage zur Psychoanalyse aus den Jahren 1907-1926. (Abraham, Karl.) Leipzig, 1921.

Phil 6968.4.3 Klinische Psychiatrie. 3. Aufl. (Schüle, H.) Leipzig, 1886.

Phil 6962.5.5 Klinische Vorlesungen über Psychiatrie. v.1-2. (Meynert, T.) Wien, 1889-90.

Phil 3160.9.85 Klink, Siegfried. Das Prinzip des Unbewussten bei Carl Gustav Carus. Tübingen, 1933.

Phil 3492.42.5 Klinke, Willibald. Kant for everyman. N.y., 1962.

Phil 5648.15 Klinkenberg, E. Der Raumsinn der Haut. Inaug. Diss. Bonn, 1883.

Phil 850.14 Klippel, M. Philosophie et poésie: Les origines. Paris, 1925.

Phil 5760.2 Klippel, T. Determinismus und Strafe. Berlin, 1890.

Phil 3450.15.90 Klitzner, Julius. Hieronymus Hiruhaim: zum deutschen Geist im Barock Böhmens. Prag, 1943.

Phil 4757.1.30 Kliuch very. (Gershenzon, M.O.) Peterburg, 1922.

Phil 8092.19 Klivar, Miroslav. Estetika nových umeni. Vyd. 1. Praha, 1970.

Phil 8685.16 Klockhoff, D. Om den pantheistiska esthetiken. Academisk ävhandling. Upsala, 1864.

Phil 3450.18.200 Klösters, Joseph. Die "Kritische Ontologie" Nicolai Hartmanns und ihre Bedeutung für das Erkenntnisproblem. Inaug. Diss. Fulda, 1927.

Phil 310.589.8 Klofáč, Jaroslav. Materialistické pojetí dějin. Vyd. 3. Praha, 1962.

Phil 310.589 Klofáč, Jaroslav. O rozporech ve společnostii. Praha, 1962.

Phil 2905.1.580 Klohr, Olof. Beiträge zur Deutung von Teilhard de Chardin. Berlin, 1966.

Phil 9495.164.5 Klomps, H. Ehemoral und Jansenismus. Köln, 1964.

Phil 8960.12 Klomps, Heinrich. Tradition und Fortschritt in der Moraltheologie: die grundsätzliche Bedeutung der Kontroverse zwischen Jansenismus und Probabilismus. Köln, 1963.

Phil 7060.105 Die Klopf- und Spussgeister. (Berthelen, K.A.) Zittau, 1864.

Phil 5593.42.5 Klopfer, Bruno. The Rorschach technique; a manual for a projective method of personality diagnosis. Yonkers-on-Hudson, 1942.

Phil 4803.360.30 Klopot z istnieniem. (Elzenberg, Henryk.) Kraków, 1963.

Phil 3552.290 Klopp, O. Zur Ehrenrettung von Leibniz. Berlin, 1878.

Phil 3160.9.95 Kloppe, Wolfgang. Erinnerungen an Carl Gustav Carus. Berlin, 1969.

Phil 3640.780 Klossowski, Pierre. Nietzsche et le cercle vicieux. Paris, 1969.

Phil 8665.5 Klostermann, E. Späte Vergeltung aus der Geschichte der Theodicee. Strassburg, 1916.

Phil 5090.12.2 Klotz, Hans. Der philosophische Beweis. 2. Aufl. Berlin, 1969.

Phil 8700.18 Klotz, John William. Genes. Saint Louis, 1959.

Phil 3195.6.113 Kluback, William. Philosophy of history. N.Y., 1956.

Phil 185.67.5 Klubertanz, G.P. Introduction to the philosophy of being. N.Y., 1955.

Phil 185.67 Klubertanz, G.P. The philosophy of human nature. N.Y., 1953.

Phil 9560.57 Klubertanz, George Peter. Habits and virtues. N.Y., 1965.

Phil 5590.330 Kluckhohn, Clyde. Personality in nature, society, and culture. 1. ed. N.Y., 1948.

Phil 5590.105.2 Kluckhohn, Clyde. Personality in nature, society and culture. 2. ed. N.Y., 1967.

Phil 5590.105 Kluckhohn, Clyde. Personality in nature. 2. ed. N.Y., 1953.

Phil 5820.5 Klüver, H. Behavior mechanisms in monkeys. Chicago, 1933.

Phil 8885.30 Klug, J. Die Tiefen der Seele. Paderborn, 1926.

Phil 3415.82 Kluge, A. Philosophische Fragmente...Hartmann's Philosophie. Breslau, 1875-77. 2v.

Phil 6680.6.3 Kluge, C.A.F. Versuch einer Darstellung dis animalischen Magnetismus. Berlin, 1818.

Phil 3625.13.90 Kluge, Fritz. Die Philosophie der Mathematik und Naturwissenschaft bei Aloys Müller. Inaug. Diss. Leipzig, 1935.

Phil 6680.8 Kluge, G. Zhivotnyi magnitizm. Sankt Peterberg, 1818.

Phil 3010.7 Klugen, A. von. Die Absage an die Romantik in der Zeit nach den Weltkriege. Berlin, 1938.

Phil 8620.60 Kluger, Rivkah Schärf. Satan in the Old Testament. Evanston, 1967.

Phil 9070.35 Klugheit vereind mit Tugend. (Eskartshausen, K. von.) Brünn, 1791.

Phil 4769.1.125 Klum, Edith. Natur, Kunst und Liebe in der Philosophie Vladimir Solov'evs. München, 1965.

Phil 5643.105 Kluver, H. Visual mechanisms. Lancaster, 1942.

Htn Phil 1955.6.90F* Klyce, S. Dewey's suppressed psychology. Winchester, Mass., 1928.

Phil 8700.9 Klyce, S. Sins of science. Boston, 1925.

Phil 291.2F Klyce, Scudder. Universe. Winchester, Mass., 1921.

Phil 9410.5.3 The knack of it. 2. ed. (Loomis, Charles.) N.Y., 1908.

Phil 5722.78 The knack of using your subconscious mind. (Williams, John K.) Scarsdale, N.Y., 1952.

Htn Phil 7054.124* Knaggs, Samuel T. Human fads, foibles, fallacies. Sydney, 1898.

Phil 7054.175 Knapp, C. Richard. The newest Bible demonstrated by nature. Grass Valley, Calif., n.d.

Phil 5250.84 Knapp, Franz. Das geistige Leben der Person in den persönlichkeitspsychologischen Schichttheorien. Inaug. Diss. Heidelberg? 1967?

Phil 6960.1 Knapp, P.C. The insanity of doubt. Baltimore, 1890.

Phil 6120.9 Knapp, Sheldon. Towards a new era in healing. London, 1926.

Phil 1540.8 Knappe, O.F. The scholastic theory of the species sensibilis. Washington, 1915.

Phil 3415.83 Knauer, G. Das Facit aus Eduard von Hartmann's Philosophie des Unbewussten. Berlin, 1873.

Phil 3010.10 Knauer, Rudolf. Der Voluntarismus. Berlin, 1907.

Phil 1710.1 Knauer, V. Geschichte der Philosophie mit besonderer Berücksichtung der Neuzeit. Wien, 1876.

Phil 1710.1.2 Knauer, V. Geschichte der Philosophie mit besonderer Berücksichtung der Neuzeit. 2e Aufl. Wien, 1882.

Phil 5220.3 Knauer, V. Grundlinien zur Aristotelisch-Thomistischen Psychologie. Wien, 1885.

Phil 810.3 Knauer, Vincenz. Die haupt Probleme der Philosophie. Wien, 1892.

Phil 5050.16 Knauss, G. Gegenstand und Umgreifendes. Basel, 1954.

Phil 5020.5 Kneale, William Calvert. The development of logic. Oxford, 1962.

Phil 5020.5.10 Kneale, William Calvert. The development of logic. Oxford, 1968.

Phil 5125.20 Kneale, William Calvert. Probability and induction. Oxford, 1949.

Phil 5125.20.1 Kneale, William Calvert. Probability and induction. Reprint. Oxford, 1966.

Phil 8610.834.5 Kneeland, A. National hymns. Boston, 1836.

Phil 8635.6 Kneib, P. Die Beweise für die Unsterblichkeit der Seele. Freiburg, 1903.

Phil 5760.6 | Kneib, Philipp. Die Willensfreiheit und die innere Verantwortlichkeit. Mainz, 1898.

Phil 8590.11.2 | Kneib, Philipp. Wissen und Glauben. 2. Aufl. Mainz, 1905.

Phil 978.37 | Kneisel, R. Die Lehre von der Seelenwanderung. Leipzig, 1889.

Phil 5421.20.120 | Kneutgen, Johannes. Der Mensch, ein kriegerisches Tier. Stuttgart, 1970.

Phil 3850.16.85 | Knevels, Wilhelm. Simmels Religionstheorie. Leipzig, 1920.

Phil 3830.4 | Kniat, Joseph. Spinoza's Ethik gegenüber der Erfahrung. Posen, 1888.

Phil 185.56 | Kniepf, Albert. Theorie der Geisteswerthe. Leipzig, 1892.

Phil 6990.25 | Kniga chudes. (Bushenskii, N.) Pesch', 1860.

Phil 310.290 | Kniga dlia chteniia po marksistsko filosofii. (Rozental', Mark M.) Moskva, 1960.

Phil 9513.2 | Knigge, A. von. Über den Umgang mit Menschen. Pt.1-3. Hildburghausen, 1830.

Phil 9513.2.5 | Knigge, A. von. Über den Umgang mit Menschen. 3. Aufl. pt.1-3. Hannover, 1790.

Phil 8885.17 | Knigge, Adolf. Practical philosophy of social life. 1st American ed. Lansingburgh, 1805.

Phil 3640.285 | Kniggendorf, W. Friedrich Nietzsche - der Deutsche! Erfurt, 1938.

Phil 3640.260 | Knight, A.H.J. Some aspects of the life and work of Nietzsche. Cambridge, 1933.

Phil 7010.7 | Knight, David C. The ESP reader. N.Y., 1969.

Phil 3830.2 | Knight, E. Spinoza, essays by Land, Fischer, Vloten, and Renan. London, 1882.

Phil 1750.485A | Knight, E.W. Literature considered as philosophy. London, 1957.

Phil 1710.6 | Knight, Everett. The objective society. London, 1959.

Phil 1710.6.2 | Knight, Everett. The objective society. N.Y., 1959.

Phil 8960.9 | Knight, F.H. The economic order and religion. N.Y., 1945.

Phil 3640.347 | Knight, George W. Christ and Nietzsche. London, 1948.

Phil 8665.1 | Knight, H. The being and attributes of God. London, 1747.

Phil 2493.100 | Knight, Isabel F. The geometric spirit; the Abbe de Condillac and the French Enlightenment. New Haven, 1968.

Phil 5790.10 | Knight, James Allen. For the love of money. Philadelphia, 1968.

Phil 6960.2 | Knight, P.S. Beobachtungen...des Irrseyns. Koln, 1829.

Phil 8411.7.5 | Knight, R.P. An analytical inquiry into the principles of taste. 2. ed. London, 1805.

Phil 8411.7.6 | Knight, R.P. An analytical inquiry into the principles of taste. 3. ed. London, 1806.

Phil 8411.7.10 | Knight, R.P. An analytical inquiry into the principles of taste. 4. ed. London, 1808.

Phil 5250.42 | Knight, Rex. A modern introduction to psychology. 5. ed. London, 1957.

Phil 2225.5.115 | Knight, Thomas Stanley. Charles Peirce. N.Y., 1965.

Phil 185.7 | Knight, W. Essays in philosophy. Boston, 1890.

Phil 8411.7.15 | Knight, W. The philosophy of the beautiful. N.Y., 1891-93. 2v.

Phil 185.7.5 | Knight, W. Studies in philosophy and literature. London, 1879.

Phil 185.7.9 | Knight, W. Varia; studies on problems of philosophy and ethics. London, 1901.

Phil 8635.8 | Knight, W.A. Aspects of theism. London, 1893.

Phil 2050.88.15 | Knight, William. Hume. Edinburgh, 1905.

Phil 2050.88 | Knight, William. Hume. Philadelphia, 1886.

Phil 176.41.5 | Knight, William. Lord Monboddo. London, 1900.

Phil 1750.370 | Knittermeyer, H. Dit Philosophie der Existenz von der Renaissance bis zur Gegenwart. Wien, 1952.

Phil 3801.491 | Knittermeyer, H. Schelling und die romantische Schule. München, 1929.

Phil 8590.19 | Knittermeyer, Heinrich. Die philosophie und das Christentum. Jena, 1927.

Phil 705.11.5 | Knittermeyer, Hinrich. Der Mensch der Erkenntnis. Hamburg, 1962.

Phil 705.11 | Knittermeyer, Hinrich. Der Terminus transszendental in seiner historischen Entwickelung bis zu Kant. Inaug. Diss. Marburg, 1920.

VPhil 2255.1.140 | Knjazeva-Adamović, Svetlana. Filozofija Bertranda Russella: strasno traženje izvesnosti. Zagreb, 1966.

Phil 7050.10 | The "knockings"Exposed. (Diotrephes.) N.Y., 1850. 3 pam.

Phil 3310.1.125 | Knoodt, Peter. Anton Günther. Wien, 1881. 2v.
Phil 3310.1.127 | Knoodt, Peter. Günther und Blemens. Wien, 1853-54.

Phil 3425.320 | Knoop, Bernhard. Hegel und die Franzosen. Stuttgart, 1941.

Phil 6321.53.10 | Knots. (Laing, Roland David.) London, 1970.
Phil 9070.41 | Knots and crosses. (Roche, A.) Dublin, 1943.
Phil 9350.1 | Knott, Laura A. Vesper talks to girls. Boston, 1916.
Phil 2035.82A | Know the truth. Hamilton's theory. (Jones, J.H.) N.Y., 1865.

Phil 5255.42 | Know thyself; a study in mental qualities. (Potts, John.) Philadelphia, 1935.

Phil 7059.18 | Know thyself, o man! (Gallion, D.A.) Keokuk, Iowa, 1865.
Phil 9035.85 | Know thyself. (Carr, William.) N.Y., 1944.
Phil 5246.18 | Know your own mind...book of practical psychology. (Glover, William.) Cambridge, 1915.

Phil 337.27 | The knower and the known. (Grene, Marjorie.) N.Y., 1966.
Phil 8893.36 | Knowing and acting. (Smith, J.A.) Oxford, 1910.
Phil 346.20.15 | Knowing and being. (Polanyi, Michael.) London, 1969.
Phil 196.12 | Knowing and being. (Veitch, John.) Edinburg, 1889.
Phil 1955.6.32A | Knowing and the known. (Dewey, John.) Boston, 1949.
Phil 1955.6.33 | Knowing and the known. (Dewey, John.) Boston, 1960.
Phil 350.2 | Knowledge, belief and certitude. (Turner, F.S.) London, 1900.

Phil 342.14 | Knowledge, belief and opinion. (Aaron, John.) N.Y., 1930.
Phil 186.16.15 | Knowledge, life and reality. (Ladd, G.T.) New Haven, 1918.

Phil 331.40 | Knowledge, mind and nature. (Aune, Bruce.) N.Y., 1967.
Phil 3270.13.21 | Knowledge. (Frank, Erich.) Chicago, 1955.
Phil 353.27 | Knowledge. (Weigel, Gustave.) Englewood Cliffs, N.J., 1961.

Phil 337.35 | Knowledge and belief. (Griffiths, A. Phillips.) London, 1967.

Phil 338.40 | Knowledge and belief. (Hintikka, K.J.J.) Ithaca, 1962.
Phil 343.30 | Knowledge and certainty. (Malcolm, N.) Englewood Cliffs, 1963.

Phil 70.94 | Knowledge and experience. (Oberlin Colloguium in Philosophy, 3d, Oberlin College, 1962.) Pittsburgh, Pa. 1962

Phil 1885.94.2 | Knowledge and experience in the philosophy of F.H. Bradley. (Eliot, T.S.) London, 1964.

Phil 1885.94 | Knowledge and experience in the philosophy of F.H. Bradley. (Eliot, T.S.) N.Y., 1964.

Phil 338.44.1 | Knowledge and interests. (Habermas, Jürgen.) Boston, 1971.

Phil 179.3.41 | Knowledge and life. (Eucken, R.) N.Y., 1914.
Phil 346.16 | Knowledge and perception. (Prichard, H.A.) Oxford, 1950.
Phil 5041.20.8 | Knowledge and reality. (Bosanquet, B.) London, 1885.
Phil 185.59 | Knowledge and society. N.Y., 1938.
Phil 720.18 | Knowledge and truth. (Reid, Louis A.) London, 1923.
Phil 7080.44 | Knowledge exchanged; phenomenon of sleep. (Fish, Luther S.) Cheveland, 1920.

Phil 346.29 | Knowledge of actions. (Powell, Betty.) London, 1967[1966]
Phil 8584.2 | The knowledge of divine things from revelation. (Ellis, J.) London, 1743.

Phil 8584.2.2 | The knowledge of divine things from revelation. (Ellis, J.) London, 1747.

Phil 8584.2.3 | The knowledge of divine things from revelation. (Ellis, J.) London, 1771.

Phil 8674.12 | Knowledge of God. (Trueblood, D.E.) N.Y., 1939.
Phil 3120.30.79 | The knowledge of man. (Buber, Martin.) N.Y., 1965.
Phil 341.35 | Knowledge of other minds. Lahore, 1959.
Phil 186.73 | The knowledge of reality. (Lutosławski, W.) Cambridge, 1930.

Phil 978.49.17 | Knowledge of the higher worlds. 3d English ed. (Steiner, R.) London, 1937.

Phil 978.49.16 | Knowledge of the higher worlds and its attainment. (Steiner, R.) N.Y., 193-?

Phil 332.21 | Knowledge of the individual. (Burgh, W.G.) London, 1939.
Phil 8877.33.5 | The knowledge of the world and the attainments. (Callieres, F. de.) Dublin, 1774.

Phil 1030.5A | Knowledge triumphant; the concept of knowledge in medieval Islam. (Rosenthal, Franz.) Leiden, 1970.

Phil 530.11.15.5 | Knowles, David. The English mystical tradition. London, 1961.

Phil 530.11.15 | Knowles, David. The English mystics. London, 1927.
Phil 1515.3 | Knowles, David. The evolution of medieval thought. Baltimore, 1962.

Phil 525.247 | Knowles, David. What is mysticism? London, 1967.
Phil 8590.9 | Knowles, E.R. The supremacy of the spiritual. Boston, 1895.

Htn | Phil 8590.9.2* | Pamphlet box. Knowles, E.R. The supremacy of the spiritual.
Phil 5590.554 | Knowles, Henry P. Personality and leadership behavior. Reading, Mass., 1971.

Phil 5330.28 | Knowlson, T.S. The secret of concentration. 1st. ed. N.Y., 1931.

Phil 185.19 | Knowlson, T.S. A thought book on Socratic method. London, 1920?

Phil 5425.26 | Knowlson, Thomas S. Originality, a popular study of creative mind. Philadelphia, 1918.

Phil 6120.11 | Knowlton, C. Two remarkable lectures. Boston, 1833.
Phil 9075.22 | Knowlton, Pitt G. Origin and nature of conscience. Oberlin, 1897.

Phil 185.71 | Knox, Crawford. The idiom of contemporary thought. London, 1956.

Phil 2070.80A | Knox, H.V. The philosophy of William James. London, 1914.
Phil 5760.8 | Knox, Howard V. The will to be free. London, 1924.
Phil 3492.40.2 | Knox, Israel. The aesthetic theories of Kant. N.Y., 1958.
Phil 8885.52 | Knox, Malcolm. Action. London, 1968.
Phil 8590.20 | Knox, Raymond C. Religion and the American dream. N.Y., 1934.

Phil 8885.7 | Knox, V. Essays, moral and literary. London, 1808. 3v.

Phil 185.43 | Knox,H.V. The evolution of truth and other essays. London, 1930.

Phil 575.64 | Knudson, A.C. The philosophy of personalism. N.Y., 1927.
Phil 8590.28 | Knudson, A.C. Present tendencies in religious thought. N.Y., 1924.

Phil 5627.148 | Knudson, A.C. The vaiidity of religious experience. N.Y., 1937.

Phil 5050.15 | Knutzen, M. Elementa philosophiae rationalis seu logicae. Regiomonti, 1747.

Phil 665.58.5 | Knutzen, Martin. Philosophische Abhandlung von der immateriellen Natur der Seele. Königsberg, 1744.

VPhil 3640.766 | Ko je Niče. (Grlić, Danko.) Beograd, 1969.
Phil 3801.496.5 | Ko Ktanck, Anton Mirko. Schelling-Studien. München, 1965.
Phil 7150.58 | Kobler, Arthur. The end of hope. N.Y., 1964.
Phil 5648.6 | Kobylecki, S Wahrnehmbarkeit plötzlicher Drückveranderungen. Leipzig, 1905.

Phil 165.150 | Koch, Adrienne. Philosophy for a time of crisis. N.Y., 1959.

Phil 2520.110 | Koch, Anton. Die Psychologie Descartes. München, 1881.
Phil 5400.42.5 | Koch, Bernhard. Experimentelle Untersuchungen. Leipzig, 1913.

Phil 5592.5 | Koch, Charles. The tree test. Bern, 1952.
Phil 5627.80 | Koch, E. Die Psychologie in der Religionswissenschaft. Freiburg, 1896.

Phil 341.2 | Koch, Emil. Das Bewusstsein der Transcendenz. Halle an der Saale, 1895.

Phil 8885.33 | Koch, Gregor. Das menschliche Leben. Ensiedeln, 1916.
Phil 8665.9.5 | Koch, H.G. The abolition of God. Philadelphia, 1963.
Phil 8665.9 | Koch, H.G. Abschaffung Tottes? Stuttgart, 1961.
Phil 8092.2 | Koch, Hans. Marxismus und Asthetik. Berlin, 1962.
Phil 185.22.6 | Koch, J.L.A. Grundriss der Philosophie. 2e Aufl. Göppingen, 1885.

Phil 6960.3 | Koch, J.L.A. Die psychopathischen Minderwertigkeiten. Ravensburg, 1891-93. 3v.

Phil 185.22 | Koch, J.L.A. Die Wirchlichkeit und ihre Erkenntnis. Göppingen, 1886.

Phil 341.15 | Koch, Julius L. Erkenntnistheoretische Untersuchaungen. Göppingen, 1883.

Phil 5374.27 | Koch, Julius L.A. Vom Bewusstsein in Zustanden sogennanten Bewusstlosigkeit. Stuttgart, 1877.

Phil 5592.10 | Koch, Karl. Der Baumtest. 2. Aufl. Bern, 1954.
Phil 5592.10.3 | Koch, Karl. Der Baumtest. 3. Aufl. Bern, 1957.
Phil 5238.100 | Koch, Sigmund. Psychology. v.2-6. v.1 lost. N.Y., 1959. 5v.

Phil 3425.621 | Koch, Traugott. Differenz und Versöhnung; eine Interpretation der Theologie G.W.F. Hegels nach seiner "Wissenschaft der Logik." 1. Aufl. Gütersloh, 1967.

Phil 5520.616 | Kocha, lubi, szanuje. Wyd. 1. (Wierzbicka, Anna.) Warszawa, 1971.

Phil 8700.14.5 | Kocher, Paul Harold. Science and religion in Elizabethan England. N.Y., 1969.

Phil 8700.14 | Kocher, Paul Harold. Science and religion in Elizabethan England. San Marino, Calif., 1955.

Phil 5274.4 | Kochergin, A.N. Problemy modelirovaniia psikhicheskoi deiatel'nosti. Photoreproduction. Moskva, 1969. 2v.

Phil 5520.706 | Kochergin, Al'bert N. Modelirovanie myshleniia. Moskva, 1969.

Phil 3450.19.250 | Kockelmans, A. Martin Heidegger. Teilt, 1962.

Phil 3450.11.380   Kockelmans, Joseph John. Edmund Husserl's phenomenological psychology. Pittsburgh, 1967.

Phil 3450.11.395   Kockelmans, Joseph John. A first introduction to Husserl's phenomenology. Pittsburgh, 1967.

Phil 3450.19.253   Kockelmans, Joseph John. Martin Heidegger. Pittsburgh, 1965.

Phil 583.8   Kockelmans, Joseph John. Phenomenology and physical science. Pittsburgh, 1966.

Phil 583.8.5   Kockelmans, Joseph John. Phenomenology and the natural sciences: essays and translations. Evanston, 1970.

Phil 4803.454.60   Kodeks prawodawstwa społecznego absolutnego. (Hoene-Wroński, Józef Maria.) Warszawa, 1923.

Phil 5374.33   Kodis, J. Zur Analyse des Apperceptions begriffes. Berlin, 1893.

Phil 3808.89.5   Koeber, R. von. Die Philosophie Arthur Schopenhauers. Heidelberg, 1888.

Phil 3808.89   Koeber, R. von. Schopenhauer's Erlösungslehre. Leipzig, 1881?

Phil 3415.91.5   Koeber, Raphael. Das philosophische System Eduard von Hartmann's. Breslau, 1884.

Phil 8411.26   Koebner, R. Vom Schönen und seiner Wahrheit. Berlin, 1957.

Phil 4580.31   Køffding, Harald. Formel logik. København, 1884.

Phil 3565.124   Kögel, Fritz. Lotzes Aesthetik. Göttingen, 1886.

Phil 8590.12   Köhler, Friedrich. Kulturwege und Erkenntnisse. Leipzig, 1916. 2v.

Phil 1540.1   Koehler, H.O. Realismus und Nominalismus. Gotha, 1858.

Phil 8590.37   Koehler, Hans. Theologische Anthropologie; die biblische Sicht des Menschen und der Mensch der Gegenwart. München, 1967.

Phil 19.10   Köhler, M.F. Jahrbücher der Philosophie. Berlin, 1913. 3v.

Phil 3552.263   Köhler, Paul. Der Begriff der Repräsentation bei Leibniz. Bern, 1913.

Phil 8590.14   Köhler, R. Der Begriff a priori in der modernen Religionsphilosophie. Leipzig, 1920.

Phil 3492.36   Köhler, W. Kant. Berlin, 1913.

Phil 8599.19.109   Köhler, Walther. Ernst Troeltsch. Tübingen, 1941.

Phil 341.7   Köhler, Watther. Geist und Freiheit. Tübingen, 1914.

Phil 5250.15.16   Köhler, Wolfgang. Dynamics in psychology. N.Y., 1940.

Phil 5250.15.17   Köhler, Wolfgang. Dynamische Zusammenhänge in der Psychologie. Bern, 1958.

Phil 5250.15.11   Köhler, Wolfgang. Gestalt psychology. N.Y., 1929.

Phil 5250.15.15   Köhler, Wolfgang. Gestalt psychology. N.Y., 1929.

Phil 5250.15.15.10

Phil 5250.15.15.5   Köhler, Wolfgang. Gestalt psychology. N.Y., 1947.

Phil 5820.4.15   Köhler, Wolfgang. Gestalt psychology. N.Y., 1947.

  Köhler, Wolfgang. L'intelligence des singes supérieurs. Paris, 1927.

Phil 5820.4.10   Köhler, Wolfgang. Intelligenzprüfungen an Menschenaffen. 2. Aufl. Berlin, 1921.

Phil 5820.4.5   Köhler, Wolfgang. The mentality of apes. London, 1925.

Phil 735.118.2   Köhler, Wolfgang. The place of value in a world of facts. N.Y., 1959.

Phil 5250.15.18   Köhler, Wolfgang. The task of Gestalt psychology. Princeton, 1969.

NEDL Phil 497.2.9   Köhlerglaube und Wissenschaft...Wagner. (Vogt, C.) Giessen, 1856.

Phil 9495.160.15   Koehn-Behrens, Charlotte. Eros at bay; the illusion of modern love. London, 1962.

Phil 185.80   Koelbel, Gerhard. Über die Einsamkeit. München, 1960.

Phil 3085.6.85   Koelker, A. Alardus Amstelredamus en Cornelius Crocus. Nijmegen, 1963.

Phil 5627.86   Köllner, G. Histoire de la vie et de la conversion de Guillaume Köllner. Geneve, 1823.

Phil 1540.92   Koelner Mediaevistentagung. Universalismus und Partikularismus in Mittelalter. Berlin, 1968.

Phil 270.15   Koenig, E. Entwickelung des Casualproblems. Leipzig, 1888.

Phil 5643.121   Koenig, E. Experimentelle Beiträge zur Theorie des binokularen Einfach- und Tefensehens. Meisenheim, 1962.

Phil 3492.8   König, E. Kant und die Naturwissenschaft. Braunschweig, 1907.

Phil 185.8   Koenig, E. La science du vrai. Paris, 1844.

Phil 3915.85   König, Edmund. Wilhelm Wundt. Stuttgart, 1901.

Phil 3915.85.5   König, Edmund. Wilhelm Wundt als Psycholog und als Philosoph. Stuttgart, 1902.

Phil 3492.43   Koenig, Ernst. Arzt und Ärztliches bei Kant. Kitzingen, 1954.

Phil 185.63   König, J. Sein und Denken. Halle, 1937.

Phil 5250.21   König, Josef. Der Begriff der Intuition. Halle, 1926.

Phil 8590.4   Koenig, Julius. Religion a curse! Why? N.Y., 1915.

Phil 6315.2.315   Koenig, K. Die Schicksale Sigmund Freuds und J. Breners. Stuttgart, 1962.

Phil 575.29   König, Karl. Rhythmus, Religic.., Persönlichkeit. Jena, 1908.

Phil 3415.101   König, N. Die metaphysische Begründung der Ethik in Eduard von Hartmanns philosophischen System. Leipzig, 1910.

Phil 8120.5   König, René. Die naturalistische Asthetik in Frankreich und ihre Auflösung. Leipzig, 1930.

Phil 8120.4   König, René. Die naturalitistische Asthetik in Frankreich und ihre Auflösung. Borna, 1931.

Phil 5250.14   Königbauer, J. Grundzüge der Psychologie und Logik. 2. Aufl. Regensburg, 1893.

Phil 7082.182   Das Königreich der Träume. (Pongracz, Marion.) Wien, 1963.

Phil 3492.21   Königsberg. Universität. Immanuel Kant. Leipzig, 1924.

Phil 3492.41   Königsberg Universität. Zur Erinnerung an Immanuel Kant. Halle, 1904.

Phil 8677.18   Können wir ohne Gottesglauben Leben? (Werfel, Franz.) Berlin, 1932.

Phil 9495.129   Kønsmoral og livslykke. 3. opl. (Muller, J.P.) København, 1910.

Phil 185.48   Köppen, Friedrich. Darstellung des Wesens der Philosophie. Nürnberg, 1810.

Htn Phil 3801.494*   Köppen, Friedrich. Schellingslehre. Hamburg, 1803.

Phil 3801.494.2   Köppen, Friedrich. Schellingslehre. Hamburg, 1803.

Phil 5820.1   Körner, F. Instinkt und freier Wille. Leipzig, 1875.

Phil 5820.1.5   Körner, F. Instinkt und freier Wille. 2. Aufl. Leipzig, 1878.

Phil 5250.9   Körner, F. Die Seele und ihre Thätigkeiten. 2. Aufl. Leipzig, 1890.

Phil 485.1.5   Körner, F. Thierseele und Menschengeist. Leipzig, 1872.

Phil 8885.8   Koerner, H.J.A. Natur-Ethik. Hamburg, 1873. 2v.

Phil 3255.81   Körner, Hermann. Studien zur geistesgeschichtlichen Stellung S. Francks. Breslau, 1935.

Phil 5627.230   Koerner, Margot. Religionspsychopathologische Untersuchungen. Mainz, 1959.

Phil 5080.6   Koerner, S. Conceptual thinking. Cambridge, Eng., 1955.

Phil 5075.8   Koerner, Stephan. Categorical frameworks. Oxford, 1970.

Phil 3492.44   Körner, Stephan. Kant. Harmondsworth, 1955.

Phil 3492.44.5   Koerner, Stephan. Kant. Harmondsworth, 1960.

Phil 185.104   Koerner, Stephan. What is philosophy? London, 1969.

Phil 7069.62.25   Koervey, E.M. Wege Zum Licht; Erlebnisse und Gespräche mit mystikern. Garmisch-Partenkirchen, 1962.

Phil 6128.27   Körper und Geist. (Scheffler, H.) Braunschweig, 1862.

Phil 5710.18   Körperbau und Charakter. (Kretschmer, Ernst.) Berlin, 1961.

Phil 6125.20   Körperbau und Charakter. Inaug. Diss. (Polen, Laura.) Leipzig, 1928.

Phil 6120.8   Körperbau und Charakter. 3. Aufl. (Kretschmer, E.) Berlin, 1922.

Phil 5710.16   Körperbau und Charakter. 20. Aufl. (Kretschmer, Ernst.) Berlin, 1951.

Phil 298.2   Das Körpergesetz. (Rosley, Carl.) San Francisco, 19- .

Phil 5400.16   Das körperliche Gefühl. (Kröner, E.) Breslau, 1887.

Phil 5251.20.9   Die körperlichen Ausserungen psychischer Zustände. (Lehmann, Alfred.) Leipzig, 1899-1905. 4v.

Phil 6951.25   Körperliches Kranksein als Folge seelischer Gleichgewichtsstörungen. (Boss, M.) Bern, 1940.

Phil 6328.10.10   Das Körperschema...Bewusstsein des eigenen Körpers. (Schilder, Paul.) Berlin, 1923.

Phil 3450.18.190   Koerschgen, Hans. Über die Raumlehre Nicolai Hartmanns und ihre Bezlehungen zur modernen Mathematik und Physik. Köln, 1959?

Phil 2805.94   Köster, Adolph. Die Ethik Pascal. Tübingen, 1907.

Phil 2805.94.3   Köster, Adolph. Die Ethik Pascal. Inaug.-Diss. Tübingen, 1908.

Phil 3492.24   Köster, Adolph. Der Junge Kant. Berlin, 1914.

Phil 5465.137   Koestler, Arthur. The act of creation. London, 1964.

Phil 5465.137.5   Koestler, Arthur. The act of creation. N.Y., 1964.

Phil 5250.80   Koestler, Arthur. The ghost in the machine. London, 1967.

Phil 8411.3   Köstlin, K. Asthetik. pt.1-2. Tübingen, 1869.

Phil 8411.3.5   Köstlin, K. Prolegomena zur Asthetik. Tübingen, 1889.

Phil 8835.1   Köstlin, K.R. Geschichte der Ethik. Tübingen, 1887.

Phil 3425.235   Köstlin, K.R. Hegel. Tübingen, 1870.

Phil 3246.270   Koestlin, Karl. Fichte; ein Lebensbild. Tübingen, 1862.

Phil 5250.7.10   Koffka, K. Beiträge zur Psychologie der Gestalt. Leipzig, 1919.

Phil 5250.7.19   Koffka, K. Principles of Gestalt psychology. London, 1935.

Phil 5250.7.15   Koffka, K. Principles of Gestalt psychology. N.Y., 1935.

Phil 5250.7   Koffka, K. Zur Analyse der Vorstellungen und ihre Gesetze. Leipzig, 1912.

Phil 396.22   Kofler, Leo. Perspektiven des revolutionären Humanismus. Reinbek, 1968.

Phil 8430.89   Kofman, Sarah. L'enfance de l'art. Paris, 1970.

Phil 4710.140   Kogan, Iu.Ia. Ocherki po istorii russkoi ateisticheskoi mysli XVIII v. Moskva, 1962.

Phil 4761.4.80   Kogan, Iu.Ia. Prosvetitel' XVIII veka Ia.P. Kozel'skii. Moskva, 1958.

Phil 4710.148   Kogan, Leonid A. Krepostnye vol'nodumtsy, XIX vek. Moskva, 1966.

Phil 8411.38.5   Kogan, Lev Naumovich. Iskusstvo i my. Moskva, 1970.

Phil 8411.38   Kogan, Lev Naumovich. Khudozhestvennyi vkus. Moskva, 1966.

Phil 5620.22   Kogan, Zuce. Essentials in problem solving. Chicago, 1951.

Phil 5875.30   Die kognitive Orientierung des Kindes. (Kreitler, Hans.) München, 1967.

Phil 4762.1.39   Kohanskii, A.S. Lossky's theory of knowledge. Nashville, 1936.

Phil 5649.25   Kohl, Kurt. Zum Problem der Sensumotorik. Frankfurt, 1956.

Phil 3640.161   Kohler, F.P. Friedrich Nietzsche. Leipzig, 1921.

Phil 5643.27   Kohler, J. Der simultane Farben- und Helligkeitskontrast. Leipzig, 1903.

Phil 2523.90   Kohler, Oskar. Die Logik des Destutt de Tracy. Inaug.-Diss. Borna, 1931.

Phil 3910.128   Kohlmeyer, Ernst. Kosmos und Kosmonomie bei Christian Wolff. Göttingen, 1911.

Phil 2138.84   Kohn, Benno. Untersuchungen über das Causalproblem. Wien, 1881.

Phil 720.42   Kohn, David. More than truth. N.Y., 1956.

Phil 5330.2   Kohn, H.E. Zur Theorie der Aufmerksamkeit. Halle, 1894.

Phil 3120.30.85.2   Kohn, Hans. Martin Buber, sein Werk und seine Zeit. Köln, 1961.

Phil 3120.30.85   Kohn, Hans. Martin Buber. Hellerau, 1930.

Phil 6320.7   Kohnstamm, O. Erscheinungsformen der Seele. München, 1927.

Phil 8411.9   Kohnstamm, O. Kunst als Ausdruckstätigkeit; biologische Voraussetzungen der ästhetik. München, 1907.

Phil 5760.13   Kohnstamm, Philipp A. Vrije wil of determinisme. Haarlem, 1947.

X Cg Phil 3850.1.96   Kohut, Adolph. David Friedrich Strauss als Denker und Erzieher. Leipzig, 1908.

Phil 3235.109   Kohut, Adolph. Ludwig Feuerbach, sein Leben und seine Werke. Leipzig, 1909.

Phil 2880.8.157   Kohut, Karl. Was ist Literatur? Marburg, 1965.

Phil 1124.5   He koinonikē filosofia tōn arkhaion Hellēnon. (Tsatsos, K.) Athenai, 1938.

Phil 1810.3   Koitko, D. Iu. Ocherki sovremennoi anglo-amerikanskoi filosofii. Moskva, 1936.

Phil 850.45   Koje've, Alexandre. Essai d'une histoire raisonnée de la philosophie païenne. Paris, 1968.

Phil 3425.321.10   Kojève, Alexandre. Hegel; eine Vergegenwäitigung. Stuttgart, 1958.

Phil 3425.321   Kojève, Alexandre. Introduction à la lecture de Hegel. Paris, 1947.

Phil 3425.321.5   Kojève, Alexandre. Introduction to the reading of Hegel. N.Y., 1969.

Phil 3801.493   Koktanek, A.M. Schellings erste münchner Vorlesung. Inaug. Diss. München, 1959.

Phil 3801.496   Koktanek, A.M. Schellings Seinslehre und Kierkegaard. München, 1962.

Phil 165.365   Koktanek, Anton Mirko. Philosophischer Eros im Wandel der Zeit. München, 1965.

Phil 3830.7   Kołakowski, L. Jednostka i mieskończono. Warszawa, 1958.

Phil 600.59.5   Kołakowski, Leszek. The alienation of reason; a history of positivist thought. Garden City, N.Y., 1968.

Phil 600.59   Kołakowski, Leszek. Filozofia pozytywistyczna. Warszawa, 1966.

Phil 3492.30   Kolb, Victor. Immanuel Kant: der modernen Zeit. 2. Aufl. Wien, 1919.

Phil 8980.495.5 — Kolbanovskii, Viktor N. Kommunisticheskaia moral' i byt. Moskva, 1955.

Phil 365.19.60 — Kolbe, F.C. A Catholic view of holism. N.Y., 1928.

Phil 3255.82 — Kolbenheyer, Christiane. Die Mystik des Sebastian Franck von Wörd. Inaug-Diss. Würzburg, 1935.

Phil 185.40 — Kolbenheyer, E.G. Die Bauhütte. München, 1925.

Phil 185.40.5 — Kolbenheyer, E.G. Die Philosophie de Bauhütte. Wien, 1952.

Phil 5643.58 — Kolbenheyer, E.G. Die sensorielle Theorie der optischen Raumempfindung. Leipzig, 1905.

Phil 5620.32 — Kolenda, K. The freedom of reason. San Antonio, 1964.

Phil 5585.260 — Kolers, Paul A. Recognizing patterns; studies in living and automatic systems. Cambridge, 1968.

Phil 310.495 — Kolianskii, N.N. Mir i dusha. Frankfurt am Main? 1953.

Phil 6320.3 — Kollarits, Jenö. Charakter und Nervosität. Berlin, 1912.

Phil 4803.495.220 — Kollataj, Hugo. Porządek fizyczno-moralny oraz Pomysty do dzieta Porządek fizyczno-moralny. Warszawa, 1955.

Phil 3640.340 — Kollektivistisches in der Philosophie Nietzsches. (Brin, Slata G.R.) Basel, 1948.

Phil 3210.69 — Kollektivmasslehre. (Fechner, G.T.) Leipzig, 1897.

Phil 8411.40 — Kollen, Horace Meyer. Liberty, laughter, and tears. De Kalb, 1968.

Phil 5425.62 — Koller, A.H. The Abbé Du Bos - his advocacy of the theory of climate. Champaign, 1937.

Phil 3552.259 — Kolls. Zur Chronologie der leibnizischen Abhandlung "De vera methodo philosphiae et theologiae". Schönberg, 1906.

Phil 3120.2.110 — Kolman, E. Bernard Bol'tsano. Moskva, 1955.

Phil 3120.2.112 — Kolman, E. Bernard Bolzano. Berlin, 1963.

Phil 185.32 — Kolmark P. Utkast til en systematisk afhandling i theoretiska och practiska philosophien. Stockholm, 1799.

Phil 9495.130.10 — Kolnai, Aurel. Sexualethik. Paderborn, 1930.

Phil 960.253 — Komarov, N. Ideologicheskie techeniia sovremennoi Indii. Moskva, 1965.

Phil 291.11 — Komarov, V.N. Kosmos, log i vechnost' mira. Moskva, 1963.

Phil 270.150 — Komarov, Viktor N. Zagadka budushchego. Moskva, 1971.

Phil 850.50 — Komarova, Vera Ia. K tekstologicheskomu analizn antichnoi filosofi. Leningrad, 1969.

Phil 5525.72 — Komicheskoe. (Borev, Iurii B.) Moskva, 1970.

Phil 5525.13 — Komik und Humor. (Lipps, T.) Hamburg, 1898.

Phil 5525.8 — Das Komische. (Ueberhorst, K.) Leipzig, 1896-1900. 2v.

Phil 5525.33 — Das Komische. (Ziegler, J.) Leipzig, 1900.

Phil 55.5 — Komisya do badania historji filozofji w Polsce archivum. (Polska Akademia Umiejętności.) Krakowie. 1-6,1915-1935 5v.

Phil 5520.628 — Komlev, Nikolai G. Komponenty soderzhatel'noi struktury slova. Moskva, 1969.

Phil 3425.265A — Kommentar zu den grundlegenden Abschnitten von Hegels Phänomenologie des Geistes. (Nink, Caspar.) Regensburg, 1931.

Phil 3484.2.15 — Kommentar zu Immanuel Kant's Kritik. (Cohen, H.) Leipzig, 1907.

Phil 3484.2.16A — Kommentar zu Immanuel Kant's Kritik. 2. Aufl. (Cohen, H.) Leipzig, 1917.

Phil 3484.2.17 — Kommentar zu Immanuel Kant's Kritik. 3. Aufl. (Cohen, H.) Leipzig, 1920.

Phil 3494.13.20 — Kommentar zu Kants ethischen und religionsphilosophischen Hauptschriften. (Messer, A.) Leipzig, 1929.

Phil 3484.13 — Kommentar zu Kant's Kritik der reinen Vernunft. (Cornelius, Hans.) Erlangen, 1926.

Phil 3494.13.15 — Kommentar zu Kants Kritik der reinen Vernunft. (Messer, A.) Stuttgart, 1923.

Phil 3495.12 — Kommentar zu Kants Kritik der reinen Vernunft. (Nink, Casper.) Frankfurt, 1930.

Phil 3503.1.2 — Kommentar zu Kants Kritik der reinen Vernunft. 2. Aufl. (Vaihinger, H.) Stuttgart, 1922. 2v.

Phil 3482.5.5 — Kommentar zu Kants Prologomena. (Apel, Max.) Leipzig, 1923.

Phil 3482.5.3 — Kommentar zu Kants "Prologomena". (Apel, Max.) Schöneberg, 1908.

Phil 3837.15 — Kommentar zu Spinozas Ethik. v.1-2. (Robinson, Lewis.) Leipzig, 1928.

Phil 8980.180 — Kommunist nravstvennost'. (Avraamov, D.) Moskva, 1963.

Phil 310.628 — Kommunisticheskaia Akademiia, Moscow. Institut Filosofii. Materialy nauchnoi sessii. Moskva, 1934.

Phil 8980.495.5 — Kommunisticheskaia moral' i byt. (Kolbanovskii, Viktor N.) Moskva, 1955.

Phil 8980.329 — Kommunisticheskaia moral' i voinskii dolg. (Dmitrenko, A.P.) Moskva, 1960.

Phil 8980.572.15 — Kommunisticheskaia moral' i voinskii dolg. (Milovidov, Arsenii S.) Moskva, 1971.

Phil 8980.386 — Kommunisticheskaia nravntvennost'. (Fedorenko, I.H.) Kiev, 1958.

Phil 310.608 — Kommunisticheskaia Partiia. Sovetskogo Soiuza. Zaochnaia Vysshaia Partiinaia Shkola. Katedra Marksistsko-Leninskoi Filosofii. Marksistsko-leninskaia filosofiia. Moskva, 1965.

Phil 8980.616 — Kommunisticheskaia Partiia Sovetskogo Soiuza. Novosibirskaia Vysshaia Partiinaia Shkola. Kategorii marksistsko-leninskoi etiki. Moskva, 1965.

Phil 8980.850 — Kommunisticheskii ideal i nravstvennoe razvitie lichnosti. (Tselikova, Ol'ga P.) Moskva, 1970.

Phil 8980.275.10 — Kommunistychnyi ideal i diisnist'. (Chevkashyn, D.S.) Kharkiv, 1970.

Phil 8980.495.10 — Kommunizm i lichnost! Moskva, 1964.

Phil 9245.140 — Kommunizm i problema schast'ia. (Korneva, Mariia N.) Moskva, 1970.

Phil 3745.18 — Die Komödie der Wahrheit. 10 essays. (Perls, Hugo.) Bern, 1967.

Phil 310.654 — Kompaneets, Aleksei I. Leninskaia filosofiia i progress fizicheskikh nauk. Moskva, 1967.

X Cg Phil 8961.1 — Kompendium der theologischen Moral. (Less, G.) Göttingen, 1767.

Phil 5066.172 — Kompleksnaia logika. (Zinov'ev, Aleksandr A.) Moskva, 1970.

Phil 6319.1.181 — Komplex. (Jacobi, Jolan.) Zürich. 1957.

Phil 5585.34 — Komplextheorie und Gestalttheorie. (Müller, Georg E.) Göttingen, 1923.

Phil 5520.628 — Komponenty soderzhatel'noi struktury slova. (Komlev, Nikolai G.) Moskva, 1969.

Phil 9065.3 — Der Kompromiss als ethisches Problem. (Steubing, Hans.) Gütersloh, 1955.

Phil 9065.4 — Der Kompromiss als Problem der Gesellschaft. (Joehr, W.A.) Tübingen, 1958.

Phil 8980.495 — Kon, I.S. Moral kommunisticheskaia i moral' burzhvaznaia. Moskva, 1960. 2 pam.

Phil 8171.100.5 — Konan, Uladzimir M. Demokraticheskaia estetika Belorussi (1905-1917 gg). Minsk, 1971.

Phil 8171.100 — Konan, Uladzimir M. Razvitstsio estetychnai dumki u Belarusi. Minsk, 1968.

Phil 4800.22.10 — Koncepcja nauki w pozytywizmie polskim. (Skarbek, Janusz.) Wrocław, 1968.

Phil 5760.9 — Konczewska, H. Contingence, liberté et la personnalité humaine. Paris, 1937.

Phil 5760.9.5 — Konczewska, H. Contingence, liberté et la personnalité humaine. Thèse. Paris, 1937.

Phil 185.62 — Konczewska, H. Le problème de la substance. Paris, 1937.

Phil 5250.33 — Konczewski, C. La pensée préconsciente. Paris, 1939.

Phil 5520.658 — Konczewski, C. La psychologie dynamique et la pensée vécue. Paris, 1970.

Phil 5004.1 — Kondakov, Nikolai I. Logicheskii slovar'. Moskva, 1971.

Phil 5050.26 — Kondakov, Nikolai I. Vvedenie v logiku. Moskva, 1967.

Phil 410.82 — Konechnoe i beskonechnoe. (Viderskii, Vladimir I.) Moskva, 1966.

Phil 4807.4 — Konference o dějinách české filosofie, Liblice, 1958. Filosofie v dějinách českého národa. Vyd. 1. Praha, 1958.

Phil 5425.106 — Konferentsiia po Problemam Sposobnostei, Leningrad, 1960. Problemy sposobnostei. Moskva, 1962.

Phil 176.69.80 — Konferenz über Fragen der Blochschen Philosophie. Ernst Blochs Revision des Marxismus. Berlin, 1957.

Phil 8622.12 — Der Konflikt. (Jakob, J.) Basel, 1952.

Phil 193.59.20A — Der Konflikt der modernen Kultur. 2. Aufl. (Simmel, G.) München, 1921.

Phil 5251.53 — Konflikt-Psychologie. (Lückert, Heinz Rolf.) München, 1957.

Phil 5477.14 — Konflikt und Entscheidung. (Hövmann, H.) Göttingen, 1960.

Phil 5593.63.5 — Konflikt und Konfliktschicksal. (Brückner, Peter.) Bern, 1963.

Phil 8409.3 — Konflikti v estetichnogo. (Iastrebova, Nataliia.) Sofiia, 1964.

Phil 5365.4 — Konfliktmtivation und Examen. (Fisch, Rudolf.) Meisenheim am Glan, 1970.

Phil 815.4 — Konformismus eine Philosophie der normatwen Werte. (Pfordten, Otto.) Heidelberg, 1910-13.

Phil 70.98 — Kongres Psihologa Jugoslavije, 2d, Zagerb, 1964. Materijali. Zagreb, 1964.

Phil 8960.15 — Kongress der Deutschsprachigen Moraltheologen, Freiburg, Germany, 1963. Moraltheologie und Bibel. Paderborn, 1964.

Phil 70.9 — Kongress für Experimentelle Psychologie. Bericht. Jena. 10,1927

Phil 70.15 — Kongress für Synthetische Lebensforschung. Verhandlungsbericht. Prag, 1937.

Phil 5643.29 — Konig, Arthur. Gesammelte Abhandlungen der physiologischen Optik. Leipzig, 1903.

Phil 5050.11 — Konig, Julius. Neue Grundlagen der Logik Arithmetic. Leipzig, 1914.

Phil 2045.126 — Konijnenburg, Willem van. Thomas Hobbes' Leviathan. Proefschrift. Assen, 1945.

Phil 310.90 — Konimunisticheskaia Partiia Sovetskogo Soiuza Vysshaia Partiinaia Shkola. Kajedra dialektiki i istoricheskogo materializme. Moskva. 1-3,1958-1963+ 3v.

Phil 8893.120 — Konkrete Ethik. (Schoellgen, W.) Düsseldorf, 1961.

Phil 8980.496 — Kononenko, E.V. O krasote dushevnoi. Moskva, 1959.

Phil 6120.24 — Konorski, Jerzy. Integrative activity of the brain; an interdisciplinary approach. Chicago, 1967.

Phil 8879.35 — Konsequenzen der Naturwissenschaft. (Elken, Robert.) Kassel, 1963.

Phil 5756.12 — Die Konsequenzen und Inkonsequenzen des Determinismus. (Groos, Helmut.) München, 1931.

Phil 585.315 — Konservative Evolution. (Riedweg, Franz.) München, 1968.

Phil 8586.36.65 — Konservative politische Romantik. (Strohm, Theodor.) Berlin, 1961.

Phil 5238.238 — Konspekt lektsii po psikhologii. v.3. (El'kin, David G.) Odessa, 1966.

Phil 3270.8.80 — Konstantin Frantz' Jugendjahre und erste Schriften. (Stamm, E.) Heidelberg, 1907.

Phil 310.9A — Konstantinov, F.V. Istoricheskii materializm. Izd. 2. Moskva, 1954.

Phil 8412.15 — Konsten och tiden. (Lindholm, C.) Stockholm, 1950.

Phil 8419.60 — Konstforskning. (Sandstroem, Sven.) Stockholm, 1965.

Phil 978.49.615 — Die Konstitution der Allgemeinen anthroposophischen Gesellschaft und der freien Hochschule. (Steiner, R.) Dornach, 1966.

Phil 3450.11.450 — Die Konstitution des transzendenten Etevas im Vollzug des Sehens. (Wewel, Meinolf.) Düsseldorf, 1968.

Phil 3160.10.90 — Konstitution und Gegenstand im logistischen Neuposivitismus Rudolf Carnaps. Inaug. Diss. (Burg, Josef.) Leipzig, 1933.

Phil 3850.18.135 — Konthock, K. Max Scheler. Berlin, 1934.

Phil 3489.16 — Kontinuiteten i Kants filosofiske udviklingsgang. (Høffding, H.) Kjøbenhavn, 1893.

Phil 1845.3.100 — Konvitz, Milton R. On the nature of value; the philosophy of Samuel Alexander. N.Y., 1946.

Phil 1504.11.6 — Der Konzeptualismus. v.11, pt.6. (Dreiling, R.) Münster, 1913.

Phil 8090.10 — Koopmann, Helmut. Beiträge zur Theorie der Künste im 19. Jahrhundert. Frankfurt, 1971-

Phil 310.335 — Kopnin, P.V. Dialektika kak logika. Kiev, 1961.

Phil 5250.75 — Kopnin, P.V. Problemy myshleniia v sovremennoi nauke. Moskva, 1964.

Phil 1810.6 — Kopnin, Pavel V. Sovremennaia burzhuaznaia filosofiia SShA. Kiev, 1966.

Phil 310.639 — Kopnin, Pavel V. Vvedenie v marksistskuiu gnoseologiia. Kiev, 1966.

Phil 2905.1.140 — Kopp, Josef Vital. Entstehung und Zukunft des Menschen. Luzern, 1961.

Phil 3552.89 — Koppehl, H. Die Verwandtschaft Leibizens mit Thomas von Aquino. Jena, 1892.

Phil 8590.25 — Koppelmann, W. Der Erlösungs- und Heilsgedanke von freisinnig protestantischen Standpunkt. Bonn, 1925.

Phil 3492.9 — Koppelmann, W. Die Ethic Kants. Berlin, 1907.

Phil 8885.12 — Koppelmann, W. Kritik des sittlichen Bewusstzeins vom philosophische und historische Standpunkt. Berlin, 1904.

Phil 5050.9 — Koppelmann, W. Untersuchungen zur Logik Gegenwart. Berlin, 1913-18. 2v.

Phil 185.26 — Koppelmann, W. Weltanschauungsfragen. 2e Aufl. Berlin, 1922.

Phil 810.15 — Kopper, J. Reflexion und Raisonnement im ontologischen Gottesbeweis. Köln, 1962.

Phil 5190.35 — Korchyns'ka, H. Try abo chotyry zakony diialektyky. Miunkhen, 1964.

Phil 5170.13 — Korcik, Antoni. Teoriia sylogizmu zdań asertorycznych u azystotelesa. Lublin, 1948.

Phil 2100.4.30 — Koren, H.J. An introduction to the philosophy of animate nature. St. Louis, 1955.

Phil 291.8.5   Koren, Henry. An introduction to the philosophy of nature. Pittsburg, 1960.

Phil 291.8   Koren, Henry. Readings in the philosophy of nature. Westminster, Md., 1958.

Phil 4803.799.25   Korespondencja Jana Śniadeckiego; listy z Krakowa. (Śniadecki, Jan.) Krakow, 1932-54. 2v.

Phil 5250.12.3   Korfattet taenke-og sjaelelaere. 3. udg. (Kroman, Kristian.) København, 1899.

Phil 5250.12   Korfattet taenke-og sjaelelaere. 5. udg. (Kroman, Kristian.) København, 1914.

Phil 9560.60   Korff, Wilhelm. Ehre, Prestige, Gewissen. Köln, 1966.

Phil 4972.5.20   Korn, Alejandro. De San Agustín a Bergson. Buenos Aires, 1959.

Phil 4972.5.10   Korn, Alejandro. Ensayos críticos. Buenos Aires, 193-.

Phil 1710.16   Korn, Alejandro. Estudios de filosofía contemporánea. 1st ed. Buenos Aires, 1963.

Phil 4972.5.15   Korn, Alejandro. Obras. La Plata, 1938-40. 3v.

Phil 4972.5.5   Korn, Alejandro. Obras completas. Buenos Aires, 1949.

Phil 4960.250   Korn, Alejandro. El pensamiento argentino. Buenos Aires, 1961.

VPhil 1135.191   Kornatowski, Wiktor. Zarys driejów mysli politycznej starożytnosii. Wyd. 1. Warsawa, 1968.

Phil 5068.28   Korneeva, Anna I. Kritika neopoz, vzgliadov na prizodu poznaniia. Moskva, 1962.

Phil 5068.29   Korneeva, Anna I. Leninskaia kritika malchizma i bor'ba protiv sovremennogo idealizma. Moskva, 1971.

Phil 9245.140   Korneva, Mariia N. Kommunizm i problema schast'ia. Moskva, 1970.

Phil 3625.1.139   Kornfeld, H. Moses Mendelssohn und die Aufgabe der Philosophie. Berlin, 1896.

Phil 8411.16   Kornfeld, M. L'énigme du beau. Paris, 1942.

Phil 8411.30   Kornienko, V.S. O sushchnosti esteticheskogo poznaniia. Novosibirsk, 1962.

Phil 8411.42   Kornienko, Vasilii S. O zakonakh krasoty. Khar'kov, 1970.

Phil 5250.35   Kornilov, K.N. Psikhologiia. Moskva, 1941.

Phil 5250.35.2   Kornilov, K.N. Psikhologiia. Moskva, 1946.

Phil 5250.35.3   Kornilov, K.N. Psikhologiia. Izd. 8. Moskva, 1948.

Phil 8885.18.20   Koröman, Kristian. Begrebet "det etiske". København, 1903.

Phil 8885.18.5   Koröman, Kristian. Ethik. Leipzig, 1904.

Phil 730.35   Korotkova, Galina P. Printsipy tselostnosti. Leningrad, 1968.

Phil 5850.228   Korrelation oder Wertigkeit? Inaug. Diss. (Helke, J.W.) Leipzig, 1935.

Phil 5243.19   Korrelative Beziehungen zwischen Elementarenvergleichsleistungen. Inaug. Diss. (Damm, Hermann.) Leipzig, 1914.

Phil 1705.4.8   Kort inledning till nyare filosofia historia. (Fischer, K.) Stockholm, 1866.

Phil 4580.35.7   Kort oversigt over den nyere filosofis historie. 7e ed. (Høffding, Harald.) Kjøbenhavn, 1919.

Phil 4580.35.9   Kort oversigt over den nyere filosofis historie. 9e ed. (Høffding, Harald.) Kjøbenhavn, 1925.

Phil 107.1   Kort woordenboek van wijsgeerige kunstlermen. (Wynaendts Francken, C.J.) Haarlem 1925.

Phil 3822.4.10   Korte, dog waaragtige levens-beschrijving van Benedictus de Spinoza. (Colerus, Johannes.) Amsterdam, 1705[1910]

Phil 3819.40   Korte verhandeling van God. (Spinoza, Benedictus de.) Amsterdam, 1869.

Phil 818.10   Kortfattet fremstilling ad filosofiens historie. 3. Opl. (Scholten, J.H.) Kjøbenhavn, 1886.

Phil 5253.7   Kortfattet sjaelelaere. (Naesgaard, S.) København, 1919.

Phil 5253.7.2   Kortfattet sjaelelaere. (Naesgaard, S.) København, 1928.

Phil 1810.1   Kortholti, C. De tribus impostoribus magnis liber. Hamburgi, 1701.

Phil 6114.9   Die kortikalen Erregungen. (Ebbecke, Ulrich.) Leipzig, 1919.

Phil 185.42   Kortmulder, R.J. Metaphysicia der rede. Amsterdam, 1925.

Phil 6320.4   Kortsen, K.K. De psykiske spaltninger. København, 1916.

Phil 2070.93   Kortsen, K.K. William James' filosofi. København, n.d.

Phil 185.45   Korzybski, A. Time-binding; the general theory. N.Y., 1924. 2 pam.

Phil 5520.96.15   Korzybski, Alfred. General semantics seminar, 1937. 2. ed. Lakeville, Conn., 1964.

Phil 5520.96.10   Korzybski, Alfred. Science and sanity. Lakeville, Conn., 1933.

Phil 5520.96.01   Pamphlet box. Korzybski, Alfred. Language and thought.

Phil 310.255   Kosanović, I. Dijalektički materijalizam. 4. vyd. Sarajevo, 1959.

Phil 310.256   Kosanović, I. Istoriski materijalizam. 3. izd. Sarajevo, 1960.

Phil 3549.30   Kosegarten, Chritian. Memnens Bildsäule in Briefen au Ida von Kosegarten. Berlin, 1799.

Phil 310.585   Kosichev, A.D. Bor'ba marksizma-leninizma s ideologiei anarkhizma i sovremennost'. Moskva, 1964.

Phil 310.599.2   Kosík, Karel. Dialektika konkrétního. 2. Vyd. Praha, 1965.

Phil 978.49.155   Kosmische und menschliche Geschichte. (Steiner, R.) Dornach, 1933-34. 5v.

Phil 978.49.157   Kosmische und menschliche Geschichte. (Steiner, R.) Dornach, 1964. 4v.

Phil 299.32   Das kosmische Weltbild. (Sterneder, Hans.) Freiburg, 1969.

Phil 1135.28   Die kosmischen Systeme der Griechen. (Gruppe, O.F.) Berlin, 1851.

Phil 285.1   Kosmogonie. (Ehrenfils, C.) Jena, 1916.

Phil 282.6   Kosmologische Gedanken. (Baratsch, W.) Leipzig, 1911.

Phil 282.6.2   Kosmologische Gedanken. 2. ed. (Baratsch, W.) Leipzig, 1912.

Phil 291.11   Kosmos, log i vechnost' mira. (Komarov, V.N.) Moskva, 1963.

Phil 705.22   Kosmos Atheos. (Pannwitz, R.) München, 1926.

Phil 303.6   Kosmos die Weltentwickelung. (Wolff, H.) Leipzig, 1890.

Phil 4845.227.32   Ho kosmos toü pneumatos. 2. ed. (Papanoutsos, Euangelos.) Athēna, 1953-56. 3v.

Phil 285.6.5   Kosmos und Geschichte. (Eliade, Mircea.) Hamburg, 1966[1953]

Phil 3910.128   Kosmos und Kosmonomie bei Christian Wolff. (Kohlmeyer, Ernst.) Göttingen, 1911.

Phil 291.5   Kosmos und Menschenwesen im Spiegel der platonischen Körper. (Kaiser, Wilhelm.) Basel, 1930.

Phil 4803.522.80   Kosmowska, J.W. Karol Libelt jako działacz polityczny i społeczny, ur. 1807 um. 1875. Poznań, 1918.

Phil 8980.496.10   Kosolapov, S.M. Nravstvennye printsipy stroitelia kommunizma. Moskva, 1962.

Phil 8980.496.5   Kosolapov, S.M. Voprosy vospitaniia trudiashchikhsia v dukhe kommunisticheskoi nravstvennosti. Moskva, 1961.

Phil 4803.496.30   Kossak, Jerzy. Bunt na kolanach. Warszawa, 1960.

Phil 5650.32   Kostelijk, P.J. Theories of hearing. Leiden, 1950.

Phil 8672.19   Kostenne, P. La foi des athées. Paris, 1953.

Phil 5250.6   Kostyleff, N. La crise de la psychologie expérimentale. Paris, 1911.

Phil 6120.5   Kostyleff, N. Mécanisme cérébral de la pensée. Paris, 1914.

Phil 665.18   Kostyleff, Nicolas. Les substituts de l'âme. Paris, 1906.

Phil 8141.2   Kőszegi, L. Präparation zu einer Rom-zentrischen Ästhetik. Detmold, 1959.

Phil 4803.495.20   Kotakowski, Leszek. Kultura i fetysze; zbiór rozpraw. Wyd. 1. Warszawa, 1967.

Phil 4803.495.21   Kotakowski, Leszek. Traktat über die Sterblichkeit der Vernunft. München, 1967.

Phil 4803.497.35   Kotarbiński, Tabeusz. Sprawność i błąd. Warszawa, 1956.

Phil 8610.960   Kotarbiński, Tad. Przykład indywidualny kształtowania sie postawy wolnomys'licielskiej. Warszawa, 1960.

Phil 185.49   Kotarbiński, Tadeusz. Elementy. Lwów, 1929.

Phil 185.49.2   Kotarbiński, Tadeusz. Elementy teorii poznania. Wyd. 2. Wrocław, 1961.

Phil 185.49.5   Kotarbiński, Tadeusz. Gnosiology; the scientific approach to the theory of knowledge. 1. English ed. Oxford, 1966.

Phil 4803.497.30   Kotarbiński, Tadeusz. Hasło dobrej roboty. Wyd. 1. Warszawa, 1968.

Phil 5020.10   Kotarbiński, Tadeusz. Leçons sur l'histoire de la logique. Warszawa, 1965.

Phil 4803.497.45   Kotarbiński, Tadeusz. Medytacje o życiu godziwym. Warszawa, 1966.

Phil 5250.70   Kotarbiński, Tadeusz. Osnova primena prakseologije. Beograd, 1961.

Phil 5250.78   Kotarbiński, Tadeusz. Praxiology; an introduction to the sciences of efficient action. 1. English ed. Oxford, 1965.

Phil 4803.497.6   Kotarbiński, Tadeusz. Studia z zakresu filozofii, etyki i nauk społecznych. Wrocław, 1970.

Phil 5250.79.4   Kotarbiński, Tadeusz. Traktat o dobrej robocie. Wyd. 4. Wrocław, 1969.

Phil 4803.497.25   Kotarbiński, Tadeusz. Wybór pism. Warszawa, 1957-58. 2v.

Phil 4803.497.40   Kotarbiński, Tadeusz. Wykłady z dziejów logiki. Łódź, 1957.

Phil 7069.08.50   Kotik, N. Die Emanation der psychophysischen Energie. Wiesbaden, 1908.

Phil 8980.497   Kotov, L.I. Razuitie nravstvennykh ubezhdenii i privychek v protsesse kommunisticheskogo vospitaniia. Moskva, 1961.

Phil 5425.100   Kotsovsky, D. Tragödie des Genius. München, 1959.

Phil 5585.217   Kottenhoff, H. Was ist richtiges Sehen mit Umkehrbillen. Meisenheim am Glan, 1961.

Phil 3801.495   Kotzias, Nikolaos. Skellighios iti oligha tina peri ton vion ke tis filosofias aftou. Athena, 1855.

Phil 5875.75   Koupernir, Cyrille. Développement neuro-psychique du nourrisson. 1. ed. Paris, 1968.

Phil 5590.447.2   Kovalev, Aleksandr G. Psikhologiia lichnosti. 2. izd. Moskva, 1965.

Phil 8980.497.20   Kovalev, S.M. Rabotat' i zhit' po kommunisticheski. Moskva, 1961.

Phil 310.4.3   Kovalgin, V.M. Dialekticheskii materializm o zakonakh nauki. Minsk, 1958.

Phil 310.400   Kovalgin, V.M. Marksistskaia filosofiia protiv idealizma i metafiziki. Minsk, 1961.

Phil 5635.45   Kovalgin, V.M. Problema oshchushchenii i reflektornaia teoriia. Minsk, 1959.

Phil 5635.45.5   Kovalgin, V.M. Reflektornaia teoriia oskchushchenii. Minsk, 1963.

Phil 575.248   Kovály, Pavel. Americký personalismus; příspěvek k rozboru krize současného buržoazního myšlení. Praha, 1962.

Phil 3808.109A   Kowalewski, A. Arthur Schopenhauer und seine Weltanschaung. Halle, 1908.

Phil 187.52.80   Kowalewski, A. Die Philosophie des Bewusstseins von Friedrich Michelis. Berlin, 1897.

Phil 1930.4.81   Kowalewski, Arnold. Kritische Analyse von Arthur Colliers Clavis Universalis. Inaug. Diss. Griefswald, 1897.

Phil 4803.282.80   Kowalski, Kazimierz Józef. Filozofja Augusta Hr. Cieszkowskiego w świetle zasad filozofji. Poznań, 1929.

Phil 4803.497.230   Kowalski, Kazimierz Józef. Podstawy filozofji. Guiezano, 1930.

Phil 575.261   Koy, Igor S. Sotsiologiia lichnosti. Moskva, 1967.

Phil 2520.161   Koyré, A. Descartes und die Scholastik. Bonn, 1923.

Phil 2520.161.10   Koyré, A. Entretiens sur Descartes. N.Y., 1944.

Phil 2520.161.5   Koyré, A. Essai sur l'idée de Dieu...chez Descartes. Paris, 1922.

Phil 4710.2   Koyré, A. Etudes sur l'histoire de la pensée philosophique en Russie. Paris, 1950.

Phil 185.96   Koyré, Alexandre. Etudes d'histoire de la pensée philosophique. Paris, 1961.

Phil 291.7   Koyré, Alexandre. From the closed world to the infinite universe. Baltimore, 1957.

Phil 3010.8   Koyré, Alexandre. Mystiques. Paris, 1955.

Phil 3110.92   Koyré, Alexandre. La philosophie de Jacob Boehme. Thèse. Paris, 1929.

Phil 3110.92.5   Koyré, Alexandre. La philosophie de Jakob Boehme. Paris, 1929.

Phil 3255.90   Koyré, Alexandre. Sebastien Franck. Paris, 1932.

Phil 1170.17   Koytsogiannopoyloy, D.I. Hellēnikē philosophia kai christianikon dogma. Athens, 1960.

Phil 3450.19.405   Koza, Joachim. Das Problem des Grundes in Heideggers Auseinandersetzung mit Kant. Ratingen, 1967.

Phil 4809.497.30   Kozák, Jan Blahoslav. Věda a duch. Praha, 1938.

VPhil 5250.81   Kozielecki, Józef. Zagadnienia psychologii myślenia. Wyd. 1. Warszawa, 1966.

Phil 5250.29   Kozlowski, W.M. Thought considered as action and the logical axioms. N.Y., 1927.

Phil 4800.4   Kozlowski, Władysław M. Les idées françaises dans la philosophie nationale et la poésie patriotique de la Bologne. Grenoble, 1923.

Phil 4803.497.420   Kozlowski, Władysław M. Szkice filozoficzne. Warszawa, 1900.

Phil 3480.85.3   De kracht van den wil in het beheerschen van ziekelijke aandoeningen. 3. druk. (Kant, Immanuel.) Leeuwarden, 1885.

Phil 303.2   Die Kräfte der unorganischen Natur. (Werther, C.A.) Dessau, 1852.

Phil 3120.55.105   Kraenzle, Karl. Utopie und Ideologie. Bern, 1970.

Phil 400.99   Kränzlin, Gerhard. Die Philosophie vom unendlichen Menschen. Leipzig, 1936.

Phil 400.99.5   Kränzlin, Gerhard. Das System des Panhumanismus. Zürich, 1949.

Phil 6960.5.5   Kraepelin, E. Clinical psychiatry. N.Y., 1902.

Phil 6960.5.7   Kraepelin, E. Clinical psychiatry. N.Y., 1904.

Phil 6960.5.12 Kraepelin, E. Einfuhrung in die psychiatrische Klenik. Leipzig, 1905.

Phil 6960.5.11 Kraepelin, E. Einfuhrung in die psychiatrische Klenik dreissez Vorlesungen. Leipzig, 1901.

Phil 6960.5.15 Kraepelin, E. One hundred years of psychiatry. N.Y., 1962.

Phil 6960.5 Kraepelin, E. Psychiatrie. Leipzig, 1896.

Phil 6960.5.3 Kraepelin, E. Psychiatrie. Leipzig, 1909-15. 4v.

Phil 5250.18 Kraepelin, Emil. Om sjalsarbete. Stockholm, 1894.

Phil 5250.18.10 Kraepelin, Emil. Über die Beeinflussung einfacher psychischer Vorgänge durch einige Arzneimittel. Jena, 1892.

Phil 3640.202 Kräutlein, Jonathan. Friedrich Nietzsches Morallehre. Leipzig, 1926.

Phil 6680.2 Krafft-Ebing, R. von. Eine experimentelle Studie. Stuttgart, 1888.

Phil 6960.4 Krafft-Ebing, R. von. Lehrbuch der Psychiatrie. Stuttgart, 1893.

Phil 6960.4.3 Krafft-Ebing, R. von. Lehrbuch der Psychiatrie. 3. Aufl. Stuttgart, 1888.

Htn Phil 6978.12.10 Krafft-Ebing, Richard. Die Melancholie. Erlangen, 1874.

Htn Phil 7075.7.8* Krafft-Ebing, Richard von. Psychopathia sexualis. Stuttgart, 1893.

Phil 3010.5 Kraft, J. Von Husserl zu Heidegger. Leipzig, 1932.

Phil 3010.5.2 Kraft, J. Von Husserl zur Heidegger. 2. Aufl. Frankfurt, 1957.

Phil 185.55.2 Kraft, Julius. Die Unmöglichkeit der Geisteswissenschaft. Frankfurt, 1957.

Phil 185.55 Kraft, Julius. Die Unmöglichkeit der Geisteswissenschaft. Leipzig, 1934.

Phil 2905.1.560 Kraft, Ralph Wayne. The relevance of Teilhard. Notre Dame, 1968.

Phil 6980.398.40 Kraft, Thomas. De jeudgpsychiatriche diensten in Nederland. Utrecht, 1960.

Phil 735.114 Kraft, V. Die Grundlagen einer wissenschaftlichen Wertlehre. Wien, 1937.

Phil 735.114.5 Kraft, V. Die Grundlagen einer wissenschaftlichen Wertlehre. 2. Aufl. Wien, 1951.

Phil 341.32 Kraft, Victor. Erkenntnislehre. Wien, 1960.

Phil 185.65 Kraft, Viktor. Einführung in die Philosophie. Wien, 1950.

Phil 5068.16A Kraft, Viktor. Der Wiener Kreis. Wien, 1950.

Phil 5068.16.2 Kraft, Viktor. Der Wiener Kreis. Der Ursprung des Neopositivismus. Ein Kapitel der jüngsten Philosophiegeschichte. 2. Aufl. Wien, 1968.

Phil 3120.30.125 Kraft, Werner. Gespräche mit Martin Buber. München, 1966.

Phil 5460.7 Kraft-Ebing, R. Die Sinnesdelirien. Erlangen, 1864.

Phil 6680.2.3 Kraft-Ebing, R. von. Hypnotische Experimente. Stuttgart, 1893.

Phil 476.3.4.10 Kraft och materia. (Büchner, L.) Stockholm, 1869.

Phil 3425.81 Kraft und Stoff...Hegel'schen Prämissen. (Chlebik, F.) Berlin, 1873.

Phil 476.3.1 Kraft und Stoff. (Büchner, L.) Frankfurt, 1855.

Phil 476.3.2.5 Kraft und Stoff. (Büchner, L.) Frankfurt, 1858.

Phil 476.3 Kraft und Stoff. (Büchner, L.) Frankfurt, 1859.

Phil 476.3.2.4 Kraft und Stoff. (Büchner, L.) Frankfurt, 1898.

Phil 476.3.2 Kraft und Stoff. (Büchner, L.) Leipzig, 1867.

Phil 9070.65 Kraines, S.H. Live and help live. N.Y., 1951.

Phil 6120.19 Kraines, S.H. Managing your mind. N.Y., 1943.

Phil 4803.498.20 Krajewski, Władysław. Szkice filozofczne. Wyd. 1. Warszawa, 1963.

Phil 2115.105 Krakowski, E. Les sources médiévales de la philosophie de Locke. Paris, 1915.

Phil 2115.106 Krakowski, E. Les sources médiévales de la philosophie de Locke. Thèse. Paris, 1915.

Phil 810.8 Krakowski, Edouard. La philosophie gardienne de la cité de Plotin à Bergson. Paris, 1964.

Phil 4805.5 Král, Josef. Ceskoslovenská filosofie. Praha, 1937.

Phil 4809.524.80 Král, Josef. Studie o G.A. Lindnerovi. Bratislava, 1930.

Phil 185.25 Kralik, R. Weltweisheit. v.1-3. Wien, 1896.

Phil 185.25.5 Kralik, R. Weltwissenschaft. Wien, 1896.

Phil 5250.16 Kramar, W. Neue Grundlagen zur Psychologie des Denkens. Brünn, 1914.

Phil 6320.19 Kramer, Charles. La frustration. Neuchâtel, 1959.

Phil 6980.398.20 Kramer, Edith. Art therapy in a children's community. Springfield, 1958.

Phil 8960.6 Kramer, H.G. The indirect voluntary, or Voluntarium in causa. Diss. Washington, 1935.

Phil 3640.252 Kramer, H.G. Nietzsche and Rousseau. Inaug. Diss. Borna, 1928.

Phil 8960.7 Kramer, J.W. The right road. N.Y., 1891.

Phil 8885.32 Kramer, Morris. Song of the optimist. N.Y., 1926.

Phil 5190.2 Kramp, Leo. Das Verhältnis von Urteil und Satz. Bonn, 1916.

Phil 9245.132 Kramp, Willy. Über die Freude; zwei Betrachtungen. Hamburg, 1968.

Phil 3195.15.81 Krampf, W. Hugo Dingler. München, 1956.

Phil 3195.15.80 Krampf, W. Die Philosophie Hugo Dinglers. München, 1955.

Phil 6320.9.5 Kranefeldt, W.M. Secret ways of the mind. N.Y., 1932.

Phil 5545.169 Das kranke Gedachtnis. (Ranachburg, P.) Leipzig, 1911.

Phil 3640.273 Der kranke Nietzsche. (Nietzsche, Frau Franziska O.) Wien, 1937.

Phil 6968.3 Die Krankheiten, Storüngen, menschlichen Seele. (Schubert, G.H. yon.) Stuttgart, 1845.

Phil 2520.92 Krantz, É. Essai sur l'esthétique de Descartes. Paris, 1882.

Phil 6980.398* Krapf, E. Eduardo. Tomas de Aquino y la psicopatología. Buenos Aires, 1943.

Phil 341.20 Krapice, M.A. Realizm ludzkiego poznania. Poznań, 1959.

Phil 185.85 Krąpiec, M.A. Teoria analogii bytu. Lublin, 1959.

Phil 8590.13.5 Krarup, F.C. Religionsfilosofi. København, 1921.

Phil 310.640 Krasnoiarsk, Siberia (City). Gosudarstvennyi Pedagogicheskii Institut. Kafedra Filosofii. Voprosy teoreticheskogo nasledstva V.I. Lenina. Krasnoiarsk, 1966.

Phil 8980.498 Krasnor, Iu. M. O kul'ture povedeniia molodogo cheloveka. Moskva, 1962.

Phil 8171.5 Krasota i dobro. (Apresian, Grant Z.) Moskva, 1966.

Phil 6128.75 Krasota truda. (Sartakov, S.V.) Moskva, 1961.

VPhil 95.4 Kratki slovar' po filosofii. Moskva, 1966.

Phil 95.4.2 Kratki slovar' po filosofii. Izd.2. Moskva, 1970.

Phil 95.5 Kratkii anglo-russkii filosofskii slovar'. Moskva, 1969.

Phil 102.5 Kratkii filosofskii slovar'. (Rozental, Mark Moiseevich.) Moskva, 1939.

Phil 102.5.2 Kratkii filosofskii slovar'. (Rozental, Mark Moiseevich.) Moskva, 1940.

Phil 102.5.3 Kratkii filosofskii slovar'. Izd. 3. (Rozental', Mark Moiseevich.) Moskva, 1951.

Phil 102.5.5 Kratkii filosofskii slovar'. Izd. 4. (Rozental', Mark Moiseevich.) Leningrad, 1954.

Phil 808.4 Kratkii ocherk istorii filosofii. 2e Izd. (Iovchuk, Mikhail T.) Moskva, 1969.

Phil 5028.4 Kratkii ochesk istorii obshchei i matemaficheskoi logiki v Rossii. (Stiazhkin, N.I.) Moskva, 1962.

NEDL Phil 8980.2 Kratkii slovar' po etike. (Drobnitskii, Oleg G.) Moskva, 1965.

Phil 310.558 Kratkii uchebnik istoricheskogo materializma. (Fingert, B.A.) Leningrad, 1930.

Phil 4761.3.30 Kratkoe poniatie o cheloveke. n.p., 18-?

Phil 810.7 Kratochvii, J. Rukovet filosofie. Brno, 1939.

Phil 5400.76 Kratz, H. Asthetik. Gütersloh, 1891.

Phil 3830.5 Kratz, H. Spinoza's Ansicht über den Zweckbegriff. Newied, 1871.

Phil 9558.48 Kraus, Annie. Über den Hochmut. Frankfurt, 1966.

Phil 3549.18 Kraus, Annie. Vom Wesen und Ursprung der Dummheit. Köln, 1961.

Phil 341.42 Kraus, Hermann. Der Geist als Materie in Gehirnphysiologie und Kausalitätstheorie. Nurnberg, 1963.

Phil 185.60.10 Kraus, O. Selbstdarstellung. Leipzig, 1929.

Phil 185.60 Kraus, O. Wege und Abwege der Philosophie. Prag, 1934.

Phil 735.116 Kraus, O. Die Werttheorien; Geschichte und Kritik. Brünn, 1937.

Phil 3850.27.97 Kraus, Oskar. Albert Schweitzer. London, 1943.

Phil 3850.27.95 Kraus, Oskar. Albert Schweitzer. 2. Aufl. Berlin, 1929.

Phil 3625.9.80 Kraus, Oskar. Anton Marty; sein Leben und seine Werke. Halle, 1916.

Phil 3120.8.81 Kraus, Oskar. Franz Brentano. München, 1919.

Phil 3120.8.82 Kraus, Oskar. Franz Brentanos Stellung zur Phänomenologie und Gegenstandstheorie. Leipzig, 1924.

Phil 1850.119 Kraus, Oskar. Der Machtgedanke und der Friedensidee in des Philosophie des Engländer, Bacon und Bentham. Leipzig, 1926.

Phil 1865.151A Kraus, Oskar. Zur Theorie des Wertes. Halle, 1901.

Phil 672.12 Krause, A. Die Gesetze der menschlichen Herzens. Lahr, 1876.

Phil 3492.2.5 Krause, A. Immanuel Kant wider Kuno Fischer. Lahr, 1884.

Phil 3492.2A Krause, A. Kant und Helmholtz. Lahr, 1878.

Phil 3492.2.10 Krause, A. Die letzten Gendanken Immanuel Kants. Hamburg, 1902.

Phil 3492.2.15 Krause, A. Populäre Darstellung von Immanuel Kant's Kritik der reinen Vernunft. Lahr, 1881.

Phil 3492.2.17 Krause, A. Populäre Darstellung von Immanuel Kant's Kritik der reinen Vernunft. 2. Aufl. Hamburg, 1911.

Phil 6945.50 Krause, Elliott Arthur. Factors related to length of mental hospital stay. Boston, 1966?

Phil 3525.61 Krause, K.C.F. Abriss des Systemes der Logik. Göttingen, 1828.

Phil 3525.45 Krause, K.C.F. Abriss des Systemes der Philosophie. Göttingen, 1825.

Phil 8411.5.5 Krause, K.C.F. Compendio de estética traducido del aleman. Sevilla, 1939.

Phil 3525.86.5 Krause, K.C.F. Dei Briefwechsel Karl Christian Friedrich Krauses. Leipzig, 1903.

Phil 3525.30 Krause, K.C.F. Emporleitende Theil der Philosophie. Prag, 1869.

Phil 3525.35 Krause, K.C.F. Erneute Vernunftkritik. Prag, 1868.

Phil 3525.60 Krause, K.C.F. Grundriss der historischen Logik. Jena, 1803.

Phil 3525.20.2 Krause, K.C.F. Handschriftlicher Nachlass; Anthropologie. Göttingen, 1848.

Phil 3525.20 Krause, K.C.F. Handschriftlicher Nachlass; Logik. Göttingen, 1836.

Phil 3525.20.4 Krause, K.C.F. Handschriftlicher Nachlass; Rechtsphilosophie. Leipzig, 1874.

Phil 3525.20.3 Krause, K.C.F. Handschriftlicher Nachlass; Religionsphilosophie. Dresden, 1834-43. 2v.

Phil 3525.55 Krause, K.C.F. Ideal de la humanidad para la vida. 2. ed. Madrid, 1871.

Phil 8411.5 Krause, K.C.F. Karl Christian Friedrich Krause's Abriss der Asthetik oder der Philosophie des schönen Kunst. Göttingen, 1837.

Phil 3525.75 Krause, K.C.F. Lebenlehre. 2. Aufl. Leipzig, 1904.

Phil 3525.86 Krause, K.C.F. Pädagogischen Gedenken K.C.F. Krauses in ihrem Zusammenhange mit seiner Philosophie Dargestellt. Inaug. Diss. Leipzig, 1911.

Phil 3525.70 Krause, K.C.F. System der Sittenlehre. Bd.1. Leipzig, 1810.

Phil 3525.50 Krause, K.C.F. Das Urbild der Menschheit. Göttingen, 1851.

Phil 3525.65 Krause, K.C.F. Vorlesung über psychische Anthropologie. Leipzig, 1905.

Phil 3525.40 Krause, K.C.F. Vorlesungen über das System der Philosophie. Göttingen, 1828.

Phil 5050.7 Krause, K.H. Versuchplanmässiger und Naturgemässer unmittelbarer Denkübungen. Halle, 1844. 3v.

Phil 3525.88 Die Krause'sche Philosophie. (Hohlfeld, P.) Jena, 1879.

Phil 3525.80 El Krausismo. (Atienza y Medrano, A.) Madrid, 1887.

Phil 4312.5A El krausismo español. 1. ed. (Lopez Morillas, Juan.) México, 1956.

Phil 4960.265 Los krausistas argentinos. (Roig, Arturo Andres.) Puebla, Mexico, 1969.

Phil 5250.30 Krauss, S. Der seelische Konflikt; Psychologie und existentiale Bedeutung. Stuttgart, 1933.

Phil 2855.2.95 Krauss, S. Théodule Ribots Psychologie. Jena, 1905.

Phil 2515.16 Krauss, W. Cartaud de la Villate. Berlin, 1960. 2v.

Phil 3195.6.190 Krausser, Peter. Kritik der endlichen Vernunft. Frankfurt, 1968.

Phil 341.20 Krausser, Peter. Untersuchungen über den grundsatzlichen Auspruch der Wahrnehmung. Meisenheim am Glan, 1959.

Phil 6978.12 Kraussold, Karl. Melancholie und Schuld. Stuttgart, 1884.

Phil 95.3 Krauth, C.P. Vocabulary of the philosophical sciences. N.Y., 1878.

Phil 1930.18.85 Krauth, Lothar. Die Philosophie Carnaps. Wien, 1970.

Phil 5645.49 Kravkou, S.V. Tsvetovoe zrenie. Moskva, 1951.

Phil 4803.108.90 Krawczyk, Zbigniew. Socjologia Edwarda Abramowskiego. Warszawa, 1965.

Phil 4595.1.31 Krebs, C. Handling og iaggttagelse. København, 1913.

Phil 1504.5.5 Krebs, E. Meister Dietrich. v.5, pt.5-6. Münster, 1906.

Phil 1504.11.3 Krebs, E. Theologie und Wissenschaft nach der Lehre. v.11, pt.3-4. Münster, 1912.

Phil 7140.106 Krebs, Stanley le Fevre. The law of suggestion. 1st ed. Chicago, 1906.

Phil 5250.45.2 Krech, David. Elements of psychology. N.Y., 1965.

Phil 3425.101 Kredenburch, W.C.A. De staatsleer van Hegel. Utrecht, 1896.

Phil 185.16.5 Kreibig, J.C. Die intellektuellen Funktionen. Wien, 1909.

Phil 735.89A Kreibig, J.C. Psychologische Grundlegung eines Systems der Wert-Theorie. Wien, 1902.

Phil 645.16 Kreibig, J.K. Geschichte und Kritik des ethischen Skepticismus. Wien, 1896.

Phil 5330.29 Kreibig, Josef C. Die Aufmerksamkeit. Wien, 1897.

Phil 5640.125 Kreibig, Josef K. Die Sinne des Menschen. 3. Aufl. Leipzig, 1917.

Phil 8080.24 Kreis, Friedrich. Die Autonomie des Ästhetischen in der neuren Philosophie. Tübingen, 1922.

Phil 165.300 Kreise um Schopenhauer. (Emge, Carl August.) Wiesbaden, 1962.

Phil 5066.268 Kreisel, Georg. Elements of mathematical logic. Amsterdam, 1967.

Phil 185.102 Kreiser, Lothar. Untersuchungen zur Möglichkeit Habilitationsschrift. Leipzig?, 1967?

Phil 487.1.4 Der Kreislauf des Lebens. (Moleschott, J.) Giessen, 1875-87. 2v.

Phil 487.1.3 Der Kreislauf des Lebens. (Moleschott, J.) Mainz, 1855.

Phil 8590.17 Kreiss. Theophilosophie. Berlin, 1880.

Phil 5875.30 Kreitler, Hans. Die kognitive Orientierung des Kindes. München, 1967.

Phil 6960.16 Kreitler, Hans. Die wellanscharlie Orienterung der Schizophrenen. München, 1965.

Phil 1710.3.5 Krejčí, F. Filosofie posledních let před válkou. 2. vyd. Praha, 1930.

Phil 1710.3 Krejčí, F. O filosofii přítomnosti. V Praze, 1904.

Phil 5250.25 Krejčí, F.V. Základy vědeckého systému psychologie. Praha, 1929.

Phil 4809.498.30 Krejčí, František. Pozitivní etika jakožto mravanka na základě přirozeném. Praha, 1922.

Phil 8665.10 Krejčí, Jaroslav. Teleologický, kosmologický, a etický důkaz existence Boha v neotomismu. Vyd. 1. Praha, 1967.

Phil 185.47 Kremer, Josef. Einleitung in die Philosophie. Graz, 1931.

Phil 3492.27.5 Kremer, Josef. Kritik der Vernunftkritik. Erfurt, 1925.

Phil 3492.27 Kremer, Josef. Vorwärts zu Kant! Erfurt, 1924.

Phil 1170.20 Kremer, Klaus. Die neuplatonische Seinsphilosophie und ihre Wirkung auf Thomas von Aquin. Leiden, 1966.

Phil 630.23 Kremer, René. Le néo-réalisme américain. Louvain, 1920.

Phil 630.23.10 Kremer, René. La théorie de la connaissance chez les néo-réalistes anglais. Louvain, 1928.

Phil 3425.445 Kremer-Garietti, Angèle. La pensée de Hegel. Paris, 1957.

Phil 3640.510 Kremer-Marietti, Angèle. Thèmes et structures dans l'oeuvre de Nietzsche. Paris, 1957.

Phil 5250.60 Kremers, Johan. Scientific psychology and naive psychology. Nijmegen, 1960.

Phil 291.16 Kremianskii, Viktor I. Strukturnze urovni zhivoi materii. Moskva, 1969.

Phil 4710.148 Krepostnye vol'nodumtsy, XIX vek. (Kogan, Leonid A.) Moskva, 1966.

Phil 3850.18.83 Kreppel, F. Die Religionsphilosophie Max Schelers. Inaug. Diss. München, 1926.

Phil 6159.10 Kreppel, Gisela Richters. Die psychischen Phänomene im Schwellenbereich des Meshalin. Inaug. Diss. Bonn, 1964.

Phil 8885.38 Kresge, E.E. The search for a way of life. N.Y., 1950.

Phil 8980.498.25 Krešić, Ljubinka. Etičko-humanisticki problemi socijalizma. Beograd, 1964.

Phil 3492.35 Kress, Rudolf. Die soziologischen Gedanken Kants in Zusammenhang seiner Philosophie. Berlin, 1929.

Phil 8050.64 Krestovskaia, L.A. La laideur dans l'art à travers les âges. Paris, 1947.

Phil 6680.1.25 Kretschmar, F. Die Seherin von Prevorst. Weinsberg, 1929.

Phil 400.14 Kretschmer, E. Die Ideale und die Seele. Leipzig, 1900.

Phil 6120.8 Kretschmer, E. Körperbau und Charakter. 3. Aufl. Berlin, 1922.

Phil 6320.6.3 Kretschmer, E. Medizinische Psychologie. 3. Aufl. Leipzig, 1926.

Phil 6320.6.20 Kretschmer, E. Mensch und Lebensgrund. Tübingen, 1966.

Phil 6120.8.7 Kretschmer, E. Physique and character. N.Y., 1926.

Phil 6120.8.10 Kretschmer, E. Physique and character. 2d ed. N.Y., 1970.

Phil 6960.7 Kretschmer, E. Der sensitive Beziehungwahn. Berlin, 1918.

Phil 6320.6.15 Kretschmer, E. A text book of medical psychology. London, 1934.

Phil 5425.47.3 Kretschmer, Ernst. Geniale Menschen. 5. Aufl. Berlin, 1958.

Phil 6615.12.5 Kretschmer, Ernst. Hysteria. N.Y., 1926.

Phil 6615.12.3 Kretschmer, Ernst. Hysterie, reflex und instikt. 3. Aufl. Leipzig, 1944.

Phil 5710.18 Kretschmer, Ernst. Körperbau und Charakter. Berlin, 1961.

Phil 5710.16 Kretschmer, Ernst. Körperbau und Charakter. 20. Aufl. Berlin, 1951.

Phil 5425.47.5 Kretschmer, Ernst. The psychology of men of genius. London, 1931.

Phil 6615.12 Kretschmer, Ernst. Über hysterie. Leipzig, 1923.

Phil 8635.9 Kretzenbacher, Leopold. Die Seelenwaage. Klagenfurt, 1958.

Phil 3640.242 Kretzer, Eugen. Friedrich Nietzsche. Leipzig, 1895.

Phil 185.37 Kreyenbühl, J. Die Bedeutung der Philosophie für die Erfahrungswissenschaften. Heidelberg, 1885.

Phil 5627.69 Kriebel, O.S. Conversion and religious experience. Pennsburg, Pa., 1907.

Phil 3625.12.80 Krieg, Max. Fritz Mauthners Kritik der Sprache. München, 1914.

Phil 6120.16 Krieg, Wendell J.S. Functional neuroanatomy. Philadelphia, 1942.

Phil 8590.35 Krieger, Evelina. Abgrund und Gründe. Versuch einer Philosophie christlicher Positivität. Graz, 1966.

Phil 8520.60 Krieger, Evelina. Grenzwege. Freiburg, 1968.

Phil 5865.10 Kriekemans, Albert. Genetische Psychologie, systematischen historisch. v.1,7,9,12. Tielt, 1965- 4v.

Phil 2045.165 Kriele, Martin. Die Herausforderung der Verfassungsstaates; Hobbes und englische Juristen. Neuwied, 1970.

Phil 5640.18 Kries, J. von. Allgemeine Sinnesphysiologie. Leipzig, 1923.

Phil 3492.26 Kries, J. von. Immanuel Kant und seine Bedeutung für die Naturforschung der Gegenwart. Berlin, 1924.

Phil 5374.9.9 Kries, Johannes. Über die materiellen Grundlagen der Bewusstseins-Erscheinungen. Tübingen, 1901.

Phil 5643.56 Kries, Johannes von. Die Gesichts-Empfindungen und ihre Analyse. Leipzig, 1882.

Phil 5050.10 Kries, Johannes von. Logik. Tübingen, 1916.

Phil 4941.9 Kriezes, T.A. To Ellinikon ethnos ke i sighxroni epoxi. Athena, 1964.

Phil 900.27 Krikorian, Sergei. Sovremennaia filosofskaia i sotsiologicheskaia mysl' stran vostoka. Moskva, 1965.

Phil 1020.39 Krikorian, Sergei. Srednevekovaia filosofiia narodov Blizhnego i Srednego Vostoka. Moskva, 1966.

Phil 1760.10 Krikorien, Yervant H. Contemporary philosophic problems, selected readings. N.Y., 1959.

Phil 3493.18 Kring Kants "Tugendlehre". (Lewan, Axel.) Lund, 1930.

Phil 185.69 Krings, H. Fragen und Aufgaben der Ontologie. Tübingen, 1954.

Phil 1540.82 Krings, Hermann. Ordo. Halle, 1941.

Phil 705.50 Krings, Hermann. Transzendentale Logik. München, 1964.

Phil 5250.19 Krinns-psykologi och krinnlig logik. (Key, Ellen.) Stockholm, 1896.

Phil 8411.29A Kris, Ernst. Psychoanalytic exploration in art. London, 1953.

Phil 1135.18 Krische, A.B. Die theologischen Lehren der griechischen Denker. Göttingen, 1840.

Phil 3007.12 Krise der Freiheit. (Hommes, Jakob.) Regensburg, 1958.

Phil 8877.64.5 Krise der Weltanschauung. (Coudenhove-Kalergi, R.N.) Wien, 1923.

Phil 3450.11.275 Die Krise des a priori in der Transzendentalen. (Eley, Lathan.) Den Haag, 1762.

Phil 400.93 Die Krise des Idealismus. (Liebert, Arthur.) Zürich, 1936.

Phil 5627.110 Krisen katholischer Frömmigkeit. (Heinsius, Wilhelm.) Berlin, 1925.

Phil 6320.5 Krishaber, M. De la névropathie cérebro-cardiaque. Paris, 1873.

Phil 185.70 Krishna, Daya. The nature of philosophy. Calcutta, 1955.

Phil 960.42 Krishnachandra, B. Studies in Vedantism. Calcutta, 1909.

Phil 978.59.65 Krishnamarti, J. Talks in Europe, 1968. Wassenaar, 1920.

Phil 978.59.5 Krishnamurti, J. At the feet of the master. Chicago, 1927?

Phil 978.59.7 Krishnamurti, J. Authentic notes of discussions and talks given by Kris at Ojai and Sarabia. Hollywood, 1940.

Phil 978.59.42 Krishnamurti, J. Commentaries on living. London, 1957.

Phil 978.59.40 Krishnamurti, J. Commentaries on living. London, 1959.

Phil 978.59.41 Krishnamurti, J. Commentaries on living. N.Y., 1956.

Phil 978.59.44 Krishnamurti, J. Commentaries on living. 1st ed. N.Y., 1960.

Phil 978.59.22 Krishnamurti, J. Discussions with Krishnamurti in Europe, 1965. London, 1966.

Phil 978.59.55 Krishnamurti, J. Education and the significance of life. N.Y., 1953.

Phil 978.59.35 Krishnamurti, J. The first and last freedom. London, 1954.

Phil 978.59.50 Krishnamurti, J. Freedom from the known. 1st ed. N.Y., 1969.

Phil 978.59.2 Krishnamurti, J. The kingdom of happiness. N.Y., 1930.

Phil 978.59.45 Krishnamurti, J. Life ahead. London, 1963.

Phil 978.59.20 Krishnamurti, J. Life in freedom. N.Y., 1928.

Phil 978.59.60 Krishnamurti, J. The only revolution. London, 1970.

Phil 978.59.10 Krishnamurti, J. The pool of wisdom; Who brings the truth; By what authority and three poems. Eerde, 1928.

Phil 978.59.14 Krishnamurti, J. The search. N.Y., 1927.

Phil 978.59.15 Krishnamurti, J. The search. N.Y., 1927[1928]

Phil 978.59.8 Krishnamurti, J. The song of life. Ommen, 1931.

Phil 978.59.30 Krishnamurti, J. Talks, Ojai, California. Ojai, California, 1950.

Phil 978.59.70 Krishnamurti, J. Talks and dialogues, Saanen 1968. Wassenaar, 1970.

Phil 978.59.72 Krishnamurti, J. Talks and discussions at Brockwood Park, 1969. Wassenaar, 1970.

Phil 978.59.74 Krishnamurti, J. Talks with American students, 1968. Wassenaar, 1970.

Phil 978.59.125 Krishnamurti, sa vie, sa parole. (Bercou, Lydia.) n.p., 1969.

Phil 978.59.105 Krishnamurti. (Matwani, Kewal.) Madras, 1957.

Phil 978.59.110 Krishnamurti. (Methorst-Kuiper, A.) Amsterdam, 1961.

Phil 978.59.97 Krishnamurti. (Suares, Carlo.) Paris, 1933.

Phil 978.59.100 Krishnamurti. 2d ed. (Fouéré, René.) Bombay, 1954.

Phil 978.59.115 Krishnamurti and the experience. (Dhopeshwarkar, A.D.) Bombay, 1956.

Phil 978.59.95 Krishnamurti and the world crisis. (Heber, Lilly.) London, 1935.

Phil 20.1 Krisis der Psychoanalyse. Leipzig. 1,1928

Phil 705.14 Krisis der transzendentalen Wahrheit im anfang. (Plessner, H.) Heidelberg, 1918.

Phil 8593.21 Die Krisis des Cristentums. (Nestle, Wilhelm.) Stuttgart, 1947.

Phil 1750.310 Die Krisis des Existentialismus. (Siebers, G.) Hamburg, 1949.

Phil 8592.22.6 Die Krisis im Christentum. 2. Aufl. (Mach, Franz.) Dresden, 1908.

Phil 1750.65 De krisis van de burgerlijke moraal. (Flam, Leopold.) Antwerpen, 1956.

Phil 4010.2 Kristeller, P.O. Eight philosophers of the Italian Renaissance. Stanford, 1964.

Phil 1630.15 Kristeller, P.O. La tradizione aristotelica nel Rinascimento. Padova, 1962.

Phil 4110.1.89 Kristeller, Paul Oskar. The philosophy of Marsilio Ficino. Gloucester, Mass., 1964.

Phil 8958.1 Kristendomen och det etiska behovet. (Ideström, A.) Stockholm, 1918.

Phil 8590.30 Kristensen, William. The meaning of religion. The Hague, 1960.

Phil 8950.10 Kristikunnan kouluss. (Aula, Olari.) Porvoo, 1964.

Phil 8598.80 Den kristna människouppfattningen. (Silen, S.) Stockholm, 1938.

Phil 5272.22 Kristof, Walter. Untersuchungen zur Theorie psychologischen Messens. Meisenheim, 1969.

Phil 8980.838 Kriterii nravstvennogo progressa. (Titarenko, Aleksandr I.) Moskva, 1967.

Phil 3492.55 Kriticheskii analiz filosofii Kanta. (Karapetian, H.A.) Erevan, 1958.

Phil 3850.56 'n Kritiese studie van die wysbegeerte van H.G. Stoker vanuit die standpunt van H. Dooye weerd. (Malan, Daniel Johannes.) Amsterdam, 1968.

Phil 3085.7.45 Kritik: kleine Schriften zur Gesellschaft. 1. Aufl. (Adorno, Theodor W.) Frankfurt, 1971.

Phil 705.12 Kritik af subjektivismen. (Phalén, Adolf K.) Uppsala, 1910.

Phil 5421.20.140 Kritik der Anthropologie. (Lepenies, Wolf.) München, 1971.

Phil 3195.6.190 Kritik der endlichen Vernunft. (Krausser, Peter.) Frankfurt, 1968.

Phil 5762.4 Kritik der Freiheitstheorien. (Mack, Joseph.) Leipzig, 1906.

Phil 5250.31 Eine Kritik der Ganzheitstheorien. (Kastein, G.W.) Leiden, 1937.

Phil 803.12 Kritik der historischen Vernunft. (Dempf, Alois.) Wien, 1957.

Phil 3486.2 Kritik der Kantischen Antinomienlehre. (Erhardt, Franz.) Cöthen, 1888.

Phil 3484.16   Kritik der Kantischen Erkenntnislehre. (Christiansen, B.)
                 Hanau, 1911.
Phil 3487.1   Kritik der Kantischen Philosophie. (Fischer, Kuno.)
                 München, 1883.
Phil 3487.1.2   Kritik der Kantischen Philosophie. 2. Aufl. (Fischer,
                 Kuno.) Heidelberg, 1892.
Phil 3850.16.89 Kritik der Lebensphilosophie Georg Simmels. (Fabian, W.)
                 Breslau, 1926.
Phil 5130.2   Kritik der logischen Konstanten. (Lenk, Hans.)
                 Berlin, 1968.
Phil 1750.98   Kritik der neueren Ontologie. (Haag, Karl Hanz.)
                 Stuttgart, 1960.
Phil 1750.100   Kritik der neueren Ontololgie. (Haag, Karl Hanz.)
                 Stuttgart, 1960.
Phil 8590.15   Kritik der neukantischen religionsphilosophie der
                 Gegenwart. (Kesseler, Kurt.) Leipzig, 1920.
Phil 193.77   Kritik der Philosophie. (Schmitt, Eugen H.)
                 Leipzig, 1908.
Phil 3549.2.92   Kritik der Philosophie des Grafen H. Keyserling. Diss.
                 (Vondran, Hugo.) Erlangen, 1927.
Phil 8411.19   Kritik der Philosophie des Schönen. (Kulke, Eduard.)
                 Leipzig, 1906.
Phil 3480.45.7   Kritik der praktischen Vernunft. (Kant, Immanuel.)
                 Berlin, 1869.
Phil 3480.30.3.2A Kritik der praktischen Vernunft. (Kant, Immanuel.)
                 Leipzig, 1878?
Phil 8888.6   Kritik der praktischen Vernunft. (Nelson, Leonard.)
                 Leipzig, 1917.
Phil 3480.45.10 Kritik der praktischen Vernunft. 3. Aufl. (Kant,
                 Immanuel.) Heidelberg, 1882. 2 pam.
Phil 3480.45.15 Kritik der praktischen Vernunft. 7. Aufl. (Kant,
                 Immanuel.) Leipzig, 1920.
Phil 3480.45.16 Kritik der praktischen Vernunft. 9. Aufl. (Kant,
                 Immanuel.) Leipzig, 1929.
Phil 3480.45.18 Kritik der praktischen Vernunft als Prüfung der tätigen
                 Vernunft. 3. Aufl. (Kant, Immanuel.) Lübeck, 1919.
Phil 3480.45.17 Kritik der praktischen Vernunft als Prüfung der tätigen
                 Vernunft. 4. Aufl. (Kant, Immanuel.) Lübeck, 1922.
Phil 3480.45.25 Kritik der praktischen Vernunft nebst Grundlegung zur
                 Metaphysik der Sitten. (Kant, Immanuel.) Leipzig, 1925.
Phil 5244.13   Kritik der Psychologie als Wissenschaft. (Ehrenberg,
                 Hans.) Tübingen, 1910.
Phil 3100.85   Kritik der Psychologie von Beneke. Inaug-Diss. (Weber,
                 Adalbert.) Weimar, 1872.
Phil 8110.6   Die Kritik der rationalcn Asthetik in England im
                 achtzehnten Jahrhundert. (Wallace,H.B.) Jena, 1912.
Phil 331.2   Kritik der Reinen Erfahrung. (Avenarius, R.)
                 Leipzig, 1888.
Phil 331.2.5   Kritik der Reinen Erfahrung. (Avenarius, R.)
                 Leipzig, 1907.
Phil 3480.30.10 Kritik der reinen Vernunft. (Kant, Immanuel.)
                 Berlin, 1868-69.
Phil 3480.30.5A Kritik der reinen Vernunft. (Kant, Immanuel.)
                 Berlin, 1889.
Phil 3480.30.45 Kritik der reinen Vernunft. (Kant, Immanuel.)
                 Berlin, 1928.
Phil 3480.30.15 Kritik der reinen Vernunft. (Kant, Immanuel.)
                 Halle, 1899?
Phil 3480.30.5.5 Kritik der reinen Vernunft. (Kant, Immanuel.)
                 Hamburg, 1889.
Phil 3480.30.56 Kritik der reinen Vernunft. (Kant, Immanuel.)
                 Heldeberg, 1884.
Phil 3480.30.7   Kritik der reinen Vernunft. (Kant, Immanuel.) Kiel, 1881.
Phil 3480.30.8   Kritik der reinen Vernunft. (Kant, Immanuel.)
                 Leipzig, 1853.
Phil 3480.30.9   Kritik der reinen Vernunft. (Kant, Immanuel.)
                 Leipzig, 1868.
Phil 3480.30.4   Kritik der reinen Vernunft. (Kant, Immanuel.)
                 Leipzig, 1878.
Phil 3480.30.20 Kritik der reinen Vernunft. (Kant, Immanuel.)
                 Leipzig, 1920.
Phil 3480.30.27 Kritik der reinen Vernunft. (Kant, Immanuel.)
                 Leipzig, 1925.
Phil 3480.30.29 Kritik der reinen Vernunft. (Kant, Immanuel.)
                 Leipzig, 1926.
Phil 3480.30.40 Kritik der reinen Vernunft. (Kant, Immanuel.)
                 Lübeck, 1926.
Phil 3480.30.35 Kritik der reinen Vernunft. (Kant, Immanuel.)
                 München, 1920.
Phil 3480.30.44 Kritik der reinen Vernunft. (Kant, Immanuel.)
                 Stuttgart, 1904.
Phil 3480.32.65 Kritik der reinen Vernunft. (Kant, Immanuel.)
                 Wiesbaden, 1956-64. 6v.
Phil 3480.30.3   Kritik der reinen Vernunft. 2. Verb. Aufl. (Kant,
                 Immanuel.) Leipzig, 1877.
Phil 3480.30.6   Kritik der reinen Vernunft. 5. Aufl. (Kant, Immanuel.)
                 Berlin, 1900.
Phil 3480.30.18 Kritik der reinen Vernunft. 10. Aufl. (Kant, Immanuel.)
                 Leipzig, 1913.
Phil 3480.30.25 Kritik der reinen Vernunft. 12. Aufl. (Kant, Immanuel.)
                 Leipzig, 1922.
Phil 3805.175   Kritik der Schleiermacherschen Glaubenslehre. (Rosenkranz,
                 Karl.) Königsberg, 1836.
Phil 185.48.25   Kritik der Schrift Darstellung des Wesens der Philosophie.
                 (Schafberger, F.) Nürnberg, 1813.
Phil 2885.105   Kritik der Taineschen Kunsttheorie. (Schlaf, Johannes.)
                 Wien, 1906.
Phil 3850.13.30 Kritik der theoritischen Philosophie. (Schulze, G.E.)
                 Hamburg, 1801. 2v.
Phil 338.48   Kritik der transzendentalphilosophischen Erkenntnistheprie.
                 (Hoeres, Walter.) Stuttgart, 1969.
Phil 3480.50.40 Kritik der Urtheilskraft für Uneingeweihte. (Kant,
                 Immanuel.) Berlin, 1804.
Phil 3480.50.10A Kritik der Urtheilskraft. (Kant, Immanuel.)
                 Leipzig, 1878?
Phil 3480.50.22 Kritik der Urtheilskraft. (Kant, Immanuel.)
                 Stuttgart, 1925.
Phil 3480.50.13A Kritik der Urtheilskraft. 3. Aufl. (Kant, Immanuel.)
                 Leipzig, 1902.
Phil 3480.50.15 Kritik der Urtheilskraft. 5. Aufl. (Kant, Immanuel.)
                 Leipzig, 1922.
Phil 3492.27.5   Kritik der Vernunftkritik. (Kremer, Josef.) Erfurt, 1925.
Phil 197.54   Kritik der Weltanschauungen. (Weber, Maximilian.)
                 Langensalza, 1926.
Phil 5520.103   Kritik der Wissenschaft. (Winkler, R.) Wien, 1950.
Phil 299.12   Kritik der wissenschaftlichen Erkenntnis. (Schoeler, H.
                 von.) Leipzig, 1898.
Phil 3425.84.10 Kritik des Bewusstseins. (Gabler, G.A.) Leiden, 1901.

Phil 3549.2.79.15 Kritik des Denkens. (Keyserling, Hermann.)
                 Innsbruck, 1948.
Phil 353.13   Kritik des Erkennens. (Wendel, Georg.) Bonn, 1914.
Phil 735.87   Kritik des Gefühls. (Vetter, A.) Prien, 1923.
Phil 9245.30   Kritik des Hedonismus. (Gomperz, H.) Stuttgart, 1898.
Phil 348.6   Die Kritik des Intellects. (Ratzenhofer, Gustav.)
                 Leipzig, 1902.
Phil 535.25   Kritik des Nihilismus. (Mayer, Ernst.) München, 1958.
Phil 9430.14   Kritik des philosophischen Pessimismus der neuesten Zeit.
                 (Weygoldt, G.P.) Leiden, 1875.
Phil 5700.4   Kritik des psychoanalytischen Symbolbegriffs. 1. Aufl.
                 (Lorenzer, Alfred.) Frankfurt, 1970.
Phil 8885.12   Kritik des sittlichen Bewusstzeins vom philosophische und
                 historische Standpunkt. (Koppelmann, W.) Berlin, 1904.
Phil 2490.182   Kritik liner Soziologie der Ordnung: Organismus und System
                 bei Comte, Spencer und Parsons. 1. Aufl. (Kellermann,
                 Paul.) Freiburg, 1967.
Phil 4515.96   Kritik öfver den Boströmska filosofien. v.1-2. (Borelius,
                 J.J.) Stockholm, 1859-60.
Phil 3480.52   Kritik of judgment. (Kant, Immanuel.) London, 1892.
Phil 3495.13   Kritik über die metaphysischen Aufangsgründe der
                 Rechtslehre des I. Kant. (Nehr, J.G.) Nürnberg, 1798.
Phil 3500.3   Kritik über Kant's Subjektivität und Apriorität des Raumes
                 und der Zeit. (Scherer, G.) Frankfurt, 1871.
Phil 187.22   Kritik und Kurze Darlegung der exacten Natur-Philosophie.
                 (Mühry, A.) Göttingen, 1882.
Phil 182.140   Kritik und Leben. v.2. (Hammacher, Klaus.) München, 1969.
Phil 3640.195.5 Die Kritik und mein "Fall Nietzsche". (Schlaf, Johannes.)
                 Leipzig, 1907.
Phil 165.382   Kritik und Metaphysik; Studien. (Kaulbach, Friedrich.)
                 Berlin, 1966.
Phil 3640.38   Kritik und Zukunft der Kultur. (Nietzsche, Friedrich.)
                 Zürich, 1933.
Phil 75.75   Kritika burzhuaznoi i reformistskoi filosofii i sotsiologii
                 epokhi imperializma. (Akademiia Nauk SSSR.)
                 Fundamental'naia Biblioteka Obshchestvennykh Nauk.)
                 Moskva, 1967.
Phil 2280.5.155 Kritika filosofii amerikanskogo kriticheskogo realizma.
                 (Endovitskii, V.D.) Moskva, 1968.
Phil 5055.30   Kritika na logicheskite vuzgledi na burzhoaznite filosofi v
                 Bulgariia. (Penev, Mikho.) Sofiia, 1958.
Phil 5068.28   Kritika neopoz, vzgliadov na prirodu poznaniia. (Korneeva,
                 Anna I.) Moskva, 1962.
Phil 5520.650   Kritika osnovnykh idei estestvoznaniia. Photoreproduction.
                 (Bervi, Vasilii V.) Sankt-Peterburg, 1904.
Phil 4769.1.45   Kritika otvlechennykh nachal. (Solov'ev, V.S.)
                 Moskva, 1880.
Phil 5520.185   Kritika semanticheskogo idealizma. (Narskii, I.S.)
                 Moskva, 1956.
Phil 8400.55   Kritika sovremennoi burzhuaznoi estetiki. Moskva, 1968.
Phil 1750.545   Kritika sovremennoi burzhuaznoi filosofii. (Moscow.
                 Akademiia Obshchestvennykh Nauk.) Moskva, 1959.
Phil 1750.645   Kritika sovremennoi burzhuaznoi filosofii i sotsiologii.
                 (Moscow. Akademiia Obshchestvennykh Nauk.) Moskva, 1961.
Phil 1750.646   Kritika sovremennoi burzhuaznoi filosofii i sotsiologii.
                 (Moscow. Akademiia Obshchestvennykh Nauk.) Moskva, 1963.
Phil 1717.22   Kritika sovremennoi burzhuaznoi ideologii. (Russia, 1917.
                 Ministerstvo vysshego Obrazovaniia.) Petrozavodsk, 1963.
Phil 1704.1.10   Kritika sovremennoi burzruaznoi filosofii. (Ermolenko,
                 D.V.) Moskva, 1959.
Phil 8828.5   Kritika sovremennykh burzhuaznykh eticheskikh kontseptsii.
                 (Drobnitskii, Oleg G.) Moskva, 1967.
Phil 8893.125   Kritika sovremennykh burzhuaznykh filosofsko-esteticheskikh
                 system. (Shvartsman, Klara Aronovna.) Moskva, 1961.
Phil 1870.150   Kritika subektivno-idealisticheskoi filosofii D. Berkli.
                 (Bogomolov, A.S.) Moskva, 1959.
Phil 585.110   Kritika teorii biologizatsii cheloveka. (Gal'perin, S.I.)
                 Leningrad, 1960.
Phil 1750.862   Kritika va neotomizma. (Radev, R.) Sofiia, 1970.
Phil 4822.8   Kritikata na Dimitur Blagoev na neokantianstvoto v
                 Bulgariia po vuprosite na filosofiiata. (Andreev, Kosta.)
                 Sofiia, 1968.
Phil 5258.76.10 Kritiken af min psychologi svar til mine kritikere.
                 (Starcke, C.N.) Kjøbenhavn, 1916.
Phil 4815.368.30 Kritikus objectiv metaphysíka. (Erösdi, Mihály.)
                 Budapest, 1885.
Phil 400.50   Het kritisch idealisme. (Ovink, B.J.H.) Utrecht, 1913.
Phil 1930.4.81   Kritische Analyse von Arthur Colliers Clavis Universalis.
                 Inaug. Diss. (Kowalewski, Arnold.) Griefswald, 1897.
Phil 3565.83   Kritische Bemerkungen zu Lotze's Seelenbegriff. (Powers,
                 J.H.) Göttingen, 1892.
Phil 5325.10.5   Kritische Bemerkungen zur Associationstheorie. Teil 1.
                 (Popp, Walter.) Leipzig, 1913.
Phil 179.7   Kritische Einführung in die Philosophie. (Eisler, R.)
                 Berlin, 1905.
Phil 3425.91   Kritische Erläuterungen des Hegel's...Systems.
                 (Rosenkranz, K.) Königsberg, 1840.
Phil 3790.4.87   Kritische Erörterungen über Rickert. Diss. (Bloch, Ernst.)
                 Ludwigshafen, 1909.
Phil 3495.6.5   Die kritische Ethik bei Kant, Schilles und Fries. (Nelson,
                 Leonard.) Göttingen, 1914.
Phil 3482.3   Kritische excurse im Gebiete der Kant-Forschung. (Arnoldt,
                 Emil.) Köningsburg, 1894.
Phil 665.17   Kritische Geschichte der Ideale. (Svoboda, A.V.)
                 Leipzig, 1886.
Phil 803.2   Kritische Geschichte der Philosophie. 2d Aufl. (Dühring,
                 E.) Berlin, 1873.
Phil 803.2.3   Kritische Geschichte der Philosophie. 3e Aufl. (Dühring,
                 E.) Leipzig, 1878.
Phil 3415.55   Kritische Grundlegung der trancedentalen Realismus.
                 (Hartmann, Eduard von.) Berlin, 1875.
Phil 400.40   Der kritische Idealismus. (Rauschenberger, W.)
                 Leipzig, 1918.
Phil 400.20   Der kritische Idealismus und die reine Logik. (Jerusalem,
                 W.) Wien, 1905.
Phil 5253.8   Die kritische Methode und das Verhaltnis der Psychologie
                 zur Philosophie. (Nelson, Leonard.) Göttingen, 1904.
Phil 1750.115.155 Kritische ondervraging van de fenomenologische rede.
                 (Hoeven, Johannes van der.) Amsterdam, 1963.
Phil 3450.18.200 Die "Kritische Ontologie" Nicolai Hartmanns und ihre
                 Bedeutung für das Erkenntnisproblem. Inaug. Diss.
                 (Klösters, Joseph.) Fulda, 1927.
Phil 8585.31   Kritische Philosophie und Dialektischen Theologie.
                 Proefschrift. (Franken, J.C.) Amsterdam, 1932.
Phil 630.33   Der kritische Realismus. (Messer, August.)
                 Karlsruhe, 1923.
Phil 3260.152.5 Die kritische Rechtsphilosophie bei Fries. (Fraenkel,
                 Georg.) Göttingen, 1912.

Phil 8050.59   Kritische studien zur Ästhetik der Gegenwart. (Spitzer, Hugo.) Wien, 1897.

Phil 3450.28.15   Kritische Theorie. (Horkheimer, Max.) Frankfurt, 1968. 2v.

Phil 3625.28.31   Kritische Theorie der Offenbarung. (Maass, Johann Gebhard Ehrenreich.) Bruxelles, 1969.

Phil 5460.5   Kritische und klinische Betrachtungen im Gebiete der Sinnestäuschungen. (Kandinsky, V.) Berlin, 1885.

Phil 6135.1   Kritische Untersuchung über das Wesen der vernünstigen Geist-Seele. (Zukrigl, J.) Regensburg, 1854.

Phil 5525.1   Kritische Untersuchungen. (Keppler, J.F.) Cilli, 1792.

Phil 3625.5.40   Kritische Untersuchungen über den menschlichen Geist. (Atlas, S.) Leipzig, 1797.

Phil 1050.15.9   Kritische Untersuchungen zu Levi hen Gersons (Ralbag) Widerlegung des Aristotelischen Zeitbegriffes. Inaug. Diss. (Karo, Jakob.) Leipzig, 1935.

Phil 3415.72   Kritische Wanderungen durch die Philosophie der Gegenwart. (Hartmann, Eduard von.) Leipzig, 1889.

Phil 4575.94   Kritisk exposition of Benjamin Höijers. (Leufren, E.J.) Upsala, 1897.

Phil 8905.32   Kritisk forskerholdning i etikk og religionsfilosofi. (Nome, John.) Oslo, 1970.

Phil 2270.115   Kritisk framställning af Herbert Spencer's "Principles of Psychology". Akademisk afhandling. (Thyren, Johan.) Lund, 1883.

Phil 3483.4   Kritisk framställning of Kants frihetslära. (Boström, G.) Lund, 1897.

Phil 3245.83   Kritiska anmärkningar vid I.H. Fichtes ethiska grundsatzer. (Swahn, F.O.B.) Lund, 1856.

Phil 3483.34   Kritiska studier till Kants transcendentala ästetik. (Bendixson, A.) Upsala, 1885.

Phil 3494.26   Kritizismus: Eine Sammlung...Neu-Kantianismus. (Myrho, F.) Berlin, 1926.

Phil 3491.5   Der Kritizismus Kants. (Jansen, B.) München, 1925.

Phil 9430.6   Kritk des Pessimismus. (Küssner, G.) Halle, 1888.

Phil 8411.34   Krivskovskii, Nikolai I. Logika krasoty. Minsk, 1965.

Phil 176.13   Krizis burzhuaznogo soznaniia. (Baskin, M.P.) Moskva, 1962.

Phil 291.18   Kroeber, Günter. Der Gesetzesbegriff in der Philosophie und den Einzelwissenschaften. Berlin, 1968.

Phil 1135.188   Kroeber, Günter. Wissenschaft und Weltanschauung in der Antike. Berlin, 1966.

Phil 6060.86   Kroeber-Keneth, Ludwig. L. Kroeber-Keneth's Buch der Graphologie. 1. Aufl. Düsseldorf, 1968.

Phil 3492.4   Kroeger, A.E. Immanuel Kant. New Haven, 1872.

Phil 8590.40   Kroeger, Athanasius. Mensch und Person. Recklinghausen, 1968.

Phil 400.49   Kröger, Otto. Die Philosophie des reinen Idealismus. Bonn, 1921.

Phil 400.49.10   Kröger, Otto. Die Weltanschauung des absoluten Idealismus. Harz, 1909.

Phil 3640.286   Kroekel, F. Europas Selbsbesinnung durch Nietzsche. München, 1929.

Phil 5250.4.5   Kroell, H. Die Aufbau der menschlichen Seele. Leipzig, 1900.

Phil 5250.4   Kroell, H. Die Seele im Lichte des Monismus. Strassburg, 1902.

Phil 5400.16   Kröner, E. Das körperliche Gefühl. Breslau, 1887.

Phil 1710.4   Kröner, Franz. Die Anarchie der philosophischen Systeme. Leipzig, 1929.

Phil 185.9   Krönig, Prof. Das Dasein Gottes. Berlin, 1874.

Phil 9045.16   Krogh, Matthias B. Om Kierlighed til faedrenelandet. Trondhiem, 1801.

Phil 735.265   Krohn, Sven. Totuus, arvo ja ihminen. Porvoo, 1967.

Phil 3805.182   Kroker, P. Die Tugendlehre Schleiermachers. Erlangen, 1889.

Phil 9590.17.5   Krol', L.I. Osnovaniia biosofii. v.1-2. Kaunas, 1937.

Phil 9590.17   Krol', L.I. Vvedenie v biosofiia. Kaunas, 1937.

Phil 1504.12.2   Kroll, J. Die Lehren des Hermes Trismegistos. v.12, pt.2-4. Münster, 1914.

Phil 8885.18   Kroman, Krist. Etik I. København, 1904.

Phil 5250.12.15   Kroman, Kristian. Grundtraek af sjaelelaeren. 6. udg. København, 1920.

Phil 5250.12.17   Kroman, Kristian. Grundtraek af sjaelelaeren. 7. udg. København, 1928.

Phil 5250.12.3   Kroman, Kristian. Korfattet taenke-og sjaelelaere. 3. udg. København, 1899.

Phil 5250.12   Kroman, Kristian. Korfattet taenke-og sjaelelaere. 5. udg. København, 1914.

Phil 8665.27   Kromer, Klaus. Gott und Welt in der klassischen Metaphysik. Stuttgart, 1969.

Phil 8885.45   Kron, Helmut. Ethos und Ethik. Frankfurt, 1960.

Phil 3640.314   Kronenberg, M. Friedrich Nietzsche und seine Herrenmoral. München, 1901.

Phil 400.23   Kronenberg, M. Geschichte der deutschen Idealismus. München, 1909. 2v.

Phil 3492.13   Kronenberg, M. Kant; sein Leben und sein Lehre. 5. Aufl. München, 1918.

Phil 3492.13.6   Kronenberg, M. Kant; sein Leben und sein Lehre. 6. Aufl. München, 1922.

Phil 3492.13.3   Kronenberg, M. Kant. München, 1897.

Phil 3492.13.2   Kronenberg, M. Kant. 2. Aufl. München, 1904.

Phil 3492.13.5   Kronenberg, M. Kant. 4. Aufl. München, 1910.

Phil 8885.31   Kronenberg, Moritz. Ethische Präludien. München, 1905.

Phil 3010.14   Kronenberg, Moritz. Moderne Philosophen; Porträts und Charakteristiken. München, 1899.

Phil 3010.3   Kroner, R. Von Kant bis Hegel. Tübingen, 1921-24. 2v.

Phil 3010.3.2   Kroner, R. Von Kant bis Hegel. v.1-2. Tübingen, 1961.

Phil 8622.2.5   Kroner, Richard. Between faith and thought: reflections and suggestions. N.Y., 1966.

Phil 3549.11.5   Kroner, Richard. Freiheit und Gnade. Tübingen, 1969.

Phil 3492.18.5   Kroner, Richard. Kant's Weltanschauung. Chicago, 1956.

Phil 3492.18   Kroner, Richard. Kants Weltanschauung. Tübingen, 1914.

Phil 8622.2   Kroner, Richard. The primacy of faith. N.Y., 1943.

Phil 3549.11   Kroner, Richard. The religious function of imagination. New Haven, 1941.

Phil 185.41   Kroner, Richard. Die Selbstverwirklichung des Geistes. Tübingen, 1928.

Phil 810.11   Kroner, Richard. Speculation and revelation in the history of philosophy. London, 1952.

Phil 6315.2.325   Kronfeld, A. Über die psychologischen Theorien Freuds und verwandte Anschauungen. Leipzig, 1912.

Phil 9035.64   Kronfeld, Arthur. Lehrbuch der Charakterkunde. Berlin, 1932.

Phil 6960.6.7   Kronfeld, Arthur. Psychotherapie, Charakterlehre, Psychoanalyze, Hynose, Psychogogik. 2. Aufl. Berlin, 1925.

Phil 6960.6.5   Kronfeld, Arthur. Psychotherapie. Berlin, 1924.

Phil 6960.6   Kronfeld, Arthur. Das Wesen der psychiatrischen Erkenn. Berlin, 1920.

Phil 6060.16   Kronsbein, W. Die physiologischen und psychologischen Beziehungen zwischen Sprache und Schrift. Weinsberg, 191-?

VPhil 3425.620   Kroński, Tadeusz. Hegel. wyd. 2. Warszawa, 1966.

Phil 4803.500.20   Kroński, Tadeusz. Rozwazania wokól Hegla. Warszawa, 1960.

Htn   Phil 6100.10*   Kronthal, P. Schnitte durch das centrale Nervensystem des Menschen. Berlin, 1892.

Phil 8835.5   Krook, Dorothea. Three traditions of moral thought. Cambridge, Eng., 1959.

Phil 8835.2.5   Kropotkin, Petr Alekseevich. Ethics; origin and development. N.Y., 1924.

Phil 8835.2.6   Kropotkin, Petr Alekseevich. Ethics; origin and development. N.Y., 1968.

Phil 810.9   Kropp, Gerhard. Von Lao-Tse zu Sartre. Berlin, 1953.

Phil 575.92   Krout, M.H. Major aspects of personality. Chicago, 1933.

Phil 6980.400   Krout, M.H. Psychology. Minneapolis, 1956.

Phil 8125.36   Krudewig, B. Das Groteske in der Ästhetik seit Kant. Bergisch, 1934.

Phil 5643.89.80   Krudewig, M. Die Lehren von der visuelfen Wahrnehmung und Vorstellung. Meisenheim, 1953.

Phil 974.3.122.2   Krueck, M.J. Wir Erlebten Rudolf Steiner. 2. Aufl. Stuttgart, 1957.

Phil 9550.4   Krueger, F. Der Begriff des Absolut Wertvollen. Leipzig, 1898.

Phil 185.51   Krueger, F. Ganzheit und Form. Berlin, 1932.

Phil 8885.29   Krueger, Felix. Der Begriff des absolut Wertvollen. Leipzig, 1898.

Phil 5250.13.20   Krueger, Felix. Beobachtungen über zweiklänge. Leipzig, 1900-08. 10 pam.

Phil 5250.13.5   Krueger, Felix. Ist Philosophie ohne Psychologie möglich? Eine Erwiderung. München, 1896.

Phil 5250.13.9   Krueger, Felix. Neue psychologische Studien. München. 1926-1939 23v.

Phil 5400.200   Krueger, Felix. Über das Gefühl. Darmstadt, 1967.

Phil 5250.13   Krueger, Felix. Über Entwicklungspsychologie. Leipzig, 1915.

Phil 5250.13.25   Krueger, Felix. Zur Philosophie und Psychologie der Ganzheit. Berlin, 1953.

Phil 8633.1.26   Krüger, E. Immortality of man. Cambridge, 1927.

Phil 3552.370   Krueger, G. Leibniz als Friedensstifter. Wiesbaden, 1947.

Phil 1750.166.80   Krueger, Gerhard. Abendländische Humanität. Stuttgart, 1953.

Phil 810.10   Krueger, Gerhard. Grundfragen der Philosophie. Frankfurt, 1958.

Phil 3492.37   Krüger, Gerhard. Philosophie und Moral in der Kantischen Kritik. Tübingen, 1931.

Phil 3010.15   Krueger, Gustav. Die Religion der Goethezeit. Tübingen, 1931.

Phil 3415.94   Krüger, Gustav. Der Vitalismus Eduard von Hartmanns und seine philosophischen Grundlagen. Inaug. Diss. Schwerin, 1911.

Phil 185.66   Krueger, H. Zwischen Dekadenz und Erneuerung. Frankfurt, 1953.

Phil 3425.615   Krueger, H.J. Theologie und Aufklärung. Stuttgart, 1966.

Phil 8060.8   Krueger, J. Ästhetik der Antike. Berlin, 1964.

Phil 3552.486   Krueger, Lorenz. Rationalismus und Entwurf einer universalen Logik bei Leibniz. Frankfurt, 1969.

Phil 665.108   Krueger, Walter. Metaphysische Praxis als Schlüssel zur geistigen Welt. Freiburg, 1968.

Phil 185.10.30   Krug, W.T. De humanitate in philosophando rite servanda. Vitebergae, 1800.

Phil 1115.2   Krug, W.T. Geschichte der Philosophie alter Zeit. Leipzig, 1827.

Phil 8411.25   Krug, W.T. Geschmackslehre oder Ästhetik. Wien, 1818. 2v.

Phil 185.10   Krug, W.T. Handbuch der Philosophie. Leipzig, 1828.

Phil 185.10.15   Krug, W.T. Handbuch i philosophien. Stockholm, 1831.

Htn   Phil 3801.498*   Krug, W.T. Schelling und Hegel. Leipzig, 1835.

Phil 341.4   Krug, W.T. Versuch einer systematischen Enzyklopädie. Whittenberg, 1796.

Phil 95.2   Krug, Wilhelm Traugott. Allgemeines Handwörterbuch der philosophischen Wissenschaften. Leipzig, 1827. 5v.

Phil 95.2.2A   Krug, Wilhelm Traugott. Allgemeines Handwörterbuch der philosophischen Wissenschaften. 2e Aufl. Leipzig, 1832-38. 5v.

Phil 3528.58   Krug, Wilhelm Traugott. Briefe über die Wissenschaftslehre. Bruxelles, 1968.

Phil 3528.37   Krug, Wilhelm Traugott. Bruchstücke aus meiner Lebensphilosophie. v.1-2. Berlin, 1800-01.

Phil 3528.60.1   Krug, Wilhelm Traugott. Entwurf eines neuen Organon's der Philosophie. Meissen, 1801. Bruxelles, 1969.

Phil 3528.40   Krug, Wilhelm Traugott. Fundamentalphilosophie. Leipzig, 1827.

Phil 3528.40.5   Krug, Wilhelm Traugott. Fundamentalphilosophie. 2. Aufl. Züllichan, 1819.

Phil 3528.10   Krug, Wilhelm Traugott. Gesammelte Schriften. Braunschweig, 1830-45. 12v.

Phil 185.10.2   Krug, Wilhelm Traugott. Handbuch der Philosophie und der philosophischen Literatur. v.1-2. Düsseldorf, 1969.

Phil 3528.35.2   Krug, Wilhelm Traugott. System der praktischen Philosophie. Königsberg, 1830-38. 2v.

Phil 3528.35.5   Krug, Wilhelm Traugott. System der praktischen Philosophie. Wien, 1818.

Phil 3528.35   Krug, Wilhelm Traugott. System der praktischen Philosophie. 2. Aufl. Königsberg, 1817-19. 3v.

Phil 3528.30.2   Krug, Wilhelm Traugott. System der theoretischen Philosophie. Königsberg, 1806-18. 2v.

Phil 3528.30   Krug, Wilhelm Traugott. System der theoretischen Philosophie. Königsberg, 1823-33. 3v.

Phil 3528.50   Krug, Wilhelm Traugott. Über altes und neues Christenthum. Leipzig, 1836.

Phil 3528.45   Krug, Wilhelm Traugott. Universalphilosophische Vorlesungen für Gebildete beiderlei Geschlechts. Neustadt, 1831.

Phil 3528.55.2   Krug, Wilhelm Traugott. Der Widerstreit der Vernunft mit sich Selbst in der Versöhnungslehre. Bruxelles, 1968.

Phil 3120.2.115   Krug und Bolzano. (Zimmermann, J.) Sulzbach, 1837.

Phil 8665.30   Kruger, Klaus. Der Gottesbegriff der spekulativen Theologie. Berlin, 1970.

Phil 7150.42   Kruijt, Cornuijtus Simon. Zilfmoord. Assen, 1960.

Phil 818.39   Kruispaaie van die filosofie. (Smuts, Johannes Petrus.) Kaapstad, 1968.

Phil 3425.515   Kruithof, J. Het uitgangspunt van Hegel's ontologie. Brugge, 1959.

Phil 6020.2.3   Krukenberg, H. Der Gesichtsausdruck des Menschen. 3. und 4. Aufl. Stuttgart, 1923.

Phil 341.16.5 — Kruse, F.V. Erkendelseslaeren og naturvidenskabens grundbegreber. København, 1960.

Phil 341.16.10 — Kruse, F.V. Erkenntnis und Wertung; das Grundproblem. Berlin, 1960.

Phil 341.16 — Kruse, F.V. The foundation of human thought. London, 1949.

Phil 2050.208 — Kruse, F.V. Hume's philosophy in his principal work, a treatise of human nature, and in his essays. London, 1939.

Phil 6320.30 — Kruse, Friedrich. Die Anfänge des menschlichen Seelenlebens. Stuttgart, 1969.

Phil 4352.1.103 — Kruse, Paul. Die pädagogischen Elemente in der Philosophie des Jakob Balmes. Inaug. Diss. Neuherberg, 1935.

Phil 4756.1.35 — Krushenie kumirov. (Frank, Semen L.) Berlin, 1924.

Phil 5066.264 — Krushenie metafizicheskoi kontseptsii univeral'nosti predmetnoi oblasti v logike. (Biriukov, Boris Vl.) Moskva, 1963.

Phil 1710.5.10 — Krutch, Joseph W. The measure of man. 1. ed. Indianapolis, 1954.

Phil 1710.5.3 — Krutch, Joseph W. The modern temper. N.Y., 1929.

Phil 1710.5.5 — Krutch, Joseph W. The modern temper. N.Y., 1930.

Phil 8980.501 — Krutova, Ol'ga Natanouna. Chelovek i moral'. Moskva, 1970.

Phil 4710.30 — Kruzhkov, U.S. O russkoi klassicheskoi filosofii XIX v. Moskva, 1945.

Phil 2494.83 — Krynska, S. Entwicklung und Fortschritt nach Condorcet und A. Comte. Diss. Bern, 1908.

Phil 331.31 — Krytyka ludzkiego poznania. Wyd.1. (Adamczyk, S.) Lublin, 1962.

Phil 575.160 — Krytyka personalistyczna. (Terlecki, Tymon.) Londyn, 1957.

Phil 8665.25 — Kryvelev, A.I. O dokazatel'stvakh bytiia Bozhiia. Moskva, 1960.

Phil 8700.16 — Kryvelev, I.A. Sovremennoe bogoslov'e i nauka. Moskva, 1959.

Phil 8520.70 — Kryvelev, Iosif A. Religioznaia kartina mira i ee bogoslovskaia modernizatsiia. Moskva, 1968.

Phil 2885.112 — Krzemień-Ojak, Slaw. Taine. Wyd. 1. Warszawa, 1966.

Phil 1750.140 — Krzesinski, André. Une nouvelle philosophie de l'immanence. Paris, 1931.

Phil 4803.570.80 — Ksiądz Konstanty Michalski, 1879-1947. Wyd. 1. (Usovicz, Aleksandr.) Kraków, 1949.

Phil 165.361 — Księga pamiątkowa ku czci prof. W. Heinricha. Kraków, 1927.

Phil 165.170 — Ksiega pamiątkowa ku uczczeniu czterdziestolecia pracy nauczycielskiej. Warszawa, 1959.

Phil 165.169 — Ksiega pamiątkowa ku uczczeniu piętnastolecia pracy nauczycielskiej w Uniwersytecie Warszawskim profesora Tadeusza Kotarbińskiego. Warszawa, 1934.

Phil 3492.6 — Kuberka, F. Kant's Lehre von der Sinnlichkeit. Halle, 1905.

Phil 310.650.3 — Kubeš, Miloslav. Člověk, svět a filosofie. Vyd. 3. Praha, 1968.

Phil 6320.17A — Kubie, L.S. Neurotic distortion of the creative process. Lawrence, 1958.

Phil 2138.114.2 — Kubitz, O.A. Development of John S. Mill's system of logic. Urbana, 1932.

Phil 2138.114 — Kubitz, O.A. Development of John S. Mill's system of logic. Thesis. Urbana, 1932.

Phil 8411.23 — Kublanov, B.G. Esteticheskoe chuvstvo i iskusstvo. L'vov, 1956.

Phil 8411.2 — Kubler, George. The shape of time; remarks on the history of things. New Haven, 1962.

Phil 5650.17 — Kucharski, P. Recherches sur l'exitabilité auditive. Thèse. Paris, 1928.

Phil 5590.544 — Kucher, Volodymyr. Zorzumiite samykh sebe. Kanada, 1969.

Phil 8592.122.25 — Kucherenko, Gennadii S. Sud'ba "Zaveshchaniia" zhana mel'e v XVIII veke. Moskva, 1968.

Phil 8411.37 — Kucherenko, Georgii A. Esteticheskoe mnogoobrazie iskusstva sotsialisticheskogo realizma. Moskva, 1966.

Phil 87.12.5 — Kücük felsefesözlügü. (Cuvillier, Armand.) Ankara, 1944.

Phil 4110.11.35 — Kuczyńska, Alicja. Filozofia i seoria piękna Marsilia Ficina. Wyd. 1. Warszawa, 1970.

Phil 9070.109 — Kuczyński, Janusz. Filozofia życia. Wyd. 1. Warszawa, 1965.

Phil 3640.714 — Kuczyński, Janusz. Zmierzch mies zczaństwa. Warszawa, 1967.

Phil 4803.502.20 — Kuczyński, Janusz. Zyć i filozofować. Wyd. 1. Warszawa, 1969.

Phil 3425.586 — Kuderowicz, Z. Doktryna moralna mlodego Hegla. Warszawa, 1962.

VPhil 3195.6.180 — Kuderowicz, Zbigniew. Dilthey. Warszawa, 1967.

VPhil 3195.6.175 — Kuderowicz, Zbigniew. Światopogląd a zycie u Dilhteya. Warszawa, 1966.

VPhil 185.99 — Kudriavtsev-Platonov, Viktor D. Vvedenie v filosofiiu. Izd. 7. Sergiev Posad, 1908.

Phil 3425.605 — Kudrna, J. Studie k Hegel om pojetí historie. Praha, 1964.

Phil 3549.28.30 — Kudszus, Hans. Zaworte, Neimworte, Aphorismen. 1. Aufl. Frankfurt, 1970.

Phil 5790.2.15 — Kuebler-Ron, Elisabeth. On death and dying. N.Y., 1969.

Phil 5262.4.50 — Der Kückfall in die Methodenkrise der Psychologie. (Wellek, Albert.) Göttingen, 1959.

Phil 3805.167 — Kügelgen, C. von. Schleiermachers Reden und Kants Predigten. Leipzig, 1901.

Phil 3492.32 — Kügelgen, C.W. von. Die Bibel bei Kant. Leipzig, 1904.

Phil 3492.32.5 — Kügelgen, C.W. von. Immanuel Kant Auffassung von der Bibel und seine Auslegung derselben. Leipzig, 1896.

Phil 8620.36 — Kühler, Hans. Das Problem der Theodizee. Inaug. Diss. Bonn, 1929.

Phil 735.82 — Kühn, Lenore. Die Autonomie der Werte. Berlin, 1926-31. 2v.

Phil 1145.22 — Kühn, O. Sittlichen Ideen der Griechen. Leipzig, 1888.

Phil 3195.8.85 — Kühne, A. Der Religionsphilosoph Georg F. Daumer. Inaug. Diss. Berlin, 1936.

Phil 185.29 — Kühne, B. Die höchste Aufgabe der Philosophie. Einsiedeln, 1880.

Phil 9070.58 — Kuehne, O. Lebenskunst und Lebensgemeinschaft in Gesellschaft und Wirtschaft. Berlin, 1954[1958] 2v.

Phil 2050.94 — Kühne, R. Uber das Verhältniss der Hume'schen und Kantischen Erkenntnisstheorie. Berlin, 1878.

Phil 1115.1 — Kühnemann, E. Grundlehren der Philosophie. Berlin, 1899.

Phil 3492.19 — Kühnemann, E. Kant. München, 1923-24. 2v.

Phil 3549.9.90 — Kühnemann, E. Mit unbefangener Stirn. Heilbronn, 1937.

Phil 3830.3 — Kühnemann, E. Uber die Grundlagen der Lehre des Spinoza. Halle, 1902.

Phil 3492.70.2 — Kühnemann, Eugen. Kants und Schillers Begründung der Ästhetik. Marburg, 1895.

Phil 3492.70 — Kühnemann, Eugen. Kants und Schillers Begründung der Ästhetik. München, 1895.

Phil 2490.124 — Kühnert, H. August Comtes Verhältnis zur Kunst. Leipzig, 1910.

Phil 2730.89 — Kühtmann, A. Maine de Biran. Bremen, 1901.

Phil 185.12.7 — Külpe, O. Einleitung in die Philosophie. Leipzig, 1895.

Phil 185.12.4 — Külpe, O. Einleitung in die Philosophie. 4. Aufl. Leipzig, 1907.

Phil 185.12.5 — Külpe, O. Einleitung in die Philosophie. 5. Aufl. Leipzig, 1910.

Phil 185.12.8 — Külpe, O. Einleitung in die Philosophie. 6. Aufl. Leipzig, 1913.

Phil 341.5 — Külpe, O. Erkenntnistheorie und Naturwissenschaft. Leipzig, 1910.

Phil 8411.13 — Külpe, O. Grundlagen der Ästhetik. Leipzig, 1921.

Phil 3492.7 — Külpe, O. Immanuel Kant. Leipzig, 1907.

Phil 185.12 — Külpe, O. Introduction to philosophy. London, 1897.

Phil 3010.2 — Külpe, O. Die Philosophie der Gegenwart in Deutschland. Leipzig, 1905.

Phil 3010.2.5 — Külpe, O. Die Philosophie der Gegenwart in Deutschland. Leipzig, 1911.

Phil 3010.2.26 — Külpe, O. The philosophy of the present in Germany. N.Y., 1913.

Phil 630.7A — Külpe, O. Die Realisierung. Leipzig, 1912. 3v.

Phil 185.12.20 — Pamphlet vol. Külpe, O. Über das Problem der Willensfreiheit. 10 pam.

Phil 5250.2.5 — Külpe, Oswald. Grundriss der Psychologie. Leipzig, 1893.

Phil 5250.2 — Külpe, Oswald. Outlines of psychology. London, 1895.

Phil 5250.2.3A — Külpe, Oswald. Outlines of psychology. London, 1921.

Phil 5250.2.8 — Külpe, Oswald. Vorlesungen über Psychologie. Leipzig, 1920.

Phil 5250.2.9 — Külpe, Oswald. Vorlesungen über Psychologie. 2. Aufl. Leipzig, 1922.

Phil 672.216 — Kuemmel, F. Über den Begriff der Zeit. Tübingen, 1962.

Phil 341.39 — Kuemmel, Friedrich. Platon und Hegel zur ontologischen Begründung des Zirkels in der Zeit. Tübingen, 1968.

Phil 3450.9.80 — Ein Künder neuer Lebenswege...R.M. Holzapfel. (Zbinden, H.) Jena, 1923.

Phil 5247.22 — Das Künftige Jahrhundert der Psychologie. (Heymans, G.) Leipzig, 1911.

Phil 8587.30 — Die künftige Religion. (Horneffer, Ernst.) Leipzig, 1909.

Phil 5068.53 — Küng, Gaide. Ontologie und logistische Analyse der Sprache. Wien, 1963.

Phil 5068.53.1 — Küng, Gaide. Ontology and the logistic analysis of language. Dordrecht, 1967.

Phil 6320.10.5 — Künkel, Fritz. Die Arbeit am Charakter. Schwerin, 1939.

Phil 9035.59.15 — Künkel, Fritz. Charakter, Einzelmensch und Gruppe. Leipzig, 1933.

Phil 9035.59.9 — Künkel, Fritz. Charakter, Wachstum und Erziehung. 2. Aufl. Leipzig, 1934.

Phil 9035.59.20 — Künkel, Fritz. Charakter. Leipzig, 1932.

Phil 6320.10 — Künkel, Fritz. Conquer yourself. N.Y., 1936.

Phil 9035.59.5 — Künkel, Fritz. Einfuhrung in die Charakterkunde auf individualpsychologischer Grundlage. 2. Aufl. Leipzig, 1929.

Phil 9035.59.7 — Künkel, Fritz. Einfuhrung in die Charakterkunde auf individualpsychologischer Grundlage. 8. Aufl. Leipzig, 1939.

Phil 5250.39 — Künkel, Fritz. In search of maturity. N.Y., 1944.

Phil 9035.58 — Künkel, Fritz. Let's be normal! N.Y., 1929.

Phil 9035.59.30 — Künkel, Fritz. Vitale Dialektik. Leipzig, 1929.

Phil 291.6 — Künkel, H. Das Gesetz deines Lebens. Jena, 1933.

Phil 185.64 — Künkel, H. Die Lebensalter. Jena, 1939.

Phil 3850.1.84 — Kuenkler, Heinrich. Zum Gedächtnis an David Friedrich Strauss. Wiesbaden, 1898.

Phil 9450.25 — Künneth, W. Politik zwischen Dämon und Gott. 1. Aufl. Berlin, 1954.

Phil 5593.63 — Künsler, W. Über Blutdeutungen im Rorschachschen Formdeutversuch. Bern, 1963.

Phil 5841.18.2 — Der Künstler; Ansatze zu einer Sexualpsychologie. 2. - 3. Aufl. (Rank, Otto.) Wien, 1918.

Phil 5841.18.4 — Der Künstler. 4. Aufl. (Rank, Otto.) Leipzig, 1925.

Phil 8080.20 — Künstler und Interpret; zur Modernen Ästhetik. (Hermann, Rolf-Dieter.) Bern, 1967.

Phil 3808.154 — Das künstlerische in der Aprache Schopenhauers. (Hochfeld, Sophus.) Leipzig, 1912.

Phil 974.3.3 — Das Künstlerische in seiner Weltmission. (Steiner, Rudolf.) Dornach, 1961.

Phil 5465.39 — Die künstlerische Phantasie. (Nussberger, M.) München, 1935.

Phil 3640.251 — Die künstlerischen Mittel der Darstellung in Nietzsches "Zarathustra". (Gerhard, H.F.) Berlin, 1896.

Phil 8404.21 — Künstlerisches und rationalisiertes Sehen. (Doucher, Hans.) München, 1967.

Phil 5780.15.20 — Die künstlich gesteuerte Seele. (Thomas, Klaus.) Stuttgart, 1970.

Phil 6671.16 — Der künstlich Hervorgerufene Somnambulismus. (Beaunis, H.) Leipzig, 1889.

Phil 3492.50.5 — Küpenberg, Max. Der Begriff der Pflicht in Kants vorkritischen Schriften. Innsbruck, 1927.

Phil 3492.50 — Küpenberg, Max. Ethische Grundfragen...Ethikvorselung Kants. Innsbruck, 1929.

Phil 3492.3 — Küpffer, C. Der Schädel Immanuel Kant's. Braunschweig, 1881?

Phil 9558.14 — Küppers, L. Psychologische Untersuchungen über die Lüge. Inaug. Diss. Duburg-Erft, 1928.

Phil 7150.14 — Kürten, O. Statistik des Selbstmordes im Königreich Sachsen. Leipzig, 1913.

Phil 3850.18.90 — Kürth, Herbert. Das Verhältnis von Ethik und Ästhetik bei Max Scheler. Diss. Leipzig, 1929.

Phil 9430.6 — Küssner, G. Kritk des Pessimismus. Halle, 1888.

Phil 8411.41 — Kuezyńska, Alicja. Przemiany wyobraźni. Wyd. 1. Warszawa, 1969.

Phil 6980.403 — Kugelmass, I.N. The management of mental deficiency in children. N.Y., 1954.

Phil 5238.140 — Kuhlen, Raymond. Psychological studies of human development. N.Y., 1952.

Phil 4065.99.2 — Kuhlenbeck, L. Bruno. 2e Aufl. Leipzig, 1899.

Phil 8590.23 — Kuhlmann, G. Theologische Anthropologie im Abriss. Tübingen, 1935.

Phil 978.67 — Kuhn, Alvin Boyd. Theosophy. N.Y., 1930.

Phil 1750.350.2 — Kuhn, H. Begegnung mit dem Nichts. Tübingen, 1950.

Phil 1750.350 — Kuhn, H. Encounter with nothingness. London, 1951.

Phil 3549.21 — Kuhn, H. Das Sein und das Gute. München, 1962.

Phil 978.93 — Kuhn, Hans. Es Ist an der Zeit. Nürnberg, 1965.

Phil 3425.578 — Kuhn, Helmut. Die Kulturfunktion der Kunst. Berlin, 1931. 2v.

Phil 8411.28.5 — Kuhn, Helmut. Schriften zur Ästhetik. München, 1966.

Phil 185.100   Kuhn, Helmut. Traktat über die Methode der Philosophie. München, 1966.

Phil 8411.28   Kuhn, Helmut. WesenUnd Wirken des Kunstwerks. München, 1960.

Phil 1930.10.82   Kuhn, M. Arno. Morris Raphael Cohen. N.Y., 1957.

Phil 5593.54.5   Kuhn, Roland. Maskendeutungen im Rorschachschen Versuch. 2. Aufl. Basel, 1954.

Phil 5425.112   Kuhn-Foelix, August. Vom Wesen des genialen Menschen. Zürich, 1968.

Phil 410.9   Kuhns, Levi O. The sense of the infinite. N.Y., 1908.

Phil 8411.22   Kuhr, Victor. Ästhetisches Erleben und kunstlerisches Schaffen. Stuttgart, 1929.

Phil 3492.39.5   Kuhrke, Walter. Kants Wohnhaus. 2. Aufl. Königsberg, 1924.

Phil 6634.5   Kuijper, Siem. Einge especten vom vrij en dwangmatig herhalen. Hilversum, 1963.

Phil 1020.4.40   Kuksewicz, Zdzislaw. Averroïsme bolonais au XIVe siècle. Wroclaw, 1965.

Phil 1020.4.41   Kuksewicz, Zdzislaw. De siger de Bredant à Jacques de Plaisance. Wroclaw, 1968.

Phil 4800.24   Kuksewicz, Zdzislaw. Z dziejów filosofii na Uniwersytecie Krakowskim w XV wieku. Wroclaw, 1965.

Phil 4710.40   Kulchitskii, Aleksandr. Die marxistisch-sowjetische Konzeption des Menschen. München, 1956.

Phil 3549.26   Kulenkampff, Arend. Antinomie und Dialektik. Stuttgart, 1970.

Phil 5760.4   Kulew, T. Das Probleme der Willensfreiheit und der Grundbegriffe der Strafrechts. Sofia, 1906.

Phil 8411.19   Kulke, Eduard. Kritik der Philosophie des Schönen. Leipzig, 1906.

Phil 5203.30   Kullman, Siv-Aino. Törster Husén. Tryckataskrifter 1940-1965. Stockholm, 1966.

Phil 8412.18   A különösség mintesztétikai kategória. (Lukács, György.) Budapest, 1957.

Phil 5050.12   Kulpe, Oswald. Vorlesungen über Logik. Leipzig, 1923.

Phil 3120.15.97.5   Kultur. (Bickel, Lothar.) Zürich, 1956.

Phil 4655.1.35   Kultur och filosofi i deras förhällande till hvarandra. (Wikner, Pontus.) Stockholm, 1869.

Phil 3790.14   Kultur und Barbarei. 2e Aufl. (Reinwald, J.G.) Mainz, 1828.

Phil 5440.31   Kultur und Ertartung. (Bumke, O.) Berlin, 1922.

Phil 2150.22.30   Kultur und Gesellschaft. (Marcuse, Herbert.) Frankfurt, 1965. 2v.

Phil 9450.61   Kultura, politika in morala. (Rus, Vojan.) Maribor, 1969.

Phil 8400.57   Kul'tura chuvstv. Moskva, 1968.

Phil 4803.495.20   Kultura i fetysze; zbiór rozpraw. Wyd. 1. (Kotakowski, Leszek.) Warszawa, 1967.

Phil 8410.9   Kul'tura i stil'. (Joffe, Jeremiia I.) Leningrad, 1927.

RRC   Phil 8980.330   Kul'tura povedeniia sovetskogo molodogo cheloveka. Izd. 3. (Dodon, Larisa L.) Leningrad, 1957.

Phil 5238.8   Die kulturelle Bedeutung der komplexen Psychologie. (Psychologischer Club, Zürich.) Berlin, 1935.

Phil 4630.4.40   Kulturen och tiden. (Ruin, Waldemar.) Helsingfors, 1920.

Phil 8887.75.5   Kulturethik. (Messner, J.) Innsbruck, 1954.

Phil 3425.578   Die Kulturfunktion der Kunst. (Kuhn, Helmut.) Berlin, 1931. 2v.

Phil 3200.8.5   Kulturgeschichtliche Autobiographie. (Ehrlich, W.) Tübingen, 1961.

Phil 4650.1.35   Kulturidealism. (Vannérus, Allen.) Stockholm, 1903.

Phil 20.6   Kulturphilosophische und philosophiegeschichtliche Studien. Würzburg. 1-3,1937-1938 3v.

Phil 9455.17   Kulturpropaganda. (Rühlmann, Paul.) Charlottenburg, 1919.

Phil 8590.12   Kulturwege und Erkenntnisse. (Köhler, Friedrich.) Leipzig, 1916. 2v.

Phil 530.20.55   Die Kulturwerte der deutschen Mystik des Mittelalters. (Grabmann, M.) Augsburg, 1923.

Phil 8411.23.5   Kulvanov, B.G. Gnoseologicheskaia priroda literatury i iskusstva. L'vov, 1958.

Phil 7060.256   Kummerich, M. Gespenster und Spuk. Ludwigshafenam Bodensee, 1921.

Phil 8411.39   Kuncheva, L.I. Esteticheskoe i eticheskoe v zhizni i v iskusstve. Moskva, 1968.

Phil 1750.605   Kundschafter der Existenztiefe. (Pfleger, Karl.) Frankfurt, 1959.

Phil 8430.40   Kundt und Sittlichkeit. (Thode, H.) Heidelberg, 1906.

Phil 3492.33   Kunhardt, H. I. Kants Grundlegung zur Metaphysik der Sitten. Lübeck, 1800.

Phil 530.20.67   Kunisch, H. Das Wort "Grund" in der Sprache der deutschen Mystik des 14. und 15. Jahrhunderts. Inaug.-Diss. Osnabrück, 1929.

Phil 3270.1.82   Kuno Fischer. (Sosnioski, M.E.V.) Breslau, n.d.

Phil 3270.1.84   Kuno Fischer: Rede...seine 100. Geburstages. (Hoffmann, E.) Heidelberg, 1924.

Phil 3270.1.80   Kuno Fischer Gedächtnisrede. (Windelband, W.) Heidelberg, 1907.

Phil 3270.1.81   Kuno Fischer und der litterarhistorische Methode. (Falken, H.N.) Berlin, 1892.

Phil 3487.1.10   Kuno Fischer und sein Kant. (Trendelenburg, A.) Leipzig, 1869.

Phil 4630.4.30   Kunskap och ideal. (Ruin, Waldemar.) Helsingfors, 1886.

Phil 4650.1.39   Kunskapslära. (Vannérus, Allen.) Stockholm, 1905.

Phil 4600.2.39   Kunskapslivet. 3e uppl. (Larsson, Hans.) Stockholm, 1920.

Phil 3915.158   Kunskapsteoretiska studier med särskild hänsyn till Wundts äsikt. (Svensson, P.I.K.) Lund, 1904.

Phil 3120.15.30   Kunst, Philosophie, Mystik, Gesammelte Anfsätze. (Brunner, Constantin.) Zürich, 1940.

Phil 3120.55.25   Die Kunst, Schiller zu sprechen und andere literarische Aufsätze. (Bloch, Ernst.) Frankfurt, 1969. 14v.

Phil 8125.37   Kunst- und Dichtungstheorien zwischen Aufklärung und Klassik. (Nivelle, A.) Berlin, 1960.

Phil 8125.37.2   Kunst- und Dichtungstheorien zwischen Aufklärung und Klassik. 2. Aufl. (Nivelle, A.) Berlin, 1971.

Phil 8411.9   Kunst als Ausdruckstätigkeit; biologische Voraussetzungen der ästhetik. (Kohnstamm, O.) München, 1907.

Phil 978.49.143   Die Kunst der Rezitation und Deklamation. 2. Aufl. (Steiner, R.) Dornach, 1967.

Phil 5520.56   Die Kunst des begrifflichen Denkens. (Jordan, Leo.) München, 1926.

Phil 200.15.5   Die Kunst des Kritisieren. (Zerle, Herbert.) Berlin, 1957.

Phil 8402.66   Kunst eller kaos? (Baekkelund, Kjell.) Oslo, 1969.

Phil 978.49.610   Kunst im Lichte der Mysterienweisheit. (Steiner, R.) Dornach, 1966.

Phil 3450.29.90   Die Kunst in christlicher Daseinsverantwortung nach Theodor Haecker. Thesis. (Eid, Volker.) Würzburg, 1968.

Phil 6020.1   Die Kunst in der Liebe und Freundschaft. Pesth, 1816.

Phil 8430.12   Die KunstIn ihrer Beziehung. (Dreher, Eugen.) Berlin, 1878.

Phil 3915.154   Die Kunst nach Wilhelm Wundt. (Bernstein, Xenja.) Nürnberg, 1914.

Phil 8886.76   Kunst og etik. (Loegstrup, K.E.C.) Kobenhavn, 1961.

Phil 8413.35   Kunst og idé. (Medlöe, Jon.) Oslo, 1965.

Phil 3425.692   Kunst und Freiheit. (Horn, András.) Den Haag, 1969.

Phil 8416.26   Kunst und Illusion. (Pap, Julius.) Leipzig, 1914.

Phil 8092.13   Kunst und Koexistenz. (Fischer, Ernst.) Reinbek, 1966.

Phil 3640.688   Kunst und Künstlerexistenz bei Nietzsche und Thomas Mann. (Puetz, Heinz Peter.) Bonn, 1963.

Phil 8408.38   Kunst und Kult. (Halder, A.) Freiburg, 1964.

Phil 978.49.340   Kunst und Kunsterkuntniss. (Steiner, R.) Dornach, 1961.

Phil 8416.11.10   Kunst und Literatur. (Plekhanov, Georgii Valentinovich.) Berlin, 1955.

Phil 8414.11   Kunst und schöpferisches Unbewusstes. (Neumann, E.) Zürich, 1954.

Phil 2885.110   Die Kunstphilosophie von H.A. Taine. (Zeitler, Julius.) Leipzig, 1901.

Phil 8419.33   Kunstschöpfer und Kunstschaffen. (Saitschick, R.) Marburg, 1957.

Phil 8125.8   Das Kunstschone und chacaktivstische von Winckelmann bis Friedrich Schlegel. Inaug. Diss. (Denk, Ferdinand.) München, 1925.

Phil 97.2.5   Kunstsprache der kritischen Philosophie. (Mellin, G.S.A.) Jena, 1798.

Phil 8423.14   Das Kunstwerk als Organismus. (Waetzoldt, W.) Leipzig, 1905.

Phil 8406.13   Kunstwissenschaftliche Grundfragen. (Frey, Dagobert.) Wien, 1946.

Phil 8400.22   Die Kunstwissenschaft der Gegenwart in Selbstdarstellungen. (Jahn, Johannes.) Leipzig, 1924.

Phil 8407.21   Kunstwissenschaftliche Studien. (Grosse, Ernst.) Tübingen, 1900.

Phil 6120.14   Kuntz, A. The autonomic nervous system. Philadelphia, 1934.

Phil 5760.7   Kuntz, Leo F. Education of the will in the light of modern research. Diss. Washington, D.C., 1927.

Phil 835.6   Kuntze, Friedrich. Erkenntnistheorie. München, 1927.

Phil 3625.5.87   Kuntze, Friedrich. Die Philosophie Salomon Maimons. Heidelberg, 1912.

Phil 5520.73   Kunz, H. Zur Phänomenologie und Analyse des Ausdrucks. Basel, 1934.

Phil 3801.499   Kunz, Hans. Schellings Gedichte und dichtischer Pläne. Zürich, 1955.

Phil 5250.50   Kunz, Hans. Über den Sinn und die Grenzen des psychologischen Erkennens. Zürich, 1957.

Phil 8430.31   Kunzle, Magnus. Ethik und Asthetik. Freiburg, 1910.

Phil 930.56   Kuo, Mo-jo. Bronzovij vek. Moskva, 1959.

Phil 930.62   Kuo, Mo-jo. Filosofy drevnego kitaia. Moskva, 1961.

Phil 8411.33   Kupareo, Raimundo. Tratado de estetica. v.1- Santiago de Chile, 1964-

Phil 5627.115   Kupky, Oscar. The religious development of adolescents. N.Y., 1928.

Phil 6120.21   Kupper, H.I. Back to life. N.Y., 1945.

Phil 8885.56   Kupperman, Joel J. Ethical knowledge. London, 1970.

Phil 341.34   Kurazhkovskaia, E.A. Dialektika protsessa poznaniia. Moskva, 1960.

Phil 396.12.2   Kurella, Alfred. Das Eigene und das Fremde. Neue Beiträge zum sozialist. Humanismus. 2. Aufl. Berlin, 1970.

Phil 310.140   Kurella, Alfred. Der Mensch als Schöpfer seiner Selbst. Berlin, 1958.

Phil 6980.14.100   Kurge Geschichte der Psychiatrie. (Ackerknecht, E.H.) Stuttgart, 1957.

Phil 310.554.2   Kurs istoricheskogo materializma. 2. Izd. (Kelle, Vladislav Zh.) Moskva, 1969.

Phil 310.575   Kurs marksistskoi filosofii. (Spizkin, A.G.) Moskva, 1963.

Phil 310.525   Kursanov, G.A. Dialekticheskii materializm o poniatii. Moskva, 1963.

Phil 1810.5   Kursanov, G.A. Gnoseologiia sovremennaia pragmatizma. Moskva, 1958.

Phil 400.121.5   Kursanov, Georgii A. Sovremennia idealisticheskaia gnoseologiia. Moskva, 1968.

Phil 400.121   Kursanov, Georgii A. Sovremennyi ob"ektivnyi idealizm. Moskva, 1960.

Phil 3415.97   Kurt, N. Wahrheit und Dichtung in den Hauptlehren Eduard von Hartmann's. Leipzig, 1894.

Phil 5760.3   Kurt, N. Die Willensprobleme. Weimar, 1902.

Phil 5251.41.90   Kurt Lewin, une théorie du change dans les sciences de l'homme. (Kaufmann, Pierre.) Paris, 1968.

Phil 3585.13.90   Kurth, Hans. Die Weltdeutung Mathilde Ludendorffs. München, 1932.

Phil 3808.194   Kurth, K.O. Arthur Schopenhauer. Kitzingen, 1952.

Phil 341.18   Kurth, R. Vonden Grenzen des Wissens. München, 1953.

Phil 5270.2   Kurtz, Kenneth Hassett. Foundations of psychological research. Boston, 1965.

Phil 1830.54   Kurtz, Paul W. American thought before 1900. 1st ed. N.Y., 1966.

Phil 5760.14   Kurtz, Paul W. Decision and the condition of man. Seattle, 1965.

Phil 735.134   Kurtz, Paul W. The problems of value theory. Thesis. N.Y., 1952.

Phil 801.5.15   Kurtze Fragen aus der philosophischen Historie. (Brucker, J.) Ulm, 1731-36. 7v.

Phil 8697.11   Kurtze Fragen von den natürlichen Dingen. (Hoffmann, J.G.) Halle, 1757.

Phil 3010.11   Kurucz, J. Die Opposition der Jugendbrücken. Saar, 1958.

Phil 3270.6.80   Kurz, August. Über Christian Gabriel Fischers vernünftige Gedanken von der Natur. Inaug. Diss. Halle, 1908.

Phil 1135.230   Kurz, Dietrich. Akpibeia. Göppingen, 1970.

Phil 3819.41.15   Kurze Abhandlung von Gott dem Menschen und seinen Glück. (Spinoza, Benedictus de.) Leipzig, 1922.

Phil 8597.3.15   Kurze auch dem Laien verstandliche Verantwortung wider die Beschuldigungen. (Blasche, J.C.) Jena, 1778.

Phil 5055.6   Kurze Darstellung des Hauptinhalts der Logik. (Püllenberg, Johann.) Coblenz, 1854.

Phil 3805.33.10   Kurze Darstellung des theologischen Studiums. (Schleiermacher, Friedrich.) Berlin, 1811.

Phil 5642.20   Kurze Einführung in die Farbe-Ton-Forschung. (Anschütz, Georg.) Leipzig, 1927.

Phil 3428.37   Kurze Encyklopädie der Philosophie. (Herbart, J.F.) Halle, 1841.

Phil 3842.3   Kurze Erklarung Ethic von Spinoza. (Wahle, R.) Wien, 1899.

Phil 8050.21.2   Kurze Geschichte der Ästhetik. (Ovsiannikov, M.F.) Berlin, 1966.

Phil 1719.1   Kurze pragmatische Geschichte der neueren Philosophie. (Thilo, C.A.) Göthen, 1874.

Phil 3494.33 Kurze und deutliche Darstellung des Kantischen Systemes. (Metz, Andreas.) Bamberg, 1795.

Phil 818.16 Kurzer Abriss der Geschichte der Philosophie. (Snell, P.L.) Giessen, 1819. 2v.

Phil 3500.57 Kurzer Entwurf der unausstehlichen Ungereimtheiten der Kantischen Philosophie. (Stattler, B.) n.p., 1791.

Phil 70.1.3.2 Kurzer Gesamt-Bericht die Tätigkeit in der Sektionen und allgemeinen Sitzungen. (International Congress of Philosophy, 3rd, Heidelberg, 1908.) Heidelberg. 1908

Phil 3819.41 Kurzer Tractat von Gott. (Spinoza, Benedictus de.) Freiburg, 1881.

Phil 6328.11 Kurzes Lehrbuch der Psychoanalyse. (Stollenhoff, H.) Stuttgart, 1926.

Phil 5258.50 Kurzgefaszte empirische Psychologie. (Schuchter, Josef.) Wien, 1902.

Phil 5259.45 Kurzzeitige nacheffekte unserer Wahrnehmungen. (Thurner, Franz K.) Berlin, 1961.

Phil 9560.64 Kuş, Nuri. Güneş batidan doğmustur. Kütahya, 1970.
Phil 3460.84 Kusch, E. C.G.J. Jacobi und Helmholtz auf dem Gymnasium. Potsdam, 1896.

Phil 6315.2.425 Kushner, Martin D. Freud, a man obsessed. Philadelphia, 1967.

Phil 185.106 Kuspit, Donald Burton. The philosophical life of the senses. N.Y., 1969.

Phil 70.3.75 Kussmann, Thomas. Achtzehnte Internationale Kongress für Psychologie in Moskau, 1966. Göttingen, 1967.

Phil 5520.27.2 Kussmaul, A. Die Störungen der Sprache. Leipzig, 1887.
Phil 3808.112.15 Kusten, Wallebald. Züruck zu Schopenhauer. Berlin, 1910.
VPhil 310.704 Kusý, Miroslav. Marxistická filozofia. 2. Vyd. Bratislava, 1969.

Phil 310.55 Kutasov, D.A. V chem sostoit osnovnoi vopros filosofii. Moskva, 1958.

Phil 8885.24 Kutna, G. Egoismus und Altruismus als Grundlage des Sittlichen. Berlin, 1903.

Phil 3450.11.230 Kutschera, Franz. Über das Problem des Angangs der Philosophie im Spätwerk Edmund Husserl. München, 1960.
Phil 5050.24 Kutschera, Franz von. Die Antinomien der Logik. Freiburg, 1969.

Phil 5050.25 Kutschera, Franz von. Elementare Logik. Wien, 1967.
Phil 3492.28 Kutter, Hermann. Im Anfang war die Tat: Versuch einer Orientierung in der Philosophie Kants. Basel, 1924.

Phil 3492.76 Kuypers, Karel. Immanuel Kant. Baarn, 1966.
Phil 3549.24 Kuypers, Karel. Verspreide Geschriften. Assen, 1968. 2v.

Phil 2050.190 Kuypers, M.S. Studies in the eighteenth-century background of Hume's empiricism. Minneapolis, 1930.

Phil 5066.277 Kuzichev, Aleksandr S. Diagrammy Venna. Moskva, 1968.
Phil 310.637 Kuz'min, Vsevolod P. Kategoriia mery v marksistskoi dialektike. Moskva, 1966.

Phil 4065.186 Kuznetsov, Boris G. Dzhordano Bruno i genesis klassicheskoi nauki. Moskva, 1970.

Phil 2410.1 Kuznetsov, Vitalii N. Frantsuzskaia burzhuaznaia filosofiia dvadtsatogo veka. Moskva, 1970.

Phil 2880.8.255 Kuznetsov, Vitalii N. Zhan-Pol Sartr i ekzistentsializm. Moskva, 1969.

Phil 8411.21 Kuznitzky, G. Die Seinssymbolik des Schönen und die Kunst. Berlin, 1932.

Phil 7069.06.15 Kvaran, E.H. Dularfull fyrirbrigd Reykjavik, 1906.
Phil 7069.17.29 Kvaran, E.H. Líf og daudi. Reykjavik, 1917.
Phil 7069.05.12 Kvaran, E.H. Samband viðframlida menn. Reykjavik, 1905.
Phil 7069.19.152 Kvaran, E.H. Trú og sannanir. Reykjavik, 1919.
Phil 5220.6 Kvasov, Dmitrii G. Fiziologicheskaia shkola I.P. Pavlova. Leningrad, 1967.

Phil 3552.229 Kvêt, F.B. Leibnitz und Comenius. Prag, 1857.
Phil 3552.229.5 Kvêt, F.B. Leibnitz'ens Logik. Prag, 1857.
Phil 3010.9 Kvochow, Christian C. von. Die Entscheidung. Stuttgart, 1958.

Phil 3549.22 Kwant, R.C. Critique; its nature and function. Pittsburgh, 1967.

Phil 3549.20 Kwant, R.C. Mens en kritiek. Utrecht, 1962.
Phil 1750.115.175 Kwant, Remigius Cornelis. Phenomonology of expression. Pittsburgh, 1969.

Phil 2750.20.80 Kwant, Remigius Cornelis. De fenomenologie van Merleau-Ponty. Utrecht, 1962.

Phil 2750.20.110 Kwant, Remigius Cornelis. From phenomenology to metaphysics. Pittsburgh, 1966.

Phil 2750.20.82 Kwant, Remigius Cornelis. Mens en expressie, in het licht van de wijsbegeerte van Merleau-Ponty. Utrecht, 1968.

Phil 585.65 Kwant, Remy C. Encounter. Pittsburgh, 1960.
Phil 585.66 Kwant, Remy C. Wijsbegeerte van de ontmoeting. Utrecht, 1959.

Phil 20.5 Kwartalnik filozoficzny. Kraków. 1-18,1923-1949 11v.
Phil 20.3 Kwartalnik psychologiczny. Poznán. 1-6,1930-1935 6v.
Phil 75.55 Kwee, Swan Liat. Bibliography of humanism. Utrecht, 1957.
Phil 310.692 Kybernetik, Information, Widerspiegelung. (Kirschenmann, Peter.) München, 1969.

Phil 5520.656 Kybernetische Analysen geistigen Prozesse. Berlin, 1968.
Phil 5145.3 Kyburg, Henry E. Studies in subjective probability. N.Y., 1964.

Phil 2050.113 Kydd, Rachel M. Reason and conduct in Hume's treatise. London, 1946.
Phil 5050.17 Kyle, William M. The elements of deductive logic. 4th ed. Brisbane, 1957.

Phil 185.11.5 Kym, A.L. Metaphysische Untersuchungen. München, 1875.
Phil 185.11 Kym, A.L. Die Weltanschauungen. Zürich, 1854.
Phil 8620.26 Kym, Arnold L. Das Problem des Bösen. München, 1878.
Phil 3492.31 Kynast, R. Kant: sein System als Theorie des Kulturbewusstseins. München, 1928.

Phil 341.13 Kynast, R. Das Problem der Phänomenologie. Breslau, 1917.
Phil 185.39 Kynast, R. Ein Weg zur Metaphysik. Leipzig, 1927.
Phil 5068.65 Kyserling, Arnold. Der Wiener Denkstil: Mach, Carnap. Graz, 1965.

Phil 486.6 L, B.L. Matter and energy. London, 1887.
Phil 3235.111 L. Feuerbach; en monografi. (Starcke, C.N.) Kjøbenhavn, 1883.

Phil 6060.86 L. Kroeber-Keneth's Buch der Graphologie. 1. Aufl. (Kroeber-Keneth, Ludwig.) Düsseldorf, 1968.

Phil 5374.244 L.S.D. on campus. (Young, Warren R.) N.Y., 1966.
Phil 2055.5.90 L.T. Hobhouse; his life and work. (Hobson, John A.) London, 1931.

Phil 4803.536.20 L zagadnień logiki i filozofii; pisma wybrane. (Lukasiewicz, Jan.) Warszawa, 1961.

Phil 3425.120 La dottrina dello stato di G.F.G. Hegel. (Levi, Giuseppe.) Pavia, 1880-84.

Phil 2415.12A La libertinage érudit dans la première mortié du XVII siècle. v.1-2. (Pintard, René.) Paris, 1943.

Phil 5042.5.5 La logique. 2e éd. (Crousaz, J.P. de.) Amsterdam, 1720. 3v.

Phil 8843.6 La metafisica nella morale moderna. (Scotti, Giulio.) Milano, 1903.
Phil 2705.81.2 La Mettrie. (Du Bois-Reymond, E.) Berlin, 1875.
NEDL Phil 2705.81 La Mettrie. (Du Bois-Reymond, E.) Berlin, 1875.
Phil 8404.12 La mission de l'art. (Delville, Jean.) Bruxelles, 1900.
Phil 1750.450.5 La notion de liberte dans l'existentialisme positif de Nicola Abbagnano. (Simona, Maria.) Fribourg, 1962.
Phil 1750.144A La notion de renaissance dans l'histoire de la philosophie. (Bréhier, Émile.) Oxford, 1934.
Phil 672.123 La notion d'espace. (Nys, Désiré.) Bruxelles, 1922.
Phil 6053.2.1 La science de la main. The science of the hand. (Arpentigny, Casimir Stanislas d'.) London, 1886.
Phil 2270.132 La vita di H. Spencer, ed "I primi principii". (Sacerdote, S.) Torino, 1907.
Phil 400.4 Laas, E. Idealistische und Positivistische. Berlin, 1879-1884. 3v.
Phil 3493.1 Laas, E. Kants Analogien der Erfahrung. Berlin, 1876.
Phil 3493.1.5 Laas, E. Kants Stellung in der Geschichte des Conflicts zwischen Glauben und Wissen. Berlin, 1882.
Phil 7069.39.57 Labadié, Jean. Aux frontières de l'au-dela. Paris, 1939.
Phil 3808.90.1 Laban, Ferdinand. Die Schopenhauer-Literatur. N.Y., 1970.
Phil 5051.20 Labanca, B. Della dialettica. v.1-2. Firenze, 1874.
Phil 8591.33 Labanca, B. Della religione e della filosofia cristiana. Pt.2. Torino, 1888.
Phil 4285.1.95 Labanca, B. Sopra Giacomo Zabarella. Napoli, 1878.
Phil 4160.1.33 Labanca, Baldassare. Della filosofia razionale. 2a ed. Firenze, 1868. 2v.
Phil 4160.1.40 Labanca, Baldassare. Il mio testamento. Agnone, 1913.
Phil 4160.1.85 Labanca, Baldassare. Ricordi autobiografici. Agnone, 1913.
Phil 8961.5 La Barre, A. La morale d'après St. Thomas. Paris, 1911.
Phil 6159.16.1 La Barre, Weston. The peyote cult. Hamden, 1964.
Phil 3425.675 Labarriere, Pierre Jean. Structures et mouvement dialectique dans la phenoménologie de l'esprit de Hegel. Paris, 1968.
Phil 2733.104 Labbas, Lucien. La grace et la liberté dans Malebranche. Paris, 1931.
Phil 2733.104.15 Labbas, Lucien. La grace et la liberté dans Malebranche. Thèse. Paris, 1931. 2 pam.
Phil 2733.104.10 Labbas, Lucien. L'idée de science dans Malebranche et son originalité. Paris, 1931.
Phil 9075.5 Labbé, J. La conscience. Paris, 1868.
Phil 9070.42 Label your luggage. (Nash, R.S.J.) Dublin, 1943.
Phil 8591.22 La Belle, Alfred. Essai sur l'origine des cults. Paris, 1880.
Phil 6021.5 La Bellière, C. de. La physionomie raisonnée. Lyon, 1681.
Phil 292.9 Laberenne, P. L'origine des mondes. Paris, 1936.
Phil 2520.194 Laberthonnière, L. Études sur Descartes. Paris, 1935. 2v.
Phil 8591.27 Laberthonnière, L. Le réalisme chrétien et l'idealisme grec. Paris, 1904.
Phil 8591.27.6 Laberthonniere, Lucien. Le réalisme chrétien, précédé de essais de philosophie religieuse. Paris, 1966.
Phil 8591.27.5 Laberthonniere, Lucien. Il realismo cristiano e l'idealismo greco. Firenze, 1922.
Phil 2725.22 Laberthounière, L. Oeuvres. Paris, 1937.
Phil 45.1 Laboratorio di Psicologia Sperimentale, Florence. Istituto di Studi Superiori. Ricerche psicologia. Firenze. 1-2,1905-1907
Phil 5249.7.5.3 Laboratory equipment for psychological experiments. (Judd, C.H.) N.Y., 1907.
Phil 7069.39.9 Laboratory investigations into psychic phenomena. (Carrington, H.) Philadelphia, 1939.
Phil 5252.72 A laboratory manual in general experimental psychology. (Munn, Norman L.) Pittsburgh, 1934.
Phil 5249.7.5.2 Laboratory manual of psychology. (Judd, C.H.) N.Y., 1907.
Phil 5246.47 Laboratory studies in psychology. (Guilford, Joy Paul.) N.Y., 1934.
Phil 2520.147 Labordère, Marcel. Une profession de foi cartésienne. Paris, 1919.
Phil 665.62 Laborier-Tradens, A. Le bonheur est en nous-mêmes. Paris, 1931.
Phil 4065.103 Labriola, Arturo. Giordano Bruno. Roma, 1924?
Phil 4065.103.5 Labriola, Arturo. Giovanni Bovio e Giordano Bruno. Napoli, 1911.
Phil 9230.11 Labrousse, Louis. De l'exception de jeu. Paris, 1897.
Phil 6321.16 Laburu, J.A. de. Anormalidades del caracter. Montevideo, 1941.
Phil 5520.514 The labyrinth of language. (Black, Max.) N.Y., 1968.
Phil 6321.51 Lacan, Jacques. Écrits. Paris, 1966.
Phil 5520.525 Lacan, Jacques. The language of the self. Baltimore, 1968.
Phil 6321.51.10 Lacan, le symbolique et l'imaginaire. (Palmier, Jean Michel.) Paris, 1969.
Phil 5761.18 Lacape, R.S. La notion de liberté et la crise du déterminisme. Paris, 1935.
Phil 3831.16 Lacharrière, R. Études sur la théorie démocratique. Paris, 1963.
Phil 2725.11.30 Lachelier, Jules. Du fondement de l'induction. Paris, 1871.
Phil 2725.11.31 Lachelier, Jules. Études sur le syllogisme. Paris, 1907.
Phil 2725.11.20 Lachelier, Jules. La nature. 1e éd. Paris, 1955.
Phil 2725.11.15 Lachelier, Jules. Oeuvres. Paris, 1933. 2v.
Phil 2725.11.75 Lachelier, Jules. The philosophy of Jules Lachelier. The Hague, 1960.
Phil 3493.20 Lachièze-Rey, P. L'idéalisme Kantien. Thèse. Paris, 1931.
Phil 3493.20.5 Lachièze-Rey, P. L'idéalisme Kantien. Thèse. 2. éd. Paris, 1950.
Phil 2725.21 Lachièze-Rey, P. Le moi, le monde et Dieu. Paris, 1938.
Phil 3831.15 Lachièze-Rey, P. Les origines cartésiennes du Dieu de Spinoza. Thèse. Paris, 1932.
Phil 8961.10 Lachmann, J.J. Religion og ethik. Kjobenhavn, 1897.
Phil 2885.84.5 Lacombe, Paul. La psychologie des individus et des societés chez Taine. Paris, 1906.
Phil 2885.84 Lacombe, Paul. Taine historien et sociologue. Paris, 1909.
Phil 2805.335 Lacombe, R.E. L'apologétique de Pascal. Paris, 1958.
Phil 2475.1.284 Lacombe, R.E. La psychologie bergsonienne; étude critique. Paris, 1933.
Phil 2725.2.81 Lacordaire, H. Considérations sur le système philosophique de M. de Lamennais. Paris, 1834.
Phil 8666.1 Lacordaire, P.J.B.H.D. God. London, 1870.
Phil 3493.40 Lacorte, Carmelo. Kant. Ancora un episodio dell' alianza di religione e filosofia. Urbino, 1969.
Phil 3425.485 Lacorte, Carmelo. Il primo Hegel. Firenze, 1959.
Phil 8666.9 Lacour, J.B. Dieu et la création. Paris, 1866.
NEDL Phil 12.1.5 La critique philosophique. Supplemente. La critique religieuse. Paris. 1878-1885 7v.

Author and Title Listing

Phil 1750.760 — Lacroix, Jean. Histoire et mystère. Tournai, 1962.
Phil 3493.44.3 — Lacroix, Jean. Kant et le Kantisme. 3. éd. Paris, 1969.
Phil 2725.24 — Lacroix, Jean. Marxisme, existentialisme, personnalisme. Paris, 1950.
Phil 2477.6.150 — Lacroix, Jean. Maurice Blondel. Paris, 1963.
Phil 8666.21.5 — Lacroix, Jean. The meaning of modern atheism. N.Y., 1966.
Phil 2411.9 — Lacroix, Jean. Panorama de la philosophie française contemporaine. Paris, 1966.
Phil 2490.140 — Lacroix, Jean. La sociologie d'Auguste Comte. Paris, 1956.
Phil 2490.140.5 — Lacroix, Jean. La sociologie d'Auguste Comte. 2. éd. Paris, 1961.
Phil 3831.18 — Lacroix, Jean. Spinoza et le problème du salut. Paris, 1970.
Phil 5400.94.5 — Lacroze, R. L'angoisse et l'émotion. Paris, 1938.
Phil 5400.94 — Lacroze, R. L'angoisse et l'émotion. Paris, 1938.
Phil 5251.70 — Lacroze, René. Eléments d'anthropologie. Paris, 1966.
Phil 5465.38.5 — Lacroze, René. La fonction de l'imagination. Paris, 1938.
Phil 5465.38 — Lacroze, René. La fonction de l'imagination. Paris, 1938.
Phil 2730.116 — Lacroze, René. Maine de Biran. 1. éd. Paris, 1970.
Phil 6315.6 — L'activité psychique. (Forel, Auguste.) Genève, 1919.
Phil 186.79.5 — Lacuria, P.F.G. Les harmonies de l'être exprimées par les nombres. v.1-2. Paris, 1899.
Phil 9430.34 — Lacy, B.F. Pessimism. Philadelphia, 1920.
Phil 2270.141.5 — Lacy, William M. An examination of the philosophy of the unknowable as expounded by Herbert Spencer. Philaldelphia, 1883.
Phil 2270.141 — Lacy, William M. Examination of the philosophy of the unknowable as expounded by Herbert Spencer. Philadelphia, 1912.
Phil 6681.1 — Ladame, P. La névrose hypnotique. Paris, 1881.
Phil 5251.1.20 — Ladd, G.T. Descriptive psychology, N.Y., 1898.
Phil 5251.1.15.3 — Ladd, G.T. Elements of physiological psychology. London, 1889.
Phil 5251.1.15 — Ladd, G.T. Elements of physiological psychology. N.Y., 1887.
NEDL Phil 5251.1.15.8 — Ladd, G.T. Elements of physiological psychology. N.Y., 1896.
Phil 5251.1.18 — Ladd, G.T. Elements of physiological psychology. N.Y., 1911.
Phil 5251.1.22 — Ladd, G.T. Elements of physiology, psychology. N.Y., 1911.
Phil 186.16 — Ladd, G.T. Introduction to philosophy. N.Y., 1890.
Phil 186.16.15 — Ladd, G.T. Knowledge, life and reality. New Haven, 1918.
Phil 5251.1.16 — Ladd, G.T. Outlines of physiological psychology. N.Y., 1896.
Phil 342.1 — Ladd, G.T. Philosophie of knowledge. N.Y., 1897.
Phil 8886.17 — Ladd, G.T. Philosophy of conduct. N.Y., 1902.
Phil 5251.1.5 — Ladd, G.T. Philosophy of mind. N.Y., 1895.
Phil 5251.1.2 — Ladd, G.T. Primer of psychology. N.Y., 1894.
Phil 5251.1.10 — Ladd, G.T. Psychology descriptive and explanatory. N.Y., 1895.
Phil 186.16.5 — Ladd, G.T. Theory of reality. N.Y., 1899.
Phil 720.9 — Ladd, G.T. What can I know? N.Y., 1914.
Phil 9120.7 — Ladd, G.T. What ought I to do? N.Y., 1915.
Phil 5070.9 — Ladd, G.T. What should I believe? London, 1915.
Phil 575.23 — Ladd, George T. Secret of personality. N.Y., 1918.
Phil 8110.2 — Ladd, H.A. With eyes of the past. N.Y., 1928.
Phil 8701.15 — Ladd, H.O. The trade of scientific thought away from religious beliefs. Boston, 1909.
Phil 1145.79 — Lade biosas. Studien zur ältesten Ethik bei den Griechen. (Wehrli, Fritz.) Leipzig, 1931.
Phil 186.85 — Ladet, F. Méditations sur l'omnitude. Paris, 1936.
Htn Phil 1845.1.30* — The ladies calling. (Allestree, Richard.) Oxford, 1673.
Htn Phil 9340.6* — The ladies calling. (Allestree, Richard.) Oxford, 1673.
Phil 9351.13 — The ladies' companion...politeness of manners. 2d. ed. Brookfield, 1826.
NEDL Phil 9351.1.3 — Ladies library. London, 1714. 3v.
Phil 9351.1 — Ladies library. London, 1722.
NEDL Phil 9351.1.2 — Ladies library. London, 1751. 3v.
Phil 7084.24 — The lady of the hare, being a study in the healing power of dreams. (Layard, John Willoughby.) London, 1944.
Phil 8430.47 — Ladyhina, Aryadna B. Iskusstvo i sovremennost'. Minsk, 1964.
Phil 9167.3.9F — The lady's new-years gift, or Advice to a daughter. (Halifax, G.S.) Kensington, 1927.
Phil 9351.7.2 — Lady's pocket library. Philadelphia, 1792.
Phil 9351.7 — Lady's pocket library. Philadelphia, 1797.
Phil 9351.7.4 — Lady's pocket library. 4th ed. Philadelphia, 1809.
Phil 9340.5 — The lady's preceptor. (Ancourt, Abbe d'.) London, 1743.
Phil 9342.7 — Lady's present. (Cummings, A.I.) Boston, 1856.
Phil 5203.2 — Laehr, H. Die Literatur der Psychiatrie, Neurologie und Psychologie. v.1-3. Berlin, 1900. 4v.
Phil 4650.1.37 — Lära och lif. (Vannérus, Allen.) Stockholm, 1904.
Phil 5051.15.5 — Laerebog i den objektive logik. (Lyng, Georg V.) Christiania, 1881.
Phil 4655.1.45 — Lärobok i anthropologien. (Wikner, Pontus.) Upsala, 1870.
Phil 4630.2.36 — Lärobok i den formella logiken. (Rein, T.) Helsingfors, 1886.
Phil 5041.36.5 — Lärobok i den formella logiken. 4. Uppl. (Borelius, J.J.) Lund, 1882.
Phil 5058.34 — Lärobok i logik af Gustaf Sjöberg och Gustaf Klingberg. (Sjoberg, Gustaf.) Stockholm, 1887.
Phil 5050.5.15 — Lärobok i logiken. (Kiesewetter, J.G.C.C.) Abo, 1806.
Phil 5258.72.5 — Lärobok i psykologi. (Scheele, Frans von.) Stockholm, 1899.
Phil 260.9 — Lafaist, M. Dissertation sur la philosophie atomistique. Paris, 1833.
Phil 2880.8.216 — Lafarge, René. Jean-Paul Sartre: his philosophy. Notre Dame, 1970.
Phil 2880.8.215 — Lafarge, René. La philosophie de Jean Paul Sartre. Toulouse, 1967.
Phil 5520.433 — Laffal, Julius. Pathological and normal language. N.Y., 1965.
Phil 8701.18 — Laffey, C. Religion and science. London, 1940.
Phil 600.41 — Laffitte, P. Les grandes types de l'humanité. Paris, 1875-76. 2v.
Phil 186.66 — Laffitte, Pierre. Cours de philosophie première. Paris, 1889-1894. 2v.
Phil 2725.2.15 — Laffitte, Pierre. Cours philosophique sur l'histoire générale de l'humanité; discours d'ouverture, ordre et progrès. Paris, 1859.
Phil 2725.2.10 — Laffitte, Pierre. Moral positiva, sua necessidade atual. Rio de Janeiro, 1938.
Phil 3450.19.450 — Laffoucrière, Odette. Le destin de la pensée et la mort de Dieu selon Heidegger. La Haye, 1968.
Phil 5251.54 — Lafitte, Paul. The person in psychology. N.Y., 1957.
Phil 5051.7A — Lafleur, P.T. Illustrations of logic. Boston, 1899.

Phil 1200.24 — Lafon, R. Les stoïciens. Paris, n.d.
Phil 2477.1.100 — LaFontaine, A.P. La philosophie d'E. Boutroux. Paris, 1920.
Phil 6681.2 — Lafontaine, C. L'art de magnétiser. Paris, 1886.
Phil 6681.2.5 — Lafontaine, C. Mémoires d'un magnétiseur. Paris, 1866. 2v.
Phil 186.61 — Lafora, G.R. Don Juan, Los milagros y otros ensayos. Madrid, 1927.
Phil 1116.1 — Laforet, N.J. Histoire de la philosophie ancienne. Bruxelles, 1866. 2v.
Phil 6121.20 — La Forge, Louis de. Traité de l'esprit de l'homme. Amsterdam, n.d.
Phil 6121.20.5 — La Forge, Louis de. Traité de l'esprit de l'homme. Genève, 1725.
Phil 6121.20.3 — La Forge, Louis de. Traité de l'esprit de l'homme. Paris, 1666.
Phil 6321.12.15 — Laforgue, R. Au dela du scientisme. Genève, 1963.
Phil 6321.12.5 — Laforgue, R. Clinical aspects of psychoanalysis. London, 1938.
Phil 6321.12.10 — Laforgue, R. Psychopathologie de l'échec. Paris, 1944.
Phil 7084.4.15 — Laforgue, René. Le rêve et la psychanalyse. Paris, 1926.
Phil 2805.249.5 — Lafuma, Louis. Controverses pascaliennes. Paris, 1952.
Phil 2805.249.10 — Lafuma, Louis. Histoire des Pensées de Pascal. Paris, 1954.
Phil 2805.249A — Lafuma, Louis. Trois pensées inédites de Pascal. Paris, 1945.
Phil 5270.24 — Lagache, Daniel. L'unité de la psychologie. 2. éd. Paris, 1969.
Phil 5241.75.80 — La Garanderie, Antoine de. Le dynamisme des structures inconscientes dans la psychologie d'Albert Burloud. Louvain, 1969.
Phil 600.13 — Lagarrigue, J. Lettres sur le positivisme. Vincennes, 1886.
Phil 2490.134 — Lagarrigue, L. La paz del mundo y la alianza universal de las doctrinas. Santiago de Chile, 1940.
Phil 2490.132 — Lagarrigue, L. Politique internationale. Paris, 1928.
Phil 5400.74 — Lagerborg, R. Das Gefühlsproblem. Leipzig, 1905.
Phil 8886.19 — Lagerborg, R. La morale publique. Paris, 1903.
Phil 8886.19.5 — Lagerborg, R. Moralens vasen. Helsingfors, 1900.
Phil 342.8 — Lagerborg, R. Vetenskapliga vanföreställningars. Helsingfors, 1920.
Phil 4600.7.30 — Lagerborg, Rolf. Invita Minerva. Stockholm, 1918.
Phil 4600.6.2 — Lagerwall, A. Skrifter. Göteborg, 1921.
Phil 3493.10 — Lagerwall, A. Transscendentalfilosofiens problem och metod hos Kant. Göteborg, 1904.
Phil 4110.3.86 — La Giovine Calabria. Giornale, Catanzaro. Per Francesco Fiorentino nella inaugurazione del monumento in Catanzaro. Catanzaro, 1889.
Phil 2725.14.100 — Lagneau, Jules. Célèbres leçons et fragments. 2. éd. Paris, 1964.
Phil 186.24 — Lagos, C.D. La doctrina de los siglos. Santiago, 1910.
VPhil 9590.37 — Lagrange, Charles Henri. Mathématique de l'histoire, géométrie et cinématique. Bruxelles, 1900.
Phil 8591.16 — La Grasserie, R. de. De la psychologie des religions. Paris, 1899.
Phil 8886.57 — Lagresille, Henry. Monde moral, l'ordre des fins et des progrès. Paris, 1911.
Phil 5520.45 — Laguna, Grace A. de. Speech; its function and development. New Haven, 1927.
Phil 186.25 — Laguna, T. de. Dogmatism and evolution. N.Y., 1910.
Phil 8886.25 — Laguna, T. de. Introduction to the science of ethics. N.Y., 1914.
Phil 3425.216 — Lagus, R.E. De Hegeliana philosophiam juris tractandi ratione. Helsingforsiae, 1852.
Phil 4580.115 — La Harpe, J. La réligion comme conservation de la valeur dans ses rapports avec...H. Høffding. Lausanne, 1920.
Phil 5051.31 — LaHarpe, J. de. La logique de l'assertion pure. Paris, 1950.
Phil 2515.22.20 — LaHarpe, Jacqueline Ellen Violette de. Jean-Pierre de Crousaz et le conflit des idées au siècle des lumières. Genève, 1955.
Phil 8886.31 — La Hautière, E. de. Cours élémentaire de philosophie morale. 2. ed. Paris, 18- .
Phil 186.71 — La Hautière, E. de. Philosophie. Paris, 1895.
Phil 1133.48 — Lahaye, Robert. La philosophie ionienne, l'Ecole de Mileti Thales, Anaxemandre, Anaximène, Héraclite d'Ep'hèse. Paris, 1966.
Phil 575.251 — Lahbabi, Mohamed Aziz. De l'être à la personne. 1. éd. Paris, 1954.
Phil 2475.1.345 — Lahbabi, Mohamed Aziz. Liberté ou libération? Aubier, 1956.
Phil 2805.189 — Lahorque, P.M. Le réalisme de Pascal. Paris, 1923.
Phil 8610.963 — Lahoz Lainez, Bienvenido. El destino humano en el realismo introspectivo. Madrid, 1963.
Phil 2725.10.30 — Lahr, Charles. Cours de philosophie. 23e éd. Paris, 1920. 2v.
Phil 8961.6 — Lahy, J.M. La morale de Jésus. Paris, 1911.
Phil 6949.369 — Laiblin, Wilhelm. Märchenforschung und Tiefenpsychologie. Darmstadt, 1969.
Phil 8725.20 — Laïcité, liberté et vérité. (Jouguelet, Pierre.) Tournai, 1970.
Phil 8050.64 — La laideur dans l'art à travers les âges. (Krestovskaia, L.A.) Paris, 1947.
Phil 8125.28 — Laienurtheil über bildende Kunst bei den Alten. (Birt, Theodor.) Marburg, 1902.
Phil 6321.10 — Laignel-Lavastine, Maxime. Concentric method in the diagnosis of psychoneurotics. London, 1931.
Phil 5421.10.15 — Lain Entralgo, Pedro. La espera y la esperanza. Madrid, 1957.
Phil 5421.10.16 — Lain Entralgo, Pedro. La espera y la esperanza. 2. ed. Madrid, 1958.
Phil 1711.9 — Laín Entralgo, Pedro. Teoría y realidad del otro. Madrid, 1961. 2v.
Phil 2050.203 — Laing, B.M. David Hume. London, 1932.
Phil 8886.35 — Laing, B.M. A study in moral problems. London, 1922.
NEDL Phil 1850.105 — Laing, F.H. Lord Bacon's philosophy examined. London, 1877.
Phil 2880.8.143 — Laing, R.D. Reason and violence. London, 1964.
Phil 6321.53.10 — Laing, Roland David. Knots. London, 1970.
Phil 6321.53 — Laing, Roland David. The politics of experience. N.Y., 1967.
Phil 6961.19.5 — Laing, Ronald David. The divided self; a study. Chicago, 1960.
Phil 6976.17 — Laing, Ronald David. Sanity, madness and family: families of schizophrenics. 2. ed. London, 1970.
Phil 6961.19 — Laing, Ronald David. The self and others. London, 1961.
Phil 6961.19.2 — Laing, Ronald David. Self and others. 2. ed. London, 1969.

Phil 8701.7.2 Laing, Samuel. Modern science and modern thought. 2. ed. London, 1885.
Phil 5850.254 Lainz, Ronald David. Interpersonal perception. London, 1966.
Phil 5545.220 Laird, Donald. Techniques for efficient remembering. N.Y., 1960.
Phil 5850.253.10 Laird, Donald A. The dynamics of personal efficiency. 1. ed. N.Y., 1961.
Phil 5850.253.5 Laird, Donald A. Increasing personal efficiency. N.Y., 1925.
Phil 5850.253 Laird, Donald A. Increasing personal efficiency. N.Y., 1925.
Phil 186.96 Laird, J. The limits of speculative humanism. London, 1940.
Phil 8886.45.15 Laird, John. An enquiry into moral nations. London, 1935.
Phil 2045.115 Laird, John. Hobbes. London, 1934.
Phil 2050.198 Laird, John. Hume's philosophy of human nature. N.Y., 1932.
Phil 735.92 Laird, John. The idea of value. Cambridge, Eng., 1929.
Phil 342.14 Laird, John. Knowledge, belief and opinion. N.Y., 1930.
Phil 8666.14 Laird, John. Mind and deity. London, 1941.
Phil 186.69 Laird, John. Modern problems in philosophy. London, 1928.
Phil 8886.45.10 Laird, John. Morals and western religion. London, 1931.
Phil 5761.21 Laird, John. On human freedom. London, 1947.
Phil 6121.23 Laird, John. Our minds and their bodies. London, 1925.
Phil 575.24 Laird, John. Problems of the self. London, 1917.
Phil 8886.45 Laird, John. A study in moral theory. N.Y., 1926.
Phil 630.22 Laird, John. A study in realism. Cambridge, 1920.
Phil 8666.13 Laird, John. Theism and cosmology. London, 1940.
Phil 4688.110.32 Laisve ir būtist. (Girnius, Juozas.) Brooklyn, 1953.
Phil 8633.1.22 Lake, Kirsopp. Immortality and the modern mind. Cambridge, 1922.
Phil 8633.1.22.3 Lake, Kirsopp. Immortality and the modern mind. Cambridge, 1922.
Phil 3425.375 Lakebrink, Bernhard. Hegels dialektische Ontologie und die thomistische Analektik. Köln, 1955.
Phil 1750.552.5 Lakebrink, Bernhard. Klassische Metaphysik. Freiburg, 1967.
Phil 3425.712 Lakebrink, Bernhard. Studien zur Metaphysik Hegels. Freiburg, 1969.
Phil 5400.126 Lakobson,P.M. Psikhologiia chuvstv. Moskva, 1956.
Phil 1850.117.5 Lalande, A. L'interpretation de la nature dans le Valerius terminus. Mâcon, 1901.
Phil 1850.117 Lalande, A. Quid de mathematica senserit Baconus. Thesis. Lutetiae, 1899.
Phil 5620.24 Lalande, A. La raison et les normes. Paris, 1948.
Phil 96.3 Lalande, A. Vocabulaire technique et critique de la philosophie. Paris, 1926. 2v.
Phil 96.4.8 Lalande, A. Vocabulaire technique et critique de la philosophie. Paris, 1960.
Phil 96.4 Lalande, A. Vocabulaire technique et critique de la philosophie. 4. ed. Paris, 1932. 3v.
Phil 365.31.5 Lalande, André. La dissolution opposée a l'évolution dans les sciences physiques et morales. Paris, 1899.
Phil 365.31.15 Lalande, André. Les illusions évolutionnistes. Paris, 1930.
Phil 8886.37 Lalande, André. Précis raisonné de morale pratique. 2. ed. Paris, 1909.
Phil 8886.37.5 Lalande, André. Précis raisonné de morale pratique. 3. ed. Paris, 1930.
Phil 150.5 Lalande, André. Sur la critique et la fixation du langage philosophique. Paris, 19- . 2 pam.
Phil 5125.13 Lalande, André. Les théories de l'induction et de l'expérimentation. Paris, 1929.
Phil 186.125 Lalande, André. Vocabulaire technique et critique de la philosophie. 6. ed. Paris, 1951.
Phil 5251.2 Lallebasque. Introduzione alla filosofia naturale di pensiero. Lugano, 1824.
Phil 8430.18 Lalo, C. L'art et la morale. Paris, 1922.
Phil 8430.18.5 Lalo, C. L'arte et la vie sociale. Paris, 1921.
Phil 8412.6.10 Lalo, Charles. L'art et la vie. Paris, 1946-47. 3v.
Phil 8412.6.5 Lalo, Charles. L'expression de la vie dans l'art. Paris, 1933.
Phil 8412.6 Lalo, Charles. Notions d'esthétique. Paris, 1925.
Phil 8886.1 Lalor, J. Money and morals. London, 1852.
Phil 1750.166.85.5 Laloup, Jean. Communauté des hommes. 4e éd. Tournai, 1957.
Phil 1750.166.85 Laloup, Jean. Hommes et machines. Tournai, 1953.
Phil 2750.10.111 LaLumia, Joseph. The ways of reason; a critical study of the ideas of Emile Meyerson. N.Y., 1966.
Phil 5761.13 La Luzerne, C.G. de. Dissertation sur la liberté de l'homme. Langres, 1808.
Phil 5628.55.6 Lama, Friedrich. Therese Neumann; a stigmatist of our days. Milwaukee, 1929.
Phil 3493.46 Lamacchio, Ada. La filosofia della religione in Kant. Mandeiria, 1969-
Phil 811.6 Lamanna, E. Paolo. Manuale di storia della filosofia ad uso delle scuole. Firenze, 1928. 2v.
Phil 811.16 Lamanna, E. Paolo. Storia della filosofia. Firenze, 1961. 6v.
Phil 96.5 Lamanna, E.P. Dizionario di termini filosofia. Firenze, 1951.
Phil 3493.13.5 Lamanna, E.P. Il fondamento morale...secondo Kant. Firenze, 1916.
Phil 3493.13 Lamanna, E.P. Kant. Milano, 1926. 2v.
Phil 8591.19 Lamanna, E.P. La religione nella vita dello spirito. Firenze, 1914.
Htn Phil 2725.5.30* Lamarck, J.B. Philosophie zoologique. Paris, 1809. 2v.
Phil 186.44 Lambeck, G. Philosophische Propädeutik. Leipzig, 1919.
Phil 342.11.5 Lambek, C. Essay on the foundation of cognition. Copenhagen, 1935.
Phil 186.49.5 Lambek, C. Growth of the mind in relation to culture. Copenhagen, 1936.
Phil 186.49 Lambek, C. Indledning til kulturens filosofi. København, 1908.
Phil 5051.18 Lambek, C. Om psychologische beviser. København, 1909.
Phil 5251.28 Lambek, C. Psyckologiske studier. Supplementhefte til tidsschrift for aandskultur. København, 1904.
Phil 8591.26 Lambek, C. Religionen och nutidsmänniskan. Stockholm, 1924.
Phil 5251.28.7 Lambek, C. The structure of our apprehension of reality. Copenhagen, 1933.
Phil 186.91 Lambek, C. Studies in the dynamic coherence. Copenhagen, 1938.
Phil 342.11 Lambek, C. Track af vor erkendelses psykologi. København, 1925.
Phil 365.14 Lambek, C. Udkast til en sjaelelig bevaegelseslaere. København, 1901-1906.
Phil 8886.2 Lambert, C. Le système du monde moral. Paris, 1862.
Phil 7069.28.45 Lambert, Helen C.S. A general survey of psychical phenomena. N.Y., 1928.
Phil 186.82 Lambert, Henri. Hypothèse sur l'évolution physique et métaphysique de l'énergie. Bruxelles, 1935.
Phil 5051.1 Lambert, J.H. Neues organon Gedanken. Leipzig, 1764. 2v.
Phil 3585.1.40 Lambert, Johann Heinrich. Anlage zur Architectonic oder Theorie. Riga, 1771. 2v.
Phil 3585.1.30 Lambert, Johann Heinrich. Logische und philosophische Abhandlungen. Berlin, 1782-87. 2v.
Phil 3585.1.35 Lambert, Johann Heinrich. Philosophische Schriften. Reprografischer Nachdruck. v.1-4,6-7,9. Hildesheim, 1965- 7v.
Phil 5039.24 Lambert, Karel. The logical way of doing things. New Haven, 1969.
Phil 8663.3.88 Lambert, L.A. Ingersoll's Christmas sermon delivered by Rev. L.A. Lambert. Akron, 1898.
Phil 8663.3.90 Lambert, L.A. Tactics of infidels. Buffalo, 1887.
Phil 5875.5 Lambert, Wallace E. Children's views of foreign peoples. N.Y., 1966.
Phil 8886.49 Lamblardie. Traité élémentaire de métaphysique et de morale. Brunswick, 1801.
Phil 2725.8.82 Lame, D. Étude sur la philosophie de Laromiguiere. Guéret, 1864.
Phil 4080.3.147 Lameere, Jean. L'esthétique de Benedetto Croce. Paris, 1936.
Phil 2725.2.47 Lamenais, F.R. de. Parole d'un credente. Bruxelles, 1834. 3 pam.
Phil 2725.2.48 Lamenais, F.R. de. Parole d'un credente. Italia, 1834.
Phil 2725.2.37 Lamenais, F.R. de. Paroles d'un croyant. 7. éd. Paris, 1834.
Phil 2725.2.39 Lamenais, F.R. de. Paroles d'un croyant. 9. éd. Paris, 1834.
Phil 2725.2.49 Lamenais, F.R. de. The words of a believer. London, 1834.
Phil 2725.2.82 Lamennais, F.R. de. Catalogue de livres rares et precieux provenant de la bibliothèque de M.F. de la Mennais. Paris, 1836.
Phil 2725.2.33 Lamennais, F.R. de. De la famille et de la propriété. Paris, 1848.
Phil 2725.2.66 Lamennais, F.R. de. Défense de l'essai sur l'indifférence. Paris, 1828.
Phil 2725.2.35 Lamennais, F.R. de. Discussions critiques, et pensées diverses sur la religion et la philosophie. Paris, 1841.
Phil 2725.2.73 Lamennais, F.R. de. Les erreurs. Bruxelles, n.d.
Phil 2725.2.30 Lamennais, F.R. de. Esquisse d'une philosophie. Paris, 1840-1846. 4v.
Phil 2725.2.77 Lamennais, F.R. de. Essai d'un système de philosophie catholique. Rennes, 1954.
Phil 2725.2.57 Lamennais, F.R. de. Essai sur l'indifférence en matière de religion. Paris, 1819-20. 2v.
Phil 2725.2.59 Lamennais, F.R. de. Essai sur l'indifférence en matière de religion. Paris, 1828. 5v.
Phil 2725.2.61 Lamennais, F.R. de. Essai sur l'indifférence en matière de religion. Paris, 1843. 4v.
Phil 2725.2.83 Lamennais, F.R. de. Études et notice biographique. Paris, 1835.
Phil 2725.2.31 Lamennais, F.R. de. Grundriss einer Philosophie. v.1-3. Paris, 1841. 3v.
Phil 2725.2.54 Lamennais, F.R. de. Il libro del popolo. n.p., n.d. 2 pam.
Phil 2725.2.53 Lamennais, F.R. de. Il libro del popolo. v.1-2. Firenze, 1848.
Phil 2725.2.65 Lamennais, F.R. de. Libro per il popolo. Milano, 1874.
Htn Phil 2725.2.52* Lamennais, F.R. de. Le livre du peuple. Paris, 1838.
Phil 2725.2.34 Lamennais, F.R. de. M. Lamennais réfuté par lui-même. Paris, 1841.
Phil 2725.2.46 Lamennais, F.R. de. Palabras de un creyente. 8. ed. Paris, 1834.
Htn Phil 2725.2.40* Lamennais, F.R. de. Paroles d'un croyant. Bruxelles, 1834.
Htn Phil 2725.2.36* Lamennais, F.R. de. Paroles d'un croyant. Paris, 1834.
Phil 2725.2.41.5 Lamennais, F.R. de. Paroles d'un croyant. Paris, 1949.
Phil 2725.2.41 Lamennais, F.R. de. Les Paroles d'un croyant. Thèse. Paris, 1949.
Phil 2725.2.55 Lamennais, F.R. de. The people's own book. Boston, 1839.
Phil 2725.2.70 Lamennais, F.R. de. Questions politiques et philosophiques. v.1-2. Paris, 1840.
Phil 2725.2.75 Lamennais, F.R. de. Una voce di prigione. Genova, 1850.
Phil 2725.2.76 Lamennais, F.R. de. Une voix de prison. Paris, 1954.
Phil 2725.2.52.5 Lamennais, F.R. de. Das Volksbuch von Félicité de Lamennais. Leipzig, 1905.
Phil 2725.2.43 Lamennais, F.R. de. Worte eines Gläubigen. Hamburg, 1834.
Phil 2725.2.110 Lamennais, ses amis et le mouvement des idées à l'époque romantique, 1824-1834. (Derre, Jean R.) Paris, 1962.
Phil 2725.2.101 Lamennais. (Treves, P.) Milano, 1934.
Phil 2725.2.115 Lamennais and England. (Roe, William.) Oxford, 1966.
Phil 2725.2.50 Pamphlet vol. Lamennais' Paroles d'un croyante. 7 pam.
Htn Phil 2705.40* La Mettrie, Julien Offray de. Histoire naturelle de l'ame. La Haye, 1745.
Htn Phil 2705.30* La Mettrie, Julien Offray de. L'homme machin. v.1-2. Leyde, 1748.
Phil 2705.35 La Mettrie, Julien Offray de. L'homme machine, suivi de l'Art de jouir. Paris, 1921.
Phil 2705.35.6 La Mettrie, Julien Offray de. L'homme machine. Paris, 1966.
Phil 2705.35.5A La Mettrie, Julien Offray de. L'homme machine. Princeton, 1960.
Phil 2705.37 La Mettrie, Julien Offray de. Man a machine. Chicago, 1927.
Phil 2705.31 La Mettrie, Julien Offray de. Man a machine. v.1-2. London, 1752.
Phil 2705.30.55 La Mettrie, Julien Offray de. Der Mensch eine Maschine. Leipzig, 1909.
Htn Phil 2705.15* La Mettrie, Julien Offray de. Oeuvres philosophiques. London, 1751.
Phil 2705.45 La Mettrie, Julien Offray de. Un pamphlet médical au XVIIIe siècle. Thèse. Paris, 1931.
Phil 2705.20 La Mettrie, Julien Offray de. Textes choisis. Paris, 1954.
Phil 8591.42 Lamm, H. The relation of concept and demonstration in the ontological argument. Chicago, 1940.
Phil 2280.5.140 Lamont, C. The enduring impact of G. Santayana. N.Y., 1964.
Phil 2280.5.115 Lamont, Corliss. Dialogue on George Santayana. N.Y., 1959.

Phil 1955.6.145   Lamont, Corliss. Dialogue on John Dewey. N.Y., 1959.
Phil 5761.24.1   Lamont, Corliss. Freedom of choice affirmed. Boston, 1969.
Phil 5761.24   Lamont, Corliss. Freedom of choise affirmed. N.Y., 1967.
Phil 1750.166.20   Lamont, Corliss. Humanism as a philosophy. N.Y., 1949.
Phil 1750.166.21   Lamont, Corliss. Humanism as a philosophy. 2nd ed. N.Y., 1949.
Phil 8636.8.5   Lamont, Corliss. The illusion of immortality. N.Y., 1935.
Phil 8636.8.7   Lamont, Corliss. The illusion of immortality. 2. ed. N.Y., 1950.
Phil 8636.8.10   Lamont, Corliss. The illusion of immortality. 3. ed. N.Y., 1959.
Phil 2120.8.30   Lamont, Corliss. The independent mind. N.Y., 1951.
Phil 8636.8   Lamont, Corliss. Issues of immortality. N.Y., 1932.
Phil 1750.166.24   Lamont, Corliss. The philosophy of humanism. 4th ed. N.Y., 1957.
Phil 1750.166.23   Lamont, Corliss. The philosophy of humanism. 5th ed. N.Y., 1965.
Phil 2020.86   Lamont, W.D. Introduction to Green's moral philosophy. London, 1934.
Phil 735.140   Lamont, W.D. The value judgement. Edinburgh, 1955.
Phil 8886.65   Lamont, William D. The principles of moral judgement. Oxford, 1946.
Htn   Phil 3110.88*   Lamotte-Fouqué, Friedrich. Jakob Böhme. Greiz, 1831.
Phil 8412.30   Lamouche, A. Esthétique. Paris, 1961.
Phil 8886.78   Lamouche, André. D'une morale de l'amour à une sociologie de la raison. Paris, 1963. 2v.
Phil 5021.5   Lamouche, André. Logique de la simplicité. Paris, 1959.
Phil 5251.62   Lamouche, André. Psychologie. Paris, 1957.
Phil 186.147   Lamouche, André. Rythmologie universelle et metaphysique de l'harmonie. Paris, 1966. 2v.
Phil 4752.2.80   Lampert, Evengu. Nicolas Berdyaev and the new middle ages. London, 194-.
Phil 6321.49.2   Lampl de Groot, Jeanne. The development of the mind. London, 1966.
Phil 6321.49   Lampl de Groot, Jeanne. The development of the mind. N.Y., 1965.
Phil 4200.2.20   Lamprecht, F. Zur Theorie der humanistischen Geschichtsschreibung. Zürich, 1950.
Phil 9530.55   Lamprecht, H. Erfolg und Gesellschaft. München, 1964.
Phil 3552.294   Lamprecht, J.F. Leben des Freyherrn Gottfried Wilhelm von Leibnitz au das licht Gestellet. Berlin, 1740.
Phil 3552.294.5   Lamprecht, J.F. Vita del Signore Barone Goffredo G. di Leibnitz. Roma, 1787.
X Cg   Phil 2115.114   Lamprecht, S.P. The moral and political philosophy of John Locke. N.Y., 1918.
Phil 2115.114.5   Lamprecht, S.P. The moral and political philosophy of John Locke. N.Y., 1962.
Phil 186.109   Lamprecht, S.P. Nature and history. N.Y., 1950.
Phil 811.15   Lamprecht, S.P. Our philosophical traditions. N.Y., 1955.
Htn   Phil 8701.9.5*   Lamy, Bernard. Entretiens sur les sciences dans lesquels on apprend comment l'on doit étudier les sciences. Bruxelles, 1684.
Phil 8701.9.7   Lamy, Bernard. Entretiens sur les sciences dans lesquels on apprend comment l'on doit étudier les sciences. 3. éd. Lyon, 1706.
Phil 8701.9   Lamy, Bernard. Entretiens sur les sciences dans lesquels on apprend comment l'on doit étudier les sciences. Lyon, 1724.
Phil 8701.9.9   Lamy, Bernard. Entretiens sur les sciences dans lesquels on apprend comment l'on doit étudier les sciences. Paris, 1966.
Phil 2725.20   Lamy, G. De principiis rerum. Paris, 1669.
Phil 5643.122   Lamy, P. Le mystere de la vision. Paris, 1964.
Phil 7039.12   Lancaster, Evelyn. The final face of Eve. N.Y., 1958.
Phil 7069.66.15   Lance, Pierre. Le spiritualisme athée. Paris, 1966.
Phil 8886.59   Lancre, P. de. Tableau de l'inconstance et instabilité de toutes choses. Paris, 1607.
Phil 3280.86   Land, J.P.N. Arnold Geulincx te Leiden. Amsterdam, 1887.
Phil 3280.85   Land, J.P.N. Arnold Geulincx und seine Philosophie. Haag, 1895.
Phil 3960.12   Land, Jan P.N. De wijsbegeerte in de Nederlanden. 's Gravenhage, 1899.
Phil 8886.39   Landau, L.R. System der gesammten Ethik. Band 1-2. Berlin, 1877-78.
Phil 270.61A   Landau, M.A. Ul'mskaia noch': filosofi slucnaia. N'iu Iork, 1953.
Phil 9070.21.10   Landau, Rom. Human relations. London, 1948.
Phil 9070.21   Landau, Rom. Letter to Andrew. London, 1943.
Phil 5520.21.15   Landauer, Gustav. Skepsis und Mystik. Berlin, 1903.
Phil 8412.38   L'Andelyn, Charles de. Esthétique. Neuchâtel, 1964.
Phil 2520.211   Landermy, P.C.R. Descartes y su vida, su obra, su pensamiento. México, 1940.
Phil 8610.895   Landers, C.M. The skeptics defense against all Christian or other priests. Rochester, 1895.
Phil 342.26   Landesman, Charles. The foundations of knowledge. Englewood Cliffs, 1970.
Phil 9410.6.2   Landesmann, H. Der grundlose Optimismus. Dresden, 1897.
Phil 292.22   Landesmann, Heinrich. Der Naturgenuss. Berlin, 1876.
Phil 310.15   Landesverband Nordshein-West-Tälischer Geschichte. Historie Materialismus und europäisches Geschichtsdenken. 1. Aufl. Düsseldorf, 1954.
Phil 3450.11.122   Landgrabe, Ludwig. Edmund Husserl zum Gednachtnis. Prag, 1938.
Phil 3450.11.128   Landgrabe, Ludwig. Phänomenologie und Metaphysik. Hamburg, 1949.
Phil 3450.11.129   Landgrabe, Ludwig. Der Weg der Phäramenologie. Gütersloh, 1963.
Phil 165.370   Landgrebe, Ludwig. Beispiela. Den Haag, 1965.
Phil 1711.6.5   Landgrebe, Ludwig. Major problems in contemporary European philosophy. N.Y., 1966.
Phil 1750.115.130   Landgrebe, Ludwig. Phänomenologie und Geschichte. 1. Aufl. Gütersloh, 1968.
Phil 1711.6   Landgrebe, Ludwig. Philosophie der Gegenwart. Bonn, 1952.
Phil 186.54s   Landino, C. Camaldonensische Gespräche. Jena, 1927.
Htn   Phil 186.54*   Landino, C. Disputationum Camaldulensium. Bk. 4. Argentoraci, 1508.
Phil 6961.16   Landis, C. Modern society and mental diseases. N.Y., 1938.
Phil 5590.11   Landis, Carney. Personality and sexuality of the handicapped woman. N.Y., 1942.
Phil 5400.92   Landis, Carney. Studies of emotional reactions. n.p., 1924.
Phil 6321.25   Landis, Carney. Text book of abnormal psychology. N.Y., 1946.
Phil 8412.9   Landmann, E. Grundzüge einer Lehre vom Schönen. Basel, 1940.
Phil 8412.9.5   Landmann, E. Die Lehre vom Schönen. Wien, 1952.

Phil 705.16   Landmann, E. Die Transcendenz des erkennens. Berlin, 1923.
Phil 3640.384   Landmann, M. Geist und Leben. Bonn, 1951.
Phil 3585.25   Landmann, M. Der Mensch als Schöpfer und Geschäpf der Kultur. München, 1961.
Phil 3640.384.5   Landmann, M. Zum Stil des Zarathustra. n.p., 1944.
Phil 585.120   Landmann, Michael. De homine. Freiburg, 1962.
Phil 1135.194   Landmann, Michael. Ursprungsbild und Schöpfertat. München, 1966.
Phil 8886.3   Landmann, R. Hauptfragen der Ethik. Leipzig, 1874.
Phil 6390.2   Landmann, S. Die Mehrheit geistiger Persönlichkeiten in einem Individuum. Stuttgart, 1894.
Phil 8591.21   Landmark, J.D. Erkjendelses-teortisk religionsfilosofi. København, 1908.
Phil 165.27   Landmarks for beginners in philosophy. (Edman, Irwin.) N.Y., 1948?
Phil 8708.10.5   Landmarks in the struggle between science and religion. (Simpson, James Y.) N.Y., 1925?
Phil 5871.50   Landolf, Peter. Kind ohne Vater. Bern, 1968.
Phil 186.1   Landon, E. Le spiritualisme. Paris, 1872.
Phil 2520.136   Landormy, Paul. Descartes. 5e éd. Paris, 1917?
Phil 5251.39   Landquist, J. Människokunskap. Stockholm, 1920.
Phil 5761.11   Landquist, J. Viljan. Stockholm, 1908.
Phil 4600.1.35   Landquist, John. Essayer. Stockholm, 1913.
Phil 4600.1.31   Landquist, John. Filosofiska essayer. Stockholm, 1906.
Phil 4600.1.40   Landquist, John. Det levande forflutna. Stockholm, 1919.
Phil 8886.41   Landry, Adolph. Principes de morale rationnelle. Paris, 1906.
Phil 1540.16   Landry, Bernard. L'idée de chrétienté chez les scolastiques du XIIIe siècle. Paris, 1929.
Phil 3640.363   Landry, H. Friedrich Nietzsche. Berlin, 1931.
Phil 6021.1   Landsberg, I. Wahrsagekunst aus der menschlichen Gestalt. Berlin, 1895.
Phil 8612.31   Landsberg, P.L. Die Erfahrung des Todes. Luzern, 1937.
Phil 705.13   Landström, Gustaf. Locke och Kant. Uppsala, 1900.
Phil 4515.94   Landström, Gustaf. Om tänkaren Kristofer Jakob Boström och hans filosofi. Stockholm, 1903.
Phil 811.1.3   Landtman, G. Inledning till det filosofiska tänkandet. Helsingfors, 1920.
Phil 3493.11   Landtman. Immanuel Kant. Stockholm, 1922.
Phil 7069.20.205   Lane, Anne W. Life in the circles. N.Y., 1920.
Phil 7069.20.200   Lane, Anne W. To walk with God. N.Y., 1920.
Phil 187.32.80   Lane, Charles A. Montgomery's philosophy of vital organization. Chicago, 1909.
Phil 720.88   Lane, Gilles. Être et langage; essai sur la recherche de l'objectivité. Paris, 1970.
Phil 8701.11   Lane, H.H. Evolution and Christian faith. Princeton, 1923.
Phil 680.25   Lane, Michael. Introduction to structuralism. N.Y., 1970.
Phil 680.26   Lane, Michael. Structuralism: a reader. London, 1970.
Phil 1020.36   Lane-Poole, Stanley. Essay on the brotherhood of purity. Lahore, 1954.
Phil 8886.24.9   Lanessan, J.I. de. L'idéal moral du matérialisme et la guerre. Paris, 1918.
Phil 8886.24.5   Lanessan, J.I. de. La morale des religions. Paris, 1905.
Phil 8886.24   Lanessan, J.I. de. La morale naturelle. Paris, 1908.
Phil 930.26   Lanessan, J.M. La morale des philosophies chinois. Paris, 1896.
Phil 9351.15   Lanfear, (Mrs.). Letters to young ladies on their entrance into the world. London, 1824.
Phil 5251.17   Lanfeld, H.S. Elementry laboratory course in psychology. Boston, 1916.
Phil 1730.8   Lanfrey, Pierre. L'église et les philosophes au dix-huitième siècle. Paris, 1855.
Phil 1730.8.3   Lanfrey, Pierre. L'église et les philosophes au dix-huitième siècle. Paris, 1879.
Phil 270.17.5   Lang, Albert. Aphoristische Betrachtungen über das Kausalproblem. Köln, 1909.
Phil 270.17   Lang, Albert. Das Kausalproblem. Köln, 1904.
Phil 2730.88   Lang, Albert. Maine de Biran und die neuere Philosophie. Köln, n.d.
Phil 8591.12   Lang, Albert. Making of religion. London, 1898.
Phil 8591.12.2   Lang, Albert. Making of religion. 2. ed. London, 1900.
Phil 8591.12.5   Lang, Albert. Wesen und Wahrheit der Religion. München, 1957.
Phil 5593.66.5   Lang, Alfred. Rorschach-Bibliographie, 1921-1964. Bern, 1966.
Phil 7068.97.5   Lang, Andrew. The book of dreams and ghosts. London, 1897.
Phil 7068.94.5   Lang, Andrew. Cock Lane and common-sense. London, 1894.
Phil 3120.30.100   Lang, Bernhard. Martin Buber und das dialogische Leben. Bern, 1963.
Phil 5374.67   Lang, Ernst Hildegard. Das wahre Wesen und Wirken des Bewusstseins in seiner normalen und anormalen Erscheinungen. München, 1960.
Phil 8701.6   Lang, O. Am Wendepunkt der Ideen. Wien, 1909.
Phil 5627.131   Lang, Wyatt. A study of conversion. London, 1931.
Phil 6400.11   Le langage, la parole et les aphasies. (Ferrand, Auguste.) Paris, 1894.
Phil 5520.17   Le langage. (Leroy, E.B.) Paris, 1905.
Phil 735.79.1   Le langage affectif et les jugements de valeur. (Vaucher, G.) Paris, 1925.
Phil 735.79   Le langage affectif et les jugements de valeur. Thèse. (Vaucher, G.) Paris, 1925.
Phil 5520.380   Langage et contexte. (Slama-Cazacu, T.) 's-Gravenhage, 1961.
Phil 5520.41   Le langage et la pensée. (Delacroix, H.) Paris, 1924.
Phil 5520.41.3   Le langage et la pensée. 2. éd. (Delacroix, H.) Paris, 1930.
Phil 5520.37   Le langage et la verbomanie. (Lourié, Ossip.) Paris, 1912.
Phil 5520.54   Langage et pensée, vie et matière. (Buyssens, T.) Brasschaat, 1928.
Phil 6400.1   Le langage intérieur. (Ballet, G.) Paris, 1886.
Phil 5520.30   Le langage intérieur et les paraphasies. (Saint-Paul, Georges.) Paris, 1904.
Phil 6619.10   Le langage musical et ses troubles hystériques. (Ingenieros, José.) Paris, 1907.
Phil 575.88   Langan, Hubert E. The philosophy of personalism and its educational applications. Diss. Washington, D.C., 1935.
Phil 3450.19.175   Langan, Thomas. The meaning of Heidegger. N.Y., 1959.
Phil 2750.20.105   Langan, Thomas. Merleau-Ponty's critique of reason. New Haven, 1966.
Phil 6121.36   Langdon-Davies, I. Man: the known and unknown. London, 1968.
Phil 585.95   Langdon-Davies, J. On the nature of man. N.Y., 1961.
Phil 9495.155   Langdon Davies, J. Sex, sin and sanity. London, 1954.
Phil 292.7   Langdon-Davies, John. Man and his universe. N.Y., 1930.

Phil 292.7.5   Langdon-Davies, John. Man comes of age. 1st ed. N.Y., 1932.

Phil 8412.33   Lange, A.K. Problems of art. N.Y., 1957.

Phil 672.6   Lange, C.C.L. Die geschichtliche Entwickelung des Bewegungsbegriffes. Leipzig, 1886.

Phil 5403.5   Lange, C.G. Bidrag til nydelsernes fysiologi som grundlag for en rationel aestetik. Kjobenhavn, 1899.

Phil 5400.50.20A   Lange, C.G. The emotions. Baltimore, 1922.

Phil 5400.50.6   Lange, C.G. Die Gemüthsbewegungen. 2e Aufl. Würzburg, 1910.

Phil 5400.50   Lange, C.G. Om sindsbevaegelser. Kjobenhavn, 1885.

Phil 5400.50.5   Lange, C.G. Über Gemüthsbewegungen. Leipzig, 1887.

Phil 4655.1.85   Lange, Dagmar M. Pontus Wikner som vitter författare. Nora, 1946.

Phil 4769.1.96   Lange, E.M. Solowjew. Mainz, 1923.

Phil 3900.1.82   Lange, F.A. Friedrich Ueberweg. Berlin, 1871.

Phil 486.1   Lange, F.A. Geschichte des Materialismus. Iserlohn, 1873-75. 2v.

Phil 486.1.6A   Lange, F.A. Geschichte des Materialismus. 3e Aufl. Iserlohn, 1876-77. 2v.

Phil 3428.81   Lange, F.A. Die Grundlegung der mathematische Psychologie. Duisburg, 1865.

NEDL Phil 486.1.5.3   Lange, F.A. History of materialism. Boston, 1879-81. 3v.

Phil 486.1.5   Lange, F.A. History of materialism. London, 1877. 3v.

Phil 486.1.5.7A   Lange, F.A. History of materialism and criticism of its importance. v.1-3. 3rd ed. London, 1925.

Phil 486.1.5.9   Lange, F.A. History of materialism and criticism of its present importance. Photoreproduction. Boston, 1880-81. 3v.

NEDL Phil 486.1.5.8   Lange, F.A. The history of materialism and criticism of its present importance. v.1-3. 3rd ed. N.Y., 1925.

Phil 5051.2   Lange, F.A. Logische Studien. Iserlohn, 1877.

Phil 8886.4   Lange, J. Medicina mentis. London, 1715.

Phil 186.160   Lange, John. The cognitivity paradox. Princeton, 1970.

Phil 8412.31   Lange, K. von. Das Wesen der Kunst. Berlin, 1901. 2v.

Phil 8412.22   Lange, K. von. Das Wesen der Kunst. Berlin, 1907. 2v.

Phil 5374.7.5   Lange, K.M. Apperception. Boston, 1893.

Phil 5374.7.6   Lange, K.M. Apperception. Boston, 1894.

Phil 5374.7   Lange, K.M. Über Apperception. Plauen, 1879.

Phil 3565.108   Lange, Paul. Die Lehre vom Instinkte bei Lotze und Darwin. Berlin, 1896.

Phil 5425.44.4   Lange, Wilhelm. Genie, Irrsinn und Ruhm. München, 1967.

Phil 5425.44.3   Lange, Wilhelm. Genie, Irrsinn und Ruhm. 3. Aufl. München, 1942.

Phil 5425.44.25   Lange, Wilhelm. Genie, Irrsinn und Ruhm. 4. Aufl. München, 1956.

Phil 5425.44   Lange, Wilhelm. Genie-Irrsinn und Ruhm. München, 1928.

Phil 5425.44.5   Lange, Wilhelm. Das Genie-Problem; eine Einführung. München, 1931.

Phil 5425.44.10   Lange, Wilhelm. Das Genie-Problem. 3. Aufl. München, 1941.

Phil 5425.44.23   Lange, Wilhelm. Genies als Problem. 2. Aufl. München, 1941.

Phil 3640.353   Lange, Wilhelm. Nietzsche, Krankheit und Wirking. Hamburg, 1948.

Phil 5425.44.15   Lange, Wilhelm. The problem of genius. London, 1931.

Phil 2490.106   L'Ange-Huet, J. De methode der positieve filosofie volgens Auguste Comte. Leiden, 1866.

Phil 270.25   L'Ange Huet, J. Nieuwe oplossing van een oud vraagstuk. Leiden, 1872.

Phil 5251.4   Langel, A. Les problèmes. Paris, 1873.

Phil 5251.4.5   Langel, A. Les problèmes de la vie. Paris, 1867.

Phil 3625.8.92   Langen, S.G. Leben Georg Friedrich Meiers. Halle, 1778.

Phil 3428.93   Langenbeck, H. Die theoretische Philosophie Herbarts und seiner Schule. Berlin, 1867.

Phil 5790.30   Langenheder, Werner. Ansatz zu einer allgemeinen Verhaltenstheorie in der Sozialwissenschaften. Köln, 1968.

Phil 2805.185   Langenskjold, Agnes. Blaise Pascal. Uppsala, 1922.

Phil 186.97   Langer, Mrs. S.K. Philosophy in a new key. Cambridge, Mass., 1942.

Phil 186.97.2   Langer, Mrs. S.K. Philosophy in a new key. 2d ed. Cambridge, Mass., 1951.

Phil 186.97.5   Langer, Mrs. S.K. Philosophy in a new key. 3d ed. Cambridge, Mass., 1957.

Phil 186.72   Langer, Mrs. S.K. The practice of philosophy. N.Y., 1930.

Phil 3640.233   Langer, Norbert. Das Problem der Romantik bei Nietzsche. Münster, 1929.

Phil 5251.3   Langer, P. Die Grundlagen der Psychophysik. Jena, 1876.

Phil 5251.3.5   Langer, P. Psychophysische Streitfragen. Ohrdruf, 1893.

Phil 5051.27A   Langer, S.K. (Mrs.). An introduction to symbolic logic. Boston, 1937.

Phil 5066.52.2   Langer, S.K.K. An introduction to symbolic logic. 2nd ed. N.Y., 1953.

Phil 6121.42   Langer, Susanne K. Mind; an essay on human feeling. Baltimore, 1967-

Phil 2120.11.30   Langer, Susanne Katherina (Knauth). Philosophical sketches. Baltimore, 1962.

Phil 8412.40   Langer, Susanne Katherina Knauth. Feeling and form; a theory of art developed from philosophy in a new key. N.Y., 1953.

Phil 5850.255   Langer, W.C. Psychology and human living. N.Y., 1943.

Phil 3160.9.83   Langewisch, Eva. Das teleologische Prinzip bei Carl Gustav Carus. Inaug. Diss. Würzburg, 1927.

Phil 8412.23.2   Langfeld, Herbert Sidney. The aesthetic attitude. N.Y., 1920.

Phil 8412.23.3   Langfeld, Herbert Sidney. The aesthetic attitude. Port Washington, N.Y., 1967.

Phil 6961.17.5   Langfeldt, G. The prognosis in schizophrenia. Copenhagen, 1937.

Phil 6961.17   Langfeldt, G. The schizophreniform states. Copenhagen, 1939.

Phil 3850.27.165   Langfeldt, Gabriel. Albert Schweitzer. London, 1960.

Phil 3850.27.166   Langfeldt, Gabriel. Albert Schweitzer. N.Y., 1960.

Phil 8961.21   Langfeldt, Gabriel. Den gylne regel og andre humanisticke moralnormer. Oslo, 1966.

Phil 5821.9   Langfeldt. Tier- und Menschenverstand. München, 1909.

Phil 2225.18   Langford, Thomas A. Intellect and hope; essays in the thought of Michael Polanyi. Durham, 1968.

Phil 5548.101   Langkjaer, Asger. Contributions to a general normalogy, or Theory of purpose-setting. København, 1961.

Phil 7072.15   Langley, Noel. Edgar Cayce on reincarnation. N.Y., 1968.

Phil 665.96   Langre, Michel de. Ame humaine et science moderne. Paris, 1963.

Phil 6321.45   Langstroth, Lovell. Structure of the ego. Stanford, Calif., 1955.

Phil 5520.75.5A   Language, meaning and maturity. 1. ed. (ETC., a Review of General Semantics.) N.Y., 1954.

Phil 180.86   Language, mind and value. (Findlay, J.N.) London, 1963.

Phil 338.47   Language, minds, and knowledge. (Hoffman, Robert.) N.Y., 1970.

Phil 3925.16.145   Language, persons, and belief studies in Wittgenstein's Philosophical investigations. (High, Dallas.) N.Y., 1967.

Phil 5520.430   Language, thought and comprehension. (Hotopf, W.H.N.) London, 1965.

Phil 175.38.4   Language, truth and logic. (Ayer, Alfred J.) London, 1938.

Phil 175.38.15A   Language, truth and logic. (Ayer, Alfred J.) N.Y., 1952.

Phil 1905.33.30   Language. (Banerje, N.V.) London, 1963.

Phil 5520.240   Language. N.Y., 1957.

Phil 5520.620   Language: selected readings. (Oldfield, Richard Charles.) Harmondsworth, 1968.

Phil 583.6   Language and being: an analytic phenomenology. (Erickson, Stephen A.) New Haven, 1970.

Phil 5520.113   Language and communication. 1. ed. (Miller, G.A.) N.Y., 1951.

Phil 5520.632   Language and illumination. (Engel, S. Morris.) The Hague, 1969.

Phil 5520.101   Language and intelligence. (Holloway, J.) London, 1951.

Phil 6400.20.2   Language and language disturbances. (Goldstein, Kurt.) N.Y., 1948.

Phil 5520.406   Language and magic. (Izutsu, T.) Tokyo, 1956.

Phil 5520.477   Language and natural theology. (Clarke, Bowman L.) The Hague, 1966.

Phil 5520.582   Language and ontology. (Kaminsky, Jack.) Carbondale, 1969.

Phil 5520.97A   Language and philosophy. (Black, M.) Ithaca, 1949.

Phil 5520.728   Language and psychology. (Blumenthal, Arthur L.) N.Y., 1970.

Phil 5520.351   Language and the discovery of reality; a developmental psychology of cognition. (Church, Joseph.) N.Y., 1961.

Phil 5520.160   Language and the pursuit of truth. (Wilson, John.) Cambridge, Eng., 1956.

Phil 5360.25   Language and thinking; a philosophical introduction. (Alexander, Hubert Griggs.) Princeton, N.J., 1966.

Phil 5520.423   Language and thought. (Carroll, John B.) Englewood Cliffs, N.J., 1964.

Phil 6960.12   Language and thought in schizophrenia. (Kasanin, J.S.) Berkeley, 1944.

Phil 6400.36   Language behavior and psychopathology. (Vetter, Harold J.) Chicago, 1969.

Phil 6971.5   Language behavior in schizophrenia. (Vetter, Harold T.) Springfield, Ill., 1968.

Phil 6400.32   Language disturbance and intellectual functioning. (Lubin, Carl Kenneth.) The Hague, 1967.

Phil 5520.325.10   Language et connaissance. (Schaff, Adam.) Paris, 1969.

Phil 5055.23   Language et logique. (Prot, Marcel.) Paris, 1949.

Phil 5520.76A   Language habits in human affairs. (Lee, Irving J.) N.Y., 1941.

Phil 5520.75   Language in action. (Hayakawa, S.I.) N.Y., 1941.

Phil 5520.75.2   Language in action. (Hayakawa, S.I.) N.Y., 1941.

Phil 5520.140   Language in relation to a unified theory of the structure of human behavior. (Pike, Kenneth Lee.) Glendale, Calif., 1954.

Phil 5520.140.2   Language in relation to a unified theory of the sturcture of human behavior. 2. ed. (Pike, Kenneth Lee.) The Hague, 1967.

Phil 5520.88   Language in society. (Lewis, Morris M.) London, 1947.

Phil 5520.155   Language meaning. 1. ed. (Nesbit, F.L.) N.Y., 1955.

Phil 8413.36   The language of art and art criticism. (Margolis, Joseph.) Detroit, 1965.

Phil 5645.16   The language of color. (Luckiesh, M.) N.Y., 1918.

Phil 680.15   The language of criticism and the science of man. (Macksey, Richard.) Baltimore, 1970.

Phil 5400.198   The language of emotion. (Davitz, Joel Robert.) N.Y., 1969.

Phil 8897.73   The language of ethics. (Wellman, Carl.) Cambridge, 1961.

Phil 1630.45   The language of history in the Renaissance. (Struever, Nancy S.) Princeton, N.J., 1970.

Phil 5066.253   The language of logic. (Freudenthal, Hans.) Amsterdam, 1966.

Phil 8882.68   The language of morals. (Hare, Richard Mervyn.) Oxford, 1952.

Phil 5520.265   The language of psychology. (Mandler, George.) N.Y., 1959.

Phil 672.15.10   A language of space. (Hinton, Charles H.) London, 1906.

Phil 5520.525   The language of the self. (Lacan, Jacques.) Baltimore, 1968.

Phil 8598.110.20   Language of the self. (Schuon, Frithjof.) Madras, 1959.

Phil 672.242   The language of time. (Gale, Richard.) London, 1968.

Phil 735.124.5   The language of value. (Lepley, Ray.) N.Y., 1957.

Phil 5520.530   Language within language; immediacy, a channel in verbal communication. (Wiener, Morton.) N.Y., 1968.

Phil 8587.69   Languages, standpoints, attitudes. (Hodges, H.A.) London, 1953.

Phil 2030.6.5A   Languages of art. (Goodman, Nelson.) Indianapolis, 1968.

Phil 6125.32   Languages of the brain. (Pribram, Karl H.) Englewood Cliffs, 1971.

Phil 5066.229   Languages with expressions of infinite length. (Karp, Carol R.) Amsterdam, 1964.

Phil 5520.61.10   La langue, le sens, la pensée. (Serrus, Charles.) Paris, 1941.

Phil 735.244   Langweg, R. Das Phänomen der Wertblindheit. Lingen-Ems, 1961?

Phil 5251.21   Langwieser, Karl. Der Bewusstseinsmechanismus. Leipzig, 1897.

Phil 3640.765   Lannoy, Joris C. Dionysos of God. Brugge, 1968.

Phil 3640.414A   Lannoy, Joris C. Nietzsche, ou L'histoire d'un égocentrisme athée. Paris, 1952.

Phil 665.92   LaNoë, François de. L'appel de l'esprit. Paris, 1960.

Phil 9070.27   Lansing, Florence. The builder. N.Y., 1909.

Phil 6321.8   Lanteirès, André. Essai descriptif sur les troubles psychopathiques avec lucidités d'esprit. Paris, 1885.

Phil 1750.755   Lanteri-Laura, G. La psychiatrie phénoménologique. Paris, 1963.

Phil 720.90   Lanteri-Laura, Georges. Structures subjectives du champ transcendantal. Thèse. Paris, 1968.

Phil 971.8   Lantier, Jacques. La théosophie. Paris, 1970.

Phil 2295.85   Lantoine, Albert. Un précurseur de la franc-maçonnerie, John Toland, 1670-1722. Paris, 1927.

Phil 4080.8.87   Lantrua, A. La filosofia di Augusto Conti. Padova, 1955.

Phil 8886.62   Lanz, H. In quest of morals. Stanford, 1941.

Phil 4260.147   Lanza, Franco. Saggi di poetica vichiana. Varese, 1961.

Phil 552.3   Lanza del Vasto, Joseph Jean. Les quatre fléaux. Paris, 1971.

Phil 8416.22   Laokoon; kunstheoretische Essays. (Pudor, H.) Leipzig, 1902.

Phil 8402.35   Laokoon-studien. (Blümner, Hugo.) Freiburg, 1881-82.

Phil 2070.135   Lapan, A. The significance of James' essay. Thesis. N.Y., 1936.

Phil 8666.7   La Paquerie, J. Les arguments de l'athéisme. Paris, 1909.

Phil 4472.1.30   Lapas de Gusmão. Virtudes e defeitas dos homens. Lisboa, 1957.

Phil 8060.3   Lapcević, Draguicha. La philosophie de l'art classique. Paris, 1927.

Phil 8961.15   Łapicki, B. Etyczna kultura starożytnego Rzymu. Łódź, 1958.

Phil 5761.4.2   Lapie, P. Logique de la volonté. Paris, 1902.

Phil 5761.1   La Placette, J. Eclaircissemens...difficultez...liberté. Amsterdam, 1709.

Phil 8886.27   Laplaigne, H. Morale d'un égoiste; essai de morale sociale. Paris, 1900.

Phil 6321.60   Laplanche, Jean. Vie et mort en psychanalyse. Paris, 1970.

Phil 2520.206   La Plata. Universidad Nacional. Escritos en honor de Descartes. La Plata, 1938.

Phil 4972.5.80   La Plata. Universidad Nacional. Estudios sobre Alejandro Korn. La Plata, 1963.

Phil 5360.10   Laporte, J.M.F. Le problème de l'abstraction. Paris, 1940.

Phil 270.50   Laporte, Jean. L'idee de necessité. Paris, 1941.

Phil 2520.344   Laporte, Jean. Le rationalisme de Descartes. Paris, 1950.

Phil 1504.6.2   Lappe, J. Nicolaus von Autrecourt. v.6, pt.2. Münster, n.d.

Phil 9070.1   Lappin, M.M. Let us talk about you. N.Y., 1940.

Phil 6681.6.5   Lapponi, Guiseppe. Hypnotism and spiritism...travel. 2. ed. N.Y., 1915.

Phil 6681.6.3   Lapponi, Guiseppe. Iypnotismo e spiritismo. 3. ed. Roma, 1907.

Phil 8412.26   Laprade, V. Questions d'art et de morale 2. éd. Paris, 1864.

Phil 8412.4   Laprade, Victor de. Histoire du sentiment de la nature. Paris, 1882.

Phil 8886.21.5   La Primaudaye, P. de. L'Académie française. v.1-4. Saumur, 1613.

Htn   Phil 8886.21.3*   La Primaudaye, P. de. L'Académie française. 3. ed. London, 1594. 2v.

Htn   Phil 8886.21.2*   La Primaudaye, P. de. L'Académie française. 3. ed. Paris, 1582.

Htn   Phil 8886.21*   La Primaudaye, P. de. The French Academie. London, 1586.

Htn   Phil 8886.21.7*   La Primaudaye, P. de. Suite de l'Académie française. Paris, 1580.

Htn   Phil 8886.21.12*   La Primaudaye, P. de. The third volume of the French Academie. London, 1601.

Phil 186.46   Lapshin', I. Filosofia izobreteniia. Praga, 1924. 2v.

Phil 4762.4.30   Lapshin, I.I. La synergie spirituelle. Praha, 1935.

Phil 2835.35   La Ramée, P. de. Dialectique (1555). Genève, 1964.

Phil 3425.250   Larenz, Karl. Hegels Zurechnungslehre und der Begriff der objektiven Zurechnung. Leipzig, 1927.

Phil 5593.45   Large scale Rorschach techniques. 1. ed. (Erickson, Mary R.) Springfield, Ill., 1945.

Phil 3270.12.115   Largeault, Jean. Logique et philosophie chez Frege. Paris, 1970.

Phil 5251.25   Larguier des Bancels, Jean. Introduction à la psychologie. Paris, 1921.

Phil 5585.11.11F   La Rive, Lucien de. Sur la collection des sensations. Genève, 1888.

Phil 6121.38   La Rivière, A. L'homme et le complexe normal. Paris, 1961.

Phil 665.34   Larkin, E.L. The matchless altar of the soul. Los Angeles, 1916.

Phil 8870.8   Larned, J.N. A multitude of counselors. Boston, 1901.

Phil 8870.9   Larned, J.N. A primer of right and wrong. Boston, 1902.

Phil 5590.42   Larned, Josephus N. A study of greatness in men. Boston, 1911.

Phil 5040.11   Lärobok i logiken for elementar-undervisningen. (Afzelius, F.G.) Upsala, 1852.

Phil 4762.3.80   Laroche, P.G. Ossip-Leurié (L'homme et l'oeuvre). Paris, 1934.

Phil 2725.36.30   LaRochefoucauld, Edmée. Pluralité de l'être. Paris, 1957.

Phil 176.213   La Rochefoucauld, Edmée de Fels. La nature et l'esprit. Paris, 1965.

Phil 5251.30   Laromiguiere, P. Leçons de philosophie, ou Essai sur les facultés de l'ame. Paris, 1815-18. 2v.

Phil 5251.30.5   Laromiguiere, P. Leçons de philosophie:sur les principles de l'intelligence. 5. ed. Paris, 1833. 2v.

Phil 2493.87.5   Laromiguiere, P. Paradoxes de Condillac. Paris, 1825.

Phil 2725.8.85   Laromiguière et son école. (Alfaric, Prosper.) Paris, 1929.

Phil 2805.178   Laros, M. Das Glaubensproblem bei Pascal. Düsseldorf, 1918.

Phil 2280.5.90   Larrabee, H.A. George Santayana. pt.1-2. n.p., 1931.

Phil 5620.31   Larrabee, H.A. Reliable knowledge. Boston, 1964.

Phil 186.68   Larrabee, Harold A. What philosophy is. N.Y., 1928.

Phil 2805.495   Larraillet, Paul. Pascal et le problème de la destinée. Paris, 1970.

Phil 9558.30   Larrañaga, T. De materia gravi in furto apud theologos saeculorum XVI et XVII. Romae, 1960.

Phil 4957.25   Larrayo, Francisco. Historía de las doctrinas filosóficas en Latinoamérica. 1. ed. México, 1968.

Phil 4374.5.80   Larroya, Francisco. El romanticismo filosófico observaciones a la weltanschauung de Joaquin Xirau. Mexico, 1941.

Phil 735.119   Larroyo, F. La filosofía de los valores. México, 1936.

Phil 8886.63   Larroyo, F. Los principios de la ética social. 4. ed. Mexico, 1941.

Phil 575.105   Larroyo, Francisco. Exposición y crítica del personalismo espiritualista de nuestro tiempo. México, 1941.

Phil 4957.5   Larroyo, Francisco. La filosofía americana, su razón y su sinrazón de ser. Mexico, 1958.

Phil 5051.44.4   Larroyo, Francisco. Lecciones de lógica y etica. 4. ed. México, 1970.

Phil 2045.96   Larsen, Eduard. Thomas Hobbes' filosofi. København, 1891.

Phil 8510.25   Larsen, H. Martensen. Jesus und die Religionsgeschichte. Freiburg, 1898. 3 pam.

Phil 6121.30   Larson, Christian I. Your forces and how to use them. N.Y., 1912.

Phil 8663.3.97   Larson, O.P. American infidel. 1. ed. N.Y., 1962.

Phil 585.394   Larson, Victor E. Man: who-whence; a layman's attempt at a logical synthesis. N.Y., 1967.

Phil 4600.2.48   Larsson, Hans. Filosofien och politiken. Stockholm, 1915.

Phil 4600.2.50   Larsson, Hans. Gränsen mellan sensation och emotion. 2e uppl. Lund, 1911.

Phil 1116.3   Larsson, Hans. Den grekiska filosofien. Stockholm, 1921.

Phil 4600.2.37   Larsson, Hans. Hemmabyarna världsbetraklelser i femton kapitel. Stockholm, 1916.

Phil 4600.2.32   Larsson, Hans. Ideer och makter. 2. uppl. Lund, 1909.

Phil 4600.2.52   Larsson, Hans. Den intellektuella askadningens filosofi. Stockholm, 1920.

Phil 4600.2.45   Larsson, Hans. Intuition. 3e uppl. Stockholm, 1910.

Phil 4600.2.46   Larsson, Hans. Intuition. 4e uppl. Stockholm, 1920.

Phil 4600.2.44   Larsson, Hans. Intuitionsproblemet. Stockholm, 1912.

Phil 3493.7   Larsson, Hans. Kants deduktion av kategorierna. 2. uppl. Lund, 1914.

Phil 3493.7.5   Larsson, Hans. Kants transscendentala deduktion af kategorierna. Lund, 1914.

Phil 4600.2.39   Larsson, Hans. Kunskapslivet. 3e uppl. Stockholm, 1920.

Phil 4515.100   Larsson, Hans. Minnesteckning över Christopher Jacob Boström. Stockholm, 1931.

Phil 4600.2.33   Larsson, Hans. Nagot om den fria viljan. n.p., n.d.

Phil 4600.2.30   Larsson, Hans. Postscriptum. Stockholm, 1944.

Phil 4600.2.40   Larsson, Hans. Psykologi paa Dansk red Stig Bredstrup. København, 1914.

Phil 4600.2.53   Larsson, Hans. Reflexioner för dagen. Lund, 1911.

Phil 4600.2.36   Larsson, Hans. Studier och meditationer. 4e uppl. Lund, 1912.

Phil 4600.2.38   Larsson, Hans. Under världskrisen. Stockholm, 1920.

Phil 4600.2.34   Larsson, Hans. Viljans frihet. Lund, 1899.

Phil 4600.2.35   Larsson, Hans. Viljans frihet. Lund, 1910.

Phil 2520.17.5   La Rue, D.W. Mental hygiene. N.Y., 1930.

Phil 7150.8   La Rue, F.A.H. Du suicide. Québec, 1859.

Phil 3001.19   Las sources mystiques de la phlosophie romantique allemande. (Benz, Ernst.) Paris, 1968.

Phil 1116.5   Lasacco, Michele. Introduzione alla storia della filosofia greca e appendice di testi tradotti. Bari, 1929.

Phil 186.101   Lasaga y Travieso, J.I. Manual de introducción a la filosofia de acuerdo. 2. ed. Facs. 1-8. La Habana, 1944-1946.

Phil 186.83   LaSalle, A. de. La balance naturelle, ou Essai sur une loi universelle appliquée aux sciences. Londres, 1788. 2v.

Phil 270.52   Le lasard et la destinée. (Sageret, Jules.) Paris, 1927.

Phil 2725.15.30   Lasbax, E. La dialectique et le rythme de l'univers. Paris, 1925.

Phil 3831.9.3   Lasbax, Émile. La hiérarchie dans l'univers chez Spinoza. Thèse, Paris, 1919.

Phil 8620.32   Lasbax, Émile. Le problème du mal. Paris, 1919.

Phil 1535.33   La Scala, Puis. Cursus philosophicus ad usum seminariorum. Parisiis, 1910. 2v.

Phil 4959.405   Láscaris Comneno, Constantino. Desarrollo de las ideas filosóficas en Costa Rica. Costa Rica, 1964.

Phil 1711.15   Láscaris Comneno, Constantino. Estudios de filosofía moderna. 1. ed. San Salvador, 1966.

Phil 4959.5   Lascaris Comneno, Constantino. Historia de las ideas en Centroamerica. 1. ed. San José de Costa Rica, 1970.

Phil 7069.29.50   Lascelles, (pseud.). Beyond, a continuation of the seekers. London, 1929.

Phil 6051.15   La Seer, E.J. Illustrated palmistry. N.Y., 1904.

Phil 5066.241   Laserna, Mario. Klassenlogik und formale Einteilung der Wissenschaft. Berlin, 1963?

Phil 9245.19   Laserre, J.P. de. Le tombeau des délices du monde. Brusselles, 1632.

Phil 8961.4   La Serre. La vie heureuse, ou L'homme content. Paris, 1693.

Phil 6121.28   Lashley, K.S. Experimental analysis of instinctive behavior. Lancaster, Pa., 1938.

Phil 6121.27   Lashley, K.S. Integrative functions of the cerebral cortex. Baltimore, 1933.

Phil 5251.58A   Lashley, K.S. The neuropsychology of Lashley. N.Y., 1960.

Phil 5400.84   Lashley, K.S. Studies in the dynamics of behavior. Chicago, 1932.

Phil 5400.84.6   Lashley, K.S. The thalamus and emotion. Lancaster, 1938.

Phil 6121.39A   Lashley, Karl S. Brain mechanisms and intelligence. N.Y., 1963.

Phil 5500.5   Lask, E. Die Lehre vom Urteil. Tübingen, 1912.

Phil 5051.5   Lask, E. Die Logik der Philosophie und die Kategorienlehre. Tübingen, 1911.

Phil 3246.172   Lask, Emil. Fichtes Idealismus und die Geschichte. Tübingen, 1914.

Phil 3585.30   Lask, Emil. Gesammelte Schriften. Tübingen, 1923. 3v.

Phil 186.45   Lasker, E. Die Philosophie des Unvollendbar. Leipzig, 1919.

Phil 525.264.1   Laski, Marghanita. Ecstasy; a study of some secular and religious experiences. N.Y., 1968.

Phil 1830.17.5   Laslett, Peter. Philosophy, politics, and society, third series. N.Y., 1967.

Phil 1830.17   Laslett, Peter. Philosophy. Oxford, 1956. 2v.

Phil 3585.12.90   Lassahn, Rudolf. Das Selbsterständnis der Pädagogik Theodor Litts. Wuppertal, 1968.

Phil 3246.335   Lassahn, Rudolf. Studien zur Wirkungsgeschichte Fichtes als Pädagoge Habilitationsschrift. Heidelberg, 1970.

Phil 6681.8   Lassaigne, Auguste. Memoires d'un magnétism. Paris, 1851.

Phil 2730.110   Lassaigne, Jean. Maine de Biran, homme politique. Paris, 1958.

Phil 3425.240   Lassalle, F. Die hegelsche und rosenkranzsche Logik. Leipzig, 1927.

Phil 6990.3   Lasserre, H. Les épisodes miraculeux de Lourdes. Paris, 1884.

Phil 6990.3.7   Lasserre, H. Notre-Dame de Lourdes. Paris, 1869.

Phil 6990.3.5   Lasserre, H. Our lady of Lourdes. N.Y., 1904.

Phil 3640.216   Lasserre, Pierre. Les idées de Nietzsche sur la musique. Paris, 1919?

Phil 3640.216.10   Lasserre, Pierre. Les morale de Nietzsche. Paris, 1902.

Phil 292.3   Lassivitz, Kurd. Seelen und Ziele. Beiträge zum Weltverständnis. Leipzig, 1908.

Phil 8735.18   Lasson, A. De causis finalibus. Berolini, 1874.

Phil 3415.104   Lasson, A. Die Entwickelung der religiösen...nach Eduard von Hartmann. Halle, 1883.

Phil 5545.182   Lasson, Adolf. Das Gedächtnis. Berlin, 1894.

Phil 3246.227   Lasson, Adolf. Johann Gottlieb Fichte im Verhältniss zu Kirche und Staat. Berlin, 1863.

Phil 5051.11   Lasson, Adolf. Der Satz vom Widerspruch. Halle, 1885.

Phil 186.42   Lasson, Adolf. Zeitliches und Zeitloses. Leipzig, 1890.

Phil 3425.108.7   Lasson, G. Beiträge zur Hegelforschung. Berlin, 1919-21. 2v.

Phil 3425.108.10   Lasson, G. Einführung in Hegels Religionsphilosophie. Leipzig, 1930.

Phil 3425.108.5   Lasson, G. Hegel; handschriftliche Zusätze zu seiner Rechtsphilosophie. Leipzig, 1914. 3v.

Author and Title Listing

Phil 3425.108A   Lasson, G. Hegel...Gedankenwelt in Auszügen aus seine Werken. Stuttgart, 1906.

Phil 6321.9.6   Lasswell, H.D. Psychology and politics. Chicago, 1934.

Phil 6321.9.8   Lasswell, H.D. Psychopathology and politics. N.Y., 1960.

Phil 3210.28   Lasswitz, K. Gustav Theodor Fechner. Stuttgart, 1902.

Phil 3493.4   Lasswitz, K. Die Lehre Kants von der Idealität. Berlin, 1883.

Phil 3210.81.2   Lasswitz, Kurd. Gustav Theodor Fechner. Stuttgart, 1896.

Phil 3210.81   Lasswitz, Kurd. Gustav Theodor Fechner. Stuttgart, 1910.

Phil 3493.8   Last, E. Mehr Licht! Berlin, 1879.

Phil 3493.8.5   Last, E. Die realistische und die idealistische Weltanschauung entwickelt an Kants Idealität von Zeit und Raum. Leipzig, 1884.

Phil 978.6.91   The last four lives of Annie Besant. (Nethercot, A.H.) London, 1963.

Phil 6128.30   The last lap. (Starrett, D.W.) Boston, 1915.

Phil 7069.19.10   Last letters from the living dead man. (Barker, Elsa.) N.Y., 1919.

Phil 1200.16   The last pagan. (Thompson, J.W.) Chicago, 1917.

Htn   Phil 2045.77F*   Last sayings. (Hobbes, Thomas.) London, 1680.

Phil 8631.15   The last things. (Guardini, R.) London, 1954.

Phil 8662.5.9   The last trial for atheism in England. 5. ed. (Holyoake, George Jacob.) London, 1878.

Phil 4112.80   Lastrucci, V. Pasquale Galluppi; studio critico. Firenze, 1890.

Phil 9035.52   Lasurski, A. Über das Studium der Individualität. Leipzig, 1912.

Phil 2120.13   Laszlo, Ervin. Beyond scepticism and realism. The Hague, 1966.

Phil 2120.13.5   Laszlo, Ervin. Essential society; an ontological reconstruction. The Hague, 1963.

Phil 2340.10.240   Laszlo, Ervin. La métaphysique de Whitehead: recherche des prolongements anthropologiques. La Hague, 1970.

Phil 4710.19   Laszlo, Ervin. Philosophy in the Soviet Union. Dordrecht, 1967.

Phil 6121.55   Laszlo, Ervin. System, structure, and experience. N.Y., 1969.

Phil 5790.45   Latané, Bibb. The unresponsive bystander: why doesn't he help? N.Y., 1970.

Phil 5627.107.20   The late Liz. (Behanna, Gertrude Florence.) N.Y., 1957.

Phil 5627.107.20.5   The late Liz. (Behanna, Gertrude Florence.) N.Y., 1968.

Phil 1020.4.20   Der lateinische Awerroismus des 13 Jahrhunderts. (Grabmann, M.) München, 1931.

Phil 3450.19.270A   The later Heidegger and theology. (Robinson, J.M.C.) N.Y., 1963.

Phil 1930.8.105   The later philosophy of R.G. Collingwood. (Donagan, Alan.) Oxford, 1962.

Phil 3925.16.86   The later philosophy of Wittgenstein. (Pole, David.) London, 1958.

Phil 5051.3   Latham, R.G. Logic..application to language. London, 1856.

Phil 8636.4   Lathbury, C. The great morning. Minneapolis, 1911.

Htn   Phil 7150.20*   Lathrop, Joseph. Two sermons on the atrocity of suicide. Suffield, 1805.

Phil 9400.5   Lathrop, S.G. Fifty years and beyond. Chicago, 1881.

Phil 5520.63   Latif, Israil. The physiological basis of linguistic development. Diss. Lancaster, Pa., 1934.

NEDL   Phil 2050.97   Latimer, J.E. Immediate perception as held by Reid and Hamilton. Leipzig, 1880.

Phil 4363.3.80   Latour, A. de. Don Miguel de Manara. Paris, 1857.

Phil 5374.65   Latour, M. Autour des fondements de l'être et du connaître selon l'analyse psychologique. Paris, 1949. 2v.

Phil 5400.29   Latour, Marius. Premiers principes d'une théorie générale des émotions. Paris, 1912.

Phil 5400.29.5   Latour, Marius. Premiers principes d'une théorie générale des émotions. Paris, 1935.

Phil 5400.29.15   Latour, Marius. Premiers principes d'une théorie générale des émotions. Observations complémentaires. 3me série. Bayonne, 1937.

Phil 5400.29.25   Latour, Marius. Premiers principes d'une théorie générale des émotions. Observations complémentaires. 5me série. Bayonne, 1937.

Phil 5400.29.20   Latour, Marius. Premiers principes d'une théorie générale des émotions. Observations complémentaires. 4me série. Bayonne, 1937.

Phil 5525.56   Latour, Marius. Le problème du rire et du réel. Paris, 1956.

Phil 2477.10.90   Latreille, C. Francisque Bouillier. Paris, 1907.

Phil 525.47   Latta, R. The old mysticism and the new pluralism. Glasgow, 1902.

Phil 5051.24A   Latta, Robert. The elements of logic. London, 1929.

Phil 525.40   Latteo, Ernesto. Il misticismo. Torino, 1908.

Phil 8666.12   Lattey, Cuthbert. God. London, 1931.

Phil 6321.1   Lattimore, E.L. Some illustrative clinic cases. Thesis. Menasha, 1916.

Phil 3280.91   Lattre, Alain de. L'Occasionalisme d'Arnold Geulincx. Paris, 1967.

Phil 410.79   Latzin, H. Analysis des Unendlichen im Psychischen und Physischen. Wien, 1931.

Phil 3195.9.81   Lau, Hamann. Eugen Dühring als Religionsphilosoph. Inaug. Diss. Lübeck, 1907.

Phil 8583.11.90   Lau, Paul. August Dorners Religionsphilosophie. Inaug. Diss. Königsberg, 1928.

Htn   Phil 186.33*   Lau, Theodor L. Meditationes philosophicae de Deo, mundo, homine. Frankfurt, 1717.

Phil 7069.69.40   Laubscher, Barend Jacob Frederick. In quest of the unseen. 1st ed. N.Y., 1969.

Phil 2120.9.30   Laucks, I.F. A speculation in reality. N.Y., 1953.

Phil 8886.40   Laudatio, Giorgio. La giustizia e la morale. Trani, 1902.

Phil 3310.1.130   Lauden, V.J.C. Peter Franz Knoodt als Philosoph. Elberfeld, 1920.

Phil 1135.100   Laudowicz, Felix. Wesen und Ursprung der Lehre von der Präexistenz der Seele und von der Seelenwanderung in der griechischen Philosophie. Berlin, 1898.

Phil 3425.588   Lauener, H. Die Sprache in der Philosophie Hegels. Berlin, 1962.

Phil 3493.42   Lauener, Henri. Hume und Kant. Bern, 1969.

Phil 978.49.805   Lauer, H.E. Klassik. Basel, 1950.

Phil 978.49.805.5   Lauer, H.E. Die zwölf Sumie des Menschen. Basel, 1953.

Phil 974.3.91   Lauer, Hans E. Rudolf Steiners Anthroposophie in Weltanschauungskampfe der Gegenwart. 8. Aufsätze. Basel, 1927.

Phil 974.3.90   Lauer, Hans E. Rudolf Steiner's Lebenswerk. Basel, 1926.

Phil 978.96   Lauer, Hans Erhard. Die Anthroposophie und die Zukunft des Christentums. Stuttgart, 1966.

Phil 5251.76   Lauer, Hans Erhard. Die Rätsel der Seele: Tiefenpsychologie und Anthroposophie. 2. Aufl. Freiburg, 1964.

Phil 978.96.5   Lauer, Hans Erhard. Der Mensch in den Entscheidungen unseres Jahrhunderts. Freiburg, 1968.

Phil 835.2   Lauer, Hans Erhard. Die Wiedergeburt der Erkenntnis in der Entwicklungsgeschichte. Freiburg, 1946.

Phil 5628.54.4   Lauer, Nikolaus. Barbara Pfister, eine pfälzische Stigmatisierte. 4. Aufl. Speyer, 1964.

Phil 3450.11.135   Lauer, Quentin. La genèse de l'intentionalité dans la philosophie de Husserl. Paris, 1954.

Phil 3450.11.140   Lauer, Quentin. Phénoménologie, existence. Paris, 1955.

Phil 3450.11.142   Lauer, Quentin. Phénoménologie de Husserl. 1st ed. Paris, 1955.

Phil 3450.11.142.5A   Lauer, Quentin. The triumph of subjectivity. N.Y., 1958.

Phil 6121.2.10   Laugel, A. Om själens problemer. Stockholm, 1869.

Phil 6121.2   Laugel, A. Les problèmes de l'âme. Paris, 1868.

Phil 186.18.9   Laugel, Auguste. Los problemas de la naturaleza. Barcelona, 18- ?

Phil 186.18.5   Laugel, Auguste. Les problèmes de la nature. Paris, 1864.

Phil 6121.3.3   Laugel, T. Mind and brain. N.Y., 1869. 2v.

Phil 5525.32.5   Laughing: an essay. (Armstrong, M.) London, 1928.

Phil 5525.32   Laughing: an essay. (Armstrong, M.) N.Y., 1928.

Phil 5525.70   Laughing and crying; a study of limits of human behavior. (Plessner, Helmuth.) Evanston, 1970.

Phil 6321.58   Laughlin, Henry Prather. The ego and its defenses. N.Y., 1970.

Phil 2475.1.69.6   Laughter. (Bergson, Henri.) London, 1911.

Phil 5525.54   Laughter and the sense of humor. (Bergler, Edmund.) N.Y., 1956.

Phil 6315.2.91   Laumonier, J. Le freudisme; exposé et critique. Paris, 1925.

Phil 2520.165   Launay, Louis de. Descartes. Paris, 1923.

Phil 3493.19   Laupichler, Max. Die Grundzüge der materialen Ethik Kants. Berlin, 1931.

Phil 811.1   Laurent, P.M. Résumé de l'histoire de la philosophie. Paris, 1826.

Phil 6990.3.110   Laurentin, René. Les apparitions de Lourdes. Paris, 1966.

Phil 6990.3.90   Laurentin, René. Lourdes. Paris, 1961. 6v.

Phil 6990.3.92   Laurentin, René. Lourdes. 2. ed. Paris, 1957. 7v.

Phil 5525.28   Laurentius, A.P. Dialogus pulcherrimus et utilissimus. Marpurgi, 1606.

Phil 2138.96   Lauret, Henri. Philosophie de Stuart Mill. Thèse. Neufchâteau, 1885.

Phil 1811.1   Laurie, H. Scottish philosophy. Glasgow, 1902.

Phil 9530.32   Laurie, Ossip. L'arrivisme. Paris, 1929.

Phil 8886.5.5   Laurie, S.S. Ethica: or The ethics of reason. London, 1885.

Phil 315.1   Laurie, S.S. Metaphysica nova et vetusta. London, 1884.

Phil 8836.1   Laurie, S.S. Notes, expository and critical, on certain British theories of morals. Edinburgh, 1868.

Phil 8886.5   Laurie, S.S. On the philosophy of ethics. Edinburgh, 1866.

Phil 186.19   Laurie, S.S. Synthetica. London, 1906. 2v.

Phil 8412.8.5   Laurila, K.S. Ästhetische Streitfragen. Helsinki, 1934.

Phil 8412.8.10   Laurila, K.S. Estetiikhan peruskysymyksia. Porvoo, 1919.

Phil 2475.1.231   Laurila, K.S. La théorie du comique de M.H. Bergson. Helsinki, 1929.

Phil 8591.75   Laurila, K.S. Vapaamielisyys. Helsingissä, 1917.

Phil 8412.8   Laurila, K.S. Versuch einer Stellungnahme zu den Hauptfragen der Kunstphilosophie. Helsingfors, 1903.

Phil 5585.291   Laurondeau, Monique. The development of the concept of space in the child. N.Y., 1970.

Phil 5585.290   Laurondeau, Monique. La premières notions spatiales de l'enfant. Neuchâtel, 1968.

Phil 3640.420   Lauscher, A. Friedrich Nietzsche. Essen, 1909.

Phil 8589.25   Láusterité et la vie morale. (Jankélévetch, V.) Paris, 1956.

Phil 3493.48   Lauter, Josef. Untersuchungen zur Sprache von Kants Kritik der reinen Vernunft. Köln, 1966.

Phil 720.70   Lauth, Reinhard. Die absolute Ungeschichtlichkeit der Warhheit. Stuttgart, 1966.

Phil 705.54.5   Lauth, Reinhard. Begriff. München, 1967.

Phil 8886.91   Lauth, Reinhard. Ethik in ihrer Grundlage aus Prinzipien entfaltet. Stuttgart, 1969.

Phil 705.54   Lauth, Reinhard. Zur Idee der Transzendentalphilosophie. München, 1965.

Phil 5650.22.10   Lautheit und Lärn. (Sader, Manfred.) Göttingen, 1966.

Phil 6961.7   Lauze, Charles A. La psychose hallucinatoire chronique. Thèse. Paris, 1914.

Phil 5251.32   La Vaissière, J. de. Elements of experimental psychology. St. Louis, 1926.

Phil 7074.5   Laval. L'heure des révélations; le livre des temps. Montpellier, 1969.

Phil 2730.84   LaValette, Monbrun A. de. Essai de biographie historique...Maine de Biran. Paris, 1914.

Phil 2805.165   La Vallette-Monbrun, A. de. Maine de Biran, critique et disciple de Pascal. Paris, 1914.

Phil 6032.5   Lavater, der Menschenkenner. 1. Aufl. (Waldemar, Charles.) Zürich, 1960.

Htn   Phil 3625.1.160*   Lavater, J.C. Antwort an den herrn Moses Mendelssohn zu Berlin. Berlin, 1770.

Htn   Phil 8886.6*   Lavater, J.C. Aphorisms on man. Boston, 1790.

Phil 6021.2.4   Lavater, Johann Caspar. Essays on physiognomy. London, n.d.

Phil 6021.2   Lavater, Johann Caspar. Essays on physiognomy. London, 1789. 3v.

Htn   Phil 6021.2.1F*   Lavater, Johann Caspar. Essays on physiognomy. London, 1789-98. 5v.

Phil 6021.2.2   Lavater, Johann Caspar. Essays on physiognomy. London, 1797. 3v.

Phil 6021.2.3   Lavater, Johann Caspar. Essays on physiognomy. London, 1840.

Htn   Phil 6021.2.5*   Lavater, Johann Caspar. Essays on physiognomy. 1st American ed. Boston, 179-?

Phil 6021.2.12   Lavater, Johann Caspar. Essays on physiognomy. 17th ed. London, 18- .

Htn   Phil 6021.2.8*   Lavater, Johann Caspar. Physiognomische Fragmente. Winterthur, 1783.

Phil 6021.2.18   Lavater, Johann Caspar. Physiognomische Fragmente zur Beförderung der Menschenkenntnis und Menschenliebe. Zürich, 1968- 4v.

X Cg   Phil 6021.2.59   Lavater, Johann Caspar. The physiognomist's own book. Philadelphia, 1841.

Phil 6021.2.10   Lavater, Johann Caspar. La physiognomonie. Paris, 1841.

Phil 6021.2.6   Lavater, Johann Caspar. Physiognomy. London, 1792.

Author and Title Listing

	Phil 6021.2.15	Lavater, Johann Caspar. Physionomie portative. Paris, 1806. 2v.
	Phil 6021.2.55	Lavater, Johann Caspar. The pocket Lavater. Hartford, 18- .
Htn	Phil 7060.2*	Lavater, L. De spectris. Genevae, 1580.
	Phil 7060.2.2	Lavater, L. De spectris. Lugduni Batavorum, 1659.
	Phil 7060.2.3	Lavater, L. De spectris. Lugduni Batavorum, 1687.
Htn	Phil 7060.2.5*	Lavater, L. Of ghostes and spirites walking by night. London, 1572.
Htn	Phil 7060.2.7*	Lavater, L. Of ghostes and spirites walking by night. London, 1596.
	Phil 7060.2.15	Lavater, L. Of ghostes and spirites walking by nyght. London, 1929.
	Phil 6021.2.85	Lavaters physiognomische...Kunst. (Steinbrucker, C.) Berlin, 1915.
	Phil 6021.2.87	Lavaters physiognomische Fragmente. (Janentzky, C.J.C.) Halle, 1916.
	Phil 6990.14	LaVausserie. Apparitions de la St. Vierge à deux jeunes enfants. Paris, 1873.
	Phil 1145.75	Lavell, C.F. Evolution of Greek moral education. Kingston, 1911.
	Phil 2725.35.60	Lavelle, Louis. La conscience de soi. Paris, 1933.
	Phil 2725.35.55	Lavelle, Louis. De l'acte. Paris, 1937.
	Phil 2725.35.50	Lavelle, Louis. De l'être. Paris, 1928.
	Phil 2725.35	Lavelle, Louis. De l'intimité spirituelle. Paris, 1955.
	Phil 5585.32	Lavelle, Louis. La dialectique du monde sensible. Strasbourg, 1921.
	Phil 5585.32.3	Lavelle, Louis. La dialectique du monde sensible. Thèse. Strasbourg, 1921. 2 pam.
	Phil 2725.35.20	Lavelle, Louis. Du temps et de l'eternité. Paris, 1945.
	Phil 2725.35.65	Lavelle, Louis. Introduction à l'ontologie. 1. éd. Paris, 1947.
	Phil 2725.35.70	Lavelle, Louis. Manuel de méthodologie dialectique. Paris, 1962.
	Phil 2725.35.30	Lavelle, Louis. Le moi et son destin. Paris, 1936.
	Phil 2725.35.5	Lavelle, Louis. Morale et religion. Paris, 1960.
	Phil 186.65.35	Lavelle, Louis. Panorama des doctrines philosophiques. Paris, 1967.
	Phil 5585.33	Lavelle, Louis. La perception visuelle de la profondeur. Strasbourg, 1921.
	Phil 2725.35.40	Lavelle, Louis. La présence totale. Paris, 1934.
	Phil 2725.35.10	Lavelle, Louis. Psychologie et spiritualité. Paris, 1967.
	Phil 186.65.30	Lavelle, Louis. Science, esthétique, métaphysique. Paris, 1967.
	Phil 315.16	Lavergne, Bernard. Individualisme contre autoritarisme. Paris, 1959.
	Phil 4120.4.82	La Via, G. L'idealismo attuale di Giovanni Gentile. Trani, 1925.
	Phil 4080.3.190	LaVia, Pietro. Mente e realtà; il pensiero di Benedetto Croce. Firenze, 1947. 2v.
	Phil 850.22	LaVia, V. Il problema della fondazione della filosofia e l'oggettivismo antico. 2. ed. Roma, 1946.
	Phil 400.104	La Via, Vincenzo. Idealismo e filosofia. Messina, 1942.
	Phil 8412.16	La Via, Vincenzo. L'umanità dell'arte. Roma, 1924.
	Phil 7069.03.45	Lavius Egyptus. (Spivey, T.S.) Cincinnati, 1903. 2v.
	Phil 8591.28	Lavollée, R. Raison et foi. Paris, 1926.
	Phil 8416.42	Lavovo e conoscenza nell'arte. (Prestipino, Giuseppe.) Napoli, 1967.
	Phil 3640.349	Lavrin, Janko. Nietzsche; an approach. London, 1948.
	Phil 292.11	Lavrov, A.S. V poiskakh istiny. Paris, 1940.
	Phil 8591.1	Law, E. Considerations...theory of religion. Cambridge, 1755.
	Phil 8591.1.3	Law, E. Considerations...theory of religion. Cambridge, 1765.
	Phil 8591.1.2	Law, E. Considerations...theory of religion. Cambridge, 1765.
	Phil 8952.12	Law, liberty and love. (Cary-Elwes, C.F.) N.Y., 1951.
	Phil 5258.193	Law, liberty and psychiatry. (Szasz, Thomas Stephen.) N.Y., 1963.
Htn	Phil 2128.80.2*	Law, William. Remarks on...the fable of the bees. Cambridge, 1844.
	Phil 2128.80	Law, William. Remarks on...the fable of the bees. Cambridge, 1844.
	Phil 2128.80.5	Law, William. Remarks on...the fable of the bees. London, 1724.
Htn	Phil 2120.2.30*	Law, William. A serious call to a devout and holy life. London, 1729.
	Phil 8959.4	Law and love. (Jessof, T.E.) London, 1940.
	Phil 70.97	Law and philosophy. (New York. Institute of Philosophy.) N.Y., 1964.
	Phil 194.21.7	The law and the word. (Troward, Thomas.) N.Y., 1919.
	Phil 7069.31.50	Law governing mediumship. (Wells, Helen B.) N.Y., 1931.
	Phil 298.18	The law in nature and anxiety-superior. (Remits, E.) Ottawa, 1962.
	Phil 298.18.5	The law in nature and the dynamics of openness. (Remits, E.) Ottawa, 1965.
	Phil 176.84	The law of being. (Bonlnois, Helen.) London, 1920.
	Phil 9590.2	The law of biogenesis. (Moore, J.H.) Chicago, 1914.
	Phil 8691.10	The law of human life; scriptures in the light of science. (Brookshire, E.V.) N.Y., 1916.
	Phil 8882.21.15	The law of love and love as a law. (Hopkins, M.) N.Y., 1885.
	Phil 8882.21.12	The law of love and love as a law. 3rd ed. (Hopkins, M.) N.Y., 1871.
	Phil 6117.42	The law of mental medicine. (Hudson, T.J.) Chicago, 1903.
	Phil 6128.41	The law of mentalism. 26th ed. (Segno, A.V.) Los Angeles, 1902.
	Phil 6117.22	The law of mind in action. (Holmes, F.L.) N.Y., 1919.
Htn	Phil 2925.2.35*	The law of nations. v.1-2. (Vattel, Emmerich.) London, 1760[1759].
	Phil 8896.17	The law of nature, or Principles of morality. (Volney, C.F.C.) Philadelphia, 1796.
	Phil 7060.28	Law of psychic phenomena. (Hudson, T.J.) Chicago, 1893.
	Phil 7068.96.7.9	The law of psychic phenomena. 30. ed. (Hudson, Thomson J.) Chicago, 1905.
	Phil 6115.17	Law of rhythmic breath. (Fletcher, E.A.) N.Y., 1908.
	Phil 6051.21	The law of scientific hand reading. (Benham, William G.) N.Y., 1901.
	Phil 193.98	The law of struggle. (Segal, Hyman.) N.Y., 1918.
	Phil 7140.106	The law of suggestion. 1st ed. (Krebs, Stanley le Fevre.) Chicago, 1906.
	Phil 5374.153	The law of vital transfusion and the phenomenon of consciousness. (Reed, Charles J.) San Francisco, 1921.
	Phil 8886.26	Lawätz, H.W. Über die Tugenden und Laster...des Menschen. Flensburg, 1789-1792. 3v.
	Phil 9010.19	Lawful amusements. (Burder, George.) London, 1805.

	Phil 342.30	Ławniczak, Włodzimierz. O uzasadniającej roli analogii na przykładzie wnioskowań z zakresu historii sztaki. Poznań, 1971.
Htn	Phil 9495.126*	Lawrence, D.H. Pornography and obscenity. N.Y., 1930.
	Phil 6321.5.10	Lawrence, David Herbert. Fantasia of the unconscious. N.Y., 1930.
	Phil 6321.5.8.2	Lawrence, David Herbert. Fantasia of the unconscious and Psychoanalysis and the unconscious. London, 1971.
	Phil 6321.5A	Lawrence, David Herbert. Psycho-analysis and its unconscious. N.Y., 1921.
X Cg	Phil 6049.05	Lawrence, E. The science of palmistry. London, 1905.
	Phil 7054.184	Lawrence, E. Spiritualism among civilised and savage races. London, 1921.
	Phil 7068.74.10	Lawrence, Jas. Angel voices from the spirit world. Cleveland, 1874.
	Phil 5251.50	Lawrence, Merle. Studies in human behavior. Princeton, 1949.
	Phil 2340.10.135	Lawrence, N.M. Whitehead's philosophical development. Berkeley, 1956.
	Phil 186.3	Laws, S.S. Metaphysics. Columbia, Mo., 1879.
	Phil 5052.22	The laws of discursive thought. (McCosh, James.) London, 1870.
	Phil 5052.22.3	The laws of discursive thought. (McCosh, James.) N.Y., 1870.
	Phil 2125.57	The laws of discursive thought. (McCosh, James.) N.Y., 1876.
	Phil 5400.45.15	Laws of feeling. (Paulhan, Frédéric.) London, 1930.
	Phil 3488.39	Laws of freedom. (Gregor, Mary J.) N.Y., 1963.
	Phil 9220.2.20	Laws of friendship human and devine. (King, H.C.) N.Y., 1919.
	Phil 5262.36.10	Laws of human nature. (Wheeler, R.H.) N.Y., 1932.
	Phil 1135.157	The laws of motion in ancient thought. (Cornford, F.M.) Cambridge, Eng., 1931.
	Phil 8693.5.70	The laws of nature...reply to Professor Drummond. (Cockburn, S.) London, 1886.
	Phil 6049.00.7	The laws of scientific hand reading. (Benham, W.G.) N.Y., 1912.
	Phil 310.225.5	The laws of social development. (Glezerman, G.E.) Moscow, 196-?
	Phil 5041.15.2	The laws of thought. (Boole, George.) Chicago, 1916.
	Phil 5041.15.3	The laws of thought. (Boole, George.) Chicago, 1940.
Htn	Phil 5041.15.1*	The laws of thought. (Boole, George.) London, 1854.
	Phil 5041.15	The laws of thought. (Boole, George.) London, 1854.
	Phil 8672.4	The laws of thought. (Robertson, A.) London, 1865.
	Phil 1955.6.190	Lawson, D.E. John Dewey and the world view. Carbondale, 1964.
Htn	Phil 2045.104*	Lawson, George. An examination of the political part of Mr. Hobbs his Leviathan. London, 1657.
	Phil 5535.56	Lawson, Philippe Reed. Learning and behavior. N.Y., 1960.
	Phil 9400.13	Lawton, George. Aging successfully. N.Y., 1946.
	Phil 7069.32.50	Lawton, George. The drama of life after death. N.Y., 1932.
	Phil 9171.5	Lawton, R.O. The making of a home. Boston, 1914.
	Phil 7060.114	The lawyer's ghost. London, 17- ?
	Phil 5045.19.2	The lawyer's logic, 1588. (Fraunce, Abraham.) Menston, Eng., 1969.
	Phil 6321.2.3	Lay, Wilfrid. Man's unconcious conflict. N.Y., 1919.
	Phil 6321.2.5	Lay, Wilfrid. Man's unconcious conflict. N.Y., 1921.
	Phil 7084.24	Layard, John Willoughby. The lady of the hare, being a study in the healing power of dreams. London, 1944.
	Phil 8886.6.10	Laycock, F.U. Motives of mankind. London, 1907.
	Phil 6121.3.2	Laycock, T. Mind and brain. Edinburgh, 1860. 2v.
	Phil 6125.21	The layman looks at doctors. (Pierce, S.W.) N.Y., 1929.
	Phil 182.77	A layman to his sons. (Hanan, F.) London, 1924.
	Phil 8709.4	A layman's apology. (Tucker, G.M.) Boston, 1913.
	Phil 1750.757	A layman's introduction to religious existentialism. (Borowitz, Eugene B.) Philadelphia, 1965.
Htn	Phil 8624.3*	Layton, Henry. Arguments and replies. London, 1703. 7 pam.
Htn	Phil 8624.2*	Layton, Henry. A search after souls. n.p., 1706.
	Phil 6980.413	Lazarus, Arnold A. Behavior therapy and beyond. N.Y., 1971.
	Phil 3585.7.90	Lazarus, der Begründer der Volkerpsychologie. (Leicht, Alfred.) Leipzig, 1904.
	Phil 186.4	Lazarus, M. Ideale Fragen. Berlin, 1878.
	Phil 5251.10	Lazarus, M. Das Leben der Seele. Berlin, 1876. 3v.
	Phil 5821.8	Lazarus, M. Über die Reize des Spiels. Berlin, 1883.
	Phil 5251.10.9	Lazarus, M. Über Tact, Kunst, Freundschaft und Sitten. 3e Aufl. Berlin, 1896.
	Phil 9035.5	Lazarus, M.E. Comparative psychology and universal analogy. Vegetable portraits of character. N.Y., 1851.
	Phil 5590.422	Lazarus, Richard. Adjustment and personality. N.Y., 1961.
	Phil 5590.422.5	Lazarus, Richard. Patterns of adjustment and human effectiveness. N.Y., 1968.
	Phil 6121.41	Lazarus, Richards. Psychological stress and the coping process. N.Y., 1966.
	Phil 3585.7.92	Lazarusstudien. (Leicht, Alfred.) Meissen, 1912.
	Phil 972.9	Lazenby, C. The work of the masters. London, 1917.
	Phil 186.120.4	Lazerowitz, M. Philosophy and illusion. London, 1968.
	Phil 186.120	Lazerowitz, M. The structure of metaphysics. London, 1955.
	Phil 186.120.2	Lazerowitz, M. The structure of metaphysics. N.Y., 1955.
	Phil 186.120.5	Lazerowitz, M. Studies in metaphilosophy. London, 1964.
	Phil 5590.448.2	Lazurskii, Aleksandr F. Klassifikatsiis lichnosti. 2. izd. Moskva, 1923.
	Phil 3493.24	Lazzarini, Renato. Dalla religione naturale prekantiani alla religione morale di Kant. Roma, 1942.
	Phil 4160.5.230	Lazzarini, Renato. Valore e religione nell'orizzonte esistenziale. Padova, 1965.
	Phil 4160.5.30	Lazzerini, Virgilio. Annotaziori per un nuovo criticismo. Milano, 1965.
	Phil 2725.12.81	Le Sage als Vorkämpfer der Atomistik. Inaug. Diss. (Stosz, Wilhelm.) Halle, 1884.
	Phil 6322.60	Le temps vécu. (Minkowski, Eugène.) Neuchâtel, 1968.
	Phil 3640.490	Lea, F.A. The tragic philosopher. London, 1957.
	Phil 186.145	Lea, Frank A. A defence of philosophy. London, 1962.
	Phil 978.8.2	Leadbeater, C.W. The christian creed. 2nd ed. London, 1904.
	Phil 6681.14	Leadbeater, C.W. Clairvoyance. 2d ed. London, 1903.
	Phil 978.8.25	Leadbeater, C.W. Dreams; what they are and how they are caused. 4th ed. London, 1908.
	Phil 978.8.30	Leadbeater, C.W. Invisible helpers. London, 1899.
	Phil 978.8.15	Leadbeater, C.W. Man visible and invisible. N.Y., 1903.
	Phil 978.8.9	Leadbeater, C.W. Outline of theosophy. London, 1902.
	Phil 978.8.11	Leadbeater, C.W. Outline of theosophy. London, 1915.
	Phil 978.8.10	Leadbeater, C.W. Outline of theosophy. 2d ed. Chicago, 1903.

Phil 978.8.35   Leadbeater, C.W. Reincarnation; a lecture. Harrogate, 1903.

Phil 978.8.19   Leadbeater, C.W. Textbook of theosophy. Chicago, 1925.

Phil 8886.13   Leadbeater, M. Cottage dialogues. Richmond, 1811.

Phil 5590.16   Leadership and isolation. (Jennings, Helen H.) N.Y., 1943.

Phil 7069.19.155   Leaf, Horace. What is this spiritualism? N.Y., 1919.

Phil 8886.66   Leake, C.D. Can we agree? Austin, 1950.

Phil 1905.22.80   Lean, Martin. Sense - perception and matter. London, 1953.

Phil 1750.146   Leander, F. Humanism and naturalism. Göteborg, 1937.

Phil 4582.4.83   Leander, P.H.J. Svar på kritik af ett kompetensutlåtande. Lund, 1898.

Phil 4515.86   Leander, P.J.H. Boströms lära om guds ideer. Lund, 1886.

Phil 4600.3.31   Leander, P.J.H. Om substansbegreppet hos Cartesius, Spinoza och Liebnitz. Akademisk afhandling. Lund, 1862. 2 pam.

Phil 4060.2.80   Leão Hebreu, filósofo. (Carvalho, Joaqium de.) Coimbra, 1918.

Phil 5535.42   Learning, memory, and conceptual processes. (Kintsch, Walter.) N.Y., 1970.

Phil 5545.94   Learning, remembering, and forgetting. (Conference on Learning, Remembering and Forgetting.) Palo Alto, 1965-

Phil 5545.205   Learning, remembering and knowing. (Meredith, Patrick.) N.Y., 1961.

Phil 5535.56   Learning and behavior. (Lawson, Philippe Reed.) N.Y., 1960.

Phil 5829.11   Learning and instinct in animals. (Thorpe, W.H.) London, 1956.

Phil 21.17   Learning and motivation. N.Y. 1,1970+

Phil 6998.6   Learning foundations of behavior therapy. (Kanfer, Frederick H.) N.Y., 1970.

Phil 333.6   The learning process. Theory of knowledge. (Coursault, J.H.) N.Y., 1907.

Phil 5535.46   Learning theory and mental development. (Estes, William Kaye.) N.Y., 1970.

Phil 5251.36   Leary, Daniel Bell. Modern psychology, normal and abnormal. Philadelphia, 1928.

Phil 342.20   Leary, Lewis. The unity of knowledge. Garden City, N.Y., 1955.

Phil 5590.220   Leary, Timothy. Interpersonal diagnosis of personality. N.Y., 1957.

Phil 5374.234.30   Leary, Timothy Francis. High priest. N.Y., 1968.

Phil 6155.4.5   Leary, Timothy Francis. The politics of ecstasy. N.Y., 1968.

Phil 6155.4.10   Leary, Timothy Francis. The psychedelic experience. New Hyde Park, 1964.

Phil 6155.4   Leary, Timothy Francis. Psychedelic prayers after the tao te ching. Kerhonkson, 1966.

Phil 8886.30   Leathes, Stanley. The foundations of morality. London, 1882.

Phil 6315.1.80   The leaven of love. (De Forest, Izette.) Hamden, Conn., 1954.

Phil 6315.1.14   The leaven of love. (De Forest, Izette.) London, 1926.

Phil 2805.208   Leavenworth, I. The physics of Pascal. N.Y., 1930.

Phil 7069.27.15   Leaves from a psychic note-book. (Dallas, H.A.) London, 1927.

Phil 2035.83   Leaves from my writing desk. London, 1872.

Phil 6121.25   Leavitt, C.F. Leavitt-science. Chicago, 19- .

Phil 6121.25   Leavitt-science. (Leavitt, C.F.) Chicago, 19- .

Phil 5070.23   Lebacqz, Joseph. Certitude et volonté. Bruges, 1962.

Phil 2475.1.480   Lebacqz, Joseph. De l'identique au multiple. Québec, 1968.

Phil 5761.23   Lebacqz, Joseph. Libre arbitre et jugement. Paris, 1960.

Phil 292.6   LeBel, J.A. Cosmologie rationnelle. Le Mans, 1925.

Phil 8693.14   Leben, Natur, Religion. 2. Aufl. (Dessauer, F.) Bonn, 1926.

Phil 3120.15.97.10   Das Leben - eine Aufgabe. (Bickel, Lothar.) Zürich, 1959.

Phil 3195.14.45   Leben als Symbol. (Dacqué, Edgar.) München, 1928.

Phil 3835.5   Leben Benedikt's von Spinoza. (Philipson, M.) Braunschweig, 1790.

Phil 6520.7   Das Leben der ekstatischen und stigmatischen Christina von Stommeln. (Wollersheim, T.) Köln, 1859.

Phil 5628.52.5   Leben der Gottseligen Anna Katharina Emmerich. (Schmöger, Karl Erhard.) Freiburg, 1885.

Phil 812.13   Das Leben der Philosophen. (Moog, W.) Berlin, 1932.

Phil 5251.10   Das Leben der Seele. (Lazarus, M.) Berlin, 1876. 3v.

Phil 3822.4.15   Das Leben des Benedict von Spinoza. (Colerus, Johannes.) Frankfurt, 1733.

Phil 3822.4.25   Das Leben des Benedict von Spinoza. (Colerus, Johannes.) Heidelberg, 1952.

Phil 3552.294   Leben des Freyherrn Gottfried Wilhelm von Leibnitz au das licht Gestellet. (Lamprecht, J.F.) Berlin, 1740.

Phil 1075.1.5   Leben des Heiligen David von Thessalonilke. (Rose, Valentin.) Berlin, 1887.

Phil 7082.134   Das Leben des Traums. (Scheruer, Karl Albert.) Berlin, 1861.

Phil 3640.88   Das Leben Friedrich Nietzsche's. (Förster-Nietzsche, E.) Leipzig, 1895. 2v.

Phil 3625.8.92   Leben Georg Friedrich Meiers. (Langen, S.G.) Halle, 1778.

Phil 306.2.2   Das Leben im Weltall. (Zehnder, Ludwig.) Tübingen, 1910.

Phil 5762.32   Leben ist Willkür. (Marx, Otto.) Hamburg, 1962.

Phil 3110.173   Das Leben Jakob Böhmes. (Peuckert, W.E.) Jena, 1924.

Phil 5411.10   Leben mit dem Hass. (Haesler, Alfred A.) Reinbeck, 1969.

Phil 3808.169.10   Leben mit Schopenhauer. (Hübscher, Arthur.) Frankfurt, 1966.

Phil 3805.85   Leben Schleiermachers. (Dilthey, Wilhelm.) Berlin, 1870.

Phil 3805.85.2   Leben Schleiermachers. 2. Aufl. (Dilthey, Wilhelm.) Berlin, 1922.

Phil 3640.755   Leben und Denken. (Volkmann-Schluck, Karl Heinz.) Frankfurt, 1968.

Phil 480.2   Das Leben und die todte Natur. (Flentje, L.) Cassel, 1866.

Phil 197.58   Leben und Erkennen. (Wolff, Gustav.) München, 1933.

Phil 3120.2.96   Leben und Geistige. (Winter, J.) Halle, 1949.

Phil 288.8   Leben und Lebensform. (Häberlin, Paul.) Basel, 1957.

Phil 3625.1.90   Leben und Meinungen M. Mendelssohn. (Schütz, F.W. von.) Hamburg, 1787.

Htn   Phil 3801.606*   Leben und Meinungen Sempronius Gundibert's. (Nicolai, F.) Berlin, 1798.

Phil 2050.83   Leben und Philosophie David Hume's. (Jodl, F.) Halle, 1872.

Phil 3090.27   Leben und theosophische Werke. v.1-2. (Baader, Franz von.) Stuttgart, 1886-87.

Phil 21.20   Leben und Weltenschauung; Beiträge zu geistiger Lebensgestaltung und Weltschau von Denkern aller Zeiten. Monatsschrift. Godesberg. 1-10,1926-1935 10v.

Phil 3552.462.5   Leben und Werk von Gottfried Wilhelm Leibniz. (Mueller, Kurt.) Frankfurt, 1969.

Phil 8643.26   Leben wir nach unseren Tode weiter? (Stern-Gwiazdowski, H. von.) Leipzig, 1896.

Phil 303.9.3   Das Lebendige all; idealistische Weltanschauung. (Wille, Bruno.) Hamburg, 1905.

Phil 3450.11.310   Lebendige Gegenwart. (Held, Klaus.) Köln, 1963.

Phil 3450.11.311   Lebendige Gegenwart. Thesis. (Held, Klaus.) Den Haag, 1966.

Phil 6315.2.190   Lebendige Psychoanalyse. (Riemann, Fritz.) München, 1956.

Phil 3900.2.5   Das Lebendige und das Goettliche. (Unger, Erich.) Jerusalem, 1966.

Phil 7060.45   Die Lebendigen und die Toten. (Kleinpaul, R.) Leipzig, 1898.

Phil 165.328   Lebendiger Realismus. (Hartmann, Klaus.) Bonn, 1962.

Phil 978.49.640   Lebendiges Naturerkennen. (Steiner, R.) Dornach, 1966.

Phil 3425.109   Lebendiges und Totes in Hegels Philosophie. (Croce, B.) Heidelberg, 1909.

Phil 3525.75   Lebenlehre. 2. Aufl. (Krause, K.C.F.) Leipzig, 1904.

Phil 3160.9   Lebens Erinnerungen und Denkwürdigkeiten. (Carus, Karl Gustav.) Weimar, 1966. 2v.

Phil 3415.89.5   Das Lebens Werk Eduard von Hartmanns. (Drews, A.) Leipzig, n.d.

Phil 9400.27   Der Lebensabend. 1. Aufl. (Bartholody, E Mendelssohn.) Gütersloh, 1958.

Phil 185.64   Die Lebensalter. (Künkel, H.) Jena, 1939.

Phil 193.59.15   Lebensanschauung; vier...Kapitel. (Simmel, G.) München, 1918.

Phil 818.9   Lebensanschauungen Alter und neuer Denker. (Sawicki, Franz.) Paderborn, 1923. 3v.

Phil 8829.2   Die Lebensanschauungen der grossen Denker. (Eucken, Rudolf.) Leipzig, 1890.

Phil 8829.2.2   Die Lebensanschauungen der grossen Denker. (Eucken, Rudolf.) Leipzig, 1897.

Phil 8829.2.5   Die Lebensanschauungen der grossen Denker. (Eucken, Rudolf.) Leipzig, 1905.

Phil 8829.2.7   Die Lebensanschauungen der grossen Denker. 12. Aufl. (Eucken, Rudolf.) Leipzig, 1918.

Phil 8829.2.8   Der Lebensanschauungen der grossen Denker. 13e und 14e Aufl. (Eucken, Rudolf.) Berlin, 1919.

Phil 8829.2.8.2   Die Lebensanschauungen der grossen Denker. 20. Aufl. (Eucken, Rudolf.) Berlin, 1950.

Phil 1718.24   Lebensanschauungen moderner Denker. (Sawicki, F.) Paderborn, 1949-1952. 2v.

Phil 1145.32   Die Lebensauffassung der griechischen Philosophen. (Gomperz, H.) Jena, 1904.

Phil 3195.6.95   Lebensbegriff und Lebenskategorie. Inaug. Diss. (Hennig, J.) Aachen, 1934.

Phil 3790.11.85   Lebensbeschreibung, von ihm selbst. (Reimarus, J.A.H.) Hamburg, 1814.

Phil 5425.78   Lebensbild des Talents. (Scheffler, K.) Berlin, 1948.

Phil 3195.10.30   Lebenserinnerungen. (Driesch, H.) Basel, 1951.

Phil 179.3.75   Lebenserinnerungen. (Eucken, R.) Leipzig, 1921.

Phil 179.3.75.25   Lebenserinnerungen. (Eucken, R.) Stockholm, 1921.

Phil 510.133   Die Lebenserscheinungen. (Jordan, H.) Leipzig, 1911.

Phil 5258.74.4   Lebensformen; geisteswissenschaftliche Psychologie und Ethik der Personlichkeit. 4. Aufl. (Spranger, Eduard.) Halle, 1924.

Phil 3475.3.67   Lebensfragen der deutschen Politik. (Jaspers, Karl.) München, 1963.

Phil 9165.3.6   Lebensführung. (Foerster, F.W.) Berlin, 1962.

Phil 3625.5.78.2   Lebensgeschichte. (Atlas, S.) Berlin, 1792-93. 2 pam.

Phil 3625.5.78   Lebensgeschichte. (Atlas, S.) München, 1911.

Phil 4065.117   Die Lebensgeschichte Giordano Bruno's. (Sigwart, C.) Tübingen, 1880.

Phil 8590.16   Der Lebensglaube. (Key, Ellen.) Berlin, 1906.

Phil 3745.8   Lebenshilfe. (Pfannwitz, Rudolf.) Zürich, 1938.

Phil 745.5   Die "Lebenskraft" in der Schriften des Vitalisten und ihrer Gegner. (Noll, Alfred.) Leipzig, 1914.

Phil 9165.3   Lebenskunde, ein Buch für Knaben und Mädchen. (Foerster, F.W.) Berlin, 1907.

Phil 9070.134   Die Lebenskunst nach den Inschriften des Tempels zu Delphi. (Carus, Karl Gustav.) Stuttgart, 1968.

Phil 9070.58   Lebenskunst und Lebensgemeinschaft in Gesellschaft und Wirtschaft. (Kuehne, O.) Berlin, 1954[1958] 2v.

Phil 6120.18   Lebensmächte. (Klatt, F.) Jena, 1939.

Phil 745.12   Die Lebensphilosophie. (Bollnow, Otto F.) Berlin, 1958.

Phil 197.29   Lebensphilosophie und Lebenskunst. (Walthoffen, H. Walter von.) Wien, 1907.

Phil 3850.16.96   Lebensphilosophie und Religion bei Georg Simmel. (Mueller, H.) Berlin, 1960.

Phil 3552.425   Lebensquellen der deutschen Metaphysik. (Lion, Ferdinand.) Frankfurt, 1960.

Phil 2411.7   Lebensquellen französischer Metaphysik. (León, Ferdinand.) Hamburg, 1949.

Phil 8418.22   Lebensstufe und Kunstwerk, ihre Symbolik und ihre Foringesetze. 1. Aufl. (Ruefenacht, E.) Zürich, 1960.

Phil 974.3.120   Lebenswege mit Rudolf Steiner. (Strakosch, A.) Strasbourg, 1947.

Phil 3808.72   Lebensweisheit. (Schopenhauer, Arthur.) Berlin, 1943.

Phil 1750.115.200   Lebensweisheit. (Brand, Gerd.) Berlin, 1971.

Phil 3450.11.265   Lebenswelt und Geschichte. (Hohl, Hubert.) Areiburg, 1962.

Phil 5350.3   Die Lebenswende als Reifungskrisis. (Dobler, u.) München, 1961.

Phil 3485.5   Das Lebenswerk Immanuel Kants. 4. Aufl. (Döring, W.O.) Lübeck, 1917.

Phil 9530.54   Lebhar, G.M. The use of time. 3. ed. N.Y., 1958.

Phil 486.2   Leblais, A. Matérialisme et spiritualisme. Paris, 1865.

Phil 5051.32   Leblanc, H. An introduction to deductive logic. N.Y., 1955.

Phil 5145.2   Leblanc, Hugues. Statistical and inductive probabilities. Englewood Cliffs, 1962.

Phil 5066.251   Leblanc, Hugues. Techniques of deductive inference. Englewood Cliffs, 1966.

Phil 5135.3   Le Bon, Gustave. Les opinions et les croyances. Paris, 1911.

Phil 5070.14   Le Bon, Gustave. La vie des vérités. Paris, 1917.

Phil 8961.7   Le Bosquet, John E. The war within. Boulder, Col., 1911.

Phil 2070.127   Le Breton, M. La personnalité de William James. Paris, 1911.

Phil 2070.127.5   Le Breton, M. La personnalité de William James. Paris, 1929.

Htn   Phil 6021.6*   Le Brun, Charles. Conference sur l'expression générale et particuliere des passions. Verone, 1751.

Phil 3493.52 — Lebrun, Gérard. Kant et la mort de la métaphysique. Paris, 1970.
Phil 5170.10 — Lebzeltern, G. Der Syllogismus. Graz, 1948.
Phil 5640.8 — Le Cat, C.N. A physical essay on the senses. London, 1750.
Phil 5640.8.5 — Le Cat, C.N. Traité des sens. Rouen, 1740.
Phil 4362.5 — Lecciones de filosofía. (Lloreus y Barba, F.J.) Barcelona, 1920. 3v.
Phil 196.28 — Lecciones de filosofía. (Varela, F.) Havana, 1940.
Phil 4983.5.20 — Lecciones de filosofía. 5. ed. (Varela, Félix.) Habana, 1961. v.
Phil 5057.15 — Lecciones de lógica dictadas en el Colegio. 2nd ed. (Restrepo-Hernandez, J.) Bogota, 1914.
Phil 5051.44.4 — Lecciones de lógica y etica. 4. ed. (Larroyo, Francisco.) México, 1970.
Phil 1535.29 — Lecciones de metafísica y ética. 2. ed. (Carrasquilla, R.M.) Bogotá, 1918.
Phil 181.80 — Lecciones preliminares de filosofia. (Garcia Morente, Manuel.) Tucuman, 1938.
Phil 5246.6 — Lecciones sumarias de psicología. (Giner de los Rios, Francisco.) Midrid, 1877.
Phil 672.18 — Lechalas, G. Étude sur l'espace et le temps. Paris, 1910.
Phil 8412.7 — Lechalas, G. Études esthétiques. Paris, 1902.
Phil 2050.93 — Lechartier, G. David Hume. Paris, 1900.
Phil 186.143 — Lechat, Jean. Analyse et synthèse. Paris, 1962.
Phil 1905.10.95 — LeChevalier, C. Ethique et idéalisme. Paris, 1963.
Phil 2515.12 — LeChevalier, Charles. La confidence et la personne humaine. Aubier, 1960.
Phil 5041.16.80 — LeChevalier, Charles. La pensée morale de Bernard Bosanquet. Paris, 1963.
Phil 3552.301 — Le Chevallier, L. La morale de Leibniz. Paris, 1933.
Phil 8520.4A — Lechler, G.V. Geschichte des Englischen Deismus. Stuttgart, 1881.
Phil 6965.3.90 — Lechler, Walther Helmut. Neue Ergebnisse in der Forschung über Philippe Pinel. München, 1960.
Phil 8412.32 — Lechner, R. The aesthetic experience. Chicago, 1953.
Phil 6121.34 — Lechuga, Z.G. La higiene mental en México. México, 1937.
Phil 8836.2.18 — Lecky, E. A memoir of W.E.H. Lecky. London, 1909.
Phil 5590.22 — Lecky, Prescott. Self-consistency; a theory of personality. N.Y., 1945.
Phil 8836.2 — Lecky, W.E.H. History of European morals. London, 1869. 2v.
Phil 8836.2.11 — Lecky, W.E.H. History of European morals. N.Y., 1913. 2v.
Phil 8836.2.13 — Lecky, W.E.H. History of European morals. N.Y., 1926. 2v.
Phil 8836.2.5 — Lecky, W.E.H. History of European morals. v.1. N.Y., 1876.
Phil 8836.2.6 — Lecky, W.E.H. History of European morals. 3. ed. N.Y., 1897. 2v.
Phil 623.1.5 — Lecky, W.E.H. History of the rise and influence of the spirit of rationalism in Europe. London, 1865. 2v.
Phil 623.1A — Lecky, W.E.H. History of the rise and influence of the spirit of rationalism in Europe. N.Y., 1866. 2v.
Phil 623.1.20 — Lecky, W.E.H. History of the rise and influence of the spirit of rationalism in Europe. v.1-2. London, 1910.
Phil 623.1.7 — Lecky, W.E.H. History of the rise and influence of the spirit of rationalism in Europe. N.Y., 1968. 2v.
Phil 8886.14.5 — Lecky, W.E.H. The map of life. London,1899.
Phil 8886.14 — Lecky, W.E.H. The map of life. N.Y., 1899.
Phil 8886.14.2 — Lecky, W.E.H. The map of life. N.Y., 1901.
Phil 8836.2.15 — Lecky, W.E.H. A survey of English ethics. London, 1903.
Phil 8836.2.20 — Lecky, W.E.H. A Victorian historian. London, 1947.
Phil 8836.2.80 — Lecky. (Auchmuty, J.J.) London, 1945.
Phil 6321.55 — Leclaire, Serge. Psychanalyser, un essai sur l'ordre de l'inconscient et la pratique de la lettre. Paris, 1968.
Phil 2340.10.148 — Leclerc, Ivor. The relevance of Whitehead. London, 1961.
Phil 2340.10.145 — Leclerc, Ivor. Whitehead's metaphysics. London, 1958.
Htn Phil 2115.82.1* — LeClerc, J. The life and character of Mr. John Locke. London, 1706.
Htn Phil 2115.82* — LeClerc, J. The life and character of Mr. John Locke. London, 1706-13.
Phil 186.5.6 — LeClerc, J. Logica, ontologia, et pneumatologia. 4. ed. Cambridge, 1704.
Phil 186.5.5 — LeClerc, J. Logica, sive Ars ratiocinandi. London, 1692. 3 pam.
Phil 186.5.2 — LeClerc, J. Opera philosophica. Amsterdam, 1722. 4v.
Phil 186.5 — LeClerc, J. Opera philosophica. v.1-4. Amsterdam, 1698. 3v.
Htn Phil 2725.6.31* — LeClerc, Jean. Five letters concerning the inspiration of the Holy Scriptures. London, 1690.
Phil 6021.4 — LeClerc, S. Caractères des passions. Paris, n.d.
Phil 8886.74 — Leclercq, Francois. Propos sur la morale et la science. Paris, 1959.
Phil 8886.23.5 — Leclère, A. L'éducation morale rationnelle. Paris, 1909.
Phil 8886.23 — Leclère, A. La morale rationnelle. Paris, 1909.
Phil 525.48 — Leclère, A. Le mysticisme catholique et l'âme de Dante. Paris, 1906.
Phil 186.21 — Leclére, A. Pragmatisme, modernisme, protestantisme. Paris, 1909.
Phil 342.10 — Leclère, Albert. Essai critique sur le droit d'affirmer. Paris, 1901.
Phil 1133.11 — Leclère, Albert. La philosophie grecque avant Socrate. Paris, 1908.
Phil 585.153 — Leclerq, J. La révolution de l'homme au XXe siècle. Tournai, 1963.
Phil 5051.9 — Lecomte, A. La logique populaire. Paris, 1832.
Phil 486.3 — Lecomte, F.D. L'âme. Paris, 1869.
Phil 365.47.10 — Lecomte du Noüy, Pierre. L'avenir de l'esprit. Gallimard, 1941.
Phil 365.47.15 — Lecomte du Noüy, Pierre. L'avenir de l'esprit. N.Y., 1943.
Phil 365.47.17 — Lecomte du Noüy, Pierre. La dignité humaine. N.Y., 1944.
Phil 365.47.18 — Lecomte du Noüy, Pierre. La dignité humaine. N.Y., 1947.
Phil 8701.21 — Lecomte du Nouy, Pierre. Human destiny. N.Y., 1947.
Phil 8881.42.15 — La leçon des moeurs contemporaines. 2e éd. (Gaultier, Paul.) Paris, 1930.
Phil 2655.6.30 — Leçon inaugurale faite le jeudi 19 déc. 1963. (Hyppolite, J.) Nougent-le-Rotrou, 1964.
Phil 6971.3 — Leçons cliniques...maladies mentales. (Voisin, A.) Paris, 1883.
Phil 6968.5.10 — Leçons cliniques sur les maladies. (Séglas, J.) Paris, 1895.
Phil 6962.1 — Leçons cliniques sur les maladies mentales. (Magnan, V.) Paris, 1882-91.
Phil 6962.1.2 — Leçons cliniques sur les maladies mentales. 2. éd. (Magnan, V.) Paris, 1893.
Phil 6681.12 — Leçons cliniques sur les principaux phenomènes de l'hypnotisme. (Luys, J.) Paris, 1890.

Phil 6619.2 — Leçons cliniques sur l'hystérie et l'hypnotisme faites à l'hôpital Saint André de Bordeaux. (Pitres, Albert.) Paris, 1891. 2v.
X Cg Phil 8876.21 — Les leçons de la sagesse. (Bonnaire, L. de.) Paris, 1750-51. 3v.
Phil 5042.16 — Leçons de logique. (Charma, A.) Paris, 1840.
Phil 5057.22 — Leçons de logique. (Robert, Arthur.) Québec 1914.
Phil 5047.15 — Leçons de logique et de morale. (Hourticq, R.) Paris, 19-?
Phil 5043.33 — Leçons de logique formelle. v.1-3. (Dopp, Joseph.) Louvain, 1949-50. 2v.
Phil 3480.60 — Leçons de metaphysique. (Kant, Immanuel.) Paris, 1843.
Phil 8881.4 — Leçons de morale. (Gellert, C.F.) Utrecht, 1772. 2v.
Phil 8892.21 — Leçons de morale. (Robert, A.) Quebec, 1915.
Phil 8887.2.5 — Leçons de morale. 17. ed. (Marion, H.) Paris, 1917.
Phil 5251.30 — Leçons de philosophie, ou Essai sur les facultés de l'ame. (Laromiguiere, P.) Paris, 1815-18. 2v.
Phil 176.228 — Leçons de philosophie. (Balmes, Raymond.) Paris, 1965-66. 2v.
Phil 187.31 — Leçons de philosophie. (Malapert, P.) Paris, 1907-1908. 2v.
Phil 192.1 — Leçons de philosophie. (Rabier, E.) Paris, 1886. 2v.
Phil 192.32 — Leçons de philosophie. (Roustan, D.) Paris, 1912.
Phil 187.31.7 — Leçons de philosophie. v.1. 6. éd.; v.2. 7. ed. (Malapert, P.) Paris, 1916-1918. 2v.
Phil 192.1.9 — Leçons de philosophie. 9e éd. (Rabier, E.) Paris, 1912.
Phil 5251.30.5 — Leçons de philosophie:sur les principes de l'intelligence. 5. ed. (Laromiguiere, P.) Paris, 1833. 2v.
Phil 5257.19 — Leçons de psychologie. (Robert, Arthur.) Québec, 1915.
Phil 5257.19.3 — Leçons de psychologie. 3. éd. (Robert, Arthur.) Québec, 1921.
Phil 5257.15 — Leçons de psychologie et de philosophie. 3. éd. (Rey, A.) Paris, 1911.
Phil 735.16 — Leçons de sociologie sur l'évolution des valeurs. (Bougle, Celestin C.) Paris, 1922.
Phil 192.25 — Leçons élémentaires de psychologie et de philosophie. (Rey, A.) Paris, 1908.
Phil 5245.14 — Leçons élémentaires de psychologie. (François, A.) Paris, 1897.
Phil 6956.3 — Leçons orales phrénopathies. (Guislain, J.) Paris, 1880. 2v.
Phil 3425.60.3 — Leçons sur la philosophie de la religion. pt.1-5. (Hegel, Georg Wilhelm Friedrich.) Paris, 1954-59. 3v.
Phil 3425.40.25 — Leçons sur la philosophie de l'histoire. (Hegel, Georg Wilhelm Friedrich.) Paris, 1937.
Phil 6125.6 — Leçons sur la physiologie...du système nerveux. (Poincaré, E.L.) Paris, 1873-6. 3v.
Phil 2255.1.145 — Leçons sur la première philosophie de Russell. (Vuillemin, Jules.) Paris, 1968.
Phil 6121.7.21 — Leçons sur la structure et les maladies du système nerveux. (Luys, J.) Paris, 1875.
Phil 6115.8 — Leçons sur les fonctions motrices du cerveau et sur l'épilepsie cérébrale. (François-Franck, C.) Paris, 1887.
Phil 296.6 — Leçons sur les hypotheses cosmogoniques. (Poincaré, H.) Paris, 1911.
Phil 296.6.2 — Leçons sur les hypotheses cosmogoniques. 2. ed. (Poincaré, H.) Paris, 1913.
Phil 6952.23 — Leçons sur les localisations dans les maladies du cerveau. (Charcot, J.M.) Paris, 1876.
Phil 1750.301 — Leçons sur l'existentialisme. 4e éd. (Verneaux, R.) Paris, 1964.
Phil 1750.300 — Leçons sur l'existentialisme et ses formes principales. (Verneaux, R.) Paris, 1949.
Phil 5020.10 — Leçons sur l'histoire de la logique. (Kotarbiński, Tadeusz.) Warszawa, 1965.
Phil 6127.9 — Leçons sur l'histologie du système nerveux. pt.1-2. (Ranvier, L.) Paris, 1878.
Phil 186.17 — Le Conte, J. Man's place in nature. N.Y., 1878.
Phil 8701.5 — Le Conte, J. Religion and science. N.Y., 1874.
Phil 5643.15 — Le Conte, J. Sight. N.Y., 1881.
Phil 6321.13 — Leconte, M. Conflits sociaux et psychoses. Paris, 1938.
Phil 2905.1.655 — Lecourt, Jacques. Cari Gustav Jung et Pierre Teilhard de Chardin. Goële, 1970.
Phil 292.10 — Lecourturier, H. La cosmosphie. Paris, 1850.
Phil 6681.16.5 — Le Cron, L.M. Experimental hypnosis. N.Y., 1954.
Phil 8580.14 — Lectiones philosophiae. v.2. (Alvarez, Joachim.) Vallisoleti, 1868-69. 3 pam.
Phil 9050.2 — A lecture...on the influences of great cities. (Scott, Rev. Dr.) San Francisco, 1854.
Phil 9230.8 — A lecture before Boston young men's societies on the subject of lotteries. (Gordon, G.W.) Boston, 1833.
Phil 3482.14 — Lecture de Kant. (Alexandre, Michel.) Paris, 1961.
Phil 340.8 — La lecture de l'expérience. (Jonckheere, A.) Paris, 1958.
Phil 5258.122 — Lecture demonstrations for general psychology. (Scheidemann, N.V.) Chicago, 1939.
Phil 6322.11 — Lecture on diseases of the nervous system. (Mitchell, S.W.) Philadelphia, 1881.
Phil 1750.1 — Lecture on nature and objects of modern philosophy. (Leib, J.R.) Philadelphia, 1830-39. 3 pam.
Phil 6676.4 — Lecture on the magnetism of the human body. (Gibbes, R.W.) Columbia, 1843.
Phil 6682.14 — A lecture on the phenomena of dreams, mesmerism, clairvoyance. (Millington, T.S.) London, 1852?
Phil 5832.2 — Lectures...psychology: thought, action. (Wilson, W.D.) Ithaca, 1871.
Htn Phil 181.24* — Lectures. (Gifford, A.) Frankfurt, n.d.
Phil 27.92 — Lectures. (Royal Institute of Philosophy.) London. 1,1966+ 3v.
Phil 5242.15 — Lectures and addresses before departments of psychology and pedagogy...20 anniversary. (Clark University, Worcester, Mass.) Worcester, 1910.
Phil 3925.16.25 — Lectures and conversations on asthetics. (Wittgenstein, Ludwig.) Berkeley, 1966.
Phil 177.14A — Lectures and essays. (Clifford, W.K.) London, 1879. 2v.
X Cg Phil 177.14.2 — Lectures and essays. 2nd ed. (Clifford, W.K.) London, 1886.
Phil 8602.14 — Lectures and essays on natural theology and ethics. (Wallace, W.) Oxford, 1898.
Phil 8589.5 — Lectures and miscellanies. (James, H.) Redfield, N.Y., 1852.
Phil 8876.29 — Lectures for the people. (Brown, H.S.) Philadelphia, 1859.
Phil 6972.14.30 — Lectures in psychiatry. (White, William Alanson.) N.Y., 1928.

Phil 8877.18.2 — Lectures morales et civiques. (Compayré, J.G.) Paris, 1883.

Phil 2885.32 — Lectures on art. 1st series. (Taine, Hippolyte Adolphe.) N.Y., 1875.

Phil 2885.32.5A — Lectures on art. 2nd series. (Taine, Hippolyte Adolphe.) N.Y., 1889.

Phil 2885.34.16A — Lectures on art. 3d ed. 1st series. (Taine, Hippolyte Adolphe.) N.Y., 1875. 2v.

Phil 9178.3 — Lectures on domestic duties. (Smith, D.D.) Portland, 1837.

Phil 3480.67.75 — Lectures on ethics. (Kant, Immanuel.) London, 1930.

Phil 8598.88.2 — Lectures on Godmanhood. (Solov'ev, Vladimir Sergeevich.) London, 1948.

Phil 1110.1.5 — Lectures on Greek philosophy. v.2. (Ferrier, J.F.) Edinburgh, 1866.

Phil 1110.1.6 — Lectures on Greek philosophy. 2nd ed. (Ferrier, J.F.) Edinburgh, 1875.

Phil 807.2 — Lectures on history of philosophy. (Hegel, G.W.F.) London, 1892-96. 3v.

Phil 3915.55.5A — Lectures on human and animal psychology. (Wundt, Wilhelm.) London, 1894.

Phil 3915.55.7 — Lectures on human and animal psychology. (Wundt, Wilhelm.) London, 1896.

Phil 187.27.5 — Lectures on humanism. (Mackenzie, J.S.) London, 1907.

Phil 5264.1 — Lectures on intellectual philosophy. (Young, J.) Glasgow, 1835.

Phil 6952.23.5 — Lectures on localization in diseases of the brain. (Charcot, J.M.) N.Y., 1878.

Phil 5053.8 — Lectures on logic. (Newman, F.W.) Oxford, 1838.

Phil 5052.7 — Lectures on logic. Photoreproduction. (Moberly, Charles Edward.) Oxford, 1848.

Phil 5545.21.5 — Lectures on memory culture. (Pick, E.) N.Y., 1899.

Phil 6968.9 — Lectures on mental disease. (Stearns, H.P.) Philadelphia, 1893.

Phil 5942.1 — Lectures on mental science. (Weaver, G.S.) N.Y., 1852.

Phil 5942.1.5 — Lectures on mental science according to the philosophy of phrenology. (Weaver, G.S.) N.Y., 1852.

Phil 2035.40 — Lectures on metaphysics and logic. (Hamilton, William.) Boston, 1859-60. 2v.

Phil 2035.40.5 — Lectures on metaphysics and logic. (Hamilton, William.) Boston, 1860.

Phil 2035.40.3 — Lectures on metaphysics and logic. (Hamilton, William.) Edinburgh, 1859. 4v.

Phil 2035.40.10 — Lectures on metaphysics and logic. (Hamilton, William.) N.Y., 1880.

Phil 3017.5 — Lectures on modern idealism. (Royce, J.) New Haven, 1964.

Phil 2250.45A — Lectures on modern idealism. (Royce, Josiah.) New Haven, 1919.

Phil 2250.45.5 — Lectures on modern idealism. (Royce, Josiah.) New Haven, 1923.

Phil 5922.4.40 — Lectures on moral philosophy. (Combe, George.) Boston, 1836.

Phil 5922.4.41 — Lectures on moral philosophy. (Combe, George.) Boston, 1840.

Phil 8897.20 — Lectures on moral philosophy. (Witherspoon, J.) Philadelphia, 1822.

Phil 8897.20.5 — Lectures on moral philosophy. (Witherspoon, J.) Princeton, 1912.

Phil 8882.21.5.3 — Lectures on moral science. (Hopkins, M.) Boston, 1865.

Phil 8599.8 — Lectures on natural and revealed religion. (Tunstall, J.) London, 1765.

Phil 8582.5 — Lectures on natural theology. (Chadbourne, P.A.) N.Y., 1867.

Phil 187.4 — Lectures on philosophy. (Maguire, J.) London, 1885.

Phil 2150.18.50 — Lectures on philosophy. (Moore, George Edward.) London, 1966.

Phil 1890.30.2 — Lectures on philosophy of human mind. (Brown, T.) Andover, 1822. 3v.

Phil 1890.30.4 — Lectures on philosophy of human mind. (Brown, T.) Edinbrugh, 1846. 4v.

Phil 1890.30 — Lectures on philosophy of human mind. (Brown, T.) Edinburgh, 1820. 4v.

Phil 1890.30.3.5 — Lectures on philosophy of human mind. (Brown, T.) Hallowell, 1831.

Phil 1890.30.5 — Lectures on philosophy of human mind. (Brown, T.) London, 1860.

Phil 1890.30.3 — Lectures on philosophy of human mind. (Brown, T.) Philadelphia, 1824. 3v.

Phil 5921.1.5 — Lectures on phrenology. (Broussais, F.J.V.) London, 1847.

Phil 5922.4 — Lectures on phrenology. (Combe, George.) N.Y., 1839.

Phil 5923.2 — Lectures on phrenology. (Dean, Amos.) Albany, 1834.

Phil 5922.4.3 — Lectures on phrenology. 3. ed. (Combe, George.) N.Y., 1847.

Phil 7069.62.15 — Lectures on physical research. (Broad, Charlie.) London, 1962.

Phil 6980.135 — Lectures on psychoanalytic psychiatry. (Brill, Abraham A.) N.Y., 1946.

Phil 1807.4 — Lectures on recent trends in American philosophy. (Hocking, William E.) Claremont, 1941.

Phil 9351.5 — Lectures on relations and middle aged. (Linsley, J.H.) Hartford, 1828.

Phil 7054.137 — Lectures on spiritualism. (Tiffany, Joel.) Cleveland, 1851.

Phil 8897.14.9 — Lectures on systematic morality. (Whewell, W.) London, 1846.

Phil 8661.2.3 — Lectures on the atheistic controversy. (Godwin, B.) Boston, 1835.

Phil 8661.2 — Lectures on the atheistic controversy. (Godwin, B.) London, 1834.

Phil 8600.1 — Lectures on the bases of religious belief. (Upton, C.B.) London, 1894.

Phil 6956.1 — Lectures on the diagnosis of disease of the brain. (Gowers, W.R.) London, 1885.

Phil 5400.25 — Lectures on the elementary psychology of feeling and attention. (Titchener, E.B.) N.Y., 1908.

Phil 5400.25.5 — Lectures on the elementary psychology of feeling and attention. (Titchener, E.B.) N.Y., 1924.

Phil 8843.1.5 — Lectures on the ethics of T.H. Green. (Sidgwick, Henry.) London, 1902.

NEDL Phil 5259.5.10A — Lectures on the experimental psychology of the thought-processes. (Titchener, E.B.) N.Y., 1909.

Phil 5259.5.10.5 — Lectures on the experimental psychology of the thought-processes. (Titchener, E.B.) N.Y., 1926.

Phil 188.10 — Lectures on the five-foot shelf of books. 4. Philosophy. (Neilson, W.A.) N.Y., 1913.

Phil 8877.26 — Lectures on the formation of character. (Clark, T.M.) Hartford, 1852.

Phil 1106.7 — Lectures on the history of ancient philosophy. (Butler, W.A.) Cambridge, 1856. 2v.

Phil 1106.7.5 — Lectures on the history of ancient philosophy. (Butler, W.A.) Philadelphia, 1857. 2v.

Phil 8592.15 — Lectures on the origin and growth of religion. (Müller, F.M.) London, 1880.

Phil 8592.15.2 — Lectures on the origin and growth of religion. (Müller, F.M.) N.Y., 1879.

Phil 8592.15.4 — Lectures on the origin and growth of religion. 2. ed. (Müller, F.M.) London, 1878.

Phil 8661.1 — Lectures on the origin and growth of the conception of God. (Goblet D'Alviella, E.) London, 1892.

Phil 3500.19 — Lectures on the philosophy of Kant. (Sidgwich, H.) London, 1905.

Phil 3552.320 — Lectures on the philosophy of Leibniz. (Joseph, H.W.B.) Oxford, 1949.

Phil 3425.60.5 — Lectures on the philosophy of religion. (Hegel, Georg Wilhelm Friedrich.) London, 1895. 3v.

Phil 3425.60.6 — Lectures on the philosophy of religion. (Hegel, Georg Wilhelm Friedrich.) N.Y., 1962. 3v.

Phil 9341.4 — Lectures on the sphere and duties of woman. (Burnap, G.W.) Baltimore, 1841.

Phil 2496.40.6 — Lectures on the true, the beautiful, and the good. (Cousin, Victor.) N.Y., 1855.

Phil 2496.40.5 — Lectures on the true, the beautiful and the good. (Cousin, Victor.) N.Y., 1854.

Phil 2496.40.10 — Lectures on the true, the beautiful, and the good. (Cousin, Victor.) N.Y., 1854.

Phil 6327.17.10 — Lectures on war neuroses. (Ross, Thomas Arthur.) London, 1941.

Phil 9341.2.2 — Lectures to young men. (Beecher, H.W.) Boston, 1850.

Phil 9341.2.10 — Lectures to young men. (Beecher, H.W.) Edinburgh, 1887.

Phil 9341.2.6 — Lectures to young men. (Beecher, H.W.) N.Y., 1856.

Phil 9341.2.5 — Lectures to young men. (Beecher, H.W.) Salem, 1846.

Phil 9341.4.5 — Lectures to young men. (Burnap, G.W.) Baltimore, 1840.

Phil 9344.2 — Lectures to young men. (Eliot, W.G.) St. Louis, 1852.

Phil 9347.1 — Lectures to young men. (Hawes, J.) Boston, 1856.

Phil 9347.1.2 — Lectures to young men. (Hawes, J.) Hartford, 1832.

Phil 9351.6 — Lectures to young men. (Livermore, A.A.) Boston, 1846.

Htn Phil 9351.2* — Lectures to young men. N.Y., 1892.

Phil 9344.2.3 — Lectures to young men. 6th ed. (Eliot, W.G.) Boston, 1856.

Phil 9344.2.5 — Lectures to young women. (Eliot, W.G.) Boston, 1860.

Phil 8612.7 — LeDantec, F. Le problème de la mort et la conscience universelle. Paris, 1917.

Phil 8612.7.5 — LeDantec, F. Le problème de la mort et la conscience universelle. Paris, 1917.

Phil 8666.6.5 — Le Dantec, Félix. L'athéisme. Paris, 1912.

Phil 186.76.15 — Le Dantec, Félix. Le conflit. 6e ed. Paris, 1913.

Phil 186.76 — Le Dantec, Félix. Contre la métaphysique; questions de méthode. Paris, 1912.

Phil 186.76.5 — Le Dantec, Félix. Le déterminisme biologique et la personnalité consciente. Paris, 1897.

Phil 4363.3.85 — Lede, Luis Perez de Guzman y Sanjuan. Discurso de la verdad. Bilboa, 1954.

Phil 342.2 — Leder, H. Untersuchungen über Augustins Erkenntnistheorie. Warburg, 1901.

Phil 8666.15 — Lederer, Julius. Gott und Teufel im 20. Jahrhundert. 4. Aufl. Berlin, 1910?

Phil 3831.1 — Ledinský, F. Die Philosophie Spinoza's. Budweis, 1871.

Phil 8591.55 — Lee, Atkinson. Groundwork of the philosophy of religion. London, 1946.

Phil 6681.9.2 — Lee, Edwin. Animal magnetism. London, 1849.

Phil 6681.9 — Lee, Edwin. Animal magnetism. 3d ed. London, 1843. 2 pam.

Phil 7060.86 — Lee, F.G. Glimpses of the supernatural. London, 1875.

Phil 7060.86.5 — Lee, F.G. Lights and shadows. London, 1894.

Phil 2150.15.80 — Lee, G.C. George Herbert Mead. N.Y., 1945.

Phil 9575.5 — Lee, G.S. Inspired millionaires...America. Northampton, 1908.

Phil 186.20 — Lee, G.S. The voice of the machines. Northampton, 1906.

Phil 8591.23 — Lee, Gerald S. The shadow Christ. N.Y., 1896.

Phil 8412.20 — Lee, H.L. Perception and aesthetic value. N.Y., 1938.

Phil 5066.200 — Lee, Harold Newton. Symbolic logic. N.Y., 1961.

Phil 2115.4F — Lee, Henry. Anti-scepticism: or notes upon...Mr. Lock's essay. London, 1702.

Phil 5520.109 — Lee, I.J. How to talk with people. N.Y., 1952.

Phil 5520.76A — Lee, Irving J. Language habits in human affairs. N.Y., 1941.

Phil 8886.60 — Lee, James W. The making of a man. St. Louis, 1899.

Phil 8701.20 — Lee, John H. Are science and religion at strife? Evanston, 1945.

Phil 1711.10 — Lee, Otis. Existence and inquiry, a study of thought in the modern world. Chicago, 1949.

Phil 978.81 — Lee, Pi-cheng. An outline of Karma. n.p., 1941?

Phil 5620.36 — Lee, Wayne. Decision, theory and human behavior. N.Y., 1971.

Phil 6945.2 — Leech, J. Suggestion of the law of the lunacy. London, 1852.

Phil 5051.13 — Leechman, John. Logic. 4th ed. London, 1864.

Phil 3925.16.285 — Leeds, England. University. Department of Philosophy. A Witttgenstein workbook. Berkeley, 1970.

Phil 5465.23 — Leeming, B.C. Imagination, mind's dominant power. N.Y., 1926.

Phil 186.86 — Leendertz, W. Dogma en existentie. Amsterdam, 1933.

Phil 186.86.10 — Leendertz, W. Ratio en existentie. Amsterdam, 1936.

Phil 5761.16 — Leenhardt, Henry. Le déterminisme des lois de la nature et la réalité. Thèse. Montpellier, 1930.

Phil 3925.11.70 — Leenhouwen, Albinus. Ungesicherheit und Wagnis. Essen, 1964.

Phil 3790.4.83 — Leenmans, H.A. De logica der geschiedeniswetenschap's van H. Rickert. 's Gravenhage, 1924.

Phil 5590.300 — Leeper, Robert. Toward understanding human personalities. N.Y., 1959.

Phil 2053.81 — De Leer van den Zedelijken zin bij Hutcheson. (Boerma, N.W.) n.p., n.d.

Phil 3525.91 — De leer van God bij Schelling, Hegel en Krause. (Opzoomer, C.W.) Leiden, 1846.

Phil 5251.7.7 — Leerbaek der empirische zielkunde. (Lindner, G.A.) Zutphen, 18- .

Phil 3915.47.25 — Leerboek der zielkunde. (Wundt, Wilhelm.) Amsterdam, 1898?

Phil 7069.20.210 — Lees, Robert James. Through the mists. London, 1920.

Phil 8591.60 — Leese, Kurt. Ethische und religiöse Grundfragen im Denken der Gegenwart. Stuttgart, 1956.

Phil 3425.231 — Leese, Kurt. Die Geschichtsphilosophie Hegels. Berlin, 1922.

Phil 400.79 — Leese, Kurt. Philosophie und Theologie im Spätidealismus. Berlin, 1929.

Phil 5643.78 — Leeser, Otto. Über Linien- und Flächenvergleichung. Inaug. Diss. Leipzig, 1915.

Phil 4210.165 — Leetham, C.R. Rosmini. London, 1957.

Phil 8430.44 — Leeuw, G. van der. Sacred and profane beauty. N.Y., 1963. 10v.

Phil 5643.165 — Leeuwerberg, Emanuel Laurens Jan. Structural information of visual pattern. The Hague, 1968.

Phil 978.120 — Leevwen, A.J.H. van. Ganesha. Amsterdam, 1969.

Phil 186.63 — Le Fébure, L.F.H. Essai sur l'organisation du monde physique et moral. Commercy, 1806.

Phil 5465.148 — Lefebve, Maurice Jean. L'image fascinante et le surréel. Paris, 1965.

Phil 2520.228 — Lefebvre, H. Descartes. Paris, 1947.
Phil 3640.281.5 — Lefebvre, H. Nietzsche. Mexico, 1940.
Phil 3640.281 — Lefebvre, H. Nietzsche. Paris, 1939.
Phil 2805.259 — Lefebvre, H. Pascal. Paris, 1949. 2v.
Phil 680.50 — Lefebvre, Henri. Au-delà du structuralisme. Paris, 1971.
Phil 2725.37.35A — Lefebvre, Henri. Critique de la vie quotidienne. 2e éd. Paris, 1958-68. 2v.

Phil 1750.181 — Lefebvre, Henri. L'existentialisme. Paris, 1946.
Phil 5051.42 — Lefebvre, Henri. Logique formelle, logique dialectique. 2e éd. Paris, 1969.

Phil 408.6 — Lefebvre, Henri. Le manifeste différentialiste. Paris, 1970.

Phil 2725.37.40 — Lefebvre, Henri. Métaphilosophie; prolégomènes. Paris, 1965.

Phil 2725.37.30 — Lefebvre, Henri. La somme et le reste. Paris, 1959. 2v.

Phil 811.2.5 — Lefèvre, A. La Philosophie. 2e ed. Paris, 1884.
Phil 811.2 — Lefèvre, A. Philosophy. London, 1879.
Phil 2477.6.87 — Lefévre, Frédéric. L'itinéraire philosophique de M. Blondel. Paris, 1928.

Phil 8886.20 — Lefèvre, G. Obligation morale et idéalisme. Paris, 1894.
Phil 400.36 — Lefèvre, Georges. Obligation morale et idéalisme. Thèse. Paris, 1894.

Phil 2880.8.86 — Lefevre, Luc J. L'existentialiste est-il un philosophe? Paris, 1946. 2v.

Phil 2520.255.20 — Lefèvre, Roger. La bataille du "cogito". 1. éd. Paris, 1960.

Phil 2520.255.10 — Lefèvre, Roger. Le criticisme de Descartes. 1. éd. Paris, 1958.

Phil 2520.255.5 — Lefèvre, Roger. L'humanisme de Descartes. Paris, 1957.
Phil 2520.255.15 — Lefèvre, Roger. La métaphysique de Descartes. 1. éd. Paris, 1959.

Phil 2520.353 — Lefèvre, Roger. La pensée existentielle de Descartes. Paris, 1965.

Phil 2520.255 — Lefèvre, Roger. La vocation de Descartes. v.1-3. Paris, 1956-1957. 2v.

Phil 1516.4 — Leff, Gordon. Medieval thought. Harmondsworth, 1958.
Phil 4210.230 — Leffere sulla spiritualitá rosminiana. (Verondini, Enrico.) Milano, 1966.

Phil 3493.3 — Lefkovits, M. Die Staatslehre auf Kantischer Grundlage. Bern, 1899.

Phil 2411.8 — LeFlamanc, Auguste. Les utopies prérévolutionnaires et la philosophie du XVIIIe siècle. Brest, 1933.

Phil 4630.2.45 — Lefnadsminnen. (Rein, T.) Helsingfors, 1918.
Phil 2805.93 — Lefranc, A. Défense de Pascal...est-il un faussaire? Paris, 1906.

Phil 8412.3 — Lefrancq, J. Oser penser. Neuchâtel, 1961.
Phil 6111.70.5 — Left-handed man in a right-handed world. (Barsley, Michael.) London, 1970.

Phil 6125.15 — Lefthandedness. (Parson, B.S.) N.Y., 1924.
Phil 5068.86 — The legacy of logical positivism. Baltimore, 1969.
Phil 6965.3.95 — The legacy of Philippe Pinel. (Riese, Walter.) N.Y., 1969.

Phil 6315.2.305 — The legacy of Sigmund Freud. (Arlow, J.A.) N.Y., 1956.
Phil 5374.24.5 — Legahn, August F. Entricklungsgeschichte des Bewusstseins. Leipzig, 1914.

Phil 9495.25 — Legalized prostitution. (Woodruff, C.E.) Boston, 1862.
Phil 8591.13 — LeGallienne, R. The religion of a literary man. N.Y., 1893.

Phil 585.404 — Légaut, Marcel. L'homme à la recherche de son humanité. Paris, 1971.

Phil 4073.34 — Legazioni ai Maomettani. (Campanella, Tommaso.) Firenze, 1960.

Phil 2419.2 — La légende des "philosophes". (Tornezy, Albert.) Paris, 1911.

Phil 1135.153 — Legendorum philosophorum veterum praecepta nonnulla et exemplum. (Garve, C.) Leipzig, 1770.

Phil 6681.5 — Leger, J. Animal magnetism. N.Y., 1846.
Phil 6155.26 — Legewie, Heiner. Persönlichkeitstheorie und Psychopharmaka. Meisenheim, 1968.

Phil 8420.7 — La legge del bello. (Trudu, Luciano.) Padova, 1962.
Phil 5241.19 — La legge del tempo. (Buccola, G.) Milano, 1883.
Phil 8415.10.3 — La legge della come legge universale della natura. 3. ed. (Ottaviano, Carmelo.) Padova, 1970.

Phil 2255.1.110 — Leggett, H.W. Bertrand Russell. London, 1949.
Phil 2255.1.111 — Leggett, H.W. Bertrand Russell. N.Y., 1950.
Phil 6957.6 — Legisation on insanity. (Harrison, G.L.) Philadelphia, 1884.

Phil 1750.166.280 — Legitimo, Gianfranco. Nuovo umanesimo sociale. Torino, 1968.

Phil 2725.9.86 — LeGoff, François. De la philosophie de l'abbé de Lignac. Paris, 1863.

Htn Phil 2725.16.30* — Legouis, Émile. Histoire de la littérature anglaise. Paris, 1924.

Phil 9171.4.8 — Legouvé, E. Les pères et les enfants. Enfance et adolescence. 16. éd. Paris, 1867.

Phil 9171.4.12 — Legouvé, E. Les pères et les enfants. La jeunesse. 13. éd. Paris, 1869.

Phil 811.17 — Legowicz, J. Zarys historii filozofii. Warszawa, 1964.
Phil 850.31 — Legowiiz, J. Filozofia okresu sosarstwa rzymekiego. Warszawa, 1962.

NEDL Phil 5425.37 — Legrain, M. Les dégénérés. Paris, 1895.
Phil 6961.1 — Legrain, M. Du délire chez les dégénérés. Paris, 1886.
Htn Phil 5821.11* — Legrand, A. Dissertatio de carentia sensus et cognitionis in brutis. London, 1675.

Htn Phil 2725.3* — LeGrand, A. An entire body of philosophy. London, 1694.
Htn Phil 2725.3.35* — LeGrand, A. Institutio philosophiae. London, 1678.
Htn Phil 2725.3.30* — LeGrand, A. Institutio philosophiae. London, 1680.
Phil 1133.50 — Legrand, Gérard. La pensée des présocratiques. Paris, 1970.

Phil 6400.15 — Legroux, A. De l'aphasie. Thèse. Paris, 1875.
Phil 2805.465 — Le Guern, Michel. L'image dans l'oeuvre de Pascal. Paris, 1969.

Phil 2725.2.35.5 — Le Guillou, Louis. Les discussions critiques. Paris, 1967.

Phil 8591.45 — Leh, L.L. Christianity reborn. N.Y., 1928.
Phil 310.395 — Lehév, Iwere. Iyöväenluohan maailmankatsomus. Helsinki, 1959.

Phil 51.3 — Lehigh University. Studies psychology series. Bethlehem, Pa.

Phil 5465.180 — Lehman, Harvey Christian. Age and achievement. Princeton, 1953.

Phil 3808.122 — Lehman, Rudolf. Schopenhauer und die Entwickelung der monistischen Weltanschauung. Berlin, 1892.

Phil 5645.24 — Lehmann, A. Farvernes elementare aestetik. Kjøbenhavn, 1884.

Phil 5400.15 — Lehmann, A. Die Hauptgesetze des menschlichen Gefühlslebens. Leipzig, 1892.

Phil 5400.15.2 — Lehmann, A. Die Hauptgesetze des menschlichen Gefühlslebens. 2. Aufl. Leipzig, 1914.

Phil 6681.3 — Lehmann, A. Die Hypnose. Leipzig, 1890.
Phil 5325.22 — Lehmann, A. Om gedenkelse. Kjøbenhavn, 1888.
Phil 5850.256 — Lehmann, A. Størst unbytte af legemligt og aandeligt arbejde. København, 1919.

Phil 5251.20 — Lehmann, Alfred. Grundzüge der Psychophysiologie. Leipzig, 1912.

Phil 5251.20.15 — Lehmann, Alfred. Den individuelle sjaelelige udrikling. København, 1920.

Phil 5251.20.9 — Lehmann, Alfred. Die körperlichen Äusserungen psychischer Zustände. Leipzig, 1899-1905. 4v.
Phil 5251.20.5 — Lehmann, Alfred. Lehrbuch der psychologischen Methodik. Leipzig, 1906.

Phil 5251.20.20 — Lehmann, Alfred. Uppfostran till arbete. Stockholm, 1920.
Phil 3808.91 — Lehmann, E. Die verschiedenartigen Elemente der Schopenhauer'schen Willenslehre. Strassburg, 1889.

Phil 525.22.2 — Lehmann, Edvard. Mystik in Heidentum und Christentum. 2e Aufl. Leipzig, 1918.

Phil 3011.3.15 — Lehmann, G. Die deutschen Philosophie der Gegenwart. Stuttgart, 1943.

Phil 3011.3 — Lehmann, G. Geschichte der nachkantischen Philosophie. Berlin, 1931.

Phil 3011.3.10 — Lehmann, G. Die Ontologie der Gegenwart in ihren Grundgestalten. Halle, 1933.

Phil 575.69 — Lehmann, G. Über Einzigkeit und Individualität. Leipzig, 1926.

Phil 3493.54 — Lehmann, Gerhard. Beiträge zur Geschichte und Interpretation der Philosophie Kants. Berlin, 1969.
Phil 186.58 — Lehmann, Gerhard. Über Einzigkeit und Individualität. Leipzig, 1926.

Phil 186.59 — Lehmann, Gerhard. Vorschule der Metaphysik. Berlin, 1927.
Phil 5465.175 — Lehmann, Günther Kurt. Phantasie und Künstlerische Arbeit. Berlin, 1966.

Phil 3493.22 — Lehmann, Otto. Über Kant's Principien der Ethik und Schopenhauer's Beurteilung derselben. Greifswald, 1880.

Phil 8961.17 — Lehmann, P.L. Ethics in a Christian context. 1. ed. N.Y., 1963.

Phil 186.36.4 — Lehmann, R. Lehrbuch der philosophischen Propädeutik. 4. Aufl. Berlin, 1917.

Phil 186.36.5 — Lehmann, R. Lehrbuch der philosophischen Propädeutik. 5. Aufl. Leipzig, 1922.

Phil 3808.92 — Lehmann, R. Schopenhauer. Berlin, 1894.
Phil 3831.13 — Lehmans, J.B. Spinoza. Würzburg, 1864.
Phil 1516.3.5 — Lehmen, Alfonso. Lehrbuch der Philosophie. Freiburg, 1923.

Phil 1516.3 — Lehmen, Alfonso. Lehrbuch der Philosophie. 4e Aufl. n.p., 1912-19. 4v.

Phil 8961.11 — Lehmkuhl, A. Theologia moralis. Freiburg, 1888. 2v.
Phil 2880.2.90 — Lehner, Felix. Freiheit in Wirtschaft, Staat und Religion: die Philosophie der Gesellschaft von Charles Secrétan. Zürich, 1967.

Phil 8656.7.20 — Lehr-Sätze von der Atheisterey und dem Aberglauben mit gelehrten Anmerckungen erläutert. 2. Aufl. (Buddeus, J.F.) Jena, 1723.

Phil 3552.54 — Lehr-Satze über die Monadologie. (Leibniz, Gottfried Wilhelm.) Franckfurt, 1720.

Phil 6115.11.12 — Lehrbuch der ärtlichen Seelenkunde. (Feuchtersleben, E.F.V.) Wien, 1845.

Phil 5246.14.5 — Lehrbuch der allegemeinen Psychologie. 2. Aufl. (Geyser, J.) Munster, 1912.

Phil 8879.16.2 — Lehrbuch der allgemeinen Ethik. 2e Aufl. (Eisler, Julius.) Wien, 1912.

Phil 6329.10 — Lehrbuch der allgemeinen Kinderpsychiatrie. (Tramer, Moritz.) Basel, 1945.

Phil 5051.16.6 — Lehrbuch der allgemeinen Logik. 6e Aufl. (Lindner, Gustav A.) Wien, 1914.

Phil 5257.3 — Lehrbuch der allgemeinen Psychologie. (Rehmke. J.) Hamburg, 1894.

Phil 9035.64 — Lehrbuch der Charakterkunde. (Kronfeld, Arthur.) Berlin, 1932.

Phil 8951.5 — Lehrbuch der christlichen Sittenlehre. v.1-2. (Bruch, J.F.) Strassburg, 1829-32.

Phil 1535.1.25 — Lehrbuch der Elemente der Philosophie. v.1-4. (Balmes, Jaime.) Regensburg, 1861.

Phil 5251.7 — Lehrbuch der empiriochen Psychologie. (Lindner, G.A.) Wien, 1872.

Phil 5251.7.3 — Lehrbuch der empiriochen Psychologie. 9. Aufl. (Lindner, G.A.) Wien, 1889.

Phil 5590.534 — Lehrbuch der empirischen Persönlichkeitsforschung. (Herrmann, T.) Göttingen, 1969.

Phil 5243.9 — Lehrbuch der empirischen Psychologie. (Irbal, M.) Wien, 1885.

Phil 5245.21 — Lehrbuch der experimentellen Psychologie. (Fröbes, Joseph.) Freiburg, 1917. 2v.

Phil 5245.21.2A — Lehrbuch der experimentellen Psychologie. 2. und 3. Aufl. (Fröbes, Joseph.) Freiburg, 1922-1923. 2v.

Phil 6972.2 — Lehrbuch der Gehirnkrankheiten. v.1-2. (Wernicke, C.) Kassel, 1881.

Phil 1707.1.15 — Lehrbuch der Geschichte der neueren Philosophie. (Höffding, H.) Leipzig, 1907.

Phil 801.8 — Lehrbuch der Geschichte der Philosophie. (Buhle, T.G.) Göttingen, 1796-1804. 8v.

Phil 822.2.4.5 — Lehrbuch der Geschichte der Philosophie. (Windelband, W.) Genf, 1945?

Phil 822.2.4 — Lehrbuch der Geschichte der Philosophie. (Windelband, W.) Tübingen, 1935.

Phil 822.2.4.7 — Lehrbuch der Geschichte der Philosophie. (Windelband, W.) Tübingen, 1957.

Phil 822.2.3 — Lehrbuch der Geschichte der Philosophie. 3. Aufl. (Windelband, W.) Tübingen, 1903.

Phil 6688.18 — Lehrbuch der Hypnose. (Schilder, Paul.) Wien, 1926.

Phil 6319.1.209 — Lehrbuch der komplexen Psychologie C.G. Jungs. (Meier, Carl A.) Zürich, 1968.

Phil 3500.91 — Lehrbuch der Kritik des Geschmack. (Snell, Christian.) Leipzig, 1795.

Phil 8414.6 — Lehrbuch der Kunstwissenschaft zum Gebrance bei Vorlesungen. (Nüsslein, F.A.) Landshut, 1819.

Phil 5045.1 — Lehrbuch der Logik. (Fischer, Friedrich.) Stuttgart, 1838.

Phil 5045.9 — Lehrbuch der Logik. (Fischhaber, G.C.F.) Stuttgart, 1818.

Phil 5051.21 — Lehrbuch der Logik. (Loeive, J.H.) Wien, 1881.

Phil 5065.1A — Lehrbuch der Logik. (Zuhen, Theodor.) Bonn, 1920.

Phil 5053.5.2 — Lehrbuch der Logik. 2e Aufl. (Nitsche, Adolf.) Innsbruck, 1890.

Phil 5058.31.5 — Lehrbuch der Logik in psychologisierender Darstellung. (Stöhr, Adolf.) Leipzig, 1910.

Phil 3745.1.40 — Lehrbuch der Logik und Metaphysik. (Platner, E.) Leipzig, 1795.

Phil 5066.56 — Lehrbuch der Logistik. (Dürr, K.) Basel, 1954.

Phil 5258.7.10 — Lehrbuch der Menschen- und Seelenkunde. (Schubert, G.H. von.) Erlangen, 1838.

Phil 6964.1.6 — Lehrbuch der Nervenkrankheiten. 6. Aufl. (Oppenheim, H.) Berlin, 1913. 2v.

Phil 803.8 — Lehrbuch der Philosophie. (Dressoir, M.) Berlin, 1925. 2v.

Phil 3450.30 — Lehrbuch der Philosophie. (Hessen, Johannes.) München, 1947-50. 3v.

Phil 1516.3.5 — Lehrbuch der Philosophie. (Lehmen, Alfonso.) Freiburg, 1923.

Phil 1535.11 — Lehrbuch der Philosophie. (Stöckl, A.) Mainz, 1876. 2v.

Phil 1535.11.8 — Lehrbuch der Philosophie. (Stöckl, A.) Mainz, 1905-12. 2v.

Phil 3450.30.10 — Lehrbuch der Philosophie. 2e Aufl. v.3. (Hessen, Johannes.) München, 1950-

Phil 1516.3 — Lehrbuch der Philosophie. 4e Aufl. (Lehmen, Alfonso.) n.p., 1912-19. 4v.

Phil 5257.4 — Lehrbuch der philosophisch propädeutischen Psychologie und der formalen Logik. 2. Aufl. (Reinhold, E.C.) Jena, 1839.

Phil 180.40 — Lehrbuch der philosophischen Propädeutik. (Finckh, T.) Heidelberg, 1909.

Phil 181.1 — Lehrbuch der philosophischen Propädeutik. (Gabler, G.A.) Erlangen, 1827.

Phil 181.1.2 — Lehrbuch der philosophischen Propädeutik. (Gabler, G.A.) Erlangen, 1827.

Phil 186.36.4 — Lehrbuch der philosophischen Propädeutik. 4. Aufl. (Lehmann, R.) Berlin, 1917.

Phil 186.36.5 — Lehrbuch der philosophischen Propädeutik. 5. Aufl. (Lehmann, R.) Leipzig, 1922.

Phil 176.53.7 — Lehrbuch der philosophischen Vorkenntnisse. (Bouterwek, F.) Göttingen, 1820.

Phil 176.53.2 — Lehrbuch der philosophischen Wissenschaften. (Bouterwek, F.) Göttingen, 1820. 2v.

Phil 3100.46 — Lehrbuch der pragmatischen Psychologie. (Beneke, F.E.) Berlin, 1853.

Phil 8880.40 — Lehrbuch der praktischen Philosophie. (Feder, J.G.H.) Göttingen, 1770.

Phil 6960.4 — Lehrbuch der Psychiatrie. (Krafft-Ebing, R. von.) Stuttgart, 1893.

Phil 6960.4.3 — Lehrbuch der Psychiatrie. 3. Aufl. (Krafft-Ebing, R. von.) Stuttgart, 1888.

Phil 3100.50 — Lehrbuch der Psychologie. (Beneke, F.E.) Berlin, 1861.

Phil 5244.10.6 — Lehrbuch der Psychologie. (Elsenhans, Theodor.) Tübingen, 1920.

Phil 5246.4 — Lehrbuch der Psychologie. (George, S.) Berlin, 1854.

Phil 5249.8 — Lehrbuch der Psychologie. (Jerusalem, W.) Wien, 1902.

Phil 5249.5 — Lehrbuch der Psychologie. (Jodl, Friedrich.) Stuttgart, 1896.

Phil 5258.61.3 — Lehrbuch der Psychologie. (Schilling, Gustav, of Giessen.) Langensalza, 1913.

Phil 5258.65 — Lehrbuch der Psychologie. (Schindler, Ferdinand.) Troppau, 1913.

Phil 5261.1 — Lehrbuch der Psychologie. (Volkmann, W.) Göthen, 1875-76. 2v.

Phil 5261.1.3 — Lehrbuch der Psychologie. (Volkmann, W.) Göthen, 1884-8. 2v.

Phil 5262.2.5 — Lehrbuch der Psychologie. (Waitz, T.) Braunschweig, 1849.

Phil 5261.1.2 — Lehrbuch der Psychologie. v.1-2. (Volkmann, W.) Göthen, 1884-85.

Phil 5249.5.5 — Lehrbuch der Psychologie. 2. Aufl. v.1-2. (Jodl, Friedrich.) Stuttgart, 1903.

Phil 5257.26.8 — Lehrbuch der Psychologie. 3. Aufl. (Rüegg, H.R.) Bern, 1876.

Phil 5244.10.9 — Lehrbuch der Psychologie. 3e Aufl. (Elsenhans, Theodor.) Tübingen, 1937-1938.

Phil 5249.8.10 — Lehrbuch der Psychologie. 4. Aufl. (Jerusalem, W.) Wien, 1907.

Phil 5251.20.5 — Lehrbuch der psychologischen Methodik. (Lehmann, Alfred.) Leipzig, 1906.

Phil 5243.8 — Lehrbuch der Psychology. (Dittes, F.) Wien, 1873.

Phil 6968.22 — Lehrbuch der psychopathologischen untersuchungs Methoden. (Sommer, Robert.) Berlin, 1899.

Phil 5850.274 — Lehrbuch der Psychotechnik. (Moede, Walther.) Berlin, 1930.

Phil 8598.9 — Lehrbuch der Religionsphilosophie. (Siebeck, Hermann.) Freiburg, 1893.

Phil 5593.57 — Lehrbuch der Rorschach-Psychodiagnostik. 2. Aufl. (Bohm, E.B.) Bern, 1957.

Phil 5252.66 — Lehrbuch der Seelenwissenschaft. (Musmann, J.G.) Berlin, 1827.

Phil 6317.14 — Lehrbuch der Storungen des Seelenlehre. v.1-2. (Heinroth, D.F.C.A.) Leipzig, 1818.

Phil 182.17.15 — Lehrbuch der theoretischen Philosophie. (Hillebrand, J.) Mainz, 1826.

Phil 7084.12.1 — Lehrbuch der Traumanalyse. 1. Aufl. (Schultz-Hencke, Harald.) Stuttgart, 1968.

Phil 6060.27.5 — Lehrbuch der wissenschaftlichen Graphologie. (Lungspeer, A.S.L.) Leipzig, 1929.

Phil 812.14 — Lehrbuch des Geschichte der Philosophie. v.1-2. (Marbach, G.O.) Leipzig, 1838-41.

Phil 3428.30 — Lehrbuch zur Einleitung in die Philosophie. (Herbart, J.F.) Königsberg, 1837.

Phil 192.2 — Lehrbuch zur Einleitung in die Philosophie. (Rabus, L.) Erlangen, 1887-1895. 2v.

Phil 3428.30.5 — Lehrbuch zur Einleitung in die Philosophie. 2. Aufl. (Herbart, J.F.) Königsberg, 1821.

Phil 3428.30.55 — Lehrbuch zur Einleitung in die philosophie. 4. Aufl. (Herbart, J.F.) Leipzig, 1912.

Phil 186.40.5 — Lehrbuch zur Einleitung in die Philosophie. 5e Aufl. (Lichtenfels, Johann.) Wien, 1863.

Phil 3428.44 — Lehrbuch zur Psychologie. (Herbart, J.F.) Hamburg, 1900.

Phil 3428.43 — Lehrbuch zur Psychologie. (Herbart, J.F.) Königsberg, 1816.

Phil 3428.43.5 — Lehrbuch zur Psychologie. 3. Aufl. (Herbart, J.F.) Leipzig, 1887.

Phil 1504.10.6 — Die Lehre Anselms von Canterbury. v.10, pt.6. (Baeumker, F.) Münster, 1912.

Phil 1505.1 — Lehre der Scholastiker von der Synteresis. (Appel, H.) Rostock, 1891.

Phil 3110.24 — Die Lehre des deutschen Philosophen J. Böhme. (Böhme, J.) München, 1844.

Phil 3838.12 — Die Lehre des Spinoza. (Schlüter, C.B.) Münster, 1836.

Phil 3495.5 — Die Lehre Kants...Vermorst. (Noiré, L.) Mainz, 1882.

Phil 3493.4 — Die Lehre Kants von der Idealität. (Lasswitz, K.) Berlin, 1883.

Phil 3822.2 — Die Lehre Spinoza's. (Camerer, T.) Stuttgart, 1877.

Phil 3822.2.10 — Die Lehre Spinozas. 2. Aufl. (Camerer, T.) Stuttgart, 1914.

Phil 3790.4.81 — Die Lehre vom Bewusstsein bei Heinrich Rickert. Inaug. Diss. (Schlunke, Otto.) Leipzig, 1911.

Phil 9035.72 — Die Lehre vom Charakter. (Heiss, Robert.) Berlin, 1936.

Phil 672.132 — Die Lehre vom diskreten Raum in der neueren Philosophie. (Poppovich, N.M.) Wien, 1922.

Phil 8837.7 — Die Lehre vom Erlaubten in der Geschichte der Ethic seit Schleier Macher. (Mayer, Gottlob.) Leipzig, 1899.

Phil 5761.7 — Die Lehre vom freien Willen. (Luthardt, C.E.) Leipzig, 1863.

Phil 1504.7.6 — Die Lehre vom göttlichen Willen. v.7, pt.6. (Grünfeld, A.) Münster, 1909.

Phil 1540.14 — Die Lehre vom Human Naturale bei Thomas Aquin, Bonaventura und Duns Scotus. Inaug. Diss. (Heuel, Meinolf.) Koblenz, 1927.

Phil 3494.12.10 — Die Lehre vom inneren Sinn bei Kant. (Monzel, Alois.) Bonn, 1913.

Phil 3565.108 — Die Lehre vom Instinkte bei Lotze und Darwin. (Lange, Paul.) Berlin, 1896.

Phil 1135.80 — Die Lehre vom Logos. (Heinze, M.) Oldenburg, 1872.

Phil 186.14 — Die Lehre vom Menschen. (Lindemann, H.S.) Zürich, 1844.

Phil 3120.8.45 — Die Lehre vom Nrichtigen Urteil. (Brentano, Franz.) Bern, 1956.

Phil 8735.20.5 — Lehre vom richtigen Verhältniss zu den Schöpfungswerken und die durch öffentliche Einführung derselben allein zu bewürkende allgemeine Menschenglückung. (Ziegenhagen, F.H.) Braunschweig, 1799.

Phil 8412.9.5 — Die Lehre vom Schönen. (Landmann, E.) Wien, 1952.

Phil 196.11.9 — Die Lehre vom Sein. (Varnbüler, Theodore.) Leipzig, 1883.

Phil 1707.29 — Die Lehre vom Sein in der modernen Philosophie. (Haag, Karl Heinz.) Frankfurt, 1963.

Phil 4210.114 — Die Lehre vom sentimento fondamentale bei Rosmini nach ihrer Anlage. Inaug. Diss. (Schwaiger, Georg.) Fulda, 1914.

Phil 3552.103 — Die Lehre vom Uebel. (Willareth, O.) Strassburg, 1898.

Phil 5500.5 — Die Lehre vom Urteil. (Lask, E.) Tübingen, 1912.

Phil 5250.1 — Die Lehre vom Wissen. (Kirchmann, J.H. von.) Berlin, 1871.

Phil 7069.24.42 — Die Lehre von den Gedankenwellen. 2.-3. Aufl. (Giese, F.) Leipzig, 1924.

Phil 176.73.2 — Die Lehre von den Geistigen und vom Volk. 2. Aufl. (Brunner, Constantin.) Potsdam, 1927. 2v.

Phil 176.73.3 — Die Lehre von den Geistigen und vom Volk. 3. Aufl. (Brunner, Constantin.) Stuttgart, 1962. 2v.

Phil 176.73 — Die Lehre von den Geistigen und vom Volke. (Brunner, Constantin.) Berlin, 1908. 2v.

Phil 5643.176 — Lehre von den Gesichtsempfindungen auf Grund hinterlassener Aufzeichnungen. (Hillebrand, Franz.) Wien, 1929.

Phil 338.15 — Die Lehre von den Ideen. (Heyder, Carl.) Frankfurt am Main, 1874.

Phil 3552.282 — Die Lehre von den kleinen Vorstellungen bei Leibniz. (Hohenemser, E.) Heidelberg, 1899.

Phil 5400.21 — Die Lehre von den Leidenschaften. (Schutz, L.H.) Hagen, 1901.

Phil 2520.98 — Die Lehre von den Sinnesqualitäten...Descartes. (Schwarz, H.) Halle, 1894.

Phil 332.8 — Die Lehre von Denken zur Ergänzung. v.1-3. (Bastian, Adolf.) Berlin, 1902-05.

Phil 1504.3.4 — Die Lehre von der Anfangslosigkeit. v.3, pt.4. (Worms, M.) Münster, 1900.

Phil 5330.6.5 — Die Lehre von der Aufmerksamkeit. (Braunschweiger, D.) Leipzig, 1899.

Phil 5330.10 — Die Lehre von der Aufmerksamkeit. (Dürr, E.) Leipzig, 1907.

Phil 8643.6 — Die Lehre von der bedingten Unsterblichkeit in ihren Entstehung geschichtlichen Entwickelung. (Seebach, E.) Krefeld, 1898.

Phil 3850.27.75 — Die Lehre von der Ehrfurcht von dem Leben. (Schweitzer, A.) München, 1966.

Phil 343.1 — Die Lehre von der Erkenntniss. (Mayer, A.) Leipzig, 1875.

Phil 3808.167 — Die Lehre von der Freiheit bei Kant und Schopenhauer. Inaug. Diss. (Siedel, K.G.) Erlangen, 1888.

Phil 5258.108 — Die Lehre von der Gestalt. (Scheerer, M.) Berlin, 1931.

Phil 5016.1 — Die Lehre von der Identität in der deutschen Logik-Wissenschaft seit Lotze. Inaug. Diss. (Göldel, R.W.) Leipzig, 1935.

Phil 3915.53 — Die Lehre von der Muskelbewegung. (Wundt, Wilhelm.) Braunschweig, 1858.

Phil 665.94 — Die Lehre von der Präexistenz der Menschlichen Seelen. (Bruch, Johann Friedrich.) Strassburg, 1859.

Phil 1135.90 — Die Lehre von der praktischen Vernunft. (Walter, J.) Jena, 1874.

Phil 3850.25.80 — Die Lehre von der psychologischen Kausalität in der Philosophie Ludwig Strümpells. Inaug. Diss. (Schmidt, Hugo.) Leipzig, 1907.

Phil 978.37 — Die Lehre von der Seelenwanderung. (Kneisel, R.) Leipzig, 1889.

Phil 5330.1.15 — Die Lehre von der sinnlichen Aufmerksamkeit. Inaug. Diss. (Pilzecker, A.) München, 1889.

Phil 8640.2 — Die Lehre von der Unsterblichkeit der Seele. (Perdelwitz, R.) Leipzig, 1900.

Phil 5772.4 — Die Lehre von der Willensfreiheit des Menschen. (Wolański, L.T.) Münster, 1868.

Phil 807.16 — Die Lehre von der Zweckbestimmung der Menschen. (Heinemann, Fritz.) Breslau, 1926.

Phil 4200.1.81 — Die Lehre von der zweifachen Wahrheit bei Petrus Pomponatius. Inaug. Diss. (Betzendörfer, Walter.) Tübingen, 1919.

Phil 5760.1   Die Lehre von Primat des Willens. (Kahl, W.)
               Strassburg, 1886.
Phil 3022.5   Die Lehre von Sündenfall in der Philosophie Schellings.
               Inaug. Diss. (Wimmershoff, H.) Selingen, 1934.
Phil 3260.40   Lehren der Liebe des Glaubens. (Fries, J.F)
               Heidelberg, 1823.
Phil 5057.7   Die Lehren der reinen Logik. (Rösling, C.L.) Ulm, 1826.
Phil 1504.12.2 Die Lehren des Hermes Trismegistos. v.12, pt.2-4. (Kroll,
               J.) Münster, 1914.
Phil 270.53   Die Lehren vom Zufall. (Windelband, W.) Berlin, 1870.
Phil 5643.89.80 Die Lehren von der visuelfen Wahrnehmung und Vorstellung.
               (Krudewig, M.) Meisenheim, 1953.
Phil 672.1   Die Lehren von Raun, Zeit, und Mathematik. v.1-2.
               (Baumann, J.J.) Berlin, 1868-69.
Phil 5520.640 Lehrer, Adrienne. Theory of meaning. Englewood Cliffs,
               N.J., 1970.
Phil 5761.25   Lehrer, Keith. Freedom and determinism. N.Y., 1966.
Phil 3940.2.35 Das Lehrgespräch vom Allgemeinen Menschen in Lieben
               Abenden. (Ziegler, L.) Hamburg, 1956.
Phil 978.86   Lehrs, Ernst. Man or matter. London, 1951.
Phil 978.86.2 Lehrs, Ernst. Man or matter. 2d. ed. London, 1958.
Phil 978.86.7 Lehrs, Ernst. Mensch und Materie. 2. Aufl.
               Frankfurt, 1966.
Phil 8601.11   Lei das contrastes. (Veiga, Antonio D.A.) Porto, 1928.
Phil 1750.1   Leib, J.R. Lecture on nature and objects of modern
               philosophy. Philadelphia, 1830-39. 3 pam.
Phil 5225.3   Leib-Seele-Linheit. (Prinzhorn, H.) Frankfurt, 1927.
Phil 6132.29   Das Leib-Seele-Problem. (Wenzl, Aloys.) Leipzig, 1933.
Phil 3963.2   Das Leib-Seele-Problem in der Philosophie Hollands im 19.
               und 20. Jahrhundert. (Stien, Hendrik.) Lengerich, 1937.
Phil 6113.19   Leib und Seele. (Driesch, Hans.) Leipzig, 1916.
Phil 6114.4   Leib und Seele. (Eisler, R.) Leipzig, 1906.
Phil 6117.38   Leib und Seele. (Häberlin, Paul.) Bern, 1927.
Phil 6128.2   Leib und Seele. (Schaller, J.) Weimar, 1858.
Phil 6128.12   Leib und Seele. Der Entwicklungs gedanke. (Stumpf, C.)
               Leipzig, 1903.
Phil 6128.2.2 Leib und Seele. 2. Aufl. (Schaller, J.) Weimar, 1856.
Phil 6113.19.3 Leib und Seele. 3. Aufl. (Driesch, Hans.) Leipzig, 1923.
Phil 3565.106 Leib und Seele bei Fechner und Lotze als vertretern Zweier
               massgebenden Weltanschauungen. (Simon, Theodor.)
               Göttingen, 1894.
Phil 6128.34   Leib und Seele in ihrem verhältnis Zueinander. (Sommer,
               George.) Leipzig, 1920.
Phil 6114.11   Leib und Seele nach ihrem Begriff und ihrem Verhaltniss zur
               Einander. (Erdmann, J.E.) Halle, 1837.
Phil 8972.5   Der Leib und sein Recht im Christentum. (Walter, Franz.)
               Donauwörth, 1910.
Phil 6961.18   Leibbrand, Werner. Der Wahnsinn. Freiburg, 1961.
Phil 3246.185 Leibholz, G. Fichte und der demokratischen Gedanke.
               Freiburg, 1921.
Phil 3235.124 Leiblichkeit und Gesellschaft. (Bochmuell, Klaus.)
               Göttingen, 1961.
Phil 3552.415 Leibnits i ego vek. (Guerrier, V.I.) Sankt
               Peterburg, 1868.
Phil 3831.2   Leibnitz, G.W. A refutation...Spinoza. Edinburgh, 1855.
Phil 3552.322.5 Leibnitz and the seventeenth century revolution. (Meyer,
               R.W.) Cambridge, Eng., 1952.
Phil 3552.254 Leibnitz considéré comme historien de la philosophie.
               Thèse. (Bertereau, A.) Paris, 1843.
Phil 3552.133 Leibnitz ett forëbud till Kant. Akademisk afhandling.
               (Bolin, Wilhelm.) Helsingfors, 1864.
Phil 4260.99   Il Leibnitz gindicato da G.B. Vico. (Ferrari, G.M.)
               n.p., n.d.
Phil 3552.299 Leibnitz Stellung zur Offenbarung. (Dieckhoff, A.W.)
               Rostock, 1888.
Phil 3552.93   Leibnitz und Baumgarten. (Schmidt, J.) Halle, 1875.
Phil 3552.229 Leibnitz und Comenius. (Kvĕt, F.B.) Prag, 1857.
Phil 3428.155.15 Leibnitz und Herbart. (Zimmerman, R.) Wien, 1849.
Phil 3552.231 Leibnitz und Newton. (Durdik, Josef.) Halle, 1869.
Phil 3552.229.5 Leibnitz'ens Logik. (Kvĕt, F.B.) Prag, 1857.
Phil 3552.120 Leibnitz's Stellung zur katholischen Kirche. (Kirchner,
               Friedrich.) Berlin, 1874.
Phil 3552.86.15 Leibniz, Descartes et Spinoza. (Foucher de Careil,
               Alexandre.) Paris, 1862.
Phil 3552.430 Leibniz, G.W. Confessio philosophi. Paris, 1961.
Phil 3552.431 Leibniz, G.W. Confessio philosophi. Ein Dialog.
               Frankfurt, 1967.
Phil 3552.405.5 Leibniz, G.W. Fragmente zur Logik. Berlin, 1960.
Phil 3552.405 Leibniz, G.W. Polemika G. Leibnitsa i S. Klarka po
               voprosam filosofii i estesvoznaniia, 1715-1716 gg.
               Leningrad, 1960.
Phil 3552.445 Leibniz, G.W. The preface to Leibniz' Novissima Sinica.
               Honolulu, 1957.
Phil 3552.33   Leibniz, Gottfried. Politische Schriften. v.1-2.
               Wien, 1966-67.
Phil 3552.56   Leibniz, Gottfried Wilhelm. Abhandlung über die beste
               philosophische Ausdrucksweise. Berlin, 1916.
Htn Phil 3552.55* Leibniz, Gottfried Wilhelm. Ars Combinatoria.
               Francofurti, 1690.
Phil 3552.77   Leibniz, Gottfried Wilhelm. Der Briefwechsel.
               Hannover, 1889.
Phil 3552.78   Leibniz, Gottfried Wilhelm. Briefwechsel zwischen Leibniz,
               Arnould, und dem Landgrafen Earnst von Hessen-Rheinfels.
               Hannover, 1846.
Phil 3552.71   Leibniz, Gottfried Wilhelm. A collection of papers.
               London, 1717.
Htn Phil 3552.71.1* Leibniz, Gottfried Wilhelm. A collection of papers.
               London, 1717.
Phil 3552.52   Leibniz, Gottfried Wilhelm. Confessio philosophi.
               Paris, 1961.
Phil 3552.77.20 Leibniz, Gottfried Wilhelm. Correspondance de Leibniz avec
               l'électrice Sophie de Brunswick-Lunebourg. Hanovre, 1874.
               3v.
Phil 3552.78.15 Leibniz, Gottfried Wilhelm. Correspondance Leibnitz-Clarke
               présenté d'après les manuscrits originaux des
               bibliothèques de Hanovre et de Londres. 1. éd.
               Paris, 1957.
Htn Phil 3552.64* Leibniz, Gottfried Wilhelm. De la tolérance des religions.
               Paris, 1692.
Phil 3552.23.5 Leibniz, Gottfried Wilhelm. Deutsche Schriften.
               Berlin, 1838-40. 2v.
Phil 3552.23   Leibniz, Gottfried Wilhelm. Deutsche Schriften.
               Leipzig, 1916. 2v.
Phil 3552.51.15 Leibniz, Gottfried Wilhelm. Discorso di metafisica "Hortus
               conclusus". Napoli, 1934.
Phil 3552.51.10 Leibniz, Gottfried Wilhelm. Discours de métaphysique.
               Paris, 1929.

Phil 3552.51.12 Leibniz, Gottfried Wilhelm. Discours de métaphysique et
               Correspondance aves Arnauld. Paris, 1957.
Phil 3552.51   Leibniz, Gottfried Wilhelm. Discourse on metaphysics.
               Chicago, 1927.
Phil 3552.51.8 Leibniz, Gottfried Wilhelm. Discourse on metaphysics. La
               Salle, 1962.
Phil 3552.51.7 Leibniz, Gottfried Wilhelm. Discourse on metaphysics.
               Manchester, 1953.
Htn Phil 3552.50* Leibniz, Gottfried Wilhelm. Disputatio metaphysica.
               Lipsiae, 1663.
Htn Phil 3552.74* Leibniz, Gottfried Wilhelm. Epistolae ad diversos. Cum
               annotationibus suis primum divulgavit christian.
               Lipsiae, 1734-42. 4v.
Phil 3552.23.10 Leibniz, Gottfried Wilhelm. Ermahnung anu die Deutschen.
               Darmstadt, 1967.
Htn Phil 3552.60* Leibniz, Gottfried Wilhelm. Essai de Theodicée.
               Amsterdam, 1710. 3 pam.
Phil 3552.61   Leibniz, Gottfried Wilhelm. Essais de Theodicée.
               Paris, 1720.
Phil 3552.60.10 Leibniz, Gottfried Wilhelm. Essais de Theodicée.
               Paris, 1962.
Phil 3552.60.5 Leibniz, Gottfried Wilhelm. Essais de Theodicée sur la
               bonté de Dieu. Amsterdam, 1720.
Phil 3552.68   Leibniz, Gottfried Wilhelm. Exposition sur la religion.
               Paris, 1819.
Phil 3552.53   Leibniz, Gottfried Wilhelm. Den förutbestämda harmonien.
               Stockholm, 1927.
Phil 3552.28   Leibniz, Gottfried Wilhelm. Geist des Herrn von Leibniz.
               Wittenburg, 1775. 2v.
Phil 3552.35   Leibniz, Gottfried Wilhelm. General investigations
               concerning the analysis of concepts and truths.
               Athens, 1968.
Phil 3552.31   Leibniz, Gottfried Wilhelm Leibniz;
               Gott, Geist, Güte. Gütersloh, 1947.
Phil 3552.67.30 Leibniz, Gottfried Wilhelm. Grundwahrheiten der
               Philosophie. Frankfurt, 1962.
Phil 3552.24   Leibniz, Gottfried Wilhelm. Hauptschriften zur Grundelung
               der Philosophie. Leipzig, 1904-06. 2v.
Phil 3552.24.5.3 Leibniz, Gottfried Wilhelm. Hauptschriften zur Grundelung
               der Philosophie. 3. Aufl. Hamburg, 1966. 2v.
Phil 3552.57A Leibniz, Gottfried Wilhelm. Die Hauptwerke. 3. Aufl.
               Stuttgart, 1949.
Phil 3552.21.5 Leibniz, Gottfried Wilhelm. Kleine Schriften zur
               Metaphysik. Frankfurt, 1965.
Phil 3552.21   Leibniz, Gottfried Wilhelm. Kleinere philosophische
               Schriften. Jena, 1740.
Phil 3552.22   Leibniz, Gottfried Wilhelm. Kleinere philosophische
               Schriften. Leipzig, 1883.
Phil 3552.54   Leibniz, Gottfried Wilhelm. Lehr-Satze über die
               Monadologie. Franckfurt, 1720.
Phil 3552.28.5 Leibniz, Gottfried Wilhelm. Leibniz als Denker.
               Leipzig, 1863.
Phil 3552.78.80 Leibniz, Gottfried Wilhelm. The Leibniz-Arnauld
               correspondence. Manchester, 1967.
Phil 3552.78.25 Leibniz, Gottfried Wilhelm. Leibniz' bref till
               Sparfrenfelt. n.p., n.d.
Phil 3552.29.35 Leibniz, Gottfried Wilhelm. Leibniz et la racine de
               l'existence. Par+s, 1962.
Phil 3552.78.40 Leibniz, Gottfried Wilhelm. Leibniz korrespondiert mit
               Paris. Hamburg, 1940.
Phil 3552.78.5 Leibniz, Gottfried Wilhelm. Leibniz und Landgraf E. von
               Hessen-Rheinfels...Briefwechsel. v.1-2. Frankfurt, 1847.
Phil 3552.73   Leibniz, Gottfried Wilhelm. Leibnizens geschichtliche
               Aufsätze und Gedichte. Hannover, 1847.
Phil 3552.78.50 Leibniz, Gottfried Wilhelm. Lettres de Leibniz à Arnauld.
               1. éd. Paris, 1952.
Phil 3552.78.30 Leibniz, Gottfried Wilhelm. Lettres et fragments inédits
               sur les problèmes philosophiques. Paris, 1934.
Phil 3552.19.5 Leibniz, Gottfried Wilhelm. Lettres et opuscules inédits.
               Paris, 1854.
Phil 3552.73.5 Leibniz, Gottfried Wilhelm. Logical papers. Oxford, 1966.
Phil 3552.79.25 Leibniz, Gottfried Wilhelm. Metaphysische Abhandlung.
               Hamburg, 1958.
Phil 3552.66.11 Leibniz, Gottfried Wilhelm. La monadologia. Milano, 1926.
Phil 3552.66.16 Leibniz, Gottfried Wilhelm. La monadologia. Torino, 1929.
NEDL Phil 3552.66 Leibniz, Gottfried Wilhelm. La monadologie, avec étude et
               notes. Paris, 1900.
Phil 3552.67   Leibniz, Gottfried Wilhelm. La monadologie. Paris, 1881.
Phil 3552.67.3 Leibniz, Gottfried Wilhelm. La monadologie. Paris, 1883.
Phil 3552.63.30 Leibniz, Gottfried Wilhelm. La monadologie. Paris, 1952.
Phil 3552.67.15 Leibniz, Gottfried Wilhelm. Monadologie. Wien, 1847.
Phil 3552.66.13 Leibniz, Gottfried Wilhelm. Monadologie. 2. Ausg.
               Stuttgart, 1954.
Phil 3552.67.5 Leibniz, Gottfried Wilhelm. La monadologie. 5. éd.
               Paris, n.d.
Phil 3552.67.40 Leibniz, Gottfried Wilhelm. Monadology, and other
               philosophical essays. Indianapolis, 1965.
Phil 3552.65   Leibniz, Gottfried Wilhelm. The monadology. Oxford, 1898.
Phil 3552.65.10 Leibniz, Gottfried Wilhelm. The monadology of Leibniz.
               Los Angeles, 1930.
Phil 3552.39.5 Leibniz, Gottfried Wilhelm. Neue Abhandlungen über den
               menschlichen verstand. Frankfurt, 1961. 2v.
Phil 3552.39   Leibniz, Gottfried Wilhelm. Neue Abhandlungen über den
               menschlichen verstand. 3e Aufl. Leipzig, 1915.
Phil 3552.40A Leibniz, Gottfried Wilhelm. New essays concerning human
               understanding. N.Y., 1896.
Phil 3552.40.5 Leibniz, Gottfried Wilhelm. New essays concerning human
               understanding. 3rd ed. La Salle, 1949.
Phil 3552.41.5 Leibniz, Gottfried Wilhelm. Nouveaux essais sur
               l'entendement humain. Paris, 1886.
Phil 3552.41   Leibniz, Gottfried Wilhelm. Nouveaux essais sur
               l'entendement humain. Paris, 1899.
Phil 3552.41.10 Leibniz, Gottfried Wilhelm. Nouveaux essais sur
               l'entendement humain. Paris, 1966.
Phil 3552.76   Leibniz, Gottfried Wilhelm. Nouvelles lettres.
               Paris, 1857.
Phil 3552.42   Leibniz, Gottfried Wilhelm. Nové úvahy o lidské soudnosti
               od auktora Systému předzjednané harmonie. Praha, 1932.
Phil 3552.18.10 Leibniz, Gottfried Wilhelm. Oeuvres, publiées pour la
               première fois d'après les manuscrits. v.2-7. N.Y., 1969.
               7v.
Phil 3552.16   Leibniz, Gottfried Wilhelm. Oeuvres. Paris, 1842-45.
               2v.
Phil 3552.17   Leibniz, Gottfried Wilhelm. Oeuvres. Paris, 1859-75.
               7v.
Phil 3552.9   Leibniz, Gottfried Wilhelm. Oeuvres choisies.
               Paris, 1939.

Author and Title Listing

Phil 3552.10 Leibniz, Gottfried Wilhelm. Oeuvres philosophiques. Amsterdam, 1765.
Htn Phil 3552.10.2* Leibniz, Gottfried Wilhelm. Oeuvres philosophiques. Amsterdam, 1765.
Phil 3552.18 Leibniz, Gottfried Wilhelm. Oeuvres philosophiques. v.2. Paris, 1866.
Phil 3552.18.5 Leibniz, Gottfried Wilhelm. Oeuvres philosophiques. 2e éd. Paris, 1900. 2v.
Phil 3552.11 Leibniz, Gottfried Wilhelm. Opera omnia. Genevae, 1768. 6v.
Phil 3552.24.25 Leibniz, Gottfried Wilhelm. Opera philosophica. Aalen, 1959.
Phil 3552.15 Leibniz, Gottfried Wilhelm. Opera philosophica. v.1-2. Berolini, 1839-40.
Phil 3552.29.25 Leibniz, Gottfried Wilhelm. Opere filosofiche; estratti. Bologna, 1929.
Phil 3552.26 Leibniz, Gottfried Wilhelm. Opere varie. Bari, 1912.
Phil 3552.30.10 Leibniz, Gottfried Wilhelm. Opuscula philosophica selecta. Paris, 1939.
Phil 3552.19 Leibniz, Gottfried Wilhelm. Opuscules et fragments inédits. Paris, 1903.
Phil 3552.30.15 Leibniz, Gottfried Wilhelm. Opuscules philosophiques choisis. Paris, 1954.
Phil 3552.20 Leibniz, Gottfried Wilhelm. Opusculum adscititio titulo Systema theologicum inscriptum. Lutetiae Parisiorum, 1845.
Htn Phil 3552.29* Leibniz, Gottfried Wilhelm. Otium hanoueranum sive Miscellanea. Lipsiae, 1718.
Htn Phil 3552.29.2* Leibniz, Gottfried Wilhelm. Otium hanoueranum sive Miscellanea. Lipsiae, 1718.
Phil 3552.32 Leibniz, Gottfried Wilhelm. Philosophical papers and letters. Chicago, 1956. 2v.
Phil 3552.32.2 Leibniz, Gottfried Wilhelm. Philosophical papers and letters. 2nd ed. Dordrecht, 1969.
Phil 3552.25 Leibniz, Gottfried Wilhelm. Philosophical works. New Haven, 1890.
Phil 3552.25.2 Leibniz, Gottfried Wilhelm. Philosophical works. 2nd ed. New Haven, 1908.
Phil 3552.34 Leibniz, Gottfried Wilhelm. Philosophical writings. London, 1956.
Phil 3552.10.15 Leibniz, Gottfried Wilhelm. Philosophische Werke nach Rapspens Sammlung. Halle 1778-80. 2v.
Phil 3552.14 Leibniz, Gottfried Wilhelm. Die philosophischen Schriften. Berlin, 1875-90. 7v.
Phil 3552.63.40 Leibniz, Gottfried Wilhelm. Plädoyer fur Gottes Gottheit. 1. Aufl. Berlin, 1947.
Phil 3552.78.35 Leibniz, Gottfried Wilhelm. Principes de la nature et de la grace fondés en raison. Paris, 1954.
Htn Phil 3552.30.5* Leibniz, Gottfried Wilhelm. Principia philosophica. Lipsiae, 1728.
Phil 3552.59 Leibniz, Gottfried Wilhelm. Protegée; ou De la formation et des révolutions du globe. Paris, 1859.
Phil 3552.70 Leibniz, Gottfried Wilhelm. Recueil...Pieces...Leibniz. Lausanne, 1759. 2v.
Htn Phil 3552.45* Leibniz, Gottfried Wilhelm. Réfutation inédite de Spinoza. Paris, 1854.
Phil 3552.12 Leibniz, Gottfried Wilhelm. Sämtliche Schriften und Briefe. v.1, pt.1-8. Darmstadt, 1923-50. 8v.
Phil 3552.79.30 Leibniz, Gottfried Wilhelm. Saggi filosofici e lettere. Bari, 1963.
Phil 3552.27 Leibniz, Gottfried Wilhelm. Schäpferische Vernunft. Marbrug, 1951.
Phil 3552.78.10 Leibniz, Gottfried Wilhelm. Sechzehn ungedruckte Briefe. Zürich, 1844.
Phil 3552.36 Leibniz, Gottfried Wilhelm. Selections. N.Y., 1951.
Htn Phil 3552.58* Leibniz, Gottfried Wilhelm. Summi polyhistoris Godefridi Guilielmi Leibntii Protogaea. Goettingae, 1749.
Phil 3552.69.30 Leibniz, Gottfried Wilhelm. System der Theologie. Mainz, 1820.
Phil 3552.69 Leibniz, Gottfried Wilhelm. A system of theology. London, 1850.
Phil 3552.63.20 Leibniz, Gottfried Wilhelm. Tentamina theodicaeae de bonitate Dei libertate hominis et origine mali. Francofurti, 1719.
Phil 3552.63.25 Leibniz, Gottfried Wilhelm. Tentamina theodicaeae de bonitate Dei libertate hominis et origine mali. Tubingae, 1771.
Phil 3552.72 Leibniz, Gottfried Wilhelm. Textes inédits d'après les manuscrits de la Bibliothèque provinciale. Paris, 1948. 2v.
Phil 3552.62 Leibniz, Gottfried Wilhelm. Theodicaea. Paris, 1726.
Phil 3552.62.10 Leibniz, Gottfried Wilhelm. Theodicée. Hannover, 1744.
Htn Phil 3552.63* Leibniz, Gottfried Wilhelm. Theodicee. Hannover, 1763.
Phil 3552.63.15 Leibniz, Gottfried Wilhelm. Die Theodicee. Leipzig, 1883. 2v.
Phil 3552.63.10 Leibniz, Gottfried Wilhelm. Theodicy. New Haven, 1952.
Phil 3552.69.20 Leibniz, Gottfried Wilhelm. Theologisches System. Tübingen, 1860.
Phil 3552.67.20 Leibniz, Gottfried Wilhelm. Vernunftprinzipien der Natur und der Gnade. Hamburg, 1956.
Phil 3552.38 Leibniz, Gottfried Wilhelm. Welträtsel und Lebensharmonie. Wiesbaden, 1949.
Phil 3552.24.20 Leibniz, Gottfried Wilhelm. Werke. Stuttgart, 1949.
Phil 3552.13 Leibniz, Gottfried Wilhelm. Die Werke von Leibniz gemäss seinem handschriftlichen Nachlasse in der Königlichen Bibliothek zu Hannover. Hannover, 1864-84. 11v.
Phil 3552.336.5 Leibniz; initiation à sa philosophie. (Belaval, Yvor.) Paris, 1962.
Phil 3552.253.5 Leibniz, sa vie, son oeuvre. (Cresson, André.) Paris, 1946.
Phil 3552.253.8 Leibniz, sa vie, son oeuvre. 3. éd. (Cresson, André.) Paris, 1958.
Phil 3552.307A Leibniz; ses idées sur l'organisation des relations internationales. (Schrecker, Paul.) London, 1937.
Phil 3552.125.5 Leibniz, zu seinen Zweihundertzahrigen. (Wundt, Wilhelm.) Leipzig, 1917.
Phil 3552.480 Leibniz, 1646-1716, aspects de l'homme et de l'oeuvre. (Journées, Leibniz.) Paris, 1968.
Phil 3552.451 Leibniz, 1646-1716. (Newman, L.M.) London, 1966.
Phil 3552.79 Pamphlet vol. Leibniz. 14 pam.
Phil 3552.79.5 Pamphlet box. Leibniz.
Phil 3552.108 Leibniz. (Archambault, P.) Paris, n.d.
Phil 3552.265 Leibniz. (Brunswig, A.) Wien, 1925.
Phil 3552.279 Leibniz. (Carr, H.W.) London, 1929.
Phil 3552.449 Leibniz. (Cione, Edmondo.) Napoli, 1964.
Phil 3552.314 Leibniz. (Drago del Boca, S.) Milano, 1946.
Phil 3552.315 Leibniz. (Guggenberger, Alois.) Stuttgart, 1947.
Phil 3552.122 Leibniz. (Halbwachs, Maurice.) Paris, 1907.
Phil 3552.122.5 Leibniz. (Halbwachs, Maurice.) Paris, 1929.
Phil 3552.380 Leibniz. (Holz, Hans H.) Stuttgart, 1958.
Phil 3552.332 Leibniz. (Huber, Kurt.) München, 1951.
Phil 3552.316 Leibniz. (Kanthack, K.H.) Berlin, 1946.
Phil 3552.92.5 Leibniz. (Merz, J.T.) Edinburgh, 1907.
Phil 3552.355 Leibniz. (Merz, J.T.) N.Y., 1948.
Phil 3552.92A Leibniz. (Merz, J.T.) Philadelphia, 1884.
Phil 3552.324 Leibniz. (Pape, Ingetrud.) Stuttgart, 1949.
Phil 3552.478 Leibniz. (Peursen, Cornelis Anthonie van.) Baarn, 1966.
Phil 3552.478.1 Leibniz. (Peursen, Cornelis Anthonie van.) London, 1969.
Phil 3552.121 Leibniz. (Piat, C.) Paris, 1915.
Phil 3552.129 Leibniz. (Pichler, Hans.) Graz, 1919.
Phil 3552.352 Leibniz. (Saw, R.L.) Harmondsworth, Eng., 1954.
Phil 3552.260 Leibniz. (Schmalenbach, H.) München, 1921.
Phil 3552.289 Leibniz. (Stammler, G.) München, 1930.
Phil 3552.452 Leibniz. (Totok, Wilhelm.) Hannover, 1966.
NEDL Phil 3552.79.2 Pamphlet vol. Leibniz. German dissertations, 1909-1929. 15 pam.
Phil 3552.79.3 Pamphlet box. Leibniz. German dissertations.
Phil 3552.350 Leibniz. Il congresso internazionale di filosofia, Roma, 1946. (Archivio di Filosofia.) Roma, 1947.
Phil 3552.464.5.2 Leibniz. Logik und Metaphysik. 2. Aufl. (Martin, Gottfried.) Berlin, 1967.
Phil 3552.464 Leibniz: logique et métaphysique. (Martin, Gottfried.) Paris, 1966.
Phil 3552.28.5 Leibniz als Denker. (Leibniz, Gottfried Wilhelm.) Leipzig, 1863.
Phil 3552.115 Leibniz als Ethiker. (Beneke, H.F.) Erlangen, 1891.
Phil 3552.370 Leibniz als Friedensstifter. (Krueger, G.) Wiesbaden, 1947.
Phil 3552.130 Leibniz als Gegner der Gelehrteneinseitigkeit. (Mahnke, D.) Stade, 1912.
Phil 3552.296.10 Leibniz als Verfasser von Zwölf Anonymen. (Pfleiderer, Edmund.) Leipzig, 1870.
Phil 3552.238 Leibniz' Apriorismus. (Silberstein, Adela.) Weimar, 1902.
Phil 3552.291 Leibniz-Archiv. Darmstadt. 1-3 3v.
Phil 3552.78.80 The Leibniz-Arnauld correspondence. (Leibniz, Gottfried Wilhelm.) Manchester, 1967.
Phil 3552.109 Leibniz as a politician. (Ward, A.W.) Manchester, 1911.
Phil 3552.462 Leibniz-Bibliographie; die Literatur über Leibniz. (Mueller, Kurt.) Frankfurt, 1967.
Phil 3552.78.25 Leibniz' bref till Sparfrenfelt. (Leibniz, Gottfried Wilhelm.) n.p., n.d.
Phil 3552.375A The Leibniz-Clarke correspondence. (Clarke, Samuel.) Manchester, 1956.
Phil 3552.447 Leibniz' cosmological synthesis. (Tymiernniecka, A.T.) Assen, 1964.
Phil 3552.400 Leibniz critique de Descartes. (Belaval, Yvon.) Paris, 1960.
Phil 3552.360 Leibniz e la logica formale. (Barone, F.) Torino, 1955.
Phil 3552.302 Leibniz erkolcatana. (Tirtsch, Gergely.) Balassagyarmat, 1898.
Phil 3552.395 Leibniz et la dynamique. (Costabel, Pierre.) Paris, 1960.
Phil 3552.390 Leibniz et la querelle du pur amour. (Naert, Emilienne.) Paris, 1959.
Phil 3552.29.35 Leibniz et la racine de l'existence. (Leibniz, Gottfried Wilhelm.) Par+s, 1962.
Phil 3552.305 Leibniz et les démonstrations mathématiques de l'existence de Dieu. (Iwanicki, Joseph.) Strasbourg, 1933.
Phil 3552.305.5 Leibniz et les démonstrations mathématiques de l'existence de Dieu. Thèse. (Iwanicki, Joseph.) Strasbourg, 1933.
Phil 3552.86.5 Leibniz et les deux sophies. (Foucher de Careil, Alexandre.) Paris, 1876.
Phil 3552.112.5 Leibniz et l'organisation religieuse. (Baruzi, Jean.) Paris, 1907.
Phil 2730.91 Leibniz et Maine de Biran. Thèse. (Robef, E.) Paris, 1925.
Phil 3552.86.10 Leibniz et Pierre-le-Grand. (Foucher de Careil, Alexandre.) Paris, 1874.
Phil 3552.312 Leibniz et Spinoza. (Friedmann, G.) Paris, 1946.
Phil 3552.312.2 Leibniz et Spinoza. (Friedmann, G.) Paris, 1962.
Phil 3552.110 Die Leibniz-Handschriften. (Bodemann, E.) Hannover, 1895.
Phil 3552.114 Leibniz historien. (Davillé, L.) Paris, 1909.
Phil 2401.15 Leibniz in France. (Barber, W.H.) Oxford, 1955.
Phil 3552.275 Leibniz in seiner Stellung zur tellurischen Physik. (Schmoger, F.) München, 1901.
Phil 3552.78.40 Leibniz korrespondiert mit Paris. (Leibniz, Gottfried Wilhelm.) Hamburg, 1940.
Phil 3552.86 Leibniz la philosophie juive et la cabale. (Foucher de Careil, Alexandre.) Paris, 1861.
Phil 3552.267 Leibniz' Philosophie. (Caspari, Otto.) Leipzig, 1870.
Phil 3552.111 Leibniz' System. (Cassirer, E.) Marburg, 1902.
Phil 3552.111.15 Leibniz' Theodicee. (Rydberg, Viktor.) Leipzig, 1903.
Phil 3552.441 Leibniz und Baumgarten als Begründer der deutschen Aesthetik. (Meyer, H.G.) Halle, 1874.
Phil 3552.338 Leibniz und das Reich der Gnade. (Hildebrandt, Kurt.) Haag, 1953.
Phil 3552.317 Leibniz und die deutsche Gegenwart. (Litt, Theodore.) Wiesbaden, 1946.
Phil 3552.322 Leibniz und die europäische Ordnungskrise. (Meyer, R.W.) Hamburg, 1948.
Phil 3552.127.5 Leibniz und die religiöse Wiedervereinigung Deutschlands. 2. Aufl. (Kiefl, Franz X.) München, 1925.
Phil 3552.273 Leibniz und die Scholastik. Inaug. Diss. (Jasper, Joseph.) Münster, 1898-99.
Phil 3552.474 Leibniz und die Versöhnung der Konfessionen. (Schering, Ernst.) Stuttgart, 1966.
Phil 3552.296.15 Leibniz und Geulinx mit besonderer Beziehung auf ihr beiderseitiges Uhrengleichniss. (Pfleiderer, Edmund.) Tübingen, 1884.
Phil 3552.130.5 Leibniz und Goethe. (Mahnke, D.) Erfurt, 1924.
Phil 3552.81 Leibniz und Herbart über die Freiheit des menschlichen Willens. (Braeutigam, L.) Heidelberg, 1882.
Phil 3552.78.5 Leibniz und Landgraf E. von Hessen-Rheinfels...Briefwechsel. v.1-2. (Leibniz, Gottfried Wilhelm.) Frankfurt, 1847.
Phil 3552.328 Leibniz und sein Russland. (Richter, L.) Berlin, 1946.
Phil 3552.119.5 Leibniz und seine Zeit. (Grote, Ludwig.) Hannover, 1869.
Phil 3552.96 Leibniz und Spinoza. (Stein, L.) Berlin, 1890.
Phil 3552.461 Leibniz und Wir. (Robinet, André.) Göttingen, 1967.
Phil 3552.79.20 Leibniz zu seinem 300. Geburtstag. 1-7. Berlin, 1946-52.
Phil 3552.75 Leibnizens Briefwechsel...Bernstorff. Hannover, 1882.
Phil 3552.73 Leibnizens geschichtliche Aufsätze und Gedichte. (Leibniz, Gottfried Wilhelm.) Hannover, 1847.
Phil 3552.246 Leibnizens Rechtfertigung des Uebels. (Urbach, B.) Prag, 1901.
Phil 3552.227 Leibnizens Streit gegen Locke. (Thilly, Frank.) Heidelberg, 1891.

Phil 3552.130.10   Leibnizens Synthese von Universalmathematik und Individualmethaphysik. (Mahnke, D.) Halle, 1925.

Phil 2295.90   Leibnizenz kritik der Religionsphilosophie von John Toland. Abhandlung. (Muff, Margrit.) Affoltern, 1940.

Phil 3552.83.5   Leibniz's new essays concerning the human understanding. (Dewey, J.) Chicago, 1902.

Phil 3552.94.5   Leibniz's Psychologie. (Kirchner, Friedrich.) Cöthen, 1875.

Phil 3552.94   Die Leibniz'sche Philosophie. (Schwarz, H.) Jena, 1888.

Phil 3552.105   Der leibnizsche Substanzbegriff. (Rall, H.F.) Halle, 1899.

Phil 3552.102   Der leibnizsche Substanzbegriff. (Werckmeister, Walther.) Halle, 1899.

Phil 3850.18.175   Das Leibphänomen. (Lorscheid, B.) Bonn, 1962.

Phil 5066.232.20   Leicester, England. University. Summer School in Mathematical Logic. Sets, models and recursion theory. Amsterdam, 1967.

Phil 3585.7.90   Leicht, Alfred. Lazarus, der Begründer der Volkerpsychologie. Leipzig, 1904.

Phil 3585.7.92   Leicht, Alfred. Lazarusstudien. Meissen, 1912.

Phil 2250.90   Leidecker, K.F. Josiah Royce and Indian thought. N.Y., 1931.

Phil 3903.3.105   Leidel, A. Die Philosophie des Als Ob und das Leben Festschrift. Berlin, 1932.

Phil 3640.701   Leider, Kurt. Friedrich Nietzsche. Lübeck, 1963.

Phil 705.20   Leider, Kurt. Das Transzendentale. Königsberg, 1925.

Phil 6121.40   Leiderman, P.H. Psychological approaches to social behavior. Manford, 1964.

Phil 50.35   Leidiniai. (Kaunas. Universitetas. Teologijos-Filosofijos Fakultetas.) Kaunas. 8-18 2v.

Phil 8599.19.100   Leidreiter, Erich. Troeltsch und die Absolutheit des Christentums. Inaug. Diss. Mahrungen, 1927.

NEDL Phil 8591.3   Leifchild, J.R. The higher ministry of nature. London, 1872.

Phil 21.7   Leiftur. Reykjavik. 1,1915

Phil 5221.8   Leigh, D. The historical development of British psychiatry. Oxford, 1961.

Phil 186.28   Leighton, J.A. The field of philosophy. Columbus, Ohio, 1918.

Phil 186.28.5   Leighton, J.A. The field of philosophy. 4.ed. N.Y., 1930.

Phil 8886.68   Leighton, J.A. The individual and the social order. N.Y., 1927.

Phil 8591.24   Leighton, J.A. Religion, and the mind of to-day. N.Y., 1924.

Phil 8666.5   Leighton, J.A. Typical modern conceptions of God. N.Y., 1901.

Phil 705.48   Leighton, Walter Leatherbee. French philosophers and New England transcendentalism. Charlottesville, 1908.

Phil 8412.42   Leijonhiel, Christer. Colours, forms and art. Studies in differential aesthetic psychology. Akademisk avhandling. Stockholm, 1967.

Phil 176.69.80.5   Leipzig. Universität. Ernst Blochs Revision des Marxismus. Berlin, 1957.

Phil 3001.3   Leipziger Philosophen. (Brasch, M.) Leipzig, 1894.

Phil 5525.12.5   Leir, Giulio A. Il comico. Genova, 1913.

Phil 635.2   Leisegang, Dieter. Die drei Potenzen der Relation. Inaug. Diss. Frankfurt, 1969.

Phil 2520.245   Leisegang, G. Descartes Dioptrik. Meisenheim am Glan, 1954.

Phil 186.67   Leisegang, H. Denkformen. Berlin, 1928.

Phil 186.67.3   Leisegang, H. Denkformen. 2. Aufl. Berlin, 1951.

Phil 186.67.5   Leisegang, H. Einführung in die Philosophie. Berlin, 1951.

Phil 186.67.8   Leisegang, H. Einführung in die Philosophie. 3. Aufl. Berlin, 1956.

Phil 1116.4   Leisegang, H. Griechische Philosophie von Thales bis Platon. Breslau, 1922.

Phil 1116.4.5   Leisegang, H. Hellenistische Philosophie von Aristoteles bis Plotin. Breslau, 1923.

Phil 3585.15   Leisegang, H. Meine Weltanschaunng. Berlin, 1951.

Phil 1750.630   Leist, Fritz. Existenz im Nichts. München, 1961.

Phil 186.152   Leist, Fritz. Über Leben, Lüge and Liebe. Freiburg, 1966.

Phil 971.10   Leiste, Heinrich. Ein Beitrag zur anthroposophischen Hochschulfrage. Dornach, 1970.

Phil 3120.11.84   Leiste, Heinrich. Die Charakterologie von Julius Bahnsen. Diss. Köln, 1928.

Phil 6114.17   Der Leistungs kräftige Mensch. (Espenschied, Richard.) Hamburg, 1957.

Phil 5548.148   Leistungsbedürfnis und soziale Umwelt. (Vontobel, Jacques.) Bern, 1970.

Phil 9290.10   Leisure, how to enjoy it. (Simnett, William E.) London, 1946.

Phil 190.80.6   Leisure, the basis of culture. (Pieper, Josef.) N.Y., 1964.

Phil 9362.18.5   Leisure hours. 3d ed. (Wakefield, P. Bell (Mrs.).) London, 1798-1801. 2v.

Phil 8666.8   Leitch, A. Ethics of theism. Edinburgh, 1868.

Phil 5251.72   Leite, Dante M. Psicologia diferencial. São Paulo, 1966.

Phil 3850.13.60   Leitfaden der Entwickelung der philosophischen Prinzipien. (Schulze, G.E.) Göttingen, 1813.

Phil 6316.4   Leitfaden der experimentellen Psychopathologie. (Gregor, Adalbert.) Berlin, 1910.

Phil 5058.31   Leitfaden der Logik in psychologisierender Darstellung. 2e Aufl. (Stöhr, Adolf.) Leipzig, 1915.

Phil 8897.44   Leitfaden der Moral. 2. Aufl. (Woffny, F.) Leipzig, 1903.

Phil 5265.1   Leitfaden der physiologischen Psychologie. (Ziehen, Theodor.) Jena, 1891.

Phil 5265.1.3   Leitfaden der physiologischen Psychologie. (Ziehen, Theodor.) Jena, 1908.

Phil 5265.1.2   Leitfaden der physiologischen Psychologie. 3. Aufl. (Ziehen, Theodor.) Jena, 1896.

Phil 5265.1.4   Leitfaden der physiologischen Psychologie. 5. Aufl. (Ziehen, Theodor.) Jena, 1900.

Phil 5265.1.4.2   Leitfaden der physiologischen Psychologie. 7. Aufl. (Ziehen, Theodor.) Jena, 1906.

Phil 5265.1.4.3   Leitfaden der physiologischen Psychologie. 10. Aufl. (Ziehen, Theodor.) Jena, 1914.

Phil 5265.1.4.5   Leitfaden der physiologischen Psychologie. 12. Aufl. (Ziehen, Theodor.) Jena, 1924.

Phil 6962.10.5   Leitfaden der Psychiatrie. (Mendel, Emanuel.) Stuttgart, 1902.

Phil 5249.11   Leitfaden der Psychologie. (Jander, E.) Leipzig, 1908.

Phil 5251.8.5   Leitfaden der Psychologie. (Lipps, T.) Leipzig, 1903.

Phil 343.4.6   Die Leitgedanken einer naturwissenschaftlichen Erkenntnislehre und ire Aufnahme durch die Zeitenossen. (Mach, E.) Leipzig, 1919.

Phil 8886.22   Leith, W.C. Apologia diffidentis. London, 1908.

Phil 5251.52   Leithauser, J.C. Das unbekannte Ich. Berlin, 1955.

Phil 5627.124   Leitner, Hans. Psychologie jugendlicher Religiosität innerhalb des deutschen Methodismus. München, 1930.

Phil 5627.124.5   Leitner, Hans. Psychologie jugendlicher Religiosität innerhalb des deutschen Methodismus. Inaug. Diss. München, 1930.

Phil 4210.74   Leitsätze für Christen von Antonio Rosmini. (Rosmini-Serbati, Antonio.) Einsiedeln, 1964.

Phil 2115.51.10   Leitung des Verstandes. (Locke, J.) Heidelberg, 1883.

Phil 6111.16.5   Die Leitungsbahnen im Gehirn und Rückenmark. (Bechterew, W. von.) Leipzig, 1899.

Phil 6115.6.9   Die Leitungsbahnen im Gehirn und Rückenmark. (Flechsig, P.) Leipzig, 1876.

Phil 525.49   Lejeune, Paul. Introduction à la vie mystique. Paris, 1899.

Phil 525.49.5   Lejeune, Paul. An introduction to the mystical life. London, 1915.

Phil 5467.4   Lejins, Peter P. The concept of imitation. Part of thesis. Chicago, 1942.

Phil 530.15.5   Le Jonvello, H. Une mystique bretonne aux XVIIe siècle. Paris, 1913.

Phil 4513.8.31   Lek och allvar. (Aspelin, Gunnar.) Lund, 1968.

Phil 310.120   Lektsii po dialekticheskom materializme. (Ai, Ssu-ch'i.) Moskva, 1959.

Phil 8400.41   Lektsii po marksistsko-leninskoi estetike. (Kagan, Moisei S.) Leningrad, 1963- 3v.

Phil 8400.41.2   Lektsii po marksistsko-leninskoi estetike. Izd. 2. (Kagan, Moisei S.) Leningrad, 1971.

Phil 8980.159.5   Lektsii po marksistskoi etiki. v.1-. (Arkhangel'skii, Leonid M.) Sverdlovsk, 1969.

Phil 2020.82   Leland, A.P. Educational theory...T.H. Green. N.Y., 1911.

Phil 5761.3   Leland, C.G. Have you a strong will? London, 1899.

Phil 5761.3.2   Leland, C.G. Have you a strong will? London, 1902.

Phil 5761.3.3   Leland, C.G. Have you a strong will? London, 1903.

Phil 5761.3.10   Leland, C.G. Have you a strong will? N.Y., 1919.

Phil 5545.18   Leland, C.G. Mastery of memorizing. Harrisburg, 1890-91.

Phil 5761.3.5   Leland, C.G. The mystic will. Chicago, 1907.

Phil 5761.3.7   Leland, C.G. The mystic will. Chicago, 1907.

Phil 8520.5   Leland, J. A view of the principal deistical writers. London, 1754-56. 3v.

Htn Phil 8520.5.3*   Leland, J. A view of the principal deistical writers. London, 1757. 2v.

Phil 8520.5.2   Leland, J. A view of the principal deistical writers. London, 1954.

Phil 8520.5.3.10   Leland, J. A view of the principal deistical writers. 5. ed. London, 1766. 2v.

Phil 8520.5.4   Leland, J. A view of the principal deistical writers. 5. ed. London, 1798. 2v.

Phil 8599.4.97   Leland, John. An answer to a book intituled, Christianity as old as the creation. 2. ed. London, 1740. 2v.

Phil 8599.4.95   Leland, John. An answer to a late book intituled, Christianity as old as the creation. Dublin, 1733. 2v.

VPhil 5255.11.10   A lelektan alapelvei. (Pikler, Gyula.) Budapest, 1909.

Phil 720.16   Lelesz, H. La conception de la vérité. Thèse. Paris, 1921.

Phil 5051.26   LeLeu, Louis. La logique; l'art de penser. Paris, 1930.

Phil 4582.1.81   Leljeqvist, E. Marginalanmärkningar till Docenten Herrlins skrift "Filosofi och fackvetenskap". Göteborg, 1905.

Phil 8636.6   Le Long, Jean. Saint Athanase, ou Traité de la nature. Middelburg, 1645.

Phil 8666.19   Lelong, Michel. Pour un dialogue avec les athées. Paris, 1965.

Htn Phil 7060.6*   Le Loyer, P. Des spectres ou apparitions et visions. Angers, 1586.

Phil 7060.6.7   Le Loyer, P. Discours des spectres, ou visions. Paris, 1608.

Phil 7060.6.3   Le Loyer, P. Discours et histoires des spectres, visions et apparitions des spirits. Paris, 1605.

Htn Phil 7060.6.5*   Le Loyer, P. Treatise of specters. London, 1605.

Phil 2805.83   Lelut, L.F. L'amulette de Pascal. Paris, 1846.

Phil 6121.22.2   Lélut, L.F. Physiologie de la pensée. 2. éd. Paris, 1862. 2v.

Phil 5931.1   Lélut, L.F. Qu'est-ce que la phrénologie...Gall. Paris, 1836.

Phil 186.6   Lemaire, C. Initiation à la philosophie. Paris, 1843. 2v.

Phil 5640.26   Lemaire, J. Étude sur la connaissance sensible des objets extérieurs. Liege, 1921.

Phil 342.6   Lemaire, J. Notes complementiares sur une thèorie de la connaissance sensible. Bruges, 1923.

Phil 1850.107   Lemaire, Paul. François Bacon. Paris, 1913.

Phil 5421.25.50   Lemaire, Ton. De tederheid. Gedachten over de liefde. Utrecht, 1968.

Phil 5642.13   Lemaitre, A. Audition colorée et phénomènes connexes. Paris, 1901.

Phil 720.27   Lemaitre, C. L'amour du vrai. Louvain, 1929.

Phil 525.135   Lemaître, S. Textes mystiques d'Orient et d'Occident. Paris, 1955.

Phil 575.89   Lemarié, O. Essai sur la personne. Paris, 1936.

Phil 8886.53   Lemarie, O. La morale privée. Paris, 1932.

Phil 3493.23   Lembke, B. Immanuel Kants Geld-Theorie. Danzig, 1933.

Phil 8412.24   Lemcke, Carl von. Populäre Ästhetik. Leipzig, 1879.

Phil 2705.86   Lemée, Pierre. Offray de la Mettrie. Saint-Servan, 1925.

Phil 5465.170   Le Men, Jean. L'espace figuratif et les structures de la personnalité, une épreuve clinique originale. Paris, 1966. 2v.

Htn Phil 9510.3*   Le Mercier, A. A treatise against detraction. Boston, 1733.

Phil 1750.854   Leminizm i sovremennze problemy istoriko-filosofskoi nauki. Moskva, 1970.

Phil 8412.25   Lemke, Carl von. Populäre Ästhetik. 4. Aufl. Leipzig, 1873.

Phil 8961.18   Lemme, Ludwig. Christliche Ethik. Berlin, 1905. 2v.

Phil 9035.18   Lemmon, G.J. Eternal building, or The making of manhood. N.Y., 1899.

Phil 1540.74   Lemny, Richard. Abu Ma'shar and Lah'n Aristoteliaram. Beirut, 1962.

Phil 6961.2   Lemoine, A. L'aliéné devant la philosophie, la morale et la société. Paris, 1865.

Phil 6121.4   Lemoine, A. L'âme et le corps. Paris, 1862.

Phil 6021.3   Lemoine, A. De la physiognomie et de parole. Paris, 1865.

Phil 2733.105   LeMoine, A. Des vérités éternelles selon Malebranche. Paris, 1936.

Phil 2733.105.5   LeMoine, A. Des vérités éternelles selon Malebranche. Thèse. Marseille, 1936.

Phil 3850.2.80A   Lemoine, A. Le vitalisme et l'animisme de Stahl. Paris, 1864.

Phil 2465.81 — Lemoine, Albert. Charles Bonnet de Genève. Thèse. Paris, 1850.
Phil 7080.30 — Lemoine, Albert. Du sommeil au point de vue physiologique et psychologique. Paris, 1855.
Phil 186.7 — Lemoine, J.J. Les trois voyageurs. Paris, 1819.
Phil 5648.2 — Lemon, J.S. The skin considered as an organ of sensation. Gardner, Mass., 1896.
Phil 8701.23 — Lemonnyer, Antoine. La révélation primitive, et les données actuelles de la science. Paris, 1914.
Phil 9351.4 — Lemontey, P.E. Raison, folie. Bruxelles, 1830. 2v.
Phil 186.158 — Lemos, Ramon M. Experience, mind, and value. Leiden, 1969.
Phil 6360.6 — Lempp, Reinhart. Eine Pathologie der psychischen Entwicklung. Bern, 1967.
Phil 8630.6.4 — Le lendemain de la mort. 4e éd. (Figuier, L.) Paris, 1872.
Phil 3801.516 — Lendi-Wolff, Christian. Friedrich Wilhelm Joseph von Schelling. Bad Ragaz, 1954.
Phil 8886.54 — Lenglart, Marcel. Essai sur les conditions du progrès moral. Paris, 1934.
Phil 7060.5 — Lenglet, Dufresnoy N. Traité historique et dogmatique...apparitions. Avignon, 1751. 2v.
Phil 5520.43 — El lenguaje interior y los trastornos de la palabra. (Mouchet, Enrique.) La Plata, 1923.
Phil 6121.26 — Lenhossék, Mihaly. Der Feinere bau des Nervensystems im Lichte neuester Forschungen. Berlin, 1893.
Phil 6121.16 — Lenhossék, Mihaly. Untersuchungen über Leidenschaften und Gemüthsaffekten als Ursachen. Pesth, 1804.
Phil 3493.25 — Leni di Spadafora, F. Kant nel realismo. Paris, 1953.
Phil 3425.300 — Lenin, V.I. Cahiers sur la dialectique de Hegel. Paris, 1938.
Phil 3425.300.5 — Lenin, V.I. Hefte zu Hegels Dialektik. München, 1969.
Phil 310.794 — Lenin i niakoi problemi na marksistkata filosofiia. Sofiia, 1970.
Phil 1750.850 — Lenin kak istorik filosofii. (Protasenko, Zoia M.) Leningrad, 1969.
Phil 3425.34.32 — Lenin o nauke logiki Gegelia. (Tavadze, I.K.V.I.) Tbilisi, 1959.
Phil 8400.32 — Leningrad. Gosudarstvennyi Institut Istorii Iskusstv. Zadachi i metody izucheniia iskusstv. Peterburg, 1924.
Phil 8505.8 — Leningrad. Muzei Istorii Religii i Ateizma. Ezhegodnik. Moskva. 1,1957+ 6v.
Phil 8505.8.10 — Leningrad. Muzei Istorii Religii i Ateizma. Istoriia papstva i inkvizitsii. Moskva, 1959.
Phil 8505.8.25 — Leningrad. Muzei Istorii Religii i Ateizma. Muzei istorii religii i ateizma. Leningrad, 1965.
Phil 8505.8.15 — Leningrad. Muzei Istorii Religii i Ateizma. Nauka i religiia. Moskva, 1961.
Phil 8505.8.20 — Leningrad. Muzei Istorii Religii i Ateizma. Proiskhozhdenie religii. Moskva, 1962.
Phil 310.485 — Leningrad. Universitet. Filosofskie voprosy sovremennogo ucheniia o dvizhenii v prirode. Leningrad, 1962.
Phil 310.475 — Leningrad. Universitet. Nekotorye voprosy dialekticheskii materializma. Leningrad, 1962.
Phil 310.595 — Leningrad. Universitet. Rasprostranenie idei marksistskoi filosofii v Evrope. Leningrad, 1964.
Phil 4710.154 — Leningrad. Universitet. Filosofskii Fakul'tet. Materialy k nauchnoi sessii, posviashchennoi 50-letiiu Velikoi Oktiabr'skoi sotsialisticheskoi revoliutsii. Leningrad, 1967.
Phil 310.465 — Leningrad. Universitet. Filosofskii Fakultet. Voprosy marksistskoi sotsiologii. Leningrad, 1962.
Phil 310.772 — Leninism, filosofskie traditsii i sovremennost'. (Iovchuk, Mikhail T.) Moskva, 1970.
Phil 310.702 — Leninizm i filosofskie problemy sovremennosti. Moskva, 1970.
Phil 4710.147 — Leninizm i progressivnye traditsii russkoi obshchestvennoi mysli. (Novikov, Avraam I.) Leningrad, 1965.
Phil 310.776 — Leninizum, filosofiia, ideologicheska borba. (Iribadzhakov, Nikolai.) Sofiia, 1970.
Phil 310.654 — Leninskaia filosofiia i progress fizicheskikh nauk. (Kompaneets, Aleksei I.) Moskva, 1967.
Phil 349.90 — Leninskaia kontseptsiia poniatiia i evoliutsiia poniatiia "vid". (Sadovskyi, Grigorii I.) Minsk, 1970.
Phil 310.792 — Leninskaia kontseptsiia razvitiia. Gor'kii, 1970.
Phil 5068.29 — Leninskaia kritika malchizma i bor'ba protiv sovremennogo idealizma. (Korneeva, Anna I.) Moskva, 1971.
Phil 310.710 — Leninskaia teoriia na otrazhenieto i sovremennostta. Sofiia, 1969.
Phil 310.716 — Leninskii etap v razvitii marksistskoi filosofii; sbornik nauchnykh rabot kafedry filosofii. Dnepropetrovsk, 1969.
Phil 310.590 — Leninskii printsip ob"ektivnosti v poznanii. (Uvarov, A.I.) Tomsk, 1963.
Phil 8980.516 — Leninskoe eticheskoe nasledstvo i sovremennost. Tambov, 1971.
Phil 8980.898 — Leninskoe teoreticheskoe nasledie i nekotorye voprosy marksistskoi etiki. Moskva, 1970.
Phil 5425.94 — Lenk, Emil. Das Liebesleben des Genies. 2. Aufl. Badeburg, 1926.
Phil 5130.2 — Lenk, Hans. Kritik der logischen Konstanten. Berlin, 1968.
Phil 3850.18.160 — Lenk, Kurt. Von der Ohnmacht des Geistes. Tübingen, 1959.
Phil 6980.416 — Lennard, H.L. The anatomy of psychotherapy. N.Y., 1960.
Phil 5520.421 — Lenneberg, E.H. New directions in the study of language. Cambridge, 1964.
Phil 5592.60 — Lennep, Johanna Elisabeth van. Beleving en verbeelding in het tekenen. Amsterdam, 1958.
Phil 6536.9 — Lennox, W.G. Science and seizures. N.Y., 1941.
Phil 130.2 — Lenoël, L. Les philosophes de l'antiquité. Paris, 1864.
Phil 4011.2 — Lenoir, E. Trois novateurs. Paris, 1939.
Phil 1711.2 — Lenoir, R. Les historiens de l'esprit humain. Paris, 1926.
Phil 2493.89 — Lenoir, Raymond. Condillac. Paris, 1924.
Phil 3831.14 — Lénström, C.J. De principiis philosophiae practicae Spinozae. Gevaliae, 1843.
Phil 8430.20 — Lénström, C.J. Om konstens förhållande till religionen. Upsala, 1842.
Phil 4080.3.480 — Lentini, Giacinto. Croce e Gramsci. Palermo, 1967.
Phil 5625.101.5 — Le Ny, Jean François. Apprentissage et activités psychologiques. Paris, 1967.
Phil 5625.101 — Le Ny, Jean François. Le conditionnement. Paris, 1961.
Phil 1750.354 — Lenz, Joseph. Der moderne deutsche und französische Existentialismus. 2e Aufl. Trier, 1951.
Phil 5627.68 — Léo, A. Etude psychologique sur la prière d'après deux enquêtes américaines. Thèse. Cahors, 1905.
Phil 2530.84 — Leo, Werner. Diderot als Kunstphilosophie. Inaug.-Diss. Erlangen, 1918.

Phil 8831.12 — Leo grandes doctrines morales. (Grégoire, François.) Paris, 1958.
Phil 4060.2.82 — Leo Hebraeus, ein jüdischer Philosoph. (Zimmels, B.) Breslau, 1886.
Phil 4060.2.40 — Leo Hebraeus. Dialoghi d'amore. Bari, 1929.
Phil 4060.2.42 — Leo Hebraeus. Dialoghi d'amore. Heidelberg, 1929.
Htn Phil 4060.2.33* — Leo Hebraeus. Dialoghi di amore. Vinegia, 1552.
Phil 4060.2.55 — Leo Hebraeus. Dialogos de amor. Madrid, 1949. 2v.
Htn Phil 4060.2.35* — Leo Hebraeus. Los dialogos de amor. Venetia, 1568.
Htn Phil 4060.2.37* — Leo Hebraeus. Los dialogos de amor. Venetia, 1572.
Phil 4060.2.38 — Leo Hebraeus. Diálogos de amor. 1. ed. Romano, 1953.
Phil 4060.2.50 — Leo Hebraeus. The philosophy of love. London, 1937.
Phil 640.4 — Leo XIII and the new scholasticism. (Watzlaurk, Joseph.) Cebu City, 1966.
Phil 3831.7 — Léon, Albert. Les éléments cartésiens. Paris, 1907.
Phil 2411.7 — León, Ferdinand. Lebensquellen französischer Metaphysik. Hamburg, 1949.
Phil 811.8 — Leon, M. The comedy of human philosophy. Boston, 1932.
X Cg Phil 535.35 — Leon, Philip. Beyond belief and unbelief. London, 1965.
Phil 3246.92.5 — Léon, Xavier. Fichte et son temps. Paris, 1922-24. 2v.
Phil 3246.92 — Léon, Xavier. La philosophie de Fichte, ses rapports avec la conscience contemporaine. Paris, 1902.
Phil 2477.11.90 — Léon Brunschvicg. (Carbonara, C.) Napoli, 1930.
Phil 2477.11.94 — Léon Brunschvicg ou l'idéalisme à hauteur d'homme. (Deschoux, Marcel.) Paris, 1969.
Phil 2800.1.87 — Léon Ollé-Laprune, l'homme et le penseur. (Fonsegrive, Georges.) Paris, 1912.
Phil 2800.1.88 — Léon Ollé-Laprune. (Blondel, M.) Paris, 1923.
Phil 3425.778 — Léonard, Andre. La foi chez Hegel. Paris, 1970.
Phil 6854.2 — Leonard, Calista V. Understanding and preventing suicide. Springfield, Ill., 1967.
Phil 7069.29.5 — Leonard and Soule experiments in psychical research. (Allison, Lydia W.) Boston, 1929.
Phil 3665.5.95 — Leonard Nelson zum Gedächtnis. (Specht, Minna.) Frankfurt, 1959.
Phil 402.18 — Leonardi, Franco. Sociologia dell'ideologia. Catania, 1969.
Phil 5251.64 — Leonhard, Karl. Biologische Psychologie. Leipzig, 1962.
Phil 6021.15 — Leonhard, Karl. Der menschliche Ausdruck. Leipzig, 1968.
Phil 3525.83 — Leonhardi, Hermann. Karl C.F. Krause's Leben und Lehre. Leipzig, 1902.
Phil 3525.84 — Leonhardi, Hermann. Karl Christian Friedrich Krause als philosophischer Denker Gewürdigt. Leipzig, 1905.
Phil 6681.13 — Leonidas (pseud.). Stage hypnotism. Chicago, 1901.
Phil 4110.2.85 — Leonij, Lorenzo. Notizie della vita di Marianna Florenzi Waddington. Todi, 1865.
Phil 5520.707 — Leon'tev, Aleksei A. Iazyk, rech', rechevaia deiatel'nost'. Moskva, 1969.
Phil 5520.595 — Leont'ev, Aleksei A. Psikholingvisticheskie edinitsy v porozhdenie rechevogo vyskazyvaniia. Moskva, 1969.
Phil 5520.510 — Leont'ev, Aleksei A. Psikholingvistika. Leningrad, 1967.
Phil 5251.68 — Leont'ev, Aleksei N. Problemy razvitiia psikhiki. Moskva, 1959.
Phil 5374.239 — Leont'ev, Aleksei N. Problemy razvitiia psikhiki. 2. izd. Moskva, 1965.
Phil 3831.8 — Leopold, J.H. Ad Spinozae opera posthuma. Hagae, 1902.
Phil 3850.21.91 — Leopold Schmid's Leben und Denken. (Schroeder, B.) Leipzig, 1871.
Phil 5421.20.140 — Lepenies, Wolf. Kritik der Anthropologie. München, 1971.
Phil 9330.10 — Lepenies, Wolf. Melancholie und Gesellschaft. Thesis. Frankfurt, 1969.
Phil 5330.36 — Leplat, Jacques. Attention et incertitude dans les travaux de surveillance et d'inspection. Paris, 1968.
Phil 735.124.5 — Lepley, Ray. The language of value. N.Y., 1957.
Phil 735.124A — Lepley, Ray. Value; a cooperative inquiry. N.Y., 1949-50.
Phil 8612.52.10 — Lepp, Ignace. La mort et ses mystères. Paris, 1966.
Phil 1750.375 — Lepp, Ignace. La philosophie Chrétiennie de l'existance. Paris, 1953.
Phil 8666.22 — Lepp, Ignace. Psychoanalyse de l'atéisme moderne. Paris, 1961.
Phil 8886.79 — Lepp, Ignance. La morale nouvelle. Paris, 1963.
Phil 1750.280 — Lepp, Ignoce. Existence et existentialismes. Paris, 1947.
Phil 8591.34 — Le Prince de Beaumont, Marie. Les americaines, ou La preuve de la religion chrétienne par les lumières naturelles. 1.é. Lyon, 1770. 6v.
Phil 3585.1.90 — Lepsius, J. Johann Heinrich Lambert; eine Darstellung seiner kosmologischen und philosophischen Leistungen. München, 1881.
Phil 6990.37 — Le Quien de la Neufville, Charles Jacques. Nouvelles prennes contre le faux miracle de migne approuvé à Rome. Paris, 1828.
Phil 6990.37.5 — Le Quien de la Neufville, Charles Jacques. Vains efforts de plusieurs évêques. Paris, 1830.
Htn Phil 186.8* — Lequier, J. La recherche d'une première vérité. Saint-Cloud, 1865.
Phil 2725.13.32.1 — Lequier, Jules. La liberté. Paris, 1936.
Phil 2725.13.32 — Lequier, Jules. La liberté. Thèse. Paris, 1936.
Phil 2725.13.34 — Lequier, Jules. La recherche d'une première vérité. Paris, 1924.
Phil 9045.17 — Lequinio, J.M. Philosophie du peuple. Paris, 1796.
Phil 2530.88.2 — Lerel, A.C. Diderots Naturphilosophie. Wien, 1950.
Phil 2530.88 — Lerel, A.C. Diderots Naturphilosophie. Wien, 1950.
Phil 900.15 — Le Renard, A. L'Orient et sa tradition. Paris, 1952.
Phil 4362.2 — Leret, Carlos. La Trinidad, principio fundamental del universo. Madrid, 1938.
Phil 2411.1 — Lerminier, E. De l'influence de la philosophie du XVIIIe siècle. Paris, 1833.
Phil 5850.343 — Lerne menschen Kennen und Behandeln. (Sonnet, André.) Freiburg, 1959.
Phil 5535.4 — Lernen, Gedächtnis, Verhalten. (Foppa, Klaus.) Köln, 1965.
Phil 5811.13 — Das Lernen des Hundes. Inaug. Diss. (Baudouin, Charles.) Berlin, 1909.
Phil 5535.64 — Lernen und Erfahrung. (Buck, Günther.) Stuttgart, 1967.
Phil 5535.48 — Der Lernprozess. Anthropologie, Psychologie, Biologie des Lernens. Freiburg, 1969.
Phil 5865.5.45 — Die Lernpsychologie Jean Piagets. (Montada, Leo.) Stuttgart, 1970.
Phil 1535.38 — LeRohellec, J. Problèmes philosophiques. Paris, 1932.
Phil 1915.81 — Le Rossignol, J.E. Ethical philosophy of Samuel Clarke. Leipzig, 1894.
Phil 9351.9 — Le Roup, Hugues. Nos filles qu'en ferons-nous? 5. ed. Paris, 1898.
Phil 1811.2.5 — Leroux, E. Bibliographie méthodique du pragmatisme américain. Thèse. n.p., 1922.
Phil 1811.2.10 — Leroux, E. La philosophie anglaise classique. Paris, 1951.

Phil 1811.2   Leroux, E. Le pragmatisme américain et anglais. Paris, 1923.

Phil 1811.2.2   Leroux, E. Le pragmatisme américain et anglais. Thèse. Paris, 1922.

Phil 2496.81.2   Leroux, P. Réfutation de l'eclectisme. Paris, 1839.

Phil 2496.81   Leroux, P. Réfutation de l'eclectisme. Paris, 1841.

Phil 2672.81   Leroux, Pierre. De la mutilation d'un écrit posthume de Théodore Jouffroy. Paris, 1843.

Htn   Phil 8591.4*   Leroux, Pierre. De l'humanité. Paris, 1860. 2v.

Phil 8591.4.5   Leroux, Pierre. Du christianisme et de son origine democratique. pt.1-2. Boussac, 1848.

Phil 2050.229   Leroy, A.L. David Hume. 1. éd. Paris, 1953.

Phil 2115.197   Leroy, A.L. Locke, sa vie. Paris, 1964.

Phil 2050.193   Leroy, André. La critique et la religion chez David Hume. Paris, 1931.

Phil 2050.193.5   Leroy, André. La critique et la religion chez David Hume. Thèse. Paris, 1929.

Phil 1870.138   Leroy, André Louis. George Berkeley. Paris, 1959.

Phil 5821.1.5   Leroy, Charles Georges. Lettres philosophiques sur l'intelligence et la perfectibilité des animaux. Paris, 1802.

Phil 5821.1.10   Leroy, Charles Georges. Lettres sur les animaux. Nuremberg, 1781.

Phil 5821.1   Leroy, Charles Georges. Lettres sur les animaux. Paris, 1862.

Phil 2475.1.115   LeRoy, E. The new philosophy of Henri Berguson. N.Y., 1913.

Phil 2475.1.113   LeRoy, E. Une philosophie nouvelle Henri Bergson. Paris, 1912.

Phil 5627.75   Leroy, E.B. Interprétation psychologique des visions intellectuelles. Paris, 1907.

Phil 5520.17   Leroy, E.B. Le langage. Paris, 1905.

Phil 2725.30.30   LeRoy, Edouard. Essai d'une philosophie première. Paris, 1956- 2v.

Phil 365.27   LeRoy, Edouard. L'exigence idéaliste et le fait de l'évolution. Paris, 1927.

Phil 365.27.5   LeRoy, Edouard. Les origines humaines et l'évolution de l'intelligence. Paris, 1928.

Phil 186.70   LeRoy, Edouard. La pensée intuitive. Paris, 1929.

Phil 8666.11   Le Roy, Edouard. Le problème de Dieu. Paris, 1930.

Phil 5545.72   Leroy, Eugène B. Etude sur l'illusion de fausse reconnaissance. Paris, 1898.

Phil 3552.98   Leroy, G.V. Die philosophische Probleme...Leibniz und Clarke. Mainz, 1893.

Phil 2730.96   LeRoy, Georges. L'expérience de l'effort et de la grace chez Maine de Biran. Paris, 1937.

Phil 2730.96.5   LeRoy, Georges. L'expérience de l'effort et de la grace chez Maine de Biran. Thèse. Paris, 1937.

Phil 2805.330   LeRoy, Georges. Pascal. 1. éd. Paris, 1957.

Phil 2493.92   LeRoy, Georges. La psychologie de Condillac. Paris, 1937.

Phil 2493.92.5   LeRoy, Georges. La psychologie de Condillac. Thèse. Paris, 1937.

Phil 2520.174   Leroy, Maxime. Descartes le philosophie au masque. Paris, 1929. 2v.

Phil 2520.174.5   Leroy, Maxime. Descartes social. Paris, 1931.

Phil 7069.28.50   Leroy, O. La lévitation. Paris, 1928.

Phil 5401.28   Leroy, Paul. Angst und Lachen. Wien, 1954.

Phil 2905.1.90   Leroy, Pierre. Pierre Teilhard de Chardin tel que je l'ai connu. Paris, 1958.

Phil 7055.173   Leroy, Roger. Un voyant au XXe siècle: Dieudonné. Paris, 1965.

Phil 5590.95.6   Lersch, Philipp. Aufbau der Person. 6. Aufl. München, 1954.

Phil 5590.95.7   Lersch, Philipp. Aufbau der Person. 7. Aufl. München, 1956.

Phil 5590.95.9   Lersch, Philipp. Aufbau der Person. 9. Aufl. München, 1964.

Phil 5590.95   Lersch, Philipp. Der Aufbau des Charakters. Leipzig, 1938.

Phil 5590.95.3   Lersch, Philipp. Der Aufbau des Charakters. 3. Aufl. Leipzig, 1948.

Phil 585.320   Lersch, Philipp. Der Mensch als Schnittpunkt. München, 1969.

Phil 6321.46   Lertora, A.C. Re-fundamentacion de la psiquiatria. Buenos Aires, 1963.

Phil 5252.153   Les compléments amodaux des structures perceptives. (Michotte, A.E.) Louvain, 1964.

Phil 2805.33   Les provinciales. (Pascal, Blaise.) Berlin, 1878.

Phil 6135.8   Les théories des milieux et la pédagogie mesologique. (Zaniewski, R.) Tournai, 1952.

Phil 3831.6   Lesbazeilles, P. De logica Spinozae. Paris, 1883.

Phil 1750.16   Leschbrand, A. Substanzbegriff in der neueren Philosophie. Rostock, 1895.

Phil 9245.29   Lescoeur, Louis. La science du bonheur. Paris, 1873.

Phil 8636.5.5   Lescoeur, Louis. A vida futura; conferencias. Lisboa, 1877.

Phil 5520.320   Lesen und Benennen in Reaktionsversuch. (Pfeil, Alfred.) Frankfurt, 1959.

Phil 186.56   Le Senne, R. Introduction à la philosophie. Paris, 1925.

Phil 186.56.5   Le Senne, R. Introduction à la philosophie. Paris, 1939.

Phil 186.56.10   Le Senne, R. Obstacle et valeur. Paris, 1934.

Phil 9120.162   Le Senne, René. Le devoir. Paris, 1930.

Phil 2725.25.20   LeSenne, René. LeSenne ou le Combat pour la spiritualisation. Paris, 1968.

Phil 9558.15   Le Senne, René. Le mensonge et la caractère. Paris, 1930.

Phil 9558.15.2   Le Senne, René. Le mensonge et la caractère. Thèse. Paris, 1930.

Phil 8886.64   Le Senne, René. Traité de morale générale. 1. ed. Paris, 1942.

Phil 2725.25.20   LeSenne ou le Combat pour la spiritualisation. (LeSenne, René.) Paris, 1968.

Phil 342.7   Leser, Hermann. Einfuhrung in die Grundprobleme der Erkenntnistheorie. Leipzig, 1911.

Phil 600.62   Lesevich, Vladimir V. Opyt kriticheskago izsledovaniia osnovonachal pozitivnoi filosofii. Sanktpeterburg, 1877. 2 pam.

X Cg   Phil 8666.4*   Leslie, Charles. A short and easie method with the deists. 8. ed. v.1-3. London, 1723.

Phil 7054.181.15   Leslie, John. Nature and super-nature. Aberdeen, 1820.

Phil 8701.10   Leslie, John. Revelation and science. Aberdeen, 1921.

Phil 1811.3.5   Les logiciens anglais contemporains. 5e éd. (Liard, Louis. Les logiciens anglais contemporains.'57 1811.3.5 44's.) Paris, 1907.

Phil 8412.17   Lesparre, A. de G. Essai sur le sentiment esthétique. Paris, 1921.

Phil 8735.17   Lesparre, A. de G. L'idée de finalité. Paris, 1916.

X Cg   Phil 8961.1   Less, G. Kompendium der theologischen Moral. Göttingen, 1767.

Phil 7150.33   Less, G. Vom Selbstmorde. Göttingen, 1786.

Phil 8666.2   Lesser, F.C. Testaceo-Theologia. Leipzig, 1756.

Phil 8666.2.5   Lesser, F.C. Theologie des insects. La Hague, 1742.

Htn   Phil 3585.3.30*   Lessing, G.E. Zur Geschichte und Literatur. Braunschweig, 1777.

Phil 186.52   Lessing, T. Philosophie als Tat. Göttingen, 1914.

Phil 3850.5.95   Lessing, Theodor. African Spir's Erkenntnislehre. Inaug. Diss. Giessen, 1900.

Phil 3585.14.10   Lessing, Theodor. Gesammelte Schriften in zehn Bäuden. Prag, 1935.

Phil 3640.220   Lessing, Theodor. Nietzsche. Berlin, 1925.

Phil 3808.179   Lessing, Theodor. Schopenhauer, Wagner, Nietzsche. München, 1906.

Phil 735.14   Lessing, Theodor. Studien zur Wertaxiomatik. 2e Ausg. Leipzig, 1914.

Phil 3585.14.5   Lessing, Theodor. Die verfluchte Kultur. München, 1921.

Phil 5247.13.33   Lessings Huarte-Übersetzung, 1752. (Franzbach, Martin.) Hamburg, 1965.

Htn   Phil 8591.17.8*   Lessius, Leonardus. Sir Walter Rawleigh's ghost. London, 1651.

Phil 8836.4   Lessona, Marco. La storia della filosofia morale; studio. Torino, 1888.

Phil 8886.33   Lessona, Marco. L'utilità e il senso morale. Torino, 1886.

Phil 7069.33.50   Lessons in etheric and electric vibratory law. (Wells, Helen B.) N.Y., 1933. 6 pam.

Phil 8897.10   Lessons in ethics. pt.1. (Wells, K.G.) Boston, 1882.

Phil 8882.18.5   Lessons in life. (Holland, J.G.) N.Y., 1861.

Phil 5059.12   Lessons in logic. (Turner, W.) Washington, 1911.

Phil 5247.36   Lessons in psychology. (Hannahs, E.H.) Albany, 1908.

Phil 1535.30   Lessons in scholastic philosophy. (Shallo, Michael.) Philadelphia, 1916.

Phil 6674.7   Lessons in the mechanics of personal magnetism. (Edgerley, W.J.) Washington, D.C., 1888.

Phil 8886.7   Lessons on the subject of right and wrong. Boston, 1864.

Phil 7140.125   Lestchinski, A. Essai médico-psychologique sur l'autosuggestion. Neuchâtel, 1924.

Phil 8587.32.91   Lester-Garland, L.V. The religious philosophy of Baron F. von Hügel. N.Y., 1933.

Phil 2905.1.69.1   Let me explain. (Teilhard de Chardin, Pierre.) London, 1970.

Phil 2255.1.36   Let the people think. 2nd ed. (Russell, Bertrand Russell.) London, 1961.

Phil 7074.20.6   Let us in. (Burke, Jane R.) N.Y., 1931.

Phil 7074.20.5   Let us in. 1st ed. (Burke, Jane R.) N.Y., 1931.

Phil 9070.1   Let us talk about you. (Lappin, M.M.) N.Y., 1940.

Phil 6961.3.2   Letchworth, W.P. The insane in foreign countries. N.Y., 1889.

Phil 2750.13.100   Lê Thanh Tri. L'idée de la participation chez Gabriel Marcel. Fribourg? 1959.

Phil 7069.67.10   Lethbridge, Thomas. A step in the dark. London, 1967.

Phil 7162.265   Lethbridge, Thomas C. E.S.P.; beyond time and distance. London, 1965.

Phil 3493.26   Letocart, M. La morale Kantienne. Bruxelles, 1954.

Phil 5625.75.115   Letopis' zhizni i deiatel'nosti akademika I.P. Pavlova. Leningrad, 1969.

Phil 8886.8.2   Letourneau, C. L'évolution de la morale. Paris, 1887.

Phil 8886.8   Letourneau, C. L'évolution de la morale. Paris, 1894.

Phil 5400.6.3   Letourneau, C. Physiologie des passions. Paris, 1868.

Phil 5400.6.2   Letourneau, C. Physiologie des passions. 2. éd. Paris, 1878.

Phil 8599.40   Le Trocquer, René. Homme, qui suis-je? Paris, 1957.

Phil 9035.58   Let's be normal! (Künkel, Fritz.) N.Y., 1929.

Phil 5643.44   Letter, word, and mind blindness. (Hinshelwood, J.) London, 1900.

Htn   Phil 177.15*   Letter...concerning natural experimental philosophy. (Casaubon, M.) Cambridge, 1669.

Phil 5922.4.15   Letter...Francis Jeffrey. (Combe, George.) Edinburgh, 1826-29. 2 pam.

Phil 9230.7   Letter...to Lieutenant General B. Tarleton. (Venault de charmilly.) London, 1810.

Phil 8882.10.15   Letter. (Hildreth, R.) Boston, 1844.

Htn   Phil 2262.76*   Letter concerning enthusiasm. (Shaftesbury, A.A.C.) London, 1708-09. 4 pam.

Phil 2262.59A   Letter concerning enthusiasm. (Shaftesbury, A.A.C.) Paris, 1930.

Htn   Phil 2115.70*   Letter concerning toleration. (Locke, J.) London, 1689.

Phil 2115.70.20   A letter concerning toleration. (Locke, J.) The Hague, 1963.

Phil 2050.77.25   A letter from a gentleman to his friend in Edinburgh (1745). Facsimile. (Hume, David.) Edinburgh, 1967.

Phil 8581.14.5   A letter in answer to a book...entitled Christianity not mysterious. (Browne, Peter.) London, 1697.

Phil 5627.106   A letter of a friend. Chicago, 1928.

Phil 9351.11   A letter of advice to a young gentleman. (Lingard, R.) N.Y., 1907.

Phil 9167.1   A letter of advice to his grandchildren. (Hale, M.) Boston, 1817.

Phil 8595.15.50   Letter of Thomas Paine to lawyer Erskine. (Paine, Thomas.) n.p., 18- .

Phil 665.13   A letter on praeexistence to Richard Baxter. (Glanvill, Joseph.) Osceola, 1890.

Phil 8581.18   A letter to a deist. (Balguy, J.) London, 1730-38. 7 pam.

Phil 9490.6   Letter to an undergraduate. (Forbes, W.C.) n.p., 1904.

Phil 9070.21   Letter to Andrew. (Landau, Rom.) London, 1943.

Phil 6668.1   Pamphlet vol. Letter to Brigham on animal magnetism. 7 pam.

Phil 2128.61   A letter to Dion. (Mandeville, B.) Liverpool, 1954.

Htn   Phil 1870.81*   A letter to Dion Bp. Berkeley on Alciphron. (Mandeville, B.) London, 1732.

Htn   Phil 1915.70*   Letter to Dodwell. (Clarke, Samuel.) London, 1708-13. 9 pam.

Phil 6688.5   Letter to Dr. Brigham on animal magnetism. (Stone, W.L.) N.Y., 1837.

Phil 5062.6.55   A letter to Dr. Whately. (Smart, B.H.) London, 1852.

Htn   Phil 2115.73*   A letter to Edward, Lord Bishop of Worcester. (Locke, J.) London, 1697.

Phil 9070.18   A letter to my son. By a solider's mother. 1st ed. N.Y., 1942.

Htn   Phil 8657.11*   A letter to the Rev. A. Cumming attempting to show him that it is not blasphemy to say, no man can love God. (Croswell, A.) Boston, 1831. 2 pam.

Phil 4115.98   Una lettera inedita a Taparelli d'Azeglio. (Gioberti, V.) Roma, 1923.

Phil 2725.2.95   Lettera intorno alle dottrine filosofiche e politiche del sig. di Lamennais. (Gioberti, V.) Lucca, 1845. 2 pam.

Phil 2725.2.95.2 — Lettera intorno alle dottrine filosofiche e religiose del sig. di Lamennais. (Gioberti, V.) Milano, 1971.
Phil 2115.70.16 — Lettera sulla tolleranza. (Locke, J.) Firenze, 1961.
Phil 4160.41.35 — Letteratura, arte, filosofia. (Librizzi, Carmelo.) Padova, 1969.
Phil 7069.30.2.15 — Letteratura d'Oltretomba. (Bozzano, Ernesto.) Città della Pieve, 1930.
Phil 4210.62 — Letteratura e arti belle. pt.1-2. (Rosmini-Serbati, Antonio.) Intra, 1870-73.
Phil 4080.3.255 — Letterature Moderne. Benedetto Croce. Milano, 1953.
Phil 4073.75 — Lettere. (Campanella, Tommaso.) Bari, 1927.
Phil 4200.5.30 — Lettere. (Pusci, F.) Firenze, 1955. 2v.
Phil 3819.77 — Lettere. (Spinoza, Benedictus de.) Lanciano, 1938. 2v.
Phil 4225.8.68 — Lettere dalla campagna, e scritti affini. 2. ed. (Sciacca, Michele Federico.) Milano, 1966.
Phil 4114.75 — Lettere familiari. (Genovesi, Antonio.) Venezia, 1844. 2v.
Phil 4112.40 — Lettere filosofiche. (Galluppi, Pasquale.) Firenze, 1833.
Phil 4112.39.5 — Lettere filosofiche. (Galluppi, Pasquale.) Firenze, 1842.
Htn Phil 4112.39* — Lettere filosofiche. (Galluppi, Pasquale.) Messina, 1827.
Phil 4112.40.2 — Lettere filosofiche. (Galluppi, Pasquale.) Napoli, 1838.
Phil 4114.50 — Lettere filosofiche. (Genovesi, Antonio.) Napoli, 1785.
Phil 4112.40.6 — Lettere filosofiche. 2a ed. (Galluppi, Pasquale.) Firenze, 1925.
Phil 4112.40.7 — Lettere filosofiche e lezioni di logica e metafisica. (Galluppi, Pasquale.) Torino, 1925?
Phil 4115.76 — Lettere inedite di V. Gioberti e P. Galluppi. (Gioberti, V.) Roma, 1920.
Phil 4170.9.30 — Lettere inedito di S. Mancino a V. Coasin. (Mancino, Salvatore.) Palermo, 1936.
Phil 4210.93 — Lettere intorno al nuovo paggio sull'origine delle idea dell'ab. A. Rosmini-Serbati. Modena, 1843. 2 pam.
Phil 2130.40 — Letters, lectures and reviews. (Mansel, H.L.) London, 1873.
Phil 5240.3.2 — Letters...laws of man's nature. (Atkinson, H.G.) Boston, 1851.
Phil 5240.3 — Letters...laws of man's nature. (Atkinson H.G.) London, 1851.
Phil 5241.1 — Letters...philosophy...human mind. (Bailey, S.) London, 1855.
Phil 5241.1.2 — Letters...philosophy...human mind. (Bailey, S.) London, 1858.
Phil 2050.76 — Letters. (Hume, David.) Edinburgh, 1841.
Phil 2050.75 — Letters. (Hume, David.) Oxford, 1888.
Phil 2050.77.15 — Letters. (Hume, David.) Oxford, 1932. 2v.
Phil 8663.3.75 — Letters. (Ingersoll, Robert G.) N.Y., 1951.
Phil 2070.75A — Letters. (James, William.) Boston, 1920. 2v.
Phil 2250.25 — Letters. (Royce, Josiah.) Chicago, 1970.
Phil 2262.75 — Letters. (Shaftesbury, A.A.C.) London, 1750.
Phil 197.12.5A — Letters. (Wright, C.) Cambridge, 1877.
Phil 6315.2.67 — Letters. 1st. ed. (Freud, Sigmund.) N.Y., 1960.
Htn Phil 6682.3.12* — Letters à M. Vicq-d'Azyr. (Mesmer, F.A.) Bruxelles, 1784.
Phil 5255.3 — Letters concerning mind. (Petvin, J.) London, 1750.
Phil 8403.6 — Letters concerning taste. 3. ed. (Cooper, John G.) London, 1757.
Phil 8403.6.4 — Letters concerning taste. 4th ed. (Cooper, John.) London, 1771.
Htn Phil 2115.70.5* — Letters concerning toleration. (Locke, J.) London, 1765.
Phil 6687.9 — Letters d'un magnétiseur. (Ricard, J.J.A.) Paris, 1843.
Phil 9359.3 — Letters from a father to a son. (Thurston, D.) Portland, 1858.
Phil 9340.1 — Letters from a father to his son. (Aikin, J.) London, 1794-1800. 2v.
Htn Phil 9340.1.2* — Letters from a father to his son. (Aikin, J.) Philadelphia, 1794.
Htn Phil 9340.1.5* — Letters from a father to his son. (Aikin, J.) Philadelphia, 1796.
Phil 9528.2 — Letters from a father to his son in college. (Miller, S.) Philadelphia, 1852.
Phil 7069.18.10 — Letters from a living dead man. (Barker, Elsa.) N.Y., 1918.
X Cg Phil 9358.1 — Letters from a mother...daughter. (Sargent, J.A.) Boston, n.d.
Phil 2905.1.30 — Letters from a traveler. (Teilhard de Chardin, Pierre.) London, 1962.
Htn Phil 9351.8*A — Letters from an elder to a younger brother. Boston, 1810.
Phil 2905.1.60 — Letters from Egypt. (Teilhard de Chardin, Pierre.) N.Y., 1965.
Phil 7069.30 — Letters from eternity. (Behr, Hermann.) N.Y., 1930.
Phil 7069.17.50 — Letters from Harry and Helen. (White, Mary Blount.) N.Y., 1917.
Phil 6322.45 — Letters from Jenny. (Masterson, Jenny Gove.) N.Y., 1965.
Phil 3925.16.135 — Letters from Ludwig Wittgenstein with a memoir. (Engelmann, Paul.) Oxford, 1967.
Phil 978.40 — Letters from the teacher. (Curtiss, F.H.) Denver, 1909?
Phil 7069.17.40 — The letters of a woman who wa. (Robertson, Helen F.) Minneapolis, 1917.
Phil 2050.80.9A — Letters of eminent persons to Hume. (Burton, J.H.) Edinburgh, 1849.
Phil 2138.76A — Letters of John Stuart Mill. (Mill, John S.) London, 1910. 2v.
Phil 6315.2.26.6 — The letters of Sigmund Freud and Arnold Zweig. (Freud, Sigmund.) London, 1970.
Phil 6315.2.26.5 — The letters of Sigmund Freud and Arnold Zweig. (Freud, Sigmund.) N.Y., 1970.
Phil 2070.75.3A — The letters of William James. (James, William.) Boston, 1920. 2v.
Phil 2070.75.5 — The letters of William James. v.1-2. (James, William.) Boston, 1926.
Phil 2070.75.15 — The letters of William James and Théodore Flournoy. (James, William.) Madison, 1966.
Phil 9342.9 — Letters on female character. (Cary, V. (Mrs.).) Richmond, 1830.
Phil 8888.5 — Letters on life. (Nicoll, W.R.) N.Y., 1901.
Phil 5058.28.15 — Letters on logic, to a young man. (Smith, Henry B.) Philadelphia, 1920.
Phil 6682.2 — Letters on mesmerism. (Martineau, H.) N.Y., 1845.
Phil 978.74.25 — Letters on occult meditation. 2d ed. (Bailey, A.A. (Mrs.).) N.Y., 1926.
Phil 8893.20 — Letters on practical subjects. (Sprague, W.B.) Hartford, 1822.
Phil 8590.10.7 — Letters on the greatness and simplicity of the Christian faith. (King, Henry C.) Boston, 1906.
Phil 8581.4 — Letters on the grounds and objects of religious knowledge. (Beard, J.R.) London, 1856. 2v.
Phil 9342.2.12 — Letters on the improvement of the mind. (Chapone, H. (Mrs.).) Boston, 1809.

Phil 9342.2.9 — Letters on the improvement of the mind. (Chapone, H. (Mrs.).) London, 1815.
Phil 9342.2.10 — Letters on the improvement of the mind. (Chapone, H. (Mrs.).) London, 1819.
Phil 9342.2.4 — Letters on the improvement of the mind. (Chapone, H. (Mrs.).) London, 1822.
Phil 9342.2 — Letters on the improvement of the mind. (Chapone, H. (Mrs.).) London, 1830.
Phil 9342.2.8 — Letters on the improvement of the mind. (Chapone, H. (Mrs.).) N.Y., 1827.
Htn Phil 9342.2.7* — Letters on the improvement of the mind. (Chapone, H. (Mrs.).) Philadelphia, 1786.
X Cg Phil 9342.2.6 — Letters on the improvement of the mind. (Chapone, H. (Mrs.).) Philadelphia, 1816.
Htn Phil 9342.2.11* — Letters on the improvement of the mind. (Chapone, H. (Mrs.).) Portland, 17- ?
Htn Phil 9342.2.3* — Letters on the improvement of the mind. v.1-2. (Chapone, H. (Mrs.).) Hagerstown, 1819.
Htn Phil 9342.2.2* — Letters on the improvement of the mind. v.1-2. (Chapone, H. (Mrs.).) N.Y., 1793.
Phil 9342.2.5 — Letters on the improvement of the mind. 2. ed. (Chapone, H. (Mrs.).) London, 1773. 2v.
Phil 9171.2.3 — Letters on the moral and religious duties of parents. Boston, 1844.
Phil 9171.2 — Letters on the moral and religious duties of parents. Boston, 1860.
Phil 978.7.5 — Letters that have helped me. (Judge, W.Z.) N.Y., 1891.
Phil 978.7.9 — Letters that have helped me. 4th ed. (Judge, W.Z.) N.Y., 1891.
Phil 6676.5 — Letters to a candid inquirer on animal magnetism. (Gregary, William.) London, 1851.
Phil 8634.4 — Letters to a missionary. (Johnston, R.F.) London, 1918.
Phil 9171.3 — Letters to a mother. Boston, 1831.
Phil 6312.5 — Letters to a neurologist. 2nd series. (Collins, J.) N.Y., 1910.
Phil 9341.7.5 — Letters to a young lady. (Bennett, J.) London, 1803. 2v.
Phil 9341.7 — Letters to a young lady. (Bennett, J.) Philadelphia, 1818.
Htn Phil 9362.2* — Letters to a young lady. (West, J. (Mrs.).) N.Y., 1806.
Htn Phil 9362.2.2* — Letters to a young man. (West, J. (Mrs.).) Charlestown, 1803.
Phil 2648.43.10 — Letters to Eugenia. (Holbach, Paul Henri T.) Boston, 1870.
Phil 3819.63 — Letters to friend and foe. (Spinoza, Benedictus de.) N.Y., 1966.
Phil 2225.5.27 — Letters to Lady Welby. Photoreproduction. (Peirce, C.S.) New Haven, 1953.
Phil 2905.1.29.5 — Letters to Léontine Zanta. (Teilhard de Chardin, Pierre.) London, 1969.
Phil 9178.2.2 — Letters to mothers. (Sigourney, L.H.) Hartford, 1838.
Phil 9178.2 — Letters to mothers. (Sigourney, L.H.) N.Y., 1839.
Phil 1915.70.5 — Letters to Mr. Dodwell. (Clarke, Samuel.) London, 1731.
Phil 2255.7.20 — Letters to my God. (Runes, Dagobert D.) N.Y., 1958.
Phil 2255.7 — Letters to my son. (Runes, Dagobert D.) N.Y., 1949.
Phil 2255.7.3 — Letters to my teacher. (Runes, Dagobert D.) N.Y., 1961.
Htn Phil 2295.24* — Letters to Serena. (Toland, John.) London, 1704.
Phil 8882.18.9 — Letters to the Joneses. (Holland, J.G.) N.Y., 1863.
Phil 2905.1.28 — Letters to two friends, 1926-1952. (Teilhard de Chardin, Pierre.) N.Y., 1968.
Phil 9351.15 — Letters to young ladies on their entrance into the world. (Lanfear, (Mrs.).) London, 1824.
Phil 9358.8.2 — Letters to young men. 2d ed. (Sprague, W.B.) Albany, 1845.
Phil 6687.8 — Lettre à la société exegétique...magnétisme animal. (Rosenmüller, J.G.) Leipzig, 1788.
Phil 6673.2.15 — Lettre à l'auteur d'un ouvrage intitulé: superstitions et prestiges des philosophies du dix-huitième siècle. (Deleuze, J.P.F.) Paris, 1818.
Htn Phil 6682.3.14* — Lettre à M. le comte de C. (Mesmer, F.A.) Paris? 1784.
Phil 2403.1.50 — Lettre à M.P. Damiron sur un article de son essai sur l'histoire de la philosophie en France au dix-neuvième siècle. (Massias, N.) Paris, 1828.
Phil 6671.23 — Lettre de M.L.B.D.B....sur l'existence du magnétisme animal. (Bormes, Baron de.) Genève, 1784.
Phil 2805.402 — Lettre de Mr. l'abbé...à Eudoxe. (Daniel, Gabriel.) Cologne, 1698-99.
Phil 3838.29 — Lettre d'un ami du sens commun à un Hollandois. (Delouit.) Utrecht, 1809.
Htn Phil 6671.24* — Lettre d'un médicin. (Bergasse, N.) Bordeaux, 1784.
Phil 2520.204 — Lettre d'un philosophie à un cartesien de ses amis. (Rochon, Antoine.) Paris, 1672.
Htn Phil 2915.74* — Lettre philosophique. (Voltaire, F.M.A. de.) Berlin, 1774.
Htn Phil 6669.4* — Lettre sur la découverte du magnetisme. (Hervier, C.) Pekin, 1784.
Phil 2115.70.25 — Lettre sur la tolérance. 1. éd. (Locke, J.) Montréal, 1964.
Htn Phil 6682.13* — Lettre sur le magnétisme animal. (Montjore, C.F.L.) Philadelphia, 1784.
Htn Phil 2530.35* — Lettre sur les aveugles. (Diderot, Denis.) Londres, 1749.
Phil 2855.9.35 — Lettre sur les chimpanzés. (Rosset, Clément.) Paris, 1966.
Htn Phil 2530.40* — Lettre sur les sourds et muets. (Diderot, Denis.) n.p., 1751.
Phil 3450.12.100 — Lettre sur l'homme et ses rapports. (Hemsterhuis, F.) New Haven, 1964.
Phil 1750.166.30.5 — Lettre sur l'humanisme. (Heidegger, Martin.) Paris, 1957.
Phil 9358.9 — Lettres à Claude. (Saint-Jacques, F.) Québec, 1916.
Phil 2490.78 — Lettres à des positivistes anglais. (Comte, Auguste.) London 1889. 2v.
Phil 3850.1.102 — Lettres à Gambetta...sur le dernier ouvrage de Strauss. (Plasman, L.C. de.) Paris, 1877.
Phil 2905.1.29 — Lettres à Léontine Zanta. (Teilhard de Chardin, Pierre.) Bruges, 1965.
Phil 176.111 — Lettres à Mélisande. (Benda, Julien.) Paris, 1926.
Phil 9070.119 — Lettres à mes fils. 5. éd. (Onimus, Jean.) Paris, 1965.
Htn Phil 6682.3.11* — Lettres à messieure les auteurs du journal de Paris et à M. Franklin. (Mesmer, F.A.) n.p., 1784.
Phil 3640.76.16 — Lettres à Peter Gast. (Nietzsche, Friedrich.) Monaco, 1958. 2v.
Phil 2490.78.10 — Lettres à Richard Congreve. (Comte, Auguste.) London, 1889.
Phil 3484.19 — Lettres à Sergio Solmi sur la philosophie de Kant. (Chartier, Emile.) Paris, 1946.
Phil 817.14.5 — Lettres à Zoé sur l'histoire des philosophies. (Reinach, S.) Paris, 1926. 3v.

Phil 2490.72   Lettres d'Auguste Comte à divers. v.1-2. (Comte, Auguste.) Paris, 1902-05. 3v.

Phil 2490.74   Lettres d'Auguste Comte à J.S. Mill. (Comte, Auguste.) Paris, 1877.

Phil 2490.73   Lettres d'Auguste Comte à M. Valat. (Comte, Aguste.) Paris, 1870.

Phil 2805.32.30   Les lettres de Blaise Pascal. (Pascal, Blaise.) Paris, 1922.

Phil 2520.76.55   Lettres de Descartes. (Descartes, René.) Paris, 1724-25. 6v.

Phil 3552.78.50   Lettres de Leibniz à Arnauld. 1. éd. (Leibniz, Gottfried Wilhelm.) Paris, 1952.

Phil 2750.8.50   Lettres de Mr. de Maupertuis. (Maupertuis, P.L.M. de.) Dresden, 1752.

Phil 2905.1.55   Lettres d'Egypte, 1905-1908. (Teilhard de Chardin, Pierre.) Paris, 1963.

Phil 2905.1.73   Lettres d'Hastings et de Paris, 1908-1914. (Teilhard de Chardin, Pierre.) Paris, 1965.

Phil 2805.30.6   Lettres écrites à un provincial. (Pascal, Blaise.) Paris, 1842.

Phil 2805.30.5   Lettres écrites à un provincial. (Pascal, Blaise.) Paris, 1885-86. 2v.

Phil 9420.10   Lettres et discours sur les passions. (Siegfried, R.) Paris, 1925.

Phil 3552.78.30   Lettres et fragments inédits sur les problèmes philosophiques. (Leibniz, Gottfried Wilhelm.) Paris, 1934.

Phil 3552.19.5   Lettres et opuscules inédits. (Leibniz, Gottfried Wilhelm.) Paris, 1854.

Htn   Phil 6682.3.13*   Lettres guéri. (Mesmer, F.A.) London, 1784.

Phil 3090.62   Lettres inédites. (Baader, Franz von.) Paris, 1942-51. 4v.

Phil 2115.76   Lettres inédites. (Locke, J.) La Haye, 1912.

Phil 2138.75   Lettres inédites. (Mill, John S.) Paris, 1899.

Phil 2490.76.15   Lettres inédites à C. de Blignières. (Comte, Auguste.) Paris, 1932.

Phil 3850.5.100   Lettres inédites au professeur. (Spir, Afrikan.) Neuchâtel, 1948.

Phil 3090.61   Lettres inédites de Franz von Baader. Thèse. (Baader, Franz von.) Paris, 1942.

Phil 3819.71   Lettres inédites en français. (Spinoza, Benedictus de.) Paris, 1884.

Htn   Phil 2520.76.3*   Lettres ou sont traitées les plusieurs belles questions de la morale. (Descartes, René.) Paris, 1657.

Htn   Phil 2520.76*   Lettres ou sont traitées les plusieurs belles questions touchant la morale. (Descartes, René.) Paris, 1663. 2v.

Htn   Phil 2520.76.5*   Lettres ou sont traitées les plusieurs belles questions touchant la morale. v.1-3. (Descartes, René.) Paris, 1666-67.

Phil 2477.6.40   Lettres philosophiques. (Blondel, Maurice.) Paris, 1961.

Phil 4112.41   Lettres philosophiques. (Galluppi, Pasquale.) Paris, 1844.

Htn   Phil 2295.65*   Lettres philosophiques. (Toland, John.) London, 1768.

Phil 2915.75   Lettres philosophiques. (Voltaire, F.M.A. de.) Paris, 1909. 2v.

Phil 2915.75.2   Lettres philosophiques. (Voltaire, F.M.A. de.) Paris, 1918.

Phil 6025.2   Lettres philosophiques sur les physionomies. (Pernetti, J.) La Haie, 1746.

Phil 5821.1.5   Lettres philosophiques sur l'intelligence et la perfectibilité des animaux. (Leroy, Charles Georges.) Paris, 1802.

Phil 6673.10   Lettres physiologiques...sur le magnétisme. (Dupau, Jean A.) Paris, 1826.

Phil 292.1   Lettres physiques et morales sur l'histoire...terre. (Luc, J.A. de.) Paris, 1779. 6v.

Phil 2805.32.25   Les lettres provinciales. (Pascal, Blaise.) Manchester, 1920.

Phil 2477.6.89   Lettres reçues à propos de la communication de M. Blondel. (Castelli, Enrico.) Marseille, 1933.

Phil 2520.76.65   Lettres sur la morale. (Descartes, René.) Paris, 1935.

Phil 2515.5.97   Lettres sur la philosophie première. 1. éd. (Chartier, Emile.) Paris, 1955.

Htn   Phil 6668.4*   Lettres sur le magnetis. n.p., 178-. 3 pam.

Phil 6677.16   Lettres sur le magnétisme animal. (Holsbéek, H. von.) Bruxelles, 1863.

Phil 600.13   Lettres sur le positivisme. (Lagarrigue, J.) Vincennes, 1886.

Phil 2262.55   Lettres sur l'enthousiasme de milord Shaftesbury. (Shaftesbury, A.A.C.) London, 1761.

Phil 5821.1.10   Lettres sur les animaux. (Leroy, Charles Georges.) Nuremberg, 1781.

Phil 5821.1   Lettres sur les animaux. (Leroy, Charles Georges.) Paris, 1862.

Phil 1705.8   Letture su la storia della filosofia moderna. (Franchi, Ausonio.) Milano, 1863. 2v.

Phil 5425.36   Letzte Wahrheiten. (Bleibtreu, K.) Leipzig, 1894.

Phil 8643.40   Die letzte Zeit. (Staudinger, Josef.) Innsbruck, 1955.

Phil 2050.185   Die letzten Fundamente der Hume'schen Erkenntnistheorie. (Radakovic, K.) Graz, 1925.

Phil 3480.100   Die letzten Gedanken. (Kant, Immanuel.) Hamburg, 1902.

Phil 3492.2.10   Die letzten Gendanken Immanuel Kants. (Krause, A.) Hamburg, 1902.

Phil 2070.114   Leuba, J.H. The immediate apprehension of God according to William James and W.E. Hocking. n.p., 1924?

Phil 8886.44   Leuba, J.H. The psycho-physiology of the moral imperative. n.p., 1897.

Phil 5627.20.5   Leuba, J.H. The psychological origin and the nature of religion. London, 1909.

Phil 5627.20.6   Leuba, J.H. The psychological origin and the nature of religion. London, 1921.

Phil 5627.20   Leuba, J.H. A psychological study of religion. N.Y., 1912.

Phil 5627.20.7   Leuba, J.H. The psychology of religious mysticism. London, 1925.

Phil 5627.20.10   Leuba, J.H. Studies in the psychology of religious phenomena. Worcester, 1896.

Phil 8636.2   Leuba, James H. The belief in God and immortality. Boston, 1916.

Phil 5460.8   Leubuscher, R. Über die Entstehung der Sinnestäuschung. Berlin, 1852.

Phil 8897.8   Die Leuchte des Diogenes. (Weishaupt, A.) Regensburg, 1804.

Phil 5251.22   Leuchtenberger, G. Houptbegriffe der Psychologie. Berlin, 1899.

Phil 5465.15   Leuchtenberger, G. Die Phantasie ihr Wesen. Erfurt, 1894.

Phil 8586.20   Leuchtende fakel zum allgemeinen Glaubensbekenntniss aller Religionen. Frankfurt, 1784.

Phil 21.15   Leuchter; Weltanschauung von Lebensgestaltung. Darmstadt. 1919-1926 7v.

Phil 21.22   Der Leuchter. Darmstadt. 1930-1931//

Phil 4575.94   Leufren, E.J. Kritisk exposition of Benjamin Höijers. Upsala, 1897.

Phil 8591.39   Leufvén, E. Det religiösa kunskapsproblemet. Uppsala, 1914.

Phil 5821.10   Leuret, F. Anatomie comparée du système nerveux. Paris, 1839.

Phil 5761.19   Leuridan, Charles. L'idée de la liberté morale. Paris, 1936.

Phil 4762.2.90   Lev Mikhailovich Lopatin. (Ognev, A.I.) Petrograd, 1922.

Phil 7085.5   Levade, L. A true account of a natural sleep walker. Edinburgh, 1792.

Phil 8591.6   Levallois, J. Deisme et christianisme. Paris, 1866.

Phil 4600.1.40   Det levande forflutna. (Landquist, John.) Stockholm, 1919.

Phil 525.62   Levasti, A. I mistici. Firenze, 1925. 2v.

Phil 530.35.15   Levasti, A. Mistici del duecento e del trecento. Milano, 1935.

Phil 5520.300   Levels of knowing and existence. (Weinberg, Harry.) N.Y., 1959.

Phil 195.8   Leven en dood. (Utrecht. Rijks Universiteit. Utrechts Universiteits fonds.) Haarlem, 1961.

Phil 7042.8.2   Leven in meervoud. 2. druk. (Berg, Jan Hendrik van den.) Nijkerk, 1963.

Phil 179.35   Levensaspecten. (Esser, Pieter H.) Zutphen, 1946.

Phil 3821.7   Levenschets van Baruch de Spinoza. (Betz, H.J.) 's Gravenhage, 1876.

Phil 3821.8   Levensleer naar de beginselen van Spinoza. (Bierens de Haan, J.D.) 's Gravenhage, 1900.

Phil 3790.34   Levenstijdperken van de naan. (Ruemke, Henricus Cornelius.) Amsterdam, 1968.

Phil 575.51.42   Levensvormen. (Breukers, Eugenio Marie Josephine.) Roermond, 1947.

Phil 8412.5   Lévêque, C. La science du beau, ses principes, ses applications et son histoire. 2. éd. Paris, 1872. 2v.

Phil 186.9   Lévêque, J.C. La science de l'invisible. Paris, 1865.

Phil 5325.27   Lévêque, R. L'éclosion des pensées. Paris, 1938.

Phil 5325.156   Lévêque, R. L'éclosion des pensées. Thèse. Strasbourg, 1938.

Phil 2515.4.99   Lévêque, R. L'élément historique dans...Cournot. Paris, 1938.

Phil 2515.4.100   Lévêque, R. L'élément historique dans la connaissance humaine d'après Cournot. Thèse. Strasbourg, 1938.

Phil 2725.45   Lévêque, R. Unité et diversité. Paris, 1963.

Phil 3831.11   Lévêque, Raphail. Le problème de la vérité dans la philosophie de Spinoza. Strasbourg, 1923.

Htn   Phil 5051.19*   Lever, Ralph. The arte of reason. London, 1573.

Phil 2725.35.100   Levert, Paul. L'être et le réel selon Louis Lavelle. Paris, 1960.

Phil 2725.44   Levert, Paule. L'idée de commencement. Paris, 1961.

Phil 2775.6.80   Levert, Paule. Jean Nabert; ou, L'exigence absolue. Paris, 1971.

Phil 1535.23   Levesque, l'abbé. Précis de philosophie. Paris, 1912.

Phil 8886.51.5   Levesque, M. Cours élémentaire de morale. Paris, 1801.

Phil 850.1   Levesque de Bruiquy, J. Histoire de la philosophie payenne. La Haye, 1724.

Phil 5402.4   Levesque de Pouilly, L.J. Theorie des sentimens agreables. Paris, 1748.

Phil 5402.4.2   Levesque de Pouilly, L.J. Theorie des sentimens agreables. Paris, 1774.

Phil 5402.4.5   Levesque de Pouilly, L.J. Theory of agreeable sensations. Boston, 1812.

Phil 1145.45   Levi, A. Delitto e pena nel pensiero dei Greci. Torino, 1903.

Phil 4011.1   Levi, A. Saggio di una bibliografia filosofia italiana. Bologna, 1908.

Phil 165.90   Levi, A.W. Varieties of experience. N.Y., 1957.

Phil 672.126   Levi, Adolfo. Il concetto del tempo. Milano, 1919.

Phil 1870.97   Levi, Adolfo. La filosofia di Giorgio Berkeley. Torino, 1922.

Phil 2045.112   Levi, Adolfo. La filosofia di Thommaso Hobbes. Milano, 1929.

Phil 2411.4   Levi, Adolfo. L'indeterminismo nella filosofia francese contemporanea. Firenze, 1904.

Phil 1850.123   Levi, Adolfo. Il pensiero di Francesco Bacone. Torino, 1925.

Phil 645.28   Levi, Adolfo. Sceptica. Torino, 1921.

Phil 1300.20   Levi, Adolfo. Storia della filosofia romana. Firenze, 1949.

Phil 1195.20   Levi, Adolfo. Storia della sofistica. Napoli, 1966.

Phil 1711.7   Levi, Albert. Philosophy and the modern world. Bloomington, 1959.

Phil 1750.166.240   Levi, Albert William. Humanism and politics. Bloomington, 1969.

Phil 75.16   Levi, Alessandro. Bibliografia filosofica italiana, 1914-15. Roma, 1919.

Phil 8865.372   Levi, Anthony. French moralists; the theory of the passions, 1585-1649. Oxford, 1964.

Htn   Phil 8595.16.15*   Levi, David. Defence of Old Testament. N.Y., 1797.

Phil 4065.100   Levi, David. Giordano Bruno. Torino, 1887.

Phil 9171.6   Levi, G. Autobiografia di un padre di famiglia. Firenze, 1868.

Phil 4215.1.89   Levi, G. Del carattere meglio determinante la filosofia di Romagnosi. Parma, 1885.

Phil 3425.120   Levi, Giuseppe. La dottrina dello stato di G.F.G. Hegel. Pavia, 1880-84.

VPhil 6980.518   Levi, Vladimir L'. Okhota za mysl'iu. Moskva, 1967.

Phil 6980.518.2   Levi, Vladimir L'. Okhota za mysl'iu. Izd. 2. Moskva, 1971.

Phil 2045.53   Leviatano. (Hobbes, Thomas.) Bari, 1911-12. 2v.

Phil 2045.53.10   Il leviatano. (Hobbes, Thomas.) Messina, 1930.

Htn   Phil 2045.47.5*   Leviathan, sive de materia civitatis. (Hobbes, Thomas.) London, 1678.

Phil 2045.49.5   Leviathan. (Hobbes, Thomas.) Amstelodami, 1670.

Phil 2045.49   Leviathan. (Hobbes, Thomas.) Amsterdam, 1667.

Phil 2045.52.5   Leviathan. (Hobbes, Thomas.) Cambridge, 1935.

Htn   Phil 2045.48*   Leviathan. (Hobbes, Thomas.) London, 1651.

Htn   Phil 2045.48.5F*   Leviathan. (Hobbes, Thomas.) London, 1651.

Phil 2045.51.9   Leviathan. (Hobbes, Thomas.) London, 1894.

Phil 2045.52.15   Leviathan. (Hobbes, Thomas.) London, 1940.

Phil 2045.52.25   Leviathan. (Hobbes, Thomas.) London, 1947.

NEDL   Phil 2045.50.2   Leviathan. (Hobbes, Thomas.) Oxford, 1881.

Phil 2045.50.9   Leviathan. (Hobbes, Thomas.) Oxford, 1909.

Phil 2045.52.20   Leviathan. (Hobbes, Thomas.) Oxford, 1946.

Phil 2045.52.27	Leviathan. (Hobbes, Thomas.) Oxford, 1957.
Phil 2045.52.28	Leviathan. (Hobbes, Thomas.) Oxford, 1967.
Phil 2045.54	Leviathan. (Hobbes, Thomas.) Paris, 1921.
Phil 2045.54.5	Leviathan. Part I. (Hobbes, Thomas.) Chicago, 1949.
Phil 2045.51.3A	Leviathan. 3rd ed. (Hobbes, Thomas.) London, 1887.
Htn Phil 2045.87*	Leviathan drawn out with a hook. (Rosse, A.) London, 1653.
Phil 2138.160	Leviathan och folkviljan. (Nyman, Alf.) Stockholm, 1948.
Phil 8400.34	Levich, M. Aesthetics and the philosophy of criticism. N.Y., 1963.
Phil 6961.11	Levillain, F. La neurasthénie. Paris, 1891.
Phil 3831.17	Levin, Dan. Spinoza, the young thinker who destroyed the past. N.Y., 1970.
Phil 3450.11.465	Levin, David Michael. Reason and evidence in Husserl's phenomenology. Evanston, 1970.
Phil 342.28	Levin, Grigorii Aronovich. V.I. Lenin i sovremennye problemy teorii poznaniia. Minsk, 1970. 9v.
Phil 5520.550	Levin, Poul. Semantik. København, 1968.
Phil 3120.30.115	Levin-Goldschmidt, Hermann. Abschied von Martin Buber. Köln, 1966.
Phil 811.20	Levin-Goldschmidt, Hermann. Dialogik; Philosophie auf dem Boden der Neuzeit. Frankfurt, 1964.
Phil 3160.3.95	Levin-Goldschmidt, Hermann. Hermann Cohen und Martin Buber. Genève, 1946.
Phil 535.5	Levin-Goldschmidt, Hermann. Der Nihilismus im Licht einer kritischen Philosophie. Thayngen, 1941.
Phil 2725.42.5	Levinas, Emannuel. Totality and infinity. Pittsburgh, Pennsylvania, 1969.
Phil 3450.11.98.5	Levinas, Emmanuel. En découvrant l'existence avec Husserl et Heidegger. Paris, 1949.
Phil 3450.11.98.6	Levinas, Emmanuel. En découvrant l'existence avec Husserl et Heidegger. Paris, 1967.
Phil 3450.11.97	Levinas, Emmanuel. La théorie de l'institution dans la phénoménologie de Husserl. Paris, 1930.
Phil 3450.11.98	Levinas, Emmanuel. La théorie de l'institution dans la phénoménologie de Husserl. Thèse. Paris, 1930.
Phil 2725.42	Levinas, Emmanuel. Totalité et l'infini. La Haye, 1961.
Phil 5221.1	Levine, A.J. Current psychologies. Cambridge, 1940.
Phil 1050.24	Levine, I. Faithful rebels; a study in Jewish speculative thought. London, 1936.
Phil 5722.10	Levine, I. The unconscious. N.Y., 1923.
Phil 8886.47	Levine, Israel. Reasons and morals. Glasgow, 1924.
Phil 5590.424	Levine, Louis. Personal and social development. N.Y., 1963.
Phil 6321.18	Levine, M. Psychotherapy in medical practice. N.Y., 1942.
Phil 6961.20	Levinson, Daniel Jacob. Patienthood in the mental hospital. Boston, 1964.
Phil 3120.30.165	Levinson, Nathan P. Martin Buber. Frankfurt, 1966. 2v.
Phil 5590.442	Levita, David Joël de. The concept of identity. Paris, 1965.
Phil 6321.50	Levitas, G.B. The world of psychoanalysis. N.Y., 1965.
Phil 7069.28.50	La lévitation. (Leroy, O.) Paris, 1928.
Phil 5251.65	Levitov, N.D. O psikhicheskikh sostoianiiakh cheloveka. Moskva, 1964.
Phil 5590.530.3	Levitov, Nikolai D. Psikologiia kharaktera. 3. izd. Moskva, 1969.
Phil 5590.441	Levitov, Nikolai D. Voprosy psikhologii kharaktera. Moskva, 1952.
Phil 186.113	Levitskii, S.A. Osnovy organicheskogo mirovozzreniia. n.p., 1946.
Phil 5761.22	Levitskii, S.H. Tragediia svobody. Frankfurt, 1958.
Phil 4710.159	Levitskii, Sergei A. Ocherki po istorii russkoi filosofskoi i obshchestvennoi mysli. Frankfurt, 1968.
Phil 5421.10.20	Levitt, Eugene Elmer. The psychology of anxiety. Indianapolis, 1967.
Phil 8881.46	Levjathan; ricerche sulla natura morale dell'uomo. (Garello, Luigi.) Torino, 1910.
Phil 3850.1.98	Lévy, Albert. David Frédéric Strauss, la vie et l'oeuvre. Paris, 1910.
Phil 3235.82	Lévy, Albert. La philosophie de Feuerbach. Thèse. Paris, 1904.
Phil 5251.43	Lévy, Albert. Le sens intime en psychologie. Bruxelles, 1896.
Phil 3640.86	Levy, Albert. Stirner et Nietzsche. Paris, 1904.
Phil 7140.5	Lévy, Alfred. La psychose d'influence. Thèse. Paris, 1914.
Phil 974.3.65	Lévy, Eugène. Rudolf Steiners Weltanschauung und ihre Gegner. 3. Aufl. Berlin, 1926?
Phil 3011.4	Levy, H. Die Hegel-Renaissance in der deutschen Philosophie. Charlottenburg, 1927.
Phil 8423.20	Levy, Hanna. Henri Wölfflin; sa théorie, ses prédécesseurs. Rottweil, 1936.
Phil 3493.5	Levy, Heinrich. Kants Lehre vom Schematismus der reinen Verstandesbegriffe. Teil I. Halle, 1907.
Phil 342.4	Levy, Heinrich. Uber die apriorischen Elemente. Leipzig, 1914.
Phil 5251.42	Levy, Hyman. Thinking. London, 1936.
Phil 1182.54	Lévy, Isidore. Recherches esséniennes et pythagoriciennes. Genève, 1965.
Phil 5585.340	Lévy, Jean Claude. Le temps psychologique. Paris, 1969.
Phil 8591.25.2	Lévy, L.G. Une religion rationnelle et laïque. 2. éd. Dijon, 1904.
Phil 5590.540	Levy, Leon Harris. Conception of personality; theories and research. N.Y., 1970.
Phil 5761.9	Lévy, Paul Émile. L'éducation rationelle de la volonté. 10e éd. Paris, 1917.
Phil 5761.9.5	Lévy, Paul Émile. The rational education of the will. 9. ed. Philadelphia, 1920.
Phil 5761.9.12	Lévy, Paul Emile. Le traitement moral. Paris, 1927.
Phil 186.105	Lévy-Bruhe, L. Les carnets. 1. ed. Paris, 1949.
Phil 8886.29	Lévy-Bruhl, L. Ethics and moral science. London, 1905.
Phil 2411.2	Lévy-Bruhl, L. History of modern philosophy in France. London, 1899.
Phil 9470.2	Lévy-Bruhl, L. L'idée de responsabilité. Paris, 1884.
Phil 8886.29.5	Lévy-Bruhl, L. La morale et la science des moeurs. 5. ed. Paris, 1913.
Phil 2490.88.10	Lévy-Bruhl, L. Die Philosophie August Comte's. Leipzig, 1902.
Phil 2490.88	Lévy-Bruhl, L. La philosophie d'Auguste Comte. Paris, 1900.
Phil 2490.88.3	Lévy-Bruhl, L. La philosophie d'Auguste Comte. 3. éd. Paris, 1913.
Phil 3460.88	Lévy-Bruhl, L. La philosophie de Jacobi. Paris, 1894.
NEDL Phil 2490.88.5	Lévy-Bruhl, L. The philosophy of Auguste Comte. N.Y., 1903.
Phil 3425.106	Lévy-Bruhl, L. La théorie de l'état dans Hegel. Paris, 1889.
Phil 5875.15	Lévy-Schoen, Ariane. L'image d'autrui chez l'enfant. Paris, 1964.
Phil 5875.20	Lévy-Schoen, Ariane. Sur le développement de la connaissance d'autrui. Thèse. Paris, 1964.
Phil 6321.43	Lévy-Valensi, E. Le dialoge psychanalytique. Paris, 1962.
Phil 6321.47	Lévy-Valensi, E. Les rapports intersubjectifs en psychanalyse. Paris, 1962.
Phil 5585.141	Lévy-Valensi, Elaine Amado. Le temps dans la vie psychologique. Paris, 1965.
Phil 5520.578	Lévy-Valensi, Eliane Amado. La communication. 1.éd. Paris, 1967.
Phil 8886.84	Lévy-Valensi, Eliane Amado. Le temps dans la vie morale. Paris, 1968.
Phil 3011.5	Lewalter, E. Spanisch-Jesuisitische und Deutsch-Lutherische Metaphysik des 17. Jahrhunderts. Hamburg, 1935.
Phil 3493.18	Lewan, Axel. Kring Kants "Tugendlehre". Lund, 1930.
Phil 5821.6	Lewandowsky, M. Die Funktionen des zentralen Nervensystems. Jena, 1907.
Phil 2138.90	Lewels, Max. John Stuart Mill. Münster, 1902.
Phil 811.3.2	Lewes, G.H. A biographical history of philosophy. London, 1857.
Phil 811.3.5	Lewes, G.H. The biographical history of philosophy. London, 1875.
Phil 811.3.6	Lewes, G.H. The biographical history of philosophy. N.Y., 1859.
Phil 811.3	Lewes, G.H. A biographical history of philosophy. v.1-4. London, 1845-46. 9v.
Phil 2490.81	Lewes, G.H. Comte's philosophy of the sciences. London, 1853.
Phil 2490.81.5	Lewes, G.H. Comte's philosophy of the sciences. London, 1871.
Phil 811.3.3	Lewes, G.H. History of philosophy. 3d ed. London, 1867. 2v.
Phil 5251.6.5.2	Lewes, G.H. The physical basis of mind. Boston, 1891.
Phil 5251.6.5	Lewes, G.H. The physical basis of mind. London, 1893.
Phil 5251.6.2.6	Lewes, G.H. Problems of life and mind. 1st series. London, 1874-75. 2v.
Phil 5251.6.3	Lewes, G.H. Problems of life and mind. 1st-3rd series. London, 1874. 5v.
Phil 5251.6.4.5	Lewes, G.H. Problems of life and mind. 3rd series. Boston, 1879-80. 2v.
Phil 5251.6.4	Lewes, G.H. The study of psychology. London, 1879.
Phil 7060.78.5	Lewes, M.L. The queer side of things. London, 1923.
Phil 7060.78	Lewes, M.L. Stranger than fiction. London., 1911.
VPhil 3425.676	Lewica Heglowska. wyd. 1. (Panasiuk, R.) Warszawa, 1969.
Phil 7084.34	Lewin, Bertram David. Dreams and the uses of regression. N.Y., 1958.
Phil 3549.8.130	Lewin, James. Geist und Seele. Berlin, 1931.
Phil 5251.41A	Lewin, Kurt. A dynamic theory of personality. N.Y., 1935.
Phil 5761.14.10	Lewin, Kurt. Die Entwicklung des experimentellen Willenspsychologie. Leipzig, 1929.
Phil 5251.41.25	Lewin, Kurt. Field theory in social science. 1st ed. N.Y., 1951.
Phil 5251.41.9	Lewin, Kurt. Principles of topological psychology. 1st ed. N.Y., 1936.
Phil 5251.41.15A	Lewin, Kurt. Resolving social conflicts. 1st ed. N.Y., 1948.
Phil 5761.14	Lewin, Kurt. Vorsatz Wille und Bedürfnis. Berlin, 1926.
Phil 486.4	Lewins, R. Life and mind. Lewes, 1877.
Phil 6060.32	Lewinson, T.S. Handwriting analysis. N.Y., 1942.
Phil 9420.12	Lewis, C.S. The four loves. London, 1960.
Phil 342.13.5A	Lewis, Clarence I. An analysis of knowledge and value. La Salle, Ill., 1946.
Phil 342.13A	Lewis, Clarence I. Mind and the world-order. N.Y., 1929.
Phil 342.13.10A	Lewis, Clarence I. Mind and the world-order. N.Y., 1956.
Phil 5051.10.2	Lewis, Clarence I. A survey of symbolic logic. Berkeley, 1918.
Phil 5051.10.14	Lewis, Clarence I. A survey of symbolic logic. N.Y., 1960.
Phil 5051.10.10	Lewis, Clarence I. Symbolic logic. N.Y., 1932.
Phil 5051.10.12	Lewis, Clarence I. Symbolic logic. 2nd ed. N.Y., 1959.
Phil 8886.86	Lewis, Clarence I. Values and imperatives. Stanford, Calif., 1969.
Phil 2120.18	Lewis, Clarence Irving. Collected papers. Stanford, 1970.
Phil 8666.16.5	Lewis, Clive Staples. Beyond personality; the Christian idea of God. London, 1945.
Phil 8591.44.10	Lewis, Clive Staples. The case for Christianity. N.Y., 1944.
Phil 8591.44.11	Lewis, Clive Staples. The case for Christianity. N.Y., 1945.
Phil 8961.13	Lewis, Clive Staples. Christian behaviour. London, 1943.
Phil 8961.13.10	Lewis, Clive Staples. Christian behaviour. N.Y., 1944.
Phil 8591.44.45	Lewis, Clive Staples. Christian reflections. London, 1967.
Phil 8591.44.15A	Lewis, Clive Staples. The great divorce. N.Y., 1946.
Phil 8591.44.12	Lewis, Clive Staples. More Christianity. N.Y., 1960.
Phil 5402.21.10	Lewis, Clive Staples. The problem of pain. London, 1943.
Phil 8591.44.5A	Lewis, Clive Staples. The screwtape letters. N.Y., 1943.
Phil 8591.44.8	Lewis, Clive Staples. The screwtape letters. N.Y., 1943.
Phil 8591.44.6	Lewis, Clive Staples. The screwtape letters and Screwtape proposes a toast. London, 1961.
Phil 8591.44.35	Lewis, Clive Staples. They asked for a paper. London, 1962.
Phil 8591.44.20	Lewis, Clive Staples. Transposition, and other addresses. London, 1949.
Phil 8591.44.25	Lewis, Clive Staples. The weight of glory. N.Y., 1949.
Phil 8591.44.30	Lewis, Clive Staples. The world's last night. 1. ed. N.Y., 1960.
Phil 9351.10	Lewis, D. Our girls. N.Y., 1871.
Phil 5520.571	Lewis, David Kellogg. Convention; a philosophical study. Cambridge, 1969.
Phil 5251.56	Lewis, Don. Quantitative methods in psychology. N.Y., 1960.
Phil 9390.2	Lewis, E. Dissertation on oaths. Philadelphia, 1838.
Phil 9390.2.5	Lewis, E. Observations on legal and judicial oaths. v.1-2. Philadelphia, 1846-59.
Phil 2520.230	Lewis, G. L'individualité selon Descartes. Paris, 1950.
Phil 2520.230.2	Lewis, G. L'individualité selon Descartes. Thèse. Paris, 1950.
Phil 2520.230.10	Lewis, G. Le problème de l'inconscient et le cartesianisme. 1. éd. Paris, 1950.
Phil 2520.230.20	Lewis, G. René Descartes. Paris, 1953.
Phil 9455.5	Lewis, G.C. An essay on the influence of authority in matters of opinion. London, 1894.
Phil 5135.2	Lewis, G.C. An essay on the influence of authority opinion. London, 1849.

Phil 6420.10 Lewis, George Andrew. The practical treatment of stammering and stuttering. Detroit, 1902.
Phil 8886.28 Lewis, George Edward. Pay your fare. N.Y., 1914.
Phil 7054.21 Lewis, H.C. The alleged physical phenomena of spiritualism. Boston, 1887.
Phil 8666.18 Lewis, Hymel D. Our experience of God. London, 1959.
Phil 5520.402 Lewis, Hywel D. Clarity is not enough. London, 1963.
Phil 5520.402.2 Lewis, Hywel D. Clarity is not enough. N.Y., 1963.
Phil 7082.142.5 Lewis, Hywel David. Dreaming and experience. London, 1968.
Phil 6121.60 Lewis, Hywel David. The elusive mind; based on the first series of the Gifford lectures. London, 1969.
Phil 8591.80 Lewis, Hywel David. Philosophy of religion. London, 1965.
Phil 8636.7 Lewis, Jason. The anastasis of the dead. Boston, 1860.
Phil 2255.1.95 Lewis, John. Bertrand Russell: philosopher and humanist. London, 1968.
Phil 811.9 Lewis, John. Introduction to philosophy. London, 1937.
Phil 2120.6.30 Lewis, John. Marxism and modern idealism. London, 1944.
Phil 310.8 Lewis, John. Marxism and the irrationalists. London, 1955.
Phil 8591.30 Lewis, John. The passion for life. New Haven, 1928.
Phil 8663.3.95 Lewis, Joseph. Ingersoll the magnificent. N.Y., 1957.
Phil 5520.88 Lewis, Morris M. Language in society. London, 1947.
Phil 6980.419 Lewis, Nolan don Carpentier. A short history of psychiatric achievement. N.Y., 1941.
Phil 6980.419.5 Lewis, Nolan don Carpentier. Wartime psychiatry; a compendium. N.Y., 1954.
Phil 5500.6 Lewis, T.A. Judgment as belief. Baltimore, 1910.
Phil 8701.2.4 Lewis, Tayler. Faith, the life of science. Albany, 1838.
Phil 8701.2.15 Lewis, Tayler. Nature, progress, ideas. Schenectady, 1850.
Phil 8701.2.2 Lewis, Tayler. Six days of creation. 2nd ed. Schenectady, 1855.
Phil 6121.17 Lewis, W. Bevan. The human brain. London, 1882.
Phil 6961.10 Lewis, W.B. A text-book of mental diseases. Philadelphia, 1890.
Phil 672.140 Lewis, Wyndham. Time and Western man. N.Y., 1928.
Phil 8520.29 Lewkowitz, A. Religiöse Denker der Gegenwart. Berlin, 1923.
Phil 2150.18.90 Lewy, C. G.E. Moore on the naturalistic fallacy. London, 1964.
Phil 103.1 Lexicon peripateticum philosophico theologicum. (Signorrello, N.) Neapoli, 1872.
Phil 87.15 Lexicon philosophicum. 2. Aufl. (Chauvin, Étienne.) Dusseldorf, 1967.
Phil 97.10 Lexicon philosophicum terminorum philosophis usitatorum. (Micraelius, Johann.) Düsseldorf, 1966.
Phil 80.1 Lexicon rationale. (Chauvin, E.) Rotterdam, 1692.
Phil 3821.32 Lexicon Spinozanum. (Boschavini, Emilia Giancotti.) La Haye, 1970.
Phil 8815.5 Lexikon der christlichen Moral. (Hoermann, Karl.) Innsbruck, 1969.
Phil 1750.115.95 Lexington. Conference on Pure and Applied Phenomenology. Phenomenology of will and action. Chicago, 1967.
Phil 1020.8.21 Lexique de la langue...d'Ibn Sina. (Goichon, A.M.) Paris, 1938.
Phil 86.1 Lexique de philosophie. (Bertrand, A.) Paris, 1892.
Phil 2905.1.195 Lexique Teilhard de Chardin. (Cuénot, Claude.) Paris, 1963.
Phil 811.24 Ley, Hermann. Geschichte der Aufklärung und des Atheismus. Berlin, 1966- 3v.
Phil 486.10 Ley, Hermann. Studie zur Geschichte des Materialismus im Mittelalter. Berlin, 1957.
Phil 1730.36 Leyden, Wolfgang von. Seventeenth-century metaphysics. N.Y., 1968.
Phil 5251.57 Leyden. Universiteit. De toekomst der psychologie. Leiden, 1960.
Phil 5460.2 Leyendecker, Herbert. Zur Phänomenologie der Täuschungen. Inaug. Diss. Halle, 1913.
Phil 5460.2.3 Leyendecker, Herbert. Zur Phänomenologie der Täuschungen. 1. Teil. Halle, 1913.
Phil 7054.121 Leymarie, P.G. Proces des spirites. Paris, 1875.
Phil 8886.61.5 Leys, W.A.R. Ethics and policy decisions. N.Y., 1952.
Phil 8886.61 Leys, W.A.R. Ethics and social policy. N.Y., 1941.
Phil 2725.38.5 Leyvraz, Jean Pierre. Phénoménologie de l'expérience. La Haye, 1970.
Phil 2725.38 Leyvraz, Jean Pierre. Le temple et le Dieu. Paris, 1960.
Phil 5649.46 Lézine, Iréne. Les étopes de l'intelligence sensori-motrice. Paris, 1969.
Phil 6128.37 Leziomi di fisiologia sperimentale sul sistema nervoso. 2. ed. (Schiff, M.) Firenze, 1873.
Phil 4210.250 La lezione liturgica di Antonio Rosmini. (Quacguarelli, Antonio.) Milano, 1970.
Phil 4080.3.498 Lezioni crociane. (Trieste. Università Facoltà di Lettere e Filosofia.) Trieste, 1967.
Phil 5057.16 Lezioni di algebra della logica. (Re, Alfonso del.) Napoli, 1907.
Phil 177.105.2 Lezioni di filosofia. (Calogero, G.) Torino, 1960. 3v.
Phil 194.19 Lezioni di filosofia. v.1-3. (Tarozzi, Giuseppe.) Torino, 1896-1898.
Phil 177.105 Lezioni di filosofia. v.2-3. (Calogero, G.) Roma, 1946. 2v.
Phil 4112.45 Lezioni di logica e metafisica. v.1-4. (Galluppi, Pasquale.) Milano, 1845-46. 2v.
Phil 3489.26 Lezte aeusserungen Kant's von einem seiner Tischgenossen. (Hasse, J.G.) Königsberg, 1804.
Phil 2805.212 Lhermet, J. Pascal et la Bible. Thèse. Paris, 1931?
Phil 6121.24 Lhermitte, J. Les fondements biologiques de la psychologie. Paris, 1925.
Phil 6321.14 L'hermitte, J.J. L'image de notre corps. Paris, 1939.
Phil 7080.42 Lhermitte, J.J. Le sommeil. Paris, 1931.
Phil 6830.4 Li digenerazioni psico-sessuali. (Venturi, Silvio.) Torino, 1892.
Phil 5021.1 Liard, L. Les logiciens anglais contemporains. Paris, 1878.
Phil 186.10 Liard, L. La science positive. Paris, 1879.
Phil 186.10.5 Liard, L. La science positive. 5. ed. Paris, 1905.
Phil 2520.122 Liard, Louis. Descartes. 3e éd. Paris, 1911.
Phil 1811.3.5 Liard, Louis. Les logiciens anglais contemporains.'57 1811.3.5 44's. Les logiciens anglais contemporains. 5e éd. Paris, 1907.
Phil 5051.17.9 Liard, Louis. Logique. 9e éd. Paris, 1917?
Phil 186.39 Liard, Louis. Wissenschaft und Metaphysik. Leipzig, 1911.
Phil 186.115 Liat, W.S. Methods of comparative philosophy. Leiden, 1955.
Phil 4803.522.5 Libelt, Karol. Estetyka czyli umnictwo piękne. v.1-2. Petersburg, 1854. 3v.
Phil 4803.522.20 Libelt, Karol. Feleton polityczno-literacki. Poznań, 1846.
Phil 4803.522.15 Libelt, Karol. Filozofia i krytyka. Wyd. 2. v.1-6. Poznań, 1874-75. 3v.
Phil 4803.522.30 Libelt, Karol. Pisma o oświacie i wychowaniu. Wrocław, 1971.
Phil 4803.522.10 Libelt, Karol. Pisma promniejsze. Poznań, 1849-51. 6v.
Phil 4803.522.35 Libelt, Karol. Samowładztwo rozumu i objawy filozofii słowiańskiej. Warszawa, 1967.
Phil 6121.29 Liber, B. Your mental health. N.Y., 1940.
Htn Phil 176.31* Liber...vetaribus rarum principia. (Browne, R.) London, 1678.
Phil 665.22 Liber de anima. (Scheibler, Christoph.) Francofurti, 1665.
Phil 1504.18 Der "liber de consonanci a nature et gracie." v.18, pt.1. (Michel, K.) Münster, 1915.
Htn Phil 1106.5.5* Liber de vita et moribus philosophorum. (Burley, W.) Tübingen, 1886.
Htn Phil 4938.2.30* Liber egregius de unitate ecclesiae. (Hus, J.) n.p., n.d.
Phil 2115.205 The liberal politics of John Locke. (Seligen, Martin.) London, 1968.
Phil 3585.11 Der Liberalismus als Fordering. (Liebert, Arthur.) Zürich, 1938.
Phil 1535.5.10 Liberatore, M. Della conoscenza intellectuale. 2e ed. Roma, 1873-74. 2v.
Phil 1535.5 Liberatore, M. Elementi di filosofia. Livorno, 1852.
Phil 1535.5.15 Liberatore, M. Institutiones philosophicae. v.1-3. 10th ed. Romae, 1857.
Phil 4080.3.58 Liberismo e liberalismo. (Croce, Benedetto.) Milano, 1957.
Phil 5762.34 La libertà. (Martinetti, Piero.) Torino, 1965.
Phil 2138.40.25 La libertà. (Mill, John S.) Torino, 1925.
Phil 4080.3.320 La liberta come fondamento dello stato. (Iofrida, Vincenzo.) Milano, 1959.
Phil 4225.8.65 La libertà e il tempo. (Sciacca, Michele Federico.) Milano, 1965.
Phil 440.6 Libertá e responsabilitá. (Centro di Studi Filosofici di Gallarate.) Padova, 1967.
Phil 2880.8.104 La libertà esistenziale in Jean Paul Sartre. (Stefoni, M.) Milano, 1949.
Phil 3821.25 La libertà umana. (Benincá, A.) Caravate, 1952.
Phil 5769.8 La libertà umana e la critica del determinismo. (Tarozzi, G.) Bologna, 1936.
Phil 5752.8 La libertà umana nella filosofia contemporanea. (Cavallo, V.) Napoli, 1933.
Phil 4357.10 La libertad. (García Lahiguera, Fernando.) Valencia, 1961.
Phil 8958.5 Libertad. (Izu Loiteque, Gofronia.) Venezuela, 1944.
Phil 3492.38 De libertate morali ex ratione Kantiana. (Kleuker, Johann.) Osnabrugi, 1789.
Phil 70.18 La liberté; actes. (Congrès des Sociétés de Philosophie de Langue Française, 4th, Neuchâtel, 1949.) Neuchâtel. 1949
Phil 4979.41.30 La liberté; choix, amour, création. (Rio, Manuel.) Paris, 1961.
Phil 2725.13.32.1 La liberté. (Lequier, Jules.) Paris, 1936.
Phil 5765.6 La liberté. (Piat, Clodius.) Paris, 1894-95. 2v.
Phil 2725.13.32 La liberté. Thèse. (Lequier, Jules.) Paris, 1936.
Phil 2520.116.5 La liberté chez Descartes et la théologie. (Gilson, E.) Paris, 1913.
Phil 8592.26 La liberté de conscience. (Marillier, Léon.) Paris, 1890.
Phil 5753.14 La liberté de la volonté. 1. éd. (Daudin, H.) Paris, 1950.
Phil 5755.3 La liberté et le déterminisme. (Fouillée, A.) Paris, 1872.
Phil 5755.3.2 La liberté et le déterminisme. 2. éd. (Fouillée, A.) Paris, 1884.
Phil 9150.24 La liberté et le déterminisme rapports avec la théorie de l'évolution. Thèse. (Sarolea, Charles.) Bruxelles, 1893.
Phil 2520.430 Liberté et raison. v. 1- (Gabaude, Jean Marc.) Toulouse, 1970-
Phil 3246.306 La liberté humaine dans la philosophie de Fichte. (Philonenko, Alexis.) Paris, 1966.
Phil 8896.5 La liberté intérieure. (Vietinghoff, Jeanne de.) Paris, 1912.
Phil 2475.1.345 Liberté ou libération? (Lahbabi, Mohamed Aziz.) Aubier, 1956.
Phil 2750.28.30 La liberté spirituelle. (Maudoussat, G.) Paris, 1959.
Phil 525.14 Les libertins spirituels. (Schmidt, C.) Bale, 1876.
Phil 8411.40 Liberty, laughter, and tears. (Kollen, Horace Meyer.) De Kalb, 1968.
Phil 9050.3 Liberty and a living. 2nd ed. (Hubert, P.G.) N.Y., 1904.
Phil 8705.4.5 Liberty and life. (Powell, E.P.) Chicago, 1889.
Phil 5752.1 Liberty and necessity. (Carleton, H.) Philadelphia, 1857.
Phil 8591.86 Libizzi, Carmelo. Religione e vita. Padova, 1966.
Phil 8886.82 Libnizzi, Carmelo. Il pro e il contro: considerazioni morali. Padova, 1967.
Phil 7061.5 Library catalogue of the Society for Psychical Research. (Society for Psychical Research, London.) Glasgow, 1927.
Phil 75.92 Library of Congress. General Reference and Bibliography Division. Philosophical periodicals. Washington, 1952.
Phil 2150.6.01 The library of H. Münsterberg. (Münsterberg, H.) n.p., n.d.
Phil 8610.842 The Library of reason. London. 1-22
Phil 29.27.2 Library of theoria. Lund. 1-11 4v.
Phil 5751.13 Le libre arbitre. (Boufflers, S.) Paris, 1808.
Phil 5763.1 Le libre arbitre. (Naville, E.) Genève, 1898.
Phil 5761.23 Libre arbitre et jugement. (Lebacqz, Joseph.) Paris, 1960.
Phil 8610.871.25 Libre examen. 5. éd. (Viardot, L.) Paris, 1877.
Phil 176.21 Libre philosophie. (Bersot, P.E.) Paris, 1868.
Phil 2115.49.20 Libri IV de intellectu humano. (Locke, J.) Lipsiae, 1709.
Phil 2115.49.25 Libri IV de intellectu humano. (Locke, J.) Lipsiae, 1741.
Phil 4265.6.90 Librizzi, C. La filosofia di B. Varisco. Catania, 1936.
Phil 4265.6.80 Librizzi, C. Il pensiero di B. Varisco. Padova, 1942.
Phil 4011.3 Librizzi, C. Il risorgimento filosofica in Italia. Padova, 1952. 2v.
Phil 4011.3.5 Librizzi, C. Lo spiritualismo religioso nell'età del Risorgimento italiano. Catania, 1955.
Phil 8412.37 Librizzi, Carmelo. Conoscenza e arte. Padova, 1962.
Phil 8666.24.2 Librizzi, Carmelo. Immanenza e trascendenza. 2. ed. Padova, 1966.
Phil 4160.41.35 Librizzi, Carmelo. Letteratura, arte, filosofia. Padova, 1969.
Phil 186.146 Librizzi, Carmelo. Morale e conoscenza; saggi critici. Padova, 1961.
Phil 4160.41.30 Librizzi, Carmelo. Morale e religione. Padova, 1962.

Phil 2725.2.54   Il libro del popolo. (Lamennais, F.R. de.) n.p., n.d. 2 pam.

Phil 2725.2.53   Il libro del popolo. v.1-2. (Lamennais, F.R. de.) Firenze, 1848.

Htn   Phil 8890.43*   Libro della vita civile. (Palmieri, Matteo.) n.p., 15- .

Phil 21.5   Il libro pensiero. Milano. 1-11,1866-1876   8v.

Phil 2725.2.65   Libro per il popolo. (Lamennais, F.R. de.) Milano, 1874.

Phil 6400.8   Licções sobre as localisações cerebraes. (Bianchi, Leonardo.) Rio de Janeiro, 1899.

Phil 300.15   Lichaam en wereld. (Tollenaere, M. de.) Brugge, 1967.

Phil 9070.112   Lichnoe dostoianie i lichnoe destoinstvo. (Feofanov, Iurii V.) Moskva, 1966.

Phil 6322.44   Lichnost' i nevrozy. (Miasishchev, V.N.) Leningrad, 1960.

Phil 8980.851.5   Lichnost' i obshchestvo. (Tugarinov, Vasilii P.) Moskva, 1965.

Phil 9513.42   Lichnost i sotsial'no-nravstvennye otnosheniia vobshchestve. Photoreproduction. Pskov, 1968.

Phil 575.253   Lichnost' i trud. (Platonov, Konstantin K.) Moskva, 1965.

Phil 5590.564   Lichnost' kak sotsiologicheskaia problema. (Dantov, Tasbolat M.) Alma-Ata, 1970.

Phil 575.292   Lichnost' llaaz asennost! (Slobodianuz, Sergei S.) Moskva, 1971.

Phil 5590.475   Lichnost' pri sotsializme. Moskva, 1968.

Phil 5645.57   Licht und Farbe. (Heimendahl, E.) Berlin, 1961.

Phil 487.1.5   Licht und Leben. (Moleschott, J.) Frankfurt, 1856.

Phil 3640.106.4   Lichtenberger, H. Friedrich Nietzsche. Dresden, 1900.

Phil 3640.106.5   Lichtenberger, H. Friedrich Nietzsche. 2e Aufl. Dresden, 1900.

Phil 3640.106A   Lichtenberger, H. The gospel of superman. N.Y., 1912.

Phil 3640.106.2   Lichtenberger, H. The gospel of superman. N.Y., 1926.

Phil 3640.105   Lichtenberger, H. La philosophie de Nietzsche. 3e éd. Paris, 1912.

Phil 3640.105.5   Lichtenberger, H. Die Philosophie Friedrich Nietzsches. Dresden, 1899.

Phil 9035.69   Lichtenfels, H. Die christliche Religion in ihrer Bedeutung für dieCharaktererziehung. Kallmünz, 1934.

Phil 186.40.5   Lichtenfels, Johann. Lehrbuch zur Einleitung in die Philosophie. 5e Aufl. Wien, 1863.

Phil 5251.9   Lichthorn, C. Die Erforschung der physiologische Naturgesetze. Breslau, 1875.

Phil 1050.27   Lichtigfeld, A. Philosophy and revelation in the work of contemporary Jewish thinkers. London, 1937.

Phil 1050.27.5   Lichtigfeld, A. Twenty centuries of Jewish thought. London, 1937.

Phil 5645.31   Der Lichtsinn augenloser Tiere. (Nagel, W.A.) n.p., 1896-1908. 7 pam.

Phil 3415.19   Lichtstrahlen aus Eduard von Hartmann's sämmtlichen Werken. (Hartmann, Eduard von.) Berlin, 1881.

Phil 3808.21   Lichtstrahlen aus seinen Werken. (Schopenhauer, Arthur.) Leipzig, 1867.

Phil 6121.12.5   Lickley, J.D. The nervous system. N.Y., 1919.

Phil 310.415   Lid a osobnost v dějinách. (Cvekl, Jiří.) Praha, 1961.

Phil 2280.5.107   Lida, R. Belleza, arte y poesía en la estética de Santayana. Tucumán, 1943.

Phil 672.120.50   Liddell, Anna F. Alexander's space, time and deity. Chapel Hill, 1925?

Phil 8591.7   Liddon, H.P. Some elements of religion. London, 1872.

Phil 8591.7.10   Liddon, H.P. Some elements of religion. 10. ed. London, 1894.

Phil 186.26   Liddy, Ray Balmer. Relation of science and philosophy. Thesis. Toronto, 1914?

Phil 4600.4.45   Lidforss, Bengt. Bengt Lidforss i urral. Stockholm, 1965.

Phil 4600.4.30   Lidforss, Bengt. Dagsbilder. Malmö, 1917.

Phil 4600.4.32   Lidforss, Bengt. Fragment och miniatyrer. 2. uppl. Malmö, 1912.

Phil 4600.4.38   Lidforss, Bengt. Modärna apologeter. Malmö, 1911.

Phil 4600.4.35   Lidforss, Bengt. Onda makter och goda. Malmö, 1909.

Phil 4600.4.40   Lidforss, Bengt. Polemiska inlägg. Malmö, 1913.

Phil 4805.15   Lidová přísloví s logického hlediska. (Zich, Otakar.) Praha, 1956.

Phil 4809.814.30   Lidský smysl kultury. Vyd. 1. (Sviták, Ivan.) Praha, 1968.

Phil 5590.485   Lidz, Theodore. The person: his development throughout the life cycle. N.Y., 1968.

Phil 3090.85   Lieb, Fritz. Franz Baaders Jugendgeschichte...von Baaders. München, 1926.

Phil 165.280   Lieb, Irwin C. Experience, existence and good. Carbondale, 1961.

Phil 5252.18.54   Das Lieb-Seele-Problem bei George Trumbull Ladd und William McDougall. Inaug. Diss. (Fochtman, V.A.) München, 1928.

Phil 3210.83   Liebe, R. Fechner's Metaphysik. Greifswald, 1903.

Phil 3210.83.2   Liebe, R. Fechner's Metaphysik. Leipzig, 1903.

Phil 8957.20   Liebe als sittliche Grundkraft und ihre Fehlformen. 3. Aufl. (Heinen, Wilhelm.) Basel, 1968.

Phil 6328.2.35   Das liebe Ich. (Stekel, Wilhelm.) Berlin, 1913.

Phil 9495.12   Die liebe Platons. (Friedlander, B.) Berlin, 1909.

Phil 3805.169   Liebe und Ehe in Schleiermachers Kreis. (Steinberg, Julius.) Dresden, 1921.

Phil 3850.18.30A   Liebe und Erkenntnis. (Scheler, Max.) Bern, 1955.

Phil 5421.25.10   Liebe und Feindschaft. (Helwig, Paul.) München, 1964.

Phil 5421.20.105   Liebe und Hass. (Eibl-Eibesfeld, Irenäus.) München, 1970.

Phil 5811.5.5   Liebe und Leibes- Leben in der Thierwelt. (Büchner, L.) Berlin, 1879.

Phil 818.30   Liebe zum Wissen. (Strobach, W.) Wien, 1957.

Phil 6681.4   Liébeault, A.A. Du sommeil et des états analogues. Paris, 1866.

Phil 6681.4.15   Liébeault, A.A. Étude sur le zoomagnétisme. Paris, 1883.

Phil 6681.4.5   Liébeault, A.A. Le sommeil provoqué et les etats analogues. Paris, 1889.

Phil 6681.4.10   Liébeault, A.A. Thérapeutique suggestive, son mécanisme, propriétés du sommeil provoqué. Paris, 1891.

Phil 1135.32   Liebeck, H. Quaestiones Duae de Philosophia Graecorum. Halle, 1872.

Phil 1135.30   Liebeck, H. Untersuchungen zur Philosophie der Griechen. Halle, 1873.

Phil 1135.31   Liebeck, H. Untersuchungen zur Philosophie der Griechen. 2nd ed. Freiburg, 1888.

Phil 5401.12   Liebeck, O. Das Unbekannte und die Angst. Leipzig, 1928.

Phil 9351.3   Lieber, F. Character of the gentleman. Philadelphia, 1864.

Phil 9450.1   Lieber, F. Manual of political ethics. Boston, 1838-39. 2v.

Phil 9450.1.2   Lieber, F. Manual of political ethics. Boston, 1839. 2v.

Phil 5051.29   Lieber, Lillian R. Mits, wits and logic. 1st ed. N.Y., 1947.

Phil 5051.29.3   Lieber, Lillian R. Mits, wits and logic. 3d ed. N.Y., 1960.

Phil 1135.172   Lieberg, Godo. Geist und Lust. Tübingen, 1959.

Phil 1711.1   Liebert, A. Die geistige Krisis der Gegenwart. Berlin, 1923.

Phil 735.17   Liebert, A. Das Problem der Geltung. 2e Aufl. Leipzig, 1920.

Phil 186.93   Liebert, A. Von der Pflicht der Philosophie in unserer Zeit. Zürich, 1938.

Phil 8886.43   Liebert, Arthur. Ethik. Berlin, 1924.

Phil 186.35.15   Liebert, Arthur. Geist und Welt der Dialektik. Berlin, 1929.

Phil 3493.17   Liebert, Arthur. Kants Ethik. Berlin, 1931.

Phil 400.93   Liebert, Arthur. Die Krise des Idealismus. Zürich, 1936.

Phil 3585.11   Liebert, Arthur. Der Liberalismus als Fordering. Zürich, 1938.

Phil 3585.11.30   Liebert, Arthur. Der universale Humanismus. Zürich, 1946.

Phil 186.35.5   Liebert, Arthur. Wie ist kritische Philosophie überhaupt möglich? Leipzig, 1919.

Phil 186.35.7   Liebert, Arthur. Wie ist kritische Philosophie überhaupt möglich? Leipzig, 1923.

Phil 6328.27   Die Liebesfähigkeit. 2e Aufl. (Speer, Ernst.) München, 1937.

Phil 5425.94   Das Liebesleben des Genies. 2. Aufl. (Lenk, Emil.) Badeburg, 1926.

Phil 6849.2   Liebesunfähigkeit bie Frauen und ihre Behandlung. (Schumann, Hans Joachim von.) München, 1969.

Phil 7140.134   Liebetrau, U. Macht und Geheimnis der Suggestion. Basel, 1951.

Phil 1850.91F   Liebig, J.F. von. Rede in der...(F. Bacon...Geschichte...Naturwissenschaften). München, 1863.

Phil 3120.4.80   Liebing, H. Zurschen Orthodoxie und Aufklärung. Tubingen, 1961.

Phil 5590.26.5   Liebman, Joshua Loth. Hope for man. N.Y., 1966.

Phil 5590.26A   Liebman, Joshua Loth. Peace of mind. N.Y., 1946.

Phil 3640.495   Liebmann, K. Friedrich Nietzsche. München, 1943.

Phil 186.12.5   Liebmann, O. Gedanken und Thatsachen. Strassburg, 1882-1899. 2v.

Phil 186.12.11   Liebmann, O. Die Klimax der Theorieen. Strassburg, 1884.

Phil 5761.2   Liebmann, O. Über den individuellen Beweis für die Freiheit. Stuttgart, 1866.

Phil 186.12.8   Liebmann, O. Über philosophische Tradition. Strassburg, 1883.

Phil 186.12   Liebmann, O. Zur Analysis der Wirklichkeit. Strassburg, 1876.

Phil 3493.6   Liebmann, Otto. Kant und die Epigonen. Berlin, 1912.

Phil 3640.209   Liebmann, W. Nietzsche für und gegen Vaihinger. München, 1923.

Phil 3552.277   Liebniz: zum Gedächtnis seines. 200. Jahrigen Todestages. Hannover, 1916.

Phil 5520.425   Liebrucks, Bruno. Sprache und Bewusstsein. Frankfurt, 1964. 5v.

Phil 2515.2.125   Liebscher, H. Charron und sien Werk, "de la Sagesse". Leipzig, 1890.

Phil 3552.126   Lieder, F.W.C. Friedrich Spie and the théodicée of Leibniz. Urbana, 1912.

Phil 3011.10   Liedman, Sven Eric. Det organiska livet i tysk debatt, 1795-1845. Thesis. Land, 1966.

Phil 3493.35   Liedtke, Max. Der Begriff der reflektierenden Urteilskraft in Kants Kritik der reinen Vernunft. Hamburg, 1964.

Phil 2520.144   Liedtke, V. De Beweise für das dasein Gottes. Heidelberg, 1893.

Phil 9558.35   Liegen met en zonder opzet. (Berg, Robert Frederik.) Utrecht, 1961.

Phil 1711.1.5   Liehert, A. Zur Kritik der Gegenwart. Langensalza, 1927.

Phil 3890.10.90   Liehrich, H. Die historische Wahrheit bei Ernst Troeltsch. Diss. Giessen, 1937.

Phil 5485.2   Lienert, Gustav Adolf. Belastung und Regression. Meisenheim am Glan, 1964.

Phil 6961.9.5   Liepmann, Hugo. Drei Aufsätze aus dem Aprariegebut. Berlin, 1908.

Phil 8412.36   Lier, Henri. Les arts de l'espace. 3. éd. Tournai, 1963.

Phil 7069.68.65   Lietaert, Peerbolte, Maarten. Psychocybernetica. Amsterdam, 1968.

Phil 21.21   Lietuvos TSR aukštuju mokyklu mokslo darbai filosofija. Vilnius. 1-3   2v.

Phil 4369.2.80   Le livre d'origine, du philosophe Francisco Sanchez. (Cazac, H.P.) Bordeaux, 1903.

Phil 7069.17.29   Líf og daudi. (Kvaran, E.H.) Reykjavik, 1917.

Phil 5255.47A   Life; a psychological survey. 1st ed. (Pressey, Sidney Leavitt.) N.Y., 1939.

Phil 5400.42   Life, emotion, and intellect. (Andrews, Cyril B.) London, 1913.

Phil 187.165   Life; its dimensions. (MacIver, R.M.) N.Y., 1960.

Phil 365.12.7   Life, mind and spirit. (Morgan, Conwy L.) N.Y., 1925.

Htn   Phil 2045.78.5F*   Life. (Hobbes, Thomas.) London, 1680.

Htn   Phil 2050.82.3*   Life. (Hume, David.) London, 1777. 5 pam.

Htn   Phil 2050.82.2*   Life. (Hume, David.) London, 1777.

Phil 8890.17   Life. (Platt, J.) N.Y., 1889.

Phil 5925.2.13   Life: its science, laws...improvement. (Fowler, O.S.) Boston, 1871.

Phil 2262.77   Life. Unpublished letters. (Shaftesbury, A.A.C.) London, 1900.

Phil 8632.8.5   Life after death. (Hyslop, J.H.) N.Y., 1919.

Phil 7060.98   Life after death. London, 1758.

Phil 7069.61.30   A life after death. 1. ed. (Harlow, Samuel R.) Garden City, 1961.

Phil 6311.39   Life against death. 1st ed. (Brown, Norman Oliver.) Middletown, Conn., 1959.

Phil 978.59.45   Life ahead. (Krishnamurti, J.) London, 1963.

Phil 6953.3   Life among lunatics. (Derby, J.B.) Boston, 1839.

Phil 6750.231   Life among the lowbrows. (Wembridge, Eleanor H.R.) Boston, 1931.

Htn   Phil 2115.82.1*   The life and character of Mr. John Locke. (LeClerc, J.) London, 1706.

Htn   Phil 2115.82*   The life and character of Mr. John Locke. (LeClerc, J.) London, 1706-13.

Phil 2050.80A   Life and correspondence of Hume. (Burton, J.H.) Edinburgh, 1846. 2v.

Phil 8615.5.5   Life and destiny. (Adler, Felix.) N.Y., 1905.

Phil 7069.19.90   Life and destiny. (Denis, Léon.) N.Y., 1919.

Phil 9590.26   Life and finite individuality. (Carr, H.W.) London, 1918.

Phil 176.108   Life and I. (Bradford, Gamaliel.) Boston, 1928.

Phil 5816.5   Life and immortality. (Gentry, Thomas G.) Philadelphia, 1897.

Phil 7054.11   Life and labor in the spirit world. (Shelhamer, M.F.) Boston, 1885.

Phil 8893.14.3   Life and labour. (Smiles, Samuel.) Chicago, 1891.

Phil 8893.14   Life and labour. (Smiles, Samuel.) London, 1887.

Phil 8893.14.2   Life and labour. (Smiles, Samuel.) N.Y., 1888.

Phil 6122.27 Life and law. 1st ed. (Maule, G.E.) Ogden, 1908.
NEDL Phil 2055.2.80 Life and letters. (Hinton, James.) London, 1885.
Phil 1870.84.3 Life and letters of George Berkeley. (Fraser, Alexander Campbell.) Oxford, 1871.
Phil 2270.96 Life and letters of Herbert Spencer. (Duncan, D.) N.Y., 1908. 2v.
NEDL Phil 2115.93.10 The life and letters of John Locke. (King, Peter.) London, 1858.
Phil 8882.29 Life and love and peace. (Hall, B.) N.Y., 1909.
Phil 510.1.12 Life and matter. A criticism of Prof. Haeckel's riddle. (Lodge, Oliver.) N.Y., 1906.
Phil 510.1.13.5 Life and matter. 2nd ed. (Lodge, Oliver.) London, 1912.
NEDL Phil 2520.51 Life and meditations. (Descartes, René.) London, 1878.
Phil 486.4 Life and mind. (Lewins, R.) Lewes, 1877.
Phil 1930.7.80 Life and philosophy. (Chamberlin, R.V.) Salt Lake City, 1925.
Phil 1930.6.125 The life and philosophy of Edward Caird. (Jones, Henry.) Glasgow, 1921.
Phil 9590.40 Life and teaching of the masters of the Far East. (Spalding, Baird Thomas.) Los Angeles, California, 1944. 5v.
Phil 4065.93 Life and teachings of Giordano Bruno, 1548-1600. (Turnbull, C.) San Diego, 1913.
Phil 8876.103 Life and the conditions of survival. (Brooklyn Ethical Association.) Chicago, 1895.
Phil 177.83 Life and the student. (Coaley, C.H.) N.Y., 1927.
Phil 3850.27.197 The life and thought of Albert Schweitzer. (Picht, Werner.) N.Y., 1964.
Phil 5251.29 Life and word. (Lloyd, R.E.) London, 1924.
Phil 2150.1.80 Life and work of George Sylvester Morris. (Wenley, R.M.) N.Y., 1917.
Phil 7069.30.25 Life and work of Mrs. Piper. (Piper, Alta L.) London, 1929.
Phil 6315.2.151 The life and work of Sigmund Freud. (Jones, Ernest.) London, 1961.
Phil 6315.2.150A The life and work of Sigmund Freud. 1st ed. (Jones, Ernest.) N.Y., 1953. 3v.
Phil 600.7.100 The life and works of Émile Littré. (Aquarone, Stanislas.) Leyden, 1958.
Phil 1850.126 The life and writings of Francis Bacon. Edinburgh, 1837.
Phil 4260.109 The life and writings of Giambattista Vico. (Adams, Henry P.) London, 1935.
Phil 178.31 Life as reality. (Dewing, A.S.) N.Y., 1910.
Phil 9400.11 Life at eighty as I see it. (Flake, A.) Nashville, 1944.
Phil 5627.134.25 Life began yesterday. (Foot, Stephen.) N.Y., 1935.
Phil 9530.31.5 Life begins at forty. (Pitkin, Walter B.) N.Y., 1932.
Phil 8951.25 Life begins with love. (Barrett, E.B.) Dublin, 1953.
Phil 7069.28.70 Life beyond death, with evidence. 1st ed. (Thomas, Charles D.) London, 1937.
Phil 7069.44.45 Life beyond death. (Abhedânanda.) Calcutta, 1944.
Phil 8643.11 Life beyond death. (Savage, M.J.) N.Y., 1899.
Phil 7069.26.15 The life beyond the veil. (Owen, G.V.) London, 1926. 2v.
Phil 5627.15.11 Life changers. (Begbie, H.) N.Y., 1927.
Phil 4872.109.2 The life divine. (Ghose, Aurobindo.) N.Y., 1949.
Phil 4872.109.3 The life divine. 3rd ed. (Ghose, Aurobindo.) N.Y., 1965.
Phil 8647.4 Life eternal. (Wright, T.F.) Boston, 1885.
Phil 8633.1.5 Life everlasting. (Fiske, J.) Boston, 1900.
Phil 8630.3.6A Life everlasting. (Fiske, J.) Boston, 1901.
Phil 665.55 Life everlasting and psychic evolution. (Fringe, J.W.) London, 1919.
Phil 672.159 Life here and now; conclusions derived from an examination of the sense of duration. (Ponsonby, A.P.) London, 1936.
Phil 6302.5 Life history research in psychopathology. Minneapolis, 1970.
Phil 978.59.20 Life in freedom. (Krishnamurti, J.) N.Y., 1928.
Phil 187.51 Life in mind and conduct. (Maudsley, Henry.) London, 1902.
Phil 7069.20.205 Life in the circles. (Lane, Anne W.) N.Y., 1920.
Phil 8592.3 Life in the making. (Macdonald, L.B.) Boston, 1911.
Phil 9500.1 Life in the sick-room. (Martineau, H.) Boston, 1844.
Phil 9500.1.2 Life in the sick-room. 2d American ed. (Martineau, H.) Boston, 1845.
Phil 8626.28 Life in the world unseen. (Borgia, Anthony V.) London, 1956.
Phil 8631.8 The life indeed. (Genung, John F.) Boston, 1921.
Phil 8602.30 Life more abundant. (Wood, Henry.) Boston, 1905.
Phil 8599.28 Life negation; an Indian study of Christ. (Tampoe, A.McG. Coomarasamy.) London, 19- .
Phil 2266.165A Life of Adam Smith. (Rae, John.) N.Y., 1965.
Phil 4210.83.5 Life of Antonio Rosmini-Serbati. (MacWalter, G.S.) London, 1883.
Phil 4210.107.5 The life of Antonio Rosmini-Serbati. (Pagani, G.B.) London, 1907.
Phil 4210.83 Life of Antonio Rosmini-Serbati. 2 ed. (Lockhart, W.) London, 1886. 2v.
Phil 3808.100A Life of Arthur Schopenhauer. (Wallace, W.) London, 1890.
Phil 3808.100.5 Life of Arthur Schopenhauer. (Wallace, W.) N.Y., 1890.
Phil 8587.32.115 The life of Baron von Hügel. (Bedoyere, M. de la.) London, 1951.
Phil 3822.4.6A The life of Benedict de Spinoza. (Colerus, Johannes.) London, 1706.
Htn Phil 3822.4.5* The life of Benedict de Spinoza. (Colerus, Johannes.) London, 1706.
Phil 1870.108 The life of Bishop Berkeley. (Norton, John N.) N.Y., 1861.
Phil 2050.212.5 The life of David Hume. (Mossner, E.C.) Austin, 1954.
Phil 3805.81 The life of F.D.E. Schleiermacher. London, 1860. 2v.
Phil 1850.97 The life of Francis Lord Bacon. (Sortain, J.) London, n.d.
Phil 3640.96 Life of Friedrich Nietzsche. (Halévy, D.) N.Y., 1911.
Phil 1870.124 The life of George Berkeley. (Luce, Arthur A.) London, 1949.
Phil 5922.4.50 The life of George Combe. (Gibbon, C.) London, 1878. 2v.
Phil 4065.92.3 Life of Giordano Bruno. (Frith, I.) Boston, 1887.
Phil 4065.92 Life of Giordano Bruno. (Frith, I.) London, 1887.
Phil 3552.91 Life of Godfrey William von Leibnitz. (Mackie, J.M.) Boston, 1845.
Phil 3500.12A Life of Immanuel Kant. (Stuelsenberg, J.) London, 1882.
Phil 182.44.5 The life of Jehoshua, the prophet of Nazareth. (Hartmann, F.) Boston, 1889.
Phil 182.44 The life of Jehoshua, the prophet of Nazarette. (Hartmann, F.) London, 1909.
Phil 2115.91A The life of John Locke. (Bourne, H.R.F.) London, 1876. 2v.
Phil 2115.91.2A The life of John Locke. (Bourne, H.R.F.) N.Y., 1876. 2v.

Phil 2115.92.90 Life of John Locke. (King, Peter.) London, 1829.
Phil 2115.93A Life of John Locke. (King, Peter.) London, 1830. 2v.
Phil 2138.82.5 Life of John Stuart Mill. (Courtney, W.S.) London, 1889.
Phil 2138.82.7A Life of John Stuart Mill. (Courtney, W.S.) London, 1889.
Phil 2138.124 The life of John Stuart Mill. (Packe, M.) London, 1954.
Phil 2218.80 The life of Joseph Priestley. (Corry, J.) Birmingham, 1804.
Phil 2115.90.4 Life of Locke. (Fowler, T.) London, n.d.
Phil 2880.1.82 The life of Louis C. de Saint-Martin. (Waite, Arthur E.) London, 1901.
Phil 2805.30.27 The life of Mr. Paschal with his letters relating to the Jesuits. (Pascal, Blaise.) London, 1765-66. 2v.
Phil 3640.88.5 Life of Nietzsche. (Förster-Nietzsche, E.) N.Y., 1912-15. 2v.
Htn Phil 3110.87* The life of one Jacob Boehmen. London, 1644.
Phil 8881.4.9 The life of Professor C.F. Gellert. (Douglas, M.) London, 1810. 3v.
Phil 1955.8.30 The life of reason. (DeBurgh, William G.) London, 1949.
Phil 193.49A Life of reason. (Santayana, G.) N.Y., 1905. 5v.
Phil 193.49.1 Life of reason. (Santayana, G.) N.Y., 1906. 5v.
Phil 2280.5.88 The life of reason. (Santayana, George.) N.Y., 1954.
Phil 193.49.3 The life of reason. v.1,3-5. (Santayana, G.) N.Y., 1924-1925. 4v.
Phil 193.49.2 The life of reason. v.2-3. (Santayana, G.) N.Y., 1921. 2v.
Phil 193.49.4 The life of reason. v.3. (Santayana, G.) N.Y., n.d.
Htn Phil 2150.5.80* Life of Sir Thomas More, by his great-grandson. (More, Thomas.) London, 1726.
Phil 5628.11.1 The life of St. Mary Magdalene of Pazzi, a Carmelite nun. (Puccini, Vincenzo.) London, 1687.
Phil 8582.55 The life of the mind. (Cailliet, Émile.) N.Y., 1942.
Phil 179.3.21 The life of the spirit. (Eucken, R.) London, 1909.
Phil 8887.37.90 The life of the spirit. (Mabie, H.W.) N.Y., 1900.
Phil 5627.60.7 The life of the spirit and the life of today. (Underhill, E.) London, 1922.
Phil 5627.60.5 The life of the spirit and the life of today. (Underhill, E.) N.Y., 1926.
Phil 5627.60 The life of the spirit and the life of today. 3d ed. (Underhill, E.) London, 1923.
Phil 5865.12 Life-span developmental psychology. N.Y., 1970.
Phil 5938.12 Life story and experiences of a phrenologist. (Severn, J.M.) Brighton, Eng., 1929.
Phil 6053.4 Life studies in palmistry. (Oxenford, Ina.) London, 1899.
Phil 8581.3 Life theories. (Beale, L.S.) London, 1871.
Phil 192.41 Life understood from a scientific and religious point of view. 4th ed. (Rawson, F.L.) London, 1917.
Phil 298.9 Life understood from a scientific and religious point of view. 7. ed. (Rawson, F.) London, 1947.
Phil 5401.15 Life without fear. (Fletcher, J.P.) N.Y., 1939.
Phil 7068.95.10 Life work of Mrs. Cora L.V. Richmond. (Barrett, Harrison D.) Chicago, 1895.
Phil 974.4.35 The life works of Mrs. Besant. (Gay, S.E.) London, 1913?
Phil 179.3.29 Life's basis and life's ideal. (Eucken, R.) London, 1911.
Phil 978.50 Life's mysteries unveiled. (Ferrier, John T.) London, 1923.
Phil 298.2.10 Life's reality. (Rosley, Carl.) Hayward, 1932.
Phil 8877.35 Life's tangled thread. (Carpenter, W.B.) London, 1912.
Phil 6316.8.25 Life's unknown ruler...teaching of George Groddeck. (Taylor, H.M.) London, 1935. 2v.
Phil 3850.10.50 Lifrets philosophie. (Schlegel, Friedrich von.) Stockholm, 1834.
Phil 5780.22A Lifton, Robert. Thought reform and the psychology of totalism. N.Y., 1961.
Phil 8892.31 Lifvets konst. (Ritter, T.H.) Stockholm, 1906.
Phil 1516.2 Ligeard, H. La théologie scolastique. Paris, 1908.
Phil 5374.54 Light, a philosophy of consciousness. (Weir, A.) Oxford, 1932.
Phil 21.9 Light. London. 64,1944+
NEDL Phil 21.9 Light. London. 1881-1931
Phil 7069.14.10 Light and colors. (Colville, William J.) N.Y., 1914.
Phil 1802.14 Light and enlightenment. (Colie, Rosalie L.) Cambridge, 1957.
Phil 21.2 Light and life. Glasgow. 1885-1887+ 2v.
Phil 525.235 The light and the gate. (Johnson, R.C.) London, 1964.
Phil 8740.8 The light and the rainbow. (Graef, Hilda C.) London, 1959.
Phil 7069.31.25 The light and the word. London, 1931.
Phil 7069.18.130A The light beyond. (Maeterlinck, Maurice.) N.Y., 1918.
Phil 960.36 Light from the East. (Arunáchalam, P.) London, 1927.
Phil 7054.62.2 Light from the spirit world. (Hammond, Charles.) N.Y., 1852.
Phil 7054.70 Light in the valley: my experience of spiritualism. (Crosland, N.) London, 1857.
Phil 525.46 The light of mysticism. (Elkinton, J.) Philadelphia, 1907.
Phil 2300.30.5 Light of nature pursued. (Tucker, Abraham.) Cambridge, 1831. 4v.
Phil 2300.30.2 Light of nature pursued. (Tucker, Abraham.) London, 1768. 5v.
Phil 2300.30 Light of nature pursued. (Tucker, Abraham.) London, 1768-77. 7v.
Phil 2300.30.3 Light of nature pursued. (Tucker, Abraham.) London, 1805. 7v.
Phil 8610.911 The light of reason. (Indiana Rationalist Association.) Indianapolis, Ind., 1911.
Phil 181.78 The light of the mind. (Gattell, B.B.) Philadelphia, 1938.
Phil 7069.17.30 Light on the future. London, 1917.
Phil 7054.20 Light on the hidden way. Boston, 1886.
Phil 978.15.4 Light on the path. (Cook, M.C.) Boston, 1889.
Phil 978.15.2 Light on the path. (Cook, M.C.) Chicago, Ill., n.d.
Phil 978.15.4.5 Light on the path. (Cook, M.C.) N.Y., 18- .
Phil 978.15.3 Light on the path. (Cook, M.C.) N.Y., 1886?
Phil 978.15 Light on the path. (Cook, M.C.) Point Loma, California, 1897.
Phil 9070.9 Lighted candles. (Shurtleft, A.D.K.) Boston, 1939.
Phil 9070.44 The lighted pathway. (Chamberlain, F.E.) Los Angeles, Calif., 1943.
Phil 5051.14 Lightfoot, John. Logic and education. London, 1899.
Phil 186.31 Lightfoot, John. Studies in philosophy. Edinburgh, 1888.
Phil 186.48.10 Lighthall, W.D. The person of evolution. Montreal, 1930.
Phil 186.48.11 Lighthall, W.D. The person of evolution. Toronto, 1933.
Phil 186.48.5 Lighthall, W.D. Superpersonalism, the outer consciousness. Montreal, 1926.
Phil 186.48.2 Pamphlet box. Lighthall, W.D.
Phil 7060.86.5 Lights and shadows. (Lee, F.G.) London, 1894.

X Cg Phil 9172.1 — Lights and shadows of domestic life. (Moody, C.C.P.) Boston, 1846.

Phil 7052.5 — Lights and shadows of spiritualism. (Home, D.D.) London, 1878.

Phil 4851.10A — Lights on contemporary Moslem philosophy. (Amin, Osman.) Cairo, 1958.

Phil 5627.142 — Ligon, E.M. The psychology of Christian personality. N.Y., 1936.

Phil 5821.12 — Ligon, Ernest M. A comparative study of certain incentives in the learning of the white rat. Diss. Baltimore, 1929.

Phil 5251.11 — Liguet, G.H. Idée générales de psychologie. Paris, 1906.

Phil 4120.4.120 — Liguori, Ersilia. La pedagogia come scienza filosofica di Giovanni Gentile. Padova, 1951.

Phil 2477.1.136 — Liguori-Barbieri, E. La filosofia di Émile Boutroux. Pisa, 1926.

Phil 6122.80 — Likvidiraneto na protivopolozhnostta mezhdu umstveniia i fizicheokiia trud. (Mikhailov, S.) Sofiia, 1959.

Phil 292.5 — Lilburne, H.A. The psychology of the atom. London, 1924.

Phil 342.9 — Liljeckrantz, B. Ur världoförklaringarnas och kunskapsteoriernas urkunder. Stockholm, 1921.

Phil 4610.7.87 — Liljedal, E. Vitalis Norström. Stockholm, 1917-18. 2v.

Phil 4575.95 — Liljekrantz, B. Benjamin Höijer. Lund, 1912.

Phil 186.55.5 — Liljekrantz, B. Verklighetsproblemet i den antika filosofien. Göteborg, 1915.

Phil 7060.144 — Liljencrants, Johan. Spiritism and religion. Diss. Lynchburg, Va., 1918.

Phil 3625.11.82 — Liljequist, E. Meinongs allmänna värdeteori. Göteborg, 1904.

Phil 1850.114 — Liljeqvist, E. Om Francis Bacon filosofi med särskild hänsyn till det etiska problemet. Uppsala, 1893.

Phil 1195.7 — Liljeqvist, Efraim. Antik och modern sofistik. Göteborg, 1896.

Phil 4515.85.5 — Liljeqvist, Efraim. Boströms äldsta latinska dissertationer. Thesis. Lund, 1915.

Phil 4515.85 — Liljeqvist, Efraim. Om Boströms äldsta skrifter. Göteborg, 1897.

Phil 4210.123F — Lilla, V. Le fonti del sistema filosofico di Antonio Rosmini. Milano, 1897.

Phil 7054.50 — Lillie, Arthur. Modern mystics and modern magic. N.Y., 1894.

Phil 7054.50.2 — Lillie, Arthur. The worship of Satan in modern France. London, 1896.

Phil 8886.72 — Lillie, William. An introduction to ethics. 3. ed. London, 1957.

Phil 192.3.8 — Lilliput lectures. (Rands, W.B.) London, 1871.

Phil 6158.50 — Lilly, John Cunningham. The center of the cyclone. N.Y., 1972.

Phil 6121.62.1 — Lilly, John Cunningham. Programming and metaprogramming in the human biocomputer. Berkeley, 1970.

Phil 5921.8.5 — Lilly, W.S. Ancient religion and modern thought. 2. ed. London, 1885.

Phil 8591.8 — Lilly, W.S. The great enigma. N.Y., 1892.

Phil 8886.18 — Lilly, W.S. On right and wrong. London, 1892.

Phil 8886.36 — Lilly, William S. An invisible kingdom. London, 1919.

Phil 3425.664.2 — Lim, Sok-Zin. Der Begriff der Arbeit bei Hegel. 2. Aufl. Bonn, 1966.

Phil 6021.10 — Lima Fulza, G. La faccia e l'anima. Milano, 1875.

Phil 2266.114 — Limentani, L. La morale della simpatia; saggio sopra l'etica di Adamo Smith. Genova, 1914.

Phil 8886.32 — Limentani, Ludovico. I presupposti formali...etica. Genova, 1913.

Phil 365.3 — A limit to evolution. (Mivart, St. G.) London? 1884.

Phil 9470.1 — The limitations of human responsibility. (Wayland, F.) Boston, 1838.

Phil 9470.1.2 — The limitations of human responsibility. (Wayland, F.) N.Y., 1838.

Phil 190.34 — I limiti del determinismo scientifico. (Petrone, Igino.) Modena, 1900.

Phil 3499.31 — I limiti del trascendentale in Kant. (Rigobello, A.) Milano, 1963.

Phil 801.17 — I limiti della storia della filosofia. (Bodrero, E.) Roma, 1919.

Phil 5240.16 — I limiti dell'esperimento in psicologia. (Alfonso, N.R.) Roma, 1905.

Phil 400.12 — Limits of evolution. (Howison, G.H.) N.Y., 1901.

Phil 400.12.3 — Limits of evolution. 2nd ed. (Howison, G.H.) N.Y., 1905.

Phil 1865.22 — The limits of jurisprudence defined. (Bentham, Jeremy.) N.Y., 1945.

Phil 5828.17 — The limits of learning ability in kittens. (Shuey, A.M.) Worcester, 1931.

Phil 5815.5 — The limits of learning ability in rhesus monkeys. Thesis. (Fjeld, Harriett A.) Worcester, Mass., 1934.

Phil 5827.11 — Limits of learning ability in the white rat and the guinea pig. Diss. (Riess, Bernard F.) Worcester, Mass., 1934.

Phil 193.130 — The limits of purpose and other essays. (Stocks, J.L.) London, 1932.

Phil 176.210 — The limits of reason. (Boas, George.) London, 1961.

Phil 2130.45 — The limits of religious thought. 1st American ed. (Mansel, H.L.) Boston, 1859.

Phil 2130.45.10 — The limits of religious thought. 1st American ed. (Mansel, H.L.) Boston, 1875.

Phil 2130.45.5 — The limits of religious thought. 3rd ed. (Mansel, H.L.) London, 1859.

Phil 5042.35 — The limits of science. (Chwistek, Leon.) London, 1948.

Phil 186.96 — The limits of speculative humanism. (Laird, J.) London, 1940.

Phil 8663.3.35 — The limits of toleration. (Ingersoll, Robert G.) N.Y., 1889.

Phil 930.39 — Lin, Mou-Sheng. Men and ideas; an informal history of Chinese political thought. N.Y., 1942.

Phil 186.88 — Lin, Yu-t'ang. The importance of living. N.Y., 1937.

Phil 6961.6.2 — Lincoln, D.F. Sanity of mind. N.Y., 1901.

Phil 7084.28.5 — Lincoln, Jackson Steward. The dream in primitive cultures. London, 1935.

Phil 7069.00.28 — L'inconnu, The unknown. (Flammarion, C.) N.Y., 1900.

Phil 3850.27.113 — Lind, Emil. Albert Schweitzer. Bern, 1948.

Phil 3850.27.113.5 — Lind, Emil. Ein Meister der Menscheit Albert Schweitzer. Bühl, 1954.

Phil 3850.27.112 — Lind, Emil. Die Universalmenschen Goethe und Schweitzer. Neustadt, 1947.

Phil 3493.9.5 — Lind, Paul von. Immanuel Kant und Alexander von Humboldt. Inaug. Diss. Erlangen, 1897.

Phil 3493.9 — Lind, Paul von. Eine unsterbliche Entdeckung Kants. Leipzig, 1898.

Phil 3915.40.2.2 — Lindan, Hans. Namenverzeichniss und Sachregister zu Wundt's Logik. 2. Aufl. Stuttgart, 1902.

Phil 3246.99 — Lindau, Hans. Johann Gottlieb Fichte und der neuere Socialismus. Berlin, 1900.

Phil 3246.99.10 — Lindau, Hans. Johann Gottlieb Fichtes Lehren von Staat und Gesellschaft in ihrem Verhältnis zum neueren Sozialismus. n.p., 1899.

Phil 3246.99.5 — Lindau, Hans. Die Schriften zu Johann Gottlieb Fichte's Atheismusstreit. München, 1912.

Phil 8520.25 — Lindau, Hans. Die Theodicee im 18 Jahrhundert. Leipzig, 1911.

Phil 5645.44 — Lindberg, Bengt J. Experimental studies of colour and non-colour attitudes in school children and adults. Copenhagen, 1938.

Phil 3831.5 — Linde, A. van der. Benedictus Spinoza. Gravenhage, 1871.

Phil 3831.3 — Linde, A. van der. Spinoza. Göttingen, 1862.

Phil 5871.5.5 — Lindeman, Bard. The twins who found each other. N.Y., 1969.

Phil 186.87 — Lindemann, H.A. Weltgeschehen und Welterkenntnis. Baden, 1931.

Phil 5051.4 — Lindemann, H.S. Die Denkkunde oder die Logik. Solothurn, 1846.

Phil 186.14 — Lindemann, H.S. Die Lehre vom Menschen. Zürich, 1844.

Phil 3525.81 — Lindemann, H.S. Uebersichtliche Darstellung des Lebens und der Wissenschaftlehre K.C.F. Krause's. München, 1839.

Phil 978.49.910 — Lindenberg, Christoph. Individualismus und offenbare Religion. Stuttgart, 1970.

Phil 9500.5 — Lindenberg, Wladimir. Gespräche am Krankenbett. München, 1959.

Phil 5627.259.10 — Lindenberg, Wladimir. Mysterium der Begegnung. München, 1959.

Phil 8636.10 — Lindhardt, P.G. Helvedes strategi. n.p., 1958.

Phil 8412.15 — Lindholm, C. Konsten och tiden. Stockholm, 1950.

Phil 3808.93 — Lindner, E.O. Arthur Schopenhauer. Berlin, 1863.

Phil 186.13 — Lindner, G.A. Einleitung in das Studium der Philosophie. Wien, 1866.

Phil 5251.7.7 — Lindner, G.A. Leerbaek der empirische zielkunde. Zutphen, 18- .

Phil 5251.7 — Lindner, G.A. Lehrbuch der empiriochen Psychologie. Wien, 1872.

Phil 5251.7.3 — Lindner, G.A. Lehrbuch der empiriochen Psychologie. 9. Aufl. Wien, 1889.

Phil 5251.7.5 — Lindner, G.A. Manual of empirical psychology. Boston, 1889.

Phil 5403.4.5 — Lindner, Gustav. Lyckans problem. Stockholm, 1869.

Phil 5403.4 — Lindner, Gustav. Das Problem des Glücks. Wien, 1864.

Phil 5403.4.10 — Lindner, Gustav. Zahada štěsti. Praha, 1931.

Phil 5051.16.6 — Lindner, Gustav A. Lehrbuch der allgemeinen Logik. 6e Aufl. Wien, 1914.

Phil 811.22 — Lindner, Herbert. Der Entwicklungsgang des philosophischen Denkens. Berlin, 1966.

Phil 5070.24 — Lindner, Herbert. Der Zweifel und seine Grenzen. Berlin, 1966.

Phil 6321.40 — Lindner, R.M. The fifty minute hour. N.Y., 1955.

Phil 6321.35 — Lindner, R.M. Prescription for rebellion. London, 1953.

Phil 5594.156A — Lindquist, Everet F. Design and analysis of experiments in psychology and education. Boston, 1956.

Phil 3805.160 — Lindroth, H. Schleiermachers religionsbegrepp. Thesis. Uppsala, 1926.

Phil 8701.24 — Lindroth, Hjalmer. Filosofiska och teologiska essayer. Stockholm, 1965.

Phil 6121.11 — Lindsay, A.A. Mind the transformer, the new psychology. 7. ed. Los Angeles, 1911.

Phil 9240.5 — Lindsay, A.D. The good and the clever. Cambridge, 1945.

Phil 3493.21 — Lindsay, A.D. Kant. London, 1934.

Phil 2475.1.83 — Lindsay, A.D. The philosophy of Bergson. London, 1911.

Phil 8701.19 — Lindsay, A.D. Religion, science, and society in the modern world. New Haven, 1943.

Phil 8961.12 — Lindsay, A.D. The two moralities: our duty to God and society. London, 1940.

Phil 2120.10.20 — Lindsay, A.D.L. Selected addresses. Cumberland, 1957.

Phil 9351.16.2 — Lindsay, A.R.B. What is worth while? N.Y., 1893.

Phil 8591.38 — Lindsay, Eric. Losing religion to find it. London, 1935.

Phil 186.23 — Lindsay, J. The fundamental problems of metaphysics. Edinburgh 1910.

Phil 5070.7 — Lindsay, J. The psychology of belief. Edinburgh, 1910.

Phil 630.11 — Lindsay, James. A philosophical system of theistic idealism. Edinburgh, 1917.

Phil 8591.18 — Lindsay, James. Recent advances in theistic philosophy of religion. Edinburgh, 1897.

Phil 811.10 — Lindsay, James. Studies in European philosophy. Edinburgh, 1909.

Phil 186.57 — Lindsay, Norman. Creative effort. 1. ed. London, 1924.

Phil 5821.2 — Lindsay, W.L. Mind in the lower animals. London, 1879. 2v.

Phil 5821.2.3 — Lindsay, W.L. Physiology and pathology of mind in the lower animals. Edinburgh, 1871.

Htn Phil 9351.12* — Lindsley, Philip. Baccalaureate address. Nashville, 1827.

Phil 5251.34.15 — Lindworsky, J. Experimental psychology. London, 1931.

Phil 5627.147.5 — Lindworsky, J. The psychology of asceticism. London, 1936.

Phil 5251.34.10 — Lindworsky, J. Theoretical psychology. St. Louis, 1932.

Phil 5251.34.3 — Lindworsky, J. Theoretische Psychologie in Umriss. 3. Aufl. Leipzig, 1926.

Phil 5761.10.15 — Lindworsky, J. The training of the will. Milwaukee, 1929.

Phil 5761.10 — Lindworsky, J. Der Wille, seine Erscheinung und seine Beherrschung. Leipzig, 1919.

Phil 5761.10.2 — Lindworsky, J. Der Wille, seine Erscheinung und seine Beherrschung. 2. Aufl. Leipzig, 1921.

Phil 8961.8 — Lindwurm, A. Die metaphysische Wurzel die christlichen Ethik. Berlin, 1872.

Phil 5548.50 — Lindzey, Gardner. Assessment of human motives. N.Y., 1958.

Phil 5548.50.2 — Lindzey, Gardner. Assessment of human motives. N.Y., 1964.

Phil 8408.14 — Lineamenti d'estetica fondati sul problema gnoseologico. (Hammond, Robert.) Aleppo, 1926.

Phil 8403.25 — Lineamenti di estetica. 1. ed. (Castelfranco, G.) Firenze, 1950.

Phil 181.57.10 — Lineamenti di filosofia. (Galli, Gallo.) Bologna, 1935.

Phil 4070.3 — Lineamenti di filosofia dell'azione. (Brunello, B.) Modena, 1938.

Phil 645.22 — Lineamenti di filosofia scetica. (Rensi, Giuseppe.) Bologna, 1919.

Phil 645.22.2 — Lineamenti di filosofia scetica. (Rensi, Giuseppe.) Bologna, 1921.

Phil 193.168 — Lineamenti di metalogica. (Scarlata, G.P.) Padova, 1951.

Phil 5257.11.15 — Lineamenti di psicologia. (Royce, Josiah.) Bari, 1928.

Author and Title Listing

Phil 811.7   Lineamenti di storia della filosofia. (Losacco, Michele.) Napoli, 1931.

Phil 8418.35   Lineamenti di una storia della poetica e dell'estetica. (Ruschioni, Ada.) Milano, 1966.

Phil 1955.6.107   Líneas fundamentales de la filosofía de John Dewey. (Mendoza de Montero, A.) Buenos Aires, 1940.

Phil 4120.9.30   Linee fondamentali d'une filosofia dello spirito. (Galli, Gallo.) Torino, 1961.

Phil 8404.6   Linee per una fenomenologia dell'arte. (Diano, Carlo.) Venezia, 1956.

Phil 800.8   Linei fondamentali di storia della filosofia. v.1-3. (Aquilanti, F.) Milano, 1938-40. 2v.

Phil 196.8.20   Lines de filosofia critica. 2a ed. (Varisco, B.) Roma, 1931.

Phil 8620.54   Ling, Trevor. The significance of Satan. London, 1961.

Phil 8591.84   Ling, Trevor Oswald. Buddha, Marx, and God: some aspects of religion in the modern world. N.Y., 1966.

Phil 9351.11   Lingard, R. A letter of advice to a young gentleman. N.Y., 1907.

Phil 9150.22   Lingle, T.W. Die Bedeutung der Entwickelungsgeschichte. Leipzig, 1899.

Phil 8591.81   Lings, Martin. Ancient beliefs and modern superstitions. London, 1964.

Phil 8591.83   Lings, Martin. Ancient beliefs and modern superstitions. 1. ed. London, 1965.

Htn   Phil 8879.6.2*   Lingua, sive, de linguae. (Erasmus, D.) Basileae, 1547.

Phil 8879.6A   Lingua, sive, de linguae. (Erasmus, D.) Lugdunum Batavorum, 1641.

Phil 5520.122   Linguaggia comune e linguaggi scientifici. (Preti, Giulio.) Roma, 1953.

Phil 5520.440   Linguaggio, scienza e filosofia. 2. ed. (Pasquinelli, Alberto.) Bologna, 1964.

Phil 150.15   Il linguaggio dei filosofi. (Ranzoli, C.) Padova, 1911.

Phil 3925.16.170   Linguaggio di esperienza in Ludwig Wittgenstein. (Gargani, Aldo Giorgio.) Firenze, 1966.

Phil 4200.9.35   Linguaggio e interpetrazione. (Pucci, Raffaele.) Napoli, 1966.

Phil 2493.94   Linguaggio e mondo umano in Condillac. (Salvucci, Pasquale.) Urbino, 1957.

Phil 5520.434   Linguaggio e salvezza. (Mancini, Italo.) Milano, 1964.

Phil 337.10   Der Linguismus und die Erkenntnistheorie der Verweisungen. (Goldschmidt, W.) Zürich, 1936.

Phil 5650.4   Linguistic lapses. (Wells, F.L.) N.Y., 1906.

Phil 5520.463   The linguistic turn; recent essays in philosophical method. (Rorty, Richard.) Chicago, 1967.

Phil 5520.449.5   Linguistica cartesiana. (Chomsky, Noam.) Madrid, 1969.

Phil 325.20   Linguistica ed empirismo nel Seicento inglese. (Formigari, Lia.) Bari, 1970.

Phil 5520.487   Linguistics in philosophy. (Ventler, Zeno.) Ithaca, 1967.

Phil 5520.605   Linguistique et philosophie. (Gilson, Etienne.) Paris, 1969.

Phil 5251.44.7   Link, Henry C. The rediscovery of man. N.Y., 1939.

Phil 5850.258.4   Link, Henry C. The return to religion. N.Y., 1937.

Phil 5850.258.5   Link, Henry C. The way to security. Garden City, 1951.

Phil 2050.186   Linke, Paul. David Humes Lehre vom Wissen. Diss. Leipzig, 1901.

Phil 5585.29   Linke, Paul F. Grundlagen der Wahrnehmungslehre. München, 1918.

Phil 5585.29.2   Linke, Paul F. Grundlagen der Wahrnehmungslehre. 2. Aufl. München, 1928.

Phil 3011.7   Linke, Paul F. Niedergangserscheinungen in der Philosophie der Gegenwart. München, 1961.

Phil 342.5   Linke, Paul F. Die phänomenale Sphäre und das Bewusstsein. Halle an der Saale, 1912.

Phil 7069.35.51F   Linking the spaces. (Wells, Helen B.) N.Y., 1935. 2 pam.

Phil 5585.285   Links en rechts in waarneming en beleving. Proefschrift. (Zwaan, Evert Joost.) Utrecht, 1965.

Phil 5643.120   Die Links-Rechts-Polarisation des phaenomenalen Raumes. (Meer, H.C. von der.) Groningen, 1959.

Phil 186.92   Lins, I.M.de B. Escolas filosoficas. Rio, 1939.

Phil 600.58   Lins, Ivan Monteiro de Barros. História do positivismo no Brasil. São Paulo, 1964.

Phil 4973.7   Lins, Mario. Foundations of social determinism. Rio de Janeiro, 1959.

Phil 5585.100   Linschoten, J. Strukturanalyse der binokularen Tiefenwahrnehmung. Groningen, 1956.

Phil 5251.66   Linschoten, Johannes. Idolen van de psycholoog. Utrecht, 1964.

Phil 2070.145.5   Linschoten, Johannes. On the way toward a phenomenological psychology; the psychology of William James. Pittsburgh, 1968.

Phil 2070.145   Linschoten, Johannes. Op weg naar een fenomenologische psychologie. Utrecht, 1959.

X Cg   Phil 7075.140   Linsert, Richard. Kabale und Liebe. Berlin, 1931.

Phil 5520.137   Linsky, Leonard. Refering. London, 1967.

Phil 5520.135A   Linsky, Leonard. Semantics and the philosophy of language. Urbana, Ill., 1952.

Phil 9351.5   Linsley, J.H. Lectures on relations and middle aged. Hartford, 1828.

Phil 486.25   Linssen, Robert. Spiritualité de la matière. Paris, 1966.

Phil 7054.54.5   Linton, Charles. The healing of the nations. 2. ed. N.Y., 1855.

Phil 7054.54.7   Linton, Charles. The healing of the nations. 2. series. Philadelphia, 1864.

Phil 5590.19.1   Linton, Ralph. The cultural background of personality. N.Y., 196-?

Phil 5520.117   Lintsbakh, Ia. Printsipy filosofskogo iazyka. Petrograd, 1916.

Phil 303.12.25   Lintz, E.J. The unity of the universe. Fribourg, 1939.

Phil 342.15   Lion, Alene. Anaknises and the a priori. Oxford, 1935.

Phil 8591.35   Lion, Aline. The idealistic conception of religion. Oxford, 1932.

Phil 8412.29   Lion, Ferdinand. Die Geburt der Aphrodite. Heidelberg, 1955.

Phil 3552.425   Lion, Ferdinand. Lebensquellen der deutschen Metaphysik. Frankfurt, 1960.

Phil 9400.4A   Lionberger, I.H. The felicities of sixty. Boston, 1922.

Phil 930.58   Liou, Kia-hway. L'ésprit synthétique de la Chine. Paris, 1961.

Phil 4803.468.80   Lipkowski, Otton. Józefa Joteyko. Wyd. 1. Warszawa, 1968.

Phil 5251.12   Lipmann, O. Grundriss der Psychologie für Juristen. Leipzig, 1908.

Phil 9558.45   Lipmann, Otto. Die Lüge Sprach- und literaturwissenschaftlicher und entwicklungschichtlicher Betrachtung. Leipzig, 1927.

Phil 4960.255   Lipp, Solomon. Three Argentine thinkers. N.Y., 1969.

Phil 400.66   Lippa, L. von. Der Aufstieg von Kant zu Goethe. Berlin, 1921.

Phil 7068.88.20   Lippitt, F.J. Physical proof of another life. Washington, 1888.

Phil 6980.424   Lippman, Hyman. Treatment of the child in emotional conflict. N.Y., 1956.

Phil 5635.10   Lippmann, F. Du déterminisme psychologique. Strasbourg, 1909.

Phil 8886.50.6   Lippmann, W. A preface to morals. London, 1931.

Phil 8886.50   Lippmann, W. A preface to morals. N.Y., 1929.

Phil 8886.50.3   Lippmann, W. A preface to morals. N.Y., 1929.

Phil 8886.50.5   Lippmann, W. A preface to morals. N.Y., 1931.

Phil 8412.21   Lippold, F. Bausteine zu einer Asthetik der inneren Form. München, 1920.

Phil 6121.10   Lipps, G.F. Grundriss der psychophysik. Leipzig, 1909.

Phil 5761.5   Lipps, G.F. Das Problem der Willensfreiheit. Leipzig, 1912.

Phil 6121.10.5   Lipps, G.F. Die psychischen Massmethoden. Braunschweig, 1906.

Phil 186.38   Lipps, Gottlob F. Mythenbildung und Erkenntnis. Leipzig, 1907.

Phil 5590.145   Lipps, Hans. Die menschliche Natur. Frankfurt, 1941.

Phil 210.20   Lipps, Hans. Untersuchungen zu einer Hermeneutischen Logik. 2. Aufl. Frankfurt, 1959.

Phil 342.12   Lipps, Hans. Untersuchungen zur Phänomenologie der Erkenntnis. v.1-2. Bonn, 1927-28.

Phil 5520.92   Lipps, Hans. Die Verbindlichkeit der Sprache. Frankfurt, 1944.

Phil 3585.17   Lipps, Hans. Die Wirklichkeit des Menschen. Frankfurt, 1954.

Phil 8886.15   Lipps, T. Die ethischen Grundfragen. Hamburg, 1899.

Phil 8886.15.6   Lipps, T. Die ethischen Grundfragen. 2e Aufl. Hamburg, 1905.

Phil 5051.30   Lipps, T. Grundzüge der Logik. Hamburg, 1893.

Phil 5525.13   Lipps, T. Komik und Humor. Hamburg, 1898.

Phil 5251.8.5   Lipps, T. Leitfaden der Psychologie. Leipzig, 1903.

Phil 5251.8.15   Lipps, T. Psychological studies. 2d ed. Baltimore, 1926.

Phil 5251.8.25   Lipps, T. Psychologie der Komik. n.p., 1888-1906. 23 pam.

Phil 5251.8.7   Lipps, T. Psychologische Studien. Heidelberg, 1885.

Phil 5251.8.8   Lipps, T. Psychologische Studien. Leipzig, 1905.

Phil 5251.8   Lipps, T. Seelenlebens. Bonn, 1883.

Phil 8412.10   Lipps, Theodor. Asthetik; Psychologie des Schönen und der Kunst. Hamburg, 1903-06. 2v.

Phil 5374.10   Lipps, Theodor. Einheiten und Relationen. Leipzig, 1902.

Phil 186.37   Lipps, Theodor. Philosophie und Wirklichkeit. Heidelberg, 1908.

Phil 5761.12   Lipps, Theodor. Vom Fühlen, Wollen und Denken. Leipzig, 1902.

Phil 5761.12.3   Lipps, Theodor. Vom Fühlen, Wollen und Denken. 3. Aufl. Leipzig, 1926.

Phil 8412.10.5   Lipps, Theodor. Von der Form des ästhetischen Apperception. Halle, 1902.

Phil 2045.109   Lips, Julius. Die Stellung des Thomas Hobbes zu den politischen Parteien der grossen englischen Revolution. Leipzig, 1927.

Phil 510.13.5   Lipsius, Friedrich R. Einheit der Erkenntnis und Einheit des Seins. Leipzig, 1913.

Phil 186.41   Lipsius, Friedrich R. Naturphilosophie und Weltanschauung. Leipzig, 1918.

Phil 510.13   Lipsius, Friedrich R. Die Religion des Monismus. Berlin, 1907.

Phil 1200.1   Lipsius, J. Manuductionis ad stoicam philosophiam. Antverpriae, 1604.

Phil 1200.1.5   Lipsius, J. Manuductionis ad stoicam philosophiam. Lugduni Batavorum, 1644.

Htn   Phil 2725.7.30*   Lipsius, Justus. Manuductionis ad stoicam. Antverpiae, 1604.

Phil 5251.24   Liqueno, Jose M. Compendio de psicologia contemporanea. Córdoba, 1919.

Phil 3640.61   La lirica di Nietzsche. (Nietzsche, Friedrich.) Messina, 1948.

Phil 3801.522   Lisco, Heinrich. Geschichtsphilosophie Schellings, 1792-1809. Inaug. Diss. Jena, 1884.

Phil 3425.495   De list de rede in de geschiedenisfilosofie van Hegel. (Beerling, R.F.) Arnhem, 1959.

Phil 75.32   List of books in the New York Public Library relating to philosophy. (New York. Public Library.) N.Y., 1908.

Phil 6327.21.30   Listen little man. (Reich, Wilhelm.) N.Y., 1948.

Phil 23.24   Listener's notebook. (National Advisory Council on Radio in Education.) Chicago. 1931-1932

Phil 5330.38   Listening and attention. (Moray, Neville.) Baltimore, 1969.

Phil 5643.32   Listing, J.B. Beitrag zur physiologischen Optik. Leipzig, 1905.

Phil 8880.16.2   The listner. (Fry, Caroline.) Philadelphia, 1832. 2v.

Phil 8880.16   The listner. (Fry, Caroline.) Philadelphia, 1833. 2v.

Phil 8080.4   Listowel, William Francis Hare. A critical history of modern aesthetics. London, 1933.

Phil 8080.4.5   Listowel, William Francis Hare. Modern aesthetics. N.Y., 1967.

Phil 4803.454.32   Lit do piezy o maglacej potrzebie obechej spelnienia religli. (Hoene-Wroński, Józef Maria.) Warszawa, 1928.

Phil 75.21   Literarische Berichte. (Deutsche Philosphische Gesellschaft.) Erfurt. 8-26 19v.

Phil 75.20   Literarische Berichte aus dem Gebiete der Philosophie. Sonder Druck von Heft 9/10. Erfurt, 1926.

Phil 974.3.10   Das literarische Lebenswerk Rudolf Steiners. (Picht, C.S.) Dornach, 1926.

Phil 8893.83.25   Die literarische Stellung des Protestanten zu dem Katholicen. (Salat, Jakob.) Laudshut, 1831.

Phil 2138.153   The literary criticism of J.S. Mill. (Sharpless, F. Parvin.) The Hague, 1967.

Phil 8589.5.5A   Literary remains. (James, H.) Boston, 1885.

Phil 8110.4   Literatur- und Kunstkritik in ihren Wechselbeziehungen. (Thielke, K.L.F.) Halle, 1935.

Phil 5203.2   Die Literatur der Psychiatrie, Neurologie und Psychologie. v.1-3. (Laehr, H.) Berlin, 1900. 4v.

Phil 8416.11.5   Literatura i estetika. (Plekhanov, Georgii Valentinovich.) Moskva, 1958.

Phil 188.24   Literature, philosophy and the social sciences; essays in existentialism and phenomenology. (Natanson, M.) The Hague, 1962.

Phil 7082.30.5   The literature and curiosities of dreams. (Grant, Alexander Henley.) London, 1865. 2v.

Phil 1750.485A   Literature considered as philosophy. (Knight, E.W.) London, 1957.

Phil 8625.2   Literature of the doctrine of a future life. (Abbot, Ezra.) Cambridge? 1862?

Phil 8625.2.5   The literature of the doctrine of a future life. (Abbot, Ezra.) N.Y., 1871.

Phil 176.160   Literaturmetaphysik. 1. Aufl. (Bense, Max.) Stuttgart, 1950.

Phil 5203.7   Literatuurlijsten en atlas. (Spek, J. van der.) Groningen, 1927.

Phil 960.244   Litman, Aleksei D. Filosofskaia mysl' nezavisimoi Indii. Moskva, 1966.

Phil 342.17   Litt, Theodor. Denken und Sein. Stuttgart, 1948.

Phil 186.60.15   Litt, Theodor. Einleitung in die Philosophie. Leipzig, 1933.

Phil 186.60   Litt, Theodor. Erkenntnis und Leben. Leipzig, 1923.

Phil 3425.346   Litt, Theodor. Hegel. Heidelberg, 1953.

Phil 3493.16   Litt, Theodor. Kant und Herder als Deuter der Geistigen Welt. Leipzig, 1930.

Phil 3493.16.5   Litt, Theodor. Kant und Herder als Deuter der Geistigen Welt. 2. Aufl. Heidelberg, 1949.

Phil 186.60.20   Litt, Theodor. Mensch und Welt. München, 1948.

Phil 8591.41   Litt, Theodor. Protestantisches Geschichtswussteins. Leipzig, 1939.

Phil 3585.12   Litt, Theodor. Die Selbsterkenntnis des Menschen. Leipzig, 1938.

Phil 3585.12.5   Litt, Theodor. Die Selbsterkenntnis des Menschen. 2. Aufl. Hamburg, 1948.

Phil 186.60.10   Litt, Theodor. Wissenschaft, Bildung, Weltanschauung. Leipzig, 1928.

Phil 3552.317   Litt, Theodore. Leibniz und die deutsche Gegenwart. Wiesbaden, 1946.

Phil 2805.29   Litterae provinciales. (Pascal, Blaise.) Helmaestadt, 1664.

Phil 8412.27   Little, J.S. What is art? London, 1884.

Phil 5051.33   Little, W.W. Applied logic. Boston, 1955.

Phil 3210.67.5   Little book of life after death. (Fechner, G.T.) Boston, 1912.

Phil 193.49.20   Little essays drawn from writings of George Santayana. (Santayana, G.) N.Y., 1920.

Phil 193.49.23   Little essays drawn from writings of George Santayana. (Santayana, G.) N.Y., 1924.

Phil 9178.1   The little family. v.1-2. (Sanders, C.E.) Haverhill, n.d.

Phil 8875.9   Little Jeremiads. (Albertson, Ralph.) Lewiston, 1903.

Phil 21.6   Little journeys to the homes of great philosophers. (Hubbard, Elbert.) East Aurora, n.d.

Phil 5211.7   The little world of man. (Bamborough, J.B.) London, 1952.

Phil 1516.1.2   Littlejohn, J.M. Political theory of the schoolmen. College Springs, 1894.

Phil 600.7   Littré, Emile. De la philosophie positive. v.1-2. Paris, 1845.

Phil 600.7.5   Littré, Emile. Fragments de philosophie positive et de sociologie. Paris, 1876.

Phil 600.7.1   Littré, Emile. Paroles de philosophie positive. Paris, 1859.

Phil 600.7.2   Littré, Emile. Paroles de philosophie positive. Paris, 1863.

Phil 600.7.3   Littré, Emile. La science au point de vue philosophique. Paris, 1873.

Phil 2490.83.2   Littré, M.P.E. Auguste Comte et la philosophie positive. Paris, 1864.

Phil 600.7.105   Littré devant Dieu. (Six, J.F.) Paris, 1962.

Phil 2750.11.88   Liturgie et contemplation. (Maritain, Jacques.) Bruges, 1959.

Phil 8643.31   Litwell, Constance. Seek paradise. London, 1948.

Phil 5548.120   Litwin, George Henry. Motivation and organizational climate. Boston, 1968.

VPhil 2725.2.120   Litwin, Jakub. Eseję o dialogach wewnętrznych: Diderot, Lamennais. Warszawa, 1967.

Phil 5410.5   Litwinski, Léon. La psychologie de l'ingratitude. Bruxelles, 1964.

Phil 5401.18   Litwinski, Léon de. La timidité constitutionnelle et ses formes passive et active. Lisbonne, 1944.

Phil 3235.128   Liudvig Feierbakh. (Bykhovskii, Bernard E.) Moskva, 1967.

Phil 3235.81.20   Liudvig Feierbakh. 2. izd. (Engels, Friedrich.) Geneva, 1905.

Phil 175.60   Liudyna i svitohliad. (Akademiia Nauk URSR, Kiev. Institut Filosofii.) Kyiv, 1963.

Phil 8951.32   Liv, fellesskap, tjeneste. (Boeckman, Peter Wilhelm.) Oslo, 1970.

Phil 7020.2   Liv efter döden? (Jacobson, Nils-Olof.) Salna, 1971.

Phil 8422.12   Liv og kunst. (Vedel, V.) København, 1949. 2v.

Phil 9070.65   Live and help live. (Kraines, S.H.) N.Y., 1951.

Phil 1730.16   Lively, Jack. The enlightenment. London, 1966.

Phil 7069.68.30   The lively ghosts of Ireland. (Holzer, Hans W.) London, 1968.

Phil 9351.6   Livermore, A.A. Lectures to young men. Boston, 1846.

Phil 5590.292   Lives in progress. 2. ed. (White, Robert Winthrop.) N.Y., 1966.

Phil 1801.1   Lives of philosophers of the time of George III. (Brougham, H.) London, 1855.

Phil 5886.10   Lives through the years. 1st ed. (Williams, Richard Hays.) N.Y., 1965.

Phil 4600.5.31   Livets bejakande. (Ljunglund, L.) Stockholm, 1914.

Phil 8897.52.5   Livets grundvardier. (Wilkens, C.) København, 1909.

Phil 8878.44   Livets vardiproblemer. (Dam, Axel.) København, 1921.

Phil 8633.1.20   Living again. (Brown, Charles R.) Cambridge, 1920.

Phil 194.45.5   Living and knowing. (Tomlin, E.W.F.) London, 1955.

Phil 1750.166.35   Living as a humanist. (Blackham, H.J.) London, 1957.

Phil 818.27   Living biographies of great philosophers. (Schnittkind, H.T.) Garden City, 1941.

Phil 178.12.17   Living by the spirit. (Dresser, H.W.) N.Y., 1901.

Phil 8643.13   Living for the future. (Slater, J.R.) Boston, 1916.

Phil 9070.28   Living in crisis. (Wilkins, Ernest Hatch.) Boston, 1937.

Phil 8602.27   Living issues in religious thought. (Wood, Herbert G.) London, 1924.

Phil 5374.48   The living mind. (Fite, Warner.) N.Y., 1930.

Phil 186.94A   Living philosophies. N.Y., 1931.

Phil 8602.12   The living present and the dead past. (Wright, H.C.) Boston, 1865.

Phil 7069.28.90   Living secrets. (Valdry, Luma.) London, 1928.

Phil 6310.1.106   The living symbol. (Adler, Gerhard.) N.Y., 1961.

Phil 2520.52.70   The living thoughts of Descartes. (Descartes, René.) Philadelphia, 1947.

Phil 6315.2.52   The living thoughts of Freud. (Freud, Sigmund.) N.Y., 1941.

Phil 3480.25.55   The living thoughts of Kant. (Kant, Immanuel.) N.Y., 1940.

Phil 3640.73   The living thoughts of Nietzsche. (Nietzsche, Friedrich.) London, 1946.

Phil 3640.277A   The living thoughts of Nietzsche. (Nietzsche, Friedrich.) N.Y., 1939.

Phil 2805.25.50A   The living thoughts of Pascal. (Pascal, Blaise.) N.Y., 1940.

Phil 3819.29.30   The living thoughts of Spinoza. (Spinoza, Benedictus de.) N.Y., 1939.

Phil 3808.176   Living thoughts presented by Thomas Mann. (Schopenhauer, Arthur.) N.Y., 1939.

Phil 2175.5.30   Living time and the integration of the life. (Nicoll, Maurice.) London, 1953.

Phil 1750.166.200   The living tradition. (Hadas, Moses.) N.Y., 1967.

Phil 305.1   The living universe. (Younghusband, F.E.) N.Y., 1933.

Phil 8589.14.5   A living universe (Hibbert lectures, 1923). (Jacks, L.P.) N.Y., 1924.

Phil 7069.19.160   Living waters. N.Y., 1919.

Phil 6962.36   Living with mental illness. (Mills, Enid.) London, 1962.

Phil 7069.30.11   Livingston, Marjorie. The new Nuctemeron (The twelve hours of Apollonius of Tyana). London, 1930.

Phil 9161.2   Livre de lecture courante des devoirs des enfants. (Beleze, G.L.G.) Paris, 1855.

Phil 9163.2   Livre de mes fils. (Doumer, P.) Paris, 1906.

Phil 8592.62   Le livre des certitudes admirables. (Magre, M.) Avignon, 1941.

Phil 7054.37   Le livre des esprits. (Rivail, H.L.D.) Paris, 1857.

Phil 7054.37.15   Le livre des esprits. 15. ed . (Rivail, H.L.D.) Paris, 1866.

Htn   Phil 2725.2.52*   Le livre du peuple. (Lamennais, F.R. de.) Paris, 1838.

Phil 5593.66.15   Livret de cotation des formes dans le Rorschach d'après une compilation des cotations de H. Rorschach. (Beizmann, Cécile.) Paris, 1966.

Phil 8886.58   Livry, Hypolite. Reflexions morales et probablement fort inutiles. Paris, 1807.

Phil 9070.126   Livsåskådning och religion. (Husén, Torsten.) Stockholm, 1968.

Phil 585.178   Livsåskådningar. (Aaberg, Thorsten.) Stockholm, 1965.

Phil 165.250   Livsanskuelse gennem tiderne. (Marcus, Aage.) København, 1955-58. 10v.

Phil 9070.106   Livsforståelse moralloven livets ophør. (Jørgensen, T.G.) København, 1964.

Phil 3640.217   Livsproblemet hos Nietzsche. (Rosen, Hugo.) Stockholm, 1923.

Phil 4973.41   Lizarte Martínez, Angel. Dios, espíritu y materia; esencia. 2. ed. Montevideo, 1944.

Phil 4225.15.90   Lizzio, Maria. Marxismo e metafisica. Catania, 1968.

Phil 978.72.5   Ljumgström, O. Theosophy. n.p., n.d. 6 pam.

Phil 8050.41   Ljunggren, G. Framställning af de förnämsta esthetiska systemerna. Lund, 1856. 2v.

Phil 8050.43   Ljunggren, G. Några punkter ur läran om det natursköna. Lund, 1852.

Phil 4515.93   Ljunghoff, Johannes. Christopher Jacob Boström Sveriges Platon. Uppsala, 1916.

Phil 4600.5.31   Ljunglund, L. Livets bejakande. Stockholm, 1914.

Phil 978.72   Ljungström, O. Graded lessons in theosophy. Lund, 1935.

Htn   Phil 978.72.10*   Ljungström, O. A philosophical overhaul. Lund, 1937.

Phil 3450.19.180   Llambías de Azevedo, Juan. El antiguo y el nuevo Heidegger y un dialogo con el. Montevideo, 1958.

Phil 4351.5.80   Llanos, Alfredo. Carlos Astrada. Buenos Aires, 1962.

Phil 2520.315   Llanos, Alfredo. El problema del voluntarismo en Descartes. Bahia Blanca, 1960.

Phil 9351.14   Llonu, Lastenia Lurriva de. Cartas a mi hijo. Lima, 1919.

Phil 4362.5   Lloreus y Barba, F.J. Lecciones de filosofia. Barcelona, 1920. 3v.

Phil 400.10   Lloyd, A.H. Dynamic idealism. Chicago, 1898.

Phil 645.8   Lloyd, A.H. The will to doubt. London, 1907.

Phil 6681.15   Lloyd, B. Layton. Hypnotism in the treatment of disease. London, 1934.

Phil 1135.184   Lloyd, Geoffrey Ernest Richard. Polarity and analogy. Cambridge, Eng., 1966.

Phil 8886.9   Lloyd, J. Duty and faith. Manchester, 1884.

Phil 9240.1   Lloyd, R.B. The mastery of evil. London, 1941.

Phil 5251.29   Lloyd, R.E. Life and word. London, 1924.

X Cg   Phil 9430.8   Lloyd, R.J. Pessimism, a study in contemporary sociology. Liverpool, 1880.

Phil 5251.13   Lloyd, W.E. Psychology, normal and abnormal. Los Angeles, 1908.

Phil 5251.13.2   Lloyd, W.E. Psychology, normal and abnormal. N.Y., 1910.

Phil 8430.6   Lo bello y la buena a la luz. (Benaz, Manuel.) Buenos Aires, 1933.

Phil 3480.35.5   Lo dissertatio de 1770, sobre la forma y los principios del mundo sensible y del inteligible. (Kant, Immanuel.) Madrid, 1961.

Phil 4374.5.30   Lo fugaz y lo eterno. (Xirau, Joaquín.) Mexico, 1942.

Phil 8886.73.5   Lo que sabemos de moral. (López Aranguren, José Luis.) Madrid, 1967.

Phil 181.45.80   Lo spirito come atto puro in Giovanni Gentile. (Orsi, Domenico d'.) Padova, 1957.

Phil 5203.37   Loattit, Chauncey McKinley. Handbook of psychological literature. Bloomington, Ind., 1932.

Phil 4710.3   Lobkowicz, Nikolaus. Das Widerspruchsprinzie in der neueren sowjetischen Philosophie. Reidel, 1959.

Phil 8961.2   Lobstein, P. Die Ethik Calvins. Strassburg, 1877.

Htn   Phil 7060.7.5*   Loca infesta, hoc est, de infestes. (Thyraeus, P.) London, 1599.

Phil 6115.6.5   Localisation der geistigen Vorgänge. (Flechsig, P.) Leipzig, 1896.

Phil 6129.5   Localisations cérébelleuses. (Thomas, André.) Paris, 1914.

Phil 575.90   Lochman, M. Inner life of humanity. Pt.1. n.p., 1936.

Phil 3110.55.35   Die lochteure Pforte. (Böhme, J.) Berlin, 1921.

Phil 2115.196   Locke, Berkeley, Hume. (Morris, C.R.) London, 1963.

Phil 2115.132   Locke, Berkeley, Hume. (Reininger, R.) München, 1922.

Phil 6121.50   Locke, Don. Myself and others; a study in our knowledge of minds. Oxford, 1968.

Phil 573.6   Locke, Don. Perception and our knowledge of the external world. London, 1967.

Phil 2115.45.2   Locke, J. An abridgment of Mr. Locke's Essay concerning human understanding. Boston, 1794.

Phil 2115.45.5   Locke, J. An abridgment of Mr. Locke's Essay concerning human understanding. Glasgow, 1744.

Htn   Phil 2115.45*   Locke, J. An abridgment of Mr. Locke's Essay concerning human understanding. London, 1700.

Htn   Phil 2115.44*   Locke, J. An abridgment of Mr. Locke's Essay concerning humane understanding. London, 1696.

Phil 2115.78A   Locke, J. An account of Mr. Lock's religion. London, 1700.

Phil 2115.27   Locke, J. The beauties of Locke. London, n.d.

Phil 2115.70.7   Locke, J. Ein Brief über Toleranz. Hamburg, 1957.

Htn	Phil 2115.77.5F*	Locke, J. Catalogue of Locke's library. Ms. photostat. n.p., n.d.
Htn	Phil 2115.77F*	Locke, J. Catalogus librorum. Ms. photostat. n.p., n.d.
Htn	Phil 2115.25*	Locke, J. Collection of several pieces. London, 1720.
Htn	Phil 2115.64*	Locke, J. A common-place book to the Holy Bible. London, 1697.
	Phil 2115.64.20	Locke, J. A common-place book to the Holy Bible. 3d ed. London, 1725.
	Phil 2115.64.25	Locke, J. A common-place book to the Holy Bible. 4th ed. London, 1738.
	Phil 2115.65	Locke, J. A commonplace book to the Holy Bible. London, 1824.
	Phil 2115.65.25	Locke, J. A commonplace book to the Holy Bible. 5th London ed. N.Y., 18- ?
	Phil 2115.50	Locke, J. The conduct of the understanding. Boston, 1825.
	Phil 2115.50.10	Locke, J. The conduct of the understanding. Cambridge, 1781.
	Phil 2115.51.7	Locke, J. The conduct of the understanding. N.Y., 1966.
	Phil 2115.51A	Locke, J. The conduct of the understanding. Oxford, 1881.
	Phil 2115.50.2	Locke, J. The conduct of the understanding. v.1-2. Boston, 1828.
	Phil 2115.50.3	Locke, J. The conduct of the understanding. v.1-2. Boston, 1831.
	Phil 2115.51.6	Locke, J. The conduct of the understanding. 5th ed. Oxford, 1901.
	Phil 2115.75.9	Locke, J. The correspondence of John Locke and Edward Clarke. Cambridge, 1927.
	Phil 2115.75.10	Locke, J. The correspondence of John Locke and Edward Clarke. London, 1927.
Htn	Phil 2115.75.11*	Locke, J. Correspondence of John Locke and Edward Clarke. Editor's ms. for Cambridge edition. n.p., n.d.
	Phil 2115.29.125F	Locke, J. De intellectu humano. Ed. 4a. London, 1701.
	Phil 2115.51.20	Locke, J. Della guida dell'intelligenza nella ricerca della veritá. Lanciano, 1927.
	Phil 2115.70.15	Locke, J. Epistola su la tolleranza. Lanciano, 1920. 2v.
	Phil 2115.48.2	Locke, J. Essai philosophique concernant l'entendement humaine. Amsterdam, 1700.
	Phil 2115.48.7	Locke, J. Essai philosophique concernant l'entendement humaine. Amsterdam, 1735.
	Phil 2115.48.12	Locke, J. Essai philosophique concernant l'entendement humaine. Amsterdam, 1755.
	Phil 2115.48.5	Locke, J. Essai philosophique concernant l'entendement humaine. La Haye, 1714.
	Phil 2115.48.10	Locke, J. Essai philosophique concernant l'entendement humaine. Abrégé. Genève, 1741.
	Phil 2115.48.15	Locke, J. Essai philosophique concernant l'entendement humaine. Abrégé. Upsal, 1792.
	Phil 2115.48.11	Locke, J. Essai philosophique concernant l'entendement humaine. 4e éd. Amsterdam, 1742.
	Phil 2115.48.14	Locke, J. Essai philosophique concernant l'entendement humaine. 5e éd. Paris, 1799? 4v.
	Phil 2115.36.30	Locke, J. Essay concerning human understanding. Cambridge, 1931.
Htn	Phil 2115.36.31*	Locke, J. Essay concerning human understanding. Cambridge, 1931.
	Phil 2115.47.5	Locke, J. Essay concerning human understanding. Chicago, 1917.
	Phil 2115.36.31.12	Locke, J. Essay concerning human understanding. Chicago, 1956.
	Phil 2115.32.5	Locke, J. Essay concerning human understanding. Edinburgh, 1798. 3v.
	Phil 2115.30.3	Locke, J. Essay concerning human understanding. London, 1716. 2v.
	Phil 2115.30	Locke, J. Essay concerning human understanding. London, 1726. 2v.
	Phil 2115.30.2	Locke, J. Essay concerning human understanding. London, 1748. 2v.
	Phil 2115.31	Locke, J. Essay concerning human understanding. London, 1753. 2v.
	Phil 2115.32	Locke, J. Essay concerning human understanding. London, 1791. 2v.
	Phil 2115.34.15	Locke, J. Essay concerning human understanding. London, 1823. 3v.
	Phil 2115.35.25	Locke, J. Essay concerning human understanding. London, 1870.
	Phil 2115.36.31.10	Locke, J. Essay concerning human understanding. London, 1947.
	Phil 2115.36	Locke, J. Essay concerning human understanding. Oxford, 1894. 3v.
	Phil 2115.36.25A	Locke, J. Essay concerning human understanding. Oxford, 1924.
	Phil 2115.35.15	Locke, J. Essay concerning human understanding. Philadelphia, 1849.
	Phil 2115.35.17	Locke, J. Essay concerning human understanding. Philadelphia, 185-?
	Phil 2115.35.19A	Locke, J. Essay concerning human understanding. Philadelphia, 185-?
	Phil 2115.36.35	Locke, J. Essay concerning human understanding. An early draft. Oxford, 1936.
Htn	Phil 2115.36.32*	Locke, J. Essay concerning human understanding. Photostat copy of Locke's original ms. n.p., n.d.
	Phil 2115.34.2	Locke, J. Essay concerning human understanding. v.1,3: 1st American ed. Boston, 1803-06. 3v.
	Phil 2115.32.3A	Locke, J. Essay concerning human understanding. v.1-2,3. London, 1795. 2v.
	Phil 2115.35	Locke, J. Essay concerning human understanding. v.1-2. N.Y., 1824.
	Phil 2115.33	Locke, J. Essay concerning human understanding. v.1-3. Edinburgh, 1801.
	Phil 2115.31.5	Locke, J. Essay concerning human understanding. v.2. Edinburgh, 1765.
	Phil 2115.30.4	Locke, J. Essay concerning human understanding. v.2. London, 1735.
NEDL	Phil 2115.34.5	Locke, J. Essay concerning human understanding. v.2. 2nd American ed. Boston, 1813.
	Phil 2115.34	Locke, J. Essay concerning human understanding. 1st American ed. Boston, 1803. 3v.
Htn	Phil 2115.34.3*	Locke, J. Essay concerning human understanding. 2nd American ed. Brattleboro, Vt., 1806. 3v.
Htn	Phil 2115*	Locke, J. Essay concerning human understanding. 2nd American ed. Brattleboro, Vt., 1806. 3v.
	Phil 2115.34.9	Locke, J. Essay concerning human understanding. 24th ed. London, 1817.
	Phil 2115.35.5	Locke, J. Essay concerning human understanding. 25th ed. London, 1825.
Htn	Phil 2115.2.1F*	Locke, J. An essay concerning humane understanding. London, 1690.
Htn	Phil 2115.2*	Locke, J. An essay concerning humane understanding. London, 1690.
Htn	Phil 2115.2.2*A	Locke, J. An essay concerning humane understanding. 2nd ed. London, 1694.
Htn	Phil 2115.2.3F*	Locke, J. An essay concerning humane understanding. 2nd ed. London, 1694.
Htn	Phil 2115.2.5F*	Locke, J. An essay concerning humane understanding. 3rd ed. London, 1695.
Htn	Phil 2115.2.7F*	Locke, J. An essay concerning humane understanding. 4th ed. London, 1700.
Htn	Phil 2115.2.9F*	Locke, J. An essay concerning humane understanding. 5th ed. London, 1706.
Htn	Phil 2115.60*	Locke, J. Essay for the understanding of St. Paul's epistles. Boston, 1820.
	Phil 2115.60.2	Locke, J. Essay for the understanding of St. Paul's epistles. Boston, 1820.
	Phil 2115.72	Locke, J. Essays on the law of nature. Oxford, 1954.
	Phil 2115.75.2	Locke, J. Familiar letters. London, 1742.
	Phil 2115.75	Locke, J. Familiar letters. London, 1742.
	Phil 2115.75.3	Locke, J. Familiar letters. London, 1830.
	Phil 2115.29	Locke, J. La filosofia di G. Locke. Firenze, 1920-21. 2v.
	Phil 2115.51.10	Locke, J. Leitung des Verstandes. Heidelberg, 1883.
Htn	Phil 2115.70*	Locke, J. Letter concerning toleration. London, 1689.
	Phil 2115.70.20	Locke, J. A letter concerning toleration. The Hague, 1963.
Htn	Phil 2115.73*	Locke, J. A letter to Edward, Lord Bishop of Worcester. London, 1697.
	Phil 2115.70.16	Locke, J. Lettera sulla tolleranza. Firenze, 1961.
Htn	Phil 2115.70.5*	Locke, J. Letters concerning toleration. London, 1765.
	Phil 2115.70.25	Locke, J. Lettre sur la tolérance. 1. éd. Montréal, 1964.
	Phil 2115.76	Locke, J. Lettres inédites. La Haye, 1912.
	Phil 2115.49.20	Locke, J. Libri IV de intellectu humano. Lipsiae, 1709.
	Phil 2115.49.25	Locke, J. Libri IV de intellectu humano. Lipsiae, 1741.
	Phil 2115.69	Locke, J. Locke's travels in France. Cambridge, 1953.
	Phil 2115.74.15	Locke, J. O forgripelize. Stockholm, 1726.
	Phil 2115.48.25	Locke, J. Oeuvres de Locke et Leibnitz. Paris, 1839.
Htn	Phil 2115.20*	Locke, J. Oeuvres diverses. Rotterdam, 1710.
	Phil 2115.19	Locke, J. Oeuvres philosophiques de Locke. Paris, 1821-25. 7v.
	Phil 2115.68	Locke, J. Of civil government and toleration. London, 1950.
	Phil 2115.67	Locke, J. On politics and education. N.Y., 1947.
	Phil 2115.62.10	Locke, J. A paraphrase and notes on epistle of St. Paul. Cambridge, 1832.
Htn	Phil 2115.62.2*	Locke, J. A paraphrase and notes on epistle of St. Paul. London, 1707.
	Phil 2115.62	Locke, J. A paraphrase and notes on epistle of St. Paul. London, 1823.
	Phil 2115.27.5	Locke, J. Philosophical beauties. N.Y., 1828.
	Phil 2115.14	Locke, J. Philosophical works. London, 1877. 2v.
	Phil 2115.14.7	Locke, J. Philosophical works. London, 1892. 2v.
	Phil 2115.46	Locke, J. Philosophy of Locke in extracts. N.Y., 1891.
Htn	Phil 2115.15*	Locke, J. Posthumous works. London, 1706.
Htn	Phil 2115.15.5*	Locke, J. Posthumous works. London, 1706.
	Phil 2115.45.40	Locke, J. I principi dell'illuminismo eclettico, estratti dal "Saggio sull'intelligenza umano". Torino, 1927.
Htn	Phil 2115.58.5*	Locke, J. The reasonableness of Christianity. Boston, 1811.
Htn	Phil 2115.58*	Locke, J. The reasonableness of Christianity. London, 1695.
	Phil 2115.58.9	Locke, J. The reasonableness of Christianity. London, 1836.
Htn	Phil 2115.73.5*	Locke, J. Reply to the Lord Bishop of Worcester's answer to his letter. London, 1697.
Htn	Phil 2115.73.7*	Locke, J. Reply to the Lord Bishop of Worcester's answer to his second letter. London, 1699.
	Phil 2115.61	Locke, J. Scritti editi e inediti sulla tolleranza. Torino, 1961.
	Phil 2115.26	Locke, J. Selections. Chicago, 1928.
	Phil 2115.74.50	Locke, J. Some familiar letters between Mr. Locke and his friends. London, 1708.
Htn	Phil 2115.71*	Locke, J. Some thoughts concerning education. London, 1693.
Htn	Phil 2115.70.2*	Locke, J. A third letter for toleration. London, 1692.
	Phil 2115.21	Locke, J. Two tracts on government. Cambridge, Eng., 1967.
Htn	Phil 2115.74*	Locke, J. Two treatises of government. London, 1690.
	Phil 2115.49.30	Locke, J. Über den menschlichen Verstand. Berlin, 1962. 2v.
	Phil 2115.49.15	Locke, J. Über den menschlichen Verstand. Leipzig, 1897. 2v.
	Phil 2115.49.13	Locke, J. Versuch über den menschlichen Verstand. Berlin, 1872-73. 2v.
	Phil 2115.49.10	Locke, J. Versuch über den menschlichen Verstand. Jena, 1795. 3v.
	Phil 2115.49	Locke, J. Versuch über den menschlichen Verstand. Leipzig, 1913. 2v.
Htn	Phil 2115.49.5*	Locke, J. Versuch vom menschlichen Verstand. Altenburg, 1757.
	Phil 2115.49.8	Locke, J. Vom menschlichen Verstande. Mannheim, 1791.
	Phil 2115.1.6F	Locke, J. Works. London, 1659. 3v.
	Phil 2115.10	Locke, J. Works. London, 1801. 10v.
	Phil 2115.10.5A	Locke, J. Works. London, 1812. 10v.
	Phil 2115.11	Locke, J. Works. London, 1823. 10v.
	Phil 2115.12	Locke, J. Works. London, 1854. 2v.
	Phil 2115.13	Locke, J. Works. London, 1876.
	Phil 2115.11.2	Locke, J. Works. London, 1893. 10v.
	Phil 2115.1	Locke, J. Works. 1st ed. v.1,3. London, 1714. 2v.
	VPhil 2115.1.1	Locke, J. Works. 2nd ed. London, 1722. 3v.
	VPhil 2115.1.2	Locke, J. Works. 3rd ed. London, 1727. 3v.
	VPhil 2115.1.3	Locke, J. Works. 4th ed. v.1,3. London, 1740. 2v.
	Phil 2115.1.3	Locke, J. Works. 4th ed. v.2. London, 1740.
	VPhil 2115.1.5F	Locke, J. Works. 6th ed. London, 1759. 3v.
	Phil 2115.1.8F	Locke, J. Works. 8th ed. London, 1777. 4v.
	Phil 2115.74.10	Locke, J. Zwei Abhandlungen über Regierung. Halle, 1906.
	Phil 2115.197	Locke, sa vie. (Leroy, A.L.) Paris, 1964.
	Phil 2115.99	Locke. (Alexander, S.) London, 1908.
	Phil 2115.168.5	Locke. (Cranston, M.W.) London, 1961.
	Phil 2115.90	Locke. (Fowler, T.) London, 1880.
	Phil 2115.90.3	Locke. (Fowler, T.) N.Y., 1880?
	Phil 2115.90.7	Locke. (Fowler, T.) N.Y., 1899.
	Phil 2115.92	Locke. (Fraser, A.C.) Edinburgh, 1890.
	Phil 2115.92.2A	Locke. (Fraser, A.C.) Philadelphia, 1890.
	Phil 2115.215	Locke and Berkeley: a collection of ciritical essays. (Martin, Charles Burton.) London, 1968.

Phil 1870.113	Locke and Berkeley's commonplace book. (Aaron, Richard I.) Aberdeen, 1931. 2 pam.
Phil 2115.146	Locke and scepticism. (Hofstadter, A.) N.Y., 1935.
Phil 2115.225	Locke and the compass of human understanding; a selective commentary on the Essay. (Yolton, John W.) Cambridge, Eng., 1970.
Phil 2115.164	Locke e i suoi problemi. (Ricci Garotti, Loris.) Urbino, 1961.
Phil 2115.122	Locke e il sensismo francese. (Ferrari, M.) Modena, 1900.
Phil 2115.131	Locke en Spinoza over de tolerantie. (Tex, Jan den.) Amsterdam, 1926.
Phil 2115.230	The Locke newsletter. Heslington, York, Eng. 1,1970+
Phil 705.13	Locke och Kant. (Landström, Gustaf.) Uppsala, 1900.
Phil 2115.172	Locke on war and peace. (Cox, Richard H.) Oxford, 1960.
Phil 2115.125	Locke's bewijs voor het bestaan van God. (Burger, D.) Amersfoort, 1872.
Phil 2115.5	Locke's Lehre. (Hartenstein, G.) Leipzig, 1861.
Phil 2115.69	Locke's travels in France. (Locke, J.) Cambridge, 1953.
Phil 2115.136	Locke's Verhältnis zu Descartes. Diss. (Sommer, R.) Berlin, 1887.
Phil 2115.86	Locke's writings and philosophy. (Tagart, E.) London, 1855.
Phil 4210.83	Lockhart, W. Life of Antonio Rosmini-Serbati. 2. ed. London, 1886. 2v.
Phil 4210.83.2	Lockhart, W. An outline of the life of...Antonio Rosmini. London, 1856.
Phil 4210.83.3	Lockhart, W. Vie d'Antonio Rosmini-Serbati. Paris, 1889.
Phil 2115.109	Lockii et Liebnitii de cognitione humana. Inaug.-Diss. (Quaebicker, R.) Halis Saxonium, 1868.
Phil 1845.16	Locutionary and illocutionary acts. (Furberg, M.) Göteborg, 1963.
Phil 486.15	Lodetti, Milka. La matière imaginaire. Paris, 1959.
Phil 510.1.12	Lodge, Oliver. Life and matter. A criticism of Prof. Haeckel's riddle. N.Y., 1906.
Phil 510.1.13.5	Lodge, Oliver. Life and matter. 2nd ed. London, 1912.
Phil 7069.30.12	Lodge, Oliver Joseph. Conviction of survival. London, 1930.
Phil 8701.4.13	Lodge, Oliver Joseph. Faith and knowledge, April, 1902. London, 19- .
Phil 8636.05	Lodge, Oliver Joseph. The immortality of the soul. Boston, 1908.
Phil 8701.4.3.5	Lodge, Oliver Joseph. Man and the universe. N.Y., 1920.
Phil 8701.4.3	Lodge, Oliver Joseph. Man and the universe. 9. ed. London, 1911.
Phil 7069.30.12.5	Lodge, Oliver Joseph. Phantom walls. N.Y., 1930.
Phil 7069.16.40	Lodge, Oliver Joseph. Raymond. N.Y., 1916.
Phil 8701.4.7	Lodge, Oliver Joseph. Reason and belief. N.Y., 1910.
Phil 8701.4.9	Lodge, Oliver Joseph. Reason and belief. 5. ed. London, 1911.
Phil 8701.4	Lodge, Oliver Joseph. Science and immortality. N.Y., 1908.
Phil 8701.4.2	Lodge, Oliver Joseph. Science and immortality. N.Y., 1914.
Phil 8701.4.5	Lodge, Oliver Joseph. The substance of faith allied with science. London, 1915.
Phil 8701.4.4	Lodge, Oliver Joseph. The substance of faith allied with science. N.Y., 1907.
Phil 7069.10.19	Lodge, Oliver Joseph. The survival of man. N.Y., 1909.
Phil 7069.10.20	Lodge, Oliver Joseph. The survival of man. London, 1910.
Phil 7069.16.41	Lodge, Oliver Joseph. The survival of man. 7. ed. London, 1916.
Phil 7069.12.51	Lodge, Oliver Joseph. La survivance humaine. 3. ed. Paris, 1912.
Phil 186.111	Lodge, R.C. Applied philosophy. London, 1951.
Phil 186.84	Lodge, R.C. The questioning mind. N.Y., 1937.
Phil 5051.12	Lodge, Rupert C. An introduction to modern logic. Minneapolis, 1920.
Phil 2115.115	Lodge, Rupert C. The meaning...of...philosophy of John Locke. Minneapolis, 1918.
Phil 525.234	Lodyzhenskii, M.V. Svet nezrimyi. Izd. 2. Petrograd, 1915.
Phil 5821.4.5	Loeb, J. Comparative physiology of the brain and comparative psychology. N.Y., 1900.
Phil 5821.4	Loeb, J. Einleitung...Gehirnphysiologie...Psychologie. Leipzig, 1899.
Phil 5416.2	Loeb, Robert H. The sins of bias. N.Y., 1970.
Phil 6980.429.5	Loebsacu, T. Die unheimlichen Moglichkeiten oder die Manipulierte Seele. Düsseldorf, 1967.
Phil 2138.100	Löchen, Arne. Om J. Stuart Mills logik. Kristiania, 1885.
Phil 6961.22	Loechen, Yngvar. Idealer og realiteter i et psykiatrisk sykehus. Oslo, 1970.
Phil 8886.76	Loegstrup, K.E.C. Kunst og etik. Kobenhavn, 1961.
Phil 3493.50	Loegstrup, Knud Ejler Christian. Kants Kritik af erkendelsen og refleksionen. København, 1970.
Phil 3493.33	Loegstrup, Kocud Ejler Christian. Kants aestetik. København, 1965.
Phil 4260.106	Löhde, Hermann. Giambattista Vico und das Problem der Bildung. Inaug. Diss. Erlangen, 1932.
Phil 186.135	Loehrich, R.R. Modus operandi. McHenry, Ill., 1956.
Phil 7084.40	Loehrich, Rolf Rudolf. Oneirics and psychosomatics. McHenry, Ill., 1953.
Phil 5051.21	Loeive, J.H. Lehrbuch der Logik. Wien, 1881.
Phil 8591.29	Lönborg, Sven. Religion och vetenskap. Stockholm, 1914.
Phil 4080.3.465	Lönne, Karl-Egon. Benedetto Croce als Kritiker seiner Zeit. Tübingen, 1967.
Phil 3850.27.220	Loennebo, M. Albert Schweitzers etisk-religiösa iderl. Stockholm, 1964.
Phil 5258.77.5	Loeren om de menneskelige Folelser. (Sibbern, F.C.) Kjøbenhavn, 1885.
Phil 8980.529	Loeser, Franz. Deontik, Planung und Leitung der moralischen Entwicklung. Berlin, 1966.
Phil 5821.14	Loeser, Johann A. Die Psychologie des Emotionalen. Berlin, 1931.
Phil 3492.15.5	Die lösung der widersprüche des Dasiens. (Kesseler, Kurt.) Bunzlau, 1909.
Phil 3246.95.9	Loewe, Johann H. Die Philosophie Fichte's. Stuttgart, 1862.
Phil 5761.15	Loewe, Johann H. Die speculative Idee der Freiheit. Prag, 1890.
Phil 3100.125	Löwenberg, Adolf. Friedrich Edward Beneke. Berlin, 1901.
Phil 8701.14	Loewenberg, B.J. The controversy over evolution in New England, 1859-1873. n.p., 1935.
Phil 8412.11	Loewenberg, J. Dialogues from Delphi. Berkeley, 1949.
Phil 2250.105A	Loewenberg, J. Royce's synoptic vision. n.p., 1955.
Phil 2120.15	Loewenberg, Jacob. Thrice-born. N.Y., 1968.
Phil 6321.4	Loewenfeld, L. Pathologie und Therapie de Neurasthenie und Hysterie. Wiesbaden, 1894.
Phil 5841.14	Loewenfeld, Leopold. Sexualleben und Nervenleiden. Wiesbaden, 1906.
Phil 5390.4	Loewenfeld, Leopold. Über die Dummheit. Wiesbaden, 1909.
Phil 8591.10	Löwenhardt, E. Uber Gott, Geist und Unsterblichkeit. Wolgast, 1875.
Phil 3831.4	Loewenhardt, S.E. Benedict von Spinoza. Berlin, 1872.
Phil 3585.1.100F	Loewenhaupt, Friedrich. Johann Heinrich Lambert. Mülhausen, 1943?
Phil 6321.30.10	Loewenstein, R. Christians and Jews. N.Y., 1951.
Phil 6321.30.5	Loewenstein, R. Drives, affects, behavior. N.Y., 1953.
Phil 6321.30	Loewenstein, R. Psychoanalyse de l'antisémitisme. 1. éd. Paris, 1952.
Phil 6315.2.245	Loewenstein, Rudolph Maurice. Freud. N.Y., 1951.
Phil 811.5	Loewenthal, E. Geschichte der Philosophie im Umriss. Berlin, 1896.
Phil 486.7	Löwenthal, E. System und Geschichte des Naturalismus. Leipzig, 1863.
Phil 510.27	Loewenthal, Eduard. Der Bankrott der Darwin-Haeckel'schen Entwicklungstheories und die Krönung des monistischen Gebäudes. Berlin, 1900.
Phil 5761.6	Loewenthal, N. Physiologie des freien Willens. Leipzig, 1843.
Phil 5545.157	Loewenton, E. Versuche über das Gedächtnis. Inaug. Diss. Dorpat, 1893.
Phil 3493.32	Löwisch, Dieter-Jürgen. Immanuel Kant und David Hume's, dialogues concerning natural religion. Bonn, 1964.
Phil 8886.67	Löwith, K. Das Individuum in der Rolle des Mitmenschen. München, 1928.
Phil 3011.8.2	Loewith, Karl. From Hegel to Nietzsche: the revolution in nineteenth century thought. 1st ed. N.Y., 1964.
Phil 585.235	Loewith, Karl. Gott, Mensch und Welt in der Metaphysik von Descartes bis zu Nietzsche. Göttingen, 1967.
Phil 3050.6	Loewith, Karl. Die Hegelsche Linke; Texte aus den Werken. Stuttgart, 1962.
Phil 3640.261	Löwith, Karl. Kierkegaard und Nietzsche. Frankfurt am Main, 1933.
Phil 3640.261.10	Löwith, Karl. Nietzsches Philosophie der ewigen Wieder kehr des Gleichen. Stuttgart, 1956.
Phil 3640.261.5A	Löwith, Karl. Nietzsches Philosophie der ewigen Wiederkunft des Gleichen. Berlin, 1935.
Phil 3011.8A	Loewith, Karl. Von Hegel bis Nietzsche. Zürich, 1941.
Phil 8591.65	Loewith, Karl. Wissen, Glaube und Skepsis. Göttingen, 1956.
Phil 8591.65.5	Loewith, Karl. Zur Kritik der Christlichen Überlieferung. Stuttgart, 1966.
Phil 6980.429	Loewnau, H.W. Reifungskrisen im Kindes- und Jugendalter. Göttingen, 1961.
VPhil 165.409	Løwne zagadnienia filozofii. v.3. Warszawa, 1966.
Phil 8591.82	Lofland, John. Doomsday Cult; a study of conversion proselytization, and maintenance of faith. Englewood Cliffs, 1966.
Phil 1885.90	Lofthouse, W.F. F.H. Bradley. London, 1949. 2v.
Phil 9171.8	Lofthouse, William F. Ethics and the family. London, 1912.
Phil 7159.260	Logan, Daniel. The reluctant prophet. 1st ed. Garden City, N.Y., 1968.
Phil 292.4	Logan, J.D. Three papers reprinted. n.p., 1897-99.
VPhil 3450.11.490	Logar, Cene. Fenomenologija analiza in kritika filosofije Edmunda Husserla. Ljubljana, 1970.
Phil 5066.235	Logic, computing machines, and automation. (Hilton, Alice Mary.) Cleveland, 1964.
Phil 5042.20	Logic, deductive and inductive. (Crumley, T.) N.Y., 1926.
Phil 5045.2.15	Logic, deductive and inductive. (Fowler, Thomas.) Oxford, 1904-05.
Phil 5047.8.8	Logic, deductive and inductive. (Hibben, J.G.) N.Y., 1910[1905].
Phil 5057.9	Logic; deductive and inductive. (Read, C.) London, 1898.
Phil 5058.33.4	Logic, inductive and deductive. (Subrahmanyam, A.) Madras, 1916.
Phil 70.82	Logic, methodology and philosophy of science. Amsterdam. 1,1962+ 3v.
Phil 5040.4.4	Logic, or The art of thinking. (Arnauld, Antoine.) Edinburgh, 1850.
Phil 5040.4.2	Logic, or The art of thinking. (Arnauld, Antoine.) London, 1717.
Phil 5040.4.3	Logic, or The art of thinking. (Arnauld, Antoine.) London, 1723.
Phil 5041.16	Logic, or The morphology of knowledge. (Bosanquet, B.) Oxford, 1888. 2v.
Phil 5041.16.2A	Logic, or The morphology of knowledge. (Bosanquet, B.) Oxford, 1911. 2v.
Phil 5043.6	Logic; or The science of inference. (Devey, Joseph.) London, 1854.
Phil 5170.18	Logic, physics and metaphysics. (Bradley, Raymond.) Auckland, 1967.
Phil 5043.16.3A	Logic; the theory of inquiry. (Dewey, J.) N.Y., 1938.
Phil 5044.8	Logic, theoretical and applied. (Evans, D.L.) Garden City, 1937.
Phil 5005.1	Pamphlet vol. Logic, 1896-1910.
Phil 5005.3	Pamphlet vol. Logic, 1901-1908. 5 pam.
Phil 5051.3	Logic..application to language. (Latham, R.G.) London, 1856.
Phil 5005.4	Pamphlet vol. Logic. 35 pam.
Phil 5005.6	Pamphlet box. Logic.
Phil 5040.25	Logic. (Ambrose, A.) N.Y., 1961.
Phil 5041.3	Logic. (Bain, Alexander.) London, 1870. 2v.
Phil 5042.9	Logic. (Croke, J.L.O.) London, 1906.
Phil 5046.6.1	Logic. (Gatry, A.J.A.) LaSalle, Ill., 1944.
Phil 3425.32	Logic. (Hegel, Georg Wilhelm Friedrich.) Oxford, 1874.
Phil 5049.16.1	Logic. (Johnson, William Ernest.) N.Y., 1964. 3v.
Phil 3565.31	Logic. (Lotze, Hermann.) Oxford, 1884.
Phil 5052.6	Logic. (Minto, William.) N.Y., 1894.
Phil 5058.94	Logic. (Ruge, Arnold.) London, 1913.
Phil 5058.21	Logic. (Salmon, W.) Englewood, 1963.
NEDL Phil 5062.4.11	Logic. (Smith, G.H.) N.Y., 1901.
Phil 5062.4.25	Logic. (Watts, S.) Edinburgh, 1807.
NEDL Phil 5062.4.9	Logic. (Watts, S.) London, 17- .
Phil 5062.4.11.5	Logic. (Watts, S.) London, 1802.
Phil 5062.15.5	Logic. (Watts, S.) London, 1813.
Phil 3910.66	Logic. (Wilson, W.D.) Ithaca, N.Y., 1872.
Phil 5046.50	Logic. (Wolff, Christian von.) London, 1770.
	Logic: a comprehensive introduction. (Guttenplan, Samuel D.) N.Y., 1971.
Phil 5041.90	Logic: a dialogue. (Bierman, Arthur Kalmer.) San Francisco, 1964.
Phil 5005.7	Pamphlet box. Logic. German dissertations.
Phil 5005.5	Pamphlet vol. Logic. German pamphlets and dissertations, 1910-1922. 11 pam.

Phil 5049.16A — Logic. pt.1. (Johnson, William Ernest.) Cambridge, Eng., 1921-24. 3v.
Phil 5058.28.50 — Pamphlet box. Logic. Smith, Henry B.
Phil 3425.32.2 — Logic. 2nd ed. (Hegel, Georg Wilhelm Friedrich.) Oxford, 1892.
Phil 5058.13 — Logic. 2nd ed. (Sigwart, H.C.W.) London, 1895. 2v.
Htn Phil 5062.6.7.7 — Logic. 2nd ed. (Whately, Richard.) London, 1852.
Htn Phil 5062.4.10* — Logic. 3rd American ed. (Watts, S.) Exeter, 1806.
Phil 5051.13 — Logic. 4th ed. (Leechman, John.) London, 1864.
Phil 5058.13.5 — Logic. 5e aufl. (Sigwart, H.C.W.) Tübingen, 1924. 2v.
Htn Phil 5062.4.12* — Logic. 6th American ed. (Watts, S.) Boston, 1819.*
Phil 5049.3.4 — Logic (science primers). (Jevons, W.S.) N.Y., 1880.
Phil 5049.3.6 — Logic (science primers). (Jevons, W.S.) N.Y., 1884.
Phil 5049.3.7 — Logic (science primers). (Jevons, W.S.) N.Y., 1885.
Phil 5047.9.5 — Logic and argument. (Hyslop, J.H.) N.Y., 1907.
Phil 165.466 — Logic and art. Indianapolis, 1972.
Phil 5015.2 — Logic and dialecta in the Soviet Union. (Filipor, R.P.) N.Y., 1952.
Phil 5051.14 — Logic and education. (Lightfoot, John.) London, 1899.
Phil 5041.65 — Logic and effective argument. (Bilsky, Manuel.) N.Y., 1956.
Phil 5042.23.8 — Logic and epistemology. (Cotter, Anthony C.) Boston, 1940.
Phil 5042.23.5 — Logic and epistemology. 2nd ed. (Cotter, Anthony C.) Boston, 1931.
Phil 5066.195.5 — Logic and foundations of science. (E.W. Beth Memorial Colloquium, Institut Henri Poincaré, 1964.) Dordrecht, 1968.
Phil 720.10 — Logic and imagination in the perception of truth. (Stoner, J.R.) N.Y., 1910.
Phil 2255.1.75 — Logic and knowledge. (Russell, Bertrand Russell.) London, 1956.
Phil 165.305 — Logic and language. Holland, 1962.
Phil 5047.43 — Logic and language. 1st ed. (Huppé, B.J.) N.Y., 1956.
Phil 5520.100.10 — Logic and language. 2. ser. (Flew, A.G.N.) Oxford, 1953.
Phil 5058.45 — Logic and nature. (Swabey, Marie.) N.Y., 1930.
Phil 5058.65 — Logic and nature. 2nd ed. (Swabey, M.) N.Y., 1955.
Phil 187.97 — Logic and other nonsense. (McCrossan, J.D.) London, 1895.
Phil 5066.36.15 — Logic and psychology. (Piaget, Jean.) Manchester, Eng., 1953.
Phil 5068.18.10 — Logic and reality. (Bergmann, Gustav.) Madison, 1964.
Phil 3552.448 — Logic and reality in Leibniz's metaphysics. (Parkinson, George H.R.) Oxford, 1965.
Phil 5050.14 — Logic and reasoning. (Keeling, S.V.) London, 1929.
Phil 5017.6 — Logic and rhetoric in England. (Howell, W.S.) N.Y., 1961.
Phil 5017.5 — Logic and rhetoric in England. (Howell, W.S.) Princeton, 1956.
Phil 5058.53A — Logic and scientific methods. (Searles, Herbert L.) N.Y., 1948.
Phil 5058.53.5 — Logic and scientific methods. 2. ed. (Searles, Herbert L.) N.Y., 1956.
Phil 8890.48 — Logic and the bases of ethics. (Prior, A.N.) Oxford, 1949.
Phil 175.40.5 — Logic and the cosmic order. (Anderson, L.F.) N.Y., 1939.
Phil 185.68.5 — Logic and the nature of reality. (Kattsoff, L.O.) The Hague, 1956.
Phil 5042.10.5 — Logic as the science of the pure concept. (Croce, B.) London, 1917.
Phil 5047.40 — Logic cases for philosophy, 1919-1920. (Harvard University. Department of Philosophy.) Cambridge, Mass., 1920.
Phil 5066.232 — Logic Colloquiam, 8th, Oxford, 1963. Formal systems and recursive functions. Amsterdam, 1965.
Phil 5066.280 — Logic Colloquiam, 11th, Hannover, 1966. Contributions to mathematical logic; proceedings of the logic colloquium, Hannover, 1966. Amsterdam, 1968.
Phil 5041.3.5 — Logic deductive and inductive. (Bain, Alexander.) N.Y., 1887.
Phil 5062.29.5 — Logic for living. (Williams, Henry H.) N.Y., 1951.
Phil 5066.50.5 — Logic for mathematicians. (Rosser, J.B.) N.Y., 1953.
Phil 5046.3 — Logic for the million. (Gilbart, J.W.) London, 1860.
Phil 5046.3.5 — Logic for the million. 5th ed. (Gilbart, J.W.) London, 1857.
Phil 5052.39 — Logic for the millions. (Mander, Alfred E.) N.Y., 1947.
Phil 5058.24.10 — Logic for use. (Schiller, F.C.S.) London, 1929.
Phil 5058.46.15 — Logic in practice. (Stebbing, Lizzie S.) London, 1934.
Phil 5058.46.30 — Logic in practice. 4. ed. (Stebbing, Lizzie S.) London, 1954.
Phil 5058.48 — Logic in theory and practice. (Shaw, Charles G.) N.Y., 1935.
Phil 5049.11.2 — Logic inductive and deductive. (Jones, A.L.) N.Y., 1909.
Phil 5195.2 — Logic machines and diagrams. (Gardner, Martin.) N.Y., 1958.
Phil 5047.17 — The logic of argument. (Hoag, C.G.) Haverford, 1909.
Phil 8599.33 — The logic of belief. 1. ed. (Trueblood, D.E.) N.Y., 1942.
Phil 2475.1.195 — Logic of Bergson's philosophy. (Peckham, George W.) N.Y., 1917.
Phil 5061.1.9 — The logic of chance. (Venn, J.) London, 1866.
Phil 5061.1.8 — The logic of chance. (Venn, J.) London, 1876.
X Cg Phil 5061.1.11 — The logic of chance. (Venn, J.) London, 1888.
Phil 5061.1.11 — The logic of chance. (Venn, J.) London, 1888.
Phil 5190.42 — The logic of commands. (Rescher, Nicholas.) London, 1966.
Phil 2493.30.6 — The logic of Condillac. (Condillac, Étienne Bonnot.) Philadelphia, 1809.
Phil 5052.26 — The logic of conduct. (Mackaye, James.) N.Y., 1924.
Phil 630.25 — The logic of contemporary English realism. Thesis. (Hawes, R.P.) N.Y., 1923.
Phil 5066.269 — The logic of decision and action. Pittsburgh, 1966.
Phil 5043.21 — The logic of definition. (Davidson, William L.) London, 1885.
Phil 5042.22A — The logic of discovery. (Carmichael, R.D.) Chicago, 1930.
Phil 5068.80 — The logic of empirical theories. (Przelecki, Marian.) London, 1969.
Phil 9035.68 — The logic of human character. (Whitby, Charles J.) London, 1905.
Phil 2045.146 — The logic of Leviathan; the moral and political theory of Thomas Hobbes. (Gauthier, David Peter.) Oxford, 1969.
Phil 5255.43A — The logic of modern psychology. (Pratt, Carroll C.) N.Y., 1939.
Phil 8879.28 — The logic of moral discourse. (Edwards, Paul.) Glencoe, Ill., 1955.
Phil 2055.9.35 — The logic of perfection. (Hartshorne, Charles.) LaSalle, Ill., 1962.
Phil 5590.135 — The logic of personality. (Mayo, B.) London, 1952.
Phil 5055.40 — The logic of power. (Poern, Ingmar.) Oxford, 1970.
Phil 1955.6.120 — The logic of pragmatism. (Thayer, H.S.) N.Y., 1952.

Phil 8897.84 — The logic of preference, an essay. (Wright, G.H. von.) Edinburgh, 1963.
Phil 5049.28 — The logic of relationship. (Johnston, Frederick S.) N.Y., 1968.
Phil 5000.5 — Logic of relatives. (Pierce, C.S.) Cambridge, 1870.
Phil 5520.446 — The logic of religion. (Bocheński, Innocentius M.) N.Y., 1965.
Phil 8602.22 — The logic of religion. Diss. (Watson, A.C.) Chicago, 1918.
Phil 8592.35.10 — The logic of religious thought. (Milburn, R.G.) London, 1929.
Phil 193.106 — The logic of self-realization. (Stuart, H.W.) Berkeley, 1904.
Phil 3160.12.40 — The logic of the humanities. (Cassirer, Ernst.) New Haven, 1961.
Phil 2175.4.30 — The logic of the sciences and the humanities. (Northrop, F.S.C.) N.Y., 1947.
Phil 5722.7 — The logic of the unconscious mind. (Bradley, M.K.) London, 1920.
Phil 5772.6 — The logic of will. (Wodehouse, Helen.) London, 1908.
Phil 5061.8 — Logica, cui praemittitur. (Vries, Joseph de.) Friburgi, 1952.
Phil 5068.84 — Logica, linguaggio e sociologia. (Statera, Gianni.) Torino, 1967.
Phil 5043.38 — Logica, norme, azione. (DiBernardo, Giuliano.) Trento, 1969.
Phil 2493.30.20 — La lógica, o Los primeros elementos del arte de pensar. (Condillac, Étienne Bonnot.) Caracas, 1959.
Phil 186.5.6 — Logica, ontologia, et pneumatologia. 4. ed. (LeClerc, J.) Cambridge, 1704.
Phil 186.5.5 — Logica, sive Ars ratiocinandi. (LeClerc, J.) London, 1692. 3 pam.
Phil 5055.15 — Logica, usui juniorum. (Plenning, J.) Holmiae, 1746.
Phil 5041.38 — La logica. (Bertini, G.M.) Roma, 1880.
Phil 2493.30 — La lógica. (Condillac, Étienne Bonnot.) Caracas, 1812.
Phil 5043.26 — La logica. (Donati, P.) Forli, 1920.
Phil 4114.40 — La logica. (Genovesi, Antonio.) Napoli, 1790.
Phil 5049.9 — Logica. (Jevons, W.S.) Milano, 1920.
Phil 5054.3.5 — Lógica. (Orti y Lara, J.M.) Madrid, 1885.
Phil 5055.36 — Logica. (Paulus Venetus.) Hildesheim, 1970.
Phil 4210.23 — Logica. (Rosmini-Serbati, Antonio.) Intra, 1867.
Phil 4210.23.2 — Logica. (Rosmini-Serbati, Antonio.) Torino, 1853.
Phil 165.155 — Logica. Neuchâtel, 1959.
Phil 5046.32 — Lógica. 7. ed. (Garcia Tuduri, R.) Habana, 1959.
Phil 3450.24.10 — Logica als leer van zuivere rede. Deel. 1. (Hessing, Jacob.) Bussum, 1941.
Phil 4200.7.06 — Logica et tractatus de sensu composito et diviso. (Pergulensis, Paulus.) St. Bonaventure, 1961.
Phil 5042.10 — Logica come scienza del concetto puro. (Croce, B.) Bari, 1909.
Phil 5042.10.4 — Logica come scienza del concetto puro. 4a ed. (Croce, B.) Bari, 1920.
Phil 5042.10.3 — Logica come scienza del concetto puro. 5a ed. (Croce, B.) Bari, 1928.
Phil 5042.10.6 — Logica come scienza del concetto puro. 7. ed. (Croce, B.) Bari, 1947.
Phil 5061.5 — Logica come scienza positiva. (Volpe, G. della.) Messina, 1950.
Phil 5061.5.2 — Logica come scienza positiva. 2. ed. (Volpe, G. della.) Messina, 1956.
Phil 180.84.5 — La logica della filosofia. (Franchini, Raffaello.) Napoli, 1967.
Phil 2477.6.110 — La logica della vita morale in Maurice Blondel. (Salvo, Franco.) Palermo, 1942.
Phil 3790.4.83 — De logica der geschiedeniswetenschap's van H. Rickert. (Leenmans, H.A.) 's Gravenhage, 1924.
Phil 3425.105.15 — La logica di Hegel. (Hibben, J.G.) Torino, 1910.
Phil 3425.297 — La logica di Hegel. (Pelloux, L.) Milan, 1938.
Phil 2138.149 — La logica di J. Stuart Mill e la problematica eticosociale. (Arata, Fidia.) Milano, 1964.
Phil 5068.58 — Logica e analisi. Scritti di P. Filiasi Carcano (et al.). Padova, 1966.
Phil 5058.85 — Logica e dialettica. (Sichirollo, Livio.) Milano, 1957.
Phil 3450.11.255 — Logica e esperienza in Husserl. (Melandri, Enzo.) Bologna, 1960.
Phil 4080.18.85 — Logica e metafisica nel pensiero di Guido Calogero. (Raggiunti, Renzo.) Firenze, 1963.
Phil 4225.1.32 — Logica e metafisica. (Spaventa, Bertrando.) Bari, 1911.
Phil 5069.2 — Logica ed esperienz. (Spisoni, Franco.) Milano, 1967.
Phil 5040.20.5 — Lógica elemental. 4a ed. (Aragón, G.A.) Habana, 1926.
Phil 5052.16 — Logica elementare. (Marchisini, A.) Firenze, 1917.
Phil 5055.20 — Logica formale...modelli meccanici. (Pastore, Annibale.) Torino, 1906.
Phil 3425.668 — Logica hegeliana e filosofia contemporanea. (Massolo, Arturo.) Firenze, 1967.
Phil 5058.39 — Logica Martini. (Smiglecki, Marcin.) Oxonii, 1658.
Phil 5066.110 — Lógica matemática. (Ferrater Mora, José.) México, 1955.
Phil 5027.2 — Logica modernorum. (Rijh, Lambertus.) Assen, 1962. 3v.
Phil 2477.6.120 — La logica morale in Maurice Blondel. (Bonicelli, B.M.) Torino, 1950.
Phil 5041.44 — Logica of Denkleer. 3e druk. (Beysens, J.T.) Hilversum, 1923?
Htn Phil 5000.3* — Logica pamph. v.1-3. (Monti, Panfilo.) Venice, 1512.
Phil 5066.273 — La logica simbolica. (Agazzi, Evandro.) Brescia, 1964.
Phil 5066.324 — Logica simbolica e diritto. (Amato, Nicolò.) Milano, 1969.
Phil 3493.38 — La logica trascendentale Kantiana. (Lugarini, Leo.) Milano, 1960.
Phil 5042.12 — Logica vetus et nova. 2a ed. (Clauberg, Johann.) Amsterdam, 1658.
Phil 5061.4.5 — Lógica viva. (Vaz Ferreira, Carlos.) Montevideo, 1920.
Phil 5061.4.15 — Lógica viva (adaptación prática y didáctica). (Vaz Ferreira, Carlos.) Buenos Aires, 1945.
Phil 5040.30 — La lógica y el hombre. (Alejandro, Jose Maria de.) Madrid, 1970.
Phil 5057.30 — Lógica y nóciones de teoria del concimiento. 2. ed. (Romero, Francisco Argentine.) Buenos Aires, 1939.
Phil 5057.30.5 — Lógica y nóciones de teoria del concimiento. 5. ed. (Romer, Francisco Argentine.) Buenos Aires, 1942.
Htn Phil 5042.17* — Logicae, libri quinque. (Crakanthorp, R.) London, 1622.
Phil 5058.1 — Logicae artis compend. (Sandersono, R.) Oxoniae, 1741.
Htn Phil 5062.5* — Logicae institutiones. (Wendelin, M.F.) Amstelrodami, 1654.
Phil 5042.17.3 — Logicae libri quinque. 3a ed. (Crakanthorp, R.) Oxoniae, 1670.
Phil 5060.5 — Logicae seu philosophiae rationalis elementa. 6. ed. (Ubahgs, G.C.) Lovanii, 1860.

Phil 5040.12 — Logicae systema harmonicum. (Alstedius, J.H.) Herbonae Nassoviorum, 1614.
Phil 348.16 — Logical analysis of fictionalism with respect to the theory of truth. (Roque Pascual, R.) Chicago, Ill., 1940.
Phil 2255.1.90 — The logical atomism of Bertrand Russell. Diss. (Benjamin, A.C.) Champaign, Ill., 1927?
NEDL Phil 5051.8 — Logical compendium. Glasguae, 1756.
Phil 8878.11.13 — Logical conditions of a scientific treatment of morality. (Dewey, John.) Chicago, 1903.
Phil 2250.10 — Logical essays. (Royce, Josiah.) Dubuque, Iowa, 1951.
Phil 5125.24.6 — Logical foundations of probability. 2nd ed. (Carnap, Rudolf.) Chicago, 1962.
Phil 5047.11.4 — Logical investigations. 2nd ed. (Husserl, Edmund.) N.Y., 1970. 2v.
Phil 3552.73.5 — Logical papers. (Leibniz, Gottfried Wilhelm.) Oxford, 1966.
Phil 5055.1 — Logical papers. (Pierce, C.S.) n.p., n.d.
Phil 325.6 — Logical positivism, pragmatism and scientific empiricism. (Morris, C.W.) Paris, 1937.
Phil 5058.46.10A — Logical positivism and analysis. (Stebbing, Lizzie S.) London, 1933.
Phil 5043.3.10 — Logical praxis. (Day, Henry N.) N.Y., 1876.
Phil 5125.21.5 — The logical problem of induction. 2nd ed. (Wright, G.H. von.) N.Y., 1957.
Phil 5125.21.7 — The logical problem of induction. 2nd ed. (Wright, G.H. von.) Oxford, 1957.
Phil 333.12.2 — The logical structure of the world. (Carnap, Rudolf.) Berkeley, 1967.
Phil 5049.19 — Logical studies. (Joachim, Harold H.) Oxford, 1948.
Phil 5062.38 — Logical studies. (Wright, G.H. von.) London, 1957.
Phil 5042.21.14.5A — The logical syntax of language. (Carnap, Rudolf.) London, 1954.
Phil 5042.21.14.10 — The logical syntax of language. (Carnap, Rudolf.) London, 1967.
Phil 5042.21.14 — The logical syntax of language. (Carnap, Rudolf.) N.Y., 1937.
Phil 5875.30.5 — Logical thinking in children; research based on Piaget's theory. (Sigel, Irving Edward.) N.Y., 1968.
Phil 5039.24 — The logical way of doing things. (Lambert, Karel.) New Haven, 1969.
Phil 5055.20.5 — Logicalia. (Pastore, Annibale.) Padova, 1957.
Phil 5042.70 — Logicheskaia fraza i predlozhenie. (Chesnokov, P.V.) Rostov-na-Donu, 1961.
Phil 5520.513 — Logicheskaia semantika i modal'naia logika. Moskva, 1967.
Phil 5066.252 — Logicheskaia struktura nauchnogo znaniia. (Tavanets, P.V.) Moskva, 1965.
Phil 672.238 — Logicheskie funktsii kategorii prostranstva i vremeni. (Pavlov, Vasilii T.) Kiev, 1966.
Phil 5066.135 — Logicheskie issledovaniia. (Akademiia Nauk SSSR. Institut Filosofii.) Moskva, 1959.
Phil 410.85 — Logicheskie problemy abstraktsii beskonechnosti i osushchestvimosti. (Petron, Iurii A.) Moskva, 1967.
Phil 5004.1 — Logicheskii slovar'. (Kondakov, Nikolai I.) Moskva, 1971.
Phil 5021.1 — Les logiciens anglais contemporains. (Liard, L.) Paris, 1878.
Htn Phil 5062.4.2* — Logick. (Watts, S.) London, 1725.
NEDL Phil 5062.4.6 — Logick. (Watts, S.) London, 1786.
NEDL Phil 5062.4.8.5 — Logick. (Watts, S.) London, 1801.
Htn Phil 5062.4.8* — Logick. 2nd American ed. (Watts, S.) Newburyport, 1796.
NEDL Phil 5062.4.3 — Logick. 6th ed. (Watts, S.) London, 1736.
Phil 5062.4.3.5 — Logick. 8th ed. (Watts, S.) London, 1745.
NEDL Phil 5062.4.4 — Logick. 9th ed. (Watts, S.) London, 1751.
NEDL Phil 5062.4.5 — Logick. 10th ed. (Watts, S.) London, 1755.
Phil 5062.4.5.2 — Logick. 12th ed. (Watts, S.) London, 1763.
Htn Phil 5062.4.7* — Logick. 16th ed. (Watts, S.) Philadelphia, 1789.
Phil 5011.6.10 — Logico-philosophical studies. (Bocheński, I.M.) Dordrecht, 1962.
Phil 5058.98 — Logics without existence assumptions. (Schock, Rolf.) Uppsala, 1968.
Phil 5045.5 — Logik, die Lehre von Denken. (Friedlaender, S.) Berlin, 191-?
Phil 3565.30.30 — Logik, drei Bücher vom Denken. 2e Aufl. (Lotze, Hermann.) Leipzig, 1928.
Phil 5045.15 — Logik; ein Lehrbuch. 2. Aufl. (Fischl, J.) Graz, 1952[1946].
Phil 338.21 — Logik, Mathematik und Naturerkennen. (Hahn, Hans.) Wien, 1933.
Phil 5057.17 — Logik, oder Philosophie als Wissenslehre. (Rehmke, Johannes.) Leipzig, 1918.
Phil 5040.4 — Logik, or The art of thinking. (Arnauld, Antoine.) London, 1702.
Phil 5052.25 — Logik, Psychologie und Psychologismus. (Moog, Willy.) Halle, 1919.
Phil 5052.44.7 — Logik, vetenskapsteori, argumentationsanalys. 2. tryckningen. (Marc-Wogau, Konrad.) Stockholm, 1969.
Phil 5041.21 — Die Logik...Verhaltniss zur philosophische Geschichte betrachter. (Braniss, C.J.) Berlin, 1823.
Phil 5041.72 — Logik. (Brunstaed, Friedrich.) München, 1933.
Phil 5041.50 — Logik. (Burkamp, W.) Berlin, 1932.
Phil 5042.14 — Logik. (Commer, Ernst.) Paderborn, 1897.
Phil 5044.1A — Logik. (Erdmann, B.) Halle, 1892.
Phil 5045.16 — Logik. (Fogarasi, Béla.) Berlin, 1956.
Phil 5045.7.3 — Logik. (Freytag, Bruno baron von.) Stuttgart, 1955-67. 2v.
Phil 5046.19 — Die Logik. (Grassmann, R.) Stettin, 1900.
Phil 5047.19 — Logik. (Harms, Friedrick.) Leipzig, 1886.
Htn Phil 3480.70* — Logik. (Kant, Immanuel.) Königsberg, 1800.
Phil 3480.70.1 — Logik. (Kant, Immanuel.) Königsberg, 1801.
Phil 3480.70.2 — Logik. (Kant, Immanuel.) Reutlingen, 1801.
Phil 5050.10 — Logik. (Kries, Johannes von.) Tübingen, 1916.
Phil 3565.64 — Logik. (Lotze, Hermann.) Leipzig, 1843.
Phil 5055.21.5 — Logik. (Pauler, Akás.) Berlin, 1929.
Phil 5055.16 — Logik. (Pfänder, A.) Halle, 1921.
Phil 5058.4 — Die Logik. (Schlötel, W.) Göttingen, 1854.
Phil 5058.9 — Logik. (Seydel, R.) Leipzig, 1866.
Phil 5058.12.2 — Logik. (Sigwart, H.C.W.) Freiberg, 1889-1893. 2v.
Phil 5058.12 — Logik. (Sigwart, H.C.W.) Tübingen, 1873-78. 2v.
Phil 5058.29 — Logik. (Stadler, A.) Leipzig, 1912.
Phil 5058.30 — Logik. (Störring, Gustav.) Leipzig, 1916.
Phil 5059.9 — Logik. (Troxler, I.P.V.) Stuttgart, 1829-30. 3v.
Phil 3915.40 — Logik. (Wundt, Wilhelm.) Stuttgart, 1880-83. 2v.
Phil 3915.40.2 — Logik. (Wundt, Wilhelm.) Stuttgart, 1893-95. 3v.
Phil 3425.309 — Logik. Als Commentar und Ergänzung zu Hegels Wissenschaft der Logik. (Werder, K.) Berlin, 1841.
Phil 5047.32 — Logik: eine Systematik der logischen Probleme. (Honecker, M.) Berlin, 1927.

Phil 5047.49 — Logik. Klassik og moderne. (Hartnack, Justus.) København, 1968.
Phil 3480.70.20 — Logik. 2. Aufl. (Kant, Immanuel.) Leipzig, 1876.
Phil 3494.19.15 — Logik. 2. Aufl. (Marcus, Ernst.) Herford, 1911.
Phil 5055.16.5 — Logik. 2. aufl. (Pfänder, A.) Halle, 1929.
Phil 5055.13.2 — Logik. 2. Aufl. (Poetter, F.C.) Gütersloh, 1887.
Phil 5044.1.2 — Logik. 2e Aufl. (Erdmann, B.) Halle, 1907.
Phil 5047.14.10 — Logik. 2e Aufl. (Höfler, Alois.) Wien, 1922.
Phil 3480.70.3 — Logik. 3. Aufl. (Kant, Immanuel.) Leipzig, 1920.
Phil 5055.16.6 — Logik. 3. Aufl. (Pfänder, A.) Tübingen, 1963.
Phil 3915.40.3 — Logik. 3. Aufl. (Wundt, Wilhelm.) Stuttgart, 1906-08. 3v.
Phil 5044.1.3 — Logik. 3e Aufl. (Erdmann, B.) Berlin, 1923.
Phil 3915.40.4 — Logik. 4. Aufl. (Wundt, Wilhelm.) Stuttgart, 1919-21. 3v.
Phil 5058.18A — Die Logik als Aufgabe. (Driesch, H.) Tübingen, 1913.
Phil 5041.57 — Logik als Erfahrungswissenschaft. (Baumgarten, Arthur.) Kaunas, 1939.
Phil 5046.1 — Die Logik als Wissenschaftslehre Dargestellt. (George, L.) Berlin, 1868.
Phil 5055.11.5 — Die Logik auf dem Scheidewege. (Palágyi, Melchior.) Berlin, 1903.
Phil 3504.48 — Die Logik bei Kant. Inaug. Diss. (Wickenhagen, Ernst.) Jena, 1869.
Phil 5421.10.10 — Die Logik der Angst. (Silva-Tarouca, Amadeo.) Innsbrucke, 1953.
Phil 5027.4 — Die Logik der Neuzeit. (Risse, Wilhelm.) Stuttgart, 1964- 2v.
Phil 5051.25 — Logik der Philosophie. (Lünemann, Arthur.) Wien, 1929.
Phil 5051.5 — Die Logik der Philosophie und die Kategorienlehre. (Lask, E.) Tübingen, 1911.
Phil 177.28A — Logik der reinen Erkenntnis. (Cohen, Hermann.) Berlin, 1902. 3v.
Phil 5055.18.5 — Die Logik der Seele. (Pichler, Hans.) Erfurt, 1927.
Phil 3925.16.225 — Die Logik der seelischen Ereignisse. Thesis. (Giegel, Hans Joachim.) Frankfurt, 1969.
Phil 3120.60.30 — Logik der Tatsachen. (Buchheim, Karl.) München, 1959.
Phil 5046.25 — Logik der Weltanschauung. 1. Aufl. (Gabriel, Leo.) Graz, 1949.
Phil 2523.90 — Die Logik des Destutt de Tracy. Inaug.-Diss. (Kohler, Oskar.) Borna, 1931.
Phil 5722.17 — Die Logik des Unbewussten. (Petraschek, K.O.) München, 1926. 2v.
Phil 5047.35 — Logik des Widerspruchs. (Heiss, Robert.) Berlin, 1932.
Phil 5052.44.2 — Logik for nybörjare. 2. uppl. (Marc-Wogau, Konrad.) Stockholm, 1967.
Phil 2115.195 — Die Logik John Lockes'. (Martinak, E.) Halle, 1894.
Phil 4650.1.43 — Logik och vetenskapslära. (Vannérus, Allen.) Stockholm, 1918.
Phil 5057.3.5 — Die Logik oder die allgemeine Denkformenlehre. (Reinhold, Ernest.) Jena, 1827.
Phil 5160.6 — Logik og argumenter. (Espersen, Jon.) København, 1969.
Phil 4466.2.80 — Die Logik Petrus Fonseca's mit Ausschluss des Sprachlogischen. Inaug. Diss. (Uedelhofen, M.) Bonn, 1914.
Phil 5058.37.5 — Logik sem taenkelaere. 2. udg. (Sibbern, F.C.) Kjöbenhavn, 1835.
Phil 5043.23 — Logik til brug under laereruddannelsen paa seminarierne. (Dam, Axel.) København, 1915.
Phil 3310.5.33 — Logik und Erkenntnisstheorie. (Gutberlet, C.) Münster, 1882.
Phil 5052.28 — Logik und Erkenntnistheorie. 2. abd. (Maier, H.) Tübingen, 1918.
Phil 5041.35 — Logik und Erkentnistheorie. Facsimile. (Baumgartner, M.) n.p., 1905-06.
Phil 5066.65 — Logik und Existenz. (Menne, Albert.) Meisenheim/Glan, 1954.
Phil 5045.8 — Logik und Metaphysik. (Feder, J.G.H.) Göttingen, 1769.
Phil 5045.8.5 — Logik und Metaphysik. (Feder, J.G.H.) Wien, 1779.
Phil 192.2.5 — Logik und Metaphysik. (Rabus, L.) Erlangen, 1868.
Phil 5062.28 — Logik und Metaphysik. (Weissborn, G.) Halle, 1850.
Phil 182.1.10 — Logik und Nötik. 9e und 10e Aufl. (Hagemann, G.) Freiburg, 1915.
Phil 5062.23 — Logik und Sprachphilosophie. (Wolff, Hermann.) Berlin, 1880.
Phil 5062.23.5 — Logik und Sprachphilosophie. (Wolff, Hermann.) Leipzig, 1883.
Phil 5043.11 — Logik und Wissenschaftstheorie. (Dühring, E.K.) Leipzig, 1878.
Phil 5050.5.5 — Logik zum Gebrauch für Schulen. (Kiesewetter, J.G.C.C.) Leipzig, 1832.
Phil 4772.10 — Logika, kak chast' teorii poznaniia. 2. izd. (Vvedenskii, A.I.) Sankt Peterburg, 1912.
Phil 5040.22 — Logika. (Asmus, V.F.) Moskva, 1947.
Phil 5046.27 — Logika. (Gorskii, D.D.) Moskva, 1956.
Phil 5049.24 — Logika. (Jelenský, Šimon.) Praha, 1926.
Phil 5051.23.4 — Logika. (Losskiĭ, N.O.) Berlin, 1923.
Phil 5058.55 — Logika. (Strogovich, M.S.) Moskva, 1949.
Phil 5046.38 — Logika. v.1- (Gokieli, Levan P.) Tbilisi, 1965. 2v.
Phil 5045.16.2 — Logika. 2. kiadás. (Fogarasi, Béla.) Budapest, 1953.
Phil 8900.10 — Logika deontyczna jako formalizacja rozumowań normalywnych. Wyd. 1. (Ziemba, Zdzisław.) Warszawa, 1969.
Phil 3425.597 — Logika dialektika i teoriia poznaniia Gegelia. (Shinkaruk, V.I.) Kiev, 1964.
Phil 8411.34 — Logika krasoty. (Krivskovskii, Nikolai I.) Minsk, 1965.
Phil 5066.212 — Logika nauki. (Zinov'ev, Aleksandr A.) Moskva, 1971.
Phil 5051.22 — Logika ogolna czyli Teorja poznania i logika formalna. (Lutosławski, W.) London, 1906.
Phil 5040.19.5 — Logika pragmatyczna. (Adjukiewicz, Kazimierz.) Warszawa, 1965.
Phil 5066.210 — Logika vyskazyvanii i teorii vyvoda. (Zinov'ev, Aleksandr A.) Moskva, 1962.
Phil 5055.34 — Logikē. (Papanoutsos, Euangelos.) Athéna, 1970.
Phil 5058.90 — Logikens Uppkomst och Väsen. (Saarnio, Uuno.) Helsingfors, 1957.
Phil 5051.26 — La logique; l'art de penser. (LeLeu, Louis.) Paris, 1930.
Phil 186.78 — Logique, morale, métaphysique. (Luquet, G.H.) Paris, 1931.
Phil 5040.4.4.7 — La logique, ou L'art de penser. (Arnauld, Antoine.) Paris, 1965.
Phil 5011.4 — La logique. (Boll, Marcel.) Paris, 1935.
Phil 2493.30.10 — Logique. (Condillac, Etienne Bonnot.) Paris, 1789.
Phil 2493.30.2 — Logique. (Condillac, Étienne Bonnot.) Paris, 1821.
Phil 5046.6 — Logique. (Gratry, A.J.A.) Paris, 1868. 2v.
Phil 3480.70.5 — Logique. (Kant, Immanuel.) Paris, 1840.
Phil 5058.57 — Logique. (Sesmat, A.) Paris, 1950.
Phil 5059.5 — Logique. (Tiberghein, G.) Paris, 1865. 2v.

Phil 3425.31 Logique. v.1-2. (Hegel, Georg Wilhelm Friedrich.) Paris, 1859.
Phil 3480.70.6 Logique. 2. éd. (Kant, Immanuel.) Paris, 1862.
Phil 5051.17.9 Logique. 9e éd. (Liard, Louis.) Paris, 1917?
Phil 331.15 Logique apprentissage et probabilité. (Apostel, Léo.) Paris, 1959.
Phil 5055.2 Logique classique. (Perrard, M.J.F.) Paris, 1860.
Phil 5066.240 Logique contemporaine et formalisation. (Martin, Roger.) Paris, 1964.
Phil 2493.30.15 Logique de Condillac à l'usage des élèves des prytanées. v.1-2. (Condillac, Étienne Bonnot.) Paris, 1802. 2v.
Phil 3425.99 La logique de Hegel. (Noël, G.) Paris, 1897.
Phil 3450.11.190 La logique de Husserl. (Bachelard, Suzanne.) Paris, 1957.
Phil 5055.8 La logique de la contradiction. (Paulhan, F.) Paris, 1911.
Phil 197.71 Logique de la philosophie. (Weil, Eric.) Paris, 1950.
Phil 5021.5 Logique de la simplicité. (Lamouche, André.) Paris, 1959.
Phil 5761.4.2 Logique de la volonté. (Lapie, P.) Paris, 1902.
Phil 176.72 La logique de l'absolu. (Braun, Edmond.) Paris, 1887.
Phil 5051.31 La logique de l'assertion pure. (LaHarpe, J. de.) Paris, 1950.
NEDL Phil 3552.106 La logique de Leibniz. (Couturat, L.) Paris, 1901.
Phil 5115.1 La logique de l'hypothèse. (Naville, J.E.) Paris, 1880.
Phil 5053.3 Logique de l'identité...contradiction. (Naville, A.) Genève, 1909.
Phil 5040.3.5 Logique de Port Royal. (Arnauld, Antoine.) Paris, 1854.
Phil 5040.3.9 Logique de Port Royal. (Arnauld, Antoine.) Paris, 1861.
Phil 5040.3.12 Logique de Port Royal. (Arnauld, Antoine.) Paris, 1869.
NEDL Phil 5040.3.15 Logique de Port Royal. (Arnauld, Antoine.) Paris, 1878.
Phil 5040.3.18 Logique de Port-Royal. Facsimile. (Arnauld, Antoine.) Lille, 1964.
Phil 5041.3.10 Logique déductive et inductive. 3e éd. (Bain, Alexander.) Paris, 1894. 2v.
Phil 735.86 La logique des jugements de valeur. (Goblot, E.) Paris, 1927.
Phil 5400.18.9 La logique des sentiments. 2. éd. (Ribot, T.) Paris, 1907.
Phil 5400.18.12 La logique des sentiments. 5. éd. (Ribot, T.) Paris, 1920.
Phil 270.56 Logique du pari. (Segond, J.L.P.) Paris, 1938.
Phil 21.19 Logique et analyse. Louvain. 1,1958+ 7v.
Phil 5055.29.10 Logique et argumentation. (Perelman, Chaim.) Bruxelles, 1968.
Phil 5046.42 Logique et connaissance. (Grize, Jean Blaise.) Genève, 1965.
Phil 3425.319.10 Logique et existence. 1. ed. (Hyppolite, Jean.) Paris, 1953.
Phil 254.2 La logique et le monde sensible. (Vuillemin, Jules.) Paris, 1971.
Phil 1200.52 La logique et l'épistémalogie des stoïciens. (Virieux, A.) Lausanne, 1950.
Phil 5057.34 Logique et métalogique. (Roure, Marie Louise.) Paris, 1957.
Phil 187.154 Logique et morale. (Mucchielli, Roger.) Paris, 1955.
Phil 192.25.9 Logique et morale. 4. ed. (Rey, A.) Paris, 1916.
Phil 5585.135 Logique et Perception. Logique et perception. Paris, 1958.
Phil 5585.135 Logique et perception. (Logique et Perception.) Paris, 1958.
Phil 3270.12.115 Logique et philosophie chez Frege. (Largeault, Jean.) Paris, 1970.
Phil 3425.606 Logique et religion chrétiene dans la philosophie de Hegel. (Bruaire, Claude.) Paris, 1964.
Phil 5051.42 Logique formelle, logique dialectique. 2e éd. (Lefebvre, Henri.) Paris, 1969.
Phil 5051.6.13 Logique formelle. (Luquet, G.H.) Paris, 1925.
Phil 5047.11.15 Logique formelle et logique transcendantale. (Husserl, Edmund.) Paris, 1957.
Phil 5042.55 La logique moderne. 1. éd. (Chauveneau, Jean.) Paris, 1957.
Phil 5051.9 La logique populaire. (Lecomte, A.) Paris, 1832.
Phil 5041.49 Logique positive; essai d'un théorie nouvelle de la connaissance. (Bonnot, Lucien.) Dijon, 1930.
Phil 3425.35 Logique subjective. (Hegel, Georg Wilhelm Friedrich.) Paris, 1854.
Phil 5066.227 Logiques construites par une methode de déduction naturelle. (Dopp, J.) Louvain, 1962.
Phil 5011.6.5 Logisch-philosophische Studien. (Bochénski, I.M.) Freiburg, 1959.
Phil 5040.16 Das logische; seine Gesetze und Kategorien. (Anderson, Louis.) Leipzig, 1929.
Phil 5047.30 Der logische Algorithmus. (Hontheim, J.) Berlin, 1895.
Phil 333.12 Der logische Aufbau der Welt. (Carnap, Rudolf.) Berlin, 1928.
Phil 3425.270 Die logische Frage in Hegel's System. (Trendelenburg, A.) Leipzig, 1843.
Phil 5068.54.5 Der logische Positivismus. (Übersetzung aus den Techechischen). (Ruml, Vladimir.) Berlin, 1965.
Phil 5068.20 Der logische Positivismus und das Existenzproblem der höheren Ideen. (Simàn, B.) Tel-Aviv, 1950.
Phil 8831.2 Die logische rechtvaadiging der zedelijkheid bij Fichte, Schelling en Hegel. Proefschrift. (Goedewaagen, T.) Amsterdam, 1923.
Phil 5052.38.5 Logische Schriften. (Mally, Ernst.) Dordrecht, 1971.
Phil 8893.90 Logische Struktur des emotionalen Ich. Diss. (Staehr, V. von.) Saalfeld, 1934.
Phil 9035.62 Die logische Struktur des Typusbegriffes. Inaug. Diss. (Seiterich, Eugen.) Freiburg, 1930.
Phil 5051.2 Logische Studien. (Lange, F.A.) Iserlohn, 1877.
Phil 5042.21.9A Logische Syntax der Sprache. (Carnap, Rudolf.) Wien, 1934.
Phil 5190.60 Logische und methodologische Probleme der wissenschaftlichen Erklärung. (Patel, Peter.) München, 1965.
Phil 3585.1.30 Logische und philosophische Abhandlungen. (Lambert, Johann Heinrich.) Berlin, 1782-87. 2v.
Phil 3270.12.45 Logische Untersuchungen. (Frege, Gottlob.) Göttingen, 1966.
Phil 5047.11 Logische Untersuchungen. (Husserl, Edmund.) Halle, 1900.
Phil 3890.1.42 Logische Untersuchungen. (Trendelenburg, A.) Berlin, 1840. 2v.
Phil 5047.11.3 Logische Untersuchungen. v. 1-2, pt. 1-2. (Husserl, Edmund.) Tübingen, 1968[1913]. 3v.
Phil 3890.1.41 Logische Untersuchungen. 2. Aufl. (Trendelenburg, A.) Leipzig, 1862. 3v.
Phil 5047.11.2 Logische Untersuchungen. 2. Aufl. v. 1-2, pt. 1-2. (Husserl, Edmund.) Halle, 1913. 3v.

Phil 3890.1.45A Logische Untersuchungen. 3. Aufl. (Trendelenburg, A.) Leipzig, 1870. 2v.
Phil 5055.3 Logisches Kausalgesetz. (Planck, K.C.) Nördlingen, 1877.
Phil 4515.101 Den logiska strukturen hos Boströms filosofi. (Wedberg, A.) Uppsala, 1937.
Phil 5066.24 Logistiek geformaliseerde logica. (Feys, Robert.) Antwerpen, 1944.
Phil 5068.92 Logistischer Positivismus. (Petzäll, Åke.) Göteborg, 1931.
Phil 21.4 Logos; mezhdumarodnyi ezhegodnik. Praga. 1-2,1912-1913
Phil 21.12 Logos; revista de la mesa redonda. Mexico.
Phil 5520.32 Logos; Ursprung und Wesen der Begriffe. (Noiré, Ludwig.) Leipzig, 1885.
Phil 3120.30.76 Logos. (Buber, Martin.) Heidelberg, 1962.
Phil 21.11 Logos. Kaunas.
Phil 21.1 Logos. Tübingen. 1910-1943 23v.
Phil 21.3 Logos: rivista internazionale di filosofia. Napoli. 1914-1943 18v.
Phil 3450.11.335 Il logos di Husserl. (Sancipriano, Mario.) Torino, 1962.
Phil 3745.8.5 Logos eidos, bios. (Pfannwitz, Rudolf.) München, 1930.
Phil 4845.227.30 Ho logos kai ho anthrōpos. (Papanoutsos, Euangelos.) Athena, 1971.
Phil 8595.56.5 Logos-meditatsiia drevnei tserkvi. (Pozov, A.) Miunkhen, 1964.
Phil 1750.359 Logos und Existenz. (Frankl, V.C.) Wien, 1951.
Phil 1135.82 Die Logoslehre von Heraklit bis Origenes. (Kelber, Wilhelm.) Stuttgart, 1958.
Phil 6969.12 Logotherapy and the Christian faith. (Tweedie, D.F.) Grands Rapids, 1961.
Phil 8412.35 Logroscimo, G. Teoria dell'arte e della critica. Padova, 1962.
Phil 3450.19.130 Logstrup, K.E.C. Kierkegaards und Heideggers Existenzanalyse und ihr Verhaltnis. 1-3. Aufl. Berlin, 1950.
Phil 2805.221 Lohde, Richard. Die Anthropologie Pascals. Halle, 1936.
Phil 3475.3.160 Lohff, Wenzel. Glaube und Freiheit. Gütersloh, 1957.
Phil 177.75 La loi de relation et l'erreur séparatiste en science et en philosophie. (Choisnard, Paul.) Paris, 1923.
Phil 600.40 La loi des trois états. Thèse. (Mathis, René.) Nancy, 1924.
Phil 2490.118.10 La loi des trois etats dans la philosophie d'Auguste Comte. (Uta, Michel.) Bourg, 1928.
Phil 8876.62.3 La loi morale fondée sur l'etude comparée des deux natures de l'homme. (Barbier, Louise.) Paris, 1884.
Phil 8896.17.5 La loi naturelle. (Volney, C.F.C.) Paris, 1934.
Phil 298.1 Les lois de Dieu. (Richard, C.) Paris, 1862.
Phil 5467.6 Les lois de l'imitation; étude sociologique. 4. éd. (Tarde, Gabriel.) Paris, 1904.
Phil 190.24 Lois de l'univers. (Perreaux, L.-G.) Paris, 1877. 2v.
Phil 2733.100 Les lois du choc des corps d'après Malebranche. (Mouy, P.) Paris, 1927.
Phil 2733.100.2 Les lois du choc des corps d'après Malebranche. Thèse. (Mouy, P.) Paris, 1927.
Phil 2750.33.30 Les lois du tragique. (Monnerot, Jules.) Paris, 1969.
Phil 8677.11.5 Lois et mystères de la création. (Weill, Alexandre.) Paris, 1896.
Phil 5520.4 Les lois psychologiques du symbolisme. (Ferrero, G.) Paris, 1895.
Phil 5627.22 Les lois psychophysiologique du développement des religions. (Binet-Sangle, Charles.) Paris, 1907.
Phil 8430.19 Loisel, A. L'expérience esthétique et l'ideal chrétien. Paris, 1909.
Phil 8886.90 Loiser, Burton M. Custom, law, and morality: conflict and continuity in social behavior. 1st ed. Garden City, 1969.
Phil 5545.38 Loisette, A. Assimilative memory. N.Y., 1896.
Phil 5545.38.25 Pamphlet box. Loisette, Alphonse.
Phil 5545.38.26 "Loisette" exposed. (Fellows, G.S.) N.Y., n.d.
Phil 8591.20.5 Loisy, Alfred. Autour d'un petit livre. Paris, 1903.
Phil 8591.20.12 Loisy, Alfred. Autres mythes à propos de la religion. Paris, 1938.
Phil 8886.38.8 Loisy, Alfred. La crise morale. Paris, 1937.
Phil 8701.8 Loisy, Alfred. De la discipline intellectuelle. Paris, 1919.
Phil 8886.38 Loisy, Alfred. La morale humaine. Paris, 1923.
Phil 8886.38.5 Loisy, Alfred. La morale humaine. 2. ed. Paris, 1928.
Phil 8591.20 Loisy, Alfred. La religion. Paris, 1917.
Phil 8591.20.2 Loisy, Alfred. La religion. 2. éd. Paris, 1924.
Phil 8591.20.9 Loisy, Alfred. Religion et l'humanité. Paris, 1926.
Phil 2475.1.245 Loisy, Alfred. Y a-t-il deux sources de la religion et de la morale? Paris, 1933.
Phil 1928.31.2 Loix de la nature. (Cumberland, R.) Leiden, 1757.
Phil 310.700 Lojacono, Giorgio. L'ideología marxista. Roma, 1968. 3v.
Phil 6117.24 Lokalisations-Psychologie. Die Lokalisationstheorie. 2. Aufl. (Hirth, George.) München, 1895.
Phil 6130.1 Das Lokalisationsgesetz. (Uschakoff, J.) Helsingfors, 1900.
Phil 6130.1.2 Das Lokalisationsgesetz. (Uschakoff, J.) Leipzig, 1900.
Phil 5820.3 Lola, or The thought and speech of animals. (Kindermann, H.) London, 1922.
Phil 186.89.5 Lolli, E. La conception inductive de la vie. Paris, 1937.
Phil 6681.11 Lombard, A. Les dangers du magnétisme animal. Paris, 1819.
Phil 5850.259 Lombard, G.F.F. Behavior in a selling group. Boston, 1955.
Phil 4080.3.195 Lombardi, A. La filosofia di Benedetto Croce. Roma, 1946.
Phil 186.80 Lombardi, F. L'esperienza e l'uomo. Firenze, 1935.
Phil 8886.56 Lombardi, F. Il mondo degli uomini. Firenze, 1935.
Phil 4011.4 Lombardi, Franco. La filosofia italiana negli ultimi cento anni. Asti, 1958?
Phil 4160.66.12 Lombardi, Franco. Scritti; saggi. v.10-13. Firenze, 1965-4v.
Phil 4160.66.12.2 Lombardi, Franco. Scritti; saggi. v.11- 2. ed. Firenze, 1970-
Phil 4160.66.14 Lombardi, Franco. Scritti. Opere. Firenze, 1963- 6v.
Phil 4960.210.2 Lombardo Toledano, Vicente. Las corrientes filosóficas en la vida de México. 2. ed. México, 1963.
Phil 4973.5.6 Lombardo Toledano, Vicente. Escritos filosóficos. México, 1975.
Phil 8886.10 Lombarès, M. de. Du gout ou de la passion du bien-être matériel. Montauban, 1860?
Phil 3493.14 Lomber, Wilhelm. Die Gratistätte Immanuel Kants auf Grund authentischen Quellen dargestellt. Königsberg, 1924.
Phil 3493.14.5 Lomber, Wilhelm. Immanuel Kants letzte Lebensjahre und Tod. Königsberg, 1923.
Phil 5425.4.15 Lombroso, C. Entartung und Genie. Leipzig, 1894.
Phil 6060.3 Lombroso, C. Grafologia. Milano, 1895.

Phil 5425.4.5   Lombroso, C. L'homme de génie. Paris, 1889.
Phil 7060.31   Lombroso, C. Inchiesta sulla trasmissione del pensiero. Torino., 1891.
NEDL   Phil 5425.4.9   Lombroso, C. The man of genius. London, 1891.
Phil 5425.4   Lombroso, C. L'uomo di genio. Torino, 1894.
Phil 7082.106   Lomer, Georg. Der Traumspiegel. München, 1918.
Phil 6681.7   Lonbert, J.B. Le magnétisme et le sommambulisme. Paris, 1844.
Phil 7069.09.7   Lonbroso, Cesare. After death - what? Boston, 1909.
X Cg   Phil 6321.15   London, L.S. Mental therapy. N.Y., 1937. 2v.
Phil 5780.25   London, Perry. Behavior control. 1. ed. N.Y., 1969.
Phil 51.5   London. University. Council for Psychical Research. Bulletin. London.
Phil 1865.185.2   London. University. University College Library. Catalogue of the manuscripts of Jeremy Bentham in the Library of University College. London, 1937.
Phil 1865.185   London. University. University College Library. Catalogue of the manuscripts of Jeremy Bentham in the Library of University College. 2nd ed. London, 1962.
Phil 1865.183   London. University. University College Library. Jeremy Bentham, bicentenary celebrations. London, 1948.
Phil 21.16   London. University. University College Psychological Laboratory. Collected papers. London. 1-10 5v.
Phil 6952.16   The London-citizen...sent...to...madhouse. 2. ed. (Cruden, Alexander.) London, 17- .
Phil 7068.73.10   London Dialectical Society. Report on spiritualism of the committee of the London Dialectical Society. London, 1873.
Phil 5418.4   Loneliness; a study of the human condition. (Mannin, Ethel Edith.) London, 1966.
Phil 8665.2   The lonely God. (Kernahan, C.) London, n.d.
Phil 342.18.2   Lonergan, Bernard J.F. Insight. N.Y., 1964.
Phil 6321.6   Long, C.E. Collected papers on the psychology of phantasy. N.Y., 1921.
Phil 3475.3.215   Long, Eugene Thomas. Jaspers and Bultmenn. Durham, 1968.
Phil 1135.162   Long, Herbert S. A study of the doctrine of metempsychocis in Greece. Thesis. Princeton, 1948.
Phil 7069.59.40   Long, Max Freedom. Psychometric analysis. Vista, Calif., 1959.
Phil 2050.180   Long, William J. Über Hume's Lehre von den Ideen. Inaug. Diss. Heidelberg, 1897.
Phil 7069.45   Long distance calling. (Barnes, M.S.) N.Y., 1945.
Phil 5520.255   Longebaugh, T. General semantics. 1. ed. N.Y., 1957.
Phil 7054.166   Longley, Mary. Teachings...from the spirit world. Chicago, 1908.
Phil 4260.90   Longo, Michele. Giambattista Vico. Torino, 1921.
Phil 8886.48   Longo, P. Etica umana. Torino, 1924.
Phil 4265.3.85   Longoni, L. Il sistema filosofico di Hegel...sulla pena di morte di A. Vera. Milano, 1863.
Phil 3640.279   Lonsbach, R.M. Friedrich Nietzsche und die Juden. Stockholm, 1939.
Phil 510.1.27   Loofs, F. Anti-Haeckel. 3rd ed. London, 1904.
Phil 6682.3.85   Look, Maria van. Franz Anton Mesmer, Reinhold Schneider. Freiburg, 1969.
Phil 6323.15   Look before you leap. (Nelson, John.) Washington, D.C., 1954.
Phil 6750.267   The look of competence; stigma in the lives of the mentally retarded. (Edgerton, Robert B.) Berkeley, 1967.
Phil 6316.8.13   The look of the it. (Groddeck, Georg.) N.Y., 1961.
Phil 6112.17   A look upward. (Clark, Susie C.) Boston, 1899.
Phil 5251.38   Loomans, Charles. De la connaissance de soi-même. Bruxelles, 1880.
Phil 1885.86A   Loomba, R.M. Bradley and Bergson. Lucknow, 1937.
Phil 9410.5.3   Loomis, Charles. The knack of it. 2. ed. N.Y., 1908.
Phil 6121.18.5   Loomis, E. Occult science library; seven essays. Chicago, 1898.
Phil 6121.18   Loomis, E. Seven essays on the subject of your practical forces on the subject of practical occultism. Chicago, 1897.
Phil 186.107   Loos, A. The nature of man, his world. N.Y., 1950.
Htn   Phil 2045.90*   Loose remarks on certain positions to be found in Mr. Hobbes's Philosophical rudiments of government and society. 2nd ed. (Graham, C.M.) London, 1769.
Phil 6961.12   Loosmore, W.C. Nerves and the man. N.Y., 1921.
Phil 5400.69   Loosmore, W.C. Ourselves and our emotions. London, 1928.
Phil 4762.2.30   Lopatin, Lev M. Filosofskiia kharakteristiki i rechi. Moskva, 1911.
Phil 4967.20.85   Lopes de Maltos, C. O pensamento de Farias Brito. São Paulo, 1962.
Phil 96.6   Lopes de Mattos, Carlos. Vocabulario filosófico. Sao Paulo, 1957.
Phil 9513.20   Lopez, Aranguren, José Luis. Moral y sociedad. Madrid, 1965.
Phil 9450.56   López Aranguren, J.L. Etica y política. Madrid, 1963.
Phil 8886.73   López Aranguren, José Luis. Etica. Madrid, 1958.
Phil 8886.73.2   López Aranguren, José Luis. Etica. 2. ed. Madrid, 1959.
Phil 8886.73.5   López Aranguren, José Luis. Lo que sabemos de moral. Madrid, 1967.
Phil 8886.73.10   López Aranguren, José Luis. Teoria y sociedad. Barcelona, 1970.
Phil 6980.431   López Ibor, Juan. La agonía del psicoanalisis. 3. ed. Madrid, 1961.
Phil 4312.5A   Lopez Morillas, Juan. El krausismo español. 1. ed. México, 1956.
Phil 4312.8   Lopez Quintas, Alfonso. Filosofía española contemporánea; temas y autores. Madrid, 1970.
Phil 1740.28   López Quintás, Alfonso. Pensadores cristianos contemporáneos. v.1- Madrid, 1968-
Phil 6321.11   Lorand, Sándor. Psycho-analysis today. London, 1933.
Phil 6321.11.10   Lorand, Sándor. Psycho-analysis today. N.Y., 1944.
Phil 6321.11.15   Lorand, Sándor. Technique of psychoanalytic therapy. N.Y., 1946.
Phil 8701.13   Lorbeer, Floyd Irwing. A message of light, containing scientifc foundation for religion. Los Angeles, 1927.
Phil 8701.13.5   Lorbeer, Floyd Irwing. Philosophy of light. Los Angeles, 1932.
Phil 8701.1   Lord, D.N. Geognosy, or The facts and principles of geology against theories. N.Y., 1855.
Phil 8701.17   Lord, Eleazar. The epoch of creation. N.Y., 1851.
Phil 5272.5   Lord, Frederick M. Estimating true-score distributions in psychological testing. Princeton, 1967.
Phil 5401.5   Lord, H.G. The psychology of courage. Boston, 1918.
Phil 8965.4.5   Lord Bacon not the author of The Christian paradoxes. (Palmer, Herbert.) Edinburgh, 1865.
NEDL   Phil 1850.105   Lord Bacon's philosophy examined. (Laing, F.H.) London, 1877.
Phil 7069.36.20   Lord Halifax's ghost book. 3. ed. (Halifax, Charles L.W.) London, 1936.
Phil 176.41.5   Lord Monboddo. (Knight, William.) London, 1900.

Phil 186.22   Lorensen, C. Essay on positive theology or a new system of philosophy. Waterbury, 1899.
Phil 175.13.9   Lorenz, B. Die Philosophie A.M. Ampères. Berlin, 1908.
Phil 3635.90   Lorenz, Heinrich. Dr P.J. Möbius als Philosoph. Inaug. Diss. Wiesbaden, 1894.
Phil 5251.67   Lorenz, Konrad Zacharias. Evolution and modification of behavior. Chicago, 1965.
Phil 5421.20.21   Lorenz, Konrad Zacharias. On aggression. N.Y., 1966.
Phil 5421.20.20   Lorenz, Konrad Zacharias. Das sogenannte Böse. 2. Aufl. Wien, 1964.
Phil 258.10   Lorenz, Kuno. Elemente der Sprachkritik; eine Alternative zum Dogmatismus und Skeptizismus in der analytischen Philosophie. 1. Aufl. Frankfurt am Main, 1970.
Phil 8961.19   Lorenz, Willy. Der Gentleman und der Christ. Wien, 1967.
Phil 978.124   Lorenzen, Iwer Thor. Evolution durch Inkarnation und Metamorphose. Hamburg, 1969.
Phil 5051.46.4   Lorenzen, Paul. Formale Logik. 4. Aufl. Berlin, 1970.
Phil 5068.82   Lorenzen, Paul. Normative logic and ethics. Mannheim, 1969.
Phil 5700.4   Lorenzer, Alfred. Kritik des psychoanalytischen Symbolbegriffs. 1. Aufl. Frankfurt, 1970.
Phil 5520.53.2   Lorimer, F. The growth of reason. N.Y., 1929.
Phil 5876.20   Lorimier, Jacques de. Le projet de vie de l'adolescent, identité psychosociale et vocation. Paris, 1967.
Phil 735.252   Loring, L.M. Two kinds of values. London, 1966.
Phil 5325.155   Loring, Mildred W. Methods of studying controlled word associations. Baltimore, 1919.
Phil 2190.5   Lornay, Stephen Clark. Ockham. LaSalle, Ill., 1938.
Phil 3493.2   Lorquet, N.H.A. Discussion des Antinomies Kantiennes. Paris, 1841.
Phil 3850.18.175   Lorscheid, B. Das Leibphänomen. Bonn, 1962.
Phil 3850.18.145   Lorschield, Bernhard. Max Schelers Phänomenologie des Psychischen. Bonn, 1957.
Phil 7140.6   Loryea, J.H. Is man a free agent? London, 1902.
Phil 178.84   Los fundamentos metafisicos del orden moral. 3. ed. (Derisi, Octavio Nicolas.) Madrid, 1969.
Phil 487.3   Los vom Materialismus! (Mayer, Adolf.) Heidelberg, 1906.
Phil 477.11   Los von Materialismus! (Coudenhove-Kalergi, R.N.) Wien, 1931.
Phil 811.7   Losacco, Michele. Lineamenti di storia della filosofia. Napoli, 1931.
Phil 3801.529   Losacco, Michele. Schelling. Milano, 1914?
Phil 3499.1.5   Lose blätter aus Kants nach lass, Mitgetheit von Rudolf Reicke. (Kant, Immanuel.) Königsberg, 1889-98.
Phil 3480.27.5   Lose Blätter aus Kants Nachloss. (Kant, Immanuel.) Königsberg, 1889-98.
Phil 8062.8   Losev, Aleksei F. Istoriia antichnoi estetiki. Moskva, 1963.
Phil 8412.39   Losev, Aleksei F. Istoriia esteticheskikh kategorii. Moskva, 1965.
Phil 5051.37   Losev, Aleksei F. Muzyka kak predmet logiki. Moskva, 1927.
Phil 5535.22   Losifeseu, Marius. Random processes and learning. Berlin, 1969.
Phil 8591.38   Losing religion to find it. (Lindsay, Eric.) London, 1935.
Phil 5790.2.5   The loss of loved ones. (Moriarty, David M.) Springfield, 1967.
Phil 5051.40   Lossada, Luis de. Institutiones dialecticae, vulgo summulae, ad primam partem philosophici cursus pertinentes. Salmanticae, 1721.
Phil 96.1   Lossius, J.C. Neues Philosophie Real-Lexikon. Erfurt, 1803-06. 4v.
Phil 342.3   Losskii, N. Die Grundlegung des Intuitivismus. Halle, 1908.
Phil 342.3.10   Losskii, N. L'intuition, la matière et la vie. Paris, 1928.
Phil 342.3.5   Losskii, N. The intuitive basis of knowledge. London, 1919.
Phil 5251.23.5   Losskii, N.O. Chuvstvennaia, intellektual'naia i misticheskaia intuitsiia. Paris, 1938.
Phil 4710.12   Losskii, N.O. Dialekticheskii materializm v SSSR. Paris, 193-?
Phil 5251.23   Losskii, N.O. Die Grundlehren der Psychologie. Leipzig, 1904.
Phil 5051.23.7   Losskii, N.O. Handbuch der Logik, Übersetzung von W. Sesemann. Leipzig, 1927.
Phil 4710.35A   Losskii, N.O. History of Russian philosophy. N.Y., 1951.
Phil 186.64.10   Losskii, N.O. Intellectual intuition and ideal being. Praha, 1934.
Phil 5051.23.4   Losskiĭ, N.O. Logika. Berlin, 1923.
Phil 5251.74   Losskii, N.O. Principles of voluntaristic psychology. n.p., 1935. 2v.
Phil 186.99   Losskii, N.O. Tipy mirovozzrenii. Parizh, 1931.
Phil 186.156   Losskii, N.O. Types of world views; an introduction to metaphysics. Typescript. n.p., n.d.
Phil 8886.69   Losskii, N.O. Usloviia absoliutnogo dobra. Parizh, 1949.
Phil 186.64   Losskii, N.O. The world as an organic whole. London, 1928.
Phil 745.10   Losskii, Nikolai O. Materiia i zhizn'. Berlin, 1923.
Phil 5490.5   Losskii, Nikolai O. Sensory, intellectual and mystical intuition. v.1-2. n.p., n.d.
Phil 735.107   Losskii, Nikolai O. Value and existence. London, 1935.
Phil 4762.1.38   Losskii, Nikolai Onufrievich. Obshchedostupnoe vvedenie v filosofiiu. Frankfurt, 1956.
Phil 4762.1.42   Losskii, Nikolai Onufrievich. Philosophical essays. n.p., 1941.
Phil 4762.1.35   Losskii, Nikolai Onufrievich. Sbornik zadach po logike. Praga, 1924.
Phil 4762.1.37   Losskii, Nikolai Onufrievich. Svoboda voli. Paris, n.d.
Phil 4762.1.36   Losskii, Nikolai Onufrievich. Vospominaniia. München, 1968.
Phil 4762.1.30   Losskii, Nikolai Onufrievich. Vvedenie v filosofiiu. Petrograd, 1918.
Phil 4762.1.90   Losskij's erkenntnistheoretischer Intuitionismus. Inaug. Diss. (Polanowska, Fejga.) Berlin, 1931.
Phil 5761.17.5   Lossky, N.O. Freedom of will. London, 1932.
Phil 8550.508   Lossky, Nikolai O. Slavonic religious philosophy. n.p., n.d.
Phil 4762.1.39   Lossky's theory of knowledge. (Kohanskii, A.S.) Nashville, 1936.
Phil 525.246   The lost dimension. (Fausset, Hugh I'Anson.) London, 1966.
Phil 1801.6   The lost world of Thomas Jefferson. (Boorstin, D.J.) N.Y., 1948.
Phil 3850.27.120   Lotar, Peter. Von Sinn des Lebens. Strasbourg, 1951.
Phil 5251.27   Lothian, A.J.D. An outline of psychology for education. London, 1923.

Phil 7069.67.60 Lots-Poole, Marietta. Strange dreams and their portents and other reflections Brentwood, 1967.
Phil 3831.10 Lotsij, M.C.L. Spinoza's wijsbegeerte. Utrecht, 1888-?
Phil 3246.200 Lott, F.C. Festrede zur Saecularfeier Fichtes. Wien, 1862.
Phil 349.54 La lotta per la scienza. 1. ed. (Semerari, Giuseppe.) Milano, 1965.
Phil 8961.16 Lottin, O. Etudes de morale histoire et doctrine. Gembloux, 1961.
Phil 5221.5 Lottin, Odon. Psychologie et morale aux XIIe et XIIIe siècles. v.1-6. Louvain, 1942. 8v.
Phil 185.52 The lotus path. (King, Mrs. E.D.) Los Angeles, 1917.
Phil 976.5 Lotusblueten. Leipzig. 4-99,1893-1900// 16v.
Phil 3493.27 Lotz, J.B. Kant und die Scholastik Heute. Pullach, 1955.
Phil 3640.410 Lotz, J.B. Zwischen Seligkeit und Verdamnis. Frankfurt, 1953.
Phil 3585.28.5 Lotz, Johannes Baptist. Ich, du, wir. 1. Aufl. Frankfurt, 1968.
Phil 3585.28 Lotz, Johannes Baptist. Der Mensch im Sein. Freiburg, 1967.
Phil 8591.87 Lotz, Johannes Baptist. Neue Erkenntnisprobleme in Philosophie und Theologie. Freiburg, 1968.
Phil 3585.28.20 Lotz, Johannes Baptist. Ontologia. Barcinone, 1963.
Phil 1750.552.15 Lotz, Johannes Baptist. Sein und Existenz. Freiburg, 1965.
Phil 1135.245 Lotz, Johannes Baptist. Die Stufen der Liebe; Eros, Phila, Agape. 1. Aufl. Frankfurt, 1971.
Phil 3585.28.10 Lotz, Johannes Baptist. Das Urteil und das Sein. München, 1957.
Phil 8125.38 Lotze, H. Geschichte der Aesthetik in Deutschland. München, 1868.
Phil 3565.51.50 Lotze, Hermann. Das Dasein der Seele. Leipzig, 1929?
Phil 8125.24 Lotze, Hermann. Geschichte der Aesthetik in Deutschland. München. 1848.
Phil 3565.58 Lotze, Hermann. Grundtraek af religionsfilosofien. København, 1886.
Phil 8412.19.5 Lotze, Hermann. Grundzüge der Ästhetik; Diktate aus den Vorlesungen. 2. Aufl. Leipzig, 1888.
Phil 3565.65 Lotze, Hermann. Grundzüge der Logik. Leipzig, 1883.
Phil 3565.65.5 Lotze, Hermann. Grundzüge der Logik und Encyklopädie der Philosophie. 3e Aufl. Leipzig, 1891.
Phil 3565.45.5A Lotze, Hermann. Grundzüge der Metaphysik. Leipzig, 1883.
Phil 3565.45.12 Lotze, Hermann. Grundzüge der Metaphysik. 2. Aufl. Leipzig, 1887.
Phil 3565.60 Lotze, Hermann. Grundzüge der Naturphilosophie. Leipzig, 1882.
Phil 3565.60.2 Lotze, Hermann. Grundzüge der Naturphilosophie. 2. Aufl. Leipzig, 1889.
Phil 3565.35.2 Lotze, Hermann. Grundzüge der praktischen Philosophie. Leipzig, 1882.
Phil 3565.35 Lotze, Hermann. Grundzüge der praktischen Philosophie. 3. Aufl. Leipzig, 1899.
Phil 3565.69 Lotze, Hermann. Grundzüge der Psychologie. Leipzig, 1881.
Phil 3565.72 Lotze, Hermann. Grundzüge der Religionsphilosophie. 2e Aufl. Leipzig, 1884.
Phil 8412.19 Lotze, Hermann. Grundzuge der Ästhetik. 3. Aufl. Leipzig, 1906.
Phil 3565.10 Lotze, Hermann. Kleine Schriften. Leipzig, 1885-91. 4v.
Phil 3565.31 Lotze, Hermann. Logic. Oxford, 1884.
Phil 3565.30.30 Lotze, Hermann. Logik, drei Bücher vom Denken. 2e Aufl. Leipzig, 1928.
Phil 3565.64 Lotze, Hermann. Logik. Leipzig, 1843.
Htn Phil 3565.68.1* Lotze, Hermann. Medicinische Psychologie. Leipzig, 1852.
Phil 3565.68 Lotze, Hermann. Medicinische Psychologie. Leipzig, 1852.
Phil 3565.31.2 Lotze, Hermann. Metaphysic. Oxford, 1884.
Phil 3565.31.4 Lotze, Hermann. Metaphysic. 2. ed. Oxford, 1887. 2v.
Phil 3565.45 Lotze, Hermann. Metaphysik. Leipzig, 1841.
Phil 3565.45.10 Lotze, Hermann. Metaphysik. Leipzig, 1879.
Phil 3565.31.15 Lotze, Hermann. Métaphysique. Paris, 1883.
Phil 3565.51.10 Lotze, Hermann. Microcosmo. Pavia, 1911-16. 2v.
Phil 3565.51 Lotze, Hermann. Microcosmos. N.Y., 1885. 2v.
Phil 3565.51.1 Lotze, Hermann. Microcosmos. v.1-2. N.Y., 1886.
Phil 3565.51.4 Lotze, Hermann. Microcosmos. v.1-2. N.Y., 1897.
Phil 3565.51.2 Lotze, Hermann. Microcosmos. v.1-2. 2. ed. N.Y., 1885.
Phil 3565.50 Lotze, Hermann. Mikrokosmus. Leipzig, 1869-72. 3v.
Phil 3565.50.5 Lotze, Hermann. Mikrokosmus. v.1-3. Leipzig, 1885-1896. 2v.
Phil 3565.50.6 Lotze, Hermann. Mikrokosmus. 6e Aufl. Leipzig, 1923. 3v.
Phil 3565.32.5 Lotze, Hermann. Outline of aesthetics. Boston, 1886.
Phil 3565.32.1.3 Lotze, Hermann. Outline of Metaphysic. Boston, 1884.
Phil 3565.32 Lotze, Hermann. Outline of Metaphysic. Boston, 1886.
Phil 3565.32.3 Lotze, Hermann. Outline of practical philosophy. Boston, 1885.
Phil 3565.32.4 Lotze, Hermann. Outline of psychology. Boston, 1886.
Phil 3565.70 Lotze, Hermann. Outline of psychology. Minneapolis, 188-?
Phil 3565.51.5 Lotze, Hermann. An outline of the Microcosmos. Oberlin, 1895.
Phil 3565.32.5.5 Lotze, Hermann. Outlines of logic and of encyclopaedia of philosophy. Boston, 1887.
Phil 3565.32.6 Lotze, Hermann. Outlines of logic and of encyclopaedia of philosophy. Boston, 1892.
Phil 3565.68.5 Lotze, Hermann. Principes généraux de psychologie physiologique. Paris, 1876.
Phil 3565.55 Lotze, Hermann. Streitschriften. Leipzig, 1857.
Phil 3565.30 Lotze, Hermann. System der Philosophie. Leipzig, 1874-79. 2v.
Phil 3565.30.25 Lotze, Hermann. System der Philosophie. Leipzig, 1912. 2v.
Phil 3565.30.3A Lotze, Hermann. System der Philosophie. 2e Aufl. Leipzig, 1880-84. 2v.
Phil 8412.19.15 Lotze, Hermann. Über Bedingungen der Kunstschönheit. Göttingen, 1847.
Phil 8412.19.10 Lotze, Hermann. Über den Begriff der Schonhëit. Göttingen, 1845.
Phil 3565.74 Lotze, Hermann. Der Zusammenhang der Dinge. Berlin, 191-?
Phil 3011.1 Lotze, R.H. Geschichte der deutschen Philosophie - Kant. Leipzig, 1882.
Phil 3565.120 Lotze als Anthropologe. (Seibert, F.) Wiesbaden, 1900.
Phil 3565.124 Lotzes Aesthetik. (Kögel, Fritz.) Göttingen, 1886.
Phil 3565.108.5 Lotze's Gedanken zur den Principienfragen der Ethik. (Tienes, Alfred.) Heidelberg, 1896.
Phil 3565.81 Lotze's Philosophie. (Hartmann, K.R.E.) Leipzig, 1888.
Phil 3565.117 Lotze's philosophische Weltanschauung nach ihren Grundzügen. (Pfleiderer, E.) Berlin, 1882.
Phil 3565.78 Lotze's philosophische Weltanschauungen nach ihren Grundzugen. (Pfleiderer, E.) Berlin, 1882. 5 pam.
Phil 3565.114 Lotzes religionsfilosofi. (Rosenquist, G.G.) Helsingfors, 1889.
Phil 3565.128 Lotze's religionsphilosophische Gedanken im Lichte der göttichen Offenbarung. (Bartell, Fr., pastor.) Hannover, 1884.
Phil 3565.129 Lotzes Stellung zum Occasionalismus. (Tuch, Ernst.) Berlin, 1897.
Phil 3565.132 Lotze's system of philosophy. (Santayana, George.) Bloomington, 1971.
Phil 3565.109 Lotze's theory of reality. (Thomas, Evan E.) London, 1921.
Phil 186.29 Louage, Augustin. A course of philosophy. 4. ed. N.Y., 1895.
Phil 5251.16 Louden, D.M. van. Onderzoek naar den duur der eenvoudige psychische processen v.n. bij de Psychosen. Amsterdam, 1905.
Phil 4065.86 Louis, G. Giordano Bruno. Berlin, 1900.
Phil 1135.24 Louis, M. Doctrines religieuses. Paris, 1909.
Phil 2880.1.85 Louis C. de Saint-Martin et le Martinisme. (Amadou, R.) Paris, 1946.
Phil 2515.1.80 Louis Couturat (1868-1914). Coulomniers, 191-?
Phil 2725.1.80 Louis de la Forge. (Seyfarth, H.) Jena, 1887.
Phil 5628.51 Louise Lateau. (Warlomont, Evariste.) Bruxelles, 1875.
Phil 5628.51.10 Louise Lateau: her stigmas and ecstasy. (Rohling, August.) N.Y., 1879.
Phil 811.26 Louisgrand, Jean. De Lucrèce à Camus, littérature et philosophie comme réflexion sur l'homme. Paris, 1970.
Phil 6953.18 Louisiana. Southeast Louisiana Hospital, Mandeville. Psychotherapy with schizophrenics. Baton Rouge, 1961.
Phil 525.61.5 Louismet, S. La contemplation chrétienne. Paris, 1923.
Phil 525.38.2 Louismet, S. Miracle et mystique. 2e ed. Paris, 1923.
Phil 6990.3.52 Lourdes, Konnersreuth oder Gallspach? (Mayer, L.) Schopfheim, 1932.
Phil 6990.3.19 Lourdes. (Benson, R.H.) St. Louis, 1914.
Phil 6990.3.90 Lourdes. (Laurentin, René.) Paris, 1961. 6v.
Phil 6990.42 Lourdes. (Saunders, E.) N.Y., 1940.
Phil 6990.3.55 Lourdes: hier, aujourd'hui, demain. (Barbé, Daniel.) Paris, 1893.
Phil 6990.3.54 Lourdes: yesterday, today and tomorrow. (Barbé, Daniel.) Baden, 1893.
Phil 6990.3.92 Lourdes. 2. ed. (Laurentin, René.) Paris, 1957. 7v.
Htn Phil 6990.3.27* Lourdes depuis 1858 jusqu'à nos jours. (Boissarie, P.G.) Paris, 1894.
Phil 6990.3.116 Lourdes et Fatima. (Bettez, Norbert Marie.) Montréal, 1967.
Phil 6990.3.25 Lourdes und seine Geschichte vom medizinischen Standpunkte. 2. ed. (Boissarie, P.G.) Augsburg, 1892.
Phil 4472.89.30 Lourencao, Eduardo. Heterodoxia. Coimbra, 1967. 2v.
Phil 4710.5 Lourié, Osip. La philosophie russe contemporaine. Paris, 1902.
Phil 4710.5.2A Lourié, Osip. La philosophie russe contemporaine. 2. ed. Paris, 1905.
Phil 5520.37.5 Lourié, Ossip. La graphomanie. Paris, 1920.
Phil 5520.37 Lourié, Ossip. Le langage et la verbomanie. Paris, 1912.
Phil 51.1 Louvain. Université. Institute Supérieuse de Philosophe. Annales. Louvain. 1-5,1912-1924 5v.
Phil 51.1.5 Louvain. Université. Laboratoire de Psychologie Experimentale. Travaux. Louvain.
Phil 2750.18.80 Louvain. Université Catholique. Jubilé Albert Michotte. Louvain, 1947.
Phil 75.11 Louvain. Université Catholique. Institut Supérieur de Philosophie. Sommaire idéologique. Bruxelles. 1-20,1895-1914 4v.
Phil 5238.12 Louvain. Université Catholique. Institute Supérieur de Philosophie. Miscellanea psychologica Albert Michotte. Louvain, 1947.
Phil 5251.46 Loux, Samuel. Man and his fellowmen. London, 1945.
Phil 4466.1.80 Louzada de Magalhaes, J.J. Silvestre Pinheiro Ferreira. Bonn, 1881.
Phil 4809.447.90 Loužil, Jaromír. Ignác Jan Hanuš. Vyd. 1. Praha, 1971.
Phil 8612.21 Lovatelli, E. Thanatos. Roma, 1888.
Phil 3640.684 Love, F.R. Young Nietzsche and the Wagnerian experience. Chapel Hill, 1963.
Phil 5400.166 Love, hate, fear, anger and the other lively emotions. (Callwood, J.) Garden City, 1964.
Phil 6320.11 Love, hate and reparation. (Klein, M.) London, 1937.
Phil 5251.33 Love, Mary C. Human conduct and the law. Menasha, 1925.
Phil 7069.44.25 Love after death. (Desmond, S.) London, 1944.
Phil 6322.19.10 Love against hate. 1st ed. (Menninger, Karl Augustus.) N.Y., 1942.
Phil 9240.22 Love almighty and ills unlimited. 1st ed. (Farrer, Austin.) Garden City, N.Y., 1961.
Phil 9495.17 Love and parentage. (Fowler, O.S.) N.Y., 1855.
Phil 9165.6.5 Love and parentage. 40th ed. (Fowler, O.S.) N.Y., 1869.
Phil 5841.22 Love and power. (Rosenfels, Paul.) N.Y., 1966.
Phil 9495.167 Love and sexuality. 1st ed. (Ryan, Mary Perkins.) N.Y., 1967.
Phil 5421.25.60 Love and will. 1. ed. (May, Rollo.) N.Y., 1969.
Phil 9345.11 Love and you. (Friend, N.E. (Mrs.).) N.Y., 1933.
Phil 2005.12 The love of anxiety, and other essays. 1st ed. (Frankel, Charles.) N.Y., 1945.
Phil 486.8 Lovecchio, Antonino. Filosofia della prassi e filosofia dello spirito. Palmi, 1928.
Phil 1711.8A Lovejoy, A.D. Reflections on human nature. Baltimore, 1961.
Phil 2475.1.135 Lovejoy, A.O. Bergson and romantic evolutionism. Berkeley, 1913.
Phil 292.8A Lovejoy, A.O. The great chain of being. Cambridge, Mass., 1936.
Phil 292.8.5 Lovejoy, A.O. The great chain of being. Cambridge, Mass., 1957.
Phil 292.8.6 Lovejoy, A.O. The great chain of being. Cambridge, Mass., 1961.
Phil 186.140 Lovejoy, A.O. The reason, the understanding and time. Baltimore, 1961.
Phil 315.6A Lovejoy, A.O. The revolt against dualism. Chicago, 1930.
Phil 315.6.3 Lovejoy, A.O. The revolt against dualism. La Salle, Ill., 1955.
Phil 2120.12.30 Lovejoy, A.O. The thirteen pragmatisms. Baltimore, 1963.
Phil 811.11A Lovejoy, Arthur O. Essays in the history of ideas. Baltimore, 1948.
Phil 9410.7 Lovejoy, Arthur O. Optimism and romanticism. n.p., 1927.
Phil 1850.84.2 Lovejoy, B.G. Francis Bacon. London, 1888.
Phil 5535.30 Lovejoy, Elijah. Attention in discrimination learning; a point of view and a theory. San Francisco, 1968.
Phil 7069.30.13 Lovejoy, H.T. Talks with the invisible. Sunderland, 1930.
Phil 5821.16 Lovenz, Konrad Zacharias. Antriebe tierischen und menschlichen Verhaltens. München, 1968.

Phil 9495.168.20   Lovers in marriage. (Evely, Louis.) N.Y., 1968.
Phil 6311.47   Love's body. (Brown, Norman Oliver.) N.Y., 1966.
Phil 6321.17   Low, A.A. Secret of self-help in psychiatric aftercare. v.1-3. Chicago, 1943.
X Cg   Phil 6321.3.2   Low, Barbara. Psycho-analysis. London, 1920.
Htn   Phil 2115.130*   Lowde, J. Moral essays; wherein some of Mr. Locks and Monsir. Malbranch's opinions are briefly examin'd. York, 1699.
Htn   Phil 186.30*   Lowde, James. A discourse concerning the nature of man. London, 1694.
Phil 6321.56   Lowe, Gordon Robb. Personal relationships in psychological disorders. Harmondsworth, 1969.
Phil 2340.10.170   Lowe, Victor A. Understanding Whitehead. Baltimore, 1962.
Phil 2340.10.120A   Lowe, Victor A. Whitehead and the modern world. Boston, 1950.
Phil 8886.11   Lowell, A.C. (Mrs.). Seed-grain for thought and discussion. Boston, 1856. 2v.
Phil 9455.4   Lowell, A.L. Public opinion in war and peace. Cambridge, 1923.
Phil 8886.52   Lowell, Abbot L. Conflicts of principle. Cambridge, 1932.
Phil 1880.43.2   Lowell lectures...metaphysics...science. (Bowen, F.) Boston, 1849.
Phil 1880.43   Lowell lectures...metaphysics...science. (Bowen, F.) Boston, 1849.
Phil 8693.5.40   Lowell lectures on the ascent of man. 13th ed. (Drummond, H.) N.Y., 1906.
Phil 5402.44   Lowen, Alexander. Pleasure: a creative approach to life. N.Y., 1970.
Phil 3425.78A   Lowenberg, Jacob. Hegel's Entwürfe zur Enzyklopädie und Propadentik. Leipzig, 1912.
Phil 3425.78.10   Lowenberg, Jacob. Hegel's phenomenology. La Salle, Ill., 1965.
Phil 342.19   Lowenberg, Jacob. Reason and the nature of things. La Salle, Ill., 1959.
Phil 5599.95   The Lowenfeld world technique. 1. ed. (Bowyer, Laura Ruth.) Oxford, N.Y., 1970.
Phil 3425.245   Lowenstein, Julius. Hegels Staatsidee. Berlin, 1927.
Phil 3450.19.118A   Lowith, Carl. Heidegger. Frankfurt, 1953.
Phil 5070.1.2   Lowndes, R. Introduction...philosophy of primary beliefs. London, 1865.
Phil 5070.1   Lowndes, R. Introduction...philosophy of primary beliefs. London, 1865.
NEDL   Phil 1925.80   Lowrey, C.E. Philosophy of Ralph Cudworth. N.Y., 1884.
Phil 6980.433   Lowrey, Lawson G. Psychiatry for social workers. N.Y., 1946.
Phil 6980.433.2   Lowrey, Lawson G. Psychiatry for social workers. 2. ed. N.Y., 1952.
Phil 5070.12   Lowrié, Ossip. Croyance religieuse et croyance intellectuelle. Paris, 1908.
Phil 6321.20   Lowy, Samuel. New directions in psychology toward individual happiness and social progress. N.Y., 1945.
Phil 7082.188.1   Lowy, Samuel. Psychological and biological foundations of dream-interpretation. London, 1946.
Phil 9390.14   Loyalty by oath. (Hoffman, H.B.) Wallingford, 1957.
Phil 6158.20   LSD, man and society. 1st ed. Middletown, 1967.
Phil 6158.45   LSD. (Alpert, Richard.) N.Y., 1966.
Phil 6158.5   LSD: the consciousness-expanding drug. (Solomon, David.) N.Y., 1964.
Phil 6983.2   LSD psychotherapy; an explosion of psychedelic and psycholytic therapy. (Caldwell, William Vernon.) N.Y., 1968.
Phil 5722.24.5   Lubac, Émile. Le cycle de l'inconscient. Paris, 1934.
Phil 5251.19   Lubac, Émile. Esquisse d'un système de psychologie rationnelle. Paris, 1903.
Phil 5722.24   Lubac, Emile. Les niveaux de conscience et d'inconscient et leurs intercommunications. Paris, 1929.
Phil 5722.24.10   Lubac, Emile. Présent conscient et cycles de durée. Paris, 1936.
Phil 8701.22   Lubac, H. de. The discovery of God. N.Y., 1960.
Phil 8666.17.11   Lubac, Henri de. The drama of atheist humanism. Cleveland, 1969.
Phil 8666.17.7   Lubac, Henri de. Le drame de l'humanisme athée. Paris, 1963.
Phil 8666.17.10   Lubac, Henri de. Le drame de l'humanisme athée. 3. éd. Paris, 1945.
Phil 8666.17.6   Lubac, Henri de. Le drame de l'humanisme athée. 6. éd. Paris, 1959.
Phil 2905.1.180.7   Lubac, Henri de. L'éternel féminin, étude sur un texte du père Teilhard de Chardin. Paris, 1968.
Phil 2905.1.180.6   Lubac, Henri de. The faith of Teilhard de Chardin. London, 1965.
Phil 2905.1.180   Lubac, Henri de. La pensée religieuse du père Teilhard de Chardin. Paris, 1962.
Phil 2905.1.180.5   Lubac, Henri de. La prière du père Teilhard de Chardin. Paris, 1964.
Phil 2905.1.180.5.2   Lubac, Henri de. La prière du père Teilhard de Chardin. Paris, 1968.
Phil 2905.1.410   Lubac, Henri de. Teilhard, missionnaire et apologiste. Toulouse, 1966.
Phil 342.16   Lubboch, J.W. Remarks on the classification of the different branches of human knowledge. London, 1838.
Phil 2045.114   Łubieński, Z. Die Grundlagen des ethisch-politischen Systems von Hobbes. München, 1932.
Phil 6400.32   Lubin, Carl Kenneth. Language disturbance and intellectual functioning. The Hague, 1969.
Phil 21.18   Lublin, Poland. Universytitu Marii Curie. Annales. Skodowskiej. 3,1948+ 5v.
Phil 186.43   Lublinski, Samuel. Die Humanität als Mysterium. Jena, 1907.
Phil 3493.15   Lubnichi, Naum. Critique des eléments fondamentaux de la doctrine Kantienne. Paris, 1929.
Phil 292.1   Luc, J.A. de. Lettres physiques et morales sur l'histoire...terre. Paris, 1779. 6v.
Phil 1850.85   Luc, J.A. de. Précis de la philosophie de Bacon. Paris, 1802. 2v.
Phil 165.310   Lucas, Eric. What is a man. London, 1962.
Phil 486.5   Lucas, F. Le procès du matérialisme. Paris, 1867.
Phil 8663.3.89   Lucas, H.M. View of Lambert's "Notes on Ingersoll." N.Y., 1909.
Phil 384.25   Lucas, John Randolph. The freedom of the will. Oxford, 1970.
Phil 6121.14.5   Lucas, Keith. The conduction of the nervous impulse. London, 1917.
Htn   Phil 9245.4*   Lucas, R. An enquiry after happiness. London, 1704.
NEDL   Phil 9245.4.2   Lucas, R. An enquiry after happiness. London, 1717. 2v.

Phil 9245.4.3   Lucas, R. An enquiry after happiness. London, 1753. 2v.
Phil 9245.4.4   Lucas, R. An enquiry after happiness. pt.1. Edinburgh, 1754.
Phil 9245.4.5   Lucas, R. An enquiry after happiness. v.1-2. London, 1764.
Phil 5790.35   Lucas, Rex H. Men in crisis; a study of a mine disaster. N.Y., 1969.
Phil 4075.86   Lucas Dubreton, D. Le monde enchanté de la Renaissance. Paris, 1954.
Phil 2475.1.206   Luce, A.A. Bergson's doctrine of intuition. London, 1922.
Phil 1955.7.90   Luce, A.A. Charles Frederick D'Arcy, 1859-1938. London, 1938.
Phil 486.9   Luce, A.A. Sense without matter, or Direct perception. Edinburgh, 1954.
Phil 1870.115   Luce, Arthur A. Berkeley and Malebranche. London, 1934.
Phil 1870.115.10   Luce, Arthur A. Berkeley's immaterialism. London, 1945.
Phil 1870.115.15   Luce, Arthur A. The dialectic of immaterialism. London, 1963.
Phil 1870.124   Luce, Arthur A. The life of George Berkeley. London, 1949.
Phil 7080.56   Luce, Gay Gaer. Sleep. N.Y., 1966.
Phil 5352.5   Luce, Robert. Individual choice behavior. N.Y., 1959. 2v.
Phil 5251.60   Luce, Robert D. Development in mathematical psychology. Glencoe, 1960.
Phil 5251.60.10   Luce, Robert D. Handbook of mathematical psychology. N.Y., 1963. 2v.
Phil 5272.3   Luce, Robert D. Readings in mathematical psychology. N.Y., 1963-65. 2v.
Phil 3425.228   Lucia, V. de. L'Hegel in Italia. Vasto, 1888.
Phil 6121.6   Luciani, L. Die Functions-Localisation die Grosshirnrinde. Leipzig, 1886.
Phil 6121.6.5   Luciani, L. Das Keinhirn. Leipzig, 1893.
Phil 4115.92   Luciani, P. Gioberti e la filosofia nuova italiana. Napoli, 1866-72. 3v.
Phil 8591.70   Luciano Laberthmière. (Bonafede, Giulio.) Palermo, 1958.
Phil 7060.131   Lucidité et intuition. (Osty, Eugène.) Paris, 1913.
Phil 2725.46   Lucien Lévy-Bruhl, sa vie, son oeuvre. (Cazeneuve, J.) Paris, 1963.
Phil 21.8   Lucifer. Point Loma, Calif. 68,1948 2v.
Phil 575.110   Lucka, E. Grenzen der Seele. Berlin, 1916.
Phil 3905.80   Lucka, E. Otto Weininger: sein Werk und Persönlichkeit. Wien, 1905.
Phil 5465.13   Lucka, Emil. Die Phantasie. Wien, 1908.
Phil 8701.12   Luckey, L.W.A. Whence comest thou? Whither goest thou? Boston, 1927.
Phil 5645.16   Luckiesh, M. The language of color. N.Y., 1918.
Phil 5645.21   Lucky, Bertha. The specific brightness of colors. Lincoln, 1916.
Phil 2630.2.125   Łuczewski, Kazimierz. Das Problem der Religion in der Philosophie Guyaus. Posen, 1915.
Phil 8080.14   Ludács, G. Adalékok az estétika történetehez. Budapest, 1953.
Phil 8080.14.5   Ludács, G. Beitrage zur Geschichte der Ästhetik. Berlin, 1954.
Phil 811.12   Ludat-Deniselle, A. Von Thales bis Heidegger. Ratingen, 1952.
Phil 186.98   Ludendorff, M.S. Ist das Leben sinnlose Schinderei? München, 1935.
Phil 8591.43   Ludendorff, Mathilde S. Aus der Gotterkenntnis meinerwerke. München, 1935.
Phil 8591.43.5   Ludendorff, Mathilde S. In den Gegilden der Gottoffenbarung. Pähl, 1959.
Phil 3585.13.30   Ludendurff, Mathilde. Statt Heiligenschein oder Hexenzeichen mein Leben. v.2- München, 193- 5v.
Phil 6046.61   Ludicrum chiromanticum praetorii seu thesaurus chiromantiae. (Praetorius, J.) Jenae, 1661.
Phil 7069.67.55   Ludlam, Harry. The restless ghosts of Ladye Place, and other true hauntings. London, 1967.
Phil 8423.8.25   Ludolf Wienberg als jungdeutscher Asthetiker und Kunstkritiker. (Schweizer, V.) Leipzig, 1896.
Phil 5525.37   Ludovici, A.M. Secret of laughter. London, 1932.
Phil 3640.98   Ludovici, Anthony M. Nietzsche, his life and works. London, 1910.
Phil 3640.98.20   Ludovici, Anthony M. Nietzsche, his life and works. London, 1916.
Phil 3640.98.5   Ludovici, Anthony M. Nietzsche and art. London, 1911.
Phil 3640.98.9   Ludovici, Anthony M. Who is to be master of the world? Edinburgh, 1914.
Phil 186.77.5   Ludovici, August. Denkfibel; der Gegensatz als Richtmass. 2e Aufl. München, 1929.
Phil 3552.90   Ludovici, C.G. Ausfuhrlicher...Historie der leibnitzischen Philosophie. Leipzig, 1737. 2v.
Phil 3910.84   Ludovici, Karl G. Sammlung Auszüge der sämmtlichen Wegen der Wolffischen Philosophie. Pt.1-2. Leipzig, 1737-38.
Phil 2805.29.3   Ludovici Montaltii Litterae provinciales. 6. éd. (Pascal, Blaise.) Coloniae, 1700. 2v.
Htn   Phil 4073.35*   Ludovico iusto XIII; Atheismus Tsiumphatus. (Campanella, Tommaso.) Parisiis, 1636.
Phil 186.50.10   Ludowici, A. Denkfibel; die Lehre vom organischen Gegensatz. München, 1927.
Phil 186.50   Ludowici, A. Das genetische Prinzip. München, 1913.
Phil 186.50.2   Ludowici, A. Spiel und Widerspiel. 2. Ausg. München, 1917.
Phil 186.50.20   Ludowici, A. Zugleich. München, 1933.
Phil 8412.28   Ludvig sju dialoger om idé. (Lundegårdh, H.) Stockholm, 1913.
Phil 3493.12   Ludwich, A. Zur Kantfeier der Albertina. Regimontii, 1889.
Phil 9558.42   Ludwig, Arnold M. The importance of lying. Springfield, Ill, 1965.
Phil 3110.172   Ludwig, Else. Jakob Böhme, der Görlitzer Mystiker. 2. Aufl. Bad Smiedeberg, 1924.
Phil 6315.2.132   Ludwig, Emil. Doctor Freud. N.Y., 1947.
Phil 6315.2.131   Ludwig, Emil. Der entzauberte Freud. 9. Aufl. Zürich, 1946.
Phil 3246.340   Ludwig, Karl Friedrich Ernst. Freymüthige Gedanken über Fichte's Appellation gegen die Anklage des Atheismus und deren Veranlassung. Bruxelles, 1968.
Phil 2138.147   Ludwig, M. Die Sozialethik des John Stuart Mill. Zürich, 1963.
Phil 7060.79   Ludwig, W. Spaziergänge eines Wahrheitssuchers. Leipzig, 1899.
Phil 4070.8.80   Ludwig Buzorinis. (Heuser, H.) München, 1961.
Phil 3235.109   Ludwig Feuerbach, sein Leben und seine Werke. (Kohut, Adolph.) Leipzig, 1909.
Phil 3235.84   Ludwig Feuerbach. (Bolin, Wilhelm.) Stuttgart, 1891.

Phil 3235.81.5 Ludwig Feuerbach. (Engels, Friedrich.) Chicago, 1903.
Phil 3235.81.35 Ludwig Feuerbach. (Engels, Friedrich.) Chicago, 1906.
Phil 3235.81.12 Ludwig Feuerbach. (Engels, Friedrich.) Wien, 1927.
Phil 3235.134 Ludwig Feuerbach. (Gagen, Michael von.) München, 1970.
Phil 3235.88 Ludwig Feuerbach. (Starcke, Carl N.) Stuttgart, 1885.
Phil 3235.118 Ludwig Feuerbach. 1. éd. (Arvon, Henri.) Paris, 1957.
Phil 3235.110 Ludwig Feuerbach. 2. Aufl. Photoreproduction. (Jodl, F.) Stuttgart, 1921.
Phil 3235.81.30 Ludwig Feuerbach. 3. Aufl. (Engels, Friedrich.) Berlin, 1952.
Phil 3235.81.25 Ludwig Feuerbach and the end of classical German philosophy. (Engels, Friedrich.) Moscow, 1949.
Phil 3235.81.27 Ludwig Feuerbach and the end of classical German philosophy. (Engels, Friedrich.) Moscow, 1950.
Phil 3235.81.15 Ludwig Feuerbach and the outcome of classical German philosophy. (Engels, Friedrich.) N.Y., 1935.
Phil 3235.81.17 Ludwig Feuerbach and the outcome of classical German philosophy. (Engels, Friedrich.) N.Y., 1941.
Phil 3235.81.24 Ludwig Feuerbach et la fin de la philosophie classique allemande. (Engels, Friedrich.) Paris, 1945.
Phil 3235.83 Ludwig Feuerbach og kristendommen. (Schat Petersen, L.W.) København, 1883.
Phil 3235.81.8 Ludwig Feuerbach und der Ausgang der klassischen deutschen Philosophie. 5. Aufl. (Engels, Friedrich.) Stuttgart, 1910.
Phil 3235.81.9 Ludwig Feuerbach und der Ausgang der klassischen deutschen Philosophie. 6. Aufl. (Engels, Friedrich.) Stuttgart, 1919.
Phil 3235.80 Ludwig Feuerbach's Moralphilosophie. (Meyer, M.) Berlin, 1899.
Phil 3235.116 Ludwig Feuerbach's Philosophie. (Ran, Albrecht.) Leipzig, 1882.
Phil 3235.112 Ludwig Feuerbachs Philosophie. (Rawidowicz, Simon.) Berlin, 1931.
Phil 3235.112.2 Ludwig Feuerbachs Philosophie. 2. Aufl. (Rawidowicz, Simon.) Berlin, 1964.
Phil 3235.15 Ludwig Feuerbachs sämmtliche Werke. (Feuerbach, Ludwig.) Stuttgart, 1903-11. 10v.
Phil 3549.8.120 Ludwig Klages im Memoriam. (Hager, Wilhelm.) München, 1957.
Phil 3549.8.105 Ludwig Klages seine Lebenslehre und das Vitalismusproblem. (Bartels, Enno.) Meisenheim, 1953.
Phil 3549.8.110 Ludwig Klages und seine Lebensphilosophie. (Wandrey, Conrad.) Leipzig, 1933.
Phil 3549.8.140 Ludwig Klages Werk und Wirkung. (Kasdorff, Hans.) Bonn, 1969.
Phil 2880.1.83 Ludwig von Saint-Martin. (Claassen, J.) Stuttgart, 1891.
Phil 3925.16.84 Ludwig Wittgenstein. (Malcolmi, Norman.) London, 1958.
Phil 3925.16.260 Ludwig Wittgenstein. (Pear, David Francis.) N.Y., 1970.
Phil 3925.16.98 Ludwig Wittgenstein. (Peursen, Cornelis Anthonie van.) Baarn, 1965.
Phil 3925.16.98.1 Ludwig Wittgenstein: an introduction to his philosophy. (Peursen, Cornelis Anthonie van.) London, 1969.
Phil 3925.16.295 Ludwig Wittgenstein: Briefe und Begegnungen. (Engelmann, Paul.) Wien, 1970.
Phil 3425.598 Luebbe, Hermann. Die Hegelsche Rechte. Stuttgart, 1962.
Phil 8725.6 Luebbe, Hermann. Säkularisierung. Freiburg, 1965.
Phil 4356.2.81 Lueben, Robert. Sebastian Fox Morzillo und seine erkenntnistheoretische Stellung zur Naturphilosophie. Inaug. Diss. Bonn, 1911.
Phil 3450.19.160 Lüble, Hermann. Bibliographie der Heidegger. Literatur, 1917-1955. Meisenheim am Glan, 1957.
Phil 5467.10 Lueck, Helmut E. Soziale Aktivierung. Köln, 1969.
Phil 5251.53 Lückert, Heinz Rolf. Konflikt-Psychologie. München, 1957.
Phil 5590.452 Lückert, Heinz Rolf. Die Problematik der Persönlichkeitsdiagnostik. München, 1965.
Phil 6121.9 Lueddeckens, F. Rechts und Linkshändigkeit. Leipzig, 1900.
Phil 735.8 Lüdemann, H. Das Erkennen und die Werturteile. Leipzig, 1910.
Phil 2050.108 Lüers, Adolf. David Humes religionsphilosophische Anschauungen. Berlin, 1901.
Phil 9558.1 Die Lüge. (Heinroth, J.C.A.) Leipzig, 1834.
Phil 9558.8 Lüge im Urteil der neuesten deutschen Ethiker. Inaug. Diss. (Jakobovits, J.) Paderborn, 1914.
Phil 9558.45 Die Lüge Sprach- und literaturwissenschaftlicher und entwicklungsgeschichtlicher Betrachtung. (Lipmann, Otto.) Leipzig, 1927.
Phil 3210.88 Lülmann, C. Monismus und Christentum bei G.T. Fechner. Berlin, 1917.
Phil 5051.25 Lünemann, Arthur. Logik der Philosophie. Wien, 1929.
Phil 5645.48 Lüscher, Max. Die Farbe als psychologisches Untersuchungsmittel. St. Gallen, 1949.
Phil 5599.52 Luescher, Max. The Lüscher color test. N.Y., 1969.
Phil 5599.52 The Lüscher color test. (Luescher, Max.) N.Y., 1969.
Phil 5592.165 Der Lüscher Test. (Max Luescher-Institut für Medizinsche Psychologie.) Hergiswil, 1960.
Phil 8591.32 Lütgert, Wilhelm. Natur und geist Gottes; Vorträge zur Ethik. Leipzig, 1910.
Phil 3805.205 Luetgert, Wilhelm. Schleiermacher. Berlin, 1934.
Phil 935.11 Lüth, Paul. Die japanische Philosophie. Tübingen, 1944.
Phil 3850.18.86 Lützeler, Heinrich. Der Philosoph Max Scheler. Bonn, 1947.
Htn Phil 2705.85* Luface, Elie. L'homme plus que machine. Londres, 1748.
Phil 186.154 Lugarini, Leo. Filosofia e metafisica. Urbino, 1964.
Phil 3493.38 Lugarini, Leo. La logica trascendentale Kantiana. Milano, 1950.
Phil 400.56 Lugaro, E. Idealismo filosofico e realismo politico. Bologna, 1920.
Phil 6961.15 Lugaro, E. La psichiatria tedesca. Firenze, 1916.
Phil 4260.117 Luginbühl, Johannes. Die Axiomatik bei Giambattista Vico. Bern, 1946.
Phil 3585.19 Lugmayer, Karl. Philosophie der Person. Salzburg, 1956.
Phil 292.20 Lugones, Leopoldo. El tamaño del espacio. Buenos Aires, 1921.
Phil 672.26 Luguet, Henry. Étude sur la notion d'espace d'après Descartes. Thèse. Paris, 1875.
Phil 4110.4.99 Luigi Ferri. (Barzellotti, G.) Roma, 1895.
Phil 4110.4.93 Luigi Ferri. (Cantoni, Carlo.) Roma, 1895.
Phil 4110.4.102 Luigi Ferri. (Tauro, G.) Roma, 1896.
Phil 4200.1.6 Luigi Ferri: la psicologia di Pietro Pomponazzi. (Fiorentino, F.) Napoli, 1877.
Phil 8583.41.20 Luijk, Henk van. Philosophie du fait chrétien. Paris, 1964.
Phil 3585.20.20 Luijpen, Wilhelmus Anonius Maria. Phenomenology and metaphysics. Pittsburgh, 1965.
Phil 3585.20.5 Luijpen, Wilhelmus Antonius Maria. Existential phenomenology. Pittsburgh, 1960.

Phil 3585.20 Luijpen, Wilhelmus Antonius Maria. Existentiële fenomenologie. Utrecht, 1959.
Phil 3585.20.10 Luijpen, Wilhelmus Antonius Maria. Fenomenologie en atheisme. Utrecht, 1963.
Phil 3585.20.22 Luijpen, Wilhelmus Antonius Maria. Fenomenologie en metafysica. Utrecht, 1966.
Phil 1750.115.55 Luijpen, Wilhelmus Antonius Maria. De fenomenologie is een humorisme. Amsterdam, 1961.
Phil 3585.20.30 Luijpen, Wilhelmus Antonius Maria. Fenomenologie van het natuurrecht door W. Luijpen. Utrecht, 1969.
Phil 3585.20.6 Luijpen, Wilhelmus Antonius Maria. A first introduction to existential phenomenology. Pittsburgh, 1969.
Phil 3585.20.4 Luijpen, Wilhelmus Antonius Maria. Nieuwe inleiding tot de existentiële fenomenologie. Utrecht, 1969.
Phil 3585.20.15 Luijpen, Wilhelmus Antonius Maria. Phenomenology and atheism. Pittsburgh, 1964.
Phil 1750.115.56 Luijpen, Wilhelmus Antonius Maria. Phenomenology and humanism. Pittsburg, 1966.
Phil 3585.20.25 Luijpen, Wilhelmus Antonius Maria. Phenomenology of natural law. Pittsburgh, 1967.
Phil 4372.1.97 Luis Vives. (Marañón, G.) Madrid, 1942.
Phil 4372.1.130 Luis Vives y el pacifismo. (Riba y García, Carlos.) Zaragoza, 1933.
Phil 4372.1.85 Luis Vives y la filosofía del renacimiento. (Bonilla y San Martín, D.A.) Madrid, 1903.
Htn Phil 9171.7.5* Luján, Pedro de. Colo os matrimoniales. Toledo, 1563.
Phil 5525.68 Luk, Oleksandr N. O chuvstve iumora i ostroumii. Moskva, 1968.
Phil 3011.6.5 Lukács, G. La destruction de la raison. Paris, 1958-59. 2v.
NEDL Phil 1750.45 Lukács, G. Az ész troufasztása. Budapest, 1954.
Phil 3425.322 Lukács, G. Der junge Hegel. Zürich, 1948.
Phil 3011.6 Lukács, G. Die Zerstörung der Vernunft. Berlin, 1954.
Phil 1750.405.5 Lukacs, G.S. Existentialisme ou Marxisme. 2e éd. Paris, 1961.
Phil 1750.405 Lukacs, G.S. Existentialismus oder Marxismus? Berlin, 1951.
Phil 8412.18.5 Lukács, Georg. Über die (Beson derheit) als Kategorie der Asthetik. Neuwied, 1967.
Phil 8412.18 Lukács, György. A különösség mintesztétikai kategória. Budapest, 1957.
Phil 292.2 Lukas, F. Die Grundbegriffe...Kösmogonien. Leipzig, 1893.
Phil 5821.5 Lukas, F. Psychologie der niedersten Tiere. Wien, 1905.
Phil 978.49.695 Das Lukas-Evangelium. Ein Zyklus von zehn Vorträgen. 6. Aufl. (Steiner, R.) Dornach, 1968.
Phil 5051.28.5 Lukasiewicz, Jan. Elements of mathematical logic. 2nd ed. Oxford, 1964.
Phil 5051.28 Lukasiewicz, Jan. Elementy logiki matematycznej. Warszawa, 1929.
Phil 4803.536.20 Lukasiewicz, Jan. L zagadnień logiki i filozofii; pisma wybrane. Warszawa, 1961.
Phil 5051.28.10 Lukasiewicz, Jan. Selected works. Amsterdam, 1970.
Phil 5585.4 Lukens, H.T. Die Vorstellungsreihen. Gütersloh, 1892.
Phil 4769.1.92 Luk'ianov, S.M. O Vl. S. Solov'eve v ego molodye gody. Kniga 3. Vyp. I. Petrograd, 1921. 2v.
Phil 8182.2 Lukić, Sveta. Umetnost i kriterijumi. Beograd, 1964.
Phil 8400.33 Lukin, Iu.B. Prekrasnoe i zhizn'. Moskva, 1962.
Phil 7059.15 Lulu Hurst...writes her biography. (Atkinson, Lulu Hurst.) Rome, Ga., 1897.
Phil 7054.143 Lum, Dyer D. The "spiritual" delusion. Philadelphia, 1873.
Phil 186.75 Lumbreras, Pedro. Estudios filosóficos. Madrid, 1930.
Phil 3493.29 Lumia, Giuseppe. La dottrina Kantiana del diritto e dello stato. Milano, 1960.
Phil 553.2 Lumière, commencement, liberté. Thèse. (Misrahi, Robert.) Paris, 1969.
Phil 2733.38 Lumière et mouvement de l'esprit. (Malebranche, Nicolas.) Paris, 1962.
Phil 530.15.40 Lumière éternelle. (Paillard, Etienne.) Paris, 1944.
Phil 6677.19 La lumière sur le magnétisme. (Hont, A.E.) Neuchâtel, 1880.
Phil 8587.40 Luminous bodies here and hereafter (the shining ones). (Hallock, C.) N.Y., 1906.
Phil 6400.13 The Lumleian lectures on some problems in connection with aphasia and new speech defects. (Bastian, H.C.) n.p., 1897.
Phil 8412.43 Lunacharskii, Anatolii V. Osnovy pozitivnoi estetiki. Moskva, 1923.
Phil 8666.23 Lunacharskii, Anatolii V. Pochemu nel'zia verit' v boga. Moskva, 1965.
Phil 6957.3 Lunacy: Its past and its present. (Hill, R.G.) London, 1870.
Phil 6945.9 Lunacy reform. v.1-4. (Seguin, E.C.) N.Y., 1879-
Phil 402.4 Lund, Erik. De europäiske ideers historie. 2. opl. Gyldendal, 1963.
Phil 5251.35.9 Lund, F.H. Psychology: an empirical study of behavior. N.Y., 1933.
Phil 5251.35 Lund, F.H. Psychology: the science of mental activity. N.Y., 1927.
Phil 5400.79 Lund, Frederick H. Emotions of men. N.Y., 1930.
Phil 5400.79.5 Lund, Frederick H. Emotions of men. N.Y., 1939.
Phil 6536.10 Lundborg, Herman B. Die progressive myoklonus-epilepsie. Upsala, 1903.
Phil 8412.28 Lundegårdh, H. Ludvig sju dialoger om idé. Stockholm, 1913.
Phil 8412.14 Lundholm, H. The aesthetic sentiment. Cambridge, 1941.
Phil 5251.51 Lundholm, H. God's failure or man's folly? Cambridge, 1949.
Phil 5070.21 Lundholm, H. The psychology of belief. Durham, 1936.
Phil 6961.14 Lundholm, Helge. The manic-depressive pychosis. Durham, N.C., 1931.
Phil 6961.13 Lundholm, Helge. Schizophrenia. Durham, N.C., 1932.
Phil 1865.170 Lundin, Hilda G. The influence of J. Bentham on English democratic development. Iowa City, 1920.
Phil 5590.506 Lundin, Robert William. Personality; a behavioral analysis. N.Y., 1969.
Phil 6060.27.5 Lungspeer, A.S.L. Lehrbuch der wissenschaftlichen Graphologie. Leipzig, 1929.
Phil 5251.31 Lungwitz, H. Die Entdeckung der Seele. Leipzig, 1925.
Phil 6690.1 L'union Protectrice. Appel à tous les partisans et amis du magnétisme. 2e éd. Paris, 1850.
Phil 180.54 L'universo come guioco. (Fersen, Alessandro.) Modena, 1936.
Phil 186.74 Lunn, A.H.M. The flight from reason. N.Y., 1931.
Phil 8591.50 Lunn, Arnold. Good gorilla. London, 1944.
Phil 8886.80.2 Lunn, Arnold. The new morality. London, 1967.
Phil 5627.166 Lunn, Arnold. Now I see. N.Y., 1938.

Phil 8701.16 — Lunn, Arnold. Science and the supernatural; a correspondence between Arnold Lunn and J.B.S. Haldane. N.Y., 1935.

Phil 5401.14 — Lunn, H.K. Courage; an anthology. London, 1939.
Phil 6961.4 — Lunt, Adeline T.P. Behind the bars. Boston, 1871.
Phil 7054.83 — Lunt, George. Boston Courier report of the proceedings of professed spiritual agents and mediums. Boston, 1859. 2 pam.

Phil 5535.20 — Lunzer, Eric Anthony. Development in learning. London, 1968- 3v.

Phil 3850.16.100 — Luongo, M.R. Il relativismo di G. Simmel e de Pirandello. Napoli, 1955?

Phil 186.81.5 — Lupasco, Stéphane. Du devenir logique et de l'affectivité. v.1-2. Paris, 1935-1936. 2v.

Phil 186.81 — Lupasco, Stéphane. Du devenir logique et de l'affectivité. v.1-2. Thèse. Paris, 1935.

Phil 186.81.10 — Lupasco, Stéphane. Qu'est-ce qu'une structure? Paris, 1967.

Phil 3493.30 — Luperini, Cesuce. Spazio e materia in Kant. Firenze, 1961.

Phil 186.103 — Luporini, C. Filosofi vecchi e nuovi. Firenze, 1947.
Phil 1711.5 — Luppal, I.K. Istoriko-filosofskie etiudy. Moskva, 1935.
Phil 8591.40 — Lupton, D. Religion says you can. Boston, 1938.
Phil 8591.37 — Lupus, J. Le traditionalisme et le rationalisme. Liége, 1858. 3v.

Phil 5051.6.5 — Luquet, G.H. Eléments de logique formelle. Paris, 1909.
Phil 5051.6 — Luquet, G.H. Essai d'une logique systematique et simplifiée. Lille, 1913.

Phil 186.78 — Luquet, G.H. Logique, morale, métaphysique. Paris, 1931.
Phil 5051.6.13 — Luquet, G.H. Logique formelle. Paris, 1925.
Htn Phil 6990.38* — Luquet, J.F.O. Abrege de la notice sur la vie et les vertus d'Anna Maria Taigi. Rome, 1851.

Phil 5261.15 — The lure of superiority. (Vaughan, W.F.) N.Y., 1928.
Phil 177.129 — The lure of wisdom. (Collins, J.D.) Milwaukee, 1962.
Phil 5251.40.5A — Luria, A.R. The nature of human conflicts. N.Y., 1932.
Phil 6121.45.2 — Luria, Aleksandr Romanovich. Higher cortical functions in man. N.Y., 1966.

Phil 6121.45.5 — Luria, Aleksandr Romanovich. Human brain and psychological processes. N.Y., 1966.

Phil 6961.8 — Lurié, Aron. Multiple Sklerose mit amnestischer Aphasie. Inaug. Diss. Königsberg, 1914.

Phil 5545.235 — Luriiâ, Aleksandr R. The mind of a mnemonist. N.Y., 1968.
Phil 5545.236 — Luriiâ, Aleksandr R. Une prodigieuse mémoire. Neuchâtel, 1970.

Phil 6400.34 — Luriia, Aleksandr Romanovich. Traumatic aphasia. The Hague, 1970.

Phil 5850.260 — Lurton, D.E. Make the most of your life. London, 1945.
Phil 9245.45 — Lush, Samuel Beryl. Six roads to happiness. N.Y., 1930.
Phil 4780.2 — Lushchytski, I.N. Narysy pa historyi hramadska-palitychnai i filosofskai dumki u Belarusi u drukoi palavine XIX veku. Minsk, 1958.

Phil 8980.537 — Lushchytski, I.N. Osnovy marksistko-leninskoi etiki. Minsk, 1965.

Phil 6121.13 — Lussana, F. Fisiologia dei centri nervosi encefalici. Padova, 1871. 2v.

Htn Phil 7075.6.7* — Lussuria e castità. (Orsi, Alberto.) Milano, 1913.
Phil 9245.26 — Die Lust als socialethisches Entwickelungsprincip. (Dudoc, J.) Leipzig, 1900.

Phil 5525.39 — Lust und Leid im Witz; sechs psychoanalytische Studien. (Reik, Theodor.) Wien, 1929.

Phil 812.11 — A luta pela liberdade no pensamento europeu. (Macedo, Newton de.) Coimbra, 1930.

Phil 310.725 — Lutai, Vadlen Stepanovich. O metode postroeniia sistemy dialekticheskogo materializma. Kiev, 1970.

Phil 1145.97 — Luthardt, C.E. Die antike Ethik in ihrer geschichtlichen Entwicklung als Einleitung in die Geschichte der christlichen Moral. Leipzig, 1887.

Phil 8961.3 — Luthardt, C.E. Geschichte der christlichen Ethik. Leipzig, 1888-93. 2v.

Phil 5761.7 — Luthardt, C.E. Die Lehre vom freien Willen. Leipzig, 1863.

Phil 186.53.5 — Luthardt, C.E. De moderna verldsåsigterna. Lund, 1880.
Phil 2055.7.90 — Luther, A.R. Existence as dialectical tension. The Hague, 1968[1969]

Phil 7069.26.12 — Luther, F. Der Okkultismus. Leipzig, 1926.
Htn Phil 3585.4.33* — Luther, Martin. Etliche schöne Predigten. n.p., 1533.
Htn Phil 3585.4.31* — Luther, Martin. Ob man für dem Sterben fliehen muge. Wittenberg, 1527.

Htn Phil 3585.4.30* — Luther, Martin. Theologia Deütsch. n.p., 1519.
Htn Phil 3585.4.32* — Luther, Martin. Vermanug an die Geistlichen. Wittemberg, 1531.

Htn Phil 3585.4.34* — Luther, Martin. Warnung. Nürnberg, 1556.
Phil 3110.91 — Luther und Böhme. (Bornkamm, H.) Bonn, 1925.
Phil 3483.8.5 — Luther und Kant. (Bauch, Bruno.) Berlin, 1904.
Phil 3492.16 — Luther und Kant. (Katzer, Ernst.) Giessan, 1910.
Phil 5768.14 — Die Lutherische Lehre vom Unvermögen des Freyen Willens zur Höheren. (Sartorius, E.) Göttingen, 1821.

Phil 8586.35 — Lutherische Metaphysik. (Grohmann, W.) Leipzig, 1904.
NEDL Phil 186.73.20 — Lutosławski, W. Iskierki Warszawskie. Ser. 1. Warszawa, 1911.

Phil 186.73 — Lutosławski, W. The knowledge of reality. Cambridge, 1930.

Phil 5051.22 — Lutosławski, W. Logika ogolna czyli Teorja poznania i logika formalna. London, 1906.

Phil 575.82 — Lutosławski, W. El personalismo. Madrid, 1887.
X Cg Phil 4777.536.100 — Lutosławski, W. Postannictwo polskiego narodu. Warszawa, 1939. (Changed to XP 5137, 3/20/72)

Phil 5761.8.5 — Lutosławski, W. Rozwójpotęgi woli przez psychofizyczne ćiviczenia. Warszawa, 1910.

Phil 575.8 — Lutosławski, W. Über die Grundvoraussetzungen und Consequenzen der individualistischen Weltanschauung. Helsingfors, 1898.

Phil 5761.8 — Lutosławski, W. Volenté et liberté! Paris, 1913.
Phil 665.41 — Lutosławski, W. The world of souls. London, 1924.
Phil 186.73.10 — Lutosławski, W. Wykłady jagiellońskie. Kraków, 1901-1902. 2v.

X Cg Phil 4777.536.80 — Pamphlet box. Lutosławski, W.
Phil 4803.537.40 — Lutosławski, Wincenty. Eine Bekehrung. Kempten, 19- .
Phil 4803.537.30 — Lutosławski, Wincenty. Iskierki warszawskie. Warszawa, 1911.

Phil 4803.537.45F — Lutosławski, Wincenty. Jeden łatwy zywot. Dzięgielów? 1926.

Phil 4803.537.37 — Lutosławski, Wincenty. Pewniki polityki polskiej. Wyd. 2. W Szamotułach, 1926.

Phil 665.7.5 — Lutosławski, W. Nieśmiertelność duszy i wolność woli. Warszawa, 1909.

Phil 665.7.7 — Lutosławski, W. Pre-existence and reincarnation. London, 1928.

Phil 665.7 — Lutosławski, W. Seelenmacht; Abriss einer zeitgemässen Weltanschauung. Leipzig, 1899.

Phil 9240.4 — La lutte contre le mal. (Clamageran, J.J.) Paris, 1897.
Phil 1504.6.4 — Lutz, E. Die Psychologie bonaventuras. v.6, pt.4-5. Münster, 1909.

Phil 6681.10 — Lutzebourg. Nouveaux extraits des journaux d'un magnétiseur. Strasbourg, 1788.

Phil 8622.57 — Lutzenberger, H. Das Glaubensproblem in der Religionsphilosophie. München? 1962.

X Cg Phil 7075.152 — Luvandowski, Herbert. Ferne Lände, fremde Sitten. 1. Aufl. Stuttgart, 1958.

Htn Phil 665.12* — Lux orientalis. (Glanvill, Joseph.) London, 1662.
Phil 2515.18.5 — La luxure et la mort. (Caraco, Albert.) Lausanne, 1968.
Phil 6121.7 — Luys, J. The brain and its functions. N.Y., 1882.
Phil 6121.7.3 — Luys, J. Le cerveau et ses fonctions. Paris, 1876.
Phil 6121.7.9 — Luys, J. Des actions réflexes du cerveau. Paris, 1874.
Phil 6121.7.12 — Luys, J. Das Gehirn. Leipzig, 1877.
Htn Phil 6100.13* — Luys, J. Iconographie photographique des centres nerveux. Texte et atlas. Paris, 1873. 2v.

Phil 6681.12 — Luys, J. Leçons cliniques sur les principaux phenomènes de l'hypnotisme. Paris, 1890.

Phil 6121.7.21 — Luys, J. Leçons sur la structure et les maladies du système nerveux. Paris, 1875.

Phil 6121.7.5 — Luys, J. Recherches sur le système nerveux. Paris, 1865. 2v.

Phil 6961.5 — Luys, J. Traité clinique et pratique des maladies mentales. Paris, 1881.

Phil 5400.38 — Luys, Jules. Les émotions chez les sujets en état d'hypnotisme. Paris, 1887.

Phil 3585.32 — Luyten, Norbert Alfons. Ordo rerum. Freiburg, 1969.
Phil 2905.1.385 — Luyten, Norbert Alfons. Teilhard de Chardin. Fribourg, 1965.

Htn Phil 5761.20* — Luzac, E. Essai sur la liberté de produire ses sentimens. n.p., 1749.

Phil 978.49.310 — Luzifer-Gnosis, 1903-1908. (Steiner, R.) Dornach, 1960.
Phil 1135.56 — Lwellengrebel, J.G.H. Veterum de Elementis Placita. Rhenum, 1844.

Phil 186.15 — Lyall, W. Intellect, the emotions and moral nature. Edinburgh, 1855.

Phil 7069.45.25 — Lychgate. (Dowding, H.C.T.) London, 1945.
Phil 5403.4.5 — Lyckans problem. (Lindner, Gustav.) Stockholm, 1869.
Phil 4520.1.31 — Lyckovägar. (Blomquist, G.) Stockholm, 1916.
Phil 8877.66 — Lykkens smil. (Crane, Anker.) København, 1922.
Htn Phil 2120.3.30* — Lyly, John. Euphues and his England. London, 1588.
Phil 8591.36 — Lyman, E.W. The meaning and truth of religion. N.Y., 1933.

Phil 8633.1.28 — Lyman, E.W. The meaning of selfhood and faith in immortality. Cambridge, 1928.

Phil 8591.36.10 — Lyman, E.W. Religion and the issues of life. N.Y., 1943.
Phil 7080.6 — Lyman, H.M. Insomnia and other disorders of sleep. Chicago, 1885.

Phil 8886.34 — Lynch, Arthur. Ethics, an exposition of principles. London, 1922.

Phil 5251.18.5 — Lynch, Arthur. Principles of psychology. London, 1923.
Phil 5251.18 — Lynch, Arthur. Psychology; a new system. London, 1912. 2v.

Phil 186.142 — Lynch, W.F. The integrating mind. N.Y., 1962.
Phil 5421.35.5 — Lynch, William F. Images of hope. Baltimore, 1965.
Phil 5414.20.2 — Lynd, Helen Merrell. On shame and the search for identity. N.Y., 1958.

Phil 5066.255 — Lyndon, Roger C. Notes on logic. Princeton, N.J., 1966.
Phil 186.51 — Lyng, G.W. Philosophische Studien. n.p., 1877.
Phil 5051.15 — Lyng, Georg V. Grundtankernes system. v.1-3. Christiania, 1882-1887.

Phil 5051.15.5 — Lyng, Georg V. Laerebog i den objektive logik. Christiania, 1881.

Htn Phil 3801.539* — Lyng, Georg V. Studier over Schelling. Thesis. Christiania, 1866.

Phil 5871.114 — Lynn, David Brandon. Parental and sex-role identification. Berkeley, Calif., 1969.

Phil 5651.9 — Lynn, Richard. Attention, arousal, and the orientation reaction. 1. ed. Oxford, 1966.

Phil 5896.5 — Lynn, Richard. Personality and national character. 1. ed. Oxford, 1971.

Phil 400.5 — Lyon, G. L'idéalisme en Angleterre. Paris, 1888.
Phil 2045.80 — Lyon, G. La philosophie de Hobbes. Paris, 1893.
Phil 6121.15 — Lyon, I.L.R. The wonders of life. N.Y., 1910.
Phil 5401.32 — Lyon, Josette. L'angoisse. Paris, 1957.
Phil 186.34 — Lyon, Otto. Das Pathos der Resonanz. Leipzig, 1900.
Phil 9530.27 — Lyons, Albert E. The self-starter. Boston, 1924.
Phil 2262.91 — Lyons, Alexander. Shaftesbury's ethical principle of adaptation to universal harmony. N.Y., 1909?

Phil 9550.18 — Lyons, David. Forms and limits of utilitarianism. Oxford, 1965.

Phil 6321.48 — Lyons, Joseph. Psychology and the measure of man. N.Y., 1963.

Htn Phil 8591.11* — Lyons. The infallibility of human judgement. London, 1724.

Phil 1750.38 — Lyotard, Jean François. La phénoménologie. 3e éd. Paris, 1959.

Phil 1750.38.6 — Lyotard, Jean François. La phénoménologie. 6e éd. Paris, 1967.

Phil 1750.655 — The lyrical existentialists. 1. ed. (Hanna, Thomas.) N.Y., 1962.

Phil 2905.1.100 — Le lyrisme et la mystique dans les oeuvres du Pierre Teilhard de Chardin. (Talhonët, Jean de.) Paris, 1959.

Phil 9495.2 — Lyttelton, E. Training of the young in laws of sex. London, 1900.

Phil 7069.31.27 — Lyttelton, Edith B. Our superconscious mind. London, 1931.

Phil 7069.31.28 — Lyttelton, Edith B. Our superconscious mind. N.Y., 1931.
Htn Phil 8636.9* — Lyttelton, W.H. Scripture revelations of the life of man after death. 3. ed. London, 1876.

Phil 8610.919.30 — Lyttleton, Edward. The parson and the atheist. London, 1919.

Phil 8881.26.28 — M. Guyaus Moral. Inaug. Diss. (Schwartz, E.J.) Strassburg, 1909.

Phil 2725.2.69 — M. l'abbé F. de Lamennais réfuté. (Flottes, J.B.M.) Paris, 1825.

Phil 2725.2.34 — M. Lamennais réfuté par lui-même. (Lamennais, F.R. de.) Paris, 1841.

Phil 600.7.86 — M. Littré et Auguste Comte. 2e éd. (Poéy, Andrés.) Paris, 1880.

Phil 600.7.90 — M. Littré et le positivisme. (Caro, Elme.) Paris, 1883.
Phil 3625.1.87 — M. Mendelssohn's Verdienste und die Bildung seines Volkes. (Guttenstein, B.) Heidelberg, 1829.

Phil 4796.96.80 — M.F. Akhundov i russkaia revolutsionno-demokraticheskaia estetika. (Kasumov, Mekhbaly Mamedovich.) Baku, 1954.

Phil 9070.32   A ma életművészete. (Perlaky, Lajos.) Budapest, 193-?

Phil 4075.79.25   Ma vie. (Cardano, Girolamo.) Paris, 1936.

Phil 6315.2.73   Ma vie et la psychanalyse. 23. éd. (Freud, Sigmund.) Paris, 1949.

Phil 187.61   Maack, F. Naturforschung und Philosophie. Kiel, 1896.

Phil 2115.167   Maag, Urs. Die psychologischen Ansichten John Lockes. Aarau, 1960.

Phil 575.276   Maaloee, Erik. Egenskab og faellesskab. København, 1969.

Phil 187.84   Maar, Jean. Le fondement de la philosophie. Paris, 1925.

Phil 9560.7.9   Maarse, Jan. Een psychologische en zebekundige studie over de hegrippen eer en eergevoel. Proefschrift. Amsterdam, 1936.

Phil 5400.87   Maas, J.G.E. Versuch über die Leidenschaften. Halle, 1805-07. 2v.

Phil 3625.28.31   Maass, Johann Gebhard Ehrenreich. Kritische Theorie der Offenbarung. Bruxelles, 1969.

Phil 5465.190   Maass, Johann Gebhard Ehrenreich. Versuch über die Einbildungskraft. Bruxelles, 1969.

Phil 5545.250   al-Ma'ayirji, Muhammad Ismat. Die postmentalen Erregungen als struktureller Faktor beim Lernen. Thesis. St. Margrethen, 1964.

Phil 585.214   Maaz, Wilhelm. Selbstschöpfung oder Selbstintegration des Menschen. Münster, 1967.

Phil 8887.124   Mabbott, John David. An introduction to ethics. London, 1966.

Phil 8965.2.5   Mabie, H.W. Ethics and the Garger neighborhood, 1914. Philadelphia, 1914.

Phil 8887.37.90   Mabie, H.W. The life of the spirit. N.Y., 1900.

Phil 8887.38.5   Mabie, H.W. Works and days. N.Y., 1902.

Phil 6122.65   Mabille, P. Initiation à la connaissance de l'homme. Paris, 1949.

Phil 3552.274   Mabilleau, L. De perfectione apud Leibnitium. Thesim. Paris, 1861.

Phil 4080.1.80   Mabilleau, L. Étude historique...Cesare Cremonini. Paris, 1881.

Phil 260.2A   Mabilleau, S. Histoire de la philosophie atomistique. Paris, 1895.

Phil 7123.2   Mabru, G. Les magnetiseurs, jugés par eux-mêmes. Paris, 1858.

Phil 6420.34   McAllister, Anne H. Clinical studies in speech therapy. London, 1937.

Phil 5822.7   McAllister, W.G. A further study of the delayed reaction in the albino rat. Baltimore, 1932.

Phil 8413.12   McAlpen, Colin. Hermara, a study in compatative aesthetics. London, 1915.

Phil 6322.42A   Macalpine, Ida. Schizophrenia, 1677. London, 1956.

Phil 1850.113.3   Macaulay, Thomas Babington. Essay on Bacon. Oxford, 19- .

Phil 6962.28   McAuley, W.F. The concept of schizophrenia. N.Y., 1954.

Phil 8667.19   McAuliffe, A.T. Some modern non-intellectual approaches to God. Washington, D.C., 1934.

Phil 8887.78   MacBeath, A. Experiments in living. London, 1952.

Phil 8702.1   Macbriar, R.M. Geology and geologists. London, 1843.

Phil 575.59   McBride, Peter. The riddle of personality: mechanism or mystery? London, 1926.

Phil 8667.15   McCabe, J. The existence of God. London, 1913.

Phil 7069.20.220   McCabe, J. Spiritualism. N.Y., 1920.

Phil 623.16   McCabe, Joseph. A biographical dictionary of modern rationalists. London, 1920.

Phil 5822.6   McCabe, Joseph. The evolution of mind. London, 1910.

Phil 510.1.17   McCabe, Joseph. Haeckel's critics answered. London, 1903.

Phil 510.1.18   McCabe, Joseph. Haeckel's critics answered. London, 1910.

Phil 623.16.5   McCabe, Joseph. A rationalist encyclopaedia. London, 1948.

Phil 8701.4.50   McCabe, Joseph. The religion of Sir Oliver Lodge. London, 1914.

Phil 8592.47   McCabe, Joseph. Story of religious controversy. Boston, 1929.

Phil 8610.923.10   McCabe, Joseph. The twilight of the gods. London, 1923.

Phil 4983.5.95   McCadden, Joseph James. Father Varela. N.Y., 1969.

Phil 5066.265   McCall, Storrs. Polish logic, 1920-1939 papers. Oxford, 1967.

Phil 487.4   Maccall, William. The newest materialism. London, 1873.

Phil 1930.8.90   McCallum, R.B. Robin George Collingwood, 1889-1943. London, 1943.

Phil 187.145   MacCallum, Reid. Initiation and design, and other essays. Toronto, 1953.

Phil 1750.135   MacCampbell, D. Irving Babbitt. n.p., 1935.

Phil 2280.5.99   MacCampbell, D. Santayana's debt to New England. n.p., 1935.

Phil 5762.17   McCarthy, R.C. The measurement of conation. Chicago, 1926.

Phil 6122.59   McCarthy, R.C. Safeguarding mental health. N.Y., 1937.

Phil 187.57   McCarty, R.J. An essay in practical philosophy: relations of wisdom and purpose. Kansas City, Mo., 1922.

Phil 5590.325   McCary, James Leslie. Psychology of personality. N.Y., 1956.

Phil 3525.90   MacCauley, Clay. Karl Christian Friedrich Krause. Berkeley, Calif., 1925.

Phil 8702.2.9   McCausland, D. Adam and the adamite. London, 1872.

Phil 8702.2   McCausland, D. Sermons in stones. London, 1873.

Phil 8702.2.5   McCausland, D. Shinar. London, 1867.

Phil 5548.5A   McClelland, D.C. The achievement nature. N.Y., 1953.

Phil 5590.80   McClelland, D.C. Personality. N.Y., 1951.

Phil 5590.82.2   McClelland, D.C. Personality. N.Y., 1963.

Phil 5548.5.5   McClelland, D.C. The roots of consciousness. Princeton, N.J., 1964.

Phil 5548.125   McClelland, David Clarence. Motivating economic achievement. N.Y., 1969.

Phil 8887.134   McCloskey, H.J. Meta-ethics and normative ethics. The Hague, 1969.

Phil 2138.180   McCloskey, Henry John. John Stuart Mill: a critical study. London, 1971.

Phil 5052.27   McClure, M.T. An introduction to the logic of reflection. N.Y., 1925.

Phil 1750.20   McClure, M.T. Study of realistic movement in contemporary philosophy. Staunton, 1912.

Phil 1133.28   McClure, Matthew T. The early philosophers of Greece. N.Y., 1935.

Phil 5052.12   MacColl, H. Symbolic logic and its applications. London, 1906.

Phil 1190.4   Maccoll, N. Greek sceptics from Pyrrho to Sextus. London, 1869.

Phil 1750.767   MacColl, Sylvia. Structure and development of phenomenal reality. N.Y., 1965.

Phil 5627.30   McComas, Henry Clay. Psychology of religious sects. N.Y., 1912.

Phil 7054.173   McComb, Samuel. The future life in the light of modern inguiry. N.Y., 1919.

Phil 6122.30   McComb, Samuel. The power of self suggestion. N.Y., 1909.

Phil 6122.75   MacConaill, Michael A. Bodily structure and the will. London, 1960.

Phil 8887.37   McConnell, R.M. Duty of altruism. N.Y., 1910.

Phil 8592.2   McConnell, S. Christianity. N.Y., 1912.

Phil 8637.6.5   McConnell, S.D. The evolution of immortality. N.Y., 1902.

Phil 8592.49   McCormac, H. Aspirations from the inner, the spiritual life. London, 1860.

Phil 187.1   M'Cormac, H. Philosophy of human nature. London, 1837.

Phil 1812.1   McCosh, J. The Scottish philosophy. N.Y., 1875.

Phil 2125.62.5   McCosh, James. Christianity and positivism. N.Y., 1871.

Phil 2125.62   McCosh, James. Christianity and positivism. N.Y., 1874.

Phil 2125.45.7   McCosh, James. A criticism of the critical philosophy. N.Y., 1884.

Phil 2125.55   McCosh, James. The emotions. N.Y., 1880.

Phil 2138.85   McCosh, James. An examination of Mr. J.S. Mill's philosophy. London, 1866.

NEDL Phil 2138.85.2   McCosh, James. An examination of Mr. J.S. Mill's philosophy. N.Y., 1866.

Phil 2125.30   McCosh, James. First and fundamental truths. N.Y., 1889.

Phil 8709.2.50   McCosh, James. Ideas in nature overlooked by Dr. Tyndall. N.Y., 1875.

Phil 2125.52   McCosh, James. Intuitions of the mind. London, 1860.

Phil 2125.52.5   McCosh, James. Intuitions of the mind. 3rd ed. N.Y., 1874.

Phil 5052.22   McCosh, James. The laws of discursive thought. London, 1870.

Phil 5052.22.3   McCosh, James. The laws of discursive thought. N.Y., 1870.

Phil 2125.57   McCosh, James. The laws of discursive thought. N.Y., 1876.

Phil 2125.65.5   McCosh, James. Method of divine government. Edinburgh, 1852.

Phil 2125.65   McCosh, James. Method of divine government. N.Y., 1851.

Phil 2125.65.4   McCosh, James. Method of divine government. N.Y., 1855.

Phil 2125.65.7   McCosh, James. Method of divine government. 2nd ed. Edinburgh, 1850.

Phil 2125.73   McCosh, James. Our moral nature, being a brief system of ethics. N.Y., 1892.

Phil 2125.40   McCosh, James. Philosophical papers. N.Y., 1869.

Htn Phil 2125.75*   McCosh, James. Philosophy of reality: should it be favored by America? N.Y., 1894.

Phil 2125.50   McCosh, James. Psychology: the cognitive powers. N.Y., 1886.

Phil 2125.50.2   McCosh, James. Psychology: the cognitive powers. N.Y., 1889.

Phil 2125.50.5   McCosh, James. Psychology: the cognitive powers. N.Y., 1906.

Phil 2125.50.3   McCosh, James. Psychology: the motive powers. N.Y., 1888.

Phil 2125.66   McCosh, James. The supernatural in relation to the natural. Cambridge, Eng., 1862.

Phil 2125.35   McCosh, James. The tests of the various kinds of truth. N.Y., 1891.

Phil 2125.60   McCosh, James. Typical forms and special ends in creation. Edinburgh, 1857.

Phil 735.128   McCracken, D.J. Thinking and valuing. London, 1950.

Phil 40.3   MacCracken, H.M. A propaganda of philosophy; a history of the American Institute of Christian Philosophy, 1881-1914. N.Y., 1914.

Phil 7069.67.40   McCreery, Charles. Science, philosophy and E.S.P. London, 1967.

Phil 187.97   McCrossan, J.D. Logic and other nonsense. London, 1895.

Phil 8667.2   Macculloch, J. Proofs and illustrations of the attributes of God. London, 1837. 3v.

Phil 1812.4   MacCunn, J. Six radical thinkers. London, 1907.

Phil 1812.4.5   MacCunn, J. Six radical thinkers. London, 1910.

Phil 1812.4.10   MacCunn, J. Six radical thinkers. N.Y., 1964.

Phil 9045.14   MacCunn, John. Ethics of citizenship. Glasgow, 1894.

Phil 5252.61.2   MacCurdy, J.T. Common principles in psychology and physiology. Cambridge, 1928.

Phil 5252.61   MacCurdy, J.T. Common principles in psychology and physiology. N.Y., 1928.

Phil 6322.8   MacCurdy, J.T. Problems in dynamic psychology. Cambridge, 1923.

Phil 6322.8.5   MacCurdy, J.T. The psychology of emotion; morbid and normal. London, 1925.

Phil 9380.6   MacCurdy, J.T. The structure of morale. Cambridge, Eng., 1943.

Phil 1750.23   McCutcheon, Roger Philip. The present-day relevance of eighteenth-century thought. Washington, 1956.

Phil 5890.2   McDaniel, James Winnard. Physical disability and human behavior. N.Y., 1969.

Phil 8413.6   M'Dermot, Martin. A critical dissertation on nature and principles of taste. London, 1823.

Phil 7158.715   MacDermot, Violet. The cult of the seer in the ancient Middle East. Berkeley, 1971.

Phil 6322.10   Macdonald, A. Abnormal man. Washington, D.C., 1893.

Phil 5425.6   Macdonald, A. Genius and insanity. Lewes, 1892.

Phil 1517.6   Macdonald, A.J. Authority and reason in the early middle ages. London, 1933.

Phil 1050.23   Macdonald, D.B. The Hebrew philosophical genius. Princeton, 1936.

Phil 8663.3.91   McDonald, E.M. Col. Robert G. Ingersoll as he is. N.Y., 1910?

Phil 8610.929.15   MacDonald, G.E. Fifty years of freethought. v.1. pt.1-2. N.Y., 1929-31. 2v.

Phil 8592.3   Macdonald, L.B. Life in the making. Boston, 1911.

Phil 2030.8   Macdonald, Lauchlin D. John Grote. The Hague, 1966.

Phil 187.96   McDonald, M.F. Brief readings in philosophy. Brooklyn, 1931.

Phil 8637.17   McDonald, N.T. The dawn beyond the sunset. London, 1929.

Phil 7060.133   McDonald, Neil T. The Belledoon mysteries, 1830-40. 3. ed. Wallaceburg, Ont., n.d.

Phil 8887.46   MacDonald, Normand. Maxims and moral reflections. N.Y., 1827.

Phil 6122.17   MacDonald, R. Mind, religion and health. N.Y., 1908.

Phil 9035.57   McDonough, M.R. The empirical study of character. Diss. Washington, 1929.

Phil 5110.1   MacDougall, C.D. Hoaxes. N.Y., 1940.

Phil 6980.464   McDougall, Joyce. Dialogue with Sammy; a psycho-analytical contribution to the understanding of a child psychosis. London, 1969.

Phil 5252.23.5   MacDougall, R. The general problems of psychology. N.Y., 1922.

Phil 5252.23.20   MacDougall, R. The physical characteristics of attention. n.p., 1896-1904. 15 pam.

Phil 5252.23   Pamphlet box. MacDougall, R. Minor writings.

Phil 9035.49   McDougall, W. Character and the conduct of life. N.Y., 1927.
Phil 6322.14A   McDougall, W. Outline of abnormal psychology. N.Y., 1926.
Phil 6322.14.25   McDougall, W. Psychopathologie funktioneller Störungen. Leipzig, 1931.
Phil 6122.13.5   McDougall, William. Body and mind. N.Y., 1911.
Phil 6122.13.11   McDougall, William. Body and mind. 4th ed. London, 1918.
Phil 6122.13.13   McDougall, William. Body and mind. 6th ed. London, 1923.
Phil 5252.18.30   McDougall, William. A contribution towards an improvement in psychological method. n.p., 1898-1914. 8 pam.
Phil 5252.18.25   McDougall, William. The energies of men. N.Y., 1933.
Phil 8887.57   McDougall, William. Ethics and some modern world problems. N.Y., 1924.
Phil 5252.18.37   McDougall, William. The frontiers of psychology. N.Y., 1934.
Phil 5252.18.8   McDougall, William. The group mind. Cambridge, 1920.
Phil 5252.18.8.3   McDougall, William. The group mind. N.Y., 1920.
Phil 5252.18.8.2   McDougall, William. The group mind. 2d ed. N.Y., 1920.
Phil 5252.18.6   McDougall, William. An introduction to social psychology. Boston, 1926.
Phil 5252.18.5.4   McDougall, William. An introduction to social psychology. 3d ed. London, 1910.
Phil 5252.18.3   McDougall, William. An introduction to social psychology. 15th ed. Boston, 1923.
Phil 487.6.3   McDougall, William. Modern materialism and emergent evolution. N.Y., 1929.
Phil 487.6.5   McDougall, William. Modern materialism and emergent evolution. 2. ed. London, 1934.
Phil 5252.18.15   McDougall, William. Outline of psychology. N.Y., 1923.
Phil 5252.18.16   McDougall, William. Outline of psychology. N.Y., 1926.
Phil 6122.13.3   McDougall, William. Physiological psychology. London, 1918.
Phil 6315.2.109   McDougall, William. Psycho-analysis and social psychology. London, 1936.
Phil 5252.18.13   McDougall, William. Psychologi. København, 1926.
Phil 5252.18.12   McDougall, William. Psychology, the study of behavior. London, 1912.
Phil 5252.18.11A   McDougall, William. Psychology, the study of behavior. N.Y., 1912.
Phil 5252.18.12.10   McDougall, William. Psychology. 2d ed. London, 1952.
Phil 5252.18.35   McDougall, William. Religion and the sciences of life. London, 1934.
Phil 5252.18.38   McDougall, William. The riddle of life. London, 1938.
Phil 7069.67.65   McDougall, William. William McDougall: explorer of the mind. N.Y., 1967.
Phil 630.18   McDowall, A.S. Realism, a study in art and thought. London, 1918.
Phil 5252.60   McDowall, R.J.S. The mind. N.Y., 1927.
Phil 5252.60.12   McDowall, R.J.S. Sane psychology. 2d ed. London, 1944.
Phil 8413.21   McDowall, S.A. Beauty and the beast; an essay in evolutionary aesthetic. Cambridge, Mass., 1920.
Phil 3450.19.525   MacDowell, João Augusto A. Amazonas. A gênese da ontologia fundamental de Martin Heidegger. São Paulo, 1970.
Phil 5222.7   Mace, C.A. Current trends in British psychology. London, 1953.
Phil 1830.20   Mace, Cecil Alec. British philosophy in the mid-century. London, 1957.
Phil 1830.20.2   Mace, Cecil Alec. British philosophy in the mid-century. 2nd ed. London, 1966.
Phil 187.107   MacEachran, John M. Pragmatismus; eine neue Richtung der Philosophie. Leipzig, 1910.
Phil 4363.5.31   Macedo, J.A. de. Cartas filosoficas a Attico. Lisboa, 1815.
Phil 812.11   Macedo, Newton de. A luta pela liberdade no pensamento europeu. Coimbra, 1930.
Phil 1712.16   McElroy, H.C. Modern philosophers. N.Y., 1950.
Phil 7069.20.230   McEvilly, Mary A. Meslom's messages from the life beyond. N.Y., 1920.
Phil 7069.20.232   McEvilly, Mary A. To woman from Meslom. N.Y., 1920.
Phil 293.9   McEwen, J.W. An essay on creation. Philadelphia, 1900.
Phil 6322.29.5   MacFadden, B. StrengtheningThe nerves. N.Y., 1928.
Phil 9495.35.15   Macfadden, B.A. The virile powers of superb manhood. London, 1896.

Htn   Phil 8592.58*   M'Farland, Asa. An oration, produced before the Phi Beta Kappa,...Hanover, Aug. 25, 1802. Hanover, 1802.
Phil 3494.74   McFarland, John D. Kant's concept of teleology. Edinburgh, 1970.
Phil 6322.29   McFarland, R.A. Miscellaneous papers on abnormal psychology. n.p., n.d.
Phil 6322.29.3   McFarland, R.A. Psycho-physiological studies at high altitude in the Andes. Baltimore, 1937.
Phil 5643.104A   McFarland, R.A. Studies of visual fatigue. Boston, 1942.
Phil 7080.39   MacFarlane, A.W. Insomnia and its therapeutics. N.Y., 1891.
Phil 5052.18   Macfarlane, Alexander. Principles of the algebra of logic. Edinburgh, 1879.
Phil 8887.138   McGann, Thomas F. Ethics: theory and practice. Chicago, 1971.
Phil 8637.21   McGavin, E.C. Paradise revisited. Boston, 1937.
Phil 9070.111   McGee, Charles Douglas. The recovery of meaning; an essay on the good life. N.Y., 1966.
Phil 600.43   McGee, John Edwin. A crusade for humanity. London, 1931.
Phil 8592.32   McGiffert, A.C. The rise of modern religous ideas. N.Y., 1922.
Phil 5400.116   McGill, V.J. Emotions and reason. Springfield, 1954.
Phil 3808.161   McGill, Vivian J. Schopenhauer; pessimist and pagan. N.Y., 1931.
Phil 9245.120   McGill, Vivian Jerauld. The idea of happiness. N.Y., 1967.
Phil 52.3   McGill University. Department of philosophy. Papers, 1-4. Montreal, 1896-99.

NEDL   Phil 3425.98   McGilvary, E. Principle and method of the Hegelian dialectic. Berkeley, 1897.
Phil 2150.19.30   McGilvary, E.B. Toward a perspective realism. LaSalle, Ill., 1956.
Phil 2070.133   McGilvary, Evander B. The fringe of William James's psychology, the basis of logic. n.p., 1911.
Phil 8887.60   McGinley, A.A. The profit of love. N.Y., 1907.
Phil 6155.16   McGlothlin, William Herschel. Hallucinogenic drugs: a perspective with special reference to peyote and cannalis. Santa Monica, 1964.
Phil 187.178   McGlynn, James. A metaphysics of being and God. Englewood Cliffs, 1966.
Phil 960.29   McGovern, W.M. A manual of Buddhist philosophy. London, 1923.
Phil 8887.125   McGrath, Patrick. The nature of moral judgement: a study in contemporary moral philosophy. London, 1967.

Phil 8622.10   MacGregor, G. Doubt and faith. London, 1951.
Phil 8887.80   MacGregor, G. Les frontières de la morale et de la religion. Thèse. Paris, 1952.
Phil 8592.106   MacGregor, Geddes. The hemlock and the cross. Philadelphia, 1963.
Phil 8592.105   MacGregor, Geddes. Introduction to religious philosophy. London, 1960.
Phil 7069.30.17   MacGregor, Helen. The psychic faculties and their development. London, 1930.
Phil 5052.1   McGregor, P. A system of logic. N.Y., 1862.
Phil 343.4.5   Mach, E. La connaissance et l'erreur. Paris, 1908.
Phil 343.4   Mach, E. Erkenntnis und Irrtum. Leipzig, 1905.
Phil 343.4.3   Mach, E. Erkenntnis und Irrtum. 2. Aufl. Leipzig, 1906.
Phil 343.4.6   Mach, E. Die Leitgedanken meiner naturwissenschaftlichen Erkenntnislehre und ire Aufnahme durch die Zeitenossen. Leipzig, 1919.
Phil 672.17   Mach, E. Space and geometry. Chicago, 1906.
Phil 5635.5.5   Mach, Ernst. Die Analyse der Empfindungen. Jena, 1900.
Phil 5635.5.6   Mach, Ernst. Die Analyse der Empfindungen. 6. Aufl. Jena, 1911.
Phil 5635.5.9   Mach, Ernst. The analysis of sensations. Chicago, 1914.
Phil 5635.5.8   Mach, Ernst. The analysis of sensations on the relation of the physical to the psychical. N.Y., 1959.
Phil 5635.5.4   Mach, Ernst. Beiträge zur Analyse de Empfindungen. Jena, 1886.
Phil 5635.5.2   Mach, Ernst. Contributions to the analysis of the sensations. Chicago, 1897.
Phil 5635.5.10   Mach, Ernst. Contributions to the analysis of the sensations. Chicago, 1910.
Phil 5635.5.7   Mach, Ernst. Grundlinien der Lehre vom den Bewegungsempfindungen. Leipzig, 1875.
Phil 5762.12.5   Mach, F.J. Die Willensfreiheit des Menschen. Paderborn, 1894.
Phil 8592.22.6   Mach, Franz. Die Krisis im Christentum. 2. Aufl. Dresden, 1908.
Phil 8592.22   Mach, Franz. Das religions- und Weltproblem. 2. Aufl. Dresden, 1904. 2v.
Phil 187.180   Machado Bandeira de Mello, Lydio. Crítica cosmológica da física quântica. Belo Horizonte, 1969.
Phil 978.108   Der Macher bim Ich. (Ballmer, R.) Besazio, 1967.
Phil 6480.200.5   Les machinations de la nuit. (Becker, Raymond de.) Paris, 1965.
Phil 6132.41   The machinery of the brain. (Wooldridge, Dean E.) N.Y., 1963.
Phil 8980.546   Machovec, Milan. Smysl lidského života. Praha, 1965.
Phil 3625.3.88   Mach's empirio-pragmatism in physical science. (Weinberg, Carlton Berenda.) N.Y., 1937.
Phil 3625.3.82   Machs Erkenntnistheorie. (Reinhold, Ferdinand.) Leipzig, 1908.
Phil 343.4.9   Die Machsche Erkenntnistheorie. (Schultz, R.) Berlin, n.d.
Phil 4196.85   Die Macht des Bildes. (Raith, Werner.) München, 1967.
Phil 5520.390   Die Macht des Wortes. (Segerstedt, T. Torgnysson.) Zürich, 1946.
Phil 5425.54.5   Macht und Geheimnis der Dummheit. (Guerster, Eugen.) Zürich, 1967.
Phil 7140.134   Macht und Geheimnis der Suggestion. (Liebetrau, H.) Basel, 1951.
Phil 3090.91   Macht und Gewalt in der Philosophie Franz von Baaders. (Helberger-Frobenius, Sebastian.) Bonn, 1969.
Phil 8957.13   Macht und Ohnmacht der Religion. (Haering, Bernhard.) Salzburg, 1956.
Phil 3503.20   Macht und Ohnmacht der Vernunft. Zur Einführung in die Philosophie Kants. (Varga, Alexander von.) München, 1967.
Phil 193.160   Macht und Ohnmacht des Geistes. (Szilasi, Wilhelm.) Bern, 1946.
Phil 8875.16   Macht und Pflicht. (Aall, Anathon.) Leipzig, 1902.
Phil 9240.16   Macht und Wirklichkeit des Bösen. München, 1958.
Phil 1850.119   Der Machtgedanke und der Friedensidee in der Philosophie der Engländer, Bacon und Bentham. (Kraus, Oskar.) Leipzig, 1926.
Phil 6319.9   Machtwille und Minderwertigkeitsgefuhl. (Jahn, Ernst.) Berlin, 1931.
Phil 343.55   McInerny, Ralph M. Studies in analogy. The Hague, 1969.
Phil 343.6   Macintosh, D.C. Problem of knowledge. N.Y., 1915.
Phil 8592.48.5   Macintosh, D.C. The problem of religious knowledge. N.Y., 1940.
Phil 8592.48.10   Macintosh, D.C. The reaction against metaphysics in theology. Chicago, 1911.
Phil 8592.48.7   Macintosh, D.C. The reasonableness of Christianity. N.Y., 1926.
Phil 8592.48   Macintosh, D.C. Religious realism. N.Y., 1931.
Phil 8592.48.3   Macintosh, D.C. Theology as an empirical science. N.Y., 1919.
Phil 165.438   MacIntosh, John James. The business of reason. London, 1969.
Phil 2150.22.135   MacIntyre, Alasdair C. Herbert Marcuse: and exposition and a polemic. N.Y., 1970.
Phil 310.803   MacIntyre, Alasdair C. Marxism and Christianity. N.Y., 1968.
Phil 8667.30   MacIntyre, Alasdair C. The religious significance of atheism. N.Y., 1969.
Phil 8837.17   MacIntyre, Alasdair C. A short history of ethics. N.Y., 1966.
Phil 402.22   MacIntyre, Alasdair Chalmers. Against the self-images of the age: essays on ideology and philosophy. London, 1971.
Phil 4065.87   McIntyre, J.S. Giordano Bruno. London, 1903.
Phil 187.185   MacIver, R.M. Life; its dimensions. N.Y., 1960.
Phil 9245.60A   MacIver, R.M. The pursuit of happiness. N.Y., 1955.
Phil 672.215   MacIver, Robert Morrison. The challenge of the passing years. N.Y., 1u962.
Phil 5762.4   Mack, Joseph. Kritik der Freiheitstheorien. Leipzig, 1906.
Phil 1865.186   Mack, Mary P. Jeremy Bentham; an odyssey of ideas. London, 1963.
Phil 1865.186.2   Mack, Mary P. Jeremy Bentham. N.Y., 1963.
Phil 343.23   Mack, R.D. The appeal to immediate experience. N.Y., 1945.
Phil 8592.64   Mackay, A. Heritage and destiny. N.Y., 1943.
Phil 9550.8   Mackaye, J. The happiness of nations. N.Y., 1915.
Phil 8887.64   MacKaye, James. Convictionism versus non-convictionism. n.p., 1928.
Phil 293.18   McKaye, James. Dynamic universe. N.Y., 1931.
Phil 5052.26   Mackaye, James. The logic of conduct. N.Y., 1924.
Phil 5465.80   McKellar, Peter. Imagination and thinking. London, 1957.
Phil 5640.3.5   M'Kendrick, J.G. The physiology of the senses. N.Y., 1907.

Phil 5402.25   McKenna, A.G. Les réactions psycho-physiologiques à la douleur. Louvain, 1963.

Phil 7069.68.25   MacKenzie, Andrew. Frontiers of the unknown: the insights of psychical research. London, 1968.

Phil 7069.66.25   Mackenzie, Andrew. The unexplained; some strange cases in psychical research. London, 1966.

Phil 9560.54   Mackenzie, C. On moral courage. London, 1962.

Phil 5655.6   McKenzie, Dan. Aromatics and the soul. London, 1923.

Phil 8887.59.10   Mackenzie, G. Essays upon several moral subjects. London, 1713.

Htn   Phil 9352.1*   Mackenzie, G. Moral gallantry. Edinburgh, 1669. 2 pam.

Phil 9352.1.5   Mackenzie, G. Moral gallantry. London, 1685.

Phil 8610.899.25   MacKenzie, G.L. Brimstone ballads and other verse. London, 1895.

Phil 8413.18   MacKenzie, G.S.B. An essay on some subjects connected with taste. Edinburgh, 1817.

Htn   Phil 9515.4*   Mackenzie, George. Moral essay, preferring solitude to public employment. London, 1685.

Htn   Phil 9560.16*   Mackenzie, George. The moral history of frugality. London, 1691.

Phil 8702.3   Mackenzie, H. Evolution illuminating the Bible. London, 1891.

Phil 8702.3.5   Mackenzie, H. Modern science unlocking the Bible. London, 1892.

Phil 5627.161   McKenzie, J.G. Psychology, psychotherapy and evangelicalism. London, 1940.

Phil 7069.16.65   McKenzie, J.H. Spirit intercourse. 5th ed. London, 1916.

Phil 665.40   Mackenzie, J.N. Landseer. The universal medium; a new interpretation of the soul. London, 1922.

Phil 187.27.13   Mackenzie, J.S. Cosmic problems. London, 1931.

Phil 187.27.9   Mackenzie, J.S. Elements of constructive philosophy. London, 1917.

Phil 2150.8.79   Mackenzie, J.S. John Stuart Mackenzie. London, 1936.

Phil 187.27.5   Mackenzie, J.S. Lectures on humanism. London, 1907.

Phil 8887.1.3   Mackenzie, J.S. A manual of ethics. 3rd ed. London, 1897.

Phil 8887.59   Mackenzie, J.S. A manual of ethics. 4. ed. London, 1910.

Phil 8887.1.4   Mackenzie, J.S. A manual of ethics. 4th ed. N.Y., 1901.

Phil 8887.1.15   Mackenzie, J.S. A manual of ethics. 6th ed. London, 1948.

Phil 187.27   Mackenzie, J.S. Outlines of metaphysics. London, 1902.

Phil 735.78   Mackenzie, J.S. Ultimate values in the light of contemporary thought. London, 1924.

Phil 5414.35   McKenzie, John. Guilt. London, 1962.

Phil 8837.8   McKenzie, John. Hindu ethics. London, 1922.

Phil 5252.77   Mackenzie, M. The human mind. Philadelphia, 1941.

Phil 3425.116   Mackenzie, Millicent Hughes. Hegel's educational theory and practice. Photoreproduction. London, 1909.

Phil 7082.194   Mackenzie, Norman Jan. Dreams and dreaming. N.Y., 1965.

Phil 8633.1.29   Mackenzie, W.D. Man's consciousness of immortality. Cambridge, 1929.

Phil 3832.11A   McKeon, R. The philosophy of Spinoza. N.Y., 1928.

Phil 2150.13A   McKeon, Richard P. The philosophic bases of art and criticism. Chicago? 1944.

Phil 1560.10   McKeon, Richard P. Selections from medieval philosophers. N.Y., 1929-1930. 2v.

Phil 2150.13.6   McKeon, Richard P. Thought, action and passion. Chicago, 1968.

Phil 5252.47   McKerrow, J.C. The appearance of mind. London, 1923.

Phil 187.94   McKerrow, J.C. Novius organum. London, 1931.

Phil 3552.91   Mackie, J.M. Life of Godfrey William von Leibnitz. Boston, 1845.

Phil 5252.41   McKim, William D. A study for the times. N.Y., 1920.

Phil 6122.60.5   McKinney, Fred. Psychology of personal adjustment. 2d ed. N.Y., 1949.

Phil 8622.76   McKinnon, Alastair. Falsification and belief. The Hague, 1970.

Phil 8592.108   MacKinnon, D.M. The borderlands of theology. Cambridge, Eng., 1961.

Phil 8887.95   Mackinnon, D.M. A study in ethical theory. London, 1957.

Phil 5252.91   MacKinnon, D.W. Experimental studies in psychodynamics. Cambridge, 1948. 2v.

Phil 8837.1.4   Mackintosh, James. A general view of the progress of ethical philosophy. Edinburgh, 1837.

Phil 8837.1.2   Mackintosh, James. A general view of the progress of ethical philosophy. Philadelphia, 1832.

Phil 8837.1.3   Mackintosh, James. A general view of the progress of ethical philosophy. Philadelphia, 1834.

Phil 3425.104A   Mackintosh, R. Hegel and Hegelianism. Edinburgh, 1903.

Phil 2020.87   McKirachan, John C. The temporal and eternal in the philosophy of Thomas H. Green. Thesis. Ann Arbor, 1941.

Phil 680.15   Macksey, Richard. The language of criticism and the science of man. Baltimore, 1970.

Phil 5330.42.5   Mackworth, Jane F. Vigilance and attention; a signal detection approach. Harmondsworth, 1970.

Phil 5330.42   Mackworth, Jane F. Vigilance and habituation: a new psychological approach. Harmondsworth, 1969.

Phil 5052.19   McLachlan, D.B. Reformed logic. London, 1892.

Phil 5650.22   McLachlan, Norman W. Noise. London, 1935.

Phil 8962.20   Maclagan, W.G. The theological frontier of ethics. N.Y., 1961.

Phil 1905.12.90   McLarney, James J. The theism of Edgar S. Brightman. Diss. Washington, 1936.

Phil 5627.264.20   McLaughlin, Barry. Nature, grace and religious development. N.Y., 1964.

Phil 8962.16   McLaughlin, P.J. The church and modern science. N.Y., 1957.

Phil 1133.54   McLean, George F. Ancient Western philosophy: the Hellenic emergence. N.Y., 1971.

Phil 75.74   McLean, George F. An annotated bibliography of philosophy in Catholic thought, 1900-1964. N.Y., 1967.

Phil 75.74.5   McLean, George F. A bibliography of Christian philosophy and contemporary issue. N.Y., 1967.

Phil 2115.147.2   MacLean, K. John Locke and English literature of the eighteenth century. N.Y., 1962.

Phil 2115.147   MacLean, K. John Locke and English literature of the eighteenth century. New Haven, 1936.

Phil 5052.13   Macleane, D. Reason, thought and language. London, 1906.

Phil 8592.73   MacLeish, Norman. The nature of religious knowledge. N.Y., 1938.

Phil 187.79   MacLeod, A.H.D. Sur diverses questions se présentant dans l'étude du concept de réalité. Paris, 1927.

Phil 187.79.2   MacLeod, A.H.D. Sur diverses questions se présentant dans l'étude du concept de réalité. Paris, 1927.

Phil 343.37F   MacLeod, Andries Hugo Donald. De psykiska företeelsernas förhallande till rum och tid. Stockholm, 1964.

Phil 7060.60   M'Leod, D. Treatise on the second sight. Edinburgh, 1763.

Phil 5645.35   MacLeod, R.B. An experimental investigation of brightness constancy. N.Y., 1932.

Phil 8413.9   McMahon, Amos. The meaning of art. N.Y., 1930.

Phil 8050.72   McMahon, Amos. Preface to an American philosophy of art. Chicago, 1945.

Phil 1750.132A   McMahon, Francis E. Humanism of Irving Babbitt. Diss. Washington, D.C., 1931.

Phil 187.2   MacMahon, J.H. Treatise on metaphysics. London, 1860.

Phil 2880.8.287   McMahon, Joseph H. Humans being; the world of Jean-Paul Sartre. Chicago, 1971.

Phil 2150.14.30   McMahon, T.E. A Catholic looks at the world. N.Y., 1945.

Phil 9245.5   Macmillan, M. The promotion of general happiness. London, 1890.

Phil 3494.10   Macmillan, R.A.C. Crowning phase of critical philosophy...Kant. London, 1912.

Phil 575.100   McMorrow, G.J. A metaphysical study on the individual and the person. Diss. Notre Dame, 1940.

Phil 165.337   McMullin, Ethan. The concept of matter. Notre Dame, Indiana, 1963.

Phil 165.337.5   McMullin, Ethan. The concept of matter in Greek and medieval philosophy. Notre Dame, 1965.

Phil 6750.220   MacMurchy, H. The almosts, a study of the feeble minded. Boston, 1920.

Phil 5620.17   Macmurray, John. Reason and emotion. London, 1935.

Phil 5620.28   Macmurray, John. Reason and emotion. 2. ed. N.Y., 1962.

Phil 8702.28   MacMurray, John. Religion, art, and science. Liverpool, 1961.

Phil 575.165   Macmurray, John. The self as agent. London, 1957. 2v.

Phil 5627.144.1   Macmurray, John. The structure of religious experience. Hamden, Conn., 1971.

Phil 8592.75   McMurrin, S.M. The patterns of our religious faiths. Salt Lake City, 1954.

Phil 6962.38   Macnab, Francis A. Estrangement and relationship. Bloomington, 1966.

Phil 2050.223   MacNabb, Donald George Cecil. David Hume. London, 1951.

Phil 2050.223.2   MacNabb, Donald George Cecil. David Hume. 2nd ed. Oxford, 1966.

Phil 7140.116.50   Macnaghten, H. Emile Coué, the man and his work. N.Y., 1922.

Phil 8887.54   McNair, G.H. Timely lessons on today's living. Newport, Vt., 1922.

Phil 5520.16   MacNamara, N.C. Human speech; its physical basis. N.Y., 1909.

Phil 5822.10   MacNamara, N.C. Instinct and intelligence. London, 1915.

Phil 5649.22   McNeill, H. Motor adaptation and accuracy. Louvain, 1934.

Phil 2477.6.160   McNeill, John J. The Blondelian synthesis; a study of the influence of German philosophical sources on the formation of Blondel's method and thought. Leiden, 1966.

Phil 2045.142   McNeilly, F.S. The anatomy of Leviathan. London, 1968.

Phil 7080.7   Macnish, R. Philosophy of sleep. N.Y., 1834.

Phil 3450.19.395   Macomber, William B. The anatomy of disillusion; Martin Heideggers notion of truth. Evanston, 1967.

Phil 2270.91A   Macpherson, H. Spencer and Spencerism. N.Y., 1900.

Phil 5222.20   McPherson, Marion White. Problems and procedures in oral histories of the Archives of the History of American Psychology. Akron, 1967.

Phil 8592.116   McPherson, Thomas. The philosophy of religion. London, 1965.

Phil 5190.10   MacPherson, William. The psychology of persuasion. London, 1920.

Phil 5190.10.1   MacPherson, William. The psychology persuasion. N.Y., 192-?

Phil 8520.44   Macquarrie, J. Twentieth century religious thought. London, 1963.

Phil 8702.4   MacQueary, H. The evolution of man and Christianity. N.Y., 1890.

Phil 7069.08.24   Macrae, Norman. Highland second-sight. Dingwall, 1908?

Phil 3425.39   Macran, H.S. Hegel's doctrine of formal logic. Oxford, 1912.

Htn   Phil 182.13*   Macrocosm and microcosm. (Helmont, F.M. van.) London, 1685.

Phil 3832.19   McShea, Robert J. The political philosophy of Spinoza. N.Y., 1968.

Phil 187.56.4   McTaggart, J.M.E. Dare to be wise. London, 1910.

Phil 187.56.9   McTaggart, J.M.E. Introduction to the study of philosophy. Cambridge, Eng., 190-.

Phil 187.56   McTaggart, J.M.E. The nature of existence. Cambridge, Eng., 1921-1927. 2v.

Phil 187.56.5   McTaggart, J.M.E. Philosophical studies. London, 1934.

Phil 8592.21.5   McTaggart, J.M.E. Some dogmas of religion. London, 1930.

Phil 3425.100.9   McTaggart, John McTaggart Ellis. A commentary on Hegel's logic. Cambridge, 1910.

Phil 3425.100.5A   McTaggart, John McTaggart Ellis. Studies in Hegelian cosmology. Cambridge, 1901.

Phil 3425.100.2   McTaggart, John McTaggart Ellis. Studies in the Hegelian dialectic. 2. ed. Cambridge, 1922.

Phil 3425.100.2.1   McTaggart, John McTaggart Ellis. Studies in the Hegelian dialectic. 2. ed. N.Y., 1964.

Phil 187.122   MacTaggart, M. Man, mind and psychology. London, 1940.

Phil 187.43   McTaggart, William. Absolute relativism. London, 1887.

Phil 187.3   Macvicar, J.G. Sketch of a philosophy. v.1-4. London, 1868-1874.

Phil 8413.10   MacVicar, John. The philosophy of the beautiful. Edinburgh, 1855.

Phil 4210.83.5   MacWalter, G.S. Life of Antonio Rosmini-Serbati. London, 1883.

Phil 2475.1.226   MacWhannel, J. Criticism of the philosophy of Bergson. Edinburgh, 1928.

Phil 2490.170   The "mad" philosopher. 1st ed. (Sokoloff, Boris.) N.Y., 1961.

Phil 6952.4   A mad world and its inhabitants. (Chambers, J.) N.Y., 1877.

Phil 974.2.60   Madame Blavatsky. (Symonds, John.) London, 1959.

Phil 5055.21.10   Madarászné Zsigmond Anna. A tiszta logika alapkérdesei. Budapest, 1965.

Phil 4363.12   Madariaga, Salvador de. Portrait of a man standing. London, 1968.

Phil 2905.1.275   Madaule, J. Initiation à Teilhard de Chardin. Paris, 1963.

Phil 4769.9.21   Maday, J. Wladimir Sergejewitsch Solowjew. Düsseldorf, 1961.

Phil 5822.4A   Máday, Stefan. Psychologie des Pferdes und der Dressur. Berlin, 1971.

Phil 1182.40   Maddalena, A. I Pitagorici. Bari, 1954.

Phil 1133.49   Maddalena, Antonio. Ionici; testimonianze e frammenti. Introduzione. 1. ed. Firenze, 1963.

Phil 1117.10   Maddalena, Antonio. Sulla cosmologia ionica da talete a eraclita. Padova, 1940.

Phil 2340.18.80   Madden, E. Chauncey Wright and the foundations of pragmatism. Seattle, 1963.

Phil 1812.20 — Madden, Edward Harry. Civil disobedience and moral law in nineteenth century American philosophy. Seattle, 1968.

Phil 5252.158 — Madden, Edward Harry. Philosophical problems of psychology. N.Y., 1922.

Phil 3246.330 — Mader, Johann Karl. Fichte, Feierbach, Marx. Wien, 1968.

Phil 187.73F — Madiedo, M.M. Una gran revolucion, ó La razon del hombre juzgada por sí misma. Caracas, 1876.

Phil 293.1 — Madiis, H. de. Le plan de la creation. Paris, 1864.

Phil 5520.114 — Madinier, G. Conscience et signification. 1. éd. Paris, 1953.

Phil 9075.45 — Madinier, G. La conscience morale. Paris, 1954.

Phil 2725.14.95 — Madinier, G. Vers une philosophie réflexive. Neuchâtel, 1960.

Phil 2750.14 — Madinier, Gabriel. Conscience et amour. Paris, 1938.

Phil 2750.15 — Madinier, Gabriel. Conscience et mouvement. Paris, 1938.

Phil 2750.15.1 — Madinier, Gabriel. Conscience et mouvement. Thesis. Paris, 1938.

Phil 6315.2.280 — Madison, P. Freud's concept of repression and defense, its theoretical and observational language. Minneapolis, 1961.

Phil 6955.23 — Madness and civilization. (Foucault, Michel.) N.Y., 1965.

Phil 6967.25 — Madness in society. (Rosen, George.) London, 1968.

Phil 5412.20 — Madow, Leo. Anger. N.Y., 1972.

Phil 75.60 — Madrid. Universidad. Facultad de Filosofía y Letras. Sumarios y extractos de las tesis doctorales en las secciones de filosofía y pedagogía. 1940-1950

Phil 70.110 — Madrid. Universidad. Seminario de Metafísica. Anales del Seminario de Metafísica. Madrid, 1967.

Phil 5252.175 — Madsen, K.B. Almen psykologi. 3. opl. v.1-2. København, 1968.

Phil 5222.22 — Madsen, K.B. Moderne psykologiske teorier. 2. oplag. København, 1969.

Phil 5222.22.5 — Madsen, K.B. Psykologiens udvikling. København, 1970.

Phil 5548.95.4 — Madsen, Kaj Berg. Theories of motivation; a comparative study. 4. ed. Kent, Ohio, 1968.

Phil 5548.95 — Madsen, Kaj Berg. Theories of motivation. Copenhagen, 1959.

Phil 9515.3.96 — Maduschka, Leo. Das Problem der Einsamkeit in 18 Jahrhundert. Weimar, 1933.

Phil 9515.3.95 — Maduschka, Leo. Das Problem der Einsamkeit in 18 Jahrhundert. Inaug. Diss. Murnan, 1932.

Phil 8430.27 — Mächte der Gestaltung; vom künstlerischen, philosophischen und religiösen Sein. (Ruefenacht, E.) Zürich, 1957.

Phil 7082.154 — Maeder, Alphonse. The dream problem. N.Y., 1916.

Phil 6322.5 — Maeder, Alphonse. Heilung und Entwicklung im Seelenleben. Zürich, 1918.

Phil 6980.447 — Maeder, Alphonse. Der Psychotherapeut als Paktnei. Zürich, 1957.

Phil 8962.28 — Maehl, Sibylle. Quadriga virtutum. Köln, 1969.

Phil 3120.7.81 — Mäinlander, ein neuer Messias. (Seiling, Max.) München, 1888.

Phil 972.18 — Maendl, Hans. Vom Geist des Nordens. Stuttgart, 1966.

Phil 5360.1 — Maennel, B. Über abstraktion. Gütersloh, 1890.

Phil 6951.24 — Männer zwischen 15 und 25. (Braatøy, T.) Oslo, 1934.

Phil 3246.35.12 — Männeskans bestammelse. (Fichte, Johann Gottlieb.) Stockholm, 1923.

Phil 5627.266.25 — Människan och makterna. (Bjoerkhen, John.) Stockholm, 1966.

Phil 8634.2.5 — Människans odödlighet. (James, William.) Stockholm, 1908.

Phil 5251.39 — Människokunskap. (Landquist, J.) Stockholm, 1920.

Phil 6060.58 — Männlichkeit und Weiblichkeit im Spiegel. (Reichert, G.) Heidelberg, 1962.

Phil 3832.8 — Mänoloff, P. Willensfreiheit und Erziehungsmöglichkeit Spinoza. Diss. Bern, 1904.

Phil 5258.72 — Det mänskliga själslifvet. (Scheele, Frans von.) Stockholm, 1896.

Phil 6316.6 — Det mänskliga själslivet i belysning av sinnessjukläkarens erfarenhet. (Gadelius, Bror.) Stockholm, 1921-24. 4v.

Phil 6949.369 — Märchenforschung und Tiefenpsychologie. (Laiblin, Wilhelm.) Darmstadt, 1969.

Phil 1145.78 — Märcker, F.A. Das Princip des Bösen nach den Begriffen den Griechen. Berlin, 1842.

Phil 187.125 — Märker, F. Sinn und Gesetze des Lebens. Berlin, 1938.

Phil 6022.4.5 — Märker, Friedrich. Autokraten und Demokraten. Erlenbach, 1931.

Phil 6022.4 — Märker, Friedrich. Symbolik der Gesichtsformen. Erlenbach, 1933.

Phil 6022.4.10 — Märker, Friedrich. Typen; Grundlagen der Charakterkunde. Erlenbach, 1931.

Phil 4510.10 — Märre skrifter. Stockholm. 1-45,1908-1917 9v.

Phil 1850.86 — Maestre, J. de. Examen de la philosophie de Bacon. Paris, 1836. 2v.

Phil 815.36 — Maestri di ieri. (Petruzzellis, Nicola.) Napoli, 1970.

Phil 177.76 — Maestri e problemi di filosofia. (Calò, G.) Torino, 1924. 2v.

Phil 7069.18.130A — Maeterlinck, Maurice. The light beyond. N.Y., 1918.

Phil 665.93 — Maeztu, Ramiro de. Defensa del espíritu. Madrid, 1958.

Htn — Phil 176.123.5* — Maffei, G.C. Scala naturale. Venice, 1573.

Phil 22.1 — Magazin zur Erfahrungsseelenkunde. Berlin. 1-10,1783-1793 10v.

Phil 5374.35 — Mager, Alois. Die Enge des Bewusstseins. Stuttgart, 1920.

Phil 525.125 — Mager, Alois. Mystik als seelische Wirklichkeit. Graz, 1947.

Phil 3425.203.5 — Mager, K.W.E. Popular framstallning af Hegelska philosofeska. Stockholm, 1843.

Phil 4080.3.435 — Mager, Wolfgang. Benedetto Croces literarisches und politisches Interesse an der Geschichte. Koln, 1965.

Phil 9245.128 — Maggal, Moshe M. Acres of happiness. 1st ed. N.Y., 1967.

Phil 2805.310 — Maggioni, Mary J. The pensées of Pascal. Washington, 1950.

Phil 3246.180 — Maggiore, G. Fichte. Castello, 1921.

Phil 187.80 — Maggiore, G. L'unita del mondo nel sistema del penšiero. Palermo, 1913.

Phil 960.30 — I maggiori sistemi filosofici indiani. (Belloni-Filippi, F.) Milano, 1914.

Phil 4073.39.5 — Magia e grazia. (Campanella, Tommaso.) Roma, 1957.

Phil 6671.10.10 — Magic, witchcraft, animal magnetism. (Braid, James.) London, 1852.

Phil 5627.259.5 — Magic and religion. (Vetter, George.) London, 1959.

Phil 5850.335.10 — The magic of psychic power. (Schwartz, David J.) West Nyack, N.Y., 1965.

Phil 978.77.2 — The magic presence. (King, G.R.) Chicago, 1935.

NEDL — Phil 7054.6.3 — The magic staff; an autobiography. (Davis, A.J.) N.Y., 1857.

Phil 7069.24.25 — A magician among the spirits. (Houdini, Harry.) N.Y., 1924.

Phil 5627.225 — Magie des extremes. Bruges, 1952.

Phil 6980.770 — La magie du dession. (Vinchon, Jean.) Paris, 1959.

Phil 6980.114 — Magie und Wunder in der Heilkunde. (Bitter, Wilhelm.) Stuttgart, 1959.

Phil 165.270 — Magill, F.N. Masterpieces of world philosophy in summary form. 1st ed. N.Y., 1961.

Htn — Phil 187.5* — Magirus, J. Physiologiae peripateticae. Francofurti, 1610.

Phil 22.46 — Magjar pszichologiai szemle. Budapest. 9,1936+ 13v.

Phil 2905.1.310 — Magloire, G. Teilhard de Chardin. Paris, 1964.

Phil 2905.1.155 — Magloire, George. Présence de Pierre Teilhard de Chardin. Paris, 1961.

Phil 6962.1.10 — Magnan, V. Le délire chronique à évolution systématique. Paris, 1892.

Phil 6962.1 — Magnan, V. Leçons cliniques sur les maladies mentales. Paris, 1882-91.

Phil 6962.1.2 — Magnan, V. Leçons cliniques sur les maladies mentales. 2. éd. Paris, 1893.

Phil 6962.1.3 — Magnan, V. Psychiatrische Vorlesungen. v.2-6. Leipzig, 1892-93.

Phil 6962.1.5 — Magnan, V. Recherches sur les centres nerveux. 2. série. Paris, 1893.

Phil 2725.25.95 — Magnani, Giovanni S.I. Itinerario al valore in R. Le Senne. Roma, 1971.

Phil 9035.38 — The magnet. (Churchill, L.A.) N.Y., 1903.

Phil 22.9 — The magnet. N.Y.

Htn — Phil 6672.9.17* — Magnetic magic. (Cahagnet, L.) n.p., 1898.

Phil 6673.17.10 — Le magnétime animal. (Delboeuf, J.) Paris, 1889.

Phil 22.11 — Le magnétiseur spiritualiste. Paris. 1-2,1849-1851

Phil 7123.2 — Les magnetiseurs, jugés par eux-mêmes. (Mabru, G.) Paris, 1858.

Phil 6673.17 — Magnétiseurs et médecins. (Delboeuf, J.) Paris, 1890.

Phil 6672.9 — Magnétisme, arcanes de vie future. (Cahagnet, L.) Paris, 1848.

Phil 6672.9.15 — Magnétisme; encyclopédie magnétique. v.1-6. (Cahagnet, L.) Paris, 1854-62. 3v.

Phil 6671.2 — Le magnétisme animal. (Barety, A.) Paris, 1887.

Phil 6671.7 — Le magnétisme animal. (Binet, A.) Paris, 1887.

Phil 6671.9 — Le magnétisme animal. (Bottey, F.) Paris, 1886.

Phil 6682.12 — Le magnétisme animal. (Morand, J.S.) Paris, 1889.

Phil 6672.12 — Magnétisme et hypnotisme. (Cullere, A.) Paris, 1886.

Phil 6681.7 — Le magnétisme et le sommambulisme. (Lonbert, J.B.) Paris, 1844.

Phil 6688.13 — Magnétisme et magnétothérapie. (Szapary, Franz von.) Paris, 1853.

Phil 6682.21 — Le magnétisme humain. (Moutin, Lucien.) Paris, 1907.

Phil 6673.4.21 — Le magnétisme opposé a la médecine. (Du Potet, J. de S.) Paris, 1840.

Phil 6673.16 — Magnétisme personnel ou psychique. (Durville, H.) Paris, 1905.

Phil 6682.15 — Le magnétisme traduit en cour d'assises. Paris, 1845.

Phil 6676.8 — Il magnetismo animale. (Guidi, Franc.) Milano, 1860.

Phil 6682.8 — Il magnetismo animale. (Morselli, E.A.) Torino, 1886.

Phil 6671.17 — Magnetismo e ipnotismo. 2. ed. (Belfiore, Giulio.) Milano, 1903.

Phil 6674.1 — Der Magnetismus in Verhältnisse zur Natur und Religion. (Ennemoser, J.) Stuttgart, 1842.

Phil 7108.388 — Der Magnetismus mit seinen mystischen Verirrungen. (Avé-Lallemant, F.C.B.) Leipzig, 1881.

Phil 6692.9 — Der Magnetismus und die allgemeine Weltsprache. (Wesermann, N.M.) Creveld, 1822.

Phil 6676.1 — Magnetismus und Hypnotismus. (Gessman, G.) Wien, 1887.

Htn — Phil 2045.95.2* — Magni philosophi Thomae Hobbes malmesburiensis vita. (Blackburne, Richard.) London, 1682.

Phil 6682.22 — Magnia, E. L'art et hypnose. Genève, 1905?

Phil 6682.1 — Magnin, P. Étude clinique et expérimentale sur l'hypnotisme. Paris, 1884.

Phil 4170.18.30 — Magnini, Carlomagno. Introduzione alla critica della scienza. Bologna, 1969.

Phil 8592.112 — Magnino, B. Illuminismo e cristianesimo. Brescia, 1960. 3v.

Phil 1712.15 — Magnino, Bianca. Alle origini della crisi contemporanea. Roma, 1946.

Phil 6122.96.2 — Magnun, Horace. The waking brain. 2. ed. Springfield, Ill., 1963.

Phil 2520.405 — Magnus, Bernd. Cartesian essays; a collection of critical studies. The Hague, 1969.

Phil 3450.19.540 — Magnus, Bernd. Heidegger's metahistory of philosophy: amor fati, being and truth. The Hague, 1970.

Phil 7069.20.240 — Magnussen, Julius. God's smile. N.Y., 1920.

Phil 8962.11 — Magoon, E.L. Proverbs for the people. Boston, 1849.

Phil 5590.17 — Magoun, F.A. Balanced personality. N.Y., 1943.

Phil 5850.264.25 — Magoun, F.A. The teaching of human relations. Boston, 1959.

Phil 8592.62 — Magre, M. Le livre des certitudes admirables. Avignon, 1941.

Phil 187.4 — Maguire, T. Lectures on philosophy. London, 1885.

Phil 293.2 — Magy, F. De la science et de la nature. Paris, 1865.

Phil 5620.3 — Magy, F. La raison et l'âme. Paris, 1877.

Phil 8177.5 — A magyar esztétikai irodolan történeto. (Mitrovics, Gyula.) Debrecen, 1928.

Phil 22.44 — Magyar filozofiai szemle. Budapest. 1+ 14v.

Phil 75.47 — Magyar nyelvu filozófiai kézirutók a Széchenyi Könyitárban. (Joó, Tibor.) Budapest, 1940.

Phil 5203.14 — Magyar pszichológiai irodalom 1945-66. (Benedek, László.) Budapest, 1967.

Phil 2520.93 — Mahaffy, J.P. Descartes. Edinburgh, 1880.

Phil 2520.93.2.5 — Mahaffy, J.P. Descartes. Edinburgh, 1884.

Phil 2520.93.3 — Mahaffy, J.P. Descartes. Philadelphia, 1881.

Phil 3494.1 — Mahaffy, J.P. Kant's critical philosophy. v.1,3. London, 1872. 2v.

Phil 7068.55.14 — Mahan, A. Modern mysteries, explained and exposed. Boston, 1885.

Phil 7054.107 — Mahan, A. Modern mysteries explained and exposed. Boston, 1855.

Phil 5252.2 — Mahan, A. System of intellectual philosophy. N.Y., 1847.

Phil 5252.2.5 — Mahan, A. System of mental philosophy. 4th ed. Chicago, 1886.

Phil 5762.7 — Mahan, Asa. Doctrine of the will. N.Y., 1846.

Phil 5052.35 — Mahan, Asa. The science of logic. N.Y., 1857.

Phil 1535.6.20 — Maher, Michael. Psychology. 6th ed. v.5. London, 1909.

Phil 5871.55 — Mahler, Margaret S. On human symbiosis and the vicissitudes of individuation. N.Y., 1969-

Phil 3552.130 — Mahnke, D. Leibniz als Gegner der Gelehrteneinseitigkeit. Stade, 1912.

Phil 3552.130.5 — Mahnke, D. Leibniz und Goethe. Erfurt, 1924.

Phil 3552.130.10 — Mahnke, D. Leibnizens Synthese von Universalmathematik und Individualmethaphysik. Halle, 1925.

Phil 525.82 — Mahnke, D. Unendliche Sphäre und Allmittelpunkt. Halle, 1937.

Phil 187.62   Mahnke, D. Der Wille zur Ewigkeit. Halle, 1917.

Phil 2520.365   Mahnke, Detlef. Des Aufbau des philosophischen Wissens nach René Descartes. München, 1967.

Phil 7084.14   Mahoney, Maria F. The meaning in dreams and dreaming. 1st ed. N.Y., 1966.

Phil 1812.9   Mahony, M.J. History of modern thought, the English, Irish and Scotch schools. N.Y., 1933.

Phil 7072.10   Mahony, Patrick. Unsought visitors; a book of visitations. v.1-2. N.Y., 1953. 2v.

Phil 4803.558.20   Mahrburg, Adam. Pisma filozoficzne. Warszawa, 1914. 2v.

Phil 5590.520   Mahrer, Alvin. New approaches to personality classification. N.Y., 1970.

Phil 1540.28   Maier, A. An der Grenze von Scholastik und Naturwissenschaft. 2. Aufl. Roma, 1952.

Phil 1517.8   Maier, A. Ausgehedes Mittelalter. Roma, 1964. 2v.

Phil 1517.7   Maier, A. Metaphysische Hintergrunde der spatscholastischen Naturphilosophie. Roma, 1955.

Phil 3625.18.30   Maier, A. Zwei Grundprobleme der scholastischen Naturphilosophie. 2. Aufl. Roma, 1951.

Phil 1712.27   Maier, Anneliese. Zwei Untersuchungen zur nachscholastischen Philosophie. 2e Aufl. Roma, 1968.

Phil 293.30   Maier, Anneliese. Zwischen Philosophie und Mechanik. Roma, 1958.

Phil 5052.28   Maier, H. Logik und Erkenntnistheorie. 2. abd. Tübingen, 1918.

Phil 5400.37   Maier, H. Psychologie des emotionalen Denkens. Tübingen, 1908.

Phil 8520.13   Maier, Heinrich. An der Grenze der Philosophie. Photoreproduction. Tübingen, 1909.

Phil 187.75   Maier, Heinrich. Philsophie der Wirklichkeit. Tübingen, 1926-1935. 3v.

Phil 3494.42   Maier, J. On Hegel's critique of Kant. N.Y., 1939.

Phil 5822.9   Maier, Norman Raymond Frederick. Principles of animal psychology. N.Y., 1935.

Phil 5822.9.2   Maier, Norman Raymond Frederick. Principles of animal psychology. N.Y., 1964.

Phil 5850.264   Maier, Norman Raymond Frederick. Psychology in industry. Boston, 1946.

Phil 5822.9.10   Maier, Norman Raymond Frederick. Studies of abnormal behavior in the rat. N.Y., 1939.

Phil 2750.20.135   Maier, Willi. Das Problem der Leiblichkeit bei Jean Paul Sartre und Maurice Merleau-Ponty. Tübingen, 1964.

Phil 5762.20   Maillant, Claude. Cultivez votre volonté. Paris, 1960.

Phil 293.10.2   Maillard, Louis. Quand la lumiére fut. Les cosmogonies anciennes...modernes. Paris, 1922-23. 2v.

Phil 6990.8.5   Maillard, Mary. An exact relation of the wonderful cure of Mary Maillard. London, 1730.

Htn   Phil 6990.8*   Maillard, Mary. A true relation of the wonderful cure of Mary Maillard. London, 1694.

Phil 293.8.2   Maillet, Benoît de. Telliamed. La Haye, 1755. 2v.
Phil 293.8.4   Maillet, Benoît de. Telliamed. La Haye, 1755. 2v.
Phil 293.8.6   Maillet, Benoît de. Telliamed. London, 1750.
Phil 293.8.8   Maillet, Benoît de. Telliamed. Urbana, 1968.
Htn   Phil 293.8.15*   Maillet, Benoît de. Telliamed. The world explained. Baltimore, 1797.

Phil 293.8   Maillet, Benoît de. Telliamed. v.1-2. Amsterdam, 1748.
Phil 5400.8   Maillet, E. De l'essence des passions. Paris, 1877.
Phil 1750.115.195   Mailov, Anatolii Il'ich. Opisanie i ob''iasnenie. Tashkent, 1969.

Phil 97.1   Maimon, S. Philosophisches Wörterbuch. Berlin, 1791.
Phil 3625.5.79   Maimon, Salomon. Autobiography. London, 1954.
Phil 3625.5.2   Maimon, Salomon. Gesammelte Werke. Hildesheim, 1965. 6v.

Phil 3625.5.78.10   Maimon, Salomon. Salomon Maimon. Boston, 1888.
Phil 3625.5.30   Maimon, Salomon. Über die Progressen der Philosophie. Bruxelles, 1969.

Phil 3625.5.34   Maimon, Salomon. Versuch einer neuen Logik, oder Theorie. Berlin, 1794.

Phil 3625.5.35   Maimon, Salomon. Versuch einer neuen Logik, oder Theorie. Berlin, 1912.

Phil 1050.12   Maimonides and Halevi. (Wolfson, Harry A.) Philadelphia, 1912.

Phil 1718.25.1   Main currents in contemporary German, British, and American philosophy. (Stegmüller, W.) Bloomington, 1970.

Phil 179.3.7.4   Main currents of modern thought. (Eucken, R.) London, 1912.

Phil 6111.67   La main et l'esprit. (Brun, J.) Paris, 1963.
Phil 187.160   The main problems of philosophy. (Maitra, Sushil.) Calcutta, 1957. 2v.

Phil 5627.27.5   Mainage, T. Introduction à la psychologie des convertis. Paris, 1913.

Phil 5627.27   Mainage, T. La psychologie de la conversion. Paris, 1915.
Phil 8592.118   Mainberger, G. Widerspruch und Zuversicht. Olten, 1967.
Phil 2805.165   Maine de Biran, critique et disciple de Pascal. (La Vallette-Monbrun, A. de.) Paris, 1914.

Phil 2730.110   Maine de Biran, homme politique. (Lassaigne, Jean.) Paris, 1958.

Phil 2730.21   Maine de Biran, Pierre. De l'existence, textes inédits. Paris, 1966.

Phil 2730.45   Maine de Biran, Pierre. Essai de restitution de l'écrit...L'apperception immédiate. Thèse. Paris, 1908.

Phil 2730.35   Maine de Biran, Pierre. Influence de l'habitude. Paris, 1803.

Phil 2730.35.3   Maine de Biran, Pierre. Influence de l'habitude sur la faculté de penser. 1e éd. Paris, 1954.

Phil 2730.35.5   Maine de Biran, Pierre. The influence of habit on the faculty of thinking. Baltimore, 1929.

Phil 2730.60.2   Maine de Biran, Pierre. Journal. Neuchâtel, 1954. 3v.

Phil 2730.60   Maine de Biran, Pierre. Journal intime. 5e éd. Paris, 1927-1931. 2v.

Phil 2730.55   Maine de Biran, Pierre. Mémoire sur la décomposition de la pensée. v.1-2. Paris, 1952.

Phil 2730.40   Maine de Biran, Pierre. Mémoire sur les perceptions obscures. Paris, 1920.

Phil 2730.50   Maine de Biran, Pierre. Nouvelles considerations sur les rapports du physique et du moral de l'homme. Paris, 1834.

Phil 2730.15   Maine de Biran, Pierre. Oeuvres. Paris, 1920-1939. 12v.

Phil 2730.11   Maine de Biran, Pierre. Oeuvres inédites. Paris, 1859. 3v.

Phil 2730.10   Maine de Biran, Pierre. Oeuvres philosophiques. Paris, 1841. 4v.

Phil 2730.30   Maine de Biran, Pierre. Science et psychologie. Paris, 1887.

Phil 2730.108   Maine de Biran, reformer. (Hallie, P.P.) Cambridge, 1959.
Phil 2730.86   Maine de Biran. (Amendola, G.) Firenze, 1911.

Phil 2730.82   Maine de Biran. (Couailhac, M.) Paris, 1905.
Phil 2730.95   Maine de Biran. (Delbos, Victor.) Paris, 1931.
Phil 2730.89   Maine de Biran. (Kühtmann, A.) Bremen, 1901.
Phil 2730.80   Maine de Biran. (Naville, E.) Paris, 1857.
Phil 2730.116   Maine de Biran. 1. éd. (Lacroze, René.) Paris, 1970.
Phil 2730.80.5   Maine de Biran. 3e éd. (Naville, E.) Paris, 1877.
Phil 2730.88   Maine de Biran und die neuere Philosophie. (Lang, Albert.) Köln, n.d.

Phil 2730.81   Maine de Biran's philosophy of will. (Truman, N.E.) N.Y., 1904.

Phil 2730.104   Maine der Biran. (Funke, Gerhard.) Bonn, 1947.
Phil 6122.54   Mainini, Carlos. Téorica del sistema nervioso. n.p., 1901.

Phil 8110.16   Mainusch, Herbert. Romantische Ästhetik. Habilitationsschrift. Bad Homburg, 1969.

Phil 2805.78   Maire, Albert. Bibliographie générale des oeuvres de Blaise Pascal. Paris, 1925-27. 5v.

Phil 2805.176   Maire, Albert. Essai sur la psychologie de Blaise Pascal. Paris, 1922.

Phil 2805.77   Maire, Albert. L'oeuvre scientifique de Blaise Pascal. Paris, 1912.

Phil 2475.1.249   Maire, Gilbert. Bergson, mon maître. 6e éd. Paris, 1935.
Phil 5465.130   Maire, Gilbert. Les instants privilégiés. Aubier, 1962.
Phil 2070.131   Maire, Gilbert. William James et le pragmatisme religieux. Paris, 1933.

Phil 6750.267.5   Maire, Luce. Les enfants de nulle part. Paris, 1967.
Phil 5240.30.2   Mairet, Philippe. A.B.C. of Adler's psychology. N.Y., 1929.

Phil 8702.36   Mairlot, Edouard. Science et foi chrétienne. Bruxelles, 1968.

Phil 7039.2.2   Mais, Charles. The surprising case of Rachel Baker who prays and preaches in her sleep. v.1-2. 2d ed. N.Y., 1814.

Phil 6312.32   Mais la terre est sacrée. (Choisy, Maryse.) Genève, 1968.
Phil 187.147   Maisels, Misha. Thought and truth. N.Y., 1956.
Phil 5400.136   Maisonneuve, Jean. Les sentiments. 4. ed. Paris, 1957.
Phil 5400.136.5   Maisonneuve, Jean. Les sentiments. 5. ed. Paris, 1960.
Phil 5592.85   Maistriaux, Robert. L'intelligence et le caractère. Paris, 1959.

Phil 1750.11.15   Maitra, S.K. The neo-romantic movement in contemporary philosophy. Thesis. Calcutta, 1922.

Phil 187.160   Maitra, Sushil. The main problems of philosophy. Calcutta, 1957. 2v.

Phil 8837.10   Maitra, Sushil Kumar. The ethics of the Hindus. Calcutta, 1925.

Phil 1523.10   Les maîtres chrétiens de nos pensées et de nos vies. (Simard, G.) Ottawa, 1937.

Phil 1750.4   Les maîtres de la pensée moderne. (Janet, P.) Paris, 1888.

Phil 1108.6   Les maîtres de vérité dans le Grèce archaique. (Detienne, Marcel.) Paris, 1967.

Phil 8884.4.17   The majesty of calmness. (Jordan, W.G.) N.Y., 1900.
Phil 9070.30   Major, Clare Tree. How to develop your will-power. N.Y., 1920.

Phil 5252.86   Major, David R. The elements of psychology. Columbus, 1913.

Phil 3494.14   Major, David R. The principle of teology. Ithaca, N.Y., 1897.

Phil 410.80   Major, John. Le traité "De l'infini" de Jean Muir. Paris, 1938.

Phil 6990.43   Major, R.H. Faiths that healed. N.Y., 1940.
Phil 575.92   Major aspects of personality. (Krout, M.H.) Chicago, 1933.

Phil 5477.5   Major forms of inhibition in man. (Skaggs, Ernest B.) Chicago, 1931.

Phil 1711.6.5   Major problems in contemporary European philosophy. (Landgrebe, Ludwig.) N.Y., 1966.

Phil 6615.6.7   The major symptoms of hysteria. 2. ed. (Janet, Pierre.) N.Y., 1920.

Phil 6615.6.8   The major symptoms of hysteria. 2. ed. (Janet, Pierre.) N.Y., 1920.

Phil 801.28.5   The major traditions of European philosophy. (Boas, George.) N.Y., 1929.

Phil 4959.245.5   Major trends in Mexican philosophy. (México (City). Universidad Nacional. Consejo Técnico de Humanidades.) Notre Dame, 1966.

Phil 978.49.295   Major writings. 1. ed. (Steiner, R.) Englewood, 1959- 6v.

Phil 8403.30   The majority report on art. (Carey, Arthur.) Newport, R.I., 1927.

Phil 310.205   Makarov, A.D. Dialekticheskii materializm. Moskva, 1960.
Phil 310.390   Makarov, Aleksei D. Istoriko-filosofskoe vvedenie v kursu dialektiki i istoricheskogo materializma. Moskva, 1961.

Phil 310.390.2   Makarov, Aleksei D. Istoriko-filosofskoe vvedenie v kursu marksistsko-leninskoi filosofii. 2. Izd. Moskva, 1967.

Phil 8980.552   Makarova, N.F. Pogovorim o zhizni i sehe. Moskva, 1961.
Phil 6816.5   Make inferiorities and superiorities work for you. (Kahn, Samuel.) Ossining, N.Y., 1954.

Phil 5850.260   Make the most of your life. (Lurton, D.E.) London, 1945.
Phil 9070.10   Make up your mind. (Wilson, M.) N.Y., 1940.
Phil 2630.11.8   Make your mind work for you. (Guitton, Jean.) N.Y., 1958.
Phil 8954.3   Maker of men. (Eddy, S.) N.Y., 1941.
Phil 9035.68.5   Makers of man, a study of human initiative. (Whitby, Charles J.) London, 1911.

Phil 130.9   Makers of the modern mind. 2nd ed. (Neill, T.P.) Milwaukee, 1958.

Phil 735.250   Makiguchi, Tsunesaburo. Philosophy of value. Tokyo, 1964.
Phil 6132.4.20   Making life better. (Worcester, Elwood.) N.Y., 1933.
Phil 8885.47   Making moral decisions. (Kattsoff, Louis Osgood.) The Hague, 1965.

Phil 9171.5   The making of a home. (Lawton, R.O.) Boston, 1914.
Phil 8886.60   The making of a man. (Lee, James W.) St. Louis, 1899.
Phil 2905.1.36   The making of a mind. (Teilhard de Chardin, Pierre.) London, 1965.

Phil 5425.88   The making of a scientist. (Roe, Anne.) N.Y., 1953.
Phil 4757.2.97   The making of man. (Walker, K.M.) London, 1963.
Phil 5242.55   The making of modern mind. (Carmichael, L.) Houston, 1956.

Phil 8591.12   Making of religion. (Lang, Albert.) London, 1898.
Phil 8591.12.2   Making of religion. 2. ed. (Lang, Albert.) London, 1900.
Phil 5850.385.19   Making our minds behave. (Walsh, W.S.) N.Y., 1935.
Phil 9362.14   Making the most of ourselves. (Wilson, Calvin D.) Chicago, 1909.

Phil 5022.5   Makovel'skii, Aleksandr O. Istoriia logiki. Moskva, 1967.
Phil 187.6.2   Makowski, J. Metaphysica. Amsterdam, 1651.
Phil 187.6   Makowski, J. Metaphysica. n.p., n.d.
Phil 978.49.350   Makrokosmos uund Mikrokosmos. (Steiner, R.) Dornach, 1962.

Phil 5241.57.10   Makten i vår själ. (Baudouin, C.) Stockholm, 1925.

Phil 9240.26 — Le mal. (Journet, Charles.) Bruges? 1961.
Phil 585.205 — Le mal de la culture. (Gabriel, Mesmin.) Port-au-Prince, 1962.
Phil 8620.21 — Mal et ses origines. (Bruyssel, Ernest van.) Paris, 1911.
Phil 5052.46 — Mała encyklopedia logiki. Wrocław, 1970.
Phil 6323.3 — Les malades dits imaginaires. (Nathan, Marcel.) Paris, 1931.
Phil 5545.22.2 — Les maladies de la mémoire. (Ribot, T.) Paris, 1881.
Phil 5545.22 — Les maladies de la mémoire. (Ribot, T.) Paris, 1881.
Phil 5545.181.5 — Les maladies de la mémoire. 3. éd. (Delay, Jean Paul Louis.) Paris, 1961.
Phil 6440.5 — Les maladies de la mémoire. 5e ed. (Delay, Jean.) Paris, 1970.
Phil 5545.65.10 — Les maladies de la mémoire et de l'imagination. (Dugas, L.) Paris, 1931.
Phil 6327.46 — Les maladies de la personnalité. (Ribot, Théodule.) Paris, 1885.
Phil 6327.46.7 — Les maladies de la personnalité. 7. éd. (Ribot, Théodule.) Paris, 1897.
Phil 8876.145 — Les maladies de la vertu. (Berge, André.) Paris, 1960.
Phil 5767.1 — Les maladies de la volonté. (Ribot, T.) Paris, 1883.
Phil 6313.6 — Les maladies de l'esprit et les asthénies. (Deschamps, Albert.) Paris, 1919.
Phil 5651.6 — Les maladies de l'orientation et de l'equilibre. (Grasset, Joseph.) Paris, 1901.
Phil 5627.201 — Les maladies du sentiment religieux. (Murisier, Ernest.) Paris, 1901.
Phil 5628.50.10 — Maladies et facultés diverses des mystiques. (Charbonnier, Nestor.) Bruxelles, 1875.
Phil 1870.90 — Malan, D.F. Het idealisme van Berkeley. Utrecht, 1905.
Phil 3850.56 — Malan, Daniel Johannes. 'n Kritiese studie van die wysbegeerte van die Stoker vanuit die standpunt van H.G. Dooye weerd. Amsterdam, 1968.
Phil 9035.26 — Malapert, P. Le caractère. Paris, 1902.
Phil 3832.6 — Malapert, P. De Spinozae politica. Thesis. Paris, 1897.
Phil 9035.26.2 — Malapert, P. Les éléments du caractère. 2e éd. Paris, 1906.
Phil 187.31 — Malapert, P. Leçons de philosophie. Paris, 1907-1908. 2v.
Phil 187.31.7 — Malapert, P. Leçons de philosophie. v.1 6. ed.; v.2. 7. ed. Paris, 1916-1918. 2v.
Phil 6327.46.20 — Le malattie della personalità. (Ribot, Théodule.) Milano, 1923.
Phil 343.30 — Malcolm, N. Knowledge and certainty. Englewood Cliffs, 1963.
Phil 7082.142 — Malcolm, Norman. Dreaming. London, 1959.
Phil 5252.168 — Malcolm, Norman. Problems of mind. N.Y., 1971.
Phil 3925.16.84 — Malcolmi, Norman. Ludwig Wittgenstein. London, 1958.
Phil 2733.61.2 — Malebranche, Nicolas. Conversations chrétiennes. Paris, 1702.
Phil 2733.61.7 — Malebranche, Nicolas. Conversations chrétiennes. Paris, 1929.
Phil 2733.61 — Malebranche, Nicolas. Conversations chrêtiennes. Rotterdam, 1685.
Phil 2733.61.5 — Malebranche, Nicolas. Conversations chrétiennes dans lesquelles on justifie la vérité de la religion. Thèse. Paris, 1929.
Htn   Phil 2733.30.6* — Malebranche, Nicolas. De inquirenda veritate. Genevae, 1685.
Phil 2733.29 — Malebranche, Nicolas. De la recherche de la vérité. Paris, 1676-78. 3v.
Phil 2733.29.30 — Malebranche, Nicolas. De la recherche de la vérité. Paris, 1935. 2v.
Phil 2733.30.4 — Malebranche, Nicolas. De la recherche de la vérité. Paris, 1945. 2v.
Phil 2733.29.35 — Malebranche, Nicolas. De la recherche de la vérité. Paris, 1962. 2v.
NEDL Phil 2733.30.2 — Malebranche, Nicolas. De la recherche de la vérité. v.2. Paris, 1886.
Phil 2733.30 — Malebranche, Nicolas. De la recherche de la vérité. v.2. Paris, 1886.
Phil 2733.29.20 — Malebranche, Nicolas. De la recherche de la vérité. 2e éd. Paris, 1675. 2v.
Phil 2733.29.10 — Malebranche, Nicolas. De la recherche de la vérité. 4e éd. v.1-2. Amsterdam, 1688.
Phil 2733.29.3 — Malebranche, Nicolas. De la recherche de la vérité. 7e éd. v.1-2. Paris, 1721.
Phil 2733.36.10 — Malebranche, Nicolas. Dialogues on metaphysics and on religion. London, 1923.
Phil 2733.60 — Malebranche, Nicolas. Entretien d'un philosophe chrétien. Paris, 1708.
Phil 2733.60.5 — Malebranche, Nicolas. Entretien d'un philosophe chrétien et d'un philosophe chinois. Paris, 1936.
Phil 2733.60.7 — Malebranche, Nicolas. Entretien d'un philosophe chrétien et d'un philosophe chinois. Thèse. Marseille, 1936.
Phil 2733.36.4 — Malebranche, Nicolas. Entretiens sur la métaphysique. Paris, 1721. 2v.
Phil 2733.36 — Malebranche, Nicolas. Entretiens sur la métaphysique. Paris, 1871.
Phil 2733.36.5 — Malebranche, Nicolas. Entretiens sur la métaphysique. v.1-2. Paris, 1922.
Phil 2733.30.20 — Malebranche, Nicolas. Erforschung der Wahrheit. München, 1914.
Phil 2733.6.2 — Malebranche, Nicolas. Father Malebranche, his treatise...Search after truth. 2d ed. London, 1700.
Phil 2733.38 — Malebranche, Nicolas. Lumière et mouvement de l'esprit. Paris, 1962.
Phil 2733.64 — Malebranche, Nicolas. Malebranche et Leibniz. Thèse. Paris, 1955.
Phil 2733.41 — Malebranche, Nicolas. Méditations chrétiennes. Paris, 1928.
Htn   Phil 2733.39* — Malebranche, Nicolas. Meditations chrétiennes et métaphysiques. Lyon, 1707.
Phil 2733.40 — Malebranche, Nicolas. Méditations métaphysiques. Paris, 1841.
Phil 2733.43 — Malebranche, Nicolas. Méditations pour se disposer à l'humilité et à la pénitence. Paris, 1944.
Phil 2733.4 — Malebranche, Nicolas. Oeuvres. Paris, 1842. 2v.
Phil 2733.4.5 — Malebranche, Nicolas. Oeuvres. Paris, 1859. 2v.
Phil 2733.3 — Malebranche, Nicolas. Oeuvres. v.1-4. Paris, 1871. 2v.
Phil 2733.5 — Malebranche, Nicolas. Oeuvres complètes. Paris, 1837. 2v.
Phil 2733.5.5 — Malebranche, Nicolas. Oeuvres complètes. Paris, 1938.
Phil 2733.5.11 — Malebranche, Nicolas. Oeuvres complètes. Paris, 1970.
Phil 2733.5.10 — Malebranche, Nicolas. Oeuvres complètes. v.1-20. Paris, 1958-63. 21v.

Phil 2733.45 — Malebranche, Nicolas. Pensiere metafisici. Lanciano, 1911.
Htn   Phil 2733.66* — Malebranche, Nicolas. Reflections sur la primation physique. Paris, 1715.
Htn   Phil 2733.57* — Malebranche, Nicolas. Réponse du Père Malebranche à la troisième lettre de Mr. Arnauld. Amsterdam, 1704.
Htn   Phil 2733.31* — Malebranche, Nicolas. Search after truth. London, 1694-95. 2v.
Htn   Phil 2733.55.5* — Malebranche, Nicolas. Traité de la nature et de la grace. Amsterdam, 1680. 2 pam.
Phil 2733.67 — Malebranche, Nicolas. Traité de la nature et de la grâce. Paris, 1958. 2v.
Phil 2733.55.10 — Malebranche, Nicolas. Traité de la nature et de la grace. Rotterdam, 1712. 2 pam.
Htn   Phil 2733.65.1* — Malebranche, Nicolas. Traité de l'amour de Dieu. Lyon, 1707.
Phil 2733.65 — Malebranche, Nicolas. Traité de l'amour de Dieu. Paris, 1922.
Htn   Phil 2733.50.3* — Malebranche, Nicolas. Traité de morale. Lyon, 1697. 2v.
Htn   Phil 2733.50* — Malebranche, Nicolas. Traité de morale. pt.1-2. Rotterdam, 1684.
Htn   Phil 2733.6.1F* — Malebranche, Nicolas. Treatise...Search for truth. Oxford, 1694.
Htn   Phil 2733.50.5* — Malebranche, Nicolas. A treatise of morality. pt.1-2. London, 1699.
Phil 2733.55 — Malebranche, Nicolas. A treatise of nature and grace. London, 1695. 2 pam.
Htn   Phil 2733.56* — Malebranche, Nicolas. Trois lettres...la defense de Mr. Arnauld. Rotterdam, 1685.
Phil 2733.107 — Malebranche; sa vie, son oeuvre, avec un exposé de sa philosophie. 1e éd. (Ducassé, Pierre.) Paris, 1942.
Phil 2733.79 — Pamphlet box. Malebranche.
Phil 2733.98 — Malebranche. (Bonavino, C.) Milano, 1926.
Phil 2733.94.10 — Malebranche. (Gouhier, Henri.) Paris, 1929.
Phil 2733.106.5 — Malebranche. (Guéroult, Martial.) Paris, 1955. 3v.
Phil 2733.85 — Malebranche. (Joly, H.) Paris, 1901.
Phil 2733.86 — Malebranche. (Martin, J.) Paris, 1912.
Phil 2733.78.2 — Malebranche. (Vidgrain, Joseph.) Paris, n.d.
Phil 2733.82 — Malebranche en Zijne Bestrijders. (Cruse, P.J.) Utrecht, 1891.
Phil 2733.109 — Malebranche et la quiétisme. (Montcheuil, Y. de.) Paris, 1946.
Phil 2733.64 — Malebranche et Leibniz. Thèse. (Malebranche, Nicolas.) Paris, 1955.
Phil 2733.125 — Malebranche l'homme et l'oeuvre, 1638-1715. (Journées Malebranche, Paris, 1965.) Paris, 1967.
Phil 2733.108 — Malebranche nel terzo centenario della nascita. Milano, 1938.
Phil 2733.89 — Malebranches Lehre von der Erkenntnis in psychologischer Hinsicht. Inaug.-Diss. (Spehner, Edmund.) Borna, 1915.
Phil 8413.44 — Malecki, Herbert. Spielräume. Frankfurt, 1969.
Phil 3820.3.5 — Maledictus und Benedictus: Spinoza. (Altkirchi, Ernst.) Leipzig, 1924.
Phil 510.155 — Malenovskii, A.A. Empiriomonizm. v.1-3. S'ankt Peterburg, 1905-06.
Phil 8658.17.80 — Malevez, Léopold. Transcendence de Dieu et création des valeurs. Paris, 1958.
Phil 5279.5 — Malewski, Andrzej. Verhalten und Interaktion. Tübingen, 1967.
Phil 5252.74 — Malgand, W. De l'action à la pensée. Paris, 1935.
Phil 5252.74.5 — Malgand, W. Devant la réalité. 1. éd. Paris, 1953.
Phil 3425.257 — La malheur de la conscience dans la philosophie de Hegel. (Wahl, Jean A.) Paris, 1929.
Phil 3450.33.12 — Maliandi, Ricardo G. Wertobjektivität und Realitätserfahrung. Bonn, 1966.
Phil 4710.141 — Malinin, V.A. Osnovnye problemy kritiki idealisticheskoi istorii russkoi filosofii. Moskva, 1963.
Phil 4752.1.30 — Malinovskii, Aleksandr A. Allgemeine Organisationslehre Tektologie. Berlin, 1926-28. 2v.
Phil 4752.1.32 — Malinovskii, Aleksandr A. Filosofiia zhivogo opyta. Moskva, 1920.
Phil 4763.1.30 — Malinovskii, V.F. Izbrannye obshchestvenno-politicheskie sochineniia. Moskva, 1958.
Phil 1712.12 — Malisoff, William M. A calendar of doubts and faiths. N.Y., 1930.
Phil 960.147 — Malkani, G.R. Ajñana. London, 1933.
Phil 187.49.5 — Malkani, G.R. Metaphysics of energy. Amalner, 1920.
X Cg Phil 187.49 — Malkani, G.R. The problem of nothing. Amalner, 1918.
Phil 2050.254 — Mall, Rom Adhar. Humes Bild vom Menschen. Köln, 1963.
Phil 2050.280 — Mall, Rom Adhar. Hume's concept of man. Bombay, 1967.
Phil 2905.1.450 — Mallemann, René de. Notice sur la vie et les travaux de Pierre Teilhard de Chardin. Paris, 1962.
Phil 187.7 — Mallet, C.A. Études philosophiques. Paris, 1844. 2v.
Phil 1117.4 — Mallet, Charles. Histoire de la philosophie ionienne. Paris, 1842.
Phil 1210.6 — Mallet, Charles. Histoire de l'école de Mégare et des écoles d'Élis et d'Érétrie. Paris, 1845.
Phil 6962.23 — Mallet, Raymond. La démence. Paris, 1935.
Phil 187.143.5 — Mallik, B.K. The real and the negative. London, 1940.
Phil 187.143 — Mallik, B.K. Related multiplicity. Oxford, 1952.
Phil 4872.187.30 — Mallik, Basanta Kumar. The towering wave. London, 1953.
Phil 8887.30 — Mallock, W.H. Is life worth living? N.Y., 1879.
Phil 8702.7.5 — Mallock, W.H. The reconstruction of belief. London, 1905.
Phil 8702.7.7 — Mallock, W.H. The reconstruction of religious belief. N.Y., 1905.
Phil 8702.7.2 — Mallock, W.H. Religion as a credible doctrine. N.Y., 1903.
Phil 8667.10 — Mallock, William H. Atheism and the value of life. London, 1884.
Phil 293.24 — Mally, E. Erlebnis und Wirklichkeit. Leipzig, 1935.
Phil 5052.38 — Mally, Ernst. Gegenstandstheoretische Grundlagen der Logik und Logistik. Leipzig, 1912.
Phil 5762.15 — Mally, Ernst. Grundgesetze des Sollens. Graz, 1926.
Phil 5052.38.5 — Mally, Ernst. Logische Schriften. Dordrecht, 1971.
Phil 4972.5.50 — Malmurca Sánchez, Ernesto. Para una posición argentina. La Plata, 1940.
Phil 8413.34 — Malraux, Q. The voices of silence. Garden City, 1935.
Phil 5873.2 — Malrieu, Philippe. Les émotions et la personnalité de l'enfant. Thèse. Paris, 1952.
Phil 5873.2.2 — Malrieu, Philippe. Les émotions et la personnalité de l'enfant. 2. éd. Paris, 1967.
Phil 187.41 — Malter, Mrs. M.P. The world process. Fresno, Cal., 1914.
Phil 187.104 — Maltese, F. Il problema morale. Vittoria, 1896.
Phil 310.150 — Mal'tsev, V.I. Bor'ba v SSSR protiv mekhanitsizma. Moskva, 1959.

Phil 310.151   Mal'tsev, V.I. Marksistskaia dialektika i sovremennyi mekhanitsizm. Moskva, 1962.

Phil 310.100   Mal'tsev, V.I. Problemy dialekticheskoi logikii. Moskva, 1959.

Phil 2805.191   Malvy, A. Pascal et le problème de la croyance. Paris, 1923.

Phil 3640.179   Malwida vom Meysenburg und Friedrich Nietzsche. (Binder, Elsa.) Berlin, 1917.

Phil 8413.39   Malygin, Vladimir A. O vozvyshennom v mire estetiki. Leningrad, 1966.

Phil 6962.30   Malzberg, Benjamin. Migration and mental disease. N.Y., 1956.

Phil 343.56   Mamardashvili, M.K. Formy i soderzhanie mephleniia. Moskva, 1968.

Phil 4795.8   Mamedov, Sheidabek Faradzhievich. Razvitie filosofskoi mysli v Azerbaidzhane. Moskva, 1965.

Phil 3850.16.92   Mamelet, A. Le relativisme philosophique chez G. Simmel. Paris, 1914.

Phil 3494.27   Mamiani, T. Della psicologia di Kant. Roma, 1877.

Phil 8637.16   Mamiani della Rovere, T. Mario Pagano, ovvero Della immortalità. Parigi, 1845.

Phil 4170.7.30   Mamiani della Rovere, Terenzio. Compendio e sintesi della propriafilosofia. Torino, 1876.

Phil 4170.7.33   Mamiani della Rovere, Terenzio. Confessioni di un metafisico. Firenze, 1865. 2v.

Phil 4170.7.43   Mamiani della Rovere, Terenzio. Critica delle rivelazioni. Roma, 1873.

Phil 4170.7.40   Mamiani della Rovere, Terenzio. Della religione positiva e perpetua. Milano, 1880.

Phil 4170.7.35   Mamiani della Rovere, Terenzio. Dell'ontologia e del metodo. Parigi, 1841.

Phil 4170.7.36   Mamiani della Rovere, Terenzio. Dell'ontologia e del metodo. 2a ed. Firenze, 1843.

Phil 4170.7.37   Mamiani della Rovere, Terenzio. Dell'ontologia e del metodo. 2a ed. Firenze, 1848.

Phil 4170.7.46   Mamiani della Rovere, Terenzio. Dialoghi di scienza prima. Parigi, 1846.

Phil 4170.7.50   Mamiani della Rovere, Terenzio. Discorso proemiale letto li 10 nov. 1850. Genova, 1850.

Phil 4170.7.60   Mamiani della Rovere, Terenzio. Le meditazioni cartesiane rinnovate nel seccolo XIX. Firenze, 1869.

Phil 4170.7.52   Mamiani della Rovere, Terenzio. Nuovo discorso proemiale. Genova, 1852.

Phil 4170.7.48   Mamiani della Rovere, Terenzio. Lo Spedalieri. Roma, 1894.

Phil 4012.1   Mamiani di Rovere, T. Del rinnovamento della filosofia antica italiana. Milano, 1836.

Phil 4012.1.3   Mamiani di Rovere, T. Del rinnovamento della filosofia antica italiana. Parigi, 1834.

Phil 4012.1.4   Mamiani di Rovere, T. Del rinnovamento della filosofia antica italiana. 3. ed. Firenze, 1836.

Phil 4012.1.5   Mamiani di Rovere, T. Sei lettere...intorno al libro filosofia antica italiana. Parigi, 1838.

Phil 4012.1.7   Mamiani di Rovere, T. Sei lettere...intorno al libro filosofia antica italiana. 2. ed. Firenze, 1842.

Phil 4170.7.93   Mamini, C. Diagnosi comparativa della filosofia di Rosmini e di Mamiani. Bologna, 1860.

Phil 5535.3   Mammalian learning and behavior. (Smith, David D.) Philadelphia, 1965.

Phil 585.171   Man, as the ontological mean. (Endres, Josef.) N.Y., 1965.

Phil 4980.3   Man; his life, his education, his happiness. (Silva Mello, Antonio da.) N.Y., 1956.

Phil 187.122   Man, mind and psychology. (MacTaggart, M.) London, 1940.

Phil 5245.45.6   Man, morals and society. (Flügel, John Carl.) Harmondsworth, 1962.

Phil 5245.45.2   Man, morals and society. (Flügel, John Carl.) London, 1945.

Phil 5245.45.5   Man, morals and society. (Flügel, John Carl.) N.Y., 1955.

Phil 3790.15.30   Man, mutable and immutable. (Riezler, K.) Chicago, 1950.

Phil 2175.4.35   Man, nature and God. (Northrop, F.S.C.) N.Y., 1962.

Phil 176.149   Man, the problem-solver. (Benjamin, Harold.) Boston, 1930.

Phil 9341.5   A man. (Bell, J.D.) Philadelphia, 1860.

Phil 5246.68   Man: divine or social. (Guirdham, Arthur.) London, 1960.

Phil 487.5.10   Man: mind or matter? (Mayer, Charles L.) Boston, 1951.

Phil 585.55   Man: the bridge. (Winkler, Franz E.) N.Y., 1960.

Phil 6121.36   Man: the known and unknown. (Langdon-Davies, I.) London, 1960.

Phil 8584.11.2   Man. What? Whence? Whither? 2. ed. (Evans, Robert C.T.) Chatham, 1923.

Phil 585.394   Man: who-whence; a layman's attempt at a logical synthesis. (Larson, Victor E.) N.Y., 1967.

Phil 177.55   Man - God's masterpiece. (Crowell, Frank.) N.Y., 1916.

Phil 270.7.2   Man a creative first cause. (Hazard, R.G.) Boston, 1883.

Phil 270.7   Man a creative first cause. (Hazard, R.G.) Boston, 1883.

Htn   Phil 270.7.3*   Man a creative first cause. (Hazard, R.G.) Boston, 1883.

Phil 2705.37   Man a machine. (La Mettrie, Julien Offray de.) Chicago, 1927.

Phil 2705.31   Man a machine. v.1-2. (La Mettrie, Julien Offray de.) London, 1752.

Phil 8637.5   Man a soul. (Muzzey, A.B.) Boston, 1842.

Phil 7150.31   Man against himself. (Menninger, Karl Augustus.) N.Y., 1938.

Phil 585.151   Man against mass society. (Marcel, Gabriel.) Chicago, 1962.

Phil 5421.20.45   Man and aggression. (Montagu, Ashley.) London, 1968.

Phil 5832.4   Man and beast, here and hereafter. (Wood, J.G.) N.Y., n.d.

Phil 5809.102   Man and beast: comparative social behavior. Washington, 1971.

Phil 6112.42   Man and civilization: control of the mind. (California. University Medical Center.) N.Y., 1961.

Phil 2905.1.340   Man and cosmos. (Chauchard, Paul.) N.Y., 1965.

Phil 190.43   Man and his affairs from an engineering point of view. (Polakov, W.N.) Baltimore, 1925.

Phil 585.163   Man and his becoming. (Phenix, Philip H.) New Brunswick, N.J., 1964.

Phil 8657.8   Man and his Divine Father. (Clarke, J.C.C.) Chicago, 1900.

Phil 182.18   Man and his dwelling place. (Hinton, J.) N.Y., 1859.

Phil 5251.46   Man and his fellowmen. (Loux, Samuel.) London, 1945.

Phil 193.75   Man and his future. (Sedgwick, W.) Philadelphia, 1913.

Phil 8664.5   Man and his God. (Jernegan, P.F.) n.p., 1927.

Phil 8581.75   Man and his lifebelts. (Bell, E.T.) N.Y., 1938.

Phil 9590.24   Man and his meaning. (Milum, John P.) London, 1945.

Phil 6111.6.2   Man and his relations:...influence of the mind on the body. (Brittan, S.B.) N.Y., 1864.

Phil 6111.6   Man and his relations:...influence of the mind on the body. (Brittan, S.B.) N.Y., 1868.

Phil 8595.29   Man and his religion. (Prideaux, Sherburne P.T.) London, 1930.

Phil 6319.1.71A   Man and his symbols. (Jung, C.G.) London, 1964.

Phil 287.5   Man and his universe. (Grant Watson, E.L.) London, 1940.

Phil 292.7   Man and his universe. (Langdon-Davies, John.) N.Y., 1930.

Phil 735.263   Man and his values. (Werkmeister, William H.) Lincoln, 1967.

Phil 5259.7.30   Man and his works. (Thorndike, E.L.) Cambridge, 1943.

Phil 585.370   Man and his world; a Marxian view. (Sviták, Ivan.) N.Y., 1970.

Phil 310.620   Man and law. (Szabó, András.) Budapest, 1965.

Phil 482.6   Man and materialism. 1st ed. (Hoyle, Fred.) N.Y., 1956.

Phil 8709.20   Man and matter. (Taylor, F.S.) N.Y., 1953?

Phil 175.44   Man and metaphysics. (Adams, George P.) N.Y., 1948.

Phil 8882.73   Man and morals. (Hawkins, Denis J.B.) London, 1960.

Phil 8643.23   Man and the attainment of immortality. 2. ed. (Simpson, J.Y.) London, 1923.

Phil 178.12.25   Man and the divine order. (Dresser, H.W.) N.Y., 1903.

Phil 8627.9   Man and the spiritual world. (Chambers, A.) Philadelphia, 1900.

Phil 8600.3.5   Man and the supernatural. (Underhill, E.) London, 1927.

Phil 8600.3   Man and the supernatural. (Underhill, E.) N.Y., 1928.

Phil 178.22.25   Man and the universe. (Driesch, H.) London, 1929.

Phil 8701.4.3.5   Man and the universe. (Lodge, Oliver Joseph.) N.Y., 1920.

Phil 8701.4.3   Man and the universe. 9. ed. (Lodge, Oliver Joseph.) London, 1911.

Phil 5421.25.45   The man and the woman; psychology of human love. (Evory, John J.) N.Y., 1968.

Phil 672.190   Man and time. (Eranos-Jahrbuch.) N.Y., 1957.

Phil 672.221   Man and time. (Priestley, J.B.) London, 1964.

Phil 525.131   Man and transformation. (Eranos-Jahorbuch.) N.Y., 1964.

Phil 9357.5   Man and woman, equal but different. (Reed, James.) Boston, 1870.

Phil 22.54   Man and world. State College, Pa. 1,1968+ 3v.

Phil 8887.40   Man as a moral and accountable being. (Mudie, Robert.) London, 1840.

Phil 187.141A   Man as interpreter. 1st ed. (Mumford, L.) N.Y., 1950.

Phil 5257.27.10   Man as psychology sees him. (Robinson, E.S.) N.Y., 1934.

Phil 805.13   Man at the crossroads. (Ferrater Mora, José.) Boston, 1957.

Phil 7069.56.20   Man being revealed. 1. ed. (Davis, S.E.) N.Y., 1956.

Phil 292.7.5   Man comes of age. 1st ed. (Langdon-Davies, John.) N.Y., 1932.

Phil 8702.19.5   Man does not stand alone. (Morrison, Abraham C.) N.Y., 1946.

Phil 2750.32.35   Man faces his destiny. (Mayer, Charles Leopold.) London, 1968.

Phil 8880.48A   Man for himself. (Fromm, Erich.) N.Y., 1947.

Phil 8887.40.5   Man in his relations to society. (Mudie, Robert.) London, 1840.

Phil 8434.6   Man in the landescape. (Shepard, Paul.) N.Y., 1967.

Phil 1750.134   Man in the new humanism. Thesis. (Killeen, M.V.) Washington, D.C., 1934.

Phil 476.3.7   Man in the past, present and future. (Büchner, L.) London, 1872.

Phil 476.3.9   Man in the past, present and future. (Büchner, L.) N.Y., 1894.

Phil 6317.19.5   The man in the street and the new psychology. (Howden, R.A.) London, 1935.

Phil 6327.21.80   Man in the trap. (Baker, Elsworth.) N.Y., 1967.

Phil 288.21   Man in the universe. (Hoyle, Fred.) N.Y., 1966.

Phil 181.87.5   Man in time. (Guitton, Jean.) Notre Dame, Ind., 1966.

Phil 5841.2   Man is a sexual being. (Maxey, Wallace de Ortega.) Fresno, Calif., 1958.

Phil 7069.18.112   Man is a spirit. (Hill, John Arthur.) N.Y. 1918.

Phil 197.42.3   Man limitless. 3d. ed. (Wilson, F.B.) N.Y., 1905.

Phil 1712.26   Man-made morals. 1st ed. (Marnell, William Henry.) Garden City, N.Y., 1966.

Phil 7069.29.7   Man made perfect. (Beatty, Mabel.) Lonodon, 1929.

Phil 2050.243   The man of (almost) independent mind. (Grieve, C.M.) Edinburgh, 1962.

NEDL Phil 5425.4.9   The man of genius. (Lombroso, C.) London, 1891.

Phil 5425.15.27   The man of genius. (Türck, H.) London, 1923.

X Cg   Phil 9245.44   The man of the future. (Calder, Alexander.) London, 1872.

Phil 6128.13.10   Man on his nature. (Sherrington, C.S.) Cambridge, Eng., 1946.

Phil 6128.13.9A   Man on his nature. (Sherrington, C.S.) Cambridge, 1940.

Phil 6128.13.11   Man on his nature. (Sherrington, C.S.) N.Y., 1941.

Phil 8581.120   Man on his own. (Bloch, Ernst.) N.Y., 1970.

Phil 978.86   Man or matter. (Lehrs, Ernst.) London, 1951.

Phil 978.86.2   Man or matter. 2d ed. (Lehrs, Ernst.) London, 1958.

Phil 8587.2.5   Man primeval. (Harris, J.) Boston, 1849.

Phil 9470.4   Man responsible for his dispositions, opinions, and conduct. (Taylor, Isaac.) London, 1840.

Phil 7069.60.10   Man the immortal. (East, John.) London, 1960.

Phil 1750.361   Man the lonely. (Straelen, H. van.) Tokyo, 1952.

Phil 8592.61   Man unfit to govern man, by a citizen of London. London, 1833.

Phil 978.8.15   Man visible and invisible. (Leadbeater, C.W.) N.Y., 1903.

Phil 8887.41   A man worth while. (Meakin, J.P.) Rahway, N.J., 1913.

Phil 525.68   Manacarda, A. Verso una nuova mistica. Bologna, 1922.

Phil 7080.13   Manaceïne, M. de. Sleep, its physiology, pathology, hygiene and psychology. London, 1897.

Phil 1955.6.205   Mañach, Jorge. Dewey y el pensamiento americano. Madrid, 1959.

Phil 6965.1   Management of lunatics. (Parkman, G.) Boston, 1817-18. 2 pam.

Phil 9380.1   The management of men. (Munson, E.L.) N.Y., 1921.

Phil 6980.403   The management of mental deficiency in children. (Kugelmass, I.N.) N.Y., 1954.

Htn   Phil 8887.29*   The management of the tongue. (Montlosier, F.D. de R.) Boston, 1814.

Phil 6120.19   Managing your mind. (Kraines, S.H.) N.Y., 1943.

Phil 4363.3.95   Mañara. (Tassara y Sangian, Luz.) Sevilla, 1959.

Phil 4363.3.38   Manara Vicentelo de Leca, M. de. Discurso de la verdad dedicado á la Imperial Majestad de Dios. Zaragoza, 1967.

Phil 4363.3.35   Manara Vincentelo de Leca, M. de. Discurso de la verdad dedicado á la Imperial Majestad de Dios. Madrid, 1878.

Phil 8962.24   Manaranche, André. Y a-t-il une éthique sociale chrétienne? Paris, 1969.

Phil 2725.11.100   Manchaussat, Gaston. L'idéalisme de Lachelier. Paris, 1961.

Phil 3499.26.5   Mancherley zur Geschichte der metacritischen Invasion. (Rink, Friedrich T.) Bruxelles, 1969.

Phil 9352.13   Manchester, R.E. The Saturday letters. Cuyahoga Falls, 1937.

Phil 9352.13.5   Manchester, R.E. The Saturday letters. Cuyahoga Falls, 1938.

Phil 9070.12   Manchester, R.E. The Saturday letters. Cuyahooga Falls, 1941.

Phil 8887.65   Mancini, F.O. Riflessioni per la vita morale civile. Parma, 1706.

Phil 1200.43   Mancini, Guido. L'etica stoica da Zenone a Crisippo. Padova, 1940.

Phil 1750.560.20   Mancini, Italo. Filosofi esistenzialisti. Urbino, 1964.

Phil 5520.434   Mancini, Italo. Linguaggio e salvezza. Milano, 1964.

Phil 187.8   Mancino, S. Elementi di filosofia. Palermo, 1846. 2v.

Phil 4170.9.30   Mancino, Salvatore. Lettere inedito di S. Mancino a V. Coasin. Palermo, 1936.

Phil 9070.118   Mandelbaum, Bernard. Choose life. N.Y., 1968.

Phil 8887.85   Mandelbaum, M.H. The phenomenology of moral experience. Glencoe, Ill., 1955.

Phil 343.33   Mandelbaum, M.H. Philosophy, science, and sense perception. Baltimore, 1964.

Phil 1735.16   Mandelbaum, Maurice H. History, man, and reason; a study in nineteenth-century thought. Baltimore, 1971.

Phil 165.85   Mandelbaum, Maurice H. Philosophic problems. N.Y., 1957.

Phil 165.86   Mandelbaum, Maurice H. Philosophic problems. N.Y., 1961.

Phil 165.86.2   Mandelbaum, Maurice H. Philosophic problems. N.Y., 1966.

Phil 8030.7   Mandel'shtam, Roza S. Marksistskoe iskusstvovedenie. Moskva, 1929. Ann Arbor, 1965.

Phil 5252.75   Mander, A.E. Psychology for everyman. London, 1939.

Phil 5052.39   Mander, Alfred E. Logic for the millions. N.Y., 1947.

Phil 2128.40A   Mandeville, B. Bernard de Mandeville's Bienenfabel. Diss. Halle, 1886. 2v.

Phil 2128.60   Mandeville, B. Enquiry into the origin of honour. London, 1732.

Htn   Phil 2128.60.2*   Mandeville, B. Enquiry into the origin of honour. v.1-2. London, 1725-32.

Htn   Phil 2128.50*   Mandeville, B. La fable des abeilles. London, 1750. 2v.

Htn   Phil 2128.33.12*   Mandeville, B. Fable of the bees. Edinburgh, 1755. 2v.

Htn   Phil 2128.27*   Mandeville, B. Fable of the bees. London, 1714.

Htn   Phil 2128.28*   Mandeville, B. Fable of the bees. London, 1723.

Phil 2128.30   Mandeville, B. Fable of the bees. London, 1725.

Phil 2128.31   Mandeville, B. Fable of the bees. London, 1728-29. 2v.

Phil 2128.32   Mandeville, B. Fable of the bees. London, 1729-32. 2v.

Phil 2128.43   Mandeville, B. Fable of the bees. London, 1934.

Phil 2128.45   Mandeville, B. Fable of the bees. N.Y., 1962.

Phil 2128.41A   Mandeville, B. Fable of the bees. Oxford, 1924. 2v.

Phil 2128.33.5   Mandeville, B. Fable of the bees. Pt.II. London, 1730.

Phil 2128.29   Mandeville, B. Fable of the bees. 3rd ed. London, 1724.

Htn   Phil 2128.65*   Mandeville, B. Free thoughts on religion. London, 1720.

Phil 2128.61   Mandeville, B. A letter to Dion. Liverpool, 1954.

Htn   Phil 1870.81*   Mandeville, B. A letter to Dion Bp. Berkeley on Alciphron. London, 1732.

Phil 2128.55   Mandeville, B. Il paradosso Mandeville. Firenze, 1958.

Phil 2128.84   Mandevilles Bienenfabel. (Stammler, B.) Berlin, 1918.

Phil 5520.265   Mandler, George. The language of psychology. N.Y., 1959.

Phil 5238.202   Mandler, J.M. Thinking. N.Y., 1964.

Phil 2045.93   Mandolfo, R. Saggi per la storia della morale utilitaria. Verona, 1903-04.

Phil 4060.5.85   Mandolfo, Santo. I positivisti italiani. Anuilli, 1966.

Phil 3850.18.215   Mandrioni, Héctor Delfor. Max Scheler; un estudio sobre el concepto de espíritu en el formalismu de Max Scheler. Buenos Aires, 1965.

Phil 5643.160   Mandy-van Moerbeke, Marie Paule. Movement apparent et préparation perceptive. Louvain, 1967.

Phil 5052.43   Maneev, A.K. Predmet formal'noi logiki i dialektika. Minsk, 1964.

Phil 672.270   Maneev, Aleksei K. Preemstvennost' v razoitii kategorii prostranstva, vremeni i dvizheniia. Minsk, 1971.

Phil 1712.23   Mañero Mañero, Salvador. El humanismo. Madrid, 1963.

Phil 8876.157   Manevi limler metadu olorok anlama. (Biroud, K.) Ankara, 1960.

Phil 4210.210   Manganelli, Maria. Persona e personalità nell'antropologia di Antonio Rosmini. Milano, 1967.

Phil 8610.902.36   Mangasarian, M.M. A new catechism. 2. ed. Chicago, 1902.

Phil 5822.5   Mangold, Ernst. Hypnose und Katalepsie bei Tieren. Jena, 1914.

Phil 6049.67   Mangoldt, Ursula von. Das grosse Buch der Hand. Weilheim, 1967.

Phil 8612.40   Mangoldt, Ursula von. Der Tod als Antwort auf das Leben. München, 1957.

Phil 6049.61   Mangoldt, Ursula von. Zeichen des Schicksals im Bild der Hand. Olten, 1961.

Phil 5052.32   Manheim, Ernst. Zur Logik des Konkreten Begriffs. München, 1930.

Phil 6961.14   The manic-depressive pychosis. (Lundholm, Helge.) Durham, N.C., 1931.

Phil 1506.9   Manière d'enseigner la philosophie scolastique. (Barbedette, D.) Paris, 1936.

Phil 177.74   Das Manifest der Vernunft. 3e Aufl. (Clemens, F.) Berlin, 1875.

Phil 9230.10A   A manifest detection of the most vyle and detestable use of dice play. (Walker, Gilbert.) London, 1850.

Phil 5592.30   Manifest structure analysis. (DuMas, F.M.) Missoula, Montana, 1955.

Phil 2940.1.90   Manifestation en l'honneur de Monsieur Maurice de Wulf, 7 mars 1934. Louvain, 1934.

Phil 408.6   Le manifeste différentialiste. (Lefebvre, Henri.) Paris, 1970.

Phil 3235.20   Manifestes philosophiques; textes choisis. (Feuerbach, Ludwig.) Paris, 1960.

Phil 5475.12   Manipulation des Menschen als Schicksal und Bedrohung. (Portmann, Adolf.) Zürich, 1969.

Phil 5241.155   Mankind. (Berg, Charles.) London, 1962.

Phil 3425.746   Man'kovski, Boris S. Uchenie Gegelia o gosudarstve i sovremennost. Moskva, 1970.

Phil 4803.555.32   Mankowski, Mieczysław. Złoty dar człowieka. Wyd. 2. Kraków, 1912.

Phil 187.95   Manley, R.M. Synthetic philosophy. Cleveland, Ohio, 1931.

Phil 9560.5   Manliness in the scholar. (Storrs, R.S.) N.Y., 1883.

Phil 2115.88   Manly, G.W. Contradictions in Locke's theory of knowledge. Leipzig, 1885.

Phil 5252.151   Mann, J.H. Frontiers of psychology. N.Y., 1963.

Phil 165.372   Mann, Jesse Aloysius. Perspectives on reality; readings in metaphysics. N.Y., 1966.

Phil 5350.8   Mann, John Harvey. Changing human behavior. N.Y., 1965.

Phil 6985.10   Mann, John Harvey. Encounter; a weekend with intimate strangers. N.Y., 1970.

Phil 3640.836   Mann, Thomas. Nietzsches Philosophie im Lichte unserer Erfahrung. Berlin, 1948.

Phil 3808.174A   Mann, Thomas. Schopenhauer. Stockholm, 1938.

Phil 1200.40   Mann, W. Beitrag zur Kenntnis der Sozial- und Staats-philosophischen Anschauungen der Hauptvertreter der neueren Stoa. Inaug. Diss. Halle (Saale), 1936.

Phil 7069.19.163   Mann, Walter. The follies and frauds of spiritualism. London, 1919.

Phil 487.7   Mann, Walter. Modern materialism. London, 1921.

Phil 187.44.7   Mann, William E. A new theory of evolution. Walpole, Mass., 1923.

Phil 187.44.9   Mann, William E. A new theory of evolution. Walpole, Mass., 1924.

Phil 187.44   Mann, William E. Theories about the truth of things. Franklin, Mass., 1919.

Phil 187.44.5   Mann, William E. The truth of things. Boston, 1922.

Phil 3246.233   Der Mann der Tat; eine Fichtebiographie. (Döring, W.O.) Lübeck, 1926.

Phil 400.97   Mann und Frau im deutschen Idealismus. Inaug. Diss. (Kellner, Eva.) Berlin, 1937.

Phil 187.102   Mannarino, G. La ragion d'essere della filosofia. Catanzaro, 1931.

Phil 4582.3.32   Mannens ynglingaålder. (Hwasser, Israel.) Upsala, 1856.

Phil 5520.260   Mannerisms of speech and gestures in everyday life. (Feldman, Sandor S.) N.Y., 1959.

Phil 8894.8.15   Manners. 2d ed. (Toussaint, F.V.) London, 1752.

Phil 812.5   Mannheimer, A. Geschichte der Philosophie in übersichthcher Darstellung. v.1-3. Frankfurt, 1903-08.

Phil 5418.4   Mannin, Ethel Edith. Loneliness; a study of the human condition. London, 1966.

Phil 5421.25.55   Mannin, Ethel Edith. Practitioners of love: some aspects of the human phenomenon. London, 1969.

Phil 7069.67   Manning, A.G. Helping yourself with E.S.P. West Nyack, 1967.

Phil 1865.196   Manning, David John. The mind of Jeremy Bentham. London, 1968.

Phil 8685.5   Manning, J.M. Half truths and the truth. Boston, 1872.

Phil 4260.153   Manno, Ambrogio G. Lo storicismo di G.B. Vico. Napoli, 1965.

Phil 3450.19.440   Manno, Ambrogio Giacomo. Esistenza de essere in Heidegger. Napoli, 1967.

Phil 3450.19.370   Manno, Mario. Heidegger e la filosofia. Roma, 1962.

Phil 5762.14   Manno, R. Heinrich Hertz - für die Willensfreiheit? Leipzig, 1900.

Phil 5871.20   Mannoni, Maud. L'enfant arriéré et sa mère. Paris, 1964.

Phil 6315.2.465   Mannoni, O. Freud. 1st American ed. N.Y., 1971.

Phil 5520.64   Mannoury, G. Les deux pôles de l'esprit. Amsterdam, 1932.

Phil 3494.22   Manns, Richard. Die Stellung des Substanzbegriffes. Inaug. Diss. Bonn, 1887.

Phil 5222.6   Manoll, A. La psychologie expérimentale en Italie. Paris, 1938.

Phil 4369.7.5   Manrique, Gervasio. Sanz del Rio. Madrid, 1935.

Phil 2130.50   Man's conception of eternity. (Mansel, H.L.) London, 1854.

Phil 8612.64   Man's concern with death. London, 1968.

Phil 8633.1.29   Man's consciousness of immortality. (Mackenzie, W.D.) Cambridge, 1929.

Htn   Phil 665.4*   Man's dignity. (Ramesey, W.) London, 1661.

Phil 978.85   Man's eternal biography; three essays on life and death. (Poppelbaum, H.) N.Y., 1945.

Phil 2340.11.40   Man's freedom. (Weiss, Paul.) New Haven, 1950.

Phil 6120.22   Man's hidden resources. (Kent, Caron.) Melbourne, Arkansas, 1962?

Phil 8626.17   Man's immortality proved by study of his natural constitution. (Bromberg, F.G.) Mobile, Ala., 1929.

Phil 2630.6.85   Man's invincible surmise; a personal interpretation of Bovarysm. (Spring, Gerald M.) N.Y., 1968.

Phil 8655.10   Man's knowledge of God. (Armstrong, R.A.) London, 1886.

Phil 8876.34   Man's moral mature. (Bucke, R.M.) N.Y., 1879.

Htn   Phil 8624.1*   Man's mortallitie. (Overton, R.) Amsterdam, 1644-97. 7 pam.

Phil 585.156   Man's physical and spiritual nature. (Collingwood, F.J.) N.Y., 1963.

Phil 6322.26.5   Man's picture of his world. (Money-Kyrle, R.E.) London, 1961.

Phil 186.17   Man's place in nature. (Le Conte, J.) N.Y., 1878.

Phil 193.23.5   Man's place in the cosmos. (Seth Pringle-Pattison, A.) N.Y., 1897.

Phil 193.23.7   Man's place in the cosmos. 2d ed. (Seth Pringle-Pattison, A.) Edinburgh, 1902.

Phil 978.17   Man's place in the universe. London, 1902.

Phil 8708.11   Man's position in the universe. (Sedgwick, William.) London, 1902.

Phil 5421.6   Man's quest for security; a symposium. (Faulkner, Edwin Jerome.) Lincoln, 1966.

Phil 5252.95A   Man's search for himself. (May, Rollo.) N.Y., 1953.

Phil 6110.3   Man's supreme inheritance. (Alexander, F.M.) London, 1910.

Phil 6110.3.1   Man's supreme inheritance. (Alexander, F.M.) N.Y., 1918.

Phil 7069.21.60   Man's survival after death. (Tweedale, Charles L.) N.Y., 1921?

Phil 7060.151.5   Man's survival after death. 2. ed. (Tweedale, C.L.) London, 1920.

Phil 6321.2.3   Man's unconcious conflict. (Lay, Wilfrid.) N.Y., 1919.

Phil 6321.2.5   Man's unconcious conflict. (Lay, Wilfrid.) N.Y., 1921.

Phil 6117.49   Man's unconquerable mind. (Highet, G.) N.Y., 1954.

Phil 365.48   Man's unknown journey. (Bulford, S.) London, 1941.

Phil 8882.26.9   A man's value to society. (Hillis, N.D.) Edinburgh, 1901.

Phil 8662.17   Man's vision of God, and the logic of theism. (Hartshorne, Charles.) Chicago, 1941.

Phil 177.102   Man's way, a first book in philosophy. 1st ed. (Cobb, Henry V.Z.) London, 1942.

Phil 2130.40   Mansel, H.L. Letters, lectures and reviews. London, 1873.

Phil 2130.45   Mansel, H.L. The limits of religious thought. 1st American ed. Boston, 1859.

Phil 2130.45.10   Mansel, H.L. The limits of religious thought. 1st American ed. Boston, 1875.

Phil 2130.45.5   Mansel, H.L. The limits of religious thought. 3rd ed. London, 1859.

Phil 2130.50   Mansel, H.L. Man's conception of eternity. London, 1854.

Phil 2130.30   Mansel, H.L. Metaphysics. Edinburgh, 1860.

Phil 2130.31   Mansel, H.L. Metaphysics. N.Y., 1871.

Phil 2130.60   Mansel, H.L. Philosophy of the conditioned. London, 1866.

Phil 2035.84   Mansel, H.L. Philosophy of the conditioned. London, 1866.

Phil 2130.35.3   Mansel, H.L. Prolegomena logica. Boston, 1860.

Phil 2130.35   Mansel, H.L. Prolegomena logica. Oxford, 1851.

Phil 2130.35.2A   Mansel, H.L. Prolegomena logica. 2nd ed. Oxford, 1860.

Author and Title Listing

Phil 2130.33 — Mansel, H.L. Psychology; the test of moral and metaphysical philosophy. Oxford, 1855.

Phil 8592.30 — Mansel, H.L. A second letter to professor Goldwin Smith. Oxford, 1862.

Phil 2880.8.101 — Manser, Anthony Richards. Sartre: a philosophic study. London, 1966.

Phil 178.30.7 — The mansions of philosophy. (Durant, William.) Garden City, 1941.

Phil 178.30.5 — The mansions of philosophy. (Durant, William.) N.Y., 1929.

Phil 4260.165 — Manson, Richard. The theory of knowledge of Giambattista Vico. Hamden, Conn., 1969.

Phil 450.4 — Mansuy, Michel. Études sur l'imagination de la vie. Paris, 1970.

Phil 2477.15.95 — Mansuy, Michel. Gaston Bachelard et les élements. Paris, 1967.

Phil 3832.15 — Mansveld, M. Adversus anonymun theologs-politicum. Amstelaedami, 1674.

Phil 5222.10 — Manswrov, N.S. Sovremennaia curzhuazhaia psikhologiia. Moskva, 1962.

Phil 812.21 — Mantague, W. Great visions of philosophy. La Salle, Ill., 1950.

Htn Phil 7075.11.5* — Mantegazza, P. Gli amori degli uomeni. Milano, 1886.

Phil 5402.3.15 — Mantegazza, P. L'anima delle cose. Torino, 1921.

NEDL Phil 5300.1 — Mantegazza, P. Atlante della espressione del dolore. Firenze, 1876.

Phil 8413.20 — Mantegazza, P. Epikur; Physiologie des Schönen. Jena, 1891.

Phil 5402.3 — Mantegazza, P. Le estase umane. Milano, 1887. 2v.

Phil 5402.3.5 — Mantegazza, P. Fisiologia del dolore. Firenze, 1880.

Phil 5411.5.4 — Mantegazza, P. Fisiologia dell'odio. 4a ed. Milano, 1889.

Phil 6022.1.8 — Mantegazza, P. Physiognomik und Mimik. v.1-2. Leipzig, 1890.

Phil 6022.1.7.5 — Mantegazza, P. Physiognomy and expression. 3rd ed. London, 1904.

Phil 5411.5.10 — Mantegazza, P. Die Physiologie des Hasses. Jena, 1889.

Phil 5402.3.10 — Mantegazza, P. Physiologie du plaisir. Paris, 1886.

Phil 6022.1 — Mantegazza, P. La physionomie. Paris, 1885.

Phil 7076.14 — Mantegazza, Paolo. Die Ekstasen des Menschen. Jena, 1888.

Phil 5252.73 — Mantell, U. Aktualgenetische Untersuchungen an Situationsdarstellungen. Inaug. Diss. München, 1936.

Phil 8637.23 — Manthey, Franz. Das Problem der Erlösung in den Religionen der Menschheit. Hildesheim, 1964.

Phil 3640.470 — Manthey-Zorn, Otto. Dionysus. Amherst, 1956.

Phil 5222.2 — Mantorani, Giuseppe. Psicologia fisiologica. 2. ed. Milano, 1905.

Phil 196.27.5 — Manual de filosofía. (Vasconcelos, J.) Mexico, 1940.

Phil 178.81 — Manual de filosofíe. (Delavigne, A.) Bucuresti, 1846.

Phil 806.38 — Manual de historia de la filosofía. 3. ed. (Gonzalez Alvarez, Angel.) Madrid, 1964.

Phil 186.101 — Manual de introducción a la filosofía de acuerdo. 2. ed. Facs. 1-8. (Lasaga y Travieso, J.I.) La Habana, 1944-1946.

Phil 6945.5 — A manual for attendants in hospitals for the insane. (Curwen, J.) Philadelphia, 1851.

Phil 960.29 — A manual of Buddhist philosophy. (McGovern, W.M.) London, 1923.

Phil 6048.85.1 — A manual of cheirosophy. 10th ed. (Heron-Allen, Edward.) London, 1885.

Phil 6360.10 — Manual of child psychopathology. N.Y., 1972.

Phil 5040.6.2 — Manual of elementary logic. (Atwater, L.H.) Philadelphia, 1867.

Phil 5040.6 — Manual of elementary logic. (Atwater, L.H.) Philadelphia, 1867.

Phil 5251.7.5 — Manual of empirical psychology. (Lindner, G.A.) Boston, 1889.

Phil 8887.1.3 — A manual of ethics. 3rd ed. (Mackenzie, J.S.) London, 1897.

Phil 8887.59 — A manual of ethics. 4. ed. (Mackenzie, J.S.) London, 1910.

Phil 8887.1.4 — A manual of ethics. 4th ed. (Mackenzie, J.S.) N.Y., 1901.

Phil 8887.1.15 — A manual of ethics. 6th ed. (Mackenzie, J.S.) London, 1948.

Phil 6956.15 — A manual of first aid for mental health. (Green, Sidney L.) N.Y., 1955.

Phil 8827.7 — A manual of Hindu ethics. 3rd ed. (Chandavarkar, G.A.) Poona, 1925.

Phil 5246.44 — A manual of human culture. (Garvey, M.A.) London, 1866.

Phil 5059.11 — A manual of logic. (Turrell, H.J.) London, 1870.

Phil 5262.13 — Manual of mental and physical tests. (Whipple, G.M.) Baltimore, 1910.

Phil 5262.13.2 — Manual of mental and physical tests. Pt. 1-2. (Whipple, G.M.) Baltimore, 1914-15. 2v.

Phil 5925.6 — A manual of mental science for teachers and students. (Fowler, J.A.) London, 1897.

Phil 1517.3 — A manual of modern scholastic philosophy. 2nd ed. (Mercier, Désiré.) London, 1917. 2v.

Phil 1517.3.5 — A manual of modern scholastic philosophy. 3rd ed. (Mercier, Désiré.) London, 1928. 2v.

Phil 8880.8 — A manual of moral philosophy. (Fleming, W.) London, 1867.

Phil 8880.8.2 — A manual of moral philosophy. (Fleming, W.) London, 1870.

Phil 8890.9 — A manual of moral philosophy. (Peabody, A.P.) N.Y., 1873.

NEDL Phil 8882.1 — A manual of morals. (Hall, A.) Andover, 1848.

Phil 8882.1.2 — A manual of morals. (Hall, A.) Boston, 1850.

Phil 5926.1.10 — Manual of phrenology...system of Dr. Gall. Philadelphia, 1835.

Phil 9450.1 — Manual of political ethics. (Lieber, F.) Boston, 1838-39. 2v.

Phil 9450.1.2 — Manual of political ethics. (Lieber, F.) Boston, 1839. 2v.

Phil 6967.11.15 — Manual of psychiatry. 3. ed. (Rogues de Fursac, J.) N.Y., 1913.

Phil 5258.27.2 — A manual of psychology. (Stout, G.F.) N.Y., 1899.

Phil 5258.27 — A manual of psychology. v.1-2. (Stout, G.F.) London, 1898-99.

Phil 5258.27.1 — A manual of psychology. 2d ed. (Stout, G.F.) London, 1901.

Phil 5258.27.9 — A manual of psychology. 3. ed. (Stout, G.F.) London, 1913.

Phil 5258.27.10 — A manual of psychology. 4th ed. (Stout, G.F.) London, 1929.

Phil 7059.6 — Manual of psychometry. (Buchanan, J.R.) Boston, 1885.

VPhil 5203.26 — Manual of reference sources in psychology. (Ostvold, Harald.) St. Louis? 1949.

Phil 819.1.13A — Manual of the history of philosophy. (Tennemann, W.G.) London, 1852.

Phil 819.1.12 — Manual of the history of philosophy. (Tennemann, W.G.) Oxford, 1832.

Phil 6967.12 — Manual of the nervous diseases. (Romberg, M.H.) London, 1853. 2v.

Phil 5245.2.2 — A manual of the physiology of mind. (Fearn, J.) London, 1829.

Phil 6951.4.5 — A manual psychological medicine...insanity. (Bucknill, J.C.) London, 1858.

Phil 6951.4.6 — A manual psychological medicine...insanity. (Bucknill, J.C.) London, 1879.

Phil 5649.20 — Manual skill. (Cox, John William.) Cambridge, Eng., 1934.

Phil 6111.55 — Manual skills and the measurement of handedness. (Beck, L.J.) Worcester, 1936.

Phil 5243.36.15 — Manual to accompany Fundamentals of general psychology. (Dashiell, J.F.) Boston, 1931.

Phil 187.105 — Manuale di filosofia. (Melillo, F.) Napoli, 1873.

Phil 811.6 — Manuale di storia della filosofia ad uso delle scuole. (Lamanna, E. Paolo.) Firenze, 1928. 2v.

Phil 1506.2 — Manuale philosophiae scholasticae. (Blanc, Elie.) Lugduni, 1901. 2v.

Phil 8050.68 — Manualetto d'estetica. (Zonta, Giuseppe.) Torino, 1925.

Phil 5059.8 — Manuductio ad logicam. (Trieu, A.R.P.P.D.) Oxoniae, 1662.

Htn Phil 2725.7.30* — Manuductionis ad stoicam. (Lipsius, Justus.) Antverpiae, 1604.

Phil 1200.1 — Manuductionis ad stoicam philosophiam. (Lipsius, J.) Antverpriae, 1604.

Phil 1200.1.5 — Manuductionis ad stoicam philosophiam. (Lipsius, J.) Lugduni Batavorum, 1644.

Phil 2412.12A — Manuel, F.E. The prophets of Paris. Cambridge, 1962.

Phil 6673.4.5 — Manuel de l'étudiant magnétiseur. 3e éd. (Du Potet, J. de S.) Paris, 1854.

Phil 6673.4.7 — Manuel de l'étudiant magnétiseur. 5e éd. (Du Potet, J. de S.) Paris, 1887.

Phil 801.4 — Manuel de l'histoire de la philosophie. (Bouillier, F.) Paris, 1845.

Phil 819.1.7 — Manuel de l'histoire de la philosophie. (Tennemann, W.G.) Paris, 1829. 2v.

Phil 819.1.8 — Manuel de l'historie de la philosophie. (Tennemann, W.G.) Paris, 1839. 2v.

Phil 1535.25 — Manuel de logique. (Bensa, A.M.) Paris, 1855.

Phil 2725.35.70 — Manuel de méthodologie dialectique. (Lavelle, Louis.) Paris, 1962.

Phil 8892.34 — Manuel de morale. (Renauld, J.F.) Paris, 1920.

Phil 177.72 — Manuel de philosophie. (Cuvillier, Armand.) Paris, 1927. 2v.

Phil 184.2 — Manuel de philosophie. (Jacques, A.) Paris, 1855.

Phil 184.2.2 — Manuel de philosophie. (Jacques, A.) Paris, 1857.

Phil 187.12 — Manuel de philosophie. (Matthiae, A.H.) Paris, 1837.

Phil 184.2.9 — Manuel de philosophie. 9. ed. (Jacques, A.) Paris, 1883.

Phil 1122.1 — Manuel de philosophie ancienne. (Renouvier, C.B.) Paris, 1844. 2v.

Phil 1717.1 — Manuel de philosophie moderne. (Renouvier, C.B.) Paris, 1842.

Phil 8876.12 — Manuel de philosophie morale. (Bautain, L.E.M.) Paris, 1866.

Phil 8881.9 — Manuel de philosophie morale. (Gilson, B.) Louvain, 1883.

Phil 6327.3 — Manuel de psychiatrie. (Rogues de Fursac, J.) Paris, 1917.

Phil 6967.11.6 — Manuel de psychiatrie. 6. éd. (Rogues de Fursac, J.) Paris, 1923.

Phil 5246.43.10 — Manuel de psychologie. (Guillaume, Paul.) Paris, 1944.

Phil 5259.5.16 — Manuel de psychologie. (Titchener, E.B.) Paris, 1922.

Phil 818.10.5 — Manuel d'histoire comparée de la philosophie et de la religion. (Scholten, J.H.) Paris, 1861.

Phil 2445.1.30 — Manuel du philosophe. (Azaïs, Pierre H.) Paris, 1816.

Phil 6963.7 — Manuel élémentaire de psychiatrie. (Nathan, M.) Paris, 1930.

Phil 6980.652.8 — Manuel de psychiatry. 6. ed. (Rosanoff, A.J.) N.Y., 1927.

Phil 6334.5 — A manuel of psychotherapy. (Yellowlees, H.) London, 1923.

Phil 6955.13.10 — Manuel pour l'étude des maladies du système nerveaux. (Fleury, M. de.) Paris, 1904.

Phil 5592.140 — Manuel pour l'examen psychologique de l'enfant. (Zazzo, René.) Neuchâtel, 1960.

Phil 5245.50 — Manuel pratique de psychologie experimentale. 1. éd. (Fraisse, Paul.) Paris, 1956.

Phil 805.6.2 — Manuele di storia della filosofia. (Fiorentino, F.) Torino, 1924. 2v.

Phil 5649.34 — Manuele varrdigheid; cen oriëntatie. Proefschrift. (Both, Frans Jacob.) Groningen, 1967.

Phil 6980.717.30 — The manufacture of madness. 1st ed. (Szazs, Thomas Stephen.) N.Y., 1970.

Htn Phil 4170.1.30* — Manuzio, Paolo. De gli elementi. Venetia, 1557.

Phil 6327.12.60 — The many faces of sex. (Reik, Theodor.) N.Y., 1966.

Phil 8635.12 — Many lifetimes. 1. ed. (Kelsey, Denys.) Garden City, N.Y., 1967.

Phil 7069.43.10 — Many mansions. (Dowding, H.C.T.) London, 1943.

Phil 5066.50 — Many-valued logics. (Rosser, J.B.) Amsterdam, 1952.

Phil 7055.211 — Many voices; the autobiography of a medium. (Garrett, Eileen Jeanette Lyttle.) N.Y., 1968.

Phil 720.60 — Manzana Martinez de Marañon, José. Objektivität und Wahrheit. Vitoria, 1961.

Phil 720.63 — Manzana Martinez de Marañon, José. Objektivität und Wahrheit. Vitoria, 1961.

Phil 8413.8 — Manzari, A. Principii di estetica. Napoli, 1908.

Phil 9550.14 — Manzoni, A. Del sistema che fonda la morale sull utilità. Firenze, 1925.

Phil 4372.1.105 — Manzoni, Bruno. Vives. Lugano, 1960.

Phil 3120.1.80 — Maosherr, T. J.A.E. Biedermann. Jena, 1893.

Phil 8886.14.5 — The map of life. (Lecky, W.E.H.) London,1899.

Phil 8886.14 — The map of life. (Lecky, W.E.H.) N.Y., 1899.

Phil 8886.14.2 — The map of life. (Lecky, W.E.H.) N.Y., 1901.

Phil 7069.64.30 — The map of ghost. The realm of ghost. London, 1902.

Phil 3640.170 — Maquiarelo y Nietzsche. (Rodriguez Aniceto, N.) Madrid, 1919.

Phil 286.7 — A maquina do mundo. (Faria Gersão Ventura, Augusta.) Porto, 1944.

Phil 8592.72 — Marain, L. Humanism as the next step. Boston, 1954.

Phil 4372.1.97 — Marañón, G. Luis Vives. Madrid, 1942.

Htn Phil 2750.3.30* — Marat, Jean Paul. A philosophical essay on man. v.1-2. London, 1773.

Phil 6985.15 — Marathon 16. (Shepard, Martin.) N.Y., 1970.

Phil 325.8 — Maravall, Jose Antonio. Las origenes del empirismo en el pensamiento político español del siglo XVII. Granada, 1947.

Phil 3832.18 — Marbach, G.O. Gedächtnissrede auf Benedict von Spinoza. Halle, 1831.

Phil 812.14 — Marbach, G.O. Lehrbuch des Geschichte der Philosophie. v.1-2. Leipzig, 1838-41.

Htn Phil 3801.546* — Marbach, G.O. Schelling, Hegel, Cousin und Krug. Leipzig, 1835.

Phil 5252.34   Marbe, K. Grundzüge der forensischen Psychologie. München, 1913.

Phil 187.50   Marbe, Karl. Die Gleichförmigkeit in der Welt. München, 1916-1919. 2v.

Phil 187.50.6   Pamphlet vol. Marbe, Karl. Die Schwankungen der Gesichtsempfindungen. 15 pam.

Phil 310.790   Marc, Alexandre. De la méthodologie à la dialectique. Paris, 1970.

Phil 2750.21   Marc, André. Dialectique de l'affirmation. Paris, 1952.

Phil 2750.25   Marc, André. L'être et l'esprit. Paris, 1958.

Phil 2750.30.30   Marc, André. Raison et conversion chrétienne. Paris, 1961.

Phil 4605.74.31   Marc-Wogan, Konrad. Filosofiska dis Kussioner. Stockholm, 1967.

Phil 6315.2.415   Marc-Wogan, Konrad. Freuds psykoanalys, presentation och kritik. Stockholm, 1967.

Phil 4582.4.100   Marc-Wogan, Konrad. Studier till Axel Hägerströms filosofi. Stockholm, 1968.

Phil 3494.38   Marc-Wogau, K. Untersuchungen zur Raumlehre Kants. Inaug. Diss. Lund, 1932.

Phil 5052.44.7   Marc-Wogau, Konrad. Logik, vetenskapsteori, argumentationsanalys. 2. tryckningen. Stockholm, 1969.

Phil 5052.44.2   Marc-Wogau, Konrad. Logik för nybörjare. 2. uppl. Stockholm, 1967.

Phil 187.93.10   Marcel, Gabriel. Being and having. Westminster, 1949.

Phil 2750.19.32   Marcel, Gabriel. Creative fidelity. N.Y., 1964.

Phil 2750.19.30   Marcel, Gabriel. Le declin de la sagesse. Paris, 1954.

Phil 2750.19.31   Marcel, Gabriel. The decline of wisdom. London, 1954.

Phil 1750.758   Marcel, Gabriel. La dignité humaine et ses assises existentielles. Paris, 1964.

Phil 2750.13.30   Marcel, Gabriel. Du refus à l'invocation. 11. éd. Paris, 1956.

Phil 187.93.5   Marcel, Gabriel. Être et avoir. Paris, 1935.

Phil 2750.19.39   Marcel, Gabriel. The existential background of human dignity. Cambridge, 1963.

Phil 2750.19.42   Marcel, Gabriel. Fragments philosophiques 1909-1914. Louvain, 1962.

Phil 2750.19.26   Marcel, Gabriel. L'homme problématique. Paris, 1955.

Phil 2750.19.25   Marcel, Gabriel. Les hommes contre l'humain. Paris, 1951.

Phil 187.8.5   Marcel, Gabriel. Homo viator. London, 1951.

Phil 187.8.7   Marcel, Gabriel. Homo viator. Paris, 1952.

Phil 187.93   Marcel, Gabriel. Journal métaphysique. Paris, 1927.

Phil 585.151   Marcel, Gabriel. Man against mass society. Chicago, 1962.

Phil 3120.30.185   Marcel, Gabriel. Martin Buber. L'homme et le philosophe. Bruxelles, 1968.

Phil 2750.19.20   Marcel, Gabriel. Men against humanity. London, 1952.

Phil 187.93.3   Marcel, Gabriel. Metaphysical journal. London, 1952.

Phil 2250.94   Marcel, Gabriel. La métaphysique de Royce. Paris, 1945.

Phil 2750.19.35   Marcel, Gabriel. El misterio ontologico. Tucumán, 1959.

Phil 2750.19.10   Marcel, Gabriel. Le mystère de l'être. Paris, 1951. 2v.

Phil 2750.19.5   Marcel, Gabriel. The mystery of being. Chicago, 1950-51. 2v.

Phil 2750.19   Marcel, Gabriel. The mystery of being. London, 1950. 2v.

Phil 2750.19.42.5   Marcel, Gabriel. Philosophical fragments, 1904. Notre Dame, Ind., 1965.

Phil 1750.215   Marcel, Gabriel. The philosophy of existence. London, 1948.

Phil 2750.19.37   Marcel, Gabriel. The philosophy of existentialism. 2nd ed. N.Y., 1962.

Phil 187.93.15   Marcel, Gabriel. Position et approches concrètes du mystére ontologique. Louvain, 1949.

Phil 2750.19.43   Marcel, Gabriel. Pour une sagesse tragique et son au-delà. Paris, 1968.

Phil 2250.94.5   Marcel, Gabriel. Royce's metaphysics. Chicago, 1956.

Phil 343.17   Marcel, Victor. De l'activité purement immanente. Thèse. Nancy, 1932.

Phil 2520.190   Marcel, Victor. Étendue et conscience. Thèse. Nancy, 1932.

Phil 850.26   Marcer, S.A.B. Earliest intellectual man's idea of the cosmos. London, 1957.

Phil 5401.40   March, Hans. Verfolgung und Angst in ihren leib-seelischen Auswirkungen. Stuttgart, 1960.

Phil 5252.20   March, J.L. A theory of mind. N.Y., 1908.

Phil 5627.134.30F   The march of events, Oxford, 1935. (Oxford Group.) Oxford, 1935.

Phil 8693.15   The march of life. (Dewart, E.H. (Mrs.).) Boston, 1929.

Phil 800.7   The march of philosophy. (Alpern, Henry.) N.Y., 1933.

Phil 8592.122.20   Marchal, Jean. L'étrange figure du curé Meslier, 1664-1729. Charleville, 1957.

Phil 9075.32.10   Marchal, Victor. La coscienza quale dev'essere. Torino, 1932.

Phil 5653.7   Marchand, L. Le goût. Paris, 1903.

Phil 600.29   La marche de l'humanité et les grands hommes d'après la doctrine positive. (Bombard, Émile.) Paris, 1900.

Phil 4070.6.80   Marchello, G. Felice Battaglia. Torino, 1953.

Phil 1750.590   Marchello, Giuseppe. La crisi del concetto filosofico. Milano, 1959.

Phil 187.83   Marchesini, A. L'imaginazione creatrice nella filosofia. Torino, 1905.

Phil 600.28   Marchesini, G. La crisi del positivismo...filosofico. Torino, 1898.

Phil 4170.6.30   Marchesini, G. La dottrina positiva delle idealità. Roma, 1913.

Phil 4170.6.40   Marchesini, G. Le finzioni dell'anima. Bari, 1905.

Phil 4060.1.81   Marchesini, G. Roberto Ardigo, l'uomo e l'umanista. Firenze, 1922.

Phil 187.45   Marchesini, G. Saggio sulla naturale unità del pensiero. Firenze, 1895.

Phil 4170.6.35   Marchesini, G. Il simbolismo nella conoscenza. Torino, 1901.

Phil 4060.1.82   Marchesini, G. Lo spirito evangelico di Roberto Ardigo. Bologna, 1919.

Phil 9550.12   Marchesini, G. La teoria dell'utile. Milano, 1900.

Phil 4060.1.83   Marchesini, G. La vita e il pensiero di Roberto Ardigo. Milano, 1907.

Phil 5252.32   Marchesini, Giovanni. Psicologia elementare, ad uso dei licei. pt.1-3. Firenze, 1916. 2v.

Phil 9495.160.5   Marchi, L. de. Senso e civiltà. p.2. ed. Bari, 1960.

Phil 3494.36   Marchi, Vittore. La filosofia morale di Emmanuel Kant. Roma, 1931.

Phil 9161.7   Marching manward. (Beck, Frank O.) N.Y., 1913.

Phil 5421.10.25   Marchisa, Ernestina. Ansietà e carenze affettive. Napoli, 1968.

Phil 5052.16   Marchisini, G. Logica elementare. Firenze, 1917.

Phil 187.101   Marci von Kronland, J.M. Philosophia vetus restituta. Francofurti, 1676.

Phil 3450.19.112   Marcia, Renè. Martin Heidegger und die Existenzialphilosophie. Bad Ischl, 1949.

Phil 4012.12   Marciano, Francesco. Storia della filosofia italiana. Roma, 1959.

Phil 2630.7.90   Marcireau, J. René Guenon et son oeuvre. Poitiers, 1946.

Phil 3494.17   Marck, S. Kant und Hegel. Tübingen, 1917.

Phil 1750.615   Marck, Siegfried. Die Aufhebung des Irrationalismus. Wilhelmshaven, 1958.

Phil 5022.1   Marck, Siegfried. Die Dialektik in der Philosophie der Gegenwart. v.1-2. Tübingen, 1929-31.

Phil 1730.12   Marck, Siegfried. Das Jahrhundert der Aufklärung. Leipzig, 1923.

Phil 8962.22.5   Marck, Wilhelm Henricus Marie van der. Grundzüge einer christlichen Ethik. Düsseldorf, 1967.

Phil 8962.22   Marck, Wilhelm Henricus Marie van der. Toward a Christian ethic. Westminster, 1967.

Phil 5252.70   Marconi, A. Oggetto ed uficio della psicologia. Milano, 1915.

Phil 3925.16.300   Marconi, Diego. Il mito del linguaggio scientifico. Studi su Wittgenstein. Milano, 1971.

Phil 4369.2   Marcos Coujáles, B. Miguel Sabuco. Madrid, 1923.

Phil 2750.10.110   Marcucci, Silvestro. Emile Meyerson. Torino, 1962.

Phil 3415.98   Marcus, A. Hartmann's inductive Philosophie im Chassidismus. Wien, 1888.

Phil 165.250   Marcus, Aage. Livsanskuelse gennem tiderne. København, 1955-58. 10v.

Phil 8887.58   Marcus, E. Das Gesetz der Vernunft und die ethischen Strömungen der Gegenwart. Herford, 1907.

Phil 8887.58.10   Marcus, E. Das Rätsel der Sittlichkeit und seine Lösung. München, 1932.

Phil 3494.19.35   Marcus, Ernst. Aus den Tiefen der Erkennens...Kants. München, 1925.

Phil 3494.19.40   Marcus, Ernst. Die Bewersführung in der Kritik der reinen Vernunft. Essen, 1914.

Phil 3494.19.25   Marcus, Ernst. Die exakte Aufdeckung des Fundaments der Sittlichkeit und Religion...Kant. Leipzig, 1899.

Phil 3494.19.30   Marcus, Ernst. Kants Revolutionsprinzip (Kopernikanisches Prinzip). Herford, 1902.

Phil 3494.19.5   Marcus, Ernst. Kants Weltgebäude. München, 1917.

Phil 3494.19.6   Marcus, Ernst. Kants Weltgebäude. 2. Aufl. München, 1920.

Phil 3494.19.2   Marcus, Ernst. Der kategorische Imperativ. München, 1921.

Phil 3494.19.15   Marcus, Ernst. Logik. 2. Aufl. Herford, 1911.

Phil 3494.19.10   Marcus, Ernst. Die Zeit- und Raumlehre Kants. München, 1927.

Phil 510.21   Marcus, Hugo. Die Philosophie des Monopluralismus. Berlin, 1907.

Phil 510.1.29   Marcus, S.P. Monism? London, 1907.

Phil 4605.1.80   Marcus Jacob Monrad. (Christophersen, Halfdan.) Oslo, 1959.

Phil 2490.121   Marcuse, A. Die Geschichtsphilosophie Auguste Comtes. Inaug.-Diss. Stuttgart, 1932.

Phil 6682.24   Marcuse, F.L. Hypnosis through the world. Springfield, Ill., 1964.

Phil 3425.292   Marcuse, H. Hegels Ontologie und die Grundlegung einer Theorie der Geschichtlichkeit. Frankfurt, 1932.

Phil 3425.292.5   Marcuse, H. Reason and revolution; Hegel and the use of social theory. London, 1941.

Phil 3425.292.12   Marcuse, H. Reason and revolution; Hegel and the use of social theory. 2nd ed. Boston, 1960.

Phil 3425.292.10A   Marcuse, H. Reason and revolution; Hegel and the use of social theory. 2nd ed. N.Y., 1963.

Phil 6315.2.310.5   Marcuse, Herbert. Eros and civilization; a philosophical inquiry into Freud. Boston, 1966.

Phil 6315.32   Marcuse, Herbert. Eros and civilization. Boston, 1955.

Phil 6315.2.310.3   Marcuse, Herbert. Eros and civilization. N.Y., 1962.

Phil 6315.2.310.10   Marcuse, Herbert. Eros et civilization. Paris, 1963.

Phil 2150.22.35   Marcuse, Herbert. An essay on liberation. Boston, 1969.

Phil 2150.22.42   Marcuse, Herbert. Five lectures. Boston, 1970.

Phil 2150.22.40.2   Marcuse, Herbert. Ideen zu einer kritischen Theorie der Gesellschaft. 2e Aufl. Frankfurt, 1969.

Phil 2150.22.30   Marcuse, Herbert. Kultur und Gesellschaft. Frankfurt, 1965. 2v.

Phil 2150.22.38   Marcuse, Herbert. Negations; essays in critical theory. Boston, 1968.

Phil 6322.55   Marcuse, Herbert. Psychoanalyse und Politik. Frankfurt, 1968.

Phil 3625.21   Marcuse, L. Aus den Papieren eines bejahrten Philosophie-Studenten. München, 1964.

Phil 9430.35   Marcuse, L. Pessimismus. Hamburg, 1953.

Phil 9245.58   Marcuse, L. Die Philosophie des Glücks. Zürich, 1949.

Phil 6315.2.180   Marcuse, L. Sigmund Freud. Hamburg, 1956.

Phil 1812.11A   Marcuse, Ludwig. Amerikanisches Philosophieren. Hamburg, 1959.

Phil 2150.22.100   Marcuse, vida e obra. (Doria, Francisco Antônjo.) Rio de Janeiro, 1969.

Phil 2150.22.125   Marcuse et la critique de la civilisation américaine. (Ambacher, Michel.) Paris, 1969.

Phil 9352.7.15   Marden, O.S. Architects of fate. Boston, 1895.

Phil 9352.7.17   Marden, O.S. The optimistic life. N.Y., 1907.

Phil 9352.7.3   Marden, O.S. Pushing to the front. Boston, 1895.

Phil 9352.7.7   Marden, O.S. Pushing to the front. Petersburg, N.Y., 1911.

Phil 9245.28.10   Marden, Orison S. Arbetsglädje-livsglädje. Stockholm, 1912.

Phil 6122.35   Marden, Orison S. Every man a king. N.Y., 1906.

Phil 9530.25   Marden, Orison S. He can who thinks he can. N.Y., 1908.

Phil 9245.28   Marden, Orison S. The joys of living. N.Y., 1913.

Phil 6122.34.3   Marden, Orison S. Peace, power and plenty. N.Y., 1909.

Phil 9530.25.5   Marden, Orison S. Prosperity, how to attract it. N.Y., 1922.

Phil 9530.25.10   Marden, Orison S. Success. Boston, 1897.

Phil 6122.97   Mardersptein, I.G. Otrazhenie v khudozhestvennoi literature ucheniia o fiziologii golovnogo mozga. Tashkent, 1962.

Phil 2725.2.67   Maréchal, C. La Mennais. Paris, 1925.

Phil 2725.2.89   Maréchal, C. La Mennais. Paris, 1925.

Phil 525.37   Maréchal, J. Dalla percezione sensible all'intuizione mistica. Firenze, 1913.

Phil 525.37.5   Maréchal, J. Études sur la psychologie des mystiques. v.1-2. Bruges, 1924-37.

Phil 343.8   Maréchal, J. Le point de départ de la métaphysique. v.1-5. Bruges, 1922-47. 3v.

Phil 2750.23.30   Maréchal, Joseph. A Maréchal reader. N.Y., 1970.

Phil 2750.23   Maréchal, Joseph. Mélanges Joseph Maréchal. Bruxelles, 1950. 2v.

Phil 1712.13   Maréchal, Joseph. Précis d'histoire de la philosophie moderne. Louvain, 1933.

Phil 1712.13.2　Maréchal, Joseph. Précis d'histoire de la philosophie moderne. 2e éd. Bruxelles, 1951.
Phil 8667.21　Maréchal, P.S. La fable de Christ dévoilée. Paris, 1794.
Phil 8667.52　Maréchal, Pierre. Culte et loix d'une société d'hommes sans Dieu. Paris, 1967.
Phil 2750.23.80　Maréchal e Kant. (Casula, Mario.) Roma, 1955.
Phil 2750.23.30　A Maréchal reader. (Maréchal, Joseph.) N.Y., 1970.
Phil 6990.60　Marert, Léonce. Nouvelle histoire de Lourdes. Paris, 1955.
Phil 8685.6　Maret, H.L.C. Essai sur le panthéisme. Paris, 1841.
Phil 8592.8　Maret, H.L.C. Théodicée chrétienne. Paris, 1844.
Phil 812.1　Maret, H.S.C. Philosophie et religion. Paris, 1856.
Phil 5252.37　Marett, R.R. Psychology and folk-lore. N.Y., 1920.
Phil 5252.83　Marf, Gustav. Grundriss der Psychologie. Bern, 1943.
Phil 6060.31　Margadant, S.V. Eine tiefenpsychologische Grundlage zur Klages'chen Graphologie. Amsterdam, 1938.
Phil 5238.199　Margarete Eberhardt, zum 18. August, 1961. Hamburg, 1961.
Phil 8887.121　Margenau, H. Ethics and science. Princeton, 1964.
Phil 5762.36　Margenau, Henry. Scientific indeterminism and human freedom. Latrobe, Pa., 1968.
Phil 8592.5　Margerie, A. de. Théodicée. Paris, 1865. 2v.
Phil 2885.83　Margerie, Amédée de. H. Taine. Paris, 1894.
Phil 2412.1　Margerie, M.A. Philosophie contemporaine. Paris, 1870.
Phil 7069.25.10　Margery, Harvard veritas. (Richardson, Mark Wyman.) Boston, 1925.
Phil 7069.25.9A　Margery - Harvard - Veritas; a study in psychics. (Richardson, Mark Wyman.) Boston, 1925.
Phil 7069.28.4　The Margery mediumship. (Bird, J. Malcolm.) N.Y., 1928.
Phil 7069.25.11.5　The Margery mediumship. (Crandon, Le R.G.) n.p., 1930.
Phil 7069.25.12.5　The "Margery" mediumship. N.Y., 1931.
Phil 7069.25.12.10　The "Margery" mediumship. N.Y., 1932. 2 pam.
Phil 7069.25.5A　"Margery" the medium. (Bird, J. Malcolm.) Boston, 1925.
Phil 4582.1.81　Marginalanmärkningar till Docenten Herrlins skrift "Filosofi och fackvetenskap" (Leljeqvist, E.) Göteborg, 1905.
Phil 3494.15.3　Marginalien und Register zu Kants Kritik der Erkenntnisvermögen. Pt. 1-2. (Mellin, G.S.A.) Gotha, 1900-02.
Htn　Phil 3494.15*　Marginalien und Register zu Kants Kritik der Erkenntnissvermögen. (Mellin, G.S.A.) Züllichau, 1794.
Phil 3494.15.10　Marginalien und Register zu Kants metaphysischen Anfangsgründen der Sittenlehre. Pt.1-2. (Mellin, G.S.A.) Jena, 1801[1800]
Phil 8400.29　Margolis, J. Philosophy looks at the arts. N.Y., 1962.
Phil 8413.36　Margolis, Joseph. The language of art and art criticism. Detroit, 1965.
Phil 6980.458.5　Margolis, Joseph. Psychotherapy and morality. N.Y., 1966.
Phil 8887.136　Margolis, Joseph Zalman. Values and conduct. Oxford, 1971.
Phil 9070.114　Margolius, Hans. Aphorismen zur Ethik. Heidelberg, 1957.
Phil 3120.8.96　Margolius, Hans. Die Ethic Franz Brentanos. Leipzig, 1929.
Phil 8887.69　Margolius, Hans. Grundlegung zur Ethik. Berlin, 1936.
Phil 9070.114.5　Margolius, Hans. Notes on ethics. Miami, 1947.
Phil 8887.129　Margolius, Hans. System der Ethik. Freiburg, 1967.
Phil 3494.55　Marguard, Odo. Skeptische Methode im Blick auf Kant. Freiburg, 1958.
Phil 6122.43　Marguardt, H. Der Mechanismus der Seele. Holstein, 1921.
Phil 3494.40　Marheinecke, P. De potiori vi quam ad commutandam. Erlangae, 1805.
Htn　Phil 3801.545*　Marheinecke, P. Zur Kritik der Schellingschen Offenbarungsphilosophie. Berlin, 1843.
Phil 3425.273　Marheineke, Philipp. Einleitung in die öffentlichen Vorlesungen über die Bedeutung der hegelschen Philosophie in der christlichen Theologie. Berlin, 1842.
Phil 8702.17　Maria, R. de. Religione e scienza. Palermo, 1936.
Phil 9166.4.5　Le mariage au point de vue chrétien. 2. éd. (Gasparin, A.E.) Paris, 1844.
Phil 4265.3.80　Mariano, R. Augusto Vera. Napoli, 1887.
Phil 4265.2.31　Mariano, R. Le bellezze della fede ne misteri. Milano, 1867. 3v.
Phil 4065.109　Mariano, R. Giordano Bruno: la vita e l'uomo. Roma, 1881.
Phil 4012.3　Mariano, R. La philosophie contemporaine. Paris, 1868.
Phil 2630.1.85　Marias Aguilera, J. La filosofía del Padre Gratry. 2. ed. Buenos Aires, 1948.
Phil 812.19　Marias Aguilera, J. San Anselmo y el insensato. Madrid, 1944.
Phil 585.400　Marías Aguilera, Julián. Antropología metafísica. Madrid, 1970.
Phil 4363.7.10　Marias Aguilera, Julián. Ensayos de convivencia. Buenos Aires, 1955.
Phil 4363.7.33　Marias Aguilera, Julián. Ensayos de teoria. 3. ed. Madrid, 1966.
Phil 4313.5　Marias Aguilera, Julian. La escuela de Madrid. Buenos Aires, 1959.
Phil 4313.5.10　Marias Aguilera, Julian. Filosofía actual, y Existencialismo en España. Madrid, 1955.
Phil 4363.7.25　Marías Aguilera, Julián. Historia de la filosofía. 19. ed. Madrid, 1966.
Phil 4363.7.5　Marias Aguilera, Julián. Idea de la metafísica. Buenos Aires, 1954.
Phil 4363.7.6　Marias Aguilera, Julián. Idée de la métaphysique. Toulouse, 1969.
Phil 4363.7.20　Marias Aguilera, Julián. Nuevos ensayos de filosofía. 2. ed. Madrid, 1968.
Phil 4363.7.2　Marias Aguilera, Julián. Obras. Madrid, 1958-60. 8v.
Phil 4313.5.5　Marias Aguilera, Julian. El oficio del pensamiento. Madrid, 1958.
Phil 4363.7　Marias Aguilera, Julián. Reason and life. New Haven, 1956.
Phil 4363.7.15　Marias Aguilera, Julián. El tiempo que ni vuelve ni tropieza. Barcelona, 1964.
Phil 187.139　Marias Aquilera, J. El tema del hombre. Madrid, 1943.
Phil 8592.38　Mariavé, Henry. Le philosophe suprême. v.2. Montpellier, 1925-26. 2v.
Phil 365.22　Marichal, H. Essai de philosophie évolutive. Bruxelles, 1891.
Phil 6962.14　Marie, A. La demence. Paris, 1906.
Phil 5627.123　Marie, Auguste. Mysticisme et folie. Paris, 1907.
Phil 6322.3　Marie, Auguste. Traité international de psychologie pathologique. Paris, 1910-12. 3v.
Phil 974.3.160　Marie Steiner von Sivers, Mitarbeiterin von Rudolf Steiner. (Savitch, Marie.) Dornach, 1965.
Phil 530.20.110　Marienwerder, Johannes. Vita Dorotheae Montoviensis. Graz, 1964.

Phil 2475.1.305　Marietti, A. Les formes du mouvement chez Bergson. Le Puy, 1953.
Phil 8592.26　Marillier, Léon. La liberté de conscience. Paris, 1890.
Phil 6682.9　Marin, Carmen. Endemoniada de Santiago. Valparaiso, 1857.
Phil 8612.45　Marin, Edgar. L'homme et la mort dans l'histoire. Paris, 1951.
Phil 6322.25　Marin, J. Ensayos freudianos. Santiago de Chile, 1938.
Phil 5628.50.15　Marin, Paul. Coup d'oeil sur les thaumaturges et les médiums du XIXe siècle. Paris, 1891.
Phil 187.34　Marin, V. Elementos de la filosofía del espiritu humano. Santiago, 1834.
Phil 187.34.5　Marin, V. Elementos de la filosofia del espiritu humano. 3d ed. Santiago, 1872.
Phil 293.17　Marin de Carranrais, E. de. Études sur les origines. Paris, 1876.
Phil 4473.1.30　Marinho, José. Teoria do ser e da verdade. Lisboa, 1961.
Phil 4120.149　Marini, Cesare. Grambattista Vico al cospetto del secolo XIX. Napoli, 1852.
Phil 3195.6.185　Marini, Giuliano. Dilthey e la comprensione del mondo umano. Milano, 1965.
Phil 4110.3.80　Marino, L. Gli elementi di filosofia del professore Francesco Fiorentino. Napoli, 1878.
Phil 4012.2　Mario. I nostri filosofi contemporanei; rivista. Napoli, 1862.
Phil 8637.16　Mario Pagano, ovvero Della immortalità. (Mamiani della Rovere, T.) Parigi, 1845.
Phil 7069.50.10　Marion, Frederick. In my mind's eye. 1. ed. N.Y., 1950.
Phil 8887.2　Marion, H. De la solidarité morale. Paris, 1880.
Phil 8887.2.5　Marion, H. Leçons de morale. 17. ed. Paris, 1917.
Phil 2115.134.5　Marion, Henri. J. Locke: sa vie et son oeuvre. Paris, 1878.
Phil 2115.134　Marion, Henri. J. Locke: sa vie et son oeuvre. 2e éd. Paris, 1893.
Phil 6122.9　Marique, J.M.L. Recherches expérimentales sur le mécanisme de fonctionnement des centres psychomoteurs du Cerveau. Bruxelles, 1885.
Phil 7150.95　Maris, Ronald W. Social forces in urban suicide. Homewood, 1969.
Phil 400.28.5　Marischini, G. La dottrina positiva delle idealità. Roma, 1913.
Phil 8413.33　Maritain, J. Art and scholasticism. N.Y., 1962.
Phil 5052.36　Maritain, J. An introduction to logic. London, 1937.
Phil 187.60.7　Maritain, J. An introduction to philosophy. London, 1937.
Phil 2750.11.84　Maritain, Jacques. Antimoderne. Paris, 1922.
Phil 2750.11.75　Maritain, Jacques. Approaches to God. 1st ed. N.Y., 1954.
Phil 2750.11.89　Maritain, Jacques. Art and poetry. N.Y., 1943.
Phil 2750.11.85　Maritain, Jacques. Art et scolastique. 3. éd. Paris, 1935.
Phil 2750.11.85.4　Maritain, Jacques. Art et scolastique. 4. éd. Paris, 1965.
Phil 2475.1.128　Maritain, Jacques. Bergsonian philosophy and Thomism. N.Y., 1955.
Phil 2750.11.62　Maritain, Jacques. Carnet de notes. Paris, 1965.
Phil 2750.11.20　Maritain, Jacques. Challenges and renewals. Notre Dame, 1966.
Phil 2750.11.58　Maritain, Jacques. Christianisme et démocratie. N.Y., 1943.
Phil 2750.11.58.5　Maritain, Jacques. Christianity and democracy. N.Y., 1944.
Phil 2750.11.49A　Maritain, Jacques. Confession de foi. N.Y., 1941.
Phil 2750.11.42A　Maritain, Jacques. Court traité de l'existence et de l'existent. Paris, 1947.
Phil 2750.11.45A　Maritain, Jacques. Le crépuscule de la civilisation. Montreal, 1941.
Phil 2750.11.37.5　Maritain, Jacques. De Bergson à Thomas d'Aquin. N.Y., 1944.
Phil 2750.11.37　Maritain, Jacques. De Bergson à Thomas d'Aquin. Paris, 1944.
Phil 2750.11.41　Maritain, Jacques. De la grâce et de l'humanité de Jèsus. Bruges, 1967.
Phil 2750.11.43.5　Maritain, Jacques. De la philosophie chrétienne. Paris, 1933.
Phil 2750.11.56　Maritain, Jacques. De la vie d'oraison. Paris, 1947.
Phil 2750.11.38　Maritain, Jacques. De l'Église du Christ; la personne de l'Église et son personnel. Paris, 1970.
Phil 2750.11.48.10　Maritain, Jacques. The degree of knowledge. N.Y., 1938.
Phil 2750.11.64　Maritain, Jacques. Dieu et la permission du mal. Paris, 1964.
Phil 2750.11.48.15　Maritain, Jacques. Distinguer pour unir. Paris, 1932.
Phil 2750.11.48.20　Maritain, Jacques. Distinguer pour unir. 4. éd. Paris, 1946.
Phil 2750.11.48.5　Maritain, Jacques. Distinguish to unite. London, 1959.
Phil 2750.11.48　Maritain, Jacques. Distinguish to unite. N.Y., 1959.
Phil 2750.11.72　Maritain, Jacques. The dream of Descartes. N.Y., 1944.
Phil 2750.11.61　Maritain, Jacques. The education of man. Garden City, 1962.
Phil 2750.11.59　Maritain, Jacques. Éléments de philosophie. Paris, 1921-23. 2v.
Phil 2750.11.43　Maritain, Jacques. An essay on Christian philosophy. N.Y., 1955.
Phil 2750.11.40　Maritain, Jacques. Existence and the existent. N.Y., 1948.
Phil 2750.11.67　Maritain, Jacques. Freedom in the modern world. London, 1935.
Phil 2750.11.54　Maritain, Jacques. Humanisme intégral. Paris, 1936.
Phil 2750.11.54.5　Maritain, Jacques. Integral humanism. N.Y., 1968.
Phil 2750.11.52　Maritain, Jacques. An introduction to philosophy. London, 1930.
Phil 2750.11.88　Maritain, Jacques. Liturgie et contemplation. Bruges, 1959.
Phil 2750.11.148　Maritain, Jacques. Moral philosophy. N.Y., 1964.
Phil 2750.11.55　Maritain, Jacques. Neuf leçons sur les notions premières de la philosophie morale. Paris, 1951.
Phil 2750.11.41.1　Maritain, Jacques. On the grace and humanity of Jesus. N.Y., 1969.
Phil 2750.11.79　Maritain, Jacques. On the philosophy of history. N.Y., 1957.
Phil 2750.11.83　Maritain, Jacques. On the use of philosophy. Princeton, N.J., 1961.
Phil 2750.11.44　Maritain, Jacques. Le paysan de la Garonne. Paris, 1966.
Phil 2750.11.44.2　Maritain, Jacques. The peasant of the Garonne. 1. éd. N.Y., 1968.
Phil 2750.11.47.5　Maritain, Jacques. The person and the common good. N.Y., 1947.

Phil 2750.11.47 — Maritain, Jacques. La personne et le bien commun. Paris, 1947.
Phil 2750.11.81 — Maritain, Jacques. Le philosophe dans la cité. Paris, 1960.
Phil 2475.1.125 — Maritain, Jacques. La philosophie Bergsonienne. Paris, 1914.
Phil 2475.1.126 — Maritain, Jacques. La philosophie Bergsonienne. 2. éd. Paris, 1930.
Phil 2750.11.66 — Maritain, Jacques. La philosophie de la nature. Paris, 1936.
Phil 2750.11.149 — Maritain, Jacques. La philosophie morale. Paris, 1960.
Phil 2750.11.60 — Maritain, Jacques. Pour une philosophie de l'éducation. Paris, 1959.
Phil 2750.11.53 — Maritain, Jacques. A preface to metaphysics. N.Y., 1940.
Phil 2750.11.65 — Maritain, Jacques. Quatre essais sur l'esprit dans sa condition charnelle. Paris, 1939.
Phil 2750.11.65.3 — Maritain, Jacques. Quatre essais sur l'esprit dans sa condition charnelle. Paris, 1956.
Phil 2750.11.63 — Maritain, Jacques. Questions de conscience. Paris, 1938.
Phil 2750.11.50 — Maritain, Jacques. Raison et raisons. 10. éd. Paris, 1947.
Phil 2750.11.70 — Maritain, Jacques. The range of reason. London, 1953.
Phil 2750.11.70.5 — Maritain, Jacques. The range of reason. N.Y., 1961.
Phil 2750.11.33 — Maritain, Jacques. Ransoming the time. N.Y., 1941.
Phil 2750.11.35 — Maritain, Jacques. Redeeming the time. London, 1943.
Phil 2750.11.80A — Maritain, Jacques. Reflections on America. N.Y., 1958.
Phil 2750.11.82 — Maritain, Jacques. Reflexions sur l'Amérique. Paris, 1958.
Phil 2750.11.69 — Maritain, Jacques. Reflexions sur l'intelligence et sur sa vie propre. Paris, 1931?
Phil 2750.11.87 — Maritain, Jacques. La responsibilité de l'artiste. Paris, 1961.
Phil 2750.11.86 — Maritain, Jacques. The responsibility of the artist. N.Y., 1960.
Phil 2750.11.76 — Maritain, Jacques. Scholasticism and politics. N.Y., 1940.
Phil 2750.11.57.5 — Maritain, Jacques. Science and wisdom. N.Y., 1940.
Phil 2750.11.57 — Maritain, Jacques. Science et sagesse. Paris, 1935.
Phil 2750.11.74 — Maritain, Jacques. Sept leçons sur l'être. Paris, 1934?
Phil 2750.11.68 — Maritain, Jacques. La signification de l'athéisme contemporain. Paris, 1949.
Phil 2750.11.78 — Maritain, Jacques. The social and political philosophy of Jacques Maritain. N.Y., 1955.
Phil 2750.11.51 — Maritain, Jacques. Some reflections on culture and literature. Chicago, 1933.
Phil 2750.11.140 — Maritain, Jacques. Son oeuvre philosophique. Paris, 1949?
Phil 2750.11.72.5 — Maritain, Jacques. Le songe de Descartes. Paris, 1932.
Phil 2750.11.91 — Maritain, Jacques. Le songe de Descartes. Paris, 1965.
Phil 2750.11.73 — Maritain, Jacques. Théonas. 2. éd. Paris, 1925.
Phil 2750.11.71.10 — Maritain, Jacques. Three reformers: Luther, Descartes, Rousseau. Paris, 1929?
Phil 2412.4.7 — Maritain, Jacques. Trois réformateurs; Luther, Descartes, Rousseau. Paris, 1939.
Phil 2750.11.71.5 — Maritain, Jacques. Trois réformateurs: Luther-Descartes-Rousseau. Paris, 1925. 2v.
Phil 2750.11.71A — Maritain, Jacques. Trois réformateurs: Luther-Descartes-Rousseau. Paris, 1925.
Phil 2750.11.77 — Maritain, Jacques. Truth and human fellowship. Princeton, 1957.
Phil 2750.11.45.5 — Maritain, Jacques. The twilight of civilization. N.Y., 1943.
Phil 2750.11.190 — Maritain, politica e ideologia; revolución cristiana en la Argentina. (Martinez Paz, Fernando.) Buenos Aires, 1966.
Phil 2750.11.105 — Maritain. (Podellaro, N.) Brescia, 1953.
Phil 2750.11.145 — Maritain en notre temps. (Bars, Henry.) Paris, 1959.
Phil 2750.11.120 — Maritain on the nature of man in a Christian democracy. (Michener, N.W.) Hull, 1955.
Phil 2750.11.215 — Maritain umano e metafisico. (Riccio, Franco.) Trapani, 1968.
Phil 2750.11.170 — Maritain's theory of poetic intuition. (Sullivan, S.M.) Fribourg, 1964.
Phil 3494.46 — Maritz, M. Studien zum pflichtbegriff in Kants Kritischer Ethik. Lund, 1951.
NEDL Phil 1158.15.3 — Marius the Epicurean. (Pater, Walter.) London, 1891.
Phil 1158.15.5 — Marius the Epicurean. (Pater, Walter.) London, 1893.
Phil 1158.15.7 — Marius the Epicurean. (Pater, Walter.) London, 1895.
Phil 1158.15.10 — Marius the Epicurean. (Pater, Walter.) London, 1897.
Phil 1158.15.14A — Marius the Epicurean. (Pater, Walter.) London, 1910. 2v.
Phil 1158.15.15A — Marius the Epicurean. (Pater, Walter.) N.Y., 1930. 2v.
Phil 1158.15.2 — Marius the Epicurean. 2. ed. (Pater, Walter.) London, 1885. 2v.
Phil 1158.15.12 — Marius the Epicurean. 4th ed. (Pater, Walter.) London, 1904. 2v.
Phil 1158.15.13 — Marius the Epicurean. 4th ed. (Pater, Walter.) London, 1907. 2v.
Phil 187.120 — Markakis, A. A new philosophy and the philosophical sciences. N.Y., 1940. 2v.
Phil 5465.210 — Markov, Mark E. Iskusstvo nak protsess. Moskva, 1970.
Phil 310.659.7 — Marković, Mihajlo. Dijalektička teorija značenja. 2. izd. Beograd, 1971.
VPhil 310.659 — Marković, Mihajlo. Humanizam i dijalektika. Beograd, 1967.
Phil 187.98 — Markovics, J.M. Assertiones ex universa philosophia. Pestini, 1802? 2 pam.
Phil 5401.60 — Marks, Issac M. Fears and phobias. N.Y., 1969.
Phil 5401.6 — Marks, J. Courage today and tomorrow. N.Y., 1919.
Phil 5425.43 — Marks, Jeannette. Genius and disaster. London, 1928.
Phil 7106.5 — Marks, Robert. The story of hypnotism. N.Y., 1947.
Phil 5850.386.5 — The marks of a clear mind. (Wiggam, A.E.) N.Y., 1933.
Phil 8581.113.5 — Marksist i kršćanin. (Bošnjak, Branko.) Zagreb, 1969.
Phil 310.60.5 — Marksistko-leninskaia filosofii i estestroznaniia. (Fataliev, K.M.) Moskva, 1960.
Phil 8980.581.10 — Marksistko-leninskaia filosofiia. (Moscow. Vsesoiuznyi Zaochnyi Politekhunicheskii Institut.) Moskva, 1965.
Phil 310.151 — Marksistskaia dialektika i sovremennyi mekhanitsizm. (Mal'tsev, V.I.) Moskva, 1962.
Phil 8422.18 — Marksistskaia estetika i problemy realizma. (Vaiman, Semen T.) Moskva, 1964.
Phil 8980.787.20 — Marksistskaia etika; khrestomatiia. (Russia (1917-   ). Upravlenie Prepodavaniia Obshchestvennykh Nauk.) Moskva, 1961.
Phil 310.400 — Marksistskaia filosofiia protiv idealizma i metafiziki. (Kovalgin, V.M.) Minsk, 1961.
Phil 310.7.10 — Marksistskaia filosofiia v poznavalnosti mira. (Golovakha, I.P.) Kiev, 1955.

Phil 310.540 — Marksistskaia logika kak dialektika i teoriia poznaniia. (Gabriel'ian, G.G.) Erevan, 1963.
Phil 310.13 — Marksistskii filosofskii materializm. (Danilenko, D.I.) Moskva, 1953.
Phil 310.7.5 — Marksistskii filosofskii materializm. (Vostrikov, A.V.) Moskva, 1954.
Phil 310.3.10 — Marksistsko-leninskaia dialektika. (Rozhin, V.P.) Leningrad, 1957.
Phil 8400.61 — Marksistsko-leninskaia estetika. (Ovsiannikov, Mkikhail F.) Moskva, 1966.
Phil 310.608 — Marksistsko-leninskaia filosofiia. (Kommunisticheskaia Partiia. Sovetskogo Soiuza. Zaochnaia Vysshaia Partiinaia Shkola. Katedra Marksistsko-Leninskoi Filosofii.) Moskva, 1965.
VPhil 310.608.5 — Marksistsko-leninskaia filosofiia. Moskva, 1967. 2v.
Phil 310.608.7 — Marksistsko-leninskaia filosofiia. Moskva, 1971. 2v.
Phil 310.587.2 — Marksistsko-leninskaia filosofiia. 2. Izd. Moskva, 1966.
Phil 310.587.3 — Marksistsko-leninskaia filosofiia. 3. Izd. Moskva, 1968.
Phil 310.601 — Marksistsko-leninskaia filosofiia i sotsiologiia v SSSR i evropeiskikh sotsialisticheskikh stranakh. (Akademiia Nauk SSSR. Institut Filosofii.) Moskva, 1965.
Phil 8030.7 — Marksistskoe iskusstvovedenie. Moskva, 1929. (Mandel'shtam, Roza S.) Ann Arbor, 1965.
Phil 310.210 — Marksistskoe ponimanie predmeta filosofii i pozitivizm. (Narskii, I.S.) Moskva, 1959.
Phil 310.445 — Marksizm i egzystencjalizm. (Schaff, Adam.) Warszawa, 1961.
Phil 8610.929.40 — Marksizm i religiia. (Berdiaev, N.A.) Paris, 1929.
Phil 310.626 — Marksizm-leninizm, teoreticheskaia osnova stroitel'stva kommunizma. Moskva, 1965.
Phil 3494.25 — Markull, G. Ueber Glauben und Wissen. Progr. Danzig, 1884.
Phil 8837.11 — Markum, Leo. Mrs. Grundy. N.Y., 1930.
Phil 978.49.325 — Das Markus-Evanqelium. (Steiner, R.) Dornach, 1960.
Phil 6980.458 — Marlet, J.J.C. De psychiater en zijn pratkijk. Utrecht, 1962.
Phil 8612.25 — Marminia, A. L'idée de la mort et de l'eternité. Paris, 1865.
Phil 6322.46 — Marmorston, Jessie. Psychoanalysis and the human situation. 1st ed. N.Y., 1964.
Phil 5520.720 — Marmy, Emile. La philosophie du signe. Fribourg, 1969.
Phil 1712.26 — Marnell, William Henry. Man-made morals. 1st ed. Garden City, N.Y., 1966.
Phil 5535.24 — Marnet, Otto. Soziales Lernen; das Problem der Lertheorien in der Sozialpsychologie. Zürich, 1968.
Phil 2340.1.80 — Maron, M.E. Norbert Wiener. Santa Monica, Calif., 1965.
Phil 4080.3.425 — Marone, Gherardo. Ensayo sobre el pensamiento de Benedetto Croce. Buenos Aires, 1946.
Phil 5068.70 — Maros dell'Oro, Angiolo. Il pensiero scientifico in Italia negli anni 1930-1960. Cremona, 1963.
Phil 3494.2 — Marquardt, A. Kant und Crusius. Kiel, 1885.
Phil 525.105.5 — Marquette, Jacques de. Confessions d'un mystique contemporain. Paris, 1949.
Phil 525.105 — Marquette, Jacques de. Introduction to comparative mysticism. N.Y., 1949.
Phil 4987.89.85 — Marquinez Argote, Germán. En torno a Zubiri. Madrid, 1965.
Phil 6842.2.5 — The Marquis and the Chevalier. (Cleugh, James.) London, 1951.
X Cg Phil 7075.135 — The marquis and the chevalier. (Cleugh, James.) London, 1951.
Phil 6842.2 — The marquis de Sade. (Dawes, C.R.) London, 1927.
X Cg Phil 7075.9 — Le Marquis de Sade et son temps. (Bloch, Iwan.) Berlin, 1901.
Phil 4080.3.220 — Marra, Dara. Conversazioni con Benedetto Croce su alcuni libri della sua biblioteca. Milano, 1952.
Phil 5401.9 — Marrel, P. Les phobies. Paris, 1895.
Phil 9165.5 — Marriage, its ethic and religion. (Forsyth, P.T.) London, 1912.
Phil 5440.15 — Marriage and disease. (Strahan, S.A.K.) London, 1892.
Phil 5440.2 — Marriage and heredity. (Nisbet, J.F.) London, 1889.
Phil 9495.14.2 — Marriage and the sex problem. (Foerster, F.W.) London, 1911.
Phil 9495.14 — Marriage and the sex problem. (Foerster, F.W.) N.Y., n.d.
Phil 9169.1.5 — The marriage ring. (James, J.A.) Boston, 1842?
Phil 9165.2 — The married state. (Foster, J.) Hartford, 18- .
Phil 5052.40 — Marriott, J.W.O.E.D. Some hints on arguing. London, 1948.
Phil 5251.41.95 — Marrow, Alfred Jay. The practical theorist; the life and work of Kurt Lewin. N.Y., 1969.
Phil 3120.55.82 — Marsch, Wolf. Hoffen worauf? Hamburg, 1963.
Phil 3425.625 — Marsch, Wolf Dieter. Gegenwart Christi in der Gesellschaft; eine Studie zu Hegels Dialektik. München, 1965.
Phil 6122.28 — Marschik, S. Geist und Seele. Berlin, 1906.
Htn Phil 293.11* — Marsh, E.G. An oration on the truth of the Mosaic history of the creation. Hartford, 1798.
Phil 6122.16.2 — Marsh, H.D. Diurnal course of efficiency. N.Y., 1906.
Phil 6122.16 — Marsh, H.D. Diurnal course of efficiency. N.Y., 1906.
Phil 2520.345 — Marshall, D.J. Physik und Metaphysik bei Descartes. München? 1961.
Phil 3850.27.230 — Marshall, George. An understanding of Albert Schweitzer. N.Y., 1966.
Phil 3850.27.230.5 — Marshall, George N. Schweitzer; a biography. 1st ed. Garden City, 1971.
Phil 8592.17 — Marshall, H.K. Instinct and reason. N.Y., 1898.
Phil 5374.43 — Marshall, H.R. Consciousness. London, 1909.
Phil 8887.48 — Marshall, H.R. Mind and conduct. N.Y., 1919.
Phil 5402.11 — Marshall, H.R. Pain, pleasure, and aesthetics. N.Y., 1894.
Phil 8413.11 — Marshall, Henry. Aesthetic principles. N.Y., 1895.
Phil 8413.11.5 — Marshall, Henry. The beautiful. London, 1924.
Phil 1117.1.2 — Marshall, John. Short history of Greek philosophy. London, 1891.
Phil 1117.1.3 — Marshall, John. Short history of Greek philosophy. London, 1898.
Phil 6155.8 — Marshall, William. The art of ecstasy. Don Mills, 1967.
Phil 310.587 — Marsistsko-leninskaia filosofiia; uchebnoe posobie. Moskva, 1964.
Phil 6122.21 — Marston, W.M. Essentials of mental healing. Boston, 1887.
Phil 5400.66 — Marston, W.M. Emotions of normal people. London, 1928.
Phil 5252.64 — Marston, W.M. Integrative psychology. London, 1931.
Phil 4080.32 — Martano, Giuseppe. La filosofia dell'esperienza di Cleto Carbonara. Napoli, 1965.
Phil 8413.4 — Martano, Giuseppe. La conoscenza sensibile nel razionalismo moderno. Napoli, 1960.
Phil 343.28 — Martel, K. Podstawowe zagadnienia marksistowskiej teorii poznania. Warszawa, 1961.

VPhil 3450.11.385   Martel, Karol. U podstaw fenomenologii Husserla. Warszawa, 1967.

Phil 8962.1   Martensen, H.L. Christian ethics. Edinburgh, 1873.
Phil 8962.1.5   Martensen, H.L. Christian ethics. Edinburgh, 1881. 2v.
Phil 3110.85.5   Martensen, Hans L. Jacob Böhme. Leipzig, 1882.
Phil 3110.85.10   Martensen, Hans L. Jacob Boehme. London, 1949.
Phil 3110.85   Martensen, Hans L. Jacob Böhme. Photoreproduction. London, 1885.
Phil 8413.23   Martha, C. La délicatesse dans l'art. Paris, 1884.
Phil 1350.6   Martha, Constant. Etudes morales sur l'antiquité. Paris, 1883.
Phil 1350.6.3   Martha, Constant. Etudes morales sur l'antiquité. Paris, 1896.
Phil 1350.5   Martha, Constant. Les moralistes sous l'Empire romain. Paris, 1866.
Phil 1350.5.4   Martha, Constant. Les moralistes sous l'Empire romain. 4e éd. Paris, 1881.
Phil 8685.7   Martha-Beker, F. Spiritualisme et panthéisme. Paris, 1867.
Phil 1517.4   Martigné, P. de. La scolastique et les traditions franciscaines. Paris, 1888.
Phil 8637.13   Martin, A.W. Faith in a future life. N.Y., 1916.
Phil 8887.56.5   Martin, A.W. A philosophy of life and its spiritual values. N.Y., 1923.
Phil 3640.305.10   Martin, A.W.O. von. Nietzsche und Burckhardt; zwei geistige Welten im Dialog. 3e Aufl. Basel, 1945.
Phil 5762.13   Martin, Alfred H. An experimental study of the factors and types of voluntary choice. N.Y., 1922.
Phil 8615.14.5   Martin, Alfred W. Consolations. N.Y., 1931.
Phil 8615.14   Martin, Alfred W. Deity, duty, destiny; selections from addresses. N.Y., 1916.
Phil 8615.14.15   Martin, Alfred W. What human life is for. n.p., 19- .
Phil 7069.18.132   Martin, Alfred Wilhelm. Psychic tendencies of to-day. N.Y., 1918.
Phil 3525.85   Martin, B.R. Karl Christian Friedrich Krause's Leben, Lehre und Bedeutung. Leipzig, 1885.
Htn   Phil 130.1*A   Martin, Benjamin. Biographia philosophica. London, 1764.
Phil 8592.110   Martin, C.B. Religious belief. Ithaca, N.Y., 1959.
Phil 8592.60   Martin, Cecil Percy. The decline of religion. London, 1940.
Phil 2115.215   Martin, Charles Burton. Locke and Berkeley: a collection of ciritical essays. London, 1968.
Phil 8725.12   Martin, David. The religious and the secular. London, 1969.
Phil 6945.35   Martin, Denis V. Adventure in psychiatry. Oxford, 1962.
Phil 5762.5   Martin, E. Psychologie de la volonté. Paris, 1913.
Phil 8637.22   Martin, E. Reincarnation, the ring of return. New Hyde Park, N.Y., 1963.
Phil 5252.58.2   Martin, E.D. Psychology. N.Y., 1924.
Phil 5252.58   Martin, E.D. Psychology. pt.1-20. N.Y., 1924.
Phil 5627.187   Martin, Everett D. The mystery of religion. N.Y., 1924.
Phil 187.9   Martin, F. La perception extérieure. Paris, 1894.
Phil 9450.11   Martin, Félix. La morale républicaine. Paris, 1912.
Phil 2190.10   Martin, G. Wilhelm von Ockham. Berlin, 1949.
Phil 187.156   Martin, Gottfried. Einleitung in die allgemeine Metaphysik. Köln, 1957.
Phil 3494.45   Martin, Gottfried. Immanuel Kant. Köln, 1951.
Phil 3494.45.4   Martin, Gottfried. Immanuel Kant. 4. Aufl. Berlin, 1969.
Phil 187.156.5   Martin, Gottfried. An introduction to general metaphysics. London, 1961.
Phil 3494.45.5A   Martin, Gottfried. Kant's metaphysics and theory of science. Manchester, Eng., 1955.
Phil 3552.464.5.2   Martin, Gottfried. Leibniz. Logik und Metaphysik. 2. Aufl. Berlin, 1967.
Phil 3552.464   Martin, Gottfried. Leibniz: logique et métaphysique. Paris, 1966.
Phil 3494.45.10   Martin, Gottfried. Sachindex zu Kants Kritik der reinen Vernunft. Berlin, 1967.
Phil 5625.116   Martin, Irene. The genesis of the classical conditioned response. 1. ed. Oxford, 1969.
Phil 2733.86   Martin, J. Malebranche. Paris, 1912.
Phil 8702.5   Martin, J.L. Anti-evolution: Girardeau vs. Woodrow. Memphis, Tenn.? 1888.
Phil 2050.221   Martin, John J. Shaftesbury's und Hutcheson's Verhältnis zu Hume. Inaug. Diss. Halle, 1905.
Phil 5722.6   Martin, L. Ein experimenteller Beitrag zur Erforschung. Leipzig, 1915.
Phil 10.5   Martin, L.A. Annuaire philisophique. Paris, 1-5,1864-1868 5v.
Phil 8837.2   Martin, L.A. Histoire de la morale. Paris, 1859.
Htn   Phil 5252.62.5*   Martin, L.J. Psychology of aesthetics. n.p., 1905-1907. 4 pam.
Phil 5252.62   Martin, L.J. Zur Analyse der Unterschiedsempfindlichkeit. Leipzig, 1899.
Phil 5545.62   Martin, M.A. Transfer effects of practice in cancellation tests. N.Y., 1915.
Phil 5252.40   Martin, Otto. Zur Psychologie des Verstehens wissenschaftlicher Texte. Inaug. Diss. Freiburg, 1914.
Phil 5722.35   Martin, P.W. Experiment in depth. London, 1955.
Phil 5520.413   Martin, R.M. Intension and decision. Englewood Cliffs, N.J., 1963.
Phil 5068.34   Martin, R.M. Truth and denotation. London, 1958.
Phil 5066.145   Martin, Richard M. The notion of analytic truth. Philadelphia, 1959.
Phil 5070.30   Martin, Richard Milton. Belief, existence, and meaning. N.Y., 1969.
Phil 2477.8.81   Martin, Robert. Alfred Binet. Thèse. Paris, 1924.
Phil 5190.72   Martin, Robert L. The paradox of the liar. New Haven, 1970.
Phil 5066.240   Martin, Roger. Logique contemporaine et formalisation. Paris, 1964.
Phil 812.22   Martin, S.G. A history of philosophy. N.Y., 1947.
Phil 6990.3.43   Martin, Stuart. The secret of Lourdes. London, 1926.
Phil 5252.5   Martin, T. Zetemata dianoetika. Liverpool, 1821.
Phil 293.3   Martin, T.H. Philosophie spiritualiste de la nature. Paris, 1849. 2v.
Phil 187.10   Martin, T.H. Les sciences et la philosophie. Paris, 1869.
Phil 8637.1   Martin, T.H. La vie future. Paris, 1870.
Phil 2520.120   Martin, W.A.P. The Cartesian philosophy before Descartes. Peking, 1888.
Phil 187.148   Martin, W.O. The order and integration of knowledge. Ann Arbor, 1957.
Phil 187.158   Martin, William O. Metaphysics and ideology. Milwaukee, 1959.
Phil 6022.2   Martin, William W. Our noses. London, 1893.
Phil 3120.30.200   Martin Buber; an intimate portrait. (Hodes, Aubrey.) N.Y., 1971.

Phil 3120.30.83   Martin Buber, Jewish existentialist. (Diamand, Malcolm L.) N.Y., 1960.
Phil 3120.30.135   Martin Buber, nebräischer Humanismus. (Schaeder, Grete.) Gottingen, 1966.
Phil 3120.30.71   Martin Buber, philosophe de la relation. (Buber, Martin.) Paris, 1968.
Phil 3120.30.170   Martin Buber, profeta del diálogo. (Pilosof, Nelson.) Montevideo, 1965.
Phil 3120.30.85.2   Martin Buber, sein Werk und seine Zeit. (Kohn, Hans.) Köln, 1961.
Phil 3120.30.95   Martin Buber. (Beek, Martinus Adrianus.) Baarn, 1964.
Phil 3120.30.82   Martin Buber. (Cohen, A.A.) London, 1957.
Phil 3120.30.82.1   Martin Buber. (Cohen, A.A.) N.Y., 1957.
Phil 3120.30.175   Martin Buber. (Dujoune, León.) Buenos Aires, 1966[1965]
Phil 3120.30.80   Martin Buber. (Friedman, M.S.) Chicago, 1955.
Phil 3120.30.88   Martin Buber. (Goldstein, Walter Benjamin.) Jerusalem, 1967.
Phil 3120.30.85   Martin Buber. (Kohn, Hans.) Hellerau, 1930.
Phil 3120.30.165   Martin Buber. (Levinson, Nathan P.) Frankfurt, 1966. 2v.
Phil 3120.30.145   Martin Buber. (Smith, Ronald Gregor.) Richmond, 1967.
Phil 3120.30.185   Martin Buber. L'homme et le philosophe. (Marcel, Gabriel.) Bruxelles, 1968.
Phil 3120.30.95.5   Martin Buber: personalist and prophet. (Beek, Martinus Adrianus.) Westminster, 1968.
Phil 3120.30.195   Martin Buber: sein Denken und Wirken. (Rosenblueth, Pinchas Erich.) Hannover, 1968.
Phil 3120.30.91   Martin Buber and Christianity. (Balthasar, Hans von.) London, 1961.
Phil 3120.30.190   Martin Buber in Selbstzeugnissen und Bilddokumenten. (Wehr, Gerhard.) Reinbek, 1968.
Phil 3120.30.100   Martin Buber und das dialogische Leben. (Lang, Bernhard.) Bern, 1963.
Phil 3120.30.180   Martin Buber's ontology. (Wood, Robert E.) Evanston, 1969.
Phil 8592.100   Martin-Deslias, N. L'invention divine. Paris, 1957.
Phil 2905.1.108   Martin-Deslias, Noël. Un aventurier de l'esprit, Pierre Teilhard de Chardin. Paris, 1963.
Phil 3195.2.85   Martin Deutinger. (Deutinger, Martin.) München, 1938.
Phil 3195.2.120   Martin Deutinger. (Endres, Joseph A.) Mainz, 1906.
Phil 3195.2.80   Martin Deutinger als Ethiker. (Sattel, G.) Paderborn, 1908.
Phil 3195.2.79   Martin Deutingers Gotteslehre. (Sattel, G.) Regensburg, 1905.
Phil 3195.2.95   Martin Deutinger's Leben und Schriften. (Kastner, Lorenz.) München, 1875.
Phil 3450.19.340   Martin Heidegger, 26 September 1959. Messkirch, 1959.
Phil 3450.19.365   Martin Heidegger. (Colombo, Arrigo.) Bologna, 1964.
Phil 3450.19.150   Martin Heidegger. (Grene, Marjorie.) London, 1957.
Phil 3450.19.38   Martin Heidegger. (Heidegger, Martin.) Frankfurt, 1969.
Phil 3450.19.250   Martin Heidegger. (Kockelmans, A.) Teilt, 1962.
Phil 3450.19.253   Martin Heidegger. (Kockelmans, Joseph John.) Pittsburgh, 1965.
Phil 3450.19.145   Martín Heidegger als godsdienstwijsgeer. (Raessingh, Karel Hendrik.) Assen, 1956.
Phil 3450.19.310   Martin Heidegger and the pre-Socratics. (Seidel, G.J.) Lincoln, 1964.
Phil 3450.19.470   Martin Heidegger im Gespräch. München, 1970.
Phil 3450.19.445   Martin Heidegger on being human. (Schmitt, Richard.) N.Y., 1969.
Phil 3450.19.112   Martin Heidegger und die Existenzialphilosophie. (Marcia, Renè.) Bad Ischl, 1949.
Phil 3450.19.355   Martin Heidegger und Thomas von Aquin. (Meyer, Hans.) München, 1964.
Phil 3450.19.190   Martin Heidegger zum siebzigsten Geburtstag. (Neshe, Günther.) Pfullingen, 1959.
Phil 3450.19.110   Martin Heideggers Einfluss auf die Wissenschaften aus Anlass seines Sechzig sun Geburtstages verfasst Carlos Astrada. (Heidegger, Martin.) Bern, 1949.
Phil 3850.18.185   Martin-Izquierdo, Honorio. Das religiöse Apriori bei Max Scheler. Bonn, 1964.
Phil 3549.5.90   Martin Knutzen und seine Zeit. (Erdmann, B.) Leipzig, 1876.
Phil 343.32   Martin Scheerer Memorial Meetings on Cognitive Psychology. University of Kansas, 1962. Cognition: theory, research, promise. N.Y., 1964.
Phil 2115.95   Martinak, E. Die Logik John Lockes'. Halle, 1894.
Phil 3625.11.80   Martinak, E. Meinong als Mensch und als Lehrer. Graz, 1925.
Phil 5520.6   Martinak, E. Psychologische Untersuchungen zur Bedeutungslehre. Leipzig, 1901.
Phil 2115.108   Martinak, E. Zur Logik Lockes. Graz, 1887.
Phil 2905.1.355   Martinazzo, Eusebio. Teilhard de Chardin. Romae, 1965.
Phil 2138.105   Martinazzoli, A.L. La teorica dell'individualismo secondo J.S. Mill. Milano, 1905.
Phil 8887.3   Martineau, H. How to observe. Morals and manners. London, 1838.
Phil 8887.3.3   Martineau, H. How to observe. Morals and manners. N.Y., 1838.
Phil 8887.3.2   Martineau, H. How to observe. Morals and manners. N.Y., 1838.
Phil 6682.2   Martineau, H. Letters on mesmerism. N.Y., 1845.
Phil 9500.1   Martineau, H. Life in the sick-room. Boston, 1844.
Phil 9500.1.2   Martineau, H. Life in the sick-room. 2d American ed. Boston, 1845.
Phil 187.11.2   Martineau, J. Essays. Boston, 1866. 2v.
Phil 187.11   Martineau, J. Essays. Boston, 1866-1868. 2v.
Phil 187.11.9   Martineau, J. Essays. N.Y., 1875. 2v.
Phil 487.2.2   Martineau, J. Modern materialism. Boston, 1876.
Phil 487.2   Martineau, J. Modern materialism. London, 1876.
Phil 487.2.5   Martineau, J. Religion affected by modern materialism. London, 1876-78. 2 pam.
Phil 487.2.6   Martineau, J. Religion affected by modern materialism. N.Y., 1875.
Phil 3832.1A   Martineau, J. A study of Spinoza. London, 1882.
Phil 8887.4.13   Martineau, J. Tides of the spirit. Boston, 1905.
Phil 8887.4   Martineau, J. Types of ethical theory. Oxford, 1885.
Phil 8887.4.5   Martineau, J. Types of ethical theory. v.1-2. 3. ed. Oxford, 1891.
Phil 8887.4.2   Martineau, J. Types of ethical theory. 2. ed. Oxford, 1886. 2v.
Phil 8887.4.3   Martineau, J. Types of ethical theory. 2. ed. Oxford, 1886. 2v.
Phil 8887.4.10   Martineau, J. Types of ethical theory. 3. ed. Oxford, 1891. 2v.
Phil 8592.6.8   Martineau, James. Inter Amicos. London, 1901.
Phil 8592.6.12   Martineau, James. The new affinities of faith. Boston, 1869.

Phil 8592.6.11 Martineau, James. The new affinities of faith. London, 1869.

Phil 8592.6.20 Martineau, James. The relation between ethics and religion. London, 1881.

Phil 8592.6.2 Martineau, James. Study of religion. London, 1900. 2v.

Phil 8592.6 Martineau, James. Study of religion. Oxford, 1888. 2v.

Phil 8592.6.3 Martineau, James. A study of religion. Oxford, 1888. 2v.

Phil 8592.6.4 Martineau, James. A study of religion. 1. American ed. Oxford, 1888. 2v.

Htn Phil 2150.2.30* Martineau, James. Types of ethical theory. Oxford, 1885. 2v.

Phil 8887.5 Martinelli, V. Istoria critica della vita civile. Napoli, 1764. 2v.

Phil 9290.3 Martinet, J.F. Zeemans handboek. Amsterdam, 1781.

Phil 4170.10.30 Martinetti, P. Il compito della filosofia e altri saggi inediti ed editi. 1. ed. Torino, 1951.

Phil 5762.34 Martinetti, Piero. La libertà. Torino, 1965.

Phil 4170.10.80 Martinetti. (Sciacca, Michele F.) Brescia, 1943.

Phil 4363.11 Martinez, Martin. Philosophia sceptica. Madrid, 1730.

Phil 8887.74 Martínez de Trujillo, Maria. Meditaciones morales. México, 1948.

Phil 8887.74.5 Martínez de Trujillo, Maria. Moral meditations. N.Y., 1954.

Phil 3640.692 Martinez Estrada, E. Nietzsche. Buenos Aires, 1947.

Phil 75.62 Martínez Gómez, Luis. Bibliografía filosófica. Barcelona, 1961.

Phil 2750.11.190 Martinez Paz, Fernando. Maritain, politica e ideologia; revolución cristiana en la Argentina. Buenos Aires, 1966.

Phil 8413.27 Martini, Miro. La deformazione estetica. Milano, 1955.

Phil 4215.1.100 Martino, R. de. Saggio su G.D. Romagnosi. Napoli, 1887.

Phil 5404.4 Martinon, Jean Pierre. Les métamorphoses du désir et l'oeuvre. Paris, 1970.

Phil 4815.558.85 Martinovics élete. (Fraknói, Vilmos.) Budapest, 1921.

Phil 4815.558.80 Martinovicsnak istentagadó elveket hirdetó, imént fölfedezett francia munkája. (Fraknói, Vilmos.) Budapest, 1920.

Phil 1200.53 Martinozzoli, F. Parataxeis. 1st ed. Firenze, 1953.

Phil 5722.71 Martins, D. Do inconsciente. Braga, 1964.

Phil 585.145 Martins, D. Mistério do homen. Braga, 1961.

Phil 1750.695 Martins, Diamantino. Existencialismo. Braga, 1955.

Phil 4473.78.30 Martins, Diamantino. Filosofia da plenitude. Braga, 1966.

Phil 8667.26 Martins, Diamantino. O problema de Deus. Braga, 1957.

Phil 343.40 Martins, Diamantino. Teoria do conhecimento. Braga, 1957.

Phil 8550.420 Martins, Mário. Correntes da filosofia religiosa em Braga dos séculos IV-VII. Porto, 1950.

Phil 9560.27.5 Martinus, Dumiensis. Volgarizzamento della forma di onesta vita. Napoli, 1863.

Phil 5238.2 Martius, Götz. Beiträge zur Psychologie und Philosophie. Leipzig, 1905.

Phil 2070.151 Martland, T. The metaphysics of William James and John Dewey. N.Y., 1963.

Phil 8592.40 Pamphlet box. Martsynkovskii, V.F. Philosophy of religion.

Phil 187.68 Marty, Anton. Gesammelte Schriften. Halle, 1916-1918. 2v.

Phil 672.124 Marty, Anton. Raum und Zeit. Halle, 1916.

Phil 8725.18 Marty, Martin E. The modern schism. 1. ed. N.Y., 1969.

Phil 5520.288 Martynov, Viktor V. Kibernetika, semiotika, lingvistika. Minsk, 1966.

Phil 130.4 Les martyrs de la libre pensée. 2. éd. (Barni, Jules.) Paris, 1880.

Phil 5400.89 Marucci, A. Le passioni nella filosofia e nell'arte. Torino, 1932.

Phil 5762.8 Marucci, Achille. La volontà. Roma, 1903.

VPhil 6400.31 Maruszewski, Mariusz. Afazja. Wyd. 1. Warszawa, 1966.

Phil 7080.8 Marvaud, J.L.A. Le sommeil et l'insomnie. Paris, 1881.

Phil 5816.12 Marvels and mysteries of instinct. 3rd ed. (Garratt, G.) London, 1862.

Phil 8592.67 Marvin, D.E. The church and her prophets. N.Y., 1909.

Phil 2490.129 Marvin, F.S. Comte, the founder of sociology. London, 1936.

Phil 187.26.5 Marvin, W.T. A first book in metaphysics. N.Y., 1912.

Phil 812.4 Marvin, W.T. The history of European philosophy. N.Y., 1917.

Phil 187.26 Marvin, W.T. Introduction to systematic philosophy. N.Y., 1903.

Phil 6990.2 Marx, J. History of the robe of Jesus Christ. Philadelphia, 1845.

Phil 3425.372 Marx, Karl. Critique of Hegel's 'Philosophy of right.' Cambridge, Eng., 1970.

Phil 5252.152 Marx, M.H. Systems and theories in psychology. N.Y., 1963.

Phil 5238.170 Marx, Melvin Herman. Psychological theory. N.Y., 1961.

Phil 5252.155 Marx, Melvin Herman. Theories in contemporary psychology. N.Y., 1965.

Phil 5821.1.15 Marx, Moses. Charles Georges Leroy und seine "Lettres philosophiques." Strassburg, 1898.

Phil 5762.32 Marx, Otto. Leben ist Willkür. Hamburg, 1962.

Phil 3450.19.230 Marx, Werner. Heidegger und die Tradition. Stuttgart, 1961.

Phil 187.186 Marx, Werner. Vernunft und Welt. The Hague, 1970.

Phil 310.445.10 Marx oder Sartre? (Schaff, Adam.) Wien, 1964.

Phil 450.10 Marxiaten-Lennisten über den Sinn des Lebens. (Steiner, Hans Friedrich.) Essen, 1970.

Phil 310.803 Marxism and Christianity. (MacIntyre, Alasdair C.) N.Y., 1968.

Phil 310.596 Marxism and existentialism. 1. ed. (Adajnyk, Walter.) Garden City, N.Y., 1965.

Phil 2120.6.30 Marxism and modern idealism. (Lewis, John.) London, 1944.

Phil 8980.165 Marxism and moral concepts. (Ash, William F.) N.Y., 1964.

Phil 6324.7 Marxism and psycho-analysis. (Osbert, Reuben.) London, 1965.

Phil 2880.8.275 Marxism and the existentialists. (Aron, Raymond.) N.Y., 1970.

Phil 310.8 Marxism and the irrationalists. (Lewis, John.) London, 1955.

Phil 5520.436.5 Marxism and the linguistic philosophy. (Cornforth, Maurice Campbell.) London, 1965.

Phil 5520.436 Marxism and the linguistic philosophy. (Cornforth, Maurice Campbell.) N.Y., 1965.

Phil 310.643.1 Marxism in the twentieth century. (Garaudy, Roger.) London, 1970.

Phil 2725.24 Marxisme, existentialisme, personnalisme. (Lacroix, Jean.) Paris, 1950.

Phil 310.643 Marxisme du XXe siècle. (Garaudy, Roger.) Paris, 1966.

Phil 310.447 Marxisme et existentialisme. (Schaff, Adam.) Paris, 1962.

Phil 3425.716 Il marxismo e Hegel. (Colletti, Lucio.) Bari, 1969.

Phil 4225.15.90 Marxismo e metafisica. (Lizzio, Maria.) Catania, 1968.

Phil 8092.2 Marxismus und Ästhetik. (Koch, Hans.) Berlin, 1962.

Phil 8982.2 Marxismus und Ethik. 1. Aufl. (Vega, Rafael de la.) Frankfurt am Main, 1970.

Phil 2880.8.58 Marxismus und Existentialismus. (Sartre, Jean Paul.) Reinbeck, 1964.

Phil 310.784 Marxismus und Geschichte. (Fleischer, Helmut.) Frankfurt, 1969.

Phil 1750.116 Marxist-Non-Marxist Humanist Dialogue, 2d, Herceg-Novi, 1969. Tolerance and revolution. Beograd, 1970.

Phil 8676.5 Les marxistes et la religion. (Verret, Michel.) Paris, 1961.

Phil 8676.5.3 Les marxistes et la religion. 3. éd. (Verret, Michel.) Paris, 1966.

Phil 310.698 Marxisticka' dialektika a neotomizmus. Vyd. 1. (Tomášek, Ladislav.) Bratislava, 1967.

VPhil 310.704 Marxistická filozofia. 2. Vyd. (Kusý, Miroslav.) Bratislava, 1969.

Phil 4805.25 Marxisticko-leninská filosofie v Československu mezi dvěma světovými válkami. Vyd. 1. (Strohs, Slavomil.) Praha, 1962.

Phil 310.672 Marxisticko-leninská teorie tříd a třídního boje. Vyd. 1. (Sedlák, Jaromír.) Praha, 1959.

Phil 5625.75.90 Die marxistisch-leninistische Widerspiegelungstheorie und die Lehre Pawlows. (Kiselinchev, A.) Berlin, 1957.

Phil 4710.40 Die marxistisch-sowjetische Konzeption des Menschen. (Kulchitskii, Aleksandr.) München, 1956.

Phil 310.668 Marxistische Philosophie. Berlin, 1967.

Phil 1535.37 Marxuach, F. Compendium dialecticae, critical et ontologial. Barcinone, 1926.

Phil 7054.163 Mary Anne Carew; wife, mother, spirit. (Petersilea, Carlyle.) London, 1893.

Phil 7069.48.12 Mary Baker Eddy, her communications from beyond the grave to Harold Horwood. (Roberts, Ursula.) London, 1964.

Phil 5241.184.80 Mary Everest Boole; a pioneer student of the unconscious. (Dummer, Ethel Sturges.) n.p., 19- ?

Phil 365.41 Mary Frederick, Sister. Religion and evolution since 1859. Diss. Notre Dame, 1934.

Phil 7054.81.15 Mary Jane; or spiritualism chemically explained. (Guppy, Samuel.) London, 1863.

Phil 5628.11.6 Mary Minima, Sister. Seraph among angels; the life of St. Mary Magadalene de' Pazzi. Chicago, 1958.

Phil 7039.6A Mary Reynolds: a case of double consciousness. (Mitchell, Silas Weir.) Philadelphia, 1889.

Phil 7054.187 Mary S. Vanderbilt, a twentieth century seer. (Cadwallader, Mary E.) Chicago, 1921.

Phil 5850.267 Maryland. Conference on Military Contributions to Methology. New methods in applied psychology. College Park, 1947.

Phil 5590.345 Marzi, Alberto. La personalitá nell'etá evolutiva. Firenze, 1959.

Phil 196.24 Mas espiritu, meuos materia. (Veale, César.) Buenos Aires, 1931.

Phil 9575.15 Masani, Rustom Pestonji. The role of wealth in society. Bombay, 1956.

Phil 8962.12 Masaryk, J.G. The immortal soul in danger. London, 1941.

Phil 2050.104 Masaryk, T.G. David Hume's Skepsis. Wien, 1884.

Phil 187.114 Masaryk, T.G. Die Ideale der Humanität. Wien, 1902.

Phil 187.114.5 Masaryk, T.G. The ideals of humanity and How to work. London, 1938.

Phil 187.114.10 Masaryk, T.G. Ideály humanitní. Praha, 1901.

Phil 8592.57.5 Masaryk, T.G. Modern man and religion. London, 1938.

Phil 8592.57 Masaryk, T.G. Moderní člověk a náboženství. Praha, 1934.

Phil 2050.104.5 Masaryk, T.G. Počet pravděpodobnosti a Humova skepse. Praha, 1883.

Phil 6854.6 Masaryk, Tomáš Gottigue. Der Selbstmord als sociale Massenerscheinung des modernen Civilisation. Wien, 1881.

Phil 6854.6.5 Masaryk, Tomáš Gottigue. Suicide and the meanings of civilization. Chicago, 1970.

Phil 8667.22.10 Mascall, E.L. Existence and analogy. London, 1949.

Phil 8667.22 Mascall, E.L. He who is; a study in traditional theism. London, 1943.

Phil 8592.90 Mascall, E.L. The importance of being human. N.Y., 1958.

Phil 8584.19 La mascarada cristiana. (Espinosa, G.) Santiago de Chile, 1940.

Phil 8050.76 Mascello, Leonardo. Aestheticà di silencio. Rio de Janeiro, 1919.

Phil 4180.2 La maschera e il volto della nostra società. (Nobile-Ventura, Attilio.) Milano, 1965.

Phil 349.20 Die Maschinen-Theorie des Lebens. (Schultz, Julius.) Göttingen, 1909.

Phil 349.20.5 Die Maschinen-Theorie des Lebens. 2. Aufl. (Schultz, Julius.) Leipzig, 1929.

Phil 8887.62 Masci, F. Coscienza, volontà, libertà. Lanciano, 1884.

Phil 4170.4.31 Masci, F. Pensiero e conoscenza. Torino, 1922.

Phil 5252.45 Masci, Filippo. El materialismo psicofisico. Napoli, 1901.

Phil 187.72 Masci, Filippo. Elementi di filosofia per le scuole secondarie. Napoli, 1899-1904. 2v.

Phil 8592.44 Masci, Filippo. L'idealismo indeterminista. Napoli, 1898.

Phil 187.72.5 Masci, Filippo. Intelletualismo e pragmatismo. Napoli, 1911.

Phil 5252.45.5 Masci, Filippo. Introduzione generale alla psicologia. Milano, 1926.

Phil 812.30 Mascia, Carmin. A history of philosophy. Paterson, N.J., 1957.

Phil 9590.28 Masferrer, A. Ensayo sobre el destino. San Salvador, 1963.

Phil 8685.22 Masferrer, A. Helios. San Salvador, 1963.

Phil 5585.228 Mashhour, M. Psychophysical relations in the perception of velocity. Stockholm, 1964.

Phil 8667.35 Masi, Giorgio. Dalla religione degli dei alla religione dell'uomo. Milano, 1967.

Phil 8702.26 Masi, R. Religione. Brescia, 1958.

Phil 6825.2.2 The mask of sanity. 2. ed. (Cleckley, Hervey Milton.) St. Louis, 1950.

Phil 3640.290 Maske und Scham bei Nietzsche. Diss. (Furstenthal, Achim.) Basel, 1940.

Phil 575.145 Die Masken der Siecle. (Kern, Hans.) Leipzig, 194-.

Phil 5593.54.5 Maskendeutungen im Rorschachschen Versuch. 2. Aufl. (Kuhn, Roland.) Basel, 1954.

Phil 6328.42 Masks of love and life. (Sachs, Hanns.) London, 1957.

Phil 1865.193 Maślinśka, Hallna. Bentham i jcgo system ctyczny. Warszawa, 1964.

Phil 6322.27A Maslow, A.H. Principles of abnormal psychology. N.Y., 1941.

Phil 5548.98   Maslow, Abraham Harold. Motivation and personality. 2. ed. N.Y., 1970.

Phil 5627.264.5   Maslow, Abraham Harold. Religions, values and peak-experiences. Columbus, Ohio, 1964.

Phil 5548.100   Maslow, Abraham Harold. Toward a psychology of being. Princeton, 1962.

Phil 5548.100.2   Maslow, Abraham Harold. Toward a psychology of being. 2. ed. Princeton, 1968.

Phil 3925.16.275   Maslow, Alexander. A study in Wittgenstein's Tractatus. Berkeley, 1961.

Phil 5252.115   Maslow, Paul. Intuition versus intellect. N.Y., 1957.

Phil 5593.45.5   Maslow, Paul. Rorschach psychology. Brooklyn, 1945.

Phil 4012.5   Masnovo, A. Il neo-tomismo in Italia (origini e prime vicende). Milano, 1923.

Phil 1517.5.5   Masnovo, Amato. Da Guglielmo d'Auvergne. 2. ed. Milano, 1946. 3v.

Phil 1517.5   Masnovo, Amato. Da Guglielmo d'Auvergne a San Tomaso d'Aquino. Milano, 1930. 2v.

Phil 187.90   Masnovo, Amato. Problemi di metafisica e di criteriologia. Milano, 1930.

Phil 4080.3.85   Masnovo, Omero. L'estetica di Benedetto Croce. Parma, 1914.

Phil 6323.8   Le masochisme. 2. éd. (Nacht, Sacha.) Paris, 1948.

Phil 6322.24   Mason, E.C. Why we do it? St. Louis, 1937.

Phil 978.41   Mason, E.L. The discovery of discoveries. n.p., n.d.

Phil 293.21   Mason, F.B. (Mrs.). The great design. N.Y., 1935.

Phil 8592.52.5   Mason, Francis. The contents of the history of ancient paganism. London, 1747.

Phil 8610.964.10   Mason, Gabriel Richard. What I believe. v.1-2. N.Y., 1964?

Phil 8702.10   Mason, Henry M. The relation between religion and science. n.p., 1839.

Phil 8887.6.25   Mason, J. Peri tou gnôthi sauton. Korphoi, 1821.

Phil 8887.6   Mason, J. Self-knowledge. London, 1745.

Phil 8887.6.2   Mason, J. Self-knowledge. London, 1753.

Phil 8887.6.3   Mason, J. Self-knowledge. London, 1755.

Phil 8887.6.4.5   Mason, J. Self-knowledge. London, 1794.

Phil 8887.6.10   Mason, J. Self-knowledge. London, 1824.

Phil 8887.6.5   Mason, J. Self-knowledge. Portland, 1807.

Htn   Phil 8887.6.4*   Mason, J. Self-knowledge. Worcester, Mass., 1789.

Phil 8887.6.6   Mason, J. A treatise on self-knowledge. Boston, 1809.

Phil 8887.6.9   Mason, J. A treatise on self-knowledge. London, 1821.

Phil 8887.6.7   Mason, J. A treatise on self-knowledge. Montpelier, 1813.

Phil 8887.6.15   Mason, J. A treatise on self-knowledge. N.Y., 1943.

Htn   Phil 8887.6.6.5*   Mason, J. A treatise on self-knowledge. Newburyport, 1812.

Phil 8887.6.9.5   Mason, J. A treatise on self-knowledge. 3. ed. Boston, 1822.

Phil 8887.6.12   Mason, J. A treatise on self knowledge. 4th ed. Boston, 1826.

Phil 187.71   Mason, J.W.T. Creative freedom. N.Y., 1926.

Phil 5525.58   Mason, Michael. The centre of hilarity. London, 1959.

Phil 5253.11   Mason, Phillips. The X of psychology. Cambridge, 1940.

Phil 7068.97.30   Mason, R.O. Telepathy and the subliminal self. N.Y., 1897.

Phil 7068.97.34   Mason, R.O. Telepathy and the subliminal self. N.Y., 1899.

Phil 6682.11   Mason, Rufus O. Hypnotism and suggestion in theraputics. N.Y., 1911.

Phil 3120.62.30   Mass und Vermesserheit des Menschen. (Bollnow, Otto Fredrich.) Göttingen, 1962.

Phil 575.150   Massa, Eugenio. I fondamenti metafisici "dignitas hominis". Torino, 1954.

Phil 52.7.12   Massachusetts. Society for Mental Hygiene. Monthly bulletin. Boston. 1-19,1922-1940 2v.

Phil 52.7.25   Massachusetts. Society for Mental Hygiene. Publication. 1-45 2v.

Phil 52.7.15   Massachusetts. Society for Mental Hygiene. Report of the Boston Mental Hygiene Survey. Boston.

Phil 52.7.5   Massachusetts. Society for Social Hygiene. Bulletin. Boston. 1-15,1931-1945

Phil 52.7   Massachusetts. Society for Social Hygiene. Bulletin. Boston. 1918-1920

Phil 6309.2   Massachusetts Commission on Lunacy. Insanity and idiocy in Massachusetts; report of the Commission on lunacy, 1855. Cambridge, 1971.

Phil 3246.243   Massalo, A. Fichte e la filosofia. Firenze, 1948.

Phil 6122.24   Massalongo, Robert. Mielopatia da fulmine. Napoli, 1891.

Phil 9150.18   Massebieau, Eugéne. De principe de la morale. Thèse. Alençon, 1886.

Phil 6315.2.44   Massenpsychologie und Ich-Analyse. (Freud, Sigmund.) Leipzig, 1921.

Htn   Phil 5380.77*   Massenpsychologie und Ich-Analyse. (Freud, Sigmund.) Leipzig, 1921.

Phil 4974.5   Massera, José P. Estudios filosóficos. v.12. Montevideo, 1954.

Phil 5252.81A   Masserman, J.H. Behavior and neurosis. Chicago, 1943.

Phil 5252.81.2   Masserman, J.H. Behavior and neurosis. N.Y., 1964.

Phil 6980.459   Masserman, Jules Hymen. Principles of dynamic psychiatry. London, 1946.

Phil 9513.35   Masses, morale et machines. (Huant, Ernest.) Paris, 1967.

Phil 2825.15.80   Masset, Pierre. La dialectique de la conscience chez Jacques Paliard. Paris, 1959.

Phil 2150.22.140   Masset, Pierre. La pensée de Herbert Marcuse. Toulouse, 1969.

Phil 4195.83   Massetani, D.G. La filosofia cabbalistica di Giovanni Pico. Empoli, 1897.

Phil 7068.87.20   Massey, C.C. Zöllner. London, 1887.

Phil 7068.71.8   Massey, G. Concerning spiritualism. London, 1871.

Phil 5066.318   Massey, Gerald J. Understanding symbolic logic. N.Y., 1970.

Phil 2403.1.50   Massias, N. Lettre à M.P. Damiron sur un article de son essai sur l'histoire de la philosophie en France au dix-neuvième siècle. Paris, 1828.

Phil 2750.7.37   Massias, Nicolas. Principe de la philosophie psycho-physiologique sur lequel repose la science de l'homme. Paris, 1829.

Phil 2750.7.35   Massias, Nicolas. Traité de philosophie psycho-physiologique. Paris, 1830.

Phil 2750.7.39   Pamphlet vol. Massias, Nicolas. Philosophical essays. 4 pam.

Phil 2115.151   Massie, J. An essay on...Mr. Locke. London, 1750.

Phil 2115.152   Massie, J. Observations. London, 1760.

Phil 8962.13   Massimi, Massimo. Catholic morality. Paterson, 1943.

Phil 2490.174   Massing, Otwin. Fortschritt und Gegenrevolution. Die Gesellschaftslehre Comtes in ihrer sozialen Funktion. Stuttgart, 1966.

Phil 2805.420   Massis, Henri. Le réalisme de Pascal. St.-Felicien-en-Vivarais, 1924.

Phil 2805.415   Massis, Henri. Troisième centenaire de la mort de Pascal. Paris, 1962.

Phil 4610.7.38   Masskultur. (Norström, V.) Stockholm, 1910.

Phil 4210.144   Massolo, A. Il problema dell'individuo nella filosofia di A. Rosmini. Palermo, 1934.

Phil 3494.44   Massolo, Arturo. Introduzione alla analitica Kantiaña. Serie 2. Firenze, 1946.

Phil 3425.668   Massolo, Arturo. Logica hegeliana e filosofia contemporanea. Firenze, 1967.

Phil 3425.510   Massolo, Arturo. Prime ricerche di Hegel. Urbino, 1959.

Phil 3801.560   Massolo, Arturo. Il primo Schelling. Firenze, 1953.

Phil 1812.2.5   Masson, D. Recent British philosophy. London, 1865.

Phil 1812.2.2   Masson, D. Recent British philosophy. London, 1867.

Phil 1812.2   Masson, D. Recent British philosophy. London, 1866.

Phil 187.106   Masson, T.L. The city of perfection. N.Y., 1927.

Phil 8837.15   Masson-Ourel, Paul. La morale et l'histoire. 1. éd. Paris, 1955.

Phil 812.9.5   Masson-Oursel, Paul. Comparative philosophy. N.Y., 1926.

Phil 960.31.2   Masson-Oursel, Paul. Esquisse d'une histoire de la philosophie indienne. Thèse. Paris, 1923.

Phil 960.31   Masson-Oursel, Paul. Esquisse d'une histoire de la philosophie indienne. Thèse. Paris, 1923.

Phil 187.131   Masson-Oursel, Paul. Le fait métaphysique. Paris, 1941.

Phil 812.9   Masson-Oursel, Paul. La philosophie comparée. Paris, 1923.

Phil 812.9.2   Masson-Oursel, Paul. La philosophie comparée. Thèse. Paris, 1923.

Phil 3494.35   Massonius, M. Ueber Kant's Transscendentale Aesthetik. Diss. Leipzig, 1890.

Phil 5222.12   Massucco Costa, Angiola. Psicologia sovietica. Torino, 1963.

Phil 3640.830   Massuh, Victor. Nietzsche y el fin de la religión. Buenos Aires, 1969.

Phil 5465.162   The master game; pathways to higher consciousness beyond the drug experience. (De Ropp, Robert S.) N.Y., 1968.

Phil 176.59   The master-key. (Blair, D.) Wimbledon, 1914.

Phil 6117.40   The master key. (Haanel, C.F.) St. Louis, 1919.

Phil 5850.108.5   Mastering your own mind. (Alexander, James.) N.Y., 1931.

Phil 165.270   Masterpieces of world philosophy in summary form. 1st ed. (Magill, F.N.) N.Y., 1961.

Phil 6155.6   Masters, Robert E.L. The varieties of psychedelic experience. 1st ed. N.Y., 1966.

Phil 193.51   The masters of fate...the power of the will. (Shaler, S.P.) N.Y., 1906.

Phil 9530.10   Masters of the situation. (Tilley, W.J.) Chicago, 1887.

Phil 6322.45   Masterson, Jenny Gove. Letters from Jenny. N.Y., 1965.

Phil 9240.1   The mastery of evil. (Lloyd, R.B.) London, 1941.

Phil 5401.7   The mastery of fear. (Walsh, W.S.) N.Y., 1924.

Phil 5545.18   Mastery of memorizing. (Leland, C.G.) Harrisburg, 1890-91.

Phil 6112.20   The mastery of nervousness based upon self-reeducation. (Carroll, Robert S.) N.Y., 1917.

Phil 6112.20.2   The mastery of nervousness based upon self-reeducation. 2nd ed. (Carroll, Robert S.) N.Y., 1918.

Phil 9495.133.10   Mastery of sex through psychology and religion. (Weatherhead, L.D.) N.Y., 1934.

Phil 9495.133.5   Mastery of sex through psychology and religion. 2d ed. (Weatherhead, L.D.) London, 1931.

Phil 6115.31   Mastery of stress. (Funkenstein, D.H.) Cambridge, Mass., 1957.

Phil 960.166   Masui, J. Approaches de l'Inde. Tours? 1949.

Phil 3246.304   Masullo, Aldo. La comunitá come fondamento. Napoli, 1965.

Phil 585.265   Masullo, Aldo. Il senso del fondamento. Napoli, 1967.

Phil 175.50   Matafzika ogólna czyli ontologia. (Adamczyk, S.) Lublin, 1960.

Phil 3565.84   Matagrin, A. Essai sur l'esthétique de Lotze. Paris, 1901.

Phil 5850.356.10   Matalon, Benjamin. L'analyse hiérarchique. Paris, 1965.

Phil 187.137   Matchette, F.J. Outline of a metaphysics. N.Y., 1949.

Phil 665.34   The matchless altar of the soul. (Larkin, E.L.) Los Angeles, 1916.

Phil 5593.68   Matejek, Georg. Zur Frage quantitativer und qualitativer Anderungen einiger Rorschach-Kategorien im Schulalter. Weinheim, 1968.

Phil 5066.230   Matematicheskaia logika i teoriia mnozhestv. (Kharin, N.N.) Moskva, 1963.

Phil 5066.266   Matematicheskaia teoriia logicheskogo vyvoda. (Jdel'son, A.V.) Moskva, 1967.

Phil 3801.406.20   Matematismo e spinozismo nel primo Schelling. (Frigo, Gianfranco.) Padova, 1969.

Phil 2750.19.120   Matera, Rocco. Problematico e meta-problematico in Gabriel Marcel. Bari, 1969.

Phil 70.81   La materia. v.2. (Reunion de Aproximacion Filosofica Cuntifica.) Zaragoza, 1961.

Phil 491.2   Materia (appunti di critica). (Quarto di Palo, A.) Roma, 1968.

Phil 180.30   Materia e sensazione. (Fazio-Allmayer, V.) Milano, 1913.

Phil 3489.1   Materialen zur Geschichte der critischen Philosophie. (Hausius, K.G.) Leipzig, 1793. 2v.

Phil 7069.14.60   Materialisationsphaenomene. (Schrenck von Notzing, Albert.) München, 1914.

Phil 7069.14.61   Materialisationsphaenomene. 2. ed. (Schrenck von Notzing, Albert.) München, 1923.

Phil 482.4   Die Materialisierung des Geistes. (Haering, T.L.) Tübingen, 1919.

Phil 487.8   Materialism; the scientific basis. (Mins, H.F.) N.Y., 1934.

Phil 476.5   Materialism. (Bliven, Eliza M.) n.p., n.d.

Phil 182.111   Materialism. (Haldane, J.S.) London, 1932.

Phil 477.9   Materialism: has it been exploded?...debate. (Cohen, Chapman.) London, 1928.

Phil 492.5   Materialism. 2nd ed. (Roy, M.N.) Calcutta, 1951.

NEDL Phil 2668.35.5   The materialism of the present day. (Janet, Paul A.R.) London, 1866.

Phil 477.9.5   Materialism re-stated. (Cohen, Chapman.) London, 1927.

Phil 477.6   Matérialisme, vitalisme, rationalisme. (Cournot, A.A.) Paris, 1875.

Phil 477.6.5   Matérialisme, vitalisme, rationalisme. (Cournot, A.A.) Paris, 1923.

Phil 2668.35   Le matérialisme contemporain. (Janet, Paul A.R.) Paris, 1875.

Phil 3009.1   Le matérialisme contemporaine...Allem. (Janet, P.) Paris, 1864.

Phil 493.1   Le matérialisme de masque. (Simonin, A.H.) Paris, 1878.

Phil 492.1   Le matérialisme et la nature. (Renaud, H.) Paris, 1870.

Phil 480.3 Le matérialisme et la phrénologie. (Forichon, L.) Paris, 1840.
Phil 477.2 Le matérialisme et la science. (Caro, E.M.) Paris, 1867.
Phil 477.2.5 Le matérialisme et la science. 2e éd. (Caro, E.M.) Paris, 1868.
Phil 486.2 Matérialisme et spiritualisme. (Leblais, A.) Paris, 1865.
Phil 1135.183 Le materialisme gréco-romain. (Cogniot, Georges.) Paris, 1964.
Phil 490.4.10 Le matérialisme militant (materialismus militans). (Plekhanov, G.V.) Paris, 1930.
Phil 2477.15 Le matérialisme rationnel. (Bachelard, Gaston.) Paris, 1953.
Phil 310.567 Materialismo dialectico. (Troise, Emilio.) Buenos Aires, 1938.
Phil 310.603 Il materialismo dialettico e storico. (Silipo, Luigi.) Padova, 1962.
Phil 480.6 O materialismo em face da sciencia. (Fernandez de Santanna, M.) Lisboa, 1899. 2v.
Phil 480.1 Il materialismo storico. (Ferraris, C.F.) Palermo, 1897.
Phil 7068.74.15 Het materialismus, het spiritismus. 2. druk. (Polak, M.S.) Amsterdam, 1874.
Phil 478.3 Der Materialismus. (Dreher, Eugen.) Berlin, 1892.
Phil 476.3.50 Der Materialismus. (Frauenstadt, J.) Leipzig, 1856.
Phil 310.580 Materialismus dialectic si stiintele contemporane ale naturii. (Academia Republicii Populare Romine. Biblioteca.) Bucuresti, 1963.
Phil 497.9.2 Der Materialismus im Verhältnis zu Religion und Moral. 2e Aufl. (Wollny, F.) Leipzig, 1902.
Phil 490.4.10.12 Materialismus militans (voinstvuiushchii materializm). Izd. 2. (Plekhanov, G.V.) Moskva, 1931.
Phil 3120.15.35 Materialismus und Idealismus. (Brunner, Constantin.) Köln, 1959.
Phil 1845.17 A materialist theory of the mind. (Armstrong, David M.) London, 1968.
Phil 488.1 Les matérialistes de l'antiquité. (Nizan, Paul.) Paris, 1936.
Phil 488.1.5 Les matérialistes de l'antiquité. (Nizan, Paul.) Paris, 1965.
Phil 2430.6 Les materialistes français de 1750 à 1800. (Desné, Roland.) Paris, 1965.
Phil 310.705 Materialisticheskaia dialektika. (Furman, Aleksei E.) Moskva, 1969.
Phil 4768.1 Materialisticheskaia dialektika. (Rozental', M.M.) Moskva, 1937.
Phil 310.430 Materialisticheskaia dialektika kak logika i teoria poznaniia. (Cherkesov, V.I.) Moskva, 1962.
Phil 490.9 Materialisticheskoe mirovozrenie i teoriia poznaniia russkikh revoliutsionnikh demokratov. (Pantin, Igor' K.) Moskva, 1961.
Phil 310.589.8 Materialistické pojetí dějin. Vyd. 3. (Klofáč, Jaroslav.) Praha, 1962.
Phil 310.95 Materialistische Dialektik. (Ogiermann, H.A.) München, 1958.
Phil 496.1 Die materialistische Epoche des neunzehnten Jahrhunderts. (Volkmann, P.) Leipzig, 1909.
Phil 978.49.245 Der materialistische Erkenntnisimpuls und seine Bedeutung für die ganze Menscheitsentwicklung. (Steiner, R.) Basel, 1953.
Phil 337.16.5 Die materialistische Erkenntnistheorie. (Garaudy, Roger.) Berlin, 1960.
Phil 978.49.255 Die materialistische Weltanschauung des neunzehnten Jahrhunderts. (Steiner, R.) Basel, 1955.
Phil 3235.122 Die materialistishe Philosophie Ludwig Feuerbachs. 1. Aufl. (Esin, Ivan M.) Berlin, 1956.
Phil 7068.86.40 Materialized apparitions. (Brackett, E.A.) Boston, 1886.
Phil 7069.08.12 Materialized apparitions. (Brackett, E.A.) Boston, 1908.
Phil 3235.81.29 Materializm Feierbakha. (Gabaraev, S.S.) Tbilisi, 1955.
VPhil 310.694 Materializm historyezny. (Ochocki, Aleksander.) Warszawa, 1969.
Phil 4769.6.81 Materializm I.M. Sechenova. (Belov, P.T.) Moskva, 1963.
Phil 310.17 Materializm i religiia. (Baskin, M.P.) Moskva, 1955.
Phil 481.2 Materializm v svete sovremennoi nauki. (Glagolev, B.) Frankfurt, 1946.
Phil 310.629 Materializmus proti holizmu. (Filová, Elena.) Bratislava, 1963.
Phil 176.43 Materials for thinking. (Burdon, W.) London, 1820. 2v.
Phil 70.103 Materialy. (Iubileinaia Nauchnaia Sessiia Vuzov Ural'skoi zony, Sverdlovsk.) Sverdlovsk, 1967?
Phil 310.623 Materialy. (Soveshchanie po Sovremennym Problemam Materialisticheskoi Dialektiki.) Moskva, 1966. 4v.
Phil 4710.149 Materialy. (Zonal'naia Nauchnaia Konferentsiia po Filosofskim Naukam, 2d, Perm', 1965.) Perm', 1965.
Phil 487.9 Materialy dlia razoblacheniia materialisticheskago nigilizma. Photoreproduction. Sankt Peterburg, 1864.
Phil 22.53 Materiały do historii filozofii średniowiecznej w Polsce. Wrocław. 1,1970+
Phil 5520.509 Materialy k konferentsii "Iazyk kak znakovaia sistema osobogo roda. Moskva, 1967.
Phil 4710.154 Materialy k nauchnoi sessii, posviashchennoi 50-letiiu Velikoi Oktiabr'skoi sotsialisticheskoi revoliutsii. (Leningrad. Universitet. Filosofskii Fakul'tet.) Leningrad, 1967.
Phil 5520.457 Materialy kollokviuma po eksperimental'noi fonetike i psikhologii rechi. (Moscow. Pervyi Moskovskii Gosudarstvennyi Pedagogicheskii Institut Inostrannykh iazykov.) Moskva, 1966.
Phil 310.628 Materialy nauchnoi sessii. (Kommunisticheskaia Akademiia, Moscow. Institut Filosofii.) Moskva, 1934.
Phil 960.240 Materialy po istorii indiiskoi filosofii. (Piatigorskii, A.M.) Moskva, 1962.
Phil 1020.34 Materialy poistorii progressivnoi obshchestvennoi filosofskoi mysl v Uzbekistane. (Akademiia Nauk Uzbekskoi SSR, Tashkend. Otdel Filosofii i Prava.) Tashkent, 1957.
Phil 22.52 Materiały prakseologiczne. Warszawa. 20,1965+ 3v.
Phil 70.118 Materialy V Zonal'noi Konferentsii Psikhologov Pribaltiki. (Zonal'naia Konferentsiia Psikhologov Pribaltiki, 5th, Tartu, Kääriku, 1968.) Tartu, 1968.
Phil 4655.3.30 Materie eller ande? 3. uppl. (Waerland, Are.) Uppsala, 1919.
Phil 197.34.10 Materie nie ohne Geist. (Wille, Bruno.) Berlin, 1901.
Phil 4710.11.5 Materie und Bewusstsein. 5. Aufl. (Khaskhachikh, F.I.) Berlin, 1957.
NEDL Phil 6111.12.15 Materie und Gedächtnis. (Bergson, Henri.) Jena, 1919.
Phil 315.19 Materie und Geist. (Vries, Joseph de.) München, 1970.
Phil 4650.1.59 Materiens värld. (Vannérus, Allen.) Stockholm, 1925.
Phil 310.597 Materiia i poznanie. (Polikarov, A.) Sofiia, 1961.
Phil 4710.11 Materiia i soznanie. (Khaskhachikh, F.I.) Moskva, 1951.
Phil 745.10 Materiia i zhizn'. (Losskii, Nikolai O.) Berlin, 1923.
Phil 70.98 Materijali. (Kongres Psihologa Jugolsavije, 2d, Zagerb, 1964.) Zagreb, 1964.
Phil 3790.12.81 Matern Reuss. (Motsch, Karl E.) Freiburg, 1932.
Phil 9179.3 Maternal instinct, or Love. (Toner, J.M.) Baltimore, 1864.
Phil 5066.231 Mates, Benson. Elementary logic. N.Y., 1965.
Phil 310.517 Matetialisticheskaia dialektika i metody estestvennykh nauk. Moskva, 1968.
Phil 4372.1.90 Mateu y Llopez, F. Catálogo de la exposición bibliográfica celebrada con motivo del IV centenario de la muerte de Luis Vives. Barcelona, 1940.
Phil 2520.220 Mateu y Llopis, Felipe. Descartes. Barcelona, 1945.
Phil 150.10 Mateucci, Arturo. Vocabolarietto di termini filosofici. Milano, 1925.
Phil 5252.65 Mathaei, Rupprecht. Das Gestaltproblem. München, 1929.
Phil 5066.34 The mathematical analysis of logic. (Boole, George.) Oxford, 1948.
Phil 8419.53 The mathematical basis of the arts. (Schillinger, J.) N.Y., 1948.
Phil 5066.85 Mathematical interpretation of formal systems. (Wiskundig Genootschap. Amsterdam.) Amsterdam, 1955.
Phil 5066.300 Mathematical logic; a first course. (Robbin, Joel W.) N.Y., 1969.
Phil 5066.125 Mathematical logic. (Goodstein, R.L.) Leicester, 1957.
Phil 5066.261 Mathematical logic. (Kleene, Stephen Cole.) N.Y., 1967.
Phil 5066.11.7 Mathematical logic. (Quine, Willard van Orman.) Cambridge, Mass., 1951.
Phil 5066.11 Mathematical logic. (Quine, Willard van Orman.) N.Y., 1940.
Phil 5066.263 Mathematical logic. (Shoenfield, Joseph R.) Reading, Mass., 1967.
Phil 5238.70 Mathematical models of human behavior. (Dunlap and Associates, Stanford, Conn.) Stanford, 1955.
Phil 8664.1 Mathematical principles of theology. (Jack, R.) London, 1747.
Phil 5246.9.8A The mathematical psychology of Gratry and Boole. (Boole, M.E.) London, 1897.
Phil 5272.8 Mathematical solutions for psychological problems. (Gulliksen, Harold.) n.p., 1958.
Phil 5066.284 Mathematics and logic. (Kac, Mark.) N.Y., 1968.
Phil 5066.7 Mathematics-deductive theory of rate learning. New Haven, 1940.
Phil 281.3 Mathematik als Grundlage der Weltanschauung. (Alexejeff, W.G.) Jurjew, 1903.
VPhil 9590.37 Mathématique de l'histoire, géométrie et cinématique. (Lagrange, Charles Henri.) Bruxelles, 1900.
Phil 2494.87 La mathématique sociale du marquis de Condorcet. 1. éd. (Granger, Gilles Gaston.) Paris, 1956.
Phil 2520.310 Mathématiques et métaphysique de Descartes. (Vuillemin, Jules.) Paris, 1960.
Phil 5066.160 Mathematische Gesetze der Logik. (Schmidt, H.A.) Berlin, 1960.
Phil 3260.39 Die mathematische Naturphilosophie. (Fries, J.F.) Heidelberg, 1822.
Phil 349.5 Die mathematischen Elemente der Erkenntnisstheorie. (Schmitz-Dumont, O.) Berlin, 1878.
Phil 2520.346 Le mathématisme de Descartes. (Allard, J.L.) Ottawa, 1963.
Htn Phil 8667.4* Mather, C. The Christian philosopher. London, 1721.
Htn Phil 9352.2* Mather, C. Daughters of Zion. n.p., 1691?
Phil 8887.7.2 Mather, C. Essays to do good. Dover, 1826.
Phil 8887.7.4 Mather, C. Essays to do good. London, 1816.
Htn Phil 9010.14* Mather, Cotton. A serious address. Boston, 1726.
Phil 8413.19 Mather, F.J. Concerning beauty. Princeton, 1935.
Phil 8702.16.5 Mather, K.F. Crusade for life. Chapel Hill, N.C., 1949.
Phil 8702.16A Mather, K.F. Science in search of God. N.Y., 1928.
Phil 8702.16.2 Mather, K.F. Science in search of God. N.Y., 1928.
Phil 9352.12 Mather, Persis (pseud.). The counsels of a worldly godmother. Boston, 1905.
Phil 3832.22 Matheron, Alexandre. Individu et communauté chez Spinoza. Paris, 1969.
Phil 193.225 Mathesis Universalis. (Scholz, H.) Stuttgart, 1961.
Phil 8592.68 Mathews, B. Through tragedy to triumph. N.Y., 1939.
Phil 7055.108 Mathias, Julio. Don Luis de Alderete y Soto. Málaga, 1965.
Phil 6962.17 Mathieu, A. Neurasthénie. Paris, 1892.
Phil 2750.26.30 Mathieu, Guy. Science du bonheur. Paris, 1957.
Phil 6990.4 Mathieu, P.F. Histoire des miracules et des convulsionnaires de Saint-Médard. Paris, 1864.
Phil 2905.1.585 Mathieu, Pierre Louis. La pensée politique et économique de Teilhard de Chardin. Paris, 1969.
Phil 3494.61 Mathieu, V. La filosofia trascendentale. Torino, 1958.
Phil 2475.1.350 Mathieu, Vittorio. Bergson. Torino, 1954.
Phil 343.50 Mathieu, Vittorio. Il problema dell'esperienza. Trieste, 1963.
Phil 5411.7 Mathis, René. La haine. Thèse. Nancy, 1927.
Phil 600.40 Mathis, René. La loi des trois états. Thèse. Nancy, 1924.
Phil 282.5.5 Matho, or, The cosmotheoria puerilis. (Baxter, A.) London, 1745. 2v.
Phil 282.5 Matho; sive, Cosmotheoria puerilis. (Baxter, A.) London, 1746.
Phil 583.14 Mathur, Dinesh Chandra. Naturalistic philosophies of experience. St. Louis, 1971.
Phil 75.69 Matica Slovenská, Turčiansky sv. Martin. Bibliografický Odbor. Bibliografia filozofíckéj Knižnej tvorby na Slovensku. Martin, 1965.
Phil 5052.21 Matičević, Stephan. Zur Grundlegung der Logik. Wien, 1909.
Phil 2475.1.60.6 Matière et mémoire. (Bergson, Henri.) Genève, 1946.
X Cg Phil 6111.12 Matière et mémoire. (Bergson, Henri.) Paris, 1900.
Phil 2475.1.60 Matière et mémoire. 7. éd. (Bergson, Henri.) Paris, 1911.
Phil 2475.1.60.2 Matière et mémoire. 8. éd. (Bergson, Henri.) Paris, 1912.
Phil 2475.1.60.4 Matière et mémoire. 36. éd. (Bergson, Henri.) Paris, 1941.
Phil 486.15 La matière imaginaire. (Lodetti, Milka.) Paris, 1959.
Phil 8407.41 Matiéres et formes. (Gilson, Étienne.) Paris, 1964.
Phil 293.25.5 Matisse, G. L'incohérence universelle. 1. éd. Paris, 1953.
Phil 293.25 Matisse, G. La philosophie de la nature. Paris, 1938. 3v.
Phil 6122.42 Matisse, Georges. L'intelligence et le cerveau. Paris, 1909.
Phil 7069.30.14 Matla, J.L.W.P. La solution du mystère de la mort. La Haye, 1930.
Phil 672.214 Matoré, Georges. L'espace humain. Paris, 1962.
Phil 5925.3.20 Matrimony. (Fowler, O.S.) Philadelphia, 1841.
Phil 6119.9 The matrix of the mind. (Jones, F. Wood.) Honolulu, 1928.

Phil 8170.4 Matsa, Ivan. Khudozhestvennoe nasledie i estetickeskoe vospitanie. Moskva, 1959.
Phil 8092.17 Matsa, Ivan L. Problemy khudozhestvennoi kul'tury XX veka. Moskva, 1966.
Phil 5238.215 Matson, Floyd W. Being, becoming and behavior; the psychological sciences. N.Y., 1967.
Phil 6980.460 Matte Blanco, Ignacio. Estudios de psicología dinámica. Santiago de Chile, 1955.
Phil 5252.102 Matte Blanco, Ignacio. La psíquica y la naturaleza humana. Santiago, 1954.
Phil 2520.216 Mattei, André. L'homme de Descartes. Paris, 1940.
Phil 4073.89 Mattei, R. de. La politica di Campanella. Roma, 1927.
Phil 4073.90 Mattei, R. de. Studi Campanelliani. Firenze, 1934.
Phil 8887.8.5 Matter, J. De l'affaiblissement des idées. Paris, 1841.
Phil 9450.2 Matter, J. De l'influence des moeurs sur le lois. Paris, 1832.
Phil 812.2 Matter, J. Histoire de la philosophie. Paris, 1854.
Phil 8887.8 Matter, J. La morale, ou La philosophie des moeurs. Paris, 1860.
Phil 8592.7 Matter, J. La philosophie de la religion. Paris, 1857. 2v.
Phil 530.15.37 Matter, Jacques. Le mysticisme en France au temps de Fénelon. 2e éd. Paris, 1865.
Phil 530.15.3 Matter, Jacques. Le mysticisme en France au temps de Fénelon. 2e éd. Paris, 1865.
Phil 2880.1.87 Matter, Jacques. Saint-Martin. 2. ed. Paris, 1862.
Htn Phil 3801.544* Matter, Jacques. Schelling, ou La philosophie de la nature. Paris, 1845.
Phil 3801.544.2 Matter, Jacques. Schelling, ou La philosophie de la nature. Paris, 1845.
Phil 182.49.5 Matter, life, mind and God. (Hoernlé, R.F.A.) London, 1923.
Phil 184.26.5A Matter, life and value. (Joad, C.E.M.) London, 1929.
Phil 8708.28.2 Matter, mind and man. (Sinott, Edmund Ware.) N.Y., 1962.
Phil 177.93 Matter, spirit and living intellect. (Carneades, D.) London, 1936.
Phil 192.42 Matter, spirit and the cosmos. (Redgrove, H.S.) London, 1916.
Phil 8708.28 Matter. 1. ed. (Sinnott, Edmund Ware.) N.Y., 1957.
Phil 477.14 Matter and becoming. (Connell, Richard J.) Chicago, 1966.
Phil 486.6 Matter and energy. (L, B.L.) London, 1887.
Phil 1135.190 Matter and infinity in the Presocratic school and Plato. (Sinnige, Theo G.) Assen, 1968.
Phil 2475.1.61.4A Matter and memory. (Bergson, Henri.) London, 1919.
Phil 2475.1.61 Matter and memory. (Bergson, Henri.) N.Y., 1911.
Phil 2475.1.61.2 Matter and memory. (Bergson, Henri.) N.Y., 1912.
Phil 6125.13 Matter and spirit. (Pratt, J.B.) N.Y., 1922.
Phil 3494.43 Mattern, C.D. Personal freedom within the third antimony. Thesis. Philadelphia, 1941.
Phil 5822.3 Matthes, B. Betrachtungen über Wirbelthiere. Dresden, 1861.
Phil 3832.4 Matthes, Ewald. Die Unsterblichkeitslehre des Benedictus Spinoza. Inaug. Diss. Heidelberg, 1892.
Phil 8592.69 Matthes, H. Christus-Religion oder philosophische Religion? Göttingen, 1925.
Phil 6322.40 Matthew, A.V. Depth psychology and education. Kolhapur, 1944.
Phil 1812.8 Matthews, K. British philosophers. London, 1943.
Phil 8633.1.33 Matthews, Shailer. Immortality and the cosmic process. Cambridge, 1933.
Phil 8667.17 Matthews, W.R. God in Christian experience. N.Y., 193-?
Phil 8667.17.7 Matthews, W.R. The purpose of God. London, 1935.
Phil 8592.31 Matthews, W.R. Studies in Christian philosophy. London, 1921.
Phil 8887.32 Matthia, C. Systema ethicum. Marpurgi, 1626.
Phil 187.12 Matthiae, A.H. Manuel de philosophie. Paris, 1837.
Phil 525.64 Mattiesen, Emil. Der jenseitige Mensch. Berlin, 1925.
Phil 4080.3.500 Mattioli, Raffaele. Fedeltà a Croce. Milano, 1966.
Phil 8637.20.5 Mattison, H. The immortality of the soul. 2d ed. Philadelphia, 1866.
Phil 9010.11 Mattison, H. Popular amusements. N.Y., 1867?
Phil 7054.23 Mattison, H. The rappers. N.Y., n.d.
Phil 7054.23.5 Mattison, H. Spirit-rapping unveiled. N.Y., 1855.
Phil 7054.23.3 Mattison, H. Spirit rapping unveiled. N.Y., 1953.
Phil 2070.50 Máttur manna. (James, William.) Reykjavík, 1925.
Phil 6332.40 The maturational processes and the facilitating environment. (Winnicott, Donald Woods.) London, 1965.
Phil 6124.5 The mature mind. (Overstreet, H.A.) N.Y., 1949.
Phil 3425.213 Maturi, S. L'idea di Hegel. Napoli, 1891.
Phil 4170.5.30 Maturi, S. Introduzione alla filosofia. Bari, 1913.
Phil 4065.108 Maturi, Sebastiano. Bruno e Hegel. Firenze, 1926.
Phil 7069.20.250 Maturin, Edith Money. Rachel comforted. N.Y., 1920.
Phil 978.59.105 Matwani, Kewal. Krishnamurti. Madras, 1957.
Phil 3552.326 Matzat, H.L. Gesetz und Freiheit. Köln, 1948.
Phil 260.12 Mau, Jergen. Zum Problem des Infinitesimalen bei den antiken Atomisten. Berlin, 1957.
Phil 5252.150 Mauchart, I.D. Neues allgemeines Repertorium. Leipzig, 1802-03.
Phil 5875.145 Mauco, Georges. L'inconscient et la psychologie de l'enfant. 1. éd. Paris, 1970.
Phil 5415.11 Maucorps, P.H. Empathies et connaissance d'autrui. Paris, 1965.
Phil 8887.9 Maude, J.E. The foundations of ethics. N.Y., 1887.
Phil 7069.65.20 Maudiut, Jacques A. Aux fontières de l'irrationnel. Paris, 1965.
Phil 2750.28.30 Maudoussat, G. La liberté spirituelle. Paris, 1959.
Phil 6122.1.10 Maudsley, H. The physiology and pathology of the mind. 2. ed. London, 1868.
Phil 6122.1 Maudsley, H. Body and mind. London, 1870.
Phil 6122.1.3 Maudsley, H. Body and mind. N.Y., 1871.
Phil 6122.1.5 Maudsley, H. Body and mind. N.Y., 1873.
Phil 6122.1.4 Maudsley, H. Body and mind. N.Y., 1895.
Phil 5762.1 Maudsley, H. Body and will. London, 1883.
Phil 7068.86.50 Maudsley, H. Natural causes and supernatural seemings. London, 1886.
Phil 6122.1.17 Maudsley, H. Natural causes and supernatural seemings. London, 1897.
Phil 6122.1.19 Maudsley, H. Organic to human; psychology and sociology. London, 1916.
Phil 6962.2.6 Maudsley, H. The pathology of mind. London, 1895.
Phil 6962.2.9A Maudsley, H. The pathology of mind. N.Y., 1880.
Phil 6122.1.11 Maudsley, H. The physiology and pathology of the mind. N.Y., 1867.
Phil 6122.1.14 Maudsley, H. The physiology of mind. N.Y., 1872.
Phil 6122.1.13 Maudsley, H. The physiology of mind. N.Y., 1878.
Phil 6122.1.15 Maudsley, H. The physiology of mind. 3d ed. pt.1. London, 1876.

Phil 6962.2 Maudsley, H. Responsibility in mental disease. N.Y., 1874.
Phil 6962.2.3 Maudsley, H. Die Zurechnungsfähigkeit der Geisteskranken. Leipzig, 1875.
Phil 187.51 Maudsley, Henry. Life in mind and conduct. London, 1902.
Phil 6322.22 Mauerhofer, Hugo. Der schizoid-dämonische Charakter. Leipzig, 1930.
Phil 187.116 Maugé, F. L'esprit et le réel dans les limites du nombre et de la grandeur. Paris, 1937.
Phil 187.116.4 Maugé, F. L'esprit et le réel perçu. Paris, 1937.
Phil 187.78 Maugeri, P. Antonino. Corso di lezioni di filosofia razionale. Catania, 1865-1866. 2v.
Phil 6122.27 Maule, G.E. Life and law. 1st ed. Ogden, 1908.
Phil 2412.3 Maumus, Vincent. Les philosophes contemporains. Paris, 1891.
Phil 2050.206 Maund, Costance. Hume's theory of knowledge. London, 1937.
Phil 2750.8.35 Maupertuis, P.L.M. de. Essai de philosophie morale. Berlin, 1749.
Phil 2750.8.37 Maupertuis, P.L.M. de. Essai de philosophie morale. Londres, 1750.
Phil 2750.8.50 Maupertuis, P.L.M. de. Lettres de Mr. de Maupertuis. Dresden, 1752.
Phil 2750.8.79 Pamphlet box. Maupertuis, P.L.M. de.
Phil 2750.8.89 Maupertuis. (Brunet, Pierre.) Paris, 1929. 2v.
Phil 2750.8.87 Maupertuis. Thèse. (Brunet, Pierre.) Paris, 1929. 2 pam.
Phil 3425.617 Maurer, R.K. Hegel und das Ende der Geschichte. Stuttgart, 1965.
Phil 2805.214 Mauriac, F. Blaise Pascal et sa soeur Jacqueline. Paris, 1931.
Phil 2805.418 Mauriac, François. La rencontre avec Pascal. Paris, 1926.
Phil 3494.3 Maurial, E. Le scepticisme...Scepticisme de Kant. Montpellier, 1856.
Phil 3494.3.2 Maurial, E. Le scepticisme...Scepticisme de Kant. Supplément. Paris, 1857.
Phil 8962.3 Maurice, F.D. Epistles of Saint John. London, 1867.
Phil 8592.4.5 Maurice, F.D. Sequel to the inquiry, what is revelation? Cambridge, 1860.
Phil 8887.10 Maurice, F.D. Social morality. London, 1869.
Phil 9075.6 Maurice, J.F.D. The conscience. London, 1872.
Phil 812.3.3.5 Maurice, J.F.D. Mediaeval philosophy. London, 1870.
Phil 812.3.3 Maurice, J.F.D. Mediaeval philosophy. 2d ed. London, 1859.
Phil 812.3.4 Maurice, J.F.D. Modern philosophy. London, 1862.
Phil 812.3 Maurice, J.F.D. Moral and metaphysical philosophy. London, 1850.
Phil 812.3.9 Maurice, J.F.D. Moral and metaphysical philosophy. London, 1873. 2v.
Phil 812.3.2 Maurice, J.F.D. Moral and metaphysical philosophy. 2d ed. London, 1854.
Phil 8877.38 Maurice, the philosopher. (Cooke, H.P.) Cambridge, 1912.
Phil 2477.6.150 Maurice Blondel. (Lacroix, Jean.) Paris, 1963.
Phil 2477.6.99 Maurice Blondel. 2e éd. (Valensin, A.) Paris, 1934.
Phil 2477.6.81 Maurice Blondel's philosophy of action. (Gilbert, K.) Chapel Hill, 1924.
Phil 2750.20.120 Maurice Merleau-Ponty. (Derossi, Giorgio.) Torino, 1965.
Phil 2175.5.80 Maurice Nicoll. (Pogson, Beryl.) London, 1961.
Phil 5520.480.2 Mauro, Tullio de. Introduzione alla semantica. 2. ed. Bari, 1966.
Phil 2515.5.95 Maurois, André. Alain. Paris, 1950.
Phil 8887.71.5 Maurois, André. Un art de vivre. Paris, 1939.
Phil 8887.71 Maurois, André. The art of living. 5. ed. N.Y., 1940.
Phil 8887.71.10 Maurois, André. Sentiments et coutumes. 56. ed. Paris, 1934.
Phil 8413.30 Mauron, C. Aesthetics and psychology. London, 1935.
Phil 600.15 Maurras, C. L'avenir d'intelligence. Paris, 1909.
Phil 2490.96 Maurras, Charles. L'avenir de l'intelligence. 2e éd. Paris, 1917.
Phil 7080.9 Maury, L.F.A. Le sommeil et les rêves. Paris, 1861.
Phil 7080.9.3 Maury, L.F.A. Le sommeil et les rêves. Paris, 1865.
Phil 8962.2 Maushach, J. Christentum und Weltmoral. Münster, 1897.
Phil 8667.25 Mauthner, F. Der Atheismus und seine Geschichte im Abendlande. Stuttgart, 1922-23. 4v.
Phil 97.3 Mauthner, F. Wörterbuch der Philosphie. München, 1910. 2v.
Phil 5520.25 Mauthner, Fritz. Beiträge zu einer Kritik der Sprache. 2. Aufl. Stuttgart, 1906.
Phil 3832.5.5 Mauthner, Fritz. Spinoza; eine Umriss seine Lebens und Wirkens. Dresden, 1921.
Phil 3832.5 Mauthner, Fritz. Spinoza. Berlin, 1906.
Phil 3832.5.7 Mauthner, Fritz. Spinoza. 16. Aufl. Dresden, 1922.
Phil 5643.23 Mauthner, L. Gehirn und Auge. Wiesbaden, 1881.
Phil 5520.25.1 Mauthner's Critique of language. (Weiler, Gershon.) Cambridge, Eng., 1970.
Phil 2515.10.10 Le Mauvais démiurge. (Cioran, Émile M.) Paris, 1969.
Phil 9075.35.5 La mauvaise conscience. (Jankélévitch, Vladimir.) Paris, 1933.
Phil 9075.74 La mauvaise conscience. (Jankélévitch, Vladimir.) Paris, 1966.
Phil 9240.2.5 Maux présents et foi chrétienne. 2. éd. (Simard, Georges.) Montréal, 1941.
Phil 8887.49 Mauxion, Marcel. Essai sur les éléments et l'évolution. Paris, 1904.
Phil 2412.10.2 Mauzi, Robert. L'idée du bonheur dans la littérature et la pensée françaises. 2e éd. Paris, 1965.
Phil 8667.50 Mavrodes, George I. Belief in God; a study in the epistemalogy of religion. N.Y., 1970.
Phil 1135.181 Maw, Jürgen. Isonomia. Berlin, 1964.
Phil 525.57 Maw, M.B. Buddhist mysticism. Thèse. Bordeaux, 1924.
Phil 3195.11.90 Max Dessoir Mensch und Werk. (Hermann, C.) Stuttgart, 1929.
Phil 3450.7.81 Max Heinze. (Eleutheropulos, A.) Leipzig, 1909.
Phil 5592.165 Max Luescher-Institut für Medizinische Psychologie. Der Lüscher Test. Hergiswil, 1960.
Phil 3850.18.142 Max Scheler; Bibliographie. (Hartmann, Wilfried.) Stuttgart, 1963.
Phil 3850.18.215 Max Scheler; un estudio sobre el concepto de espíritu en el formalismu de Max Scheler. (Mandrioni, Héctor Delfor.) Buenos Aires, 1965.
Phil 3850.18.205 Max Scheler, 1874-1928; an intellectual portrait. (Staude, John Raphael.) N.Y., 1967.
Phil 3850.18.190 Max Scheler. (Frings, Manfred S.) Pittsburgh, 1965.
Phil 3850.18.130 Max Scheler. (Hessen, J.) Essen, 1948.
Phil 3850.18.82 Max Scheler. (Kerler, D.H.) Ulm, 1917.
Phil 3850.18.135 Max Scheler. (Konthock, K.) Berlin, 1948.
Phil 3850.18.92 Max Scheler. (Nota, J.) Utrecht, 1947.

Phil 3850.18.80 Max Scheler als Ethiker. (Wittmann, Michael.) Düsseldorf, 1923.

Phil 3850.18.87 Max Schelers Auffassung. Diss. Photoreproduction. (Neive, Heinrich.) Würzburg, 1928.

Phil 3850.18.84 Max Schelers Persönlichkeitsidee. Diss. (Hügelmann, H.) Leipzig, 1927.

Phil 3850.18.81 Max Schelers Phänomenologie der Religion. (Geyser, Joseph.) Freiburg, 1924.

Phil 3850.18.220 Max Schelers Phänomenologie des Fühlens. (Rutishauser, Bruno.) Bern, 1969.

Phil 3850.18.145 Max Schelers Phänomenologie des Psychischen. (Lorschield, Bernhard.) Bonn, 1957.

Phil 5841.2 Maxey, Wallace de Ortega. Man is a sexual being. Fresno, Calif., 1958.

Phil 5643.84 Maxfield, F.N. An experiment in linear space perception. Princeton, 1913.

Phil 8878.6 The maxims...of Agogos. (Davy, C.W.) Boston, 1844.

Phil 8877.20 Maxims. (Counsel, E.) Melbourne, 188-?

Phil 8877.20.2 Maxims. 2nd ed. (Counsel, E.) Melbourne, 1892.

Phil 8887.46 Maxims and moral reflections. (MacDonald, Normand.) N.Y., 1827.

Phil 5594.158 Maxwell, A.E. Experimental design in psychology and the medical sciences. London, 1958.

Phil 7069.03.35 Maxwell, J. Les phénomènes psychiques. Paris, 1903.

Phil 7054.159 Maxwell, Joseph. Un récent procès spirite. Bordeaux, 1904.

Phil 3494.76 May, Joseph Austin. Kant's concept of geography and its relation to recent geographical thought. Toronto, 1970.

Phil 5238.85 May, Rollo. Existence. N.Y., 1958.

Phil 5238.88.2 May, Rollo. Existential psychology. 2d ed. N.Y., 1969.

Phil 5421.25.60 May, Rollo. Love and will. 1. ed. N.Y., 1969.

Phil 5252.95A May, Rollo. Man's search for himself. N.Y., 1953.

Phil 5401.26A May, Rollo. The meaning of anxiety. N.Y., 1950.

Phil 5252.96 May, Rollo. Psychology and the human dilemma. Princeton, 1967.

Phil 4959.205 Mayagoitia, David. Ambiente filosófico de la Nueva España. México, 1945.

Phil 343.1 Mayer, A. Die Lehre von der Erkenntniss. Leipzig, 1875.

Phil 510.135 Mayer, A. Die monistische Erkenntnislehre. Leipzig, 1882.

Phil 5460.3 Mayer, A. Die Sinnestäuschungen. Wien, 1869.

Phil 5252.56 Mayer, A. Zur Seelenfrage. Mainz, 1866.

Phil 487.3 Mayer, Adolf. Los vom Materialismus! Heidelberg, 1906.

Phil 487.5 Mayer, Charles L. L'homme, esprit ou matière?. Paris, 1949.

Phil 8887.91 Mayer, Charles L. In quest of a new ethics. Boston, 1954.

Phil 487.5.10 Mayer, Charles L. Man: mind or matter? Boston, 1951.

Phil 8887.90 Mayer, Charles L. La morale de l'avenir. Paris, 1953.

Phil 2750.32.30 Mayer, Charles Leopold. L'homme face à son destin. Paris, 1964.

Phil 2750.32.35 Mayer, Charles Leopold. Man faces his destiny. London, 1968.

Phil 535.25 Mayer, Ernst. Kritik des Nihilismus. München, 1958.

Phil 812.20 Mayer, F. A history of ancient and medieval philosophy. N.Y., 1950.

Phil 6322.33 Mayer, Felix. Dynamische Tiefenspsychologie. Bern, 1953.

Phil 5520.275 Mayer, Felix. Schöpferische Sprache und Rhythmus. Berlin, 1959.

Phil 2150.16.40 Mayer, Frederick. Education and the good life. Washington, 1957.

Phil 2150.16.30 Mayer, Frederick. Essentialism. London, 1950.

Phil 1712.17A Mayer, Frederick. A history of modern philosophy. N.Y., 1951.

Phil 2150.16.45 Mayer, Frederick. New perspectives for education. Washington, 1962.

Phil 2150.16.35 Mayer, Frederick. Patterns of a new philosophy. Washington, 1955.

Phil 8837.7 Mayer, Gottlob. Die Lehre vom Erlaubten in der Geschichte der Ethic seit Schleier Macher. Leipzig, 1899.

Phil 343.12 Mayer, J.V. Der welthistorische Prozess als die unzige Grundlage der Philosophie. Freiburg, 1857.

Phil 7054.15 Mayer, John (Mrs). Further communications from the world of spirits. N.Y., 1861.

Phil 6990.3.52 Mayer, L. Lourdes, Konnersreuth oder Gallspach? Schopfheim, 1932.

Phil 97.4 Mayer, M.B. A primary glossary of psychological and philosophical terms. N.Y., 1932.

Phil 3246.215 Mayer, Otto. Fichte über das Volk. Leipzig, 1913.

Phil 8667.12 Mayer, P. Der teleologische Gottesbeweis und der Darwinismus. Mainz, 1901.

Phil 3425.121 Mayer-Moreau, K. Hegels Socialphilosophie. Tübingen, 1910.

Phil 2045.160 Mayer-Tasch, Peter Cornelius. Autonomie und Autorität; Rousseau in den Spuren von Hobbes? Neuwied, 1968.

Phil 2045.137 Mayer-Tasch, Peter Cornelius. Thomas Hobbes und das Widerstandsrecht. Mainz? 1964.

Phil 9070.142 Mayeroff, Milton. On caring. 1st American ed. N.Y., 1971.

Phil 6315.2.99 Maylan, Charles E. Freuds tragischer Komplex. 2e Aufl. München, 1929.

Phil 2805.84 Maynard, M.U. Pascal, sa vie et son charactère. Paris, 1850. 2v.

Htn Phil 5640.29* Mayne, Zachary. Two dissertations concerning sense and the imagination. London, 1728.

Phil 5590.135 Mayo, B. The logic of personality. London, 1952.

Phil 8887.100 Mayo, Bernard. Ethics and the moral life. London, 1958.

Phil 5585.82A Mayo, Elton. Achieving sanity in the modern world. Cambridge, Mass., 194-?

Phil 2150.17.94A Mayo, Elton. Excerpts from civilization - the perilous adventure. Cambridge, Mass. 19- .

Phil 2150.17.95A Mayo, Elton. Notes on a lecture on equilibrium. Cambridge, 1946?

Phil 2675.2.80 Mayo, Elton. Some notes on the psychology of Pierre Janet. Cambridge, 1948.

Phil 6100.1 Mayo, H. A series of engravings...brain...in man. London, 1827.

Phil 7060.137 Mayo, Herbert. Popular superstitions. 3. ed. Philadelphia, 1852.

Phil 6962.3 Mayo, T. Elements of pathology of human mind. London, 1838.

Phil 1117.2.7 Mayor, J.B. A sketch of ancient philosophy. Cambridge, Eng., 1889.

Phil 1117.2A Mayor, J.B. Sketch of ancient philosophy. Cambridge, 1881.

Phil 1117.2.5 Mayor, J.B. Sketch of ancient philosophy. Cambridge, 1885.

Phil 187.144 Mayor, R.J.G. Reason and common sense. London, 1951.

Phil 8411.7 Mayoux, J.J. Richard Payne Knight et le pittoresque essai sur phase esthétique. Paris, 1932.

Phil 812.43 Mayr, Franz Karl. Geschichte der Philosophie. Kevelaer, 1966.

Phil 2340.10.155 Mays, Wolfe. The philosophy of Whitehead. London, 1959.

Phil 343.26 Mayz Vallenilla, E. Ontologia del conocimiento. Caracas, 1960.

Phil 3195.6.114 Mayz Vallenilla, Ernesto. La idea de estructura psiquica in Dilthey. Caracas, 1949.

Phil 3494.64 Mayz Vallenilla, Ernesto. El problema de la nada en Kant. Madrid, 1965.

Phil 4351.4.20 La maza de fraga sobre los filosofastros liberales del día. (Alvarado, Francisco.) Madrid, 1812.

Phil 187.184 Maziarski, Stanisław. Prolegomena do filozofii przyrody inspiracji arystotelesowsko-tomistycznej. Lublin, 1969.

Phil 270.115 Mazierski, S. Determinizm i indet w aspekcie fizykalrym i filozoficznym. Lublin, 1961.

Phil 8887.45 Mazumdar, A.K. Outlines of moral philosophy. Culcutta, 1915.

Phil 2520.94 Mazure, P.A. Etudes du Cartésianisme. Paris, 1828.

Phil 8637.14 Mazzantini, C. La speranza nell immortalità. Torino, n.d.

Phil 812.42 Mazzantini, Carlo. Filosofia e storia della filosofia, 1933-1959. Torino, 1960.

Phil 5762.26 Mazzantini, Carlo. Il problema filosofico del "libero arbitrio" nelle controversie teologiche del secolo XIII. Torino, 1965.

Phil 3450.19.485 Mazzantini, Carlo. Il tempo e quattro saggi su Heidegger. Parma, 1969.

Phil 4190.2.80 Mazzarella, Pasquale. Ira finito e infinito; saggio sul pensiero di Carmelo Ottaviano. Padova, 1961.

Phil 4170.14 Mazzilli, Stefano. I sommi problemi. Padova, 1963. 2v.

Phil 8520.31 The McAlpin collection of British history and theology. (Gillett, C.R.) N.Y., 1924.

Phil 2125.77 McCosh bibliography. (Dulles, J.H.) Princeton, 1895.

Phil 5252.18.50 McDougall's social psychology anticipated by 100 years. (Hollander, B.) n.p., 1924.

Phil 2150.15.95 Mead, G.H. The social psychology of George Herbert Meal. Chicago, 1956.

Phil 8592.27 Mead, G.R.S. Quests old and new. London, 1913.

Phil 5252.71 Mead, George H. The definition of the psychical. Chicago, 1903.

Phil 1712.14A Mead, George H. Movements of thought in the nineteenth century. Chicago, 1936.

Phil 187.100.5 Mead, George H. The philosophy of the act. Chicago, 1938.

Phil 187.100 Mead, George H. The philosophy of the present. Chicago, 1932.

Phil 2150.15.30 Mead, George Herbert. George Herbert Mead. N.Y., 1968.

Phil 2150.15.20 Mead, George Herbert. Selected writings. Indianapolis, 1964.

Phil 187.133 Mead, Hunter. Types and problems of philosophy. N.Y., 1946.

Phil 2205.83 Meadley, G.W. Memoirs of William Paley, D.D. Sunderland, 1809. 2 pam.

Phil 8887.41.5 Meakin, F. Function, feeling, and conduct. N.Y., 1910.

Phil 8887.41 Meakin, J.P. A man worth while. Rahway, N.J., 1913.

Phil 2115.115 The meaning...of...philosophy of John Locke. (Lodge, Rupert C.) Minneapolis, 1918.

Phil 194.56 Meaning and action. (Thayer, Horace Standish.) Indianapolis, 1968.

Phil 8598.133 The meaning and end of religion. (Smith, W.C.) N.Y., 1963.

Phil 5068.18.5 Meaning and existence. (Bergmann, Gustav.) Madison, 1960.

Phil 5520.108 Meaning and interpretation. (California. University. Philosophical Union.) Berkeley, 1950.

Phil 344.5 Meaning and knowledge. (Nagel, Ernest.) N.Y., 1965.

Phil 6312.24 The meaning and measurement of neuroticism and anxiety. (Cattell, Raymond.) N.Y., 1961.

Phil 8586.4 The meaning and method of life. (Gould, George M.) N.Y., 1893.

Phil 5520.570 Meaning and mind. (Terwilliger, Robert F.) N.Y., 1968.

Phil 5520.121.2 Meaning and necessity. (Carnap, Rudolf.) Chicago, 1964.

Phil 6980.293 The meaning and practice of psychotherapy. (Fisher, Vivian Ezra.) N.Y., 1950.

Phil 8602.50 Meaning and purpose. (Walker, K.M.) London, 1944.

Phil 5520.746 Meaning and truth: an inaugural lecture delivered before the University of Oxford on 5 November 1969. (Strawson, Peter Frederick.) Oxford, 1970.

Phil 5520.412 Meaning and truth in religion. (Christian, W.A.) Princeton, 1964.

Phil 8408.36.2 Meaning and truth in the art. (Haspers, John.) Hamden, Connecticut, 1946.

Phil 8408.36 Meaning and truth in the arts. (Haspers, John.) Chapel Hill, 1947.

Phil 3925.16.160 Meaning and truth in Wittgenstein's Tractatus. (Morrison, James.) The Hague, 1968.

Phil 8591.36 The meaning and truth of religion. (Lyman, E.W.) N.Y., 1933.

Phil 179.3.27.15 The meaning and value of life. (Eucken, R.) London, 1909.

Phil 525.30.2 The meaning and value of mysticism. 2nd ed. (Herman, E.) London, 1916.

Phil 585.188 Meaning for man. (Chambliss, Rollin.) N.Y., 1966.

Phil 7084.14 The meaning in dreams and dreaming. 1st ed. (Mahoney, Maria F.) N.Y., 1966.

Phil 5401.26A The meaning of anxiety. (May, Rollo.) N.Y., 1950.

Phil 8407.14.10 The meaning of art. (Gaultlier, Paul.) Philadelphia, 1914.

Phil 8413.9 The meaning of art. (McMahon, Amos.) N.Y., 1930.

Phil 8419.28 The meaning of beauty, a theory of aesthetics. (Stace, W.T.) London, 1929.

Phil 8598.29 The meaning of Christianity. 2. ed. (Spencer, F.A.M.) London, 1914.

Phil 7040.43 The meaning of despair. (Gaylin, Willard.) N.Y., 1968.

Phil 7082.72.15 The meaning of dreams. (Coriat, Isador Henry.) Boston, 1915.

Phil 7082.72.5 The meaning of dreams. (Graves, Robert.) London, 1924.

Phil 7082.72.20 The meaning of dreams. (Hall, Calvin Springer.) N.Y., 1953.

Phil 7082.72.10 The meaning of dreams. (Roback, Abraham Aaron.) n.p., 193-

Phil 8620.51 The meaning of evil. (Journet, C.) N.Y., 1963.

Phil 190.81 The meaning of existence. (Pontifex, Mark.) London, 1953.

Phil 5790.50 The meaning of gifts. (Tournier, Paul.) Richmond, Va., 1970.

Phil 8662.7 The meaning of God in human experience. (Hocking, W.E.) New Haven, Conn., 1912.

Phil 8662.7.6A The meaning of God in human experience. (Hocking, W.E.) New Haven, Conn., 1924.

Phil 8662.7.5 The meaning of God in human experience. (Hocking, W.E.) New Haven, 1923.

Phil 8878.23.4   The meaning of good. 4th ed. (Dickinson, G.L.)
N.Y., 1907.

Phil 3450.19.175   The meaning of Heidegger. (Langan, Thomas.) N.Y., 1959.

Phil 8595.38   The meaning of human existence. (Paul, Leslie A.)
London, 1949.

Phil 8633.1.36.5   The meaning of immortality in human experience. (Hocking,
W.E.) N.Y., 1957.

Phil 365.40   The meaning of life. (Joad, C.E.N.) London, 1928.

Phil 6990.3.100   The meaning of Lourdes. (Izard, Francis.) London, 1939.

Phil 4769.1.70   The meaning of love. (Solov'ev, V.S.) London, 1945.

Phil 8592.80   The meaning of man. (Mouroux, Jean.) N.Y., 1952.

Phil 5520.35   The meaning of meaning. (Ogden, Charles K.) London, 1923.

Phil 5520.35.10   The meaning of meaning. (Ogden, Charles K.) N.Y., 1936.

Phil 5520.35.3   The meaning of meaning. 3. ed. (Ogden, Charles K.)
N.Y., 1930.

Phil 5520.35.7   The meaning of meaning. 5. ed. (Ogden, Charles K.)
London, 1938.

Phil 5520.35.5   The meaning of meaning. 5. ed. (Ogden, Charles K.)
N.Y., 1938.

Phil 5520.35.8   The meaning of meaning. 7. ed. (Ogden, Charles K.)
N.Y., 1945.

Phil 5520.35.9   The meaning of meaning. 8. ed. (Ogden, Charles K.)
N.Y., 1953.

Phil 5520.35.12   The meaning of meaning. 8. ed. (Ogden, Charles K.)
N.Y., 1956.

Phil 8408.45   The meaning of modern art. (Harries, Karsten.)
Evanston, 1968.

Phil 8666.21.5   The meaning of modern atheism. (Lacroix, Jean.)
N.Y., 1966.

Phil 525.69   The meaning of mysticism. (Riley, I.W.) N.Y., 1930.

Phil 7069.66.5   The meaning of personal existence. (Osborn, Arthur
Walter.) London, 1966.

Phil 5590.548   The meaning of persons. (Tournier, Paul.) N.Y., 1957.

Phil 6325.11   The meaning of psychoanalysis. (Peck, Martin W.)
N.Y., 1931.

Phil 5254.2   The meaning of psychology. (Ogden, C.K.) N.Y., 1926.

Phil 8590.30   The meaning of religion. (Kristensen, William.) The
Hague, 1960.

Phil 8877.65.20A   The meaning of right and wrong. (Cabot, Richard C.)
N.Y., 1933.

Phil 8877.65.22   The meaning of right and wrong. (Cabot, Richard C.)
N.Y., 1936.

Phil 8633.1.28   The meaning of selfhood and faith in immortality. (Lyman,
E.W.) Cambridge, 1928.

Phil 1200.62   The meaning of stoicism. (Edelstein, Ludwig.)
Cambridge, 1966.

Phil 194.23   The meaning of terms 'existence' and 'reality'.
(Thalheimer, A.) Princeton, 1920.

Phil 4752.2.72   The meaning of the creative act. (Berdiaev, Nikolai
Aleksandrovich.) N.Y., 1955.

Phil 8615.2.3   The meaning of the ethical movement, fifth anniversary
address. (Sheldon, Walter L.) St. Louis, 1891.

Phil 5627.134.60   The meaning of the groups. (Spencer, F.A.M.)
London, 1934.

Phil 8888.12   The meaning of the moral life. (Nevins, W.N.) N.Y., 1930.

Phil 2475.1.63   The meaning of the war. (Bergson, Henri.) London, 1915.

Phil 184.3.22.5A   The meaning of truth. (James, W.) N.Y., 1914.

Phil 2070.28   The meaning of truth. (James, William.) N.Y., 1914.

Phil 3195.6.50   Meanings in history. (Dilthey, Wilhelm.) London, 1961.

Phil 97.6   Means, B.W. Selected glossary of philosophical terms.
Hartford, Connecticut, 1943.

Htn   Phil 9358.2.5*   Means and ends, or Self-training. (Sedgwick, C.)
Boston, 1839.

Phil 9172.5   Means without living. Boston, 1837.

Phil 585.360   The measure of a man. 1st ed. (Williams, Gershom Antonio.)
Toronto, 1970.

Phil 1710.5.10   The measure of man. 1. ed. (Krutch, Joseph W.)
Indianapolis, 1954.

Phil 5259.11.5   Measure your mind. (Trabue, M.R.) Garden City, 1921.

Phil 5272.12   The measurement and prediction of judgment and choice.
(Bock, R. Darrell.) San Francisco, 1968.

Phil 5592.171   Measurement in personality and cognition. (Messick, S.)
N.Y., 1962.

Phil 5330.12   The measurement of attention. (Geissler, L.R.)
n.p., 1909.

Phil 5330.24   The measurement of attention. (Woodrow, H.)
Princeton, 1914.

Phil 5762.17   The measurement of conation. (McCarthy, R.C.)
Chicago, 1926.

Phil 5400.64   The measurement of emotional reactions. (Wechsler, David.)
N.Y., 1925.

Phil 5650.42   The measurement of hearing. (Hirsh, Ira Jean.)
N.Y., 1952.

Phil 5520.190   The measurement of meaning. (Osgood, C.E.) Urbana, 1957.

Phil 6316.30   The measurement of psychological states through the content
analysis of verbal behavior. (Gottschalk, Louis.)
Berkeley, 1969.

Phil 8837.16   Méautis, Georges. Mes pélerinages de l'âme. Paris, 1959.

Phil 6120.5   Mécanisme cérébral de la pensée. (Kostyleff, N.)
Paris, 1914.

Htn   Phil 6000.2*   Mécanisme de la physionomie humaine. (Duchenne, Guillaume
B.) Paris, 1876.

Phil 7069.23.19   Le mécanisme de la survie. (Rutot, A.) Paris, 1923.

Phil 5400.23   Le mécanisme des émotions. (Sollier, P.) Paris, 1905.

Phil 5374.154   Le mécanisme du courant de la conscience. (Peucesco, M.G.)
Paris, 1922.

Phil 5374.154.2   Le mécanisme du courant de la conscience. Thèse.
(Peucesco, M.G.) Paris, 1921.

Phil 6116.30   Mécanisme et intelligence. (Goër de Herve, Jacques de.)
Paris, 1969.

Phil 9075.55   Les mécanismes cerebraux de la prise de conscience.
(Chauchord, Paul.) Paris, 1956.

Phil 5545.91   Les mécanismes de la mémoire en rapport avec ses objects.
(Wallon, H.) Paris, 1951.

Phil 5520.610   Les mécanismes du comportement verbal. (Ehrlich,
Stéphane.) Paris, 1968.

Phil 5585.195   Les mécanismes perceptifs. (Piaget, Jean.) Paris, 1961.

Phil 5722.8.5   Les mécanismes subconscients. (Dwelshauvers, G.)
Paris, 1925.

Phil 5374.36   Il meccanismo della coscienza. (Pavese, R.) Milano, 1922.

Phil 4060.7   Un meccanismo umano. (Acari, P.) Milano, 1909.

Phil 5875.130   Mecham, Merlin J. Development of audiolinguistic skills in
children. St. Louis, 1969.

Phil 6132.41.5   Mechanical man. (Wooldridge, Dean E.) N.Y., 1968.

Phil 665.59.5   Die Mechanik der Seele. 3e Aufl. (Weidenbach, H.)
Mannheim, 1931.

Phil 6131.3   Die Mechanik des Geisteslebens. (Verworn, M.)
Leipzig, 1910.

Phil 5259.14   Die Mechanik des Seelenlebens. (Theone, Alois S.)
Bonn, 1911.

Phil 510.23   Der mechanische Monismus. (Gutberlet, C.)
Paderborn, 1893.

Phil 193.44   Mechanism and personality. (Shoup, F.A.) Boston, 1891.

Htn   Phil 6117.5*A   Mechanism in thought and morals. (Holmes, O.W.)
Boston, 1871.

Phil 6117.5.7   Mechanism in thought and morals. (Holmes, O.W.)
Boston, 1879.

Phil 6117.5.6   Mechanism in thought and morals. (Holmes, O.W.)
Boston, 1882.

Phil 7069.27.38   The mechanism of death. (Sherrill, E.P.) Boston, 1927.

Phil 5242.11   The mechanism of man. (Cox, E.W.) London, 1876. 2v.

Phil 5520.588   The mechanism of mind. (De Bono, Edward.) N.Y., 1969.

Phil 6111.35   The mechanism of the brain. (Bianchi, L.) Edinburgh 1922.

Phil 5650.15   The mechanism of the cochlea. (Wilkinson, G.)
London, 1924.

Phil 5257.51   The mechanism of thought. (Rosett, Joshua.) N.Y., 1939.

Phil 9035.23   Mechanisms of character formation. (White, William A.)
N.Y., 1916.

Phil 5545.246   Mechanisms of memory. (John, Erwin Roy.) N.Y., 1967.

Phil 5585.195.5   The mechanisms of perception. (Piaget, Jean.)
London, 1969.

Phil 6122.43   Der Mechanismus der Seele. (Marguardt, H.)
Holstein, 1921.

Phil 510.5.15   Der Mechanismus des menschlichen Denkens. (Ruckhaber,
Erich.) Brackwede, 1911.

Phil 8735.13   Mechanismus und Teleologie. (Erhart, Franz.)
Leipzig, 1890.

Phil 5421.30   Mechanu, David. Students under stress. N.Y., 1962.

Phil 3260.86   Mechler, W. Die Erkenntnislehre bei Fries. Inaug. Diss.
Berlin, 1911.

Phil 187.28.13   Mechnikov, I.I. Beiträge zur einer optimistischen
Weltauffassung. München, 1908.

Phil 187.28.11   Mechnikov, I.I. Essais optimistes. Paris, 1907.

Phil 187.28.22   Mechnikov, I.I. Etiudy o prirode cheloveka. Izd. 2.
Moskva, 1905.

Phil 187.28.15   Mechnikov, I.I. Ėtiudy optimizma. Moskva, 1907.

Phil 187.28.2   Mechnikov, I.I. Études sur la nature humaine.
Paris, 1903.

Phil 187.28   Mechnikov, I.I. Études sur la nature humaine. 2. ed.
Paris, 1903.

Phil 187.28.3   Mechnikov, I.I. Études sur la nature humaine. 5. ed.
Paris, 1917.

Phil 187.28.7   Mechnikov, I.I. Nature of man. London, 1938.

Phil 187.28.6.7   Mechnikov, I.I. Nature of man. N.Y., 1911.

Phil 187.28.25   Mechnikov, I.I. Sorok let iskaniia ratsional'nago
mirovozzreniia. Moskva, 1913.

Phil 187.28.4   Mechnikov, I.I. Studien über die Natur des Menschen.
Leipzig, 1904.

Phil 187.28.8   Mechnikov, I.I. Studier öfver människans natur.
Stockholm, 1906.

Phil 2475.1.198   Meckauer, Walter. Der Intuitionismus und seine Elemente
bei Henri Bergson. Leipzig, 1917.

Phil 5022.2   Meckies, H. Beiträge zur Geschichte des
Induktionsproblems. Münster, 1933.

Phil 8887.51   Mecklin, John M. An introduction to social ethics.
N.Y., 1920.

Phil 9440.1   Med ideali in resniönostjo. Ljubljana, 1970.

Phil 5051.28.15   Med logiko in filozofijo. (Jermen, Frane.)
Ljubljana, 1971.

Phil 8598.76   Meddelelser af indholdet af et skrivt fra aaret. v.1-2.
(Sibbern, F.C.) Kjøbenhavn, 1858-72.

Phil 6675.2   La médecine d'imagination. (Féré, C.) Paris, 1886.

Phil 6959.1.20   La médecine psychologique. (Janet, Pierre.) Paris, 1923.

Phil 8897.21   Les médecins moralistes. (Woillez, C.T.R.) Paris, 1862.

Phil 60.2   Mededeelingen. (Utrecht. Rijksuniversiteit. Psychologisch
Laboratorium.) Utrecht. 1-7,1924-1933 3v.

Phil 3846.10   Mededeslingen. (Rijnsburg, Netherlands. Spinozahuis.)
Leiden. 1,1934+ 3v.

Phil 6682.18   Medeiros e Albuquerque, J.J. de C. da C. O hypnotismo. 3.
ed. Rio de Janeiro, 1926.

Phil 4570.1.83   Meden, Carl. Om Grubbes deduktion af rättsbegreppet.
Uppsala, 1869.

Phil 1524.2   The mediaeval mind. (Taylor, H.O.) London, 1911. 2v.

Phil 1524.2.15A   The mediaeval mind. 4th ed. (Taylor, H.O.) Cambridge,
Mass., 1949. 2v.

Phil 530.11.22   The mediaeval mystics of England. (Colledge, Eric.)
N.Y., 1961.

Phil 525.233   Mediaeval mystique tradition and S. John of the Cross.
London, 1954.

Phil 812.3.3.5   Mediaeval philosophy. (Maurice, J.F.D.) London, 1870.

Phil 812.3.3   Mediaeval philosophy. 2d ed. (Maurice, J.F.D.)
London, 1859.

Phil 1527.1.17   Mediaeval philosophy illustrated from the system of Thomas
Aquinas. (Wulf, M. de.) Cambridge. 1922.

Phil 4800.10   Mediaevalia philosophica polonorum. Warszawa. 1,1958+

Phil 7068.63.35   Les médiateurs et les moyens de la magie. (Gougenot des
Mousseaux, H.R.) Paris, 1863.

Phil 5258.40   Mediation; the function of thought. (Sullivan, H.)
Andover, 1871.

Phil 6129.1   Medical aspects of mental dicipline. (Phomson, W.H.)
N.Y., 1890.

Phil 22.2   Medical critic and psychological journal. London.
2-3,1862-1863 2v.

Phil 6967.3.2   Medical inquiries...diseases...mind. (Rush, B.)
Philadelphia, 1830.

Phil 6967.3.5   Medical inquiries...diseases...mind. 5. ed. (Rush, B.)
Philadelphia, 1835.

Phil 5190.1   Medical logic. (Oesterlen, F.) London, 1855.

Phil 5258.124.5   Medical psychology. (Schilder, Paul.) N.Y., 1953.

Phil 6322.6.5   Medical psychology and psychological research. (Mitchell,
T.W.) London, 1922.

Phil 6310.4.10   The medical value of psychoanalysis. (Alexander, Franz G.)
N.Y., 1936.

Phil 6959.1.15   Les médications psychologiques. (Janet, Pierre.)
Paris, 1919. 3v.

Phil 8886.4   Medicina mentis. (Lange, J.) London, 1715.

Phil 3890.2.30   Medicina mentis. (Tschirnhaus, E.W. von.) Lipsiae, 1695.

Phil 6115.13   Medicine and the mind. (Fleury, D.M. de.) London, 1900.

Phil 3565.68   Medicinische Psychologie. (Lotze, Hermann.)
Leipzig, 1852.

Htn   Phil 3565.68.1*   Medicinische Psychologie. (Lotze, Hermann.)
Leipzig, 1852.

Phil 720.40   Medicus, F. Menschlichkeit. Zürich, 1951.

Phil 3246.93.5   Medicus, Fritz. Fichtes Leben. Leipzig, 1914.

Phil 5762.16   Medicus, Fritz. Die Freiheit des Willens und ihre Grenzen.
Tübingen, 1926.

Phil 8413.14   Medicus, Fritz. Grundfragen der Ästhetik. Jena, 1917.
Phil 3246.93A   Medicus, Fritz. Johann Gottlieb Fichte; Dreizehn Vorlesungen gehalten and der Universität Halle. Berlin, 1905.
Phil 3625.17.30   Medicus, Fritz. Das mythologische in der Religion. Erlenbach, 1944.
Phil 187.135   Medicus, Fritz. Natur und Geist. Erlenback-Zurich, 1946.
Phil 187.135.5   Medicus, Fritz. Vom überzeitlichen in der Zeit. Zürich, 1954.
Phil 8402.12.5   Medida estetica. (Birkhoff, G.D.) Rosario, 1945.
Phil 1750.156   Medieval humanism. (Walsh, Gerald G.) N.Y., 1942.
Phil 1540.30   Medieval logic. (Böhner, P.) Chicago, 1952.
Phil 1540.30.2   Medieval logic. (Böhner, P.) Manchester, 1952.
Phil 6307.332   Medieval minds; mental health in the Middle Ages. (Graham, Thomas F.) London, 1967.
Phil 1504.27   Medieval philosophical texts in translation. Milwaukee. 6-19+ 8v.
Phil 1507.7   Medieval philosophy. (Copleston, F.C.) London, 1952.
Phil 1507.7.2   Medieval philosophy. (Copleston, F.C.) N.Y., 1952.
Phil 1523.14   Medieval philosophy. (Shapiro, Herman.) N.Y., 1964.
Phil 1560.18   Medieval philosophy: from St. Augustine to Nicolas of Cusa. (Wippel, John F.) N.Y., 1969.
Phil 1516.4   Medieval thought. (Leff, Gordon.) Harmondsworth, 1958.
Phil 1511.3.23   Medieval universalism and its present value. (Gilson, Etienne.) N.Y., 1937.
Phil 3808.126.2   Medilch, P. La theorie de l'intelligence chez Schopenhauer. Paris, 1923.
Phil 8667.11   Medina, Juan J. La cruzada del error. Sevilla, 1879.
Phil 8592.39   Medina, Juan J. Cuadros disolventes. Sevilla, 1881.
Phil 8592.42   Medina. Conjunto de las doctrinas y filosofías del siglo comparadas con los conocimientos modernos. Madrid, 1872.
Phil 1507.9   Medioevo monastico e scolastico. (Cilento, Vicenzo.) Milano, 1961.
Phil 4479.2.30   Meditação sobre a cultura. (Santos, Delfin.) Lisboa, 1946.
Phil 8887.74   Meditaciones morales. (Martínez de Trujillo, Maria.) México, 1948.
Phil 2520.53.10   Meditações metafisicas. (Descartes, René.) Coimbra, 1930.
Phil 978.49.870   Meditation als Erkenntnisweg. (Buehler, W.) Stuttgart, 1962.
Phil 8583.43.5   Meditation im christlichen Dasein. (Dessauer, Philipp.) München, 1968.
Phil 2520.52.80   Meditationen über die erste Philosophie. (Descartes, René.) Hamburg, 1956.
Phil 2520.53.4   Meditationen über die Grundlagen der Philosophie. 4e Aufl. (Descartes, René.) Leipzig, 1915.
Phil 2520.13.14   Meditationeo de prima philosophia. (Descartes, René.) Amsterdam, 1685.
Phil 2520.52.20   Meditationes de prima philosophia. (Descartes, René.) Amstelodami, 1644.
Phil 2520.52.25   Meditationes de prima philosophia. (Descartes, René.) Amstelodami, 1650. 3 pam.
Phil 2520.52.26   Meditationes de prima philosophia. (Descartes, René.) Amstelodami, 1654.
Phil 2520.52.27   Meditationes de prima philosophia. (Descartes, René.) Amstelodami, 1678.
Phil 2520.52.28   Meditationes de prima philosophia. (Descartes, René.) Amstelodami, 1698. 3 pam.
Phil 2520.52.60   Meditationes de prima philosophia. (Descartes, René.) Amsterdam, 1657. 5 pam.
Phil 2520.14   Meditationes de prima philosophia. (Descartes, René.) Amsterdam, 1685.
Phil 2520.14.9   Meditationes de prima philosophia. (Descartes, René.) München, 1901.
Phil 2520.52.32   Meditationes de prima philosophia. (Descartes, René.) Paris, 1944.
Htn   Phil 2520.52.17*   Meditationes de prima philosophia. 2a ed. (Descartes, René.) Amstelodami, 1642. 2 pam.
Phil 2520.14.2   Meditationes de prima philosophia. 2e. Aufl. (Descartes, René.) München, 1912.
Phil 2520.52.8   Les méditationes métaphysiques. 2e éd. (Descartes, René.) Paris, 1661.
Phil 2520.52.10   Les méditationes métaphysiques. 3e éd. (Descartes, René.) Paris, 1673.
Phil 177.25   Meditationes philosophicae. (Canz, Israel Gottlieb.) Tubingae, 1750.
Htn   Phil 186.33*   Meditationes philosophicae de Deo, mundo, homine. (Lau, Theodor L.) Frankfurt, 1717.
Phil 3095.51   Meditationes philosophicae de nonnullis ad poema pertinentibus. (Baumgarten, A.G.) Halae, 1735.
Phil 3552.285   Meditationes philosophicas. (Alstrin, Eric.) Upsala, 1731.
Phil 2520.50.5   The meditations, and selections from the Principles of René Descartes. (Descartes, René.) n.p., 1968.
Phil 2520.52.75   Méditations. 4. éd. (Descartes, René.) Paris, 1952.
Phil 182.67.5   Méditations cartésiennes. (Husserl, Edmund.) Paris, 1931.
Phil 2733.41   Méditations chrétiennes. (Malebranche, Nicolas.) Paris, 1928.
Htn   Phil 2733.39*   Méditations chrétiennes et métaphysiques. (Malebranche, Nicolas.) Lyon, 1707.
Phil 181.21   Méditations critiques. (Gruyer, L.A.) Paris, 1847.
Phil 8881.23.15   Méditations et études morales. (Guizot, F.P.G.) Paris, 1864.
Phil 8598.78   Meditations in season on the elements of Christian philosophy. (Schneider, H.W.) N.Y., 1938.
Phil 2630.1.35   Méditations inédites. (Gratry, Auguste.) Paris, 1926.
Htn   Phil 2520.52.7*   Les méditations métaphysics. (Descartes, René.) Paris, 1647.
Phil 2520.52.35   Les méditations métaphysiques. (Descartes, René.) Paris, 1724. 2v.
Phil 2733.40   Méditations métaphysiques. (Malebranche, Nicolas.) Paris, 1841.
Phil 8894.6.5   Méditations morales. (Tissot, Joseph.) Paris, 1860.
Phil 9354.1   Meditations of a young man. (Olcott, Gage.) Boston, 1914.
Phil 8887.12   Méditations philogiques et morales. (Mercier, A.D.) Paris, 1835.
Phil 2733.43   Méditations pour se disposer à l'humilité et à la pénitence. (Malebranche, Nicolas.) Paris, 1944.
Phil 9075.50   Meditations pour une éthique de la personne. 1st éd. (Bastide, G.) Paris, 1953.
Phil 8586.34.5   Méditations sur la religion chrétienne. (Guizot, F.P.G.) Paris, 1866-1868. 3v.
Phil 8586.34.3   Méditations sur l'essence de la religion. (Guizot, F.P.G.) Paris, 1866.
Phil 8586.34.2   Méditations sur l'essence de la religion chrétienne. 1e série. (Guizot, F.P.G.) Paris, 1864.
Phil 8586.34   Méditations sur l'essence de la religion chrétienne. 1e série. (Guizot, F.P.G.) Paris, 1864.

Phil 176.138   Méditations sur l'existence. (Berdiaev, Nikolai A.) Paris, 1936.
Phil 186.85   Méditations sur l'omnitude. (Ladet, F.) Paris, 1936.
Phil 978.49.545   Meditative Betrachtungen und Anleitungen zur Vertiefung der Heilkunst. (Steiner, R.) Dornach, 1967.
Phil 4200.6.30   Meditazione critiche. (Petruzzellis, Nicola.) Napoli, 1960.
Phil 4170.7.60   Le meditazioni cartesiane rinnovate nel seccolo XIX. (Mamiani della Rovere, Terenzio.) Firenze, 1869.
Phil 1955.6.235   Meditazioni deweyane. (Filograsso, Nando.) Urbino, 1968.
Phil 2520.52.50   Meditazioni filosofiche. (Descartes, René.) Torino, 1927.
Phil 4115.53   Meditazioni filosofiche inedite. (Gioberti, V.) Firenze, 1909.
Phil 4114.47   Meditazioni filosofiche sulla religione e sulla morale. (Genovesi, Antonio.) Bassano, 1783.
Phil 1870.165   Meditazioni su Berkeley. (Testa, Aldo.) Bologna, 1965.
Phil 4073.116   Meditazioni su Campanella. (Testa, Aldo.) Bologna, 1965.
Phil 2520.241   Le meditizioni di Cartesio. (Nardi, Bruno.) Roma, 1952.
Phil 7054.45.50   Le médium D.D. Home. (Gardy, Louis.) Genève, 189-.
Phil 7054.45.60   Das medium D.D. Home. (Tischner, R.) Leipzig, 1925.
Phil 7054.149   Mediumistic experiences of John Brown. 3. ed. (Brown, John.) San Francisco, 1897.
Phil 7054.106   Mediums and mediumship. (Hazard, T.R.) Boston, 1872.
Phil 7054.106.2   Mediums and mediumship. (Hazard, T.R.) Boston, 1873.
Phil 7069.02.12   Mediums of the 19th century. (Podmore, Frank.) N.Y., 1963. 2v.
Phil 7069.00.53   Mediumship and its laws. 3. ed. (Tuttle, Hudson.) Chicago, 1900.
Phil 7069.41.4   The mediumship of Jack Webber. (Edwards, Harry.) N.Y., 1941.
Phil 7055.256   The mediumship of Mrs. Leonard. (Smith, Susy.) New Hyde Park, N.Y., 1964.
Phil 6320.6.3   Medizinische Psychologie. 3. Aufl. (Kretschmer, E.) Leipzig, 1926.
Phil 8413.35   Medlöe, Jon. Kunst og idé. Oslo, 1965.
VPhil 5401.51   O medo no seculo XX. (Alvarez, Martins d'.) Rio de Janeiro, 1964.
Phil 8430.10   Meduse et cie. (Caillais, Roger.) Paris, 1960.
Phil 5625.103   Medvedev, N.M. Teoriia otrazheniia i ee estestvenno-nauchnoe obosnovanie. Moskva, 1963.
Phil 8980.564   Medynskii, Grigorii A. Trudnaia kniga. Moskva, 1964.
Phil 4803.497.45   Medytacje o życiu godziwym. (Kotarbiński, Tadeusz.) Warszawa, 1966.
Phil 9070.48   Meehan, Francis Joseph D. The temple of the spirit. N.Y., 1948.
Phil 187.88   Meek, Charles. The will to function. Bisley, 1929.
Phil 7150.63F   Meer, Fatima. Suicide in Durban. Durban, 1964.
Phil 5643.120   Meer, H.C. von der. Die Links-Rechts-Polarisation des phaenomenalen Raumes. Groningen, 1959.
Phil 5252.36.2   Meerkatz. Einführung in die Psychologie. 2. Aufl. Halle, 1919.
Phil 5780.16   Meerlo, A.M. The rape of the mind. 1. ed. Cleveland, 1956.
Phil 5520.106   Meerloo, A.M. Conversation and communication. N.Y., 1952.
Phil 5520.106.5   Meerloo, A.M. Het web van menselijke en sociale relaties. Den Haag, 1962.
Phil 5465.172   Meerloo, Joost Abraham Maurits. Creativity and eternization. Assen, 1967.
Phil 7069.68.50   Meesters van het verborgene. (Bunge, H.) Amsterdam, 1968.
Phil 1701.11   The meeting of extremes in contemporary philosophy. (Bosanquet, Bernard.) London, 1921.
Phil 8583.35.5   The meeting of love and knowledge. 1. ed. (D'Arcy, M.C.) N.Y., 1957.
Phil 7069.19.130   The meeting of the spheres. (Herbine, Charlotte G.) N.Y., 1919.
Phil 5421.20.100   Megargee, Edwin I. The dynamics of aggression. N.Y., 1970.
Phil 5590.457   Megargee, Edwin I. Research in clinical assessment. N.Y., 1966.
Phil 1750.105   Meglio, Gaetano. Prospettive filosofiche. Padova, 1966.
Phil 7082.94   Mégroz, Rodolphe Louis. The dream world. N.Y., 1939.
Phil 8592.113   Mehl, R. The condition of the Christian philosopher. London, 1963.
Phil 8962.30   Mehl, Roger. Ethique catholique et éthique protestante. Neuchâtel, 1970.
Phil 1712.18   Mehl, Roger. Images de l'homme. Genève, 1953.
Phil 1712.18.2   Mehl, Roger. Images of man. Richmond, 1965.
Phil 2490.126   Mehlis, G. Die Geschichtsphilosophie Auguste Comtes. Leipzig, 1909.
Phil 525.78   Mehlis, G. Die Mystik. München, 1927.
Phil 8887.52   Mehlis, Georg. Probleme der ethik. Tübingen, 1918.
Phil 3801.565   Mehlis, Georg. Schellings Geschichtsphilosophie in den Jahren 1799-1804. Heidelberg, 1906.
Phil 8592.23   Mehlis, Goerg. Einfuhrung in ein System...Religions. Tübingen, 1917.
Phil 3493.8   Mehr Licht! (Last, E.) Berlin, 1879.
Phil 5590.483   Mehrabian, Albert. An analysis of personality theories. Englewood Cliffs, N.J., 1968.
Phil 1020.6   Mehren, A.F. Correspondance philosophique d'Ibn Sab'in. Florence, 1879.
Phil 6390.2   Die Mehrheit geistiger Persönlichkeiten in einem Individuum. (Landmann, S.) Stuttgart, 1894.
Phil 3640.515   Mehring, Franz. Friedrich Nietzsche. Berlin, 1957.
Phil 812.16   Mehring, Franz. Zur Geschichte der Philosophie. Berlin, 1931?
Phil 187.85   Mehring, G. Grundzüge der speculativen Kritik. Heilbronn, 1844.
Phil 5252.6   Mehring, G. Philosophische-Kritische Grundsätze der Selbsterkenntniss. Stuttgart, 1857.
Phil 3450.19.475   Mehta, Jarava Lal. The philosophy of Martin Heidegger. Varanasi, 1967.
Phil 1812.15   Mehta, Ved P. Fly and the fly-bottle. 1. ed. Boston, 1962.
Phil 4170.12   Mei, F. Storia e significato del superuomo. Milano, 1962.
Phil 4170.12.10   Mei, Flavio. Eroicità ed ereticalità della filosofia. Milano, 1968.
Phil 3808.235   Mei, Flavio. Etica e politica nel pensiero di Schopenhauer. Milano, 1966.
Phil 4170.12.5   Mei, Flavio. La missione del filosofo. Milano, 1964.
Phil 3640.740   Mei, Flavio. Tramonto della ragione. Milano, 1967.
Phil 6319.1.208   Meier, Carl A. Jung and analytical psychology. Newton, Mass., 1959.
Phil 6319.1.209   Meier, Carl A. Lehrbuch der komplexen Psychologie C.G. Jungs. Zürich, 1968.
Phil 3801.563   Meier, F. Die Idee der Transzendentalphilosophie. Winterthur, 1961.
Phil 3625.8.62   Meier, Georg Friedrich. Auszug aus der Vernunftlehre. Halle, 1752.

Author and Title Listing

Phil 3625.8.31 Meier, Georg Friedrich. Betrachtung über den Fehler der menschlichen Tugenden. Halle, 1755.

Phil 3625.8.57 Meier, Georg Friedrich. Beweis: dass' keine Materie dencken Könne. 2e Aufl. Halle, 1751. 7 pam.

Phil 3625.8.58 Meier, Georg Friedrich. Beweis dass die menschliche Seele ewig Lebt. Halle, 1751.

Phil 3625.8.55 Meier, Georg Friedrich. Beweiss: das keine Materie dencken Könne. Halel, 1742.

Phil 3625.8.38 Meier, Georg Friedrich. Gedancken von der Ehre. Halle, 1746.

Phil 3625.8.41 Meier, Georg Friedrich. Gedanken vom philosophischen Predigen. Halle, 1762.

Phil 3625.8.30 Meier, Georg Friedrich. Gedanken von Scherzen. Halle, 1754.

Phil 3625.8.25 Meier, Georg Friedrich. Georg Friedrich Meiers Metaphysik. v.1-4. Halle, 1755-59. 3v.

Phil 3625.8.50 Meier, Georg Friedrich. Philosophische Betrachtungen über die chrislichen Religion. v.1-7. Halle, 1761-66. 2v.

Phil 3625.8.42 Meier, Georg Friedrich. Philosophische Sittenlehre. Halle, 1762. 2v.

Phil 3625.8.43 Meier, Georg Friedrich. Philosophische Sittenlehre. 2. Aufl. Halle, 1762-66. 5v.

Phil 3625.8.60 Meier, Georg Friedrich. Vernenftlehre. 2e Aufl. Halle, 1762.

Phil 3625.8.52 Meier, Georg Friedrich. Versuch einer Allegemeinen Auslegungskunst. Dusseldorf, 1965.

Phil 3625.8.35 Meier, Georg Friedrich. Versuch einer Erklärung des Nachtwandelns. Halle, 1758.

Phil 3625.8.65 Meier, Georg Friedrich. Vertheidigung der christlichen Religion. 2e Aufl. Halle, 1749.

Phil 7067.48.10 Meier, George F. Vertheidigung der Gedanken von Gespenstern. Halle im Magdeburgischen, 1748.

Phil 2520.143 Meier, M. Descartes und die Renaissance. München, n.d.

Phil 5252.55 Meier, M. Der Seelenbegriff in der modernen Psychologie. München, n.d.

Phil 8430.39 Meier, N.C. Art in human affairs. N.Y., 1942.

Phil 5627.119 Meige, Henry. Les possédées noires. Paris, 1894.

Phil 6631.5 Meige, Henry. Der Tic. Leipzig, 1903.

Phil 7140.113 Meijer, A.F. Experimenten omtrent suggestibilteit bij senuw- en zielszieken. Amsterdam, 1919.

Phil 3832.10.15 Meijer, W. Spinoza, een levensbeeld. Amsterdam, 1915.

Phil 3832.10 Meijer, W. Spinozana 1897-1922. Heidelberg, 1922.

Phil 187.91 Meiklejohn, A. Philosophy. Chicago, 1926.

Phil 418.5 Meiland, Jack W. The nature of intention. London, 1970.

Phil 408.4 Meiland, Jack W. Talking about particulars. London, 1970.

Phil 187.146 Meimberg, R. Über die Einseitigkeit. Berlin, 1951.

Phil 735.175 Meimberg, Rudolf. Alternativen der Ordnung. Berlin, 1956.

Phil 6315.2.118 Mein Dank an Freud; offener Brief an S. Freud zu seinem 75. Geburtstag. (Andreas-Salomé, L.) Wien, 1931.

Phil 3195.7.80 Mein Leben. (Deussen, Paul.) Leipzig, 1922.

Phil 974.3 Mein Lebensgang. (Steiner, Rudolf.) Geotheanum, 1925.

Phil 974.3.6 Mein Legebensgang. (Steiner, Rudolf.) Dornach, 1962.

Phil 8643.7 Mein Recht auf Leben. (Spitta, H.) Tübingen, 1900.

Phil 3549.8.135 Mein Weg zu Ludwig Klages. (Chidani, Shichiro.) Hamburg, 1967.

Phil 2050.192 Meinardus, H. David Hume als Religionsphilosoph. Inaug. Diss. Coblenz, 1897.

Phil 3640.219 Meine Beziehungen zu Nietzsche. (Spitteler, Carl.) München, 1908.

Phil 9530.60.2 Meine Daktor-Dissertation...die Revolution der Begabten. 2. Aufl. (Grossmann, Gustav.) München, 1964.

Phil 3270.1.83 Meine Erfahrungen mit Kuno Fischer. (Türck, Hermann.) Jena, 1895.

Phil 3120.8.31 Meine Letzten wünsche für Oesterreich. (Brentano, Franz.) Stuttgart, 1895.

Phil 177.42 MeineLösung der Welträtsel. (Christiansen, H.) Wiesbaden, 1914.

Phil 6115.6.12 Meine myelogenetische Hirnlehre. (Flechsig, P.) Berlin, 1927.

Phil 3780.79 Meine Reform der hegelschen Philosophie. (Rosenkranz, Karl.) Königsberg, 1852.

Phil 3585.15 Meine Weltanschaunng. (Leisegang, H.) Berlin, 1951.

Phil 193.230 Meine Weltansicht. (Schroedinger, Erwin.) Hamburg, 1961.

Phil 75.28 Meiner, Felix. Philosophischer Handkatalog. 1er Nachtrag über die Jahre 1927/28. Leipzig, 1928.

Phil 8837.3 Meiners, C. Allgemeine kritische Geschichte der ältern und neuern Ethik. Göttingen, 1800-01. 2v.

Phil 1117.3 Meiners, C. Geschichte des Ursprungs. Lemzo, 1781-82.

Phil 1117.3.5 Meiners, C. Histoire de l'origine...der sciences dans la Grèce. Paris, 1799. 5v.

Phil 1117.3.10 Meiners, C. Vermischte philosophische Schriften. Leipzig, 1775. 3v.

Phil 5252.93 Meinertz, Josef. Moderne Seinsprobleme in ihrer Bedeutung für die Psychologie. Heidelberg, 1948.

Phil 187.150 Meinertz, Josef. Philosophie. München, 1958.

Phil 5090.9 Meinhandl, F. Über Urteilswahrheit. Leipzig, 1923.

Phil 343.5.19 Meinong, A. Gesammelte Abhandlungen. Leipzig, 1913. 2v.

Phil 9550.3 Meinong, A. Psychologisch-ethische Untersuchungen zur Werth-Theorie. Graz, 1874.

Phil 343.5 Meinong, A. Über Annahmen. Leipzig, 1902.

Phil 343.5.2 Meinong, A. Über Annahmen. 2. Aufl. Leipzig, 1910.

Phil 343.5.15 Meinong, A. Über die Erfahrungsgrundlagen unseres Wissens. Berlin, 1906.

Phil 343.5.9 Meinong, A. Über die Stellung der Gegenstand Theorie im System der Wissenschaften. Leipzig, 1907.

Phil 343.5.25 Meinong, A. Über Möglichkeit und Wahrscheinlichkeit. Leipzig, 1915.

Phil 5585.15 Meinong, A. Untersuchungen zur Gegenstandstheorie und Psychologie. Leipzig, 1904.

Phil 270.33 Meinong, A. Zum Erweise des allgischen Kausalgesetzes. Wien, 1918.

Phil 9550.3.5 Meinong, A. Zur Grundlegung der allgemeinen Werth-Theorie. Graz, 1923.

Phil 3625.11 Meinong, Alexius. Gesamtausgabe. Herausgeber: Rudolf Haller und R. Kindinger. Graz, 1968- 3v.

Phil 3625.22 Meinong, Alexius. Philosophenbriefe aus den wissenschaftlichen Korrespondez mit Franz Brentano. Graz, 1965.

Phil 3625.11.80 Meinong als Mensch und als Lehrer. (Martinak, E.) Graz, 1925.

Phil 3625.11.82 Meinongs allmänna värdeteori. (Liljequist, E.) Göteborg, 1904.

Phil 3625.11.85 Meinong's theory of objects. (Findlay, J.N.) London, 1933.

Phil 3625.11.86 Meinong's theory of objects and values. 2. ed. (Findlay, J.N.) Oxford, 1963.

Phil 3832.3 Meinsma, K.O. Spinoza en zijn kring. 's Gravenhage, 1896.

Phil 3832.3.15 Meinsma, K.O. Spinoza und sein Kreis. Berlin, 1909.

Htn Phil 3910.34* Meinung von dem Wesen der Seele. (Wolff, Christian von.) Leipzig, 1727.

Phil 2725.2.103 Meinvielle, Jules. De Lamennais à Maritain. Paris, 1956.

Phil 8592.120 Meinvielle, Julio. Un progresismo vergonzante. Buenos Aires? 1967.

Phil 4580.118 Meis, Hans. Darstellung und Würdigung der Ethik Harald Høffdings. Inaug. Diss. Obersassel, 1928.

Phil 343.19 Meisner, E. Erkenntniskritische Weltanschauung. Leipzig, 1936.

Phil 3805.200 Meisner, Heinrich. Schleiermachers Lehrjahre. Berlin, 1934.

Phil 3494.31 Meissinger, K.A. Kant und die deutsche Aufgabe. Frankfurt, 1924.

Phil 3910.134.1 Meissner, Heinrich Adam. Philosophischer Lexicon aus Christian Wolffs sämtlichen deutschen Schriften. Düsseldorf, 1970.

Phil 6990.52 Meist, Paul. Les cinquant-quatre miracles de Lourdes au jugement du drait canon. Paris, 1958.

Phil 8637.2 Meister, J.H. Euthanasie. Paris, 1809.

Phil 3850.27.113.5 Ein Meister der Menscheit Albert Schweitzer. (Lind, Emil.) Bühl, 1954.

Phil 1504.5.5 Meister Dietrich. v.5, pt.5-6. (Krebs, E.) Münster, 1906.

Phil 3110.90 Meister Jacob Böhme. (Wernicke, A.) Braunschweig, 1898.

Phil 9070.48.5 Der Meister und sein Jünger. (Iranschähr, H.K.) Olten, 1948-1950. 2v.

Phil 4961.615 Mejia Valera, Manuel. Fuentes para la história de la filosofía en el Perú. Lima, 1963.

Phil 2045.108 Den mekaniske naturopfattelse hos Thomas Hobbes. (Brandt, Frithiof.) København, 1921.

Phil 22.42.5 Mekarski, S. Myśl filozoficzna Romunristow w Polsce. Londyn, 1953.

Phil 3475.3.240 Mekkes, Johan Peter Albertus. Teken en motief der creatuur. Amsterdam, 1965.

Phil 3832.13 Melames, S.M. Spinoza and Buddha. Chicago, Ill., 1933.

Phil 6978.12.10 Die Melancholie. (Krafft-Ebing, Richard.) Erlangen, 1874.

Phil 9330.10 Melancholie und Gesellschaft. Thesis. (Lepenies, Wolf.) Frankfurt, 1969.

Phil 6978.12.15 Melancholie und Manie. (Binswanger, Ludwig.) Pfullingen, 1960.

Phil 6978.12 Melancholie und Schuld. (Kraussold, Karl.) Stuttgart, 1884.

Phil 6978.12.20 Melancholie und Todestriebe. (Biran, Sigmund.) München, 1961.

Phil 9330.1 The melancholy of Stephen Allard. (Smith, Garnet.) N.Y., 1895.

Htn Phil 5052.31* Melanchthon, Philipp. Erotemata dialectices. Lipsiae, 1559. 2 pam.

Phil 6978.12.5 La mélancolie. (Raubinovitch, Jacques.) Paris, 1897.

Phil 3450.11.255 Melandri, Enzo. Logica e esperienza in Husserl. Bologna, 1960.

Phil 165.434A Mélanges à la mémoire de Charles de Koninck. Québec, 1968.

Phil 1540.27 Mélanges Auguste Pelzer. Louvain, 1947.

Phil 175.6.20 Mélanges de littérature et de philosophie. (Ancillon, F.) Paris, 1809. 2v.

Phil 165.95 Mélanges de philosophie grecque. Paris, 1956.

Phil 1050.5 Mélanges de philosophie Juive et Arabe. (Munk, S.) Paris, 1859.

Phil 1050.5.5 Mélanges de philosophie Juive et Arabe. (Munk, S.) Paris, 1927.

Phil 2855.6.80 Mélanges de théologie et de philosophie offerts à Arnold Reymond. Lausanne, 1940.

Phil 193.3.5 Mélanges d'histoire, de morale. (Saisset, E.E.) Paris, 1859.

Phil 2750.23 Mélanges Joseph Maréchal. (Maréchal, Joseph.) Bruxelles, 1950. 2v.

Phil 165.145.5 Mélanges offerts à Étienne Gilson de l'Académie Française. Toronto, 1959.

Phil 176.25 Mélanges philosophiques. (Bordas-Demoulin, Jean B.) Paris, 1846.

Phil 2672.29 Mélanges philosophiques. (Jouffroy, Théodore S.) Paris, 1833.

Phil 2672.30 Mélanges philosophiques. (Jouffroy, Théodore S.) Paris, 1838.

Phil 4265.3.37 Mélanges philosophiques. (Vera, A.) Paris, 1862.

Phil 2672.30.5 Mélanges philosophiques. 4e éd. v.1-2. (Jouffroy, Théodore S.) Paris, 1866.

Phil 8050.74 Melchers, H. Von Kunst und Künstlern. München, 1953.

Phil 2280.22.80 Melchert, Norman P. Realism, materialism, and the mind: the philosophy of Roy Wood Sellars. Springfield, Ill., 1968.

Phil 2750.22.85 Melchione, Vuceolio. Il metodo di Mounier altri saggi. Milano, 1960.

Phil 4120.1.81 Melchiorre Gioia e la sua dottrina politica. (Semprini, G.) Genova, 1934.

Phil 8887.77 Melden, A.I. Essays in moral philosophy. Seattle, 1958.

Phil 8887.77.5 Melden, A.I. Essays in moral philosophy. Seattle, 1958.

Phil 8870.15.2 Melden, A.I. Ethical theories. 2nd ed. N.Y., 1955.

Phil 9070.70 Melden, Abraham. Rights and right conduct. Oxford, 1959.

Phil 5762.24 Melden, Abraham Irving. Free action. London, 1964.

Phil 5330.40 Meldman, Monte Jay. Diseases of attention and perception. 1st ed. Oxford, 1970.

Phil 8592.122.30 Mel'e. (Porshnev, Boris F.) Moskva, 1964.

Phil 665.26 Melegari, Dora. Il destarsi delle anime. Milano, 1915.

Phil 3494.60 Meleschenko, Z.N. Neokantianstvo kak filosofskaia osnova revizionizma. Leningrad, 1960.

Phil 3012.5 Meleshchenko, Zoia N. Nemctskaia filosofiia XIX - nachala XX vv. Leningrad, 1965.

Htn Phil 3450.3.30* Meletemata philosophica. (Heereboord, Adriani.) Amsterdam, 1680.

Htn Phil 182.10.3* Meletemata philosophica. (Heereboort, A.) Amsterdam, 1665.

Phil 182.10A Meletemata philosophica. (Heereboort, A.) Amsterdam, 1680.

Phil 3160.3.98 Melher, Jehuda. Hermann Cohen's philosophy of Judaism. N.Y., 1968.

Phil 5190.24.5 Melhwish, George. The paradoxical universe. Bristol, Eng., 1959.

Phil 3832.14 Meli, Fausto. Spinoza e due antecedenti italiani dello Spinozismo. Firenze, 1934.

Phil 187.105 Melillo, F. Manuale di filosofia. Napoli, 1873.

Phil 812.15 Melillo, F. Preliminari alla storia della filosofia. Napoli, 1858.

Phil 310.260 Meliukhin, S.I. O dialektike razvitiia neorganicheskoi prirody. Moskva, 1960.

Phil 1750.330 Il mella e il problema dell'uomo. 1st ed. (Paci, Enzo.) Torino, 1950.

Phil 1117.5 — Melli, G. La filosofia greca. Firenze, 1922.
Phil 3808.107.5 — Melli, Giuseppe. La filosofia di Schopenhauer. Firenze, 1905.
Phil 97.2 — Mellin, G.S.A. Encyclopädisches Wörterbuch der Philosophie. Leipzig, 1797. 6v.
Phil 97.2.5 — Mellin, G.S.A. Kunstsprache der kritischen Philosophie. Jena, 1798.
Phil 3494.15.3 — Mellin, G.S.A. Marginalien und Register zu Kants Kritik der Erkenntnisvermögen. Pt. 1-2. Gotha, 1900-02.
Htn Phil 3494.15* — Mellin, G.S.A. Marginalien und Register zu Kants Kritik der Erkentnissvermögen. Züllichau, 1794.
Phil 3494.15.10 — Mellin, G.S.A. Marginalien und Register zu Kants metaphysichen Anfangsgründen der Sittenlehre. Pt.1-2. Jena, 1801[1800].
Phil 8328.2.2 — Mello, Mario Vieira de Mello. Desenvolvimento e cultura. 2. ed. Rio de Janeiro, 1970.
Phil 6122.2 — Mello Moraes, Alexandre José de. Physiologia das paixões e affecões. Rio de Janeiro, 1854-55. 3v.
Phil 8592.41 — Mellone, S.H. Back to realities. London, 1928.
Phil 1712.11 — Mellone, S.H. The dawn of modern thought. London, 1930.
Phil 8637.10 — Mellone, S.H. The immortal hope. Edinburgh, 1910.
Phil 5052.9.9 — Mellone, S.H. An introductory text-book of logic. 9th ed. Edinburgh, 1917.
Phil 5252.17 — Mellone, Sydney Herbert. Elements of psychology. Edinburgh, 1907.
Phil 8592.28 — Mellor, Stanley. Religion as effected by modern science philosophy. London, 1914.
Phil 2115.139 — Mellring, J.G. Specimen academicum. Upsaliae, 1792.
Phil 187.170 — Mel'nykov, V.M. Do pytannia pro pryrodu filosofs'kykh kategorii. Kyiv, 1959.
Phil 3640.635 — Melo, R. de. Considerações sobre Frederico Nietzsche. Coimbra, 1961.
Phil 585.198 — Melo, Roneu de. O homem contemporâneo. Lisboa, 1965.
Phil 177.84 — The melody of life. (Clark, S.C.) N.Y., 1902.
Phil 293.27 — Melsen, A.G.M. van. The philosophy of nature. Pittsburg, 1953.
Phil 187.177 — Melsen, Andreas Gerardus Maria van. Evolution and philosophy. Pittsburgh, 1965.
Phil 8887.132 — Melsen, Andreas Gerardus Maria van. Physical science and ethics. Pittsburgh, 1967.
Phil 2150.15.96 — Meltzer, Bernard. The social psychology of George Herbert Mead. Kalamazoo, Michigan, 1964.
Phil 6980.466 — Meltzoff, Julian. Research in psychotherapy. 1. ed. N.Y., 1970.
Phil 6682.10.2 — Melvelle, John. Crystal-gazing and the wonders of clairvoyance. London, 1910.
Phil 6682.10 — Melvelle, John. Crystal-gazing and the wonders of clairvoyance. London, 1910.
Phil 575.149 — Mel'vil', Iu.K. Amerikanskii personalizm-filosofiia imperialisticheskoi reaktsii. Moskva, 1954.
Phil 1812.5.10 — Mel'vil', Iu.K. Amerikanskii pragmatizm. Moskva, 1957.
Phil 2225.5.160 — Mel'vil', Iurii K. Charlz Pirs i pragmatizm. Moskva, 1968.
Phil 3246.80.5 — Melzer, Ernst. Die Unsterblichkeitstheorie. Neisse, 1881.
Phil 9515.3.90 — Melzer, Friso. J.G. Zimmermann's "Einsamkeit". Inaug. Diss. Breslau, 1930.
Phil 2150.11 — Melzer, J.H. An examination of critical monism. Ashland, 1937.
Phil 97.5 — Melzer, J.H. Guide to philosophical terminology. Ashland, Ohio, 1938.
Htn Phil 293.4* — Memma, G.M. Sostanza et forma del mondo. Venice, 1545. 4v.
Phil 3549.30 — Memnens Bildsäule in Briefen au Ida von Kosegarten. (Kosegarten, Christian.) Berlin, 1799.
Phil 3246.84 — Memoir. (Smith, W.) Boston, 1846.
Phil 6952.7.30 — A memoir of John Conolly. (Clark, James.) London, 1869.
Phil 6952.7.35 — A memoir of John Conolly. (James, E.) London, 1869?
Phil 5627.88 — Memoir of Mrs. Joanna Turner. 1. American ed. (Wells, Mary.) N.Y., 1827.
Htn Phil 1980.2.80* — Memoir of Ralph Wlado Emerson. (Cabot, J.E.) Boston, 1887. 2v.
Phil 8407.36 — A memoir of the late Rev. William Gilpin. Lymington, 1851.
Phil 5938.7.20 — A memoir of the life and philosophy of Spurzheim. 1st American ed. (Carmichael, A.) Boston, 1833.
Phil 8836.2.18 — A memoir of W.E.H. Lecky. (Lecky, E.) London, 1909.
Phil 2035.88.5 — Memoir of William Hamilton. (Veitch, J.) Edinburgh, 1869.
Phil 5545.264 — La mémoire, comment l'acquérer, comment la conserver. (Tocquet, Robert.) Paris, 1968.
Phil 5545.2 — La mémoire. (Biervliet, J.J. von.) Gand, 1893.
Phil 5545.260 — La Mémoire. 1. éd. (Association de Psychologie Scientifique de Langue Française.) Paris, 1970.
Phil 5545.50.5 — La mémoire au point de vue physiologique. (Verneuil, Henri.) Paris, 1888.
Phil 5545.158.5 — La mémoire collective. 1. éd. (Halbwachs, Maurice.) Paris, 1950.
Phil 6682.3.4 — Mémoire du magnetisme animal. (Mesmer, F.A.) n.p., 1781. 4 pam.
Phil 8878.7.20 — Memoire en faveur de Dieu. (Delisle de Sales, J.B.C.I.) Paris, 1802.
Phil 3552.435 — Mémoire et conscience de soi selon Leibniz. (Naert, Emilienne.) Paris, 1961.
Phil 5545.67 — Mémoire et habitude. (Henry, Charles.) Paris, 1911.
Phil 5545.1 — Mémoire et imagination. (Arréat, L.) Paris, 1895.
Phil 5545.242 — Mémoire et intelligence. (Piaget, Jean.) Paris, 1968.
Phil 5545.175 — La mémoire et la vie. (Augier, E.) Paris, 1939.
Phil 5545.65 — La mémoire et l'oubli. (Dugas, L.) Paris, 1917.
Phil 2475.1.76 — Memoire et vie. 1e éd. (Bergson, Henri.) Paris, 1957.
Phil 2730.55 — Mémoire sur la décomposition de la pensée. v.1-2. (Maine de Biran, Pierre.) Paris, 1952.
Htn Phil 6682.3.7* — Mémoire sur la dicouverte du magnetisme animal. (Mesmer, F.A.) Genève, 1799.
Phil 1075.1 — Memoire sur la vie et les ouvrages de David. (Neumann, C.F.) Paris, 1829.
Phil 2733.99 — Mémoire sur la vision en Dieu de Malebranche. (Bouillier, F.) Orleans, 1852?
Phil 2730.40 — Mémoire sur les perceptions obscures. (Maine de Biran, Pierre.) Paris, 1920.
Phil 7060.95 — Mémoire sur les récits d'apparitions. (Hauréau, M.B.) Paris, 1875.
Phil 8658.1.5 — Memoire sur Naigeon et accessoirement sur Sylvain Maréchal et Delalande. (Damiron, J.P.) Paris, 1857.
NEDL Phil 48.5 — Mémoires. (Institut Général Psychologique.) Paris. 1-5+ 5v.
Phil 2465.85 — Mèmoires autobiographiques de Charles Bonnet de Genève. Thèse. (Bonnet, Charles.) Paris, 1948.
Phil 6681.2.5 — Mémoires d'un magnétiseur. (Lafontaine, C.) Paris, 1866. 2v.

Phil 6681.8 — Memoires d'un magnétism. (Lassaigne, Auguste.) Paris, 1851.
Phil 2403.1.5 — Memoires pour servir á l'histoire...philosophie au XVIIIe siècle. (Damiron, J.P.) Paris, 1858. 2v.
Phil 6685.9.5 — Mémoires pour servir à l'histoire et à l'etablissement du magnétisme animal. 3. éd. (Puységur, Armand Marie Jacques de Chastenet.) Paris, 1820.
Phil 1900.80 — Memoirs...Joseph Butler D.C.L. (Bartlett, T.) London, 1839.
Phil 2218.81 — Memoirs. (Priestley, Joseph.) London, 1805-07. 2v.
Phil 2218.81.2 — Memoirs. (Priestley, Joseph.) London, 1806. 2v.
Phil 62.1 — Memoirs. (Society for Philosophical Inquiry, Washington, D.C.) Lancaster, Pa. 1-4,1893-1927+
Phil 1870.75 — Memoirs. 2nd ed. (Berkeley, G.) London, 1784.
Phil 3850.27.35 — Memoirs of childhood and youth. 1st American ed. (Schweitzer, A.) N.Y., 1949.
Phil 8670.16 — The memoirs of God. (Papini, G.) Boston, 1926.
Phil 3625.1.44 — Memoirs of Moses Mendelssohn. (Samuels, M.) London, 1825.
Phil 3625.1.45 — Memoirs of Moses Mendelssohn. 2. ed. (Samuels, M.) London, 1827.
Phil 6968.32 — Memoirs of my nervous illness. (Schreben, Daniel P.) London, 1955.
Htn Phil 2115.116* — Memoirs of the life...of Mr. John Locke. London, 1742.
Phil 2205.83 — Memoirs of William Paley, D.D. (Meadley, G.W.) Sunderland, 1809. 2 pam.
Phil 7054.43.20 — Memorabilia. (Pioda, Alfredo.) Bellinzona, 1891.
Phil 5545.69.5 — La memoria. (Dandolo, Giovanni.) Messina, 1903.
Phil 4112.75 — Una memoria. (Galluppi, Pasquale.) Padova, 1957.
Phil 5545.160 — Memoria e associazione nella scuola cartesiana. (Mondolfo, R.) Firenze, 1900.
Phil 5545.13.2 — Memoria technica. (Grey, R.) Dublin, 1796.
Phil 5545.13 — Memoria technica. (Grey, R.) London, 1730.
Phil 5545.13.3 — Memoria technica. (Grey, R.) London, 1806.
Phil 5545.32 — Memoria technica. 3. ed. (Johnson, L.D.) Boston, 1847.
Phil 3790.11.90 — Memoriae J.A.H. Reimari. (Ebeling, C.D.) Hamburgi, 1815.
Htn Phil 6946.8420* — Memorial to Legislative Assembly of Nova Scotia (concerning confinement of insane persons). (Dix, D.L.) Halifax? 1850.
Phil 3450.13.90 — Memoriam Heusdii. (Kist, N.C.) Lugduni Batavorum, 1839.
Phil 7069.20 — Memorias de un fraile. (Almasque, Jose A.) Habana, 192-?
Phil 70.100.5 — Memorias del XIII congreso internacional de filosofía, México. (International Congress of Philosophy, 13th, México, 1963.) México. 1-10 10v.
Phil 4006.2.20 — Memorie italiane e problemi della filosofia e della vita. (Gentile, G.) Firenze, 1936.
Phil 184.3.30 — Memories and studies. (James, W.) London, 1911.
Phil 184.3.30.5A — Memories and studies. (James, W.) N.Y., 1912.
Phil 184.3.30.10 — Memories and studies. (James, W.) N.Y., 1968.
Phil 5425.2.18 — Memories of my life. (Galton, F.) London, 1908.
Phil 5425.2.20 — Memories of my life. (Galton, F.) N.Y., 1909.
Phil 2905.1.295 — Memories of Teilhard de Chardin. (Terra, Helmut de.) London, 1964.
Phil 7054.190 — Memories of the supernatural in east and west. (Holmes, W.H.G.) London,, 1941.
Phil 3110.81 — Memoris...Jacob Behrnen. (Okely, F.) Northampton, 1780.
Phil 5545.6 — Memory. (Colegrove, F.W.) N.Y., 1900.
Phil 5545.5.7A — Memory. (Ebbinghaus, H.) N.Y., 1913.
Phil 5545.5.9 — Memory. (Ebbinghaus, H.) N.Y., 1964.
Phil 5545.190 — Memory. (Hunter, I.M.L.) Harmondsworth, 1957.
Phil 5545.17 — Memory. (Kay, D.) London, 1888.
Phil 5545.17.3 — Memory. (Kay, D.) N.Y., 1888.
Phil 5545.224 — Memory. (Smith, Brian.) London, 1966.
Phil 5545.23 — Memory. (Stokes, W.) London, 1888.
Phil 5545.167 — Memory. By an ignorant student. London, 1928.
Phil 5545.800.-.999 —

Pamphlet box. Memory. Chronological file.

Phil 5545.240 — Memory and attention. (Norman, Donald A.) N.Y., 1968[1969]
Phil 5545.27 — Memory and its cultivation. (Edridge-Green, F.W.) N.Y., 1897.
Phil 5545.21 — Memory and its doctors. (Pick, E.) London, 1888.
Phil 5545.232 — The memory system of the brain. (Young, John Zachary.) Berkeley, 1966.
NEDL Phil 5545.50 — Memory systems. 1. American ed. (Middleton, A.E.) N.Y., 1888.
Phil 5545.165 — Memory training, its law and their application to practical life. pts.1-5. (Pelman, Christopher L.) Chicago, 1903.
Phil 5545.7 — Memory training. (Evans, W.L.) N.Y., 1889.
Phil 9346.10A — Men, women and God. (Gray, Arthur Herbert.) N.Y., 1922.
Phil 2750.19.20 — Men against humanity. (Marcel, Gabriel.) London, 1952.
Phil 930.39 — Men and ideas; an informal history of Chinese political thought. (Lin, Mou-Sheng.) N.Y., 1942.
Phil 8842.7 — Men and morals. (Riley, Isaac.) Garden City, 1929.
Phil 182.128 — Men and nations. (Halle, L.J.) Princeton, 1962.
Phil 197.61.15 — Men and tendencies. (Watkin, E.I.) London, 1937.
Phil 6315.15 — Men and their motives. (Flügel, G.C.) London, 1934.
Phil 5790.35 — Men in crisis; a study of a mine disaster. (Lucas, Rex H.) N.Y., 1969.
Phil 6980.336.5 — Men under stress. (Grinker, Roy R.) Philadelphia, 1945.
Phil 8893.97 — Men wanted. (Smith, F.B.) N.Y., 1911.
Phil 525.95 — Men who have walked with God. (Cheney, Sheldon.) N.Y., 1945.
Phil 7069.45.5 — Men who wouldn't stay dead. (Clark, Ida C.G.) N.Y., 1945.
Phil 7069.20.260 — The menace of spiritualism. (O'Donnell, Elliot.) Chicago, 1920.
Phil 7069.20.261 — The menace of spiritualism. (O'Donnell, Elliot.) London, 1920.
Phil 5590.440 — Menaker, Esther. Ego in evolution. N.Y., 1965.
Phil 5249.2.95 — Ménard, A. Analyse et critique des principes de la psychologie. Paris, 1911.
Phil 5249.2.81 — Ménard, A. Analyse et critique des principes de la psychologie de W. James. Paris, 1911.
Phil 1145.11 — Ménard, L. De la morale avant les philosophes. Paris, 1860.
Phil 1145.12 — Ménard, L. De la morale avant les philosophes. 2e éd. Paris, 1863.
Phil 8610.875 — Ménard, Louis. Catéchisme religieux des libres penseurs. Paris, 1875.
Phil 6060.28 — Menard, Pierre. L'écriture et le subsconsient. Paris, 1931.
Phil 75.82 — Menchaca, José. Diccionario bio-bibliográfico de filósofos. Bilbao, 1965.
Phil 8837.13 — Mencken, H.L. Treatise on right and wrong. N.Y., 1934.
Htn Phil 3640.90* — Mencken, Henry. Philosophy of Friedrich Nietzsche. Boston, 1908.
Phil 3640.90 — Mencken, Henry. Philosophy of Friedrich Nietzsche. Boston, 1908.

X Cg   Phil 3640.90.3   Mencken, Henry. Philosophy of Friedrich Nietzsche. 3d ed. Boston, 1913.

Phil 1750.465   Mende, Georg. Studien über die Existenzphilosophie. Berlin, 1956.

Phil 8980.566   Mende, Georg. Treiheit und Verantwortung. Berlin, 1958.

Phil 6060.38   Mendel, A.O. Personality in handwriting. N.Y., 1947.

NEDL   Phil 23.4   Mendel, E. Neurologisches Centralblatt. Leipzig, 1884-93. 10v.

Phil 6962.10.5   Mendel, Emanuel. Leitfaden der Psychiatrie. Stuttgart, 1902.

Phil 6962.10   Mendel, Emanuel. Text-book of psychiatry. Philadelphia, 1907.

Phil 8637.3   Mendelsohn, M. Phädon oder über die Unsterblichkeit der Seele. Berlin, 1821.

Phil 8667.5   Mendelssohn, M. Morgenstunden. Berlin, 1786.

Htn   Phil 8667.3*   Mendelssohn, M. Morgenstunden oder Vorlesungen uber das Daseyn Gottes. Berlin, 1785.

Htn   Phil 3625.1.47*   Mendelssohn, Moses. An die Freunde Lessings. Berlin, 1786.

Htn   Phil 3625.1.55*   Mendelssohn, Moses. An die Freunde Lessings. Berlin, 1786.

Phil 3625.1.42A   Mendelssohn, Moses. Brautbriefe. Berlin, 1936.

Phil 3625.1.43   Mendelssohn, Moses. Briefe. Berlin, 1892.

Phil 3625.1.10   Mendelssohn, Moses. Gesammelte Schriften. Leipzig, 1843-45. 8v.

Phil 3625.1.15A   Mendelssohn, Moses. Gesammelte Schriften. v.1-3,7,11,16. Berlin, 1929-32. 6v.

Phil 3625.1.58A   Mendelssohn, Moses. Jerusalem, and other Jewish writings. N.Y., 1969.

Htn   Phil 3625.1.35*   Mendelssohn, Moses. Kleine philosophische Schriften. Berlin, 1789.

Phil 3625.1.53   Mendelssohn, Moses. Moses Mendelssohn. Berlin, 1929.

Phil 3625.1.49   Mendelssohn, Moses. Moses Mendelssohn. Berlin, 1929.

Phil 3625.1.48   Mendelssohn, Moses. Moses Mendelssohn. Leipzig, 1883.

Phil 3625.1.7   Mendelssohn, Moses. Moses Mendelssohn's sämmtliche Werke. Wien, 1838.

Phil 3625.1.20   Mendelssohn, Moses. Opere filosofiche. Parma, 1800. 2v.

Htn   Phil 3625.1.38*   Mendelssohn, Moses. Phädon. Berlin, 1767.

Phil 3625.1.39   Mendelssohn, Moses. Phädon. Berlin, 1768.

Phil 3625.1.39.15   Mendelssohn, Moses. Phädon. London, n.d. 2 pam.

X Cg   Phil 3625.1.39.3   Mendelssohn, Moses. Phädon. 3. Aufl. Berlin, 1769.

Phil 3625.1.39.4   Mendelssohn, Moses. Phédon. Amsterdam, 1773.

Phil 3625.1.39.9   Mendelssohn, Moses. Phédon. Amsterdam, 1821.

Phil 3625.1.39.11   Mendelssohn, Moses. Phédon. Leipzig, 1869.

Phil 3625.1.39.5A   Mendelssohn, Moses. Phédon. 4. Aufl. Amsterdam, 1776.

Phil 3625.1.30   Mendelssohn, Moses. Philosophische Schriften. Berlin, 1777. 2v.

Phil 3625.1.31A   Mendelssohn, Moses. Philosophische Schriften. Carlsruhe, n.d.

Phil 3625.1.32   Mendelssohn, Moses. Philosophische Schriften. v.1-2. Carlsruhe, 1780.

Phil 3625.1.26   Mendelssohn, Moses. Philosophische Schriften. Verb. Aufl. Berlin, 1771.

Phil 3625.1.5   Mendelssohn, Moses. Sämmtliche Werke. Wien, 1838. 3v.

Htn   Phil 3625.1.40*   Mendelssohn, Moses. Schreiben an den Herrn Diaconus Lavater. Berlin, 1770-87. 3 pam.

Phil 3625.1.25   Mendelssohn, Moses. Schriften zur Philosophie. Leipzig, 1880.

Phil 3625.1.109   Mendelssohn, sa vie et ses oeuvres. (Schwab, Moise.) Paris, 1868.

Phil 3625.1.185   Mendelssohn Gedenkfeier der Jüdischen Gemeinde zu Berlin am 8, Sept. 1929. (Baeck, Leo.) Berlin, 1929.

Phil 3625.1.190   Mendelssohn Mózes, a zsidó Sokrates. (Stadler, Károly.) Szekesfehérvárott, 1895.

Phil 3625.1.135   Mendelssohn und Lessing. 2e Aufl. (Ritter, I.H.) Berlin, 1886.

Phil 3625.1.117   Mendelssohn's character and philosophy of religion. (Rothman, W.) n.p., 1929.

Phil 4313.2   Mendez Bejarano, M. Historia de la filosofía en España hasta el siglo XX. Madrid, 192-.

Phil 2490.171   Mendieta y Núñez, L. Homenajes: Augusto Comte. 1. ed. México, 1961.

Phil 5052.20   Mendive, José. Elementos de lógica. 2a ed. Valladolid, 1887.

Phil 3625.1.56   Mendlssohn, Moses. Moses Mendelssohn; eine Auswahl aus seinen Schriften und Briefen. Frankfurt, 1912.

Phil 22.27   Mendoza, Argentine Republic (City). Universidad Nacional de Cuyo. Institute de Psicologia Experimental. Publicaciones. Mendoza. 1943-1945

Htn   Phil 1535.13*   Mendoza, P.H. de. Disputationes de universa philosophia. Lugduni, 1617.

Phil 1955.6.107   Mendoza de Montero, A. Líneas fundamentales de la filosofía de John Dewey. Buenos Aires, 1940.

Phil 4309.5   Menendez Pelayo y la filosofía española. (Iriarte, Joaquin S.J.) Madrid, 1947.

Phil 9590.13   Menendez Samara, A. Fanatismo y misticismo. México, 1940.

Phil 4352.1.89   Menendez y Pelayo, D.M. Das palabras sobre centenario de Balmes. Vich, 1910.

Phil 4313.1   Menéndez y Pelayo, M. Discurso leído en la universidad central. Madrid, 1889.

Phil 4363.4.30   Menéndez y Pelayo, M. Ensayos de crítica filosófica. Madrid, 1918.

NEDL   Phil 8145.2   Menendez y Pelayo. Historia de las ideas. Madrid, 1890.

Phil 812.8   Mener, J.B. Geschichte der Philosophie zum Gebrauche. Bonn, 1882.

Phil 5252.140   Menert, Evžen. Fysiologický základ logického myšlení. Praha, 1960.

Phil 2750.24.30   Menetrier, Jacques. L'homme quelconque. Paris, 1959.

Phil 4974.24   Menezes, O. Raízes pré-socráticas do pensamento atual. Ceará, 1958.

Phil 6122.61.5   Meng, H. Praxis der seelischen Hygiene. Basel, 1943.

Phil 6122.61   Meng, H. Seelischer Gesundheitschutz. Basel, 1939.

Phil 5585.95   Mengenvergleich und Übung. (Becker, Egon.) Frankfurt, 1957.

Phil 8887.67   Menger, Karl. Moral, Wille und Weltgestaltung. Wien, 1934.

Phil 5279.25.2   De mening van de psycholoog. 2. druk. (Geer, Johannes Petrus van de.) Haarlem, 1968.

Phil 3833.6   Meniţescu, Joan. Die Affectenlehre Spinoza's. Leipzig, 1887.

Phil 2725.2.67   La Mennais. (Maréchal, C.) Paris, 1925.

Phil 2725.2.89   La Mennais. (Maréchal, C.) Paris, 1925.

Phil 5052.45   Menne, Albert. Einführung in die Logik. Bern, 1966.

Phil 5066.65   Menne, Albert. Logik und Existenz. Meisenheim/Glan, 1954.

Phil 5245.70   Menneshe kundskab. (From, Franz.) København, 1959. 2v.

Phil 4585.1.31   Menneskelig kvintessens. (Ibsen, Sigurd.) Kristiania, 1911.

Phil 4635.2.34F   Den menneskelige tänkning. (Starcke, C.N.) Kopenhagen, 1916.

Phil 182.36.17   Den menneskelige tanke. (Höffding, H.) Kjobenhavn, 1910.

Phil 5247.70   Mennesker og andre dyr. (Hoejgaard, Mogens.) København, 1959.

Phil 5827.12   Mennesker og Høns. (Rubin, E.) København, 1937.

Phil 9513.48   Mennesket i samfunnet. En sosialetikk. (Aukrust, Tor.) Oslo, 1965-

Phil 1750.166.45   Mennesket i tiden. København, 1950.

Phil 8882.46   Mennesket og moralen. (Horn, E.F.B.) Malling, 1877.

Phil 8634.2.7   Menneskets udødelighed. (James, William.) Kjøbenhavn, 1918.

Phil 2733.101   Mennicken, Peter. Die Philosophie des Nicolas Malebranche. Leipzig, 1927.

Phil 6322.32.5   Menninger, Karl Augustus. Theory of psychoanalytic technique. N.Y., 1958.

Phil 6322.19   Menninger, Karl Augustus. The human mind. N.Y., 1930.

Phil 6322.19.2   Menninger, Karl Augustus. The human mind. N.Y., 1930.

Phil 6322.19.5   Menninger, Karl Augustus. The human mind. 2d ed. N.Y., 1937.

Phil 6322.19.7   Menninger, Karl Augustus. The human mind. 3d ed. N.Y., 1945.

Phil 6322.19.10   Menninger, Karl Augustus. Love against hate. 1st ed. N.Y., 1942.

Phil 7150.31   Menninger, Karl Augustus. Man against himself. N.Y., 1938.

Phil 6322.19.15   Menninger, Karl Augustus. The vital balance. N.Y., 1963.

Phil 6322.32   Menninger, W.C. Social change and scientific progress. Portland, 1951.

Phil 52.10   Menninger Clinic. Bulletin. Topeka, Kan. 15,1951+ 19v.

Phil 184.15.3   Menniskan. (Jochnick, W.) Stockholm, 1881. 5 pam.

Phil 4514.1.40   Mennikans naturlif i dess förhållande de till det andliga lifvet. (Borelius, J.J.) Stockholm, 1855.

Phil 8880.42   Menniskans sedliga lif. (Franck, A.) Stockholm, 1870.

Phil 9120.10.5   Mennikors aprioriska. (Cederschiöld, F.) Lund, 1828.

Phil 5525.36   Menon, V.K.K. A theory of laughter. London, 1931.

Phil 3500.35.5   Menon oder Versuch in Gesprächen. (Snell, F.W.D.) Mannheim, 1789.

Phil 3500.35.7   Menon oder Versuch in Gesprächen. 2. Aufl. (Snell, F.W.D.) Mannheim, 1796.

Phil 5238.190   Der Mens als Persönlichkeit und Problem. (Herlrich, E.) München, 1963.

Phil 8599.17   Mens creatrix. v.1-2. (Temple, William.) London, 1917.

Phil 2750.20.82   Mens en expressie, in het licht van de wijsbegeerte van Merleau-Ponty. (Kwant, Remigius Cornelius.) Utrecht, 1968.

Phil 22.48   Mens en kosmos. Deventer. 17,1961+ 5v.

Phil 3549.20   Mens en kritiek. (Kwant, R.C.) Utrecht, 1962.

Phil 3790.22   Mens en werk. (Riessen, Hendrick van.) Amsterdam, 1962.

Phil 1707.24   De mens in tweeotrijd. (Hoenderdaal, G.J.) Arnhem, 1956.

Phil 8677.15   Die mens naar die beeld van God. (Walmarans, H.P.) Purmerend, 1932.

Phil 5070.26   Der Mensch, das Wesen der Zukunft. (Mynarek, Hubertus.) München, 1968.

Phil 5421.20.120   Der Mensch, ein kriegerisches Tier. (Kneutgen, Johannes.) Stuttgart, 1970.

Phil 585.345   Der Mensch, eine philosophische Anthropologie. (Haeberlin, Paul.) Zürich, 1969.

Phil 3488.26   Mensch, Gemeinschaft und Welt in der Philosophie Immanuel Kants. (Goldmann, L.) Zürich, 1945.

Phil 365.53   Der Mensch, seine Abstammung und Gesittung. (Rolle, Friedrich.) Frankfurt, 1866.

Phil 476.3.5   Der Mensch. (Büchner, L.) Leipzig, 1872.

Phil 3915.148   Der Mensch. (Klenke, Friedrich.) Graz, 1908.

Phil 3745.15   Mensch. (Przywara, Erich.) Nürnberg, 1959.

Phil 5257.3.10   Der Mensch. (Rehmke, J.) Leipzig, 1928.

Phil 585.196   Der Mensch: Sinnziel der Weltentwicklung. Inaug. Diss. (Mynarek, Hubertus.) München, 1967.

Phil 5871.106   Der Mensch als Anfang. (Ulrich, Ferdinand.) Benziger, 1970.

Phil 585.320   Der Mensch als Schnittpunkt. (Lersch, Philipp.) München, 1969.

Phil 310.140   Der Mensch als Schöpfer seiner Selbst. (Kurella, Alfred.) Berlin, 1958.

Phil 3585.25   Der Mensch als Schöpfer und Geschäpf der Kultur. (Landmann, M.) München, 1961.

Phil 177.51   Der Mensch als Selbstjweck. (Carneri, Bartolomeo.) Wien, 1877.

Phil 5520.58   Der Mensch als Symbol. (Groddeck, Georg.) Wien, 1933.

Phil 585.416   Der Mensch als Wissender und Glaubender. Inaug. Diss. (Schleissheimer, Bernhard.) Wien, 1970.

Phil 705.11.5   Der Mensch der Erkenntnis. (Knittermeyer, Hinrich.) Hamburg, 1962.

Phil 1750.565   Der Mensch der Zukunft. (Hollenbach, Johannes.) Frankfurt, 1970.

Phil 2705.30.55   Der Mensch eine Maschine. (La Mettrie, Julien Offray de.) Leipzig, 1909.

Phil 7082.118   Mensch en droom. (Dietz, Paul Antoine.) Leiden, 1935.

Phil 3210.58   Der Mensch im Kosmos. (Fechner, G.T.) Berlin, 1949.

Phil 3585.28   Der Mensch im Sein. (Lotz, Johannes Baptist.) Freiburg, 1967.

Phil 187.108.5   Der Mensch im Sein. (Müller, G.E.) Stuttgart, 1938.

Phil 978.96.5   Der Mensch in den Entscheidungen unseres Jahrhunderts. (Lauer, Hans Erhard.) Freiburg, 1968.

Phil 5352.10   Der Mensch in der Entscheidung. (Thomae, Hans.) München, 1960.

Phil 8598.96.5   Der Mensch in der Fragik. (Sellmair, Josef.) München, 1948.

Phil 5850.127.5   Der Mensch in der Gruppe. (Battegay, Raymond.) Bern, 1967- 3v.

Phil 6980.112.20   Der Mensch in der Psychiatrie. (Binswanger, L.) Pfullingen, 1957.

Phil 1750.95   Der Mensch in der technischen Welt. (Engelhardt, Wolf von.) Köln, 1957.

Phil 585.5   Der Mensch in seinem Dasein. (Siegmund, Georg.) Freiburg, 1953.

Phil 4080.36   Der Mensch in seinem ursprünglichen Sein nach der Lehre Landulfs von Neapel. (Grocholl, Wolfgang.) München, 1969.

Phil 978.49.605   Der Mensch in seinem Zusammenhange mit dem Kosmos. v.5-6,9. (Steiner, R.) Dornach, 1967- 5v.

Phil 3500.106   Der Mensch ist Person. (Schwartlaender, Johannes.) Stuttgart, 1968.

Phil 7069.59.25   Der Mensch ist voller Geheimnisse. (Sonnet, Andre.) Berlin, 1959.

Phil 8631.1.5   Der Mensch nach Leib, Seele und Geist. (Göschel, C.F.) Leipzig, 1856.

Phil 8672.22   Mensch ohne Gott. (Rohde, Hubert.) Freiburg, 1961.

Phil 5058.47.5   Mensch und Begriff. (Schingnitz, Werner.) Leipzig, 1935.

Phil 585.418   Der Mensch und das Ganze. (Riedel, Maximilian.) München, 1969.

Phil 9575.7   Der Mensch und das Geld. (Ebersberg, Luise.) Wien, 1826.

Phil 2905.1.565   Der Mensch und die Evolution; Teilhard de Chardins philosophische Anthropologie. (Gosztonyi, Alexander.) München, 1968.

Phil 8581.102   Der Mensch und die ewigen Hintergründe. (Barthel, Ernst.) München, 1939.

Phil 301.5   Der Mensch und die Natur. (Uexkuell, T. von.) Bern, 1953.

Phil 197.65.10   Der Mensch und die Philosophie. 2. Aufl. (Wust, Peter.) Münster, 1947.

Phil 6127.16   Der Mensch und die Seele. (Reich, E.) Berlin, 1872.

Phil 178.22.20   Der Mensch und die Welt. (Driesch, H.) Leipzig, 1928.

Phil 3549.8.92   Mensch und Erde. (Klages, Ludwig.) München, 1920.

Phil 3549.8.35   Mensch und Erde. (Klages, Ludwig.) Stuttgart, 1956.

Phil 3549.2.35   Mensch und Erde in Darstellungen. (Keyserling, Hermann.) Darmstadt, 1927.

Phil 3850.18.5   Mensch und Geschichte. (Scheler, Max.) Zürich, 1929.

Phil 8582.56   Mensch und Gott. (Chamberlain, H.S.) München, 1921.

Phil 1117.14   Mensch und Kosmos im ihrer Zusammengehörigkeit bei den frühen griechischen Denkern. (Michaelides, Konstantinos.) München? 1961?

Phil 6320.6.20   Mensch und Lebensgrund. (Kretschmer, E.) Tübingen, 1966.

Phil 978.86.7   Mensch und Materie. 2. Aufl. (Lehrs, Ernst.) Frankfurt, 1966.

Phil 1750.166.115   Mensch und Menschlichkeit. Stuttgart, 1950.

Phil 8590.40   Mensch und Person. (Kroeger, Athanasius.) Recklinghausen, 1968.

Phil 3120.30.37   Der Mensch und sein Gebild. (Buber, Martin.) Heidelberg, 1955.

Phil 5590.140   Der Mensch und sein Lebenswerkzeug. (Pfahler, G.) Stuttgart, 1954.

Phil 193.91.2   Der Mensch und sein Ziel. 2. Aufl. (Saitschick, R.) München, 1922.

Phil 5811.15.25   Mensch und Tier. (Buytendijk, Frederik Jacobus Johannes.) Hamburg, 1958.

Phil 525.130   Mensch und Wandlung. (Froebe-Kapteyn, Olga.) Zürich, 1955.

Phil 186.60.20   Mensch und Welt. (Litt, Theodor.) München, 1948.

Phil 179.3.65   Mensch und Welt. 3e Aufl. (Eucken, R.) Leipzig, 1923.

Phil 6319.1.186   Mensch und Welt bei C.G. Jung. (Walder, P.) Zürich, 1951.

Phil 197.32   Mensch und Wirklichkeit. (Weidenbach, Oswald.) Giessen, 1907.

Phil 585.85F   Der Mensch zwischen Atom und Universum. (Grünsteidl, Edmund.) Wien, 1958?

Phil 585.213   Der mensch zwischen Übernatur und Unternatur. (Boehler, Walther.) Nürnberg, 1966.

Phil 3482.12   Der Menschen als Bürger zweier Welten. (Antonopoulos, Georg.) Bonn, 1958.

Phil 3549.2.50   Menschen als Sinnbilder. (Keyserling, Hermann.) Darmstadt, 1926.

Phil 6125.29   Menschen Formen. (Germany. Heer Inspection des Personalprüfwesens.) Berlin, 1941.

Phil 185.3   Menschen-Kenntnis oder Anthropologie. (Keyserlingh, H. von.) Berlin, 1827.

Phil 5832.3.9   Menschen und Tierseele. (Wasmann, E.) Köln, 1906.

Phil 5832.3.13   Menschen und Tierseele. 5. Aufl. (Wasmann, E.) Köln, 1910.

Phil 165.340A   Menschenbild und Lebensführung. (Besch, L.) München, 1963.

Phil 978.49.685   Menschenfragen und Weltenantworten. 1. Aufl. (Steiner, R.) Dornach, 1969.

Phil 176.115.50   Menschengeest. (Bierens de Haan, J.D.) Amsterdam, 1926.

Phil 182.94.82   Der Menschengeist und das Sein. (Guggenberger, Alois.) Krailling vor München, 1942.

Phil 978.49.390   Menschengeschichte im Lichte der Geistesforschung. (Steiner, R.) Berlin, 1962.

Phil 6025.9   Das Menschengesicht. 2. Aufl. (Picard, Max.) München, 1929.

Phil 9035.53.5   Menschenkenntnis. 2. Aufl. (Adler, Alfred.) Leipzig, 1928.

Phil 9035.53.6   Menschenkenntnis. 5. Aufl. (Adler, Alfred.) Zürich, 1947.

Phil 5252.38.20   Menschenkenntnis und Menschenbehandlung. (Müller-Freienfels, R.) Berlin, 1951.

Htn   Phil 3480.40.50*   Menschenkunde oder philosophische Anthropologie. (Kant, Immanuel.) Leipzig, 1831.

Phil 3480.40.52   Menschenkunde oder philosophische Anthropologie. (Kant, Immanuel.) Quedlinburg, 1838.

Phil 7140.126   Menschenleiden als Lebensgeheimnis...Autosuggestion. (Graeter, Karl.) Kandern, 1926.

Phil 978.49.315   Menschenschichsale und Völkerschicksale. (Steiner, R.) Dornach, 1960.

Phil 497.2   Menschenschöpfung und Seelensubstanz. (Wagner, R.) Göttingen, 1854.

Phil 978.49.408   Menschenwesen, Menschenschicksal und Weltentwicklunz. 3. Aufl. (Steiner, R.) Dornach, 1966.

Phil 978.49.278   Menschheitsentwicklung und Christus-Erkenntnis. (Steiner, R.) Dornach, 1967.

Phil 5627.95.15   Mensching, Gustav. Gut und Böse im Glauben der Völker. Leipzig, 1941.

Phil 5627.95.17   Mensching, Gustav. Gut und Böse im Glauben des Völker. 2. Aufl. Stuttgart, 1950.

Phil 5627.95   Mensching, Gustav. Die heilige Schweigen. Giessen, 1926.

Phil 5627.95.5   Mensching, Gustav. Das heilige Wort. Bonn, 1937.

Phil 5627.95.10   Mensching, Gustav. Die Idee der Sünde. Leipzig, 1931.

Phil 5627.271.5   Mensching, Gustav. Topos und Typos; Motive und Strukturen religiösen Lebens. Bonn, 1971.

Phil 3450.33.5   Die Menschkeit am Scheideweg. (Hildebrand, D. von.) Regensburg, 1955.

Phil 6315.2.93   Die Menschkeitsproblematik der Freudschen Psychoanalyse. (Michaëlis, Edgar.) Leipzig, 1925.

Phil 6315.2.94   Die Menschkeitsproblematik der Freudschen Psychoanalyse. 2. Aufl. (Michaëlis, Edgar.) Leipzig, 1931.

Phil 585.45   Das Menschliche. (Buytendijk, F.J.J.) Stuttgart, 1958.

Phil 5548.112   Der menschliche Antrieb. Psychologie und Psychopathologie. (Kages, Wolfgang.) Stuttgart, 1967.

Phil 7069.26.90   Die menschliche Aura. Psychologie und experimentelle Erforschung. 2.-3. Aufl. (Feerhow, F.) Leipzig, 1926.

Phil 6021.15   Der menschliche Ausdruck. (Leonhard, Karl.) Leipzig, 1968.

Phil 5520.581   Das menschliche Begreifen und seine Grenzen. (Rossi, Eduard.) Bonn, 1968.

Phil 6311.38   Menschliche Beziehungen. (Bertine, Eleanor.) Zürich, 1957.

Phil 9035.96   Der menschliche Charakter in Wertung und Forschung. (Betzendahl, Walter.) Paderborn, 1956.

Phil 5058.7.5   Das menschliche Denken. (Schuppe, W.) Berlin, 1870.

Phil 334.5   Das menschliche Erkennen. (Dorner, August.) Berlin, 1887.

Phil 585.255   Menschliche Existenz und moderne Welt. Ein internationales Symposon zum Selbstverständnis des heutigen Menschen. (Schwarz, Richard.) Berlin, 1967. 2v.

Phil 182.36.15   Der menschliche Gedanke. (Höffding, H.) Leipzig, 1911.

Phil 6116.8   Die menschliche Geistestätigkeit in der Weltentwicklung. (Giss, A.J.) Leipzig, 1910.

Phil 8879.31   Menschliche Grundhaltungen. (Endres, Josef.) Salzubrg, 1958.

Phil 193.150   Das menschliche Ich und die Kultur; der psychische Dynamismus und seine Gestabtung der Welt. (Spakovski, A.) Novi Sad, 1939.

Phil 8885.33   Das menschliche Leben. (Koch, Gregor.) Ensiedeln, 1916.

Phil 5241.88   Der menschliche Lebenslauf als psychologisches Problem. (Bühler, Charlotte M.) Leipzig, 1933.

Phil 5241.88.5   Der menschliche Lebenslauf als psychologisches Problem. 2. Aufl. (Bühler, Charlotte M.) Göttingen, 1959.

Phil 8876.22   Das menschliche Mitgefühl. (Bösch, I.M.) Winterthur, 1891.

Phil 5590.145   Die menschliche Natur. (Lipps, Hans.) Frankfurt, 1941.

Phil 575.130   Die menschliche Persönlichkeit in Anlehnung an Zinzendorfsche Gedanken. (Tietzen, Hermann.) Stuttgart, 1922.

Phil 5520.44   Die menschliche Rede. (Ammann, H.J.F.) Lahr, 1925-28. 2v.

Phil 978.49.600   Die menschliche Seele in ihrem Zusammenhang mit göttlich-geistigen Individualitäten. (Steiner, R.) Dornach, 1966.

Phil 978.49.450   Menschliche und menschheitliche Entwicklungswahrheiten. (Steiner, R.) Dornach, 1964.

Phil 175.12   Der menschliche Weltbegriff. (Avenarius, R.) Leipzig, 1891.

Phil 5768.1   Der menschliche Wille. (Schneider, G.H.) Berlin, 1882.

Phil 5750.8   Die menschliche Willensfreiheit im Lehrsystem des Thomas von Aquin und Johannes Duns Scotus. (Auer, Johannes.) München, 1938.

Phil 5751.9   Das menschliche Wollen. (Bessmer, Julius.) Freiburg, 1915.

Phil 5400.17   Die menschlichen und tierischen Gemütsbewegungen. (Steinitzer, M.) München, 1889.

Phil 3640.11.2   Menschliches, allzumenschliches sein Buch für freie Geister. (Nietzsche, Friedrich.) Leipzig, 1886.

Phil 3640.17.3   Menschliches, Allzumenschliches; ein Buch für freie Geister. (Nietzsche, Friedrich.) Stuttgart, 1960.

Phil 3640.47   Menschliches, Allzumenschliches; ein Buch für freie Geister. v.1-2. (Nietzsche, Friedrich.) Stuttgart, 1954.

Phil 720.40   Menschlichkeit. (Medicus, F.) Zürich, 1951.

Phil 180.56   Menschsein als Aufgabe. (Fischer-Mampoteng, F.C.) Heidelberg, 1928.

Phil 585.212.2   Menschsein als Auftrag. 2. Aufl. (Jones, Arthur.) Bern, 1967.

Phil 450.6   Menschsein ohne Illusionen. (Gradman, Hans.) München, 1970.

Phil 9560.23   Mensing, C. An activity analysis of the four cardinal virtues. Diss. Washington, 1929.

Phil 5249.15   Menskligheten vitigaste frågor. v.1-2. (Jochnick, W.) Stockholm, 1880-81.

Phil 5325.21   Le mensonge du monde. (Paulhan, Fr.) Paris, 1921.

Phil 9558.15   Le mensonge et la caractère. (Le Senne, René.) Paris, 1930.

Phil 9558.15.2   Le mensonge et la caractère. Thèse. (Le Senne, René.) Paris, 1930.

Phil 5243.16   Les mensonges de la vie intérieure. 2e éd. (Dromard, Gabriel.) Paris, 1914.

Phil 5558.9   Les mensonges du caractère. (Paulhan, F.) Paris, 1905.

Phil 6327.20   Mental abnormality and crime. (Radzinowicz, Leon.) London, 1944.

Phil 6325.6   Mental abnormality and deficiency. (Pressey, Sidney L.) N.Y., 1926.

Phil 5360.13   Mental acts. (Geach, P.T.) N.Y., 1957.

Phil 6122.64   Mental adjustments. (Muhlbery, W.) Cincinnati, O., 1944.

Phil 6332.2.7   Mental adjustments. (Wells, F.L.) N.Y., 1920.

Phil 6332.2.9   Mental adjustments. (Wells, F.L.) N.Y., 1922.

Phil 5440.9   Mental and moral heredity in royalty. (Woods, F.A.) N.Y., 1906.

Phil 5440.9.5   "Mental and moral heredity in royalty" - Woods. (Spillman, W.J.) Lancaster, 1909.

Phil 5425.21   Mental and physical decadence. (Roscoe, T.G.) London, 1914.

Phil 6805.4   Mental conflicts and personality. (Sherman, Mandel.) N.Y., 1938.

Phil 6114.5.12   A mental-cure illustrated influence of the mind on the body. (Evans, W.F.) Boston, 1884.

Phil 6750.234   Mental defect. (Penrose, Lionel S.) N.Y., 1934.

Phil 6750.12   Mental defectives in Virginia. (Virginia. State Board of Charities and Corrections.) Richmond, 1915.

Phil 6750.18   Mental deficiency (Amentia). (Tredgold, A.F.) N.Y., 1908.

Phil 6750.18.5   Mental deficiency (Amentia). 2d ed. (Tredgold, A.F.) N.Y., 1914.

Phil 6750.18.12   Mental deficiency (Amentia). 4.ed. (Tredgold, A.F.) N.Y., 1922.

Phil 6750.18.15   Mental deficiency (Amentia). 5th ed. (Tredgold, A.F.) N.Y., 1929.

Phil 5241.3.8   Mental development. 2. ed. (Baldwin, J.M.) N.Y., 1897.

Phil 6955.4.5   Mental disease. (Folsom, C.F.) n.p., 1886.

Phil 6969.1   Mental diseases...modern treatment. (Talcott, S.H.) N.Y., 1901.

Phil 6320.14   Mental disorders in later life. (Kaplan, Oscar J.) Stanford, Calif., 1945.

Phil 9341.12   Mental efficiency. (Bennett, Arnold.) N.Y., 1911.

Phil 9341.12.5   Mental efficiency and other hints to men and women. (Bennett, Arnold.) London, 1912.

Phil 6111.47   Mental effort. (Benedict, F.G.) Washington, 1933.

Phil 6129.6   The mental element in the treatment of disease. (Taylor, E.W.) Boston, 1891.

Phil 5827.1   Mental evolution in animals. (Romanes, G.J.) London, 1883.

Phil 5827.1.3A   Mental evolution in animals. (Romanes, G.J.) N.Y., 1884.

Phil 5827.1.6   Mental evolution in man, origin of human faculty. (Romanes, G.J.) N.Y., 1889.

Phil 5827.1.5   Mental evolution in men. (Romanes, G.J.) London, 1888.

Phil 6972.19.5   Mental examiners handbook. 2. ed. (Wells, Frederick L.) N.Y., 1945.

Phil 5240.5   Mental fatigue - 1908. (Abelson, R.) Leipzig, 1908.

Phil 6110.20   Mental fatique. (Arai, T.) N.Y., 1912.

Phil 5247.16.22 Mental growth and decline. (Hollingworth, H.L.) N.Y., 1928.
Phil 5545.20.5 Mental gymnastics, or lessons on memory. 4. ed. (Miller, Adam.) Chicago, 1886.
Phil 5545.20 Mental gymnastics. (Miller, Adam.) Chicago, 1886.
Phil 6135.4.5A Mental healers. (Zweig, Stefan.) N.Y., 1932.
Phil 6132.6 Mental healing. (Whipple, L.E.) N.Y., 1907.
Phil 6945.12 Mental health. (Ruggles, A.H.) Baltimore, 1934.
Phil 22.14 Mental health. Baltimore. 1,1923
Phil 6959.6 Mental health and social policy. (Jones, Kathleen.) London, 1960.
Phil 6963.8 Mental health and social welfare. (National Conference on Social Welfare.) N.Y., 1961.
Phil 6140.10 Mental health and the community; problems, programs and strategies. (Shore, Milton F.) N.Y., 1969.
Phil 6127.30 Die Mental Health Bewegung. (Reimann, Helga.) Tübingen, 1967.
Phil 22.18 Mental health bulletin. Danville. 5-16,1928-1939
Phil 6127.25 Mental health in modern society. (Rennie, T.A.C.) N.Y., 1948.
Phil 6110.21 Mental health in the United States. (American Academy of Political and Social Science.) Philadelphia, 1953.
Phil 6946.1.10 Mental health in the United States. (Ridenour, Nina.) Cambridge, 1961.
Phil 6980.32 Mental health manpower trends. (Albee, George.) N.Y., 1959.
Phil 6327.36A Mental health of the poor. (Riessman, Frank.) London, 1964.
Phil 6980.328 Mental health or mental illness? (Glasser, William.) N.Y., 1960.
Phil 22.26 Mental health sentinal. Boston. 1940-1942
Phil 6945.45 The mental hospital. (Stanton, Alfred Hodgin.) N.Y., 1954.
Phil 6103.3 Pamphlet box. Mental hygiene, mind cure.
Phil 6120.20 Mental hygiene. (Klein, David B.) N.Y., 1944.
Phil 6321.7.5 Mental hygiene. (La Rue, D.W.) N.Y., 1930.
Phil 6122.58 Mental hygiene. (Mikesell, W.H.) N.Y., 1939.
Phil 6127.1 Mental hygiene. (Ray, J.) Boston, 1863.
Phil 6128.8.3 Mental hygiene. (Sweetser, W.) N.Y., 1843.
Phil 6128.8 Mental hygiene. (Sweetser, W.) N.Y., 1850.
Phil 22.12 Mental Hygiene. Concord. 1-30,1917-1946 31v.
Phil 70.2 Mental Hygiene Conference and Exhibit. Proceedings, 1911. N.Y., 1912.
Phil 6112.32 Mental hygiene for community nursing. (Clarke, Eric K.) Minneapolis, 1942.
Phil 6120.13 Mental hygiene for effective living. (Kirkpatrick, E.A.) N.Y., 1934.
Phil 6111.49 Mental hygiene in the community. (Bassett, Clara.) N.Y., 1934.
Phil 6951.5.15 The mental hygiene movement. (Beers, C.W.) N.Y.? 1921.
Phil 6951.5.53 The mental hygiene movement. (National Committee for Mental Hygiene.) N.Y., 1938.
Phil 6952.26 The mental hygiene movement from the philanthropic standpoint. (Hanover Bank, New York.) N.Y., 1939.
Phil 22.23 Mental hygiene news. New Haven.
Phil 6945.14 Mental hygiene with special reference to the migration of the people. (Treadway, Walter L.) Washington, 1925.
Phil 6946.1.20 Mental illness; progress and prospects. (Felix, Robert Hanna.) N.Y., 1967.
Phil 6968.26 Mental illness. (Stern, Edith M.) N.Y., 1942.
Phil 6946.40 Mental illness in the urban Negro community. (Parker, Seymour.) N.Y., 1966.
Phil 5465.182 Mental imagery. (Richardson, Alan.) London, 1969.
Phil 5465.182.1 Mental imagery. (Richardson, Alan.) N.Y., 1969.
Phil 5465.151 Mental imagery in the child; a study of the development of imaginal representation. (Piaget, Jean.) London, 1971.
Phil 5244.19 Mental life. (Edgell, B.) London, 1926.
Phil 5257.34.5 The mental life. (Ruckmick, C.A.) N.Y., 1928.
Phil 5834.1.9A Mental life of monkeys and apes. (Yerkes, R.M.) Cambridge, 1916.
Phil 6954.3 Mental maladies. (Esquirol, Etienne.) Philadelphia, 1845.
Phil 5262.12 The mental man. (Wenzlaff, G.G.) N.Y., 1909.
Phil 6117.12 Mental medicine. (Huckel, O.) N.Y., 1909.
Phil 6114.5.4 Mental medicine. 6. ed. (Evans, W.F.) Boston, 1881.
Phil 6114.5.7 Mental medicine. 15th ed. (Evans, W.F.) Boston, 1885.
Phil 6956.2.5 Mental pathology and therapeutics. (Griesinger, W.) London, 1867.
Phil 8880.2 Mental perceptions. (Ferris, S.) London, 1807.
Phil 5247.6.1 Mental philosophy. (Haven, J.) Boston, 1872.
Phil 5260.1.3 Mental philosophy. (Upham, T.C.) N.Y., 1869. 2v.
Phil 5260.1.15 Mental philosophy. v.2. (Upham, T.C.) N.Y., 1875.
Phil 6117.6 Mental physiology. (Hyslop, T.B.) Philadelphia, 1895.
Phil 5425.114.1 Mental prodigies. (Barlow, F.) N.Y., 1969.
Phil 7069.30.30.2 Mental radio. (Sinclair, Upton B.) N.Y., 1930.
Phil 7069.30.30 Mental radio. (Sinclair, Upton B.) N.Y., 1930.
Phil 5241.2 Mental science. (Bain, A.) N.Y., 1868.
Phil 5241.2.2 Mental science. (Bain, A.) N.Y., 1873.
Phil 5241.2.5 Mental science. (Bain, A.) N.Y., 1880.
Phil 6952.5 The mental status of guiteau. (Channing, W.) Cambridge, 1882.
Phil 6684.1.5 Mental suggestion. v.1-4. (Ochorowicz, J.) N.Y., 1891.
X Cg Phil 6321.15 Mental therapy. (London, L.S.) N.Y., 1937. 2v.
Phil 5259.9 The mental traits of sex. (Thompson, H.B.) Chicago, 1903.
Phil 7084.38 La mentalité haitienne et le domaine du rêve. (Hyppolite, Michelson Paul.) Port-au-Prince, 1965.
Phil 6115.22 Mentality and freedom. (Fairburn, W.A.) N.Y., 1917.
Phil 5820.4.5 The mentality of apes. (Köhler, Wolfgang.) London, 1925.
Phil 6945.17.2 The mentally ill in America. 2. ed. (Deutsch, Albert.) N.Y., 1960.
Phil 6945.17.3 The mentally ill in America. 2. ed. (Deutsch, Albert.) N.Y., 1962.
Phil 6750.223.15 The mentally retarded in society. (Davies, S.P.) N.Y., 1959.
Phil 4210.94 La mente di Antonio Rosmini. (Pestalozza, A.) Milano, 1855.
Phil 4215.1.80.5 La mente di G.D. Romagnosi. (Ferrari, Giuseppe.) Milano, 1913.
Phil 4215.1.80 La mente di G.D. Romagnosi. (Ferrari, Giuseppe.) Prato, 1839.
Phil 4260.81 La mente di Giambattista Vico. (Ferrari, G.) Milano, 1837.
Phil 4080.3.190 Mente e realtà; il pensiero di Benedetto Croce. (LaVia, Pietro.) Firenze, 1947. 2v.
Phil 6115.18.6.5 Menticulture, or The ABC of true living. (Fletcher, Horace.) Chicago, 1897.
Phil 6115.18.7 Menticulture. (Fletcher, Horace.) Chicago, 1898.
Phil 6115.18.7.5 Menticulture. (Fletcher, Horace.) Chicago, 1898.

Phil 9357.8.5 Mentor's letters, addresses to youth. 3d ed. (Rack, E.) Bath, 1778.
Phil 5252.46.5 Mentré, F. Espèces et variétés d'intelligences. Thèse. Paris, 1920.
Phil 5252.46 Mentré, F. Espèces et variétés d'intelligences. Thèse. Paris, 1920.
Phil 2515.4.97 Mentré, F. Pour qu'on lise Cournot. Paris, 1927.
Phil 5258.210 Mentre il secolo muore. (Sighele, Scipio.) Milano, 1899.
Phil 5650.3 Mentz, P. Die Wirkung akustischer Sinnesreize auf Puls und Athmung. Leipzig, 1895.
Phil 5875.65.10 Menýuk, Paula. The acquisition and development of language. Englewood Cliffs, 1971.
Phil 3494.21 Menzel, A. Kants Kritik der reinen Vernunft. Berlin, 1922.
Phil 1117.12 Menzel, Adolf. Hellenika. Baden, 1938.
Phil 3494.18 Menzer, Paul. Kants Lehre von der Entwicklung in Natur und Geschichte. Berlin, 1911.
Phil 187.46 Menzer, Paul. Weltanschauungsfragen. Stuttgart, 1918.
Phil 510.1.21 Menzi, Theodor. Ernst Haeckels Welträtsel oder der Neomaterialismus. Zürich, 1901.
Phil 4605.2.31 Menzinger, A. Fra før Kant. København, 1918.
Phil 2493.96 Meoli, Umberto. Il pensiero economico del Condillac. Milano, 1761.
Phil 3832.9 Meozzi, A. Le dottrine politiche e religiose di B. Spinoza. Arezzo, 1915.
Phil 4655.1.83 Mer om och af Pontus Wikner. (Kjellberg, Elis.) Upsala, 1913.
Phil 192.76 Le meraviglio del mondo. (Rosa, Gabriele.) Milano, 1851.
Phil 2475.1.203 Mercanti, Pietro. Il pensiero filosofico cotemporaneo e la psicologia del Bergson. Roma, 1919?
Phil 1750.155 Mercati, G. Ultimi contributi alla storia degli umanisti. pt.1-2. Città del Vaticano, 1939.
Phil 8887.35 Mercer, A.G. Notes of an outlook on life. London, 1899.
Phil 8612.10 Mercer, Edward. Why do we die? London, 1919.
Phil 8887.11 Mercer, M. Popular lectures on ethics. Petersburg, 1841.
VPhil 978.114 Merchant, Francis. The golden hoard. Houston, 1959.
Phil 575.260 Merchant, Francis. A search for identity. Salem, 1967.
Phil 8887.12 Mercier, A.D. Méditations philogiques et morales. Paris, 1835.
Phil 6682.20 Mercier, A.D. La vérité du magnétisme, prouvée par les faits. Paris, 1829.
Phil 343.60 Mercier, André. Erkenntnis und Wirklichkeit. Bern, 1968.
Phil 5052.14 Mercier, C. A new logic. London, 1912.
Phil 5710.8.3 Mercier, C.A. Human temperaments; studies in character. 3. ed. London, 1923?
Phil 5252.15 Mercier, C.A. Psychology normal and morbid. London, 1901.
Phil 6962.4 Mercier, C.A. Sanity and insanity. London, 1890.
Phil 7069.19.165 Mercier, C.A. Spirit experiences. London, 1919.
Phil 6962.4.4 Mercier, C.A. A text-book of insanity. London, 1902.
Phil 6962.4.5 Mercier, C.A. A text-book of insanity. London, 1914.
Phil 6122.31 Mercier, Charles A. The nervous system and the mind. London, 1888.
Phil 270.43 Mercier, Charles A. On causation, with a chapter on belief. London, 1916.
Phil 7069.17.31 Mercier, Charles A. Spiritualism and Sir Oliver Lodge. London, 1917.
Phil 187.25 Mercier, D. Cours de philosophie. 3e éd. v.1. Louvain, 1902.
Phil 187.25.2 Mercier, D. Cours de philosophie. 3e éd. v.2. Louvain, 1902.
Phil 187.25.4 Mercier, D. Cours de philosophie. 4e éd. v.4. Louvain, 1900.
Phil 187.25.3 Mercier, D. Cours de philosophie. 6e éd. v.3. Louvain, 1903.
Phil 187.25.5 Mercier, D. Curso de philosophia. v.1. Logica. v.3. Psychologia. Vizeu, 1904. 2v.
Phil 5222.1 Mercier, D. Les origines de la psychologie contemporaine. Paris, 1897.
Phil 5222.1.5 Mercier, D. The origins of contemporary psychology. N.Y., 1918.
Phil 1517.3 Mercier, Désiré. A manual of modern scholastic philosophy. 2nd ed. London, 1917. 2v.
Phil 1517.3.5 Mercier, Désiré. A manual of modern scholastic philosophy. 3rd ed. London, 1928. 2v.
Phil 187.23 Mercier, E. De la certitude. Paris, 1844.
Phil 1750.133A Mercier, L.J.A. Challenge of humanism. N.Y., 1933.
Phil 1750.166.5 Mercier, Louis J.A. American humanism and the new age. Milwaukee, 1948.
Phil 585.115 Mercier, R. La réhabilitation de la nature humaine. Villemomble, 1960.
Phil 8630.13 Mercy and judgment. (Farrar, F.W.) London, 1881.
Phil 2630.11.15 Une mère dans sa vallée. (Guitton, Jean.) Paris, 1961.
Phil 5545.205 Meredith, Patrick. Learning, remembering and knowing. N.Y., 1961.
Phil 8887.13.5 Meres, F. Palladis tamia. N.Y., 1938.
Htn Phil 8887.13* Meres, F. Wits commonwealth. pt. 2. London, 1634.
Phil 2805.237 Merezhkovskii, Dimitrii S. Pascal. Paris, 1941.
Phil 293.12 Merezhkovskii, K.S. Fragments du "Schema d'une nouvelle philosophie de l'univers". Genève, 1920.
Phil 6400.4 Meringer, R. Versprechen und Verlesen. Stuttgart, 1895.
Phil 1145.90 Merit and responsibility. (Adkins, Arthur.) Oxford, 1960.
Phil 1145.90.1 Merit and responsibility. (Adkins, Arthur.) Oxford, 1960[1970]
Phil 3552.298 Merkel, Franz R. G.W. Leigniz und die China Mission. Leipzig, 1920.
Phil 3850.6.81 Merkel, Franz R. Der Naturphilosoph Gotthilf Heinrich Schubert und die deutsche Romantik. München, 1913.
Phil 525.145 Merkel, Rudolph Franz. Die Mystik im Kulturleben der Völker. Hamburg, 1940.
Phil 1730.26 Merker, Nicolao. L'illuminismo tedesco. Bari, 1968.
Phil 3425.602 Merker, Nicolas. Le origini della logica hegeliana. Milano, 1961.
Phil 5628.53 Merkt, Josef. Die Wundmale des heiligen Franziskus von Assisi. Leipzig, 1910.
Phil 525.231 Merlan, P. Monopsychism, mysticism. The Hague, 1963.
Phil 1170.11.3 Merlan, Philip. From Platonism to Neoplatomism. 3rd ed. The Hague, 1969.
Phil 1170.11 Merlan, Philip. From Platonism to Neoplatonism. The Hague, 1953.
Phil 1170.11.2 Merlan, Philip. From Platonism to Neoplatonism. 2nd ed. The Hague, 1960.
Phil 8413.2 Merle, Pierre. Pour une clinique d'art. Paris, 1962.
Phil 310.16.5 Merlean-Ponty, Maurice. Les aventures de la dialectique. Paris, 1961.
Phil 2750.20.115 Merleau-Ponty, existentialist of the social world. (Rabil, Albert.) N.Y., 1967.
Phil 293.33 Merleau-Ponty, Jacques. Cosmologie du XXe siècle. Paris, 1965.

Phil 5252.85 Merleau-Ponty, M. La structure du comportement. 1. ed. Paris, 1942.
Phil 5252.85.5 Merleau-Ponty, M. La structure du comportement. 3. ed. Paris, 1955.
Phil 5252.85.10A Merleau-Ponty, M. The structure of behavior. Boston, 1963.
Phil 2750.20.10 Merleau-Ponty, Maurice. Eloge de la philosophie. Paris, 1953.
Phil 2750.20.11 Merleau-Ponty, Maurice. Eloge de la philosophie. Paris, 1962.
Phil 2750.20.15 Merleau-Ponty, Maurice. In praise of philosophy. Evanston, 1963.
Phil 1750.115.25 Merleau-Ponty, Maurice. Phénoménologie de la perception. Paris, 1945.
Phil 1750.115.26 Merleau-Ponty, Maurice. Phénoménologie de la perception. Paris, 1945.
Phil 1750.115.28 Merleau-Ponty, Maurice. Phenomenology of perception. London, 1966.
Phil 812.35 Merleau-Ponty, Maurice. Les philosophes célébres. Paris, 1956.
Phil 2750.20.35 Merleau-Ponty, Maurice. The primacy of perception. Evanston, 1964.
Phil 2750.20.60 Merleau-Ponty, Maurice. La prose du monde. Paris, 1969.
Phil 2750.20.50 Merleau-Ponty, Maurice. Résumés de cours, Collège de France, 1952-1960. Paris, 1968.
Phil 1750.115.125 Merleau-Ponty, Maurice. Les sciences de l'homme et la phénoménologie. Paris, 1965.
Phil 2750.20.20 Merleau-Ponty, Maurice. Sens et non-sens. Paris, 1948.
Phil 2750.20.24 Merleau-Ponty, Maurice. Sense and non-sense. Evanston, 1964.
Phil 2750.20.30 Merleau-Ponty, Maurice. Signes. Paris, 1960.
Phil 2750.20.32 Merleau-Ponty, Maurice. Signs. Evanston, 1964.
Phil 2750.20.50.5 Merleau-Ponty, Maurice. Themes from the lectures at the Collège de France, 1952-1960. Evanston, 1970.
Phil 2750.20.55 Merleau-Ponty, Maurice. L'union de l'âme et du corps chez Malebranche, Biran et Bergson. Paris, 1968.
Phil 2750.20.45 Merleau-Ponty, Maurice. The visible and the invisible. Evanston, 1968.
Phil 2750.20.40A Merleau-Ponty, Maurice. Le visible et l'invisible. Paris, 1964.
Phil 2750.20.95 Merleau-Ponty. (Bakker, Reinout.) Bearn, 1965.
Phil 2750.20.100 Merleau-Ponty. (Barral, Mary Rose.) Pittsburgh, 1965.
Phil 2750.20.90 Merleau-Ponty. (Rofinet, A.) Paris, 1963.
Phil 2750.20.145 Merleau-Ponty. (Tilliette, Xavier.) Paris, 1970.
Phil 2750.20.105 Merleau-Ponty's critique of reason. (Langan, Thomas.) New Haven, 1966.
Phil 5710.21 Merlin, V.S. Ocherk teori temperamenta. Moskva, 1964.
Phil 5252.154 Merlin, Vol'f S. Tipologicheskie issledovaniia po psikhologii lichnosti i po psikhologii truda. Perm', 1964.
Phil 4080.3.201 Merlotti, Eric. L'intention spéculative de Benedetto Croce. (Filosofia dello spirito). Neuchâtel, 1970.
Phil 2905.1.510 Mermod, Denis. La morale chez Teilhard. Paris, 1967.
Phil 2630.7.105 Meroz, Lucien. René Guénon, ou La sagesse initiatique. Paris, 1962.
Phil 3494.9 Merren, R. Über der Bedeutung v. Leibniz...für Kant. Leipzig, 1908.
Phil 22.60 Merrill-Palmer quarterly of behavior and development. Detroit. 4,1957+ 12v.
Phil 8592.18 Merriman, H.B. Religio pictoris. Boston, 1899.
Phil 6122.52 Merriman, H.B. (Mrs.). What shall make us whole? Boston, 1888.
Phil 8887.43 Merrington, E.N. Morales et religions. Paris, 1909.
Phil 9075.37 Merrington, E.N. The possibility of a science of casuistry. Sydney, 1902.
Phil 575.21 Merrington, E.N. The problem of personality. London, 1916.
Phil 2520.191 Merrylees, W.A. Descartes. Melbourne, 1934.
Phil 8887.61 Mersch, Emile. L'obligation morale, principe de liberté. Louvain, 1927.
Phil 187.65.5 Merten, J. Grundriss der Metaphysik. Trier, 1848.
Phil 187.65 Merten, J. Die Hauptfragen der Metaphysik in Verbindung mit der Speculation. Trier, 1840.
Phil 2750.9.30 Merten, O. Des limites de la philosophie. Paris, 1896.
Phil 1712.3 Merten, O. L'état présent de la philosophie. Namur, 1907.
Phil 5070.17 Mertens, Paul. Zur Phänomenologie des Glaubens. Inaug. Diss. Fulda, 1927.
Phil 343.9 Merton, Adolf. Gedanken über Grundprobleme der Erkenntnistheorie. München, 1916.
Phil 5850.271 Merton, R.K. The focused interview. Glencoe, Ill., 1956.
Phil 5252.105 Mertsalov, V.S. K issledovaniiu problem psikhologicheskoi voiny; sbornik statei. Miunkhen, 1955.
Phil 7069.65.25 Les merveilles du spiritualisme. (Crouzet, Jean-Philippe.) Paris, 1965.
Phil 7060.61 La merveilleuse hystorie de l'esprit de Lyon. Paris, 1887.
Phil 7068.65.2 Le merveilleux dans le Jansénisme, le magnétisme, le méthodisme et le baptisme américains. (Blanc, H.) Paris, 1865.
Phil 6313.2 Le merveilleux scientifique. (Durand, J.P.) Paris, 1894.
Phil 5325.13 Mervoyer, P.M. Étude sur l'association des idées. Paris, 1864.
Phil 1812.5 Merwe, A.J. van der. Het zondebegrip in de engelsche evolutionislische wijsbegeerte. Utrecht, 1925.
Phil 7068.96.40 Mery, Gaston. La voyante de la rue de Paradis. Paris, 1896.
Phil 2840.100 Méry, Marcel. La critique du christianisme chez Renouvier. Thèse. Paris, 1952. 2v.
Phil 1712.2 Merz, J.T. History of European thought, 19th century. Edinburgh, 1896-1914. 4v.
Phil 1712.2.4 Merz, J.T. History of European thought, 19th century. Edinburgh, 1904. 2v.
Phil 1712.2.3A Merz, J.T. History of European thought, 19th century. v.1-3. Edinburgh, 1907-1912. 2v.
Phil 1712.2.5 Merz, J.T. A history of European thought in the nineteenth century. Edinburgh, 1912-27. 4v.
Phil 1712.2.6 Merz, J.T. A history of European thought in the nineteenth century. N.Y., 1965. 4v.
Phil 3552.92.5 Merz, J.T. Leibniz. Edinburgh, 1907.
Phil 3552.355 Merz, J.T. Leibniz. N.Y., 1948.
Phil 3552.92A Merz, J.T. Leibniz. Philadelphia, 1884.
Phil 8702.9 Merz, J.T. Religion and science. Edinburgh, 1915.
Phil 187.47 Merz, John T. A fragment on the human mind. Edinburgh, 1919.
Phil 5825.7.2 Mes deux chats. 2. éd. (Perez, Bernard.) Paris, 1900.
Phil 2138.79.9 Mes mémoires: histoire de ma vie et de mes idées. 2e éd. (Mill, John S.) Paris, 1875.
Phil 8837.16 Mes pélerinages de l'âme. (Méautis, Georges.) Paris, 1959.
Phil 310.19 Mesaventures de l'anti-Marxisme. Paris, 1956.
Phil 7082.122 Meseguer, Pedro. El secreto de los sueños. Madrid, 1956.
Phil 8592.122 Meslier, Jean. Oeuvres complètes. Paris, 1970- 2v.
Phil 8592.122.5 Meslier, Jean. Le testament de Jean Meslier. Amsterdam, 1864. 3v.
Phil 7069.20.230 Meslom's messages from the life beyond. (McEvilly, Mary A.) N.Y., 1920.
Phil 6682.3.10 Mesmer, F.A. Aphorismes de Mesmer. 3. éd. Paris, 1785.
Htn Phil 6682.3.12* Mesmer, F.A. Letters à M. Vicq-d'Azyr. Bruxelles, 1784.
Htn Phil 6682.3.14* Mesmer, F.A. Lettre à M. le comte de C. Paris? 1784.
Htn Phil 6682.3.11* Mesmer, F.A. Lettres à messieure les auteurs du journal de Paris et à M. Franklin. n.p., 1784.
Htn Phil 6682.3.13* Mesmer, F.A. Lettres guéri. London, 1784.
Phil 6682.3.4 Mesmer, F.A. Mémoire du magnetisme animal. n.p., 1781. 4 pam.
Htn Phil 6682.3.7* Mesmer, F.A. Mémoire sur la dicouverte du magnetisme animal. Genève, 1799.
Phil 6682.3.2 Mesmer, F.A. Mesmerism. London, 1948.
Phil 6682.3 Mesmer, F.A. Mesmerismus. Berlin, 1814.
Phil 6682.3.5 Mesmer, F.A. Précis historique des faits relatifs au magnétisme. London, 1781.
Phil 6671.6 Mesmer, le magnétism animal. (Bersot, P.E.) Paris, 1879.
Phil 6671.12 Mesmer and Swedenborg. (Bush, G.) N.Y., 1847.
Phil 6691.2 Mesmer et son secret. (Vinchon, Jean.) Paris, 1936.
Htn Phil 6685.10* Mesmer justifié. (Paulet, J.J.) Constance, 1784.
Phil 6677.7 Mesmeric experiences. (Hall, Spencer T.) London, 1845.
Phil 6671.3 The mesmeric mania. (Bennett, J.H.) Edinburgh, 1851.
Phil 6688.16 Mesmerism, or The new school of arts. (Staite, Opie.) London, 1844.
Phil 7068.77.1 Mesmerism, spiritualism,...historically and scientifically considered. (Carpenter, William B.) London, 1877.
Phil 7068.77 Mesmerism, spiritualism,...historically and scientifically considered. (Carpenter, William B.) N.Y., 1877.
Phil 6685.6 Mesmerism, spiritualism. (Putnam, A.) Boston, 1872.
Phil 6679.1 Mesmerism, with hints for beginners. (James, John.) London, 1879.
Phil 6682.3.2 Mesmerism. (Mesmer, F.A.) London, 1948.
Phil 6677.9 Mesmerism. 1st American ed. (Hall, Charles R.) N.Y., 1845.
Phil 6685.7 Mesmerism and christian science...history of mental healing. (Podmore, F.) Philadelphia, 1909.
Phil 6688.8.2 Mesmerism and its opponents. (Sandby, G.) London, 1844.
Phil 6688.8 Mesmerism and its opponents. 2. ed. (Sandby, G.) London, 1848.
Phil 7108.372 Mesmerism and the end of the Enlightenment in France. (Darnton, Robert.) Cambridge, 1968.
Phil 6674.4 Mesmerism in India. (Esdaile, James.) Hartford, 1847.
Phil 6689.2.5 Mesmerism proved true. (Townehend, C.H.) London, 1854.
Phil 6682.3 Mesmerismus. (Mesmer, F.A.) Berlin, 1814.
Phil 6688.12 Mesmerismus und Hypnotismus. (Sturm, G.) Leipzig, n.d.
Phil 6680.3 Mesmer's Leben und Lehre. (Kiesewetter, C.) Leipzig, 1893.
Phil 2805.263A Mesnard, Jean. Pascal, l'homme et l'oeuvre. Paris, 1951.
Phil 2805.421 Mesnard, Jean. Pascal. Bruges, 1965.
Phil 2805.263.2 Mesnard, Jean. Pascal. London, 1952.
Phil 2805.421.1 Mesnard, Jean. Pascal. University, 1969.
Phil 2805.422 Mesnard, Jean. Pascal et les Roannez. Bruges, 1965. 2v.
Phil 2520.196.10 Mesnard, Pierre. Descartes, ou Le combat pour la vérité. Paris, 1966.
Phil 2520.196 Mesnard, Pierre. Essai sur la morale de Descartes. Paris, 1936.
Phil 2520.196.5 Mesnard, Pierre. Essai sur la morale de Descartes. Thèse. Paris, 1936.
Phil 7085.1 Mesnet, E. De l'automatisme. Paris, 1874.
Phil 6682.4 Mesnet, E. Outrages à la pudeur....Somnambulisme. Paris, 1894.
Phil 3640.234 Mess, Friedrich. Nietzsche der Gesetzgeber. Leipzig, 1930.
Phil 190.102 Le message d'Amédée Ponceau. (Barraud, Jean.) Paris, 1962.
Phil 7054.186 The message of Anne Simon. (Simon, Otto J.) Boston, 1920.
Phil 8701.13 A message of light, containing scientifc foundation for religion. (Lorbeer, Floyd Irwing.) Los Angeles, 1927.
Phil 8870.5 The message of man. (Coit, Stanton.) London, 1905.
Phil 6129.7 The message of mysticism in spiritual healing. (Trumper, Henry.) London, 1933.
Phil 7069.40.12 A message to a troubled world. (Eaton, A.K.) Clarmont, Calif., 1940.
Phil 9347.2.3 A message to Garcia. (Hubbard, E.) East Aurora, 1899.
Phil 9347.2.13 A message to Garcia. (Hubbard, E.) n.p., 192-.
Phil 9347.2 A message to Garcia. (Hubbard, E.) N.Y., 1900.
Htn Phil 9347.2.5* A message to Garcia. (Hubbard, E.) N.Y., 1906.
Phil 178.12.33 A message to the well. (Dresser, H.W.) N.Y., 1910.
Phil 7054.79 Messages from the superior state. (Hewitt, S.C.) Boston, 1853.
Phil 7057.8.15 Messages on healing understood to have been dictated by William James. (Burke, Jane Revere.) N.Y., 1936.
Phil 2477.11.91 Messaut, J. La philosophie de Léon Brunschvicg. Paris, 1938.
Phil 2905.1.70 La messe sur le monde. (Teilhard de Chardin, Pierre.) Paris, 1965.
Phil 365.32 Messenger, E.C. Evolution and theology. N.Y., 1932.
Phil 5585.47 Messenger, J. Franklin. Perception of number. Thesis. N.Y., 1903.
Phil 5252.28.5 Messer, A. Empfindung und Denken. Leipzig, 1908.
Phil 8887.53 Messer, A. Ethik. Leipzig, 1918.
Phil 8887.53.4 Messer, A. Ethik. Leipzig, 1925.
Phil 1712.5 Messer, A. Geschichte der Philosophie. Leipzig, 1913.
Phil 1712.5.2 Messer, A. Geschichte der Philosophie vom Beginn der Neuzeit zum Ende des 18. Jahrhunderts. Leipzig, 1912.
Phil 1712.5.4 Messer, A. Geschichte der Philosophie vom Beginn der Neuzeit zum Ende des 18. Jahrhunderts. Leipzig, 1920.
Phil 1712.5.4.10 Messer, A. Geschichte der Philosophie vom Beginn der Neuzeit zum Ende des 18. Jahrhunderts. 6e und 7e Aufl. Leipzig, 1923.
Phil 3625.15.87 Messer, A. Glauben und Wissen. 3. Aufl. München, 1924.
Phil 3494.13.5 Messer, A. Immanuel Kants Leben und Philosophie. Stuttgart, 1924.
Phil 3494.13 Messer, A. Kant's Ethik. Leipzig, 1904.
Phil 3494.13.20 Messer, A. Kommentar zu Kants ethischen und religionsphilosophischen Hauptschriften. Leipzig, 1929.
Phil 3494.13.15 Messer, A. Kommentar zu Kants Kritik der reinen Vernunft. Stuttgart, 1923.
Phil 1712.5.10 Messer, A. Die Philosophie der Gegenwart. Leipzig, 1927.
Phil 1712.5.5 Messer, A. Die Philosophie der Gegenwart. 3e Aufl. Leipzig, 1913.
Phil 5252.28 Messer, A. Psychologie. Stuttgart, 1914.
Phil 5252.28.2 Messer, A. Psychologie. 2. Aufl. Stuttgart, 1920.

Phil 8887.53.10 Messer, A. Sittenlehre. Leipzig, 1920.
Phil 735.81 Messer, August. Deutsche Wertphilosophie der Gegenwart. Leipzig, 1926.
Phil 343.7 Messer, August. Einführung in die Erkenntnistheorie. Leipzig, 1912.
Phil 5252.120 Messer, August. Einführung in die Psychologie und die psychologischen Richtungen der Gegenwart. 2. Aufl. Leipzig, 1931.
Phil 3640.162 Messer, August. Erläuterungen zu Nietzsches Zarathustra. Stuttgart, 1922.
Phil 3246.179 Messer, August. Fichte. Leipzig, 1920.
Phil 812.6 Messer, August. Geschichte der Philosophie in Atlertum und Mittelalter. Leipzig, 1919.
Phil 630.33 Messer, August. Der kritische Realismus. Karlsruhe, 1923.
Phil 5762.11.2 Messer, August. Das Problem der Willensfreiheit. Göttingen, 1911.
Phil 5762.11 Messer, August. Das Problem der Willensfreiheit. 2. Aufl. Göttingen, 1918.
Phil 665.7.15 Messer, Max. Die moderne Seele. 3e Aufl. Leipzig, 1903.
Phil 2045.91 Messer, W.A. Das Verhältnis von Sittengesetz...bei Hobbes. Mainz, 1893.
Phil 4803.454.30 Messianisme; ou Réforme absolue du savoir humain. (Hoene-Wroński, Józef Maria.) Paris, 1847. 3v.
Phil 4803.454.35 Messianisme; philosophie absolue. (Hoene-Wroński, Józef Maria.) Paris, 1876.
Phil 4803.454.50 Messianisme, union finale de la philosophie et de la religion. (Hoene-Wroński, Józef Maria.) Paris, 1831.
Phil 3120.30.92 Das Messiasproblem bei Martin Buber. (Hammerstein, Franz von.) Stuttgart, 1958.
Phil 5592.171 Messick, S. Measurement in personality and cognition. N.Y., 1962.
Phil 5272.11 Messmethoden der Psychologie. (Sixtl, Friedrich.) Weinheim, 1967.
Phil 8887.75.10 Messner, J. Ethik. Innsbruck, 1955.
Phil 8887.75.5 Messner, J. Kulturethik. Innsbruck, 1954.
Phil 8887.76 Messner, J. Das Naturrecht. Innsbruck, 1950.
Phil 8887.75 Messner, J. Social ethics; natural law in the modern world. St. Louis, 1949.
Phil 5822.4.10 Messner, J. Widersprüche in der menschlichen Existenz. Innsbruck, 1952.
Phil 343.34 Mesthene, Emmanuel G. How language makes us know. The Hague, 1964.
Phil 310.609 Mesto istoricheskogo materializma v sisteme nauk. (Verbin, Andrei.) Moskva, 1965.
Phil 4363.14 Mestre, Antonio. Ilustración y reforma de la Iglesia. Valencia, 1968.
Phil 4958.210 Mestre, José Manuel. De la filosofía en la Habana. Habana, 1862.
Phil 4974.27.20 Mestre, Jose Manuel. Obras. Habana, 1965.
Phil 5756.14 La mesure de notre liberté. (Gardet, Louis.) Tunis, 1946.
Phil 5592.182 La mésure des attitudes. (Debaty, Pol.) Paris, 1967.
Phil 8887.134 Meta-ethics and normative ethics. (McCloskey, H.J.) The Hague, 1969.
Phil 2520.358.4 Meta-meditations; studies in Descartes. (Sesonske, Alexander.) Belmont, Calif., 1967[1965].
Phil 3120.69.30 Metabletica van de materie. (Berg, Jan Hendrik van den.) Nijkerk, 1968.
Phil 8667.54 Metadologicheski problemi na ateizma. (Mizor, Nikolai.) Sofiia, 1970.
Phil 3801.194 Metafiscia e rivelazione nella filosofia positiva di Schelling. (Bausola, Adriano.) Milano, 1965.
Phil 8893.43.10 Metafisica, scienza e moralità. (Sarlo, Francisco de.) Roma, 1898.
Phil 175.54 Metafisica. (Abraches, Cassiano.) Braga, 1956.
Phil 178.55 La metafisica. (Donati, G.) Savignano, 1921.
Phil 190.104 Metafisica classica e pensiero moderno. (Padovani, U.A.) Milano, 1961.
Phil 2655.3.105 La metafisica critica di Octave Hamelin. (Deregibus, Arturo.) Torino, 1968.
Phil 3480.62 Metafisica de Kant. (Kant, Immanuel.) Madrid, 1877.
Phil 1540.43 Metafísica de la Edad Media. (Dempf, Alois.) Madrid, 1957.
Phil 3480.66.51 La metafisica dei costumi. v.1-2. (Kant, Immanuel.) Torino, 1923-25.
Phil 3808.112.13 La metafisica del bello e dei costumi di...Schopenhauer. (Covotti, Aurelio.) Napoli, 1934.
Phil 189.19 Metafisica del concreto. (Ottaviano, C.) Roma, 1929.
Phil 4225.9 Metafisica della forma. (Stefanini, Luigi.) Padova, 1949.
Phil 5590.160 Metafisica della persona. (Stefanini, L.) Padova, 1950.
Phil 193.183 Metafisica dell'arte e altri saggi. (Stefanini, Luigi.) Padova, 1948.
Phil 190.42 La metafisica dell'esperienza. (Pelazza, A.) Bergamo, 1907.
Phil 4073.120.5 La metafisica di Tommaso Campanella. (Femiano, Salvatore Beniamino.) Milano, 1968.
Phil 3500.96 Metafisica e critica in Kant. (Santinello, Giovanni.) Bologna, 1965.
Phil 190.112 Metafisica e pensiero. (Pavese, Roberto.) Padova, 1967.
Phil 192.100 Metafisica e scientismo. (Rinerso, Emmanuele.) Napoli, 1957.
Phil 4000.15 Metafisica e spiritualisti italiani contemporanei. (Alberghi, Sante.) Milano, 1960.
Phil 165.67 Metafisica ed esperienza religiosa. (Archivio di Filosofia.) Roma, 1956.
Phil 181.128.10 Metafisica natural estabilizada y problematica. (Garcia Bacca, J.D.) Mexico, 1963.
Phil 1135.158 La metafisica presofistica. (Gentile, M.) Padova, 1939.
Phil 188.16.10 Metafisica y ciencia. (Nuñez Requeiro, M.) Buenos Aires, 1941.
Phil 4829.749.30 Metafizika i ćudoredje. (Rodin, Davor.) Zagreb, 1971.
Phil 3501.13 Metafizika predpolozheniia poznaniia opyt preodolevaniia Kanta. (Trubetskoi, E.) Moskva, 1917.
Phil 3837.11 Metafizika Spinozy. (Robinson, L.) Sankt Peterburg, 1913.
Phil 1135.125 Metafizika v drevnei Gretsii. (Trubetskoi, S.) Moskva, 1890.
Phil 181.66.5 Metafizikai világnézet. (Gruenhut, Ladislaus.) Baja? 1934.
Phil 2520.330 Metafysica en fysica bij Descartes. (Hoeven, Pieter van der.) Gorinchem, 1961.
Phil 4650.1.53 Metafysik. (Vannérus, Allen.) Lund, 1914.
Phil 5069.4 Metakritik der formalen Logik. (Eley, Lothar.) Den Haag, 1969.
Phil 8965.16 La metamorfosi dell'etica medioevale. (Piergiovanni, Enzo.) Bologna, 1967.
Phil 5404.4 Les métamorphoses du désir et l'oeuvre. (Martinon, Jean Pierre.) Paris, 1970.
Phil 5590.280.5 Metamorphosis. (Schachtel, Ernest G.) London, 1963.
Phil 5590.280 Metamorphosis. (Schachtel, Ernest G.) N.Y., 1959.

Phil 2340.19.30 The metamorphosis of metaphysics. (Wisdom, John.) London, 1961?
Phil 2725.37.40 Métaphilosophie; prolégomènes. (Lefebvre, Henri.) Paris, 1965.
Phil 182.4.10 Metaphilosophie. (Harms, F.) Leipzig, 1895.
Phil 22.61 Metaphilosophy. Oxford, England. 1,1970+
Phil 3565.31.2 Metaphysic. (Lotze, Hermann.) Oxford, 1884.
Phil 3565.31.4 Metaphysic. 2. ed. (Lotze, Hermann.) Oxford, 1887. 2v.
Phil 182.19.11 Metaphysic of experience. (Hodgson, S.H.) London, 1898. 4v.
Htn Phil 3480.67.70* The metaphysic of morals, divided into metaphisical elements of law and of ethics. v.1-2. (Kant, Immanuel.) London, 1799.
Phil 1885.80 The metaphysic of Mr. F.H. Bradley. (Rashdall, H.) London, 1912.
Phil 3095.35.5 Metaphysica. (Baumgarten, A.G.) Halae, 1739.
Phil 3095.35 Metaphysica. (Baumgarten, A.G.) Halae, 1757.
Phil 4073.62F Metaphysica. (Campanella, Tommaso.) Torino, 1961.
Phil 187.6.2 Metaphysica. (Makowski, J.) Amsterdam, 1651.
Phil 187.6 Metaphysica. (Makowski, J.) n.p., n.d.
Phil 190.90 Metaphysica. (Peters, Johannes Arnold Josef.) Utrecht, 1957.
Phil 3095.40 Metaphysica. 7th ed. (Baumgarten, A.G.) Halae, 1779.
Phil 176.119 Metaphysica generalis. (Baron, K.) Londini, 1657?
Phil 179.30 Metaphysica generalis in usum scholarum. (Esser, Gerard.) Techny, Ill., 1933.
Phil 315.1 Metaphysica nova et vetusta. (Laurie, S.S.) London, 1884.
Phil 193.32.3 Metaphysicae. (Stahli, D.) Bredae, 1650.
Phil 193.38 Metaphysicae. v.1-4. (Storchenau, S.) Venice, 1819-1820. 2v.
Htn Phil 3480.36* Metaphysicae cum geometria junctae usus in philosophiam naturicam. (Kant, Immanuel.) Regiomonti, 1756.
Phil 2053.52 Metaphysical synopsis. (Hutcheson, F.) n.p., 1742.
Phil 5520.506 Metaphysical analysis. (Yolton, John W.) Toronto, 1967.
Phil 194.49 Metaphysical beliefs. (Taulmin, St. E.) London, 1957.
Phil 52.8 Metaphysical Club, Boston. Calendar. Boston, n.d.
Phil 3480.67.110 The metaphysical elements of justice. (Kant, Immanuel.) Indianapolis, 1965.
Phil 185.6 Metaphysical essays. (Kirwan, R.) London, 1809.
Phil 185.6.5 Metaphysical essays. (Kirwan, R.) London, 1809.
Phil 3480.81.4.1 Metaphysical foundations of natural science. (Kant, Immanuel.) Indianapolis, 1970.
Phil 177.21 Metaphysical inquiry. (Cory, Isaac P.) London, 1833-37.
Phil 187.93.3 Metaphysical journal. (Marcel, Gabriel.) London, 1952.
NEDL Phil 22.3 Metaphysical magazine. N.Y. 1-20,1895-1907 6v.
Phil 3790.8.80 The metaphysical presuppositions of Ritschl. (Keirstead, W.C.) Chicago, 1905.
Phil 1955.6.128 The metaphysical presuppositions of the philosophy of John Dewey. Thesis. (Battle, J.J.) Fribourg, 1951.
Phil 52.9A The metaphysical society. (Brown, A.W.) N.Y., 1947.
Phil 575.100 A metaphysical study on the individual and the person. Diss. (McMorrow, G.J.) Notre Dame, 1940.
Phil 2045.55 Metaphysical system. (Hobbes, Thomas.) Chicago, 1910.
Phil 2045.27A The metaphysical system of Hobbes. (Hobbes, Thomas.) Chicago, 1905.
Phil 190.2 Metaphysical tracts by English philosophers of the 18th century. (Parr, S.) London, 1837.
Phil 3480.61 Metaphysical works. (Kant, Immanuel.) London, 1836.
Phil 1020.8.12 Metaphysics compendium...Latinum...N. Carame. (Ibn Sina.) Roma, 1926.
Phil 177.60 Metaphysische Gespräche. (Conrad-Martius, Hedwig.) Halle, 1921.
Phil 185.42 Metaphysicia der rede. (Kortmulder, R.J.) Amsterdam, 1925.
Phil 190.90.5 Metaphysics; a systematic survey. (Peters, Johannes Arnold Josef.) Pittsburgh, 1963.
Phil 2150.20.30 Metaphysics, man and freedom. (Murty, K. Satchidananda.) N.Y., 1963.
Phil 165.364 Metaphysics; readings and reappraisals. (Kennick, William E.) Englewood Cliffs, N.J., 1966.
Phil 5068.56.5 Metaphysics, reference, and language. (Cornman, James W.) New Haven, 1966.
Phil 140.18 Pamphlet vol. Metaphysics, 1893-1910. 6 pam.
Phil 175.58 Metaphysics. (Ando, Takatuna.) Hague, 1963.
Phil 176.27 Metaphysics. (Bowne, B.P.) N.Y., 1882.
Phil 176.27.5 Metaphysics. (Bowne, B.P.) N.Y., 1882.
Phil 176.27.2 Metaphysics. (Bowne, B.P.) N.Y., 1898.
Phil 177.128.2 Metaphysics. (Coreth, Emerich.) N.Y., 1968.
Phil 2035.51 Metaphysics. (Hamilton, William.) Cambridge, 1861.
Phil 2035.51.9 Metaphysics. (Hamilton, William.) Cambridge, 1864.
Phil 2075.7.35 Metaphysics. (Jordan, Elijah.) Evanston, Ill., 1956.
Phil 186.3 Metaphysics. (Laws, S.S.) Columbia, Mo., 1879.
Phil 2130.30 Metaphysics. (Mansel, H.L.) Edinburgh, 1860.
Phil 2130.31 Metaphysics. (Mansel, H.L.) N.Y., 1871.
Phil 187.16 Metaphysics. (Miller, J.) N.Y., 1877.
Phil 197.23 Metaphysics. (Woodbridge, F.J.E.) N.Y., 1908.
Phil 325.22 Metaphysics and British empiricism. (Armstrong, Robert L.) Lincoln, 1970.
Phil 1845.10.5 Metaphysics and common sense. (Ayer, Alfred Jules.) London, 1969.
Phil 70.94.5 Metaphysics and explanation. (Oberlin Colloquium in Philosophy, 5th, Oberlin College, 1964.) Pittsburgh, Pa. 1966
Phil 3270.15.31 Metaphysics and historicity. (Frackenheim, Emil L.) Milwaukee, 1961.
Phil 187.158 Metaphysics and ideology. (Martin, William O.) Milwaukee, 1959.
Phil 177.122 Metaphysics and man. (Collins, William B.) Dubuque, 1959.
Phil 178.76 Metaphysics and religious language. (Dilley, Frank B.) N.Y., 1964.
Phil 8669.6 Metaphysics and the existence of God. (O'Brien, Thomas C.) Washington, 1960.
Phil 1750.848 Metaphysics and the philosophy of science. (Buchdahl, G.) Oxford, 1969.
Phil 181.74.5 Metaphysics in modern times. (Gilson, E.) Chicago, 1940.
Phil 193.234 A metaphysics of authentic existentialism. (Sweeney, Leo.) Englewood Cliffs, N.J., 1965.
Phil 187.178 A metaphysics of being and God. (McGlynn, James.) Englewood Cliffs, 1966.
Phil 1870.116 The metaphysics of Berkeley critically examined in the light of modern philosophy. (Kaveeshwar, G.W.) Mandleshwar, 1933.
Phil 2520.350 The metaphysics of Descartes. (Beck, Leslie John.) Oxford, 1965.
Phil 187.49.5 Metaphysics of energy. (Malkani, G.R.) Amalner, 1920.
NEDL Phil 3480.66.3 The metaphysics of ethics. 3. ed. (Kant, Immanuel.) Edinburgh, 1871.

Phil 2138.82   Metaphysics of John Stuart Mill. (Courtney, W.S.) London, 1879.

Phil 5068.18.2   The metaphysics of logical positivism; papers. 2. ed. (Bergmann, Gustav.) Madison, 1967.

Phil 1905.34   Metaphysics of natural complexes. (Buchler, Justus.) N.Y., 1966.

Phil 192.22   The metaphysics of nature. (Read, C.) London, 1905.

Phil 182.82   The metaphysics of pragmatism. (Hook, Sidney.) Chicago, 1927.

Phil 2035.51.15   The metaphysics of Sir William Hamilton. (Hamilton, William.) Boston, 1872.

Phil 2035.51.19   The metaphysics of Sir William Hamilton. (Hamilton, William.) Boston, 1877[1861]

Phil 6112.14   Metaphysics of the nature and in the conception of the soul. (Clements, J.) Boston, 1909.

Phil 1512.2   Metaphysics of the school. (Harper, Thomas.) London, 1879. 3v.

Phil 2520.124   Metaphysics of the supernatural as illustrated by Descartes. (Kahn, Lina.) N.Y., 1918.

Phil 735.122   The metaphysics of value. (Sreenivasa Iyengar, K.R.) Mysore, 1942.

Phil 2070.151   The metaphysics of William James and John Dewey. (Martland, T.) N.Y., 1963.

Phil 3850.72.2   Metaphysik, Skepsis, Wissenschaft. 2. Aufl. (Stegmueller, Wolfgang.) Berlin, 1969.

Phil 3085.3.31   Metaphysik. (Apelt, E.F.) Leipzig, 1857.
Phil 3095.45   Metaphysik. (Baumgarten, A.G.) Halle, 1766.
Phil 177.128   Metaphysik. (Coreth, Emerich.) Innsbruck, 1961.
Phil 178.22.7   Metaphysik. (Driesch, H.) Breslau, 1924.
Phil 3200.8   Metaphysik. (Ehrlich, W.) Tübingen, 1955.
Phil 179.2   Metaphysik. (Erhardt, F.) Leipzig, 1894.
Phil 180.92   Metaphysik. (Fasel, Georg K.) Duisburg, 1969.
Phil 3310.5.31   Die Metaphysik. (Gutberlet, C.) Münster, 1880.
Phil 185.3.5   Metaphysik. (Keyserlingh, H. von.) Heidelberg, 1818.
Phil 3565.45   Metaphysik. (Lotze, Hermann.) Leipzig, 1841.
Phil 3565.45.10   Metaphysik. (Lotze, Hermann.) Leipzig, 1879.
Phil 192.38   Metaphysik. (Runze, Georg.) Leipzig, 1905.
Phil 193.102   Metaphysik. (Schenach, G.) Innsbruck, 1856.
Phil 197.14.5   Metaphysik. (Wentscher, Max.) Berlin, 1928.
Phil 192.58   Die Metaphysik: eine fiktion. (Roretz, Karl.) Wien, 1927.
Phil 197.30   Metaphysik. v.1-2. (Weber, Theodor.) Gotha, 1888-1891.
Phil 176.140.5   Metaphysik. 3. Aufl. (Baur, Ludwig.) München, 1935.
Phil 176.143   Metaphysik als beobachtende Wissenschaft. (Bräuer, Ernst Wasa.) Berlin, 1934.

Phil 193.99   Metaphysik als exakte Wissenschaft. Pt.1-3. (Schneider, H.) Leipzig, 1919-1921.

Phil 182.11.10   Die Metaphysik als Grundwissenschaft. (Helfferich, A.) Hamburg, 1846.

Phil 176.76   Metaphysik als Lehre vom Vorbewussten. Bd.I. (Bilharz, Alfons.) Wiesbaden, 1897.

Phil 193.225.7   Metaphysik als strenge Wissenschaft. 2. Aufl. (Scholz, H.) Darmstadt, 1965.

Phil 197.63.7   Metaphysik als Weg von den Grenzen der Wissenschaft au die Grenzen der Religion. 2. Aufl. (Wenzl, Aloys.) Graz, 1956.

Phil 178.37.10   Metaphysik als Wissenschaft vom Letzten. (Dingler, Hugo.) München, 1929.

Phil 1020.8.9   Die metaphysik Ayicennas. (Ibn Sina.) Halle, 1907-09.
Phil 3100.82   Die Metaphysik Benekes. (Wandschneider, A.) Berlin, 1903.
Phil 3826.12   Die Metaphysik der Ethik Spinozas im Quellenlichte der Kabbalah. (Gelbraus, Samuel.) Wien, 1917.

Phil 3450.33.7   Metaphysik der Gemeinsheaft. (Hildebrand, D. von.) Regensburg, 1955.

Phil 8583.20   Metaphysik der Geschichte. (Denkmann, D.K.) Leipzig, 1914.

Phil 284.6.10   Metaphysik der Natur. (Driesch, Hans.) München, 1926.
Phil 1707.8.6   Metaphysik der Neuzeit. (Heimsoeth, H.) München, 1967.
Htn   Phil 3480.63*   Die Metaphysik der Sitten. (Kant, Immanuel.) Königsberg, 1797.

Phil 3480.63.15   Metaphysik der Sitten. (Kant, Immanuel.) Leipzig, 1870.
Phil 8892.60   Metaphysik der sittlichen Werte. 1. Aufl. (Reding, Marcel.) Düsseldorf, 1949.

Phil 192.70   Metaphysik der Wirklichkeit. (Reininger, Robert.) Wien, 1931.

Phil 192.70.5   Metaphysik der Wirklichkeit. 2. Aufl. (Reininger, Robert.) Wien, 1947. 2v.

Phil 1123.7   Metaphysik des Altertums. (Stenzel, Julius.) München, 1931.

Phil 5400.112   Metaphysik des Fühlens. 4. Aufl. (Haecker, T.) München, 1950.

Phil 196.23   Metaphysik des Ich. (Vowinckel, E.) Berlin, 1924.
Phil 187.86   Metaphysik des Irrationalen. (Müller-Freienfels, R.) Leipzig, 1927.

Phil 4110.1.85   Metaphysik des Marsilius Ficinus. Inaug. Diss. (Hobert, Werner.) Koblenz, 1930.

Phil 1540.40   Metaphysik des Mittelalters. (Dempf, Alois.) München, 1930.

Phil 5520.67   Metaphysik des Wortes. Inaug. Diss. (Bruns, L.) Bonn, 1937.

Phil 187.152   Metaphysik einst und jetzt. (Moser, Simon.) Berlin, 1958.
Phil 3428.80   Die Metaphysik Herbarts. (Capesius, J.) Leipzig, 1878.
Phil 3200.8.15   Metaphysik im erkenntniskritischen Grundriss. (Ehrlich, W.) Halle, 1924.

Phil 3450.4.90   Metaphysik im Horizont der Theologie Wilhelm Herrmanns. (Fischer-Appelt, Peter.) München, 1965.

Phil 70.75.2A   Die Metaphysik im Mittelalter, ihr Ursprung und ihre Bedeutung. (Congrès International de Philosophie Médiévale, 2d, Cologne, 1961.) Berlin. 1963

Phil 182.66   Die Metaphysik in der modernen Physiologie. (Hauptmann, C.) Jena, 1894.

Phil 182.91   Metaphysik oder verstehende Sinnwissenschaft? (Hofmann, P.) Berlin, 1929.

Phil 3808.87.5   Metaphysik und Asketik. (Hecker, M.F.) Bonn, 1896.
Phil 3160.6.85   Metaphysik und Kritik bei Christian August Crusius. (Heimsoeth, H.) Berlin, 1926.

Phil 282.7.16   Metaphysik und Naturwissenschaften. (Becher, Erich.) München, 1926.

Phil 3425.702   Metaphysik und Politik. (Ritta, Joachim.) Frankfurt, 1969.

Phil 8612.78   Metaphysik und Tod. (Fink, Eugen.) Stuttgart, 1969.
Phil 3565.31.15   Métaphysique. (Lotze, Hermann.) Paris, 1883.
Phil 196.1   La métaphysique. (Vacherot, E.) Paris, 1858. 2v.
Phil 175.2.8   Métaphysique considérée comme science. (Alaux, J.E.) Paris, 1879.

Phil 2520.255.15   La métaphysique de Descartes. 1. éd. (Lefèvre, Roger.) Paris, 1959.

Phil 3565.86   La métaphysique de Hermann Lotze. (Schoen, H.) Paris, 1902.

Phil 3485.32   La métaphysique de Kant. (Destutt de Tracy, Antoine Louis Claude.) Bruxelles, 1968.

Phil 3485.19.2   La métaphysique de Kant. Thèse. (Daval, Roger.) Paris, 1950.

Phil 3485.19   La métaphysique de Kant. 1. éd. (Daval, Roger.) Paris, 1950.

Phil 2266.43.5   La métaphysique de l'âme. (Smith, Adam.) Paris, 1764. 2v.

Phil 2725.35.80   La métaphysique de l'être dans la philosophie de Louis Lavelle. (Ecole, Jean.) Louvain, 1957.

Phil 2477.6.125   La métaphysique de l'être dans la philosophie de Maurice Blondel. (École, Jean.) Louvains, 1959.

Phil 178.46.80   La métaphysique de Paul Decoster. (Gerard, Jacques.) Paris, 1945.

Phil 2555.7.90   La métaphysique de Paul Decoster et la science. (Cochet, M.A.) Bruges, 1937.

Phil 2250.94   La métaphysique de Royce. (Marcel, Gabriel.) Paris, 1945.
Phil 2340.10.240   La métaphysique de Whitehead: recherche des prolongements anthropologiques. (Laszlo, Ervin.) La Hague, 1970.

Phil 8599.44   La métaphysique du christianisme. (Tresmontant, Claude.) Paris, 1961.

Phil 8599.44.10   La métaphysique du christianisme. (Tresmontant, Claude.) Paris, 1964.

Phil 196.1.2   La métaphysique et de science. 2d ed. (Vacherot, E.) Paris, 1863.

Phil 2515.8.80   Métaphysique et intuition; le message de Jacques Chevalier. (Guy, Alain.) Paris, 1940.

Phil 192.106   La métaphysique et le langage. (Rougier, Louis.) Paris, 1960.

Phil 70.90   La métaphysique et l'ouverture. (Gonseth, Ferdinand.) Paris, 1960.

Phil 6311.46   Métaphysique et psychanalyse. 2. éd. (Benoit, Hubert.) Paris, 1964.

Phil 180.7   Métaphysique et psychologie. (Flournoy, T.) Genève, 1890.
Phil 180.7.2   Métaphysique et psychologie. 2. éd. (Flournoy, T.) Genève, 1919.

Phil 177.47   La métaphysique et sa méthode. (Cellarier, Felix.) Paris, 1914.

Phil 530.105.5   A métaphysique of mysticism. (Govindácárya, Alkondavilli.) Mysore, 1923.

Phil 181.71.10   La métaphysique orientale. 2. ed. (Guénon, R.) Paris, 1945.

Phil 3552.79.25   Metaphysische Abhandlung. (Leibniz, Gottfried Wilhelm.) Hamburg, 1958.

Htn   Phil 3480.81*   Metaphysische Anfangsgründe der Jugendlehre. (Kant, Immanuel.) Königsberg, 1797.

Phil 3480.81.3   Metaphysische Anfangsgründe der Jugendlehre. 2. Aufl. (Kant, Immanuel.) Königsberg, 1803.

Phil 3480.81.5   Metaphysische Anfangsgründe der Jugendlehre. 2. Aufl. (Kant, Immanuel.) Kreuznach, 1800.

Htn   Phil 3480.81.2*   Metaphysische Anfangsgründe der Jugendlehre. 2. Aufl. (Kant, Immanuel.) Kreuznach, 1800.

Phil 3480.81.4   Metaphysische Anfangsgründe der Naturwesenschaft. (Kant, Immanuel.) Leipzig, 1914.

Phil 3480.55.12   Metaphysische Anfangsgründe der Naturwissenschaft. (Kant, Immanuel.) Frankfurt, 1794.

Phil 3480.55.15   Metaphysische Anfangsgründe der Naturwissenschaft. (Kant, Immanuel.) Grätz, 1796. 3 pam.

Phil 3480.55   Metaphysische Anfangsgründe der Naturwissenschaft. (Kant, Immanuel.) Leipzig, 1800.

Phil 3480.56A   Metaphysische Anfangsgründe der Naturwissenschaft. (Kant, Immanuel.) Leipzig, 1900.

Htn   Phil 3480.55.2*   Metaphysische Anfangsgründe der Naturwissenschaft. (Kant, Immanuel.) Riga, 1786.

Phil 3480.55.4   Metaphysische Anfangsgründe der Naturwissenschaft. (Kant, Immanuel.) Riga, 1787.

Phil 3480.67.50.5   Metaphysische Anfangsgrunde der Rechtslehre. (Kant, Immanuel.) Frankfurt, 1797.

Htn   Phil 3480.67.50*   Metaphysische Anfangsgrunde der Rechtslehre. (Kant, Immanuel.) Königsberg, 1797.

Htn   Phil 3480.67.51*   Metaphysische Anfangsgrunde der Rechtslehre. 2. Aufl. (Kant, Immanuel.) Königsberg, 1798.

Phil 3415.101   Die metaphysische Begründung der Ethik in Eduard von Hartmanns philosophischen System. (König, N.) Leipzig, 1910.

Phil 182.90   Die metaphysische Form. (Herrigel, E.) Tübingen, 1929.
Phil 3504.16.5   Die metaphysische Grundanschauung Kants. (Wolff, Hermann.) Leipzig, 1870.

Phil 1517.7   Metaphysische Hintergrunde der spatscholastischen Naturphilosophie. (Maier, A.) Roma, 1955.

Phil 665.108   Metaphysische Praxis als Schlüssel zur geistigen Welt. (Krueger, Walter.) Freiburg, 1968.

Phil 1135.50   Metaphysische Theorie der griechischen Philosophie. (Weisz, C.O.M.) Rostock, 1873.

Phil 3501.24   Metaphysische und transzendentale Dynamik in Kants opus postumum. (Tuschling, Burkhard.) Berlin, 1971.

Phil 185.11.5   Metaphysische Untersuchungen. (Kym, A.L.) München, 1875.
Phil 3552.276   Die metaphysische Unvollkommenheit...bei Augustin und Leibniz. Inaug. Diss. (Trepte, Adolf.) Halle, 1889.

Phil 8961.8   Die metaphysische Wurzel die christlichen Ethik. (Lindwurm, A.) Berlin, 1872.

Phil 3640.590   Die metaphysischen und anthropologischen Voraussetzungen der Politik bei Friedrich Nietzsche. (Hohn, Hans.) Bonn, 1959.

Phil 3552.120.5   Die metaphysischen Voraussetzungen. (Class, Gustav.) Tübingen, 1874.

Phil 190.3.12   De metaphysiska problemen. (Paulsen, F.) Stockholm, 1904.
Phil 4803.454.55   Metapolityke. (Hoene-Wroński, Józef Maria.) Warszawa, 1923.

Phil 8581.61   Das Metareligiöse. (Bauhofer, O.) Leipzig, 1930.
Phil 2880.6   Le métaverbe. (Sauvage-Jousse, P.) Paris, 1928.
Phil 8887.14   Metcalf, D. An enquiry into...moral obligation. Boston, 1860.

Phil 9455.7   Metcalf, Thomas. An address to the Phi Beta Kappa Society of Brown University, Sept. 5, 1832. Boston, 1833.

Phil 5590.270   Metelli, Fabio. Le dottrine caratterologiche di Ernest Kretschmer e Gerarhd Pfahler. Padova, 1958.

Phil 8633.1.17   Metempsychosis. (Moore, G.F.) Cambridge, 1914.
Phil 5649.32   Metheny, Eleanor. Movement and meaning. N.Y., 1968.
Phil 2520.36   The method, meditation and selections. (Descartes, René.) Edinburgh, 1897.

Phil 5254.7A   Method and theory in experimental psychology. (Osgood, C.E.) N.Y., 1956.

Phil 5500.65   Method effects in absolute and comparative judgment. Proefschrift. (Hofstee, Willem Karel Bernard.) Groningen, 1967.

Phil 8879.34   Method in ethical theory. (Edel, A.) London, 1963.

Phil 5265.6   Method in experimental psychology. (Zimny, George.) N.Y., 1961.

Phil 182.113   Method in metaphysics. (Henle, R.J.) Milwaukee, 1951.

Phil 2520.238   The method of Descartes. (Beck, L.J.) Oxford, 1952.

Phil 2125.65.5   Method of divine government. (McCosh, James.) Edinburgh, 1852.

Phil 2125.65   Method of divine government. (McCosh, James.) N.Y., 1851.

Phil 2125.65.4   Method of divine government. (McCosh, James.) N.Y., 1855.

Phil 2125.65.7   Method of divine government. 2nd ed. (McCosh, James.) Edinburgh, 1850.

Phil 5058.2.2   The method to science. (Sargent, J.) London, 1696.

Phil 3246.50   Méthode...a la vie bienheureuse. (Fichte, Johann Gottlieb.) Paris, 1845.

Phil 2520.188   La méthode de Descartes et son application à la métaphysique. (Serrus, Charles.) Paris, 1933.

Phil 2520.188.5   La méthode de Descartes et son application à la métaphysique. Thèse. (Serrus, Charles.) Paris, 1933.

Phil 281.13   Méthode de la philosophie de la nature. (Ambacher, Michel.) Paris, 1961.

Phil 2730.97   La méthode de réflexion chez Maine de Biran. (Fessard, G.) Paris, 1938.

Phil 2520.113   Die Methode der Erkenntnis bei Descartes. (Heimsoeth, H.) Giessen, 1912.

Phil 353.4   Die Methode der Gestaltanalyse. (Weinhandl, F.) Leipzig, 1923.

Phil 2490.106   De methode der positieve filosofie volgens Auguste Comte. (L'Ange-Huet, J.) Leiden, 1866.

Phil 2490.130   Méthode et intuition chez Auguste Comte. Thèse. (Ducassé, P.) Paris, 1939.

Phil 3120.8.115   Méthode et métaphysique selon Franz Brentano. (Gilson, Lucie.) Paris, 1955.

Phil 2905.1.160   Méthode et principes du père Teilhard de Chardin. (Blanchard, Julien P.) Paris, 1961.

Phil 3450.18.135   Die Methode in der Philosophie Nicolai Hartmanns. 1e Aufl. (Hülsmann, Heinz.) Düsseldorf, 1959.

Phil 2475.1.194   La méthode intuitive de M. Bergson. (Penido, M.T.L.) Genève, 1918.

Phil 2490.52   La méthode positive en seize leçons. (Comte, Auguste.) Paris, 1917.

Phil 600.50   La méthode positive et l'intuition comtienne. (Ducassé, Pierre.) Paris, 1939.

Phil 6060.7.7   Méthode pratique de graphologie. (Michon, J.H.) Paris, 1899.

Phil 6315.2.111   La méthode psychanalytique et la doctrine freudienne. v.1-2. Thèse. (Dalbiez, R.) Paris, 1936.

Phil 192.28.8.5   Méthode scientifique en philosophie. (Russell, B.) Paris, 1929.

Phil 2655.3.93   La méthode synthétique d'Hamelin. (Beck, Leslie J.) Paris, 1935.

Phil 6109.4   Methoden der Aktivierungsforschung. (Schoenpflug, Wolfgang.) Bern, 1969.

Phil 8893.11.22   Die Methoden der Ethick. v.1-2. (Sidgwick, H.) Leipzig, 1909.

Phil 5259.15.10   Die Methoden der psychologischen Forschung. (Tumarkin, Anna.) Leipzig, 1929.

Phil 5270.28   Methodenprobleme der kulturvergleichenden Psychologie. (Eckensberger, Lutz H.) Saarbrücken, 1970.

Phil 400.73   Les méthodes de l'idéalisme scientifique. (Dwelshauvers, G.) Paris, 1892. 2 pam.

Phil 1020.80   Les méthodes d'exegèse. (Hanafi, Hasan.) Le Caire, 1965.

Phil 5592.145   Les méthodes projectives. (Anzieu, D.) Paris, 1960.

Phil 5592.148   Les méthodes projectives. 3e éd. (Anzieu, D.) Paris, 1970.

Phil 5257.64.5   Les méthodes quantitatives en psychologie. (Reuchlin, Maurice.) Paris, 1962.

Phil 5625.1   Die Methodik der Enforschung der bedingten Reflexe. (Podkopaev, N.A.) München, 1926.

Phil 978.49.145.5   Methodik und Wesen der Sprachgestaltung. (Steiner, R.) Dornach, 1955.

Phil 5425.45   Die methodische Entwicklung der Talente und des Genies. (Hock, Alfred.) Leipzig, 1920.

Phil 978.49.360   Methodische Grundlagen der Anthroposophie. (Steiner, R.) Dornach, 1961.

Phil 5270.20   Methodisches Denken in der Psychologie. (Schneewind, Klaus Alfred.) Bern, 1969.

Phil 5262.23   Methodisches Lehrbuch der Psychologie. (Walsemann, Hermann.) Potsdam, 1905.

Phil 2225.16.80   Methodologie als Erkenntnistheorie. (Wellmer, Albrecht.) Frankfurt, 1967.

Phil 4080.3.370   Methodologie et spéculation esthétique. (Svenaeus, G.) Lund, 1961.

Phil 5246.38   Methodologische und experimentelle Beiträge zur Quantitätslehre. (Geiger, Moritz.) Leipzig, 1907.

Phil 22.40   Methodos; Revista trimestrale di methodologi e di logica simbolica. Milano. 2,1950+ 11v.

Phil 5042.50   Methods and criteria of reasoning. (Crawshay-Williams, Rupert.) London, 1957.

Phil 6316.15   The methods and experience of psychoanalysis. (Goerres, Albert.) London, 1962.

Phil 178.12.19   Methods and problems of spiritual healing. (Dresser, H.W.) N.Y., 1899.

Phil 7118.5   Methods and uses of hypnosis and self-hypnosis. (Hollander, Bernard.) Hollywood, Calif. 1966.

Phil 5330.1   Methods for mind training. (Aiken, C.) N.Y., 1889.

Phil 5330.1.3   Methods for mind training. (Aiken, C.) N.Y., 1897.

Phil 5590.310   Methods in personality assessment. (Stern, George G.) Glencoe, Ill., 1956.

Phil 186.115   Methods of comparative philosophy. (Liat, W.S.) Leiden, 1955.

Phil 5041.92   The methods of contemporary thought. (Bocheński, Innocentius M.) Dordrecht, 1965.

Phil 8893.11.2   The methods of ethics. (Sidgwick, H.) London, 1874.

Phil 8893.11   The methods of ethics. (Sidgwick, H.) London, 1874.

Phil 8893.11.15   The methods of ethics. (Sidgwick, H.) London, 1922.

Htn Phil 2280.1.30*   The methods of ethics. (Sidgwick, Henry.) London, 1874.

Phil 8893.11.10   The methods of ethics. Supplement to 1. ed. Photoreproduction. (Sidgwick, H.) London, 1877.

Phil 8893.11.6   The methods of ethics. 6. ed. (Sidgwick, H.) London, 1801.

Phil 8893.11.17   The methods of ethics. 7. ed. (Sidgwick, H.) London, 1930.

Phil 6312.18   Methods of group psychotherapy. (Corsini, R.J.) N.Y., 1957.

Phil 349.11   Methods of knowledge. (Smith, Walter.) N.Y., 1899.

Phil 5056.1.15   Methods of logic. (Quine, Willard Van Orman.) N.Y., 1950.

Phil 5056.1.22   Methods of logic. (Quine, Willard Van Orman.) N.Y., 1953.

Phil 5056.1.20   Methods of logic. (Quine, Willard Van Orman.) N.Y., 1959.

Phil 5056.1.23   Methods of logic. (Quine, Willard Van Orman.) N.Y., 1964.

Phil 5240.43   Methods of psychology. (Andrews, T.G.) N.Y., 1948.

Phil 5325.155   Methods of studying controlled word associations. (Loring, Mildred W.) Baltimore, 1919.

Phil 5834.1.5   Methods of studying vision in animals. (Yerkes, R.M.) Cambridge, n.d.

Phil 978.59.110   Methorst-Kuiper, A. Krishnamurti. Amsterdam, 1961.

Phil 1750.640   Metod analiza v sovremennoi burzhuaznoi filosofii. (Begiashvili, A.F.) Tbilisi, 1960.

Phil 5400.162   Metod K.S. Stanislavskogo i fiziologiia emotsii. (Simonov, P.V.) Moskva, 1962.

Phil 3425.127   Metoda Hegla i zasady filosofii spekulatywej. (Żółtowski, A.) Krakow, 1910.

Phil 3425.520   Metoda si sistem la Hegel. (Gulian, C.I.) Bucuresti, 1957. 2v.

Phil 4352.1.135   Metodalogía filosófica de Balmes. (Solaguren, Celestino.) Madrid, 1961.

Phil 310.674.2   Metodicheskoe posobre po filosofii. Izd. 2. Moskva, 1968.

Phil 5625.1.5.3   Metodika izucheniia uslovnykn refleksov. 3. izd. (Podkopaev, N.A.) Moskva, 1952.

Phil 8884.15.5   Il metodo dell'economica pura nell'etica. (Juvalta, E.) Pavia, 1907.

Phil 2750.22.85   Il metodo di Mounier altri saggi. (Melchione, Vuceolio.) Milano, 1960.

Phil 4080.3.405.5   Il metodo e la critica di Benedetto Croce. (Puppo, Mario.) Milano, 1964.

Phil 1750.785   O método fenomenológico; estudo para a determinação do seu valor filosófico. (Soveral, Eduardo S.) Porto, 1965.

Phil 1750.670   Il metodo fenomenologico e la fondazione della filosofia. (Valori, Paolo.) Roma, 1959.

Phil 1730.14   Il metodo geometrico nella filosofia del Seicento. (DeAngelis, Eurico.) Pisa, 1964.

Phil 6125.12   Le metodo nello studio del fenomeno biopsichio. (Panizza, M.) Roma, 1901.

Phil 5593.52   Il metodo psicodiagnostico de Rorschach. (Pergola, Elio de.) Roma, 1952.

Phil 183.4   Il metodo secondo dialogo filosofico. (Isola, I.G.) Modena, 1871.

Phil 194.62   Metodologia del pensamiento mágico. (Trias, Eugenio.) Bercelona, 1970.

Phil 5068.44   La metodologia nel rinnovarsi del pensiero. (Filiasi Carcano, Paolo.) Napoli, 1957.

Phil 5270.16   Metodologicheskie i teoreticheskie problemy psikhologii. Moskva, 1969.

Phil 334.10   Metodologicheskie problemy teoreticheskogo i istoricheskogo poznaniia. (Dobriianov, Velichko S.) Moskva, 1968.

Phil 190.100   Métodos y principios filosóficos. (Oromi, Miguel.) Madrid, 1960.

Phil 6028.6   La metoposcopia, overo comensuratione delle linea della fronte. (Spontane, Ciro.) Venetia, 1626.

Phil 6012.5F   Metoposcopia libris tredecim. (Cardano, Girolamo.) Lutetiae, 1658.

Phil 1133.21   Metpon; étude sur l'idée de mesure dans la philosophie antésocratique. Thèse. (Moulard, A.) Angers, 1923.

Phil 5257.80   Metric analysis of ordinal data in psychology. Proefschrift. (Roskam, Edwarda Elias Charles Iben.) Voorschoten, 1968.

Phil 6315.2.170   Mette, Alexander. Sigmund Freud. Berlin, 1956.

Phil 6315.2.170.3   Mette, Alexandre. Sigmund Freud. 3. Aufl. Berlin, 1958.

Phil 3640.435   Mette, H.J. Der handschriftliche Nachlass Friedrich Nietzsches. Leipzig, 1932.

Phil 3640.436   Mette, H.J. Sachlicher Vorbericht zur Gesamtausgabe der Werke Friedrich Nietzsches. n.p., 193-?

Phil 2705.84   La Mettrie. (Boissier, Raymond.) Paris, 1931.

Phil 2705.84.2   La Mettrie. Thèse. (Boissier, Raymond.) Paris, 1931.

Phil 3494.33.5   Metz, Andreas. Darstellung der Hauptmomente der Elementarlehre der Kantischen Kritik der reinen Vernunft. Pt. 1-2. Bamberg, 1802.

Phil 3494.33   Metz, Andreas. Kurze und deutliche Darstellung des Kantischen Systemes. Bamberg, 1795.

Phil 5643.76   Metz, Bernhard. Über die pseudoskopische Ablenkung paralleler Linien. Marburg, 1882.

Phil 2050.01   Metz, Rudolf. Bibliographie der Hume-Literatur. Erfurt, 1928.

Phil 2050.188   Metz, Rudolf. David Hume: Leben und Philosophie. Stuttgart, 1929.

Phil 1812.6.5   Metz, Rudolf. England und die deutsche Philosophie. Stuttgart, 1941.

Phil 1870.101   Metz, Rudolf. George Berkeley Leben und Lehre. Stuttgart, 1925.

Phil 1812.6A   Metz, Rudolf. Die philosophischen Strömungen der Gegenwart in Grossbritannien. Leipzig, 1935. 2v.

Phil 6051.3   Metz, V. de. Hand-book of modern palmistry. N.Y., 1885?

Phil 6048.83.2   Metz, V. de. Handbook of modern palmistii. 2. ed. N.Y., 1883.

Phil 5402.40   Metz, Willem. Het verschijnsel pijn. Proefschrift. Haarlem, 1964.

Phil 8620.47   Metzger, A. Freiheit und Tod. Tübingen, 1955.

Phil 705.49   Metzger, Arnold. Dämonie und Transzendenz. Pfullingen, 1964.

Phil 705.49.5   Metzger, Arnold. De Einzelne und der Einsame. Pfullingen, 1967.

Phil 585.285   Metzger, Arnold. Existentialismus und Sozialismus. Pfullingen, 1968.

Phil 343.10.5   Metzger, Arnold. Phänomenologie und Metaphysik. Halle an der Saale, 1933.

Phil 343.10   Metzger, Arnold. Untersiechungen zur Frage die Differenz der Phänomenologie und des Kantianismus. Jena, 1915.

Phil 8702.18   Metzger, H. Atraction universelle et religion naturelle. Paris, 1938. 3v.

Phil 3494.47   Metzger, J.D. Aeusserungen über Kant. Königsberg, 1804.

Phil 5643.97   Metzger, W. Gesetze des Sehens. Frankfurt, 1936.

Phil 5252.100   Metzger, W. Psychologie. 2. Aufl. Darmstadt, 1954.

Phil 3801.566   Metzger, Wilhelm. Die Epochen der Schellingschen Philosophie von 1795 bis 1802. Heidelberg, 1911.

Phil 3494.37   Metzger, Wilhelm. Untersuchungen zur Sitten - und Rechtslehre Kants und Fichtes. Heidelberg, 1912.

Phil 5465.121   Metzger, Wolfgang. Schöpferische Freiheit. 2. Aufl. Frankfurt, 1962.

Phil 812.40   Metzke, Erwin. Coincidentia oppositorum. Witten, 1961.

Phil 97.12   Metzke, Erwin. Handlexikon der Philosophie. Heidelberg, 1948.

Phil 3780.90   Metzke, Erwin. Karl Rosenkranz und Hegel. Leipzig, 1929.

Phil 3450.19.125   Meulen, J.A. van der. Heidegger und Hegel. Groningen, 1953.

Phil 3425.470   Meulen, Jan van der. Hegel. Hamburg, 1958.

Phil 5545.46   Meumann, E. Ökonomie und Technik des Gedächtnisses. Leipzig, 1908.

Phil 5545.49.3A   Meumann, E. The psychology of learning. N.Y., 1913.

Phil 8080.3 Meumann, Ernst. Einführung in die Ästhetik der Gegenwart. Leipzig, 1908.
Phil 8080.16 Meumann, Ernst. A estética contemporânea. 3. ed. Coimbia, 1930.
Phil 5762.9 Meumann, Ernst. Intelligenz und Wille. 3. Aufl. Leipzig, 1920.
Phil 5762.9.4 Meumann, Ernst. Intelligenz und Wille. 4. Aufl. Leipzig, 1925.
Phil 325.5 Meurer, W. Gegen den Empirismus. Leipzig, 1925.
Phil 343.14 Meurer, W. Ist Wissenschaft überhaupt Möglich? Leipzig, 1920.
Phil 343.14.10 Meurer, W. Selbsterkenntnis. Berlin, 1931.
Phil 310.200 Meurers, Joseph. Wissenschaft im Kollektiv. München, 1959.
Phil 3832.12 Meurling, H. Fullkomlighetsbegreppet i Spinozas filosofi. Diss. Uppsala, 1928.
Phil 4752.2.170 Meusel, Joachim. Geschichtlichkeit und Mystik im Denken Nikolaj Berdjayews. Berlin? 1962?
Phil 310.712 Meuterei auf den Knien. (Dahm, Helmut.) Olten, 1969.
Phil 4513.4.43 Mexethma philosophicum de subordinatione veritatum. (Asp, Matthia.) Upsaliae, 1733.
Phil 22.30 México (city). Colegio de México a la Historia del Pensamiento Hispano-Americano. Contribuciones. Mexico. 2-3 2v.
Phil 4959.245 México (City). Universidad Nacional. Consejo Técnico de Humanidades. Estudios de historía de la filosofía en México. 1. ed. México, 1963.
Phil 4959.245.5 México (City). Universidad Nacional. Consejo Técnico de Humanidades. Major trends in Mexican philosophy. Notre Dame, 1966.
NEDL Phil 22.35 México (city). Universidad Nacional. Facultad de Filosofía y Estudios Superiores. Centro de Estudios Filosoficos. Boletin bibliografico. Mexico.
Phil 52.12 Mexico (City). Universidad Nacional. Facultad de Filosofía y Letras. Anuario de filosofía.
Phil 22.62 Mexico (City). Universidad Nacional. Facultad de Filosofía y Letras. Anuario psicologia. Mexico. 1-3,1962-1964//
Phil 5401.49 Mexico (City). Universidad Nacional. Facultad de Filosofía y Letras. La esencia del valor. México, 1964.
Phil 2475.1.270 Mexico City. Universidad Nacional. Facultad de Filosofía y Estudios Superiores. Centro de Estudios Filosóficos. Homenaje a Bergson. México, 1941.
X Cg Phil 9590.14 Meximas de buena educación. (Spetien Montero y Austri, P.A.) México, 1828.
Phil 6046.65 Mey, Philipp. La chiromancie medicinale. La Haye, 1665.
Phil 3494.24 Meydenbauer, A. Kant oder Laplace? Marburg, 1880.
Phil 6980.489 Meyer, Adolf. Psychobiology. Springfield, 1957.
Phil 8887.105 Meyer, Arthur E. Mind, matter, and morals. 1st. ed. N.Y., 1957.
Phil 5222.11 Meyer, Donald Burton. The positive thinkers. 1. ed. Garden City, N.Y., 1965.
Phil 2655.1.81 Meyer, E. Der Philosoph Franz Hemsterhuis. Breslau, 1893.
Phil 293.6 Meyer, E.H. Die eddische Kosmogonie. Freiburg, 1891.
Phil 7054.173.15 Meyer, F.B. The modern craze of spiritualism. London, 1919.
Phil 2475.1.288 Meyer, François. La pensée de Bergson. Grenoble, 1944.
Phil 3246.79.50 Meyer, Friedrich. Eine Fichte-Sammlung. Leipzig, 1921.
Phil 6122.22 Meyer, G.H. Untersuchungen Psychologie der Nervenfaser. Tübingen, 1843.
Phil 5052.42 Meyer, H. Le rôle médiateur de la logique. Assen, 1956.
Phil 3552.441 Meyer, H.G. Leibniz und Baumgarten als Begründer der deutschen Aesthetik. Halle, 1874.
Phil 1750.660 Meyer, H.J. Die Technisierung der Welt. Tübingen, 1961.
Phil 1117.6 Meyer, Hans. Geschichte der alten Philosophie. München, 1925.
Phil 1133.10 Meyer, Hans. Geschichte der Lehre von den Keimkräften von der Stoa bis zum Ausgang der Patristik. Bonn, 1914.
Phil 3450.19.355 Meyer, Hans. Martin Heidegger und Thomas von Aquin. München, 1964.
Phil 3625.20.30 Meyer, Hans. Systematische Philosophie. Paderborn, 1955. 4v.
Phil 8592.85 Meyer, Hans. Weltanschauungsprobleme der Gegenwart. 1. Aufl. Recklinghausen, 1956.
Phil 5252.52 Meyer, Hans. Zur Psychologie der Gegenwart. Köln, 1909.
Phil 6962.32 Meyer, Henry F. An experiment in mental patient rehabilitation. N.Y., 1959.
Phil 6682.5 Meyer, J.A.G. Natur. Gotha, 1839.
Phil 187.13 Meyer, J.B. Philosophische Zeitfragen. Bonn, 1874.
Phil 3808.99 Meyer, J.B. Weltelend und Weltschmerz. Bonn, 1872.
Phil 6122.3 Meyer, J.B. Zum streit über Leib und Seele. Hamburg, 1856.
Phil 8592.9 Meyer, J.F. von. Wahrnehmungen einer Seherin. v.1-2. Hamburg, 1827-28.
Phil 3494.20 Meyer, Jürgen B. Kant's Psychologie. Berlin, 1870.
Phil 3235.80 Meyer, M. Ludwig Feuerbach's Moralphilosophie. Berlin, 1899.
Phil 3832.2 Meyer, M. Die Tugendlehre Spinoza's. Fleusburg, 1885.
Phil 5252.42 Meyer, M.F. Psychology of the other one. Columbia, 1921.
Phil 5252.42.15 Meyer, M.F. Über Tonverschmelzung. n.p., 1898-1913. 20 pam.
Phil 6322.17 Meyer, Max F. Abnormal psychology. Columbia, 1927.
Phil 8837.9 Meyer, R.M. Le mouvement moral vers 1840. Paris, 1913.
Phil 3552.322.5 Meyer, R.W. Leibnitz and the seventeenth century revolution. Cambridge, Eng., 1952.
Phil 3552.322 Meyer, R.W. Leibniz und die europäische Ordnungskrise. Hamburg, 1948.
Phil 3640.127 Meyer, Richard M. Nietzsche. München, 1913.
Phil 9075.39 Meyer, Rudolf. Der Protest des Gewissens in der Philosophie. Zürich, 1941.
Phil 5252.26.10 Meyer, Semi. Die geistige Wirklichkeit. Stuttgart, 1925.
Phil 5252.26 Meyer, Semi. Probleme der Entwicklung des Geistes. Leipzig, 1913.
Phil 8413.25 Meyer, T.A. Ästhetik. Stuttgart, 1923.
Phil 5762.6 Meyer, W. Die Wahlfreiheit des Willens in ihrer Nichtigkeit. Gotha, 1886.
Phil 1150.11A Meyer, W.A. Hypatia von Alexandria. Heidelberg, 1886.
Phil 270.19 Meyer-Pforzheim, C.W. Der Kausalitätsbegriff. Hamburg, 1914.
Phil 6962.9 Meyerhof, O. Beiträge zur psychologischen Theorie der Geistesstörungen. Göttingen, 1910.
Phil 8735.56 Meyers, A.M. Die Ursachen aller geschaffenen Dinge. Limburg, 1963?
Phil 187.113 Meyerson, É. Essais. Paris, 1936.
Phil 343.16.25 Meyerson, Émile. Du cheminement de la pensée. Paris, 1931. 3v.
Phil 343.16.15 Meyerson, Émile. Identität und Wirklichkeit. Leipzig, 1930.
NEDL Phil 343.16 Meyerson, Émile. Identité et réalité. Paris, 1908.
Phil 343.16.5 Meyerson, Émile. Identité et réalité. 2. éd. Paris, 1912.
Phil 343.16.11 Meyerson, Émile. Identité et réalité. 4. éd. Paris, 1932.
Phil 343.16.12 Meyerson, Émile. Identité et réalité. 5. éd. Paris, 1951.
Phil 343.16.10 Meyerson, Émile. Identity and reality. London, 1930.
Phil 343.16.16 Meyerson, Émile. Identity and reality. N.Y., 1962.
Phil 2750.10.79 Pamphlet box. Meyerson, Emile.
Phil 5252.166 Meyerson, Ignace. Les fonctions psychologiques et les oeuvres. Thèse. Paris, 1948.
Phil 6962.5.5 Meynert, T. Klinische Vorlesungen über Psychiatrie. v.1-2. Wien, 1889-90.
Phil 6962.5 Meynert, T. Psychiatrie. Wien, 1884.
Phil 5252.27 Meynert, T. Sammlung von populär- wissenschaftlichen Vorträgen über den bau und die leistungen des gehirns. Wien, 1892.
Phil 6122.44 Meynert, T. Zur Mechanik des Gehirnbaues. Wien, 1874.
Phil 400.124 Meynier, Philippe. Essai sur l'idéalisme moderne. Paris, 1957.
Phil 7150.40 Meyuard, L. Le suicide. Paris, 1958.
Phil 5252.159 Meza, César. Mimo, dependencia, depresión, alcoholismo. 1. ed. Guatemala, 1967.
Phil 8887.34 Mezes, S.E. Ethics descriptive and explanatory. N.Y., 1901.
Phil 735.230 Mezing, Otto O. A grammar of human values. Pittsburgh, 1961.
Phil 196.22 Mi segunda dimension. (Vincenzi, Moises.) San José, 1928.
Phil 4225.3.89 La mia conversione dal Rosmini a S. Tommaso. (Sichirollo, G.) Padova, 1887.
Phil 6682.19 Mialle, S. Exposé par ordre alphabétique des cures. Paris, 1826. 2v.
Phil 5467.8 Miami. University. Symposium on Social Behavior, 1st, 1967. Social facilitation and imitative behavior. Boston, 1968.
Phil 5625.124 Miami Symposium on the Prediction of Behavior. Aversive stimulation. Coral Gables, Fla., 1968.
Phil 343.38 Miani, Vincenzo. Problemi di gnoseologia e metafisica. Zürich, 1966.
Phil 97.7 Miano, V. Dizionario filosofico. Torino, 1963.
Phil 6322.44 Miasishchev, V.N. Lichnost' i nevrozy. Leningrad, 1960.
Phil 5822.12 Miatto, A. Istinto e società animale. Firenze, 195-?
Phil 1750.115.87 Micallef, John. Philosophy of existence. N.Y., 1969.
Phil 4369.2.90 Miccolis, Salvatore. Francesco Sanchez. Bari, 1965.
Phil 4012.6 Miceli di Serradileo, R. Filosofia. Verona, 1937.
Phil 4012.6.10 Miceli di Serradileo, R. La filosofia italiana actual. Buenos Aires, 1940.
Phil 4012.6.5 Miceli di Serradileo, R. La philosophie contemporaine en Italie. Paris, 1939.
Phil 187.151 Miceli di Serradileo, Riccardo. Introduzione alla filosofia. Roma, 1957.
Phil 4170.8.90 Il Miceli ovvero dell'ente uno e reale. (Giovanni, V. di.) Palermo, 1864.
Phil 6315.2.93 Michaëlis, Edgar. Die Menschkeitsproblematik der Freudschen Psychoanalyse. Leipzig, 1925.
Phil 6315.2.94 Michaëlis, Edgar. Die Menschkeitsproblematik der Freudschen Psychoanalyse. 2. Aufl. Leipzig, 1931.
Phil 1117.14 Michaelides, Konstantinos. Mensch und Kosmos im ihrer Zusammengehörigkeit bei den frühen griechischen Denkern. München? 1961?
Phil 7080.32 Michaelis, A.O. Der Schlaf nach seinerBedeutung. Leipzig, 1894.
Phil 3494.34 Michaelis, C.F. Über die settliche Natur und Bestimmung des Menschen. v.1-2. Leipzig, 1796-97.
Phil 3808.171 Michaelis, G. Arthur Schopenhauer. Leipzig, 1937.
Phil 4818.571.20 Michăilescce, Ştefan C. Pagini filozofice alese. Bucureşti, 1955.
Phil 4803.879.95 Michał wiszniewski. (Dybiec, Julian.) Wrocław, 1970.
Phil 1517.10 Michalski, Konstanty. La philosophie au XIVe siècle; six études. Frankfurt, 1969.
Phil 3494.29 Michalsky, O. Kant's Kritik der reinen Vernunft und Herder's Metakritik. Diss. Breslau, 1883.
Phil 1750.430 Michalson, Carl. Christianity and the existentialists. N.Y., 1956.
Phil 187.53 Michaltschew, Dimitri. Philosophische Studien. Leipzig, 1909.
Phil 8887.73 Michaud, Félix. Science et morale. Paris, 1941.
Phil 5400.132 Michaud, H. La sensibilité. Lyon, 1954?
Phil 2750.29.30 Michaud, Humbert. Analyse de la révolution moderne. Paris, 1968?
Phil 2805.230 Michaut, Gustave. Pascal, Molière, Musset; essais de critique et de psychologie. Paris, 1942.
Phil 7082.2 Michaux, Henri. Façons d'endormi, façons d'éveillé. Paris, 1969.
Phil 6322.47 Michel, André. L'école freudienne devant la musique. Paris, 1965.
Phil 8430.36 Michel, E. Der Weg zum Mythos. Jena, 1919.
Phil 575.210 Michel, Ernst. Der Prozess "Gesellschaft contra Person". Stuttgart, 1959.
Phil 2138.101 Michel, Henry. De Stuarti Millii individualismo. Thesis. Parisiis, 1895.
Phil 1504.18 Michel, K. Der "liber de consonanci a nature et gracie." v.18, pt.1. Münster, 1915.
Phil 4065.170 Michel, Paul. La caemologie de Giordano Bruno. Paris, 1962.
Phil 8887.68 Michel, Virgil. Philosophy of human conduct. Minneapolis, 1936.
Phil 3640.287 Michel, W. Nietzsche in unserern Jahrhundert. Berlin, 1939.
Phil 4225.8.75 Michele F. Sciacca in occasione del trenta anno di cattedra universitaria, 1938-1968. Milano, 1968.
Phil 8413.42 Michelés, Panagiótés Andreau. Études d'esthétique. Paris, 1967.
Phil 5252.54 Michelet, C.L. Anthropologie und Psychologie. Berlin, 1840.
Phil 3425.229.10 Michelet, C.L. Einleitung in Hegel's philosophische Abhandlungen. Berlin, 1832.
Phil 3012.1.5 Michelet, C.L. Entwickelungsgeschichte der neuesten deutschen Philosophie. Berlin, 1843.
Phil 3012.1 Michelet, C.L. Geschichte...Philosophie in Deutschland. Berlin, 1837-38. 2v.
Phil 3425.229.15 Michelet, C.L. Hegel, der unwiderlegte Weltphilosoph. Leipzig, 1870.
Phil 3425.229 Michelet, C.L. Hegel und der Empirismus. Berlin, 1873.
Phil 2270.89 Michelet, C.L. Herbert Spencer's System der Philosophie. Halle, 1882.
Htn Phil 3801.570.10* Michelet, Carl L. Entwickelungsgeschichte der neuesten deutschen Philosophie...Schelling. Berlin, 1843.
Phil 3801.570.2 Michelet, Carl L. Schelling und Hegel. Berlin, 1839.
Htn Phil 3801.570*A Michelet, Carl L. Schelling und Hegel. Berlin, 1839.
Phil 8667.9 Michelet, Georges. Dieu et l'agnosticisme contemporaine. 3. éd. Paris, 1912.

Phil 3625.2.6   Michelet, K.L. Naturrecht oder Rechts-Philosophie als die praktische Philosophie. Berlin, 1866. Bruxelles, 1968. 2v.

Phil 187.14   Michelet, K.L. Das System der Philosophie. Berlin, 1876-1881. 5v.

Phil 3625.2   Michelet, K.L. Wahrheit aus meinem Leben. Berlin, 1884.
Phil 1560.15   Michelet, Marcel. Le Rhin Mystique de Maitre Eckert à Thomas à Kempis. Paris, 1960.

Phil 2750.2.80   Michelet, naturaliste. (Van der Elst, Robert.) Paris, 1914.

Phil 812.7   Michelis, F. Geschichte der Philosophie von Thales. Braumsberg, 1865.

Phil 3494.4   Michelis, F. Kant vor und nach dem Jahre 1770. Braunsberg, 1871.

Phil 3850.8.81   Michelis, F. Staudenmaier's Wissenschaftliche Leistung. Freiburg, 1877.

Phil 187.52   Michelis, Friedrich. Die Philosophie des Bewusstseins. Bonn, 1877.

Phil 7084.4.20   Micheloud, Pierrette. Dictionnaire psychanalytique des rêves. Paris, 1957.

Phil 2750.11.120 Michener, N.W. Maritain on the nature of man in a Christian democracy. Hull, 1955.

Phil 52.1   Michigan. University. Philosophical papers. Ann Arbor. 1-4

Phil 4809.796.80 Michňáková, Irena. Augustin Smetana. Praha, 1963.
Phil 6060.7.7   Michon, J.H. Méthode pratique de graphologie. Paris, 1899.

Phil 5585.248   Michon, John Albertus. Timing in temporal tracking. Proefschrift. Essen, 1967.

Phil 5252.153   Michotte, A.E. Les compléments amodaux des structures perceptives. Louvain, 1964.

Phil 270.62.5   Michotte, A.E. La perception de la causalité. Louvain, 1946.

Phil 270.62A   Michotte, A.E. La perception de la causalité. 2. ed. Louvain, 1954.

Phil 270.62.10   Michotte, A.E. The perception of causality. London, 1963.
Phil 5585.211   Michotte, Albert. Causalité, permanence et réalité phénoménales. Louvain, 1962.

Phil 6122.41   Micklem, E.R. Miracles and the new psychology. Oxford, 1922.

Phil 97.10   Micraelius, Johann. Lexicon philosophicum terminorum philosophis usitatorum. Düsseldorf, 1966.

Phil 8667.14   Micrandu, J. Disputatio philosophica de contemplatione mortis. Stockholmiae, 1684.

Phil 32.2   The microcosm. N.Y.
Phil 3565.51.10   Microcosmo. (Lotze, Hermann.) Pavia, 1911-16. 2v.
Phil 3565.51   Microcosmos. (Lotze, Hermann.) N.Y., 1885. 2v.
Phil 3565.51.19   Microcosmos. v.1-2. (Lotze, Hermann.) N.Y., 1886.
Phil 3565.51.4   Microcosmos. v.1-2. (Lotze, Hermann.) N.Y., 1897.
Phil 3565.51.2   Microcosmos. v.1-2. 2. ed. (Lotze, Hermann.) N.Y., 1885.
Phil 6113.14F   Microscopic anatomy...of the spinal cord. (Dean, J.) Cambridge, 1861.

Phil 7060.111.19 Middelton, Jessie A. Another grey ghost book. London, 1915.

Phil 8612.47   Midden in het leven. (Sikken, Willem.) Kampen, 1960.
NEDL Phil 5545.50 Middleton, A.E. Memory systems. 1. American ed. N.Y., 1888.

Phil 7060.111.15 Middleton, Jessie A. The grey ghost book. London, 1915.
Phil 6122.95   The Midtown Manhattan study. N.Y., 1962. 2v.
Phil 8170.8   Miedzy tradycja a wizja przyszłości. (Morawski, Stefan.) Warszawa, 1964.

Phil 5725.5   Międzynarodowego Sympozjum Poświęcone Psychologia Rozumienia, Krakow, 1965. Psychologia rozumienia. Warszawa, 1968.

Phil 2805.460   Miel, Jan. Pascal and theology. Baltimore, 1969.
Phil 5592.173   Mields, J. Diagnostische Möglichkeiten der Intelligenz-Beurteilung. Heidelberg, 1962.

Phil 8050.84   Miele, Franco. Teoria e storia dell'estetica. Milano, 1965.

Phil 6122.24   Mielopatia da fulmine. (Massalongo, Robert.) Napoli, 1891.

Phil 2190.20   Miethke, Jürgen. Ockhams Weg zur Sozialphilosophie. Berlin, 1969.

Phil 2750.17.30   Mieville, Henri L. Condition de l'homme. Genève, 1959.
Phil 8637.18   Mifflin, Mildred. Out of darkness into light. Shelbyville, 1888.

Phil 187.15   Migeot, A. Philosophiae elementa. Carolopoli, 1784. 2v.

Phil 6672.8   Mighty curative powers of mesmerism. (Caperu, T.) London, 1851.

Phil 308.6   Migliorini, Ermanno. Critica, oggetto e logica. Firenze, 1968.

Phil 5403.3   Mignard, M. La joie passive. Paris, 1909.
Phil 6962.18   Mignard, Maurice. L'unité psychique et les troubles mentaux. Paris, 1928.

Phil 2496.83   Mignet,M. Notice historique sur la vie...de Victor Cousin. Paris, 1869.

Phil 1517.1   Mignon, A. Les origines de la scolastique. Paris, n.d. 2v.

Phil 2805.30.800 Mignone, C. Rensi, Leopardi e Pascal. Milano, 1954.
Phil 3808.175   Mignosi, P. Schopenhauer. Brescia, 1934.
Phil 187.74   Mignosi, Pietro. Critica dell'identita. Palermo, 1926.
Phil 400.70   Mignosi, Pietro. L'idealismo. Milano, 1927.
Phil 1200.67.2   Mignucci, Mario. Il significato della logica stoica. 2. edizione riveduta. Bologna, 1967.

Phil 1200.67   Mignucci, Mario. Il siguificato della logica stoica. Bologna, 1965.

Phil 6962.30   Migration and mental disease. (Malzberg, Benjamin.) N.Y., 1956.

Phil 4363.2.40   Miguel de Molinos, siglo XVII. (Entrambasaguas y Pena, J. de.) Madrid, 1935?

Phil 4363.2.85   Miguel de Molinos en Valencia y Roma, nuevos datas biográficos. (Sanchez-Castañer, Francisco.) Valencia, 1965.

Phil 4369.2   Miguel Sabuco. (Marcos Coujáles, B.) Madrid, 1923.
Phil 1750.82   Mihalich, J.C. Existentialism and Thomism. N.Y., 1960.
Phil 2150.24.30   Mika, Lumir Victor. Thinker's handbook. Columbia, Mo., 1947.

VPhil 4012.13   Mikecin, Vjekoslav. Suvremena talijanska filozofija. Zagreb, 1966.

Phil 6122.58   Mikesell, W.H. Mental hygiene. N.Y., 1939.
Phil 6315.2.295   Mikhailov, Feliks T. Za porogom soznaniia; kriticheskii ocherk freidizma. Moskva, 1961.

Phil 5585.234   Mikhailov, Feliks T. Zagadka chelovecheskogo Ia. Moskva, 1964.

Phil 6122.80   Mikhailov. Likvidiraneto na protivopolozhnostta mezhdu umstveniia i fizicheokiia trud. Sofiia, 1959.

Phil 1133.41   Mikhailova, Engelina N. Ioniiskaia filosofiia. Moskva, 1966.

Phil 2050.250   Mikhalenko, Iu.P. Filosofiia D. Iuma. Moskva, 1962.
Phil 8980.572.10 Mikhalevich, Aleksandr Vl. Front dushi. Kiev, 1970.
Phil 8980.572   Mikhalevich, Aleksandr Vl. Izmeniat'sia. Moskva, 1964.
Phil 8980.572.5   Mikhalevich, Aleksandr Vl. Sporiu. Moskva, 1968.
Phil 1750.25   Mikolaj Hill. Studjum z histoiji filozofji atomistycznej. (Heitzman, M.) Krakow, 192-?

Phil 293.15   Mikos, J. Hypothesen über einige kosmologische und geologische Momente. Leipzig, 1895.

Phil 8702.15   Mikos, J. Eine wissenschaftliche Wellanschauung auf religiöser Grundlage. Leipzig, 1896.

Phil 3565.50   Mikrokosmus. (Lotze, Hermann.) Leipzig, 1869-72. 3v.
Phil 3565.50.5   Mikrokosmus. v.1-3. (Lotze, Hermann.) Leipzig, 1885-1896. 2v.

Phil 3565.50.6   Mikrokosmus. 6e Aufl. (Lotze, Hermann.) Leipzig, 1923. 3v.

Phil 8980.572.30 Miladinović, Milan M. Moralno-politicki lik komunista Vojvodine u NOR-u i revoluciji. Beograd, 1971.

Phil 6990.3.33   O milagre e a critica moderna on a immaculada conceição de Lourdes. (Senna Freitas, José J. de.) Braga, 1873.

Phil 6990.13   El milagro. 2. ed. (Mir y Noguera, Juan.) Barcelona, 1915. 3v.

Phil 52.11   Milan. Università. Instituto di Storia della Filosofia. Pubblicazioni. Milan. 1,1951+ 11v.

Phil 3425.358   Milan. Universita Cattolica del Sacro Cuare. Hegel nel centenario. Milano, 1932.

Phil 70.10.8   Milan. Università Cattolica del Sacro Cuore. Faculta di Filosofia. Relazione e cumunicazioni presentate al Congresso Nazionale di Filosofia. Milano, 1935. 2v.

Phil 22.56   Milan. Università Cattolica del Sacro Cuore. Institutadi filosofia. Contributi. Milano. 1,1969+

Phil 5238.4   Milan. Università Cattolica del Sacro Cuore. Laboratorio di Psicologia di Biologia. Contributi. Milano. 1-29 26v.

Phil 3832.16   Milan. Universita Cattolica del Sacro Cuore-Facolta di Filosofia. Spinoza nel terzo centenario della sua nascita. Milano, 1934.

Phil 7069.22.17   Milburn, L.M. The classic of spiritism. N.Y., 1922.
Phil 8592.35.10   Milburn, R.G. The logic of religious thought. London, 1929.

Phil 8592.35   Milburn, R.G. The theology of the real. London, 1925.
Phil 9515.3.99   Milch, W. Die Einsamkeit. Frauenfeld, 1937.
Phil 5545.56   Miles, E.H. How to remember without memory systems or with them. London, 1901.

Phil 8592.10   Miles, J.W. Philosophic theology. Charleston, 1849.
Phil 5932.2   Miles, L. Phrenology. Philadelphia, 1835.
Phil 5545.19   Miles, Pliny. American mnemotechny. N.Y., 1848.
Phil 5545.19.5   Miles, Pliny. Mnemotechny, or art of memory. 1. English ed. London, 1850.

Phil 5068.38   Miles, Thomas R. Religion and the scientific outlook. London, 1959.

Phil 5762.10   Milesi, G.B. La negazione del libero arbitrio ed il criterio del giusto. Milano, 1894.

Phil 5548.150   Milestones in motivation; contributions to the psychology of drive and purpose. (Russell, Wallace Addison.) N.Y., 1970.

Phil 2115.133   Milhac, F. Essai sur les idées religieuses de Locke. Thèse. Genève, 1886.

Phil 2475.1.475   Milhand, Jean. A Bergson, la patrie reconnaissante. Paris, 1967.

Phil 5090.7   Milhaud, G. Essai sur les conditions et les limites. 3e éd. Paris, 1912.

Phil 2840.89   Milhaud, G. La philosophie de Charles Renouvier. Paris, 1927.

Phil 5090.7.5   Milhaud, G. Le rationnel. Paris, 1898.
Phil 2520.138   Milhaud, G.S. Descartes savant. Paris, 1921.
Phil 2520.138.5   Milhaud, G.S. Num Cartesii methodus tantum valeat in suo opere illustrando quantum ipse senserit. Thesis. Montpellier, 1894.

Phil 2490.97   Milhaud, Gaston. Le positivisme et le progrès de l'esprit. Paris, 1902.

Phil 8962.32   Milhaven, John Giles. Toward a new Catholic morality. Garden City, 1970.

Phil 6967.10   Military psychiatry in peace and war. (Read, C. Stanford.) London, 1920.

Phil 2138.170   Mill, a collection of critical essays. (Schneewind, Jerome B.) Notre Dame, 1969.

Phil 5252.7A   Mill, J. Analysis of the phenomena of human mind. London, 1829. 2v.

Phil 5252.7.2   Mill, J. On the mind. London, 1869. 2v.
Phil 2035.80.6   Mill, J.S. Examination...Hamilton's philosophy. Boston, 1865. 2v.

Phil 2035.80.2.10 Mill, J.S. Examination...Hamilton's philosophy. Boston, 1868. 2v.

Phil 2035.80A   Mill, J.S. Examination...Hamilton's philosophy. London, 1865.

Phil 2035.80.2   Mill, J.S. Examination...Hamilton's philosophy. 3rd ed. London, 1867.

Phil 2035.80.2.5 Mill, J.S. Examination...Hamilton's philosophy. 3rd ed. London, 1867.

Phil 2035.80.8   Mill, J.S. Examination...Hamilton's philosophy. 6th ed. London, 1889.

Phil 2035.80.40   Mill, J.S. Eine Prüfung der Philosophie Sir William Hamiltons. Halle, 1908.

Phil 8837.1.15   Mill, James. A fragment on Mackintosh. London, 1835.
Phil 8837.1.16   Mill, James. A fragment on Mackintosh. London, 1870.
Htn Phil 2138.79.4* Mill, John S. Autobiography. London, 1873.
X Cg Phil 2138.79.6 Mill, John S. Autobiography. N.Y., 1874.
Phil 2138.79.10.3 Mill, John S. Autobiography. N.Y., 1887.
Phil 2138.79.8.4 Mill, John S. Autobiography. N.Y., 1944.
Phil 2138.79.8.5 Mill, John S. Autobiography. N.Y., 1957.
Phil 2138.79.8.6 Mill, John S. Autobiography. N.Y., 1969.
Phil 2138.79.10.5 Mill, John S. Autobiography. Early draft. Urbana, 1961.
Phil 2138.02A   Mill, John S. Bibliography of the published writings of J.S. Mill. Evanston, Ill., 1945.

Phil 2138.11   Mill, John S. Collected works. v.2,3, 4(2), 5(2), 10,12,13. Toronto, 1963. 9v.

Phil 2138.53   Mill, John S. Considerations on representative government. N.Y., 1958.

Phil 2138.38.5   Mill, John S. Dissertations and discussions. v.2-5. v.1 rejected 1972. N.Y., 1873-75. 4v.

Phil 2138.54   Mill, John S. Essays on politics and culture. Garden City, 1962.

Phil 2138.55   Mill, John S. The ethics of John Stuart Mill. Edinburgh, 1897.

Phil 2138.30A   Mill, John S. An examination of Hamilton's philosophy. Boston, 1865. 2v.

Htn	Phil 2138.30.2*	Mill, John S. An examination of Hamilton's philosophy. London, 1865.
	Phil 2138.40.14	Mill, John S. Die Freiheit. Leipzig, 1928.
	Phil 2138.40.16	Mill, John S. Die Freiheit (On Liberty) Übers. 3. Aufl. Darmstadt, 1970.
	Phil 2138.2	Mill, John S. Gesammelte Werke. v.1-3, 4-6, 7-9, 10-12. Leipzig, 1869-80. 4v.
Htn	Phil 2138.65*	Mill, John S. Inaugural address to...University of St. Andrews. London, 1867.
	Phil 2138.35.12	Mill, John S. Die inductive Logik. Braunschweig, 1849.
	Phil 2138.79.12	Mill, John S. John Mill's boyhood visit to France. Toronto, 1960.
	Phil 2138.23	Mill, John S. John Stuart Mill; a selection of his works. N.Y., 1966.
	Phil 2138.76A	Mill, John S. Letters of John Stuart Mill. London, 1910. 2v.
	Phil 2138.75	Mill, John S. Lettres inédites. Paris, 1899.
	Phil 2138.40.25	Mill, John S. La libertà. Torino, 1925.
	Phil 2138.79.9	Mill, John S. Mes mémoires: histoire de ma vie et de mes idées. 2e éd. Paris, 1875.
	Phil 2138.77.6	Mill, John S. Mill on Bentham and Coleridge. London, 1967.
	Phil 2138.45A	Mill, John S. Nature, the utility of religion and theism. London, 1874.
	Phil 2138.45.12	Mill, John S. Nature, the utility of religion and theism. London, 1874.
	Phil 2138.45.15	Mill, John S. Nature, the utility of religion and theism. Westmead, Eng., 1969.
	Phil 2138.40.15	Mill, John S. Om friheten. Upsala, 1881.
	Phil 2138.77.5	Mill, John S. On Bentham and Coleridge. N.Y., 1962.
	Phil 2138.40.7	Mill, John S. On liberty. London, 19- .
Htn	Phil 2138.40.1*	Mill, John S. On liberty. London, 1859.
	Phil 2138.40	Mill, John S. On liberty. London, 1859.
	Phil 2138.40.2.5	Mill, John S. On liberty. London, 1871.
	Phil 2138.40.3	Mill, John S. On liberty. London, 1874.
	Phil 2138.40.3.2	Mill, John S. On liberty. London, 1875.
	Phil 2138.40.4	Mill, John S. On liberty. London, 1878.
	Phil 2138.40.47	Mill, John S. On liberty. London, 190-?
	Phil 2138.40.10	Mill, John S. On liberty. London, 1903.
	Phil 2138.40.8	Mill, John S. On liberty. N.Y., 19- .
	Phil 2138.40.6	Mill, John S. On liberty. N.Y., 1895.
	Phil 2138.40.35	Mill, John S. On liberty. N.Y., 1947.
	Phil 2138.40.46	Mill, John S. On liberty. N.Y., 1956.
	Phil 2138.40.42	Mill, John S. On liberty. Considerations on representative government. Oxford, 1946.
	Phil 2138.40.2.2	Mill, John S. On liberty. 2nd ed. Boston, 1863.
	Phil 2138.41	Mill, John S. On social freedom. N.Y., 1941.
	Phil 2138.20	Mill, John S. The philosophy of John Stuart Mill. N.Y., 1961.
	Phil 2138.48	Mill, John S. Philosophy of scientific method. N.Y., 1950.
	Phil 2138.40.45	Mill, John S. Prefaces to liberty. Boston, 1959.
	Phil 2138.25	Mill, John S. The spirit of the age. Chicago, 1942.
X Cg	Phil 2138.37	Mill, John S. The student's handbook...of Mill's...logic. London, 1870.
	Phil 2138.37.15	Mill, John S. The student's handbook...of Mill's logic. London, 1891.
Htn	Phil 2138.60*	Mill, John S. The subjection of women. London, 1869.
	Phil 2138.35.10	Mill, John S. System der deductiven und inductiven Logik. Leipzig, 1872. 3 pam.
	Phil 2138.35.8	Mill, John S. System der deductiven und inductiven Logik. 2e Aufl. Braunschweig, 1862-63. 2v.
	Phil 2138.35.6	Mill, John S. System der deductiven und inductiven Logik. 4e Aufl. v.1-2. Braunschweig, 1877.
Htn	Phil 2138.35.1*	Mill, John S. A system of logic. London, 1843. 2v.
	Phil 2138.35.4	Mill, John S. A system of logic. London, 1886.
	Phil 2138.35.5	Mill, John S. A system of logic. London, 1896.
	Phil 2138.35.5.3	Mill, John S. A system of logic. London, 1898.
	Phil 2138.35.5.10	Mill, John S. A system of logic. London, 1911.
	Phil 2138.35.20	Mill, John S. A system of logic. London, 1965.
NEDL	Phil 2138.35.3	Mill, John S. A system of logic. N.Y., 1869.
NEDL	Phil 2138.35.2	Mill, John S. A system of logic. 3rd ed. London, 1851. 2v.
	Phil 2138.35.3.15A	Mill, John S. A system of logic. 8th ed. London, 1872. 2v.
	Phil 2138.35.3.19	Mill, John S. A system of logic. 8th ed. N.Y., 1874.
	Phil 2138.35.3.23	Mill, John S. A system of logic. 8th ed. N.Y., 1881.
	Phil 2138.45.10	Mill, John S. Three essays on religion. London, 1925.
	Phil 2138.45.2	Mill, John S. Three essays on religion. N.Y., 1874.
X Cg	Phil 2138.45.5	Mill, John S. Three essays on religion. N.Y., 1884.
	Phil 2138.45.20	Mill, John S. Tre religions-filosofiska afhandlingar. Stockholm, 1883.
	Phil 2138.40.13	Mill, John S. Über die Freiheit. Frankfurt, 1860. 4 pam.
	Phil 2138.46	Mill, John S. Über Religion. Berlin, 1875.
	Phil 2138.50.21	Mill, John S. Utilitarianism. Belmont, Calif., 1969.
	Phil 2138.50.8	Mill, John S. Utilitarianism. Chicago, 1906.
Htn	Phil 2138.50.4*	Mill, John S. Utilitarianism. London, 1863.
	Phil 2138.50.20	Mill, John S. Utilitarianism. N.Y., 1953.
	Phil 2138.50.5	Mill, John S. Utilitarianism. 4th ed. London, 1871.
	Phil 2138.50.6	Mill, John S. Utilitarianism. 12th ed. London, 1895.
	Phil 2138.50.17	Mill, John S. L'utilitarisme. Paris, 1883.
	Phil 2490.84.20	Mill, John Stuart. Auguste Comte and positivism. Ann Arbor, 1965.
	Phil 2490.84.15	Mill, John Stuart. Auguste Comte and positivism. London, 1908?
	Phil 2490.84.10	Mill, John Stuart. Auguste Comte et le positivisme. 2. éd. Paris, 1879.
	Phil 2490.84.6	Mill, John Stuart. The positive philosophy of Auguste Comte. N.Y., 1873.
	Phil 2490.41.2.2	Mill, John Stuart. The positive philosophy of Auguste Comte. N.Y., 1873.
	Phil 2490.84.4	Mill, John Stuart. The positive philosophy of Auguste Comte. N.Y., 1887.
	Phil 8685.8	Mill, W.H. Observations...pantheistic principles. Cambridge, 1855.
	Phil 2138.80	Mill and Carlyle. (Alexander, P.P.) Edinburgh, 1866.
	Phil 2138.126	Mill and his early critcs. (Rees, John C.) Leicester, 1956.
	Phil 2138.146	Mill and liberalism. (Cowling, M.) Cambridge, Eng., 1963.
	Phil 2138.150	The Mill news letter. Toronto. 1,1965+
	Phil 2138.77.6	Mill on Bentham and Coleridge. (Mill, John S.) London, 1967.
	Phil 343.31	Millán Puellas, A. La función social de los saberes liberales. Madrid, 1961.
	Phil 5875.80	Millar, Susanna. The psychology of play. Harmondsworth, 1968.
	Phil 7159.152	Millard, Joseph. Edgar Cayce, mystery man of miracles. N.Y., 1956.
	Phil 1750.166.255	Millas, Orlando. El humanismo científico de los comunistas. Santiago de Chile, 1968.
	Phil 1050.4.25	Millás y Vallicrosa, José María. Sêlomó Ibn Gabirol como poeta y filósofo. Madrid, 1945.
	Phil 6688.24	The millennium: the goodtime coming. (Sheldon, William.) Springfield, 1862.
	Phil 6122.56	Miller, A.G. Train development. N.Y., 1909.
	Phil 5545.20.5	Miller, Adam. Mental gymnastics, or lessons on memory. 4. ed. Chicago, 1886.
	Phil 5545.20	Miller, Adam. Mental gymnastics. Chicago, 1886.
	Phil 8592.13	Miller, Andrew. The problem of theology in modern thought. London, 1909.
	Phil 5270.30	Miller, Arthur G. The social psychology of psychological research. N.Y., 1971.
	Phil 8702.20	Miller, C.W. A scientist's approach to religion. N.Y., 1947.
	Phil 5190.10.20	Miller, Clyde R. The process of persuasion. Firenze, 1907.
	Phil 9380.8	Miller, D.C. The morale of adults. Thesis. Menasha, Wis., 1940.
	Phil 2340.10.99	Miller, D.L. The philosophy of A.N. Whitehead. Minneapolis, 1938.
	Phil 5762.19	Miller, David L. Modern science and human freedom. Austin, 1959.
	Phil 5867.30	Miller, David LeRoy. Gods and games; toward a theology of play. N.Y., 1970.
	Phil 6962.25	Miller, E. The neurosis in war. N.Y, 1940.
	Phil 3494.11.10	Miller, E.M. The basis of freedom: a study of Kant's theory. Sydney, 1924.
	Phil 3494.11.5	Miller, E.M. Moral action and natural law in Kant. Melbourne, 1911.
	Phil 3494.11.15A	Miller, E.M. Moral law and the highest good; a study of Kant's doctrine. Melbourne, 1928.
	Phil 5252.87	Miller, Edmond M. Brain capacity and intelligence. Sydney, 1926.
	Phil 5520.113	Miller, G.A. Language and communication. 1. ed. N.Y., 1951.
	Phil 5252.125A	Miller, George. Plans and the structure of behavior. N.Y., 1960.
	Phil 5252.141A	Miller, George A. Psychology, the science of mental life. N.Y., 1962.
	Phil 7082.44.1	Miller, Gustavus Hindman. Ten thousand dreams interpreted; or, What's in a dream. Chicago, 1931.
	Phil 343.20	Miller, H. History and science. Berkeley, 1939.
	Phil 8702.6	Miller, H. The testimony of the rocks. Boston, 1857.
	Phil 8702.6.25	Miller, H. The two records: The mosaic and the geological. Boston, 1854.
	Phil 8592.66	Miller, Hugh. Christian truth in history. N.Y., 1941.
	Phil 812.18	Miller, Hugh. An historical introduction to modern philosophy. N.Y., 1947.
	Phil 6322.4	Miller, Hugh C. Functional nerve disease. London, 1920.
	Phil 6322.4.5	Miller, Hugh C. The new psychology and the parent. N.Y., 1923.
	Phil 6322.4.7	Miller, Hugh C. The new psychology and the preacher. London, 1924.
	Phil 6322.4.15	Miller, Hugh C. Psycho-analysis and its derivations. London, 1933.
	Phil 8637.8	Miller, J. Are souls immortal? 3rd ed. Princeton, N.J., 1887.
	Phil 187.16	Miller, J. Metaphysics. N.Y., 1877.
	Phil 9560.29	Miller, J.R. The beauty of kindness. N.Y., 1905.
	Phil 5066.105	Miller, J.W. Exercises in introductory symbolic logic. Montreal? 1955.
	Phil 5722.25	Miller, James G. Unconsciousness. N.Y., 1942.
	Phil 5052.37	Miller, James N. The structure of Aristotelian logic. London, 1938.
	Phil 9352.14	Miller, James R. Girls: faults and ideals. N.Y., 1892.
	Phil 2475.1.165	Miller, L.H. Bergson and religion. N.Y., 1916.
	Phil 3805.270	Miller, Marlin E. Der Ubergang. 1. Aufl. Gütersloh, 1970.
	Phil 5252.78A	Miller, N.E. Social learning and imitation. New Haven, 1941.
	Phil 5252.78.5	Miller, N.E. Social learning and imitation. New Haven, 1953.
	Phil 3494.53A	Miller, Oscar W. The Kantian thing-in-itself. N.Y., 1956.
	Phil 575.235	Miller, Reinhold. Persönlichkeit und Gemeinschaft zur Kritik der neothomistischen Persönlichkeitsauffassung. Berlin, 1916.
	Phil 9528.2	Miller, S. Letters from a father to his son in college. Philadelphia, 1852.
	Phil 8702.34	Miller, Samuel Howard. Religion in a technical age. Cambridge, 1968.
	Phil 8667.16	Miller, T.A. The mind behind the universe. N.Y., 1928.
	Phil 5252.22	Miller, T.E. The psychology of thinking. N.Y., 1909.
	Phil 44.2	Miller, W. The "philosophical". A short history of the Edinburgh Philosophical Institution. Edinburgh, 1949.
	Phil 6122.63	Miller, W.H. How to relax. N.Y., 1944.
	Phil 3455.1.01	Miller, Wilhelm A. Isenkrahe-Bibliographie. 3e Aufl. Berlin, 1927.
Htn	Phil 2150.3.30*	Miller, William. Evidence from Scripture...the second coming of Christ. Troy, 1838.
	Phil 3790.4.90	Miller-Rostoska, A. Das Individuelle als Gegenstand der Erkenntnis. Winterthur, 1955.
	Phil 2138.107	Millet, J. An Millius veram mathematicorum axiomatum originem invenerit. Paris, 1867.
	Phil 5642.9	Millet, J. Audition colorée. Paris, 1892.
	Phil 2520.95.5	Millet, J. Descartes; son histoire depuis 1637. Paris, 1876.
	Phil 2520.95	Millet, J. Histoire de Descartes avant 1637. Paris, 1867.
	Phil 3832.24	Millet, Louis. La pensée de Spinoza. Paris, 1970.
	Phil 680.30	Millet, Louis. Le structuralisme. Paris, 1970.
	Phil 2725.11.95	Millet, Louis. Le symbolisme dans la philosophie. Paris, 1959.
	Phil 6834.1	Millett, Antony P.U. Homosexuality; a bibliography of literature published since 1959 and available in New Zealand. Wellington, 1967.
	Phil 1135.44	Milliaud, G. Les philosophes-geometres de la Gréce. Paris, 1900.
	Phil 510.14	Milliet, J. Paul. Remarques sur la monadologie. Paris, 1907.
	Phil 5252.21	Milliet, J.P. La dynamis et les trois ames. Paris, 1908.
	Phil 8702.13	Millikan, R.A. Evolution in science and religion. New Haven, 1927.
	Phil 6682.14	Millington, T.S. A lecture on the phenomena of dreams, mesmerism, clairvoyance. London, 1852?
	Phil 3808.129	Millioud, Maurice. Étude critique système philosophique de Schopenhauer. Lausanne, 1893.

Phil 3832.17   Millner, Simond. The face of Benedictus Spinoza. N.Y., 1946.

Phil 6122.20   Mills, A.W. Practical metaphysics. Chicago, 1896.
Phil 8592.11   Mills, B.F. Twentieth century religion. Boston, 1898.
Phil 6122.4   Mills, C.K. Toner lectures, IX. Mental overwork. Washington, 1885.
Phil 6962.12   Pamphlet box. Mills, C.K. Minor writings.
Phil 6967.3.25   Mills, Charles K. Benjamin Rush and American psychiatry. n.p., 1886.
Phil 1812.16   Mills, Charles W. Sociology and pragmatism. N.Y., 1964.
Phil 6962.36   Mills, Enid. Living with mental illness. London, 1962.
Phil 5251.1.30   Mills, Eugene S. George Trumbull Ladd: pioneer American psychologist. Cleveland, 1969.
Phil 6122.39   Mills, James P. Illumination; spiritual healing. N.Y., 1916.
Phil 5822.2   Mills, W. The nature and development of animal intelligence. London, 1898.
Phil 2138.115   Mill's logic of the moral sciences. Diss. (Castell, A.) Chicago, 1936.
Phil 9550.16   Mills' utilitarianism. (Plamenatz, J.P.) Oxford, 1949.
Phil 3494.62   Milmed, Bella Kussy. Kant and current philosophical issues. N.Y., 1961.
Phil 1812.14   Milne, A.J.M. The social philosophy of English idealism. London, 1962.
Phil 8637.11   Milne, J. Napier. The dream that comes true. London, 1919.
Phil 5640.144   Milne, Lorus J. The senses of animals and men. N.Y., 1962.
Phil 6990.29   Milner, John. Authentic documents relative to the cure of Winefrid White. 3. ed. London, 1806.
Phil 6322.65   Milner, Marion Blackett. The hands of the living god. London, 1969.
Phil 9495.160   Miłość i odpowiedzialność. (Wojtyka, Karol.) Lublin, 1960.
Phil 8980.572.15   Milovidov, Arsenii S. Kommunisticheskaia moral' i voinskii dolg. Moskva, 1971.
Phil 8837.14   Miloyévitch, Voukossava. La théorie des passions du P. Senault et la morale chrétienne en France au XVIIe siècle. Thèse. Paris, 1934.
Phil 5420.16   Milsen, G. Studies in self-confrontation. Copenhagen, 1962.
Phil 9245.41   Miltenberger, W.F. De felicitate. Washington, D.C., 1914.
Phil 8962.9   Miltner, C.C. The elements of ethics. N.Y., 1931.
Htn Phil 2150.4.30*   Milton, Joannis. Angli pro populo anglicano defensio. Londini, 1651.
Phil 9590.24   Milum, John P. Man and his meaning. London, 1945.
Phil 187.115   Milville, H.L. Vers une philosophie de l'esprit ou de la totalité. Lausanne, 1937.
Phil 6028.5   Die Mimik des Denkens. (Sanctis, Sante de.) Halle, 1906.
Phil 6000.4   Die Mimik des Menschen auf grundvoluntarischer Psychologie. (Hughes, Henry.) Frankfurt, 1900.
Phil 6025.1   Mimik und Physiognomik. (Piderit, Leo.) Detmold, 1886.
Phil 6012.1   La mimique. (Cuyer, E.) Paris, 1902.
Phil 6953.8   La mimique ches les aliénés. (Dromard, Gabriel.) Paris, 1909.
Phil 5252.159   Mimo, dependencia, depresión, alcoholismo. 1. ed. (Meza, César.) Guatemala, 1967.
Phil 1182.20   Minar, Edwin L. Early Pythagorean politics and theory. Baltimore, 1942.
Phil 6113.30   Mind, a social phenomenon. (Doran, F.S.A.) N.Y., 1953.
Htn Phil 22.4.8*   Mind; a unique review of ancient philosophy (a parody). London, 1901.
Phil 6121.42   Mind; an essay on human feeling. (Langer, Susanne K.) Baltimore, 1967-
Phil 5234.2   Mind, brain and adaptation in the nineteenth century. (Young, Robert Maxwell.) Oxford, 1970.
Phil 1930.8.120   Mind, History, and dialectic: the philosophy of R.G. Collingwood. (Mink, Louis O.) Bloomington, 1969.
Phil 5242.28   Mind; its origin and goal. (Cutten, George.) New Haven, 1925.
Phil 165.376   Mind, matter, and method. (Feyerabend, Paul.) Minneapolis, 1966.
Phil 8887.105   Mind, matter, and morals. 1st. ed. (Meyer, Arthur E.) N.Y., 1957.
Phil 5247.56   Mind, mechanism and adaptive behavior. (Hull, C.L.) Lancaster, 1937.
Phil 6335.15   Mind, medicine and man. (Zilboorg, Gregory.) N.Y., 1943.
Phil 6311.19   Mind, medicine and metaphysics. (Brown, William.) London, 1936.
Phil 5585.75   Mind, perception and science. (Brain, W.R.) Oxford, 1951.
Phil 6122.17   Mind, religion and health. (MacDowall, R.) N.Y., 1908.
Phil 6132.27   Mind, thought and cerebration. (Wilder, Alexander.) n.p., 188-?
Phil 5252.60   The mind. (McDowall, R.J.S.) N.Y., 1927.
Phil 5255.27   The mind. (Pyne, John K.) N.Y., 1926.
Phil 22.4   Mind. London. 1,1876+ 80v.
X Cg Phil 22.4   Mind. London. 5-16
Htn Phil 22.4.6*   Mind. London. 1876-1910 35v.
NEDL Phil 22.7   Mind. N.Y. 1-17,1897-1906 16v.
Phil 510.147   Mind: creative and dynamic. (Russell, C.W.) N.Y., 1932.
Phil 22.4.3   Mind. Index to new series. v. 1-12. London, 1904.
Phil 5258.124   Mind: perception and thought in their constructive aspects. (Schilder, Paul.) N.Y., 1942.
Phil 5590.125   The mind alive. (Overstreet, H.A.) N.Y., 1954.
Phil 6103.2   Pamphlet vol. Mind and body. 23 pam.
Htn Phil 6103.5*   Pamphlet box. Mind and body. 5 pam.
Phil 6103   Pamphlet box. Mind and body.
Phil 6111.1   Mind and body. (Bain, A.) London, 1873.
Phil 6111.1.2   Mind and body. (Bain, A.) N.Y., 1873.
Phil 6111.1.5   Mind and body. (Bain, A.) N.Y., 1874.
Phil 6113.19.9   Mind and body. (Driesch, Hans.) N.Y., 1927.
Phil 6103.10   Pamphlet box. Mind and body. German dissertations.
Phil 6121.3.3   Mind and brain. (Laugel, A.) N.Y., 1869. 2v.
Phil 6121.3.2   Mind and brain. (Laycock, T.) Edinburgh, 1860. 2v.
Phil 6111.48   Mind and brain in thought and reason process. (Bowman, A.) London, 1930.
Phil 193.61   Mind and brain with other studies. (Sopote, M.) Oxford, n.d.
Phil 8887.48   Mind and conduct. (Marshall, H.R.) N.Y., 1919.
Phil 3905.84   The mind and death of a genius. (Abrahamsen, David.) N.Y., 1946.
Phil 8666.14   Mind and deity. (Laird, John.) London, 1941.
Phil 6132.9   Mind and health. (Weaver, E.E.) N.Y., 1913.
Phil 8953.8.3   The mind and heart of love, lion and unicorn. (D'Arcy, Martin Cyrile.) London, 1954.
Phil 8953.8.2   The mind and heart of love, lion and unicorn. (D'Arcy, Martin Cyrile.) N.Y., 1947.

Phil 8953.8   The mind and heart of love. (D'Arcy, Martin Cyrile.) London, 1945.
Phil 5440.26   Mind and heredity. (Kellogg, V.L.) Princeton, 1923.
Phil 5245.33   Mind and its body. (Fox, Charles.) London, 1931.
Phil 5241.69   The mind and its mechanism. (Bonsfield, Paul.) London, 1927.
Phil 5241.66.5   The mind and its place. (Broad, C.D.) N.Y., 1927.
Phil 5241.66   The mind and its place in nature. (Broad, C.D.) London, 1925.
Phil 5243.30   Mind and its place in nature. (Drake, Durant.) N.Y., 1925.
Phil 5259.13.15   Mind and life. (Tansley, A.G.) London, 1952.
Phil 6111.7   Mind and matter. (Brodie, B.) N.Y., 1857.
Phil 6128.59   Mind and matter. (Schroedinger, Erwin.) Cambridge, Eng., 1958.
Phil 193.128   Mind and matter. (Stout, G.F.) N.Y., 1931.
Phil 6127.14   Mind and medicine. 2d ed. (Rivers, W.H.R.) Manchester, 1920.
Phil 510.2   Mind and motion and monism. (Romanes, G.J.) N.Y., 1895.
Phil 1828.6   Mind and nature; a study of the naturalistic philosophies of Cohen. (Delaney, Cornelius F.) Notre Dame, Ind., 1969.
Phil 353.15   Mind and nature. (Weyl, H.) Philadelphia, 1934.
Phil 5241.28.13   Mind and personality. (Brown, W.) London, 1926.
Phil 6111.14.6   The mind and the brain. (Binet, A.) London, 1907.
Phil 8584.18   Mind and the mystery. (Eustace, C.J.) N.Y., 1937.
Phil 2418.5   The mind and the sword. (Stein, Jay W.) N.Y., 1961.
Phil 8660.13   Mind and the universal frame. (Fitzpatrick, M.S.) Dublin, 1935.
Phil 342.13A   Mind and the world-order. (Lewis, Clarence I.) N.Y., 1929.
Phil 342.13.10A   Mind and the world-order. (Lewis, Clarence I.) N.Y., 1956.
Phil 6116.7   Mind and work. (Gulick, L.H.) N.Y., 1908.
Phil 5850.279.7   Mind and work. (Myers, Charles S.) London, 1920.
Phil 5247.32   Mind as a force. (Harford, C.F.) London, 1924.
Phil 5258.91   Mind as behavior and studies in empirical idealism. (Singer, Edgar A.) Columbus, Ohio, 1924.
Phil 5465.126   The mind as nature. 1. ed. (Eiseley, Loren.) N.Y., 1962.
Phil 5722.26   The mind at mischief. (Sadler, W.S.) N.Y., 1929.
Phil 187.29.5   Mind at the crossways. (Morgan, C.L.) N.Y., 1930.
Phil 5257.29   The mind at work. (Rhodes, G.) London, 1914.
Phil 8667.16   The mind behind the universe. (Miller, T.A.) N.Y., 1928.
Phil 6109.2   The mind-brain identity theory. (Borst, Clive Vernon.) N.Y., 1970.
Phil 2475.1.46   Mind energy. (Bergson, Henri.) London, 1920.
Phil 6132.35   Mind explorers. (Winkler, J.K.) N.Y., 1939.
Phil 5254.3.7   The mind goes forth. 1st. ed. (Overstreet, H. Allen.) N.Y., 1956.
Phil 6980.105   The mind in action. (Berne, Eric.) N.Y., 1947.
Phil 5246.42   The mind in action. (Garnett, Arthur C.) London, 1931.
Phil 5246.42.5   The mind in action. (Garnett, Arthur C.) N.Y., 1932.
Phil 5246.32.5   The mind in action. (Green, G.H.) London, 1923.
Phil 5811.5   Mind in animals. (Büchner, L.) London, 1880.
Phil 6962.37   The mind in chains. (Moore, W.) N.Y., 1955.
Phil 6317.19   The mind in conflict. (Howden, R.A.) London, 1931.
Phil 5241.110   Mind in everyday affairs. (Barnard, Chester Irving.) Princeton, 1936.
Phil 5817.5   Mind in evolution. (Hobhouse, L.T.) London, 1901.
Phil 5817.5.2   Mind in evolution. (Hobhouse, L.T.) London, 1915.
Phil 5817.5.5   Mind in evolution. 3d ed. (Hobhouse, L.T.) London, 1926.
Phil 5817.3   Mind in man and animals. (Henslow, G.) London, 1853-81. 2 pam.
Phil 8674.1   Mind in matter. (Tait, J.) London, 1884.
Phil 22.22   Mind in nature. Chicago.
Phil 5821.2   Mind in the lower animals. (Lindsay, W.L.) London, 1879. 2v.
Phil 6675.13   Mind "magic". (Fox, Alfred J.) N.Y., 1937.
Phil 6951.22   A mind mislaid. (Brown, H.C.) N.Y., 1937.
Phil 5834.1.15   The mind of a gorilla. (Yerkes, R.M.) Worcester, Mass., 1926.
Phil 5545.235   The mind of a mnemonist. (Luriiâ, Aleksandr R.) N.Y., 1968.
Phil 1865.196   The mind of Jeremy Bentham. (Manning, David John.) London, 1968.
Phil 6951.23   The mind of man. (Bromberg, W.) N.Y., 1937.
Phil 5251.30.3   The mind of man. "Ethical series." (Spiller, G.) London, 1902.
Phil 2280.5.110A   The mind of Santayana. (Butler, Richard.) Chicago, 1955.
Phil 5811.15.10A   The mind of the dog. (Buytendijk, Frederik Jacobus Johannes.) Boston, 1936.
Phil 8598.82   The mind of the maker. (Sayers, Dorothy L.) London, 1941.
Phil 8598.82.5   The mind of the maker. (Sayers, Dorothy L.) N.Y., 1941.
Phil 9575.8   The mind of the millionaire. (Atwood, Albert W.) N.Y., 1926.
Phil 7069.60   Mind power. 1. ed. (Nagel, E.W.) N.Y., 1960.
Phil 22.17   Mind power plus. St. Louis, Mo. 1-11
Phil 7069.59.10   The mind readers. (Soal, Samuel G.) London, 1959.
Phil 6951.5.5.7   A mind that found itself. (Beers, C.W.) Garden City, 1925.
Phil 6951.5.6   A mind that found itself. (Beers, C.W.) Garden City, 1929.
Phil 6951.5.7   A mind that found itself. (Beers, C.W.) Garden City, 1933.
Phil 6951.5.8   A mind that found itself. (Beers, C.W.) Garden City, 1937.
Phil 6951.5.3   A mind that found itself. (Beers, C.W.) N.Y., 1908.
NEDL Phil 6951.5.2   A mind that found itself. 2. ed. (Beers, C.W.) N.Y., 1912.
Phil 6951.5.4.2   A mind that found itself. 4. ed. (Beers C.W.) N.Y., 1920.
Phil 6951.5.5   A mind that found itself. 5. ed. (Beers, C.W.) N.Y., 1921.
Phil 6951.5.52   A mind that found itself and its author. (American Foundation for Mental Hygiene, Inc.) N.Y., 193-.
Phil 6951.5.50   A mind that found itself and its author. N.Y., 1924.
Phil 575.80   A mind that was different. (Thompson, Dow.) Wellston, 1932.
Phil 6121.11   Mind the transformer, the new psychology. 7. ed. (Lindsay, A.A.) Los Angeles, 1911.
Phil 7069.48   Mind to mind. (Warcollier, R.) N.Y., 1948.
Phil 4580.15   Mindre arbejder. Rǽkke 1-2. (Høffding, Harald.) København, 1899-1905.
Phil 6957.19   The minds and nerves of soldiers. (Hanes, E.L.) Pasadena, Calif., 1941.
Phil 6311.28   Minds in distress. (Bridger, A.E.) London, 1913.
Phil 6950.12   Minds that came back. (Alvarez, W.C.) Philadelphia, 1961.
Phil 22.37   Minerva. Buenos Aires. 1-2,1944-1945
Phil 1504.7   Minges, P. Der angebliche Exzessive Realismus Dons Scotus. v.7, pt.1. Münster, 1908.

Phil 1504.5.4   Minges, Parthenius. Ist duns scotus indeterminist? v.5, pt.4. Münster, 1905.

Phil 3085.4.31   Minima Moralia. (Adorno, F.W.) Berlin, 1951.

Phil 1504.32   Minio-Palvello, Lorenzo. Twelfth century logic. Roma, 1956- 2v.

Phil 8615.23   A ministry to man. 1. ed. (Hohoff, Tay.) N.Y., 1959.

Phil 1930.8.120   Mink, Louis O. Mind, History, and dialectic: the philosophy of R.G. Collingwood. Bloomington, 1969.

Phil 293.23   Minkowski, E. Vers une cosmologie. Paris, 1936.

Phil 6322.60   Minkowski, Eugène. Le temps vécu. Neuchâtel, 1968.

Phil 1850.128   Minkowski, Helmut. Einordnung, Wesen und Aufgaben...des Francis Bacon. Leyde, 1933.

Phil 575.225   Minkus, P.A. Philosophy of the person. Oxford, 1960.

Phil 5870.6   Minnesota. Symposia on Child Psychology. Papers. Minneapolis. 1,1967+ 3v.

Phil 52.2   Minnesota. University. Department of Philosophy. Papers. Minneapolis, 1893-

Phil 4515.100   Minnesteckning över Christopher Jacob Boström. (Larsson, Hans.) Stockholm, 1931.

Phil 705.68   The minor and later transcendentalists; a symposium. Hartford, 1969.

Phil 6132.34   Minor mental maladjustments in normal people. (Wallin, J.E.W.) Durham, N.C., 1939.

Phil 8876.97   The minor moralist. (Bell, F.O.) London, 1903.

Phil 178.12.05   Pamphlet box. Minor writings.

Phil 5374.56   Minot, C.S. The problem of consciousness in its biological aspects. N.Y., 1902.

Phil 487.8   Mins, H.F. Materialism; the scientific basis. N.Y., 1934.

Phil 1860.10.4   The minstrel. Works 10. (Beattie, James.) Philadelphia, 1809.

Phil 5052.6   Minto, William. Logic. N.Y., 1894.

Phil 2045.132A   Mintz, Samuel. The hunting of Leviathan. Cambridge, 1962.

Phil 5545.159   Minuet. (Herrlin, Axel.) Stockholm, 1917.

Phil 9230.13.5F   Minutes of evidence...first 24 days, Thursday, 30 June, 1932-Thursday, 23 February, 1933. Pt.1-24. (Great Britain. Commission on Lotteries and Betting, 1932-33.) London, 1932-33.

Phil 62.5   Minutes of the Vienna Psychoanalytic Society. (Wiener, P.V.) N.Y., 1962- 2v.

Phil 5465.206   Minuty poeticheskikh vdokhnovenii. (Mironov, Alekseĭ V.) Iavoslavl', 1970.

Phil 4006.4   Il mio contributo alla filosofia neoscolastica. (Gemelli, A.) Milano, 1926.

Phil 4160.1.40   Il mio testamento. (Labanca, Baldassare.) Agnone, 1913.

Phil 3494.66.2   Miotti, Peter. Über die Nichtigkeit der Kantische Grundsätze in der Philosophie...Logik von Professor Kreil. Facsimile. Bruxelles, 1968.

Phil 3494.28   Miotti. Uiber die Falschheit und Gottlosigkeit des Kantischen System. Augsburg, 1802.

Phil 3494.28.5   Miotti. Uiber die Falschheit und Gottlosigkeit des Kantischen System. Wien, 1801.

Phil 8702.14   Mir, Miguel. Harmonia entre a sciencia a fé. v.2. Coimbra, 1892.

Phil 310.495   Mir i dusha. (Kolianskii, N.N.) Frankfurt am Main? 1953.

Phil 4769.8.20   Mir kak tseloe. 2. izd. (Strakhov, N.N.) Sankt Peterburg, 1892.

Phil 735.264   Mir ozhivshikh predmetov. (Drobnitskii, Oleg G.) Moskva, 1967.

Phil 6990.13   Mir y Noguera, Juan. El milagro. 2. ed. Barcelona, 1915. 3v.

Phil 6322.28.5   Mira y López, E. Doctrinas psicoanaliticas. Buenos Aires, 1963.

Phil 6322.28   Mira y López, E. Psychiatry in war. 1st ed. N.Y., 1943.

Phil 5252.80   Mira y Lopez E. Problemas psicologicos actuales. Buenos Aires, 1940.

Phil 2655.2.80   Mirabaud, R. Charles Henry et l'idéalisme scientifique. Paris, 1926.

Phil 3625.1.147   Mirabeau, H.G.R. Sur la réforme politique des Juifs. Bruxelles, 1788.

Phil 3625.1.145   Mirabeau, H.G.R. Sur Moses Mendelssohn. Leipzig, 1853.

Phil 8413.31   Mirabent, F. De la bellesa. v.5. Barcelona, 1936.

Phil 8110.13   Mirabent, F. La estética inglesa del siglo XVIII. Barcelona, 1927.

Phil 4363.8   Mirabeut Vilaplana, Francisco. Estudios estéticos. Barcelona, 1957. 2v.

Phil 6990.28   Miracle and its philosophical presuppositions. (Tennant, F.R.) Cambridge, 1925.

Phil 525.38.2   Miracle et mystique. 2e ed. (Louismet, S.) Paris, 1923.

Phil 6990.20   Le miracle et ses suppléances. (Poulpiquet, E.) Paris, 1914.

Phil 7069.07.9   Le miracle moderne. 4. ed. (Bois, Jules.) Paris, 1907.

Phil 8587.58   The miracle of answered prayers. (Hallimond, J.G.) N.Y., 1916.

Phil 7069.54.25   The miracle on the wall. (Porten, Harry.) Eastbourne, Eng., 1954.

Htn   Phil 6990.40*   Miracles, no violations of the law of nature. (Blount, Charles.) London, 1683.

Phil 6990.23   Miracles; their physical possibility. (Taylor, William F.) Liverpool, 1868.

Phil 6990.32   Miracles and medicine. (Allen, Simeon C.) Boston, 1929.

Phil 7068.96.10   Miracles and modern spiritualism. (Wallace, Alfred R.) London, 1896.

Phil 6122.41   Miracles and the new psychology. (Micklem, E.R.) Oxford, 1922.

Phil 5753.5   Les miracles de la volonté. (Duchatel, Edmond.) Paris, 1914.

Phil 6990.17   Miracles in the light, science and history. (Huelster, A.) Chicago, 19- .

Phil 6990.11   Miracles of healing. (Waddle, C.W.) n.p., 1909.

Phil 6990.21   Pamphlet vol. Miracles of Prince Hohenlore. 10 pam.

Htn   Phil 6990.40.5*   Miracles work's. (Browne, T.) London, 1683.

Phil 8583.35   Mirage and truth. (D'Arcy, M.C.) N.Y., 1935.

Phil 8876.51.9   Le mirage de la vertu. (Bayet, Albert.) Paris, 1912.

Phil 6129.4   Mirage of the nervous system. (Thompson, J.J.) n.p., 1914.

Phil 6990.61   Mirakelbücker bayerischer Wallfahrtsorte. (Bach, H.) Möhrendorf, 1963.

Phil 6400.9   Mirallie, C. De l'aphasie sensorielle. Paris, 1896.

Phil 4012.4   Miranda, L. Die Hegel a Croce e da Jellinek a Chiovenda. Bari, 1921.

Phil 2725.30.80   Miranda, Maria do Carmo Tavares de. Théorie de la vérité chez Edouard LeRoy. Paris, 1957.

Phil 3494.5   Mirbt, E.S. Kant und seine Nachfolger. Jena, 1841.

Phil 3494.5.5   Mirbt, E.S. Kant's Philosophie. Jena, 1851.

Phil 187.48   Mirbt, Ernst. Was heisst Philosophiren und was 1st Philosophie? Jena, 1839.

Phil 5052.48.2   Miro, Quesada Cantuarias. Iniciación lógica. 2. ed. Lima, 1969.

Phil 3450.11.120   Miro Quesada, F. Sentido del movimiento. Lima, 1941.

Phil 396.14   Miro Quesada, Francisco. Humanismo y revolución. Lima, 1969.

Phil 270.49   Miró Quesada, Oscar. El problema de la libertad y la ciencia. Lima, 1945.

Phil 5465.206   Mironov, Alekseĭ V. Minuty poeticheskikh vdokhnovenii. Iavoslavl', 1970.

Phil 4769.1.101   Mirosozertsanie Vl. Solov'eva. (Skobtsov, E.) Paris, 1929.

Phil 4769.1.105   Mirosozertsanie Vl.C. Solov'eva. v.1-2. (Truhetskoĭ, E.N.) Moskva, 1913.

Phil 4769.6.82   Mirovozzrenie I.M. Sechenova. (Kaganov, V.) Moskva, 1943.

Phil 4751.2.80   Mirovozzrenie M.A. Antonovicha. (Peunova, M.N.) Moskva, 1960.

Phil 4753.4   Mirovozzrenie i nauchnoe poznanie. (Chernovolenko, Vilen F.) Kiev, 1970.

Htn   Phil 9355.1.5*   A mirror for the female sex. (Pilkington, M.) Hartford, 1799.

Phil 9355.1.2   A mirror for the female sex. (Pilkington, M.) London, 1798.

Phil 9355.1   A mirror for the female sex. (Pilkington, M.) London, 1804.

Phil 8582.75   The mirror of language. (Colish, Marcia L.) New Haven, 1968.

Phil 5925.4   The mirror of nature...science of phrenology. (Fletcher, J.) Boston, 1838.

Phil 9035.50   A mirror of personality. (Vance, J.G.) London, 1927.

Phil 530.15.20   The mirror of simple souls. London, 1927.

Phil 190.59   The mirror of your soul. (Palumbo, A.) Boston, 1935.

Phil 7068.63   Mirville, J.E. Pneumatologie. Des esprits. v. 2-6. Paris, 1863-68. 5v.

Phil 7068.54   Mirville, J.E. Pneumatologie des esprits. 3. ed. Paris, 1854.

Phil 7068.63.5   Mirville, J.E. Question des esprits et de leurs manifestations diverses. Paris, 1863.

Phil 7068.55   Mirville, J.E. Questions des esprits; ses progrès dans la science. Paris, 1855.

Phil 6975.5.2   Mis quinientos locos; memorias del director de un manicomio. 2. ed. (Zaglul, Antonio.) Santo Domingo, 1966.

Phil 1713.5   Misao kao odraz vremens. (Nikolajević, Sietamir B.) Beograd, 1971.

Phil 5232.4   The misbehaviorists. (Wickham, H.) N.Y., 1928.

Phil 9375.7   Mis'c., or Sundry discourses concerning trade. London, 1712.

Phil 4983.5.6   Miscelanea filosófica. (Varela, Félix.) Habana, 1944.

Phil 801.5.20   Miscellanea historiae philosophicae literariae criticae. (Brucker, J.) Augustae Vindelicorum, 1748.

Htn   Phil 8657.15.3*   Miscellanea philo-theologica, or God and man. (Church, Henry.) London, 1638.

Htn   Phil 8657.15*   Miscellanea philo-theologica, or God and man. (Church, Henry.) London, 1937.

Phil 5238.12   Miscellanea psychologica Albert Michotte. (Louvain. Université Catholique. Institute Supérieur de Philosophie.) Louvain, 1947.

Phil 140.16   Pamphlet vol. Miscellanee filosofiche. 10 pam.

Phil 4120.4.79   Pamphlet box. Miscellaneous pamphlets.

Phil 6322.29   Miscellaneous papers on abnormal psychology. (McFarland, R.A.) n.p., n.d.

Phil 8800.1   The miscellaneous works. (Hyde, E.) London, 1751.

Phil 2295.15   Miscellaneous works. (Toland, John.) London 1747. 2v.

Htn   Phil 8877.15.5*   Miscellanies in five essays. (Collier, Jeremy.) London, 1694.

Phil 1124.4   Miscellanies in prose and verse. (Taylor, Thomas.) London, 1805.

Phil 1870.70   Miscellany containing several tracts on various subjects. (Berkeley, G.) London, 1752.

Phil 2805.42.6A   Miscelleneous writings. (Pascal, Blaise.) London, 1849.

Phil 850.23.2   Misch, G. The dawn of philosophy. Cambridge, 1951.

Phil 850.23   Misch, G. The dawn of philosophy. Cambridge, 1951.

Phil 3195.6.109   Misch, Georg. Vom Lebens- und Gedankenkreis Wilhelm Diltheys. Frankfurt, 1947.

Phil 812.10   Misch, Georg. Der Weg in die Philosophie. Leipzig, 1926.

Phil 812.10.5   Misch, Georg. Der Weg in die Philosophie. 2. Aufl. München, 1950.

Phil 5590.457.5   Mischel, Walter. Personality and assessment. N.Y., 1968.

Phil 522.53   Mischer. Psychologische Fragen. Stendal, 1884.

Phil 530.35.7   Misciattelli, Piero. L'Italia mistica. Firenze, 1932.

Phil 530.35F   Misciattelli, Piero. Misticismo senese. Firenze, 1966.

Phil 530.35.5   Misciattelli, Piero. The mystics of Siena. Cambridge, Eng., 1929.

Phil 8612.86   Miseriae regum. Diss. (Bornscheuer, Lothar.) Berlin, 1968.

Phil 3625.3.94   Mises, R. Ernst Mach. 's-Gravenhage, 1938.

Phil 5068.5   Mises, R.E. von. Kleines Lehrbuch des Positivismus. The Hague, 1939.

Phil 5068.5.5A   Mises, R.E. von. Positivism. Cambridge, 1951.

Phil 5252.135   Misiak, H. The philosophical roots of scientific psychology. N.Y., 1961.

Phil 5222.13   Misiak, Henryk. Catholics in psychology. N.Y., 1954.

Phil 4368.2.85   Mision y pensamiento de Francisco Romero. 1. ed. (Rodriguez Acala, Hugo.) Mexico, 1959.

Phil 1750.726   El misoneísmo y la modernidad cristiana en el siglo XVIII. (Gonzalez Casanova, Pablo.) México, 1948.

Phil 553.2   Misrahi, Robert. Lumière, commencement, liberté. Thèse. Paris, 1969.

Phil 3832.20   Misrahi, Robert. Spinoza; présentation, choix et traduction des textes. 2. ed. Paris, 1966.

Phil 8965.13.20   Missbrauch der Sprache, Missbrauch der Macht. (Pieper, Josef.) Zürich, 1970.

NEDL   Phil 7054.7   The missing link in modern spiritualism. (Underhill, A. Leah.) N.Y., 1885.

Phil 6117.9   La mission de la physiologie expérimentale. (Héger, P.) Bruxelles, 1899.

Phil 960.137.25   The mission of philosophy. (Hiriyanna, M.) Mysore, 1960.

Phil 4170.12.5   La missione del filosofo. (Mei, Flavio.) Milano, 1964.

Phil 52.5   Missouri. University. Studies. Philosophie and education series. Columbia, 1911.

Phil 9490.7.2   Mistakes of educated men. (Hart, J.S.) Philadelphia, 1862.

Phil 8663.3.87   The mistakes of R.G. Ingersoll on nature and God. (Edgett, G.W.) Boston, 1881.

Phil 4115.100   I misteri di Demofilo. (Sordi, Serafino.) Milano, 1850. 3 pam.

Phil 6673.9   I misteri svelati dello ipnotismo. (Donati, Alberto.) Roma, 1886.

Phil 585.145   Mistério do homen. (Martins, D.) Braga, 1961.

	Phil 2750.19.35	El misterio ontologico. (Marcel, Gabriel.) Tucumán, 1959.
	Phil 525.79	La mistica dell'avenire. (Vellani, Giovanni E.) Modena, 1936.
	Phil 3485.12	La mistica kantiana. (Drago, Pietro C.) Messina, 1929.
	Phil 525.113	I mistice medievali. (Bertin, G.) Milano, 1944.
	Phil 525.62	I mistici. (Levasti, A.) Firenze, 1925. 2v.
	Phil 530.35.15	Mistici del duecento e del trecento. (Levasti, A.) Milano, 1935.
	Phil 525.40	Il misticismo. (Latteo, Ernesto.) Torino, 1908.
	Phil 525.92	El misticismo como instrumento de investigación de la verdad. (Brenes Mesen, R.) San José de Costa Rica, 1921.
	Phil 525.67	Il misticismo medioevale. (Buonaiuti, E.) Pinerolo, 1928.
	Phil 525.5.15	Il misticismo moderno. (Troilo, E.) Torino, 1899.
	Phil 525.6	El misticismo ortodoxo en sus relaciones con la filosofia. (Gutiérrez, Marcelino.) Valladolid, 1886.
	Phil 530.35F	Misticismo senese. (Misciattelli, Piero.) Firenze, 1966.
	Phil 525.99	Los místicos. (Serrano Plaja, A.) Buenos Aires, 1943.
	Phil 530.40.15	Los místicos españoles. (Rousselot, P.) Barcelona, 1907. 2v.
	Phil 530.40.45	Místicos españoles. (Santullano, Luis.) Madrid, 1934.
	Phil 525.250	Mistisizmin ana hatlari. (Sunar, Cavit.) Ankara, 1966.
	Phil 4769.1.65	Mistitsizm v nauke. (Chicherin, Boris N.) Moskva, 1880.
	Phil 4215.1.103	Mistrali, Dario. G.D. Romagnosi. Borgo San Donnino, 1907.
	Phil 5240.29	La misura in psicologia sperimentale. (Aliotta, A.) Firenze, 1905.
	Phil 2475.1.262	The misuse of mind. (Stephen, Karin.) N.Y., 1922.
	Phil 2475.1.205	The misuse of the mind. (Stephen, Karin.) London, 1922.
	Phil 3085.7.80	Mit Beiträgen von Kurt Oppens. (Adorno, Theodor W.) Frankfurt, 1968.
	Phil 9515.3.80	Mit dem Herrn [von] Zimmermann. (Bahrat, Karl F.) n.p., 1790.
	Phil 3549.9.90	Mit unbefangener Stirn. (Kühnemann, E.) Heilbronn, 1937.
	Phil 2475.1.230	Mitchell, A. Studies in Bergson's philosophy. Lawrence, 1914-
	Phil 8592.119	Mitchell, Basil. Neutrality and commitment: an inaugural lecture delivered before the University of Oxford on 13 May, 1968. Oxford, 1968.
	Phil 5330.16	Mitchell, David. Influence of distractions on the formation of judgments in lifted weight experiments. Princeton, 1914.
	Phil 1117.7	Mitchell, E.M. (Mrs.). A study of Greek philosophy. Chicago, 1891.
	Phil 7230.2	Mitchell, G.W. X+Y=Z, or The sleeping preacher. N.Y., 1877.
	Phil 8592.53	Mitchell, H.B. Talks on religion. N.Y., 1908.
	Phil 6322.20	Mitchell, John K. Self help for nervous women. Philadelphia, 1909.
	Phil 8586.64.80	Mitchell, Phillip Marshall. Vilhelm Grønbech. En indføring. København, 1970.
	Phil 6122.12	Mitchell, S.W. Fat and blood. Philadelphia, 1884.
	Phil 6322.11	Mitchell, S.W. Lecture on diseases of the nervous system. Philadelphia, 1881.
	Phil 7039.6A	Mitchell, Silas Weir. Mary Reynolds: a case of double consciousness. Philadelphia, 1889.
	Phil 6322.6.5	Mitchell, T.W. Medical psychology and psychological research. London, 1922.
	Phil 6322.6.10	Mitchell, T.W. Problems in psychopathology. London, 1927.
	Phil 6322.6	Mitchell, T.W. The psychology of medicine. London, 1921.
	Phil 5252.16	Mitchell, W. Structure and growth of the mind. London, 1907.
	Phil 293.16	Mitchell, William. Nature and feeling. Adelaide, 1929.
	Phil 187.110	Mitchell, William. The place of minds in the world. London, 1933.
	Phil 187.110.5	Mitchell, William. The quality of life. London, 1935?
	Phil 8080.7	I miti delle Poetiche. (Ballo, Guido.) Milano, 1959.
	Phil 310.310	Mitin, M.B. Filosofiia i sovremennost'. Moskva, 1960.
	Phil 4710.75	Mitin, M.B. Filosofskaia nauka v SSSR za 25 let. Moskva, 1943.
	Phil 310.798	Mitin, Mark B. V.I. Lenin i aktual'nye problemy filosofii. Moskva, 1971.
	Phil 3925.16.300	Il mito del linguaggio scientifico. Studi su Wittgenstein. (Marconi, Diego.) Milano, 1971.
	Phil 4080.9.39	Il mito del realismo. (Carlini, Armando.) Firenze, 1936.
	Phil 8601.8	Mito e scienza saggio. (Vignoli, Tito.) Milano, 1879.
	Phil 5052.24.6	Mitra, A.C. The principles of logic deductive and inductive. Calcutta, 1922. 2v.
	Phil 8887.44	Mitra, Ambika C. The elements of morals. 2. ed. Calcutta, 1914.
	Phil 960.129	Mitra, K.N. Pessimism and life's ideal: the Hindu outlook. Madras, 1926.
	Phil 8177.5	Mitrovics, Gyula. A magyar esztétikai irodolan történeto. Debrecen, 1928.
	Phil 2520.180	Mitrovitch, R. La théorie des sciences chez Descartes d'après sa géométrie. Thèse. Paris, 192-?
	Phil 5051.29	Mits, wits and logic. 1st ed. (Lieber, Lillian R.) N.Y., 1947.
	Phil 5051.29.3	Mits, wits and logic. 3d ed. (Lieber, Lillian R.) N.Y., 1960.
	Phil 6322.38	Mitscherlich, A. Entfaltung des Psychoanalyse. Stuttgart, 1956.
	Phil 5421.20.80	Mitscherlich, Alexander. Bis hierher und nicht weiter. München, 1969.
	Phil 5421.20.85	Mitscherlich, Alexander. Die Idee des Friedens und die menschliche Aggressivität. Frankfurt, 1969.
	Phil 3640.402	Mittasch, A. Friedrich Nietzsche als Naturphilosoph. Stuttgart, 1952.
	Phil 1511.1.15	Mittelalterliches Geistesleben. (Grabmann, M.) München, 1926-36. 3v.
	Phil 5374.14	Mittenzwey, K. Über abstrahierende Apperception. Leipzig, 1907.
	Phil 293.22.5	Mittere, Albert. Wesensartwandel und Artensystem der physikalischen Körperwelt. Bressanone, 1936. 3v.
	Phil 293.22	Mitterer, Albert. Das Rinzen der alten Stoff-Form-Metaphysik mit der heutigen Stoff-Physik. Innsbruck, 1935.
	Phil 343.2	Mivart, G. The groundwork of science. N.Y., 1898.
	Phil 5620.4	Mivart, S.G. Origin of human reason. London, 1889.
	Phil 187.17.9	Mivart, St. G. The helpful science. N.Y., 1895.
	Phil 365.3	Mivart, St. G. A limit to evolution. London? 1884.
	Phil 187.17	Mivart, St. G. Nature and thought. London, 1882.
	Phil 187.17.5	Mivart, St. G. On truth. London, 1889.
	Phil 8667.54	Mizor, Nikolai. Metadologicheski problemi na ateizma. Sofiia, 1970.
	Phil 4520.8.50	Mjarnason, Ágúst. Rannsókn dularfullra fyrirbrigd. Reykjavík, 1914.
	Phil 974.2.70	Mme. Blatavsky defended. (Harris, Iverson L.) San Diego, 1971.
	Phil 5592.155	An MMPI handbook. (Dahistrom, W.G.) Minneapolis, 1960.
	Phil 5545.54.10	The mneme. (Semon, R.) Leipzig, 1921.
	Phil 5545.54	Die Mneme als erhaltendes Prinzip im Wechsel des organischen Gesehens. 3. Aufl. (Semon, R.) Leipzig, 1911.
	Phil 5545.54.15	Mnemic psychology. (Semon, R.) N.Y., 1923.
	Phil 5545.54.5	Die mnemischen Empfindungen. (Semon, R.) Leipzig, 1909.
	Phil 5545.53	Mnemonics. (D., T.W.) N.Y., 1844.
	Phil 5545.81	Mnemonics. (Pike, Robert.) Boston, 1848.
	Phil 5545.80	Mnemonics applied to acquisition of knowledge. (Pike, Robert, Jr.) Boston, 1844.
	Phil 5545.64	Mnemosyne, Organ für Gedächtniskunst. Leipzig, 1883-1885.
	Phil 5545.176	Das mnemotechnische Schrifttum. (Hajdu, H.) Wien, 1936.
	Phil 5545.19.5	Mnemotechny, or art of memory. 1. English ed. (Miles, Pliny.) London, 1850.
Htn	Phil 7069.11.45*	Moberly, C.A.E. An adventure. London, 1911.
	Phil 7069.11.48	Moberly, C.A.E. An adventure. 4th ed. London, 1931.
	Phil 5052.7	Moberly, Charles Edward. Lectures on logic. Photoreproduction. Oxford, 1848.
	Phil 1750.21	Le mobilisme moderne. (Chide, A.) Paris, 1908.
	Phil 7140.132	Mobilizing the mid-brain. (Pierce, Frederick.) N.Y., 1924.
	Phil 5252.39.2	Mobius, P. Die Hoffnungslosigkeit allen Psychologie. Halle, 1907.
	Phil 6322.1.10	Mobius, P.J. Über den Begriff der Hysterie und andere Vorwürfe vorwegend psychologischer Art. Leipzig, 1894.
	Phil 6322.1.5	Mobius, P.J. Vermischte Aufsätze. Leipzig, 1898.
	Phil 343.15	Mochi, Alberto. La connaissance scientifique. Paris, 1927.
	Phil 343.15.5	Mochi, Alberto. De la connaissance à l'action. Paris, 1928.
	Phil 4769.1.103	Mochul'skiĭ, K. Vladimir Solov'ev; zhizn' i uchenie. Paris, 1936.
	Phil 4769.1.104	Mochul'skiĭ, K. Vladimir Solov'ev. 2. izd. Parizh, 1951.
	Phil 4600.4.38	Modärna apologeter. (Lidforss, Bengt.) Malmö, 1911.
	Phil 5066.24.5	Modal logics. (Feys, Robert.) Louvain, 1965.
	Phil 5047.12	The modalist, or The laws of rational conviction. (Hamilton, E.J.) Boston, 1891.
	Phil 5500.7	La modalité du jugement. Thèse. (Brunschvicg, Léon.) Paris, 1897.
	Phil 5500.7.3	La modalité du jugement. 3.éd. (Brunschvicg, Léon.) Paris, 1964.
	Phil 3450.18.130	Die Modallehre Nicolai Hartmanns. (Feuerstein, R.) Köln? 1957.
	Phil 3425.680	Das Modalproblem und die historische Handlung. (Rollwage, Jürgen.) München, 1969.
	Phil 6111.63	A model of the mind. (Blum, Gerald S.) N.Y., 1961.
	Phil 9070.36	Modelando el porvenir. (Garcia, Garia.) Lima, 1944.
	Phil 8881.77	Le modèle en morale. (Gobry, Ivan.) Paris, 1962.
	Phil 5590.463	Les modèles de la personnalité en psychologie. 9e symposium de l'association de psychologie scientifique de langue française. (Association de Psychologie Scientifique de Langue Française.) Paris, 1965.
	Phil 5274.2	Les modêles et la formalisation du comportement. (Colloque International sur les Modèles et la Formalisation du Comportement, Paris, 1965.) Paris, 1967.
	Phil 5520.706	Modelirovanie myshleniia. (Kochergin, Al'bert N.) Moskva, 1969.
	Phil 5274.5	Modelirovanie psikhicheskoi deiatel'nosti. Moskva, 1969.
	Phil 6322.50	Modell, Arnold H. Object love and reality. N.Y., 1968.
	Phil 6322.51	Modell, Arnold H. Object love and reality: an introduction to a psychoanalytic theory of object relations. London, 1969.
	Phil 1905.32.30	Models and metaphores. (Black, Max.) N.Y., 1962.
	Phil 5467.7	Models and mystery. (Ramsey, I.T.) London, 1964.
	Phil 5066.314	Models for modalities. (Hintikka, Kaarlo Jaakko Johani.) Dordrecht, Holland, 1969.
	Phil 5643.140	Models for the perception of speech and visual form; proceedings of a symposium. Cambridge, 1967.
	Phil 5350.6	Models of change and response uncertainty. (Coleman, James Samuel.) Englewood Cliffs, N.J., 1964.
	Phil 5520.638	Models of thinking. (George, Frank Honywill.) London, 1970.
	Phil 4160.5.280	Modenato, Francesca. Intenzionalità e storia in Renato Lazzarini. Bologna, 1967.
	Phil 8893.74	Modern; romantik och etik. (Sandström, A.) Stockholm, 1898.
	Phil 8080.4.5	Modern aesthetics. (Listowel, William Francis Hare.) N.Y., 1967.
NEDL	Phil 7054.123	Modern American spiritualism. (Britten, Emma H.) N.Y., 1870.
	Phil 7054.123.2	Modern American spiritualism. 4th ed. (Britten, Emma H.) N.Y., 1870.
	Phil 6980.504	Modern attitudes in psychiatry. (New York Academy of Medicine.) N.Y., 1946.
	Phil 8643.30	Modern belief in immortality. (Smyth, Newman.) N.Y., 1910.
	Phil 8400.28.3	A modern book of esthetics. 3. ed. (Rader, M.M.) N.Y., 1962.
	Phil 8580.30A	Modern Christian revolutionaries. (Attwater, D.) N.Y., 1947.
	Phil 7054.81	Modern Christian spiritualism. Philadelphia, 1863.
	Phil 8610.875.25	Modern Christianity, a civilized heathenism. (Pullen, H.W.) Boston, 1875.
	Phil 8610.875.27	Modern Christianity, a civilized heathenism. (Pullen, H.W.) N.Y., 1879.
	Phil 8610.875.30	Modern Christianity, a civilized heathenism. (Pullen, H.W.) N.Y., 1901.
	Phil 1717.6	Modern classical philosophers. (Rand, Benjamin.) Boston, 1908.
	Phil 1717.6.3A	Modern classical philosophers. (Rand, Benjamin.) Boston, 1908.
	Phil 1717.6.6A	Modern classical philosophers. (Rand, Benjamin.) Boston, 1936.
	Phil 1717.6.5A	Modern classical philosophers. 2nd ed. (Rand, Benjamin.) Boston, 1924.
	Phil 6323.7.2	Modern clinical psychiatry. 2d ed. (Noyes, Arthur P.) Philadelphia, 1939.
	Phil 6323.7.5	Modern clinical psychiatry. 5th ed. (Noyes, Arthur P.) Philadelphia, 1958.
	Phil 8583.24	A modern conception of religion. (Deyo, M.L.) Binghamton, 1933.
	Phil 6328.54	Modern concepts of psychoanalysis. (Salzman, Leon.) N.Y., 1962.
	Phil 7054.173.15	The modern craze of spiritualism. (Meyer, F.B.) London, 1919.
	Phil 7054.58	Modern diabolism; commonly called modern spiritualism. (Williamson, M.J.) N.Y., 1873.
	Phil 5058.46.25	A modern elementary logic. (Stebbing, Lizzie S.) London, 1943.

Phil 1718.5	Modern European philosophy. (Snider, Denton J.) Saint Louis, 1904.
Phil 7069.54.5	Modern experiments in telepathy. (Soal, Samuel G.) New Haven, 1954.
Phil 2406.2	Modern French philosophy. (Gunn, J.A.) London, 1922.
Phil 2406.2.2	Modern French philosophy. (Gunn, J.A.) N.Y., 1922.
Phil 665.106	Modern Greek philosophers on the human soul. (Cavarnos, Constantine.) Belmont, 1967.
Phil 4843.2	Modern Greek thought. (Cavarnos, Constantine Peter.) Belmont, Mass., 1969.
Phil 4870.16	Modern ideological struggle for the ancient philosophical heritage of India. (Anikeev, Nikolai Petrovich.) Calcutta, 1969.
Phil 4870.12	Modern Indian thought; a philosophical survey. (Naravane, Vishwanath S.) Bombay, 1964.
Phil 8610.801.5	Modern infidelity considered. (Hall, Robert.) Philadelphia, 1853.
Phil 8881.75	A modern introduction to ethics. (Garvin, Lucius.) Boston, 1953.
Phil 5041.70	A modern introduction to logic. (Blyth, J.W.) Boston, 1957.
Phil 5058.46	A modern introduction to logic. (Stebbing, Lizzie S.) London, 1930.
Phil 5058.46.3	A modern introduction to logic. 2. ed. (Stebbing, Lizzie S.) N.Y., 1933.
Phil 5058.46.7	A modern introduction to logic. 7. ed. (Stebbing, Lizzie S.) London, 1961.
Phil 165.324	A modern introduction to metaphysics. (Drennen, D.) N.Y., 1962.
Phil 8887.110.10	A modern introduction to moral philosophy. (Montefiore, Alan.) London, 1964.
Phil 8887.110.5	A modern introduction to moral philosophy. (Montefiore, Alan.) N.Y., 1959.
Phil 165.105	A modern introduction to philosophy. (Edwards, Paul.) Glencoe, Illinois, 1957.
Phil 165.105.2	A modern introduction to philosophy. (Edwards, Paul.) N.Y., 1965.
Phil 5250.42	A modern introduction to psychology. 5. ed. (Knight, Rex.) London, 1957.
Phil 8630.7	Modern light on immortality. 2. ed. (Frank, Henry.) Boston, 1909.
Phil 7069.35.10	Modern loaves and fishes. (Haley, P.S.) San Francisco, 1935.
Phil 6951.16	The modern malady. (Bennett, C.) London, 1890.
Phil 8592.57.5	Modern man and religion. (Masaryk, T.G.) London, 1938.
Phil 6319.1.43	Modern man in search of a soul. (Jung, C.G.) N.Y., 1947.
Phil 8581.36	Modern man's religion. (Brown, Charles R.) N.Y., 1911.
Phil 6124.7	Modern materialism; readings on mind-body identity. (O'Connor, John.) N.Y., 1969.
Phil 487.7	Modern materialism. (Mann, Walter.) London, 1921.
Phil 487.2.2	Modern materialism. (Martineau, J.) Boston, 1876.
Phil 487.2	Modern materialism. (Martineau, J.) London, 1876.
Phil 493.6.5	Modern materialism. (Seely, Charles Sherlock.) N.Y., 1960.
Phil 487.6.3	Modern materialism and emergent evolution. (McDougall, William.) N.Y., 1929.
Phil 487.6.5	Modern materialism and emergent evolution. 2. ed. (McDougall, William.) London, 1934.
Phil 1717.14	The modern mind. (Roberts, Michael.) London, 1937.
Phil 7068.55.14	Modern mysteries, explained and exposed. (Mahan, A.) Boston, 1885.
Phil 7054.107	Modern mysteries explained and exposed. (Mahan, A.) Boston, 1855.
Phil 525.87.5	Modern mystics. 1st ed. (Younghusband, F.E.) N.Y., 1935.
Phil 7054.50	Modern mystics and modern magic. (Lillie, Arthur.) N.Y., 1894.
Phil 7054.118.5	Modern nirvanaism. (Danmar, William.) Jamaica, 1921.
Phil 7054.118	Modern nirvanaism. (Danmar, William.) N.Y., 1914.
Phil 8581.59	The modern notion of faith. Diss. (Bauer, Joachim M.) Washington, 1930.
Phil 1707.1.13	Modern philosophers. (Höffding, H.) London, 1915.
Phil 1712.16	Modern philosophers. (McElroy, H.C.) N.Y., 1950.
Phil 1701.1.2	Modern philosophy. (Bowen, F.) N.Y., 1877.
Phil 1701.1	Modern philosophy. (Bowen, F.) N.Y., 1877.
Phil 812.3.4	Modern philosophy. (Maurice, J.F.D.) London, 1862.
Phil 1717.8.5A	Modern philosophy. (Ruggiero, G. de.) London, 1921.
Phil 1701.1.3	Modern philosophy. 2nd ed. (Bowen, F.) N.Y., 1877.
Phil 2270.80	Modern physical fatalism. (Birks, T.R.) London, 1876.
Phil 8595.40	The modern predicament. (Paton, H.J.) London, 1955.
Phil 8957.6	Modern problems and Christian ethics. (Hocking, William J.) London, 1898.
Phil 186.69	Modern problems in philosophy. (Laird, John.) London, 1928.
Phil 7069.29.45	Modern psychic mysteries. (Hack, Gwendolyn Kelley.) London, 1929.
Phil 7069.19.40	Modern psychical phenomena. (Carrington, Hereward.) N.Y., 1919.
Phil 6311.7	Modern Psychoanalyse, katholische, beichte und pädagogik. (Bopp, L.) Kempten, 1923.
Phil 5251.36	Modern psychology, normal and abnormal. (Leary, Daniel Bell.) Philadelphia, 1928.
Phil 5255.45	Modern psychology. (Pennsylvania. University. Bicentennial Conference.) Philadelphia, 1941.
Phil 6323.6	Modern psychology in practice. (Neustatter, W.L.) Philadelphia, 1937.
Phil 8580.16.10	Modern religious cults. (Atkins, Gaius G.) N.Y., 1923.
Phil 8725.18	The modern schism. 1. ed. (Marty, Martin E.) N.Y., 1969.
Phil 22.24F	The modern schoolman. St. Louis, Mo. 11-19,1933-1942 6v.
Phil 22.24	The modern schoolman. St. Louis, Mo. 20,1942+ 18v.
Phil 5762.19	Modern science and human freedom. (Miller, David L.) Austin, 1959.
Phil 8701.7.2	Modern science and modern thought. 2. ed. (Laing, Samuel.) London, 1885.
Phil 2475.1.415	Modern science and the illusions of Professor Bergson. (Elliots, Hugh Samuel Roger.) London, 1912.
Phil 8702.3.5	Modern science unlocking the Bible. (Mackenzie, H.) London, 1892.
Phil 1511.3.14	A modern social philosophy. (Gunn, W.W.) Cutting, 1937.
Phil 6961.16	Modern society and mental diseases. (Landis, C.) N.Y., 1938.
Phil 7069.20.298	Modern spiritism. (Schofield, A.T.) London, 1920.
Phil 7069.09.17	Modern spiritism. 2. ed. (Raupert, John G.) St. Louis, 1909.
Phil 7054.40	Modern spiritualism; or Opening way. (Hall, T.B.) Boston, 1883.
Phil 7054.90	Modern spiritualism. (Constantine, T.C.) Manchester, 1858.
Phil 7069.02.11	Modern spiritualism. (Podmore, Frank.) London, 1902. 2v.
Phil 7069.28.75	Modern spiritualism. (Thurston, Herbert.) St-Louis, 1928.
Phil 7054.115	Modern spiritualism: its facts and fanaticisms. (Capron, Eliab W.) Boston 1855.
Phil 7054.137.3	Modern spiritualism compared with Christianity. (Tiffany, Joel.) Warren, Ohio, 1855.
Phil 9075.11	Modern study of conscience. (Huckel, O.) Philadelphia, 1907.
Phil 6980.355	Modern svensk psykiatri under redaktion av Gunnar Holmberg. (Holmberg, Gunnar.) Stockholm, 1908.
Phil 8632.9	A modern symposium. (Harrison, Frederic.) Detroit, 1878.
Phil 1710.5.3	The modern temper. (Krutch, Joseph W.) N.Y., 1929.
Phil 1710.5.5	The modern temper. (Krutch, Joseph W.) N.Y., 1930.
Phil 189.22.5	The modern theme. (Ortega y Gasset, José.) London, 1931.
Phil 4365.2.38	The modern theme. (Ortega y Gasset, José.) N.Y., 1933.
Phil 1719.2	Modern theories in philosophy and religion. (Tullock, J.) Edinburgh, 1884.
Phil 8602.16	Modern theories of religion. (Waterhouse, E.S.) London, 1910.
Phil 5722.13	Modern theories of the unconscious. (Northbridge, W.L.) London, 1924.
Phil 8893.79	A modern theory of ethics. (Stapledon, W.O.) London, 1929.
Phil 22.5	Modern Thinker. 1-2,1870-1872
Phil 193.95	Modern thinkers and present problems. (Singer, Edgar A.) N.Y., 1923.
Phil 1750.106	Modern Thomistic philosophy. (Phillips, Richard P.) London, 1934-40. 2v.
Phil 8712.10	Modern thought and crisis in belief. (Wenley, R.M.) N.Y., 1909.
Phil 6957.7.5	The modern treatment of mental disorders. (Hart, Bernard.) Manchester, 1918.
Phil 9550.1	Modern utilitarianism. (Birks, T.R.) London, 1874.
Phil 186.53.5	De moderna verldsåsigterna. (Luthardt, C.E.) Lund, 1880.
Phil 5870.90	Die moderne Elternschule. (Clauser, Günter.) Freiburg, 1969.
Phil 5865.6.2	Moderne Entwicklungspsychologie. 2. Aufl. (Oerter, Rolf.) Donauwörth, 1968.
Phil 5238.45	Moderne Entwicklungsychologie. Berlin, 1956.
Phil 735.108	Die moderne ethische Wertphilosophie. (Störring, G.) Leipzig, 1935.
Phil 1713.4	Moderne filosofer. (Naess, Arne.) Stockholm, 1965.
Phil 5041.58.7	Moderne logica. 2. druk. (Beth, Evert Willem.) Assen, 1967.
Phil 7069.21.43	Der moderne Okkultismus in Lichte des Experiments! (Kirchhoff, P.) Köln, 1921.
Phil 9430.29	Der moderne Pessimismus. (Golther, L. von.) Leipzig, 1878.
Phil 9430.11	Der moderne Pessimismus. (Schädelin, K.F.E.) Bern, 1878.
Phil 9430.27	Der moderne Pessimismus. (Voigt, G.) Heilbronn, 1889.
Phil 3010.14	Moderne Philosophen; Porträts und Charakteristiken. (Kronenberg, Moritz.) München, 1899.
Phil 1707.1.9	Moderne Philosophen. (Höffding, H.) Leipzig, 1905.
Phil 180.22	Moderne Philosophie. (Frischeisen-Köhler, M.) Stuttgart, 1907.
Phil 5240.53	Moderne Physik und Tiefenpsychologie. (Anrich, Ernst.) Stuttgart, 1963.
Phil 3415.71	Moderne Probleme. (Hartmann, Eduard von.) Leipzig, 1886.
Phil 3415.71.2	Moderne Probleme. 2. Aufl. (Hartmann, Eduard von.) Leipzig, 1888.
Phil 1717.9	Moderne Propheten. (Rösener, Karl.) München, 1907.
Phil 5247.17	Die moderne Psychologie. (Hartmann, E.) Leipzig, 1901.
Phil 5257.37	Der moderne psychophysische Parallelismus. Inaug. Diss. (Reiff, Paul.) Heilbronn, 1901.
Phil 5222.22	Moderne psykologiske teorier. 2. oplag. (Madsen, K.B.) København, 1969.
Phil 5330.6.2	Die moderne psysiologische Psychologie...Aufmerksamkeit. (Heinrich, W.) Leipzig, 1895.
Phil 5330.6	Die moderne psysiologische Psychologie...Aufmerksamkeit. (Heinrich, W.) Zürich, 1899.
Phil 665.7.15	Die moderne Seele. 3e Aufl. (Messer, Max.) Leipzig, 1903.
Phil 5258.96.5	Die moderne Seelenlehre; Begabungsforschung und Berufsberatung. 3. Aufl. (Schulze, Rudolf.) Leipzig, 1921.
Phil 5252.93	Moderne Seinsprobleme in ihrer Bedeutung für die Psychologie. (Meinertz, Josef.) Heidelberg, 1948.
Phil 7069.06.7	Die moderne Spuk- und Geisterglaube. (Hennig, R.) Hamburg, 1906.
Phil 8583.12	Moderne Versuche eines Religionsersatzes. (Drustowitz, H.) Heidelberg, 1886.
Phil 176.110	Die moderne Weltanschauung. (Becker, Carl.) Berlin, 1911.
Phil 735.243	Die moderne Wertethik. (Wittmann, M.) Münster, 1940.
Phil 5757.17	Moderne Willensziele. (Hilbert, Gerhard.) Leipzig, 1911.
Phil 6120.1	Die modernen Theorien über Verhältnis von Leib und Seele. (Klein, A.) Breslau, 1906.
Phil 8667.45	Moderner Atheismus und Moral. Freiburg, 1968.
Phil 8592.57	Moderní člověk a náboženství. (Masaryk, T.G.) Praha, 1934.
Phil 4809.727.35	Moderní věda. (Rádl, Emanuel.) Praha, 1926.
Phil 197.20	Modernism according to the law of sensual impression. (Wright, A.L.) Albany, 1910.
Phil 8586.32	Modernity and the churches. (Gardner, P.) London, 1909.
Phil 8092.16	Modernizm bez maski. (Gus, Mikhail S.) Moskva, 1966.
Phil 2340.11.50	Modes of being. (Weiss, Paul.) New Haven, 1956. 2v.
Phil 2340.10.98A	Modes of thought. (Whitehead, Alfred North.) N.Y., 1938.
Phil 2340.10.98.5	Modes of thought. (Whitehead, Alfred North.) N.Y., 1956.
Phil 960.138	Modi, P.M. Aksara, a forgotten chapter in the history of Indian philosophy. Inaug. Diss. Baroda, 1932.
Phil 5057.24	Die Modification en des Logik. (Rosenkranz, Karl.) Leipzig, 1846.
Phil 8950.8	Modo para vivir eternamento. (Arrese y Ontiveros, Pedro Alexandro de.) Madrid, 1710.
Phil 186.135	Modus operandi. (Loehrich, R.R.) McHenry, Ill., 1956.
Phil 3200.16.30	Moe obrashchenie. 2. izd. (Ebner, Felix.) Moskva, 1903.
Phil 3120.15.90	Moebius, A. Constantin Brunners Lehre, das Evangelium. Berlin, 1910.
Phil 6122.10	Möbius, P.J. Das Nervensystem des Menschen. Leipzig, 1880.
Phil 6322.1.15	Möbius, P.J. Die Nervosität. 3e Aufl. Leipzig, 1906.
Phil 6322.1	Möbius, P.J. Stachyologie, weitere vermischte Aufsätze. Leipzig, 1909.
Phil 5932.3	Möbius, P.J. Über die Anlage zur Mathematik. Leipzig, 1900.
Phil 3808.102	Möbius, P.J. Über Schopenhauer. Leipzig, 1899.
Phil 3635.6	Möbius, Paul. Ausgewählte Werke. Leipzig, 1905-11. 8v.

Phil 9495.33   Moechialogie, traité des péchés contre les sixième et neuvième commandements du décalogue. 4th ed. (Debreyne, P.J.C.) Paris, 1868.

Phil 5850.274   Moede, Walther. Lehrbuch der Psychotechnik. Berlin, 1930.

Phil 3850.27.180   Møde med Albert Schweitzer. (Rode, Ebbe.) København, 1959.

Phil 3450.18.150   Möglichkeit und Notwendigkeit. (Beck, Heinrich.) Pullach, 1961.

Phil 3850.24.90   Die Möglichkeit der Gotteserkenntnis in der Philosophie Gideon Spickers. Diss. (Beuschlein, K.) Würzburg, 1914.

Phil 346.4   Möglichkeit und Widerspruschlosigkeit. (Pichler, H.) Leipzig, 1912.

Phil 182.94.16   Möglichkeit und Wirklichkeit. (Hartmann, N.) Berlin, 1938.

Phil 3450.19.225   Möglichkeit und Wirklichkeit bei M. Heidegger. (Mueller-Lauter, W.) Berlin, 1960.

Phil 6980.321   Möglichkeiten moderner Psychotherapien. (Gesellschaft zur Örderung Tiefenpsychologischer und Psychotherapeutischer Forschung und Weiterbildung in München.) Göttingen, 1967.

Phil 180.49   Der Möglichkeitsgedanke. (Faust, August.) Heidelberg, 1931-1932. 2v.

Phil 1750.356   Möller, J. Existenzialphilosophie und katholische Theologie. Baden-Baden, 1952.

Phil 2880.8.130   Moeller, Joseph. Absurdes sein? Stuttgart, 1959.

Phil 3425.342   Möller, Joseph. Der Geist und das Absolute. Paderborn, 1951.

Phil 9070.100   Moeller, Orla. At vaere ung. København, 1962.

Phil 8592.33   Møller, Otto. Noget om determinisme og frihed. Kjøbenhavn, 1893.

Phil 3625.5.91   Moeltzner, A. Salomon Maimons erkenntnistheoretische Verbesserungsveruche der Kantischen Philosophie. Inaug. Diss. Greifswald, 1889.

Phil 9075.77   Mönks, Franz. Gewetens groei en gewetens functie. Nijmogen, 1967.

Phil 3552.311   Mönnich, Conrad Willem. De natuurlijke kennis gods bij Leibniz. Rotterdam, 1942.

Phil 3494.70.2   Mörchen, Hermann. Die Einbildungskraft bei Kant. 2. Aufl. Tübingen, 1970.

Phil 8413.24   Moerth, L. Was ist Schön? Eine ästhetische Studie. München, 1913?

Phil 3450.18.175   Moeslang, Alois. Finalität. Freiburg, 1964.

Htn   Phil 8894.8.2   Les moeurs. (Toussaint, F.V.) Amsterdam, 1763.

Htn   Phil 8894.8.5*   Les moeurs. pt. 3. (Toussaint, F.V.) Amsterdam, 1748.

Htn   Phil 8894.8.3*   Les moeurs. pt.1-2,3. (Toussaint, F.V.) Aux Indes, 1749.

Htn   Phil 8894.8*   Les moeurs. 4th ed. (Toussaint, F.V.) n.p., 1749.

Phil 8881.42.9   Les moeurs du temps. 3e éd. (Gaultier, Paul.) Paris, 1928.

Phil 8413.22   Moffat, J.C. An introduction to the study of aesthetics. Cincinnati, 1856.

Phil 8592.70   Moffatt, J. The thrill of tradition. London, 1944.

Phil 4210.130   Moglia, A. I suareziani e l'abate Rosmini. Piacenza, 1882.

Phil 4170.2.80   Pamphlet box. Moglia, Agostino.

Phil 310.699   Mognénost čovjeka. (Petrović, Gajo.) Zagreb, 1969.

Phil 3425.574   Mogućnost, nužnost, slučajnost, stvarnost. (Focht, I.) Sarajevo, 1961.

Phil 3450.11.315   Mohanty, J.N. Edmund Husserl's theory of meaning. The Hague, 1964.

Phil 3450.18.125   Mohanty, J.N. Nicolai Hartmann and Alfred North Whitehead. Calcutta, 1957.

Phil 418.16   Mohanty, Jitendra Nath. The concept of intentionality. St. Louis, 1971.

Phil 583.12   Mohanty, Jitendra Nath. Phenomenology and ontology. Den Haag, 1970.

Phil 8092.9   Moholy-Nagy, L. Vision in motion. Chicago, 1956.

Phil 6122.48   Mohr, Fritz. Psychophysische Behandlungs-Methoden. Leipzig, 1925.

Phil 8962.21   Mohr, R. Die christliche Ethik im Lichte der Ethnologie. München, 1954.

Phil 2725.21   Le moi, le monde et Dieu. (Lachièze-Rey, P.) Paris, 1938.

Phil 2725.35.30   Le moi et son destin. (Lavelle, Louis.) Paris, 1936.

Phil 8702.11   Moigno, F.N.M. Un pequeño libro de actualidad. Puerto Rico, 1884.

Phil 8667.7   Moisant, Xavier. Dieu. Paris, 1907.

Phil 6315.2.79.10   Moïse et la monothéisme. 8 éd. (Freud, Sigmund.) Paris, 1948.

Phil 2750.22.80   Moix, Candide. Emmanuel Mounier. Paris, 1960.

Phil 583.18   Mokrejš, Antonín. Fenomenologie a problém intersubjektivity. 1. Vyd. Praha, 1969.

Phil 270.31   Mokrzycki, G. Relativisierung des Kausalitätsbegriffes. Leipzig, 1922.

Phil 8413.38   Molchanova, Albina S. Na vkus, na tsvet. Moskva, 1966.

Phil 8887.70   Molé, L.M. Essai de morale et de politique. Paris, 1791.

Phil 8430.3.5   Moles, Abraham A. Information theory and esthetic perception. Urbana, 1966.

Phil 8430.3   Moles, Abraham A. Théorie de l'information et perception esthétique. Paris, 1958.

Phil 487.1.10   Moleschott, J. La circulation de la vie. Paris, 1866.

Phil 487.1   Moleschott, J. De Kreislauf des Lebens. Mainz, 1857.

Phil 487.1.4   Moleschott, J. Der Kreislauf des Lebens. Giessen, 1875-87. 2v.

Phil 487.1.3   Moleschott, J. Der Kreislauf des Lebens. Mainz, 1855.

Phil 487.1.5   Moleschott, J. Licht und Leben. Frankfurt, 1856.

Phil 8622.70   Molevez, Léopold. Pour une théologie de la foi. Paris, 1969.

Phil 8592.114   Molina, Antonio de. Excercicios espirituales de las excelencias, provecho y necesidad. Barcelona, 1702.

Phil 4363.6.10   Molina, E. Confesión filosófica y llamado de superación a la América Hispana. Santiago, 1942.

Phil 4363.6   Molina, E. De lo espiritual. Concepcion, 1937.

Phil 2630.2.133   Molina, Enrique. Dos filosofos contemporaneos; Guyau-Bergson. Santiago de Chile, 1925.

Phil 3640.312   Molina, Enrique. Nietzsche, dionisíaco y asceta. Santiago, 1944.

Phil 2475.1.265   Molina, Enrique. Proyecciones de la intuición. Santiago de Chile, 1935.

Phil 4974.50.2   Molina, Enrique. Tragedia y realización del espíritu. 2. ed. Santiago, 1953.

Phil 1750.715   Molina, Fernando. Existentialism as philosophy. N.Y., 1962.

Phil 4080.3.145   Molina, G. Saggio su Benedetto Croce. Genova, 1928.

Phil 2050.267   Molinari, Ernesto. L'utopia controllata. Milano, 1964.

Phil 8592.50.5   Molinari, G. de. Religion. 2. ed. London, 1894.

Phil 4363.2.37   Molinos, M. de. Golden thoughts from the spiritual guide. N.Y., 1883.

Phil 4363.2.5   Molinos, M. de. Guia espiritual. Barcelona, 1906.

Htn   Phil 4363.2.30*   Molinos, M. de. The spiritual guide. Venice, 1688.

Phil 4363.2.36   Molinos, M. de. The spiritual guide of Michael de Molinos. London, 191-?

Phil 4363.2.35   Molinos, M. de. The spiritual guide of Michael de Molinos. Philadelphia, 1897.

Phil 4363.2.80A   Molinos the quietist. (Bigelow, John.) N.Y., 1882.

Htn   Phil 4363.2.81*   Molinos the quietist. (Bigelow, John.) N.Y., 1882.

Phil 8887.115   Molitor, Arnulf. Zum Formalismus in der neueren Ethik. Wien, 1960.

Phil 2520.195   Molitor, Emil. Über die Realitätstheorie Descartes'. Inaug.-Diss. Mayen, 1935.

Phil 7069.25.20   Moll, A. Der Spiritismus. Stuttgart, 1925.

Htn   Phil 7075.8*   Moll, Albert. Die conträre Sexualempfindung. Berlin, 1891.

X Cg   Phil 7075.8.3   Moll, Albert. Die conträre Sexualempfindung. Berlin, 1899.

Phil 6682.6.3   Moll, Albert. Hypnotism. London, 1892.

Phil 6682.6.9   Moll, Albert. Hypnotism. London, 1909?

Phil 6682.6.15   Moll, Albert. Hypnotism. 2. ed. London, 1890.

Phil 6682.6.4   Moll, Albert. Hypnotism. 4th ed. London, 1898.

Phil 2750.16.30   Molle, G. van. La connaissance dialectique et l'expérience existentielle. Liège, 1945.

Phil 2555.7.93   Molle, Germaine van. La philosophie de Paul Decoster. Bruxelles, 1940.

Phil 1750.166.175   Mollenauer, Robert. Introduction to modernity. Austin, 1965.

Phil 3494.48   Mollowitz, Gerhard. Kants Platosuffassung. Berlin, 1935.

Phil 310.562   Molnár, Erik. Les antécédents idéologiques du matérialisme historique. Budapest, 1965.

Phil 2636.88   Momdzhian, Khashik. Helvitius, ein streitbarer Atheist das 18. Jahrhunderts. Berlin, 1959.

Phil 2636.88.5   Momdzhian, Khashik. La philosophie d'Helvétius. Moscow, 1959.

Phil 3425.762   Moment et processus. (Palma, Norman.) Paris, 1970-

Phil 8612.57   The moment of truth. (Boros, Ladislaus.) London, 1965.

Phil 1117.16   Momenti del pensiero greco e cristiano. (Mondolfo, Rodolfo.) Napoli, 1964.

Phil 7069.67.80   Momenti e problemi dello spiritualismo. (Dollo, Corrado.) Padova, 1968.

Phil 7069.23.45   Momentous memoirs. (Wright A.A.) Boston, 1923.

Phil 8610.884.10   Momerie, A.W. Agnosticism. 2. ed. Edinburgh, 1887.

Phil 8592.12   Momerie, A.W. The basis of religion. Edinburgh, 1886.

Phil 8667.6   Momerie, A.W. Belief in God. Edinburgh, 1888.

Phil 575.2   Momerie, A.W. Personality. Edinburgh, 1879.

Phil 575.2.5   Momerie, A.W. Personality. Edinburgh, 189-?

Phil 575.2.2   Momerie, A.W. Personality. 3rd ed. Edinburgh, 1886.

Phil 575.2.3   Momerie, A.W. Personality. 4th ed. Edinburgh, 1889.

Phil 293.19   Momo, Giovanni. Sulla proposizione il mondo va da se. Lucca, 1827.

Phil 8887.135   Momov, Vasil M. Nravstvenata norma i neinata realizatsiia. Sofiia, 1969.

Phil 8400.25   Mon, Franz. Movens; Dokumente und Analysen zur Dichtung. Wiesbaden, 1960.

Phil 176.227   Mon moi dans l'être. (Balthasar, Nicolas J.J.) Louvain, 1946.

Phil 2880.1.65   Mon portrait historique et philosophique. (Saint-Martin, L.C.) Paris, 1961.

Phil 8592.20   Monaco, C. La ragione naturale. Caserta, 1888.

Phil 187.77   Monaco, Nicolao. Praelectiones metaphysicae specialis. Romae, 1917-1920. 3v.

Phil 510.153   Die Monade. (Cramer, Wolfgang.) Stuttgart, 1954.

Phil 182.134   Monade und Begriff. Der Weg von Leibniz zu Hegel. (Horn, Joachim Christian.) Wien, 1965.

Phil 510.22   Monaden und Weltphantasie. (Frohschammer, J.) München, 1879.

Phil 3552.116   De monadenleer van Leibniz. (Ritter, P.H.) Leiden, 1882.

Phil 510.145   Die Monadenlehre und ihre Beziehung zur griechischen Philosophie. (Penzler, Martin.) Minden, 1878.

Phil 3552.135   Monadlärans uppkomst. (Svahn, Oscar.) Lund, 1863.

Phil 3552.66.11   La monadologia. (Leibniz, Gottfried Wilhelm.) Milano, 1926.

Phil 3552.66.16   La monadologia. (Leibniz, Gottfried Wilhelm.) Torino, 1929.

NEDL Phil 3552.66   La monadologie, avec étude et notes. (Leibniz, Gottfried Wilhelm.) Paris, 1900.

Phil 3552.67   La monadologie. (Leibniz, Gottfried Wilhelm.) Paris, 1881.

Phil 3552.67.3   La monadologie. (Leibniz, Gottfried Wilhelm.) Paris, 1883.

Phil 3552.63.30   La monadologie. (Leibniz, Gottfried Wilhelm.) Paris, 1952.

Phil 3552.67.15   Monadologie. (Leibniz, Gottfried Wilhelm.) Wien, 1847.

Phil 3552.66.13   Monadologie. 2. Ausg. (Leibniz, Gottfried Wilhelm.) Stuttgart, 1954.

Phil 3552.67.5   La monadologie. 5. éd. (Leibniz, Gottfried Wilhelm.) Paris, n.d.

Phil 3499.3   Die monadologischen...Bestimmungen...Kant's. (Riedel, O.) Hamburg, 1884.

Phil 3552.67.40   Monadology, and other philosophical essays. (Leibniz, Gottfried Wilhelm.) Indianapolis, 1965.

Phil 3552.65   The monadology. (Leibniz, Gottfried Wilhelm.) Oxford, 1898.

Phil 3552.65.10   The monadology of Leibniz. (Leibniz, Gottfried Wilhelm.) Los Angeles, 1930.

Phil 5400.185   Monakow, Constantin. The emotions, morality and the brain. Washington, 1925.

Phil 6962.13   Monakow, Constantin von. Gehirnpathologie. 2. Aufl. Wien, 1905. 2v.

Phil 6322.21   Monakow, Constantin von. Introduction biologique à l'étude de la neurologie et de la psychopathologie. Paris, 1928.

Phil 4073.36   Monarchia Messiae. (Campanella, Tommaso.) Torino, 1960.

Phil 22.10   Monatsschrift für Kriminalpsychologie und Strafrecht. Heidelberg. 3-11,1906-1915 9v.

Phil 176.41   Monboddo, James Barnet. Ancient metaphysics. v.1-6. Edinburgh, 1779-99. 7v.

Phil 5052.8   Monck, W.H.S. An introduction to logic. Dublin, 1880.

Phil 3494.6   Monck, W.H.S. Introduction to the critical philosophy. Dublin, 1874.

Phil 2035.85   Monck, W.H.S. Sir William Hamilton. English philosopher. London, 1881.

Phil 5643.17   Monck, W.H.S. Space and vision. Dublin, 1872.

Phil 6322.30   Moncrieff, A.A. Psychology in general practice. London, 1945.

Phil 9172.4.2   Moncrieff, A.H. A book about boys. 2. ed. Edinburgh, 1868.

Phil 8402.36   Il monda sensbile. (Baratono, A.) Milano, 1934.

Phil 6962.22   Mondain, Paul. Les fous satisfaits. Paris, 1933.

Htn   Phil 2520.62.5*   Le monde. (Descartes, René.) Paris, 1664.

Phil 8956.18   Un monde ambigu. (Gaboury, Placide.) Montréal, 1968.

Phil 3808.35.28   Le monde comme volonté et comme représentation. 8. éd. v.3. (Schopenhauer, Arthur.) Paris, 1943.

Phil 5465.21   Le monde des images; suite de l'hérédo. (Daudet, Léon.) Paris, 1919.

Phil 7082.152.2   Le monde des rêves. 2. éd. (Simon, Paul Max.) Paris, 1888.

Phil 4075.86   Le monde enchanté de la Renaissance. (Lucas Dubreton, D.) Paris, 1954.

Phil 8661.3   Monde et Dieu. (Guilbert, A.V.F.) Paris, 1879.

Phil 3450.19.535   Monde et être chez Heidegger. (Cauturier, Fernand.) Montréal, 1971.

Phil 2855.9.30   Le monde et ses remèdes. (Rosset, Clément.) Paris, 1964.

Phil 177.27   La monde extérieur. (Cochin, D.) Paris, 1895.

Phil 8886.57   Monde moral, l'ordre des fins et des progrès. (Lagresille, Henry.) Paris, 1911.

Phil 6673.1   Le monde prophétique. (Delaage, M.H.) Paris, 1853.

Phil 3808.38.5   Il mondo come volontà e rappresentazione. 2. ed. (Schopenhauer, Arthur.) Bari, 1920-21. 2v.

Phil 8886.56   Il mondo degli uomini. (Lombardi, F.) Firenze, 1935.

Phil 4007.5   Il mondo della sicurezza; Ardigo, Labriola, Croce. (Guerra, Augusto.) Firenze, 1963.

Phil 802.11   Il mondo delle idee. pt. 1a, 2a. (Capone Braga, G.) Città di Cástello, 1928-33. 2v.

Phil 2250.43.5   Il mondo e l'individuo. (Royce, Josiah.) Bari, 1913-14. 4v.

Phil 1712.9   Mondolfo, R. Il dubbio metodico e la storia della filosofia. Padova, 1908.

Phil 1630.21   Mondolfo, R. Figure e idee della filosofia del Rinascimento. Firenze, 1963.

NEDL Phil 1135.154.5   Mondolfo, R. El infinitio en el pensamiento de la antiguedad clasica. Buenos Aires, 1952.

Phil 1135.154   Mondolfo, R. L'infinito nel pensiero dei Greci. Firenze, 1934.

Phil 1135.154.10   Mondolfo, R. L'infinito nel pensiero dell'antichita classica. Firenze, 1956.

Phil 5545.160   Mondolfo, R. Memoria e associazione nella scuola cartesiana. Firenze, 1900.

Phil 812.25   Mondolfo, R. Problemi e metodi di ricerca nella storia della filosofia. Firenze, 1952.

Phil 1117.8.5   Mondolfo, Rodolfo. La camprensione del soggeho. 1. ed. Firenze, 1958.

Phil 4012.7.5   Mondolfo, Rodolfo. Da Ardigò a Gramsci. Milano, 1962.

Phil 812.41.2   Mondolfo, Rodolfo. En los origenes de la filosofia. 2. ed. Buenos Aires, 1960.

Phil 4012.7   Mondolfo, Rodolfo. La filosofia politica de Italia en el siglo XIX. Buenos Aires, 1942.

Phil 1117.16   Mondolfo, Rodolfo. Momenti del pensiero greco e cristiano. Napoli, 1964.

Phil 1145.83   Mondolfo, Rodolfo. Moralistas griegos. Buenos Aires, 1941.

Phil 1117.8.10   Mondolfo, Rodolfo. El pensamiento antiguo. Buenos Aires, 1942. 2v.

Phil 1117.8.18   Mondolfo, Rodolfo. Il pensiero antico. 3. ed. Firenze, 1961.

Phil 4060.1.88   Mondolfo, Rodolfo. Il pensiero di Roberto Ardigo. Mantova, 1908.

Phil 1117.8   Mondolfo, Rodolfo. Problemi del pensiero antico. Bologna, 1935.

Phil 2493.90   Mondolfo, Rodolfo. Un psicologo associazionista: E.B. de Condillac. Bologna, 1923.

Phil 187.42   Mondolfo, Rodolfo. Saggi per la storia della morale utilitaria. Verona, 1903. 2 pam.

Phil 5403.16   Monedero Gil, Carmelo. La alegría. Madrid, 1970.

Phil 5401.11   Mones, L. Why be afraid? Boston, 1931.

Phil 2905.1.395   Monestier, André. Teilhard ou Marx? Paris, 1965.

Phil 5421.15.20   Money, power, and sex. (Stewart, David A.) N.Y., 1965.

Phil 6951.27   Money and emotional conflicts. 1. ed. (Bergler, E.) Garden City, 1951.

Phil 8886.1   Money and morals. (Lalor, J.) London, 1852.

Phil 9375.6   Money hunger. (Wood, H.A.W.) N.Y., 1908.

X Cg   Phil 7075.127   Money-Kyrle, R.E. The development of the sexual impulses. London, 1932.

Phil 6322.26.5   Money-Kyrle, R.E. Man's picture of his world. London, 1961.

Phil 9450.24   Money-Kyrle, R.E. Psychoanalysis and politics. N.Y., 1951.

Phil 6322.26   Money-Kyrle, R.E. Superstition and society. London, 1939.

Phil 402.8   Mongardini, Carlo. Storia del concetto di ideologia. Roma, 1968.

Phil 2885.114   Mongardini, Carlo. Storia e sociologia nell'opera di H. Taine. Milano, 1965.

Phil 510.1.1.5   Monism. (Haeckel, Ernst.) London, 1894.

Phil 510.1.1.7   Monism. (Haeckel, Ernst.) London, 1895.

Phil 510.1.29   Monism? (Marcus, S.P.) London, 1907.

Phil 22.6.5   Monism: its scope and review of The Monist. (Carus, P.) Chicago, 1890-1891.

Phil 510.6A   Monism and meliorism. (Carus, P.) N.Y., 1885.

Phil 510.8   Monism as the goal of civilization. (Ostwald, W.) Hamburg, 1913.

Phil 6116.15   The monism of man. (Gorton, D.A.) N.Y., 1893.

Phil 510.10   Le monisme matérialiste. (Saulze, J.B.) Paris, 1911.

Phil 510.140   Monisme vitaliste. (Cassaigneau, M.) Paris, 1925.

Phil 4065.111   Il monismo teosofico di G.B. (Acanfora-Venturelli, R.) Palermo, 1893.

Phil 510.19.2   Monismus, Monistenbund, Radikalismus und Christentum. 2e Aufl. (Weiss, Bruno.) Breme, 1908.

Phil 22.6.15   Der Monismus. Berlin. 1-7,1906-1912 5v.

Phil 510.1.1   Der Monismus als Band zwischen Religion und Wissenschaft. 6e Aufl. (Haeckel, Ernst.) Bonn, 1893.

Phil 510.139   Der Monismus dargestellt in Beiträgen seiner Vertreter. v.1-2. Jena, 1908.

Phil 510.144   Monismus in alter und neuer Zeit. (Wendland, J.) Basel, 1908.

Phil 3210.88   Monismus und Christentum bei G.T. Fechner. (Lülmann, C.) Berlin, 1917.

Phil 510.24   Monismus und Monotheismus. (Wobbermin, Georg.) Tübingen, 1911.

Phil 510.16   Der Monismus und seine Ideale. (Unold, Johannes.) Leipzig, 1908.

Phil 510.125.4   Monismus und Theologie. 4e Aufl. (Flügel, D.) Gotha, 1914.

Phil 22.6   The monist. Chicago. 1890-1891+ 51v.

Phil 22.6.3   The monist. Complete index. v.1-17. Chicago, 1908.

Phil 510.135   Die monistische Erkenntnislehre. (Mayer, A.) Leipzig, 1882.

Phil 8968.6   Monistische Ethik. (Stern, M.L.) Leipzig, 1911.

Phil 510.9   Der monistische Gedanke. (Noiré, Ludwig.) Leipzig, 1875.

Phil 510.3   Monistische Gottes und Weltanschuung. (Sack, J.) Leipzig, 1899.

Phil 22.6.20   Das monistische Jahrhundert. Leipzig. 1-4,1912-1915 6v.

Phil 510.132   Die monistische Philosophie. (Rosenthal, L.A.) Berlin, 1880.

Phil 510.4   Monistische Philosophie von Spinoza bis auf unserer Tage. (Reichenau, W.) Köln, 1884.

Phil 630.39   Der monistische Realismus im amerikanischen Denken. Inaug. Diss. (Heacock, Roger.) Berlin? 1933.

Phil 7060.34   Die monistische Seelenlehre. (Du Prel, C.F.) Leipzig, 1888.

Phil 510.8.5   Monistische Sonntagspredigten. Series 1-3,4. (Ostwald, W.) Leipzig, 1911-13. 2v.

Phil 510.11   Monistische Weltanschauung, (Olivier, J. von.) Leipzig, 1906.

Htn   Phil 5041.26*   Monitio logica, or An abstract and translation of Burgersdicius his Logick. (Burgersdijck, Franco.) London, 1697.

Phil 1712.24   Moniuszko, Antoni. Aczyistość i synteza. Warszawa, 1962.

Phil 7109.195   Moniz, Egas. O padre Faria na história do hipnotismo. Lisboa, 1925.

Phil 4475.1.80   Moniz Barreto, G. Oliveira Martins: estudo de psicologia. Paris, 1892.

Phil 510.157   Monizm kak printsip dialekticheskoi logiki. (Naumenko, Lev K.) Alma-Ata, 1968.

Phil 8110.3   Monk, S.H. The sublime; a study of critical theories in 18th century England. Ann Arbor, 1960.

Phil 4195.100   Monnerjahn, E. Giovanni Pico della Mirandola. Wiesbaden, 1960.

Phil 2750.33.30   Monnerot, Jules. Les lois du tragique. Paris, 1969.

Phil 6122.66   Monnier, Marcel. L'organisation des fonctions psychiques. Neuchâtel, 1951.

Phil 8520.17   Monod, Albert. De Pascal à Chateaubriand. Paris, 1916.

Phil 8667.18   Monod, Victor. Dieu dans l'univers. Thèse. Paris, 1933.

Phil 8667.13   Monod, W. Un athée. Neuchâtel, 1904.

Phil 41.8   Monógrafias psicológicas. (Buenos Aires. Universidad. Instituto de Filosofia. Sección de Psicología.)

Phil 14.21   Monograph. (Experimental Psychology Society.) Cambridge. 1,1961+ 3v.

Phil 23.26   Monograph. (New York. Psychoanalytic Institute. Ernst Kris Study Group.) 1,1965+

Phil 7080.31   A monograph on sleep and dream. (Cox, E. William.) London, 1878.

Phil 40.5   Monograph series. (Australasian Association of Psychology and Philosophy.) Sidney.

Phil 22.50   Monographien und Studien zur Konflikt-Psychologie. Konflikt-Anahyse. München. 1-6+ 6v.

Phil 22.19   Monographien zur Grundlegung der philosophischen Anthropologie und Wirklichkeitsphilosophie. Berlin. 1-4,1929-1930 4v.

Phil 22.38   Monographien zur philosophischen Forschung. Reutlingen. 1,1947+ 48v.

VPhil 5205.13   Pamphlet box. Monographs in psychology and anthropology.

Phil 330.3   Pamphlet vol. Monographs on epistemology. 4 pam.

Phil 3805.40   Monologen. (Schleiermacher, Friedrich.) Berlin, 1800.

Phil 3805.41   Monologen. (Schleiermacher, Friedrich.) Berlin, 1868.

Phil 3805.45   Monologen nebst den Vorarbeiten. 2. Aufl. (Schleiermacher, Friedrich.) Leipzig, 1914.

Phil 821.6   Monólogos e diálogos. (Vita, Luís Washington.) São Paulo, 1964.

Phil 525.231   Monopsychism, mysticism. (Merlan, P.) The Hague, 1963.

Phil 6132.21   Die Monotonie der Arbeit. (Winkler, H.) Leipzig, 1922.

Phil 8413.15   Monrad, M.J. Æsthetik. Christiania, 1889-90. 2v.

Phil 4605.1.49   Monrad, M.J. Denkrichtungen der neueren Zeit. Bonn, 1879.

Phil 4605.1.41   Monrad, M.J. Om det skjønne. Christiania, 1873.

Phil 4605.1.36   Monrad, M.J. Philosophisk propaedentik. 5. opl. Christiania, 1896.

Phil 4605.1.46   Monrad, M.J. Tankeretninger i den nyere tid. 2 opl. Christiania, 1884.

Phil 4605.1.31   Monrad, M.J. Tro og viden. Kristiania, 1892.

Phil 5052.11   Monrad, M.J. Udsigt over den høiere logik. Christiania, 1881.

Phil 187.21   Pamphlet box. Monrad, M.T. Philosophical pamphlets. 6 pam.

Phil 5252.33.5   Monrad, Marcus. Psychologie; grundrids til brug. Christiania, 1892.

Phil 6122.49.3   Monrad-Krohn, G. The clinical examination of the nervous system. 3d ed. London, 1926.

Htn   Phil 6100.11*   Monro, A. Three treatises. On the brain, the eye and the ear. Edinburgh, 1797.

Phil 6122.25FA   Monro, Alexander. Observations on the structure of the nervous system. Edinburgh, 1783. 2v.

Phil 5525.44   Monro, David Hector. Argument of laughter. Carlton, Victoria, 1951.

Phil 5525.44.5   Monro, David Hector. Argument of laughter. Notre Dame, 1963.

Phil 8887.123   Monro, David Hector. Empiricism and ethics. Cambridge, Eng., 1967.

Phil 7054.75   Monroe, L.B. A revelation from heaven. Boston, 1851.

Phil 6322.70   Monroe, Russell R. Episodic behavioral disorders. Cambridge, 1970.

Phil 5593.47   Mons, Walter E. Principles and practise of the Rorschach personality test. London, 1947.

Phil 365.36   Monsarrat, K.W. Desire and creation. Liverpool, 1932.

Phil 187.118.10   Monsarrat, K.W. Human desires and their fulfilment. Liverpool, 1950.

Phil 187.118   Monsarrat, K.W. Human powers and their relations. Liverpool, 1938.

Phil 5252.110   Monsarrat, K.W. On human thinking. London, 1955.

Phil 187.118.5   Monsarrat, K.W. Thoughts, deeds and human happiness. London, 1944.

Phil 4757.2.80   Monsieur Gurdjieff. (Pauwels, L.) Paris, 1954.

Phil 2520.305   Monsieur Réné Descartes en son temps. (Frédérix, Pierre.) Paris, 1959.

Phil 8702.22   Monsma, John C. The evidence of God in an expanding universe. N.Y., 1958.

Phil 5865.5.45   Montada, Leo. Die Lernpsychologie Jean Piagets. Stuttgart, 1970.

Phil 5421.20.45   Montagu, Ashley. Man and aggression. London, 1968.

Phil 2020.84   Montagné, Paul. Un radical religieux. v.1-2. Thèse. Toulouse, 1927.

Phil 1135.75   Montagni, G.R. L'evoluzione presocratica. Castello, 1912.

Phil 293.7   Montagu, A. Cours de philosophie scientifique. Paris, 1879.

Phil 293.7.2   Montagu, A. Cours de philosophie scientifiques et ses conséquences sociales. 2. ed. Paris, 1881.

Htn Phil 8637.9.3* Montagu, H. Contemplatio mortis, and immortalitatis. London, 1631.

Htn Phil 8637.9* Montagu, H. Contemplatio mortis, and immortalitatis. London, 1638.

Phil 525.32 Montague, M.P. Twenty minutes of reality. N.Y., 1917.

Phil 8592.45.6 Montague, W.P. Belief unbound. Freeport, N.Y., 1970.

Phil 8592.45 Montague, W.P. Belief unbound. New Haven, 1930.

Phil 8633.1.32 Montague, W.P. The chances of surviving death. Cambridge, 1934.

Phil 5374.22 Montague, W.P. Consciousness a form of energy. N.Y., 19-? 2 pam.

Phil 187.33.5 Montague, W.P. Introductory course in philosophy. Syllabus. N.Y., 1920.

Phil 187.33.10 Montague, W.P. The ways of things: a philosophy of knowledge, nature, and value. N.Y., 1940.

Phil 343.13A Montague, William P. The ways of knowing. London, 1925.

Htn Phil 2750.5.30* Montaigne, Michel de. Les essais. Lyon, 1595.

Htn Phil 2750.5.35* Montaigne, Michel de. Essayes or Morall, politike, and militarie discourses. 3d ed. London, 1632.

Phil 187.87 Montalto, F. L'intuizione e la verità di fatto saggio; psicologico-metafisico. Roma, 1924.

Phil 187.87.5 Montalto, F. L'intuizione e la verità di fatto saggio; psicologico-metafisico. 2. ed. Roma, 1930.

Phil 52.4 Montana. University. Psychological series. Missoula, 1908.

Phil 4012.9 Montanari, Fausto. Riserve su l'umanesimo. Milano, 1943.

Phil 8612.59 Montanden, Raoul. La mort, cette in connue. Neuchâtel, 1948.

Phil 4080.3.285 Montano, Rocco. Arte. 1. ed. Napoli, 1951.

Phil 9070.148 Montapert, Alfred Armand. The supreme philosophy of man; the laws of life. Englewood Cliffs, N.J., 1970.

Phil 2733.109 Montcheuil, Y. de. Malebranche et la quiétisme. Paris, 1946.

Phil 187.112 Monteath, K.M. The philosophy of the past. York, 1936.

Phil 1350.11 Montée, P. Le stoïcisme à Rome. Paris, 1865.

Phil 9358.19 La montée des jeunes dans la communauté des genérations. (Semaines Sociales de France. 48th, Reims, 1961.) Lyon, 1962.

Phil 8887.110.10 Montefiore, Alan. A modern introduction to moral philosophy. London, 1964.

Phil 8887.110.5 Montefiore, Alan. A modern introduction to moral philosophy. N.Y., 1959.

Phil 9145.7.5 Montegazza, P. The Tartuffian age. Boston, 1890.

Phil 4372.1.140 Montegú, Bernardo. Filosofía del humanismo de Juan Luis Vives. Madrid, 1961.

Phil 8610.877.17 Monteil, Edgar. The freethinker's catechism. N.Y., 19-?

Phil 8610.877.15 Monteil, Edgar. The freethinker's catechism. N.Y., 19-?

Phil 2520.212 Monteiro de Barros Lius, Ivan. Descartes. Rio de Janeiro, 1940.

Phil 7082.108 Monteith, Mary E. A book of true dreams. London, 1929.

Htn Phil 2750.6.30* Montesquieu, Charles Louis de Secondat. Considerations sur les causes de la grandeur des Romains et de leur décadence. Amsterdam, 1734.

Phil 5252.48 Montet, C. de. Les problemes fondamentaux de la psychologie medical. Berne, 1922.

Phil 5252.49 Montet, C. de. Psychologie et development de l'enfance à la vieillesse. Berne, 1922.

Phil 5252.49.5 Montet, C. de. Le relativisme psychologique et la recherche médicale. Paris, 1926.

Phil 4957.15 Montevideo. Universidad. Facultad de Humanidades y Ciencias. Aportes a una bibliografía anotada de historia de las ideas en América. Montevideo, 1964.

Phil 4983.1.79 Montevideo. Universidad. Facultad de Humanidades y Ciencias. Bibliografía de Carlos Vaz Ferreira. Montevideo, 1962.

Phil 3494.7 Montgomery, E. Die Kant'sche Erkenntnisslehre. München, 1871.

Phil 187.32 Montgomery, E. Philosophical problems. N.Y., 1907.

Phil 187.32.5 Montgomery, E. Vitality and organization of protoplasm. Austin, Texas, 1904.

Phil 343.3 Montgomery, G.R. The place of values. Bridgeport, 1903.

Phil 8962.6 Montgomery, G.R. The unexplored self. N.Y., 1910.

Phil 9560.3 Montgomery, G.w. Illustrations of the law of kindness. Utica, 1841.

Phil 7159.173 Montgomery, Ruth S. A gift of prophecy: the phenomenal Jeane Dixon. N.Y., 1965.

Phil 7077.2 Montgomery, Ruth Shick. A world beyond. N.Y., 1971.

Phil 187.32.80 Montgomery's philosophy of vital organization. (Lane, Charles A.) Chicago, 1909.

Phil 52.7.12 Monthly bulletin. (Massachusetts. Society for Mental Hygiene.) Boston. 1-19,1922-1940 2v.

Phil 4170.13 Monti, G.F. Anima brutorum secundum sanioris. Neapoli, 1742.

Htn Phil 5000.3* Monti, Panfilo. Logica pamph. v.1-3. Venice, 1512.

Phil 2475.1.325 Montiani, Oddino. Bergson e il suo umanismo integrale. Padova, 1957.

Htn Phil 6682.13* Montjore, C.F.L. Lettre sur le magnétisme animal. Philadelphia, 1784.

Phil 8887.28 Montlosier, F.D. de R. Des mysteres de la vie humaine. v.1-2. Bruxelles, 1829. 2v.

Htn Phil 8887.29* Montlosier, F.D. de R. The management of the tongue. Boston, 1814.

Phil 5722.23.10 Montmasson, J.M. Invention and the unconscious. London, 1931.

Phil 5722.23.2 Montmasson, J.M. Le rôle de l'inconscient dans l'invention scientifique. Thèse. Bourg, 1928.

Phil 2840.87 Montpellier. Université. Inauguration d'un buste de C. Renouvier le 4 mai 1911. Montpellier, 1911.

Phil 4371.10 Montseny y Carret, Juan. La evolución de la filosofía en España. Barcelona 1968.

Phil 4371.5 Montseny y Carret, Juan. La evolución de la filosofía en España. v.1-2. Barcelona, 1934.

Phil 3494.12 Monzel, Alois. Die historischen Voraussetzungen,...der Kantischen Lehre. Bonn, 1912.

Phil 3494.12.10 Monzel, Alois. Die Lehre vom inneren Sinn bei Kant. Bonn, 1919.

Phil 5258.69 Mood in relation to performance. (Sullivan, E.T.) N.Y., 1922.

X Cg Phil 9172.1 Moody, C.C.P. Lights and shadows of domestic life. Boston, 1846.

Phil 8637.4 Moody, L. The problem of life and immortality. Boston, 1872.

Phil 812.13 Moog, W. Das Leben der Philosophen. Berlin, 1932.

Phil 3012.3 Moog, Willy. Die deutsche Philosophie des 20. Jahrhunderts. Stuttgart, 1922.

Phil 3246.178 Moog, Willy. Fichte über den Krieg. Darmstadt, 1917.

Phil 3425.262 Moog, Willy. Hegel und die hegelische Schule. München, 1930.

Phil 3494.23 Moog, Willy. Kants Ansichten über Krieg und Frieden. Leipzig, n.d.

Phil 5052.25 Moog, Willy. Logik, Psychologie und Psychologismus. Halle, 1919.

Phil 75.17 Moog, Willy. Philosophie. Gotha, 1921.

Phil 187.66 Moog, Willy. Das Verhältnis der Philosophie zu den Einzel-Wissenschaften. Halle, 1919.

Phil 960.141 Mookerjee, S. The Buddhist philosophy of universal flux. Calcutta, 1935.

Phil 2905.1.380 Mooney, Christopher F. Teilhard de Chardin and the mystery of Christ. London, 1966.

Phil 2905.1.377 Mooney, Christopher F. Teilhard de Chardin et le mystère du Christ. Paris, 1966.

Phil 5465.158 Mooney, Ron Lawler. Explorations in creativity. 1. ed. N.Y., 1967.

Phil 6304.2 Moor, Lise. Glossaire de psychiatrie. Paris, 1966.

Phil 2115.6 Moore, A.W. Existence, meaning, and reality in Locke's essay. Chicago, 1903.

Phil 187.39A Moore, A.W. Pragmatism and its critics. Chicago, 1910.

Phil 165.17 Moore, C.A. Essays in East-West philosophy. Honolulu, 1951.

Phil 187.127 Moore, C.F. The challenge of life. N.Y., 1925.

Phil 812.23 Moore, Charles A. Philosophy - East and West. Princeton, 1944.

Phil 8633.1.18 Moore, Clifford H. Pagan ideas of immortality. Cambridge, 1918.

Phil 8637.15 Moore, Clifford Herschel. Ancient beliefs in the immortality of the soul. N.Y., 1931.

Phil 1812.12 Moore, E.C. American pragmatism. N.Y., 1961.

Phil 187.121 Moore, E.C. The essence of the matter. Berkeley, 1940.

Phil 8592.55A Moore, Edward C. The nature of religion. N.Y., 1936.

Phil 8520.18.2 Moore, Edward C. An outline of the history of Christian thought since Kant. London, 1912.

Phil 2225.5.120A Moore, Edward C. Studies in the philosophy of Charles Sanders Peirce. 2nd series. Amherst, 1964.

Phil 2070.152 Moore, Edward Carter. William James. N.Y., 1966.

Phil 2730.114 Moore, Francis Charles Timothy. The psychology of Maine de Biran. Oxford, 1970.

Phil 6122.5.3 Moore, G. Der Beruf des Körpers in Beziehung auf den Geist. Leipzig, 1850.

Phil 5252.8 Moore, G. Power of the soul. London, 1845.

Phil 6122.5 Moore, G. The use of the body in relation to the mind. N.Y., 1847.

Phil 187.59 Moore, G.E. Philosophical studies. London, 1922.

Phil 8633.1.17 Moore, G.F. Metempsychosis. Cambridge, 1914.

Phil 343.21A Moore, George E. Proof of an external world. London, 1939.

Phil 8887.21.7 Moore, George Edward. Commonplace book, 1919-1953. London, 1962.

Phil 8887.21.10 Moore, George Edward. Ethics. N.Y., 1912.

Phil 2150.18.50 Moore, George Edward. Ethics. N.Y., 1965.

Phil 2150.18.35 Moore, George Edward. Lectures on philosophy. London, 1966.

NEDL Phil 8887.21.2 Moore, George Edward. Philosophical papers. London, 1959.

Phil 8887.21.2 Moore, George Edward. Principia ethica. Cambridge, Eng., 1922.

Phil 8887.21.3 Moore, George Edward. Principia ethica. Cambridge, Eng., 1922.

Phil 8887.21.4 Moore, George Edward. Principia ethica. Cambridge, Eng., 1929.

Phil 8887.21.6 Moore, George Edward. Principia ethica. Cambridge, Eng., 1954.

Phil 2150.18.30 Moore, George Edward. Principia ethica. Cambridge, Eng., 1959.

Phil 9590.2 Moore, George Edward. Some main problems of philosophy. London, 1953.

Phil 8887.55 Moore, J.H. The law of biogenesis. Chicago, 1914.

Phil 9352.4 Moore, J.H. The new ethics. London, 1909.

Phil 5627.154 Moore, J.H. Young gentleman and lady's monitor. London, 1794.

Phil 5252.43 Moore, J.M. Theories of religious experience. Thesis. N.Y., 1938.

Phil 5252.43.5 Moore, J.S. The foundations of psychology. Princeton, 1921.

Phil 187.82 Moore, J.S. The foundations of psychology. 2d ed. Princeton, 1933.

Phil 8637.12 Moore, J.S. Rifts in the universe. New Haven, 1927.

Phil 9540.12 Moore, Justin H. The world beyond. N.Y., 1920.

Phil 7069.44.10 Moore, Katharine. The spirit of tolerance. London, 1964.

Phil 8413.5 Moore, M.G. Things I can't explain. London, 1944.

Phil 5252.50.10 Moore, T.S. Armour for aphrodite. London, 1929.

Phil 5252.50 Moore, T.V. Cognitive psychology. Chicago, 1939.

Phil 5252.50.2 Moore, T.V. Dynamic psychology. Philadelphia, 1924.

Phil 6962.21 Moore, T.V. Dynamic psychology. 2d ed. Philadelphia, 1926.

Phil 8837.6 Moore, T.V. The essential psychoses and their fundamental syndromes. Baltimore, 1933.

Phil 5649.14 Moore, T.V. Historical introduction to ethics. N.Y., 1915.

Phil 6962.37 Moore, T.V. A study in reaction time and movement. Diss. Washington, 1904.

Phil 8702.8 Moore, W.L. The mind in chains. N.Y., 1955.

Phil 5100.5 Moore, W.U. The cosmos and the creeds. London, 1903.

Phil 7069.11.50 Moore, William H. Frequent fallacies. Boston, 1931.

Phil 7069.13.30 Moore, William U. Glimpses of the next state (the education of an agnostic). London, 1911.

Phil 8592.36 Moore, William U. The voices. London, 1913.

Phil 2150.18.45 Moore, Willis L. Spiritual gravity of the cosmist. Pasadena, 1926.

Phil 8125.12 Moore and Ryle: two ontologists. (Addis, Laird.) Iowa City, 1965.

Phil 8125.12.5 Moos, Paul. Die deutsche Ästhetik der Gegenwart. Berlin, 1919.

Phil 8612.90 Moos, Paul. Die deutsche Ästhetik der Gegenwart. Berlin, 1931.

Phil 3428.87 Moos, Peter von. Consolatio; Studien zur mittellateinischen Trostliteratur über den Tod und zum Problem der christlichen Trauer. München, 1971-

Phil 5052.4 Moosherr, T. Herbarts Metaphysik. Basel, 1898.

Phil 8980.435 Mora, J.J. de. Cursos de lojica y etica segun la escuela de Edinburgo. Lima, 1832.

Phil 4463.5 Moraal, marxisme en ethiek in de sowietunie. (Graaf, Johannes de.) Hilversum, 1967.

Phil 293.14 Moraes, Manuel. Cartesianismo em Portugal: Antonio Cordeiro. Braga, 1966.

Moraes Carvalho, A.A. de. Le problème de l'univers. Lisbonne, 1920.

Author and Title Listing

	Phil 8667.20	Morais, H.M. Deism in eighteenth century America. N.Y., 1934.
	Phil 8667.20.5	Morais, H.M. Deism in eighteenth century America. N.Y., 1960.
	Phil 8882.43	Moral, religion og videnskab. (Hansen, Hans C.) Kjøbenhavn, 1890.
	Phil 8887.67	Moral, Wille und Weltgestaltung. (Menger, Karl.) Wien, 1934.
	Phil 3494.11.5	Moral action and natural law in Kant. (Miller, E.M.) Melbourne, 1911.
	Phil 8893.78	Moral adventure. (Streeter, Burnett.) N.Y., 1929.
	Phil 337.17	Moral aesthetic and religious insight. (Greeve, T.M.) New Brunswick, N.J., 1957.
	Phil 8890.12.2	Moral and literary dissertations. (Percival, T.) Dublin, 1786.
	Phil 8890.12.3	Moral and literary dissertations. (Percival, T.) Philadelphia, 1806.
	Phil 8890.12	Moral and literary dissertations. (Percival, T.) Warrington, 1784.
	Phil 812.3	Moral and metaphysical philosophy. (Maurice, J.F.D.) London, 1850.
	Phil 812.3.9	Moral and metaphysical philosophy. (Maurice, J.F.D.) London, 1873. 2v.
	Phil 812.3.2	Moral and metaphysical philosophy. 2d ed. (Maurice, J.F.D.) London, 1854.
	Phil 8953.7	Moral and pastoral theology. 3. ed. (Davis, H.) N.Y., 1938. 4v.
	Phil 8882.23	Moral and political dialogues. (Hurd, R.) London, 1760.
	Phil 2050.59.25	Moral and political philosophy. (Hume, David.) N.Y., 1948.
	Phil 2266.20	Moral and political philosophy. (Smith, Adam.) N.Y., 1948.
	Phil 2050.252	The moral and political philosophy of David Hume. (Stewart, J.B.) N.Y., 1963.
X Cg	Phil 2115.114	The moral and political philosophy of John Locke. (Lamprecht, S.P.) N.Y., 1918.
	Phil 2115.114.5	The moral and political philosophy of John Locke. (Lamprecht, S.P.) N.Y., 1962.
	Phil 2045.1	Moral and political works. (Hobbes, Thomas.) London, 1750.
	Phil 8972.10	Moral and social questions arranged for high school religious discussion groups and study clubs. (Wyse, Alexander.) Paterson, 1943.
	Phil 575.45	The moral and social significance of the conception of personality. (Heath, Arthur G.) Oxford, 1921.
	Phil 9050.6	Moral aspects of city life. 2d ed. (Chapin, E.H.) N.Y., 1854.
	Phil 8615.1.15	Moral aspiration and song. (Salter, W.M.) Philadelphia, 1905.
	Phil 2035.80.17	Moral causation, or Notes on Mr. Mill's notes to the chapter on freedom in the 3rd edition of his examination of Sir W. Hamilton's philosophy. (Alexander, P.P.) Edinburgh, 1868.
	Phil 2035.80.18	Moral causation. Notes on Mr. Mill's examination. 2nd ed. (Alexander, P.P.) Edinburgh, 1875.
	Phil 8980.193	The moral challenge of Communism. (Barton, William Ernest.) London, 1966.
	Phil 8893.28	The moral class book. (Sullivan, W.) Boston, 1831.
	Phil 8893.28.3	The moral class book. (Sullivan, W.) Boston, 1833.
	Phil 9172.2	The moral class book. Photoreproduction. London, 1856.
	Phil 9430.15	Die Moral des Pessimismus. (Hartsen, F.A. von.) Leipzig, n.d.
	Phil 9430.15.5	Die Moral des Pessimismus. (Hartsen, F.A. von.) Nordhausen, 1874.
	Phil 5875.70	Moral development: a psychological study of moral growth from childhood to adolescence. (Kay, William.) London, 1968.
	Phil 8877.70	Moral e economia politica. (Carlos, M.) Rio de Janeiro, 1941.
	Phil 9575.10	A moral e o capitalismo. (Du Lassage, Henri.) Pôrto, 19-
	Phil 8890.26.5	The moral economy. (Perry, R.B.) N.Y., 1909.
Htn	Phil 9515.4*	Moral essay, preferring solitude to public employment. (Mackenzie, George.) London, 1685.
	Phil 8888.2	Moral essayes. (Nicole, P.) London, 1696. 2v.
Htn	Phil 2115.130*	Moral essays; wherein some of Mr. Locks and Monsir. Malbranch's opinions are briefly examin'd. (Lowde, J.) York, 1699.
Htn	Phil 8893.64*	Moral essays and discourses upon several subjects. (Shannon, F.B.) London, 1690.
	Phil 8882.4	Moral evolution. (Harris, G.) Boston, 1896.
	Phil 8893.57.10	Moral experience, an outline of ethics for class-teaching. (Sturt, Henry.) London, 1928.
	Phil 5769.3	Moral freedom reconciled with causation. (Travis, H.) London, 1865.
Htn	Phil 9352.1*	Moral gallantry. (Mackenzie, G.) Edinburgh, 1669. 2 pam.
	Phil 9352.1.5	Moral gallantry. (Mackenzie, G.) London, 1685.
Htn	Phil 9560.16*	The moral history of frugality. (Mackenzie, George.) London, 1691.
	Phil 8882.87	Moral-hvad er det? (Henningsen, N.) København, 1962.
	Phil 8897.7	The moral ideal. (Wedgwood, J.) London, 1888.
	Phil 8897.7.2	The moral ideal. (Wedgwood, J.) London, 1889.
	Phil 8881.17	The moral ideals. (Grote, J.) Cambridge, 1876.
	Phil 8844.4	The moral ideals of our civilization. (Tsanoff, R.A.) N.Y., 1942.
	Phil 3310.6.80	Die Moral in der Politik bei Christian Grane. Inaug. Diss. (Stolleis, Michael.) München, 1967.
	Phil 9050.8	The moral influence, dangers and duties connected with great cities. (Todd, John.) Northampton, 1841.
NEDL	Phil 8890.2.2	The moral instructor. pt. 2. (Palmer, T.H.) Boston, 1846.
	Phil 8890.2.5	The moral instructor. pt.1. (Palmer, T.H.) Boston, 1853.
	Phil 8890.2	The moral instructor. pt.1. (Palmer, T.H.) Philadelphia, 1841.
	Phil 8890.2.3	The moral instructor. pt.3. (Palmer, T.H.) Boston, 1874.
	Phil 8890.2.4	The moral instructor. pt.4. (Palmer, T.H.) Boston, 1851.
Htn	Phil 8894.25.5*	The moral instructor. 2d ed. (Torrey, Jesse, Jr.) Albany, 1819.
	Phil 8897.96	Moral integrity: inaugural lecture in the Chair of Philosophy delivered at King's College, London, 9 May 1968. (Winch, Peter.) Oxford, 1968.
	Phil 5850.326	The moral issues involved in applied psychology. (Roback, A.A.) n.p., 1917.
	Phil 8892.65	Moral judgement. (Raphael, D. Daiches.) London, 1955.
	Phil 8980.252.3	Moral' kak ee ponimaiut kommunisty. Izd. 3. (Bychkova, N.V.) Moskva, 1966.
	Phil 8884.25	Moral knowledge. (Johnson, Oliver Adolph.) Hague, 1966.
	Phil 8980.495	Moral kommunisticheskaia i moral' burzhvaznaia. (Kon, I.S.) Moskva, 1960. 2 pam.
	Phil 3480.67.80A	The moral law, or Kant's Groundwork of the metaphysic of morals. (Kant, Immanuel.) London, 1947?
	Phil 3480.67.100	The moral law. (Kant, Immanuel.) London, 1961.
	Phil 3480.67.90	The moral law. (Kant, Immanuel.) N.Y., 1950.
	Phil 8882.27	The moral law - theory and practice of duty. (Hamilton, E.J.) N.Y., 1902.
	Phil 8892.30	Moral law and civil law; parts of the same thing. (Ritter, Eli F.) N.Y., 1896.
	Phil 8892.30.2	Moral law and civil law; parts of the same thing. (Ritter, Eli F.) Westerville, Ohio, 1910.
	Phil 3494.11.15A	Moral law and the highest good; a study of Kant's doctrine. (Miller, E.M.) Melbourne, 1928.
	Phil 8876.93	Moral laws. (Brightman, E.S.) N.Y., 1933.
	Phil 8887.16	The moral library. Boston, 1796.
	Phil 8878.25	The moral life; a study in genetic ethics. (Davies, A.E.) Baltimore, 1909.
	Phil 8884.25.5	The moral life. (Johnson, Oliver Adolph.) London, 1969.
	Phil 8893.37	The moral life and moral worth. (Sorley, W.R.) Cambridge, Eng., 1911.
	Phil 8896.20	The moral life and the ethical life. (Vivas, E.) Chicago, 1950.
	Phil 8887.74.5	Moral meditations. (Martínez de Trujillo, Maria.) N.Y., 1954.
	Phil 8887.17	The moral mirror. Philadelphia, 1813.
	Phil 8880.5	The moral monitor. v.2. (Fiske, N.) Worcester, Mass., 1801.
	Phil 8884.23	Moral nerve and the error of literary verdicts. (Jordan, Furneaux.) London, 1901.
	Phil 9120.161.20	Moral obligations. (Prichard, H.A.) Oxford, 1949.
	Phil 8875.5	Moral order and progress. (Alexander, S.) London, 1889.
	Phil 8656.9.2	The moral order of the World. (Bruce, A.B.) N.Y., 1899.
	Phil 9490.15	Moral para intelectuales. (Vaz Ferreira, C.) La Plata, 1957.
	Phil 8881.7	Moral pathology. (Giles, A.E.) London, 1895.
	Phil 8887.18	The moral philosopher. (Morgan, T.) London, 1737-39. 2v.
	Phil 8887.18.3	The moral philosopher. v.1, 2. ed. (Morgan, T.) London, 1738-40. 3v.
	Phil 8952.15	Moral philosophy. (Crofts, Ambrose M.) Dublin, 1960.
	Phil 8880.43.5	Moral philosophy. (Fairchild, J.H.) Oberlin, Ohio, 1869.
	Phil 8880.18.5	Moral philosophy. (Fite, Warner.) N.Y., 1925.
	Phil 8882.5.2	Moral philosophy. (Haven, J.) Boston, 1874.
	Phil 2672.36	Moral philosophy. (Jouffroy, Théodore S.) N.Y., 1862.
	Phil 2750.11.148	Moral philosophy. (Maritain, Jacques.) N.Y., 1964.
	Phil 8890.9.2	Moral philosophy. (Peabody, A.P.) Boston, 1887.
	Phil 1535.6.14	Moral philosophy. 4th ed. (Rickaby, Joseph.) London, 1919.
	Phil 2050.262	The moral philosophy of David Hume. (Broiles, R. David.) The Hague, 1964.
	Phil 1870.175	The moral philosophy of George Berkeley. (Olscamp, Paul J.) The Hague, 1970.
	Phil 2250.113	The moral philosophy of Josiah Royce. (Fuss, Peter Lawrence.) Cambridge, 1965.
	Phil 2280.5.105	Moral philosophy of Santayana. (Munitz, M.K.) N.Y., 1939.
	Phil 2070.34	The moral philosophy of William James. (James, William.) N.Y., 1969.
	Phil 8876.117	The moral point of view. (Baier, Kurt.) Ithaca, 1958.
	Phil 8876.117.2	The moral point of view. (Baier, Kurt.) N.Y., 1967.
	Phil 2725.2.10	Moral positiva, sua necessidade atual. (Laffitte, Pierre.) Rio de Janeiro, 1938.
	Phil 8890.66	Moral practices. (Phillips, Dewi Zephaniah.) London, 1966[1970]
	Phil 8964.4	Moral principles. (O'Rahilly, Alfred.) Cork, 1948.
	Phil 8870.13	Moral principles of action. 1st ed. (Anshen, R.N.) N.Y., 1952.
	Phil 8831.5	Moral progess; being the Frazer lecture delivered within the University of Glasgow on 18th April 1944. (Ginsberg, M.) Glasgow, 1944.
	Phil 8893.35	Moral razonada. (Spínola, R.) Guatemala, 1900.
	Phil 8876.164	Moral reasoning. (Beardsmore, R.W.) London, 1969.
	Phil 7084.32	Moral reflections in a real dream. London, 1708.
NEDL	Phil 8876.2	Moral science. (Bain, A.) N.Y., 1869.
	Phil 8897.49	The moral self; its nature and development. (White, A.K.) London, 1923.
	Phil 8893.68	The moral self: an introduction to the science of ethics. (Sherman, C.L.) Boston, 1927.
	Phil 8876.89	Moral sense. (Bonar, J.) London, 1930.
	Phil 8892.58	The moral sense. (Raphael, D. Daiches.) London, 1947.
	Phil 2262.85	Moral sense und Moral-Prinzip bei Shaftesbury. Inaug. Diss. (Rehorn, F.) Bonn, 1882.
	Phil 8955.10	Moral situation. (Fotion, Nicholas G.) Yellow Springs, 1968.
	Phil 8887.20	Moral sketches. (More, H.) Boston, 1819.
	Phil 8887.20.3	Moral sketches. (More, H.) London, 1819.
	Phil 8890.5.50	Moral standards. 2. ed. (Patterson, C.H.) N.Y., 1957.
	Phil 8880.55	Moral strategy. (Feibleman, James.) The Hague, 1967.
	Phil 8887.27	The moral teacher. (Muzzey, A.B.) N.Y., 1839.
	Phil 8967.2	The moral teaching of the New Testament. (Row, C.A.) London, 1873.
	Phil 8880.36	Moral theory. An introduction to ethics. (Field, G.C.) London, 1922.
	Phil 8891.4	The moral theory of evolutionary naturalism. (Quillian, W.F.) New Haven, 1945.
	Phil 3791.06	Moral und Dogma. (Riehl, Alois.) n.p., 1871-92. 5 pam.
	Phil 8980.213	Moral und Gesellschaft. (Bittighoefer, Bernd.) Berlin, 1968.
	Phil 8881.82	Moral und Hypemoral. (Gehlen, Arnold.) Frankfurt, 1969.
	Phil 179.3.70	Moral und Lebensanschauung. 2. Aufl. (Eucken, R.) Leipzig, 1917.
	Phil 8955.13.5	Moral und Moraltheologie nach dem Konzil. (Fuchs, Josef.) Freiburg, 1969.
	Phil 8965.1	Moral und Religion. (Pfeiderer, O.) Leipzig, 1872.
	Phil 8879.15	Moral values. (Everett, W.G.) N.Y., 1918.
	Phil 630.13	Moral values and the idea of God. (Sorley, W.R.) Cambridge, 1918.
	Phil 630.13.7	Moral values and the idea of God. 2nd ed. (Sorely, W. R.) N.Y., 1921.
	Phil 8878.9	Moral views of commerce, society and politics. (Dewey, O.) N.Y., 1838.
	Phil 2520.340	Moral y libertad en Descartes. (Pousa, Narciso.) La Plata, 1960.
	Phil 9513.20	Moral y sociedad. (Lopez, Aranguren, José Luis.) Madrid, 1965.
	Phil 8870.29	Moral zwischen Anspruch und Verantwortung. (Boeckle, Franz.) Düsseldorf, 1964.

Phil 8880.68   Moralbegrundelse og logik. (Fink, Hans.) København, 1970.
Phil 8881.26.21   La morale, l'art...d'après Guyau. (Fouillée, A.) Paris, 1909.
Phil 8887.8   La morale, ou La philosophie des moeurs. (Matter, J.) Paris, 1860.
Phil 2725.23.90   La morale...de M. Lucien Levy-Bruhl. (Chang Chi Chang.) Lyon, 1937.
Phil 8878.46   La morale. (Donati, G.) Forli, 1918.
Phil 8881.58   Morale. (Goddard, H.C.) N.Y., 1918.
Phil 8882.39   Morale. (Hall, G. Stanley.) N.Y., 1920.
Phil 8896.9   La morale. (Véron, Eugène.) Paris, 1884.
Phil 8881.39   La morale: la moralé théologique. (Guyot, Yves.) Paris, 1883.
Phil 8878.22.2   La morale. Théorie psycho-sociologique d'une conduite rationnelle. 2. ed. (Duprat, G.L.) Paris, 1912.
Phil 8831.1   La morale anglaise contemporaine. (Guyau, M.J.) Paris, 1878.
Phil 1145.82   La morale antique. (Robin, L.) Paris, 1938.
Phil 8878.29   La morale basée sur la démographie. (Dumont, Arsène.) Paris, 1901.
Phil 2905.1.510   La morale chez Teilhard. (Mermod, Denis.) Paris, 1967.
Phil 8965.6   Morale chrétienne. (Pictet, Benedict.) Genève, 1710. 2v.
Phil 8962.17   Morale chrétienne et morale marxiste. Paris, 1960.
Phil 8962.18   Morale cristiana ed esigenre contemporanee. Milano, 1957.
Phil 8876.4   La morale dans la démocratie. (Barni, J.) Paris, 1868.
Phil 8961.5   La morale d'après St. Thomas. (La Barre, A.) Paris, 1911.
Phil 2520.100   La morale de Descartes. (Touchard, G.) Paris, 1898.
Phil 2520.275   La morale de Descartes. 1. ed. (Rodis-Lewis, Geneviève.) Paris, 1957.
Phil 2520.276   La morale de Descartes. 3e ed. (Rodis-Lewis, Geneviève.) Paris, 1970.
Phil 2725.17.90   La morale de Félix Le Dantec (1869-1917). Thèse. (Bonnet, Georges.) Poitiers, 1930.
Phil 3280.83   La morale de Geulincx. (Terraillon, E.) Paris, 1912.
Phil 8961.6   La morale de Jésus. (Lahy, J.M.) Paris, 1911.
Phil 3482.15   La morale de Kant. (Alquié, Ferdinand.) Paris, 1965.
Phil 3484.9   La morale de Kant. (Cresson, André.) Paris, 1904.
Phil 3503.12   La morale de Kant. 1. éd. (Vialatoux, J.) Paris, 1956.
Phil 8877.29   La morale de la raison theorique. (Cresson, Andre.) Paris, 1903.
Phil 8887.90   La morale de l'avenir. (Mayer, Charles L.) Paris, 1953.
Phil 8951.3   La morale de l'église et la morale naturelle. (Boutteville, M.L.) Paris, 1866.
Phil 3552.301   La morale de Leibniz. (Le Chevallier, L.) Paris, 1933.
Phil 8951.11   La morale de l'évangile comparée. (Bautain, Louis E.) Paris, 1855. 2 pam.
Phil 8884.14   La morale de l'honneur. (Jeudon, L.) Paris, 1911.
Phil 8884.7   La morale de l'impératif catégorique et la morale du bonheur. (Janssens, E.) Louvain, 1921.
Phil 9255.5   La morale de l'ironie. 2. éd. (Paulhan, Frederic.) Paris, 1914.
Phil 3640.216.10   Les morale de Nietzsche. (Lasserre, Pierre.) Paris, 1902.
Phil 8870.11   Morale de savants d'Hippocrate à Einstein. (Felseneer, Jean.) Bruxelles, 1946.
Phil 3842.6   La morale de Spinoza. (Worms, René.) Paris, 1892.
Phil 3845.3   La morale de Spinoza. (Zac, Sylvain.) Paris, 1959.
Phil 3845.3.2   La morale de Spinoza. 2. éd. (Zac, Sylvain.) Paris, 1966.
Phil 2266.114   La morale della simpatia; saggio sopra l'etica di Adamo Smith. (Limentani, L.) Genova, 1914.
Phil 8430.94   La morale dell'artista. (Bono, Pierluigi.) Milano, 1969.
Phil 1158.5   La morale d'Epicure. (Guyau, M.) Paris, 1878.
Phil 2270.74.35   La morale des différents peuples et la morale personnelle. (Spencer, Herbert.) Paris, 1896.
Phil 8826.5   La morale des gaulois. (Bayet, Albert.) Paris, 1930.
Phil 336.1.6   Morale des idées-forces. (Fouillée, A.) Paris, 1908.
Phil 336.1.7   Morale des idées-forces. 2. ed. (Fouillée, A.) Paris, 1908.
Phil 930.26   La morale des philosophies chinois. (Lanessan, J.M.) Paris, 1896.
Phil 8887.24   La morale des poètes. (Moustalon.) Paris, 1816.
Phil 8886.24.5   La morale des religions. (Lanessan, J.I. de.) Paris, 1905.
Phil 1200.6   La morale des stoiciens. (Favre, Jules.) Paris, 1888.
Phil 2270.101   La morale di Herbert Spencer. (Traina, Tommaso.) Torino, 1881.
Phil 9245.32   La morale du bonheur. (Piat, Clodius.) Paris, 1910.
Phil 8952.21   Morale du cerveau. (Chauchard, P.) Paris, 1962.
Phil 8886.27   Morale d'un égoïste; essai de morale sociale. (Laplaigne, H.) Paris, 1900.
Phil 186.146   Morale e conoscenza; saggi critici. (Librizzi, Carmelo.) Padova, 1961.
Phil 4210.202   Morale e politica in Rosmini. (Cuciuffo, Michele.) Milano, 1967.
Phil 4160.41.30   Morale e religione. (Librizzi, Carmelo.) Padova, 1962.
Phil 3808.62   Morale e religione. (Schopenhauer, Arthur.) Torino, 1921.
Phil 4580.62   Morale essai sur les principes théoriques. (Høffding, Harald.) Paris, 1903.
Phil 8881.16   La morale et la loi de l'histoire. (Gratry, A.J.A.) Paris, 1871. 2v.
Phil 8886.29.5   La morale et la science des moeurs. 5. ed. (Lévy-Bruhl, L.) Paris, 1913.
Phil 8837.15   La morale et l'histoire. 1. éd. (Masson-Ourel, Paul.) Paris, 1955.
Phil 9075.21   Morale et moralité. (Sollier, Paul.) Paris, 1912.
Phil 8967.10   Morale et perfection. (Ranwez, E.) Tournai, 1959.
Phil 9450.23   Morale et politique. (Claparède, Edouard.) Neuchâtel, 1947.
Phil 2725.35.5   Morale et religion. (Lavelle, Louis.) Paris, 1960.
Phil 8880.25   Morale et société. 4e ed. (Fonsegrive, George.) Paris, 1908.
Phil 8880.60   Morale et tyrannies. (Fernand-Laurent, Camille J.) Paris, 1967.
Phil 8878.36.8   Morale fondée sur les lois de la nature. 3e éd. (Deshumbert, Marius.) Paris, 191-.
Phil 8893.100   La morale fouillée dans ses fondements. (Boissière, P.) Paris, 1866.
Phil 8890.58   Morale generale. (Palazzini, Pietro.) Brescia, 1961.
Phil 8968.22   Morale humaine, morale chrétienne. (Semaine des Intellectuels Catholiques, 1966.) Paris, 1966.
Phil 8886.38   La morale humaine. (Loisy, Alfred.) Paris, 1923.
Phil 8886.38.5   La morale humaine. 2. ed. (Loisy, Alfred.) Paris, 1928.
Phil 8877.19   La morale indépendante. (Coignet, C.) Paris, 1869.
Phil 8888.9   Morale induttiva. (Nobili-Vitelleschi, F.) Roma, 1882-91. 4v.
Phil 3493.26   La morale Kantienne. (Letocart, M.) Bruxelles, 1954.
Phil 3500.28   Morale Kantienne et morale humaine. (Sartiaux, F.) Paris, 1917.

Phil 8876.51.19   La morale laïque et ses adversaires. 4e éd. (Bayet, Albert.) Paris, 1925.
Phil 8971.4   La morale monastique du XIe au XVIe siècle. (Vandenbroucke, Francois.) Louvain, 1966.
Phil 8886.24   La morale naturelle. (Lanessan, J.I. de.) Paris, 1908.
Phil 8886.79   La morale nouvelle. (Lepp, Ignance.) Paris, 1963.
Phil 9380.8   The morale of adults. Thesis. (Miller, D.C.) Menasha, Wis., 1940.
Phil 8826.5.10   La morale paienne a l'époque gallo-romaine. (Bayet, Albert.) Paris, 1931.
Phil 600.30   La morale positive. (Clavel, Adolphe.) Paris, 1873.
Phil 9245.38   La morale positive et le bonheur. (Grimanelli, P.) Paris, 1924.
Phil 9070.110   Une morale pour notre temps. (Oraison, Marc.) Paris, 1964.
Phil 8877.102   Une morale pour un monde en mutation. (Coste, René.) Gembloux, 1969.
Phil 8894.14   Morale pratique. 3e éd. (Troufleau, L.) Paris, 1913.
Phil 9045.21   Morale privata e morale politica. (Sighele, Seipio.) Milano, 1913.
Phil 8886.53   La morale privée. (Lemarie, O.) Paris, 1932.
Phil 8886.19   La morale publique. (Lagerborg, R.) Paris, 1903.
Phil 8886.23   La morale rationnelle. (Leclère, A.) Paris, 1908.
Phil 8890.30   Morale religieuse et morale laïque. (Ecole des Hautes Études Sociales.) Paris, 1914.
Phil 9450.11   La morale républicaine. (Martin, Félix.) Paris, 1912.
Phil 8951.12   La morale sans Dieu. (Broglie, L'abbé de.) Paris, 1903.
Phil 8882.69   Morale sans péché. (Hesnard, Angelo.) Paris, 1954.
Phil 8962.15   Morale sans péché? Paris, 1955.
Phil 8876.51   La morale scientifique. 2e ed. (Bayet, Albert.) Paris, 1907.
Phil 8881.26.18   La morale selon Guyau. (Aslan, G.) Paris, 1906.
Phil 3483.84   La morale selon Kant et selon Marx. (Besse, Guy.) Paris, 196-.
Phil 9495.128   La morale sexuelle. (Wylm, Antoine.) Paris, 1907.
Phil 1200.65   La Morale sociale des derniers stoïciens, Sénèque, Epictète et Marc Aurèle. (Bodson, Arthur.) Paris, 1967.
Phil 1200.8   La morale stoïcienne. (Chollet, A.) Paris, n.d.
Phil 1200.72   La morale stoïcienne. (Rodis-Lewis, Geneviève.) Paris, 1970.
Phil 8877.76.5   La morale supérieure. (Colesanti, Giulio.) Paris, 1940.
Phil 8877.60.10   Morale théorique et notions historiques. 10e éd. (Chabot, Charles.) Paris, 1925.
Phil 8881.64   Morale théorique et science des moeurs. (Gurvitch, Georges.) Paris, 1937.
Phil 8881.64.2   Morale théorique et science des moeurs. 2. éd. (Gurvitch, Georges.) Paris, 1948.
Phil 8952.10   La morale universelle. (Chassanis.) Paris, 1791.
Htn Phil 2648.49*   La morale universelle. (Holbach, Paul Henri T.) Amsterdam, 1776. 3v.
Phil 2648.50   La morale universelle. (Holbach, Paul Henri T.) Tours, 1792. 3v.
Phil 9550.11   La morale utilitaire. (Carran, Ludovic.) Paris, 1875.
Phil 2138.89F   La morale utilitaria dello Stuart Mill. (Zuccante, G.) Milano, 1899.
Phil 5062.27   "Moralens matematik". (Wadstein, E.A.) Stockholm, 1888.
Phil 8897.28.5   Moralens uppkomst och utveckling. (Westermarck, E.) Stockholm, 1916.
Phil 8886.8.10   Moralens utveckling: fri bearbetning efter Letourneau. (Key, Ellen.) Stockholm, 1903.
Phil 8886.19.5   Moralens vasen. (Lagerborg, R.) Helsingfors, 1900.
Phil 5190.80   Morales Encina, Carlos. Técnica de la persuasión. Santiago de Chile, 1969.
Phil 8887.43   Morales et religions. (Merrington, E.N.) Paris, 1909.
Phil 3018.13   Morales et religions nouvelles en Allemagne. (Seillière, E.) Paris, 1927.
Phil 8879.20   Moralfilosofiens elementer. (Enberg, L.M.) Stockholm, 1831.
Phil 8877.59   Moralische Betrachtungen. (Clemmens, H.W.) Stuttgart, 1761.
Phil 8878.17   Moralische Briefe. (Dusch, J.J.) Leipzig, 1772. 2v.
Phil 8882.53   Moralische Briefe. (Horwicz, Adolf.) Magdebourg, 1878.
Phil 8878.17.5   Moralische Briefe. v.2. (Dusch, J.J.) Wien, 1771.
Phil 8880.41   Die moralische Idee. (Flake, Otto.) München, 1921.
Phil 5753.2   Die moralische Statistik. (Drobisch, M.W.) Leipzig, 1867.
Phil 5043.10.3   Die moralische Statistik und die menschliche Willens Freiheit. (Drobisch, Moritz Wilhelm.) Leipzig, 1867.
Htn Phil 8881.4.5*   Moralische Vorlesungen. v. 1-3. (Gellert, C.F.) Leipzig, 1770.
Phil 8589.5.15   Moralism and Christianity, or Man's experience and destiny, in three lectures. (James, H.) N.Y., 1850.
Phil 3487.3.3   Le moralisme de Kant et l'amoralisme contemporain. (Fouillée, Alfred.) Paris, 1921.
Phil 3487.3.2   Le moralisme de Kant et l'amoralisme contemporain. 2. éd. (Fouillée, Alfred.) Paris, 1905.
Phil 22.25   The moralist. London. 1,1823
Phil 1145.83   Moralistas griegos. (Mondolfo, Rodolfo.) Buenos Aires, 1941.
Phil 9346.2   Le moraliste de la jeunesse. (Girot.) London, 1801.
Phil 2262.50   Die Moralisten, eine philosophische Rhapsodie. (Shaftesbury, A.A.C.) Jena, 1910.
Phil 2262.51   Moralisterna, en filosofisk rhapsodi. (Shaftesbury, A.A.C.) Stockholm, 1926.
Phil 180.8   Moralistes et philosophes. (Franck, A.) Paris, 1872.
Phil 1350.5   Les moralistes sous l'Empire romain. (Martha, Constant.) Paris, 1866.
Phil 1350.5.4   Les moralistes sous l'Empire romain. 4e éd. (Martha, Constant.) Paris, 1881.
Htn Phil 2262.49*   The moralists. (Shaftesbury, A.A.C.) London, 1709.
Phil 4120.8.35   La moralità. (Guzzo, Augusto.) Torino, 1950.
Phil 8430.15   Moralità dell'arte. (Fazio-Allmayer, V.) Firenze, 1953.
Phil 8893.19   Moralität und Religion. (Spir, A.) Leipzig, 1874.
Phil 193.31.8   Moralität und Religion. 4e aufl. (Spir, A. von.) Leipzig, 1909.
Phil 9502.9   La moralité professionnelle des origines à nos jours. (Prevet, François.) Paris, 1956. 2v.
Phil 8969.11   Morality and beyond. (Tillich, Paul.) N.Y., 1963.
Phil 3491.10   Morality and freedom in...Kant. (Jones, W.T.) London, 1940.
Phil 8877.100   Morality and moral reasoning; five essays in ethics. (Casey, John.) London, 1971.
Phil 193.130.15   Morality and purpose. (Stocks, J.L.) N.Y., 1969.
Phil 8882.57   Morality and reality. (Howe, E.G.) London, 1934.
Phil 8885.4   Morality and religion. (Kidd, J.) Edinburgh, 1895.
Phil 8897.92   Morality and the emotions: an inaugural lecture. (William, Bernard Arthur Owen.) London, 1966.
Phil 8870.24   Morality and the language of conduct. (Castaneda, H.) Detroit, 1963.

Phil 9550.20 Morality and utility. (Narveson, Jan.) Baltimore, 1967.
Phil 8893.28.8 Morality as a religion. (Sullivan, W.R.) London, 1898.
Phil 9495.155.10 Morality fair. (Williamson, Geoffrey.) London, 1955.
Phil 8955.11 The morality gap. (Furfey, Paul Hanly.) N.Y., 1968.
Phil 2475.1.505 Morality in evolution: the moral philosophy of Henri Bergson. (Callagher, Idella J.) The Hague, 1970.
Phil 8897.66 Morality in the making. (Whitney, R.E.) N.Y., 1929.
Phil 8957.13.20 Morality is for persons. (Haering, Bernhard.) N.Y., 1971.
Phil 8881.50 The morality of nature. (Gibson, R.W.) N.Y., 1923.
Phil 9450.3 The morality of public men. (Harcourt, W.G.G.V.V.) London, 1852.
Phil 9450.3.2 The morality of public men. 2. ed. (Harcourt, W.G.G.V.V.) London, 1853.
Phil 9490.20 The morality of scholarship. (Frye, Northrop.) Ithaca, 1967.
Phil 8889.10 The morality of self-interest. (Olson, Robert Goodwin.) N.Y., 1965.
Phil 9010.18 The morality of social pleasures. (Fowler, Montague.) London, 1910.
Phil 8980.472.5 Morálka dnes a zajtra. (Kánský, Jiří.) Bratislava, 1963.
Phil 8980.252 Moral'kak ee ponimaiut kommunisty. (Bychkova, N.V.) Moskva, 1962.
Phil 8980.252.2 Moral'kak ee ponimaiut kommunisty. 2. izd. (Bychkova, N.V.) Moskva, 1960.
Phil 8980.572.30 Moralno-politicki lik komunista Vojvodine u NOR-u i revoluciji. (Miladinović, Milan M.) Beograd, 1971.
Phil 8964.7 Moralnośc życia Społecznego. (Olejnik, Stanisław.) Warszawa, 1970.
Phil 8980.8 Moral'nye oblik stroitelia kommunizma. (Akademiia nauk SSSR. Kafedra Filosofii.) Moskva, 1964.
Phil 8980.895.5 Moral'nyi oblik sovetskogo rabochego. (Zhuravkov, M.G.) Moskva, 1966.
Phil 8980.579 Moral'nyi rodeks stroitelia kommunizma. Moskva, 1964.
Phil 8877.50.15 Moralphilosophie. (Cathrein, Victor.) Leipzig, 1924. 2v.
Phil 8881.12.10 Moralphilosophie. (Gizycki, G.) Leipzig, n.d.
Phil 8893.138 Moralphilosophie. (Sibben, Frederik Christian.) Kjobenhavn, 1878.
Phil 8893.83 Die Moralphilosophie. 3. Aufl. (Salat, Jakob.) München, 1821.
Phil 2490.119 Die Moralphilosophie Auguste Comte's Versuch einer Darstellung und Kritik. (Schaefer, Albert.) Basel, 1906.
Phil 3890.6.83 Die Moralphilosophie von Tetens. (Schinz, Max.) Leipzig, 1906.
Phil 8893.53.5 Moralphilosophische Streitfragen. (Störring, Gustav.) Leipzig, 1903.
Phil 2280.1.93 Das Moralprinzip bei Sidgwick und bei Kant. (Bernays, Paul.) Göttingen, 1910.
Phil 9495.167.5 Moralpsykologi og sexualmoral. (Bjerg, Kresten.) København, 1967.
Phil 8962.26 Morals, law, and authority. Dayton, Ohio, 1969.
Phil 8962.26.1 Morals, law and authority. Dublin, 1969.
Phil 8878.22 Morals: a treatise on the psycho-sociological bases of ethics. (Duprat, G.L.) London, 1903.
Phil 8971.2.5 Morals and man. (Vann, Gerald.) N.Y., 1960.
Phil 8877.80 Morals and man in the social sciences. (Casserley, J.V.L.) London, 1951.
Phil 9358.6 Morals and manners. (Shearer, W.J.) N.Y., 1904.
Phil 8888.7 Morals and the evolution of man. (Nordau, Max.) London, 1922.
Phil 8886.45.10 Morals and western religion. (Laird, John.) London, 1931.
Phil 8893.110 Morals for mankind. (Schneider, Herbert W.) Columbia, 1960.
Phil 8882.59 Morals for moderns. (Habas, R.A.) N.Y., 1939.
Phil 8882.30 Morals in evolution. (Hobhouse, L.T.) London, 1908. 2v.
Phil 8832.3.5 Morals in evolution. 5th ed. (Hobhouse, L.T.) London, 1925.
Phil 8960.14 Morals in free society. (Keeling, Michael.) London, 1967.
Phil 8842.6 Morals in review. (Rogers, A.K.) N.Y., 1927.
Phil 8842.11 Morals in world history. (Robertson, Archibald M.A.) London, 1945.
Phil 8893.31.5 The morals of evolution. (Savage, M.J.) Boston, 1881.
Phil 8893.81 Morals of tomorrow. (Sockman, R.W.) N.Y., 1931.
Phil 8832.6 Morals since 1900. (Heard, Gerald.) London, 1950.
Phil 8894.31 Moralsjukdomen. (Törngren, P.H.) Stockholm, 1940.
Phil 8956.20.80 Der Moraltheologe Joseph Geishüttner (1763-1805), I. Kant und J.G. Fichte. (Derungs, Ursicin.) Regensburg, 1969.
Phil 8960.15 Moraltheologie und Bibel. (Kongress der Deutschsprachigen Moraltheologen, Freiburg, Germany, 1963.) Paderborn, 1964.
Phil 8957.16 Moraltheologisch Erkenntniss- und Methodenlehre. (Hofmann, Rudolf.) München, 1963.
Phil 6682.12 Morand, J.S. Le magnétisme animal. Paris, 1889.
Phil 343.45.5 Morandini, Francesco. Critica. 5. ed. Romae, 1963.
Phil 4210.149.3 Morando, Dante. Antonio Rosmini. Brescia, 1958.
Phil 4210.149 Morando, Dante. Rosmini. 2a ed. Brescia, 1945.
Phil 187.117 Morando, G. Corso elementare di filosofia. Milano, 1898-1899. 3v.
Phil 4210.124 Morando, G. Esame critico delle XL proposizioni rosminiane condaunate dalla S.R.U. inquisizione. Milano, 1905.
Phil 5252.31 Morando, G. Psicologia. 2a. ed. Voghera, 1915.
Phil 6122.14 Morat, J.P. Physiology of the nervous system. Chicago, 1906.
Phil 5252.156 Morávek, Milan. Otázky vzniku a povahy psychiky. Praha, 1965.
Phil 3640.615 Morawa, Hans. Sprache und Stil von Nietzsches Zarathustra. München, 1958.
Phil 3552.470 Morawietz, Kurt. Gottfried Wilhelm Leibniz. Hannover, 1962.
Phil 8170.8 Morawski, Stefan. Miedzy tradycja a wizja przyszłości. Warszawa, 1964.
Phil 8125.26 Morawski, Stefan. Rozwáj myśli. Warszawa, 1957.
Phil 8088.8 Morawski, Stefan. Studia z historii myśli estetycznej XVII:i XIX wieku. Warszawa, 1961.
Phil 5330.38 Moray, Neville. Listening and attention. Baltimore, 1969.
Phil 8430.26 Moray y arte. (Salicrú Puigvert, C.) Barcelona, 1960.
Phil 6315.3.2 Morbid fears and compulsions, their psychology. (Frink, H.W.) London, 1921.
Phil 6315.3 Morbid fears and compulsions, their psychology. (Frink, H.W.) N.Y., 1918.
Phil 7080.10 More, C.H. On going to sleep. London, 1868.
Htn Phil 8667.8* More, G. A demonstration of God in his workes. London, 1598.
Phil 8887.20 More, H. Moral sketches. Boston, 1819.
Phil 8887.20.3 More, H. Moral sketches. London, 1819.
Phil 9184.1 More, H. The young bride at home. Boston, 1836.
Htn Phil 8962.4.5* More, Hannah. Christian morals. 1st American ed. N.Y., 1813.
Htn Phil 8962.4.6* More, Hannah. Christian morals. 2nd American ed. N.Y., 1813.
Htn Phil 2145.65* More, Henry. Antidote against atheisme. London, 1653.
Htn Phil 2145.1* More, Henry. Collection...philosophical writings. London, 1662.
Htn Phil 2145.2.2* More, Henry. Collection...philosophical writings. London, 1712.
Phil 2145.2 More, Henry. Collection...philosophical writings. 4th ed. London, 1712.
Htn Phil 2145.60* More, Henry. Divine dialogues. London, 1668. 2v.
Htn Phil 2145.61* More, Henry. Divine dialogues. London, 1713.
Htn Phil 2145.48.5* More, Henry. Enchiridion ethicum. Amstelodami, 1679.
Htn Phil 2145.49.5* More, Henry. Enchiridion ethicum. Amstelodami, 1695.
Htn Phil 2145.49* More, Henry. Enchiridion ethicum. Amstelodami, 1695.
Phil 2145.50 More, Henry. Enchiridion ethicum. London, 1711.
Phil 2145.55A More, Henry. Enchiridion ethicum. N.Y., 1930.
Htn Phil 2145.40* More, Henry. Enchiridion metaphysicum. London, 1671.
Htn Phil 2145.70* More, Henry. The immortality of the soul. London, 1659.
Htn Phil 2150.5.31* More, Henry. The immortality of the soul. London, 1659.
Phil 2145.15 More, Henry. Philosophical writings. N.Y., 1925.
Phil 1133.22 More, Paul E. Hellenistic philosophies (From the death of Socrates to A.D. 451). Princeton, 1923.
Htn Phil 2150.5.30* More, Thomas. De optimo reipublicae statu, deque nova insula Utopia. Basileae, 1518.
Htn Phil 2150.5.80* More, Thomas. Life of Sir Thomas More, by his great-grandson. London, 1726.
Htn Phil 2150.5.10* More, Thomas. Workes. London, 1557.
Phil 8626.28.5 More about life in the world unseen. (Borgia, Anthony V.) London, 1958.
Phil 6980.112.10 More about psychiatry. (Binger, C.A.L.) Chicago, 1949.
Phil 8591.44.12 More Christianity. (Lewis, Clive Staples.) N.Y., 1960.
Phil 7060.92.45 More haunted houses of London. (O'Donnell, Elliot.) London, 1920.
Phil 5421.25.65 More loves than one. (Rosenberg, Stuart E.) N.Y., 1963.
Phil 9530.43 More power to you. (Barton, Bruce.) N.Y., 1917.
Phil 720.42 More than truth. (Kohn, David.) N.Y., 1956.
Phil 5627.15.9 More twice-born men. (Begbie, H.) N.Y., 1923.
Phil 1135.159 Moreau, J. L'âme du monde de Platon aux Stoiciens. Thèse. Paris, 1939.
Phil 5585.185 Moreau, J. L'horizon des esprits. Paris, 1960.
Phil 187.92 Moreau, J. Perspectives sur les relativités humaines. 2. ed. Paris, 1929.
Phil 5762.23 Moreau, J. Problèmes et pseudo-problèmes du déterminisme physique, biologique, psychologique. Paris, 1964.
Phil 6962.16 Moreau, J.J. Un chapitre oublié de la pathologie mentale. Paris, 1850.
Phil 6322.12 Moreau, J.J. La psychologie morbide. Paris, 1859.
Phil 2412.2 Moreau, Jacob N. Nouveau mémoire pour servir à l'histoire des Cacouacs. Amsterdam, 1757. 2 pam.
Phil 7150.16 Moreau, Jacques. Du suicide chez les enfants. Thèse. Paris, 1906.
Phil 582.4 Moreau, Joseph. La conscience et l'être. Paris, 1958.
Phil 3494.68 Moreau, Joseph. Le Dieu des philosophes. Paris, 1969.
Phil 3832.26 Moreau, Joseph. Spinoza et le spinozisme. 1. éd. Paris, 1971.
Phil 3552.358 Moreau, Joseph. L'univers leibnizien. Paris, 1956.
Htn Phil 7075.5.2* Moreau, P. Des aberrations du sens génésique. 2. ed. Paris, 1880.
Phil 6962.7 Moreau, P. Les excentriques. Paris, 1894.
Phil 6750.5 Moreau, P. Fous et Bouffons. Paris, 1888.
Phil 6682.17 Moreau, P.G. L'hypnotisme. Paris, 1891.
Phil 6962.6 Moreau-Christopie, L.M. De la mortalité et de la folie. Paris, 1839.
Phil 187.19 Moreau de St. Elier, L. Les songes physiques. Amsterdam, 1781.
Phil 812.17 Moreira da Sá, A. Os precursores de Desartes. Lisboa, 1944.
Phil 3640.840A Morel, Georges. Nietzsche; Introduction à une première lecture. Paris, 1970-71. 3v.
Phil 8667.40 Morel, Georges. Problèmes actuels de religion. Paris, 1968.
Phil 5252.9 Morell, J.D. Elements of psychology. pt. 1. Photoreproduction. London, 1853.
Phil 5052.41 Morell, J.D. Handbook of logic. London, 1866.
Phil 1712.1 Morell, J.D. Historical and critical...philosophy, XIX century. London, 1846. 2v.
Phil 1712.1.2 Morell, J.D. Historical and critical...philosophy, XIX century. N.Y., 1848.
Phil 1712.1.6 Morell, J.D. Historical and critical...philosophy, XIX century. N.Y., 1856.
Phil 5252.9.5 Morell, J.D. Introduction to mental philosophy. London, 1862.
Phil 187.20.5 Morell, J.D. Philosophical fragments. London, 1878.
Phil 8592.14.2 Morell, J.D. The philosophy of religion. London, 1849.
Phil 8592.14 Morell, J.D. The philosophy of religion. N.Y., 1849.
Phil 187.20 Morell, J.O. Philosophical tendencies of the age. London, 1848.
Phil 2115.81 Morell, T. Notes and annotations on Locke. London, 1794.
Phil 293.26 Morelli, C. Lo sviluppo del mondo nelle principali teorie filosofiche. Avellino, 1892.
Phil 5627.6.85 Morelli, G. La realtà dello spirito. Milano, n.d.
Phil 8962.7 Moren, Thorbjörn. Sedeläran i sammandrag. Stockholm, 1823.
Phil 3494.16.5 Morente, M.G. La estética de Kant. Thesis. Madrid, 1912.
Phil 3494.16 Morente, M.G. La filosofía de Kant. Madrid, 1917.
Phil 7060.65 Moreton, A. Secrets of the invisible world disclos'd. London, 1735.
Phil 7060.65.5 Moreton, A. Secrets of the invisible world disclos'd. London, 1740.
Phil 8702.32 Moretti, Jean. Biologie et réflexion chrétienne. Paris, 1967.
Phil 5627.215.10 Moretti-Costanzi, Teodorice. L'estetica pia. Bologna, 1966.
Phil 187.182 Moretti-Costanzi, Teodorico. L'ora della filosofia. Bologna, 1968.
Phil 8702.12.5 Moreux, T. Les confins de la science et de la foi. Paris, 1925. 2v.
Phil 8581.81.80 Morgan, A.E. The philosophy of Edward Bellamy. N.Y., 1945.
Phil 2150.23 Morgan, Arthur Ernest. Observations. Yellow Springs, 1968.
Phil 1955.2.80 Pamphlet box. De Morgan, Augustus.
Phil 575.87 Morgan, B.S. Individuality in a collective world. N.Y., 1935.
Phil 5822.1.15 Morgan, C.L. Animal behaviour. London, 1900.
Phil 5822.1.20 Morgan, C.L. The animal mind. N.Y., 1930.
Phil 187.29.15A Morgan, C.L. The emergence of novelty. London, 1933.
Phil 5822.1.10A Morgan, C.L. Habit and instinct. London, 1896.

Phil 5822.1.25 Morgan, C.L. Instinct and experience. N.Y., 1912.
Phil 187.29 Morgan, C.L. The interpretation of nature. Bristol, 1905.
Phil 187.29.3 Morgan, C.L. The interpretation of nature. N.Y., 1906.
Phil 5822.1A Morgan, C.L. Introduction to comparative psychology. London, 1884.
Phil 5822.1.3 Morgan, C.L. Introduction to comparative psychology. London, 1894.
Phil 187.29.5 Morgan, C.L. Mind at the crossways. N.Y., 1930.
Phil 9150.2 Morgan, C.L. The springs of conduct. London, 1885.
Htn Phil 8592.59* Morgan, Caesar. A demonstration that true philosophy has no tendency to undermine divine revelation. Cambridge, 1787.
Phil 5252.82.13 Morgan, Clifford Thomas. Introduction to psychology. 3d ed. N.Y., 1966.
Phil 5252.82.2A Morgan, Clifford Thomas. Physiological psychology. 2. ed. N.Y., 1950.
Phil 5252.82.3 Morgan, Clifford Thomas. Physiological psychology. 3. ed. N.Y., 1965.
Phil 365.12 Morgan, Conwy L. Emergent evolution. London, 1923.
Phil 365.12.7 Morgan, Conwy L. Life, mind and spirit. N.Y., 1925.
Phil 8622.60 Morgan, E.K. The ordeal of wonder. London, 1964.
Phil 575.268 Morgan, George W. The human predicament and dissolution and wholeness. Providence, 1968.
Phil 5330.17 Morgan, H.H.B. The overcoming of distraction and other resistances. N.Y., 1916.
Phil 5252.97 Morgan, J.J.B. Psychology. N.Y., 1947.
Phil 5252.67 Morgan, John J.B. An introduction to psychology. N.Y., 1927.
Phil 6122.55 Morgan, John J.B. Keeping a sound mind. N.Y., 1934.
Phil 6322.16.9 Morgan, John J.B. The psychology of abnormal people. 2d ed. N.Y., 1936.
Phil 6322.16.5 Morgan, John J.B. The psychology of abnormal people with educational applications. N.Y., 1935.
Phil 8887.18 Morgan, T. The moral philosopher. London, 1737-39. 2v.
Phil 8887.18.3 Morgan, T. The moral philosopher. v.1, 2. ed. London, 1738-40. 3v.
Phil 8887.18.5 Morgan, T. Physico-theology. London, 1741.
Phil 8887.19 Morgan, T.C. Sketches of the philosophy of morals. London, 1822.
Phil 5627.120 Morgan, William Joseph. La psychologie de la religion dans l'Amérique. Thèse. Paris, 1928.
Phil 3120.55.30 Das Morgen im Heute; eine Auswahl. (Bloch, Ernst.) Frankfurt, 1960.
Phil 3640.17.4 Morgenröte. (Nietzsche, Friedrich.) Stuttgart, 1952. 2v.
Phil 8667.5 Morgenstunden. (Mendelssohn, M.) Berlin, 1786.
Htn Phil 8667.3* Morgenstunden oder Vorlesungen uber das Daseyn Gottes. (Mendelssohn, M.) Berlin, 1785.
Phil 6962.19 Morgenthaler, Walter. Die Pflege der Gemüts- und Geisteskranken. Bern, 1930.
Phil 6962.19.5 Morgenthaler, Walter. Die Pflege der Gemüts- und Geisteskranken. 4. Aufl. Bern, 1941.
Phil 22.21 Morgunn; tímarit um andleg mál. Reykjavík. 1-9,1920-1928 2v.
Phil 5790.2.5 Moriarty, David M. The loss of loved ones. Springfield, 1967.
Phil 585.414 Morichon, René. Entretiens sur la destinée humaine. Limoges, 1970.
Phil 3925.16.150 Morick, Harold. Wittgenstein and the problem of other minds. N.Y., 1967.
Phil 6682.7 Morin, A.S. Du magnétisme. Paris, 1860.
Phil 8612.45.2 Morin, Edgar. L'homme et la mort. Paris, 1970.
Phil 293.32 Morin, Gérard. Vie et cosmos. Paris, 1962.
Phil 293.28 Morin, J.A. The serpent and the satellite. N.Y., 1953.
Phil 2750.12.90 Morin et les démonstrations mathématiques de l'existence de Dieu. (Iwanicki, J.) Paris, 1936.
Phil 6962.11 Morison, A. Physiognomik der Geisteskrankheiten. Leipzig, 1853.
Phil 8592.19 Morison, J.C. The service of man. London, 1887.
Phil 9560.52 Morisset, B. Le syllogisme prudentiel. Laval, 1961.
Phil 735.272 Moritz, Manfred. Inledning i värdeteori. 2. uppl. Lund, 1968.
Phil 3585.7.86 Moritz Lazarus. (Münz, Bernhard.) Berlin, 1900.
Phil 3195.1.80 Moritz Wilhelm Drobisch. (Neubert-Drobisch, W.) Leipzig, 1902.
Phil 4115.83 Morkos, D. Spiegazione analitica della formola ideale di V. Gioberti. Torino, 1865.
Phil 8413.41 Morkrejs, Antonín. Umění, skutečnost, poznání. Praha, 1966.
Phil 9560.4 Morley, C. The power of kindness. N.Y., 1851.
Phil 575.170 Morley, Felix. Essays on individuality. Philadelphia, 1958.
Phil 4075.80 Morley, H. Jerome Cardan. v.2. London, 1854.
Phil 9065.1 Morley, J. On compromise. London, 1877.
Phil 9065.1.5 Morley, J. On compromise. London, 1898.
Phil 9065.1.15 Morley, J. On compromise. London, 1933.
Phil 8413.17 Mormone, R. Avviamento alla critica d'arte. Napoli, 1954.
Phil 5585.175 The morning notes of Adelbert Ames, Jr. (Ames, Adelbert.) New Brunswick, N.J., 1960.
Phil 575.26 Moroney, Timothy. The idea of personality. Diss. Washington, 1919.
Phil 343.24 Morot, E. La pensée negative. Thèse. Paris, 1947.
Phil 525.107 Morot-Sir, E. Philosophie et mystique. Thèse. Paris, 1948.
Phil 310.235 Moroz, K.V. Dialekticheskii materializm, ideinoe oruzoiie bor'by za Kommunizm. Moskva, 1960.
Phil 7080.38 Morpheus, or The future of sleep. (Fraser-Harris, D.F.) London, 1928.
Phil 6315.4 Der Morphinismus, Kokainismus, Alkoholismus und Saturnismus. (Friedländer, A.) Jena, 1913.
Phil 6951.2 La morphinomanie. (Ball, B.) Paris, 1888.
Phil 5253.6 The morphologic aspect of intelligence. (Naccarati, S.) N.Y., 1921.
Phil 5258.152.10 Morphologie des seelischen Geschehens. (Salber, Wilhelm.) Ratingen, 1965.
Phil 3195.6.200 Morphologie und Hermeneutik. (Rodi, Frithjof.) Stuttgart, 1969.
Phil 8092.10 Morpurgo Taghabue, G. L'esthétique contemporaine. Milan, 1960.
Phil 3640.102 Morr, P.M. Nietzsche. Boston, 1912.
Phil 8592.124 Morra, Gianfranco. Dio senza Dio. Bologna, 1970.
Phil 585.169 Morra, Gianfranco. La riscoperta del sacro. Bologna, 1964.
Phil 4215.3.85 Morra, Gianfranco. Scetticismo e misticismo nel pensiero di Giuseppe Rensi. Siracuse, 1958.
Phil 665.84 Morreale de Castro, Margherita. Versiones españolas de animus y anima. Granada? 1957.

Phil 4351.3 Morreale deCastro, M. Pedro Simon Abril. Madrid, 1949.
Phil 5520.417 Morric, C.W. Signification and significance. Cambridge, 1964.
Phil 5374.2 Morrill, J.S. Self-consciousness of noted persons. Boston, 1887.
Phil 8413.26 Morris, B. The aesthetic process. Evanston, 1943.
Phil 8887.120 Morris, B. Philosophical aspects of culture. Yellow Springs, Ohio, 1961
Phil 5052.34 Morris, C.R. Idealistic logic. London, 1933.
Phil 2115.196 Morris, C.R. Locke, Berkeley, Hume. London, 1963.
Phil 325.6 Morris, C.W. Logical positivism, pragmatism and scientific empiricism. Paris, 1937.
Phil 735.160 Morris, C.W. Varieties of human value. Chicago, 1956.
Phil 8592.63.10 Morris, Charles W. The open self. N.Y., 1948.
Phil 8592.63 Morris, Charles W. Paths of life, prepace to a world religion. N.Y., 1942.
Phil 5520.84A Morris, Charles W. Signs, language and behavior. N.Y., 1946.
Phil 5252.68.5 Morris, Charles W. Six theories of mind. Chicago, 1959.
Phil 8702.21 Morris, D.L. Possibilities unlimited. 1. ed. N.Y., 1952.
Phil 5822.14 Morris, Desmond. The biology of art. London, 1962.
Phil 5822.14.5 Morris, Desmond. The biology of art. N.Y., 1962.
Phil 5252.170 Morris, Desmond. Intimate behaviour. London, 1971.
Phil 5252.157A Morris, Desmond. The naked ape; a zoologist's study of the human animal. 1. ed. N.Y., 1967.
Phil 1812.3 Morris, G.S. British thought and thinkers. Chicago, 1880.
Phil 3425.102A Morris, G.S. Hegel's philosophy of the state. Chicago, 1887.
Phil 3494.8 Morris, G.S. Kant's Critique of pure reason. Chicago, 1882.
Phil 2070.141 Morris, Lloyd R. William James; the message of a modern mind. N.Y., 1950.
Phil 2070.141.5 Morris, Lloyd R. William James; the message of a modern mind. N.Y., 1969.
Phil 596.2 Morris, Louis W. Polarity; a philosophy of tensions among values. Chicago, 1956.
Phil 1930.10.82 Morris Raphael Cohen. (Kuhn, M. Arno.) N.Y., 1957.
Phil 187.129 Morrish, Furze. Outline of metaphysics. London, 194-.
Phil 5627.185 Morrish, Furze. The ritual of higher magic. London, 1947?
Phil 7054.151 Morrison, A.B. Spiritualism and necromancy. Cincinnati, 1873.
Phil 8702.19.5 Morrison, Abraham C. Man does not stand alone. N.Y., 1946.
Phil 6750.224 Morrison, B.M. A study of the major emotions in persons of defective intelligence. Berkeley, 1924.
Phil 978.25 Morrison, D. The open door of the soul. Boston, 1908.
Phil 3925.16.160 Morrison, James. Meaning and truth in Wittgenstein's Tractatus. The Hague, 1968.
Phil 7076.22 Morrison, Paul Guerrant. The place of the ecstatic trance in the ideal of the good life. Chicago, 1932.
Htn Phil 6990.36* Morry, A. de. Discours d'un miracle avenu en la Basse Normandie. Paris, 1598.
Phil 7069.51.10 Mors et vita. (Aron, Robert.) Paris, 1951.
Phil 5401.4 Morse, J. The psychology and neurology of fear. Worcester, 1907.
Phil 7072.6.10 Morse, James Johnson. Spirit photography. Manchester, 1909.
Phil 7150.9.5 Morselli, H. Suicide. N.Y., 1882.
Phil 4065.83 Morselli, E. Giordano Bruno. Torino, 1888.
Phil 5052.30 Morselli, E. Principios de lógica. Buenos Aires, 1928.
Phil 7069.08.40 Morselli, E. Psicologia e "spiritismo". Torino, 1908. 2v.
Phil 6682.8 Morselli, E.A. Il magnetismo animale. Torino, 1886.
Phil 400.27.9 Morselli, Emilio. Il fondamento dell' idealismo etico. Livorno, 1911.
Phil 8612.59 La mort, cette in connue. (Montanden, Raoul.) Neuchâtel, 1948.
Phil 8612.61 La mort. (Jankélévitch, Valdimir.) Paris, 1966.
Phil 972.20 La mort de Canopus. (Panet, Edmond.) Paris, 1970.
Phil 8612.52.10 La mort et ses mystères. (Lepp, Ignace.) Paris, 1966.
Phil 7069.20.130 La mort et son mystère. (Flammarion, Camille.) Paris, 1920-1921. 2v.
Phil 1695.10 La morte della filosofia dopo Hegel e le correnti del pensiero contemporaneo. Roma, 1958.
Phil 400.94.15 La morte dell'idealismo. (Parente, A.) Napoli, 1937.
Phil 4225.8.34.2 Morte e immortalità. 2. ed. (Sciacca, Michele Federico.) Milano, 1962.
Phil 4225.8.34 Morte ed immortalità. (Sciacca, Michele Federico.) Milano, 1959.
Phil 5252.51 Mortensen, M. Grundrids af psykologi og paedogogik. 2. utg. København, 1901.
Phil 2905.1.515 Mortier, Jeanne M. Avec Teilhard de Chardin, vues ardentes. Paris, 1967.
Phil 8592.46 Mortier, Lowis. Le problème de la vie. Paris, 1872.
Phil 1730.28 Mortier, Roland. Clartés et ombres du siècle des lumières. Etudes sur le 18e siècle littéraire. Genève, 1969.
Phil 2805.345 Mortimer, Ernest. Blaise Pascal. London, 1959.
Phil 8610.902.25 Mortimer, G. The new morality. London, 1902.
Phil 8887.22 Morton, E. A key to true happiness. Hudson, Ohio, 1854.
Phil 6325.8.80 Morton Prince and abnormal psychology. (Taylor, William Sentman.) N.Y., 1928.
Phil 3494.39 Mortzfeldt, J.C. Fragmente aus Kants Leben. Königsberg, 1802.
Phil 7055.386 Mosaic; a psychic autobiography. (Woods, Margaret.) London, 1968.
Phil 8712.22 The mosaic account of creation. (Warring, C.B.) N.Y., 1875.
Phil 8706.1 The mosaic cosmogony. (Quarterman, J.) n.p., n.d.
Phil 8705.5 The mosaic theory of the solar or planetary system. (Pye, S.) London, 1766.
Htn Phil 170.2* Mosaicall philosophy. (Fludd, Robert.) London, 1659.
Phil 8887.23 Mosby, E.F. The ideal life. Cincinnatti, Ohio, 1877.
Phil 5068.102 Moscato, Alberto. Intenzionalità e dialettica. Firenze, 1969.
Phil 2805.417 Moscato, Alberto. Pascal. Milano, 1963.
Phil 343.65 Moscato, Alberto. Ricerche sulla struttura della conoscenza formale. Milano, 1962.
Phil 5075.5 Moschetti, A.M. L'unità come categoria. Milano, 1952. 2v.
Phil 3625.3.84 Moschetti, L. Fenomenismo e relativismo nel pensiero di E. Mach. Genova, 1923.
Phil 6322.48 Moscovici, Serge. La psychanalyse, son image et son public. Paris, 1961.
Phil 310.12.12 Moscow. Akademiia Obshchestvennogo Nauk. Programmy po istorii filosofii. Moskva, 1958.
Phil 1750.545 Moscow. Akademiia Obshchestvennykh Nauk. Kritika sovremennoi burzhuaznoi filosofii. Moskva, 1959.

Phil 1750.645 — Moscow. Akademiia Obshchestvennykh Nauk. Kritika sovremennoi burzhuaznoi filosofii i sotsiologii. Moskva, 1961.

Phil 1750.646 — Moscow. Akademiia Obshchestvennykh Nauk. Kritika sovremennoi burzhuaznoi filosofii i sotsiologii. Moskva, 1963.

Phil 8980.581 — Moscow. Akademiia Obshchestvennykh Nauk. Voprosy marksistko-leninskoi etiki. Moskva, 1962.

Phil 5203.15 — Moscow. Gosudarstvennaia Biblioteka SSSR. Imeni V.I. Lenina. Kak nauka ob"iasniaet psikhologicheskoi deiatel'nosti cheloveka. Moskva, 1954.

Phil 310.70 — Moscow. Gosudarstvennaia Biblioteka SSSR imeni V.I. Lenina. Chto chitat' po filosofii. Moskva, 1958.

Phil 8667.29 — Moscow. Gosudarstvennaia Biblioteka SSSR Imeni V.I. Lenina. Osnovy nauchnogo ateizma. Moskva, 1966.

Phil 8980.580 — Moscow. Gosudarstvennaia Bibiblioteka SSSR. Imeni V.I. Lenina. Chto chitat' o kommunisticheskoi morali. Moskva, 1955.

Phil 310.591 — Moscow. Institut Povyshennoi Kvalifikatsii Prepodovatelei Obshchestvennykh Nauk. Kafedra Dialekticheskogo i Istoricheskogo Materializma. Voprosy istoricheskogo materializma i nauchnogo kommunizma. Moskva, 1964.

Phil 310.12.10 — Moscow. Kafedra. Akadamiia Obshchestvennogo Nauk. Programma kursa dialekticheskogo i istori cheskogo materializma. Moskva, 1956.

Phil 310.545 — Moscow. Moskovskii Institut Inzhenerov Zheleznogo Transporta. Nekotorye voprosy teorii poznaniia dialekticheskogo materializma. Moskva, 1962.

Phil 5520.457 — Moscow. Pervyi Moskovskii Gosudarstvennyi Pedagogicheskii Institut Inostrannykh iazykov. Materialy kollokviuma po eksperimental'noi fonetike i psikhologii rechi. Moskva, 1966.

Phil 4710.7 — Moscow. Universitet. Filosofskii Fakul'tet. Iz istorii russkoi filosofii, sbornik. Leningrad, 1949.

Phil 4710.7.5 — Moscow. Universitet. Filosofskii Fakul'tet. Iz istorii russkoi filosofii, sbornik. Moskva, 1951.

Phil 4710.7.5.2 — Moscow. Universitet. Filosofskii Fakul'tet. Iz istorii russkoi filosofii, sbornik. Moskva, 1952.

Phil 4710.7.7 — Moscow. Universitet. Filosofskii Fakul'tet. Iz istorii russkoi filosofii, XVIII-XIX vv. Moskva, 1952.

Phil 4802.4 — Moscow. Universitet. Filosofskii fakultet. Izbrannye proizvedeniia progressivnykh pol'skikh myslitelei. Moskva, 1956-58. 3v.

Phil 4710.7.10A — Moscow. Universitet. Filosofskii Fakul'tet. Izbrannye proizvedeniia russkikh myslitelei vtoroi poloviny XVIII v. Leningrad, 1952. 2v.

Phil 5022.4 — Moscow. Universitet. Filosofskii Fakul'tet. Ocherki po istorii logiki v Rossii. Moskva, 1962.

Phil 8670.20.2 — Moscow. Universitet. Kafedra Istorii i Teorii Ateizma. Osnovnye voprosy nauchnogo ateizma. 2. izd. Moskva, 1966.

Phil 1712.22 — Moscow. Universitet Filosoficheskii Fakul'tet. Protiv sovremennoi burzhuaznoi filosofii. Moskva, 1963.

Phil 8980.581.10 — Moscow. Vsesoiuznyi Zaochnyi Politekhunicheskii Institut. Marksistko-leninskaia filosofiia. Moskva, 1965.

Phil 7060.156 — Moser, F. Spuk. Baden bei Zürich, 1950.

Phil 2045.111 — Moser, H. Thomas Hobbes: seine logische Problematik. Bern, 1923.

Phil 8887.127 — Moser, Shia. Absolutism and relativism in ethics. Springfield, 1968.

Phil 187.152 — Moser, Simon. Metaphysik einst und jetzt. Berlin, 1958.

Phil 187.152.5 — Moser, Simon. Philosophie und Gegenwart. Meisenheim am Glan, 1960.

Phil 6122.68 — Moser, Ulrich. Psychologie der Arbeitswahl und der Arheitsstörungen. Bern, 1953.

Phil 5627.11 — Moses, J. Pathological aspects of religions. Worcester, 1906.

Phil 6962.35 — Moses, Paul Joseph. Die Stimme der Neurose. Stuttgart, 1956.

Phil 6962.35.1 — Moses, Paul Joseph. The voice of neurosis. N.Y., 1954.

Phil 7068.94.45 — Moses, W.S. Spirit teachings. London, 1894.

Phil 7054.8 — Moses, William S. Higher aspects of spiritualism. London, 1880.

Phil 7077.4 — Moses, William S. Psychography. London, 1878.

Phil 7077.4.2 — Moses, William S. Psychography. 2d ed. London, 1882.

Phil 7054.8.5 — Moses, William S. Spirit identity. London, 1879.

Phil 8712.1 — Moses and modern science. (Weaver, G.O.) Cincinnati, 1872.

Phil 3625.1.129 — Moses Mendelssohn, critic and philosopher. (Walter, Hermann.) N.Y., 1930.

Phil 3625.1.56 — Moses Mendelssohn; eine Auswahl aus seinen Schriften und Briefen. (Mendelssohn, Moses.) Frankfurt, 1912.

Phil 3625.1.113 — Moses Mendelssohn. (Goldstein, L.) Konigsberg, 1904.

Phil 3625.1.107 — Moses Mendelssohn. (Kayserling, M.) Leipzig, 1862.

Phil 3625.1.53 — Moses Mendelssohn. (Mendelssohn, Moses.) Berlin, 1929.

Phil 3625.1.49 — Moses Mendelssohn. (Mendelssohn, Moses.) Berlin, 1929.

Phil 3625.1.48 — Moses Mendelssohn. (Mendelssohn, Moses.) Leipzig, 1883.

Phil 3625.1.150 — Moses Mendelssohn. (Zarek, O.) Amsterdam, 1936.

Phil 3625.1.180 — Moses Mendelssohn als Mensch. (Richter, Johann Andreas Lebrecht.) Dessau, 1829.

Phil 3625.1.139 — Moses Mendelssohn und die Aufgabe der Philosophie. (Kornfeld, H.) Berlin, 1896.

Phil 3625.1.175 — Moses Mendelssohn und die Dink. (Holdheim, Samuel.) Berlin, 1859.

Phil 3625.1.105 — Moses Mendelssohn und seine Familie. (Kahut, Adolf.) Dresden, 1886.

Phil 3625.1.153 — Moses Mendelssohn zur 200 jahrigen Wiederkehr seines Gehertstages. (Encyclopaidia Judaica.) Berlin, 1929.

Phil 3625.1.195 — Moses Mendelssohn's philosophische und religiöse Grundsätze mit Hinblick auf Lessing. (Kayserling, Meyer.) Leipzig, 1856.

Phil 3625.1.7 — Moses Mendelssohn's sämmtliche Werke. (Mendelssohn, Moses.) Wien, 1838.

Phil 4710.79 — Moskalenko, F.Ia. Gnoseologicheskoe soderzhanie logicheskikh form i metodov. Kiev, 1960.

Phil 4710.78 — Moskalenko, F.Ia. Uchenie ob induktivnykh vyrodakh v istorii russkoi logiki. Kiev, 1955.

Phil 5850.277 — Moss, F.A. Applications of psychology. Boston, 1929.

Phil 6962.20 — Moss, Fred August. Foundations of abnormal psychology. N.Y., 1932.

Phil 2475.1.310 — Mossé-Bastide, R.M. Bergson. Paris, 1955.

Phil 2475.1.360 — Mossé-Bastide, Rose Marie. Bergson et Plotin. 1. éd. Paris, 1959.

Phil 2475.1.360.5 — Mossé-Bastide, Rose Marie. Bergson et Plotin. 1. éd. Thèse. Paris, 1959.

Phil 187.81 — Mossig, T. Wirklichkeit. Leipzig, 1927.

Phil 1900.91 — Mossner, E.C. Bishop Butler and the age of reason. N.Y., 1936.

Phil 2050.212 — Mossner, E.C. The forgotten Hume, le bon David. N.Y., 1943.

Phil 2050.212.5 | Phil 6122.7.4 | Phil 6122.7 — Mossner, E.C. The life of David Hume. Austin, 1954.

Mosso, A. Die Ermüdung. Leipzig, 1892.

Mosso, A. La fatigue intellectuelle et physique. Paris, 1894.

X Cg — Phil 6122.7.3.5 | Phil 5401.1.10 | Phil 5401.1.12 | Phil 5401.1 | Phil 5401.1.5 | Phil 6122.7.5 — Mosso, A. Fatique. N.Y., 1904.

Mosso, A. Fear. London, 1896.

Mosso, A. Die Furcht. Leipzig, 1889.

Mosso, A. La paura. Milano, 1884.

Mosso, A. La peur. Paris, 1886.

Mosso, A. Psychic processes and muscular exercise. n.p., 1899. 2 pam.

Phil 6122.7.15 — Mosso, A. La température du cerveau, études thermometriques. Turin, 1895.

Phil 6122.7.9 — Mosso, A. Uber den Kreislauf des Blutes. Leipzig, 1881.

Phil 5052.29 — Mosso, Pietro. Principii di logica del potenziamento. Torino, 1924.

Phil 7069.41.5 — The most haunted house in England. (Price, Harry.) London, 1941.

Htn — Phil 7060.13.5* | Phil 672.266 — A most strange and dreadful apparition. London, 1680.

Mostepanenko, Aleksandr M. Problema universal'nosti osnovnykh svoistv prostranstva i vremeni. Leningrad, 1969.

Phil 5066.312 — Mostowski, Andrzej. Constructable sets with applications. Warszawa, 1969.

Phil 5066.254 — Mostowski, Andrzej. Thirty years of foundational studies. Oxford, 1966.

Phil 5790.2 — The mother, anxiety, and death: the catastrophic death complex. (Rheingold, Joseph Cyrus.) London, 1967.

Phil 9171.1.5 — A mother's advice to her son and daughter. (De Lambert, A.T. de M. de C.) Haverhill, 1814.

Phil 9171.1 — A mother's advice to her son and daughter. (De Lambert, A.T. de M. de C.) London, 1800.

Phil 9171.1.2 — A mother's advice to her son and daughter. (De Lambert A.T. de M. de C.) Boston, 1814.

Phil 9344.3.5 — Mothers of England. (Ellis, S.S.) N.Y., 1844. 7 pam.

Htn — Phil 187.54.9F* | Phil 187.54 — Motion, George. Diagram of the celestial city. n.p., n.d.

Motion, George. Fragments of philosophy: Democracy. Nelson, B.C., 1920.

Phil 187.54.5F | Phil 5066.145 — Pamphlet box. Motion, George. Fragments of philosophy.

The motion of analytic truth. (Martin, Richard M.) Philadelphia, 1959.

Phil 5548.125 — Motivating economic achievement. (McClelland, David Clarence.) N.Y., 1969.

Phil 5548.75.5 — Motivation, Persönlichkeit, Umwelt. (Toman, Walter.) Göttingen, 1968.

Phil 5548.60 — Motivation. (Bindra, Dalbir.) N.Y., 1959.

Phil 5548.65 — La motivation. 1. éd. (Association de Psychologie Scientifique de Langue Française.) Paris, 1959.

Phil 5548.83 — La motivation à l'avancement professionnel. (Iff, Werner.) Paris, 1962.

Phil 5548.90 — Motivation and emotion. (Young, Paul Thomas.) N.Y., 1961.

Phil 5548.120 — Motivation and organizational climate. (Litwin, George Henry.) Boston, 1968.

Phil 5548.98 — Motivation and personality. 2. ed. (Maslow, Abraham Harold.) N.Y., 1970.

Phil 5548.102 — Motivation and social interaction. (Harvey, O.J.) N.Y., 1963.

Phil 5590.10 — Motivation and visual factors; individual studies of college students. Hanover, 1942.

Phil 5548.105 — Die Motivation menschlichen Handelns. (Thomae, Hans.) Köln, 1965.

Phil 5548.80 — The motivation of behavior. (Brown, J.S.) N.Y., 1961.

Phil 5264.3 — Motivation of behavior. (Young, P.T.) N.Y., 1936.

Phil 5264.3.5 — Motivation of behavior. (Young, P.T.) N.Y., 1950.

Phil 5867.5 — Motivations in play, games and sports. (Slovenko, Ralph.) Springfield, 1967.

Phil 3549.10.5 — Motive; essays. (Kassner, Rudolf.) Berlin, 1906.

Phil 5548.85A — Motives in fantasy, action, and society. (Atkinson, John W.) Princeton, 1958.

Phil 5548.85.2 — Motives in fantasy, action, and society. (Atkinson, John W.) Princeton, 1968.

Phil 8886.6.10 — Motives of mankind. (Laycock, F.U.) London, 1907.

Phil 8416.13 — Motivos de estética. 2. ed. (Pagano, José L.) Buenos Aires, 1941.

Phil 5649.22 — Motor adaptation and accuracy. (McNeill, H.) Louvain, 1934.

Phil 900.9 — Motora, Y. An essay on Eastern philosophy. Leipzig, 1905.

Phil 5520.46 — Die motorischen Wortvorstellungen. (Dodge, Raymond.) Halle, 1896.

Phil 1712.28 — Motroshilova, Nelli V. Poznanie i obshchestvo. Moskva, 1969.

Phil 3450.19.305 — Mots, mythes et réalité dans la philosophie de Heidegger. (Wahl, J.A.) Paris, 1961.

Phil 3790.12.81 — Motsch, Karl E. Matern Reuss. Freiburg, 1932.

Phil 2150.1.130 — Mott, F.J. The crisis of opinion. Boston, 1944.

Phil 6122.70 — Mott, Francis. The nature of the self. London, 1959.

Phil 6122.26 — Mott, Frederick Walker. Nature and nurture in mental development. N.Y., 1915.

Phil 7150.6 — Motta, Emilio. Bibliografia del suicidio. Bellinzona, 1890.

Phil 8413.32 — Mottier, G. Le phémomène de l'art. Parisè 1936.

Phil 5440.40 — Mottram, Vernon Henry. The physical basis of personality. Harmondsworth, 1944.

Phil 5548.55 — Motywy postępowania. (Ossowska, M.) Warszawa, 1958.

Phil 8060.7 — Motz, H. Uber die Empfindung der Naturschönheit bei den Alten. Leipzig, 1865.

Phil 575.16 — Mouchet, E. Examen del concepto de identidad. Buenos Aires, 1910.

NEDL — Phil 5252.79 — Mouchet, E. Percepción instinto y razon. Buenos Aires, 1941.

Phil 5520.43 — Mouchet, Enrique. El lenguaje interior y los trastornos de la palabra. La Plata, 1923.

Phil 1750.382 — Mougin, Henri. La sainte famille existentialiste. Paris, 1947.

Phil 8702.24 — Mouiren, Trophine. La création. Paris, 1961.

Phil 1133.21 — Moulard, A. Metpon; étude sur l'idée de mesure dans la philosophie antésocratique. Thèse. Angers, 1923.

Phil 343.21 — Mouloud, N. Formes structurées et modes productifs. Paris, 195-?

Phil 575.147 — Mounier, E. Be not afraid. London, 1951.

Phil 575.146.10 — Mounier, E. The character of man. London, 1956.

Phil 2750.22 — Mounier, E. Mounier et sa generation. Paris, 1956.

Phil 2750.22.5 — Mounier, E. Ouevres. Paris, 1961. 5v.

Phil 575.146.5 — Mounier, E. Personalism. London, 1952.

Phil 575.146 — Mounier, E. Le personnalisme. Paris, 1950.

Phil 2750.22.30   Mounier, E. La petite peur du XXe siècle. Neuchâtel, 1959.

Phil 1750.230   Mounier, Emman. Existentialist philosophies. London, 1948.

Phil 1750.225   Mounier, Emman. Introduction aux existentialismes. Paris, 1947.

Phil 2750.22   Mounier et sa generation. (Mounier, E.) Paris, 1956.

Phil 5520.750   Mounin, Georges. Introductions à la sémiologie. Paris, 1971.

Phil 8893.18   The mountaineer. (Speece, C.) Staunton, 1823.

Phil 5252.88   Mourad, Youssef. L'eveil de l'intelligence. Paris, 1939.

Phil 330.18   Mourelos, G. L'épistémologie positive et la critique. Paris, 1962.

Phil 330.18.2   Mourelos, G. L'épistémologie positive et la critique meyersonienne. Thèse. Paris, 1962.

Phil 2475.1.425   Mourélos, Giorgos. Bergson et les niveaux de realité. Paris, 1964.

Phil 2490.115   Mourgue, R. La philosophie biologique d'A.C. Lyon, 1909.

Phil 8615.8   Mourik Broekman, M.C. von. De "Deutsche Gesellschaft für ethische Kultur". n.p., 1909.

Phil 8592.80   Mouroux, Jean. The meaning of man. N.Y., 1952.

Phil 8592.81   Mouroux, Jean. Sens chrétien de l'homme. Paris, 1953.

Phil 2805.278   Moussalli, U. Le vrai visage de Blaise Pascal. Paris, 1952.

Phil 6990.50   Mousset, Albert. L'étrange histoire des convulsionnaires de Saint-Medard. Paris, 1953.

Phil 5465.196   Moustakas, Clark E. Creativity and conformity. N.Y., 1967.

Phil 5590.320   Moustakas, Clark E. The self. N.Y., 1956.

Phil 8887.24   Moustalon. La morale des poètes. Paris, 1816.

Phil 5374.275   Moutada, Leo. Über die Funktion der Mobilität in der geistigen Entwicklung. Stuttgart, 1968.

Phil 6682.21   Moutin, Lucien. Le magnétisme humain. Paris, 1907.

Phil 5649.6   Le mouvement. (Woodworth, R.S.) Paris, 1903.

Phil 2401.7   Le mouvement antipositiviste contemporain en France. Thèse. (Bonnard, A.) Paris, 1936.

Phil 5374.154.9   Mouvement et pensée. (Peucesco, M.G.) Paris, 1927.

Phil 1750.136   Le mouvement humaniste en Amerique. (Richard, Christian.) Paris, 1934.

Phil 1750.136.5   Le mouvement humaniste en Amérique et les courants de pensée similaire en France. Thèse. (Richard, Christian.) Paris, 1934.

Phil 400.28   Le mouvement idéaliste et la réaction contre la science positive. 3. ed. (Fouilleé, A.) Paris, 1913.

Phil 8837.9   Le mouvement moral vers 1840. (Meyer, R.M.) Paris, 1913.

Phil 2401.1   Le mouvement philosophique, 1748-1789. (Belin, J.P.) Paris, 1913.

Phil 1700.12   Le mouvement philosophique dan la première moitie du XVIIIe siècle. (Adam, Antoine.) Paris, 1967.

Phil 400.35   Mouw, J.A. der. Het absoluut idealisme. Leiden, 1905.

Phil 2840.90   Mouy, P. L'idée de progrès dans la philosophie de Renouvier. Paris, 1927.

Phil 2840.90.2   Mouy, P. L'idée de progrès dans la philosophie de Renouvier. Thèse. Paris, 1927.

Phil 2733.100   Mouy, P. Les lois du choc des corps d'après Malebranche. Paris, 1927.

Phil 2733.100.2   Mouy, P. Les lois du choc des corps d'après Malebranche. Thèse. Paris, 1927.

Phil 9530.62   Move ahead with possibility thinking. 1. ed. (Schuller, Robert.) Garden City, 1967.

Phil 5649.32   Movement and meaning. (Metheny, Eleanor.) N.Y., 1968.

Phil 5780.6   Movement and mental imagery. (Washburn, M.F.) Boston, 1916.

Phil 5643.160   Movement apparent et préparation perceptive. (Mandy-van Moerbeke, Marie Paule.) Louvain, 1967.

Phil 6965.28   Movement in psychotherapy; psychomotor techniques and training. (Pesso, Albert.) N.Y., 1969.

Phil 1712.14A   Movements of thought in the nineteenth century. (Mead, George H.) Chicago, 1936.

Phil 8400.25   Movens; Dokumente und Analysen zur Dichtung. (Mon, Franz.) Wiesbaden, 1960.

Phil 1140.10   Movia, Giancarlo. Anima e intelletto. Padova, 1968.

Phil 70.22.5   Il movimento di Gallarate. (Centro di Studi Filosofici Cristiani, Gallarate.) Padova. 1955

Phil 365.44   The moving tent. (Kingson, B.) Wellington, 1936.

Phil 6980.482   Mowrer, O.H. The crisis in psychiatry and religion. Princeton, N.J., 1961.

Phil 9352.10   Mowry, William A. Talks with my boys. Boston, 1885.

Phil 9352.10.5   Mowry, William A. Talks with my boys. 5th ed. N.Y., 1909.

Phil 9352.11   Moxom, P.S. The aim of life. Boston, 1894.

Phil 8593.13   Mozhet-li sovremennyi obrazovannyi, mysliashchii chelovek vierit' v bozhectvo Iisusa Khrista. 3. izd. (Nikolai, Pavel N.) Praga, 1923.

Phil 8092.24   Mozhniagun, Sergei E. O modernizme. Moskva, 1970.

Phil 410.77   Mozkowski, A. Der Abbau des "Unendlich". Berlin, 1925.

Phil 6480.192   Mozzuchelli, M. I sogni. Milano, 1954.

Phil 3705.2.86   Mr. C.W. Opzoomer als wijsgeer. (Veer, Hendrik.) Assen, 1961.

Phil 3705.2.85   Mr. C.W. Opzoomer als wijsgeer. (Veer, Hendrik.) Assen, 1961.

Htn   Phil 2045.64*   Mr. Hobbes considered in his loyalty, religion, reputation and manners. (Hobbes, Thomas.) London, 1662.

Phil 2280.1.90   Mr. Sidgwick's hedonism. (Bradley, F.H.) London, 1877.

Phil 2750.11.175   Mrówczyński, Tadeusz. Personalizm Maritaina i współczesna myśl Katolicka. Warszawa, 1964.

Phil 974.4.25   Mrs. Annie Besant. (Besterman, T.) London, 1934.

Phil 974.4.10   Mrs. Annie Besant. (West, G.) London, 1927.

Phil 8837.11   Mrs. Grundy. (Markum, Leo.) N.Y., 1930.

Phil 197.3.15   Mrs. Piozzi and Isaac Watts. (Piozzi, H.L.T. (Mrs.).) London, 1934.

Phil 5068.50   Mshvenieradze, V.V. Filosofiia reopozitivizma i semantiki. Moskva, 1961.

Phil 1712.21   Mshvenieradze, V.V. Osnovnye fecheniia sovremennoi burzhuaznoi filosofii. Kiev, 1961.

Phil 5822.4.3   Muan, N.L. Psychological development. Boston, 1938.

Phil 1718.42   Muasir Aurupa felsefesi. (Saffet, Mehmet.) Ankara, 1933.

Phil 5590.180   Mucchielli, R. Caractères et visages. Paris, 1954.

Phil 5590.350   Mucchielli, R. La caractérologie à l'âge scientifique. Neuchâtel, 1961.

Phil 5252.162   Mucchielli, Roger. Introduction à la psychologie structurale. 2. ed. Bruxelles, 1968.

Phil 187.154   Mucchielli, Roger. Logique et morale. Paris, 1955.

Phil 8592.115   Muck, Otto. Christliche Philosophie. Kevelaer, 1964.

Phil 1750.107.2   Muck, Otto. The transcendental method. N.Y., 1968.

Phil 1750.107   Muck, Otto. Die transzendentale Methode in der scholastischen Philosophie der Gegenwart. Innsbruck, 1964.

Phil 3640.156   Muckle, Friedrich. Friedrich Nietzsche und der Zusammenbruch der Kultur. München, 1921.

Phil 8637.24.2   Muderspach, L. Bag død og grav. 2. udg. København, 1927.

Phil 5627.63   Mudge, E.L. The God-experience. Cincinnati, 1923.

Phil 8887.40   Mudie, Robert. Man as a moral and accountable being. London, 1840.

Phil 8887.40.5   Mudie, Robert. Man in his relations to society. London, 1840.

Phil 974.3.123   Muecke, Johanna. Erinnerungen an Rudolf Steiner. Basel, 1955.

Phil 7080.53   Müde Menschen. (Wiedemann, Fritz.) Heidenheim, 1953.

Phil 5762.2   Müffelmann, L. Das Problem der Willensfreiheit. London, 1902.

Phil 3640.218.2   Mügge, M.A. Friedrich Nietzsche. London, 1908.

Phil 3640.218   Mügge, M.A. Friedrich Nietzsche. London, 1912.

Phil 3640.218.5   Mügge, M.A. Friedrich Nietzsche. N.Y., 1915?

Phil 3640.218.4   Mügge, M.A. Friedrich Nietzsche. 4th ed. London, 1914.

Phil 1750.520   Muehlethaler, Jakob. Existenz und Transzendenz in der gegenwärtegen Philosophie. Basel, 1958.

Phil 5875.64   Muehling, Ursel. Erstellung eines Projektiven Verfahrens zur psychologischen Untersuchung nichtsprechender und hochgradig sprechbehinderter Kinder. Köln, 1968.

Phil 187.22   Mühry, A. Kritik und Kurze Darlegung der exacten Natur-Philosophie. Göttingen, 1882.

Phil 165.2A   Muelder, Walter G. The development of American philosophy. Boston, 1940.

Phil 165.2.5   Muelder, Walter G. The development of American philosophy. 2. ed. Boston, 1960.

Phil 3808.112.20   Mülethaler, J. Die Mystik bei Schopenhauer. Berlin, 1910.

Phil 2493.82   Mülhaupt, P. Darstellung der Psychologie bei Condillac und Bonnet. Cassel, 1874.

Phil 6122.40   Müller, A. Bismarck, Nietzsche, Scheffel, Mörike; der Einfluss nervöser Zustände auf ihr Leben und Schaffen. Bonn, 1921.

Phil 735.145   Müller, A. Die Grundkategorien des Lebendigen. Meisenheim, 1954.

Phil 8413.29   Mueller, A.E. The world as spectacle, an aesthetic view of philosophy. N.Y., 1944.

Phil 3625.24   Müller, Adam H. Schriften. Neuwield, 1967. 2v.

Phil 6055.2.2   Mueller, Alfred Eugen. Weltgeschichte graphologisch Gesehen. Köln, 1965.

Phil 3625.13.19   Müller, Aloys. Schriften zur Philosophie. Bonn, 1967. 2v.

Phil 293.34   Mueller, Aloys. Die Stellung des Menschen im Kosmos. Bonn, 1948.

Phil 630.6.5   Müller, Aloys. Wahrheit und Wirklichkeit: Untersuchungen zum realistischen Wahrheitsproblem. Bonn, 1913.

Phil 3625.13.34   Müller, Aloys. Welt und Mensch in ihrem irrealen Aufbau. 4. Aufl. Leiden, 1951.

Phil 3925.16.185   Mueller, Anselm. Ontologie in Wittgensteins "Tractatus". Bonn, 1967.

Phil 2905.1.270   Mueller, Armin. Das naturphilosophische Werk Teilhard de Chardins. Freiburg, 1964.

Phil 510.1.31   Müller, D.A. Scheinchristentum und Haeckels Welträtsel. Inaug. Diss. Gotha, 1901.

Phil 1135.70   Müller, E. Die Idee der Menschheit. Leipzig, 1877.

Phil 5052.10   Müller, E. Über die Algebra der Logik. v. 1-2. Leipzig, 1900-01.

Phil 8060.2   Müller, Eduard. Geschichte der Theorie der Kunst. v.1-2. Breslau, 1834-37.

Phil 7068.89.3   Müller, Egbert. Enthüllung des Spukes von Resau. 3. Aufl. Berlin, 1889.

Phil 5252.10   Müller, F.A. Das Axiom der Psychophysik. Marburg, 1882.

Phil 6322.2   Müller, F.C. Psychologie des Bewusstseins. Leipzig, 1889.

Phil 4012.8   Mueller, F.L. La pensée contemporaine en Italie et l'influence de Hegel. Genève, 1941.

Phil 8592.15   Müller, F.M. Lectures on the origin and growth of religion. London, 1880.

Phil 8592.15.2   Müller, F.M. Lectures on the origin and growth of religion. N.Y., 1879.

Phil 8592.15.4   Müller, F.M. Lectures on the origin and growth of religion. 2. ed. London, 1878.

Phil 8592.15.5   Müller, F.M. Natural religion. London, 1889.

Phil 5520.3   Müller, F.M. Science of thought. London, 1887.

Phil 5520.3.5   Müller, F.M. Science of thought. v.2. N.Y., 1887.

Phil 8520.2   Müller, F.M. Theosophy or psychological religion. London, 1893.

Phil 3425.750   Mueller, Friedrich. Entfremdung. Berlin, 1970.

Phil 6990.3.50   Müller, G.A. Nach Lourdes. Luzern, 1909.

Phil 5252.30.9   Müller, G.E. Abriss der Psychologie. Göttingen, 1924.

Phil 187.149.5   Mueller, G.E. Dialectic; a way into and within philosophy. N.Y., 1953.

Phil 5252.30.5   Müller, G.E. Die Gesichtspunkte und der Tatsachen der psychophysischen Methodik. Wiesbaden, 1904.

Phil 187.149   Mueller, G.E. The interplay of opposites. N.Y., 1956.

Phil 5645.37   Müller, G.E. Kleine Beiträge zur Psychophysik der Farbenempfindungen. Leipzig, 1934.

Phil 187.108.5   Müller, G.E. Der Mensch im Sein. Stuttgart, 1938.

Phil 187.108   Müller, G.E. Philosophy of our uncertainties. Norman, 1936.

Phil 5252.30   Müller, G.E. Zur Grundlegung der Psychophysik. 2. Ausg. Berlin, 1879.

Phil 5330.3   Müller, G.E. Zur Theorie der sinnlichen Aufmerksamkeit. Leipzig, 1874?

Phil 3425.299   Müller, G.R. Hegel über Offenbarung. München, 1939.

Phil 5585.34   Müller, Georg E. Komplextheorie und Gestalttheorie. Göttingen, 1923.

Phil 3850.1.105   Müller, Gotthold. Identität und Immanenz; zur Genese der Theologie von David Friedrich Strauss, eine theologie- und philosophiegeschichtliche Studie. Zürich, 1968.

Phil 5585.38   Müller, Günter. Theorie des Vorstellungsverlaufs. Mannheim, 1925.

Phil 1812.7A   Müller, Gustav E. Amerikanische Philosophie. Stuttgart, 1936.

Phil 1812.7.5   Müller, Gustav E. Amerikanische Philosophie. 2. Aufl. Stuttgart, 1950[1936].

Phil 3425.525   Mueller, Gustav E. Hegel. Bern, 1959.

Phil 5520.74   Müller, H. Experimentelle Beiträge zur Analyse des Verhältnisses von Laut und Sinn. Berlin, 1935.

Phil 3140.80   Müller, H. Johannes Clauberg. Jena, 1891.

Phil 3850.16.96   Mueller, H. Lebensphilosophie und Religion bei Georg Simmel. Berlin, 1960.

Phil 5520.340   Mueller, Heinz A. Die Psychologie des Lesens. Lörrach, 1958.

Phil 5762.28   Mueller, Heinz Alfred. Spontaneität und Gesetzlichkeit. Bonn, 1967.

Phil 3850.27.175   Mueller, Herbert. Albert Schweitzer. Duisburg, 1956.

Phil 2138.125   Mueller, I.W. John Stuart Mill and French thought. Urbana, 1956.

Phil 3832.7 — Müller, J. Der Begriff die sittlichen Unvollkommenheit bei Descartes und Spinoza. Leipzig, 1890.

Htn Phil 3625.4.35 — Müller, J. Ja zur Wirklichkeit. Weilheim, 1963.

Phil 7060.20* — Müller, J. Über die phantastischen Gesichteserscheinungen. Coblenz, 1826.

Phil 3625.4.30 — Müller, J. Vom Gebeimnis des Lebens. Stuttgart, 1953. 3v.

Phil 8612.13 — Müller, J. Vom Leben und Sterben. 3. Aufl. München, 1913.

Phil 187.24 — Müller, J.G. Philosophische Aufsäze. Breslau, 1795.

Phil 8887.50.10 — Müller, Johannes. Hemmungen des Lebens. München, 193-?

Phil 8887.50.11 — Müller, Johannes. Hemmungen des Lebens. München, 1956.

Phil 8887.50.12 — Müller, Johannes. Hindrances of life. N.Y., 1909.

Phil 3494.50 — Mueller, Johannes. Kantisches Staatsdenken und der Preussische Staat. Kitzingen, 1954.

Phil 8887.50 — Müller, Johannes. Neue Wegweiser; Aufsätze und Reden. München, 1920.

Phil 6122.85 — Mueller, Johannes. Physiologie du système nerveux. 3. éd. Paris, 1840. 2v.

Phil 187.70 — Müller, Josef. System der Philosophie. Mainz, 1898.

Phil 5585.226 — Mueller, Kurt. Der Aufbau figural-optischer Phänomene bei sukzessiver Reizung. Frankfurt, 1963.

Phil 3552.462.5 — Mueller, Kurt. Leben und Werk von Gottfried Wilhelm Leibniz. Frankfurt, 1969.

Phil 3552.462 — Mueller, Kurt. Leibniz-Bibliographie; die Literatur über Leibniz. Frankfurt, 1967.

Phil 4769.1.102.5 — Müller, Ludolf. Das religionsphilosophische System Vladimir Solowjews. Berlin, 1956.

Phil 4769.1.102 — Müller, Ludolf. Solovjev und der Protestantismus. Freiburg, 1951.

Phil 7068.72 — Müller, M. Triumph of the blessed sacrament or History of Nicola Aubry. Baltimore, 1872.

Phil 1712.25 — Mueller, Max. Das christliche Menschenbild und die Weltanschauungen der Neuzeit im Breiszau. Freiburg, 1945.

Phil 1750.352 — Müller, Max. Existenzphilosophie im geistigen Leben der Gegenwart. Heidelberg, 1949.

Phil 1750.352.3 — Müller, Max. Existenzphilosophie im geistigen Leben der Gegenwart. 3e Aufl. Heidelberg, 1964.

Phil 2412.5 — Müller, Max. Die französische Philosophie der Gegenwart. Karlsruhe, 1926.

Phil 3625.26 — Müller, Max. Symbolos. München, 1967.

Phil 735.103 — Müller, Max. Über Grundbegriffe philosophischer Wertlehre. Inaug. Diss. Freiburg, 1932.

Phil 9495.168.15 — Müller, Michael. Grundlagen der Katholischen Sexualethik. Regensburg, 1968.

Phil 5374.39 — Müller, R. Das normale Bewusstsein. Leipzig, 1898.

Phil 3120.8.110 — Mueller, Richard. Franz Brentanos Lehre von den Gemütsbewegungen. Brünn, 1943.

Phil 5465.128 — Mueller, Robert E. Inventivity. N.Y., 1963.

Phil 3549.8.145 — Mueller, Roland. Das verzwistete Ich-Ludwig Klages und sein philosophisches Hauptwerk Der Geist als Widersacher der Seele. Bern, 1971.

Phil 5875.140 — Mueller, Rudolf. Entwicklung des sozialen Wertbewusstseins; eine empirische Untersuchung des sittlichen Beuresstseins bei Kindern und Jugendlichen. Thesis. Weinheim, 1968.

Phil 5222.8 — Müller, T.L. Histoire de la psychologie. Paris, 1960.

Phil 1504.19 — Müller, W. Der Staat in seinen Beziehungen zur sittlichen. v.19, pt.1. Münster, 1916.

Phil 3450.11.180 — Mueller, W.H. Die Philosophie Edmund Husserl den Grandzügen ihrer Entstefung. Bonn, 1956.

Phil 665.51A — Müller, Walter. Das Problem der Seelenschönheit im Mittelalter. Bern, 1923.

Phil 6122.29 — Müller, Wilhelm. Rede Gehalten zur Feier der akademischen Preisverteilung am 23 Juni 1898. Jena, 1898.

Phil 5425.72 — Müller, Willy. Genie und Talent. München, 1940.

Phil 5627.264.15 — Mueller-Eckhard, Hans. Das Unzerstörbare. Stuttgart, 1964.

Phil 9070.75 — Mueller-Eckhard, Hans. Weltbewältigung. Stuttgart, 1959.

Phil 5222.4.5 — Müller-Freienfelds, R. The evolution of modern psychology. New Haven, 1935.

Phil 5222.4 — Müller-Freienfels, R. Die Hauptrichtungen der gegenwärtigen Psychologie. Leipzig, 1929.

Phil 5252.38 — Müller-Freienfels, R. Das Denken und die Phantasie. Leipzig, 1916.

Phil 187.86.10 — Müller-Freienfels, R. Geheimnisse der Seele. München, 1927.

Phil 5252.38.5 — Müller-Freienfels, R. Grundzüge einer Lebenspsychologie. Leipzig, 1924-25. 2v.

Phil 343.11 — Müller-Freienfels, R. Irrationalismus. Leipzig, 1922.

Phil 5252.38.20 — Müller-Freienfels, R. Menschenkenntnis und Menschenbehandlung. Berlin, 1951.

Phil 187.86 — Müller-Freienfels, R. Metaphysik des Irrationalen. Leipzig, 1927.

Phil 187.86.15 — Müller-Freienfels, R. Mysteries of the soul. London, 1929.

Phil 8413.28 — Müller-Freienfels, R. Psychologie der Kunst. Leipzig, 1923-33. 3v.

Phil 5252.38.15 — Müller-Freienfels, R. Die Seele des Alltags. 2. Aufl. Berlin, 1925.

Phil 5252.38.10 — Müller-Freienfels, R. Tagebuch eines Psychologen. Leipzig, 1931.

Phil 575.34 — Müller-Freienfels, Richard. Persönlichkeit und Weltanschauung. Berlin, 1919.

Phil 575.34.2 — Müller-Freienfels, Richard. Persönlichkeit und Weltanschauung. 2e Aufl. Berlin, 1923.

Phil 575.34.5.2 — Müller-Freienfels, Richard. Philosophie der Individualität. 2e Aufl. Leipzig, 1923.

Phil 1740.2 — Müller-Freienfels, Richard. Die Philosophie des zwanzigsten Jahrhunderts in ihren Hauptströmungen. Berlin, 1923.

Phil 3450.19.225 — Mueller-Lauter, W. Möglichkeit und Wirklichkeit bei M. Heidegger. Berlin, 1960.

Phil 9415.5 — Mueller-Lyer, Franz. Soziologie der Leiden. München, 1914.

Phil 1750.750 — Mueller-Schwefe, Hans Rudolf. Existenzphilosophie. Zürich, 1961.

Phil 1750.750.2 — Mueller-Schwefe, Hans Rudolf. Existenzphilosophie. 2. Aufl. Göttingen, 1969.

Phil 1750.166.260 — Mueller-Schwefe, Hans Rudolf. Humanismus ohne Gott. Stuttgart, 1967.

Phil 3195.6.160 — Mueller-Vollmer, K. Towards a phenomenological theory of literature. The Hague, 1963.

Phil 978.49.835 — Muellner, L. Rudolf Steiner und Brunn am Gebirge bei Wien. Wien, 1960.

Phil 3120.30.130 — München ehrt Martin Buber. München, 1961.

Phil 52.6 — Münchener philosophische Abhandlungen. Leipzig, 1911.

Phil 22.15 — Münchener Studien zur Psychologie und Philosophie. Stuttgart. 1-5,1914-1920 5v.

Phil 3800.386.2 — Münchener Vorlesungen. (Schelling, F.W.J. von.) Leipzig, 1902.

Phil 2050.110 — Münster, O. Det Hume'ske problem. København, 1912.

Phil 2150.6.30 — Münsterberg, H. American patriotism and other social studies. N.Y., 1913.

Phil 5252.12.17 — Münsterberg, H. American problems. N.Y., 1910.

Phil 5252.12 — Münsterberg, H. Beiträge zur experimentellen Psychologie. Freiberg, 1888-92.

Phil 5850.278.15 — Münsterberg, H. Business psychology. Chicago, 1915.

Phil 735.90.5 — Münsterberg, H. The eternal values. Boston, 1909.

Phil 5252.12.9A — Münsterberg, H. Grundzüge der Psychologie. Leipzig, 1900.

Phil 5252.12.10 — Münsterberg, H. Grundzüge der Psychologie. 2. Aufl. Leipzig, 1918.

Phil 5850.278 — Münsterberg, H. Grundzüge der Psychotechnik. Leipzig, 1914.

Phil 2150.6.01 — Münsterberg, H. The library of H. Münsterberg. n.p., n.d.

Phil 5252.12.13.2 — Münsterberg, H. On the witness stand. N.Y., 1909.

Phil 5252.12.18 — Münsterberg, H. On the witness stand. N.Y., 1933.

Phil 735.90 — Münsterberg, H. Philosophie der Werte. Leipzig, 1908.

Phil 5850.278.13 — Münsterberg, H. Psicologia de la actividad industrial. Madrid, 1914.

Phil 5850.278.5 — Münsterberg, H. Psychologie und Wirtschaftsleben. Leipzig, 1912.

Phil 5850.278.7 — Münsterberg, H. Psychology and industrial efficiency. Boston, 1913.

Phil 5252.12.35 — Münsterberg, H. Psychology and social sanity. Garden City, 1914.

Phil 5252.12.45 — Münsterberg, H. Psychology general and applied. N.Y., 1914.

Htn Phil 3625.10.35* — Münsterberg, H. Science and idealism. Boston, 1906.

Phil 400.19 — Münsterberg, H. Science and idealism. Boston, 1906.

Phil 5252.12.29 — Münsterberg, H. Social studies of today. London, 1913.

Phil 8887.36 — Münsterberg, H. Der Ursprung der Sittlichkeit. Freiburg, 1889.

Htn Phil 3625.10.30* — Münsterberg, H. Verse; von Hugo Terberg. Grossenhain, 1897.

Phil 5762.3 — Münsterberg, H. Die Willenshandlung. Freiburg, 1888.

Phil 6980.484 — Münsterberg, Hugo. Psychotherapy. N.Y., 1909.

Phil 5722.12 — Münsterberg, Hugo. Subconscious phenomena. Boston, 1910.

Phil 2150.6.80 — Münsterberg, M. Hugo Münsterberg, his life and work. N.Y., 1922.

Phil 8637.7 — Münsterberg, S. The eternal life. Boston, 1905.

Phil 3270.3.83 — Münz, Bernhard. Briefe von und über Jakob Frohschammer. Leipzig, 1897.

Phil 3270.3.85 — Münz, Bernhard. Jakob Frohschammer. Breslau, 1894.

Phil 3585.7.86 — Münz, Bernhard. Moritz Lazarus. Berlin, 1900.

Phil 4810.2 — Muenz, Teodor. Filosofia slovenského osvietenstva. Vyd. 1. Bratislava, 1961.

Phil 4810.2.5 — Muenz, Teodor. Náhľady filozofov malohontstkej spoločnosti. Bratislava, 1954.

Phil 8592.37 — Münzenberger, H.C. Über die Entstehung religiöser Volksbegriffe. Göttingen, 1791.

Phil 8612.29 — Los muertos, las muertas y otras fantasmagarias. (Gómez de la Serna, R.) Madrid, 1935.

Phil 3805.171 — Müsebeck, Ernst. Schleiermacher in der Geschichte der Staatsides. Berlin, 1927.

Phil 5871.2 — Mütter-Schicksal grosser Söhne. (Skasa-Weiss, Eugen.) Oldenburg, 1966.

Phil 400.18 — Muff, Christian. Idealismus. 3e Aufl. Halle, 1902.

Phil 400.18.5 — Muff, Christian. Idealismus. 5e Aufl. Halle, 1911.

Phil 2295.90 — Muff, Margrit. Leibinenz kritik der Religionsphilosophie von John Toland. Abhandlung. Affoltern, 1940.

Phil 293.29 — Mugler, Charles. Deux thèmes de la cosmologie grecque. Paris, 1953.

Phil 6022.5 — Muhammad ibn Umar, Fakhr al-Din. La physiognomonie arabe. Thèse. Paris, 1939.

Phil 7069.30.15 — Mühl, Anita M. Automatic writing. Dresden, 1930.

Phil 6122.64 — Muhlbery, W. Mental adjustments. Cincinnati, O., 1944.

Phil 2266.83 — Muir, Ethel. The ethical system of Adam Smith. Thesis. Halifax, N.S., 1898.

Phil 187.63 — Muirhead, J.H. Contemporary British philosophy. 1st Ser. N.Y., 1924.

Phil 187.63.5 — Muirhead, J.H. Contemporary British philosophy. 2nd ser. N.Y., 1925.

Phil 187.63.8A — Muirhead, J.H. Contemporary British philosophy. 3rd ser. London, 1956.

Phil 8887.25.6 — Muirhead, J.H. The elements of ethics. London, 1910.

Phil 8887.25 — Muirhead, J.H. The elements of ethics. N.Y., 1892.

Phil 3012.2 — Muirhead, J.H. German philosophy in relation to the war. London, 1917.

Phil 2150.8.90 — Muirhead, J.H. John Stuart Mackenzie, 1860-1935. London, 1936?

Phil 8887.25.9 — Muirhead, J.H. Philosophy and life. London, 1902.

Phil 400.78 — Muirhead, J.H. The Platonic traditions in Anglo-Saxon philosophy. London, 1931.

Phil 2150.12 — Muirhead, J.H. Reflections by a journeyman in philosophy. London, 1942.

Phil 8837.12 — Muirhead, J.H. Rule and end in morals. London, 1932.

Phil 187.63.12 — Muirhead, J.H. The use of philosophy. Cambridge, 1929.

Phil 8887.72 — Mukenje, D.G. Daily meditations. N.Y., 1933.

Phil 8472.193.30 — Mukerjea, Jyoti S. Humanism. Nagpur, 19- .

Phil 525.83 — Mukerjee, R. Theory and art of mysticism. London, 1937.

Phil 585.184 — Mukerjee, Radhakamal. The community of communities. Bombay, 1966.

Phil 585.173 — Mukerjee, Radhakamal. The dimensions of human evolution. London, 1963.

Phil 735.245 — Mukerjee, Radhakamal. The dimensions of values. London, 1964.

Phil 735.126 — Mukerjee, Radhakamal. The social structure of values. London, 1950.

Phil 735.126.2 — Mukerjee, Radhakamal. The social structure of values. 2nd ed. New Delhi, 1965.

Phil 1750.166.235 — Mukerjee, Radhakamal. The way of humanism, East and West. Bombay, 1968.

Phil 343.18.9 — Mukerji, A.C. The nature of self. Allahabad, 1938.

Phil 343.18 — Mukerji, A.C. Self, thought and reality. Allahabad, 1933.

Phil 5052.23 — Mukerji, A.C. A text-book of inductive logic. Allahabad, 1919.

Phil 343.18.5 — Mukerji, A.C. Thought and reality. Allahabad, 1930.

Phil 400.45 — Mukerji, N.C. The ethical and religious philosophy of idealism. Allahabad, 1922.

Phil 7069.21.57 — Mukerji, S. Indian ghost stories. Allahabad, 1921.

Phil 2020.140 — Mukhopadhyay, Amal Kumar. The ethics of obedience; a study of the philosophy of T.H. Green. Calcutta, 1967.

Phil 5274.23 — Mulaik, Stanley A. The foundations of factor analysis. N.Y., 1971.

Phil 7069.29.61 — Muldoon, Sylvan J. The projection of the astral body. London, 1961.

Author and Title Listing

Phil 7069.51.25   Muldoon, Sylvan Joseph. The phenomena of astral projection. London, 1962.

Phil 6122.23   Mulford, P. Your forces and how to use them. N.Y., 1904. 2v.

Phil 6122.23.1   Mulford, Prntice. Your forces and how to use them. N.Y., 1888-92. 6v.

Phil 7069.38.30   Mulholland, J. Beware familiar spirits. N.Y., 1938.

Phil 6322.31.2   Mullahy, Patrick. Oedipus. N.Y., 1955.

Phil 6322.31   Mullahy, Patrick. Oedipus. 1st ed. N.Y., 1948.

Phil 6322.31.1   Mullahy, Patrick. Oedipus myth and complex. 1st ed. N.Y., 1948.

Phil 6980.485   Mullahy, Patrick. A study of interpersonal relations. N.Y., 1957.

Phil 6322.15   Mullen, J.J. Psychological factors in the pastoral treatement of scruples. n.p., 1927.

Phil 960.6   Mullens, J. Religious aspects of Hindu philosophy. London, 1860.

Phil 187.69   Muller, Aloys. Einleitung in die Philosophie. Berlin, 1925.

Phil 8702.30   Muller, C. Science and faith, co-existence or synthesis? Louvain, 1962.

Phil 960.7   Muller, F.M. The six systems of Indian philosophy. N.Y., 1899.

Phil 960.7.5   Muller, F.M. Three lectures on the Vedânta philosophy. London, 1894.

Phil 187.123   Muller, H.J. Science and criticism. New Haven, 1943.

Phil 187.38   Muller, J.B. De kennisleer van het Anglo-Amerikanisch pragmatisme. 's-Gravenhage, 1913.

Phil 9495.129   Muller, J.P. Kønsmoral og livslykke. 3. opl. København, 1910.

Phil 8413.13   Muller, Josef. Eine Philosophie des Schönen in Natur und Kunst. Mainz, 1897.

Phil 2412.6   Muller, Maurice. De Descartes à Marcel Proust. Neuchâtel, 1943.

Phil 187.99.5   Muller, Maurice. Idées et archetypes de Platon à Elie Cartan. Neuchâtel, 1959.

Phil 187.99   Muller, Maurice. Individualité, causalité, indeterminisme. Paris, 1932.

Phil 1712.20   Muller, Philippe. Itineraire philosophique. Neuchâtel, 1956.

Phil 5222.9   Muller, Philippe. La psychologie dans le monde moderne. Bruxelles, 1964.

Phil 5222.9.5   Muller, Philippe. Psychology in the modern world. N.Y., 1969.

Phil 2225.5.106   Mullin, Albert A. Philosophical comments on the philosophies of Charles S. Peirce and Ludwig Wittgenstein. Urbana, Ill., 1961.

Phil 5520.407   Multilingualism. (Vildomec, V.) Leyden, 1963.

Phil 7042.6A   Multiple personality: an experimental investigation. (Sidis, Boris.) N.Y., 1905.

Phil 5545.189   Multiple-probability learning. (Smedslund, Jan.) Oslo, 1955.

Phil 6961.8   Multiple Sklerose mit amnestischer Aphasie. Inaug. Diss. (Lurié, Aron.) Königsberg, 1914.

Phil 8870.8   A multitude of counselors. (Larned, J.N.) Boston, 1901.

Phil 22.58   Multivariate behavioral research. Fort Worth, Tex. 1,1966+

Phil 22.59   Multivariate behavioral research. Monographs. Fort Worth, Tex. 1966+

Phil 5242.64   Multivariate procedures for the behavorial sciences. (Cooley, William.) N.Y., 1962.

Phil 187.141A   Mumford, L. Man as interpreter. 1st ed. N.Y., 1950.

Phil 8430.37   Mumford, L. The role of the creative arts in comtemporary society. Durham, 1958.

Phil 9070.51.5A   Mumford, Lewis. The conduct of life. 1st ed. N.Y., 1951.

Phil 1020.38   Muminov, I.M. Iz istorii razvitiia...musli v uzbekistane. Tashkent, 1957.

Phil 8962.14   Munby, D.L. Christianity and economic problems. London, 1956.

Phil 2750.20.5   El mundo. (Touron del Pie, Eliseo.) Madrid, 1961.

Phil 4318.4   El mundo clásico en el pensamiento español contemporáneo. (Robledo, Maria N.) Madrid, 1965.

Phil 4330.5   El mundo clasico en el pensamiento español contemporaneo. Madrid, 1960.

Phil 3195.6.111   El mundo histórico social. (Roura-Parella, J.) México, 1948.

Phil 4967.20.5   O mundo interior. (Farias Brito, Raymundo de.) Rio de Janeiro, 1951.

Phil 8413.16   Mundt, Ernest. Art, form, and civilization. Berkeley, 1952.

Phil 8413.40   Mundt, Theodor. Ästhetik. Göttingen, 1966.

Phil 3425.244   Mundts und Kühnes Verhältnis zu Hegel und seinen Gegnern. (Grupe, Walter.) Halle, 1928.

Phil 9352.8.3   Munger, Theodore T. On the threshold. Boston, 1884.

Phil 9352.8.7   Munger, Theodore T. On the threshold. 26th ed. Boston, 1893.

Phil 2280.5.105   Munitz, M.K. Moral philosophy of Santayana. N.Y., 1939.

Phil 293.31.5   Munitz, Milton Karl. The mystery of existence. N.Y., 1965.

Phil 293.31   Munitz, Milton Karl. Space, time, and creation. Glencoe, 1957.

Phil 187.55.3   Muñiz, Narcisse. Problèmes de la vie. Paris, 1914.

Phil 6122.11   Munk, H. Uber die Funktionen der Grosshirnrinde. Berlin, 1881.

Phil 6122.11.2   Munk, H. Uber die Funktionen der Grosshirnrinde. 2. Aufl. Berlin, 1890.

Phil 6122.11.5   Munk, H. Untersuchungen über das Wesen. Leipzig, 1868.

Phil 1050.5   Munk, S. Mélanges de philosophie Juive et Arabe. Paris, 1859.

Phil 1050.5.5   Munk, S. Mélanges de philosophie Juive et Arabe. Paris, 1927.

Phil 1050.2   Munk, S. Philosophie und Schriftsteller der Juden. Leipzig, 1838.

Phil 5762.22   Munn, Allan M. Free will and determinism. Toronto, 1960.

Phil 5822.8   Munn, Norman L. An introduction to animal psychology. Boston, 1933.

Phil 5252.72   Munn, Norman L. A laboratory manual in general experimental psychology. Pittsburgh, 1934.

Phil 5350.7   Munn, Norman Leslie. The evolution and growth of human behavior . 2d ed. Boston, 1965.

Phil 5252.89   Munn, Norman Leslie. Psychology. Boston, 1946.

Phil 5252.89.2   Munn, Norman Leslie. Psychology. 2. ed. Boston, 1951.

Phil 5252.89.4A   Munn, Norman Leslie. Psychology. 2. ed. Boston, 1961.

Phil 5252.89.5   Munn, Norman Leslie. Psychology. 5. ed. Boston, 1966.

Phil 5790.2.10   Munnichs, Jozef M.A. Ouderdom en eindigheid. Assen, 1964.

Phil 5627.261.15   Muñoz, Jesu. Psychologia philosophica. Santander, 1961.

Phil 9035.83   Muñoz, Juan A. El caracter. México, 1912.

Phil 585.152   Muñoz Espinalt, Carlos. Saber-se entendre. Barcelona, 1961.

Phil 6750.14   Munro, Caroline S.G. The blight of the feeble-minded. Boston, 191-?

Phil 930.72   Munro, Donald J. The concept of man in early China. Stanford, 1969.

Phil 3805.97   Munro, R. Schleiermacher, personal and speculative. Paisley, 1903.

Phil 8413.7   Munro, Thomas. Scientific method in aesthetics. N.Y., 1928.

Phil 8413.7.5   Munro, Thomas. Toward science in aesthetics. N.Y., 1956.

Phil 5593.45.10   Munroe, R.L. Prediction of the adjustment and academic performance of college students. Stanford, 1945.

Phil 6322.35   Munroe, R.L. Schools of psychoanalytic thought. N.Y., 1955.

Phil 5252.11   Munsell, O.S. Psychology. N.Y., 1880.

Phil 9380.1   Munson, E.L. The management of men. N.Y., 1921.

Phil 1750.164   Munson, G.B. The dilemma of the liberated. N.Y., 1930.

Phil 2280.5.79   Munson, T.N. The essential wisdom of George Santayana. N.Y., 1962.

Phil 8592.117   Munson, Thomas N. Reflective theology; philosophical orientations in religion. New Haven, 1968.

Phil 3494.41   Munteano, B. Épisodes Kantiens en Suisse et en France sous le Directoire. Paris, 1935.

Phil 8887.122   Munz, Peter. Relationship and solitude. 1st. American ed. Middletown, Conn., 1965.

Phil 4769.1.112   Munzer, Egbert. Solovyev. London, 1956.

Phil 5252.76   Munzinger, K.F. Psychology. Denver, 1939.

Phil 5252.76.5   Munzinger, K.F. Psychology. N.Y., 1942.

Phil 6322.13   Muralt, Alexander von. Ein Pseudoprophet. München, 1920.

Phil 6322.13.5   Muralt, Alexander von. Wahnsinniger oder Prophet? Zürich, 1946.

Phil 3494.58   Muralt, André. La conscience transcendentale. Paris, 1958.

Phil 3450.11.195   Muralt, André de. L'idée de la phénoménologie. Paris, 1958.

Phil 2980.8   Muralt, André de. Philosophes en Suisse française. Neuchâtel, 1966.

Phil 8962.10   Muratori, L.A. Della carita cristiana in quanto essa è amore del prossimo. Venezia, 1736.

Phil 5465.2.5   Muratori, L.A. Della forza della fantasia umana. Venezia, 1740.

Phil 5465.2   Muratori, L.A. Trattato della forza della fantasia umana. Napoli, 1783.

Phil 5222.5A   Murchison, C.A. A history of psychology in autobiography. Worcester, 1930-36. 4v.

Phil 7069.26.13A   Murchison, C. The case for and against psychical belief. Worcester, 1927.

Phil 5252.63A   Murchison, C.A. The foundations of experimental psychology. Worcester, 1929.

Phil 5252.63.10   Murchison, C.A. Handbook of general experimental psychology. Worcester, 1934.

Phil 5203.8A   Murchison, C.A. The psychological register. v.2-3. Worcester, 1929.

Phil 5203.8   Murchison, C.A. The psychological register. v.3. Worcester, 1932.

Phil 5545.171   Murden, J.R. The art of memory. N.Y., 1818.

Phil 6327.21.20   The murder of Christ: the emotional plague of mankind. (Reich, Wilhelm.) N.Y., 1953.

Phil 8620.62.5   Murdoch, Iris. The sovereignty of good. London, 1970.

Phil 8620.62   Murdoch, Iris. The sovereignty of good over other concepts. London, 1967.

Phil 978.53   Murdoch, J. Theosophy unveiled. Madras, 1885.

Phil 8887.39   Murdoch, J.G. Economics as the basis of living ethics. Troy, 1913.

Phil 3012.4   Murdock, J. Sketches of modern philosophy. Hartford, 1842.

Phil 3425.302   Mure, G.R.G. Introduction to Hegel. Oxford, 1940.

Phil 3425.610   Mure, G.R.G. The philosophy of Hegel. London, 1965.

Phil 1812.10   Mure, G.R.G. Retreat from truth. Oxford, 1958.

Phil 3425.326A   Mure, G.R.G. A study of Hegel's logic. Oxford, 1950.

Phil 8413.37   Murian, Vasim M. Esteticheskii ideal. Moskva, 1966.

Phil 5627.201   Murisier, Ernest. Les maladies du sentiment religieux. Paris, 1901.

Phil 5585.145   Murloo, Abraham. The two faces of man. N.Y., 1954.

Phil 8416.15   Le murmure condition et destin de l'artiste. (Ponze, Francis.) Lyon, 1956.

Phil 2225.5.104   Murphey, M.G. The development of Peirce's philosophy. Cambridge, 1961.

Phil 343.22   Murphy, A.E. The uses of reason. N.Y., 1943.

Phil 187.176   Murphy, Arthur E. Reason and the common good. Englewood Cliffs, 1963.

Phil 343.35   Murphy, Arthur Edward. The theory of practical reason. La Salle, Ill., 1964[1965]

Phil 6322.18A   Murphy, Gardiner. An outline of abnormal psychology. N.Y., 1929.

Phil 5222.3.10   Murphy, Gardner. Approaches to personality. N.Y., 1932.

Phil 5222.16   Murphy, Gardner. Asian psychology. N.Y., 1968.

Phil 5252.69.10   Murphy, Gardner. A briefer general psychology. N.Y., 1935.

Phil 7069.61A   Murphy, Gardner. Challenge of psychical research. 1. ed. N.Y., 1961.

Phil 5252.69.20   Murphy, Gardner. Encounter with reality. Boston, 1968.

Phil 5252.69A   Murphy, Gardner. General psychology. N.Y., 1933.

Phil 5222.3   Murphy, Gardner. Historical introduction to modern psychology. N.Y., 1929.

Phil 5222.3.5A   Murphy, Gardner. Historical introduction to modern psychology. N.Y., 1949.

Phil 5222.3.5.2   Murphy, Gardner. An historical introduction to modern psychology. 2. ed. N.Y., 1930.

Phil 5590.260A   Murphy, Gardner. Human potentialities. N.Y., 1958.

Phil 5252.69.15   Murphy, Gardner. An introduction to psychology. N.Y., 1951.

Phil 5590.36   Murphy, Gardner. Personality. N.Y., 1947.

Phil 5252.69.25   Murphy, Gardner. Psychological thought from Pythagoras to Freud. 1st. ed. N.Y., 1968.

Phil 5252.160   Murphy, Gardner. Western psychology. N.Y., 1969.

Phil 5252.13   Murphy, J.J. Habit and intelligence. London, 1869. 2v.

Phil 5252.13.2   Murphy, J.J. Habit and intelligence. 2d. ed. London, 1879.

Phil 8592.16.2   Murphy, J.J. The scientific basis of faith. London, 1873.

Phil 5252.130   Murphy, James G. The human mind. Belfast, 1873.

Phil 3494.72   Murphy, Jeffrie G. Kant: the philosophy of right. London, 1970.

Phil 6834.10   Murphy, John. Homosexual liberation; a personal view. N.Y., 1971.

Phil 5252.84   Murphy, L.B. Emotional factors in learning. N.Y., 1945.

Phil 5252.84.2 — Murphy, L.B. Emotional factors in learning. N.Y., 1946.
Phil 5870.110 — Murphy, Lois Barclay. The widening world of childhood. N.Y., 1962.
Phil 8637.19 — Murphy, R.W. A key to the secret vault. San Francisco, 1890.
Phil 2340.6.95 — Murray, A.H. The philosophy of James Ward. Cambridge, Eng., 1937.
Phil 187.35 — Murray, D.L. Pragmatism. London, 1912.
Phil 5635.12 — Murray, E. Organic sensation. n.p., 1909.
Phil 7080.58 — Murray, Edward. Sleep, dreams, and arousal. N.Y., 1965.
Phil 4080.3.385 — Murray, G. Benedetto Croce. London, 1953.
Phil 187.119 — Murray, G. Stoic, Christian and humanist. London, 1940.
Phil 1200.15.7 — Murray, G. The stoic philosophy. London, 1918.
Phil 5590.15 — Murray, Henry A. Thematic apperception test. Cambridge, Mass., 1943. 2v.
Phil 6122.57 — Murray, J.A.C. An introduction to a Christian psycho-therapy. Edinburgh, 1938.
Phil 8962.5 — Murray, J.C. A handbook of Christian ethics. Edinburgh, 1908.
Phil 5252.14 — Murray, J.C. Handbook of psychology. Boston, 1888.
Phil 8887.26 — Murray, J.C. An introduction to ethics. Paisley, 1891.
Phil 5252.14.5 — Murray, J.C. An introduction to psychology. Boston, 1904.
Phil 2035.86 — Murray, J.C. Outline of Sir William Hamilton's philosophy. Boston, 1870.
Phil 8667.27 — Murray, J.C. The problem of God. New Haven, 1964.
Phil 6317.22.80 — Murray, M. The concepts of self acceptance and self respect in Karen Horney's theory of neurosis. n.p., n.d.
Phil 2905.1.375 — Murray, Michael Hunt. The thought of Teilhard de Chardin. N.Y., 1966.
Phil 8962.34 — Murray, Michael V. Problems in conduct. N.Y., 1963.
Phil 7069.24.31 — Murray, O. The spiritual universe. London, 1924.
Phil 8592.65 — Murray, R. Time and the timeless. London, 1942.
Phil 6122.47 — Murray, William J. The Astor lectures. N.Y., 1917.
Phil 9070.55 — Murrow, E.R. This I believe. N.Y., 1952. 2v.
Phil 8667.23 — Murry, John M. God, being an introduction to the science of metabiology. London, 1929.
Phil 5592.176 — Murstein, Bernard. Theory and research in projective techniques, emphasizing the TAT. N.Y., 1965.
Phil 2150.20.30 — Murty, K. Satchidanda. Metaphysics, man and freedom. N.Y., 1963.
Phil 270.108 — Musabaeva, N.A. Kibernetika i kategoriia prichinnosti. Alma-Ata, 1965.
Phil 270.107 — Musabaeva, N.A. Problemy prichinnosti v filosofii i giologii. Alma-Ata, 1962.
Phil 187.76 — Musatti, C.L. Analisi del concetto di realtà empirica. Castello, 1926.
Phil 5585.255 — Musatti, Cesare L. Condizioni dell'esperienza e fondazione della psicologia. Firenze, 1964.
Phil 530.30.5 — Muschg, Walter. Die Mystik in der Schweiz, 1200-1500. Frauenfeld, 1935.
Phil 530.30.10A — Muschg, Walter. Mystische Texte aus dem Mittelalter. Basel, 1943.
Phil 5649.12 — The "muscular sense". (Bastian, H.C.) London, 1887.
Phil 1750.776 — Museo de filósofos. 1. ed. (Gaos, José.) México, 1960.
Phil 197.57 — Music and meaning. (Woods, Elizabeth R.) Cambridge, 1932.
Phil 6980.674.10 — Music and medicine; inaugural lecture. (Schneider, Ulment Victor.) Johannesburg, 1964. 2v.
Phil 3850.27.102 — Music in the life of Albert Schweitzer. 1st ed. (Joy, C.R.) N.Y., 1951.
Phil 5390.12 — Musil, Robert. Über die Dummheit. Wien, 1937.
Phil 8677.21 — The Muslim attributes and the Christian trinity. (Wolfson, H.A.) Cambridge, Mass., 1956.
Phil 1020.22.5 — Muslim thought and its source. (Nadvi, Muzaffar Uddir.) Lahore, 1946.
Phil 1020.22.7 — Muslim thought and its source. 4th ed. (Nadvi, Muzaffar Uddir.) Lahore, 1960.
Phil 5252.66 — Musmann, J.G. Lehrbuch der Seelenwissenschaft. Berlin, 1827.
Phil 190.80 — Musse und Kult. (Pieper, Josef.) München, 1949.
Phil 400.82 — Mussmann, J.G. De idealismo, seu philosophia ideali. Diss. Berolini, 1826.
Phil 193.9.25 — Must philosophers disagree? (Schiller, F.C.S.) London, 1934.
Phil 1930.20 — Must we mean what we say? (Cavell, Stanley.) N.Y., 1969.
Phil 4610.12.80 — Mustelin, Olof. Hjalmar Neiglick. Helsingfors, 1966.
Htn Phil 3110.39* — Musterium magnum. (Böhme, J.) London, 1654.
Phil 8120.6A — Mustoxidi, T.M. Histoire de l'esthétique française, 1700-1900. Paris, 1920.
Phil 370.2 — Musu, Aldo M. Educazione ed esistenza. Padova, 1967.
Phil 5400.150 — Muszynski, Franz. Unsere Leidenschaften. 2. Aufl. Paderborn, 1926.
Phil 735.19 — Mutius, Gerhard von. Gedanke und Erlebnis; Umriss einer Philosophie des Wertes. Darmstadt, 1922.
Phil 575.137 — Mutius, Gerhard von. Jenseits von Person und Sache. München, 1925.
Phil 8887.63 — Mutschelle, S. Vermischte Schriften, oder philosophischen Gedanken. 2. Aufl. München, 1799. 4v.
Phil 3494.32 — Mutschelle, S. Versuch einer solchen fasslichen Darstellung der Kantischen Philosophie. München, 1803. 2v.
Phil 9500.2 — Mutterings and musings of an invalid. (Townsend, F.) N.Y., 1851.
Phil 8707.3 — The mutual relations of natural science and theology. (Rudder, W.) Philadelphia, 1869.
Phil 8430.30 — Muveszet és erkölcs. (Jaszi, Oszhai.) Budapest, 1908.
Phil 8505.8.25 — Muzei istorii religii i ateizma. (Leningrad. Muzei Istorii Religii i Ateizma.) Leningrad, 1965.
Htn Phil 8887.31* — Muzéo, G. La polvere del mutio. n.p., n.d.
Phil 310.604 — Mužík, Josef. Subjekt a objekt. Praha, 1964.
Phil 187.89 — Muzquiz, J.M. La verdadera legitimidad y el verdadero liberalismo. Habana, 1886.
Phil 5051.37 — Muzyka kak predmet logiki. (Losev, Aleksei F.) Moskva, 1927.
Phil 9352.5 — Muzzey, A.B. The blade and the ear. Boston, 1865.
Phil 9172.3 — Muzzey, A.B. The fireside: an aid to parents. Boston, 1854.
Phil 8637.5 — Muzzey, A.B. Man a soul. Boston, 1842.
Phil 8887.27 — Muzzey, A.B. The moral teacher. N.Y., 1839.
Phil 9352.5.4 — Muzzey, A.B. The young maiden. Boston, 1840.
Phil 9352.5.5 — Muzzey, A.B. The young maiden. Boston, 1841.
Phil 9352.5.5 — Muzzey, A.B. The young maiden. London, 1843.
Phil 9352.5.6 — Muzzey, A.B. The young maiden. Boston, 1843.
Phil 9352.5.10 — Muzzey, A.B. Young man's friend. Boston, 1836.
Phil 9352.5.11 — Muzzey, A.B. Young man's friend. Boston, 1838.
Phil 8615.20 — Muzzey, David S. Ethical religion. N.Y., 1943.
Phil 8615.20.10 — Muzzey, David S. Ethics as a religion. N.Y., 1951.
Phil 8615.20.12 — Muzzey, David S. Ethics as a religion. N.Y., 1967.
Phil 2280.20.30 — My brother death. 1st ed. (Sulzberger, Cyrus.) N.Y., 1961.

Phil 9352.6 — My daughter's manual. N.Y., 1837.
Phil 7069.15.50 — My experiences while out of my body and my return after many days. (Richmond, Cora L.) Boston, 1915.
Phil 5635.40 — My friends. (Boulogne, C.D.) N.Y., 1953.
Phil 7069.45.60 — My greatest story. (Swaffer, Hannen.) London, 1945.
Phil 8668.4.5 — My idea of God. (Newton, J.F.) Boston, 1927.
Phil 6325.23 — My language is me. (Parker, B.) N.Y., 1962.
Phil 1980.3.95A — My life; autobiography of Havelock Ellis. (Ellis, H.) Boston, 1939.
Phil 2280.2.75 — My life and friends. (Sully, James.) London, 1918.
Phil 7039.4.15 — My life as a dissociated personality. (Prince, Morton.) Boston, 1909.
Phil 7069.39.19 — My life as a search for the meaning of mediumship. (Garrett, Eileen Jeanette Lyttle.) London, 1939.
Phil 6112.40.15 — My life with Edgar Cayce. 1. ed. (Kahn, David E.) Garden City, 1970.
Phil 7140.116.5 — My method. (Coué, Émile.) Garden City, 1923.
Phil 8980.126 — My ne odin na svete. (Agapov, B.N.) Moskva, 1961.
Phil 2255.1.32 — My philosophical development. (Russell, Bertrand Russell.) London, 1959.
Phil 187.111 — My philosophy, by an unprofessional thinker. Oxford, 1934.
Phil 4080.3.60 — My philosophy. (Croce, Benedetto.) London, 1949.
Phil 189.20 — My philosophy of life. (Osmond, A.) Salt Lake City, 1927.
Phil 7069.23.2 — My psychic adventures. (Brid, J. Malcolm.) London, 1923.
Phil 5627.76 — My religious experience. (Collins, F.P.) Kansas City, Mo., 1901.
Phil 8610.891.10 — My religious experience. (Putnam, S.P.) N.Y., 1891.
Phil 8640.12 — My rendezvous with life. (Pickford, M.) N.Y., 1935.
Phil 4872.242.30 — My search for truth. 2nd ed. (Radhakrishnan, Sarvépalli.) Agra, 1956.
Phil 3640.77.15.10 — My sister and I. (Nietzsche, Friedrich.) N.Y., 1951.
Phil 3640.77.15.12 — My sister and I. (Nietzsche, Friedrich.) N.Y., 1953.
Phil 9352.6.7 — My son's book. N.Y., 1841.
Phil 193.230.3 — My view of the world. (Schroedinger, Erwin.) Cambridge, 1964.
Phil 6122.53 — Myers, C.S. The absurdity of any mind-body relation. London, 1932.
Phil 5252.19.8 — Myers, C.S. An introduction to experimental psychology. Cambridge, 1911.
Phil 5252.19.20 — Myers, C.S. A psychologist's point of view. London, 1933.
Phil 5252.19 — Myers, C.S. Text-book of experimental psychology. N.Y., 1909.
Phil 5252.19.3 — Myers, C.S. Text-book of experimental psychology. 3d ed. Cambridge, 1925.
Phil 5252.19.2.5 — Myers, C.S. A text book of experimental psychology with laboratory exercises. 2nd ed. pt.1. Cambridge, 1911.
Phil 5850.279.17 — Myers, Charles S. In the realm of mind. Cambridge, Eng., 1937.
Phil 5850.279.7 — Myers, Charles S. Mind and work. London, 1920.
Phil 5850.279 — Myers, Charles S. Present-day applications of psychology. 2nd ed. London, 1918.
Phil 5850.279.13 — Myers, Charles S. Psychological conceptions in other sciences. Oxford, 1929.
Phil 8592.71 — Myers, E.D. Christianity and reason. N.Y., 1951.
Phil 7069.07.25 — Myers, F.W.H. Human personality. N.Y., 1907.
Phil 5249.2.99 — Myers, F.W.H. The principles of psychology. London, 1891.
Phil 1712.19 — Myers, Francis M. The warfare of democratic ideals. Yellow Springs, Ohio, 1956.
Phil 7069.19.170 — Myers, Fred W.H. Human personality and its survival of bodily death. London, 1919.
Phil 7069.19.173 — Myers, Fred W.H. Human personality and its survival of bodily death. London, 1919.
Phil 7069.03.10 — Myers, Frederic William Henry. Human personality and its survival of bodily death. N.Y., 1903. 2v.
Phil 5545.55 — Myers, G.C. Study in incidental memory. N.Y., 1913.
Phil 165.255 — Myers, G.E. Self, religion and metaphysics. N.Y., 1961.
Phil 5590.512 — Myers, Gerald E. Self; an introduction to philosophical psychology. N.Y., 1969.
Phil 7069.10.30 — Myers, Gustavus. Beyond the borderline of life. Boston 1910.
Phil 187.175 — Myers, Henry. Systematic pluralism. Ithaca, 1961.
Phil 3425.310 — Myers, Henry Alonzo. The Spinoza-Hegel paradox. Ithaca, 1944.
Phil 6990.16 — Myers, J. Narrative of two wonderful cures. Baltimore, 1831.
Phil 8592.34 — Myers, J.H. Philosophy of faith. Syracuse, N.Y., 1896.
Phil 6962.34 — Myers, Jerome K. Family and class dynamics in mental illness. N.Y., 1959.
Phil 6957.30 — Myers, Jerome Keeley. A decade later: a follow-up of social class and mental illness. N.Y., 1968.
Phil 8837.5 — Myers, P.V. History as past ethics. Boston, 1913.
Phil 6322.23.5 — Myerson, A. The nervous housewife. Boston, 1929.
Phil 575.47 — Myerson, Abraham. The foundations of personality. Boston, 1921.
Phil 5590.18 — Myerson, Abraham. The foundations of personality. Boston, 1926.
Phil 6962.15 — Myerson, Abraham. The psychology of mental disorders. N.Y., 1927.
Phil 2750.10.106 — Myerson y la fisica moderna. (Caso, A.) México, 1939.
Phil 6405.2 — Myklebust, Helmer R. Development and disorders of written language. N.Y., 1965.
Phil 5640.139 — Mykytenko, Danylo A. Vidchuttia i diisnist'. Kyïv, 1966.
Phil 5070.26 — Mynarek, Hubertus. Der Mensch, das Wesen der Zukunft. München, 1968.
Phil 585.196 — Mynarek, Hubertus. Der Mensch: Sinnziel der Weltentwicklung. Inaug. Diss. München, 1967.
Phil 4525.2.90 — Myrberg, Otto F. Om förhållandet mellan teologi och filosofi. v.2. Upsala, 1861.
Phil 3494.26 — Myrho, F. Kritizismus: Eine Sammlung...Neu-Kantianismus. Berlin, 1926.
Phil 177.73.5 — Myself and dreams. (Constable, F.C.) N.Y., 1918.
Phil 6121.50 — Myself and others; a study in our knowledge of minds. (Locke, Don.) Oxford, 1968.
Phil 5520.305 — Myshlenie i iazyk. (Achkov, P.A.) Moskva, 1959.
Phil 5520.250 — Myshlenie i iazyk. (Spirkin, A.G.) Moskva, 1958.
Phil 5520.416 — Myshlenie i rech'. (Zhinkin, N.I.) Moskva, 1963.
Phil 8419.34 — Myśl a marmur, i inne szkice estetyczne. Wyd. 1. (Sobeski, M.) Warszawa, 1959.
Phil 22.42 — Myśl filozoficzna. Warsaw. 1952-1957 9v.
Phil 22.42.5 — Myśl filozoficzna Romunristow w Polsce. (Mekarski, S.) Londyn, 1953.
Phil 22.13 — Mysl' i slovo filosofskii ezhegodnik. Moskva, 1918-21.
Phil 5258.203 — Mysl' v deistvii. (Slavskaia, Kseniie A.) Moskva, 1968.
Phil 4803.592.20 — Mysłakowski, Zygmunt. Pisma wybrane. Wyd. 1. Warszawa, 1971.

Phil 4803.592.30   Mysłakowski, Zygmunt. Zatracone ścieżki, zagubione ślady. Wyd. 1. Warszawa, 1967.
Phil 8586.56   Mysli o religii. (Galitskaia, I.A.) Moskva, 1962.
Phil 8598.67   Mysli o religii. (Stepanov, I.) Moskva, 1922.
Phil 812.12   Myślicki, Ignacy. Historja filozofji. Warszawa, 1930.
Phil 4803.846.40   Myślini czyli catoksztalt loiki narodowéj. (Trentowski, Bronisław F.) Poznań, 1844. 2v.
Phil 5545.183   Le mystère de la mémoire. (Ellenberger, F.) Genève, 1947.
Phil 5643.122   Le mystere de la vision. (Lamy, F.) Paris, 1964.
Phil 2750.19.10   Le mystère de l'être. (Marcel, Gabriel.) Paris, 1951. 2v.
Phil 282.20   Le mystère de vivre. (Bertrand, René.) Monaco, 1957.
Phil 8657.22   Le mystère du temple. 2. éd. (Congar, M.J.) Paris, 1963.
Phil 6688.15.2   Les mystéres de la magie ou les secrets du magnetisme. 2e éd. (Ségouin, A.) Paris, 1853.
Phil 6060.9   Les mystères de l'écriture; art de juger les hommes. (Desbarrolles, A.) Paris, 1872.
Phil 7085.11.5   Mystères du sommeil et du magnétisme. 4. ed. (Debay, A.) Paris, 1845.
Phil 978.49.175   Mysterienstätten des Mittelalters. (Steiner, R.) Dornach, 1932.
Phil 978.49.635   Mysterienwahrheiten und Weihnachtsimpulse. (Steiner, R.) Dornach, 1966.
Phil 7069.50.6   Mysteries and realities of this world and the next. (Silva Mello, Antonio da.) London, 1960.
Phil 6116.4   The mysteries of human nature. (Grimes, J.S.) Boston, 1860.
Phil 6673.14   The mysteries of hypnosis. (Dubor, G. de.) N.Y., 1923.
Phil 7060.89.5   Mysteries of life, death and futurity. (Timbs, John.) N.Y., 1863.
Phil 7060.89   Mysteries of life, death and futurity. (Welby, H.) London, 1861.
Phil 978.16   The mysteries of the heart doctrine. (Tingley, K.A. (Mrs.).) Point Loma, Calif., 1902.
Phil 187.86.15   Mysteries of the soul. (Müller-Freienfels, R.) London, 1929.
Phil 974.2.30   The mysterious Madame Helena P. Blavatsky. (Robert, C.E.B.) N.Y., 1931.
Phil 6131.6.5   Mysterious phenomena of the human psyche. (Vasil'ev, Leonid L.) New Hyde Park, N.Y., 1965.
Phil 7069.07.18   Mysterious psychic forces. (Flammarion, C.) Boston, 1907.
Phil 5627.259.10   Mysterium der Begegnung. (Lindenberg, Wladimir.) München, 1959.
Phil 974.3.109   Das Mysterium des Menschen. (Jellinek, Karl.) Zürich, 1960. 2v.
Phil 3110.39.5   Mysterium magnum. (Böhme, J.) Amsterdam, 1682.
Phil 9182.8   Mysterium magnum. (Weber, L.M.) Freiburg, 1963.
Phil 8612.52   Mysterium mortis. (Boros, Ladislaus.) Olten, 1962.
Phil 8585.48   Mysterium salutis. (Feiner, Johannes.) Einsiedeln, 1965. 4v.
Phil 8620.12   The mystery; or evil and God. (Young, J.) Philadelphia, 1856.
Phil 7069.30.35   Mystery and love of apparitions. (Thompson, C.J.S.) London, 1930.
Phil 2750.19.5   The mystery of being. (Marcel, Gabriel.) Chicago, 1950-51. 2v.
Phil 2750.19   The mystery of being. (Marcel, Gabriel.) London, 1950. 2v.
Htn   Phil 6480.26*   The mystery of dreames. (Goodwin, P.) London, 1658.
Phil 7082.96   The mystery of dreams. (Stevens, William Oliver.) London, 1950.
Phil 8620.24.5   The mystery of evil. (Heyl, Paul R.) Chicago, 1920.
Phil 293.31.5   The mystery of existence. (Munitz, Milton Karl.) N.Y., 1965.
Phil 6060.19   The mystery of handwriting. (Keene, John H.) Boston, 1896.
Htn   Phil 2805.32.15*   The mystery of jesuitism. (Pascal, Blaise.) London, 1689[1679].
Phil 176.122   The mystery of life. (Burke, J.B.) London, 1931.
Phil 585.25   Mystery of man. (Jeffreys, M.V.C.) London, 1957.
Phil 190.12   The mystery of matter. (Picton, J.A.) London, 1873.
Phil 5259.19   The mystery of mind. (Troland, L.T.) N.Y., 1926.
Phil 5627.134.90   The mystery of moral re-armament. (Driberg, Tom.) N.Y., 1964.
Phil 9520.2.2   The mystery of pain. (Hinton, James.) Boston, 1886.
Phil 9520.2.3   The mystery of pain. (Hinton, James.) London, 1866.
Phil 9520.2.1   The mystery of pain. (Hinton, James.) London, 1879.
Phil 9520.2.5   The mystery of pain. (Hinton, James.) N.Y., 1914.
Phil 5627.187   The mystery of religion. (Martin, Everett D.) N.Y., 1924.
Phil 7080.16   The mystery of sleep. (Bigelow, John.) N.Y., 1903.
Phil 7080.16.5   Mystery of sleep. (Bigelow, John.) N.Y., 1924.
Phil 672.29.3   The mystery of space. (Browne, Robert T.) N.Y., 1919.
Phil 6315.50   The mystery of the androgyne. (Faithfull, Theordore.) London, 1938.
Phil 7072.3   The mystery of the human double. (Shirley, Ralph.) N.Y., 1965.
Phil 180.53   The mystery of the mind's desire. (Finley, John H.) N.Y., 1936.
Phil 8408.42   Mystetstvo, diisnist' i svoboda khudozhn'oï tvorchosti. (Hordiienko, Anatolii.) Kyïv, 1966.
Phil 8170.7   Mystetstvo i estetichne vychovannia. (Honcharenko, M.V.) Kyïv, 1963.
Phil 8411.23.10   Mystetstvo iak forma piznannia diisnosti. (Kaublanov, B.G.) Kyïv, 1867.
Phil 7054.59   Mystic hours, or spiritual experience. (Redman, G.A.) N.Y., 1859.
Phil 7069.13.10   Mystic light essays. 1st ed. (Colville, William J.) N.Y., 1913.
Phil 525.103   Mystic rebels. (Schnur, H.C.) N.Y., 1949.
Phil 7069.00.60   The mystic self. (Rayon, M.) Chicago, 1900.
Phil 525.7.10   The mystic way. (Underhill, Evelyn.) London, 1913.
Phil 3110.174   The mystic will. (Brinton, H.) N.Y., 1930.
Phil 5761.3.7   The mystic will. (Leland, C.G.) Chicago, 1907.
Phil 5761.3.5   The mystic will. (Leland, C.G.) Chicago, 1907.
Htn   Phil 2305.1.30*   The mystical initiations. (Taylor, Thomas.) London, 1787.
Phil 5628.55.11   Mystical phenomena in the life of Theresa Neumann. (Teodorowicz, Józef.) St. Louis, Mo., 1940.
Phil 1020.21   The mystical philosophy of Muhyid din-ibnul 'Arabi. (Affifi, A.E.) Cambridge, 1939.
Phil 525.18   Mysticism, an epistemological problem. (Dawkins, M.B.) New Haven, 1915.
Phil 6313.5   Mysticism, Freudianism and scientific psychology. (Dunlap, K.) St. Louis, 1920. 2v.
Phil 525.230   Mysticism. (Happold, F.C.) Baltimore, 1967.
Phil 525.140   Mysticism. (Suzuki, D.T.) N.Y., 1957.
Phil 525.51.2   Mysticism: its true nature and value. (Sharpe, A.B.) London, 1910?
Phil 525.7.1   Mysticism. 3rd ed. (Underhill, Evelyn.) N.Y., 1911.

Phil 525.7.2   Mysticism. 4th ed. (Underhill, Evelyn.) N.Y., 1912.
NEDL   Phil 525.7.3   Mysticism. 8th ed. (Underhill, Evelyn.) N.Y., 1919.
Phil 192.28.19   Mysticism and logic. (Russell, B.) N.Y., 1929.
Phil 192.28.17   Mysticism and logic and other essays. (Russell, B.) London, 1919.
Phil 525.53   Mysticism and modern life. (Buckham, J.N.) N.Y., 1915.
Phil 525.205   Mysticism and philosophy. 1st ed. (Stace, Walter T.) Philadelphia, 1960.
Phil 525.89   Mysticism and poetry. (Brockington, A.A.) London, 1934.
Phil 525.74.5   Mysticism East and West. (Otto, Rudolf.) N.Y., 1932.
Phil 525.16.5   The mysticism of William Law. (Gem, S. Harvey.) London, 1914.
Phil 525.117   Le mysticisme. (Aegerter, E.) Paris, 1952.
Phil 525.86   Mysticisme. (Cailliet E.) Cahors, 1937.
Phil 525.48   Le mysticisme catholique et l'âme de Dante. (Leclère, A.) Paris, 1906.
Phil 530.15.37   Le mysticisme en France au temps de Fénelon. 2e éd. (Matter, Jacques.) Paris, 1865.
Phil 530.15.3   Le mysticisme en France au temps de Fénelon. 2e éd. (Matter, Jacques.) Paris, 1866.
Phil 530.15.9   Le mysticisme en Normandie au XVIIe siècle. (Sourian, M.) Paris, 1923.
Phil 525.8.5   Mysticisme et domination. (Seillière, E.) Paris, 1913.
Phil 5627.123   Mysticisme et folie. (Marie, Auguste.) Paris, 1907.
Phil 525.254   Mystics and society; a point of view. (Ghose, Sisirkumar.) N.Y., 1968.
Phil 530.35.5   The mystics of Siena. (Misciattelli, Piero.) Cambridge, Eng., 1929.
Phil 530.40.47   The mystics of Spain. (Peers, E.A.) London, 1951.
Phil 525.56.5   Mystics of the Renaissance. (Steiner, R.) N.Y., 1911.
Phil 6155.22   Mystification and drug misuse; hazards in using psychoactive drugs. 1st ed. San Francisco, 1971.
Phil 525.78   Die Mystik. (Mehlis, G.) München, 1927.
Phil 525.125   Mystik als seelische Wirklichkeit. (Mager, Alois.) Graz, 1947.
Phil 3808.112.20   Die Mystik bei Schopenhauer. (Mülethaler, J.) Berlin, 1910.
Phil 3255.82   Die Mystik des Sebastian Franck von Wörd. Inaug-Diss. (Kolbenheyer, Christiane.) Würzburg, 1935.
Phil 978.49.62   Die Mystik im Aufgange des neuzeitlichen Geisteslebens und ihr Verhältnis zur modernen Weltanschauung. 3. Aufl. (Steiner, R.) Stuttgart, 1924.
Phil 978.49.60   Die Mystik im Aufgange des neuzeitlichen Geisteslebens und ihr Verhältnis zur modernen Weltanschauung. 2. Aufl. (Steiner, R.) Stuttgart, 1924.
Phil 525.44   Die Mystik im Irrsinn. (Specht, G.) Wiesbaden, 1891.
Phil 525.145   Die Mystik im Kulturleben der Völker. (Merkel, Rudolph Franz.) Hamburg, 1940.
Phil 525.155   Mystik in den Religionen der Völker. (Schloetermann, Heinz.) München, 1958.
Phil 530.30.5   Die Mystik in der Schweiz, 1200-1500. (Muschg, Walter.) Frauenfeld, 1935.
Phil 525.22.2   Mystik in Heidentum und Christentum. 2e Aufl. (Lehmann, Edvard.) Leipzig, 1918.
Phil 525.59   Die Mystik nach Wesen, Entwicklung undBedeutung. (Clemen, Carl.) Bonn, 1923.
Phil 525.58   Mystik und Rationalismus. (Janentzky, C.) München, 1922.
Phil 530.20.77   Die Mystiker und die deutsche Gesellschaft des 13. und 14. Jahrhunderts. Inaug.-Diss. (Zippel, W.) Düren, 1935.
Phil 6520.7.9   Die Mystikerin Margaretha Ebner. (Zoepf, L.) Leipzig, 1914.
Phil 530.15.5   Une mystique bretonne aux XVIIe siècle. (Le Jonvello, H.) Paris, 1913.
Phil 1504.13.2   La mystique de Ramon Lull et l'art de contemplació. v.13, pt.2-3. (Probst, J.H.) Münster, 1914.
Phil 525.73   La mystique divine. (Thulié, H.) Paris, 1912.
Phil 530.15.25   Une mystique en pays Perthois au XVIIe siècle Marie Darizy de Verget. (Jovy, Ernest.) Vitry-Le-François, 1913.
Phil 525.270   Mystique et continence. (Congrès international de psychologie religieuse, 7th, Avon, 1950.) Bruges, 1952.
Phil 8582.44   La mystique et la raison. (Colas, Émile.) Paris, 1922.
Phil 525.243   La mystique et les mystiques. (Ravier, André.) Bruges, 1965.
Phil 525.232   La mystique rhénane, Colloque de Strasbourg, 16-19 mai, 1961. (Colloque de Strasbourg, 1961.) Paris, 1963.
Phil 3010.8   Mystiques. (Koyré, Alexandre.) Paris, 1955.
Phil 530.20.105   Les mystiques allemands du XVII au XIX siècle. (Chuzeville, Jean.) Paris, 1935.
Phil 530.15.28   Mystiques de France. (Daniel-Rops, Henry.) Paris, 1941.
Phil 530.50.5   Les mystiques des Pays-Bas. (Groult, Pierre.) Louvain, 1927.
Phil 525.8   Les mystiques du néo-romantisme. (Seillière, E.) Paris, 1911.
Phil 530.40.5   Les mystiques espagnols. (Rousselot, P.) Paris, 1869.
Phil 530.35.20   Les mystiques italiens. (Chuzeville, Jean.) Paris, 1942.
Phil 525.180   Mystiques parmi nous. (Weyergans, Franz.) Paris, 1959.
Phil 3210.89   Mystische Motive in Fechners Philosophie. Inaug. Diss. (Rezazadeh-Schafagh, Sadeg.) Charlottenburg, 1928.
Phil 530.30.10A   Mystische Texte aus dem Mittelalter. (Muschg, Walter.) Basel, 1943.
Phil 525.21.2   Die mystischen Erscheinungen der menschlichen Natur. Bd.1-2. 2e Aufl. (Perty, M.) Leipzig, 1872.
Phil 525.21   Die mystischen Erscheinungen der menschlichen Natur. With supplement. (Perty, M.) Leipzig, 1861.
Phil 8589.21.2   Myth and Christianity. (Jaspers, Karl.) N.Y., 1958.
Phil 5261.2   Myth and science. (Vignoli, T.) N.Y., 1882.
Phil 6319.1.236   The myth of meaning in the work of C.G. Jung. (Jaffé, Aniela.) London, 1970.
Phil 6980.717.25   The myth of mental illness. (Szasz, Thomas Stephen.) N.Y., 1961.
Phil 5520.395   The myth of metaphor. (Turbayne, C.M.) New Haven, 1962.
Phil 176.218   The myth of simplicity. (Bunge, Mario.) Englewood Cliff, N.J., 1963.
Phil 285.6   The myth of the eternal return. (Eliade, Mircea.) N.Y., 1954.
Phil 6120.15   The myth of the mind. (Kenyon, F.) London, 1941.
Phil 285.6.1   Le myth de l'eternel retour. (Eliade, Mircea.) Paris, 1969.
Phil 8622.64   Mythe et foi. (Colloque International sur Mythe et Foi, Rome, 1966.) Paris, 1966.
Phil 181.114   Mythe et métaphysique. (Gusdorf, G.) Paris, 1953.
Phil 186.38   Mythenbildung und Erkenntnis. (Lipps, Gottlob F.) Leipzig, 1907.
Phil 1106.13   Mythologie und Metaphysik. Die Entstehung der Weltanschauungen im greichisch Altertums. (Bender, W.) Stuttgart, 1899.
Phil 3625.17.30   Das mythologische in der Religion. (Medicus, Fritz.) Erlenbach, 1944.

Phil 6480.160   Mythology of the soul. (Baynes, H.G.) Baltimore, 1940.
Phil 194.58   Mythos, Philosophie, Politik. (Topitsch, Ernst.) Freiburg, 1969.
Phil 3801.134   Der Mythos bei Schelling. (Allwohn, Adolf.) Charlottenburg, 1927.
Phil 5700.6   Der Mythos der Maschine. (Kadinsky, David.) Bern, 1969.
Phil 3450.44   Mythos und Logik im 20. Jahrhundert. (Hochgesang, Michael.) München, 1965.
Phil 3801.872.25   Mythos und Logos. (Volkmann-Schluck, Karl Heinz.) Berlin, 1969.
Phil 4215.8.35   Myths and ideals. (Ruggiero, Guido de.) London, 1946.
Phil 7069.67.20   Myths of the space age. (Cohen, Daniel.) N.Y., 1967.
Phil 8586.13   Mythus und Sage. (George, J.F.L.) Berlin, 1837.
Phil 6319.1.235   Der Mythus vom Sinn in Werk von C.G. Jung. (Jaffé, Aniela.) Zürich, 1967.
Phil 8403.12.5   N.G. Chernyshevskii ob iskusstve. (Chernyshevskii, N.G.) Moskva, 1950.
Phil 1750.166.275   Na batalho do humanismo. 2. ed. (Azevedo, Fernando de.) São Paulo, 1967.
Phil 4803.680.30   Na drogach współczesnej kultury. (Peľka-Peliński, Stanisław.) Lódz, 1946.
Phil 9495.155.5   Na poroge zrelosti. 2. izd. (Zenkovskii, V.V.) Parizh, 1955.
Phil 193.134   Na vesakh Iova. (Shestov, L.) Parizh, 1929.
Phil 8413.38   Na vkus, na tsvet. (Molchanova, Albina S.) Moskva, 1966.
Phil 5046.14   Några anmarkningar angäende den formella logiken. (Gustrin, E.F.) Lund, 1876.
Phil 4655.1.50   Några drag af kulturens offerväsen. (Wikner, Pontus.) Upsala, 1880.
Phil 184.15.5   Några grundlinjer fill filosofien. (Jochnick, W.) Stockholm, 1895.
Phil 5249.2.40   Några livsideal samt de store männen och deres omgiming. (James, William.) Stockholm, 1917.
Phil 585.245   Naar omega. Conceptie van nieuw denken. (Andriessen, J.H.) Den Haag, 1967.
Phil 8668.9   Nabert, Jean. Le désir de Dieu. Paris, 1966.
Phil 8888.13   Nabert, Jean. Eléments pour une éthique. 1st ed. Paris, 1943.
Phil 5763.3.5   Nabert, Jean. L'expérience intérieure de la liberté. Paris, 1924.
Phil 5763.3   Nabert, Jean. L'expérience intérieure de la liberté. Thèse. Paris, 1923.
Phil 585.310   Nabhani, Koribaa. Essai d'une détermination esthétique de l'humain. Thèse. Alger, 1964.
Phil 5253.6   Naccarati, S. The morphologic aspect of intelligence. N.Y., 1921.
Phil 6990.3.50   Nach Lourdes. (Müller, G.A.) Luzern, 1909.
Htn   Phil 3819.73.10F*   Nachbildung der im Jahre 1902 noch Erhaltenen...Briefe. (Spinoza, Benedictus de.) Haag, 1903.
Phil 5525.39.5   Nachdenkliche Heiterkeit. (Reik, Theodor.) Wien, 1933.
Htn   Phil 3800.385*   Nachgelassene Schriften...Vorwort von Schelling. (Steffens, Henrik.) Berlin, 1846.
Phil 8589.2.10   Nachgelassene Schriften. (Jerusalem, J.F.W.) Braunschweig, 1792-93. 2v.
Phil 3246.19   Nachgelassene Schriften. Bd.2. (Fichte, Johann Gottlieb.) Berlin, 1937.
Phil 3480.76   Das nachgelassene Werk. (Kant, Immanuel.) Lahr, 1888.
Phil 3246.15   Nachgelassene Werke. (Fichte, Johann Gottlieb.) Bonn, 1934-35. 3v.
Phil 3246.18.3.5   Nachgelassene Werke. (Fichte, Johann Gottlieb.) Bonn, 1962. 3v.
Phil 3246.18.3   Nachgelassene Werke. (Fichte, Johann Gottlieb.) Leipzig, 1924. 3v.
Phil 2880.1.25   NachgelasseneWerke. (Saint-Martin, L.C.) Münster, 1833.
Phil 3460.20   Nachlass. Ungedruckte Briefe. (Jacobi, F.H.) Leipzig, 1869.
Phil 3120.30.56   Nachlese. (Buber, Martin.) Heidelberg, 1965.
Phil 3450.19.245   Nachlese zu Heidegger. (Schneeberger, Guido.) Bern, 1962.
Phil 7060.56   Nachricht von einem gewissen Monche in Dresden. (Hilscher, M.P.C.) Dresden, 1729.
Phil 978.49.875   Nachrichten mit Veröffentlichungen aus dem Archiv. (Rudolf Steiner-Nachlassverwaltung.) Dornach. 5-11
Phil 1133.16.10   Die Nachsokratiker. (Nestle, W.) Jena, 1923. 2v.
Phil 6323.8   Nacht, Sacha. Le masochisme. 2. éd. Paris, 1948.
Phil 6323.20   Nacht, Sacha. La présence du psychanalyste. Paris, 1963.
Phil 6323.21   Nacht, Sacha. Traité de psychanalyse. Paris, 1965.
Phil 7060.36.5   Nacht Seite der Natur. v.1-2. (Crowe, C.S.) Stuttgart, 1849.
Phil 978.49.915   Nachweis der Zitate zu Rudolf Steiner Die Rätsel der Philosophie im ihrer Geschichte als Umriss Dargestellt. (Ericsson-Skopnik, Brigitte.) Dornach, 1969.
Phil 4357.12.2   El nacimiento de la intimidad, y otros estudios. 2. ed. (Carcía Hoz, Victor.) Madrid, 1970.
Phil 4960.230   Nacimiento y desarollo de la filosofía en el Rio de la Plata, 1536-1810. (Fúrlong Cárdiff, Guillermo.) Buenos Aires, 1952.
Phil 5823.2   Nadaillac, J.F.A. Intelligence et instinct. Paris, 1892.
Phil 5402.15   Nádejde, D.C. Die biologische Theorie der Lust und Unlust. Leipzig, 1908.
Phil 5125.6   Naden, Constance C.W. Induction and deduction. London, 1890.
Phil 672.254   Nadenken over de tijd. (Popma, Klaas Johan.) Amsterdam, 1954.
Phil 8414.9   Nadiani, A. Fra kaos til form. Oslo, 1949.
Phil 3425.266   Nadler, Käte. Der dialektische Widerspruch in Hegels Philosophie und das Paradoxon des Christentums. Leipzig, 1931.
Phil 1020.22.5   Nadvi, Muzaffar Uddir. Muslim thought and its source. Lahore, 1946.
Phil 1020.22.7   Nadvi, Muzaffar Uddir. Muslim thought and its source. 4th ed. Lahore, 1960.
Phil 6323.2   Naegeli, Otto. Uber den Einfluss von Rechtsansprüchen bei Neurosen. Leipzig, 1913.
Phil 3801.765   Nägra anteckningar om Schellings philosophi. (Sandberg, Sven.) Lund, 1856.
Phil 8050.43   Nägra punkter ur läran om det natursköna. (Ljunggren, G.) Lund, 1852.
Phil 3552.390   Naert, Emilienne. Leibniz et la querelle du pur amour. Paris, 1959.
Phil 3552.435   Naert, Emilienne. Mémoire et conscience de soi selon Leibniz. Paris, 1961.
Phil 3552.446   Naert, Emilienne. La pensée politique de Leibniz. Paris, 1964.
Phil 5068.40   Naese, Arne. Wie fördert man heute die empirische Bewegung? Oslo, 1956.
Phil 5253.7.5   Naesgaard, S. Begrebet som psykologisk element. København, 1924.
Phil 5253.7   Naesgaard, S. Kortfattet sjaelelaere. København, 1919.

Phil 5253.7.2   Naesgaard, S. Kortfattet sjaelelaere. København, 1928.
Phil 4635.2.92   Naesgaard, S. Starcken forsvar, metoder og resultater. København, 1917.
Phil 4635.2.90   Naesgaard, S. Starckes psykologi. København, 1916.
Phil 1713.4.2   Naess, Arne. Four modern philosophers. Chicago, 1968.
Phil 4610.10.30   Naess, Arne. Hva er filosofi? Oslo, 1965.
Phil 5520.170   Naess, Arne. Interpretation and preciseness. Oslo, 1953.
Phil 1713.4   Naess, Arne. Moderne filosofer. Stockholm, 1965.
Phil 5253.8.50   Naess, Arne. Notes on the foundation of psychology as a science. Oslo, 1960.
Phil 645.55   Naess, Arne. Scepticism. London, 1968[1969]
Phil 8620.25   Nagel, E. Das Problem der Erlösung. Basel, 1901.
Phil 7069.60   Nagel, E.W. Mind power. 1. ed. N.Y., 1960.
Phil 344.5   Nagel, Ernest. Meaning and knowledge. N.Y., 1965.
Phil 3280.87   Nagel, Karl. Das Substanzproblem bei Arnold Geulincx. Inaug. Diss. Köln, 1930.
Phil 9290.2   Nagel, O. Die Welt als Arbeit. Stuttgart, 1909.
Phil 8888.18   Nagel, Thomas. The possibility of altruism. Oxford, 1970.
Phil 5645.31   Nagel, W.A. Der Lichtsinn augenloser Tiere. n.p., 1896-1908. 7 pam.
Phil 1703.3   Nagelaten Geschriften. (Du Marchie van Voorlhnipen, H.) Arheim, 1886. 2v.
Phil 5627.139   Nagle, Urban. An empirical study of the development of religious thinking in boys from twelve to sixteen years old. Washington, 1934.
Phil 4600.2.33   Nagot on den fria viljan. (Larsson, Hans.) n.p., n.d.
Phil 9245.119   Naguib, Mohammad. Full happiness. Cairo, n.d.
Phil 1504.2.5   Nagy, A. Die philosophischen Abhandlungen. v.2, pt.5. Münster, 1897.
Phil 5053.4   Nagy, Albino. Fondamenti del calcolo logico. Napoli, 1904.
Phil 315.7   Nahile, Emilia. Il dualismo nella filosofia. Napoli, 1931.
Phil 4810.2.5   Náhl'ady filozofov malohontstkej spoločnosti. (Muenz, Teodor.) Bratislava, 1954.
Phil 8888.1.3   Nahlowsky, J.W. Allgemeine Ethik. 2. Aufl. Pleizig, 1885.
Phil 8888.1   Nahlowsky, J.W. Allgemeine praktische Philosophie. Leipzig, 1871.
Phil 8888.1.6   Nahlowsky, J.W. Die ethischen Ideen als die Waltenden Mächte. Langensalza, 1904.
Phil 5400.13   Nahlowsky, J.W. Das Gefühlsleben. Leipzig, 1884.
Phil 5643.93   Nahm, E. Uber den Vergleich von Komplexen geometrischen Gebilde und tontfreier Farben. Inaug. Diss. Frankfurt, 1930?
Phil 8414.8.11   Nahm, Milton Charles. Aesthetic experience and its presuppositions. N.Y., 1946.
Phil 8414.8   Nahm, Milton Charles. The artist as creator; an essay of human freedom. Baltimore, 1956.
Phil 5253.13   Nahoum, Charles. L'entretien psychologique. Paris, 1958.
Phil 6951.13   Die Nahrungsverweigerung der Irren. (Böttger, H.) Leipzig, 1878.
Phil 5811.10.7   La naissance de l'intelligence. (Bohn, Georges.) Paris, 1920.
Phil 3245.86   Najdanović, D. Die Geschichtsphilosophie Immanuel Hermann Fichtes. Berlin, 1940.
Phil 3245.86.2   Najdanović, D. Die Geschichtsphilosophie Immanuel Hermann Fichtes. Berlin, 1940.
Phil 4897.15   Nakamura, Hajime. A history of the development of Japanese thought from 592 to 1868. v.1-2. Tokyo, 1967.
Phil 3495.15   Nakashima, R. Kant's doctrine of the "thing-in-itself". New Haven, 1889.
Phil 5252.157A   The naked ape; a zoologist's study of the human animal. 1. ed. (Morris, Desmond.) N.Y., 1967.
Phil 5465.115   Naksianowicz-Gołaszewska, M. Twórczość a osobowość twórcy. Lublin, 1958.
Phil 8430.51   Naksianowicz-Golaszewska, Maria. Odbiorca sztuki jako krytyk. Wyd.1. Kraków, 1967.
Phil 3915.40.2.2   Namenverzeichniss und Sachregister zu Wundt's Logik. 2. Aufl. (Lindan, Hans.) Stuttgart, 1922.
Phil 4065.107.5   Namer, Émile. Les aspects de Dieu dans la philosophie de Giordano Bruno. Paris, 1926.
Phil 4065.107   Namer, Émile. Les aspects de Dieu dans la philosophie de Giordano Bruno. Thèse. Paris, 1926.
Phil 4065.107.10   Namer, Émile. Giordano Bruno, ou L'univers infini comme fondement de la philosophie moderne. Paris, 1966.
Phil 4013.10   Namer, Émile. La philosophie italienne. Paris, 1970.
Phil 285.4   The Namic philosophy. (Embry, J.) N.Y., 1951.
Phil 250.1   Nancel, N. de. Analogia microcosmi. Paris, 1611.
Phil 6683.3   Nani, Giacomo D. Trattato teorico-pratico sul magnetismo animale. Torino, 1850.
Phil 3210.59   Nanna. (Fechner, G.T.) Hamburg, 1908.
Phil 6990.18   Nanz, C.F. Die Besessenen im neuen Testament. Reutlingen, 1840.
Phil 1135.177   Napoli, G. La concezione dell'essere nella filosofia. Milano, 1953.
Phil 4112.89   Napoli, G. di. La filosofia di Pasquale Galluppi. Padova, 1947.
Phil 1614.10   Napoli, Giovanni di. Dal rinascimento all'illuminismo. Roma, 1969.
Phil 4195.107   Napoli, Giovanni di. Giovanni Pico della Mirandola. Roma, 1965.
Phil 8140.5   Napoli, Paolo. Arte e architettura in regime fascista. Roma, 1938.
Phil 4870.12   Naravane, Vishwanath S. Modern Indian thought; a philosophical survey. Bombay, 1964.
Phil 7082.110   Narayan, Ram. The dream problem. Delhi, 1917?-22. 2v.
Phil 5053.10   Narbutt, Olgierd. O pierwszym polskim podręczniku logiki. Lódz, 1958.
Phil 1614.5   Nardi, Bruno. La crisi del Rinascimento e il dubbio cortesiano. Roma, 1950-51.
Phil 2520.241   Nardi, Bruno. Le meditizioni di Cartesio. Roma, 1952.
Phil 4013.2   Nardi, Bruno. Saggi sull'aristotelismo padovana dal secolo XIV al XVI. Firenze, 1958.
Phil 1518.2   Nardi, Bruno. Studi di filosofia medievale. Roma, 1960.
Phil 4200.1.84   Nardi, Bruno. Studi su Pietro Pomponazzi. Firenze, 1965.
Phil 4210.81   Nardi, P. de. Antonio Rosmini ed i gesuiti. Torino, 1882.
Phil 2270.131   Nardi, P. de. L'assoluto inconoscibile di H. Spencer. Forlì, 1904.
Phil 4210.81.15   Nardi, P. de. La compagnia di Gesu et la recente condanna di A. Rosmini. Intra, 1888. 5 pam.
Phil 4210.81.12F   Nardi, P. de. Di Antonio Rosmini-Serbati reformatore. Forli, 1894.
Phil 4210.81.4   Nardi, P. de. La filosofia di Antonio R-S. Pt. 1. Bellinzona, 1881.
Phil 4210.81.8   Nardi, P. de. Rosmini e Kant. Forli, 1902.
Phil 2115.137   Nardi, Pietro de. Caratteri della filosofia di Giovanni Locke. Firenze, 1889.

Phil 2115.137.5   Nardi, Pietro de. Del rinnovamento delle dottrine di Gall e...di Locke. Firenze, 1890.

Phil 4655.1.55   Narkissos-sagan och platonismen. (Wikner, Pontus.) Upsala, 1880.

Phil 4803.465.86   Narodziny filozofii nauki o pracy w Polsce. Wyd. 1. (Bańka, Józef.) Warszawa, 1970.

VPhil 585.191   Narodziny nowożytnej filozofii człowieka. (Suchodolski, Bogdan.) Warszawa, 1963.

Phil 4800.22   Naroziny pozytywizmu polskiego, 1831-1864. (Skarga, Barbara.) Warszawa, 1964.

Phil 6990.16   Narrative of two wonderful cures. (Myers, J.) Baltimore, 1831.

Phil 2115.175   Narshii, I.S. Fislosofiia Dzhona Lokka. Moskva, 1960.
Phil 2255.1.114   Narskii, I.S. Filosfiia Bertrana Rassela. Moskva, 1962.
Phil 5520.185   Narskii, I.S. Kritika semanticheskogo idealizma. Moskva, 1956.

Phil 310.210   Narskii, I.S. Marksistskoe ponimanie predmeta filosofii i pozitivizm. Moskva, 1959.
Phil 310.212   Narskii, I.S. Problema protivorechiia v dialekticheskoi logike. Moskva, 1969.

Phil 5068.48   Narskii, I.S. Sovremennyi pozitivizm. Moskva, 1960.
Phil 5068.94   Narskii, Igor S. Dialekticheskoe protivorechie i logika poznaniia. Moskva, 1969.

Phil 2050.268   Narskii, Igor' S. Filosofiia Davida Iuma. Moskva, 1967.
Phil 600.57   Narskii, Igor Sergeevich. Ocherki po istorii pozitivizma. Moskva, 1960.

Phil 4800.14   Narskii, Igor' Sergeevich. Pol'skie mysliteli epokhi Vozrozhdeniia. Moskva, 1960.

Phil 600.57.10   Narskii, Igor Sergeevich. Positivismus in Vergangenheit und Gegenwart. Berlin, 1967.

Phil 9550.20   Narveson, Jan. Morality and utility. Baltimore, 1967.
Phil 4710.50.20   Narys istorii filosofii na Ukraini. (Akademiia Nauk URSR, Kiev. Instytut Filosofii.) Kyïv, 1966.

Phil 4780.2   Narysy pa historyi hramadska-palitychnai i filosofskai dumki u Belarusi u drukoi palavine XIX veku. (Lushchytski, I.N.) Minsk, 1958.

Phil 4710.55   Narysy z istorii filosofii na Ukraini. (Chizhevskii, D.) Praga, 1931.

Phil 3425.259   La nascita della dialettica Hegeliana. (Negri, Enrico de.) Firenza, 1930.

Phil 9450.17   Naše dějinné poslání; čaovas úvaha politicko-ethická. (Joklík, F.) Praha, 1919?

Phil 5374.31.5   Nasgaard, S. Bevidsthedens form. Kóbenhavn, 1922.
Phil 5374.31   Nasgaard, S. Die Form der Bewusstheit. München, 1923.
Phil 9380.4   Nash, Jay Bryan. Building morale. N.Y., 1942.
Phil 5865.8   Nash, John. Developmental psychology. Englewood Cliffs, N.J., 1970.

Phil 9070.42   Nash, R.S.J. Label your luggage. Dublin, 1943.
Htn   Phil 9050.7.5*   Nash, T. Quaternio, or A fourfold way to a happy life. London, 1633.

Htn   Phil 9050.7*   Nash, T. Quaternio, or A fourfold way to a happy life. London, 1636.

Phil 2805.276   Nasmuth, E. Die Philosophie Pascals. Heidelberg, 1949.
Phil 2805.277   Nasmuth, E. Der unbekannte Pascal. Regensburg, 1962.
Phil 1020.47   Naso, S.H. An introduction to Islamic cosmological doctrines. Cambridge, 1964.

Phil 294.1   Nason, L.H. History of the prehistoric ages. Chicago, 1880.
Phil 8703.5   Nasr, Segyed Hossein. The encounter of man and nature; the spiritual crisis of modern man. London, 1968.
Phil 8593.19   Nass, R.B. Two popular philosophic-scientific essays in the spirit of faith and religion. Brooklyn, N.Y., 1943.
Phil 1133.25   Nassauer, Kurt. Denker der hellenischen Frühzeit. Frankfurt, 1948.

Phil 5253.14   Nassefat, Mortega. Étude quantitative sur l'évolution des opérations inteslectuelles. Neuchâtel, 1963.
Phil 8888.20   Nassent, Georges. Joie, souffrance et vie morale. Paris, 1968.

Phil 1955.6.180   Nassif, F.R. En el centenario de John Dewey. La Plata, 1961.

Phil 8668.10   Nastol'naia Kniga ateista. Moskva, 1968.
Phil 6816.10.2   Natale, Nicola G. Vita segreta del complesso d'inferiorita. 2. ed. Bologna, 1961.

Phil 2880.8.122   Natanson, M. A critique of Jean Paul Sartre's ontology. Lincoln, 1951.

Phil 188.24   Natanson, M. Literature, philosophy and the social sciences; essays in existentialism and phenomenology. The Hague, 1962.

Phil 2150.15.100   Natanson, M. The social dynamics of George H. Mead. Washington, 1956.
Phil 1750.780   Natanson, Maurice Alexander. Essays in phenomenology. The Hague, 1966.

Phil 575.282   Natanson, Maurice Alexander. The journeying self; a study in philosophy and social role. Reading, Mass., 1970.
Phil 6315.2.155   Natenberg, M. The case history ⌐f Sigmund Freud. 1. ed. Chicago, 1955.

Phil 9070.146   Natesan, B. The sympathy of life. Madras, 1967.
Phil 8414.5   Natev, A. Tsel ili samotselnost na izkustvoto. Sofiia, 1960.

Phil 1850.104   Natge, Hans. Über Francis Bacons Formenlehre. Leipzig, 1891.

Phil 3565.126   Nath, Max. Die Psychologie Hermann Lotzes in ihrem Verhältnis zu Herbart. Halle, 1892.
Phil 3552.257   Nathan, Bernhard. Über das Verhältnis der leibnizischen Ethik zu Metaphysik und Theologie. Diss. Jena, 1916.

Phil 6963.7   Nathan, M. Manuel élémentaire de psychiatrie. Paris, 1930.

Phil 6323.3   Nathan, Marcel. Les malades dits imaginaires. Paris, 1931.

Phil 1955.6.119   Nathanson, J. John Dewey. N.Y., 1951.
Phil 23.24   National Advisory Council on Radio in Education. Listener's notebook. Chicago. 1931-1932
Phil 23.23   National Advisory Council on Radio in Education. Psychology series lecture. Chicago. 11-30

Phil 53.2   National Association for Study of Epilepsy and Care and Treatment of Epileptics. Transactions, 1901. Buffalo, 1901.
Phil 6963.1   National association for the protection of the insane, 1880-1882. Boston, 1880. 2v.
Phil 23.8   National committee for mental hygiene, inc.   1,1924
Phil 6123.8   National Committee for Mental Hygiene. N.Y. Division on Rehabilitation. Bibliography. Mental hygiene in industry. N.Y., 1945.

Phil 6980.598   National Committee for Mental Hygiene. Directory of psychiatric clinics in the United States. 1. ed. N.Y., 1932.

Phil 53.3F   National Committee for Mental Hygiene. Eight annual meeting (typed announcements). n.p., 1916.

Phil 6951.5.53   National Committee for Mental Hygiene. The mental hygiene movement. N.Y., 1938.
Phil 53.3.5   National Committee for Mental Hygiene. Publication. N.Y. 1-12 2v.
Phil 53.3.9   National Committee for Mental Hygiene. Publication. N.Y. 2-196 2v.
Phil 6750.15   National Conference of Charities and Corrections. Feeble-mindedness and insanity. Chicago, 1916?
Phil 6963.8   National Conference on Social Welfare. Mental health and social welfare. N.Y., 1961.
Phil 9495.37.15   National Council of Public Morals for Great and Greater Britain. Campaigns of peace. N.Y., 1919.
Phil 8610.834.5   National hymns. (Kneeland, A.) Boston, 1836.
Phil 7061.10   National Laboratory of Psychical Research, London. Short title catalogue of works...from c.1450 to 1929. London, 1929.
Phil 23.14   National laboratory of psychical research. Bulletin. London. 1-6,1931-1933
Phil 8642.6   National life in the spirit world. (Rogers, E.H.) Chelsea? 1891.
Phil 8885.10.5   National living. (King, H.C.) N.Y., 1912.
Phil 5850.281   National Research Council. Psychology for the returning serviceman. 1st ed. Washington, 1945.
Phil 75.27   National Research Council. Research Information Service. Union list of foreign serials cited in Psychological index, 1922. Washington, 1925.
X Cg   Phil 8610.875.20   National Secular Society. The secular song and hymn book. London, 1875?
Phil 978.49.660   Nationalökonomischer Kurs. 4. Aufl. (Steiner, R.) Dornach, 1965.
Phil 3915.71.2   Nationen und ihre Philosophie. (Wundt, Wilhelm.) Leipzig, 1915.
Phil 3915.71   Die Nationen und ihre Philosophie. (Wundt, Wilhelm.) Leipzig, 1916.
Phil 9495.30   The nation's morals. (Public Morals Conference, London, 1910.) London, 1910.
Phil 5585.351   NATO Advanced Study Institute, University of Thessaloniki, 1968. Contemporary problems in perception. London, 1970.
Phil 5655.15   NATO Advanced Study Institute on Theories of Odor and Odor Measurement, Istanbul, 1966. Theories of odor and odor measurement. Bebek, Istanbul, 1966.
Phil 5253.1.5   Natorp, P. Allgemeine Psychologie. Tübingen, 1912.
Phil 5253.1.9   Natorp, P. Allgemeine Psychologie. 2. Aufl. Marburg, 1910.
Phil 2520.107   Natorp, P. Descartes' Erkenntnisstheorie. Marburg, 1882.
Phil 5253.1   Natorp, P. Einleitung in die Psychologie. Freiburg, 1888.
Phil 1118.2   Natorp, Paul. Forschungen zur Geschichte der Erkenntnissproblems im Alterthum. Berlin, 1884.
Phil 3160.3.82   Natorp, Paul. Hermann Cohen. Marburg, 1918.
Phil 188.12.5   Natorp, Paul. Jemand und ich. Stuttgart, 1906.
Phil 3495.10   Natorp, Paul. Kant über Krieg und Frieden. Erlangen, 1924.
Phil 3495.10.10   Natorp, Paul. Kant und die Marburger Schule. Berlin, 1912.
Phil 188.12.20   Natorp, Paul. Philosophie: ihr Problem und ihre Probleme. Göttingen, 1911.
Phil 188.12   Natorp, Paul. Philosophische Propädeutik. Marburg, 1903.
Phil 3665.1.30   Natorp, Paul. Philosophische Systematik. Hamburg, 1958.
Phil 8593.8.2   Natorp, Paul. Religion inneralb der Grenzen. Tübingen, 1908.
Phil 5763.2   Natorp, Paul. Sozialpädagogik. Theorie der Willenserziehung. 3. Aufl. Stuttgart, 1909.
Phil 5763.2.5   Natorp, Paul. Sozialpädagogik. Theorie der Willenserziehung. 6. Aufl. Stuttgart, 1925.
Phil 188.12.9   Natorp, Paul. Vorlesungen über praktische Philosophie. Erlangen, 1925.
Phil 310.663   Natsii - narod - chelovechestvo. (Rogachev, Petr M.) Moskva, 1967.
Phil 7054.27.7   Natty, a spirit; his portrait and his life. (Putnam, A.) Boston, 1856.
Phil 5043.11.5   Natürliche Dialektik. (Dühring, E.K.) Berlin, 1865.
Phil 3235.85   Der natürliche Sittenlehre Ludwig Feuerbachs. (Wintzer, Wilhelm.) Leipzig, 1898.
Phil 165.24   Natur, Geist, Geschichte. (Hanslmeier, J.) München, 1950.
Phil 4769.1.125   Natur, Kunst und Liebe in der Philosophie Vladimir Solov'evs. (Klum, Edith.) München, 1965.
Phil 6682.5   Natur. (Meyer, J.A.G.) Gotha, 1839.
Phil 3552.236   Die Natur des Willens bei Leibniz. (Bugarski, G.M.) Leipzig, 1897.
Phil 8885.8   Natur-Ethik. (Koerner, H.J.A.) Hamburg, 1873. 2v.
Phil 285.2   Natur oder Schöpfung? (Erdmann, J.E.) Leipzig, 1840.
Phil 4610.9.31   Natur og aand. (Nielsen, R.) Kjøbenhavn, 1873. 2 pam.
Phil 1535.21   Natur-Philosophie. (Biedermann, G.) Prag, 1887-89. 3v.
Phil 193.82   Natur Philosophie als exakte Wissenschaft. (Schmitz-Dumont, A.) Leipzig, 1895.
Phil 7082.162   Die Natur und Entstehung der Träume. (Strümpell, Ludwig.) Leipzig, 1874.
Phil 476.3.20   Natur und Geist. (Büchner, L.) Frankfurt, 1857.
Phil 187.135   Natur und Geist. (Medicus, Fritz.) Erlenback-Zurich, 1946.
Phil 476.3.15   Natur und Geist. 2e Aufl. (Büchner, L.) Hamm, 1865.
Phil 8591.32   Natur und geist Gottes; Vorträge zur Ethik. (Lütgert, Wilhelm.) Leipzig, 1910.
Phil 165.410   Natur und Geschichte. Stuttgart, 1967.
Phil 283.2   Natur und Idee. (Carus, C.G.) Wien, 1861.
Phil 8402.49   Natur und Kunst. (Brinkmann, D.) Zürich, 1938.
Phil 978.49.552   Natur und Menschin geisteswissenschaftlicher Betrachtung. 2. Aufl. (Steiner, R.) Dornach, 1967.
Phil 3085.5.40   Natur und Mysterium. (Andre, H.) Einsiedeln, 1959.
Phil 8587.28   Natur und Offenbarung. 2. Aufl. (Hoppe, Edmund.) Hannover, 1904.
Phil 3801.775   Natur und Wahrheit; Untersuchungen über Entstehung...der Schellingschen Systems. (Schilling, Kurt.) München, 1934.
Phil 298.4   Die Natur und Wir. (Reinke, J.) Berlin, 1907.
Phil 4260.210   Natura e humanitas nel Giovane Vico. (Donzelli, Maria.) Napoli, 1970.
Phil 2050.230   Natura e societá in David Hume. 1. ed. (Carsi, M.) Firenze, 1953.
Phil 400.128   Natura e spirito nell'idealismo attuale. (Spisani, Franco.) Milano, 1968?
Phil 4060.1.35   Natura naturans. (Ardigo, Roberto.) Ostiglia, 1918.
Phil 8602.18.15   Natural and comparative religion. (Webb, C.C.J.) Oxford, 1912.
Phil 8892.14   Natural and social morals. (Read, Carveth.) London, 1909.
Phil 8594.13   The natural and the supernatural. (Oman, John.) N.Y., 1931.

Phil 192.54.5 A natural approach to philosophy. (Rohrbaugh, L.G.) N.Y., 1934.
Phil 8891.3 Natural basis of moral and ethics. (Quinby, L.J.) Boston, 1936.
Phil 7069.35.7 A natural bridge to cross. (Burton, Eva.) N.Y., 1935.
Phil 7068.86.50 Natural causes and supernatural seemings. (Maudsley, H.) London, 1886.
Phil 6122.1.17 Natural causes and supernatural seemings. (Maudsley, H.) London, 1897.
Phil 8877.69 Natural conduct. (Copeland, Edwin B.) Stanford, Calif., 1928.
Phil 8669.5 The natural desire for God. (O'Connor, William R.) Milwaukee, 1948.
Phil 8626.2 Natural evidence of a future life. (Bakewell, F.C.) London, 1835.
Phil 5421.20.25 The natural history of aggression. (Carthy, John D.) London, 1964.
Phil 8656.3 The natural history of atheism. (Blackie, J.S.) London, 1877.
Phil 8656.3.2 The natural history of atheism. (Blackie, J.S.) N.Y., 1878.
Phil 5405.5.2 Natural history of enthusiasm. (Taylor, I.) Boston, 1830.
Phil 5405.5.5 Natural history of enthusiasm. (Taylor, I.) London, 1830.
Phil 5405.5.3 Natural history of enthusiasm. (Taylor, I.) London, 1830.
Phil 5405.5.10 Natural history of enthusiasm. 10th ed. (Taylor, I.) London, 1845.
Phil 8620.40 The natural history of evil. (Whyte, A.G.) London, 1920.
Phil 8640.10 The natural history of hell. (Philipson, J.) N.Y., 1894.
Phil 7075.154 The natural history of love. (Hunt, Morton M.) N.Y., 1959.
Phil 5257.48 The natural history of mind. (Ritchie, Arthur D.) London, 1936.
Phil 9150.28 The natural history of our conduct. (Ritter, William E.) N.Y., 1927.
Phil 2050.67.5 The natural history of religion. (Hume, David.) Stanford, 1957.
Phil 5627.21 The natural history of religious feeling. (Cornelison, I.A.) N.Y., 1911.
Htn Phil 5400.2* Natural history of the passions. (Charleton, W.) London, 1674.
Phil 2750.11.185 Natural knowledge of God in the philosophy of Jacques Maritain. (Daly, Mary F.) Rome, 1966.
Phil 8893.13 Natural law. (Simcox, E.) London, 1877.
Phil 290.5 Natural law as controlled but not determined by experiment. Thesis. (Jaffe, Haym.) Philadelphia, 1934.
Phil 2477.1.44 Natural law in science and philosophy. (Boutroux, Émile.) London, 1914.
Phil 8693.5.10A Natural law in the spiritual world. (Drummond, H.) N.Y., 1885.
Phil 8693.5.11 Natural law in the spiritual world. (Drummond, H.) N.Y., 1887.
Phil 8693.5.14 Natural law in the spiritual world. (Drummond, H.) N.Y., 189-.
Phil 8693.5.3 Natural law in the spiritual world. (Drummond, H.) Philadelphia, 1892.
Phil 8693.5.2 Natural law in the spiritual world. 17th ed. (Drummond, H.) London, 1885.
Phil 8893.21.3 The natural laws of man. (Spurzheim, J.K.) N.Y., 1849.
Phil 7069.15.28 The natural order of spirit. (Gravies, L.C.) Boston, 1915.
Phil 177.16.9 Natural philosophie reformed by divine light. (Comenius, J.A.) London, 1651.
Phil 295.1.6 Natural philosophy. (Ostwald, W.) N.Y., 1910.
Phil 672.212 The natural philosophy of time. (Whitrow, G.J.) London, 1961.
Htn Phil 8881.67* Natural principles of rectitude. (Gros, J.D.) N.Y., 1795.
Phil 8592.15.5 Natural religion. (Müller, F.M.) London, 1889.
Phil 8598.7.3 Natural religion. (Seeley, R.) Boston, 1882.
Phil 8598.7 Natural religion. (Seeley, R.) London, 1882.
Phil 8598.10.5 Natural religion. (Simon, J.) London, 1857.
Phil 8707.21.5A Natural religion and Christian theology. (Raven, C.E.) Cambridge, Eng., 1953. 2v.
Phil 8696.7 Natural science and religion. (Gray, Asa.) N.Y., 1880.
Phil 5390.10 The natural science of stupidity. 1. ed. (Tabori, Paul.) Philadelphia, 1959.
Phil 8582.14 Natural theology. (Crombie, A.) London, 1829. 2v.
Phil 2205.30.12 Natural theology. (Paley, W.) Albany, 1803.
Phil 2205.30.9 Natural theology. (Paley, W.) Boston, 1829.
Phil 2205.30.13 Natural theology. (Paley, W.) Boston, 1831.
Phil 2205.30.5 Natural theology. (Paley, W.) Boston, 1854.
Phil 2205.30.15 Natural theology. (Paley, W.) Boston, 1857.
Phil 2205.30.18 Natural theology. (Paley, W.) Hallowell, 1819.
Htn Phil 2205.30.17* Natural theology. (Paley, W.) Hallowell, 1819.
Phil 2205.30 Natural theology. (Paley, W.) London, 1803.
Phil 2205.30.4 Natural theology. (Paley, W.) London, 1822.
Phil 2205.30.7.5 Natural theology. (Paley, W.) London, 1836. 2v.
Phil 2205.30.6 Natural theology. (Paley, W.) N.Y., n.d. 2 pam.
NEDL Phil 2205.30.11 Natural theology. (Paley, W.) Philadelphia, 1814.
Phil 2205.30.2 Natural theology. (Paley, W.) Philadelphia, 1814.
NEDL Phil 2205.30.3 Natural theology. (Paley, W.) Philadelphia, 1814.
Phil 2205.30.14 Natural theology. (Paley, W.) Trenton, N.J., 1824.
NEDL Phil 2205.30.10 Natural theology. 10th ed. (Paley, W.) London, 1805.
Phil 8599.9 Natural theology considered with reference to Lord Brougham's discourse on that subject. 2. ed. (Turton, Thomas.) Cambridge, 1836.
Phil 8599.9.5 Natural theology considered with reference to Lord Brougham's discourse on that subject. 2. ed. (Turton, Thomas.) London, 1836.
Phil 8583.43 Die naturale Meditation. (Dessauer, Philipp.) München, 1961.
Phil 4987.89.30 Naturaleza, historia, Dios. (Zubiri, Xavier.) Buenos Aires, 1948.
Phil 7069.08.27 The naturalisation of the supernatural. (Podmore, Frank.) N.Y., 1908.
Phil 531.2 Naturalism. (Pratt, James B.) New Haven, 1939.
Phil 8610.899.15 Naturalism and agnosticism. (Ward, James.) London, 1899. 2v.
Phil 8610.899.17 Naturalism and agnosticism. v.1. v.2 lost. (Ward, James.) N.Y., 1899.
Phil 5262.19.5 Naturalism and agnosticism. 4th ed. (Ward, J.) London, 1915.
Phil 165.426 Naturalism and historical understanding. (Anton, John Peter.) Albany, 1967.
Phil 8704.1.5 Naturalism and religion. (Otto, Rudolf.) London, 1907.
Phil 1750.96 Naturalism and subjectivism. (Farber, Marvin.) Springfield, Ill., 1959.
Phil 2493.88 The naturalism of Condillac. (Schaupp, Zora.) Lincoln, 1926.
Phil 2493.88.2 The naturalism of Condillac. Diss. (Schaupp, Zora.) n.p., 1925.
Phil 179.3.55 Naturalism or idealism? Photoreproduction. (Eucken, R.) Cambridge, 1912.
Phil 531.4 Le naturalisme. (Cogny, Pierre.) Paris, 1953.
Phil 1850.125 Il naturalismo e l'individualismo di F. Bacone. (Catalano, E.) Napoli, 1931.
Phil 4060.1.85 Naturalismo italiano. (Carelle, Antonio.) Padova, 1911.
Phil 1955.6.135 Naturalismo umanistico e sperimentale di John Dewey. (Verra, Valerio.) Torino, 1950.
Phil 8703.3 The naturalist: a dialogue. London, 1749. 2 pam.
Phil 583.14 Naturalistic philosophies of experience. (Mathur, Dinesh Chandra.) St. Louis, 1971.
Phil 5812.14 A naturalistic view of man. (Crile, George J.) N.Y., 1969.
Phil 5270.14 Naturalistic viewpoints in psychological research. N.Y., 1969.
Phil 8120.5 Die naturalistische Ästhetik in Frankreich und ihre Auflösung. (König, René.) Leipzig, 1930.
Phil 8876.130 Den naturalistiske sejlslutning. (Blegvad, Mogeus.) København, 1959.
Phil 8120.4 Die naturalitistische Ästhetik in Frankreich und ihre Auflösung. (König, René.) Borna, 1931.
Htn Phil 1850.74.5* The naturall and experimentall history of winds. (Bacon, Francis.) London, 1653.
Phil 284.6 Naturbegriffe und natururteile. (Driesch, Hans.) Leipzig, 1904.
Phil 299.6 Naturbetrachtung und Naturkenntnis. (Stunz, F.) Leipzig, 1904.
Phil 5627.264.20 Nature, grace and religious development. (McLaughlin, Barry.) N.Y., 1964.
Phil 7069.33.15 Nature, man and destiny. (Bull, Titus.) N.Y., 1933.
Phil 8599.17.10 Nature, man and God. (Temple, William.) London, 1935.
Phil 9362.19 Nature, man and woman. (Watts, Alan W.) N.Y., 1958.
Phil 6113.29 Nature, mind and death. (Ducasse, C.J.) La Salle, Ill., 1951.
Phil 338.26 Nature, mind of modern science. (Harris, E.E.) London, 1954.
Phil 8701.2.15 Nature, progress, ideas. (Lewis, Tayler.) Schenectady, 1850.
Phil 2138.45A Nature, the utility of religion and theism. (Mill, John S.) London, 1874.
Phil 2138.45.12 Nature, the utility of religion and theism. (Mill, John S.) London, 1874.
Phil 2138.45.15 Nature, the utility of religion and theism. (Mill, John S.) Westmead, Eng., 1969.
Phil 184.29 Nature, thought and personal experience. (Jones, W.T.) London, 1926.
Htn Phil 1980.2.30* Nature. (Emerson, R.W.) Boston, 1836.
Phil 8708.10.9 Nature. (Simpson, James Y.) New Haven, 1929.
Phil 2725.11.20 La nature. 1e éd. (Lachelier, Jules.) Paris, 1955.
Phil 978.46 The nature and aim of theosophy. (Buck, J.D.) Cincinnati, 1889.
Phil 8400.54.5 The nature and art of motion. (Keper, Gyorgy.) N.Y., 1965.
Phil 672.9.5 Nature and cognition of space and time. (Walter, J.E.) W. Newton, Pa., 1914.
Phil 8827.9 Nature and culture. (Crocker, L.) Baltimore, 1963.
Phil 5822.2 The nature and development of animal intelligence. (Mills, W.) London, 1898.
Phil 293.16 Nature and feeling. (Mitchell, William.) Adelaide, 1929.
Phil 8695.7 Nature and God. (Fulton, William.) Edinburgh, 1927.
Phil 186.109 Nature and history. (Lamprecht, S.P.) N.Y., 1950.
Phil 175.14.5 Nature and human nature. (Alexander, H.B.) Chicago, 1923.
Phil 5500.14.5 Nature and judgment. (Buchler, J.) N.Y., 1955.
Phil 177.7 Nature and man. (Carpenter, W.B.) London, 1888.
Phil 2340.11.30 Nature and man. (Weiss, Paul.) N.Y., 1947.
Phil 8620.41 The nature and meaning of evil. (Bond, C.J.) London, 1937.
Phil 197.23.10 Nature and mind. (Woodbridge, F.J.E.) N.Y., 1937.
Phil 6122.26 Nature and nurture in mental development. (Mott, Frederick Walker.) N.Y., 1915.
Phil 2270.85 Nature and reality of religion. A controversy. (Harrison, F.) N.Y., 1885.
Phil 7054.181.15 Nature and super-nature. (Leslie, John.) Aberdeen, 1820.
Phil 5520.99 The nature and technique of understanding. (Woodworth, Hugh.) Vancouver, B.C., 1949.
Phil 7054.49.4 The nature and tendency of modern spiritualism. 4. ed. (Waggoner, J.H.) Battle creek. Mich., 1872.
Phil 8707.2 Nature and the Bible. (Reusch, F.H.) Edinburgh, 1886. 2v.
Phil 1135.166 Nature and the Greeks. (Schroedinger, E.) Cambridge, Eng., 1954.
Phil 8581.16 Nature and the supernatural. (Bushnell, H.) N.Y., 1858.
Phil 8581.16.2 Nature and the supernatural. (Bushnell, H.) N.Y., 1859.
Phil 187.17 Nature and thought. (Mivart, St. G.) London, 1882.
Phil 8597.56 The nature and truth of the great religions. (Reischauer, August K.) Tokyo, 1966.
Phil 8581.67.10 Nature and values. (Brightman, E.S.) N.Y., 1945.
Phil 3492.25 La nature de l'expérience chez Kant et chez Bradley. Thèse. (Keeling, S.V.) Montpellier, 1925.
Phil 70.17 Nature des problemes en philosophie. (International Institute of Philosophy.) Paris, 1949.
Phil 337.18 La nature du psychique. 1. ed. (Gregoire, F.) Paris, 1957.
Phil 193.248 Nature et histoire; leur réalité et leur vérité. (Siegwalt, Gérard.) Leiden, 1965.
Phil 8881.22 La nature et la morale. (Guilly, E.P.) Paris, 1884.
Phil 2477.1.55 La nature et l'esprit. (Boutroux, Émile.) Paris, 1926.
Phil 176.213 La nature et l'esprit. (La Rochefoucauld, Edmée de Fels.) Paris, 1965.
Phil 2020.90 La nature et l'esprit dans la philosophie de T.H. Green. (Pucelle, Jean.) Louvain, 1960-65. 2v.
Phil 176.85.10 Nature et liberté. (Brunschvicg, L.) Paris, 1921.
Phil 8877.60 Nature et moralité. (Chabot, Charles.) Paris, 1896.
Phil 3820.8 Nature et vérité dans la philosophie de Spinoza. (Alquié, Ferdinand.) Paris, 1965.
Phil 8434.3.5 Nature for its own sake. 5th ed. (Van Dyke, J.C.) N.Y., 1908.
Phil 5253.3 La nature humaine. (Nourrisson, J.F.) Paris, 1865.
Phil 8400.39 The nature of beauty. Lahore, 1962.
Phil 193.72 The nature of being...essay in ontology. (Slesser, Henry H.) London, 1919.
Phil 5238.142 The nature of being human. (Rasey, Marie I.) Detroit, 1959.
Phil 8622.30 The nature of belief. (d'Arcy, M.C.) Dublin, 1958.
Phil 8599.21.5 The nature of belief. (Tennant, F.R.) London, 1943.

Phil 349.75   The nature of concepts, their inter-relation and role in social structure. (Stillwater Conference on the Nature of Concepts, their Structure and Social Inter-relation, Oklahoma Agricultural and Mechanical College, 1950.) Stillwater, Oklahoma, 1950.

Phil 8712.32   The nature of conflicts between science and religion. (Wood, John Karl.) Logan, 1967.

Phil 5627.107.25   The nature of conversion. (Gordon, Albert.) Boston, 1967.

Phil 5465.60   The nature of creative thinking. (Industrial Research Institute, New York.) N.Y., 1952?

Phil 8674.8.7   The nature of deity; a sequel to Personality and reality. (Turner, J.E.) London, 1927.

Phil 8620.5   The nature of evil. (James, H.) N.Y., 1855.

Phil 8620.37   The nature of evil. (Tsanoff, R.A.) N.Y., 1931.

Phil 187.56   The nature of existence. (McTaggart, J.M.E.) Cambridge, Eng., 1921-1927. 2v.

Phil 332.30   The nature of experience. (Brain, W.R.) London, 1959.

Phil 1920.1.32   The nature of explanation. (Craik, Kenneth James Williams.) Cambridge, Eng., 1952.

Phil 1920.1.30   The nature of explanation. (Craik, Kenneth James Williams.) Cambridge, 1943.

Phil 380.4   The nature of form in process. (Porter, Gene L.) N.Y., 1969.

Phil 9230.20   The nature of gambling. (Allen, David D.) N.Y., 1952.

Phil 9240.7   The nature of goodness. (Palmer, G.H.) Boston, 1903.

Phil 8890.23.16   The nature of goodness. (Palmer, G.H.) Boston, 1904.

Phil 5251.40.5A   The nature of human conflicts. (Luria, A.R.) N.Y., 1932.

Phil 5246.47.15   The nature of human intelligence. (Guilford, Joy Paul.) N.Y., 1967.

Phil 6688.30   The nature of hypnosis. (Shor, Ronald E.) N.Y., 1965.

Phil 5115.5   The nature of hypothesis. (Ashley, M.L.) Chicago, 1903.

Phil 5259.17   The nature of intelligence. (Thurstone, L.L.) London, 1924.

Phil 5258.68   The nature of "intelligence" and the principles of cognition. (Spearman, C.) London, 1923.

Phil 5258.68.2   The nature of "intelligence" and the principles of cognition. (Spearman, C.) London, 1927.

Phil 418.5   The nature of intention. (Meiland, Jack W.) London, 1970.

Phil 331.7   The nature of knowing. (Aaron, R.I.) London, 1930.

Phil 340.9   The nature of knowledge. (Jones, P. Chopin.) N.Y., 1964.

Phil 5525.23A   The nature of laughter. (Gregory, J.C.) London, 1924.

Phil 5247.29.15   The nature of learning in its relation to the living system. (Humphrey, G.) London, 1933.

Phil 197.35   The nature of life. (Webster, Florence.) N.Y., 1922.

Phil 186.107   The nature of man, his world. (Loos, A.) N.Y., 1950.

Phil 187.28.7   Nature of man. (Mechnikov, I.I.) London, 1938.

Phil 187.28.6.7   Nature of man. (Mechnikov, I.I.) N.Y., 1911.

Phil 585.143   The nature of man and the meaning of existence. (Burr, Harold S.) Springfield, 1962.

Phil 179.33.5   The nature of metaphysical thinking. (Emmet, D.M.) London, 1945.

Phil 190.84   The nature of metaphysics. (Pears, D.F.) London, 1957.

Phil 8887.125   The nature of moral judgement: a study in contemporary moral philosophy. (McGrath, Patrick.) London, 1967.

Phil 5643.138   The nature of perceptual adaptation. (Rock, Irvin.) N.Y., 1966.

Phil 5590.70   The nature of personality. (Allport, G.W.) Cambridge, Mass., 1950.

Phil 5590.71   The nature of personality. (Allport, Gordon Willard.) Cambridge, 1950.

Phil 70.112   The nature of philosophical inquiry. Notre Dame, 1970.

Phil 185.70   The nature of philosophy. (Krishna, Daya.) Calcutta, 1955.

Phil 5247.79   The nature of psychological inquiry. (Hyman, R.) Englewood Cliffs, N.J., 1964.

Phil 1920.1.35   The nature of psychology. (Craik, Kenneth James Williams.) Cambridge, Eng., 1966.

Phil 6959.4.25   The nature of psychotherapy. (Jaspers, K.) Manchester, 1964.

Phil 8592.55A   The nature of religion. (Moore, Edward C.) N.Y., 1936.

Phil 8602.34.10   The nature of religion. (Wobbermin, G.) N.Y., 1933.

Phil 8593.17   The nature of religious experience. N.Y., 1937.

Phil 8592.73   The nature of religious knowledge. (MacLeish, Norman.) N.Y., 1938.

Phil 8402.54   The nature of representation. (Bernheimer, Richard.) N.Y., 1961.

Phil 5046.34   The nature of science. (Greenwood, David.) N.Y., 1959.

Phil 343.18.9   The nature of self. (Mukerji, A.C.) Allahabad, 1938.

Phil 672.185   The nature of space. 1st ed. (Pereira, I.R.) N.Y., 1956.

Phil 5415.7.9   The nature of sympathy. (Scheler, Max.) Hamden, 1970.

Phil 5465.163   The nature of the creative process in art. (Havelka, Jaroslav.) The Hague, 1968.

Phil 5425.102   The nature of the genius. (Gemant, Andrew.) Springfield, Ill., 1961.

Phil 8875.13   The nature of the relationship between ethics and economics. (Ayres, Clarence E.) Chicago, Ill., n.d.

Phil 3246.53   Nature of the scholar. (Fichte, Johann Gottlieb.) London, 1845.

Phil 3246.53.2   Nature of the scholar. 2nd ed. (Fichte, Johann Gottlieb.) London, 1848.

Phil 575.151A   The nature of the self. (Frondizi, R.) New Haven, 1953.

Phil 6122.70   The nature of the self. (Mott, Francis.) London, 1959.

Phil 193.154   The nature of the world; an essay in phenomenalist metaphysics. (Stace, W.T.) Princeton, 1940.

Phil 288.20   The nature of things. (Hawley, Don.) N.Y., 1959.

Phil 1905.15   The nature of thought. (Blanshard, B.) N.Y., 1940. 2v.

Phil 672.246   The nature of time. (Gold, Thomas.) Ithaca, 1967.

Htn   Phil 720.11*   Nature of truth. (Brooke, R.G.) London, 1640.

Phil 720.74   The nature of truth. (Joachim, Harold Henry.) Ann Arbor, 1969.

Phil 4655.1.67   Naturens förbannelse. (Wikner, Pontus.) Upsala, 1866.

Phil 290.1   Naturens lag. (Jacobsson, M.) Stockholm, 1914.

Phil 8693.5.20   Naturens lagar och andens verld. (Drummond, H.) Stockholm, 1888.

Phil 184.50   Naturens orden; de divisione naturae. 2. Opl. (Jorn, A.) København, 1962.

Phil 1518.5   Naturer Kenntnis und politisches Handeln im Mittelalter. (Nitsche, August.) Körpen, 1967.

Phil 299.30   Naturerkenntnis und Wirklichkeit. (Sachsse, Hans.) Braunschweig, 1967.

Phil 7068.63.25   Nature's secrets or psychometric researches. Photoreproduction. (Denton, W.) London, 1863.

Phil 476.2   Naturforschung und Kulturleben. (Böhner, A.N.) Hannover, 1859.

Phil 187.61   Naturforschung und Philosophie. (Maack, F.) Kiel, 1896.

Phil 310.605   Naturforschung und Weltbild. (Guntau, Martin.) Berlin, 1964.

Phil 292.22   Der Naturgenuss. (Landesmann, Heinrich.) Berlin, 1876.

Phil 8601.4   Die Naturgeschichte der Göttes. (Vallis, R.) Leipzig, 1875.

Phil 2050.68.17   Die Naturgeschichte der Religion. (Hume, David.) Frankfurt, 1911.

Phil 5241.84   Naturgeschichte der Seele und ihres Bewusst-Werdens. (Bleuler, Eugen.) Berlin, 1921.

Phil 7082.170   Naturgeschichte des Traums. (Baege, Max Hermann.) Leipzig, 1928.

Phil 291.15   Naturgesetz, Freiheit und Wunder. (Kafka, Gustav.) Paderborn, 1940.

Phil 8893.145   Das Naturgesetz und seine dynamische Kraft. (Schmoebz, Franz Martin.) Freiburg, 1959.

Phil 193.45   Die Naturgesetze. v.1-4 and Supplement 1-3. (Scheffler, H.) Leipzig, 1876-1883. 7v.

Phil 8694.5   Naturgestez und Schöpfung. (Ewald, Günter.) Wuppertal, 1966.

Phil 8897.42   Das Naturgestz der Seele und...Freiheit. (Wyneken, Ernst F.) Heidelberg, 1906.

Phil 4610.7.33   Naturkunskapens själfbesinning. (Norström, V.) Stockholm, 1907.

Phil 3475.4   Naturleben und Geistesleben. (Jacobi, Maximilian.) Leipzig, 1851.

Phil 194.34   Naturlehre dis menschlichen Erkennens. (Troxler, I.P.V.) Aarau, 1828.

Phil 3808.130   Naturlÿke historie van den Filistijn. (Kiehl, Daniel.) 's Gravenhage, 1895.

Phil 3850.6.81   Der Naturphilosoph Gotthilf Heinrich Schubert und die deutsche Romantik. (Merkel, Franz R.) München, 1913.

Phil 282.7   Naturphilosophie. (Becher, Erich.) Leipzig, 1914.

Phil 284.5   Naturphilosophie. (Dippe, Alfred.) München, 1907.

Phil 3310.5.35   Naturphilosophie. (Gutberlet, C.) Münster, 1885.

Phil 3850.32.20   Naturphilosophie. (Spann, Othmar.) Jena, 1937.

Phil 180.32   Naturphilosophie. v.1. (Frost, Walter.) Leipzig, 1910.

Phil 3850.32.22   Naturphilosophie. 2. Aufl. (Spann, Othmar.) Graz, 1963.

Phil 2750.1.79   Die Naturphilosophie des Joannes...Magnenus. (Gusgens, J.) Bonn, 1910.

Phil 288.12   Naturphilosophie in 19. Jahrhundert. (Hennemann, Gerhard.) Freiburg, 1959.

Phil 186.41   Naturphilosophie und Weltanschauung. (Lipsius, Friedrich R.) Leipzig, 1918.

Phil 288.24   Naturphilosophie von der Spekulation zur Wissenschaft. (Hoerz, Herbert.) Berlin, 1969.

Phil 182.43.10   Naturphilosophische Betrachtungen. (Häberlin, Paul.) Zurich, 1939-1940. 2v.

Phil 5255.23   Naturphilosophische Vorlesungen über die Grundprobleme des Bewusstseins und des Lebens. (Palágyi, M.) Charlottenburg, 1907.

Phil 5255.23.2   Naturphilosophische Vorlesungen über die Grundprobleme des Bewusstseins und des Lebens. (Palágyi, M.) Leipzig, 1924.

Phil 2905.1.270   Das naturphilosophische Werk Teilhard de Chardins. (Mueller, Armin.) Freiburg, 1964.

Phil 8887.76   Das Naturrecht. (Messner, J.) Innsbruck, 1950.

Phil 8965.20   Naturrecht in der Kontroverse. (Peschke, Karlheinz.) Salzburg, 1967.

Phil 3625.2.6   Naturrecht oder Rechts-Philosophie als die praktische Philosophie. Berlin, 1866. (Michelet, K.L.) Bruxelles, 1968. 2v.

Phil 2045.67   Naturrecht und allgemeines Staatsrecht in den Anfangsgründen. (Hobbes, Thomas.) Berlin, 1926.

Phil 2115.220   Naturrecht und Politik bei John Locke. (Euchner, Walter.) Frankfurt am Main, 1969.

Phil 3425.60.17   Die Naturreligion. (Hegel, Georg Wilhelm Friedrich.) Leipzig, 1927.

Phil 8685.18   Die Naturreligion. (Rosenkranz, K.) Iserlohn, 1831.

Phil 5258.10.25   Naturstudium und Kultur. (Schultz-Schultzenstein, K.H.) Berlin, 1866.

Phil 4635.3.31   Naturvetenskap eller metafysik? (Sylwan, O.C.) Stockholm, 1881.

Phil 189.4.14F   Naturvidenskabelige skrifter. (Oersted, H.C.) København, 1920. 3v.

Phil 8707.34   Naturwissenschaft, Weltbild, Glaube. (Rohrbach, Hans.) Wuppertal, 1967.

Phil 978.94   Naturwissenschaft an der Schwelle. (Boernsen, Hans.) Stuttgart, 1964.

Phil 497.1   Naturwissenschaft und Bibel. (Wagner, J.A.) Stuttgart, 1855.

Phil 8715.3   Naturwissenschaft und christliche Offenbarung. (Zöllner, J.F.K.) Leipzig, 1881.

Phil 978.49.730   Die Naturwissenschaft und die welgeschichtliche Entwicklung der Menschheit seit dem Altertum. (Steiner, R.) Dornach, 1969.

Phil 3120.8.91   Naturwissenschaft und Metaphysik. Brünn, 1938.

Phil 3915.50   Naturwissenschaft und Psychologie. (Wundt, Wilhelm.) Leipzig, 1903.

Phil 196.4   Naturwissenschaft und Weltanschauung. 2e Aufl. (Verworn, M.) Leipzig, 1904.

Phil 3665.2.35   Die Naturwissenschaften und Materialismus. (Naumann, M.E.A.) Bonn, 1869.

Phil 3415.85   Die naturwissenschaftlichen Grundlagen der Philosophie des Unbewussten. (Schmidt, O.) Leipzig, 1877.

Phil 284.15   Naturwissenschaftliches Erkennen. (Dessauer, Friedrich.) Frankfurt, 1958.

Phil 978.105   Naturwissensehaftliche Grundfragen. (Bockemnehl, Jochen.) Dornach, 1964.

Phil 3120.11.97   De natuur. (Bolland, G.J.P.J.) Leiden, 1915.

Phil 3120.35.30   Natuurbegrip en leuen. (Bolland, G.J.P.J.) Leiden, 1917. 2 pam.

Phil 3552.311   De natuurlijke kennis gods bij Leibniz. (Mönnich, Conrad Willem.) Rotterdam, 1942.

Phil 188.21   Natzmer, G. von. Weisheit der Welt. Berlin, 1954.

Phil 813.5   Natzner, Gert von. Das Weltbild des Menschen. Berlin, 1962.

Phil 5360.19   Nauchnaia abstraktsiia i ee vidy. (Rozov, Mikhail A.) Novosibirsk, 1965.

Phil 5238.221   Nauchnaia Sessiia Posviashchennaia 50-Letiiu Velikoi Oktiabr'skoi Sotsialisticheskoi Revoliutsii, Sverdlovsk, 1967. Voprosy psikhologii. Sverdlovsk, 1967.

Phil 344.7   Nauchnoe otknjtie i ego vospriiatie. Moskva, 1971.

Phil 24.7   Nauchnye trudy. Filosofskaia seriia. (Novosibirsk Universitet.) 2,1968+

Phil 310.507   Nauchnyi kommunizm. (Afanas'ev, Viktor G.) Moskva, 1966.

Phil 8691.34   Nauchno-tekhnicheskaia revoliutsiia i modernizatsiia katolitsizma. (Babosov, Evgenii M.) Minsk, 1971.

Phil 1695.30   Nauka i filozofija. Beograd. 1,1963+

Phil 8905.34   Nauka i nravstvennost'. Moskva, 1971.

Phil 8692.27   Nauka i religiia. (Chicherin, Boris N.) Moskva, 1817.

Phil 8692.17   Nauka i religiia. (Chicherin, Boris N.) Moskva, 1901.

Phil 8505.8.15   Nauka i religiia. (Leningrad. Muzei Istorii Religii i Ateizma.) Moskva, 1961.

Phil 8709.25   Nauka oprovergaet religioznye dogmaty. (Tancher, Volodymyr K.) Kiev, 1970.

Phil 8703.4   Nauka protiv religii. v.1- Moskva, 1967. 2v.

Phil 2775.3.30   Naulin, Paul. L'itinéraire de la conscience. Paris, 1963.

Phil 3640.302   Naumann, Gustav. Zarathustra-Commentar. Leipzig, 1899-1901. 4v.

Phil 3665.2.35   Naumann, M.E.A. Die Naturwissenschaften und Materialismus. Bonn, 1869.

Phil 3665.2.31   Naumann, M.E.A. Über die Grenzen zwischen Philosophie und Naturwissenschaften. Leipzig, 1823.

Phil 510.157   Naumenko, Lev K. Monizm kak printsip dialekticheskoi logiki. Alma-Ata, 1968.

Phil 2880.8.190   Nauta, Lolle Wibe. Jean Paul Sartre. Door, 1966.

Phil 440.14   Nauta, Lolle Wibe. Vrijheid, Horizon der Geschiedenis. Nijkerk, 1966.

Phil 8050.73   Nauwelaerts, M.A.M.E. Uren van schoonheid. Antwerpen, 1960.

Phil 4959.210.5   Navarro, Bernabé. Cultura mexicana moderna en el siglo XVIII. 1. ed. México, 1964.

Phil 4959.210   Navarro, Bernabé. La introducción de la filosofía moderna en México. México, 1948.

Phil 4357.2.80   Navarro. Vida y obras de Don Francisco Giner de los Rios. 1. ed. Mexico, 1945.

Phil 5053.3   Naville, A. Logique de l'identité...contradiction. Genève, 1909.

Phil 2775.1.80   Naville, E. Ernest Naville, sa vie et sa pensée. Genève, 1913-17. 2v.

Phil 8668.1.5   Naville, E. The heavenly father. Boston, 1867.

Phil 5763.1   Naville, E. Le libre arbitre. Genève, 1898.

Phil 2730.80   Naville, E. Maine de Biran. Paris, 1857.

Phil 2730.80.5   Naville, E. Maine de Biran. 3e éd. Paris, 1877.

Phil 8668.1.10   Naville, E. Det ondas problem. Stockholm, 1872.

Phil 8668.1   Naville, E. Le père céleste. Genève, 1866.

Phil 8620.8   Naville, E. Le problème du mal. Genève, 1869.

Phil 188.11.5   Naville, Ernest. La définition de la philosophie. Genève, 1894.

Phil 188.11.10   Naville, Ernest. Les philosophies négatives. Paris, 1900.

Phil 188.11   Naville, Ernest. Les systèmes de philosophie. Paris, 1909.

Phil 5115.1   Naville, J.E. La logique de l'hypothèse. Paris, 1880.

Phil 1750.600   Naville, Pierre. Les conditions de la liberté. Paris, 1947.

Phil 2880.8.126   Naville, Pierre. L'intellectual communiste. Paris, 1956.

Phil 2648.94   Naville, Pierre. Paul Thiry d'Holbach et la philosophie scientifique au XVIIIe siècle. 2. éd. Paris, 1943.

Phil 2648.94.3   Naville, Pierre. Paul Thiry d'Holbach et la philosophie scientifique au XVIIIe siécle. Paris, 1967.

Phil 5330.8   Nayrac, J.P. Physiologie et psychologie de l'attention. Paris, 1906.

Phil 2805.91.3   Nazelle, R.J. Étude sur Alexandre Vinet critique de Pascal. Alençon, 1901.

Phil 188.20   Neal, H.H. The universe and you. Laguna Beach, Calif., 1954.

Phil 745.9   Neal, Herbert V. Vitalism and mechanism. Lancaster, Pa., 1934.

Phil 5867.25   Neale, Robert Edward. In praise of play; toward a psychology of religion. N.Y., 1969.

Phil 6990.3.106   Neame, Alan. The happening at Lourdes. London, 1968.

Phil 8963.2   Neander, A. Vorlesungen über Geschichte der christlichen Ethik. Berlin, 1864.

Phil 8430.38   Nebel, G. Das Ereignis es Schönen. Stuttgart, 1953.

Phil 1133.45   Nebel, Gerhard. Die Geburt der Philosophie. Stuttgart, 1967.

Phil 672.227   Nebel, Gerhard. Zeit und Zeiten. Stuttgart, 1965.

Phil 5548.3   Nebraska. University. Department of Psychology. Current theory and research in motivation, a symposium. Lincoln. 1954+ 15v.

Phil 8661.8.30   The necessary existence of God. (Gillespie, W.H.) Edinburgh, 1843.

Phil 5750.10   La necessità del volere e la reattività sociale. (Azzalini, Mario.) Padova, 1931.

Phil 8595.50   Necessità e sufficienza del principio cristiano. (Panese, Roberto.) Padova, 1958.

Phil 8586.41   The necessity of belief. (Gill, Eric.) London, 1936.

Phil 8582.2   The necessity of revelation. (Campbell, A.) London, 1739.

Phil 8593.15   The necessity of some of the positive institutions of ch---ty consider'd, in a letter to the minister of Moffat. London, 1731.

Phil 1158.40   Neck, Gisela. Das Problem der Zeit im Epikureismus. Inaug. Diss. Köln, 1964.

Phil 8963.1   Necker, J. Cours de morale religieuse. Paris, 1800. 3v.

Phil 4265.4.85   Necrologio di Giovanni Vailati. (Ricci, Umberto.) Roma, 1909.

Phil 7054.76   Necromancy; or a rap for the rappers. (Cooke, P.) Boston, 1857.

Phil 188.23   Nedeljković, Duš. Pragmatizm i djalektika. Beograd, 1960.

Phil 4825.10   Nedeljković, Dušan. Aperçu de la philosophie contemporaine en Yougoslavie. Beograd, 1934.

Phil 8888.17   Nedeljković, Dušan. Etika. 2. izd. Beograd, 1969.

Phil 3425.693   Nedeljković, Dušan. Hegelova estetika, Marksovi osnovi estetike i današnje estetičke perspektive. Beograd, 1970.

Phil 310.676   Nedeljkovió, Dušan. Humanizam Marksove dijalektike i dijalektike humanizma danas. Beograd, 1968.

Phil 4825.11   Nedeljkovió, Dušan. Od Heraklita do njegośa i Svetozara. Beograd, 1971.

Phil 2805.193   Nedelkovitch, D. La pensées philosophique créatrice de Pascal. Paris, 1925.

Phil 3552.460   Nedergaard-Hansen, Leif. Bayle's og Leibniz' drøftelse af theodicé-problemet; en idéhistorisk redegørelse. v.1-2. København, 1965.

Phil 23.17   Nederlandsch tijdschrift voor de psychologie en hoor grensgevieden. Amsterdam. 1,1946+ 22v.

Phil 5645.52   Nederlandse. Kleurendag. Verslag. Den Haag. 6-11

Phil 8414.10   Nédoncelle, M. Introduction à l'esthétique. Paris, 1953.

Phil 8587.32.99   Nédoncelle, M. La pensée religieuse de F. von Hügel, 1852-1925. Paris, 1935.

Phil 8587.32.101   Nédoncelle, M. La pensée religieuse de F. von Hügel, 1852-1925. Thèse. Paris, 1935.

Phil 5590.28   Nédoncelle, M. La personne humaine et la nature. 1. éd. Paris, 1943.

Phil 5627.262.10   Nédoncelle, M. Prière humaine, prière divine. Bruges, 1962.

Phil 188.25   Nédoncelle, Maurice. Conscience et logos. Paris, 1961.

Phil 575.247   Nédoncelle, Maurice. Personne humaine et nature. Paris, 1963.

Phil 8550.342.5   Nédoncelle, Maurice. La philosophie religieuse en Grand-Bretagne de 1850 à nos jours. Paris, 1934.

Phil 575.140   Nédoncelle, Maurice. La réciprocité des consciences; essai sur la nature de la personné. Thèse. Paris, 1942.

Phil 575.140.5   Nédoncelle, Maurice. Vers une philosophie de l'amour et de la personne. Aubier, 1957.

Phil 3665.8.30   Neeb, Johann. System der kritischen Philosophie auf den Satz des Bewustseyns gegründet. Bruxelles, 1968. 2v.

Phil 3495.14.5   Neeb, Johann. Über Kant's Verdienste um das Interesse der philosophiren den Vernunft. 2. Aufl. Frankfurt, 1795.

Phil 3665.3.31   Neeb, Johann. Vernunft gegen Vernunft. Frankfurt, 1797. Bruxelles, 1969.

Phil 8622.50   The need for faith in a scientifc age. (Hailsham, Quinten McG.) Glasgow, 1961.

Phil 8897.76.5   The need for roots. (Weil, Simone.) N.Y., 1952.

Phil 6980.635.40   The need to be loved. (Reik, T.) N.Y., 1963.

Phil 8090.3   Needham, Harold. Le développement de l'esthétique sociologique en France et en Angleterre au XIX siècle. Paris, 1926.

Phil 8703.2.5   Needham, Joseph. The great amphibium; four lectures. London, 1931.

Phil 8703.2.15   Needham, Joseph. History is on our side. London, 1946.

Phil 8703.2   Needham, Joseph. Science, religion and reality. N.Y., 1928.

Phil 8703.2.10   Needham, Joseph. Time: the refreshing river; essays and addresses, 1932-1942. London, 1943.

Phil 672.233   Needham, Joseph. Time and Eastern man. London, 1965.

Phil 270.29   Neef, Fritz. Kausalität und Originalität. Tübingen, 1918.

Phil 294.6   Neeff, F. Prolegomena zu einer Kosmologie. Tübingen, 1921.

Phil 2520.222   Néel, Marguerite. Descartes et la princesse Elisabeth. Paris, 1946.

Phil 5627.220   Neeser, Maurice. Du protestantisme au catholicisme. Paris, 1926.

Phil 585.100   Nef, John U. Religion and the study of man. Houston, 1961.

Phil 3915.153   Nef, Willi. Die Philosophie Wilhelm Wundts. Leipzig, 1923.

Phil 3552.242   Neff, L. Abfassungszeit von Leibnizens Unvorgreiflichen Gedanken. Durlach, 1880.

Phil 3552.242.5   Neff, L. Gottfried Wilhelm Leibniz als Sprachforscher und Etynologie. v.1-2. Heidelburg, 1870-71.

Phil 6123.3   Neff, S.S. Power through perfected ideas. Philadelphia, 1911.

Phil 98.3.2   Neff, Vladimir. Filosofiký sborník pro sannonsy neboli autigorgias. 2. vyd. Praha, 1970.

Phil 5790.25   Neff, Walter Scott. Work and human behavior. 1. ed. N.Y., 1968.

Phil 9590.3   Negación de la nueva verdad. (García, E.A.) Buenos Aires, 1929.

Phil 5045.17   Negation und Andersheit. (Flach, W.) München, 1959.

Phil 2150.22.38   Negations; essays in critical theory. (Marcuse, Herbert.) Boston, 1968.

Phil 585.270   Negative Anthropologie. (Sonnemann, Ulrich.) Reinbeck bei Hamburg, 1969.

Phil 3085.7.31   Negative Dialektik. (Adorno, Theodor W.) Frankfurt, 1966.

Phil 5190.70   Negative fact, negation and truth. (Das, Adhar Chandra.) Calcutta, 1942.

Phil 5762.10   La negazione del libero arbitrio ed il criterio del giusto. (Milesi, G.B.) Milano, 1894.

Phil 900.14   Negelein, J. Deltanschauung des indogermanischen Asiens. Erlangen, 1924.

Phil 2490.87   A neglected chapter in the life of Comte. (Schoff, W.F.) Philadelphia, 1896.

Phil 6315.2.89   A neglected complex and its relation to Freudian psychology. (Bonsfield, William A.) London, 1924.

Phil 344.4   Negley, Glenn. The organization of knowledge...philosophical analysis. N.Y., 1942.

Phil 971.6   Negner, Helena. Beiträge zur Geschichte der Weisheitsreligion. Pforzheim, 1960.

Phil 4170.3.86   Negrelli, Giorgio. Storicismo e moderatismo nel pensiero politico di Angelo Camillo de Meis. Milano, 1968.

Phil 3495.20.2   Negri, Antimo. La comunità estetica in Kant. 2. ed. Bari, 1968.

Phil 188.26   Negri, Antimo. Spirito del tempo e costume speculativo. Firenze, 1962.

Phil 2520.415   Negri, Antonio. Descartes politico o della ragionevole idealogia. Milano, 1970.

Phil 3195.6.120   Negri, Antonio. Saggi sullo storicismo tedesco. Milano, 1959.

Phil 3425.328   Negri, Enrico de. Interpretazione di Hegel. Firenze, 1943.

Phil 3425.328.1   Negri, Enrico de. Interpretazione di Hegel. Firenze, 1969.

Phil 3425.259   Negri, Enrico de. La nascita della dialettica Hegeliana. Firenze, 1930.

Phil 5592.65A   The Negro personality. (Karon, Bertram P.) N.Y., 1958.

Phil 8633.1.47   The negro spiritual speaks of life and death. (Thurman, Howard.) N.Y., 1947.

Phil 310.805   Negt, Oskar. Abram Deborin/Nikolai Bucharin: Kontroversen über dialektischen und mechanistischen Materialismus. Frankfurt, 1969.

Phil 3425.776   Negt, Oskar. Aktualität und Folgen der Philosophie Hegels. Frankfurt am Main, 1970.

Phil 2490.173   Negt, Oskar. Strukturbeziehungen Zwischen den Gesellschaftslehren Comtes und Heges. Frankfurt a.M., 1964.

Phil 813.6   Negulescu, P.P. Scrieri inedite. Bucuresti, 1969.

Phil 3495.13   Nehr, J.G. Kritik über die metaphysischen Aufangsgründe der Rechtslehre des I. Kant. Nürnberg, 1798.

Phil 5413.16   Der Neid. (Schoeck, Helmut.) Freiburg, 1966.

Phil 3495.11   Neide, P.S. Die Kantische Lehre vom Schematismus der reinen Verstandesbegriffe. Diss. Halle, 1878.

Phil 8599.19.115   Neige des Historismus. (Bodenstein, Walter.) Gütersloh, 1959.

Phil 5643.80   Neiglick, H. Zur Psychophysik des Lichtsinns. Leipzig, 1887.

Phil 5610.2   Neil, C.E. Sources of effectiveness in public speaking. Philadelphia, 1920.

Phil 5053.1   Neil, Samuel. The art of reasoning. London, 1853.

Phil 130.9   Neill, T.P. Makers of the modern mind. 2nd ed. Milwaukee, 1958.

Phil 8593.23   Neill, T.P. Religion and culture. Milwaukee, 1952.

Phil 2175.3.30   Neilson, Francis. The roots of our learning. N.Y., 1947.

Phil 188.10   Neilson, W.A. Lectures on the five-foot shelf of books. 4. Philosophy. N.Y., 1913.

Phil 5253.15   Neimark, Edith. Stimulus sampling theory. San Francisco, 1967.

Phil 3890.8.105 — Neisser, Liselotte. Christian Thomasius und seine Beziehungen zum Pietismus. Inaug. Diss. München, 1928.

Phil 5374.252 — Neisser, Ulric. Cognitive psychology. N.Y., 1967.

Htn Phil 7069.20.300* — Neither dead nor sleeping. (Sewell, May Wright.) Indianapolis, 1920.

Phil 7069.20.300 — Neither dead nor sleeping. (Sewell, May Wright.) Indianapolis, 1920.

Phil 3850.18.87 — Neive, Heinrich. Max Schelers Auffassung. Diss. Photoreproduction. Würzburg, 1928.

Phil 3640.605 — Nejedlý, Zděnek. Nietzscheova tragedie. Vinohrady, 1926.

Phil 5066.322 — Neklassicheskuia logika. Moskva, 1970.

Phil 310.722 — Nekotorye aktual'nye problemy marksistsko-leninskoi filosofii. Perm', 1968.

Phil 8879.33 — Nekotorye problemy nauchnoi etiki. (Engst, Jaroslav.) Moskva, 1960.

Phil 5590.566 — Nekotorye problemy sormirovaniia lichnosti. Krasnoiarsk, 1968.

Phil 310.475 — Nekotorye voprosy dialekticheskii materializma. (Leningrad. Universitet.) Leningrad, 1962.

Phil 310.669 — Nekotorye voprosy dialecticheskogo materializma i marksistskoi sotsiologii. Rostov-na-Donn, 1967.

Phil 310.627 — Nekotorye voprosy dialektiki izmeneniia i razvitiia. (Sviderskii, Vladimir I.) Moskva, 1965.

Phil 23.21 — Nekotorye voprosy filosofie. Nishinev. 2-4 2v.

Phil 310.616 — Nekotorye voprosy istoricheskogo materializma. (Rostov on the Don, Russia. Universitet. Kafedra Dialektichnskogo i Estoricheskogo Materializma.) Rostov-na-Donn, 1962.

Phil 310.630 — Nekotorye voprosy istoricheskogo materializma i nauchnogo kommunizma. (Sverdlin, Matvei A.) Volgograd, 1965.

Phil 310.749 — Nekotorye voprosy istoricheskogo materializma i nauchnogo kommunizma. Fergana, 1969.

Phil 8980.316 — Nekotorye voprosy marksistsko-leninskoi etiki. (Danielian, Mal'feda.) Erevan, 1962.

Phil 8400.8 — Nekotorye voprosy marksistsko-leninskoi estetiki. (Akademiia Nauk SSSR. Institut Filosofii.) Moskva, 1954.

Phil 23.32 — Nekotorye voprosy marksistsko-leninskoi filosofii. Cheliabinsk. 2,1969+

Phil 310.651 — Nekotorye voprosy marksistsko-leninskoi filosofii. Khar'kov, 1964.

Phil 310.545 — Nekotorye voprosy teorii poznaniia dialekticheskogo materializma. (Moscow. Moskovskii Institut Inzhenerov Zheleznogo Transporta.) Moskva, 1962.

VPhil 8400.58 — Některé otázky kulturní politiky a marxistické estetiky. 1. vyd. Praha, 1965.

Phil 5374.37 — Nel domonio dell' "io". (Galli, Ettore.) Milano, 1919.

Phil 4060.1.95 — Nel LXX compleanno di Roberto Ardigò. (Ghisleri, Arcangelo.) Cremona, 1898.

Phil 5246.33.5 — Nel mondo dello spirito. (Galli, Ettore.) Milano, 1919.

Phil 5246.33 — Nel mondo dello spirito. (Galli, Ettore.) Milano, 1920.

Phil 4225.5 — Nel primo centenario della morte di Nicola Spedalieri. Roma, 1899.

Phil 4060.1.98 — Nel settantesimo anniversario di Roberto Ardigò. (Groppali, A.) Torino, 1898.

Phil 6315.2.220A — Nelson, B.N. Freud and the 20th century. N.Y., 1958.

Phil 6053.12.10 — Nelson, Edith Halforel. Out of the silence. London, 194-?

Phil 7069.69.5 — Nelson, Geoffrey K. Spiritualism and society. London, 1969.

Phil 5238.175 — Nelson, Harry. Theoretical foundations of psychology. Princeton, 1959.

Phil 4065.155 — Nelson, J.C. Renaissance theory of love. N.Y., 1958.

Phil 6323.15 — Nelson, John. Look before you leap. Washington, D.C., 1954.

Phil 188.9 — Nelson, L. Ist metaphysikfreie Naturwissenschaft möglich? Göttingen, 1908.

Phil 188.9.5 — Nelson, L. Die neue Reformation. v.1-2,4. n.p., n.d. 3v.

Phil 188.9.10 — Nelson, L. Socratic method and critical philosophy. New Haven, 1949.

Phil 344.1 — Nelson, L. Über das sogenannte Erkenntnisproblem. Göttingen, 1908.

Phil 5066.220 — Nelson, Leonard. Beiträge zur Philosophie. Frankfurt, 1959.

Phil 8888.6.1 — Nelson, Leonard. Critique of practical reason. Scarsdale, 1970?

Phil 8888.6.25 — Nelson, Leonard. Ethische Methodenlehre. Leipzig, 1915.

Phil 8888.6.27 — Nelson, Leonard. Ethischer Realismus. Leipzig, 1921.

Phil 3665.5.30 — Nelson, Leonard. Fortschritte und Rückschritte der Philosophie. Frankfurt, 1962.

Phil 3665.5.2 — Nelson, Leonard. Gesammelte Schriften. v.1-8. Hamburg, 1970. 7v.

Phil 8888.6 — Nelson, Leonard. Kritik der praktischen Vernunft. Leipzig, 1917.

Phil 3495.6.5 — Nelson, Leonard. Die kritische Ethik bei Kant, Schilles und Fries. Göttingen, 1914.

Phil 5253.8 — Nelson, Leonard. Die kritische Methode und das Verhaltnis der Psychologie zur Philosophie. Göttingen, 1904.

Phil 3665.5.32 — Nelson, Leonard. Progress and regress in philosophy, from Hume and Kant to Hegel and Fries. Oxford, 1970.

Phil 8888.6.2 — Nelson, Leonard. System der philosophischen Ethik und Pädagogik. Göttingen, 1932.

Phil 8888.6.3 — Nelson, Leonard. System der philosophischen Rechtslehre und Politik. Leipzig, 1924.

Phil 8888.6.30 — Nelson, Leonard. System of ethics. New Haven, 1956.

Phil 3495.6 — Nelson, Leonard. Untersuchungen...Kantischen Erkenntnistheorie. Göttingen, 1909.

Phil 1350.12 — Nemanic, D. De stoicorum romanorum. Görz, 1880.

Phil 5385.5 — Nemberg, Herman. Curiosity. N.Y., 1961.

Phil 3012.5 — Nemtcskaia filosofiia XIX - nachala XX vv. (Meleshchenko, Zoia N.) Leningrad, 1965.

Phil 1750.166.220 — Némésis; ou, La limite. (Beaujon, Edmond.) Paris, 1965.

Phil 3001.20 — Nemetskaia burzhuaznaia filosofiia posle 1865 goda. (Bogomolov, A.S.) Moskva, 1969.

Phil 8125.40 — Nemetskaia estetika XVIII veka. (Asmus, V.F.) Moskva, 1962.

Phil 6323.18 — Nemiah, J.C. Foundations of psychopathology. N.Y., 1961.

Phil 8980.602 — Nemtsov, V.I. Volneniia, radosti, nadezoidy. Moskva, 1961.

Htn Phil 9560.18* — Nenna, Giovanni B. Il nennio, nel quale si ragiona di nobilita. Colophon, 1542.

Htn Phil 9560.18.5* — Nenna, Giovanni B. Nennio, or A treatise of nobility. London, 1595.

Phil 9560.18.6 — Nenna, Giovanni B. Nennio, or A treatise of nobility. Facsimile. Jerusalem, 1967.

Htn Phil 9560.18* — Il nennio, nel quale si ragiona di nobilita. (Nenna, Giovanni B.) Colophon, 1542.

Htn Phil 9560.18.5* — Nennio, or A treatise of nobility. (Nenna, Giovanni B.) London, 1595.

Phil 9560.18.6 — Nennio, or A treatise of nobility. Facsimile. (Nenna, Giovanni B.) Jerusalem, 1967.

Phil 2840.80 — Le néo-criticisme de Charles Renouvier. (Janssens, B.) Louvain, 1904.

Phil 8735.24 — Néo-finalisme. 1. éd. (Ruyer, R.) Paris, 1952.

Phil 1807.3 — Neo-Hegelianism. (Haldar, H.) London, 1927.

Phil 1905.10.80.2 — Le néo-hegelianisme en Angleterre. (Huang, Chia-cheng.) Paris, 1954.

Phil 1905.10.80 — Le néo-hegelianisme en Angleterre. (Huang, Chia-cheng.) Paris, 1954.

Phil 4080.3.450 — Neo-idealistic aesthetics. (Brown, Merle Elliott.) Detroit, 1966.

Phil 1170.5.3 — Neo-Platonists. Photoreproduction. 2nd ed. (Whittaker, Thomas.) Cambridge, 1928.

Phil 1170.5.5 — The Neo-Platonists. 4th ed. (Whittaker, Thomas.) Olm, 1970.

NEDL Phil 1170.5 — Neo-Platonists::Study in history of Hellenism. (Whittaker, Thomas.) Cambridge, 1901.

Phil 630.23 — Le néo-réalisme américain. (Kremer, René.) Louvain, 1920.

Phil 1750.11.15 — The neo-romantic movement in contemporary philosophy. Thesis. (Maitra, S.K.) Calcutta, 1922.

Phil 1702.6.15 — Neo-scolastica, idealismo e spiritualismo. (Olgiati, F.) Milano, 1933.

Phil 4012.5 — Il neo-tomismo in Italia (origini e prime vicende). (Masnovo, A.) Milano, 1923.

Phil 270.132 — Neobkhodimost' i sluchainost'. (Pilipenko, Nikolai V.) Moskva, 1965.

Phil 2725.50 — Il neoilluminismo etico di André Lalande. (Bertoni, Italo.) Milano, 1965.

Phil 3488.38 — Neokantianstvo. (Grigor'ian, B.T.) Moskva, 1962.

Phil 3494.60 — Neokantianstvo kak filosofskaia osnova revizionizma. (Meleschenko, Z.N.) Leningrad, 1960.

Phil 3018.40 — Neokantyzm - filozofia społeczna wraz a filozofia prawa natury o zmilnej treści. Wyd. 1. (Szyszkowka, Maria.) Warszawa, 1970.

Phil 4845.227.44 — Neollěnikě philosophia. 2. ed. v.1-2. (Papanoutsos, Euangelos.) Athena, 1956-59.

Phil 1170.6A — Neoplatonism. (Bigg, C.) London, 1895.

Phil 1170.7 — Neoplatonism in relation to Christianity; an essay. (Elsee, Charles.) Cambridge, 1908.

Phil 5068.88 — Neopositivismo, analisi del linguaggio e cibernetica. (Fano, Giorgio.) Torino, 1968.

Phil 5068.26 — Neopositivismo e scienza de diritto. (Giorgianni, Virgilio.) Roma, 1956.

Phil 5068.57 — Neopozitivizm i problemy empiricheskogo oboshovaniia nauki. (Shvyrev, Vladimir S.) Moskva, 1966.

Phil 630.31 — Il neorealismo anglo-americano. (Padovani, U.A.) Firenze, 1916.

Phil 1750.635 — Neotmizm - filosofiia sovremennoi reaktsionoi burzhuazii. (Oizerman, T.I.) Moskva, 1959.

Phil 4003.5 — I neotomisti italiani del XIX secolo. (Dezza, Paolo.) Milano, 1942-44. 2v.

Phil 8696.27 — Neotomizm. Razum. Nauka. (Garadzha, Vikton I.) Moskva, 1969.

Phil 8963.4 — Nepliuev, N.N. Polnoe sobranie sochinenii. Sankt Peterburg, 1901. 2v.

Phil 4756.1.47.1 — Nepostizhimoe. (Frank, Semen L.) München, 1971.

Phil 2805.187 — Neri, F. Un ritratto immaginario di Pascal. Torino, 1921.

Phil 1750.115.170 — Neri, Guido Davide. Prassi e conoscenza. 1. ed. Milano, 1966.

Phil 294.7 — Nernst, Walther. Zum Gültigkeitsbereich der Naturgesetze. Berlin, 1921.

Phil 6111.18.5 — Nerve control and how to gain it. (Bruce, H.A.) N.Y., 1918.

Phil 6131.4 — Nerve force. (Von Boeckmann P.) N.Y., 1919.

Phil 6120.10 — Nerve tracts of the brain and cord. (Keiller, William.) N.Y., 1927.

Phil 6951.12.5 — Die Nervenschwäche. 2. Aufl. (Beard, G.M.) Leipzig, 1883.

Phil 6122.10 — Das Nervensystem des Menschen. (Möbius, P.J.) Leipzig, 1880.

Phil 6117.14 — Nerves. (Harris, D.F.) London, 1913.

Phil 6120.12 — Nerves and personal power. (King, D.M.) N.Y., 1922.

Phil 6961.12 — Nerves and the man. (Loosmore, W.C.) N.Y., 1921.

Phil 6328.2 — Nervöse Angstzustände und ihre Behandlung. (Stekel, Wilhelm.) Berlin, 1908.

Phil 6327.45 — Der nervöse Mensch und seine Heilung. (Rattner, Josef.) Zürich, 1965.

Phil 6128.70 — Nervose. (Stuttgart. Institut für Psychotherapie und Tiefenpsychologie.) Stuttgart, 1960.

Phil 6322.1.15 — Die Nervosität. 3e Aufl. (Möbius, P.J.) Leipzig, 1906.

Phil 23.6 — Nervous and mental diseases. Chicago. 1907-1917 10v.

Phil 6972.20 — Nervous breakdown; its cause and cure. (Wolfe, Walter Béran.) N.Y., 1933.

Phil 23.6.5 — The nervous child. N.Y. 1-11,1941-1956 10v.

Phil 6322.23.5 — The nervous housewife. (Myerson, A.) Boston, 1929.

Phil 6968.12.9 — Nervous ills; their cause and cure. (Sidis, Boris.) Boston, 1922.

Phil 6121.12.5 — The nervous system. (Lickley, J.D.) N.Y., 1919.

Phil 5625.02F — Pamphlet box. Nervous system (reflex action).

Phil 5625.01 — Pamphlet box. Nervous system (reflex action).

Phil 6128.31.5 — The nervous system and its conservation. (Stiles, Percy G.) Philadelphia, 1915.

Phil 6111.26 — The nervous system and its constituent neurones. (Barker, L.F.) N.Y., 1899.

Phil 6122.31 — The nervous system and the mind. (Mercier, Charles A.) London, 1888.

Phil 6314.1 — Nervousness; its causes, treatment and prevention. (Emerson, L.E.) Boston, 1918.

Phil 5520.155 — Nesbit, F.L. Language meaning. 1. ed. N.Y., 1955.

Phil 5421.25 — Nesbitt, Michael. Friendship, love, and values. Princeton, 1959.

Phil 3450.19.190 — Neshe, Günther. Martin Heidegger zum siebzigsten Geburtstag. Pfullingen, 1959.

Phil 5365.2 — Nesswetha, Wilhelm. Formen der Reaktion auf Konflikte. Diss. Bonn, 1964.

Phil 310.145 — Nesterenko, G.I. Obshchestvennoe soznanie i ego formy. Moskva, 1959. 2 pam.

Phil 8980.604 — Nesteroo, Vladimir G. Trud i moral' v sovetskom doshchestve. Moskva, 1969.

Phil 1118.3 — Nestle, W. Griechische Weltanschauung in ihrer Bedeutung für die Gegenwart. Stuttgart, 1946.

Phil 1133.16.10 — Nestle, W. Die Nachsokratiker. Jena, 1923. 2v.

Phil 1133.16.5 — Nestle, W. Die Sokratiker. Jena, 1922.

Phil 1133.16 — Nestle, W. Die Vorsokratiker. Auschauungen, 1908.

Phil 8593.21 — Nestle, Wilhelm. Die Krisis des Cristentums. Stuttgart, 1947.

Phil 978.6.90 — Nethercot, A.H. The first five lives of Annie Besant. Chicago, 1960.

Phil 978.6.91 Nethercot, A.H. The last four lives of Annie Besant. London, 1963.

Phil 23.25 Netherlands. Rijko Psychologische Dienst. Publikaties. 's Gravenhage. 1-2 2v.

Phil 2520.96 Netter, A. Notes sur le vie de Descartes. Nancy, 1896.

Phil 5253.4 Netter, S. De l'intuition. Strasbourg, 1879.

Phil 188.7A Nettleship, R.L. Philosophical lectures and remains. London, 1897.

Phil 8888.4.2 Nettleton, T. A treatise on virtue. Edinburgh, 1774.

NEDL Phil 8888.4 Nettleton, T. A treatise on virtue. London, 1759.

Phil 8703.1 Netto. F.J. Sociabilidade natural do homem. Povoa de Varzim, 1914.

Phil 3850.46 Neu, Theodor. Bibliographie Eduard Spranger. Tübingen, 1958.

Phil 3482.2.21 Ein neu aufgefundenes Kollegheft nach Kants Vorlesung über Psysischegeographie. (Adickes, E.) Tübingen, 1913.

Phil 3270.10.31 Das neuantike Weltbild. (Flake, Otto.) Darmstadt, 1922.

Phil 8881.34.5 Neubegründung der Ethik aus ihrem Verhältnis zu den besonderen Gemeinschaftswissenschaften. (Görland, Albert.) Berlin, 1918.

Phil 293.8.75 Neubert, Fritz. Einleitung in eine kritische Ausgabe von B. de Maillets Telliamed. Berlin, 1920.

Phil 5520.404 Neubert, Q. Semantischer Positivismus in den USA. Halle, 1962.

Phil 3195.1.80 Neubert-Drobisch, W. Moritz Wilhelm Drobisch. Leipzig, 1902.

Phil 665.65 Neuburger, E. Das Verständnis der Seele im Christentum und in der psychologischen Literatur der Gegenwart. Inaug. Diss. Tübingen, 1937.

Phil 8125.30 Neudecher, Georg. Studien zur Geschichte des deutschen Asthetik seit Kant. Wurzburg, 1878.

Phil 5053.6 Neudecker, G. Grundlegung der reinen Logik. Würzburg, 1882.

Phil 3195.2.93 Neudecker, G. Der Philosoph Deutinger und ultramontane Sophistik. Würzburg, 1877.

Phil 23.9 Neudrucke zur Psychologie. 1-3,1917-1918

Phil 3552.39.5 Neue Abhandlungen über den menschlichen verstand. (Leibniz, Gottfried Wilhelm.) Frankfurt, 1961. 2v.

Phil 3552.39 Neue Abhandlungen über den menschlichen verstand. 3e Aufl. (Leibniz, Gottfried Wilhelm.) Leipzig, 1915.

Phil 6323.1 Neue Arbeiten zur Ärztlichen Psychoanalyse. Leipzig. 1-6,1924-1927 5v.

Phil 8581.2 Neue Aussichten in die Wahrheiten und Religion der Vernunft. (Basedow, J.B.) Altona, 1764. 2v.

Phil 6615.14 Neue Beiträg zur Psychologie des hysterischen Geisteszustandes. (Ranschburg, Pál.) Leipzig, 1897.

Phil 3246.265 Neue Bemerkungen zu Johann Gottlieb Fichte. (Bergner, Dieter.) Berlin, 1957.

Phil 3808.82.5 Neue Brief über die Schopenhauerische Philosophie. (Frauenstädt, C.M.J.) Leipzig, 1876.

Phil 3425.75 Neue Briefe...und Verwandtes. (Hegel, Georg Wilhelm Friedrich.) Leipzig, 1912.

Phil 3552.107 Eine neue Darstellung der leibnizischen Monadenlehre. (Dillmann, E.) Leipzig, 1891.

Phil 5043.10 Neue Darstellung der Logik. (Drobisch, Moritz Wilhelm.) Leipzig, 1851.

Phil 5043.10.4 Neue Darstellung der Logik nach ihren einfachsten Verhältnissen mit Rücksicht auf Mathematik und Naturwissenschaft. 4. Aufl. (Drobisch, Moritz Wilehlm.) Leipzig, 1875.

Phil 477.5 Neue Darstellung des Sensualismus. (Czolbe, H.) Leipzig, 1855.

Phil 1707.12 Das neue Denken. (Hevigel, H.) Berlin, 1928.

Phil 5241.34 Neue Denklehre. (Bilharz, A.) Wiesbaden, 1908.

Phil 3925.10 Neue Dialoge; zwischen Hylas und Philoneris. (Wimmer, H.A.) Heidelberg, 1938.

Phil 9245.35 Der neue Epikur, oder die Philosophie der Sittlichenwollust. Prag, 1779.

Phil 6965.3.90 Neue Ergebnisse in der Forschung über Philippe Pinel. (Lechler, Walther Helmut.) München, 1960.

Phil 8591.87 Neue Erkenntnisprobleme in Philosophie und Theologie. (Lotz, Johannes Baptist.) Freiburg, 1968.

Phil 3246.76 Neue Fichte-funde, aus der Heimat und Schweiz. (Fichte, Johann Gottlieb.) Gotha, 1919.

X Cg Phil 7075.9.5 Neue Forschungen über den Marquis de Sade. (Bloch, Iwan.) Berlin, 1904.

Phil 1750.179.15 Neue Geborgenheit. (Bollnow, O.F.) Stuttgart, 1955.

Phil 978.49.782 Die neue Geistigkeit und das Christus-Erlebnis im zwanzigsten Jahrhunderts. 2. Aufl. (Steiner, R.) Dornach, 1970.

Phil 8657.19 Der neue Gott. (Christiansen, Broder.) München, 1934.

Phil 5050.11 Neue Grundlagen der Logik Arithmetic. (Konig, Julius.) Leipzig, 1914.

Phil 5250.16 Neue Grundlagen zur Psychologie des Denkens. (Kramar, W.) Brünn, 1914.

Phil 194.18.5 Neue Grundlegung der Psychologie und Logik. (Teichmüller, G.) Breslau, 1889.

Phil 1750.745 Der neue Humanismus. (Pollak, Oscar.) Wien, 1962.

Phil 9166.8 Neue Jugend und katholischer Geist. (Guardini, R.) Mainz, 1924.

Htn Phil 3480.19.11* Neue Kleine Schriften. (Kant, Immanuel.) Berlin? 1795.

Phil 3504.16 Neue Kritik der reinen Vernunft. (Wolff, Hermann.) Leipzig, 1897.

Phil 972.12 Der neue Mensch. (Brander-Pracht, K.) Berlin, 1920.

NEDL Phil 23.10 Neue metaphysische Rundschau. Berlin. 1897-1913 20v.

Phil 3585.26 Neue nege zu Frieden und Freiheit. (Asser-Kramer, G.) Pähl/Oberbayern, 1962.

Phil 3260.35.2 Neue oder anthropologische Kritik der Vernunft. 2. Aufl. (Fries, Jakob Friedrich.) Berlin, 1935. 3v.

Phil 1860.45 Neue philosophische Versuche. (Beattie, James.) Leipzig, 1779-80. 2v.

Phil 3100.50.2 Die neue Psychologie. 2. Aufl. (Beneke, F.E.) Berlin, 1845.

Phil 3100.50.4 Die neue Psychologie. 4. Aufl. (Beneke, F.E.) Berlin, 1877.

Phil 5250.13.9 Neue psychologische Studien. (Krueger, Felix.) München. 1926-1939 23v.

Phil 672.28 Die neue Raumtheorie. (Gutberlet, Constantin.) Mainz, 1882.

Phil 188.9.5 Die neue Reformation. v.1-2,4. (Nelson, L.) n.p., n.d. 3v.

Htn Phil 3801.959* Der neue Reineke Fuchs in acht philosophischen Fabeln. (Schelling, F.W.J. von.) Stuttgart, 1844.

Phil 3801.959.2 Der neue Reineke Fuchs in acht philosophischen Fabeln. (Schelling, F.W.J. von.) Stuttgart, 1844.

Phil 3549.8.115 Die neue Schau der Seele. (Ganzoni, Werner.) Wien, 1957.

Phil 3100.51 Neue Seelenlehre. (Beneke, F.E.) Bautzen, 1854.

Phil 9495.142 Die neue Sexualmoral und das Geburtenproblem unserer Tage. (Wolf, J.) Jena, 1928.

Phil 3017.3 Neue Studien: IV Geschichte deutschen Philosophie. v.1-2. (Rosenkranz, K.) Leipzig, 1878. 3v.

Phil 1124.1.5 Neue Studien zur Geschichte der Begriffe. (Teichmüller, G.) Gotha, 1876-1879. 2v.

Phil 5585.43 Neue Theorie der Wahrnehmung und des Denkens. (Hamburger, R.) Berlin, 1927.

Phil 5811.10.5 Die neue Tierpsychologie. (Bohn, Georges.) Leipzig, 1912.

Phil 7150.50 Neue Untersuchungen zum Selbstmordproblem. (Ringel, Erwin.) Wien, 1961.

Phil 50.7 Der neue Weg; Mittelungen der Keyserling Gesellschaft für Freie Philosophie. Wiesbaden. 1-17,1950-1958

Phil 182.94.18 Neue Wege der Ontologie. (Hartmann, N.) Stuttgart, 194-.

Phil 182.94.18.3 Neue Wege der Ontologie. 3.Aufl. (Hartmann, Nicolai.) Stuttgart, 1949.

Phil 1707.10 Neue Wege der Philosophie, Geist, Leben, Existenz. (Heinemann, Fritz.) Leipzig, 1929.

Phil 8887.50 Neue Wegweiser; Aufsätze und Reden. (Müller, Johannes.) München, 1920.

Phil 182.81 Die neue Welterkenntnis. (Hart, Julius.) Leipzig, 1902.

Phil 2225.2.80 Die "neue Wirklichkeitslehre". (Jacoby, Günther.) Berlin, 1914?

Phil 8585.15 Das neue Wissen und der neue Glaube. (Frohschammer, J.) Leipzig, 1873.

Phil 2045.148 Die neue Wissenschaft des Thomas Hobbes. (Wolf, Friedrich Otto.) Stuttgart, 1969.

Phil 4260.37 Die neue Wissenschaft über die gemeinschaftliche Natur der Völker. (Vico, G.B.) München, 1924.

Phil 4260.37.1 Die neue Wissenschaft über die gemeinschaftliche Natur der Völker. (Vico, G.B.) Hamburg, 1966.

Phil 5170.6 Die neuen theorien der Kategorischen Schlüsse. (Hillebrand, F.) Wien, 1891.

Phil 3549.2.79.5 Die neuentstehende Welt. (Keyserling, Hermann.) Darmstadt, 1926.

Phil 3499.6.9 Ein neuer Paulus. (Romundt, H.) Berlin, 1886.

Phil 181.35 Ein neuer Versuch über das Wesen der Philosophie. (Garfein-Garski, Stan.) Heidelberg, 1909.

Phil 5325.14 Neuere Einsichten...Ideenassoziationen. (Sganzini, Carlo.) Bern, 1918.

Phil 7060.101 Der neuere Geisterglaube. (Schneider, Wilhelm.) Paderborn, 1882.

Phil 7069.16.25 Neuere mystik. (Grabinski, B.) Hildesheim, 1916.

Phil 1701.8 Neuere Philosophie bis Kant. 3. Aufl. (Bauch, Bruno.) Berlin, 1919.

Phil 7068.97.42 Der neuere Spiritismus in seinem Wesen dargelegt und nach seinem Werte geprüft. 2. Aufl. (Dippel, Joseph.) München, 1897.

Phil 7054.36 Der neuere Spiritualismus; sein Werth. (Fichet, I.H. von.) Leipzig, 1878.

Phil 3415.106.8 Neuere Stimmen der Kritik über Eduard von Hartmanns Werke. (Haacke, Hermann.) Leipzig 1898.

Phil 5828.5 Die neuere Tierpsychologie. (Strassen, O.Z.) Leipzig, 1908.

Phil 5257.17 Die neueren Untersuchungen über Psychologie des Denkens. (Reichwein, G.) Halle, 1910.

Phil 6111.43 Neueres über die Zentralisation der Funktionen. (Bürker, Karl.) Giessen, 1926.

Phil 5252.150 Neues allgemeines Repertorium. (Mauchart, I.D.) Leipzig, 1802-03.

Phil 8980.15 Neues Leben. 1. Aufl. (Berlin. Institut für Gesellschaftswissenschaften.) Berlin, 1957.

Phil 8968.2.5 Neues Lehrbuch der Moral. (Stäudlin, C.F.) Göttingen, 1813.

Phil 1850.50.8 Neues Organon. J.H. Kirchmann. (Bacon, Francis.) Berlin, 1870.

Phil 5051.1 Neues zu einigen Gedanken. (Lambert, J.H.) Leipzig, 1764. 2v.

Phil 96.1 Neues Philosophie Real-Lexikon. (Lossius, J.C.) Erfurt, 1803-06. 4v.

Phil 5041.14 Neues praktisches System der Logik. (Bobrik, Eduard.) Zürich, 1838.

Phil 9560.62 Neues System einer philosophischen Tugendlehre. (Abicht, Johann Heinrich.) Leipzig, 1970.

Phil 3246.290 Neues zu den politischen Anschauungen des Jungen Fichte. (Funcke, Gerhard.) Hildesheim, 1915.

Phil 3310.7.90 Die neueste Lehre Geysers über des Kausali-Tatspriuzip. (Franzelin, B.) Innsbruck, 1924.

Phil 497.4 Die neueste Vergötterung des Stoffs. (Weber, A.) Giessen, 1858.

Phil 5027.1 Der neuesten Bestrebung...Logik. (Rabus, L.) Erlangen, 1880.

Phil 2750.11.55 Neuf leçons sur les notions premières de la philosophie morale. (Maritain, Jacques.) Paris, 1951.

Htn Phil 1850.38* Neuf livres de la dignité et de l'accroissement des sciences. (Bacon, Francis.) Paris, 1632.

Phil 5590.435 Neugarten, B.L. Personality in middle and late life. N.Y., 1964.

Phil 978.49.430 Neugestaltung, des sozialen Organismus. (Steiner, R.) Dornach, 1963.

Phil 3665.9.30 Neuhaeusler, Anton Otto. Fragmente keines Vorsokratikers. München, 1968.

Phil 98.2 Neuhaeusler, Anton Otto. Grundbegriffe der philosophischen Sprache. München, 1963.

Phil 3415.42 Neukantianismus, Schopenhauerianismus. (Hartmann, Eduard von.) Berlin, 1877.

Phil 8888.14 Neumam, Erich. Tiefenpsychologie und neue Ethik. Zürich, 1954.

Phil 4769.1.89 Un Neuman Russe: Vladimir Soloviev (1853-1900). 2. ed. (Herbigny, Michel d'.) Paris, 1911.

Phil 1075.1 Neumann, C.F. Memoire sur la vie et les ouvrages de David. Paris, 1829.

Phil 8414.11 Neumann, E. Kunst und schöpferisches Unbewusstes. Zürich, 1954.

Phil 5374.163.7 Neumann, E. The origins and history of consciousness. N.Y., 1964.

Phil 5374.163 Neumann, E. Ursprungsgeschichte des Bewusstseins. 1. Aufl. Zürich, 1949.

Phil 8888.14.1 Neumann, Erich. Depth psychology and a new ethic. London, 1969.

Phil 5590.305 Neumann, Erich. Der schöpferische Mensch. Zürich, 1959.

Phil 6963.3 Neumann, H. Über die Knochenbrüche bei Geisteskranken. Berlin, 1883.

Phil 3805.188 Neumann, J. Schleiermacher. Berlin, 1936.

Phil 9035.67 Neumann, Johannes. Die Entwicklung zur sittlichen Persönlichkeit. Gütersloh, 1931.

Phil 1050.7.9 Neumark, D. Essays in Jewish philosophy. Vienna, 1929.

Phil 1050.7 Neumark, D. Geschichte der jüdischen Philosophie der Mittelalters. Berlin, 1907. 3v.
Phil 1050.16 Neumark, D. Jehuda Hallevi's philosophy in its principles. Cinncinati, 1908.
Phil 3495.7 Neumark, David. Die Freiheitslehre bei Kant. Hamburg, 1896.
Htn Phil 3500.17.10* Neun Gespräche zwischen Christian Wolff. (Schwab, J.C.) Berlin, 1798.
Phil 3549.10.45 Das neunzehnte Jahrhundert; Ausdruck und Grösse. (Kassner, Rudolf.) Erlenbach, 1947.
Phil 1170.20 Die neuplatonische Seinsphilosophie und ihre Wirkung auf Thomas von Aquin. (Kremer, Klaus.) Leiden, 1966.
Phil 5374.51 The neural energy constant. (Bostock, John.) London, 1930.
Phil 5625.112 Neural mechanisms of higher vertebrate behavior. 1st English ed. (Beritashvili, Ivan S.) Boston, 1965.
Phil 6119.2 Die Neuralanalyse. (Jaeger, G.) Leipzig, 1881.
Phil 6951.12.15 Neurasthenia (nerve exhaustion), with remarks on treatment. (Beard, G.M.) n.p., 1879?
Phil 6952.10.2 Neurasthenia and its mental symptoms. (Cowles, E.) Boston, 1891.
Phil 6961.11 La neurasthénie. (Levillain, F.) Paris, 1891.
Phil 6962.17 Neurasthénie. (Mathieu, A.) Paris, 1892.
Phil 6951.15 La neurasthénie. 2. éd. (Bouveret, L.) Paris, 1891.
Phil 6951.17 La neurasthénie ruale. (Belbèze, Raymond.) Paris, 1911.
Phil 6960.9 Der neurasthenische Angstaffect bei Zwangsvorstellungen und der primordiale Grübelzwang. (Kaan, Hanns.) Wien, 1892.
Phil 5253.10 Neurath, Otto. Einheitswissenschaft und Psychologie. Wien, 1933.
NEDL Phil 23.13 Neurobiologia. Pernambuco. 1-18 17v.
Phil 6952.15 Neurological and mental diagnosis. (Clark, L.P.) N.Y., 1908.
Phil 5838.269 The neurological basis of motivation. (Glickman, Stephen E.) N.Y., 1969.
Phil 6132.12 Neurologische Untersuchungen. (Wagner, J.R.) Göttingen, 1854.
NEDL Phil 23.4 Neurologisches Centralblatt. (Mendel, E.) Leipzig, 1884-93. 10v.
Phil 6980.775 The neurologist's point of view. (Wechsler, Israel S.) N.Y., 1945.
Phil 5753.3 Neurology of Apraxia. (Dearborn, G.V.N.) Boston, 1911.
Phil 6125.10 Le neurone et les hypothèses. (Pupin, Charles.) Paris, 1896.
Phil 5460.13 The neurophysiological aspects of hallucinations and illusory experience. (Walter, W.G.) London, 1960.
Phil 6114.15 The neurophysiological basis of mind. (Eccles, J.C.) Oxford, 1953.
Phil 6114.15.3 The neurophysiological basis of mind. (Eccles, J.C.) Oxford, 1960.
Phil 5251.58A The neuropsychology of Lashley. (Lashley, K.S.) N.Y., 1960.
Phil 6972.16 The neuroses. (Wechsler, Israel S.) Philadelphia, 1929.
Phil 6313.8.10 Neuroses and character types. (Deutsch, Helene.) London, 1965.
Phil 6319.1.34 Neurosis, dreams, reflections. (Jung, C.G.) N.Y., 1963.
Phil 6310.21 Neurosis and treatment. (Angyal, András.) N.Y., 1965.
Phil 6962.25 The neurosis in war. (Miller, E.) N.Y, 1940.
Phil 5241.97.10 The neurosis of man. (Burrow, Trigant.) London, 1949.
Phil 5401.24 Neurotic anxiety. (Schwartz, C.) N.Y., 1954.
Phil 6310.1 The neurotic constitution; individualistic psychology. (Adler, A.) N.Y., 1917.
Phil 6320.17A Neurotic distortion of the creative process. (Kubie, L.S.) Lawrence, 1958.
Phil 6316.7 The neurotic personality. (Gordon, R.G.) London, 1927.
Phil 6317.22A The neurotic personality of our time. (Horney, Karen.) N.Y., 1937.
Phil 6968.37 Neurotic styles. (Shapiro, David.) N.Y., 1965.
Phil 6668.3 Neururgie oder der thierische Magnetismus. (Robiano, Comte de.) Stuttgart, 1849.
Phil 6671.10.20 Neurypnologie. (Braid, James.) Paris, 1883.
X Cg Phil 6671.10.15 Neurypnology. (Braid, James.) London, 1899.
Phil 5250.65 Die neuscholastische und die empirische Psychologie. (Kelly, William L.) Meisenheim, 1961.
Phil 1135.29 Neustadt, E. Die religiös-philosophische Bewegung der Hellenismus. Leipzig, 1914.
Phil 6323.6 Neustatter, W.L. Modern psychology in practice. Philadelphia, 1937.
Phil 8592.119 Neutrality and commitment: an inaugural lecture delivered before the University of Oxford on 13 May, 1968. (Mitchell, Basil.) Oxford, 1968.
Phil 5066.304 Neutralizzazione dello spazio per sintesiproduttiva. 2. ed. (Spisani, Franco.) Milano, 1968.
Phil 5465.33.10 Neuvième semaine internationale de synthèse. L'invention. (Centre International de Synthèse, Paris.) Paris, 1938.
Phil 530.20.85 Neuwinger, R. Die deutsche Mystik unter besonderer Berücksichtigung des "cherubinischen Wandersmannes" Johann Schefflers. Bleicherode am Harz, 1937.
Phil 3120.67.80 Neuwinger, Rudolf. Die Philosophie Ernst Bergmanns. Stuttgart, 1938.
Phil 5215.1 Die neuzeitliche psychologische Strömungen. (Friedländer, A.A.) Lubeck, 1926.
Phil 2885.81 Nève, P. La philosophie de Taine. Paris, 1908.
Phil 23.16.5 Neve Deutsche Forschungen. Abteilung Charakterologie, psychologische und philosophische Anthropologie. Berlin. 1-17 4v.
Phil 23.16 Neve Deutsche Forschungen. Abteilung Philosophie. Berlin. 3-37 18v.
Phil 193.10.15 Neve philosophische Schriften. (Schlegel, Friedrich von.) Frankfurt, 1935.
Phil 188.17 Nevin, J.W. Human freedom and a plea for philosophy. Mercersburg, 1850.
Phil 8888.12 Nevins, W.N. The meaning of the moral life. N.Y., 1930.
Htn Phil 9173.2* Nevizanis, J. de. Sylva nuptialis. n.p., 1602.
Phil 5374.165 Nevratil, Michel. Introduction critique à une découverte de la pensée. Paris, 1954.
Phil 6957.15 La névrose d'angoisse. (Hartenberg, P.) Paris, 1902.
Phil 6681.1 La névrose hypnotique. (Ladame, P.) Paris, 1881.
Phil 6959.1.12 Les névroses. (Janet, Pierre.) Paris, 1909.
Phil 6959.1.5 Névroses et idées fixes. (Janet, Pierre.) Paris, 1898. 2v.
Phil 6317.4 Névroses et possessions diaboliques. 2. éd. (Hélat, C.) Paris, 1898.
Phil 6328.57 Névroses et psychoses au moyen age et au début des temps modernes. (Szumowski, W.) Paris, 1939.
Phil 8592.6.12 The new affinities of faith. (Martineau, James.) Boston, 1869.
Phil 8592.6.11 The new affinities of faith. (Martineau, James.) London, 1869.
Phil 1817.18 The new American philosophers. (Reck, A.J.) Baton Rouge, 1968.
Phil 8585.9 A new analogy. (Fowle, T.W.) London, 1881.
Phil 8879.18 New and old methods of ethics. (Edgeworth, F.Y.) Oxford, 1877.
Phil 192.83 A new approach to philosophy. (Rice, Cale Y.) Lebanon, Tennessee, 1943.
Phil 5590.520 New approaches to personality classification. (Mahrer, Alvin.) N.Y., 1970.
Phil 8586.39 A new argument for God. (Grant, Malcolm.) London, 1934.
Phil 5545.9 New art of memory. (Feinaigle, G. von.) London, 1812.
Phil 8408.4 New bearings in esthetics and art criticism. (Heyl, Bernard.) New Haven, 1957.
Phil 7054.174 The new black magic. (Raupert, J.G.) N.Y., 1920.
Phil 8610.902.36 A new catechism. 2. ed. (Mangasarian, M.M.) Chicago, 1902.
NEDL Phil 23.5 The new century. N.Y. 1-14,1897-1910 11v.
Phil 9400.22 New channels for the golden years. (New York (State). Legislature. Joint Committee on Problems for the Aging.) Albany? 1956.
Phil 8712.3.4 New chapters in the warfare of science. (Geology). (White, Andrew Dickson.) N.Y., 1888.
Phil 8712.3.3 New chapters in the warfare of science. (Meteorology). (White, Andrew Dickson.) N.Y., 1887.
Phil 6972.8 New chapters in the warfare of science. v.1-2. (White, A.D.) N.Y., 1889.
Phil 8400.14A The new criticism; an anthology of modern aesthetics. (Burgum, E.B.) N.Y. , 1930.
Phil 334.14 A new critique of theoretical thought. (Dooyeweerd, Herman.) Amsterdam, 1953-58. 4v.
Phil 8897.46.5 The new decalogue of science. (Wiggam, A.E.) Garden City, 1925.
Phil 8897.46 The new decalogue of science. (Wiggam, A.E.) Indianapolis, 1923.
Phil 8593.11 A new departure. Boston, 1895.
Phil 6315.46 New developments in analytical psychology. (Fordham, M.S.M.) London, 1957.
Phil 7069.55.15 New dimensions of deep analysis. (Ehrenwald, Jan.) N.Y., 1955.
Phil 6320.11.10 New directions in psycho-analysis. (Klein, M.) London, 1955.
Phil 5238.176 New directions in psychology. N.Y., 1962.
Phil 6321.20 New directions in psychology toward individual happiness and social progress. (Lowy, Samuel.) N.Y., 1945.
Phil 5520.421 New directions in the study of language. (Lenneberg, E.H.) Cambridge, 1964.
Phil 6049.01.5 New discoveries in palmistry. (Hargett, Joseph Bryant.) N.Y., 1901.
Phil 2255.4 A new earth and a new humanity. (Reiser, Oliver L.) N.Y., 1942.
Htn Phil 2225.7.32* The new education; three papers. (Fitzgerald, John J.) Boston, 1887.
Phil 5246.49 New elements from old subjects presented as the basis for a science of mind. (Gaskell, John.) Philadelphia, 1874.
Phil 9160.4 The New England family. (Allen, N.) New Haven, 1882.
Phil 1815.2 New England transcendentalism and Saint Louis Hegelianism. (Pochmann, Henry A.) Philadelphia, 1948.
Phil 672.15 A new era of thought. (Hinton, Charles H.) London, 1888.
Phil 3552.40A New essays concerning human understanding. (Leibniz, Gottfried Wilhelm.) N.Y., 1896.
Phil 3552.40.5 New essays concerning human understanding. 3rd ed. (Leibniz, Gottfried Wilhelm.) La Salle, 1949.
Phil 1750.115.180 New essays in phenomenology. Chicago, 1969.
Phil 8697.26 New essays on religious language. (High, Dallas M.) N.Y., 1969.
Phil 8881.63 A new estimate of manners and principles. pt.1-2. (Gordon, John.) Cambridge, Eng., 1760.
Phil 8887.55 The new ethics. (Moore, J.H.) London, 1909.
Phil 8893.7 The new ethics. (Sewall, F.) N.Y., 1881.
Phil 7069.11.40 New evidences in psychical research. (Hill, John A.) London, 1911.
Phil 365.43 The new evolution, being a general solution of all modern life problems, based on truth. (Kausika, N.) Nemmara, 1936.
Phil 3246.58 New exposition of the science of knowledge. (Fichte, Johann Gottlieb.) Saint Louis, 1869.
Phil 6750.7.5 New facts and remarks concerning idiocy. (Seguin, E.) N.Y., 1870.
Phil 5241.59.15 The new field of psychology. (Bentley, I.M.) N.Y., 1934.
Phil 7069.37.5A New frontiers of the mind. (Rhine, Joseph B.) N.Y., 1937.
Phil 6328.30 A new German-English psycho-analytical vocabulary. (Strachey, Alix.) Baltimore, 1943.
Phil 8955.3 A new gospel. (Fassler, A.) N.Y., 1908.
Phil 2255.1.60 New hopes for a changing world. (Russell, Bertrand Russell.) London, 1951.
Phil 2255.1.61 New hopes for a changing world. (Russell, Bertrand Russell.) N.Y., 1951.
Phil 9355.9 New horizons. (Park, John Edgar.) Norton, 1929.
Phil 23.12F The new ideal. Boston.
Phil 23.12 The new ideal. Boston. 3,1890
Phil 400.33.5 The new idealism. (Sinclair, May.) N.Y., 1922.
Phil 400.41 The new idealist movement in philosophy. (Carr, Herbert Wildon.) London, 1918.
Phil 6111.59 New ideals in healing. (Baker, R.S.) N.Y., 1909.
Phil 978.80.10 The new image. (Bragdon, C.F.) N.Y., 1928.
Phil 8893.91 The new immoralities. (Sargent, Porter E.) Boston, 1935.
Phil 9495.168.5 The new immorality. 1st ed. (Walker, Brooks R.) Garden City, 1968.
Phil 672.136.17 The new immortality. (Dunne, John W.) London, 1938.
Phil 974.4 New India, Madras. Annie Besant, servant of humanity. Madras, 1924.
Phil 8696.2 The new infidelity. (Grote, A.R.) N.Y., 1881.
Phil 3428.88 New interpretation of Herbart's psychology. (Davidson, John.) Edinburgh, 1906.
Phil 6315.2.22 New introductory lectures on psycho-analysis. (Freud, Sigmund.) N.Y., 1964.
Phil 735.195 New knowledge in human values. (Scientific Conference on New Knowledge...1st.) N.Y., 1959.
Phil 177.130 New lamps for old. (Craig, Hardin.) Oxford, 1960.
Phil 8402.28.10 The new Laocoon; an essay on the confusion of the arts. (Babbitt, Irving.) Boston, 1913.
Phil 8402.28 The new Laocoon. (Babbitt, Irving.) Boston, 1910.
Phil 8402.28.5 The new Laocoon. (Babbitt, Irving.) Boston, 1910.
Phil 5049.12 A new law of thought and its logical bearings. (Jones, E.E.C.) Cambridge, 1911.
Phil 2050.77.20 New letters. (Hume, David.) Oxford, 1954.
Phil 177.85.10 The new leviathan, or Man, society, civilization and barbarism. (Collingwood, R.G.) Oxford, 1942.

Phil 23.15 The new liberator. N.Y. 1-3 2v.
Phil 23.15F The new liberator. N.Y. 3
Phil 5627.77 The new life. (Daniels, A.H.) Worcester, 1893.
Phil 193.133 New light on fundamental problems. (Seshagiri Row, T.V.) Mylapore, Madras, 1932.
Phil 7069.21.50 The new light on immortality. (Randall, John H.) N.Y., 1921.
Phil 7069.65.30 New light on old ghosts. (Hall, Trevor H.) London, 1965.
Phil 5052.14 A new logic. (Mercier, C.) London, 1912.
Phil 8952.22 A new look at Christian morality. (Curran, Charles E.) Notre Dame, 1968.
Phil 5241.114 The new man in Soviet psychology. (Bauer, R.A.) Cambridge, Mass., 1952.
Phil 480.10 The new materialism. (Feibleman, James.) The Hague, 1970.
Phil 6115.18.9 The new menticulture. (Fletcher, Horace.) London, 1905.
Phil 6115.18.10 The new menticulture. (Fletcher, Horace.) N.Y., 1903.
Phil 193.24 The new metaphysics. (Sewall, F.) London, 1888.
Phil 8586.2 A new method of demonstrating...the four fundamental points of religion. (Gordon, T.) London, 1756.
Phil 1750.78 New method of philosophy: an introduction to radiciology. (Kittaka, Rin'ichi.) Tokyo, 1967.
Phil 5850.267 New methods in applied psychology. (Maryland. Conference on Military Contributions to Methology.) College Park, 1947.
Phil 53.4 New Mexico. University. Bulletin. Philosophical series. Albuquerque. 1
Phil 4771.5.2 A new model of the universe. 2d ed. (Uspenskii, P.D.) N.Y., 1956.
Phil 8878.28.10 The new morality. (Drake, Durant.) N.Y., 1928.
Phil 8953.15 The new morality. (Dunphy, William.) N.Y., 1967.
Phil 8886.80.2 The new morality. (Lunn, Arnold.) London, 1967.
Phil 8610.902.25 The new morality. (Mortimer, G.) London, 1902.
Phil 9495.134 The new morality. (Newsom, G.E.) N.Y., 1933.
Phil 8844.2 A new morality. (Turner, Arthur T.) London, 1904.
Phil 525.15.5 The new mysticism. 3d ed. (Curtis, Adela M.) London, 1913.
Phil 8610.913.25 The new New England primer. Newport, Vt., 1913.
Phil 7069.30.11 The new Nuctemeron (The twelve hours of Apollonius of Tyana). (Livingston, Marjorie.) London, 1930.
Phil 6132.17.15 The new old healing. (Wood, Henry.) Boston, 1908.
Phil 4926.160.30 The new perspective, an essay. (Jordan, Rudolf.) Chicago, 1951.
Phil 2150.16.45 New perspectives for education. (Mayer, Frederick.) Washington, 1962.
Phil 6312.25 New perspectives in psychoanalysis. (Columbia. University. Psychoanalytic Clinic for Training and Reaserch.) N.Y., 1965.
Phil 6320.20 New perspectives in psychoanalysis. (Kelman, Harold.) N.Y., 1965.
Phil 177.31 The new philosophy. (Crane, A.) San Francisco, 1904.
Phil 5255.1 The new philosophy. (Paine, A.W.) Bangor, 1884.
Phil 8593.1 The new philosophy. London, 1847-49. 3v.
Phil 187.120 A new philosophy and the philosophical sciences. (Markakis, A.) N.Y., 1940. 2v.
Phil 2475.1.115 The new philosophy of Henri Berguson. (LeRoy, E.) N.Y., 1913.
Phil 5241.91 A new physiological psychology. (Burridge, William.) London, 1933.
Phil 5258.94 A new primer of psychology. (Sahai, Mahajot.) London, 1928.
Phil 6951.5.17 A new project; the first International Congress on Mental Hygiene. (Beers, C.W.) N.Y., 1924.
Phil 192.20 New propositions in...philosophy. (Richards, L.S.) Plymouth, 1903.
Phil 7060.35 The new psychic studies. (Johnson, F.) N.Y., 1887.
Phil 5246.12.12 New psychology. (Gordy, J.P.) N.Y., 1902.
Phil 5258.13.10 The new psychology. (Scripture, E.W.) London, 1897.
Phil 5258.13.15 The new psychology. (Scripture, E.W.) London, 1901.
Phil 5259.13.2 The new psychology. (Tansley, A.G.) London, 1920.
Phil 5259.13.10 The new psychology. (Tansley, A.G.) N.Y., 1924.
Phil 5232.3 The new psychology and the gospel. (Wray, W.J.) London, 1926.
Phil 6322.4.5 The new psychology and the parent. (Miller, Hugh C.) N.Y., 1923.
Phil 6322.4.7 The new psychology and the preacher. (Miller, Hugh C.) London, 1924.
Phil 7082.12.5 The new psychology of dreaming. (Jones, Richard Matthew.) N.Y., 1970.
Phil 6331.1.5 The new psychology of the unconscious. (Valentine, C.W.) London, 1932.
Phil 23.27 New race. Hyderabad. 1,1965+
Phil 630.42 The new rationalism. (Spaulding, E.G.) N.Y., 1918.
Phil 365.8 New reading of evolution. (Thompson, H.C.) Chicago, 1907.
Phil 630.5.5A The new realism. (Holt, E.B.) N.Y., 1912.
Phil 630.5.7 The new realism. (Holt, E.B.) N.Y., 1922.
Phil 630.5.10 The new realism. (Holt, E.B.) N.Y., 1925.
Phil 630.30.5 New realism and old reality. (Evans, Daniel L.) Princeton, 1928.
Phil 630.28 New realism in the light of scholasticism. (Verda, Mary.) N.Y., 1926.
Phil 8581.32 The new reformation...moral and social problems. (Balmforth, R.) London, 1893.
Phil 8705.14 The new reformation. (Prepin, Michael T.) N.Y., 1927.
Phil 8597.55 The new reformation? (Robinson, John Arthur Thomas.) London, 1965.
Phil 7069.18.95 The new revelation. (Doyle, Arthur Conan.) N.Y., 1918.
Phil 7069.18.95.6 The new revelation. 6th ed. (Doyle, Arthur Conan.) London, 1918.
Phil 5055.29.5 The new rhetoric: a treatise on agrumentation. (Perelman, Chaim.) Notre Dame, Ind., 1969.
Phil 23.11 The new scholasticism. Washington, D.C. 1,1927+ 38v.
Phil 23.11.5 The new scholasticism. Index. v.1-40. Washington, 1968.
Phil 4260.34 The new science of Giambattista Vico. (Vico, G.B.) Ithaca, 1948.
Phil 4260.34.2A The new science of Giambattista Vico. (Vico, G.B.) Ithaca, 1968.
Phil 2340.10.230 New shapes of reality: aspects of A.N. Whitehead's philosophy. (Jordan, Martin.) London, 1968.
Phil 1870.155 New studies in Berkeley's philosophy. (Steinkraus, Warren Edward.) N.Y., 1966.
Phil 2520.119.5 New studies in the philosophy of Descartes. (Smith, N.K.) London, 1952.
Phil 5041.17 A new system of logic. (Bosanquet, S.R.) London, 1839.
Phil 8968.12 New Testament ethics. (Scott, Charles A.A.) Cambridge, Eng., 1930.
Phil 7054.111.2 New Testament "miracles". 2. ed. (Fowler, J.H.) Boston, 1856.
Phil 7054.111.5 New Testament "miracles". 2. ed. (Fowler, J.H.) Boston, 1859.
Phil 7068.61 New Testament of our Lord...as revised and corrected by the spirits. (Bible. New Testament. English.) N.Y., 1861.
Phil 8575.7 New themes in Christian philosophy. Notre Dame, 1968.
Phil 187.44.7 A new theory of evolution. (Mann, William E.) Walpole, Mass., 1923.
Phil 187.44.9 A new theory of evolution. (Mann, William E.) Walpole, Mass., 1924.
Phil 9150.8 A new theory of evolution. (Smith, A.W.) N.Y., 1901.
Phil 1870.60.3A A new theory of vision. (Berkeley, G.) London, 1906.
Phil 197.13.15 The new thought simplified. (Wood, H.) Boston, 1903.
Phil 6117.45 New thought terms and their meanings. (Holmes, Ernest R.) N.Y., 1942.
Phil 7068.98.30 New thoughts. (Fitler, C.H.) Philadelphia, 1898.
Phil 3450.33 The new tower of Babel. (Hildebrand, D. von.) N.Y., 1953.
Phil 5042.5 New treatise...art of thinking. (Crousaz, J.P. de.) London, 1724. 2v.
Phil 189.12 The new tyranny; mysticism, scepticism. (Oppenheimer, F.J.) N.Y., 1927.
Phil 270.2.5 A new view of causation. (Barrett, T.S.) London, 1871.
Phil 6972.3 A new view of insanity. The duality of the mind. (Wigan, A.L.) London, 1844.
Phil 585.180 New views of the nature of man. (Platt, John Rader.) Chicago, 1965.
Phil 9495.143 New vistas...religion, sex and morals. (Walton, A.H.) London, 1943.
Phil 6117.47 The new way to relax. (Roon, K.) N.Y., 1949.
Phil 6317.22.5A New ways in psychoanalysis. (Horney, Karen.) N.Y., 1939.
Phil 400.24 The new world. (Upward, A.) N.Y., 1910.
NEDL Phil 23.2 The new world. Boston. 1-9 9v.
Phil 193.101 A new world by a new vision. (Sadler, G.T.) London, 1925. 2 pam.
Phil 1710.12 The new world of philosophy. (Kaplan, A.) N.Y., 1961.
Phil 7069.53 New world of the mind. (Rhine, Joseph B.) N.Y., 1953.
Phil 6315.44 New York. Academy of Medicine. Freud and contemporary culture. N.Y., 1957.
Phil 9495.24 New York. Homeopathic Medical Society. Communication on Public Education. Second communication. Albany? 1905.
Phil 70.97 New York. Institute of Philosophy. Law and philosophy. N.Y., 1964.
Phil 23.26 New York. Psychoanalytic Institute. Ernst Kris Study Group. Monograph. 1,1965+
Phil 75.32 New York. Public Library. List of books in the New York Public Library relating to philosophy. N.Y., 1908.
Phil 5650.23 New York (City). Noise Abatement Commission. City noise. N.Y., 1930.
Phil 6123.10 New York (City). University. Institution of Philosophy. Dimensions of mind. N.Y., 1960.
Phil 9400.22 New York (State). Legislature. Joint Committee on Problems for the Aging. New channels for the golden years. Albany? 1956.
Phil 6980.504 New York Academy of Medicine. Modern attitudes in psychiatry. N.Y., 1946.
Phil 8615.6.9 New York Society for Ethical Culture. Ethical addresses. Philadelphia. 2v.
Phil 8615.6.5 New York Society for Ethical Culture. Ethical pamphlets. N.Y.
Phil 8615.6 New York Society for Ethical Culture. Year book. N.Y. 1905
Phil 8400.46 New York University. Institute of Philosophy, 7th, 1964. Art and philosophy. N.Y., 1966.
Phil 8505.10 New York University. Institute of Philosophy. Religious experience and truth. N.Y., 1961.
Phil 23.19 The New Zealand bulletin of psychology. Auckland. 1954-1955
Htn Phil 294.4.2F* Newcastle, M.L.C. Grounds of natural philosophy. 2. ed. London, 1668.
Htn Phil 294.4F* Newcastle, M.L.C. Philosophical and physical opinions. London, 1663.
Htn Phil 6123.5.2* Newcomb, C.B. All's right with the world. Boston, 1897.
Phil 6123.5 Newcomb, C.B. All's right with the world. Boston, 1897.
Phil 6123.5.5 Newcomb, C.B. Discovery of a lost trail. Boston, 1900.
Phil 188.8 Newcomb, C.B. Principles of psychic philosophy. Boston, 1908.
Phil 9353.1 Newcomb, H. How to be a lady. Boston, 1850.
Phil 9173.1 Newcomb, H. How to be a man: a book for boys. Boston, 1850.
Phil 575.120 Newcomb, Theodore Mead. Personality and social change. N.Y., 1943.
Phil 575.120.2.2 Newcomb, Theodore Mead. Personality and social change. N.Y., 1957.
Phil 5500.16 Newell, Allen. Elements of a theory of human problem solving. Santa Monica, 1957.
Phil 5500.16.5 Newell, Allen. Human problem solving. Englewood Cliffs, 1972.
Phil 188.28 Newell, Robert. The concept of philosophy. London, 1967.
Phil 8581.33 The newer religious thinking. (Beach, D.N.) Boston, 1893.
Phil 7069.10.40 The newer spiritualism. (Podmore, Frank.) London, 1910.
Phil 7054.175 The newest Bible demonstrated by nature. (Knapp, C. Richard.) Grass Valley, Calif., n.d.
Phil 487.4 The newest materialism. (Maccall, William.) London, 1873.
Phil 9035.34 Newfang, Oscar. The development of character. N.Y., 1921.
Phil 294.5 Newlyn, Herbert N. The relationship...mystical and the sensible world. London, 1918.
Phil 8593.2 Newman, F.W. Hebrew Theism, common basis of Judaism, Christianity and Mohammedism. London, 1874.
Phil 5053.8 Newman, F.W. Lectures on logic. Oxford, 1838.
Phil 8593.2.10 Newman, F.W. Phases of faith. London, 1850.
Phil 8593.2.11 Newman, F.W. Phases of faith. 3. ed. London, 1853.
Phil 8593.2.13 Newman, F.W. Phases of faith. 5. ed. London, 1858.
Phil 8593.2.9 Newman, F.W. Soul, its sorrows and its aspirations. 3. ed. London, 1852.
Phil 8593.2.5 Newman, F.W. The soul. London, 1849.
Phil 8593.2.6 Newman, F.W. The soul. London, 1853.
Phil 8593.2.8 Newman, F.W. The soul. London, 1858.
Phil 1713.3 Newman, J. A time for truth. Dublin, 1955.
Phil 6683.1 Newman, J.B. Fascination. N.Y., 1847.
Phil 5090.3.2 Newman, J.H. An essay in aid of a Grammar of assent. London, 1901.
Phil 5090.3A Newman, J.H. Grammar of assent. N.Y., 1870.
Htn Phil 2175.1.30* Newman, John H. Apologia pro vita sua. pt.1-7. London, 1864. 3 pam.
Phil 3552.451 Newman, L.M. Leibniz, 1646-1716. London, 1966.
Phil 6683.2 Newman, W. Human magnetism. London, 1845.
Phil 6683.2.2 Newman, W. Human magnetism. N.Y., 1845.
Phil 6123.1.5 Newnham, W. Essay on superstition. London, 1830.

Phil 6123.1　Newnham, W. The reciprocal influence of body and mind. London, 1842.

Htn　Phil 7066.74*　News from Puddle-Dock in London. London, 1674.
Phil 7060.117　News from the invisible world. (Tregortha, John.) Burslem, 1813.
Phil 7069.00.35　News from the invisible world. 3. ed. London, 1900.
Phil 7069.40.8　News from the new world. (Tweedale, C.L.) London, 1940.
Phil 365.35　Newsholme, H.P. Evolution and redemption. London, 1933.
Phil 55.9　Newsletter. (Parapsychology Foundation.) N.Y. 1,1953+ 5v.
Phil 5627.232　Newsletter-review. (Bucke (R.M.) Memorial Society for the Study of Religious Experience.) Montreal. 1,1966+
Phil 9495.134　Newsom, G.E. The new morality. N.Y., 1933.
Phil 7068.56　Newton, Alonzo E. Answer to charges of belief in modern revelations. Boston, 1856. 2 pam.
Phil 8668.4.5　Newton, J.F. My idea of God. Boston, 1927.
Phil 8965.15　The next day. 1st ed. (Pike, James A.) Garden City, 1959.
Phil 9150.11　The next step in evolution. (Funk, I.K.) N.Y., 1902.
Phil 1210.16F　Nexus philosophiae theorico-politécae pecipatentica. (Weis, Georg.) Prague, 1670.
Phil 6980.354　Niacin therapy in psychiatry. (Hoffer, Abram.) Springfield, Ill., 1962.
Phil 310.5.15　Niakoi aktualni problemina nauchnogo. komunizum. (Oshakov, Zhivko.) Sofiia, 1961.
Phil 5253.5　Nicati, W.M. La psychologie naturelle. Paris, 1898.
Phil 3640.825　Niče i marksizam. (Simpozium na temu Niče i Marksizam, Belgrade, 1968.) Beograd, 1969.
Phil 6023.1　Nicefaro, A. La fisonomia nell'arte e nella scienza. Firenze, 1952.

Htn　Phil 8878.15*　Nicetas feu triumphata incontinentia. (Drexelius, H.) Colonia Agrippina, 1631.
Phil 1850.87　Nichol, J. Bacon. Philadelphia, 1888-89. 2v.
Phil 4752.2.85　Nicholas Berdyaev. (Spinka, M.) Philadelphia, 1950.
Phil 1713.2　Nicholl, Donald. Recent thought in focus. N.Y., 1953.
Phil 672.11　Nichols, H. Our notions of number and space. Boston, 1894.
Phil 5585.22　Nichols, H. The psychology of time. N.Y., 1891.
Phil 294.3　Nichols, H. Treatise on cosmology. Cambridge, 1904.
Phil 8593.3.2　Nichols, I. A catechism of natural theology. Boston, 1831.
Phil 8593.3.3　Nichols, I. A catechism of natural theology. Boston, 1839.
Phil 8593.3　Nichols, I. A catechism of natural theology. Portland, 1829.
Phil 8593.4　Nichols, J.R. From whence, what, where? Boston, 1882.
Phil 8593.4.10　Nichols, J.R. Whence, what, where? Boston, 1886.
Phil 7060.52　Nichols, T.L. A biography of the brothers Davenport. London, 1864.
Phil 7054.172　Nichols, T.L. Supramundane facts. London, 1865.
Phil 735.3　Nicholson, Anne M. The concept standard. N.Y., 1910.
Phil 188.19　Nicholson, J.A. Introductory course in philosophy. N.Y., 1939.
Phil 8400.52　Die nicht mehr schönen Künste; Grenzphänomene des Asthetischen. München, 1968.
Phil 8612.37　Das Nichts und der Tod. (Berlinger, R.) Frankfurt, 1954.
Phil 310.490　Nichyk, V.M. Dialektychnyi materializm pro katenoriiu prychynnosti. Kyiv, 1960.
Phil 294.8　Nickel, E.J. Zugang zur Wicklichkeit. Freiburg, 1963.
Phil 5125.9　Nicod, Jean. Le problème logique de l'induction. Paris, 1924.
Phil 8593.18　Nicodemus (pseud.). Renaissence; an essay in faith. London, 1943.
Phil 4314.2　Nicol, Eduardo. El problema de la filosofía hispanica. Madrid, 1961.
Phil 5253.12　Nicol, Eduardo. Psicología de las situaciones vitales. Mexico, 1941.

Htn　Phil 3495.1*　Nicolai, C.F. Über...kritischen Philosophie...Kant. Berlin, 1799.

Htn　Phil 3801.606*　Nicolai, F. Leben und Meinungen Sempronius Gundibert's. Berlin, 1798.
Phil 3200.3.81　Nicolai, Friedrich. Gedächtnisschrift auf Johann August Eberhard. Berlin, 1810.
Phil 3665.7.30　Nicolai, Friedrich. Philosophische Abhandlungen. Bruxelles, 1968. 2v.
Phil 3495.2　Nicolai, G.W. Ist der Begriff des Schönen bei Kant. Kiel, 1889.
Phil 3195.6.97　Nicolai, Heinz. Wilhelm Dilthey und das Problem der dichterischen Phantasie. Inaug. Diss. München, 1934.
Phil 6123.7　Nicolai, J.F. Psicogenesis. Santiago, 1935.
Phil 3450.18.105　Nicolai Hartmann, der Denker und sein Werk. (Heimsoeth, H.) Göttingen, 1952.
Phil 3450.18.125　Nicolai Hartmann and Alfred North Whitehead. (Mohanty, J.N.) Calcutta, 1957.
Phil 3450.18.195　Nicolai Hartmann dal neokantismo all ontologia. (Sirchia, Francesco.) Milano, 1969.
Phil 3450.18.170　Nicolai Hartmann nella filosofia del novecento. (Barone, Francisco.) Torino, 1957.
Phil 3450.18.145　Nicolai Hartmann und das Ende der Ontologie. (Hanthack, K.) Berlin, 1962.
Phil 182.94.80　Nicolai Hartmann y la idea de la metafisica. (Alarco, L.F.) Lima, 1943.
Phil 3450.18.95　Nicolai Hartmanns Lehre. (Hirning, H.) Tübingen, 1937.
Phil 3450.18.115F　Nicolai Hartmanns Ontologie des idealen Seins. Thesis. (Fleischer, Helmut.) Erlangen? 1954.
Phil 2475.1.208.9　Nicolardot, F. A propos de Bergson? Paris, 1924.
Phil 2475.1.208.5　Nicolardot, F. Flore de G'nose, Laggrond, Pellis et Bergson. Paris, 1924.
Phil 5435.5　Nicolardot, F. Habitude ou train? Paris, 1922.
Phil 2475.1.208　Nicolardot, F. Un pseudonyme Bergsonien? Paris, 1923.
Phil 2150.22.120　Nicolas, André. Herbert Marcuse ou la Quête d'un univers trans-prométhéen. Paris, 1969.
Phil 1750.27　Nicolas, M. De l'eclectisme. Paris, 1840.
Phil 3640.270　Nicolas, M.P. De Nietzsche à Hitler. Paris, 1936.
Phil 188.22　Nicolas, M.P. Regards sur l'humain. Paris, 1958.
Phil 813.4　Nicolas, Michel. Introduction à l'étude de l'histoire de la philosophie. Paris, 1849-50. 2v.
Phil 4752.2.190　Nicolas Berdiaeff. (Gaith, Jérome.) Beyrouth, 1968.
Phil 4752.2.38　Nicolas Berdiaeff ou la Révolte contre l'objectivation. (Berdiaev, Nikolai Aleksandrovich.) Paris, 1967.
Phil 4752.2.140　Nicolas Berdiaev, l'homme du huitième jour. (Davy, M.M.) Paris, 1964.
Phil 4752.2.95　Nicolas Berdyaev. (Seaver, George.) London, 1950.
Phil 4752.2.80　Nicolas Berdyaev and the new middle ages. (Lampert, Evengu.) London, 194-.
Phil 2733.117　Nicolas Malebranche. (Rodis-Lewis, G.) Paris, 1963.
Phil 1504.6.2　Nicolaus von Autrecourt. v.6, pt.2. (Lappe, J.) Münster, n.d.

Phil 5823.1　Nicolaÿ, Fernand. L'âme et l'instinct; l'homme et l'animal. Paris, 1922.
Phil 6323.4.5　Nicole, J.E. Psychopathology. 2d ed. Baltimore, 1934.
Phil 6323.4.6　Nicole, J.E. Psychopathology. 4. ed. Baltimore, 1947.
Phil 8888.2　Nicole, P. Moral essayes. London, 1696. 2v.
Phil 188.2　Nicole, P. Oeuvres philosophiques et morales. Paris, 1845.
Phil 5253.20　Nicoletti, Ivan. Analisi quantitativa e programmi di ricerca in psicologia epsichiatria. Torino, 1968.
Phil 5053.7.4　Nicoli, P. Elementi di logica. Milano, 1912.
Phil 3425.385　Nicolin, F. Gründlinien einer geisteswissenschaftlichen Pädagogik bei G.W.F. Hegel. Bonn, 1955.
Phil 3425.385.2　Nicolin, F. Hegels Bildungstheorie. Bonn, 1955.
Phil 3425.14.5　Nicolin, Günther. Hegel in Berichten seines Zeitgenossen companion von to Briefe von und an Hegel. Hamburg, 1970.
Phil 4080.3.410　Nicolini, F. Benedetto Croce. Roma, 1954.
Phil 4260.123　Nicolini, F. Commento storico alla seconda Scienza nuova. Roma, 1949- 2v.
Phil 4080.3.400　Nicolini, F. Il Croce minore. Milano, 1963.
Phil 4260.124　Nicolini, F. La giovinezza di Giambattista Vico. 2. ed. Bari, 1932.
Phil 4260.124.10　Nicolini, F. La religiosità di Giambattista Vico. Bari, 1949.
Phil 4260.124.5　Nicolini, F. Saggi vichiani. Napoli, 1955.
Phil 4260.155　Nicolini, F. Vico storico. Napoli, 1967.
Phil 4080.3.170　Nicolini, Fausto. Benedetto Croce. Napoli, 1944.
Phil 4080.3.172　Nicolini, Fausto. Benedetto Croce. Torino, 1962.
Phil 7082.186　Nicoll, Maurice. Dream psychology. London, 1917.
Phil 2175.5.30　Nicoll, Maurice. Living time and the integration of the life. London, 1953.
Phil 4757.2.100　Nicoll, Maurice. Psychological commentaries on the teaching of G.I. Gurdjieff and P.D. Ouspensky. London, 1955-57. 5v.
Phil 8638.2　Nicoll, N.R. Reunion in eternity. N.Y., 1919.
Phil 8888.5　Nicoll, W.R. Letters on life. N.Y., 1901.
Phil 5425.54　Nicolle, Charles. Biologie de l'invention. Paris, 1932.
Phil 2733.119　Nicolosi, Salvatore. Causalità divina e libertà umana nel pensiero di Malebranche. Padova, 1963.
Phil 9070.57　Nicolson, Harold Georg. Good behavior. London, 1955.
Phil 9070.50.5　Nicolson, Harold Georg. Good behaviour; being a study of certain types of activity. Garden City, 1956.
Phil 5023.1　Nidditch, Peter. The development of mathematical logic. London, 1962.
Phil 8963.3　Niebuhr, R. Interpretation of Chirstian ethics. N.Y., 1935.
Phil 9513.30　Niebuhr, Reinhold. Faith and politics. N.Y., 1968.
Phil 3805.222　Niebuhr, Richard R. Schleiermacher on Christ and religion. N.Y., 1964.
Phil 3011.7　Niedergangserscheinungen in der Philosophie der Gegenwart. (Linke, Paul F.) München, 1961.
Phil 2494.80　Niedlich, J.K. Condorcet's "Esquisse d'un tableau historique". Sorai, 1907.
Phil 1750.166.185　Niel, André. Les grands appels de l'humanisme contemporain, christianisme, marxisme. Paris, 1966.
Phil 2880.8.162　Niel, André. Jean-Paul Sartre. Paris, 1966.
Phil 3425.312　Niel, Henri. De la médiation dans la philosophie de Hegel. Paris, 1945.
Phil 3425.316　Niel, Henri. De la médiation dans la philosophie de Hegel. Thèse. Madrid, 1945.
Phil 188.15　Nielsen, F.K. Sjaele-og taenkelaere i almenfattelig. 4e udg. Kjøbenhavn, 1882.
Phil 5053.7　Nielsen, R. Grundideernes logik. Kjøbenhavn, 1864-66. 2v.
Phil 4610.9.31　Nielsen, R. Natur og aand. Kjøbenhavn, 1873. 2 pam.
Phil 4610.9.35　Nielsen, R. Om personlig sanning och sann personlighet. Upsala, 1856.
Phil 8593.10　Nielsen, Rasmus. Om hindringer og betingelser for det aandelige liv i nutiden. Kjøbenhavn, 1867.
Phil 5465.22　Nielsen, Rasmus. Om phantasiens magt. Kjøbenhavn, 1876.
Phil 7069.13.32　Nielsson, H. Hví slaer pú mig? v.1-2. Reykjavik, 1913.
Phil 7069.22.45　Nielsson, H. Kirken og den psykiske Forskning. København, 1922.
Phil 9353.2　Niemeyer, J.F. Vermaechtniss an Helene von ihrem Vater. Bremen, 1794.
Phil 3495.16　Nierkaus, F. Das Problem des psychophysischen Kommersiums in der Entwicklung der Kantischen Philosophie. Köln, 1962.
Phil 3495.18　Nieschmidt, Gerd Peter. Praktische Vernunft und Ewiger Friede. München, 1965.
Phil 665.7.5　Nieśmiertelność duszy i wolność woli. (Lutosławski, W.) Warszawa, 1909.
Phil 3640.76.15　Nietsche, Friedrich. Briefe an Peter Gast. Leipzig, 1908.
Phil 3640.76.17　Nietzsche; a self-portrait from his letters. (Nietzsche, Friedrich.) Cambridge, 1971.
Phil 3640.349　Nietzsche; an approach. (Lavrin, Janko.) London, 1948.
Phil 3640.308　Nietzsche; conférences prononcées à Genève sous les auspices de la fondation Marie Gretler. Erlenbach, 1945.
Phil 3640.465　Nietzsche, critique d'art. (Hartmann, H.) Manosque, 1955.
Phil 3640.312　Nietzsche, dionisíaco y asceta. (Molina, Enrique.) Santiago, 1944.
Phil 3640.815　Nietzsche; eine christliche Besinnung. Photoreproduction. (Steinbuechel, Theodor.) Stuttgart, 1946.
Phil 3640.122　Nietzsche, Emerson, Tolstoy. (Sánchez Torres, E.) Barcelona, 1902.
Phil 3640.121.4　Nietzsche; essai de mythologie. (Bertram, Ernst.) Paris, 1932.
Phil 3808.192　Nietzsche, F.W. Schopenhauer als Erzieher. Leipzig, 1931.
Phil 3640.273　Nietzsche, Frau Franziska O. Der kranke Nietzsche. Wien, 1937.
Phil 3640.39　Nietzsche, Friedrich. Ainsi parlait Zarathustra. 29e éd. Paris, 1914.

Htn　Phil 3640.41*　Nietzsche, Friedrich. Also sprach Zarathustra. Leipzig, 19- .
Phil 3640.41.4　Nietzsche, Friedrich. Also sprach Zarathustra. Leipzig, 1905?
Phil 3640.41.8A　Nietzsche, Friedrich. Also sprach Zarathustra. Leipzig, 1909.
Phil 3640.41.15　Nietzsche, Friedrich. Also sprach Zarathustra. Stuttgart, 1943.
Phil 3640.17.6　Nietzsche, Friedrich. Also Sprach Zarathustra. Stuttgart, 1956.
Phil 3640.57A　Nietzsche, Friedrich. L'antéchrist. Paris, 1931.
Phil 3640.56　Nietzsche, Friedrich. L'antéchrist. Paris, 1931.
Phil 3640.53.5　Nietzsche, Friedrich. Der Antichrist. 2. Aufl. Berlin, 1940.
Phil 3640.42　Nietzsche, Friedrich. Asi hablaba Zarathustra. Valencia, 19- ?
Phil 3640.30.5　Nietzsche, Friedrich. Aurora. Valencia, 1910?
Phil 3640.30.9　Nietzsche, Friedrich. Aurore. 7e éd. Paris, 1912.

Phil 3640.46   Nietzsche, Friedrich. Basic writings of Nietzsche. N.Y., 1968.

Phil 3640.31.5A   Nietzsche, Friedrich. Beyond good and evil. Chicago, 1949.

Phil 3640.31A   Nietzsche, Friedrich. Beyond good and evil. N.Y., 1907.
Phil 3640.31.9   Nietzsche, Friedrich. Beyond good and evil. N.Y., 1917.
Phil 3640.31.3   Nietzsche, Friedrich. Beyond good and evil. N.Y., 1917.
Phil 3640.31.4   Nietzsche, Friedrich. Beyond good and evil. N.Y., 1924.
Phil 3640.58.20   Nietzsche, Friedrich. The birth of tragedy. N.Y., 1967.
Phil 3640.79.10   Nietzsche, Friedrich. The birth of tragedy and The genealogy of morals. 1. ed. Garden City, N.Y., 1956.

Phil 3640.77.10   Nietzsche, Friedrich. Brevier. 2. Aufl. Wien, 1951.
Phil 3640.76A   Nietzsche, Friedrich. Briefe. v.1-5. 3rd ed. Berlin, 1902. 6v.

Phil 3640.77A   Nietzsche, Friedrich. Briefwechsel mit Franz Overbeck. Leipzig, 1916.

Phil 3640.70   Nietzsche, Friedrich. The case of Wagner. Photoreproduction. Nietzsche, 1896.

Phil 3640.15.5   Nietzsche, Friedrich. Complete works. N.Y., 1964. 18v.

Phil 3640.15   Nietzsche, Friedrich. Complete works. v.1,3,7,9-10,13,18. Edinburgh, 1910-13. 7v.

NEDL Phil 3640.15   Nietzsche, Friedrich. Complete works. v.2,4-6,8,11,14-15,17. Edinburgh, 1910-13. 9v.

Phil 3640.15.2   Nietzsche, Friedrich. Complete works. v.11,16. London, 1913. 2v.

Phil 3640.15.3   Nietzsche, Friedrich. Complete works. 3. ed. v.11. N.Y., 1914.

Phil 3640.77.15   Nietzsche, Friedrich. Ecce homo. Leipzig, 1908.
Phil 3640.77.15.5   Nietzsche, Friedrich. Ecce homo. Leipzig, 1931.
Phil 3640.79.15   Nietzsche, Friedrich. Erkenntnistheoretische Schriften. Frankfurt, 1968.

Phil 3640.11.4   Nietzsche, Friedrich. Der Fall Wagner; und die Geburt der Trajödie. Leipzig, 1888.

Phil 3640.52   Nietzsche, Friedrich. Der Fall Wagner. Frankfurt, 1946.
Phil 3640.52.5   Nietzsche, Friedrich. Der Fall Wagner. Leipzig, 1931.
Phil 3640.62   Nietzsche, Friedrich. Federico Nietzsche. 3. ed. Milano, 1944.

Phil 3640.72   Nietzsche, Friedrich. Fragments sur l'énergie et la puissance. Paris, 1957.

Phil 3640.33   Nietzsche, Friedrich. Die fröhliche Wissenschaft. Leipzig, 1887.

Phil 3640.33.5   Nietzsche, Friedrich. Die fröhliche Wissenschaft. München, 1959.

Phil 3640.17.5   Nietzsche, Friedrich. Die fröhliche Wissenschaft. Stuttgart, 1956.

Phil 3640.16   Nietzsche, Friedrich. Fünf Vorreden in fünf ungeschriebenen Büchern. Berlin, 1943.

Phil 3640.43   Nietzsche, Friedrich. La gaya ciencia. Valencia, 1910?
Phil 3640.58.5   Nietzsche, Friedrich. Die Geburt der Tragödie aus dem Geiste der Musik. Leipzig, 1931.

Phil 3640.25.10   Nietzsche, Friedrich. Gedichte und Sprüche. Leipzig, 1901.

Phil 3640.25   Nietzsche, Friedrich. Gedichte und Sprüche. Leipzig, 1908.

Phil 3640.25.7   Nietzsche, Friedrich. Gedichte und Sprüche. Leipzig, 1916.

Phil 3640.12.10   Nietzsche, Friedrich. Gedichts. Leipzig, 1923.
Phil 3640.34   Nietzsche, Friedrich. The genealogy of morals. N.Y., 1918.

Phil 3640.24   Nietzsche, Friedrich. Germans, Jews and France. Newark, 1935.

Phil 3640.10.15   Nietzsche, Friedrich. Gesammelte Werke. München, 1929-29. 23v.

Phil 3640.32   Nietzsche, Friedrich. Götzen-Dämmerung. Leipzig, 1889.
Phil 3640.17.8   Nietzsche, Friedrich. Götzendämmerung. Stuttgart, 1954. 2v.

Phil 3640.35.5   Nietzsche, Friedrich. Humain, trop humain. Paris, 1899.
Phil 3640.36   Nietzsche, Friedrich. Humano, demasiado humano. Valencia, 1909?

Phil 3640.31.2   Nietzsche, Friedrich. Jenseits von Gut und Böse. Leipzig, 1886.

Phil 3640.54   Nietzsche, Friedrich. Jenseits von Gut und Böse. Leipzig, 193-.

Phil 3640.17.7   Nietzsche, Friedrich. Jenseits von Gut und Böse. Stuttgart, 1959.

Phil 3640.77.25   Nietzsche, Friedrich. The joyful wisdom. London, n.d.
Phil 3640.77.27   Nietzsche, Friedrich. Joyful wisdom. N.Y., 1960.
Phil 3640.21   Nietzsche, Friedrich. Jugendschriften. München, 1923.
Phil 3640.38   Nietzsche, Friedrich. Kritik und Zukunft der Kultur. Zürich, 1933.

Phil 3640.76.16   Nietzsche, Friedrich. Lettres à Peter Gast. Monaco, 1958. 2v.

Phil 3640.61   Nietzsche, Friedrich. La lirica di Nietzsche. Messina, 1948.

Phil 3640.73   Nietzsche, Friedrich. The living thoughts of Nietzsche. London, 1946.

Phil 3640.277A   Nietzsche, Friedrich. The living thoughts of Nietzsche. N.Y., 1939.

Phil 3640.11.2   Nietzsche, Friedrich. Menschliches, allzumenschliche sein Buch für freie Geister. Leipzig, 1886.

Phil 3640.47   Nietzsche, Friedrich. Menschliches, Allzumenschliches; ein Buch für freie Geister. v.1-2. Stuttgart, 1954.

Phil 3640.17.3   Nietzsche, Friedrich. Menschliches, Allzumenschliches; ein Buch für freie Geister. Stuttgart, 1960.

Phil 3640.17.4   Nietzsche, Friedrich. Morgenröte. Stuttgart, 1952. 2v.

Phil 3640.77.15.10   Nietzsche, Friedrich. My sister and I. N.Y., 1951.

Phil 3640.77.15.12   Nietzsche, Friedrich. My sister and I. N.Y., 1953.
Phil 3640.76.17   Nietzsche, Friedrich. Nietzsche; a self-portrait from his letters. Cambridge, 1971.

Phil 3640.14.16   Nietzsche, Friedrich. Nietzsche. Index. München, 1965.
Phil 3640.28   Nietzsche, Friedrich. Nietzsche as critic. N.Y., 1901.
Phil 3640.76.9   Nietzsche, Friedrich. Nietzsches Briefe. Leipzig, 1917.
Phil 3640.22.8   Nietzsche, Friedrich. Nietzsche's Philosophie in Selbstzeugnissen. Leipzig, 1921. 4v.

Phil 3640.22   Nietzsche, Friedrich. Nietzsche's Werke. v.2-4. Leipzig, 1931. 3v.

Phil 3640.26   Nietzsche, Friedrich. Pages choisies. 5e éd. Paris, 1899.
Phil 3640.31.15   Nietzsche, Friedrich. Par delà le bien et le mal. Paris, 1951.

Phil 3640.63   Nietzsche, Friedrich. Die Philosophie im tragischen Zeitalter der Griechen. Leipzig, 1931.

Phil 3640.63.5   Nietzsche, Friedrich. Die Philosophie im tragischen Zeitalter der Griechen. München, 1923.

Phil 3640.22.15   Nietzsche, Friedrich. Philosophy of Nietzsche. N.Y., 195-?

Phil 3640.60   Nietzsche, Friedrich. Póesies complètes. Paris, 1948.
Phil 3640.17.12   Nietzsche, Friedrich. Sämtliche Werke. Stuttgart, 1964-65. 12v.

Phil 3640.45   Nietzsche, Friedrich. Schwert des Geistes. Stuttgart, 1941.

Phil 3640.78   Nietzsche, Friedrich. Selected letters. London, 1921.
Phil 3640.78.5   Nietzsche, Friedrich. Selected letters of Friedrich Nietzsche. Chicago, 1969.

Phil 3640.58.7   Nietzsche, Friedrich. Socrates und die griechische Tragödie. München, 1933.

Phil 3640.23   Nietzsche, Friedrich. Studienausgabe in 4 Bänden. Frankfurt, 1968. 4v.

Phil 3640.40.2   Nietzsche, Friedrich. Thus spake Zararhustra. N.Y., 1908.
Phil 3640.40.12   Nietzsche, Friedrich. Thus spake Zarathustra. Chicago, 1957.

Phil 3640.40.10   Nietzsche, Friedrich. Thus spake Zarathustra. London, 1958.

Phil 3640.40.5   Nietzsche, Friedrich. Thus spake Zarathustra. N.Y., 1896.
Phil 3640.40.30   Nietzsche, Friedrich. Thus spake Zarathustra. N.Y., 1936.
Phil 3640.40.3   Nietzsche, Friedrich. Thus spake Zarathustra. 2d ed. N.Y., 1911.

Phil 3640.27.1   Nietzsche, Friedrich. Umwertung aller Werte. München, 1969. 2v.

Phil 3640.17.2   Nietzsche, Friedrich. Un zeitgemässe Betrachtungen. Stuttgart, 1955.

Phil 3640.77.5   Nietzsche, Friedrich. Unpublished letters. N.Y., 1959.
Phil 3640.17.10   Nietzsche, Friedrich. Die Unschuld des Werdens. v.1-2. Leipzig, 1931.

Phil 3640.64.5   Nietzsche, Friedrich. Unzeigemässe Betrachtungen. Leipzig, 189-?

Phil 3640.11.5   Nietzsche, Friedrich. Unzeitgemässe Betrachtungen. Leipzig, 189-?

Phil 3640.79.20   Nietzsche, Friedrich. Van vornehmen Menschen. Klosterberg, 1945.

Phil 3640.27   Nietzsche, Friedrich. Das Vermächtnis Friedrich Nietzsches. Salzburg, 1940.

Phil 3640.77.20   Nietzsche, Friedrich. La vie de Friedrich Nietzsche d'après sa correspondance. Paris, 1932.

Phil 3640.19   Nietzsche, Friedrich. Volks-Nietzsche. Berlin, 1931. 4v.

Phil 3640.63.10   Nietzsche, Friedrich. Vom Nietzen un Nachteil der Historie für das Leben. Leipzig, 1931.

Phil 3640.50   Nietzsche, Friedrich. Von neuen Freiheiten des Geistes. 1. Aufl. München, 1943.

Phil 3640.58   Nietzsche, Friedrich. Vorstufen der Geburt der Tragödie aus dem Geiste der Musik. Leipzig, 1926-28. 3v.

Phil 3640.37   Nietzsche, Friedrich. Der Wanderer und sein Schatten. Chemnitz, 1880.

Phil 3640.77.7   Nietzsche, Friedrich. Der werdende Nietzsche. München, 1924.

Phil 3640.10.2   Nietzsche, Friedrich. Werke. Leipzig, 1895-1926. 19v.
Phil 3640.10A   Nietzsche, Friedrich. Werke. Leipzig, 1896-1926. 20v.
Phil 3640.11.10A   Nietzsche, Friedrich. Werke. Leipzig, 1906-09. 11v.
Phil 3640.20   Nietzsche, Friedrich. Werke. Leipzig, 1930. 2v.
Phil 3640.14.15A   Nietzsche, Friedrich. Werke. München, 1954-56. 3v.
Phil 3640.14.10   Nietzsche, Friedrich. Werke. Salzburg, 1952. 2v.
Phil 3640.10.5   Nietzsche, Friedrich. Werke. Kritische Gesamtausgabe. Berlin, 1967. 9v.

Phil 3640.17   Nietzsche, Friedrich. Werke. v.1-11. Leipzig, 1931-59. 12v.

Phil 3640.13   Nietzsche, Friedrich. Werke und Briefe. München, 1933-49. 5v.

Phil 3640.14   Nietzsche, Friedrich. Werke und Briefe. München, 1938-42. 4v.

Phil 3640.51.10   Nietzsche, Friedrich. The will to power. N.Y., 1967.
Phil 3640.51.11   Nietzsche, Friedrich. The will to power. N.Y., 1968.
Phil 3640.51   Nietzsche, Friedrich. Der Wille zur Macht. Stuttgart, 1952.

Phil 3640.17.9   Nietzsche, Friedrich. Der Wille zur Macht. Stuttgart, 1959.

Phil 3640.65   Nietzsche, Friedrich. Zeitgemässes und Unzeitgemässes. Frankfurt, 1956.

Phil 3640.34.5   Nietzsche, Friedrich. Zur Genealogie der Moral. Leipzig, 193-.
Phil 3640.98   Nietzsche, his life and works. (Ludovici, Anthony M.) London, 1910.

Phil 3640.98.20   Nietzsche, his life and works. (Ludovici, Anthony M.) London, 1916.

Phil 3640.690   Nietzsche, homme et surhomme. (Doisy, M.) Bruxelles, 1946.

Phil 3640.840A   Nietzsche; Introduction à une première lecture. (Morel, Georges.) Paris, 1970-71. 3v.

Phil 3640.353   Nietzsche, Krankheit und Wirking. (Lange, Wilhelm.) Hamburg, 1948.

Phil 3640.351   Nietzsche; ou Le declin de l'esprit. 13e éd. (Thibon, G.) Lyon, 1948.

Phil 3640.414A   Nietzsche, ou L'histoire d'un égocentrisme athée. (Lannoy, Joris C.) Paris, 1952.

Phil 3640.480   Nietzsche, philosophe de la valeur. (Quinot, Armand.) Manosque, 1956.

Phil 3640.113   Nietzsche, poeta. (Keiper, Wilhelm.) Buenos Aires, 1911.
Phil 3640.306   Nietzsche; sa vie, son oeuvre, avec un exposé de sa philosophie. 1e éd. (Cresson, André.) Paris, 1942.

Phil 3640.708   Nietzsche; sa vie, son oeuvre. (Deleuze, Gilles.) Paris, 1965.

Phil 3640.158   Nietzsche, sa vie et sa pensée. (Andler, Charles.) Paris, 1920-31. 6v.

Phil 3640.158.4   Nietzsche, sa vie et sa pensée. (Andler, Charles.) Paris, 1958.

Phil 3640.158.3   Nietzsche, sa vie et sa pensée. 3. éd. (Andler, Charles.) Paris, 1922.

Phil 3640.208   Nietzsche, tendances et problèmes. (Barbat, V.J.) Zürich, 1911.

Phil 3640.121.3   Nietzsche; Versuch einer Mythologie. (Bertram, Ernst.) Berlin, 1929.

Phil 3640.318   Nietzsche...die Erfüllung. (Giese, Fritz.) Tübingen, 1934.

Phil 3640.257   Nietzsche. (Abraham, G.E.H.) London, 1933.
Phil 3640.257.5   Nietzsche. (Abraham, G.E.H.) N.Y., 1933.
Phil 3640.707   Nietzsche. (Bartuschat, Wolfgang.) Heidelberg? 1964.
Phil 3640.121.2   Nietzsche. (Bertram, Ernst.) Berlin, 1918.
Phil 3640.121.3.5   Nietzsche. (Bertram, Ernst.) Bonn, 1965.
Phil 3640.120A   Nietzsche. (Carus, Paul.) Chicago, 1914.
Phil 3640.366   Nietzsche. (Challaye, F.) Paris, 1950.
Phil 3640.717   Nietzsche. (Colloque Philosophique International de Royaumont, 7th, 1964.) Paris, 1967.

Author and Title Listing

Phil 3640.450 Nietzsche. (Flam, Leopold.) Bussum, 1955.
Phil 3640.167.5 Nietzsche. (Gaultier, J. de.) Paris, 1926.
Phil 3640.359 Nietzsche. (Giesz, Ludwig.) Stuttgart, 1950.
Phil 3640.250 Nietzsche. (Giorgianni, E.) Roma, 1931.
Phil 3640.275 Nietzsche. (Goedewaagen, T.) 's-Gravenhage, 1933.
Phil 3640.159.5 Nietzsche. (Grützmacher, R.H.) Leipzig, 1921.
Phil 3640.310 Nietzsche. (Guisso, Lorenzo.) Milano, 1942.
Phil 3640.96.5A Nietzsche. (Halévy, D.) Paris, 1944.
Phil 3640.620 Nietzsche. (Heidegger, M.) Pfullingen, 1961. 2v.
Phil 3640.699 Nietzsche. (Heller, E.) Frankfurt am Main, 1964.
Phil 3640.267 Nietzsche. (Jaspers, Karl.) Berlin, 1936.
Phil 3640.355 Nietzsche. (Jungen, F.) Frankfurt, 1949.
Phil 3640.101.5 Nietzsche. (Kennedy, J.M.) London, 1914.
Phil 3640.281.5 Nietzsche. (Lefebvre, H.) Mexico, 1940.
Phil 3640.281 Nietzsche. (Lefebvre, H.) Paris, 1939.
Phil 3640.220 Nietzsche. (Lessing, Theodor.) Berlin, 1925.
Phil 3640.692 Nietzsche. (Martinez Estrada, E.) Buenos Aires, 1947.
Phil 3640.127 Nietzsche. (Meyer, Richard M.) München, 1913.
Phil 3640.102 Nietzsche. (Morr, P.M.) Boston, 1912.
Phil 3640.336 Nietzsche. (Reyburn, Hugh A.) London, 1948.
Phil 3640.168 Nietzsche. (Römer, H.) Leipzig, 1921. 2v.
Phil 3640.570.5 Nietzsche. (Roeschl, Herbert.) Paris, 1960.
Phil 3640.160 Nietzsche. (Schacht, W.) Bern, 1901.
Phil 3640.394A Nietzsche. (Société Française d'Études Nietzschéennes.) Paris, 1950.
Phil 3640.206 Nietzsche. (Tissi, Silvio.) Milano, 1926.
Phil 3640.199 Nietzsche. (Vetter, A.) München, 1926.
Phil 3640.388 Nietzsche. (Würzbach, F.) Berlin, 1942.
Phil 3640.267.4 Nietzsche: an introduction to the understanding of his philosophical activity. (Jaspers, Karl.) Tucson, 1965.
Phil 3640.14.16 Nietzsche. Index. (Nietzsche, Friedrich.) München, 1965.
Phil 3640.368.3 Nietzsche: philosopher, psychologist, antichrist. (Kaufmann, Walter Arnold.) Cleveland, 1964.
Phil 3640.368.4 Nietzsche: philosopher, psychologist, antichrist. 3. ed. (Kaufmann, Walter Arnold.) Princeton, N.J., 1968.
Phil 3640.17.11 Nietzsche. Register. (Oehler, R.) Stuttgart, 1943.
Phil 3640.213.5 Nietzsche: sein Leben und seine Lehre. (Heckel, K.) Leipzig, 1922.
Phil 3640.213 Nietzsche: sein Leben und seine Lehre. (Heckel, K.) Leipzig, 1922.
Phil 3640.703 Nietzsche: the man and his philosophy. (Hollingsdale, Reginald J.) London, 1965.
Phil 3640.282.1 Nietzsche. 1. ed. (Brinton, Clarence Crane.) N.Y., 1965.
Phil 3640.334 Nietzsche. 2e Aufl. (Flake, Otto.) Baden-Baden, 1947.
Phil 3640.267.3 Nietzsche. 2e Aufl. (Jaspers, Karl.) Berlin, 1947.
Phil 3640.357 Nietzsche als Ausnahme. (Götz, K.A.) Freiburg, 1949.
Phil 3640.200.25 Nietzsche als Bildner der Persönlichkeit. (Oehler, Richard.) Leipzig, 1911?
Phil 3640.183 Nietzsche als Erzieher. (Havenstein, M.) Berlin, 1922.
Phil 3640.98.15 Nietzsche als Künstler. (Eckertz, Erich.) München, 1910.
Phil 3640.124 Nietzsche als Moralist und Schriftsteller. (Horneffer, Auguet.) Jena, 1906.
Phil 3640.244 Nietzsche als Philosoph. (Vaihinger, Hans.) Berlin, 1902.
Phil 3640.126.4 Nietzsche als Philosoph. 4e Aufl. (Vaihinger, Hans.) Berlin, 1916.
Phil 3640.406 Nietzsche als Prophet und das Geheimnis des Übermenschen. (Wiser, Edwin.) Affaltern, 1953.
Phil 3640.98.5 Nietzsche and art. (Ludovici, Anthony M.) London, 1911.
Phil 3640.378 Nietzsche and Christian ethics. (Thompson, R.M.) London, 1951.
Phil 3640.396 Nietzsche and the French. (Williams, W.D.) Oxford, 1952.
Phil 3640.109 Nietzsche and the ideals of modern Germany. (Stewart, H.L.) London, 1915.
Phil 3640.236 Nietzsche apostata, oder die Philosophie des Argernisses. (Fischer, Hugo.) Erfurt, 1931.
Phil 3640.28 Nietzsche as critic. (Nietzsche, Friedrich.) N.Y., 1901.
Phil 3640.706 Nietzsche as philosopher. (Danto, Arthur Coleman.) N.Y., 1965.
Phil 3640.259 Nietzsche de goede Europeaan. (Visser, H.L.A.) Zutphen, 1933.
Phil 3640.430 Nietzsche der Atheist und Anti-christ. 4e Aufl. (Siegmund, G.) Paderborn, 1946.
Phil 3640.855 Nietzsche der falsche Prophet. (Schmidt, Otto Ernst.) Leipzig, 1914.
Phil 3640.234 Nietzsche der Gesetzgeber. (Mess, Friedrich.) Leipzig, 1930.
Phil 3640.163.7 Nietzsche der Philosoph des Heroismus. (Weichelt, Hans.) Leipzig, 1924.
Phil 3640.240A Nietzsche der Philosoph und Politiker. (Baeumler, Alfred.) Leipzig, 1931.
Phil 3640.240.3 Nietzsche der Philosoph und Politiker. 3e Aufl. (Baeumler, Alfred.) Leipzig, 1937.
Phil 3640.555 Nietzsche devant ses contemporains. (Bianquis, Genevieve.) Monaco, 1959.
Phil 3640.726 Nietzsche e la letteratura francese. (Vaglia, Anna Teresa.) Brescia, 1967.
Phil 3640.650 Nietzsche éducateur. (Baroni, C.) Paris, 1961.
Phil 3640.295 Nietzsche el conquistador. (Arevalo Martinez, R.) Guatemala, 1943.
Phil 3640.730 Nietzsche en España. (Sobejano, Gónzalo.) Madrid, 1967.
Phil 3640.230 Nietzsche en France; l'influence de Nietzsche sur la pensée française. (Bianquis, G.) Paris, 1929.
Phil 3640.255 Nietzsche en stalie. 15. éd. (Pourtalès, Guy de.) Paris, 1929.
Phil 3640.630 Nietzsche et DuBos. (Savounet, Marie.) Paris, 1960.
Phil 3640.475 Nietzsche et Gide. (Drain, Henri.) Paris, 1932.
Phil 3640.670 Nietzsche et la Philosophie. (Deleuze, Gilles.) Paris, 1962.
Phil 3640.167.2 Nietzsche et la réforme philosophique. 2. éd. (Gaultier, J. de.) Paris, 1904.
Phil 3640.570 Nietzsche et la solitude. (Roeschl, Herbert.) Manosque, 1958.
Phil 3640.805 Nietzsche et l'au-delà de la liberté; Nietzsche et les écrivains français de 1930 à 1960. (Boudot, Pierre.) Paris, 1970.
Phil 3640.780 Nietzsche et le cercle vicieux. (Klossowski, Pierre.) Paris, 1969.
Phil 3640.164 Nietzsche et les théories biologiques contemporaines. 2. éd. (Richter, Claire.) Paris, 1911.
Phil 3640.117.5 Nietzsche et l'immoralisme. (Fouillée, Alfred E.) Paris, 1902.
Phil 3640.117 Nietzsche et l'immoralisme. 3e éd. (Fouillée, Alfred E.) Paris, 1913.
Phil 3640.686 Nietzsche et Valéry. (Gaède, E.) Paris, 1962.
Phil 3640.209 Nietzsche für und gegen Vaihinger. (Liebmann, W.) München, 1923.
Phil 3640.680 Nietzsche in der Hispania; ein Beitrag zur hispanischen Kultur- und Geistesgeschichte. (Rukser, Udo.) Bern, 1962.

Phil 3640.810 Nietzsche in England, 1890-1914. (Thatcher, David S.) Toronto, 1970.
Phil 3640.287 Nietzsche in unserm Jahrhundert. (Michel, W.) Berlin, 1939.
Phil 3640.249 Der Nietzsche-Kultus; eine Kritik. (Tönnies, Ferdinand.) Leipzig, 1897.
Phil 3640.342 Nietzsche och tredje riket. (Johnsson, Milker.) Stockholm, 1943.
Phil 3640.116A Nietzsche the thinker; a study. (Salter, William M.) N.Y., 1917.
Phil 3640.116.2 Nietzsche the thinker; a study. (Salter, William M.) N.Y., 1968.
Phil 3640.709 Nietzsche und Bismarck. (Schieder, Theodor.) Krefeld, 1963.
Phil 3640.305.10 Nietzsche und Burckhardt; zwei geistige Welten im Dialog. 3e Aufl. (Martin, A.W.O. von.) Basel, 1945.
Phil 3640.247 Nietzsche und Christus. (Jesinghaus, W.) Berlin, 1913.
Phil 3640.267.5 Nietzsche und das Christentum. (Jaspers, Karl.) Hameln, 1946.
Phil 3640.253 Nietzsche und das gegenwärtige Geistesleben. (Beckenhaupt, D.) Leipzig, 1931.
Phil 3640.307 Nietzsche und das Labyrinth. (Roos, Carl Nissen.) Copenhagen, 1940.
Phil 3640.445 Nietzsche und das Problem der dichterischen Sprache. (Olzien, Otto H.) Berlin, 1941.
Phil 3640.298 Nietzsche und das Recht. (Kassler, K.) München, 1941.
Phil 3640.229 Nietzsche und das XX Jahrhundert. (Prinzhorn, Hans.) Heidelberg, 1928.
Phil 3640.280 Nietzsche und der Nationalsozialismus. 2e Aufl. (Härtle, H.) München, 1939.
Phil 3640.238 Nietzsche und die Frauen. (Brann, H.W.) Leipzig, 1931.
Phil 3640.416 Nietzsche und die poetische Lüge. (Bindschedler, M.B.) Basel, 1954.
Phil 3640.800 Nietzsche und die Rhetorik. (Goth, Joachim.) Tübingen, 1970.
Phil 3640.94.5 Nietzsche und die Romantik. (Joël, Karl.) Jena, 1905.
Phil 3640.94.6 Nietzsche und die Romantik. 2. Aufl. (Joël, Karl.) Jena, 1923.
Phil 3640.90.7 Nietzsche und die Schweiz. (Bernoulli, Carl A.) Leipzig, 1922.
Phil 3640.246 Nietzsche und die Vergeltungsidee. (Kerler, D.H.) Ulm, 1910.
Phil 3640.398 Nietzsche und die Verwandlung des Menschen. (Pannwitz, Rudolf.) Amsterdam, 1939.
Phil 3640.505 Nietzsche und die Verwandlung des Menschen. (Pannwitz, Rudolf.) Amsterdam, 1943.
Phil 3640.262 Nietzsche und George. (Rosengarth, W.) Leipzig, 1934.
Phil 3640.158.5 Nietzsche und Jakob Burckhardt. (Andler, Charles.) Basel, 1926.
Phil 3640.198.15 Nietzsche und Klages. Inaug. Diss. (Ellermann, H.) Hamburg, 1933.
Phil 3640.252 Nietzsche und Rousseau. Inaug. Diss. (Kramer, H.G.) Borna, 1928.
Phil 3640.393 Nietzsche und sein Zarathustra in psychiatrischer Beleuchtung. (Kesselring, M.) Aehren Verlag, 1954.
Phil 3640.157 Nietzsche und Strindberg. (Strecker, Karl.) München, 1921.
Phil 3640.258 Nietzsche und Wagner. (Dippel, P.G.) Bern, 1934.
Phil 3640.184 Nietzsche und Wagner. (Griesser, Luitpold.) Wien, 1923.
Phil 3640.159.15 Nietzsche und wir Christen. (Grützmacher, R.H.) Berlin, 1910.
Phil 3640.418 Nietzsche vivant. (Dournes, P.) n.p., 1948.
Phil 3640.121.5 Nietzsche-Vorträge. (Horneffer, Ernst.) Leipzig, 1920.
Phil 3640.88.10 The Nietzsche-Wagner correspondence. (Förster-Nietzsche, E.) N.Y., 1921.
Phil 3640.830 Nietzsche y el fin de la religión. (Massuh, Victor.) Buenos Aires, 1969.
Phil 3640.605 Nietzscheova tragedie. (Nejedlý, Zdeněk.) Vinohrady, 1926.
Phil 3640.76.5 Nietzsche, Friedrich. Friedrich Nietzsches Briefe an Mutter und Schwester. Leipzig, 1909. 2v.
Phil 3640.79.100 Nietzscheregister. (Oehler, Richard.) Leipzig, 1926.
Phil 3640.79.105 Nietzscheregister. (Oehler, Richard.) Stuttgart, 1943.
Phil 3640.79.107 Nietzscheregister. (Oehler, Richard.) Stuttgart, 1965.
Phil 3640.81 Nietzsches Asthetik. (Zeitler, Julius.) Leipzig, 1900.
Phil 3640.560 Nietzsches Atheismus und das Christentum. (Welke, Bernhard.) Darmstadt, 1958.
Phil 3640.97 Nietzsches Bild. (Fischer, W.) München, 1911.
Phil 3640.76.9 Nietzsches Briefe. (Nietzsche, Friedrich.) Leipzig, 1917.
Phil 3640.122.5 Nietzsche's Erkenntnistheorie und Metaphysik. (Eisler, Rudolf.) Leipzig, 1902.
Phil 3640.197 Nietzsches estetik. (Ekman, Karl.) Helsingfors, 1920.
Phil 3640.408 Nietzsches grosser Mittag. (Schlechta, Karl.) Frankfurt, 1954.
Phil 3640.232 Nietzsches Idee der Kultur. (Brock, Werner.) Bonn, 1930.
Phil 3640.485 Nietzsches Ideen zur Geschichte des Christentum wider der Kirche. (Benz, Ernst.) Leiden, 1956.
Phil 3640.520 Nietzsches Kampf gegen den göttlichen Zwang. (Klein, Werner.) Stuttgart, 1940.
Phil 3640.186 Nietzsches Kampf um den Sinn des Lebens. (Reininger, R.) Wien, 1922.
Phil 3640.770 Nietzsches Kritik des Ich-denke. (Dickopp, Karl-Heinz.) Bonn, 1965.
Phil 3640.713 Nietzsches Kunde vom Tode Gottes. (Siegmund, Georg.) Berlin, 1964.
Phil 3640.84 Nietzsches Lehre. (Ewald, Oscar.) Berlin, 1903.
Phil 3640.725 Nietzsches Lehre vom Verbrecher. Inaug. Diss. (Stobbe, Erhard.) Marburg, 1964.
Phil 3640.190.30 Nietzsches Metaphysik. (Bélart, Hans.) Berlin, 1904.
Phil 3640.180 Nietzsches Persönlichkeit und Lehre. (Spindler, Josef.) Stuttgart, 1913.
Phil 3640.83 Nietzsches Philosophie. (Drews, Arthur.) Heidelberg, 1904.
Phil 3640.682 Nietzsches Philosophie. (Heftrich, Eckhard.) Frankfurt, 1962.
Phil 3640.374 Nietzsches Philosophie. (Schoeck, H.) Tübingen, 1948.
Phil 3640.174 Nietzsche's Philosophie. 2. Aufl. (Düringer, Adelbert.) Leipzig, 1906.
Phil 3640.785 Nietzsches Philosophie. 2e Aufl. (Fink, Eugen.) Köln, 1968.
Phil 3640.261.10 Nietzsches Philosophie der ewigen Wieder kehr des Gleichen. (Löwith, Karl.) Stuttgart, 1956.
Phil 3640.261.5A Nietzsches Philosophie der ewigen Wiederkunft des Gleichen. (Löwith, Karl.) Berlin, 1935.
Phil 3640.836 Nietzsches Philosophie im Lichte unserer Erfahrung. (Mann, Thomas.) Berlin, 1948.
Phil 3640.22.8 Nietzsche's Philosophie in Selbstzeugnissen. (Nietzsche, Friedrich.) Leipzig, 1931. 4v.

Phil 3640.245 Nietzsches Philosophie und das neutige Christentum. (Düringer, Adelbert.) Leipzig, 1907.

Phil 3640.200 Nietzsches philosophisches Werden. (Oehler, Richard.) München, 1926.

Phil 3640.222 Nietzsches Professur in Basel. (Stroux, Johannes.) Jena, 1925.

Phil 3640.580 Nietzsches Raatsauffassung. (Binder, J.) Göttingen, 1925.

Phil 3640.433 Nietzsches religiöse Entwicklung. (Augustin, G.) Stuttgart, 1936.

Phil 3640.247.5 Nietzsches Stellung zu Weib. 3e Aufl. (Jesinghaus, W.) Leipzig, 1907.

Phil 3640.325 Nietzsches Stellung zur christlichen Demut. Inaug. Diss. (Hauff, R. von.) Tübingen, 1939.

Phil 3640.284 Nietzsches "System" in seinen Grundbegriffen. (Heintel, E.) Leipzig, 1939.

Phil 3640.178.5 Nietzsches Welt und Lebensanschauung. (Ritschl, Otto.) Freiburg, 1899.

Phil 3640.178 Nietzsches Welt und Lebensanschauung. 2. Aufl. (Ritschl, Otto.) Leipzig, 1899.

Phil 3640.165 Nietzsches Weltkampf mit Sokrates und Plato. (Hildebrandt, K.) Dresden, 1922.

Phil 3640.22 Nietzsche's Werke. v.2-4. (Nietzsche, Friedrich.) Leipzig, 1931. 3v.

Phil 3640.239 Nietzsches Wirkung und Erbe. (Rauch, Karl.) Berlin, 1930.

Phil 3640.299 Nietzsches Würdigung des Menschen. (Umland, Karl.) Würzburg, 1930.

Phil 3640.274 Nietzsches Zarathustra; Gehalt und Gestalt. (Siegel, Carl.) München, 1938.

Phil 3640.235 Nietzsches Zusammenbruch. (Podach, Erich F.) Heidelberg, 1930.

Phil 3585.20.4 Nieuwe inleiding tot de existentiële fenomenologie. (Luijpen, Wilhelmus Antonius Maria.) Utrecht, 1969.

Phil 2475.1.211 "De nieuwe wijsbegeerte." Een studie over Henri Bergson. (Hoogveld, J.E.H.J.) Utrecht, 1915.

Phil 5053.2 Nieuwenhuis, Jacobi. Initia philosophiae logicae. Lugdunum Batavorum, 1831.

Phil 3665.4.30 Nieuwenlijt, B. Gronden van zekerheid of Die regte betooguyse der wiskundigen. Amsterdam, 1728.

Phil 8668.2 Nieuwentijt, B. L'existence de Dieu. Paris, 1725.

Phil 8593.5.7 Nieuwentyt, B. Het regt gebruik der werelt beschouwingen. 4. druk. Amsterdam, 1725.

NEDL Phil 8593.5 Nieuwentyt, B. The religious philosopher. London, 1719. 3v.

Phil 8593.5.2 Nieuwentyt, B. The religious philosopher. London, 1730. 3v.

Phil 8586.36.80 Nievergelt, Hans-Ulrich. Hutorität und Begegnung. Zürich, 1963.

Phil 270.25 Nieuwe oplossing van een oud vraagstuk. (L'Ange Huet, J.) Leiden, 1872.

Phil 8593.20.5 Nigg, Walter. Prophetische Denker. Zürich, 1957.
Phil 8593.20.2 Nigg, Walter. Religiöse Denker. Berlin, 1952.
Phil 8593.20 Nigg, Walter. Religiöse Denker. Bern, 1942.
Phil 7060.36 Night side of nature. (Crowe, C.S.) London, n.p.
Phil 7060.36.7 The night-side of nature. (Crowe, C.S.) N.Y., 1853.
Phil 8888.3 Nihell, L. Rational self-love. Limerick, 1770.
Phil 535.16 Nihilism, its origin and nature, with a Christian answer. 1st ed. (Thielicke, H.) N.Y., 1961.

Phil 535.45 Nihilism: a philosophical essay. (Rosen, Stanley.) New Haven, 1969.

Phil 1955.6.125 The nihilism of John Dewey. (Crosser, P.K.) N.Y., 1955.
Phil 535.40 Nihilisme en cultuur. (Goudsblom, Johan.) Amsterdam, 1960.
Phil 535.30 Nihilismus. (Arendt, Dieter.) Köln, 1970.
Phil 535.15 Der Nihilismus. (Thielicke, H.) Tübingen, 1950.
Phil 535.5 Der Nihilismus im Licht einer kritischen Philosophie. (Levin-Goldschmidt, Hermann.) Thayngen, 1941.

Phil 535.10 Der Nihilismus und die Welt. (Pannwitz, R.) Nürnberg, 1951.

Phil 4520.8.36 Níjtánda öldin. (Bjarnason, Ágúst.) Reykjavík, 1906.
Phil 344.6 Nikitin, Evgenii P. Ob"iasnenie - funktsiia nauki. Moskva, 1970.

Phil 8593.13 Nikolai, Pavel N. Mozhet-li sovremennyi obrazovannyi, mysliashchii cheloviek vierit' v bozhectvo Iisusa Khrista. 3. izd. Praga, 1923.

Phil 4756.2.35 Nikolai Fedorovich Fedorov i sovremennost'. v.1-3. (Ostromirov, A.) Kharbin, 1928.

Phil 4757.4 Nikolai Iakovlevich Grot v ocherkakh, vospominaniiakh i pis'makh tovarishchei. Sankt Peterburg, 1911.

Phil 1713.5 Nikolajević, Sietamir B. Misao kas odraz vremens. Beograd, 1971.

Phil 2733.93 Nikolaus Malebranche. (Stieler, Georg.) Stuttgart, 1925.
Phil 1750.115.75 Nikolov, Elit I. Fenomenologiia i estetika. Sofiia, 1965.
Phil 2630.2.129 Nilsson, A. Guyaus estetik. Lund, 1909.
Phil 8593.22 Nilsson, M.P. Fondamenti di scienza delle religioni. 1. ed. Firenze, 1950.

Phil 5590.195 Ninck, M. Schicksal und Charakter. Wien, 1956.
Phil 6536.5 Ninde, F.W. The application of the auditory memory test to two thousand institut'l epileptics. West Chester, 1924?

Phil 3246.190 Nindelband, N. Fichte's Idee des deutschen Staates. Tübingen, 1921.

Phil 8423.11 Nine basic arts. (Weiss, Paul.) Carbondale, 1961.
Phil 1560.12 Nine medieval thinkers. (O'Donnell, J. Reginald.) Toronto, 1955.

Phil 8967.7.5 Nine modern moralists. (Ramsey, Paul.) Englewood, 1962.
Phil 9150.23 Nineteenth century evolution and after. (Dawson, M.) N.Y., 1923.

Phil 4962.5 Niñez y filosofía. (Abad Carretero, Luis.) México, 1957.
Phil 344.3 Nink, Caspar. Grundlegung der Erkenntnistheorie. Frankfurt am Main, 1930.

Phil 3425.265A Nink, Caspar. Kommentar zu den grundlegenden Abschnitten von Hegels Phänomenologie des Geistes. Regensburg, 1931.

Phil 3495.12 Nink, Casper. Kommentar zu Kants Kritik der reinen Vernunft. Frankfurt, 1930.

Phil 8668.6 Nink, Gaspar. Philosophische Gotteslehre. München, 1948.
Phil 8581.10.9 The ninth Bridgewater treatise. 2. ed. (Babbage, C.) London, 1838.

Phil 8581.11 The ninth Bridgewater treatise. 2. ed. (Babbage, C.) London, 1838.

Phil 8832.4A Nippon shindo ron; or, The national ideals of the Japanese people. (Hibino, Yutaka.) Cambridge, Eng., 1928.

Phil 8520.20 Nirenstein, S. The problem of the existence of God, in Maimonides, Alanus and Averroes. Philadelphia, 1924.

Phil 6123.6 Nisbet, J.F. The human machine. London, 1899.
Phil 5425.3 Nisbet, J.F. Insanity of genius. London, 1891.
Phil 5440.2 Nisbet, J.F. Marriage and heredity. London, 1889.
Phil 1955.6.215 Nissen, Lowell. John Dewey's theory of inquiry and truth. The Hague, 1966.

Phil 3552.283 Nithack, A. Darstellung und Kritik der Lehre Leibniz' von der menschlichen Wahlfreiheit. Inaug. Diss. Halle, 1893.

Phil 801.27.20 Nitjánda äldin. (Bjarnason, A.) Reykjavik, 1906.
Phil 5053.5.2 Nitsche, Adolf. Lehrbuch der Logik. 2e Aufl. Innsbruck, 1890.

Phil 5635.23 Nitsche, Adolf. Versuch einer einheitlichen Lehre von der Gefühlin. Innsbruck, 1886.

Phil 1518.5 Nitsche, August. Naturer Kenntnis und politisches Handeln im Mittelalter. Körpen, 1967.

Phil 5870.117 Nitschke, Alfred. Das verwaiste Kind der Natur. 2. Aufl. Tübingen, 1968.

Phil 3640.711 Nitsshe. (Solov'ev, Evgenii A.) Sankt Peterburg, 1902.
Phil 9450.45 Nitze, P.H. The recovery of ethics. N.Y., 1960.
Phil 8888.11 Nivard, M. Ethica. Paris, 1928.
Phil 8881.74 Les niveaux de la vie morale. 1. éd. (Gobry, Ivan.) Paris, 1956.

Phil 5590.458 Niveaux d'aspiration et d'expectation. (Robaye, Francine.) Paris, 1957.

Phil 5722.24 Les niveaux de conscience et d'inconscient et leurs intercommunications. (Lubac, Émile.) Paris, 1929.

Phil 175.59 Les niveaux de l'être la connaissance et le mal. (Amado Levy-Valensi, E.) Paris, 1962.

Phil 6125.30 Niveaux de tension et contrôle de l'activité. (Perron, Roger.) Paris, 1961.

Phil 8125.37 Nivelle, A. Kunst- und Dichtungstheorien zwischen Aufklärung und Klassik. Berlin, 1960.

Phil 8125.37.2 Nivelle, A. Kunst- und Dichtungstheorien zwischen Aufklärung und Klassik. 2. Aufl. Berlin, 1971.

Phil 8125.37.5 Nivelle, A. Les théories esthétiques en Allemagne de Baumgarten à Kant. Paris, 1955.

Phil 8980.610F Nivison, A. S. Communist ethics and Chinese tradition. Cambridge, Mass., 1954.

Phil 2775.2.30 Nizan, Paul. Les chiens de garde. Paris, 1960.
Phil 488.1 Nizan, Paul. Les matérialistes de l'antiquité. Paris, 1936.

Phil 488.1.5 Nizan, Paul. Les matérialistes de l'antiquité. Paris, 1965.

Phil 4180.1 Nizzoli, Mario. De veris principiis et vera ratione philosophandi contra pseudophilosophos. Roma, 1956. 2v.

Phil 7055.388 No mundo de Chico Xavier. (Barbosa, Elia.) São Paulo, 1968.

Phil 9495.164.10 No new morality. (Rhymes, D.A.) Indianapolis, Ind., 1964.
Htn Phil 665.5* No praexistence. (Warren, E.) London, 1667.
Phil 8598.12.9 No refuge but in truth. (Smith, Goldwin.) N.Y., 1909.
Phil 978.39 No revelation infallible. (Hume, A.C.) Calcutta, 1883.
Phil 3013.2 Noack, H. Deutsche Geisteswelt. Darmstadt, 1955. 2v.
Phil 8593.24 Noack, H. Sprache und Offenbarung. Gütersloh, 1960.
Phil 1750.732 Noack, Hermann. Die Philosophie Westeuropus. Basel, 1962.
Phil 8610.853 Noack, L. Die Freidenker in der Religion. pt.3. Bern, 1853-55.

Phil 813.3 Noack, L. Geschichte der Philosophie. Weimar, 1853.
Phil 3495.8 Noack, L. I. Kant's Auferstehung aus dem Grabe. Leipzig, 1861.

Phil 98.1 Noack, L. Philosophie-Geschichtliches Lexikon. Leipzig, 1879.

Phil 188.3 Noack, L. Propädeutik der Philosophie. Weimar, 1854.
Phil 525.12.7 Noack, Ludwig. Die christliche Mystik. Königsberg, 1853.
Phil 3246.203 Noack, Ludwig. Johann Gottlieb Fichte nach seinen Leben, Lehren und Wirken. Leipzig, 1862.

Phil 3425.263 Noack, Ludwig. Der Religions begriff Hegel's. Darmstadt, 1845.

Htn Phil 3801.612* Noack, Ludwig. Schelling und der Philosophie des Romantik. Berlin, 1859. 2v.

Phil 3801.612.2 Noack, Ludwig. Schelling und der Philosophie des Romantik. v.1-2. Berlin, 1859.

Phil 2225.1.80 Noah Porters Erkenntnislehre. (Judd, W.B.) Jena, 1897.
Phil 5258.202 Nobel Conference, 3d, Gustavus Adolphus College, 1967. The human mind. Amsterdam, 1967.

Phil 585.280 Nobel Conference, 4th, Gustavus Adolphus College. The uniqueness of man. Amsterdam, 1969.

Phil 5465.198 Nobel Conference, 6th, Gustavus Adolphus College, 1970. Creativity. Amsterdam, 1970.

Phil 9245.39 Nobile, Flamineo. De hominis felicitate libri treo. Lucae, 1563.

Phil 4225.8.80 Nobile-Ventura, Attilio. Crisi dell'uomo e conquista. Milano, 1958.

Phil 4180.2 Nobile-Ventura, Attilio. La maschera e il volto della nostra società. Milano, 1965.

Phil 4225.8.102 Nobile-Ventura, Attilio. Colloquio con Michele Federico Sciacca. Milano, 1966.

Phil 4080.17.5 Nobile Ventura, O.M. Filosofia e religione in un metafisico laico. 1. ed. Milano, 1951.

Phil 8888.9 Nobili-Vitelleschi, F. Morale induttiva. Roma, 1882-91. 4v.

Phil 9560.15 Nobilta commune, et heroica penser nuova é curiosa. (Zuccolo, L.) Venetia, 1625.

Phil 6123.2 Noble, D. The brain and its physiology. London, 1846.
Phil 1813.5 Noble, D.W. The paradox of progressive thought. Minneapolis, 1958.

Phil 5933.1 Noble, Daniel. An inquiry into the claims of phrenology, to rank among the sciences. Manchester, 1837.

Phil 365.20A Noble, Edmund. Purposive evolution. N.Y., 1926.
Phil 960.17.5 Noble, M.E. Kali the mother. London, 1900.
Phil 960.17 Noble, M.E. Religion and dharma. London, 1915.
Phil 8668.8 Noce, Augusto del. Il problema dell'ateismo. 2. ed. Bologna, 1964.

Phil 2520.352 Noce, Augusto del. Riforma cattolica e filosofia moderna. Bologna, 1965.

Phil 192.79 Nociones de alta critica. (Restrepo, D.) Manziales, 1937.
Phil 184.14 Nociones de filosofia. (Jourdain, Charles.) Valparaiso, 1870.

Phil 5061.2 Nociones de lógica. (Varona, E.J.) Habana, 1902.
Phil 8892.20 Nociones fundamentales de ética ó filosofía moral. (Riego, Julio del.) Madrid, 1903.

Phil 805.20 Noções de história da filosofia. (Franca, Leonel.) Rio de Janeiro, 1967.

Phil 978.14 Nodern priestess of Isis. (Solovef, V.S.) London, 1895.
Phil 3425.99 Noël, G. La logique de Hegel. Paris, 1897.
Phil 2515.6 Noël, J. Un philosophie belge, Colins. Mons, 1909.
Phil 630.47 Noël, L. Le réalisme immédiat. Louvain, 1938.
Phil 8638.1 Noel, R. Philosophy of immortality. London, 1882.
Phil 6750.26 Noel, R.R. Physical basis of mental life. London, 1873.
Phil 2270.113 Nöll, Heinrich. Intentionalität, Reaktivität und Schwachsinn. Halle, 1909.

VPhil 337.29 Nörregård, Jens. Studier over Spencer, Lotze og Grundtvig. København, 1890.

Phil 6331.7 Le noeu suprême de Socrate. (Viard, Marcel.) Paris, 1953.

Phil 2905.1.665 — Nogare, Pedro Dalle. Pessoa e amor segundo Teilhard de Chardin. São Paulo, 1970.

Phil 8592.33 — Noget om determinisme og frihed. (Møller, Otto.) Kjøbenhavn, 1893.

Phil 5374.158 — Nogué, J. Essai sur l'activité primitive du moi. Paris, 1936.

Phil 5374.158.5 — Nogué, J. Essai sur l'activité primitive du moi. Thèse. Paris, 1936.

Phil 5640.41 — Nogué, Jean. Esquisse d'un système des qualités sensibles. Paris, 1943.

Phil 5585.64 — Nogué, Jean. La signification du sensible. Paris, 1936.

Phil 5585.64.5 — Nogué, Jean. La signification du sensible. Thèse. Paris, 1936.

Phil 4967.20.80 — Nogueira, A. Farias Brito e a filosofia do espírito. Rio de Janeiro, 1962.

Phil 5525.65 — Nohain, Jean. Histoire du rure à travers le monde. Paris, 1965.

Phil 8050.75 — Nohl, H. Die ästhetische Wirklichkeit; eine Einfuhrung. 2. Aufl. Frankfurt, 1954.

Phil 188.18 — Nohl, H. Einführung in die Philosophie. Frankfurt, 1935.

Phil 188.18.5 — Nohl, H. Einführung in die Philosophie. 5. Aufl. Frankfurt, 1953.

Phil 9035.79 — Nohl, Herman. Charakter und Schicksal. Frankfurt, 1938.

Phil 5545.193 — Nohl, Johanna. Erinnerung und Gedächtnis. Langensalza, 1932.

Phil 6750.6 — Noir, J. Étude sur les tics. Paris, 1893.

Phil 813.2.5 — Noiré, L. Die Entwickelung der abendländischen Philosophie Critik der reinen Vernunft. Mainz, 1883.

Phil 3495.5 — Noiré, L. Die Lehre Kants...Vermorst. Mainz, 1882.

Phil 813.2.3 — Noiré, L. A sketch...development of philosophical thought. London, 1908.

Phil 188.4 — Noire, L. Die Welt als Entwicklung des Geistes. Leipzig, 1874.

Phil 510.9.6 — Noiré, Ludwig. Aphorismen zur monistischen Philosophie. 2. ed. Mainz, 1884.

Phil 270.20 — Noiré, Ludwig. Die Doppelnatur der Causalität. Leipzig, 1875.

Phil 510.9.10 — Noiré, Ludwig. Einleitung und Begründung einer monistischen Erkenntnis-Theorie. Mainz, 1877.

Phil 510.9.11 — Noiré, Ludwig. Einleitung und Begründung einer monistischen Erkenntnis-Theorie. 2e Ausg. Mainz, 1884.

Phil 5520.32 — Noiré, Ludwig. Logos; Ursprung und Wesen der Begriffe. Leipzig, 1885.

Phil 510.9 — Noiré, Ludwig. Der monistische Gedanke. Leipzig, 1875.

Phil 5520.32.5 — Noiré, Ludwig. Origin of language and logos theory. 2. ed. Chicago, 1899.

Phil 5650.22 — Noise. (McLachlan, Norman W.) London, 1935.

Phil 5650.50 — Noise and man. (Burns, William.) London, 1968.

Phil 8888.8 — Nolan, Preston M. Pertinent and impertinent. Chicago, 1923.

Phil 3495.4 — Nolen, D. Critique de Kant. Paris, 1875.

Phil 3552.281 — Nolen, Désiré. Quid Leibniz uis Aristoteli debuerit. Parisiis, 1875.

Phil 2805.201 — Nolhac, P. de. Pascal en Auvergne. Saint-Felicien-en-Vivarais, 1925.

Phil 745.5 — Noll, Alfred. Die "Lebenskraft" in der Schriften der Vitalisten und ihrer Gegner. Leipzig, 1914.

Phil 3640.422 — Noll, B. Zeitalter der Feste. Bonn, 1947.

Phil 3665.6.30 — Noll, Baldwin. Philosophie und Politik. Bonn, 1953.

Phil 3640.440 — Noll, Baldwin. Das Wesen von Friedrich Nietzsches Idealismus. Köln, 1940.

Phil 3450.19.242 — Noller, Gerhard. Heidegger und die Theologie. München, 1967.

Phil 3450.19.240 — Noller, Gerhard. Sein und Existenz. München, 1962.

Phil 8414.7 — Nolte, Fred O. Art and reality. Lancaster, 1942.

Phil 6323.26 — Nolte, Helmut. Psychoanalyse und Soziologie. Bern, 1970.

Phil 5253.9 — Noltenius, F. Die Gefühlswerte. Leipzig, 1927.

Phil 5066.26.5 — Nomalogical statements and admissable operations. (Reichenbach, H.) Amsterdam, 1954.

Phil 1182.30 — Le nombre d'or. v.1-2. (Ghyks, M.C.) Paris, 1952.

Phil 8905.32 — Nome, John. Kritisk forskerholdning i etikk og religionsfilosofi. Oslo, 1970.

Phil 1540.9 — Die nominalisirende Psychologie der Scholastik des späteren Mittelalters. (Werner, Karl.) Wien, 1882.

Phil 1504.8.5 — Der Nominalismus in der Frühscholastik. v.8, pt.5. (Reiners, J.) Münster, n.d.

Phil 3018.11 — Nominalismus und Realismus in der neuesten deutschen Philosophie. (Spitzer, Hugo.) Leipzig, 1876.

Phil 630.64 — Nominalistic systems. (Eberle, Rolf A.) Dordrecht, 1970.

Phil 5057.32 — Nomological statements and admissible operations. (Reichenbach, Hans.) Amsterdam, 1954.

Phil 1145.85 — Nomos und physis. (Heinimann, Felix.) Basel, 1945.

Phil 4803.454.65F — Nomothétique messianique. (Hoene-Wroński, Józef Maria.) Paris, 1881.

Phil 5058.28.9 — Non-Aristotelian logic. (Smith, Henry B.) Philadelphia, 1919.

Phil 1980.6 — Non-linguistic philosophy. (Ewing, Alfred Cyril.) London, 1968.

Phil 8586.8.5 — The non-religion of the future. (Guyau, M.J.) London, 1897.

Phil 5125.32 — Nondeductive inference. (Ackermann, Robert John.) London, 1966.

Phil 4215.3.83 — Nonis, Piero. La scepsi etica di Giuseppe Rensi. Roma, 1957.

Phil 8593.7 — Nonnotte, Claude. Dictionnaire philosophique de la religion. n.p., 1772. 4v.

Phil 3745.9 — De noodzaak. (Poortman, J.J.) Assen, 1936.

Phil 5031.1 — De noodzakelijkheid eener christelijke logica. (Vollenhoven, D.H.T.) Amsterdam, 1932.

Phil 5875.90 — Nooteboom, Wilhelmina E. Some psychological aspects of the chorcatiform syndrome: development of the intelligence. Assen, 1967.

Phil 1813.10 — Norak, Michael. American philosophy and the future. N.Y., 1968.

Phil 9035.101 — Norakidze, Vladimir. Tipy kharaktera i fiksirovannaia ustanovka. Tbilisi, 1966.

Phil 9035.111 — Norakidze, Vladimir G. Temperament lichnosti i fiksiorovannaia ustanovka. Tbilisi, 1970.

Phil 2340.1.80 — Norbert Wiener. (Maron, M.E.) Santa Monica, Calif., 1965.

Phil 5627.156 — Norborg, S. Varieties of Christian experience. Minneapolis, 1938.

Phil 2250.91 — Norborg, Sven. Josiah Royce. Oslo, 1934.

Phil 5425.7.10 — Nordau, M. Degeneration. 2. ed. N.Y., 1895.

Phil 5425.7.12 — Nordau, M. Degeneration. 4. ed. N.Y., 1895.

Phil 5425.7.12.5 — Nordau, M. Degeneration. 5. ed. London, 1895.

NEDL Phil 5425.7.13 — Nordau, M. Degeneration. 6. ed. London, 1895.

Phil 5425.7.5 — Nordau, M. Dégénérescence. Paris, 1894. 2v.

Phil 5425.7.3 — Nordau, M. Entartung. 2. Aufl. Berlin, 1893. 2v.

Phil 8888.7.10 — Nordau, Max. La biologie de l'éthique. Paris, 1930.

Phil 8888.7 — Nordau, Max. Morals and the evolution of man. London, 1922.

Phil 2055.1.81 — Norden, Joseph. Die Ethik Henry Homes. Inaug. Diss. Halle, 1895.

Phil 188.14.5 — Nordenholz, A. Scientologie. München, 1934.

Phil 188.14.7 — Nordenholz, A. Scientologie. München, 1937.

Phil 188.14 — Nordenholz, A. Welt als Individuation. Leipzig, 1927.

Phil 23.18.5 — Nordisk Psykologi. Register, 1949-1960. København, n.d.

Phil 23.18 — Nordisk psykologi. København. 1,1949+ 9v.

Phil 5520.310 — Nordisk Sommeruniversitet. Betydningsproblemer. Oslo, 1954.

Phil 2520.141 — Nordlindh, Arvid. Descates' lära om känslan. Akademisk afhaudling. Upsala, 1897.

Phil 672.142 — Nordmann, Charles. Notre maître le temps. Paris, 1924.

Phil 672.142.5 — Nordmann, Charles. The tyranny of time. London, 1925.

Phil 5640.20 — Nordvall, A.L. Psykologiska studier. Stockholm, 1885.

Phil 3833.3 — Nordwall, A.L. De Spinozismi initiis aphorismi. Upsaliae, 1852.

Phil 8888.10 — Nordwall, Adolf L. Om ethikens problem och de vigtigaste försäken att lösa detsamma. Upsala, 1852.

Phil 3425.222 — Norelius, G. Grunddragen af Hegels filosofi och ästetik. Norrköping, 1893.

Phil 3495.8.5 — Norelius, G. Om Kants sedelära. Upsala, 1889.

Phil 4372.1.135 — Noreña, Carlos G. Juan Luis Vives. The Hague, 1970.

Phil 3833.5 — Norinder, A.V. Försök till en framställning, af Spinozismens nufvidsatser. Upsala, 1851.

Phil 8668.3 — Norlin, C. Etude laique de la notion de Dieu. Paris, 1906.

Phil 8897.85 — Norm and action. (Wright, G.H. von.) London, 1963.

Phil 5520.642 — Norm and order; an investigation into logic, semantics, and the theory of law and morals. (Brkić, Jovan.) N.Y., 1970.

Phil 3120.40.50 — De norm der waarheid is in ons-zelf. (Bierens de Haan, J.D.) Utrecht, 1897.

Phil 8955.4 — The norm of morality. Diss. (Flynn, V.S.) Washington, 1928.

Phil 5886.20 — Normal aging: reports from the Duke longitudinal study, 1955-1969. (Duke University. Center for the Study of Aging and Human Development.) Durham, N.C., 1970.

Phil 5259.28 — The normal person. (Torrey, D.C.) Jaffrey, New Hampshire, 1927.

Phil 5374.39 — Das normale Bewusstsein. (Müller, R.) Leipzig, 1898.

Phil 5243.50 — Der normale Mensch im Urteil der Psychiatrie. (Dobbelstein, Herman.) Einsiedeln, 1955.

Phil 177.54 — La normalienne en philosophie. (Corbeil, S.) Montreal, 1914.

Phil 5648.5 — Normaltäuschungen in der Lagewahrnehmung. (Spearman, C.) Leipzig, 1905.

Phil 7053.344 — Norman, Diana. Tom Corbett's stately ghosts of England. N.Y., 1970.

Phil 5545.240 — Norman, Donald A. Memory and attention. N.Y., 1968[1969]

Phil 9215.2 — Norman, Richard. Reasons for actions: a critique of utilitarian rationality. Oxford, 1971.

Phil 735.240 — Normative discourse. (Taylor, Paul.) Englewood, 1961.

Phil 5068.82 — Normative logic and ethics. (Lorenzen, Paul.) Mannheim, 1969.

Phil 3450.39.30 — Die Normen des Seins. (Hirsch, Wolfgang.) Amsterdam, 1959?

Phil 8889.8.10 — Normy moralne. (Ossowska, Maria.) Warszawa, 1970.

Phil 585.410 — Nornengast, Urda. Der androgyne Mensch. Bellnhausen, 1970.

Phil 188.5.2 — Norris, J. Essay towards the theory of the world. London, 1701-1704. 2v.

Htn Phil 2175.2.55* — Norris, John. An essay towards the theory of the ideal or intelligible world. pt.1-2. London, 1701-04. 2v.

Htn Phil 2175.2.40* — Norris, John. An essay towards the theory of the world. London, 1701. 2v.

Phil 8638.3 — Norris, John. A philosophical discourse...natural immortality. London, 1708.

Htn Phil 2175.2.35* — Norris, John. The picture of love unveil'd. 4. ed. London, 1744.

Htn Phil 2175.2.49* — Norris, John. Reflections on the conduct of human life. London, 1690.

Htn Phil 2175.2.45* — Norris, John. Reflections on the conduct of human life. 2nd ed. London, 1691-93. 2 pam.

Htn Phil 2175.2.30* — Norris, John. The theory and regulation of love. Oxford, 1688.

Phil 5520.71 — Norris, Tom C. Thought and speech. London, 1938.

Phil 4215.1.87 — Norsa, Achille. Il pensiero filosofico di Giandomenico Romagnosi. Milano, 1930.

Phil 5325.46 — Norske ord-assosiasjonsnormer. (Håseth, Kjell Johan.) Oslo, 1969.

Phil 4610.7.85 — Norström, V. Brev, 1889-1916. Stockholm, 1923.

Phil 4610.7.18 — Norström, V. Hvad är sanning. Göteborg, 1899.

Phil 4610.7.35 — Norström, V. Hvad vi behöfva. Stockholm, 1901.

Phil 4610.7.38 — Norström, V. Masskultur. Stockholm, 1910.

Phil 4610.7.33 — Norström, V. Naturkunskapens självbesinning. Stockholm, 1907.

Phil 4610.7.50 — Norström, V. Den nyaste människan. Stockholm, 1906.

Phil 4610.7.32 — Norström, V. Om natursammanhang och frihet. Göteborg, 1895.

Phil 4610.7.31 — Norström, V. Om pligt, frihet och förnuft. Upsala, 1891.

Phil 4610.7.40 — Norström, V. Om viljans frihet. Stockholm, 1917.

Phil 4610.7.15 — Norström, V. Religion och tanke. Stockholm, 1912.

Phil 4610.7.25 — Norström, V. Religion och Gedanke. Lund, 1932.

Phil 4610.7.45 — Norström, V. Tal och tankar. Stockholm, 1919.

Phil 4610.7.13 — Norström, V. Tankar och forskningar. Stockholm, 1915.

Phil 4610.7.10 — Norström, V. Tankeliner. Stockholm, 1906.

Phil 3640.194 — Norström, Vitalis. Friedrich Nietzsche. Stockholm, 1901.

Phil 4610.7.88 — Norströmiana. (Akesson, Elof.) Stockholm, 1924.

Phil 5722.13 — Nortbridge, W.L. Modern theories of the unconscious. London, 1924.

Phil 9495.39.5 — Northcote, Hugh. Christianity and sex problems. Philadelphia, 1906.

Phil 9495.39 — Northcote, Hugh. Christianity and sex problems. 2d ed. Philadelphia, 1916.

Phil 930.37 — Northern Pacific Railroad Company. The story of the Monad. St. Paul, Minn., 1933.

Phil 2175.4.30 — Northrop, F.S.C. The logic of the sciences and the humanities. N.Y., 1947.

Phil 2175.4.35 — Northrop, F.S.C. Man, nature and God. N.Y., 1962.

Phil 9450.30 — Northrop Filmer, Stuart C. The complexity of legal and ethical experience. 1. ed. Boston, 1959.

Phil 3495.9 — Northwestern University. Evanston, Illinois. Immanuel Kant. Chicago, 1925.

Phil 70.36 — Nortisk Psykologmøte. Förhandlingar. 1947-1956 4v.

Phil 9035.32 — Norton, Carol. Studies in character. Boston, 1906.

Phil 1870.108 Norton, John N. The life of Bishop Berkeley. N.Y., 1861.
Phil 1900.92 Norton, William J. Bishop Butler, moralist and divine. New Brunswick, 1940.
Phil 1721.3 Nos encruzilhadas do pensamento. (Veloso, A.) Porto, 1956.
Phil 9351.9 Nos filles qu'en ferons-nous? 5. ed. (Le Roup, Hugues.) Paris, 1898.
Phil 3850.27.265 Nosik, Boris M. Shveitser. Moskva, 1971.
Phil 3833.2 Nossig, Alfred. Ueber die bestimmende Ursache des Philosophirens. Stuttgart, 1895.
Phil 3501.20 La nostalgie de la Grèce à l'aube de l'idéalisme allemand. (Taminiaux, Jacques.) La Haye, 1967.
Phil 175.43.10 La nostalgie de l'être. (Alquié, Ferdinand.) Paris, 1950.
Phil 175.43.11 La nostalgie de l'être. Thèse. (Alquié, Ferdinand.) Paris, 1950.
Phil 5240.51 El nostre caracter. (Abella Gibert, D.) Barcelona, 1961.
Phil 4012.2 I nostri filosofi contemporanei; rivista. (Mario, A.) Napoli, 1862.
Phil 8740.4 Not by bread alone. 2. ed. (Dun, Angus.) N.Y., 1942.
Phil 6316.25 Die Not des Lebens und ihre Überwindung. (Goraber, Gustav Hans.) Bern, 1966.
Phil 9528.1 Not in the curriculum. N.Y., 1903.
Phil 978.49.185 Die not Nach dem Christus. (Steiner, R.) Dornach, 1942.
Phil 1865.60 Not Paul, but Jesus. (Bentham, Jeremy.) Camden, 1917.
Htn Phil 1865.60.5* Not Paul, but Jesus. (Bentham, Jeremy.) London, 1823.
Phil 3850.18.92 Nota, J. Max Scheler. Utrecht, 1947.
Phil 8092.22 Notas para la polémica sobre realismo. (Bignami, Ariel.) Buenos Aires, 1969.
Phil 23.20 Notas y estudios de filosofia. San Miguel de Tucuman. 3-5,1953-1954 3v.
Phil 5150.1.5 Notational relativity. (Sheffer, H.M.) n.p., 1926?
Phil 5066.12.10 Notations de logique mathématique. (Peano, G.) Turin, 1894.
Phil 4080.3.235 Note biografiche di Benedetto Croce. (Franchini, R.) Torino, 1953.
Phil 193.109 Note e problemi di filosofia contemporanea. (Schiattarella, R.) Palermo, 1891.
Phil 1050.14 Note on Crescas's definition of time. (Wolfson, Harry A.) Philadelphia, 1919.
Phil 6331.2 Note sopra la originalitá del pensiero. (Vivante, Leone.) Roma, 1924?
Phil 6331.2.3 Note sopra la originalità del pensiero. (Vivante, Leone.) Roma, 1925.
Phil 1135.193 Note sul realismo nel pensiero dei Greci. (Carbonara Naddei, Mirella.) Napoli, 1965.
Phil 2475.1.255 Note sur M. Bergson et la philosophie bergsonienne. 6e éd. (Péguy, Charles.) Paris, 1935.
Phil 4120.4.110 Note sur pensiero di Giovanni Gentile. (Spirito, Ugo.) Firenze, 1954.
Phil 3925.16.15A Notebooks. (Wittgenstein, Ludwig.) Oxford, 1961. 2v.
Phil 7069.28.85 Noted witnesses for psychic occurrences. (Prince, Walter Franklin.) N.Y., 1963.
Phil 8836.1 Notes, expository and critical, on certain British theories of morals. (Laurie, S.S.) Edinburgh, 1868.
Phil 2115.81 Notes and annotations on Locke. (Morell, T.) London, 1794.
Phil 525.16.9 Notes and materials for an adequate biography of...William Law. (Walton, C.) London, 1854.
Phil 6670.1 Notes and studies... philosophy of animal magnetism. (Ashburner, J.) London, 1867.
Phil 342.6 Notes complementiares sur une thèorie de la connaissance sensible. (Lemaire, J.) Bruges, 1923.
Phil 48.5.10 Notes et documents concernant l'oeuvre, 1900-1921. (Institut Général Psychologique.) Paris, 1921.
Phil 9353.3 Notes for boys...on morals, mind and manners. London, 1885.
Phil 5042.21.17 Notes for symbolic logic. (Carnap, Rudolf.) Chicago, 1937.
Phil 8894.1 Notes from life. (Taylor, H.) Boston, 1853.
Phil 5249.2.89 Notes in psychology. (Jastrow, J.) Madison, 1912.
Phil 8887.35 Notes of an outlook on life. (Mercer, A.G.) London, 1899.
Phil 2150.17.95A Notes on a lecture on equilibrium. (Mayo, Elton.) Cambridge, 1946?
Phil 2520.223 Notes on Descartes' règles pour la direction de l'esprit. (Jacob, S.M.) London, 1948.
Phil 9070.114.5 Notes on ethics. (Margolius, Hans.) Miami, 1947.
Phil 8714.1 Notes on evolution and Christianity. (Yorke, J.F.) N.Y., 1883.
Phil 4075.83 Notes on life and writings of Gironimo Cardano. (Cumston, Charles Greene.) Boston, 1902.
Phil 5066.255 Notes on logic. (Lyndon, Roger C.) Princeton, N.J., 1966.
Phil 5253.8.50 Notes on the foundation of psychology as a science. (Naess, Arne.) Oslo, 1960.
Phil 6331.2.5 Notes on the originality of thought. (Vivante, Leone.) London, 1927.
Phil 8401.32 Notes on the synthesis of form. (Alexander, C.W.J.) Cambridge, 1964.
Phil 2490.100 Notes sur Auguste Comte. (Deroisin, Hippolyte P.) Paris, 1909.
Phil 2520.193 Notes sur la première partie des principes de la philosophie de Descartes. (Alquié, F.) Paris, 1933.
Phil 2520.96 Notes sur le vie de Descartes. (Netter, A.) Nancy, 1896.
Phil 1020.15 Notes sur les philosophes arabes. (Bouyges, P.M.) Beyrouth, 1921.
Phil 5425.2.13 Noteworthy families (Modern science). (Galton, F.) London, 1906.
Phil 1540.78 Nothdurft, Kalus Dieter. Studien zum Einfluss Senecas auf die Philosophie und Theologie des 12. Jahrhunderts. Leiden, 1963.
Phil 672.136.25 Nothing dies. (Dunne, John W.) London, 1940.
Phil 7069.58.10 Nothing so strange. 1. ed. (Ford, Arthur.) N.Y., 1958.
Phil 6123.4 Nothnagel, H. Topische Diagnostik der Gehirnkrankheiten. Berlin, 1879.
Phil 6963.5 Nothnagel, H. Über die Localisation der Gehirnkrankheiten. Wiesbaden, 1887.
Phil 2480.82 Notice historique et philosophique sur la vie. (Peisse, L.) Paris, 1844.
Phil 2496.83 Notice historique sur la vie...de Victor Cousin. (Mignet, M.) Paris, 1869.
Phil 2477.19.80 Notice sur la vie et les travaux de Gaston Berger, 1896-1960. (Gouhier, Henri.) Paris, 1962.
Phil 2725.11.83 Notice sur la vie et les travaux de Jules Lachelier. (Brunschvicg, L.) Paris, 1921.
Phil 2905.1.450 Notice sur la vie et les travaux de Pierre Teilhard de Chardin. (Mallemann, René de.) Paris, 1962.
Phil 2490.85 Notice sur l'oeuvre et sur la vie d'Auguste Comte. (Robinet, J.F.) Paris, 1860.

Phil 4110.4.95 Notice sur Luigi Ferri. (Dejob, Charles.) Versailles, 1896.
Phil 2555.9.30 La notion d'a priori. 1. éd. (Dufrenne, Mikel.) Paris, 1959.
Phil 1182.53 La notion de daimôn dans le pythagorisme ancien. (Detienne, M.) Paris, 1963.
Phil 1135.63 Notion de droit naturel. (Burle, E.) Trevoux, 1908.
Phil 5241.94 La notion de fait psychique. Thèse. (Blanché, Robert.) Paris, 1934.
Phil 2725.35.115 La notion de la liberté partjcipée dans la philosophie de Louis Lavelle. (Quito, Emérita.) Fribourg, 1969.
Phil 5761.18 La notion de liberté et la crise du déterminisme. (Lacape, R.S.) Paris, 1935.
Phil 5829.9.5 La notion de l'instinct et ses bases scientifiques. (Thomas, Maurice.) Paris, 1936.
Phil 184.35.5 La notion de substance. (Jolivet, Régis.) Paris, 1929.
Phil 184.35 La notion de substance. (Jolivet, Régis.) Paris, 1929.
Phil 672.123.10 La notion de temps. 2e éd. (Nys, Désiré.) Louvain, 1923.
Phil 705.74 La notion de transcendance; son sens, son évolution. (Piclin, Michel.) Paris, 1969.
Phil 735.1 La notion de valeur. (Berguer, G.) Genève, 1908.
Phil 720.13 La notion de vérité dans la "philosophie nouvelle". (Tonquédec, J. de.) Paris, 1908.
Phil 801.34 La notion d'existence. (Baillot, A.F.) Paris, 1954.
Phil 2070.82 La notion d'expérience d'après William James. (Reverdin, H.) Genève, 1913.
Phil 2750.10.105 La notion d'irrationnel chez Emile Meyerson. Thèse. (Bonnard, A.) Paris, 1936.
Phil 1135.93 Notion du Necessaire chez Aristote. (Chevalier, Jacques.) Paris, 1915.
Phil 165.346 The notion of existence. (Rasheed, A.) Lahore, 1959.
Phil 2555.9.31A The notion of the a priori. (Dufrenne, Mikel.) Evanston, Ill., 1966.
Phil 5043.33.10 Notions de logique formelle. (Dopp, Joseph.) Louvain, 1965.
Phil 8875.25 Notions de morale générale. (Alquié, F.) Paris, 1933.
Phil 184.21.9 Notions de philosophie. (Jourdain, Charles.) Paris, 1865.
Phil 184.21.15 Notions de philosophie. 15e ed. (Jourdain, Charles.) Paris, 1875.
Phil 3837.9 Les notions d'essence...de Spinoza. (Rivaud, Albert.) Paris, 1906.
Phil 8412.6 Notions d'esthétique. (Lalo, Charles.) Paris, 1925.
Phil 4520.2.32 Notionum ethicarum quas formales dicunt, dialexis critica. Diss. Pt.1-2. (Biberg, N.F.) Upsaliae, 1823-24.
Phil 3200.14 Notizen, Tagebücher, Lebenserinnerungen. v.1-2,3. (Ebner, Ferdinand.) München, 1963. 2v.
Phil 4080.10.85 Notizia degli scritti e del pensiere filosofico di Pietro Ceretti. (Ercole, P. d'.) Torino, 1866.
Phil 4215.1.95 Notizia di G.D. Romagnosi. 2a ed. (Cantù, Cesare.) Prato, 1840.
Phil 4215.1.82 Notizia storica di Gian Domenico Romagnosi. (Stiattesi, Andrea.) Firenze, 1878.
Phil 4110.2.85 Notizie della vita di Marianna Florenzi Waddington. (Leonij, Lorenzo.) Todi, 1865.
Phil 8668.7 Noto, Antonio di. L'evidenza di Dio nella filosofia del secolo XIII. Padova, 1958.
Phil 6990.3.7 Notre-Dame de Lourdes. (Lasserre, H.) Paris, 1869.
Phil 6990.3.20 Notre-Dame de Lourdes. (Rebsomen, A.) Paris, 1925.
Phil 23.22 Notre Dame journal of formal logic. Notre Dame, Ind. 1,1960+ 7v.
Phil 672.142 Notre maître le temps. (Nordmann, Charles.) Paris, 1924.
Phil 8657.14.5 Notre Père. (Cieszkowski, August D.) Paris, 1906.
Phil 4757.2.105 Nott, C.S. Teachings of Gurdjieff. London, 1961.
Phil 188.30 Nott, Kathleen. Philosophy and human nature. London, 1970.
Phil 5625.108 Notterman, Joseph M. Dynamics of response. N.Y., 1965.
Phil 5768.19 Notwendigkeit in Natur- und Kulturwissenschaft. (Stammler, Gerhard.) Halle, 1926.
Phil 5066.10 Noue lezioni di logica simbolica. (Bochénski, I.M.) Roma, 1938.
Phil 4210.22 Nouovo saggio sull'origine delle idee. (Rosmini-Serbati, Antonio.) Milano, 1836-37. 3v.
Phil 188.6 Nourrisson, J.F. Histoire et philosophie. Paris, 1860.
Phil 5253.3 Nourrisson, J.F. La nature humaine. Paris, 1865.
Phil 2805.85 Nourrisson, J.F. Pascal physicien et philosophe. Paris, 1885.
Phil 2805.85.5 Nourrisson, J.F. Pascal physicien et philosophe. Défense de Pascal. Paris, 1888.
Phil 294.2 Nourrisson, J.F. Philosophies de la nature. Paris, 1887.
Phil 3833.1 Nourrisson, J.F. Spinoza et la naturalisme contemporain. Paris, 1866.
Phil 813.1 Nourrisson, J.F. Tableau des progrès de la pensée humaine. Paris, 1858.
Phil 813.1.2 Nourrisson, J.F. Tableau des progrès de la pensée humaine. Paris, 1867.
Phil 813.1.7 Nourrisson, J.F. Tableau des progrès de la pensée humaine. 7e éd. Paris, 1886.
Phil 3552.113 Nourrisson, M. La philosophie de Leibniz. Paris, 1860.
Phil 23.29 Noûs; nihil philosophici a nobis alienum putamus. Detroit. 1,1967+ 5v.
Phil 184.9 Nouveau cours de philosophie. (Joly, H.) Paris, n.d.
Phil 2905.1.195.5 Nouveau lexique Teilhard de Chardin. (Cuénot, Claude.) Paris, 1968.
Phil 2412.2 Nouveau manuale mour servir à l'histoire des Cacouacs. (Moreau, Jacob N.) Amsterdam, 1757. 2 pam.
Htn Phil 2605.3.30* Le nouveau monde. (Fourier, C.) Paris, 1829.
Phil 525.17 Le nouveau mysticisme. (Paulhan, F.) Paris, 1891.
Phil 180.68.5 Nouveau précis de philosophie a l'usage des candidats au baccalauréat. (Foulquié, Paul.) Paris, 1955. 3v.
Phil 196.1.8 Le nouveau spiritualisme. (Vacherot, E.) Paris, 1884.
Phil 5243.29.10 Nouveau traité de psychologie. v.1-8. (Dumas, George.) Paris, 1930-36. 7v.
Phil 5635.4 Nouveau traité des sensations. (Guillaume, J.A.M.) Paris, 1876. 2v.
Phil 87.13 Nouveau vocabulaire philosophique. 2. éd. (Cuvillier, Armand.) Paris, 1957.
Phil 180.8.5 Nouveaux essais de critique philosophique. (Franck, A.) Paris, 1890.
Phil 3552.41.5 Nouveaux essais sur l'entendement humain. (Leibniz, Gottfried Wilhelm.) Paris, 1886.
Phil 3552.41 Nouveaux essais sur l'entendement humain. (Leibniz, Gottfried Wilhelm.) Paris, 1899.
Phil 3552.41.10 Nouveaux essais sur l'entendement humain. (Leibniz, Gottfried Wilhelm.) Paris, 1966.
Phil 6681.10 Nouveaux extraits des journaux d'un magnétiseur. (Lutzebourg.) Strasbourg, 1788.
Phil 2496.31 Nouveaux fragmens philosophiques. (Cousin, Victor.) Paris, 1828.

Phil 2672.30.2   Nouveaux mélanges philosophiques. (Jouffroy, Théodore S.) Paris, 1842.

Phil 2672.30.3   Nouveaux mélanges philosophiques. 2e éd. (Jouffroy, Théodore S.) Paris, 1861.

Phil 5643.6   Nouvel essai sur la lumière et les couleurs. (Déal, J.N.) Paris, 1827.

Phil 6060.72   Nouvelle graphologie pratique. (Salberg, Renée de.) Paris, 1967?

Phil 6990.60   Nouvelle histoire de Lourdes. (Marert, Léonce.) Paris, 1955.

Phil 3552.100   La nouvelle monadologie. (Renouvier, Charles.) Paris, 1899.

Phil 5520.96.80   Une nouvelle orientation. (Bulla de Villaret, H.) Paris, 1945.

Phil 1750.140   Une nouvelle philosophie de l'immanence. (Krzesinski, André.) Paris, 1931.

Phil 5811.10   La nouvelle psychologie animale. (Bohn, Georges.) Paris, 1911.

Phil 23.30   Nouvelle revue de psychanalyse. Paris. 1,1970+

Phil 8587.1   Nouvelle théologie philosophique. (Hannotin, E.) Paris, 1846. 2v.

Phil 2270.102   Les nouvelles bases de la morale d'après Herbert Spencer. (Blanc, Elie.) Lyon, 1881.

Phil 2730.50   Nouvelles considerations sur les rapports du physique et du moral de l'homme. (Maine de Biran, Pierre.) Paris, 1834.

Phil 2520.88.30   Nouvelles difficultez proposees par un peripateticien. (Daniel, Gabriel.) Paris, 1693.

Phil 2401.5   Nouvelles études d'histoire de la philosophie. (Boutroux, E.) Paris, 1927.

Phil 5241.21.5   Nouvelles études familières de psychologie et de morale. (Bouillier, F.C.) Paris, 1887.

Phil 8827.3.7   Nouvelles études morales sur le temps présent. (Caro, E.M.) Paris, 1869.

Phil 477.7   Les nouvelles formules du matérialisme. (Cros, Antoine.) Paris, 1897.

Phil 6127.7.10   Les nouvelles idées sur la structure du système nerveux. (Ramón y Cajal, S.) Paris, 1895.

Phil 3552.76   Nouvelles lettres. (Leibniz, Gottfried Wilhelm.) Paris, 1857.

Phil 2490.70   Nouvelles lettres inédites. (Comte, Auguste.) Paris, 1939.

Phil 8890.28   Nouvelles orientations de la morale. (Palhoriès, F.) Paris, 1911.

Phil 6990.37   Nouvelles prennes contre le faux miracle de migne approuvé à Rome. (Le Quien de la Neufville, Charles Jacques.) Paris, 1828.

Phil 189.26   Nouvelles questions philosophiques. (Oegger, G.) Tubingue, 1835.

Phil 8878.20   Nouvelles recherches sur l'esthetique et la morale. (Durand, J.P.) Paris, 1900.

Phil 2520.242.5   Nouvelles réflexions sur la preuve ontologique de Descartes. (Gueroult, Martial.) Paris, 1955.

Phil 4215.1.81   Nova, Alessandro. Delle censure dell'abate A. Rosmini-Serbati contro la dottrina religiosa di G.D Romagnosi. Milano, 1842.

Htn   Phil 4200.2.10*   Nova de universis philosophia. (Patrizzi, F.) Venetiis, 1593.

Phil 4478.1.30   Nova filosofia cristă. (Rocha, Germano da Costa.) Lisboa, 1961?

Phil 488.2   Novack, George Edward. The origins of materialism. 1st ed. N.Y., 1965.

Phil 75.67   Novaia sovetskaia literatura po filosofii. Moskva. 1965+ 7v.

Phil 1750.777   Novak, George Edward. Existentialism versus Marxism. N.Y., 1966.

Phil 8593.25   Novak, Michael. Ascent of the mountain. 1. ed. N.Y., 1971.

Phil 8176.2   Novák, Mirko. Česká estetika. Praha, 1941.

Phil 3495.17   Novák, Mirko. Kanův kriticismus a problém hodnoty. V Bratislave, 1936.

Phil 8414.14   Novák, Mirko. Od skutečnosti ku uměni. Praha, 1965.

Phil 8080.83   Novák, Mirko. Otázky estetiky v přítainnosti i minulosti. Praha, 1963.

Phil 8414.13   Novak, Mirko. Základy vědy o umění, se zvláštním zřením k vědeckému studiu hudby. Praha, 1928.

Phil 4829.616.30   Novaković, Staniša. Problem metafizike u savremenoj analitickoj filozofiji. Beograd, 1967.

Phil 2733.88   Novaro, Mario. Die Philosophie des Nicolaus Malebranche. Berlin, 1893.

Phil 3552.42   Nové úvahy o lidské soudnosti od auktora Systému předjednané harmonie. (Leibniz, Gottfried Wilhelm.) Praha, 1932.

Phil 6980.516   Noveck, Simon. Judaism and psychiatry. N.Y., 1956.

Phil 1700.9   Noveishie priemy zashchity starogo mira. (Akademiia Nauk SSSR. Institut Filosofii. Sektor Sovremennoi Burzhuaznoi Filosofii i Sotsiologii Stran Zapada.) Moskva, 1962.

Phil 1695.23   Novelle initiation philosophique. (Gaboriau, F.) Tournai, 1962. 6v.

Phil 4013.5   Noventa, Giacomo. Nulla di nuova. 1. ed. Milano, 1960.

Phil 6323.24   Novey, Samuel. The second look: the reconstruction of personal history in psychiatry and psychoanalysis. Baltimore, 1968.

Phil 400.122   Novgorodtsev, P.I. Problemy idealizma. Moskva, 1903.

Phil 3925.16.255   Novielli, Valeria. Wittgenstein e la filosofia. Bari, 1969.

VPhil 1705.13   Novija filozofija Zapada i odabrani telestovi. (Filipović, Vladimir.) Zagreb, 1968.

Phil 5253.21   Novik, Il'ia B. Filosofskie voprosy modelirovaniia psikhiki. Moskva, 1969.

Phil 310.215   Novikov, A.I. Bor'ba marksizma-leninizma protiv sovremennogo filosofskogo revizionizma. Leningrad, 1959.

Phil 4710.147   Novikov, Avraam I. Leninizm i progressivnye traditsii russkoi obshchestvennoi mysli. Leningrad, 1965.

Phil 9245.118   Novikov, Mikhail I. O schast'e. Moskva, 1965.

Phil 5066.226   Novikov, P.S. Elements of mathematical logic. Edinburgh, 1964.

Phil 310.470   Novinskii, I.I. Poniatie sviazi v marksistskoi filosofii. Moskva, 1961.

Phil 187.94   Novius organum. (McKerrow, J.C.) London, 1931.

Phil 5238.178   Novosibirsk. Gosudartvennyi Pedagogicheskii Institut. Voprosy psikhologii. Omsk, 1965.

Phil 24.7   Novosibirsk Universitet. Nauchnye trudy. Filosofskaia seriia. 2,1968+

Phil 8430.85   Novozhilova, Larisa I. Sotsiologiia iskusstva. Leningrad, 1968.

Phil 1850.51   The novum organon. (Bacon, Francis.) Oxford, 1855.

Phil 5062.8   Novum organon renovatum. (Whewell, W.) London, 1858.

Phil 1850.50.10   Novum organum. (Bacon, Francis.) Glasguae, 1803.

Phil 1850.50.25   Novum organum. (Bacon, Francis.) Lanciano, 1928.

Phil 1850.50.13A   Novum organum. (Bacon, Francis.) London, 1905.

Htn   Phil 1850.50.6*   Novum organum. (Bacon, Francis.) Lugdunum Batavorum, 1650. 2 pam.

Phil 1850.50.11   Novum organum. (Bacon, Francis.) Oxonii, 1813.

Phil 1850.50.12   Novum organum. (Bacon, Francis.) St. Louis, 1901.

Phil 1850.50.9   Novum organum. (Bacon, Francis.) Wirceburgi, 1779.

Phil 1850.50.5A   Novum organum. Rev. A. Johnson. (Bacon, Francis.) London, 1859.

Phil 1850.50.3   Novum organum. T. Fowler. (Bacon, Francis.) Oxford, 1878.

Phil 1850.50.2   Novum organum. T. Fowler. (Bacon, Francis.) Oxford, 1878.

Phil 1850.50.4   Novum organum. T. Fowler. 2nd ed. (Bacon, Francis.) Oxford, 1889.

Htn   Phil 1850.50.7*   Novum organum. 2a ed. (Bacon, Francis.) Amsterdam, 1660.

Phil 310.621   Nový, Lubomír. Filosofie v neklidné době. Praha, 1965.

Phil 310.754   Novye filosofskie aspekty elementno-strukturnykh otnoshenii. (Svidenskii, Vladimir I.) Leningrad, 1970.

Phil 23.28   Novye issledovaniia v psikhologii i vozrastnoi fiziologii. Moskva. 1,1970+

Phil 5627.166   Now I see. (Lunn, Arnold.) N.Y., 1938.

Phil 9400.30   Now or never. (Blanton, S.) Englewood Cliffs, N.J., 1959.

VPhil 2475.1.470   Nowa filozofja. (Romanowski, Henryk.) Lublin, 1929.

Phil 8888.15   Nowell-Smith, P.H. Ethics. Melbourne, 1954.

Phil 4065.172   Nowicki, A. Centralne Kategorie filozofii Giordana Bruna. Warszawa, 1962.

Phil 4265.1.95   Nowicki, Andrzej. Centralne kategorie filozofii Vaniniego. Wyd. 1. Warszawa, 1970.

Phil 4013.7   Nowicki, Andrzej. Filozofia włoskiego odrodzenia. Warszawa, 1967.

Phil 8668.5   Noyes, A. The unknown god. London, 1937.

Phil 6323.7.2   Noyes, Arthur P. Modern clinical psychiatry. 2d ed. Philadelphia, 1939.

Phil 6323.7.5   Noyes, Arthur P. Modern clinical psychiatry. 5th ed. Philadelphia, 1958.

Phil 8414.15.2   Noyes, Carleton E. The gate of appreciation. Boston, Mass., 1907.

Phil 8593.6   Noyes, R.K. Views of religion. Boston, 1906.

Phil 6963.2   Noyes, W. Paranoia. Baltimore, 1888-89.

Phil 3425.666.2   La nozione di alienazione in Hegel, Feuerbach e Marx. 2. ed. (Parinetto, Luciano.) Milano, 1969.

Phil 4060.10.80   La nozione di possibilità nel pensiero di Nicola Abbagnano. (Travaglia, Sandro.) Padova, 1969.

Phil 4210.116.5   Nozioni di ontologia. 2a ed. (Buroni, Giuseppe.) Torino, 1878.

Phil 5259.22   Nozioni di psicologia. (Tarozzi, G.) Bologna, 1925.

Phil 125.1   Nozioni elementari di logica. (Chicchitti-Suriani.) Torino, 1887.

Phil 8887.135   Nravstvenata norma i neinata realizatsiia. (Momov, Vasil M.) Sofiia, 1969.

Phil 8980.616.5   Nravstvennoe razvitie lichnosti. Moskva, 1969.

Phil 8881.33   Nravstvennoe soznanie cheloviechestva. (Gorodenskii, N.) Sergiev, 1903.

Phil 8980.131   Nravstvennost' i religiia. (Akademiia Nauk SSSR. Institut Filosofii.) Moskva, 1964.

Phil 8980.496.10   Nravstvennye printsipy stroitelia kommunizma. (Kosolapov, S.M.) Moskva, 1962.

Phil 8980.895.10   Nravstvennye printsipy stroitelia kommunizma. (Zhuravkov, M.G.) Moskva, 1965.

Phil 8980.676   Nravstvennye tsennosti nachego sovremennika. (Pavlova, Liia Jakovlevna.) Moskva, 1971.

Phil 8980.785.20   Nravstvennyi oblik razvedchikov budushchego. (Shcherbak, F.N.) Leningrad, 1961.

Phil 9513.41   Nravstvennyi progress. (Titarenko, Aleksandr I.) Moskva, 1969.

Phil 8980.131.5   Nravstvennyi progressi religiia. (Anisimov, Sergei F.) Moskva, 1965.

Phil 184.7   Nuces philosophicae, or The philosophy of things. (Johnson, Edward.) London, 1842.

Phil 5068.56.25   Nuchelmans, Gabriël. O verzicht van de analytische wijsbegeeste. Utrecht, 1969.

Phil 5068.56.20   Nuchelmans, Gabriël. Proeven van analytisch filosofesen. Hilversum, 1967.

Phil 4752.2.150   Nucho, Fuad. Berdyaev's philosoophy. London, 1967.

Phil 5643.30   Nuel, J.P. La vision. Paris, 1904.

Phil 3425.42   Nürnberger Schriften. (Hegel, Georg Wilhelm Friedrich.) Leipzig, 1938.

Phil 8414.6   Nüsslein, F.A. Lehrbuch der Kunstwissenschaft zum Gebrance bei Vorlesungen. Landshut, 1819.

Phil 75.34   Nuestra bibliográfica de la filosofía católica. (Buenos Aires. Colegio Máximo.) Buenos Aires, 1939.

Phil 585.60   Nueva filosofia de la naturaleza del hombre. (Sabuco de Nantes Barrera, O.) Madrid, 1728.

Phil 3640.442   Una nueva imagen del hombre a través de Nietzsche y Freud. (Weyland, M.) Buenos Aires, 1953.

Phil 346.28   Nuevi principi di epistemología. (Pasquinelli, Alberto.) Milano, 1964.

Phil 8892.43   El nuevo mundo moral ó La nueva vida del hombre. (Ruiz Gómez, J.E.) Madrid, 1892.

Phil 195.5   Nuevos ensayos de critica filosofica. (Urmeneta, F. de.) Barcelona, 1953.

Phil 4363.7.20   Nuevos ensayos de filosofía. 2. ed. (Marias Aguilera, Julián.) Madrid, 1968.

Phil 196.29   Nuevos prolegómenos a la metafisica. (Vassallo, Angel.) Buenos Aires, 1938.

Phil 2805.207   La nuit de Gethsémani. (Shestor, Lev.) Paris, 1923.

Phil 4013.5   Nulla di nuova. 1. ed. (Noventa, Giacomo.) Milano, 1960.

Phil 2520.138.5   Num Cartesii methodus tantum valeat in suo opere illustrando quantum ipse senserit. Thesis. (Milhaud, G.S.) Montpellier, 1894.

Phil 3425.217   Num recte et vere de Spinozismo judicavit Hegelius? (Wennerberg, J.) Upsaliae, 1848.

Phil 7072.6   The number "spirit" photograph case. (Gerry, Elbridge T.) N.Y., 1869.

Phil 5841.10   Nun, witch, playmate; the Americanization of sex. 1st ed. (Richardson, Herbert Warren.) N.Y., 1971.

Phil 6323.5.3   Nunberg, Hermann. Allgemeine Neurosenlehre. Bern, 1959.

Phil 6323.5   Nunberg, Hermann. Allgemeine Neurosenlehre auf psychoanalytischer Gundlage. Bern, 1932.

Phil 6323.5.6   Nunberg, Hermann. Practice and theory of psychoanalysis. N.Y., 1960. 2v.

Phil 1865.191   Nuñez, T. Sistema de la ciencia social. Salamanca, 1820.

Phil 8414.12   Nunez de Arenas, I. Elementos filosóficos de la literatura. Madrid, 1858.

Phil 4364.1.70   Núñez Regueiro, M. On the knowledge and progress of oneself. Rosario, 1941.

Phil 8593.16   Núñez Regueiro, Manuel. Suma contra una nueva edad media. Rosario, 1938.

Phil 188.16.10   Nuñez Requeiro, M. Metafisica y ciencia. Buenos Aires, 1941.
Phil 188.16   Nuñez Requeiro, M. Tratado de metalogica. Rosario, 1936.
Phil 5272.6   Nunnally, Jum Clarence. Psychometric theory. N.Y., 1967.
Phil 4961.918   Nuño, Alicia de. Ideas sociales del positivismo en Venezuela. Caracas, 1969.
Phil 1750.778   Nuño Montes, Juan Antonio. Sentido de la filosofía contemporánea. Caracas, 1965.
Phil 3501.7   Nuova critica della morale Kantiana. (Trivero, Camillo.) Milano, 1914.
Phil 287.7   La nuova filosofia della natura in Germania. (Geymonat, Ludovico.) Torino, 1934.
Phil 4115.25   Nuova protologia brani scelti da tutte le sue opere. (Gioberti, V.) Bari, 1912. 2v.
Phil 23.7   La nuova scienza. Todi. 1-6 2v.
Phil 5255.13   Nuova teorica fisiologica della conoscenza. (Panizza, Mario.) Roma, 1899.
Phil 4080.3.47   Nuove pagini sparse. (Croce, Benedetto.) Napoli, 1948-49. 2v.
Phil 4080.3.47.2   Nuove pagini sparse. 2. ed. (Croce, Benedetto.) Bari, 1966. 2v.
Phil 4190.1.45   Nuove vedute logiche. (Orestano, Francesco.) Milano, 1939.
Phil 4070.1.90   I nuovi auspizi all'Italia e le confessioni di Ausonio Franchi. Genova, 1852.
Phil 4080.8.35   Nuovi discorsi del tempo o famiglia, patria e Dio. (Conti, Augusto.) Firenze, 1896-97. 2v.
Htn   Phil 4073.81*   Nuovi documenti su T. Campanella. (Berti, D.) Roma, 1881.
Phil 5255.13.5   I nuovi elemente della psicofisiologia. (Panizza, Mario.) Roma, 1898.
Phil 4190.1.30   Nuovi princèpi. (Orestano, Francesco.) Milano, 1939.
Phil 189.16   Nuovi principi. (Orestano, F.) Roma, 1925.
Phil 4080.3.48.2   Nuovi saggi di estetica. 2. ed. (Croce, Benedetto.) Bari, 1926.
Phil 4260.91.5   Nuovi studi sulla filosofia civile di G.B. Vico. (Donati, Benvenuto.) Firenze, 1936.
Phil 176.232   Nuovo corso di filosofia a norma del Concilio Vaticano II. (Bogliolo, Luigi.) Roma, 1969- 2v.
Phil 4170.7.52   Nuovo discorso proemiale. (Mamiani della Rovere, Terenzio.) Genova, 1852.
Phil 103.4.5   Nuovo dizionario di coltura filosofica e scientifica. (Semprini, G.) Torino, 1952.
Phil 400.74   Il nuovo idealismo inglese ed americano. (Abbagnano, N.) Napoli, 1927.
Phil 4018.3   Il nuovo idealismo italiano. (Spirito, Ugo.) Roma, 1923.
Phil 4080.3.127   Il nuovo idealismo italiano di Benedetto Croce. 2a ed. (Zacchi, Angelo.) Roma, 1925.
Phil 1850.50.26   Nuovo organo. (Bacon, Francis.) Firenze, 1938.
Phil 1850.50.23   Nuovo organo delle scienze. (Bacon, Francis.) Bassano, 1788.
Phil 5246.25.5   Nuovo orizzonti della psicologia sperimentale. 2. ed. (Gemelli, Agostino.) Milano, 1923.
Phil 4190.1.40   Il nuovo realismo. (Orestano, Francesco.) Milano, 1939.
Phil 630.14   Il nuovo realismo contemporaneo. (Cesca, Giovanni.) Verona, 1883.
Phil 4210.22.10   Nuovo saggio sull'origine delle idee. 3. ed. (Rosmini-Serbati, Antonio.) Bari, 1948.
Phil 4018.4   Il nuovo spiritualismo in Italia. (Simoni, M.) Napoli, 1936.
Phil 6684.3   Nuovo studi sull'ipnotismo. (Ottolenghi, S.) Torino, 1889.
Phil 1750.166.195   Nuovo umanesimo. (Spirito, Ugo.) Roma, 1964.
Phil 1750.166.280   Nuovo umanesimo sociale. (Legitimo, Gianfranco.) Torino, 1968.
Phil 5870.60   The nursery years. (Isaacs, Susan (Fairhurst).) N.Y., 1968.
Phil 6951.7   Nursing the insane. (Barrus, C.) N.Y., 1908.
Phil 5465.39   Nussberger, M. Die künstlerische Phantasie. München, 1935.
Phil 665.42.5   Nutids själavård; om största utbytet av själens gåvor. (Feilberg, Ludvig.) Stockholm, 1917.
Phil 9410.8   Nutrimento, L. La definizione del bene in relazione al problema dell'ottimismo. Padova, 1936.
Phil 9179.8   Nuts for boys for crack. (Todd, J.) N.Y., n.d.
Phil 4791.2   Nutsubidze, Shalva Isakovich. Istoriia gruzinskoi filosofii. Tbilisi, 1960.
Phil 6323.10   Nuttin, Jozef. Psychanalyse et conception spiritualiste de l'homme. 2. ed. Louvain, 1955.
Phil 6323.12   Nuttin, Jozef. Psychoanalyse und Personlichkeit. Freiburg, 1956.
Phil 5223.10   Nuttin, Jozef. Psychology in Belgium. Louvain, 1961.
Phil 5535.28.5   Nuttin, Jozef. Reward and punishment in human learning: elements of a behavior theory. N.Y., 1968.
Phil 5590.454   Nuttin, Jozef. La structure de la personnalité. Paris, 1965.
Phil 5535.28   Nuttin, Jozef. Tâche réussite et échec. Louvain, 1953.
Phil 5223.1   Nuttin, Jozef. Tendences nouvelles dans la psychologie contemporaine. Louvain, 1951.
Phil 5223.5   Nuttin, Jozef. Tôche relussité et échec. Bruxelles, 1953.
Phil 8672.18.3   Nuzhna li vera v Boga. 3. izd. (Reusner, M.A.) Moskva, 1923.
Phil 270.130   Nužnost i sloboda. (Šešić, Bogdan.) Beograd, 1963.
Phil 4620.3   Nýall. (Pétursss, Helgi.) Reykjavík, 1919.
Phil 4620.1   Nýall Nokkur íslenzk drög til heimsfraeði og liffraeði (Pétursss, Helgi.) Reykjavík, 1922.
Phil 4610.7.50   Den nyaste människan. (Norström, V.) Stockholm, 1906.
Phil 4515.81.5   Nyblâeus, A. Bidrag till en karakteristik af den Boströmska filosofien. Lund, 1892.
Phil 4515.81   Nyblâeus, A. Tvänne uppsatser om den Boströmska filosofien. Lund, 1889.
Phil 3425.204   Nyblaeus, Axel. Ar en practisk philosophi möjlig efter Hegels verldsåsigt? Lund, 1855.
Phil 3425.251   Nyblaeus, Axel. Bidrag till granskning af den Hegelska dialektiken och dess princip "Motsägelsen". Upsala, 1851.
Phil 8593.14   Nyblaeus, Axel. Om religionens betydelse och förhållande till philosophen. pt.1-4. Upsala, 1853.
Phil 4610.6.31   Nyblaeus, Axel. Om straffrätten. Lund, 1852.
Phil 4610.6.2   Nyblaeus, Axel. Trenne religiousfilosfiska uppsatser. 2. uppl. Lund, 1874.
Phil 4508.4   Nyblaseus, Axel. Den filosofiska forskningen i Sverige. Lund, 1873-97. 3v.
Phil 4580.36   Den nyere filosofis historie. (Høffding, Harald.) København, 1894-95. 2v.
Phil 4580.36.3   Den nyere filosofis historie. v.1-10. (Høffding, Harald.) København, 1921-22. 2v.
Phil 8963.5   Nygren, A. Agape and Eros. London, 1953.
Phil 8593.9   Nygren, A. Religiöst apriori. Lund, 1921.
Phil 188.13   Nyman, A. Kämpande intelligens. Malmö, 1911.

Phil 4600.2.80   Nyman, Alf. Hans Larsson. Stockholm, 1945.
Phil 2138.160   Nyman, Alf. Leviathan och folkviljan. Stockholm, 1948.
Phil 672.123   Nys, Désiré. La notion d'espace. Bruxelles, 1922.
Phil 672.123.10   Nys, Désiré. La notion de temps. 2e éd. Louvain, 1923.
Phil 8593.12   Nyström, A. Gyldene ord ur mensklighetens allmänna religion. 2. uppl. Stockholm, 1880.
Phil 2490.101   Nyström, A. Positivism. Stockholm, 1879.
Phil 600.37   Nyström, Anton. Den gamla tiden inför den nya. Stockholm, 1875.
Phil 600.37.5   Nyström, Anton. Positivismen och Herbert Spencer. Stockholm, 1887.
Phil 8654.116   O bogu i o człowieku. Warszawa, 1968.
Phil 4803.454.95   O cenę absolutu; rzecz o Hoene-Wrońskim. (Ujejski, Józef.) Warszawa, 1925.
Phil 5525.68   O chuvstve iumora i ostroumii. (Luk, Oleksandr N.) Moskva, 1968.
Phil 4761.2.30   O comnenii, nauke i vere. (Karsavin, L.P.) Berlin, 1925.
Phil 9035.45.20   O conceptie americana despre caracter. (Todoranu, D.) Cluj, 1933.
Phil 310.6   O dialekticheskii materializme; sbornik statei. (Institut Filosofii. Akadamiia Nauk SSSR.) Moskva, 1952.
Phil 310.117   O dialektike elementov i struktury v ob"ektivnom mire i v poznanii. (Sviderskii, Vladimir Io.) Moskva, 1962.
Phil 310.615   O dialektike protsessa poznaniia prirody i kibernetika. (Vislobokov, Aleksei Dmitrievich.) Moskva, 1965.
Phil 310.260   O dialektike razvitiia neorganicheskoi prirody. (Meliukhin, S.I.) Moskva, 1960.
Phil 8665.25   O dokazatel'stvakh bytiia Bozhiia. (Kryvelev, A.I.) Moskva, 1960.
Phil 4803.462.21   O dziele literackim. (Ingarden, Roman.) Warszawa, 1960.
Phil 1710.3   O filosofii přítomnosti. (Krejčí, F.) V Praze, 1904.
Phil 2115.74.15   O forgripelipe. (Locke, J.) Stockholm, 1726.
Phil 310.670   O historickén materialismu. Vyd. 1. (Zelený, Jindřich.) V Praze, 1960.
VPhil 8735.59   O kategoriiakh "tsel'", "sredstvo", "rezul'tat". (Trubnikov, Nikolai N.) Moskva, 1968.
Phil 4769.1.130   O khristianskom edinstve. (Solov'ev, V.S.) Briussell, 1967.
Phil 8416.5   O khudozhestvennom obraze. (Papennyi, Z.S.) Moskva, 1961.
Phil 8402.65   O kiczu. Wyd. 6. (Banach, Andrzej.) Kraków, 1968.
Phil 672.225   O kierunku upływu czasu. (Szumilewicz, Irena.) Warszawa, 1964.
Phil 8980.630   O kommunisticheskoi etike. (Obshchestvo pro Rasprostran.) London, 1962.
Phil 8980.392   O kommunisticheskoi morali. (Filonovich, Pavel G.) Moskva, 1963.
Phil 4769.5   O konechnom ideale. (Setnitskii, N.A.) Kharbin, 1932.
Phil 8980.496   O krasote dushevnoi. (Kononenko, E.V.) Moskva, 1959.
Phil 9355.13   O kul'ture molodogo rabochego. (Postovoitov, V.K.) Moskva, 1960.
Phil 8980.498   O kul'ture povedeniia molodogo cheloveka. (Krasnor, Iu. M.) Moskva, 1962.
Phil 960.252   O materialisticheskikh traditsiiakh v indiiskoi filosofii. (Anikeev, Nikolai P.) Moskva, 1965.
Phil 310.725   O metode postroeniia sistemy dialekticheskogo materializma. (Lutai, Vadlen Stepanovich.) Kiev, 1970.
Phil 8092.24   O mnimom materializme russkoi nauki i filosofii. (Zen'kovskii, V.V.) Miunkhen, 1956.
Phil 8980.780.5   O modernizme. (Mozhniagun, Sergei E.) Moskva, 1970.
Phil 8980.673   O moral'nom avtoritete. (Semenov, Mikhail N.) Alma-Ata, 1967.
Phil 4768.2.7   O moral'nom oblike sovetskogo cheloveka. (Panferov, F.I.) Moskva, 1960.
Phil 4761.2.35   O myshlenii i putiakh ego issledovaniia. (Rubinshtein, Sergei L.) Moskva, 1958.
VPhil 178.79   O nachalakh. (Karsavin, L.P.) Berlin, 1925.
Phil 4803.313.35   O narzedziach i przedmiotach poznamia. Wyd. 1. (Dambska, Izydora.) Warszawa, 1967.
Phil 8876.91   O naukach humanistycznych. (Czezowski, Tadeusz.) Toruń, 1969.
Phil 3120.2.35   O naznachenii cheloveka. (Berdiaev, N.A.) Parizh, 1931.
Phil 310.118   O nejlepším státě. (Bolzano, Bernard.) Praha, 1952.
  O nekotorykh formakh protivorechivosti v ob"ektivnom mire. (Sviderskii, Vladimir Io.) Leningrad, 1968.
Phil 352.11   O nekotorykh osnovnykh voprosakh marks - leninskoi gnoseologii. (Vardapetian, K.) Erevan, 1963.
Phil 8980.785   O nekotorykh voprosakh kommunisticheskoi morali. (Shariia, P.A.) Moskva, 1951.
Phil 8408.30.5   O některých otázkách estetiky Otakara Hostinskéko. (Sádecký, Z.) Praha, 1956.
Phil 5053.10   O pierwszym polskim podręczniku logiki. (Narbutt, Olgierd.) Lódź, 1958.
Phil 4580.37   O plevelse og tydning religionsfilosofiske studier. (Høffding, Harald.) Kjøbenhavn, 1918.
Phil 1707.22   O plysningstiden. (Holm, Søren.) Kjøbenhavn, 1959.
Phil 3120.2.30   O pokroku a dobročinnosti. (Bolzano, Bernard.) Praha, 1951.
Phil 310.375   O povtoriaemosti v protsesse razoitiia. (Kechov, B.M.) Moskva, n.d.
Phil 4710.80   O poznovaemosti mira. (Khaskhachikh, F.I.) Moskva, 1946.
Phil 8422.17   O předmětu a metodě estetǎky a obecne teorie umění. (Volek, Jaroslav.) Praha, 1963.
Phil 8735.55   O prichinnosti i tselesoobraznosti v zhivoi prirode. (Frolov, I.T.) Moskva, 1961.
Phil 8407.43   O prirode esteticheskogo tvorchestva. (Gol'dentrikht, Semen S.) Moskva, 1966.
Phil 1195.18   O prirode sofistiki. (Osipova, Valentina.) Erevan, 1964.
Phil 5251.65   O psikhicheskikh sostoianiiakh cheloveka. (Levitov, N.D.) Moskva, 1964.
Phil 3480.32.67   O pus Postumum. (Kant, Immanuel.) Berlin, 1936.
Phil 575.142   O rabstve i svobode cheloveka. (Berdiaev, N.A.) Paris, 194-.
Phil 8405.7   O reaktsionnoi sushchnosti. (Egorov, A.G.) Moskva, 1961.
Phil 400.110   O reaktsionnoi sushchnosti idealizma. (Cherkashin, P.P.) Moskva, 1953.
Phil 8669.7   O religii; khrestomatiia. Moskva, 1963.
Phil 8595.19   O religii. (Plekhanov, G.) Moskva, 1923.
Phil 349.43   O roli abstraktsii v poznanii. (Stempkovskaia, V.I.) Moskva, 1959.
Phil 353.32   O roli kategorii sushchnost' i iavlenie v poznanii. (Vakhtomin, N.K.) Moskva, 1959.
Phil 310.589   O rozporech ve společnostii. (Klofáč, Jaroslav.) Praha, 1960.
Phil 4710.30   O russkoi klassicheskoi filosofii XIX v. (Kruzhkov, U.S.) Moskva, 1968.
Phil 7150.34   O samoubiistvie. (Berdiaev, N.A.) Paris, 1931.
Phil 9245.118   O schast'e. (Novikov, Mikhail I.) Moskva, 1965.

Phil 8980.770.5 O sociajalističkom moralu. (Savez Komunista Srbije. Univerzitetski Komitet.) Beograd, 1964.

Phil 630.56 O socialistickom realizme. (Bakoš, Mik.) Bratislava, 1952.

Phil 4759.1.35 O soprotivlenii zlu siloiu. (Il'in, I.A.) Berlin, 1925.

Phil 8015.2 O sovremennoi burzhuaznoi estetike. Moskva. 2,1965+

Phil 8411.30 O sushchnosti esteticheskogo poznaniia. (Kornienko, V.S.) Novosibirsk, 1962.

Phil 8409.4 O sushchnosti krasoty. (Ivanov, Pavel L.) Moskva, 1967.

Phil 175.61 O sushchnosti zhizni. (Akademiia Nauk SSSR. Nauchnyi Sovet po Filosofskim Voprosam Estestvoznaniia.) Moskva, 1964.

Phil 8419.62 O svobode tvorchestva. (Shamota, Mykolaz.) Moskva, 1966.

Phil 8980.851 O tsennostiakh zhizni i kul'tury. (Tugarinov, Vasilii P.) Leningrad, 1960.

Phil 8408.30 O umění. (Hostinsky, Otakar.) Praha, 1956.

Phil 4803.313.30 O uniwersytecie i studiach uniwersyteckick. (Czezowski, Tadeusz.) Toruń, 1946.

Phil 342.30 O uzasadniającej roli analogii na przykładzie wnioskowań z zakresu historii sztaki. (Ławniczak, Włodzimierz.) Poznań, 1971.

Phil 5068.56.25 O verzicht van de analytische wijsbegeeste. (Nuchelmans, Gabriël.) Utrecht, 1969.

Phil 310.610 O vidakh protivorechii. (Horbach, U.I.) Minsk, 1964.

Phil 4769.1.92 O Vl. S. Solov'eve v ego molodye gody. Kniga 3. Vyp. I. (Luk'ianov, S.M.) Petrograd, 1921. 2v.

Phil 8413.39 O vozvyshennom v mire estetiki. (Malygin, Vladimir A.) Leningrad, 1966.

Phil 8411.42 O zakonakh krasoty. (Kornienko, Vasilii S.) Khar'kov, 1970.

Phil 310.415.5 O zákonech dějin. (Cvekl, Jiři.) Praha, 1957.

Phil 5545.215 O zakonomernostiakh elementarnoi poznavatel'noi deiatel'nosti. (Antsyferova, L.I.) Moskva, 1961.

Phil 1145.15 Oakeley, Frederick. Remarks upon Aristotelian and Platonic ethics. Oxford, 1837.

Phil 1145.74 Oakeley, Hilda D. Greek ethical thought. London, 1925.

Phil 575.68 Oakeley, Hilda D. A study in the philosophy of personality. London, 1928.

Phil 189.23 Oakeshott, Michael. Experience and its modes. Cambridge,Eng., 1933.

Phil 180.70.5 Oase des Glücks. (Fink, Eugen.) Freiburg, 1957.

Phil 585.266 Ob idolakh i idealakh. (Il'enkov, Eval'd V.) Moskva, 1968.

Htn Phil 3585.4.31* Ob man für dem Sterben fliehen muge. (Luther, Martin.) Wittenberg, 1527.

Phil 310.750 Ob otnoshenii marksistski-leninskoi filosofii k estestrosnamiu. (Iurova, Inna L.) Moskva, 1970.

Htn Phil 3801.779* Ob Schelling? ob Schmitt? (Seuberg, J.A.) Mainz, 1845.

Phil 178.54.5 L'obbietto della filosofia e la verità. (Dandolo, G.) Padova, 1894.

Phil 310.778 Ob"ektirnye zakony istorii i nauchnoe rukovodstov obshchestvom. (Simpozium po Teme Ob"ektivnye Zakony Istorii i Nauchnoe Rukovodstov Obshchestvom, Moscow, 1967.) Moskva, 1970.

Phil 4720.5 Ob"ektivnoe i sub"ektivnoe v poznanii i prakticheskoi deiatel'nosti. (Zuev, Ivan E.) Moskva, 1969.

Phil 3640.425 Obenauer, K.J. Friedrich Nietzsche der erkstatische Nihilist. Jena, 1924.

Phil 3496.4 Obereit, J.H. Beobachtungen über die Quelle der Metaphysik. Meiningen, 1791.

Phil 70.94 Oberlin Colloquium in Philosophy, 3d, Oberlin College, 1962. Knowledge and experience. Pittsburgh, Pa. 1962

Phil 70.94.5 Oberlin Colloquium in Philosophy, 5th, Oberlin College, 1964. Metaphysics and explanation. Pittsburgh, Pa. 1966

Phil 70.94.6 Oberlin Colloquium in Philosophy, 6th, Oberlin College, 1965. Art, mind, and religion; proceedings. Pittsburgh. 1967

Phil 70.94.8 Oberlin Colloquium in Philosophy, 8th, Oberlin College, 1967. Perception and personal identity. Cleveland. 1969

Phil 70.94.10 Oberlin Colloquium in Philosophy. Society, revolution and reform; proceedings. Cleveland, 1971.

Phil 6324.4 Oberndorf, Clarence. A history of psychoanalysis in America. N.Y., 1953.

Phil 6124.1 Obersteiner, H. Anleitung beim Studium des Baues der nervösen Centratorgane. Leipzig, 1888.

Phil 3705.7 Oberth, Hermann. Stoff und Leben. Remagen, 1959.

Phil 8415.9 Oberti, Elisa, Contributi all'analisi estetica. Milano, 1962.

Phil 3450.19.135 Oberti, Elisa. L'estetica nel pensiero di Heidegger. Milano, 1955.

Phil 8415.9.5 Oberti, Elisa. Estetica teoria dell'oggetto artistico come presenz evidenziata. Milano, 1962.

Phil 8415.9.10 Oberti, Elisa. Per una fondazione fenomenologica della conoscitività dell'arte. Milano, 1968.

Phil 344.6 Ob"iasnenie - funktsiia nauki. (Nikitin, Evgenii P.) Moskva, 1970.

Phil 193.49.45A Obiter dicta. (Santayana, G.) N.Y., 1936.

Phil 9530.8 An object in life. (Schmidt, F.L.) N.Y., 1889.

Phil 6322.50 Object love and reality. (Modell, Arnold H.) N.Y., 1968.

Phil 6322.51 Object love and reality: an introduction to a psychoanalytic theory of object relations. (Modell, Arnold H.) London, 1969.

Phil 8580.27 The object of Christian worship. Thesis. (Aldwinckle, M.R.F.) Strasbourg, 1938.

Phil 8897.90.5 The object of morality. (Warnock, Geoffrey James.) London, 1971.

Phil 5590.200 The object relations technique. (Phillipson, H.) London, 1955. 2v.

Phil 9495.8 Objecte der sinnlichen Wahrnehmung. (Drossbach, M.) Halle, 1865.

Phil 1750.166.145 Objections to humanism. (Blackham, H.J.) London, 1963.

Phil 5923.1 Objections to phrenology. (Drummond, D.) Calcutta, 1829.

Phil 6312.11.5 Objective and experimental psychiatry. 2. ed. (Cameron, Donald E.) N.Y., 1941.

Phil 6319.1.204 The objective psyche. (Fordham, M.S.M.) London, 1958.

Phil 630.27 Objective reality. (Roberts, George L.) London, 1925.

Phil 1710.6 The objective society. (Knight, Everett.) London, 1959.

Phil 1710.6.2 The objective society. (Knight, Everett.) N.Y., 1959.

Phil 531.8 Objectivism and the study of man. (Skjeroheim, Hans.) Oslo, 1959.

Phil 1145.81 Het objectiviteitsbeginsel in de oudste Grieksche ethik. (Wal, L.G.) Groningen, 1934.

Phil 335.8 Objectivity. (Earle, William A.) N.Y., 1955.

Phil 338.39 Objectivity and reason. (Harris, E.E.) Johannesburg, 1955.

Phil 8423.10 The objectivity of the judgment of aesthetic value. (Walsh, Dorothy.) Lancaster, 1936.

Phil 720.2 Objectivity of truth. (Stokes, G.J.) London, 1884.

Phil 3475.3.145 Objekt und Transzendenz bei Jaspers. (Armbruster, Ludwig.) Innsbruck, 1957.

Phil 356.3 Die objektive Geltung Slogik und der Immanenzge Danke. (Zocher, Rudolf.) Tübingen, 1925.

Phil 3475.3.120 Objektive Norm. Inaug. Diss. (Grunert, P.L.) Bonn, 1953.

Phil 353.14 Objektivität, voraussetzungslose Wissenschaft und wissenschaftliche Wahrheit. (Weidauer, F.) Leipzig, 1935.

Phil 1511.4 Das Objektivität-Prinzip der aristotelisch-scholastische Philosophie. (Glossner, M.) Regensburg, 1880.

Phil 720.60 Objektivität und Wahrheit. (Manzana Martinez de Marañon, José.) Vitoria, 1961.

Phil 720.63 Objektivität und Wahrheit. (Manzana Martinez de Marañon, José.) Vitoria, 1961.

Phil 3500.21 L'objet de la métaphysique selon Kant. (Sentroul, C.) Louvain, 1905.

Phil 5585.54 L'objet de la perception. Thèse. (Duret, René.) Paris, 1929.

Phil 5585.54.2 L'objet de la perception. Thèse. (Duret, René.) Paris, 1929.

Phil 5460.14.5 Les objets dans la folie. (Faure, Henri.) Paris, 1965. 2v.

Phil 9120.185 Obligation; a social theory. (Ross, Ralph Gilbert.) Ann Arbor, 1970.

Phil 8887.61 L'obligation morale, principe de liberté. (Mersch, Émile.) Louvain, 1927.

Phil 8886.20 Obligation morale et idéalisme. (Lefèvre, G.) Paris, 1894.

Phil 400.36 Obligation morale et idéalisme. Thèse. (Lefèvre, Georges.) Paris, 1894.

Phil 8881.45 L'obligation morale raisonnée. (Gomer, A. de.) Paris, 1913.

Phil 5545.66 L'oblio; saggio sull'attività selettiva della coscienza. (Renda, A.) Torino, 1910.

Phil 4368.1.80 La obra del filósofo español Diego Ruiz. (Rigau, P.) Paris, 1913.

Phil 4979.65.30 Obra filosófica. (Romero, Sylvio.) Rio de Janeiro, 1969.

Phil 4803.727.80 La obra psicológica de Radecki, 1910-35. (Cáceres, Alfredo.) Montevideo, 1936.

Phil 3850.18.120F La obra sociologica de Max Scheler. (Povina, Alfredo.) Cordoba, 1941.

Phil 4972.5.15 Obras. (Korn, Alejandro.) La Plata, 1938-40. 3v.

Phil 4363.7.2 Obras. (Marias Aguilera, Julián.) Madrid, 1958-60. 8v.

Phil 4974.27.20 Obras. (Mestre, Jose Manuel.) Habana, 1965.

Phil 4983.1.5 Obras. v.1-25. (Vaz Ferreira, Carlos.) Montevideo, 1957. 20v.

Phil 4374.5.20 Obras. 1. ed. (Xirau, Joaquín.) Mexico, 1963.

Phil 4352.1.55 Obras completas. (Balmes, Jaime.) Madrid, 1948- 8v.

Phil 4970.1.11 Obras completas. (Ingenieros, José.) Buenos Aires, 1962. 8v.

Phil 4972.5.5 Obras completas. (Korn, Alejandro.) Buenos Aires, 1949.

Phil 4368.3.5 Obras completas. (Rouges, Alberto.) Tucumán, 1960.

Phil 4980.52.30 Obras completas. (Silva, Vicente Ferreira da.) São Paulo, 1964. 2v.

Phil 4372.1.1A Obras completas. (Vives, Juan Luis.) Madrid, 1947-48. 2v.

Phil 4357.2.3 Obras completas. v.1-19. (Giner de los Rios, Francisco.) Madrid, 1916-27. 15v.

Phil 1020.7.2 Obras escogidas. (Asin Palacios, M.) Madrid, 1946.

Phil 4340.5 Obras escogidas de filosófos. (Castro y Rossi, Adolf de.) Madrid, 1953.

Phil 4351.4 Obras escogidas del filosofo rancio. (Alvarado, Francisco.) Madrid, 1912.

Phil 4963.6 Obras filosóficas. (Barreto, Luís Pereira.) São Paulo, 1967.

Phil 4360.2 Obras filosoficas. 2. ed. (Joannes XXI.) Barcelona, 1961.

Phil 4356.3 Obras selectas. (Ferrater Mora, José.) Madrid, 1967. 2v.

Phil 4372.1.36 Obras sociales y políticas. (Vives, Juan Luis.) Madrid, 1960.

Phil 4769.10 Obretaet li metafizika vtoroe dykhanie. (Skvortsov, Lev V.) Moskva, 1966.

Phil 6964.6 O'Brien, Barbara (pseud.). Operators and things: the inner life of a schizophrenic. Cambridge, Mass., 1958.

Phil 525.237 O'Brien, E. Varieties of mystic experience, an anthology and interpretation. 1st ed. N.Y., 1964.

Phil 3640.254 O'Brien, Edward J. Son of the morning; a portrait of F. Nietzsche. N.Y., 1932.

Phil 365.33 O'Brien, J.A. Evolution and religion. N.Y., 1932.

Phil 6964.3.5 O'Brien, John D. An outline of psychiatry. 2. ed. St. Louis, Mo., 1935.

Phil 8669.6 O'Brien, Thomas C. Metaphysics and the existence of God. Washington, 1960.

Phil 6950.1 Observation...insanity, lunacy or madness. v.1-2. (Arnold, T.) Leicester, 1782-86.

Phil 5190.25 Observation and protocolstatement. (Schultzer, B.) Copenhagen, 1938.

Phil 6972.1 Observationes...affectibus capitis. (Wepferi, J.J.) Scaphusii, 1727.

Phil 6968.8.6 Observations...mind...insanity. (Spurzheim, J.K.) Boston, 1833.

Phil 6968.8.5 Observations...mind...insanity. (Spurzheim, J.K.) London, 1817.

Phil 8581.13.15 Observations...natural theology by H. Lord Brougham. (Wallace, T.) London, 1835.

Phil 8685.8 Observations...pantheistic principles. (Mill, W.H.) Cambridge, 1855.

Phil 6990.4.2 Observations. (Bonnaire, Louis de.) n.p., 1773. 2 pam.

Phil 2115.152 Observations. (Massie, J.) London, 1760.

Phil 2150.23 Observations. (Morgan, Arthur Ernest.) Yellow Springs, 1968.

Phil 2218.83 Observations. (Pures, J.) Philadelphia, 1797.

Phil 2218.84 Observations. v.1-2. (Palmer, J.) London, 1779.

Phil 8897.48 Observations of a progressive religionist. (Wirpel, Aaron.) Cleveland, 1923.

Phil 5921.2.5 Observations on Dr. Barclay's ojections. (Combe, A.) Edinburgh, 1823.

Phil 8434.2.15 Observations on forest scenery. (Gilpin, W.) Edinburgh, 1834.

Phil 9390.2.5 Observations on legal and judicial oaths. v.1-2. (Lewis, E.) Philadelphia, 1846-59.

Htn Phil 2038.30* Observations on man. (Hartley, D.) London, 1749. 2v.

Phil 2038.31 Observations on man. (Hartley, D.) London, 1791. 3v.

Phil 2038.32 Observations on man. (Hartley, D.) London, 1801. 3v.

Phil 2038.33 Observations on man. (Hartley, D.) London, 1834.

Phil 2038.34 Observations on man. v.1-2. (Hartley, D.) Gainesville, Fla., 1966.

Phil 6965.9 Observations on maniacal disorders. (Pargeter, William.) Reading, Eng., 1792.

Phil 6115.5 Observations on mental phenomena. (Fisher, W.S.) Philadelphia, 1851.

Phil 6128.20 Observations on nervous system. (Swan, Joseph.) London, 1822.

Phil 6134.1 Observations on scientific study of human nature. (Youmans, E.L.) N.Y., 1867.

Phil 8669.2 Observations on the chronology of scripture. (Franklin, Maria.) N.Y., 1795.

Phil 2218.85.5 Observations on the emigration of Joseph Priestley. (Cobbett, William.) Philadelphia, 1794.

Phil 2218.85 Observations on the emigration of Joseph Priestley. London, 1794.

Phil 3480.82.8 Observations on the feeling of the beautifull and sublime. (Kant, Immanuel.) Berkeley, 1960.

Phil 5257.2.2 Observations on the growth of the mind. (Reed, S.) Boston, 1829.

Phil 5257.2 Observations on the growth of the mind. (Reed, S.) Boston, 1838.

Phil 5257.2.5 Observations on the growth of the mind. 5th ed. (Reed, S.) Boston, 1859.

Phil 6119.1.5 Observations on the localisation of movements in the cerebral hemispheres. (Jackson, J.H.) n.p., n.d.

Phil 9390.6 Observations on the nature of oaths. (Douglas, Robert.) Edinburgh, 1783.

Phil 6122.25FA Observations on the structure of the nervous system. (Monro, Alexander.) Edinburgh, 1783. 2v.

Phil 7054.73.9 Observations on the theological mystery...spirit rappings. Hartford, 1851.

Htn Phil 7230.1* Observations on trance. (Braid, J.) London, 1850.

Phil 5827.4 Observations physiques et morales sur l'instinct des animaux. (Reimarus, Hermann Samuel.) Amsterdam, 1770. 2v.

Phil 181.21.10 Observations sur le dieu-monde de M. Vacherot et de M. Tiberghien. (Gruyer, L.A.) Paris, 1860.

Phil 477.3 Observations sur le livre "Système de la nature". (Castillon, J. de.) Berlin, 1771.

Phil 5816.7 Observations sur les instincts de l'homme et l'intelligence des animaux. (Gay, Henri.) Paris, 1878.

Phil 2403.3 Observations sur les Savans incredules. (DeLuc, J.F.) Genève, 1762.

Phil 822.11 Obsessions and convictions of the human intellect. (Westaway, F.W.) London, 1938.

Phil 5627.34.5 Les obsessions dans la vie religieuse. Thèse. (Perrier, Louis.) Montpellier, 1905.

Phil 6959.1.9A Les obsessions et la psychasthénie. (Janet, Pierre.) Paris, 1903. 2v.

Phil 4762.1.38 Obshchedostupnoe vvedenie v filosofiiu. (Losskii, Nikolai Onufrievich.) Frankfurt, 1956.

Phil 960.245 Obshchestvenno-politicheskaia i filosofskaia mysl' Indii. (Akademiia Nauk SSSR. Institut Narodov Azii.) Moskva, 1966.

Phil 310.145 Obshchestvennoe soznanie i ego formy. (Nesterenko, G.I.) Moskva, 1959. 2 pam.

Phil 8980.630 Obshchestvo pro Rasprostran. O kommunisticheskoi etike. London, 1962.

Phil 54.5 Obshchestvo Psikhologov, Moscow, 1. S"ezd, 1959. Tezisy dokladov, 29 iiunia -4 iiulia 1959 g. v.1-3. Moskva, 1959.

Phil 8980.770 Obshchie metody nravstvennogo vospitaniia. (Sarich, A.L.) Moskva, 1956.

Phil 186.56.10 Obstacle et valeur. (Le Senne, R.) Paris, 1934.

Phil 8060.5 O'Callaghan, J. Las tres categorías estéticas de la cultura clásica. Madrid, 1960.

Phil 3549.2.100 Ocampo, Victoria. El viajero y una de sus sombras; Keyserling en mis memorias. Buenos Aires, 1951.

Phil 8696.3 Occasional papers. (Gardiner, F.) Middletown, Conn., 1881. 3 pam.

Phil 57.14F Occasional papers. (Rhodes University, Grahamstown, South Africa. Department of Philosophy.) Grahamstown. 1,1965+

Phil 8595.9 Occasional thoughts...astronomer, nature, revelation. (Pritchard, C.) London, 1889.

Phil 3280.91 L'Occasionalisme d'Arnold Geulincx. (Lattre, Alain de.) Paris, 1967.

Phil 1540.24 L'occasionalismo e il suo sviluppo nel pensiero de N. Malebranche. (DeMatteis, F.) Napoli, 193-.

Phil 7069.20.259 Occult diary. Chicago, 1920.
Phil 7060.81 Occult experiences. (Reichel, W.) London. n.d.
Phil 978.68.5 Occult glossary. (Purucker, G. de.) London, 1933.
Phil 7054.29 Occult revelations in prose and verse. (Tindall, A.F.) London, n.d.

Phil 7060.76 Occult science in India. (Jacolliot, Louis.) N.Y., 1908.
Phil 6121.18.5 Occult science library; seven essays. (Loomis, E.) Chicago, 1898.

Phil 978.9.10 The occult world. (Sinnett, A.P.) Boston, 1882.
Phil 7060.113 Occultism and common sense. (Willson, Beckles.) London, 1908.

Phil 7069.09.30 Occultism and common-sense. (Willson, Beckles.) N.Y., 1908?

Phil 7069.21.47 Occultism and modern science. (Oesterreich, T.K.) London, 1923.

Phil 7060.69 L'occultisme: hier et aujourd'hui. (Grasset, J.) Montpelier, 1908.

Phil 525.25 Occultists and mystics of all ages. (Shirley, Ralph.) London, 1920.

Phil 7069.01.5 The occultist's handbook. Chicago, 1901.
Phil 7069.08.30 An occultist's travels. (Reichel, Willy.) N.Y., 1908.
Phil 978.7.3 The ocean of theosophy. (Judge, W.Z.) Point Loma, Calif., 1926[1923]

Phil 978.7.2 The ocean of theosophy. 2nd ed. (Judge, W.Z.) N.Y., 1893.
Htn Phil 2055.4.30F* The oceana of James Harrington. (Harrington, James.) Dublin, 1737.

Phil 3850.18.165 Ocena możliwości zbudowania etyki chresc. (Wojtyła, K.B.) Lublin, 1959.

Phil 4803.896.20 Oceny i normy. (Znamierowski, Czesław Stanisław.) Warszawa, 1957.

Phil 5415.10 Ochanine, D. La sympathie. Paris, 1938.
Phil 1075.6 Ocherk istorii armianskoi mysli. (Gabriel'ian, Genri.) Erevan, 1962.

Phil 8839.5 Ocherk istorii etiki. Moskva, 1969.
Phil 1108.4 Ocherk istorii filosofii klassicheskoi Gretsii. (Dynnik, M.A.) Moskva, 1936.

Phil 310.677 Ocherk marksistskoi filosofii. (Iakhot, Ovshii O.) Moskva, 1968.

Phil 4680.312 Ocherk razvitiia progressivnoi filosofskoi iobshchestvenno-politicheskoi mysli v Latvii. (Valeskalns, Peteris.) Riga, 1967.

Phil 4769.4.5 Ocherk razvitiia russkoi filosofii. (Shpet, Gustav.) Petrograd, 1922.
Phil 5710.21 Ocherk teori temperamenta. (Merlin, V.S.) Moskva, 1964.
Phil 310.1.8 Ocherki istorii dialektiki v novoi filosofii. 2. izd. (Asmus, Valentin F.) Moskva, 1929. 2 pam.

Phil 8050.21 Ocherki istorii esteticheskikh uchenii. (Ovsiannikov, M.F.) Moskva, 1963.

Phil 4882.1 Ocherki istorii filosofskoi i obshchestvenno-politicheskoi mysli v Turkmenistane. Ashkhabad, 1970.

Phil 310.683 Ocherki istorii marksistsko-leninskoi filosofii v Belorussii, 1919-1968. Minsk, 1968.

Phil 8090.4 Ocherki istorii marksistskoi estetiki. (Trofimov, P.S.) Moskva, 1963.

Phil 6980.363.5 Ocherki istorii otechestvennoi psikhiatrii. (Iudin, Tikhon I.) Moskva, 1951.

Phil 5237.516.5 Ocherki istorii psikhologicheskikh vozznenii v Rossii v XI-XVIII vekakh. (Sokolov, Mikhail V.) Moskva, 1963.
Phil 310.340 Ocherki logiki istoricheskogo issledovaniia. (Grushin, B.H.) Moskva, 1961.

Phil 8400.13 Ocherki marksistsko-leninskoi estetiki. (Akademiia Khudozhestv SSSR. Institut Teorii i Istorii Iskusstva.) Moskva, 1956.

Phil 8400.15 Ocherki marksistsko-leninskoi estetiki. (Akademiia Khudozhestv SSSR. Institut Teorii i Istorii Iskusstva.) Moskva, 1960.

Phil 8980.463 Ocherki marksistsko-leninskoi etiki. (Ivanov, Vladimir G.) Leningrad, 1963.

Phil 4710.151 Ocherki po etike velikikh russkih revoliutsionnykh demokratov. (Aznaurov, Artem A.) Baku, 1964.
Phil 4795.10 Ocherki po istorii Azerbaidzhanskoi filosofii. (Akademiia nauk Azerbaidzhanskoi SSR, Baku. Sektor filosofii.) Baku, 1966.

Phil 4710.17A Ocherki po istorii filosoficheskoi i obshchestvenno-politicheskoi mysli narodov SSSR. (Akademiia Nauk SSSR. Institut Filosofii.) Moskva, 1955. 2v.

Phil 1819.5 Ocherki po istorii filosofii i sotsiologii Anglii XIX v. (Trakhtenberg, O.V.) Moskva, 1959.
Phil 5022.4 Ocherki po istorii logiki v Rossii. (Moscow. Universitet. Filosofskii Fakul'tet.) Moskva, 1962.
Phil 1701.45 Ocherki po istorii noveishei i sovremennoi burzhuaznoi filosofii. (Bakradze, K.S.) Tbilisi, 1960.
Phil 6980.286 Ocherki po istorii otechestvennoi psikhiatrii, vtoria polovina XVIII. (Fedotov, D.D.) Moskva, 1957.
Phil 4795.6 Ocherki po istorii peredovoi filosofskoi i obshchestvenno-politicheskoi mysli azerbaidzhanskogo naroda v XIX veke. (Kasumov, Mekhbaly Mamedovich.) Baku, 1959.
Phil 600.57 Ocherki po istorii pozitivizma. (Narskii, Igor Sergeevich.) Moskva, 1960.
Phil 4710.140 Ocherki po istorii russkoi ateisticheskoi mysli XVIII v. (Kogan, Iu.Ia.) Moskva, 1962.
Phil 4710.159 Ocherki po istorii russkoi filosofskoi i obshchestvennoi mysli. (Levitskii, Sergei A.) Frankfurt, 1968.
Phil 5237.516 Ocherki po istorii russkoi psikhologii. Moskva, 1957.
Phil 5210.5 Ocherki po istorii russkoi psikhologii XVII i XIX v. (Anan'ev, B.G.) Moskva, 1947.
Phil 1020.49 Ocherki po istorii tadzhikskoi filosofii. (Bogoutdinov, Alautin M.) Stalinabad, 1961.
Phil 1524.5 Ocherki po istorii zapadno-evropeiskoi Srednevekovoi filosofii. (Traktenberg, O.V.) Moskva, 1957.
Phil 8980.861 Ocherki po marksistsko-leninskoi etike. (Utkin, S.S.) Moskva, 1962.
Phil 8665.20 Ocherki po nauchnomu ateizmu. (Karliak, A.S.) Minsk, 1961.
Phil 4710.4.10 Ocherki russkoi filosofii. (Jakovenko, B.) Berlin, 1922.
Phil 1810.3 Ocherki sovremennoi anglo-amerikanskoi filosofii. (Koitko, D. Iu.) Moskva, 1936.
VPhil 310.694 Ochocki, Aleksander. Materializm historyezny. Warszawa, 1969.

Phil 6684.1 Ochorowicz, J. De la suggestion mentale. Paris, 1887.
Phil 6684.1.5 Ochorowicz, J. Mental suggestion. v.1-4. N.Y., 1891.
Phil 6124.5 Ochs, Sidney. Elements of neurophysiology. N.Y., 1965.
Phil 2190.5 Ockham. (Lornay, Stephen Clark.) LaSalle, Ill., 1945.
Phil 2190.20 Ockhams Weg zur Sozialphilosophie. (Miethke, Jürgen.) Berlin, 1969.
Phil 189.1 O'Connell, J. Vestiges of civilization. N.Y., 1851.
Phil 8583.28.10 O'Connor, D.A. The relation between religion and culture according to C. Dawson. Montreal, 1952.
Phil 814.6 O'Connor, Daniel J. A critical history of Western philosophy. N.Y., 1964.
Phil 189.28 O'Connor, E.M. Potentiality and energy. Diss. Washington, 1939.
Phil 6124.7 O'Connor, John. Modern materialism; readings on mind-body identity. N.Y., 1969.
Phil 5850.288.5 O'Connor, Johnson. Psychometrics. Cambridge, Mass., 1934.
Phil 5238.160 O'Connor, N. Recent Soviet psychology. N.Y., 1961.
Phil 8669.5 O'Connor, William R. The natural desire for God. Milwaukee, 1948.
Htn Phil 182.29* Octavum renata. (Heidfeld, J.) Herbornae Nassoviorum, 1621.

Phil 9560.56 Od filantropii do human i humanizmu. 2. wyd. (Sinko, Tadeuz.) Warszawa, 1960.
Phil 4825.11 Od Heraklita do njegoša i Svetozara. (Nedeljković, Dušan.) Beograd, 1971.

Phil 1715.13 Od Lockea do Ayera. (Petrović, Gajo.) Beograd, 1964.
Phil 1701.56 Od realizmu k iracionalizmu; zo súčasnej západnej filozofie. 1. vyd. (Podnár, Ján.) Bratislava, 1966.
Phil 8414.14 Od skutečnosti ku umění. (Novák, Mirko.) Praha, 1965.
Phil 8692.26 Od víry k vědě. (Čížek, Fr.) Praha, 1961.
Phil 8430.51 Odbiorca sztuki jako krytyk. Wyd.1. (Naksianowicz-Golaszewska, Maria.) Kraków, 1967.
Phil 8964.2 Oddone, Andrea. Teoria degli atti umani. Milano, 1933.
Phil 8415.3 Odebrecht, R. Gefühl und schöpferische Gestaltung. Berlin, 1929.
Phil 8415.3.5 Odebrecht, R. Grundlegung einer ästhetischen Wertheorie. Berlin, 1927-
Phil 3705.4 Odebrecht, R. Welterlebnis. Berlin, 1938.
Phil 3496.5 Odebrecht, Rudolf. Form und Geist. Berlin, 1930.
Phil 5250.13.80 Odebrecht, Rudolf. Gefühl und Ganzheit. Berlin, 1929.
Phil 99.2 Odebrecht, Rudolf. Kleines philosophiches Wörterbuch. Berlin, 1909.
Phil 99.1 Odebrecht, Rudolf. Kleines philosophisches Wörterbuch. Berlin, 1908.
Phil 3805.180 Odebrecht, Rudolf. Schleiermachers System der Ästhetik. Berlin, 1932.
Phil 3640.201 Odenwald, T. Friedrich Nietzsche und der heutige Christentum. Giessen, 1926.
Phil 6100.18 Odette, Laffoneriere. L'ame et le corps. Paris, 1961.

Phil 4803.454.74F Odezwa do naródov slawianskich wzgledem przeznaczeń świata. (Hoene-Wroński, Józef Maria.) Paryz, 1848.
Phil 5401.44 Odier, Charles. Anxiety and magic thinking. N.Y., 1956.
Phil 8905.22 Odier, Charles. Les deux sources, consciente et inconsciente, de la vie morale. 2. éd. Neuchâtel, 1968.
Phil 9070.49.5 Odier, Charles. Les deux sources consciente et inconsciente de la vie morale. 2d éd. Neuchâtel, 1947.
Phil 6324.2 Odier, Charles. Étude psychoanalytique. Le complex d'Oedipe. Genève, 1925.
Phil 6687.1.9 Odisch-magnetische Briefe. (Reichenback, C.) Stuttgart, 1852.
Phil 7060.92.19 O'Donnell, Elliot. Animal ghosts. London, 1913.
Phil 7060.92.47 O'Donnell, Elliot. The Banshee. London, 1920.
Phil 7060.92.29 O'Donnell, Elliot. Bona-fide adventures with ghosts. Bristol, 1908.
Phil 7060.92.20 O'Donnell, Elliot. By ways of ghost-land. London, 1911.
Phil 7060.92.55 O'Donnell, Elliot. Confessions of a ghost hunter. London, 1928.
Phil 7060.92.60 O'Donnell, Elliot. Family ghosts and ghostly phenomena. 1st ed. N.Y., 1934.
Phil 7069.29.70 O'Donnell, Elliot. Famous curses. London, 1929.
Phil 7060.92.9 O'Donnell, Elliot. Ghostly phenomena. London, n.d.
Phil 7060.92.57 O'Donnell, Elliot. Ghosts of London. London, 1932.
Phil 7069.51.5 O'Donnell, Elliot. Ghosts with a purpose. London, 1951.
Phil 7060.92.25 O'Donnell, Elliot. Haunted highways and byways. London, 1914.
Phil 7060.92.15 O'Donnell, Elliot. Haunted houses of London. London, 1909.
Phil 7060.92.35 O'Donnell, Elliot. Haunted places in England. London, 1919.
Phil 7069.57.5 O'Donnell, Elliot. Haunted waters. London, 1957.
Phil 7069.20.260 O'Donnell, Elliot. The menace of spiritualism. Chicago, 1920.
Phil 7069.20.261 O'Donnell, Elliot. The menace of spiritualism. London, 1920.
Phil 7060.92.45 O'Donnell, Elliot. More haunted houses of London. London, 1920.
Phil 7060.92.61 O'Donnell, Elliot. Phantoms of the night. London, 1956.
Phil 7060.92.5 O'Donnell, Elliot. Some haunted houses. London, 1908.
Phil 7060.92.41 O'Donnell, Elliot. Twenty years' experience as a ghost hunter. London, 1916.
Phil 1560.12 O'Donnell, J. Reginald. Nine medieval thinkers. Toronto, 1955.
Phil 5655.7 L'odorat. (Zwaardemaker, H.) Paris, 1925.
Phil 5655.9 Odors and the sense of smell. (Airkem, Inc.) N.Y., 1952.
Phil 8408.41 Odraz, izraz. (Hadživasilev, Mito.) Skopje, 1958.
Phil 3640.595.5 Oduev, S.F. Reaktsionnaia sushchnost' nitssheanstva. Moskva, 1959.
Phil 3640.595.5 Oduev, S.F. Tropami Zaratustry. Moskva, 1971.
Phil 1750.115.190 Odvažnost izricanja; fenomenologije životnih formi. (Prohić, Kasim.) Zagreb, 1970.
Phil 2496.79.10 Ody, Hermann. Victor Cousin. Saarbrücken, 1953.
Phil 3801.465.5 L'odyssée de la conscience dans la dernière philosophie de Schelling. (Jankélévitch, V.) Paris, 1933.
Phil 3801.465 L'odyssée de la conscience dans la dernière philosophie de Schelling. Thèse. (Jankélévitch, V.) Paris, 1932.
Phil 182.107 Odysseus oder die Zukunft der Philosophie. (Heinemann, F.) Stockholm, 1939.
Phil 3910.60 Oeconomica. (Wolff, Christian von.) Halae, 1754.
Phil 6980.557 Oedipe africain. (Ortigues, Marie.) Paris, 1966.
Phil 6322.31.2 Oedipus. (Mullahy, Patrick.) N.Y., 1955.
Phil 6322.31 Oedipus. 1st ed. (Mullahy, Patrick.) N.Y., 1948.
Phil 6315.2.86 Der Ödipus-Komplex der Freudschen Psychoanalyse. (Schmidt, Wilhelm.) Berlin, 1929.
Phil 6322.31.1 Oedipus myth and complex. 1st ed. (Mullahy, Patrick.) N.Y., 1948.
Phil 189.26 Oegger, G. Nouvelles questions philosophiques. Tubingue, 1835.
Phil 530.20.86 Oehl, W. Deutsche Mystikerbriefe. München, 1931.
Phil 165.339 Oehler, K. Einsichten. Frankfurt a.M., 1962.
Phil 3640.221 Oehler, Max. Den Manen Friedrich Nietzsches. München, 1921.
Phil 3640.17.11 Oehler, R. Nietzsche. Register. Stuttgart, 1943.
Phil 3640.200.15 Oehler, Richard. Friedrich Nietzsche und die deutsche Zukunft. Leipzig, 1935.
Phil 3640.200.9 Oehler, Richard. Friedrich Nietzsche und die Vorsokratiker. Leipzig, 1904.
Phil 3640.200.25 Oehler, Richard. Nietzsche als Bildner der Persönlichkeit. Leipzig, 1911?
Phil 3640.79.100 Oehler, Richard. Nietzscheregister. Leipzig, 1926.
Phil 3640.79.105 Oehler, Richard. Nietzscheregister. Stuttgart, 1943.
Phil 3640.79.107 Oehler, Richard. Nietzscheregister. Stuttgart, 1965.
Phil 3640.200 Oehler, Richard. Nietzsches philosophisches Werden. München, 1926.
Phil 5643.9 L'oeil et l'oreille. (Egger, V.) Paris, 1886.
Phil 5545.46 Ökonomie und Technik des Gedächtnisses. (Meumann, E.) Leipzig, 1908.
Phil 8422.7.30 Oelmueller, W. Friedrich T. Vischer und das Problem der nachhegelschen Ästhetik. Stuttgart, 1959.
Phil 3030.6 Oelmueller, W. Die unbefriedigte Aufklärung. Frankfurt, 1969.
Phil 5465.29 Ölzelt-Newin, A. Über Phantasie-Vorstellungen. Graz, 1889.
Phil 5400.46 Oelzelt-Newin, A. Über sittliche Dispositionen. Graz, 1892.
Phil 4655.1.40 Öppet sändebref till teologisk tidskrift. (Wikner, Pontus.) Upsala, 1881.
Phil 3480.80.125 Az örök héke. (Kant, Immanuel.) Budapest, 1918.
Phil 189.4.10 Oersted, H.C. Der Geist in der Natur. München, 1850-1851. 2v.
Phil 189.4 Oersted, H.C. Gesammelte Schriften. Leipzig, 1850-1851. 6v.
Phil 189.4.14F Oersted, H.C. Naturvidenskabelige skrifter. København, 1920. 3v.
Phil 189.4.2 Oersted, H.C. Samlede og efterladte skrifter. v.1-3, 4-6, 7-9. Kjøbenhavn, 1851-1852. 3v.
Phil 189.4.12 Oersted, H.C. The soul in nature. London, 1852.
Phil 1870.114 Oertel, Hans. George Berkeley und die englische Literatur. Halle, 1934.
Phil 5865.6.2 Oerter, Rolf. Moderne Entwicklungspsychologie. 2. Aufl. Donauwörth, 1968.
Phil 8415.7.4 Oeser, C. Briefe an eine Jungfrau über die Hauptgegenstände der Ästhetik. 4. Aufl. Leipzig, 1852.
Phil 8415.7.13 Oeser, C. Briefe an eine Jungfrau über die Hauptgegenstände der Ästhetik. 13. Aufl. Leipzig, 1872.
Phil 3801.637 Oeser, Erhard. Die antike Dialektik in der Spätphilosophie Schellings. Wein, 1965.

Phil 189.33 Østerberg, Dag. Forståelsesformer. Et filosofisk bidrag. Oslo, 1966.
Phil 3246.229 Oestereich, H. Freiheitsides und Rechtsbegriff in der Philosophie von Johann Gottlieb Fichte. Jena, 1935.
Phil 8889.5 Oesterle, J.A. Ethics. Englewood Cliffs, N.J., 1957.
Phil 5190.1 Oesterlen, F. Medical logic. London, 1855.
Phil 3014.1A Oesterreich, K. Die deutsche Philosophie inder zweiten Halfte des neunzehnten Jahrhund. Tübingen, 1910.
Phil 575.14 Oesterreich, K. Die Phänomenologie des Ich in ihren Grundproblem. Leipzig, 1910.
Phil 5627.71 Oesterreich, T.K. Einfürung in die Religionspsychologie. Berlin, 1917.
Phil 7069.21.47 Oesterreich, T.K. Occultism and modern science. London, 1923.
Phil 7069.21.45 Oesterreich, T.K. Der Okkultismus im modernen Weltbild. 3. Aufl. Dresden, 1923.
Phil 3705.6.20 Oesterreich, Trangott K. Trangott Konstanin Österreich. Stuttgart, 1954.
Phil 8964.6 Oesterreichisches Seelsorge-Institut. Weihnachts-Seelsorgertagung, 1959. Der Christ und die Weltwirklichkeit. Wien, 1960.
Phil 2730.15 Oeuvres. (Maine de Biran, Pierre.) Paris, 1920-1939. 12v.
Phil 8423.7 L'oeuvre d'art et la beauté. (Wulf, M. de.) Louvain, 1920.
Phil 8401.16 L'oeuvre d'art vivant. (Appin, Adolph.) Genève, 1921.
Phil 6315.2.455 L'oeuvre de Freud et son importance pour le monde moderne. (Hesnard, Angelo.) Paris, 1960.
Phil 6319.1.220 L'oeuvre de Jung. (Baudouin, C.) Paris, 1963.
Phil 3497.25 L'oeuvre de Kant. (Philonenko, Alexis.) Paris, 1969-
Phil 2805.22 L'oeuvre de Pascal. (Pascal, Blaise.) Argenteuil, 1936.
Phil 190.85 L'oeuvre de philosophie. (Piguet, Jean C.) Neuchâtel, 1960.
Phil 4080.15.81 L'oeuvre inachevée de Mario Calderoni. (Renauld, J.F.) n.p., n.d.
Phil 6315.2.129 L'oeuvre paradoxale de Freud. 1. éd. (Cové, M.) Paris, 1945.
Phil 4803.454.5 L'oeuvre philosophique de Hoené Wronski. (Hoene-Wroński, Józef Maria.) Paris, 1933-36. 2v.
Phil 2477.2.25 Oeuvre posthumes. (Bordas-Demoulin, J.B.) Paris, 1861. 2v.
Phil 6312.14 Oeuvre psychiatrique. v.1-2. (Clerambault, G.G.) Paris, 1942. 2v.
Phil 2655.2.85 L'oeuvre psychobiophysique. (Warrain, F.) Paris, 1931.
Phil 2655.2.86 L'oeuvre psychobiophysique. 2 éd. (Warrain, F.) Paris, 1938.
Phil 2905.1.7 L'oeuvre scientifique. (Teilhard de Chardin, Pierre.) Olten, 1971.
Phil 2805.77 L'oeuvre scientifique de Blaise Pascal. (Maire, Albert.) Paris, 1912.
Phil 2805.416 L'oeuvre scientifique de Pascal. Paris, 1964.
Phil 2805.40 Oeuvres; Les pensées. (Pascal, Blaise.) Paris, 1830.
Phil 3552.18.10 Oeuvres, publiées pour la première fois d'après les manuscrits. v.2-7. (Leibniz, Gottfried Wilhelm.) N.Y., 1969. 7v.
Phil 2445.3.1 Oeuvres. (André, Yves.) Paris, 1766-67. 4v.
Phil 1850.23 Oeuvres. (Bacon, Francis.) Dijon, 1800. 3v.
Phil 2480.10 Oeuvres. (Cabanis, P.J.G.) Paris, 1823. 5v.
Phil 2493.10 Oeuvres. (Condillac, Étienne Bonnot.) Paris, 1798. 23v.
Phil 2520.16 Oeuvres. (Descartes, René.) Paris, 1824-26. 11v.
Phil 2520.19.4 Oeuvres. (Descartes, René.) Paris, 1844.
Phil 2520.19.4.5 Oeuvres. (Descartes, René.) Paris, 1850.
Phil 2520.19.3 Oeuvres. (Descartes, René.) Paris, 1860.
Phil 2520.19.5 Oeuvres. (Descartes, René.) Paris, 1865.
Phil 2520.19.7 Oeuvres. (Descartes, René.) Paris, 1868.
Phil 2725.22 Oeuvres. (Laberthounière, L.) Paris, 1937.
Phil 2725.11.15 Oeuvres. (Lachelier, Jules.) Paris, 1933. 2v.
Phil 3552.16 Oeuvres. (Leibniz, Gottfried Wilhelm.) Paris, 1842-45. 2v.
Phil 3552.17 Oeuvres. (Leibniz, Gottfried Wilhelm.) Paris, 1859-75. 7v.
Phil 2733.4 Oeuvres. (Malebranche, Nicolas.) Paris, 1842. 2v.
Phil 2733.4.5 Oeuvres. (Malebranche, Nicolas.) Paris, 1859. 2v.
Phil 2805.10 Oeuvres. (Pascal, Blaise.) La Haye, 1779. 5v.
NEDL Phil 2805.17 Oeuvres. (Pascal, Blaise.) Paris, 1914-23. 14v.
Phil 2805.21 Oeuvres. (Pascal, Blaise.) Paris, 1928-29. 6v.
Phil 3819.12 Oeuvres. (Spinoza, Benedictus de.) Paris, 1842.
Phil 3819.12.2 Oeuvres. (Spinoza, Benedictus de.) Paris, 1861.
Phil 3819.12.3 Oeuvres. (Spinoza, Benedictus de.) Paris, 1872. 3v.
Phil 2275.20 Oeuvres. (Stewart, D.) Bruxelles, 1829. 5v.
Phil 2275.22 Oeuvres. (Stewart, D.) Paris, 1829. 2v.
Phil 2905.1.5 Oeuvres. (Teilhard de Chardin, Pierre.) Paris, 1956-10v.
Phil 4260.25 Oeuvres. (Vico, G.B.) Paris, 1835. 2v.
Phil 2520.32.15 Oeuvres. v.1,2,6,8 (pt.1-2), 9 (pt.1-2), 10-11. (Descartes, René.) Paris, 1964. 11v.
Phil 2262.2 Les oeuvres. v.1-3. (Shaftesbury, A.A.C.) Genève, 1769.
Phil 2733.3 Oeuvres. v.1-4. (Malebranche, Nicolas.) Paris, 1871. 2v.
Phil 2475.1.5 Oeuvres. 1e éd. (Bergson, Henri.) Paris, 1959.
Phil 2475.1.8 Oeuvres. 3. éd. (Bergson, Henri.) Paris, 1970.
Phil 2520.19.11 Oeuvres choisies. (Descartes, René.) Paris, 1865.
Htn Phil 2520.19.9* Oeuvres choisies. (Descartes, René.) Paris, 1865.
Phil 2520.26.2 Oeuvres choisies. (Descartes, René.) Paris, 1876.
Phil 2520.26 Oeuvres choisies. (Descartes, René.) Paris, 1877.
Phil 3552.9 Oeuvres choisies. (Leibniz, Gottfried Wilhelm.) Paris, 1939.
Phil 2490.29 Oeuvres choisis. (Comte, Auguste.) Paris, 1943.
Phil 2636.10 Oeuvres complètes. (Helvétius, C.A.) London, 1777. 2v.
Phil 2636.12 Oeuvres complètes. (Helvétius, C.A.) Paris, 1793. 5v.
Phil 2636.12.2 Oeuvres complètes. (Helvétius, C.A.) Paris, 1793-97. 10v.
Phil 2733.5 Oeuvres complètes. (Malebranche, Nicolas.) Paris, 1837. 2v.
Phil 2733.5.5 Oeuvres complètes. (Malebranche, Nicolas.) Paris, 1938. 2v.
Phil 2733.5.11 Oeuvres complètes. (Malebranche, Nicolas.) Paris, 1970.
Phil 8592.122 Oeuvres complètes. (Meslier, Jean.) Paris, 1970-2v.
Phil 2805.13 Oeuvres complètes. (Pascal, Blaise.) Bruges, 1964-
Phil 2805.12 Oeuvres complètes. (Pascal, Blaise.) Paris, 1858.
Phil 2805.19 Oeuvres complètes. (Pascal, Blaise.) Paris, 1926. 2v.
Phil 2240.20 Oeuvres complètes. (Reid, Thomas.) Paris, 1828-36. 6v.

Phil 3819.12.4 Oeuvres complètes. (Spinoza, Benedictus de.) Paris, 1954.
Phil 2630.11.30 Oeuvres complètes. v.1-2. (Guitton, Jean.) Paris, 1966.
Htn Phil 2636.10.7* Oeuvres complètes. v.1-2. (Helvétius, C.A.) London, 1781.
Phil 2733.5.10 Oeuvres complètes. v.1-20. (Malebranche, Nicolas.) Paris, 1958-63. 21v.
Phil 2636.11 Oeuvres complètes. v.3-7. (Helvétius, C.A.) Deuxponts, 1784. 5v.
Phil 2805.15 Oeuvres de Blaise Pascal. (Pascal, Blaise.) Paris, 1886-95. 2v.
Phil 2520.19 Oeuvres de Descartes. (Descartes, René.) Paris, 1897. 12v.
Phil 2520.19.2 Oeuvres de Descartes. Suppl. Index général. (Descartes, René.) Paris, 1913.
Phil 2115.48.25 Oeuvres de Locke et Leibnitz. (Locke, J.) Paris, 1839.
Phil 2438.17 Oeuvres de Messire Antoine Arnauld. v.1-43. (Arnauld, Antoine.) Paris, 1964. 38v.
Phil 3819.15 Oeuvres de Spinoza. (Spinoza, Benedictus de.) Paris, 1914. 2v.
Phil 2496.5 Oeuvres de Victor Cousin. (Cousin, Victor.) Bruxelles, 1840-41. 3v.
Htn Phil 2115.20* Oeuvres diverses. (Locke, J.) Rotterdam, 1710.
Phil 8120.10 Les oeuvres et les lumières. (Brincourt, A.) Paris, 1955.
Phil 2520.31 Oeuvres et lettres. (Descartes, René.) Paris, 1937.
Phil 2730.11 Oeuvres inédites. (Maine de Biran, Pierre.) Paris, 1859. 3v.
Phil 2520.17 Oeuvres morales et philosophiques. (Descartes, René.) Paris, n.d.
Phil 2520.17.5 Oeuvres morales et philosophiques. (Descartes, René.) Paris, 1879.
Htn Phil 1850.27.5* Les oeuvres morales et politiques. (Bacon, Francis.) Paris, 1633. 2v.
Htn Phil 1850.27.3* Les oeuvres morales et politiques. (Bacon, Francis.) Paris, 1637.
Htn Phil 1850.27* Les oeuvres morales et politiques. (Bacon, Francis.) Paris, 1637.
Phil 2515.20 Oeuvres philosophiques, avec une étude bio-bibliographique. (Cordemoy, Géraud de.) Paris, 1968.
Phil 1850.26.5 Oeuvres philosophiques, morales et politiques. (Bacon, Francis.) Paris, 1811.
Phil 2445.3.3 Oeuvres philosophiques. (André, Yves.) Paris, 1843.
Phil 2438.15 Oeuvres philosophiques. (Arnauld, Antoine.) Paris, 1843.
Phil 2438.16 Oeuvres philosophiques. (Arnauld, Antoine.) Paris, 1843.
Phil 1850.25 Oeuvres philosophiques. (Bacon, Francis.) Paris, 1834. 3v.
Phil 176.34 Oeuvres philosophiques. (Buffier, Claude.) Paris, 1843.
Phil 1915.14 Oeuvres philosophiques. (Clarke, Samuel.) Paris, 1843.
Phil 2493.21 Oeuvres philosophiques. (Condillac, Étienne Bonnot.) Paris, 1795. 2v.
Phil 2493.22 Oeuvres philosophiques. (Condillac, Étienne Bonnot.) Paris, 1947-51. 3v.
Phil 2520.15 Oeuvres philosophiques. (Descartes, René.) Paris, 1835. 4v.
Phil 2520.32.10 Oeuvres philosophiques. (Descartes, René.) Paris, 1963- 2v.
Phil 2530.15 Oeuvres philosophiques. (Diderot, Denis.) Bruxelles, 1829. 6v.
Phil 2530.15.5 Oeuvres philosophiques. (Diderot, Denis.) Paris, 1956.
Phil 182.14 Oeuvres philosophiques. (Hemsterhuis, F.) Paris, 1792. 2v.
Phil 182.14.1 Oeuvres philosophiques. (Hemsterhuis, F.) Paris, 1809. 2v.
Htn Phil 2705.15* Oeuvres philosophiques. (La Mettrie, Julien Offray de.) London, 1751.
Phil 3552.10 Oeuvres philosophiques. (Leibniz, Gottfried Wilhelm.) Amsterdam, 1765.
Htn Phil 3552.10.2* Oeuvres philosophiques. (Leibniz, Gottfried Wilhelm.) Amsterdam, 1765.
Phil 2730.10 Oeuvres philosophiques. (Maine de Biran, Pierre.) Paris, 1841. 4v.
Phil 192.9 Oeuvres philosophiques. (Riambourg, J.B.) Paris, 1846. 3v.
Phil 4265.1.15 Oeuvres philosophiques. (Vanini, Lucilio, afterwards Giulio Cesare.) Paris, 1842.
Phil 3552.18 Oeuvres philosophiques. v.2. (Leibniz, Gottfried Wilhelm.) Paris, 1866.
Phil 182.14.2 Oeuvres philosophiques. v.3. (Hemsterhuis, F.) Leuwarde, 1850.
Phil 2480.15 Oeuvres philosophiques. 1. éd. (Cabanis, P.J.G.) Paris, 1956. 2v.
Phil 3552.18.5 Oeuvres philosophiques. 2e éd. (Leibniz, Gottfried Wilhelm.) Paris, 1900. 2v.
Phil 2050.20 Oeuvres philosophiques choisies. (Hume, David.) Paris, 1912. 2v.
Phil 2050.20.5 Oeuvres philosophiques choisies. (Hume, David.) Paris, 1930.
Phil 2115.19 Oeuvres philosophiques de Locke. (Locke, J.) Paris, 1821-25. 7v.
Phil 1850.26 Oeuvres philosophiques et morales. (Bacon, Francis.) Paris, 1797. 2v.
Phil 188.2 Oeuvres philosophiques et morales. (Nicole, P.) Paris, 1845.
Phil 2045.15 Oeuvres philosophiques et politiques. (Hobbes, Thomas.) Neufchatel, 1787. 2v.
Phil 5258.165 Oeuvres philosophiques et psychologiques choisies. (Sechenov, Ivan M.) Moscou, 1957.
Phil 2520.18A Oeuvres philosophiques publiées. (Descartes, René.) Paris, 1852.
Phil 6311.52 Oeuvres psychanalytiques. (Bouvet, Maurice.) Paris, 1967-68. 2v.
Htn Phil 8400.35 Of art: Plato to Picasso. (Gallatin, A.E.) N.Y., 1945.
Htn Phil 1955.3.30* Of bodies and of man's soul. (Digby, Kenelm.) London, 1669.
Phil 2115.68 Of civil government and toleration. (Locke, J.) London, 1950.
Phil 5765.12 Of clouds and clocks. (Popper, Karl R.) St. Louis, 1966.
Htn Phil 7060.2.5* Of ghostes and spirites walking by night. (Lavater, L.) London, 1572.
Htn Phil 7060.2.7* Of ghostes and spirites walking by night. (Lavater, L.) London, 1596.
Phil 7060.2.15 Of ghostes and spirites walking by nyght. (Lavater, L.) London, 1929.
Phil 2255.7.5 Of God, the devil and the Jews. (Runes, Dagobert D.) N.Y., 1952.
Phil 9245.2 Of happiness in its relations to work and knowledge. (Forbes, J.) London, 1850.
Phil 9560.35 Of honour. (Ashley, Robert.) San Marino, 1947.
Phil 3800.340.25 Of human freedom. (Schelling, F.W.J. von.) Chicago, 1936.
Phil 5125.4 Of induction. (Whewell, W.) London, 1849.

Phil 9255.17 Of irony, especially in drama. (Sedgewick, Garrett G.) Toronto, 1935.
Phil 9255.17.5 Of irony, especially in drama. (Sedgewick, Garrett G.) Toronto, 1948.
Phil 1865.28 Of laws in general. (Bentham, Jeremy.) London, 1970.
Htn Phil 2045.63* Of libertie and necessity. (Hobbes, Thomas.) London, 1654.
Phil 8969.3 Of magnanimity and charity. (Traherne, Thomas.) N.Y., 1942.
Phil 6112.29 Of meditation and health. (Curtis, A.M.) London, 1910.
Phil 8581.21 Of religion. (Bowker, R.R.) Boston, 1903.
Phil 299.27 Of stars and men. (Shapley, Harlow.) Boston, 1958.
Phil 299.27.5 Of stars and men. (Shapley, Harlow.) Boston, 1964.
Htn Phil 1850.33.5* Of the advancement and proficiencie of learning. (Bacon, Francis.) London, 1674.
Phil 1850.35.12 Of the advancement of learning. 5th ed. (Bacon, Francis.) Oxford, 1920.
Htn Phil 4931.1.30* Of the citie of God. (Augustinus, S.) London, 1610.
Phil 8880.23 Of the doctrine of morality in its relation to grace of redemption. (Fairbairn, R.B.) N.Y., 1887.
Phil 8582.17 Of the light of nature. (Culverwel, N.) Edinburgh, 1857.
Htn Phil 9230.4.5* Of the nature and use of lots. (Gataker, T.) London, 1619.
Htn Phil 9230.4* Of the nature and use of lots. (Gataker, T.) London, 1627.
Phil 8602.6 Of the plurality of worlds. (Whewell, W.) London, 1853.
Htn Phil 8602.7* Of the principles and duties of natural religion. (Wilkins, J.) London, 1698-99.
Htn Phil 8602.7.2* Of the principles and duties of natural religion. (Wilkins, J.) London, 1710.
Phil 1850.34.3 Of the proficience and advancement of learning. (Bacon, Francis.) London, 1828.
Phil 1850.34.5 Of the proficience and advancement of learning. (Bacon, Francis.) London, 1838.
Phil 1850.35A Of the proficience and advancement of learning. (Bacon, Francis.) London, 1851.
Phil 1850.35.1 Of the proficience and advancement of learning. (Bacon, Francis.) London, 1861.
Phil 176.215 Of the seer and the vision. (Brent, Duncan.) Amsterdam, 1967.
Phil 1905.9.30 Of the soul of the world of particular souls. (Burthogge, R.) London, 1699.
Phil 6834.6 Of those alone. (Hutton, Robert.) London, 1958.
Htn Phil 2515.2.40* Of wisdom, three books. (Charron, P.) London, 1651.
Htn Phil 2515.2.33* Of wisdome. (Charron, P.) London, 1630.
Htn Phil 2515.2.41* Of wisdome. (Charron, P.) London, 1670.
Phil 8597.58 Offenarung und Uberlieferung. (Rahner, Karl.) Freiburg, 1965.
Phil 193.254 Offenheit und Perspektive. (Stuettgen, Albert.) Warendorf, 1966.
Phil 5876.18 Offer, Daniel. The psychological world of the teen-ager. N.Y., 1969.
Phil 1865.53 Official aptitude maximized. (Bentham, Jeremy.) London, 1830.
Phil 5545.63 Offner, Max. Das Gedächtnis. Berlin, 1909.
Phil 5545.63.5 Offner, Max. Das Gedächtnis. Berlin, 1913.
Phil 5545.63.2 Offner, Max. Das Gedächtnis. 2. Aufl. Berlin, 1911.
Phil 5764.3 Offner, Max. Willensfreiheit, Zurechnung, und Verantwortung. Leipzig, 1904.
Phil 2705.86 Offray de la Mettrie. (Lemée, Pierre.) Saint-Servan, 1925.
Phil 4313.5.5 El oficio del pensamiento. (Marias Aguilera, Julian.) Madrid, 1958.
Phil 5764.4 Ofstad, H. An inquiry into the freedom of decision. Oslo, 1961.
Phil 8889.9F Ofstad, Harald. Innføring i moralfilosofi. Stockholm, 1964.
Phil 384.30 Ofstad, Harald. Two new studies in moral philosophy. Stockholm, 1967.
Phil 9550.17 Ofstad, Harald. Upartiskhet og utilitarisme. Stockholm, 1962.
Phil 6990.7 Ofte van Goeden Will. (Duffel, O.L.V. van.) Antwerpen, 1717.
Phil 5254.2.15 Ogden, C.K. The ABC of psychology. Harmondsworth, 1944.
Phil 8415.5A Ogden, C.K. The foundations of aesthetics. London, 1922. 2v.
Phil 5254.2 Ogden, C.K. The meaning of psychology. N.Y., 1926.
Phil 1865.176.5 Ogden, Charles K. Jeremy Bentham 1832-2032...Bentham centenary lecture...on June 6th, 1930. London, 1932.
Phil 5520.35 Ogden, Charles K. The meaning of meaning. London, 1923.
Phil 5520.35.10 Ogden, Charles K. The meaning of meaning. N.Y., 1936.
Phil 5520.35.3 Ogden, Charles K. The meaning of meaning. 3. ed. N.Y., 1930.
Phil 5520.35.7 Ogden, Charles K. The meaning of meaning. 5. ed. London, 1938.
Phil 5520.35.5 Ogden, Charles K. The meaning of meaning. 5. ed. N.Y., 1938.
Phil 5520.35.8 Ogden, Charles K. The meaning of meaning. 7. ed. N.Y., 1945.
Phil 5520.35.9 Ogden, Charles K. The meaning of meaning. 8. ed. N.Y., 1953.
Phil 5520.35.12 Ogden, Charles K. The meaning of meaning. 8. ed. N.Y., 1956.
Phil 5520.35.15.5 Ogden, Charles K. Opposition; a linguistic and psychological analysis. Bloomington, 1967.
Phil 8110.8 Ogden, Henry. English taste in landscape. Washington, 1955.
Phil 8889.4 Ogden, John. Elements of ethical science. Bismarck, N.D., 1891.
Phil 5254.1 Ogden, R.M. An introduction to general psychology. N.Y., 1914.
Phil 8415.8A Ogden, R.M. The psychology of art. N.Y., 1938. 2v.
Phil 5545.33 Ogden, R.M. Untersuchungen über den Einfluss der Geschwindigkeit des lauten Lesens. Leipzig, 1903.
Phil 5650.13 Ogden, Robert M. Hearing. N.Y., 1924.
Phil 6964.4 Ogdon, J.A.H. The kingdom of the lost. London, 1947.
Phil 1200.29 Ogereau, F. Essai sur le système philosophique des stoïciens. Paris, 1885.
Phil 4210.191 L'oggettivita in Antonio Rosmini. (Giacon, Carlo.) Milano, 1960.
Phil 180.84 L'oggetto della filosofia. (Franchini, Raffaello.) Napoli, 1876.
Phil 5252.70 Oggetto ed uficio della psicologia. (Marconi, A.) Milano, 1875.
Phil 2520.320 Oggione, Emilio. Cartesio. Bologna, 1959.
Phil 1750.535 Oggioni, Emilio. L'esistenzialismo. Bologna, 1956.
Phil 3450.11.435 Oggioni, Emilio. La fenomenologia di Husserl e il pensiero contemporaneo. Bologna, 1963.

Phil 1714.4 Oggioni, Emilio. Filosofia e psicologia nel pensiero postromantico. Bologna, 1955.

Phil 310.95 Ogiermann, H.A. Materialistische Dialektik. München, 1958.

Htn Phil 189.2* Ogilvie, J. Philosophical essays. Philadelphia, 1816.

Phil 575.3 Oginski, T. Die Idee der Person. Breslau, 1853.

Phil 4762.2.90 Ognev, A.I. Lev Mikhailovich Lopatin. Petrograd, 1922.

Phil 7069.35.20 O'Hare, Elizabeth. Universal knowledge; the road home. N.Y., 1935.

Phil 6324.1 O'Higgins, H. The secret springs. N.Y., 1920.

Phil 1930.5.80 O'higgins, James. Anthony Collins; the man and his works. The Hague, 1970.

Phil 24.3 Ohio. State University. Department of Psychology. Contributions in psychology. Columbus. 8-12,1927-1934

Phil 165.75 Ohio State University, Columbus. Department of Philosophy. Perspectives in philosophy. Columbus, 1953.

Phil 8594.1 Ohlert, A.L.J. Religionsphilosophie. Leipzig, 1835.

Phil 6805.10 Ohm, August. Persönlichkeitswandlung unter Freiheitsentzug. Berlin, 1964.

Phil 8401.37 Ohne Leitbild. (Adorno, Theodor W.) Frankfurt, 1967.

Phil 5585.25 Das Ohrlabyrinth als Organ der mathematischen Sinne fur Raum und Zeit. (Cyon, Elie von.) Berlin, 1908.

Phil 3552.266 Ohse, Jakob. Untersuchungen über den Substansbegriff bei Leibniz. Inaug.-Diss. Dorpat, 1888.

Phil 1145.53 Oikeios, etairos, epitedeios, filos; bejdtrage tot de kennis van de terminologie. (Eernstman, J.P.A.) Groningen, 1932.

Phil 8957.22 Oikeus ja uskonnolliset totuudet. (Hermanson, Robert Fredrik.) Porvoossa, 1921.

Phil 1714.1 Oischinger, J.N.P. Speculative Entwicklung...neueren Philosophie. Schaffhaussen, 1853-4. 2v.

Phil 3425.535 Oiserman, Teodor. Die Philosophie Hegels. 1. Aufl. Berlin, 1959.

Phil 310.460 Oizerman, T.I. Formirovanie filosofii marksizma. Moskva, 1962.

Phil 1750.635 Oizerman, T.I. Neotmoizm - filosofiia sovremennoi reaktsionoi burzhuazii. Moskva, 1959.

Phil 814.4 Oizerman, T.I. Osnovnye etapy razvitiia domarksistskoi filosofii. Moskva, 1957.

Phil 189.34 Oizerman, Teodor I. Problemy istoriko-filosofskoi nauki. Moskva, 1969.

Phil 1750.560.30 Oizerman, Teodor I. Sovremennyi ekzistensialism. Moskva, 1966.

Phil 1714.6 Oizerman, Teodor I. Zur Geschichte der vormarxschen Philosophie. Berlin, 1960.

Phil 1750.768 Oizerman, Teodor Il'ich. Die Entfremdung als historische Kategorie. Berlin, 1965.

Phil 8657.14 Ojcze-nasz. (Cieszkowski, August D.) Paryż, 1848.

Phil 8657.14.15 Ojcze-nasz. (Cieszkowski, August D.) Poznań, 1899-1906. 4v.

Phil 8657.14.10 Ojcze-nasz. v.1-3. (Cieszkowski, August D.) Poznań, 1922-23.

Phil 260.14 Okál, M. Grécki atomisti a epikuros. Bratislava, 1953.

Phil 3110.81 Okely, F. Memoris...Jacob Behrnen. Northampton, 1780.

VPhil 6980.518 Okhota za mysl'iu. (Levi, Vladimir L'.) Moskva, 1967.

Phil 6980.518.2 Okhota za mysl'iu. Izd. 2. (Levi, Vladimir L'.) Moskva, 1971.

Phil 978.49.173 Die okkulte Bewegung im Neunzehnten Jahrhundert und ihre Beiziehung zur Weltkultur. 3. Aufl. (Steiner, R.) Dornach, 1969.

Phil 974.3.8 Die okkulten Grundlagen der Bhagavad Gita. 3. Aufl. (Steiner, Rudolf.) Dornach, 1962.

Phil 978.49.585 Okkultes Lesen und okkultes Hören. 4. Aufl. (Steiner, R.) Dornach, 1967.

Phil 7069.26.12 Der Okkultismus. (Luther, F.) Leipzig, 1926.

Phil 7069.22.91 Okkultismus. (Wulff, E.) Dresden, 1922.

Phil 7069.21.45 Der Okkultismus im modernen Weltbild. 3. Aufl. (Oesterreich, T.K.) Dresden, 1923.

Phil 7069.26.80 Okkultismus und Spiritismus. (Baerwald, R.) Berlin, 1926.

Phil 7069.26.9 Okkultismus und Wissenschaft. (Hellwig, A.) Stuttgart, 1926.

Phil 3890.14 Das Oknosprinzip. (Treher, W.) München, 1962.

Phil 3834.3 Oko, Adolph S. The Spinoza bibliography. Boston, 1964.

Phil 4710.170 Okulov, Aleksandr F. Sovetskaia filosofskaia nauka i ee problemy. Moskva, 1970.

Phil 1955.6.112 Okun, Sid. John Dewey; a Marxian critique. Chicago, 1942.

Phil 1750.786 Olafson, Frederick. Principles and persons. Baltimore, 1967.

Phil 8893.75 Olbie, ou Essai sur les moyens de reformer. (Say, J.B.) Paris, 1799-1800.

Phil 9354.1 Olcott, Gage. Meditations of a young man. Boston, 1914.

Phil 978.11 Olcott, H.S. Collection of lectures on theosophy and archaic religions. Madras, 1883.

Phil 972.5 Olcott, H.S. Old diary leaves; Story of theosophy. N.Y., 1895.

Phil 7054.47 Olcott, H.S. People from the other world. Hartford, 1875.

Phil 5243.15.9 Old and new viewpoints in psychology. (Dunlap, K.) St. Louis, 1925.

Phil 8709.16 The old Bible and the new science. 2. ed. (Thomas, J.B.) N.Y., 1877.

Phil 189.7 Old criticism and new pragmatism. (O'Sullivan, J.M.) Dublin, 1909.

Phil 972.5 Old diary leaves; Story of theosophy. (Olcott, H.S.) N.Y., 1895.

Phil 8708.16 Old faith and new knowledge. (Snowden, J.H.) N.Y., 1928.

Phil 3850.1.36 The old faith and the new. (Strauss, D.F.) London, 1873.

Phil 3850.1.37 The old faith and the new. v.1-2. (Strauss, D.F.) N.Y., 1873.

Phil 9590.6 The old faiths perish. (Hudson, J.W.) N.Y., 1939.

Phil 194.4 Old-fashioned ethics. (Thornton, W.T.) London, 1873.

Phil 8692.3.5 Old lamps and new light of science. (Coutts, John.) London, 1911.

Phil 978.80 Old lamps for new. (Bragdon, C.F.) N.Y., 1925.

Phil 525.47 The old mysticism and the new pluralism. (Latta, R.) Glasgow, 1902.

Phil 9400.2 Old people. (Paine, Harriet E.) Boston, 1910.

Phil 9355.7 Old tales and modern ideals. (Phillips, John H.) N.Y., 1905.

Phil 8633.1.37 The old Teutonic idea of the future life. (Kittredge, George.) Cambridge, 1937.

Phil 8598.70 Old truths and modern progress. (Slack, Robert.) London, 1856.

Phil 6990.46 Olden, R. Propheten in deutscher Krise. Berlin, 1932.

Phil 960.120 Oldenberg, Hermann. Vorwissenschaftliche Wissenschaft die Weltanschauung der Brahamana. Göttingen, 1919.

Phil 7060.9 Oldenburg, F. Om gjenfard eller gjengangere. Kjobenhavn, 1818.

Phil 179.3.125 Oldendorff, Paul. Von deutscher Philosophie des Lebens. Langensalza, 1916.

Phil 3842.8 The oldest biography of Spinoza. (Wolf, Abraham.) London, 1927.

Phil 189.25 Oldfield, C.H. The kingdoms of the spirit. London, 1924.

Phil 5054.1 Oldfield, J. An essay towards the improvement of reason. London, 1707.

Phil 5850.291 Oldfield, R.C. The psychology of the interview. London, 1941.

Phil 5850.291.3 Oldfield, R.C. The psychology of the interview. 3rd ed. London, 1947.

Phil 5520.620 Oldfield, Richard Charles. Language: selected readings. Harmondsworth, 1968.

Phil 814.1 Oldham, A. An introduction to the study of philosophy. Dublin, 1909.

Phil 3425.635 Oldrini, Guido. Gli Hegeliani di Napoli. Milano, 1964.

Phil 3425.678 Oldrini, Guido. Il primo hegelismo Italiano. Firenze, 1969.

Phil 5548.20 Olds, James. The growth and structure of motives. Glencoe, Ill., 1956.

Phil 1020.14A O'Leary, DeLacy. Arabic thought and its place in history. London, 1922.

Phil 1020.14.5 O'Leary, DeLacy. Arabic thought and its place in history. London, 1939.

Phil 8964.7 Olejnik, Stanisław. Moralność życia Społecznego. Warszawa, 1970.

Phil 4710.50.55 Oleksiuk, Myroslav M. Borot'ba filosofs'kykh techii na zakhidnoukraïns'kykh zemliak u 20-30kh rokakh XX st. L'viv, 1970.

Phil 5520.419 Oleron, P. Les activités intellectuelles. Paris, 1964.

Phil 5274.18 Oléron, Pierre. Les composantes de l'intelligence d'après les recherches factorielles. Paris, 1957.

Phil 165.22 Offener Horizont. (Piper, K.) München, 1953.

Phil 1714.3 Olgiati, F. L'anima dell'umanesimo e del rinascimento. Milano, 1924.

Phil 4080.3.240 Olgiati, F. Benedetto Croce e lo storicismo. Milano, 1953.

Phil 1119.5 Olgiati, F. I fondamenti della filosofia classica. 2. ed. Milano, 1953.

Phil 1870.107 Olgiati, F. L'idealismo di G. Berkeley. Milano, 1926.

Phil 1702.6.15 Olgiati, F. Neo-scolastica, idealismo e spiritualismo. Milano, 1933.

Phil 630.45 Olgiati, F. Il realismo. Milano, 1936.

Phil 2520.186 Olgiati, Francesco. Cartesio. Milano, 1934.

Phil 2520.186.10 Olgiati, Francesco. La filosofia di Descartes. Milano, 1937.

Phil 2475.1.149 Olgiati, Francesco. La filosofia di Enrico Bergson. Torino, 1914.

Phil 3552.288 Olgiati, Francesco. Il significato storico di Leibniz. Milano, 1929.

Phil 1400.10 Olhler, Klaus. Antike Philosophie und byzan tinisches Mittelalter. München, 1969.

Phil 8594.5.5 Oliphant, L. Scientific religion. Buffalo, 1889.

Phil 8594.5.2 Oliphant, L. Scientific religion. 2. ed. Edinburgh, 1888.

Phil 295.4 Oliveira, I. de. Introduction du sens cosmique en philosophie. Paris, 1962.

Phil 9470.3 Oliveira Guimarães, José Joaquim d'. De morali responsabilitate. Conimbrigae, 1901.

Phil 4475.1.80 Oliveira Martins: estudo de psychologia. (Moniz Barreto, G.) Paris, 1892.

Phil 9245.6 Oliver, B.L. Hints for an essay on the pursuit of happiness. Chicago, 1818.

Phil 9070.19.2 Oliver, J.R. The ordinary difficulties of everyday people. N.Y., 1935.

Phil 5401.13.10 Oliver, John R. Fear. N.Y., 1931.

Phil 6964.2 Oliver, John R. Pastoral psychiatry and mental health. N.Y., 1932.

Phil 6964.2.6 Oliver, John R. Psychiatry and mental health. N.Y., 1933.

Phil 3120.30.160 Oliver, Roy. The wanderer and the way. Ithaca, N.Y., 1968.

Phil 189.30 Oliver, W.D. Theory of order. Yellow Springs, Ohio, 1951.

Phil 7080.20 Oliver, William. A relation of a very extraordinary sleeper. London, 1707.

Phil 6310.1.95 Oliver Brachfield, F. Les sentiments d'infériorité. Genève, 1945.

Phil 3460.96 Olivetti, Marco M. L'esito teologico della filosofia del linguaggio di Jacobi. Padova, 1970.

Phil 189.10 Olivier, Aimé. De l'absolu. Paris, 1887.

Phil 6684.4 Olivier, J. Traité de magnétisme. Paris, 1854.

Phil 510.11 Olivier, J. von. Monistische Weltanschauung, Leipzig, 1906.

Phil 3496.6 Olivier, Paul. Zum Willinsproblem bei Kant und Reinhold. Berlin, 1941.

Phil 8889.1 Ollé-Laprune, L. De la certitude morale. Paris, 1880.

Phil 2920.1.80 Ollé-Laprune, L. Étienne Vacherot. Paris, 1898.

Phil 2733.83 Ollé-Laprune, L. La philosophie de Malebranche. Paris, 1870. 2v.

Phil 1714.2 Ollé-Laprune, L. La philosophie et le temps présent. 5e éd. Paris, 1908

Phil 8889.1.15 Ollé-Laprune, L. Le prix de la vie. 43. ed. Paris, 1921.

Phil 5620.13.3 Ollé-Laprune, L. La raison et le rationalisme. 3. éd. Paris, 1906.

Phil 8889.1.10 Ollé-Laprune, L. Les sources de la paix intellectuelle. 7. ed. Paris, 1916.

Phil 2672.80 Ollé-Laprune, L. Théodore Jouffroy. Paris, 1899.

Phil 8594.6 Ollé-Laprune, L. La vitalite chrétiene. Paris, 1914.

Phil 7060.90 Ollier, Charles. Fallacy of ghosts, dreams and omens. London, 1848.

Phil 2115.97 Ollion, H. La philosophie générale de John Locke. Paris, 1909.

Phil 9230.25 Olmsted, Charlotte. Heads, I win; tails, you lose. N.Y., 1962.

Phil 9490.2 Olney, R. The scholar in politics. Philadelphia, 1896.

Phil 1870.175 Olscamp, Paul J. The moral philosophy of George Berkeley. The Hague, 1970.

Phil 4065.110 Olschki, L. Giordano Bruno. Bari, 1927.

Phil 1750.710 Olson, Robert. An introduction to existentialism. N.Y., 1962.

Phil 8889.10 Olson, Robert Goodwin. The morality of self-interest. N.Y., 1965.

Phil 575.4 Olssen, W.W. Personality. N.Y., 1882.

Phil 5645.40 Olsson, G.F. Experimentelle Untersuchungen. Stockholm, 1938.

Phil 2150.18.100 Olthuis, James H. Facts, values and ethics. Assen, 1968.

Phil 960.13 Oltramare, P. La formule bouddhique des douze causes. Geneve, 1909.

Phil 8594.11 Oltramare, P. La religion et la vie de l'esprit. Paris, 1925.

Phil 960.140 — Oltramare, Paul. L'histoire des idées theosophiques dans l'Inde. Paris, 1906-23. 2v.

Phil 193.166 — Oltre i cinque sensi. (Società Italiana di Metapsichica.) Torino? 1952.

Phil 3483.48 — Oltre la critica. (Barié, G.E.) Milano, 1929.

Phil 5520.33 — Oltuszewski, W. Psychologie und Philosophie der Sprache. Berlin, 1901.

Phil 6060.33 — Olyanova, N. What does your handwriting reveal? N.Y., 1929.

Phil 189.8 — Olzelt-Newin, A. Kleinere philosophische Schriften. Leipzig, 1903.

Phil 3640.445 — Olzien, Otto H. Nietzsche und das Problem der dichterischen Sprache. Berlin, 1941.

Phil 260.8 — Om atomismen. (Dahlbäck, Carl J.) Stockholm, 1857.

Phil 4655.1.38 — Om auktoritet och sjelfständighet. (Wikner, Pontus.) Upsala, 1872.

Phil 8893.59 — Om autonoma och heteronoma moralprinciper. (Svensson, P.K.) Lund, 1904.

Phil 5757.10 — Om begrebet frihed en filosofisk afhandling. (Hansen, H.C.) Kristiania, 1896.

Phil 8879.22 — Om begreppet sedlighet. (Edfeldt, H.) Upsala, 1877.

Phil 5421.15.35 — Om bildandet av dyader. (Trost, Jan.) Uppsala, 1966.

Phil 4515.92 — Om Boströmianismen. (Dons, Waldemar.) Christiania, 1874.

Phil 4515.85 — Om Boströms äldsta skrifter. (Liljeqvist, Efraim.) Göteborg, 1897.

Phil 4515.83 — Om Boströms ideelära. (Edfeldt, Hans.) Uppsala, 1884.

Phil 8879.19 — Om de etiska grundbegreppen. (Edfeldt, Hans.) Upsala, 1894.

Phil 8892.82 — Om de mens. (Roscam Abbing, Pieter Johan.) Leiden, 1968.

Phil 6114.13 — Om de uvilkaarlige livsyttringers forhold til de vilkaarlige. (Eschricht, D.F.) Kjøbenhavn, 1845.

Phil 4630.2.40 — Om den filosofiska methoden. (Rein, T.) Helsingfors, 1868.

Phil 5620.15 — Om den förnuftiga känslan. (Jönsson, A.) Lund, 1868.

Phil 5757.15 — Om den menneskelige Frihed. (Heiberg, J.L.) Kiel, 1824.

Phil 4640.1.30 — Om den menneskelige natur. (Treschow, N.) København, 1812.

Phil 4582.4.35 — Om den moraliska känslan och driften sasom förnuftiga. (Hägerström, Axel.) Upsala, 1895.

Phil 5938.4 — Om den nöiagtige bestemmelse. (Simesen, R.J.) Kjøbenhavn, 1846.

Phil 8685.16 — Om den pantheistiska esthetiken. Academisk ävhandling. (Klockhoff, D.) Upsala, 1864.

Phil 4515.98 — Om den svenske tänkaren Boström. (Wikner, P.) Göteborg, 1888.

Phil 6317.13 — Om det abnorme. (Halberg, F.) København, 1907.

Phil 5420.3.31 — Om det absoluta förnuftet. (Björkman, N.O.) Stockholm, 1888.

Phil 5055.12 — Om det kvantitativa betraktelsesättet i logiken. (Phalen, A.K.) Uppsala, 1911.

Phil 8597.43 — Om det personligas betydelse. (Rudin, W.) Upsala, 1885?

Phil 4508.7 — Om det personligt andliga. (Adelborg, Gustaf Otto.) Stockholm, 1907.

Phil 8581.46 — Om det religiöse i dets enhed met det humane. (Brochner, Hans.) Kjöbenhavn, 1869.

Phil 4605.1.41 — Om det skjønne. (Monrad, M.J.) Christiania, 1873.

Phil 8612.20 — Om døden; en almenfattelig fremstelling. (Block, Oscar.) Kobenhavn, 1903. 2v.

Phil 8626.8.5 — Om döden och uppstandeken fran cellärans synpunkt. (Björklund, Gustaf.) London, 1910.

Phil 7082.58 — Om drömmen. (Hedenius, Per.) Stockholm, 1880.

Phil 4655.1.30 — Om egenskapen och närgränsande tankeföremál. (Wikner, Pontus.) Upsala, 1880.

Phil 4650.1.47 — Om erfarenheten ett kunskapstheoretiskt studieförsök. Akademisk afhandling. (Vannérus, Allen.) Stockholm, 1890.

Phil 8888.10 — Om ethikens problem och de vigtigaste försäken att lösa detsamma. (Nordwall, Adolf L.) Upsala, 1852.

Phil 1802.3 — Om filosofien i Amerika. (Carlson, J.S.) Upsala, 1895.

Phil 3425.200.10 — Om filosofiens supremati enligt Hegelska systemet. (Borelius, J.J.) Lund, 1852.

Phil 8589.15 — Om förhållandet mellan religion och moral. (Jacobsson, M.) Stockholm, 1917.

Phil 4525.2.90 — Om förhållandet mellan teologi och filosofi. v.2. (Myrberg, Otto F.) Upsala, 1861.

Phil 5440.23 — Om förvärfvade egenskapers ärftlighet. (Retzius, Gustaf.) Stockholm, 1895.

Phil 1850.114 — Om Francis Bacon filosofi med särskild hänsyn till det etiska problemet. (Liljeqvist, E.) Uppsala, 1893.

Phil 3900.1.83 — Om Friedrich Ueberwegs "System der logik". (Hallmer, Lars.) Lund, 1877.

Phil 2138.40.15 — Om friheten. (Mill, John S.) Upsala, 1881.

Phil 5325.22 — Om gedenkelse. (Lehmann, A.) Kjøbenhavn, 1888.

Phil 7060.9 — Om gjenfard eller gjengangere. (Oldenburg, F.) Kjobenhavn, 1818.

Phil 4570.1.83 — Om Grubbes deduktion af rättsbegreppet. (Meden, Carl.) Uppsala, 1869.

Phil 5055.14.5 — Om grundformerna i den reella logiken. (Pira, Karl.) Stockholm, 1907.

Phil 4580.64 — Om grundlaget for den humane ethik. (Høffding, Harald.) Kjøbenhavn, 1876.

Phil 8593.10 — Om hindringer og betingelser for det aandelige liv i nutiden. (Nielsen, Rasmus.) Kjøbenhavn, 1867.

Phil 3245.82 — Om Immanuel Hermann Fichte's teism och etik. (Ambrosius, J.M.) Lund, 1882.

Phil 8587.38 — Om intolerance, isaer i henseende til religios overbevisning. (Heegaard, P.S.V.) Kjobenhavn, 1878.

Phil 2138.100 — Om J. Stuart Mills logik. (Löchen, Arne.) Kristiania, 1885.

Phil 5255.20 — Om känslolagar. (Petrini, Edvard.) Upsala, 1900.

Phil 3495.8.5 — Om Kants sedelära. (Norelius, G.) Upsala, 1884.

Phil 9045.16 — Om Kierlighed til faedrenelandet. (Krogh, Matthias B.) Trondhiem, 1801.

Phil 8430.20 — Om konstens förhållande till religionen. (Lénström, C.J.) Upsala, 1842.

Phil 4515.88 — Om kunskapen; studier. (Kalling, P.) Upsala, 1875.

Phil 4630.2.39 — Om kunskapens möjlighet. (Rein, T.) Helsingfors, 1867.

Phil 665.42 — Om ligeløb og Kredsning i Sjaelelivet. (Feilberg, Ludvig.) Kjøbenhavn, 1896.

Phil 5043.24 — Om logikens studium vid elementarläroverken. (Dahlbäck, Carl J.) Umea, 1864.

Phil 4515.87.2 — Om menistrarne i den konstitutionela monarkier. enligt Boströms statslära. (Sahlin, K.Y.) Uppsala, 1877.

Phil 4515.87 — Om ministrarne i den konstitutionela monarkien enligt Boströms statslära. (Sahlin, K.Y.) Uppsala, 1877.

Phil 5244.18 — Om moralens oprindelse. (Ellefsen, Olaf.) Kristiania, 1893.

Phil 4582.4.33 — Om moraliska föreställningars sanning. (Hägerström, Axel.) Stockholm, 1911.

Phil 5243.26 — Om muligheden af formel opdragelse af de intellektuelle evner. (Dam, Axel.) København, 1912.

Phil 4610.7.32 — Om natursammanhang och frihet. (Norström, V.) Göteborg, 1895.

Phil 182.70 — Om opdragelse. 4e Opl. v.1-2. (Heegaard, S.) Kjøbenhavn, 1893.

Phil 4610.9.35 — Om personlig sanning och sann personlighet. (Nielsen, R.) Upsala, 1856.

Phil 5465.22 — Om phantasiens magt. (Nielsen, Rasmus.) Kjøbenhavn, 1876.

Phil 4635.8.31 — Om philosophiens begreb. (Sibbern, F.C.) Kjøbenhavn, 1843.

Phil 4610.7.31 — Om pligt, frihet och förnuft. (Norström, V.) Upsala, 1891.

Phil 8882.54 — Om praktiska filosofiens grundbegrepp och deras inre förhållande till hvarandra. (Hollander, A.G.) Lund, 1855.

Phil 5051.18 — Om psychologische beviser. (Lambek, C.) København, 1909.

Phil 5261.11 — Om psykisk energi. (Vannérus, A.) Stockholm, 1896.

Phil 8612.72 — Om rätten att dö. (Fagerberg, Holsten.) Stockholm, 1967.

Phil 4515.50 — Om religion, vishet och dygd. (Boström, C.J.) Stockholm, 1943.

Phil 8593.14 — Om religionens betydelse och förhållande till philosophen. pt.1-4. (Nyblaeus, Axel.) Upsala, 1853.

Phil 7060.154 — Om satanismen. (Kaarsberg, H.S.) Kjøbenhavn, 1896.

Phil 5400.50 — Om sindsbevaegelser. (Lange, C.G.) Kjøbenhavn, 1885.

Phil 5640.19 — Om sinnesrörelsernas fysiologi och psykologi. (Abrutz, Sydney.) Upsala, 1901.

Phil 665.43.2 — Om själens helsa. 2e uppl. (Beskow, B. von.) Stockholm, 1867.

Phil 665.43 — Om själens helsa. 4e uppl. (Beskow, B. von.) Stockholm, 1880.

Phil 6121.2.10 — Om själens problemer. (Laugel, A.) Stockholm, 1869.

Phil 5240.31 — Om själslifvets studium på fysiologisk grundval. (Alrutz, S.G.L.R.) Stockholm, 1899.

Phil 5250.18 — Om sjalsarbete. (Kraepelin, Emil.) Stockholm, 1894.

Phil 4610.6.31 — Om straffrätten. (Nyblaeus, Axel.) Lund, 1852.

Phil 4600.3.31 — Om substansbegreppet hos Cartesius, Spinoza och Liebnitz. Akademisk afhandling. (Leander, P.J.H.) Lund, 1862. 2 pam.

Phil 5415.3 — Om sympatiska känslor. (Petrini, E.) Upsala, 1900.

Phil 4515.94 — Om tänkaren Kristofer Jakob Boström och hans filosofi. (Landström, Gustaf.) Stockholm, 1903.

Phil 8656.18 — Om teismen. (Burman, E.O.) Upsala, 1886.

Phil 4582.3.31 — Om vår tids ungdom. (Hwasser, Israel.) Upsala, 1842.

Phil 4610.7.40 — Om viljans frihet. (Norström, V.) Stockholm, 1917.

Phil 4515.82 — Om viljefrihetsläran i Boströms definitiva filosofi. (Hellström, Carl.) Uppsala, 1919.

Phil 5769.7 — Om viljens frihed. (Teisen, N.) Kjøbenhavn, 1904.

Phil 8893.77 — Om vilkoren för möjligheten al praktisk philosophi. (Sahlin, Karl Y.) Lund, 1855.

Phil 4080.3.330 — Omaggio a Benedetto Croce. Torino, 1953.

Phil 3450.11.85 — Omaggio a Husserl. (Paci, Enzo.) Milano, 1960.

Phil 4170.16.10 — Omaggio a Rodolfo Mondolfo. Urbino, 1963.

Phil 4260.42 — Omaggio a Vico di A. Corsano, Paolo Romi, A.M. Jacobelli Inoldi. Napoli, 1968.

Phil 2750.19.110 — O'Malley, John B. The fellowship of being; an essay on the concept of person in the philosophy of Gabriel Marcel. The Hague, 1966.

Phil 8594.13.10 — Oman, John. Honest religion. Cambridge, Eng., 1941.

Phil 8594.13 — Oman, John. The natural and the supernatural. N.Y., 1931.

Phil 1750.435 — L'ombre de Dieum. 1e éd. (Sourian, E.) Paris, 1955.

Phil 177.26.5 — L'ombre de Socrate. (Choraux, C.) Paris, 1878.

Phil 4065.32.20 — Le ombre delle idee. (Bruno, Giordano.) Catania, 1901.

Phil 5599.85 — Ombredane, André. L'exploration de la mentalité des noirs, le Congo T.A.T. Paris, 1969.

Phil 24.9 — Omega; an international journal for the psychological study of dying, death, bereavement, suicide and other lethal behaviors. Westport, Conn., 1,1970+

Phil 310.592 — Omel'ianovskyi, M.E. Dialektika v naukahi o nezhivoi prirode. Moskva, 1964.

Phil 7069.56.25 — Omez, Réginald. Supranormal ou surnaturel. Paris, 1956.

Phil 7069.00.37 — Omni Victis (pseud.) Super-physical projection. n.p., 19- ?

Phil 6311.5.5 — The omnipotent self. (Bousfield, Paul.) London, 1923.

Phil 8882.90.5 — Den omoraliska anständigheten. (Hedenius, Ingemar.) Stockholm, 1969.

Phil 177.9 — L'omu nun l'usu di la ragiuni. (Catara-Lettieri, Antonio.) Messina, 1869.

Phil 356.5 — Omverdens problemet. (Zinkernagel, Peter.) København, 1957.

Phil 8615.1.7 — On a foundation for religion. (Salter, W.M.) Boston, 1879. 17 pam.

Phil 5421.20.21 — On aggression. (Lorenz, Konrad Zacharias.) N.Y., 1966.

Phil 365.28 — On an evolutionist theory of axioms. (Wilson, J.C.) Oxford, 1912.

Phil 6315.2.79.15 — On aphasia. (Freud, Sigmund.) London, 1953.

Phil 8406.14 — On art and connoisseurship. (Friedländer, Max J.) London, 1942.

Phil 8402.7 — On beauty; three discourses delivered in the University of Edinburgh. (Blackie, J.S.) Edinburgh, 1858.

Phil 6980.650.35 — On becoming a person. (Rogers, Carl Ransom.) Boston, 1961.

Phil 8601.12 — On being human; St. Thomas and Mr. Aldous Huxley. (Vann, Gerald.) N.Y., 1934.

Phil 9070.34.5 — On being human. (Wilson, W.) N.Y., 1916.

Phil 5592.177 — On being mindful of man, essay toward a proactive psychology. (Bonner, Hubert.) Boston, 1965.

Phil 2138.77.5 — On Bentham and Coleridge. (Mill, John S.) N.Y., 1962.

Phil 9070.142 — On caring. 1st American ed. (Mayeroff, Milton.) N.Y., 1971.

Phil 270.43 — On causation, with a chapter on belief. (Mercier, Charles A.) London, 1916.

Phil 6317.1 — On certain conditions of nervous derangement. (Hammond, W.A.) N.Y., 1881.

Phil 6317.1.2 — On certain conditions of nervous derangement. 3d ed. (Hammond, W.A.) N.Y., 1883.

Phil 3925.16.35A — On certainty. (Wittgenstein, Ludwig.) Oxford, 1969.

Phil 6310.23 — On character and libido development. (Abraham, Karl.) N.Y., 1966.

Phil 9065.1 — On compromise. (Morley, J.) London, 1877.

Phil 9065.1.5 — On compromise. (Morley, J.) London, 1898.

Phil 9065.1.15 — On compromise. (Morley, J.) London, 1933.

Phil 6315.2.21 — On creativity and the unconscious. (Freud, Sigmund.) N.Y., 1958.

Phil 6671.11 — On darlingism, misnamed electro-biology. (Buchanan, A.) London, 1851.

Phil 5790.2.15 — On death and dying. (Kuebler-Ron, Elisabeth.) N.Y., 1969.

Phil 5500.32 — On decision-making in large organizations. (Jones, William.) Santa Monica, 1964.

	Phil 5725.2	On development of the understanding. (Wedgwood, H.) London, 1848.
	Phil 7042.4	On double consciousness. (Binet, Alfred.) Chicago, 1890.
	Phil 7042.4.1	On double consciousness. (Binet, Alfred.) Chicago, 1896.
	Phil 7042.4.2	On double consciousness. (Binet, Alfred.) Chicago, 1905.
	Phil 7082.74	On dreams. (Archer, William.) London, 1935.
	Phil 6480.23.13	On dreams. (Freud, Sigmund.) London, 1924.
	Phil 7082.8.5	On dreams. (Freud, Sigmund.) N.Y., 1952.
	Phil 8407.12	On education in the principles of art. (Greswell, R.) Oxford, 1844.
	Phil 5520.130	On expressive language. (Clark University, Worcester, Massachusetts. Conference on Expressive Language Behavior.) Worcester, Mass., 1955.
	Phil 9530.50	On facing the world. (Halle, L.J.) N.Y., 1950.
	Phil 6110.16	On failure of brain-power. (Althaus, J.) London, 1883.
	Phil 5066.11.25	On functions of relations. (Quine, Willard van Orman.) Santa Monica, 1949.
	Phil 5850.221.15	On fundamental measurement in psychology. (Goude, G.) Stockholm, 1962.
	Phil 7080.10	On going to sleep. (More, C.H.) London, 1868.
	Phil 3494.42	On Hegel's critique of Kant. (Maier, J.) N.Y., 1939.
	Phil 5761.21	On human freedom. (Laird, John.) London, 1947.
	Phil 3808.31.5	On human nature; essays. (Schopenhauer, Arthur.) London, 1957.
	Phil 3808.31.2	On human nature. (Schopenhauer, Arthur.) London, 1897.
	Phil 5871.55	On human symbiosis and the vicissitudes of individuation. (Mahler, Margaret S.) London, 1969-
	Phil 5252.110	On human thinking. (Monsarrat, K.W.) London, 1955.
	Phil 7060.21	On illusions of the senses. Photoreproduction. (Paterson, Robert.) Edinburgh, 1867.
	Phil 8631.13	On immortality. (Grenfell, W.T.) Boston, 1912.
	Phil 8630.11	On immortality of the soul. (Foerster Lecture.) N.Y. 1933+
	Phil 5832.14	On instinct and intelligence. Thesis. (Wyman, Eva May.) Philadelphia, 1931.
NEDL	Phil 2885.31.1	On Intelligence. (Taine, Hippolyte Adolphe.) N.Y., 1871.
	Phil 2885.31.3	On intelligence. (Taine, Hippolyte Adolphe.) N.Y., 1875. 2v.
	Phil 2885.31.6	On intelligence. (Taine, Hippolyte Adolphe.) N.Y., 1889. 2v.
	Phil 2885.31	On intelligence. pt. 1-2. (Taine, Hippolyte Adolphe.) London, 1871.
	Phil 3120.30.32	On Judaism. (Buber, Martin.) N.Y., 1967.
	Phil 332.36	On knowing. (Bruner, J.S.) Cambridge, 1962.
	Phil 2138.40.7	On liberty. (Mill, John S.) London, 19- .
	Phil 2138.40	On liberty. (Mill, John S.) London, 1859.
Htn	Phil 2138.40.1*	On liberty. (Mill, John S.) London, 1859.
	Phil 2138.40.2.5	On liberty. (Mill, John S.) London, 1871.
	Phil 2138.40.3	On liberty. (Mill, John S.) London, 1874.
	Phil 2138.40.3.2	On liberty. (Mill, John S.) London, 1875.
	Phil 2138.40.4	On liberty. (Mill, John S.) London, 1878.
	Phil 2138.40.47	On liberty. (Mill, John S.) London, 190-?
	Phil 2138.40.10	On liberty. (Mill, John S.) London, 1903.
	Phil 2138.40.8	On liberty. (Mill, John S.) N.Y., 19- .
	Phil 2138.40.6	On liberty. (Mill, John S.) N.Y., 1895.
	Phil 2138.40.35	On liberty. (Mill, John S.) N.Y., 1947.
	Phil 2138.40.46	On liberty. (Mill, John S.) N.Y., 1956.
	Phil 2138.40.42	On liberty. Considerations on representative government. (Mill, John S.) Oxford, 1946.
	Phil 2138.40.2.2	On liberty. 2nd ed. (Mill, John S.) Boston, 1863.
	Phil 3210.67.9	On life after death. (Fechner, G.T.) Chicago, 1914.
	Phil 3210.67.10	On life after death. (Fechner, G.T.) Chicago, 1945.
	Phil 3210.67.12	On life after death. (Fechner, G.T.) N.Y., 1943.
	Phil 8876.1	On man. (Bagshaw, W.) London, 1833. 2v.
	Phil 5545.37.5	On memory and specific energies of the nervous system. 2. ed. (Hering, Ewald.) Chicago, 1897.
	Phil 5545.37.10	On memory and the specific energies of the nervous system. 4. ed. (Hering, Ewald.) Chicago, 1905.
	Phil 5270.6	On method: toward a reconstruction of psychological investigation. 1st ed. (Bakan, David.) San Francisco, 1967.
	Phil 7060.104	On miracles and modern spiritualism. (Wallace, A.R.) London, 1875.
	Phil 9560.54	On moral courage. (Mackenzie, C.) London, 1962.
	Phil 2270.84.5A	On Mr. Spencer's data of ethics. (Guthrie, M.) London, 1884.
	Phil 2270.84	On Mr. Spencer's formula of evolution. (Guthrie, M.) London, 1878.
	Phil 2270.84.8	On Mr. Spencer's unification of knowledge. (Guthrie, M.) London, 1882.
	Phil 6972.5	On obscure diseases of the brain. (Winslow, E.) London, 1860.
	Phil 6972.5.2	On obscure diseases of the brain. (Winslow, F.) Philadelphia, 1860.
	Phil 6968.30	On obsession, a clinical and methodological study. (Straus, Erwin.) N.Y., 1948.
	Phil 6951.18	On paralysis from brain disease. (Bastian, H.C.) N.Y., 1875.
	Phil 1750.115.205	On phenomenology and social relations. (Schutz, Alfred.) Chicago, 1970.
	Phil 176.170	On philosophical style. (Blanshard, B.) Bloomington, 1954.
	Phil 3480.52.15	On philosophy in general. (Kant, Immanuel.) Calcutta, 1935.
	Phil 2477.15.22	On poetic imagination and reverie; selections from the works of Gaston Bachelard. (Bachelard, Gaston.) Indianapolis, 1971.
	Phil 2115.67	On politics and education. (Locke, J.) N.Y., 1947.
	Phil 3805.31.6	On religion. (Schleiermacher, Friedrich.) N.Y., 1955.
	Phil 3805.31.5	On religion. (Schleiermacher, Friedrich.) N.Y., 1958.
	Phil 9470.14	On responsibility. (Fingarette, Herbert.) N.Y., 1967.
	Phil 8886.18	On right and wrong. (Lilly, W.S.) London, 1892.
	Phil 8712.35	On science, necessity, and the love of God. (Weil, Simone.) London, 1968.
	Phil 5648.9	On sensations from pressure and impact. (Griffing, H.) N.Y., 1895.
	Phil 5414.20.2	On shame and the search for identity. (Lynd, Helen Merrell.) N.Y., 1958.
	Phil 7082.10	On Sigmund Freud's dreams. (Grinstein, Alexander.) Detroit, 1968.
	Phil 5635.19F	On small differences of sensation. (Peirce, C.S.) n.p., 18- ?
	Phil 2138.41	On social freedom. (Mill, John S.) N.Y., 1941.
	Phil 5585.315	On social perception. (Jaspars, Joseph Maria Franciscus.) Leiden, 1966.
	Phil 6972.18	On some disorders. (West, Charles.) Philadelphia, 1871.
	Phil 2070.31	On some Hegelisms. (James, William.) London, 1882.
	Phil 5249.2.38	On some of life's ideals. (James, William.) N.Y., 1900.

	Phil 5070.2	On some of the characteristics of belief; scientific and religious. (Venn, J.) London, 1870.
	Phil 3825.2	On Spinozistic immortality. (Fullerton, G.S.) Philadelphia, 1899.
	Phil 8708.4	On the absence of real opposition between science and revelation. (Stokes, G.G.) London, 1884?
	Phil 8590.2.2	On the adaption of external nature, physical condition, Man. (Kidd, J.) Philadelphia, 1883.
X Cg	Phil 8590.2	On the adaption of external nature, physical condition of man. (Kidd, J.) London, 1852.
	Phil 3120.30.38	On the Bible; eighteen studies. (Buber, Martin.) N.Y., 1968.
	Phil 5535.36	On the biology of learning. N.Y., 1969.
	Phil 5240.8	On the consciousness of the universal. Thesis. (Aveling, Francis.) London, 1912.
	Phil 6945.3	On the construction, organization and general arrangements of hospitals for the insane. (Kirkbride, T.S.) Philadelphia, 1854.
	Phil 6945.20	On the construction, organization and general arrangements of hospitals for the insane. 2. ed. (Kirkbride, T.S.) Philadelphia, 1880.
	Phil 193.145	On the contented life. (Singer, E.A.) N.Y., 1936.
	Phil 7060.100	On the cosmic relations. (Holt, H.) Boston, 1914. 2v.
	Phil 7069.15.30	On the cosmic relations. (Holt, Henry.) Boston, 1915. 2v.
	Phil 5865.5.9	On the development of memory and identity. (Piaget, Jean.) Worcester, 1968.
	Phil 4195.39	On the dignity of man. (Pico della Mirandola, Giovanni.) Indianapolis, 1965.
	Phil 8644.8	On the doctrine of personal identity. (Tucker, C.C.) London, 1909.
	Phil 9161.6	On the duties of the young. (Blair, H.) London, 1794.
	Phil 8876.20	On the employment of time. (Bolton, R.) London, 1754.
	Phil 3850.18.45	On the eternal in man. (Scheler, Max.) N.Y., 1960.
	Phil 9150.4	On the ethics of naturalism. (Sorley, W.R.) London, 1885.
	Phil 9150.4.3	On the ethics of naturalism. 2. ed. (Sorley, W.R.) London, 1904.
	Phil 8897.14.16	On the foundations of morals. (Whewell, W.) Cambridge, n.d.
	Phil 8897.14.15	On the foundations of morals. (Whewell, W.) N.Y., 1839.
	Phil 3808.51.7	On the fourfold root of the principle of sufficient reason. (Schopenhauer, Arthur.) London, 1903.
	Phil 3808.51.6	On the fourfold root of the principle of sufficient reason and on the will in nature; two essays. (Schopenhauer, Arthur.) London, 1891.
	Phil 5751.1	On the freedom of the human will. (Bockshammer, G.F.) Andover, 1835.
	Phil 5926.1.6	On the functions of the brain. (Gall, F.J.) Boston, 1835. 6v.
	Phil 6112.15.5	On the functions of the cerebellum. (Combe, G.) Edinburgh, 1838.
	Phil 6115.23	On the functions of the cerebrum. (Frany, Shepherd I.) N.Y., 1907.
	Phil 8420.11	On the genesis of the aesthetic categories. (Tafts, James.) Chicago, 1902.
	Phil 2750.11.41.1	On the grace and humanity of Jesus. (Maritain, Jacques.) N.Y., 1969.
	Phil 6315.2.56	On the history of the psychoanalytic movement. (Freud, Sigmund.) N.Y., 1966.
	Phil 8583.4.2	On the improvement of society by the diffusion of knowledge. (Dick, T.) Glasgow, 1833.
	Phil 8583.4.3	On the improvement of society by the diffusion of knowledge. (Dick, T.) N.Y., 1836.
	Phil 3819.39.7	On the improvement of the understanding. (Spinoza, Benedictus de.) N.Y., 1958.
	Phil 1850.106	On the inductive philosophy. (Finch, A. Elley.) London, 1872.
	Phil 4364.1.70	On the knowledge and progress of oneself. (Núñez Regueiro, M.) Rosario, 1941.
	Phil 9240.13	On the knowledge of good and evil. (Rice, P.B.) N.Y., 1955.
	Phil 5066.115	On the logic of 'better'. (Halldén, Sören.) Lund, 1957.
	Phil 6116.16F	On the mammalian nervous system. (Gotch, Francis.) London, 1891.
	Phil 178.30.10	On the meaning of life. (Durant, William.) N.Y., 1932.
	Phil 5252.7.2	On the mind. (Mill, J.) London, 1869. 2v.
NEDL	Phil 6128.26.5	On the minute structure and functions of the spinal cord. (Schroeder van der Kolk, J.L.C.) London, 1859.
	Phil 6113.32	On the mysterious leap from the mind to the body. (Deutsch, Felix.) N.Y., 1959.
	Phil 8598.72	On the nature and grounds of religious belief. (Stocks, J.L.) London, 1934.
	Phil 978.6.3	On the nature and the existence of God. (Besant, Annie.) London, 1875.
	Phil 585.95	On the nature of man. (Langdon-Davies, J.) N.Y., 1961.
	Phil 2255.7.10	On the nature of man. (Runes, Dagobert D.) N.Y., 1956.
	Phil 960.270	On the nature of man and society, and other essays. 1st ed. (Seneviratne, M.J.) Colombo, 1967.
	Phil 7150.105	On the nature of suicide. 1st ed. San Francisco, 1969.
	Phil 1845.3.100	On the nature of value; the philosophy of Samuel Alexander. (Konvitz, Milton R.) N.Y., 1946.
	Phil 6111.10.15	On the neural processes underlying attention and volition. (Bastian, H.C.) London, 1893.
	Phil 5585.50	On the non-visual perception of the length of lifted rods. Thesis. (Hoisington, Louis B.) Worcester, Mass., 1920.
	Phil 8894.17.15	On the open road. (Trine, Ralph W.) N.Y., 1908.
	Phil 5620.18	On the origin of reason. (Zoul, L.) N.Y., 1938.
Htn	Phil 1955.1.30*	On the origin of species. (Darwin, Charles.) London, 1859.
	Phil 8064.2	On the perception of natural beauty by the ancients and moderns. (Wiseman, N.) London, 1856.
	Phil 5649.13	On the perception of small differences. (Fullerton, G.S.) Philadelphia, 1892.
	Phil 7082.158	On the phenomena of dreams. (Dendy, Walter Cooper.) London, 1832.
	Phil 7054.102.2	On the phenomena of modern spiritualism. 2. ed. (Hayden, William B.) Boston, 1855. 2 pam.
	Phil 197.6.5	On the philosophy of discovery. (Whewell, W.) London, 1860.
	Phil 8886.5	On the philosophy of ethics. (Laurie, S.S.) Edinburgh, 1866.
	Phil 2750.11.79	On the philosophy of history. (Maritain, Jacques.) N.Y., 1957.
	Phil 960.3.2	On the philosophy of the Vedânta in its relations to occidental metaphysics. (Deussen, P.) Bombay, 1893.
	Phil 8691.12.5.5	On the power, wisdom and goodness of God. (Chalmers, Thomas.) London, 1839. 2v.

Phil 8691.12.5   On the power, wisdom and goodness of God. (Chalmers, Thomas.) London, 1865.

Phil 6112.3   On the principles of aesthetic medicine. (Catlow, P.) London, 1867.

Phil 5421.15.12   On the problem of empathy. 2d ed. (Stein, Edith.) The Hague, 1970.

Phil 8615.15   On the religious frontier. (Chubb, Percival.) N.Y., 1931.

Phil 8585.11   On the religious ideas. (Fox, W.J.) London, 1849.

Phil 8709.21   On the resolution of science and faith. (Thomas, W.) N.Y., 1946.

Phil 5810.3.2   On the senses, instincts, and intelligence of animals. 2nd ed. (Avebury, John L.) London, 1889.

Phil 346.27   On the sources of knowledge and of ignorance. (Popper, Karl Raimund.) London, 1960.

Phil 9035.2   On the study of character. (Bain, A.) London, 1861.

Phil 5170.15   On the syllogism, and other logical writings. (DeMorgan, Augustus.) London, 1966.

Phil 8612.54   On the theology of death. (Rahner, Karl.) Freiburg, 1964.

Phil 410.8   On the theory of the infinite in modern thought. (Jourdain, E.F.) London, 1911.

Phil 9352.8.3   On the threshold. (Munger, Theodore T.) Boston, 1884.

Phil 9352.8.7   On the threshold. 26th ed. (Munger, Theodore T.) Boston, 1893.

Phil 178.12.49   On the threshold of the spiritual world. (Dresser, H.W.) N.Y., 1919.

Phil 7060.82.4   On the threshold of the unseen. (Barrett, W.F.) London, 1917.

Phil 7069.19.15   On the threshold of the unseen. (Barrett, William F.) N.Y., 1919.

Phil 7060.82.5   On the threshold of the unseen. 3. ed. (Barrett, W.E.) London, 1918.

Htn   Phil 6967.4*   On the treatment of the insane. (Randall, J.R.) n.p., n.d.

Phil 2750.11.83   On the use of philosophy. (Maritain, Jacques.) Princeton, N.J., 1961.

Phil 184.3.41   On the vital reserves. (James, W.) N.Y., 1922.

Phil 2340.20.30   On the way to myself: communications to a friend. (Wolff, Charlotte.) London, 1969.

Phil 2070.145.5   On the way toward a phenomenological psychology; the psychology of William James. (Linschoten, Johannes.) Pittsburgh, 1968.

Phil 8663.1   On the whole doctrine of final causes. (Irons, W.J.) London, 1836.

Phil 5520.500   On the wisdom of words. (Wagner, Geoffrey A.) Princeton, 1968.

Phil 5252.12.13.2   On the witness stand. (Münsterberg, H.) N.Y., 1909.

Phil 5252.12.18   On the witness stand. (Münsterberg, H.) N.Y., 1933.

Phil 8692.8   On true relations of scientific thought and religious belief. (Cotterill, H.) London, 1878.

Phil 187.17.5   On truth. (Mivart, St. G.) London, 1889.

Phil 730.36   On universals. (Wolterstorff, Nicholas Paul.) Chicago, 1970.

Phil 7080.5.5   On wakefulness. (Hammond, W.A.) Philadelphia, 1866.

Phil 6315.2.20.15   On war, sex and neurosis. (Freud, Sigmund.) N.Y., 1947.

Phil 5585.227   Oñativia, O.V. Dimensiones de la percepcion. Tucuman, 1963.

Phil 4769.1.50   Det onda. Tre samtal. (Solov'ev, V.S.) Stockholm, 1918.

Phil 4600.4.35   Onda makter och goda. (Lidforss, Bengt.) Malmö, 1909.

Phil 4513.1.40   Det ondas problem. (Ahlberg, A.) Stockholm, 1923.

Phil 8668.1.10   Det ondas problem. (Naville, E.) Stockholm, 1872.

Phil 8692.19   Het onderscheidingsvermogen voor toonintensiteiten. (Deenik, Arie.) Leiden, 1906.

Phil 8407.50   Onderzoek en phantasie. (Geel, Jacobus.) Leiden, 1838.

Phil 5592.175   Onderzoek naar de kleurintentionaliteit. (Smits, Willem C.M.) Nijmegen, 1964.

Phil 5251.16   Onderzoek naar den duur der eenvoudige psychische processen v.n. bij de Psychosen. (Louden, D.M. van.) Amsterdam, 1905.

Phil 6619.14   Onderzoekingen over de aandachtsbepaling bij gezonden en zielszieken. (Godefroy, Jan C.L.) Groningen, 1915?

Phil 5243.48   Les ondes cérébrales et la psychologie. (Delay, Jean P.L.) Paris, 1942.

Phil 814.2.5   Ondes Reggio, V. Sulla necessità della instaurazione. 2a ed. Palermo, 1861.

Phil 860.10   One and many in Presocratic philosophy. (Stokes, Michael C.) Washington, 1971.

Phil 1885.82   The one and the many...Bradley's "Appearance and reality". Diss. (Pounder, R.M.) Cambridge, 1928.

Phil 2905.1.595   The one and the many. (Gray, Donald P.) N.Y., 1969.

Phil 5627.165   One fight more. (Thornhill, Alan.) London, 1943.

Phil 7069.44.35   One hundred cases for survival after death. (Baird, A.T.) N.Y., 1944.

Phil 8598.13   One hundred theses, foundations of human knowledge. (Snell, M.M.) Washington, 1891.

Phil 6980.38.2   One hundred years of American psychiatric Association, 1844-1944. (American Psychiatric Association.) N.Y., 1945.

Phil 8525.10   One hundred years of freethought. (Tribe, David H.) London, 1967.

Phil 6960.5.15   One hundred years of psychiatry. (Kraepelin, E.) N.Y., 1962.

Phil 8707.22   One man's mind. (Rowland, J.) London, 1952.

Phil 6980.127   One mind. (Bond, Earl Clanford.) N.Y., 1958.

Phil 9182.7   One operation and another. (Wicks, Robert R.) N.Y., 1939.

Phil 5627.134.12   One thing I know. (Russell, A.J.) N.Y., 1933.

Phil 7074.20   The one way. (Burke, Jane R.) N.Y., 1922.

Phil 7074.20.1   The one way. (Burke, Jane R.) N.Y., 1923.

Phil 190.18.25A   One world in the making. 1st ed. (Perry, R.B.) N.Y., 1945.

Phil 165.145   O'Neil, Charles J. An Etienne Gilson tribute presented by his North American students. Milwaukee, 1959.

Phil 9495.168.10   O'Neil, Robert P. Sexuality and moral responsibility. Washington, 1968.

Phil 5254.8   O'Neil, William Matthew. An introduction to method in psychology. 2d. ed. Parkville, 1962.

Phil 7069.44.40   O'Neill, Herbert V. Spiritualism as spiritualists have written of it. London, 1944.

Phil 295.2   O'Neill, John. Cosmology; an introduction to the philosophy of matter. London, 1923.

Phil 2750.20.140   O'Neill, John. Perception, expression, and history. Evanston, 1970.

Phil 345.5   O'Neill, Reginald. Theories of knowledge. Englewood Cliffs, N.J., 1960.

Phil 7084.40   Oneirics and psychosomatics. (Loehrich, Rolf Rudolf.) McHenry, Ill., 1953.

Phil 7081.2   Oneirocritica Americana. (Weiss, Harry Bischoff.) N.Y., 1944.

Phil 5024.1   Öner, Nécoti. Fromsy sosydojiokuluna góre mokhyinmensei. Ankara, 1965.

Phil 5592.174   Ong, Jin. The opposite form procedure in inventory construction and research. 1. ed. N.Y., 1965.

Phil 2835.84   Ong, Walter J. Ramus, method and the decay of dialogue. Cambridge, 1958. 2v.

Htn   Phil 2835.84.5*A   Ong, Walter J. Ramus and Talon inventory. Cambridge, 1958.

Phil 2835.84.5   Ong, Walter J. Ramus and Talon inventory. Cambridge, 1958.

Phil 5520.489   Ong, Walter Jackson. The presence of the word. New Haven, 1967.

Phil 189.29A   Onians, R.B. The origins of European thought about the body, the mind, the soul. Cambridge, Eng., 1951.

Phil 189.29.2   Onians, R.B. The origins of European thought about the body, the mind, the soul. 2. ed. Cambridge, Eng., 1954.

Phil 2905.1.210   Onimus, J. Pierre Teilhard de Chardin. Paris, 1963.

Phil 9070.119   Onimus, Jean. Lettres à mes fils. 5. éd. Paris, 1965.

Phil 9070.43   Onis y Sanchez, F. de. Disciplina y rebeldia. San José, Costa Rica, 1917.

Phil 978.59.60   The only revolution. (Krishnamurti, J.) London, 1970.

Phil 4225.1.90   Onoranze funebri a Bertrando Spaventa. Napoli, 1883.

Phil 4110.3.83   Onoranze funebri a Francesco Fiorentino. Napoli, 1885.

Phil 4112.86   Onori funebri che alla memoria di Pasquale Galluppi. (Cursi, C.M.) Napoli, 1847.

Phil 176.162   Onsocratische gesprekken. (Beerling, R.F.) Amsterdam, 1949.

Phil 24.8   The Ontario psychologist. Toronto. 1,1969+ 2v.

Phil 1750.540   Ontbinding en protest. (Flam, Leopold.) Antwerpen, 1959.

Phil 8884.19   De ontkenning der moraal. (Jelgersma, D.G.) Amsterdam, 1896.

Phil 4215.4.80   L'ontognoseologia di Cesare Ranzoli. (Gentiluomo, D.) Padova, 1951.

Phil 3585.28.20   Ontologia. (Lotz, Johannes Baptist.) Barcinone, 1963.

Phil 178.67   Ontologia. 9. ed. (Donat, Josef.) Oeniponte, 1940.

Phil 343.26   Ontologia del conocimiento. (Mayz Vallenilla, E.) Caracas, 1960.

Phil 1750.840   Ontología del siglo XX: Husserl. (Riu, Federico.) Caracas, 1960.

Phil 8401.28   Ontologia dell'arte. (Apollonio, M.) Brescia, 1961.

Phil 2880.8.295   L'ontologia di Jean Paul Sartre. (Cavaciuti, Santino.) Milano, 1969.

Phil 4200.6.80   Ontologia e assiologia critica nel pensiero di Nicola Petruzzellis. (Firrito, Giovanni.) Napoli, 1967.

Phil 2905.1.640   L'ontologia fenomenologica di Teilhard de Chardin. (Straniero, Giorgio.) Milano, 1969.

Phil 3450.19.91   La ontologia fundamental de Heidegger. (Wagner de Peyna, A. de.) Buenos Aires, 1939.

Phil 3450.19.104   La ontologia fundamental de Heidegger. (Wagner de Reyna, A.) Buenos Aires, 1939.

Phil 8670.21   The ontological argument. (Plantinga, Alvin.) Garden City, N.Y., 1965.

Phil 5066.11.50   Ontological relativity, and other essays. (Quine, Willard van Orman.) N.Y., 1969.

Phil 178.13   Ontologie. (Dupont, A.H.H.) Louvain, 1875.

Phil 182.74   Ontologie. (Hugonin, F.) Paris, 1856-1857. 2v.

Phil 193.162   Ontologie. (Steenberghen, F.) Louvain, 1946.

Phil 3640.845   L'ontologie de Nietzsche. (Boudot, Pierre.) Paris, 1971.

Phil 3011.3.10   Die Ontologie der Gegenwart in ihren Grundgestalten. (Lehmann, G.) Halle, 1933.

Phil 193.170   Die Ontologie der Kultur. (Samuel, Otto.) Berlin, 1956.

Phil 3200.8.20   Ontologie des Bewusstseins. (Ehrlich, W.) Zürich, 1940.

Phil 3140.82   Die Ontologie des J. Clauberg. (Brosch, P.) Greifswald, 1926.

Phil 197.70   Ontologie des Lebendigen. (Woltereck, Richard.) Stuttgart, 1940.

Phil 193.220   Ontologie du langage. (Siewerth, Gustav.) Bruges, 1958.

Phil 3925.16.185   Ontologie in Wittgensteins "Tractatus". (Mueller, Anselm.) Bonn, 1967.

Phil 3483.88   Die Ontologie Kants. Ihr Grundriss in der Transzendentalphilosophie. Habilitationsschrift. (Blaha, Ottokar.) Salzburg, 1967.

Phil 1540.87   Ontologie oder Metaphysik? Die Diskussion über den Gegenstand der Metaphysik im 13. und 14. Jahrhundert. Habilitationeschrift. (Zimmermann, Albert.) Leiden, 1965[1966].

Phil 3450.19.265   L'ontologie phénoménologique de Heidegger. (Chapelle, Albert.) Paris, 1962.

Phil 5068.53   Ontologie und logistiche Analyse der Sprache. (Küng, Gaide.) Wien, 1963.

Phil 672.235   Ontologische Beiträge zum Raum-Zeit-Problem. (Hoelling, Joachim.) Freiburg? 1965.

Phil 1750.747   Die ontologische Betrachtungsweise. (Zinzen, A.) Meisenheim, 1963.

Phil 8662.24   Der ontologische Gottesbeweis. (Henrich, Dieter.) Tübingen, 1960.

Phil 8672.7   Der ontologische Gottesbeweis. (Runze, G.) Halle, 1882.

Phil 337.9   Die ontologischen Grundlagen der neueren Erkenntnislehre. (Günther, E.) Halle, 1933.

Phil 4115.110   L'ontologismo di Vincenzo Gioberti; antologia sistematica. (Portale, Vincenzo.) Cosenza, 1968.

Phil 177.91   Ontology; or The theory of being. (Coffey, Peter.) London, 1914.

Phil 180.76   Ontology. (Feibleman, James.) Baltimore, 1951.

Phil 193.43.5   Ontology. (Swedenborg, E.) Boston, 1901.

Phil 193.43   Ontology. Photoreproduction. (Swedenborg, E.) Philadelphia, 1880.

Phil 5068.53.1   Ontology and the logistic analysis of language. (Küng, Gaide.) Dordrecht, 1967.

Phil 5015.3   De onturkkeling van het logisch denken. (Feys, Robert.) Antwerpen, 1949.

Phil 3450.11.225   De ontwikkelingsgang in het denken van Husserl. (Boer, Theodorus de.) Assem, 1966.

Phil 3475.3.40   Die ontwort on Sigrid Undset. (Jaspers, Karl.) Konstang, 1947.

Phil 4080.3.380   Onufrio, Salvatore. La politica nel pensiero di Benedetto Croce. Milano, 1962.

Phil 1750.734   De onverzoenlijken. (Flam, L.) St. Niklaas, 1959.

Phil 8594.2.9   Onze godsdienst. (Opzoomer, C.W.) Amsterdam, 1874.

Phil 3850.52.40   Onze nonger naar oprechtheid. (Stallaert, L.) Brugge, 1965.

Phil 1106.12   De oorsprong der grieksche wijsbegeerte. 3e uitg. (Bolland, G.J.P.J.) Leiden, 1921.

Phil 353.5   De oorsprong en de grenzen der kennis. 2e Druk. (Wijck, B.H.C.K. van der.) Groningen, 1863.

Phil 2070.145   Op weg naar een fenomenologische psychologie. (Linschoten, Johannes.) Utrecht, 1959.

Phil 3790.22.5   Op wijsgerige wegen. (Riessen, Hendrick van.) Wageningen, 1963.

Phil 282.24   Op zoek naar identiteit. (Berger, Herman.) Nijmegen, 1968.

Phil 178.48   Opdragelsens hovedopgaver. 3. udg. (Dam, Axel.) Kobenhavn, 1923.

Phil 182.71   Opdragelseslaere. (Hansen, O.) Kjobenhavn, 1898.

Phil 5335.6   The open and closed mind. (Rokeach, Milton.) N.Y., 1960.

Phil 3120.11.95   Open brief aan den heer K.J.A.M. Schaepman. (Bolland, G.J.P.J.) Leiden, 1899.

Phil 24.1   The open court. Chicago. 1-50 31v.

Phil 978.25   The open door of the soul. (Morrison, D.) Boston, 1908.

Phil 282.10   The open secret; a study of life's deeper forces. (Bixby, J.T.) Boston, 1912.

Phil 197.39   The open secret. (Whitby, C.J.) London, 1912.

Phil 8592.63.10   The open self. (Morris, Charles W.) N.Y., 1948.

Phil 7069.20.120   The open vision. (Dresser, Horatio W.) N.Y., 1920.

Phil 7069.32.12   The opening of the door. (Christie, Anne.) Boston, 1932.

Phil 3819.10.10   Opera, im Auftrag der Heidelberg Akademie der Wissenschaften Herausgegeben. (Spinoza, Benedictus de.) Heidelberg, 1925. 4v.

Htn   Phil 4932.2.30F*   Opera. (Bernard de Clairvaux, St.) n.p., 1508.

Phil 4075.1F   Opera. (Cardano, Girolamo.) Lugduni, 1663. 10v.

Htn   Phil 4110.1.30F*   Opera. (Ficino, Marsilio.) Basileae, 1576. 2v.

Htn   Phil 4196.5*   Opera. (Pico, G.F.) n.p., 1508.

Htn   Phil 4200.1.10*   Opera. (Pomponazzi, Pietro.) Basileae, 1567.

Phil 3480.10   Opera ad philosophiam criticam. (Kant, Immanuel.) Leipzig, 1796-98. 4v.

Phil 2490.104   L'opera di Augusto Comte, in occasione del primo centenario della sua nascita. (Fornelli, N.) Milano, 1898.

Phil 4080.3.445   L'opera di Benedetto Croce. (Borsari, Silvano.) Napoli, 1964.

Phil 5251.41.80   L'opera di Kurt Lewin nella psicologia contemporanea. (Ossicuri, Adriano.) Messina, 1960.

Phil 4195.106A   L'opera e il pensiero di Giovanni Pico della Mirandola nella storia dell'umanesimo. (Convegno Internazionale per il V Centenario della Nascita di Giovanni Pico della Mirandola, Mirandola, 1963.) Firenze, 1965.

Phil 4080.3.160   L'opera filosofica...di Benedetto Croce. (Cione, Edmondo.) Bari, 1942.

Phil 4818.298.15   Opera filozofice. (Conta, Vasile.) Bucureşti, 1967.

Phil 4065.12A   Opera latine. v. 1-3. (Bruno, Giordano.) Neapoli, 1879-91. 6v.

Phil 5000.4F   Opera logica. 16a ed. (Zabarella, Giacomo.) Tarvisii, 1604.

Phil 2520.13.20   Opera omnia, novem tomis comprehensa. (Descartes, René.) Amstelodami, 1692. 9v.

VPhil 1850.1F   Opera omnia. (Bacon, F.) Frankfort, 1664-68.

VPhil 1850.1.2F   Opera omnia. (Bacon, F.) Frankfort, 1665.

VPhil 1850.1.7F   Opera omnia. (Bacon, F.) Hafniae, 1694.

VPhil 1850.1.8F   Opera omnia. (Bacon, F.) Lipsiae, 1694.

Phil 1850.1.4F   Opera omnia. (Bacon, F.) London, 1730. 2v.

VPhil 1850.1.3F   Opera omnia. (Bacon, F.) London, 1730 4v.

Phil 2610.2   Opera omnia. (Gassendi, P.) Florentiae, 1727. 6v.

Phil 3552.11   Opera omnia. (Leibniz, Gottfried Wilhelm.) Genevae, 1768. 6v.

Htn   Phil 4195.5*   Opera omnia. (Pico della Mirandola, Giovanni.) Basileae, 1573. 2v.

Phil 4195.3F   Opera omnia. (Pico della Mirandola, Giovanni.) Reggio, 1506.

Phil 4225.23.15   Opera omnia. (Stellini, J.) Patavii, 1778-79. 4v.

Phil 4372.1.5   Opera omnia. (Vives, Juan Luis.) London, 1964. 8v.

Phil 3140.1   Opera omnia philosophica. Reprint. (Clauberg, Johann.) Hildesheim, 1968. 2v.

X Cg   Phil 2520.11   Opera philosophica. (Descartes, René.) Francofurti, 1656-58.

Phil 2520.10.25   Opera philosophica. (Descartes, René.) Francofurti, 1692.

Phil 3280.10   Opera philosophica. (Geulincx, A.) Hagae, 1891. 3v.

Phil 2045.10.5   Opera philosophica. (Hobbes, Thomas.) Aalen, 1961. 5v.

Htn   Phil 2045.3*   Opera philosophica. (Hobbes, Thomas.) Amstelodami, 1668. 2v.

Phil 2045.12   Opera philosophica. (Hobbes, Thomas.) London, 1839-45. 5v.

Phil 2045.10   Opera philosophica. (Hobbes, Thomas.) London, 1839-45. 5v.

Phil 186.5.2   Opera philosophica. (LeClerc, J.) Amsterdam, 1722. 4v.

Phil 3552.24.25   Opera philosophica. (Leibniz, Gottfried Wilhelm.) Aalen, 1959.

Phil 4369.2.86   Opera philosophica. (Sanches, Francisco.) Coimbra, 1955.

Phil 3552.15   Opera philosophica. v.1-2. (Leibniz, Gottfried Wilhelm.) Berolini, 1839-40.

Phil 186.5   Opera philosophica. v.1-4. (LeClerc, J.) Amsterdam, 1698. 3v.

Phil 2520.10.8   Opera philosophica. 4a ed. (Descartes, René.) Amsterdam, 1664.

Phil 2520.10.10   Opera philosophica. 4a ed. (Descartes, René.) Amsterdam, 1664.

Htn   Phil 2520.10.9*   Opera philosophica. 4a ed. (Descartes, René.) Amsterdam, 1664.

Htn   Phil 2520.10.16*   Opera philosophica. 5a ed. (Descartes, René.) Amsterdam, 1672.

Htn   Phil 2520.10.15*   Opera philosophica. 5a ed. (Descartes, René.) Amsterdam, 1672.

Phil 2520.10.20   Opera philosophica. 5a ed. (Descartes, René.) Amsterdam, 1677-78. 2v.

Phil 3819.10.2   Opera philosophische omnia. v.3. (Spinoza, Benedictus de.) Stuttgardiae, 1830.

Htn   Phil 3819.10.11*   Opera posthuma. Pt.2. (Spinoza, Benedictus de.) Amstelodami, 1677.

Phil 4195.6F   Opera quae extant omnia. (Pico della Mirandola, Giovanni.) Basileae, 1601.

Phil 3819.10   Opera quae supersunt omnia. (Spinoza, Benedictus de.) Ienae, 1802. 2v.

Phil 3819.10.3   Opera quae supersunt omnia. (Spinoza, Benedictus de.) Lipsiae, 1843-46. 3v.

Phil 3819.10.4   Opera supersunt omnia supplementum. (Spinoza, Benedictus de.) Amstelodami, 1862.

Phil 3819.10.8   Opera quotquot reperta sunt. (Spinoza, Benedictus de.) Hagae, 1882-83. 2v.

Phil 3819.10.9   Opera quotquot reperta sunt. 2. ed. (Spinoza, Benedictus de.) Hagae, 1895-96. 3v.

Phil 3819.10.9.3   Opera quotquot reperta sunt. 3. ed. v.1-4. (Spinoza, Benedictus de.) Hagae, 1913-14. 2v.

Phil 5520.115   Operational philosophy. 1. ed. (Rapoport, A.) N.Y., 1953.

Phil 5058.5   Der Operationskries der Logikkalkuls. (Schröder, E.) Leipzig, 1877.

Phil 6964.6   Operators and things: the inner life of a schizophrenic. (O'Brien, Barbara (pseud.).) Cambridge, Mass., 1958.

Phil 4065.11   Opere. (Bruno, Giordano.) Gottinga, 1888. 2v.

Phil 4065.10A   Opere. (Bruno, Giordano.) Lipsia, 1830. 2v.

Phil 4265.1.18   Opere. (Vanini, Lucilio, afterwards Giulio Cesare.) Lecce, 1912. 2v.

Phil 4260.17   Opere. (Vico, G.B.) Bari, 1914. 6v.

Phil 4260.16   Opere. (Vico, G.B.) Milano, 1953.

Phil 4260.17.10   Opere. (Vico, G.B.) Milano, 1959.

Phil 4115.14   Opere. v. 1-16. (Gioberti, V.) Napoli, 1845- 7v.

Phil 4120.4.11   Opere. v. 1-28,30-38,42. (Gentile, Giovanni.) Firenze, 1942. 36v.

Phil 4210.10   Opere. v.1, 9-10, 11-12, 15. (Rosmini-Serbati, Antonio.) Napoli, 1842-47. 4v.

Phil 4260.12   Opere. v.1-4. (Vico, G.B.) Napoli, 1840-41. 5v.

Phil 4260.15   Opere. v.1-6. (Vico, G.B.) Milano, 1854- 3v.

Phil 4080.14.2   Opere. v.1-7. (Celesia, Paolo.) Roma, 1923-30. 8v.

Phil 4265.2.10   Opere. v.1-13. (Ventura da Raulica, G.) Napoli, 1856-64. 11v.

Phil 4060.4.2   Opere complete. (Aliotta, Antonio.) Roma, 1947. 7v.

Phil 4265.8.2   Opere complete. (Sciacca, Michele Federico.) Milano, 1952-56. 7v.

Phil 4070.9.1   Opere complete: saggi, scritti inediti, opere minori, recensioni. (Bozzetti, Giuseppe.) Milano, 1966. 3v.

Phil 4065.28   Opere di G. Bruno e di T. Campanella. (Bruno, Giordano.) Milano, 1956.

Phil 4215.1.10   Opere di G.D. Romagnosi. Pt. 1-2. Milano, 1841. 16v.

Phil 4265.1.20   Le opere di Giulio Cesare Vanini e le loro fonti. (Vanini, Lucilio, afterwards Giulio Cesare.) Milano, 1933-34. 2v.

Phil 4215.1.30   Opere di Romagnosi. (Romagnosi, G.D.) Milano, 1957.

Phil 4210.12   Opere edite e inedite. (Rosmini-Serbati, Antonio.) Roma, 1934-63. 42v.

Phil 4210.8   Opere edite e inedite. v.5, 11-14, 20, 27-30. (Rosmini-Serbati, Antonio.) Milano, 1837. 10v.

Phil 4115.12   Opere edite e inedite. v. 1-7, 13. (Gioberti, V.) Brusselle, 1843-44. 6v.

Phil 3552.29.25   Opere filosofiche; estratti. (Leibniz, Gottfried Wilhelm.) Bologna, 1929.

Phil 4060.1.2   Opere filosofiche. (Ardigo, Roberto.) Padova, 1901-13. 11v.

Phil 3625.1.20   Opere filosofiche. (Mendelssohn, Moses.) Parma, 1800. 2v.

Phil 4065.13   Opere italiane. (Bruno, Giordano.) Bari, 1907. 2v.

Phil 4120.1.10   Opere minori. (Gioja, Melchiorre.) Lugano, 1832-37. 17v.

Phil 4080.10.60   Opere postume. (Ceretti, Pietro.) Torino, 1890.

Phil 4120.1.8   Opere principali. (Gioja, Melchiorre.) Lugano, 1838-40. 16v.

Htn   Phil 3552.26   Opere varie. (Leibniz, Gottfried Wilhelm.) Bari, 1912.

Htn   Phil 1850.1.10*   Operum moralium et civilium tomus. (Bacon, F.) London, 1638.

Phil 9510.1.5   Opie, A.A. (Mrs.). Detraction displayed. N.Y., 1828.

NEDL   Phil 9510.1   Opie, A.A. (Mrs.). Detraction displayed. Philadelphia, 1828.

NEDL   Phil 9558.13   Opie, Amelia A. (Mrs.). Illustrations of lying, in all its branches. 2. ed. Boston, 1826.

Phil 5380.3.3   L'opinion et la foule. 3rd éd. (Tarde, G.) Paris, 1910.

Phil 5590.210.2   Opinions and personality. (Smith, M.B.) N.Y., 1964.

Phil 5135.3   Les opinions et les croyances. (Le Bon, Gustave.) Paris, 1911.

Phil 3850.1.43   The opinions of Professor D.F. Strauss. (Strauss, D.F.) London, 1844.

Phil 1750.115.195   Opisanie i ob''iasnenie. (Mailov, Anatolii Il'ich.) Tashkent, 1969.

Phil 8594.7   Opitz, H.G. Das Christentum im Freilichte. Leipzig, 1911.

Phil 189.9.5   Opitz, H.G. Grundriss einer Seinswissenschaft. v.1-2. Leipzig, 1897-1899.

Phil 189.9   Opitz, H.G. Die Philosophie der Zukunft. Leipzig, 1910.

Phil 3480.82.25   Opmerkingen over het gevoll van Schoone en Vorheveve. (Kant, Immanuel.) Sneck, 1919.

Phil 3850.10.85   Oppenburg, Ursula. Quellenstudien zu Friedrich Schlegels Übersetzungen aus dem Sanskrit. Diss. Narburg, 1965.

Phil 5545.96   Oppenheim, Abraham Naftali. Questionnaire design and attitude measurement. N.Y., 1966.

Phil 6964.1.6   Oppenheim, H. Lehrbuch der Nervenkrankheiten. 6. Aufl. Berlin, 1913. 2v.

Phil 189.12   Oppenheim, F.J. The new tyranny; mysticism, scepticism. N.Y., 1927.

Phil 5635.27   Oppenheimer, Z. Physiologie des Gefühls. Heidelberg, 1899.

Phil 396.18   Oppermann, Hans. Humanismus. Darmstadt, 1970.

Phil 9528.5   Oppermann, W. Schulfeierstunden. Leipzig, 1923.

Phil 9450.18   Oppler, A.C. Ethics in public administration. Cambridge, 1942.

Phil 5485.4   Opplevelse, erfaring og intelligens. (Raaheim, Kjell.) Bergen, 1969.

Phil 1350.13.5   Oppormann, Hans. Römische Wertbegriffe. Darmstadt, 1967.

Phil 5592.174   The opposite form procedure in inventory construction and research. 1. ed. (Ong, Jin.) N.Y., 1965.

Phil 3425.230   Opposite things. (Sturge, M.C.) Bristol, 1927.

Phil 5520.35.15.5   Opposition; a linguistic and psychological analysis. (Ogden, Charles K.) Bloomington, 1967.

Phil 3010.11   Die Opposition der Jugendbrücken. (Kurucz, J.) Saar, 1958.

Phil 194.43   L'opposition universelle. (Tardé, G.) Paris, 1897.

Phil 4772.1   Opravdanie zla. (Veideman, A.) Riga, 1939.

Phil 2520.133   Oprescu, Georg. Descartes' Erkenntnislehre. Inaug.-Diss. Göttingen, 1889.

Phil 8828.8   Opskorting van die etiese? Thesis. (Du Plessis, Pieter Gert Wessel.) Potchefstroom, 1965.

Phil 5643.124   Optical illusion. (Jolansky, Samuel.) N.Y., 1964.

Phil 5643.21   Optical illusions of motion. (Bowditch, H.P.) Cambridge, 1882.

Phil 6115.18   Optimism; a real remedy. (Fletcher, Horace.) Chicago, 1908.

Phil 8581.64   Optimism, the lesson of ages. (Blood, B.P.) Boston, 1860.

Phil 9410.2   Optimism. (Keller, Helen.) N.Y., 1903.

Phil 9410.7   Optimism and romanticism. (Lovejoy, Arthur O.) n.p., 1927.

Phil 1900.45   The optimism of Butler's "analogy". (Holland, H.S.) Oxford, 1908.

Phil 960.139   L'optimisme dans la pensée indienne. Thèse. (Syed, M.H.) n.p., 1932.

Phil 3808.117   L'optimisme de Schopenhauer. (Rzewuski, S.) Paris, 1908.

Phil 9410.1   Der Optimismus als Weltanschauung. (Duboc, K.J.) Bonn, 1881.

Phil 9430.30   Optimismus und Pessimismus. (Gass, W.) Berlin, 1876.

Phil 1050.18 Der Optimismus und Pessimismus in der jüdischen Religionsphilosophie. (Gortein, H.) Berlin, 1890.
Phil 9352.7.17 The optimistic life. (Marden, O.S.) N.Y., 1907.
Phil 5643.8.10 Optique physiologique. (Helmholtz, H.) Paris, 1867.
Htn Phil 6045.83F* Opus mathematicum cheiromantis. (Taisnier, Joannes.) Coloniae, 1583.
Htn Phil 6045.62F* Opus mathematicum octs libros complectens. (Taisnier, Joannes.) Coloniae, 1562.
Phil 8951.13 Opus theologicum morale in Busernbaum Medullam. 3.ed. (Ballerini, A.) Prati, 1898-1901. 7v.
Phil 4073.39 Opuscali inediti. (Campanella, Tommaso.) Firenze, 1951.
Phil 4210.45 Opuscali morali. (Rosmini-Serbati, Antonio.) Milano, 1841.
Phil 4114.71 Opuscoli e lettere familiari. (Genovesi, Antonio.) Venezia, 1827.
Phil 4215.1.25 Opuscoli filosofici. (Romagnosi, G.D.) Lanciano, 1923.
Phil 8587.51.10 Opuscula. (Haecker, T.) Olten, 1949.
Phil 3552.30.10 Opuscula philosophica selecta. (Leibniz, Gottfried Wilhelm.) Paris, 1939.
Phil 2520.30 Opuscula posthuma. (Descartes, René.) Amsterdam, 1701.
Htn Phil 1850.76* Opuscula varia posthuma, philosophica, civilia, et theologica. (Bacon, Francis.) Londini, 1658.
Phil 2490.12 Opuscules de philosophie sociale. (Comte, Auguste.) Paris, 1883.
Phil 3552.19 Opuscules et fragments inédits. (Leibniz, Gottfried Wilhelm.) Paris, 1903.
Phil 2805.73 Opuscules et lettres. (Pascal, Blaise.) Paris, 1955.
Phil 181.21.5 Opuscules philosophiques. (Gruyer, L.A.) Bruxelles, 1851.
Phil 2805.70 Opuscules philosophiques. (Pascal, Blaise.) Paris, 1864.
Phil 2805.72 Opuscules philosophiques. (Pascal, Blaise.) Paris, 1887.
Phil 3552.30.15 Opuscules philosophiques choisis. (Leibniz, Gottfried Wilhelm.) Paris, 1954.
Phil 3552.20 Opusculum adscititio titulo Systema theologicum inscriptum. (Leibniz, Gottfried Wilhelm.) Lutetiae Parisiorum, 1845.
Phil 5054.2.2 Opyoomer, C.W. Het weyen der kennis. 2e druk. Amsterdam, 1867.
Phil 8980.191.5 Opyt izlozheniia sistemy marksistskoi etiki. (Bandzeladze, Gela.) Tbilisi, 1963.
Phil 600.62 Opyt kriticheskago izsledovaniia osnovonachal pozitivnoi filosofii. (Lesevich, Vladimir V.) Sanktpeterburg, 1877. 2 pam.
Phil 2520.128 Opzoomer, C.W. Cartesius. Amsterdam, 1861.
Phil 8594.2.5 Opzoomer, C.W. De godsdienst. Amsterdam, 1864.
Phil 3525.91 Opzoomer, C.W. De leer van God bij Schelling, Hegel en Krause. Leiden, 1846.
Phil 8594.2.9 Opzoomer, C.W. Onze godsdienst. Amsterdam, 1874.
Phil 8594.3 Opzoomer, C.W. Order. n.p., 1885.
Phil 8594.3.2 Opzoomer, C.W. Order. n.p., 1885.
Phil 8594.2 Opzoomer, C.W. Die Religion. Elberfeld, 1868.
Phil 8594.2.15 Opzoomer, C.W. De vrucht der godsdienst. 3. druk. Amsterdam, 1868.
Phil 189.15.5 Opzoomer, C.W. De waarheid en hare kenbronnen. Amsterdam, 1859.
Phil 189.15 Opzoomer, C.W. De wijsbegeerte, den mensch met zich zelvon verzoenende. Leiden, 1846.
Phil 187.182 L'ora della filosofia. (Moretti-Costanzi, Teodorico.) Bologna, 1968.
Phil 8610.841 The oracle of reason. Bristol, Eng. 1-2,1841-1843 2v.
Phil 8610.841.3 The oracle of reason. Bristol, Eng. 1-18
Phil 9530.52 Orage, A.R. The active mind. N.Y., 1954.
Phil 3640.100A Orage, A.R. Friedrich Nietzsche. Chicago, 1911.
Phil 8964.4 O'Rahilly, Alfred. Moral principles. Cork, 1948.
Phil 9070.110 Oraison, Marc. Une morale pour notre temps. Paris, 1964.
Phil 5254.9 Oraison, Mark. Illusion and anxiety. N.Y., 1963.
Phil 3805.252 Oranje, Leendert. God en wereld. Kampen, 1968.
Phil 3450.41 Oratio de summae veritatis cognoscendae ratione atque via. (Haekstra, Sytze.) Amstelodami, 1857.
Htn Phil 8592.58* An oration, produced before the Phi Beta Kappa,...Hanover, Aug. 25, 1802. (M'Farland, Asa.) Hanover, 1802.
Phil 9245.22 An oration...before...Phi Beta Kappa Society. (Dickson, Henry S.) New Haven, 1842.
Phil 8892.8 An oration...enquiry into the influence of physical causes upon the moral faculty. (Rush, Benjamin.) Philadelphia, 1786.
Phil 4195.38 Oration on the dignity of man. (Pico della Mirandola, Giovanni.) Chicago, 1956.
Htn Phil 8663.3.31* An oration on the Gods. (Ingersoll, Robert G.) Peoria, 1872.
Htn Phil 293.11* An oration on the truth of the Mosaic history of the creation. (Marsh, E.G.) Hartford, 1798.
Phil 295.6 Orban, A.P. Les dénominations du monde chez les premiers auteurs chrétiens. Nijmegen, 1970.
Phil 5625.75.105 Orbeli, Leon A. Vospominaniia o I.P. Pavlove. Leningrad, 1966.
Phil 5058.92 Ord och Mängd. (Saarnio, Uuno.) Helsingfors, 1960.
Phil 8587.57 The ordeal of western civilization. (Hutchinson, Paul.) Boston, 1933.
Phil 8622.60 The ordeal of wonder. (Morgan, E.K.) London, 1964.
Phil 8712.30 Order, goodness, glory. (Whitehouse, Walter.) London, 1960.
Phil 8594.3 Order. (Opzoomer, C.W.) n.p., 1885.
Phil 8594.3.2 Order. (Opzoomer, C.W.) n.p., 1885.
Phil 315.17 Order and counter-order. (Waterston, G.C.) N.Y., 1966.
Phil 1523.11 Order and disorder; a study of mediaeval principles. (Slesser, Henry H.) London, 1945.
Htn Phil 8878.4.5* Order and growth. (Davies, J.L.) London, 1891.
Phil 187.148 The order and integration of knowledge. (Martin, W.O.) Ann Arbor, 1957.
Phil 8735.6A The order of nature. (Henderson, L.J.) Cambridge, 1917.
Phil 8735.6.5A The order of nature. (Henderson, L.J.) Cambridge, 1925.
Phil 8595.7 The order of nature. (Powell, B.) London, 1859.
Phil 5190.10.26 The order of presentation in persuasion. (Yale University. Institute of Human Relations.) New Haven, 1961.
Phil 9070.19.2 The ordinary difficulties of everyday people. (Oliver, J.R.) N.Y., 1935.
Phil 5520.555 Ordinary language; essays in philosophical method. (Chappell, Vere Claiborne.) Englewood Cliffs, N.J., 1964.
Phil 8880.45 L'ordine ed i fatti morali. (Falco, Francesco.) Alessandria, 1874.
Phil 680.5 Ordnung und Chaos. (Jaeggi, Urs.) Frankfurt, 1968.
Phil 178.22 Ordnungslehre. (Driesch, H.) Jena, 1912.
Phil 178.22.2 Ordnungslehre. (Driesch, H.) Jena, 1923.
Phil 193.175 Ordnungslehre. (Schmidt, Franz.) München, 1956.
Phil 1540.82 Ordo. (Krings, Hermann.) Halle, 1941.
Phil 3585.32 Ordo rerum. (Luyten, Norbert Alfons.) Freiburg, 1969.
Phil 165.25 Ordre, désordre, lumière. Paris, 1952.
Phil 9495.170.10 L'ordre et le sexe. (Caraco, Albert.) Lausanne, 1970.
Phil 8876.85 L'ordre social et l'ordre moral. (Bertauld, Alfred.) Paris, 1874.
Phil 4075.85 Ore, Oystein. Cardano, the gambling scholar. Princeton, 1953.
Phil 5650.18 L'orecchio. (Tullio, Pietro.) Bologna, 1928.
Phil 5254.4 Oreg, J. Gondslkodastan az eggetemesitö (inductiv) s lehozó (deductiv) módazer alapján. Nagy Köros, 1877.
Phil 54.2 Oregon. University. Publications. Psychology series. Eugene. 1929-1935
Phil 24.4 Oregon. University. Studies in psychology. Eugene. 1-3,1943-1959 3v.
Phil 24.5 Oregon. University. Studies in psychology. Eugene. 2,1955
Phil 9495.42 Oregon Social Hygiene Society. Bulletin. Portland.
Phil 9354.2.5 O'Reilly, B. True men as we need them. 4th ed. N.Y., 1882.
Phil 3834.1 Orelli, J.C. von. Spinoza's Leben und Lehre. Aurau, 1843.
Phil 189.16 Orestano, F. Nuovi principi. Roma, 1925.
Phil 4073.99 Orestano, F. Tommaso Campanella. Roma, 1940.
Phil 3496.3 Orestano, F. Der Tugendbegriff bei Kant. Inaug. Diss. Palermo, 1901.
Phil 8889.3 Orestano, F. I valori umani. Milan, 1907.
Phil 189.16.5 Orestano, F. Verità dimostrate. Napoli, 1934.
Phil 4190.1.35 Orestano, Francesco. Idee econcetti. Milano, 1939.
Phil 3640.85.5 Orestano, Francesco. Le idee fondamentali de F. Nietzsche. Palermo, 1903.
Phil 4190.1.45 Orestano, Francesco. Nuove vedute logiche. Milano, 1939.
Phil 4190.1.30 Orestano, Francesco. Nuovi princèpi. Milano, 1939.
Phil 4190.1.40 Orestano, Francesco. Il nuovo realismo. Milano, 1939.
Phil 8889.3.7 Orestano, Francesco. Prolegomeni alla scienza del bene e del mali. Roma, 1915.
Phil 165.55 Organ, F.W. The examined life. Boston, 1956.
Phil 960.246 Organ, T.W. The self in Indian philosophy. London, 1964.
Phil 5635.12 Organic sensation. (Murray, E.) n.p., 1909.
Phil 6122.1.19 Organic to human; psychology and sociology. (Maudsley, H.) London, 1916.
Phil 3450.34 Organik. (Heske, Franz.) Berlin, 1954.
Phil 9075.10 L'organisation de la conscience morale. (Delvolve, Jean.) Paris, 1906.
Phil 6122.66 L'organisation des fonctions psychiques. (Monnier, Marcel.) Neuchâtel, 1951.
Phil 5643.136 L'organisation perceptive: son rôle dans l'évolution des illusion optico-géométrique. (Vurpillot, Eliane.) Paris, 1963.
Phil 5241.140 Organisches Denken. (Birnbaum, W.) Tübingen, 1960.
Phil 6317.21.104 Der Organism der Seele. 4. Aufl. (Heyer, Gustav R.) München, 1959.
Phil 6317.21.5 The organism of the mind. (Heyer, Gustav R.) N.Y., 1934.
Phil 196.11.5 Der Organismus der Allvernunft und das Leben der Menschheit in Ihm. (Varnbüler, Theodore.) Prag, 1891.
Phil 182.17.10 Der Organismus der philosophischen Idee. (Hillebrand, J.) Dresden, 1842.
Phil 182.11 Der Organismus der Wissenschaft. (Helfferich, A.) Leipzig, 1856.
Phil 5238.20 Organization and pathology of thought. (Rapaport, D.) N.Y., 1951.
Phil 344.4 The organization of knowledge...philosophical analysis. (Negley, Glenn.) N.Y., 1942.
Phil 5545.254.2 The organization of recall; proceedings. (International Interdisciplinary Conference on Learning, Remembering and Forgetting.) N.Y., 1967.
Phil 24.6 Organizational behavior and human performance. N.Y. 1,1966+ 3v.
Phil 5250.34.5 Organizing and memorizing. (Katona, George.) N.Y., 1949.
Phil 333.1 Organon der Erkenntniss. (Carus, C.G.) Leipzig, 1856.
Phil 197.1 Organon der menschlichen Erkenntniss. (Wagner, J.) Ulm, 1851.
Phil 5058.26 Organon of science. (Stinson, J.H.) Eureka, Calif., 1879.
Phil 6310.1.93 Orgler, Hertha. Alfred Adler, the man and his work. London, 1939.
Phil 6310.1.103 Orgler, Hertha. Alfred Adler, the man and his work. 3d ed. London, 1963.
Phil 6310.1.100 Orgler, Hertha. Alfred Adler. Wien, 1956.
Phil 6324.8 Örgü, Halis. Kampleksler ve insanlar. Istanbul, 1969.
Phil 9558.10 L'orgueil humain. 2. éd. (Zyromski, Ernest.) Paris, 1905.
Phil 8080.2 Oribe, Emilia. Tres ideales esteticos. Montevideo, 1958.
Phil 189.24 Oribe, Emilio. Teoría del nous. Buenos Aires, 1934.
Phil 189.24.5 Oribe, Emilio. Teoría del nous. Buenos Aires, 1944.
Phil 900.15 L'Orient et sa tradition. (Le Renard, A.) Paris, 1952.
Phil 705.23 The Orient in American transcendentalism. (Christy, Arthur.) N.Y., 1932.
Phil 705.23.2 The Orient in American transcendentalism. (Christy, Arthur.) N.Y., 1963.
Phil 1135.150 Orient und griechische Philosophie. (Hopgner, T.) Leipzig, 1925.
Phil 54.3 Oriental Esoteric Society, Washington, D.C. Bulletin. Washington. 11-16,1915-1920 4v.
Phil 900.11 Oriental philosophy. (Grant, Francis.) N.Y., 1936.
Phil 970.2 Pamphlet box. Oriental theosophy.
Phil 970.4 Pamphlet box. Oriental theosophy.
Phil 970.6 Pamphlet box. Oriental theosophy.
Phil 970.15F Pamphlet box. Oriental theosophy.
Phil 970.3 Pamphlet box. Oriental theosophy.
Phil 1702.6 Orientamenti della filosofia conteporanea. (Carlini, A.) Roma, 1931.
Phil 814.5 Orientamenti filosofici e pedagogico. Milano, 1962. 4v.
Phil 5651.4 L'orientation. (Bomier, Pierre.) Paris, 1900.
Phil 5827.8.5 L'orientation lointaine et la reconnaissance des lieux. (Rabaud, E.) Paris, 1927.
Phil 5815.6 The orientation of animals. (Fraenkel, G.S.) Oxford, Eng., 1940.
Phil 5811.24 L'orientation spatiale chez l'animal, ses indices et ses repères. (Blancheteau, Marc.) Paris, 1969.
Phil 8876.82 L'orientazione psicologica dell'etica e della filosofia del diritto. (Bonucci, A.) Perugia, 1907.
Phil 180.78 Orientazioni metafisiche. (Forest, Aimé.) Milano, 1960.
Phil 5651.3 Die Orientierung; die Physiologie. (Hartmann, F.) Leipzig, 1902.
Phil 3450.19.170 El origen de la obra de arte y la verdad en Heidegger. (Soler Grimma, Francisco.) Bogota, 1953.
Phil 4365.2.35 Origen y epílogo de la filosofía. (Ortega y Gasset, José.) Mexico, 1960.
Phil 325.8 Las origenes del empirismo en el pensamiento político español del siglo XVII. (Maravall, Jose Antonio.) Granada, 1947.
Phil 8897.28.3 The origin and development...moral ideas. (Westermarck, E.) London, 1908-12. 2v.

Phil 8897.28 The origin and development...moral ideas. 2nd ed. (Westermarck, E.) London, 1906-17. 2v.

Phil 6315.2.12 The origin and development of psychoanalysis. (Freud, Sigmund.) Chicago, 1955.

Phil 8897.28.20 The origin and development of the moral ideas. 2nd ed. (Westermarck, E.) London, 1924-26.

Phil 6327.18 The origin and function of culture. (Roheim, Geza.) N.Y., 1943.

Phil 8843.4 The origin and growth of moral instinct. (Sutherland, A.) London, 1898. 2v.

Phil 9075.22 Origin and nature of conscience. (Knowlton, Pitt G.) Oberlin, 1897.

Phil 5400.32 The origin and nature of the emotions. (Crile, George W.) Philadelphia, 1915.

Phil 3425.103 The origin and significance of Hegel's logic. (Baillie, J.B.) London, 1901.

Phil 5374.21 The origin of consciousness. (Strong, Charles A.) London, 1918.

Phil 5620.4 Origin of human reason. (Mivart, S.G.) London, 1889.

Phil 4210.50 The origin of ideas. (Rosmini-Serbati, Antonio.) London, 1883-84. 3v.

Phil 8876.41 Origin of knowledge of right and wrong. (Brentano, Franz.) London, 1902.

Phil 5520.32.5 Origin of language and logos theory. 2. ed. (Noiré, Ludwig.) Chicago, 1899.

Phil 4365.2.36 The origin of philosophy. 1st ed. (Ortega y Gasset, José.) N.Y., 1967.

Phil 960.18 The origin of subjectivity in Hindu thought. (Kitch, Ethel May.) Chicago, 1917.

Phil 8656.2 The origin of the laws of nature. (Beckett, E.) London, 1879.

Phil 8403.22 The origin of the sense of beauty. (Clay, Felix.) London, 1908.

Phil 8628.4 An original essay on the immateriality and immortality of the human soul. (Drew, Samuel.) London, 1819.

Htn Phil 8628.4.2* An original essay on the immateriality and immortality of the human soul. 1st American ed. (Drew, Samuel.) Baltimore, 1810.

Phil 3489.4 Originalität über die kritische Philosophie. (Heydenreich, C.H.) Leipzig, 1793.

Phil 5425.26 Originality, a popular study of creative mind. (Knowlson, Thomas S.) Philadelphia, 1918.

Phil 8596.1 L'origine de la religion. (Quetin, M.A.) Montauban, 1903.

Phil 8673.7 L'origine de l'idée de Dieu. pt.1. (Schmidt, Wilhelm.) Paris, 1910.

Phil 5258.70.5 L'origine dei fenomeni psichici e il loro significato biologico. 2. ed. (Sergi, G.) Torino, 1904.

Phil 1523.6.5 Le origine del neo-tomismo. (Saitta, Giuseppe.) Bari, 1912.

Phil 1106.17 L'origine dell'intellettualismo. (Bartolone, Félippi.) Palermo, 1959.

Phil 178.9.3 Origine des découvertes. 3e éd. (Dutens, Louis.) Louvain, 1796.

Phil 178.9.4 Origine des découvertes. 4e éd. (Dutens, Louis.) Paris, 1812.

Phil 292.9 L'origine des mondes. (Laberenne, P.) Paris, 1936.
Phil 286.1 L'origine du monde. (Faye, H.A.E.) Paris, 1884.
Phil 190.16.5 Les origines. 3e éd. (Pressensé, E. de.) Paris, 1883.
Phil 3831.15 Les origines cartésiennes du Dieu de Spinoza. Thèse. (Lachièze-Rey, P.) Paris, 1932.
Phil 5374.20 Origines de la connaissance. (Turró, R.) Paris, 1914.
Phil 5246.35 Les origines de la pensée. (Giran, Paul.) Paris, 1923.
Phil 8520.40 Les origines de la philosophie chrétienne. (Tresmontant, C.) Paris, 1962.

Phil 5222.1 Les origines de la psychologie contemporaine. (Mercier, D.) Paris, 1897.

Phil 1517.1 Les origines de la scolastique. (Mignon, A.) Paris, n.d. 2v.

Phil 5590.536.4 Les origines du caractère chez l'enfant. 4. éd. (Wallon, Henri.) Paris, 1970.

Phil 2805.216 Les origines du mouvement antijanseniste. Thèse. (Réguron, Paule.) Grenoble, 1934.

Phil 2880.2.85 Les origines et l'évolution de la pensée de Charles Secrétan. (Grin, Edmond.) Lausanne, 1930.

Phil 365.27.5 Les origines humaines et l'évolution de l'intelligence. (LeRoy, Édouard.) Paris, 1928.

Phil 482.5 Les origines judéo-chrétiennes du matérialisme contemporain. (Huré, Jules.) Paris, 1928.

Phil 5068.56.15 Le origini del metodo analitico. (Crescini, Angelo.) Udine, 1965.

Phil 4080.3.215 Le origini del pensiero di Benedetto Croce. 1. ed. (Corsi, Mario.) Firenze, 1951.

Phil 817.27 Origini del pensiero europeo. (Roncuzzi, Alfredo.) Milano, 1964.

Phil 848.4 Le origini della dialettica. (Franchini, Raffaello.) Napoli, 1961.

Phil 848.4.2 Le origini della dialettica. 2. ed. (Franchini, Raffaello.) Napoli, 1965.

Phil 4006.2.5A Le origini della filosofia contemporanea in Italia. v. 1-3. (Gentile, G.) Messina, 1917-21. 4v.

Phil 3425.602 Le origini della logica hegeliana. (Merker, Nicolas.) Milano, 1961.

Phil 623.21 Le origini dello irrazionalismo contemporaneo. (Aliotta, A.) Napoli, 1968.

Phil 5374.163.7 The origins and history of consciousness. (Neumann, E.) N.Y., 1964.

Phil 5222.1.5 The origins of contemporary psychology. (Mercier, D.) N.Y., 1918.

Phil 189.29A The origins of European thought about the body, the mind, the soul. (Onians, R.B.) Cambridge, Eng., 1951.

Phil 189.29.2 The origins of European thought about the body, the mind, the soul. 2. ed. (Onians, R.B.) Cambridge, Eng., 1954.

Phil 5421.25.76 The origins of love. (Suttie, Ian Dishart.) N.Y., 1966.
Phil 488.2 The origins of materialism. 1st ed. (Novack, George Edward.) N.Y., 1965.

Phil 6980.348.50 Origins of modern psychiatry. (Harms, Ernest.) Springfield, 1967.

Phil 2225.5.155 The origins of pragmatism: studies in the philosophy of Charles Sanders Peirce and William James. (Ayer, Alfred Jules.) London, 1968.

The origins of psycho-analysis. 1st ed. (Freud, Sigmund.) N.Y., 1954.

Phil 6332.26 Origins of psychosomatic and emotional disturbances. (Wenar, Charks.) N.Y., 1962.

Phil 338.41 The origins of science. (Hutten, Ernest.) London, 1962.
Phil 8876.40 Az orkölcsi törvény alkalmazása. (Bodnai, Zsigmond.) Budapest, 1896.

Phil 2805.211 Orliac, Jehanne d'. Le coeur humain, inhumain, surhumain de Blaise Pascal. Paris, 1931.

Phil 310.295 Orlov, V.V. Dialekticheskii materializm i psikhofiziologicheskaia problema. Perm, 1960.

Phil 345.6 Orlov, V.V. Osobennosti chuvstvennogo poznaniia. Perm, 1962.

Phil 5585.325 Orme, John Edward. Time, experience and behavior. London, 1969.

Phil 2905.1.335 Ormea, Ferdinando. Pierre Teilhard de Chardin. 2. ed. Torino, 1964.

Phil 189.6 Ormond, A.T. Basal concepts in philosophy. N.Y., 1894.
Phil 189.6.5 Ormond, A.T. Concepts of philosophy. N.Y., 1906.
Phil 345.1 Ormond, A.T. Foundations of knowledge. London, 1900.
Phil 8594.8 Ormond, A.T. The philosophy of religion. Princeton, N.J., 1922.

Phil 189.27 Oro, A.M. dell'. Protologia; preludio al sapere. Milano, 1937.

Phil 310.11 Oroli narodnogo max i lichnosti v istorii. (Bol'shukhin, A.A.) Gor'kii, 1955.

Phil 1750.675 Oromi, Miguel. Introducción a la filosofía esencialista. Madrid, 1961.

Phil 190.100 Oromi, Miguel. Métodos y principios filosóficos. Madrid, 1960.

Phil 3890.1.83 Orphal, H. Die religionsphilosophischen Anschauungen Trendelenburg's. Eisleben, 1891.

Phil 8594.15 Orr, J. The Christian view of God and the world. 8. ed. N.Y., 1907.

Phil 8594.4 Orr, J. The theory of religion. London, 1762.
Phil 2050.101.3A Orr, James. David Hume and his influence on philosophy and theology. Edinburgh, 1903.

Phil 2050.101 Orr, James. David Hume and his influence on philosophy and theology. N.Y., 1903.

Phil 8669.1.5 Orr, John. English deism. Grand Rapids, 1934.
Phil 8669.1 Orr, John. Theism. London, 1857.
Phil 5254.6 Orr, T.V. Applied mental efficiency. Chicago, 1913.
Phil 1750.166.190 Orrego, Antenor. Hacia un humanismo americano. Lima, 1966.

Phil 4365.1.5 Ors y Rovira, E. d'. Aprendizaje y heroismo. Madrid, 1915.

Phil 4365.1.10 Ors y Rovira, E. d'. Grandeza y servidumbre de la intelegencia. Madrid, 1919.

Htn Phil 7075.6.3* Orsi, Alberto. La donna nuda. 3. ed. Milano, 1912.
Htn Phil 7075.6.7* Orsi, Alberto. Lussuria e castità. Milano, 1913.
Phil 2340.10.140 Orsi, Concetta. La filosofia dell'organismo di A.N. Whitehead. Napoli, 1955.

Phil 181.45.80 Orsi, Domenico d'. Lo spirito come atto puro in Giovanni Gentile. Padova, 1957.

Phil 1714.5 Orsi, Domenico d'. Saggi varii di filosofia moderna e contemporanea. Padova, 1962.

Phil 1714.5.5 Orsi, Domenico d'. Il tramonto della filosofia moderna. Padova, 1962.

Phil 1714.5.8 Orsi, Domenico d'. Il tramonto della filosofia moderna. 3. ed. Padova, 1970.

Phil 4372.3.85 Ortega, Euselio. Francisco de Valles, el Divino. Madrid, 1914.

Phil 4365.2.33A Ortega y Gasset, José. Concord and liberty. 1st ed. N.Y., 1946.

Phil 4365.2.42 Ortega y Gasset, José. Ideas y creencias. Buenos Aires, 1940.

Phil 189.22.5 Ortega y Gasset, José. The modern theme. London, 1931.
Phil 4365.2.38 Ortega y Gasset, José. The modern theme. N.Y., 1933.
Phil 4365.2.35 Ortega y Gasset, José. Origen y epílogo de la filosofía. Mexico, 1960.

Phil 4365.2.36 Ortega y Gasset, José. The origin of philosophy. 1st ed. N.Y., 1967.

Phil 4365.2.41 Ortega y Gasset, José. Some lessons in metaphysics. 1st ed. N.Y., 1969.

Phil 4365.2.40 Ortega y Gasset, José. Unas lecciones de metafísica. Madrid, 1966.

Phil 4368.2.50 Ortega y Gasset y el problema de la jefatura espiritual. (Romero, Francisco.) Buenos Aires, 1960.

Phil 8594.14 Ortegat, Paul. Philosophie de la religion. Bruxelles, 1938.

Phil 8594.14.5 Ortegat, Paul. Philosophie de la religion. Gembloux, 1948. 2v.

Phil 1540.22 Orth, Albert. Untersuchungen zu Prinzipien Fragen der scholastischen Erkenntnistheorie. Bahenhausen, 1933.

Phil 3450.11.410 Orth, Ernst Wolfgang. Bedeutung, Sim, Gegenstand. Thesis. Bonn, 1967.

Phil 6124.2 Orth, H. Disputatio philosophica. Jenae, 1674.
Phil 5224.1 Orth, Johannes. Der psychologische Begriff des Unbewuzten in der Schelling'schen Schule. Heidelberg, 1914.

Phil 5245.75 L'orthogenèse lumaine. (Ferrière, A.) Neuchâtel, 1959.
Phil 5054.3.5 Orti y Lara, J.M. Lógica. Madrid, 1885.
Phil 5520.401 Ortigues, E. Le discours et le symbole. Paris, 1962.
Phil 6980.557 Ortigues, Marie. Oedipe africain. Paris, 1966.
Phil 75.79 Ortloff, Johann Andreas. Handbuch der Literatur der Geschichte der Philosophie. Düsseldorf, 1967.

Phil 3496.2 Ortner, F. Kant in Österreich und Vincenz. Klagenfurt, 1904.

VPhil 2490.176 Ortodoksja i rewizja w pozytywizmie francuskim. (Skarga, Barbara.) Warszawa, 1967.

Phil 189.31 Ortuzar Arriaga, M. El ser y la accion en la dimension humana. Madrid, 1961.

Phil 8669.9 Ortuzar Arriaga, Martin. Los prenotandos del conocimiento natural de Dios. Madrid, 1963.

Phil 8889.7 Osbert, Reuben. Humanism and moral theory. London, 1959.
Phil 6324.7 Osbert, Reuben. Marxism and psycho-analysis. London, 1965.

Phil 3450.11.125A Osborn, A. Edmund Husserl. 2d ed. Cambridge, 1949.
Phil 5465.59 Osborn, A.F. Applied imagination. N.Y., 1953.
Phil 5465.57.10 Osborn, A.F. Wake up your mind. N.Y., 1952.
Phil 5465.57 Osborn, A.F. Your creative power. N.Y., 1951.
Phil 3805.177 Osborn, A.R. Schleiermacher and religious education. London, 1934.

Phil 2200.10 Osborn, Arthur W. The expansion of awareness. Reigate, 1967.

Phil 7069.66.5 Osborn, Arthur Walter. The meaning of personal existence. London, 1966.

Phil 8704.2.5 Osborn, H.F. The earth spaks to Bryan. N.Y., 1925.
Phil 8704.2 Osborn, H.F. Evolution and religion. N.Y., 1923.
Phil 5254.5 Osborn, John K. A comparison of reactions to personality and achievement test items. Diss. Ann Arbor, 1936.

Phil 8964.3 Osborne, A.R. Christian ethics. London, 1940.
Phil 974.5.10 Osborne, Arthur. Ramana Maharshi and the path of self-knowledge. London, 1970.

Phil 8415.4 Osborne, H. Theory of beauty; an introduction to aesthetics. N.Y., 1953.

Phil 735.102 Osborne, Harold. Foundations of the philosophy of value. Cambridge, 1933.
Phil 4225.8.62 L'oscuramento dell'intelligenza. (Sciacca, Michele Federico.) Milano, 1970.
Phil 8412.3 Oser penser. (Lefrancq, J.) Neuchâtel, 1961.
Phil 5520.190 Osgood, C.E. The measurement of meaning. Urbana, 1957.
Phil 5254.7A Osgood, C.E. Method and theory in experimental psychology. N.Y., 1956.
Phil 6400.22 Osgood, Charles E. Approaches to the study of aphasia. Urbana, 1963.
Phil 6684.2.3 Osgood, H. Therapeutic value of suggestion. Boston, 1890.
Phil 9174.1.8 Osgood, S. American boys and girls. N.Y., 1867.
Phil 9174.1 Osgood, S. The hearth-stone. N.Y., 1854.
NEDL Phil 9174.1.3 Osgood, S. The hearth-stone. N.Y., 1854.
Phil 9174.1.2 Osgood, S. The hearth-stone. N.Y., 1876.
VPhil 310.5.10 Oshakov, Zhivko. Istoricheskiiat materializum. Sofiia, 1958.
Phil 310.5.12 Oshakov, Zhivko. Istoricheskiiat materializum i sotsiologiiatu. 2. izd. Sofiia, 1970.
Phil 310.5.15 Oshakov, Zhivko. Niakoi aktualni problemina nauchnogo. komunizum. Sofiia, 1961.
Phil 4752.2.120 Osipov, N. Kleveta druzei. Miunkhen, 1958.
Phil 4800.16 Osipova, Elena Vladimirovna. Filosofiia pol'skogo Prosveshcheniia. Moskva, 1961.
Phil 1195.18 Osipova, Valentina. O prirode sofistiki. Erevan, 1964.
Phil 1135.16 Osiris und Sokrates. (Plessing, F.V.L.) Berlin, 1783.
Phil 8633.1.6.5 Osler, W. Science and immortality. Boston, 1904.
Phil 9490.10 Osler, W. A way of life. London, 1918.
Phil 5655.4 Osmics; the science of smell. (Kenneth, J.H.) Edinburgh, 1922.
Phil 189.20 Osmond, A. My philosophy of life. Salt Lake City, 1927.
Phil 5250.70 Osnova primena prakseologije. (Kotarbiński, Tadeusz.) Beograd, 1961.
Phil 9590.17.5 Osnovaniia biosofii. v.1-2. (Krol', L.I.) Kaunas, 1937.
Phil 735.286 Osnovaniia logiki otsenok. (Ivin, Aleksandr A.) Moskva, 1970.
Phil 8170.5.9 Osnovni vuprosi na estetikata. 2. izd. (Pavlov, T.D.) Sofiia, 1949-
Phil 8170.6 Osnovni vuprosi na marksistko-leninskata estetika. 3. izd. (Pavlov, T.D.) Sofiia, 1958.
Phil 310.20 Osnovnoto v Michurinskoto uchenie v svetlinata na dialekticheskii materializm. (Pavlov, Todor D.) Sofia, 1955.
Phil 4710.65 Osnovnye cherty russkoi klassicheskoi filosofii XIX v. (Jovchuk, M.T.) Moskva, 1945.
Phil 5520.622 Osnovnye edinitsy iazyka i myshleniia. (Chernokov, Petr V.) Rostov-na-Donu, 1966.
Phil 814.4 Osnovnye etapy razvitiia domarksistskoi filosofii. (Oizerman, T.I.) Moskva, 1957.
Phil 1712.21 Osnovnye fecheniia sovremennoi burzhuaznoi filosofii. (Mshvenieradze, V.V.) Kiev, 1961.
Phil 310.425 Osnovnye kategorii i zakony materialisticheskoi dialektiki. (Vorob'ev, L.V.) Moskva, 1962.
Phil 4791.6 Osnovnye mirovozzrencheskie napravleniia v feodal'noi Gruzii. (Khidasheli, Shalva Vasil'evich.) Tbilisi, 1962.
Phil 1700.8 Osnovnye napravleniia burzhuaznoi filosofii i sotsiologii XX veka. (Aseev, I.A.) Leningrad, 1961.
Phil 5240.54 Osnovnye napravleniia issledovanii psikhologii myshleniia v kapitalisticheskikh stranakh. (Akademiia Nauk SSSR. Institut Filosofii.) Moskva, 1966.
Phil 5520.652 Osnovnye podkhody k modelirovaniia psikhiki i evristicheskomu programmirovaniiu. Moskva, 1968.
Phil 5520.596 Osnovnye problemy iazyka i myshleniia. (Sotnikian, Pogos A.) Erevan, 1968.
Phil 4710.141 Osnovnye problemy kritiki idealisticheskoi istorii russkoi filosofii. (Malinin, V.A.) Moskva, 1963.
Phil 8670.20 Osnovnye voprosy nauchnogo ateizma. (Pantskhawa, I.D.) Moskva, 1962.
Phil 8670.20.2 Osnovnye voprosy nauchnogo ateizma. 2. izd. (Moscow. Universitet. Kafedra Istorii i Teorii Ateizma.) Moskva, 1966.
Phil 310.617.5 Osnovnye zakony dialektiki. (Sheptulin, Aleksandr P.) Moskva, 1966.
Phil 310.180 Osnovnye zakony i kategorii materialisticheskoi dialektiki. (Andreev, I.D.) Moskva, 1959.
Phil 310.125 Osnovnye zotkony materialisticheskoi dialektiki. (Siusiukalov, B.I.) Moskva, 1958.
Phil 8595.56 Osnovy drevne-tserkovnoi antropologii. (Pozov, A.) Madrid, 1965. 2v.
Phil 310.505 Osnovy filosofskikh znanii. 2. izd. (Afanas'ev, Viktor G.) Moskva, 1962.
Phil 310.506 Osnovy filosofskikh znanii. 3. izd. (Afanas'ev, Viktor G.) Moskva, 1965.
Phil 8605.10 Osnovy khristianskoi filosofii. (Zen'kovskii, V.V.) Frankfurt, 1960.
Phil 8980.787 Osnovy kommunisticheskoi morali. (Shishkin, Aleksandr F.) Moskva, 1955.
Phil 5066.211 Osnovy logicheskoi teorii nauchnykh znanii. (Zinov'ev, Aleksandr A.) Moskva, 1967.
Phil 8980.537 Osnovy marksistko-leninskoi etiki. (Lushchytski, I.N.) Minsk, 1965.
Phil 8400.17 Osnovy marksistsko-leninskoi estetiki. (Berestnev, V.F.) Moskva, 1960.
Phil 8170.3 Osnovy marksistsko-leninskoi estetiki. (Sakharova, E.M.) Moskva, 1961.
Phil 8980.386.5 Osnovy marksistsko-leninskoi etiki. (Fedorenko, I.H.) Kiev, 1965.
Phil 310.6.7 Osnovy marksistsko-leninskoi filosofii. Moskva, 1971.
Phil 8980.787.15 Osnovy marksistskoi etiki. (Shishkin, Aleksandr F.) Moskva, 1961.
Phil 310.245 Osnovy marksistskoi filosofii. (Afanas'ev, V.G.) Moskva, 1960.
Phil 310.6.5 Osnovy marksistskoi filosofii. (Akadamiia Nauk SSSR. Institut Filosofii.) Moskva, 1958.
Phil 310.6.6 Osnovy marksistskoi filosofii. Izd. 2. (Akadamiia Nauk SSSR. Institut Filosofii.) Moskva, 1964.
Phil 310.543 Osnovy marksistskoi logiki. (Kaprielian, Henri.) Erevan, 1968.
Phil 8980.659 Osnovy marksysts'ko-lenińskoi etyky. Chernivtsi, 1962.
Phil 8667.29 Osnovy nauchnogo ateizma. (Moscow. Gosudarstvennaia Biblioteka SSSR Imeni V.I. Lenina.) Moskva, 1966.
Phil 8674.14 Osnovy nauchnogo ateizma. (Tugov, Iu.M.) Moskva, 1959.
Phil 8669.8 Osnovy nauchnogo ateizma. (Yaroslavl', Russia (City). Gosudarstvennyi Pedagogicheskii Institut. Kafedra Filosofii.) Iaroslavl', 1963.
Phil 8655.20 Osnovy nauchnogo ateizma. 3. izd. (Akademiia Nauk SSSR. Institut Filosofii.) Moskva, 1964.
Phil 186.113 Osnovy organicheskogo mirovozzreniia. (Levitskii, S.A.) n.p., 1946.
Phil 8412.43 Osnovy pozitivnoi estetiki. (Lunacharskii, Anatolii V.) Moskva, 1923.
Phil 331.20 Osnovy teorii poznaniia. (Andreev, Ivan D.) Moskva, 1959.
Phil 345.6 Osobennosti chuvstvennogo poznaniia. (Orlov, V.V.) Perm, 1962.
Phil 8980.330.5 Osoboe mnenie. (Dobrovol'skii, Eugenii N.) Moskva, 1967.
VPhil 5590.558 Osobowość. Wyd. 1. (Gerstmann, Stanisław.) Warszawa, 1970.
Phil 575.254 Osobowość i własność. (Jaroszewski, Tadeusz M.) Warszawa, 1965.
Phil 3808.158 Osservazioni critiche alla filosofia di Arturo Schopenhauer. (Zuccante, G.) Milano, 1929.
Phil 1850.129 Ossi, M.M. Saggio su Francesco Bacon. Napoli, 1935.
Phil 5251.41.80 Ossicuri, Adriano. L'opera di Kurt Lewin nella psicologia contemporanea. Messina, 1960.
Phil 4762.3.80 Ossip-Leurié (L'homme et l'oeuvre). (Laroche, P.G.) Paris, 1934.
Phil 8082.4 Ossola, Carlo. Autunno del Rinascimento. Firenze, 1971.
Phil 5548.55 Ossowska, M. Motywy postępowania. Warszawa, 1958.
Phil 8889.8.10 Ossowska, Maria. Normy moralne. Warszawa, 1970.
Phil 8889.8.5 Ossowska, Maria. Social determinants of moral ideas. Philadelphia, 1970.
Phil 8889.8 Ossowska, Maria. Socjologia moralności. Warszawa, 1963.
Phil 8889.8.2 Ossowska, Maria. Socjologia moralności 2. wyd. Warszawa, 1969.
Phil 8415.2 Ossowski, S. U podstaw estetyki. Wyd. 3. Warszawa, 1958.
Phil 5651.8 Oster, Wilhelm. Struktur-psychologische Untersuchungen über die Leistung des Zeitsinns. Inaug. Diss. Würzburg, 1937.
Phil 5628.50 Ostermann, Petrus. Commentarius iuridicus ad L. Stigmata, C. de Fabricensibus. Coloniae Agripinae, 1629.
Phil 3428.95.2 Ostermann, W. Die Hauptsächlichstein der Herbartschen Psychologie. 2. Aufl. Oldenburg, 1894.
Phil 5330.18 Ostermann, W. Das Interesse. 3e Aufl. Oldenburg, 1912.
Phil 4080.3.245 Osterwalder, T. Die Philosophie Benedetto Croces als moderne Ideenlehre. Berne, 1954.
Phil 525.97.5 Ostkirche und Mystik. 2. Aufl. (Arsen'ev, N.S.) München, 1943.
Phil 1504.6 Ostler, H. Die Psychologie. v.6, pt.1. Münster, 1906.
Phil 345.4 Ostler, H. Die Realität der Aussenwelt. Paderborn, 1912.
Phil 6324.6 Oston, Mortimer. Drugs in psychoanalysis and psychopathology. N.Y., 1962.
Phil 7069.70.10 Ostrander, Sheila. Psychic discoveries behind the Iron Curtain. Englewood Cliffs, 1970.
Phil 4783.1 Ostrianyn, Danylo Kh. Rozvytok materialistychnoi filosofii na Ukrainii. Kyiv, 1971.
Phil 4756.2.35 Ostromirov, A. Nikolai Fedorovich Fedorov i sovremennost'. v.1-3. Kharbin, 1928.
VPhil 5203.26 Ostvold, Harald. Manual of reference sources in psychology. St. Louis? 1949.
Phil 345.2 Ostwald, N. Die Wissenschaft. Leipzig, 1911.
Phil 2490.93 Ostwald, W. Auguste Comte. Leipzig, 1914.
Phil 5425.24 Ostwald, W. Grosse Männer. Leipzig, 1909.
Phil 8633.1.8 Ostwald, W. Individuality and immortality. Boston, 1906.
Phil 510.8 Ostwald, W. Monism as the goal of civilization. Hamburg, 1913.
Phil 510.8.5 Ostwald, W. Monistische Sonntagspredigten. Series 1-3,4. Leipzig, 1911-13. 2v.
Phil 295.1.6 Ostwald, W. Natural philosophy. N.Y., 1910.
Phil 8633.1.8.5 Ostwald, W. Personlighet och odödlighet. Stockholm, 1911.
Phil 735.6 Ostwald, W. Die Philosophie der Werte. Leipzig, 1913.
Phil 489.1A Ostwald, W. Überwindung des wissenschaftlichen Materialismus. Leipzig, 1895.
Phil 295.09 Ostwald, W. Vorlesungen über Naturphilosophie. Leipzig, 1902.
Phil 295.1 Ostwald, W. Vorlesungen über Naturphilosophie. 2. Aufl. Leipzig, 1902.
Phil 5645.20 Ostwald, Wilhelm. Die Farbenlehre. v.1-2,4. Leipzig, 1918-22. 3v.
Phil 5645.20.2 Ostwald, Wilhelm. Die Farbenlehre. 2. Aufl. Leipzig, 1921.
Phil 5645.4.25 Ostwald, Wilhelm. Goethe, Schopenhauer und die Farbenlehre. Leipzig, 1918.
Phil 8704.3 Ostwald, Wilhelm. Wissenschaft contra Gottesglauben. Leipzig, 1960.
Phil 7069.32.30 Osty, E. Les pouvoirs inconnus de l'esprit sur la matière. Paris, 1932.
Phil 7069.23.10 Osty, Eugène. La connaissance supra-normale. Paris, 1923.
Phil 7060.131 Osty, Eugène. Lucidité et intuition. Paris, 1913.
Phil 7069.23.11 Osty, Eugène. Supernormal faculties in man. London, 1923.
Phil 189.7 O'Sullivan, J.M. Old criticism and new pragmatism. Dublin, 1909.
Phil 2193.30 Oswald, J. An appeal to common sense in behalf of religion. Edinburgh, 1766-72. 2v.
Phil 2193.30.2 Oswald, J. An appeal to common sense in behalf of religion. London, 1768-72. 2v.
Phil 8525.15 Ot Erazma Potterdamskogo do Bertrana Rassela. Moskva, 1966.
Phil 5130.4 Ot formal'noi logiki k dialektike. (Antonov, Georgii V.) Moskva, 1971.
Phil 5044.10 Ot Gegelia k Dzhennago. (Efiroo, S.A.) Moskva, 1960.
Phil 8408.30.10 Otakara Hostinského esthetika. (Hostinský, Otakar.) Praha, 1921.
Phil 7082.128 Otaola, J.R. de. El análisis de los sueños. Barcelona, 195-?
Phil 8050.83 Otázky estetiky v přítainnosti i minulosti. (Novák, Mirko.) Praha, 1963.
Phil 5252.156 Otázky vzniku a povahy psychiky. (Morávek, Milan.) Praha, 1965.
Phil 4751.3.6 Otdel'nyia stranitsy. (Aikhenval'd, Iu.I.) Moskva, 1910.
Phil 8602.38.10 Other dimensions. (Welby-Gregory, Victoria.) London, 1931.
Phil 6111.70 The other hand; an investigation into the sinister history of left-handedness. 1st ed. (Barsley, Michael.) N.Y., 1967.
Phil 353.21.5 Other minds. (Wisdom, John.) Berkeley, 1968.
Phil 353.21 Other minds. (Wisdom, John.) Oxford, 1952
Phil 5627.81 The other paraclete. (Thompson, J.B.) n.p., 1897.
Phil 7055.310 The other side. (Pike, James Albert.) Garden City, 1968.
Phil 8627.13 The other side of death. (Cohen, Chapman.) London, 1922.
Phil 7069.20.290 "The other side of God's door". (Robertson, Mabel N.) London, 1920.
Phil 7069.64.10 The other side of the mind. (Stone, W.C.) Englewood Cliffs, 1964.
Phil 3850.32 Othmar Spanns Philosophie. (Räber, H.) Jena, 1937.

Phil 7080.55   Othmer, Ekkehard. Persönlichkeit und Schlafverhalten. Meisenheim, 1965.

Htn   Phil 3552.29.2*   Otium hanoueranum sive Miscellanea. (Leibniz, Gottfried Wilhelm.) Lipsiae, 1718.

Htn   Phil 3552.29*   Otium hanoueranum sive Miscellanea. (Leibniz, Gottfried Wilhelm.) Lipsiae, 1718.

Phil 310.764   Otnoshenie material'nogo i ideal'nogo v obshchestve kak problema istoricheskogo materializma. (Barulin, Vladimir S.) Barnaul, 1970.

Phil 5360.15   Otnosheniia mezhdu poniatiiami. (Pavlov, V.T.) Kiev, 1961.

Phil 310.690   Otobrazhenie v nezhivoi prirode. (Ukraintsev, Boris S.) Moskva, 1969.

Phil 6122.97   Otrazhenie v khudozhestvennoi literature ucheniia o fiziologii golovnogo mozga. (Mardersptein, I.G.) Tashkent, 1962.

Phil 3425.90   Ott, A. Hegel et la philosophie allemande. Paris, 1844.
Phil 400.43   Ott, Aguste. Critique de l'idéalisme et du criticisme. Paris, 1883.
Phil 189.18   Ott, Auguste. De la raison. Paris, 1873.
Phil 3425.274   Ott, Emil. Die Religionsphilosophie Hegels. Berlin, 1904.
Phil 3450.19.220   Ott, Heinrich. Denken und Sein. Zollikon, 1959.
Phil 4080.7.80   Ottario Colecchi, un filosofo da riscoprire. (Cristallini, Alessandro.) Padova, 1968.

Phil 3552.342   Ottaviano, C. Le basi fisico-metafische della filosofia di Leibniz. Padova, 1952.
Phil 400.94   Ottaviano, C. Critica dell'idealismo. Napoli, 1936.
Phil 400.94.3   Ottaviano, C. Critica dell'idealismo. 3. ed. Padova, 1960.
Phil 189.19   Ottaviano, C. Metafisica del concreto. Roma, 1929.
Phil 8415.10.3   Ottaviano, Carmelo. La legge della come legge universale della natura. 3. ed. Padova, 1970.
Phil 4190.1.90   Ottaviano, Carmelo. Il pensiero di Francesco Orestano. Palermo, 1933.
Phil 4190.2.30   Ottaviano, Carmelo. La tragicita del reale. Padova, 1964.
Phil 4752.2.195   L'ottavo giorno della creazione. Saggio su N. Berdjaev. (Déchet, Ferruccio.) Milano, 1969.
Phil 1119.1   Otten, Alois. Einleitung in die Geschichte der Philosophie. Paderborn, 1895.
Phil 5926.1.35   Ottin, N.J. Précis analytique et raisonné du système du docteur Gall. Bruxelles, 1835.
Phil 8964.1   Ottley, Robert L. Christian ideas and ideals. London, 1916.
Phil 3565.115   Otto, Clemens. Hermann Lotze über das Unbewusste. Labes, 1900.
Phil 5764.1   Otto, F.W. Die Freiheit des Menschen. Gütersloh, 1872.
Phil 5374.260   Otto, Herbert Arthur. Ways of growth. N.Y., 1968.
Phil 189.11   Otto, M.C. Things and ideals. N.Y., 1924.
Phil 2880.8.134   Otto, Maria. Rene und Freiheit. Freiburg, 1961.
Phil 2200.1   Otto, Max Carl. The human enterprise. N.Y., 1940.
Phil 2200.5A   Otto, Max Carl. Science and the moral life. N.Y., 1949.
Phil 3496.1   Otto, R. Kantisch-Fries'sche Religionsphilosophie. Tübingen, 1909.
Phil 8669.3.5   Otto, Rudolf. The idea of the holy. London, 1928.
Phil 525.74.5   Otto, Rudolf. Mysticism East and West. N.Y., 1932.
Phil 8704.1.5   Otto, Rudolf. Naturalism and religion. London, 1907.
Phil 8594.10   Otto, Walter F. Der Geist der Antike und die christliche Welt. Bonn, 1923.
Phil 6327.4.60   Otto Rank Association. Journal. Doylestown. 1,1966+ 2v.
Phil 3905.92   Otto Weininger, der Mensch, sein Werk und sein Leben. (Klaren, Georg.) Wien, 1924.
Phil 3905.80   Otto Weininger: sein Werk und Persönlichkeit. (Lucka, E.) Wien, 1905.
Phil 3905.86   Otto Weiningers Tod. 2. Aufl. (Swoboda, H.) Wien, 1923.
Phil 3905.88   Otto Weiningers und sein Werk. (Dallago, Carl.) Innsbruck, 1912.
Phil 6684.3   Ottolenghi, S. Nuovo studi sull'ipnotismo. Torino, 1889.
Phil 4225.8.79   Ottonello, Pier Paolo. Bibliografia di M.F. Sciacca. Milano, 1969.
Phil 4190.3.30   Ottonello, Pier Paolo. Dialogo e silenzio. Milano, 1967.
Phil 4210.225   Ottonello, Pier Paolo. L'essere iniziale nell'ontologia di Rosmini. Milano, 1967.
Phil 7068.36.20   Ottway, T. The spectre. London, 1836.
Phil 189.17   Où chercher le réel? Paris, 1927.
Phil 7069.26.50   Où en est la métapsychique. (Heuzé P.) Paris, 1926.
Phil 8620.64   Où est le mal? (Barreau, Jean Claude.) Paris, 1969.
Phil 5790.2.10   Ouderdom en eindigheid. (Munnichs, Jozef M.A.) Assen, 1964.
Phil 2750.22.5   Ouevres. (Mounier, E.) Paris, 1961. 5v.
Phil 2905.1.670   Ouince, René d'. Un prophète en procès. Paris, 1970. 2v.
Phil 525.52   Oulmont, Charles. Le verger, le temple et la cellule. Paris, 1912.
Phil 6320.11.25   Our adult world. (Klein, M.) N.Y., 1963.
Phil 6310.4.15.5A   Our age of unreason. (Alexander, Franz G.) Philadelphia, 1951.
Phil 7069.22.5   Our American adventure. (Doyle, Arthur Connan.) N.Y., 1923.
Phil 8666.18   Our experience of God. (Lewis, Hymel D.) London, 1959.
Phil 5401.8   Our fear complexes. (Williams, E.H.) London, 1924.
Phil 8643.15   Our future existence. (Shaw, Fred G.) London, 1912.
Phil 9351.10   Our girls. (Lewis, D.) N.Y., 1871.
Phil 8585.30   Our gods on trial. (Floyd, William.) N.Y., 1931.
Phil 8705.4.2   Our heredity from God. 2. ed. (Powell, E.P.) N.Y., 1888.
Phil 7069.17.13   Our hidden forces. (Boirac, Émile.) N.Y., 1917.
Phil 2280.7.30   Our human truths. (Schiller, F.C.S.) N.Y., 1939.
Phil 5400.99   Our hunches; the effect of emotions on our lives and habits. (Foster, George S.) N.Y., 1942.
Phil 6317.22.20   Our inner conflict. (Horney, Karen.) N.Y., 1945.
Phil 7069.43.5   Our invisible friends. (Allen, Maurice.) N.Y., 1943.
Phil 338.38   Our knowledge of fact and value. (Halt, Everett W.) Chapel Hill, 1961.
Phil 575.52.15   Our knowledge of one another. (Webb, C.C.J.) London, 1930.
Phil 5258.100   Our knowledge of other minds. (Spencer, Willard Wylie.) New Haven, 1930.
Phil 582.6   Our knowledge of other selves. (Chatterjee, Margaret.) Bombay, 1963.
Phil 1750.115.65   Our knowledge of other selves. (Chatteyee, Margaret.) Bombay, 1963.
Phil 8882.115   Our knowledge of right and wrong. (Harrison, Jonathan.) London, 1971.
Phil 192.28.9   Our knowledge of the external world. (Russell, B.) Chicago, 1914.
Phil 5080.5   Our knowledge of universals. (Aaron, Richard I.) London, 1945.
Phil 6990.3.75   Our Lady of Lourdes. (Deery, Joseph.) Dublin, 1958.

Phil 6990.3.5   Our lady of Lourdes. (Lasserre, H.) N.Y., 1904.
Phil 5520.245   Our language and our world. 1. ed. (ETC., a Review of General Semantics.) N.Y., 1959.
Phil 8627.9.3   Our life after death. (Chambers, A.) Philadelphia, 1902.
Phil 8634.5   Our life beyond. (Jones, John Daniel.) Boston, 1914.
Phil 7069.17.10   Our living dead. (Bates, Emily K.) London, 1917.
Phil 92.1   Our minds and our motives. (Hugon, Paul D.) N.Y., 1928.
Phil 6121.23   Our minds and their bodies. (Laird, John.) London, 1925.
Phil 2125.73   Our moral nature, being a brief system of ethics. (McCosh, James.) N.Y., 1892.
Phil 6112.20.5   Our nervous friends. (Carroll, Robert S.) N.Y., 1919.
Phil 1701.17   Our new ways of thinking. (Boas, George.) N.Y., 1930.
Phil 6022.2   Our noses. (Martin, William W.) London, 1893.
Phil 672.11   Our notions of number and space. (Nichols, H.) Boston, 1894.
Phil 8615.5.23   Our part in this world. (Adler, Felix.) N.Y., 1946.
Phil 6328.7   Our phantastic emotions. (Slade, T. Kenrick.) London, 1923.
Phil 811.15   Our philosophical traditions. (Lamprecht, S.P.) N.Y., 1955.
Phil 1750.129   Our present philosophy of life. (Belgion, Montgomery.) London, 1929.
Phil 6049.34   Our revealing hands. (Jaquin, Noel.) N.Y., 1934.
Phil 7069.24.5   Our second American adventure. (Doyle, Arthur Conan.) Boston, 1924.
Phil 7069.31.27   Our superconscious mind. (Lyttelton, Edith B.) London, 1931.
Phil 7069.31.28   Our superconscious mind. (Lyttelton, Edith B.) N.Y., 1931.
Phil 5710.9   Our temperaments; their study and teaching. 2. ed. (Stewart, A.) London, 1892.
Phil 5710.14   Our temperaments. (Stewart, A.) London, 1887.
Phil 5245.84   Our troubled selves. (Fromme, Allan.) N.Y., 1967.
Phil 5722.9   Our unconscious mind and how to use it. (Pierce, Frederick.) N.Y., 1922.
Phil 7059.22   Our unseen guest. N.Y. 1920.
Phil 8627.9.9   Ourself after death. (Chambers, A.) Chicago, 191-.
Phil 5400.69   Ourselves and our emotions. (Loosmore, W.C.) London, 1928.
Phil 575.60.5   Ourselves and reality. (Braham, Ernest G.) London, 1929.
Phil 8581.24.5   Ourselves and the universe. (Brierley, J.) N.Y., 1905.
Phil 8669.4   Oursler, F. Why I know there is a God. 1. ed. Garden City, N.Y., 1950.
Phil 8637.18   Out of darkness into light. (Mifflin, Mildred.) Shelbyville, 1888.
Phil 8951.17   Out of the rut, a layman's point of view. (Birchard, Ford G.) Boston, 1931.
Phil 6053.12.10   Out of the silence. (Nelson, Edith Halforel.) London, 194-?
Phil 9070.11   Out of the wilderness. (Hostel, G.) N.Y., 1940.
Phil 6112.40.20   The outer limits of Edgar Cayce's power. 1. ed. (Cayce, Edgar Evans.) N.Y., 1971.
Phil 5440.29   Outhit, M.C. A study of the resemblance of parents and children in general intelligence. Thesis. N.Y., 1933.
Phil 5213.1.9A   Outline...history of psychology. (Dessoir, M.) N.Y., 1912.
Phil 75.44   An outline and a bibliography of Chinese philosophy. (Chan, Wing-Tsit.) Hanover, N.H., 1953.
Phil 930.44   An outline and a bibliography of Chinese philosophy. (Chan, Wing-tsit.) Hanover, 1955.
Phil 930.44.2   An outline and annotated bibliography of Chinese philosophy. (Chan, Wing-tsit.) New Haven, 1961.
Phil 3504.7   An outline introduction of Kant's Critique of pure reason. (Wenley, R.M.) N.Y., 1897.
Phil 3504.7.5   An outline introduction of Kant's Critique of pure reason. (Wenley, R.M.) N.Y., 1907.
Phil 6319.1.216   Outline of a Jungian aesthetics. (Philipson, M.H.) Evanton, 1963.
Phil 187.137   Outline of a metaphysics. (Matchette, F.J.) N.Y., 1949.
Htn   Phil 5041.37*   Outline of a new system of logic. (Bentham, G.) London, 1827.
Phil 8582.13   An outline of a system of natural theology. (Crabbe, G.) London, 1840.
Phil 5643.11.10   Outline of a theory of the light sense. (Hering, E.) Cambridge, 1964.
Phil 6311.3   An outline of abnormal psychology. (Bridges, J.W.) Columbus, 1919.
Phil 6313.11   Outline of abnormal psychology. (Drake, R.M.) N.Y., 1936.
Phil 6322.14A   Outline of abnormal psychology. (McDougall, W.) N.Y., 1926.
Phil 6322.18A   An outline of abnormal psychology. (Murphy, Gardiner.) N.Y., 1929.
Phil 6311.3.2   An outline of abnormal psychology. 2d ed. (Bridges, J.W.) Columbus, 1921.
Phil 6311.3.3   An outline of abnormal psychology. 3rd ed. (Bridges, J.W.) Columbus, 1925.
Phil 3565.32.5   Outline of aesthetics. (Lotze, Hermann.) Boston, 1886.
Phil 2520.210   An outline of Descartes' philosophy. Cambridge, 1938.
Phil 8877.51   An outline of evolutionary ethics. (Cohen, C.) London, 1896.
Phil 5066.9   An outline of formal logic. Pt.1. (Cooley, J.C.) Cambridge, 1939.
Phil 5245.41   An outline of general psychology. (Fryer, D.) N.Y., 1936.
Phil 5246.37   Outline of general psychology. (Gault, Robert H.) N.Y., 1925.
Phil 5257.45   An outline of genetic psychology according to the theory of inherited mind. (Rattray, Robert F.) London, 1931.
Phil 978.81   An outline of Karma. (Lee, Pi-cheng.) n.p., 1941?
Phil 2115.104   An outline of Locke's ethical philosophy. (Curtis, M.M.) Leipzig, 1890.
Phil 5041.30   An outline of logic. (Bode, B.H.) N.Y., 1910.
Phil 5046.5   An outline of logic or the use of teachers and students. 2d ed. (Garden, F.) London, 1871.
Phil 5247.11.7   An outline of man; or, The body and mind in one system. (Hopkins, A.) N.Y., 1889.
Phil 3565.32.1.3   Outline of Metaphysic. (Lotze, Hermann.) Boston, 1884.
Phil 3565.32   Outline of Metaphysic. (Lotze, Hermann.) Boston, 1886.
Phil 187.129   Outline of metaphysics. (Morrish, Furze.) London, 194-.
Phil 6111.58   An outline of neurology and its outlook. (Buzzard, E.F.) London, 1929.
Phil 6952.24   An outline of neuropathology for students of general medicine. (Cobb, Stanley.) Cambridge, 1929.
Phil 978.49.19   An outline of occult science. (Steiner, R.) Chicago, Ill., 1922.
Phil 192.28.20.2   An outline of philosophy. (Russell, B.) London, 1956.
Phil 197.2.2   Outline of philosophy with notes. 2d ed. (Watson, J.) Glasgow, 1898.

Phil 3565.32.3 — Outline of practical philosophy. (Lotze, Hermann.) Boston, 1885.

Phil 6965.15 — Outline of psychiatric case-study. (Preu, P.W.) N.Y., 1939.

Phil 6964.3.5 — An outline of psychiatry. 2. ed. (O'Brien, John D.) St. Louis, Mo., 1935.

Phil 6331.5 — An outline of psychoanalysis. (Van Teslaar, J.S.) N.Y., 1925.

Phil 6315.2.8.20 — An outline of psychoanalysis. 1st. ed. (Freud, Sigmund.) N.Y., 1949.

Phil 6113.11 — An outline of psychobiology. (Dunlap, Knight.) Baltimore, 1914.

Phil 6113.11.2 — An outline of psychobiology. 2d ed. (Dunlap, Knight.) Baltimore, 1917.

Phil 3565.32.4 — Outline of psychology. (Lotze, Hermann.) Boston, 1886.

Phil 3565.70 — Outline of psychology. (Lotze, Hermann.) Minneapolis, 188-?

Phil 5252.18.15 — Outline of psychology. (McDougall, William.) N.Y., 1923.

Phil 5252.18.16 — Outline of psychology. (McDougall, William.) N.Y., 1926.

Phil 5259.18 — Outline of psychology. (Tapy, George H.) Crawfordsville, 19- ?

Phil 5259.5.5 — An outline of psychology. (Titchener, E.B.) N.Y., 1897.

Phil 5251.27 — An outline of psychology for education. (Lothian, A.J.D.) London, 1923.

Phil 5041.6 — An outline of Rede-Craft (Logic). (Barnes, William.) London, 1880.

Phil 2035.86 — Outline of Sir William Hamilton's philosophy. (Murray, J.C.) Boston, 1870.

Phil 365.10 — Outline of the evolution-philosophy. (Cazalles, Emile.) N.Y., 1875.

Phil 8520.18.2 — An outline of the history of Christian thought since Kant. (Moore, Edward C.) London, 1912.

Phil 332.7 — An outline of the idealistic construction of experience. (Baillie, T.B.) London, 1906.

Phil 4210.83.2 — An outline of the life of...Antonio Rosmini. (Lockhart, W.) London, 1856.

Phil 3565.51.5 — An outline of the Microcosmos. (Lotze, Hermann.) Oberlin, 1895.

Phil 5059.4.2 — Outline of the necessary laws of thought. (Thomson, W.) Cambridge, 1859.

Phil 5059.4 — Outline of the necessary laws of thought. (Thomson, W.) London, 1849.

Phil 5059.4.3 — Outline of the necessary laws of thought. (Thomson, W.) N.Y., 1879.

Phil 5059.4.4 — Outline of the necessary laws of thought. 4th ed. (Thomson, W.) London, 1857.

Phil 2515.4.101 — An outline of the philosophy of Antoine-Augustin Cournot. (Floss, S.W.) Philadelphia, 1941.

Phil 3834.2 — An outline of the philosophy of Spinoza. Boston, 1939.

Phil 960.3.4.5 — Outline of the Vedânta system of philosophy. (Deussen, P.) Cambridge, 1906.

Phil 960.3.4A — Outline of the Vedânta system of philosophy. 2d ed. (Deussen, P.) N.Y., 1906.

Phil 978.8.9 — Outline of theosophy. (Leadbeater, C.W.) London, 1902.

Phil 978.8.11 — Outline of theosophy. (Leadbeater, C.W.) London, 1915.

Phil 978.8.10 — Outline of theosophy. 2d ed. (Leadbeater, C.W.) Chicago, 1903.

Phil 960.43.2 — An outline scheme for a history of Indian philosophy. (Belvalkar, S.K.) Poona, 1919. 2v.

Phil 5258.99 — An outline sketch. (Stanley, H.M.) Chicago, 1899.

Phil 5247.11.3 — An outline study of man. (Hopkins, M.) N.Y., 1883.

Phil 2494.42 — Outlines...historical...progress...human mind. (Condorcet, M.J.A.N.) Baltimore, 1802.

NEDL Phil 2494.41 — Outlines...historical...progress...human mind. (Condorcet, M.J.A.N.) Philadelphia, 1796.

Phil 6027.1.5 — Outlines...physiognomy. (Redfield, J.W.) N.Y., 1849.

Phil 5049.2 — Outlines. Philosophy. Education. Logic. (Jardine, George.) Glasgow, 1818.

Phil 5247.16.5 — Outlines for applied and abnormal psychology. (Hollingworth, H.L.) N.Y., 1914.

Phil 5247.16 — Outlines for experimental psychology. (Hollingworth, H.L.) N.Y., 1914.

Phil 8878.11.2 — Outlines of a critical theory of ethics. (Dewey, John.) N.Y., 1957.

Phil 8878.11.3 — Outlines of a critical theory of ethics. (Dewey, John.) N.Y., 1969.

Phil 197.38 — Outlines of a philosophy of life. (Widgery, A.G.) London, 1923.

Phil 8598.24.7 — Outlines of a philosophy of religion. (Sabatier, Auguste.) N.Y., 1902.

Phil 180.5 — Outlines of analogical philosophy. (Field, G.) London, 1839. 2v.

Phil 286.2.3 — Outlines of cosmic philosophy. (Fiske, J.) Boston, 1874. 2v.

Htn Phil 286.2*A — Outlines of cosmic philosophy. (Fiske, J.) Boston, 1875. 2v.

Phil 286.2.9 — Outlines of cosmic philosophy. (Fiske, J.) Boston, 1902. 4v.

Phil 286.2.15 — Outlines of cosmic philosophy. (Fiske, J.) Boston, 1916. 4v.

Phil 286.2.2 — Outlines of cosmic philosophy. (Fiske, J.) London, 1874. 2v.

Phil 286.2.5 — Outlines of cosmic philosophy. 11. ed. (Fiske, J.) Boston, 1890. 2v.

Phil 8843.1.7 — Outlines of history of ethics for English readers. (Sidgwick, Henry.) Boston, 1960.

Phil 1130.5.2 — Outlines of history of Greek philosophy. (Zeller, Eduard.) London, 1886.

Phil 1130.5.5 — Outlines of history of Greek philosophy. (Zeller, Eduard.) London, 1895.

Phil 1130.5.9 — Outlines of history of Greek philosophy. (Zeller, Eduard.) London, 1922.

Phil 1130.5 — Outlines of history of Greek philosophy. (Zeller, Eduard.) N.Y., 1886.

Phil 1130.5.4 — Outlines of history of Greek philosophy. (Zeller, Eduard.) N.Y., 1889.

Phil 1130.5.3 — Outlines of history of Greek philosophy. (Zeller, Eduard.) N.Y., 1890.

Phil 1130.5.17 — Outlines of history of Greek philosophy. 13th ed. (Zeller, Eduard.) London, 1931.

Phil 1130.5.15 — Outlines of history of Greek philosophy. 13th ed. (Zeller, Eduard.) London, 1931.

Phil 960.3.9 — Outlines of Indian philosophy. (Deussen, P.) Berlin, 1907.

Phil 960.137 — Outlines of Indian philosophy. (Hiriyanna, M.) London, 1932.

Phil 804.1 — Outlines of lectures on history of philosophy. (Elmendorf, J.J.) N.Y., 1876.

Phil 176.82 — Outlines of logic, psychology and ethics. (Baker, Arthur.) London, 1891.

Phil 5046.9.5 — Outlines of logic. (Gilmore, J.H.) N.Y., 1888.

Phil 5046.9 — Outlines of logic. (Gilmore, J.H.) Rochester, 1876.

Phil 5044.5.10 — Outlines of logic and metaphysics. 4th rev. ed. (Erdmann, J.E.) London, 1896.

Phil 3565.32.5.5 — Outlines of logic and of encyclopaedia of philosophy. (Lotze, Hermann.) Boston, 1887.

Phil 3565.32.6 — Outlines of logic and of encyclopaedia of philosophy. (Lotze, Hermann.) Boston, 1892.

Phil 187.27 — Outlines of metaphysics. (Mackenzie, J.S.) London, 1902.

Phil 5069.6 — Outlines of modern legal logic. (Tammelo, Ilmar.) Wiesbaden, 1969.

Phil 8887.45 — Outlines of moral philosophy. (Mazumdar, A.K.) Culcutta, 1915.

Phil 2275.70 — Outlines of moral philosophy. (Stewart, D.) Edinburgh, 1893.

Phil 8875.4.15 — Outlines of moral science. (Alexander, A.) N.Y., 1858.

Phil 5938.6 — Outlines of phrenology. (Spurzheim, Johann Gaspar.) Boston, 1832.

Phil 5938.6.2 — Outlines of phrenology. 2nd ed. (Spurzheim, Johann Gaspar.) Boston, 1833.

Phil 5938.6.3 — Outlines of phrenology. 3rd ed. (Spurzheim, Johann Gaspar.) Boston, 1834.

Phil 5938.6.5 — Outlines of phrenology. 3rd ed. (Spurzheim, Johann Gaspar.) Boston, 1834.

Phil 5251.1.16 — Outlines of physiological psychology. (Ladd, G.T.) N.Y., 1896.

Phil 6972.14.13 — Outlines of psychiatry. 13. ed. (White, William Alanson.) Washington, 1932.

Phil 5247.10.6 — Outlines of psychology. (Höffding, H.) London, 1892.

Phil 5247.10.8 — Outlines of psychology. (Höffding, H.) London, 1904.

Phil 5250.2 — Outlines of psychology. (Külpe, Oswald.) London, 1895.

Phil 5250.2.3A — Outlines of psychology. (Külpe, Oswald.) London, 1921.

Phil 5257.11A — Outlines of psychology. (Royce, Josiah.) N.Y., 1903.

Phil 5257.11.5 — Outlines of psychology. (Royce, Josiah.) N.Y., 1906.

Phil 5257.11.3 — Outlines of psychology. (Royce, Josiah.) N.Y., 1908.

Phil 5258.25.4 — Outlines of psychology. (Sully, J.) London, 1920.

Phil 5258.25.2 — Outlines of psychology. (Sully, J.) N.Y., 1885.

Phil 5258.25.3.5 — Outlines of psychology. (Sully, J.) N.Y., 1900.

Phil 3915.47 — Outlines of psychology. (Wundt, Wilhelm.) Leipzig, 1897.

Phil 3915.47.2 — Outlines of psychology. (Wundt, Wilhelm.) Leipzig, 1902.

Phil 3915.47.3 — Outlines of psychology. 3rd ed. (Wundt, Wilhelm.) Leipzig, 1907.

Phil 5258.25.3 — Outlines of psychology. 6th ed. (Sully, J.) London, 1889.

Phil 5725.1 — Outlines of the history and formation of...understanding. (Ellis, W.) London, 1847.

Phil 8843.3 — Outlines of the history of ethics. (Samson, G.W.) Washington, 1861.

Phil 5627.118 — Outlines of the psychology of religion. (Dresser, Horatio W.) N.Y., 1929.

Phil 5048.1 — Outlines of theoretical logic. (Ingleby, C.M.) Cambridge, 1856.

Phil 497.10.5 — The outlook of science. 2nd ed. (Worrall, R. L.) N.Y., 1946.

Phil 9050.4.5 — The outlook to nature. (Bailey, L.H.) N.Y., 1911.

Phil 6682.4 — Outrages à la pudeur....Somnambulisme. (Mesnet, E.) Paris, 1894.

Phil 5247.67 — Outside readings in psychology. (Hartley, Eugene Leonard.) N.Y., 1950.

Phil 8693.9 — The outskirts of physical science. (Dale, T. Nelson.) Boston, 1884.

Phil 6319.5 — Outwitting our nerves. (Jackson, Josephine A.) N.Y., 1921.

Phil 6119.11 — Outwitting our nerves. (Jackson, Josephine Agnes.) N.Y., 1921.

Phil 6119.11.5 — Outwitting our nerves. 2d ed (Jackson, Josephine Agnes.) N.Y., 1932.

Phil 3450.11.205 — L'ouvrage posthume de Husserl. (Wahle, Jean A.) Paris, 1957. 2v.

Phil 189.13 — Ouy, A. Cahier d'études philosophiques. v.1-2. Paris, 1924-1925.

Phil 672.129 — Over de vierde dimensie. (Weitzenböck, R.) Groningen, 1923.

Phil 193.169 — Over de wijsgeerige verwondering. (Schilfgaarde, P. von.) Assen, 1948.

Phil 3425.202 — Over het onderscheid tusschen de wetenschap van Hegel en de wijsheid van Bolland. (Pen, K.J.) Leiden, 1915.

Phil 6315.2.8 — Over psychoanalyse. (Freud, Sigmund.) Leiden, 1912.

Phil 1519.1 — Overbeck, Franz. Vorgeschichte und Jugend der mittelalterlichen Scholastek. Basel, 1917.

Phil 5330.17 — The overcoming of distraction and other resistances. (Morgan, H.H.B.) N.Y., 1916.

Phil 7080.46 — Overcoming sleeplessness. (Weschcke, Charles.) St. Paul, 1935.

Phil 6420.40 — Overcoming stammering. (Pellman, Charles.) N.Y., 1947.

Phil 345.3 — Overhuber, H.E. Die Geltungsgrundlagen metaphysischer Urteile. München, 1928.

Phil 5254.3 — Overstreet, H. Allen. About ourselves. N.Y., 1927.

Phil 5254.3.5 — Overstreet, H. Allen. The great enterprise. 1st. ed. N.Y., 1952.

Phil 5254.3.7 — Overstreet, H. Allen. The mind goes forth. 1st. ed. N.Y., 1956.

Phil 189.21.3 — Overstreet, H.A. The enduring guest. N.Y., 1931.

Phil 5850.299 — Overstreet, H.A. Influencing human behavior. N.Y., 1925.

Phil 5850.299.5 — Overstreet, H.A. Influencing human behavior. N.Y., 1925.

Phil 6124.5 — Overstreet, H.A. The mature mind. N.Y., 1949.

Phil 5590.125 — Overstreet, H.A. The mind alive. N.Y., 1954.

Phil 9290.9 — Overstreet, Harry A. A guide to civilized loafing. N.Y., 1934.

Htn Phil 8624.1* — Overton, R. Man's mortallitie. Amsterdam, 1644-97. 7 pam.

Phil 1119.2.21 — Overzicht der grieksche wijsbegeerte. 2e druk (Ovink, B.J.H.) Zutphen, 1906.

Phil 400.50 — Ovink, B.J.H. Het kritisch idealisme. Utrecht, 1913.

Phil 1119.2.21 — Ovink, B.J.H. Overzicht der griekscke wijsbegeerte. 2e druk. Zutphen, 1906.

Phil 3425.500 — Ovsiannikov, M.F. Filosofiia Gegelia. Moskva, 1959.

Phil 8050.21.2 — Ovsiannikov, M.F. Kurze Geschichte der Ästhetik. Berlin, 1966.

Phil 8050.21 — Ovsiannikov, M.F. Ocherki istorii esteticheskikh uchenii. Moskva, 1963.

Phil 8400.61 — Ovsiannikov, Mkikhail F. Marksistsko-leninskaia estetika. Moskva, 1966.

Phil 5520.50 — Owen, E.T. Interrogative thought and the means of its expression. Madison, 1904.

Phil 7069.26.15 — Owen, G.V. The life beyond the veil. London, 1926. 2v.

Phil 7069.27.30   Owen, G.V. Problems which perplex. London, 1927.
Phil 645.3   Owen, J. Evenings with skeptics. N.Y., 1881. 2v.
NEDL Phil 2414.1   Owen, J. The skeptics of the French renaissance. London, 1893.
Phil 4014.1   Owen, J. Skeptics of the Italian Renaissance. Photoreproduction. London, 1893.
Phil 7060.27.5   Owen, R.D. The debatable land between this world and the next. N.Y., 1872.
Phil 7060.27.3   Owen, R.D. Footfalls on the boundary of another world. Philadelphia, 1865.
Phil 189.32   Owens, Joseph. An elementary Christian metaphysics. Milwaukee, 1963.
Phil 1119.6   Owens, Joseph. A history of ancient Western philosophy. N.Y., 1959.
Phil 5280.5   Owens, Thomas J. Phenomenology and intersubjectivity. The Hague, 1971.
Phil 1750.455.10   The owl and the nightingale. (Kaufmann, W.A.) London, 1963.
Phil 3425.5   The owl of Minerva. Tallahassee. 1,1969+
Phil 6051.7   Oxenford, I. The complete palmist. Chicago, 1902.
Phil 6053.4   Oxenford, Ina. Life studies in palmistry. London, 1899.
Phil 2475.1.223   Oxenstierna, G. Tids- och intuitionsproblemen i Bergson's filosofi. Thesis. Uppsala, 1926.
Phil 8889.2.2   Oxenstjerna, J.T. Pensées, réflexions et maximes morales. Paris, 1825. 2v.
Phil 8889.2.3   Oxenstjerna, J.T. Pensées. v.1-2. Paris, 1774.
Phil 8889.2.4   Oxenstjerna, J.T. Pensées. v.1-2. Rouen, 1782.
Phil 8889.2   Oxenstjerna, J.T. Pensées sur divers sujets. Francfort, 1736. 2v.
Htn Phil 2115.96*   Oxford and Locke. (Grenville.) London, 1829.
Phil 5850.145   Oxford essays on psychology. (Brown, William.) London, 1948.
Phil 5627.134.30F   Oxford Group. The march of events, Oxford, 1935. Oxford, 1935.
Phil 5627.134.15   The Oxford Group international house party. Oxford, 1934.
Phil 5627.134.100   Pamphlet box. Oxford Group movement.
Phil 5627.134   The Oxford group movement. (Henson, H.H.) N.Y., 1933.
Phil 189.14   Pamphlet vol. Oxford lectures on philosophy, 1910-1923. 8 pam.
Phil 7054.185   Oxley, William. Angelic revelations concerning the origin, ultimation and destiny of the human spirit. Manchester, 1875-83. 4v.
Phil 8964.5   Oyen, Hendrik van. Evangelische Ethik. Basel, 1952. 2v.
Phil 814.3   Oyen, Hendrik van. Philosophia. v.1-2. Utrecht, 1947-49. 2v.
Phil 310.225   Ozakonakh obskchestvennogo razvitiia. (Glezerman, G.E.) Moskva, 1960.
Phil 5421.10.30   Özcan, Mehmed Tevfik. Angoisse (sikinti). Ankara, 1966.
Phil 5590.550   Özgü, Halis. Şahsiyet. 2. b. Istanbul, 1969.
Phil 4080.40   L'ozio, la contemplazione, il giuoco, la tecnica. (Cardone, Domenico Antonio.) Roma, 1968.
Phil 8415.6   Ozzòla, L. L'arte come conoscenza degli individuali. Roma, 1928.
Phil 1535.8   P. Institutiones philosophiae. Parisiis, 1868. 2v.
Phil 2630.1.82   Le P. Gratry; sa vie et ses oeuvres. 7e ed. (Perraud, A.) Paris, 1933.
Phil 2835.89   P. Ramus, professeur au Collège de France. Sa vie. (Desmaze, Charles.) Genève, 1970.
Phil 3270.4.84   P.J.A. Feuerbachs politische. (Hartmann, Richard.) Berlin, 1961.
Phil 3246.263   Ein paar Worte zur Belehrung. (Gruner, C.G.) Jena, 1799.
Phil 57.1   Pabblicazioni. (Rome. Universita. Scuola di Filosofia.) Roma. 1-17 14v.
Phil 2270.99   Pace, E. Das Relativitätsprincip bei Herbert Spencer. Leipzig, 1891.
Phil 5247.55   Pacemakers. (Hoggland, H.) N.Y., 1935.
Phil 3270.5.80   Pachaly, E. J.G.H. Feders Erkenntnistheorie und Metaphysik. Inaug. Diss. Leipzig, 1906.
Phil 5425.33   Pacheco, Albino Augusto. Degenerescencia. Diss. inaug. Coimbra, 1901.
Phil 9175.4   Pacheco, R. Cartas a mi esposa. Santiago de Chile, 1878.
Phil 600.20   Pacheu, Jules. Du positivisme au mysticisme. 2e éd. Paris, 1906.
Phil 5627.58   Pacheu, Jules. L'expérience mystique et l'activité subconciente. Paris, 1911.
Phil 1750.330.5   Paci, Enzo. Ancora sull'esistenzialismo. Torino, 1956.
Phil 1750.330.10   Paci, Enzo. Dall'esistenzialismo al relazionismo. Messina, 1957.
Phil 1750.480   Paci, Enzo. Esistenzialismo e storicismo. 1. ed. Milano, 1950.
Phil 1715.7   Paci, Enzo. La filosofia contemporanea. 1. ed. Milano, 1957.
Phil 2340.10.215   Paci, Enzo. La filosofia di Whitehead e i problemi del tempo e della struttura. Milano, 1965.
Phil 3450.11.87   Paci, Enzo. La formazione del pensiero di Husserl e il problema della costituzione della natura materiale e della natura animale. Milano, 1967.
Phil 1750.765   Paci, Enzo. Funzione delle scienze e significato dell'uomo. Milano, 1963.
Phil 4260.126   Paci, Enzo. Ingens sylva. 1. ed. Milano, 1949.
Phil 1750.330   Paci, Enzo. Il mella e il problema dell'uomo. 1st ed. Torino, 1950.
Phil 3450.11.85   Paci, Enzo. Omaggio a Husserl. Milano, 1960.
Phil 3450.11.86   Paci, Enzo. Il problema del tempo nella fenomenologia di Husserl. Milano, 1960.
Phil 1750.752   Paci, Enzo. I problemi dell'economic e la fenomenologia. Milano, 1963.
Phil 4200.8.30   Paci, Enzo. Relazioni e significati. v.1-2. Milano, 1965. 3v.
Phil 1133.32   Paci, Enzo. Storia del pensiero presocratico. Torino, 1957.
Phil 1750.820   Paci, Enzo. Tempo e relazione. Milano, 1965.
Phil 25.136   Pacific philosophy forum. Stockton, Califorina. 1,1962+ 5v.
Phil 2255.1.180   Il pacifismo nella dottrina politico-pedagogica di Bertrand Russell. (Rizzacasa, Aurelio.) Bologna, 1969.
Phil 815.34   Pacini, Dante. Crise filosófica do século atual. Rio de Janeiro, 1969.
Phil 190.114   Pacini, Dante. Sinteses e hipóteses de ser-humano. Rio de Janeiro, 1967.
Phil 2138.124   Packe, M. The life of John Stuart Mill. London, 1954.
Phil 3246.302   Die Padagogik Johann Gottlieb Fichtes. (Schuffenhauer, H.) Berlin, 1963.
Phil 3450.19.235   Padellaro De Angelis, Rosa. Heidegger e il problema Kantiano. Torino, 1960.
Phil 1135.180   Padellaro De Angelis, Rosa. Il problema cosmologica e l'antivomia unomalteplice. Milano, 1962.

Phil 5425.34.3   Padovan, A. Il genio. 3. ed. Milano, 1923.
Phil 8595.33.5   Padovani, U.A. Cultura e critianesimo. Milano, 1964.
Phil 8595.33   Padovani, U.A. La filosofia della religione e il problema della vita. Milano, 1937.
Phil 8890.56   Padovani, U.A. Filosofia e morale. Padova, 1960.
Phil 165.28   Padovani, U.A. Grande antologia filosofica. Milano, 1954. 16v.
Phil 190.104   Padovani, U.A. Metafisica classica e pensiero moderno. Milano, 1961.
Phil 630.31   Padovani, U.A. Il neorealismo anglo-americano. Firenze, 1916.
Phil 3808.168   Padovani, Umberto A. Arturo Schopenhauer. Milano, 1934.
Phil 7109.195   O padre Faria na história do hipnotismo. (Moniz, Egas.) Lisboa, 1925.
Phil 4265.2.94   Il padre Ventura e la filosofia. (Rémusat, Charles.) Milano, 1853.
Phil 4265.2.93   Il padre Ventura e la filosofia. (Rémusat, Charles.) Milano, 1853.
Phil 3120.55.60   Pädagogica. 1.Aufl. (Bloch, Ernst.) Frankfurt, 1971.
Phil 2115.117   Die Pädagogik des John Locke. (Getschmann, W.) Köthen, 1881.
Phil 3805.89   Die Pädagogik Schleiermachers. (Wickert, R.) Leipzig, 1907.
Phil 3805.166   Die Pädagogik Schleiermachers im Lichte seiner und unserer Zeit. (Diebow, Paul.) Halle, 1894.
Phil 3805.163   Die Pädagogik und Philosophie Schleiermachers in ihren Bezienungen zu J.J. Tousseau. Inaug. Diss. (Strobel, Anton.) n.p., 1927.
Phil 3195.6.210   Die Pädagogik Wilhelm Diltheys. (Herrmann, Ulrich.) Göttingen, 1971.
Phil 176.238   Der pädagogische Beruf der Philosophie. (Boehme, Guenther.) München, 1968.
Phil 4352.1.103   Die pädagogischen Elemente in der Philosophie des Jakob Balmes. Inaug. Diss. (Kruse, Paul.) Neuherberg, 1935.
Phil 3525.86   Pädagogischen Gedenken K.C.F. Krauses in ihrem Zusammenhange mit seiner Philosophie Dargestellt. Inaug. Diss. (Krause, K.C.F.) Leipzig, 1911.
Phil 2070.86   Paetz, W. Die erkenntnis-theoretischen Grundlagen von William James "The Varieties of Religious Experience." Eilenburg, 1907.
Phil 8633.1.18   Pagan ideas of immortality. (Moore, Clifford H.) Cambridge, 1918.
Phil 4210.107.5   Pagani, G.B. The life of Antonio Rosmini-Serbati. London, 1907.
Phil 4210.107   Pagani, G.B. Vita di Antonio Rosmini scritta da un sacerdote dell'istituto della carità. Rovereto, 1959. 2v.
Phil 190.45   Pagani, Silvio. Umanismo antivitale. Milano, 1925.
Phil 8581.43.3   Paganism, Christianity, Judaism; a confession of faith. (Brod, M.) University, 1970.
Phil 192.94   Paganisme ou christianisme. (Rideau, E.) Tournai, 1953.
Phil 2880.8.300   Pagano, Giacoma Maria. Sartre e la dialettica. Napoli, 1970.
Phil 8416.13   Pagano, José L. Motivos de estética. 2. ed. Buenos Aires, 1941.
Phil 4112.82   Pagano, V. Galluppi e la filosofia italiana. Napoli, 1897.
Phil 190.44   Page, Harvey L. Section I. Auto-philosophy founded on the straight and the curve; the 4 and the 9 of Pythagoras. San Antonio, 1927.
Phil 7076.24   Pagenstecher, Gustav. Aussersinnliche Wahrnehmung. Halle, 1924.
Phil 6325.7   Pagès, Louis. Affectivité et intelligence: étude psycho-pathologique. Paris, 1926.
Phil 6325.7.2   Pagès, Louis. Affectivité et intelligence: étude psycho-pathologique. Thèse. Paris, 1926.
Phil 3640.26   Pages choisies. 5e éd. (Nietzsche, Friedrich.) Paris, 1899.
Phil 2520.218   Les pages immortelles de Descartes. (Descartes, René.) Paris, 1942.
Phil 2520.218.5   Les pages immortelles de Descartes. (Descartes, René.) Paris, 1961.
Phil 2805.25.52   Les pages immortelles de Pascal, choisies et expliquées par F. Mauriac. (Pascal, Blaise.) N.Y., 1941.
Phil 5255.24   Paget, Violet. Proteus or The future of intelligence. London, 1925.
Phil 190.51   Paget, Violet. Vital lies. London, 1912. 2v.
Phil 7069.09.10   Paget, Walburga v.H. Colloquies with an unseen friend. London, 1909.
Phil 4060.8.83   Paggiaro, L. La filosofia di Francesco Acri. Padova, 1953.
Phil 8595.57   Paggiaro, Luigi. L'esperienza religiosa. Padova, 1964.
Phil 4964.67   Una página de historia en la naciente filosofia argentina y otros ensayos criticos. (Coviello, Alfredo.) Tucumán, 1941.
Phil 3425.109.15   Una pagina sconosciuta degli ultimi mesi della vita di Hegel. (Croce, B.) Bari, 1950.
Phil 196.35   Paginas filosofias. (Villoro, Luis.) Mexico, 1962.
Phil 8402.68   Pagine di estetica. (Brissoni, Armando.) Padova, 1968.
Phil 4115.23   Pagine scelte, edite ed inedite. (Gioberti, V.) Torino, 1922.
Phil 4060.1.23   Pagine scelte. (Ardigo, Roberto.) Genova, 1913.
Phil 4818.571.20   Pagini filozofice alese. (Micháilescce, Ştefan C.) Bucureşti, 1955.
Phil 4080.3.475   Pagliano Ungari, Graziella. Croce in Francia; ricerche sulla fortuna dell'opera crociana. Napoli, 1967.
Phil 8446.2   Pagliaro, Antonino. Ironia e verità. Milano, 1970.
Phil 2270.136   Pagnone, A. Le intuizioni morali e l'eredità nello Spencer. Torino, 1897.
Phil 9150.4.9   Pagnone, Annibale. L'eredità organica e la formazione delle idealità morale. Torino, 1904.
Phil 6955.14   Pahological anatomy of nervous centres. (Fox, E.L.) London, 1874.
Phil 9343.9   Paige, Elbridge G. Short patent sermons. N.Y., 1845.
Phil 530.15.40   Paillard, Etienne. Lumière éternelle. Paris, 1944.
Phil 4960.640   Paim, Antônio. A filosofia da escola do Recife. Rio de Janeiro, 1966.
Phil 4960.640.5   Paim, Antônio. História das idéias filosóficas no Brasil. São Paulo, 1967.
Phil 5402.39   Pain; a psychophysiological analysis. (Sternbach, Richard A.) N.Y., 1968.
Phil 5402.11   Pain, pleasure, and aesthetics. (Marshall, H.R.) N.Y., 1894.
Phil 365.46   Pain, sex and time. (Heard, G.) N.Y., 1939.
Phil 5402.42   Pain and emotion. (Trigg, Roger.) Oxford, 1970.
Phil 5402.23   Pain and pleasure. (Szasz, T.S.) N.Y., 1957.
Phil 8735.25   The pain of this world and the providence of God. (D'Arcy, M.C.) London, 1952.

Phil 5255.1 Paine, A.W. The new philosophy. Bangor, 1884.
Phil 9355.8 Paine, Harriet E. Girls and women. Boston, 1890.
Phil 9400.2 Paine, Harriet E. Old people. Boston, 1910.
Phil 8705.1 Paine, M. A discourse on the soul and the principle of instinct. N.Y., 1848. 4 pam.
Phil 8705.1.2 Paine, M. A discourse on the soul and the principle of instinct. N.Y., 1848. 4 pam.
Phil 8705.1.5 Paine, M. A review of theoretical geology. N.Y., 1856.
Phil 8595.16 Paine, Thomas. Age of reason. London, 1795.
Phil 8595.15.18 Paine, Thomas. The age of reason. N.Y., 1896.
Phil 8595.15.19 Paine, Thomas. Age of reason. N.Y., 1898.
Phil 8595.15.23 Paine, Thomas. Age of reason. N.Y., 194-?
Phil 8595.15.24 Paine, Thomas. The age of reason. N.Y., 1951.
Htn Phil 2225.3.30* Paine, Thomas. The age of reason. Paris, 1794.
Htn Phil 8595.15.5* Paine, Thomas. Age of reason. Investigation of true and fabulous theology. Boston, 1794. 4 pam.
Phil 8595.15.17 Paine, Thomas. Age of reason. Investigation of true and fabulous theology. Boston, 1875. 2 pam.
Phil 8595.15.9A Paine, Thomas. Age of reason. Investigation of true and fabulous theology. London, 1852.
Htn Phil 8595.15.16* Paine, Thomas. Age of reason. Investigation of true and fabulous theology. n.p., n.d. 5 pam.
Phil 8595.15.7 Paine, Thomas. Age of reason. Investigation of true and fabulous theology. pt.1-2. 2d ed. Boston, 1795.
Htn Phil 8595.15.8* Paine, Thomas. Age of reason. Investigation of true and fabulous theology. pt.1-2. London, 1796.
Htn Phil 8595.15.6* Paine, Thomas. The age of reason. Pt.1. Paris, 1794.
Htn Phil 2225.3.35* Paine, Thomas. Examination of...passages in the New Testament. N.Y., n.d.
Phil 8595.15.50 Paine, Thomas. Letter of Thomas Paine to lawyer Erskine. n.p., 18- .
Htn Phil 8595.15.28* Paine, Thomas. La siècle de la raison. Paris, 1794.
Phil 8595.15.30 Paine, Thomas. Siècle de la raison. pt.2. Paris, 1795-96.
Phil 8595.15.3.5 Paine, Thomas. The theological works. Boston, 1834.
Phil 8595.15.4 Paine, Thomas. Theological works. Boston, 1858.
Phil 8595.15.4.3 Paine, Thomas. Theological works. Chicago, 19- ?
Phil 8595.15.4.10 Paine, Thomas. Theological works. London, 1819.
Phil 8595.15.2 Paine, Thomas. Theological works. London, 1824.
Phil 8595.15.2.5 Paine, Thomas. The theological works. London, 1827.
Phil 8595.15.4.5 Paine, Thomas. Theologische Werke. v.1-4,6. Philadelphia, 1851.
Htn Phil 8595.16.13* Paine's second part of The age of reason answered. (Tytler, James.) Salem, 1796.
Phil 5535.6 Paired-associates learning; the role of meaningfulness, similarity. (Goss, Albert E.) N.Y., 1965.
Phil 2880.8.102 Paissac, H. Le dieu de Sartre. Grenoble, 1950.
Phil 270.129 Pakistan. Philosophical Congress, 7th, Dacca, Pakistan, 1960. Symposia on basic human values and causality. Lahore, 1960?
Phil 70.95 Pakistan Philosophical Congress. Proceedings. 1,1954+ 6v.
Phil 25.125 The Pakistan philosophical journal. Lahore. 1,1957+ 3v.
Phil 960.172 Pal, B.C. An introduction to the study of Hinduism. 2. ed. Calcutta, 1951.
Phil 525.266 Palabra y silencio. 1. ed. (Xirau, Ramón.) México, 1968.
Phil 2725.2.46 Palabras de un creyente. 8. ed. (Lamennais, F.R. de.) Paris, 1834.
Phil 190.103 Palacios, L.E. Filosofía del saber. Madrid, 1962.
Phil 5255.23 Palágyi, M. Naturphilosophische Vorlesungen über die Grundprobleme des Bewusstseins und des Lebens. Charlottenburg, 1907.
Phil 5255.23.2 Palágyi, M. Naturphilosophische Vorlesungen über die Grundprobleme des Bewusstseins und des Lebens. Leipzig, 1924.
Phil 5585.42 Palágyi, M. Wahrnehmungslehre. Leipzig, 1925.
Phil 3497.12 Palágyi, Melchiar. Kant und Bolzano. Halle, 1902.
Phil 5055.11.5 Palágyi, Melchior. Die Logik auf dem Scheidewege. Berlin, 1903.
Phil 5055.11 Palágyi, Melchior. Der streit der Psychologisten. Leipzig, 1902.
Phil 9430.22 Palante, Georges. Pessimisme et individualisme. Paris, 1914.
Phil 2630.4.90 Palante, Georges. La philosophie du Bovarysme. Paris, 1924.
Phil 2520.175 Palau, J.Y. Descartes y el idealismo subjetivista moderno. Barcelona, 1927.
Phil 8965.17 Palazzini, Pietro. Casus conscientiae. Torino, 1958. 2v.
Phil 8965.17.2 Palazzini, Pietro. Casus conscientiae. 2. ed. Torino, 1964. 2v.
Phil 8890.58 Palazzini, Pietro. Morale generale. Brescia, 1961.
Phil 7150.35 Palazzo, D. Il suicidio sotto l'aspetto fisiopatologico. Napoli, 1953.
Phil 5425.40 Palcos, Alberto. El genio; ensayo sobre su génesis. Buenos Aires, 1920.
Phil 2905.1.615 La paleogeografia in Teilhard de Chardin. (Imbrighi, Gastone.) L'Aguila, 1967.
Phil 2205.40.30 Paley, W. Grundsätze der Moral und Politik. Leipzig, 1787. 2v.
Phil 2205.30.12 Paley, W. Natural theology. Albany, 1803.
Phil 2205.30.9 Paley, W. Natural theology. Boston, 1829.
Phil 2205.30.13 Paley, W. Natural theology. Boston, 1831.
Phil 2205.30.5 Paley, W. Natural theology. Boston, 1854.
Phil 2205.30.15 Paley, W. Natural theology. Boston, 1857.
Phil 2205.30.18 Paley, W. Natural theology. Hallowell, 1819.
Htn Phil 2205.30.17* Paley, W. Natural theology. Hallowell, 1819.
Phil 2205.30 Paley, W. Natural theology. London, 1803.
Phil 2205.30.4 Paley, W. Natural theology. London, 1822.
Phil 2205.30.7.5 Paley, W. Natural theology. London, 1836. 2v.
Phil 2205.30.6 Paley, W. Natural theology. N.Y., n.d. 2 pam.
NEDL Phil 2205.30.3 Paley, W. Natural theology. Philadelphia, 1814.
Phil 2205.30.2 Paley, W. Natural theology. Philadelphia, 1814.
NEDL Phil 2205.30.11 Paley, W. Natural theology. Philadelphia, 1814.
Phil 2205.30.14 Paley, W. Natural theology. Trenton, N.J., 1824.
NEDL Phil 2205.30.10 Paley, W. Natural theology. 10th ed. London, 1805.
Phil 2205.40.15 Paley, W. Paley's moral philosophy. London, 1859.
Phil 2205.40.13 Paley, W. Paley's moral philosophy. N.Y., 1828.
Phil 2205.40.2 Paley, W. Principles of moral and political philosophy. Boston, 1795.
Phil 2205.40.2.5 Paley, W. Principles of moral and political philosophy. Boston, 1801.
Phil 2205.40.4 Paley, W. Principles of moral and political philosophy. Boston, 1810.
Phil 2205.40.5 Paley, W. Principles of moral and political philosophy. Boston, 1811.
Phil 2205.40.6 Paley, W. Principles of moral and political philosophy. Boston, 1815.
Phil 2205.40.11 Paley, W. Principles of moral and political philosophy. Boston, 1827.
Phil 2205.40.7 Paley, W. Principles of moral and political philosophy. Boston, 1830. 2v.
Phil 2205.40.14 Paley, W. The principles of moral and political philosophy. Boston, 1831. 2v.
Htn Phil 2205.39* Paley, W. Principles of moral and political philosophy. London, 1785.
Phil 2205.1 Paley, W. Principles of moral and political philosophy. London, 1785.
Phil 2205.39.5 Paley, W. Principles of moral and political philosophy. London, 1786.
Phil 2205.40.3 Paley, W. Principles of moral and political philosophy. London, 1804. 2v.
Phil 2205.40.8 Paley, W. Principles of moral and political philosophy. N.Y., 1817.
Phil 2205.40.10 Paley, W. Principles of moral and political philosophy. N.Y., 1824.
Phil 2205.40 Paley, W. Principles of moral and political philosophy. Paris, 1788.
Phil 2205.40.9 Paley, W. Principles of moral and political philosophy. v.1-2. Boston, 1828.
Phil 2205.40.8.5 Paley, W. Principles of moral and political philosophy. 11th American ed. Boston, 1825.
Phil 2205.31 Paley, W. Theologia naturale. Roma, 1808.
Phil 2205.10 Paley, W. Works. Boston, 1810-12. 5v.
Phil 2205.11.5 Paley, W. Works. Cambridge, 1830. 6v.
Phil 2205.12 Paley, W. Works. Edinburgh, 1833.
Phil 2205.13 Paley, W. Works. London, 1823. 5v.
Phil 2205.11 Paley, W. Works. London, 1825. 5v.
Phil 2205.13.15 Paley, W. Works. London, 1838. 4v.
Phil 2205.15 Paley, W. Works. London, 1851.
Phil 2205.14 Paley, W. Works. Philadelphia, 1850.
Phil 2205.10.5 Paley, W. Works. v.1,3-5. Boston, 1812. 4v.
Phil 2205.30.7 Paley, W. Natural theology. London, 1836. 2v.
Phil 2205.40.15 Paley's moral philosophy. (Paley, W.) London, 1859.
Phil 2205.40.13 Paley's moral philosophy. (Paley, W.) N.Y., 1828.
Phil 2205.84.5 Paley's natural theology refuted in his own words. (Holyoake, G.J.) London, 1851.
Htn Phil 8890.1* Palfreyman, T. A treatise of moral philosophy. London?, 1564?
Phil 815.9 Palhariés, F. Vies et doctrines des grands philosophes à travers les âges. Paris, 1928. 3v.
Phil 4115.89 Palhories, F. Gioberti. Paris, 1929.
Phil 8890.28 Palhoriès, F. Nouvelles orientations de la morale. Paris, 1911.
Phil 4210.108 Palhoriès, F. La philosophie de Rosmini. Thèse. Paris, 1908.
Phil 4210.108.5 Palhoriès, F. Rosmini. Paris, 1908.
Phil 4112.81 Palhoriès, F. La theorie idéologique de Galluppi. Paris, 1909.
Phil 5585.71 Paliard, J. Pensée implicite et perception visuelle. Paris, 1949.
Phil 2825.15 Paliard, J. Profondeur de l'âme. Paris, 1954.
Phil 5374.161 Paliard, J. Théorème de la connaissance. Paris, 1938.
Phil 5255.25.5 Paliard, Jacques. Intuition et réflexion. Thèse. Paris, 1925.
Phil 2730.90 Paliard, Jacques. Le raisonnement selon Maine de Biran. Paris, 1925.
Phil 2730.90.5 Paliard, Jacques. Le raisonnement selon Maine de Biran. Thèse. Paris, 1925.
Phil 281.9.10 Palimodia manifesta. Sevilla, 1792?
Phil 8887.13.5 Palladis tamia. (Meres, F.) N.Y., 1938.
Phil 100.5 Pallares, Eduardo. Diccionario de filosofía. 1. ed. México, 1964.
Phil 3640.166 Pallarès, V. de. Le crépuscule d'une idole, Nietzsche, nietzschéisme, nietzscheens. Paris, 1910.
Phil 9450.55 Pallas athene. (Freyer, Hans.) Jena, 1935.
Phil 4060.4.85 Pallavicini, Gian Luigi. Il pensiero di Antonio Aliotta. Napoli, 1968.
Phil 2475.1.239 Pallière, Aimé. Bergson et le Judaïsme. Paris, 1933.
Phil 3425.762 Palma, Norman. Moment et processus. Paris, 1970-
Phil 5255.66 Palmade, G. L'unité des science humaines. Paris, 1961.
Phil 8890.46 Palmer, E. Principles of nature. London, 1823.
Phil 8890.46.5 Palmer, E. Principles of nature. 3. ed. N.Y., 1806.
Phil 7069.27.33 Palmer, E.C. The riddle of spiritualism. London, 1927.
Phil 8640.5 Palmer, Fred. Winning of immortality. London, 1910.
Phil 8890.23.7A Palmer, G.H. The field of ethics. Boston, 1901.
Phil 8890.23.9 Palmer, G.H. Field of ethics. Boston, 1902.
Phil 8890.23 Palmer, G.H. The glory of the imperfect. Boston, 1891.
Phil 8890.23.5 Palmer, G.H. The glory of the imperfect. Boston, 1915.
Phil 8890.23.3 Palmer, G.H. The glory of the imperfect. N.Y., 1898.
Phil 9240.7 Palmer, G.H. The nature of goodness. Boston, 1903.
Phil 8890.23.16 Palmer, G.H. The nature of goodness. Boston, 1904.
Phil 5765.4A Palmer, G.H. The problem of freedom. Boston, 1911.
Phil 8890.23.21 Palmer, George H. Altruism. N.Y., 1920.
Phil 8633.1.15 Palmer, George H. Intimations of immortality in the sonnets of Shakespeare. Boston, 1912.
Htn Phil 2225.7.30* Palmer, George H. The teacher. Boston, 1908.
Phil 6325.17 Palmer, H.A. The philosophy of psychiatry. N.Y., 1952.
Phil 8965.4.5 Palmer, Herbert. Lord Bacon not the author of The Christian paradoxes. Edinburgh, 1865.
Phil 2218.84 Palmer, J. Observations. v.1-2. London, 1779.
Phil 2415.8 Palmer, R.R. Catholics and unbelievers in eighteenth century France. Princeton, 1939.
Phil 210.5 Palmer, Richard E. Hermeneutics; interpretation theory in Schleiermacher, Dilthey, Heidegger, and Gadamer. Evanston, 1969.
NEDL Phil 8890.2.2 Palmer, T.H. The moral instructor. pt. 2. Boston, 1846.
Phil 8890.2.5 Palmer, T.H. The moral instructor. pt.1. Boston, 1853.
Phil 8890.2 Palmer, T.H. The moral instructor. pt.1. Philadelphia, 1841.
Phil 8890.2.3 Palmer, T.H. The moral instructor. pt.3. Boston, 1874.
Phil 8890.2.4 Palmer, T.H. The moral instructor. pt.4. Boston, 1851.
Phil 5425.61 Palmer, William J. Genius. Los Angeles, 1937.
Phil 5838.266 Palmeri, R. The sources of instinctive life, and A theory of mental functioning. N.Y., 1966.
Phil 165.45 Palmeró, J. La philosophie par les textes. Paris, 1955.
Phil 5592.95 Palmés, F.M. Como informar sobre la personalidad propria. Barcelona, 1958.
Phil 5255.40 Palmés, F.M. Psicología. Barcelona, 1928.
Phil 3450.19.490 Palmier, Jean Michel. Les écrits politiques de Heidegger. Paris, 1968.
Phil 6321.51.10 Palmier, Jean Michel. Lacan, le symbolique et l'imaginaire. Paris, 1969.
Phil 2150.22.110 Palmier, Jean Michel. Présentation d'Herbert Marcuse. Paris, 1969.
Htn Phil 8890.43* Palmieri, Matteo. Libro della vita civile. n.p., 15- .

Phil 6049.09   Palmistry made easy. (Gratz, Thomas Donelson.) Philadelphia, 1909.

Phil 3835.7   Palmodo, Kurt. Der Freiheitsbegriff in der Lehre Spinozas. Weiden, 1920.

Phil 348.4.80   Palmoe, E. Indledning til filosofi som grundvidenskab efter Johs. København, 1954.

Phil 7069.40.15   Palmstierna, E.K. Widening horizons. London, 1940.

Phil 8595.35   Palmstierna, E.K. The world's crisis and faiths. London, 1942.

Phil 5401.34   Palou, Jean. La peur dans l'histoire. Paris, 1958.

Phil 2340.10.165   Palter, Robert M. Whitehead's philosophy of science. Chicago, 1960.

Phil 190.59   Palumbo, A. The mirror of your soul. Boston, 1935.

Phil 2880.8.120   Palumbo, Giovanni. La filosofia esistenziale di Jean Paul Sartre. Palermo, 1953.

Phil 4265.1.80   Palumbo, R. Giulio Cesare Vanini e i suo tempi. Napoli, 1878.

Phil 4807.6F   Památník na oslavu padesátiletého panovnického jubilea jeho veličenstva císaře a krále Františka Josefa I. (Česká akademie věd a umění.) Praha, 1898.

Phil 1850.151   Pamer, C. Bacon von Verulam und seine Stellung in der Geschichte der Philosophie. Triest, 1888.

Phil 5545.223   Pamięc jako właściwość poszczególnych analizatorów. (Włodarski, Z.) Warszawa, 1964.

Phil 4803.799.95   Pamiętniki o Janie Śniadeckim. (Baliński, Michał.) Wilno, 1865. 2v.

Phil 59.3.6   Pamphlet. (Theosophical Society in America. Oriental Department.) N.Y. 1891-1897 2v.

Phil 2705.45   Un pamphlet médical au XVIIIe siècle. Thèse. (La Mettrie, Julien Offray de.) Paris, 1931.

Phil 974.3.9   Pamphlet box. Pamphlets on Steiner.

Phil 6980.573   Pan-African Psychiatric Conference, 1st, Abeokuta, 1961. First Pan-African psychiatric conference. Ibadan, 1962?

Phil 4961.140   Pan American Union. Fuentes de la filosofía latinoamericana. Washington, 1967.

Phil 1955.6.117   Pan American Union. Division of Philosophy, Letters and Sciences. John Dewey en sus noventa años. Washington, 1949.

Phil 197.10   Pan-Gnosticism. (Winter, N.) N.Y., 1895.

Phil 3497.20   Panaev, I. Ras"iskateli istinyi: I. Kant. Sankt Peterburg, 1878.

VPhil 3425.676   Panasiuk, R. Lewica Heglowska. wyd. 1. Warszawa, 1969.

Phil 960.250   Pandeya, R.C. The problem of meaning in Indian philosophy. 1. ed. Delhi, 1963.

Phil 9175.1   Pandolfini, A. Trattato del governo della famiglia. Milano, 1802.

Phil 9175.1.8   Pandolfini, A. Trattato del governo della famiglia. Milano, 1829.

Phil 8595.50   Panese, Roberto. Necessità e sufficienza del principio cristiano. Padova, 1958.

Phil 972.20   Panet, Edmond. La mort de Canopus. Paris, 1970.

Phil 8980.673   Panferov, F.I. O moral'nom oblike sovetskogo cheloveka. Moskva, 1960.

Phil 5520.756   Panfilov, Vladimir Z. Vzaimootnoshenie iazyka i myshleniia. Moskva, 1971.

Phil 284.1   The Panidèa. (Durfee, J.) Boston, 1846.

Phil 1750.166.180   Panikkar, Raimundo. Humanismo y cruz. Madrid, 1963.

Phil 8705.13   Panin, Ivan. The writings of Ivan Panin. New Haven, 1918.

Phil 6125.12.3   Panizza, M. La fisiologia del sistema nervoso. Roma, 1897.

Phil 6125.12   Panizza, M. Le metodo nello studio del fenomeno biopsichio. Roma, 1901.

Phil 5255.13   Panizza, Mario. Nuova teorica fisiologica della conoscenza. Roma, 1899.

Phil 5255.13.5   Panizza, Mario. I nuovi elemente della psicofisiologia. Roma, 1898.

Phil 296.14   Panizza, O. Der Illusionismus und die Rettung. Leipzig, 1895.

Phil 6980.573.5   Pankow, Gisela. Gesprengte Fesseln der Psychose. München, 1968.

Phil 585.260   Pannenberg, Wolfhart. Was ist der Mensch? Die Anthropologie der Gegenwart im Lichte der Theologie. Göttingen, 1962.

Phil 585.260.3   Pannenberg, Wolfhart. Was ist der Mensch? Die Anthropologie der Gegenwart in Lichte der Theologie. 3e Aufl. Göttingen, 1968.

Phil 705.22   Pannwitz, R. Kosmos Atheos. München, 1926.

Phil 535.10   Pannwitz, R. Der Nihilismus und die Welt. Nürnberg, 1951.

Phil 3640.398   Pannwitz, Rudolf. Nietzsche und die Verwandlung des Menschen. Amsterdam, 1939.

Phil 3640.505   Pannwitz, Rudolf. Nietzsche und die Verwandlung des Menschen. Amsterdam, 1943.

Phil 8407.38   Panofsky, E. Galileo as a critic of the arts. The Hague, 1954.

Phil 8050.79   Panofsky, E. Idea. 2. Aufl. Berl'., 1960.

Htn   Phil 1865.35*   Panopticon. (Bentham, Jeremy.) Dublin, 1791.

Phil 1865.19   Panopticon. (Bentham, Jeremy.) London, 1812-17. 4 pam.

Phil 4960.625.10   Panorama da filosofia no Brasil. (Vita, Luís Washington.) Pôrto Alegre, 1969.

Phil 8125.2   Panorama de la estética clásica-romántica alemana. (Guerrero, Luis.) La Plata, 1934.

Phil 4958.205   Panorama de la filosofía cubana. (Piñera Llera, Humberto.) Washington, 1960.

Phil 4958.510   Panorama de la filosofía en Santo Domingo. (Cordero, Armando.) Santo Domingo, 1962.

Phil 4957.55   Panorama de la filosofía iberoamericana actual. (Villegas, Abelardo.) Buenos Aires, 1963.

Phil 2411.9   Panorama de la philosophie française contemporaine. (Lacroix, Jean.) Paris, 1966.

Phil 5210.20   Panorama de la psicología en el Perú. (Alarcón, Reynaldo.) Lima, 1968.

Phil 186.65.35   Panorama des doctrines philosophiques. (Lavelle, Louis.) Paris, 1967.

Phil 4960.605.25   Panorama of the history of philosophy in Brazil. (Cruz Costa, João.) Washington, 1962.

Phil 184.45   Le panpsychisme vital. (Jeandidier, A.) Paris, 1954.

Phil 5401.50   Panse, Friedrich. Angst und Schreck in klinisch psychologischer und sozialmedizinischer Sicht. Stuttgart, 1952.

Phil 3497.26   Pantaleo, Pasquale. La direzione coscienza-intenzione nella filosofia di Kant e Husserl. Bari, 1967.

Phil 4065.119   Il panteismo di Giordano Bruno. (Fiorentino, F.) Napoli, 1861.

Phil 8685.15   Pantheism, and the value of life. Thesis. (Urquhart, W.S.) London, 1919.

Phil 8685.11.5   Pantheism, its story and significance. (Picton, J.A.) London, 1905.

Phil 8685.14   Pantheism. (Amryc, C.) n.p., 1898.

Phil 2905.1.485   Panthéisme, action, oméga chez Teilhard de Chardin. (Dussault, Gabriel.) Bruges, 1967.

Phil 8685.4   Der Pantheismus. (Jäsche, G.B.) Berlin, 1826-32. 3v.

Htn   Phil 2295.39*   Pantheisticon, sive formula celebrandae sodalitatis Socraticae. (Toland, John.) Cosmopoli, 1720.

Phil 2295.40.5   Das Pantheistikon. (Toland, John.) Leipzig, 1897.

Phil 490.9   Pantin, Igor' K. Materialisticheskoe mirovozrenie i teoriia poznaniia russkikh revoliutsionnikh demokratov. Moskva, 1961.

Phil 310.75   Pantskhava, I.D. Dialekticheskii materializm. Moskva, 1958.

Phil 190.107   Pantskhava, Il'ia D. Chelovek, ego zhizn' i bessmertie. Moskva, 1967.

Phil 8670.20.5   Pantskhawa, I.D. Istoriia i teoriia ateizma. Moskva, 1962.

Phil 8670.20   Pantskhawa, I.D. Osnovnye voprosy nauchnogo ateizma. Moskva, 1962.

Phil 5643.39   Panum, P.L. Physiologische Untersuchungen über das Sehen mit zwei Augen. Kiel, 1858.

Phil 9530.45.5   Panzer, Martin. It's your future. N.Y., 1943.

Phil 3552.444   Panzer, Ursula. Die Phänomenalität der Res Extensa bei Leibniz. Köln, 1962.

Phil 4210.128   Paoli, A. Lo Schopenhauer e il Rosmini. Roma, 1878.

Phil 2050.105   Paoli, Alessandro. Hume e il principio di causa. Napoli, 1882.

Phil 3808.120   Paoli, Alessandro. Lo Schopenhauer e il Rosmini. Roma, 1878.

Phil 4210.82   Paoli, F. Della vita di Antonio Rosmini-Serbati. Torino, 1880-84. 2v.

Phil 346.6   Paoli, Giulio C. Considerazioni filosofiche sulla dottrina della conoscenza. Milano, 1911.

Phil 8890.3   Paolino. Trattato de regimine rectoris. Vienna, 1868.

Phil 346.19   Pap, Arthur. Analytische Erkenntnistheorie. Wien, 1955.

Phil 190.78   Pap, Arthur. Elements of analytic philosophy. N.Y., 1949.

Phil 346.19.5   Pap, Athur. Semantics and necessary truth. New Haven, 1958.

Phil 8416.26   Pap, Julius. Kunst und Illusion. Leipzig, 1914.

Phil 400.85.5   Papafava, N. L'attualismo considerazioni. Milano, 1932.

Phil 815.33   Papalexandrou, K. Synoptike historia tes philosophias. 3. ed. Athens, 1969.

Phil 4845.227.34   Papanoutsos, Euangelos. Epikaira kai anepikaira. Athena, 1962.

Phil 4845.227.38   Papanoutsos, Euangelos. Hē ēthikē syneidēsē kai tä problēmatä tes. Athena, 1962.

Phil 4845.227.32.3   Papanoutsos, Euangelos. The foundations of knowledge. Albany, 1968.

Phil 4845.227.32.2   Papanoutsos, Euangelos. Gnosiologia. 2. ed. Athena, 1962.

Phil 4845.227.32   Papanoutsos, Euangelos. Ho kosmos toū pneumatos. 2. ed. Athēna, 1953-56. 3v.

Phil 5055.34   Papanoutsos, Euangelos. Logikē. Athēna, 1970.

Phil 4845.227.30   Papanoutsos, Euangelos. Ho logos kai ho anthrōpos. Athena, 1971.

Phil 4845.227.44   Papanoutsos, Euangelos. Neollēnikē philosophia. 2. ed. v.1-2. Athena, 1956-59.

Phil 4845.227.36   Papanoutsos, Euangelos. Philosophia kai paideia. Athena, 1958.

Phil 4845.227.40   Papanoutsos, Euangelos. Philosophika problemata. Athena, 1964.

Phil 5255.82   Papanoutsos, Euangelos. Psychologia. Athēnai, 1970.

Phil 1750.166.117   Paparelli, Gioacchino. Tra umanesimo e reforma. Napoli, 1964.

Phil 3552.324   Pape, Ingetrud. Leibniz. Stuttgart, 1949.

Phil 346.30   Pape, Ingetrud. Tradition und Transformation der Modalitat Habilitationschrift. Hamburg, 1966-

Phil 176.236   El papel de la filosofía en el conjunto del saber. (Bueno Martinez, Gustavo.) Madrid, 1970.

Phil 5585.218   El papel del cuerpo en la percepción. (Galindez, J.) Tucuman, 1963.

Phil 8416.5   Papennyi, Z.S. O khudozhestvennom obraze. Moskva, 1961.

Phil 52.3   Papers, 1-4. (McGill University. Department of philosophy.) Montreal, 1896-99.

Phil 5870.6   Papers. (Minnesota. Symposia on Child Psychology.) Minneapolis. 1,1967+ 3v.

Phil 52.2   Papers. (Minnesota. University. Department of Philosophy.) Minneapolis, 1893-

Phil 55.8   Papers. (Psychological Society of Great Britain.) London. 1875-1876

Phil 9350.3.7   Papers for thoughtful girls. (Keddie, H.) Boston, 1864.

Phil 510.01   Papers from the Monist. n.p., n.d.

Phil 5520.77   Papers from the second American congress on general semantics, August, 1941. (American Congress on General Semantics.) Chicago, 1943.

Phil 2250.80   Papers in honor of Josiah Royce on his sixtieth birthday. Lancaster, Pa., 1916.

Phil 25.157   Papers in psychology. Belfast. 1,1967+

Htn   Phil 5055.1.15*   Papers on logic. (Pierce, C.S.) n.p., 1867?

Phil 338.8   Papers on logic and epistemology. v.1-6. (Hocking, William E.) N.Y., 1905.

Phil 6319.2.2   Papers on psycho-analysis. (Jones, Ernest.) London, 1918.

Phil 6319.2.6   Papers on psycho-analysis. (Jones, Ernest.) N.Y., 1913.

Phil 6319.2.1   Papers on psycho-analysis. (Jones, Ernest.) N.Y., 1919.

Phil 6319.2.4   Papers on psycho-analysis. 4th ed. (Jones, Ernest.) Baltimore, 1938.

Phil 6319.2.4.5   Papers on psycho-analysis. 5th ed. (Jones, Ernest.) Boston, 1961.

Phil 6319.2.4.6   Papers on psycho-analysis. 5th ed. (Jones, Ernest.) Boston, 1967.

Phil 735.7   Papers on the theory of value. (Hocking, William E.) Lancaster, Pa., 1908. 2 pam.

Phil 5066.103   Papers on time and tense. (Prior, Arthur Norman.) Oxford, 1968.

Phil 70.3.35   Papers read to the Xth International Congress of Psychology at Copenhagen, 1932. (International Congress of Psychology, 10th, Copenhagen, 1932.) The Hague. 1935

Phil 4070.7.80   Papi, Fulveo. Il pensiero di Antonio Banfi. Firenze, 1961.

Phil 3497.28   Papi, Fulvio. Cosmologia e civilta. Urbino, 1969.

Phil 3850.1.75   Der papier-Reisende. (Strauss, D.F.) Weimar, 1907.

Phil 3015.1   Papillault, G. Science française, scolastique allemande. Paris, 1917.

Phil 1715.1   Papillen, Fernand. Histoire de la philosophie moderne. Paris, 1876. 2v.

Phil 5055.22   Papineau, Arthur B. Philosophy II and III in Harvard College. Cambridge, 1889.

Phil 1870.105   Papini, G. Giorgio Berkeley. Milano, 1908.
Phil 8670.16   Papini, G. The memoirs of God. Boston, 1926.
Phil 190.20.7   Papini, Giovanni. L'altra metà. 3a ed. Firenze, 1919.
Phil 190.20.8   Papini, Giovanni. L'altra metà. 4a ed. Firenze, 1922.
Phil 1715.2.10   Papini, Giovanni. Gli amanti de Sofia, 1902-1918. Firenze, 1942.
Phil 1715.2   Papini, Giovanni. Il crepuscolo dei filosofi. Milano, 1906.
Phil 1715.2.5   Papini, Giovanni. Le crepuscule des philosophes. Paris, 1922.
Phil 190.20.4   Papini, Giovanni. Pragmatismo, 1903-1911. 2. ed. Firenze, 1920.
Phil 190.20.3   Papini, Giovanni. Sul pragmatismo. Milano, 1913.
Phil 2880.8.260   Papone, Annagrazia. Esistenza e corporeità in Sartre. Firenze, 1969.
Phil 2138.135   Pappe, H. O. John Stuart Mill and the Harriet Taylor myth. Melbourne, 1960.
Phil 1190.5.5   Pappenheim, E. Der angebliche Heraklitismus des Skeptikers. Berlin, 1889.
Phil 1190.5   Pappenheim, E. Die Tropen der griechischen Skeptiker. Berlin, 1885.
Phil 4070.10.30   Papuli, Giovanni. Girdamo Balduino. Manduzia, 1967.
Phil 25.61   Papyaus. Le Caire.
Phil 2705.80   Paquet, H.R.R. Essai sur La Mettrie. Paris, 1873.
Phil 3640.31.15   Par delà le bien et le mal. (Nietzsche, Friedrich.) Paris, 1951.
Phil 4960.272   Para la historia de las ideas argentinas. 1. ed. (Vazela Dominiguez de Ghioldi, Delfina.) Buenos Aires, 1952.
Phil 585.159   Para una nueva idea del hombre y de la antropología filosófica. (Virasoro, M.A.) Tucuman, 1963.
Phil 4972.5.50   Para una posición argentina. (Malmurca Sánchez, Ernesto.) La Plata, 1940.
Phil 8881.24   Parables for school and home. (Garrison, W.P.) N.Y., 1897.
Phil 8637.21   Paradise revisited. (McGavin, E.C.) Boston, 1937.
Phil 4357.8   La paradoja del filósofo. (Caragorri, P.) Madrid, 1959.
Phil 4080.12.65   I paradossi del senso comune. (Castelli, Enrico.) Padova, 1970.
Phil 2128.55   Il paradosso Mandeville. (Mandeville, B.) Firenze, 1958.
Phil 353.31   Paradox and discovery. (Wisdom, John.) N.Y., 1965.
Phil 9558.50   The paradox of cruelty. 1. ed. (Hallie, Phillip Paul.) Middletown, Conn., 1969.
Phil 5246.77   The paradox of pleasure and relativity. (Garan, D.G.) N.Y., 1963.
Phil 1813.5   The paradox of progressive thought. (Noble, D.W.) Minneapolis, 1958.
Phil 5190.72   The paradox of the liar. (Martin, Robert L.) New Haven, 1970.
Phil 5525.35   The paradoxe of the ludicrous. (Seward, Samuel S.) Stanford, 1930.
Phil 1819.7   Paradoxe de la pensée anglaise au XVIIe siècle. (Tedeschi, Paul.) Paris, 1961.
Phil 8875.3.15   Paradoxe sur l'incertitude vanité et abus des sciences. (Agrippa von Nettesheim, Heinrich Cornelius.) n.p., 1603.
Phil 8875.3.16   Paradoxe sur l'incertitude vanité et abus des sciences. (Agrippa von Nettesheim, Heinrich Cornelius.) n.p., 1603.
Phil 3255.83   Das Paradoxen als Ausdrucksform der spekulativen Mystik Sebastian Francks. Inaug-Diss. (Klemm, Karl.) Leipzig, 1937.
Phil 5190.24.15   The paradoxes. (Toensma, E.) Assen, 1969.
Phil 2493.87.5   Paradoxes de Condillac. (Laromiguiere, P.) Paris, 1825.
Phil 410.11   Les paradoxes de l'infini. (Borel, Emile.) Paris, 1946.
Phil 410.6.10.2   Paradoxes of the infinite. (Bolzano, B.) London, 1950.
Phil 410.6.10   Paradoxes of the infinite. (Bolzano, B.) New Haven, 1950.
Phil 5402.9   Paradoxical pain. (Harlin, R.M.) Boston, 1916.
Phil 8644.1.5   Paradoxical philosophy. (Tait, P.G.) London, 1879.
Phil 5190.24.5   The paradoxical universe. (Melhwish, George.) Bristol, Eng., 1959.
Phil 410.6.5   Paradoxien des Unendlichen. (Bolzano, B.) Leipzig, 1920.
Htn   Phil 177.78*   Paradoxo ou Sentença, philosophica contra opinão do vulgo. (Cointha, Jean des Boulez.) Lixboa, 1866.
Phil 7069.33.45   Paragnosie en "Einfuehlen". Proefschrift. (Tenhaeff, W.H.C.) Bussum, N.H., 1933.
Phil 182.7   Paragraphen für den Unterricht in der Philosophie. (Hassler, K.D.) Ulm, 1832.
Phil 182.7.2   Paragraphen für den Unterricht in der Philosophie. 2. Aufl. (Hassler, K.D.) Ulm, 1852.
Phil 5520.598   Parain, Brice. Petite métaphysique de la parole. Paris, 1969.
Phil 1750.830.10   Parain-Vial, Jeanne. Analyses structurales et idéologies structuralistes. Toulouse, 1969.
Phil 6127.8.5   Parallelism of mind and body. (Rogers, A.K.) Chicago, 1899.
Phil 6127.8   Parallelism of mind and body. (Rogers, A.K.) Chicago, 1899.
Phil 5520.61   Le parallélisme logico-grammatical. Thèse. (Serrus, Charles.) Paris, 1933.
Phil 817.15   Der Parallelismus der Alten und neuen Philosophie. (Reichlin-Meldegg, K.) Leipzig, 1866.
Phil 348.7.3   Les paralogismes du rationalisme. Thèse. (Rougier, Louis.) Paris, 1920.
Phil 623.30   Paranjpye, Raghunath Purushottam. Rationalism in practice. Calcutta, 1935.
Phil 6968.5   Paranoia, systematized delusions. (Séglas, J.) N.Y., 1888.
Phil 6963.2   Paranoia. (Noyes, W.) Baltimore, 1888-89.
Phil 7069.44.17   Paranormal cognition in human psychology. (Bendit, L.J.) London, 1944.
Phil 2115.62.10   A paraphrase and notes on epistle of St. Paul. (Locke, J.) Cambridge, 1832.
Htn   Phil 2115.62.2*   A paraphrase and notes on epistle of St. Paul. (Locke, J.) London, 1707.
Phil 2115.62   A paraphrase and notes on epistle of St. Paul. (Locke, J.) London, 1823.
Phil 6322.41   The parapraxis in the Haizmann case of Sigmund Freud. (Vandendriessche, Gaston.) Louvain, 1955.
Phil 6331.10   The parapraxis in the Haizmann case of Sigmund Freud. (Vandendriessche, Gaston.) Louvain, 1965.
Phil 25.99   Parapsicologia; rivista internazionale di studi, di ricerche ed orientamenti del pensiero relativo. Roma. 1,1955
Phil 55.11   Parapsychological Association. Proceedings. Bruges. 1957-1964+ 5v.
Phil 25.135   Parapsychological monographs. N.Y. 1-6 3v.
Phil 7010.5.1   Parapsychologie; ihre Ergebnisse und Probleme. (Bender, Hans.) Bremen, 1970.
Phil 7069.59.15   Parapsychologie, paragnosie. (Visser, B.J.J.) Roermond, 1959.

Phil 7069.54.15   La parapsychologie. (Amadou, Robert.) Paris, 1954.
Phil 7069.43.20   Parapsychologie. (Driesch, Hans.) Zürich, 1943.
Phil 7030.2   Parapsychologie. (Tenhaeff, Wilhelm H.C.) Antwerpen, 1968.
Phil 7010.5   Parapsychologie. Entwicklung, Ergebnisse, Probleme. (Bender, Hans.) Darmstadt, 1966.
Phil 7069.43.22   Parapsychologie. 3. Aufl. (Driesch, Hans.) Zürich, 1952.
Phil 7069.25.15   Parapsychologische Erkenntnisse. (Gruber, K.) München, 1925.
Phil 3808.63.20   Parapsychologische Schriften. (Schopenhauer, Arthur.) Basel, 1961.
Phil 7069.56.15   Parapsychologische woordentolk. (Dietz, Paul A.) Den Haag, 1956.
Phil 7069.28.35   Die parapsychologischen Erscheinungen. 2. Aufl. (Jaeschke, Willy K.) Leipzig, 1928.
Phil 7069.57   Parapsychology, F. Proceedings of four conferences. N.Y., 1957.
Phil 7069.57.16   Parapsychology, frontier science of the mind. 2. ed. (Rhine, Joseph B.) Springfield, 1962.
Phil 7026.2   Parapsychology. (Pratt, Joseph G.) N.Y., 1966.
Phil 7069.57.15   Parapsychology. (Rhine, Joseph B.) Springfield, Ill., 1957.
Phil 7028.2   Parapsychology. (Rýzl, Milan.) N.Y., 1970.
Phil 25.90   Parapsychology bulletin. Durham, N.C. 1,1946+ 3v.
Phil 55.9   Parapsychology Foundation. Newsletter. N.Y. 1,1953+ 5v.
Phil 55.10   Parapsychology Foundation. Report on five years of activities. N.Y., 1959.
Phil 7069.65.10   Parapsychology Foundation. Ten years of activities. N.Y., 1965.
Phil 7069.65.15   Parapsychology from Duke to FRNM. (Rhine, Joseph B.) Durham, 1965.
Phil 25.170   Parapsychology review. N.Y. 1,1970+
Phil 7010.10   Parapsychology today. 1. ed. (Rhine, Joseph Banks.) N.Y., 1968-
Phil 1200.53   Parataxeis. 1st ed. (Martinozzoli, F.) Firenze, 1953.
Phil 5825.6.4   Pardies, Ignace. Discours de la connaissance des bestes. 4. éd. Paris, 1896.
Phil 8890.34   Pardines, Maurice. Critique des conditions de l'action. Paris, 1970. 2v.
Phil 4080.3.139   Pardo, Ferruccio. La filosofia teoretica di Benedetto Croce. Napoli, 1928.
Phil 346.18   Pardo, R. Del origen a la escencia del conocimiento. Buenos Aires, 1954.
Phil 2675.4.30   Le pardon. (Jankélévitch, Vladimir.) Paris, 1967.
Phil 5875.150   Pareek, Udai Narain. Developmental patterns in reactions to frustration. N.Y., 1965.
Phil 5871.114   Parental and sex-role identification. (Lynn, David Brandon.) Berkeley, Calif., 1969.
Htn   Phil 9160.1.9*   Parental duties in the promotion of early piety. (Abbott, Jacob.) London, 1836.
Phil 400.94.15   Parente, A. La morte dell'idealismo. Napoli, 1937.
Phil 4080.3.175   Parente, Alfredo. Il pensiero politico di Benedetto Croce e u nuovo liberalismo. 2. ed. Napoli, 1944.
Phil 575.84   Parenthood and civilization. (Donahue, G.H.) Boston, 1931.
Phil 5871.80   Les parents, les inconnus. (Baroni, Christophe.) Genève, 1969.
Phil 5871.90   Parents and children in history. (Hunt, David.) N.Y., 1970.
Phil 2520.168   Parenty, Henri. Les tourbillons de Descartes et la science moderne. Paris, 1903.
Phil 4210.141.5   Parere intorno alle dottrine ed alle opere di Antonio Rosmini-Serbati. (Trullet, Angelo) Modena, 1882.
Phil 4120.8.40   Parerga. (Guzzo, Augusto.) Torino, 1956.
Phil 3808.60.8   Parerga en Paralipomena. (Schopenhauer, Arthur.) Amsterdam, 1908. 2v.
Phil 3808.60.30   Parerga et Paralipomena: fragments sur l'histoire de la philosophie. (Schopenhauer, Arthur.) Paris, 1912.
Phil 3808.60   Parerga und Paralipomena. (Schopenhauer, Arthur.) Berlin, 1862.
Phil 3808.60.2   Parerga und Paralipomena. v.1-2. (Schopenhauer, Arthur.) Berlin, 1851.
Phil 190.50   Paret, Hans. Der dialektische Ursprung der Glückseligkeit. Berlin, 1925.
Phil 400.117   Pareyson, L. L'estetica dell'idealismo tedesco. Torino, 1950.
Phil 3246.255   Pareyson, L. Fichte. Torino, 1950.
Phil 8416.8.15   Pareyson, Luigi. Conversazioni di estetica. Milano, 1966.
Phil 1750.340.8   Pareyson, Luigi. Esistenza e persona. 3. ed. Torino, 1966.
Phil 8416.12   Pareyson, Luigi. Estética. Torino, 1954.
Phil 8416.8   Pareyson, Luigi. L'estetica e i suoi problemi. Milano, 1961.
Phil 2805.445   Pareyson, Luigi. L'etica di Pascal; corso di filiosfia morale dell'anno accademico 1965-1966. Torino, 1966.
Phil 8416.8.12   Pareyson, Luigi. I problemi dell'estetica. 2. ed. Milano, 1966.
Phil 1750.340   Pareyson, Luigi. Studi sull'esistenzialismo. 2. ed. Firenze, 1950.
Phil 8416.8.5   Pareyson, Luigi. Theoria dell'arte; saggi di estetica. Milano, 1965.
Phil 6965.9   Pargeter, William. Observations on maniacal disorders. Reading, Eng., 1792.
Phil 2805.370.5   Le Pari de Pascal. (Brunet, Georges.) Paris, 1956.
Phil 3425.666.2   Parinetto, Luciano. La nozione di alienazione in Hegel, Feuerbach e Marx. 2. ed. Milano, 1969.
Phil 346.26   París, Carlos. Ciencia. Santiago, 1957.
Phil 2520.01   Paris. Bibliothèque National. Département des Imprimés. Catalogue des ouvrages de Descartes. Paris, 1909.
Phil 2520.227   Paris. Bibliotheque Nationale. Descartes. Paris, 1937.
Phil 4372.1.95   Paris. Bibliotheque Nationale. Vives. Paris, 1942.
Phil 2655.3   Paris. Ecole Libre des Sciences Politiques. Élie Halévy. Paris, 1937.
Phil 5645.53   Paris. Ecole Pratique des Hautes Études. Problèmes. Paris, 1957.
Phil 815.32   Paris. Institut Catholique. Faculte de Philosophie. Histoire de la philosophie et metaphysique. Paris, 1955.
Phil 2805.325   Paris. Musée National des Granges de Port-Royal. Pascal et les provinciales. Paris, 1956.
Phil 6965.14   Paris. Université. Faculté de Medecine. Rapport de Mm. Cosnier, Maloet, Darcet, [and others]...nouveau méthode d'adminster l'électricité...maladies nerveuses. Paris, 1783.
Phil 3450.11.75   The Paris lectures. (Husserl, Edmund.) The Hague, 1964.
Phil 4065.88.12   Paris Zezin, Luis. Fray Giordano Bruno y su tiempo. 2a ed. Madrid, 1886.

462

Author and Title Listing

Phil 8595.20 Pariser, E. Einführung in die Religions-Psychologie. Halle, 1914.
Phil 5460.6 Parish, E. Hallucinations and illusions. London, 1897.
Phil 7068.94.15 Parish, Edmond. Über die Trugwahrnehmung. Leipzig, 1894.
Phil 7054.91 Parisi, G. Two appeals to the leaders of spiritualism. Florence, 1871.
Phil 2270.100 Parisot, E. Herbert Spencer. Paris, n.d.
Htn Phil 190.67* Parité de la vie et de la mort. n.p., n.d.
Phil 3450.2.87 Paritzky, J.E. Franz Hemsterhuis, seine Philosophie und ihr Einfluss auf dei deutschen Romantiker. Berlin, 1926.
Phil 2255.1.127 Park, J. Bertrand Russell on education. Columbus, 1963.
Phil 9355.9 Park, John Edgar. New horizons. Norton, 1929.
Phil 5627.84 Park, M. Remarkable vision and death bed experience of Ada Park. Pulaski, N.Y., 1882.
Phil 2218.89 Park, Mary Cathryne. Joseph Priestley and the problem of pantiscocracy. Philadelphia, 1947.
Phil 2218.88 Park, Mary Cathryne. Joseph Priestley and the problem of pantiscocracy. Diss. Philadelphia, 1947.
Phil 525.60 Parke, Jean. The immaculate perception. N.Y., 1927.
Phil 6325.23 Parker, B. My language is me. N.Y., 1962.
Phil 8705.11 Parker, Benjamin. A survey of six days work of creation. London, 1745.
Phil 2225.10 Parker, D.H. Experience and substance. Ann Arbor, 1941.
Phil 735.170 Parker, D.H. The philosophy of value. Ann Arbor, 1957.
Phil 8416.29 Parker, de W.H. The principles of aesthetics. Boston, 1920.
Phil 735.97 Parker, DeWitt H. Human values. N.Y., 1931.
Phil 190.26 Parker, DeWitt H. Self and nature. Cambridge, 1917.
Phil 8622.86 Parker, Francis H. Reason and faith revisited. Milwaukee, 1971.
Phil 7069.16.50 Parker, Frank E. Christian wisdom. Cambridge, Mass., 1916.
Phil 8416.30 Parker, H.W. The spirit of beauty; essays, scientific and aesthetic. N.Y., 1888.
Phil 8595.21 Parker, S. A demonstration of the divine authority of the law of nature. London, 1681.
Phil 8670.3 Parker, S. Disputationes de Deo. London, 1678.
Phil 6946.40 Parker, Seymour. Mental illness in the urban Negro community. N.Y., 1966.
Phil 8595.1.3 Parker, T. A discourse of matters pertaining to religion. Boston, 1842.
Phil 8595.1 Parker, T. A discourse of matters pertaining to religion. Boston, 1847.
Phil 8595.1.2 Parker, T. A discourse of matters pertaining to religion. Boston, 1856.
Phil 8595.1.4A Parker, T. A discourse of matters pertaining to religion. Boston, 1907.
Phil 8595.1.6 Parker, T. Sermons of Theism, Atheism, and the popular theology. Boston, 1853.
Phil 8595.1.7 Parker, T. Sermons of Theism, Atheism, and the popular theology. Boston, 1856.
Phil 6834.15 Parker, William. Homosexuality: a selective bibliography of over 3000 items. Metuchen, N.J., 1971.
Phil 190.68 Parkes, Henry B. The pragmatic test; essays on the history of ideas. San Francisco, 1941.
Phil 8670.15 Parkes, J.W. God and human progress. Harmondsworth, Eng., 1944.
Phil 9175.3 Parkes, W. Domstic duties. N.Y., 1829.
Phil 8416.24 Parkhurst, H.H. Beauty; an interpretation of art and the imaginative life. 1st ed. N.Y., 1930.
Phil 630.15 Parkhurst, Helen. Recent logical realism. Thesis. Bryn Mawr, 1917.
Phil 8890.4 Parkhurst, J.L. Elements of moral philosophy. Boston, 1832.
Phil 3835.8 Parkinson, G.H.R. Spinoza's theory of knowledge. Oxford, 1854.
Phil 3552.448 Parkinson, George H.R. Logic and reality in Leibniz's metaphysics. Oxford, 1965.
Phil 7069.35.70 Parkman, Frances. Dedication; being later letters from the writer of "Reality". Boston, 1935.
Phil 7069.38.65 Parkman, Frances. Vision, being the continuation of "Reality" and "Dedication". Boston, 1938.
Phil 6965.1 Parkman, G. Management of lunatics. Boston, 1817-18. 2 pam.
Phil 9530.26 Parlette, R.A. A book of rejoicing, big business. Chicago, 1917.
Phil 9035.37 Parlette, R.A. The university of hard knocks. Chicago, 1917.
Phil 5825.3 Parmelee, M. The science of human behavior. N.Y., 1913.
Phil 1133.5 Parmenidas, anaxagorae, protagore principia. (Reesema, W.S.) Lugduni, 1840.
Phil 5643.148 Parmenter, Ross. The awakened eye. 1. ed. Middletown, Conn., 1968.
Phil 2340.10.225 Parmentier, Alix. La philosophie de Whitehead. Paris, 1968.
Phil 310.658 Parniuk, Mikhail A. Determinizm dialekticheskogo materializma. Kiev, 1967.
Phil 8890.41.10 Parodi, D. Les bases psychologiques de la vie morale. Paris, 1928.
Phil 190.63 Parodi, D. En quête d'un philosophie. Paris, 1935.
Phil 190.63.7 Parodi, D. En quête d'une philosophie; la conduite humaine et les valeurs idéales. Paris, 1939.
Phil 8890.41 Parodi, D. Le problème morale et la pensée contemporaine. 2. ed. Paris, 1921.
Phil 2415.5.10 Parodi, Dominique. Du positivisme à l'idéalisme. Paris, 1930. 2v.
Phil 2415.5 Parodi, Dominique. La philosophie contemporaine en France. Paris, 1919.
Phil 2415.5.2 Parodi, Dominique. La philosophie contemporaine en France. Paris, 1920.
Phil 5520.110 La parole. 1. éd. (Gusdorf, George.) Paris, 1955.
Phil 4210.121F Parole dette da N. Zucchi per l'inaugurazione del monumento ad Antonio Rosmini in Milano. (Zucchi, N.) n.p., 1896.
Phil 2725.2.47 Parole d'un credente. (Lamenais, F.R. de.) Bruxelles, 1834. 3 pam.
Phil 2725.2.48 Parole d'un credente. (Lamenais, F.R. de.) Italia, 1834.
Phil 5520.1 La parole intérieure. (Egger, V.) Paris, 1881.
Phil 600.7.1 Paroles de philosophie positive. (Littré, Émile.) Paris, 1859.
Phil 600.7.2 Paroles de philosophie positive. (Littré, Émile.) Paris, 1863.
Htn Phil 2725.2.40* Paroles d'un croyant. (Lamennais, F.R. de.) Bruxelles, 1834.
Htn Phil 2725.2.36* Paroles d'un croyant. (Lamennais, F.R. de.) Paris, 1834.
Phil 2725.2.41.5 Paroles d'un croyant. (Lamennais, F.R. de.) Paris, 1949.
Phil 2725.2.41 Les Paroles d'un croyant. Thèse. (Lamennais, F.R. de.) Paris, 1949.
Phil 2725.2.37 Paroles d'un croyant. 7. éd. (Lamenais, F.R. de.) Paris, 1834.
Phil 2725.2.39 Paroles d'un croyant. 9. éd. (Lamenais, F.R. de.) Paris, 1834.
Phil 3850.5.8 Paroles d'un sage. (Spir, Afrikan.) Paris, 1938.
Phil 4316.1 Parpal y Marques, C. Antecedentes de la escuela filosófica Catalana del siglo XIX. Barcelona, 1914.
Phil 190.83 Parpert, F. Philosophie der Einsamkeit. München, 1955.
Phil 190.2 Parr, S. Metaphysical tracts by English philosophers of the 18th century. London, 1837.
Phil 9550.6 Parris, M. Total utility and the economic judgment. Philadelphia, 1909.
Phil 6125.15 Parson, B.S. Lefthandedness. N.Y., 1924.
Phil 8610.919.30 The parson and the atheist. (Lyttleton, Edward.) London, 1919.
Phil 672.222 Parsons, E. Time devoured. London, 1964.
Phil 5645.15 Parsons, J.H. Introduction to study of colour vision. Cambridge, 1915.
Phil 5585.39A Parsons, John H. An introduction to the theory of perception. Cambridge, 1927.
Phil 575.246 Parsons, Talcott. Social structure and personality. N.Y., 1964.
Phil 5465.37 La part de l'imagination. (Biervliet, J.J. van.) Paris, 1937.
Phil 8620.43 La part du diable. (Rougemont, Denis de.) N.Y., 1942.
Phil 8620.43.3 La part du diable. (Rougemont, Denis de.) N.Y., 1944.
Phil 3004.3 Die Parteiung der Philosophie. (Ehrenberg, Hans.) Leipzig, 1911.
Phil 2725.35.85 La participation à l'être. (Sargi, Bechara.) Paris, 1957.
Phil 9355.12 Parting advice to a youth on leaving his Sunday school. N.Y., 1833.
Phil 177.72.5 Partis pris sur l'art. (Cuvillier, Armand.) Paris, 1956.
Phil 70.89 Parts and wholes. (Hayden Colloquium on Scientific Concept and Method, M.I.T.) N.Y., 1963.
Phil 2406.4A The party of humanity. 1st ed. (Gay, P.) N.Y., 1963.
Phil 2477.6.175 Parys, Jean M. van. La vocation de la liberté. Paris, 1968.
Phil 2805.36 Pascal, Blaise. Cartas escritas a un provincial. Paris, 1849.
Phil 2805.35 Pascal, Blaise. Las celebres cartas provinciales. Madrid, 1846.
Phil 2805.65 Pascal, Blaise. Deux pièces imparfaites sur la grâce et le concile de trente. Paris, 1947.
Phil 2805.55 Pascal, Blaise. Discours sur les passions de l'amour. Paris, 1900.
Phil 2805.74 Pascal, Blaise. Entretien avec de Saci sur Épictète et Montaigne. Paris, 1875.
Phil 2805.74.10 Pascal, Blaise. Entretien avec M. de Saci. 2. éd. Aix, 1946.
Phil 2805.74.20 Pascal, Blaise. L'entretien de Pascal et Sacy. Paris, 1960.
Phil 2805.24 Pascal, Blaise. Fragments philosophiques. Paris, 1875.
Phil 2805.25 Pascal, Blaise. Fragments philosophiques. Paris, 1876.
Phil 2805.44 Pascal, Blaise. Gedanken. Leipzig, 1881.
Phil 2805.50 Pascal, Blaise. L'homme et l'oeuvre. Paris, 1956.
Phil 2805.33 Pascal, Blaise. Les provinciales. Berlin, 1878.
Phil 2805.32.30 Pascal, Blaise. Les lettres de Blaise Pascal. Paris, 1922.
Phil 2805.30.6 Pascal, Blaise. Lettres écrites à un provincial. Paris, 1842.
Phil 2805.30.5 Pascal, Blaise. Lettres écrites à un provincial. Paris, 1885-86. 2v.
Phil 2805.32.25 Pascal, Blaise. Les lettres provinciales. Manchester, 1920.
Phil 2805.30.27 Pascal, Blaise. The life of Mr. Paschal with his letters relating to the Jesuits. London, 1765-66. 2v.
Phil 2805.29 Pascal, Blaise. Litterae provinciales. Helmaestadt, 1664.
Phil 2805.25.50A Pascal, Blaise. The living thoughts of Pascal. N.Y., 1940.
Phil 2805.29.3 Pascal, Blaise. Ludovici Montaltii Litterae provinciales. 6. éd. Coloniae, 1700. 2v.
Phil 2805.42.6A Pascal, Blaise. Miscelleneous writings. London, 1849.
Htn Phil 2805.32.15* Pascal, Blaise. The mystery of jesuitism. London, 1689[1679].
Phil 2805.22 Pascal, Blaise. L'oeuvre de Pascal. Argenteuil, 1936.
Phil 2805.40 Pascal, Blaise. Oeuvres; Les pensées. Paris, 1830.
Phil 2805.10 Pascal, Blaise. Oeuvres. La Haye, 1779. 5v.
NEDL Phil 2805.17 Pascal, Blaise. Oeuvres. Paris, 1914-23. 14v.
Phil 2805.21 Pascal, Blaise. Oeuvres. Paris, 1928-29. 6v.
Phil 2805.13 Pascal, Blaise. Oeuvres complètes. Bruges, 1964-
Phil 2805.12 Pascal, Blaise. Oeuvres complètes. Paris, 1858. 2v.
Phil 2805.19 Pascal, Blaise. Oeuvres complètes. Paris, 1926. 2v.
Phil 2805.15 Pascal, Blaise. Oeuvres de Blaise Pascal. Paris, 1886-95. 2v.
Phil 2805.73 Pascal, Blaise. Opuscules et lettres. Paris, 1955.
Phil 2805.70 Pascal, Blaise. Opuscules philosophiques. Paris, 1864.
Phil 2805.72 Pascal, Blaise. Opuscules philosophiques. Paris, 1887.
Phil 2805.25.52 Pascal, Blaise. Les pages immortelles de Pascal, choisies et expliquées par F. Mauriac. N.Y., 1941.
Phil 2805.26 Pascal, Blaise. Pascal; ein brevier seiner Schriften. Stuttgart, 1908.
Phil 2805.45 Pascal, Blaise. Pascal. Paris, 1946.
Phil 2805.46 Pascal, Blaise. Pascal. Paris, 1947.
Phil 2805.26.7 Pascal, Blaise. Pascal de l'esprit géométrique. Paris, 1871.
Phil 2805.30.30 Pascal, Blaise. Pascal et les provinciales. Paris, 1956.
Phil 2805.272 Pascal, Blaise. Pascal par lui-même. Paris, 1952.
Phil 2805.40.45 Pascal, Blaise. Pascal's apology for religion. Cambridge, Eng., 1942.
Phil 2805.42.25 Pascal, Blaise. Pascal's Pensées. Mt. Vernon, 1946?
Phil 2805.43 Pascal, Blaise. Pensamientos. Zaragoza, 1790.
Phil 2805.40.2A Pascal, Blaise. Pensées, fragments et lettres. Paris, 1844. 2v.
Phil 2805.40.33 Pascal, Blaise. Pensées, opuscules et lettres. Paris, 1873. 2v.
Htn Phil 2805.39* Pascal, Blaise. Pensées...sur la religion. Paris, 1670.
Phil 2805.40.10 Pascal, Blaise. Pensées...sur la religion. Paris, 1725.
Phil 2805.40.11 Pascal, Blaise. Pensées...sur la religion. Paris, 1734.
Phil 2805.40.12 Pascal, Blaise. Pensées...sur la religion. Paris, 1748.
Phil 2805.40.18 Pascal, Blaise. Pensées. Fribourg, 1896.
Phil 2805.42.11 Pascal, Blaise. The pensées. Harmondsworth, 1961.
Phil 2805.42.37 Pascal, Blaise. Pensées. London, 1943.
Phil 2805.42.27 Pascal, Blaise. Pensées. London, 1947.
Phil 2805.42.30 Pascal, Blaise. Pensées. London, 1950.
Phil 2805.42.50 Pascal, Blaise. Pensées. N.Y., 1962.
Htn Phil 2805.39.5* Pascal, Blaise. Pensées. Paris, 1670.
Htn Phil 2805.39.2* Pascal, Blaise. Pensées. Paris, 1670.

Phil 2805.40.13.15   Pascal, Blaise. Pensées. Paris, 1842.
Phil 2805.40.37   Pascal, Blaise. Pensées. Paris, 1852.
Phil 2805.40.3   Pascal, Blaise. Pensées. Paris, 1854.
Phil 2805.40.29   Pascal, Blaise. Pensées. Paris, 186-.
Phil 2805.40.34   Pascal, Blaise. Pensées. Paris, 1869.
NEDL Phil 2805.40.14   Pascal, Blaise. Pensées. Paris, 1874.
Phil 2805.40.7   Pascal, Blaise. Les pensées. Paris, 1877-79. 2v.
Phil 2805.40.15   Pascal, Blaise. Pensées. Paris, 1897.
Phil 2805.40.17A   Pascal, Blaise. Pensées. Paris, 1904. 3v.
Phil 2805.40.19   Pascal, Blaise. Pensées. Paris, 1907.
Phil 2805.40.23   Pascal, Blaise. Pensées. Paris, 1924.
Phil 2805.40.38   Pascal, Blaise. Pensées. Paris, 1934.
Phil 2805.42.35   Pascal, Blaise. Pensées. Paris, 1942.
Phil 2805.42.40   Pascal, Blaise. Pensées. Paris, 1958. 2v.
Phil 2805.42.45   Pascal, Blaise. Pensées. Paris, 1960. 2v.
Phil 2805.42.55   Pascal, Blaise. Pensées. Paris, 1962.
Phil 2805.42.58   Pascal, Blaise. Pensées. Paris, 1966.
Phil 2805.40.6   Pascal, Blaise. Pensées. Tours, 1873.
Phil 2805.40.5   Pascal, Blaise. Pensées. Tours, 1873.
Phil 2805.40.16   Pascal, Blaise. Pensées. v.1-2. Paris, 1812.
Phil 2805.40.4A   Pascal, Blaise. Pensées. v.1-2. Paris, 1866.
Phil 2805.40.4.3   Pascal, Blaise. Pensées. 2e éd. v.1-2. Paris, 1866. 2v.
Phil 2805.40.22   Pascal, Blaise. Pensées choisies. 2. éd. Paris, 1882.
Phil 2805.40.21   Pascal, Blaise. Pensées choisies. 6e éd. Paris, 1876.
Phil 2805.40.30   Pascal, Blaise. Pensées contenant les lettres et opuscules. Paris, 1861.
Phil 2805.40.13   Pascal, Blaise. Pensées de Blaise Pascal. Paris, 1817. 2v.
Phil 2805.40.13.5   Pascal, Blaise. Pensées de Blaise Pascal. Paris, 1829.
Phil 2805.40.13.10   Pascal, Blaise. Pensées de Blaise Pascal. Paris, 1839.
Phil 2805.40.6.5   Pascal, Blaise. Pensées de Blaise Pascal. Paris, 1873.
Phil 2805.40.32   Pascal, Blaise. Pensées de Pascal. Paris, 1866.
Phil 2805.40.28   Pascal, Blaise. Les pensées et oeuvres choisies. Paris, 1937.
Phil 2805.40.36   Pascal, Blaise. Pensées et opuscules. 6. éd. Paris, 1912.
Phil 2805.40.35   Pascal, Blaise. Pensées et opuscules. 11e éd. Paris, 1923.
Phil 2805.40.31   Pascal, Blaise. Pensées sur la religion. Paris, 1951. 3v.
Phil 2805.40.39   Pascal, Blaise. Pensées sur la religion. v.1-2. Paris, 1948[1947]
Phil 2805.40.50   Pascal, Blaise. Pensées sur la religion et sur quelques autres sujets. Monaco, 1962.
Phil 2805.40.20   Pascal, Blaise. Pensées sur la vérité de la religion chrétienne par J. Chevalier. 2. éd. Paris, 1925. 2v.
Phil 2805.31   Pascal, Blaise. Première, quatrième et treizième lettres provinciales. Paris, 1882.
Phil 2805.31.2   Pascal, Blaise. Première, quatrième et treizième lettres provinciales. Paris, 1885.
Phil 2805.31.5   Pascal, Blaise. Les première, quatrième et treizième lettres provinciales. 13. éd. Paris, 188-.
Phil 2805.32.2   Pascal, Blaise. The provincial letters. Cambridge, Eng., 1880.
Phil 2805.32.6.20   Pascal, Blaise. The provincial letters. London, 1889.
Phil 2805.32.5   Pascal, Blaise. The provincial letters. N.Y., 1828.
Phil 2805.32.4   Pascal, Blaise. The provincial letters. N.Y., 1850.
Phil 2805.32.6   Pascal, Blaise. The provincial letters. N.Y., 1856.
Phil 2805.32   Pascal, Blaise. Provincial letters. N.Y., 1859.
Phil 2805.32.7   Pascal, Blaise. The provincial letters. 1st Canadian ed. Toronto, 19- ?
Phil 2805.30.9   Pascal, Blaise. Les provinciales. Amsterdam, 1734. 3v.
Htn Phil 2805.28*   Pascal, Blaise. Les provinciales. Cologne, 1657.
Htn Phil 2805.30.16*   Pascal, Blaise. Les provinciales. Cologne, 1657.
Htn Phil 2805.29.5*   Pascal, Blaise. Les provinciales. Cologne, 1685.
Phil 2805.30.11   Pascal, Blaise. Les provinciales. Leiden? 1761. 4v.
Htn Phil 2805.32.11*   Pascal, Blaise. Les provinciales. London, 1657.
Htn Phil 2805.32.12*   Pascal, Blaise. Les provinciales. London, 1658.
Phil 2805.30.21   Pascal, Blaise. Les provinciales. Mexico, 1841.
Phil 2805.30.15   Pascal, Blaise. Les provinciales. Paris, 1815. 2v.
Phil 2805.30.7   Pascal, Blaise. Les provinciales. Paris, 1816. 2v.
NEDL Phil 2805.30.12   Pascal, Blaise. Les provinciales. Paris, 1816. 2v.
Phil 2805.30.2   Pascal, Blaise. Les provinciales. Paris, 1819. 2v.
Phil 2805.30.14   Pascal, Blaise. Les provinciales. Paris, 1819. 2v.
Phil 2805.30.13   Pascal, Blaise. Les provinciales. Paris, 1851. 2v.
Phil 2805.30.25   Pascal, Blaise. Les provinciales. Paris, 1853.
Phil 2805.30.23   Pascal, Blaise. Les provinciales. Paris, 1867.
Phil 2805.30.4   Pascal, Blaise. Les provinciales. Paris, 1885. 2v.
Phil 2805.32.28   Pascal, Blaise. Provinciales. Paris, 1964.
Phil 2805.32.27   Pascal, Blaise. Les provinciales. Paris, 1965.
Phil 2805.30.19   Pascal, Blaise. Les provinciales. Strasbourg, n.d.
Htn Phil 2805.29.6*   Pascal, Blaise. Les provinciales. 6. éd. Cologne, 1666.
Htn Phil 2805.30.18*   Pascal, Blaise. Les provinciales. 7. éd. Cologne, 1669.
Phil 2805.30.26   Pascal, Blaise. Provinciales. 9. éd. Paris, 1913.
Phil 2805.32.26   Pascal, Blaise. Les provinciales écrits des curés de Paris. Paris, 1962. 2v.
Phil 2805.30.29   Pascal, Blaise. Quatorzième lettre provinciale. Paris, 1883.
Phil 2805.40.40   Pascal, Blaise. Tankar i religiösa frågor. 2. uppl. Stockholm, 1911.
Phil 2805.30.3   Pascal, Blaise. Texte primitif des Lettres provinciales. Paris, 1867.
Phil 2805.27   Pascal, Blaise. Textes inédits. Bruges, 1962.
X Cg Phil 2805.41.15   Pascal, Blaise. Thoughts, letters, and opuscules. N.Y., 1861.
Htn Phil 2805.41*   Pascal, Blaise. Thoughts, meditations, and prayers, touching matters moral and divine. London, 1688.
Phil 2805.42.2   Pascal, Blaise. The thoughts of Blaise Pascal. London, 1888.
Phil 2805.42.9   Pascal, Blaise. The thoughts of Blaise Pascal. London, 1904.
Htn Phil 2805.42.4*   Pascal, Blaise. Thoughts on religion. London, 1704.
NEDL Phil 2805.42.7   Pascal, Blaise. Thoughts on religion. London, 1825.
Phil 2805.42.3   Pascal, Blaise. Thoughts on religion. London, 1836.
Phil 2805.42.5   Pascal, Blaise. Thoughts on religion and other curious subjects. London, 1749.
Phil 2805.40.25   Pascal, Blaise. Thoughts on religion and philosophy. London, 1894.
Htn Phil 2805.60*   Pascal, Blaise. Traité de l'equilibre. Paris, 1663.
Phil 2805.26   Pascal; ein brevier seiner Schriften. (Pascal, Blaise.) Stuttgart, 1908.
Phil 8890.39   Pascal, G. de. Philosophie morale et sociale. Paris, 1894.

Phil 2805.226.5   Pascal; genius in the light of scripture. (Cailliet, E.) Philadelphia, 1945.
Phil 2515.5.93   Pascal, Georges. La pensée d'Alain. Paris, 1946.
Phil 5850.304   Pascal, Gerald. Behaviorial change in the clinic. N.Y., 1959.
Phil 2805.227   Pascal, La Rochefoucauld, Bossuet. (Deschanel, E.A.E.M.) Paris, 1885.
Phil 2805.263A   Pascal, l'homme et l'oeuvre. (Mesnard, Jean.) Paris, 1951.
Phil 2805.230   Pascal, Molière, Musset; essais de critique et de psychologie. (Michaut, Gustave.) Paris, 1942.
Phil 2805.182   Pascal, mondain et amoureux. (Chamaillard, E.) Paris, 1923.
Phil 2805.229.5   Pascal; sa vie, son oeuvre, avec un exposé de sa philosophie. 2e éd. (Cresson, André.) Paris, 1942.
Phil 2805.229.8   Pascal; sa vie, son oeuvre, avec un exposé de sa philosophie. 5. éd. (Cresson, André.) Paris, 1962.
Phil 2805.84   Pascal, sa vie et son caractère. (Maynard, M.U.) Paris, 1850. 2v.
Phil 2805.409   Pascal, sa ville et son temps. (Clermont-Ferrand. Musée du Ranquet.) Clermont-Ferrand, 1962.
Phil 2805.413A   Pascal; testes du tricentenaire. Paris, 1963.
Phil 2805.245   Pascal. (Andreas, Peter.) Strasbourg, 1946.
Phil 2805.103   Pascal. (Archambault, P.) Paris, n.d.
Phil 2805.219   Pascal. (Bishop, M.) N.Y., 1930.
Phil 2805.203   Pascal. (Bornhausen, K.) Basel, 1920.
Phil 2805.92.7   Pascal. (Boutroux, E.) Manchester, 1902.
Phil 2805.92   Pascal. (Boutroux, E.) Paris, 1900.
Phil 2805.419   Pascal. (Brooms, Jack Howard.) N.Y., 1966.
Phil 2805.192.10A   Pascal. (Brunschvicg, L.) Paris, 1932.
Phil 2805.226.6   Pascal. (Cailliet, E.) N.Y., 1961.
Phil 2805.395   Pascal. (Chaigne, Louis.) Paris, 1962.
Phil 2805.177.5A   Pascal. (Chevalier, J.) N.Y., 1930.
NEDL Phil 2805.177   Pascal. (Chevalier, J.) Paris, 1922.
Phil 2805.106   Pascal. (Hatzfeld, A.) Paris, 1901.
Phil 2805.267   Pascal. (Holden, P.G.) London, 1951.
Phil 2805.259   Pascal. (Lefebvre, H.) Paris, 1949. 2v.
Phil 2805.237   Pascal. (Merezhkovskii, Dimitrii S.) Paris, 1941.
Phil 2805.421   Pascal. (Mesnard, Jean.) Bruges, 1965.
Phil 2805.263.2   Pascal. (Mesnard, Jean.) London, 1952.
Phil 2805.421.1   Pascal. (Mesnard, Jean.) University, 1969.
Phil 2805.417   Pascal. (Moscato, Alberto.) Milano, 1963.
Phil 2805.45   Pascal. (Pascal, Blaise.) Paris, 1946.
Phil 2805.46   Pascal. (Pascal, Blaise.) Paris, 1947.
Phil 2805.87   Pascal. (Souriau, M.) Paris, 1898.
Phil 2805.98   Pascal. (St. Cyres, S.H.N.) London, 1909.
Phil 2805.98.10   Pascal. (St. Cyres, S.H.N.) N.Y., 1910.
Phil 2805.284.5   Pascal. (Steinmann, Jean.) London, 1965.
Phil 2805.284   Pascal. (Steinmann, Jean.) Paris, 1954.
Phil 2805.284.2   Pascal. (Steinmann, Jean.) Paris, 1962.
Phil 2805.390   Pascal. (Terzi, Carlo.) Bergamo, 1960.
Phil 2805.86.5   Pascal. (Tulloch, J.) Edinburgh, 1878.
Phil 2805.86   Pascal. (Tulloch, J.) Edinburgh, 1878.
Phil 2805.251   Pascal. (Tytgat, J.) Gand, 1948.
Phil 2805.305   Pascal. (Vansina, Dirk.) Bussum, 1954.
Phil 2805.391   Pascal. (Vloemans, A.) Den Haag, 1962.
Phil 2805.412   Pascal. Barcelona, 1964.
Phil 2805.197   Pascal: saggio d'interpretazione storica. (Gentile, F.) Bari, 1927.
Phil 2805.202.1   Pascal: the man and the message. (Soltau, R.H.) Westport, 1970.
Phil 2805.330   Pascal. 1. éd. (LeRoy, Georges.) Paris, 1957.
Phil 2805.92.3   Pascal. 3. éd. (Boutroux, E.) Paris, 1903.
Phil 2805.400   Pascal. 3. éd. (Sciacca, M.F.) Milan, 1962.
Phil 2805.92.9   Pascal. 5. éd. (Boutroux, E.) Paris, 1912.
Phil 2805.239   Pascal and Kierkegaard. (Patrick, D.G.M.) London, 1947. 2v.
Phil 2805.280   Pascal and the mystical tradition. (Fletcher, F.T.H.) Oxford, 1954.
Phil 2805.179   Pascal and the Port Royalists. (Clark, William.) Edinburgh, 1902.
Phil 2805.460   Pascal and theology. (Miel, Jan.) Baltimore, 1969.
Phil 2805.26.7   Pascal de l'esprit géométrique. (Pascal, Blaise.) Paris, 1871.
Phil 2805.393   Pascal e Nietzsche. Padova, 1962.
Phil 2805.291   Pascal écrivain. (Demorest, Jean.) Paris, 1937.
Phil 2805.201   Pascal en Auvergne. (Nolhac, P. de.) Saint-Felicien-en-Vivarais, 1925.
Phil 2805.175   Pascal en Poitou et les Poitevins. (Roux, Marie.) Paris, 1919.
Phil 2805.212   Pascal et la Bible. Thèse. (Lhermet, J.) Paris, 1931?
Phil 2805.440   Pascal et la liturgie. (Sellier, Philippe.) Paris, 1966.
Phil 2805.320   Pascal et la souffrance. (Jerphagnon, L.) Paris, 1956.
Phil 2805.274   Pascal et le libertin. (Rennes, J.) Paris, 1950.
Phil 2805.191   Pascal et le problème de la croyance. (Malvy, A.) Paris, 1923.
Phil 2805.495   Pascal et le problème de la destinée. (Larraillet, Paul.) Paris, 1970.
Phil 2805.270   Pascal et Leibniz. (Guitton, Jean.) Paris, 1951.
Phil 2805.107   Pascal et les Pascalins d'après des documents contemporains. (Griselle, E.) Fribourg, 1908.
Phil 2805.325   Pascal et les provinciales. (Paris. Musée National des Granges de Port-Royal.) Paris, 1956.
Phil 2805.30.30   Pascal et les provinciales. (Pascal, Blaise.) Paris, 1956.
Phil 2805.422   Pascal et les Roannez. (Mesnard, Jean.) Bruges, 1965. 2v.
Phil 2805.194   Pascal et l'expérience du Puy-de-Dome. Thèse. (Arsovitch, R.) Montpellier, 1925.
Phil 2805.410   Pascal et l'homme moderne. (Ronnet, G.) Paris, 1963.
Phil 2805.257   Pascal et notre coeur. 6. éd. (Daniel-Rops, Henry.) Strasbourg, 1949.
Phil 2805.386F   Pascal et Port Royal. Paris, 1962.
Phil 2805.480   Pascal et Saint Augustin. (Sellier, Philippe.) Paris, 1970.
Phil 2805.111.5   Pascal et Saint Ignace. (Jovy, Ernest.) Paris, 1923.
Phil 2805.315   Pascal et ses précurseurs. (Julien Eymard d'Angers.) Paris, 1954.
Phil 2805.95   Pascal et son temps. (Strowski, F.) Paris, 1907-22. 3v.
Phil 2805.455   Pascal et Teilhard, témoins de Jésus-Christ. (Pontet, Maurice.) Paris, 1968.
Phil 2805.90   Pascal l'homme, l'oeuvre, l'influence. (Giraud, V.) Fribourg, 1898.
Phil 2805.90.3   Pascal l'homme, l'oeuvre, l'influence. (Giraud, V.) Paris, 1905.
Phil 2805.190   Pascal mathématicien et physicien. (Picard, Émile.) Paris, 1923.

Phil 2805.111.10   Pascal n'a pa inventé le haquet, démonstration lexicographique. (Jovy, Ernest.) Paris, 1923.
Phil 2805.272   Pascal par lui-même. (Pascal, Blaise.) Paris, 1952.
Phil 2805.85   Pascal physicien et philosophe. (Nourrisson, J.F.) Paris, 1885.
Phil 2805.85.5   Pascal physicien et philosophe. Défense de Pascal. (Nourrisson, J.F.) Paris, 1888.
Phil 2805.40.55   Pascal présent, 1662-1962. Clermont, 1962.
Phil 2805.104   Pascal sa vie religieuse. (Petitot, H.) Paris, 1911.
Phil 2805.89   Pascal sein Leben und seine Kämpfe. (Dreydorff, J.G.) Leipzig, 1870.
Phil 2805.213   Pascal traducteur de la Bible. Thèse. (Antoniadis, S.) Leyde, 1930.
Phil 2805.40.45   Pascal's apology for religion. (Pascal, Blaise.) Cambridge, Eng., 1942.
Phil 2805.200   Pascal's Leben und der Geist seiner Schriften. (Reuchlin, H.) Stuttgart, 1840.
Phil 2805.42.25   Pascal's Pensées. (Pascal, Blaise.) Mt. Vernon, 1946?
Phil 2805.268   Pascal's unfinished Apology. (Hubert, M.L., Sister.) New Haven, 1952.
Phil 6325.16   Paschal, Franklin C. The Witmer cylinder test. Hershey, Pa., 1918.
Phil 346.22   Pasck, Alan. Experience and the analytic. Chicago, 1958.
Phil 3497.22   Pascol, Georges. La pensée de Kant. 2. éd. Paris, 1957.
Phil 8890.32   Pascot, Giovanni. Scienze ausiliarie della morale. Udine, 1903.
Phil 4366.79.30   Pascual Ferrández, Antonio. Ensayos. Barcelona, 1961. 20v.
Phil 4803.281.80   Pasenkiewicz, Kazimierz. Pierwsze systemy semantyki Leona Chwistka. Krakow, 1961.
Htn   Phil 4200.3.30*   Pasi, Bartholomeo. Tariffa. Vinetia, 1540.
Phil 8416.44   Pasi, Isak. Esteticheski studii. Sofiia, 1970.
Phil 3835.9   Pasig, Walter. Spinozas Rationalismus und Erkenntnislehre im Lichte. Leipzig, 1892.
VPhil 5225.11   Pasłuszha, Yózet. Historia psychologii. Lublin, 1971.
Phil 2605.1.81   Pasmanik, D. Alfred Fouillées psychischen Monismus. Bern, 1899.
Phil 4112.80   Pasquale Galluppi; studio critico. (Lastrucci, V.) Firenze, 1890.
Htn   Phil 4112.83*   Pasquale Galluppi giacobino. (Arnone, N.) Napoli, 1912.
Htn   Phil 9560.24*   Pasquali, C. Virtutes et vitia. Parisiis, 1615.
Htn   Phil 9355.10*   Pasquier, N. Le gentilhomme. Paris, 1611. 3 pam.
Phil 5066.140   Pasquinelli, Alberto. Introduzione alla logica simbolica. Torino, 1957.
Phil 5520.440   Pasquinelli, Alberto. Linguaggio, scienza e filosofia. 2. ed. Bologna, 1964.
Phil 346.28   Pasquinelli, Alberto. Nuevi principi di epistemología. Milano, 1964.
Phil 8707.15   Passages from the scientist's Bible. (Rodger, James George.) Washington, 1931.
Phil 6685.1   Passavant, J.K. Untersungen und der Lebensmagnetismus. Frankfurt, 1821.
Phil 8598.23   Passing and permanent in religion. (Savage, M.J.) N.Y., 1901.
Phil 197.25.7   The passing of evolution. (Williams, C.L.) Berkeley, 1912.
Phil 5825.5   The passing of the phantoms. (Patten, Charles J.) London, 1924.
Phil 2050.263   Passion and value in Hume's Treatise. (Ardal, Páll S.) Edinburgh, 1966.
Phil 720.64   Passion de la vérité. (Borne, Étienne.) Paris, 1962.
Phil 8591.30   The passion for life. (Lewis, John.) New Haven, 1928.
Phil 8598.51   The passion for reality. (Scudder, D.) N.Y., 1910.
Phil 974.4.15   The passionate pilgrim. (Williams, Gertrude M.) London, 1932.
Phil 974.4.13   The passionate pilgrim. (Williams, Gertrude M.) N.Y., 1931.
Htn   Phil 2520.60*   Passiones animae. (Descartes, René.) Amstelodami, 1650.
Htn   Phil 2520.60.1*   Passiones animae. (Descartes, René.) Amstelodami, 1650.
Htn   Phil 2520.60.5*   Passiones animae. (Descartes, René.) Amstelodami, 1664.
Phil 5400.89   Le passioni nella filosofia e nell'arte. (Marucci, A.) Torino, 1932.
Phil 5400.7   Les passions. (Frédault, F.) Paris, n.d.
Phil 2520.61.15   Les passions de l'âme. (Descartes, René.) Paris, 1726.
Phil 2520.61.16   Les passions de l'âme. (Descartes, René.) Paris, 1955.
Htn   Phil 2520.61.12*   Les passions de l'âme. (Descartes, René.) Rouen, 1651.
Phil 5400.71   Les passions humaines. (Joussain, A.) Paris, 1928.
Phil 2225.8   The passions of life. (Paterson, William R.) London, 1938.
Phil 5400.86.5   The passions of the human soul. (Fourier, C.) London, 1851. 2v.
Htn   Phil 5400.10.2*   The passions of the minde in generall. (Wright, Thomas.) London, 1604.
Htn   Phil 5400.10*   The passions of the minde in generall. (Wright, Thomas.) London, 1604.
Htn   Phil 5400.10.5*   The passions of the minde in generall. (Wright, Thomas.) London, 1630.
Phil 180.52   Passivity and rationalization. (Fialko, N.M.) N.Y., 1935.
Phil 180.52.5   Passivnost'. (Fialko, N.M.) Paris, 1927.
Phil 3915.152   Passkönig, Oswald. Die Psychologie Wilhelm Wundts. Leipzig, 1912.
Phil 1925.84   Passmore, J.A. Ralph Cudworth. Cambridge, Eng., 1951.
Phil 2050.227.1   Passmore, John A. Hume's intentions. N.Y., 1968.
Phil 1715.6.5   Passmore, John Arthur. A hundred years of philosophy. London, 1962.
Phil 1715.6.7   Passmore, John Arthur. A hundred years of philosophy. 2nd ed. London, 1966.
Phil 585.365   Passmore, John Arthur. The perfectibility of man. London, 1970.
Phil 190.95   Passmore, John Arthur. Philosophical reasoning. London, 1961.
Phil 5066.102   Past, present and future. (Prior, Arthur Norman.) Oxford, 1967.
Phil 8894.29   Past and future of ethics. (Tuker, M.A.R.) London, 1938.
Phil 978.18.3   The past revealed. (Goffield, E.C.) Boston, 1905.
Phil 3210.84   Pastor, Willy. Im GeisteFechners. Leipzig, 1901.
Phil 6964.2   Pastoral psychiatry and mental health. (Oliver, John R.) N.Y., 1932.
Phil 5627.266.15   Pastoralpsychologische Studien. (Griesl, Gottfried.) Innsbruck, 1966.
Phil 8400.26   Pastore, A. Introduzione alla metafisica della poesia. Padova, 1957. 2 pam.
Phil 4200.4.30   Pastore, A. Il pensiero puro. Milano, 1913.
Phil 5170.3   Pastore, A. Sillogismo e proporzione. Milano, 1910.
Phil 4200.4.35   Pastore, A. Il solipsismo. Torino, 1924.
Phil 5055.20   Pastore, Annibale. Logica formale...modelli meccanici. Torino, 1906.
Phil 5055.20.5   Pastore, Annibale. Logicalia. Padova, 1957.

Phil 270.24   Pastore, Annibale. Il problema della causalità con particolare reguardo alla teoria del metodo sperimentale. Torino, 1921. 2v.
Phil 5643.174   Pastore, Nicholas. Selective history of theories of visual perception: 1650-1950. N.Y., 1971.
Phil 5590.34   Pastori, Giuseppina. Il substrato biologico della personalità. Brescia, 1916.
Phil 9070.38   Pastor's psychology. (Hopkinson, A.W.) London, 1944.
Phil 5255.58   Pastuszka, J. Charakter cztowieka. Lublin, 1959.
Phil 5255.58.5   Pastuszka, J. Charakter cztowieka. Lublin, 1962.
Phil 665.90   Pastuszka, J. Dusza ludzka, jej istnienie i natura. Lublin, 1947.
Phil 2266.82   Paszkowski, W. Adam Smith als Moralphilosoph. Halle, 1890.
Phil 5190.60   Patel, Peter. Logische und methodologische Probleme der wissenschaftlichen Erklärung. München, 1965.
Htn   Phil 8890.24*   Pater, W. Conclusion: an essay. N.Y., 1898.
NEDL   Phil 1158.15.5   Pater, Walter. Marius the Epicurean. London, 1891.
Phil 1158.15.3   Pater, Walter. Marius the Epicurean. London, 1891.
Phil 1158.15.5   Pater, Walter. Marius the Epicurean. London, 1893.
Phil 1158.15.7   Pater, Walter. Marius the Epicurean. London, 1895.
Phil 1158.15.10   Pater, Walter. Marius the Epicurean. London, 1897.
Phil 1158.15.14A   Pater, Walter. Marius the Epicurean. London, 1910. 2v.
Phil 1158.15.15A   Pater, Walter. Marius the Epicurean. N.Y., 1930.
Phil 1158.15.2   Pater, Walter. Marius the Epicurean. 2. ed. London, 1885. 2v.
Phil 1158.15.12   Pater, Walter. Marius the Epicurean. 4th ed. London, 1904. 2v.
Phil 1158.15.13   Pater, Walter. Marius the Epicurean. 4th ed. London, 1907. 2v.
Phil 8691.4   Pater mundi. 1st series. (Burr, E.F.) Boston, 1870.
Phil 8691.4.2   Pater mundi. 2nd series. (Burr, E.F.) Boston, 1873.
Phil 6980.575.5   Paterson, A.S. Electrical and drug treatment in psychiatry. Amsterdam, 1963.
Phil 4065.184   Paterson, Antoinette Mann. The infinite worlds of Giordano Bruno. Springfield, 1970.
Phil 5255.38   Paterson, D.G. Physique and intellect. N.Y., 1930.
Phil 7060.21   Paterson, Robert. On illusions of the senses. Photoreproduction. Edinburgh, 1867.
Phil 2225.8   Paterson, William R. The passions of life. London, 1938.
Phil 9245.130   The path of darkness. (Harper, Ralph.) Cleveland, 1968.
Phil 525.77   The path of the eternal wisdom. 2d ed. (Cordelier, John.) London, 1912.
Phil 970.5   Pamphlet box. The path series.
Phil 3850.27.103   The path to reconstruction...Albert Schweitzer's philosophy of civilization. (Russell, L.M.) London, 1941.
Phil 3850.27.103.5   The path to reconstruction. (Russell, L.M.) London, 1943.
Phil 1750.733   Patha, Frederick. Existentialist thinkers and thought. N.Y., 1962.
Phil 5258.26   Pathetism. (Sunderland, La Ray.) Boston, 1847.
Phil 6950.3   Pathological, practical researches, diseases...brain. (Abercrombie, J.) Philadelphia, 1831.
Phil 5520.433   Pathological and normal language. (Laffal, Julius.) N.Y., 1965.
Phil 5627.11   Pathological aspects of religions. (Moses, J.) Worcester, 1906.
Phil 6642.5   Pathologie de la mémoire. 1. éd. (Barbizet, Jacques.) Paris, 1970.
Phil 6313.12   Pathologie de l'imagination et de l'émotivité. (Dupré, E.) Paris, 1925.
Phil 6360.6   Eine Pathologie der psychischen Entwicklung. (Lempp, Reinhart.) Bern, 1967.
Phil 6400.23   Pathologie du langage. (Hekaen, Henry.) Paris, 1965.
Phil 181.160   Pathologie en therapie der filosofie. (Gans, Abraham.) Wassenaar, 1968.
Phil 6321.4   Pathologie und Therapie de Neurasthenie und Hysterie. (Loewenfeld, L.) Wiesbaden, 1894.
Phil 6956.2   Die Pathologie und Therapie der psychischen Krankheiten. (Griesinger, W.) Braunschweig, 1871.
Htn   Phil 6956.2.2*   Die Pathologie und Therapie der psychischen Krankheiten. (Griesinger, W.) Stuttgart, 1867.
Phil 6313.1.5   Die pathologische Lüge und die psychisch abnormen Schwindler. (Delbrück, A.) Stuttgart, 1891.
Phil 6968.20   The pathology and therapeutics of mental diseases. (Schroeder van der Kolk, J.L.K.) London, 1870.
Phil 6962.2.6   The pathology of mind. (Maudsley, H.) London, 1895.
Phil 6962.2.9A   The pathology of mind. (Maudsley, H.) N.Y., 1880.
Phil 186.34   Das Pathos der Resonanz. (Lyon, Otto.) Leipzig, 1900.
Phil 8592.63   Paths of life, prepace to a world religion. (Morris, Charles W.) N.Y., 1942.
Phil 6132.28   Paths to power. (Wilson, Floyd B.) N.Y., 1901.
Phil 182.35.2   The pathway to reality. (Haldane, Richard B.) London, 1905.
Phil 182.35.3   The pathway to reality. (Haldane, Richard B.) London, 1926.
Phil 8581.53.5   Pathways to certainty. (Brown, William A.) N.Y., 1930.
Phil 7069.16.60   Patience Worth; a psychic mystery. (Worth, Patience.) N.Y., 1916.
Phil 6961.20   Patienthood in the mental hospital. (Levinson, Daniel Jacob.) Boston, 1964.
Phil 585.165   Patka, Frederick. Value and existence. N.Y., 1964.
Phil 6968.15   La patologia mentale im rapporto. (Sailo, Francesco.) Milano, 1908.
Phil 6335.20   Patologiia myshleniia. (Zeigarnik, B.V.) Moskva, 1962.
Phil 8840.2   Paton, H.J. Fashion and philosophy. Oxford, 1937.
Phil 8890.42   Paton, H.J. The good will. London, 1927.
Phil 2225.12   Paton, H.J. In defence of reason. London, 1951.
Phil 8595.40   Paton, H.J. The modern predicament. London, 1955.
Phil 3497.19.5   Paton, Herbert J. The categorical imperative. London, 1946.
Phil 3497.19.10   Paton, Herbert J. Kant on friendship. London, 1956.
Phil 3497.19   Paton, Herbert J. Kant's metaphysic of experience. London, 1936. 2v.
Phil 5255.46   Paton, S. Human behavior. N.Y., 1921.
X Cg   Phil 6965.5   Paton, Stewart. Psychiatry. Philadelphia, 1905.
Phil 6125.14   Paton, Stewart. Signs of sanity and the principles of mental hygiene. N.Y., 1922.
Phil 9045.9   Patria! Livro da Mocidade. (Varela, Alfredo.) Rio de Janeiro, 1900.
Htn   Phil 2005.5.30*   Patriarcha. (Filmer, Robert.) London, 1680.
Phil 2805.239   Patrick, D.G.M. Pascal and Kierkegaard. London, 1947. 2v.
Phil 190.56   Patrick, G.T.W. Introduction to philosophy. Boston, 1924.
Phil 190.56.5   Patrick, G.T.W. Introduction to philosophy. London, 1935.
Phil 6125.9.3   Patrick, G.T.W. The psychology of relaxation. Boston, 1916.

Phil 6125.9 Patrick, G.T.W. The psychology of relaxation. Boston, 1916.
Phil 5255.41 Patrick, G.T.W. What is the mind? N.Y., 1929.
Phil 1850.153 Patrick, J.M. Francis Bacon. London, 1961.
Phil 1190.9 Patrick, Mary M. The Greek sceptics. N.Y., 1929.
Phil 1828.6.20 Patrick Romanelli e l'odierno naturalismo statunitense. 1. ed. (Crescenzo, Giovanni de.) Firenze, 1966.
Phil 1512.7 Patristische und scholastische Philosophie. (Hessen, John.) Breslau, 1922.
Phil 5330.21.5 Patriži, M.L. La graphique psychométrique de l'attention. Turin, 1895.
Phil 5625.69 Patrizi, M.L. I riflessi vascolari nelle membra e nel cervello dell'uomo. Reggio-Emilia, 1897.
Phil 5330.21 Patrizi, M.L. Il tempo di reazione semplice. Reggio-Emilia, 1897.
Phil 4200.2.30 Patrizzi, F. L'amorosa filosofia di F. Patrizzi. Firenze, 1963.
Htn Phil 4200.2.10* Patrizzi, F. Nova de universis philosophia. Venetiis, 1593.
Phil 4200.2.79 Pamphlet box. Patrizzi, F.
Phil 9045.12 Patrjotyzm i objawy Jego u niektórych narodów. (Chojeckiego, E.) Paryz, 1870.
Phil 5465.160 Patron Miranda, Joaquin R. La tecnica divina: el movimiento. Campeche, 1945.
Phil 1520.4 Patru, G.A. De la philosophie du moyen âge. Paris, 1848.
Phil 1850.122 Patru, G.A. Esprit et méthode de Bacon en philosophie. Paris, 1854.
Phil 2880.8.180 Patte, Daniel. L'athéisme d'un chrétien; ou Un chrétien à l'écoute de Sartre. Paris, 1965.
Phil 5825.5 Patten, Charles J. The passing of the phantoms. London, 1924.
Phil 8890.45 Patten, Simon N. Economic causes of moral progress. Philadelphia, 1892.
Htn Phil 8595.16.5* Patten, William. Christianity the true theology. Warren, 1795.
Phil 9245.51 Patter, Charles F. Technique of happiness. N.Y., 1935.
Phil 5590.380 Pattern and growth in personality. (Allport, G.W.) N.Y., 1961.
Phil 5585.5 Pattern recognition. N.Y. 1,1968+ 3v.
Phil 2150.16.35 Patterns of a new philosophy. (Mayer, Frederick.) Washington, 1955.
Phil 5590.422.5 Patterns of adjustment and human effectiveness. (Lazarus, Richard.) N.Y., 1968.
Phil 9240.32 Patterns of good and evil. (Gotshalk, D.W.) Urbana, 1963.
Phil 960.272.5 Patterns of Indian thought. (Chethimattam, John B.) Maryknoll, N.Y., 1971.
Phil 8592.75 The patterns of our religious faiths. (McMurrin, S.M.) Salt Lake City, 1954.
Phil 5585.238 Patterns of redundancy. (Staniland, Alan Charles.) Cambridge, Eng., 1966.
Phil 310.636 Patterns of Soviet thought. (DeGeorge, Richard T.) Ann Arbor, 1966.
Phil 6125.17 Patterson, C.B. Dominion and power. 2d ed. N.Y., 1902.
Phil 6125.17.5 Patterson, C.B. The will to be well. 5th ed. N.Y., 1906.
Phil 8890.5.50 Patterson, C.H. Moral standards. 2. ed. N.Y., 1957.
Phil 5125.11 Patterson, C.H. Problems in logic. N.Y., 1926.
Phil 6980.575 Patterson, Charles H. Counseling and psychotherapy. N.Y., 1959.
Phil 5055.17.5 Patterson, Charles H. Principles of correct thinking. Minneapolis, 1936.
Phil 5055.17 Patterson, Charles H. Problems in logic. N.Y., 1926.
Phil 8890.5 Patterson, J.S. Conflict in nature and life. N.Y., 1883.
Phil 8595.62 Patterson, Robert Leet. A philosophy of religion. Durham, 1970.
Phil 8673.6.2 Pattison, A. The idea of God. 2. ed. N.Y., 1920.
Phil 5055.38 Patzig, Günther. Sprache und Logik. Göttingen, 1970.
Phil 1815.5 Paul, L.A. The English philosophers. London, 1953.
Phil 8595.38 Paul, Leslie A. The meaning of human existence. London, 1949.
Phil 6325.21 Paul, Louis. Psychoanalytic clinical interpretation. N.Y., 1963.
Phil 3497.16 Paul, Ludwig. Kant's Lehre vom Idealen Christus. Kiel, 1869.
Phil 960.149.5 Paul, N.C. A treatise on the Yoga philosophy. 3d ed. Bombay, 1888.
Phil 7069.30.4 Paul in Athens (the scripts of Cleophas). (Cummins, G.D.) London, 1930.
Phil 3450.42 Paul Leopold Hoffner als Philosophie. (Ball, Thomas.) Mainz? 194-?
Phil 3665.1.85 Paul Natorp som repraesentant for den kritiske idealisme. (Jørgensen, J.F.) København, 1918.
Phil 3790.10.91 Paul Rée's Lehre vom Gewissen. Thesis. (Bertele, H.) München, 1927.
Phil 2855.11.80 Paul Ricoeur. (Philibert, Michel André Jean.) Paris, 1971.
Phil 2648.94.3 Paul Thiry d'Holbach et la philosophie scientifique au XVIIIe siécle. (Naville, Pierre.) Paris, 1967.
Phil 2648.94 Paul Thiry d'Holbach et la philosophie scientifique au XVIIIe siécle. 2. éd. (Naville, Pierre.) Paris, 1943.
Phil 3890.9.90 Paul Vital Ignoz Troxlers Leben und Philosophie. Diss. (Gamper, J.) Bern, 1907.
Phil 190.48 Pauler, A. von. Grundlagen der Philosophie. Berlin, 1925.
Phil 5055.21.5 Pauler, Akás. Logik. Berlin, 1929.
Phil 8890.44 Pauler, Akós. Az ethikai megismerés természete. Budapest, 1907.
Phil 5080.4 Pauler, Akos. A fogalom problémája a teozta logikaban. Budapest, 1915.
Htn Phil 6685.10.5* Paulet, J.J. L'antimagnétisme, ou origine. Loudres, 1784.
Htn Phil 6685.10* Paulet, J.J. Mesmer justifié. Constance, 1784.
Phil 575.9 Paulham, F. Les caractères. Paris, 1902.
Phil 5255.2 Paulhan, F. L'activité mentale. Paris, 1889.
Phil 5255.2.2 Paulhan, F. L'activité mentale. 2. éd. Paris, 1913.
Phil 5255.2.12 Paulhan, F. Analystes et esprits synthétiques. Paris, 1902.
Phil 5520.60 Paulhan, F. La double fonction du langage. Paris, 1929.
Phil 5255.2.6 Paulhan, F. Esprits logiques et esprits faux. Paris, 1914.
Phil 5545.36 Paulhan, F. La fonction de la mémoire. Paris, 1904.
Phil 5055.8 Paulhan, F. La logique de la contradiction. Paris, 1911.
Phil 9558.9 Paulhan, F. Les mensonges du caractère. Paris, 1905.
Phil 525.17 Paulhan, F. Le nouveau mysticisme. Paris, 1891.
Phil 6125.7.5 Paulhan, F. La physiologie de l'esprit. 5. éd. Paris, 1910.
Phil 5360.6 Paulhan, F. Les puissances de l'abstraction. Paris, 1928.
Phil 5325.21 Paulhan, Fr. Le mensonge du monde. Paris, 1921.
Phil 5400.45.15 Paulhan, Frédéric. Laws of feeling. London, 1930.
Phil 9255.5 Paulhan, Frederic. La morale de l'ironie. 2. éd. Paris, 1914.

Phil 5400.45.9 Paulhan, Frédéric. Les phénomènes affectifs et les lois de leur apparition. 3d éd. Paris, 1912.
Phil 5400.45 Paulhan, Frédéric. Les transformations sociales des sentiments. Paris, 1920.
Phil 5590.85 Pauli, R. Der Pauli-Test. 2. Aufl. München, 1951.
Phil 5255.31 Pauli, R. Psychologisches Praktikum. Jena, 1920.
Phil 5255.31.10 Pauli, R. Über psychische Gesetzmässigkeit. Jena, 1920.
Phil 5255.3.5 Pauli, Richard. Psychologisches Praktikum. 6. Aufl. Stuttgart, 1957.
Phil 5590.85 Der Pauli-Test. 2. Aufl. (Pauli, R.) München, 1951.
Phil 190.66 Paullier, W. Ciencia, filosofia y laicismo. Buenos Aires, 1937. 2v.
Phil 5627.231.2 Pauls, Theodor. Pietismus. 2. Aufl. Frankfurt, 1931.
Phil 190.3.2 Paulsen, F. Einleitung in die Philosophie. Berlin, 1892.
Phil 190.3.3 Paulsen, F. Einleitung in die Philosophie. 3e Aufl. Berlin, 1895.
Phil 190.3.8.5 Paulsen, F. Inleiding tot de wijsbegeerte. Amsterdam, 1910.
Phil 190.3.7 Paulsen, F. Introduction to philosophy. 2. American ed. N.Y., 1928.
Phil 190.3.7.5 Paulsen, F. Introduction to philosophy. 2. American ed. N.Y., 1930.
Phil 190.3.8 Paulsen, F. Introduzione alla filosofia. Milano, 1911.
Phil 190.3.12 Paulsen, F. De metaphysiska problemen. Stockholm, 1904.
Phil 190.3.9 Paulsen, F. Philosophia militans. 3e und 4e Aufl. Berlin, 1908.
Phil 9430.17 Paulsen, F. Schopenhauer und Naturgeschichte des Pessimismus. Berlin, 1900.
Phil 8890.6 Paulsen, F. Symbolae ad systemata philosophiae moralis. Berolini, 1871.
Phil 8890.6.5 Paulsen, F. System der Ethik. Berlin, 1889.
Phil 8890.6.6 Paulsen, F. System der Ethik. Berlin, 1896-97. 2v.
Phil 8890.6.7 Paulsen, F. System der Ethik. Stuttgart, 1903. 2v.
Phil 8890.6.5.8 Paulsen, F. System der Ethik. 2. Aufl. Berlin, 1891.
Phil 8890.6.5.9 Paulsen, F. System der Ethik. 3. Aufl. Berlin, 1894. 2v.
Phil 8890.6.8 Paulsen, F. System der Ethik. 11. und 12. Aufl. Stuttgart, 1921. 2v.
Phil 8890.6.11 Paulsen, F. System of ethics. N.Y., 1899.
Phil 8890.6.9 Paulsen, F. System of ethics. N.Y., 1899.
Phil 8890.6.15 Paulsen, F. Zur Ethik und Politik. Berlin, 19- . 2v.
Phil 8890.6.17 Paulsen, F. Zur Ethik und Politik. Berlin, 19- ? 2v.
Phil 8890.6.12 Paulsen, F. Zur Ethik und Politik. v.1-2. Berlin, n.d.
Phil 3745.5.85 Paulsen, Friedrich. Aus meinen Leben. Jena, 1909.
Phil 3497.3.4.5 Paulsen, Friedrich. Immanuel Kant; his life and doctrine. N.Y., 1963.
Phil 3497.3A Paulsen, Friedrich. Immanuel Kant. Stuttgart, 1898.
Phil 3497.3.5 Paulsen, Friedrich. Immanuel Kant. 4. Aufl. Stuttgart, 1904.
Phil 3497.3.6 Paulsen, Friedrich. Immanuel Kant. 6. Aufl. Stuttgart, 1920.
Phil 3497.3.7 Paulsen, Friedrich. Kant. Milano, 1914.
Phil 3497.3.9 Paulsen, Friedrich. Kant der Philosophie des Protestantismus. Berlin, 1899.
Phil 3497.3.19 Paulsen, Friedrich. Kants Verhaltnis zur Metaphysik. Berlin, 1900.
Phil 3497.3.15 Paulsen, Friedrich. Versuch...Kantischen Erkenntnisstheorie. Leipzig, 1875.
Phil 3497.3.23 Paulsen, Friedrich. Was uns Kant sein kann? Leipzig, 1881.
Phil 5635.8 Paulsen, J. Das Problem der Empfindung. Giessen, 1907.
Phil 3415.90 Paulus, H. Die Gottesbeweise Eduard von Hartmanns. Würzburg, 1907.
Htn Phil 3801.669* Paulus, H.E.G. Die endlich offenbar Gewordene positive Philosophie der Offenbarung. Darmstadt, 1843.
Phil 3801.669.2 Paulus, H.E.G. Die endlich offenbar Gewordene positive Philosophie der Offenbarung. Darmstadt, 1843.
Htn Phil 3801.749.10* Paulus, H.E.G. Entdeckungen über des Entdeckungen unserer neuesten Philosophen. Bremen, 1835.
Htn Phil 3801.669.10* Paulus, H.E.G. Vorläufige Appellation...Contra das Philosophie...Schelling. Darmstadt, 1843.
Phil 5255.72 Paulus, Jean. Les fondements théoriques et méthodologiques de la psychologie. Bruxelles, 1965.
Phil 3450.10.80 Paulus van Hermert, als godgeleerde en als wijsgeer. Proefschrift. (Groenewegen, H.J.) Amsterdam, 1889.
Phil 5055.36 Paulus Venetus. Logica. Hildesheim, 1970.
Phil 9075.26 Pauly, Karl. Zur Theorie des Gewissens. Inaug. Diss. Greifswald, 1913.
Phil 3475.3.155 Paumen, Jean. Raison et existence chez Karl Jaspers. Bruxelles, 1958.
Phil 2725.25.90 Paumen, Jean. Le spiritualisme existentiel de René LeSenne. Paris, 1949.
Phil 5401.1 La paura. (Mosso, A.) Milano, 1884.
Phil 8595.58 Paus, Ansgar. Religiöser Erkenntnisgrund. Leiden, 1966.
Phil 5643.50 Pauwels, Friedrich. Beiträge zur Lehre vom optischen Zeitsinn. Inaug. Diss. Frieburg, 1911?
Phil 4757.2.80 Pauwels, L. Monsieur Gurdjieff. Paris, 1954.
Phil 2750.11.225 Pavan, Antonio. La formazione del pensiero di J. Maritain. Padova, 1967.
Phil 8595.41 Pavelkin, P.A. Chto takoe religiia; besedy. Moskva, 1956.
Phil 400.68 Pavese, R. L'idea e il mondo. Torino, 1925.
Phil 5374.36 Pavese, R. Il meccanismo della coscienza. Milano, 1922.
Phil 5055.27.3 Pavese, Roberto. Commento alla logica sintetica. Padova, 1963.
Phil 5055.27 Pavese, Roberto. Compendio di logica sintetica. Padova, 1954.
Phil 296.15 Pavese, Roberto. Fisica e metafisica. Padova, 1964[1965]
Phil 190.112 Pavese, Roberto. Metafisica e pensiero. Padova, 1967.
Phil 440.10 Pavidovich, Vsevolod E. Grani svobody. Moskva, 1969.
Phil 5625.75.3 Pavlov, Ivan P. Conditioned reflexes. London, 1928.
Phil 5625.75A Pavlov, Ivan P. Conditioned reflexes. Oxford, 1927.
Phil 5625.75.40 Pavlov, Ivan P. Essays in psychology and psychiatry. N.Y., 1962.
Phil 5625.75.20 Pavlov, Ivan P. Experimental psychology. N.Y., 1957.
Phil 5625.75.5 Pavlov, Ivan P. Izbrannye trudy. Moskva, 1950.
Phil 5625.75.2 Pavlov, Ivan P. Polnoe sobranie trudov. v.2-5. Moskva, 1946. 4v.
Phil 5625.75.35 Pavlov, Ivan P. Psychopathology and psychiatry. Moscow, 1962?
Phil 5625.75.15 Pavlov, Ivan P. Les reflexes conditionelles. Paris, 1927.
Phil 5625.75.25 Pavlov, Ivan P. Selected works. Moscow, 1955.
Phil 5625.75.45 Pavlov, Ivan P. Vorlesungen über die Arbeit der Grosshirnhemisphären. Lenogiz, 1932.
Phil 5625.75.30 Pavlov, Ivan P. The work of the digestive glands. London, 1910.

Phil 310.5 — Pavlov, T. Ravnosmetka na edna idealistko reaktsionii filosofiia. Sofiia, 1953.

Phil 8170.5.9 — Pavlov, T.D. Osnovni vuprosi na estetikata. 2. izd. Sofiia, 1949-

Phil 8170.6 — Pavlov, T.D. Osnovni vuprosi na marksistko-leninskata estetika. 3. izd. Sofiia, 1958.

Phil 310.20 — Pavlov, Todor D. Osnovnoto v Michurinskoto uchenie v svetlinata na dialekticheskii materializm. Sofiia, 1955.

Phil 310.20.5 — Pavlov, Todor D. Teoriiata na otrazhenieto i nashata suvremennost. Sofiia, 1961.

Phil 4824.676.30 — Pavlov, Todor Dimitrov. Izkustvoiživot. Sofiia, 1953.

Phil 5360.15 — Pavlov, V.T. Otnosheniia mezhdu poniatiiami. Kiev, 1961.

Phil 672.238 — Pavlov, Vasilii T. Logicheskie funktsii kategorii prostranstva i vremeni. Kiev, 1966.

Phil 5232.9 — Pavlov and Freud. (Wells, H.K.) N.Y., 1956. 2v.

Phil 5625.75.87 — Pavlov and his school. (Frolov, I.P.) London, 1937.

Phil 8980.676 — Pavlova, Liia Jakovlevna. Nravstvennye tsennosti nachego sovremennika. Moskva, 1971.

Phil 5625.75.100 — Pavlov's typology. (Gray, Jeffrey Alan.) N.Y., 1964.

Phil 8430.90 — Pavlovskii, Boris V. U istokov sovetskoi khudozhestvennoi kritiki. Leningrad, 1970.

Htn Phil 8890.7* — Pavonio, F. Summa ethicae. Oxonii, 1633.

Phil 310.740 — Pawelzig, Gerd. Dialektik der Entwicklung objektiver Systeme. 1. Aufl. Berlin, 1970.

Phil 336.1.15 — Pawlicki, S. A. Fouillée's Neue Theorie der Ideenlorëfts. Wien, 1893.

Phil 5274.16 — Pawlik, Kurt. Dimensionen des Verhaltens. Bern, 1968.

Phil 9400.25 — Pax, Schweyerische Lebensmensecherungsgesellschaft, Basel. Der Weg, ins Altern. Basel, 1958.

Phil 8505.9 — Pax Romana, International Catholic Movement for Intellectual and Cultural Affairs. Foi et technique. Paris, 1960.

Phil 2205.32 — Paxton, J. Illustrations of Paley's natural theology. Boston, 1827.

Phil 8886.28 — Pay your fare. (Lewis, George Edward.) N.Y., 1914.

Phil 8890.8 — Payne, G. Elements of mental and moral science. London, 1828.

Phil 9558.10.20 — Payne, R. The wanton nymph. London, 1951.

Phil 9558.10.5 — Payne, Robert. Hubris. N.Y., 1960.

Phil 3850.27.150 — Payne, Robert. The three worlds of Albert Schweitzer. N.Y., 1957.

Phil 4768.5 — Payne, T.R. S.L. Rubinstein and the philosophical foundations of Soviet psychology. Dordrecht, 1969.

Phil 1122.4 — Payot, E. Les auteurs philosophiques, grecs. Paris, 1898.

Phil 5070.5 — Payot, J. De la croyance. Paris, 1896.

Phil 9245.33 — Payot, Jules. La conquête du bonheur. Paris, 1921.

Phil 8890.29 — Payot, Jules. Cours de morale. 9. ed. Paris, 1914.

Phil 5765.2 — Payot, Jules. L'éducation de la volonté. Paris, 1900.

Phil 5765.2.3 — Payot, Jules. L'éducation de la volonté. Paris, 1912.

Phil 5765.2.4 — Payot, Jules. L'éducation de la volonté. Paris, 1941.

Phil 5765.2.9 — Payot, Jules. The education of the will. N.Y., 1909.

Phil 5765.2.9.5 — Payot, Jules. The education of the will. N.Y., 1910.

Phil 9245.33.10 — Payot, Jules. Erövringen av lyckan. Stockholm, 1923.

Phil 5765.2.5 — Payot, Jules. Die Erziehung des Willens. Leipzig, 1901.

Phil 5765.2.10 — Payot, Jules. Le travail intellectuel et la volonté. Paris, 1919.

Phil 5765.2.11 — Payot, Jules. Le travail intellectuel et la volonté. Paris, 1920.

Phil 5765.2.20 — Payot, Jules. Will-power and work. 2. ed. N.Y., 1921.

Phil 2750.11.44 — Le paysan de la Garonne. (Maritain, Jacques.) Paris, 1966.

Phil 2490.134 — La paz del mundo y la alianza universal de las doctrinas. (Lagarrigue, L.) Santiago de Chile, 1940.

Phil 3450.11.295 — Pazanin, A. Das Problem der Philosophie als strenger Wissenschaft. Köln, 1962.

Phil 9035.6 — Peabody, A.P. Building a character. Boston, 1887.

Phil 8965.10 — Peabody, A.P. Christian morals. Boston, 1886.

Phil 8595.2 — Peabody, A.P. Christianity the religion of nature. Boston, 1864.

Phil 8890.9.5 — Peabody, A.P. The immutable right. Boston, 1858.

Phil 8890.9 — Peabody, A.P. A manual of moral philosophy. N.Y., 1873.

Phil 8890.9.2 — Peabody, A.P. Moral philosophy. Boston, 1887.

Phil 600.8 — Peabody, A.P. The positive philosophy. Boston, 1867.

Phil 8965.11 — Peabody, F.G. The Christian life in the modern world. N.Y., 1914.

Phil 8965.3 — Peabody, F.G. Jesus Christ and the Christian character. N.Y., 1905.

Phil 9400.6 — Peabody, F.G. The privileges of old age. Cambridge, 1931.

Phil 6685.2 — Peabody, J.R. World of wonders. Boston, 1838.

Phil 6122.34.3 — Peace, power and plenty. (Marden, Orison S.) N.Y., 1909.

Phil 9245.9.75 — Peace and happiness. (Avebury, John Lubbock.) N.Y., 1909.

Phil 5850.330 — Peace and power within. (Russell, W.L.) Houston, Texas, 1951.

Phil 5850.330.5 — Peace and power within. (Russell, W.L.) N.Y., 1954.

Phil 5590.26A — Peace of mind. (Liebman, Joshua Loth.) N.Y., 1946.

Htn Phil 2225.4.30* — Peacham, Henry. The compleat gentleman. London, 1622.

Phil 9355.2.7 — Peacham, Henry. The complete gentleman. N.Y., 1962.

Htn Phil 9355.2.9* — Peacham, Henry. The truth of our times. London, 1638.

Phil 9355.2.10 — Peacham, Henry. The truth of our times. N.Y., 1942.

Phil 9355.2 — Peacham, Henry. The worth of a penny. London, 1667.

Phil 9355.2.5 — Peachman, Henry. The compleat gentleman. London, 1906.

Phil 8582.35.9 — The peak in Darien...an octave of essays. (Cobbe, F.P.) Boston, 1882.

Phil 5850.305A — Peale, N.V. The power of positive thinking. N.Y., 1955.

Phil 9070.108 — Peale, Norman Vincent. Sin, sex and self control. 1st ed. Garden City, 1965.

Phil 5066.12.5 — Peano, G. Arithmétique. Turin, 1898.

Phil 5066.12 — Peano, G. Aritmetica generale e algebra elementare. Torino, 1902.

Phil 5066.12.10 — Peano, G. Notations de logique mathématique. Turin, 1894.

Phil 5066.12.15 — Peano, G. I principii di geometria logicamente esposti. Torino, 1889.

Phil 3925.16.260 — Pear, David Francis. Ludwig Wittgenstein. N.Y., 1970.

Phil 5520.235 — Pear, T.H. Personality, appearance and speech. London, 1957.

Phil 5627.163 — Pear, T.H. Religion and contemporary psychology. London, 1937.

Phil 5455.155 — Pear, T.H. Remembering and forgetting. London, 1922.

Phil 5585.13 — Pearce, H.J. Über den Einfluss von Nebenreizen. Leipzig, 1903.

Phil 2050.253.5 — Pears, D.F. David Hume. London, 1966.

Phil 5765.11 — Pears, D.F. Freedom and the will. London, 1966.

Phil 190.84 — Pears, D.F. The nature of metaphysics. London, 1957.

Phil 2255.1.130A — Pears, David Francis. Bertrand Russell and the British tradition in philosophy. London, 1967.

Phil 5500.45 — Pears, David Francis. Predicting and deciding. London, 1964.

Phil 346.38 — Pears, David Francis. What is knowledge? N.Y., 1971.

Phil 2225.14 — Pearson, A.N. A search for knowledge. Melbourne, 1889.

Phil 2205.80 — Pearson, Edward. Annotations on the practical part of Dr. Paley's Principles of moral and political philosophy. Ipswich, 1801.

Phil 2205.80.5 — Pearson, Edward. Remarks on the theory of morals in which is contained an examination of the theoretical part of Dr. Paley's Principles of moral and political philosophy. Ipswich, 1804.

Phil 5878.10 — Pearson, Gerald Hamilton Jeffrey. Adolescence and the conflict of generations. N.Y., 1958.

Phil 365.5 — Pearson, K. Chances of death...studies in evolution. London, 1897. 2v.

Phil 8610.888 — Pearson, Karl. The ethic of freethought. London, 1888.

Phil 8610.888.3A — Pearson, Karl. The ethic of freethought. 2. ed. London, 1901.

Phil 1145.92 — Pearson, L.I.C. Popular ethics in ancient Greece. Stanford, Calif., 1962.

Phil 190.21 — Pearson, N. Some problems of existence. London, 1907.

Phil 8610.854.15 — Pearson, Thomas. Infidelity. N.Y., 1854.

Phil 2750.11.44.2 — The peasant of the Garonne. 1. éd. (Maritain, Jacques.) N.Y., 1968.

Phil 5238.130 — Peatman, J.G. Festschrift for Gardner Murphy. N.Y., 1960.

Phil 4073.43 — Il peccato originale. (Campanella, Tommaso.) Roma, 1960.

Phil 2750.19.95 — Peccorini Letona, Francisco. Gabriel Marcel. Barcelona, 1959.

Phil 4476.1.30 — Pecegueiro, Jose. Problemas da ciencia e da filosofia contemporanea. Coimbra, 1966.

Phil 190.5 — Peck, J.S. The ultimate generalization. N.Y., 1876.

Phil 6325.11 — Peck, Martin W. The meaning of psychoanalysis. N.Y., 1931.

Phil 2475.1.195 — Peckham, George W. Logic of Bergson's philosophy. N.Y., 1917.

Phil 6328.2.20 — Peculiarities of behavior. (Stekel, Wilhelm.) N.Y., 1924. 2v.

Phil 4120.4.120 — La pedagogia come scienza filosofica di Giovanni Gentile. (Liguori, Ersilia.) Padova, 1951.

Phil 4080.3.495 — Pedagogia crociana. (Alfieri, Vittorio Enzo.) Napoli, 1967.

Phil 4120.4.47 — La pedagogia di G. Gentile. v.1-2. (Puglisi, F.) Catania, 1953-54.

Phil 2750.11.115 — La pedagogia di Jacques Maritain. (Cassata, M.L.) Palermo, 1953.

Phil 5710.20 — Die Pedanterie. (Sacherl, Karl.) Göttingen, 1957.

Phil 8705.15 — Pedder, Henry C. Issues of the age. N.Y., 1874.

Phil 5645.38 — Peddie, William. Colour vision. London, 1922.

Phil 4210.132 — Pederzolli, G. La filosofia di Antonio Rosmini. Roveroto, 1887.

Phil 525.23 — Pedrick, Katharine F. How to make perfection appear. Boston, 1919.

Phil 525.23.5 — Pedrick, Katharin F. Du moyen de manifester la perfection. Paris, 1921.

Phil 4351.3 — Pedro Simon Abril. (Morreale deCastro, M.) Madrid, 1949.

Phil 3450.11.101.50 — Pedroli, Guido. La fenomenologia di Husserl. Torino, 1958.

Phil 4210.137F — Pedrotti, Pietro. Discorso...per Antonio Rosmini. Roveroto, 1937.

Phil 7069.04.60 — Peebles, J.M. The demonism of the ages. Battle Creek, Mich., 1904.

Phil 7054.42 — Peebles, J.M. The practical of spiritualism. Chicago, 1868.

Phil 7054.167 — Peebles, J.M. Seers of the ages, embracing spiritualism. Boston, 1869.

Phil 7054.167.10 — Peebles, J.M. Spirit mates, their origin and destiny. Battle Creek, 1909.

Phil 2270.190 — Peel, John David Yeadon. Herbert Spencer; the evolution of a sociologist. London, 1971.

Phil 298.14 — The peep-hole of the present. (Roth, Samuel.) N.Y., 1945.

Phil 7069.15.20 — Peeps into the psychic world. (Crawford, Mary MacDermont.) Philadelphia, 1915.

Phil 530.40.47 — Peers, E.A. The mystics of Spain. London, 1951.

Phil 530.40.25 — Peers, E.A. Spanish mysticism. London, 1924.

Phil 530.40.27 — Peers, E.A. Studies of the Spanish mystics. London, 1927-30. 2v.

Phil 530.40.27.5 — Peers, E.A. Studies of the Spanish mystics. 2nd ed. London, 1951-60. 3v.

Phil 6132.7.6 — Peg along. (Walton, G.L.) Philadelphia, 1915.

Phil 8705.22 — Pégand, Georges. Ascèse et science. Paris, 1963.

Phil 8595.55 — Pegis, Anton C. Christian philosophy and intellectual freedom. Milwaukee, 1960.

Phil 190.76 — Pegis, Anton C. Essays in modern scholasticism in honor of John F. McCormick. Westminster, Md., 1944.

Phil 2475.1.255 — Péguy, Charles. Note sur M. Bergson et la philosophie bergsonienne. 6e éd. Paris, 1935.

Phil 3850.52.35 — Peilingen. (Stallaert, L.) Rotterdam, 1956. 3v.

Phil 9035.71 — Peillaube, E. Caractère et personnalité. Paris, 1935.

Phil 5545.47 — Peillaube, E. Les images. Paris, 1910.

Phil 5360.7 — Peillaube, E. Théorie des concepts. Paris, n.d.

Phil 3110.84.5 — Peip, A. Jakob Böhme, der deutsche Philosoph. Hamburg, 1862.

Phil 3110.84 — Peip, A. Jakob Böhme der deutsche Philosoph. Leipzig, 1860.

Phil 2225.5.30 — Peirce, C.S. Chance, love, and logic. N.Y., 1923.

Phil 2225.5.35 — Peirce, C.S. Chance, love, and logic. N.Y., 1949.

Phil 2225.5.10A — Peirce, C.S. Collected papers. Cambridge, 1931. 8v.

Phil 2225.5.50A — Peirce, C.S. Collected papers. v.1-6. Cambridge, 1960. 3v.

Phil 2225.5.20 — Peirce, C.S. Essays in the philosophy of science. N.Y., 1957.

Phil 2225.5.27 — Peirce, C.S. Letters to Lady Welby. Photoreproduction. New Haven, 1953.

Phil 5635.19F — Peirce, C.S. On small differences of sensation. n.p., 18-?

Phil 2225.5.25 — Peirce, C.S. The philosophy of Peirce; selected writings. London, 1940.

Phil 2225.5.55.5 — Peirce, C.S. Über die Klarheit unserer Gedanken. Frankfurt, 1968.

Phil 2225.5.40 — Peirce, C.S. Values in a universe of chance. Stanford, 1958.

Phil 2225.5.130 — Peirce. (Buczyńska, Hanna.) Warszawa, 1965.

Phil 2225.5.93 — Peirce and pragmatism. (Gallie, W.B.) Harmondsworth, 1952.

Phil 2225.5.175 — Peirce e i problemi dell'interpretazione. (Salanitro, Niccolò.) Roma, 1969.

Phil 2225.5.170 — Peirce's theory of abduction. (Fann, K.T.) The Hague, 1970.

Phil 2225.5.135 — Peirce's theory of signs as foundation for pragmatism. (Fitzgerald, John J.) The Hague, 1966.

Phil 5545.44 — Peiron, Henri. L'évolution de la mémoire. Paris, 1910.
Phil 190.47 — Peiser, Fritz. Systematische Philosophie in leichtfasslicher Darstellung. Berlin, 1923.
Phil 2480.82 — Peisse, L. Notice historique et philosophique sur la vie. Paris, 1844.
Phil 4829.680.30 — Pejović, Danilo. Protiv struje. Zagreb, 1965.
Phil 1715.18 — Pejović, Danilo. Sistem i egzistencija. Zagreb, 1970.
Phil 3497.8 — Pekelharing, C. Kant's Teleologie. Gröningen, 1916.
Phil 190.46 — Peladan, J. Traité des antinomies. Paris, 1901.
Phil 190.42 — Pelazza, A. La metafisica dell'esperienza. Bergamo, 1907.
Phil 5058.7.18 — Pelazza, Amelio. Guglielmo Schuppe e la filosofia dell'immanerza. Milano, 1914.
Phil 3850.7.81 — Pelazza, Aurelio. W. Schuppe and the immanent philosophy. London, 1915.
Phil 5520.748 — Pelc, Jerzy. Semiotyka polska, 1894-1969. Warszawa, 1971.
Phil 5520.748.2 — Pelc, Jerzy. Studies in functional logical semiotics of natural language. The Hague, 1971.
Phil 815.30 — The Pelican history of European thought. v.1,4. Harmondsworth, Middlesex, 1968. 2v.
Phil 5229.2 — The Pelican history of psychology. (Thomson, Robert.) Harmondsworth, 1968.
Phil 5765.8 — Pelikán, F. Entstehung und Entwicklung der Kontingentismus. Berlin, 1915.
Phil 4710.25.5 — Pelikán, Ferdinand. Aus der philosophischen Riffamationsliteratur. Prag, 1934.
Phil 2050.200 — Pelikán, Ferdinand. Fikcionalism novověké filosofie zvláště u Humea a Kanta. Praha, 1928.
Phil 4710.25 — Pelikán, Ferdinand. Současná filosofie u Slovanů. Praha, 1932.
Phil 5275.10 — Pelikán, Pavel. Homo informationicus, réflexions sur l'homme et l'informatique. Nancy, 1967.
Phil 4803.680.30 — Pełka-Peliński, Stanisław. Na drogach współczesnej kultury. Łódz, 1946.
Phil 735.95 — Pell, Orlie A.H. Value theory and Criticism. Thesis. N.Y., 1930.
Phil 600.7.79 — Pellarin, Charles. Essai critique sur la philosophie positive. Paris, 1864.
Htn Phil 6025.8* — Pellegrini, A. I segni de la natura ne l'huomo. Venetia, 1569.
Phil 4170.10.85 — Pellegrino, U. Religione ed educazione nell'idealismo trascendente di Piero Martinetti. Brescia, 1956.
Phil 8581.45.20 — Pellegrino di Roma. (Buonaiuti, Ernesto.) Bari, 1964.
Phil 5360.9 — Pellet, R. Des premières perceptions du concret à la conception de l'abstrait. Thèse. Lyon, 1938.
Htn Phil 8670.4* — Pelling, E. A discourse concerning the existence of God. London, 1696.
Phil 190.6 — Pellissier, P.A. Précis d'un cours complet de philosophie élémentaire. Paris, 1873. 2v.
Phil 6420.40 — Pellman, Charles. Overcoming stammering. N.Y., 1947.
Phil 3425.297 — Pelloux, L. La logica di Hegel. Milan, 1938.
Phil 6325.9 — Pelman, Carl. Psychische Grenzzustände. 3. Aufl. Bonn, 1912.
Phil 5545.165 — Pelman, Christopher L. Memory training, its law and their application to practical life. pts.1-5. Chicago, 1903.
Phil 5545.165.25 — Pelman Institute of America. Pelmanism. Lesson 1,3-12. N.Y., 1924.
Phil 5850.306 — Pelman Institute of America. Scientific mind training. N.Y., 1924.
Phil 5850.306.5 — Pelman Institute of America. Scientific mind training. N.Y., 1927.
Phil 5545.165.25 — Pelmanism. Lesson 1,3-12. (Pelman Institute of America.) N.Y., 1924.
Phil 1750.166.170 — Pelo humanismo ameaçado. (Amoroso Lima, Alcew.) Rio de Janeiro, 1965.
Phil 75.45 — Pelzer, A. Répertoires d'incipit pour la littérature latine philosophique. Roma, 1951.
Phil 1520.6 — Pelzer, Auguste. Études d'histoire littéraire sur la scolastique médiévale. Louvain, 1964.
Phil 672.164 — Pemartin, J. Introducción a una filosofía de lo temporal. Sevilla, 1937.
Htn Phil 190.7* — Pemble, W. De Formarum origine. Cantabrigia, 1631.
Phil 3425.202 — Pen, K.J. Over het onderscheid tusschen de wetenschap van Hegel en de wijsheid van Bolland. Leiden, 1915.
Phil 1750.835 — Penati, Giancarlo. Introduzione alla filosofia come metocultura. Milano, 1968.
Phil 8705.2 — Pendleton, W.N. Science a witness for the Bible. Philadelphia, 1860.
Phil 8595.24 — Penel, Raymond. Qu'est-ce que la vérité? Paris, 1926.
Phil 8595.60 — Penelhum, Terence. Religion and rationality. 1. ed. N.Y., 1971.
Phil 8640.16 — Penelhum, Terence. Survival and disembodied existence. London, 1970.
Phil 7054.6.18 — The penetralia, being harmonial answers. 3. ed. (Davis, A.J.) Boston, 1857.
Phil 5055.30 — Penev, Mikho. Kritika na logicheskite vuzgledi na burzhoaznite filosofi v Bulgariia. Sofiia, 1958.
Phil 4822.6 — Penev, Mikho. Za religiozno-idealisticheskata sŭshtnost na bŭlgarskata burzhoazno filosofiia. Sofiia, 1964.
Phil 6536.11 — Penfield, W. Epilepsy and cerebral localization. 1st ed. Springfield, 1941.
Phil 6125.28 — Penfield, Wilder. Speech and brain-mechanisms. N.J., 1959.
Phil 2475.1.194 — Penido, M.T.L. La méthode intuitive de M. Bergson. Genève, 1918.
Phil 1870.92 — Penjon, A. Étude sur vie et les oeuvres philosophiques de G. Berkeley. Paris, 1878.
Phil 815.7 — Penjon, A. Précis d'histoire de la philosophie. Paris, 1896.
Phil 3552.124 — Penjon, Auguste. De infinito apud Leibnitium. Thesis. Paris, 1878.
Phil 8705.8 — Penn, G. A comparative estimate of the mineral and mosaical geology. London, 1822.
Phil 8890.10.5 — Penn, W. Früchte der Einsamkeit. Friedensthal, 1803.
Phil 8890.10 — Penn, W. Fruits of solitude, in reflections and maxims. N.Y., 1813.
Phil 4015.3 — Pennisi, S. Intorno allo stato e ai bisogni attuali della filosofia teoretica in Italia. Firenze, 1862. 3v.
Phil 190.57 — Pamphlet vol. Pennisi-Mauro, A. Il principio della sapienza. 3 pam.
Phil 5627.55 — Pennock, Gilbert L. The consciousness of communion with God. New Brunswick, N.J., 1914.
Phil 6750.16 — Pennsylvania. Commission on Segregation, Care and Treatment of the Feebleminded and Epileptic Persons. Report of the commission. Harrisburg, 1913.
Phil 9400.40 — Pennsylvania. Governor's White House Conference Committee on Aging. Subcommittee reports. Harrisburg, 1960.
Phil 1830.50 — Pennsylvania. State University. Philosophy Department. Essays in philosophy. University Park, Penn., 1962.

Phil 55.1 — Pennsylvania. University. Public series in philosophy. Philadelphia. 1-4 2v.
Phil 5255.45 — Pennsylvania. University. Bicentennial Conference. Modern psychology. Philadelphia, 1941.
Phil 8595.34A — Pennsylvania. University. Bicentennial Conference. Religion and the modern world. Philadelphia, 1941.
Phil 6325.15 — Pennsylvania. University. Bicentennial Conference. Therapeutic advances in psychiatry. Philadelphia, 1941.
Phil 7060.102 — Pennsylvania. University. Seybert Commission for Investigating Modern Spiritualism. Preliminary report. Philadelphia, 1887.
Phil 7060.102.2 — Pennsylvania. University. Seybert Commission for Investigating Modern Spiritualism. Preliminary report. Philadelphia, 1887.
Phil 7068.87.9.5 — Pennsylvania. University. Seybert Commission for Investigating Modern Spiritualism. Preliminary report. Philadelphia, 1895.
Phil 7069.20.270 — Pennsylvania. University. Seybert Commission for Investigating Modern Spiritualism. Preliminary report. Philadelphia, 1920.
Phil 55.1.10 — Pennsylvina. University. Laboratory of Neuropathology. Contributions. Philadelphia, 1905. 5v.
Phil 3110.86 — Penny, A.J. Jacob Boehme. London, 1912.
Phil 3110.85.50 — Penny. A.J. An introduction to the study of Jacob Boehme's writings. N.Y., 1901.
Phil 8890.11 — Penrose, John M.A. An inquiry chiefly on principles of religion. London, 1820.
Phil 6750.234 — Penrose, Lionel S. Mental defect. N.Y., 1934.
Phil 9450.10 — Pensa, Henri. De la morale politique. Paris, 1910.
Phil 3015.4 — Pensa, M. Il pensiero tedesco. Bologna, 1938.
Phil 1740.28 — Pensadores cristianos contemporáneos. v.1- (López Quintás, Alfonso.) Madrid, 1968-
Phil 4967.20.85 — O pensamento de Farias Brito. (Lopes de Maltos, C.) São Paulo, 1962.
Phil 4960.660 — Pensamento filosófico brasileiro na atualidade. (Buggenhagen, Erich Arnold von.) São Paulo, 1968.
Phil 25.77 — Pensamiento, revista de investigacion e informacion filosofica. Madrid. 4,1948+ 22v.
Phil 25.77.5 — Pensamiento, revista de investigacion filosofica. Indices generales, 1945-60. Madrid, n.d. 2v.
Phil 1117.8.10 — El pensamiento antiguo. (Mondolfo, Rodolfo.) Buenos Aires, 1942. 2v.
Phil 4960.250 — El pensamiento argentino. (Korn, Alejandro.) Buenos Aires, 1961.
Phil 4961.116 — El pensamiento colombiano en el siglo XIX. (Jaramillo Uribe, Jaime.) Bogotá, 1964.
Phil 4368.4 — El pensamiento de Amor Ruibal. (Baliñas, Carlos A.) Madrid, 1968.
Phil 4967.5.80 — El pensamiento de Guillermo Francovich. (Zelada C., Alberto.) Sucre, 1966.
Phil 4957.10 — Pensamiento de lengua española. (Gaos, José.) México, 1945.
Phil 4225.8.95 — El pensamiento de Michele Federico Sciacca; homenaje, 1908-1958. Buenos Aires, 1959.
Phil 4307.1 — Pensamiento español. (Gaos, José.) México, 1945.
Phil 4372.1.87 — El pensamiento filosófico de Juan Luis Vives. (Gutiérrez, Alberto.) Buenos Aires, 1940.
Phil 4958.505 — El pensamiento filosófico en Santo Domingo. (Sánchez, Juan Francisco.) Ciudad Trujillo, 1956?
Phil 4357.2.85 — El pensamiento filsofico de Giner. (Villalopos, José.) Sevilla, 1969.
Phil 4352.1.165 — Pensamiento histórico cristiano. 1. ed. (Sáiz Barberá, Juan.) Madrid, 1967.
Phil 4080.3.530 — El pensamiento histórico de Benedetto Croce. (Dujovne, León.) Buenos Aires, 1968.
Phil 4959.220 — El pensamiento mexicano en los siglos XVI y XVII. (Gallegos Rocafull, José Manuel.) México, 1951.
Phil 4330.10 — El pensamiento tradicional en la España del siglo XVIII, 1700-1760. (Puy, Francisco.) Madrid, 1966.
Phil 4316.3 — El pensamiento tradicional en la España del siglo XVIII, 1700-1760. (Puy Munãoz, Francisco.) Madrid, 1966.
Phil 6127.7.20 — El pensamiento vivo de Cajal. (Ramón y Cajal, S.) Buenos Aires, 1941.
Phil 4357.2.31 — El pensamiento vivo de Giner de los Rios. (Giner de los Rios, Francisco.) Buenos Aires, 1949.
Phil 3483.55 — El pensamiento vivo de Kant. (Benda, Julien.) Buenos Aires, 1939.
Phil 4326.1 — Pensamiento y poesía en la vida española. (Zambrano, M.) México, 1939.
Phil 2805.43 — Pensamientos. (Pascal, Blaise.) Zaragoza, 1790.
Phil 4000.17 — I pensatori della seconda metà del secolo XIX. (Alliney, G.) Milano, 1942.
Phil 3425.356 — La pensée, religieuse du jeune Hegel. (Asveld, Paul.) Louvain, 1953.
Phil 5241.90 — La pensée. (Blondel, M.) Paris, 1934. 2v.
Phil 25.69 — La pensée. Paris. 1,1944+ 5v.
Phil 180.19 — La pensée. 2e éd. (Fouillée, Alfred.) Paris, 1911.
Phil 5241.90.5 — La pensée. 4. éd. (Blondel, M.) Paris, 1948.
Phil 3018.19 — La pensée allemande de Luther à Nietzsche. (Spenlé, J.E.) Paris, 1934.
Phil 1806.2 — La pensée anglo-saxonne depuis 1900. 1e éd. (Ginestier, Paul.) Paris, 1956.
Phil 850.11 — La pensée antique (de Moise à Marcaurèle). (Fabre, Joseph.) Paris, 1902.
Phil 1526.4 — Le pensée au moyen âge. (Vignaux, Paul.) Paris, 1938.
Phil 3552.112 — La pensée chretienne...Leibniz. (Baruzi, Jean.) Paris, 1909.
Phil 5241.75.12 — La pensée conceptuelle. Thèse. (Burloud, Albert.) Paris, 1927.
Phil 5258.92.2 — La pensée concrète. Thèse. (Spaier, A.) Paris, 1927.
Phil 8586.55.5 — Pensée constructive et réalités spirituelle. (Guerin, Pierre.) Paris, 1934.
Phil 1706.2 — La pensée contemporaine. (Gaultier, P.) Paris, 1911.
Phil 196.25 — La pensée contemporaine. (Veuthy, L.) Paris, 1938.
Phil 4012.8 — La pensée contemporaine en Italie et l'influence de Hegel. (Mueller, F.L.) Genève, 1941.
Phil 2515.5.93 — La pensée d'Alain. (Pascal, Georges.) Paris, 1946.
Phil 5241.75 — La pensée d'après les recherches experimentales de H.J. Watt, de Messer et de Bühler. (Burloud, Albert.) Paris, 1927.
Phil 5241.75.2 — La pensée d'après les recherches experimentales de H.J. Watt, de Messer et de Bühler. (Burloud, Albert.) Paris, 1927.
Phil 2490.184.5 — La pensée d'Auguste Comte. (Arnaud, Pierre.) Paris, 1969.
Phil 2475.1.288 — La pensée de Bergson. (Meyer, François.) Grenoble, 1944.
Phil 6315.2.140.5 — La pensée de Freud. (Pesch, Edgar.) Paris, 1960.
Phil 6315.2.140 — La pensée de Freud et la psychanalyse. (Pesch, Edgar.) Paris, 1946.

Phil 2280.5.108   La pensée de George Santayana. (Duron, J.) Paris, 1950.
Phil 2280.5.108.2   La pensée de George Santayana. Thèse. (Duron, J.) Paris, 1950.
Phil 3425.445   La pensée de Hegel. (Kremer-Garietti, Angèle.) Paris, 1957.
Phil 2475.1.111   La pensée de Henri Bergson. (Desaymard, J.) Paris, 1912.
Phil 2150.22.140   La pensée de Herbert Marcuse. (Masset, Pierre.) Toulouse, 1969.
Phil 3497.22   La pensée de Kant. 2. éd. (Pascol, Georges.) Paris, 1957.
Phil 1850.143   La pensée de Lord Bacon. (Schuhl, P.) Paris, 1949.
Phil 2730.118   La pensée de Maine de Biran. (Holda, Bernard.) Paris, 1970.
Phil 2825.5   La pensée de Maurice Pradines. (Grappe, André.) Paris, 1938.
Phil 3640.316   La pensée de Nietzsche. (Baranger, William.) Paris, 1946.
Phil 3808.29.25   La pensée de Schopenhauer. (Schopenhauer, Arthur.) Paris, 1918.
Phil 3832.24   La pensée de Spinoza. (Millet, Louis.) Paris, 1970.
Phil 3625.3.85   La pensée d'Ernst Mach. (Bouvier, Robert.) Paris, 1923.
Phil 1133.50   La pensée des présocratiques. (Legrand, Gérard.) Paris, 1970.
Phil 2905.1.365   La pensée du Père Teilhard de Chardin. (Rideau, Émile.) Paris, 1965.
Phil 177.26   La pensée et l'amour. (Choraux, C.) Paris, 1869.
Phil 6111.33   La pensée et le cerveau. (Bastide, Jules.) Paris, 1886.
Phil 5759.6   La pensée et le libre arbitre. (Jakubisiak, A.) Paris, 1936.
Phil 2475.1.65.4   La pensée et le mouvant. (Bergson, Henri.) Genève, 1946.
Phil 2475.1.65   La pensée et le mouvant. 5. éd. (Bergson, Henri.) Paris, 1934.
Phil 2475.1.65.2   La pensée et le mouvant. 12. éd. (Bergson, Henri.) Paris, 1941.
Phil 178.78   La pensée et le réel, antique de l'ontologie. (Delhomme, Yeanne.) Paris, 1967.
Phil 5245.37   Pensée et re-création. (Fauré-Fremiet, P.) Paris, 1934.
Phil 2520.353   La pensée existentielle de Descartes. (Lefèvre, Roger.) Paris, 1965.
Phil 337.22   Pensée formelle et sciences de l'homme. (Granger, Gilles Gaston.) Paris, 1960.
Phil 1122.6.3   La pensée grecque et les origines de l'esprit scientifique. (Robin, Léon.) Paris, 1928.
Phil 1122.6.4   La pensée grecque et les origines de l'esprit scientifique. (Robin, Léon.) Paris, 1948.
Phil 1122.6.10   La pensee hellenique des origines a epicule questions de methode. 1.ed. (Robin, Léon.) Paris, 1948.
Phil 5247.10.15   Pensée humaine. (Höffding, H.) Paris, 1911.
Phil 1750.166.50   Pensée humaniste et tradition chrétienne aux XVe et XVIe siècle. (France. Centre National de la Recherche Scientifique.) Paris, 1950.
Phil 5585.71   Pensée implicite et perception visuelle. (Paliard, J.) Paris, 1949.
Phil 5249.21.5   La pensée interieure et ses troubles. pts.1-6. (Janet, Pierre.) Paris, 1927.
Phil 186.70   La pensée intuitive. (LeRoy, Édouard.) Paris, 1929.
Phil 990.25   La pensée iranienne à travers l'histoire. Thèse. (Beroukhim, Moussa.) Paris, 1938.
Phil 4002.1   La pensée italienne au XVIe siècle. (Charbonnel, J.R.) Paris, 1919.
Phil 2905.1.470   Pensée logique et pensée politique chez Teilhard de Chardin. (Soucy, Claude.) Paris, 1967.
Phil 2520.342   La pensée métaphysique de Descartes. (Gonhier, Henri.) Paris, 1962.
Phil 1705.6   La pensée moderne. (Fabre, Joseph.) Paris, 1908.
Phil 1705.6.1   La pensée moderne [de Luther à Leibniz]. (Fabre, Joseph.) Genève, 1970.
Phil 2630.11.2   La pensée moderne et le catholicisme. v.6,7,9,10. (Guitton, Jean.) Aix, 1936. 5v.
Phil 8601.17   Pensée moderne et philosophie chrétienne. (Vancourt, Raymond.) Paris, 1957.
Phil 5041.16.80   La pensée morale de Bernard Bosanquet. (LeChevalier, Charles.) Paris, 1963.
Phil 343.24   La pensée negative. Thèse. (Morot, E.) Paris, 1947.
Phil 817.24   La pensée occidentale face à la sagesse de l'orient. (Rochedieu, Edmond.) Paris, 1963.
Phil 3640.610   La pensée philosophique de Nietzsche. (Wahl, J.A.) Paris, 1959.
Phil 2905.1.400   Pensée philosophique et religieuse du père Teilhard de Chardin. (Frenaud, Georges.) Le Chesnay, 1965.
Phil 3425.688   La pensée politique de Hegel. (Bourgeois, Bernard.) Paris, 1969.
Phil 3503.14   La pensée politique de Kant. (Vlachos, G.) Paris, 1962.
Phil 3552.446   La pensée politique de Leibniz. (Naert, Emilienne.) Paris, 1964.
Phil 2805.215   La pensée politique de Pascal. Thèse. (Demahis, E.) St. Amand, 1931.
Phil 2905.1.585   La pensée politique et économique de Teilhard de Chardin. (Mathieu, Pierre Louis.) Paris, 1969.
Phil 5250.33   La pensée préconsciente. (Konczewski, C.) Paris, 1939.
Phil 1020.28   La pensée religieus d'Avicenne. (Gardet, Louis.) Paris, 1951.
Phil 1870.121   La pensée religieuse de Berkeley. (Baladi, Naguit.) La Caire, 1945.
Phil 8587.32.99   La pensée religieuse de F. von Hügel, 1852-1925. (Nédoncelle, M.) Paris, 1935.
Phil 8587.32.101   La pensée religieuse de F. von Hügel, 1852-1925. Thèse. (Nédoncelle, M.) Paris, 1935.
Phil 3425.607   La pensée religieuse de Hegel. (Vancourt, Raymond.) Paris, 1965.
Phil 2905.1.180   La pensée religieuse du père Teilhard de Chardin. (Lubac, Henri de.) Paris, 1962.
Phil 623.24A   La pensée religieuse française de Charron à Pascal. (Busson, Henri.) Paris, 1933.
Phil 2905.1.97   La pensée scientifique de Teilhard. (Chauchard, Paul.) Paris, 1965.
Phil 8705.16   Pensée scientifique et foi chrétienne. Paris, 1953.
Phil 2905.1.175   La pensée théologique de Teilhard de Chardin. (Crespy, Georges.) Paris, 1961.
Phil 5257.66   La pensée vivante; réales et techniques de la pensée créatrice. (Rohrbach, M.A.) Paris, 1959.
Phil 5258.88   Pensée vivante et perfection formelle. Thèse. (Souriau, Étienne.) Paris, 1925.
Phil 5258.88.5   Pensée vivante et perfection formelle. 2. éd. (Souriau, Étienne.) Paris, 1952.
Phil 2520.27.5   Pensées, choisies. (Descartes, René.) Paris, 1944.
Phil 2805.40.2A   Pensées, fragments et lettres. (Pascal, Blaise.) Paris, 1844. 2v.
Phil 2805.40.33   Pensées, opuscules et lettres. (Pascal, Blaise.) Paris, 1873. 2v.

Phil 8889.2.2   Pensées, réflexions et maximes morales. (Oxenstjerna, J.T.) Paris, 1825. 2v.
Htn   Phil 2805.39*   Pensées...sur la religion. (Pascal, Blaise.) Paris, 1670.
Phil 2805.40.10   Pensées...sur la religion. (Pascal, Blaise.) Paris, 1725.
Phil 2805.40.11   Pensées...sur la religion. (Pascal, Blaise.) Paris, 1734.
Phil 2805.40.12   Pensées...sur la religion. (Pascal, Blaise.) Paris, 1748.
Phil 2805.40.18   Pensées. (Pascal, Blaise.) Fribourg, 1896.
Phil 2805.42.11   The pensées. (Pascal, Blaise.) Harmondsworth, 1961.
Phil 2805.42.37   Pensées. (Pascal, Blaise.) London, 1943.
Phil 2805.42.27   Pensées. (Pascal, Blaise.) London, 1947.
Phil 2805.42.30   Pensées. (Pascal, Blaise.) London, 1950.
Phil 2805.42.50   Pensées. (Pascal, Blaise.) N.Y., 1962.
Htn   Phil 2805.39.5*   Pensées. (Pascal, Blaise.) Paris, 1670.
Htn   Phil 2805.39.2*   Pensées. (Pascal, Blaise.) Paris, 1670.
Phil 2805.40.13.15   Pensées. (Pascal, Blaise.) Paris, 1842.
Phil 2805.40.37   Pensées. (Pascal, Blaise.) Paris, 1852.
Phil 2805.40.3   Pensées. (Pascal, Blaise.) Paris, 1854.
Phil 2805.40.29   Pensées. (Pascal, Blaise.) Paris, 186-.
Phil 2805.40.34   Pensées. (Pascal, Blaise.) Paris, 1869.
NEDL   Phil 2805.40.14   Pensées. (Pascal, Blaise.) Paris, 1874.
Phil 2805.40.7   Les pensées. (Pascal, Blaise.) Paris, 1877-79. 2v.
Phil 2805.40.15   Pensées. (Pascal, Blaise.) Paris, 1897.
Phil 2805.40.17A   Pensées. (Pascal, Blaise.) Paris, 1904. 3v.
Phil 2805.40.19   Pensées. (Pascal, Blaise.) Paris, 1907.
Phil 2805.40.23   Pensées. (Pascal, Blaise.) Paris, 1924.
Phil 2805.40.38   Pensées. (Pascal, Blaise.) Paris, 1934.
Phil 2805.42.35   Pensées. (Pascal, Blaise.) Paris, 1942.
Phil 2805.42.40   Pensées. (Pascal, Blaise.) Paris, 1958. 2v.
Phil 2805.42.45   Pensées. (Pascal, Blaise.) Paris, 1960. 2v.
Phil 2805.42.55   Pensées. (Pascal, Blaise.) Paris, 1962.
Phil 2805.42.58   Pensées. (Pascal, Blaise.) Paris, 1966.
Phil 2805.40.6   Pensées. (Pascal, Blaise.) Tours, 1873.
Phil 2805.40.5   Pensées. (Pascal, Blaise.) Tours, 1873.
Phil 8889.2.3   Pensées. v.1-2. (Oxenstjerna, J.T.) Paris, 1774.
Phil 8889.2.4   Pensées. v.1-2. (Oxenstjerna, J.T.) Rouen, 1782.
Phil 2805.40.16   Pensées. v.1-2. (Pascal, Blaise.) Paris, 1812.
Phil 2805.40.4A   Pensées. v.1-2. (Pascal, Blaise.) Paris, 1866.
Phil 2805.40.4.3   Pensées. 2e éd. v.1-2. (Pascal, Blaise.) Paris, 1866. 2v.
Phil 2805.40.22   Pensées choisies. 2. éd. (Pascal, Blaise.) Paris, 1882.
Phil 2805.40.21   Pensées choisies. 6e éd. (Pascal, Blaise.) Paris, 1876.
Phil 2805.40.30   Pensées contenant les lettres et opuscules. (Pascal, Blaise.) Paris, 1861.
Phil 2805.40.13   Pensées de Blaise Pascal. (Pascal, Blaise.) Paris, 1817. 2v.
Phil 2805.40.13.5   Pensées de Blaise Pascal. (Pascal, Blaise.) Paris, 1829.
Phil 2805.40.13.10   Pensées de Blaise Pascal. (Pascal, Blaise.) Paris, 1839.
Phil 2805.40.6.5   Pensées de Blaise Pascal. (Pascal, Blaise.) Paris, 1873.
Phil 2520.27   Pensées de Descartes sur la religion et la morale. (Descartes, René.) Paris, 1811.
Phil 3552.251.5   Pensées de Leibnitz sur la religion. (Emery, J.A.) Paris, 1803. 2v.
Phil 2805.95.10A   Les pensées de Pascal; étude et analyse. (Strowski, F.) Paris, 1930.
Phil 2805.40.32   Pensées de Pascal. (Pascal, Blaise.) Paris, 1866.
Phil 2805.365   Les pensées de Pascal en France de 1842 à 1942. (Francis, Raymond.) Paris, 1959.
Phil 3808.55   Pensées et fragments. 9. éd. (Schopenhauer, Arthur.) Paris, 1889.
Phil 3808.55.11   Pensées et fragments. 25. éd. (Schopenhauer, Arthur.) Paris, 1911.
Phil 2805.40.28   Les pensées et oeuvres choisies. (Pascal, Blaise.) Paris, 1937.
Phil 2805.40.36   Pensées et opuscules. 6. éd. (Pascal, Blaise.) Paris, 1912.
Phil 2805.40.35   Pensées et opuscules. 11e éd. (Pascal, Blaise.) Paris, 1923.
Phil 2490.63   Pensées et préceptes. (Comte, Auguste.) Paris, 1924.
Phil 2805.310   The pensées of Pascal. (Maggioni, Mary J.) Washington, 1950.
Phil 2805.193   La pensées philosophique créatrice de Pascal. (Nedelkovitch, D.) Paris, 1925.
Phil 2050.37.20   Pensées philosophiques, morales, critiques, littéraires et politiques. (Hume, David.) Londres, 1767.
Htn   Phil 2530.30*   Pensées philosophiques. (Diderot, Denis.) La Haye, 1746.
Phil 8889.2   Pensées sur divers sujets. (Oxenstjerna, J.T.) Francfort, 1736. 2v.
Phil 2805.40.31   Pensées sur la religion. (Pascal, Blaise.) Paris, 1951. 3v.
Phil 2805.40.39   Pensées sur la religion. v.1-2. (Pascal, Blaise.) Paris, 1948[1947]
Phil 2805.40.50   Pensées sur la religion et sur quelques autres sujets. (Pascal, Blaise.) Monaco, 1962.
Phil 2805.40.20   Pensées sur la vérité de la religion chrétienne par J. Chevalier. 2. éd. (Pascal, Blaise.) Paris, 1925. 2v.
Phil 175.6.15   Pensées sur l'homme, ses rapports. (Ancillon, F.) Berlin, 1829. 2v.
Phil 4825.12   Penseurs yougoslaves. (Atanasijavič, Ksenija.) Belgrade, 1937.
Phil 2733.45   Pensiere metafisici. (Malebranche, Nicolas.) Lanciano, 1911.
Phil 4115.27   Pensieri. (Gioberti, V.) Torino, 1859-60. 2v.
Phil 2725.2.91   Pamphlet vol. Pensieri di un credente. 2 pam.
Phil 9420.11   Pensieri di un solitario. Torino, 1826.
Phil 4080.3.45   Pensieri vari (ristampa). (Croce, Benedetto.) Bari, 1944.
Phil 25.115   Il pensiero. Milano. 1,1956+ 10v.
Phil 1817.15   Il pensiero americano contemporaneo. (Rossi Landi, Ferruccio.) Milano, 1958. 2v.
Phil 193.49.19   Il pensiero americano e altri saggi. (Santayana, G.) Milano, 1939.
Phil 1117.8.18   Il pensiero antico. 3. ed. (Mondolfo, Rodolfo.) Firenze, 1961.
Phil 4115.60   Il pensiero civile. (Gioberti, V.) Torino, 1901.
Phil 25.134   Il pensiero critico; problemi del nostro tempo. Milano. 1,1959+ 4v.
Phil 4340.10   Il pensiero delea rinascenza in Spagna e Portogallo. (Batlori, Miguel.) Milano, 1964.
Phil 2605.1.85   Il pensiero di Alfredo Fouillée. (Costanzi, T.M.) Napoli, 1936.
Phil 4060.4.85   Il pensiero di Antonio Aliotta. (Pallavicini, Gian Luigi.) Napoli, 1968.
Phil 4070.7.80   Il pensiero di Antonio Banfi. (Papi, Fulveo.) Firenze, 1961.
Phil 3826.8   Il pensiero di B. Spinoza. (Guzzo, Augusto.) Firenze, 1924.

Phil 3826.8.2 — Il pensiero di B. Spinoza. 2. ed. (Guzzo, Augusto.) Torino, 1964.

Phil 4265.6.80 — Il pensiero di B. Varisco. (Librizzi, C.) Padova, 1942.

Phil 2255.1.120 — Il pensiero di Bertrand Russell. (Riverro, Emmanuele.) Napoli, 1958.

Phil 2880.2.92 — Il pensiero di Charles Secrétan. (Salmona, Bruno.) Milano, 1968.

Phil 1850.123 — Il pensiero di Francesco Bacone. (Levi, Adolfo.) Milano, 1925.

Phil 4190.1.90 — Il pensiero di Francesco Orestano. (Ottaviano, Carmelo.) Palermo, 1933.

Phil 4369.2.84 — Il pensiero di Francesco Sanchez. (Giarratano, C.) Napoli, 1903.

Phil 4260.31 — Il pensiero di Giambattista Vico. (Vico, G.B.) Torino, 1959.

Phil 1955.6.25 — Il pensiero di Giovanni Dewey. (Gillio-Tos, M.T.) Napoli, 1938.

Phil 3484.26 — Il pensiero di Immanuel Kant. (Chiodí, Pietro.) Torino, 1963.

Phil 1955.6.122 — Il pensiero di John Dewey. (Pra, Mario dal.) Milano, 1952.

Phil 3925.16.180 — Il pensiero di Ludovico Wittgenstein. (Riverso, Emanuele.) Napoli, 1965?

Phil 4060.1.88 — Il pensiero di Roberto Ardigo. (Mondolfo, Rodolfo.) Mantova, 1908.

Phil 4170.5.80 — Il pensiero di Sebastiano Maturi. (Pra, Mario dal.) Milano, 1943.

Phil 4115.85 — Il pensiero di Vincenzo Gioberti. (Saitta, Giuseppe.) Messina, 1917.

Phil 4115.85.2 — Il pensiero di Vincenzo Gioberti. 2a ed. (Saitta, Giuseppe.) Firenze, 1927.

Phil 8597.54 — Pensiero e coerenza cristiana. (Riva, C.) Brescia, 1963.

Phil 4170.4.31 — Il pensiero e conoscenza. (Masci, F.) Torino, 1922.

Phil 2733.118 — Il pensiero e l'opera di Nicola Malebranche. (Banchetti, A.) Milano, 1963.

Phil 2493.96 — Il pensiero economico del Condillac. (Meoli, Umberto.) Milano, 1761.

Phil 4060.9.40 — Pensiero ed esistenza. (Antoni, Giuseppe.) Padova, 1965.

Phil 4260.111 — Il pensiero educativo di Giambattista Vico. (Fornaca, Remo.) Torino, 1957.

Phil 1750.560.5 — Il pensiero esistenzialista. (Chiodi, Pietro.) Milano, 1959.

Phil 2725.55 — Il pensiero estetico di Charles Lalo. (Cossu, Maria.) Cagliari, 1965.

Phil 2475.1.203 — Il pensiero filosofico cotemporaneo e la psicologia del Bergson. (Mercanti, Pietro.) Roma, 1919?

Phil 4140.80 — Il pensiero filosofico de Donato Jaja. (Cristallini, Alessandro.) Padova, 1970.

Phil 3480.25.40 — Il pensiero filosofico di E.K. v.1-2. (Kant, Immanuel.) Firenze, 1926-25.

Phil 4190.1.80 — Il pensiero filosofico di Francesco Orestano. (Dollo, Corrado.) Padova, 1967.

Phil 4215.1.87 — Il pensiero filosofico di Giandomenico Romagnosi. (Norsa, Achille.) Milano, 1930.

Phil 4235.9.80 — Il pensiero filosofico di Guiseppe Tarozzi. (Fiorensoli, Dario.) Padova, 1964.

Phil 2270.114 — Il pensiero filosofico di Herbert Spencer. (Dallari, Gino.) Torino, 1904.

Phil 3499.42 — Il pensiero filosofico di Kant, ovvero problemi di critica Kantiana. (Ruvo, Vincenzo de.) Paris, 1969.

Phil 4170.10.90 — Il pensiero filosofico di Piero Martinetti. (Romano, F.) Padova, 1959.

Phil 2250.85 — Il pensiero filosofico e morale di Josiah Royce. (Galgano, Maria.) Roma, 1921.

Phil 2115.200 — Il pensiero filosofico e pedagogico di G. Locke. (Rosa, Pasquale.) Napoli, 1965.

Phil 332.29 — Il pensiero filosofico ed il suo fondamento. (Bologna, Italo.) Milano, 1957.

Phil 1721.8 — Il pensiero filosofico odierno. (Dalori, Paolo.) Roma, 1959.

Phil 2115.235 — Il pensiero giovanile di John Locke. (Baldini, Artemio Enzo.) Milano, 1969.

Phil 4210.68 — Il pensiero giuridico e politico di Antonio Rosmini. (Rosmini-Serbati, Antonio.) Firenze, 1962.

Phil 1111.13 — Il pensiero greco. (Galli, Dario.) Padova, 1954.

Phil 75.88 — Il pensiero greco. Orientamenti bibliografici a cura di Francesco Adorno. (Adorno, Francesco.) Bari, 1969.

Phil 75.88.5 — Il pensiero greco-romano e il cristianesimo. 1. ed. (Adorno, Francesco.) Bari, 1970.

Phil 4006.2.18 — Il pensiero italiano del rinascimento. 3. ed. (Gentile, G.) Firenze, 1940.

Phil 1600.20 — Il pensiero italiano del Rinascimento e il tempo Nostro. (Centro di studi umanistici di Montepulciano.) Firenze, 1970.

Phil 4006.2.15 — Il pensiero italiano del secolo XIX. (Gentile, G.) Milano, 1928.

Phil 4018.6.5 — Il pensiero italiano nell'età del Risorgimento. 2. ed. (Sciacca, M.F.) Milano, 1963.

Phil 4018.5 — Il pensiero italiano nell'umanesimo e nel Rinascimento. (Saitta, G.) Bologna, 1949. 3v.

Phil 4018.5.2 — Il pensiero italiano nell'umanesimo e nel Rinascimento. 2. ed. (Saitta, G.) Firenze, 1961. 3v.

Phil 1718.29 — Il pensiero moderno. (Sciacca, Michele Federico.) Brescia, 1949.

Phil 25.41 — Il pensiero nuovo. Roma. 1-3,1898-1899

Phil 817.26 — Il pensiero occidentale. v.1-3. (Riverso, E.) Napoli, 1964.

Phil 4080.3.390 — Il pensiero politico di Benedetto Croce. (Garosci, A.) Torino, 1962.

Phil 4080.3.175 — Il pensiero politico di Benedetto Croce e un nuovo liberalismo. 2. ed. (Parente, Alfredo.) Napoli, 1944.

Phil 4200.4.30 — Il pensiero puro. (Pastore, A.) Milano, 1913.

Phil 8605.2 — Il pensiero religioso. (Zoppola, G.) Lugano, 1911. 2 pam.

Phil 3808.170 — Il pensiero religioso di Arturo Schopenhauer. (Costa, Alessandro.) Roma, 1935.

Phil 4265.2.90 — Il pensiero religioso di P.G. Ventura. (Cristofoli, A.) Milano, 1927.

Phil 4002.7 — Il pensiero religioso italiano dall'umanesimo al giurisdizionalismo. (Corsano, A.) Bari, 1937.

Phil 5068.70 — Il pensiero scientifico in Italia negli anni 1930-1960. (Maros dell'Oro, Angiolo.) Cremona, 1964.

Phil 2725.2.125 — Il pensiero socio-politico di Lamennais. (Zadei, Guido.) Napoli, 1969.

Phil 4372.1.110 — Il pensiero ssicologico e morale di G.L. Vives. (Sancipriano, M.) Firenze, 1958.

Phil 3015.4 — Il pensiero tedesco. (Pensa, M.) Bologna, 1938.

Phil 2475.1.207 — Pentimalli, G.H. Bergson. Torino, 1920.

Phil 8900.2 — Il pentimento e la morale ascentica. (Zini, Zino.) Torino, 1902.

Phil 3808.121.5 — Penzig, Rudolph. Arthur Schopenhauer und die menschliche Willensfreiheit. Halle, 1879.

Phil 510.145 — Penzler, Martin. Die Monadenlehre und ihre Beziehung zur griechischen Philosophie. Minden, 1878.

Phil 3450.19.400 — Penzo, Giorgio. L'unità del pensiero in Martin Heidegger; una ontologia estetica. Padova, 1965.

Phil 5066.308 — Penzov, Inrii E. Elementy matematicheskoi logiki i teorii mnozhestva. Saratov, 1968.

Phil 8670.14 — The people and the presence. (Pythian-Adams, W.J.) London, 1942.

Phil 7054.47 — People from the other world. (Olcott, H.S.) Hartford, 1875.

Phil 5520.85 — People in guandaries. (Johnson, Wendel.) N.Y., 1946.

Phil 2725.2.55 — The people's own book. (Lamennais, F.R. de.) Boston, 1839.

Phil 978.49.830 — Peoppig, Fred. Schicksalswege zu Rudolf Steiner. 2. Aufl. Stuttgart, 1955.

Phil 3425.550 — Peperzak, Adrien. La jeune Hegel et la vision morale du monde. La Haye, 1960.

Phil 1715.12 — Pepi, Sergio. Umanismo logico. Roma, 1963.

Phil 530.11.20 — Pepler, Conrad. The English religious heritage. Saint Louis, 1958.

Phil 8416.34 — Pepper, S.C. Aesthetic quality, a contextualistic theory of beauty. N.Y., 1938.

Phil 8416.34.5 — Pepper, S.C. The basis of criticism in the arts. Cambridge, 1945.

Phil 8416.9 — Pepper, Stephen. The work of art. Indiana, 1955.

Phil 735.180 — Pepper, Stephen C. The sources of value. Berkeley, 1958.

Phil 190.69 — Pepper, Stephen C. World hypotheses; a study of evidence. Berkeley, 1942.

Phil 2225.11.10 — Pepper, Stephen Coburn. Concept and quality; a world hypothesis. La Salle, 1967.

Phil 2225.11 — Pepper, Stephen Coburn. A digest of purposive values. Berkeley, 1947.

Phil 8890.52 — Pepper, Stephen Coburn. Ethics. N.Y., 1960.

Phil 2225.11.5 — Pepper, Stephen Coburn. World hypotheses. Berkeley, 1957.

Phil 3745.20 — Peprzak, Adrien T.B. Gronden en Grenzen. Haarlem, 1966.

Phil 8702.11 — Un pequeño libro de actualidad. (Moigno, F.N.M.) Puerto Rico, 1884.

Phil 4210.5 — Per Antonio Rosmini nel 1o centenario dalla sua nascita. (Rosmini-Serbati, Antonio.) Milano, 1897. 2v.

Phil 4110.3.86 — Per Francesco Fiorentino nella inaugurazione del monumento in Catanzaro. (La Giovine Calabria. Giornale, Catanzaro.) Catanzaro, 1889.

Phil 4065.121 — Per Giordano Bruno dal 1876 al 1889. (Comandini, A.) Roma, 1889.

Phil 5014.1 — Per la storia della logica. (Enriques, Federigo.) Bologna, 1922.

Phil 4235.4.81 — Per le solenni onoranze al filosofo Vincenzo Tedeschi Paterno Castello. (Catania. R. Scuola Normale Maschile Superiore.) Catania, 1892.

Phil 7054.152 — Per lo spiritismo. 2. ed. (Brofferio, Angelo.) Milano, 1893.

Phil 175.68 — Per o contro l'uomo. (Abbagnano, Nieda.) Milano, 1968.

Phil 3246.294 — Per un innovamento nella interpretazione della filosofia Fichtiana. (Severino, Emanuele.) Brescia, 1968.

Phil 8690.3 — Per un nuovo patto fra le scienze e la religione. (Anzoletti, Luisa.) Milano, 1899.

Phil 1750.756 — Per un umanesimo scientifico. (Brancatisano, F.) Firenze, 1963.

Phil 192.56 — Per una concezione attivistica della filosofia. (Rossi, M.M.) Bologna, 1927.

Phil 8586.33 — Per una fede. (Graf, A.) Milano, 1906.

Phil 8415.9.10 — Per una fondazione fenomenologica della conoscitività dell'arte. (Oberti, Elisa.) Milano, 1968.

Phil 4080.27 — Per una metafisica concreta. (Crescini, Angelo.) Padova, 1963.

Phil 8092.12 — Per un'estetica mondana. (Barilli, Renato.) Bologna, 1964.

Phil 5628.12 — Perales y Gutiérrez, Arturo. El supernaturalismo de Santa Teresa y la filosofia médica. Madrid, 1894.

Phil 8705.3 — Perce, W.R. Geneses and modern science. N.Y., 1897.

Phil 349.47 — Perceiving, sensing, and knowing. 1. ed. (Swartz, Robert Jason.) Garden City, N.Y., 1965.

Phil 5585.90 — Perceiving. (Chisholm, R.M.) Ithaca, 1957.

NEDL Phil 5252.79 — Percepción instinto y razon. (Mouchet, E.) Buenos Aires, 1941.

Phil 5593.57.5 — Perceptanalysis. (Piotrowski, Z.) N.Y., 1957.

Phil 5643.145 — Perception; a seminar conducted by the Philosophy Department of Sri Venkateswara University, 1964. Bombay, 1966.

Phil 2750.20.140 — Perception, expression, and history. (O'Neill, John.) Evanston, 1970.

Phil 630.12A — Perception, physics and reality. (Broad, Charles D.) Cambridge, 1914.

Phil 573.4 — Perception, understanding and society. (Chambers, Frank P.) London, 1961.

Phil 5585.01 — Pamphlet box. Perception.

Phil 5585.80 — La perception. (Association de Psychologie Scientifique de Langue Française.) Paris, 1955.

Phil 5585.72 — Perception. (Blake, R.R.) N.Y., 1951.

Phil 5585.240 — Perception. (Forgus, Ronald H.) N.Y., 1966.

Phil 5585.229 — Perception. (Hochberg, Julian E.) Englewood Cliffs, N.J., 1964.

Phil 5585.214 — Perception. (Jordan, Nehemiah.) Santa Monica, 1961.

Phil 5585.58.5 — Perception. (Price, Henry H.) London, 1954.

Phil 5585.58.7 — Perception. (Price, Henry H.) London, 1964.

Phil 5585.05 — Pamphlet box. Perception. German dissertations.

Phil 8412.20 — Perception and aesthetic value. (Lee, H.L.) N.Y., 1938.

Phil 5650.34 — Perception and communication. (Broadbent, D.E.) N.Y., 1958.

Phil 2340.10.200 — Perception and cosmology in Whitehead's philosophy. (Schmidt, Paul Frederic.) New Brunswick, 1967.

Phil 5585.212 — Perception and motion; analysis of space-structured behavior. (Smith, Karl.) Philadelphia, 1962.

Phil 573.6 — Perception and our knowledge of the external world. (Locke, Don.) London, 1967.

Phil 70.94.8 — Perception and personal identity. (Oberlin Colloquium in Philosophy, 8th, Oberlin College, 1967.) Cleveland. 1969

Phil 25.151 — Perception and psychophysics. Goleta, California. 1,1966+ 6v.

Phil 5585.225 — Perception and the conditioned reflex. (Sokolov, E.N.) Oxford, 1963.

Phil 573.2 — Perception and the physical world. (Armstrong, David M.) London, 1961.

Phil 1715.3.5A   Perry, R.B. The present conflict of ideals. N.Y., 1918.
Phil 1715.3.8A   Perry, R.B. The present conflict of ideals. N.Y., 1922.
Phil 1715.3.2   Perry, R.B. Present philosophical tendencies. London, 1912.
Phil 2225.2.30A   Perry, R.B. Realms of value. Cambridge, Mass., 1954.
Phil 8595.12   Perry, R.B. Religion and mere morality. Boston, 1906.
Phil 190.18.5   Perry, R.B. Studies in theory of knowledge. n.p., 1900-1910.
Phil 2070.129.5A   Perry, R.B. The thought and character of William James. Boston, 1935. 2v.
Phil 2070.129.7A   Perry, R.B. The thought and character of William James. Cambridge, 1948.
Phil 2070.129   Perry, R.B. William James. Boston? 1910.
Phil 190.18.20   Pamphlet vol. Perry, R.B. Miscellaneous essays. 14 pam.
Phil 2070.01A   Perry, Ralph B. Annotated bibliography of writings of William James. N.Y., 1920.
Phil 9400.10   Perry, Ralph B. Plea for an age movement. N.Y., 1942.
Phil 735.20.12   Perry, Ralph Barton. General theory of value. Cambridge, Mass., 1954.
Phil 735.20.5A   Perry, Ralph Barton. General theory of value. N.Y., 1926.
Phil 815.5   Perry, Rufus L. Sketch of philosophical systems. n.p., n.d.
Phil 6325.26   Perry, Stewart Edmond. The human nature of science; researchers at work in psychiatry. N.Y., n.d.
Phil 1540.29   Persecution and the art of writing. (Strauss, Leo.) Glencoe, Ill., 1952. 2v.
Phil 632.8   Persephone: a study of two worlds. (Streatfeild, D.) London, 1959.
Phil 5350.10   Persistence and change: Bennington College and its students after twenty-five years. N.Y., 1967.
Phil 5645.9   Persistence of vision in color blind subjects. (Allen, Frank.) n.p., 1902.
Phil 177.33.7   The persistent problems of philosophy. (Calkins, Mary Whiton.) N.Y., 1936.
Phil 177.33.3   The persistent problems of philosophy. 3d ed. (Calkins, Mary Whiton.) N.Y., 1912.
Phil 735.256   The persistent quest for values: what are we seeking? (Hatcher, Harlan Henthorne.) Columbia, 1966.
Phil 338.14   Die persönliche Denkthätigkeit. (Hoppe, J.I.) Würzburg, 1880.
Phil 3625.11.90   Persönliche Erinnerungen an Alexius Meinong. (Benndorf, H.) Graz, 1951.
Phil 8670.6   Der persönliche Gott und Welt. (Poetter, F.C.) Elberfeld, 1875.
Phil 3549.8.90   Persönlichkeit. (Klages, Ludwig.) Potsdam, 1927.
Phil 3808.24.15   Die Persönlichkeit und das Werk. (Schopenhauer, Arthur.) Leipzig, 1925.
Phil 575.138   Persönlichkeit und Form. (Stiefel, Kurt.) Zürich, 1943.
Phil 575.235   Persönlichkeit und Gemeinschaft zur Kritik der neothomistischen Persönlichkeitsauffassung. (Miller, Reinhold.) Berlin, 1916.
Phil 5627.258.5   Persönlichkeit und Religiosität. (Potempa, Rudolf.) Göttingen, 1958.
Phil 575.65   Persönlichkeit und Schicksal. (Rohracher, H.) Wien, 1926.
Phil 7080.55   Persönlichkeit und Schlafverhalten. (Othmer, Ekkehard.) Meisenheim, 1965.
Phil 575.34   Persönlichkeit und Weltanschauung. (Müller-Freienfels, Richard.) Berlin, 1919.
Phil 575.34.2   Persönlichkeit und Weltanschauung. 2e Aufl. (Müller-Freienfels, Richard.) Berlin, 1923.
Phil 5255.44.2   Persönlichkeits-Psychologie. 2. Aufl. (Prinzhorn, H.) Heidelberg, 1958.
Phil 6319.8   Die Persönlichkeitsanalyse. (Zolowicz, E.) Leipzig, 1926.
Phil 5255.44   Persönlichkeitspsychologie. (Prinzhorn, H.) Leipzig, 1932.
Phil 6155.26   Persönlichkeitstheorie und Psychopharmaka. (Legewie, Heiner.) Meisenheim, 1968.
Phil 5590.490   Die Persönlichkeitsveränderung im Sinne der Deformierung noch schwerer Hungerdystrophie. (Reuter, Jürgen Paul.) Bonn, 1966.
Phil 6980.305   Persönlichkeitswandel. (Frankenstein, C.) München, 1964.
Phil 6805.10   Persönlichkeitswandlung unter Freiheitsentzug. (Ohm, August.) Berlin, 1964.
Phil 5590.230   Person, Charakter, Persönlichkeit. (Arnold, Wilhelm.) Göttingen, 1957.
Phil 5590.485   The person: his development throughout the life cycle. (Lidz, Theodore.) N.Y., 1968.
Phil 5238.228   Person als Prozess. Bern, 1968.
Phil 5853.6.5   Person and counselor. (Johnson, Paul Emanuel.) Nashville, 1967.
Phil 176.94.5   Person and reality. (Brigtman, E.S.) N.Y., 1958.
Phil 2750.11.47.5   The person and the common good. (Maritain, Jacques.) N.Y., 1947.
Phil 8656.27.5   The person God is. (Bertocci, Peter Anthony.) N.Y., 1970.
Phil 5251.54   The person in psychology. (Lafitte, Paul.) N.Y., 1957.
Phil 8581.60   The person in religion. Thesis. (Burkart, Anna D.) Philadelphia, 1930.
Phil 5400.105   The person in the body. (Hinsie, L.E.) N.Y., 1945.
Phil 186.48.10   The person of evolution. (Lighthall, W.D.) Montreal, 1930.
Phil 186.48.11   The person of evolution. (Lighthall, W.D.) Toronto, 1933.
Phil 185.90   Person og tänkning. (Kemp, Peter.) København, 1960.
Phil 5585.125   Person perception and interpersonal behavior. (Tagiuri, Renato.) Stanford, 1958.
Phil 5585.125.3   Person perception and interpersonal behavior. (Tagiuri, Renato.) Stanford, 1965.
Phil 5627.245.2   The person reborn. (Tournier, Paul.) N.Y., 1966.
Phil 575.286   Person und Dasein. Zur Frage der Ontologie des Wertseins. (Frings, Manfred S.) Den Haag, 1969.
Phil 5590.528   Person und Gemeinschaft. (Duesberg, Hans.) Bonn, 1970.
Phil 3665.5.90   Person und Handlung in der Ethik Leonard Nelsons. Inaug. Diss. (Hauer, Eugen.) Bonn, 1928.
Phil 575.155   Person und Persönlichkeit. (Stauenhagen, K.) Göttingen, 1957.
Phil 575.148   Person und Psychotherapie. (Gent, Werner.) Göttingen, 1951.
Phil 193.53   Person und Sache. (Stern, L.W.) Leipzig, 1906- 2v.
Phil 193.53.2   Person und Sache. (Stern, L.W.) Leipzig, 1923-1924. 3v.
Phil 4080.21   La persona e il tempo. 1. ed. pt. 1. (Caracciolo, A.) Arona, 1955.
Phil 4210.210   Persona e personalità nell'antropologia di Antonio Rosmini. (Manganelli, Maria.) Milano, 1967.
Phil 8580.34   Persona ed evidenza nella prospettiva classica. (Arata, C.) Milano, 1963.
Phil 1145.100   La persona umana nella morale dei Greci. (Banchetti, Silvestro.) Milano, 1966.

Phil 3640.272   Persona y destino. (Gil Salguero, L.) Buenos Aires, 1934.
Phil 9530.47   Personal achievements. (Coffee, John R.) N.Y., 1932.
Phil 5850.176   Personal adjustment. 1. ed. (Dunlap, Knight.) N.Y., 1946.
Phil 5590.235.2A   Personal adjustment. 2. ed. (Jourard, Sidney Marshall.) N.Y., 1963.
Phil 9400.23   Personal adjustments in old age. (Cavan, R.S.) Chicago, 1949.
Phil 5590.424   Personal and social development. (Levine, Louis.) N.Y., 1963.
Phil 5548.115   Personal causation. (DeCharms, Richard.) N.Y., 1968.
Phil 5590.190   Personal character and cultural milieu. (Haring, D.G.) N.Y., 1949.
Phil 8885.36   Personal ethics. (Kirk, K.E.) Oxford, 1934.
Phil 3494.43   Personal freedom within the third antimony. Thesis. (Mattern, C.D.) Philadelphia, 1941.
Phil 400.13   Personal idealism; philosophical essays of members of Oxford University. (Sturt, H.) London, 1902.
Phil 575.185   Personal identity and survival. (Broad, Charlie P.) London, 1958.
Phil 6671.13.5   Personal influence. (Barnes, W.A.) Boston, 1906.
Phil 346.20.3   Personal knowledge. (Polanyi, Michael.) Chicago, 1960.
Phil 346.20   Personal knowledge. (Polanyi, Michael.) London, 1958.
Phil 346.20.4   Personal knowledge towards a post-critical philosophy. (Polanyi, Michael.) Chicago, 1968[1958]
Phil 7069.00.80   Personal magnetism...by a diplomat. n.p., 19- ?
Phil 6671.13   Personal magnetism and clairvoyance. 4th ed. (Barnes, W.A.) Boston, 1900.
Phil 978.5.7   Personal memoirs of H.P. Blavatsky. (Blavatsky, H.P.) London, 1937.
Phil 9490.5   Personal power counsels to college men. (Tucker, W.J.) Boston, 1910.
Phil 6111.46   Personal problems for men and women. (Bowman, Karl M.) N.Y., 1931.
Phil 6129.8   Personal problems of everyday life. (Travis, L.E.) N.Y., 1941.
Phil 630.44   Personal realism. (Pratt, James B.) N.Y., 1937.
Phil 6321.56   Personal relationships in psychological disorders. (Lowe, Gordon Robb.) Harmondsworth, 1969.
Phil 8588.2.5   Personal religion and the life of devotion. (Inge, W.R.) London, 1924.
Phil 8587.50   Personal religious beliefs. (Harper, W.A.) Boston, 1937.
Phil 8612.88   Der personal verstandene Tod. (Wiplinger, Fridolin.) Freiburg, 1970.
Phil 8622.35   Der personale Glaube. (Cirne-Lima, Carlos.) Innsbruck, 1959.
Phil 575.135   Personalidad y caracter. (Bañuelos García, M.) Madrid, 1942.
Phil 5590.20   La personalidad y el carácter. (Delgado, Honoria.) Lima, 1943.
Phil 5590.444   Personalisation. (Edelweiss, Malomar Lund.) Wien, 1964.
Phil 176.27.12   Personalism. (Bowne, B.P.) Boston, 1908.
Phil 575.146.5   Personalism. (Mounier, E.) London, 1952.
Phil 176.27.8   Personalism and the problems of philosophy. (Flewelling, R.T.) N.Y., 1915.
Phil 574.2   Personalisme en democratisering. (Janssens, Louis.) Brussel, 1957.
Phil 575.82   El personalismo. (Lutosľawski, W.) Madrid, 1887.
Phil 574.4   Personalismo filosofico. (Stefanini, Luigi.) Brescia, 1962.
Phil 2750.22.120   Personalismo obrero. (Diaz, Carlos.) Madrid, 1969.
Phil 4210.197   Il personalismo rosminiano. (Zolo, Danilo.) Brescia, 1963.
Phil 575.85   Personalismul energetic. (Rădulescu-Motru, C.) Bucuresti, 1927.
Phil 574.6.5   Personalism in Philosophie und Theologie. (Haering, Bernhard.) München, 1968.
Phil 575.32   Personalismus und Realismus. (Dreyer, Hans.) Berlin, 1905.
Phil 175.37   Personalistische Philosophie. (Adolph, Heinrich.) Leipzig, 1931.
Phil 5590.345   La personalità nell'età evolutiva. (Marzi, Alberto.) Firenze, 1959.
Phil 6313.7   La personalité humaine. (Delmas, F. Achille.) Paris, 1925.
Phil 5590.506   Personality; a behavioral analysis. (Lundin, Robert William.) N.Y., 1969.
Phil 575.91A   Personality; a psychological interpretation. (Allport, G.W.) N.Y., 1937.
Phil 5520.235   Personality, appearance and speech. (Pear, T.H.) London, 1957.
Phil 5590.418   Personality, dynamics and development. (Sarnoff, Irving.) N.Y., 1962.
Phil 5241.79.10   Personality, many in one. (Bridges, J.W.) Boston, 1932.
Phil 5592.194   Personality; measurement of dimensions. 1. ed. (Horst, Paul.) San Francisco, 1968.
Phil 575.57.10   Personality, the crux of social intercourse. (Roback, A.A.) Cambridge, Mass., 1931.
Phil 5590.02   Pamphlet box. Personality.
Phil 5590.01   Pamphlet box. Personality.
Phil 5590.405   Personality. (Baughman, E.E.) Englewood Cliffs, N.J., 1962.
Phil 575.17   Personality. (Carus, P.) Chicago, 1911.
Phil 575.58   Personality. (Gordon, R.G.) London, 1926.
Phil 575.58.3   Personality. (Gordon, R.G.) N.Y., 1928.
Phil 5590.265   Personality. (Guilford, J.P.) N.Y., 1959.
Phil 575.19   Personality. (Jevons, F.B.) N.Y., 1913.
Phil 5590.80   Personality. (McClelland, D.C.) N.Y., 1951.
Phil 5590.82.2   Personality. (McClelland, D.C.) N.Y., 1963.
Phil 575.2   Personality. (Momerie, A.W.) Edinburgh, 1879.
Phil 575.2.5   Personality. (Momerie, A.W.) Edinburgh, 189-?
Phil 5590.36   Personality. (Murphy, Gardner.) N.Y., 1947.
Phil 575.4   Personality. (Olssen, W.W.) N.Y., 1882.
Phil 575.57.11   Personality. (Roback, A.A.) London, 1931.
Phil 5590.468   Personality. (Sarason, Irwin G.) N.Y., 1966.
Phil 9070.24   Personality. (Spillman, Harry Collins.) N.Y., 1919.
Phil 5590.240   Personality. (Thorpe, Louis Peter.) Princeton, 1958.
Phil 5257.49   Personality: its development and hygiene. (Richmond, W.V.) N.Y., 1937.
Phil 5590.524   Personality: theory, assessment, and research. (Pervin, Lawrence A.) N.Y., 1970.
Phil 575.2.2   Personality. 3rd ed. (Momerie, A.W.) Edinburgh, 1886.
Phil 575.2.3   Personality. 4th ed. (Momerie, A.W.) Edinburgh, 1889.
Phil 7040.40   Personality and arousal; a psychophysiological study of psychiatric disorder. (Claridge, Gordon S.) Oxford, 1967.
Phil 5590.457.5   Personality and assessment. (Mischel, Walter.) N.Y., 1968.
Phil 5590.429   Personality and behavior. (Gordon, J.E.) N.Y., 1963.

Phil 5590.415 — Personality and decision processes. (Brim, Orville Gilbert.) Stanford, 1962.

Phil 5590.14 — Personality and economic background. (Davidson, Helen H.) N.Y., 1943.

Phil 7118.10 — Personality and hypnosis. (Hilgard, Josephine Rohrs.) Chicago, 1970.

Phil 575.60 — Personality and immortality in post Kantian thought. (Braham, Ernest G.) London, 1926.

Phil 5590.554 — Personality and leadership behavior. (Knowles, Henry P.) Reading, Mass., 1971.

Phil 6311.27 — Personality and mental illness, psychiatric diagnosis. (Bowlby, John.) N.Y., 1942.

Phil 5548.35 — Personality and motivation structure and measurement. (Cattell, R.B.) Yonkers-on-Hudson, N.Y., 1957.

Phil 5896.5 — Personality and national character. 1. ed. (Lynn, Richard.) Oxford, 1971.

Phil 5590.275 — Personality and persuasibility. (Janis, Irving L.) New Haven, 1959.

Phil 5590.2.1 — Personality and problems of adjustment. (Young, Kimball.) N.Y., 1941.

Phil 5590.2 — Personality and problems of adjustment. (Young, Kimball.) N.Y., 1941.

Phil 6313.20 — Personality and psychotherapy. 1st. ed. (Dallard, John.) N.Y., 1950.

Phil 8674.8 — Personality and reality. (Turner, J.E.) N.Y., 1926.

Phil 575.78 — Personality and reason. (Crutcher, Roberta.) London, 1931.

Phil 8581.67 — Personality and religion. (Brightman, E.S.) N.Y., 1934.

Phil 5241.28.20 — Personality and religion. (Brown, W.) London, 1946.

Phil 5590.11 — Personality and sexuality of the handicapped woman. (Landis, Carney.) N.Y., 1942.

Phil 575.120 — Personality and social change. (Newcomb, Theodore Mead.) N.Y., 1943.

Phil 575.120.2.2 — Personality and social change. (Newcomb, Theodore Mead.) N.Y., 1957.

Phil 575.215A — Personality and social encounter. (Allport, G.W.) Boston, 1960.

Phil 5590.370 — Personality and social interaction. (Dalton, R.H.) Boston, 1961.

Phil 5242.46.5 — Personality and social psychology. (Cattell, R.B.) San Diego, 1964.

Phil 5590.426 — Personality and social systems. (Smelser, Neil Joseph.) N.Y., 1963.

Phil 5590.426.2 — Personality and social systems. 2. ed. (Smelser, Neil Joseph.) N.Y., 1970.

Phil 7040.22A — Personality and the behavior disorders. (Hunt, Joseph M.) N.Y., 1944. 2v.

Phil 575.22 — Personality and the Christian ideal. (Buckham, John W.) Boston, 1909.

Phil 5590.9.3 — Personality and the cultural pattern. (Plant, James S.) N.Y., 1939.

Phil 8876.156 — Personality and the good. (Bertocci, Peter.) N.Y., 1963.

Phil 5750.7 — Personality and will. (Aveling, Francis.) N.Y., 1931.

Phil 5592.55 — Personality assessment procedures. (Allen, Robert M.) N.Y., 1958.

Phil 5590.431A — Personality change. (Symposium on Personality Change, University of Texas.) N.Y., 1964.

Phil 6327.23 — Personality changes after operations on the frontal lobes. (Rylander, G.) Copenhagen, 1939.

Phil 6312.16.5 — Personality development and psychopathology. (Cameron, N.) Boston, 1963.

Phil 5590.445 — Personality dynamics. (Sappenfield, Bert Reese.) N.Y., 1961.

Phil 5242.58 — Personality dynamics and effective behavior. (Coleman, J.C.) Chicago, 1960.

Phil 6128.77 — Personality dynamics and mental health. (Schneiders, Alexander A.) N.Y., 1965.

Phil 6659.2 — Personality in arterial hypertension. (Binger, Carl A.L.) N.Y., 1945.

Phil 6060.38 — Personality in handwriting. (Mendel, A.O.) N.Y., 1947.

Phil 5590.435 — Personality in middle and late life. (Neugarten, B.L.) N.Y., 1964.

Phil 5590.330 — Personality in nature, society, and culture. 1. ed. (Kluckhohn, Clyde.) N.Y., 1948.

Phil 5590.105.2 — Personality in nature, society and culture. 2. ed. (Kluckhohn, Clyde.) N.Y., 1967.

Phil 5590.105 — Personality in nature. 2. ed. (Kluckhohn, Clyde.) N.Y., 1953.

Phil 5590.50 — Personality in theory and practice. (Roback, A.A.) Cambridge, Mass., 1950.

Phil 6317.18.10 — Personality information and action. (Healy, William.) N.Y., 1938.

Phil 6332.10 — Personality maladjustments and mental hygiene. 1st ed. (Wallin, John E.W.) N.Y., 1935.

Phil 6849.4 — The personality of a child molester. (Bell, Alan P.) Chicago, 1971.

Phil 7069.47.30 — The personality of man. (Tyrrell, George N.M.) W. Drayton, 1948.

Phil 5590.453 — Personality research; a book of readings. (Byrne, Donn Erwin.) Englewood Cliffs, N.J., 1966.

Phil 6316.14 — Personality structure and human interaction. (Guntrip, H.J.S.) London, 1961.

Phil 6316.14.5 — Personality structure and human interaction. (Guntrip, H.J.S.) N.Y., 1961.

Phil 5592.196 — Personality structure and measurement. (Eysenck, Hans Jurgen.) London, 1969.

Phil 2750.11.175 — Personalizm Maritaina i wspólczesna mysl Katolicka. (Mrówczyński, Tadeusz.) Warszawa, 1964.

Phil 6116.14 — Personified unthinkables, an argument against physical causation. (Grimké, S.S.) Ann Arbor, 1884.

Phil 181.110 — Personlichkeit und Geschichte. (Gunther, H.R.G.) Augsburg, 1947.

Phil 8633.1.8.5 — Personlighet och oddlighet. (Ostwald, W.) Stockholm, 1911.

Phil 5250.32.5 — Personlighetens psykologi. (Kaila, Eino.) Helsingfors, 1935.

Phil 6327.46.18 — Personlighetens sjukdomar. (Ribot, Théodule.) Stockholm, 1892.

Phil 4580.33.5 — Personlighetsprincipen i filosofin. (Høffding, Harald.) Stockholm, 1911.

Phil 575.146 — Le personnalisme. (Mounier, E.) Paris, 1950.

Phil 575.31 — Le personnalisme suivi d'une étude sur la perception extrême. (Renouvier, Charles.) Paris, 1903.

Phil 5590.250 — La personnalité; sa structure. (Boll, Marcel.) Paris, 1958.

Phil 2070.127 — La personnalité de William James. (Le Breton, M.) Paris, 1928.

Phil 2070.127.5 — La personnalité de William James. (Le Breton, M.) Paris, 1929.

Phil 5627.262 — Personnalité et vie religieuse chez l'adolescent. (Rochedieu, Edmond.) Neuchâtel, 1962.

Phil 3488.24 — La personnalité morale d'après Kant. Thèse. (Gračanin, G.) Paris, 1929.

Phil 2750.11.47 — La personne et le bien commun. (Maritain, Jacques.) Paris, 1947.

Phil 2905.1.200.5 — La personne et le drame humain chez Teilhard de Chardin. (Barthélemy-Madaule, Madeleine.) Paris, 1967.

Phil 575.13 — La personne humaine. (Piat, C.) Paris, 1897.

Phil 575.13.2 — La personne humaine. 2e éd. (Piat, C.) Paris, 1913.

Phil 5590.28 — La personne humaine et la nature. 1. éd. (Nédoncelle, M.) Paris, 1943.

Phil 575.247 — Personne humaine et nature. (Nédoncelle, Maurice.) Paris, 1963.

Phil 1701.21 — La personne incarnée, étude sur la phénoménologie et la philosophie existentialiste. (Brunner, Auguste.) Paris, 1947.

Phil 8595.30F — Persons, Lee C. The religion of the beautiful. Miami, 1932?

Phil 1815.3.5 — Persons, S. American minds. N.Y., 1958.

Phil 1815.3 — Persons, S. Evolutionary thought in America. New Haven, 1950.

Phil 8595.37 — Persons, Stow. Free religion. New Haven, 1947.

Phil 2280.5.87 — Persons and places. (Santayana, George.) London, 1944.

Phil 2280.5.85A — Persons and places. v.1,3. (Santayana, George.) N.Y., 1944-53. 2v.

Phil 575.205 — De persoon. (Wilde, Arie de.) Assen, 1951.

Phil 575.54 — De persoonlijkheidsidee bij meisterl Ekhart, Leibniz en Goethe. (Wolf, H.) Amsterdam, 1920.

Phil 165.315 — Perspectief; feestbundel. Kampen, 1961.

Phil 3837.16 — La perspective finale de l'éthique et le problème de la coherence du Spinozisme. (Rousset, Bernard.) Paris, 1968.

Phil 2920.2.35 — La perspective métaphysique. (Vallin, Georges.) Paris, 1958.

Phil 2406.3 — Perspectives de l'homme. 2e éd. (Garaudy, Roger.) Paris, 1960.

Phil 6360.5 — Perspectives in child psychopathology. (Rie, Herbert E.) Chicago, 1971.

Phil 6140.15 — Perspectives in community mental health. (Bindman, Arthur J.) Chicago, 1969.

Phil 5590.514.5 — Perspectives in personal construct theory. (Bannister, Donald.) London, 1970.

Phil 5590.340.5 — Perspectives in personality research. (David, Henry Philip.) N.Y., 1960.

Phil 165.75 — Perspectives in philosophy. (Ohio State University, Columbus. Department of Philosophy.) Columbus, 1953.

Phil 5238.120 — Perspectives in psychological theory. (Kaplan, Bernard.) N.Y., 1960.

Phil 5406.2 — Perspectives on human deprivation: biological, psychological, and sociological. (United States. National Institute of Child Health and Human Development.) Washington, 1968.

Phil 2225.5.125 — Perspectives on Peirce. (Bernstein, Richard J.) New Haven, 1965.

Phil 5190.43 — Perspectives on persuasion. (Fotheringham, Wallace C.) Boston, 1966.

Phil 165.372 — Perspectives on reality; readings in metaphysics. (Mann, Jesse Aloysius.) N.Y., 1966.

Phil 187.92 — Perspectives sur les relativités humaines. 2. ed. (Moreau, J.) Paris, 1929.

Phil 190.31 — Perspektive und Symbol in Philosophie und Rechtswissenschaft. (Pollack, Walter.) Berlin, 1912.

Phil 396.22 — Perspektiven des revolutionären Humanismus. (Kofler, Leo.) Reinbek, 1968.

Phil 559.2 — Perspektiven des Seins. (Schmida-Wöllersdorfer, Susanna.) München, 1968. 2v.

Phil 2905.1.296 — Perspektiven Teilhard de Chardins. (Terra, Helmut de.) München, 1966.

Phil 5190.85 — Persuasion; how opinions and attitudes are changed. (Abelson, Herbert Irving.) N.Y., 1959.

Phil 5190.85.2 — Persuasion; how opinions and attitudes are changed. 2nd ed. (Karlins, Marvin.) N.Y., 1970.

Phil 5190.90 — Persuasion: theory and practice. (Andersen, Kenneth E.) Boston, 1971.

Phil 6315.52 — Persuasion and healing. (Frank, J.D.) London, 1961.

Phil 5190.24.10 — The pertinence of the paradox. (Slaatte, Howard Alexander.) N.Y., 1968.

Phil 8888.8 — Pertinent and impertinent. (Nolan, Preston M.) Chicago, 1923.

Phil 5825.1 — Perty, J.A.M. Über das Seelenleben der Thiere. Leipzig, 1876.

Phil 525.21.2 — Perty, M. Die mystischen Erscheinungen der menschlichen Natur. Bd.1-2. 2e Aufl. Leipzig, 1872.

Phil 525.21 — Perty, M. Die mystischen Erscheinungen der menschlichen Natur. With supplement. Leipzig, 1861.

Phil 490.2 — Perty, M. Über die Bedeutung der Anthropologie. Bern, 1853.

Phil 6046.57 — Peruchio. La chiromance. Paris, 1657.

Phil 6046.57.5 — Peruchio. La chiromance. Paris, 1663.

Phil 6980.289.5 — Perversionen, Psychosen, Charakterstörungen. (Fenichel, Otto.) Darmstadt, 1967.

Phil 2415.10 — Pervicax (pseud.). Les infiltrations germaniques dans la pensée française. Paris, 1945.

Phil 5590.524 — Pervin, Lawrence A. Personality: theory, assessment, and research. N.Y., 1970.

Phil 5047.12.3 — Perzeptionalismus und Modalismus. (Hamilton, E.J.) N.Y., 1911.

Phil 8430.53 — Pesce, Domenico. Apollineo e dionisiaco nella storia del classicismo. Napoli, 1968.

Phil 1955.6.133 — Pesce, Domenico. Il concetto dell'arte in Dewey e in Berensoni. 1. ed. Firenze, 1956.

Phil 8140.7 — Pesce, Domenico. L'estetica dopo Croce. Firenze, 1962.

Phil 1135.185 — Pesce, Domenico. Idea, numero e anima. Padova, 1961.

Phil 9560.7.7 — Pescetti, Orlando. Dell'onore dialoghi tre. Verona, 1624.

Phil 1750.173 — Pesch, Edgar. L'existentialisme. Paris, 1946.

Phil 6315.2.140.5 — Pesch, Edgar. La pensée de Freud. Paris, 1960.

Phil 6315.2.140 — Pesch, Edgar. La pensée de Freud et la psychanalyse. Paris, 1946.

Phil 6315.2.140.8 — Pesch, Edgar. Pour connaître la pensée de Freud. Évreux, 1970.

Phil 8595.36 — Pesch, T. Christliche Lebensphilosophie. 20. bis 22. Aufl. Freiburg, 1923.

Phil 1535.9.5 — Pesch, T. Institutiones logicae et ontologicae quas secundum principia S. Thomae Aguinatis. Friburgi, 1914.

Phil 1535.9 — Pesch, T. Institutiones philosophiae naturalis. Friburgi, 1880.

Phil 3497.13   Pesch, T. Kant et la science moderne. Paris, 1894.
Phil 3497.13.6   Pesch, T. Le kantisme et ses erreurs. Paris, 1897.
Phil 296.8.3   Pesch, Tilmann. Die grossen Welträtsel. Freiburg, 1907. 2v.
Phil 8965.20   Peschke, Karlheinz. Naturrecht in der Kontroverse. Salzburg, 1967.
VPhil 575.255   Pešić-Golubović, Zagorka. Problemi savremene teorije ličnosti. Beograd, 1966.
Phil 9430.3.2   El pesimismo en el siglo XIX. (Caro, E.M.) Madrid, 1878.
Phil 5643.106   Peskin, James Charles. The regeneration of visual purple in the living animal. Thesis. N.Y., 1942.
Phil 5055.9   Peslöüan, C.L. de. Les systèmes logiques et la logistique. Paris, 1909.
X Cg Phil 9430.8   Pessimism, a study in contemporary sociology. (Lloyd, R.J.) Liverpool, 1880.
Phil 9430.34   Pessimism. (Lacy, B.F.) Philadelphia, 1920.
Phil 9430.12   Pessimism. (Sully, J.) London, 1877.
Phil 9430.12.2   Pessimism. 2. ed. (Sully, J.) N.Y., 1891.
Phil 960.129   Pessimism and life's ideal: the Hindu outlook. (Mitra, K.N.) Madras, 1926.
Phil 9430.28   Le pessimisme. (Jouvin, Léon.) Paris, 1892.
Phil 9430.3.1   Le pessimisme au XIX siècle. 2. éd. (Caro, E.M.) Paris, 1880.
Phil 9430.3   Le pessimisme au XIX siècle. 4. éd. (Caro, E.M.) Paris, 1889.
Phil 9430.22   Pessimisme et individualisme. (Palante, Georges.) Paris, 1914.
Phil 9430.3.10   Pessimismen i nittonde arhundradet. (Caro, E.M.) Stockholm, 1880.
Phil 900.7   Pessimismo orientale. (Pizzi, Italo.) Bari, 1902.
Phil 3808.210   Il pessimismo romantico nel mondo di Schopenhauer. 1. ed. (Biscardo, R.) Bolzano, 1955.
Phil 8583.11.15   Pessimismus...Nietzsche und Naturalismus. (Dorner, A.) Leipzig, 1911.
Phil 9430.4   Der Pessimismus. (Huber, J.W.) München, 1876.
Phil 9430.35   Pessimismus. (Marcuse, L.) Hamburg, 1953.
Phil 9430.5   Der Pessimismus. (Plümacher, O.) Heidelberg, 1888.
Phil 9430.16   Der Pessimismus. (Taubert, A.) Berlin, 1873.
Phil 9430.13   Der Pessimismus. (Trautz, T.) Karlsruhe, 1876.
Phil 5421.10.3   Der Pessimismus im Lichte einer höheren Weltauffassung. (Friedlaender, Julius.) Berlin, 1893.
Phil 3808.178   Der Pessimismus Schopenhauers und das Wert Problem. (Rasche, F.) Crimmitschau, 1924.
Phil 9430.21   Der Pessimismus und das Tragische in Kunst und Leben. (Vögele, Albert.) Freiburg, 1910.
Phil 9430.24.2   Der Pessimismus und der Sittenlehre. (Sommer, Hugo.) Berlin, 1883.
Phil 3808.133   Der Pessimismus und die Ethik Schopenhauers. (Kiy, Victor.) Berlin, 1866.
NEDL Phil 9430.1   Der Pessimismus und die Sittenlehre. (Bacmeister, A.) Gütersloh, 1882.
Phil 9430.9   Der Pessimismus und die Sittenlehre. (Rehmke, J.) Leipzig, 1882.
Phil 3415.102   Pessimistische Religionsphilosophie der Gegenwart. (Rintelen, F.J. von.) München, 1924.
Phil 6965.28   Pesso, Albert. Movement in psychotherapy; psychomotor techniques and training. N.Y., 1969.
Phil 4977.5   Pessoa, Fernando. Textos filosóficos. Lisboa, 1968. 2v.
Phil 2905.1.665   Pessoa e amor segundo Teilhard de Chardin. (Nogare, Pedro Dalle.) São Paulo, 1970.
Phil 9430.36   Pessymizm romantyzm a podstawy chrześcijaństwa. v.1-2. (Zdziechowski, M.) Krakow, 1915.
Phil 1535.10   Pestalozza, A. Elementi di filosofia. Milano, 1857. 2v.
Phil 4210.94   Pestalozza, A. La mente di Antonio Rosmini. Milano, 1855.
Phil 4210.142.5   Pestalozza, A. Le postille di un anonimo. Milano, 1850.
Phil 8890.13   Pestel, F.G. Fundamenta jurisprudentae naturalis. Lugdunum Batavorum, 1777.
Phil 575.294   Petander, Karl. Västerlandet inför personlighetstanken. Uppsala, 1969.
Phil 8640.3   Petavel-Olliet, E. Le problème de l'immortalité. Paris, 1891-92. 2v.
Phil 365.16   Petavel-Olliff, E. Le plan de Dieu dans l'évolution. Lausanne, 1894.
Phil 1135.104   Peter, C.L. von. Problem des Zufalls in der griechischen Philosophie. Berlin, 1909.
Phil 2490.127   Peter, J. Auguste Comtes Bild vom Menschen. Inaug.-Diss. Stuttgart, 1936.
Phil 3310.1.130   Peter Franz Knoodt als Philosoph. (Lauden, V.J.C.) Elberfeld, 1920.
Phil 5627.134.57   Peter Howard: life and letters. (Wolrige Gordon, Anne.) London, 1969.
Phil 2835.82   Peter Ramus and educational reforms of the 16th century. (Graves, F.P.) N.Y., 1912.
Phil 3925.11.80   Peter Wust, filosofo espiritualista de nuestro tiempo. (Aleorta, José Ignacio.) Bilbao, 1965.
Phil 3925.11.50   Peter Wust. (Schmidt, R.H.) Saarbrücken, 1954.
Phil 5520.718   Peterfalvi, Jean Michel. Introduction à la psycholinguistique. 1. éd. Paris, 1970.
Phil 5520.732   Peterfalvi, Jean Michel. Recherches experimentales sur le symbolisme phonétique. Paris, 1970.
Phil 5255.33.10   Petermann, B. The gestalt theory and the problem of configuration. London, 1932.
Phil 5255.33   Petermann, B. Die Wertheimer-Koffka-Köhlersche Gestalttheorie und das Gestaltproblem. Leipzig, 1929.
Phil 5286.15   Petermann, Bruno. Das Gestaltproblem in der Psychologie im Lichte analytischer Besimmung. Leipzig, 1931.
Phil 5225.2   Petermann, Bruno. Die Wertheimer-Koffka-Köhlersche Gestalttheorie und das Gestaltproblem systematische und kritisch Dargestellt. Leipzig, 1928.
Phil 4757.2.110   Peters, Arthur A. Boyhood with Gurdjieff. N.Y., 1964.
Phil 4757.2.115   Peters, Arthur A. Gurdjieff remembered. London, 1965.
Phil 190.10   Peters, C. Willenswelt und Weltwille. Leipzig, 1883.
Phil 5850.308   Peters, C.C. Human conduct. N.Y., 1918.
Phil 2805.253   Peters, F.E. Blaise Pascal. Hamburg, 1946.
Phil 1120.4   Peters, Francis E. Greek philosophical terms; a historical lexicon. N.Y., 1967.
Phil 190.90   Peters, Johannes Arnold Josef. Metaphysica. Utrecht, 1957.
Phil 190.90.5   Peters, Johannes Arnold Josef. Metaphysics; a systematic survey. Pittsburgh, 1963.
Phil 6965.8   Peters, John C. A treatise on nervous derangements. N.Y., 1854.
Phil 8640.8   Peters, M.C. After death - what? N.Y., 1908.
Phil 5548.30   Peters, R.S. The concept of motivation. London, 1958.
Phil 5548.30.2   Peters, R.S. The concept of motivation. 2. ed. London, 1967.

Phil 4260.103   Peters, Richard. Der Aufbau der Weltgeschichte bei Giambattista Vico. Stuttgart, 1929.
Phil 2045.128   Peters, Richard. Hobbes. Harmondsworth, 1956.
Phil 6325.13   Peters, W. Die Beziehungen der Psychologie zur Medizin. Würzburg, 1913.
Phil 5440.28.5   Peters, Wilhelm. Über Vererbung psychischer Fähigkeiten. Leipzig, 1915.
Phil 5440.28   Peters, Wilhelm. Die Vererbung geistiger Eigenschaften und die psychische Constitution. Leipzig, 1964.
Phil 3585.1.85   Peters, Wilhelm S. Johann Heinrich Lamberts Konzeption einer Geometrie auf einer imaginären Kugel. Bonn, 1961.
Phil 270.16   Petersen, J. Kausalität Determinismus. München, 1909.
Phil 974.3.175   Petersen, Klaus. Rudolf Steiner. Berlin, 1968.
Phil 3015.3   Petersen, Peter. Geschichte der aristotelischen Philosophie in protestantischen Deutschland. Leipzig, 1921.
Phil 3890.1.85   Petersen, Peter. Die Philosophie Friedrich Adolf Trendelenburgs. Hamburg, 1913.
Phil 3915.161   Petersen, Peter. Wilhelm Wundt und seine Zeit. Stuttgart, 1925.
Phil 1828.14   Petersen, Richard J. Scottish common sense in America, 1768-1850. Thesis. Ann Arbor, 1972.
Phil 3450.11.360   Petersen, Uwe. Das Verhältnis von Theorie und Praxis...Husserls. Heidelberg, 1964.
Phil 7054.163   Petersilea, Carlyle. Mary Anne Carew; wife, mother, spirit. London, 1893.
Phil 5850.309   Petersohn, F. Projektive Tests und Fahrtüchtigkeit. Hamburg, 1962.
Phil 6325.30   Peterson, Donald Robert. The clinical study of social behavior. N.Y., 1968.
Phil 585.392   Peterson, Forrest H. A philosophy of man and society. N.Y., 1970.
Phil 1980.3.90   Peterson, Houston. Havelock Ellis, philosopher of love. Boston, 1928.
Phil 5650.6   Peterson, J. Combination tones and other related auditory phenomena. Chicago, 1908.
Phil 5825.4   Peterson, Joseph. The effect of length of blind alleys on maze learning. N.Y., 1917.
Phil 5765.7   Peterson, Julius. Willensfreiheit, moral und strafrecht. München, 1905.
Phil 9230.15   Peterson, V.W. Gambling, should it be legalized? Chicago, Ill., 1945.
Phil 6685.12   Petetin, J.H.D. Electricité animale. Paris, 1808.
Phil 2648.80   Petifils, E. Socialiste-révolution au commencement du XVIII siècle. Paris, 1908.
Phil 8620.49   Petit, François. Le problème du mal. Paris, 1958.
Phil 2520.176   Petit, Henri. Images; Descartes et Pascal. Paris, 1930.
Phil 2520.435   Petit, Léon. Descartes et la princesse Elisabeth. Paris, 1969.
Phil 102.5.12   Petit dictionnaire philosophique. (Rozental, Mark Moiseevich.) Moscow, 1955.
Htn Phil 2805.205*   Petit-Didier, M. Apologie des lettres provinciales de Louis de Montalte. Delft, 1697-98.
Htn Phil 2805.205.5*   Petit-Didier, M. Apologie des lettres provinciales de Louis de Montalte. Pt.1-4. Delft, 1697-98. 2v.
Phil 5926.1.28   Le petit Docteur Gall. (David, A.) Paris, 1869?
Phil 6025.10   Petit-Douxciel, A. Speculum physionomicum. Langres, 1648.
Phil 6021.2.50   Le petit Lavater français. (David, Alexandre.) Paris, 1857.
Phil 5041.48   Petit traité de logique formelle. (Baudry, L.) Paris, 1929.
Phil 87.12   Petit vocabulaire de la langue philosophique. (Cuvillier, Armand.) Paris, 1925.
Phil 1750.185   Petite histoire de "l'existentialisme". (Wahl, Jean André.) Paris, 1947.
Phil 802.14   Petite histoire des grandes philosophies. (Challaye, F.) Paris, 1942.
Phil 5520.598   Petite métaphysique de la parole. (Parain, Brice.) Paris, 1969.
Phil 2750.22.30   La petite peur du XXe siècle. (Mounier, E.) Neuchâtel, 1959.
Phil 190.30   Die "Petites Perceptions" im System von Leibniz. (Strahm, Hans.) Bern, 1930.
Phil 2805.104   Petitot, H. Introduction à la philosophie. Paris, 1914.
Phil 2668.55   Petitot, H. Pascal sa vie religieuse. Paris, 1911.
Phil 8658.1   Petits éléments de morale. (Janet, Paul A.R.) Paris, 1870.
Phil 296.1   Petits traites...de la providence. (Damiron, J.P.) Paris, 1849.
Phil 3497.11   Petöcz, M. Ansicht der Welt. Leipzig, 1838.
Phil 5722.17   Petras, Otto. Der Begriff des Bösen in Kants Kritizismus. Leipzig, 1913.
Phil 9430.33   Petraschek, K.O. Die Logik des Unbewussten. München, 1926. 2v.
Phil 5400.81   Petraschek, K.O. Die Rechtsphilosophie des Pessimismus. München, 1929.
Phil 3805.168   Petrazycki, L. Wstęp do nauki prawa i moralności. Warszawa, 1930.
Phil 315.10   Petrelli, C.M.J. In Schleiermacherianam christianae fidei expositionem. Diss. Upsaliae, 1840.
Phil 5255.12   Pétrement, Simone. Le dualisme chez Platon. Paris, 1947.
Phil 4210.129   Petrescu, Nicolaus. Die Denkfunktion der Verneinung. Leipzig, 1914.
Phil 4210.129.5   Petri, Giuseppe. Lo dottrine di Antonio Rosmini...ed altri esaminate da Giuseppe Petri. Torino, 1878.
Phil 6685.3   Petri, Giuseppe. Risposta ad alcuni appunti...sul libro A. Rosmini ed i neoscolastici. Torino 1879.
Phil 1504.8.4   Petri, J.G. Der thierische magnetismus. Tlmenau, 1824.
Phil 5049.15.10   Petri Compostellani. v.8, pt.4. (Soto, P.B.) Münster, 1912.
Phil 5049.15.15   Petri hispani summulae logicales. (Alcala, P. de.) Venetiis, 1572.
Phil 5402.35   Petri hispani summulae logicales. (Joannes XXI, Pope.) Torino, 1947.
Phil 6325.27   Petrie, Asenath. Individuality in pain and suffering. Chicago, 1967.
Phil 5374.255   Petrilowitsch, Nikolaus. Charakterstudien. Basel, 1969.
Phil 6980.583.2   Petrilowitsch, Nikolaus. Das Gewissen als Problem. Darmstadt, 1966.
Phil 6309.4   Petrilowitsch, Nikolaus. Probleme der Psychotherapie alternder Menschen. 2. Aufl. Basel, 1968.
Phil 5590.472   Petrilowitsch, Nikolaus. Psychologie der abnormen Persönnlichkeiten. Darmstadt, 1968.
Phil 346.15   Petrilowitsch, Nikolaus. Zur Psychologie der Persönlichkeit. Darmstadt, 1967.
Phil 5415.3   Pétrin, Jean. Connaissance spéculative et connaissance pratique. Ottawa, 1948.
   Petrini, E. Om sympatiska känslor. Upsala, 1900.

Phil 5255.20 Petrini, Edvard. Om känslolagar. Upsala, 1900.
Phil 530.35.25 Petrocchi, Giorgio. Ascesi e mistica trecentesca. Firenze, 1957.
Phil 410.85 Petron, Iurii A. Logicheskie problemy abstraktsii beskonechnosti i osushchestvimosti. Moskva, 1967.
Phil 8890.37.5 Petrone, Igino. Ascetica. Milano, 1918.
Phil 8890.37 Petrone, Igino. Etica. Milano, 1918.
Phil 3640.181 Petrone, Igino. F. Nietzsche e L. Tolstoi. Napoli, 1902.
Phil 190.34 Petrone, Igino. I limiti del determinismo scientifico. Modena, 1900.
Phil 365.15 Petronievics, B. L'évolution universelle. Paris, 1921.
Phil 346.7 Petronievics, B. Prinzipien der Erkenntnislehre. Berlin, 1900.
Phil 1750.166.155 Petrosian, M.J. Gumanizm; opyt filosofskoeich i potsial issled problemy. Moskva, 1964.
Phil 8890.63 Petrov, Erik F. Egoizm. Moskva, 1969.
Phil 8615.18 Petrović, E. U znaku preporoda. Odjek Vivodićevoj pokreta. Sarajevo, 1928.
Phil 310.699 Petrović, Gajo. Mognénost čovjeka. Zagreb, 1969.
Phil 1715.13 Petrović, Gajo. Od Lockea do Ayera. Beograd, 1964.
Phil 5325.19 Pétrovitch, D. L'association des idées obéitelles à des lois? Thèse. Caen, 1920.
Phil 5225.5 Petrovskii, Artur V. Istoriia sovetskoi psikhologii. Moskva, 1967.
Phil 3085.10.81 Petrus Apherdianus, ludimagister ca. 1510-1580. (Graaf, Bob de.) Nieuwkoop, 1968.
Phil 1504.8.3 Petrus Damiani. v.8, pt.3. (Endres, J.A.) Münster, 1910.
Phil 5628.13 Petrus de Dacia. Vita Christinae Stumbelensis edibit Johannes Paukon. Gotoburgi, 1896.
Phil 2835.87 Petrus Ramus en de wiskunde. (Verdonk, Johannes Jacobus.) Assen, 1966.
Phil 5625.115 Petrushevskii, Stefan A. Dialektika reflektornykh protsessov. Moskva, 1967.
Phil 8416.16 Petruzzellis, N. Filosofia dell'arte. 2. ed. Mazara, 1952.
Phil 8416.16.2 Petruzzellis, N. Filosofia dell'arte. 3. ed. Napoli, 1964.
Phil 815.36 Petruzzellis, Nicola. Maestri di ieri. Napoli, 1970.
Phil 4200.6.30 Petruzzellis, Nicola. Meditazione critiche. Napoli, 1960.
Phil 4200.6.32.2 Petruzzellis, Nicola. Problemi e aporie del pensiero contemporaneo. 2. ed. Napoli, 1970.
Phil 8640.14 Petry, Ray C. Christian eschatology and social thought. N.Y., 1956.
Phil 2725.13.80 Petterlini, Arnaldo. Jules Lequier e il problema della liberta. Milano, 1969.
Phil 7068.94.35 Pettis, O.G. Autobiography by Jesus of Nazareth. Washington, 1894.
Phil 8670.13 Petty, Orville A. Common sense and God. New Haven, 1936.
Phil 4620.1.5 Péturss, Helgi. Erlendar Greiner. Reykjavík, 1955.
Phil 4620.5 Péturss, Helgi. Nýall. Reykjavík, 1919.
Phil 4620.1 Péturss, Helgi. Nýall Nokkur íslenzk drög til heimsfraeð og liffraeð Reykjavík, 1922.
Phil 4620.3.5 Péturss, Helgi. Sannyall. Reykjavík, 1943.
Phil 5255.3 Petvin, J, Letters concerning mind. London, 1750.
Phil 5068.592 Petzäll, Åke. Logistischer Positivismus. Göteborg, 1931.
Phil 2050.85 Petzholtz, E. Die Hauptpunkte der Humeschen Erkenntnislehre. Berlin, 1895.
Phil 346.2 Petzoldt, J. Einführung in die Philosophie der reinen Erfahrung. v.1-2. Leipzig, 1900.
Phil 296.7.2 Petzoldt, J. Das Weltproblem vom Standpunkte. 2. Aufl. Leipzig, 1912.
Phil 600.16 Petzoldt, Joseph. Das Weltproblem vom positivistische Standpunkte aus. Leipzig, 1906.
Phil 5374.154 Peucesco, M.G. Le mécanisme du courant de la conscience. Paris, 1922.
Phil 5374.154.2 Peucesco, M.G. Le mécanisme du courant de la conscience. Thèse. Paris, 1921.
Phil 5374.154.9 Peucesco, M.G. Mouvement et pensée. Paris, 1927.
Phil 3255.92 Peuckert, W.C. Sebastian Franck. München, 1943.
Phil 3110.173 Peuckert, W.E. Das Leben Jakob Böhmes. Jena, 1924.
Phil 4751.2.80 Peunova, M.N. Mirovozzrenie M.A. Antonovicha. Moskva, 1960.
Phil 5401.1.5 La peur. (Mosso, A.) Paris, 1886.
Phil 5401.34 La peur dans l'histoire. (Palou, Jean.) Paris, 1958.
Phil 5401.53.2 La peur et l'angoisse, phénomène central de la vie et de son évolution. 2e éd. (Diel, Paul.) Paris, 1968.
Phil 1750.250 Peursen, C.A. van. Riskante philosophie. Amsterdam, 1948.
Phil 6125.31 Peursen, Cornelis Anthonie van. Body, soul, spirit; a survey of the body-mind problem. London, 1966.
Phil 3552.478 Peursen, Cornelis Anthonie van. Leibniz. Baarn, 1966.
Phil 3552.478.1 Peursen, Cornelis Anthonie van. Leibniz. London, 1969.
Phil 3925.16.98 Peursen, Cornelis Anthonie van. Ludwig Wittgenstein. Baarn, 1965.
Phil 3925.16.98.1 Peursen, Cornelis Anthonie van. Ludwig Wittgenstein: an introduction to his philosophy. London, 1969.
Phil 190.110 Peursen, Cornetis A. van. Feiten, waarden, gebeurtenissen. Een deiktische ontologie. Hilversum, 1965[1966].
Phil 4803.537.37 Pewniki polityki polskiej. Wyd. 2. (Lutosławski, Wincenty.) W Szamotułach, 1883.
Phil 6685.4 Peyen, C. Progress of animal magnetism. Boston, 1837.
Phil 6159.16.1 The peyote cult. (La Barre, Weston.) Hamden, 1964.
Phil 6159.15 The peyote story. (Roseman, Bernard.) Hollywood, Calif., 1966.
Phil 190.11 Pezzani, A. Une philosophie nouvelle. Paris, 1872.
Phil 8890.15 Pezzani, A. Principes supérieurs de la morale. Paris, 1859.
Phil 190.116 Pezzani, André. Exposé d'un nouveau système philosophique. Paris, 1847.
Phil 5255.8 Pfänder, A. Einführung in die Psychologie. Leipzig, 1904.
Phil 5255.8.2 Pfänder, A. Einführung in die Psychologie. 2. Aufl. Leipzig, 1920.
Phil 5055.16 Pfänder, A. Logik. Halle, 1921.
Phil 5055.16.5 Pfänder, A. Logik. 2. aufl. Halle, 1929.
Phil 5055.16.6 Pfänder, A. Logik. 3. Aufl. Tübingen, 1963.
Phil 5765.3 Pfänder, A. Phänomenologie des Wollens. Leipzig, 1900.
Phil 190.79 Pfänder, A. Philosophie der Lebensziele. Göttingen, 1948.
Phil 5255.8.15 Pfänder, A. Die Seele des Menschen. Halle, 1933.
Phil 3745.10.15 Pfaender, Alexander. Phänomenologie des Wollens; eine psychologische Analuse. 3. Aufl. München, 1963.
Phil 3745.10.10 Pfaender, Alexendar. Phenomenology of willing and motivation and other phaenomenologica. Evanston, 1967.
Phil 490.5 Pfaff, A.B.I.F. Die Entwicklung der Welt auf atomischer Grundlage. Heidelberg, 1883.
Phil 7080.36 Pfaff, E.R. Das Traumleben und seine Deutung. Leipzig, 1868.
Phil 5590.140 Pfahler, G. Der Mensch und sein Lebenswerkzeug. Stuttgart, 1954.

Phil 5870.40 Pfahler, Gerhard. Die zwölf wichtigsten Jahre des Lebens. München, 1967.
Phil 1905.10.90 Pfannenstill, Bertil. Bernard Bosanquet's philosophy of the state. Inaug.-Diss. Lund, 1936.
Phil 3745.8 Pfannwitz, Rudolf. Lebenshilfe. Zürich, 1938.
Phil 3745.8.5 Pfannwitz, Rudolf. Logos eidos, bios. München, 1930.
Phil 5272.18 Pfanzogl, Johann. Theory of measurement. Würzburg, 1968.
Phil 8965.1 Pfeiderer, O. Moral und Religion. Leipzig, 1872.
Phil 3640.372 Pfeie, H. Friedrich Nietzsche und die Religion. Regensburg, 1948.
Phil 3778.91 Pfeifer, A. Die Philosophie der Kantperiode Karl Leonhard Reinholds. Inaug. Diss. W. Elberfeld, 1935.
Phil 260.6 Pfeifer, X. Die Controverse und der Beharren der Elemente. Dellingen, 1879.
Phil 2610.115 Pfeiffer, Adalbert. Die Ethik des Peter Gassendi. Inaug.-Diss. Borna, 1908.
Phil 530.20.5 Pfeiffer, Franz. Deutsche Mystiker des vierzehnten Jahrhunderts. Leipzig, 1845. 2v.
Phil 530.20.9 Pfeiffer, Franz. Deutsche Mystiker des vierzehnten Jahrhunderts. v.2. Göttingen, 1914.
Phil 530.20.7 Pfeiffer, Franz. Deutsche Mystiker des vierzehnten Jahrhunderts. 2e Aufl. Göttingen, 1907. 2v.
Phil 1715.14 Pfeiffer, Johannes. Gegen den Strom. Itzehoe, 1964.
Phil 3450.19.95.5 Pfeiffer, Johannes S. Existenz und Offenbarung. Berlin, 1966.
Phil 3450.19.95 Pfeiffer, Johannes S. Existenzphilosophie; eine Einführung in Heidegger und Jaspers. Leipzig, 1933.
Phil 3450.19.95.3 Pfeiffer, Johannes S. Existenzphilosophie. 3e Aufl. Hamburg, 1952.
Phil 5520.320 Pfeiffer, Alfred. Lesen und Benennen in Reaktionsversuch. Frankfurt, 1959.
Phil 3745.12 Pfeil, Hans. Überwindung des Massenmenschen durch echte Philosophie. 1. Aufl. Graz, 1956.
Phil 5627.112 Pfennigsdorf, Emil. Der religiöse Wille. 2. Aufl. Leipzig, 1927.
Phil 5825.2 Das Pferd des Herrn von Osten. (Pfungst, Oskar.) Leipzig, 1907.
Phil 5255.19 Pfister, O. Zur Psychologie des philosophischen Denkens. Bern, 1923.
Phil 5411.6 Pfister, Oskar. Analytische Untersuchungen über die Psychologie des Hasses und der Versöhnung. Leipzig, 1910.
Phil 6325.1.35 Pfister, Oskar. Die Behandlung schwer erziehlbarer und abnormer Kinder. Bern, 1921.
Phil 5627.168 Pfister, Oskar. Das Christentum und die Angst; eine religions-psychologische, historische und religionshygienische Untersuchung. Zürich, 1944.
Phil 6325.1.16 Pfister, Oskar. Expressionism in art. N.Y., 1923.
Phil 6325.1.10 Pfister, Oskar. Psycho-analysis in the service of education. London, 1922.
Phil 6325.1.20 Pfister, Oskar. Psychoanalyse und Weltanschauung. Leipzig, 1928.
Phil 6325.1.3 Pfister, Oskar. The psychoanalytic method. London, 1915.
Phil 6325.1 Pfister, Oskar. The psychoanalytic method. N.Y., 1917.
Phil 6325.1.25 Pfister, Oskar. Religiosität und Hysterie. Leipzig, 1928.
Phil 6325.1.17 Pfister, Oskar. Some applications of psychoanalysis. London, 1923.
Phil 6325.1.40 Pfister, Oskar. Vermeintliche Nullen und angebliche Musterkinder. Bern, 1921.
Phil 6325.1.5 Pfister, Oskar. Wahrheit und Schönheit in der Psychoanalyse. Zürich, 1918.
Phil 5765.5 Pfister, Oskar. Die Willensfreiheit. Berlin, 1904.
Phil 6325.1.30 Pfister, Oskar. Zum Kampf um die Psychoanalyse. Wien, 1920.
Phil 978.98 Die Pflanze als Lichtsinnesorgan der Erde. (Grohmann, Gerbert.) Stuttgart, 1962.
Phil 6962.19 Die Pflege der Gemüts- und Geisteskranken. (Morgenthaler, Walter.) Bern, 1930.
Phil 6962.19.5 Die Pflege der Gemüts- und Geisteskranken. 4. Aufl. (Morgenthaler, Walter.) Bern, 1941.
Phil 1750.150 Die Pflege der Philosophie. (Jansen, B.) Fulda, 1938.
Phil 1750.605 Pfleger, Karl. Kundschafter der Existenztiefe. Frankfurt, 1959.
Phil 2050.84 Pfleiderer, E. Empirismus und Skepsis...Hume's. Berlin, 1874.
Phil 9245.8 Pfleiderer, E. Eudämonismus und Egoismus. Leipzig, 1880.
Phil 3565.117 Pfleiderer, E. Lotze's philosophische Weltanschauung nach ihren Grundzügen. Berlin, 1882.
Phil 3565.78 Pfleiderer, E. Lotze's philosophische Weltanschauungen nach ihren Grundzugen. Berlin, 1882. 5 pam.
Phil 3280.81 Pfleiderer, E. Verzeichniss der Doctoren. Tübingen, 1882.
Phil 9245.8.5 Pfleiderer, E. Zur Ehrenrettung des Eudämonismus. Tübingen, 1879.
Phil 3552.296 Pfleiderer, Edmund. Gottfried Wilhelm Leibniz. Leipzig, 1870.
Phil 3497.17 Pfleiderer, Edmund. Kantischer Kritizismus und englische Philosophie. Halle, 1881.
Phil 3552.296.10 Pfleiderer, Edmund. Leibniz als Verfasser von Zwölf Anonymen. Leipzig, 1870.
Phil 3552.296.15 Pfleiderer, Edmund. Leibniz und Geulinx mit besonderer Beziehung auf ihr beiderseitiges Uhrengleichniss. Tübingen, 1884.
Phil 8595.4.11 Pfleiderer, O. Philosophy and development of religion. N.Y., 1894. 2v.
Phil 8595.4.10 Pfleiderer, O. The philosophy of religion. London, 1886-88. 4v.
Phil 8595.4 Pfleiderer, O. Die Religion. Leipzig, 1869. 2v.
Phil 8595.4.5 Pfleiderer, O. Die Religion. 2. Aufl. v.1-2. Leipzig, 1878.
Phil 8595.4.13 Pfleiderer, O. Religion and historic faiths. N.Y., 1907.
Phil 8595.4.12 Pfleiderer, O. Religion und Religionen. München, 1906.
Phil 8595.4.2 Pfleiderer, O. Religionsphilosophie. Berlin, 1878.
Phil 8595.4.2.2 Pfleiderer, O. Religionsphilosophie. 2. Aufl. Berlin, 1883-84. 2v.
Phil 8595.4.3 Pfleiderer, O. Religionsphilosophie. 3. Aufl. Berlin, 1896.
Phil 8595.4.15 Pfleiderer, O. Über das Verhältnis der Religionsphilosophie. Berlin, 1906.
Htn Phil 3801.685*A Pfleiderer, Otto. Friedrich Wilhelm Joseph Schelling. Stuttgart, 1875.
Phil 8595.4.113 Pfleiderer als Relionsphilosophie. (Gastrow, Paul.) Berlin, 1913.
Phil 9120.157 Pflicht oder Lust? (Radcke, Fritz.) Langensalza, 1917.
Phil 9490.9 Die Pflichten der Intelligenten. (Trisca, P.C.) Jena, 1911.
Htn Phil 6103.8* Pflüger, E. Die sensorischen Functionen des Rückenmarks. Berlin, 1853. 5 pam.
Phil 8735.7 Pflüger, E.F.W. Die teleologische Mechanik der lebendigen Natur. 2. Aufl. Bonn, 1877.

Phil 2475.1.355   Pflug, Günther. Henri Bergson. Berlin, 1959.

Phil 3552.300   Pflugbell, R. Der Begriff der ewigen Wahrheiten bei Leibniz. Inaug. Diss. Leipzig, 1902.

Phil 310.190   Pfoh, Werner. Philosophie und Gesellschaft. Berlin, 1958.

Phil 8890.38   Pfordten, O. Ethik. Berlin, 1919.

Phil 5500.4   Pfordten, O.F. von. Versuch einer Theorie von Urteil und Begriff. Heidelberg, 1906.

Phil 815.4   Pfordten, Otto. Konformismus eine Philosophie der normatwen Werte. Heidelberg, 1910-13.

Phil 190.37   Pfordten, Otto. Vorfragen der Naturphilosophie. Heidelberg, 1907.

Phil 3808.119.5   Pfordten, T. von der. Staat und Recht bei Schopenhauer. München, 1916.

Phil 978.49.65   Die Pforte der Einweihung (Initiation). (Steiner, R.) Dornach, 1925.

Phil 2150.15.86   Pfuetze, P.E. Self, society, existence. N.Y., 1961.

Phil 5825.2.5   Pfungst, Oskar. Clever Hans; the horse of Mr. von Osten. N.Y., 1965.

Phil 5825.2   Pfungst, Oskar. Das Pferd des Herrn von Osten. Leipzig, 1907.

Phil 3625.1.85   Der Phädo Platos und Mendelssohns. Inaug. Diss. (Biltz, Otto.) Berlin, 1897.

Htn   Phil 3625.1.38*   Phädon. (Mendelssohn, Moses.) Berlin, 1767.

Phil 3625.1.39   Phädon. (Mendelssohn, Moses.) Berlin, 1768.

Phil 3625.1.39.15   Phädon. (Mendelssohn, Moses.) London, n.d. 2 pam.

X Cg   Phil 3625.1.39.3   Phädon. 3. Aufl. (Mendelssohn, Moses.) Berlin, 1769.

Phil 8637.3   Phädon oder über die Unsterblichkeit der Seele. (Mendelsohn, M.) Berlin, 1821.

Phil 735.244   Das Phänomen der Wertblindheit. (Langweg, R.) Lingen-Ems, 1961?

Phil 3450.19.79.5   Das Phänomen des Todes im Denken Heideggers und in der Lehre Buddhas. (Chandra, Subhash.) Köln, 1965.

Phil 5767.15   Das Phänomen des Wollens. (Rohner, Peter.) Bern, 1964.

Phil 342.5   Die phänomenale Sphäre und das Bewusstsein. (Linke, Paul F.) Halle an der Saale, 1912.

Phil 341.6   Der Phänomenalismus. (Kleinpeter, Hans.) Leipzig, 1913.

Phil 2045.82   Der Phänomenalismus des T. Hobbes. (Wille, B.) Kiel, 1888.

Phil 582.2   Der Phänomenalismus und seine Schwierigkeiten. (Stegmueller, Wolfgang.) Darmstadt, 1969.

Phil 3552.444   Die Phänomenalität der Res Extensa bei Leibniz. (Panzer, Ursula.) Köln, 1962.

Phil 165.452   Phaenomenologie, Rechtsphilosophie, Jurisprudenz. Frankfurt, 1969.

Phil 1750.115.100   Phänomenologie- Metaphysik oder Methode? (Funke, Gerhard.) Bonn, 1966.

Phil 525.123.2   Phänomenologie der Mystik. 2. Aufl. (Walther, G.) Olten, 1955.

Phil 8587.62   Phänomenologie der Religion. Proefschrift. (Hirschmann, Eva.) Würzburg, 1940.

Phil 3425.72.90   Phänomenologie des Geistes. (Hegel, Georg Wilhelm Friedrich.) Leipzig, 1907.

Phil 3425.73   Phänomenologie des Geistes. (Hegel, Georg Wilhelm Friedrich.) Leipzig, 1907.

Phil 3425.73.2.5   Phänomenologie des Geistes. (Hegel, Georg Wilhelm Friedrich.) Leipzig, 1937. 2v.

Phil 3425.73.2   Phänomenologie des Geistes. 2. Aufl. (Hegel, Georg Wilhelm Friedrich.) Berlin, 1841.

Phil 3425.73.1   Phänomenologie des Geistes. 2. Aufl. (Hegel, Georg Wilhelm Friedrich.) Leipzig, 1921.

Phil 3425.73.2.10   Phänomenologie des Geistes. 6. Aufl. (Hegel, Georg Wilhelm Friedrich.) Hamburg, 1952.

Phil 3425.264   Phänomenologie des Geistes und der Staat. (Busse, Martin.) Berlin, 1931.

Phil 575.14   Die Phänomenologie des Ich in ihren Grundproblem. (Oesterreich, K.) Leipzig, 1910.

Phil 8407.32   Phänomenologie des Kitsches. (Giesz, L.) Heidelberg, 1960.

Phil 65.2   Phänomenologie des sittlechen Bewusstens. 3 Aufl. (Hartmann, E.V.) Berlin, 1924.

Phil 3415.65   Phänomenologie des sittlichen Bewussten. (Hartmann, Eduard von.) Berlin, 1879.

Phil 3415.65.2   Phänomenologie des sittlichen Bewusstseins. 3. Aufl. (Hartmann, Eduard von.) Berlin, 1924.

Phil 3745.10.15   Phänomenologie des Wollens; eine psychologische Analuse. 3. Aufl. (Pfaender, Alexander.) München, 1963.

Phil 5765.3   Phänomenologie des Wollens. (Pfänder, A.) Leipzig, 1900.

Phil 1750.166.95   Phänomenologie en natuurwetenschap. (Hulst, H.C von.) Utrecht, 1953.

Phil 3450.11.305   Phänomenologie und Egologie. (Broekman, J.M.) Den Haag, 1963.

Phil 1750.115.130   Phänomenologie und Geschichte. 1. Aufl. (Landgrebe, Ludwig.) Gütersloh, 1968.

Phil 192.71   Phänomenologie und menschliche Existenz. (Reiner, Hans.) Halle, 1931.

Phil 3450.11.128   Phänomenologie und Metaphysik. (Landgrabe, Ludwig.) Hamburg, 1949.

Phil 343.10.5   Phänomenologie und Metaphysik. (Metzger, Arnold.) Halle an der Saale, 1933.

Phil 672.135   Phänomenologie und Metaphysik der Zeit. (Volkelt, Johannes.) München, 1925.

Phil 8602.36   Phänomenologie und Religion. (Winkler, R.) Tübingen, 1921.

Phil 3450.19.76   Phänomenologie und Theologie. (Heidegger, Martin.) Frankfurt, 1970.

Phil 8426.3   Die phänomenologische Ästhetik nach Grundsätzen und bisherigen Ergebnissen kritisch Dargestellt. (Ziegenfuss, W.) Borna, 1927.

Phil 3002.1.9   Phänomenologische Blätter. (Chalybäus, H.) Kiel, 1840.

Phil 3425.115   Phalén, A. Das Erkenntnisproblem in Hegels Philosophie. Upsala, 1912.

Phil 5055.12   Phalen, A.K. Om det kvantitativa betraktelsesättet i logiken. Uppsala, 1911.

Phil 346.12   Phalén, Adolf. Beitrage zur Klärung des Begriffs. Uppsala, 1913.

Phil 2050.111   Phalén, Adolf. I. Hume's psykologiska härledning av kausalitetsförestälningenII. Hypotesen om det omedvetna i empirisk psykologi. Uppsala, 1914.

Phil 705.12   Phalén, Adolf K. Kritik af subjektivism. Uppsala, 1910.

Phil 672.33   Phalén, Adolf K. Uber die Relativität der Raum- und Zeitbestimmungen. Uppsala, 1922.

Phil 8448.11.7   Phanomenologie des Kitsches. 2. Aufl. (Giesz, Ludwig.) München, 1971.

Phil 6051.11   Phanos (pseud.) Elements of hand-reading. London, 1903.

Phil 5465.16   Die Phantasie. (Glogan, Gustav.) Halle, 1884.

Phil 5465.13   Die Phantasie. (Lucka, Emil.) Wien, 1908.

Phil 5465.41   Phantasie - ewiger Born. (Rumpf-Thevenot, Theodor Richard.) Zürich, 1943.

Phil 5245.12   Die Phantasie als Grundprincip des Weltprocesses. (Frohschammer, J.) München, 1877.

Phil 5465.15   Die Phantasie ihr Wesen. (Leuchtenberger, G.) Erfurt, 1894.

Phil 5465.178   Phantasie und Intelligenz bei Jugendlichen. (Ewert, Otto Maximilian.) Weinheim, 1967.

Phil 5465.175   Phantasie und Künstlerische Arbeit. (Lehmann, Günther Kurt.) Berlin, 1966.

Phil 3270.3.95   Phantasie Wahrheit und Erkenntnis. Inaug. Diss. (Fried, Günther.) Tübingen, 1929.

Phil 7068.86.20A   Phantasms of the living. (Gurney, Edmund.) London, 1886. 2v.

Phil 7069.18.100   Phantasms of the living. (Gurney, Edmund.) London, 1918.

Phil 7069.62.10   Phantasms of the living. (Sidgwick, Eleanor Mildred.) N.Y., 1962.

Phil 7069.30.12.5   Phantom walls. (Lodge, Oliver Joseph.) N.Y., 1930.

Phil 7067.46.25   The phantom world. (Calmet, Augustin.) London, 1850.

Phil 7067.46.26   The phantom world. (Calmet, Augustin.) Philadelphia. 1850.

Phil 7060.92.61   Phantoms of the night. (O'Donnell, Elliot.) London, 1956.

Phil 5046.37   Pharus intellectus, sive logica. (Grosser, S.) Lipsiae, 1703.

Phil 1809.4   Phases of American culture. (Jesuit Philosophical Association of the Eastern States.) Freeport, 1969.

Phil 8593.2.10   Phases of faith. (Newman, F.W.) London, 1850.

Phil 8593.2.11   Phases of faith. 3. ed. (Newman, F.W.) London, 1853.

Phil 8593.2.13   Phases of faith. 5. ed. (Newman, F.W.) London, 1858.

Phil 3625.1.39.4   Phédon. (Mendelssohn, Moses.) Amsterdam, 1773.

Phil 3625.1.39.9   Phédon. (Mendelssohn, Moses.) Amsterdam, 1821.

Phil 3625.1.39.11   Phédon. (Mendelssohn, Moses.) Leipzig, 1869.

Phil 3625.1.39.5A   Phédon. 4. Aufl. (Mendelssohn, Moses.) Amsterdam, 1776.

Phil 5400.57   Phelan, G.B. Feeling experience and its modalities. London, 1925.

Phil 2750.11.90   Phelan, G.B. Jacques Maritain. N.Y., 1937.

Htn   Phil 525.10*   Phelipeaux, J. Relation de l'origine, du progrès...du quiétisme. Ste. Ménehould, 1732.

Phil 8640.4   Phelps, E.S. The struggle for immortality. Boston, 1889.

Phil 8595.22   Phelps, William L. Adventures and confessions. N.Y., 1926.

Htn   Phil 9245.37*   Phelps, William L. Happiness. N.Y., 1927.

Phil 9245.37.2   Phelps, William L. Happiness. N.Y., 1927.

Phil 8413.32   Le phémomène de l'art. (Mottier, G.) Parisè 1936.

Phil 585.163   Phenix, Philip H. Man and his becoming. New Brunswick, N.J., 1964.

Phil 7068.93.26   Les phénomèmes psychiques occultes. 2. ed. (Coste, A.) Montpellier, 1895.

Phil 7069.51.25   The phenomena of astral projection. (Muldoon, Sylvan Joseph.) London, 1962.

Phil 7069.20.303   Phenomena of materialisation; a contribution to the investigation of mediumistic telepastics. (Schrenck von Notzing, Albert.) London, 1920.

Phil 7054.99   Phenomena of the "spiritual rappings". Boston, 1852.

Phil 181.27   Le phénomène; esquisse de philosophie générale. (Gourd, J.J.) Paris, 1888.

Phil 7054.157   Le phénomène spirite. 5. ed. (Delanne, Gabriel.) Paris, 1897.

Phil 5400.45.9   Les phénomènes affectifs et les lois de leur apparition. 3d éd. (Paulhan, Frédéric.) Paris, 1912.

Phil 7069.03.25   Les phénomènes d'autoscopie. (Sollier, P.) Paris, 1903.

Phil 7069.19.27   Les phénomènes de hantise. (Bozzano, E.) Paris, 1913.

Phil 7060.147   Les phénomènes dits de matérialisation. (Alexandre Bisson, J.) Paris, 1914.

Phil 525.81   Les phénomènes mystiques distingués de leurs contrefaçons humaines et diaboliques. (Farges, Albert.) Paris, 1920.

Phil 7069.03.35   Les phénomènes psychiques. (Maxwell, J.) Paris, 1903.

Phil 2840.96   Le phénoménisme de Charles Renouvier. Thèse. (Wang, Tsun-Sheng.) Lyon, 1935.

Phil 1750.50   The phenomenological approach to psychiatry. (Berg, J.H. van der.) Springfield, Ill., 1955.

Phil 1750.115.50   The phenomenological movement. (Spiegelberg, Herbert.) Hague, 1960. 2v.

Phil 5258.114.10   Phenomenological psychology. (Straus, Erwin.) N.Y., 1966.

Phil 5043.11.140   Phénoménologie, existence. (Lauer, Quentin.) Paris, 1955.

Phil 1750.115.30A   La phénoménologie. (Jeanson, F.) Paris, 1951.

Phil 1750.38   La phénoménologie. 3e éd. (Lyotard, Jean François.) Paris, 1959.

Phil 1750.38.6   La phénoménologie. 6e éd. (Lyotard, Jean François.) Paris, 1967.

Phil 1750.115.115   La phénoménologie au départ, Husserl, Heidagger, Gaboriau. (Rollin, France.) Paris, 1967.

Phil 3450.11.142   Phénoménologie de Husserl. 1st ed. (Lauer, Quentin.) Paris, 1955.

Phil 1750.115.25   Phénoménologie de la perception. (Merleau-Ponty, Maurice.) Paris, 1945.

Phil 1750.115.26   Phénoménologie de la perception. (Merleau-Ponty, Maurice.) Paris, 1945.

Phil 3425.73.20   La phénoménologie de l'esprit. (Hegel, Georg Wilhelm Friedrich.) Paris, 1939-41. 2v.

Phil 2725.38.5   Phénoménologie de l'expérience. (Leyvraz, Jean Pierre.) La Haye, 1970.

Phil 8404.4   Phénoménologie de l'expérience esthétique. (Dufrenne, Michel.) Paris, 1953.

Phil 3450.11.390   La phénoménologie des "Recherches logiques" de Husserl. (Schérer, René.) Paris, 1967.

Phil 2477.19.30   Phénoménologie du temps et prospective. (Berger, G.) Paris, 1964.

Phil 1750.35   La phénoménologie et la foi. (Vancourt, R.) Tournai, 1953.

Phil 1750.115.35   Phénoménologie et materialisme dialectique. (Trân-Dúc-Thao.) Paris, 1951.

Phil 8583.41.5   Phénoménologie et religion. 1. éd. (Duméry, Henry.) Paris, 1958.

Phil 3450.11.145   Phénoménologie et vérité. (Waelhens, A. de.) Paris, 1953.

Phil 3585.20.15   Phenomenology and atheism. (Luijpen, Wilhelmus Antonius Maria.) Pittsburgh, 1964.

Phil 1750.115.85   Phenomenology and existentialism. Baltimore, 1967.

Phil 1750.115.56   Phenomenology and humanism. (Luijpen, Wilhelmus Antonius Maria.) Pittsburg, 1966.

Phil 5280.5   Phenomenology and intersubjectivity. (Owens, Thomas J.) The Hague, 1971.

Phil 3585.20.20   Phenomenology and metaphysics. (Luijpen, Wilhelmus Anonius Maria.) Pittsburgh, 1965.

Phil 583.12   Phenomenology and ontology. (Mohanty, Jitendra Nath.) Den Haag, 1970.

Phil 583.8   Phenomenology and physical science. (Kockelmans, Joseph John.) Pittsburgh, 1966.

Phil 1750.101   Phenomenology and science in contemporary European thought. (Tymieniecka, Anna Teresa.) N.Y., 1962.

Phil 165.450 — Phenomenology and social reality. The Hague, 1970.
Phil 3450.11.55 — Phenomenology and the crisis of philosophy. (Husserl, Edmund.) N.Y., 1965.
Phil 1750.736 — Phenomenology and the human scientific ideal. (Straser, S.) Pittsburg, 1963.
Phil 583.8.5 — Phenomenology and the natural sciences: essays and translations. (Kockelmans, Joseph John.) Evanston, 1970.
Phil 180.44A — Phenomenology as a method and as a philosophical discipline. (Farber, M.) n.p., 1928.
Phil 1750.115.90 — Phenomenology in America. Chicago, 1967.
Phil 3450.11.470 — The phenomenology of Husserl. (Elveton, R.O.) Chicago, 1970.
Phil 3450.11.35 — The phenomenology of internal time-consciousness. (Husserl, Edmund.) Bloomington, 1964.
Phil 3425.73.5 — The phenomenology of mind. (Hegel, Georg Wilhelm Friedrich.) London, 1910.
Phil 3425.73.8A — The phenomenology of mind. 2nd ed. (Hegel, Georg Wilhelm Friedrich.) London, 1955.
Phil 3425.73.9 — The phenomenology of mind. 2nd ed. (Hegel, Georg Wilhelm Friedrich.) London, 1961.
Phil 3425.73.10A — The phenomenology of mind. 2nd ed. (Hegel, Georg Wilhelm Friedrich.) London, 1966.
Phil 8887.85 — The phenomenology of moral experience. (Mandelbaum, M.H.) Glencoe, Ill., 1955.
Phil 3585.20.25 — Phenomenology of natural law. (Luijpen, Wilhelmus Antonius Maria.) Pittsburgh, 1967.
Phil 1750.115.28 — Phenomenology of perception. (Merleau-Ponty, Maurice.) London, 1966.
Phil 1750.115.80 — The phenomenology of the social world. (Schutz, Alfred.) Evanston, Ill., 1967.
Phil 1750.115.95 — Phenomenology of will and action. (Lexington. Conference on Pure and Applied Phenomenology.) Chicago, 1967.
Phil 3745.10.10 — Phenomenology of willing and motivation and other phaenomenologica. (Pfaender, Alexandar.) Evanston, 1967.
Phil 2075.8 — The phenomenon of life. 1st ed. (Jonas, Hans.) N.Y., 1966.
Phil 2905.1.10 — The phenomenon of man. (Teilhard de Chardin, Pierre.) N.Y., 1959.
Phil 8587.42 — Phénoméologie et philosophie religieuse. Thèse. (Hering, Jean.) Strasbourg, 1925.
Phil 1750.115.175 — Phenomonology of expression. (Kwant, Remigius Cornelis.) Pittsburgh, 1969.
Phil 2905.1.12 — The phenomonon of man. (Teilhard de Chardin, Pierre.) N.Y., 1965.
Phil 25.137 — Philadelphia Associates for Psychoanalysis. Bulletin. Philadelphia. 15,1965+ 7v.
Phil 55.4.5 — Philadelphia Neurological Society. Proceedings of the 30th anniversary, November 27-28, 1914. Philadelphi? 1915.
Htn Phil 530.11.16* — Philadelphian Society, London. Propositions. London, 1697.
Phil 8610.821 — Philanthropos [pseud.]. The character of a priest. London, 1821. 2 pam.
Phil 5525.16 — Philbert, Louis. Le rire. Paris, 1883.
Phil 585.380 — Philibert, Michel André Jean. Les échelles d'âge dans la philosophie. Thèse. Paris, 1968.
Phil 2855.11.80 — Philibert, Michel André Jean. Paul Ricoeur. Paris, 1971.
Phil 346.3 — Philip, A. The dynamic foundation of knowledge. London, 1913.
Phil 346.3.5 — Philip, A. Essays towards a theory of knowledge. London, 1915.
Phil 6965.2 — Philip, A.P.W. Treatise on the more obscure affections of the brain. London, 1835.
Phil 6319.1.202 — Philip, Howard Littleton. Jung and the problem of evil. London, 1958.
Phil 5421.25.35 — Philipp, Wolfgang. Die Dreigestalt der Liebe. 1. Aufl. Konstanz, 1967.
Phil 8520.65 — Philipp, Wolfgang. Das Zeitalter der Ausklärung. Bremen, 1963.
Phil 1750.149 — Philippard, L. Connais-toi toi-même. Paris, 1937.
Phil 6685.14 — Philippe, Anthelme Philippe. Vie et paroles du maitre. Lyon, 1959.
Phil 5465.12 — Philippe, Jean. L'image mentale; évolution et dissolution. Paris, 1903.
Phil 190.55 — Philippe, Oscar. L'inconditionalité de la philosophie. Paris, 1932.
Phil 190.55.5 — Philippe, Oscar. L'inconditionalité de la philosophie. Thèse. Nancy, 1932.
Phil 2905.1.660 — Philippe de la Trinité, Father. Pour et contre Teilhard de Chardin, penseur religieux. Saint-Cénéré, 1970.
Phil 2905.1.345 — Philippe de la Trinité, Father. Rome et Teilhard de Chardin. Paris, 1964.
Phil 8670.5 — Philipps, J.T. Dissertatio historico-philosophica de atheismo. London, 1716.
Phil 8670.5.5 — Philipps, J.T. Dissertationes historicae quatuor. London, 1735.
Phil 8670.5.10 — Philipps, J.T. Historia atheismi. Altdorfi Noricorum, 1713. 3 pam.
Phil 1140.7 — Philippson, L. Hylē anthrōpinē. Berolini, 1831.
Phil 8595.32 — Philips, Vivian. The churches and modern thought. London, 1906.
Phil 8595.32.7 — Philips, Vivian. Concerning progressive revelation. London, 1936.
Phil 8595.32.5 — Philips, Vivian. Concerning progressive revelation. London, 1936.
Phil 8595.25A — Philips Brooks House Association. Harvard University. Religion and modern life. N.Y., 1927.
Phil 8640.10 — Philipson, J. The natural history of hell. N.Y., 1894.
Phil 3835.5 — Philipson, M. Leben Benedikt's von Spinoza. Braunschweig, 1790.
Phil 6319.1.216 — Philipson, M.H. Outline of a Jungian aesthetics. Evanton, 1963.
Phil 8400.16 — Philipson, Morris. Aesthetics today. Cleveland, 1961.
Phil 5255.30 — Phillips, D.E. An elementary psychology. Boston, 1927.
Phil 8890.66 — Phillips, Dewi Zephaniah. Moral practices. London, 1966[1970]
Phil 6980.587 — Phillips, Ewing. Psychotherapy. Englewood Cliffs, 1956.
Phil 3850.27.235 — Phillips, Herbert M. Albert Schweitzer, prophet of freedom. Evanston, Ill., 1957.
Phil 3850.27.160 — Phillips, Herbert M. Safari of discovery. N.Y., 1958.
Phil 6980.687 — Phillips, J.H. Psychoanalyse und Symbolik. Bern, 1962.
Phil 9355.7 — Phillips, John H. Old tales and modern ideals. N.Y., 1905.
Phil 5593.53 — Phillips, L. Rorschach interpretation. N.Y., 1953.
Phil 5400.96 — Phillips, M. The education of the emotions. London, 1937.
Phil 1750.106 — Phillips, Richard P. Modern Thomistic philosophy. London, 1934-40. 2v.
Phil 8705.7 — Phillips, S.L. Agreement of evolution and Christianity. Washington, 1904.

Phil 8595.11 — Phillips, S.L. The testimony of reason. Washington, 1903.
Phil 5590.200 — Phillipson, H. The object relations technique. London, 1955. 2v.
Htn Phil 4946.1.30* — Philo Iudaeus. De vita Mosis. Paris, 1554.
Phil 6046.77 — Philologemata abstrusa de pollice. v.1-2. (Praetonius, J.) Quedlinburgi, 1677.
Phil 6990.19.5 — Philomythus, an antidote against credulity. (Abbott, E.A.) London, 1891.
Phil 3246.306 — Philonenko, Alexis. La liberté humaine dans la philosophie de Fichte. Paris, 1966.
Phil 3497.25 — Philonenko, Alexis. L'oeuvre de Kant. Paris, 1969-
Phil 3497.24 — Philonenko, Alexis. Théorie et praxis dans la pensée morale et politique de Kant et de Fichte en 1793. Paris, 1968.
Phil 3195.2.93 — Der Philosoph Deutinger und ultramontane Sophistik. (Neudecker, G.) Würzburg, 1877.
Phil 2655.1.81 — Der Philosoph Franz Hemsterhuis. (Meyer, E.) Breslau, 1893.
Phil 3525.82 — Der Philosoph K.C.F. Krause als Erzieher. (Ranft, M.) Halle, 1907.
Phil 3850.18.86 — Der Philosoph Max Scheler. (Lützeler, Heinrich.) Bonn, 1947.
Phil 3850.1.83 — Der Philosoph Strauss. (Ulrici, H.) Halle, 1873.
Phil 2520.280 — Der Philosoph und die Königin. (Behn, Irene.) Freiburg, 1957.
Phil 3640.210 — Philosoph und Edelmensch. (Salis-Marschlins, M. von.) Leipzig, 1897.
Phil 3460.98 — Philosoph und Literat der Goethezeit. (Friedrich, Heinrich Jacobi.) Frankfurt, 1971.
Phil 8705.9 — Philosopha sacra: or The principles of natural philosophy. (Pike, S.) London, 1753.
Phil 2825.10 — Le philosophe. St. Louis, 1948.
Phil 2555.2.80 — Un philosophe amateur, essai biographique sur Léon Dumont. (Büchner, A.) Paris, 1884.
Phil 2750.11.81 — Le philosophe dans la cité. (Maritain, Jacques.) Paris, 1960.
Phil 181.73.10 — Le philosophe et la théologie. (Gilson, E.) Paris, 1960.
Htn Phil 2915.30* — Le philosophe ignorant. (Voltaire, F.M.A. de.) n.p., 1766.
Phil 8592.38 — Le philosophe suprême. v.2. (Mariavé, Henry.) Montpellier, 1925-26. 2v.
Phil 89.1.15 — Philosophen - Lexikon. (Eisler, R.) Berlin, 1912.
Phil 130.6 — Philosophen der Gegenwart. (Hubscher, Arthur.) München, 1949.
Phil 92.3 — Philosophen Lexikon. Lief. 1-6. (Hauer, E.) Berlin, 1937.
Phil 130.8 — Philosophenbilden. (Thieme, Karl.) Basel, 1952.
Phil 3625.22 — Philosophenbriefe aus den wissenschaftlichen Korrespondez mit Franz Brentano. (Meinong, Alexius.) Graz, 1965.
Phil 130.14 — Philosophengalerie. (Geldsetzer, L.) Düsseldorf, 1967.
Phil 193.163.3 — Philosophenspiegel; die Hauptlehren der Philosophie begrifflich und geschichtlich dargestellt. 3. Aufl. (Spann, Othmar.) Graz, 1970.
Phil 193.163 — Philosophenspiegel. 2. Aufl. (Spann, O.) Wien, 1950.
Phil 184.32 — Philosophenwege. (Joël, K.) Berlin, 1901.
Phil 25.53 — The philosopher. London.
Phil 181.73.15 — The philosopher and theology. (Gilson, E.) N.Y., 1962.
Phil 308.4 — The philosopher critic. (Scholes, Robert E.) Tulsa, Okla., 1970.
Phil 2520.236 — A philosopher for the modern university. (Sykes, L.C.) Leicester, 1951.
Phil 176.148 — The philosopher in chaos. (Brownell, B.) N.Y., 1941.
Phil 291.9 — A philosopher looks at science. (Kemeny, John G.) Princeton, N.J., 1959.
Phil 1955.6.106 — The philosopher of the common man; essays in honor of John Dewey to celebrate his 80th birthday. N.Y., 1940.
Phil 1980.4A — Philosophers holiday. (Edman, Irwin.) N.Y., 1938.
Phil 1123.8 — Philosophers in Hades. (Smith, T.V.) Chicago, Ill., 1932.
Phil 2005.9.32 — Philosophers lead sheltered lives. (Feibleman, James.) London, 1952.
Phil 930.64 — The philosophers of China. (Day, A.B.) N.Y., 1962.
Phil 1106.19 — The philosophers of Greece. (Brumbaugh, Robert S.) N.Y., 1964.
Phil 165.384 — Philosophers of process. (Browning, Douglas.) N.Y., 1965.
Phil 192.74 — Philosophers on holiday. (Robertson, A.) London, 1933.
Phil 197.38.5 — A philosopher's pilgrimage. (Widgery, A.G.) N.Y., 1961.
Phil 1980.4.15 — Philosopher's quest. (Edman, Irwin.) N.Y., 1947.
Phil 822.13 — The philosopher's way. (Wahl, Jean A.) N.Y., 1948.
Phil 2430.3 — Les philosophes. (Torrey, Norman L.) N.Y., 1960.
Phil 1504.50F — Les philosophes belges. Louvain. 1-15,1902-1941 12v.
Phil 812.35 — Les philosophes célèbres. (Merleau-Ponty, Maurice.) Paris, 1956.
Phil 2419.1.3 — Les philosophes clasiques du XIXe siècle. (Taine, Hippolyte Adolphe.) Paris, 1868.
Phil 1707.1.11 — Philosophes contemporains. (Höffding, H.) Paris, 1908.
Phil 2412.3 — Les philosophes contemporains. (Maumus, Vincent.) Paris, 1891.
Phil 2750.19.105 — Philosophes contemporains. (Tilliette, X.) Paris, 1962.
Phil 1750.770 — Philosophes d'aujourd'hui en présence du droit. Paris, 1965.
Phil 130.2 — Les philosophes de l'antiquité. (Lenoël, L.) Paris, 1864.
Phil 960.200 — Les philosophes de l'Inde. 1. ed. (Challaye, Felicien.) Paris, 1956.
Phil 165.235 — Philosophes du dix neuvième siècle. (Comoth, R.) Bruxelles, 1960.
Phil 2980.8 — Philosophes en Suisse française. (Muralt, André de.) Neuchâtel, 1966.
Phil 4307.2 — Les philosophes espagnols d'hier et d'aujourd'hui. (Guy, Alain.) Toulouse, 1956. 2v.
Phil 150.25 — Les philosophes et leur langage. (Belaval, Y.) Paris, 1952.
Phil 807.19 — Philosophes et savantes. (Humbert, Pierre.) Paris, 1953.
Phil 2401.8 — Philosophes et savants français du XXe siècle. (Baruzi, Jean.) Paris, 1926. 3v.
Phil 2415.6 — Philosophes et savants français du XXe siècle. Paris. 1-5,1926-1930 5v.
Phil 2415.2 — Les philosophes françâis contemporains. (Poitou, E.L.) Paris, 1864.
Phil 2428.12 — Les philosophes français d'aujourd'hui. 2. éd. (Trotignon, Pierre.) Paris, 1970.
Phil 2403.10 — Les philosophes français d'aujourd'hui par eux-mêmes. (Deledalle, Gérard.) Paris, 1964?
Phil 2419.1 — Les philosophes français du XIXe siècle. (Taine, Hippolyte Adolphe.) Paris, 1857.
Phil 2419.1.2 — Les philosophes français du XIXe siècle. (Taine, Hippolyte Adolphe.) Paris, 1860.
Phil 2419.1.2.5 — Les philosophes français du XIXe siècle. (Taine, Hippolyte Adolphe.) Paris, 1966.

Phil 1135.44 Les philosophes-geometres de la Gréce. (Milliaud, G.)
Paris, 1900.
Phil 1705.5 Philosophes modernes. (Franck, A.) Paris, 1879.
Phil 4817.5 Philosophes roumains contemporains. (Academia Republicii
Socialiste România, Bucharest.) Bucureşti, 1958.
Phil 25.56 Philosophia; philosophorum nostri temporis vox universa.
Belgradi. 1-3,1936-1938 3v.
Phil 25.191 Philosophia; phylosophical quarterly of Israel. Jerusalem.
1,1971+
Phil 25.83 Philosophia. Mendoza. 2-9 9v.
Phil 814.3 Philosophia. v.1-2. (Oyen, Hendrik van.)
Utrecht, 1947-49. 2v.
Phil 25.149F Philosophia Arhusiensis. Aarhus. 3,1965+
Phil 5028.1 Philosophia Christiana cum antiqua et nova comparata.
(Sanseverino, G.) Neapoli, 1862-66. 3v.
Phil 5228.4 Philosophia christianacum antigua et nova comparata.
(Sanseverino, G.) Neapoli, 1862-66. 3v.
Htn Phil 193.7* Philosophia compendiosa. (Scheiblero, C.) Oxoniae, 1639.
Htn Phil 193.7.2* Philosophia compendiosa. (Scheiblero, C.) Oxoniae, 1639.
Phil 3910.77 Philosophia definitiva. (Baumeister, F.C.)
Vitembergae, 1767.
Phil 4843.8 Hē philosophia en Helladi apo tēs Anostaseōs tou ethnous.
(Kissabou, Maria I.) Athena, 1951.
Phil 4355.5 Philosophia entis sensibilis. (Echarri, Jaime.)
Romae, 1959.
Phil 3095.30 Philosophia generalis. (Baumgarten, A.G.) Halae, 1770.
Htn Phil 181.32* Philosophia generalis in duas partes disterminata. (Gale,
Theophilus.) London, 1676.
Phil 804.8 Philosophia historiaja. (Ertsei, D.) Debreczen, 1825.
Phil 4845.227.36 Philosophia kai paideia. (Papanoutsos, Euangelos.)
Athena, 1958.
Htn Phil 177.53* Philosophia libera. Ed. 2a. (Carpenter, Nathaniel.)
Oxoniae, 1622.
Phil 190.3.9 Philosophia militans. 3e und 4e Aufl. (Paulsen, F.)
Berlin, 1908.
Phil 197.21 Philosophia moralis. v.2. (Wendelino, M.F.) n.p., n.d.
Phil 8952.14 Philosophia moralis in usum scholarum. (Cathrein, Victor.)
Friburgi, 1959.
Phil 3910.55 Philosophia moralis suie ethica. (Wolff, Christian von.)
Halae, 1750-53. 5v.
Htn Phil 170.2.5F* Philosophia moysaica. (Fludd, Robert.) Goudae, 1638.
Phil 4960.645 A philosophia no Brasil. (Roméro, Sylvio.) Pôrto
Alegre, 1878.
Phil 817.18 Philosophia perennis. (Rintelen, F.J. von.)
Regensburg, 1930. 2v.
Phil 192.67 Philosophia perennis. (Rintelen, Fritz J. von.)
Regensburg, 1930. 2v.
Htn Phil 8696.13* Philosophia pia. (Glanvill, Joseph.) London, 1671.
Phil 3910.54 Philosophia practica. (Wolff, Christian von.)
Francofurti, 1738-39. 2v.
Phil 3910.54.5 Philosophia practica. (Wolff, Christian von.)
Veronae, 1739-42. 2v.
Phil 3910.29 Philosophia prima. (Wolff, Christian von.)
Francofurti, 1730.
Phil 3910.30 Philosophia prima suie ontologia. (Wolff, Christian von.)
Francofurti, 1736.
Phil 3910.2 Philosophia rationalis suie logica. (Wolff, Christian
von.) Helmstadia, 1746.
Phil 3910.1 Philosophia rationalis suie logica. (Wolff, Christian
von.) Veronae, 1735.
Phil 176.11.10 Philosophia recens controversa complexa definitiones
theoremata. (Baumeister, F.C.) Vratislaviae, 1766.
Phil 25.55 Philosophia reformata. Amsterdam. 1,1936+ 14v.
Phil 25.55.3 Philosophia reformata. Register, v.1-20,1936-1955.
n.p., n.d.
Phil 4363.11 Philosophia sceptica. (Martinez, Martin.) Madrid, 1730.
Phil 1500.3 Philosophia scholastica. (Vinas, M. de.) Genuae, 1709.
3v.
Phil 4110.13.30 Philosophia sensuum mechanica methodice tractata atque ad
usus academicos accommodata. (Fortunato da Brescia.)
Venetiis, 1756.
Phil 1500.2 Philosophia thomistica salisburgensis. (Bobenstuber, P.L.)
Augusta Vindelicorum, 1724.
Phil 193.25.4 Philosophia ultima. (Shields, C.W.) N.Y., 1888-1889.
3v.
Phil 193.25 Philosophia ultima. (Shields, C.W.) Philadelphia, 1861.
Phil 187.101 Philosophia vetus restituta. (Marci von Kronland, J.M.)
Francofurti, 1676.
Phil 187.15 Philosophiae elementa. (Migeot, A.) Carolopoli, 1784.
2v.
Phil 2053.40 Philosophiae moralis. v.1-3. (Hutcheson, F.)
Glasgow, 1742.
Phil 176.242 A philosophiai tudományok encyclopaediája. (Bihari,
Péter.) Budapest, 1875.
Phil 1050.10.10 Philosophical essays. (Husik, I.) Oxford, 1952.
Phil 25.66F Philosophic abstracts. N.Y. 1-54,1940-1954 4v.
Phil 25.66 Philosophic abstracts. N.Y. 2+
Phil 25.66.2 Philosophic abstracts. Index, 1-2,1939-1950. N.Y., n.d.
Phil 175.4 Philosophic and scientific ultimatum. (Allibaco, W.A.)
N.Y., 1864.
Phil 2150.13A The philosophic bases of art and criticism. (McKeon,
Richard P.) Chicago? 1944.
Phil 8894.24 The philosophic basis of moral obligation; a study in
ethics. (Turner, J.E.) London, 1924.
Phil 5270.12 Philosophic foundations of genetic psychology and Gestalt
psychology. (Gobar, Ash.) The Hague, 1969.
Phil 735.12 The philosophic function of value. (Blechman, Nathan.)
Boston, 1918.
Phil 176.168.5 Philosophic inquiry. (Beck, Lewis White.) Englewood
Cliffs, N.J., 1958.
Phil 176.168 Philosophic inquiry. (Beck, Lewis White.) N.Y., 1953.
Phil 165.85 Philosophic problems. (Mandelbaum, Maurice H.)
N.Y., 1957.
Phil 165.86 Philosophic problems. (Mandelbaum, Maurice H.)
N.Y., 1961.
Phil 165.86.2 Philosophic problems. (Mandelbaum, Maurice H.)
N.Y., 1966.
Phil 25.195 Philosophic research and analysis; a bimonthly information
and news journal. Boulder, Colo. 4,1971+
Phil 42.4.5 Philosophic studies. (Chicago. University.) Chicago.
1-10 2v.
Phil 8592.10 Philosophic theology. (Miles, J.W.) Charleston, 1849.
Phil 8589.10 Philosophic thought and religion. (Jones, David A.)
London, 1919.
Phil 2405.5.2 Philosophic thought in France and the United States. 2. ed.
(Farber, Marvin.) Albany, 1968.
Phil 8426.7 Philosophic turnings. (Ziff, Paul.) Ithaca, N.Y., 1966.

Phil 193.123.5 The philosophic way of life. (Smith, Thomas V.)
Chicago, 1929.
Phil 193.123.8 The philosophic way of life in America. 2d. ed. (Smith,
Thomas V.) N.Y., 1943.
Phil 25.88 Philosophica slovaca. Bratislava. 1,1946+ 19v.
Phil 177.25.10 Philosophicae Leibnitianae. (Canz, Israle Gottlieb.)
Francofurti, 1749.
Phil 44.2 The "philosophical". A short history of the Edinburgh
Philosophical Institution. (Miller, W.) Edinburgh, 1949.
Phil 4873.10 Philosophical activity in Pakistan. (Smet, Richard V. de.)
Lahore, 1961.
Phil 165.13 Philosophical analysis. (Black, M.) Ithaca, 1950.
Phil 181.140.2 Philosophical analysis. (Gorovitz, Samuel.) N.Y., 1967.
Phil 1720.5 Philosophical analysis. (Urmson, J.O.) Oxford, 1956.
Phil 1845.3.95 Philosophical and literary pieces. (Alexander, Samuel.)
London, 1939.
Htn Phil 294.4F* Philosophical and physical opinions. (Newcastle, M.L.C.)
London, 1663.
Phil 5770.1 A philosophical and practical treatise on the will.
(Uphan, T.C.) Portland, 1834.
Phil 8602.16.5 The philosophical approach to religion. (Waterhouse, E.S.)
London, 1933.
Phil 182.30 Philosophical arrangements. (Harris, J.) London, 1775.
Phil 8887.120 Philosophical aspects of culture. (Morris, B.) Yellow
Springs, Ohio, 1961.
Phil 25.131 Philosophical Association; Amravate. Journal. Nagpur.
2v.
Phil 8662.16 The philosophical bases of theism. (Hicks, G.D.)
London, 1937.
Phil 8602.15 The philosophical basis of religion. (Watson, J.)
Glasgow, 1907.
Phil 8662.3 The philosophical basis of Theism. (Harris, S.)
N.Y., 1883.
Phil 2115.27.5 Philosophical beauties. (Locke, J.) N.Y., 1828.
Phil 75.56 Philosophical books. Leicester. 1,1960+ 4v.
Phil 8893.21 Philosophical catechism...natural laws of man. (Spurzheim,
J.K.) Boston, 1832.
Phil 8893.21.2 Philosophical catechism...natural laws of man. (Spurzheim,
J.K.) Boston, 1835.
Phil 5938.6.43 Philosophical catechism of the natural laws of man.
(Spurzheim, Johann Gaspar.) Boston, 1833.
Phil 1870.73.18 Philosophical commentaries generally called the commonplace
book. (Berkeley, G.) London, 1944.
Phil 2225.5.106 Philosophical comments on the philosophies of Charles S.
Peirce and Ludwig Wittgenstein. (Mullin, Albert A.)
Urbana, Ill., 1961.
Phil 3480.127 Philosophical correspondence. (Kant, Immanuel.)
Chicago, 1967.
Phil 1718.7.5 Philosophical currents of the present day. (Stein,
Ludwig.) Calcutta, 1918-19. 2v.
Phil 106.1.7 A philosophical dictionary. (Voltaire, Francois Marie
Arouet de.) London, 1824. 6v.
Phil 106.1.20 Philosophical dictionary. (Voltaire, Francois Marie Arouet
de.) N.Y., 1969. 2v.
Phil 106.1.6 The philosophical dictionary. v.1-2. (Voltaire, Francois
Marie Arouet de.) London, 1819.
Phil 2915.70 Philosophical dictionary of M. de Voltaire. (Voltaire,
F.M.A. de.) N.Y., 1830.
Phil 960.131 The philosophical discipline. (Jha, Gangānātha.)
Calcutta, 1928.
Phil 8638.3 A philosophical discourse...natural immortality. (Norris,
John.) London, 1708.
Phil 7082.126.1 Philosophical discourse on the nature of dreams.
(Saalfeld, Adam Friedrich William.) London, 1764.
Phil 197.12A Philosophical discussions. (Wright, C.) N.Y., 1877.
Phil 175.9.8 Philosophical dissertations. (Argens, J.B.) London, 1753.
2v.
Phil 1928.35 A philosophical enquiry into the laws of nature.
(Cumberland, R.) Dublin, 1750.
Htn Phil 6115.12* A philosophical enquiry into the nature, origin, and extent
of animal motion. (Farr, Samuel.) London, 1771.
Phil 8402.14.2 A philosophical enquiry into the origin of our ideas. 3rd
ed. (Burke, E.) London, 1761.
Phil 8402.14.7 A philosophical enquiry into the origin of our ideas of the
sublime and beautiful. (Burke, E.) Philadelphia, 1806.
Phil 8402.14.5 A philosophical enquiry into the origin of our ideas of the
sublime and beautiful. (Burke, E.) N.Y., 1829.
Phil 8402.14.10 A philosophical enquiry into the origin of our ideas of the
sublime and beautiful. (Burke, E.) Baltimore, 1833.
Phil 8402.14A A philosophical enquiry into the origin of our ideas of the
sublime and beautiful. 6th ed. (Burke, E.) London, 1770.
Htn Phil 8602.2* A philosophical essay. (Ward, S.) Oxford, 1667.
Phil 7060.25 Philosophical essay on credulity and superstition.
(Blakeman. R.) N.Y., 1849.
Htn Phil 2750.3.30* A philosophical essay on man. v.1-2. (Marat, Jean Paul.)
London, 1773.
Phil 165.400 Philosophical essays, dedicated to Gunnar Aspelin on the
occasion of his sixty-fifth birthday, the 23rd of September
1963. Lund, 1963.
Phil 1845.10 Philosophical essays. (Ayer, Alfred Jules.) London, 1954.
Phil 176.118 Philosophical essays. (Balfour, James.) Edinburgh, 1768.
Phil 176.222 Philosophical essays. (Bouwsma, O.K.) Lincoln,
Nebraska, 1965.
Phil 4872.55.220 Philosophical essays. (Damle, Prabhakar R.) Bombay, 1954.
Phil 960.28.5 Philosophical essays. (Daqupta, S.) Calcutta, 1941.
Phil 4762.1.42 Philosophical essays. (Losskii, Nikolai Onufrievich.)
n.p., 1941.
Htn Phil 189.2* Philosophical essays. (Ogilvie, J.) Philadelphia, 1816.
Phil 192.28.5A Philosophical essays. (Russell, B.) London, 1910.
Phil 192.28.6 Philosophical essays. (Russell, B.) N.Y., 1967.
Htn Phil 2275.59* Philosophical essays. (Stewart, D.) Edinburgh, 1810.
Phil 2275.60 Philosophical essays. (Stewart, D.) Philadelphia, 1811.
Htn Phil 197.3* Philosophical essays. (Watts, T.) London, 1733.
Phil 2050.35.85 Philosophical essays. 1st American ed. (Hume, David.)
Philadelphia, 1817. 2v.
Htn Phil 2050.34.25* Philosophical essays concerning human understanding. 2nd
ed. (Hume, David.) London, 1750.
Htn Phil 2050.34.27* Philosophical essays concerning human understanding. 2nd
ed. (Hume, David.) London, 1751.
Phil 190.61A Philosophical essays for A.N. Whitehead. London, 1936.
Phil 2280.14.80 Philosophical essays in honor of Edgar Arthur Singer, Jr.
Philadelphia, 1942.
Phil 177.40 Philosophical essays in honor of J.E. Creighton. (Sabine,
George H.) N.Y., 1917.
Phil 3450.11.115A Philosophical essays in memory of Edmund Husserl. (Farber,
Marvin.) Cambridge, 1940.

Phil 2340.8.80   Philosophical essays presented to John Watson. (Kingston, Ontario. Queen's University. Faculty of Arts.) Kingston, 1922.

Phil 3475.3.205   Philosophical faith and revelation. (Jaspers, Karl.) N.Y., 1967.

Phil 41.7   The philosophical forum; an annual published by the Boston University of Philosophical Club. Boston. 1-16,1943-1959 3v.

Phil 8581.84   Philosophical foundations of faith. (Bradshaw, M.J.) N.Y., 1941.

Phil 960.157   Philosophical foundations of India. (Bernard, Theos.) London, 1945.

Phil 2750.19.42.5   Philosophical fragments, 1904. (Marcel, Gabriel.) Notre Dame, Ind., 1965.

Phil 187.20.5   Philosophical fragments. (Morell, J.D.) London, 1878.

Phil 8581.91   The philosophical heritage of the Christian faith. (Bosley, Harold A.) Chicago, 1944.

Phil 1819.2   Philosophical ideas in the United States. (Townsend, H.G.) N.Y., 1934.

Phil 6319.1.200   The philosophical implication of C.G. Jung's individuation process. (Gruesen, J.J.) Washington, 1956.

Phil 8586.38   Philosophical implications of Christianity. (Grensted, L.W.) Oxford, 1930.

Phil 5752.2A   Philosophical inquiry...human liberty. (Collins, A.) London, 1717.

Phil 5752.2.3   Philosophical inquiry...human liberty. (Collins, A.) London, 1735.

Phil 5752.2.10   Philosophical inquiry...human liberty. (Collins, A.) London, 1890.

Phil 193.144   Philosophical inquiry. (Steeksma, J.) London, 1935.

Phil 8402.14.20   A philosophical inquiry into the origin of our ideas of the sublime and beautiful. (Burke, E.) London, 1958.

Phil 1760.20   Philosophical interrogations. 1. ed. (Rome, Sydney C.) N.Y., 1964.

Phil 8881.29   A philosophical introduction to ethics. (Gibson, W.R.B.) London, 1904.

Phil 3925.16.2   Philosophical investigations. (Wittgenstein, Ludwig.) N.Y., 1953.

Phil 3925.16   Philosophical investigations. (Wittgenstein, Ludwig.) Oxford, 1953.

Phil 3925.16.3   Philosophical investigations. 3rd ed. (Wittgenstein, Ludwig.) N.Y., 1968[1958]

Phil 3925.16.3.1   Philosophical investigations. 3rd ed. (Wittgenstein, Ludwig.) Oxford, 1968.

Phil 3925.16.3.2   Philosophical investigations. 3rd ed. (Wittgenstein, Ludwig.) Oxford, 1968.

Phil 188.7A   Philosophical lectures and remains. (Nettleship, R.L.) London, 1897.

Phil 2520.78.45   Philosophical letters. (Descartes, René.) Oxford, 1970.

Phil 6025.6   Philosophical letters on physiognomy. London, 1751.

Phil 75.13.5   Philosophical library for the American continent. (Rand, Benjamin.) Cambridge, 1904.

Phil 185.106   The philosophical life of the senses. (Kuspit, Donald Burton.) N.Y., 1969.

Phil 5039.28   Philosophical logic. (Davis, J.W.) Dordrecht, 1969.

Phil 2417.2A   Philosophical miscellanies...Cousin, Jouffray. (Ripley, G.) Boston, 1838. 2v.

Phil 288.15.5   The philosophical nature of physical bodies. (Hoenen, Peter.) West Baden Springs, Ind., 1955.

Phil 150.01   Pamphlet box. Philosophical nomenclature.

Phil 5640.14   Philosophical observations on the senses. (Elliott, John.) London, 1780.

Phil 193.49.9   Philosophical opinion in America. (Santayana, G.) London, 1918. 2v.

Phil 2240.61   Philosophical orations of Thomas Reid. (Reid, Thomas.) Aberdeen, 1937.

Htn   Phil 978.72.10*   A philosophical overhaul. (Ljungström, O.) Lund, 1937.

Phil 2477.1.06   Philosophical pamphlets, 1888-1909. (Boutroux, Emile.) Paris, 1888-1909.

Phil 140.10   Pamphlet vol. Philosophical pamphlets. 8 pam.

Phil 140.11   Pamphlet vol. Philosophical pamphlets.

Phil 140.12   Pamphlet vol. Philosophical pamphlets. 16 pam.

Phil 140.12.2   Pamphlet vol. Philosophical pamphlets. 16 pam.

Phil 140.12.3   Pamphlet vol. Philosophical pamphlets. 11 pam.

Phil 140.12.4   Pamphlet vol. Philosophical pamphlets. 11 pam.

Phil 140.8   Pamphlet vol. Philosophical pamphlets. 6 pam.

Phil 140.7   Pamphlet vol. Philosophical pamphlets. 6 pam.

Phil 140.6   Pamphlet vol. Philosophical pamphlets. 10 pam.

Htn   Phil 140.3*   Pamphlet vol. Philosophical pamphlets. 9 pam.

Htn   Phil 140.2*   Pamphlet vol. Philosophical pamphlets. 8 pam.

Phil 140.9   Pamphlet vol. Philosophical pamphlets. 16 pam.

Htn   Phil 140.4*   Pamphlet vol. Philosophical pamphlets. 6 pam.

Phil 140.5   Pamphlet vol. Philosophical pamphlets. 7 pam.

Phil 2477.1.07   Philosophical pamphlets. (Boutroux, Emile.) Paris, 1904-05. 2 pam.

Phil 175.52   Philosophical papers. (Austin, John L.) Oxford, 1961.

Phil 2125.40   Philosophical papers. (McCosh, James.) N.Y., 1869.

Phil 52.1   Philosophical papers. (Michigan. University.) Ann Arbor. 1-4

Phil 2150.18.35   Philosophical papers. (Moore, George Edward.) London, 1959.

Phil 57.14   Philosophical papers. (Rhodes University, Grahamstown, South Africa. Department of Philosophy.) Grahamstown. 3,1967+

Phil 4655.4.30   Philosophical papers. (Wedberg, Anders.) Stockholm, 1968-

Phil 175.52.2   Philosophical papers. 2d ed. (Austin, John L.) Oxford, 1970.

Phil 3552.32   Philosophical papers and letters. (Leibniz, Gottfried Wilhelm.) Chicago, 1956. 2v.

Phil 3552.32.2   Philosophical papers and letters. 2nd ed. (Leibniz, Gottfried Wilhelm.) Dordrecht, 1969.

Phil 75.92   Philosophical periodicals. (Library of Congress. General Reference and Bibliography Division.) Washington, 1952.

Phil 3850.18.40   Philosophical perspectives. (Scheler, Max.) Boston, 1958.

Phil 193.252   Philosophical perspectives. (Sellars, Wilfrid.) Springfield, 1967.

Phil 193.260   Philosophical pictures. (Shibles, Warren.) Dubuque, 1969.

Phil 176.156   The philosophical predicament. (Barnes, W.) London, 1950.

Phil 5058.41   The philosophical presuppositions of mathematical logic. Thesis. (Smart, Harold R.) N.Y., 1925.

Phil 8597.1   The philosophical principles of natural and revealed religion. (Ramsay, A.M.) Glasgow, 1748-49. 2v.

Phil 8582.8   Philosophical principles of religion. v.1-2. (Cheyne, G.) London, 1915-16.

Phil 182.131   Philosophical problems. (Hartnack, J.) Copenhagen, 1962.

Phil 187.32   Philosophical problems. (Montgomery, E.) N.Y., 1907.

Phil 5066.171   Philosophical problems. (Zinov'ev, Aleksandr A.) Dordrecht, 1963.

Phil 5039.22   Philosophical problems in logic. Dordrecht, 1970.

Phil 5252.158   Philosophical problems of psychology. (Madden, Edward Harry.) N.Y., 1922.

Phil 672.219   Philosophical problems of space and time. 1st ed. (Gruenbaum, A.) N.Y., 1963.

Phil 5243.60   Philosophical psychology. 2d ed. (Donceel, Joseph.) N.Y., 1961.

Phil 25.85   The philosophical quarterly. 1,1950+ 18v.

Phil 25.40   The philosophical quarterly. Calcutta. 1,1925+ 31v.

Phil 193.23.9   The philosophical radicals and other essays. (Seth Pringle-Pattison, A.) Edinburgh, 1907.

Phil 190.95   Philosophical reasoning. (Passmore, John Arthur.) London, 1961.

Phil 192.13.5   Philosophical remains. (Robertson, G.C.) London, 1894.

Phil 25.1   The philosophical review. Boston. 1+ 80v.

Phil 25.1.5   The philosophical review. Index, 1892-1926. N.Y., n.d.

Phil 5252.135   The philosophical roots of scientific psychology. (Misiak, H.) N.Y., 1961.

Htn   Phil 2045.60*   Philosophical rudiments concerning goverment and society. (Hobbes, Thomas.) London, 1651.

Phil 2120.11.30   Philosophical sketches. (Langer, Susanne Katherina (Knauth).) Baltimore, 1962.

Phil 735.5   Philosophical status of values. (Dashiell, J.F.) N.Y., 1913.

Phil 2280.16.80   Philosophical studies; essays in memory of L. Susan Stebbing. (Aristotelian Society for the Systematic Study of Philosophy, London.) London, 1948.

Phil 3310.14   Philosophical studies. (Gomperz, H.) Boston, 1953.

Phil 187.56.5   Philosophical studies. (McTaggart, J.M.E.) London, 1934.

Phil 187.59   Philosophical studies. (Moore, G.E.) London, 1922.

Phil 192.10.5   Philosophical studies. (Ritchie, D.G.) London, 1905.

Phil 194.11.25   Philosophical studies. (Taylor, A.E.) London, 1934.

Phil 25.132   Philosophical studies. Maynoach, Ire. 2,1954+ 12v.

Phil 165.21   Philosophical studies in honor of the very Reverend Ignatius Smith. (Ryan, J.K.) Westminster, Maryland, 1952.

Phil 935.12   Philosophical studies of Japan. Tokyo. 1,1959+ 3v.

Phil 8951.4   Philosophical study of Chrisian ethics. (Barbour, G.F.) Edinburgh, 1911.

Phil 525.63   A philosophical study of mysticism. (Bennett, C.A.) New Haven, 1923.

Phil 525.63.5   A philosophical study of mysticism. (Bennett, C.A.) New Haven, 1931.

Phil 5241.116   A philosophical study of the human mind. (Barrell, Joseph.) N.Y., 1954.

Phil 4210.41   The philosophical system. (Rosmini-Serbati, Antonio.) London, 1882.

Phil 630.11   A philosophical system of theistic idealism. (Lindsay, James.) Edinburgh, 1917.

Phil 182.117   Philosophical systems. (Hall, E.W.) Chicago, 1960.

Phil 187.20   Philosophical tendencies of the age. (Morell, J.O.) London, 1848.

Phil 150.26   Philosophical terminology in Arabic and Persian. (Afnan, Soheil.) Leiden, 1964.

Phil 8599.21   Philosophical theology. (Tennant, F.R.) Cambridge, 1928-30. 2v.

Phil 177.20   Philosophical theories. (Cornwallis, C.F.) Philadelphia, 1846.

Phil 353.29   Philosophical theory and psychological fact. (Wallraff, C.F.) Tucson, 1961.

Phil 176.223   Philosophical thinking. (Beardsley, Monroe Curtis.) N.Y., 1965.

Htn   Phil 8628.3.3*   Philosophical touchstone. (Ross, Alexander.) London, 1645.

Phil 9420.2.5   Philosophical treatise...passions. v.1-2. (Cogan, T.) Bath, 1802.

Phil 9420.2.7   Philosophical treatise...passions. v.1-2. (Cogan, T.) Boston, 1821.

Phil 9420.2.6   Philosophical treatise...passions. v.1-2. (Cogan, T.) London, 1813.

Phil 2055.6   A philosophical treatise. (Harris, G.) London, 1876. 2v.

Phil 2651.40   Philosophical treatise concerning the weakness of human understanding. (Huet, Pierre Daniel.) London, 1728.

Phil 1718.29.10   Philosophical trends in the contemporary world. (Sciacca, Michele Federico.) Notre Dame, 1964.

Phil 8585.35A   Philosophical understanding and religious truth. 1st ed. (Frank, Erich.) London, 1945.

Phil 1850.10   Philosophical works. (Bacon, Francis.) London, 1737. 3v.

Phil 2520.22   Philosophical works. (Descartes, René.) N.Y., 1955. 2v.

Phil 1990.10A   Philosophical works. (Ferrier, J.F.) Edinburgh, 1875. 3v.

Phil 2050.10   Philosophical works. (Hume, David.) Edinburgh, 1826. 4v.

Phil 2050.11A   Philosophical works. (Hume, David.) Edinburgh, 1854. 4v.

Phil 3552.25   Philosophical works. (Leibniz, Gottfried Wilhelm.) New Haven, 1890.

Phil 2115.14   Philosophical works. (Locke, J.) London, 1877. 2v.

Phil 2115.14.7   Philosophical works. (Locke, J.) London, 1892. 2v.

Phil 1990.10.5   Philosophical works. v.2. (Ferrier, J.F.) Edinburgh, 1881.

Phil 1110.1.7   Philosophical works. v.2. (Ferrier, J.F.) Edinburgh, 1888.

Phil 3552.25.2   Philosophical works. 2nd ed. (Leibniz, Gottfried Wilhelm.) New Haven, 1908.

Phil 2520.22.5   The philosophical works of Descartes. (Descartes, René.) London, 1967. 2v.

Phil 1870.22   Philosophical writings. (Berkeley, G.) Edinburgh, 1952.

Phil 1905.9.6   The philosophical writings. (Burthogge, R.) Chicago, 1921.

Phil 2520.44   Philosophical writings. (Descartes, René.) Edinburgh, 1954.

Phil 2520.23A   Philosophical writings. (Descartes, René.) N.Y., 1958.

Phil 3552.34   Philosophical writings. (Leibniz, Gottfried Wilhelm.) London, 1956.

Phil 2145.15   Philosophical writings. (More, Henry.) N.Y., 1925.

Phil 2340.18.30   Philosophical writings. (Wright, Chauncey.) N.Y., 1958.

Htn   Phil 9358.11*   Philosophicall essayes...advises to ladyes. (Sprigg, William.) London, 1657.

Phil 191.4   Philosophie, das anthropokosmische System. (Quisling, Jörgen.) Berlin, 1936.

Phil 190.62   Die Philosophie; ihre Geschichte und ihre Systematik. Abt. 1,5,7,9,10,12,14,15. Bonn, 1934-1935. 8v.

Phil 2477.9.84   Philosophie, manuscrit inédit. (Bernard, Claude.) Paris, 19- .

Phil 176.82.5 Philosophie, Metaphysik und Einzelforschung. (Bender, Hedwig.) Leipzig, 1897.

Phil 184.30 Philosophie; questions complémentaires. (Janet, P.) Paris, 1925.

Phil 184.30.5 Philosophie; questions complémentaires. 5e éd. (Janet, P.) Paris, 1936.

Phil 8697.23 Philosophie, Religion, moderne Naturwissenschaft. (Hennemann, Gerhard.) Witten, 1955.

Phil 8598.135.10 Philosophie, Theologie, Ideologie. (Schlette, Heinz Robert.) Köln, 1968.

Phil 353.10 Philosophie, Welt und Wirklichkeit. (Weinmann, R.) München, 1922.

Phil 2605.1.80 La philosophie...d'Alfred Fouillée. (Guyau, Augustin.) Paris, 1913.

Phil 175.13 Philosophie. (Ampère, A.M.) Paris, 1870.

Phil 176.10 Philosophie. (Baumann, Julius J.) Leipzig, 1872.

Phil 1701.24 Die Philosophie. (Bense, Max.) Frankfurt a.M., 1951.

X Cg Phil 2401.6 La philosophie. (Bergson, H.) Paris, 1915.

Phil 2477.9.84.2 Philosophie. (Bernard, Claude.) Paris, 1954.

Phil 88.10 Philosophie. (Diemer, Alwin.) Frankfurt, 1958.

Phil 3200.6 Die Philosophie. (Eschenmayer, C.A.) Erlangen, 1803.

Phil 75.31 Philosophie. (Fock, G.) Leipzig, 1936.

Phil 184.19.10 Philosophie. (Jaspers, K.) Berlin, 1932. 3v.

Phil 186.71 Philosophie. (La Hautière, E. de.) Paris, 1895.

Phil 187.150 Philosophie. (Meinertz, Josef.) München, 1958.

Phil 75.17 Philosophie. (Moog, Willy.) Gotha, 1921.

Phil 192.39 Philosophie. (Rée, Paul.) Berlin, 1903.

Phil 3800.65 Philosophie. (Schelling, F.W.J. von.) Berlin, 1918?

Phil 2915.40 La philosophie. (Voltaire, F.M.A. de.) Paris, 1848.

Phil 100.15 La philosophie. Paris, 1969.

Phil 179.26 Philosophie: allgemeine Weltanschauung. (Eleutheropulos, A.) Zürich, 1911.

Phil 180.48.10 Philosophie: ein unlösbares Problem. (Freund, Ludwig.) München, 1933.

Phil 188.12.20 Philosophie: ihr Problem und ihre Probleme. (Natorp, Paul.) Göttingen, 1911.

Phil 192.21.5 Philosophie: ihr Wesen, ihre Probleme. (Rickert, H.) Leipzig, 1912.

Phil 5046.6.2 Philosophie. Logique. (Gatry, A.J.A.) Paris, 1855. 2v.

Phil 1504.2.2 Die Philosophie. v.2, pt.2. (Doctor, Max.) Münster, 1895.

Phil 1504.2.4 Die Philosophie. v.2, pt.4. (Baumgartner, M.) Münster, 1896.

Phil 811.2.5 La Philosophie. 2e ed. (Lefèvre, A.) Paris, 1884.

Phil 184.30.15 Philosophie. 8e éd. (Janet, P.) Paris, 1929.

Phil 175.13.9 Die Philosophie A.M. Ampères. (Lorenz, B.) Berlin, 1908.

Phil 176.58 La philosophie affective. (Bourdeau, J.) Paris, 1912.

Phil 3000.6 La philosophie allemande. (Arvon, Henri.) Paris, 1970.

Phil 2999.2 La philosophie allemande au XIXe siècle. Paris, 1912.

Phil 3552.287 La philosophie allemande au XVII siècle. (Boutroux, Emile.) Paris, 1929.

Phil 331.2.12 Philosophie als Denken der Welt Gemäss dem Prinzip des kleinsten Kraftmasses. (Avenarius, R.) Leipzig, 1876.

Phil 331.2.13 Philosophie als Denken der Welt Gemäss dem Prinzip des kleinsten Kraftmasses. 3. Aufl. (Avenarius, R.) Berlin, 1917.

Phil 585.170 Philosophie als Erfahrungswissenschaft. (Wein, Hermann.) Den Haag, 1965.

Phil 348.4 Philosophie als Grundwissenschaft. (Rehmke, J.) Leipzig, 1910.

Phil 348.4.2 Philosophie als Grundwissenschaft. 2. Aufl. (Rehmke, J.) Leipzig, 1929.

Phil 180.12.10 Die Philosophie als Idealwissenschaft und System. (Frohschammer, J.) München, 1884.

Phil 185.35 Philosophie als Kunst. (Keyserling, H.) Darmstadt, 1920.

Phil 185.35.2 Philosophie als Kunst. 2. Aufl. (Keyserling, H.) Darmstadt, 1922.

Phil 3450.11.48 Philosophie als strenge Wissenschaft. (Husserl, Edmund.) Frankfurt am Main, 1965.

Phil 186.52 Philosophie als Tat. (Lessing, T.) Göttingen, 1914.

Phil 176.76.5 Philosophie als Universalwissenschaft. (Bilharz, Alfons.) Wiesbaden, 1912.

Phil 197.63.5 Philosophie als Weg von den Grenzen der Wissenschaft au die Grenzen der Religion. (Wenzl, Aloys.) Leipzig, 1939.

Phil 177.8.15 Philosophie als Wissenschaft. (Carus, Paul.) Chicago, 1911.

Phil 182.6.10 Die Philosophie als Wissenschaft. (Hartsen, F.A.) Heidelberg, 1876.

Phil 193.105 Die Philosophie am Scheidewege. (Schultz, J.) Leipzig, 1922.

Phil 70.91 La philosophie analytique. Paris, 1962.

Phil 1106.2 La philosophie ancienne. (Benard, Charles.) Paris, 1885.

Phil 1127.4 La philosophie ancienne et la critique historique. (Waddington, Charles.) Paris, 1904.

Phil 1811.2.10 La philosophie anglaise classique. (Leroux, E.) Paris, 1951.

Phil 1807.8 La philosophie anglaise et américaine. (Hutin, Serge.) Paris, 1958.

Phil 1107.8 La philosophie antique. 4e ed. (Cresson, André.) Paris, 1957.

Phil 1020.23 La philosophie arabe dans l'Europe mediévale. (Quadri, G.) Paris, 1947.

Phil 3808.89.5 Die Philosophie Arthur Schopenhauers. (Koeber, R. von.) Heidelberg, 1888.

Phil 3808.121 Die Philosophie Arthur Schopenhauers. (Tschofen, Johann.) München, 1879.

Phil 1710.7 La philosophie au milieu du 20e siècle. (Klibasky, Raymond.) Firenze, 1958. 4v.

Phil 1526.4.5 Philosophie au moyen-âge. (Vignaux, Paul.) Paris, 1958.

Phil 1511.3.5 La philosophie au moyen âge. v.2. (Gilson, Étienne.) Paris, 1922.

Phil 1511.3.7 La philosophie au moyen âge. 2e éd. (Gilson, Etienne.) Paris, 1944.

Phil 1706.11 La philosophie au tournant de notre temps. (Flam, Leopold.) Bruxelles, 1961.

Phil 1540.35.5 La philosophie au XIIe siècle. (Steenberghen, Fernand van.) Louvain, 1966.

Phil 1517.10 La philosophie au XIVe siècle; six études. (Michalski, Konstanty.) Frankfurt, 1969.

Phil 3120.22.10 Philosophie auf Posten, Schriften 1916-21. (Blüher, Hans.) Heidelberg, 1928.

Phil 2490.88.10 Die Philosophie August Comte's. (Lévy-Bruhl, L.) Leipzig, 1902.

Phil 2515.6 Un philosophie belge, Colins. (Noel, J.) Mons, 1909.

Phil 4080.3.245 Die Philosophie Benedetto Croces als moderne Ideenlehre. (Osterwalder, T.) Berne, 1954.

Phil 2475.1.125 La philosophie Bergsonienne. (Maritain, Jacques.) Paris, 1914.

Phil 2475.1.126 La philosophie Bergsonienne. 2. éd. (Maritain, Jacques.) Paris, 1930.

Phil 2490.115 La philosophie biologique d'A.C. (Mourgue, R.) Lyon, 1909.

Phil 3120.19.90 Die Philosophie Bruno Bauchs, als Ausdruck germanischer Geisteshaltung. (Keller, E.) Stuttgart, 1935.

Phil 1930.18.85 Die Philosophie Carnaps. (Krauth, Lothar.) Wien, 1970.

Phil 930.60 La philosophie chinoise. 2. ed. (Chow, Yih-ching.) Paris, 1961.

Phil 196.2 La philosophie chrétienne. (Ventura de Raulica, G.) Paris, 1861. 3v.

Phil 1508.3 La philosophie chrétienne au Moyen Âge. (Delhaye, Philippe.) Paris, 1959.

Phil 4752.2.100 La philosophie chrétienne en Russie. (Porret, Eugene.) Neuchâtel, 1944.

Phil 1750.375 La philosophie Chrêtiennie de l'existance. (Lepp, Ignace.) Paris, 1953.

Phil 3450.11.45 La philosophie comme science rigoureuse. Thèse. (Husserl, Edmund.) Paris, 1954.

Phil 812.9 La philosophie comparée. (Masson-Oursel, Paul.) Paris, 1923.

Phil 812.9.2 La philosophie comparée. Thèse. (Masson-Oursel, Paul.) Paris, 1923.

Phil 2493.86 Die Philosophie Condillacs. Inaug.-Diss. (Saltykow, W.) Bern, 1901.

Phil 194.28 La philosophie constructive. (Tassy, E.) Paris, 1921.

Phil 2412.1 Philosophie contemporaine. (Margerie, M.A.) Paris, 1870.

Phil 4012.3 La philosophie contemporaine. (Mariano, R.) Paris, 1868.

Phil 1701.20.7 La philosophie contemporaine en Europe. 2. éd. (Bochénski, J.M.) Paris, 1951.

Phil 2415.5 La philosophie contemporaine en France. (Parodi, Dominique.) Paris, 1919.

Phil 2415.5.2 La philosophie contemporaine en France. (Parodi, Dominique.) Paris, 1920.

Phil 4012.6.5 La philosophie contemporaine en Italie. (Miceli di Serradileo, R.) Paris, 1939.

Phil 2475.1.490 La philosophie dans la cité technique. (Ebacher, Roger.) Québec, 1968.

Phil 8691.18 La philosophie dans ses rapports avec les sciences et la religion. (Barthélemy-Saint-Hilaire, J.) Paris, 1889.

Phil 2490.88 La philosophie d'Auguste Comte. (Lévy-Bruhl, L.) Paris, 1900.

Phil 2490.88.3 La philosophie d'Auguste Comte. 3. éd. (Lévy-Bruhl, L.) Paris, 1913.

Phil 1020.8.23 La philosophie d'Avicenne et son influence in Europe médévale. (Goichon, A.M.) Paris, 1944.

Phil 2477.1.100 La philosophie d'E. Boutroux. (LaFontaine, A.P.) Paris, 1920.

Phil 185.40.5 Die Philosophie de Bauhütte. (Kolbenheyer, E.G.) Wien, 1952.

Phil 2475.1.169 Philosophie de Bergson. (Höffding, Harald.) Paris, 1916.

Phil 2465.90 La philosophie de Charles Bonnet de Genève. Thèse. 1e éd. (Savioz, R.) Paris, 1948. 4v.

Phil 2840.89 La philosophie de Charles Renouvier. (Milhaud, G.) Paris, 1927.

Phil 2840.81 Philosophie de Charles Renouvier. (Séailles, G.) Paris, 1905.

Phil 2880.2.82 La philosophie de Charles Secrétan. (Pillon, F.) Paris, 1898.

Phil 2477.9.85 La philosophie de Claude Bernard. (Sertillanges, A.G.) Paris, 1944.

Phil 2050.109 La philosophie de David Hume. (Compayré, Gabriel.) Paris, 1873.

Phil 3235.82 La philosophie de Feuerbach. Thèse. (Lévy, Albert.) Paris, 1904.

Phil 3246.92 La philosophie de Fichte, ses rapports avec la conscience contemporaine. (Léon, Xavier.) Paris, 1902.

Phil 1850.103 Philosophie de François Bacon. (Adam, Charles.) Paris, 1890.

Phil 3640.119 La philosophie de Frédéric Nietzsche. (Huan, Gabriel.) Paris, 1917.

Phil 2750.13 La philosophie de Gabriel Marcel. (Corte, Marcel de.) Paris, 1937.

Phil 2610.100.5 La philosophie de Gassendi. (Bloch, Olivier René.) La Haye, 1971.

Phil 2610.81 Philosophie de Gassendi. (Thomas, P. Felix.) Paris, 1889.

Phil 3549.2.87 La philosophie de H. Keyserling. 6. éd. (Boucher, M.) Paris, 1927.

Phil 2885.80.5 La philosophie de H. Taine. (Barzellotti, G.) Paris, 1900.

Phil 3450.19.260 La philosophie de Heidegger. (Corvez, Maurice.) Paris, 1961.

Phil 3450.22 La philosophie de Heymass. (Gerritsen, T.J.C.) Paris, 1938.

Phil 3450.22.1 La philosophie de Heymass. Thèse. (Gerritsen, T.J.C.) Paris, 1938.

Phil 2045.80 La philosophie de Hobbes. (Lyon, G.) Paris, 1893.

Phil 3110.92 La philosophie de Jacob Boehme. Thèse. (Koyré, Alexandre.) Paris, 1929.

Phil 3460.88 La philosophie de Jacobi. (Lévy-Bruhl, L.) Paris, 1894.

Phil 3110.92.5 La philosophie de Jakob Boehme. (Koyré, Alexandre.) Paris, 1929.

Phil 2630.3.84 La philosophie de Jean-Jacques Gourd. (Reymond, M.) Chambéry, 1949.

Phil 2880.8.215 La philosophie de Jean Paul Sartre. (Lafarge, René.) Toulouse, 1967.

Phil 2725.11.81A La philosophie de Jules Lachelier. (Séailles, G.) Paris, 1920.

Phil 2725.13.90 La philosophie de Jules Lequier. (Grenier, Jean.) Paris, 1936.

Phil 2725.13.91 La philosophie de Jules Lequier. Thèse. (Grenier, Jean.) Paris, 1936.

Phil 3483.35 La philosophie de Kant. (Boutroux, Émile.) Paris, 1926.

Phil 3484.3 Philosophie de Kant. (Cousin, V.) Paris, 1857.

Phil 3485.6 La philosophie de Kant. (Desdouits, T.) Paris, 1876.

Phil 3483.9 Philosophie de Kant. Examen de la Critique du jugement. (Barni, J.) Paris, 1850.

Phil 3483.9.10 Philosophie de Kant. Examen des fondements de la métaphysique des moeurs. (Barni, J.) Paris, 1851.

Phil 3503.2 Philosophie de Kant. v.1-2. (Villers, C.) Metz, 1801.

Phil 193.21 La philosophie de la liberté. (Secrétan, C.) Paris, 1849. 2v.

Phil 193.21.2 La philosophie de la liberté. 2e ed. (Secrétan, C.) Paris, 1866.

Phil 8580.37 Philosophie de la nature. (Aubert, Jean-Marie.) Paris, 1965.

Phil 2750.11.66 La philosophie de la nature. (Maritain, Jacques.) Paris, 1936.

Phil 293.25   La philosophie de la nature. (Matisse, G.) Paris, 1938. 3v.

Phil 2905.2.30   La philosophie de la nature. v. 1-2. (Tonguèdec, J.) Paris, 1956. 4v.

Phil 1135.60   Philosophie de la nature chez les anciens. (Huit, C.) Paris, 1901.

Phil 177.35.5   Philosophie de la pratique. (Croce, Benedetto.) Paris, 1911.

Phil 176.207   Philosophie de la qualité. (Barraud, Jean.) Paris, 1956.

Phil 193.14   Philosophie de la raison pure. (Schoebel, C.) Paris, 1865.

Phil 3483.5   La philosophie de la religion. (Bridel, P.) Lausanne, 1876.

Phil 3850.18.150   La philosophie de la religion. (Dupuy, Maurice.) Paris, 1959.

Phil 8586.11   Philosophie de la religion. (Gourd, J.J.) Paris, 1911.

Phil 3425.60   Philosophie de la religion. (Hegel, Georg Wilhelm Friedrich.) Paris, 1876-78. 2v.

Phil 8592.7   La philosophie de la religion. (Matter, J.) Paris, 1857. 2v.

Phil 8594.14   Philosophie de la religion. (Ortegat, Paul.) Bruxelles, 1938.

Phil 8594.14.5   Philosophie de la religion. (Ortegat, Paul.) Gembloux, 1948. 2v.

Phil 8601.2   Philosophie de la religion (Éléments). (Véry, P.) Paris, 1858.

Phil 3850.18.151   La philosophie de la religion chez Max Scheler. (Dupuy, Maurice.) Paris, 1959.

Phil 5635.34   Philosophie de la sensation. (Pradines, M.) Paris, 1928-34. 3v.

Phil 735.132   Philosophie de la valeur. (Ruyer, R.) Paris, 1952.

Phil 193.10.9   Philosophie de la vie. (Schlegel, Friedrich von.) Paris, 1838.

Phil 2402.9.5   La philosophie de la vie au XVIIIe siècle. (Callot, E.) Paris, 1965.

Phil 5767.11A   Philosophie de la volonté. Photoreproduction. (Ricoeur, Paul.) Paris, 1950. 2v.

Phil 2555.8.30   Philosophie de la volonté. 1. éd. (Darbon, André.) Paris, 1951.

Phil 2750.20   Un philosophe de l'ambiguité. (Waelhens, A. de.) Louvain, 1951.

Phil 2725.2.85   La philosophie de Lamennais. (Janet, Paul A.R.) Paris, 1890.

Phil 8120.9   Philosophie de l'art; ou, Alchimie contre histoire. (Bopp, Léon.) Paris, 1954.

Phil 2885.34.5   Philosophie de l'art. (Taine, Hippolyte Adolphe.) Paris, 1865.

Phil 2885.34A   Philosophie de l'art. (Taine, Hippolyte Adolphe.) Paris, 1881. 2v.

Phil 2885.34.8   Philosophie de l'art. 8. éd. (Taine, Hippolyte Adolphe.) Paris, 1895?

Phil 8060.3   La philosophie de l'art classique. (Lapcević, Draguicha.) Paris, 1927.

Phil 8062.5   Philosophie de l'art en Grèce. (Taine, H.A.) Paris, 1869.

Phil 6060.2   La philosophie de l'écriture. (Deschamps, L.) Paris, 1892.

Phil 8598.24.9   Philosophie de l'effort. (Sabatier, Auguste.) Paris, 1908.

Phil 3552.95   La philosophie de Leibnitz. (Secretan, C.) Genève, 1840.

Phil 3552.113   La philosophie de Leibniz. (Nourrisson, M.) Paris, 1860.

Phil 2477.11.93   La philosophie de Léon Brunschvicg. (Deschoux, Marcel.) Paris, 1949.

Phil 2477.11.91   La philosophie de Léon Brunschvicg. (Messaut, J.) Paris, 1938.

Phil 2477.11.98   La philosophie de Léon Brunschvicg. Thèse. (Deschoux, Marcel.) Paris, 1949.

Phil 3425.95.4   Philosophie de l'esprit. (Véra, A.) Paris, 1867-69. 2v.

Phil 176.85.20   La philosophie de l'esprit. 1. éd. (Brunschvicg, L.) Paris, 1949.

Phil 192.85.5.2   Philosophie de l'être. 2. ed. (Raeymaeker, Louis de.) Louvain, 1947.

Phil 2070.35   Philosophie de l'expérience. (James, William.) Paris, 1917.

Phil 808.2   La philosophie de l'histoire de la philosophie. (Istituto di Studi Filosofici, Rome.) Roma, 1956.

Phil 3415.31   Philosophie de L'inconscient. (Hartmann, Eduard von.) Paris, 1877. 2v.

Phil 2725.19.95   La philosophie de l'institutio. (Gagnebin, S.) St.-Blaise, 1944.

Phil 2115.102.4   Philosophie de Locke. 4e éd. (Cousin, V.) Paris, 1861.

Phil 284.14   Philosophie de l'univers. (Dupont de Nemours, P.S.) Paris, 1792.

Phil 176.5.51   La philosophie de M. Balfour. (Rey, J.) Paris, 1897.

X Cg Phil 2475.1.145   La philosophie de M. Bergson. 2e ed. (Farges, Albert.) Paris, 1914.

Phil 2496.80   La philosophie de M. Cousin. (Alaux, J.E.) Paris, 1864.

Phil 2475.1.105   La philosophie de M. Henri Bergson. (Gillouin, R.) Paris, 1911.

Phil 2475.1.106   La philosophie de M. Henri Bergson. (Gillouin, R.) Paris, 1911.

Phil 2880.4.80   La philosophie de M. Sully Prudhomme. (Hérnon, Camille.) Paris, 1907.

Phil 2730.92   La philosophie de Maine de Biran. (Gérard, J.) Paris, 1876.

Phil 2733.94.6   La philosophie de Malebranche. (Gouhier, Henri.) Paris, 1948.

Phil 2733.83   La philosophie de Malebranche. (Ollé-Laprune, L.) Paris, 1870. 2v.

Phil 2733.94   La philosophie de Malebranche et son expérience religieuse. (Gouhier, Henri.) Paris, 1926.

Phil 2733.94.5   La philosophie de Malebranche et son expérience religieuse. Thèse. (Gouhier, Henri.) Paris, 1926. 2 pam.

Phil 3450.19.96.10   La philosophie de Martin Heidegger. 3e éd. (Waelhens, A. de.) Louvain, 1948.

Phil 3850.18.153   La philosophie de Max Scheler. (Dupuy, Maurice.) Paris, 1959. 2v.

Phil 3850.18.152   La philosophie de Max Scheler. 1. éd. (Dupuy, Maurice.) Paris, 1959. 2v.

Phil 3640.704   La philosophie de Nietzsche. (Fink, Eugen.) Paris, 1965.

Phil 3640.105   La philosophie de Nietzsche. 3e éd. (Lichtenberger, H.) Paris, 1912.

Phil 2555.7.93   La philosophie de Paul Decoster. (Molle, Germaine van.) Bruxelles, 1940.

Phil 4210.108   La philosophie de Rosmini. Thèse. (Palhoriès, F.) Paris, 1908.

Phil 2120.1.80   La philosophie de S.S. Laurie. (Remacle, G.) Bruxelles, 1909.

Phil 337.6   Philosophie de Saint Thomas. La connaissance. (Gardair, M.J.) Paris, 1895.

Phil 9420.8   Philosophie de Saint Thomas. Les passions et la volonté. (Gardair, J.) Paris, 1892.

Phil 9560.12   Philosophie de Saint Thomas. Les passions et la volonté. (Gardair, J.) Paris, 1901.

Phil 3808.94   La philosophie de Schopenhauer. (Ribot, T.) Paris, 1874.

Phil 3808.94.10   La philosophie de Schopenhauer. 12. éd. (Ribot, T.) Paris, 1909.

Phil 2138.96   Philosophie de Stuart Mill. Thèse. (Lauret, Henri.) Neufchâteau, 1885.

Phil 2885.81   La philosophie de Taine. (Nève, P.) Paris, 1908.

Phil 2340.10.225   La philosophie de Whitehead. (Parmentier, Alix.) Paris, 1968.

Phil 5249.2.28A   La philosophie de William James. (Flournoy, T.) St. Blaise, 1911.

Phil 2555.6.90   Die Philosophie Debrye's. Inaug.-Diss. (Weber, Georg.) Augsburg, 1926.

Phil 2477.1.139   La philosophie d'Émile Boutroux. (Schyns, M.) Paris, 1924.

Phil 1020.2   Die Philosophie der Araber im X. Jahrhunderts. v.1-2,4-6,9,12-13. (Dieterici, F.) Leipzig, 1876-1895. 10v.

Phil 1750.141A   Die Philosophie der Aufklärung. (Cassirer, Ernst.) Tübingen, 1932.

Phil 197.34   Philosophie der Befreiung. (Wille, Bruno.) Berlin, 1894.

Phil 210.65   Philosophie der Beschreibung. (Kaulbach, Friedrich.) Köln, 1968.

Phil 8583.16   Die Philosophie der Bibel. 2. Aufl. (Deussen, Paul.) Leipzig, 1919.

Phil 3625.1.165   Philosophie der Dicht Kunst. (Richter, Liselotte.) Berlin, 1948.

Phil 298.8   Die Philosophie der Eimmaligkeit. (Richter, G.) Wien, 1928-32. 3v.

Phil 190.83   Philosophie der Einsamkeit. (Parpert, F.) München, 1955.

Phil 192.67.5   Philosophie der Endlichkeit. (Rintelen, Fritz J. von.) Meisenheim, 1951.

Phil 332.44   Philosophie der Erkenntnis; das Vorverständnis und die Erfahrung des Neuen. (Bollnow, Otto Friedrich.) Stuttgart, 1970.

Phil 331.8   Philosophie der Erkenntnisse. Pt.1-2. (Abicht, J.H.) Bayreuth, 1791.

Phil 176.40   Philosophie der Erlösung. (Batz, P.) Berlin, 1876-86. 2v.

Phil 176.40.5   Die Philosophie der Erlösung. 2e Aufl. (Batz, P.) Berlin, 1879.

Phil 332.25.2   Philosophie der Erscheinung. 2. Aufl. (Barth, Heinrich.) Basel, 1966-

Phil 5768.9.95   Die Philosophie der Freiheit. (Steiner, Rudolf.) Berlin, 1894.

Phil 5768.10.5   Die Philosophie der Freiheit. (Steiner, Rudolf.) Berlin, 1921.

Phil 9245.27   Die Philosophie der Freude. (Zerbst, Max.) Leipzig, 191-.

Phil 3000.4   Die Philosophie der Gegenwart. (Aster, E. Von.) Leiden, 1935.

Phil 1701.14   Die Philosophie der Gegenwart. (Brasch, Moritz.) Leipzig, 1888.

Phil 1740.18   Die Philosophie der Gegenwart. (Edmaier, Alois.) Aschaffenburg, 1970.

Phil 3006.4   Die Philosophie der Gegenwart. (Gronau, Gotthard.) Langensalza, 1920-22. 2v.

Phil 1711.6   Philosophie der Gegenwart. (Landgrebe, Ludwig.) Bonn, 1952.

Phil 1712.5.10   Die Philosophie der Gegenwart. (Messer, A.) Leipzig, 1927.

Phil 1718.27   Die Philosophie der Gegenwart. (Schneider, F.) München, 1953.

Phil 25.12   Die Philosophie der Gegenwart. Heidelberg. 1-5,1908-1912 5v.

Phil 1717.5.2   Philosophie der Gegenwart. 2e Aufl. (Riehl, Alois.) Leipzig, 1904.

Phil 1712.5.5   Die Philosophie der Gegenwart. 3e Aufl. (Messer, A.) Leipzig, 1913.

Phil 3010.2   Die Philosophie der Gegenwart in Deutschland. (Külpe, O.) Leipzig, 1905.

Phil 3010.2.5   Die Philosophie der Gegenwart in Deutschland. (Külpe, O.) Leipzig, 1911.

Phil 25.12.10   Die Philosophie der Gegenwart in Selbstdarstellungen. Leipzig. 1-7 7v.

Phil 804.15   Philosophie der Geschichte der Philosophie. (Ehrlich, Walter.) Bad Ragaz, 1965.

Phil 193.215   Philosophie der Geschichten. (Schapp, Wilhelm.) Leer, 1959.

Phil 1108.2   Philosophie der Griechen. (Deussen, P.) Leipzig, 1911.

Phil 1135.47   Die Philosophie der Griechen. (Kalthoff, A.) Berlin, 1901.

Phil 1130.2   Die Philosophie der Griechen. (Zeller, Eduard.) Leipzig, 1869-79. 3v.

Phil 1130.1   Die Philosophie der Griechen. (Zeller, Eduard.) Tubingen, 1856-68. 5v.

Phil 1130.2.6   Die Philosophie der Griechen. Register. (Zeller, Eduard.) Leipzig, 1882.

Phil 1130.2.11   Die Philosophie der Griechen. v. 1,3-6. (Zeller, Eduard.) Leipzig, 1892. 5v.

Phil 1130.2.5   Die Philosophie der Griechen. v. 1-2,4-5. (Zeller, Eduard.) Leipzig, 1876-81. 4v.

Phil 1130.2.9   Die Philosophie der Griechen. v.2. (Zeller, Eduard.) Leipzig, 1892.

Phil 1130.2.15   Die Philosophie der Griechen. 6e Aufl. (Zeller, Eduard.) Leipzig, 1919-23. 6v.

Phil 960.161   Die Philosophie der Inder. (Glasenapp, H. von.) Stuttgart, 1949.

Phil 575.34.5.2   Philosophie der Individualität. 2e Aufl. (Müller-Freienfels, Richard.) Leipzig, 1923.

Phil 3778.91   Die Philosophie der Kantperiode Karl Leonhard Reinholds. Inaug. Diss. (Pfeifer, A.) W. Elberfeld, 1935.

Phil 482.3   Die Philosophie der Kraft. (Hessen, Robert.) Stuttgart, 1913.

Phil 8407.6.10   Philosophie der Kunst. (Gentile, G.) Berlin, 1934.

Phil 190.79   Philosophie der Lebensziele. (Pfänder, A.) Göttingen, 1948.

Phil 974.7   Die Philosophie der Liebe. v.1-2. (Bolt, Ernst.) Berlin, 1927.

Phil 5043.29   Philosophie der Logik und Arithmetik. (Dingler, Hugo.) München, 1931.

Phil 3260.82   Philosophie der Mathematik. (Bliedner, E.) Jena, 1904.

Phil 3625.13.90 Die Philosophie der Mathematik und Naturwissenschaft bei Aloys Müller. Inaug. Diss. (Kluge, Fritz.) Leipzig, 1935.

Phil 3246.66 Philosophie der Maurerei. (Fichte, Johann Gottlieb.) Leipzig, 1923.

Phil 1526.2 Die Philosophie der Mittelalters. 2e Aufl. (Verweyen, Johannes M.) Berlin, 1926.

Phil 1200.7 Die Philosophie der mittleren Stoa. (Schmekel, A.) Berlin, 1892.

Phil 525.1 Die Philosophie der Mystik. (Du Prel, C.F.) Leipzig, 1885.

Phil 525.1.2 Die Philosophie der Mystik. 2e Aufl. (Du Prel, Karl.) Leipzig, 1910.

Phil 3800.280 Philosophie der Mythologie. (Schelling, F.W.J. von.) Darmstadt, 1957. 2v.

Phil 182.94.17 Philosophie der Natur. (Hartmann, N.) Berlin, 1950.

Phil 193.17 Philosophie der Naturwissenschaft. (Schultze, F.) Leipzig, 1881.

Phil 5520.624 Die Philosophie der normalen Sprache. (Savigny, Eike von.) Frankfurt, 1969.

Phil 3585.19 Philosophie der Person. (Lugmayer, Karl.) Salzburg, 1956.

Phil 3483.42 Philosophie der praktischen Vernunft. (Barth, Heinrich.) Tübingen, 1927.

Phil 672.144 Philosophie der Raum-Zeit-Lehre. (Reichenbach, H.) Berlin, 1928.

Phil 8598.3 Philosophie der Religion. (Schaumann, J.C.G.) Halle, 1793.

Phil 1618.2 Die Philosophie der Renaissance. (Riekel, August.) München, 1925.

Phil 1050.4 Die philosophie der Soloman ibn Gabirol. (Guttmann, J.) Göttingen, 1889.

Phil 5520.403 Philosophie der Sprache. (Siewerth, Gustav.) Einsiedeln, 1962.

Phil 333.5.9 Philosophie der symbolischen Formen. (Cassirer, Ernst.) Berlin, 1923-29. 3v.

Phil 333.5.10 Philosophie der symbolischen Formen. Index. (Cassirer, Ernst.) Berlin, 1931.

Phil 3018.36 Philosophie der Tat. (Stuke, H.) Stuttgart, 1963.

Phil 8693.20.15 Die Philosophie der Technik. (Tuchel, K.) Frankfurt, 1964.

Phil 165.160 Philosophie der Toleranz. Graz, 1959.

Phil 190.64 Philosophie der tragischen Strukturen. (Pohl, Joachim.) Wien, 1935.

Phil 735.90 Philosophie der Werte. (Münsterberg, H.) Leipzig, 1908.

Phil 735.6 Die Philosophie der Werte. (Ostwald, W.) Leipizig, 1913.

Phil 165.11 Philosophie der Wirklichkeitsmäke. Wien, 1949.

Phil 3235.60 Philosophie der Zukunft. (Feuerbach, Ludwig.) Stuttgart, 1922.

Phil 189.9 Die Philosophie der Zukunft. (Opitz, H.G.) Leipzig, 1910.

Phil 193.104.2 Philosophie der Zukunft. 2e Aufl. (Sauer, W.) Stuttgart, 1926.

Phil 193.104 Philosophie der Zukunft eine Grundlegung der Kultur. (Sauer, W.) Stuttgart, 1923.

Phil 3246.177 Die Philosophie des Absoluten in der Fichteschen Wissenschaftslehre. Inaug. Diss. (Kerler, Dietrich H.) Ansbach, 1917.

Phil 3903.3.30 Die Philosophie des Als Ob. (Vaihinger, Hans.) Berlin, 1911.

Phil 3903.3.34 Die philosophie des Als Ob. 2. Aufl. (Vaihinger, Hans.) Leipzig, 1924.

Phil 3903.3.33 Die Philosophie des Als Ob. 3. Aufl. (Vaihinger, Hans.) Leipzig, 1918.

Phil 3903.3.90 Die Philosophie des "Als-Ob" und...Rechtswissenschaft. (Strauch, W.) München, 1923.

Phil 3903.3.105 Die Philosophie des Als Ob und das Leben Festschrift. (Leidel, A.) Berlin, 1932.

Phil 1112.3 Die Philosophie des Altertums. (Hönigwald, R.) München, 1917.

Phil 288.4 Die Philosophie des Bewussten. (Hahn, Otto.) Tubingen, 1887.

Phil 187.52 Die Philosophie des Bewusstseins. (Michelis, Friedrich.) Bonn, 1877.

Phil 187.52.80 Die Philosophie des Bewusstseins von Friedrich Michelis. (Kowalewski, A.) Berlin, 1897.

Phil 3160.9.80 Die Philosophie des Carl Gustav Carus. (Kern, Hans.) Berlin, 1926.

Phil 5046.13 Philosophie des Denkens. (Gruber, F.X.) Bern, 1842.

Phil 3007.7.2A Die Philosophie des deutschen Idealismus. 2. Aufl. (Hartmann, N.) Berlin, 1960.

Phil 2445.2.6 Philosophie des deux Ampère. (Barthélemy-Saint-Hilaire, J.) Paris, 1866.

Phil 348.5 Philosophie des Erkennens. (Reininger, R.) Leipzig, 1911.

Phil 2275.40 Philosophie des facultés actives et morales de l'homme. v.1-2. (Stewart, D.) Paris, n.d.

Phil 1535.21.2 Philosophie des Geistes. (Biedermann, G.) Prag, 1886.

Phil 182.17 Philosophie des Geistes. (Hillebrand, J.) Heidelberg, 1835-1836. 2v.

Phil 178.44 Philosophie des Gemüths. (Delff, Heinrich K.H.) Husum, 1893.

Phil 182.12 Eine Philosophie des gesunden Menschenverstandes. (Hellenbach, L.B.) Wien, 1876.

Phil 9245.58 Die Philosophie des Glücks. (Marcuse, L.) Zürich, 1949.

Phil 3549.2.90 Die Philosophie des Grafen Keyserling. (Adolph, H.) Stuttgart, 1927.

Phil 2262.83 Die Philosophie des Grafen von Shaftesbury. (Spicker, G.) Freiburg, 1872.

Phil 1020.18.5 Die Philosophie des Islam. (Horten, M.) München, 1923.

Phil 1050.21 Die Philosophie des Judentums. (Guttmann, J.) München, 1933.

Phil 3552.114.5A Die Philosophie des Jungen Leibnitz. (Kabitz, Willy.) Heidelberg, 1909.

Phil 3195.6.35 Die Philosophie des Lebens. (Dilthey, Wilhelm.) Frankfurt, 1946.

Phil 1750.122.2 Die Philosophie des Lebens. (Rickert, H.) Tübingen, 1922.

Htn Phil 193.10.10* Philosophie des Lebens. (Schlegel, Friedrich von.) Wien, 1828.

Phil 2475.1.152 Eine Philosophie des Lebens. (H. Bergson). (Keller, Adolf.) Jena, 1914.

Phil 1504.13 Die Philosophie des Macrobius. v.13, pt.1. (Schedler, M.) Münster, 1916.

Phil 299.26 Philosophie des Materie. 1. Aufl. (Schöndorfer, Ulrich A.) Graz, 1954.

Phil 1750.270.10 Philosophie des menschlichen Konflikts. (Abbagnano, Nicola.) Hamburg, 1957.

Phil 176.152 Die Philosophie des Metaphorischen. (Biese, Alfred.) Hamburg, 1893.

Phil 1511.1.10 Die Philosophie des Mittelalters. (Grabmann, M.) Berlin, 1921.

Phil 1523.12.5 Philosophie des Mittelalters. (Steenberghen, F.) Bern, 1950.

Phil 1508.1.2 Die Philosophie des Mittelalters. 2. Aufl. (Deussen, Paul.) Leipzig, 1919.

Phil 196.16 Philosophie des Möglichen. (Verweyen, J.M.) Leipzig, 1913.

Phil 510.21 Die Philosophie des Monopluralismus. (Marcus, Hugo.) Berlin, 1907.

Phil 2733.101 Die Philosophie des Nicolas Malebranche. (Mennicken, Peter.) Leipzig, 1927.

Phil 2733.88 Die Philosophie des Nicolaus Malebranche. (Novaro, Mario.) Berlin, 1893.

Phil 1504.3.5 Die Philosophie des Petrus Lombardus. v.3, pt.5. (Espenberger, J.N.) Münster, 1901.

Phil 672.130 Die Philosophie des Raumes. (Herbertz, R.) Stuttgart, 1912.

Phil 672.151 Die Philosophie des Raumes und der Zeit. (Gent, Werner.) Bonn, 1926.

Phil 672.151.2 Die Philosophie des Raumes und der Zeit. 2. Aufl. v.1-2. (Gent, Werner.) Hildesheim, 1962.

Phil 400.49 Die Philosophie des reinen Idealismus. (Kröger, Otto.) Bonn, 1921.

Phil 1504.18.4 Die Philosophie des Robert Grosseteste. v.18, pt.4-6. (Baur, L.) Münster, n.d.

Phil 8413.13 Eine Philosophie des Schönen in Natur und Kunst. (Muller, Josef.) Mainz, 1897.

Phil 300.6 Philosophie des schöpferischen. (Tramer, Moritz.) Bern, 1957.

Phil 3415.73.5 Philosophie des Schonen. 2. Aufl. (Hartmann, Eduard von.) Berlin, 1924.

Phil 3824.2 Die Philosophie des Spinoza. (Erhardt, Franz.) Leipzig, 1908.

Phil 978.49.680 Die Philosophie des Thomas von Aquino. 3. Aufl. (Steiner, R.) Dornach, 1967.

Phil 3415.30.1 Philosophie des Unbewussten. (Hartmann, Eduard von.) Berlin, 1869.

Phil 3415.30.15 Philosophie des Unbewussten. 2. Aufl. (Hartmann, Eduard von.) Leipzig, 1923. 3v.

Phil 3415.30.1.2 Philosophie des Unbewussten. 4. Aufl. (Hartmann, Eduard von.) Berlin, 1872.

Phil 3415.30 Philosophie des Unbewussten. 5. Aufl. (Hartmann, Eduard von.) Berlin, 1873.

Phil 3415.30.3 Philosophie des Unbewussten. 6. Aufl. (Hartmann, Eduard von.) Berlin, 1874.

Phil 3415.30.2 Philosophie des Unbewussten. 8. Aufl. (Hartmann, Eduard von.) Berlin, 1878. 2v.

Phil 3415.30.9 Philosophie des Unbewussten. 9. Aufl. (Hartmann, Eduard von.) Berlin, 1882.

Phil 186.45 Die Philosophie des Unvollendbar. (Lasker, E.) Leipzig, 1919.

Phil 338.45 Philosophie des Verstehens. (Haering, Theodor Lorenz.) Tübingen, 1963.

Phil 1740.2 Die Philosophie des zwanzigsten Jahrhunderts in ihren Hauptströmungen. (Müller-Freienfels, Richard.) Berlin, 1923.

Phil 1740.6 Die Philosophie des 20. Jahrhunderts. (Hessen, Johannes.) Rottenburg, 1951.

Phil 2636.88.5 La philosophie d'Helvétius. (Momdzhian, Khashik.) Moscow, 1959.

Phil 175.9.2 La philosophie du Bon-Sens. (Argens, J.B.) La Haye, 1755. 3v.

Phil 175.9 La philosophie du Bon-Sens. (Argens, J.B.) La Haye, 1765. 2v.

Phil 2668.60 Philosophie du bonheur. (Janet, Paul A.R.) Paris, 1864.

Phil 2630.4.90 La philosophie du Bovarysme. (Palante, Georges.) Paris, 1924.

Phil 8951.11.5 Philosophie du Christianisme. (Bautain, Louis E.) Paris, 1835. 2v.

Phil 6111.85 Philosophie du corps. (Bruaire, Claude.) Paris, 1968.

Phil 9120.1 Philosophie du devoir. (Ferraz, M.) Paris, 1869.

Phil 1730.4 La philosophie du dix-huitième siècle dévoilée par elle-même. (Gourju, Pierre.) Paris, 1816. 2v.

Phil 8583.41.20 Philosophie du fait chrétien. (Luijk, Henk van.) Paris, 1964.

Phil 1506.10 La philosophie du moyen âge. (Brehser, Emile.) Paris, 1949.

Phil 9045.17 Philosophie du peuple. (Lequinio, J.M.) Paris, 1796.

Phil 8885.26 Philosophie du sens commun. (Kleffler, Henri.) Paris, 1894-95. 3v.

Phil 1750.5 La philosophie du signe. (Roberty, E. de.) Paris, 1891.

Phil 5520.720 La philosophie du signe. (Marmy, Emile.) Fribourg, 1969.

Phil 9290.8 La philosophie du travail. (Arvon, Henri.) Paris, 1961.

Phil 193.112 La philosophie du travail. (Seailles, G.) Paris, 1923.

Phil 1735.4 Philosophie du XIXe siècle. (Guepin, Anec.) Paris, 1854.

Phil 303.10 Philosophie d'un ignorant. (Wälte, Théodore.) Genève, 1914.

Phil 1802.2 Philosophie écossaise. 3e éd. (Cousin, V.) Paris, 1857. 2 pam.

Phil 3450.11.180 Die Philosophie Edmund Husserl den Grandzügen ihrer Entstefung. (Mueller, W.H.) Bonn, 1956.

Phil 200.9 La philosophie effective. (Zafiropulo, J.) Paris, 1931.

Phil 1801.2 La philosophie en Amériqe depuis les origine jusqu'à nos jours, 1607-1900. (Van Becelaere, L.) N.Y., 1904.

Phil 2400.2 La philosophie en France. (Adam, C.) Paris, 1894.

Phil 2417.1 La philosophie en France au XIXe siècle. (Ravaisson, J.G.F.) Paris, 1868.

Phil 2409.2 La philosophie en France pendant la révolution. (Joyau, Emmanuel.) Paris, 1893.

Phil 180.80 La philosophie en question. (Fougeyrollas, Pierre.) Paris, 1960.

Phil 3120.67.80 Die Philosophie Ernst Bergmanns. (Neuwinger, Rudolf.) Stuttgart, 1938.

Phil 332.25 Philosophie Erscheinung. (Barth, Heinrich.) Basel, 1947. 2v.

Phil 8662.22 Philosophie et athéisme. (Hills, Ernest.) Paris, 1923.

Phil 2050.264 Philosophie et esthétique chez David Hume. (Brunet, Oliver.) Paris, 1965.

Phil 3195.6.135 Philosophie et histoire chez W. Dilthey. (Suter, Jean F.) Bale, 1960.

Phil 2805.109 La philosophie et l'apologétique de Pascal. (Janssens, Edgard.) Louvain, 1906.

Phil 1714.2 La philosophie et le temps présent. 5e éd. (Ollé-Laprune, L.) Paris, 1908

Phil 1722.12.5 La philosophie et les experiences naturelles. (Waelkens, Alphonse de.) La Haye, 1961.

Phil 75.23 La philosophie et les philosophes. (Hoffmans, Jean.) Bruxelles, 1920.

Phil 8581.95   La philosophie et l'esprit chrétien. (Blondel, Maurice.) Paris, 1944.

Phil 525.107   Philosophie et mystique. Thèse. (Morot-Sir, E.) Paris, 1948.

Phil 2730.113   Philosophie et phénoménologie du corps. (Henry, Michel.) Paris, 1965.

Phil 2402.2   Philosophie et philosophes. (Caro, E.M.) Paris, 1888.

Phil 3808.60.10   Philosophie et philosophes. 2. éd. (Schopenhauer, Arthur.) Paris, 19- .

Phil 850.14   Philosophie et poésie: Les origines. (Klippel, M.) Paris, 1925.

Phil 8582.54   Philosophie et religion. (Chauvet-Dusoul, F.) Paris, 1941-42. 5v.

Phil 8585.12   Philosophie et religion. (Franck, A.) Paris, 1869.

Phil 812.1   Philosophie et religion. (Maret, H.S.C.) Paris, 1856.

Phil 8597.66   Philosophie et religion. (Riet, Georges van.) Louvain, 1970.

Phil 196.32   La philosophie et sa structure. v.1,3. (Vancourt, R.) Paris, 1953. 2v.

Phil 165.220   La philosophie et ses problèmes. Lyon, 1960.

Phil 801.33   La philosophie et son passé. (Bréhier, É.) Paris, 1940.

Phil 2630.12   Philosophie et spiritualité. (Geiger, Louis Bertrand.) Paris, 1963. 2v.

Phil 4004.1   La philosophie expérimentale en Italie. (Espinas, Alfred.) Paris, 1880.

Phil 3246.95.9   Die Philosophie Fichte's. (Loewe, Johann H.) Stuttgart, 1862.

Phil 4520.4.31   Philosophie för olarde. (Bastholm, Christopher.) Lund, 1795.

Phil 1535.1   Philosophie fondamentale. (Balmès, Jaime.) Paris, 1852. 3v.

Phil 75.26   La philosophie française contemporaine. (Alcan, Felix.) Paris, 1926.

Phil 2409.1.5   La philosophie française contemporaine. (Janet, P.) Paris, 1879.

Phil 1817.3.9   La philosophie française en Amérique. (Riley, I.W.) Paris, 1919.

Phil 2418.4   La philosophie française contemporaine et sa genèse de 1789 à nos jours. (Sève, L.) Paris, 1962.

Phil 3120.8.98   Die Philosophie Franz Brentanos. (Kastil, A.) München, 1951.

Phil 3200.10   Die Philosophie Franz Erhardts. (Goldmund, M.) Leipzig, 1937.

Phil 3890.1.85   Die Philosophie Friedrich Adolf Trendelenburgs. (Petersen, Peter.) Hamburg, 1913.

Phil 3640.105.5   Die Philosophie Friedrich Nietzsches. (Lichtenberger, H.) Dresden, 1899.

Phil 810.8   La philosophie gardienne de la cité de Plotin à Bergson. (Krakowski, Edouard.) Paris, 1946.

Phil 2115.97   La philosophie générale de John Locke. (Ollion, H.) Paris, 1909.

Phil 98.1   Philosophie-Geschichtliches Lexikon. (Noack, L.) Leipzig, 1879.

Phil 1127.5.3   La philosophie grecque. (Werner, Charles.) Paris, 1938.

Phil 1133.11   La philosophie grecque avant Socrate. (Leclère, Albert.) Paris, 1908.

Phil 2630.2.122   Die Philosophie Guyaus. (Bergmann, Ernst.) Leipzig, 1912.

Phil 3425.535   Die Philosophie Hegels. 1. Aufl. (Oiserman, Teodor.) Berlin, 1959.

Phil 3425.315   Die Philosophie Hegels als kontemplative Gotteslehre. (Il'in, Ivan A.) Bern, 1946.

Phil 3195.13.90   Die Philosophie Hugo Delffs als Begründung einer theistischen Idealrealismus im Sinne christlicher Weltanschauung. Inaug. Diss. (Hamm, Anton.) Bottrop, 1934.

Phil 3195.15.83   Die Philosophie Hugo Dinglers. (Gorn, Erhard.) Dusseldorf, 1960.

Phil 3195.15.80   Die Philosophie Hugo Dinglers. (Krampf, W.) München, 1955.

Phil 1722.2.5   Die Philosophie im Beginn des Zwanzigsten. (Windelband, W.) Heidelberg, 1904.

Phil 1722.2.7   Die Philosophie im Beginn des Zwanzigsten. Jahrhunderts. 2e Aufl. (Windelband, W.) Heidelberg, 1907.

Phil 1722.2.8   Die Philosophie im Beginn des zwanzigsten Jahrhunderts. (Windelband, W.) Heidelberg, 1907.

Phil 3022.3.2   Die Philosophie im deutschen Geistesleben des 19. Jahrhunderts. (Windlband, Wilhelm.) Tübingen, 1909.

Phil 3022.3   Die Philosophie im deutschen Geistesleben des 19. Jahrhunderts. 2e Aufl. (Windlband, Wilhelm.) Tübingen, 1909.

Phil 3022.3.3   Die Philosophie im deutschen Geistesleben des 19. Jahrhunderts. 3. Aufl. (Windlband, Wilhelm.) Tübingen, 1927.

Phil 1703.2.3   Die Philosophie im ersten Drittel des 19. Jahrhunderts. (Drews, Arthur.) Berlin, 1920.

Phil 1703.2   Die Philosophie im ersten Drittel des 19. Jahrhunderts. (Drews, Arthur.) Leipzig, 1912.

Phil 900.1   Die Philosophie im Fortgang. v.1-4. (Windischmann, C.J.H. von.) Bonn, 1827-34. 3v.

Phil 196.44   Philosophie im Grundriss. (Vries, Joseph de.) Würzburg, 1969.

Phil 1703.2.10   Die Philosophie im lekten Drittel des 19. Jahrhunderts. (Drews, Arthur.) Berlin, 1921.

Phil 1718.30   Philosophie im Mittelpunkt. (Silva-Tarouca, Amadeo.) Graz, 1957.

Phil 3640.63.5   Die Philosophie im tragischen Zeitalter der Griechen. (Nietzsche, Friedrich.) München, 1923.

Phil 3640.63   Die Philosophie im tragischen Zeitalter der Griechen. (Nietzsche, Friedrich.) Leipzig, 1931.

Phil 193.36   Philosophie im Umriss. (Steudel, A.) Stuttgart, 1871-1884. 6v.

Phil 807.16.5   Die Philosophie im XX Jahrhundert. (Heinemann, Fritz.) Stuttgart, 1959.

Phil 1703.2.5   Die Philosophie im zweiten Drittel des 19. Jahrhunderts. (Drews, Arthur.) Berlin, 1913.

Phil 1703.2.6   Die Philosophie im zweiten Drittel des 19. Jahrhunderts. (Drews, Arthur.) Berlin, 1922.

Phil 3245.84   Die Philosophie Immanuel Hermann Fichtes. (Herrmann, H.A.) Berlin, 1928.

Phil 3501.1.5   Die Philosophie Immanuel Kant. (Thiele, G.) Halle, 1882.

Phil 8715.4   Philosophie in Begegnung mit Religion und Wissenschaft. (Zocher, Rudolf.) München, 1955.

Phil 630.26   Die Philosophie in der Gegenwart. (Grün, Karl.) Leipzig, 1876.

Phil 2980.10   Philosophie in der Schweiz. Erlenbach, 1946.

Phil 2402.3   Philosophie in Frankreich. (Carove, F.M.) Göttingen, 1827. 2v.

Phil 2050.91   Das Philosophie in Humes Geschichte von England. (Goebel, H.) Marburg, 1897.

Phil 807.4   Die Philosophie in ihrer Geschichte. (Harms, F.) Berlin, 1878-81. 2v.

Phil 3425.22   Philosophie in wörtlichen Auszügen. (Hegel, Georg Wilhelm Friedrich.) Berlin, 1843.

Phil 1133.48   La philosophie ionienne, l'École de Mileti Thales, Anaxemandre, Anaximène, Héraclite d'Ep'hèse. (Lahaye, Robert.) Paris, 1966.

Phil 4013.10   La philosophie italienne. (Namer, Émile.) Paris, 1970.

Phil 4002.2   La philosophie italienne contemporaine. (Conti, Augusto.) Paris, 1865.

Phil 4018.7   La philosophie italienne contemporaine. (Sciacca, M.F.) Lyon, 1953.

Phil 3428.89.5   Der philosophie J.F. Herbart. (Flügel, Otto.) Leipzig, 1905.

Phil 1865.200   La philosophie juridique de Jeremy Bentham. (el Shakankiri, Mohamed Abd el-Hadi.) Paris, 1970.

Phil 3482.13   Die Philosophie Kants. (Asmus, V.F.) Berlin, 1960.

Phil 3120.30.110   Die Philosophie Martin Bubers. (Anzenbacher, Arno.) Wien, 1965.

Phil 3850.18.140   Die Philosophie Max Schelers in ihren Beziehungen zu Eduard von Hartmann. (Hartmann, Wilfried.) Düsseldorf, 1956.

Phil 1514.2   La philosophie médiévale. (Jeanneau, E.) Paris, 1963.

Phil 8893.83.16   Die Philosophie mit obskuranten und Sophisten in Kampfe. Nachtrag: Auch die Aufklärung. (Salat, Jakob.) Ulm, 1802.

Phil 1717.7   La philosophie moderne. (Rey, A.) Paris, 1908.

Phil 1718.10   La philosophie moderne. (Sortais, Gaston.) Paris, 1921-22.

Phil 1722.10   La philosophie moderne. (Werner, Charles.) Paris, 1954.

Phil 8876.12.5   Philosophie morale. (Bautain, L.E.M.) Paris, 1842. 2v.

Phil 2750.11.149   La philosophie morale. (Maritain, Jacques.) Paris, 1960.

Phil 8840.4   Philosophie morale. (Perelman, Chaim.) Bruxelles, 1967.

Phil 8897.83   Philosophie morale. (Weil, Eric.) Paris, 1961.

Phil 2250.87   La philosophie morale de Josiah Royce. (Aronson, M.J.) Paris, 1927.

Phil 2250.87.2   La philosophie morale de Josiah Royce. Thèse. (Aronson, M.J.) Paris, 1927.

Phil 8875.12   Philosophie morale et politique. (Alaux, J.E.) Paris, 1893.

Phil 8890.39   Philosophie morale et sociale. (Pascal, G. de.) Paris, 1894.

Phil 2523.85   La philosophie morale et sociale de Destutt de Tracy, 1754-1836. (Cruet, Jean.) Tours, 1909.

Phil 1020.9   La philosophie Musulmane. (Gauthier, L.) Paris, 1900.

Phil 2880.1.81   La philosophie mystique...Saint-Martin. (Franck, A.) Paris, 1866.

Phil 299.8   Philosophie naturelle. (Soury, Jules.) Paris, 1882.

Phil 3960.18   La philosophie néerlandaise au siècle d'ov. (Dibon, Paul.) Paris, 1954.

Phil 190.11   Une philosophie nouvelle. (Pezzani, A.) Paris, 1872.

Phil 2475.1.113   Une philosophie nouvelle Henri Bergson. (LeRoy, E.) Paris, 1912.

Phil 342.1   Philosophie of knowledge. (Ladd, G.T.) N.Y., 1897.

Phil 1706.1.13   La philosophie officielle et la philosophie. (Gaultier, Jules de.) Paris, 1922.

Phil 2340.10.126   La philosophie organique de Whitehead. Thèse. 1e éd. (Cesselin, Felix.) Paris, 1950.

Phil 2340.10.125   La philosophie organique de Whitehead. 1e éd. (Cesselin, Felix.) Paris, 1950.

Phil 165.45   La philosophie par les textes. (Palmeró, J.) Paris, 1955.

Phil 2805.276   Die Philosophie Pascals. (Nasmuth, E.) Heidelberg, 1949.

Phil 2475.1.192   Une philosophie pathétique. (Benda, Julien.) Paris, 1913.

Phil 2475.1.192.5   Une philosophie pathétique. (Benda, Julien.) Paris, 1914.

Phil 2496.35   Philosophie populaire. (Cousin, Victor.) Paris, 1848.

Phil 2490.41.5   La philosophie positive. (Comte, Auguste.) Paris, 1880-81. 2v.

NEDL Phil 25.2   La philosophie positive. Paris. 1-15,1867-1875

Phil 25.2   La philosophie positive. Paris. 16-29,1876-1882 7v.

Phil 1750.570   Une philosophie pour notre temps. (Benitez, Claros.) Beirut? 1961.

Phil 1750.560.25   Une philosophie pour notre temps. (Habachi, René.) Beirut? 1961.

Phil 3485.7   La philosophie pratique de Kant. (Delbos, Victor.) Paris, 1905.

Phil 184.39.5   Philosophie première. 1. ed. (Jankélévitch, V.) Paris, 1954.

Phil 176.97   Philosophie Propädeutik für Gymnasien und höhere Bildingssanstalten. (Biese, Franz.) Berlin, 1845.

Phil 3790.7.81   Die Philosophie Raoul Richters. (Hasse, Heinrich.) Leipzig, 1914.

Phil 2475.1.294   La philosophie religieuse de Bergson. (Adolphe, Lydie.) Paris, 1946.

Phil 2840.82   La philosophie religieuse de C. Renouvier. (Arnal, A.) Paris, 1907.

Phil 2750.13.90   La philosophie religieuse de Gabriel Marcel. (Bernard, M.) Le Puy, 1952.

Phil 3491.5.15   La philosophie religieuse de Kant. (Jansen, B.) Paris, 1934.

Phil 3483.96   La philosophie religieuse de Kant. Thèse. (Bruch, Jean Louis.) Paris, 1968.

Phil 8520.6   Philosophie religieuse de la théologie naturelle. (Rémusat, C.F.M.) Paris, 1864.

Phil 1050.15   Philosophie religieuse de Léi-ben-Gerson. (Weil, Isidore.) Paris, 1868.

Phil 3805.98   La philosophie religieuse de Schleiermacher. (Cramaussel, E.) Genève, 1909.

Phil 1802.1   La philosophie religieuse en Angleterre. (Carrau, L.) Paris, 1888.

Phil 8550.342.5   La philosophie religieuse en Grand-Bretagne de 1850 à nos jours. (Nédoncelle, Maurice.) Paris, 1934.

Phil 8597.8.2   Philosophie religieuse terre et ciel. (Reynaud, J.E.) Paris, 1858.

Phil 8597.8   Philosophie religiuse terre et ciel. (Reynaud, J.E.) Paris, 1854.

Phil 4710.5   La philosophie russe contemporaine. (Lourié, Osip.) Paris, 1902.

Phil 4710.5.2A   La philosophie russe contemporaine. 2. ed. (Lourié, Osip.) Paris, 1905.

Phil 3625.5.87   Die Philosophie Salomon Maimons. (Kuntze, Friedrich.) Heidelberg, 1912.

Phil 8877.58.5   Philosophie scientifique et philosophie morale. 3. ed. (Challaye, F.) Paris, 1927.

Phil 1515.2   La philosophie scolastique. (Kleutgen, R.P.) Paris, 1868-70. 4v.

Phil 1750.103   La philosophie scolastique au XXe siècle. Critique
néo-scotiste du Thomisme. (Compagnion, Jean.)
Paris, 1916.

Phil 3007.1.5   Die Philosophie seit Kant. (Harms, F.) Berlin, 1876.

Phil 3007.1.7   Die Philosophie seit Kant. (Harms, F.) Berlin, 1879.

Phil 1750.12   Philosophie sensualiste au XVIIIe siècle. (Cousin, V.)
Paris, 1866.

Phil 2262.82   Die Philosophie Shaftesbury's. (Gizycki, G. von.)
Leipzig, 1876.

Phil 2840.84   La philosophie sociale de Renouvier. (Picard, Roger.)
Paris, 1908.

Phil 2490.98.7   Philosophie sociale et religion d'Auguste Comte. (Caird,
Edward.) Paris, 1907.

Phil 4720.2   La philosophie soviétique et l'Occident. (Jeu, Bernard.)
Paris, 1969.

Phil 3830.11   Die Philosophie Spinozas. (Kaim, J.R.) München, 1921.

Phil 3831.1   Die Philosophie Spinoza's. (Ledinský, F.) Budweis, 1871.

Phil 3838.8   Die Philosophie Spinoza's. 2. Aufl. (Stern, Jakob.)
Stuttgart, 1894.

Phil 3838.8.5   Die Philosophie Spinoza's. 3. Aufl. (Stern, Jakob.)
Stuttgart, 1908.

Phil 2855.6.25   Philosophie spiritualiste. (Reymond, A.) Lausanne, 1942.
2v.

Phil 293.3   Philosophie spiritualiste de la nature. (Martin, T.H.)
Paris, 1849. 2v.

Phil 4805.10   La philosophie tchécoslovaque contemporaine. (Iakovenko,
Boris V.) Prague, 1935.

Phil 176.7   La philosophie terrestre. (Barsalou-Fromenty, Gustave.)
Geneva, 1876.

Phil 2855.2.97   Le philosophe Théodule Ribot. (Dugas, L.) Paris, 1924.

Phil 192.108   La philosophie tragique. (Rosset, Clément.) Paris, 1960.

Phil 3500.7   Philosophie transcendantale...Kant. (Schön, L.F.)
Paris, 1831.

Phil 3625.5.93   La philosophie transcendantale de Salomon Maimon.
(Gueroult, M.) Paris, 1929.

Phil 3625.5.94   La philosophie transcendantale de Salomon Maimon. Thèse.
(Gueroult, M.) Paris, 1929.

Phil 8582.7   Philosophie und Christenthum. (Chalybäus, H.M.)
Kiel, 1853.

Phil 3415.100   Philosophie und Christentum. (Schüz, A.) Stuttgart, 1884.

Phil 8590.19   Die philosophie und das Christentum. (Knittermeyer,
Heinrich.) Jena, 1927.

Phil 1109.1   Philosophie und der Lebensauffassung der Griechtens.
(Eleutheropulos, A.) Berlin, 1900-01. 2v.

Phil 1109.1.5   Die Philosophie und der sozialen Zustande (materielle und
ideele Entwicklung) des Greichentums. 3e Aufl.
(Eleutheropulos, A.) Zürich, 1915.

Phil 165.185   Philosophie und deristliche Existenz. (Huber, Gerhard.)
Basel, 1960.

Phil 70.26.7   Die Philosophie und die Frage nach dem Fortschritt.
(Deutscher Kongress für Philosophie, 7th, Münster, 1962.)
München. 1964

Phil 1704.2.5   Die Philosophie und die Lebensauffassung der
germanisch-romanischen Völker. (Eleutheropulos, A.)
Berlin, 1901.

Phil 165.405   Die Philosophie und die Wissenschaften. Simon Moser zum 65.
Geburtstag. Meisenheim am Glan, 1967.

Phil 182.50   Philosophie und Einzelwissenschaften. (Herbertz, Richard.)
Bern, 1913.

Phil 187.152.5   Philosophie und Gegenwart. (Moser, Simon.) Meisenheim am
Glan, 1960.

Phil 25.29   Philosophie und Geschichte. Tübingen. 1-67,1922-1940
70v.

Phil 310.190   Philosophie und Gesellschaft. (Pfoh, Werner.)
Berlin, 1958.

Phil 3120.55.80   Philosophie und Gesellschaft im Denken Ernst Blochs.
(Buetow, H.G.) Berlin, 1963.

Phil 25.39   Philosophie und Leben. Leipzig. 1-9,1925-1933

Phil 3492.37   Philosophie und Moral in der Kantischen Kritik. (Krüger,
Gerhard.) Tübingen, 1931.

Phil 3850.1.80   -Philosophie und Naturwiss...D.F. Strauss. (Reuschle, C.G.)
Bonn, 1874.

Phil 510.134   Philosophie und Naturwissenschaft. (Dieterich, K.)
Tübingen, 1875.

Phil 288.5   Philosophie und Naturwissenschaft. (Hartung, G.)
n.p., n.d.

Phil 193.160.5   Philosophie und Naturwissenschaft. (Szilasi, Wilhelm.)
Bern, 1961.

Phil 3475.3.66   Philosophie und Offenbarungsglaube. (Jaspers, Karl.)
Hamburg, 1963.

Phil 193.152   Philosophie und Pädagogik. (Spanzini, Carlo.) Bern, 1936.

Phil 3450.23   Philosophie und Pädagogik Paul Häberlins in ehren
Wandlungen. Diss. (Kamm, P.) Zürich, 1938.

Phil 3665.6.30   Philosophie und Politik. (Noll, Baldwin.) Bonn, 1953.

Phil 3915.38   Philosophie und Psychologie. (Wundt, Wilhelm.)
Leipzig, 1902.

Phil 197.80   Philosophie und Reflexion. (Wagner, Hans.) München, 1959.

Htn   Phil 3800.220*   Philosophie und Religion. (Schelling, F.W.J. von.)
Tübingen, 1804.

Phil 960.164.5   Philosophie und Religion Indiens. (Zimmer, H.R.)
Zürich, 1961.

Phil 1050.2   Philosophie und Schriftsteller der Juden. (Munk, S.)
Leipzig, 1852.

Phil 4595.3.31   Philosophie und Spezialforschung. (Karitz, Anders.)
Lund, 1932.

Phil 1135.160   Philosophie und sprachlicher Ausdruck. (Fritz, K. von.)
N.Y., 1938.

Phil 8597.26   Philosophie und Theologie. (Rabus, Leonhard.)
Erlangen, 1876.

Phil 3805.186   Philosophie und Theologie bei Schleiermacher. (Flückiger,
Felix.) Basel, 1947?

Phil 1526.1   Philosophie und Theologie im Mittelalter. (Verweyen,
Johannes M.) Berlin, 1911.

Phil 400.79   Philosophie und Theologie im Spätidealismus. (Leese,
Kurt.) Berlin, 1929.

Phil 705.72   Philosophie und Transzendenz. (Struve, Wolfgang.)
Freiburg, 1969.

Phil 3475.3.42   Philosophie und Welt. (Jaspers, Karl.) München, 1958.

Phil 186.37   Philosophie und Wirklichkeit. (Lipps, Theodor.)
Heidelberg, 1908.

Phil 3475.3.58   Philosophie und Wissenschaft. (Jaspers, Karl.)
Zürich, 1949.

Phil 3018.12   Die Philosophie unserer Zeit. (Schaller, J.)
Leipzig, 1837.

Phil 672.260   Een philosophie van de tijd. (Tollenaere, M. de.)
Leuven, 1952.

Phil 2496.86   Die Philosophie Victor Cousins. (Fuchs, C.E.)
Berlin, 1847.

Phil 400.99   Die Philosophie vom unendlichen Menschen. (Kränzlin,
Gerhard.) Leipzig, 1936.

Phil 331.2.9   Philosophie von Avenarius' Biomechanische. (Raab, F.)
Leipzig, 1912.

Phil 1707.5   Die Philosophie von der Renaissance bis Kant. (Hönigswald,
R.) Berlin, 1923.

Phil 4668.121.80   Die Philosophie von G.I. Hartman. (Harva, Uno.)
Turku, 1935.

Phil 2270.138   Die Philosophie von Herbert Spencer. (Weber, Reinhard H.)
Darmstadt, 1892.

Phil 331.2.25   Die Philosophie von Richard Avenarius. (Suter, Jules.)
Zurich, 1910.

Phil 2070.84.5   Die Philosophie von William James. (Flournoy, T.)
Tübingen, 1930.

Phil 1750.732   Die Philosophie Westeuropus. (Noack, Hermann.)
Basel, 1962.

Phil 3915.153   Die Philosophie Wilhelm Wundts. (Nef, Willi.)
Leipzig, 1923.

Htn   Phil 2725.5.30*   Philosophie zoologique. (Lamarck, J.B.) Paris, 1809.
2v.

Phil 804.10   Philosophiegeschichte und geschichtlicher Septizismus.
(Ehrhardt, Walter E.) Bern, 1967.

Phil 3450.19.425   Philosophiegeschichtliche Voraussetzungen der
Heideggerschen Ontologie. (Huch, Kurt Jürgen.)
Frankfurt, 1967.

Phil 805.7   Die philosophiegeschichtliche Wahrheit. Inaug. Diss.
(Freudenberg, G.) Berlin, 1921.

Phil 3007.6   Philosophien i Tydskland efter Hegel. (Høffding, H.)
Kjøbenhavn, 1872.

Phil 801.18.3   Philosophiens historie i Grundrids. (Brøchner, Hans.)
Kjøbenhavn, 1873-74.

Phil 8595.45   Philosophies chrétiennes. Paris, 1955.

Phil 294.2   Philosophies de la nature. (Nourrisson, J.F.)
Paris, 1887.

Phil 1750.530   Les philosophies de l'existence. (Sérouya, Henri.)
Paris, 1957.

Phil 1750.189   Les philosophies de l'existence. (Wahl, Jean André.)
Paris, 1954.

Phil 960.284   Les philosophies de l'Inde. (Filliozat, Jean.)
Paris, 1970.

Phil 960.135   Les philosophies indiennes, les systèmes. v.1-2.
(Grousset, René.) Paris, 1931.

Phil 8965.9   Les philosophies morales du temps présent. (Porret, James
A.) Genève, 1897.

Phil 188.11.10   Les philosophies négatives. (Naville, Ernest.)
Paris, 1900.

Phil 8400.3A   Philosophies of beauty, from Socrates to R. Bridges.
(Carritt, E.F.) N.Y., 1931.

Phil 848.10   Philosophies of essence; an examination of the category of
essence. (DeGrood, David H.) Groningen, 1970.

Phil 1750.189.5   Philosophies of existence: an introduction to the basic
thought of Kierkegaard. (Wahl, Jean André.) London, 1969.

Phil 960.164   Philosophies of India. (Zimmer, H.R.) N.Y., 1951.

Phil 5520.654   Philosophies of language in eighteenth-century France.
(Juliard, Pierre.) The Hague, 1970.

Phil 8598.140   Philosophies of religion. (Sahakian, William S.)
Cambridge, 1965.

Phil 510.126   Les philosophies pluralistes. (Wahl, Jean.) Paris, 1920.

Phil 510.126.3   Les philosophies pluralistes. Thèse. (Wahl, Jean.)
Paris, 1920.

Phil 185.36   Philosophiká. (Kaïres, Theophilos.) Athens, 1910.

Phil 4845.227.40   Philosophika problemata. (Papanoutsos, Euangelos.)
Athena, 1964.

Phil 25.129   Philosophike-Schole Episticoniki epetires.
(Thessalonike-Panepistémion.) 1,1927+ 10v.

Phil 182.43.15   Philosophin perennis. (Häberlin, Paul.) Berlin, 1952.

Phil 2515.9.30   Philosophis des moeurs contemporaines. (Corte, Marcel de.)
Bruxelles, 1945.

Phil 3030.8   Philosophisch-politische Profile. 7. Aufl. (Habermas,
Jürgen.) Frankfurt, 1971.

Phil 665.58.5   Philosophische Abhandlung von der immateriellen Natur der
Seele. (Knutzen, Martin.) Königsberg, 1744.

Phil 7067.47   Philosophische Abhandlung von Gespenstern. (Wegner, George
W.) Berlin, 1747.

Phil 178.34   Philosophische Abhandlungen. (Dreher, Eugen.)
Berlin, 1903.

Phil 3450.7.80   Philosophische Abhandlungen. (Heinze, Max.) Berlin, 1906.

Phil 3665.7.30   Philosophische Abhandlungen. (Nicolai, Friedrich.)
Bruxelles, 1968. 2v.

Phil 25.54   Philosophische Abhandlungen. Frankfurt. 1,1935+ 29v.

Phil 3850.9.90   Philosophische Abhandlungen Christoph Sigwart zu seine 70.
Geburtstage gewidmet. Tübingen, 1900.

Phil 3450.8.80   Philosophische Abhandlungen dem Andenken Rudolf Haymns.
Halle, 1902.

Phil 3160.3.80   Philosophische Abhandlungen H. Cohen zum 70sten Geburtstag
dargebracht. Berlin, 1912.

Phil 585.421   Philosophische Anthrologie. (Groethuysen, Bernhard.)
München, 1931.

Phil 585.75   Philosophische Anthropologie. (Bruning, Walther.)
Stuttgart, 1960.

Phil 585.30   Philosophische Anthropologie. (Ehrlich, Walter.)
Tübingen, 1957.

Phil 1750.110   Philosophische Anthropologie. (Hengslenberg, Hans Eduard.)
Stuttgart, 1957.

Phil 585.160   Philosophische Anthropologie. (Rothacker, Erich.)
Bonn, 1964.

Phil 3745.1.31   Philosophische Aphorismen. (Platner, E.) Leipzig, 1776.

Phil 3745.1.30A   Philosophische Aphorismen. (Platner, E.)
Leipzig, 1793-1800. 2v.

Phil 3808.20.10   Philosophische Aphorism. (Schopenhauer, Arthur.)
Leipzig, 1924.

Phil 25.25   Philosophische Arbeiten. Gieszen. 1-21+ 18v.

Phil 182.58   Philosophische Aufsätze. (Hebler, Carl.) Leipzig, 1869.

Phil 3475.3.225   Philosophische Aufsätze. (Jaspers, Karl.)
Frankfurt, 1951.

Phil 190.33   Philosophische Aufsätze. (Philosophische Gesellschaft zu
Berlin.) Berlin, 1904.

Phil 200.2   Philosophische Aufsätze. (Zeller, E.) Leipzig, 1887.

Phil 187.24   Philosophische Aufsäze. (Müller, J.G.) Breslau, 1795.

Phil 3925.16.20   Philosophische Bemerkungen; aus dem Nachlass.
(Wittgenstein, Ludwig.) Oxford, 1964.

Phil 299.18   Philosophische Betrachtungen der Natur. (Snell, Karl.)
Dresden, 1839.

Phil 3625.8.50   Philosophische Betrachtungen über die christlichen Religion.
v.1-7. (Meier, Georg Friedrich.) Halle, 1761-66. 2v.

Phil 5090.12.2   Der philosophische Beweis. 2. Aufl. (Klotz, Hans.)
Berlin, 1969.

Phil 180.50 Philosophische Bibliotek. v.1-4. (Feder, J.G.H.) Göttingen, 1788-1791. 2v.

Phil 3120.16.30 Philosophische Briefe an meine Schwester. (Brastberger, G.U.) Halle, 1779.

Phil 3235.75 Philosophische Charakterentwicklung. v.1-2. (Feuerbach, Ludwig.) Leipzig, 1874.

Phil 365.29 Philosophische Consequenzen der Lamarck-Darwin. (Gizycki, G. von.) Leipzig, 1876.

Phil 176.19.5 Philosophische Darstellung der Harmonien des Weltalls. (Berger, J.E.) Altona, 1808.

Phil 193.30.80 Der philosophische Dialog als literarisches Kunstwerk. (Wildbalz, A.) Bern, 1952.

Phil 3925.3.35 Philosophische Dogmatik oder Philosophie des Christenthums. (Weisse, Christian Hermann.) Leipzig, 1855-62. 3v.

Phil 193.125.5 Philosophische Einübung in die Theologie. (Söhngen, G.) Freiburg, 1955.

Phil 3665.3.80 Der philosophische Entwicklungsgang des Johannes Neeb 1767-1843. (Jentgens, Gerhard.) Düsseldorf, 1922.

Phil 3925.8.81 Der philosophische Entwicklungsgang von Joseph Weber. (Trefzger, Hermann.) Freiburg, 1933.

Phil 3890.9.88 Philosophische Enzyklopädie und Methodologie der Wissenschaften. (Troxler, I.P.V.) Beromünster, 1956.

Phil 3790.9.30 Die philosophische Erbsunde; Was in ich? (Rehmke, J.) Marburg, 1924.

Phil 193.31.17 Philosophische Essays. (Spir, A. von.) Stuttgart, 18- .

Phil 8892.76 Die philosophische Ethik. (Reiner, Hans.) Heidelberg, 1964.

Phil 25.43 Philosophische forschungsberichte. Berlin. 1-36,1930-1955 18v.

Phil 178.22.30 Philosophische Forschungswege. (Driesch, H.) Leipzig, 1930.

Phil 3415.43 Philosophische Fragen. (Hartmann, Eduard von.) Leipzig, 1885.

Phil 179.18 Philosophische Fragen der Gegenwart. (Ettlinger, Max.) Kempten, 1911.

Phil 3415.82 Philosophische Fragmente...Hartmann's Philosophie. (Kluge, A.) Breslau, 1875-77. 2v.

Phil 178.22.35 Philosophische Gegenwartsfragen. (Driesch, H.) Leipzig, 1933.

Phil 8584.13 Der philosophische Gehalt der religiösen Dogmatik. (Emge, Carl A.) München, 1929.

Phil 817.11 Das philosophische Genie und seine Rasseabstammung. (Rauschenberger, W.) Frankfurt, 1922.

Phil 3850.37 Das philosophische Gesamtwerk im Auszug. (Spann, Othmar.) Wien, 1950.

Phil 190.33 Philosophische Gesellschaft zu Berlin. Philosophische Aufsätze. Berlin, 1904.

Phil 11.1 Philosophische Gesellschaft zu Berlin. Verhandlungen. v.1-21. Leipzig, 1875-82. 2v.

Phil 3450.33.10 Philosophische Gespräche. (Hartmann, N.) Göttingen, 1954.
Phil 3790.13 Philosophische Gespräche. (Raab, F.) Berlin, 1937.
Phil 193.30 Philosophische Gespräche. (Solger, K.W.F.) Berlin, 1817.
Phil 184.19.25 Der philosophische Glaube. (Jaspers, K.) München, 1948.
Phil 3475.3.78 Der philosophische Glaube Angesichts der Offenbarung. (Jaspers, Karl.) München, 1962.

Phil 8668.6 Philosophische Gotteslehre. (Nink, Gaspar.) München, 1948.

Phil 8520.19 Das philosophische Gottesproblem in seinen wichtigsten Auffassungen. (Geyser, Joseph.) Bonn, 1899.

Phil 176.69.15 Philosophische Grundfragen. (Bloch, Ernst.) Frankfurt, 1961.

Phil 5062.16 Die philosophische Grundlagen der Wissenschaften. (Weinstein, B.) Leipzig, 1906.

Phil 200.13 Die philosophische Grundlehre. (Zocher, R.) Tübingen, 1939.

Phil 6328.20 Philosophische Grundprobleme der psychoanalytischen Psycholgie. (Szalai, Alex.) Budapest, 1935.

Phil 3925.2.95 Philosophische Grunzgänge. (Weischedel, Wilhelm.) Stuttgart, 1967.

Phil 8878.26 Philosophische Güterlehre. (Döring, A.) Berlin, 1888.
Phil 25.34 Philosophische Hefte. Berlin. 1-5,1928-1936 2v.
Phil 822.20 Die philosophische Hintertreppe. (Weishedel, Wilhelm.) München, 1966.

Phil 400.51 Der philosophische Idealismus und das Grundproblem der Erkenntnistheorie. (Jünemann, F.) Neisse, 1913. 4v.

Phil 1709.1.2 Die philosophische Krisis derGegenewart. 2e Aufl. (Joël, Karl.) Leipzig, 1919.

Phil 1709.1 Die philosophische Krisis der Gegenwart. (Joël, Karl.) Leipzig, 1914.

Phil 3791.35.2A Der philosophische Kritcismus. 2e Aufl. (Riehl, Alois.) Leipzig, 1908.

Phil 3791.35 Der philosophischeKriticismus. v.1-2. (Riehl, Alois.) Leipzig, 1876-1887.

Phil 5252.6 Philosophische-Kritische Grundsätze der Selbsterkenntniss. (Mehring, G.) Stuttgart, 1857.

Phil 3791.35.3 Der philosophische Kritizismus. (Riehl, Alois.) Leipzig, 1924-1926. 3v.

Phil 193.59.5 Philosophische Kultur. (Simmel, G.) Leipzig, 1911.
Phil 672.30 Die philosophische Lehre von Zeit und Raum. (Schneid, Mathias.) Mainz, 1886.

Phil 180.36 Philosophische Leitbegriffe. (Fetzer, K.A.) Tübingen, 1884.

Phil 25.138 Philosophische Lesehefte. Wien. 1,1957+ 8v.
Phil 75.19 Die philosophische Literatur. (Herbertz, R.) Stuttgart, 1912.

Phil 75.5 Die philosophische Literatur der Deutschen. (Gumposh, V.P.) Regensburg, 1851.

Phil 5049.20.5 Philosophische Logik. (Jaspers, Karl.) München, 1958.
Phil 3808.53 Philosophische Meschenkunde. (Schopenhauer, Arthur.) Stuttgart, 1957.

Phil 194.40 Die philosophische Methode. (Thyssen, Johannes.) Halle, 1930.

Phil 25.4 Philosophische Monatschafte. Berlin. 1-30,1868-1894 30v.

Phil 1750.118 Philosophische Motive im neuzeitlichen Humanismus. (Hönigswald, R.) Breslau, 1918.

Phil 525.54 Die philosophische Mystik des Mittelalters. (Bernhart, J.) München, 1912.

Phil 192.12.15 Philosophische Paradoxa. (Ritter, Heinrich.) Leipzig, 1867.

Phil 25.164 Philosophische Perspektiven; ein Jahrbuch. Frankfurt. 1,1969+ 2v.

Phil 3925.3.45 Das philosophische Problem der Gegenwart. (Weisse, Christian Hermann.) Leipzig, 1842.

Phil 3552.98 Die philosophische Probleme...Leibniz und Clarke. (Leroy, G.V.) Mainz, 1893.

Phil 182.36 Philosophische Probleme. (Höffding, H.) Leipzig, 1903.

Phil 181.40.5 Philosophische Profile. (Gleichen-Russwurm, A. von.) Stuttgart, 1922.

Phil 193.94 Philosophische Propadeutik. (Schulte-Tigges, A.) n.p., n.d. 3 pam.

Phil 3850.12.31 Philosophische Propädentik. (Stoy, Karl V.) Leipzig, 1869.

Phil 177.3 Philosophische Propädeutik. (Calinich, E.A.E.) Dresden, 1847.

Phil 5047.14.5 Philosophische Propädeutik. (Höfler, Alois.) Prag, 1890.
Phil 182.20 Philosophische Propädeutik. (Hoffmann, K.) Passan, 1872.
Phil 186.44 Philosophische Propädeutik. (Lambeck, G.) Leipzig, 1919.
Phil 188.12 Philosophische Propädeutik. (Natorp, Paul.) Marburg, 1903.

Phil 197.18.5 Philosophische Propädeutik. (Willmann, O.) Freiburg, 1912-1914. 3v.

Phil 200.3.5 Philosophische Propaedeutik. (Zimmerman, R.) Wien, 1867.
Phil 182.75 Philosophische Propädeutik. 2. Aufl. (Hollenberg, W.) Elberfeld, 1875.

Phil 193.96 Philosophische Propädeutik in neuster Literatur. (Schneidkunz, H.) Halle, 1917.

Phil 193.79 Philosophische Reden. (Schnyder, Otto.) Zürich, 1916.
Phil 193.69 Philosophische Reden und Vorträge. (Stumpf, K.) Leipzig, 1910.

Phil 350.8.2 Der philosophische Relativismus. 2. Aufl. (Thyssen, Johannes.) Bonn, 1947.

Phil 25.93.3 Philosophische Rundschau;...Beiträge. Tübingen. 1-5 2v.

Phil 25.93 Philosophische Rundschau, eine Vierteljahresschrift für philosophische Kritik. Tübingen. 1,1953+ 14v.

Phil 182.14.10 Philosophische Schriften. (Hemsterhuis, F.) Karlsruhe, 1912. 2v.

Phil 3625.1.30 Philosophische Schriften. (Mendelssohn, Moses.) Berlin, 1777. 2v.

Phil 3625.1.31A Philosophische Schriften. (Mendelssohn, Moses.) Carlsruhe, n.d.

Htn Phil 3800.50*A Philosophische Schriften. (Schelling, F.W.J. von.) Landshut, 1809.

Phil 3585.1.35 Philosophische Schriften. Reprografischer Nachdruck. v.1-4,6-7,9. (Lambert, Johann Heinrich.) Hildesheim, 1965- 7v.

Phil 5045.6.3 Philosophische Schriften. System der Logik und Metaphysik. 3e Aufl. (Fischer, Kuno.) Heidelberg, 1909.

Phil 182.52 Philosophische Schriften. v.1-2,4. (Hoffmann, Franz.) Erlangen, 1868-1877. 3v.

Phil 3625.1.32 Philosophische Schriften. v.1-2. (Mendelssohn, Moses.) Carlsruhe, 1780.

Phil 3625.1.26 Philosophische Schriften. Verb. Aufl. (Mendelssohn, Moses.) Berlin, 1771.

Phil 3090.20 Philosophische Schriften und Aufsätze. v.1-2. (Baader, Franz von.) Münster, 1831-33.

Phil 400.42 Der philosophische Sinn. (Schmidt, F.J.) Göttingen, 1912.
Phil 8884.20 Philosophische sittenlehre. (Jakob, L.H.) Halle, 1794.
Phil 3625.8.42 Philosophische Sittenlehre. (Meier, Georg Friedrich.) Halle, 1762. 2v.

Phil 3805.93 Philosophische Sittenlehre. (Schleiermacher, Friedrich.) Berlin, 1870.

Phil 8830.1 Die philosophische Sittenlehre. v.1-2. (Feuerlein, E.) Tübingen, 1857-59.

Phil 3625.8.43 Philosophische Sittenlehre. 2. Aufl. (Meier, Georg Friedrich.) Halle, 1762-66. 5v.

Phil 3120.10.80 Philosophische Streifzüge an deutschen Hochschulen. (Theile, Günther.) Berlin, 1904.

Phil 1718.7 Die philosophische Strömungen der Gegenwart. (Stein, Ludwig.) Stuttgart, 1908.

Phil 2401.3.12 Philosophische Strömungen der Gegenwart in Frankreich. (Benrubi, Isaac.) Leipzig, 1928.

Phil 1717.8.10 Philosophische Strömungen des zivanzigsten Jahrhunderts. (Ruggiero, G. de.) Köln, 1949.

Phil 186.51 Philosophische Studien. (Lyng, G.W.) n.p., 1877.
Phil 187.53 Philosophische Studien. (Michaltschew, Dimitri.) Leipzig, 1909.

Phil 25.84 Philosophische Studien. Berlin. 1-2,1949-1951 2v.
Phil 25.5 Philosophische Studien. Leipzig. 1-20,1881-1903 20v.
Phil 25.5.5 Philosophische Studien. Index, 1-20. Leipzig, n.d.
Phil 3791.75 Philosophische Studien aus 4 Jahrzehnten. (Riehl, Alois.) Leipzig, 1925.

Phil 3850.33 Philosophische Studien zum Begriff der Entscheidung. Inaug. Diss. (Schramm, A.) Berlin, 1940.

Phil 3415.91.5 Das philosophische System Eduard von Hartmann's. (Koeber, Raphael.) Breslau, 1884.

Phil 2218.87 Das philosophische System Joseph Priestleys. (Sigsbee, Ray A.) Heidelberg, 1912.

Phil 3665.1.30 Philosophische Systematik. (Natorp, Paul.) Hamburg, 1958.
Phil 150.1 Philosophische Terminologie. (Tönnies, F.) Leipzig, 1906.
Phil 8893.88 Philosophische Tugendlehre. (Schulze, G.E.) Göttingen, 1817.

Phil 5241.80 Philosophische und naturwissenschaftliche Grundlagen der Psychologie. (Bernhard, E.A.) Berlin, 1930.

Phil 25.31 Philosophische und psychologische Arbeiten. Langensalza. 1-15,1921-1932 15v.

Phil 178.24.5 Philosophische und theologische Vorlesungen. v.1-7. (Daub, Carl.) Berlin, 1838-44. 8v.

Htn Phil 3800.340* Philosophische Untersuchungen über das Wesen der menschlichen Freiheit. (Schelling, F.W.J. von.) Reutlingen, 1834.

Phil 8402.14.15 Philosophische Untersuchungen über den Ursprung unsrer Begriffe vom Erhaben und Schönen. (Burke, E.) Riga, 1773.

Phil 182.50.5 Das philosophische Urerlebnis. (Herbertz, Richard.) Bern, 1921.

Phil 5259.6 Philosophische Versuche über die menschliche Natur. (Tetens, J.N.) Leipzig, 1777. 2v.

Htn Phil 193.10* Philosophische Vorlesungen. (Schlegel, Friedrich von.) Bonn, 1836-37. 2v.

Phil 50.1 Philosophische Vorträge. (Kantgesellschaft.) Berlin. 1-31,1912-1928 3v.

Phil 3850.18.20A Philosophische Weltanschauung. (Scheler, Max.) Bern, 1954.

Phil 193.127 Philosophische Weltanschauung. (Scheler, Max.) Bonn, 1929.

Phil 8520.15.3 Die philosophische Weltanschauung. 2. Aufl. (Carriere, Moriz.) Leipzig, 1887. 2v.

Phil 3120.2.80 Das philosophische Werk Bernard Bolzanos. (Bergmann, H.) n.p., 1909.

Phil 1870.15 Philosophische Werke. (Berkeley, G.) Leipzig, 192-. 3v.

Phil 2630.2.10 Philosophische Werke. (Guyau, J.M.) Leipzig, 1912-1914. 6v.

Phil 2520.32   Philosophische Werke. v.1-2. (Descartes, René.) n.p., n.d.

Phil 3552.10.15   Philosophische Werke nach Rapspens Sammlung. (Leibniz, Gottfried Wilhelm.) Halle 1778-80. 2v.

Phil 25.18   Philosophische Wochenschrift und Literatur-Zeitung. v.1-7. Leipzig, 1906-07. 7v.

Phil 187.13   Philosophische Zeitfragen. (Meyer, J.B.) Bonn, 1874.

Phil 1504.2.5   Die philosophischen Abhandlungen. v.2, pt.5. (Nagy, A.) Münster, 1897.

Phil 5241.74   Die philosophischen Anfangsgründe der Psychologie. (Brockdorff, Cay L.G.C.) Heldesheim, 1905.

Phil 990.26   Die philosophischen Ansichten von Razi und Tusi. (Horten, Max.) Bonn, 1910.

Phil 336.12   Die philosophischen Grundlagen der wissenschaftlichen Erkenntnis. (Fischer, Anton.) Wien, 1947.

Phil 336.12.2   Die philosophischen Grundlagen der wissenschaftlichen Erkenntnis. 2. Aufl. (Fischer, Anton.) Wien, 1967.

Phil 3665.1.79   Die philosophischen Grundlagen von Natorps Sozialpadagogik. (Gschwind, H.) Leipzig, 1920.

Phil 720.25   Die philosophischen Grundlagen von Wahrheit, Wirklichkeit, Wert. (Stern, Alfred.) München, 1932.

Phil 510.143   Die philosophischen Hauptströmungen im Monistenbund. Inaug. Diss. (Herzberg, L.) Leipzig, 1928.

Phil 3480.17   Die philosophischen Hauptvorlesungen. (Kant, Immanuel.) München, 1924.

Phil 3160.6.30   Die philosophischen Hauptwerke. v.1-3. (Crusius, Christian August.) Hildesheim, 1964- 3v.

Phil 1504.10.4   Die philosophischen Lehren. v.10, pt.4. (Guttmann, J.) Münster, 1911.

Phil 25.86   Philosophischen Literaturanzeiger. 1,1949+ 19v.

Phil 3120.2.87   Die philosophischen Problem in Dr. Bolzano's "Erbauungsreden". Inaug. Diss. (Frank, Paul.) Pritzwalk, 1926.

Phil 3552.14   Die philosophischen Schriften. (Leibniz, Gottfried Wilhelm.) Berlin, 1875-90. 7v.

Phil 3246.71   Die philosophischen Schriften zum Atheismusstreit. (Fichte, Johann Gottlieb.) Leipzig, 1910.

Phil 1812.6A   Die philosophischen Strömungen der Gegenwart in Grossbritannien. (Metz, Rudolf.) Leipzig, 1935. 2v.

Phil 1707.6   Die philosophischen Stromungen der Gegenwart. (Hessen, Johannes.) München, 1923.

Phil 3805.84   Die philosophischen Voraussetzingen von Schleiermachers Determinismus. (Esselborn, F.W.) Ludwigshafen, 1897.

Phil 3007.3   Die philosophischen Weltanschauungen. 5. Aufl. (Heussner, Alfred.) Göttingen, 1919.

Phil 1504.9   Die philosophischen Werke des Robert Grosseteste. v.9. (Baur, L.) Münster, 1912.

Phil 25.38   Philosophischer Anzeiger. Bonn. 1-4,1925-1930 4v.

Phil 165.365   Philosophischer Eros im Wandel der Zeit. (Koktanek, Anton Mirko.) München, 1965.

Phil 185.30   Ein philosophischer Gedankengang. (Kann, A.) Wien, 19- .

Phil 75.28   Philosophischer Handkatalog. 1er Nachtrag über die Jahre 1927/28. (Meiner, Felix.) Leipzig, 1928.

Phil 3425.654   Philosophischer Idealismus. (Haag, Karl Heinz.) Frankfurt, 1967.

Phil 3910.134.1   Philosophischer Lexicon aus Christian Wolffs sämtlichen deutschen Schriften. (Meissner, Heinrich Adam.) Düsseldorf, 1970.

Phil 176.2   Philosophischer Nachlasz. (Bäggesen, Jens.) Zürich, 1858. 2v.

Phil 3475.3.190   Philosophischer und christlicher Glaube. (Horn, H.) Essen, 1961.

Phil 510.26   Philosophischer und naturwissenschaftlicher Monismus. (Stern, M.L.) Leipzig, 1885.

Phil 25.37F   Philosophischer Weltanzeiger. Berlin, n.d.

Phil 3486.18.2   Philosophisches Archiv. (Eberhard, John.) Bruxelles, 1968. 2v.

Phil 25.14   Philosophisches Jahrbuch. Fulda. 1+ 69v.

Phil 25.3   Philosophisches Journal. Neu-Strelite. 1-10,1795-1800 10v.

Phil 178.17   Philosophisches Lesebuch. (Dessoir, Max.) Stuttgart, 1903.

Phil 178.17.3   Philosophisches Lesebuch. (Dessoir, Max.) Stuttgart, 1910.

Phil 804.7   Philosophisches Lesebuch. (Ettlinger, M.) München, 1925.

Phil 165.440   Philosophisches Lesebuch. (Gadamer, Hans Georg.) Frankfurt a.M., 1965- 3v.

Phil 165.14   Philosophisches lesebuch. (Glockner, H.) Stuttgart, 1949-50. 2v.

Phil 165.5   Philosophisches Lesebuch zum Gebrauch an höheren Schulen und zum Selbststudium. (Schmid, Bastian.) Leipzig, 1906.

Phil 90.3   Philosophisches Real-Lexikon. (Furtmair, M.) Augsburg, 1853.

Phil 4210.40   Philosophisches System. (Rosmini-Serbati, Antonio.) Regensburg, 1879.

Phil 3310.20   Philosophisches Tagebuch. (Geyer, H.F.) Freiburg, 1969. 3v.

Phil 1870.73.13   Philosophisches Tagebuch (commonplace book). (Berkeley, G.) Leipzig, 1926.

Phil 125.4   Philosophisches Wörterbuch. (Reiner, Julius.) Leipzig, 1912.

Phil 103.3   Philosophisches Wörterbuch. (Schmidt, Heinrich.) Leipzig, 1912.

Phil 103.3.30   Philosophisches Wörterbuch. (Schmidt, Heinrich.) N.Y., 1945.

Phil 103.3.25   Philosophisches Wörterbuch. (Schmidt, Heinrich.) Stuttgart, 1943.

Phil 103.7   Philosophisches Wörterbuch. (Stockhammer, Morris.) Köln, 1967.

Phil 104.2.2   Philosophisches Wörterbuch. 2. Aufl. (Thornmeyer, P.) Leipzig, 1920.

Phil 104.2.3   Philosophisches Wörterbuch. 3e Aufl. (Thornmeyer, P.) Leipzig, 1922.

Phil 85.5   Philosophisches Wörterbuch. 4. Aufl. (Apel, Max.) Berlin, 1953.

Phil 100.10.4   Philosophisches Wörterbuch. 4. Aufl. Leipzig, 1966.

Phil 86.6   Philosophisches Wörterbuch. 5. Aufl. (Brugger, Walter.) Freiburg 1953.

Phil 100.10.7   Philosophisches Wörterbuch. 7.-Aufl. Berlin, 1970. 2v.

Phil 103.3.20   Philosophisches Wörterbuch. 9. Aufl. (Schmidt, Heinrich.) Leipzig, 1934.

Phil 103.3.30.5   Philosophisches Wörterbuch. 11. Aufl. (Schmidt, Heinrich.) Stuttgart, 1951.

Phil 103.3.30.10   Philosophisches Wörterbuch. 13. Aufl. (Schmidt, Heinrich.) Stuttgart, 1955.

Phil 103.3.31   Philosophisches Wörterbuch. 14. Aufl. (Schmidt, Heinrich.) Stuttgart, 1957.

Phil 97.1   Philosophisches Wórterbuch. (Maimon, S.) Berlin, 1791.

Phil 193.117   Philosophisk elementar-curs. 1. Psycologi; 2. Logik; 3. Rättslära. (Snellman, J.W.) Stockholm, 1837-1840. 3 pam.

Phil 4605.1.36   Philosophisk propaedentik. 5. opl. (Monrad, M.J.) Christiania, 1896.

Phil 25.62   Philosophiskt archiv og repertorium. Kjöbenhavn, n.d.

Phil 176.214   Philosophy; an introduction. (Bochénski, I.M.) Dordrecht, 1963.

Phil 193.47.2   Philosophy; its scope and relations. (Sidgwick, Henry.) N.Y., 1968.

Phil 193.47   Philosophy, its scope and relations. Photoreproduction. (Sidgwick, H.) London, 1902.

Phil 338.16   Philosophy, or The science of truth. (Haig, J.) London, 1861.

Phil 1830.17.5   Philosophy, politics, and society, third series. (Laslett, Peter.) N.Y., 1967.

Phil 1955.6.50   Philosophy, psychology and social practice. (Dewey, John.) N.Y., 1963.

Phil 900.2   Philosophy, qabbala and vedánta. (Fluegel, M.) Baltimore, 1902.

Phil 165.373   Philosophy, religion, and the coming world civilization. (Rouner, Leroy S.) The Hague, 1966.

Phil 192.116   Philosophy, science, and other essays. 1st. ed. (Rahman, F.) Lahore, 1961.

Phil 343.33   Philosophy, science, and sense perception. (Mandelbaum, M.H.) Baltimore, 1964.

Phil 1630.23.5   Philosophy, technology, and the arts in the early modern era. (Rossi, Paolo.) N.Y., 1970.

Phil 978.112   Philosophy, theosophy, parapsychology, some essays. (Poortman, Johannes Jocobus.) Leyaen, 1965[1964]

Phil 140.31F   Pamphlet box. Philosophy, 1847-1926.

Phil 140.30   Pamphlet vol. Philosophy, 1847-1926. 24 pam.

Htn   Phil 140.19*   Pamphlet vol. Philosophy, 1877-1916. 9 pam.

Phil 140.26   Pamphlet vol. Philosophy, 1880-1909. 6 pam.

Phil 140.20   Pamphlet vol. Philosophy, 1880-1909. 6 pam.

Phil 140.15   Pamphlet vol. Philosophy. 9 pam.

Phil 140.60   Pamphlet vol. Philosophy. 4 pam.

Phil 140.51   Pamphlet vol. Philosophy. 5 pam.

Phil 140.32.5   Pamphlet vol. Philosophy. 7 pam.

Phil 140.52   Pamphlet vol. Philosophy. 7 pam.

Phil 140.68   Pamphlet vol. Philosophy. 5 pam.

Phil 143.102F   Pamphlet vol. Philosophy. 12 pam.

Phil 143.101F   Pamphlet vol. Philosophy. 48 pam.

Phil 176.135   Philosophy. (Barrett, Clifford.) N.Y., 1935.

Phil 176.48   Philosophy. (Butler, N.M.) N.Y., 1908.

Phil 176.48.3   Philosophy. (Butler, N.M.) N.Y., 1938.

Phil 42.3   Philosophy. (California. University. Publications.) Berkeley. 1-30,1904-1957 15v.

Phil 2035.20   Philosophy. (Hamilton, William.) N.Y., 1853.

Phil 2035.65   Philosophy. (Hamilton, William.) N.Y., 1855.

Phil 184.26.25   Philosophy. (Joad, C.E.M.) London, 1944.

Phil 1830.17   Philosophy. (Laslett, Peter.) Oxford, 1956. 2v.

Phil 811.2   Philosophy. (Lefèvre, A.) London, 1879.

Phil 187.91   Philosophy. (Meiklejohn, A.) Chicago, 1926.

Phil 190.18.9   Philosophy. (Perry, R.B.) n.p., 1915.

Phil 2255.1.30A   Philosophy. (Russell, Bertrand Russell.) N.Y., 1927.

Phil 165.456   Philosophy. (Wolff, Robert Paul.) Englewood Cliffs, 1971.

Phil 1815.9   Philosophy. Englewood Cliffs, N.J., 1964.

Phil 143.1   Pamphlet vol. Philosophy. A - Alr. 34 pam.

Phil 143.91   Pamphlet vol. Philosophy. A - D. 37 pam.

Phil 143.2   Pamphlet vol. Philosophy. Als - Arp. 38 pam.

Phil 6400.01   Pamphlet box. Philosophy. Aphasia.

Phil 143.3   Pamphlet vol. Philosophy. Arr - Bai. 19 pam.

Phil 143.4   Pamphlet vol. Philosophy. Bak - Bat. 24 pam.

Phil 143.5   Pamphlet vol. Philosophy. Bau - Ben. 23 pam.

Phil 143.6   Pamphlet vol. Philosophy. Ben - Bla. 30 pam.

Phil 143.7   Pamphlet vol. Philosophy. Bla - Bol. 22 pam.

Phil 143.8   Pamphlet vol. Philosophy. Bol - Bra. 30 pam.

Phil 143.9   Pamphlet vol. Philosophy. Bra - Bro. 20 pam.

Phil 143.10   Pamphlet vol. Philosophy. Bru - By. 33 pam.

Phil 143.11   Pamphlet vol. Philosophy. C - Car. 23 pam.

Phil 143.12   Pamphlet vol. Philosophy. Cas - Ch. 25 pam.

Phil 143.13   Pamphlet vol. Philosophy. Cl - Cla. 18 pam.

Phil 1915.75   Pamphlet vol. Philosophy. Clarke, Samuel. 5 pam.

Phil 1915.76   Pamphlet vol. Philosophy. Clarke, Samuel. 4 pam.

Phil 143.14   Pamphlet vol. Philosophy. Cle - Cou. 32 pam.

Phil 140   Pamphlet box. Philosophy. Collected biography and tracts.

Phil 5080.01   Pamphlet box. Philosophy. Concepts.

Phil 143.15   Pamphlet vol. Philosophy. Cow - Day. 25 pam.

Phil 143.16   Pamphlet vol. Philosophy. Dea - Dex. 26 pam.

Phil 143.17   Pamphlet vol. Philosophy. Die - Dre. 30 pam.

Phil 143.18   Pamphlet vol. Philosophy. Dru - Em. 29 pam.

Phil 143.92   Pamphlet vol. Philosophy. E - G. 21 pam.

Phil 6520.01   Pamphlet box. Philosophy. Ecstasy and stigmatism.

Phil 143.19   Pamphlet vol. Philosophy. En - Fal. 29 pam.

Phil 1798   Pamphlet box. Philosophy. English.

Phil 2045.79   Pamphlet box. Philosophy. English. Hobbes. German dissertations.

Phil 2050.79.2   Pamphlet box. Philosophy. English. Hume, David.

Phil 2050.79   Pamphlet vol. Philosophy. English. Hume, David. German dissertations. 19 pam.

Phil 2070.79.6   Pamphlet box. Philosophy. English. James, William.

Phil 2070.79.5   Pamphlet vol. Philosophy. English. James, William. 4 pam.

Phil 2070.03   Pamphlet box. Philosophy. English. James, William.

Phil 2070.79   Pamphlet vol. Philosophy. English. James, William. German dissertations. 6 pam.

Phil 2075.1.79   Pamphlet box. Philosophy. English. Joachim, H.H.

Phil 2120.7.79   Pamphlet box. Philosophy. English. Laird, John. Works by and about.

Phil 2120.8.35   Pamphlet vol. Philosophy. English. Lamont, Corliss. 7 pam.

Phil 2115.79.5   Pamphlet box. Philosophy. English. Locke, J.

Phil 2115.79   Pamphlet vol. Philosophy. English. Locke, J. German dissertations.

Phil 2125.45.2   Pamphlet box. Philosophy. English. McCosh, James.

Phil 2138.79.10   Pamphlet box. Philosophy. English. Mill, John S.

Phil 2138.79.11F   Pamphlet box. Philosophy. English. Mill, John S.

Phil 2150.6.07F   Pamphlet vol. Philosophy. English. Münsterberg, H. 18 pam.

Phil 2150.6.06   Pamphlet vol. Philosophy. English. Münsterberg, H. 41 pam.

Phil 2150.6.08   Pamphlet vol. Philosophy. English. Münsterberg, H. 3 vols. 85 pam.

Phil 2150.10.79   Pamphlet box. Philosophy. English. Murray, Henry A.

Phil 2225.5.07F   Pamphlet vol. Philosophy. English. Peirce, C.S. 3 pam.

Call No.	Description
Phil 2225.5.06	Pamphlet vol. Philosophy. English. Peirce, C.S. 9 pam.
Phil 2225.2.79	Pamphlet box. Philosophy. English. Perry, R.B.
Phil 2218.01	Pamphlet box. Philosophy. English. Priestley, Joseph.
Phil 2255.2.80	Pamphlet box. Philosophy. English. Robertson, George Croom.
Phil 2250.79	Pamphlet box. Philosophy. English. Royce, Josiah. Biography.
Phil 2255.1.80	Pamphlet box. Philosophy. English. Russell, Bertrand Russell.
Phil 2280.10.79	Pamphlet box. Philosophy. English. Sanford, Robert Nevitt.
Phil 2280.7.79	Pamphlet box. Philosophy. English. Schiller, F.C.S.
Phil 2280.9.79	Pamphlet box. Philosophy. English. Schroeder, Theodore.
Phil 2262.78	Pamphlet box. Philosophy. English. Shaftesbury, A.A.C.
Phil 2280.11.79	Pamphlet box. Philosophy. English. Shevach, B.J., and Kendig, Isabel.
Phil 2280.1.79	Pamphlet box. Philosophy. English. Sidgwick, Henry.
Phil 2268.2.79	Pamphlet box. Philosophy. English. Smith, Carl Ellsworth.
Phil 2270	Pamphlet box. Philosophy. English. Spencer, Herbert.
Phil 2270.78	Pamphlet box. Philosophy. English. Spencer, Herbert.
Phil 2280.12.79	Pamphlet box. Philosophy. English. Stevens, Stanley Smith.
Phil 2280.13.79	Pamphlet box. Philosophy. English. Swenson, David F.
Phil 2305.3.79	Pamphlet box. Philosophy. English. Taylor, Alfred E., 1869-1945.
Phil 2340.9.79	Pamphlet box. Philosophy. English. Whewell, William.
Phil 2340.10.80	Pamphlet box. Philosophy. English. Whitehead, Alfred North.
Phil 2340.1.79	Pamphlet box. Philosophy. English. Wiener, Norbert.
Phil 2340.7.01	Pamphlet box. Philosophy. English. Wilson, William Dexter.
Phil 1798.1	Pamphlet box. Philosophy. English
Phil 6536.01	Pamphlet box. Philosophy. Epilepsy.
Phil 143.20	Pamphlet vol. Philosophy. Fal - Fis. 31 pam.
Phil 6750.01	Pamphlet box. Philosophy. Feebleminded.
Phil 143.21	Pamphlet vol. Philosophy. Fis - Fol. 32 pam.
Phil 143.22	Pamphlet vol. Philosophy. For - Fri. 30 pam.
Phil 2398	Pamphlet box. Philosophy. French.
Phil 2520.79.5	Pamphlet box. Philosophy. French and Belgian. Descartes.
Phil 2520.79	Pamphlet vol. Philosophy. French and Belgian. Descartes. German dissertations, 1881-1912. 19 pam.
Phil 2655.1.79	Pamphlet box. Philosophy. French and Belgian. Hemsterhuis, François.
Phil 2672.79	Pamphlet box. Philosophy. French and Belgian. Jouffroy, Théodore Simon.
Phil 2800.1.80	Pamphlet box. Philosophy. French and Belgian. Ollé-Laprune.
Phil 2725.8.80	Pamphlet box. Philosophy. French and Beligian. Laromiguière, Pierre.
Phil 143.23	Pamphlet vol. Philosophy. Fro - Gat. 31 pam.
Phil 143.24	Pamphlet vol. Philosophy. Gat - Glo. 28 pam.
Phil 3090.79	Pamphlet box. Philosophy. German.
Phil 3120.5.80	Pamphlet box. Philosophy. German. Bratuschick, Ernst.
Phil 2998.01	Pamphlet box. Philosophy. German and Dutch.
Phil 3120.2.79	Pamphlet box. Philosophy. German and Dutch. Bolzano, Bernard.
Phil 3160.2.79	Pamphlet box. Philosophy. German and Dutch. Carneri, B.
Phil 3160.1.79	Pamphlet box. Philosophy. German and Dutch. Class, Gustav.
Phil 3160.3.79	Pamphlet box. Philosophy. German and Dutch. Cohen, Hermann.
Phil 3195.2.78	Pamphlet box. Philosophy. German and Dutch. Deutinger, Martin.
Phil 3200.2.80	Pamphlet box. Philosophy. German and Dutch. Ebbinghaus, Hermann.
Phil 3200.3.80	Pamphlet box. Philosophy. German and Dutch. Eberhard, Johann August.
Phil 3200.4.80	Pamphlet box. Philosophy. German and Dutch. Erdmann, Benno.
Phil 3210.27	Pamphlet vol. Philosophy. German and Dutch. Fechner, G.T. 5 pam.
Phil 3210.80	Pamphlet box. Philosophy. German and Dutch. Fechner, G.T. German dissertations.
Phil 3235.79.5	Pamphlet box. Philosophy. German and Dutch. Feuerbach, Ludwig.
Phil 3235.79	Pamphlet box. Philosophy. German and Dutch. Feuerbach, Ludwig. German dissertations.
Htn Phil 3246.32*	Pamphlet vol. Philosophy. German and Dutch. Fichte, Johann Gottlieb. 5 pam.
Phil 3246.79.5	Pamphlet box. Philosophy. German and Dutch. Fichte, Johann Gottlieb.
Phil 3246.79	Pamphlet vol. Philosophy. German and Dutch. Fichte, Johann Gottlieb. 13 pam.
Phil 3246.79.3	Pamphlet vol. Philosophy. German and Dutch. Fichte, Johann Gottlieb. German dissertations. 14 pam.
Phil 3246.79.4	Pamphlet box. Philosophy. German and Dutch. Fichte, Johann Gottlieb. German dissertations.
Phil 3246.79.2	Pamphlet vol. Philosophy. German and Dutch. Fichte, Johann Gottlieb. German dissertations. 15 pam.
Phil 3260.79	Pamphlet box. Philosophy. German and Dutch. Fries, J.F.
Phil 3310.1.80	Pamphlet box. Philosophy. German and Dutch. Günther, Anton.
Phil 3425.79.5	Pamphlet box. Philosophy. German and Dutch. Hegel, Georg Wilhelm Friedrich.
Phil 3425.79.2	Pamphlet box. Philosophy. German and Dutch. Hegel, Georg Wilhelm Friedrich. German dissertations. 13 pam.
Phil 3425.79.3	Pamphlet box. Philosophy. German and Dutch. Hegel, Georg Wilhelm Friedrich. German dissertations.
Phil 3425.79	Pamphlet vol. Philosophy. German and Dutch. Hegel, Georg Wilhelm Friedrich. German dissertations. 18 pam.
Phil 3425.06	Pamphlet box. Philosophy. German and Dutch. Hegel, Georg Wilhelm Friedrich. Minor writings.
Phil 3428.79	Pamphlet box. Philosophy. German and Dutch. Herbart, J.F. German dissertations.
Phil 3460.79	Pamphlet box. Philosophy. German and Dutch. Jacobi, F.H.
Phil 3549.8.79	Pamphlet box. Philosophy. German and Dutch. Klages, Ludwig. Miscellaneous pamphlets.
Phil 3549.6.80	Pamphlet box. Philosophy. German and Dutch. Knoodt, Franz Peter. Miscellaneous pamphlets.
Phil 3525.79	Pamphlet box. Philosophy. German and Dutch. Krause, K.C.F.
Phil 3525.06	Pamphlet box. Philosophy. German and Dutch. Krause, K.C.F. Minor writings.
Phil 3549.4.80	Pamphlet box. Philosophy. German and Dutch. Kulpa, Oswald. Miscellaneous pamphlets.
Phil 3585.7.80	Pamphlet box. Philosophy. German and Dutch. Lazarus, Moritz.
Phil 3585.5.80	Pamphlet box. Philosophy. German and Dutch. Leonhardi, Hermann Karl von.
Phil 3585.6.80	Pamphlet box. Philosophy. German and Dutch. Lott, Karl Franz.
Phil 3565.79.5	Pamphlet box. Philosophy. German and Dutch. Lotze.
Phil 3565.79	Pamphlet vol. Philosophy. German and Dutch. Lotze. German dissertations. 21 pam.
Phil 3565.79.3	Pamphlet vol. Philosophy. German and Dutch. Lotze. German dissertations. 4 pam.
Phil 3565.79.2	Pamphlet vol. Philosophy. German and Dutch. Lotze. German dissertations. 17 pam.
Phil 3565.79.4	Pamphlet box. Philosophy. German and Dutch. Lotze. German dissertations.
Htn Phil 3625.3.78*	Pamphlet box. Philosophy. German and Dutch. Mach, Ernst.
Phil 3625.5.80	Pamphlet box. Philosophy. German and Dutch. Maimon, Salomon.
Phil 3625.1.80	Pamphlet box. Philosophy. German and Dutch. Mendelssohn, Moses.
Phil 3665.1.70	Pamphlet box. Philosophy. German and Dutch. Natorp, Paul.
Phil 3640.79.5	Pamphlet vol. Philosophy. German and Dutch. Nietzsche, Friedrich.
Phil 3640.79.4	Pamphlet box. Philosophy. German and Dutch. Nietzsche, Friedrich.
Phil 3640.79.3	Pamphlet box. Philosophy. German and Dutch. Nietzsche, Friedrich. German dissertations.
Phil 3640.79	Pamphlet vol. Philosophy. German and Dutch. Nietzsche, Friedrich. German dissertations. 1901-1915. 17 pam.
Phil 3640.79.2	Pamphlet box. Philosophy. German and Dutch. Nietzsche, Friedrich. German dissertations. 1913-1932. 12 pam.
Phil 3640.79.55	Pamphlet vol. Philosophy. German and Dutch. Nietzsche-Gesellschaft.
Phil 3745.5.79	Pamphlet box. Philosophy. German and Dutch. Paulsen, F.
Phil 3745.2.80	Pamphlet box. Philosophy. German and Dutch. Ploucquet, G.
Phil 3745.3.06F	Pamphlet box. Philosophy. German and Dutch. Prantl, Carl von.
Phil 3745.3.80	Pamphlet box. Philosophy. German and Dutch. Prantl, Carl von.
Phil 3850.4.80	Pamphlet box. Philosophy. German and Dutch. Sailor, J.M. 2 pam.
Phil 3850.11.80	Pamphlet box. Philosophy. German and Dutch. Schegk, J.
Phil 3850.14.80	Pamphlet box. Philosophy. German and Dutch. Schell, Herman.
Phil 3801.1	Pamphlet box. Philosophy. German and Dutch. Schelling. Biography and criticism.
Phil 3801.5	Pamphlet box. Philosophy. German and Dutch. Schelling. Biography and criticism. Dissertations, 1908-1913. 10 pam.
Phil 3801.6	Pamphlet box. Philosophy. German and Dutch. Schelling. Biography and criticism. Dissertations.
Phil 3805.79.5	Pamphlet box. Philosophy. German and Dutch. Schleiermacher, Friedrich.
Phil 3805.79	Pamphlet vol. Philosophy. German and Dutch. Schleiermacher, Friedrich. 12 pam.
Phil 3805.79.3	Pamphlet box. Philosophy. German and Dutch. Schleiermacher, Friedrich. German dissertations.
Phil 3805.79.2	Pamphlet box. Philosophy. German and Dutch. Schleiermacher, Friedrich. German dissertations. 12 pam.
Phil 3808.79	Pamphlet vol. Philosophy. German and Dutch. Schopenhauer, Arthur. 18 pam.
Phil 3808.79.5	Pamphlet box. Philosophy. German and Dutch. Schopenhauer, Arthur.
Phil 3808.79.4	Pamphlet box. Philosophy. German and Dutch. Schopenhauer, Arthur. German dissertations.
Phil 3808.79.3	Pamphlet vol. Philosophy. German and Dutch. Schopenhauer, Arthur. German dissertations. 15 pam.
Phil 3808.79.2	Pamphlet vol. Philosophy. German and Dutch. Schopenhauer, Arthur. German dissertations. 20 pam.
Phil 3850.6.80	Pamphlet box. Philosophy. German and Dutch. Schubert, G.H.
Phil 3850.28.80	Pamphlet box. Philosophy. German and Dutch. Siebeck, Hermann. Paris.
Phil 3850.9.80	Pamphlet box. Philosophy. German and Dutch. Sigivart, Christoph.
Phil 3850.16.79	Pamphlet box. Philosophy. German and Dutch. Simmel, Georg. German dissertations.
Phil 3819.79.2	Pamphlet vol. Philosophy. German and Dutch. Spinoza, Benedictus de. 15 pam.
Phil 3819.79	Pamphlet vol. Philosophy. German and Dutch. Spinoza, Benedictus de. 14 pam.
Phil 3819.79.3	Pamphlet vol. Philosophy. German and Dutch. Spinoza, Benedictus de.
Phil 3819.79.5	Pamphlet box. Philosophy. German and Dutch. Spinoza, Benedictus de. German dissertations.
Phil 3842.13.15	Pamphlet vol. Philosophy. German and Dutch. Spinoza. Biographie and criticism. Wolfson, H.A. 4 pam.
Phil 3850.5.80	Pamphlet box. Philosophy. German and Dutch. Spir, African von.
Phil 3850.1.79	Pamphlet box. Philosophy. German and Dutch. Strauss, D.F.
Phil 3890.5.80	Pamphlet box. Philosophy. German and Dutch. Tennemann, Wilhelm G.
Phil 3890.8.79	Pamphlet box. Philosophy. German and Dutch. Thomasius, Christian.
Phil 3890.4.80	Pamphlet vol. Philosophy. German and Dutch. Trahudorf, Karl Friedrich Eusebius.
Phil 3895.80	Pamphlet box. Philosophy. German and Dutch. Ulrici, H. 2 pam.
Phil 3903.1.80	Pamphlet vol. Philosophy. German and Dutch. Volkelt, Johannes.
Phil 3925.1.79	Pamphlet box. Philosophy. German and Dutch. Wagner, J.J.
Phil 3925.2.80	Pamphlet box. Philosophy. German and Dutch. Wasmann, Erich
Phil 3925.6.79	Pamphlet box. Philosophy. German and Dutch. Windelband, W.
Phil 3910.84.5	Pamphlet vol. Philosophy. German and Dutch. Wolff, Christian von. 4 pam.
Phil 3910.78	Pamphlet box. Philosophy. German and Dutch. Wolff, Christian von.
Phil 3915.79.5	Pamphlet box. Philosophy. German and Dutch. Wundt, Wilhelm.
Phil 3915.79	Pamphlet vol. Philosophy. German and Dutch. Wundt, Wilhelm. German dissertations. 14 pam.
Phil 3915.79.2	Pamphlet box. Philosophy. German and Dutch. Wundt, Wilhelm. German dissertations.
Phil 140.13	Pamphlet vol. Philosophy. German dissertations. 15 pam.
Phil 140.35	Pamphlet box. Philosophy. German dissertations.
Phil 2998.4	Pamphlet box. Philosophy. German dissertations.
Phil 2998.3	Pamphlet vol. Philosophy. German dissertations. 11 pam.
Phil 7060.01	Pamphlet box. Philosophy. Ghosts and hypnotism.
Phil 143.25	Pamphlet vol. Philosophy. Go - Gom. 24 pam.
Phil 143.26	Pamphlet vol. Philosophy. Goo -Gro. 18 pam.
Phil 1100.5	Pamphlet box. Philosophy. Greek and Roman.
Phil 143.27	Pamphlet vol. Philosophy. Gro - Gu. 28 pam.
Phil 143.28	Pamphlet vol. Philosophy. H - Ham. 37 pam.
Phil 143.93	Pamphlet vol. Philosophy. H - Hue. 34 pam.
Phil 143.29	Pamphlet vol. Philosophy. Han - Has. 27 pam.
Phil 143.30	Pamphlet vol. Philosophy. Hat - Hel. 29 pam.
Phil 143.31	Pamphlet vol. Philosophy. Hel - Heu. 27 pam.
Phil 143.32	Pamphlet vol. Philosophy. Hey - Hir. 23 pam.
Phil 143.33	Pamphlet vol. Philosophy. Hir - Hol. 28 pam.
Phil 143.34	Pamphlet vol. Philosophy. Hol - How. 24 pam.
Phil 143.35	Pamphlet vol. Philosophy. Hoz - Jac. 32 pam.
Phil 143.94	Pamphlet vol. Philosophy. Hum - Kr. 30 pam.
Phil 6668.800.-.999	Pamphlet box. Philosophy. Hypnotism.

Htn Phil 6669.01PF*   Pamphlet box. Philosophy. Hypnotism.
Phil 5115.01   Pamphlet box. Philosophy. Hypothesis.
Phil 6720.01   Pamphlet box. Philosophy. Hysteria.
Phil 3998.6   Pamphlet vol. Philosophy. Italian philosophers. Biographical pamphlets. 9 pam.
Phil 3998.4   Pamphlet vol. Philosophy. Italian philosophical pamphlets. 39 pam.
Phil 3998.5   Pamphlet vol. Philosophy. Italian philosophy. 7 pam.
Phil 143.36   Pamphlet vol. Philosophy. Jac - Jer. 24 pam.
Phil 143.37   Pamphlet vol. Philosophy. Jes - Kae. 24 pam.
Phil 143.38   Pamphlet vol. Philosophy. Kae - Kel. 30 pam.
Phil 143.39   Pamphlet vol. Philosophy. Kel - Kin. 28 pam.
Phil 143.40   Pamphlet vol. Philosophy. Kir - Kn. 29 pam.
Phil 143.41   Pamphlet vol. Philosophy. Ko - Kra. 28 pam.
Phil 143.42   Pamphlet vol. Philosophy. Kra - Ky. 32 pam.
Phil 143.95   Pamphlet vol. Philosophy. Ku - Me. 39 pam.
Phil 143.43   Pamphlet vol. Philosophy. L - Lan. 19 pam.
Phil 143.44   Pamphlet vol. Philosophy. Lan - Las. 25 pam.
Phil 143.45   Pamphlet vol. Philosophy. Lay - Lei. 29 pam.
Phil 143.46   Pamphlet vol. Philosophy. Lei - Lic. 24 pam.
Phil 143.47   Pamphlet vol. Philosophy. Lie - Ll. 27 pam.
Phil 143.48   Pamphlet vol. Philosophy. Lo - Ly. 26 pam.
Phil 143.49   Pamphlet vol. Philosophy. M - McG. 16 pam.
Phil 143.50   Pamphlet vol. Philosophy. Mach - Mar. 31 pam.
Phil 143.51   Pamphlet vol. Philosophy. Mas - Mel. 32 pam.
Phil 143.52   Pamphlet vol. Philosophy. Mer - Min. 31 pam.
Phil 143.96   Pamphlet vol. Philosophy. Mi - Par. 20 pam.
Phil 143.53   Pamphlet vol. Philosophy. Min - Mol. 23 pam.
Phil 3998.3   Pamphlet vol. Philosophy. Miscellanee filosofiche. 17 pam.
Phil 3998.2   Pamphlet vol. Philosophy. Miscellanee filosofiche. 15 pam.
Phil 140.40   Pamphlet box. Philosophy. Miscellaneous pamphlets.
Phil 140.45   Pamphlet vol. Philosophy. Miscellaneous pamphlets. 6 pam.
Phil 140.32   Pamphlet box. Philosophy. Miscellaneous pamphlets.
Phil 140.66   Pamphlet vol. Philosophy. Modern. 20th Century (Russian). 8 pam.
Phil 143.54   Pamphlet vol. Philosophy. Mol - Moo. 20 pam.
Phil 143.55   Pamphlet vol. Philosophy. Mor - Mui. 30 pam.
Phil 9380.02   Pamphlet box. Philosophy. Morale.
Phil 9380.01   Pamphlet box. Philosophy. Morale.
Phil 143.56   Pamphlet vol. Philosophy. Mun - Nat. 34 pam.
Phil 143.57   Pamphlet vol. Philosophy. Nat - Nu. 27 pam.
Phil 143.58   Pamphlet vol. Philosophy. O - Op. 28 pam.
Phil 9390.01   Pamphlet box. Philosophy. Oaths.
Phil 9400.01   Pamphlet box. Philosophy. Old age.
Phil 8624   Pamphlet box. Philosophy. On immortality. 3 pam.
Phil 143.59   Pamphlet vol. Philosophy. Or - Pau. 29 pam.
Phil 143.97   Pamphlet vol. Philosophy. Par - Pot. 23 pam.
Phil 2805.79   Pamphlet box. Philosophy. Pascal, Blaise. German dissertations.
Phil 143.60   Pamphlet vol. Philosophy. Pau - Pet. 24 pam.
Phil 143.61   Pamphlet vol. Philosophy. Pet - Pfe. 13 pam.
Phil 143.62   Pamphlet vol. Philosophy. Pfl - Pil. 34 pam.
Phil 143.63   Pamphlet vol. Philosophy. Pio - Pur. 23 pam.
Phil 4400.01   Pamphlet box. Philosophy. Portuguese.
Phil 143.98   Pamphlet vol. Philosophy. Pr - Sha. 39 pam.
Phil 5240.9   Pamphlet box. Philosophy. Psychology.
Phil 5240.10   Pamphlet box. Philosophy. Psychology.
Phil 5243.47   Pamphlet box. Philosophy. Psychology. General. Diven, Kenneth.
Phil 5247.60.01   Pamphlet box. Philosophy. Psychology. Holway, Alfred H.
Phil 5249.2.80   Pamphlet box. Philosophy. Psychology. James, William.
Phil 143.64   Pamphlet vol. Philosophy. Put - Ran. 25 pam.
Phil 143.65   Pamphlet vol. Philosophy. Rap - Rei. 15 pam.
Phil 143.66   Pamphlet vol. Philosophy. Rei - Rit. 27 pam.
Phil 8612.01   Pamphlet box. Philosophy. Religion.
Phil 143.67   Pamphlet vol. Philosophy. Rob -Roy. 35 pam.
Phil 143.68   Pamphlet vol. Philosophy. Ru - Scha. 25 pam.
Phil 140.57   Pamphlet vol. Philosophy. Russian. 7 pam.
Phil 140.56   Pamphlet vol. Philosophy. Russian. 4 pam.
Phil 4710.02   Pamphlet vol. Philosophy. Russian. 5 pam.
Phil 4710.04   Pamphlet vol. Philosophy. Russian. 4 pam.
Phil 4710.01   Pamphlet vol. Philosophy. Russian. 6 pam.
Phil 4710.03   Pamphlet vol. Philosophy. Russian. 5 pam.
Phil 143.69   Pamphlet vol. Philosophy. Scha - Schl. 17 pam.
Phil 143.70   Pamphlet vol. Philosophy. Schm - Schr. 30 pam.
Phil 1501.2   Pamphlet box. Philosophy. Scholastic and mystic.
Phil 1501   Pamphlet box. Philosophy. Scholastic and mystic.
Phil 143.71   Pamphlet vol. Philosophy. Schr - Schu. 13 pam.
Phil 143.72   Pamphlet vol. Philosophy. Schu - Sel. 25 pam.
Phil 143.73   Pamphlet vol. Philosophy. Set - Sie. 25 pam.
Phil 143.99   Pamphlet vol. Philosophy. She - St. 26 pam.
Phil 143.74   Pamphlet vol. Philosophy. Sie - Sm. 33 pam.
Phil 7080.01   Pamphlet box. Philosophy. Sleep.
Phil 143.75   Pamphlet vol. Philosophy. So - Spe. 27 pam.
Phil 270.01   Pamphlet box. Philosophy. Special. Causation. 2 pam.
Phil 280.01   Pamphlet box. Philosophy. Special. Cosmology.
Phil 400.01   Pamphlet box. Philosophy. Special. Idealism.
Phil 410.01   Pamphlet box. Philosophy. Special. Infinite.
Phil 474.1   Pamphlet box. Philosophy. Special. Materialism.
Phil 525.01   Pamphlet box. Philosophy. Special. Mysticism. General.
Phil 575.01   Pamphlet box. Philosophy. Special. Personality.
Phil 600.01   Pamphlet vol. Philosophy. Special. Positivism. 10 pam.
Phil 600   Pamphlet box. Philosophy. Special. Positivism.
Phil 623.01   Pamphlet box. Philosophy. Special. Rationalism.
Phil 630.02   Pamphlet box. Philosophy. Special. Realism.
Phil 630.01   Pamphlet box. Philosophy. Special. Realism.
Phil 645.01   Pamphlet box. Philosophy. Special. Scepticism.
Phil 672.01   Pamphlet box. Philosophy. Special. Space and time.
Phil 705.01   Pamphlet box. Philosophy. Special. Transcendentalism.
Phil 720.01   Pamphlet box. Philosophy. Special. Truth and error.
Phil 735.01   Pamphlet box. Philosophy. Special. Values.
Phil 745.01   Pamphlet box. Philosophy. Special. Vitalism.
Phil 143.76   Pamphlet vol. Philosophy. Spi - Ste. 18 pam.
Phil 143.77   Pamphlet vol. Philosophy. Ste - Sto. 25 pam.
Phil 143.78   Pamphlet vol. Philosophy. Str - Stu. 27 pam.
Phil 143.79   Pamphlet vol. Philosophy. Swi - Tho. 29 pam.
Phil 143.100   Pamphlet vol. Philosophy. T - Z. 26 pam.
Phil 143.80   Pamphlet vol. Philosophy. Thu - Tr. 29 pam.
Phil 143.81   Pamphlet vol. Philosophy. Ts - Up. 21 pam.
Phil 143.82   Pamphlet vol. Philosophy. Ur - Vil. 15 pam.
Phil 184.19.11   Philosophy. v.1-. Translation. (Jaspers, K.) Chicago, 1969-71. 3v.
Phil 143.83   Pamphlet vol. Philosophy. Vil - Wan. 28 pam.
Phil 143.84   Pamphlet vol. Philosophy. Wat - Wei. 20 pam.
Phil 143.85   Pamphlet vol. Philosophy. Wei - Wey. 16 pam.

Phil 143.86   Pamphlet vol. Philosophy. Wh - Wil. 23 pam.
Phil 143.87   Pamphlet vol. Philosophy. Wil - Wir. 27 pam.
Phil 143.88   Pamphlet vol. Philosophy. Wit - Woo. 20 pam.
Phil 143.89   Pamphlet vol. Philosophy. Woo - Wy. 22 pam.
Phil 143.90   Pamphlet vol. Philosophy. Y - Z. 20 pam.
Phil 812.23   Philosophy - East and West. (Moore, Charles A.) Princeton, 1944.
Phil 140.69   Pamphlet vol. Philosophy (Russian). 8 pam.
Phil 140.63   Pamphlet vol. Philosophy (Russian). 5 pam.
Phil 140.59   Pamphlet vol. Philosophy (Russian). 4 pam.
Phil 140.67   Pamphlet vol. Philosophy (Russian). 7 pam.
Phil 140.64   Pamphlet vol. Philosophy (Russian). 4 pam.
Phil 165.30   Philosophy and analysis. (Analysis. Oxford, England.) N.Y., 1954.
Phil 193.231.2   Philosophy and and scientific realism. (Smart, J.) N.Y., 1963.
Phil 978.49.110   Philosophy and anthroposophy. (Steiner, R.) London, 1928.
Phil 184.49   Philosophy and argument. (Johnstone, Henry Webb.) State College, Pa., 1959.
Phil 3808.127   Philosophy and Christianity; an introduction to the works of Schopenhauer. (Irvine, David.) London, 1907.
Phil 165.354   Philosophy and Christianity. Kampen, 1965.
Phil 178.38.40   Philosophy and civilization. (Dewey, John.) N.Y., 1931.
Phil 1527.1.15   Philosophy and civilization in the Middle Ages. (Wulf, M. de.) Princeton, 1922.
Phil 1527.1.16   Philosophy and civilization in the Middle Ages. (Wulf, M. de.) Princeton, 1922-24.
Phil 177.133   Philosophy and co-existence. (Corradi, Gemma.) Leyden, 1966.
Phil 8575.10   Philosophy and contemporary man. Washington, 1968.
Phil 70.88   Philosophy and culture. 1. ed. (East-West Philosopher Conference.) Honolulu, 1962.
Phil 8595.4.11   Philosophy and development of religion. (Pfleiderer, O.) N.Y., 1894. 2v.
Phil 182.19   Philosophy and experience. (Hodgson, S.H.) London, 1885.
Phil 179.33   Philosophy and faith. (Emmet, D.M.) London, 1936.
Phil 185.57A   Philosophy and history. (Klibansky, Raymond.) Oxford, 1936.
Phil 188.30   Philosophy and human nature. (Nott, Kathleen.) London, 1970.
Phil 4800.20   Philosophy and ideology. (Jordan, Zbigniew A.) Dordrecht, 1963.
Phil 186.120.4   Philosophy and illusion. (Lazerowitz, M.) London, 1968.
Phil 818.34   Philosophy and its history. (Smart, Hawed.) La Salle, 1962.
Phil 193.147.5   Philosophy and its significance in contemporary civilization. (Silverman, H.L.) Boston, 1946.
Phil 1845.11   Philosophy and language. (Ayer, Alfred Jules.) Oxford, 1960.
Phil 8887.25.9   Philosophy and life. (Muirhead, J.H.) London, 1902.
Phil 4872.55.20   Philosophy and life and other papers. (D'Andrade, Joseph C.P.) Bombay, 1952.
Phil 1750.95.10   Philosophy and linguistic analysis. (Charlesworth, Maxwell John.) Pittsburgh, 1959.
Phil 193.157   Philosophy and living. v.1-2. (Stapledon, Olaf.) Harmondsworth, Eng., 1939.
Phil 5042.21.15   Philosophy and logical syntax. (Carnap, Rudolf.) London, 1935.
Phil 5520.311   Philosophy and ordinary language. (Caton, Charles.) Urbana, Ill., 1963.
Phil 25.70   Philosophy and phenomenological research. Buffalo. 1,1940+ 22v.
Phil 177.24   Philosophy and physical science. (Curtis, M.M.) Cleveeland, 1892.
Phil 2255.1.40   Philosophy and politics. (Russell, Bertrand Russell.) London, 1947.
Phil 1145.37   Philosophy and popular morals in ancient Greece. (Dobbs, A.E.) Dublin, 1907.
Phil 197.93   Philosophy and psychoanalysis. (Wisdom, John.) Oxford, 1964.
Phil 4200.1.80   Philosophy and psychology of...Pomponazzi. (Douglas, A.H.) Cambridge, 1910.
Phil 5635.35   The philosophy and psychology of sensation. (Hartshorne, C.) Chicago, 1934.
Phil 25.187   Philosophy and public affairs. Princeton. 1,1971+
Phil 8587.76   Philosophy and religion. (Haegerstroem, Axel.) London, 1964.
Phil 182.18.8   Philosophy and religion. (Henton, J.) London, 1881.
Phil 192.27   Philosophy and religion. (Rashdall, H.) London, 1909.
Phil 8602.65   Philosophy and religion. (Wilson, J.) London, 1961.
Phil 8599.34.5   Philosophy and religious belief. (Thomas, George Finger.) N.Y., 1970.
Phil 1050.27   Philosophy and revelation in the work of contemporary Jewish thinkers. (Lichtigfeld, A.) London, 1937.
Phil 193.231   Philosophy and scientific realism. (Smart, J.) London, 1963.
Phil 178.30   Philosophy and social problem. (Durant, William.) N.Y., 1917.
Phil 8597.28   Philosophy and the Christian experience. (Richmond, W.) Oxford, 1922.
Phil 8602.18.20   Philosophy and the Christian religion. (Webb, C.C.J.) Oxford, 1920.
Phil 8596.2   Philosophy and the cross. (Quick, O.C.) London, 1931.
Phil 493.6   Philosophy and the ideological conflict. (Seely, Charles Sherlock.) N.Y., 1953.
Phil 176.230   Philosophy and the meaning of life. (Britton, Karl.) London, 1969.
Phil 1711.7   Philosophy and the modern world. (Levi, Albert.) Bloomington, 1959.
Phil 193.132   Philosophy and the ordinary man. (Samuel, Herbert S.) London, 1932.
Phil 5259.58   Philosophy and the science of behavior. (Turner, Merle.) N.Y., 1967.
Phil 181.102   Philosophy and the social order. (Geiger, G.R.) Boston, 1947.
Phil 2477.1.63   Philosophy and war. (Boutroux, Émile.) London, 1916.
Phil 2477.1.64   Philosophy and war. (Boutroux, Émile.) N.Y., 1916.
Phil 75.15   Philosophy as a science. (Carus, P.) Chicago, 1909.
Phil 178.65   Philosophy as a science. (Ducasse, C.J.) N.Y., 1941.
Phil 180.10A   Philosophy as absolute science. (Frothingham, Ephraim L.) Boston, 1864.
Phil 180.20   Philosophy as scientia scientarum. (Flint, Robert.) N.Y., 1904.
Htn Phil 140.25PF*   Pamphlet vol. Philosophy broadsides.
Phil 178.59   Philosophy by ways of the sciences. (Dotterer, Ray H.) N.Y., 1929.
Phil 25.89   Philosophy East and West; a journal of Oriental and comparative thought. Honolulu. 1,1951+ 9v.

Phil 165.150   Philosophy for a time of crisis. (Koch, Adrienne.) N.Y., 1959.

Phil 184.26.20   Philosophy for our time. (Joad, C.E.M.) London, 1940.

Phil 810.5   Philosophy for plain people. (Kaunitz, M.M.) N.Y., 1926.

Phil 493.5   Philosophy for the future. (Sellars, R.W.) N.Y., 1949.

Phil 5055.22   Philosophy II and III in Harvard College. (Papineau, Arthur B.) Cambridge, 1889.

Phil 186.97   Philosophy in a new key. (Langer, Mrs. S.K.) Cambridge, Mass., 1942.

Phil 186.97.2   Philosophy in a new key. 2d ed. (Langer, Mrs. S.K.) Cambridge, Mass., 1951.

Phil 186.97.5   Philosophy in a new key. 3d ed. (Langer, Mrs. S.K.) Cambridge, Mass., 1957.

Phil 1800.3A   Philosophy in America. (Anderson, P.P.) N.Y., 1939.

Phil 1830.53   Philosophy in America. (Black, Max.) London, 1965.

Phil 2520.28A   Philosophy in extracts from his writings. (Descartes, René.) N.Y., 1892.

Phil 182.5.9   Philosophy in outline. (Harris, W.T.) N.Y., 1883.

Phil 2340.11.60   Philosophy in process. (Weiss, Paul.) Carbondale, 1963-64. 5v.

Phil 807.11   Philosophy in relation to its history. (Hodgson, Shadworth H.) London, 1880.

Phil 193.148.5   Philosophy in revolution. (Selsam, H.) N.Y., 1957.

Phil 75.77   Philosophy in South Africa, 1950-1962. (Dawe, Harold G.A.) Cape Town, 1964.

Phil 1806.5   Philosophy in the mass age. (Grant, George.) N.Y., 1960.

Phil 1512.14   Philosophy in the Middle Ages. (Hyman, Arthur.) N.Y., 1967.

Phil 1526.4.10   Philosophy in the Middle Ages. (Vignaux, Paul.) N.Y., 1959.

Phil 4710.19   Philosophy in the Soviet Union. (Laszlo, Ervin.) Dordrecht, 1967.

Phil 1695.15   Philosophy in the twentieth century. (Barrett, William.) N.Y., 1962. 4v.

Phil 8400.29   Philosophy looks at the arts. (Margolis, J.) N.Y., 1962.

Phil 2340.10.99   The philosophy of A.N. Whitehead. (Miller, D.L.) Minneapolis, 1938.

Phil 182.101.7   The philosophy of a biologist. (Haldane, J.S.) Oxford, 1935.

Phil 182.101.5A   The philosophy of a biologist. (Haldane, J.S.) Oxford, 1935.

Phil 8628.2   The philosophy of a future state. (Dick, T.) N.Y., 1829.

Phil 8628.2.5   The philosophy of a future state. (Dick, T.) N.Y., 1831.

Phil 8628.2.2   The philosophy of a future state. (Dick, T.) Philadelphia, 1843.

Phil 8693.1.2   The philosophy of a future state. (Dick, T.) Philadelphia, 1845. 2 pam.

Phil 8629.2   The philosophy of a future state. (English, C.D.) Philadelphia, 1885.

Phil 8696.19   The philosophy of a scientist. (Gordon, Ronald G.) London, 1947.

Phil 1717.24   The philosophy of actuality. (Rouche, Gerhard Albin.) Fort Hare, 1963.

Phil 2340.10.101A   The philosophy of Alfred North Whitehead. (Schilpp, Paul A.) Evanston, 1941.

Phil 2340.10.127   The philosophy of Alfred North Whitehead. 2nd ed. (Schilpp, Paul A.) N.Y., 1951.

Phil 1930.11.30   The philosophy of analogy and symbolism. (Cargill, S.T.) London, 1946?

Phil 1105.1   Philosophy of ancient Greece. (Anderson, W.) Edinburgh, 1791.

Phil 960.4.5   The philosophy of ancient India. (Garbe, Richard.) Chicago, 1897.

Htn   Phil 6685.11*   The philosophy of animal magnetism. Philadelphia, 1837.

Phil 8404.8.5   The philosophy of art. (Ducasse, Curt.) Toronto, 1929.

Phil 8406.8   The philosophy of art. (Frothingham, A.L.) Princeton, 1894.

Phil 8407.24   The philosophy of art. (Griggs, Edward.) N.Y., 1913.

Phil 3425.56.15   The philosophy of art. (Hegel, Georg Wilhelm Friedrich.) Edinburgh, 1886.

Phil 3425.56.25   The philosophy of art. (Hegel, Georg Wilhelm Friedrich.) N.Y., 1879.

Phil 2885.34.12   The philosophy of art. Photoreproduction. (Taine, Hippolyte Adolphe.) London, 1867.

Phil 2885.34.10   The philosophy of art. Photoreproduction. 2. ed. (Taine, Hippolyte Adolphe.) N.Y., 1873.

Phil 3903.3.43   The philosophy of "As if"; a system of the theoretical, practical and religious fictions of mankind. 2. ed. (Vaihinger, Hans.) London, 1968.

Phil 3903.3.40   The philosophy of "As if". (Vaihinger, Hans.) London, 1924.

NEDL   Phil 2490.88.5   The philosophy of Auguste Comte. (Lévy-Bruhl, L.) N.Y., 1903.

Phil 192.85.5.5   The philosophy of being. (Raeymaeker, Louis de.) St. Louis, 1961.

Phil 4080.3.80   The philosophy of Benedetto Croce. (Carr, Herbert Wildon.) London, 1917.

Phil 4080.3.81   The philosophy of Benedetto Croce. (Carr, Herbert Wildon.) N.Y., 1969.

Phil 4080.3.360   The philosophy of Benedetto Croce. 1st ed. (DeGennaro, Angelo A.) N.Y., 1961.

Phil 2475.1.83   The philosophy of Bergson. (Lindsay, A.D.) London, 1911.

Phil 2475.1.129   The philosophy of Bergson. (Russell, B.) Cambridge, 1914.

Phil 2255.1.100   The philosophy of Bertrand Russell. (Schilpp, Paul A.) Evanston, Ill., 1944.

Phil 2255.1.102   The philosophy of Bertrand Russell. (Schilpp, Paul A.) Evanston, Ill., 1946.

Phil 2255.1.103   The philosophy of Bertrand Russell. (Schilpp, Paul A.) N.Y., 1951.

Phil 1905.22.79   The philosophy of C.D. Broad. (Schilpp, Paul.) N.Y., 1959.

Phil 2120.4.95   The philosophy of C.I. Lewis. 1. ed. Facsimile. (Schilpp, Paul A.) La Salle, 1968.

Phil 2475.1.185   The Philosophy of change. (Carr, Herbert W.) London, 1914.

Phil 720.5   Philosophy of change. (Rhodes, D.P.) N.Y., 1909.

Phil 9035.39   The philosophy of character. (Pierce, Edgar.) Cambridge, 1924.

Phil 5627.78   Philosophy of Christian experience. 3d series. (Foster, R.S.) N.Y., 1890.

Phil 8586.15   Philosophy of Christianity. (Graham, Bothwell.) Columbia, 1917.

Phil 182.39   Philosophy of common sense. (Harriman, F.) N.Y., 1907.

Phil 182.39.5   The philosophy of common sense. (Harrison, F.) London, 1907.

Phil 8602.70   The philosophy of compassion. (Wynne-Tyson, Esmé.) London, 1962.

Phil 8886.17   Philosophy of conduct. (Ladd, G.T.) N.Y., 1902.

Phil 9495.29.10   The philosophy of conflict. 2nd series. (Ellis, Havelock.) Boston, 1919.

Phil 9495.29.5   The philosophy of conflict. 2nd series. (Ellis, Havelock.) London, 1919.

Phil 284.12   The philosophy of creation. (Dole, George Henry.) N.Y., 1906.

Phil 2050.210   The philosophy of David Hume. (Smith, N.K.) London, 1941.

Phil 1750.205   The philosophy of decadentism; a study in existentialism. (Bobbio, Norberto.) Oxford, 1948.

Phil 2520.179   The philosophy of Descartes. (Gibson, A.B.) London, 1932.

Phil 9430.18   The philosophy of despair. (Jordan, D.S.) San Francisco, 1902.

Phil 9430.10.4   The philosophy of disenchantment. (Saltus, Edgar.) N.Y., 1885.

Phil 9161.8   The philosophy of domestic life. (Byford, W.H.) Boston, 1869.

Phil 1050.14.5   The philosophy of Don Hasdai Crescas. (Waxman, Meyer.) N.Y., 1920.

Phil 3450.11.116   Philosophy of Edmund Husserl...development of his phenomenology. (Welch, E.P.) N.Y., 1941.

Phil 187.32.85   The philosophy of Edmund Montgomery. (Keeton, Morris.) Dallas, 1950.

Phil 8581.81.80   The philosophy of Edward Bellamy. (Morgan, A.E.) N.Y., 1945.

Phil 9558.40   The philosophy of egoism. (Walker, James L.) Denver, 1905.

Phil 6673.3.5   The philosophy of electrical psychology. (Dods, J.B.) N.Y., 1850.

Phil 6673.3.6   The philosophy of electrical psychology. (Dods, J.B.) N.Y., 1852.

Phil 2477.1.135   The philosophy of Emil Boutroux. Thesis. (Crawford, L.S.) Charlotteville, 1924.

Phil 4570.4.81   The philosophy of Erik Gustaf Geijer. (Spongberg, V.H.) Rock Island, 1945.

Phil 3160.12.7   The philosophy of Ernst Cassirer. (Schilpp, Paul.) N.Y., 1958.

Phil 8620.9   The philosophy of evil. Philadelphia, 1845.

Phil 283.1   Philosophy of evolution. (Carpenter, S.H.) Madison, 1874.

Phil 3195.6.45   Philosophy of existence. (Dilthey, Wilhelm.) N.Y., 1957.

Phil 1750.215   The philosophy of existence. (Marcel, Gabriel.) London, 1948.

Phil 1750.115.87   Philosophy of existence. (Micallef, John.) N.Y., 1969.

Phil 2750.19.37   The philosophy of existentialism. 2nd ed. (Marcel, Gabriel.) N.Y., 1962.

Phil 3460.85   The philosophy of F.H. Jacobi. (Crawford, A.W.) N.Y., 1905.

Phil 8592.34   Philosophy of faith. (Myers, J.H.) Syracuse, N.Y., 1896.

Phil 3425.56.30   The philosophy of fine art. (Hegel, Georg Wilhelm Friedrich.) London, 1920. 4v.

Phil 197.61   A philosophy of form. (Watkin, E.I.) London, 1935.

Phil 197.61.10   A philosophy of form. (Watkin, E.I.) London, 1950.

Phil 1850.139   The philosophy of Francis Bacon. (Anderson, Fulton H.) Chicago, 1948.

Phil 1850.160   The philosophy of Francis Bacon. (Bacon, F.V.) Liverpool, 1964.

Phil 1850.118   The philosophy of Francis Bacon. (Broad, C.D.) Cambridge, Eng., 1926.

Phil 5768.10   The philosophy of freedom. (Steiner, Rudolf.) London, 1916.

Phil 5768.10.3   The philosophy of freedom. (Steiner, Rudolf.) London, 1964.

Phil 3640.95   Philosophy of Friedrich Nietzsche. (Broene, J.) n.p., n.d.

Phil 3640.90   Philosophy of Friedrich Nietzsche. (Mencken, Henry.) Boston, 1908.

Htn   Phil 3640.90*   Philosophy of Friedrich Nietzsche. (Mencken, Henry.) Boston, 1908.

Phil 3640.114   Philosophy of Friedrich Nietzsche. Photoreproduction. (Thilly, F.) N.Y., 1905.

X Cg   Phil 3640.90.3   Philosophy of Friedrich Nietzsche. 3d ed. (Mencken, Henry.) Boston, 1913.

Phil 187.59.80   The philosophy of G.E. Moore. (Schilpp, P.A.) Evanston, 1942.

Phil 187.59.82   The philosophy of G.E. Moore. 2. ed. (Schilpp, P.A.) N.Y., 1952.

Phil 2280.5.106.2   The philosophy of George Santayana. 2nd ed. (Schilpp, P.A.) N.Y., 1951.

Phil 4260.85   The philosophy of Giambattista Vico. (Croce, B.) London, 1913.

Phil 4260.85.8   The philosophy of Giambattista Vico. (Croce, B.) N.Y., 1964.

Phil 1106.3.5   The philosophy of Greece. (Benn, A.W.) London, 1898.

Phil 6060.8   The philosophy of handwriting. (Salamanea, F. de.) London, 1879.

Phil 9245.18   The philosophy of happiness. (Joslyn, R.) Elgin, n.d.

Phil 6132.24   The philosophy of health. no.1-3. (White, H.P.) Kalamazoo, Mich., 1901.

Phil 3425.20   The philosophy of Hegel. (Hegel, Georg Wilhelm Friedrich.) N.Y., 1953.

Phil 3425.610   The philosophy of Hegel. (Mure, G.R.G.) London, 1965.

Phil 3425.199A   The philosophy of Hegel. (Stace, N.J.) London, 1924.

Phil 2636.82.3   The philosophy of Helvetius. (Grossman, Mordecai.) N.Y., 1926.

Phil 2636.82   Philosophy of Helvetius. Thesis. (Grossman, Mordecai.) N.Y., 1926.

Phil 8589.5.30   The philosophy of Henry James, Sr. (Young, F.H.) N.Y., 1951.

Phil 8589.5.40   Philosophy of Henry James. (Kellogg, J.A.) N.Y., 1883.

Phil 2270.90.5   The philosophy of Herbert Spencer; being an examination of the first principles of his system. New York, 1881. Photoreproduction. (Bowne, Borden Parker.) Ann Arbor, Michigan, 1970.

Phil 2270.90   The philosophy of Herbert Spencer. (Bowne, B.P.) N.Y., n.d.

Phil 2270.90.2   The philosophy of Herbert Spencer. (Bowne, B.P.) N.Y., 1881.

Phil 3425.40.5.6   The philosophy of history. (Hegel, Georg Wilhelm Friedrich.) N.Y., 1900.

Phil 3425.40.5.9A   The philosophy of history. (Hegel, Georg Wilhelm Friedrich.) N.Y., 1944.

Phil 3425.40.5.10A   The philosophy of history. (Hegel, Georg Wilhelm Friedrich.) N.Y., 1956.

Phil 3195.6.113   Philosophy of history. (Kluback, William.) N.Y., 1956.

Phil 2045.25   Philosophy of Hobbes in extracts and notes from his philosophy. (Hobbes, Thomas.) Minneapolis, 1903.

Phil 8887.68   Philosophy of human conduct. (Michel, Virgil.) Minneapolis, 1936.

Phil 178.29	Philosophy of human life. (Dean, Amos.) Boston, 1839.
Phil 5241.20	The philosophy of human nature. (Buchanan, Joseph.) Richmond, 1812.
Phil 5241.20.2	The philosophy of human nature. (Buchanan, Joseph.) Weston, Mass., 1970.
Phil 185.67	The philosophy of human nature. (Klubertanz, G.P.) N.Y., 1953.
Phil 187.1	Philosophy of human nature. (M'Cormac, H.) London, 1837.
Phil 338.10.5	The philosophy of humanism. (Haldane, R.B.) New Haven, 1922.
Phil 1750.166.24	The philosophy of humanism. 4th ed. (Lamont, Corliss.) N.Y., 1957.
Phil 1750.166.23	The philosophy of humanism. 5th ed. (Lamont, Corliss.) N.Y., 1965.
Phil 2050.71A	Philosophy of Hume. (Hume, David.) N.Y., 1893.
Phil 400.71	A philosophy of ideals. (Brightman, E.S.) N.Y., 1928.
Phil 8638.1	Philosophy of immortality. (Noel, R.) London, 1882.
Phil 960.282	The philosophy of India and its impact on American thought. (Riepe, Dale Maurice.) Springfield, 1970.
Phil 8893.85	The philosophy of indifference. (Stone, M.A.) Providence, 1931.
Phil 176.44	The philosophy of individuality. (Blackwell, A.B.) N.Y., 1893.
Phil 288.15.10	The philosophy of inorganic compounds. (Hoenen, Peter.) West Baden Springs, Ind., 1960.
Phil 5811.6	The philosophy of instinct and reason. (Bushnan, J.S.) Edinburgh, 1837.
Phil 8582.41	The philosophy of integration. (Crawford-Frost, W.A.) Boston, 1906.
Phil 2138.123	The philosophy of J.S. Mill. (Anschutz, R.P.) Oxford, 1953.
Phil 2750.11.100A	The philosophy of Jacques Maritain. (Fecher, C.A.) Westminster, 1953.
Phil 2340.6.95	The philosophy of James Ward. (Murray, A.H.) Cambridge, Eng., 1937.
Phil 2880.8.20A	The philosophy of Jean Paul Sartre. (Sartre, Jean Paul.) N.Y., 1965.
Phil 178.38.10	The philosophy of John Dewey. (Dewey, John.) N.Y., 1928.
Phil 1955.6.95	The philosophy of John Dewey. (Feldman, W.T.) Baltimore, 1934.
Phil 1955.6.96	The philosophy of John Dewey. (Feldman, W.T.) Baltimore, 1934.
Phil 1955.6.101	The philosophy of John Dewey. (Schilpp, P.A.) Evanston, 1939.
Phil 1955.6.102	The philosophy of John Dewey. 2d ed. (Schilpp, P.A.) N.Y., 1951.
Phil 182.101.20	The philosophy of John Scott Haldane. (Sampson, A.H.) Philadelphia, 1938.
Phil 2138.20	The philosophy of John Stuart Mill. (Mill, John S.) N.Y., 1961.
Phil 2250.70	The philosophy of Josiah Royce. (Royce, Josiah.) N.Y., 1971.
Phil 2725.11.75	The philosophy of Jules Lachelier. (Lachelier, Jules.) The Hague, 1960.
Phil 3482.1	Philosophy of Kant. (Adamson, R.) Edinburg, 1879.
Phil 3484.3.5	Philosophy of Kant. (Cousin, V.) London, n.d.
Phil 3480.25.10	The philosophy of Kant. (Kant, Immanuel.) Glasgow, 1927.
Phil 3480.25.50A	The philosophy of Kant. (Kant, Immanuel.) N.Y., 1949.
Phil 3480.25.5	The philosophy of Kant. 2d ed. (Kant, Immanuel.) Glasgow, 1923.
Phil 3489.36	The philosophy of Kant and our modern world. (Hendel, C.W.) N.Y., 1957.
Phil 3480.25	Philosophy of Kant as contained in extracts. (Kant, Immanuel.) N.Y., 1888.
Phil 3480.25.2	Philosophy of Kant as contained in extracts. (Kant, Immanuel.) N.Y., 1891.
Phil 3504.3.5	The philosophy of Kant explained. (Watson, J.) Glasgow, 1908.
Phil 3475.3.140.5	The philosophy of Karl Jaspers. 1st ed. (Schilpp, P.A.) N.Y., 1957.
Phil 337.24	The philosophy of knowledge. (Gallagher, K.T.) N.Y., 1964.
Phil 5520.418	Philosophy of language. (Alston, W.) Englewood Cliffs, N.J., 1964.
Phil 5520.447	The philosophy of language. (Katz, Jerrold J.) N.Y., 1966.
Phil 5525.19.2	The philosophy of laughter and smiling. 2. ed. (Vasey, George.) London, 1877.
Phil 3480.67.105	The philosophy of law. (Kant, Immanuel.) Edinburgh, 1887.
Phil 3552.454	The philosophy of Leibniz. (Rescher, Nicholas.) Englewood Cliffs, N.J., 1967.
Phil 8598.75	Philosophy of life; with an appendix on the Bible. (Smith, Abbot Edes.) Norwood, 1938.
Phil 930.41	Philosophy of life. (Chen, Li-Fu.) N.Y., 1948.
Phil 8881.59	The philosophy of life. (Goodman, R.M.) Marietta, Ga., 1863.
Phil 193.10.6	Philosophy of life. (Schlegel, Friedrich von.) London, 1847.
Phil 193.10.7	Philosophy of life. (Schlegel, Friedrich von.) N.Y., 1848.
Phil 8887.56.5	A philosophy of life and its spiritual values. (Martin, A.W.) N.Y., 1923.
Phil 8701.13.5	Philosophy of light. (Lorbeer, Floyd Irwing.) Los Angeles, 1932.
Phil 1955.10.30	The philosophy of live. 2nd ed. (Davis, Charles G.) Chicago, 1906.
Phil 8893.135	A philosophy of living. (Sathaye, S.G.) N.Y., 1963.
Phil 2115.46	Philosophy of Locke in extracts. (Locke, J.) N.Y., 1891.
Phil 5011.5	The philosophy of logic, 1880-1908. (Bowne, G.D.) The Hague, 1966.
Phil 5055.42	Philosophy of logic. (Putnam, Hilary.) N.Y., 1971.
Phil 5056.1.25	Philosophy of logic. (Quine, Willard Van Orman.) Englewood Cliffs, N.J., 1970.
Phil 5068.67	Philosophy of logical construction. 1st ed. (Ganguli, Hermanta Kumar.) Calcutta, 1963.
Phil 8960.8	The philosophy of love. (Kenmare, D. (pseud.).) London, 1942.
Phil 4060.2.50	The philosophy of love. (Leo Hebraeus.) London, 1937.
Phil 8892.12.9	The philosophy of loyalty. (Royce, J.) N.Y., 1908.
Phil 8892.12.10	The philosophy of loyalty. (Royce, J.) N.Y., 1908.
Phil 8892.12.4	The philosophy of loyalty. (Royce, J.) N.Y., 1908.
Phil 8892.12.15A	The philosophy of loyalty. (Royce, J.) N.Y., 1920.
Phil 8892.12.20A	The philosophy of loyalty. (Royce, J.) N.Y., 1924.
Phil 3235.132	The philosophy of Ludwig Feuerbach. (Kamenka, Eugene.) London, 1970.
Phil 2733.116	The philosophy of Malebranche. (Rome, B.K.) Chicago, 1963.

Phil 4170.7.96	Pamphlet vol. The philosophy of Mamiani della Rovere, Terenzio. 3 pam.
Phil 310.445.4	A philosophy of man. (Schaff, Adam.) London, 1963.
Phil 585.392	A philosophy of man and society. (Peterson, Forrest H.) N.Y., 1970.
Phil 4110.1.89	The philosophy of Marsilio Ficino. (Kristeller, Paul Oskar.) Gloucester, Mass., 1964.
Phil 3120.30.150	The philosophy of Martin Buber. 1st ed. (Schilpp, Paul Arthur.) La Salle, 1967.
Phil 3450.19.475	The philosophy of Martin Heidegger. (Mehta, Jarava Lal.) Varanasi, 1967.
Phil 8592.6.80	The philosophy of Martineau in relation to the idealism of the present day. (Jones, Henry.) London, 1905.
Phil 3246.66.5	Philosophy of masonry. (Fichte, Johann Gottlieb.) Seattle, 1945.
Phil 5545.30	The philosophy of memory. (Smith, D.T.) Louisville, Ky., 1899.
Phil 6132.6.5	The philosophy of mental healing. (Whipple, L.E.) N.Y., 1893.
Phil 333.20	The philosophy of mind. (Chappell, Vere C.) Englewood Cliffs, 1962.
Phil 5251.1.5	Philosophy of mind. (Ladd, G.T.) N.Y., 1895.
Phil 585.340	Philosophy of mind. (Shaffer, Jerome A.) Englewood Cliffs, N.J., 1968.
Phil 5750.1	Philosophy of mind in volition. (Allyn, J.) Oberlin, 1851.
Phil 7054.122	Philosophy of modern miracles. N.Y., 1850.
Phil 8893.15	The philosophy of morals. (Smith, Alexander.) London, 1835. 2v.
Phil 192.28.28	The philosophy of Mr. B*rtr*nd R*ss*ll. (Jourdain, P.) London, 1918.
Phil 7054.140	Philosophy of mysterious agents. (Rogers, E.C.) Boston, 1853.
Phil 7060.24	Philosophy of mystery. (Dendy, W.B.) London, 1841.
Phil 7060.24.5	Philosophy of mystery. (Dendy, W.B.) N.Y., 1845.
Phil 525.2	Philosophy of mysticism. (Du Prel, Karl.) London, 1889. 2v.
Phil 525.26	The philosophy of mysticism. (Watkin, Edward Ingram.) London, 1920.
Phil 8589.1	The philosophy of natural theology. (Jackson, W.) London, 1874.
Phil 283.20	Philosophy of nature. (Collingwood, Francis.) Englewood Cliffs, N.J., 1961.
Phil 293.27	The philosophy of nature. (Melsen, A.G.M. van.) Pittsburg, 1953.
Phil 280.5	Pamphlet vol. Philosophy of nature 1905-1911. 5 pam.
Phil 5751.7.3	The philosophy of necessity. 3. ed. (Bray, Charles.) London, 1889.
Phil 3640.104	Philosophy of Nietzsche. (Chatterton-Hill, G.) London, 1912.
Phil 3640.22.15	Philosophy of Nietzsche. (Nietzsche, Friedrich.) N.Y., 195-?
Phil 3640.108	The philosophy of Nietzsche. (Wolf, A.) London, 1915.
Phil 3640.722	The philosophy of Nietzsche in the light of Thomistic principles. 1st ed. (Jette, Celine.) N.Y., 1967.
Phil 187.108	Philosophy of our uncertainties. (Müller, G.E.) Norman, 1936.
Phil 2230.5A	The philosophy of P.P. Quimby. (Dresser, A.G.) Boston, 1895.
Phil 2225.5.25	The philosophy of Peirce; selected writings. (Peirce, C.S.) London, 1940.
Phil 575.64	The philosophy of personalism. (Knudson, A.C.) N.Y., 1927.
Phil 575.88	The philosophy of personalism and its educational applications. Diss. (Langan, Hubert E.) Washington, D.C., 1935.
Phil 630.9.10	The philosophy of physical realism. (Sellars, R.W.) N.Y., 1932.
Phil 4265.1.41	A philosophy of potentiality. (Vivante, Leone.) London, 1955.
Phil 6325.17	The philosophy of psychiatry. (Palmer, H.A.) N.Y., 1952.
NEDL Phil 1925.80	Philosophy of Ralph Cudworth. (Lowrey, C.E.) N.Y., 1884.
Phil 199.4	A philosophy of reality. (Young, E.L.) Manchester, 1930.
Htn Phil 2125.75*	Philosophy of reality: should it be favored by America? (McCosh, James.) N.Y., 1894.
Phil 182.19.5	Philosophy of reflection. (Hodgson, S.H.) London, 1878. 2v.
Phil 2240.35	The philosophy of Reid...in the "Inquiry into the human mind". (Reid, Thomas.) N.Y., 1892.
Phil 8735.01	Pamphlet box. Philosophy of religion.
Phil 8510.20	Pamphlet vol. Philosophy of religion. 6 pam.
Htn Phil 8510.2*	Pamphlet vol. Philosophy of religion. 13 pam.
Phil 8510.1	Pamphlet vol. Philosophy of religion. 6 pam.
Htn Phil 8510.5*	Pamphlet vol. Philosophy of religion. 9 pam.
Phil 8510	Pamphlet box. Philosophy of religion.
Phil 8510.15	Pamphlet vol. Philosophy of religion. 12 pam.
Htn Phil 8510.2.2*	Pamphlet vol. Philosophy of religion. 13 pam.
Phil 8510.7	Pamphlet box. Philosophy of religion.
Phil 8581.20	Philosophy of religion. (Bascom, J.) N.Y., 1876.
Phil 4515.36	Philosophy of religion. (Boström, C.J.) New Haven, 1962.
Phil 8581.67.5	A philosophy of religion. (Brightman, E.S.) N.Y., 1940.
Phil 8583.4	The philosophy of religion. (Dick, T.) Brookfield, Mass., 1829.
Phil 8584.10	The philosophy of religion. (Edwards, D.M.) N.Y., 1924.
Phil 8586.10.17	The philosophy of religion. (Galloway, G.) N.Y., 1927.
Phil 8632.2	The philosophy of religion. (Höffding, H.) London, 1906.
Phil 8591.80	Philosophy of religion. (Lewis, Hywel David.) London, 1965.
Phil 8592.116	The philosophy of religion. (McPherson, Thomas.) London, 1965.
Phil 8592.14.2	The philosophy of religion. (Morell, J.D.) London, 1849.
Phil 8592.14	The philosophy of religion. (Morell, J.D.) N.Y., 1849.
Phil 8594.8	The philosophy of religion. (Ormond, A.T.) Princeton, N.J., 1922.
Phil 8595.62	A philosophy of religion. (Patterson, Robert Leet.) Durham, 1970.
Phil 8595.4.10	The philosophy of religion. (Pfleiderer, O.) London, 1886-88. 4v.
Phil 8591.14	The philosophy of religion. (Sadd, G.T.) N.Y., 1905. 2v.
Phil 8598.98	Philosophy of religion. (Sheen, Fulton John.) Dublin, 1952.
Phil 8598.137	Philosophy of religion. (Smith, John E.) N.Y., 1965.
Phil 8510.3	Pamphlet vol. Philosophy of religion. German dissertations. 13 pam.
Phil 8510.8	Pamphlet box. Philosophy of religion. German dissertations.
Phil 8655.8.10	Pamphlet box. Philosophy of religion. God.
Phil 8654.01	Pamphlet box. Philosophy of religion. God.

Phil 8583.4.18   The philosophy of religion. v.1-2. (Dick, T.) Philadelphia, 1845.

Phil 8510.6.1   Pamphlet vol. Philosophy of religion. 1848-1929. 19 pam.

Htn   Phil 8510.6*   Pamphlet vol. Philosophy of religion. 1883-1912. 6 pam.

Phil 8520.8   The philosophy of religion in England and America. (Caldecott, Alfred.) N.Y., 1901.

Phil 5627.62   The philosophy of religious experience. Thesis. (Waterhouse, E.S.) London, 1923.

Phil 3425.71   Philosophy of right. (Hegel, Georg Wilhelm Friedrich.) London, 1896.

Phil 3425.71.11   Philosophy of right. (Hegel, Georg Wilhelm Friedrich.) Oxford, 1967.

Phil 1930.18.80   The philosophy of Rudolf Carnap. (Schilpp, Paul.) La Salle, 1887.

Phil 3625.5.95   The philosophy of Salomon Maimon. (Bergmann, Hugo.) Jerusalem, 1967.

Phil 1845.3.105   The philosophy of Samuel Alexander. (Brettschneider, B.D.) N.Y., 1964.

Phil 193.49.50   The philosophy of Santayana; selections. (Santayana, G.) N.Y., 1936.

Phil 2280.5.25   The philosophy of Santayana. (Santayana, George.) N.Y., 1953.

Phil 2280.5.106   The philosophy of Santayana. (Schilpp, P.A.) Evanston, 1940.

Phil 4872.242.80   The philosophy of Sarvepalli Radhakrishnan. (Schilpp, Paul A.) N.Y., 1952.

Phil 3805.183   The philosophy of Schleiermacher. (Brandt, R.B.) N.Y., 1941.

Phil 3808.60.50   The philosophy of Schopenhauer. (Schopenhauer, Arthur.) N.Y., 1956.

Phil 270.2   Philosophy of science...on cause and effect. (Barrett, T.S.) London, 1872.

Phil 493.6.10   The philosophy of science. (Seely, Charles Sherlock.) N.Y., 1964.

Phil 2138.48   Philosophy of scientific method. (Mill, John S.) N.Y., 1950.

Phil 9590.12   The philosophy of silence. (Greene, Alice.) N.Y., 1940.

Phil 2120.5   The philosophy of Sir Oliver Lodge. Thesis. (Cooper, B.S.) Nashville, 1934.

Phil 2035.86.35   The philosophy of Sir William Hamilton. (Rasmussen, S.V.) Copenhagen, 1925.

Phil 7080.7   Philosophy of sleep. (Macnish, R.) N.Y., 1834.

Phil 9515.6   A philosophy of solitude. (Powys, J.C.) N.Y., 1933.

Phil 672.144.3   The philosophy of space and time. (Reichenbach, H.) N.Y., 1958.

Phil 8658.2   The philosophy of special providences. (Davis, A.J.) Boston, 1856.

Phil 3832.11A   The philosophy of Spinoza. (McKeon, R.) N.Y., 1928.

Phil 3819.35.3   Philosophy of Spinoza. (Spinoza, Benedictus de.) N.Y., 1892.

Phil 3819.35   Philosophy of Spinoza. (Spinoza, Benedictus de.) N.Y., 1894.

Phil 3819.29A   The philosophy of Spinoza. (Spinoza, Benedictus de.) N.Y., 1927.

Phil 3842.13A   The philosophy of Spinoza. (Wolfson, H.A.) Cambridge, 1934. 2v.

Phil 3842.13.2   The philosophy of Spinoza. v.1-2. (Wolfson, H.A.) N.Y., 1958.

Phil 3821.21   The philosophy of Spinoza and Brunner. (Bernard, Walter.) N.Y., 1934.

Phil 8598.53   The philosophy of spirit. (Snaith, John.) London, 1914.

Phil 6111.17   Philosophy of spirits in relation to matter. (Burnett, C.M.) London, 1850.

Phil 7054.6.5   The philosophy of spiritual intercourse. (Davis, A.J.) N.Y., 1851.

Phil 7069.16.30   The philosophy of spiritualism. (Kates, George W.) Boston, 1916.

Phil 333.5.12A   The philosophy of symbolic forms. (Cassirer, Ernst.) New Haven, 1953- 3v.

Phil 2477.9.81   The philosophy of the Abbé Bautain. (Horton, W.M.) N.Y., 1926.

Phil 187.100.5   The philosophy of the act. (Mead, George H.) Chicago, 1938.

Phil 2275.39   Philosophy of the active and moral poweers. (Stewart, D.) Cambridge, 1849.

Htn   Phil 2275.38*A   Philosophy of the active and moral powers. (Stewart, D.) Boston, 1828. 2v.

Phil 2275.39.2   Philosophy of the active and moral powers. (Stewart, D.) Boston, 1858.

Phil 2275.38.2   Philosophy of the active and moral powers. v.1-2. (Stewart, D.) Boston, 1828.

Phil 8423.22   Philosophy of the arts. (Weitz, M.) Cambridge, 1950.

Phil 2496.40.15   The philosophy of the beautiful. (Cousin, Victor.) London, 1848.

Phil 8403.8.10   The philosophy of the beautiful. (Cousin, Victor.) N.Y., 1849.

Phil 8411.7.15   The philosophy of the beautiful. (Knight, W.) N.Y., 1891-93. 2v.

Phil 8413.10   The philosophy of the beautiful. (MacVicar, John.) Edinburgh, 1855.

Phil 585.325   The philosophy of the body. (Spicker, Stuart F.) Chicago, 1970.

Phil 8585.1.5   The philosophy of the Christian religion. (Fairbairn, A.M.) London, 1905.

Phil 2130.60   Philosophy of the conditioned. (Mansel, H.L.) London, 1866.

Phil 2035.84   Philosophy of the conditioned. (Mansel, H.L.) London, 1866.

Phil 1750.141.3A   The philosophy of the enlightenment. (Cassirer, Ernst.) Princeton, N.J., 1951.

Phil 1707.2A   Philosophy of the enlightenment. (Hibben, J.G.) N.Y., 1910.

Phil 3120.55.50   A philosophy of the future. (Bloch, Ernst.) N.Y., 1970.

Phil 8831.4   Philosophy of the good life. (Gore, Charles.) London, 1930.

Phil 493.2   Philosophy of the great unconscious. (Stevens, S.E.) Boston, 1908.

Phil 410.1.2   The philosophy of the infinite. (Calderwood, H.) Cambridge, 1861.

Phil 410.1   The philosophy of the infinite. (Calderwood, H.) Edinburgh, 1854.

Phil 410.4.5   The philosophy of the infinite. (Swedenborg, E.) Boston, 1848.

Phil 8875.1   The philosophy of the moral feelings. (Abercrombie, J.) N.Y., 1833.

Phil 8875.1.3   The philosophy of the moral feelings. (Abercrombie, J.) N.Y., 1839.

Phil 8956.4   A philosophy of the moral nature of man. (Gooding, W.M.) Newark, 1877.

Phil 187.112   The philosophy of the past. (Monteath, K.M.) York, 1936.

Phil 575.225   Philosophy of the person. (Minkus, P.A.) Oxford, 1960.

Phil 177.35.9   Philosophy of the practical. (Croce, Benedetto.) London, 1913.

Phil 187.100   The philosophy of the present. (Mead, George H.) Chicago, 1932.

Phil 3010.2.26   The philosophy of the present in Germany. (Külpe, O.) N.Y., 1913.

Phil 177.107   A philosophy of the real and the possible. (Costello, H.T.) N.Y., 1954.

Phil 1715.3.9A   Philosophy of the recent past. (Perry, R.B.) N.Y., 1926.

Phil 178.12.26   Philosophy of the spirit. (Dresser, H.W.) N.Y., 1908.

Phil 7054.62.5   Philosophy of the spirit world. (Hammond, Charles.) N.Y., 1853.

Phil 3415.32.16   Philosophy of the unconcious. (Hartmann, Eduard von.) N.Y., 1931.

Phil 3415.32.15   Philosophy of the unconcious. (Hartmann, Eduard von.) N.Y., 1931.

Phil 3415.32.8   Philosophy of the unconcious. 2nd ed. (Hartmann, Eduard von.) London, 1893. 2v.

Phil 3415.32.2   Philosophy of the unconscious. (Hartmann, Eduard von.) London, 1884. 3v.

Phil 3415.32   Philosophy of the unconscious. (Hartmann, Eduard von.) London, 1884. 3v.

Phil 960.3.7   The philosophy of the Upanishads. (Deussen, P.) Edinburgh, 1906.

Phil 960.3.8   The philosophy of the Upanishads. (Deussen, P.) Edinburgh, 1908.

Phil 960.3.8.5   The philosophy of the Upanishads. (Deussen, P.) N.Y., 1966.

Phil 5767.11.5   Philosophy of the will. v.2, pt. 1. (Ricoeur, Paul.) Chicago, 1965-

Phil 8656.8.5   Philosophy of theism. (Bowne, B.P.) N.Y., 1887.

Phil 8660.5.2   Philosophy of theism. (Fraser, A.C.) N.Y., 1895.

Phil 8660.5   Philosophy of theism. 2. ed. (Fraser, A.C.) Edinburgh, 1899.

Phil 8660.5.3   Philosophy of theism. 2. series. (Fraser, A.C.) N.Y., 1896.

Phil 2020.80.2A   Philosophy of Thomas Hill Green. 2nd ed. (Fairbrother, W.H.) London, 1900.

Phil 735.250   Philosophy of value. (Makiguchi, Tsunesaburo.) Tokyo, 1964.

Phil 735.170   The philosophy of value. (Parker, D.H.) Ann Arbor, 1957.

Phil 735.91.5   Philosophy of value. Diss. (Ward, Leo Richard.) N.Y., 1930.

Phil 2340.10.97A   The philosophy of Whitehead. (Das, Ras-Vihari.) London, 1938.

Phil 2340.10.155   The philosophy of Whitehead. (Mays, Wolfe.) London, 1959.

Phil 3195.6.94.5   The philosophy of Wilhelm Dilthey. (Hodges, Herbert A.) London, 1952.

Phil 2070.25.5   The philosophy of William James, selected from his chief works. (James, William.) N.Y., 194-.

Phil 2070.25.7   The philosophy of William James, selected from his chief works. (James, William.) N.Y., 1953.

Phil 2070.84A   Philosophy of William James. (Flournoy, T.) N.Y., 1917.

Phil 2070.80A   The philosophy of William James. (Knox, H.V.) London, 1914.

Phil 3925.16.95   The philosophy of Wittgenstein. (Pitcher, George Willard.) Englewood Cliffs, 1964.

Phil 3903.5.31   The philosophy of wonder. (Verhoeven, Cornelius Wilhelmus Maria.) N.Y., 1972.

Phil 25.179   Philosophy today. N.Y. 1,1968+

Phil 185.5   Philosophy without assumptions. (Kirkman, T.P.) London, 1876.

Phil 182.62.10   Philosophy without metaphysics. (Holmes, Edmond.) London, 1930.

Phil 2405.10   La philosopie catholique en France au XIX siècle avant la renaissance Thomiste et dans son rapporrt avecelle. (Foucher, Louis.) Paris, 1955.

Phil 75.87   Philosphie; chronique annuelle. Paris. 1,1939+ 8v.

Phil 75.22   Philosphie. Antiquarists-Katalog 159/160. (Cohen, F.) Bonn, 1927.

Htn   Phil 4946.2.30F*   Philostratus. Quae supersunt omnia. Lipsiae, 1709.

Htn   Phil 4065.30*   Philothei Jordani. (Bruno, Giordano.) Paris, 1582.

Phil 6315.2.175   Philp, Howard Littleton. Freud and religious belief. London, 1956.

Phil 7069.15.40   Philpott, Anthony J. The quest for Dean Bridgman Conner. London, 1915.

Phil 187.75   Philsophie der Wirklichkeit. (Maier, Heinrich.) Tübingen, 1926-1935. 3v.

Phil 1817.9   La philsophie française en Amérique. (Riley, I.W.) Paris, n.d.

Phil 7069.27.50   Phineas speaks. (Doyle, Arthur Conan.) London, 1927.

Phil 6315.9.2   Phisiologische Praktikum für Mediziner. 2. Aufl. (Fuchs, R.F.) Wiesbaden, 1912.

Phil 5401.20F   Phobia. (Vassos, John.) N.Y., 1931.

Phil 5401.9   Les phobies. (Marrel, P.) Paris, 1895.

Phil 181.106   Phoenix and turtle. (Gilby, Thomas.) London, 1950.

Phil 6129.1   Phomson, W.H. Medical aspects of mental dicipline. N.Y., 1904.

Phil 7060.152   La photographie et l'étude des phénomènes psychiques. (Fontenay, G. de.) Paris, 1912.

Phil 5645.36   A photometric study of the perception of object color. (Henneman, R.H.) N.Y., 1935.

Phil 1802.6   Phrases of thought in English. (Carré, M.H.) Oxford, 1949.

Phil 25.20   The phreno-magnet and mirror of nature. London, 1843.

Phil 5545.10.10   Phreno-mnemotechny. (Fauvel-Gourand, F.) n.p., 1844.

Phil 5545.10   Phreno-mnemotechny. v.1-2. (Fauvel-Gourand, F.) N.Y., 1844.

Phil 5545.10.5   Phreno-mnemotechny dictionary. pt.1. (Fauvel-Gourand, F.) N.Y., 1844.

Phil 25.17.5   The phrenological almanac and physiological guide. N.Y. 1845-1854

Phil 5938.12.5   Phrenological Institution, Brighton. The boy - what will he become? Hove, 1929.

Phil 25.59   The phrenological magazine. London.

Phil 5938.8   Phrenologie in und ausserhalb Deutschland. (Struve, Gustav von.) Heidelberg, 1843.

Phil 5938.9   Phrenologische Bilder. (Scheve, G.) Leipzig, 1874.

Phil 5938.6.30   Phrenology, in connection with the study of physiognomy. (Spurzheim, Johann Gaspar.) Boston, 1833.

Phil 5923.3   Phrenology. (Davies, John D.) New Haven, 1955.

Phil 5932.2   Phrenology. (Miles, L.) Philadelphia, 1835.

Phil 5938.6.11   Phrenology. (Spurzheim, Johann Gaspar.) Boston, 1834. 2v.

Phil 5938.6.23 Phrenology. (Spurzheim, Johann Gaspar.) London, 1825?
Phil 5910.15F Pamphlet box. Phrenology. Charts, numbered I, II, IV-XXI. Descriptions in German.
Phil 5938.6.24 Phrenology. pt.1. (Spurzheim, Johann Gaspar.) London, 1826.
Phil 5938.6.10 Phrenology. v.1-2. (Spurzheim, Johann Gaspar.) Boston, 1832.
Phil 5938.6.12 Phrenology. 5th American ed. (Spurzheim, Johann Gaspar.) Boston, 1838.
Phil 5918.00.-.99 Pamphlet box. Phrenology. 19th century.
Phil 5919.00.-.99 Pamphlet box. Phrenology. 20th century.
Phil 5935.1 Phrenology and the scriptures. (Pierpont, J.) N.Y., 1850.
Phil 5910.5 Pamphlet vol. Phrenology pamphlets. London, 1821. 3 pam.
Phil 5925.3.11 Phrenology proved. (Fowler, O.S.) N.Y., 1838.
Phil 5925.3.10 Phrenology proved. (Fowler, O.S.) N.Y., 1839.
Phil 5922.1 Phrenology vindicated and antiphrenology unmasked. (Caldwell, C.) N.Y., 1838.
Phil 25.103 Phronesis; a journal for ancient philosophy. Assen. 1,1961+ 5v.
Phil 5640.37 Phusis, Maurice (pseud.). Classification universelle systématique et coordonnée des connaissances humaines. Paris, 1934.
Phil 6028.8 Phyisiognomik. (Stoehr, Coelestinus.) Coburg, 1804. 2v.
Phil 5246.45 Phyloanalysis. (Galt, William.) London, 1933.
Htn Phil 177.16* Physicae. (CJ.A.) Amsterdaam, 1645.
Phil 6131.5 Physical and moral enquiry. (Vere, James A.) London, 1778.
Phil 8626.7 Physical basis of immortality. (Blackwell, A.B.) N.Y., 1876.
Phil 5253.2 Physical basis of mental life. (Noel, R.R.) London, 1873.
Phil 5251.6.5.2 The physical basis of mind. (Lewes, G.H.) Boston, 1891.
Phil 5251.6.5 The physical basis of mind. (Lewes, G.H.) London, 1893.
Phil 6115.20 The physical basis of mind and morals. (Fitch, Michael H.) Chicago, 1914.
Phil 5440.40 The physical basis of personality. (Mottram, Vernon Henry.) Harmondsworth, 1944.
Phil 5252.23.20 The physical characteristics of attention. (MacDougall, R.) n.p., 1896-1904. 15 pam.
Phil 5398.5 Physical control of the mind. (Delgado, José M.R.) N.Y., 1969.
Phil 5374.57 The physical dimensions of consciousness. (Boring, E.G.) N.Y., 1933.
Phil 6132.40 Physical disability; a psychological approach. (Wright, B.A.) N.Y., 1960.
Phil 5890.2 Physical disability and human behavior. (McDaniel, James Winnard.) N.Y., 1969.
Phil 5640.8 A physical essay on the senses. (Le Cat, C.N.) London, 1750.
Phil 8876.5 Physical ethics. (Barratt, A.) London, 1869.
Phil 6032.1 Physical expression its modes. (Warner, F.) N.Y., 1886.
Phil 6115.33 The physical foundations of the psyche. (Fair, Charles.) Middletown, 1963.
Phil 7054.33 The physical in spiritualism. (Samson, G.W.) Philadelphia, 1880.
Phil 282.1 Physical metempiric. (Barratt, A.) London, 1883.
Phil 2280.5.91 Physical order and moral liberty. (Santayana, George.) Nashville, 1969.
Phil 525.115 The physical phenomena of mysticism. (Summers, M.) N.Y., 1950.
Phil 525.119 The physical phenomena of mysticism. (Thurston, H.) Chicago, 1952.
Phil 7069.07.10 The physical phenomena of spiritualism. (Carrington, Hereward.) Boston, 1907.
Phil 7069.08.16 The physical phenomena of spiritualism. (Carrington, Hereward.) Boston, 1908.
Phil 7069.07.12 The physical phenomena of spiritualism. 2. ed. (Carrington, Hereward.) Boston, 1908.
Phil 7069.07.13 The physical phenomena of spiritualism. 3. ed. (Carrington, Hereward.) N.Y., 1920.
Phil 7068.88.20 Physical proof of another life. (Lippitt, F.J.) Washington, 1888.
Phil 630.14.501 Physical realism. (Case, Thomas.) London, 1888.
Phil 8887.132 Physical science and ethics. (Melsen, Andreas Gerardus Maria van.) Pittsburgh, 1967.
Phil 5643.94 Physical Society of London. Report of a joint discussion on vision. London, 1933.
Phil 8644.2 Physical theory of another life. (Taylor, Isaac.) N.Y., 1836.
Phil 8644.2.2 Physical theory of another life. 2. ed. (Taylor, Isaac.) N.Y., 1836.
Phil 8644.2.3 Physical theory of another life. 3. ed. (Taylor, Isaac.) London, 1847.
Phil 178.12.40 A physician to the soul. (Dresser, H.W.) N.Y., 1908.
Phil 9495.28 The physician's answer. (Exner, M.J.) N.Y., 1913.
Phil 6314.3.2 A physician's problems. (Elam, C.) Boston, 1869.
Phil 6314.3 A physician's problems. (Elam, C.) London, 1869.
Phil 6687.1.2 Physico-physiological researches. (Reichenback, C.) N.Y., 1851.
Phil 8658.4.6 Physico-theology. (Derham, W.) London, 1714.
Phil 8658.4.7 Physico-theology. (Derham, W.) London, 1716.
Phil 8887.18.5 Physico-theology. (Morgan, T.) London, 1741.
Phil 8658.4.9 Physico-theology. 7. ed. (Derham, W.) London, 1727.
Phil 5640.5 Physics and philosophy of the senses. (Wyld, R.S.) London, 1875.
Phil 400.21 The physics of idealism. (Hinman, E.L.) Lincoln, 1906.
Phil 2805.208 The physics of Pascal. (Leavenworth, I.) N.Y., 1930.
Phil 2520.345 Physik und Metaphysik bei Descartes. (Marshall, D.J.) München? 1961.
Phil 7069.20.145 Physikalisch-mediumistische Untersuchungen. (Grunewald, F.) Pfullingen, 1920.
Phil 288.7 Die physikalische Energie und die Brücke. (Hartung, J.F.) Obersalzbrunn, 1928.
Phil 7069.25.14 Der physikalische Mediumismus. (Gulat-Wellenburg, W.K.H.) Berlin, 1925.
Phil 7069.20.301 Physikalische Phaenomene des Mediumismus. (Schrenck von Notzing, Albert.) München, 1920.
Phil 3915.69 Die physikalischen Axiome und ihre Beziehung zum Causal Princip. (Wundt, Wilhelm.) Erlangen, 1866.
Phil 194.16 Physio-Psychics. (Thayer, H.D.) Philadelphia, 1914.
Htn Phil 6045.55* Physiognomiae et chiromantiae compendium. (Cocles, B.) Argentorati, 1555.
Phil 6016.1 Physiognomica et chiromantica specialia. (Goclenius, R.) Marpurgi Cattorum, 1621.
Phil 6020.4.5 Physiognomik. (Kassner, Rudolf.) München, 1932.
Phil 6020.4.6 Physiognomik. (Kassner, Rudolf.) Wiesbaden, 1951.
Phil 6962.11 Physiognomik der Geisteskrankheiten. (Morison, A.) Leipzig, 1853.
Phil 6022.1.8 Physiognomik und Mimik. v.1-2. (Mantegazza, P.) Leipzig, 1890.
Htn Phil 6021.2.8* Physiognomische Fragmente. (Lavater, Johann Caspar.) Winterthur, 1783.
Phil 6021.2.18 Physiognomische Fragmente zur Beförderung der Menschenkenntnis und Menschenliebe. (Lavater, Johann Caspar.) Zürich, 1968- 4v.
Phil 6028.3 Physiognomische Studien. (Schack, S.) Jena, 1881.
Phil 6028.3.2 Physiognomische Studien. 2e Aufl. (Schack, S.) Jena, 1890.
Htn Phil 6025.7* Physiognomisches Cabinet für Freunde und Schüler der Menschenkenntniss. pt.1-2. Leipzig, 1777-78.
X Cg Phil 6021.2.59 The physiognomist's own book. (Lavater, Johann Caspar.) Philadelphia, 1841.
Phil 6025.4.3 Physiognomoniae collestis libri sex. (Porta, G.B.) Argentorati, 1606. 2 pam.
Phil 6025.4.5 Physiognomoniae collestis libri sex. (Porta, G.B.) Ursellis, 1601-08. 2 pam.
Phil 6021.2.10 La physiognomonie. (Lavater, Johann Caspar.) Paris, 1841.
Phil 6022.5 La physiognomonie arabe. Thèse. (Muhammad ibn Umar, Fakhr al-Din.) Paris, 1939.
Htn Phil 6012.4* Physiognomy. (Clubbe, J.) London, 1763.
Phil 6021.2.6 Physiognomy. (Lavater, Johann Caspar.) London, 1792.
Phil 6022.1.7.5 Physiognomy and expression. 3rd ed. (Mantegazza, P.) London, 1904.
Phil 6028.1.5 Physiognomy illustrated. (Simms, J.) N.Y., 1887.
Phil 6122.2 Physiologia das paixões e affeções. (Mello Moraes, Alexandre José de.) Rio de Janeiro, 1854-55. 3v.
Htn Phil 187.5* Physiologiae peripateticae. (Magirus, J.) Francofurti, 1610.
Phil 8401.18 Physiological aesthetics. (Allen, Grant.) N.Y., 1877.
Phil 5653.8 Physiological and behavioral aspects of taste. (Kare, M.R.) Chicago, 1961.
Phil 5520.63 The physiological basis of linguistic development. Diss. (Latif, Israil.) Lancaster, Pa., 1934.
Phil 5400.206 Physiological correlates of emotion. N.Y., 1970.
Phil 6117.44 Physiological psychology. (Hathaway, S.R.) N.Y., 1942.
Phil 6122.13.3 Physiological psychology. (McDougall, William.) London, 1918.
Phil 5252.82.2A Physiological psychology. 2. ed. (Morgan, Clifford Thomas.) N.Y., 1950.
Phil 5252.82.3 Physiological psychology. 3. ed. (Morgan, Clifford Thomas.) N.Y., 1965.
Phil 6672.10 Physiologie, médecine et métaphysique. (Charpignon, J.) Paris, 1848.
Phil 5374.200 Physiologie de la conscience. 4. éd. (Chauchard, P.) Paris, 1959.
Phil 6121.22.2 Physiologie de la pensée. 2. éd. (Lélut, L.F.) Paris, 1862. 2v.
Phil 5753.6 Physiologie de la volonté. (Dallemagne, Jules.) Paris, 1898.
Phil 6125.7.5 La physiologie de l'esprit. 5. éd. (Paulhan, F.) Paris, 1910.
Phil 5643.3 Physiologie der Netzhaut. (Aubert, H.R.) Breslau, 1865.
Phil 5258.46 Physiologie der Seele. (Spamer, K.) Stuttgart, 1877.
Phil 6128.36 Physiologie der Seele. (Spamer, Karl.) Stuttgart, 1877.
Phil 5761.6 Physiologie des freien Willens. (Loewenthal, N.) Leipzig, 1843.
Phil 5635.27 Physiologie des Gefühls. (Oppenheimer, Z.) Heidelberg, 1899.
X Cg Phil 5653.6 Physiologie des Geschmacks. (Brillat-Savarin, A.) Leipzig, 18- .
Phil 5643.5 Physiologie des Gesichtssinnes. (Classen, A.) Braunschweig, 1876.
Phil 5411.5.10 Die Physiologie des Hasses. (Mantegazza, P.) Jena, 1889.
Phil 5249.10 Physiologie des menschlichen Denkens. (Jessen, Peter.) Hannover, 1872.
Phil 5400.6.3 Physiologie des passions. (Letourneau, C.) Paris, 1868.
Phil 5400.6.2 Physiologie des passions. 2. éd. (Letourneau, C.) Paris, 1878.
Phil 5400.36 Physiologie des passions. 2e éd. (Alibert, J.L.) Paris, 1827. 2v.
Phil 8402.43 Physiologie des Schönen. (Byk, S.) Leipzig, 1878.
Phil 5402.3.10 Physiologie du plaisir. (Mantegazza, P.) Paris, 1886.
Phil 9480.1 Physiologie du ridicule. (Gay, M.F.S.) Bruxelles, 1833.
Phil 8881.8 Physiologie du sentiment. (Gilliot, A.) Paris, 1848. 2v.
Phil 6122.85 Physiologie du système nerveux. 3. éd. (Mueller, Johannes.) Paris, 1840. 2v.
Phil 5330.8 Physiologie et psychologie de l'attention. (Nayrac, J.P.) Paris, 1906.
Phil 5525.17 Die Physiologie und Psychologie des Lachens. (Hecker, Ewald.) Berlin, 1873.
Phil 978.49.560 Physiologisch-therapeutisches auf Grundlage der Geisteswissenschaft and zur Therapie und Hygiene. (Steiner, R.) Dornach, 1965.
Phil 5247.23.8 Physiologische oder experimentelle Psychologie am Gymnasium? (Höfler, Alois.) Wien, 1898.
Phil 5651.1 Physiologische Studien...Orientierung. (Aubert, H.R.) Tübingen, 1888.
Phil 5585.48 De physiologische tijd bij psychische processen. Proefschrift. (Jaager, Johan J. de.) Utrecht, 1865.
Phil 5643.39 Physiologische Untersuchungen über das Sehen mit zwei Augen. (Panum, P.L.) Kiel, 1858.
Htn Phil 5643.8* Physiologischen Optik. v.1 and Atlas. (Helmholtz, H.) Leipzig, 1867. 2v.
Phil 6060.16 Die physiologischen und psychologischen Beziehungen zwischen Sprache und Schrift. (Kronsbein, W.) Weinsberg, 191-?
Phil 5925.2.2 Physiology, animal and mental. (Fowler, O.S.) N.Y., 1853. 3 pam.
Phil 6117.18 Physiology and pathology of cerebral circulation. (Hill, Leonard.) London, 1896.
Phil 5821.2.3 Physiology and pathology of mind in the lower animals. (Lindsay, W.L.) Edinburgh, 1871.
Phil 6122.1.11 The physiology and pathology of the mind. (Maudsley, H.) N.Y., 1867.
Phil 6122.1.10 The physiology and pathology of the mind. 2. ed. (Maudsley, H) London, 1868.
Phil 6320.1.9 Physiology of attitude. (Kempf, E.J.) n.p., 1935.
Phil 8419.17 The physiology of beauty. (Sewell, Arthur.) London, 1931.
Phil 9495.18.5 The physiology of marriage. (Fowler, O.S.) Boston, 1860.
Phil 6122.1.14 The physiology of mind. (Maudsley, H.) N.Y., 1872.
Phil 6122.1.13 The physiology of mind. (Maudsley, H.) N.Y., 1878.
Phil 6122.1.15 The physiology of mind. 3d ed. pt.1. (Maudsley, H.) London, 1876.

Phil 6115.27   Physiology of the nervous system. (Fulton, J.F.) London, 1938.

Phil 6115.27.5   Physiology of the nervous system. (Fulton, J.F.) London, 1939.

Phil 6122.14   Physiology of the nervous system. (Morat, J.P.) Chicago, 1906.

VPhil 6115.27.7   Physiology of the nervous system. 2. ed. (Fulton, J.F.) London, 1943.

Phil 6115.27.15   Physiology of the nervous system. 3. ed. (Fulton, J.F.) N.Y., 1949.

Phil 5640.3.5   The physiology of the senses. (M'Kendrick, J.G.) N.Y., 1907.

Phil 490.1.6   Physiology of the soul and instinct. N.Y., 1872.

Phil 490.1.5   Physiology of the soul and instinct. N.Y., 1872.

Phil 5640.38   Physiology of the special senses. (Greenwood, Major.) London, 1910.

Phil 6022.1   La physionomie. (Mantegazza, P.) Paris, 1885.

Phil 6028.3.10   La physionomie chez l'homme. (Schack, S.) Paris, 1887.

Phil 6017.1.2   Physionomie et caractère. (Hartenberg, Paul.) Paris, 1911.

Htn   Phil 6025.4.25*   La physionomie humaine. (Porta, G.B.) Rouen, 1655.

Phil 6021.2.15   Physionomie portative. (Lavater, Johann Caspar.) Paris, 1806. 2v.

Phil 6021.5   La physionomie raisonnée. (La Bellière, C. de.) Lyon, 1681.

Phil 6120.8.7   Physique and character. (Kretschmer, E.) N.Y., 1926.

Phil 6120.8.10   Physique and character. 2d ed. (Kretschmer, E.) N.Y., 1970.

Phil 5255.38   Physique and intellect. (Paterson, D.G.) N.Y., 1930.

Phil 801.23.15   La physique du vingtième siècle et la philosophie. (Brunschvicg, L.) Paris, 1936.

Phil 3503.11   Physique et métaphysique Kantiennes. 1. éd. (Vuillemin, Jules.) Paris, 1955.

Phil 3480.101.2   Physische Geographie. (Kant, Immanuel.) Leipzig, 1803-07. 2v.

Htn   Phil 3480.101*   Physische Geographie. v.1-2. (Kant, Immanuel.) Königsberg, 1802.

Phil 5255.51.8   Piaget, J. La psychologie de l'intelligence. 3. ed. Paris, 1952.

Phil 346.17.5   Piaget, Jean. Biologie et connaissance, essai sur les relations entre les régulations organiques et les processus cognitifs. Paris, 1967.

Phil 5865.5.22   Piaget, Jean. The child's conception of time. London, 1969.

Phil 5066.36.20   Piaget, Jean. Classes, relations et nombres. Paris, 1942.

Phil 5066.36.10   Piaget, Jean. Essai sur les transformations des óperations logiques. 1. ed. Paris, 1952.

Phil 5865.5.20   Piaget, Jean. Genetic epistomology. N.Y., 1970.

Phil 5465.150   Piaget, Jean. L'image mentale chez l'enfant, étude sur le développement. Paris, 1966.

Phil 190.106.5   Piaget, Jean. Insights and illusions of philosophy. Translation. 1st American ed. N.Y., 1971.

Phil 346.17   Piaget, Jean. Introduction à l'épistémologie génétique. 1. éd. Paris, 1950. 3v.

Phil 5066.36.15   Piaget, Jean. Logic and psychology. Manchester, Eng., 1953.

Phil 5585.195   Piaget, Jean. Les mécanismes perceptifs. Paris, 1961.

Phil 5585.195.5   Piaget, Jean. The mechanisms of perception. London, 1969.

Phil 5545.242   Piaget, Jean. Mémoire et intelligence. Paris, 1968.

Phil 5465.151   Piaget, Jean. Mental imagery in the child; a study of the development of imaginal representation. London, 1971.

Phil 5865.5.9   Piaget, Jean. On the development of memory and identity. Worcester, 1968.

Phil 5865.5.4   Piaget, Jean. La psychologie de l'enfant. Paris, 1966.

Phil 5875.175   Piaget, Jean. Psychologie et épistémologie. Paris, 1970.

Phil 5255.51   Piaget, Jean. The psychology of intelligence. N.Y., 1950.

Phil 5865.5.5   Piaget, Jean. The psychology of the child. N.Y., 1969.

Phil 190.106   Piaget, Jean. Sagesse et illusions de la philosophie. Paris, 1965.

Phil 5865.5.6   Piaget, Jean. Six études de psychologie. Genève, 1964.

Phil 5865.5.7   Piaget, Jean. Six psychological studies. N.Y., 1967.

Phil 1750.830.8   Piaget, Jean. Le structuralisme. 3e éd. Paris, 1968.

Phil 5066.36   Piaget, Jean. Traité de logique. Paris, 1949.

Phil 5865.5.30   Piaget: a practical consideration. 1st ed. (Helmore, Geoffrey Anthony.) N.Y., 1969.

Phil 5865.5.25   Piaget and knowledge. (Furth, Hans G.) Englewood Cliffs, 1969.

Phil 3450.11.355   Piana, G. Esistenza e storia negli inediti di Husserl. Milano, 1965.

Phil 1750.783   Piana, Giovanni. I problemi della fenomenologia. 1. ed. Milano, 1966.

Phil 2070.140   Piane, A.L. delle. William James. Montevideo, 1943.

Phil 4769.1.115   Piaskovskii, N.Ia. Kak myslil Vladimir Solov'ev o voskresenie. Moskva, 1901.

Phil 8640.7.2   Piat, A. La destinée de l'homme. 2. éd. Paris, 1912.

Phil 3497.6   Piat, C. L'idée ou Critique du Kantisme. Paris, n.d.

Phil 3552.121   Piat, C. Leibniz. Paris, 1915.

Phil 575.13   Piat, C. La personne humaine. Paris, 1897.

Phil 575.13.2   Piat, C. La personne humaine. 2e éd. Paris, 1913.

Phil 8965.8   Piat, Clodius. Idées directrices de la morale chrétienne. Paris, 1917.

Phil 190.28   Piat, Clodius. Insuffisance des philosophies de l'intuition. Paris, 1908.

Phil 5255.14   Piat, Clodius. L'intellect actif. Thèse. Paris, 1890.

Phil 346.5   Piat, Clodius. L'intelligence et la vie. Paris, 1915.

Phil 5765.6   Piat, Clodius. La liberté. Paris, 1894-95. 2v.

Phil 9245.32   Piat, Clodius. La morale du bonheur. Paris, 1910.

Phil 960.240   Piatigorskii, A.M. Materialy po istorii indiiskoi filosofii. Moskva, 1962.

Phil 4195.105   Pic de la Mirandole, 1463-94. (Gautier-Vignal, L.) Paris, 1937.

Phil 4195.82   Pic de la Mirandole en France, 1485-1488. (Dorez, Léon.) Paris, 1897.

Phil 2520.192   Picard, Émile. Une édition nouvelle du discours de la méthode de Descartes. Paris, 1934.

Phil 2805.190   Picard, Émile. Pascal mathématicien et physicien. Paris, 1923.

Phil 5400.63   Picard, Ernest. Problème de la vie affective. Paris, 1926.

Phil 735.77   Picard, Maurice. Values immediate and contributory and their interrelation. N.Y., 1920.

Phil 8670.17.2   Picard, Max. The flight from God. London, 1951.

Phil 8670.17   Picard, Max. Die Flucht vor Gott. 2. Aufl. Erlenbach, 1935.

Phil 6025.9.10   Picard, Max. Die Grenzen der Physiognomik; mit 30 Bildtafeln. Erlenbach, 1937.

Phil 6025.9.5   Picard, Max. The human face. London, 1931.

Phil 6025.9   Picard, Max. Das Menschengesicht. 2. Aufl. München, 1929.

Phil 9560.10.20   Picard, Max. The world of silence. London, 1948.

Phil 2840.84   Picard, Roger. La philosophie sociale de Renouvier. Paris, 1908.

Phil 1520.2.5   Picavet, F. Essais sur l'histoire générale et comparée des theologies et des philosophies médiévales. Paris, 1913.

Phil 1520.2   Picavet, F. Histoire...des philosophies médiévales. Paris, 1905.

Phil 2415.4   Picavet, F. Les idealogues. Paris, 1891.

Phil 8416.35   Piccardt, K.L. Het wezen der kunst. Amsterdam, 1937.

Phil 7069.68.55   Piccardt, Karel. De bovenzinnelijke wereld. Amsterdam, 1968.

Phil 1750.585   Piccardt, Karel. Wijsbegeerte in verval. Amsterdam, 1959.

Phil 190.40.2   Piccoli, V. Introduzione alla filosofia. 2a ed. Milano, 1924.

Phil 4015.2   Piccoli, V. Storia della filosofia italiano. Torino, 1924.

Phil 4115.86.5   Piccoli, Valentino. L'estetica di Vincenzo Gioberti. Milano, 1917.

Phil 4115.86   Piccoli, Valentino. Vincenzo Gioberti. Roma, 1923.

Phil 103.4   Piccolo dizionario di coltura filosofica e scientifica. (Semprini, G.) Milano, 1931.

Phil 5190.4.15F   Piccolomineus, F. De rerum definitionibus liber unus. Venetiis, 1600.

Phil 8890.34.5   Piccolomineus, F. Universa philosophia de moribus. Francofurti, 1627.

Htn   Phil 8890.35F*   Piccolomineus, F. Universa philosophia de moribus. Venetiis, 1583.

Htn   Phil 296.10*   Piccolomini, A. Della filosofia naturale. Venetia, 1585. 2v.

Htn   Phil 8890.22.10*   Piccolomini, A. Della institutione di tutta la vita. Vinegia, 1552.

Htn   Phil 8890.21*   Piccolomini, A. Della institutione morale, libri XII. Venetia, 1560. (Transferred to Houghton Library 31/1/72)

Htn   Phil 8890.21.5*   Piccolomini, A. Della institutione morale, libri XII. Venetia, 1594. (Transferred to Houghton Library 31/1/72)

Htn   Phil 8890.22*   Piccolomini, A. Della institutione morale. Venetia, 1575. (Transferred to Houghton Library 31/1/72)

Htn   Phil 5055.19*   Piccolomini, A. L'instrumento de la filosofia. Roma, 1561.

Phil 190.41   Pichard, P. Doctrine du réel. Paris, 1889.

Phil 3552.119   Pichler, A. Die Theologie des Leibniz. München, 1869. 2v.

Phil 346.4   Pichler, H. Möglichkeit und Widerspruschlosigkeit. Leipzig, 1912.

Phil 346.4.5   Pichler, H. Uber die Erkennbarkeit. Wien, 1909.

Phil 730.34   Pichler, Hans. Ganzheit und Gemeinschaft. Wiesbaden, 1967.

Phil 8890.36   Pichler, Hans. Grundzüge einer Ethik. Graz, 1919.

Phil 3552.129   Pichler, Hans. Leibniz. Graz, 1919.

Phil 5055.18.5   Pichler, Hans. Die Logik der Seele. Erfurt, 1927.

Phil 5055.18   Pichler, Hans. Zur Logik der Gemeinschaft. Tübingen, 1924.

Phil 974.3.10   Picht, C.S. Das literarische Lebenswerk Rudolf Steiners. Dornach, 1926.

Phil 3850.27.195   Picht, Werner. Albert Schweitzer. Hamburg, 1960.

Phil 3850.27.197   Picht, Werner. The life and thought of Albert Schweitzer. N.Y., 1964.

Phil 6400.12   Pick, A. Uber das Sprachverständnis. Leipzig, 1909.

Phil 6965.10   Pick, Arnold. Studien über motorische Apraxie. Leipzig, 1905.

Phil 5545.21.5   Pick, E. Lectures on memory culture. N.Y., 1899.

Phil 5545.21   Pick, E. Memory and its doctors. London, 1888.

Phil 8640.12   Pickford, M. My rendezvous with life. N.Y., 1935.

Phil 6125.24.4   Pickford, Mary. Why not try God? N.Y., 1934.

Phil 2415.7   Pickman, Edward M. Collapse of the scholastic hierarchy in 17th century France. Boston, 1931.

Phil 705.74   Piclin, Michel. La notion de transcendance; son sens, son évolution. Paris, 1969.

Phil 2750.11.230   Pico, Cesar E. Carta a Jacques Maritain sobre la colaboración de los católicos con los movimientos de tipo fascista. Buenos Aires, 1937.

Phil 4196.30   Pico, G.F. Le epistole de imitation di G. Pico. Firenze, 1954.

Htn   Phil 4196.5*   Pico, G.F. Opera. n.p., 1508.

Phil 4195.10   Pico della Mirandola, Giovanni. Ausgewählte Schriften. Jena, 1905.

Htn   Phil 4195.30*   Pico della Mirandola, Giovanni. Conclusiones nongentae. n.p., 1532.

Phil 4195.37   Pico della Mirandola, Giovanni. De dignitate hominis. Bad Homburg, 1968.

Phil 4195.36.5   Pico della Mirandola, Giovanni. La dignità dell'uomo. Matera, 1963.

Phil 4195.36.2   Pico della Mirandola, Giovanni. Dignità dell'uomo. 2. ed. Firenze, 1943.

Phil 4195.36   Pico della Mirandola, Giovanni. Dignità dell'uomo. 3. ed. Firenze, 1945.

Phil 4195.34   Pico della Mirandola, Giovanni. Disputationes adversus astrologiam divinatricem. Firenze, 1946-52. 2v.

Phil 4195.40.5   Pico della Mirandola, Giovanni. Ioannis Pici Mirandulae...vita. Modena, 1963.

Phil 4195.7F   Pico della Mirandola, Giovanni. Joannes Pieus Mirandulanus Opera omnia. Torino, 1971.

Phil 4195.39   Pico della Mirandola, Giovanni. On the dignity of man. Indianapolis, 1965.

Htn   Phil 4195.5*   Pico della Mirandola, Giovanni. Opera omnia. Basileae, 1573. 2v.

Phil 4195.3F   Pico della Mirandola, Giovanni. Opera omnia. Reggio, 1506.

Phil 4195.6F   Pico della Mirandola, Giovanni. Opera quae extant omnia. Basileae, 1601.

Phil 4195.38   Pico della Mirandola, Giovanni. Oration on the dignity of man. Chicago, 1956.

Phil 4195.32   Pico della Mirandola, Giovanni. Le sette sposizioni. Pescia, 1555.

Htn   Phil 1135.26F*   Picodella Mirandola, G.F. Examen vanitatis doctrinae gentium et veritatis Christianae disciplinae. Mirandulae, 1520.

Phil 8965.6   Pictet, Benedict. Morale chrétienne. Genève, 1710. 2v.

Phil 490.3   Pictet, Raoul. Étude critique du matérialisme et du spiritualisme. Genève, 1897.

Phil 3835.2   Picton, Allanson. Spinoza, handbook to the Ethics. London, 1907.

Phil 190.12   Picton, J.A. The mystery of matter. London, 1873.

Phil 8685.11.5   Picton, J.A. Pantheism, its story and significance. London, 1905.

Phil 8685.11   Picton, J.A. The religion of the universe. London, 1904.

Phil 6990.45   A pictorial history of Lourdes. (Boyle, J.L.) Philadelphia, 1940.

Phil 817.28F   Pictorial history of philosophy. (Runes, Dagobert.) N.Y., 1965.

Phil 5058.20   Picture logic. (Swinburne, A.J.) London, 1881.

Htn Phil 2340.3.31*   The picture of love. 4th ed .v.1-2. (Waring, Robert.) London, 1744.

Htn Phil 2175.2.35*   The picture of love unveil'd. 4. ed. (Norris, John.) London, 1744.

Phil 8434.4   The picturesque. (Hussey, C.) London, 1927.

Phil 5525.38.2   Piddington, Ralph. The psychology of laughter. 2. ed. N.Y., 1963.

Phil 6025.1   Piderit, Leo. Mimik und Physiognomik. Detmold, 1886.

Phil 6125.1   Piderit, T. Gehirn und Geist. Leipzig, 1868.

Phil 5403.2   Piderit, Theodor. Die Theorie des Glücks. Leipzig, 1867.

Phil 5876.10   Piel, Jacques. Analyse des formes prises par la socialité des adolescent dans le cadre de leurs loisis. Bruxelles, 1968.

Phil 5255.60   Piela, Franz. Die Psychologie. Köln, 1959.

Phil 8416.6   Piemonteal, Filippo. Problemi di filosofia dell'arte. Torino, 1952.

Phil 8416.19   Piemontese, F. L'intelligenza nell'arte. Milano, 1955.

Phil 4210.220   Piemontese, Filippo. La dottrina del sentimento fondamentale nella filosofia di A. Rosmini. Milano, 1966.

Phil 6125.19   Pieper, Gustav. Das geistige Heilverfahren. Magdeburg, 1929.

Phil 9450.26   Pieper, J. Uber del Gerechtigkeit. München, 1953.

Phil 9560.66   Pieper, Josef. Auskunft über die Tugenden. Zürich, 1970.

Phil 3745.14.15   Pieper, Josef. Belief and faith. N.Y., 1963.

Phil 8612.68.5   Pieper, Josef. Death and immortality. N.Y., 1969.

Phil 8965.13.15   Pieper, Josef. The four cardinal virtues. N.Y., 1965.

Phil 3745.14.5   Pieper, Josef. Glück und Kontemplation. 1. Aufl. München, 1957.

Phil 8965.13.10   Pieper, Josef. Justice. London, 1957.

Phil 3745.14   Pieper, Josef. Kleines Lesebuch von den Tugenden des menschlichen Herzens. 5. Aufl. München, 1957.

Phil 190.80.6   Pieper, Josef. Leisure, the basis of culture. N.Y., 1964.

Phil 8965.13.20   Pieper, Josef. Missbrauch der Sprache, Missbrauch der Macht. Zürich, 1970.

Phil 190.80   Pieper, Josef. Musse und Kult. München, 1949.

Phil 8965.13   Pieper, Josef. Prudence. N.Y., 1959.

Phil 8890.62   Pieper, Josef. Reality and the good. Chicago, 1967.

Phil 1520.5.10   Pieper, Josef. Scholasticism. N.Y., 1960.

Phil 1520.5.5   Pieper, Josef. Scholastik. München, 1960.

Phil 8612.68   Pieper, Josef. Tod und Vusterblichkeit. München, 1968.

Phil 8965.13.5   Pieper, Josef. Über die Gerechtigkeit. 1. Aufl. München, 1953.

Phil 190.80.25   Pieper, Josef. Verteidigungsrede für die Philosophie. München, 1966.

Phil 8965.13.15.5   Pieper, Josef. Das Viergespann; Klugheit, Gerechtigkeit, Tapferkeit, Mass. München, 1964.

Phil 1520.5   Pieper, Josef. Wahrheit der Dinge. München, 1947.

Phil 190.80.10   Pieper, Josef. Was heisst akademisch? München, 1952.

Phil 190.80.15   Pieper, Josef. Was heisst philosophieren? 3. Aufl. München, 1956.

Phil 190.80.20   Pieper, Josef. Die Wirklichkeit und das Gute. 6. Aufl. München, 1956.

Phil 5585.12   Pierce, A.H. Studies in auditory and visual space perception. N.Y., 1901.

Phil 7054.88   Pierce, A.P. Extracts from unpublished volumes. Boston, 1868.

Phil 5000.5   Pierce, C.S. Logic of relatives. Cambridge, 1870.

Phil 5055.1   Pierce, C.S. Logical papers. n.p., n.d

Htn Phil 5055.1.15*   Pierce, C.S. Papers on logic. n.p., 1867?

Phil 5055.1.5A   Pierce, C.S. Studies in logic. Boston, 1883.

Htn Phil 5055.1.9*   Pierce, C.S. Three papers on logic. n.p., 1867?

Phil 7054.87   Pierce, David. The revelation...twenty-one days' entrancement. Bangor, 1857.

Phil 9035.39   Pierce, Edgar. The philosophy of character. Cambridge, 1924.

Phil 7082.64.5   Pierce, Frederick. Dreams and personality. N.Y., 1931.

Phil 7140.132   Pierce, Frederick. Mobilizing the mid-brain. N.Y., 1924.

Phil 5722.9   Pierce, Frederick. Our unconscious mind and how to use it. N.Y., 1922.

Phil 6125.21   Pierce, S.W. The layman looks at doctors. N.Y., 1929.

Phil 8595.14   Piercy, B.H. Facts and fancies. London, 1913.

Phil 8595.14.5   Piercy, B.H. Superstition and common sense. London, 1912.

Phil 258.5   Pieretti, Antonio. Analisi linguistica e metafisica. Milano, 1968.

Phil 8965.16   Piergiovanni, Enzo. La metamorfosi dell'etica medioevale. Bologna, 1967.

Phil 3850.27.145   Pierhal, Jean. Albert Schweitzer. N.Y., 1957.

Phil 3425.450   Piérola, R.A. Hegel y la estatica. Tucumán, 1956.

Phil 182.67.80   Pierola, Raul A. Apuntes dispersos sobre fenomenologia. Santa Fe, 1943.

Phil 7080.25   Pieron, H. Le problème physiologique du sommeil. Paris, 1912.

Phil 5640.43   Piéron, Henri. Aux sources de la connaissance la sensation. 3. éd. Paris, 1945.

Phil 6125.18   Piéron, Henri. Le cerveau et la pensée. Paris, 1923.

Phil 5643.98   Piéron, Henri. La connaissance sensorielle et les problèmes de la vision. Paris, 1936.

Phil 5825.9   Piéron, Henri. De l'actinie à l'homme. Paris, 1958. 2v.

Phil 5255.18.15   Piéron, Henri. Le développment mental et l'intelligence. Paris, 1929.

Phil 5255.18.10   Piéron, Henri. Principles of experimental psychology. London, 1929.

Phil 5255.18.20   Piéron, Henri. Les problémes fondamentaux de la psychophysique dans la science actuelle. Paris, 1951.

Phil 5255.18.5   Piéron, Henri. Psychologie experimentale. Paris, 1927.

Phil 5640.130.2   Piéron, Henri. La sensation. 2. éd. Paris, 1957.

Phil 5648.19   Piéron, Henri. Les sensibilités cutanées. v.1-3. Paris, 1928-32.

Phil 6125.18.5   Piéron, Henri. Thought and the brain. London, 1927.

Phil 5850.310   Piéron, Henri. Traité de psychologie appliquée. Paris, 1949- 7v.

Phil 5643.123   Piéron, Henri. La vision en lumière intermittente. Paris, 1961.

Phil 5204.12.2   Piéron, Henri. Vocabulaire de la psychologie. 2. éd. Paris, 1957.

Phil 5204.12.3   Piéron, Henri. Vocabulaire de la psychologie. 3. éd. Paris, 1963.

Phil 5935.1   Pierpont, J. Phrenology and the scriptures. N.Y., 1850.

Phil 2450.81.5A   Pierre Bayle. (Dibon, Paul.) Amsterdam, 1959.

Phil 2450.81   Pierre Bayle. (Feuerback, L.A.) Ansbach, 1838.

Phil 2450.81.2   Pierre Bayle. 2. Aufl. (Feuerback, L.A.) Leipzig, 1848.

Phil 2515.2.95   Pierre Chanet; une psychologie de l'instinct. Thèse. (Piohetta, J.B.) Paris, 1937.

Phil 2651.83   Pierre-Daniel Huet, 1630-1721. (Tolmer, L.) Bayeux, 1949.

Phil 2610.84   Pierre Gassendi. Thèse. (Andrieux, L.) Paris, 1927.

Phil 2725.4.81   Pierre Leroux. (Thomas, P. F.) Paris, 1904.

Phil 2725.4.85   Pierre Leroux and his philosophy in relation to literature. (Evans, David O.) n.p., 1929.

Phil 2725.4.87   Pierre Leroux et ses oeuvres. (Raillard, Célestin.) Chateauroux, 1899.

Phil 2905.1.315   Pierre Teilhard de Chardin. (Colomer, Eusebi.) Barcelona, 1961.

Phil 2905.1.82   Pierre Teilhard de Chardin. (Cristiani, Léon.) London, 1960.

Phil 2905.1.210   Pierre Teilhard de Chardin. (Onimus, J.) Paris, 1963.

Phil 2905.1.335   Pierre Teilhard de Chardin. 2. ed. (Ormea, Ferdinando.) Torino, 1964.

Phil 2905.1.575   Pierre Teilhard de Chardin in Selbstzeugnissen und Bilddokumenten. (Hemkben, Johannes.) Reinbek, 1966.

Phil 2905.1.90   Pierre Teilhard de Chardin tel que je l'ai connu. (Leroy, Pierre.) Paris, 1958.

Phil 2905.1.435   Pierre Teilhard de Chardin y otros ensayos. (Briones Toledo, Hernán.) Santiago de Chile, 1966.

Phil 5414.15A   Piers, Gerhart. Shame and guilt. Springfield, Ill., 1953.

Phil 2725.35.90   Piersol, Wesley. La valeur dans la philosophie de Louis Lavelle. Paris, 1959.

Phil 8416.31   Pierson, A. Schöhiedszon en levenswijsheid. Arnhem, 1886.

Phil 4803.281.80   Pierwsze systemy semantyki Leona Chwistka. (Pasenkiewicz, Kazimierz.) Krakow, 1961.

Phil 4800.8   Piérwsze zasady krytyki powszechnéj. v.1-2. (Tyszyński, Aleksander.) Warszawa, 1870.

Phil 1107.5   I piesocratici; saggi. (Covotti, Aurelio.) Napoli, 1934.

Phil 8610.804   Piestre, J.L. Les crimes de la philosophie. Paris, 1804.

Phil 5590.526   Pieter, Józef. Wstęp do nauki o osobowości. Katowice, 1948.

Phil 5627.231.2   Pietismus. 2. Aufl. (Pauls, Theodor.) Frankfurt, 1931.

Phil 4170.11.80   Pietrangeli, Alfonso. Filippo Maxi e il suo neocriticismo. Padova, 1962.

Phil 4080.10.88   Pietro Ceretti. (Alemanni, V.) Milano, 1904.

Phil 4115.106   Pietro Luciani e il giobertismo. (Crescenzo, G. de.) Napoli, 1960.

Phil 4200.1.83   Pietro Pomponazzi. (Ardigò, R.) Mantova, 1869.

Phil 4200.1.82   Pietro Pomponazzi. (Fiorentino, F.) Firenze, 1868.

Phil 665.39   Pietropaolo, F. L'anima nel mondo greco e romano nel medio evo e nella filosofia moderna. Roma, 1898.

Phil 6685.8   Pigeaire, Jules. Puissance de l'électricité animale. Paris, 1839.

Phil 4120.4.50   Piglianu, A. Giovanni Gentile. Sassari, 1953.

Phil 4225.8.90   Pignoloni, Emilio. Genesi e sviluppo del rosminianesimo nel pensiero di Michele F. Sciacca. Milano, 1964. 2v.

Phil 190.85   Piguet, Jean C. L'oeuvre de philosophie. Neuchâtel, 1960.

Phil 2825.25   Piguet, Jean Claude. De l'esthétique à la métaphysique. La Haye, 1959.

Phil 5360.18   Pikas, Anatol. Abstraction and concept formation. Cambridge, 1944.

Phil 8685.13   Pike, G.R. The divine drama; the manifestation of God. N.Y., 1899.

Phil 8965.15   Pike, James A. The next day. 1st ed. Garden City, 1959.

Phil 7055.310   Pike, James Albert. The other side. Garden City, 1968.

Phil 5520.140   Pike, Kenneth Lee. Language in relation to a unified theory of the structure of human behavior. Glendale, Calif., 1954.

Phil 5520.140.2   Pike, Kenneth Lee. Language in relation to a unified theory of the structure of human behavior. 2. ed. The Hague, 1967.

Phil 8620.53   Pike, Nelson. God and evil. Englewood Cliffs, 1764.

Phil 8670.22   Pike, Nelson craft. God and timelessness. N.Y., 1970.

Phil 5545.80   Pike, Robert, Jr. Mnemonics applied to acquisition of knowledge. Boston, 1844.

Phil 5545.81   Pike, Robert. Mnemonics. Boston, 1848.

Phil 8705.9   Pike, S. Philosopha sacra: or The principles of natural philosophy. London, 1753.

Phil 490.6   Pikler, G. Das Grundgesetz alles neuro-psychologischen Lebens. Leipzig, 1900.

Phil 5255.11.9   Pikler, Gyula. Das Beharren und die Gegensätzlichkeit des Erlebens. Stuttgart, 1908.

Phil 5640.125.7   Pikler, Gyula. Hypothesenfreie Theorie der Gegenfarben. Leipzig, 1919.

VPhil 5255.11.10   Pikler, Gyula. A lektan alapelvei. Budapest, 1909.

Phil 5640.125.5   Pikler, Gyula. Sinnesphysiologische Untersuchungen. Leipzig, 1917.

Phil 5374.17.5   Pikler, Gyula. Die Stelle des Bewusstseins in der Natur. Leipzig, 1910.

Phil 5255.11   Pikler, Gyula. The psychology of belief in objective existence. pt.1. London, 1890.

Phil 5640.125.10   Pikler, Gyula. Theorie der Empfindungsqualität als Abbildes des Reizes. Leipzig, 1922.

Phil 5640.125.9   Pikler, Gyula. Theorie der Empfindungsstärke und Insbesondere des Weberschen Gesetzes. Leipzig, 1920.

Phil 5640.125.8   Pikler, Gyula. Theorie der Konsonanz und Dissonanz. Leipzig, 1919.

Phil 5640.125.15   Pikler, Gyula. Theorie des Gedächtnisses. Leipzig, 1926.

Phil 5255.11.5   Pikler, Gyula. Zwei Vorträge über dynamische Psychologie. Leipzig, 1908.

Phil 3585.10.91   Pikler, Julius. Uber Theodor Lipps' Versuch einer Theorie des Willens. Leipzig, 1908.

Phil 5255.64   Pikunas, J. Psychology of human development. N.Y., 1961.

Phil 8416.40   Pilar, Ivo. Secesija. Zagreb, 1898.

Phil 8640.13   Pilcher, C.V. The hereafter in Jewish and Christian thought. London, 1940.

Phil 6990.3.85   Pilerinage spirituel à Lourdes. (Combes, André.) Paris, 1959.

Phil 8878.35   The pilgrim of the infinite. (Davies, William.) London, 1894.

Phil 7054.62   Pilgrimage of Thos. Paine. (Hammond, Charles.) N.Y., 1852.

Phil 8580.16   Pilgrims of the lonely road. (Atkins, Gaius G.) N.Y., 1913.

Phil 270.132   Pilipenko, Nikolai V. Neobkhodimost' i sluchainost'. Moskva, 1965.

Htn Phil 9355.1.5*   Pilkington, M. A mirror for the female sex. Hartford, 1799.

Phil 9355.1.5   Pilkington, M. A mirror for the female sex. London, 1798.

Phil 9355.1   Pilkington, M. A mirror for the female sex. London, 1804.

Phil 8705.18   Pilkington, Roger. World without end. London, 1961.

Phil 2880.2.82   Pillon, F. La philosophie de Charles Secrétan. Paris, 1898.

Phil 5330.7.7   Pillsbury, W.B. Attention. London, 1921.

Phil 5255.7.5   Pillsbury, W.B. The essentials of psychology. N.Y., 1915.

Phil 5255.7.8 Pillsbury, W.B. The essentials of psychology. N.Y., 1925.
Phil 5255.7 Pillsbury, W.B. Fundamentals of psychology. N.Y., 1916.
Phil 5255.7.15 Pillsbury, W.B. Handbook of general psychology. N.Y., 1942.
Phil 5225.1A Pillsbury, W.B. The history of psychology. N.Y., 1929.
Phil 5620.7 Pillsbury, W.B. The psychology of reasoning. N.Y., 1910.
Phil 6325.12 Pillsbury, Walter B. An elementary psychology of the abnormal. 1. ed. N.Y., 1932.
Phil 5520.51A Pillsbury, Walter B. The psychology of language. N.Y., 1928.
Phil 8416.33 Pilo, Mario. Estetica lexioni sur bello. 2. ed. Milano, 1921.
Phil 3120.30.170 Pilosof, Nelson. Martin Buber, profeta del diálogo. Montevideo, 1965.
Phil 5330.1.15 Pilzecker, A. Die Lehre von der sinnlichen Aufmerksamkeit. Inaug. Diss. München, 1889.
Phil 815.6A Pim, Herbert M. Short history of Celtic philosophy. Dundalk, 1920.
Phil 9175.6 Pimentel Castello-Branco, B.B. Regimento saudavel. Lisboa, 1750.
Phil 8416.39 Pimienta, Gustave. Évidences. Paris, 1965.
Phil 978.70 Pinchin, Edith F. The bridge of the gods in Gaelic mythology. London, 1934.
Phil 8965.18 Pinckaers, Servais. Le renouveau de la morale. Tournai, 1964.
Phil 6965.3 Pinel, Philippe. Traité médico-philosophique sur l'aliénation mentale. Paris, 1809.
Phil 6965.3.5 Pinel, Philippe. Treatise on insanity. Sheffield, 1806.
Phil 6965.3.80 Pamphlet box. Pinel, Philippe.
Phil 4958.205 Piñera Llera, Humberto. Panorama de la filosofía cubana. Washington, 1960.
Phil 1020.19.5 Pines, Salomon. Beiträge zur islamischen Atomenlehre. Berlin, 1936.
Phil 1020.19 Pines, Salomon. Beiträge zur islamischen Atomenlehre. Inaug Diss. Berlin, 1936.
Phil 1715.10 Pinilla, Antonio. El filósofo en la sociedad actual. Lima, 1959.
Phil 6319.1.250 Pintacuda, Luigi. La psicologia religiosa di Karl Jung. Roma, 1965.
Phil 2415.12A Pintard, René. La libertinage érudit dans la première mortié du XVII siècle. v.1-2. Paris, 1943.
Phil 5890.3.1 Pintner, Rudolf. The psychology of the physically handicapped. N.Y., 1945.
Phil 8670.19 Pinto, Raphael de Souza. Deus, pensamento e universo. Curitiba, 1959.
Phil 6953.10 Pintores e poetas de Rilhafolles. (Dantas, J.) Liboa, 1900.
Phil 7054.43.20 Pioda, Alfredo. Memorabilia. Bellinzona, 1891.
Phil 5255.22 Pioger, J. La vie et la pensée. Paris, 1893.
Phil 2515.2.95 Piohetta, J.B. Pierre Chanet; une psychologie de l'instinct. Thèse. Paris, 1937.
Phil 5055.10 Piola, Giuseppe. Elementi di logica guiridica. Roma, 1894.
Phil 1817.4 Pioneer humanists. (Robertson, J.M.) London, 1907.
Phil 1930.17.80 A pioneer of the new psychology. (Irvine, E.F.) Chatham, 1963.
Phil 8110.10 Pionjärer och fullföjare. (Brunius, Teddy.) Stockholm, 1952.
Phil 3425.554 Piontkovskii, A.A. Hegels Lehre über Staat und Recht und seine Strafrechtstheorie. Berlin, 1960.
Phil 3425.554.5 Piontkovskii, A.A. Uchenie Gegelia o prave i gosudarstve i ego ugolovno-pravovaia teoriia. Moskva, 1963.
Phil 5850.311 Piorkowski, C. Beiträge zur psychologischen Methodologie der wirtschaftlichen Berufseignung. Leipzig, 1915.
Phil 5593.57.5 Piotrowski, Z. Perceptanalysis. N.Y., 1957.
Phil 8695.11 The pious scientist. (Feibleman, James.) N.Y., 1958.
Phil 1715.16 Piovani, Pietro. Conoscenza storica e coscienza morale. Napoli, 1966.
Phil 4210.175 Piovani, Pietro. La teodicea sociale di Rosmini. Padova, 1957.
Phil 4897.10.5 Piovesana, Gino K. Contemporary Japanese philosophical thought. N.Y., 1969.
Phil 4897.10 Piovesana, Gino K. Recent Japanese philosophical thought, 1862-1962. Tokyo, 1963.
Phil 197.3.15 Piozzi, H.L.T. (Mrs.). Mrs. Piozzi and Isaac Watts. London, 1934.
Phil 7069.30.25 Piper, Alta L. Life and work of Mrs. Piper. London, 1929.
Phil 346.10 Piper, H. Prinzipielle Grundlagen. Göttingen, 1916.
Phil 165.22 Piper, K. Olfener Horizont. München, 1953.
Phil 8965.12 Piper, Otto. Die Grundlagen der evangelischen Ethik. Gütersloh, 1928.
Phil 7069.17.31.15 Piper, Otto. Der Spuk. 2. Aufl. München, 1922.
Phil 3475.3.150 Piper, R.C. Karl Jaspers. München, 1958.
Phil 100.2 Piquet, Jean Claude. Vocabulaire de philosophie. Paris, 1966.
Phil 3850.9.92 Pira, Karl. Framställning och kritik af J.S. Mills, Lotzes och Sigwarts...i logiken. Stockholm, 1897.
Phil 5055.14.5 Pira, Karl. Om grundformerna i den reella logiken. Stockholm, 1907.
Htn Phil 8870.7* Pirckheimer, W. Theatrum virtutis et honoris. Nürnberg, 1606.
Phil 2477.15.100 Pire, François. De l'imagination poétique dans l'oeuvre de Gaston Bachelard. Paris, 1967.
Phil 1200.58 Pire, Georges. Stoïcisme et pedagogie. Liege, 1958.
Phil 8416.32 Pirenne, H.E. Essai sur le beau. Paris, 1924.
Phil 190.58 Pirenne, H.E. Sur l'angoisse métaphysique; essai de philosophie. Bruxelles, 1934.
Phil 7055.205.7 Pires, José. Arigó: vida, mediunidade e martírio. 2. ed. São Paulo, 1966.
Phil 5255.75 Piret, Roger. Psychologie différentielle des sexes. Paris, 1965.
Phil 2725.25.5 Pirlot, J. Destinée et valeur. Namur, 1950?
Phil 310.714 Piroschkow, Vera. Freiheit und Notwendigkeit in der Geschichte; zur Kritik des historischen Materialismus. München, 1970.
Phil 4803.108.1 Pisma. (Abramowski, Edward.) Warszawa, 1924.
Phil 4769.1.85 Pis'ma. (Solov'ev, V.S.) Sankt Peterburg, 1908-09.
Phil 4803.558.20 Pisma filozoficzne. (Mahrburg, Adam.) Warszawa, 1914. 2v.
Phil 4803.799.23 Pisma filozoficzne. (Śniadecki, Jan.) Warszawa, 1958. 2v.
Phil 4803.281.20 Pisma filozoficzne i logiczne. (Chwistek, Leon.) Warszawa, 1961-63. 2v.
Phil 8875.31 Pis'ma k neizvestnomu drugu. (Aleksandrov, R.N.) Frankfurt, 1951.
Phil 8980.428 Pis'ma k tebe. (Glebova, Tamara G.) Moskva, 1965.

Phil 4803.522.30 Pisma o oświacie i wychowaniu. (Libelt, Karol.) Wrocław, 1971.
Phil 4803.799.22 Pisma pedagogiczne. (Śniadecki, Jan.) Wrocław, 1961.
Phil 4803.522.10 Pisma promniejsze. (Libelt, Karol.) Poznań, 1849-51. 6v.
Phil 4803.799.20 Pisma rozmaite. (Śniadecki, Jan.) Wilno, 1818-22. 4v.
Phil 4803.592.20 Pisma wybrane. Wyd. 1. (Mysłakowski, Zygmunt.) Warszawa, 1971.
Phil 182.9 Pisteodicee. (Heinroths, J.) Leipzig, 1829.
Phil 5467.2 Pistolesi, G. L'imitazione; studio di psicologia. Torino, 1910.
Phil 5520.66 Pita, Enrique B. La frase infantil monopalábrica y la intelligencia. Buenos Aires, 1935.
Phil 8670.24 Pita Carpenter, Tomás. El ateismo de las masas. Madrid, 1969.
Phil 1182.40 I Pitagorici. (Maddalena, A.) Bari, 1954.
Phil 8890.25 Pitcairn, E.H. Unwritten laws of active careers. London, 1899.
Phil 3925.16.95 Pitcher, George Willard. The philosophy of Wittgenstein. Englewood Cliffs, 1964.
Phil 5640.146 Pitcher, George Willard. A theory of perception. Princeton, N.J., 1971.
Phil 720.76 Pitcher, George Willard. Truth. Englewood Cliffs, N.J., 1964.
Phil 3925.16.120 Pitcher, George Willard. Wittgenstein: the philosophical investigation. 1st ed. Garden City, N.Y., 1966.
Phil 9245.46.5 Pitkin, W.B. The psychology of happiness. N.Y., 1929.
Phil 6125.26 Pitkin, W.B. Take it easy. N.Y., 1935.
Phil 9530.31.5 Pitkin, Walter B. Life begins at forty. N.Y., 1932.
Phil 9530.31 Pitkin, Walter B. The psychology of achievement. N.Y., 1930.
Phil 5390.8 Pitkin, Walter B. A short introduction to the history of human stupidity. N.Y., 1932.
Phil 6125.16 Pitres, A. Recherches sur les lésions du centre ovale des hémisphères cérébraux. Paris, 1877.
Phil 6619.2.5 Pitres, Albert. Des anesthésies hystériques. Bordeaux, 1887.
Phil 6619.2 Pitres, Albert. Leçons cliniques sur l'hystérie et l'hypnotisme faites à l'hôpital Saint André de Bordeaux. Paris, 1891. 2v.
Phil 5825.8 Pitt, Frances. The intelligence of animals. London, 1931.
Phil 190.32 Pitt, St. George Lane-Fox. Free will and destiny. London, 1920.
Phil 978.31 The pitt and marrow of some sacred writings. (Theosophy Publishing Company.) N.Y., 1899.
Phil 8890.33 Pitt-Rivers, Goerge. Conscience and fanaticism. London, 1919.
Phil 5520.443 Pittau, Massimo. Filosofia e linguaggio. Pisa, 1962.
Phil 5520.443.5 Pittau, Massimo. Problemi di filosofia del linguaggio. Cagliari, 1967.
Phil 5592.135 Pittenger, R.E. The first five minutes. Ithaca, 1960.
Phil 8685.4.5 Pitter, A.H. Die Halb-Kantianer und der Pantheismus (veranlasst durch Jäsche's Pantheismus). Berlin, 1827.
Phil 296.3 Pivány, J.A. Entwicklungsgeschichte des Welt...Organismen. Plauen, 1877.
Phil 3450.11.480 Pivčević, Edo. Husserl and phenomenology. London, 1970.
Phil 9035.82 Piwowarczyk, W. Charakter. Kielce, 1938.
Phil 900.7 Pizzi, Italo. Pessimismo orientale. Bari, 1902.
Phil 3497.23 Plaass, Peter. Kants Theorie der Naturwissenschaft. Göttingen, 1965.
Phil 3585.1.95 De plaats van J.H. Lambert...idealisme voor Kant. (Sterkman, P.) 's-Gravenhage, 1928.
Phil 672.7 Place, C. That space is necesary being. London, 1728.
Phil 2905.1.45 La place de l'homme dans la nature. (Teilhard de Chardin, Pierre.) Paris, 1962.
Phil 5627.266.21 A place for you; psychology and religion. 1st U.S. ed. (Tournier, Paul.) N.Y., 1968.
Phil 8403.32 The place of beauty in American life. (Cabat, Walter.) N.Y., 1911.
Phil 8627.14 The place of immortality in religious belief. (Carpenter, Joseph E.) London, 1898.
Phil 187.110 The place of minds in the world. (Mitchell, William.) London, 1933.
Phil 365.37 The place of the church in evolution. (Tyler, J.M.) Boston, 1914.
Phil 7076.22 The place of the ecstatic trance in the ideal of the good life. (Morrison, Paul Guerrant.) Chicago, 1932.
Phil 5115.7 The place of the hypothesis in logic. (Crane, Esther.) Chicago, 1924.
Phil 735.118.2 The place of value in a world of facts. (Köhler, Wolfgang.) N.Y., 1959.
Phil 343.3 The place of values. (Montgomery, G.R.) Bridgeport, 1903.
Phil 8890.16 Placette, J. Essais de morale. Amsterdam, 1716-32 6v.
Phil 1135.57 Placita Graecorum. (Bouché-Leclerq, A.) Paris, 1871.
Phil 1105.3 Placitis philosophorum. (Aquilianiis, S.) Lipsiae, 1756.
Phil 9420.13 Plack, A. Die Stellung der Liebe. Landshut, 1962.
Phil 9495.167.10 Plack, Arno. Die Gesellschaft und das Böse. München, 1967.
Phil 3552.63.40 Plädoyer fur Gottes Gottheit. 1. Aufl. (Leibniz, Gottfried Wilhelm.) Berlin, 1947.
Phil 7054.162 Plain guide to spiritualism. (Clark, Uriah.) Boston, 1863.
Phil 8610.919.20 A plain man's plea for rationalism. (Gorham, C.T.) London, 1915.
Phil 6955.3 Plain talk about insanity. (Fisher, T.W.) Boston, 1872.
Phil 8881.25 Plain thoughts on the art of living. (Gladden, W.) Boston, 1868.
Phil 25.81 The plain view. London. 5,1930+ 9v.
Phil 9362.10 Plain words to young men. (Woodbury, A.) Concord, 1858.
Phil 1158.30 Le plaisir et la mort dans la philosophie d'Epicure. (Fallat, Jean.) Paris, 1951.
Phil 5402.24 Plaisir et tempérance. (Heidsieck, François.) Paris, 1962.
Phil 9550.16.5 Plamenatz, J.P. The English utilitarians. 2. ed. Oxford, 1958.
Phil 9550.16 Plamenatz, J.P. Mills' utilitarianism. Oxford, 1949.
Phil 365.16 Le plan de Dieu dans l'évolution. (Petavel-Olliff, E.) Lausanne, 1902.
Phil 293.1 Le plan de la creation. (Madiis, H. de.) Paris, 1864.
Phil 6115.6 Plan des menschlichen Gehirns. (Flechsig, P.) Leipzig, 1883.
Phil 6117.4 The plan of the central nervous system. (Hill, A.) Chicago, 1885.
Phil 7054.34.5 Planchette; or, The despair of science. (Sargent, Epes.) Boston, 1869.
Htn Phil 3801.697* Planck, Adolf. Schellings nachgelassene Werke. Erlangen, 1858.

Phil 5255.4 Planck, K.C. Anthropologie und Psychologie. Leipzig, 1874.
Phil 5055.3 Planck, K.C. Logisches Kausalgesetz. Nördlingen, 1877.
Phil 3745.6.35 Planck, K.C. Testament eines Deutschen; Philosophie der Natur und Menschheit. 3e Ausg. Jena, 1925.
Phil 3745.6.95 Planck, M. Karl Christian Planck. Stuttgart, 1950.
Phil 5765.9 Planck, Max. Kansalgesetz und Willensfreiheit. Berlin, 1923.
Phil 190.53 Planck, Max. Positivismus und reale Aussenwelt. Leipzig, 1931.
Phil 190.53.10 Planck, Max. Religion und Naturwissenschaft. Leipzig, 1938.
Phil 5125.15 Planella Guille, J. El razonamiento inductivo. Barcelona, 1929?
Phil 396.3 Planetary democracy. (Reiser, Oliver Leslie.) N.Y., 1944.
Phil 585.130 The planetary man. (Desan, Wilfrid.) Washington, 1961.
Phil 5255.4.5 Plank, K.C. Seele und Geist. Leipzig, 1871.
Phil 5252.125A Plans and the structure of behavior. (Miller, George.) N.Y., 1960.
Phil 5590.9.3 Plant, James S. Personality and the cultural pattern. N.Y., 1939.
Phil 575.75 Plant, Paul. Die Psychologie der produktiven Persönlichkeit. Stuttgart, 1929.
Phil 585.216 Plantiko, Otto. Rousseaus, Herders und Kants Theorie vom Zukunftsideal der Menschheitsgeschichte. Inaug. Diss. Greifswald, 1895.
Phil 8575.5 Plantinga, Alvin. Faith and philosophy; philosophical studies in religion and ethics. Grand Rapids, 1964.
Phil 8670.21.5 Plantinga, Alvin. God and other minds. Ithaca, 1967.
Phil 8670.21 Plantinga, Alvin. The ontological argument. Garden City, N.Y., 1965.
Phil 25.6 The plantonist. St. Louis. 1-4 3v.
Phil 310.598 Planty-Bonjour, Guy. Les categories du materialisme dialectique. Dordrecht, 1965.
Phil 310.598.2 Planty-Bonjour, Guy. The categories of dialectical materialism. Dordrecht, 1967.
Phil 8595.31 Plarity; a German Catholic's interpretation of religion. (Przywara, Erich.) London, 1935.
Phil 3850.1.102 Plasman, L.C. de. Lettres à Gambetta...sur le dernier ouvrage de Strauss. Paris, 1877.
Phil 6132.13 Plates of the thoracic and abdominal nerves. (Walters, J.G.) London, 1804.
Phil 3745.1.50 Platner, E. Anthropologie für Ärzte und Weltweise. Leipzig, 1772.
Phil 3745.1.40 Platner, E. Lehrbuch der Logik und Metaphysik. Leipzig, 1795.
Phil 3745.1.31 Platner, E. Philosophische Aphorismen. Leipzig, 1776.
Phil 3745.1.30A Platner, E. Philosophische Aphorismen. Leipzig, 1793-1800. 2v.
Phil 8670.12.5 Platner, E. Über den Atheismus. Leipzig, 1783.
Phil 1130.7 Plato and the older academy. (Zeller, Eduard.) Leipzig, 1876.
Phil 1130.7.5 Plato and the older academy. (Zeller, Eduard.) London, 1888.
Phil 338.25 Plato und Aristoteles. (Heynig, J.G.) Amberg, 1804.
Phil 341.39 Platon und Hegel zur ontologischen Begründung des Zirkels in der Erkenntnis. (Kuemmel, Friedrich.) Tübingen, 1968.
Phil 3504.27 Platon und Kant. (Wichmann, G.) Berlin, 1920.
Phil 5627.267 Platonev, Konstantin K. Psikhologiia religii. Moskva, 1967.
Phil 1802.10 The platonic renaissance in England. (Cassirer, E.) Edinburgh, 1953.
Phil 400.78 The Platonic traditions in Anglo-Saxon philosophy. (Muirhead, J.H.) London, 1931.
Phil 3552.308 Platonism, Aristotoleanism and Cabelism in the philosophy of Leibniz. (Politella, Joseph.) Philadelphia, 1938.
Phil 1925.85 Platonism and Cartesianism. (Gysi, Lydia.) Bern, 1962.
Phil 193.49.30 Platonism and the spiritual life. (Santayana, G.) N.Y., 1927.
Phil 1800.3.5 Platonism in the Midwest. (Anderson, P.P.) Philadelphia, 1963.
Phil 1170.26 Le platonisme. (Descombes, Vincent.) Paris, 1971.
Phil 3552.247 Il platonismo di Plotino, Sant'Agosinto, Cartesio, Leibniz. (Ivaldi, I.G.) Napoli, n.d.
Phil 1540.55 Platonismo medievale. (Gregory, Tullio.) Roma, 1958.
Phil 1540.96 Platonismus in der Philosophie des Mittelalters. (Beierwaltes, Werner.) Darmstadt, 1969.
Phil 1506.4 Platonismus in Mittelalter. (Baeumker, Clemens.) München, 1916.
Phil 8587.65.3 Platonismus und Prophetismus. 2. Aufl. (Hessen, Johannes.) München, 1955.
Phil 310.450 Platonov, G.V. Dialekticheskii materializm i voprosy genetiko. Moskva, 1961.
Phil 4756.6.50 Platonov, G.V. Kh.M. Fataliev. Makhachkala, 1964.
Phil 6325.22 Platonov, K.I. The word as a physiological and therapeutic factor. Moscow, 1959.
Phil 575.253 Platonov, Konstantin K. Lichnost' i trud. Moskva, 1965.
Phil 5255.70 Platonov, Konstantin Konstantinovich. Psychology as you may like it. Moscow, 1965.
Phil 8980.697 Platonov, Rostislav P. Vospitanie kommunisticheskoi soznatel'nosti. Minsk, 1970.
Phil 9530.44 Platt, C. The essence of success. London, 19- ?
Phil 9375.5 Platt, J. Business. London, 1876.
Phil 8890.17 Platt, J. Life. N.Y., 1889.
Phil 585.180 Platt, John Rader. New views of the nature of man. Chicago, 1965.
Phil 7054.85 Platt, L.L. Spiritual experience. New Haven, 1852. 2 pam.
Phil 585.135.2 Plattel, Martinus Gulielmus. Social philosophy. Pittsburgh, 1965.
Phil 585.135 Plattel, Martinus Gulielmus. Sociale wijsbegeerte. v.1-2. Utrecht, 1960-64.
Phil 7069.20.272 Platts, J. The witness. London, 1920.
Phil 5025.2 Platzeck, E.W. Von der Analogie zum Syllogismus. Paderborn, 1954.
Phil 575.30 Platzhoff-Lejeune, E. Werk und Persönlichkeit. Minden, 1903.
Phil 6998.4.2 Play therapy. (Axline, Virginia Mae.) N.Y., 1969.
Phil 6325.32 Plé, Albert. Freud et la morale. Paris, 1969.
Phil 6315.2.435 Plé, Albert. Freud et la religion. Paris, 1968?
Phil 9010.2 A plea for amusements. (Sawyer, F.W.) N.Y., 1847.
Phil 9010.2.2 A plea for amusements. (Sawyer, F.W.) N.Y., 1847.
Phil 9400.10 Plea for an age movement. (Perry, Ralph B.) N.Y., 1942.
Phil 8705.10 Plea for candor in Bible-reading. Jackson, 1878.
Phil 8685.3 A plea for pantheism. (Hittell, J.S.) N.Y., 1857.
Phil 6972.4.5 The plea of insanity in criminal cases. (Winslow, F.) Boston, 1843.

Phil 5402.44 Pleasure: a creative approach to life. (Lowen, Alexander.) N.Y., 1970.
Phil 5402.12 Pleasure and behavior. (Wells, Frederic L.) N.Y., 1924.
Phil 9245.138 Pleasure and desire: the case for hedonism reviewed. (Gosling, Justin Cyril Bertrand.) Oxford, 1969.
Phil 5402.17 Pleasure and instinct. (Burlton Allen, A.H.) London, 1930.
Phil 5402.16 Pleasure and pain. (Bousfield, P.) London, 1926.
Phil 5402.37 Pleasure and pain: a study in philosophical psychology. (Cowan, Joseph Lloyd.) London, 1968.
Phil 9245.9.2.3 The pleasures of life. (Avebury, John Lubbock.) London, 1889.
Phil 9245.9.7 The pleasures of life. (Avebury, John Lubbock.) London, 1893.
Phil 9245.9.1 The pleasures of life. (Avebury, John Lubbock.) N.Y., 1887.
Phil 9245.9.3 The pleasures of life. (Avebury, John Lubbock.) N.Y., 1893.
Phil 9245.9.4 The pleasures of life. v.1-2. (Avebury, John Lubbock.) London, 1913-14.
Phil 9010.30 Pleasures of the past. (Brooke, Iris.) London, 1955.
Phil 8430.63 Plebe, Armando. Che cosa è l'estetica sovietica. Roma, 1969.
Phil 8140.10 Plebe, Armando. L'estetica italiana dopo Croce. Padova, 1968.
Phil 8080.15 Plebe, Armando. Processo all'estetica. Firenze, 1959.
Phil 8595.19 Plekhanov, G. O religii. Moskva, 1923.
X Cg Phil 490.4.3 Plekhanov, G.V. Beiträge zur Geschichte des Materialismus. 3. Aufl. Stuttgart, 1921.
Phil 310.24 Plekhanov, G.V. The development of the monist view of history. Moscow, 1956.
Phil 490.4.7 Plekhanov, G.V. Essays in the history of materialism. London, 1934.
Phil 490.4.10 Plekhanov, G.V. Le matérialisme militant (materialismus militans). Paris, 1930.
Phil 490.4.10.12 Plekhanov, G.V. Materialismus militans (voinstvuiushchii materializm). Izd. 2. Moskva, 1931.
Phil 8416.11.22 Plekhanov, Georgii Valentinovich. Art and social life. London, 1953.
Phil 8416.11.20 Plekhanov, Georgii Valentinovich. Art and society. N.Y., 1936.
Phil 8416.11.25 Plekhanov, Georgii Valentinovich. L'art et de vie sociale (quatorze études). Paris, 1950.
Phil 8416.11 Plekhanov, Georgii Valentinovich. Iskusstvo i literatura. Moskva, 1948.
Phil 8416.11.15 Plekhanov, Georgii Valentinovich. Iskusstvo i obshchestvennaia zhizn'. Moskva, 1922.
Phil 8416.11.10 Plekhanov, Georgii Valentinovich. Kunst und Literatur. Berlin, 1955.
Phil 8416.11.5 Plekhanov, Georgii Valentinovich. Literatura i estetika. Moskva, 1958.
Phil 5055.15 Plenning, J. Logica, usui juniorum. Holmiae, 1746.
Phil 1135.16 Plessing, F.V.L. Osiris und Sokrates. Berlin, 1783.
Phil 1120.1 Plessing, F.V.L. Versuche zur Aufklärung der Philosophie des ältesten Alterthums. Leipzig, 1788-90. 3v.
Phil 585.158 Plessner, H. Conditio humana. Pfullingen, 1964.
Phil 5640.27 Plessner, H. Die Einheit der Sinne grundlinien einer Asthesiologie. Bonn, 1923.
Phil 705.14 Plessner, H. Krisis der transzendentalen Wahrheit im anfang. Heidelberg, 1918.
Phil 190.82A Plessner, H. Zwischen Philosophie und Gesellschaft. Bern, 1953.
Phil 5525.70 Plessner, Helmuth. Laughing and crying; a study of limits of human behavior. Evanston, 1970.
Phil 3745.7 Plessner, Helmuth. Die Stufen des Organischen und des Marisch; Einleitung in die philosophische Anthropologie. Berlin, 1928.
Phil 5330.14 Plethysmographic study of attention. (Stevens, H.C.) n.p., 1905.
Phil 6965.24 Plokker, J.H. Geschonden feeld. 's-Gravenhage, 1962.
Phil 75.90 Plott, John C. Sarva-darsana-sangraha; a bibliographical guide to the global history of philosophy. Leiden, 1969.
Phil 490.7 Ploucquet, G. Dissertatio de materialismo. Tubingae, 1751.
Phil 3745.2.31 Ploucquet, Gottfried. Sammlung der Schriften welche den logischen calcul Herrn Prof. Ploucquets Betreffen, mit neuen Zusäben, Frankfurt und Leipzig, 1766. Stuttgart, 1970.
Phil 190.14 Ploucquet, W.G. Commentationes philosophicae selectiores. Trajecti ad Rhenum, 1781.
Phil 296.4 Pluche, N.A. The history of the heavens. London, 1740. 2v.
Phil 3415.84 Plümacher, O. Der Kampf um's Unbewusste. Berlin, 1881.
Phil 3415.84.2 Plümacher, O. Der Kampf um's Unbewusste. Leipzig, 1890.
Phil 9430.5 Plümacher, O. Der Pessimismus. Heidelberg, 1888.
Phil 3808.134 Plümacher, G. Zwei Individualisten der Schopenhauer'schen Schule. Wien, 1881.
Phil 672.170 Plumbe, C.C. Release from time. London, 1950.
Phil 978.78 Plummer, L.G. From atom to kosmos. Point Loma, 1940.
Phil 978.78.5 Plummer, L.G. Star habits and orbits. Covina, Calif., 1944.
NEDL Phil 8685.9 Plumptre, C.E. General sketch...history of pantheism. London, 1881. 2v.
Phil 6965.20 Plunkett, Richard. Epidemiology and mental illness. N.Y., 1960.
Phil 510.28 Le pluralisme. (Rosny, J.H.) Paris, 1909.
Phil 510.126.9 The pluralist philosophies of England and America. (Wahl, Jean.) London, 1925.
Phil 184.3.23A A pluralistic universe. (James, W.) London, 1909.
Phil 184.3.24 A pluralistic universe. (James, W.) London, 1920.
Phil 2725.36.30 Pluralité de l'être. (LaRochefoucauld, Edmée.) Paris, 1957.
Phil 8602.6.2 The plurality of worlds. (Whewell, W.) Boston, 1854.
Phil 8602.6.3 The plurality of worlds. (Whewell, W.) Boston, 1855.
Phil 176.70 Pluriverse. (Blood, B.P.) Boston, 1920.
Phil 7068.63 Pneumatologie. Des esprits. v. 2-6. (Mirville, J.E.) Paris, 1863-68. 5v.
Phil 7068.54 Pneumatologie des esprits. v. 2- ed. (Mirville, J.E.) Paris, 1854.
Phil 8980.432 Po dolgu grazhdanina. (Golovan, I.P.) Moskva, 1962.
Phil 4710.50.25 Pobudova naukovoï teorii. (Akademiia Nauk URSR, Kiev.) Kyïv, 1965.
Htn Phil 9560.25* Pocaterra, A. Due dialogi della vergogna. Ferrara, 1592. 2v.
Phil 4825.16 Počeci filosofije Srba od Save do Dositeja na osnovama narodne mudrosti. (Stojković, Andrija B.) Beograd, 1970.
Phil 2050.104.5 Počet pravděpodobnosti a Humova skepse. (Masaryk, T.G.) Praha, 1883.

Phil 8666.23   Pochemu nel'zia verit' v boga. (Lunacharskii, Anatolii V.) Moskva, 1965.

Phil 1815.2   Pochmann, Henry A. New England transcendentalism and Saint Louis Hegelianism. Philadelphia, 1948.

Phil 6021.2.55   The pocket Lavater. (Lavater, Johann Caspar.) Hartford, 18- .

Phil 6021.2.53   Pocket Lavater. n.p., n.d.

Phil 3492.65   Początki Kantyzmu. (Kaczmaeck, S.) Poznań, 1961.

Phil 7069.23.25   Pod urokiem zaświatów. (Wasylewski, S.) Lwów, 1923.

Phil 3640.235.30   Podach, Erich F. Ein Blick in Notizbücher Nietzsches. Heidelberg, 1963.

Phil 3640.235.10   Podach, Erich F. L'effondrement de Nietzsche. 4e éd. Photoreproduction. Paris, 1931.

Phil 3640.235.20   Podach, Erich F. Friedrich Nietzsche und Lou Salomé. Zürich, 1938.

Phil 3640.235.25   Podach, Erich F. Friedrich Nietzsches Werke des Zusammenbruchs. Heidelberg, 1961.

Phil 3640.235.15   Podach, Erich F. Gestalten um Nietzsche. Weimar, 1932.

Phil 3640.235   Podach, Erich F. Nietzsches Zusammenbruch. Heidelberg, 1930.

Phil 2750.11.105   Podellaro, N. Maritain. Brescia, 1953.

Phil 346.34   Podhorytov, Gennadii A. Istorizm kak metod nauchnogo poznaniia. Leningrad, 1967.

Phil 5625.1   Podkopaev, N.A. Die Methodik der Enforschung der bedingten Reflexe. München, 1926.

Phil 5625.1.5.3   Podkopaev, N.A. Metodika izucheniia uslovnykn refleksov. 3. izd. Moskva, 1952.

Phil 6685.7.5   Podmore, F. From Mesmer to Christian Science. N.Y., 1964.

Phil 6685.7   Podmore, F. Mesmerism and christian science...history of mental healing. Philadelphia, 1909.

Phil 7068.94.10   Podmore, Frank. Apparitions and thought-transference. London, 1894.

Phil 7069.02.12   Podmore, Frank. Mediums of the 19th century. N.Y., 1963. 2v.

Phil 7069.02.11   Podmore, Frank. Modern spiritualism. London, 1902. 2v.

Phil 7069.08.27   Podmore, Frank. The naturalisation of the supernatural. N.Y., 1908.

Phil 7069.10.40   Podmore, Frank. The newer spiritualism. London, 1910.

Phil 7068.97.10   Podmore, Frank. Studies in psychical research. London, 1897.

Phil 7068.97.11   Podmore, Frank. Studies in psychical research. N.Y., 1897.

Phil 1701.56   Podnár, Ján. Od realizmu k iracionalizmu; zo súčasnej západnej filozofie. 1. vyd. Bratislava, 1966.

Phil 585.335   Podol'nyi, Grigor'evich. Sviaz' vremen. Moskva, 1969.

Phil 6325.25   Podolsky, Edward. Encyclopedia of aberrations. N.Y., 1953.

Phil 310.370   Podosetnik, V.M. Chto takoe dialekticheskii i istoricheskii materializm. Moskva, 1961.

Phil 310.370.5   Podosetnik, V.M. A glance at historical materialism. Moscow, 1965.

Phil 343.28   Podstawowe zagadnienia marksistowskiej teorii poznania. (Martel, K.) Warszawa, 1961.

Phil 4803.497.230   Podstawy filozofji. (Kowalski, Kazimierz Józef.) Guiezano, 1930.

Phil 3450.19.290   Poeggeler, Otto. Der Denkweg Martin Heideggers. Pfullingen, 1963.

Phil 3425.410   Poeggeler, Otto. Hegels Kritik der Romantik. Bonn, 1956.

Phil 3450.19.460   Poeggeler, Otto. Heidegger; Perspektiven zur Deutung seines Werks. Köln, 1970.

Phil 7150.85   Poeldinger, Walter. Die Abschätzung der Suizidalität. Bern, 1968.

Phil 5627.265.5   Pöll, Wilhelm. Religionspsychologie. München, 1965.

Phil 7140.133   Pöll, Wilhelm. Die Suggestion. München, 1951.

Phil 190.65   Pöll, Wilhelm. Wesen und Wesenserkenntnis. München, 1936.

Phil 3640.215A   Il poema eroico di F. Nietzsche. (Castiglioni, M.) Torino, 1924.

Phil 974.3.112   Poepping, Fred. Rudolf Steiner, der grosse Unbekannte. Wien, 1960.

Phil 7069.16.17   Pörfin á vinnuvísindum. (Finnbogason, Gudmundsr.) Reykjavik, 1916.

Phil 5055.40   Poern, Ingmar. The logic of power. Oxford, 1970.

Phil 8890.40   Pörschke, K.L. Einleitung in die Moral. Libau, 1797.

Phil 8601.20   Poesia e ontologia. (Vattimo, Gianni.) Milano, 1967.

Phil 3640.60   Pöesies complètes. (Nietzsche, Friedrich.) Paris, 1948.

Phil 1135.52   Poestion, J.C. Griechische Philosophinnen. Bremen, 1882.

Phil 8707.7.5   The poet of science and other addresses. (Rice, William N.) N.Y., 1919.

Phil 6155.2   Poetic vision and the psychedelic experience. 1st ed. (Durr, R.A.) Syracuse, 1970.

Phil 2750.11.180   The poetics of Maritain. (Rover, Thomas Dominic.) Washington, 1965.

Phil 2477.15.8   The poetics of reverie. (Bachelard, Gaston.) N.Y., 1969.

Phil 2477.15.6   The poetics of space. (Bachelard, Gaston.) N.Y., 1964.

Phil 2477.15.10   La poétique de la rêverie. (Bachelard, Gaston.) Paris, 1960.

Phil 2477.15.13   La poétique de la rêverie. 3. éd. (Bachelard, Gaston.) Paris, 1965.

Phil 2477.15.5   La poétique de l'espace. 1. éd. (Bachelard, Gaston.) Paris, 1957.

Phil 2477.15.5.2   La poétique de l'espace. 2. éd. (Bachelard, Gaston.) Paris, 1958.

Phil 8419.16   Das Poetische in der Kunst. (Schmied, W.) Nürnburg, 1960.

Phil 3805.29   Ein poetischer Brief Schleiermachers. (Schleiermacher, Friedrich.) Halle, 1917.

Phil 3450.19.64   Poetry, language, thought. 1. ed. (Heidegger, Martin.) N.Y., 1971.

Phil 8599.36   Poetry, religion, and the spiritual life. (Thomas, George Finger.) Houston, 1951.

Phil 176.106.10   Poetry and mathematics. (Buchanan, S.M.) N.Y., 1929.

Phil 2138.140   Poetry and philosophy. (Woods, Thomas.) London, 1961.

Phil 8430.46   Poetry and politics. (Adler, Mortimer Jerome.) Pittsburgh, 1965.

Phil 815.1   Poetter, F.C. Die Geschichte der Philosophie. Elberfeld, 1874.

Phil 5055.13.2   Poetter, F.C. Logik. 2. Aufl. Gütersloh, 1887.

Phil 8670.6   Poetter, F.C. Der persönliche Gott und Welt. Elberfeld, 1875.

Phil 600.7.86   Poëy, Andrés. M. Littré et Auguste Comte. 2e éd. Paris, 1880.

Phil 600.56   Poey, Andrés. El positivismo. Habana, 1960.

Phil 5850.314   Poffenberger, A.T. Applied psychology; its principles and methods. N.Y., 1927.

Phil 5255.28   Poffenberger, A.T. Experimental psychology; loose leaf laboratory manual. Chicago, 1926.

Phil 5255.28.2   Poffenberger, A.T. Experimental psychology; loose leaf laboratory manual. N.Y., 1925?

Phil 5850.314.5   Poffenberger, A.T. Principles of applied psychology. N.Y., 1942.

Phil 5643.37   Poffenberger, A.T. Reaction time to retinal stimulation. N.Y., 1912.

Phil 8897.82   Pogadanki obczajowe. (Witwicki, W.) Warszawa, 1960.

Phil 3428.161   Poggi, Alfredo. La filosofia de G.F. Herbart. Genova, 1932.

Phil 8416.37   Poggioli, Renato. Teoria dell'arte d'avanguardia. Bologna, 1962.

Phil 8416.37.5   Poggioli, Renato. The theory of the avant-garde. Cambridge, 1968.

Phil 4803.108.95   Poglądy etyczne Edwarda Abramowskiego. Wyd. 1. (Jezierski, Romuald.) Poznań, 1970.

Phil 4803.879.90   Poglądy filozoficzno-społeczne Michała Wiszniewskiego. Wyd. 1. (Bańku, Józef.) Warszawa, 1967.

Phil 4825.18   Poglavitne ideje slovenskih filozofov med sholastiko in neosholako. (Urbančič, Juan.) Ljubljana, 1971.

Phil 4777.282.10   Poglądy społeczne i ekonomiczne Augusta Cieszkowskiego. (Roszkowski, Antonio.) Poznań, 1923.

Phil 8980.552   Pogovorim o zhizni i sehe. (Makarova, N.F.) Moskva, 1961.

Phil 6110.24   Pogranichnye problemy psikhologii i fiziologii. (Akademiia Pedagogicheskikh Nauk RSFSR, Moscow. Institut Psikhologii.) Moskva, 1961.

Phil 3552.490   Pogrebyskii, Iosif B. Gotfrid Vil'gel'm Leibnits, 1646-1716. Moskva, 1971.

Phil 2175.5.80   Pogson, Beryl. Maurice Nicoll. London, 1961.

Phil 5627.267.5   Pohier, Jacques Marie. Psychologie et théologie. Paris, 1967.

Phil 8890.61   Pohl, Hermann Paul Albert. Das Gesetz. Der Morgen der Menschheit. Berlin, 1966.

Phil 190.64   Pohl, Joachim. Philosophie der tragischen Strukturen. Wien, 1935.

Phil 1200.44.2   Pohlenz, Max. Die Stoa. 2. und 4. Aufl. Göttingen, 1970. 2v.

Phil 1200.44.5   Pohlenz, Max. Stoa und Staiker. Zürich, 1950.

Phil 5545.40   Pohlmann, A. Experimentalle Beiträge zur Lehre vom Gedächtnis. Berlin, 1906.

Phil 3415.107   Pohorilles, N.E. Entwicklung und Kritik der Erkenntnistheorie Eduard von Hartmanns. Wien, 1911.

Phil 6125.6   Poincaré, E.L. Leçons sur la physiologie...du système nerveux. Paris, 1873-6. 3v.

Phil 296.6   Poincaré, H. Leçons sur les hypotheses cosmogoniques. Paris, 1911.

Phil 296.6.2   Poincaré, H. Leçons sur les hypotheses cosmogoniques. 2. ed. Paris, 1913.

Phil 5115.4.6   Poincaré, Henri. Science and hypothesis. London, 1905.

Phil 5115.4.7   Poincaré, Henri. Science and hypothesis. London, 1914.

Phil 5115.4.5   Poincaré, Henri. Science and hypothesis. N.Y., 1905.

Phil 5115.4   Poincaré, Henri. La science et l'hypothèse. Paris, 1903.

Phil 5525.64   Poinsinet de Sivry, Louis. Psychologische und physiologische Untersuchung über das Lachen. Wolfenbüttel, 1794.

Phil 177.120   Le point d'appui pris sur le néant. 1. éd. (Carré, Jean Raoul.) Paris, 1955.

Phil 343.8   Le point de départ de la métaphysique. v.1-5. (Maréchal, J.) Bruges, 1922-47. 3v.

Phil 1701.35   Point de vue sur l'Occident. (Baudry, Bernard.) Paris, 1958.

Phil 972.15   The Point Loma community in California, 1897-1942. (Greenwalt, E.A.) Berkeley, 1955.

Phil 177.8.25   The point of view: an anthology. (Carus, Paul.) Chicago, 1927.

Phil 3120.30.70   Pointing the way. (Buber, Martin.) London, 1951.

Phil 2630.1.83   Pointud-Guillemot, B. La doctrine sociale de Gratry. Thèse. Paris, 1917.

Phil 2630.1.81   Pointud-Guillemot, B. Essai sur la philosophie de Gratry. Thèse. Paris, 1917.

Phil 8595.5   Poiret, P. Cogitationum rationalium. Amsterdam, 1715.

Phil 672.154   Poirier, René. Essai sur quelques caractères des notions d'espace et de temps. Thèse. Paris, 1931.

Phil 5125.16   Poirier, René. Remarques sur la probabilité de inductions. Thèse. Paris, 1931.

Phil 190.39   Poirson, Charles. Le dynamisme absolu. Lyon, 1898.

Phil 2725.2.97   Poisson, Jacques. Le romantisme social de Lamennais. Thèse. Paris, 1931.

Phil 2415.2   Poitou, E.L. Les philosophes françis contemporains. Paris, 1864.

Phil 4759.1.45   Poiushchee serdtse. (Il'in, I.A.) Miunkhen, 1958.

Phil 2415.14   Pokhid proty rozumu. (Popovych, M.V.) Kyiv, 1960.

Phil 6060.65   Pokorny, Richard Raphael. Psychologie der Handschrift. Basel, 1968.

Phil 5055.7   Pokorny, T. Beiträge zur Logik der Urtheile und Schlüsse. Leipzig, 1901.

Phil 4710.90   Pokrovskii, S.A. Fal'sifkatsiia istorii russkoi politicheskoi mysli v sovremennoi reaktsionnoi burzhuaznoi literature. Moskva, 1957.

Phil 6125.8   Polak, A.J. Gedachten over geest. n.p., 1894.

Phil 346.11   Polak, L. Kennisleer contra materíe-realisme. Amsterdam, 1912.

Phil 3745.21   Polak, Leo. Verzamelde werken. Amsterdam, 1947.

Phil 7068.74.15   Polak, M.S. Het materialismus, het spiritismus. 2. druk. Amsterdam, 1874.

Phil 8640.9   Polak, M.S. Die Unsterblichkeitsfrage. Amsterdam, 1857.

Phil 190.43   Polakov, W.N. Man and his affairs from an engineering point of view. Baltimore, 1925.

Phil 4762.1.90   Polanowska, Fejga. Losskij's erkenntnistheoretischer Intuitionismus. Inaug. Diss. Berlin, 1931.

Phil 346.20.15   Polanyi, Michael. Knowing and being. London, 1969.

Phil 346.20.3   Polanyi, Michael. Personal knowledge. Chicago, 1960.

Phil 346.20   Polanyi, Michael. Personal knowledge. London, 1958.

Phil 346.20.4   Polanyi, Michael. Personal knowledge towards a post-critical philosophy. Chicago, 1968[1958].

Phil 346.20.5A   Polanyi, Michael. The study of man. London, 1959.

Phil 346.20.10   Polanyi, Michael. The tacet dimension. 1. ed. Garden City, N.Y., 1966.

Phil 182.126   Der polare Mensch. (Havemann, Hans.) Hannover, 1923.

Phil 9035.90   Die Polarität im Aufbau des Charakters. (Hellek, A.) Bern, 1950.

Phil 978.49.770   Die Polarität von Dauer und Entwickelung im Menschenleben. (Steiner, R.) Dornach, 1968.

Phil 1750.166.135   Polariteitsbesef als een der fundamenten van het humanisme. (Dijkhuis, P.) Assen, 1960.

Phil 596.2   Polarity; a philosophy of tensions among values. (Morris, Louis W.) Chicago, 1956.

Phil 1135.184   Polarity and analogy. (Lloyd, Geoffrey Ernest Richard.) Cambridge, Eng., 1966.

Phil 2725.30.90   Polato, Franco. Il pragmatismo epistemológico e religioso di Edouard LeRoy. 1. ed. Padova, 1959.

Phil 735.225   Pole, David. Conditions of rational inquiry. London, 1961.

Phil 3925.16.86   Pole, David. The later philosophy of Wittgenstein. London, 1958.

Phil 7069.60.20   Pole, W.T. The silent road in the light of personal experience. London, 1960.

Phil 298.12   Die Pole der Gesamtnatur. (Rieder, Albert.) Pfaffenhofen an der Ilm, 1959.

Phil 4170.7.98   Una polemica filosofica dell'1800. (Tavianini, U.) Padova, 1955.

Phil 4115.87.10   Polemica giobertiana. (Calcaterra, C.) Torino, 1923.

Phil 4225.15.85   Polemica sull'immanenza in Ugo Spirito. (Conti, O.) Milano, 1963.

Phil 4215.3.32   Polemiche antidogmatiche. (Rensi, Giuseppe.) Bologna, 1920.

Phil 3552.405   Polemika G. Leibnitsa i S. Klarka po voprosam filosofii i estesvoznaniia, 1715-1716 gg. (Leibniz, G.W.) Leningrad, 1960.

Phil 4600.4.40   Polemiska inlägg. (Lidforss, Bengt.) Malmö, 1913.

Phil 6125.20   Polen, Laura. Körperbau und Charakter. Inaug. Diss. Leipzig, 1928.

Phil 2905.1.370   Polgár, Ladislaus. Internationale Teilhard-Bibliographie. Freiburg, 1965.

Phil 8890.19   Polier de St. Germain, A. de. Du gouvernement des moeurs. Lausanne, 1785.

Phil 310.597   Polikarov, A. Materiia i poznanie. Sofiia, 1961.

Phil 9245.64   Polin, Raymond. Le bonheur considéré comme l'un des beaux-arts. Paris, 1965.

Phil 735.123   Polin, Raymond. Essai sur la compréhension des valeurs. Thèse. Paris, 1945.

Phil 2045.122   Polin, Raymond. Politique et philosophie chez Thomas Hobbes. 1. éd. Paris, 1953.

Phil 2115.190   Polin, Raymond. La politique morale de John Locke. 1e éd. Paris, 1960.

Phil 4800.28   Polish analytical philosophy. (Skolimowski, Henryk.) London, 1967.

Phil 5066.265   Polish logic, 1920-1939 papers. (McCall, Storrs.) Oxford, 1967.

Phil 25.177   Polish psychological bulletin. Warszawa. 1,1970+

Phil 9513.46   Polishchuk, Nina P. Problema moral'noho idealn. Kyïv, 1970.

Htn   Phil 9345.4*   Polite philosopher. (Forrester, J.) London, 1758.

Phil 3552.308   Politella, Joseph. Platonism, Aristoteleanism and Cabelism in the philosophy of Leibniz. Philadelphia, 1938.

Phil 190.29   Politeo, Giorgio. Scritti filosofici et letterari. Bologna, 1919.

Htn   Phil 8876.19.6*   Politeuphuia, wits common-wealth. (Bodenham, John.) London, 1650.

Htn   Phil 8876.19.7*   Politeuphuia, wits common-wealth. (Bodenham, John.) London, 1653.

Htn   Phil 8876.19.2*   Politeuphuia, wits common-wealth. (Bodenham, John.) London, 1655.

Htn   Phil 8876.19.13*   Politeuphuia, wits common-wealth. (Bodenham, John.) London, 1674.

Htn   Phil 8876.19*   Politeuphuia, wits common-wealth. (Bodenham, John.) London, 1688.

Htn   Phil 8876.19.5*   Politeuphuia. (Bodenham, John.) London, 1598.

Phil 4073.89   La politica di Campanella. (Mattei, R. de.) Roma, 1927.

Phil 4225.1.85   Politica e filosofia in Bertrando Spaventa. (Vacca, Giuseppe.) Bari, 1967.

Phil 4080.3.380   La politica nel pensiero di Benedetto Croce. (Onufrio, Salvatore.) Milano, 1962.

Phil 8599.27   The political aspects of religious development. (Thomas, E.E.) London, 1937.

Htn   Phil 2050.73*   Political discourses. (Hume, David.) Edinburgh, 1752.

Phil 9045.11   Political duties. (Sowdon, A.J.C.) Boston, 1878.

Phil 2050.59.40   Political essays. (Hook, Sidney.) N.Y., 1953.

Phil 8582.57   The political faith of our fathers. (Crawford, Benjamin F.) Carnegie, Pa., 1943.

Phil 2255.1.43   Political ideals. (Russell, Bertrand Russell.) N.Y., 1963.

Phil 9450.68   Political morality; a general theory of politics. (Haring, Philip S.) Cambridge, Mass., 1970.

Phil 2045.117   The political philosophy of Hobbes. (Strauss, Leo.) Oxford, 1936.

Phil 2045.130   The political philosophy of Hobbes. (Warrender, H.) Oxford, 1957.

Phil 3832.19   The political philosophy of Spinoza. (McShea, Robert J.) N.Y., 1968.

Phil 333.24   Political science and ideology. st ed. (Connolly, William.) N.Y., 1967.

Phil 1955.6.240   The political theory of John Dewey. (Somjee, Abdulkarim Husseinbhay.) N.Y., 1968.

Phil 1516.1.2   Political theory of the schoolmen. (Littlejohn, J.M.) College Springs, 1894.

Phil 3819.57.15A   The political works. (Spinoza, Benedictus de.) Oxford, 1958.

Phil 3120.2.120   Politické a pociálné názory Bernard Bolzano. (Seidlerová, I.) Praha, 1963.

Phil 9450.4   Politics, and the moral law. (Ruemelin, G.) N.Y., 1901.

Phil 9450.9   Politics and crowd-morality. (Christensen, A.) London, 1915.

Phil 9450.50   Politics and ethics. (Gordis, R.) Santa Barbara, Calif., 1961.

Phil 2020.88   The politics of conscience. (Richter, M.) Cambridge, 1964.

Phil 2020.89   The politics of conscience. (Richter, M.) London, 1964.

Phil 6155.4.5   The politics of ecstasy. (Leary, Timothy Francis.) N.Y., 1968.

Phil 6321.53   The politics of experience. (Laing, Roland David.) N.Y., 1968.

Phil 6140.5   The politics of mental health; organizing community mental health in metropolitan areas. N.Y., 1968.

Phil 9450.9.5   Politik og massemoral. (Christensen, A.) København, 1911.

Phil 9450.27   Politik und Ethik. (Freund, Ludwig.) Frankfurt, 1955.

Phil 9450.64   Politik und Ethik. (Wendland, Heinz Dietrich.) Darmstadt, 1969.

Phil 9450.27.2   Politik und Ethik. 2. Aufl. (Freund, Ludwig.) Gütersloh, 1961.

Phil 9450.25   Politik zwischen Dämon und Gott. 1. Aufl. (Künneth, W.) Berlin, 1954.

Phil 2045.122   Politique et philosophie chez Thomas Hobbes. 1. éd. (Polin, Raymond.) Paris, 1953.

Phil 2490.132   Politique internationale. (Lagarrigue, L.) Paris, 1928.

Phil 2115.190   La politique morale de John Locke. 1e éd. (Polin, Raymond.) Paris, 1960.

Phil 2750.11.146   La politique selon Jacques Maritain. (Bars, Henry.) Paris, 1961.

Phil 9450.20   Politische Ethik. (Gogartin, F.) Jena, 1932.

Phil 8892.42   Politische Ethik und ethische Weltanschauung. (Rolffs, Ernst.) Liepzig, 1923.

Htn   Phil 3480.78.5*   Politische Meinungen. (Kant, Immanuel.) n.p., 1794.

Htn   Phil 3480.78*   Politische Meinungen. (Kant, Immanuel.) n.p., 1796.

Phil 3450.19.345   Politische Philosophie im Denken Heideggers. (Schwan, Alexander.) Köln, 1965.

Phil 1930.8.100   Die politische Philosophie von R.G. Collingwood. (Suranyi-Unger, Nora.) München, 1960.

Phil 3425.15   Politische Schriften. (Hegel, Georg Wilhelm Friedrich.) Frankfurt am Main, 1966.

Phil 3552.33   Politische Schriften. v.1-2. (Leibniz, Gottfried.) Wien, 1966-67.

Phil 2490.175   Die politische Soziologie Auguste Comtes und ihre Differenz zur liberalen Gesellschaftstheorie Condorcets. (Steinhauer, Margarete.) Meisenheim, 1966.

Phil 3270.4.82   Die politischen Grundlagen. (Gielhammer, L.) Berlin, 1928.

Phil 4260.113   Politischer Aktivismus und sozialer Mythos. (Witzemann, Walter.) Berlin, 1935.

Phil 5520.408   Det politiska språket. 2. uppl. (Fredriksson, G.) Uppsala, 1963.

Phil 8876.107   Politsche Zeitfragen in ethischer Beleuchtung. (Börner, W.) Wien, 1935.

Phil 2475.1.299   Politzer, Georges. Le Bergsonisme. Paris, 1947.

Phil 5255.37   Politzer, Georges. Critique des fondements de la psychologie. Parjs, 1928.

Phil 2825.35   Politzer, Georges. Écrits...textes réunis par Jacques Debouzy. Paris, 1969. 2v.

Phil 2475.1.299.5   Politzer, Georges. La fin d'une parade philosophique, le Bergsonisme. Paris, 1967.

Phil 6965.26   Poljak, Leo. Graphologische Untersuchungen an den Handelschriften von Schizophren-Paranoiden und Epileptikern. Abhandlung. Tübingen, 1957.

Phil 8705.12   Pollach, Friedrich. Gesetz von der Erhaltung der Energie und der christliche Glaube. Fulda, 1913.

Phil 190.31   Pollack, Walter. Perspektive und Symbol in Philosophie und Rechtswissenschaft. Berlin, 1912.

Phil 6115.11.28   Pollak, G. The hygiene of the soul; the memoir of a physician and philosopher. N.Y., 1910.

Phil 5643.75   Pollak, G.F.X. Über den Einfluss der Gesichtsschärfe. Inaug. Diss. Dillingen, 1829.

Phil 1750.745   Pollak, Oscar. Der neue Humanismus. Wien, 1962.

Phil 6980.606.5   Pollak, Otto. Integrating sociological and psychoanalytic concepts. N.Y., 1956.

Phil 6980.606   Pollak, Otto. Social science and psychotherapy for children. N.Y., 1952.

Phil 6155.14   Polland, John C. Drugs and phantasy: the effects of LSD, psilocykin and Sernyl on college students. 1st ed. Boston, 1965.

Phil 5520.450   Pollio, Howard R. The structural basis of word association behavior. Paris, 1966.

Phil 3835.1.16.2   Pollock, F. Spinoza; his life and philosophy. 2nd ed. N.Y., 1966.

Phil 3835.1.15   Pollock, F. Spinoza. London, 1935.

Phil 3835.1.2   Pollock, F. Spinoza. 2nd ed. London, 1899.

Phil 8963.4   Polnoe sobranie sochinenii. (Nepliuev, N.N.) Sankt Peterburg, 1901. 2v.

Phil 5625.75.2   Polnoe sobranie trudov. v.2-5. (Pavlov, Ivan P.) Moskva, 1946. 4v.

Phil 3925.16.270   Polochmann, George Kimball. Terms in their proportional contexts in Wittgenstein's Tractatus; an index. Carbondale, 1962.

Phil 5039.8   Poloka Akademia Nauk. Instytut Filozofii i Socjologii. Teoria i doświadczenie. Warszawa, 1966.

Phil 600.61   Polozhitel'naia filosofiia i edinstvo nauki. (Chicherin, Boris A.) Moskva, 1892.

Phil 2225.15   Pols, E. The recognition of reason. Carbondale, 1963.

Phil 2340.10.205   Pols, Edward. Whitehead's metaphysics. Carbondale, 1967.

Phil 25.97   Polska Akademia Nauk, Warsaw. Komitet filozoficzny. Studia logica. 1-24 10v.

Phil 25.144   Polska Akademia Nauk. Zakład historii filozofii starożytnej i średniowiecznej materiały i studia. Wrocław. 3-11,1964-1969//

Phil 75.46   Polska Akademia Nauk. Komitet Filozoficzny. Bibliografia filozofii polskiej [1750-1830]. v.1,3. Warszawa, 1955. 2v.

Phil 3425.616   Polska Akademia Nauk. Zakład Historii Filozofii Nowożytnej i Myśli Społecznej. Polskie spory o Hegla, 1830-1860. Warszawa, 1966.

Phil 55.5   Polska Akademia Umiejetności. Komisya do badania historji filofozfi w Polsce archivum. Krakowie. 1-6,1915-1935 5v.

Phil 4802.2   Polska filozofja narodowa, 15 wykładow. (Straszewski, Maurycy.) Krakow, 1921.

Phil 4802.6   Polska mysl filosoficzna. (Hinz, Henryk.) Warszawa, 1964.

Phil 8581.29   Polska w apostazii cryli wtak zwanym russo-sławianismie. (Bukaty, A.) Paryż, 1842.

Phil 4803.794.30   Polski Marksizm. (Skolimowski, Henryk.) Londyn, 1969.

Phil 4800.14   Pol'skie mysliteli epokhi Vozrozhdeniia. (Narskii, Igor' Sergeevich.) Moskva, 1960.

Phil 3425.616   Polskie spory o Hegla, 1830-1860. (Polska Akademia Nauk. Zakład Historii Filozofii Nowożytnej i Myśli Społecznej.) Warszawa, 1966.

Phil 3425.645   Polsko-Czechosłowacka Sesja Naukowa, Póswięcona Recepcji Filozofii Hegle w Krajach Słowianskich, Warsaw. Der Streit um Hegel bei den Slawen; Symposium. Prag, 1967.

Phil 7069.45.15   Poltergeist over England; three centuries of mischievous ghosts. (Price, Harry.) London, 1945.

Phil 7069.40.7   Poltergeists. (Sitwell, S.) London, 1940.

Phil 7069.66.20   Poltergeists of the south. (Du Plessis, Izak David.) Cape Town, 1966.

Phil 4752.2.155   Poltoratskii, Nikolai P. Berdiaev i Rossia. N.Y., 1967.

Htn   Phil 8887.31*   La polvere del mutio. (Muzéo, G.) n.p., n.d.

Phil 8890.59   Polzer, Ignatius. Praelectiones ethicae. Olomuc, 1770.

Phil 9355.5   Pomeroy, Marcus. Sense. N.Y., 1871.

Phil 9375.3.2   Pomeroy, R.W. The young merchant. 2d ed. Boston, 1840.

Phil 2672.91   Pommier, J.J.M. Deux études sur Jouffroy et son temps. Paris, 1930.

Phil 815.2   Pompa, R.P. Sommario della storia di filosofia. Napoli, 1865.

Phil 4015.4   Pompa, Raffaele. L'Italia filosofica contemporanea. Salerno, 1875.

Phil 8640.1.10   Pomponazzi, P. De immortalitate animae. Messina, 1925.

Phil 8640.1.12   Pomponazzi, P. Tractatus de immortalitate animae. Haverford, Pa., 1938.

Htn Phil 8640.1* Pomponazzi, P. Tractatus de immortalitate animae. Paris, 1534.

Htn Phil 8640.1.15* Pomponazzi, P. Tractatus de immortalitate animae. Paris, 161-?

Phil 8640.1.5 Pomponazzi, P. Trattato sull'immortalità dell'anima. Roma, 1914.

Phil 4200.1.30 Pomponazzi, Pietro. Les causes des merveilles de la nature, ou Les enchantements. Paris, 1930.

Phil 4200.1.32 Pomponazzi, Pietro. Corsi inediti dell'insegnamento padovano. Padova, 1966.

Phil 4200.1.15 Pomponazzi, Pietro. De fato. Lucani, 1957.

Phil 4200.1.34.1 Pomponazzi, Pietro. De naturalium effectuum causis, sive, De incantationibus. Hildesheim, 1970.

Htn Phil 4200.1.10* Pomponazzi, Pietro. Opera. Basileae, 1567.

Phil 7054.95 Pond, E. Familiar spirits and spiritual manifestations. Boston, 1852.

Phil 7069.47.10 Pond, Mariam B. Time is kind. N.Y., 1947.

Phil 346.32 Pondey, Rajendra Prasad. The problem of fact. Santiniketan, 1965.

Phil 70.50.5 Ponencias y conferencias. (Semana Española de Filosofía.) Madrid. 1-9 4v.

Phil 7082.182 Pongracz, Marion. Das Königreich der Träume. Wien, 1963.

Phil 5875.25 Pongratz, Josa Maria. Zur Ontogenese des sittlichen Urteils in besonderer Antinüpfung and die einschlägige Theorie Piaget's. Inaug. Diss. Heidelberg? 1964.

Phil 5225.10 Pongratz, Ludwig Jakob. Problemgeschichte der Psychologie. Bern, 1967.

Phil 5061.6.5 Poniatie. (Voishvillo, Evgenii K.) Moskva, 1967.

Phil 5520.285 Poniatie i slovo. (Reznikov, Lazar' O.) Leningrad, 1958.

Phil 310.470 Poniatie sviazi v marksistskoi filosofii. (Novinskii, I.I.) Moskva, 1961.

Phil 310.782 Poniatiia "dvizhenie" i razvitie i ikhvol' v izuchsnii fizicheskikh protsessov. (Shchekina, Liubov' I.) Moskva, 1970.

Phil 3903.1.95 Ponnér, Jarl W. Johannes Volkelts lära am det tragiska. Lund, 1956.

Phil 5255.62 Ponomarev, Ia.A. Psikhologiia tvorcheskogo myshleniia. Moskva, 1960.

Phil 346.31 Ponomarev, Iakov A. Psikhika i intuitsiia. Moskva, 1967.

Phil 5535.12 Ponomarev, Iakov A. Znaniia, myshlenie i umstvennoe razvitie. Moskva, 1967.

Phil 8890.54 Pons, Walter. Steht uns der Himmel offen. Wiesbaden, 1960.

Phil 8890.54.2 Pons, Walter. Steht uns der Himmel offen. 2. Aufl. Wiesbaden, 1960.

Phil 672.159 Ponsonby, A.P. Life here and now; conclusions derived from an examination of the sense of duration. London, 1936.

Phil 6325.24 Pontalis, J.B. Après Freud. Paris, 1965.

Phil 8595.27 Pontanilles, E. Los dos grandes problemas de la humanidad. N.Y., 1882.

Phil 8890.68 Pontara, Giuliano. Does the end justify the means? Stockholm, 1967.

Phil 1730.32 Ponte Orvieto, Marina da. L'unità de sapere nell'illuminismo. Padova, 1968.

Phil 5068.55 Ponte Orvieto, Marina da. L'unità del sapere nel neopositivismo. Padova, 1965.

Phil 2805.455 Pontet, Maurice. Pascal et Teilhard, témoins de Jésus-Christ. Paris, 1968.

Phil 190.81 Pontifex, Mark. The meaning of existence. London, 1953.

Phil 8640.11 Ponton, M. Glimpses of the future life. London, 1873.

Phil 6325.3 Pontoppidan, Knud. Psychiatriske foreläsinger. Kjobenhavn, 1892-95.

Phil 4482.1.97 Pontos de referência. (Vieira de Almeida, Francisco.) Lisboa, 1961.

Phil 4655.1.81 Pontus Wikner. (Eklund, J.A.) Stockholm, 1903.

Phil 4655.1.84 Pontus Wikner. (Werin, A.) Lund, 1937.

Phil 4655.1.85 Pontus Wikner som vitter författare. (Lange, Dagmar M.) Nora, 1946.

Phil 8416.15 Ponze, Francis. Le murmure condition et destin de l'artiste. Lyon, 1956.

Phil 575.266 Ponzio, Augusto. La relazione interpersonale. Bari, 1967.

Phil 978.59.10 The pool of wisdom; Who brings the truth; By what authority and three poems. (Krishnamurti, J.) Eerde, 1928.

Phil 8696.4 Poole, R.S. Genesis of the earth and of man. 2. ed. London, 1860.

Phil 9359.2 Poor girl and true woman. (Thayer, W.M.) Boston, 1859.

Phil 490.8 Poortman, J.J. Achêma. v.1-2,6. Assen, 1954. 5v.

Phil 190.60.5 Poortman, J.J. De grandparadox. Assen, 1961.

Phil 3745.9 Poortman, J.J. De noodzaak. Assen, 1936.

Phil 190.60 Poortman, J.J. Tweeërlei subjectiviteit. Haarlem, 1929.

Phil 7069.39.45 Poortman, Johannes J. Drei Forträge über Philosophie und Parapsychologie. Leiden, 1939.

Phil 978.112 Poortman, Johannes Jocobus. Philosophy, theosophy, parapsychology, some essays. Leyaen, 1965[1964]

Phil 8980.707 Popelová, J. Etika. Praha, 1962.

Phil 4805.20 Popelová, Jiřina. Studie o současné české filosofii. Praha, 1946.

Phil 8712.11 The popes and science. (Walsh, J.J.) N.Y., 1911.

Phil 8712.11.2 The popes and science. (Walsh, J.J.) N.Y., 1915.

Phil 6060.80 Pophal, Rudolf. Graphologie in Vorlesungen. Stuttgart, 1965- 3v.

Phil 645.50.5 Popkin, Richard H. The history of scepticism. Assen, 1964.

Phil 645.50 Popkin, Richard H. The history of scepticism from Erasmus to Descartes. Assen, 1960.

Phil 645.50.7 Popkin, Richard H. The history of scepticism from Erasmus to Descartes. N.Y., 1964.

Phil 3745.16 Popma, Klaas. Wijsbegeerte en anthropologie. Amsterdam, 1963.

Phil 672.254 Popma, Klaas Johan. Nadenken over de tijd. Amsterdam, 1965.

Phil 5066.150 Popov, A.I. Vredenie v matematicheskuiu logiku. Leningrad, 1959.

Phil 5025.3 Popov, P.S. Istoriia logiki novogo vremeni. Moskva, 1960.

Phil 3497.21 Popov, Sergei I. Kant i Kantianstvo. Moskva, 1961.

Phil 270.133 Popov, Stoiko. Prichinnostta v obshtestvoto. Sofiia, 1964.

Phil 8890.49 Popov I.V. Estestvennyi nravstvennyi zakon. Sergiev, 1897.

Phil 680.35 Popovič, Anton. Štrukturalizmus v slovenskej vede. Martin, 1970.

Phil 2415.14 Popovych, M.V. Pokhid proty rozumu. Kyiv, 1960.

Phil 3110.176 Popp, K.R. Jakob Böhme und Issac Newton. Inaug. Diss. Leipzig, 1935.

Phil 5325.10.5 Popp, Walter. Kritische Bemerkungen zur Associationstheorie. Teil 1. Leipzig, 1913.

Phil 3095.81 Poppe, B. Alexander G. Baumgarten. Borna, 1907.

Phil 978.49.840 Poppelbaum, H. Entwicklung, Vererbung und Abstammungs. Dornach, 1961.

Phil 978.85 Poppelbaum, H. Man's eternal biography; three essays on life and death. N.Y., 1945.

Phil 190.75 Popper, J. Das Individuum und die Beertung menschlicher Existenzen. 2. Aufl. Photoreproduction. Dresden, 1920.

Phil 5765.12 Popper, Karl R. Of clouds and clocks. St. Louis, 1966.

Phil 346.27.5 Popper, Karl Raimund. Conjectures and refutations. N.Y., 1962.

Phil 346.27.8 Popper, Karl Raimund. Conjectures and refutations: the grouth of scientific knowledge. 3. ed. London, 1969.

Phil 346.27 Popper, Karl Raimund. On the sources of knowledge and of ignorance. London, 1960.

Phil 1630.30 Poppi, Antonino. Causalità e infinità nella scuola padovana dal 1480 al 1513. Padova, 1906.

Phil 4015.6 Poppi, Antonino. Introduzione all'aristotelismo padovano. Padova, 1970.

Phil 4200.1.90 Poppi, Antonio. Saggi sul pensiero inedito di Pietri Pomponazzi. Padova, 1970.

Phil 9530.39.5 Popplestone, C.E. Every man a winner. N.Y., 1936.

Phil 3497.14 Poppovich, N.M. Die Entwicklungsgeschichte der vorkritischen Raumphilosophie Kants. Wien, 1925.

Phil 672.132 Poppovich, N.M. Die Lehre vom diskreten Raum in der neueren Philosophie. Wien, 1922.

Phil 8412.24 Populäre Asthetik. (Lemcke, Carl von.) Leipzig, 1879.

Phil 8412.25 Populäre Asthetik. 4. Aufl. (Lemke, Carl von.) Leipzig, 1873.

Phil 3492.2.15 Populäre Darstellung von Immanuel Kant's Kritik der reinen Vernunft. (Krause, A.) Lahr, 1881.

Phil 3492.2.17 Populäre Darstellung von Immanuel Kant's Kritik der reinen Vernunft. 2. Aufl. (Krause, A.) Hamburg, 1911.

Phil 3425.25 Populäre Gedanken aus seinen Werker. (Hegel, Georg Wilhelm Friedrich.) Berlin, 1873.

Phil 175.5.5 Populäre Philosophie oder leichtfassliche Einfuhrung in die Weisheitslehre. (Amersin, F.) Graz, 1872.

Phil 3480.19.25 Populäre Schriften. (Kant, Immanuel.) Berlin, 1911.

Phil 6315.1.20 Populäre vorträge über Psychoanalyse. (Ferenczi, Sandor.) Leipzig, 1922.

Phil 9010.26.2 Popular amusements. (Crane, J.T.) Cincinnati, n.d.

Phil 9010.11 Popular amusements. (Mattison, H.) N.Y., 1867?

Phil 960.137.15 Popular essays in Indian philosophy. (Hiriyanna, M.) Mysore, 1952.

Phil 1145.92 Popular ethics in ancient Greece. (Pearson, L.I.C.) Stanford, Calif., 1962.

Phil 8610.884.20 Popular faith unveiled. (Hardwicke, H.J.) n.p., 1884.

Phil 3425.203.5 Popular framstallning af Hegelska philosofeska. (Mager, K.W.E.) Stockholm, 1843.

Phil 8887.11 Popular lectures on ethics. (Mercer, M.) Petersburg, 1841.

Phil 5259.29 Popular psychological fallacies. (Taylor, J.G.) London, 1938.

Phil 5257.28.9 Popular psychology. (Roback, A.A.) Cambridge, 1928.

Phil 7060.137 Popular superstitions. 3. ed. (Mayo, Herbert.) Philadelphia, 1852.

Phil 3246.25.5 Popular works. (Fichte, Johann Gottlieb.) London, 1873.

Phil 3246.26 Popular works. (Fichte, Johann Gottlieb.) London, 1889. 2v.

Phil 6105.314 Population and mental health. (World Federation for Mental Health.) Berne, 1964.

Phil 8665.23 Populiarnye lektsii po ateizmu. 2. izd. (Karpushin, Vladimir A.) Moskva, 1965.

Phil 8403.45 Por uma crítica estética. (Coutinho, Afrânio.) Rio de Janeiro, 1954.

Phil 5258.190 Pora uma psicologia na premeira pessoa. (Simões, M.B.) Lisboa, 1961.

Phil 7069.29.100 Pórdardóttir, Théodóra. Árangur reynslu minnar í dulraenum afnum. Akureyri, 1929.

Phil 8416.23 Porena, M. Che cos'é il bello? Schema d'un estetica psicologica. Milano, 1905.

Phil 5170.1 Poretsky, P. Sept lois fondamentales de la théorie des égalités logiques. Kazan, 1899.

Phil 2705.82 Poritzky, J.E. Julien Offray de La Mettrie. Berlin, 1900.

Htn Phil 9495.126* Pornography and obscenity. (Lawrence, D.H.) N.Y., 1930.

Phil 4752.2.115 Porret, Eugene. Berdiaeff. Neuchâtel, 1951.

Phil 4752.2.100 Porret, Eugene. La philosophie chrétienne en Russie. Neuchâtel, 1944.

Phil 5627.6.95A Porret, J.A. Au sujet de la conversion...théorie de Wm. James. Genève, 1907.

Phil 8965.9 Porret, James A. Les philosophies morales du temps présent. Genève, 1897.

Phil 8592.122.30 Porshnev, Boris F. Mel'e. Moskva, 1964.

Phil 5374.185 Port, Kurt. Die Enge des Bewusstseins. Esslingen, 1955.

Phil 3549.7.90 Port, Kurt. Das System der Werte. München, 1929.

Phil 5040.4.5 The Port Royal logic. (Arnauld, Antoine.) Edinburgh, 1861.

Phil 6025.4.15 Porta, G.B. La chirofisonomia overo di quelle parte della humana fisonomia. Napoli, 1677.

Htn Phil 6025.4* Porta, G.B. De humana physiognomia libri. Hanoviae, 1593.

Htn Phil 6000.1* Porta, G.B. De humana physiognomonia. Francofurti, 1586.

NEDL Phil 6025.4.8 Porta, G.B. Della fisonomia dell'huomo. Venetia, 1644.

Htn Phil 6025.4.6.5* Porta, G.B. Della fisonomia dell'huomo. Vicenza, 1615.

Htn Phil 6025.4.6F* Porta, G.B. Della fisonomia dell'huomo. Libri quattro. Napoli, 1598.

Phil 6025.4.7 Porta, G.B. Della fisonomia di tutto il corpo humano. Roma, 1637.

Phil 6025.4.9 Porta, G.B. Fisonomia dell'huomo. Venetia, 1652.

Phil 6025.4.3 Porta, G.B. Physiognomoniae collestis libri sex. Argentorati, 1606. 2 pam.

Phil 6025.4.5 Porta, G.B. Physiognomoniae collestis libri sex. Ursellis, 1601-08. 2 pam.

Htn Phil 6025.4.25* Porta, G.B. La physionomie humaine. Rouen, 1655.

Phil 4115.110 Portale, Vincenzo. L'ontologismo di Vincenzo Gioberti; antologia sistematica. Cosenza, 1968.

Phil 2415.3 Portalis, J.E.M. De l'usage et de l'abus de l'esprit philosophique durant le XVIIe siècle. Paris, 1834. 2v.

Phil 2415.3.25 Portalis, philosophes-chrétien. (Frégier, J.C.) Paris, 1861.

Phil 7069.54.25 Porten, Harry. The miracle on the wall. Eastbourne, Eng., 1955.

Phil 3497.9 Porten, M. von der. Die Grundlagen der Kantschen Philosophie. Leipzig, 1914.

Phil 346.8 Porten, Max von der. Entstehen von Empfindung und bewisstsein. Leipzig, 1910.

Phil 9175.5 Porter, Ann E. Uncle Jerry's letters to young mothers. Boston, 1854.

Phil 365.51 Porter, C. Creative personality. N.Y., 1950.

Phil 380.4 — Porter, Gene L. The nature of form in process. N.Y., 1969.

Phil 5893.4 — Porter, Judith Deborah Revitch. Black child, white child; the development of racial attitudes. Cambridge, 1971.

Phil 8890.20 — Porter, N. Elements of moral science. N.Y., 1885.
Phil 8890.20.1 — Porter, N. Elements of moral science. N.Y., 1885.
Phil 3497.2 — Porter, N. Kant's ethics. Chicago, 1886.
Phil 190.15.5 — Porter, N. Science and sentiment. N.Y., 1882.
Phil 190.15 — Porter, N. Sciences of nature vs. sciences of man. N.Y., 1871.

Phil 1870.86 — Porter, N. The two-hundredth birthday of Bishop George Berkeley. N.Y., 1885.

Phil 5255.5.9 — Porter, Noah. The elements of intellectual science. N.Y., 1872.

Phil 5255.5.6 — Porter, Noah. The human intellect. 4th ed. N.Y., 1887.
Phil 7150.60 — Porterfield, Austin Larimore. Cultures of violence; a study of the tragic man in society. Fort Worth, Texas, 1965.

Phil 6325.14 — Porteus, S.D. The practice of clinical psychology. N.Y., 1941.

Phil 6750.222 — Porteus, S.D. Studies in mental deviations. Vineland, 1922.

Phil 5592.35 — Porteus, Stanley David. The Porteus maze test manual. London, 1952.

Phil 5255.80 — Porteus, Stanley David. A psychologist of sorts. Palo Alto, 1969.

Phil 5592.37 — Porteus maze test. (Proteus, Stanley David.) Palo Alto, 1965.

Phil 5592.35 — The Porteus maze test manual. (Porteus, Stanley David.) London, 1952.

Phil 296.9 — Portig, Gustav. Die Grundzüge der monistischen und dualistischen Weltanschauung. Stuttgart, 1904.

Phil 346.9 — Portius, K.N. Ueber den Ursprung der Begriffe. Leipzig, 1848.

Phil 9495.9 — Portland (Oregon). Social Hygiene Society. Annual report. Portland, Ore. 1-4

Phil 6125.27 — Portman, Adolf. Don Quijote und Sancho Pansa vom gegenwartigen Stand der Typenlehre. Basel, 1957.
Phil 5475.12 — Portmann, Adolf. Manipulation des Menschen als Schicksal und Bedrohung. Zürich, 1969.
Phil 8416.10 — Portnoy, Julius. A psychology of art creation. Philadephia, 1942.

Phil 8881.68 — Le portrait d'un honneste homme. 2e éd. (Gaussault, Abbe.) Paris, 1694.
Phil 4363.12 — Portrait of a man standing. (Madariaga, Salvador de.) London, 1968.
Phil 1930.10.85 — Portrait of a philosopher. (Rosenfield, Leonora.) N.Y., 1962.
Phil 6319.1.266 — Portrait of Jung; an illustrated biography. (Wehr, Gerhard.) N.Y., 1971.
Phil 2805.195.5 — Portrait of Pascal. (Duclaux, A.M.F.R.) London, 1927.
Phil 2255.1.78 — Portraits from memory. (Russell, Bertrand Russell.) London, 1956.
Phil 4803.495.220 — Porządek fizyczno-moralny oraz Pomysty do dzieta Porządek fizyczno-moralny. (Kołłątaj, Hugo.) Warszawa, 1955.

Htn Phil 5765.1* — Porzio, S. An homun bonus v. malus volens fiat. Florentiae, 1551.

Htn Phil 5765.1.5* — Porzio, S. Se l'huomo diventa buono o cattivo volontariamente. Fiorenza, 1551.

Phil 346.13 — Pos, Hendrik J. Filosofie der Wetenschappen. Arnhem, 1940.

Phil 1702.3 — La position actuelle des problèmes philosophiques. (Cresson, André.) Paris, 1924.
Phil 187.93.15 — Position et approches concrètes du mystère ontologique. (Marcel, Gabriel.) Louvain, 1949.

Phil 600.36 — Den positiva filosofien i sammandrag. (Robinet, E.) Stockholm, 1889.

Phil 182.133 — The positive absolutes. (Hurtado, Manuel.) Mexico, 1963.
Phil 8892.5 — Positive Ethik. (Ratzenhofer, G.) Leipzig, 1901.
Phil 334.7 — The positive outcome of philosophy. (Dietzgen, J.) Chicago, 1906.

Phil 2490.41.4 — Die positive Philosophie. v.1-2. (Comte, Auguste.) Heidelberg, 1884.

Phil 2490.41.1.5 — The positive philosophy. (Comte, Auguste.) N.Y., 1853. 2v.

Phil 2490.41.1 — The positive philosophy. (Comte, Auguste.) N.Y., 1855.
Phil 600.8 — The positive philosophy. (Peabody, A.P.) Boston, 1867.
Phil 2490.41.2.4A — The positive philosophy. 2. ed. (Comte, Auguste.) London, 1875. 2v.

Phil 2490.84.6 — The positive philosophy of Auguste Comte. (Mill, John Stuart.) N.Y., 1873.

Phil 2490.41.2.2 — The positive philosophy of Auguste Comte. (Mill, John Stuart.) N.Y., 1873.

Phil 2490.84.4 — The positive philosophy of Auguste Comte. (Mill, John Stuart.) N.Y., 1887.

Phil 2490.105 — The positive philosophy of Auguste Comte. Thesis. (Harris, M.S.) Hartford, 1923.

Phil 7068.70.33 — Positive Pneumatologie. 2. Aufl. (Güldinstubbe, J. von.) Bern, n.d.

Phil 8580.12.2 — Positive religion. (Allen, J.H.) Boston, 1894. 5v.
Phil 8586.28 — The positive religion. (Ghose, J.C.) Calcutta, n.d.
Phil 5222.11 — The positive thinkers. 1. ed. (Meyer, Donald Burton.) Garden City, N.Y., 1965.

Phil 5261.20 — Positive versus negative instruction. (Vaughn, J.) N.Y., 1928.

Phil 3640.655 — Positives antichristentum. (Wien, Hermann.) Den Haag, 1962.

Phil 5068.5.5A — Positivism. (Mises, R.E. von.) Cambridge, 1951.
Phil 2490.101 — Positivism. (Nyström, A.) Stockholm, 1879.
Phil 1980.4.30 — Positivism in the United States. (Schneider, R.E.) Rosario, 1946.

Phil 600.21 — Le positivisme. (Cantecor, Georges.) Paris, 1904.
Phil 2490.91 — Le positivisme. (Dupuy, P.) Paris, 1911.
Phil 2138.87 — Positivisme anglais. (Taine, H.A.) Paris, 1864.
Phil 600.32 — Le positivisme dans l'action. (Deherme, G.) Paris, 1923.
Phil 600.12 — Positivisme et anarchie. (Cottin, P.) Paris, 1908.
Phil 2490.97 — Le positivisme et le progrès de l'esprit. (Milhaud, Gaston.) Paris, 1902.

Phil 25.76 — Positivisme français; histoire et sciences sociales. Boulogne, 1945

Phil 600.17 — Positivisme intégral. (Dubuisson, A.) Paris, 1910.
Phil 600.37.5 — Positivismen och Herbert Spencer. (Nyström, Anton.) Stockholm, 1887.

Phil 600.48 — Positivismo, neopositivismo y fenomenologia. (Caso, A.) México, 1941.

Phil 600.24 — Il positivismo. (Calderoni, Giuseppe.) Roma, 1900.
Phil 600.22 — El positivismo. (Estasén y Cortada, P.) Barcelona, 1877.
Phil 600.56 — El positivismo. (Poey, Andrés.) Habana, 1960.

Phil 25.7.5 — El positivismo. Buenos Aires.
Phil 25.7 — O positivismo. Porto. 1-4,1878-1882 4v.
Phil 2138.110 — Positivismo? John Stuart Mill. (Fabbricotti, Carlo A.) Firenze, 1910.

Phil 600.60 — El positivismo argentino. (Soler, Ricaurte.) Panamá, 1959.

Phil 600.35 — Il positivismo e i diritti dello spirito. (Troilo, E.) Torino, 1912.

Phil 4060.1.100 — Il positivismo e Roberto Ardigò. (Saloni, Alfredo.) Roma, 1969.

Phil 4959.230.2 — El positivismo en México. 2. ed. (Zea, Leopoldo.) México, 1953.

Phil 600.26 — El positivismo filosófico. (Gamboa, Ignacio.) Mérida, 1899.

Phil 4960.605.15 — O positivismo na república. (Cruz Costa, João.) São Paulo, 1956.

Phil 4960.610 — O positivismo no Brasil. (Torres, João Camillo de Oliveira.) Petropolis, 1943.
Phil 4960.610.2 — O positivismo no Brasil. 2. ed. (Torres, João Camillo de Oliveira.) Rio de Janeiro, 1957.
Phil 600.5 — Der Positivismus. (Brütt, M.) Hamburg, 1889.
Phil 600.57.10 — Positivismus in Vergangenheit und Gegenwart. (Narskii, Igor Sergeevich.) Berlin, 1967.
Phil 190.53 — Positivismus und reale Aussenwelt. (Planck, Max.) Leipzig, 1931.
Phil 3585.8.85 — Der Positivismus von Ernst Laas. Inaug. Diss. (Hanisch, Rudolf.) Halle, 1902.
Phil 2490.54 — The positivist calendar. (Edger, Henry.) Long Island, N.Y., 1856.
Phil 600.6 — A positivist primer. (Croly, D.G.) N.Y., 1871.
Phil 25.13 — The positivist review. London. 1-31,1893-1923 15v.
Phil 600.55 — Positivist thought in France. (Charlton, D.G.) Oxford, 1959.
Phil 4060.5.85 — I positivisti italiani. (Mandolfo, Santo.) Anuilli, 1966.
Phil 3195.9.80 — Posner, S. Abriss der Philosophie Eugen Dührings. Inaug. Diss. Breslau, 1906.
Phil 8416.38 — Pospelov, Gennadii N. Esteticheskoe i khudozhestvennoe. Moskva, 1965.

Phil 5627.119 — Les possédées noires. (Meige, Henry.) Paris, 1894.
Phil 8599.13.80 — Posselt, H. Die Religionsphilosophie Gustav Teichmüllers. Marburg, 1960.
Htn Phil 9560.30* — Possevino, G.B. Dialogo dell'honore. Venice, 1553.
Phil 5190.50 — Possibilism. (Guha Mozumdar, Roby.) Calcutta, 1966.
Phil 8702.21 — Possibilities unlimited. 1. ed. (Morris, D.L.) N.Y., 1952.
Phil 176.106 — Possibility. (Buchanan, S.M.) London, 1927.
Phil 176.106.2 — Possibility. (Buchanan, S.M.) N.Y., 1927.
Phil 9075.37 — The possibility of a science of casuistry. (Merrington, E.N.) Sydney, 1902.
Phil 8888.18 — The possibility of altruism. (Nagel, Thomas.) Oxford, 1970.
Phil 178.22.9 — The possibility of metaphysics. (Driesch, H.) London, 1924.
Phil 8635.2 — The possibility of not dying. (Kirk, H.C.) N.Y., 1883.
Phil 3625.4.81 — Post, Karl. Johannes Müllers philosophische Anschauungen. Inaug. Diss. Halle, 1905.
Phil 9450.6 — Post, Louis F. Ethics of democracy. N.Y., 1903.
Phil 7054.96 — Post, S. An exposition of modern spiritualism. N.Y., 1861.
Phil 8610.856 — Post, T.M. The skeptical era in modern history. N.Y., 1856.
Phil 7068.86.60A — Post-mortem confessions. (Putman, A.) Boston, 1886.
Phil 9575.6 — Post-Mortem use of wealth. (Remsen, D.S.) N.Y., 1911.
Phil 525.185 — Post-Reformation spirituality. (Cognet, Louis.) London, 1959.
X Cg Phil 4777.536.100 — Postannictwo polskiego narodu. (Lutosławski, W.) Warszawa, 1939. (Changed to XP 5137, 3/20/72)
Phil 7068.87.5 — Posthumous humanity. (Assier, Adolphe d'.) London, 1887.
Htn Phil 2115.15.5* — Posthumous works. (Locke, J.) London, 1706.
Htn Phil 2115.15* — Posthumous works. (Locke, J.) London, 1706.
Phil 4210.142.5 — Le postille di un anonimo. (Pestalozza, A.) Milano, 1850.
Phil 2490.41.3 — The postive philosophy. (Comte, Auguste.) London, 1896. 3v.
Le postivisme et la science expérimentale. (Broglie, Paul.) Paris, 1880-81. 2v.
Phil 600.4.5 — Postman, Leo Joseph. Psychology in the making; histories of selected research problems. N.Y., 1968.
Phil 5225.4.1 — Postman, Leo Joseph. Verbal learning and memory; selected readings. Baltimore, 1970.
Phil 5545.252 — Die postmentalen Erregungen als struktureller Faktor beim Lernen. Thesis. (al-Ma'ayirji, Muhammad Ismat.) St. Margrethen, 1964.
Phil 5545.250 — Postovoitov, V.K. O kul'ture molodogo rabocheg. Moskva, 1960.
Phil 9355.13 — Postscriptum. (Larsson, Hans.) Stockholm, 1944.
Phil 4600.2.30 — Postulates and implications. (Dotterer, Ray H.) N.Y., 1955.
Phil 178.59.5 — The postulates of revelation and of ethics. (Hill, Thomas.) Boston, 1895.
Phil 8957.5.5 — The postulates of the moral life. (Strain, J.) Cambridge, 1929.
Phil 8893.80 — Potempa, Rudolf. Persönlichkeit und Religiosität. Göttingen, 1958.
Phil 189.28 — Potentiality and energy. Diss. (O'Connor, E.M.) Washington, 1939.
Phil 665.102 — Le potenze dell'anima. (Zolla, Elémire.) Milano, 1968.
Phil 4769.7.33 — Potestas clavium. (Shestov, Lev.) Athens, Ohio, 1968.
Phil 4769.7.32 — Potestas clavium. (Shestov, Lev.) München, 1926.
Phil 8980.485 — Potrebnosti, povedenie, vospitanie. (Kiknadze, Dmitrii A.) Moskva, 1968.
Phil 9045.4 — Potte, Henry Codman. Citizen in relation in his relationship to the industrial situation. N.Y., 1902.
Phil 8595.28 — Potter, Charles F. Humanism; a new religion. N.Y., 1930.
Phil 2280.6.87 — Potter, H.C. A sermon, memorial of the Rev. Charles W. Shields. Princeton, N.J., 1905.
Phil 9355.4 — Potter, Horatio. The importance of liberal tastes and good intellectual habits. Troy, N.Y., 1837.
Phil 2225.5.150 — Potter, Vincent G. Charles S. Peirce on norms and ideals. Amherst, 1967.
Phil 8505.2 — Potter, W.J. The Free Religious Association. Boston, 1892.
Phil 8965.25 — Potterie, I. de. La vie selon l'Esprit, condition du chrétien. Paris, 1965.
Phil 6965.12 — Pottier, Claude. Réflexions sur les troubles du langage dans les psychoses paranoïdes. Thèse. Paris, 1930.
Phil 5255.42 — Potts, John. Know thyself; a study in mental qualities. Philadelphia, 1935.
Phil 525.50.5 — Poulain, A. Des graces d'oraison. 5e éd. Paris, 1906.

Phil 6990.20 Poulpiquet, E. Le miracle et ses suppléances. Paris, 1914.
Phil 1885.82 Pounder, R.M. The one and the many...Bradley's "Appearance and reality". Diss. Cambridge, 1928.
Phil 8670.11 Pounder, R.M. Some thoughts about God. Toronto, 1923.
Phil 2905.1.215 Pour comprendre Teilhard. Paris, 1962.
Phil 6315.2.140.8 Pour connaître la pensée de Freud. (Pesch, Edgar.) Évreux, 1970.
Phil 3552.336 Pour connaître la pensée de Leibniz. (Belaval, Yvor.) Paris, 1952.
Phil 2905.1.660 Pour et contre Teilhard de Chardin, pensuer religieux. (Philippe de la Trinité, Father.) Saint-Céneré, 1970.
Phil 9349.4 Pour les jeunes. (Joly, Henri.) Paris, 1919.
Phil 1504.6.6 Pour l'histoire du problème. v.6. pt.6. (Rousselot, P.) Münster, 1908.
Phil 2515.4.97 Pour qu'on lise Cournot. (Mentré, F.) Paris, 1927.
Phil 8666.19 Pour un dialogue avec les athées. (Lelong, Michel.) Paris, 1965.
Phil 9070.116 Pour un garçon de vingt ans, essai. (Simon, Pierre Henri.) Paris, 1967.
Phil 8582.65 Pour un humanisme laïc. (Chédel, André.) Neuchâtel, 1963.
Phil 1750.345 Pour un nouvel humanisme. (Rencontres Internationales.) Neuchâtel, 1949.
Phil 575.101 Pour un ordre personnaliste. (Hertel, François.) Montréal, 1942.
Phil 8413.2 Pour une clinique d'art. (Merle, Pierre.) Paris, 1962.
Phil 8876.108.5A Pour une morale de l'ambiguité. (Beauvoir, Simone de.) Paris, 1947.
Phil 8876.108.7 Pour une morale de l'ambiguité suivi de Pyraus et Cinéas. (Beauvoir, Simone de.) Paris, 1944.
Phil 2750.11.60 Pour une philosophie de l'éducation. (Maritain, Jacques.) Paris, 1959.
Phil 2750.19.43 Pour une sagesse tragique et son au-delà. (Marcel, Gabriel.) Paris, 1968.
Phil 5627.92 Pour une science de l'individuel. (Chevalier, J.) Paris, 1923.
Phil 8622.70 Pour une théologie de la foi. (Molevez, Léopold.) Paris, 1969.
Phil 8622.59 Pour une théorie rationnelle de l'acte de foi. (Broglic, Guy de.) Paris, 1963. 2v.
Phil 193.143 Pourings of a struggling soul. (Shah, R.V.) Ahmedabad, 1932.
Phil 192.98 Pourquoi des philosophes? (Revel, Jean Francois.) Paris, 1957. 2v.
Phil 192.98.2 Pourquoi des philosophes? (Revel, Jean Francois.) Paris, 1964.
Phil 192.98.3 Pourquoi des philosophes? (Revel, Jean Francois.) Utrecht, 1965. 2v.
Phil 8610.927.10 Pourquoi je ne suis pas chrétien. (Russell, Bertrand Russell.) Paris, 1964.
Phil 7059.20 Pourquoi la vie! (Denis, Léon.) Paris, 1892.
Phil 3640.255.5 Pourtalès, Guy de. Amor fati; Nietzsche in Italien. Freiburg, 1930.
Phil 3640.255 Pourtalès, Guy de. Nietzsche en stalie. 15. éd. Paris, 1929.
Phil 2520.340 Pousa, Narciso. Moral y libertad en Descartes. La Plata, 1960.
Phil 585.50 Poussière vivante. (Biot, René.) Paris, 1957.
Phil 192.102 Le pouvoir de l'esprit. (Rivier, William.) Neuchâtel, 1957.
Phil 5043.30 Pouvoir de l'esprit sur le réel. (Dialectica. Neuchâtel.) Neuchâtel, 1948.
Phil 8880.70 Pouvoir et morale. Thèse. (Fallot, Jean.) Saverne, 1967.
Phil 7069.32.30 Les pouvoirs inconnus de l'esprit sur la matière. (Osty, E.) Paris, 1932.
Phil 5425.2.7 Poverty and hereditary genius (criticism of Galton's theory). (Constable, F.C.) London, 1905.
Phil 3850.18.120F Povina, Alfredo. La obra sociologica de Max Scheler. Cordoba, 1941.
Phil 6985.20A Powdermaker, Florence. Group psychotherapy. Cambridge, 1953.
Phil 8595.7 Powell, B. The order of nature. London, 1859.
Phil 346.29 Powell, Betty. Knowledge of actions. London, 1967[1966]
Phil 3835.4.2 Powell, E.E. Spinoza and religion. Chicago, 1906.
Phil 8705.4.5 Powell, E.P. Liberty and life. Chicago, 1889.
Phil 8705.4.2 Powell, E.P. Our heredity from God. 2. ed. N.Y., 1888.
Phil 978.63 Powell, F.G.M. Studies in the lesser mysteries. London, 1913.
Phil 6125.11 Powell, Hyman R. The Emmanuel movement in a New England town. N.Y., 1909.
Phil 190.17 Powell, J.W. Truth and error. Chicago, 1898.
Phil 8965.7 Powell, John W. What is a Christian? N.Y., 1915.
Phil 7080.21 Powell, S.P. The art of natural sleep. N.Y., 1908.
Phil 2255.1.74A Power; a new social analysis. (Russell, Bertrand Russell.) N.Y., 1969.
Phil 8657.2 The power, wisdom and goodness of God. (Chalmers, T.) N.Y., 1834.
Phil 2310.1.30 Power and events. (Ushenko, A.P.) Princeton, 1946.
Phil 9450.35 Power and morality in a business society. (Selekman, Sylvia Kopald.) N.Y., 1956.
Phil 9530.57 The power of a magnetic personality. (Conklin, Bob.) West Ryack, N.Y., 1965.
Phil 978.76 The power of karma in relation to destiny. (Cannon, Alex.) London, 193-.
Phil 9560.4 The power of kindness. (Morley, C.) N.Y., 1851.
Phil 5585.236 The power of perception. (Bach, Marcus.) Garden City, 1966.
Phil 5850.305A The power of positive thinking. (Peale, N.V.) N.Y., 1955.
Phil 8884.4.13 The power of purpose. (Jordan, W.G.) N.Y., 1910.
Phil 6122.30 The power of self suggestion. (McComb, Samuel.) N.Y., 1909.
Phil 178.12.8 The power of silence. (Dresser, H.W.) Boston, 1895.
Phil 178.12.11 The power of silence. (Dresser, H.W.) N.Y., 1901.
Phil 178.12.11.9 The power of silence. 2nd ed. (Dresser, H.W.) N.Y., 1909.
Phil 178.12.9.5 The power of silence. 7th ed. (Dresser, H.W.) Boston, 1898.
Phil 7072.4 The power of the mind. (Alexander, Rolf.) London, 1965.
Htn Phil 6671.10.5* Power of the mind over the body. (Braid, James.) London, 1846.
Phil 5252.8 Power of the soul. (Moore, G.) London, 1845.
Phil 5258.41 The power of thought. (Sterrett, John D.) N.Y., 1896.
Phil 8884.4.9 The power of truth. (Jordan, W.G.) N.Y., 1902.
Phil 5757.12.6 Power of will. 55th ed. (Haddock, F.C.) Meriden, 1915.
Phil 5520.68.7 Power of words. 1. ed. (Chase, Stuart.) N.Y., 1954.
Phil 6980.347 The power tactics of Jesus Christ and other essays. (Haley, Jay.) N.Y., 1969.
Phil 6123.3 Power through perfected ideas. (Neff, S.S.) Philadelphia, 1911.
Phil 6112.2.4 Power through repose. (Call, A.P.) Boston, 1891.
Phil 6112.2.5 Power through repose. (Call, A.P.) Boston, 1893.
Phil 6112.2.8.7 Power through repose. (Call, A.P.) Boston, 1934.
Phil 5241.57 The power within us. (Baudouin, C.) N.Y., 1923.
Phil 8610.925.10 Powers, H.H. The religion of to-morrow...correspondence between H.H. Powers and William Archer. London, 1925.
Phil 3565.83 Powers, J.H. Kritische Bemerkungen zu Lotze's Seelenbegriff. Göttingen, 1892.
Phil 7069.34.7 Powers that be (the Mayfair lectures). (Cannon, Alexander.) London, 1934.
Phil 7069.34.8 Powers that be (the Mayfair lectures). (Cannon, Alexandre.) N.Y., 1935.
Phil 9400.9 Poweys, J.C. The art of growing old. London, 1944.
Phil 8595.23A Powicke, F.J. The Cambridge Platonists; a study. London, 1926.
Phil 8595.23.5A Powicke, F.J. The Cambridge Platonists. Cambridge, 1926.
Phil 9245.50.5 Powys, J.C. The art of happiness. N.Y., 1935.
Phil 9245.50.10 Powys, J.C. In defense of sensuality. N.Y., 1930.
Phil 9515.6 Powys, J.C. A philosophy of solitude. N.Y., 1933.
Phil 9245.47 Powys, Llwelyn. Impassioned day. London, 1931.
Phil 7080.35 Poyer, G.P. Contribution à la pathologie du sommeil. Le sommeil automatique. Thèse. Paris, 1914.
Phil 5440.25 Poyer, Georges. Les problèmes généraux de l'hérédité psychologique. Paris, 1921.
Phil 5440.25.3 Poyer, Georges. Les problèmes généraux de l'hérédité psychologique. Thèse. Paris, 1921. 2 pam.
Phil 4809.498.30 Pozitivní etika jakožto mravanka na základě přirozeném. (Krejčí, František.) Praha, 1922.
Phil 4809.465.30 Pozmání a život. (Jahn, Jiljí.) Praha, 1948.
Phil 1712.28 Poznanie i obshchestvo. (Motroshilova, Nelli V.) Moskva, 1969.
Phil 350.5 Poznanie i praktika. (Tomov, Kiril.) Sofiia, 1960.
Phil 332.42 Poznanie i svoboda. (Bychko, Ihor Valentynovych.) Moskva, 1969.
Phil 8595.56.5 Pozov, A. Logos-meditatsiia drevnei tserkvi. Miunkhen, 1964.
Phil 8595.56 Pozov, A. Osnovy drevne-tserkovnoi antropologii. Madrid, 1965. 2v.
Phil 600.65 Pozzo, Gianni M. Il problema della storia nel positivismo Pozzo. Padova, 1967.
Phil 845.6 Pozzo, Gianni M. Umanesimo moderno o tramonto dell'Umanesimo? Padova, 1970.
Phil 3850.5.93 Un pprécurseur. (Claparède-Spir, H.) Lausanne, 1920.
Phil 2050.257 Pra, Mario dal. Hume. Milano, 1949.
Phil 1955.6.122 Pra, Mario dal. Il pensiero di John Dewey. Milano, 1952.
Phil 4170.5.80 Pra, Mario dal. Il pensiero di Sebastiano Maturi. Milano, 1943.
Phil 630.51 Pra, Mario dal. Il realismo e il trascendente. Padova, 1937.
Phil 1190.22 Pra, Mario dal. Lo scetticismo greco. Milano, 1950.
Phil 1120.5 Pra, Mario dal. La storiografia filosofica antica. 1.ed. Milano, 1950.
Phil 960.195 Prabhavananda, Swami. Vedic religion and philosophy. Madras, 1950.
Phil 11.53 Prace. (Bydgoskie Towarzystwo naukowe. Wydział nauk Humanistycznych. Komisja Filozofii i Pedagogiki.) Bydgoszcz. 1,1969+
Phil 20.9 Prace psychologiczne. (Katowice, Poland (city). Wyzsza Szkota Pedagogiczna. Sekcja Pedagogiczna.) 1,1967+
Phil 8430.86 Pracht, Erwin. Sozialistischer Realismus-Positionen, Probleme, Perspektiven. 1. Aufl. Berlin, 1970.
Phil 6012.3 A practical and familiar view of science of physiognomy. (Cooke, Thomas.) London, 1819.
Phil 9179.7 A practical essay designed for general use. (Townsend, S.) Boston, 1783.
Phil 1855.60 Practical essays. (Bain, Alexander.) London, 1884.
Phil 8882.24 Practical ethics. (Hyde, W. De W.) N.Y., 1892.
Phil 8893.89 Practical ethics. (Samuel, Herbert.) London, 1935.
Phil 8615.4 Practical ethics. (Sidgwick, H.) London, 1898.
Phil 6060.25.10 Practical graphology. (Rice, L.G. (Mrs.).) Chicago, 1910.
Phil 6132.6.10 Practical health. (Whipple, L.E.) N.Y., 1907.
Phil 9179.1.2 Practical hints to young females. (Taylor, A. Hinton.) Boston, 1816.
Phil 9179.1 Practical hints to young females. (Taylor, A. Hinton.) London, 1815.
Phil 400.30.5 Practical idealism. (Hyde, W. De W.) N.Y., 1899.
Phil 25.52 Practical ideals. Boston.
Phil 5190.88 Practical inferences. (Hare, Richard Mervyn.) London, 1971.
Phil 6673.2.8 Practical instruction in animal magnetism. (Deleuze, J.P.F.) Providence, 1837.
Phil 5046.10 Practical logic. (Gregory, D.S.) Philadelphia, 1881.
Phil 6689.4 A practical manual of animal magnetism. (Teste, A.) London, 1843.
Phil 6967.1 Practical manual of mental medicine. (Regis, E.) Philadelphia, 1895.
Phil 6122.20 Practical metaphysics. (Mills, A.W.) Chicago, 1896.
Phil 6111.32.5 Practical methods to insure success. 31st ed. (Butler, Hiram Erastus.) Applegate, Calif., 1915.
Phil 6111.32 Practical methods to insure success. 33rd ed. (Butler, Hiram Erastus.) Applegate, Calif., 1920.
Phil 2490.95.5 Practical morals. (Ingram, John K.) London, 1904.
Phil 525.7.5.3 Practical mysticism; a little book for normal people. (Underhill, Evelyn.) N.Y., 1915.
Phil 525.7.5 Practical mysticism. (Underhill, Evelyn.) London, 1914.
Phil 6957.1 Practical observations, causes, cure insanity. (Hallaran, W.G.) Cork, 1818.
Phil 6952.11 Practical observations on insanity. (Cox, J.M.) London, 1806.
Phil 6952.11.2 Practical observations on insanity. (Cox, J.M.) Philadelphia, 1811.
Phil 7054.42 The practical of spiritualism. (Peebles, J.M.) Chicago, 1868.
Phil 6048.97.13 Practical palmistry illustrated. (Saint-Germain, C. de.) Chicago, 1897.
Phil 8885.17 Practical philosophy of social life. 1st American ed. (Knigge, Adolf.) Lansingburgh, 1805.
Phil 5925.2.5 Practical phrenology. (Fowler, O.S.) N.Y., 1844. 2 pam.
Phil 5929.1 Practical phrenology. (Jones, S.) Boston, 1836.
Phil 5257.27.6 Practical psychology; human nature in everyday life. (Robinson, E.S.) N.Y., 1927.
Phil 6675.10 Practical psychology. (Feyrer, E.C.) Springfield, Mass., 1913.
Phil 6951.9.5 Practical psychology and psychiatry. 5. ed. (Burr, Colonel Bell.) Philadelphia, 1922.
Phil 5245.25 Practical psychology for men and women. (Farnsworth, B.B.) N.Y., 1923.

Phil 9035.61.9 — Practical psychology in character development. (Allers, Rudolf.) N.Y., 1934.

Phil 3485.21 — Practical reason and morality. (Duncan, A.R.C.) London, 1957.

Phil 5620.29 — Practical reasoning. (Gauthier, Daniel Peter.) Oxford, 1963.

Phil 5620.29.2 — Practical reasoning. (Gauthier, Daniel Peter.) Oxford, 1966.

Phil 665.32 — A practical study of the soul. (Stone, M.M.) N.Y., 1901.

Phil 5251.41.95 — The practical theorist; the life and work of Kurt Lewin. (Marrow, Alfred Jay.) N.Y., 1969.

Htn Phil 9420.1* — A practical treatise...regulation...passions. (Bragge, F.) London, 1708.

Phil 6951.12.4 — Practical treatise on nervous exhaustion. 2. ed. (Beard, G.M.) N.Y., 1880.

Phil 6951.12.3 — Practical treatise on nervous exhaustion. 2. ed. (Beard, G.M.) N.Y., 1880.

Phil 6420.10 — The practical treatment of stammering and stuttering. (Lewis, George Andrew.) Detroit, 1902.

Phil 7069.20.352 — Practical views on psychic phenomena. (Wright, George E.) N.Y., 1920.

Phil 9530.28 — Practical wisdom! letters. N.Y., 1902.

Phil 8647.2 — Practice and science of religion. (Woods, J.H.) London, 1906.

Phil 6310.1.5 — The practice and theory of individual psychology. (Adler, A.) London, 1924.

Phil 6310.1.6 — The practice and theory of individual psychology. (Adler, A.) N.Y., 1932.

Phil 6323.5.6 — Practice and theory of psychoanalysis. (Nunberg, Hermann.) N.Y., 1961. 2v.

Phil 7140.116.71 — The practice of autosuggestion by the method of Emile Coué. (Brooks, C.H.) London, 1922.

Phil 7140.116.73A — The practice of autosuggestion by the method of Emile Coué. (Brooks, C.H.) N.Y., 1922.

Phil 7140.116.70 — The practice of autosuggestion by the method of Emile Coué. (Brooks, C.H.) N.Y., 1922.

Phil 7140.116.72 — The practice of autosuggestion by the method of Emile Coué. (Brooks, C.H.) N.Y., 1922.

Phil 6980.780.20 — The practice of behavior therapy. 1. ed. (Wolpe, Joseph.) N.Y., 1970.

Phil 6325.14 — The practice of clinical psychology. (Porteus, S.D.) N.Y., 1941.

Phil 6048.97.9 — The practice of palmistry. (Saint-Germain, C. de.) Chicago, 1897. 2v.

Phil 186.72 — The practice of philosophy. (Langer, Mrs. S.K.) N.Y., 1930.

Phil 8876.8 — Practische Philosophie für alle Stande. v.1-2. (Basedow, J.B.) Dessau, 1777.

Phil 5921.3F — Practische Phrenologie. (Bossard, H.) Berlin, 1851.

Phil 197.49 — Practische wijsbegeerte. 2e druk. (Wattjes, J.G.) Delft, 1926.

Phil 5421.25.55 — Practitioners of love: some aspects of the human phenomenon. (Mannin, Ethel Edith.) London, 1969.

Phil 2825.20 — Pradines, M. L'aventure de l'esprit dans les espèces. Paris, 1955.

Phil 5635.34 — Pradines, M. Philosophie de la sensation. Paris, 1928-34. 3v.

Phil 2477.20.80 — Pradines, Marie Thérèse. Georges Bastide, philosophe de la valeur. Toulouse, 1970.

Phil 5255.49 — Pradines, Maurice. Traité de psychologie générale. 1st éd. v.1-2, pt.1-2. Paris, 1943-46. 3v.

Phil 4352.1.110 — Prados y López, M. Balmes, el buen amigo de la verdad. Madrid, 1954?

Phil 126.2 — Praecepta doctrinae logicae. (Stier, J.) London, 1671.

Phil 5062.14 — Praecepta philosophiae logicae. (Wyttenback, D.) Hallae, 1820.

Phil 284.7 — Praelectiones cosmologiae. (Dario, J.M.) Paris, 1923.

Phil 8890.59 — Praelectiones ethicae. (Polzer, Ignatius.) Olomuc, 1770.

Phil 187.77 — Praelectiones metaphysicae specialis. (Monaco, Nicolao.) Romae, 1917-1920. 3v.

Phil 1535.35 — Praelectiones philosophicae. (Vallet, Pa.) Parisiis, 1878-9. 2v.

Phil 8658.15 — Praelectiones theologiae naturalis. (Descoqs, Pedro.) Paris, 1932. 2v.

Phil 197.9A — Präludien. (Windelband, W.) Freiburg, 1884.
Phil 197.9.3A — Präludien. 3. ed. (Windelband, W.) Tübingen, 1907.
Phil 197.9.4 — Präludier. (Windelband, W.) Stockholm, 1915.

Phil 8141.2 — Präparation zu einer Rom-zentrischen Ästhetik. (Kőszegi, L.) Detmold, 1959.

Phil 8665.8 — Praeter introductionem continens partem primamque est De ipso deo. (Kleutgen, J.) Ratisbonae, 1881.

Phil 6046.77 — Praetorius, J. Philologemata abstrusa de pollice. v.1-2. Quedlinburgi, 1677.

Phil 6046.61 — Praetorius, J. Ludicrum chiromanticum praetorii sen thesaurus chiromantiae. Jenae, 1661.

Phil 1135.53 — Pragmateia peri tes par Athenagorai filosofikes geoses. (Joannides, A.) Jena, 1883.

Phil 3504.13 — Pragmatic elements in Kant's philosophy. (Witter, C.E.) Chicago, 1913.

Phil 2280.7.80 — The pragmatic humanism of F.C.S. Schiller. (Abel, Reuben.) N.Y., 1955.

Phil 8664.7 — The pragmatic meaning of God. (Johann, Robert O.) Milwaukee, 1966.

Phil 2225.5.98.5 — The pragmatic philosophy of C.S. Peirce. (Thompson, M.H.) Chicago, 1953.

Phil 2225.5.98 — The pragmatic philosophy of C.S. Pierce. Part of thesis. (Thompson, M.H.) Chicago, 1945.

Phil 190.68 — The pragmatic test; essays on the history of ideas. (Parkes, Henry B.) San Francisco, 1941.

Phil 181.33 — Pragmatic theory of truth as developed by Peirce, James and Dewey. (Geyer, D.L.) n.p., 1914?

Phil 3100.45 — Pragmatische Psychologie. v.1-2. (Beneke, F.E.) Berlin, 1850.

Phil 1817.2 — Pragmatische und humanistische Strömung. (Rusk, Robert R.) Jena, 1906.

Phil 184.24 — Pragmatiska uppfostringsprinciper. (Jacobsson, M.) Lund, 1912.

NEDL Phil 184.3.16.2 — Pragmatism, a new name. (James, W.) London, 1909.
Phil 184.3.15 — Pragmatism, a new name. (James, W.) N.Y., 1907.
Phil 184.3.16 — Pragmatism, a new name. (James, W.) N.Y., 1908.
Phil 184.3.16.3 — Pragmatism, a new name. (James, W.) N.Y., 1912.
Phil 184.3.16.5 — Pragmatism, a new name. (James, W.) N.Y., 1922.
Phil 184.3.17 — Pragmatism, a new name. (James, W.) N.Y., 1928.
Phil 140.22 — Pamphlet box. Pragmatism.
Phil 140.21F — Pamphlet vol. Pragmatism.
Phil 184.3.17.5 — Pragmatism. (James, W.) N.Y., 1943.
Phil 184.3.20 — Pragmatism. (James, W.) Stockholm, 1916.
Phil 2070.27.5 — Pragmatism. (James, William.) Chicago, 1955.

Phil 2070.26 — Pragmatism. (James, William.) N.Y., 1925.
Phil 2070.27.10 — Pragmatism. (James, William.) N.Y., 1949.
Phil 187.35 — Pragmatism. (Murray, D.L.) London, 1912.
Phil 197.74 — Pragmatism. (Wells, H.K.) N.Y., 1954.
Phil 140.23 — Pamphlet box. Pragmatism. German dissertations.
Phil 1810.4 — Pragmatism and American culture. (Kennedy, Gail.) Boston, 1950.

Phil 193.63 — Pragmatism and French voluntarism. (Stebbing, L.S.) Cambridge, 1914.

Phil 177.38 — Pragmatism and idealism. (Caldwell, W.) London, 1913.
Phil 187.39A — Pragmatism and its critics. (Moore, A.W.) Chicago, 1910.
Phil 178.27 — Pragmatism and the problem of the idea. (Driscoll, John T.) N.Y., 1915.

Phil 186.21 — Pragmatisme, modernisme, protestantisme. (Leclére, A.) Paris, 1909.

Phil 182.40 — Le pragmatisme. (Hébert, A.) Paris, 1908.
Phil 184.3.18 — Le pragmatisme. (James, W.) Paris, 1911.
Phil 184.3.19 — Le pragmatisme. (James, W.) Paris, 1918.
Phil 1811.2 — Le pragmatisme américain et anglais. (Leroux, E.) Paris, 1923.

Phil 1811.2.2 — Le pragmatisme américain et anglais. Thèse. (Leroux, E.) Paris, 1922.

Phil 2120.4.90 — Le pragmatisme conceptuel de Clarence Irwing Lewis. (Devaux, P.) Paris, 1934.

Phil 176.49 — Pragmatisme et modernisme. (Bourdeau, J.) Paris, 1909.
Phil 178.71 — Pragmatisme et sociologie. (Durkheim, E.) Paris, 1955.
Phil 2418.1 — Der Pragmatisme in der modernen französischen Philosophie. (Simon, Paul M.) Paderborn, 1920.

Phil 2070.89 — Het pragmatisme van William James. (Dijk, I. van.) Groningen, 1911.

Phil 2070.85 — Het pragmatisme van William James. (Ubbink, J.G.) Arnhem, 1912.

Phil 190.20.4 — Pragmatismo, 1903-1911. 2. ed. (Papini, Giovanni.) Firenze, 1920.

Phil 177.66 — Il pragmatismo. (Chiocchetti, Emilio.) Milano, 1926.
Phil 177.57 — Il pragmatismo a cura di Giovanni Papini. (Calderoni, M.) Lanciano, 1920.

Phil 2725.30.90 — Il pragmatismo epistemológico e religioso di Edouard LeRoy. 1. ed. (Polato, Franco.) Padova, 1959.

Phil 4018.8.5 — Il pragmatismo in Italia. (Santucci, Antonio.) Bologna, 1963.

Phil 193.87 — Il pragmatismo nella filosofia contemporanea. (Spirito, U.) Firenze, 1921.

Phil 187.107 — Pragmatismus; eine neue Richtung der Philosophie. (MacEachran, John M.) Leipzig, 1910.

Phil 184.13 — Der Pragmatismus. (Jacoby, Günther.) Leipzig, 1909.
Phil 184.3.21 — Der Pragmatismus. (James, W.) Leipzig, 1908.
Phil 2070.82.5 — Der Pragmatismus von James und Schiller. (Bloch, Werner.) Leipzig, 1913.

Phil 720.24 — A pragmatist theory of truth and reality. Thesis. (Borowne, S.S.S.) Princeton, 1930.

Phil 310.456 — Pragmatistskii Izhemarksizm filosofiia antikommunizme. (Titarenko, Aleksandr I.) Moskva, 1964.

VPhil 1750.797 — Pragmatizam i savremena filozofija. (Životić, Miladin.) Beograd, 1966.

Phil 188.23 — Pragmatizm i djalektika. (Nedeljković, Duš.) Beograd, 1960.

Phil 978.6.97 — Prakasa, Sri. Annie Besant. 2d ed. Bombay, 1954.
Phil 339.10 — Prakticheskaia priroda chelovecheskogo poznaniia. (Iliadi, A.N.) Moskva, 1962.

Phil 310.345 — Praktika, kriterii istiny v nauke. Moskva, 1960.
Phil 339.5 — Praktika i ee rol' v protsese poznaniia. (Iakushevskii, I.T.) Moskva, 1961.

Phil 5043.9 — Praktisch Denklehre. (Dressler, J.G.) Bautzen, 1852.
Phil 8876.90 — Praktische Aphorismen. (Bouterwek, F.) Leipzig, 1808.
Phil 25.122 — Praktische Arbeits- und Bildungs-Psychologie. Münster.
Phil 978.49.80 — Praktische Ausbildung des Denkens. (Steiner, R.) Stuttgart, 1927.

Phil 3565.85 — Die praktische Begründung des Gottesbegriffs bei Lotze. (Kalweit, P.F.M.) Jena, 1900.

Phil 5043.7 — Praktische Logik. (Dittes, Friedrich.) Wien, 1873.
Phil 8855.4 — Praktische Philosophie. (Höffe, Otfried.) München, 1971.
Phil 185.2 — Praktische Philosophie. (Kessler, R.) Leipzig, 1691.
Phil 197.1.15 — Praktische Philosophie enthaltend Religionslehre. (Wagner, J.) Ulm, 1857.

Phil 25.32 — Praktische Psychologie. 1-4,1919-1923 4v.
Phil 5850.230.100 — Praktische Psychologie. 2. Aufl. (Holzschuher, L. von.) Seebruck am Chiemsee, 1955.

Phil 5850.385.60 — Die praktische Psychologie im Wirtschaftsleben. (Weber, Wilhelm.) Leipzig, 1927.

Phil 8876.80 — Praktische Sittenlehre. (Baumgarten, O.) Tübingen, 1921.
Phil 3495.18 — Praktische Vernunft und Ewiger Friede. (Nieschmidt, Gerd Peter.) München, 1965.

Phil 25.75 — Praktisk psykologi. Stockholm. 1-4
Phil 8416.28 — Prall, D.W. Aesthetic judgment. N.Y., 1929.
Phil 5415.9 — Prandtl, A. Die Einfühlung. Leipzig, 1910.
Phil 190.38 — Prandtl, Antonin. Einführung in die Philosophie. Leipzig, 1922.

Phil 190.38.5 — Prandtl, Antonin. Das Problem der Wirklichkeit. München, 1926.

Phil 8735.9 — Prandtl, Antonin. Über Teleologie des Geistes und über Teleologie überhaupt. Leipzig, 1915.

Phil 3015.5 — Prang, Helmut. Der Humanismus. Bamburg, 1947.
Phil 5255.76 — Prangishvili, Aleksandr S. Issledovaniia po psikhologii ustanovki. Tbilisi, 1967.

Phil 5055.5A — Prantl, C. Die Bedeutung der Logik. München, 1849.
Phil 5055.5.5 — Prantl, C. Verstehen und Beurtheilen. München, 1877.
Phil 5025.1 — Prantl, Carl von. Geschichte der Logik. Leipzig, 1855-70. 3v.

Phil 5025.1.2 — Prantl, Carl von. Geschichte der Logik. v.2. Leipzig, 1885.

Phil 5025.1.1 — Prantl, Carl von. Geschichte der Logik. v.2. 2e Aufl. Leipzig, 1855-1885.

X Cg Phil 5025.1 — Prantl, Carl von. Geschichte der Logik. v.4. Leipzig, 1855-70.

Phil 5025.1.4 — Prantl, Carl von. Geschichte der Logik im Abendlande. v.1-4. Berlin, 1957. 3v.

Phil 5025.1.3 — Prantl, Carl von. Geschichte der Logik im Abendlande. v.1-4. Graz, 1955. 3v.

Phil 9410.3 — Prantl, Carl von. Über die Berechtigung des Optimismus. München, 1879.

Phil 1120.2 — Prantl, K. Übersicht der griech-römischen Philosophie. Stuttgart, 1854.

Phil 190.19 — Prantl, Karl. Die gegenwärtige Aufgabe der Philosophie. München, 1852. 8 pam.

Phil 960.215 — Prasad, Jwala. History of Indian epistemology. 2d ed. Delhi, 1958.

Phil 960.132   Prasad, Jwala. Introduction to Indian philosophy. Allahabad, 1928.
Phil 5520.104   Prasod, Kali. The psychology of meaning. Lucknon, 1949.
Phil 1750.115.170   Prassi e conoscenza. 1. ed. (Neri, Guido Davide.) Milano, 1966.
Phil 325.2   Prat, Louis. Caractére empirique et la personne. Paris, 1906.
Phil 2840.97   Prat, Louis. Charles Renouvier. Ariège, 1937.
Phil 190.27   Prat, Louis. Contes pour les métaphysiciens. Paris, 1910.
Phil 190.27.5   Prat, Louis. L'harmonisme. Paris, 1927.
Phil 190.36   Prather, Charles E. Divine science. Denver, Col., 1915.
Phil 5041.60   Pratical logic. (Beardsley, M.C.) N.Y., 1950.
Phil 5593.70   La pratique du Rorschach. 1. éd. (Rausch de Traubenberg, Nina.) Paris, 1970.
Phil 5255.43A   Pratt, Carroll C. The logic of modern psychology. N.Y., 1939.
Phil 6125.23   Pratt, George K. Your mind and you. N.Y., 1924.
NEDL Phil 6125.23.5   Pratt, George K. Your mind and you. N.Y., 1924.
Phil 6125.13   Pratt, J.B. Matter and spirit. N.Y., 1922.
Phil 190.23   Pratt, J.B. What is pragmatism. N.Y., 1909.
Phil 190.52   Pratt, James B. Adventures in philosophy and religion. N.Y., 1931.
Phil 531.2   Pratt, James B. Naturalism. New Haven, 1939.
Phil 630.44   Pratt, James B. Personal realism. N.Y., 1937.
Phil 5627.56.4   Pratt, James B. The psychology of religious belief. N.Y., 1907.
Phil 8890.47   Pratt, James B. Reason in the art of living. N.Y., 1949.
Phil 5627.56   Pratt, James B. The religious consciousness. N.Y., 1920.
Phil 5627.56.3A   Pratt, James B. The religious consciousness. N.Y., 1927.
Phil 7026.2   Pratt, Joseph G. Parapsychology. N.Y., 1966.
Htn Phil 2050.89*   Pratt, Samuel J. An apology for life and writings of D. Hume. London, 1777.
Htn Phil 2050.89.10*   Pratt, Samuel J. Curious particulars and genuine anecdotes respecting the late Lord Chesterfield and David Hume. London, 1788.
Phil 3497.30   Prauss, Gerold. Erscheinung bei Kant. Habilitationsschrift. Berlin, 1971.
Phil 8980.459   Pravoi nravstvennost'kak reguliatory obshchestvennykh otnoshenii pri sotsializme. (Iakuba, Elena A.) Khav'kov, 1970.
Phil 4751.1.32   Pravoslavie, katolichestvo, protestantizm. (Arsen'ev, N.S.) Parizh, 1948.
Phil 4710.70.10   Pravoslavie i kul'tura. (Zen'kovskii, V.V.) Berlin, 1923.
Phil 4710.135   Pravye i levye, blizkie i dal'nie. (Bashilov, B.) Buenos Aires, 194-?
Phil 5250.78   Praxiology; an introduction to the sciences of efficient action. 1. English ed. (Kotarbiński, Tadeusz.) Oxford, 1965.
Phil 25.143   Praxis. Zagreb. 1,1965+ 6v.
Phil 25.143.5   Praxis. Jugoslovensko izdanje. Zagreb. 4,1967+ 8v.
Phil 1750.866   Praxis and action. (Bernstein, Richard Jacob.) Philadelphia, 1971.
Phil 6319.1.5.9   Praxis der Psychotherapie. v.1,3-4,6-8,11,14-16. (Jung, C.G.) Zürich, 1958.
Phil 6122.61.5   Praxis der seelischen Hygiene. (Meng, H.) Basel, 1943.
Phil 5593.66.10   Praxis des Zulliger-Tafeln- und Diapositiv-Tests und ausgewählte Aufsätze. (Zulliger, Hans.) Bern, 1966.
Phil 5042.2.5   A praxis of logic. (Collard, John.) London, 1799.
Phil 6310.1.9   Praxis und Theorie der Individual-Psychologie. 2. Aufl. (Adler, A.) München, 1924.
Phil 4770.2   Praxl, Franz. Die Rechtfertigung Gottes nach Eugen H. Trubetskoj. Inaug. Diss. München, 1967.
Phil 5627.132.5   Prayer. (Heiler, Friedrich.) London, 1932.
Phil 5627.132.7   Prayer. (Heiler, Friedrich.) N.Y., 1958.
Phil 5627.127   Prayer and its psychology. Thesis. (Hodge, Alexander.) London, 1931.
Phil 8587.2.2   The pre-Adamite earth. (Harris, J.) Boston, 1849.
Phil 8587.2.3   The pre-Adamite earth. (Harris, J.) Boston, 1850.
Phil 5015.4   Pre-dialectical logic. (Filkorn, V.) Bratislava, 1963.
Phil 665.7.7   Pre-existence and reincarnation. (Lutosławski, W.) London, 1928.
Phil 3110.163   Pre-requisites for the study of Jakob Böhme. (Barker, C.J.) London, 1920.
Phil 1133.26   The pre-Socratic philosophers. (Freeman, Kathleen.) Cambridge, Mass., 1946[1947]
Phil 1133.26.2   The pre-Socratic philosophers. (Freeman, Kathleen.) Oxford, 1946.
Phil 1135.83   The pre-Socratic use of [Psyche]. (Thomas Aquinas, Sister.) Washington, 1915.
Phil 365.57   Preachers, pedagogues, and politicians. (Gatewood, Willard B.) Chapel Hill, 1966.
Phil 8598.30   The precinct of religion in culture of humanity. (Shaw, Charles G.) London, 1908.
Phil 5926.1.35   Précis analytique et raisonné du système du docteur Gall. (Ottin, N.J.) Bruxelles, 1835.
Phil 1850.85   Précis de la philosophie de Bacon. (Luc, J.A. de.) Paris, 1802. 2v.
Phil 5041.53   Précis de logique des sciences. (Baudin, E.) Paris, 1938.
Phil 5057.10   Précis de logique évolutionniste. (Regnaud, P.) Paris, 1897.
Phil 5066.10.5   Précis de logique mathématique. (Bochénski, I.M.) Bussum, 1948.
Phil 7069.27.11   Précis de métapsychic. (Bret, Thomas.) Paris, 1927. 2v.
Phil 8892.26.8   Précis de morale. 8. ed. (Rayot, E.) Paris, 1906.
Phil 8877.56   Précis de morale rationnelle. (Courcelle-Seneuil, J.G.) Paris, 1875.
Phil 176.17   Précis de philosophie. (Bénard, Charles.) Paris, 1845.
Phil 176.17.2   Précis de philosophie. (Bénard, Charles.) Paris, 1857.
Phil 126.1   Précis de philosophie. (Bouscaillou, R.P.) Paris, 1873.
Phil 1535.23   Précis de philosophie. (Levesque, l'abbé.) Paris, 1912.
Phil 177.110   Précis de philosophie: classe de philosophie. (Cuvillier, Armand.) Paris, 1954. 2v.
Phil 180.68   Précis de philosophie. 2. ed. v.2-3. (Foulquié, Paul.) Paris, 1955.
Phil 177.103   Précis de philosophie à l'usage des candidats au baccalaureat. (Cazals de Fabel, Gabriel.) Toulouse, 1937.
Phil 194.39   Precis de philosophie fondamentale d'apres la methode d'observation. (Tourville, Henri.) Paris, 1928.
Phil 6980.43   Précis de psychodrame, introduction. 1. éd. (Aucelin Schoetzenberger, Anne.) Paris, 1966.
Phil 5244.7.9   Précis de psychologie. (Ebbinghaus, H.) Paris, 1910.
Phil 5262.20.9   Précis de psychologie. (Warren, H.C.) Paris, 1923.
Phil 5249.2.35   Précis de psychologie. 3. éd. (James, William.) Paris, 1912.
Phil 815.7   Précis d'histoire de la philosophie. (Penjon, A.) Paris, 1896.

Phil 822.18.9   Précis d'histoire de la philosophie. 9. ed. (Wulf, M.) Louvain, 1950.
Phil 1712.13   Précis d'histoire de la philosophie moderne. (Maréchal, Joseph.) Louvain, 1933.
Phil 1712.13.2   Précis d'histoire de la philosophie moderne. 2e éd. (Maréchal, Joseph.) Bruxelles, 1951.
Phil 190.6   Précis d'un cours complet de philosophie élémentaire. (Pellissier, P.A.) Paris, 1873. 2v.
Phil 6682.3.5   Précis historique des faits relatifs au magnétisme. (Mesmer, F.A.) London, 1781.
Phil 5066.10.7   A precis of mathematical logic. (Bochénski, I.M.) Dordrecht, 1959.
Phil 8886.37   Précis raisonné de morale pratique. 2. ed. (Lalande, André.) Paris, 1909.
Phil 8886.37.5   Précis raisonné de morale pratique. 3. ed. (Lalande, André.) Paris, 1930.
Phil 6311.22.5   Preconcious foundations of human experience. (Burrow, T.) N.Y., 1964.
Phil 1135.175   Precope, J. Iatrophilosophers of the Hellenic states. London, 1961.
Phil 194.33   Le precurseur. (Teste, Paulin.) Le Haye, 1912.
Phil 2295.85   Un précurseur de la franc-maçonnerie, John Toland, 1670-1722. (Lantoine, Albert.) Paris, 1927.
Phil 281.6.15   Le précurseur philosophique. (Ambacher, Michel.) Paris, 1844.
Phil 2520.97   Précurseurs et disciples de Descartes. (Saisset, Émile.) Paris, 1862.
Phil 2520.97.3   Précurseurs et disciples de Descartes. (Saisset, Émile.) Paris, 1862.
Phil 4285.1.100   Un precursore della neoscolastica. (Aliotta, S.) Noto, 1952.
Phil 812.17   Os precursores de Desartes. (Moreira da Sá, A.) Lisboa, 1944.
Phil 4302.5   Los precursores españoles de Bacon y Descartes. (Bullón y Fernández, E.) Salamanca, 1905.
Phil 5500.45   Predicting and deciding. (Pears, David Francis.) London, 1964.
Phil 5243.46   Predicting the child's development. (Dearborn, W.F.) Cambridge, Mass., 1941.
Phil 5243.46.2   Predicting the child's development. 2d rev. ed. (Dearborn, W.F.) Cambridge, Mass., 1963.
Phil 5500.48   Prediction and optimal decision. (Churchman, Charles West.) Englewood Cliffs, 1961.
Phil 7069.26.4   La prédiction de l'avenir. (Cornillier, P.E.) Paris, 1926.
Phil 5279.25.5   The prediction of performance in clinical psychology. (Kelly, Everett Lowell.) N.Y., 1966.
Phil 5593.45.10   Prediction of the adjustment and academic performance of college students. (Munroe, R.L.) Stanford, 1945.
Phil 3246.28   Predigten. (Fichte, Johann Gottlieb.) Leipzig, 1918.
Phil 3485.30   Predigten nach Kantischen Grundsätzen. (Daub, Carl.) Bruxelles, 1968.
Phil 310.410   Predmet a metoda historického materialismu. (Hrzal, L.) Praha, 1961.
Phil 8419.19   Predmet estetiki. (Stolovich, L.N.) Moskva, 1961.
Phil 5052.43   Predmet formal'noi logiki i dialektika. (Maneev, A.K.) Minsk, 1964.
Phil 310.3.12   Predmet i struktura marksistsko-leninskoi filosofii. (Rozhin, V.P.) Leningrad, 1958.
Phil 5061.6   Predmet i znachenie logiki. (Voishvillo, Evgenii K.) Moskva, 1960.
Phil 5829.16   Predystoniia obshehestva. (Tukh, Nina A.) Leningrad, 1970.
Phil 672.270   Preemstvennost' v razoitii kategorii prostranstva, vremeni i dvizheniia. (Maneev, Aleksei K.) Minsk, 1971.
Phil 8050.72   Preface to an American philosophy of art. (McMahon, Amos.) Chicago, 1945.
Phil 5421.15   Preface to empathy. (Stewart, David A.) N.Y., 1956.
Phil 3552.445   The preface to Leibniz' Novissima Sinica. (Leibniz, G.W.) Honolulu, 1957.
Phil 5042.25.5A   A preface to logic. (Cohen, Morris R.) N.Y., 1944.
Phil 2750.11.53   A preface to metaphysics. (Maritain, Jacques.) N.Y., 1940.
Phil 8886.50.6   A preface to morals. (Lippmann, W.) London, 1931.
Phil 8886.50.3   A preface to morals. (Lippmann, W.) N.Y., 1929.
Phil 8886.50   A preface to morals. (Lippmann, W.) N.Y., 1929.
Phil 8886.50.5   A preface to morals. (Lippmann, W.) N.Y., 1931.
Phil 190.77   Preface to philosophy. N.Y., 1947.
Phil 5627.132.10   A preface to prayer. 1. ed. (Heard, Gerald.) N.Y., 1944.
Phil 337.13   Prefaces to inquiry; a study in the origins and relevance of modern theories of knowledge. (Gondin, W.R.) N.Y., 1941.
Phil 2138.40.45   Prefaces to liberty. (Mill, John S.) Boston, 1959.
Phil 196.5   Prefatory lessons in a mechanical philosophy. (Van Nostrand, J.J.) Chicago, 1907.
Phil 196.5.3F   Prefatory lessons in a mechanical philosophy. (Van Nostrand, J.J.) Chicago, 1907.
Phil 530.20.25   Preger, Wilhelm. Geschichte der deutschen Mystik im Mittelalter. Leipzig, 1874-1893. 3v.
Phil 8610.911.4   Il pregiudizio religioso. (Bongini, V.) Roma, 1911.
Phil 4810.6.5   Prehl'ad od dejín slovenskej filozofie. (Várossová, Elena.) Bratislava, 1965.
Phil 11.50   Přehled nové časopisecké literatury z oblasti. filosofie, estetiky, sociologie. (Bruenn. Universita. Knihovna.) Brno. 1965+
Phil 1123.12   Il preimoginisimo dei Greci. (Stefanini, L.) Padova, 1953.
Phil 3018.1   Preisschriften...Metaphysik séet Leibnitz. (Schwab, J.C.) Berlin, 1796.
Phil 5245.34   Prejudice and impartiality. (Field, G.C.) London, 1932.
Phil 2805.399   The prejudices of Pascal. (Hay, Malcolm.) London, 1962.
Phil 8880.27   Les préjugés nécessaires. (Faguet, Émile.) Paris, 1911.
Phil 5627.269.15   Prejuicio antiprotestante y religiosidad utilitaria. (Amon, Jesus.) Madrid, 1969.
Phil 8400.33   Prekrasnoe i zhizn'. (Lukin, Iu.B.) Moskva, 1962.
Phil 181.48   Prelezioni di filosofia. (Giovanni, V. di.) Palermo, 1877.
Phil 8403.23.5   Préliminaires à l'esthétique. (Chartier, Émile.) Paris, 1939.
Phil 2605.6.31   Les preliminaires de la philosophie. (Foucou, L.) Paris, 1879.
Phil 812.15   Preliminari alla storia della filosofia. (Melillo, F.) Napoli, 1858.
Phil 5003.6A   A preliminary draft of a bibliography of contributions to modern logic. Supplement. (Weiss, Paul.) n.p., n.d.
Phil 7060.102   Preliminary report. (Pennsylvania. University. Seybert Commission for Investigating Modern Spiritualism.) Philadelphia, 1887.

Phil 7060.102.2 — Preliminary report. (Pennsylvania. University. Seybert Commission for Investigating Modern Spiritualism.) Philadelphia, 1887.

Phil 7068.87.9.5 — Preliminary report. (Pennsylvania. University. Seybert Commission for Investigating Modern Spiritualism.) Philadelphia, 1895.

Phil 7069.20.270 — Preliminary report. (Pennsylvania. University. Seybert Commission for Investigating Modern Spiritualism.) Philadelphia, 1920.

Phil 3925.16.10 — Preliminary studies for the "Philosophical investigations" generally known as the Blue and Brown books. (Wittgenstein, Ludwig.) Oxford, 1958.

Phil 3925.16.12 — Preliminary studies for the "Philosophical investigations" generally known as the Blue and Brown books. 2nd ed. (Wittgenstein, Ludwig.) Oxford, 1969.

Phil 5300.4 — A preliminary study...partial tones...of sound. (Angell, J.R.) Chicago, 1902.

Phil 5875.65 — Il prelinguaggio infantile. (Raffler Engel, Walburga von.) Paideia, 1964.

Phil 8840.3 — Prell, H.H. Das Unmittelbare in der Philosophie der Moral. Amsterdam, 1941.

Phil 5722.55 — Prelogical experience. (Tauber, Edward.) N.Y., 1959.
Phil 8062.9 — Prelude to aesthetics. (Schaper, Eva.) London, 1968.
Phil 181.70 — Preludi filosofici e politici. (Govi, Mario.) Milano, 1935.

Phil 4200.2.01 — Premec, Vladimir. Franciskus Patricijus. Beograd, 1968.
Phil 3460.90 — Premessa a Jacobi. 1. ed. (Vecchiotti, Icilio.) Roma, 1959.

Phil 2805.31 — Première, quatrième et treizième lettres provinciales. (Pascal, Blaise.) Paris, 1882.

Phil 2805.31.2 — Première, quatrième et treizième lettres provinciales. (Pascal, Blaise.) Paris, 1885.

Phil 2805.31.5 — Les première, quatrième et treizième lettres provinciales. 13. éd. (Pascal, Blaise.) Paris, 188-.

Phil 5628.10.20 — Premières [-secondes] lettres sur l'extatique de Niéderbronn et sur ses révélations. (Busson, Claude Ignace.) Besançon, 1849.

Phil 5245.15.10 — Premières leçons de psychologie expérimentale a l'usage des candidats au baccalauréat. (Foucault, Marcel.) Paris, 1930.

Phil 5585.290 — La premières notions spatiales de l'enfant. (Laurondeau, Monique.) Neuchâtel, 1968.

Phil 2520.140.8 — Les premières pensées de Descartes. (Gouhier, Henri.) Paris, 1958.

Phil 3425.40.50 — Premières publications. Thèse. (Hegel, Georg Wilhelm Friedrich.) Paris, 1952.

Phil 2477.6.30 — Les premiers écrits de Maurice Blondel. 1. éd. (Blondel, Maurice.) Paris, 1956.

Phil 2496.55.3 — Premiers essais de philosophie. 3e éd. (Cousin, Victor.) Paris, 1855.

Phil 2270.45.50 — Les premiers principes. (Spencer, Herbert.) Paris, 1871.
Phil 181.69 — Premiers principes de philosophie. (Gorce, M.M.) Paris, 1933.

Phil 5400.29 — Premiers principes d'une théorie générale des émotions. (Latour, Marius.) Paris, 1912.

Phil 5400.29.5 — Premiers principes d'une théorie générale des émotions. (Latour, Marius.) Paris, 1935.

Phil 5400.29.25 — Premiers principes d'une théorie générale des émotions. Observations complémentaires. 5me série. (Latour, Marius.) Bayonne, 1937.

Phil 5400.29.15 — Premiers principes d'une théorie générale des émotions. Observations complémentaires. 3me série. (Latour, Marius.) Bayonne, 1937.

Phil 5400.29.20 — Premiers principes d'une théorie générale des émotions. Observations complémentaires. 4me série. (Latour, Marius.) Bayonne, 1937.

Phil 4757.3.25 — Premudrost' i blagost' Bozhiia v sud'bakh mira i cheloveka; o konechnych prichinakh. 4. izd. (Golubinskii, F.A.) Sankt Peterburg, 1894.

Phil 5819.10 — Prenatal determinants of behaviour. 1. ed. (Joffe, J.M.) Oxford, 1969.

Phil 5255.34 — Prengowski, P. Le concept, le jugement et l'attention. Paris, 1930.

Phil 5057.38 — Prenlsipy dialekticheskoi logiki. (Rozental', M.M.) Moskva, 1960.

NEDL Phil 25.8 — Prenological journal. London. 1823-1847 20v.
Phil 8669.9 — Los prenotados del conocimiento natural de Dios. (Ortuzar Arriaga, Martin.) Madrid, 1963.

Phil 197.67 — Preparing the way. (World Wide Revival Prayer Movement.) Atlantic City, 1941.

Phil 8705.14 — Prepin, Michael T. The new reformation. N.Y., 1927.
Phil 3835.3 — Préposiet, Jean. Spinoza et la liberté des hommes. Paris, 1967.

Phil 5402.29 — Prescott, Frederick. The control of pain. N.Y., 1965.
Phil 6321.35 — Prescription for rebellion. (Lindner, R.M.) London, 1953.
Phil 8877.65.30 — Prescriptions. (Cabot, Richard C.) Boston, 1915.
Phil 8581.28 — Presence. (Brent, C.H.) N.Y., 1914.
Phil 575.180 — La présence d'autrui. Paris, 1957.
Phil 3425.658 — Présence de l'esthetique de Hegel. (Waldemar, George.) Paris, 1967.

Phil 2905.1.155 — Présence de Pierre Teilhard de Chardin. (Magloire, George.) Paris, 1961.

Phil 6323.20 — La présence du psychanalyste. (Nacht, Sacha.) Paris, 1963.

Phil 5520.489 — The presence of the word. (Ong, Walter Jackson.) New Haven, 1967.

Phil 2725.35.40 — La présence totale. (Lavelle, Louis.) Paris, 1934.
Phil 7054.6.6 — The present age and inner life. (Davis, A.J.) N.Y., 1855.
Phil 7054.6.8 — The present age and inner life. 3d ed. (Davis, A.J.) Boston, 1870.

Phil 8589.17 — Present and future of religion. (Joad, Cyril E.M.) London, 1930.

Phil 1715.3.5A — The present conflict of ideals. (Perry, R.B.) N.Y., 1918.
Phil 1715.3.8A — The present conflict of ideals. (Perry, R.B.) N.Y., 1922.
Phil 5722.24.10 — Présent conscient et cycles de durée. (Lubac, Émile.) Paris, 1936.

Phil 5850.279 — Present-day applications of psychology. 2nd ed. (Myers, Charles S.) London, 1918.

Phil 6952.21A — A present-day conception of mental disorders. (Campbell, C.M.) Cambridge, 1924.

Phil 8879.13.5 — Present-day ethics. (Eucken, R.C.) London, 1913.
Phil 5257.28.35 — Present day psychology. (Roback, A.A.) N.Y., 1955.
Phil 1750.23 — The present-day relevance of eighteenth-century thought. (McCutcheon, Roger Philip.) Washington, 1956.

Phil 1750.104 — Present-day thinkers and the new scholasticism. (Zybura, John. S.) Saint Louis, 1926.

Phil 8615.7 — The present duty. (Desjardins, P.) Philadelphia, 1893.
Phil 9358.13 — A present for an apprentice. 3d ed. London, 1807.

Phil 9490.1 — The present obligations of the scholar. (Adams, C.K.) Madison, Wis., 1897.
Phil 1715.3.2 — Present philosophical tendencies. (Perry, R.B.) London, 1912.
Phil 1718.8 — The present position of the phisophical sciences. (Seth, Pringle-Pattison Andrew.) Edinburgh, 1891.
Phil 8587.10 — Present religion. v.1-2. (Hennell, S.S.) London, 1865-87. 3v.
Phil 5643.69 — The present status of visual science. (Troland, L.T.) Washington, 1922.
Phil 8590.28 — Present tendencies in religious thought. (Knudson, A.C.) N.Y., 1924.
Phil 9355.11 — A present to youth and young men. Birmingham, Eng., 1891. 2v.
Phil 2150.22.110 — Présentation d'Herbert Marcuse. (Palmier, Jean Michel.) Paris, 1969.
Phil 353.2 — The presentation of reality. (Wodehouse, H.) Cambridge, 1910.
Phil 5754.1.29 — A preservative against the doctrine of fate. Boston, 1770.
Phil 58.2.5 — Presidential addresses, 1882-1911. (Society for Psychical Research, London.) Glasgow, 1912.
Phil 310.130 — Presniakov, P.V. Teoriia poznaniia dialekticheskogo materializma. Alma-Ata, 1959.
Phil 1133.35A — The presocratic philosophers. (Kirk, G.S.) Cambridge, Eng., 1957.
Phil 1133.35.4 — The presocratic philosophers. (Kirk, G.S.) Cambridge, Eng., 1962.
Phil 575.1 — Le presonnage humain. (Chantepie, É.) Paris, 1874.
Phil 190.16.5 — Pressensé, E. de. Les origines. 3e éd. Paris, 1883.
Phil 190.16.2 — Pressensé, E. de. Study of origins. 2d ed. N.Y., 1885.
Phil 190.16.10 — Pressensé, E. de. Variétés morales et politiques. Paris, 1885.
Phil 8599.16.80 — Presser, Jacob. Das Buch De tribus impostoribus. Amsterdam, 1926.
Phil 6325.6 — Pressey, Sidney L. Mental abnormality and deficiency. N.Y., 1926.
Phil 5255.47A — Pressey, Sidney Leavitt. Life; a psychological survey. 1st ed. N.Y., 1939.
Phil 8416.42 — Prestipino, Giuseppe. Lavovo e conoscenza nell'arte. Napoli, 1967.
Phil 6965.16 — Preston, G.H. Psychiatry for the curious. N.Y., 1940.
Phil 6125.25.5 — Preston, G.H. The substance of mental health. London, 1944.
Phil 6125.25 — Preston, G.H. The substance of mental health. N.Y., 1943.
Phil 181.130 — I presupposti della trascendenza. (Giannini, Giorgio.) Milano, 1959.
Phil 8886.32 — I presupposti formali...etica. (Limentani, Ludovico.) Genova, 1913.
Phil 3482.11 — I presupposti storici e teorici. (Anceschi, T.) n.p., 1955.
Phil 2270.185 — Il presupposto biologico e individualista della sociologia spenceriana. (Di Nola, Mario.) Colombo, 1965.
Phil 4080.3.30 — Il presupposto filosofico della concezione liberale Nota. (Croce, Benedetto.) Napoli, 1927.
Phil 3824.4 — Un pretendido interprete suramericano de Spinoza. (Espinosa, G.) Caracas, 1943.
Phil 2805.370 — Un prétendu traité de Pascal. (Brunet, Georges.) Paris, 1959.
Phil 3552.348 — Preti, G. Il cristianesimo universale di G.W. Leibniz. 1. ed. Roma, 1953.
Phil 2266.157 — Preti, Giulio. Alle origini dell'etica contemporanea Adamo Smith. Bari, 1957.
Phil 735.282 — Preti, Giulio. Fenomenologia del valore. Milano, 1942.
Phil 5520.122 — Preti, Giulio. Linguaggia comune e linguaggi scientifici. Roma, 1953.
Phil 6965.15 — Preu, P.W. Outline of psychiatric case-study. N.Y., 1939.
Phil 3246.325 — Preul, Reiner. Reflexion und Gefühl. Berlin, 1969.
Phil 3805.245 — Preuss, Eckhardt. Die Stellung und Bedeutung der Familie in der Pädagogik Schleiermachers. Münster? 1966?
Phil 3004.5 — Preussen und die Philosophie. (Erdmann, J.E.) Halle, 1954.
Phil 8661.45 — La preuve de Dieu et les cinq voies. (Guérard des Lauriers, Michel L.) Roma, 1966.
Phil 8640.6 — Les preuves de l'immortalité de l'âme. (Perrois, A.) Paris, 1866.
Phil 6959.3.2 — The prevention of insanity. (Jacobi, M.P.) Boston, 1880-82. 3 pam.
Phil 6959.3 — The prevention of insanity. (Jacobi, M.P.) Boston, 1882.
Phil 3915.159 — Prever, G. La filosofia di Guglielmo Wundt. Cuorgné, 1904.
Phil 9290.5 — Prevet, François. La moralité professionnelle des origines à nos jours. Paris, 1956. 2v.
Phil 2905.1.245 — La prévie, la réconciliation de la science et la foi. (Duroux, P.E.) Lyon, 1961.
Phil 333.11 — La previsione nella teoria della conoscenza. (Calderoni, M.) Milano, 1907.
Phil 4065.176 — Previti, Luigi. Giordano Bruno e i suoi tempi. Prato, 1887.
Phil 8595.8 — Prevost, J.M.C. De la déomanie au XIXe siècle. Toulouse, 1860.
Phil 8840.1.8 — Prévost-Paradol, L.A. Études sur les moralistes français. 8e éd. Paris, 1895.
Phil 365.11 — Preyer, W. Aus Natur- und Menschenleben. Berlin, 1885.
Phil 7060.33 — Preyer, W. Die Erklärung des Gedankenlesens. Leipzig, 1886.
Phil 6685.5 — Preyer, W. Der Hypnotismus. Wien, 1890.
Phil 28.2 — Preyer, W. Sammlung physiologischer Abhandlungen. Jena, 1877. 2v.
Phil 5255.29 — Preyer, W. Über die Grenzen der Tonwahrnehmung. n.p., 1876-89. 9 pam.
Phil 5585.6 — Preyer, W. Über die Grenzen des Empfindungsvermögens und des Willens. Bonn, 1868.
Phil 7080.33 — Preyer, William. Über die Ursache des Schlafes. Stuttgart, 1877.
Phil 6060.6 — Preyer, William. Zur Psychologie des Schreibens. Hamburg, 1895.
Phil 6060.6.3 — Preyer, William. Zur Psychologie des Schreibens. Leipzig, 1919.
Phil 645.37 — Preyre, A. The freedom of doubt. London, 1953.
Phil 1540.84 — Prezioso, Faustino Antonio. La species medievale e i prodromi del fenomenismo moderno. Padova, 1963.
Phil 5190.10.15 — Prezzalini, G. L'arte di persuadere. Firenze, 1907.
Phil 193.21.5 — Préзis élémentaire de philosophie. (Secrétan, C.) Lausanne, 1868.
Phil 5238.234 — Pribram, Karl H. Brain and behaviour. Harmondsworth, Middlesex, Eng., 1969. 4v.
Phil 6125.32 — Pribram, Karl H. Languages of the brain. Englewood Cliffs, 1971.

	Phil 7068.96.35	Pribytkov, V von. Aufrichtige Unterhaltungen über den Spiritismus. Leipzig, 1896?
	Phil 1750.2	Price, E.K. Some phases of modern philosophy. Philadelphia, 1872. 2 pam.
	Phil 2050.209	Price, H.H. Hume's theory of the external world. Oxford, 1940.
	Phil 5520.111A	Price, H.H. Thinking and experience. Cambridge, Mass., 1953.
	Phil 720.29	Price, H.H. Truth and corrigibility. Oxford, 1936.
	Phil 7069.36.10	Price, Harry. Confessions of a ghost-hunter. London, 1936.
	Phil 7069.36.13	Price, Harry. The haunting of Cashen's Gap. London, 1936.
	Phil 7069.41.5	Price, Harry. The most haunted house in England. London, 1941.
	Phil 7069.45.15	Price, Harry. Poltergeist over England; three centuries of mischievous ghosts. London, 1945.
	Phil 7069.30.26	Price, Harry. Rudi Schneider; a scientific example of his mediumship. London, 1930.
	Phil 5585.58.5	Price, Henry H. Perception. London, 1954.
	Phil 5585.58.7	Price, Henry H. Perception. London, 1964.
	Phil 346.14	Price, Henry H. Thinking and representation. London, 1946.
	Phil 5070.28	Price, Henry Habberley. Belief: the Gifford lectures delivered at the University of Aberdeen in 1960. London, 1969.
	Phil 2050.256.5	Price, John Valdimir. David Hume. N.Y., 1969.
	Phil 2050.256	Price, John Valdimir. The ironic Hume. Austin, 1965.
Htn	Phil 2215.30*	Price, Richard. A review of the principal questions and difficulties in morals. London, 1758.
	Phil 2215.30.2	Price, Richard. A review of the principal questions and difficulties in morals. 2d ed. London, 1769.
	Phil 2215.30.3	Price, Richard. A review of the principal questions in morals. 3d ed. London, 1787.
	Phil 9220.12	Price, W.J. Between friends. Norwood, Mass., 1934.
	Phil 8882.85	The price of morality. (Haezrahi, P.) London, 1961.
	Phil 3497.5	Prichard, H. Kant's theory of knowledge. Oxford, 1909.
	Phil 9120.161.10	Prichard, H.A. Duty and ignorance of fact. London, 1932.
	Phil 9120.161	Prichard, H.A. Duty and interest. Oxford, 1928.
	Phil 346.16	Prichard, H.A. Knowledge and perception. Oxford, 1950.
	Phil 9120.161.20	Prichard, H.A. Moral obligations. Oxford, 1949.
	Phil 6965.4	Prichard, J.C. Treatise on insanity and other disorders. Philadelphia, 1837.
	Phil 8980.780	Prichini za ostatutsite ot burzhoazniia moral v nasheto obshchestvo. (Semov, Mois I.) Sofiia, 1965.
	Phil 270.133	Prichinnostta v obshtestvoto. (Popov, Stoiko.) Sofiia, 1964.
	Phil 6980.611	Prick, Joseph Jules Guillaume. Human moods. Assen, 1968.
	Phil 9035.60	Priddle, Oamer D. Procedures in developing character controls through instructions. Thesis. Philadelphia, 1929.
	Phil 8595.29	Prideaux, Sherburne P.T. Man and his religion. London, 1930.
	Phil 7054.17	Pridham, A. The spirits tried. London, 1874.
	Phil 8400.27	Prieger, E. Anregung und metaphysische Grundlagen der Aesthetik von Alex Gottbeb Baumgarten. Berlin, 1875. 3 pam.
	Phil 2905.1.180.5	La prière du père Teilhard de Chardin. (Lubac, Henri de.) Paris, 1964.
	Phil 2905.1.180.5.2	La prière du père Teilhard de Chardin. (Lubac, Henri de.) Paris, 1968.
	Phil 5627.19	La prière-étude de psychologie religieuse. (Segond, J.) Paris, 1911.
	Phil 5627.262.10	Prière humaine, prière divine. (Nédoncelle, M.) Bruges, 1962.
	Phil 974.2.55A	Priestess of the occult, Madame Blavatsky. (Williams, G.M.) N.Y., 1946.
	Phil 672.221	Priestley, J.B. Man and time. London, 1964.
	Phil 2218.50	Priestley, Joseph. A continuation of the letters to the philosophers and politicians of France. Salem, 1795.
	Phil 2218.30	Priestley, Joseph. Disquisitions relating to matter and spirit. Birmingham, 1778-82. 3v.
	Phil 2218.29	Priestley, Joseph. Disquisitions relating to matter and spirit. 1st ed. London, 1777.
Htn	Phil 2218.45*	Priestley, Joseph. The doctrine of philosophical necessity. London, 1777.
	Phil 2218.40	Priestley, Joseph. An examination of Dr. Reid's Inquiry. 2d. ed. London, 1775.
	Phil 2218.35	Priestley, Joseph. Institutes of natural and revealed religion. 2nd ed. Birmingham, 1782. 2v.
	Phil 2218.81	Priestley, Joseph. Memoirs. London, 1805-07. 2v.
	Phil 2218.81.2	Priestley, Joseph. Memoirs. London, 1806. 2v.
	Phil 2218.47	Priestley, Joseph. A scientific autobiography of Joseph Priestley, 1733-1804. Cambridge, 1966.
	Phil 2218.55	Priestley, Joseph. Selections from his writings. University Park, 1962.
	Phil 2218.60	Priestley, Joseph. Writings on philosophy, science and politics. 1st ed. N.Y., 1965.
	Phil 2218.82	Priestley memorial. Photoreproduction. (Birmingham, England.) London, 1875.
	Phil 410.6	Přihonsky, F. B. Bolzano's Paradoxien des Unendlichen. Berlin, 1889.
	Phil 4073.45	La prima e la seconda resurrezione. (Campanella, Tommaso.) Roma, 1955.
	Phil 4080.3.35	La prima forma della estetica e della logica. (Croce, Benedetto.) Messina, 1900.
	Phil 8956.10	The primacy of charity in moral theology. (Gilleman, Gérard.) Westminster, 1959.
	Phil 8622.2	The primacy of faith. (Kroner, Richard.) N.Y., 1943.
	Phil 177.92	The primacy of metaphysics. Diss. (Casey, Joseph T.) Washington, D.C., 1936.
	Phil 2750.20.35	The primacy of perception. (Merleau-Ponty, Maurice.) Evanston, 1964.
Htn	Phil 184.1.2*	Primae philosophiae institutiones. (Jack, G.) Cantabrigia, 1649.
Htn	Phil 184.1*	Primae philosophiae institutiones. (Jack, G.) Lugdunum Batavorum, 1628.
	Phil 8673.30	Die primären Quellen des Gottesglaubens. (Schmucker, Josef.) Freiburg, 1967.
	Phil 5003.10	Primakovskii, A.P. Bibliografiia po logike. Moskva, 1955.
	Phil 8602.29	Primary facts in religious thought. (Wishart, A.W.) Chicago, 1905.
	Phil 97.4	A primary glossary of psychological and philosophical terms. (Mayer, M.B.) N.Y., 1932.
	Phil 6311.36	Primary love, and psycho-analytic technique. (Balint, Michael.) London, 1952.
	Phil 6311.36.2	Primary love, and psycho-analytic technique. (Balint, Michael.) N.Y., 1965.
	Phil 5258.114.5	The primary world of senses. (Straus, Erwin.) N.Y., 1963.
	Phil 807.15	Le primat de l'intelligence dans l'histoire de la pensée. (Habert, O.) Paris, 1926.
	Phil 4115.93	Il primato d'un popolo; Fichte e Gioberti. (Balbino, G.) Catania, 1916.
	Phil 3425.282F	Le prime categorie della logica di Hegel; memoria. (Spaventa, B.) Napoli, 1864.
	Phil 672.137	Prime linee di una teoria realistica dello spazio e del tempo. (Ranzoli, C.) Messina, 1921.
	Phil 8843.1.10	Prime livee di una storia della morale. (Sidgwick, Henry.) Torino, 1922.
	Phil 3425.510	Prime ricerche di Hegel. (Massolo, Arturo.) Urbino, 1959.
	Phil 5066.165	Primenie logiki v nauke i tekhnika. (Tavanets, P.V.) Moskva, 1960.
	Phil 6315.2.195	Primer centenario del racimiento. (Guatemala (city). Universidad Nacional.) Guatemala, 1956.
	Phil 8407.5	A primer of aesthetics. (Grudin, Louis.) N.Y., 1930.
	Phil 8402.52A	A primer of cities. (Boas, George.) Baltimore, 1937.
	Phil 9160.1.5	A primer of ethics. (Abbott, Jacob.) Boston, 1891.
	Phil 5066.9.5A	A primer of formal logic. (Cooley, J.C.) N.Y., 1942.
	Phil 6315.2.450	A primer of Freudian psychology. (Hall, Calvin S.) London, 1956.
	Phil 1106.11	A primer of Greek thought. (Boswell, F.P.) Geneva, 1923.
	Phil 672.172	A primer of higher space. (Bragdon, C.F.) Rochester, 1913.
	Phil 672.172.5	A primer of higher space. 2nd ed. (Bragdon, C.F.) N.Y., 1923.
	Phil 5058.28	A primer of logic. (Smith, Henry B.) Pulaski, 1917.
	Phil 5057.8	Primer of logical analysis. (Royce, J.) San Francisco, 1881.
Htn	Phil 2250.35*	Primer of logical analysis. (Royce, Josiah.) San Francisco, 1881.
	Phil 177.8.12A	Primer of philosophy. (Carus, Paul.) Chicago, 1893.
	Phil 192.44.2	A primer of philosophy. (Rappoport, A.S.) London, 1916.
	Phil 5241.25	Primer of psychology. (Brackenbury, L.) London, 1907.
	Phil 5251.1.2	Primer of psychology. (Ladd, G.T.) N.Y., 1894.
	Phil 5259.5A	A primer of psychology. (Titchener, E.B.) N.Y., 1898.
	Phil 8870.9	A primer of right and wrong. (Larned, J.N.) Boston, 1902.
	Phil 978.26	A primer of theosophy. (Theosophy Society in America.) Chicago, 1909.
	Phil 8630.1	A primer on the origin of knowledge. (Farlin, J.W.) Saratoga Springs, 1835.
	Phil 70.85	Primer Symposium Iberoamericano de Filosofia. (Symposium Iberoamericano de Filosofia.) Guatemala, 1961.
	Phil 850.34	Primessa storica al pensiero antico. (Cilento, Vincenzo.) Bari, 1963.
	VPhil 7072.21	Primety v svete nauki. 2. izd. (Shakhnovich, Mikhail I.) Leningrad, 1969.
	Phil 8952.9	Primi elementi di antropologia e di scienza morale. (Corte, P.A.) Torino, 1867.
	Phil 192.73	Primi passi nello studio della metafisica. 8a ed. (Rossignoli, Giovanni.) Torino, 1932.
	Phil 8420.14	Primi scritti de estetica. (Tilgher, A.) Roma, 1931.
	Phil 5241.40	I primi teoremi di psicologia. (Bocci, Balduino.) Siena, 1915.
NEDL	Phil 5627.7.8	Primitive traits in religious revivals. (Davenport, F.M.) N.Y., 1905.
	Phil 4115.81	Primo centenario di V. Gioberti. (Gioberti, V.) Torino, 1901. 2 pam.
	Phil 3425.485	Il primo Hegel. (Lacorte, Carmelo.) Firenze, 1959.
	Phil 3425.678	Il primo hegelismo Italiano. (Oldrini, Guido.) Firenze, 1969.
	Phil 175.25	Il primo passo alla filosofia. v.3. 5a ed. (Ambrosi, Luigi.) Milano, 1915.
	Phil 3801.560	Il primo Schelling. (Massolo, Arturo.) Firenze, 1953.
	Phil 7069.14.50	Primot, Alphonse. La psychologie d'une conversion du positivisme au spiritualisme. Paris, 1914.
	Phil 6325.8.15	Prince, Morton. Clinical and experimental studies in personality. Cambridge, Mass., 1929.
	Phil 6325.8.16	Prince, Morton. Clinical and experimental studies in personality. Cambridge, Mass., 1939.
	Phil 7039.4.1	Prince, Morton. The dissociation of a personality. N.Y., 1906.
	Phil 7039.4.3	Prince, Morton. The dissociation of a personality. N.Y., 1910.
	Phil 7039.4.6	Prince, Morton. The dissociation of a personality. N.Y., 1925.
	Phil 7039.4.8	Prince, Morton. The dissociation of a personality. N.Y., 1957.
	Phil 7039.4.15	Prince, Morton. My life as a dissociated personality. Boston, 1909.
	Phil 6325.8.5	Prince, Morton. The unconscious. N.Y., 1914.
	Phil 6325.8.6	Prince, Morton. The unconscious. N.Y., 1916.
	Phil 6325.8.7	Prince, Morton. The unconscious. 2d ed. N.Y., 1921.
	Phil 6325.8.8	Prince, Morton. The unconscious. 2d ed. N.Y., 1929.
	Phil 7040.6.60	Pamphlet box. Prince, Morton. Criticism.
	Phil 6325.8	Prince, Morton. Miscellaneous pamphlets on psychology. 11 pam.
	Phil 7069.16.63	Prince, W.F. The case of Patience Worth. Boston, 1927.
	Phil 7039.10	Prince, Walter Franklin. The Doris case of multiple personality. York, Pa., 1915-16. 2v.
	Phil 7069.30.28	Prince, Walter Franklin. The enchanted boundary;...psychical phenomena 1820-1930. Boston, 1930.
	Phil 7069.31.31	Prince, Walter Franklin. Human experiences. Boston, 1931.
	Phil 7069.28.85	Prince, Walter Franklin. Noted witnesses for psychic occurrences. N.Y., 1963.
	Phil 7069.25.11	Prince, Walter Franklin. A review of the Margery case. Ithaca, 1926.
	Phil 7069.26.25	Prince, Walter Franklin. The psychic in the house. Boston, 1926.
	Phil 5247.4.5	Princepes de psychologie. (Hartsen, F.A.) Paris, 1872.
	Phil 4195.87	Princeps concordiae: Pico della Mirandola. (Dulles, A.) Cambridge, 1941.
	Phil 55.2.5	Princeton contributions to philosophy. Princeton. 1898-1905+
	Phil 55.2	Princeton contributions to psychology. Princeton. 1-4,1895-1909 2v.
	Phil 5425.104	Princeton Meeting on the Recognition of Excellence, Princeton, 1959. The recognition of excellence. Washington, 1959.
	Phil 333.3	Das Princip der Infinitesimal-Methode und seine Geschichte. (Cohen, H.) Berlin, 1883.
	Phil 1145.78	Das Princip des Bösen nach den Begriffen den Griechen. (Märcker, F.A.) Berlin, 1842.
	Phil 3425.85	Princip und Methode der Philosophie. (George, L.) Berlin, 1842.
	Phil 6127.21	The principal nervous pathways. (Rasmussen, A.T.) N.Y., 1939.

Phil 8597.3.8	The principal truths of natural religion. (Reimarus, H.S.) London, 1766.	
Phil 5047.16	Les principales théories de la logique contemporaine. (Hermant, Paul.) Paris, 1909.	
Phil 184.22	Le principe constitutif de la nature organique. (Jung, E.) Paris, 1923.	
Phil 270.39.5	Le principe de causalité et ses limites. (Frank, P.) Paris, 1937.	
Phil 8893.5.5	Le principe de la morale. (Secrétan, C.) Lausanne, 1883.	
Phil 2750.7.37	Principe de la philosophie psycho-physiologique sur lequel repose la science de l'homme. (Massias, Nicolas.) Paris, 1829.	
Phil 5590.185	Principes de caractérologie. (Bourjade, Jean.) Neuchâtel, 1955.	
Phil 575.51.20	Les principes de la caractérologie. (Klages, Ludwig.) Paris, 1930.	
Phil 1870.40.25	Les principes de la connaissance humaine. (Berkeley, G.) Paris, 1920.	
Phil 5057.25	Les principes de la logique et la critique contemporaine. (Reymond, Arnold.) Paris, 1932.	
Phil 5057.25.2	Les principes de la logique et la critique contemporaine. (Reymond, Arnold.) Paris, 1957.	
Phil 2668.70	Principes de la métaphysique et de psychologie. (Janet, Paul A.R.) Paris, 1897. 2v.	
Phil 8876.57	Les principes de la morale. (Beaussire, Émile.) Paris, 1885.	
Phil 8894.6.15	Principes de la morale. (Tissot, Joseph.) Paris, 1866.	
Phil 3552.78.35	Principes de la nature et de la grace fondés en raison. (Leibniz, Gottfried Wilhelm.) Paris, 1954.	
Htn Phil 2520.39.8*	Les principes de la philosophie. (Descartes, René.) Paris, 1647.	
Htn Phil 2520.39*	Les principes de la philosophie. (Descartes, René.) Paris, 1651.	
Htn Phil 2520.39.10*	Les principes de la philosophie. (Descartes, René.) Paris, 1659.	
Phil 2520.39.3	Les principes de la philosophie. (Descartes, René.) Paris, 1668.	
Phil 2520.11.13	Les principes de la philosophie. (Descartes, René.) Paris, 1723.	
Phil 2520.39.6	Les principes de la philosophie. (Descartes, René.) Paris, 1724.	
Phil 2520.39.5	Les principes de la philosophie. (Descartes, René.) Paris, 1724.	
Phil 2520.39.16	Les principes de la philosophie. (Descartes, René.) Paris, 1950.	
Phil 2520.39.12	Les principes de la philosophie. (Descartes, René.) Rouen, 1698.	
Phil 2520.39.9	Les principes de la philosophie. (Descartes, René.) Rouen, 1706.	
Phil 2520.11.5	Les principes de la philosophie. 2e éd. (Descartes, René.) Paris, 1660.	
Phil 2520.11.10	Les principes de la philosophie. 4e éd. (Descartes, René.) Paris, 1681.	
Phil 4260.36.5	Principes de la philosophie de l'histoire. (Vico, G.B.) Bruxelles, 1835.	
Phil 4260.36A	Principes de la philosophie de l'histoire. (Vico, G.B.) Paris, 1827.	
Phil 8403.28	Les principes de la science du beau. (Chaignet, A.) Paris, 1860.	
Phil 5520.14	Principes de linguistic psychologique. (Ginneken, J. van.) Paris, 1907.	
Phil 5047.2.5	Principes de logique exposés d'après une méthode nouvelle. (Hartsen, F.A.) Paris, 1872.	
Phil 8886.41	Principes de morale rationnelle. (Landry, Adolph.) Paris, 1906.	
Phil 9450.12	Principes de morale sociale. (Deschamps, Louis.) Paris, 1903.	
Phil 176.86	Principes de philosophie. (Bertrand, A.) Paris, 1893.	
Phil 182.6	Principes de philosophie. (Hartsen, F.A.) Paris, 1877.	
Phil 2490.41.12A	Principes de philosophie positive. (Comte, Auguste.) Paris, 1868.	
Phil 5241.44.5	Principes de psychologie. (Bunge, Carlos O.) Paris, 1903.	
Phil 5850.385.15	Principes de psychologie appliquée. (Wallon, Henri.) Paris, 1930.	
Phil 9358.10	Principes des moeurs chez toutes les nations. (St. Lambert, J.F. de.) Paris, 1798. 3v.	
Phil 8403.18	Principes d'esthétique. (Coculesco, P.) Paris, 1935.	
Phil 8422.9	Principes du beau. (Vendéen, E.) Paris, 1912.	
Phil 2840.86	Les principes du droit dans la philosophie de C. Renouvier. Thèse. (Cornwell, J.) Paris, 1922?	
Htn Phil 2855.4.30*	Principes du droit politique. (Rousseau, J.J.) Amsterdam, 1762.	
Phil 600.45	Les principes du positivisme contemporain. (Halleux, Jean.) Paris, 19-?	
Phil 8612.74	Principes d'une esthétique de la mort. (Guiomar, Michel.) Paris, 1967.	
Phil 8877.58	Les principes généraux de la science et de la morale. (Challaye, F.) Paris, 1920.	
Phil 3565.68.5	Principes généraux de psychologie physiologique. (Lotze, Hermann.) Paris, 1876.	
Phil 2523.50	Principes logiques. (Destutt de Tracy, A.L.C.) Paris, 1817.	
Phil 2523.45	Principes logiques. (Destutt de Tracy, A.L.C.) Paris, 1817. 2 pam.	
Phil 3480.65.20	Principes métaphysiques de la morale. (Kant, Immanuel.) Paris, 1837.	
Phil 3480.65.23	Principes métaphysiques de la morale. 3. éd. (Kant, Immanuel.) Paris, 1854.	
Phil 3480.67.55	Principes métaphysiques du droit. (Kant, Immanuel.) Paris, 1837.	
Phil 8897.9	Principes philosophiques. (Weiss, F.R. de.) Bruxelles, 1832. 2v.	
Phil 8890.15	Principes supérieurs de la morale. (Pezzani, A.) Paris, 1859.	
Phil 1870.40.50	Principi della conoscenza umana. (Berkeley, G.) Bologna, 1925.	
Phil 8892.70	Principi della scienza morale. (Rosmini-Serbati, Antonio.) Roma, 1959.	
Phil 4210.30	Principi della scienza morale. (Rosmini-Serbati, Antonio.) Torino, 1928.	
Phil 2115.45.40	I principi dell'illuminismo eclettico, estratti dal "Saggio sull'intelligenza umano". (Locke, J.) Torino, 1927.	
Phil 8420.15	Principi di estetica. (Talia, G.B.) Venezia, 1827-28. 2v.	
Phil 2070.46.10	Principî di psicologia (estratti). (James, William.) Torino, 1928.	
Phil 5245.13	Principi di psicologia moderna. (Faggi, A.) Palermo, 1895.	

Htn Phil 4260.33*	Principi di scienza nuova. v.1-2. (Vico, G.B.) Napoli, 1744.	
Phil 4260.35.20	Principi di una scienza nuova. (Vico, G.B.) Milano, 1903.	
Phil 4260.35	Principi di una scienza nuova. (Vico, G.B.) Napoli, 1826.	
Phil 4070.7.5	Principi di una teoria della ragione. (Banfi, Antonio.) Milano, 1960.	
NEDL Phil 8887.21.2	Principia ethica. (Moore, George Edward.) Cambridge, Eng., 1922.	
Phil 8887.21.2	Principia ethica. (Moore, George Edward.) Cambridge, Eng., 1922.	
Phil 8887.21.3	Principia ethica. (Moore, George Edward.) Cambridge, Eng., 1929.	
Phil 8887.21.4	Principia ethica. (Moore, George Edward.) Cambridge, Eng., 1954.	
Phil 8887.21.6	Principia ethica. (Moore, George Edward.) Cambridge, Eng., 1959.	
Phil 2520.67	Principia philosophiae. (Descartes, René.) Amstelodami, 1692.	
Htn Phil 2520.10.5*	Principia philosophiae. (Descartes, René.) Amsterdam, 1644. 2 pam.	
Htn Phil 2520.10*	Principia philosophiae. (Descartes, René.) Amsterdam, 1650.	
Phil 2520.13.11	Principia philosophiae. (Descartes, René.) Amsterdam, 1685. 3 pam.	
Htn Phil 3552.30.5*	Principia philosophica. (Leibniz, Gottfried Wilhelm.) Lipsiae, 1728.	
Phil 1535.22	Principia philosophica. v.1-2. (Guidi, P.L.) Florentiae, 1913-14.	
Phil 3480.52.25	Principie di estetica. (Kant, Immanuel.) Bari, 1935.	
Phil 3565.116	Principien der Ethik und Religionsphilosophie Lotzes. (Vorbrodt, G.) Dessau, 1891.	
Phil 5374.32	I principii della conoscenza. (Ambrosi, L.) Roma, 1898.	
Phil 2520.39.20	I principii della filosofia. (Descartes, René.) Bari, 1914.	
Phil 4210.146	I principii della politica nella filosofia di Antonio Rosmini. (Anastasia, M.) Osimo, 1934.	
Phil 8413.8	Principii di estetica. (Manzari, A.) Napoli, 1908.	
Phil 4225.1.40	Principii di etica. (Spaventa, Bertrando.) Napoli, 1904.	
Phil 8896.11	Principii di etica. (Vivante, Lello.) Roma, 1920.	
Phil 2520.39.30	Principii di filosofia. (Descartes, René.) Napoli, 1937.	
Phil 4120.3.30	Principii di filosofia prima. (Giovanni, V. di.) Palermo, 1863. 2v.	
Phil 181.48.5	Principii di filosofia prima. (Giovanni, V. di.) Palermo, 1878. 3v.	
Phil 5066.12.15	I principii di geometria logicamente esposti. (Peano, G.) Torino, 1889.	
Phil 5052.29	Principii di logica del potenziamento. (Mosso, Pietro.) Torino, 1924.	
Phil 5040.10	Principii di logica reale. (Alfonso, N.R. d'.) Torino, 1894.	
Phil 5249.2.24	Principii di psicologia. (James, William.) Milano, 1901.	
Phil 8893.43	Principii di scienza etica. (Sarlo, Francisco de.) Milano, 1907.	
Phil 4210.29	Il principio della morale. (Rosmini-Serbati, Antonio.) Bari, 1924.	
Phil 8894.18	Il principio dell'ética e la crisi morale contemporanea; memoria. (Tarantino, Giuseppe.) Napoli, 1904.	
Phil 270.30	Il principio di causalità. (Baglioni, B.) Perugia, 1908.	
Phil 4210.192	Il principio dialettico nella filosofia di Antonio Rosmini. (Raschini, Maria A.) Milano, 1961.	
Phil 4352.1.105	Principios de filosofia de la historia. (Urmeneta, F. de.) Madrid, 1952.	
Phil 2490.41.9	Principios de filosofía positiva. (Comte, Auguste.) Santiago, 1875.	
Phil 1865.18	Principios de la ciencia social. (Bentham, Jeremy.) Salamanca, 1821.	
Phil 8886.63	Los principios de la ética social. 4. ed. (Larroyo, F.) Mexico, 1941.	
Phil 5052.30	Principios de lógica. (Morselli, E.) Buenos Aires, 1928.	
Phil 5249.2.21	Principios de psicología. (James, William.) Madrid, 1909. 2v.	
Phil 5248.2	Principios de psicología biológica. (Ingenieros, J.) Madrid, 1913.	
Phil 525.15	Principios fundamentales de la mistica. v.1-2,3. (Seisdedos Sanz, J.) Madrid, 1913. 2v.	
Phil 5041.33	Les principis du raisonment exposez en deux logiques nouvéles. (Buffier, Claude.) Paris, 1714.	
Phil 1107.4.5	Principium sapientiae. (Cornford, F.M.) Cambridge, Eng., 1952.	
Phil 4210.139	Principj della scuola Rosminiana. (Ballarini.) Milano, 1850. 2v.	
NEDL Phil 3425.98	Principle and method of the Hegelian dialectic. (McGilvary, E.) Berkeley, 1897.	
Phil 8585.20	Principle of authority in relation to certainty. (Forsyth, P.T.) London, 1912.	
Phil 575.18A	The principle of individuality and value. (Bosanquet, B.) London, 1912.	
Phil 2020.83	Principle of individuality in the philosophy of T.H. Green. (Townsend, H.G.) Lancaster, 1914.	
Phil 1750.550	The principle of sufficient reason in some scholastic systems. (Gurr, John E.) Milwaukee, 1959.	
Phil 1870.85	The principle of synthetic unity in Berkeley and Kant. (Dick, S.M.) Lowell, 1898.	
Phil 3494.14	The principle of teology. (Major, David R.) Ithaca, N.Y., 1897.	
Phil 6128.10.3	Principle of the human mind, deduced from physical laws. (Smee, Alfred.) N.Y., 1850.	
Phil 6128.10.2	Principle of the human mind, sequel to elements of electrobiology. (Smee, Alfred.) London, 1849.	
Phil 720.50	The principle of truth. (King, Peter D.) N.Y., 1960.	
Phil 8882.22	Principles, natural and supernatural morals. (Hughes, H.) London, 1890-91. 2v.	
Phil 8598.21	The principles and connexion of natural and revealed religion distinctly considered. (Sykes, A.A.) London, 1740.	
Phil 1750.786	Principles and persons. (Olafson, Frederick.) Baltimore, 1967.	
Phil 6953.14	Principles and practice of recreational theraphy for the mentally ill. (Davis, J.E.) N.Y., 1936.	
Phil 6953.14.5	Principles and practice of rehabilatation. (Davis, J.E.) N.Y., 1943.	
Phil 5593.47	Principles and practise of the Rorschach personality test. (Mons, Walter E.) London, 1947.	
Phil 193.66.9	The principles and problems of philosophy. (Sellars, Roy Wood.) N.Y., 1926.	
NEDL Phil 5041.40	Principles and problems of right thinking. (Burtt, Edwin Arthur.) N.Y., 1928.	

	Phil 5041.40.5	Principles and problems of right thinking. (Burtt, Edwin Arthur.) N.Y., 1931.
	Phil 5041.40.10	Principles and problems of right thinking. (Burtt, Edwin Arthur.) N.Y., 1938.
	Phil 5241.75.15	Principles d'une psychologie des tendances. (Burloud, Albert.) Paris, 1938.
	Phil 5257.40.5	Principles in bio-physics. (Richter, Conrad.) Harrisburg, 1927.
	Phil 3504.6.2	Principles Kantesian...philosophy. (Wirgman, T.) London, 1824.
Htn	Phil 3504.6.3*	Principles Kantesian...philosophy. 2d ed. (Wirgman, T.) London, 1832.
	Phil 176.61	Principles of a system of philosophy. (Bierbower, A.) N.Y., 1870.
	Phil 6322.27A	Principles of abnormal psychology. (Maslow, A.H.) N.Y., 1941.
	Phil 8416.29	The principles of aesthetics. (Parker, de W.H.) Boston, 1920.
	Phil 5822.9	Principles of animal psychology. (Maier, Norman Raymond Frederick.) N.Y., 1935.
	Phil 5822.9.2	Principles of animal psychology. (Maier, Norman Raymond Frederick.) N.Y., 1964.
	Phil 5829.5	Principles of animal understanding. (Toenjes, H.) N.Y., 1905.
	Phil 5058.75	Principles of applied logic. (Schipper, Edith Watson.) Dubuque, 1956.
	Phil 5850.314.5	Principles of applied psychology. (Poffenberger, A.T.) N.Y., 1942.
	Phil 8403.15	The principles of art. (Carus, Paul.) Boston, 1886.
	Phil 8403.21	The principles of art. (Collingwood, Robin George.) Oxford, 1938.
	Phil 8403.21.7	The principles of art. (Collingwood, Robin George.) Oxford, 1967.
	Phil 8419.24	The principles of beauty. (Symonds, J.A.) London, 1857.
	Phil 8419.32	The principles of beauty as manifested in nature, art, and human character. (Schimmelpenninck, Mary Anne.) London, 1859.
	Phil 5247.56.5	Principles of behavior. (Hull, C.L.) N.Y., 1943.
	Phil 2270.30.2	Principles of biology. (Spencer, Herbert.) London, 1864-67. 2v.
	Phil 5832.20	Principles of comparative psychology. (Waters, Rolland.) N.Y., 1960.
	Phil 5055.17.5	Principles of correct thinking. (Patterson, Charles H.) Minneapolis, 1936.
	Phil 3483.1.10	The principles of critical philosophy. (Beck, J.S.) London, 1797.
	Phil 8419.6F	Principles of domestic taste. (Salisbury, Edward.) New Haven, 1877.
	Phil 6980.459	Principles of dynamic psychiatry. (Masserman, Jules Hymen.) London, 1946.
	Phil 5061.1	Principles of empirical or inductive logic. (Venn, J.) London, 1889.
	Phil 5061.1.2	Principles of empirical or inductive logic. (Venn, J.) London, 1907.
	Phil 325.12	Principles of empirical realism. (Williams, Donald Cary.) Springfield, Ill., 1966.
	Phil 8876.25*	The principles of ethics. (Bowne, B.P.) N.Y., 1892.
	Phil 8876.25.5	The principles of ethics. (Bowne, B.P.) N.Y., 1893.
	Phil 8878.49	Principles of ethics. (Dunham, James.) N.Y., 1929.
	Phil 2270.73	Principles of ethics. (Spencer, Herbert.) N.Y., 1892-93. 2v.
	Phil 2270.73.3	Principles of ethics. (Spencer, Herbert.) N.Y., 1895. 2v.
	Phil 2270.73.4	Principles of ethics. (Spencer, Herbert.) N.Y., 1895-96. 2v.
	Phil 2270.73.5	Principles of ethics. (Spencer, Herbert.) N.Y., 1899.
	Phil 5255.18.10	Principles of experimental psychology. (Piéron, Henri.) London, 1929.
	Phil 5245.43	Principles of general psychology. (Freeman, E.) N.Y., 1939.
	Phil 6315.28	Principles of general psychopathology. (Fischer, S.) N.Y., 1950.
	Phil 8700.8	The principles of geology explained. (King, David.) N.Y., 1851.
	Phil 5250.7.19	Principles of Gestalt psychology. (Koffka, K.) London, 1935.
	Phil 5250.7.15	Principles of Gestalt psychology. (Koffka, K.) N.Y., 1935.
	Phil 6985.40	Principles of group treatment. (Berne, Eric.) N.Y., 1966.
	Phil 1870.40.22	The principles of human knowledge. (Berkeley, G.) London, 1942.
	Phil 6315.26A	Principles of intensive psychotherapy. (Fromm-Reichmann, F.) Chicago, 1950.
	Phil 353.1	The Principles of knowledge. (Walter, J.E.) West Newton, Pa., 1901. 2v.
Htn	Phil 1865.50.5*	Principles of legislation. (Bentham, Jeremy.) Boston, 1830.
	Phil 5068.56	The principles of linguistic philosophy. (Waismann, Friedrich.) London, 1965.
	Phil 5040.7	The principles of logic. (Aikins, H.A.) N.Y., 1902.
	Phil 5041.20	Principles of logic. (Bradley, F.H.) London, 1883.
	Phil 5041.20.3	Principles of logic. (Bradley, F.H.) N.Y., 1912.
	Phil 5049.10	Principles of logic. (Joyce, G.A.) London, 1908.
	Phil 5058.8	The principles of logic. (Schuyler, A.) Cincinnatti, n.d.
	Phil 5062.19	Principles of logic. (Williams, S.) London, n.d.
	Phil 5040.7.1	The principles of logic. 2nd ed. (Aikins, H.A.) N.Y., 1904.
	Phil 5041.20.5A	Principles of logic. 2nd ed. (Bradley, F.H.) London, 1922. 2v.
	Phil 5052.24.6	The principles of logic deductive and inductive. (Mitra, A.C.) Calcutta, 1922. 2v.
	Phil 5047.33.10	Principles of mathematical logic. (Hilbert, David.) N.Y., 1950.
	Phil 5245.4	Principles of medical psychology. (Feuchtersleben, E. von.) London, 1847.
Htn	Phil 6112.4.3*	Principles of mental psychology. (Carpenter, W.B.) London, 1881.
	Phil 6112.4.2	Principles of mental psychology. (Carpenter, W.B.) London, 1881.
	Phil 6112.4.3.5	Principles of mental psychology. (Carpenter, W.B.) N.Y., 1874.
	Phil 6112.4.9	Principles of mental psychology. 4th ed. (Carpenter, W.B.) N.Y., 1887.
	Phil 1880.40	Principles of metaphysical and ethical science. (Bowen, F.) Boston, 1855.
	Phil 8880.14	The principles of moral. v.1-2. (Fowler, T.) Oxford, 1886-87.

	Phil 2205.40.2	Principles of moral and political philosophy. (Paley, W.) Boston, 1795.
	Phil 2205.40.2.5	Principles of moral and political philosophy. (Paley, W.) Boston, 1801.
	Phil 2205.40.4	Principles of moral and political philosophy. (Paley, W.) Boston, 1810.
	Phil 2205.40.5	Principles of moral and political philosophy. (Paley, W.) Boston, 1811.
	Phil 2205.40.6	Principles of moral and political philosophy. (Paley, W.) Boston, 1815.
	Phil 2205.40.11	Principles of moral and political philosophy. (Paley, W.) Boston, 1827.
	Phil 2205.40.7	Principles of moral and political philosophy. (Paley, W.) Boston, 1830. 2v.
	Phil 2205.40.14	The principles of moral and political philosophy. (Paley, W.) Boston, 1831. 2v.
Htn	Phil 2205.39*	Principles of moral and political philosophy. (Paley, W.) London, 1785.
	Phil 2205.1	Principles of moral and political philosophy. (Paley, W.) London, 1785.
	Phil 2205.39.5	Principles of moral and political philosophy. (Paley, W.) London, 1786.
	Phil 2205.40.3	Principles of moral and political philosophy. (Paley, W.) London, 1804. 2v.
	Phil 2205.40.8	Principles of moral and political philosophy. (Paley, W.) N.Y., 1817.
	Phil 2205.40.10	Principles of moral and political philosophy. (Paley, W.) N.Y., 1824.
	Phil 2205.40	Principles of moral and political philosophy. (Paley, W.) Paris, 1788.
	Phil 2205.40.9	Principles of moral and political philosophy. v.1-2. (Paley, W.) Boston, 1828.
	Phil 2205.40.8.5	Principles of moral and political philosophy. 11th American ed. (Paley, W.) Boston, 1825.
	Phil 8800.7	Principles of moral and political science. (Ferguson, A.) Edinburgh, 1792. 2v.
	Phil 8886.65	The principles of moral judgement. (Lamont, William D.) Oxford, 1946.
	Phil 8881.11.6	The principles of moral philosophy. (Gisborne, T.) London, 1790.
	Phil 8885.42	Principles of moral philosophy. (Kimpel, B.F.) N.Y., 1960.
	Phil 8894.10	The principles of moral philosophy. (Turnbull, G.) London, 1740. 2v.
	Phil 8880.11	The principles of moral science. (Forsyth, R.) Edinburgh, 1805.
	Phil 8879.5	The principles of morality. (Ensor, G.) London, 1801.
	Phil 7054.6.30	The principles of nature, her divine revelations. 12. ed. (Davis, A.J.) N.Y., 1855.
	Phil 8890.46	Principles of nature. (Palmer, E.) London, 1823.
	Phil 7068.47	The principles of nature. 3. ed. (Davis, A.J.) N.Y., 1847.
	Phil 8890.46.5	Principles of nature. 3. ed. (Palmer, E.) N.Y., 1806.
	Phil 5585.120	Principles of perception. (Bartley, S.H.) N.Y., 1958.
	Phil 5585.295	Principles of perceptual learning and development. (Gibson, Eleanor Jack.) N.Y., 1969.
	Phil 176.205	The principles of philosophy. (Bhattacharya, H.M.) Calcutta, 1948.
	Phil 5925.3.6	The principles of phrenology and physiology. (Fowler, L.N.) N.Y., 1842.
	Phil 3915.46.6	Principles of physiological psychology. (Wundt, Wilhelm.) London, 1904.
Htn	Phil 9346.6.7*	Principles of politeness. (Chesterfield, Philip Dormer Stanhope.) Portsmouth, N.H., 1786.
	Phil 176.136	The principles of pragmatism. (Bawden, Henry H.) Boston, 1910.
	Phil 188.8	Principles of psychic philosophy. (Newcomb, C.B.) Boston, 1908.
	Phil 5241.7	The principles of psychology. (Bascom, J.) N.Y., 1869.
	Phil 5249.2.02	The principles of psychology. (James, William.) London, 1891. 2v.
	Phil 5249.2A	Principles of psychology. (James, William.) N.Y., 1890. 2v.
	Phil 5249.2.01A	Principles of psychology. (James, William.) N.Y., 1890. 2v.
Htn	Phil 5249.2*	Principles of psychology. (James, William.) N.Y., 1890. 2v.
	Phil 5249.2.1	Principles of psychology. (James, William.) N.Y., 1896. 2v.
	Phil 5249.2.3	Principles of psychology. (James, William.) N.Y., 1927.
	Phil 5250.17	Principles of psychology. (Kantor, J.R.) N.Y., 1924-26. 2v.
	Phil 5250.55	Principles of psychology. (Keller, F.) N.Y., 1950.
	Phil 5251.18.5	Principles of psychology. (Lynch, Arthur.) London, 1923.
	Phil 5249.2.99	The principles of psychology. (Myers, F.W.H.) London, 1891.
	Phil 2270.70.2	Principles of psychology. (Spencer, Herbert.) London, 1855.
	Phil 2270.70	Principles of psychology. (Spencer, Herbert.) London, 1855.
	Phil 2270.30.3	Principles of psychology. (Spencer, Herbert.) London, 1870-72. 2v.
	Phil 2270.70.5	Principles of psychology. (Spencer, Herbert.) London, 1881. 2v.
	Phil 2270.70.4.15	Principles of psychology. (Spencer, Herbert.) N.Y., 1878. 2v.
	Phil 2270.70.10	Principles of psychology. (Spencer, Herbert.) N.Y., 1894. 2v.
	Phil 2270.70.12	Principles of psychology. (Spencer, Herbert.) N.Y., 1895. 2v.
	Phil 2270.70.14	Principles of psychology. (Spencer, Herbert.) N.Y., 1901. 2v.
	Phil 2270.70.15	Principles of psychology. (Spencer, Herbert.) N.Y., 1926.
	Phil 5259.19.15A	The principles of psychology. (Troland, L.T.) N.Y., 1929. 3v.
NEDL	Phil 5249.2.01	Principles of psychology. v.2. (James, William.) N.Y., 1890.
	Phil 5249.2.2	Principles of psychology. v.2. (James, William.) N.Y., 1899.
	Phil 6959.1.25	Principles of psychotherapy. (Janet, Pierre.) N.Y., 1924.
	Phil 5057.20	The principles of reasoning. (Robinson, D.S.) N.Y., 1924.
	Phil 5057.20.2	The principles of reasoning. 2nd ed. (Robinson, D.S.) N.Y., 1930.
	Phil 5057.20.5	The principles of reasoning. 3rd ed. (Robinson, D.S.) N.Y., 1949.
	Phil 8586.10.5	Principles of religious development. (Galloway, G.) London, 1909.

Phil 5049.6 — The principles of science. (Jevons, W.S.) London, 1874. 2v.
Phil 5049.6.6 — The principles of science. (Jevons, W.S.) London, 1887.
Phil 5049.6.2.5 — The principles of science. (Jevons, W.S.) N.Y., 1874.
Phil 5049.6.18 — The principles of science. (Jevons, W.S.) N.Y., 1958.
Phil 5246.31.10 — Principles of systematic psychology. (Griffith, C.R.) Urbana, 1943.
Phil 5052.18 — Principles of the algebra of logic. (Macfarlane, Alexander.) Edinburgh, 1879.
Phil 1905.24 — Principles of the infinite philosophy. (Barnhart, F.J.C.) N.Y., 1955.
Phil 5627.90 — Principles of the interior or hidden life. (Upham, Thomas C.) London, 1874.
Phil 8893.44 — The principles of the moral empire. (Sugimori, K.) London, 1917.
Phil 5251.41.9 — Principles of topological psychology. 1st ed. (Lewin, Kurt.) N.Y., 1936.
Phil 5258.39 — Principles of understanding. (Sturt, Henry.) Cambridge, 1915.
Phil 5251.74 — Principles of voluntaristic psychology. (Losskii, N.O.) n.p., 1935. 2v.
Phil 8663.3.86.2 — Pringle, Allen. Ingersoll in Canada. 2. ed. Toronto, 1880.
Phil 2280.8.93 — Pringle-Pattison's Gifford lectures. v.1-2. (Rahder, J.) Leipzig, 1920.
Phil 8673.6.7 — Pringle-Pattison's idea of God. (Gallagher, Denis Maria.) Washington, D.C., 1933.
Phil 1750.368 — Prini, P. Esistenzialismo. Roma, 1952.
Phil 4822.4 — Prinos kum istoriiata na bulgarskata filosofska misul'. (Bunkov, Angel Iliev.) Sofiia, 1943.
Phil 5520.117 — Printsipy filosofskogo iazyka. (Lintsbakh, Ia.) Petrograd, 1916.
Phil 4768.2.9 — Printsipy i puti razvitiia psikhologii. (Rubinshtein, Sergei L.) Moskva, 1959.
Phil 310.4.5 — Printsipy periodizatsii istorii marksistsko-leninskoi filosofii. (Protasenko, Z.M.) Leningrad, 1957.
Phil 730.35 — Printsipy tselostnosti. (Korotkova, Galina P.) Leningrad, 1968.
Phil 5211.10 — Prints'pial'nye voprosy psikhologii. (Bochorishvili, A.t.) Tbilisi, 1957- 2v.
Phil 6965.18 — Prinzhorn, H. Bildnerei der Geisteskranken. Berlin, 1922.
Phil 5225.3 — Prinzhorn, H. Leib-Seele-Linheit. Potsdam, 1927.
Phil 5255.44.2 — Prinzhorn, H. Persönlichkeits-Psychologie. 2. Aufl. Heidelberg, 1958.
Phil 5255.44 — Prinzhorn, H. Persönlichkeitspsychologie. Leipzig, 1932.
Phil 575.70 — Prinzhorn, H. Um die Persönlichkeit. Bd.1. Heidelberg, 1927.
Phil 6325.10.5 — Prinzhorn, Hans. Gespräch über Psychoanalyse zwischen Frau, Dichter und Arzt. Heidelberg, 1927.
Phil 3640.229 — Prinzhorn, Hans. Nietzsche und das XX Jahrhundert. Heidelberg, 1928.
Phil 6325.10 — Prinzhorn, Hans. Psychotherapie. Leipzig, 1929.
Phil 8590.21 — Das Prinzip der Dialektik in der Theologie. Inaug. Diss. (Keller, Aaron.) Erlangen-Bruck, 1934.
Phil 284.3 — Prinzip der Entwickelung. (Dinger, H.) Jena, 1896.
Phil 3160.9.85 — Das Prinzip des Unbewussten bei Carl Gustav Carus. (Klink, Siegfried.) Tübingen, 1933.
Phil 346.10 — Prinzipielle Grundlagen. (Piper, H.) Göttingen, 1916.
Phil 5248.2.5 — Prinzipien der biologischen Psychologie. (Ingenieros, J.) Leipzig, 1922.
Phil 575.51 — Prinzipien der Charakterologie. 3e Aufl. (Klages, Ludwig.) Leipzig, 1921.
Phil 331.5 — Prinzipien der Erkenntnislehre. (Aster, Ernst von.) Leipzig, 1913.
Phil 346.7 — Prinzipien der Erkenntnislehre. (Petronievics, B.) Berlin, 1900.
Phil 3260.81 — Die Prinzipien der Ethik bei Fries. (Grape, Johannes.) Dessau, 1903.
Phil 3850.18.88 — Die Prinzipien der formalen Gesetzes Ethik Kants und der materialen Wertethik Schelers. Diss. (Herrmann, J.) Breslau, 1928.
Phil 5062.20 — Die Prinzipien der Logik. (Windelband, W.) Tübingen, 1913.
Phil 3915.69.5 — Die Prinzipien der mechanischen Naturlehre. (Wundt, Wilhelm.) Stuttgart, 1910.
Phil 2520.162 — Die Prinzipien der menschischen Erkenntniss nach Descartes. (Schmid, Paul J.) Leipzig, 187-?
Phil 2520.11.24 — Die Prinzipien der Philosophie. 3. Aufl. (Descartes, René.) Leipzig, 1908.
Phil 2520.11.25 — Die Prinzipien der Philosophie. 4e Aufl. (Descartes, René.) Leipzig, 1922.
Phil 8890.48 — Prior, A.N. Logic and the bases of ethics. Oxford, 1949.
Phil 5055.25A — Prior, Arthur N. Formal logic. Oxford, 1955.
Phil 5055.25.2 — Prior, Arthur N. Formal logic. 2nd ed. Oxford, 1962.
Phil 5066.103 — Prior, Arthur Norman. Papers on time and tense. Oxford, 1968.
Phil 5066.102 — Prior, Arthur Norman. Past, present and future. Oxford, 1967.
Phil 5066.100 — Prior, Arthur Norman. Time and modality. Oxford, 1957.
Phil 8400.60 — Priroda i funktsii esteticheskogo. Moskva, 1968.
Phil 270.141 — Priroda istoricheskoi neobkhodimosti. (Dzhioev, Otar.) Tbilisi, 1967.
Phil 8426.6 — Priroda prekrasnogo. (Zotov, Ivan A.) Moskva, 1965.
Phil 8595.9 — Pritchard, C. Occasional thoughts...astronomer, nature, revelation. London, 1889.
Phil 8595.13 — Pritchett, H.S. What is religion. Boston, 1906.
Phil 9450.58 — Private conscience - public mortality. (Inglis, B.) London, n.d.
Phil 2050.3A — Private correspondence...1761-76. (Hume, David.) London, 1820.
Phil 7069.19.180 — Private Dowding. N.Y., 1919.
Phil 5520.491 — The private language problem. (Saunders, John Turk.) N.Y., 1967.
Phil 9495.17.15 — Private lectures on perfect men, women and children. (Fowler, O.S.) N.Y., 1880.
Phil 6158.15 — The private sea; LSD and the search for God. (Braden, William.) Chicago, 1967.
Phil 5640.136.10 — Privation sensorielle et intelligence. (Hatwell, Yvette.) Paris, 1966.
Phil 5247.33 — Le privilege de l'intelligence. (Hautefeuille, F. d'.) Paris, 1923.
Phil 9400.6 — The privileges of old age. (Peabody, F.G.) Cambridge, 1931.
Phil 8889.1.15 — Le prix de la vie. 43. ed. (Ollé-Laprune, L.) Paris, 1921.
Phil 9070.31 — The prize of life. (Grenfell, W.T.) N.Y., 1914.
Phil 8416.17 — Pro, Diezo F. Tres aspectos de la cultura. Mendoza, 1942.

Phil 8610.875.10 — The pro and con of supernatural religion...together with a sketch of the life of the author. (Guild, E.E.) N.Y., 1876.
Phil 4170.16 — Pró Diego F. Rodolfo Mondolfo. v.1-2. Buenos Aires, 1967-68.
Phil 8886.82 — Il pro e il contro: considerazioni morali. (Libnizzi, Carmelo.) Padova, 1967.
Phil 5360.30 — Probabilistic concept learning. Proefschrift. (Klerk, Lein Friedrich Wolfgang de.) Leiden? 1968.
Phil 8709.5 — Probabilities; an aid to faith. (Tupper, Martin F.) N.Y., 1847.
Phil 3837.2 — The probability; a critique of Spinoza's demonstration. (Roe, E.D.) Andover, 1894.
Phil 5039.18 — Probability, confirmation, and simplicity; readings in the philosophy of inductive logic. (Foster, Marguerite H.) N.Y., 1966.
Phil 5125.20 — Probability and induction. (Kneale, William Calvert.) Oxford, 1949.
Phil 5125.20.1 — Probability and induction. Reprint. (Kneale, William Calvert.) Oxford, 1966.
Phil 5145.4 — Probability and opinion. (Byrne, Edmund F.) The Hague, 1968.
Phil 192.46 — Le probablilisme moral et la philosophie. (Richard, R.P.) Paris, 1922.
Phil 5041.28.3 — Problem; science-analysis. (Black, George A.) N.Y., 1911.
Phil 353.6 — Das Problem. (Weisengrün, P.) Leipzig, 1892.
Phil 5041.28 — Problem: science (function) analysis. (Black, George A.) N.Y., 1905.
Phil 6310.1.42 — The problem child. (Adler, A.) N.Y., 1963.
Phil 5330.19 — Das Problem der Aufmerksamkeit. (Dohrn, H.) Schleswig, 1876.
Phil 2880.8.170 — Das Problem der dialektischen Vernunft bei Jean Paul Sartre. (Sotelo, Ignacio.) Köln, 1965.
Phil 5635.8 — Das Problem der Empfindung. (Paulsen, J.) Giessen, 1907.
Phil 1050.16.5 — Das Problem der Erkenntnis in der Religions-Philosophie Jehuda Hallevis. Inaug-Diss. (Berger, Emil.) Berlin, 1915.
Phil 8620.25 — Das Problem der Erlösung. (Nagel, E.) Basel, 1901.
Phil 8637.23 — Das Problem der Erlösung in den Religionen der Menschheit. (Manthey, Franz.) Hildesheim, 1964.
Phil 8956.5 — Das Problem der Ethik...Gegenwart. (Gallwitz, Hans.) Göttingen, 1891.
Phil 8408.6.5 — Das Problem der Form in der Bildendenkunst. 6. Aufl. (Hildebrand, A.) Strassburg, 1908.
Phil 3640.241 — Das Problem der freien Rhythmen mit Bezug auf Nietzsche. (Hellenbrecht, H.) Berlin, 1931.
Phil 3640.265 — Das Problem der freien Rhythmen mit Bezug auf Nietzsche. Inaug. Diss. (Hellenbrecht, H.) Bern, 1931.
Phil 5753.8.2 — Das Problem der Freiheit. 2. Aufl. (Driesch, H.) Darmstadt, 1920.
Phil 3499.11 — Das Problem der Freiheit in Kants Erkenntnistheorie. (Ruge, Arnold.) Leipzig, 1910.
Phil 735.17 — Das Problem der Geltung. 2e Aufl. (Liebert, A.) Leipzig, 1920.
Phil 270.59 — Das Problem der Gesetzlichkeit. (Joachim, J.) Hamburg, 1949- 2v.
Phil 337.5 — Das Problem der Gewissheit. (Grung, Frants.) Heidelberg, 1886.
Phil 353.33 — Das Problem der Gewissheit. Eine erkenntnismetaphsische Studie. (Wiedmann, Franz.) München, 1966.
Phil 2050.175 — Das Problem der Gültigkeit. (Hasse, Heinrich.) Leipzig, 1919.
Phil 575.67 — Das Problem der Individualität. (Volkelt, Johannes.) München, 1928.
Phil 3845.1 — Problem der Kausalität bei Spinoza. (Zulawski, J.) Bern, 1899.
Phil 3500.88 — Das Problem der Kontingenz der Welt. (Schmucker, Josef.) Freiburg, 1969.
Phil 2750.20.135 — Das Problem der Leiblichkeit bei Jean Paul Sartre und Maurice Merleau-Ponty. (Maier, Willi.) Tübingen, 1964.
Phil 5047.36 — Das Problem der Logik als Entwicklung des Prinzips der Heterothese. (Hlučka, F.) Leipzig, 1939.
Phil 475.1 — Das Problem der Materie. v.1. (Abendroth, Robert.) Leipzig, 1889.
Phil 2305.6.30 — Das Problem der moralischen Rechtfertigung bei S.E. Toulmin. (Stark, Franz.) München, 1964.
Phil 3489.40 — Das Problem der objektiven Realität bei Kant. (Hermann, Horst.) Mainz, 1961.
Phil 70.26.6 — Das Problem der Ordnung. (Deutscher Kongress für Philosophie, 6th, München, 1960.) Meisenheim. 1962
Phil 5590.390 — Das Problem der Persönlichkeit in der amerikanischen Psychologie. (Kleiner, Fritz.) München, 1961.
Phil 341.13 — Das Problem der Phänomenologie. (Kynast, R.) Breslau, 1917.
Phil 3450.11.295 — Das Problem der Philosophie als strenger Wissenschaft. (Pazanin, A.) Köln, 1962.
Phil 2630.2.125 — Das Problem der Religion in der Philosophie Guyaus. (Łuczewski, Kazimierz.) Posen, 1915.
Phil 3640.233 — Das Problem der Romantik bei Nietzsche. (Langer, Norbert.) Münster, 1929.
Phil 7069.06.11.5 — Problem der Seelenforschung. (Hyslop, James Hervey.) Stuttgart, 1909.
Phil 665.51A — Das Problem der Seelenschönheit im Mittelalter. (Müller, Walter.) Bern, 1923.
Phil 70.26.8 — Das Problem der Sprache. (Deutscher Kongress für Philosophie, 8th, Heidelberg, 1966.) München. 1967
Phil 8520.16 — Das Problem der Theodicee. (Wegener, R.) Halle, 1909.
Phil 8620.36 — Das Problem der Theodizee. Inaug. Diss. (Kühler, Hans.) Bonn, 1929.
Phil 1050.26 — Das Problem der Theodizes in der jüdischen Religionsphilosophie des Mittelalters. Inaug. Diss. (Ehrich, J.) Breslau, 1936.
Phil 705.40 — Das Problem der Transzendenz in der Geschichte der neueren Philosophie. (Belzer, G.) Amsterdam, 1952.
Phil 8882.110 — Das Problem der Vernunftherrschaft. (Hirsch, Maximilian.) Leipzig, 1922.
Phil 5750.9 — Das Problem der Willensfreiheit. (Antweiler, A.) Freiburg, 1955.
Phil 5755.11 — Das Problem der Willensfreiheit. (Fahrion, Karl.) Heidelburg, 1904.
Phil 5756.4 — Das Problem der Willensfreiheit. (Gomperz, Heinrich.) Jena, 1907.
Phil 5761.5 — Das Problem der Willensfreiheit. (Lipps, G.F.) Leipzig, 1912.
Phil 5762.11.2 — Das Problem der Willensfreiheit. (Messer, August.) Göttingen, 1911.
Phil 5762.2 — Das Problem der Willensfreiheit. (Müffelmann, L.) London, 1902.

Phil 1540.11   Das Problem der Willensfreiheit. (Verweyen, Johannes.) Heidelberg, 1909.

Phil 5762.11   Das Problem der Willensfreiheit. 2. Aufl. (Messer, August.) Göttingen, 1918.

Phil 190.38.5   Das Problem der Wirklichkeit. (Prandtl, Antonin.) München, 1926.

Phil 672.151.10   Das Problem der Zeit. (Gent, Werner.) Hildesheim, 1965.

Phil 1158.40   Das Problem der Zeit im Epikureismus. Inaug. Diss. (Neck, Gisela.) Köln, 1964.

Phil 3425.728   Das Problem des Anfangs in Hegels Philosophie. (Schrader-Klebert, Karin.) Wien, 1969.

Phil 3488.16   Das Problem des Bewusstseins in der Philosophie Kants. (Garbeis, F.W.) Wien, 1924.

Phil 8620.26   Das Problem des Bösen. (Kym, Arnold L.) München, 1878.

Phil 9035.47   Das Problem des Charakteraufbaus. (Hoffmann, H.) Berlin, 1926.

Phil 3640.94.9   Das problem des egoistischen Perfektionismus in der Ethik Spinozas und Nietzsches. (Dernoscheck, G.A.) Annaberg, 1905.

Phil 9515.3.96   Das Problem der Einsamkeit in 18 Jahrhundert. (Maduschka, Leo.) Weimar, 1933.

Phil 9515.3.95   Das Problem der Einsamkeit in 18 Jahrhundert. Inaug. Diss. (Maduschka, Leo.) Murnan, 1932.

Phil 2138.108   Das Problem des Empirismus, dargestellt an John Stuart Mill. (Wentscher, Ela.) Bonn, 1922.

Phil 182.94.10   Das Problem des Geistigen Seins. (Hartmann, N.) Berlin, 1933.

Phil 182.94.10.5   Das Problem des geistigen Seins. 2. Aufl. (Hartmann, N.) Berlin, 1949.

Phil 5403.4   Das Problem des Glücks. (Lindner, Gustav.) Wien, 1864.

Phil 3450.19.405   Das Problem des Grundes in Heideggers Auseinandersetzung mit Kant. (Koza, Ingeborg.) Ratingen, 1967.

Phil 400.80   Das Problem des Irrationalen im wertphilosophischen Idealismus der Gegenwart. (Keller, Erich.) Berlin, 1931.

Phil 5525.7   Das Problem des Komischen. (Jahn, Franz.) Potsdam, 1904.

Phil 3415.74   Das Problem des Lebens. 2. Aufl. (Hartmann, Eduard von.) Berlin, 1925.

Phil 1718.14   Das Problem des Lebens in der heutigen Philosophie. (Stolzle, R.) Paderborn, 1922.

Phil 185.17   Das Problem des Lebens in kritischer Bearbeitung. (Kern, Berthold P.) Berlin, 1909.

Phil 9520.4.8   Das Problem des Leidens. 8. und 9. Aufl. (Keppler, Paul W.) Freiburg, 1919.

Phil 8620.35   Das Problem des Leidens in der Moral. (Keppler, Paul.) Freiburg im Breisgau, 1894.

Phil 298.16   Das Problem des Materiebegiffes. (Reitzer, Alfons.) München, 1960.

Phil 3120.30.41   Das Problem des Menschen. (Buber, Martin.) Heidelberg, 1948.

Phil 185.58   Das Problem des Nicht. (Kahl-Furthmann, G.) Berlin, 1934.

Phil 3903.3.113   Das Problem des philosophischen Skeptizismus. Diss. (Richtscheid, H.) Düsseldorf, 1935.

Phil 3425.584   Das Problem des polytechnischen Orbeitserziehung. (Reining, Richard.) Marburg, 1962.

Phil 5257.41   Das Problem des psychologischen Verstehens. (Roffenstein, G.) Stuttgart, 1926.

Phil 3495.16   Das Problem des psychophysischen Kommersiums in der Entwicklung der Kantischen Philosophie. (Nierkaus, F.) Köln, 1962.

Phil 1135.97   Das Problem des Raumes in der griechischen Philosophie bis Aristoteles. (Deichmann, C.) Halle, 1893.

Phil 353.20   Das Problem des Relativismus. (Wein, Hermann.) Berlin, 1950.

Phil 3850.18.100   Das Problem des religiösen Gegenstandes bei Max Scheler. Diss. (Hafkesbrink, H.) Gütersloh, 1930.

Phil 7080.23   Das Problem des Schlafes. (Trömmer, E.) Wiesbaden, 1912.

Phil 5250.13.87   Das Problem des seeleschen Seins. 2. Aufl. (Wellek, Albert.) Meisenheim, 1953.

Phil 3450.19.90   Das Problem des Selhstseins bei Heidegger und Kierkegaard. Diss. (Vogl, A.) Giessen, 1936.

Phil 3640.177   Das Problem des Sokrates. (Hasse, Heinrich.) Leipzig, 1918.

Phil 8612.24   Das Problem des Todes. (Schleich, Carl L.) Berlin, 1921.

Phil 8612.35   Das Problem des Todes in der Philosophie unserer Zeit. (Wach, Joachim.) Tübingen, 1934.

Phil 3585.10.82   Das Problem des tragischen bei Theodor Lipps und Johannes Volkelt. Inaug. Diss. (Ahrem, Maximilien.) Nürnberg, 1908.

Phil 8620.46   Das Problem des Übels in der Philosophie. (Billicsich, F.) Wien, 1952. 3v.

Phil 8620.31   Das Problem des Übels und die Theodicee. (Fischer, Engelbert Lorenz.) Mainz, 1883.

Phil 1135.28.20   Das Problem des Ursprungs in der Philosophie des Altertums. (Sternberg, Kurt.) Breslau, 1935.

Phil 3565.131   Das Problem des Wirkens und die monistische Weltanschauung. (Wartenberg, Mscislaw.) Leipzig, 1900.

Phil 1135.104   Problem des Zufalls in der griechischen Philosophie. (Peter, C.L. von.) Berlin, 1909.

Phil 3640.212   Das Problem Friedrich Nietzsches. (Grimm, Eduard.) Berlin, 1899.

Htn   Phil 1145.55*   A problem in Greek ethics. (Symonds, John A.) London, 1901.

Htn   Phil 9495.36*   A problem in modern ethics. (Symonds, J.A.) London, 1896.

Phil 4829.616.30   Problem metafizike u savremenoj analitickoj filozofiji. (Novaković, Staniša.) Beograd, 1967.

Phil 6315.2.43A   The problem of anxiety. (Freud, Sigmund.) N.Y., 1936.

Phil 8407.30   The problem of art; a text book of aesthetics. (Green, Peter.) London, 1937.

Phil 1811.5   The problem of certainty in English thought. (Van Leeuwen, H.G.) The Hague, 1963.

Phil 8597.20A   The problem of Christianity. (Royce, Josiah.) N.Y., 1913. 2v.

Phil 8597.20.2   The problem of Christianity. (Royce, Josiah.) N.Y., 1914.

Phil 8894.12   The problem of conduct. (Taylor, A.E.) London, 1901.

Phil 5374.56   The problem of consciousness in its biological aspects. (Minot, C.S.) N.Y., 1902.

Phil 9120.5   The problem of duty. (Dole, C.F.) N.Y., n.d.

Phil 1750.102   The problem of embodiment. (Zaner, R.M.) The Hague, 1964.

Phil 8620.20   The problem of evil. (Burton, Marion LeRoy.) Chicago, 1909.

Phil 8620.24   The problem of evil. (Gree, Peter.) London, 1920.

Phil 8620.11   The problem of evil. (Thompson, D.G.) London, 1887.

Phil 346.32   The problem of fact. (Pondey, Rajendra Prasad.) Santiniketan, 1965.

Phil 8408.6   The problem of form in painting and sculpture. (Hildebrand, A.) N.Y., 1907.

Phil 5755.16   The problem of free will. (Földesi, Tamás.) Budapest, 1966.

Phil 5765.4A   The problem of freedom. (Palmer, G.H.) Boston, 1911.

Phil 5753.17   The problem of freedom and determinism. (D'Angelo, Edward.) Columbia, 1968.

Phil 5425.44.15   The problem of genius. (Lange, Wilhelm.) London, 1931.

Phil 8656.22   The problem of God. (Brightman, E.S.) N.Y., 1930.

Phil 8667.27   The problem of God. (Murray, J.C.) New Haven, 1964.

Phil 8658.17.3   The problem of God in philosophy of religion. (Duméry, Henry.) Evanston, Ill., 1964.

Phil 8673.13   The problem of God's identity in cosmic change. (Schock, Adolph.) Chicago, 1932.

Phil 8829.2.12   The problem of human life. (Eucken, Rudolf.) N.Y., 1909.

Phil 8829.2.20   The problem of human life. (Eucken, Rudolf.) N.Y., 1924.

Phil 8644.9   The problem of immortality. (Tsanoff, R.A.) N.Y., 1924.

Phil 745.7.9A   The problem of individuality. (Driesch, H.) London, 1914.

Phil 5125.29   The problem of induction and its solution. (Katz, Jerrold J.) Chicago, 1962.

Phil 5125.18   The problem of inference. (Reade, W.H.F.) Oxford, 1938.

Phil 331.11   The problem of knowledge. (Ayer, A.J.) London, 1956.

Phil 333.5.20   The problem of knowledge. (Cassirer, Ernst.) New Haven, 1950.

Phil 343.6   Problem of knowledge. (Macintosh, D.C.) N.Y., 1915.

Phil 1818.10   The problem of knowledge in Scottish philosophy. (Segerstedt, T.T.) Lund, 1935.

Phil 6315.2.46A   The problem of lay analysis. (Freud, Sigmund.) N.Y., 1927.

Phil 8637.4   The problem of life and immortality. (Moody, L.) Boston, 1872.

Phil 5046.8   The problem of logic. (Gibson, W.R.B.) London, 1908.

Phil 175.14   The problem of metaphysics and the meaning of metaphysical explenation. Diss. (Alexander, H.B.) N.Y., 1902.

Phil 960.250   The problem of meaning in Indian philosophy. 1. ed. (Pandeya, R.C.) Delhi, 1963.

Phil 175.14.2   The problem of metaphysics and the meaning of metaphysical explenation. (Alexander, H.B.) N.Y., 1902.

Phil 6117.34   The problem of mind and body. (Han, S.J.) n.p., 1922.

Phil 5650.21   The problem of noise. (Bartlett, F.C.) Cambridge, 1934.

X Cg   Phil 187.49   The problem of nothing. (Malkani, G.R.) Amalner, 1918.

Phil 5402.21.10   The problem of pain. (Lewis, Clive Staples.) London, 1943.

Phil 575.21   The problem of personality. (Merrington, E.N.) London, 1916.

Phil 575.5   The problem of personality. (Ritchie, E.) Ithaca, N.Y., 1889.

Phil 177.63.5   Problem of philosophy. (Cunningham, G.W.) N.Y., 1935.

Phil 5258.13   Problem of psychology. (Scripture, E.W.) London, 1891.

Phil 176.14   Problem of reality. (Bax, E.B.) London, 1892.

Phil 8602.17   Problem of religion. (Wilm, Emil Carl.) Boston, 1912.

Phil 8592.48.5   The problem of religious knowledge. (Macintosh, D.C.) N.Y., 1940.

Phil 8956.7   The problem of right conduct. (Green, Peter.) London, 1931.

Phil 1050.20   The problem of space in Jewish mediaeval philosophy. (Efros, Israel I.) N.Y., 1917.

Phil 6420.14.5   The problem of stuttering. (Fletcher, John Madison.) N.Y., 1928.

Phil 8520.20   The problem of the existence of God, in Maimonides, Alanus and Averroes. (Nirenstein, S.) Philadelphia, 1924.

Phil 6400.17   The problem of the meaning of words based upon observation of aphasic patients. (Goldstein, Kurt.) Worcester, 1936.

Phil 575.284   The problem of the self. (Johnstone, Henry Webb.) University Park, 1970.

Phil 8670.9   The problem of theism. (Rigou, Arthur C.) London, 1908.

Phil 8592.13   The problem of theology in modern thought. (Miller, Andrew.) London, 1909.

Phil 672.145   The problem of time. (Gunn, J.A.) London, 1929.

Phil 179.42   The problem of tragedy. (Engel, S. Morris.) Frederiction, N.B., 1960.

Phil 720.8   The problem of truth. (Carr, H.W.) London, n.d.

Phil 3310.16.80   The problem of truth and reality in Grisebach's thought. (Rauche, G.A.) Pretoria, 1966.

Phil 730.10A   The problem of universals. (Bocheński, Innocentius M.) Notre Dame, 1956.

Phil 735.235   The problem of value. (Graham, Angus C.) London, 1961.

Phil 2050.187   Problém skutečnosti u Davida Huma. (Tvrdý, Josef.) Brno, 1925.

Phil 5500.42   Problem solving: research, method and theory. (Symposium on Cognition, 1st, Pittsburgh, 1965.) N.Y., 1966.

Phil 5772.8   Das Problem von der menschlichen Willensfreiheit. (Werner, S.) Berlin, 1914.

Phil 1135.77   Il problema antropologico. (Giannini, Giorgio.) Roma, 1965.

Phil 585.70.5   Il problema antropologico nella Filosofia Contemporanea. (Cantoni, Remo.) Milano, 1963.

RRC   Phil 5722.81   Problema bessoznatel'nogo. (Bassin, Filipp.) Moskva, 1968.

Phil 5722.70   Problema bessoznatel'nogo v psikhologii. (Bochorishvili, A.T.) Tbilisi, 1961.

Phil 3235.138   Problema bytiia i myshleniia v filosofii Liudirga Feienbakha. (Elez, Iovo.) Moskva, 1971.

Phil 585.330   Problema cheloveka v sovremennoi filosofii. Moskva, 1969.

Phil 1135.180   Il problema cosmologica e l'antivomia unomalteplice. (Padellaro De Angelis, Rosa.) Milano, 1962.

Phil 8667.26   O problema de Deus. (Martins, Diamantino.) Braga, 1957.

Phil 4983.1.85   El problema de la creencia y el intelectualismo de Vaz Ferreira. (Campo, Aníbal del.) Montevideo, 1959.

Phil 4314.2   El problema de la filosofía hispanica. (Nicol, Eduardo.) Madrid, 1961.

Phil 270.49   El problema de la libertad y la ciencia. (Miró Quesada, Oscar.) Lima, 1945.

Phil 3494.64   El problema de la nada en Kant. (Mayz Vallenilla, Ernesto.) Madrid, 1965.

Phil 4025.5   Il problema del dialogo nel pensiero italiano contemporaneo. (Zeppi, Stelio.) Firenze, 1960.

Phil 177.96   Il problema del sovraumano. (Cardone, D.A.) Firenze, 1936.

Phil 3450.11.86   Il problema del tempo nella fenomenologia di Husserl. (Paci, Enzo.) Milano, 1960.

Phil 2520.315   El problema del voluntarismo en Descartes. (Llanos, Alfredo.) Bahia Blanca, 1960.

Phil 8404.25   Il problema della bellezza e dell'arte. (Defrenza, Giuseppe.) Roma, 1967.

Phil 270.24   Il problema della causalità con particolare reguardo alla teoria del metodo sperimentale. (Pastore, Annibale.) Torino, 1921. 2v.

Phil 600.44   Il problema della conoscenza nel positivismo. (Geymonat, L.) Torino, 1931.

Phil 9075.86   Il problema della coscienza nella téologia Monastica del XII secolo. (Bertola, Ermenegildo.) Padova, 1970.

Phil 8580.33 — Il problema della demitizzazione. (Archivio di Filosofia.) Padova, 1961.

Phil 210.15 — Il problema della domanda. Padova, 1968.

Phil 5100.10 — Il problema della fallacia naturalistica. (Carcaterra, Gaetano.) Milano, 1969.

Phil 1506.13 — Il problema della filosofia cristiana. (Bogliolo, Luigi.) Brescia, 1959.

Phil 3002.5 — Il problema della filosofia da Kant a Fichte (1781-1801). (Carabellese, Pantaleo.) Palermo, 1929.

Phil 850.22 — Il problema della fondazione della filosofia e l'oggettivismo antico. 2. ed. (LaVia, V.) Roma, 1946.

Phil 8520.42 — Il problema della giustizia nel protestantesimo tedesco contemporaneo. (Zampetti, Pier L.) Milano, 1962.

Phil 645.19 — Il problema della libertà nel pensiero contemporaneo. (Calo, Giovanni.) Milano, 1906.

Phil 180.88.5 — Il problema della metafisica nel pensiero moderno. (Faggiotto, Pietro.) Padova, 1969.

Phil 8894.18.5 — Il problema della morale di fronte al positivismo ed alla metafisica. (Tarantino, Giuseppe.) Pisa, 1901.

Phil 4080.17.10 — Il problema della natura nel pensiero di Pantaleo Carabellese. (Tebaldeschi, I.) Roma, 1955.

Phil 600.65 — Il problema della storia nel positivismo Pozzo. (Pozzo, Gianni M.) Padova, 1967.

Phil 720.98 — Il problema della verità da Spinoza a Hume. (Ruvo, Vincenzo de.) Padova, 1970.

Phil 1135.167 — Il problema della vita contemplativa nel mondo greco-romano. 1. ed. (Grilli, A.) Milano, 1953.

Phil 4060.2.85 — Il problema dell'amore nell'opera di Leone Ebreo. (Fontanesi, Giuseppina.) Venezia, 1934.

Phil 4265.3.35 — Problema dell'assoluto. v.1-4. (Vera, A.) Napoli, 1872-82.

Phil 8668.8 — Il problema dell'ateismo. 2. ed. (Noce, Augusto del.) Bologna, 1964.

Phil 343.50 — Il problema dell'esperienza. (Mathieu, Vittorio.) Trieste, 1963.

Phil 8624.100 — Il problema dell'immortalità. (Archivio di Filosofia.) Roma, 1946.

Phil 4210.144 — Il problema dell'individuo nella filosofia di A. Rosmini. (Massolo, A.) Palermo, 1934.

Phil 410.78 — Il problema dell'infinito dal rinascimento a Kant. (Garofalo, Lydia.) Napoli 1931.

Phil 5242.70 — Il problema dell'unità del sapere nel comportamentismo. (Curi, Umberto.) Padova, 1967.

Phil 2520.225 — Il problema di Cartesio. (Carlini, Armando.) Bari, 1948.

Phil 4225.8.60 — Il problema di Dio e della religione nella filosofia attuale. 4. ed. (Sciacca, Michele Federico.) Milano, 1964.

Phil 510.137 — Il problema di Dio e il nuovo pluralismo. (Aliotta, A.) Città di Castello, 1924.

Phil 8673.18 — Il problema di Dio e la filosofia della immanenza. (Saitta, G.) Bologna, 1953.

Phil 8672.28 — Il problema di Dio nella filosofia occidentale. (Rizzacasa, Aurelio.) Viterbo, 1969?

Phil 5425.70 — O problema do génio; ensaio para una tesse de redução. (Veiga Azvedo, A.V.) Lisboa, 1944.

Phil 3450.11.365 — Problema ekzistentsial'nogo krizisa i transtsendental'naia fenomenologiia Edmunda Gusserlia. (Kakabadze, Zurab.) Tbilisi, 1966.

Phil 8402.29 — Il problema estetica contemporanea. (Bruno, F.) Lanclano, 1928.

Phil 8402.58 — Il problema estetico. (Bizzarri, R.) Brescia, 1954.

Phil 8408.52 — Problema estetychnoko i teoriia upravlinnia. (Havryliuk, Pedro I.) Kyïv, 1970.

Phil 8880.39 — Il problema etico. (Ferrari, G.M.) Rome, 1902.

Phil 2520.380 — Il problema etico in Cartesio. (Schiavo, Mario.) Rome, 1948?

Phil 5762.26 — Il problema filosofico del "libero arbitrio" nelle controversie teologiche del secolo XIII. (Mazzantini, Carlo.) Torino, 1965.

Phil 5520.453 — Il problema filosofico del linguaggio. (Centro di Studi Filosofici de Gallarate. 9. Convegno Annuale.) Padova, 1965.

Phil 176.102 — Il problema fondamentale dell'essere. (Bellomia Barone, F.) Ortona a Mare, 1909.

Phil 331.32 — Problema intuitsii v filosofii i matematike. (Asmus, V.F.) Moskva, 1963.

Phil 8952.23 — Il problema morale, oggi. (Comitato Cattolico Docenti Universitari.) Bologna, 1969.

Phil 187.104 — Il problema morale. (Maltese, F.) Vittoria, 1896.

Phil 4215.1.115 — Il problema morale in Romagnosi e Cattaneo. (Dentone, Adriana.) Milano, 1968.

Phil 4021.2 — Il problema morale nella filosofia italiana dell prima metà de secolo XIX. (Vanni Ronighi, S.) Milano, 1951.

Phil 8843.10 — Il problema morale nello stoicismo e nel cristianesimo. (Stefanini, L.) Torino, 1926.

Phil 9513.46 — Problema moral'noho idealn. (Polishchuk, Nina P.) Kyïv, 1970.

Phil 332.38 — Problema nachala poznaniia v B. Rassela i E. Gusserlia. (Begiashvili, Archie F.) Tbilisi, 1969.

Phil 331.41 — Problema nachala v teoreticheskom poznanii. (Abdil'din, Zhabaikhan M.) Alma-Ata, 1967.

Phil 5435.13 — Problema navyka v psikhologii. (Khodzhava, Z.I.) Tbilisi, 1960.

Phil 334.16 — Problema ob'ekta v marksysto'ko-lenins'kvi Seorii piznanoria. (Duchenko, Mykola V.) Kyïv, 1970.

Phil 5635.45 — Problema oshchushchenii i reflektornaia teoriia. (Kovalgin, V.M.) Minsk, 1959.

Phil 310.635 — Problema otrazheniia dvizheniia v logike poniatii. (Kalandarishvili, Grigorii.) Tbilisi, 1966.

Phil 2805.375 — Il problema Pascal. (Alfieri, Vittorio Enzo.) Milano, 1959.

Phil 8422.4 — Problema prekrasnogo. (Vanslov, V.V.) Moskva, 1957.

Phil 270.105.5 — Problema prichinnost v sovremeni fizike. (Akademiia Nauk SSSR. Institute Filosofii.) Moskva, 1960.

Phil 270.105 — Problema prichinnosti v sovremennoi biologie. (Akademiia Nauk SSSR. Institute Filosofii.) Moskva, 1961.

Phil 310.745 — Problema protivorechiia. (Georgiev, Filipp I.) Moskva, 1969.

Phil 310.212 — Problema protivorechiia v dialecticheskoi logike. (Narskii, I.S.) Moskva, 1969.

Phil 672.149 — Il problema psicologico del tempo. (Bonaventura, Enzo.) Milano, 1929.

Phil 6315.2.400 — El problema religioso en la historia de la psicologia médica contemporánea. (Freijo Balsebre, Enrique.) Vitoria, 1966.

Phil 5374.215 — Problema soznaniia v filosofii i estestvoznanii. (Shorokhova, E.V.) Moskva, 1961.

Phil 5041.97 — Problema subordinatsii logicheskikh form. (Bakanialze, Mamiie I.) Alma-Ata, 1968.

Phil 2905.1.650 — Il problema Teilhard de Chardin. (Canteni, Agostino.) Milano, 1969.

Phil 730.25 — Problema tselostnosti v filosofii i biologii. (Afanas'ev, V.C.) Moskva, 1964.

Phil 735.257 — Problema tsennosti v filosofii. (Akademiia Nauk SSSR. Kafedra Filosofii, Leningrad.) Leningrad, 1966.

Phil 672.266 — Problema universal'nosti osnovnykh svoistv prostranstva i vremeni. (Mostepanenko, Aleksandr M.) Leningrad, 1969.

Phil 310.742 — Problema urovnei i sistem v nauchnom poznanii. Minsk, 1970.

Phil 5545.98 — Problema uznavaniia. (Bongard, Mikhail M.) Moskva, 1967.

Phil 5190.40 — Problema vozmozhnosti i deistvitel'nosti. (Akademiia Nauk SSSR. Kafedra Filosofii, Leningrad.) Leningrad, 1964.

Phil 672.237 — Problema vremeni. (Askin, Iakov F.) Moskva, 1966.

Phil 310.632 — Problema vzaiemovidnoshennia svitohliadu i metodu v dialektychnomu materializmi. (Soldatov, Vasyl' I.) Kyïv, 1966.

Phil 5520.644 — Problema znaka i znacheniia. Moskva, 1969.

Phil 4476.1.30 — Problemas da ciencia e da filosofia contemporanea. (Pecegueiro, Jose.) Coimbra, 1966.

Phil 3450.11.270 — Problemas da fenomenologia de Husserl. (Fragata, Júlio.) Braga, 1962.

Phil 4960.220 — Problemas de la história de las ideas filosóficas en la Argentina. (Alberini, Coriolano.) La Plata, 1966.

Phil 5771.4 — Los problemas de la libertad y los del determinismo. (Vaz Ferreira, C.) Buenos Aires, 1957.

Phil 186.18.9 — Los problemas de la naturaleza. (Laugel, Auguste.) Barcelona, 18- ?

Phil 6980.289 — Problemas de ténica psicoanalitica. (Fenichel, Otto.) México, 1960.

Phil 177.37 — Problemas filosóficos. (Caso, Antonio.) México, 1915.

Phil 5252.80 — Problemas psicologicos actuales. (Mira y Lopez E.) Buenos Aires, 1940.

Phil 705.8 — Problemas trascendentales. (Tarrida del Mármol, F.) Paris, 1908.

Phil 5046.46 — Problemata logica. v.1-5. (Goclenius, Rudolph.) Frankfurt, 1967.

Phil 8407.33 — Problematica dell'arte. (Ghelli, Nino.) Roma, 1958.

Phil 2905.1.540 — La problematica di Teilhard de Chardin. (Rizzo, Enrico.) Bologna, 1965.

Phil 4225.8.105 — La problematica morale nella filosofia della integralita. 2. ed. (Dentone, Adriana.) Milano, 1966.

Phil 4210.157 — La problematica politico-sociale nel pensiero di Antonio Rosmini. (Incontro Internazionale Rosminiano, Bolzana.) Roma, 1955.

Phil 2750.19.120 — Problematico e meta-problematico in Gabriel Marcel. (Matera, Rocco.) Bari, 1969.

Phil 5590.452 — Die Problematik der Persönlichkeitsdiagnostik. (Lückert, Heinz Rolf.) München, 1965.

Phil 8590.22 — Die Problematik der Religionen. (Keilbach, W.) Paderborn, 1936.

Phil 5259.60 — La problématique de la psychologie. (Thines, Georges.) La Haye, 1968.

Phil 8407.39 — Problematyka estetiki. (Gatecki, L.) Kraków, 1962.

Phil 510.18 — Probleme. (Schoeler, Heinrich von.) Leipzig, 1900.

Phil 8735.3 — Le problème de causes finales. (Sully-Prudhomme, René F.A.) Paris, 1903.

Phil 8658.22 — Le problème de Dieu. (Delanglade, Jean.) Paris, 1960.

Phil 8666.11 — Le problème de Dieu. (Le Roy, Edouard.) Paris, 1930.

Phil 8658.17 — Le problème de Dieu en philosophie de la religion. (Duméry, Henry.) Bruges, 1957.

Phil 348.12 — Le problème de la connaissance. (Roux, Antoine.) Paris, 1930.

Phil 2475.1.228 — Le problème de la connaissance dans la philosophie de Bergson. (Jurēvičs, Pauls.) Paris, 1930.

Phil 1828.4 — Le problème de la connaissance d'autrui dans la philosophie anglaise contemporaine. (Dubois, Pierre.) Paris, 1969.

Phil 210.30 — Le problème de la conscience historique. (Gadamer, Hans Georg.) Louvain, 1963.

Phil 5750.6 — Le problème de la destinée. (Allendy, René F.) Paris, 1927.

Phil 5545.31 — La problème de la mémoire. (Sollier, P.) Paris, 1900.

Phil 193.155 — Le problème de la méthode. (Stefanesco, Marin.) Paris, 1938.

Phil 8612.12.2 — Le problème de la mort. 2. éd. (Bourdeau, L.) Paris, 1896.

Phil 8612.34 — Le problème de la mort chez M. Heidegger et J.P. Sartre. (Jolivet, Régis.) Paris, 1950.

Phil 8612.70 — Le problème de la mort dans la philosophie existentielle. (Badawi, Abdurrahman.) Le Claire, 1964.

Phil 8612.7.5 — Le problème de la mort et la conscience universelle. (LeDantec, F.) Paris, 1917.

Phil 8612.7 — Le problème de la mort et la conscience universelle. (LeDantec, F.) Paris, 1917.

Phil 176.129 — Le problème de la philosophie catholique. (Blondel, Maurice.) Paris, 1932.

Phil 8595.39 — Le problème de la philosophie chrétienne. Paris, 1949.

Phil 5402.7 — Le problème de la souffrance. (Fulliquet, G.) Genève, 1909.

Phil 185.62 — Le problème de la substance. (Konczewska, H.) Paris, 1937.

Phil 2805.223 — Le problème de la vérité chez Pascal. Thèse. (Falcucci, C.) Toulouse, 1939.

Phil 3640.715 — Le problème de la vérité dans la philosophie de Nietzsche. (Granier, Jean.) Paris, 1966.

Phil 3831.11 — Le problème de la vérité dans la philosophie de Spinoza. (Lévêque, Raphail.) Strasbourg, 1923.

Phil 720.82 — Le problème de la vérité en morale et en droit. Thése. (Kalinowski, Jerzy.) Lyon, 1967.

Phil 176.64 — Problème de la vie, essai de sociologie générale. (Bourdeau, L.) Paris, 1901.

Phil 8592.46 — Le problème de la vie. (Mortier, Lowis.) Paris, 1872.

Phil 192.78 — Le problème de la vie. (Rivier, W.) Paris, 1937.

Phil 5400.63 — Problème de la vie affective. (Picard, Ernest.) Paris, 1926.

Phil 5360.10 — Le problème de l'abstraction. (Laporte, J.M.F.) Paris, 1940.

Phil 8892.17 — Le problème de l'action. (Rodrigues, G.) Paris, 1909.

Phil 672.143 — Le problème de l'espace. (Alvarez de Toledo, A.) Paris, 1920.

Phil 2477.6.122 — Le problème de l'être dans l'ontologie de Maurice Blondel. (Ritz, Maria.) Fribourg, 1958.

Phil 2477.6.185 — Le problème de l'être et l'expérience morale chez Maurice Blondel. (Jouhaud, Michel.) Paris, 1970.

Phil 8640.3 — Le problème de l'immortalité. (Petavel-Ollief, E.) Paris, 1891-92. 2v.

Phil 2520.230.10   Le problème de l'inconscient et le cartesianisme. 1. éd. (Lewis, G.) Paris, 1950.

Phil 5039.14   Probleme de logică. Bucuresti, 1968. 3v.

Phil 1135.28.15   Le problème de l'origine et de l'eternité du monde. Thèse. (Bandry, J.) Paris, 1931.

Phil 293.14   Le problème de l'univers. (Moraes Carvalho, A.A. de.) Lisbonne, 1920.

Phil 5252.26   Probleme der Entwicklung des Geistes. (Meyer, Semi.) Leipzig, 1913.

Phil 349.23   Probleme der Erkenntnis. v.1-2. (Switalski, B.N.) Münster in Westfalen, 1923.

Phil 8887.52   Probleme der ethik. (Mehlis, Georg.) Tübingen, 1918.

Phil 193.59.30   Die Probleme der Geschichtsphilosophie. (Simmel, G.) n.p., 1892-1909. 9 pam.

Phil 5590.75   Probleme der Gesinnungsbildung. (Dürr, Otto.) Heidelberg, 1950.

Phil 8658.14   Probleme der Gotteserkenntnis. (Dyroff, Adolf.) Münster, 1928.

Phil 6060.12   Die Probleme der Graphologie. (Klages, Ludwig.) Leipzig, 1910.

Phil 6060.12.50   Probleme der Graphologie. Inaug. Diss. (Wollnik, H.) Leipzig, 1933.

Phil 8430.62   Probleme der marxistisch-leninistischen Ästhetik. (John, Erhard.) Halle, 1968.

Phil 1135.68   Das Probleme der Materie in der griechischen Philosophie. (Baeumker, C.) Münster, 1890.

Phil 1135.178   Probleme der Musse im alten Hellas. (Welskopf, E.C.) Berlin, 1962.

Phil 6328.5.5   Probleme der Mystik und ihrer Symbolik. (Silberer, Herbert.) Wien, 1914.

Phil 7016.2   Probleme der Parapsychologie. (Frei, Gebhard.) München, 1969.

Phil 182.142   Probleme der Philosophie. (Hrušovský, Igor.) Bratislava, 1970.

Phil 192.28.4   Die Probleme der Philosophie. (Russell, B.) Erlangen, 1926.

Phil 180.18.5   Die Probleme der Philosophie und ihre Lösungen historisch-critisch Dargestellt. 2.Aufl. (Flügel, D.) Cöthen, 1888.

Phil 180.18   Die Probleme der Philosophie und ihre Losungen. (Flügel, D.) Cöthen, 1906.

Phil 6980.583.2   Probleme der Psychotherapie alternder Menschen. 2. Aufl. (Petrilowitsch, Nikolaus.) Basel, 1968.

Phil 5627.102   Probleme der Religionspsychologie. 1. Teil. (Reik, Theodor.) Leipzig, 1919.

Phil 5520.12.5   Die Probleme der Sprachpsychologie. (Dittrich, O.) Leipzig, 1913.

Phil 3915.59.7   Probleme der Völkerpsychologie. 2. Aufl. (Wundt, Wilhelm.) Stuttgart, 1921.

Phil 5760.4   Das Probleme der Willensfreiheit und der Grundbegriffe der Strafrechts. (Kulew, T.) Sofia, 1906.

Phil 337.11.5   Probleme der wirklichen Bildung. (Grisebach, E.) München, 1923.

Phil 165.436   Probleme der Wissenschaftstheorie; Festschrift für Victor Kroft. Wien, 1960.

Phil 310.35   Probleme des historische Materialismus und der marxistische Sozialismus. Berlin, 1958.

Phil 5244.24.5   Probleme des höheren Seelenlebens. (Ehrenstein, Walter.) München, 1965.

Phil 6312.22   Le problème des névroses experimentales. (Cain, Jacques.) Paris, 1959.

Phil 4060.1.97   Le problème des origines. (Quadrelli, Ercole.) Gerace Marina, 1911.

Phil 5722.27   Probleme des Unbewussten. (Brinkmann, Donald.) Zürich, 1943.

Phil 1122.7   Le problème du devenir et la notion de la matière dans la philosophie grecque depuis les origines jusqu'à Theophraste. (Rivaud, Albert.) Paris, 1906.

Phil 5425.48   Le problème du génie. (Segoud, Joseph.) Paris, 1930.

Phil 8620.32   Le problème du mal. (Lasbax, Émile.) Paris, 1919.

Phil 8620.8   Le problème du mal. (Naville, E.) Genève, 1869.

Phil 8620.49   Le problème du mal. (Petit, François.) Paris, 1958.

Phil 9240.8   Le problème du mal. (Sertellanges, A.G.) Paris, 1948-1951. 2v.

Phil 8620.48   Le problème du mal. 1. éd. (Borne, Étienne.) Paris, 1958.

Phil 8620.14   Le problème du mal. 3. éd. (Bonniot, P.J. de.) Paris, 1911.

Phil 5525.56   Le problème du rire et du réel. (Latour, Marius.) Paris, 1956.

Phil 672.220   Le problème du temps. (Gonseth, F.) Neuchâtel, 1964.

Phil 3425.612   Le problème Hégélien. (Garauly, Roger.) Paris, 196-.

Phil 5125.9   Le problème logique de l'induction. (Nicod, Jean.) Paris, 1924.

Phil 8875.25.5   Le problème moral. (Alquié, F.) Paris, 1933.

Phil 8828.6   Le problème moral dans la philosophie anglaise de 1900 à 1950. (Dubois, Pierre.) Paris, 1967.

Phil 3823.6.5   Le problème moral dans la philosophie de Spinoza. (Delblos, Victor.) Paris, 1893.

Phil 1200.19   Un problème moral dans l'antiquité. (Thamin, Raymond.) Paris, 1884.

Phil 2880.8.98   Le problème moral et la pensée de Sartre. (Jeanson, Francis.) Paris, 1947.

Phil 2880.8.99   Le problème moral et la pensée de Sartre. (Jeanson, Francis.) Paris, 1965.

Phil 8827.8   Le problème moral et les philosophes. (Cresson, André.) Paris, 1933.

Phil 8890.41   Le problème morale et la pensée contemporaine. 2. ed. (Parodi, D.) Paris, 1921.

Phil 7080.25   Le problème physiologique du sommeil. (Pieron, H.) Paris, 1912.

Phil 8598.115   Probleme seines religiösen Apriori. (Schlesinger, Ruth.) Berlin, 1959.

Phil 5257.43   Probleme und Apparate zur experimentellen Pädagogik und Jugendpsychologie. (Rupp, Hans.) Leipzig, 1920.

Phil 182.41   Probleme und Grundlehren der allgemeinen Metaphysik. (Hartenstein, G.) Leipzig, 1836.

Phil 5585.270   Problemen der subliminale perceptie. (Bánřeti Fuchs, Károly Miklás.) Assen, 1964.

Phil 5251.4   Les problèmes. (Langel, A.) Paris, 1873.

Phil 5645.53   Problèmes. (Paris. Ecole Pratique des Hautes Études.) Paris, 1957.

Phil 1750.115.40   Problèmes actuels de la phénoménologie. (Breda, H.L.) Paris, 1957.

Phil 8667.40   Problèmes actuels de religion. (Morel, Georges.) Paris, 1968.

Phil 5042.13   Les problèmes de la logique. (Cordier, Paul.) Paris, 1916.

Phil 5238.67   Les problèmes de la mesure en psychologie. (Association de Psychologie Scientifique de Langue Française.) Paris, 1962.

Phil 186.18.5   Les problèmes de la nature. (Laugel, Auguste.) Paris, 1864.

Phil 192.28.3   Les problèmes de la philosophie. (Russell, B.) Paris, 1923.

Phil 178.41   Les problèmes de la philosophie et leur enchainement scientifique. (Dupont, Paul.) Paris, 1920.

Phil 5251.4.5   Les problèmes de la vie. (Langel, A.) Paris, 1867.

Phil 187.55.3   Problèmes de la vie. (Muñiz, Narcisse.) Paris, 1914.

Phil 525.70   Les problèmes de la vie mystique. (Bastide, Roger.) Paris, 1931.

Phil 5643.101   Problèmes de la vision. (Gramont, A.) Paris, 1939.

Phil 6121.2   Les problèmes de l'âme. (Laugel, A.) Paris, 1868.

Phil 8407.3   Les problèmes de l'esthétique comtemporaine. (Guyau, M.) Paris, 1884.

Phil 5125.10   Les problèmes de l'induction. (Dorolle, M.) Paris, 1926.

Phil 600.25   Problèmes de philosophie positive. (Greef, Guillaume.) Paris, 1900.

Phil 6325.18   Problèmes de psychanalyse. Paris, 1957.

Phil 5520.409   Problèmes de psycholinguistique. (Association de Psychologie Scientifique de Langue Française.) Paris, 1963.

Phil 5400.18.25   Problèmes de psychologie affective. (Ribot, T.) Paris, 1910.

Phil 348.17.5   Problèmes d'épistémologie. (Riet, G. van.) Louvain, 1960.

Phil 2668.40   Les problèmes du XIXe siècle. 2e éd. (Janet, Paul A.R.) Paris, 1873.

Phil 5762.23   Problèmes et pseudo-problèmes du déterminisme physique, biologique, psychologique. (Moreau.) Paris, 1964.

Phil 5252.48   Les problemes fondamentaux de la psychologie medical. (Montet, C. de.) Berne, 1922.

Phil 5255.18.20   Les problémes fondamentaux de la psychophysique dans la science actuelle. (Piéron, Henri.) Paris, 1951.

Phil 310.696.5   Problèmes fondamentaux du matérialisme historique. Moscou, 1968.

Phil 5440.25   Les problèmes généraux de l'hérédité psychologique. (Poyer, Georges.) Paris, 1921.

Phil 5440.25.3   Les problèmes généraux de l'hérédité psychologique. Thèse. (Poyer, Georges.) Paris, 1921. 2 pam.

Phil 3504.50.2   Problemes kantiens. 2. éd. (Weil, Eric.) Paris, 1970.

Phil 1535.38   Problèmes philosophiques. (LeRohellec, J.) Paris, 1932.

Phil 4610.9.85   Problemet om tro og viden. (Steen, H.) Kjøbenhavn, 1813.

Phil 5751.10   Problemet om viljans frihet, kritiskt och logiskt undersökt. (Bolin, W.) Helsingfors, 1868.

Phil 5225.10   Problemgeschichte der Psychologie. (Pongratz, Ludwig Jakob.) Bern, 1967.

Phil 8422.8   I problemi del gusto e dell'arte nella mente di Pietro Verri. (Carmella, S.) Napoli, 1926.

Phil 1117.8   Problemi del pensiero antico. (Mondolfo, Rodolfo.) Bologna, 1935.

Phil 1750.783   I problemi della fenomenologia. 1. ed. (Piana, Giovanni.) Milano, 1966.

Phil 4006.2   I problemi della scolastica e il pensiero italiano. (Gentile, G.) Bari, 1913.

Phil 4006.2.2   I problemi della scolastica e il pensiero italiano. 2a ed. (Gentile, G.) Bari, 1923.

Phil 1750.752   I problemi dell'economic e la fenomenologia. (Paci, Enzo.) Milano, 1963.

Phil 4110.9.30   Problemi dell'esistenzialismo. (Fabro, Cornelio.) Roma, 1945.

Phil 8416.8.12   I problemi dell'estetica. 2. ed. (Pareyson, Luigi.) Milano, 1966.

Phil 3838.28   Il problemi dello Spinozismo. (Semerari, G.) Trani, 1952.

Phil 3450.19.505   Problemi dell'Ur-Heidegger. (Garulli, Enrico.) Urbino, 1969.

Phil 4080.3.355   Problemi di critica crociana. (Viola, Italo.) Milano, 1960.

Phil 8416.18.5   Problemi di estetica e critica. (Propris, A. de.) Roma, 1954.

Phil 4080.3.33   Problemi di estetics e contributi alla storia dell'estetica italiana. (Croce, Benedetto.) Bari, 1910.

Phil 5520.443.5   Problemi di filosofia del linguaggio. (Pittau, Massimo.) Cagliari, 1967.

Phil 8416.6   Problemi di filosofia dell'arte. (Piemonteal, Filippo.) Torino, 1952.

Phil 343.38   Problemi di gnoseologia e metafisica. (Miani, Vincenzo.) Zürich, 1966.

Phil 3450.11.245   Problemi di logica. (Scrimieri, G.) Bari, 1959.

Phil 187.90   Problemi di metafisica e di criteriologia. (Masnovo, Amato.) Milano, 1930.

Phil 4070.7.50   I problemi di una estetica filosofica. (Banfi, Antonio.) Milano, 1961.

Phil 4200.6.32.2   Problemi e aporie del pensiero contemporaneo. 2. ed. (Petruzzellis, Nicola.) Napoli, 1970.

Phil 812.25   Problemi e metodi di ricerca nella storia della filosofia. (Mondolfo, R.) Firenze, 1952.

Phil 845.4   Problemi ed aspetti dell'Umanesimo. (Schiavone, Michel.) Milano, 1969.

Phil 4110.11.30   Problemi filosofia in Marsilio Ficino. (Schiavone, Michelle.) Milano, 1951.

Phil 177.86.10   Problemi filosofici. (Camera, Ugo.) Roma, 1931. 2 pam.

VPhil 310.660   Problemi filozofije marksizma. Beograd, 1967.

Phil 8896.4.9   Problemi generali di etica. (Vidari, Giovanni.) Milano, 1901.

Phil 8430.50   Problemi na khudozhestvenoto tvorchestvo. Sofiia, 1968.

Phil 5039.10   Problemi na logikata. Sofiia, 1967- 2v.

Phil 310.600   Problemi na zakonite i kategoriite na dialektikata i logikata. (Bulgarska Akademiia na Naukite, Sofia. Institut po Filosofiia. Sektsiia po Dialekticheski Materializum i Logika.) Sofiia, 1965.

VPhil 575.255   Problemi savremene teorije ličnosti. (Pešić-Golubović, Zagorka.) Beograd, 1966.

Phil 5060.6.7   The problems. (Ushenko, A.P.) Princeton, 1941.

Phil 9495.28.5   Problems and principles of sex education. (Exner, M.J.) N.Y., 1915.

Phil 5222.20   Problems and procedures in oral histories of the Archives of the History of American Psychology. (McPherson, Marion White.) Akron, 1967.

Phil 2030.6.10   Problems and projects. (Goodman, Nelson.) Indianapolis, 1972.

Phil 6158.30   The problems and prospects of LSD. Springfield, 1968.

Phil 8405.8.5   Problems and theories in modern aesthetics. (Ekman, Rolf.) Lund, 1960.

Phil 5227.7   Das Problems der Entwicklung in der neueren Psychologie. (Reinle, Rico.) Basel, 1952.

Phil 2520.85.30 Problèms du Cartesianisme. (Callot, Émile.) Annecy, 1956.
Phil 8400.31 Problems in aesthetics. (Weitz, M.) N.Y., 1959.
Phil 8962.34 Problems in conduct. (Murray, Michael V.) N.Y., 1963.
Phil 6322.8 Problems in dynamic psychology. (MacCurdy, J.T.) Cambridge, 1923.
Phil 8885.9 Problems in ethics. (Kedney, J.S.) N.Y., 1900.
Phil 5125.11 Problems in logic. (Patterson, C.H.) N.Y., 1926.
Phil 5055.17 Problems in logic. (Patterson, Charles H.) N.Y., 1926.
Phil 5247.77 Problems in measuring change. (Harris, Chester.) Madison, 1963.
Phil 5643.170 Problems in motion perception. (Cohen, Ronald L.) Uppsala, 1964.
Phil 6325.18.5 Problems in psychoanalysis. London, 1961.
Phil 5258.71 Problems in psychology. (Snow, Adolph J.) N.Y., 1923.
Phil 6322.6.10 Problems in psychopathology. (Mitchell, T.W.) London, 1927.
Phil 1200.74 Problems in stoicism. London, 1971.
Phil 5520.18 Problems in the psychology of reading. (Quantz, J.O.) Chicago, 1897.
Phil 8602.18.7 Problems in the relations of God and man. (Webb, C.C.J.) London, 1915.
Phil 3504.50 Problems kantiens. (Weil, Eric.) Paris, 1963.
Phil 8400.30A The problems of aesthetics. (Vivas, Eliseo.) N.Y., 1953.
Phil 165.13.5A Problems of analysis. (Black, Max.) Ithaca, 1954.
Phil 8412.33 Problems of art. (Lange, A.K.) N.Y., 1957.
Phil 5070.16 Problems of belief. (Schiller, F.C.S.) London, 1924.
Phil 5070.16.5 Problems of belief. (Schiller, F.C.S.) N.Y., 1924.
Phil 8878.28.2 Problems of conduct. (Drake, Durant.) Boston, 1921.
Phil 282.22 The problems of cosmology. (Bleksley, A.E.) Johannesburg, 1956.
Phil 8870.23 Problems of ethics. (Dewey, Robert E.) N.Y., 1961.
Phil 8893.84.8A Problems of ethics. (Schlick, Moritz.) N.Y., 1962.
Phil 5241.119 Problems of human pleasure and behavior. (Balint, Michael.) London, 1957.
Phil 5817.16 Problems of instinct and intelligence. (Hingston, R.W.G.) London, 1928.
Phil 333.28 Problems of knowledge and freedom: the Russell lectures. 1st ed. (Chomsky, Noam.) N.Y., 1971.
Phil 5251.6.2.6 Problems of life and mind. 1st series. (Lewes, G.H.) London, 1874-75. 2v.
Phil 5251.6.3 Problems of life and mind. 1st-3rd series. (Lewes, G.H.) London, 1874. 5v.
Phil 5251.6.4.5 Problems of life and mind. 3rd series. (Lewes, G.H.) Boston, 1879-80. 2v.
Phil 5060.6.5 The problems of logic. (Ushenko, A.P.) London, 1941.
Phil 7069.20.360 The problems of mediumship. (Zymonidas, Allessandro.) London, 1920.
Phil 1955.6.30 Problems of men. (Dewey, John.) N.Y., 1946.
Phil 5252.168 Problems of mind. (Malcolm, Norman.) N.Y., 1971.
Phil 193.128.85 Problems of mind and matter. (Wisdom, John.) Cambridge, Eng., 1934.
Phil 6328.5 Problems of mysticism and its symbolism. (Silberer, Herbert.) N.Y., 1917.
Phil 6310.1.3 Problems of neurosis. (Adler, A.) London, 1930.
Phil 978.49.135 The problems of our time. (Steiner, R.) London, 1934.
Phil 338.28 The problems of perception. (Hirst, R.J.) London, 1959.
Phil 5238.14A Problems of personality: studies presented to Dr. Morton Prince. N.Y., 1925.
Phil 5590.4 Problems of personality traits. (Schettler, C.H.) Chicago, 1940.
Phil 177.106 The problems of philosophy. (Chatterjee, S.) Calcutta, 1949.
Phil 182.28 The problems of philosophy. (Hibben, J.G.) N.Y., 1898.
Phil 182.28.2 The problems of philosophy. (Hibben, J.G.) N.Y., 1899.
Phil 182.28.3 The problems of philosophy. (Hibben, J.G.) N.Y., 1908.
Phil 182.36.6 The problems of philosophy. (Höffding, H.) N.Y., 1905.
Phil 182.36.5 The problems of philosophy. (Höffding, H.) N.Y., 1905.
Phil 182.36.7 The problems of philosophy. (Höffding, H.) N.Y., 1906.
Phil 182.38 Problems of philosophy. (Hyslop, J.H.) N.Y., 1905.
Phil 192.28 The problems of philosophy. (Russell, B.) London, 1912.
Phil 192.28.2A The problems of philosophy. (Russell, B.) N.Y., 1912.
Phil 5250.17.2A Problems of physiological psychology. (Kantor, J.R.) Bloomington, 1947.
Phil 7069.14.5 The problems of psychical research. (Carrington, Hereward.) London, 1914.
Phil 31.6.10 Problems of psychology. N.Y. 1960+
Phil 8583.14 Problems of religion. (Drake, Durant.) Boston, 1916.
Phil 5820.7 Problems of selective behavior. (Klee, James Butt.) Lincoln, 1951.
Phil 9495.149 Problems of sex. (Glasgow, M.) Boston, 1949.
Phil 672.229 Problems of space and time. (Smart, John Jamieson Carswell.) N.Y., 1964.
Phil 6750.25 Problems of subnormality. (Wallin, John E.W.) Yonkers-on-Hudson, 1917.
Phil 9415.14 Problems of suffering in religions of the world. (Bowker, John.) Cambridge, 1970.
Phil 5066.224.5 Problems of the logic of scientific knowledge. (Akademiia Nauk SSSR. Institut Filosofii.) Dordrecht, 1970.
Phil 575.24 Problems of the self. (Laird, John.) London, 1917.
Phil 8627.9.7 Problems of the spiritual. (Chambers, A.) Philadelphia, 1907.
Phil 735.134 The problems of value theory. Thesis. (Kurtz, Paul W.) N.Y., 1952.
Phil 7069.27.30 Problems which perplex. (Owen, G.V.) London, 1927.
Phil 4812.457.35 Problémy, portréty, retrospektívy. Vyd. 1. (Hrušovský, Igor.) Bratislava, 1965.
Phil 5753.15 Problemy chelovechskoi svobody. (Davidovich, Vsevolod E.) L'vov, 1967.
Phil 310.101 Problemy dialekticheskoi logiki. Alma-Ata, 1968.
Phil 310.100 Problemy dialekticheskoi logikii. (Mal'tsev, V.I.) Moskva, 1959.
Phil 5039.26 Problémy dialektiky. 1. vyd. (Bober, Juraj.) Bratislava, 1968.
Phil 25.162 Problemy differentsial'noi psikhofiziologii. Moskva. 1,1956+ 5v.
Phil 8980.712.65 Problemy dukhovnoi kul'tury i formirovaniia lichnosti. Sverdlovsk, 1970.
Phil 8402.48 Problemy estetiki. (Berestnev, V.F.) Moskva, 1958.
Phil 8430.87 Problemy estetiki i esteticheskogo vospitaniia. Moskva, 1967.
Phil 8980.131.10 Problemy etiki. (Akademiia Nauk SSSR. Institut Filosofii.) Moskva, 1964.
Phil 310.689 Problemy filosofii. Alma-Ata, 1968.
Phil 25.148 Problemy filosofii. Kyïv. 1,1966+ 4v.
Phil 4816.6 Problemy filosofii. Moskva, 1960.
Phil 25.181 Problemy filosofii i nauchnogo kommunizma. Krasnoiarsk. 3,1970+
Phil 310.688 Problemy filosofii i sotsiologii. Leningrad, 1968.
Phil 25.185 Problemy filosofii i sotsiologii. Moskva. 1,1969+
Phil 8980.712.60 Problemy formirovaniia kommunisticheskogo soznaniia. Ivanovo, 1969.
Phil 5190.41 Problemy i pseudoproblemy. (Cackowski, Zdzisław.) Warszawa, 1964.
Phil 400.122 Problemy idealizma. (Novgorodtsev, P.I.) Moskva, 1903.
Phil 5259.50 Problemy individual'nykh razlichii. (Teplov, B.M.) Moskva, 1961.
Phil 8406.23 Problemy iskusstvovedeniia: sbornik statei. (Friche, V.M.) Moskva, 1930.
Phil 310.649 Problemy istoricheskogo materializma. Dushambe. 1,1967+ 2v.
Phil 310.753 Problemy istoricheskogo materializma. Moskva, 1969.
Phil 310.198 Problemy istorii filosofskoi i sotsiologicreskoi mysli XIX veka. (Akadamiia Nauk SSSR. Institut Filosofii.) Moskva, 1960.
Phil 189.34 Problemy istoriko-filosofskoi nauki. (Oizerman, Teodor I.) Moskva, 1969.
Phil 8980.790 Problemy kategorii marksistsko-leninskoi etiki. (Simpozium Posviashchennyi 100-letiiu so Dnia Rozhdeniia V.I. Lenina, Novosibirsk? 1968?) Novosibirsk, 1968.
Phil 8092.17 Problemy khudozhestvennoi kul'tury XX veka. (Matsa, Ivan L.) Moskva, 1966.
Phil 8654.115 Problemy lichnosti v religii i ateizme. Moskva, 1969.
Phil 5066.225 Problemy logiki. (Akademiia Nauk SSSR. Institut Filosofii.) Moskva, 1963.
Phil 5040.27 Problemy logiki dialektiki poznaniia. (Akademiia Nauk Kazakhskoi SSSR, Alma-Ata. Institut Literatury i Prava.) Alma-Ata, 1963.
Phil 5055.32 Problemy logiki i teorii poznaniia. Moskva, 1968.
Phil 5066.224 Problemy logiki nauchnogo poznaniia. (Akademiia Nauk SSSR. Institut Filosofii.) Moskva, 1964.
Phil 310.421 Problemy marksistsko-leninskoi filosofii. (Iovchuk, Mikhail T.) Moskva, 1965.
Phil 5066.328 Problemy matematicheskoi logiki. Moskva, 1970.
Phil 5274.4 Problemy modelirovaniia psikhicheskoi deiatel'nosti. v.2. Photoreproduction. (Kochergin, A.N.) Moskva, 1969. 2v.
Phil 5250.75 Problemy myshleniia v sovremennoi nauke. (Kopnin, P.V.) Moskva, 1964.
Phil 5465.220 Problemy nauchnogo tvorchestva v sovremennoi psikhologii. Moskva, 1971.
Phil 8980.131.15 Problemy nravstvennogo razvitiia lichnosti. (Akmambetov, Galikhan G.) Alma-Ata, 1971.
Phil 310.686.5 Problemy otrazheniia. Moskva, 1969.
Phil 346.33 Problemy poznaniia sotsial'nykh iavlenii. Moskva, 1968.
Phil 270.107 Problemy prichinnosti v filosofii i giologii. (Musabaeva, N.A.) Alma-Ata, 1962.
Phil 5590.476 Problemy psikhologii i patopsikholozii lichnosti. (Zurabashvili, Avlipii.) Tbilisi, 1967.
Phil 5545.225 Problemy psikhologii pamiati. (Smirnov, Anatolii A.) Moskva, 1966.
Phil 5545.256 Problemy psikhologii pamiati. Khar'kov, 1969.
Phil 8980.712.50 Problemy razvitiia kommunisticheskogo soznaniia. Moskva, 1965.
Phil 5251.68 Problemy razvitiia psikhiki. (Leont'ev, Aleksei N.) Moskva, 1959.
Phil 5374.239 Problemy razvitiia psikhiki. 2. izd. (Leont'ev, Aleksei N.) Moskva, 1965.
VPhil 2750.22.110 Problemy rewolucji i socializmu we współczesnej katolickiej myśli filozoficznej. (Jędrzejczak, Klara.) Poznań, 1967.
X Cg Phil 4710.10 Problemy russkago religioznogo soznaniia. Berlin, 1924.
Phil 5066.256 Problémy sémantiky. (Tondl, Ladislav.) Praha, 1966.
Phil 5425.106 Problemy sposobnostei. (Konferentsiia po Problemam Sposobnostei, Leningrad, 1960.) Moskva, 1962.
Phil 380.6 Problemy struktuny i soderzhaniia protsessa poznaniia. (Shumilin, A.T.) Moskva, 1969.
Phil 70.100.10 Problemy teorii poznaniia i logiki. Moskva, 1968.
Phil 1504.13.2 Probst, J.H. La mystique de Ramon Lull et l'art de contemplació. v.13, pt.2-3. Münster, 1914.
Phil 4803.360.20 Proby kontaktu; eseje i studia krytyczme. (Elzenberg, Henryk.) Kraków, 1966.
Phil 8581.14.9 The procedure, extent and limits of human understanding. (Browne, Peter.) London, 1728.
Phil 8581.14.10 The procedure, extent and limits of human understanding. (Browne, Peter.) London, 1737.
Phil 9035.60 Procedures in developing character controls through instructions. Thesis. (Priddle, Oamer D.) Philadelphia, 1929.
Phil 70.12 Proceedings, Washington, D.C., May 9-10, 1930. (Conference on Individual Psychological Differences.) Washington, D.C., 1930.
Phil 70.2 Proceedings, 1911. (Mental Hygiene Conference and Exhibit.) N.Y., 1912.
Phil 6302.10 Proceedings...colloquium on personality investigation. 1st - 2nd, 1928-1929. (American Psychiatric Association. Committee on Relations with the Social Science.) Baltimore, 1929.
Phil 40.8 Proceedings. (American Catholic Philosophical Association.) Washington, D.C. 1,1926+ 15v.
Phil 40.2 Proceedings. (American Medico-Psychological Association.) St. Louis. 60,1904
Phil 40.6 Proceedings. (American Philosophical Association.) 1-25,1902-1925 4v.
Phil 58.3 Proceedings. (American Society for Psychical Research.) Boston. 1885-1889
Phil 58.3.5 Proceedings. (American Society for Psychical Research.) Boston. 1906-1927 22v.
Phil 40.1 Proceedings. (Aristotelian Society.) London. 1,1887+ 70v.
Phil 6998.3 Proceedings. (Brockton Symposium and Workshop on Behavior Therapy.) Nutley, N.J. 1,1970+
Phil 70.70 Proceedings. (Caribbean Conference for Mental Health.) San Juan. 2-3 2v.
Phil 70.8 Proceedings. (Indian philosophical congress, 1st, Calcutta, 1925.) Calcutta. 36,1927+ 4v.
Phil 48.16 Proceedings. (Institute of Psychophysical Research.) Oxford. 1,1968+ 2v.
Phil 6980.362 Proceedings. (Institute on Preventive Psychiatry, State University of Iowa.) Iowa City. 1-4 2v.
Phil 70.83 Proceedings. (International Congress of Applied Psychology, 14th, Copenhagen, 1961.) Copenhagen, 1962. 5v.
Phil 70.1.6 Proceedings. (International Congress of Philosophy, 6th, Cambridge, Mass., 1926.) N.Y. 1927
Phil 70.1.7 Proceedings. (International Congress of Philosophy, 7th, Oxford, 1930.) London. 1931

Phil 70.1.10   Proceedings. (International Congress of Philosophy, 10th, Amsterdam, 1948.) Amsterdam. 1949 2v.

Phil 70.1.11   Proceedings. (International Congress of Philosophy, 11th, Brussels, 1953.) Amsterdam. 1953 4v.

Phil 70.3.60   Proceedings. (International Congress of Psychology, 14th, Montreal, 1954.) Amsterdam. 1955

Phil 8505.6   Proceedings. (International Congress on Humanism and Ethical Culture.) Utrecht.

Phil 8505.7   Proceedings. (International Humanist and Ethical Union Regional Conference, Antwerp.)

Phil 70.95   Proceedings. (Pakistan Philosophical Congress.) 1,1954+ 6v.

Phil 55.11   Proceedings. (Parapsychological Association.) Bruges. 1957-1964+ 5v.

Phil 58.2   Proceedings. (Society for Psychical Research, London.) London. 1-49,1882-1952 43v.

Phil 58.18   Proceedings. (South African Psychologial Association.) 1,1950+

Phil 62.3   Proceedings. (Western Philosophical Association.) 1-2,1901-1902

Phil 70.3.52   Proceedings. Actes. (International Congress of Psychology, 14th, Montreal, 1954.) Amsterdam. 1955

Phil 70.3.65   Proceedings. Comptes rendus. (International Congress of Psychology, 17th, Washington, 1963.) Amsterdam. 1963

Phil 70.5   Proceedings. Philosophy and mathematics. (International Congress of Arts and Sciences, St. Louis, 1904.) Washington, 1906.

Phil 58.2.3   Proceedings. v.1, pt.2-3. (Society for Psychical Research, London.) London, 1883.

Phil 40.6.3   Proceedings and addresses. (American Philosophical Association.) 1,1927+ 9v.

Phil 70.3.25   Proceedings and papers. (International Congress of Psychology, 8th, Groningen, 1926.) Groningen. 1827

Phil 70.3.30   Proceedings and papers. (International Congress of Psychology, 9th, New Haven, 1929.) Princeton, N.J. 1930

Phil 70.3.45   Proceedings and papers. (International Congress of Psychology, 12th, Edinburgh, 1948.) Edinburgh. 1950

Phil 70.3.50   Proceedings and papers. (International Congress of Psychology, 13th, Stockholm, 1951.) Stockholm. 1952

Phil 70.3.2   Proceedings at the 2d session. (International Congress of Psychology, 2nd, London, 1892.) London. 1892

Phil 40.4.5   Proceedings of annual meeting. (American Psychological Association.) Lancaster, Pa. 26-48,1917-1940 4v.

Phil 7069.57   Proceedings of four conferences. (Parapsychology, F.) N.Y., 1957.

Phil 40.4.3   Proceedings of the annual convention. (American Psychological Association.) Washington. 74,1966+ 5v.

Phil 70.104   Proceedings of the congress. (Interamerican Congress of Philosophy, 7th, Laval University, 1967.) Quebec, 1967-68. 2v.

Phil 5465.141   Proceedings of the fifth conference, 1964. (Utah Creativity Research Conference.) N.Y., n.d. 2v.

Phil 8400.36.3   Proceedings of the third international congress on aesthetics. v. 1-2. (International Congress on Aesthetics, 3rd, Venice, 1956.) Torino, 1957.

Phil 70.83.16   Proceedings of the XVIth International Congress of Applied Psychology. (International Congress of Applied Psychology, 16th, Amsterdam, 1968.) Amsterdam, 1969.

Phil 55.4.5   Proceedings of the 30th anniversary, November 27-28, 1914. (Philadelphia Neurological Society.) Philadelphi? 1915.

Phil 5255.17   Le procès de l'intelligence. Paris, 1922.
Phil 2805.408   Procès de Pascal. (Rennes, A.) Paris, 1962.
Phil 7054.121   Proces des spirites. (Leymarie, P.G.) Paris, 1875.
Phil 486.5   Le procès du matérialisme. (Lucas, J.) Paris, 1867.
Phil 2475.1.277   El proceso filosófico de Bergson y su bibliografía. 2. ed. (Coviello, A.) Tucumán, 1941.

Phil 165.348   Process and divinity. (Reese, William L.) LaSalle, Illinois, 1964.

Phil 1750.158   Process and polarity. (Sheldon, W.H.) N.Y., 1944.
Phil 303.12.6   Process and reality; an essay in cosmology. (Whitehead, Alfred N.) N.Y., 1941.

Phil 303.12   Process and reality. (Whitehead, Alfred N.) Cambridge, Eng., 1929.

Phil 303.12.3   Process and reality. (Whitehead, Alfred N.) N.Y., 1929.
Phil 303.12.5   Process and reality. (Whitehead, Alfred N.) N.Y., 1930.
Phil 2340.10.110   Process and unreality. (Wells, Harry K.) N.Y., 1950.
Phil 5058.22.15   The process of argument. (Sidgwick, A.) London, 1893.
Phil 5360.8   The process of generalizing abstraction. Thesis. (Fisher, S.C.) Princeton, N.J., 1916.

Phil 5190.10.20   The process of persuasion. (Miller, Clyde R.) Firenze, 1907.

Phil 25.197   Process studies. Claremont, Calif. 1,1971+
Phil 9400.41   Processes of aging. (Williams, R.H.) N.Y., 1963. 2v.

Phil 4260.84   Processi...di scienza nuova in G.B. Vico. (Arcari, P.) Friburgo, 1911.

Phil 8080.15   Processo all'estetica. (Plebe, Armando.) Firenze, 1959.
Phil 4065.145   Il processo di Giordano Bruno. (Firpo, Luigi.) Napoli, 1949.

Phil 5435.16   Les processus d'adaptation; Xe symposium, Marseille, 1965. 1. éd. (Association de Psychologie Scientifique de Langue Française.) Paris, 1967.

Phil 6327.28.85   De procestheorie van C.R. Rogers. (Dijkhuis, Johannes Josephus.) Hilversum, 1964.

Phil 5440.8   Proctor, R.A. Hereditary traits. N.Y., 1882.
Phil 8084.2F   Prodi, Paolo. Ricerche sulla teorica delle arti figurative nella riforma cattalica. Roma, 1962.

Phil 5545.256   Une prodigieuse mémoire. (Luriiă, Aleksandr R.) Neuchâtel, 1970.

Phil 4803.454.51   Prodrom mesjanizmu albo filozofji absolutnej. (Hoene-Wroński, Józef Maria.) Lwów, 1921.

Htn   Phil 4635.1.30*   Prodromus philosophiae. (Swedenborg, E.) Dresdae, 1734.
Phil 5262.31.26   Productive thinking. (Wertheimer, M.) London, 1961.
Phil 5262.31.25A   Productive thinking. (Wertheimer, M.) N.Y., 1959. 2v.

Phil 346.1   Proelss, K.R. Vom Ursprung der Menschlichen Erkenntnis. Leipzig, 1913.

Phil 8416.25   Prölss, Robert. Ästhetik; Belehrungen über die Wissenschaft vom Schönen und der Kunst. 3. Aufl. Leipzig, 1904.

Phil 3450.11.80   Proeve eener ver gelijkende studie over Plato en Husserl. (Schmidt Degener, H.) Groningen, 1924.

Phil 5645.50   Proeve ener practische kleurenpsychologie. (Wal, T.O.) Amsterdam, 1954.

Phil 5480.2   Proeve van eene geschiedenis van de leer der aangeboren begrippen. (Spruijt, C.B.) Leiden, 1879.

Phil 3270.17.35   Proeven over het tragisch bewiestzijn en de geschiedenis. (Flam, Leopold.) Antwerpen, 1963.

Phil 5068.56.20   Proeven van analytisch filosopesen. (Nuchelmans, Gabriël.) Hilversum, 1967.

Phil 8408.30.15   Profesor Dr. Otakar Hostinský, 1847-1907. Praha, 1907.
Phil 2520.147   Une profession de foi cartésienne. (Labordère, Marcel.) Paris, 1919.

Phil 5262.54   The profession of psychology. (Webb, W.B.) N.Y., 1962.
Phil 8894.30   Professional and business ethics. (Taeusch, C.F.) N.Y., 1926.

Phil 5425.57   Professionalism and originality. (Hayward, F.H.) Chicago, 1917.

Phil 3100.83   Professor Dr. Eduard Beneckes Psychologie als Naturwissenschaft. (Hauffe, G.) Borna, n.d.

Phil 3310.4.80   Professor Dr. J.H. Gunning. (Semmelink, J.H.) Zeist, 1926.

Phil 6313.22   Professor Freud. (Dieren, E. van.) Baarn, 1932.
Phil 3499.6.15   Der Professorenkant. (Romundt, H.) Gotha, 1906.
Phil 8843.14   Professors and public ethics. (Smith, Wilson.) Ithaca, N.Y., 1956.

Phil 2750.22.105   Il profeta della chiesa proletaria. (Siena, Primo.) Torino, 1965.

Phil 180.72   Profielen. (Flam, Leopold.) Antwerpen, 1957.
Phil 8876.54.25   Profilo della critica blondeliana. (Crippa, R.) Milano, 1962.

Phil 4080.3.420   Profilo dell'opera di Benedetto Croce. (Focher, Ferruccio.) Cremona, 1963.

Phil 8887.60   The profit of love. (McGinley, A.A.) N.Y., 1907.
Phil 2825.15   Profondeur de l'âme. (Paliard, J.) Paris, 1954.
Phil 8401.30.5   Progetto di una sistematica dell'arte. (Anceschi, Luciano.) Milano, 1962.

Phil 8401.30.7   Progetto di una sistematica dell'arte. 2. ed. (Anceschi, Luciano.) Milano, 1966.

Phil 6961.17.5   The prognosis in schizophrenia. (Langfeldt, G.) Copenhagen, 1937.

Phil 6306.5   Progoff, Ira. The death and rebirth of psychology. N.Y., 1956.

Phil 5255.56   Progoff, Ira. Depth psychology and modern man. N.Y., 1959.

Phil 6319.1.197   Progoff, Ira. Jung's psychology and its social meaning. London, 1953.

Phil 70.2.15   Program. (International Congress on Mental Hygiene.)
Phil 2138.91   Program des königlichen Gymnasiums. (Jordan, W.) Stuttgart, 1870.

Phil 5057.18   Program zur Feier des Gedächtnisses. (Ritschl, Otto.) Bonn, n.d.

Phil 181.2   Programe d'un cours de philosophie. (Gatien-Arnoult, A.) Paris, 1835.

Phil 1200.33   Programm. (Bonnell, Karl E.) Berlin, 1864.
Phil 1145.70   Programm der koniglichen Bismarck-Gym? Pyritz, 1908.
Phil 3565.87   Programm der Realschule zu Meerane. (Bauer, C.) n.p., 1885.

Phil 182.68   Programa analitico razonado de metafisica. (Huidobro, E.) Lima, 1923.

Phil 310.12.10   Programma kursa dialekticheskogo i istori cheskogo materializma. (Moscow. Kafedra. Akadamiia Obshchestvennogo Nauk.) Moskva, 1956.

Phil 310.12.15   Programma kursa dialekticheskogo i istoricheskogo materializma. (Russia (1917-   ). Upravlenie Prepodavatel'skogo Obshchestvennogo Nauk.) Moskva, 1957.

RRC   Phil 310.12   Programma kursa dialekticheskogo i istoricheskogo materializma dlia vyshego uchebrogo zaved. (Russia (1917-   ). Upravlenie Prepodavatel'skogo Obshchestvennogo Nauk.) Moskva, 1954.

Phil 6945.40   Programmation, architecture et psychiatrie. Paris, 1967.
Phil 5520.13   Programme et méthodes de la linguistique théorique. (Sechehaye, C.A.) Paris, 1908.

Phil 6121.62.1   Programming and metaprogramming in the human biocomputer. (Lilly, John Cunningham.) Berkeley, 1970.

Phil 310.12.12   Programmy po istorii filosofii. (Moscow. Akadamiia Obshchestvennogo Nauk.) Moskva, 1968.

Phil 801.23   Le progrès de la conscience dans la philosophie. (Brunschvicg, L.) Paris, 1927. 2v.

Phil 9245.21   Progrès et bonheur. (Finot, Jean.) Paris, 1914. 2v.
Phil 8592.120   Un progresismo vergonzante. (Meinvielle, Julio.) Buenos Aires? 1967.

Phil 2775.4.80   Progress and eternal recurrence in the work of Gabriel Naudé, 1600-1650. (Curtis, D.E.) Hull, 1967.

Htn   Phil 2030.2.30*   Progress and poverty. (George, Henry.) San Francisco, 1879.

Phil 3665.5.32   Progress and regress in philosophy, from Hume and Kant to Hegel and Fries. (Nelson, Leonard.) Oxford, 1970.

Phil 5238.16   Progress de la psycotechnique. (Baumgarten, F.) Bern, 1949-

Phil 193.8   Progress der Weltgeschichte. (Schildener, H.) Greifswald, 1854.

Phil 25.133   Progress in clinical psychology. N.Y. 1,1952+ 9v.
Phil 25.166   Progress in experimental personality research. N.Y. 1,1964+ 5v.

Phil 6980.309   Progress in psychotherapy. (Fromm-Reichmann, Frieda.) N.Y., 1956.

Phil 6685.4   Progress of animal magnetism. (Peyen, C.) Boston, 1837.
Phil 819.6   The progress of philosophy. (Tyler, S.) Philadelphia, 1888.

Phil 5212.2   The progress of psychology. (Cattell, J.M.) N.Y., 1893?
Phil 585.385   De progressieven en de conservatieve mens in hermeneutisch perspectief. (Berger, Herman.) Nijmegen, 1969.

Phil 6329.18   Der progressiv, domesticierte Mensch und seine Neurosen. (Schulze, H.) München, 1964.

Phil 585.386   Progressive and conservative man. (Berger, Herman.) Pittsburgh, Pa., 1971.

Phil 8708.12   Progressive creation. (Sampson, H.E.) London, 1909. 2v.

Phil 8880.38   Progressive morality; an essay in ethics. (Fowler, Thomas.) London, 1884.

Phil 7069.35.60   The progressive Pllgrim's progress. (Wells, Helen B.) N.Y., 1935.

Phil 6119.10   Progressive relaxation. (Jacobson, Edmund.) Chicago, 1929.

Phil 1506.8.10   Progressive scholasticism. (Bruni, Gerardo.) Saint Louis, Mo., 1929.

Phil 4883.2.5   Progressivno-demokraticheskaia i marksistskaia mysl' v Kazakhstane nachala XX veka. (Beisembiev, Kasym Beisembievich.) Alma-Ata, 1965.

Phil 348.19.10   Il progresso delle conoscenze umane. (Rizzi, Erminio.) Padova, 1967.

Htn   Phil 1850.37*   Les progrez et avancement aux sciences divines et humaines. (Bacon, Francis.) Paris, 1624.

Phil 1750.445   Prohaska, L. Existentialismus und Pädagogik. Freiburg, 1955.

Phil 1750.115.190 — Prohić, Kasim. Odvaznost izricanja; fenomenologije zivotnih formi. Zagreb, 1970.

Phil 8590.32 — Proiskhozhdenie khristianstva i ego sushchnost'. (Kazhdan, AI.P.) Moskva, 1962.

Phil 8505.8.20 — Proiskhozhdenie religii. (Leningrad. Muzei Istorii Religii i Ateizma.) Moskva, 1962.

Phil 5374.205 — Proiskhozhdenie soznaniia. (Spirkin, A.G.) Moskva, 1960.

Phil 5374.210 — Proiskhozhdenie soznaniia i ego osobennosti. (Protasenia, P.F.) Minsk, 1959.

Phil 7069.29.61 — The projection of the astral body. (Muldoon, Sylvan J.) London, 1961.

Phil 5590.65 — Projective psychology. 1.ed. (Abt, L.E.) N.Y., 1950.

Phil 5850.309 — Projektive Tests und Fahrtüchtigkeit. (Petersohn, F.) Hamburg, 1962.

Phil 5876.20 — Le projet de vie de l'adolescent, identité psychosociale et vocation. (Lorimier, Jacques de.) Paris, 1967.

Phil 5625.105 — Prokasy, William Frederick. Classical conditioning, a symposium. N.Y., 1965.

Phil 8980.712 — Prokof'ev, V.I. Dve morali; moral' religioznaia i moral' kommunisticheskaia. Moskva, 1961.

Phil 3525.92 — Proksch, A. Karl Christian Friedrich Krause. Leipzig, 1880.

Phil 179.03 — Prolegomena...Einheit des Geisteslebens. (Eucken, R.) Leipzig, 1885.

Phil 3480.59 — Prolegomena and metaphysical foundations. Photoreproduction. (Kant, Immanuel.) London, 1883.

Phil 187.184 — Prolegomena do filozofii przyrody arystotelesowsko-tomistycznej. (Maziarski, Stanisław.) Lublin, 1959.

Phil 4803.454.41 — Prolegomena do mesjanizmu. (Hoene-Wroński, Józef Maria.) Lwów, 1922-25. 3v.

Phil 6111.80.5 — Prolegomena einer antropologischen Physiologie. (Buytendijk, Frederik Jacobus Johannes.) Salzburg, 1967.

Phil 3480.57.40 — Prolegomena in Sprachlicher Bearbeitung, von Emil Kühn. (Kant, Immanuel.) Gotha, 1908.

Phil 2130.35.3 — Prolegomena logica. (Mansel, H.L.) Boston, 1860.

Phil 2130.35 — Prolegomena logica. (Mansel, H.L.) Oxford, 1851.

Phil 2130.35.2A — Prolegomena logica. 2nd ed. (Mansel, H.L.) Oxford, 1860.

Phil 960.40 — Prolegomena to a history of Buddhist philosophy. (Barua, B.M.) Calcutta, 1918.

Phil 197.19.10 — Prolegomena to a new metaphysic. (Whittaker, T.) Cambridge, Eng., 1931.

Htn Phil 3480.58* — Prolegomena to any future metaphysics. (Kant, Immanuel.) Chicago, 1902.

Phil 3480.58.5 — Prolegomena to any future metaphysics. (Kant, Immanuel.) Chicago, 1926.

Phil 3480.58.22 — Prolegomena to any future metaphysics. (Kant, Immanuel.) Manchester, Eng., 1953.

Phil 3480.58.10 — Prolegomena to any future metaphysics. 3d ed. (Kant, Immanuel.) Chicago, 1912.

Phil 2020.30A — Prolegomena to ethics. (Green, T.H.) Oxford, 1883.

Phil 2020.30.2A — Prolegomena to ethics. 2d ed. (Green, T.H.) Oxford, 1884.

Phil 2020.30.3A — Prolegomena to ethics. 3d ed. (Green, T.H.) Oxford, 1890.

Phil 2020.30.4 — Prolegomena to ethics. 4th ed. (Green, T.H.) Oxford, 1899.

Phil 2020.30.5 — Prolegomena to ethics. 5th ed. (Green, T.H.) Oxford, 1924.

Phil 2020.30.15 — Prolegomena to ethics. 5th ed. (Green, T.H.) Oxford, 1929.

Phil 3425.96A — Prolegomena to Hegel's philosophy. (Wallace, W.) Oxford, 1894.

Phil 349.28A — Prolegomena to idealist theory of knowledge. (Smith, Norman K.) London, 1924.

Phil 197.98 — Prolegomena to philosophy. (Wheatley, Jon.) Belmont, Calif., 1970.

Phil 8670.8 — Prolegomena to theism. N.Y., 1910.

Phil 6111.80 — Prolegomena van een antropologische fysiologie. (Buytendijk, Frederik Jacobus Johannes.) Utrecht, 1965.

Phil 3480.57.7 — Prolegomena zu einer jeden künftigen Metaphysik. (Kant, Immanuel.) Frankfurt, 1798.

Phil 3480.57.5 — Prolegomena zu einer jeden künftigen Metaphysik. (Kant, Immanuel.) Grätz, 1795.

Htn Phil 3480.57.3* — Prolegomena zu einer jeden künftigen Metaphysik. (Kant, Immanuel.) Riga, 1783.

Htn Phil 3480.57.2* — Prolegomena zu einer jeden künftigen Metaphysik. (Kant, Immanuel.) Riga, 1783. 2 pam.

Phil 3480.57.13 — Prolegomena zu einer jeden künftigen Metaphysik. 4. Aufl. (Kant, Immanuel.) Leipzig, 1905.

Phil 3480.57.14 — Prolegomena zu einer jeden künftigen Metaphysik. 5. Aufl. (Kant, Immanuel.) Leipzig, 1913.

Phil 3480.57.15 — Prolegomena zu einer jeden künftigen Metaphysik. 6. Aufl. (Kant, Immanuel.) Leipzig, 1920.

Phil 294.6 — Prolegomena zu einer Kosmologie. (Neeff, F.) Tübingen, 1921.

Phil 5047.20 — Prolegomena zu einer realistischen Logik. (Herbertz, Richard.) Halle, 1916.

Phil 5259.15 — Prolegomena zu einer wissenschaftliche Psychologie. (Tumarkin, Anna.) Leipzig, 1923.

Phil 3480.57 — Prolegomena zur künftigen Metaphysik. (Kant, Immanuel.) Frankfurt, 1794.

Phil 8411.3.5 — Prolegomena zur Ästhetik. (Köstlin, K.) Tübingen, 1889.

Phil 182.4 — Prolegomena zur Philosophie. (Harms, F.) Braunschweig, 1852.

Phil 5258.16 — Prolégomènes a la psychogénie moderne. (Siciliani, P.) Paris, 1880.

Phil 3480.58.40 — Prolégomènes a toute métaphysique future. (Kant, Immanuel.) Paris, 1891.

Phil 3480.58.45 — Prolégomènes a toute métaphysique future. (Kant, Immanuel.) Paris, 1930.

Phil 2477.16.30 — Prolégomenes a une esthétique intégrale. (Brunet, Christian.) Paris, 1962.

Phil 8884.15.15 — Prolegomeni a una morale distinta dalla metafisica. (Juvalta, E.) Pavia, 1901.

Phil 3480.58.60 — Prolegomeni ad ogni metafisica futura. (Kant, Immanuel.) Torino, 1926.

Phil 8889.3.7 — Prolegomeni alla scienza del bene e del mali. (Orestano, Francesco.) Roma, 1915.

Phil 5058.47 — Prolegomenon zu einer Logik als Lehre von der Vergrifflichten Gegenständlichkeit. (Schingnitz, Werner.) Leipzig, 1931.

Phil 4301.1 — Prolegomenos a la unica metafisica posible. (Avelino, Andres.) Ciudad Trujillo, 1941.

Phil 801.35.5 — Prolegómenos filosóficos. (Bueno, Miguel.) México, 1963.

Phil 3480.58.70 — Prolehomena to kozhnoï maïbutn'oï metafisyky. (Kant, Immanuel.) L'viv, 1930.

Phil 2490.27 — Le prolétariat dans la societe moderne. (Comte, Auguste.) Paris, 1946.

Phil 179.3.52 — Prologomena und Epilog zu einer Philosophie des Geistlebens. (Eucken, R.) Berlin, 1922.

Phil 3425.290 — Prologue and epilogue to Hegel. (Cross, G.J.) Oxford, 1935.

Phil 4225.1.52 — Prolusione e introduzione alle lezioni di filosofia nella Università di Napoli. 2a ed. (Spaventa, Bertrando.) Napoli, 1886.

Phil 4265.3.45 — Prolusioni alla storia della filosofia. (Vera, A.) Milano, 1861.

Phil 181.34 — Promenades philosophiques. 3rd series. (Gourmont, Rémy de.) Paris, 1913. 3v.

Phil 3001.16.5 — Prometheus. (Balthasar, H.U.) Heidelburg, 1947.

Phil 180.38.10 — Prometheus: Ideen zur Philosophie der Kultur. (Freyer, Hans.) Jena, 1923.

Htn Phil 178.33* — Prometheus (les grandes crucifiés). (Duncan, R.) Paris, 1919.

Phil 9240.18 — Prometheus und die Weltübel. (Dessauer, F.J.) Frankfurt, 1959.

Phil 1750.166.270 — The promise and peril of human purpose. (Horosz, William.) Saint Louis, 1970.

Phil 2030.7 — The promise of modern life. (Gotshalk, Dilman Walter.) Yellow Springs, Ohio, 1958.

Phil 5871.30 — The promised seed; a comparative study of eminent first and later sons. (Harris, Irving D.) N.Y., 1964.

Phil 3497.15 — Promnitz, C.F. Antischrift zur Vertheidigung der Vernunft und Religion. Berlin, 1796.

Phil 9245.5 — The promotion of general happiness. (Macmillan, M.) London, 1890.

Phil 4655.1.62 — Promotionspredikan. (Wikner, Pontus.) Upsala, 1872.

Phil 5238.210.6 — Promovido pela Sociedade Interamericana de Psicologia com a cooperação de Associação Brasileira de Psicologia Aplicada. (Interamerican Congress of Psychology. 6th, Rio de Janeiro, 1959.) Rio de Janeiro, 1960.

Phil 1750.685 — Proní sešit o existencialismii. (Černý, Václav.) Phraha, 1948.

Phil 5255.54 — Pronko, N.H. Empirical foundations of psychology. N.Y., 1952.

Phil 343.21A — Proof of an external world. (Moore, George E.) London, 1939.

Phil 7054.34.10 — The proof palpable of immortality. 3. ed. (Sargent, Epes.) Boston, 1881.

Phil 7054.34.8 — The proof palpable of immortalty. (Sargent, Epes.) Boston, 1875.

Phil 8667.2 — Proofs and illustrations of the attributes of God. (Macculloch, J.) London, 1837. 3v.

Phil 8644.7 — The proofs of life after death. (Thompson, R.J.) Paris, 1906.

Phil 7069.20.70 — Proofs of the spirit world. (Chevreuil, L.) N.Y., 1920.

Phil 7054.180 — Proofs of the truth of spiritualism. (Henslow, G.) London, 1919.

Phil 7069.19.120 — The proofs of the truths of spiritualism. 2. ed. (Henslow, George.) London, 1919.

Phil 3640.172 — Proost, K.F. Friedrich, Nietzsche, zijn leven en zijn werk. Uitgave, 1920.

Phil 5043.25 — Propadeutische Logik. (Drbal, M.) Wien, 1885.

Phil 5046.4 — Propädentische Logik und Hodegetik. (Gockel, C.F.) Karlsruhe, 1839.

Phil 818.8.5 — Die Propädeutik der Geschichte. (Sigwart, H.C.W.) Tübingen, 1840.

Phil 177.2 — Propädeutik der Philosophie. (Calker, F.) Bonn, 1821.

Phil 188.3 — Propädeutik der Philosophie. (Noack, L.) Weimar, 1854.

Phil 40.3 — A propaganda of philosophy; a history of the American Institute of Christian Philosophy, 1881-1914. (MacCracken, H.M.) N.Y., 1914.

Phil 4803.454.45 — Propédeutigue messianique. v.2. (Hoene-Wroński, Józef Maria.) Paris, 1875.

Phil 3425.611 — Propédeutique philosophique. (Hegel, G.W.) Génève, 1964.

Phil 4803.454.46 — Propedeutyka mesjaniczna. v.2. (Hoene-Wroński, Józef Maria.) Warszawa, 1925.

Phil 3425.74.2 — Propédiutique philosophique. (Hegel, Georg Wilhelm Friedrich.) Paris, 1963.

Phil 3850.27.111 — Prophet in the wilderness. (Hagedorn, Hermann.) N.Y., 1947.

Phil 2905.1.670 — Un prophète en procès. (Ouince, René d'.) Paris, 1970. 2v.

Phil 6990.46 — Propheten in deutscher Krise. (Olden, R.) Berlin, 1932.

Phil 8593.20.5 — Prophetische Denker. (Nigg, Walter.) Zürich, 1957.

Phil 8581.89 — Prophets for a day of judgment. (Baker, A.E.) London, 1944.

Phil 2412.12A — The prophets of Paris. (Manuel, F.E.) Cambridge, 1962.

Phil 177.68.25 — Propos sur des philosophes. (Chartier, Émile.) Paris, 1961.

Phil 2725.13.95 — Propos sur Jules Lequier. (Callot, Emile.) Paris, 1962.

Phil 8886.74 — Propos sur la morale et la science. (Leclercq, Francois.) Paris, 1959.

Phil 8582.50.5 — Propos sur la religion. (Chartier, E.) Paris, 1938.

Phil 9245.54.5 — Propos sur le bonheur. 18e éd. (Chartier, E.) Paris, 1928.

Phil 8403.23.10 — Propos sur l'esthetique. (Chartier, Émile.) paris, 1923.

Htn Phil 2340.2.80* — Proposed for the press. (Walker, O.) Boston, 1757.

Phil 808.1 — Proposiciones relativas al porvenir de la filosofia. v.1-2. (Ingennyeros, José.) Buenos Aires, 1918.

Htn Phil 530.11.16* — Propositions. (Philadelphian Society, London.) London, 1697.

Phil 6945.4 — Propositions and resolutions of the Association of Medical Superintendents of American Institutions for the insane. (American Psychiatric Association.) Philadelphia, 1876.

Phil 176.134 — Propositions de philosophie. (Blondeau, Cyrille.) Paris, 1932.

Phil 182.122 — Proprieties and vagaries. (Hammond, A.L.) Baltimore, 1961.

Phil 8416.18 — Propris, A. de. Brevario della nuova estetica. Roma, 1951.

Phil 8416.18.5 — Propris, A. de. Problemi di estetica e critica. Roma, 1954.

Phil 8050.63 — Propris, A de. Storia degli orientamenti artistici. Roma, 1953.

Phil 4813.10 — Propylaeumok a' magyar pilosophiákoz. (Szontagh, Gusztav.) Budán, 1839.

Phil 3425.670 — Prosa der Welt: die Sprache Hegels. (Zuefle, Manfred.) Einsiedeln, 1968.

Phil 1715.11 — Prosch, H. The genesis of twentieth century philosophy. 1. ed. Garden City, N.Y., 1964.

Phil 2750.20.60 — La prose du monde. (Merleau-Ponty, Maurice.) Paris, 1969.

Phil 165.245 — Prospect for metaphysics. (Ramsey, J.T.) London, 1961.

Phil 8692.3.10 — A prospective view of the new age. (Coutts, John.) London, 1923.

Phil 8587.46   The prospects of humanism. (Hyde, Laurence.) London, 1931.
Phil 192.81   Prospects of philosophy. (Rolbiecki, J.J.) N.Y., 1939.
Phil 182.69F   Prospectus de la philosophie absolue et son développement. (Hoëné Wronski, J.M.) Paris, 1878.
Phil 9530.25.5   Prosperity, how to attract it. (Marden, Orison S.) N.Y., 1922.
Phil 4080.3.535   Prospettive crociane. (Roggerone, Giuseppe A.) Lecce, 1968.
Phil 1750.105   Prospettive filosofiche. (Meglio, Gaetano.) Padova, 1966.
Phil 4210.205   Prospettive rosminiane. (Cristaldi, Giuseppe.) Milano, 1965.
Phil 2520.123   Prost, Joseph. Essai sur l'atomisme...la philosophie cartesienne. Paris, 1907.
Phil 672.224   Prostor a čas. 2. vyd. (Tlustý, Vojtěch.) Praha, 1963.
Phil 8980.220   Prostota i skromnost'. (Bludov, Iakov S.) Kiev, 1968.
Phil 505.6   Prostranstvo mikromira. (Andreev, Edvard P.) Moskva, 1969.
Phil 8980.782   Prostye istiny. (Sevrikov, Konstantin I.) Moskva, 1969.
Phil 4761.4.80   Prosvetitel' XVIII veka Ia.P. Kozel'skii. (Kogan, Iu.Ia.) Moskva, 1958.
Phil 5055.23   Prot, Marcel. Language et logique. Paris, 1949.
Phil 5374.210   Protasenia, P.F. Proiskhozhdenie soznaniia i ego osobennosti. Minsk, 1959.
Phil 310.4.5   Protasenko, Z.M. Printsipy periodizatsii istorii marksistsko-leninskoi filosofii. Leningrad, 1957.
Phil 1750.850   Protasenko, Zoia M. Lenin kak istorik filosofii. Leningrad, 1969.
Phil 3552.59   Protegée; ou De la formation et des révolutions du globe. (Leibniz, Gottfried Wilhelm.) Paris, 1859.
Phil 8610.890   A protest against agnosticism. (Fitzgerald, P.F. (Mrs.).) London, 1890.
Phil 9075.39   Der Protest der Gewissens in der Philosophie. (Meyer, Rudolf.) Zürich, 1941.
Phil 178.14   Protest Gegen die moderne Wissenschaft. (Dietrich, K.) Hamburg, 1887.
Phil 8954.5   The Protestant ethic and modernization. (Eisenstadt, Shmuel Noah.) N.Y., 1968.
Phil 8599.14   Protestant modernism. (Torrey, D.C.) Boston, 1910.
Phil 8599.14.2   Protestant modernism. (Torrey, D.C.) N.Y., 1910.
Phil 525.249   The Protestant mystics. 1st ed. (Fremantle, Anne Jackson.) Boston, 1964.
Phil 8591.41   Protestantische Geschichtswussteins. (Litt, Theodor.) Leipzig, 1939.
Phil 3483.26   Protestantismens idé och Immanuel Kant. (Boldt, Georg.) Helsingfors, 1900.
Phil 25.49   Proteus; Blätter einer Welt. Kettwig. 1,1925
Phil 5592.37   Proteus, Stanley David. Porteus maze test. Palo Alto, 1965.
Htn   Phil 8583.3*   Proteus and Amadeus. (DeVere, Aubrey.) London, 1878.
Phil 5255.24   Proteus or The future of intelligence. (Paget, Violet.) London, 1925.
Phil 310.657   Protiv fal'sifikatorov marksistsko-leninskoi filosofii (sbornik statei). Moskva, 1967.
Phil 310.455   Protiv fal'sifikatsii filosofii marksizma progmatistami SShA. (Titarenko, Aleksandr I.) Moskva, 1961.
Phil 475.3   Protiv idealizma. (Aksel'rod, L. I.) Moskva, 1933.
Phil 8400.21   Protiv revizionizma v estetike. (Kaloshen, F.I.) Moskva, 1960.
Phil 8400.42   Protiv sovremennogo abstraktsionizma i formalizma. (Baskin, Mark P.) Moskva, 1964.
Phil 8875.32   Protiv sovremennoi burzhuaznoi etiki. (Akademiia Nauk SSSR. Institut Filosofii.) Moskva, 1965.
Phil 1712.22   Protiv sovremennoi burzhuaznoi filosofii. (Moscow. Universitet Filosoficheskii Fakul'tet.) Moskva, 1963.
Phil 3050.4   Protiv sovremennoi burzhuaznoi ideologii. Moskva, 1960.
Phil 310.607   Protiv sovremennykh burzhuaznykh fal'sifikatorov marksistsko-leninskoi filosofii. (Akademiia Nauk SSSR. Institut Filosofii.) Moskva, 1964.
Phil 4710.100   Protiv sovremennykh fal'sifikatorov istorii russkoi filosofii. (Shchipanov, I.Ia.) Moskva, 1960.
Phil 4829.680.30   Protiv struje. (Pejović, Danilo.) Zagreb, 1965.
Phil 3425.568   Protivopolozhnost' Marksistskogo i Gegelevskogo ucheniia o sozhanii. (Georgiav, F.I.) Moskva, 1961.
Phil 310.115   Protivorechivost' dvizheniia i ee proiavleniia. (Sviderskii, Vladimir Io.) Leningrad, 1959.
Phil 2150.22.97   Proto, Mario. Introduzione a Marcuse. 2. ed. Manduria, 1968.
Phil 4757.3.20   Protoierei Feodor Aleksandrovich Golubinski. (Vvedenskii, Aleksei I.) Sergiev, 1898.
Phil 4115.40.5   Protologia; estratti. (Gioberti, V.) Torino, 1924.
Phil 189.27   Protologia; preludio al sapere. (Oro, A.M. dell'.) Milano, 1937.
Phil 8980.712.20   Protopopova, A.N. V sem'e; vzaimnoe uvazhenie, zabota o detiakh. Moskva, 1962.
Phil 8426.11   Protsess esteticheskogo otrazheniia. (Zelenov, L.A.) Moskva, 1969.
Phil 5257.69   Protsess myshleniia i zakonomernosti analiza, Sinteza i obobshcheniia. (Akademiia Nauk SSSR. Institut Filosofii, Sektor Psikologii.) Moskva, 1960.
Phil 5585.85   Protsess poznaniia v obuchenii. (Smirnov, M.T.) Moskva, 1956.
Phil 8595.10   Prout, W. Chemistry, meteorology...natural theology. London, 1855.
Phil 8670.7   Prout, W. Chemistry, meteorology and the function of digestion considered with reference to natural theology. London, 1834.
Phil 8670.7.2   Prout, W. Chemistry, meteorology and the function of digestion considered with reference to natural theology. Philadelphia, 1834.
Phil 8581.10.8   Prout, William. Bridgewater treatises [8]. Chemistry, meteorology. London, 1855.
Phil 8664.9   Prouver Dieu? (Javaux, J.) Paris, 1968.
Phil 8656.30   Próva matemático da existencia de Deus. (Bandeira de Mello, L.M.) Leopoldina, 1942.
Phil 8430.29A   Provalon, Marx, Picasso. (Raphael, Max.) Paris, 1933.
Phil 8962.11   Proverbs for the people. (Magoon, E.L.) Boston, 1849.
Phil 284.13   Providence and the world-order. (D'Arcy, C.F.) London, 1932.
Phil 8604.1.2   The providence of reason: criticism. (Young, J.) London, 1860.
Phil 8604.1   The providence of reason: criticism. (Young, J.) N.Y., 1860.
Phil 8661.30   La providencia y España. (Gutiérrez, Antonio José.) San Sebastián, 1941.
Phil 5062.30.15   The province of logic; an interpretation of certain parts of Cook Wilson's "Statement and inference". (Robinson, Richard.) London, 1931.

Phil 2805.32.2   The provincial letters. (Pascal, Blaise.) Cambridge, Eng., 1880.
Phil 2805.32.6.20   The provincial letters. (Pascal, Blaise.) London, 1889.
Phil 2805.32.5   The provincial letters. (Pascal, Blaise.) N.Y., 1828.
Phil 2805.32.4   The provincial letters. (Pascal, Blaise.) N.Y., 1850.
Phil 2805.32.6   The provincial letters. (Pascal, Blaise.) N.Y., 1856.
Phil 2805.32   Provincial letters. (Pascal, Blaise.) N.Y., 1859.
Phil 2805.32.7   The provincial letters. 1st Canadian ed. (Pascal, Blaise.) Toronto, 19- ?
Phil 2805.30.9   Les provinciales. (Pascal, Blaise.) Amsterdam, 1734. 3v.
Htn   Phil 2805.28*   Les provinciales. (Pascal, Blaise.) Cologne, 1657.
Htn   Phil 2805.30.16*   Les provinciales. (Pascal, Blaise.) Cologne, 1657.
Htn   Phil 2805.29.5*   Les provinciales. (Pascal, Blaise.) Cologne, 1685.
Phil 2805.30.11   Les provinciales. (Pascal, Blaise.) Leiden? 1761.   4v.
Htn   Phil 2805.32.11*   Les provinciales. (Pascal, Blaise.) London, 1657.
Htn   Phil 2805.32.12*   Les provinciales. (Pascal, Blaise.) London, 1658.
Phil 2805.30.21   Les provinciales. (Pascal, Blaise.) Mexico, 1841.
Phil 2805.30.15   Les provinciales. (Pascal, Blaise.) Paris, 1815. 2v.
Phil 2805.30.7   Les provinciales. (Pascal, Blaise.) Paris, 1816. 2v.
NEDL   Phil 2805.30.12   Les provinciales. (Pascal, Blaise.) Paris, 1816. 2v.
Phil 2805.30.14   Les provinciales. (Pascal, Blaise.) Paris, 1819. 2v.
Phil 2805.30.2   Les provinciales. (Pascal, Blaise.) Paris, 1819. 2v.
Phil 2805.30.13   Les provinciales. (Pascal, Blaise.) Paris, 1851. 2v.
Phil 2805.30.25   Les provinciales. (Pascal, Blaise.) Paris, 1853.
Phil 2805.30.23   Les provinciales. (Pascal, Blaise.) Paris, 1867.
Phil 2805.30.4   Les provinciales. (Pascal, Blaise.) Paris, 1885. 2v.
Phil 2805.32.28   Provinciales. (Pascal, Blaise.) Paris, 1964.
Phil 2805.32.27   Provinciales. (Pascal, Blaise.) Paris, 1965.
Phil 2805.30.19   Les provinciales. (Pascal, Blaise.) Strasbourg, n.d.
Htn   Phil 2805.29.6*   Les provinciales. 6. éd. (Pascal, Blaise.) Cologne, 1666.
Htn   Phil 2805.30.18*   Les provinciales. 7. éd. (Pascal, Blaise.) Cologne, 1669.
Phil 2805.30.26   Provinciales. 9. éd. (Pascal, Blaise.) Paris, 1913.
Phil 2805.209   Les provinciales de Pascal. (Bayet, Albert.) Paris, 1929.
Phil 2805.209.5   Les provinciales de Pascal. (Bayet, Albert.) Paris, 1946.
Phil 2805.32.26   Les provinciales écrits des curés de Paris. (Pascal, Blaise.) Paris, 1962. 2v.
Phil 396.16   Provokation, Affirmation. Das Dilemma des kritischen Humanismus. (Rodi, Frithjof.) Stuttgart, 1970.
Phil 3475.3.220   Provokationen; Gespräche und Interviews. (Jaspers, Karl.) München, 1969.
Phil 6965.6   Provost, Maurice. Aliénation mentale, chez les employés de chemins de fer et de transports publics. Thèse. Paris, 1914.
Phil 2475.1.265   Proyecciones de la intuición. (Molina, Enrique.) Santiago de Chile, 1935.
Phil 9245.116   Proyecciónes espirituales del sufrimiento radiografia del dolor. (Fernández, Julio F.) San Salvador, 1964.
Phil 575.210   Der Prozess "Gesellschaft contra Person". (Michel, Ernst.) Stuttgart, 1965.
Phil 585.195   Průcha, Milan. La recontre du cogito et du marxisme. Nancy, 1965.
Phil 1750.175   Pruche, B. Existentialisme et acte d'être. Paris, 1947.
Phil 2880.8.106   Prucke, B. L'homme de Sartre. Grenoble, 1949.
Phil 8965.13   Prudence. (Pieper, Josef.) N.Y., 1959.
Phil 2805.100   Prudhomme, S. La vraie religion selon Pascal. Paris, 1905.
Phil 349.8   Prudhomme, Sully. Que Sais-je? Paris, 1896.
Phil 70.1.12.10   Prudian, Georg. Ital'ianskaia vstrecha filosov; o XII Mezhdunarodnom filosofskom Kongresse. Erevan, 1959.
Phil 3500.52   Prüfung der Kantischen Critik der reinen Vernunft. v.1-2. (Schultz, John.) Königsberg, 1789-92.
Phil 5247.13.21   Prüfung der Köpfe zu den Wissenschaften. (Huarte de San Juan, J.) Zerbst, 1752.
Htn   Phil 3625.1.100*   Prüfung der Mendelssohnschen Morgenstunden oder aller spekulativen Beweise für das Daseyn. (Jakob, Ludwig H.) Leipzig, 1786.
Phil 2035.80.40   Eine Prüfung der Philosophie Sir William Hamiltons. (Mill, J.S.) Halle, 1908.
Htn   Phil 3801.812*   Prüfung der Schellingischen Lehren von Gott. (Süskind, F.G. von.) Tübingen, 1812.
Phil 8622.58   Pruefung der Secte die an allem zweifelt. Göttingen, 1751.
Phil 6315.2.134   Pruner, Helen W. Freud, his life and his mind. N.Y., 1947.
Phil 8951.11.80   Prupard, Paul. L'abbé Louis Bautain. Tournai, 1961.
Phil 5627.268.10   Pruyser, Paul W. A dynamic psychology of religion. N.Y., 1968.
Phil 5068.80   Przelecki, Marian. The logic of empirical theories. London, 1969.
Phil 8411.41   Przemiany wyobraźni. Wyd. 1. (Kuezyńska, Alicja.) Warszawa, 1969.
Phil 4803.462.40   Przeżijni, dzieło, wartość. (Ingarden, Roman.) Kraków, 1966.
VPhil 8423.27   Przeżycie i wartość. Wyd. 1. (Wallis, Mieczysław.) Kraków, 1968.
Phil 3015.2   Przygodda, Paul. Deutsche Philosophie v.2. Berlin, 1916.
Phil 8610.960   Przykład indywidualny kształtowania sie postawy wolnomyś'licielskiej. (Kotarbiński, Tad.) Warszawa, 1960.
Phil 5465.133   Przyluski, J. Créer. Paris, 1943.
Phil 365.49   Przyluski, Jean. L'évolution humaine. Paris, 1942.
Phil 1750.166.65   Przymara, E. Humanitus. Nuinberg, 1952.
Phil 190.54   Przywara, Erich. Analogia entis. München, 1932.
Phil 1750.60   Przywara, Erich. In und Gegen. Nürnberg, 1955.
Phil 3497.18   Przywara, Erich. Kant Heute. München, 1930.
Phil 3745.15   Przywara, Erich. Mensch. Nürnberg, 1959.
Phil 8595.31   Przywara, Erich. Plarity; a German Catholic's interpretation of religion. London, 1935.
Phil 3850.18.109   Przywara, Erich. Religionsbegründung: Max Scheler, J.H. Neuman. Freiburg, 1923.
Phil 190.54.10   Przywara, Erich. Ringen der Gegenwart. Augsburg, 1929. 2v.
Phil 8670.18   Przywara, Erich. Was ist Gott; cinc Summula. Nürnberg, 1969.
Phil 665.15   Pseuchographia anthropomagica. (Carpenter, A.) London, 1652.
Phil 2475.1.208   Un pseudonyme Bergsonien? (Nicolardot, F.) Paris, 1923.
Phil 6322.13   Ein Pseudoprophet. (Muralt, Alexander von.) München, 1920.
Phil 5643.95F   Pseudoptics, the science of optical illusions. Charts. n.p., n.d.
Phil 6329.5   La psicanalisi. (Tissi, Silvio.) Milano, 1929.
Phil 5414.50   Psicanalisi della situazione atomica. (Fornari, Franco.) Milano, 1970.
Phil 6312.30   Psicanalisi e filosofia. (Centro di Studi Filosofici di Gallarate.) Padova, 1968.
Phil 25.19   Psiche, rivista di studi psicologici. v.1-4. Firenze, 1912.   4v.
Phil 6961.15   La psichiatria tedesca. (Lugaro, E.) Firenze, 1916.

Phil 7060.1.5 Psichologie ou traité de l'apparition des esprits. (Taillepied, Noël.) Paris, 1588.

Phil 5216.5 Psichologijos raidci Lietuvoje. (Gučas, Alfonsas.) Vilnius, 1968.

Phil 5590.24 Psico-cinesia, ouvero L'arte di formare il carattere. Pte. 1. (Baumann, Emilio.) Roma, 1900.

Phil 1695.25 La psicoanalisi. (Servadio, E.) Torino, 1963. 3v.

Phil 6311.32 La psicoanalisi. 4. ed. (Bonaventura, E.) Milano, 1950.

Phil 6307.408 La psicoanalisi nella cultura italiana. (David, Michel.) Torino, 1966.

Phil 7084.4 Psicoanálisis de los sueños. (Garma, Ángel.) Buenos Aires, 1940.

Phil 5520.280 Psicobiologia del lenguage. 2. ed. (Cuatrecasas, Juan.) Buenos Aires, 1958.

Phil 365.17 La psicogenesi della coscienza. (Valle, L.) Milano, 1905.

Phil 6123.7 Psicgenesis. (Nicolai, J.F.) Santiago, 1935.

Phil 9220.13 Psicolgia da Amizade. (Gonçalves Viana, M.) Porto, 1943.

Phil 5520.426 La psicolinguistica oggi. (Titone, Renzo.) Zürich, 1964.

Phil 5042.75 Psicologia, logica, dialettica. (Carbonard, Cleto.) Napoli, 1963.

Phil 5241.107 Psicologia. (Barboza, Enrique.) Lima, 1940.

Phil 5243.39 Psicología. (Delgadio, H.F.) Lima, 1933.

Phil 5255.40 Psicología. (Palmés, F.M.) Barcelona, 1928.

Phil 58.19 Psicologia. (São Paulo Brazil (City). Universidade. Faculdade de Filosofía, Ciencias e Letras.) 4-7 2v.

Phil 4210.27 Psicologia. v.1-2. (Rosmini-Serbati, Antonio.) Napoli, 1858.

Phil 5252.31 Psicologia. 2a. ed. (Morando, G.) Voghera, 1915.

Phil 5246.54 Psicología. 4. ed. (Guerrero, L.J.) Buenos Aires, 1943.

Phil 5258.125.5 Psicología. 4. ed. (Soria, T.D.) México, 1940.

Phil 5228.16 Psicología abismal del mexicano. 2. ed. (Suarez Soto, Vicente.) Puebla de Zaragoza, 1967.

Phil 5261.3.9 La psicologia contemporanea. (Villa, G.) Milano, 1911.

Phil 5261.3 La psicologia contemporanea. (Villa, G.) Torino, 1899.

Phil 9400.26 Psicologia da maturidade e da velhice. (Gonçalves Viana, Mário.) Porto, 196-.

Phil 5590.13.5 Psicologia da personalidade. 2. ed. (Kehl, R.) Rio de Janeiro, 1941.

Phil 5850.278.13 Psicologia de la actividad industrial. (Münsterberg, H.) Madrid, 1914.

Phil 4966.2 Psicología de la vocación. (Estable, C.) Montevideo, 1942.

Phil 5253.12 Psicología de las situaciones vitales. (Nicol, Eduardo.) Mexico, 1941.

Phil 5240.65 Psicología de los pueblos primitivos. (Alvarez Villar, Alfonso.) Madrid, 1969.

Phil 5255.68 Psicologia degli animali e filosofia del sentimento. (Perlenghini, A.) Genova, 1961.

Phil 5243.32 La psicologia dei testimoni. (Dattino, Giovanni.) Napoli, 1909.

Phil 9035.45.4 Psicologia del caracter. Traduccion de Santo Rubiano. (Roback, A.A.) Madrid, 192-?

Phil 7150.18 La psicología del suicidio. (Altavilla, Enrico.) Napoli, 1910.

Phil 6980.348 La psicología del yo y el problema de la adaptación. (Hartmann, Heinz.) México, 1961.

Phil 5465.4 La psicología della immaginazione. (Ambrosi, L.) Roma, 1898.

Phil 5325.2.5 La psicologia dell'associazione dall'Hobbes. (Ferri, L.) Roma, 1894.

Phil 181.158 Psicologia dell'avere. (Giorda, Renato.) Roma, 1968.

Phil 5465.4.10 La psicologia dell'immaginazione nella storia della filosofia. (Ambrosi, L.) Padova, 1959.

Phil 2270.175 La psicologia di Herbert Spencer. 2a ed. (Allievo, Giuseppe.) Torino, 1913.

Phil 4200.1.5F La psicologia di Pietro Pomponazzi. (Ferri, L.) Roma, 1876.

Phil 5251.72 Psicologia diferencial. (Leite, Dante M.) São Paulo, 1966.

Phil 5411.8 Psicologia do ódio. (Gonçalves Viana, Mário.) Porto, 196-.

Phil 5407.6 Psicologia do tédio. (Cruz Malpique, Manuel da.) Porto, 1963.

Phil 5246.25.3 Psicologia e biologia. 3. ed. (Gemelli, Agostino.) Firenze, 1913.

Phil 5258.44 Psicologia e filosophia. (Sarlo, Francesco de.) Firenze, 1918. 2v.

Phil 6319.1.195 Psicologia e religione nella concezione analitica di C.G. Jung. (Gemelli, A.) Milano, 1955.

Phil 7069.08.40 Psicologia e "spiritismo". (Morselli, E.) Torino, 1908. 2v.

Phil 5252.32 Psicologia elementare, ad uso dei licei. pt.1-3. (Marchesini, Giovanni.) Firenze, 1916. 2v.

Phil 5247.35.5 La psicologia fisica ed iperfisica di Hoenato Wronski. (Bertinaria, F.) Torino, 1877.

Phil 5222.2 Psicologia fisiologica. 2. ed. (Mantorani, Giuseppe.) Milano, 1905.

Phil 6319.1.250 La psicologia religiosa di Karl Jung. (Pintacuda, Luigi.) Roma, 1965.

Phil 5222.12 Psicologia sovietica. (Massucco Costa, Angiola.) Torino, 1963.

Phil 5258.140 Psicologia sperimental. (Sanctis, Sante de.) Roma, 1929-30. 2v.

Phil 5258.140.5 La psicologia sperimentale di Sante de Panctis. (Appecciafuoco, Romolo.) Roma, 1946.

Phil 2493.90 Un psicologo associazionista: E.B. de Condillac. (Mondolfo, Rodolfo.) Bologna, 1923.

Phil 25.68 Psicotécnica. Madrid. 1-5,1939-1955 3v.

Phil 6687.14 Psicoterapia por medio de la hipnosis. (Rodriquez, Rafael E.) Montevideo, 1944.

VPhil 5257.76 Psihologija. (Rostohar, Mihajlo.) Ljubljana, 1966.

Phil 6113.34 Psikhicheskie iavleniia i mozg. (Dubrovskii, David I.) Moskva, 1971.

Phil 346.31 Psikhika i intuitsiia. (Ponomarev, Iakov A.) Moskva, 1967.

Phil 5520.595 Psikholingvisticheskie edinitsy v porozhdenie rechevogo vyskazyvaniia. (Leont'ev, Aleksei A.) Moskva, 1969.

Phil 5520.510 Psikholingvistika. (Leont'ev, Aleksei A.) Leningrad, 1967.

Phil 5210.8 Psikhologicheskaia nauk a v SSSR. (Akademiia Pedagogicheskikh Nauk RSFSR, Moscow. Institut Psikhologii.) Moskva, 1959. 2v.

Phil 4773.5 Psikhologicheskaja kontseptsiia Anri Vallona. (Tutundzhian, Ovsep.) Erevan, 1966.

Phil 5520.698 Psikhologicheskie i psikholingvisticheskie problemy vladeniia i ovladeniia iazykom. Moskva, 1969.

Phil 5260.10.5 Psikhologicheskie issledovaniia. (Uznadze, Dmitrii N.) Moskva, 1966.

Phil 25.160 Psikhologicheskie issledovaniia. Moskva. 1,1969+

Phil 5238.211.5 Psikhologicheskie issledovaniia. Tbilisi, 1966.

Phil 5590.542 Psikhologicheskie problemy formirovaniia nravstvennykh kachestv lichnosti v podrostkovom vozraste. (Fel'dshtein, David I.) Dushanbe, 1969.

Phil 5545.99 Psikhologicheskie problemy uznavaniia. (Shekhter, Mark S.) Moskva, 1967.

Phil 5250.35 Psikhologiia. (Kornilov, K.N.) Moskva, 1941.

Phil 5250.35.2 Psikhologiia. (Kornilov, K.N.) Moskva, 1946.

NEDL Phil 5259.36 Psikhologiia. (Teplov, B.M.) Moskva, 1948.

Phil 25.46 Psikhologiia. Moskva. 1-5 3v.

Phil 5250.35.3 Psikhologiia. Izd. 8. (Kornilov, K.N.) Moskva, 1948.

X Cg Phil 4952.1.5 Psikhologiia bez vsiakoi metafiziki. (Vvedenskii, A.I.) Petrograd, 1915.

Phil 5400.126 Psikhologiia chuvstv. (Lakobson,P.M.) Moskva, 1956.

Phil 5585.170 Psikhologiia chuvstvennogo poznaniia. (Anan'ev, B.G.) Moskva, 1960.

Phil 5520.618 Psikhologiia grammatiki. Moskva, 1968.

Phil 25.145 Psikhologiia i tekhnika. Moskva. 1,1965+

Phil 5590.447.2 Psikhologiia lichnosti. 2. izd. (Kovalev, Aleksandr G.) Moskva, 1965.

Phil 5520.722 Psikhologiia myshleniia i kibernetika. (Brushlinskii, Andrei V.) Moskva, 1970.

Phil 5520.230 Psikhologiia rechi v sovetskoi psikhologicheskoi nauke za 40 let. (Raevskii, A.N.) Kiev, 1958.

Phil 5627.267 Psikhologiia religii. (Platonev, Konstantin K.) Moskva, 1967.

Phil 5255.62 Psikhologiia tvorcheskogo myshleniia. (Ponomarev, Ia.A.) Moskva, 1960.

Phil 5135.7.5 Psikhologiia ustanovki i kibernetika. (Bzhalava, Iosif T.) Moskva, 1966.

Phil 5218.5.5 Psikhologiia v XX stoletii. (Iaroshevskii, Mikhail G.) Moskva, 1971.

Phil 5627.269.5 Psikhologiia veruiushchikh i ateisticheskoe vospitanie. (Bukin, Viktor R.) Moskva, 1969.

Phil 5649.44 Psikhomotorika vzroslogo cheloveka. (Roze, Nina A.) Leningrad, 1970.

Phil 25.45 Psikhotekhnika i psikhofiziologiia. Moskva. 1-7,1928-1934 4v.

Phil 25.45.5 Psikhotekhnika i psikhofiziologiia. Moskva. 1-7,1928-1934

Phil 5590.530.3 Psikologiia kharaktera. 3. izd. (Levitov, Nikolai D.) Moskva, 1969.

Phil 5790.15 Psikoloji açisindan şahsiyette bir buud olarak içedönüküluk-Dişadönüklük. (Evrim, Selmin.) Istanbul, 1967.

Phil 6967.13 Psiquiatria penal y civil. (Ruiz Maya, M.) Madrid, 1931.

Phil 6953.6 La psiquiatría psicológica. (Delgado, Honorio F.) Lima, 1919.

Phil 6952.25 Psiquiatria social. (Cebold, Luis.) Lisboa, 1931.

Phil 5252.102 La psiquica y la naturaleza humana. (Matte Blanco, Ignacio.) Santiago, 1954.

Phil 5520.48 Le psittacisme et la pensée symbolique. (Dugas, L.) Paris, 1896.

Phil 5238.246 Psühholoogia ja kaasaeg. Tallinn, 1968.

Phil 9035.48 La psycantropie ou nouvelle théorie de l'homme. v.1-3. (Falconnet de la Bellonie.) Avignon, 1748.

Phil 6315.11 La psychanalyse, les médecins et le public. (Flournoy, Henri.) Neuchâtel, 1924.

Phil 25.105 La psychanalyse; recherche et enseignement freudiens de la Société française de psychanalyse. Paris. 1-7 6vv.

Phil 6322.48 La psychanalyse, son image et son public. (Moscovici, Serge.) Paris, 1961.

Phil 6315.2.82 La psychanalyse; theorie sexuelle de Freud. (Hesmard, Angelo.) Paris, 1924.

Phil 6311.8 La psychanalyse. (Blondel, C.) Paris, 1924.

Phil 6329.17 La psychanalyse. (This, Bernard.) Paris, 1960.

Phil 6315.2.79.25 Psychanalyse. 2. éd. (Freud, Sigmund.) Paris, 1965.

Phil 5465.132 Psychanalyse de l'artiste et de son oeuvre. (Dracoulidès, N.N.) Genève, 1952.

Phil 5870.30 La psychanalyse de l'enfant. (Smirnoff, Victor.) Paris, 1966.

Phil 5590.90 La psychanalyse de l'homme normal. (Richard, G.) Lausanne, 1951.

Phil 6311.48 La psychanalyse du feu. (Bachelard, Gaston.) Paris, 1965.

Phil 5627.257.5 Psychanalyse du symbole religieux. (Baudouin, Charles.) Paris, 1957.

Phil 6311.34.5 Psychanalyse et anthropologie. (Bonaparte, Marie.) Paris, 1952.

Phil 6311.34.10 Psychanalyse et biologie. 1. éd. (Bonaparte, M.) Paris, 1952.

Phil 6323.10 Psychanalyse et conception spiritualiste de l'homme. 2. ed. (Nuttin, Jozef.) Louvain, 1955.

Phil 9495.170.5 Psychanalyse et morale sexuelle. (Geets, Claude.) Paris, 1970.

Phil 6321.55 Psychanalyser, un essai sur l'ordre de l'inconscient et la pratique de la lettre. (Leclaire, Serge.) Paris, 1968.

Phil 6311.1.2 Psychanalysis; its theories. (Brill, A.A.) Philadelphia, 1914.

Phil 6311.1.3 Psychanalysis. 2. ed. (Brill, A.A.) Philadelphia, 1917.

Phil 25.26 Psyche; popular-wissenschaftliche Zeitschrift. Leipzig, 1858-63. 3v.

Phil 25.128 Psyche. Stuttgart. 1,1947+ 32v.

Phil 25.60 Psyche and Eros. N.Y. 1-2,1920-1921 2v.

Phil 5203.6 Psyche and Minerva. (Gunn, John A.) Melbourne, 1930.

Phil 6319.1.68 Psyche and symbol. (Jung, C.G.) Garden City, 1958.

Phil 6111.116.12 Psyche und Leben. (Bechterew, W. von.) Wiesbaden, 1908.

Phil 6155.20 Psychedelic drugs. N.Y., 1969.

Phil 6155.4.10 The psychedelic experience. (Leary, Timothy Francis.) New Hyde Park, 1964.

Phil 6155.4 Psychedelic prayers after the tao te ching. (Leary, Timothy Francis.) Kerhonkson, 1966.

Phil 5374.236 The psychedelic reader. (Psychedelic Review.) New Hyde Park, N.Y., 1965.

Phil 5374.236 Psychedelic Review. The psychedelic reader. New Hyde Park, N.Y., 1965.

Phil 6155.24 Psychedelic review. Cambridge, Mass. 1,1963+ 2v.

Phil 5421.50 Psyche's lamp. (Briffault, Robert.) London, 1921.

Phil 6980.458 De psychiater en zijn pratkijk. (Marlet, J.J.C.) Utrecht, 1962.

Phil 6962.1.3 Psychiatische Vorlesungen. v.2-6. (Magnan, V.) Leipzig, 1892-93.

Phil 6955.16 Psychiatria e hygiene mental. (Filho, Roch.) Maceló, 1936.

Phil 9380.3 Psychiatric aspects of civilian morale. (American Psychiatric Association. Military Mobilization Committee.) N.Y., 1942.

Phil 6980.259 Psychiatric aspects of modern warfare. (Ellery, R.S.) Melbourne, 1945.

	Phil 5204.20	Psychiatric dictionary, with encyclopedic treatment of modern terms. (Hinsée, Leland Earl.) N.Y., 1940.
	Phil 6980.712.5	The psychiatric interview. (Sullivan, Harry Stack.) N.Y., 1954.
	Phil 6980.779	Psychiatric interviews with children. (Witmer, Helen L.) N.Y., 1946.
	Phil 26.8	Psychiatric opinion. Framingham, Mass. 8,1971+
	Phil 6980.241	A psychiatric primer for the veteran's family and friends. (Dumas, A.G.) Minneapolis, 1945.
	Phil 6980.614	Psychiatric research papers read at the dedication of the laboratory. Cambridge, 1947.
	Phil 6960.5	Psychiatrie. (Kraepelin, E.) Leipzig, 1896.
	Phil 6960.5.3	Psychiatrie. (Kraepelin, E.) Leipzig, 1909-15. 4v.
	Phil 6962.5	Psychiatrie. (Meynert, T.) Wien, 1884.
	Phil 6975.1	Psychiatrie. (Ziehen, T.) Berlin, 1894.
	Phil 25.159	La psychiatrie de l'enfant. Paris. 1,1958+ 6v.
	Phil 6953.13	Psychiatrie et civilisation. (Damaye, Henri.) Paris, 1934.
	Phil 6971.4	La psychiatrie et les sciences de l'homme. (Villey, G.) Paris, 1938.
	Phil 140.50	Psychiatrie in de maatschappij. (Baan, P.A.H.) Groningen, 1957. 8 pam.
	Phil 6956.18	Psychiatrie in unserer Zeit. (Gebhard, Erwin.) Göttingen, 1969.
	Phil 8661.28.2	La psychiatrie morale et le problème de Dieu. (Guilhot, Jean.) Paris, 1967.
	Phil 8661.28	La psychiatrie morale et le problème de Dieu. Thesis. (Guilhot, Jean.) La Haye, 1967.
	Phil 1750.755	La psychiatrie phénoménologique. (Lanteri-Laura, G.) Paris, 1963.
	Phil 5238.150	Psychiatrie und Gesellschaft. (Ehrhardt, H.) Bern, 1958.
	Phil 6980.292	Die psychiatriochen Theorien Rudolf Arndt's. (Findl, Fritz.) München, 1960.
	Phil 6325.3	Psychiatriske foreläsinger. (Pontoppidan, Knud.) Kjobenhavn, 1892-95.
	Phil 6980.650	The psychiatrists. (Rogow, Arnold A.) N.Y., 1970.
	Phil 6980.326	A psychiatrist's views on social issues. (Ginsburg, S.W.) N.Y., 1963.
X Cg	Phil 6965.5	Psychiatry. (Paton, Stewart.) Philadelphia, 1905.
	Phil 6949.368	Psychiatry and art. (International Colloquium of Psychopathology of Expression, 4th, Washington, 1966.) Basel, 1968.
	Phil 6331.6	Psychiatry and Catholicism. 1st ed. (Van der Veldt, J.H.) N.Y., 1952.
	Phil 6331.6.2	Psychiatry and Catholicism. 2nd ed. (Van der Veldt, J.H.) N.Y., 1957.
	Phil 6964.2.6	Psychiatry and mental health. (Oliver, John R.) N.Y., 1933.
	Phil 8030.8	Psychiatry and psychology in the visual arts and aesthetics. (Kiell, Norman.) Madison, 1965.
	Phil 6328.28	Psychiatry and the war. 1st ed. (Sladen, F.J.) Baltimore, 1943.
	Phil 19.31	Psychiatry digest. Woodbourne. 1,1939+ 23v.
	Phil 6980.433	Psychiatry for social workers. (Lowrey, Lawson G.) N.Y., 1946.
	Phil 6980.433.2	Psychiatry for social workers. 2. ed. (Lowrey, Lawson G.) N.Y., 1952.
	Phil 6965.16	Psychiatry for the curious. (Preston, G.H.) N.Y., 1940.
	Phil 6314.6	Psychiatry in medical education. (Ebaugh, Franklin Gessford.) N.Y., 1942.
	Phil 6328.29.10	Psychiatry in modern warfare. (Strecker, E.A.) N.Y., 1945.
RRC	Phil 6980.383	Psychiatry in the Communist world. (Kiev, Ari.) N.Y., 1968.
	Phil 6980.710	Psychiatry in the modern world. (Strauss, E.B.) London, 1958.
	Phil 6322.28	Psychiatry in war. 1st ed. (Mira y López, E.) N.Y., 1943.
	Phil 6980.777	Psychiatry on the college campus. (Whittington, H.G.) N.Y., 1963.
	Phil 25.172	Psychic; a bimonthly magazine devoted to every aspect of psychic phenomena and related topics. San Francisco. 1,1969+
	Phil 7069.61.35	Psychic. (Van der Huok, P.) Indianapolis, 1961.
	Phil 7069.31.32	Psychic adventures in New York. (Whymant, A.N.J.) Boston, 1931.
	Phil 7069.10.10	A psychic autobiography. (Jones, Amanda T.) N.Y., 1910.
	Phil 7069.30.2	Psychic certainties. (Battersby, Henry F.P.) London, 1930.
	Phil 9590.5	Psychic dictatorship in America. (Bryan, G.B.) Los Angeles, 1940.
	Phil 7069.70.10	Psychic discoveries behind the Iron Curtain. (Ostrander, Sheila.) Englewood Cliffs, 1970.
	Phil 6317.31	Psychic energy, its source and goal. (Harding, M.E.) N.Y., 1947.
	Phil 6317.31.2	Psychic energy. 2. ed. (Harding, M.E.) N.Y., 1963.
	Phil 5261.6	The psychic factor; outline of psychology. (Van Norden, Charles.) N.Y., 1894.
	Phil 7069.30.17	The psychic faculties and their development. (MacGregor, Helen.) London, 1930.
	Phil 7069.26.25	The psychic in the house. (Prince, Walter Franklin.) Boston, 1926.
	Phil 55.3	Pamphlet box. Psychic investigation association.
	Phil 7069.68.20	Psychic investigator. 1st ed. (Holzer, Hans W.) N.Y., 1968.
	Phil 7069.67.30	Psychic phenomena, revelations and experiences. (Bradley, Dorothy Bomar.) West Nyack, 1967.
	Phil 8630.7.5	Psychic phenomena; science and immortality. 2. ed. (Frank, Henry.) Boston, 1916.
	Phil 7068.95.27	Psychic philosophy as the foundation of a religion of natural law. 2. ed. (Desertis, V.C.) London, 1901.
	Phil 6122.7.5	Psychic processes and muscular exercise. (Mosso, A.) n.p., 1899. 2 pam.
	Phil 25.24	The psychic research quarterly. London. 1-17,1920-1937 17v.
	Phil 7069.07.21	The psychic riddle. (Funk, Isaac K.) N.Y., 1907.
	Phil 7069.18.21	Psychic science. (Boirac, Émile.) London, 1918.
	Phil 25.65	Psychic science. London. 18-24,1939-1945 3v.
	Phil 7069.49.15	The psychic sense. (Bendit, Phoebe Daphne Payne.) N.Y., 1949.
	Phil 7072.20	The psychic structures at the Goligher Circle. (Crawford, William Jackson.) London, 1921.
	Phil 7069.18.132	Psychic tendencies of to-day. (Martin, Alfred Wilhelm.) N.Y., 1918.
	Phil 6953.12.5	Psychic treatment of nervous disorders. (Dubois, Paul.) N.Y., 1905.
	Phil 7069.20.365	The psychic world. (Carrington, H.) N.Y., 1937.
	Phil 7055.310.25	The psychic world of Bishop Pike. (Holzer, Hans W.) N.Y., 1970.

	Phil 7069.17.27	Psychical and supernormal phenomena. (Joire, Paul.) N.Y., 1917.
Htn	Phil 6332.1*	The psychical correlation of religious emotion and sexual desire. 2d ed. (Weir, J.) Louisville, Ky., 1897.
	Phil 6332.1.2	The psychical correlation of religious emotion and sexual desire. 2d ed. (Weir, J.) Louisville, Ky., 1897.
	Phil 7069.17.26	Psychical investigations. (Hill, John Arthur.) N.Y., 1917.
	Phil 7069.20.162	Psychical miscellanea. (Hill, John A.) London, 1919.
	Phil 7069.20.160	Psychical miscellanea. (Hill, John A.) N.Y., 1920.
	Phil 7069.19.45	Psychical phenomena. (Carrington, Hereward.) N.Y., 1919.
	Phil 7069.11.10	Psychical research. (Barrett, William F.) N.Y., 1911.
	Phil 7069.33.60	Psychical research. (Driesch, Hans.) London, 1933.
	Phil 7069.56	Psychical research. (Johnson, R.C.) N.Y., 1956.
	Phil 7069.08.22	Psychical research and the resurrection. (Hyslop, James Hervey.) Boston, 1908.
	Phil 7069.20.192	Psychical research for the plain man. (Kingsford, S.M.) London, 1920.
	Phil 7069.54.10	Psychical research today. (West, D.J.) London, 1954.
	Phil 25.10	Psychical review. Boston. 1-8
	Phil 7068.93.15	Psychics; facts and theories. (Savage, Minot J.) Boston, 1893.
	Phil 7069.35	Psychics and mediums. (Tubby, G.O.) Boston, 1935.
	Phil 3850.13.40	Psychische Anthropologie. (Schulze, G.E.) Göttingen, 1816.
	Phil 3850.13.44	Psychische Anthropologie. (Schulze, G.E.) Göttingen, 1826.
	Phil 3850.13.42	Psychische Anthropologie. 2. Aufl. (Schulze, G.E.) Göttingen, 1819.
	Phil 6980.768	Psychische bijwerkings verschijnselen van moltergan. (Verster, Justus.) Assen, 1967.
	Phil 5247.28	Die psychische Dingwelt. (Haas, Wilhelm.) Bonn, 1921.
	Phil 5258.152	Der psychische Gegenstand. (Salber, Wilhelm.) Bonn, 1959.
	Phil 6325.9	Psychische Grenzzustände. 3. Aufl. (Pelman, Carl.) Bonn, 1912.
X Cg	Phil 7075.132	Die psychische Importenz des Mannes. (Bergler, E.) Bern, 1937.
NEDL	Phil 25.30	Psychische Studien. Leipzig. 1-26,1874-1899 26v.
	Phil 5440.18	Die psychische Vererbung. (Josefovici, U.) Leipzig, 1912.
	Phil 6121.10.5	Die psychischen Massmethoden. (Lipps, G.F.) Braunschweig, 1906.
	Phil 6159.10	Die psychischen Phänomene im Schwellenbereich des Meshalin. Inaug. Diss. (Kreppel, Gisela Richters.) Bonn, 1964.
	Phil 6954.2	Die psychischen Störungen. (Emminghaus, H.) Tübingen, 1887.
	Phil 6113.15	Die psychischen Zustände. (Domrich, O.) Jena, 1849.
	Phil 7068.99.33	Psychism; analysis of things existing. 3. ed. (Gibier, P.) N.Y., 1899.
	Phil 5815.8	Le psychisme animal. (Filloux, Jean Claude.) Paris, 1959.
	Phil 7068.95.15	Le psychisme expérimental. (Erny, Alfred.) Paris, 1895.
	Phil 5812.10.5	Psychisme humain et psychisme animal. 2e ed. (Chauchard, Paul.) Paris, 1961.
	Phil 6956.11	Le psychisme inférieur. 2. éd. (Grasset, Joseph.) Paris, 1913.
	Phil 7069.11.30	Psychisms through Anvernetta Greene. (Greene, Anvernetta (pseud.).) Newark, 1911.
	Phil 25.9.9	Psychlogical review. Psychological index, 1894-1935. Lancaster, N.Y., n.d. 24v.
	Phil 6316.12.20	Psycho-analysis; a handbook for medical practitioners and students of comparitive psychology. 2d ed. (Glover, Edward.) London, 1949.
	Phil 6317.7	Psycho-analysis. (Hingley, R.H.) London, 1921.
X Cg	Phil 6321.3.2	Psycho-analysis. (Low, Barbara.) London, 1920.
	Phil 6332.9	Psycho-analysis and art. (Whitehead, George.) London, 1930.
	Phil 6328.44	Psycho-analysis and contemporary thought. (Sutherland, John D.) London, 1958.
	Phil 6322.4.15	Psycho-analysis and its derivations. (Miller, Hugh C.) London, 1933.
	Phil 6321.5A	Psycho-analysis and its unconscious. (Lawrence, David Herbert.) N.Y., 1921.
	Phil 6315.2.109	Psycho-analysis and social psychology. (McDougall, William.) London, 1936.
	Phil 6315.1.5	Psycho-analysis and the war neurosis. Photoreproduction. (Ferenczi, Sandor.) London, 1921.
	Phil 6330.1	Psycho-analysis for all. (Urbantschitsch, R.) London, 1928.
	Phil 6312.7	Psycho-analysis for normal people. (Coster, Geraldine.) London, 1926.
	Phil 6312.7.5	Psycho-analysis for normal people. 3. ed. (Coster, Geraldine.) N.Y., 1947.
	Phil 6325.1.10	Psycho-analysis in the service of education. (Pfister, Oskar.) London, 1922.
	Phil 5585.130	The psycho-analysis of artistic vision and hearing. (Ehrenzweig, Anton.) London, 1953.
	Phil 5585.130.2	The psycho-analysis of artistic vision and hearing. 2d ed. (Ehrenzweig, Anton.) N.Y., 1965.
	Phil 6313.8	Psycho-analysis of the neuroses. (Deutsch, Helene.) London, 1932.
	Phil 6321.11	Psycho-analysis today. (Lorand, Sándor.) London, 1933.
	Phil 6321.11.10	Psycho-analysis today. (Lorand, Sándor.) N.Y., 1944.
	Phil 6315.2.28	A psycho-analytic dialogue. (Freud, Sigmund.) London, 1965.
	Phil 6315.24	The psycho-analytic reader. (Fliess, R.) London, 1950.
	Phil 5257.59	Psycho-astrologische Encyclopedie. (Ram, T.) Lochem, 1950-51. 2v.
	Phil 6117.13	Psycho-biologie et energétique. (Henry, M. Charles.) Paris, 1909.
	Phil 5520.65	The psycho-biology of language. (Zipf, G.K.) Boston, 1935.
	Phil 4803.462.50	Psycho-fizjologiuzna teorja poznania i jejkrytyka. (Ingarden, Roman.) Lwów, 1930.
	Phil 5241.166	Psycho-logica. (Bijkerk, R.J.) Amsterdam, 1962.
	Phil 5203.5	Psycho-pathological references, English and American.
	Phil 6322.29.3	Psycho-physiological studies at high altitude in the Andes. (McFarland, R.A.) Baltimore, 1937.
	Phil 5926.1.18	La psycho-physiologie de Gall. Thèse. (Blondell, Charles.) Paris, 1913.
	Phil 5402.6	Psycho-physiologie de la douleur. (Ioteyko, I.) Paris, 1909.
	Phil 8886.44	The psycho-physiology of the moral imperative. (Leuba, J.H.) n.p., 1897.
	Phil 348.5.5	Das psycho-physische Problem. (Reininger, R.) Wien, 1916.
	Phil 5627.260.13	Psycho-sociologie de l'appartenance religieuse. 3. ed. (Carrier, Hervé.) Rome, 1966.
	Phil 6689.3	Psycho-therapeutics. (Tuckey, C.L.) London, 1890.
	Phil 6311.14	Die Psychoanalyse; eine Kritik. (Bumke, Oswald.) Berlin, 1931.

Phil 6309.8 — Psychoanalyse; zum 60. Geburtstag von Alexander Mitscherlich. Frankfurt am Main, 1968.

Phil 6310.3 — Die Psychoanalyse. (Aster, E.) Berlin, 1930.

Phil 6332.34 — Psychoanalyse: Geschichte, Wesen. 2. Aufl. (Wanke, Georg.) Halle, 1926.

Phil 6321.30 — Psychoanalyse de l'antisémitisme. 1. éd. (Loewenstein, R.) Paris, 1952.

Phil 8666.22 — Psychoanalyse de l'atéisme moderne. (Lepp, Ignace.) Paris, 1961.

Phil 6310.4.4 — Psychoanalyse der Gesamtpersönlichkeit. (Alexander, Franz G.) Leipzig, 1927.

Phil 6313.8.5 — Psychoanalyse der Neurosen. (Deutsch, Helene.) Wien, 1930.

Phil 6320.11.5 — Die Psychoanalyse des Kindes. (Klein, M.) Wien, 1932.
NEDL Phil 6967.1.5 — La psychoanalyse des névroses. (Regis, E.) Paris, 1914.
Phil 6311.37 — Psychoanalyse und Daseinsanalytik. (Boss, Medard.) Bern, 1957.

Phil 6315.5 — Psychoanalyse und ethik. (Furtmüller, Carl.) München, 1912.

Phil 6317.27 — Psychoanalyse und Logik. (Hermann, Imre.) Leipzig, 1924.
Phil 6323.12 — Psychoanalyse und Personlichkeit. (Nuttin, Jozef.) Freiburg, 1956.

Phil 6322.55 — Psychoanalyse und Politik. (Marcuse, Herbert.) Frankfurt, 1968.

Phil 6980.113 — Psychoanalyse und soziale Erziehung. (Bittner, Günther.) München, 1967.

Phil 6323.26 — Psychoanalyse und Soziologie. (Nolte, Helmut.) Bern, 1970.

Phil 6980.687 — Psychoanalyse und Symbolik. (Phillips, J.H.) Bern, 1962.
Phil 6325.1.20 — Psychoanalyse und Weltanschauung. (Pfister, Oskar.) Leipzig, 1928.

Phil 6328.12 — Psychoanalyse und Yoga. (Schmitz, O.A.H.) Darmstadt, 1923.

Phil 6316.13 — Psychoanalyses d'hier et d'aujourd'hui comme thérapeutiques. (Gratton, Henri.) Paris, 1955.

Phil 6317.5 — Psychoanalysis, its history, theory and practice. (Tridon, André.) N.Y., 1919.

Phil 6329.1.10 — Psychoanalysis; its history, theory and practice. (Tridon, André.) N.Y., 1920.

Phil 6329.1.9 — Psychoanalysis; its history, theory and practice. (Tridon, André.) N.Y., 1923.

Phil 7084.4.10 — Psychoanalysis, sleep and dreams. (Tridon, André.) N.Y., 1921.

Phil 6315.2.410 — Psychoanalysis; the first ten years. (Stewart, Walter A.) N.Y., 1967.

Phil 6317.38 — Psychoanalysis. (Hook, Sidney.) N.Y., 1959.
Phil 6328.17 — Psychoanalysis. (Sachs, Wulf.) London, 1934.
Phil 25.15.5 — Psychoanalysis. N.Y. 1953-1958 5v.
Phil 6329.1.3 — Psychoanalysis and behavior. (Tridon, André.) N.Y., 1920.
Phil 5238.22 — Psychoanalysis and culture. (Wilbur, G.B.) N.Y., 1951.
Phil 6316.23 — Psychoanalysis and current biological thought. (Greenfield, Norman S.) Madison, 1965.

Phil 6311.37.5 — Psychoanalysis and daseinsanalysis. (Boss, Medard.) N.Y., 1963.

Phil 6315.38 — Psychoanalysis and ethics. (Feuer, L.S.) Springfield, 1955.

Phil 6327.34 — Psychoanalysis and existential philosophy. (Ruitenbeek, H.M.) N.Y., 1962.

Phil 6315.2.57 — Psychoanalysis and faith. (Freud, Sigmund.) London, 1963.
Phil 6315.2.57.1 — Psychoanalysis and faith. (Freud, Sigmund.) N.Y., 1964.
Phil 6328.33A — Psychoanalysis and group behavior. 1st ed. (Scheidlinger, S.) N.Y., 1952.

Phil 6329.1.12 — Psychoanalysis and man's unconscious motives. (Tridon, André.) N.Y., 1924.

Phil 6328.16 — Psychoanalysis and medicine. (Stephen, Karin.) Cambridge, Eng., 1933.

Phil 6980.348.10 — Psychoanalysis and moral values. (Hartmann, Heinz.) N.Y., 1960.

Phil 9450.24 — Psychoanalysis and politics. (Money-Kyrle, R.E.) N.Y., 1951.

Phil 6980.309.5 — Psychoanalysis and psychotherapy. (Fromm-Reichmann, Frieda.) Chicago, 1959.

Phil 6315.19.16 — Psychoanalysis and religion. (Fromm, Erich.) New Haven, 1971.

Phil 6335.15.5 — Psychoanalysis and religion. (Zilboorg, Gregory.) N.Y., 1962.

Phil 6317.45 — Psychoanalysis and social research; the psychoanalytic study of the non-patient. (Hendin, Herbert.) Garden City, 1965.

Phil 6327.32 — Psychoanalysis and social science. (Ruitenbeek, H.M.) N.Y., 1962.

Phil 6319.6 — Psychoanalysis and the drama. (Jelliffe, S.E.) N.Y., 1922.

Phil 6322.46 — Psychoanalysis and the human situation. 1st ed. (Marmorston, Jessie.) N.Y., 1964.

Phil 6540.2 — Psychoanalysis and the psychic disorder of general paresis. (Hollós, Stefom.) N.Y., 1925.

Phil 25.78 — Psychoanalysis and the social sciences. London. 1-5, 1947-1958 4v.

Phil 6317.35 — Psychoanalysis as science. (Hilgard, E.R.) N.Y., 1956.
Phil 6311.12 — Psychoanalysis explained and criticized. (Baker, A.E.) London, 1926.

Phil 6315.17.8 — Psychoanalysis for teachers and parents. (Freud, Anna.) Boston, 1960.

Phil 6328.58 — Psychoanalysis in America. (Sherman, Murray Herbert.) Springfield, 1966.

Phil 6327.15.5 — Psychoanalysis of behavior; collected papers. (Rado, Sandor.) N.Y., 1956.

Phil 6327.6 — Psychoanalysis of the "reformer". (Rinaldo, Joel.) N.Y., 1921.

Phil 6310.4.5 — The psychoanalysis of the total personality. (Alexander, Franz G.) N.Y., 1930.

Phil 6325.21 — Psychoanalytic clinical interpretation. (Paul, Louis.) N.Y., 1963.

Phil 8411.29A — Psychoanalytic exploration in art. (Kris, Ernst.) London, 1953.

Phil 25.146 — The psychoanalytic forum. Beverly Hills, Calif. 1,1966+ 2v.

Phil 5593.54.20 — Psychoanalytic interpretation in Rorschach testing. (Schofer, Roy.) N.Y., 1954.

Phil 6325.1.3 — The psychoanalytic method. (Pfister, Oskar.) London, 1915.

Phil 6325.1 — The psychoanalytic method. (Pfister, Oskar.) N.Y., 1917.
Phil 6965.17 — Psychoanalytic orientation in case work. N.Y., 1944.
Phil 6310.4.35 — Psychoanalytic pioneers. (Alexander, Franz G.) N.Y., 1966.

Phil 5238.28 — Psychoanalytic psychiatry and psychology. (Austen Riggs Center, Stockbridge, Massachusetts.) N.Y., 1,1954

Phil 25.67 — Psychoanalytic quarterly. Albany, N.Y. 2,1968+ 47v.
Phil 25.67.2 — Psychoanalytic quarterly. Cumulative index, 1-35,1932-1966. n.p., n.d.

Phil 25.16 — Psychoanalytic review. N.Y. 1,1913+ 49v.
Phil 25.16.3 — Psychoanalytic review. Subject author index, v.1-18,1913-1931. Washington, n.d.

Phil 6315.2.382 — The psychoanalytic revolution. (Robert, Marthe.) London, 1966.

Phil 6328.50 — The psychoanalytic situation. (Stone, Leo.) N.Y., 1961.
Phil 25.78.10 — The psychoanalytic study of society. N.Y. 1,1960+ 3v.
Phil 5870.5 — The psychoanalytic study of the child. N.Y. 1,1945+ 23v.

Phil 6316.14.10 — Psychoanalytic theory, therapy, and the self. (Guntrip, Henry James Samuel.) N.Y., 1971.
Phil 6315.16.10 — The psychoanalytic theory of neurosis. (Fenichel, Otto.) N.Y., 1945.

Phil 6310.4.20 — Psychoanalytic threapy. (Alexander, Franz G.) N.Y., 1946.
Phil 6315.2.111.5 — Psychoanalytical method and the doctrine of Freud. v.1. v.2 lost. (Dalbiez, R.) N.Y., 1941.

Phil 25.120 — Die psychoanalytische Bewegung. Wien. 1,1929+ 4v.
Phil 6320.2 — Psychoanalytische Probleme. (Kaplan, Leo.) Leipzig, 1916.
Phil 5850.214.15 — Psychoanalytische Psychotechnik. (Giese, Fritz.) Leipzig, 1924.

Phil 6316.8.20 — Psychoanalytische Schriften zur Literatur und Kunst. (Groddeck, Georg.) Wiesbaden, 1964.

Phil 6316.8.10 — Psychoanalytische Schriften zur Psychsomatik. (Groddeck, Georg.) Wiesbaden, 1966.

Phil 6310.2.16 — Psychoanalytische Studien zur Charakterbildung und andere Schriften. (Abraham, Karl.) Frankfurt, 1969. 2v.

Phil 6315.18 — Das psychoanalytische Volksbuch. (Federn, Paul.) Bern, 1939.

Phil 6315.18.4 — Das psychoanalytische Volksbuch. 5. Aufl. (Federn, Paul.) Bern, 1957.

Phil 6980.489 — Psychobiology. (Meyer, Adolf.) Springfield, 1957.
Phil 25.23 — Psychobiology. Baltimore. 1-2,1917-1920 2v.
Phil 7069.68.65 — Psychocybernetica. (Lietaert, Peerbolte, Maarten.) Amsterdam, 1968.

Phil 5593.60 — Psychodiagnostisches Vademecum. (Bahm, Ewald B.) Bern, 1906.

Phil 6980.335.20 — Psychodrama and audience attitude change. (Greenberg, Ira A.) Beverly Hills, 1968.

Phil 6980.130 — Le psychodrame et la vie. (Baur, Pierre.) Paris, 1968.
Phil 5625.79 — Das psychogalvanische Reflexphänomen. (Veraguth, Otto.) Berlin, 1909.

Phil 7077.4 — Psychography. (Moses, William S.) London, 1878.
Phil 7077.4.2 — Psychography. 2d ed. (Moses, William S.) London, 1882.
Phil 5520.428A — Psycholinguistics; a survey of theory and research problems. (Social Science Research Committee on Linguistics and Psychology.) Bloomington, 1965.

Phil 5520.626 — Psycholinguistics. (Deese, James Earle.) Boston, 1970.
Phil 5520.758 — Psycholinguistics. (DeVito, Joseph A.) Indianapolis, 1971.

Phil 5520.365 — Psycholinguistics. (Saporta, Sol.) N.Y., 1961.
Phil 5520.736 — Psycholinguistics. (Slobin, Dan Isaac.) Glenview, Ill., 1971.

Phil 5520.560 — Psycholinguistics: experiments in spontaneous speech. (Eisler, Frieda Goldman.) London, 1968.

Phil 5520.462 — Psycholinguistics papers. (Edinburgh. University. Faculty of Social Sciences. Research Board. Conference on Psycholinguistics, 1966.) Edinburgh, 1966.

Phil 5870.65 — Psychologen over het kind. Groningen, 1968.
Phil 5252.18.13 — Psychologi. (McDougall, William.) København, 1926.
Phil 5258.76.3 — Psychologi. 3. udg. (Starcke, C.N.) København, 1923.
Phil 6317.2.10 — Psychologi och moral. 2a uppl. (Hadfield, J.A.) Stockholm, 1924.

Phil 5255.82 — Psychologia. (Papanoutsos, Euangelos.) Athēnai, 1970.
Htn Phil 3110.80* — Psychologia. (Werdenhagen, I.G.) Amsterdam, 1632.
Phil 25.95 — Psychologia. Jahrbuck. Zürich. 1955
Phil 5275.5 — Psychológia a kybernetika. (Striženec, Michal.) Bratislava, 1966.

Phil 5238.207 — Psychológia a nicktoré otázky súčasnosti. Bratislava, 1962.

Phil 3910.35 — Psychologia empirica. (Wolff, Christian von.) Francofurti, 1732.

Phil 3910.35.5F — Psychologia empirica. (Wolff, Christian von.) Veronae, 1736.

Phil 5262.60 — Psychologia metaphysica, in Usum scholarum. (Willwoll, Alexander.) Friburgi, 1952.

Phil 5627.261.15 — Psychologia philosophica. (Muñoz, Jesu.) Santander, 1961.
Htn Phil 3910.40* — Psychologia rationalis. (Wolff, Christian von.) Francofurti, 1734.

Phil 3910.40.5 — Psychologia rationalis. (Wolff, Christian von.) Veronae, 1737.

Phil 5725.5 — Psychologia rozumienia. (Międzynarodowego Sympozjum Poświęcone Psychologia Rozumienia, Krakow, 1965.) Warszawa, 1968.

Phil 6328.64 — Psychologic cues in forecasting physical illness. (Silverman, Samuel.) N.Y., 1970.

Phil 25.100 — Psychologica belgica; annales de la Société belge de psychologie. Louvain. 1,1946+ 6v.
Phil 25.35 — Psychological abstracts. Lancaster, Pennsylvania. 1,1927+ 41v.

Phil 7082.188.1 — Psychological and biological foundations of dream-interpretation. (Lowy, Samuel.) London, 1946.

Phil 6320.12 — Psychological and neurological definitions and the unconcious. (Kahn, S.) Boston, 1940.

Phil 5520.360 — Psychological and psychiatric aspects of speech and hearing. (Barbara, Dominick A.) Springfield, 1960.

Phil 6330.2 — A psychological approach to abnormal behavior. (Ullmann, Leonard P.) Englewood, Cliffs, 1969.

Phil 720.23 — The psychological approach to reality. (Aveling, Francis.) London, 1929.

Phil 5238.210 — Psychological approaches to intergroup and international understanding. (Interamerican Congress of Psychology. 3rd, Austin, Texas, 1955.) Austin, 1956.

Phil 6121.40 — Psychological approaches to social behavior. (Leiderman, P.H.) Manford, 1964.

Phil 8620.19 — The psychological aspect of...sin and salvation. (Willcox, I.L.) Oxford, 1910.

Phil 5627.24 — Psychological aspects of Christian experience. (Gill, E.H.K.) Springfield, 1915.

Phil 6110.30 — Psychological aspects of stress. Springfield, Ill., 1970.
Phil 5350.5.5 — The psychological aspects of the aging process with sociological implications. (Geist, Harold.) St. Louis, 1968.

Phil 5250.37.6 — Psychological atlas. (Katz, David.) N.Y., 1948.
Phil 25.87 — Psychological book preview. Princeton. 1-2,1951-1952 2v.

Phil 25.9.15   Psychological bulletin (literary section of Psychological Review). N.Y. 1,1904+ 73v.

Phil 25.72   Psychological clinic. Philadelphia. 1-23,1907-1935 18v.

Phil 4757.2.100   Psychological commentaries on the teaching of G.I. Gurdjieff and P.D. Ouspensky. (Nicoll, Maurice.) London, 1955-57. 5v.

Phil 5850.279.13   Psychological conceptions in other sciences. (Myers, Charles S.) Oxford, 1929.

Phil 5822.4.3   Psychological development. (Muan, N.L.) Boston, 1938.

Phil 5262.55   Psychological differentiation. (Within, Herman A.) N.Y., 1962.

Phil 5627.5   The psychological elements of religious faith. (Everett, C.C.) N.Y., 1902.

VPhil 5205.2   Pamphlet box. Psychological essays.

Phil 5520.26   The psychological experiences connected with the different parts of speech. (Rowland, Eleanor H.) Lancaster, 1907.

Phil 5241.78   Psychological experiments. (Breitwieser, Joseph V.) Colorado Springs, 1914.

Phil 5245.86   Psychological explanation. (Fodor, Jerry A.) N.Y., 1968.

Phil 5249.13.15   Psychological factors determining human behavior. (Jung, Carl G.) Cambridge, 1937.

Phil 6322.15   Psychological factors in the pastoral treatement of scruples. (Mullen, J.J.) n.p., 1927.

Phil 575.96   Psychological foundations of personality. (Thorpe, L.P.) N.Y., 1938.

Phil 5250.36A   The psychological frontiers of society. (Kardiner, Abram.) N.Y., 1945.

Phil 5886.5   Psychological functioning in the normal aging and senile aged. Basel, 1968.

Phil 6959.1.18   Psychological healing. (Janet, Pierre.) N.Y., 1925. 2v.

Phil 25.9.12   Psychological index. Abstrast references of volumes 1-35,1894-1928. Colombia, n.d. 2v.

Phil 5241.16   Psychological inquiries. (Brodie, B.C.) London, 1854.
Phil 5241.16.2   Psychological inquiries. (Brodie, B.C.) London, 1856.
Phil 5241.16.4   Psychological inquiries. (Brodie, B.C.) London, 1862.
Phil 525.20   A psychological interpretation of mysticism. Diss. (Hamilton, C.H.) Chicago, 1916.

Phil 25.130   Psychological issues. N.Y. 1,1959+ 10v.
Phil 5255.6   Psychological Laboratory. Bedford College for Women. University of London. Psychological studies. London, 1914.

Phil 6311.4.2   Psychological methods of healing. (Brown, William.) London, 1938.

Phil 25.9.5   Psychological monographs. Lancaster, N.Y. 8,1907+ 70v.

Phil 5643.100   Psychological optics. (Grant, V.W.) Chicago, 1938.
Phil 5627.20.5   The psychological origin and the nature of religion. (Leuba, J.H.) London, 1909.

Phil 5627.20.6   The psychological origin and the nature of religion. (Leuba, J.H.) London, 1921.

VPhil 5205.1   Pamphlet box. Psychological papers.
Phil 5245.22   Psychological papers. (Ferrari, G.C.) Reggio, 1896-1900.
Phil 25.173   Psychological perspectives; an interpretive review. Los Angeles. 1,1970+

Phil 5627.16   The psychological phenomenon of Christianity. (Cutten, G.B.) N.Y., 1908.

Phil 5262.19   Psychological principles. (Ward, James.) Cambridge, 1918.
Phil 5262.19.3A   Psychological principles. 2d ed. (Ward, James.) Cambridge, Eng., 1920.

Phil 6328.35   Psychological problems in mental deficiency. (Sarason, S.B.) N.Y., 1949.

Phil 6328.35.5   Psychological problems in mental deficiency. 3d ed. (Sarason, S.B.) N.Y., 1959.

Phil 5850.391   Psychological racketeers. (Yates, Dorothy H.) Boston, 1932.

Phil 5249.13.27   Psychological reflections. (Jung, Carl G.) N.Y., 1953.
Phil 5203.8A   The psychological register. v.2-3. (Murchison, C.A.) Worcester, 1929.

Phil 5203.8   The psychological register. v.3. (Murchison, C.A.) Worcester, 1932.

Phil 42.12   Psychological report. (Canterbury. University College, Christchurch, New Zealand. Department of Psychology.)

Phil 25.141F   Psychological research bulletin. Lund. 4,1964+ 2v.
Phil 5212.15   Psychological research in Communist China, 1949-1966. (Chin, Robert.) Cambridge, Mass., 1969.

Phil 5238.211   Psychological research in the U.S.S.R. Moscow, 1966.
Phil 25.9   Psychological review. Lancaster, N.Y. 1,1894+ 73v.
Phil 25.22   The psychological review. London. 1-5 5v.
Phil 25.9.6   Psychological review. Philosophical monographs. Lancaster, N.Y. 1908-1916

Phil 64.1   The psychological review and studies from Yale psychological laboratory. v.1., no.1-2 and supplement. (Yale Psychological Studies.) New Haven, n.d. 3v.

Phil 70.77   Psychological scaling: theory and applications. (Conference on Psychological Scaling, Princeton, New Jersey.) N.Y., 1960.

Phil 52.4   Psychological series. (Montana. University.) Missoula, 1908.

Phil 55.8   Psychological Society of Great Britain. Papers. London. 1875-1876

Phil 5272.24   Psychological statistics. (Courts, Frederick A.) Homewood, Ill., 1966.

Phil 6121.41   Psychological stress and the coping process. (Lazarus, Richards.) N.Y., 1966.

Phil 5246.28   Psychological studies. (Gale, Harlow.) Minneapolis, 1900.
Phil 5255.6   Psychological studies. (Psychological Laboratory. Bedford College for Women. University of London.) London, 1914.

Phil 25.57   Psychological studies. Budapest.
Phil 25.50   Psychological studies. Mysore. 1,1926
Phil 25.50.5   Psychological studies. Mysore. 1,1956+ 6v.
Phil 5238.184   Psychological studies. The Hague. 1,1961+ 6v.
Phil 5238.185   Psychological studies. Minor series. The Hague. 1,1967+
Phil 5251.8.15   Psychological studies. 2d ed. (Lipps, T.) Baltimore, 1926.

Phil 5238.140   Psychological studies of human development. (Kuhlen, Raymond.) N.Y., 1952.

Phil 5627.65   Psychological studies of religious questions. (Flower, John C.) London, 1924.

Phil 5500.33   A psychological study of problem solving. (Geer, J.P. van de.) Amsterdam, 1957.

Phil 5627.20   A psychological study of religion. (Leuba, J.H.) N.Y., 1912.

Phil 5627.152   A psychological study of religious conversion. (Jones, W.L.) London, 1937.

Phil 5520.458   A psychological study of symbolism in word association and symbolic meaning of words. (Wit, Gerard Antonius de.) Eindhoven, 1962.

Phil 6960.15   Psychological techniques in diagnosis and evaluation. (Kahn, Theodore.) N.Y., 1960.

Phil 5238.170   Psychological theory. (Marx, Melvin Herman.) N.Y., 1961.
Phil 5252.69.25   Psychological thought from Pythagoras to Freud. 1st. ed. (Murphy, Gardner.) N.Y., 1968.

Phil 5249.13   Psychological types. (Jung, Carl G.) London, 1923.
Phil 5249.13.5   Psychological types. (Jung, Carl G.) n.p., 192-.
Phil 5876.18   The psychological world of the teen-ager. (Offer, Daniel.) N.Y., 1969.

Phil 5258.149   Psychologie; Grundlagen und Aufbau. (Suter, Jules.) Frauenfeld, 1942.

Phil 5252.33.5   Psychologie; grundrids til brug. (Monrad, Marcus.) Christiania, 1892.

Phil 5258.77   Psychologie, indledet ved almindelig biologie, i sammentroengt fremstilling. (Sibbern, F.C.) Kjøbenhavn, 1856.

Phil 5275.7   Psychologie, philosophie, Menschenbild. (Domin, Georg.) Halle, 1964.

Phil 5240.7.10   Psychologie. (Anschütz, Georg.) Hamburg, 1953.
Phil 5241.102   Psychologie. (Beck, M.) Leiden, 1938.
Phil 5241.26   Psychologie. (Boucher, J.) Paris, 1908.
Phil 5242.8   Psychologie. (Cornelius, H.) Leipzig, 1897.
Phil 5243.52   Psychologie. (Daval, Simone.) Paris, 1956. 2v.
Phil 5243.5.5   La psychologie. (Delboeuf, J.R.L.) Paris, 1876.
Phil 5243.65   Psychologie. (Dirks, Heinz.) Gütersloh, 1960.
Phil 5243.17   Psychologie. (Dubot, T.) Paris, 1897.
Phil 5244.9.5   Psychologie. (Erismann, T.) Berlin, 1920.
Phil 5244.3   Psychologie. (Eschenmayer, C.A.A.) Stuttgart, 1817.
Phil 5244.4   Psychologie. (Esser, W.) Münster, 1854.
Phil 5245.70   Psychologie. (Fichte, Immanuel Hermann.) Leipzig, 1864-73. 2v.
Phil 5246.43   Psychologie. (Guillaume, Paul.) Paris, 1931.
Phil 3310.5.32   Die Psychologie. (Gutberlet, C.) Münster, 1881.
Phil 5247.25   Psychologie. (Harms, F.) Leipzig, 1897.
Phil 5249.2.13   Psychologie. (James, William.) Leipzig, 1909.
Phil 5251.62   Psychologie. (Lamouche, André.) Paris, 1957.
Phil 5252.28   Psychologie. (Messer, A.) Stuttgart, 1914.
Phil 5255.60   Die Psychologie. (Piela, Franz.) Köln, 1959.
NEDL Phil 5257.8   Die Psychologie. (Röse, F.) Göttingen, 1856.
Phil 5258.89.5   Psychologie. (Schjelderup, H.) Berlin, 1928.
Phil 5258.63   Psychologie. (Stöhr, Adolf.) Wien, 1917.
Phil 5258.144   Psychologie. (Störring, G.) Leipzig, 1923.
Phil 5243.72   Psychologie: Modell und Wirklichkeit. (Dembicki, Leo.) Bodman/Bodensee, 1969.

Phil 1504.6   Die Psychologie. v.6, pt.1. (Ostler, H.) Münster, 1906.
Phil 5246.19   Die Psychologie. 2. Aufl. (Gutberlet, C.) Münster, 1890.
Phil 5247.33.2   Die Psychologie. 2. Aufl. (Hecke, Gustav.) Braunschweig, 1919.
Phil 5252.28.2   Psychologie. 2. Aufl. (Messer, A.) Stuttgart, 1920.
Phil 5252.100   Psychologie. 2. Aufl. (Metzger, W.) Darmstadt, 1954.
Phil 5247.23.20   Psychologie. 2e Aufl. (Höfler, Alois.) Wien, 1930.
Phil 1504.4.5A   Die Psychologie Alberts des Grossen. v.4, pt.5-6. v.1 rejected 1971. (Schneider, A.) Münster, 1906.

Phil 1020.13   Die Psychologie Alhazens. (Bauer, H.) Münster, 1911.
Phil 1504.10.5   Die Psychologie Alhazens. v.10, pt.5. (Bauer, H.) Münster, n.d.

Phil 5227.2   La psychologie allemande contemporaine. (Ribot, T.) Paris, 1879.
Phil 5227.2.3   La psychologie allemande contemporaine. 2. éd. (Ribot, T.) Paris, 1885.
Phil 5249.1   Psychologie als Grundwissenschaft der Pädagogik. (Jahn, M.) Leipzig, 1883.
Phil 5249.1.2   Psychologie als Grundwissenschaft der Pädagogik. (Jahn, M.) Leipzig, 1897.
Phil 5247.39   Die Psychologie als Selbsterkenntnisslehre. (Heinroth, J.C.A.) Leipzig, 1827.
Phil 3428.47   Psychologie als Wissenschaft. (Herbart, J.F.) Königsberg, 1824. 2v.
Phil 9500.10.5   Psychologie am Krankenbett. (Hárdi, István.) Budapest, 1968.
Phil 5227.1   La psychologie anglaise contemporaine. (Ribot, T.) Paris, 1870.
Phil 5816.13   La psychologie animale. (Guillaume, P.) Paris, 1940.
Phil 2465.31   La psychologie animale de Charles Bonnet. (Claparède, E.) Genève, 1909.
Phil 5845.2   La psychologie applique en Afrique; bibliographie. (Descloitres, Claudine.) Aix-en-Provence, 1968.
Phil 5850.136   La psychologie appliquée. 3. éd. (Binois, René.) Paris, 1952.
Phil 5257.9   Psychologie as a natural science. (Raue, C.G.) Philadelphia, 1889.
Phil 1050.17   Pamphlet box. Die Psychologie bei den judischen Religions.
Phil 2475.1.284   La psychologie bergsonienne; étude critique. (Lacombe, R.E.) Paris, 1933.
Phil 1504.6.4   Die Psychologie bonaventuras. v.6, pt.4-5. (Lutz, E.) Münster, 1909.
Phil 5829.1   Psychologie comparée. (Tissot, C.J.) Paris, 1878.
Phil 5815.2.5.2   Psychologie comparée. 2e éd. (Flourens, Pierre.) Paris, 1864.
Phil 5215.5   La psychologie contemporaine. (Foulquié, Paul.) Paris, 1951.
Phil 5243.66   Psychologie contemporaine et pensée chrétienne. (Daujat, J.) Tournai, 1962.
Phil 6310.1.90   La psychologie d'Alfred Adler. (Ganz, M.) Neuchâtel, 1935.
Phil 5222.9   La psychologie dans le monde moderne. (Muller, Philippe.) Bruxelles, 1964.
Phil 5211.5   La psychologie d'aujourd'hui. (Bierviet, J.J. van.) Paris, 1927.
Phil 2493.92   La psychologie de Condillac. (LeRoy, Georges.) Paris, 1937.
Phil 2493.92.5   La psychologie de Condillac. Thèse. (LeRoy, Georges.) Paris, 1937.
Phil 2490.110   Psychologie de deux messies positivistes Saint-Simon et Auguste Comte. (Dumas, G.) Paris, 1905.
Phil 5627.27   La psychologie de la conversion. (Mainage, T.) Paris, 1915.
Phil 5627.97   La psychologie de la conversion chez les peuples noncivilisés. (Allier, Raoul.) Paris, 1925. 2v.
Phil 5246.43.5   La psychologie de la forme. (Guillaume, Paul.) Paris, 1937.
Phil 5403.9   Psychologie de la joie. (Cazeneuve, Jean.) Paris, 1952.
Phil 5627.120   La psychologie de la religion dans l'Amérique. Thèse. (Morgan, William Joseph.) Paris, 1928.
Phil 5465.28   La psychologie de la rêverie. Thèse. (Baïtch, Baïa.) Paris, 1927.
Phil 5400.118   Psychologie de la sensibilité. (Burloud, A.) Paris, 1954.
Phil 5762.5   Psychologie de la volonté. (Martin, E.) Paris, 1913.

Phil 5374.47 | Psychologie de l'apperception. (Dwelshauvers, G.) Bruxelles, 1890.
Phil 8404.11 | Psychologie de l'art. (Delacroix, Henri.) Paris, 1927.
Phil 8423.2 | La psychologie de l'art. (Weber, J. Paul.) Paris, 1961.
Phil 5325.2 | La psychologie de l'association. (Ferri, L.) Paris, 1883.
Phil 5330.4.6 | Psychologie de l'attention. (Ribot, T.) Paris, 1889.
Phil 5865.5.4 | La psychologie de l'enfant. (Piaget, Jean.) Paris, 1966.
Phil 8430.60 | Psychologie de l'esthétique. (Frances, Robert.) Paris, 1968.
Phil 6750.8 | Psychologie de l'idiot. (Sollier, P.) Paris, 1891.
Phil 5410.5 | La psychologie de l'ingratitude. (Litwinski, Léon.) Bruxelles, 1927.
Phil 5255.51.8 | La psychologie de l'intelligence. 3. ed. (Piaget, J.) Paris, 1952.
Phil 2840.94 | La psychologie de l'intelligence chez Renouvier. Thèse. (Yang, Pao-San.) Paris, 1930.
Phil 5330.25 | La psychologie de l'intérêt. Thèse. (Yeh, Ling.) Lyon, 1929.
Phil 2730.112 | La psychologie de Maine de Biran, 1766-1824. (Voutsinas, Dimitri.) Paris, 1964.
Phil 5210.2 | La psychologie de réaction en Amérique. Thèse. (Arnold, V.H.) Paris, 1926.
Phil 6309.4 | Psychologie der abnormen Persönnlichkeiten. (Petrilowitsch, Nikolaus.) Darmstadt, 1968.
Phil 6122.68 | Psychologie der Arbeitswahl und der Arheitsstörungen. (Moser, Ulrich.) Bern, 1953.
Phil 5330.4.15 | Die Psychologie der Aufmerksamkeit. 9 Aufl. (Ribot, T.) Leipzig, 1908.
Phil 5190.3 | Psychologie der Axiome. (Schultz, Julias.) Göttingen, 1899.
Phil 5811.15 | Psychologie der dieren. (Buytendijk, Frederik Jacobus Johannes.) Haarlem, 1920.
Phil 5850.385.28 | Psychologie der Fehler. 2e Aufl. (Weimer, H.) Leipzig, 1929.
Phil 5400.18.6 | Psychologie der Gefühle. (Ribot, T.) Altenburg, 1903.
Phil 5247.44 | Psychologie der Gegenwart. (Henning, Hans.) Berlin, 1925.
Phil 5643.48 | Psychologie der Gesichtsvorstellung. (Stilling, Jacob.) Berlin, 1901.
Phil 6060.65 | Psychologie der Handschrift. (Pokorny, Richard Raphael.) Basel, 1968.
Phil 1050.8 | Psychologie der Hebräer. (Cearus, F.A.) Leipzig, 1809.
Phil 3425.82 | Die Psychologie der Hegelschen Schule. (Erner, F.) Leipzig, 1842-44. 2v.
Phil 6750.259 | Psychologie der intelligenz defekte. (Busemann, Adolf.) München, 1959.
Phil 6750.259.2 | Psychologie der intelligenz Defekte. (Busemann, Adolf.) München, 1963.
Phil 5251.8.25 | Psychologie der Komik. (Lipps, T.) n.p., 1888-1906. 23 pam.
Phil 8413.28 | Psychologie der Kunst. (Müller-Freienfels, R.) Leipzig, 1923-33. 3v.
Phil 5258.28 | Psychologie der Naturvölker. (Schultze, F.) Leipzig, 1900.
Phil 187.23.7 | Die Psychologie der neuen Löwener-Schule. (Frischkopf, B.) Luzern, 1908.
Phil 5821.5 | Psychologie der niedersten Tiere. (Lukas, F.) Wien, 1905.
Phil 5590.150 | Psychologie der Persönlichkeit. (Remplein, Heinz.) München, 1954.
Phil 5590.150.5 | Psychologie der Persönlichkeit. 5. Aufl. (Remplein, Heinz.) München, 1965.
Phil 575.75 | Die Psychologie der produktiven Persönlichkeit. (Plant, Paul.) Stuttgart, 1929.
Phil 5643.55 | Psychologie der Raumwahrnehmung des Auges. (Witasek, Stephan.) Heidelberg, 1910.
Phil 5500.11 | Psychologie der Relationserfassung und des Vergleichens. (Katona, G.) Leipzig, 1924.
Phil 6968.23 | Die Psychologie der Schizophrenen und ihre Bedeutung für die Klinik der Schizophrenie. (Schneider, Carl.) Leipzig, 1930.
Phil 7140.127 | Psychologie der Selbstverteidigung in Klampf-, Not- und Krankheitzeiten. (Baerwald, Richard.) Leipzig, 1927.
Phil 5467.3 | Psychologie der Simulation. (Utitz, Emil.) Stuttgart, 1918.
Phil 5585.170.5 | Psychologie der sinnlichen Erkenntnis. (Anan'ev, B.G.) Berlin, 1963.
Phil 530.40.40 | Psychologie der Spaansche mystiek. (Brouwer, Johan.) Amsterdam, 1931.
Phil 5520.49 | Psychologie der Sprache. (Fröschels, E.) Leipzig, 1925.
Phil 5520.492 | Psychologie der Sprache. (Hoermann, Hans.) Berlin, 1967.
Phil 5520.492.2 | Psychologie der Sprache. (Hoermann, Hans.) Berlin, 1970.
Phil 7140.8.5 | Psychologie der Suggestion. (Schmidkung, Hans.) Stuttgart, 1892.
Phil 6319.1.10.5 | Die Psychologie der Übertragung. (Jung, C.G.) Zürich, 1946.
Phil 5350.1 | Psychologie der Veränderungsauffassung. (Stern, L.W.) Breslau, 1898.
Phil 5643.85 | Psychologie der waarneming. Diss. (Rutten, F.J.T.) Nijmegen, 1929.
Phil 184.19 | Psychologie der Weltanschauung. (Jaspers, K.) Berlin, 1919.
Phil 184.19.5A | Psychologie der Weltanschauung. (Jaspers, K.) Berlin, 1925.
Phil 5585.27 | Psychologie der Zeitauffassung. (Benussi, Vittorio.) Heidelberg, 1913.
Phil 5258.84 | Psychologie der Zusammenhänge und Beziehungen. (Strasser, Vera.) Berlin, 1921.
Phil 6980.712.105 | Psychologie der zwischenmenschlichen Beziehungen. (Rattner, Josef.) Olten, 1969.
Phil 5811.15.5 | Psychologie des animaux. (Buytendijk, Frederik Jacobus Johannes.) Paris, 1928.
Phil 5829.14 | Psychologie des animaux. (Thinès, Georges.) Bruxelles, 1966.
Phil 5815.8.3 | Psychologie des animaux. 3. éd. (Filloux, Jean Claude.) Paris, 1960.
Phil 5240.44 | Psychologie des Bewussten und Unbewussten. (Aeppli, E.) Zürich, 1947.
Phil 6322.2 | Psychologie des Bewusstseins. (Müller, F.C.) Leipzig, 1889.
Phil 5241.47 | Psychologie des Denkens. (Betz, W.) Leipzig, 1918.
Phil 5821.14 | Die Psychologie des Emotionalen. (Loeser, Johann A.) Berlin, 1931.
Phil 5400.37 | Psychologie des emotionalen Denkens. (Maier, H.) Tübingen, 1908.
Phil 3890.6.85 | Die Psychologie des Enkennens bei Bonnet und Tetens. (Schweig, Helmut.) Trier, 1921.
Phil 351.1 | Psychologie des Erkennens I. Leipzig, 1893 (Uphues, G.K.)

Phil 5070.15 | Psychologie des Glaubens. (Vorbrodt, Gustav.) Göttingen, 1895.
Phil 5627.236.2 | Psychologie des Gottesglaubens auf Grund literarischer Selbstzeugnisse. 2. Aufl. (Siegmond, Georg.) Münster, 1965.
Phil 5545.77 | Psychologie des grands calculateurs et joueurs d'échecs. (Binet, A.) Paris, 1894.
Phil 5249.23.5 | Psychologie des grands hommes. 2. éd. (Joly, Henri.) Paris, 1891.
Phil 336.1.5 | La psychologie des idées-forces. (Fouillée, A.) Paris, 1893. 2v.
Phil 2885.84.5 | La psychologie des individus et des sociétés chez Taine. (Lacombe, Paul.) Paris, 1906.
Phil 2225.6.80 | Die Psychologie des Johannes Pecham. Inaug. Diss. (Spettmann, P.H.) Münster, 1919.
Phil 4372.1.80 | Psychologie des Juan Luis Vives. (Hoppe, G.) Berlin, 1901.
Phil 5535.62 | Psychologie des Lernens: Methoden, Ergebnisse, Anwendungen. (Haseloff, Otto Walter.) Berlin, 1970.
Phil 5520.340 | Die Psychologie des Lesens. (Mueller, Heinz A.) Lörrach, 1958.
Phil 5246.65 | Psychologie des Mannes. (Graber, Gustav Hans.) Bern, 1957.
Phil 5400.41 | Psychologie des menschlichen Gefühlslebens. (Störring, Gustav.) Bonn, 1916.
Phil 525.29 | Psychologie des mystiques catholiques orthodoxes. (Brenier de Montmorand, Antoine F.J.H.L.M.) Paris, 1920.
Phil 525.121 | Psychologie des mystischen Bewusstseins. (Albrecht, C.) Bremen, 1951.
Phil 1504.3 | Die Psychologie des Nemesius. v.3, pt.1. (Domański, B.) Münster, 1900.
Phil 6315.12 | La psychologie des névroses. (Forel, O.L.) Genève, 1925.
Phil 5822.4A | Psychologie des Pferdes und der Dressur. (Máday, Stefan.) Berlin, 1912.
Phil 6317.48 | La psychologie des profondeurs, des origines à nos jours. (Hernfeld, Fred Farau.) Paris, 1960.
Phil 5627.74.2 | Psychologie des saints. 2. éd. (Joly, H.) Paris, 1897.
Phil 5400.18.4 | La psychologie des sentiments. (Ribot, T.) Paris, 1896.
Phil 5400.18.5 | La psychologie des sentiments. 16. éd. (Ribot, T.) Paris, 1939.
Phil 7082.18 | Psychologie des Traumbewustseins. (Bossard, Robert.) Zürich, 1951.
Phil 5722.80 | Psychologie des Unbewussten. (Drews, Arthur.) Berlin, 1924.
Phil 5768.5 | Psychologie des Willens. (Schwarz, H.) Leipzig, 1900.
Phil 2510.210 | Die Psychologie Descartes. (Koch, Anton.) München, 1881.
Phil 3120.8.120 | La psychologie descriptive selon Franz Brentano. (Gilson, Lucie.) Paris, 1955.
Phil 3890.7.81 | Die Psychologie Dieterich Liedemanns. Inaug. Diss. (Jacobskötter, A.) Erlangen, 1898.
Phil 5856.10 | La psychologie différentielle. (Reuchlin, Maurice.) Paris, 1969.
Phil 5255.75 | Psychologie différentielle des sexes. (Piret, Roger.) Paris, 1965.
Phil 25.183 | Psychologie du langage. Bruxelles. 1,1969+ 3v.
Phil 5520.59 | Psychologie du langage. Paris, 1933.
Phil 5261.23 | La psychologie du poéte. (Valdefievre, P.) Paris, 1933.
Phil 5241.17.23 | Psychologie du point de vue empirique. (Brentano, Franz.) Paris, 1944.
Phil 5620.1A | La psychologie du raisonnement. (Binet, A.) Paris, 1886.
Phil 5620.9 | Psychologie du raisonnement. (Rignano, Eugenio.) Paris, 1920.
Phil 7082.148 | La psychologie du rêve au point de une médical. (Vaschide, Nicolas.) Paris, 1920.
Phil 5525.24 | La psychologie du rire. (Dugas, L.) Paris, 1902.
Phil 5261.8 | La psychologie du témoignage. (Varendonck, J.) Gand, 1914.
Phil 5585.140 | Psychologie du temps. 1. éd. (Fraisse, Paul.) Paris, 1957.
Phil 5585.140.2 | Psychologie du temps. 2. éd. (Fraisse, Paul.) Paris, 1957.
Phil 7069.14.50 | La psychologie d'une conversion du positivisme au spiritualisme. (Primot, Alphonse.) Paris, 1914.
Phil 5627.12 | Psychologie d'une religion. (Revault D'Allonnes, G.) Paris, 1908.
Phil 5520.658 | La psychologie dynamique et la pensée vécue. (Konczewski, C.) Paris, 1970.
Phil 5627.264 | Psychologie en theologische antropologie. (Berg, J.H.) Nijkerk, 1964.
Phil 7060.135 | Psychologie énergétique. (Etchart, Carlos R.) Paris, 1914.
Phil 5252.49 | Psychologie et development de l'enfance à la vieillesse. (Montet, C. de.) Berne, 1922.
Phil 5875.175 | Psychologie et épistémologie. (Piaget, Jean.) Paris, 1970.
Phil 2605.1.83 | La psychologie et la métaphysique des idéesforces chez Alfred Fouillée. Thèse. (Gaune de Beaucourdey, E.) Paris, 1936.
Phil 5246.2 | La psychologie et la phrénologie comparées. (Garnier, A.) Paris, 1839.
Phil 5242.31 | Psychologie et métaphysique. (Challaye, F.) Paris, 1925.
Phil 5242.54 | Psychologie et métaphysique. (Château, J.) Paris, 1949.
Phil 5221.5 | Psychologie et morale aux XIIe et XIIIe siècles. v.1-6. (Lottin, Odon.) Louvain, 1942. 8v.
Phil 5275.20 | Psychologie et sous-développement. Paris, 1963.
Phil 2725.35.10 | Psychologie et spiritualité. (Lavelle, Louis.) Paris, 1967.
Phil 5627.267.5 | Psychologie et théologie. (Pohier, Jacques Marie.) Paris, 1967.
Phil 5241.9 | Psychologie experimentale. (Bautain, L.E.M.) Strasbourg, 1839. 2v.
Phil 5242.34 | Psychologie expérimentale. (Cramaussel, E.) Paris, 1925.
Phil 5255.18.5 | Psychologie experimentale. (Piéron, Henri.) Paris, 1927.
Phil 5222.6 | La psychologie expérimentale en Italie. (Manoll, A.) Paris, 1938.
Phil 25.108 | Psychologie française; bulletin trimestriel de la Société française de psychologie. Paris. 3,1958+ 10v.
Phil 5213.2 | La psychologie française contemporaine. (Dwelshauvers, Georges.) Paris, 1920.
Phil 3890.1.105 | Die Psychologie Friedrich Adolf Trendelenburgs. Inaug. Diss. (Hoffmann, Edmund.) Greifswald, 1892?
Phil 5250.11 | Psychologie générale. (Kaploun, Albert.) Lausanne, 1919.
Phil 3565.126 | Die Psychologie Hermann Lotzes in ihrem Verhältnis zu Herbart. (Nath, Max.) Halle, 1892.
Phil 3915.60 | Die Psychologie im Kampf ums Dasein. (Wundt, Wilhelm.) Leipzig, 1913.
Phil 5241.88.3 | Psychologie im Leben unserer Zeit. (Bühler, Charlotte M.) München, 1962.

Phil 5244.12.3 Psychologie im Umriss. 3e Aufl. (Eisler, Rudolf.) Leipzig, 1903.
Phil 5627.80 Die Psychologie in der Religionswissenschaft. (Koch, E.) Freiburg, 1896.
Phil 3489.3 Die Psychologie in Kant's Ethik. (Hegler, A.) Freiburg, 1891.
Phil 5247.10.13 Psychologie in Umrissen auf Grundläge der Erfahrung. (Höffding, H.) Leipzig, 1887.
Phil 5247.10.14 Psychologie in Umrissen auf Grundläge der Erfahrung. (Höffding, H.) Leipzig, 1893.
Phil 7060.129.9 La psychologie inconnue. 2. ed. (Boirac, Émile.) Paris, 1912.
Phil 5627.124 Psychologie jugendlicher Religiosität innerhalb des deutschen Methodismus. (Leitner, Hans.) München, 1930.
Phil 5627.124.5 Psychologie jugendlicher Religiosität innerhalb des deutschen Methodismus. Inaug. Diss. (Leitner, Hans.) München, 1930.
Phil 5255.53 Psychologie moderne et réflexion chrétienne. Paris, 1953.
Phil 6322.12 La psychologie morbide. (Moreau, J.J.) Paris, 1859.
Phil 5243.6 Psychologie naturelle. (Despine, P.) Paris, 1868. 3v.
Phil 5253.5 La psychologie naturelle. (Nicati, W.M.) Paris, 1898.
Phil 5241.30 La psychologie objective. (Bekhterev, V.) Paris, 1913.
Phil 3780.37 Psychologie oder die Wissenschaft vom subjectiven Geist. (Rosenkranz, Karl.) Königsberg, 1837.
Phil 6332.8 Psychologie pathologique. (Wallon, H.) Paris, 1926.
Phil 5258.70 La psychologie physiologique. (Sergi, G.) Paris, 1888.
Phil 5241.48.5 La psychologie quantitative. (Biervliet, Jules Jean van.) Gand, 1907.
Phil 5258.83 Psychologie réaliste. (Sièrebois, R.P.) Paris, 1876.
Phil 5627.266.5 Psychologie religieuse. (Vergote, Antoine.) Bruxelles, 1966.
Phil 5627.210 Psychologie und astrologische Symbolis. (Strauss, H.A.) Zürich, 1953.
Phil 5780.9 Psychologie und Besteuerung. (Conrad, H.) Stuttgart, 1928.
Phil 5258.35.5 Die Psychologie und der Personalismus. (Stern, W.) Leipzig, 1917.
Phil 8599.19.10 Psychologie und Erkenntnistheorie in der Religionswissenschaft. (Troeltsch, Ernst.) Tübingen, 1905.
Phil 5244.8 Die Psychologie und ihre Zentralstellung in der Philosophie. (Eisenmeier, J.) Halle, 1914.
Phil 5244.6 Psychologie und Logik. (Elsenhaus, T.) Leipzig, 1898.
Phil 5244.10 Psychologie und Logik. 5e Aufl. (Elsenhans, Theodor.) Berlin, 1920.
Phil 5247.40 Psychologie und Logik. 15. Aufl. (Heilmann, K.) Berlin, 1913.
Phil 6972.9 Psychologie und Pathologie der Vorstellung. (Wallaschek, R.) Leipzig, 1905.
Phil 5246.34 Psychologie und Philosophie. (Güttler, C.) München, 1896.
Phil 5520.33 Psychologie und Philosophie der Sprache. (Oltuszewski, W.) Berlin, 1901.
Phil 5760.10 Psychologie und Philosophie des Wollens. (Keller, W.) München, 1954.
Phil 25.110 Psychologie und Praxis; Zeitschrift für die Anwendurgsgebiete der Psychologie. München. 1,1956+ 5v.
Phil 5627.162 Psychologie und Psychiatrie der Conversion. (Harms, Ernst.) Leiden, 1939.
Phil 6332.16 Psychologie und Sittlichkeit. (Wolff, Konrad.) Stuttgart, 1958.
Phil 3925.3.40 Psychologie und Unsterblichkeitslehre. (Weisse, Christian Hermann.) Leipzig, 1869.
Phil 5850.278.5 Psychologie und Wirtschaftsleben. (Münsterberg, H.) Leipzig, 1912.
Phil 7082.59 Die psychologie van het droomen. (Wijnaendtsfrancken, Cornelis Johannes.) Haarlem, 1907.
Phil 8610.171 Psychologie van het ongeloof. Amsterdam. 3,193?+
Phil 6331.8 Psychologie van het onheilsvoorspellen. (Viane, Andre.) Gent, 1963.
Phil 25.150 Psychologie vekonomické praci. Praha. 1,1966+ 2v.
Phil 5241.17.25A Psychologie vom empirischen Standpunkt. (Brentano, Franz.) Hamburg, 1955.
Phil 5241.17.5 Psychologie vom empirischen Standpunkt. (Brentano, Franz.) Leipzig, 1924-25. 2v.
Phil 5258.103 Psychologie vom Standpunkt der Abhängigkeit des Erkennens von den Lebensbedürfnissen. (Szymanski, J.S.) Leipzig, 1930.
Phil 6319.1.182 Die Psychologie von C.G. Jung. (Jacobi, Jolan.) Zürich, 1945.
Phil 6319.1.183 Die Psychologie von C.G. Jung. 4. Aufl. (Jacobi, Jolan.) Zürich, 1959.
Phil 3915.152 Die Psychologie Wilhelm Wundts. (Passkönig, Oswald.) Leipzig, 1912.
Phil 5242.1.5 Psychologie zur Entwicklungsgeschichte der Seele. (Carus, C.G.) Pforzheim, 1846.
Phil 25.33 Psychologies of 1925. Worcester, 1926.
Phil 25.33.2 Psychologies of 1925. 2d ed. Worcester, 1827.
Phil 25.33.3 Psychologies of 1925. 3d ed. Worcester, 1928.
Phil 25.33.5A Psychologies of 1930. Worcester, 1930.
Phil 8876.79 Psychologikai meletai apo tou kalou. (Bizyenos, Georgios.) Athens, 1885.
Phil 5257.10 Psychologisch-ästhetische Essays. (Rubinstein, Susanna.) Heidelberg, 1877-88. 2v.
Phil 9550.3 Psychologisch-ethische Untersuchungen zur Werth-Theorie. (Meinong, A.) Graz, 1874.
Phil 6319.1.72 Psychologische Abhandlungen. (Jung, C.G.) Leipzig, 1914.
Phil 5247.12 Psychologische Analysen. v.1-2. (Horwicz, A.) Halle, 1872-78. 3v.
Phil 25.73A Psychologische Arbeiten. Leipzig. 1-9,1895-1928 9v.
Phil 5224.1 Der psychologische Begriff des Unbewuzten in der Schelling'schen Schule. (Orth, Johannes.) Heidelberg, 1914.
Phil 5246.23 Psychologische Beiträge. (Giese, Fritz.) Langensalza, 1916-
Phil 25.92 Psychologische Beiträge. Vierteljahresschrift für alle Gekiete der Psychologie. Meisenheim. 1,1953+ 11v.
Phil 5249.13.25 Psychologische Betrachtung; eine Auslese aus den Schriften. (Jung, Carl G.) Zürich, 1945.
Phil 5243.25.5 Psychologische Briefe. (Dessoir, Max.) Berlin, 1948.
Phil 5244.2 Psychologische Briefe. (Erdmann, J.E.) Leipzig, 1856.
Phil 5244.2.10 Psychologische Briefe. 3e Aufl. (Erdmann, J.E.) Leipzig, 1863.
Phil 5244.2.12 Psychologische Briefe. 5e Aufl. (Erdmann, J.E.) Leipzig, 1875.
Phil 5325.15.7 Die psychologische Diagnose des Tatbestandes. (Jung, Carl G.) Zurich, 1941.

Phil 9560.7.9 Een psychologische en zebekundige studie over de hegrippen eer en eergevoel. Proefschrift. (Maarse, Jan.) Amsterdam, 1936.
Phil 3500.6 Die psychologische Entwickelung des Apriori...Kants Kritik der reinen Vernunft. (Schneider, O.) Bonn, 1883.
Phil 25.27 Psychologische Forschung. Berlin. 1,1921+ 20v.
Phil 5258.45.5 Die psychologische Forschung und ihre Aufgabe in der Gegenwart. (Spitta, Heinrich.) Freiburg, 1889.
Phil 5252.53 Psychologische Fragen. (Mischer.) Stendal, 1884.
Phil 5850.138 Psychologische Grundlegung der praktischen Berufsberatung. (Bogen, Helmuth.) Langensalza, 1927.
Phil 735.89A Psychologische Grundlegung eines Systems der Wert-Theorie. (Kreibig, J.C.) Wien, 1902.
Phil 25.79 Psychologische Hefte der Siemens-Studien Gesellschaft für praktische Psychologie. Hannover. 1949-1952 2v.
Phil 5259.23 Psychologische hoofdstukken. (Ten Seldam, W.H.) Amsterdam, 1926.
Phil 5241.73 Psychologische methoden en begrippen. (Brugmans, H.J.) Haarlem, 1922.
Phil 25.80 Psychologische Nachrichten für die Mitglieder der Siemens-Studien-Gesellschaft für praktische Psychologie. Hannover.
Phil 5244.11 Psychologische Probleme. (Eichberg, T.) Stuttgart, 1907.
Phil 5250.23 Psychologische Probleme in der Philosophie. (Kaim, J.R.) München, 1921.
Phil 5241.88.10 Psychologische Probleme unserer Zeit. (Bühler, Charlotte M.) Stuttgart, 1968.
Phil 25.44 Psychologische Rundschan. Basel. 1-4,1929-1933 2v.
Phil 25.82 Psychologische Rundschau. Göttingen. 1,1949+ 10v.
Phil 25.91 Psychologische Schriftenreihe zur Zeitschrift der Psychologe. Schwarzenberg. 1-7,1952-1962//
Phil 5257.21 Psychologische Skizzen, von Edmund W. Rells. (Dessoir, Max.) Leipzig, 1893.
Phil 3100.65 Psychologische Skizzen. (Beneke, F.E.) Göttingen, 1825-27. 2v.
Phil 5245.65 Psychologische skizzen. (Finkelstein, Ben A.) Amsterdam, 1957.
Phil 5520.8 Psychologische Studien. (Bruchmann, K.) Leipzig, n.d.
Phil 5545.15 Psychologische Studien. (Huber, J.N.) München, 1878.
Phil 5251.8.7 Psychologische Studien. (Lipps, T.) Heidelberg, 1885.
Phil 5251.8.8 Psychologische Studien. (Lipps, T.) Leipzig, 1905.
Phil 25.17.4 Psychologische Studien. Leipzig.
Phil 25.17.3 Psychologische Studien. Leipzig. 1-7 6v.
Phil 25.17 Psychologische Studien. Leipzig. 1-10,1906-1918 10v.
Phil 5255.36 Psychologische Studien. Festschrift gewidmet Paul Ranschburg. Budapest, 1929.
Phil 5255.78 Psychologische Testtheorie. Bern, 1968.
Phil 9220.18 Een psychologische theorie van de vriendschap. Proefschrift. (Fentener van Vlissingen, Johannes.) Arnhem, 1966.
Phil 5249.13.8 Psychologische Typen. (Jung, Carl G.) Zürich, 1921.
Phil 5249.13.7 Psychologische Typen. (Jung, Carl G.) Zürich, 1925.
Phil 5249.13.9 Psychologische Typen. (Jung, Carl G.) Zürich, 1930.
Phil 5249.13.10 Psychologische Typen. (Jung, Carl G.) Zürich, 1946.
Phil 5525.64 Psychologische und physiologische Untersuchung über das Lachen. (Poinsinet de Sivry, Louis.) Wolfenbüttel, 1794.
Phil 3428.67 Psychologische Untersuchungen. (Herbart, J.F.) Göttingen, 1839-40.
Phil 6536.6 Psychologische Untersuchungen an Normalen, Schwachbegabten und Epileptikern. (Wreschner, A.) Leipzig, 1927.
Phil 9558.14 Psychologische Untersuchungen über die Lüge. Inaug. Diss. (Küppers, L.) Bedburg-Erft, 1928.
Phil 5520.6 Psychologische Untersuchungen zur Bedeutungslehre. (Martinak, E.) Leipzig, 1901.
Phil 5241.51 Psychologische Vorlesungen für Hörer aller Fakultälen. (Bumke, Oswald.) Wiesbaden, 1919.
Phil 5241.51.2 Psychologische Vorlesungen für Hörer aller Fakultälen. 2. Aufl. (Bumke, Oswald.) München, 1923.
Phil 5258.42 Psychologische Wanderungen auf Seitenwegen. (Schulz, B.) Jena, 1913.
Phil 5204.6.2 Psychologische Wörterbuch. (Giese, Fritz.) Tübingen, 1950.
Phil 2115.167 Die psychologischen Ansichten John Lockes. (Maag, Urs.) Aarau, 1960.
Phil 3640.198 Die psychologischen Errungenschaften Nietzsches. (Klages, Ludwig.) Leipzig, 1926.
Phil 3640.198.5 Die psychologischen Errungenschaften Nietzsches. 2e Aufl. (Klages, Ludwig.) Leipzig, 1930.
Phil 5655.10 Die psychologischen Grundlagen der Parfümerie. 2. Aufl. (Jellinek, Paul.) Heidelberg, 1965.
Phil 5250.37.5 Psychologischer Atlas. (Katz, David.) Basel, 1945.
Phil 5238.8 Psychologischer Club, Zürich. Die kulturelle Bedeutung der komplexen Psychologie. Berlin, 1935.
Phil 2465.33 Psychologischer Versuch. (Bonnet, Charles.) Lemgo, 1773.
Phil 5255.31 Psychologisches Praktikum. (Pauli, R.) Jena, 1920.
Phil 5255.3.5 Psychologisches Praktikum. 6. Aufl. (Pauli, Richard.) Stuttgart, 1957.
Phil 91.4 Psychologisches Wörterbuch. (Giese, Fritz.) Leipzig, 1921.
NEDL Phil 5643.12.5 Psychologish-physiologische Optik. (Hoppe, J.F.) Leipzig, 1881.
Phil 338.4 Psychologismus oder Antipsychologismus. (Heim, Karl.) Berlin, 1902.
Phil 3475.3.80 Psychologismus und Transzendentalismus bei K. Jaspers. (Feith, R.C.) Bern, 1946.
Phil 1905.14.100 Psychologist at large. (Boring, E.G.) N.Y., 1961.
Phil 5247.54 The psychologist at work. (Harrower, M.R.) London, 1937.
Phil 8404.2 The psychologist looks at art. (Danz, Louis.) London, 1937.
Phil 5255.80 A psychologist of sorts. (Porteus, Stanley David.) Palo Alto, 1969.
Phil 55.7 Psychologists League, New York. Journal. N.Y. 1-4,1937-1940 2v.
Phil 5252.19.20 A psychologist's point of view. (Myers, C.S.) London, 1933.
Phil 5262.38 Psychologia. v.1-2. (Witwicki, W.) Lwów, 1930.
Phil 1825.2 Psychologues et psychologies et psychologies d'Amérique. (Zazzo, René.) Paris, 1942.
Phil 5241.92A Psychology; a factual textbook. (Boring, E.G.) N.Y., 1935.
Phil 5251.18 Psychology; a new system. (Lynch, Arthur.) London, 1912. 2v.
Phil 5242.33 Psychology; a simplification. (Coleman, L.R.) N.Y., 1927.
Phil 5244.7.5 Psychology, an elementary text-book. (Ebbinghaus, H.) Boston, 1908.
Phil 6671.13.7 Psychology, hypnotism, personal magnatism and clairvoyance. (Barnes, W.A.) Boston, 1898.

Phil 6128.60	Psychology, morality and education. (Steenberghen, F. van.) London, 1958.
Phil 5241.79	Psychology, normal and abnormal. (Bridges, J.W.) N.Y., 1930.
Phil 5251.13	Psychology, normal and abnormal. (Lloyd, W.E.) Los Angeles, 1908.
Phil 5251.13.2	Psychology, normal and abnormal. (Lloyd, W.E.) N.Y., 1910.
Phil 5627.161	Psychology, psychotherapy and evangelicalism. (McKenzie, J.G.) London, 1940.
Phil 5248.3	Psychology, the science of behavior. (Isaacson, Robert Lee.) N.Y., 1965.
Phil 5246.17.7	Psychology; the science of human behavior. (Givler, Robert C.) N.Y., 1922.
Phil 5252.141A	Psychology, the science of mental life. (Miller, George A.) N.Y., 1962.
Phil 5252.18.12	Psychology, the study of behavior. (McDougall, William.) London, 1912.
Phil 5252.18.11A	Psychology, the study of behavior. (McDougall, William.) N.Y., 1912.
Phil 2130.33	Psychology; the test of moral and metaphysical philosophy. (Mansel, H.L.) Oxford, 1855.
VPhil 5205.11.6	Pamphlet vol. Psychology.
VPhil 5205.25	Pamphlet vol. Psychology. 22 pam.
VPhil 5205.11.8	Pamphlet vol. Psychology.
VPhil 5205.11.7	Pamphlet vol. Psychology.
VPhil 5205.11	Pamphlet vol. Psychology.
VPhil 5205.11.5	Pamphlet vol. Psychology.
VPhil 5205.3	Pamphlet box. Psychology.
VPhil 5205.26	Pamphlet vol. Psychology. 22 pam.
VPhil 5205.27	Pamphlet vol. Psychology. 20 pam.
Phil 5205.15	Pamphlet vol. Psychology. 10 pam.
Phil 5205.28	Pamphlet box. Psychology.
VPhil 5205.11.3	Pamphlet vol. Psychology.
VPhil 5205.11.1	Pamphlet vol. Psychology.
VPhil 5205.11.2	Pamphlet vol. Psychology.
VPhil 5205.11.4	Pamphlet vol. Psychology.
Phil 5210.3	Psychology. (Adams, Grace K.) N.Y., 1931.
Phil 5241.76	Psychology. (Baar, Jacob.) N.Y., 1928.
Phil 5238.232	Psychology. (Behavioral and Social Sciences Survey Committe.) Englewood Cliffs, N.J., 1970.
Phil 5241.35.2	Psychology. (Breese, B.B.) N.Y., 1921.
Phil 42.3.5	Psychology. (California. University. Publications.) Berkeley. 1-6,1910-1950 4v.
Phil 5243.7	Psychology. (Dewey, John.) N.Y., 1887.
Phil 5243.7.2	Psychology. (Dewey, John.) N.Y., 1889.
Phil 5245.55	Psychology. (Fraser, John Munro.) N.Y., 1956.
Phil 5246.29.5	Psychology. (Garrett, Henry E.) N.Y., 1950.
Phil 5246.80	Psychology. (Gilmer, Beverly von Haller.) N.Y., 1970.
Phil 5246.8	Psychology. (Granger, F.S.) London, 1891.
Phil 5247.48.5	Psychology. (Higginson, G.) N.Y., 1936.
Phil 2070.46.20A	Psychology. (James, William.) Cleveland, 1948.
Phil 5249.2.5.3	Psychology. (James, William.) N.Y., 1891.
Phil 5249.2.4A	Psychology. (James, William.) N.Y., 1892.
Phil 5249.2.11	Psychology. (James, William.) N.Y., 1893.
Phil 5249.2.6	Psychology. (James, William.) N.Y., 1900.
Phil 5249.2.6.10	Psychology. (James, William.) N.Y., 1907.
Phil 5249.2.13.5	Psychology. (James, William.) N.Y., 1909.
Phil 5249.2.5.5	Psychology. (James, William.) N.Y., 1923.
Phil 5249.2.5.10	Psychology. (James, William.) N.Y., 1961.
Phil 6980.400	Psychology. (Krout, M.H.) Minneapolis, 1956.
Phil 5252.58.2	Psychology. (Martin, E.D.) N.Y., 1924.
Phil 5252.97	Psychology. (Morgan, J.J.B.) N.Y., 1947.
Phil 5252.89	Psychology. (Munn, Norman Leslie.) Boston, 1946.
Phil 5252.11	Psychology. (Munsell, O.S.) N.Y., 1880.
Phil 5252.76	Psychology. (Munzinger, K.F.) Denver, 1939.
Phil 5252.76.5	Psychology. (Munzinger, K.F.) N.Y., 1942.
Phil 5255.26	Psychology. (Perrin, Fleming.) N.Y., 1926.
Phil 6127.13	Psychology. (Randall, F.H.) London, 1905.
Phil 5257.1	Psychology. (Rauch, F.A.) N.Y., 1840.
Phil 5257.1.2	Psychology. (Rauch, F.A.) N.Y., 1841.
Phil 5257.28.5	Psychology. (Roback, A.A.) Rahway, 1923.
Phil 4210.60	Psychology. (Rosmini-Serbati, Antonio.) London, 1886-88. 3v.
Phil 5258.6	Psychology. (Schmucker, S.S.) N.Y., 1842.
Phil 5262.9	Psychology. (Woodworth, R.S.) N.Y., 1908.
Phil 5262.9.10	Psychology. (Woodworth, R.S.) N.Y., 1924.
Phil 5262.9.15	Psychology. (Woodworth, R.S.) N.Y., 1929.
Phil 5205.35	Pamphlet vol. Psychology. (Russian). 3 pam.
Phil 25.140	Psychology. Savannah, Georgia.
Phil 5262.8.5	Psychology. A lecture. (Watt, H.J.) London, 1913.
Phil 7040	Pamphlet box. Psychology. Abnormal. Personality.
Phil 7040.01	Pamphlet box. Psychology. Abnormal. Personality.
Phil 5251.35.9	Psychology: an empirical study of behavior. (Lund, F.H.) N.Y., 1933.
Phil 5850.02	Pamphlet box. Psychology. Applied.
Phil 5242.23	Pamphlet box. Psychology. Cason, Hulsey.
Phil 5360.01	Pamphlet box. Psychology. Conception.
Phil 5380.01	Pamphlet box. Psychology. Crowds.
VPhil 5205.37	Pamphlet vol. Psychology. Dissertations. (F-K). 7 pam.
VPhil 5205.38	Pamphlet vol. Psychology. Dissertations. (L-R). 8 pam.
VPhil 5205.39	Pamphlet vol. Psychology. Dissertations. (S-Z). 8 pam.
VPhil 5205.36	Pamphlet vol. Psychology. Dissertations. (A-E). 10 pam.
Phil 5400.01	Pamphlet box. Psychology. Emotions.
Phil 5400.02	Pamphlet box. Psychology. Emotions.
Phil 5400.05	Pamphlet box. Psychology. Emotions. German dissertations.
VPhil 5205.5	Pamphlet vol. Psychology. General. 11 pam.
VPhil 5205.4	Pamphlet vol. Psychology. General experimental. 19 pam.
Phil 5249.7.2	Psychology. General introduction. (Judd, C.H.) Boston, 1917.
Phil 5249.7	Psychology. General introduction. (Judd, C.H.) N.Y., 1907.
Phil 5259.19.50	Pamphlet box. Psychology. General works.
VPhil 5205.22	Pamphlet vol. Psychology. German dissertations. 17 pam.
VPhil 5205.40	Pamphlet vol. Psychology. German dissertations. 5 pam.
VPhil 5205.21	Pamphlet vol. Psychology. German dissertations. 22 pam.
VPhil 5205.20	Pamphlet vol. Psychology. German dissertations. 21 pam.
Phil 5205.30	Pamphlet box. Psychology. German dissertations.
Phil 6060.03	Pamphlet box. Psychology. German dissertations.
Phil 6060.01	Pamphlet box. Psychology. Graphology.
Phil 5650.01	Pamphlet box. Psychology. Hearing.
Phil 5650.05	Pamphle box. Psychology. Hearing. German dissertations.
Htn Phil 6948.25*	Pamphlet box. Psychology. Insanity. Broadsides.
Phil 5258.145.2	Psychology. Instructor's manual. 1st ed. (Stager, Ross.) N.Y., 1952.
Phil 5247.16.25	Psychology: its facts and principles. (Hollingworth, H.L.) N.Y., 1928.
Phil 5251.3.50.01	Pamphlet box. Psychology. Langer, Walter C.
Phil 5520.01	Pamphlet box. Psychology. Language and thought.
Phil 5252.44.2F	Pamphlet box. Psychology. MacDonald, Arthur.
Phil 5252.44	Pamphlet box. Psychology. MacDonald, Arthur.
Phil 6930.01	Pamphlet box. Psychology. Melancholia.
Phil 6955.3.25	Pamphlet box. Psychology. Mental disease.
Phil 6954.1.25	Pamphlet box. Psychology. Mental disease.
Phil 6955.4.25	Pamphlet box. Psychology. Mental disease.
Htn Phil 6958.1.2*	Pamphlet box. Psychology. Mental disease. Letters.
Phil 6122.19	Pamphlet vol. Psychology. Mind and body. 15 pam.
Phil 6990.01	Pamphlet box. Psychology. Miraculous cures.
VPhil 5205.14	Pamphlet box. Psychology. Monographs on anomalies.
Phil 5780.01	Pamphlet box. Psychology. Movement.
Phil 5649.01	Pamphlet box. Psychology. Muscular sense.
Phil 6040.1	Pamphlet box. Psychology. Palmistry.
Phil 6051.01	Pamphlet box. Psychology. Palmistry.
Phil 6005.1	Pamphlet box. Psychology. Physiognomy.
Phil 5252.58	Psychology. pt.1-20. (Martin, E.D.) N.Y., 1924.
Phil 5648.01	Pamphlet box. Psychology. Senses.
Phil 5640.12.2	Pamphlet vol. Psychology. Senses. 10 pam.
Phil 5640.12	Pamphlet vol. Psychology. Senses. 16 pam.
Phil 5645.01	Pamphlet box. Psychology. Senses. Sight.
Phil 5645.05	Pamphlet box. Psychology. Senses. Sight. German dissertations.
Phil 5642.01	Pamphlet box. Psychology. Senses. Synaesthesia.
Phil 5655.01	Pamphlet box. Psychology. Smell.
Phil 5425.01	Pamphlet Box. Psychology. Special. Genius.
Phil 5435.01	Pamphlet box. Psychology. Special. Habit.
Phil 5440.01	Pamphlet Box. Psychology. Special. Heredity.
Phil 5465	Pamphlet vol. Psychology. Special. Imagination.
Phil 5525.01	Pamphlet box. Psychology. Special. Laughter.
Phil 7140.01	Pamphlet box. Psychology. Suggestion.
Phil 5653.1	Pamphlet box. Psychology. Taste.
Phil 5710.01	Pamphlet box. Psychology. Temperament.
Phil 2125.50	Psychology: the cognitive powers. (McCosh, James.) N.Y., 1886.
Phil 2125.50.2	Psychology: the cognitive powers. (McCosh, James.) N.Y., 1889.
Phil 2125.50.5	Psychology: the cognitive powers. (McCosh, James.) N.Y., 1906.
Phil 2125.50.3	Psychology: the motive powers. (McCosh, James.) N.Y., 1888.
Phil 5251.35	Psychology: the science of mental activity. (Lund, F.H.) N.Y., 1927.
Phil 5722.01	Pamphlet box. Psychology. Unconscious cerebration.
Phil 5238.100	Psychology. v.2-6. v.1 lost. (Koch, Sigmund.) N.Y., 1959. 5v.
Phil 5643.08	Pamphlet box. Psychology. Vision.
Phil 5643.07	Pamphlet vol. Psychology. Vision. 19 pam.
Phil 5643.01	Pamphlet vol. Psychology. Vision. 16 pam.
Phil 5643.04	Pamphlet vol. Psychology. Vision. German dissertations.
Phil 5643.03	Pamphlet vol. Psychology. Vision. German dissertations. 14 pam.
Phil 5643.02	Pamphlet vol. Psychology. Vision. German dissertations. 20 pam.
Phil 5750.01	Pamphlet vol. Psychology. Volition. 6 pam.
Phil 5750.05	Pamphlet box. Psychology. Volition. German dissertations.
Phil 5245.35	Psychology. 1. ed. (Franz, S.I.) N.Y., 1933.
Phil 5258.145	Psychology. 1st ed. (Stagner, Ross.) N.Y., 1952.
Phil 5240.5.30	Psychology. 2. ed. (Angell, J.R.) N.Y., 1905.
Phil 5252.89.2	Psychology. 2. ed. (Munn, Norman Leslie.) Boston, 1951.
Phil 5252.89.4A	Psychology. 2. ed. (Munn, Norman Leslie.) Boston, 1961.
Phil 5252.18.12.10	
NEDL Phil 5243.7.3	Psychology. 2d ed. (McDougall, William.) London, 1952.
Phil 5262.9.20	Psychology. 3d ed. (Dewey, John.) N.Y., 1896.
Phil 5240.6.2	Psychology. 3d ed. (Woodworth, R.S.) N.Y., 1935.
Phil 5262.9.25	Psychology. 4. ed. (Angell, J.R.) N.Y., 1908.
Phil 5252.89.5	Psychology. 4th ed. (Woodworth, R.S.) N.Y., 1940.
Phil 1535.6.20	Psychology. 5. ed. (Munn, Norman Leslie.) Boston, 1966.
Phil 5257.22.3	Psychology. 6th ed. v.5. (Maher, Michael.) London, 1909.
VPhil 5205.6	Psychology. 7. ed. (Ryland, F.) London, 1897.
VPhil 5205.7	Pamphlet box. Psychology. 1824-1909.
VPhil 5205.18	Pamphlet box. Psychology. 1829-1906.
VPhil 5205.8	Pamphlet vol. Psychology. 1845-1928. 27 pam.
Phil 5258.118	Pamphlet box. Psychology. 1903-1908.
Phil 7060.122	Psychology and achievement. (Society of Applied Psychology.) San Francisco, 1914.
Phil 9120.175	Psychology and common life. (Hoffman, Frank S.) N.Y., 1912.
Phil 3821.23	Psychology and ethics. (Hollingworth, H.L.) N.Y., 1949.
Phil 3821.23.2	Psychology and ethics of Spinoza. (Bidney, David.) New Haven, 1940.
Phil 5252.37	The psychology and ethics of Spinoza. 2nd ed. (Bidney, David.) N.Y., 1962.
Phil 5850.255	Psychology and folk-lore. (Marett, R.R.) N.Y., 1920.
Phil 5850.278.7	Psychology and human living. (Langer, W.C.) N.Y., 1943.
	Psychology and industrial efficiency. (Münsterberg, H.) Boston, 1913.
Phil 5257.53	Psychology and life. (Ruch, F.L.) Chicago, 1937.
Phil 5262.45.10	Psychology and life. (Weatherhead, L.D.) N.Y., 1940.
Phil 5250.17.10	Psychology and logic. (Kantor, J.R.) Bloomington, 1945. 2v.
Phil 5247.51	Psychology and modern problems. (Hadfield, J.A.) London, 1935.
Phil 6317.2	Psychology and morals. (Hadfield, J.A.) London, 1923.
Phil 6317.2.7	Psychology and morals. (Hadfield, J.A.) N.Y., 1928.
Phil 6317.2.8	Psychology and morals. 8th ed. (Hadfield, J.A.) London, 1930.
Phil 5627.56.7	Psychology and mystical experience. (Howley, John.) London, 1920.
Phil 5247.27	Psychology and natural theology. (Hill, Owen Aloysuis.) N.Y., 1921.
Phil 5401.4	The psychology and neurology of fear. (Morse, J.) Worcester, 1907.
Phil 5257.55	Psychology and personality development. (Rexroad, Carl N.) Boston, 1940.
Phil 5649.40	Psychology and physical activity. (Cratty, Bryant J.) Englewood Cliffs, 1968.
Phil 5258.112	Psychology and physiology apparatus and supplies. (Stoelting, C.H., Co., Chicago.) Chicago, 1923.
Phil 6321.9.6	Psychology and politics. (Lasswell, H.D.) Chicago, 1934.
Phil 5850.162	Psychology and practical life. (Collins, Mary.) London, 1936.
Phil 5247.1.2	Psychology and psychic culture. (Halleck, R.P.) N.Y., 1895.
Phil 5241.28.10	Psychology and psychotherapy. (Brown, W.) London, 1922.
Phil 6327.4.80	The psychology and psychotherapy of Otto Rank. (Karpf, Jay B.) N.Y., 1953.
Phil 5627.143	Psychology and religion. (Forsyth, D.) London, 1935.

Phil 6319.1.56   Psychology and religion. (Jung, C.G.) New Haven, 1955.

Phil 5627.62.10   Psychology and religion. (Waterhouse, E.S.) London, 1930.

Phil 8587.55   Psychology and religious truth. (Hughes, T.H.) London, 1942.

Phil 5241.58   Psychology and self-development. (Bennett, H.E.) Boston, 1923.

Phil 5243.7.16   Psychology and social practice. (Dewey, John.) Chicago, 1909.

Phil 5252.12.35   Psychology and social sanity. (Münsterberg, H.) Garden City, 1914.

Phil 5627.98   Psychology and the church. (Hardman, Oscar.) London, 1925.

Phil 5240.37   Psychology and the cosmic order. (Anderson, L.F.) n.p., 1939.

Phil 5850.349.50   Psychology and the day's work. (Swift, Edgar J.) N.Y., 1924.

Phil 5261.18   Psychology and the Franciscan school. (Vogel, C.L.) N.Y., 1932.

Phil 5252.96   Psychology and the human dilemma. (May, Rollo.) Princeton, 1967.

Phil 6321.48   Psychology and the measure of man. (Lyons, Joseph.) N.Y., 1963.

Phil 5258.121A   Psychology and the promethean will. (Sheldon, W.H.) N.Y., 1936.

Phil 5258.19   Psychology and the psychosis. (Snider, D.J.) St.Louis, 1896.

Phil 5241.28.7   Psychology and the sciences. (Brown, W.) London, 1924.

Phil 5241.109   Psychology and the social pattern. (Blackburn, J.M.) London, 1945.

Phil 6327.4.40A   Psychology and the soul. (Rank, Otto.) Philadelphia, 1950.

Phil 8408.50   Psychology and the visual arts: selected readings. (Hogg, James.) Harmondsworth, 1969.

Phil 8580.5   Psychology and theology. (Alliott, R.) London, 1855.

Phil 5850.135   Psychology applied. (Bingham, W.V.) n.p., 1923.

Phil 5850.166   Psychology applied. (Crane, G.W.) Chicago, 1933.

Phil 5240.4   Psychology applied to legal evidence. (Arnold, G.F.) Calcutta, 1906.

Phil 5850.228.15   Psychology applied to life and work. (Hepner, Harry W.) N.Y., 1942.

Phil 6132.18   Psychology applied to medicine. (Wells, D.W.) Philadelphia, 1907.

Phil 5262.34   Psychology as science, its problems and points of view. (Weld, Harry P.) London, 1928.

Phil 5262.34.2   Psychology as science, its problems and points of view. (Weld, Harry P.) N.Y., 1928.

Phil 5255.70   Psychology as you may like it. (Platonov, Konstantin Konstantinovich.) Moscow, 1965.

Phil 5850.102   Psychology at work. (Acilles, P.S.) N.Y., 1932.

Phil 5251.1.10   Psychology descriptive and explanatory. (Ladd, G.T.) N.Y., 1895.

Phil 5228.8   Psychology down the ages. (Spearman, C.) London, 1937. 2v.

Phil 5270.36   The psychology experiment. 2d ed. (Anderson, Barry F.) Belmont, Calif., 1971.

Phil 5241.88.3.5   Psychology for contemporary living. 1st American ed. (Bühler, Charlotte M.) N.Y., 1969.

Phil 5252.75   Psychology for everyman. (Mander, A.E.) London, 1939.

Phil 5258.116.5   Psychology for everyone. (Sprott, W.J.H.) London, 1937.

Phil 5850.340.50   Psychology for executives. (Smith, E.D.) N.Y., 1928.

Phil 5590.30   Psychology for individual education. (Raushenbush, E.) N.Y., 1942.

Phil 5850.385.65   Psychology for religious and social workers. (West, P.V.) N.Y., 1930.

Phil 5850.281   Psychology for the returning serviceman. 1st ed. (National Research Council.) Washington, 1945.

Phil 5262.21.2   Psychology from the standpoint of a behaviorist. 2d ed. (Watson, John B.) Philadelphia, 1924.

Phil 5262.21.3   Psychology from the standpoint of a behaviorist. 3d ed. (Watson, John B.) Philadelphia, 1929.

Phil 5252.12.45   Psychology general and applied. (Münsterberg, H.) N.Y., 1914.

Phil 5242.51   Psychology in action. (Clawson, J.) N.Y., 1946.

Phil 5212.5   Psychology in America. (Chin, Robert.) N.Y., 1929.

Phil 5223.10   Psychology in Belgium. (Nuttin, Jozef.) Louvain, 1961.

Phil 5210.15   Psychology in Canada. (Appley, Mortimertt.) Ottawa, 1967.

Phil 5258.34.10   Psychology in daily life. (Seashore, C.E.) N.Y., 1928.

Phil 5261.21   Psychology in everyday life. (Varnuar, W.C.) N.Y., 1938.

Phil 6322.30   Psychology in general practice. (Moncrieff, A.A.) London, 1945.

Phil 5850.264   Psychology in industry. (Maier, Norman Raymond Frederick.) Boston, 1946.

Phil 5850.385.86   Psychology in living. 3rd ed. (White, Wendell.) N.Y., 1955.

Phil 5225.4.1   Psychology in the making; histories of selected research problems. (Postman, Leo Joseph.) N.Y., 1968.

Phil 5222.9.5   Psychology in the modern world. (Muller, Philippe.) N.Y., 1969.

Phil 5238.40   Psychology in the Soviet Union. (Simon, Brian.) Stanford, Calif., 1957.

Phil 5243.24.5   Psychology in theory and application. (Dresser, H.) N.Y., 1924.

Phil 5257.82   Psychology in theory and practice. (Ringness, Thomas A.) Boston, 1959.

Phil 5850.221   Psychology in use. (Gray, John S.) N.Y., 1941.

Phil 5261.17.10   Psychology laboratory manual. (Valentine, Willard Lee.) N.Y., 1932.

Phil 5261.17.12   Psychology laboratory manual. (Valentine, Willard Lee.) N.Y., 1933.

Phil 5252.15   Psychology normal and morbid. (Mercier, C.A.) London, 1901.

Phil 5246.51   Psychology of a growing personality. (Gregg, F.M.) Lincoln, 1938.

Phil 6329.16   The psychology of abnormal behavior. (Thorpe, Louis P.) N.Y., 1961.

Phil 6322.16.9   The psychology of abnormal people. 2d ed. (Morgan, John J.B.) N.Y., 1936.

Phil 6322.16.5   The psychology of abnormal people with educational applications. (Morgan, John J.B.) N.Y., 1935.

Phil 6315.2.81   The psychology of accidents and "symtomatic actions". (Tannenbaum, S.A.) N.Y., 1924.

Phil 9530.31   The psychology of achievement. (Pitkin, Walter B.) N.Y., 1930.

Phil 6128.49   Psychology of adjustment. (Shaffer, Laurance F.) Boston, 1936.

Phil 6128.49.2   The psychology of adjustment. 2d ed. (Shaffer, Laurance F.) Boston, 1956.

Phil 5876.25.3   The psychology of adolescence; behavior and development. 3rd ed. (Horrocks, John Edwin.) Boston, 1969.

Htn   Phil 5252.62.5*   Psychology of aesthetics. (Martin, L.J.) n.p., 1905-1907. 4 pam.

Phil 5421.20.95   The psychology of aggression. (Buss, Arnold H.) N.Y., 1961.

Phil 5350.5A   The psychology of aging. (Birren, James E.) Englewood Cliffs, N.J., 1964.

Phil 5810.7.5   The psychology of animals in relation to human psychology. (Alverdes, F.) London, 1932.

Phil 6117.15   The psychology of animated nature. (Holland, G.C.) London, 1848.

Phil 5421.10.20   The psychology of anxiety. (Levitt, Eugene Elmer.) Indianapolis, 1967.

Phil 8415.8A   The psychology of art. (Ogden, R.M.) N.Y., 1938. 2v.

Phil 8416.10   A psychology of art creation. (Portnoy, Julius.) Philadephia, 1942.

Phil 5627.147.5   The psychology of asceticism. (Lindworsky, J.) London, 1936.

Phil 5325.5   The psychology of association. (Arnold, Felix.) N.Y., 1906.

Phil 5325.5.2   The psychology of association. (Arnold, Felix.) N.Y., 1906.

Phil 5330.4.7   The psychology of attention. (Ribot, T.) Chicago, 1890.

Phil 5330.4.5   Psychology of attention. (Ribot, T.) N.Y., 1889.

Phil 8408.35   The psychology of beauty. (Howes, E.D. (Mrs.).) Boston, 1905.

Phil 8893.40   The psychology of behavior. (Severn, Elizabeth.) N.Y., 1917.

Phil 6312.16   The psychology of behavior disorders. (Cameron, N.) Boston, 1947.

Phil 5070.7   The psychology of belief. (Lindsay, J.) Edinburgh, 1910.

Phil 5070.21   The psychology of belief. (Lundholm, H.) Durham, 1936.

Phil 6319.1.180   The psychology of C.G. Jung. (Jacobi, Jolan.) London, 1942.

Phil 6319.1.183.6   The psychology of C.G. Jung. (Jacobi, Jolan.) New Haven, 1962.

Phil 6319.1.185   The psychology of C.G. Jung. 5th ed. (Jacobi, Jolan.) London, 1951.

Phil 5850.348   The psychology of careers. 1st ed. (Super, D.E.) N.Y., 1957.

Phil 9035.61.5   Psychology of character. (Allers, Rudolf.) N.Y., 1931.

Phil 9035.45   The psychology of character. (Roback, A.A.) London, 1927.

Phil 9035.45.2   The psychology of character. (Roback, A.A.) N.Y., 1927.

Phil 9035.45.3   The psychology of character. (Roback, A.A.) N.Y., 1928.

Phil 9035.45.10   The psychology of character. 3. ed. (Roback, A.A.) Cambridge, Mass., 1952.

Phil 9035.45.15   The psychology of character by A.A. Roback. (Allport, G.W.) Princeton, 1927.

Phil 5627.142   The psychology of Christian personality. (Ligon, E.M.) N.Y., 1936.

Phil 5780.27   The psychology of commitment. (Kiesler, Charles A.) N.Y., 1971.

Phil 5257.28.10   The psychology of common sense. (Roback, A.A.) Cambridge, 1939.

Phil 5520.70.5   The psychology of communication. (Eisenson, J.) N.Y., 1963.

Phil 5627.29   The psychology of confession. (Roback, A.A.) Montreal, 1917.

Phil 5374.53   The psychology of consciousness. (King, C. Daly.) London, 1932.

Phil 5249.6.5   The psychology of conviction. (Jastrow, J.) Boston, 1918.

Phil 5401.5   The psychology of courage. (Lord, H.G.) Boston, 1918.

Phil 7225.2A   The psychology of day-dreams. (Varendonck, Julien.) London, 1921.

Phil 5850.385.80   The psychology of dealing with people. (White, Wendell.) N.Y., 1936.

Phil 5850.385.82   The psychology of dealing with people. (White, Wendell.) N.Y., 1941.

Phil 5245.44   The psychology of desire. (Fisher, R.A.) Saskatoon, 1930.

Phil 6480.125   The psychology of dreams. (Walsh, William S.) N.Y., 1920.

Phil 6111.60   The psychology of efficiency. (Bills, A.G.) N.Y., 1943.

Phil 5257.13   Psychology of efficiency. (Ruger, Henry A.) N.Y., 1910.

Phil 3120.65.30   The psychology of Egon Brunswik. (Hammond, Kenneth R.) N.Y., 1966.

Phil 6322.8.5*   The psychology of emotion; morbid and normal. (MacCurdy, J.T.) London, 1925.

Phil 5409.5   The psychology of expectation. (Hitchcock, C.M.) N.Y., 1903.

Phil 9380.2A   The psychology of fear and courage. (Glover, E.) Harmondsworth, Eng., 1940.

Phil 5400.90   The psychology of feeling and emotion. 1st ed. (Ruckmick, C.A.) N.Y., 1936.

Phil 6317.6   The psychology of functional neuroses. (Hallingworth, H.L.) N.Y., 1920.

Phil 5470.5   The psychology of gambling. (Bergler, Edmund.) N.Y., 1957.

Phil 5247.38   The psychology of Gestalt. (Helson, Harry.) Urbana, 1926.

Phil 6060.22   The psychology of handwriting. (French, William L.) N.Y., 1922.

Phil 6060.18   The psychology of handwriting. (Saudek, R.) London, 1925.

Phil 5403.14   The psychology of happiness. (Durand, Leo.) Blackstone, 1968.

Phil 9245.46.5   The psychology of happiness. (Pitkin, W.B.) N.Y., 1929.

Phil 5421.35.15   The psychology of hope. 1. ed. (Stotland, Ezra.) San Francisco, 1969.

Phil 6316.10   The psychology of human conflict. (Guthrie, E.R.) N.Y., 1938.

Phil 5255.64   Psychology of human development. (Pikunas, J.) N.Y., 1961.

Phil 5259.34   The psychology of human differences. (Tyler, Leona E.) N.Y., 1947.

Phil 2880.8.30   The psychology of imagination. (Sartre, Jean Paul.) N.Y., 1948.

Phil 2880.8.33   The psychology of imagination. (Sartre, Jean Paul.) N.Y., 1961.

Phil 5246.41.4   Psychology of individual differences. (Gilliland, A.R.) N.Y., 1939.

Phil 6957.7   The psychology of insanity. (Hart, Bernard.) Cambridge, 1914.

Phil 6957.7.3   The psychology of insanity. (Hart, Bernard.) Cambridge, 1921.

Phil 6957.7.4   The psychology of insanity. (Hart, Bernard.) Cambridge, 1925.

Phil 6957.7.4.10   The psychology of insanity. (Hart, Bernard.) Cambridge, 1962.

Phil 6957.7.4.7   The psychology of insanity. 4. ed. (Hart, Bernard.) N.Y., 1937.
Phil 8707.5   The psychology of inspiration. (Raymond, G.L.) N.Y., 1908.
Phil 5255.51   The psychology of intelligence. (Piaget, Jean.) N.Y., 1950.
Phil 5262.37   Psychology of intelligence and will. (Wyatt, Horace G.) London, 1930.
Phil 5590.462   The psychology of interpersonal behavior. (Argyle, Michael.) Harmondsworth, 1967.
Phil 5850.228.20   The psychology of interpersonal relations. (Heider, Fritz.) N.Y., 1958.
Phil 5850.228.20.5   The psychology of interpersonal relations. (Heider, Fritz.) N.Y., 1967.
Phil 5352.15   Psychology of judgment and choice. (Restle, Frank.) N.Y., 1961.
Phil 6319.1.214   The psychology of Jung. (Dry, Avis Mary.) London, 1961.
Phil 5520.51A   The psychology of language. (Pillsbury, Walter B.) N.Y., 1928.
Phil 5525.12   The psychology of laughter. (Sidis, B.) N.Y., 1913.
Phil 5525.12.3   The psychology of laughter. (Sidis, B.) N.Y., 1919.
Phil 5525.38.2   The psychology of laughter. 2. ed. (Piddington, Ralph.) N.Y., 1963.
Phil 5525.22   The psychology of laughter and comedy. (Grieg, J.Y.J.) London, 1923.
Phil 5545.49.3A   The psychology of learning. (Meumann, E.) N.Y., 1913.
Phil 5535.50   Psychology of learning. (Sahakian, William S.) Chicago, 1970.
Phil 25.152   The psychology of learning and motivation. N.Y. 1,1967+ 5v.
Phil 2730.114   The psychology of Maine de Biran. (Moore, Francis Charles Timothy.) Oxford, 1970.
Phil 5850.385.85   The psychology of making life interesting. (White, Wendell.) N.Y., 1939.
Phil 5520.104   The psychology of meaning. (Prasod, Kali.) Lucknon, 1949.
Phil 6322.6   The psychology of medicine. (Mitchell, T.W.) London, 1921.
Phil 5425.47.5   The psychology of men of genius. (Kretschmer, Ernst.) London, 1931.
Phil 5241.59.5   The psychology of mental arrangement. (Bentley, I.M.) Worcester, 1902.
Phil 6962.15   The psychology of mental disorders. (Myerson, Abraham.) N.Y., 1927.
Phil 6113.28.5   The psychology of mind. 2. ed. (Dercum, F.X.) Philadelphia, 1925.
Phil 5259.30   The psychology of normal people. (Tiffin, J.) Boston, 1940.
Phil 5627.36   The psychology of oriental religious experience. (Kato, Katsuji.) Menaska, Wis., 1915.
Phil 5585.205   The psychology of perception. (Dember, William Norton.) N.Y., 1961.
Phil 5585.242   The psychology of perception. (Hamlyn, David Walter.) London, 1961.
Phil 5585.213   The psychology of perception. (Vernon, Magdalen.) Harmondsworth, 1962.
Phil 6122.60.5   Psychology of personal adjustment. 2d ed. (McKinney, Fred.) N.Y., 1949.
Phil 6390.4   The psychology of personality. (Bagby, English.) N.Y., 1928.
Phil 5590.423   Psychology of personality. (Bonner, Hubert.) N.Y., 1961.
Phil 5590.325   Psychology of personality. (McCary, James Leslie.) N.Y., 1956.
Phil 575.98   Psychology of personality. (Stagner, R.) N.Y., 1937.
Phil 575.62   The psychology of personality. (Valentine, P.F.) N.Y., 1927.
Phil 5190.10   The psychology of persuasion. (MacPherson, William.) London, 1920.
Phil 182.79.5   The psychology of philosophers. (Herzberg, Alex.) London, 1929.
Phil 5875.80   The psychology of play. (Millar, Susanna.) Harmondsworth, 1968.
Phil 5402.19   The psychology of pleasantness and unpleasantness. (Beebe-Center, J.G.) N.Y., 1932.
Phil 6117.33   The psychology of power. (Hadfield, J.A.) N.Y., 1923.
Phil 6117.33.5   The psychology of power. (Hadfield, J.A.) N.Y., 1924.
Phil 5627.14   The psychology of prayer. (Strong, A.L.) Chicago, 1909.
Phil 5284.4   The psychology of private events; perspectives on covert response systems. N.Y., 1971.
Phil 5627.79   Psychology of prophecy. (Kaplan, J.H.) Philadelphia, 1908.
Phil 5610.1.15   The psychology of public speaking. (Scott, W.D.) N.Y., 1926.
Phil 5610.1   The psychology of public speaking. (Scott, W.D.) Philadelphia, 1907.
Phil 5620.1.5   The psychology of reasoning. (Binet, A.) Chicago, 1899.
Phil 5620.1.7   The psychology of reasoning. (Binet, A.) Chicago, 1907.
Phil 5620.7   The psychology of reasoning. (Pillsbury, W.B.) N.Y., 1910.
Phil 5620.9.7   Psychology of reasoning. (Rignano, Eugenio.) N.Y., 1927.
Phil 5620.12   The psychology of reasoning. Diss. (Dunn, Miriam Frances.) n.p., 1926.
Phil 6125.9.3   The psychology of relaxation. (Patrick, G.T.W.) Boston, 1916.
Phil 6125.9   The psychology of relaxation. (Patrick, G.T.W.) Boston, 1916.
Phil 5627.259.20   The psychology of religion. (Clark, W.H.) N.Y., 1959.
Phil 5627.26.5   The psychology of religion. (Coe, George A.) Chicago, 1917.
Phil 5627.192   The psychology of religion. (Grensted, L.W.) N.Y., 1952.
Phil 5627.101   The psychology of religion. (Josey, C.C.) N.Y., 1927.
Phil 5627.113.95   Psychology of religion. (Selbie, W.B.) Oxford, 1924.
NEDL Phil 5627.1   The psychology of religion. (Starbuck, E.D.) London, 1899.
Phil 5627.1   The psychology of religion. (Starbuck, E.D.) London, 1899.
Phil 5627.164   The psychology of religious awakening. (Clark, E.T.) N.Y., 1929.
Phil 5627.56.4   The psychology of religious belief. (Pratt, James B.) N.Y., 1907.
Phil 5627.17   Psychology of religious experience. (Ames, E.S.) Boston, 1910.
Phil 5627.20.7   The psychology of religious mysticism. (Leuba, J.H.) London, 1925.
Phil 5627.30   Psychology of religious sects. (McComas, Henry Clay.) N.Y., 1912.
Phil 5630.5A   The psychology of rumor. (Allport, G.W.) N.Y., 1947.
Phil 5630.5.2   The psychology of rumor. (Allport, G.W.) N.Y., 1948.

Phil 5643.107   The psychology of seeing. (Brandt, Herman F.) N.Y., 1945.
Phil 6329.4   The psychology of self-consciousness. (Turner, Julia.) London, 1923.
Phil 5858.5   The psychology of self-esteem. (Branden, Nathaniel.) Los Angeles, 1969.
Phil 9495.132   The psychology of sex. (Wexberg, Erwin.) N.Y., 1931.
X Cg Phil 7075.137   Psychology of sex relations. (Reik, T.) N.Y., 1945.
Phil 5648.11   The psychology of skill. (Book, W.F.) Missoula, Mont., 1908.
Phil 5648.11.5   The psychology of skill. (Book, W.F.) N.Y., 1925.
Phil 7080.54   The psychology of sleep. (Foulkes, David.) N.Y., 1966.
Phil 6317.23   The psychology of social movements. (Hopkins, P.) London, 1938.
Phil 5650.9A   Psychology of sound. (Watt, Henry J.) Cambridge, 1917.
Phil 672.25   Psychology of space perception. (Stevens, E.M.) New Orleans, 1915.
Phil 5520.70   Psychology of speech. (Eisenson, J.) N.Y., 1938.
Phil 5520.72   The psychology of speech. (Stinchfield, S.M.) Boston, 1928.
Phil 5520.702   The psychology of speech and language. (De Vito, Joseph A.) N.Y., 1970.
Phil 7140.2A   The psychology of suggestion. (Sidis, B.) N.Y., 1898.
Phil 6854.4   The psychology of suicide. (Shneidman, Edwin S.) N.Y., 1970.
Phil 5627.269.10   The psychology of superstition. (Johoda, Gustav.) London, 1969.
Phil 1020.4.15   The psychology of the active intellect of Averroes. Thesis. (Christ, Paul S.) Philadelphia, 1926.
Phil 292.5   The psychology of the atom. (Lilburne, H.A.) London, 1924.
Phil 5850.230.15   The psychology of the audience. (Hollingworth, H.L.) N.Y., 1935.
Phil 5865.5.5   The psychology of the child. (Piaget, Jean.) N.Y., 1969.
Phil 5627.133   Psychology of the Christian life. (Pyon, T.W.) N.Y., 1922.
Phil 5400.18   The psychology of the emotions. (Ribot, T.) London, 1897.
Phil 7069.18.20   The psychology of the future. (Boirac, Emile.) N.Y., 1918.
Phil 5850.291   The psychology of the interview. (Oldfield, R.C.) London, 1941.
Phil 5850.291.3   The psychology of the interview. 3rd ed. (Oldfield, R.C.) London, 1947.
Phil 5627.99   The psychology of the Methodist revival. (Dimond, S.G.) London, 1926.
Phil 5241.24.2A   Psychology of the moral self. (Bosanquet, B.) London, 1904.
Phil 6060.1.25   The psychology of the movements of handwriting. (Crepieux-Jamin, J.) London, 1926.
Phil 5246.20   Psychology of the normal and subnormal. (Goddard, H.H.) N.Y., 1919.
Phil 5252.42   Psychology of the other one. (Meyer, M.F.) Columbia, 1921.
Phil 5890.3.1   The psychology of the physically handicapped. (Pintner, Rudolf.) N.Y., 1945.
Phil 6951.12   Psychology of the Salem witchcraft...1697. Photoreproduction. (Beard, G.M.) N.Y., 1882.
Phil 9500.8   The psychology of the sickbed. (Berg, Jan Hendrik van den.) Pittsburgh, 1966.
Phil 5258.87   The psychology of the thinker. (Saxby, I.B.) London, 1926.
Phil 6319.1.9.5   Psychology of the unconscious. (Jung, C.G.) London, 1916.
Phil 6319.1.9A   Psychology of the unconscious. (Jung, C.G.) N.Y., 1916.
Phil 5520.714   The psychology of thinking. (Bourne, Lyle Eugene.) Englewood Cliffs, N.J., 1971.
Phil 5252.22   The psychology of thinking. (Miller, T.E.) N.Y., 1909.
Phil 5520.295   The psychology of thinking. (Thomsen, Robert.) Harmondsworth, 1959.
Phil 5520.107   The psychology of thinking. 1. ed. (Vinacke, W.E.) N.Y., 1952.
Phil 5520.128   The psychology of thought and judgment. (Johnson, D.McE.) N.Y., 1955.
Phil 5247.16.15   The psychology of thought approached through studies of sleeping and dreaming. (Hollingworth, H.L.) N.Y., 1926.
Phil 5247.16.16   The psychology of thought approached through studies of sleeping and dreaming. (Hollingworth, H.L.) N.Y., 1927.
Phil 5585.140.3   The psychology of time. (Fraisse, Paul.) N.Y., 1963.
Phil 5585.22   The psychology of time. (Nichols, H.) N.Y., 1891.
Phil 672.133   The psychology of time. (Sturt, Mary.) London, 1925.
Phil 5627.205   The psychology of unbelief. (Ruemke, H.C.) London, 1952.
Phil 5520.19   The psychology of unconventional language. (Sechrist, F.K.) n.p., n.d.
Phil 5259.7.15   The psychology of wants, interests and attitudes. (Thorndike, E.L.) N.Y., 1935.
Phil 6128.84   The psychology of work. (Scott, Donald Fletcher.) London, 1970.
Phil 5190.10.1   The psychology persuasion. (MacPherson, William.) N.Y., 192-?
Phil 5259.24.2   Psychology really simplified in terms of machinery. (Tickell, Sydney.) Cirencester, 1927.
Phil 23.23   Psychology series lecture. (National Advisory Council on Radio in Education.) Chicago. 11-30
Phil 5245.31   Psychology simplified. (Flower, J.C.) London, 1928.
Phil 5241.87   Psychology today. (Bingham, Walter V.) Chicago, 1932.
Phil 25.153   Psychology today. Del Mar, California. 1,1967+ 3v.
Phil 5627.122   Psychology's defence of the faith. (Yellowlees, David.) London, 1930.
Phil 7069.59.40   Psychometric analysis. (Long, Max Freedom.) Vista, Calif., 1959.
Phil 5246.47.6   Psychometric methods. (Guilford, Joy Paul.) N.Y., 1954.
Phil 5246.47.5A   Psychometric methods. 1. ed. (Guilford, Joy Paul.) N.Y., 1936.
Phil 5272.6   Psychometric theory. (Nunnally, Jum Clarence.) N.Y., 1967.
Phil 5850.288.5   Psychometrics. (O'Connor, Johnson.) Cambridge, Mass., 1934.
Phil 25.71   Psychometrika. Colorado Springs. 1,1936+ 32v.
Phil 25.71.6   Psychometrika. Monograph supplements. Toronto. 1,1938+
Phil 25.71.5   Psychometrika. Topical and author indexes, 1936-1945. n.p., n.d.
Phil 6960.13   Psychomotor aspects of mental disease. (King, H.E.) Cambridge, Mass., 1954.
Phil 6312.3   Psychoneuroses of war and peace. (Culpin, Millais.) Cambridge, Eng., 1920.
Phil 6313.3   Les psychonévroses et leur traitement moral. 3e éd. (Dubois, Paul.) Paris, 1909.
Phil 25.142   Psychonomic science. Goleta, Califorina. 1,1964+ 17v.
Htn Phil 7075.7.8*   Psychopathia sexualis. (Krafft-Ebing, Richard von.) Stuttgart, 1893.

Phil 11.6   Psychopathic Hospital, Boston, Mass. Contributions. 1-63,1913-1914+

Phil 6320.8   Psychopathic personalities. (Kahn, Eugen.) New Haven, 1931.

Phil 6317.24   Psychopathic states. (Henderson, D.K.) N.Y., 1939.

Phil 6960.3   Die psychopathischen Minderwertigkeiten. (Koch, J.L.A.) Ravensburg, 1891-93. 3v.

Phil 6328.14.2   Die psychopathischen Personlichkeiten. 2. Aufl. (Schneider, Kurt.) Leipzig, 1928.

Phil 6360.12   Psychopathological disorders of childhood. (Quay, Herbert Callister.) N.Y., 1972.

Phil 6305.5.5   Pamphlet box. Psychopathological references. English and American.

Phil 6968.12   Psychopathological researches. (Sidis, Boris.) N.Y., 1902.

Phil 25.155   Psychopathologie africaine. Dakar. 1,1965+ 3v.

Phil 6321.12.10   Psychopathologie de l'échec. (Laforgue, R.) Paris, 1944.

Phil 6319.15   Psychopathologie en mensbeschouwing. (Janse de Jonge, Adriaan Leendert.) Kampen, 1968.

Phil 6322.14.25   Psychopathologie funktioneller Störungen. (McDougall, W.) Leipzig, 1931.

Phil 6313.18   Psychopathologie générale. (Deshaies, Gabriel.) Paris, 1959.

Phil 6317.17.5   Psychopathology; its development and place in medicine. (Hart, Bernard.) Cambridge, 1939.

Phil 6317.17.2   Psychopathology. (Hart, Bernard.) N.Y., 1927.

Phil 6320.1.5   Psychopathology. (Kempf, E.J.) St. Louis, 1921.

Phil 6327.26   Psychopathology. (Reed, C.F.) Cambridge, Mass., 1958.

Phil 6329.20   Psychopathology. (Taylor, Frederick K.) London, 1966.

Phil 6323.4.5   Psychopathology. 2d ed. (Nicole, J.E.) Baltimore, 1934.

Phil 6323.4.6   Psychopathology. 4. ed. (Nicole, J.E.) Baltimore, 1947.

Phil 6321.9.8   Psychopathology and politics. (Lasswell, H.D.) N.Y., 1960.

Phil 5625.75.35   Psychopathology and psychiatry. (Pavlov, Ivan P.) Moscow, 1962?

Phil 6310.20   Psychopathology of communication. (American Psychopathological Association.) N.Y., 1958.

Phil 6315.2.33   Psychopathology of everyday life. (Freud, Sigmund.) London, 1914.

Phil 6315.2.33.5   Psychopathology of everyday life. (Freud, Sigmund.) London, 1917.

Phil 6315.2.33.6   Psychopathology of everyday life. (Freud, Sigmund.) N.Y., 1917.

Phil 6315.2.33.8   The psychopathology of everyday life. (Freud, Sigmund.) N.Y., 1966.

Phil 6615.10   Psychopathology of hysteria. (Fox, Charles Daniel.) Boston, 1913.

Phil 5520.636   Psychophonetik; Untersuchungen über Lautsymbolik und Motivation. (Ertel, Suitbert.) Göttingen, 1969.

Phil 5585.310   Psychophysical analysis of visual space. 1. ed. (Baird, John C.) Oxford, 1970.

Phil 5585.228   Psychophysical relations in the perception of velocity. (Mashhour, M.) Stockholm, 1964.

Phil 5246.19.10   Psychophysik. (Gutberlet, C.) Mainz, 1905.

Phil 5262.14   Psychophysik. (Wirth, W.) Leipzig, 1912.

Phil 2480.81   La psychophysiologie de Cabanis. Thèse. (Tencer, Marie.) Toulouse, 1931.

Phil 356.1   Psychophysiologische Erkenntnistheorie. (Ziehen, T.) Jena, 1898.

Phil 5590.471   Psychophysiologische Persönlichkeitsforschung. (Fahrenberg, Jochen.) Göttingen, 1967.

Phil 5245.15   La psychophysique. (Foucault, Marcel.) Paris, 1901.

Phil 6122.48   Psychophysische Behandlungs-Methoden. (Mohr, Fritz.) Leipzig, 1925.

Phil 5251.3.5   Psychophysische Streitfragen. (Langer, P.) Ohrdruf, 1893.

Phil 5257.28.15   Psychorama; a mental outlook and analysis. (Roback, A.A.) Cambridge, 1942.

Phil 7140.5   La psychose d'influence. Thèse. (Lévy, Alfred.) Paris, 1914.

Phil 6961.7   La psychose hallucinatoire chronique. Thèse. (Lauze, Charles A.) Paris, 1914.

Phil 6317.30   Psychosocial medicine. (Halliday, James.) N.Y., 1948.

Phil 6132.38   Psychosocial problems of college men. (Wedge, Bryant M.) New Haven, 1958.

Phil 5040.95.5   Psychosomatic diagnosis. (Dunbar, H.F.) N.Y., 1943.

Phil 25.63.5   Psychosomatis medicine. Monograph. Washington, D.C. 1-3 2v.

Phil 7069.15.53   Psychosophy. (Richmond, Cora L.) Chicago, 1915.

Phil 6996.5   Psychosurgery. (Freeman, Walter.) Springfield, 1942.

Phil 5850.342   La psychotechnique. (Sollier, Paul.) Bruxelles, 1935.

Phil 5246.23.9   Psychotechnisches Praktikum. (Giese, Fritz.) Halle, 1923.

Phil 6980.447   Der Psychotherapeut als Paktnei. (Maeder, Alphonse.) Zürich, 1957.

Phil 6125.5   Psychotherapeutics; a symposium. Boston, 1910.

Phil 6125.5.5   Psychotherapeutics. Boston, 1912.

Phil 6319.1.74   Psychotherapeutische Zeitfragen. (Jung, C.G.) Leipzig, 1914.

Phil 6951.29   Psychotheraphy with schizophrenia. (Brody, E.B.) N.Y., 1952.

Phil 6960.6.7   Psychotherapie, Charakterlehre, Psychoanalyze, Hynose, Psychogogik. 2. Aufl. (Kronfeld, Arthur.) Berlin, 1925.

Phil 6980.363.20   Psychotherapie. (Isserlin, Max.) Berlin, 1926.

Phil 6960.6.5   Psychotherapie. (Kronfeld, Arthur.) Berlin, 1924.

Phil 6325.10   Psychotherapie. (Prinzhorn, Hans.) Leipzig, 1929.

Phil 6967.18.2   Psychothérapie et relations humaines. (Rogers, C.R.) Louvain, 1965. 2v.

Phil 6980.650.40   Psychothérapie et relations humaines. (Rogers, Carl Ransom.) Louvain, 1962. 2v.

Phil 6980.105.10   Les psychothérapies. 1. éd. (Berge, André.) Paris, 1968.

Phil 6311.24   Psychotherapy. (Barker, L.F.) N.Y., 1940.

Phil 6992.2   Psychotherapy. (Cohen, Jacques J.) London, 1936.

Phil 6980.224   Psychotherapy. (Dick, Samuel.) Minneapolis? 1909.

Phil 6980.484   Psychotherapy. (Münsterberg, Hugo.) N.Y., 1909.

Phil 6980.587   Psychotherapy. (Phillips, Ewing.) Englewood Cliffs, 1956.

Phil 6980.674   Psychotherapy. (Schelder, Paul.) N.Y., 1951.

Phil 6980.674.25   Psychotherapy. (Schofield, William.) Englewood Cliffs, N.J., 1964.

Phil 6129.6.5   Psychotherapy. (Taylor, E.W.) Cambridge, 1926.

Phil 6132.15   Psychotherapy. (Walsh, J.J.) London, 1912.

Phil 197.90   Psychotherapy. (Watts, A.W.) N.Y., 1961.

Phil 25.139   Psychotherapy; theory, research and practice. Menasha, Wis. 1,1963+ 2v.

Phil 6980.666   Psychotherapy and counselling; studies in technique. (Sahakian, William S.) Chicago, 1969.

Phil 6980.458.5   Psychotherapy and morality. (Margolis, Joseph.) N.Y., 1966.

Phil 6332.33   Psychotherapy and the behavoral sciences. (Wolberg, Lewis Robert.) N.Y., 1966.

Phil 6980.710.80   Psychotherapy and the modification of abnormal behavior. (Strupp, Hans Herman.) N.Y., 1971.

Phil 6980.780   Psychotherapy by reciprocal inhibition. (Wolpe, Joseph.) Stanford, 1958.

Phil 6321.18   Psychotherapy in medical practice. (Levine, M.) N.Y., 1942.

Phil 70.80   Psychotherapy in the Soviet Union. (Winn, R.B.) N.Y., 1961.

Phil 6319.1.260   The psychotherapy of C.G. Jung. (Hochheimer, Wolfgang.) N.Y., 1969.

Phil 6980.699   The psychotherapy relationship. (Snyder, William U.) N.Y., 1961.

Phil 6310.9   Psychotherapy with children. (Allen, Frederick H.) N.Y., 1942.

Phil 6953.18   Psychotherapy with schizophrenics. (Louisiana. Southeast Louisiana Hospital, Mandeville.) Baton Rouge, 1961.

Phil 6980.635.25   Psychotic art. (Reitman, F.) N.Y., 1951.

Phil 6319.20   Psychotic conflict and reality. (Jacobson, Edith.) N.Y., 1967.

Phil 6327.37.1   Psychotic states. (Rosenfeld, Herbert A.) N.Y., 1966.

Phil 5251.28   Psyckologiske studier. Supplementhefte til tidsschrift for aandskultur. (Lambek, C.) København, 1904.

Phil 5865.5   Psycologie et épistémologie génétiques, thèmes piagétiens. Paris, 1966.

Phil 5690.2   Psycologie stereotyper Systeme. (Bergler, Reinhold.) Bern, 1966.

Phil 25.28   Psyke; tidskrift fär psykologisk Farskuing. Stockholm. 1906-1920 4v.

Phil 6328.22   Psykiatriske forelaesninger. (Smith, J.C.) København, 1939.

Phil 6980.346   Psykisk sjukdom: illusioner och realiteter; en teoretisk studie. (Haakanson, Kaj.) Uppsala, 1968.

Phil 343.37F   De psykiska företeelsernas förhallande till rum och tid. (MacLeod, Andries Hugo Donald.) Stockholm, 1964.

Phil 6320.4   De psykiske spaltninger. (Kortsen, K.K.) København, 1916.

Phil 6325.20   Psykoanalyse er to ting. (Psykoanalytisk diskussionsklub.) København, 1960.

Phil 6325.20   Psykoanalytisk diskussionsklub. Psykoanalyse er to ting. København, 1960.

Phil 5241.104   Psykoligi. v.1-2. (Brandt, F.) København, 1934-40.

Phil 5249.2.16   Psykologi. (James, William.) Uppsala, 1925.

Phil 5247.84.4   Psykologi. 4. uppl. (Husén, Torsten.) Stockholm, 1966.

Phil 5590.504   Psykologi för Erl. (Bouman, Jan C.) Stockholm, 1968.

Phil 5247.10.3   Psykologi i omrids paa grundlag af erfarung. 3. ed. (Höffding, H.) København, 1892.

Phil 5247.10.4   Psykologi i omrids paa grundlag af erfarung. 9. ed. (Höffding, H.) København, 1892.

Phil 5590.470   Psykologi och mentalhygien. (Weldes, Göran.) Lund, 1969.

Phil 5228.14   Psykologi og psykologar i Norge. (Skard, Ase Gruda.) Oslo, 1959.

Phil 4600.2.40   Psykologi paa Dansk red Stig Bredstrup. (Larsson, Hans.) København, 1914.

Phil 5210.1   Psykologiens historie i Norge. (Aall, A.) Kristiania, 1911.

Phil 5222.22.5   Psykologiens udvikling. (Madsen, K.B.) København, 1970.

Phil 5203.4   Psykologiske tidsskrifter; liste over ikke-nordishe tidsskrifter av psykologisk interesse på nordishe bibliioteker. Oslo.

Phil 5238.248   Psykologisk bredvielläsning. v. 1-2. (Husén, Torsten.) Stockholm, 1967.

Phil 5871.65   Psykologisk iagttagelse af børn. (Rifbjerg, Sofie.) København, 1966.

Phil 103.5   Psykologisk ordbak. 2. uppl. (Sandström, C.I.) Stockholm, 1951.

Phil 5204.10.2.1   Psykologisk-pedagogisk uppslagsbok. Supplement. Stockholm, 1956.

Phil 5204.10.2   Psykologisk-pedagogisk uppslagsbok. 2. uppl. Stockholm, 1956. 3v.

Phil 5640.20   Psykologiska studier. (Nordvall, A.L.) Stockholm, 1885.

Phil 5261.12   De psykologiska vetenskapernas system. (Vannérus, A.) Stockholm, 1907.

Phil 5047.23.5   Det psykologiske grundlag for logiske domme. (Høffding, Harald.) København, 1899.

Phil 5247.10.19   Psykologiske undersogeler. (Höffding, H.) Kjøbenhavn, 1889.

Phil 5592.160   Psykometriska och experimentalpsykologiska metoder för klinisk tillämpning. (Dureman, I.) Stockholm, 1959.

Phil 5590.451   The physiological basis of habituation. (Glaser, Eric Michael.) London, 1966.

Phil 70.63   Pubblicazione. (Instituto di Studi Filosofici.) Milano. 1940-1952 9v.

Phil 52.11   Pubblicazioni. (Milan. Università. Instituto di Storia della Filosofia.) Milan. 1,1951+ 11v.

Phil 8877.54   The public conscience. (Cox, George C.) N.Y., 1922.

Phil 9490.3   The public duty of educated men. (Curtis, G.W.) Albany, N.Y., 1878.

Phil 9045.7   Public mindedness, an aspect of citizenship. (Tucker, W.J.) Concord, 1910.

Phil 9495.30   Public Morals Conference, London, 1910. The nation's morals. London, 1910.

Phil 9455.8   Public opinion,...an oration...Connecticut Beta of Phi Beta Kappa Society, July 28, 1852. (Howe, M.A. de Wolfe.) Hartford, 1852.

Phil 9455.12   Public opinion and world politics. (Wright, Quincy.) Chicago, 1933.

Phil 9455.4   Public opinion in war and peace. (Lowell, A.L.) Cambridge, 1923.

Phil 55.1   Public series in philosophy. (Pennsylvania. University.) Philadelphia. 1-4 2v.

Phil 5627.3A   Public worship. (Hylan, J.P.) Chicago, 1901.

Phil 22.27   Publicaciones. (Mendoza, Argentine Republic (City). Universidad Nacional de Cuyo. Institute de Psicologia Experimental.) Mendoza. 1943-1945

Phil 41.3   Publicaciónes de clasicos de la filosofia. (Buenos Aires. Universidad Nacional. Instituto de Filosofia.) Buenos Aires. 3v.

Phil 41.5   Publicaciones de ensayos filosoficos. (Buenos Aires. Universidad Nacional. Instituto de Filosofia.) Buenos Aires. 1-4,1942-1945 2v.

Phil 11.18.5   Publicaciones de filosofia argentina. (Buenos Aires. University Nacional. Facultad de Filosofia y Letras.) Buenos Aires. 1-5 3v.

Phil 11.18   Publicaciones de filosofia contemporanea. (Buenos Aires. University Nacional. Facultad de Filosofia y Letras.) Buenos Aires. 1-4,1938-1945

Phil 42.7.5   Publication. (College of the Pacific. Pacific Philosophy Institute.) 1,1951+ 2v.

Phil 52.7.25 Publication. (Massachusetts. Society for Mental Hygiene.) 1-45 2v.

Phil 53.3.5 Publication. (National Committee for Mental Hygiene.) N.Y. 1-12 2v.

Phil 53.3.9 Publication. (National Committee for Mental Hygiene.) N.Y. 2-196 2v.

Phil 29.41 Publication. (Tasmania. University. Hobart. Department of Psychology.)

Phil 42.6 Publications. (Connecticut. Society for Mental Hygiene.)

Phil 7061.15 Publications. (Spiritual and Ethical Society, N.Y.) N.Y., 19- .

Phil 54.2 Publications. Psychology series. (Oregon. University.) Eugene. 1929-1935

Phil 42.7 Publications in philosophy. (College of the Pacific, Stockton, California.) Stockton. 1-3,1932-1934

Phil 61.5 Publications in psychology. (Victoria College, Wellington, New Zealand. Department of Psychology.) 5+ 5v.

Phil 58.9 Publications of the departments of philosophy and divinity. (St. Andrews University.) Glasgow, 1911.

Htn Phil 9515.5* Publick employment and active life prefered. (Evelyn, John.) London, 1667.

Phil 600.52 Publicystyka okvesu pozytywizmu. (Wojénski, T.) Wrocław, 1953.

Phil 23.25 Publikaties. (Netherlands. Rijko Psychologische Dienst.) 's Gravenhage. 1-2 2v.

Phil 4200.9.30 Pucci, Raffaele. La fenomenologia contemporanea e il problema dell'uomo. Napoli, 1963.

Phil 1750.842 Pucci, Raffaele. La filosofia e l'unità della cultura. Napoli, 1970.

Phil 4200.9.35 Pucci, Raffaele. Linguaggio e interpretazione. Napoli, 1966.

Phil 3195.6.105 Pucciarelli, E. Introduccion a la filosofia de Dilthey. Buenos Aires, 1944.

Phil 5628.11.1 Puccini, Vincenzo. The life of St. Mary Magdalene of Pazzi, a Carmelite nun. London, 1687.

Phil 1815.8 Pucelle, Jean. L'idéalisme en Angleterre. Neuchâtel, 1955.

Phil 2020.90 Pucelle, Jean. La nature et l'esprit dans la philosophie de T.H. Green. Louvain, 1960-65. 2v.

Phil 735.190 Pucelle, Jean. La source des valeurs. Lyon, 1957. 3v.

Phil 8416.22 Pudor, H. Laokoon; kunstheoretische Essays. Leipzig, 1902.

Phil 5055.6 Püllenberg, Johann. Kurze Darstellung des Hauptinhalts der Logik. Coblenz, 1854.

Phil 3497.10 Pünjer, G.C. Die Religionslehre Kants. Jena, 1874.

Phil 8520.3 Pünjer, G.C.B. Geschichte der christlichen Religionsphilosophie seit der Reformation. Braunschweig, 1880-83. 2v.

Phil 8520.32 Pünjer, G.C.B. History of the Christian philosophy of religion. Edinburgh, 1887.

Phil 3640.745 Puetz, Heinz Peter. Friedrich Nietzsche. Stuttgart, 1967.

Phil 3640.688 Puetz, Heinz Peter. Kunst und Künstlerexistenz bei Nietzsche und Thomas Mann. Bonn, 1963.

Phil 3890.8.95 Pufendoy, Samne. Briefe an Christian Thomasius. München, 1897.

Phil 4015.1 Puglia, F. Il risorgimento filosofico in Italia. Napoli, 1891.

Phil 3450.19.380 Pugliese, Orlando. Vermittlung und Kehre. Freiburg, 1965.

Phil 3425.354 Puglisi, F. L'estetica di Hegel e i suoi presupposti teoretici. Padova, 1953.

Phil 4120.4.47 Puglisi, F. La pedagogia di G. Gentile. v.1-2. Catania, 1953-54.

Phil 4120.4.115 Puglisi, Filippo. La concezione estetico-filosofica di Giovanni Gentile. Catania, 1955.

Phil 7069.59 Puharich, A. The sacred mushroom. Garden City, 1959.

Phil 4372.1.120 Puigdollers Oliver, Mariano. La filosofía española de Luis Vives. Barcelona, 1940.

Phil 6685.8 Puissance de l'électricité animale. (Pigeaire, Jules.) Paris, 1839.

Phil 8905.30 La puissance et la sagesse. (Friedmann, Georges.) Paris, 1971.

Phil 5360.6 Les puissances de l'abstraction. (Paulhan, F.) Paris, 1928.

Phil 2805.222 Puissances de Pascal. (Suarès, André.) Paris, 1923.

Phil 3835.6 Pulcini, C. L'etica di Spinoza. Genova, 1914.

Phil 8610.875.25 Pullen, H.W. Modern Christianity, a civilized heathenism. Boston, 1875.

Phil 8610.875.27 Pullen, H.W. Modern Christianity, a civilized heathenism. N.Y., 1879.

Phil 8610.875.30 Pullen, H.W. Modern Christianity, a civilized heathenism. N.Y., 1901.

Phil 9010.20 The pulpit and rostrum...unchristian amusement. N.Y., 1858.

Phil 7060.46 Puls, G. Spuls-Geschichten. Berlin, n.d.

Phil 6060.29.5 Pulver, Max. Auf Spuren des Menschen. Zürich, 1942.

Phil 5255.48 Pulver, Max. Selbsterfahrung. Zürich, 1941.

Phil 6060.29 Pulver, Max. Symbolik der Handschrift. Zürich, 1931.

Phil 6060.29.15 Pulver, Max. Trieb und Verbrechen in der Handschrift. 2e Aufl. Zürich, 1934.

Phil 5625.122 Punishment and aversive behavior. (Conference on Punishment.) N.Y., 1969.

Phil 346.36 Puntel, L. Analogie und Geschichtlichkeit. Freiburg, 1969.

Phil 4080.3.20 Punti di orientamento della filosofia moderna. (Croce, Benedetto.) Bari, 1931.

Phil 3425.370 Punti di trascendenza nell'immanentismo hegeliano alla luce della momentalita storiosofica. (Contri, Siro.) Milano, 1954.

Phil 400.58 Punto di partenza e punti di arrivo dell' "idealismo attuale". (Cicala, F.B.) Firenze, 1924.

Phil 8890.64 Punzo, Vincent C. Reflective naturalism. N.Y., 1969.

Phil 3015.6 Pupi, A. Alla soglia dell'età romantica. Milano, 1962.

Phil 3778.96 Pupi, Angelo. La formazione della filosofia di K.L. Reinhold, 1784-1794. Milano, 1966.

Phil 6125.10 Pupin, Charles. Le neurone et les hypothèses. Paris, 1896.

Phil 4080.3.405 Puppo, Mario. Croce critico e prosatore. Torino, 1953.
Phil 4080.3.405.10

Phil 4080.3.405.10 Puppo, Mario. Croce e d'annunzio, e altri saggi. Firenze, 1964.

Phil 4080.3.405.5 Puppo, Mario. Il metodo e la critica di Benedetto Croce. Milano, 1964.

Phil 2675.4.5 Le pur et l'impur. (Jankélévitch, Vladimir.) Paris, 1960.

Phil 7069.29.80 Purchas, T.A.R. The spiritual adventures of a business man. 2. ed. London, 1930.

Phil 5049.7 Pure logic. (Jevons, W.S.) London, 1864.

Phil 5049.8 Pure logic and other minor works. (Jevons, W.S.) London, 1890.

Phil 2218.83 Pures, J. Observations. Philadelphia, 1797.

Phil 9355.6 Purinton, E.E. The triumph of the man who acts. N.Y., 1920.

Phil 7068.99.40 The purity and destiny of modern spiritualism. (Hall, T.B.) Boston, 1899.

Phil 8735.58 Purpose in nature. (Canfield, John V.) Englewood Cliffs, N.J., 1966.

Phil 8667.17.7 The purpose of God. (Matthews, W.R.) London, 1935.
Phil 978.65 The purpose of theosophy. (Sinnett, Patience E.) London, 1885.

Phil 5829.10.2 Purposive behavior in animals and men. (Tolman, Edward C.) Berkeley, 1951.

Phil 5829.10 Purposive behavior in animals and men. (Tolman, Edward C.) N.Y., 1932.

Phil 365.20A Purposive evolution. (Noble, Edmund.) N.Y., 1926.

Phil 3425.247.5 Purpus, Wilhelm. Eduard von Hartmanns Kritik der dialektischen Methode Hegels. Ansbach, 1911.

Phil 3425.122 Purpus, Wilhelm. Zur Dialektik des Bewusstseins nach Hegel. Berlin, 1908.

Phil 8416.21 Purser, J.W.R. Art and truth. Glasgow, 1937.

Phil 9245.11.3 The pursuit of happiness. (Brinton, Daniel G.) Philadelphia, 1893.

Phil 9245.48 The pursuit of happiness. (Hodge, George.) N.Y., 1906.
Phil 9245.60A The pursuit of happiness. (MacIver, R.M.) N.Y., 1955.
Phil 5627.268 The pursuit of meaning. (Fobry, Joseph B.) Boston, 1968.
Phil 9380.9 The pursuit of purpose. (English, Raymond.) London, 1947.
Phil 5620.6 The pursuit of reason. (Keary, C.F.) Cambridge, 1910.
Phil 5090.1 The pursuit of truth. (Finch, A.E.) London, 1873.
Phil 6685.13 Purtscher, Nora. Doctor Mesmer. London, 1947.
Phil 978.68 Purucker, G. de. Fundamentals of the esoteric philosophy. Philadelphia, 1932.

Phil 978.68.5 Purucker, G. de. Occult glossary. London, 1933.
Phil 978.68.10 Purucker, G. de. Studies in occult philosophy. Covina, California, 1945.

Phil 4200.5.30 Pusci, F. Lettere. Firenze, 1955. 2v.
Phil 623.11 Pusey, E.B. An historical enquiry into the probable causes of the rationalist character lately predominant in the theology of Germany. London, 1828.

Phil 9352.7.3 Pushing to the front. (Marden, O.S.) Boston, 1895.
Phil 9352.7.7 Pushing to the front. (Marden, O.S.) Petersburg, N.Y., 1911.

Phil 5068.71 Pushkin, Veniamin N. Evristika-nauka o tvorcheskom myshlenii. Moskva, 1967.

Phil 4210.170 Pusineri, Giovanni. Antonio Rosmini, uomo di pensiero, di azione, di virtu. Milano, 1956.

Phil 9070.103.5 Put' dukhovnago obnovleniia. (Il'in, Ivan A.) Miunkhen, 1962.

Phil 4759.1.50 Put' k ochevidnosti. (Il'in, I.A.) Miunkhen, 1957.
Phil 5590.494 Put-offs and come-ons. (Chapman, Arthur Harry.) London, 1968.

Phil 192.75.5 Puterea sufleteasca. (Radulescu-Motin, C.) Bucuresti, 1930.

Phil 331.20.5 Puti i trudnosti poznaniia. (Andreev, Ivan D.) Moskva, 1969.

Phil 8407.34 Puti tvorchestva. (Gornfel'd, A.G.) Peterburg, 1922.
Phil 7068.86.60A Putman, A. Post-mortem confessions. Boston, 1886.
Phil 7054.27.5 Putnam, A. Agassiz and spiritualism. Boston, n.d.
Phil 7054.27.11 Putnam, A. Bible marvel workers. Boston, 1873.
Phil 7054.27 Putnam, A. Flashes of light from the spirit land. Boston, 1892.

Phil 6685.6 Putnam, A. Mesmerism, spiritualism. Boston, 1872.
Phil 7054.27.7 Putnam, A. Natty, a spirit; his portrait and his life. Boston, 1856.

Phil 7054.27.9 Putnam, A. Tipping his tables. Boston, 1873.
Phil 5255.9 Putnam, Daniel. A text book of psychology. N.Y., 1901.
Phil 5055.42 Putnam, Hilary. Philosophy of logic. N.Y., 1971.
Phil 6325.2A Putnam, J.J. Addresses on psycho-analysis. London, 1921.
Phil 5255.32.5 Putnam, J.J. Human motives. Boston, 1921.
Phil 6965.11 Putnam, J.J. Studies in neurological diagnosis. Boston, 1921.

Phil 6325.28.1 Putnam, James Jackson. James Jackson Putnam and psychoanalysis. Cambridge, 1971.

Phil 8610.894.5 Putnam, S.P. Four hundred years of freethought. N.Y., 1894.

Phil 8610.891.10 Putnam, S.P. My religious experience. N.Y., 1891.
Phil 8610.893 Putnam, S.P. Why don't he lend a hand? N.Y., 1893.
Phil 6536.13 Putnam, T.J. Convulsive seizures; how to deal with them. 2d. ed. Philadelphia, 1945.

Phil 8897.29A Putting the most into life. (Washington, B.T.) N.Y., 1906.

Phil 4330.10 Puy, Francisco. El pensamiento tradicional en la España del siglo XVIII, 1700-1760. Madrid, 1966.

Phil 4316.3 Puy Munãoz, Francisco. El pensamiento tradicional en la España del siglo XVIII, 1700-1760. Madrid, 1966.

Phil 7085.6 Puysegur, A. M.J. Recherches...sur l'homme dans l'état de somnambulisme naturel. Paris, 1811.

Phil 6685.9 Puységur, Armand Marie Jacques de Chastenet. Du magnétisme animal. Paris, 1807.

Phil 6685.9.5 Puységur, Armand Marie Jacques de Chastenet. Mémoires pour servir à l'histoire et à l'etablissement du magnétisme animal. 3. éd. Paris, 1820.

Phil 5055.31 Puzikov, Petr D. Analiticheskaia sposobnost' myshleniia. Minsk, 1965.

Phil 5257.70 A puzzling element in the notion of thinking. (Ryle, Gilbert.) London, 1958.

Htn Phil 7066.72* Pye, John. A true and perfect account of a strange and dreadful apparition. London, 1672.

Phil 8705.5 Pye, S. The mosaic theory of the solar or planetary system. London, 1766.

Phil 5409.6 Pyle, W.H. Experimental study of expectation. n.p., 1909.
Phil 5255.50 Pyle, William H. The science of human nature. Boston, 1917.

Phil 1900.83 Pynchon, T.R. Bishop Butler. N.Y., 1889.
Phil 5255.27 Pyne, John K. The mind. N.Y., 1926.
Phil 5627.133 Pyon, T.W. Psychology of the Christian life. N.Y., 1922.
Phil 1190.15 Pyrrkon et le scepticisme grec. 1. éd. (Robin, Léon.) Paris, 1944.

Phil 6980.308 The pyscho-analytical treatment of children. (Freud, Anna.) London, 1946.

Phil 25.147 Pytannia ateizmu. Kyïv. 1,1965+
Phil 7069.34.50 Pythagoras speaks. (Wells, Helen B.) N.Y., 1934.
Phil 1182.35 Pythagoras und Orpheus. 3. Aufl. (Kerenyi, K.) Zürich, 1950.

Phil 1182.15 Pythagorean politics in southern Italy. (Fritz, K.) N.Y., 1940.

Phil 1182.25 — Pythagoreans and Eleatics. (Raven, John E.) Cambridge, 1948.

Phil 8670.14 — Pythian-Adams, W.J. The people and the presence. London, 1942.

Phil 5594.161 — The Q-sort method in personality assessment. (Block, J.) Springfield, Ill., 1961.

Phil 4210.250 — Quacguarelli, Antonio. La lezione liturgica di Antonio Rosmini. Milano, 1970.

Phil 6126.5 — Quackenbos, J.D. Body and spirit. N.Y., 1916.

Phil 6686.1.5 — Quackenbos, J.D. Hypnotic therapeutics. N.Y., 1908.

Phil 8966.2 — Quacquarelli, Antonio. Il triplice frutto della vita cristiana. Roma, 1953.

Phil 42.10 — Quaderni. (Circolo Giovanile Romano di Filosofia.) 1-4, 1953-1955

Phil 4080.18.10 — Quaderno laico. (Calogero, Guido.) Bari, 1967.

Phil 2045.58 — Quadratura circuli. (Hobbes, Thomas.) n.p., 1669.

Phil 4060.1.97 — Quadrelli, Ercole. Le problème des origines. Gerace Marina, 1911.

Phil 1020.23.5 — Quadri, G. La filosofia degli arabi nel suo fiore. v.1-2. Firenze, 1939.

Phil 1020.23 — Quadri, G. La philosophie arabe dans l'Europe mediévale. Paris, 1947.

Phil 8417.2 — Quadri, G. La vita estetica, e lo sviluppo della coscienza. Firenze, 1953.

Phil 8962.28 — Quadriga virtutum. (Maehl, Sibylle.) Köln, 1969.

Phil 3552.252 — Quae fuerit prior Leibnitii philosophia. Thesis. (Hannequin, A.) Paris, 1895.

Htn Phil 4946.2.30F* — Quae supersunt omnia. (Philostratus.) Lipsiae, 1709.

Phil 2115.109 — Quaebicker, R. Lockii et Liebnitii de cognitione humana. Inaug.-Diss. Halis Saxonium, 1868.

Phil 4582.6.30 — Quaestio philosophica an philosophus passit errare? (Hermansson, J.) Upsaliae, 1728.

Phil 4235.5.30 — Le quaestiones de anima de Taddeo da Parma. (Taddeo da Parma.) Milano, 1951.

Phil 1135.32 — Quaestiones Duae de Philosophia Graecorum. (Liebeck, H.) Halle, 1872.

Phil 288.15.2 — Quaestiones noeticae de extensione corporea. (Hoenen, Peter.) Romae, 1955.

Phil 1850.115 — Qualis sapientae antiquae laudator qualis interpres Franciscus Baconus exstiterit. (Stapfer, P.) Paris, 1870.

Phil 176.71 — Le qualità del mondo fisico. (Bonaventura, E.) Firenze, 1916.

Phil 5648.14 — A qualitative and quantitative study of Weber's illusion. Thesis. (Goudge, Mabel E.) Worcester, Mass., 1918.

Phil 9035.16 — The qualities of men. (Jastrow, J.) Boston, 1910.

Phil 26.7 — Quality and quantity; European journal of methodology. Bologna. 1, 1967+

Phil 187.110.5 — The quality of life. (Mitchell, William.) London, 1935?

Phil 293.10.2 — Quand la lumiére fut. Les cosmogonies anciennes...modernes. (Maillard, Louis.) Paris, 1922-23. 2v.

Phil 3485.3 — Quando et quomodo Kantium humius. (Ducros, L.) Burgigalae, 1883.

Phil 5412.15 — Quando gli uomini perdono le staffe. (Borra, Edoardo.) Roma, 1959.

Phil 5272.10.3 — Quantitative Methoden der Psychologie. 3. Aufl. (Hofstaetter, Peter Robert.) München, 1967.

Phil 5251.56 — Quantitative methods in psychology. (Lewis, Don.) N.Y., 1960.

Phil 5274.10 — Quantitative naturalistic research. (Butler, John M.) Englewood Cliffs, 1963.

Phil 5643.88 — A quantitative study of achromatic and chromatic sensitivity from censes to periphery of the visual field. Diss. (Wentworth, H.A.) Princeton, 1930.

Phil 5635.9 — Quantitative study of rhythm. (Woodrow, H.) N.Y., 1909.

Phil 5241.115 — Quantitative theory on human behavior. (Barakin, E.W.) Santa Monica, 1952.

Phil 5247.22.5 — Quantitative Untersuchungen über der öptische Paradoxon. (Heymans, G.) n.p., 1896-1913. 13 pam.

Phil 6128.54 — Quantum reactions and associations; a theory of physical and physiological units or quanta. (Swindle, Percy Ford.) Boston, 1922.

Phil 5520.18 — Quantz, J.O. Problems in the psychology of reading. Chicago, 1897.

Phil 4210.65 — Quaranta proposizioni attribute ad A. Rosmini. (Rosmini-Werbati, Antonio.) Milano, 1889.

Phil 165.9 — Les quarante années scientifique de Theophile Boreas. Athénes, 1940. 2v.

Phil 5826.5 — Quarelli, Elena. Socrate e le bestie. Cuneo, 1958.

Phil 665.86 — Quarelli, Elena. Socrates and the animals. London, 1960.

Phil 8891.1.2 — Quarles, F. Enchiridion. London, 1856.

Phil 8891.1 — Quarles, F. Enchiridion. 1658. Reprint. London, 1568.

Phil 3484.21 — La quarta critica kantiana. (Composto, R.) Palermo, 1954.

Phil 3110.6 — Quarterly. (Jacob Boehme Society.) 1-3, 1952-1956 2v.

Phil 5203.22 — Quarterly check-list of psychology. Darien, Conn. 1, 1961+

Phil 26.3 — The quarterly journal of experimental psychology. Cambridge, England. 1, 1948+ 15v.

Phil 26.2 — The quarterly journal of psychological medicine. N.Y.

Phil 8706.1 — Quarterman, J. The mosaic cosmogony. n.p., n.d.

Phil 491.2 — Quarto di Palo, A. Materia (appunti di critica). Roma, 1928.

Phil 191.3 — Quarto Di Palo, A. Sintesi di un sistema filosofica. Roma, 1935.

Phil 5256.5 — Quastler, H. Information theory in psychology. Glencoe, 1955.

Phil 3837.13 — Quatenus doctrina quam Spinoza de fide. Thesis. (Rauh, F.) Tolosae, 1890.

Htn Phil 9050.7.5* — Quaternio, or a fourfold way to a happy life. (Nash, T.) London, 1633.

Htn Phil 9050.7* — Quaternio, or a fourfold way to a happy life. (Nash, T.) London, 1636.

Phil 2805.30.29 — Quatorzième lettre provinciale. (Pascal, Blaise.) Paris, 1883.

Phil 2750.11.65 — Quatre essais sur l'esprit dans sa condition charnelle. (Maritain, Jacques.) Paris, 1939.

Phil 2750.11.65.3 — Quatre essais sur l'esprit dans sa condition charnelle. (Maritain, Jacques.) Paris, 1956.

Phil 552.3 — Les quatre fléaux. (Lanza del Vasto, Joseph Jean.) Paris, 1971.

Phil 177.68 — Quatre-vingt et un chapitres sur l'esprit et les passions. (Chartier, Émile.) Paris, 1921.

Phil 8417.3 — Quatremère de Quincy, Antoine C. Essai sur la nature, le but et les moyens de l'imitation dans les beaux-arts. Paris, 1823.

Phil 8417.3.5 — Quatremère de Quincy, Antoine C. An essay on the nature, the end, and the means of imitation in the fine arts. London, 1837.

Phil 8417.3.20 — Quatremère de Quincy et son intervention dans les arts, 1788-1830. (Schneider, René.) Paris, 1910.

Phil 5170.5 — Quatres règles inexactes du syllogisme. (Billia, Lorenzo M.) Heidelberg, 1908?

Phil 818.35 — Quatro meditacões sobre o filósofo. (Soares, L.R.) Porto, 1963.

Phil 8419.55 — Quattro dialoghi sull'arte. (Sesti, Luigi.) Milano, 1963.

Phil 1702.8 — Le quattro epoche dello storicismo. (Ciardo, Manlio.) Bari, 1947.

Phil 6360.12 — Quay, Herbert Callister. Psychopathological disorders of childhood. N.Y., 1972.

Phil 196.36 — Que é filosofia. (Vita, Luis Washington.) São Paulo, 1965.

Phil 196.42 — Que es la ontologia. (Vazquez, Juan Adolfo.) Buenos Aires, 1964.

Phil 348.22 — Qué es la teoria Marxista del conocimiento. (Rozental, M.M.) Santiago, 1962.

Phil 1750.97 — Que l'homme soit! (Cotereau, Jean.) Paris, 1959.

Phil 8695.6 — Que l'orgueil de l'esprit est le grand écueil de la foi. (Frémont, G.) Paris, 1900.

Phil 645.35 — Que nada se sabe. (Sánchez, Francisco.) Buenos Aires, 1944.

Phil 645.35.5 — Que nada se sabe. (Sánchez, Francisco.) Madrid, 1926.

Phil 3850.27.125 — Que pense Albert Schweitzer? (Babel, Henry.) Genève, 1953.

Phil 349.8 — Que Sais-je? (Prudhomme, Sully.) Paris, 1896.

Phil 7060.78.5 — The queer side of things. (Lewes, M.L.) London, 1923.

Phil 8706.3 — Queffélec, H. La technique contre la foi? Paris, 1962.

Phil 665.110 — Queis, Karl. Wege der Seele. Wien, 1968.

Phil 352.1.5 — Die quellen der menschlichen Gewissheit. (Volkelt, J.) München, 1906.

Phil 1504.8 — Quellenbeitrage und Untersuchungen zur Geschichte. v.8, pt.1-2. (Daniels, A.) Münster, 1909.

Phil 3850.10.85 — Quellenstudien zu Friedrich Schlegels Übersetzungen aus dem Sanskrit. Diss. (Oppenburg, Ursula.) Narburg, 1965.

Phil 4114.85 — Quello che è vivo del pensiero economico di Antonio Genovesi. (Demarco, Domenico.) Napoli, 1951.

Phil 1505.3 — Quelques aspects de l'humanisme médiéval. (Association Guiellaume Bodé.) Paris, 1943.

Phil 1540.26 — Quelques aspects de l'humanisme médiéval. (Association Guillaume Bude, Paris.) Paris, 1943.

Phil 5585.223 — Quelques aspects du développement perceptif. (Francès, R.) Paris, 1962.

Phil 180.68.10 — Quelques conseils pour la dissertation. 3. ed. (Foulquié, Paul.) Paris, 1956.

Phil 6687.11 — Quelques essais de médiumnité hypnotique. (Rossi-Pagnoni, F.) Paris, 1889.

Phil 8694.3 — Quelques lettres au physicien G.L. Le Sage. (Emery, J.A.) Paris, 1916.

Phil 8423.9 — Quelques réflexions sur la conception du beau. (Waelhem, M. de.) Paris, 1958.

Phil 2885.111 — Quelques souvenirs sur H. Taine. (Begouëm, Henry.) Toulouse, 1923.

Phil 191.2 — Quensel, H. Geht es aufwärts? Cöln, 1904.

Phil 5460.10 — Quercy, Pierre. L'hallucination. Paris, 1930. 2v.

Phil 8885.54 — Querelle de la science normative, une contribution à la théorie de la science. (Kalinowski, Jerzy.) Paris, 1969.

Phil 5751.18 — La querelle des futurs contingents. (Baudry, L.) Paris, 1950.

Phil 8146.2 — Querolgavaldá, M. La escuela estetica catalana contemporanea. Madrid, 1953.

Phil 2270.97 — Quesada, E. Herbert Spencer y sus doctrinas sociológicas. Buenos Aires, 1907.

Phil 26.1 — The quest. London. 1-5, 1909-1930 23v.

Phil 960.137.5 — The quest after perfection. (Hiriyanna, M.) Madras, 1941.

Phil 960.137.8 — The quest after perfection. (Hiriyanna, M.) Mysore, 1952.

Phil 182.93.8 — Qu'est-ce que la métaphysique? (Heidegger, M.) Paris, 1937.

Phil 2270.74.30 — Qu'est-ce que la morale? (Spencer, Herbert.) Paris, 1909.

Phil 8980.417 — Qu'est-ce que la morale marxiste. (Garaudy, R.) Paris, 1963.

Phil 525.22 — Qu'est-ce que la mystique? Paris, 1925.

Phil 5931.1 — Qu'est-ce que la phrénologie...Gall. (Lélut, L.F.) Paris, 1836.

Phil 3235.50 — Qu'est-ce que la religion. (Feuerbach, Ludwig.) Paris, 1850.

Phil 8595.24 — Qu'est-ce que la vérité? (Penel, Raymond.) Paris, 1926.

Phil 1750.830 — Qu'est-ce que le structuralisme? Paris, 1968.

Phil 5766.5 — Qu'est-ce que vouloir? Paris, 1958.

Phil 186.81.10 — Qu'est-ce qu'une structure? (Lupasco, Stéphane.) Paris, 1967.

Phil 3480.67.20 — Qu'est-ceque s'orienter dans la pensée. (Kant, Immanuel.) Paris, 1959.

Phil 8410.2 — The quest for beauty. (Jarett, J.L.) Englewood Cliffs, 1957.

Phil 2055.13.30 — The quest for being. (Hook, Sidney.) N.Y., 1961.

Phil 178.38.16 — The quest for certainty. (Dewey, John.) N.Y., 1929.

Phil 178.38.15A — The quest for certainty. (Dewey, John.) N.Y., 1929.

Phil 7069.15.40 — The quest for Dean Bridgman Conner. (Philpott, Anthony J.) London, 1915.

Phil 9035.94 — The quest for identity. 1st ed. (Wheelis, Allen.) N.Y., 1958.

Phil 8879.24 — The quest for moral law. (Eby, L.S.) N.Y., 1944.

Phil 5780.23 — The quest for self-control. (Klausner, Samuel Z.) N.Y., 1965.

Phil 165.392 — The quest for the absolute. (Adelmann, Frederick.) Chestnut Hill, 1966.

Phil 9245.13 — The quest of happiness. (Hamerton, P.G.) Boston, 1897.

Phil 9245.16.2 — Quest of happiness. (Hillis, N.D.) N.Y., 1902.

Phil 822.10 — The quest of reality. (Walshe, Thomas J.) London, 1933.

Phil 9167.4 — The quest of the best. (Hyde, William de W.) N.Y., 1913.

Phil 26.1.8 — Pamphlet box. Quest society.

Phil 26.5 — Question. London. 1, 1968+ 4v.

Phil 7069.17.23 — The question: "If a man die, shall he live again?" (Clodd, Edward.) London, 1917.

Phil 7069.18.60 — The question: "If a man die, shall he live again?" (Clodd, Edward.) N.Y., 1918.

Phil 3491.12 — La question de l'homne et la fondement de la philosophie. (Julia, Didier.) Aubier, 1964.

Phil 7068.63.5 — Question des esprits et de leurs manifestations diverses. (Mirville, J.E.) Paris, 1863.

Phil 8828.1 — La question morale à la fin du XIXe siècle. (Dupuy, Paul.) Paris, 1897.

Phil 3450.19.73 — The question of being. (Heidegger, Martin.) N.Y., 1958.

Phil 6315.2.46.10 — The question of lay analysis. 1. ed. (Freud, Sigmund.) N.Y., 1950.

Phil 6990.15 — The question of miracles. (Joyce, G.H.) St. Louis, 1914.

Phil 7059.12 — The question settled. (Hull, Moses.) Boston, 1869.

Phil 193.161 — Question sur la metaphysique. (Siger de Brabant.) Louvain, 1948.

Phil 8658.24 Question vivante a un Dieu mort. (Durandeaux, Jacques.) Paris, 1967.
Phil 2050.258 La questione della vera causa in David Hume. (Brunetto, Filippo.) Bologna, 1965.
Phil 4073.104.10 Questioni Campanelliane. (Grillo, F.) Cosenza, 1961.
Phil 186.84 The questioning mind. (Lodge, R.C.) N.Y., 1937.
Phil 5545.96 Questionnaire design and attitude measurement. (Oppenheim, Abraham Naftali.) N.Y., 1966.
Phil 5592.186 Les questionnaires psychologiques. (Albou, Paul.) Paris, 1968.
Phil 2880.8.142 Questions à Jean Paul Sartre. (Garaudy, Roger.) Paris, 1960.
Phil 6688.28 Questions adressées. (Servan, J.M.A.) Padova, 1784.
Phil 365.38 Questions and answers on conscious evolution. (Bill, Annie C.B.) N.Y., 1933.
Phil 1750.390 Questions concernant l'existentialisme. 2. ed. (Gregoire, Franz.) Louvain, 1955.
Htn Phil 3110.30* Questions concerning the soul. (Böhme, J.) London, 1647.
Phil 8412.26 Questions d'art et de morale 2. éd. (Laprade, V.) Paris, 1861.
Phil 2750.11.63 Questions de conscience. (Maritain, Jacques.) Paris, 1938.
Phil 1695.33 Qüestions de filosofi, Camus, Sartre, Ortega. v.21. Barcelona, 1964.
Phil 8891.2 Questions de morale. Paris, 1900.
Phil 2477.1.50 Questions de morale et d'éducation. (Boutroux, Émile.) Paris, 1895?
Phil 8876.69 Questions de morale pratique. (Bouillier, F.) Paris, 1889.
Phil 176.17.5 Questions de philosophie. (Bénard, Charles.) Paris, 1869.
Phil 7068.55 Questions des esprits; ses progrès dans la science. (Mirville, J.E.) Paris, 1855.
Phil 12.2 Questions du temps present. Paris. 1911+ 2v.
Phil 193.74 Questions esthétiques et religeuses. (Stapfer, Paul.) Paris, 1906.
Phil 5520.399 Questions of meaning. (Antal, Laszló.) The Hague, 1963.
Phil 193.60 Questions of the day in philosophy and psychology. (Stewart, H.L.) London, 1912.
Phil 5047.18 Questions on logic. 2nd ed. (Holman, Henry.) London, 1915.
Phil 192.34 Questions on psychology, metaphysics, and ethics. (Ryland, F.) London, 1887.
Phil 8419.46 Questions on the philosophy of art. (Stone, W.F.) London, 1897.
Phil 177.81 Questions péripatéliciennes. (Cesalpino, Andrea.) Paris, 1929.
Phil 2725.2.70 Questions politiques et philosophiques. v.1-2. (Lamennais, F.R. de.) Paris, 1840.
Phil 4464.1.30 Questões actuaes de philosophia e direito. (Diniz, Almachio.) Rio de Janeiro, 1909.
Phil 8580.10 Questões fundamentaes. (Abranches, J. dos Santos.) Coimbra, 1891.
Phil 8592.27 Quests old and new. (Mead, G.R.S.) London, 1913.
Phil 8596.1 Quetin, M.A. L'origine de la religion. Montauban, 1903.
Phil 8706.4 Quevremont, Pierre. Dieu et l'homme créateur. Paris, 1965.
Phil 5360.4 Queyrat, F. L'abstraction et son rôle dans l'éducation intellectuelle. 2e éd. Paris, 1907.
Phil 1750.856 Qui est aliéné? Critique et métaphysique sociale de l'Occident. (Clavel, Maurice.) Paris, 1970.
Phil 8654.105 Qui est notre Dieu? (Journées Universitaires, 44th, Pau, France, 1967.) n.p., n.d.
Phil 2045.92 Qui fuerint saeculo XVII imprimis apud Hobbesium Anglicae solutae orationis progressus. (Chevrillon, André.) Insulae, 1893.
Phil 8596.2 Quick, O.C. Philosophy and the cross. London, 1931.
Phil 2490.111 Quid Auguste Comte de suae altatis psychologis senserit. (Dumas, G.) Lutetiae, 1900.
Phil 1850.117 Quid de mathematica senserit Baconus. Thesis. (Lalande, A.) Lutetiae, 1899.
Phil 2520.159 Quid de mundi externi existentia...Cartesius. Thesis. (Rodrigues, G.) Lutetiae Parisiorum, 1903.
Phil 3499.5.5 Quid de natura...senserit Kantius. (Ruyssen, T.) Nemausi, 1903.
Phil 3552.281 Quid Leibniz uis Aristoteli debuerit. (Nolen, Désiré.) Parisiis, 1875.
Phil 1200.35 Quid Paulus, quid stoici de virtute docuerint. (Wevers, Friedrich.) Meursae, 1876? 3 pam.
Phil 9344.10 Quiet hints to ministers' wives. (Elson, F.S.) Boston, 1934.
Phil 525.239 Der Quietismus zwischen Häresie und Orthodoxie. (Bendiscioli, Mario.) Wiesbaden, 1964.
Phil 4363.2.84 Le quiétiste espanol. (Dudon, P.) Paris, 1921.
Phil 126.5 Quiles, Ismael. Gráficos de historia de la filosofía. Buenos Aires, 1940.
Phil 2880.8.124 Quiles, Ismael. Sartre y su existencialismo. 2. ed. Buenos Aires, 1952.
Phil 9290.1 Quill, C. The American mechanic. Philadelphia, 1838.
Phil 2477.15.80 Quillet, Pierre. Bachelard. Paris, 1964.
Phil 8891.4 Quillian, W.F. The moral theory of evolutionary naturalism. New Haven, 1945.
X Cg Phil 2230.10.5 Quimby, P.P. The Quimby manuscripts. N.Y., 1921.
Htn Phil 2230.10* Quimby, P.P. The Quimby manuscripts. 1st ed. N.Y., 1921.
X Cg Phil 2230.10.5 The Quimby manuscripts. (Quimby, P.P.) N.Y., 1921.
Htn Phil 2230.10* The Quimby manuscripts. 1st ed. (Quimby, P.P.) N.Y., 1921.
Phil 8891.3 Quinby, L.J. Natural basis of moral and ethics. Boston, 1936.
Phil 5066.11.30 Quine, Willard van Orman. Commutative Boolean functions. Santa Monica, 1949.
Phil 5066.11.10A Quine, Willard van Orman. Elementary logic. Boston, 1941.
Phil 5066.11.12 Quine, Willard van Orman. Elementary logic. Cambridge, 1966.
Phil 5066.11.11 Quine, Willard van Orman. Elementary logic. N.Y., 1965.
Phil 5066.11.20 Quine, Willard van Orman. From a logical point of view. Cambridge, Mass., 1953.
Phil 5066.11.21 Quine, Willard van Orman. From a logical point of view. 2nd ed. N.Y., 1963.
Phil 5066.11.7 Quine, Willard van Orman. Mathematical logic. Cambridge, Mass., 1951.
Phil 5066.11 Quine, Willard van Orman. Mathematical logic. N.Y., 1940.
Phil 5056.1.15 Quine, Willard Van Orman. Methods of logic. N.Y., 1950.
Phil 5056.1.22 Quine, Willard Van Orman. Methods of logic. N.Y., 1953.
Phil 5056.1.20 Quine, Willard Van Orman. Methods of logic. N.Y., 1959.
Phil 5056.1.23 Quine, Willard Van Orman. Methods of logic. N.Y., 1964.
Phil 5066.11.25 Quine, Willard van Orman. On functions of relations. Santa Monica, 1949.
Phil 5066.11.50 Quine, Willard van Orman. Ontological relativity, and other essays. N.Y., 1969.
Phil 5056.1.25 Quine, Willard Van Orman. Philosophy of logic. Englewood Cliffs, N.J., 1970.
Phil 5066.276 Quine, Willard van Orman. Selected logic papers. N.Y., 1966.
Phil 5056.1.10A Quine, Willard Van Orman. A short course in logic. Cambridge, 1946.
Phil 5056.1A Quine, Willard Van Orman. A system of logistic. Cambridge, 1934.
Phil 5066.11.35 Quine, Willard van Orman. A theorem on parametric Boolean functions. Santa Monica, 1949.
Phil 5125.27A Quine, Willard van Orman. Theory of deduction. Pts.1-4. Cambridge, 1948.
Phil 5066.11.45 Quine, Willard van Orman. The ways of paradox. N.Y., 1966.
Phil 266.2 Quine, Willard Van Orman. The web of belief. N.Y., 1970.
Phil 5066.11.40A Quine, Willard van Orman. Word and object. Cambridge, 1960.
Phil 5056.1.01 Pamphlet box. Quine, Willard Van Orman. Collection of papers.
Phil 5056.1.5 Pamphlet vol. Quine, Willard Van Orman. Papers on symbolic logic. 1932-1936. 21 pam.
Phil 191.1.5 Quinet, Edgar. L'esprit nouveau. Paris, 1875.
Phil 191.1 Quinet, Edgar. L'esprit nouveau. 4. éd. Paris, 1875.
Phil 3640.480 Quinot, Armand. Nietzsche, philosophe de la valeur. Manosque, 1956.
Phil 530.20.87 Quint, J. Deutsche Mystikertexte des Mittelalters. Bonn, 1929.
Phil 530.20.95 Quint, Josef. Textbuch zur Mystik des deutschen Mittelalters. Halle, 1952.
Phil 2475.1.370 Quintanilla, Louis. Bergonismo y política. 1. ed. México, 1953.
Phil 3640.101 The quintessence of Nietzsche. (Kennedy, J.M.) London, 1909.
Htn Phil 182.29.15* Quintum renata. (Heidfeld, J.) Herbornae Nassoviorum, 1608.
Phil 4317.5 Quiroz-Martinez, Olga Victoria. La introducción de la filosofía moderna en España. 1. ed. Mexico, 1949.
Phil 191.4 Quisling, Jörgen. Philosophie, das anthropokosmische System. Berlin, 1936.
Phil 3425.227 Quist, C.J. De philosophia juris Hegeliana. Thesis. Helsingforsiae, 1853.
Phil 2725.35.115 Quito, Emérita. La notion de la liberté participée dans la philosophie de Louis Lavelle. Fribourg, 1969.
Htn Phil 5827.2* Quôd animalia bruta ratione utantur meliùs homine. (Rorario, G.) Paris, 1648.
Phil 2905.1.150 Quodlibets. (Bailly, Thomas de.) Paris, 1960.
Phil 2905.1.145 Quodlibets. (Thérines, Jacques de.) Paris, 1958.
Phil 8967.1.85 R. Rothe's speculatives System. (Roltzmann, H.J.) Freiburg, 1899.
Phil 3450.43F R.F.A. Hoernle. (Freed, Louis Franklin.) Johannesburg, 1965.
Phil 1930.8.115 R.G. Collingwood, philosophie et historien. (Shalom, Albert.) Paris, 1967.
Phil 27.32 The R.P.A. annual and ethical review. London. 1892+ 36v.
Phil 720.46 Raab, Elmar F.X. Die Wahrheit als metaphysisches Problem. Dillingen, 1959.
Phil 331.2.9 Raab, F. Philosophie von Avenarius' Biomechanische. Leipzig, 1912.
Phil 3790.13 Raab, F. Philosophische Gespräche. Berlin, 1937.
Phil 3850.27.99 Raab, Karl. Albert Schweitzer, Persönalichkeit und Denken. Inaug. Diss. Düsseldorf, 1937.
Phil 5257.24 Raaf, H. de. Die Elemente der Psychologie. 3. Aufl. Langensalza, 1908.
Phil 3428.94 Raaf, H. de. Herbarts' metafyzica, psychologie in ethiek. Groningen, 1904.
Phil 5485.4 Raaheim, Kjell. Opplevelse, erfaring og intelligens. Bergen, 1969.
Phil 2070.137 Raback, A.A. William James. Cambridge, 1942.
Phil 5827.8 Rabaud, E. How animals find their way about. Leipzig, 1928.
Phil 5827.8.5 Rabaud, E. L'orientation lointaine et la reconnaissance des lieux. Paris, 1927.
Phil 2605.5.95 Rabbe, Felix P. L'abbé Simon Foucher. Paris, 1867.
Phil 6127.11 Rabbow, Paul. Antik Schriften über Seelenheilung und Seelenleitung. Leipzig, 1914.
Phil 192.80.2 Rabeau, G. Le jugement d'existence. Paris, 1938.
Phil 192.80 Rabeau, G. Le jugement d'existence. Wetteren, 1937.
Phil 192.59 Rabeau, Gaston. Réalité et relativité. Paris, 1927.
Phil 4352.2 Rabello, Sylvio. Farias Brito. Rio de Janeiro, 1941.
Phil 4352.2.2 Rabello, Sylvio. Farias Brito. Rio de Janeiro, 1967.
Phil 3837.10 Rabenort, W.L. Spinoza as educator. N.Y., 1911.
Phil 192.1 Rabier, E. Leçons de philosophie. Paris, 1886. 2v.
Phil 192.1.9 Rabier, E. Leçons de philosophie. 9e éd. Paris, 1912.
Phil 2750.20.115 Rabil, Albert. Merleau-Ponty, existentialist of the social world. N.Y., 1967.
Phil 4761.5.80 Rabinovich, Valerii I. Revoliutsionnyi prosvetitel' F.V. Karzhaviv. Moskva, 1966.
Phil 8980.497.20 Rabotat' i zhit' po kommunisticheski. (Kovalev, S.M.) Moskva, 1961.
Phil 192.2 Rabus, L. Lehrbuch zur Einleitung in die Philosophie. Erlangen, 1887-1895. 2v.
Phil 192.2.5 Rabus, L. Logik und Metaphysik. Erlangen, 1868.
Phil 5027.1 Rabus, L. Der neuesten Bestrebung...Logik. Erlangen, 1880.
Phil 8597.26 Rabus, Leonhard. Philosophie und Theologie. Erlangen, 1876.
Phil 2905.1.120 Rabut, Oliver A. Dialogue with Teilhard de Chardin. London, 1961.
Phil 2905.1.125 Rabut, Oliver A. Teilhard de Chardin. N.Y., 1961.
Phil 5627.269 Rabut, Olivier A. L'expérience religieuse fondamentale. Paris, 1969.
Phil 8597.53 Rabut, Olivier A. Valeur spirituelle du profane. Paris, 1963.
Phil 181.23 Raccolta di opuscoli filosofici. (Gualberto, G.) Pisa, 1766. 3v.
Phil 5813.2 The raccoon: a study in animal intelligence. (Davis, H.B.) London, 1907.
Phil 2250.86 Raccuglia, Pietro. Il concetto sintetico del reale e la sua evoluzione nel pensiero di Josiah Royce. Palermo, 1920.
Phil 9575.1 The race for riches. (Arnot, W.) Philadelphia, 1853.
Phil 8892.12.5A Race questions, provincialism and other American problems. (Royce, J.) N.Y., 1908.
Phil 194.19.25 La racerca filosofica. (Tarozzi, Giuseppe.) Napoli, 1936.
Phil 7069.20.250 Rachel comforted. (Maturin, Edith Money.) N.Y., 1920.

Phil 9495.115   O racionalismo atrevido do Snr. Frederico de Ancede.
                   (Douräes Castro.) Porto, 1915.
Phil 1020.4.31   El racionalismo averroísta y el razonamiento luliano.
                   (Reyes, A.) Madrid, 1935.
Phil 4961.805.15   Racionalismo y liberalismo en el Uruguay. (Ardao, Arturo.)
                   Montevideo, 1962.
Phil 4114.80   Racioppi, G. Antonio Genovesi. Napoli, 1871.
Phil 9357.8.5   Rack, E. Mentor's letters, addresses to youth. 3d ed.
                   Bath, 1778.
Phil 6327.40   Racker, Heinrich. Transference and counter transference.
                   London, 1968.
Phil 3425.279   Rackwitz, Max. Hegels Ansicht über die Apriorität von Zeit
                   und Raum und die kantischen Kategorien. Halle, 1891.
Phil 3837.25   Rackwitz, Max. Studien über Causalität und Identität als
                   Grundprincipien des Spinozismus. Halle, 1884.
Phil 2050.185   Radakovic, K. Die letzten Fundamente der Hume'schen
                   Erkenntnistheorie. Graz, 1925.
Phil 8597.60.2   Radbruch, Gustav. Religionsphilosophie der Kultur. 2.
                   Aufl. Darmstadt, 1968.
Phil 9120.157   Radcke, Fritz. Pflicht oder Lust? Langensalza, 1917.
Phil 1122.25   Ráde, Emanuel. Dějiny filosofie. Praha, 1932-33.
                   2v.
Phil 8597.25   Rade, Martin. Die Stellung des Christentums zum
                   Geschlechtsleben. Tübingen, 1910.
Phil 5257.46   Radecki, Wacław. Tratado de psicología. Buenos
                   Aires, 1933.
Phil 8967.8   Rademacher, A. Religion und Leben. Freiburg, 1926.
Phil 3425.694   Rademaker, Hans. Hegels "objektive Logik" eine Einführung.
                   Bonn, 1969.
Phil 298.20   Rademaker, Hans. Die Welt in der Sicht der
                   wissenschaftlichen Vernunft. Bonn, 1965.
Phil 165.50   Rader, M.M. The enduring questions. N.Y., 1956.
Phil 8892.75   Rader, M.M. Ethics and the human community. N.Y., 1964.
Phil 8400.28.3   Rader, M.M. A modern book of esthetics. 3. ed.
                   N.Y., 1962.
Phil 8615.28   Radest, Howard B. Toward common ground; the study of the
                   ethical societies in the United States. N.Y., 1969.
Phil 5425.9   Radestock, P. Genie und Wahnsinn. Breslau, 1884.
NEDL Phil 7080.11 Radestock, P. Schlaf und Traum. Leipzig, 1879.
Phil 1750.862   Radev, R. Kritika va neotomizma. Sofiia, 1970.
Phil 5257.31   Radha-Krishnan, S. Essentials of psychology.
                   London, 1912.
Phil 4872.242.20   Radhakrishnan; an anthology. (Radhakrishnan, Sarvépalli.)
                   London, 1952.
Phil 8597.38.10   Radhakrishnan, S. East and West in religion.
                   London, 1933.
Phil 817.22   Radhakrishnan, S. History of philosophy. London, 1952.
                   2v.
Phil 8597.38   Radhakrishnan, S. An idealist view of life. N.Y., 1932.
Phil 960.128   Radhakrishnan, S. Indian philosophy. London, 1923.
                   2v.
Phil 8622.14   Radhakrishnan, S. Recovery of faith. 1. ed. N.Y., 1955.
Phil 960.128.10   Radhakrishnan, S. The Vedânta according to Samkara and
                   Rämänuja. London, 1928.
Phil 8597.38.15   Radhakrishnan, S. The world's unborn soul. Oxford, 1936.
Phil 585.80.2   Radhakrishnan, Sarvepalli. The concept of man.
                   London, 1960.
Phil 585.80   Radhakrishnan, Sarvepalli. The concept of man.
                   London, 1960.
Phil 4871.5   Radhakrishnan, Sarvepalli. Contemporary Indian philosophy.
                   London, 1936.
Phil 4871.5.2   Radhakrishnan, Sarvepalli. Contemporary Indian philosophy.
                   2nd ed. London, 1952.
Phil 4872.242.30   Radhakrishnan, Sarvépalli. My search for truth. 2nd ed.
                   Agra, 1956.
Phil 4872.242.20   Radhakrishnan, Sarvépalli. Radhakrishnan; an anthology.
                   London, 1952.
Phil 4872.242.22   Radhakrishnan, Sarvépalli. Radhakrishnan reader; an
                   anthology. 1st ed. Bombay, 1969.
Phil 165.20   Radhakrishnan. London, 1951.
Phil 4872.242.85   Radhakrishnan and integral experience. (Arapura, John G.)
                   London, 1966.
Phil 4872.242.22   Radhakrishnan reader; an anthology. 1st ed.
                   (Radhakrishnan, Sarvépalli.) Bombay, 1969.
Phil 4872.242.1030
                   Radhas Vamidayal. The Sär Bachan; an abstract of the
                   teachings of Swamiji Maharaj. 4th ed. Beas, 195-?
Phil 9178.9   Radiant motherhood. (Stopes, M.C.C.) N.Y., 1932.
Phil 2070.158   The radical empiricism of William James. 1st ed. (Wild,
                   John.) Garden City, N.Y., 1969.
Phil 2020.84   Un radical religieux. v.1-2. Thèse. (Montagné, Paul.)
                   Toulouse, 1927.
Phil 183.8   Radicalità e filosofia. (Incardona, Nunzio.)
                   Palermo, 1968.
Phil 4210.215   Radice, Gianfranco. Annali di Antonio Rosmini Serbati.
                   Milano, 1967. 2v.
Phil 5411.12   Radiografía del odio. (Salgado, Enrique.) Madrid, 1969.
Phil 3017.6   Rádl, E. Romantická véda. V Praze, 1918.
Phil 4809.727.35   Rádl, Emanuel. Moderní věda. Praha, 1926.
Phil 4809.727.30   Rádl, Emanuel. Uvahy vědecké a filosofické. Praha, 1914.
Phil 900.25   Rádl, Emanuel. Západ a východ; filosofia úvahy z cest.
                   Praze, 1925.
Phil 4809.727.11   Pamphlet vol. Rádl, Emanuel. Co soudím o spiritismu.
                   3 pam.
Phil 4809.727.12   Pamphlet vol. Rádl, Emanuel. Essays. 6 pam.
Phil 4710.20.5   Radloff, E. von. Russische Philosophie. Bredau, 1925.
Phil 4769.1.110   Radlov, E.L. Vladimir Solov'ev; zhizn' i uchenie. Sankt
                   Peterburg, 1913.
Phil 102.8   Radlov, Ernest L. Filosofskii slovar'. Sankt
                   Peterburg, 1904.
Phil 102.8.2   Radlov, Ernest L. Filosofskii slovar'. Izd. 2.
                   Moskva, 1913.
Phil 6327.15   Rado, Sandor. Die Kastrationsangst des Weibes.
                   Wien, 1934.
Phil 6327.15.5   Rado, Sandor. Psychoanalysis of behavior; collected
                   papers. N.Y., 1956.
Phil 4899.255.80   Radul'-Zatulovskii, Iakov B. Ando Sëëki, filosof,
                   materialist XVIII veka. Moskva, 1961.
Phil 192.75.5   Radulescu-Motin, C. Puterea sufleteasca. Bucuresti, 1930.
Phil 575.85   Rădulescu-Motru, C. Personalismul energetic.
                   Bucuresti, 1927.
Phil 6327.20   Radzinowicz, Leon. Mental abnormality and crime.
                   London, 1944.
Phil 5257.30   Radziwillowicz, P. Zagadnienia psychologji. Kraków, 1911?
Phil 2266.165A   Rae, John. Life of Adam Smith. N.Y., 1965.
Phil 3850.32   Räber, H. Othmar Spanns Philosophie. Jena, 1937.
Phil 3255.94   Raeber, Kuno. Studien zur Geschichtsbibel Sebastian
                   Francks. Basel, 1952.

Phil 3255.95   Raeber, Kuno. Studien zur Geschichtsbibel Sebastian
                   Francks. Inaug. Diss. Basel, 1952.
Phil 3475.3.135   Räber, T. Das Dasein in der Philosophie von Karl Jaspers.
                   Diss. Freiburg, 1954.
Phil 3475.3.130   Räber, T. Das Glasein in der "Philosophie" von K. Jaspers.
                   Bern, 1955.
Phil 5643.53   Raehlman, E.Zur vergleichenden Physiologie des
                   Gesichtsinnes. Jena, 1907.
Phil 3450.19.145   Raessingh, Karel Hendrik. Martin Heidegger als
                   godsdienstwijsgeer. Assen, 1956.
Phil 3805.34.10   Räthsel und Charaden. (Schleiermacher, Friedrich.)
                   Berlin, 1874.
Phil 978.49.750.8 Die Rätsel der Philosophie. 8. Aufl. (Steiner, R.)
                   Dornach, 1924.
Phil 1718.15.5   Die Rätsel der Philosophie in ihrer Geschichte. (Steiner,
                   Rudolf.) Stuttgart, 1924-26. 2v.
Phil 5722.28   Rätsel der Seele. (Spiess, Emil Jakob.) Olten, 1946.
Phil 8887.58.10   Das Rätsel der Sittlichkeit und seine Lösung. (Marcus, E.)
                   München, 1932.
Phil 7068.92.55   Das Rätsel des Menschen. (Du Prel, K.L.A.F.M.A.)
                   Leipzig, 1892.
Phil 7084.44   Rätsel des Traumes und des Zufalls. (Boehm, Arthur.)
                   Leipzig, 1920.
Phil 3120.8.140   Das Rätsel und sein Meister Franz Brentano. (Zawischa, E.)
                   n.p., 1961.
Phil 3499.13   Rätze, J.G. Herder Gegen Kant. Leipzig, 1800.
Phil 5643.13   Das räumliche Sehen. (Jaesche, E.) Stuttgart, 1879.
Phil 5520.230   Raevskii, A.N. Psikhologiia rechi v sovetskoi
                   psikhologicheskoi nauke za 40 let. Kiev, 1958.
Phil 192.85.3   Raeymaeker, Louis de. Introduction à la philosophie. 4.
                   ed. Louvain, 1956.
Phil 192.85   Raeymaeker, Louis de. Introduction to philosophy.
                   N.Y., 1948.
Phil 192.85.5.2   Raeymaeker, Louis de. Philosophie de l'être. 2. ed.
                   Louvain, 1947.
Phil 192.85.5.5   Raeymaeker, Louis de. The philosophy of being. St.
                   Louis, 1961.
Phil 192.85.10   Raeymaeker, Louis de. Riflessioni su temi filosofici
                   fondamentali. Milano, 1958.
Phil 1870.89   Raffel, Friedrich. Ist Berkeley ein Freihändler?
                   Kiel, 1904.
Phil 1817.7   Raffel, J. Die voraussetzungen Welche den empiresmus
                   Lockis. Inaug.-Diss. Berlin, 1887?
Phil 5875.65   Raffler Engel, Walburga von. Il prelinguaggio infantile.
                   Paideia, 1964.
Phil 1020.64.2   Rafi-ud-din, Muhammad. Ideology of the future. 2nd ed.
                   Karachi, 1956.
Phil 4080.3.121.20
                   Ragazzate letteraris: appunti...Croce. (Castellano, G.)
                   Napoli, 1919.
Phil 192.23   Rageot, G. Les savants et la philosophie. Paris, 1908.
Phil 4080.3.270   Raggiunti, R. La conoscenza storica. Firenze, 1955.
Phil 3450.11.445   Raggiunti, Renzo. Husserl, dalla logica alla
                   fenomenologia. Firenze, 1967.
Phil 4080.18.85   Raggiunti, Renzo. Logica e linguistica nel pensiero di
                   Guido Calogero. Firenze, 1963.
Phil 4080.18.80   Raggiunti, Renzo. Tre brevi studi: La conclusione della
                   filosofia del conoscere di Guido Calogero. Firenze, 1946.
Phil 187.102   La ragion d'essere della filosofia. (Mannarino, G.)
                   Catanzaro, 1931.
Phil 8893.99   Ragion pratica. (Sacheli, C.A.) Firenze, 1938.
Phil 27.9   La ragione; foglio ebdomadario di filosofia. Torino.
                   1-8, 1854-1857 7v.
Phil 310.758   Ragione dialettica prassi marxista e profezia cristiana.
                   (Cassa, Mario.) Milano, 1966.
Phil 8592.20   La ragione naturale. (Monaco, C.) Caserta, 1888.
Phil 4080.19   La ragione poetica. (Chiavacci, G.) Firenze, 1947.
Phil 4120.2.30   Le ragioni del fenomenismo. v. 1-3. (Guastella, Cosmo.)
                   Palermo, 1921-23. 2v.
Phil 705.28   La ragioni della trascendenza o del realismo assoluto.
                   (Troilo, E.) Venezia, 1936.
Phil 4215.3.40   Le ragioni dell'irrazionalismo. 2a ed. (Rensi, Giuseppe.)
                   Napoli, 1933.
Phil 4285.1.90   Ragnisco, P. Giacomo Zabarella il filosofo Pietro
                   Pompanazzi. Roma, 1886-87.
Phil 817.13   Ragnisco, P. Storia critica delle categorie dai primordj
                   della filosofia Greca sino ad Hagel. v.1-2. Firenze, 1871.
Phil 4215.2.83   Ragnisco, P. Tommaso Rossi e Benedetto Spinoza, saggio
                   storico-critico. Salerno, 1873.
Phil 2280.8.93   Rahder, J. Pringle-Pattison's Gifford lectures. v.1-2.
                   Leipzig, 1920.
Phil 192.116   Rahman, F. Philosophy, science, and other essays. 1st. ed.
                   Lahore, 1961.
Phil 5635.14   Rahn, Carl. Relation of sensation to other categories in
                   contemporary psychology. Princeton, 1913.
Phil 8707.12   Rahn, Carl. Science and the religious life. New
                   Haven, 1928.
Phil 8967.15.5   Rahner, Karl. The dynamic element in the church.
                   Freiburg, 1964.
Phil 8967.15   Rahner, Karl. Das Dynamische in der Kirche.
                   Freiburg, 1958.
Phil 8622.62   Rahner, Karl. Intellektuelle Redlichkeit und christlicher
                   Glaube. Wien, 1966.
Phil 8597.58   Rahner, Karl. Offenarung und Uberlieferung.
                   Freiburg, 1965.
Phil 8612.54   Rahner, Karl. On the theology of death. Freiburg, 1964.
Phil 8612.54.5   Rahnez, Karl. Zur Theologie des Todes. 5. Aufl.
                   Freiburg, 1958.
Phil 3425.564   Rahrmoser, Günter. Subjektivität und verden Glichung.
                   Gütersloh, 1961.
Phil 3246.86.5   Raich, Maria. Fichte, seine Ethik...Problem des
                   Individualismus. Tübingen, 1905.
Phil 3246.86   Raich, Maria. Fichte, seine Ethik...Problem des
                   Individualismus. Thesis. Tübingen, 1905.
Phil 5413.10   Raiga, Eugène. L'envie. Paris, 1932.
Phil 2725.4.87   Raillard, Célestin. Pierre Leroux et ses oeuvres.
                   Chateauroux, 1899.
Phil 6327.10   Raimann, Emil. Zur psychoanalyse. 2. Aufl. Berlin, 1925.
Phil 2750.19.90   Rainho, Antonio Angelo Leite. L'existencialisme de M.
                   Gabriel Marcel. Lisbonne, 1955.
Phil 8892.53   Rainsford, F.B. The Isle of Good Intent. Boston, 1936.
Phil 6990.55   Rairer, A. Essai sur la spiritualité de Bernadette.
                   Nevers, 1958.
Phil 27.52   La raison; cahiers de psychopathologie scientifique.
                   Villejuif. 4-22,1952-1958 5v.
Phil 9351.4   Raison, folie. (Lemontey, P.E.) Bruxelles, 1830. 2v.
Phil 175.2.5   La raison. (Alaux, J.E.) Paris, 1860.
Phil 5160.5.2   La raison. 2. éd. (Granger, Giles.) Paris, 1958.

Author and Title Listing

Phil 2750.30.30 — Raison et conversion chrétienne. (Marc, André.) Paris, 1961.

Phil 5041.93.10 — Raison et discours, dépense de la logique réflexive. (Blanché, Robert.) Paris, 1967.

Phil 3475.3.155 — Raison et existence chez Karl Jaspers. (Paumen, Jean.) Bruxelles, 1958.

Phil 8591.28 — Raison et foi. (Lavollée, R.) Paris, 1926.

Phil 8581.98.5 — La raison et la religion. (Brunschvicg, Léon.) Paris, 1964.

Phil 5620.10 — La raison et la vue. (Grandjean, F.) Paris, 1920.

Phil 5620.3 — La raison et l'âme. (Magy, F.) Paris, 1877.

Phil 5620.13.3 — La raison et le rationalisme. 3. éd. (Ollé-Laprune, L.) Paris, 1906.

Phil 5620.24 — La raison et les normes. (Lalande, A.) Paris, 1948.

Phil 2750.11.50 — Raison et raisons. 10. éd. (Maritain, Jacques.) Paris, 1947.

Phil 8658.17.10 — Raison et religion dans la philosophie de l'actin. (Duméry, Henry.) Paris, 1963.

Phil 196.2.5 — La raison philosophique et la raison catholique. (Ventura de Raulica, G.) Paris, 1854-1864. 4v.

Phil 3486.4 — La raison pure...essai sur la philosophie Kantienne. (Evellin, F.) Paris, 1907.

Phil 5045.12 — Le raisonnement entermes de faite dans la logique russellienne. (Feys, R.) Louvain, 1928.

Phil 5066.22 — Le raisonnement mathématique. (Daval, R.) Paris, 1945.

Phil 2730.90 — Le raisonnement selon Maine de Biran. (Paliard, Jacques.) Paris, 1925.

Phil 2730.90.5 — Le raisonnement selon Maine de Biran. Thèse. (Paliard, Jacques.) Paris, 1925.

Phil 400.55 — Les raisons de l'idéalisme. 2e éd. (Gaultier, J. de.) Paris, 1906.

Phil 5627.82 — Les raisons du coeur. (Schneider, É.) Paris, 1907.

Phil 4196.85 — Raith, Werner. Die Macht des Bildes. München, 1967.

Phil 4980.41 — Raíz y destino de la filosofía. (Sánchez Reulet, Aníbal.) Tucumán, 1942.

Phil 4974.24 — Raízes pré-socráticas do pensamento atual. (Menezes, O.) Ceará, 1958.

Phil 960.220 — Rajadhyaksha, N.D. The six systems of Indian philosophy. Bombay, 1959.

Phil 192.114 — Raju, P. Introduction to comparative philosophy. Lincoln, 1962.

Phil 960.168.2A — Raju, P.T. Idealistic thought of India. Cambridge, Mass., 1953.

Phil 960.168 — Raju, P.T. Idealistic thought of India. London, 1953.

Phil 400.95 — Raju, P.T. Thought and reality; Hegelianism and Advaita. London, 1937.

Phil 3245.87 — Rakate, Georg. Immanuel Hermann Fichte. Leipzig, 1915.

Phil 3552.105 — Rall, H.F. Der leibnizsche Substanzbegriff. Halle, 1899.

Phil 2225.2.85 — Ralph Barton Perry on education for democracy. (Steinberg, Ira Sherman.) Columbus, 1970.

Phil 1925.84 — Ralph Cudworth. (Passmore, J.A.) Cambridge, Eng., 1951.

Phil 1925.83 — Ralph Cudworth als Ethiker, Staats-Philosoph und Usthetiker auf Grund des gedruckten Schriften. Inaug. Diss. (Beyer, Joseph.) Bottrop, 1935.

Phil 2150.9 — Ralston, H.J. Emergent evolution...the philosophy of C. Lloyd Morgan. Boston, 1933.

Phil 5257.59 — Ram, T. Psycho-astrologische Encyclopedie. Lochem, 1950-51. 2v.

Phil 974.5.10 — Ramana Maharshi and the path of sell-knowledge. (Osborne, Arthur.) London, 1970.

Phil 960.15A — Rámanáthan, P. The spirit of the East contracted with spirit of the West. N.Y., 1906.

Phil 8597.21 — Rámanthán, P. The culture of the soul. N.Y., 1906.

Phil 960.278 — Ramaswami Aiyas C.P. Research Endowment Committee. A bibliography of Indian philosophy. 1. ed. Madras, 1963- 2v.

Phil 7060.94 — A rambler's recollections and reflections. (Capper, Alfred.) London, 1915.

Htn Phil 665.4* — Ramesey, W. Man's dignity. London, 1661.

Phil 672.157 — Ramige, E.A. Contemporary concepts of time and the idea of God. Boston, 1935.

Phil 5247.13.32 — Ramis Alonso, M. A propósito de examen de ingenios del Dr. Huarte. Palma de Mallorca, 1943.

Phil 3791.126 — Ramlow, Lilli. Alois Riehl und H. Spencer. Inaug. Diss. Saalfeld, 1933.

Phil 5767.12 — Ramm, T. Die Freiheit der Willensbildung. Stuttgart, 1960.

Phil 3475.3.85 — Ramming, G. Karl Jaspers und Heinrich Richert Existenzialismus und Wertphilosophie. Bern, 1948.

Phil 5421.5.5 — Ramming-Thoen, Fortunata. Das Heimweh. Thesis. Zürich, 1958.

Phil 6127.7 — Ramón y Cajal, S. Comparative study of the sensory areas. Human cortex. n.p., 1899?

Phil 6127.7.10 — Ramón y Cajal, S. Les nouvelles idées sur la structure du système nerveux. Paris, 1895.

Phil 6127.7.20 — Ramón y Cajal, S. El pensamiento vivo de Cajal. Buenos Aires, 1941.

Phil 6127.7.5 — Ramón y Cajal, S. Textura del sistema nervioso del hombre y de los Vertebrados. V.1-2. Madrid, 1899. 3v.

Phil 5525.62 — Ramondt, Marie. Studien über des Lachen. Groningen, 1962.

Phil 8050.80 — Ramos, S. Estudios de estética. México, 1963.

Phil 4979.5.30 — Ramos, Samuel. Hacia un nuevo humanismo. 1. ed. México, 1940.

Phil 5425.20 — Ramos Mejia, J.M. Los simuladores del talento. Barcelona, n.d.

Phil 720.15 — Ramousse, Gatien. Essai d'une théorie scientifique du concept de vérité. Thèse. Saint-Amand, 1909.

Phil 2053.125 — Rampendahl, R. Eine Würdigung der ethik Hutchesons. Inaug.-Diss. Leipzig, 1892.

Phil 8597.1 — Ramsay, A.M. The philosophical principles of natural and revealed religion. Glasgow, 1748-49. 2v.

Phil 348.1 — Ramsay, G. Instinct and reason. London, 1862.

Phil 7054.146 — Ramsdell, Elizabeth. Spirit life of Theodore Parker. Boston, 1870.

Phil 7054.146.5 — Ramsdell, Sarah. Spirit life of Theodore Parker. Boston, 1876.

Phil 9245.25 — Ramsey, George. An inquiry into the principles of human happiness and human duty. London, 1843.

Phil 5467.7 — Ramsey, I.T. Models and mystery. London, 1964.

Phil 8707.28 — Ramsey, I.T. Religion and science: conflict and synthesis. London, 1964.

Phil 165.245 — Ramsey, J.T. Prospect for metaphysics. London, 1961.

Phil 8967.7 — Ramsey, Paul. Basic Christian ethics. N.Y., 1950.

Phil 8967.7.5 — Ramsey, Paul. Nine modern moralists. Englewood, 1962.

Phil 7054.98.3 — Ramsey, William. Spiritualism, a satanic delusion. Peace Dale, R.I., 1856.

Phil 7054.98 — Ramsey, William. Spiritualism, a satanic delusion. Rochester, N.Y., 1857.

Phil 6128.17F — Ramström, M. Emannuel Swedenborg's investigations in natural science and the basis for his statements concerning the functions of the brain. Uppsala, 1910.

Phil 2835.81 — Ramue (Pierre de la Ramée). (Waddington, C.) Paris, 1855.

Phil 5257.62 — Ramus, Carl. Behind the scenes with ourselves. N.Y., 1931.

Phil 2835.84 — Ramus, method and the decay of dialogue. (Ong, Walter J.) Cambridge, 1958. 2v.

Htn Phil 2835.30* — Ramus, P. Dialecticae libri duo. London, 1669.

Phil 2835.84.5 — Ramus and Talon inventory. (Ong, Walter J.) Cambridge, 1958.

Htn Phil 2835.84.5*A — Ramus and Talon inventory. (Ong, Walter J.) Cambridge, 1958.

Phil 3235.116 — Ran, Albrecht. Ludwig Feuerbach's Philosophie. Leipzig, 1882.

Phil 5545.169 — Ranachburg, P. Das kranke Gedachtnis. Leipzig, 1911.

Phil 960.35A — Ranade, R.D. A constructive survey of Upanishadic philosophy. Poona, 1926.

Phil 3120.8.160 — Rancurello, Antos C. A study of Franz Brentano; his psychological standpoint and its significance in the history of psychology. N.Y., 1968.

Phil 2255.10.34 — Rand, Ayn. For the new intellectual; the philosophy of Ayn Rand. N.Y., 1961.

Phil 2255.10.32 — Rand, Ayn. Introduction to objectivist epistemology. N.Y., 1967.

Phil 2255.10.30 — Rand, Ayn. The virtue of selfishness; a new concept of egoism. N.Y., 1965.

Phil 5227.3A — Rand, B. The classical psychologists. Boston, 1912.

Phil 1870.111 — Rand, Benjamin. Berkeley's American sojourn. Cambridge, 1932.

Phil 1717.6.3A — Rand, Benjamin. Modern classical philosophers. Boston, 1908.

Phil 1717.6 — Rand, Benjamin. Modern classical philosophers. Boston, 1908.

Phil 1717.6.6A — Rand, Benjamin. Modern classical philosophers. Boston, 1936.

Phil 1717.6.5A — Rand, Benjamin. Modern classical philosophers. 2nd ed. Boston, 1924.

Phil 75.13.5 — Rand, Benjamin. Philosophical library for the American continent. Cambridge, 1904.

Phil 75.13.9 — Rand, Benjamin. Selected works on history of philosophy in English language. Boston, 1906.

Phil 125.2 — Rand, Benjamin. Tables of philosophy. Cambridge, 1882.

Phil 1527.1.6.25 — Rand, E.K. Histoire de la philosophie médiévale. v.1-2. Cambridge, Mass., 1934.

Phil 5645.14 — Rand, G. Factor...sensitivity of retina to color. Princeton, 1913.

Phil 6060.46 — Rand, H.A. Graphology. Cambridge, Mass., 1947.

Phil 6069.17.32 — Randall, Edward Caleb. The dead have never died. N.Y., 1917.

Phil 6069.19.190 — Randall, Edward Caleb. The dead have never died. N.Y., 1919.

Phil 6127.13 — Randall, F.H. Psychology. London, 1905.

Phil 575.33 — Randall, J.H. The culture of personality. N.Y., 1912.

Phil 192.40.10 — Randall, J.H. How philosophy uses its past. N.Y., 1963.

Phil 192.40 — Randall, J.H. The spirit of the new philosophy. London, 1919.

Htn Phil 6967.4* — Randall, J.R. On treatment of the insane. n.p., n.d.

Phil 1717.21 — Randall, John. The career of philosophy. N.Y., 1962. 2v.

Phil 7069.21.50 — Randall, John H. The new light on immortality. N.Y., 1921.

Phil 8707.24 — Randall, John Herman. The role of knowledge in western religion. Boston, 1958.

Phil 9177.1 — Randall, M. Reflections...duty of masters, mistresses and servants. London, 1725.

Phil 8672.1 — Randles, M. First principles of faith. London, 1884.

Phil 6687.5 — Randolph, P.B. Seership. The magnetic mirror. Toledo, 1874.

Phil 7054.84 — Randolph, P.B. The unveiling: or What I think of spiritualism. Newburyport, 1860.

Phil 8892.1 — Randolph, R. Sober thoughts on staple themes. Philadelphia, 1889.

Phil 5535.22 — Random processes and learning. (Losifeseu, Marius.) Berlin, 1969.

Phil 193.147 — Random thoughts; liberalism in life and philosophy. (Silverman, H.L.) N.Y., 1936. 2v.

Phil 192.3 — Rands, W.B. Henry Holbeach. London, 1865. 2v.

Phil 192.3.2 — Rands, W.B. Henry Holbeach. London, 1866. 2v.

Phil 192.3.8 — Rands, W.B. Lilliput lectures. London, 1871.

Phil 3525.82 — Ranft, M. Der Philosoph K.C.F. Krause als Erzieher. Halle, 1907.

Phil 2750.11.70 — The range of reason. (Maritain, Jacques.) London, 1953.

Phil 2750.11.70.5 — The range of reason. (Maritain, Jacques.) N.Y., 1961.

Phil 4260.107F — Ranieri, A. Discorso recitato il di primo anniversario del plebiscito dell'Italia meridionale. Napoli, 1861.

Phil 6327.4 — Rank, Otto. Die Bedeutung der Psychoanalyse. Wiesbaden, 1913.

Phil 6327.4.23A — Rank, Otto. Beyond psychology. Camden, 1941.

Phil 6327.4.25 — Rank, Otto. Die don Juan-Gestalt. Leipzig, 1924.

Phil 6327.4.35 — Rank, Otto. Der Doppelganger. Zürich, 1925.

Phil 6327.4.36 — Rank, Otto. The double: a psychoanalytic study. Chapel Hill, 1971.

Phil 6327.4.13 — Rank, Otto. Grundzüge einer genetischen Psychologie. v.1-2. Wien, 1927-28.

Phil 5841.18.2 — Rank, Otto. Der Künstler; Ansatze zu einer Sexualpsychologie. 2. - 3. Aufl. Wien, 1918.

Phil 5841.18.4 — Rank, Otto. Der Künstler. 4. Aufl. Leipzig, 1925.

Phil 6327.4.40A — Rank, Otto. Psychology and the soul. Philadelphia, 1950.

Phil 665.60 — Rank, Otto. Seelenglaube und Psychologie. Leipzig, 1930.

Phil 5841.18.10 — Rank, Otto. Sexualität und Schuldgefühl. Leipzig, 1926.

Phil 6327.4.9 — Rank, Otto. Technik der Psychoanalyse. Leipzig, 1926-31. 3v.

Phil 6327.4.5A — Rank, Otto. Das Trauma der Geburt. Leipzig, 1924. 2v.

Phil 6327.4.6A — Rank, Otto. The trauma of birth. London, 1929.

Phil 6327.4.7 — Rank, Otto. The trauma of birth. N.Y., 1952.

Phil 6327.4.21A — Rank, Otto. Truth and reality. N.Y., 1936.

Phil 6327.4.19 — Rank, Otto. Wahrheit und Wirklichkeit. Leipzig, 1929.

Phil 6327.4.32 — Rank, Otto. Will therapy and truth and reality. N.Y., 1936.

Phil 6327.4.30 — Rank, Otto. Will therapy and truth and reality. N.Y., 1945.

Phil 6327.4.33 — Rank, Otto. Will therapy and truth and reality. N.Y., 1950.

Phil 192.68 — Ranke, Karl E. Die Kategorien des Lebendigen. München, 1928.

Phil 8350.2   Rankin, D.H. The development and philosophy of Australian aestheticism. Melbourne, 1949.

Phil 5767.14   Rankin, K. Choice and chance. Oxford, 1961.

Phil 3850.18.195   Ranly, Ernest W. Scheler's phenomenology of community. The Hague, 1966.

Phil 3010.4   Rannengiesser, P. Dogmatismus und Skepticismus. Elberfeld, 1877.

Phil 4520.8.50   Rannsókn dularfullra fyrirbrigd. (Mjarnason, Ágúst.) Reykjavík, 1914.

Phil 5257.56   Ranschburg, Pál. Az emberi elme. Budapest, 1923. 2v.

Phil 6615.14   Ranschburg, Pál. Neue Beiträg zur Psychologie des hysterischen Geisteszustandes. Leipzig, 1897.

Phil 8707.17   Ransom, J.C. God without thunder. N.Y., 1930.

Phil 2750.11.33   Ransoming the time. (Maritain, Jacques.) N.Y., 1941.

Phil 9530.42   Ranson, J.C. The successful man. Richmond, 1887.

Phil 1155.5   Ranulf, Svend. Der eleatische satz vom widerspruch. Kjøbenhavn, 1924.

Phil 6127.9   Ranvier, L. Leçons sur l'histologie du système nerveux. pt.1-2. Paris, 1878.

Phil 8967.10   Ranwez, E. Morale et perfection. Tournai, 1959.

Phil 102.3.5   Ranzoli, C. Dizionario de scienze filosofiche. Milano, 1952.

Phil 102.3.6   Ranzoli, C. Dizionario de scienze filosofiche. 6. ed. Milano, 1963.

Phil 102.3   Ranzoli, C. Dizionario di scienze filosofiche. Milano, 1905.

Phil 102.3.2   Ranzoli, C. Dizionario di scienze filosofiche. 2a ed. Milano, 1916.

Phil 102.3.3   Ranzoli, C. Dizionario di scienze filosofiche. 3a ed. Milano, 1926.

Phil 102.3.4   Ranzoli, C. Dizionario di scienze filosofiche. 4. ed. Milano, 1943.

Phil 2270.116   Ranzoli, C. La fortuna di Herbert Spencer in Italia. Verona, 1904.

Phil 400.53   Ranzoli, C. L'idealismo e la filosofia. n.p., n.d.

Phil 150.15   Ranzoli, C. Il linguaggio dei filosofi. Padova, 1911.

Phil 672.137   Ranzoli, C. Prime linee di una teoria realistica dello spazio e del tempo. Messina, 1921.

Phil 630.38   Ranzoli, Cesare. Il realismo puro. Milano, 1932.

Phil 5238.20   Rapaport, D. Organization and pathology of thought. N.Y., 1951.

Phil 6980.631   Rapaport, David. Diagnostic psychological testing. Chicago, 1945. 2v.

Phil 5400.100   Rapaport, David. Emotions and memory. Baltimore, 1942.

Phil 5780.16   The rape of the mind. 1. ed. (Meerlo, A.M.) Cleveland, 1956.

Phil 8892.65   Raphael, D. Daiches. Moral judgement. London, 1955.

Phil 8892.58   Raphael, D. Daiches. The moral sense. London, 1947.

Phil 8870.31   Raphael, David Daiches. British moralists, 1650-1800. Oxford, 1969. 2v.

Phil 8430.29A   Raphael, Max. Provalon, Marx, Picasso. Paris, 1933.

Phil 5057.26.2   Raphael, Max. La théorie marxiste de la connaissance. Paris, 1937.

Phil 5057.26   Raphael, Max. Zur Erkenntnistheorie der konkreten Dialektik. Paris, 1934.

Phil 5520.115   Rapoport, A. Operational philosophy. 1. ed. N.Y., 1953.

Phil 6327.30   Rapoport, Robert N. Community as doctor. London, 1960.

Phil 4720.9   Rapp, Friedrich. Gesetz und Determination in der Sowjetphilosophie. Dordrecht, 1968.

Phil 3808.162   Rappaport, S. Spinoza und Schopenhauer. Berlin, 1899.

Phil 7054.23   The rappers. (Mattison, H.) N.Y., n.d.

Phil 192.44.2   Rappoport, A.S. A primer of philosophy. London, 1916.

Phil 8170.5   Rappoport, S.Kh. Tvorit' mir po zakonam krasoty. Moskva, 1962.

Phil 5643.99   Rapport aangaande het onderzoek van het gezichtsvermongen. (Donders, F.C.) Utrecht, 1877. 2 pam.

Phil 6688.23.2   Rapport confidentiel sur le magnétisme animal. 2. éd. (Scobardi, R.P.) Paris, 1839.

Phil 8956.12   Rapport de Jean Guitton sur les prix de vertu. (Guitton, Jean.) Paris, 1964.

Phil 6965.14   Rapport de Mm. Cosnier, Maloet, Darcet, [and others]...nouveau méthode d'adminstrer l'électricité...maladies nerveuses. (Paris. Université. Faculté de Medecine.) Paris, 1783.

Phil 6675.12   Rapport des commissaires chargée par le roi de l'examen du magnétisme animal. (France. Commissaires Chargée de l'Examen du Magnétisme Animal.) Paris, 1784.

Phil 5242.9   Rapport sur la terminologie psychologique. (Claparède, E.) Genève, 1909.

Phil 4210.143   Rapporti fra Kant e Rosmini. (Cheula, Pietro.) Milano, 1934.

Phil 200.5.10   I rapporti fra l'individuo e l'universo. (Zucca, Antioco.) Padova, 1937.

Phil 6675.3   Rapports...sur magnétisme animal. (Foissac, P.) Paris, 1833.

Phil 70.1.2   Rapports. (International Congress of Philosophy, 2nd, Geneva, 1904.) Genève. 1905

Phil 1135.176   Les rapports avec Autrui dans la philosophie grecque d'Aristote à Panetius. (Voelke, Andre J.) Paris, 1961.

Phil 2475.1.238   Les rapports de la matière et de l'esprit dans le bergsonisme. (Rideau, Émile.) Paris, 1932.

Phil 2475.1.238.5   Les rapports de la matière et de l'esprit dans le bergsonisme. Thèse. (Rideau, Émile.) Paris, 1932.

Phil 7028.4   Rapports du magnétisme et du spiritisme. (Rouxel.) Paris, 1892.

Phil 2480.30   Rapports du physique et du moral de l'homme. (Cabanis, P.J.G.) Paris, 1802. 2v.

Phil 2480.30.2   Rapports du physique et du moral de l'homme. (Cabanis, P.J.G.) Paris, 1805.

Phil 2480.30.5   Rapports du physique et du moral de l'homme. (Cabanis, P.J.G.) Paris, 1824. 3v.

Phil 2480.31   Rapports du physique et du moral de l'homme. (Cabanis, P.J.G.) Paris, 1843.

Phil 2480.31.5   Rapports du physique et du moral de l'homme. 8e éd. (Cabanis, P.J.G.) Paris, 1844.

Phil 70.11   Rapports et comptes rendus. (Congrés Polonais de Philosophie.) Varsovie.

Phil 70.3.15   Rapports et comptes rendus. (International Congress of Psychology, 6th, Geneva, 1909.) Genève. 1910

Phil 70.3.40   Rapports et comptes rendus. (International Congress of Psychology, 11th, Paris, 1937.) Paris. 1938

Phil 6321.47   Les rapports intersubjectifs en psychanalyse. (Lévy-Valensi, E.) Paris, 1962.

Phil 348.14   Raretz, Karl von. Au den Quellen unseres Denkens. Wien, 1937.

Phil 6060.48   Ras, M. Los artistas escriben. 1. ed. Madrid, 1954.

Phil 3808.178   Rasche, F. Der Pessimismus Schopenhauers und das Wert Problem. Crimmitschau, 1924.

Phil 1195.8   Rascher, Wilhelm. De historicae doctrinae apud sophistas maiores vesligus. Inaug. Diss. Gottingae, 1838.

Phil 4210.192   Raschini, Maria A. Il principio dialettico nella filosofia di Antonio Rosmini. Milano, 1961.

Phil 1740.24   Raschini, Maria A. Riflessioni su filosofia e cultura. Milano, 1968.

Phil 5238.142   Rasey, Marie I. The nature of being human. Detroit, 1959.

Phil 8967.3   Rashdall, H. Conscience and Christ; six lectures. London, 1916.

Phil 9075.13   Rashdall, H. Is conscience an emotion? Boston, 1914.

Phil 1885.80   Rashdall, H. The metaphysic of Mr. F.H. Bradley. London, 1912.

Phil 192.27   Rashdall, H. Philosophy and religion. London, 1909.

Phil 8892.13.5   Rashdall, Hastings. Ethics. London, 1913.

Phil 8892.13   Rashdall, Hastings. The theory of good and evil. Oxford, 1907. 2v.

Phil 8892.13.4   Rashdall, Hastings. The theory of good and evil. 2. ed. London, 1948. 2v.

Phil 8892.13.2   Rashdall, Hastings. The theory of good and evil. 2. ed. Oxford, 1924. 2v.

Phil 165.346   Rasheed, A. The notion of existence. Lahore, 1959.

Phil 3497.20   Ras"iskateli istinyi: I. Kant. (Panaev, I.) Sankt Peterburg, 1878.

Phil 3499.29   Rasker, A.J. De ethick en het probleem van het booze. Proef. Assen, 1935.

Phil 6127.21   Rasmussen, A.T. The principal nervous pathways. N.Y., 1939.

Phil 2035.86.35   Rasmussen, S.V. The philosophy of Sir William Hamilton. Copenhagen, 1925.

Phil 2035.86.30   Rasmussen, S.V. Studier over W. Hamiltons filosofi. København, 1921.

Phil 8892.79   Rašovský, Adolf. Ethos und Naturrecht. Wien, 1964.

Phil 310.595   Rasprostranenie idei marksistskoi filosofii v Evrope. (Leningrad. Universitet.) Leningrad, 1964.

Phil 3640.294   Rasse, Ehe, Zucht und Züchtung bei Nietzsche und Heute. (Endres, Hans.) Heidelberg, 1938.

Phil 3017.4   Der Rassegedanke und die neuere Philosophie. (Riecke, H.) Leipzig, 1939.

Phil 75.94   Rassegna bibliografia di storia della filosofia; recavata della riviste. Padova. 3,1968+ 2v.

Phil 2477.6.115   Rassegna di bibliografia blondeliana. (Crippà, Romeo.) Torino, 1952.

Phil 27.48   Rassegna di filosofia. Roma. 1-7,1952-1958 7v.

Phil 27.47   Rassegna di scienze filosofiche. Roma. 1,1948+ 12v.

Phil 7082.166A   Ratcliff, Arthur James John. A history of dreams. Boston, 1923.

Phil 5870.100   Ratcliffe, Tom A. The child and reality. London, 1970.

Phil 6319.1.192   Rath, Paul. Anima und Animus in der Psychologie C.G. Jung. Winterthur, 1954.

Phil 6127.23   Rathbone, J.L. Relaxation. N.Y., 1943.

Phil 3790.2.30.8   Rathenau, W. Zur Mechanik des Geistes. 8e und 9e Aufl. Berlin, 1918.

Phil 27.68   Ratio. Oxford. 1,1957+ 3v.

Phil 186.86.10   Ratio en existentie. (Leendertz, W.) Amsterdam, 1936.

Phil 8880.6   The rational, or scientific ideal of morality. (Fitzgerald, P.F.) London, 1897.

Phil 8610.900.5   Rational agnosticism. (Roberts, G.L.) n.p., n.d.

Phil 7069.40.11   Rational and scientific (Christian) spiritualism. (Redemptor Spiritual Center.) Rio de Janeiro, n.d.

Phil 175.56   The rational and the real. (Armour, Leslie.) The Hague, 1962.

Phil 5257.70.5   A rational animal. (Ryle, Gilbert.) London, 1962.

Phil 5045.14A   Rational belief. (Frye, A.M.) N.Y., 1941.

Phil 288.1   Rational cosmology. (Hickok, S.P.) N.Y., 1958.

Phil 5761.9.5   The rational education of the will. 9. ed. (Lévy, Paul Émile.) Philadelphia, 1920.

Phil 8882.30.10   The rational good. (Hobhouse, L.T.) London, 1947.

Phil 5043.27   Rational induction. (Dubs, Homer.) Chicago, 1930.

Phil 27.90   Rational living. N.Y. 1,1966+

Phil 8896.21   Rational man; a modern interpretation. (Veatch, Henry B.) Bloomington, 1962.

Phil 5643.40   Rational of the cause of cerebral vision. (Fearn, John.) London, 1830? 4 pam.

Phil 180.9   Rational philosophy. (Fraser, A.C.) Edinburgh, 1858.

Phil 5247.9   Rational psychology. (Hickok, L.P.) Auburn, 1849.

Phil 5247.9.5   Rational psychology. (Hickok, L.P.) N.Y., 1876.

Phil 8598.12.3   Rational religion. (Smith, Goldwin.) Oxford, 1861.

Phil 8888.3   Rational self-love. (Nihell, L.) Limerick, 1770.

Htn   Phil 9495.35*   Rational sex ethics. (Robie, W.F.) Boston, 1916.

Phil 2280.5.161   The rational society; a critical study of Santayana's social thought. (Singer, Beth J.) Cleveland, 1970.

Phil 8599.12   Rational theology and Christian philosophy in England in the 17th century. (Tulloch, John.) Edinburgh, 1872. 2v.

Phil 1865.42   The rationale of the reward. (Bentham, Jeremy.) London, 1830.

Phil 325.18   Rationalism, empiricism, and pragmatism: an introduction. (Aune, Bruce.) N.Y., 1970.

Phil 623.4   Rationalism. (Robertson, J.M.) London, 1912.

Phil 623.44   Rationalism and humanism. (Hobson, John Atkinson.) London, 1933.

Phil 1135.173   Rationalism in Greek philosophy. (Boas, Georje.) Baltimore, 1961.

Phil 623.30   Rationalism in practice. (Paranjpye, Raghunath Purushotam.) Calcutta, 1935.

Phil 623.28   Rationalism in theory and practice. (Robertson, A.) London, 1895.

Phil 623.2.15   Le rationalisme. (Bonarino, Cristoforo.) Bruxelles, 1855.

Phil 623.35   Het rationalisme. Den Haag, 1960.

Phil 623.25   Le rationalisme appliqué. (Bachelard, G.) Paris, 1949.

Phil 2520.344   Le rationalisme de Descartes. (Laporte, Jean.) Paris, 1950.

Phil 2340.9.94   Le rationalisme de Whewell. (Blanché, Robert.) Paris, 1935.

Phil 2340.9.93   Le rationalisme de Whewell. Thèse. (Blanché, Robert.) Paris, 1935.

Phil 623.3   Rationalisme et tradition. (Delvolvé, J.) Paris, 1910.

Phil 623.18   Rationalismens förberedelser. (Scheele, K.H.G. von.) Upsala, 1868.

Phil 1135.240   Rationalismus im Ursprung. (Stachowiak, Herbert.) Wien, 1971.

Phil 3552.486   Rationalismus und Entwurf einer universalen Logik bei Leibniz. (Krueger, Lorenz.) Frankfurt, 1969.

Phil 1750.295.5   Rationalismus und Sensibilität. (Bense, Max.) Krefeld, 1956.

Phil 623.16.5   A rationalist encyclopaedia. (McCabe, Joseph.) London, 1948.

Phil 27.26   La rationaliste. Genève. 1-9,1861-1870 9v.

Phil 165.380   Rationalität, Phänomenalität, Individualität. (Ritzel, Wolfgang.) Bonn, 1966.

Phil 5520.410   Rationality. (Bennett, J.F.) London, 1964.

Phil 5090.7.5   Le rationnel. (Milhaud, G.) Paris, 1898.

Phil 3499.23   Ratke, Heinrich. Systematisches Handlexikon zu Kants Kritik der reinen Vernunft. Leipzig, 1929.

Phil 402.20   Ratković, Radoslav. Ideoligija i politika. Beograd, 1971.

Phil 8610.967.5   Ratnathicam, Daniel S. Honest to man. Colombo, 1967.

Phil 3837.19   Ratner, J. Spinoza on God. N.Y., 1930.

Phil 1830.12   Ratner, Sidney. Vision and action. New Brunswick, N.J., 1953.

Phil 8656.46.2   Ratschow, Carl Heinz. Atheismus im Christentum? 2. Aufl. Gütersloh, 1971.

Phil 3425.744   Ratsional'noe i misticheskoe v gegelevskoi teorii iavliaiushchegosia dukha. (Golosov, Viktor F.) Krasnoiarsk, 1969.

Phil 4582.4.46   Ratten och Viljan. (Hägerström, Axel.) Lund, 1961.

Phil 3850.27.117   Ratter, Magnus C. Albert Schweitzer, life and message. Boston, 1950.

Phil 192.4   Rattier, M.S. Cours complet de philosophie. Paris, 1843-1844. 4v.

Phil 5645.70   Rattleff, Anker. Form, farve og emotioner. København, 1958.

Phil 6310.1.99   Rattner, J. Individualpsychologie. München, 1963.

Phil 5421.20.110   Rattner, Josef. Aggression und menschliche Natur. Olten, 1970.

Phil 6327.45   Rattner, Josef. Der nervöse Mensch und seine Heilung. Zürich, 1965.

Phil 6980.712.105   Rattner, Josef. Psychologie der zwischenmenschlichen Beziehungen. Olten, 1969.

Phil 6980.632   Rattner, Josef. Tiefenpsychologie und Humanismus. Zürich, 1967.

Phil 6967.20   Rattner, Josef. Das Wesen der schizophrenen Reaktion. München, 1963.

Phil 192.51   Rattray, R.F. Fundamentals. Leicester, 1925.

Phil 8597.39   Rattray, R.F. Fundamentals of modern religion. London, 1932.

Phil 5257.45   Rattray, Robert F. An outline of genetic psychology according to the theory of inherited mind. London, 1931.

Phil 8418.2   Ratzal, Friedrich. Uber Naturschilderung. München, 1904.

Phil 8892.5   Ratzenhofer, G. Positive Ethik. Leipzig, 1901.

Phil 348.6   Ratzenhofer, Gustav. Die Kritik des Intellects. Leipzig, 1902.

Phil 8622.82.2   Ratzinger, Joseph. Glaube und Zukunft. 2. Aufl. München, 1971.

Phil 5585.7   Rau, A. Empfinden und Denken. Giessen, 1896.

Phil 5585.7.5   Rau, A. Das Wesen des menschlichen Verstandus und Bewusstseins. München, 1910.

Phil 8967.4   Rau, Albrecht. Die Ethik jesu. Giessen, 1899.

Phil 6830.6.4   Rau, Hans. Die Grausamkeit mit besonder Bezugnahme auf sexualle Factoren. 4. Aufl. Berlin, 1921.

Phil 6978.12.5   Raubinovitch, Jacques. La mélancolie. Paris, 1897.

Phil 5257.1   Rauch, F.A. Psychology. N.Y., 1840.

Phil 5257.1.2   Rauch, F.A. Psychology. N.Y., 1841.

Phil 3640.239   Rauch, Karl. Nietzsches Wirkung und Erbe. Berlin, 1930.

Phil 3310.16.80   Rauche, G.A. The problem of truth and reality in Grisebach's thought. Pretoria, 1966.

Phil 720.101   Rauche, Gerhard Albin. Contemporary philosophical alternatives and the crisis of truth; a critical study of positivism, existentialism and Marxism. The Hague, 1970.

Phil 1122.15   Rauche, Gerhard Albin. A student's key to ancient Greek thought. Fort Hare, 1966.

Phil 7072.22.5   Raudive, Konstantins. Breakthrough. N.Y., 1971.

Phil 7072.22   Raudive, Konstantins. Unhorbares wird Hörbar. Ramagen, 1968.

Phil 5257.9   Raue, C.G. Psychologie as a natural science. Philadelphia, 1889.

Phil 5400.20   Rauh, F. De la méthode dans la psychologie des sentiments. Paris, 1899.

Phil 8892.18   Rauh, F. Études de morale. Paris, 1911.

Phil 3837.13   Rauh, F. Quatenus doctrina quam Spinoza de fide. Thesis. Tolosae, 1890.

Phil 5525.21   Raulin, J.M. Le rire et les exhilarants. Paris, 1900.

Phil 672.127.2   Raum, Zeit und Gott. (Rawitz, B.) Leipzig, 1923.

Phil 672.128   Raum, Zeit und Schwere. (Eddington, A.S.) Braunschweig, 1923.

Phil 3245.88   Die Raum- und Zeitlehre Immanuel Hermann Fichtes. (Serwe, Arthur.) Saarbrücken, 1959.

Phil 5640.21   Raum und Stoff. (Goering, W.) Berlin, 1876.

Phil 672.124   Raum und Zeit. (Marty, Anton.) Halle, 1916.

Phil 5811.11   Die Raumorientierung der Ameisen. (Brun, Rudolf.) Jena, 1914.

Phil 3160.12.85   Das Raumproblem in Cassirers Philosophie der Mythologie. (Gaona, Francisco.) Tübingen, 1965.

Phil 5648.15   Der Raumsinn der Haut. Inaug. Diss. (Klinkenberg, E.) Bonn, 1883.

Phil 5643.81   Die Raumvorstellung aus der Gesichtssinne. (Hasenclever, R.) Berlin, 1842.

Phil 5585.31   Die Raumwahrnehmung der Blinden. (Steinberg, Wilhelm.) München, 1920.

Phil 5648.7   Raumwahrnehmungen des Tastsinnes. (Henri, V.) Berlin, 1898.

Phil 5648.7.2   Raumwahrnehmungen des Tastsinnes. (Henri, V.) Berlin, 1898.

Phil 5257.39.2   Raup, R.B. Complacency; the foundation of human behavior. N.Y., 1925.

Phil 7054.174   Raupert, J.G. The new black magic. N.Y., 1920.

Phil 7060.72.7   Raupert, J.G. The supreme problem. Buffalo, 1910.

Phil 7069.06.20   Raupert, John G. The dangers of spiritualism. 2. ed. London, 1906.

Phil 7069.09.17   Raupert, John G. Modern spiritism. 2. ed. St. Louis, 1909.

Phil 192.26   Rausch, Alfred. Elemente der Philosophie. Halle, 1909.

Phil 192.26.3   Rausch, Alfred. Elemente der Philosophie. 3. Aufl. Halle, 1914.

Phil 5585.77   Rausch, E. Struktur und Metrik figuraloptischer Wahrnehmung. Frankfurt, 1952.

Phil 5593.70   Rausch de Traubenberg, Nina. La pratique du Rorschach. 1. éd. Paris, 1970.

Phil 1870.145   Rauschenberger, J.P. Über das Problem der Einheit un des Sinnes von Erscheinung bei Berkeley. Gernsbach, 1959.

Phil 3499.18   Rauschenberger, W. Die Antinomien Kants. Berlin, 1923.

Phil 400.40   Rauschenberger, W. Der kritische Idealismus. Leipzig, 1918.

Phil 817.11   Rauschenberger, W. Das philosophische Genie und seine Rasseabstammung. Frankfurt, 1922.

Phil 5425.32   Rauschenberger, W. Das Talent und das Genie. Frankfurt, 1922.

Phil 270.32   Rauschenberger, W. Über Identität und Kausalität. Leipzig, 1922.

Phil 3790.6.31   Rauscher, J.O. Darstellung der Philosophie. Salugan, 1891.

Phil 7060.37   Rauschink, Gottfried Peter. Gespenstersagen. Rudolstadt, 1817.

Phil 5590.30   Raushenbush, E. Psychology for individual education. N.Y., 1942.

Phil 8597.32.5   Rauwenhoff, D.L.W.E. Religionsphilosophie. 2. Aufl. Braunschweig, 1894.

Phil 4017.1   Rava, Adolfo. Descartes, Spinoza et la pensée italienne. Paris, 1927.

Phil 1735.12   Rava, Adolfo. La filosofia Europea nel secolo decimonono. Padova, 1932.

Phil 3837.30   Rava, Adolfo. Studi su Spinoza e Fichte. Milano, 1958.

Phil 2417.1   Ravaisson, J.G.F. La philosophie en France au XIXe siècle. Paris, 1868.

Phil 2855.3.83   Ravaisson et les médecins animistes et vitalistes. (Cazeneuve, Jean.) Paris, 1957.

Phil 5435.4.5   Ravaisson-Mollien, Felix. De l'habitude. Paris, 1927.

Phil 5435.4   Ravaisson-Mollien, Felix. De l'habitude. Paris, 1938.

Phil 5435.4.2   Ravaisson-Mollien, Felix. De l'habitude. 2. éd. Paris, 1957.

Htn   Phil 2855.3.30*   Ravaisson-Mollien, Felix. Essai sur la métaphysique. Paris, 1846.

Phil 2855.3.15   Ravaisson-Mollien, Félix. Testament philosophique et fragments. Paris, 1933.

Phil 8707.21.5A   Raven, C.E. Natural religion and Christian theology. Cambridge, Eng., 1953. 2v.

Phil 8707.21   Raven, C.E. Science, religion, and the future. Cambridge, Eng., 1943.

Phil 2905.1.185   Raven, Charles. Teilhard de Chardin. London, 1962.

Phil 8597.36   Raven, Charles E. The creator spirit. Cambridge, 1927.

Phil 8672.14   Raven, Charles E. Evolution and the Christian concept of God. London, 1936.

Phil 8597.36.5   Raven, Charles E. Jesus and the gospel of love. London, 1931.

Phil 1182.25   Raven, John E. Pythagoreans and Eleatics. Cambridge, 1948.

Phil 525.243   Ravier, André. La mystique et les mystiques. Bruges, 1965.

Phil 3552.01   Ravier, E. Bibliographie de la philosophie de Leibniz. Thèse. Caen, 1927.

Phil 3552.02   Ravier, E. Bibliographie des oeuvres de Leibniz. Paris, 1937.

Phil 3552.261   Ravier, E. Le système de Leibniz et le problème des rapports de la raison et de la foi. Thèse. Caen, 1927.

Phil 310.5   Ravnosmetka na edna idealistko reaktsionii filosofiia. (Pavlov, T.) Sofiia, 1953.

Phil 5590.560   Ravzvitie lichnosti v usloviiakh stroitel'stva kommunizma. Cheboksarg, 1970.

Phil 5640.40   Rawdon-Smith, A.F. Theories of sensation. Cambridge, 1938.

Phil 3235.112   Rawidowicz, Simon. Ludwig Feuerbachs Philosophie. Berlin, 1931.

Phil 3235.112.2   Rawidowicz, Simon. Ludwig Feuerbachs Philosophie. 2. Aufl. Berlin, 1964.

Phil 672.127.2   Rawitz, B. Raum, Zeit und Gott. Leipzig, 1923.

Phil 298.9   Rawson, F. Life understood from a scientific and religious point of view. 7. ed. London, 1947.

Phil 8707.8   Rawson, F.L. The evolution of the world; or, Science from a religious point of view. Garden City, 1909.

Phil 192.41   Rawson, F.L. Life understood from a scientific and religious point of view. 4th ed. London, 1917.

Phil 4870.10   Ray, Benoy Gopal. Contemporary Indian philosophers. Allahabad, 1947.

Phil 6967.5   Ray, Isaac. Contributions to mental pathology. Boston, 1873.

Phil 6945.10   Ray, Isaac. Ideal characters of officers of a hospital for the insane. Philadelphia, 1873.

Phil 6967.5.4   Ray, Isaac. Treatise of medical jurisprudence of insanity. Boston, 1838.

Phil 6967.5.10   Ray, Isaac. A treatise on the medical jurisprudence of insanity. Cambridge, 1962.

Phil 6967.5.5   Ray, Isaac. Treatise on the medical jurisprudence of insanity. 2. ed. Boston, 1844.

Phil 6967.5.8   Ray, Isaac. Treatise on the medical jurisprudence of insanity. 5. ed. Boston, 1871.

Phil 6127.1   Ray, J. Mental hygiene. Boston, 1863.

Phil 8597.2   Ray, J. Three physico-theological discourses. London, 1721.

Htn   Phil 8672.2.5*   Ray, J. The wisdom of God manifested in the works of the creation. London, 1691.

Htn   Phil 8672.2.3*A   Ray, J. The wisdom of God manifested in the works of the creation. v.1-2. London, 1704.

Htn   Phil 8672.2*   Ray, J. The wisdom of God manifested in the works of the creation. v.1-2. London, 1714.

Phil 8672.2.2   Ray, J. The wisdom of God manifested in the works of the creation. v.1-2. London, 1717.

Phil 6327.16   Ray, Marie B. Doctors of the mind; the story of the psychiatry. Boston, 1942.

Phil 6327.16.7   Ray, Marie B. Doctors of the mind, what psychiatry can do. Boston, 1946.

Phil 6127.24   Ray, Marie B. Lyons. How never to be tired, or Two lifetimes in one. Indianapolis, Ind., 1944.

Phil 960.163.5   Ray Chaudhuri, A.K. The doctrine of Maya. 2nd ed. Calcutta, 1950.

Phil 960.163.10   Ray Chaudhuri, A.K. Self and falsity in Advaita Vedanta. 1st ed. Calcutta, 1955.

Phil 4215.10.30   Raya, Gino. La fame. 2. ed. Roma, 1963.

Phil 8418.5.2   Raymond, G.L. Art in theory; an introduction to the study of comparative aesthetics. 2. ed. N.Y., 1909.

Phil 8418.6.10   Raymond, G.L. An art philosopher's cabinet. N.Y., 1915.

Phil 8418.5   Raymond, G.L. Art theory; an introduction to the study of comparative aesthetics. N.Y., 1894.

Phil 8418.6   Raymond, G.L. The essentials of aesthetics in music. N.Y., 1911.

Phil 8418.6.3   Raymond, G.L. The essentials of aesthetics in music. 3.ed. N.Y., 1921.

Phil 8430.22   Raymond, G.L. The genesis of art form. N.Y., 1893.

Phil 8430.34   Raymond, G.L. The genesis of art form. N.Y., 1893.

Phil 8707.5   Raymond, G.L. The psychology of inspiration. N.Y., 1908.

Phil 8418.4   Raymond, G.L. The representative significance of form. N.Y., 1900.

Phil 8418.4.2   Raymond, G.L. The representative significance of form. 2. ed. N.Y., 1909.

Phil 8892.24　Raymond, George L. Ethics and natural law. N.Y., 1920.
Phil 8892.24.5　Raymond, George L. Ethics and natural law. 2. ed. N.Y., 1920.
Phil 7069.16.40　Raymond. (Lodge, Oliver Joseph.) N.Y., 1916.
Phil 1504.7.4　Raymundus Lullus. v.7, pt.4-5. (Keicher, O.) Münster, 1909.
Phil 6327.2　Raynier, Julien. Les états déprésifs...chez les militaires. Thèse. Paris, 1915.
Phil 6844.2　Raynor, Darrell G. A year among the girls. N.Y., 1966.
Phil 7069.20.280　Raynor, Frank C. Through jewelled windows. London, 1920.
Phil 7069.05.15　Rayon, M. Fads or facts. Chicago, 1905.
Phil 7069.00.60　Rayon, M. The mystic self. Chicago, 1900.
Phil 8892.26.8　Rayot, E. Précis de morale. 8. ed. Paris, 1906.
Phil 5465.144　Razik, Jaher A. Bibliography of creativity; studies and related areas. Buffalo, 1965.
Phil 4210.42　Il razionalismo. (Rosmini-Serbati, Antonio.) Prato, 1882.
Phil 623.2　Il razionalismo del Popolo. (Franchi, A.) Losanna, 1861.
Phil 4070.1.65　Il razionalismo del popolo dei Ausonio Franchi. 3a ed. corretta et aumentata. (Bonavino, Cristoforo.) Milano, 1864.
Phil 1930.10.90　Il razionalismo di Morris R. Cohen. (Dereglia, A.) Torino, 1960.
Phil 3485.9　Il razionalismo religioso di E. Kant. (Dentrice di Accadia, C.) Bari, 1920.
Phil 8885.49.5　Razmisljanja o etici. (Kangrga, Milan.) Zagreb, 1970.
Phil 4983.8.90　Razón contra razón...de Enrique José de Varona. 3. ed. (Cabrera, Francisco de A.) Habana, 1893.
Phil 310.760　Razon mecanica y razon dialectica. (Tierno Galvan, Enrique.) Madrid, 1969.
Phil 5125.15　El razonamiento inductivo. (Planella Guille, J.) Barcelona, 1929?
Phil 5625.82　Razran, G.H.S. Conditioned responses in children. Thesis. N.Y., 1933.
Phil 193.150.10　Razreshenie sud'by chelovecheskoi. (Spakovski, A.) Novyi Sad, 1934.
Phil 8980.497　Razuitie nravstvennykh ubezhdenii i privychek v protsesse kommunisticheskogo vospitaniia. (Kotov, L.I.) Moskva, 1961.
Phil 8418.42　Razummyi, Vladimir A. Esteticheskoe vospitanie. Moskva, 1969.
Phil 8400.37　Razumnyi, V.A. Esteticheskoe sbornik statei. Moskva, 1964.
Phil 494.4　Razvetie materializma i ego bor'ba protiv idealizma. (Trakhtenberg, I.V.) Moskva, 1956.
Phil 260.15　Razvitie atomisticheskikh predstavlenii do nachala XIX veka. (Zubor, Vasilii P.) Moskva, 1965.
Phil 4795.8　Razvitie filosofskoi mysli v Azerbaidzhane. (Mamedov, Sheidabek Faradzhievich.) Moskva, 1965.
Phil 4822.4.5　Razvitie na filosofskata misul v Bulgariia. (Bunkov, Angel Iliev.) Sofiia, 1966.
Phil 2421.5　Razvitie obshchestvennoi mysli vo Frantsii v XVIII veke. (Volgin, V.P.) Moskva, 1958.
Phil 5235.2　Razvitie psikhologicheskoi mysli v Kazakhstane (so vtoroi poloviny XIXlveka i do nashikh dnei). (Zharikbaev, Kubigul B.) Alma-Ata, 1968.
Phil 8171.100　Razvitstsio estetychnai dumki u Belarusi. (Konan, Uladzimir M.) Minsk, 1968.
Phil 3017.7　Razzug, Aśad. Die Ansätze zu einer Kulturantnropologie in der Gegewärtigen deutschen Philosophie. Tübingen, 1963.
Phil 5057.16　Re, Alfonso del. Lezioni di algebra della logica. Napoli, 1907.
Phil 5850.227　Re-creating human nature. (Hayward, C.N.) N.Y., 1914.
Phil 6317.10　The re-creating of the individual. (Hinkle, Beatrice.) N.Y., 1923.
Phil 6321.46　Re-fundamentacion de la psiquiatria. (Lertora, A.C.) Buenos Aires, 1963.
Phil 5238.220　The reach of mind. N.Y., 1968.
Phil 7069.47.5A　The reach of the mind. (Rhine, Joseph B.) N.Y., 1947.
Phil 5643.108　Reacting and visual fatigue. (Carmichael, Leonard.) Boston, 1947.
Phil 8592.48.10　The reaction against metaphysics in theology. (Macintosh, D.C.) Chicago, 1911.
Phil 600.4　La réaction contre le positivisme. (Broglie, A.T.P.) Paris, 1894.
Phil 5834.1.20　Reaction of entomostraca to...light. (Yerkes, R.M.) n.p., 1899-1916. 44 pam.
Phil 5643.37　Reaction time to retinal stimulation. (Poffenberger, A.T.) N.Y., 1912.
Phil 5242.38　Les réactions intellectuelles élémentaires. (Cresson, André.) Paris, 1922.
Phil 5243.44　Reactions of the human machine. (Deut, John Y.) London, 1936.
Phil 5402.25　Les réactions psycho-physiologiques à la douleur. (McKenna, A.G.) Louvain, 1963.
Phil 5057.9　Read, C. Logic; deductive and inductive. London, 1898.
Phil 192.22　Read, C. The metaphysics of nature. London, 1905.
Phil 6967.10.2　Read, C. Stanford. Abnormal mental strain. London, 1920.
Phil 6967.10　Read, C. Stanford. Military psychiatry in peace and war. London, 1920.
Phil 8892.14　Read, Carveth. Natural and social morals. London, 1909.
Phil 8672.9　Read, E.A. The idea of God in relation to theology. Chicago, 1900.
Phil 8620.17　Read, H. The foot-prints of Satan. N.Y., 1874.
Phil 8418.20.10　Read, Herbert. Art and alienation: the role of the artist in society. London, 1967.
Phil 8418.20　Read, Herbert. The forms of things unknown. London, 1960.
Phil 8418.20.5　Read, Herbert. Icon and idea. Harvard, 1955.
Phil 6319.1.85　Read, Herbert. Zum 85. Geburtstag von Professor Dr. Carl Gustav Jung. Zürich, 1960.
Phil 9150.7　Read, M.S. English evolutionary ethics. N.Y., 1902.
Phil 5125.18　Reade, W.H.F. The problem of inference. Oxford, 1938.
Phil 8597.51　Reade, W.H.V. The Christian challenge and philosophy. London, 1951.
Phil 5545.254.3　Readiness to remember; proceedings of the third conference on learning, remembering, and forgetting. (International Interdisciplinary Conference on Learning, Remembering and Forgetting.) N.Y., 1969. 2v.
Phil 8587.32.25　Reading from Friedrich von Hügel. (Hügel, Friedrich von.) London, 1964.
Phil 8877.71　Reading in ethics. (Clark, Gordon H.) N.Y., 1931.
Phil 8877.71.15　Reading in ethics. 2nd ed. (Clark, Gordon H.) N.Y., 1943.
Phil 5238.194　Readings for an introduction to psychology. (King, R.A.) N.Y., 1961.
Phil 9357.3　Readings for young men. Boston, 1859.
Phil 6329.3　Readings in abnormal psychology. (Taylor, W.S.) N.Y., 1926.
Phil 5232.11　Readings in African psychology. (Wickert, F.R.) East Lansing, 1967.

Phil 165.200　Readings in ancient and medieval philosophy. (Collins, James.) Westminster, 1960.
Phil 8870.38　Readings in ethical theory. (Sellars, Wilfrid.) N.Y., 1952.
Phil 5261.17　Readings in experimental psychology. 1. ed. (Valentine, Willard Lee.) N.Y., 1931.
Phil 5590.45.20　Readings in extraversion-introversion. (Eysenck, Hans Jürgen.) London, 1970-
Phil 5238.105　Readings in general psychology. (Halmos, Paul.) London, 1959.
Phil 5257.27　Readings in general psychology. (Robinson, E.S.) Chicago, 1923.
Phil 5257.27.3　Readings in general psychology. (Robinson, E.S.) Chicago, 1929.
Phil 5039.2　Readings in logic. (Houde, Roland.) Dubuque, 1958.
Phil 5272.3　Readings in mathematical psychology. (Luce, Robert D.) N.Y., 1963-65. 2v.
Phil 6116.21　Readings in mental hygiene. (Groves, E.R.) N.Y., 1936.
Phil 5585.115　Readings in perception. (Beardslee, D.C.) Princeton, 1958.
Phil 165.402　Readings in philosophical analysis. (Feigl, Herbert.) N.Y., 1949.
Phil 175.28.2　Readings in philosophy. (Avey, A.E.) N.Y., 1924.
Phil 165.3　Readings in philosophy. (Avey, A.E.) N.Y., 1936.
Phil 5238.200　Readings in psychology. (Cohen, J.) London, 1964.
Phil 5262.36.5　Readings in psychology. (Wheeler, R.H.) N.Y., 1930.
Phil 4710.156　Readings in Russian philosophical thought. (Shein, Louis J.) The Hague, 1968.
Phil 8709.24　Readings in science and spirit. (Talafous, Camillus D.) Englewood Cliffs, N.J., 1966.
Phil 291.8　Readings in the philosophy of nature. (Koren, Henry.) Westminster, Md., 1958.
Phil 5520.480.5　Readings in the psychology of cognition. (Anderson, Richard Chase.) N.Y., 1965.
Phil 5643.125　Readings in the study of visually perceived movement. (Spigel, Irwin Myron.) N.Y., 1965.
Phil 585.295　Readings in the theory of action. (Care, Norman S.) Bloomington, 1968.
Phil 333.21　Readings in the theory of knowledge. (Canfield, J.V.) N.Y., 1964.
Phil 1695.22　Readings in twentieth century philosophy. (Alston, W.) N.Y., 1936.
Phil 5039.6　Readings on logic. (Copi, Irving M.) N.Y., 1965.
Phil 5057.28　Reajifo, F.M. Elementos de logica. Bogota, 1930.
Phil 3640.595　Reaktsionnaia sushchnost' nitssheanstva. (Oduev, S.F.) Moskva, 1959.
Phil 5401.48　Réal, Pierre. Triomphez de l'angoisse. Verviers, 1963.
Phil 176.14.10　The real, the rational and the alogical. (Bax, E.B.) London, 1920.
Phil 187.143.5　The real and the negative. (Mallik, B.K.) London, 1940.
Phil 8610.890.20　The real blasphemers. (Kelso, John R.) N.Y., 189-?
Phil 7060.254　Real ghost stories. (Stead, William T.) N.Y., 1921.
Phil 8881.27　Real life. (Gleed, J.W.) n.p., 1899.
Phil 8881.32　The real life. (Grossmann, L.) N.Y., 1914.
Phil 7059.19　Real life in the spirit land. 5. ed. (King, Maria M.) Hammonton,N.J., 1892.
Phil 2340.22.30　The real world. (Wank, Martin.) N.Y., 1970.
Phil 3425.415　Realdialektik. (Wein, Hermann.) München, 1957.
Phil 4960.650　Reale, Miguel. Filosofía em São Paulo. São Paulo, 1962.
Phil 845.2.5　Realer Humanismus. (Weinstock, Heinrich.) Heidelberg, 1955.
Phil 4981.41.100　La realidad como resultado. (Tierno Galvan, Enrique.) Rio Piedras, 1966.
Phil 5627.266　Realisation; Anthropologie in Seelsorge und Erziehung. (Goldbrunner, Josef.) Greiburg, 1966.
Phil 630.7A　Die Realisierung. (Külpe, O.) Leipzig, 1912. 3v.
Phil 3120.8.145　Realism; a critique of Brentano and Meinong. (Bergmann, Gustav.) Madison, 1967.
Phil 630.18　Realism, a study in art and thought. (McDowall, A.S.) London, 1918.
Phil 2280.22.80　Realism, materialism, and the mind: the philosophy of Roy Wood Sellars. (Melchert, Norman P.) Springfield, Ill., 1968.
Phil 630.34　Realism: an attempt to trace its origin. (Hasan, S.Z.) Cambridge, 1928.
Phil 8403.38　Realism and imagination. (Chiari, Joseph.) London, 1960.
Phil 630.53　Realism and nominalism revisited. (Veatch, Henry B.) Milwaukee, 1954.
Phil 630.55　Realism and the background of phenomenology. (Chisholm, R.M.) Glencoe, 1961.
Phil 8591.27.6　Le réalisme chrétien, précédé de essais de philosophie religieuse. (Laberthonniere, Lucien.) Paris, 1966.
Phil 8591.27　Le réalisme chrétien et l'idealisme grec. (Laberthonnière, L.) Paris, 1904.
Phil 2805.189　Le réalisme de Pascal. (Lahorque, P.M.) Paris, 1923.
Phil 2805.420　Le réalisme de Pascal. (Massis, Henri.) St.-Felicien-en-Vivarais, 1924.
Phil 8735.19　Le réalisme du principe de finalité. (Garrigou-Lagrange, Reginaldo.) Paris, 1932.
Phil 630.47　Le réalisme immédiat. (Noël, L.) Louvain, 1938.
Phil 630.1　Le réalisme métaphysique. (Thouverez, E.) Paris, 1894.
Phil 630.43　Le réalisme méthodique. (Gilson, Étienne.) Paris, 1936?
Phil 630.43.7　Réalisme thomiste. (Gilson, Étienne.) Paris, 1939.
Phil 630.45　Il realismo. (Olgiati, F.) Milano, 1936.
Phil 8591.27.5　Il realismo cristiano e l'idealismo greco. (Laberthonniere, Lucien.) Firenze, 1922.
Phil 630.51　Il realismo e il trascendente. (Pra, Mario dal.) Padova, 1937.
Phil 2477.6.118　Il realismo integrale di M. Blondel. (Crippà, Romeo.) Milano, 1954.
Phil 630.38　Il realismo puro. (Ranzoli, Cesare.) Milano, 1932.
Phil 400.60　Realismus oder Idealismus. (Heyde, Johannes E.) Leipzig, 1924.
Phil 3450.18.185　Realismus und Apriorismus in Nicolai Hartmanns Erkenntnistheorie. (Wirth, I.) Berlin, 1965.
Phil 5045.7　Der Realismus und Dastranssendenzproblem. (Freytag, Willy.) Halle, 1902.
Phil 1719.5　Realismus und moderne Philosophie. (Thyssen, Johannes.) Bonn, 1959.
Phil 1540.1　Realismus und Nominalismus. (Koehler, H.O.) Gotha, 1858.
Phil 630.2　Realistic assumptions of modern science. (Herbert, T.M.) London, 1879.
Phil 400.3　Realistic idealism in philosophy itself. (Holmes, N.) Boston, 1888. 2v.
Phil 9590.20　A realistic philosophy. (Reinhardt, K.F.) Milwaukee, 1944.
Phil 192.112　A realistic philosophy. 2d. ed. (Reinhardt, Kent F.) N.Y., 1962.

Phil 8586.47 A realistic philosophy of religion. (Garnett, A.C.) Chicago, 1942.

Phil 332.5.5 A realistic universe. (Boodin, J.E.) N.Y., 1916.

Phil 332.5.10 A realistic universe. (Boodin, J.E.) N.Y., 1931.

Phil 3791.45 Realistische Grundzüge. (Riehl, Alois.) Graz, 1870.

Phil 3493.8.5 Die realistische und die idealistische Weltanschauung entwickelt an Kants Idealität von Zeit und Raum. (Last, E.) Leipzig, 1884.

Phil 672.21 Die realistische Weltansicht und die Lehre vom Raume. (Study, E.) Braunschweig, 1914.

Phil 630.48 Realists and nominalists. (Carre, Meyrick H.) London, 1946.

Phil 345.4 Die Realität der Aussenwelt. (Ostler, H.) Paderborn, 1912.

Phil 630.35 Die Realität der Aussenwelt in der Philosophie. (Keferstein, H.) Käthen, 1883.

Phil 299.11.5 Realität und Ideelität ferner Naturkraft und Schöpfungskraft. (Scheffler, Hermann.) Braunschweig, 1897.

Phil 3425.576 Realität und Reflexion. (Braum, Hermann.) Heidelberg, 1960.

Phil 192.59 Réalité et relativité. (Rabeau, Gaston.) Paris, 1927.

Phil 8881.51 Réalités imaginatives. (Gasté, Maurice de.) Paris, 1911.

Phil 8598.57.8 Reality; a new correlation of science and religion. (Streeter, Burnett.) N.Y., 1926.

Phil 8598.57 Reality; a new correlation of science and religion. (Streeter, Burnett.) N.Y., 1926.

Phil 196.34 Reality. (Vogel, Arthur A.) London, 1959.

Phil 2340.11 Reality. (Weiss, Paul.) Princeton, 1938.

Phil 7069.33.40 Reality. Boston, 1933.

Phil 6980.222 Reality and dream. (Devereaux, G.) N.Y., 1951.

Phil 735.105 Reality and illusion. (Rothschild, R.) N.Y., 1934.

Phil 4756.1.43 Reality and man. (Frank, Semen L.) London, 1965.

Phil 510.154 Reality and monads. (Eyken, A.) Apeldoorn, 1950.

Phil 8890.62 Reality and the good. (Pieper, Josef.) Chicago, 1967.

Phil 630.10 Reality and truth. (Vance, John G.) London, 1917.

Phil 735.111 Reality and value. (Garnett, Arthur C.) New Haven, 1937.

Phil 2055.9.30 Reality as social process. (Hartshorne, Charles.) Glencoe, Ill., 1953.

Phil 7069.19.65 The reality of psychic phenomena, raps, levitations. (Crawford, William J.) N.Y., 1919.

Phil 7060.132 The reality of psychic phenomena. (Crawford, W. J.) N.Y., 1918.

Phil 8880.58 Reality or preachment; the moral crisis of our time. (Forrest, John K.) Boston, 1967.

Phil 6980.328.5 Reality therapy, a new approach to psychiatry. (Glasser, William.) N.Y., 1965.

Phil 8092.18 Realizm i khudozhestvennye iskaniia XX veka. Moskva, 1969.

Phil 341.20 Realizm ludzkiego poznania. (Krapice, M.A.) Poznań, 1959.

Phil 8407.29 The realm of art. (Goffin, Peter (pseud.).) London, 1946.

Phil 8677.8 The realm of ends, or Pluralism and theism. (Ward, James.) Cambridge, 1911.

Phil 8677.8.2 The realm of ends, or Pluralism and theism. 2. ed. (Ward, James.) Cambridge, 1912.

Phil 8677.8.3 The realm of ends, or Pluralism and theism. 3. ed. (Ward, James.) Cambridge, 1920.

Phil 193.49.35 The realm of essence: book first of Realms of being. (Santayana, G.) London, 1928.

Phil 7069.64.30 The realm of ghost. (Maple, Eric.) London, 1967.

Phil 193.49.37 The realm of matter. Book second of Realms of being. (Santayana, G.) N.Y., 1930.

Phil 197.23.5 The realm of mind. (Woodbridge, F.J.E.) N.Y., 1926.

Phil 193.49.39.8A The realm of spirit. (Santayana, G.) N.Y., 1940.

Phil 4752.2.70 The realm of spirit and the realm of Caesar. (Berdiaev, Nikolai Aleksandrovich.) London, 1952.

Phil 193.49.38 The realm of truth. (Santayana, G.) N.Y., 1938.

Phil 7069.27.20 Realms of light and healing. (Robotton.) London, 1927.

Phil 7069.19.70 Realms of the living dead. (Curtiss, Harriette A.) N.Y., 1919.

Phil 2225.2.30A Realms of value. (Perry, R.B.) Cambridge, Mass., 1954.

Phil 4756.1.42 Real'nost' i chelovek; metafizika chelovecheskogo bytiia. (Frank, Semen L.) Parizh, 1956.

Phil 282.28.2 Real'nyi mir v svete uni persal'noi seorii podoishnogo ravnovesiia. 2. izd. (Balaban, Grigorii Iu.) Hamilton, 1970.

Phil 5627.6.85 La realtà dello spirito. (Morelli, G.) Milano, n.d.

Phil 4110.6.30 Realtà e idealità. (Filippi, Liutprando.) Napoli, 1937.

Phil 8876.11.10 Realwissenschaftliche Begründung der Moral. (Baumann, Julius.) Leizpig, 1898.

Phil 8575.14 Reardon, Bernard M.G. Religious thought in the nineteenth century. Cambridge, Eng., 1966.

Phil 8885.46 Reason, action and morality. (Kemp, J.) London, 1964.

Phil 4872.247.30 Reason, romanticism and revolution. (Roy, Manendra Nath.) Calcutta, 1952-55. 2v.

Htn Phil 8580.3* Reason, the only oracle of man. (Allen, E.) Bennington, Vt., 1784.

Phil 8580.3.5 Reason, the only oracle of man. (Allen, E.) N.Y., 1836.

Phil 8580.3.2 Reason, the only oracle of man. (Allen, E.) N.Y., 1940.

Phil 186.140 The reason, the understanding and time. (Lovejoy, A.O.) Baltimore, 1961.

Phil 5052.13 Reason, thought and language. (Macleane, D.) London, 1906.

Phil 5620.16 Reason. (Whittaker, T.) Cambridge, Eng., 1934.

Phil 623.42 Reason and analysis. (Blanshard, Brand.) La Salle, Ill., 1962.

Phil 3475.3.62 Reason and anti-reason in our time. (Jaspers, Karl.) New Haven, 1952.

Phil 3475.3.61 Reason and anti-reason in our time. 1st British ed. (Jaspers, Karl.) London, 1952.

Phil 1802.8 Reason and authority in the 18th century. (Cragg, G.R.) Cambridge, Eng., 1964.

Phil 8701.4.7 Reason and belief. (Lodge, Oliver Joseph.) N.Y., 1910.

Phil 8701.4.9 Reason and belief. 5. ed. (Lodge, Oliver Joseph.) London, 1911.

Phil 187.144 Reason and common sense. (Mayor, R.J.G.) London, 1951.

Phil 8875.30 Reason and conduct. (Aichen, Henry D.) N.Y., 1962.

Phil 2050.113 Reason and conduct in Hume's treatise. (Kydd, Rachel M.) London, 1946.

Phil 5620.17 Reason and emotion. (Macmurray, John.) London, 1935.

Phil 5620.28 Reason and emotion. 2. ed. (Macmurray, John.) N.Y., 1962.

Phil 3450.11.465 Reason and evidence in Husserl's phenomenology. (Levin, David Michael.) Evanston, 1970.

Phil 3801.448.5 Reason and existence; Schelling's philosophy of history. (Hayner, Paul Collins.) Leiden, 1967.

Phil 3475.3.56.1 Reason and existenz; five lectures. (Jaspers, Karl.) London, 1956.

Phil 353.18.5 Reason and experience. (Walsh, William Henry.) Oxford, 1963.

Phil 8881.73 Reason and experience in ethics. (Ginsberg, Morris.) London, 1956.

Htn Phil 8583.26* Reason and faith. (De Costa, J.H.) Philadelphia, 1791.

Phil 8597.11.15 Reason and faith. (Rogers, H.) Boston, 1853.

Phil 8597.11.12 Reason and faith. (Rogers, H.) London, 1850.

Phil 8622.86 Reason and faith revisited. (Parker, Francis H.) Milwaukee, 1971.

Phil 8598.130 Reason and God. (Smith, J.E.) New Haven, 1961.

Phil 8876.135A Reason and goodness. (Blanshard, Brand.) London, 1961.

Phil 335.7A Reason and intuition. (Ewing, A.C.) London, 1941.

Phil 193.130.10 Reason and intuition and other essays. (Stocks, J.L.) London, 1939.

Phil 4363.7 Reason and life. (Marias Aguilera, Julián.) New Haven, 1956.

Phil 8897.80 Reason and morals. (Wilson, John.) Cambridge, Eng., 1961.

Phil 5620.01 Pamphlet box. Reason and reasoning.

Phil 1511.3.22 Reason and revelation in the Middle Ages. (Gilson, Étienne.) N.Y., 1959.

Phil 3425.292.5 Reason and revolution; Hegel and the use of social theory. (Marcuse, H.) London, 1941.

Phil 3425.292.12 Reason and revolution; Hegel and the use of social theory. 2nd ed. (Marcuse, H.) Boston, 1960.

Phil 3425.292.10A Reason and revolution; Hegel and the use of social theory. 2nd ed. (Marcuse, H.) N.Y., 1954.

Phil 2215.85 Reason and right: a critical examination of Richard Price's philosophy. (Hudson, William Donald.) London, 1970.

Phil 645.60 Reason and scepticism. (Slote, Michael A.) London, 1970.

Phil 187.176 Reason and the common good. (Murphy, Arthur E.) Englewood Cliffs, 1963.

Phil 342.19 Reason and the nature of things. (Lowenberg, Jacob.) La Salle, Ill., 1959.

Phil 2880.8.143 Reason and violence. (Laing, R.D.) London, 1964.

Phil 2215.80 Reason and virtue; a study in the ethics of Richard Price. (Cua, Antonio S.) Athens, 1966.

Phil 9070.54 The reason for living. (Wicks, R.R.) N.Y., 1934.

Phil 3425.40.30 Reason in history. (Hegel, Georg Wilhelm Friedrich.) N.Y., 1953.

Phil 8587.6 Reason in religion. (Hedge, F.H.) Boston, 1865.

Phil 8890.47 Reason in the art of living. (Pratt, James B.) N.Y., 1949.

Phil 5620.35 Reason in theory and practice. (Edgley, Roy.) London, 1969.

Phil 8598.45.5 A reasonable religion (Religio doctoris). (Sanders, Frederic W.) Boston, 1913?

Htn Phil 2115.58.5* The reasonableness of Christianity. (Locke, J.) Boston, 1811.

Htn Phil 2115.58* The reasonableness of Christianity. (Locke, J.) London, 1695.

Phil 2115.58.9 The reasonableness of Christianity. (Locke, J.) London, 1836.

Phil 8592.48.7 The reasonableness of Christianity. (Macintosh, D.C.) N.Y., 1926.

Phil 8876.55.5 The reasonalbe life, being hints for men and women. (Bennett, Arnold.) London, 1907.

Htn Phil 1930.5.95* The reasoning of Christ and his Apostles...sermons...Nov. and Dec., 1724. (Bullock, T.) London, 1725.

Phil 5832.1 The reasoning power in animals. (Watson, John S.) London, 1867.

Phil 5832.1.4 The reasoning power in animals. 2. ed. (Watson, John S.) London, 1870.

Phil 8886.47 Reasons and morals. (Levine, Israel.) Glasgow, 1924.

Phil 9215.2 Reasons for actions: a critique of utilitarian rationality. (Norman, Richard.) Oxford, 1971.

Phil 400.29 La reazione idealistica contro la scienza. (Aliotta, A.) Palermo, 1912.

Phil 822.1.30 Rebel thought. (West, H.F.) Boston, 1953.

Phil 3090.84 Reber, M. Franz von Baader und die Möglichkeit unbedingter pädagogischer Zielsetzung. Nürnburg, 1925.

Phil 7059.8 Rebman, F.J. The human aura. Storm Lake, Iowa, 1912.

Phil 2750.19.80 Rebollo Peña, A. Critica de la objetividad en el existencialism de Gabriel Marcel. Burgos, 1954.

Phil 6990.3.20 Rebsomen, A. Notre-Dame de Lourdes. Paris, 1925.

Phil 3425.780 Rebstock, Hans Otto. Hegels Auffassung des Mythos in seinen Frühschriften. Freiburg, 1971.

Phil 182.34 A rebuttal of spiritism. (Hayward, J.K.) N.Y., 1903.

Phil 525.91 Récéjac, Edonard. Essai sur les fondements de la connaissance mystique. Paris, 1897.

Phil 525.5.5 Récéjac, Edonard. Essays on the bases of mystic knowledge. London, 1899.

Phil 70.67 Recent advances in biological psychiatry. N.Y. 4,1961+ 6v.

Phil 8591.18 Recent advances in theistic philosophy of religion. (Lindsay, James.) Edinburgh, 1897.

Phil 1817.16 Recent American philosophy. (Reck, A.J.) N.Y., 1964.

Phil 1812.2.5 Recent British philosophy. (Masson, D.) London, 1865.

Phil 1812.2.2 Recent British philosophy. (Masson, D.) London, 1867.

Phil 1812.2 Recent British philosophy. (Masson, D.) N.Y., 1866.

Phil 2270.50.2 Recent discussions in science. (Spencer, Herbert.) N.Y., 1871.

Phil 2270.50 Recent discussions in science. (Spencer, Herbert.) N.Y., 1873.

Phil 672.139 Recent discussions on "Time". (Goldsbrough, G.F.) London, 1927.

Phil 5227.5 Recent experiments in psychology. 1st ed. N.Y., 1938.

Phil 4897.10 Recent Japanese philosophical thought, 1862-1962. (Piovesana, Gino K.) Tokyo, 1963.

Phil 630.15 Recent logical realism. Thesis. (Parkhurst, Helen.) Bryn Mawr, 1917.

Phil 7054.159 Un récent procès spirite. (Maxwell, Joseph.) Bordeaux, 1904.

Phil 6319.10 Recent progress in psychiatry. (Journal of Mental Science.) London. 1944

Phil 5627.121 Recent religious psychology. (Uren, A.R.) Edinburgh, 1928.

Phil 5238.160 Recent Soviet psychology. (O'Connor, N.) N.Y., 1961.

Phil 1705.11 Recent studies in philosophy and theology. (Freeman, David.) Philadelphia, 1962.

Phil 8843.5 Recent tendencies in ethics. (Sorley, W.R.) Edinburgh, 1904.

Phil 1713.2 Recent thought in focus. (Nicholl, Donald.) N.Y., 1953.

Phil 8697.6 Recent work of angelican theologians. (Hall, F.J.) Chicago, 1912.

Phil 8712.5 Recent works bearing on the relation of science to religion. (Wright, George F.) New Haven, 1877-78. 2 pam.

Phil 1135.135 Rechenberg, C.M. Entwickelung des Gottesbegriffes. Leipzig, 1872.

Phil 3475.3.75 Rechenschaft und Ausbuik. (Jaspers, Karl.) München, 1951.

Phil 5780.17   Recherche de la liberté. 1. éd. (Christoff, Daniel.) Paris, 1957.

Phil 192.31   Recherche de l'unité. (Roberty, E. de.) Paris, 1893.

Phil 8062.3   Recherche des principes d'une philosophie des arts, dits d'imitation chez Platon, Aristote et Plotin. (Grand, Y.) Lausanne, 1952.

Htn   Phil 186.8*   La recherche d'une première vérité. (Lequier, J.) Saint-Cloud, 1865.

Phil 2725.13.34   La recherche d'une première vérité. (Lequier, Jules.) Paris, 1924.

Phil 6111.2   Recherches...l'activité cérébrale. v.1-2. (Beaunie, H.E.) Paris, 1884-86.

Phil 5635.13   Recherches...sur la sensibilité. (De Seze, V.) Paris, 1786.

Phil 7085.6   Recherches...sur l'homme dans l'état de somnambulisme naturel. (Puysegur, A. M.J.) Paris, 1811.

Phil 178.9   Recherches. v.1-2. (Dutens, Louis.) Paris, 1766.

Phil 178.9.2   Recherches. 2. éd. (Dutens, Louis.) Paris, 1776. 2v.

Phil 8598.40   Recherches de la méthode qui conduit à la vérité sur nos plus grands intérêts. (Secretan, Charles.) Neuchâtel, 1857.

Phil 310.155   Recherches dialectiques. 2. éd. (Goldmann, Lucien.) Paris, 1959.

Phil 1182.54   Recherches esséniennes et pythagoriciennes. (Lévy, Isidore.) Genève, 1965.

Phil 6689.8   Recherches et doutes sur le magnetisme animal. (Thouret.) Paris, 1784.

Phil 5635.31   Recherches experimentales et cliniques sur la sensibilité. (Richet, Charles.) Paris, 1877.

Phil 6672.13   Recherches expérimentales sur quelques processus psychiques simples dans un cas d'hypnose. (Claparède, Edouard.) Genève, 1909.

Phil 5257.20   Recherches expérimentales sur la durée des actes psychiques les plus simples et sur la vitesse des courants. (Rémond, A.) Paris, 1888.

Phil 6122.9   Recherches expérimentales sur le mécanisme de fonctionnement des centres psychomoteurs du Cerveau. (Marique, J.M.L.) Bruxelles, 1885.

Phil 5520.732   Recherches experimentales sur le symbolisme phonétique. (Peterfalvi, Jean Michel.) Paris, 1970.

Phil 5300.3   Recherches expérimentales sur les fonctions des canaux semi-circulaires. Thèse. (Cyon, E. de.) Paris, 1878.

Phil 6131.1   Recherches expérimentales sur l'excitabilité électrique. (Varigny, H.C. de.) Paris, 1884.

Phil 5047.11.20   Recherches logiques. (Husserl, Edmund.) Paris, 1959. 3v.

Phil 6117.19   Recherches microscopiques sur le système nerveux. (Hannover, A.) Copenhagne, 1844.

Phil 193.1   Recherches philosophiques. (Saint-Hyacinth, T.) Rotterdam, 1743.

Phil 27.33   Recherches philosophiques. Paris. 1-6,1931-1937 6v.

Phil 2477.4.30   Recherches philosophiques sur les premiers objets des connaissances morales. (Bonald, L.G.A.) Paris, 1818. 2v.

Phil 6671.21   Recherches psychologiques...magnétisme vital. v.1-2. (Billot, G.P.) Paris, 1839.

Phil 5465.1   Recherches sur la nature et les lois de l'imagination. (Bonstetten, K.V. von.) Genève, 1807. 2v.

Phil 6100.17   Recherches sur la somatotopie sensitive dans le thalamus des singes. (Sager, O.) Harlem, 1933.

Phil 6121.7.5   Recherches sur le système nerveux. (Luys, J.) Paris, 1865. 2v.

Phil 6962.1.5   Recherches sur les centres nerveux. 2. série. (Magnan, V.) Paris, 1893.

Phil 332.23   Recherches sur les conditions de la connaissance. (Berger, Gaston.) Paris, 1941.

Phil 6125.16   Recherches sur les lésions du centre ovale des hémisphères cérébraux. (Pitres, A.) Paris, 1877.

Phil 7060.108.5   Recherches sur les phénomènes du spiritualisme. (Crookes, William.) Paris, 1886.

Phil 1870.65.5   Recherches sur les vertus de l'eau de goudron. (Berkeley, G.) Amsterdam, 1745.

Phil 1870.65.8   Recherches sur les vertus de l'eau de goudron. (Berkeley, G.) Genève, 1748.

Phil 5650.17   Recherches sur l'exitabilité auditive. Thèse. (Kucharski, P.) Paris, 1928.

Phil 5520.86.10   Rechevye refleksy. (Dobrogaev, S.M.) Moskva, 1947.

Phil 3890.8.115   Recht. (Schneiders, Werner.) Münster, 1961.

Phil 8892.77   Das Recht und die Rechtssätze. (Roschacher, E.) Winterthur, 1963.

Phil 974.3.55   Recht und Unrecht der Anthroposophie. (Schmidt, J.W.) Göttingen, 1922.

Phil 4770.2   Die Rechtfertigung Gottes nach Eugen H. Trubetskoj. Inaug. Diss. (Praxl, Franz.) München, 1967.

Phil 5769.2   Die rechtliche Willens Bestimmung. (Thomsen, H.) Kiel, 1882.

Phil 6121.9   Rechts und Linkshändigkeit. (Lueddeckens, F.) Leipzig, 1909.

Phil 3246.59   Rechtslehre vorgetragen von Ostern bis Michaelis 1812. (Fichte, Johann Gottlieb.) Leipzig, 1920.

Phil 2050.234   Die Rechtsphilosophie David Humes. (Wallenfels, Walter.) Göttingen, 1928.

Phil 9430.33   Die Rechtsphilosophie des Pessimismus. (Petraschek, K.O.) München, 1929.

Phil 3552.292   Das Rechtsprinzip bei Leibnitz. (Zimmermann, R.) Wien, 1852.

Phil 9035.110   La recindad humana. (Granell Mañiz, Manuel.) Madrid, 1969.

Phil 9179.1.5   Reciprocal duties of parents and children. (Taylor, A. Hinton.) Boston, 1825.

Phil 6123.1   The reciprocal influence of body and mind. (Newnham, W.) London, 1842.

Phil 575.140   La réciprocité des consciences; essai sur la nature de la personne. Thèse. (Nédoncelle, Maurice.) Paris, 1942.

Phil 8630.4   Récits de l'infini. (Flammarion, C.) Paris, 1873.

Phil 1817.18   Reck, A.J. The new American philosophers. Baton Rouge, 1968.

Phil 1817.16   Reck, A.J. Recent American philosophy. N.Y., 1964.

Phil 2070.157   Reck, Andrew J. Introduction to William James. Bloomington, 1967.

Phil 197.44.5   Reckoning with life. (Wilson, George A.) New Haven, 1942.

Phil 9357.6   Reclus, Elisée. L'ideal et la jeunesse. Bruxelles, 1894.

Phil 5425.104   The recognition of excellence. (Princeton Meeting on the Recognition of Excellence, Princeton, 1959.) Washington, 1959.

Phil 2225.15   The recognition of reason. (Pols, E.) Carbondale, 1963.

Phil 672.15.7   The recognition of the fourth dimension. (Hinton, Charles H.) Washington, 1902.

Phil 8598.37   The recognition of the supernatural. (Storrs, Richard S.) N.Y., 1881.

Phil 5585.260   Recognizing patterns; studies in living and automatic systems. (Kolers, Paul A.) Cambridge, 1968.

Phil 8587.47.5   The recollection. (Heard, Gerald.) Palo Alto, 1944.

Phil 6687.4   Recollection of a society clairvoyant. London, 1911.

Phil 6957.18   Recollections of an alienist. (Hamilton, A.M.) N.Y., 1916.

Phil 8695.2   The reconciliation of religion and science. (Fowle, T.W.) London, 1873.

Phil 8712.24   Reconciliation of science and religion. (Winchell, A.) N.Y., 1877.

Phil 178.38.4   Reconstruction in philosophy. (Dewey, John.) Boston, 1948.

Phil 8590.10.9   Reconstruction in theology. (King, Henry C.) N.Y., 1901.

Phil 8702.7.5   The reconstruction of belief. (Mallock, W.H.) London, 1905.

Phil 8584.6   The reconstruction of religion. (Ellwood, C.A.) N.Y., 1922.

Phil 8702.7.7   The reconstruction of religious belief. (Mallock, W.H.) N.Y., 1905.

Phil 6100.15   Reconstruction of the nuclear masses in the lower portion of the human brain-stem. (Weed, L.H.) Washington, 1914.

Phil 8615.5.20   The reconstruction of the spiritual ideal. (Adler, Felix.) N.Y., 1924.

Phil 585.195   La recontre du cogito et du marxisme. (Průcha, Milan.) Nancy, 1965.

Phil 7054.66   A record of communications from the spirit-spheres. (Ferguson, J.B.) Nashville, 1854.

Phil 5440.3   Record of family faculties. (Galton, F.) London, 1884.

Phil 6129.10   Recovery from all diseases. (Taniguchi, Masaham.) Tokyo, 1963.

Phil 6400.19   Recovery from aphasia. (Wepman, J.M.) N.Y., 1951.

Phil 8699.5   The recovery of belief. (Joad, Cyril E.M.) London, 1952.

Phil 9450.45   The recovery of ethics. (Nitze, P.H.) N.Y., 1960.

Phil 8622.14   Recovery of faith. 1. ed. (Radhakrishnan, S.) N.Y., 1955.

Phil 8587.44.15   The recovery of ideals. (Harkness, George E.) N.Y., 1937.

Phil 9070.111   The recovery of meaning; an essay on the good life. (McGee, Charles Douglas.) N.Y., 1966.

Phil 185.35.10   The recovery of truth. (Keyserling, H.) N.Y., 1929.

Phil 281.9   Recreação filosofica. (Almeida, Theodoro de.) Lisboa, 1786-1805. 10v.

Phil 5520.82   La recréation du réel et l'équivoque. (Fauré-Frémiet, P.) Paris, 1940.

Phil 3552.70   Recueil...Pieces...Leibniz. (Leibniz, Gottfried Wilhelm.) Lausanne, 1759. 2v.

Phil 7060.5.5   Recueil de dissertations...sur les apparitions. (Calmet, Augustin.) Avignon, 1751. 2v.

Htn   Phil 2520.103*   Recueil de quelques...philosophie de Descartes. (Boyle, Pierre.) Amsterdam, 1684.

Phil 6990.6   Recueil des pieces...sur les miracles. (Vialard, Felix.) Nancy, 1735.

Phil 6687.13   Recueil des pieces les plus interessantes sur le magnétisme animal. n.p., 1784.

Htn   Phil 2915.42*   Recueil necessaire. (Voltaire, F.M.A. de.) Leipsik, 1765[1766].

Phil 8610.776   Recueil nécessaire avec l'évangile de la raison. Londres, 1776.

Phil 8420.13.5   La recuperacion del objeto. v.1-2. (Torres-García, J.) Montevideo, 1965.

Phil 7069.23.5   The red octopus. (Brandt, J.v.W.) London, 1923?

Phil 400.69   Redanò, Ugo. La crisi dell'idealismo attuale. Roma, 1924.

Phil 3552.84   Rede...G.W. Leibnitz. (Encke, J.F.) Berlin, 1842.

Phil 3492.5   Rede...Jubiläums...Königreichs Preussen 18 Januar 1901. (Kaftan, J.) Berlin, 1901.

Phil 3120.30.49   Die Rede. 2. Aufl. (Buber, Martin.) Leipzig, 1920.

Htn   Phil 3800.310*   Rede an die Studierenden der Ludwig-Maximilians-Universität...29 dec. 1830. (Schelling, F.W.J. von.) München, 1831.

Phil 1750.166.165   Rede en religie in het humanisme. Amsterdam, 1962.

Phil 6122.29   Rede Gehalten zur Feier der akademischen Preisverteilung am 23 Juni 1898. (Müller, Wilhelm.) Jena, 1898.

Phil 1850.91F   Rede in der...(F. Bacon...Geschichte...Naturwissenschaften . (Liebig, J.F. von.) München, 1863.

Phil 3120.30.55   Rede das Erzieherische. (Buber, Martin.) Berlin, 1926.

Phil 5240.25.15   Rede über das Genie. (Abel, Jakob Friedrich von.) Marbach, 1955.

Htn   Phil 3800.250.5*   Rede über das Verhältniss der bildenden Künste zu der Natur. (Schelling, F.W.J. von.) Upsala, 1818.

Phil 2490.53.20   Rede über den Geist des Positivismus. (Comte, Auguste.) Hamburg, 1956.

Phil 9045.19   Rede über den Gemeingeist. (Klausen, Gottlieb E.) Altona, 1797.

Phil 9045.20   Rede über einige Hauptregeln zum wohlthätigen Einwirken auf das Zeitalter. (Siveking, Gustav A.) Hamburg, 1814.

Htn   Phil 3800.290*   Rede zum siebzigsten in öffentlicher Sitzung gefeyerten Jahrestag der K. Akademie der Wissenschaften. (Schelling, F.W.J. von.) München, 1829.

Htn   Phil 3800.320*   Rede zum zwei und Siebzigsten...Jahrestag der k. Academie der Wissenschaften. (Schelling, F.W.J. von.) München, 1831.

Htn   Phil 3800.350*   Rede zum 75. Jahrestag der k. Academie der Wissenschaften. (Schelling, F.W.J. von.) München, 1834.

Phil 2750.11.35   Redeeming the time. (Maritain, Jacques.) London, 1943.

Phil 1750.440   Redeker, Hans. Existentialisme. 2. druk. Amsterdam 1956.

Phil 8418.18   Redeker, Horst. Geschichte und Gesetze des Ästhetischen. Berlin, 1960.

Phil 8080.13   Redeker, Horst. Die Klassische Kulturkritik und das Dilemma der Dekadenz. Berlin, 1958.

Phil 3805.228   Redeker, Martin. Friedrich Schleiermacher. Berlin, 1968.

Phil 3450.4.85   Redeker, Martin. Wilhelm Herrmann im kampf Gegen den positivistische Lebensanschauung. Gotha, 1928.

Phil 7069.40.11   Redemptor Spiritual Center. Rational and scientific (Christian) spiritualism. Rio de Janeiro, n.d.

Htn   Phil 3246.55.2*   Reden an die deutsche Nation. (Fichte, Johann Gottlieb.) Berlin, 1808.

Phil 3246.55.5   Reden an die deutsche Nation. (Fichte, Johann Gottlieb.) Leipzig, n.d.

Phil 3246.55   Reden an die deutsche Nation. (Fichte, Johann Gottlieb.) Leipzig, 1824.

Phil 3246.55.3   Reden an die deutsche Nation. (Fichte, Johann Gottlieb.) Leipzig, 1872.

Phil 3246.55.6A   Reden an die deutsche Nation. (Fichte, Johann Gottlieb.) Leipzig, 1909.

Phil 3246.55.7 — Reden an die deutsche Nation. (Fichte, Johann Gottlieb.) Leipzig, 1944.

Phil 8879.14 — Reden uber wichtige Gegenstande. (Ehrenberg, F.) Leipzig, 1804.

Phil 3120.30.53 — Reden über Erziehung. (Buber, Martin.) Heidelberg, 1953.

Phil 192.30 — Reden und Aufsätze. (Rümelin, G.) Freiburg, 1881. 3v.

Phil 192.30.5 — Reden und aufsätze. (Rümelin, G.) Freiburg, 1881. 2v.

Phil 3915.56.2 — Reden und Aufsätze. 2. Aufl. (Wundt, Wilhelm.) Leipzig, 1914.

Phil 192.5 — Redern, S.E. de. Considerations sur la nature de l'homme. Paris, 1835. 2v.

Phil 5585.8 — Redern, S.E. de. Des modes accidentels de nos perceptions. Paris, 1818.

Phil 6027.1 — Redfield, J.W. Comparative physiognomy. N.Y., 1852.

Phil 6027.1.5 — Redfield, J.W. Outlines...physiognomy. N.Y., 1849.

Phil 6027.1.8 — Redfield, J.W. The twelve qualities of mind...physiognomy. no. 11. N.Y., 1850.

Phil 6127.2 — Redford, G. Body and soul. London, 1847.

Phil 2030.1.81 — Redgrove, H. Stanley. Joseph Glanvill and physical research in the seventeenth century. London, 1921.

Phil 192.42 — Redgrove, H.S. Matter, spirit and the cosmos. London, 1916.

Phil 1750.325 — Reding, M. Die Existenzphilosophie. 1e Aufl. Düsseldorf, 1949.

Phil 8892.60 — Reding, Marcel. Metaphysik der sittlichen Werte. 1. Aufl. Düsseldorf, 1949.

Phil 585.20 — The rediscovery of man. (Frank, W.D.) N.Y., 1958.

Phil 5251.44.7 — The rediscovery of man. (Link, Henry C.) N.Y., 1939.

Phil 3425.600 — Redlich, A. Die Hegelsche Logik als Selbsterfassung der Persönlichkeit. Brinkum, 1964.

Phil 6980.734 — Redlich, Fredrick. The theory and practice of psychiatry. N.Y., 1966.

Phil 1122.10 — Redlow, Götz. Theoria. Theoretische und praktische Lebensauffassung im philosophischen Denken der Antike. Berlin, 1966.

Phil 7054.59 — Redman, G.A. Mystic hours, or spiritual experience. N.Y., 1859.

Phil 1630.22 — La reductio artium ad Sacram scripturam. (Simone, F.) Torino, 1959?

Phil 8875.22 — La reduction de toutes les sciences en la connaissance de l'homme. (D'Acol.) Paris, 1668.

Phil 6327.42 — Ree, Frank van. Botsende Generaties. Assen, 1968.

Phil 6327.42.5 — Ree, Frank van. Colliding generations. Varanasi, 1970.

Phil 9075.16 — Rée, Paul. Die Entstehung des Gewissens. Berlin, 1885.

Phil 5767.5 — Rée, Paul. Die Illusion der Willensfreiheit. Berlin, 1885.

Phil 192.39 — Rée, Paul. Philosophie. Berlin, 1903.

Phil 8892.44 — Rée, Paul. Der Ursprung der moralischen Empfindungen. Chemnitz, 1877.

Phil 5465.46 — Reeb, Eugène. Les images de Taine à Binet. Thèse complementaire. Nancy, 1938.

Phil 6327.26 — Reed, C.F. Psychopathology. Cambridge, Mass., 1958.

Phil 5374.153 — Reed, Charles J. The law of vital transfusion and the phenomenon of consciousness. San Francisco, 1921.

Phil 9357.5 — Reed, James. Man and woman, equal but different. Boston, 1870.

Phil 5257.2.2 — Reed, S. Observations on the growth of the mind. Boston, 1829.

Phil 5257.2 — Reed, S. Observations on the growth of the mind. Boston, 1838.

Phil 5257.2.5 — Reed, S. Observations on the growth of the mind. 5th ed. Boston, 1859.

Phil 6400.38 — La rééduction des aphasiques. (Durieu, Colette.) Bruxelles, 1969.

Phil 165.424 — Le réel et l'irréel. Paris, 1968.

Phil 5360.26 — Reenpää, Yrjö. Wahrnehmen, Beobachten, Konstituieren. Frankfurt, 1967.

Phil 8842.3 — Rees, D. Contemporary English ethics. Leipzig, 1892.

Phil 6980.635.5 — Rees, J.R. The shaping of psychiatry by war. London, 1945.

Phil 978.55 — Rees, J.R. The threefold path to peace. N.Y., 1904.

Phil 2138.126 — Rees, John C. Mill and his early critcs. Leicester, 1956.

Phil 6127.19 — Rees, John R. The health of the mind. Cambridge, Eng., 1929.

Phil 8597.35 — Reese, Curtis W. Humanism. Chicago, 1926.

Phil 8597.35.10 — Reese, Curtis W. Humanist sermons. Chicago, 1927.

Phil 5257.78 — Reese, Ellen P. The analysis of human operant behavior. Dubuque, Iowa, 1966.

Phil 5585.280 — Reese, Hayne Waring. The perception of stimulus relations. N.Y., 1968.

Phil 6327.14 — Reese, W. L'idée de l'homme dans la neurologie contemporaine. Paris, 1938.

Phil 165.348 — Reese, William L. Process and divinity. LaSalle, Illinois, 1964.

Phil 1133.5 — Reesema, W.S. Parmenidas, anaxagorae, protagore principia. Lugduni, 1840.

Phil 5827.7 — Reeves, Cora Daisy. Discrimination of light of different wave-lengths by fish. N.Y., 1919.

Phil 5227.8 — Reeves, Joan Wynn. Body and mind in Western thought. Harmondsworth, 1958.

Phil 5227.8.10 — Reeves, Joan Wynn. Thinking about thinking. London, 1965.

Phil 5258.89 — Referat av H. Schjelderups forelaesninger over psykologi. (Schjelderup, H.) Oslo, 192-.

Phil 18.13 — Referate und Vorträge. (International Tagung für angewandte Psychopathologie.) Berlin. 1931

Phil 5046.36 — Reference and generality. (Geach, Peter.) Ithaca, N.Y., 1962.

Phil 5203.16 — Reference guide. (United States. National Institute of Mental Health.) Bethesda, Md.

Phil 5520.137 — Refering. (Linsky, Leonard.) London, 1967.

Phil 9177.1 — Reflections...duty of masters, mistresses and servants. (Randall, M.) London, 1725.

Phil 2150.12 — Reflections by a journeyman in philosophy. (Muirhead, J.H.) London, 1942.

Phil 2750.11.80A — Reflections on America. (Maritain, Jacques.) N.Y., 1958.

Phil 3270.12.110 — Reflections on Frege's philosophy. (Grossmann, Reinhardt S.) Evanston, 1969.

Phil 8672.11 — Reflections on French atheism. 2. ed. (Richards, William.) Lynn, n.d.

Phil 1711.8A — Reflections on human nature. (Lovejoy, A.D.) Baltimore, 1961.

Phil 1905.23 — Reflections on life and religion. (Baillie, J.B.) London, 1952.

Phil 193.250 — Reflections on men and ideas. (De Santillana, Giorgio.) Cambridge, 1968.

Phil 3095.51.10 — Reflections on poetry. (Baumgarten, A.G.) Berkeley, 1954.

Phil 7069.17.24 — Reflections on "Raymond". (Cook, Walter.) London, 1917.

Phil 331.9.5 — Reflections on the analogy of being. (Anderson, J.F.) The Hague, 1967.

Htn Phil 2175.2.49* — Reflections on the conduct of human life. (Norris, John.) London, 1690.

Htn Phil 2175.2.45* — Reflections on the conduct of human life. 2nd ed. (Norris, John.) London, 1691-93. 2 pam.

Phil 5238.115 — Reflections on the human venture. (Cantril, Hadley.) N.Y., 1960.

Phil 2280.21.10 — Reflections on the problem of relevance. (Schutz, Alfred.) New Haven, 1970.

Phil 6315.2.25 — Reflections on war and death. (Freud, Sigmund.) N.Y., 1918.

Htn Phil 2733.66* — Reflections sur la primation physique. (Malebranche, Nicolas.) Paris, 1715.

Htn Phil 192.6* — Reflections upon ancient and modern philosophy. London, 1678.

Htn Phil 2053.70* — Reflections upon laughter. (Hutcheson, F.) Glasgow, 1750.

Phil 5752.3.2 — Reflections upon liberty and necessity. (Corry, W.) London, 1759-63. 5 pam.

Phil 5752.3 — Reflections upon liberty and necessity. (Corry, W.) London, 1761.

Phil 8890.64 — Reflective naturalism. (Punzo, Vincent C.) N.Y., 1969.

Phil 8592.117 — Reflective theology; philosophical orientations in religion. (Munson, Thomas N.) New Haven, 1968.

Phil 5635.45.5 — Reflektornaia teoriia oskchushchenii. (Kovalgin, V.M.) Minsk, 1963.

Phil 5625.83 — Reflex action. (Fearing, F.) Baltimore, 1930.

Phil 6128.13.12 — Reflexes and motor integration; Sherrington's concept of integrative action. (Swazey, Judith Pound.) Cambridge, 1969.

Phil 5625.75.10 — Les reflexes conditionelles. (Pavlov, Ivan P.) Paris, 1927.

Phil 5850.128 — Reflexes to intelligence. (Beck, Samuel.) Glencoe, 1959.

Phil 3246.300 — Reflexion und Bildung in Fichte Wissenschaftslehre. (Schindler, I.M.T.) Bonn, 1962.

Phil 3246.300.1 — Reflexion und Bildung in Fichtes Wissenschaftslehre von 1794. 1. Aufl. (Schindler, I.M.T.) Düsseldorf, 1966.

Phil 3801.878 — Reflexion und Erfahrung. (Wild, Christoph.) Freiburg, 1968.

Phil 3246.325 — Reflexion und Gefühl. (Preul, Reiner.) Berlin, 1969.

Phil 3585.12.85 — Reflexion und Geseteltungswille. (Schlemper, Hans Otto.) Ratingen, 1964.

Phil 810.15 — Reflexion und Raisonnement im ontologischen Gottesbeweis. (Kopper, J.) Köln, 1962.

Phil 3486.1 — Reflexionen Kants zur kritischen Philosophie. (Erdmann, B.) Leipzig, 1882-84. 2v.

Phil 3483.90 — Reflexionen Kants I. Kant's Metaphysische Anfangsgründe der Tugendlehre. (Bergk, Johann Adam.) Bruxelles, 1968.

Phil 4600.2.53 — Reflexioner för dagen. (Larsson, Hans.) Lund, 1911.

Phil 8404.14.5 — Reflexions critiques sur la poésie et sur la peinture. 6. éd. (Dubos, J.B.) Paris, 1755. 3v.

Phil 5240.27 — Réflexions d'un biologiste sur l'objet...de la psychologie. (Anthony, R.) Paris, 1925.

Phil 178.8 — Réflexions et pensées. (Durand Désormeaux, Fernand.) Paris, 1884.

Phil 8612.38 — Réflexions métaphysiques sur la mort et le problème du sujet. (Echeverria, José.) Paris, 1957.

Phil 8886.58 — Reflexions morales et probablement fort inutiles. (Livry, Hypolite.) Paris, 1807.

Phil 182.22 — Réflexions philosophiques. (Holland, G.) Neuchâtel, 1775.

Phil 9070.52 — Réflexions sur la conduite de la vie. (Carrel, Alexis.) Paris, 1950.

Phil 2490.122 — Réflexions sur la pensée comtienne. (Delvolvé, Jean.) Paris, 1932.

Phil 8597.41 — Réflexions sur la religion, ou L'on établit d'une manière générale. Londres, 1801.

Phil 2750.11.82 — Reflexions sur l'Amérique. (Maritain, Jacques.) Paris, 1958.

Phil 6990.35 — Réflexions sur le miracle et les lois naturelles. (Vilar, Albert.) Clamecy, 1934.

Phil 2905.1.405 — Réflexions sur le "Phénomène humain" de Pierre Teilhard de Chardin. (Calvet, Jean.) Paris, 1966.

Phil 9558.4 — Réflexions sur les défauts d'autruy. (Villiers, Pierre.) Paris, 1690.

Phil 6965.12 — Réflexions sur les troubles du langage dans les psychoses paranoïdes. Thèse. (Pottier, Claude.) Paris, 1930.

Phil 2496.85 — Reflexions sur l'instruction synodale de Mgr. l'évêque de Poitiers. (Deschamps, A.F.) Paris, 1855.

Phil 2750.11.69 — Reflexions sur l'intelligence et sur sa vie propre. (Maritain, Jacques.) Paris, 1931?

Phil 3640.712 — Réflexions sur Nietzsche. (Garnier, Paul-Louis.) Paris, 1902.

Phil 808.3 — Die Reflexionsbestimmungen un dialektischen Denken. (Inciarte, Fernando.) Köln, 1957.

Phil 9558.10.14 — Reflexões sobre a vaidade dos homens. (Aires Ramos da Silva de Eca, M.) Rio de Janeiro, 1962.

Phil 9558.10.12 — Reflexões sobre a vaidade dos homens. (Aires Ramos da Silva de Eca, M.) São Paulo, 1942.

Phil 9558.10.10 — Reflexões sobre a vaidade dos homens. Facsimile. (Aires Ramos da Silva de Eca, M.) Rio de Janeiro, 1921.

Phil 4803.454.61 — Reforma absoluta przeto ostateczna wiedzy ludzkiej. (Hoene-Wroński, Józef Maria.) Paryz, 1891.

Phil 4065.41 — Reformation des Himmels. (Bruno, Giordano.) Leipzig, 1889.

Phil 8897.1 — Reformation of manners. (Walker, S.) London, 1711.

Phil 178.46.5 — La réforme de la conscience. (Decoster, Paul.) Bruxelles, 1919.

Phil 5052.19 — Reformed logic. (McLachlan, D.B.) London, 1892.

Phil 4307.4 — El reformismo español; Krausismo. (Gil Cremades, Juan José.) Barcelona, 1969.

Phil 9177.2 — The refuge. New Haven, 1805. 2 pam.

Phil 3831.2 — A refutation...Spinoza. (Leibnitz, G.W.) Edinburgh, 1855.

Phil 2725.2.68 — Réfutation de la doctrine. (Bouchitté, Louis Herve.) Paris, 1821.

Phil 2496.81.2 — Réfutation de l'eclectisme. (Leroux, P.) Paris, 1839.

Phil 2496.81 — Réfutation de l'eclectisme. (Leroux, P.) Paris, 1841.

Phil 1850.130 — Réfutation de l'ouvrage intitulé; ou Reponse à un ecclesiastique sur cet ouvrage. n.p., n.d.

Phil 2605.9.80 — Refutation du système de Monsr. Faidy. (Hugo, C.L.) Luxemburg, 1699.

Htn Phil 3552.45* — Réfutation inédite de Spinoza. (Leibniz, Gottfried Wilhelm.) Paris, 1854.

Phil 5750.12 — The refutation of determinism. (Ayres, Michel Richard.) London, 1968.

Phil 8661.8.35 — A refutation of Mr. U.H. Gillespie's argument a priori for the existence of a great first cause. (Barrett, R.H.) London, 1968.

Phil 8707.18   Regard, G. Etude biologique. Lausanne, 1937.
Phil 2805.231.5   Regardons vivre Blaise Pascal. 2. éd. (Valot, Stephen.) Paris, 1945.
Phil 2920.3.32   Regards. (Valensin, Auguste.) Paris, 1955-56. 3v.
Phil 8580.25   Regards catholiques sur le monde. (Auvergne, D.) Paris, 1938.
Phil 2406.6   Regards sur la pensée française, 1870-1940. (Guittoy, Jean.) Paris, 1968.
Phil 1703.16   Regards sur la philosophie contemporaine. (Duméry, Henry.) Tournai, 1957.
Phil 188.22   Regards sur l'humain. (Nicolas, M.P.) Paris, 1958.
Phil 5425.8   Regeneration. A reply to Max Nordau. N.Y., 1896.
Phil 5643.106   The regeneration of visual purple in the living animal. Thesis. (Peskin, James Charles.) N.Y., 1942.
Phil 7069.34.47   El regentador del mundo solar os da un radio de luz...julio de 1934. (Vilanova, María.) Barcelona, 1934.
Phil 3850.27.90   Regester, John D. Albert Schweitzer. N.Y., 1931.
Phil 9175.6   Regimento saudavel. (Pimentel Castello-Branco, B.B.) Lisboa, 1750.
Phil 3450.19.530   Regina, Umberto. Heidegger. Milano, 1970-
Phil 4580.38.15   Regionsphilosophie. (Høffding, Harald.) Leipzig, 1901.
Phil 6967.1   Regis, E. Practical manual of mental medicine. Philadelphia, 1895.
NEDL   Phil 6967.1.5   Regis, E. La psychoanalyse des névroses. Paris, 1914.
Htn   Phil 2520.146*   Regis, P.S. Response au livre qui a pour titre P. Danielis Huetii. Paris, 1691.
Phil 23.18.5   Register, 1949-1960. (Nordisk Psykologi.) København, n.d.
Phil 3425.56.35   Register zu Hegel's Vorlesungen über die Asthetik. (Bartsch, Heinrich.) Mainz, 1844.
Phil 3425.56.36   Register zu Hegel's Vorlesungen über die Ästhetik. (Bartsch, Heinrich.) Stuttgart, 1966.
Phil 25.14.5   Register zum philosophischen Jahrbuch. Fulda, 1912.
Phil 8876.65   La regle des devoirs. (Bonnaire, L. de.) Paris, 1758. 3v.
Phil 3428.163   Regler, Walter. Herbarts Stellung zum Eudämonismus. Leipzig, 1900.
Phil 5400.28   Les règles esthétiques et les lois du sentiment. (Dussauze, H.) Montauban, 1911.
Phil 2520.55.10   Règles pour la direction de l'esprit. (Descartes, René.) Paris, 1945.
Phil 2520.68   Regln zur des Geistes. (Descartes, René.) Leipzig, 1906.
Phil 5400.65A   Regmert, Martin L. Feelings and emotions. Worcester, Mass., 1928.
Phil 6327.1   Regnard, P. Sorcellerie, magnètisme, morphinisme. Paris, 1887.
Phil 5057.10   Regnaud, P. Précis de logique évolutionniste. Paris, 1897.
Phil 6990.31   Regnault, Félix. La genèse des miracles. Paris, 1910.
Phil 178.46   Le règne de la pensée. (Decoster, Paul.) Bruxelles, 1922.
Phil 2630.7.32   La règne de la quantité et les signes des temps. 4. ed. (Guénon, René.) Paris, 1950.
Phil 338.10.4   Le regne de la relativité. (Haldane, R.B.) Paris, 1922.
Phil 5520.754.2   Regnell, Hans. Filosofiska och språkvetenskapliga grundfrågor inom betydelseläran. 2. uppl. Stockholm, 1971.
Phil 1133.44   Regnéll, Hans. Före Sokrates. Stockholm, 1969.
Phil 348.18   Regnéll, Hans. Symbolization and fictional reference. Lund, 1949.
Phil 5057.42   Regnier, André. Les infortunes de la raison. Paris, 1966.
Phil 6687.10   Regnier, L.R. Hypnotisme et croyances anciennes. Paris, 1891.
Phil 8892.47   Regras da vida. n.p., n.d.
Phil 6313.26   Regressionen im Verhalten des Menschen. (Dejung, Beat.) Zürich, 1967.
Phil 8593.5.7   Het regt gebruik der werelt beschouwingen. 4. druk. (Nieuwentyt, B.) Amsterdam, 1725.
Phil 2520.55.12   Regulae ad directionem ingenii. (Descartes, René.) La Haye, 1966.
Phil 2520.55   Regulae ad directionem ingenii. (Descartes, René.) Torino, 1943.
Phil 2805.216.5   Réguron, Paule. De la théologie à la prière de Pascal. Thèse. Grenoble, 1934.
Phil 2805.216   Réguron, Paule. Les origines du mouvement antijanseniste. Thèse. Grenoble, 1934.
Phil 585.115   La réhabilitation de la nature humaine. (Mercier, R.) Villemomble, 1960.
Phil 3425.599   Rehm, Margarete. Hegels spekulative Deutung der Infinitesimalrechnung. Köln, 1963.
Phil 9035.17   Rehmeké, J. Zur Lehre vom Gemüt. Leipzig, 1911.
Phil 348.4.3   Rehmke, J. Anmerkungen zur Grundwissenschaft. 2. Aufl. Leipzig, 1925.
Phil 6127.6   Rehmke, J. Aussenwelt und Innenwelt, Leib und Seele. Griefswald, 1898.
Phil 5374.17   Rehmke, J. Das Bewusstsein. Heidelberg, 1910.
Phil 8892.39   Rehmke, J. Ethik als Wissenschaft. 3. Aufl. Greifswald, 1925.
Phil 3790.9.20   Rehmke, J. Gesammelte philosophische Aufsätze. Erfurt, 1928.
Phil 8892.39.5   Rehmke, J. Grundlegung der Ethic als Wissenschaft. Leipzig, 1925.
Phil 817.7   Rehmke, J. Grundriss der Geschichte der Philosophie. Berlin, 1896.
Phil 817.7.5   Rehmke, J. Grundriss der Geschichte der Philosophie. Bonn, 1959.
Phil 817.7.7   Rehmke, J. Grundriss der Geschichte der Philosophie. 5. Aufl. Frankfurt, 1965.
Phil 3790.9.80   Rehmke, J. Johannes Rehmke. Leipzig, 1921.
Phil 5257.3.10   Rehmke, J. Der Mensch. Leipzig, 1928.
Phil 9430.9   Rehmke, J. Der Pessimismus und die Sittenlehre. Leipzig, 1882.
Phil 348.4   Rehmke, J. Philosophie als Grundwissenschaft. Leipzig, 1910.
Phil 348.4.2   Rehmke, J. Philosophie als Grundwissenschaft. 2. Aufl. Leipzig, 1929.
Phil 3790.9.30   Rehmke, J. Die philosophische Erbsunde; Was in ich? Marburg, 1924.
Phil 5257.3.5   Rehmke, J. Die Seele des Menschen. Leipzig, 1902.
Phil 348.4.5   Rehmke, J. Die Welt als Wahrnehmung und Begriff. Berlin, 1880.
Phil 5257.3.25   Rehmke, Joh: Lehrbuch der allgemeinen Psychologie. (Baumann.) Göttingen, 1894.
Phil 5767.3   Rehmke, Johannes. Die Willesfreiheit. Leipzig, 1911.
Phil 5057.17   Rehmke, Johannes. Logik, oder Philosophie als Wissenslehre. Leipzig, 1918.
Phil 5257.3   Rehmke, Joh: Lehrbuch der allgemeinen Psychologie. Hamburg, 1894.
Phil 2262.85   Rehorn, F. Moral sense und Moral-Prinzip bei Shaftesbury. Inaug. Diss. Bonn, 1882.

Phil 3837.1   Rehorn, K.W.A. G.E. Lessing's Stellung zur Philosophie des Spinoza. Frankfurt, 1877.
Phil 5257.18   Rehwoldt, F. Über respiratorische Affektsymptome. Leipzig, 1911.
Phil 5425.28   Reibmayr, Albert. Die Entwicklungsgeschichte des Talentes und Genies. München, 1908. 2v.
Phil 665.37   Reich, E. Die Geschichte der Seele. Minden, 1884.
Phil 6127.16   Reich, E. Der Mensch und die Seele. Berlin, 1872.
Phil 3270.3.93   Reich, Edward. Weltanschauung und Menschenleben...Jakob Frohschammer's. Grossenhain, 1884.
Phil 3808.85.15   Reich, Emil. Schopenhauer als Philosoph der Tragödie. Wien, 1888.
Phil 6327.21.85   Reich, Ilse Ollendorff. Wilhelm Reich. N.Y., 1969.
Phil 6327.21.10   Reich, Wilhelm. Character analysis. 3. ed. N.Y., 1949.
Phil 6327.21.13   Reich, Wilhelm. Character analysis. 3. ed. N.Y., 1970.
Phil 6327.21.35   Reich, Wilhelm. Cosmic superimposition. Rangeley, Me., 1951.
Phil 6327.21.46   Reich, Wilhelm. The invasion of compulsory sex-morality. N.Y., 1971.
Phil 6327.21.30   Reich, Wilhelm. Listen little man. N.Y., 1948.
Phil 6327.21.20   Reich, Wilhelm. The murder of Christ: the emotional plague of mankind. N.Y., 1953.
Phil 6315.2.395   Reich, Wilhelm. Reich speaks of Freud. N.Y., 1967.
Phil 6327.21.41   Reich, Wilhelm. The sexual revolution. N.Y., 1971.
Phil 6327.21.40   Reich, Wilhelm. Die sexuelle Revolution. Frankfurt am Main, 1970.
Phil 6327.21.26   Reich, Wilhelm. Wilhelm Reich, biographical material. v.1. Rangeley, Me., 1953-
Phil 6327.21.25   Reich, Wilhelm. Wilhelm Reich, biographical material. v.2. Rangeley, Me., 1953-
Phil 8419.54   Das Reich der Kunst. (Schneiderfranken, J.A.) Basel, 1933.
Phil 8411.27   Das Reich des Schönen. (Kaufmann, F.) Stuttgart, 1960.
Phil 6327.38   Reich-Dörr, Marta. Zur Psychologie der falschen Anschuldigung und falschen Selbstbezichtigung. Hamburg, 1962.
Phil 8975.1   Reich Gottes. (Zwicker, Heinz.) Bern, 1948.
Phil 3120.55.100   Reich ohne Gott; zur Eschatologie Ernst Blochs. (Jager, Alfred.) Zürich, 1969.
Phil 6315.2.395   Reich speaks of Freud. (Reich, Wilhelm.) N.Y., 1967.
Phil 1200.38   Reichard, Elias C. Animi perturbationes ex mente potissimum. Magdeburgi, 1764.
Phil 3499.19   Reichardt, W. Kant's Lehre vom den synthetischen Urtheilen...Mathematik. Leipzig, 1888.
Phil 3499.17   Reiche, L.P.A. De Kanti antinomüs. Thesis. Gottingae, 1838.
Phil 1850.93   Reichel, E. Wer Schrieb das "Norum Organon" von Francis Bacon. Stuttgart, 1886.
Phil 7060.81   Reichel, W. Occult experiences. London. n.d.
Phil 7069.08.30   Reichel, Willy. An occultist's travels. N.Y., 1908.
Phil 510.4   Reichenau, W. Monistische Philosophie von Spinoza bis auf unserer Tage. Köln, 1884.
Phil 5066.26   Reichenbach, H. Elements of symbolic logic. N.Y., 1947.
Phil 5066.26.5   Reichenbach, H. Nomalogical statements and admissable operations. Amsterdam, 1954.
Phil 672.144   Reichenbach, H. Philosophie der Raum-Zeit-Lehre. Berlin, 1928.
Phil 672.144.3   Reichenbach, H. The philosophy of space and time. N.Y., 1958.
Phil 1717.17   Reichenbach, H. The rise of scientific philosophy. Berkeley, 1951.
Phil 8707.1   Reichenbach, H.G.L. Blicke in das Leben der Gegenwart. Dresden, 1856.
Phil 1717.17.7   Reichenbach, Hans. Der Aufsteig der wissenschaftlichen Philosophie. Braunschweig, 1968.
Phil 672.182   Reichenbach, Hans. The direction of time. Berkeley, 1956.
Phil 348.13   Reichenbach, Hans. Experience and prediction. Chicago, 1938.
Phil 5057.32   Reichenbach, Hans. Nomological statements and admissible operations. Amsterdam, 1954.
Phil 298.7   Reichenbach, Hans. Ziele und Wege der heutigen Naturphilosophie. Leipzig, 1931.
Phil 6687.1.15   Reichenback, C. Le fluide des magnétiseurs. Paris, 1891.
Phil 6687.1.9   Reichenback, C. Odisch-magnetische Briefe. Stuttgart, 1852.
Phil 6687.1.2   Reichenback, C. Physico-physiological researches. N.Y., 1851.
Phil 6687.1.3   Reichenback, C. Researches on magnetism, electricity. London, 1850.
Phil 6687.1.6   Reichenback, C. Der sensitive Mensch. Leipzig, 1910. 2v.
Phil 7085.4   Reichenback, C.A. Somanmbulism and cramp. N.Y., 1860.
Phil 6060.58   Reichert, G. Männlichkeit und Weiblichkeit im Spiegel. Heidelberg, 1962.
Phil 3640.79.60   Reichert, Herbert William. International Nietzsche bibliography. Chapel Hill, N.C., 1960.
Phil 3640.79.60.5   Reichert, Herbert William. International Nietzsche bibliography. Chapel Hill, 1968.
Htn   Phil 3801.734*   Reichlin-Meldegg, C.A. von. Bedenken eines süddeutschen Krebsfeindes über Schellings erste Vorlesung in Berlin. Stuttgart, 1842.
Phil 817.15   Reichlin-Meldegg, K. Der Parallelismus der Alten und neuen Philosophie. Leipzig, 1866.
Phil 5057.1   Reichlin-Meldegg, K.A.F. System der Logik. v.1-2. Wien, 1870.
Phil 3425.221   Reichlin-Meldegg, Karl A. Die Autolatrie oder Selbstanbetung. Pforzheim, 1943.
Phil 27.17   Reichl's philosophischer Almanach. Darmstadt. 1923-1927 4v.
Phil 3017.9   Reichmann, Eberhard. Die Herrschaft der Zahl. Stuttgart, 1968.
Phil 5725.4   Reichner, H. Experimentelle und kritische Beiträge zur Psychologie des Verstehens. Inaug. Diss. Leipzig, 1927.
Phil 530.20.100   Reichtum des Lebens. (Gieraths, Gundolf Maria.) Düsseldorf, 1956.
Phil 5257.17   Reichwein, G. Die neueren Untersuchungen über Psychologie des Denkens. Halle, 1910.
Phil 8967.6   Reid, A.C. Christ and the present crisis. Wake Forest, 1934.
Phil 6327.9   Reid, J. Essays on hypochondriacal and other nervous affections. Philadelphia, 1817.
Phil 2255.5   Reid, James K. Whither humanity; the philosophy of a doctor. London, 1945.
Phil 735.117   Reid, John R. A theory of value. N.Y., 1938.
Phil 8892.54   Reid, L.A. Creative morality. London, 1937.
Phil 8418.21   Reid, L.A. A study in aesthetics. London, 1931.
Phil 348.20   Reid, L.A. Ways of knowledge and experience. London, 1961.

Phil 720.18 Reid, Louis A. Knowledge and truth. London, 1923.
Htn Phil 2240.33* Reid, Thomas. Essays on the active powers of man. Edinburgh, 1788.
Phil 2240.88 Reid, Thomas. Essays on the active powers of the human mind. Cambridge, Mass., 1969.
Phil 2240.25 Reid, Thomas. Essays on the active powers of the human mind. London, 1843.
Phil 2240.49 Reid, Thomas. Essays on the intellectual and active powers of man. v.3. Dublin, 1790.
Phil 2240.60 Reid, Thomas. Essays on the intellectual powers of man. Cambridge, 1850.
Phil 2240.60.31 Reid, Thomas. Essays on the intellectual powers of man. Cambridge, 1969.
Phil 2240.59 Reid, Thomas. Essays on the intellectual powers of man. Dublin, 1786. 2v.
Htn Phil 2240.58* Reid, Thomas. Essays on the intellectual powers of man. Edinburgh, 1785.
Phil 2240.60.30 Reid, Thomas. Essays on the intellectual powers of man. London, 1941.
Phil 2240.60.3 Reid, Thomas. Essays on the intellectual powers of man. 3rd ed. Cambridge, 1852.
Htn Phil 2240.60.4* Reid, Thomas. Essays on the intellectual powers of man. 4th ed. Cambridge, 1853.
Phil 2240.60.6A Reid, Thomas. Essays on the intellectual powers of man. 6th ed. Boston, 1855.
Phil 2240.50 Reid, Thomas. Essays on the powers of the human mind. Edinburgh, 1803. 3v.
Phil 2240.30A Reid, Thomas. An inquiry into the human mind. Edinburgh, 1764.
Phil 2240.32 Reid, Thomas. An inquiry into the human mind. N.Y., 1824.
Phil 2240.30.2A Reid, Thomas. An inquiry into the human mind. 2nd ed. Edinburgh, 1765.
Phil 2240.31 Reid, Thomas. An inquiry into the human mind. 4th ed. London, 1785.
Phil 2240.20 Reid, Thomas. Oeuvres complètes. Paris, 1828-36. 6v.
Phil 2240.61 Reid, Thomas. Philosophical orations of Thomas Reid. Aberdeen, 1937.
Phil 2240.35 Reid, Thomas. The philosophy of Reid...in the "Inquiry into the human mind". N.Y., 1892.
Phil 2240.10 Reid, Thomas. Works. Charlestown, 1813-15. 4v.
Phil 2240.14 Reid, Thomas. Works. Edinburgh, 1853. 2v.
Phil 2240.12 Reid, Thomas. Works. N.Y., 1822. 3v.
Phil 8610.924 Reid, W.N. The supremacy of reason. London, 1924.
Phil 8642.4 Reid, William. Everlasting punishment and modern speculation. Edinburgh, 1874.
Phil 2240.87 Reid a Kant. (Dür, Seweryn.) Opole, 1963.
Phil 1135.163 Reidemeister, Kurt. Das Exakte denken der Griechen. Hamburg, 1949.
Phil 3790.16.30 Reidemeister, Kurt. Geist und Wirklichkeit. Berlin, 1953.
Phil 1750.395 Reidemeister, Kurt. Die Unsachlichkeit der Existenzphilosophie. Berlin, 1954.
Phil 1750.395.2 Reidemeister, Kurt. Die Unsachlichkeit der Existenzphilosophie. 2. Aufl. Berlin, 1970.
Phil 9045.75 Reidenbach, Clarence. A critical analysis of patriotism as an ethical concept. Indianpolis? 1920.
Phil 3425.720 Reidinger, Otto. Gottes Tod und Hegels Auferstehung. Berlin, 1969.
Phil 3425.111 Reiff, F. Über die Hegel'sche Dialektik. Tübingen, 1866.
Phil 3525.89 Reiff, F. Über Krause's Philosophie. n.p., n.d.
Phil 192.35 Reiff, J.F. Der Anfang der Philosophie. Stuttgart, 1840.
Phil 5767.7 Reiff, J.F. Das System der Willensbestimmungen. Tübingen, 1842.
Phil 5257.37 Reiff, Paul. Der moderne psychophysische Parallelismus. Inaug. Diss. Heilbronn, 1901.
Phil 5590.464 Reifung und Formung von Persönlichkeiten. (Tramer, Moritz.) Erlenbach, 1965.
Phil 5841.24 Reifung und Geschlecht. (Heimler, Adolf.) München, 1966.
Phil 6980.429 Reifungskrisen im Kindes- und Jugendalter. (Loewnau, H.W.) Göttingen, 1961.
Phil 8582.3.2 The reign of law. (Argyll, G.D.C.) London, 1871.
Phil 8582.3.5 The reign of law. 4. ed. (Argyll, G.D.C.) London, 1867.
Phil 8582.3.1 The reign of law. 5. ed. (Argyll, G.D.C.) N.Y., 1869.
Phil 2630.7.30 The reign of quantity and the signs of the times. (Guénon, René.) London, 1953.
Phil 338.10 The reign of relativity. (Haldane, R.B.) New Haven, 1921.
Phil 338.10.2 The reign of relativity. 2. ed. (Haldane, R.B.) London, 1921.
Phil 1200.4.3 The reign of the Stoics. (Holland, F.M.) N.Y., 1879.
Phil 6980.635.40 Reik, T. The need to be loved. N.Y., 1963.
X Cg Phil 7075.137 Reik, T. Psychology of sex relations. N.Y., 1945.
Phil 6327.12.9 Reik, Theodor. Aus Leiden Freuden. London, 1940.
Phil 5780.18 Reik, Theodor. The compulsion to confess. N.Y., 1959.
Phil 6327.12.55 Reik, Theodor. Curiosities of the self. N.Y., 1965.
Phil 5627.102.10 Reik, Theodor. Dogma und Zwangsidee eine psychoanalytische Studie zur Entwicklung der Religion. Leipzig, 1927.
Phil 5627.102.5 Reik, Theodor. Der eigene und der fremde Gott; zur Psychoanalyse der religiösen Entwicklung. Leipzig, 1923.
Phil 6327.12.40 Reik, Theodor. Fragment of a great confession. N.Y., 1949.
Phil 6315.2.115.5 Reik, Theodor. Freud als Kulturkritiker. Mit einem Briefe S. Freuds. Wien, 1930.
Phil 6315.2.115A Reik, Theodor. From thirty years with Freud. N.Y., 1940.
Phil 5525.39 Reik, Theodor. Lust und Leid im Witz; sechs psychoanalytische Studien. Wien, 1929.
Phil 6327.12.60 Reik, Theodor. The many faces of sex. N.Y., 1966.
Phil 5525.39.5 Reik, Theodor. Nachdenkliche Heiterkeit. Wien, 1933.
Phil 5627.102 Reik, Theodor. Probleme der Religionspsychologie. 1. Teil. Leipzig, 1919.
Phil 6327.12.5 Reik, Theodor. Ritual; psycho-analytical studies. London, 1931.
Phil 6327.12.7 Reik, Theodor. Ritual, psycho-analytical studies. N.Y., 1958.
Phil 6327.12.30 Reik, Theodor. Der Schrecken und andere psychoanalytische Studien. Wien, 1929.
Phil 6327.12.36 Reik, Theodor. The search within; the inner experience of a psychoanalyst. N.Y., 1968.
Phil 6327.12.35 Reik, Theodor. The search within. N.Y., 1956.
Phil 6327.12.45 Reik, Theodor. The secret self. N.Y., 1953.
Phil 6327.12.15 Reik, Theodor. Surprise and the psycho-analyst. London, 1936.
Phil 6327.12.13 Reik, Theodor. Der überraschte Psychologie. Leiden, 1935.
Phil 6327.12.50 Reik, Theodor. Voices from the inaudible. N.Y., 1964.
Phil 6327.12.25 Reik, Theodor. Wie man psychologe wird. Leipzig, 1927.
Phil 6327.12.20 Reik, Theodor. Wir Freud-Schüler. Leiden, 1936.
Phil 2225.5.165 Reilly, Francis E. Charles Peirce's theory of scientific method. N.Y., 1970.
Phil 9530.40 Reilly, William J. How to improve your human relations, by straight thinking. N.Y., 1942.
Phil 6127.30 Reimann, Helga. Die Mental Health Bewegung. Tübingen, 1967.
Phil 8597.3A Reimarus, H.S. Abhandlungen von den vornehmsten Wahrheiten der natürlichen Religion. 6. Aufl. Hamburg, 1791.
Phil 8597.3.8 Reimarus, H.S. The principal truths of natural religion. London, 1766.
Phil 5057.2 Reimarus, H.S. Die Vernunstlehre. Hamburg, 1790.
Phil 8597.3.13 Reimarus, H.S. Von dem Zwecke Jesu und seiner Jünger. Berlin, 1784.
Phil 8597.3.12 Reimarus, H.S. Von dem Zwecke Jesu und seiner Jünger. Braunschweig, 1778.
Phil 8597.3.4 Reimarus, H.S. Die Vornehmstenwahrheiten der natürlichen Religion. 4. Aufl. Hamburg, 1772.
Phil 8597.3.3 Reimarus, H.S. Die Vornehmstenwahrheiten der natürlichen Religion. 3. Aufl. Hamburg, 1766.
Phil 3790.1.80 Pamphlet box. Reimarus, H.S.
Htn Phil 5827.4.6* Reimarus, Hermann Samuel. Allgemeine Betrachtungen über die Triebe der Thiere. Hamburg, 1760.
Phil 5827.4.5 Reimarus, Hermann Samuel. Allgemeine Betrachtungen über die Triebe der Thiere. 2. Ausg. Hamburg, 1762.
Phil 5827.4.7 Reimarus, Hermann Samuel. Allgemeine Betrachtungen über die Triebe der Thiere. 3. Ausg. Hamburg, 1773. 2 pam.
Phil 5827.4 Reimarus, Hermann Samuel. Observations physiques et morales sur l'instinct des animaux. Amsterdam, 1770. 2v.
Htn Phil 3790.11.87* Reimarus, J.A.H. De vita sua commentarius. Hamburgi, 1815.
Phil 3790.11.85 Reimarus, J.A.H. Lebensbeschreibung, von ihm selbst. Hamburg, 1814.
Phil 8597.3.10 Reimarus, Johann Albert Heinrich. Über die Grunde der menschlichen Erkenntniss und der natürlichen Religion. Hamburg, 1787.
Phil 8597.3.21 Reimarus, Johann Albert Heinrich. Von dem daseyn Gottes und der menschlichen Seele. Hamburg, 1781.
Phil 8418.17.5 Reimers, N.A. Le concept du beau; essaie d'une théorie. Paris, 1930.
Phil 192.52 Rein, Doris. Hvad er kultur? Kristiania, 1916.
Phil 3160.12.80 Rein, Mercedes. Ernst Cassirer. Montevideo, 1959.
Phil 4630.2.43 Rein, T. Anteckningar i filosofi och historia. Helsingfors, 1889.
Phil 4630.2.38 Rein, T. Grunddragen af den filosofiska imputationsläran. Helsingfors, 1863.
Phil 4635.5.81.3 Rein, T. Juhana Vilhelm Snellman. Helsingissa, 1928.
Phil 4630.2.36 Rein, T. Lärobok i den formella logiken. Helsingfors, 1886.
Phil 4630.2.45 Rein, T. Lefnadsminnen. Helsingfors, 1918.
Phil 4630.2.40 Rein, T. Om den filosofiska methoden. Helsingfors, 1868.
Phil 4630.2.39 Rein, T. Om kunskapens möjlighet. Helsingfors, 1867.
Phil 4630.2.31 Rein, T. Uppsatser och tal. Helsingfors, 1903.
Phil 5257.72 Rein, Thiodolf. Sielutieteen oppikirja. Helsingissa, 1884.
Phil 3450.11.130 Reinach, Adolf. Was ist Phanomenologie. 1. Aufl. München, 1951.
Phil 817.14.5 Reinach, S. Lettres à Zoé sur l'histoire des philosophies. Paris, 1926. 3v.
Phil 5257.52 Reinbardt, J.M. Social psychology. Chicago, 1938.
Phil 978.8.35 Reincarnation; a lecture. (Leadbeater, C.W.) Harrogate, 1903.
Phil 978.51.5 Reincarnation, and other lectures. (Rogers, L.W.) Chicago, 1925.
Phil 978.60.2 Reincarnation, the hope of the world. 2d ed. (Cooper, Irving S.) Chicago, 1927.
Phil 8637.22 Reincarnation, the ring of return. (Martin, E.) New Hyde Park, N.Y., 1963.
Phil 978.45 La réincarnation. (Encausse, G.) Paris, 1912.
Phil 8632.20 Reincarnation. (Head, Joseph.) N.Y., 1961.
Phil 978.38 Reincarnation. (Walker, E.D.) Boston, 1888.
Phil 978.38.5 Reincarnation. (Walker, E.D.) Point Loma, Calif., 1923.
Phil 978.6.62 Reincarnation (Theosophical manual II). (Besant, Annie.) London, 1897.
Phil 960.150 Reincarnation and karma. (Jast, Louis S.) N.Y., 1944.
Phil 8628.10 La réincarnation des âmes selon les traditions orientales et occidentales. (Des Georges, A.) Paris, 1966.
Phil 5767.10.5 Reiner, Hans. Freiheit, Wollen und Aktivität. Leipzig, 1927.
Phil 8892.48 Reiner, Hans. Der Grund der sittlichen Bindung und das sittlich Gute. Halle, 1932.
Phil 8892.76.5 Reiner, Hans. Gut und Böse. Freiburg, 1965.
Phil 192.71 Reiner, Hans. Phänomenologie und menschliche Existenz. Halle, 1931.
Phil 8892.76 Reiner, Hans. Die philosophische Ethik. Heidelberg, 1964.
Phil 3640.185 Reiner, Julius. F. Nietzsche. Stuttgart, 1916.
Phil 3640.185.10 Reiner, Julius. Friedrich Nietzsche. 8. Aufl. Berlin, 191-.
Phil 4065.113 Reiner, Julius. Giordano Bruno und seine Weltanschauung. Berlin, 19- ?
Phil 125.4 Reiner, Julius. Philosophisches Wörterbuch. Leipzig, 1912.
Phil 8967.20 Reiners, Hermann. Grundintention und sittliches Tun. Freiburg, 1966.
Phil 1504.8.5 Reiners, J. Der Nominalismus in der Frühscholastik. v.8, pt.5. Münster, n.d.
Phil 1540.15 Reiners, Josef. Der aristotelische Realismus in der Frühscholastik. Inaug.-Diss. Bonn, 1907.
Phil 5625.117 Reinforcement and behavior. N.Y., 1969.
Phil 2905.1.570 Reinhard, Edmond. Teilhard de Chardin. Pähl, 1966.
Phil 8967.5.4 Reinhard, Franz V. System der christlichen Moral. Wittenberg, 1802-05. 3v.
Phil 8967.5.10 Reinhard, Franz V. System der christlichen Moral. Wittenberg, 1814-15. 5v.
Phil 8672.8 Reinhard, J. Gott und die Seele. Inaug. Diss. Erlangen, 1908.
Phil 3499.25 Reinhard, Walter. Über das Verhältnis von Sittlichkeit und Religion bei Kant. Bern, 1927.
Phil 3552.268 Reinhardt, Arthur. Sind es Vorzugsweise speculative oder naturwissenschaftliche Gründe. Jena, 1873.
Phil 9590.20 Reinhardt, K.F. A realistic philosophy. Milwaukee, 1944.
Phil 192.112 Reinhardt, Kent F. A realistic philosophy. 2d. ed. N.Y., 1962.
Phil 1750.360A Reinhardt, Kurt Frank. The existentialist revolt. Milwaukee, 1952.
Phil 1750.360.2 Reinhardt, Kurt Frank. The existentialist revolt. 2nd ed. N.Y., 1960.
Phil 9495.127.5 Reinheit und Jungfräulichkeit. (Hildebrand, Dietrich von.) Köln, 1927.
Phil 348.2 Reinhold, C.E. Grundzüge...Erkenntnisslehre. Schleswig, 1822.

Phil 192.7.2 Reinhold, C.E. System der Metaphysik. Jena, 1854.
Phil 192.7 Reinhold, C.E. Theorie des menschlichen Erkenntnissvermögens. Gotha, 1832-1835. 2v.
Phil 817.1 Reinhold, C.E.G. Geschichte der Philosophie. Jena, 1845. 2v.
Phil 3778.90 Reinhold, E. Karl Leonhard Reinholds Leben. Jena, 1825.
Phil 8597.6 Reinhold, E. Das Wesen der Religion. Jena, 1846.
Phil 5257.4 Reinhold, E.C. Lehrbuch der philosophisch propädeutischen Psychologie und der formalen Logik. 2. Aufl. Jena, 1839.
Phil 5057.3.5 Reinhold, Ernest. Die Logik oder die allgemeine Denkformenlehre. Jena, 1827.
Phil 5057.3 Reinhold, Ernest. Versuch einer Begrundung und neuen Darstellung der logischen Formen. Leipzig, 1819.
Phil 3625.3.82 Reinhold, Ferdinand. Machs Erkenntnistheorie. Leipzig, 1908.
Htn Phil 3801.407* Reinhold, Fichte und Schelling. (Fries, Jakob F.) Leipzig, 1803.
Phil 3246.191.5 Reinhold, Fichte und Schelling. (Fries, Jakob F.) Leipzig, 1803.
Phil 525.93 Reinhold, Hans. The soul afire. N.Y., 1944.
Phil 525.93.5 Reinhold, Hans. The soul afire. N.Y., 1960.
Phil 3778.41 Reinhold, K.L. Die alte Frage: was ist die Wahrheit? Altona, 1820.
Phil 3778.38 Reinhold, K.L. Anleitung zur Kenntniss und Beurtheilung der Philosophie in ihren sämmtlichen Lehrgebäuden. Wien, 1805.
Phil 3499.2.5 Reinhold, K.L. Auswahl der besten Aufsätze über die Kantische Philosophie. Frankfurt, 1790.
Phil 3778.6 Reinhold, K.L. Auswahl vermischter Schriften. Jena, 1796-97. 2v.
Phil 3778.32 Reinhold, K.L. Beyträge zur Berichtigung bisheriger Missverständnisse der Philosophen. Jena, 1790. 2v.
Phil 3778.30 Reinhold, K.L. Beyträge zur leichtern Übersicht des Zustandes der Philosophie. v.1-6. Hamburg, 1802. 2v.
Phil 3499.2 Reinhold, K.L. Briefe über die Kantische Philosophie. Leipzig, 1790-92. 2v.
Phil 3499.2.3 Reinhold, K.L. Briefe über die Kantische Philosophie. Leipzig, 1924.
Phil 3778.36 Reinhold, K.L. Sendschreiben an J.C. Lavater und J.G. Fichte über den Glauben an Gott. Hamburg, 1799. 3 pam.
Phil 3778.40 Reinhold, K.L. Über das fundament des philosophischen Wissens. Jena, 1791.
Phil 3499.2.10 Reinhold, K.L. Über die bisherigen Schicksale der Kantischen Philosophie. Jena, 1789.
Phil 3778.35 Reinhold, K.L. Über die Paradoxien der neuesten Philosophie. Hamburg, 1799.
Phil 3778.39 Reinhold, K.L. Verhandlungen über die Grundbegriffe und Grundsätze der Moralität. Lübeck, 1798.
Phil 5257.5 Reinhold, K.L. Versuch einer neuen Theorie des menschlichen Vorstellungs-Vermögens. Prag, 1789.
Phil 1145.102 Reinicke, Hans. Das Verhängnis der Übel im Weltbild griechischer Denker. Berlin, 1969.
Phil 3499.33 Reinig, Richard. Zur Kritik des Sowjetismus am Kritizismus Kants. Ratingen, 1964.
Phil 3425.584 Reining, Richard. Das Problem des polytechnischen Orbeitserziehung. Marburg, 1962.
Phil 3425.584.5 Reining, Richard. Zur Grundlegung der polytechnischen Bildung durch Hegel und Marx. Braunschweig, 1967.
Phil 2115.132 Reininger, R. Locke, Berkeley, Hume. München, 1922.
Phil 3640.186 Reininger, R. Nietzsches Kampf um den Sinn des Lebens. Wien, 1922.
Phil 348.5 Reininger, R. Philosophie des Erkennens. Leipzig, 1911.
Phil 348.5.5 Reininger, R. Das psycho-physische Problem. Wien, 1916.
Phil 3903.3.99 Reininger, R. Über H. Vaihingers "Philosophie des Als Ob". Leipzig, 1912.
Phil 3499.10.5 Reininger, Robert. Kant, seine Anhänger und seine Gegner. München, 1923.
Phil 3499.10.10 Reininger, Robert. Kants kritischer Idealismus. Leipzig, 1912.
Phil 3499.10 Reininger, Robert. Kants Lehre vom Unneren sinn und seine Theorie der Erfahrung. Wein, 1900.
Phil 192.70 Reininger, Robert. Metaphysik der Wirklichkeit. Wien, 1931.
Phil 192.70.5 Reininger, Robert. Metaphysik der Wirklichkeit. 2. Aufl. Wien, 1947. 2v.
Phil 8892.56 Reininger, Robert. Wertphilosophie und Ethik. Leipzig, 1939.
Phil 8892.56.5 Reininger, Robert. Wertphilosophie und Ethik. 3. Aufl. Wien, 1947.
Phil 348.26 Reinisch, Leonhard. Grenzen der Erkenntnis. Freiburg, 1969.
Phil 298.4 Reinke, J. Die Natur und Wir. Berlin, 1907.
Phil 192.33.5 Reinke, J. Die Welt als Tat. 3e Aufl. Berlin, 1903.
Phil 192.33 Reinke, J. Die Welt als That. Berlin, 1899.
Phil 298.10 Reinl, Kurt. Grundriss des Seins. München, 1958.
Phil 5227.7 Reinle, Rico. Das Problems der Entwicklung in der neueren Psychologie. Basel, 1952.
Phil 1535.36.12 Reinstadler, S. Elementa philosophiae scholasticae. 11. and 12. ed. Friburgi, 1923. 2v.
Phil 1535.36.13 Reinstadler, S. Elementa philosophiae scholasticae. 13. ed. Friburgi, 1929. 2v.
Phil 5068.96 Reintel'dt, Boris K. Zakon edinstva i bor'by protivopolzhnostei. Ioshkar-Ola, 1969.
Phil 3790.14 Reinwald, J.G. Kultur und Barbarei. 2e Aufl. Mainz, 1828.
Phil 8597.56 Reischauer, August K. The nature and truth of the great religions. Tokyo, 1966.
Phil 8597.33 Reischle, Max. Die Frage nach dem Wesen der Religion. Freiburg, 1889.
Phil 525.13 Reischle, Max. Ein Wort...über die Mystik in der Theologie. Freiburg, 1886.
Phil 3549.2.79.10 Reise durch die Zeit. (Keyserling, Hermann.) Innsbruck, 1948.
Phil 192.63 Reiser, Beat. System der Philosophie. v.1. Einsiedeln, 1920.
Phil 3120.18.90 Reiser, Joseph. Zur Erkenntnislehre Jakob Sigismund Becko. München, 1934.
Phil 1817.8 Reiser, O.L. Humanism and new world ideals. Yellow Springs, Colorado, 1933.
Phil 5057.23 Reiser, Oliver L. Humanistic logic for the mind in action. N.Y., 1930.
Phil 2255.4 Reiser, Oliver L. A new earth and a new humanity. N.Y., 1942.
Phil 2255.4.5 Reiser, Oliver L. World philosophy. Pittsburgh, 1948.
Phil 298.23 Reiser, Oliver Leslie. Cosmic humanism. Cambridge, 1966.
Phil 396.3 Reiser, Oliver Leslie. Planetary democracy. N.Y., 1944.
Phil 3549.2.75.7 Das Reisetagebuch eines Philosophen. (Keyserling, Hermann.) Darmstadt, 1956. 3v.

Phil 3549.2.75.5 Das Reisetagebuch eines Philosophen. 7. Aufl. (Keyserling, Hermann.) Darmstadt, 1923. 2v.
Phil 3808.78 Reisetagebücher aus den Jahren 1803-1804. (Schopenhauer, Arthur.) Leipzig, 1923.
Phil 348.10 Reisner, E. Das Selbstopfer der Erkenntnis. München, 1927.
Phil 8597.23.5 Reisner, Edward H. Faith in an age of fact. N.Y., 1937.
Phil 8597.23 Reisner, Edward H. Religious values and intellectual consistency. N.Y., 1915.
Phil 8633.1.14 Reisner, George A. The Egyptian conception of immortality. Boston, 1912.
Phil 5548.135 Reiss, Gretel. Der Einfluss von Erfolgs- und Misserfolgsmotivierung auf das Behalten eigener Leistungen. Inaug. Diss. Münster? 1968?
Phil 2750.11.200 Reiter, Josef. Intuition und Transzendenz. München, 1967.
Phil 5227.10 Reith, Herman. An introduction to philosophical psychology. Englewood Cliffs, N.J., 1956.
Phil 6980.635.26 Reitman, F. Insanity, art and culture. N.Y., 1959.
Phil 6980.635.25 Reitman, F. Psychotic art. N.Y., 1951.
Phil 5257.75 Reitman, Walter Ralph. Cognition and thought. N.Y., 1965.
Phil 817.17 Reitmeister, L.A. The gist of philosophy. N.Y., 1936.
Phil 298.16 Reitzer, Alfons. Das Problem des Materiebegiffes. München, 1960.
Phil 8419.26.5 Reiz ist Schönheit in Bewegung; a Rettung of Joseph Spence. (Howard, W.G.) n.p., 1909.
Phil 2270.77.20 A rejoinder to Professor Weismann. (Spencer, Herbert.) London, 1893?
Phil 7150.28 Relaçãi de hum notavel caso. Lisboa, 1755?
Phil 9558.5.10 Relaçam historia das vidas dos avarentos em que se escreve todos os seus costumes vicios. Lisboa, 17- .
Phil 7080.18.5 Relação de dous extraordinar[ios] e notaveis successos. Lisbon, 1758.
Phil 4368.2.55 Relaciones de la filosofía: la filosofía y el filósofo. (Romero, Francisco.) Buenos Aires, 1958.
Phil 8422.6 Relaciones entre lo bueno, lo bello y lo verdadero. (Valdes Rodriguez, Manuel.) Tesis, 1888.
Phil 4372.1.115 Les relacions de Juan Luis Vives amb els Anglesos i amb l'Angleterra. (Watson, Foster.) Barcelona, 1918.
Phil 187.143 Related multiplicity. (Mallik, B.K.) Oxford, 1952.
Phil 8592.6.20 The relation between ethics and religion. (Martineau, James.) London, 1881.
Phil 5649.15 Relation between magnitude of stimulus and the time of reaction. Diss. (Froeberg, Sven.) N.Y., 1907.
Phil 8583.28.10 The relation between religion and culture according to C. Dawson. (O'Connor, D.A.) Montreal, 1952.
Phil 8702.10 The relation between religion and science. (Mason, Henry M.) n.p., 1839.
Phil 8712.14 The relation between religion and science. (Woodburne, A.S.) Chicago, 1920.
Phil 8696.12 The relation between science and theology. (Gager, C.S.) Chicago, 1925.
Htn Phil 525.10* Relation de l'origine, du progrès...du quiétisme. (Phelipeaux, J.) Ste. Ménehould, 1732.
Phil 7080.20 A relation of a very extraordinary sleeper. (Oliver, William.) London, 1707.
Phil 1870.87 The relation of Berkeley's later to his early ideal. (Tower, C.V.) Ann Arbor, 1899.
Phil 6112.23 The relation of brain to mind. (Cleland, J.) Glasgow, 1882.
Phil 8591.42 The relation of concept and demonstration in the ontological argument. (Lamm, H.) Chicago, 1940.
Phil 9150.14 The relation of evolutionry theory to ethical problem. (Sanderson, J.R.) Toronto, 1912.
Phil 2138.94 The relation of inference to fact in Mill's logic. (Crawford, J.F.) Chicago, 1916.
Phil 2138.119 The relation of inference to fact in Mill's logic. (Crawford, John F.) Chicago, 1916.
Phil 2115.112A The relation of John Locke to English deism. (Hefelbower, S.G.) Chicago, 1918.
Phil 5635.24 Relation of methods of just perceptible differences and constant stimuli. (Fernberger, Samuel W.) n.p., 1912.
Phil 6115.7 The relation of our public schools to the disorders of the nervous system. (Folsom, C.F.) Boston, 1886.
Phil 5545.162 The relation of over-learning to retention. (Cuff, N.B.) Nashville, 1927.
Phil 182.19.13 The relation of philosophy to science, physical and psychological. (Hodgson, S.H.) London, 1884.
Phil 186.26 Relation of science and philosophy. Thesis. (Liddy, Ray Balmer.) Toronto, 1914?
Phil 5635.14 Relation of sensation to other categories in contemporary psychology. (Rahn, Carl.) Princeton, 1913.
Phil 5241.92.10 The relation of the attributes of sensation to the dimensions of the stimulus. (Boring, E.G.) Baltimore, 1935. 3 pam.
Phil 6952.8 Relation sur un épidémie d'hystéro-démonopathie en 1861. (Constans, A.) Paris, 1863.
Phil 6688.2 The relationale of mesmerism. (Sinnett, A.P.) Boston, 1892.
Phil 8707.9 The relations of Christianity and science. N.Y., 1863.
Phil 9045.15 The relations of education to citizenship. (Baldwin, S.E.) New Haven, 1912.
Phil 8697.4 The relations of geology to theology. (Hitchcock, C.H.) Andover, 1867.
Phil 6112.1 The relations of mind and brain. (Calderwood, H.) London, 1879.
Phil 6112.1.3 The relations of mind and brain. 3d ed. (Calderwood, H.) London, 1892.
Phil 8583.29 The relations of morality to religion. (De Burgh, William George.) London, 1935.
Phil 5240.6.15 The relations of structural and functional psychology to philosophy. (Angell, J.R.) Chicago, 1903.
Phil 338.17 Der Relationsbegriff. (Höffding, H.) Leipzig, 1922.
Phil 294.5 The relationship...mystical and the sensible world. (Newlyn, Herbert N.) London, 1918.
Phil 8887.122 Relationship and solitude. 1st. American ed. (Munz, Peter.) Middletown, Conn., 1965.
Phil 400.27 Relativer und absoluter Idealismus. (Ebbinghaus, J.) Leipzig, 1910.
Phil 270.31 Relativisierung des Kausalitätsbegriffes. (Mokrzycki, G.) Leipzig, 1922.
Phil 341.22 Relativism, knowledge and faith. (Kaufman, G.D.) Chicago, 1960.
Phil 3850.16.92 Le relativisme philosophique chez G. Simmel. (Mamelet, A.) Paris, 1914.
Phil 5252.49.5 Le relativisme psychologique et la recherche médicale. (Montet, C. de.) Paris, 1926.
Phil 3850.16.100 Il relativismo di G. Simmel e de Pirandello. (Luongo, M.R.) Napoli, 1955?

Phil 400.29.9 Relativismo e idealismo. (Aliotta, A.) Napoli, 1922.
Phil 4060.4.80 Il relativismo sperimentale di Antonio Aliotta nel suo svolgimento storico. (Gentiluomo, Domenico.) Roma, 1955.
Phil 1750.125 Relativisti contemporanei. (Tilgher, A.) Roma, 1923.
Phil 2270.99 Das Relativitätsprincip bei Herbert Spencer. (Pace, E.) Leipzig, 1891.
Phil 5249.24 Relativitätstheorie des Menschengeistes. (Jaeger, Marc A.) Zürich, 1958.
Phil 5374.41 La relativité de la conscience de soi. (Hesnard, A.) Paris, 1924.
Phil 4580.51 La relativité philosophique. (Høffding, Harald.) Paris, 1924.
Phil 8690.4 Relativity and religion. (Anthony, H.D.) London, 1927.
Phil 5246.77.5 Relativity for psychology. (Garan, D.G.) N.Y., 1968.
Phil 6127.23 Relaxation. (Rathbone, J.L.) N.Y., 1943.
Phil 70.10.8 Relazione e cumunicazioni presentate al Congresso Nazionale di Filosofia. (Milan. Universita Cattolica del Sacro Cuore. Faculta di Filosofia.) Milano, 1935. 2v.
Phil 40.12 Relazione e discussione. (Associazione Filosofica Ligure.) Milano. 1951-1952
Phil 575.266 La relazione interpersonale. (Ponzio, Augusto.) Bari, 1967.
Phil 4200.8.30 Relazioni e significati. v.1-2. (Paci, Enzo.) Milano, 1965. 3v.
Phil 6115.29 Release from nervous tension. (Fink, David H.) N.Y., 1943.
Phil 672.170 Release from time. (Plumbe, C.C.) London, 1950.
Phil 2905.1.560 The relevance of Teilhard. (Kraft, Ralph Wayne.) Notre Dame, 1968.
Phil 2340.10.148 The relevance of Whitehead. (Leclerc, Ivor.) London, 1961.
Phil 6315.2.215 Relgis, Eugen. Freud, Freudismo y las verdades sociales [a las cieñanos de su nacimiento, 6 de mayo, 1856-1956]. Montevideo, 1956.
Phil 1750.166.110 Relgis, Eugen. El humanitarismo. Buenos Aires, 1956.
Phil 5357.3 Reliability for the law of comparative judgment. (Gulliksen, Harold.) n.p., 1957. 2 pam.
Phil 5620.31 Reliable knowledge. (Larrabee, H.A.) Boston, 1964.
Phil 6111.50 The relief of pain by mental suggestion. (Batten, L.W.) N.Y., 1917.
Phil 8587.53 De religienze toekomstverwachting. (Heering, H.J.) Amsterdam, 1937.
Phil 8584.21 Religiia, vrag ravnopraviia i druzhby narodov. (Eryshev, A.A.) Kiev, 1962.
Phil 8601.6 Religiia budushchago. (Vilenkin, N.M.) Sankt Peterburg, 1905.
Phil 4756.1.48 Religiia i nauka. (Frank, Semen L.) Posev, 1959.
Phil 4829.896.30 Religija i život. (Zimmermann, Stjepan.) Zagreb, 1938.
Phil 8602.8 Religio chemici. (Wilson, G.) London, 1862.
Phil 8598.45 Religio doctoris; meditations upon life and thought. (Sanders, Frederic W.) Boston, 1913.
NEDL Phil 27.18F The religio-philosophical journal. Chicago. 1-3,1890-1893 3v.
Phil 8592.18 Religio pictoris. (Merriman, H.B.) Boston, 1899.
Phil 8597.22 Religio universalis et naturalis. Paris, 1818.
Phil 2805.115 Das religiös-ethische Ideal Pascals. (Warmuth, K.) Leipzig, 1901.
Phil 1135.29 Die religiös-philosophische Bewegung der Hellenismus. (Neustadt, E.) Leipzig, 1914.
Phil 5627.6.8 Religiös røynsle i sine ymse former. (James, William.) Øslo, 1920.
Phil 5627.266.30 Religiös roll och Kristusliv. (Hartler, Josef.) Lund, 1966.
Phil 5627.6.10 Den religiösa erfarenheten. (James, William.) Stockholm, 1906.
Phil 5627.6.11 Den religiösa erfarenheten. (James, William.) Stockholm, 1923.
Phil 5627.146 Den religiösa funktionen i människosjälen. Akademisk abhandlung. (Alm, Ivar.) Stockholm, 1936.
Phil 8591.39 Det religiösa kunskapsproblemet. (Leufvén, E.) Uppsala, 1914.
Phil 8598.49.5 Det religiösa sanningsproblemet. (Segerstedt, T.K.) Stockholm, 1912.
Phil 3850.18.185 Das religiöse Apriori bei Max Scheler. (Martin-Izquierdo, Honorio.) Bonn, 1964.
Phil 8593.20.2 Religiöse Denker. (Nigg, Walter.) Berlin, 1952.
Phil 8593.20 Religiöse Denker. (Nigg, Walter.) Bern, 1942.
Phil 8520.29 Religiöse Denker der Gegenwart. (Lewkowitz, A.) Berlin, 1923.
Phil 5627.103 Die religiöse Entwicklung der Jugend in der Reifezeit. (Bohne, G.) Leipzig, 1922.
Phil 3805.96 Die Religiöse Entwicklung Schleiermachers. (Wendland, J.) Tübingen, 1915.
Phil 5627.6.12.25 Die religiöse Erfahrung. (James, William.) Leipzig, 1907.
Phil 5627.6.13 Die religiöse Erfahrung. (James, William.) Leipzig, 1914.
Phil 5627.6.12A Religiöse erfaringer. (James, William.) København, 1906.
Phil 2070.35.10 Religiöse erfaringer en undersøgelse af det menneskelige natur. 3e udg. (James, William.) Nørregade, 1919.
Phil 5627.265 Das religiöse Erleben im Spiegel der Bildgestaltung. (Bindl, Maria Frieda.) Freiburg, 1965.
Phil 1050.4.13 Die religiöse Gedankenwelt des Salomo ibn Gabirol. Inaug. Diss. (Dreyer, Kare.) Leipzig, 1928.
Phil 8580.11 Der religiöse Glaube. (Asher, David.) Leipzig, 1860.
Phil 8581.30.4 Die religiöse Glaubenslehre. 4. ed. (Bretschneider, K.G.) Halle, 1846.
Phil 8598.41 Die religiöse Stellung der vornehmsten Denker. (Stern, Adolf.) Berlin, 1911.
Phil 4580.67 Religiöse tanketyper. (Høffding, Harald.) København, 1927.
Phil 8584.5.7 Der religiöse Wahrheitsbegriff in der Philosophie Rudolf Euckens. (Eucken, Rudolf.) Göttingen, 1910.
Phil 5627.112 Der religiöse Wille. 2. Aufl. (Pfennigsdorf, Emil.) Leipzig, 1927.
Phil 8595.58 Religiöser Erkenntnisgrund. (Paus, Ansgar.) Leiden, 1966.
Phil 6968.25 Religiøsitet og sygelige sindstilstande. 3. udg. (Schou, H.J.) København, 1928.
Phil 8593.9 Religiöst apriori. (Nygren, A.) Lund, 1921.
Phil 8583.10A Religion, a criticism and a forecast. (Dickinson, G.L.) N.Y., 1905.
Phil 8591.24 Religion, and the mind of to-day. (Leighton, J.A.) N.Y., 1924.
Phil 8702.28 Religion, art, and science. (MacMurray, John.) Liverpool, 1961.
Phil 8598.136 Religion, culture and society. (Schneider, Louis.) N.Y., 1964.
Phil 5627.196 Religion, healing and health. (Van Buskirk, J.D.) N.Y., 1952.
Phil 8597.52 Religion, humanism. Stockholm, 1942.

Phil 8691.11 La religion, la morale, et la science...quatre conference. 3. éd. (Buisson, F.) Paris, 1904.
Phil 8957.15 Religion, morality, and law. (Harding, A.L.) Dallas, 1956.
Phil 1905.22.10.2A Religion, philosophy and physical research. (Broad, C.D.) London, 1953.
Phil 1905.22.10 Religion, philosophy and physical research. (Broad, C.D.) N.Y., 1953.
Phil 2340.17.30 Religion, politics, and the higher learning. (White, Morton Gabriel.) Cambridge, 1959.
Phil 8701.19 Religion, science, and society in the modern world. (Lindsay, A.D.) New Haven, 1943.
Phil 197.1.10 Religion, Wissenschaft, Kunst und Staat in ihren Gegenseitigen Verhältnissen. (Wagner, J.) Erlangen, 1819.
Phil 8580.17 Religion. (Ames, Edward S.) N.Y., 1929.
Phil 5068.32 Religion. (Beckwith, B.P.) N.Y., 1957.
Phil 8581.100 Die Religion. (Brunner, August.) Freiburg, 1956.
Phil 8583.39 Religion. (Dunlap, Knight.) N.Y., 1946.
Phil 8586.18 Die religion. (Girgensohn, Karl.) Leipzig, 1903.
Phil 8587.8 Die Religion. (Helmersen, A. von.) Graz, 1875.
Phil 8587.13 Die Religion. (Herrmann, W.) Halle, 1879.
Phil 8591.20 La religion. (Loisy, Alfred.) Paris, 1917.
Phil 8594.2 Die Religion. (Opzoomer, C.W.) Elberfeld, 1868.
Phil 8595.4 Die Religion. (Pfleiderer, O.) Leipzig, 1869. 2v.
Phil 8598.33.3 Die Religion. (Simmel, G.) Frankfurt, 1906.
Phil 8601.1 La religion. (Vacherot, E.) Paris, 1869.
Phil 3808.27 Religion: a dialogue. (Schopenhauer, Arthur.) London, 1890.
Phil 5925.2.16 Religion: natural and revealed. 3. ed. (Fowler, O.S.) N.Y., 1844.
Phil 5925.2.16.10 Religion: natural and revealed. 10. ed. (Fowler, O.S.) N.Y., 1848.
Phil 8598.33 Die Religion. 2. Aufl. (Simmel, G.) Frankfurt, 1912.
Phil 8595.4.5 Die Religion. 2. Aufl. v.1-2. (Pfleiderer, O.) Leipzig, 1878.
Phil 8591.20.2 La religion. 2. éd. (Loisy, Alfred.) Paris, 1924.
Phil 8592.50.5 Religion. 2. ed. (Molinari, G. de.) London, 1894.
Phil 8590.4 Religion a curse! Why? (Koenig, Julius.) N.Y., 1915.
Phil 487.2.5 Religion affected by modern materialism. (Martineau, J.) London, 1876-78. 2 pam.
Phil 487.2.6 Religion affected by modern materialism. (Martineau, J.) N.Y., 1875.
Phil 8588.1 La religion al alcance de todos. 5. ed. (Ibarreta, R.H.) Madrid, 1884.
Phil 8588.1.5 La religion al alcance de todos. 35. ed. (Ibarreta, R.H.) Barcelona, 1912.
Phil 2340.11.55 Religion and art. (Weiss, Paul.) Milwaukee, 1963.
Phil 8725.10 Religion and change. (Edwards, David Lawrence.) London, 1969.
Phil 8692.2.4 Religion and chemistry. (Cooke, J.P.) N.Y., 1864.
Phil 8692.2.5 Religion and chemistry. (Cooke, J.P.) N.Y., 1880.
Phil 5627.163 Religion and contemporary psychology. (Pear, T.H.) London, 1937.
Phil 8593.23 Religion and culture. (Neill, T.P.) Milwaukee, 1952.
Phil 960.17 Religiös and dharma. (Noble, M.E.) London, 1915.
Phil 8598.141 Religion and empiricism. (Smith, John Edwin.) Milwaukee, 1967.
Phil 8843.12 Religion and ethics. Thesis. (Sheriff, W.S.) Philadelphia, 1933.
Phil 365.41 Religion and evolution since 1859. Diss. (Mary Frederick, Sister.) Notre Dame, 1934.
Phil 8581.24 Religion and experience. (Brierley, J.) N.Y., 1906.
Phil 8581.40 Religion and free will. (Benett, W.) Oxford, 1913.
Phil 8595.4.13 Religion and historic faiths. (Pfleiderer, O.) N.Y., 1907.
Phil 8581.109 Religion and humanism. (British Broadcasting Corporation.) London, 1964.
Phil 8628.7.5 Religion and immortality. (Dickinson, G.L.) Boston, 1911.
Phil 8628.7 Religion and immortality. (Dickinson, G.L.) London, 1911.
Phil 8672.10 Religion and life;...address by...faculty of Meadville Theological School. Boston, 1909.
Phil 8597.29 Religion and life; the foundations of personal religion. N.Y., 1923.
Phil 179.3.35 Religion and life. (Eucken, R.) N.Y., 1912.
Phil 8598.63 Religion and life. (Selbie, W.B.) Cambridge, 1930.
Phil 6132.4 Religion and medicine. (Worcester, Elwood.) N.Y., 1908.
Phil 6132.5 Religion and medicine. v.1-2,4,6-7. v.3,5 lost. Boston, 1908. 5 pam.
Phil 6117.50 Religion and mental health. (Hofmann, H.) N.Y., 1961.
Phil 8595.12 Religion and mere morality. (Perry, R.B.) Boston, 1906.
Phil 8595.25A Religion and modern life. (Philips Brooks House Association. Harvard University.) N.Y., 1927.
Phil 8586.10.9 Religion and modern thought. (Galloway, G.) Edinburgh, 1922.
Phil 8955.1 Religion and morality. (Fox, J.J.) N.Y., 1899.
Phil 8582.26 Religion and philosophy. (Collingwood, Robin George.) London, 1916.
Phil 3007.2.5 Religion and philosophy in Germany. (Heine, H.) Boston, 1959.
Phil 3007.2 Religion and philosophy in Germany. (Heine, H.) London, 1882.
Phil 8595.60 Religion and rationality. 1. ed. (Penelhum, Terence.) N.Y., 1971.
Phil 8582.51 Religion and reality. (Chaning-Pearce, Melville.) London, 1937.
Phil 8580.4 Religion and science; the letters of "Alpha". (Allen, S.M.) Boston, 1876.
Phil 8689.2 Pamphlet box. Religion and science.
Phil 8696.1 Religion and science. (Gibson, S.T.) London, 1875.
Phil 8697.25 Religion and science. (Habgood, J.S.) London, 1964.
Phil 8697.9 Religion and science. (Hardwick, J.C.) London, 1920.
Phil 8701.18 Religion and science. (Laffey, C.) London, 1940.
Phil 8701.5 Religion and science. (Le Conte, J.) N.Y., 1874.
Phil 8702.9 Religion and science. (Merz, J.T.) Edinburgh, 1915.
Phil 8707.16.5 Religion and science. (Russell, Bertrand Russell.) London, 1968.
Phil 8707.28 Religion and science: conflict and synthesis. (Ramsey, I.T.) London, 1964.
Phil 8689.1 Pamphlet vol. Religion and science. 1874-1926. 32 pam.
Phil 8708.18 Religion and science considered in their historical relations. (Singer, Charles.) N.Y., 1929.
Phil 5627.55.5 Religion and sex. (Cohen, Chapman.) London, 1919.
Phil 5710.6 Religion and temperament. (Stevenson, J.G.) London, 1913.
Phil 8590.20 Religion and the American dream. (Knox, Raymond C.) N.Y., 1934.
Phil 6319.1.57 Religion and the cure of souls in Jung's psychology. (Schär, Hans.) N.Y., 1950.

Phil 8591.36.10   Religion and the issues of life. (Lyman, E.W.)
                   N.Y., 1943.
Phil 8598.100   Religion and the modern mind. 1. ed. (Stace, W.T.)
                   Philadelphia, 1952.
Phil 8583.28.2   Religion and the modern state. (Dawson, Christopher H.)
                   London, 1935.
Phil 8583.28.4   Religion and the modern state. (Dawson, Christopher H.)
                   London, 1936.
Phil 8595.34A   Religion and the modern world. (Pennsylvania. University.
                   Bicentennial Conference.) Philadelphia, 1941.
Phil 5627.125   Religion and the mysterious. (Brabant, F.H.)
                   London, 1930.
Phil 5627.56.5   Religion and the new psychology. (Swisher, Walter.)
                   Boston, 1920.
Phil 8602.52   Religion and the rebel. (Wilson, Colin.) London, 1957.
Phil 645.45   Religion and the rise of scepticism. 1st ed. (Baumer,
                   Franklin.) N.Y., 1960.
Phil 5252.18.35   Religion and the sciences of life. (McDougall, William.)
                   London, 1934.
Phil 8696.26   Religion and the scientific future; reflections on myth,
                   science, and theology. 1. ed. (Gilkey, Langdon Brown.)
                   N.Y., 1970.
Phil 5068.38   Religion and the scientific outlook. (Miles, Thomas R.)
                   London, 1959.
Phil 585.100   Religion and the study of man. (Nef, John U.)
                   Houston, 1961.
Phil 8602.39   Religion and the thought of today. (Webb, c.C.J.)
                   London, 1929.
Phil 5627.140   Religion and woman. (Whitehead, George.) London, 1928.
Phil 8702.7.2   Religion as a credible doctrine. (Mallock, W.H.)
                   N.Y., 1903.
Phil 8592.28   Religion as effected by modern science philosophy.
                   (Mellor, Stanley.) London, 1914.
Phil 8590.10   Religion as life. (King, Henry C.) N.Y., 1913.
Phil 1182.45   La religion astrale des pythagoriciens. (Rongier, Louis.)
                   Paris, 1959.
Phil 8615.10   La religion basée sur la morale. 2. éd. (Hoffmann, P.)
                   Bruxelles, 1901.
Phil 5241.72   The religion called behaviorism. (Berman, Louis.)
                   N.Y., 1927.
Phil 8598.35.15   Religion coming of age. (Sellars, Roy W.) N.Y., 1928.
Phil 4580.115   La réligion conservation de la valeur dans ses
                   rapports avec...H. Høffding. (La Harpe, J.)
                   Lausanne, 1920.
Phil 8586.43.5   La religion considérée comme l'unique base du bonheur et de
                   la véritable philosophie. (Genlis, S.F.)
                   Maestricht, 1787.
Phil 8586.43   La religion considérée comme l'unique base du bonheur et de
                   la véritable philosophie. (Genlis, S.F.) Orleans, 1787.
Phil 8662.6   Religion d'amour ou Dieu existe. (Henri, P.E.)
                   Marseille, 1910.
Phil 3480.71.15   La religion dans les limites de la raison. (Kant,
                   Immanuel.) Paris, 1913.
Phil 3415.62.2   La religion de L'Avenir. (Hartmann, Eduard von.)
                   Paris, 1876.
Phil 3415.62   La religion de L'Avenir. (Hartmann, Eduard von.)
                   Paris, 1877.
Phil 8601.7   La religion de l'évolutionisme. (Vogel, W.)
                   Bruxelles, 1912.
Phil 2730.93   La religion de Maine de Biran. Thèse. (Rostan, E.)
                   Paris, 1890.
Phil 3010.15   Die Religion der Goethezeit. (Krueger, Gustav.)
                   Tübingen, 1931.
Phil 8615.1.5   Der Religion der Moral. (Salter, W.M.) Leipzig, 1885.
Phil 3415.60   Die Religion des Geistes. (Hartmann, Eduard von.)
                   Berlin, 1882.
Phil 510.13   Die Religion des Monismus. (Lipsius, Friedrich R.)
                   Berlin, 1907.
Phil 3940.4   Die Religion des Philosoph und sein Glaubenskenntniss.
                   (Zwanziger, Johann Christian.) Bruxelles, 1968.
Phil 8597.4   Die Religion des Zweiflers. Leipzig, 1874.
Phil 8581.68.5   Religion et critique. 3. éd. (Broglie, Paul.)
                   Paris, 1906.
Phil 5627.61   La religion et la foi. (Delacroix, H.) Paris, 1922.
Phil 8594.11   La religion et la vie de l'esprit. (Oltramare, P.)
                   Paris, 1925.
Phil 8591.20.9   Religion et l'humanité. (Loisy, Alfred.) Paris, 1926.
Phil 525.170   Religion et mysticisme. (Bordet, Louis.) Paris, 1959.
Phil 8587.34.2   Religion et réalité. Thèse. (Hauter, Charles.)
                   Strasbourg, 1922.
Phil 8585.33   Religion et théologie. (Fornerod, A.) Lausanne, 1932.
Phil 8601.9   Religion for all mankind. (Voysey, C.) London, 1903.
Phil 8581.78   Religion for free minds. (Bixler, J.S.) N.Y., 1939.
Phil 8583.9.10   A religion for the new day. (Dole, Charles F.)
                   N.Y., 1920.
Phil 8693.20.5   Religion im Lichte der heutigen Naturwissenschaft. 3. Aufl.
                   (Dessauer, F.) Frankfurt, 1952.
Phil 8598.68   Religion in a changing world. (Silver, Abba H.)
                   N.Y., 1930.
Phil 2055.13.35   Religion in a free society. (Hook, Sidney.)
                   Lincoln, 1967.
Phil 8702.34   Religion in a technical age. (Miller, Samuel Howard.)
                   Cambridge, 1968.
Phil 8589.7   Religion in evolution. (Jevons, Frank B.) London, 1906.
Phil 8587.45   Die Religion in ihrer dogmatischen und ihrer reinen Form.
                   (Hamburger, Leo.) München, 1930.
Phil 8585.50   Religion in philosophical and cultural perspective.
                   (Feaver, J. Clayton.) Princeton, 1967.
Phil 8696.17   Religion in science and civilization. (Gregory, R.A.)
                   London, 1940.
Phil 8602.33A   Religion in the making. (Whitehead, A.N.) N.Y., 1926.
Phil 8602.33.2   Religion in the making. (Whitehead, A.N.) N.Y., 1926.
Phil 8602.33.5   Religion in the making. (Whitehead, A.N.) N.Y., 1927.
Phil 8602.33.10   Religion in the making. (Whitehead, A.N.)
                   N.Y., 1960[1954]
Phil 2070.126   Religion in the philosophy of William James. (Bixler,
                   Julius S.) Boston, 1926.
Phil 5627.149   Religion in transition. (Ferm, V.) London, 1937.
Phil 8593.8.2   Religion inneralb der Grenzen. (Natorp, Paul.)
                   Tübingen, 1908.
Phil 3480.71.2   Die Religion innerhalb der Grenzen der blossen Vernunft.
                   (Kant, Immanuel.) Königsberg, 1784.
Htn Phil 3480.70.75* Die Religion innerhalb der Grenzen der blossen Vernunft.
                   (Kant, Immanuel.) Königsberg, 1793.
Htn Phil 3480.71.2.5* Die Religion innerhalb der Grenzen der blossen Vernunft.
                   (Kant, Immanuel.) Frankfurt, 1793.
Htn Phil 3480.71.2.6* Die Religion innerhalb der Grenzen der blossen Vernunft.
                   (Kant, Immanuel.) Frankfurt, 1793.

Phil 3480.71.2.7   Die Religion innerhalb der Grenzen der blossen Vernunft.
                   (Kant, Immanuel.) Frankfurt, 1794.
Phil 3480.71.13   Die Religion innerhalb der Grenzen der blossen Vernunft.
                   (Kant, Immanuel.) Hamburg, 1966.
Phil 3480.71.10   Die Religion innerhalb der Grenzen der blossen Vernunft. 2.
                   Aufl. (Kant, Immanuel.) Leipzig, 1875.
Phil 3480.71.4   Die Religion innerhalb der Grenzen der blossen Vernunft. 4.
                   Aufl. (Kant, Immanuel.) Leipzig, 1919.
Phil 3480.71.12   Die Religion innerhalb der Grenzen der blossen Vernunft. 5.
                   Aufl. (Kant, Immanuel.) Leipzig, 1937.
Phil 1865.66   La religion naturelle...d'apres les papiers de J. Bentham.
                   (Bentham, Jeremy.) Paris, 1875.
Phil 8598.10   La religion naturelle. 3. éd. (Simon, J.) Paris, 1857.
Phil 4610.7.15   Religion och tanke. (Norström, V.) Stockholm, 1912.
Phil 2270.134   Religion och vetenskap...Spencers. Diss. (Arfvidsson,
                   H.D.) Lund, 1894.
Phil 8591.29   Religion och vetenskap. (Lönborg, Sven.) Stockholm, 1914.
Phil 8591.13   The religion of a literary man. (LeGallienne, R.)
                   N.Y., 1893.
Phil 3210.77   Religion of a scientist. (Fechner, G.T.) N.Y., 1946.
Phil 8585.18   The religion of democracy. (Ferguson, G.) N.Y., 1900.
Phil 8615.5   The religion of duty. (Adler, Felix.) N.Y., 1905.
Phil 8587.17   The religion of geology...connected sciences. (Hitchcock,
                   E.) Boston, 1851.
Phil 600.3   Religion of humanity. (Balfour, A.T.) Edinburgh, 1888.
Phil 600.3.2   Religion of humanity. (Balfour, A.T.) London, 1888.
Phil 8585.16   The religion of humanity. (Frothingham, O.B.) N.Y., 1873.
Phil 8580.20   The religion of love. (Alexander, Mikhailovich.)
                   N.Y., 1929.
Phil 8709.8   Religion of man and ethics of science. (Tuttle, Hudson.)
                   Chicago, 1902.
Phil 7054.80   The religion of manhood. (Robinson, J.H.) Boston, 1854.
Phil 8597.15   The religion of nature. (Robinson, E.K.) London, 1906.
Htn Phil 2340.5.30* The religion of nature. (Wollaston, William.)
                   London, 1725.
Phil 8602.11   The religion of nature delineated. (Wollaston, W.)
                   London, 1724.
Htn Phil 8602.11.2.5* The religion of nature delineated. (Wollaston, W.)
                   London, 1724.
Htn Phil 8602.11.7* The religion of nature delineated. (Wollaston, W.)
                   London, 1725.
Htn Phil 8602.11.3* The religion of nature delineated. (Wollaston, W.)
                   London, 1726.
Htn Phil 8602.11.4* The religion of nature delineated. (Wollaston, W.)
                   London, 1738.
Phil 8602.11.5   The religion of nature delineated. (Wollaston, W.)
                   London, 1759.
Phil 8583.40   The religion of philosophers. (Dunham, J.H.)
                   Philadelphia, 1947.
Phil 8595.3   The religion of philosophy. (Perrin, R.S.) N.Y., 1885.
Phil 3160.3.89   Religion of reason. (Rosmarin, T.W. (Mrs.).) N.Y., 1936.
Phil 8692.10.15   The religion of science. (Carus, Paul.) Chicago, 1893.
Phil 8701.4.50   The religion of Sir Oliver Lodge. (McCabe, Joseph.)
                   London, 1914.
Phil 8581.81A   The religion of solidarity. (Bellamy, E.) Yellow
                   Springs, 1940.
Phil 8595.30F   The religion of the beautiful. (Persons, Lee C.)
                   Miami, 1932?
Phil 8615.11   The religion of the "ethical culture societies." (Gannett,
                   W.C.) Chicago, 1885.
Phil 8584.7   The religion of the future. (Eliot, C.W.) Berlin, 1909.
Phil 8584.7.5   The religion of the future. (Eliot, C.W.) Boston, 1935.
Phil 3415.63   The religion of the future. (Hartmann, Eduard von.)
                   London, 1886.
Phil 7054.48   The religion of the future. (Weil, Samuel.) Boston, 1894.
Phil 8597.30   The religion of the future and other essays. London, 1911.
Phil 494.3   The religion of the modern scientist. (Tromp, Salco U.)
                   Leiden, 1947.
Phil 8610.913.20   The religion of the open mind. (Whyte, A.G.)
                   London, 1913.
Phil 178.12.43   The religion of the spirit in modern life. (Dresser, H.W.)
                   N.Y., 1914.
Phil 8597.18   Religion of the spiritual evolution of man. Chicago, 1910.
Phil 8585.3.2   The religion of the universe. (Fellowes, R.)
                   London, 1836.
Phil 8585.3   The religion of the universe. (Fellowes, R.)
                   London, 1836.
Phil 8685.11   The religion of the universe. (Picton, J.A.)
                   London, 1904.
Phil 8586.31   The religion of thirty great thinkers. (Gehring, Albert.)
                   Boston, 1925.
Phil 8610.925.10   The religion of to-morrow...correspondence between H.H.
                   Powers and William Archer. (Powers, H.H.) London, 1925.
Phil 8581.85   Religion of tomorrow. (Boodin, J.E.) N.Y., 1943.
Phil 8961.10   Religion og ethik. (Lachmann, J.J.) Kjobenhavn, 1897.
Phil 8587.39   Religion og moral. 2. oplag. (Heiberg, J.L.)
                   Kjobenhavn, 1911.
Phil 8602.77   Religion ohne Entscheidung. 2. Aufl. (Woelber, Hans I.)
                   Göttingen, 1960.
Phil 8597.5   Religion one, even the self-same thing in all ages.
                   London, 1741.
Phil 8583.21   Religion or God? (Drown, E.S.) Cambridge, 1927.
Phil 9528.6   Religion outlines for colleges. (Cooper, John M.)
                   Washington, D.C., 1928.
Phil 8691.32   Religion ponders science. 1. ed. (Booth, E.P.)
                   N.Y., 1964.
Phil 8601.10   Religion rationalized. (Vrooman, H.) Philadelphia, 1910.
Phil 8591.25.2   Une religion rationnelle et laïque. 2. éd. (Lévy, L.G.)
                   Dijon, 1904.
Phil 8591.40   Religion says you can. (Lupton, D.) Boston, 1938.
Phil 8581.1   Religion scientifique de l'humanité. (Barthel, N.)
                   Paris, 1859.
Phil 2270.106   La religion selon Herbert Spencer. (Boutroux, É.)
                   Paris, 1905.
Phil 4610.7.25   Religion och Gedanke. (Norström, V.) Lund, 1932.
Phil 8520.23   Die Religion und ihre Grundwahrheiten in der deutschen
                   Philosophie seit Leibniz. (Straubinger, H.)
                   Freiburg, 1919.
Phil 5627.170   Religion und Individualpsychologie. (Jahn, Ernst.)
                   Wien, 1933.
Phil 8967.8   Religion und Leben. (Rademacher, A.) Freiburg, 1926.
Phil 8953.4   Religion und Moral. (Dyroff, A.) Berlin, 1925.
Phil 8897.70   Religion und Moral. (Winternitz, M.) Prag, 1922.
Phil 190.53.10   Religion und Naturwissenschaft. (Planck, Max.)
                   Leipzig, 1938.
Phil 8586.54   Religion und Offenbarung. (Guardini, Romano.)
                   Würzburg, 1958.

Phil 3120.2.97   Religion und Offenbarung in der Religionsphilosophie Bernard Bolzanos. (Winter, E.) Breslau, 1932.

Phil 3120.8.35   Religion und Philosophie. (Brentano, Franz.) Bern, 1954.

Phil 3245.55   Religion und Philosophie. (Fichte, Immanuel Hermann.) Heidelberg, 1834.

Phil 8595.4.12   Religion und Religionen. (Pfleiderer, O.) München, 1906.

Phil 3805.101   Religion und Religionen bei Schleiermacher und Hegel. (Vowinckel, Ernst.) Erlangen, 1896.

Phil 6319.1.184   Religion und Seele in der Psychologie C.G. Jung. (Schär, Hans.) Zürich, 1946.

Phil 6331.3   Religion und Seelenleiden. v. 1,2,3,6. (Verband der Vereine Katholischer Akademiker, Kevalaer.) Düsseldorf, 1926. 4v.

Phil 2262.60.2   Religion und Tugend. (Shaftesbury, A.A.C.) Leipzig, 1905.

Phil 5238.60   Religion und wissenschaftliches Heilverfahren. (Johnston, D.K.) Bahn, 1925. 7 pam.

Phil 2490.58.5   Religión universal, el amor por principio. (Comte, Auguste.) Santiago de Chile, 1944.

Phil 2490.58   La religión universal. (Comte, Auguste.) Santiago de Chile, 1938.

Phil 3480.71.5   Religion within the boundary of Pure reason. (Kant, Immanuel.) Edinburgh, 1838.

Phil 3480.71.7   Religion within the limits of reason alone. (Kant, Immanuel.) Chicago, 1934.

Phil 3480.71.8   Religion within the limits of reason alone. 2sd ed. (Kant, Immanuel.) La Salle, 1960.

Phil 8587.48   Religion without revelation. (Huxley, J.S.) N.Y., 1927.

Phil 8587.48.2   Religion without revelation. (Huxley, J.S.) N.Y., 1957.

Phil 8582.19   The religion worth having. (Carver, T.N.) Boston, 1912.

Phil 8582.19.2A   The religion worth having. (Carver, T.N.) Boston, 1912.

Phil 8582.19.5   The religion worth having. (Carver, T.N.) Los Angeles, 1940.

Phil 8597.27   Religione, materialismo, socialismo. (Rignano, Eugenio.) Bologna, 1920.

Phil 8582.47   Religione, teosofia e filosofia. (Caramella, S.) Messina, 1931.

Phil 8580.35   La religione. (Abbagnano, N.) Torino, 1961.

Phil 8702.26   Religione. (Masi, R.) Brescia, 1958.

Phil 4120.4.126   La religione: il modernismo e i rapporti tra religione e filosofia. (Gentile, Giovanni.) Firenze, 1965.

Phil 8582.72   La religione come struttura e come modo autonomo della coscienza. (Caracciolo, Alberto.) Milano, 1965.

Phil 8598.65.5   La religione d'oggi. (Sorel, G.) Lanciani, 1911.

Phil 8582.38   Religione e filosofia. (Chiocchetti, E.) Milano, 1921.

Phil 8951.10   Religione e morale, scritti varii. (Bindi, Enrico.) Firenze, 1904.

Phil 8696.10   Religione e scienza. (Gemelli, Agostino.) Milano, 1920.

Phil 8702.17   Religione e scienza. (Maria, R. de.) Palermo, 1936.

Phil 8591.86   Religione e vita. (Libizzi, Carmelo.) Padova, 1966.

Phil 4170.10.85   Religione ed educazione nell'idealismo trascendente di Piero Martinetti. (Pellegrino, U.) Brescia, 1956.

Phil 4080.3.440   La religione in Benedetto Croce. (Capanna, Francesco.) Bari, 1964.

Phil 8591.19   La religione nella vita dello spirito. (Lamanna, E.P.) Firenze, 1914.

Phil 8581.45.10   La religione nella vito dello spirito. (Buonaiuti, Ernesto.) Roma, 1926.

Phil 8585.55   La religione nell'esperienza umana. (Faggiotto, Agostino.) Padova, 1967.

Phil 8598.135   Die Religion als Thema der Theologie. (Schlette, Heinz Robert.) Freiburg, 1963.

Phil 3425.60.19   Die Religionen der geistigen Individualität. (Hegel, Georg Wilhelm Friedrich.) Leipzig, 1927.

Phil 8591.26   Religionen och nutidsmänniskan. (Lambek, C.) Stockholm, 1924.

Phil 5627.259.15   Religionen och rollerna. (Sundén, Hjalmar.) Stockholm, 1959.

Phil 5627.264.5   Religions, values and peak-experiences. (Maslow, Abraham Harold.) Columbus, Ohio, 1964.

Phil 8592.22   Das religions- und Weltproblem. 2. Aufl. (Mach, Franz.) Dresden, 1904. 2v.

Phil 3425.263   Der Religions begriff Hegel's. (Noack, Ludwig.) Darmstadt, 1845.

Phil 8647.3   Religions of the world and the world religion. (Warren, William F.) N.Y., 1911.

Phil 8520.24   Religions Philosophie. (Wobbermin, G.) Berlin, 1924.

Phil 8598.92   Religions-Philosophie auf geschichtlicher Grundlage. (Spann, Othmar.) Wien, 1947.

Phil 1504.4.4   Die religions-philosophische Lehre. v.4., pt.4. (Engelkemper, W.) Münster, 1903.

Phil 2115.161   Die religions philosophischen lehren Lockes. (Crons, E.) Halle, 1910.

Phil 3850.18.109   Religionsbegründung: Max Scheler, J.H. Neuman. (Przywara, Erich.) Freiburg, 1923.

Phil 8587.66   Religionsfilosofi. (Hägerström, A.A.T.) Stockholm, 1949.

Phil 8590.13.5   Religionsfilosofi. (Krarup, F.C.) København, 1921.

Phil 8598.48   Religionsfilosofi. (Svensson, P.K.) Lund, 1904.

Phil 4580.38.20   Religionsfilosofi. 3e ed. (Høffding, Harald.) København, 1924.

Phil 3801.837   Die religionsgeschichtliche Konstruktive in Schellings positiver Philosophie. (Tillich, Paul.) Breslau, 1910.

Phil 3497.10   Die Religionslehre Kants. (Pünjer, G.C.) Jena, 1874.

Phil 3195.8.85   Der Religionsphilosoph Georg F. Daumer. Inaug. Diss. (Kühne, A.) Berlin, 1936.

Phil 8583.19   Religionsphilosophie. (Dunkmann, D.K.) Gütersloh, 1917.

Phil 8590.15.5   Religionsphilosophie. (Kesseler, Kurt.) Leipzig, 1927.

Phil 8594.1   Religionsphilosophie. (Ohlert, A.L.J.) Leipzig, 1835.

Phil 8595.4.2   Religionsphilosophie. (Pfleiderer, O.) Berlin, 1878.

Phil 8597.31   Religionsphilosophie. (Richter, R.) Leipzig, 1912.

Phil 8598.52   Religionsphilosophie. (Steffes, J.P.) München, 1925.

Phil 8599.13   Religionsphilosophie. (Teichmüller, Gustav.) Breslau, 1886.

Phil 8587.65   Religionsphilosophie. v.1-2. (Hessen, Johannes.) Essen, 1948.

Phil 8584.3   Religionsphilosophie. v.1-3. (Eschenmayer, C.A.) Tübingen, 1818-24. 2v.

Phil 8595.4.2.2   Religionsphilosophie. 2. Aufl. (Pfleiderer, O.) Berlin, 1883-84. 2v.

Phil 8597.32.5   Religionsphilosophie. 2. Aufl. (Raμwenhoff, D.L.W.E.) Braunschweig, 1894.

Phil 8587.65.5   Religionsphilosophie. 2. Aufl. v.1-2. (Hessen, Johannes.) München, 1955.

Phil 8595.4.3   Religionsphilosophie. 3. Aufl. (Pfleiderer, O.) Berlin, 1896.

Phil 8598.92.2   Religionsphilosophie auf geschichtlicher Grundlage. 2. Aufl. (Spann, Othmar.) Graz, 1970.

Phil 8581.38   Religionsphilosophie auf modernwissenschaftlicher Grundlage. (Baumann, J.) Leipzig, 1886.

Phil 8669.3.29   Die Religionsphilosophie bei Rudolf Otto. Inaug. Diss. (Seifert, P.) Dusseldorf, 1936.

Phil 8520.15   Die Religionsphilosophie der fichteschen Schule. (Richter, Johannes.) Berlin, 1931.

Phil 8597.60.2   Religionsphilosophie der Kultur. 2. Aufl. (Radbruch, Gustav.) Darmstadt, 1968.

Phil 3195.1.81   Religionsphilosophie der Schule Herbarts, Drobisch und Hartenstein. (Flügel, Otto.) Langensalza, 1905.

Phil 8598.50   Die Religionsphilosophie des Als-Ob. (Scholz, H.) Leipzig, 1921.

Phil 3425.540   Die Religionsphilosophie des Jüngen Hegel. (Wolf, Kurt.) München, 1960.

Phil 8520.21.2   Die Religionsphilosophie des Neukantianismus. 2. Aufl. (Hessen, J.) Freiburg, 1924.

Phil 8599.13.80   Die Religionsphilosophie Gustav Teichmüllers. (Posselt, H.) Marburg, 1960.

Phil 3425.274   Die Religionsphilosophie Hegels. (Ott, Emil.) Berlin, 1904.

Phil 8598.39   Religionsphilosophie im Umriss. (Seydel, Rudolf.) Freiburg, 1893.

Phil 8550.388   Die Religionsphilosophie in Deutschland in ihren gegenwärtigen Hauptvertretern. (Siebert, Otto.) Langensalza, 1906.

Phil 3483.53   Die Religionsphilosophie Kants. (Bohatec, J.) Hamburg, 1938.

Phil 3500.34   Die Religionsphilosophie Kants. (Schweitzer, Albert.) Freiburg, 1899.

Phil 3925.9.90   Die Religionsphilosophie Karl Werners. Inaug. Diss. (Becker, J.) Bonn, 1935.

Phil 3850.18.83   Die Religionsphilosophie Max Schelers. Inaug. Diss. (Kreppel, F.) München, 1926.

Phil 8598.102   Religionsphilosophie mit Theodizee. 2. Aufl. (Straubinger, H.) Freiburg, 1949.

Phil 4769.1.102.5   Das religionsphilosophische System Vladimir Solowjews. (Müller, Ludolf.) Berlin, 1956.

Phil 3890.1.83   Die religionsphilosophischen Anschauungen Trendelenburg's. (Orphal, H.) Eisleben, 1891.

Phil 8592.43   Die religionsphilosophischen Elemente in J. David Michaelis' Dogmatik. Diss. (Hinrichs, B.) Göttingen, 1911.

Phil 4073.87   Die religionsphilosophischen Grundanschauungen des Thomas Campanella. Inaug. Diss. (Sante Felici, G.) Halle, 1887.

Phil 5627.100   Religionspsychologie. (Bruehn, W.) Breslau, 1926.

Phil 5627.265.5   Religionspsychologie. (Pöll, Wilhelm.) München, 1965.

Phil 27.23   Religionspsychologie. Wien. 1-12,1926-1952 2v.

Phil 5627.230   Religionspsychopathologische Untersuchungen. (Koerner, Margot.) Mainz, 1959.

Phil 5627.150   Religionspsykologi. (Fuglsang-Damgaard, H.) København, 1933.

Phil 8599.19.107   Religionssoziologische Grundbegriffe bei Troeltsch. (Spaleck, G.) Bleichersde, 1937.

Phil 6329.7   Die Religionstheorie der Psychoanalyse. Diss. (Trog, H.) Hamburg, 1934.

Phil 8599.19.90   Die Religionstheorie von Ernst Troeltsch. (Spiess, Emil.) Paderborn, 1927.

Phil 8643.18.2   Der religiose Unsterblichkeitsglaube. 2. Aufl. (Steinmann, Theophil.) Göttingen, 1912.

Phil 4260.124.10   La religiosità di Giambattista Vico. (Nicolini, F.) Bari, 1949.

Phil 3805.240   Religiosität und Bildung. Thesis. (Wintsch, Hans Ulrich.) Zürich, 1967.

Phil 6325.1.25   Religiosität und Hysterie. (Pfister, Oskar.) Leipzig, 1928.

Phil 8610.929.35   The religious advance toward rationalism, delivered at Conway Hall on Sept. 25, 1929. (Housman, L.) London, 1929.

Phil 8725.12   The religious and the secular. (Martin, David.) London, 1969.

Htn   Phil 192.16.5*   Religious aspect of philosophy. (Royce, Josiah.) Boston, 1885.

NEDL   Phil 192.16A   Religious aspect of philosophy. (Royce, Josiah.) Boston, 1885. (Changed to KD 55178)

Phil 960.6   Religious aspects of Hindu philosophy. (Mullens, J.) London, 1860.

Phil 2340.10.102   The religious availability of Whitehead's God. (Ely, Stephen Lee.) Madison, 1942.

Phil 5627.258   Religious behavior. (Argyle, Michael.) London, 1958.

Phil 5627.128   Religious behavior. (Trout, David McC.) N.Y., 1931.

Phil 8592.110   Religious belief. (Martin, C.B.) Ithaca, N.Y., 1959.

Phil 8580.38   Religious belief and philosophical thought. (Alston, William P.) N.Y., 1963.

Phil 8597.16   The religious conception of the world. (Rogers, A.K.) N.Y., 1907.

Phil 5627.31   Religious confessions and confessants. (Burr, Anna Robeson.) Boston, 1914.

Phil 5627.56   The religious consciousness. (Pratt, James B.) N.Y., 1920.

Phil 5627.56.3A   The religious consciousness. (Pratt, James B.) N.Y., 1927.

Phil 8575.12   Religious controversies of the nineteenth century: selected documents. (Cockshut, Anthony Oliver John.) London, 1966.

Phil 5627.107   Religious conversion. (Sanctis, S. de.) London, 1927.

Phil 8599.32   Religious corssroads. (Tsanoff, R.A.) N.Y., 1942.

Phil 9163.1   Religious courtship. (De Foe, D.) London, 1762.

Phil 8582.35.15   The religious demands of the age. (Cobbe, F.P.) Boston, 1863.

Phil 5627.115   The religious development of adolescents. (Kupky, Oscar.) N.Y., 1928.

Phil 3425.650   The religious dimension in Hegel's thought. (Fackenheim, Emil L.) Bloomington, Ind., 1968[1967]

Phil 5627.172   Religious experience; a public lecture. (Webb, Clement C.J.) London, 1945.

Phil 5627.93   Religious experience; its nature and truth. (Edward, Kenneth.) Edinburgh, 1926.

Phil 8712.17   Religious experience and scientific method. (Wieman, H.N.) N.Y., 1926.

Phil 8505.10   Religious experience and truth. (New York University. Institute of Philosophy.) N.Y., 1961.

Phil 8622.8   Religious faith, language, and knowledge. (Kimpel, B.F.) N.Y., 1952.

Phil 8589.13   Religious foundations. (Jones, R.M.) N.Y., 1923.

Phil 3549.11   The religious function of imagination. (Kroner, Richard.) New Haven, 1941.

Phil 5627.83   Religious genius. (Swetenham, L.) London, 1905.

Phil 8430.8.5   The religious influence of art. (Carpenter, Edward.) Cambridge, 1870.

Phil 8602.35.10   Religious inquiry; some explorations. (Wieman, Henry Nelson.) Boston, 1968.

Phil 5520.575 Religious language and problem of religious knowledge. (Santoni, Ronald E.) Bloomington, 1968.
Phil 8587.44.10 Religious living. (Harkness, George E.) N.Y., 1937.
Phil 5627.266.6 The religious man. (Vergote, Antoine.) Dublin, 1969.
Phil 3415.67 Religious metaphysics. (Hartmann, Eduard von.) N.Y., 1883.
Phil 9010.29 Religious novels; an argument against their use. 2d ed. (Andrews, Charles W.) N.Y., 1856.
Phil 2115.100.5 The religious opinions of John Locke. (Worcester, E.E.) Geneva, N.Y., 1889.
Phil 2115.100 The religious opinions of John Locke. Thesis. (Worcester, E.E.) Geneva, N.Y., 1889.
NEDL Phil 8593.5 The religious philosopher. (Nieuwentyt, B.) London, 1719. 3v.
Phil 8593.5.2 The religious philosopher. (Nieuwentyt, B.) London, 1730. 3v.
Phil 8602.46.5A Religious philosophy. (Wolfson, H.A.) Cambridge, 1961.
Phil 8587.32.91 The religious philosophy of Baron F. von Hügel. (Lester-Garland, L.V.) N.Y., 1933.
Phil 2250.62 The religious philosophy of Josiah Royce. (Royce, Josiah.) Syracuse, 1952.
Phil 1170.15 Religious Platonism. (Feibleman, James.) London, 1959.
Phil 5627.01 Pamphlet box. Religious psychology.
Phil 5627.05 Pamphlet box. Religious psychology. German dissertations.
Phil 8592.48 Religious realism. (Macintosh, D.C.) N.Y., 1931.
Phil 8598.31 The religious revolution of to-day. (Shotwell, James T.) Boston, 1913.
Phil 8581.12 The religious sentiment. (Brinton, D.G.) N.Y., 1876.
Phil 8667.30 The religious significance of atheism. (MacIntyre, Alasdair C.) N.Y., 1969.
Phil 8582.49 Religious thought in the eighteenth century. (Creed, J.M.) Cambridge, Eng., 1934.
Phil 8575.14 Religious thought in the nineteenth century. (Reardon, Bernard M.G.) Cambridge, Eng., 1966.
Phil 8587.17.5 Religious truth. (Hitchcock, E.) Boston, 1857.
Phil 8597.23 Religious values and intellectual consistency. (Reisner, Edward H.) N.Y., 1915.
Phil 8520.70 Religioznaia kartina mira i ee bogoslovskaia modernizatsiia. (Kryvelev, Iosif A.) Moskva, 1968.
Phil 4759.1.30 Religioznyi smysl filosofii. (Il'in, I.A.) Paris,, n.d.
Phil 3110.180 Das reliqiöse Problem der Gegenwart bei Jakob Böhme. (Baden, Hans J.) Leipzig, 1939.
Phil 8586.44 Reliquiae. (Guisan, René.) Lausanne, 1535.
Phil 7159.260 The reluctant prophet. 1st ed. (Logan, Daniel.) Garden City, N.Y., 1968.
Phil 2120.1.80 Remacle, G. La philosophie de S.S. Laurie. Bruxelles, 1909.
Htn Phil 3110.15* Remainder of books. (Böhme, J.) London, 1662.
Htn Phil 1850.18* Remaines, being essayes and severall letters. (Bacon, Francis.) London, 1648.
Phil 6111.30 Remaking a man...mental refitting. (Baylor, Courtenay.) N.Y., 1919.
Phil 5627.134.32 Remaking the world. (Buchman, Frank.) London, 1961.
Phil 5627.134.33 Remaking the world. (Buchman, Frank.) N.Y., 1949.
Phil 5752.2.15 Remark on philosophical inquiry...human liberty. (Clarke, S.) London, 1717. 2 pam.
Phil 7060.90.11 Remarkable apparitions and ghost-stories. (Day, Clarence S.) N.Y., 1848.
Phil 5627.84 Remarkable vision and death bed experience of Ada Park. (Park, M.) Pulaski, N.Y., 1882.
Htn Phil 2520.131* Remarks on...new philosophy of Descartes. (Howard, E.) London, 1701.
Htn Phil 2128.80.2* Remarks on...the fable of the bees. (Law, William.) Cambridge, 1844.
Phil 2128.80 Remarks on...the fable of the bees. (Law, William.) Cambridge, 1844.
Phil 2128.80.5 Remarks on...the fable of the bees. (Law, William.) London, 1724.
Htn Phil 8434.2* Remarks on forest scenery, and other woodland views. (Gilpin, W.) London, 1791. 2v.
Phil 8434.2.10 Remarks on forest scenery, and other woodland views. 3. ed. (Gilpin, W.) London, 1808. 2v.
Phil 5059.1 Remarks on mathematical or demonstrative reasoning. (Tagart, Edward.) London, 1837.
Phil 6674.3 Remarks on mesmerism in 1845. (Estlin, John B.) London, 1845.
Phil 342.16 Remarks on the classification of the different branches of human knowledge. (Lubboch, J.W.) London, 1838.
Phil 3925.16.4 Remarks on the foundations of mathematics. (Wittgenstein, Ludwig.) Oxford, 1956.
Phil 3925.16.5 Remarks on the foundations of mathematics. (Wittgenstein, Ludwig.) Oxford, 1964.
Phil 6111.5 Remarks on the influence of mental cultivation upon health. (Brigham, Amariah.) Hartford, 1832.
Phil 6111.5.2 Remarks on the influence of mental cultivation upon health. (Brigham, Amariah.) Boston, 1833.
Phil 8707.6 Remarks on the religious sentiments of...eminent laymen. London, 1790. 2 pam.
Phil 2205.80.5 Remarks on the theory of morals in which is contained an examination of the theoretical part of Dr. Paley's Principles of moral and political philosophy. (Pearson, Edward.) Ipswich, 1800.
Phil 8595.15.65 Remarks on the 1st part of book entitled "The age of reason." 2. ed. (Drew, Samuel.) N.Y., 1831.
Htn Phil 8610.713.20* Remarks upon a late discourse of free-thinking. (Bentley, Richard.) London, 1713. 3 pam.
Phil 8610.713.30 Remarks upon a late discourse of free-thinking. pt.3. 8th ed. (Bentley, Richard.) Cambridge, Eng., 1743.
Htn Phil 2115.129* Remarks upon an essay concerning humane understanding. (Burnet, Thomas.) London, 1697. 3 pam.
Phil 1145.15 Remarks upon Aristotelian and Platonic ethics. (Oakeley, Frederick.) Oxford, 1848.
Phil 510.14 Remarques sur la monadologie. (Milliet, J. Paul.) Paris, 1907.
Phil 5125.16 Remarques sur la probabilité de inductions. Thèse. (Poirier, René.) Paris, 1931.
Phil 8597.3.11 Remarus, Johann Albert Heinrich. Über die Gründe der menschlichen Erkenntnis und der natürlichen Religion. Bruxelles, 1968.
Phil 4195.95 Remé, Richard W. Darstellung des Inhalts der Disputationes in astrologiam. Hamburg, 1933.
Phil 5545.174.5 Remembering. (Bartlett, F.C.) Cambridge, Eng., 1964.
Phil 5545.174 Remembering. (Bartlett, F.C.) N.Y., 1932.
Phil 5545.155 Remembering and forgetting. (Pear, T.H.) London, 1922.
Phil 3499.15 Remer, G.L. Kant's Theorie der reinmoralischen Religion. Rega, 1796.
Phil 7068.84.10 Reminiscences and memories of Henry Thomas Butterworth and Nancy Irvin Wales. Lebanon, Ohio, 1886.

Phil 5938.7.15 Reminiscences of Dr. Spurzheim and George Combe. (Capen, N.) N.Y., 1881.
Phil 298.18 Remits, E. The law in nature and anxiety-superior. Ottawa, 1962.
Phil 298.18.5 Remits, E. The law in nature and the dynamics of openness. Ottawa, 1965.
Phil 5421.10 Remits, Ernest L. The feeling of superiority and anxiety-superior. Ottawa, 1955.
Phil 5257.20 Rémond, A. Recherches expérimentales sur la durée des actes psychiques les plus simples et sur la vitesse des courants. Paris, 1888.
Phil 8412.10.80 Remos, y Rubio, J.J. Las ideas estéticas de Lipps. Habana, 1925.
Phil 5590.150 Remplein, Heinz. Psychologie der Persönlichkeit. München, 1954.
Phil 5590.150.5 Remplein, Heinz. Psychologie der Persönlichkeit. 5. Aufl. München, 1965.
Phil 9575.6 Remsen, D.S. Post-Mortem use of wealth. N.Y., 1911.
Phil 3017.1 Rémusat, C. de. De la philosophie allemande. Paris, 1845.
Phil 192.8 Remusat, C. de. Essais de philosophie. Paris, 1842. 2v.
Phil 1817.1 Rémusat, C.F. Histoire de la philosophie en Angleterre. Paris, 1875. 2v.
Phil 8520.6 Rémusat, C.F.M. Philosophie religieuse de la théologie naturelle. Paris, 1864.
Phil 4265.2.93 Rémusat, Charles. Il padre Ventura e la filosofia. Milano, 1853.
Phil 4265.2.94 Rémusat, Charles. Il padre Ventura e la filosofia. Milano, 1853.
Phil 1850.88 Rémusat, Charles de. Bacon. Paris, 1858.
Phil 1607.5A Renaissance concepts of method. (Gilbert, Neal.) N.Y., 1960.
Phil 1630.2 La renaissance du stoicisme au XVIe siècle. (Zanta, Léontine.) Paris, 1914.
Phil 2915.80 Renaissance du Voltairianisme. (Saisset, E.E.) Paris, 1845.
Phil 1618.5 The Renaissance idea of wisdom. (Rice, Eugene Franklin.) Cambridge, 1958.
Phil 4065.130A The Renaissance philosophy of Giordano Bruno. (Horowitz, I.L.) N.Y., 1952.
Phil 4002.9 The Renaissance philosophy of man. (Cassirer, Ernst.) Chicago, 1948.
Phil 4002.9.5 The Renaissance philosophy of man. (Cassirer, Ernst.) Chicago, 1956.
Phil 4065.155 Renaissance theory of love. (Nelson, J.C.) N.Y., 1958.
Phil 27.10 Renaissance und Philosophie. Bonn, 1908. 13v.
Phil 8593.18 Renaissance; an essay in faith. (Nicodemus (pseud.).) London, 1943.
Phil 1020.4.5 Renan, E. Averrose et l'Averroisme. Paris, 1852.
Phil 3837.8.5 Renan, Ernest. Spinoza; conference tenue à La Haye. Paris, 1877.
Phil 3837.8 Renan, Ernest. Spinoza; Rede...gehalten im Haag. Leipzig, 1877.
Phil 8892.35 Renard, G. Des sciences physiques aux sciences morales. Paris, 1922.
Phil 9010.32 Renard, Hubert. L'automobiliste et la morale chrétienne. Paris, 1967.
Phil 3819.25 Renati des Cartes et Benedicti de Spinoza praecipua opera. (Spinoza, Benedictus de.) Lipsiae, 1843.
Htn Phil 2520.163.20* Renati des Cartes principiorum philosophial pars I, et II. (Spinoza, B. de.) Amstelodami, 1663.
Phil 2520.224.5 Renato Cartesio. (Carbonara, Cleto.) Napoli, 1965.
Phil 2520.224 Renato Cartesio e la tradizione ontologica. (Carbonara, Cleto.) Torino, 1945.
Htn Phil 2520.163.15* Renatus des Cartes beginzelen der wijsbegeerte. (Spinoza, B. de.) Amsterdam, 1664.
Phil 492.1 Renaud, H. Le matérialisme et la nature. Paris, 1870.
Phil 1750.166.120 Renaudet, Augustin. Humanisme et Renaissance. Genève, 1958.
Phil 8892.34 Renauld, J.F. Manuel de morale. Paris, 1920.
Phil 4080.15.81 Renauld, J.F. L'oeuvre inachevée de Mario Calderoni. n.p., n.d.
Phil 5238.75 Rencontre. Utrecht, 1957.
Phil 2805.418 La rencontre avec Pascal. (Mauriac, François.) Paris, 1926.
Phil 9245.62 Rencontres Internationales, Genève, 1961. Les conditions du bonheur. Neuchâtel, 1961.
Phil 1750.346 Rencontres Internationales. La connaissance de l'homme on XVe siècle. Neuchâtel, 1952.
Phil 9070.51 Rencontres Internationales. Les droits de l'esprit et les exigences sociales. Neuchâtel, 1951.
Phil 1750.345 Rencontres Internationales. Pour un nouvel humanisme. Neuchâtel, 1949.
Phil 3499.30 Renda, A. Conoscenza e moralita in Kant. Palermo, 1944.
Phil 5325.20 Renda, A. La dissociazione psicologica. Torino, 1905.
Phil 5545.66 Renda, A. L'oblio; saggio sull'attività selettiva della coscienza. Torino, 1910.
Phil 192.57 Renda, Antonio. Il criticismo: fondamenti etico-religiosi. Palermo, 1924.
Phil 192.57.5 Renda, Antonio. Valori spirituali e realtà. Messina, 1924.
Phil 585.186 Rendel, David. Earthling and Hellene; a psychological mechanism of evolution and its effect on the human race. Wimbledon, 1963.
Phil 8629.3 Rendezvous; the life that some call death. (Elliott, W.H.) London, 1942.
Phil 5827.3 Rendu, V. L'intelligence des bêtes. Paris, 1863.
Phil 2520.395 René Descartes; a biography. (Vrooman, Jack Rochford.) N.Y., 1970.
Phil 2520.129 René Descartes, eine Einführung. (Jungmann, Karl.) Leipzig, 1908.
Phil 2520.200A René Descartes. (Brunschvicg, L.) Paris, 1937.
Phil 2520.108.5 René Descartes. (Hoffmann, A.) Stuttgart, 1905.
Phil 2520.230.20 René Descartes. (Lewis, G.) Paris, 1953.
Phil 2520.285 René Descartes. (Richter, L.) Hamburg, 1942.
Phil 2520.156 René Descartes. (Starcke, C.N.) Kjøbenhavn, 1919.
Phil 2520.108.6 René Descartes. 2. Aufl. (Hoffmann, A.) Stuttgart, 1923.
Phil 2520.115 René Descartes und seine Reform der Philosophie. (Schmidt aus Schwarzenberg, X.) Nördlingen, 1859.
Phil 4818.410.80 René Fülöp-Miller's search for reality. (Vance, Wilson.) London, 1930.
Phil 2630.7.105 René Guénon, ou La sagesse initiatique. (Meroz, Lucien.) Paris, 1962.
Phil 2630.7.95 René Guenon. (Sérant, Paul.) Paris, 1953.
Phil 2630.7.90 René Guenon et son oeuvre. (Marcireau, J.) Poitiers, 1946.
Phil 2725.25 René LeSenne. (Centineo, E.) Palermo, 1952.
Phil 2880.8.134 Rene und Freiheit. (Otto, Maria.) Freiburg, 1961.

Phil 1750.635.5 Renesans scholastyki. (Jaroszewski, T.M.) Warszawa, 1961.
Phil 2805.408 Rennes, A. Procès de Pascal. Paris, 1962.
Phil 2805.274 Rennes, J. Pascal et le libertin. Paris, 1950.
Phil 8597.7 Rennie, J. Alphabet of natural theology. London, 1834.
Phil 6127.25 Rennie, T.A.C. Mental health in modern society. N.Y., 1948.
Phil 75.29 Renoir, Edmund. Bibliography of recent French philosophy, 1920. n.p. n.d.
Phil 8965.18 Le renouveau de la morale. (Pinckaers, Servais.) Tournai, 1964.
Phil 8955.13 Le renouveau de la théologie morale selon Vatican II. (Fuchs, Josef.) Paris, 1968.
Phil 197.72.5 Un renouvellement de la métaphysique. Est-il possible? (Wohl, J.A.) Paris, 1957.
Phil 3499.8 Renouvier, C. Critique de la doctrine de Kant. Paris, 1906.
Phil 2840.75 Renouvier, C.B. Correspondance de Renouvier et Secrétan. Paris, 1910.
Phil 2840.70 Renouvier, C.B. Les derniers entretiens, recueillis par Louis Prat. Paris, 1904.
Phil 2840.70.3 Renouvier, C.B. Les derniers entretiens, recueillis par Louis Prat. Paris, 1904.
Phil 2840.55 Renouvier, C.B. Les dilemmes de la métaphysique pure. Paris, 1901.
Phil 2840.30 Renouvier, C.B. Esquisse d'une classification systématique. Paris, 1885-86. 2v.
Phil 2840.40 Renouvier, C.B. Essais de critique générale. Paris, 1854-64. 4v.
Phil 2840.42 Renouvier, C.B. Essais de critique générale. Paris, 1912. 2v.
Phil 2840.41 Renouvier, C.B. Essais de critique générale. Premier essai. Paris, 1912. 2v.
Phil 2840.40.2 Renouvier, C.B. Essais de critique générale. v.1. pt.1-3; v.2, pt.1-3. Paris, 1875. 6v.
Phil 2840.60 Renouvier, C.B. Histoire et solution des problèmes métaphysiques. Paris, 1901.
Phil 1122.1 Renouvier, C.B. Manuel de philosophie ancienne. Paris, 1844. 2v.
Phil 1717.1 Renouvier, C.B. Manuel de philosophie moderne. Paris, 1842.
Phil 2840.50 Renouvier, C.B. Science de la morale. Paris, 1869. 2v.
Phil 2840.50.5 Renouvier, C.B. Science de la morale. Paris, 1908. 2v.
Phil 2840.70.5 Renouvier, C.B. As ultimas conversações. Coimbra, 1930.
Phil 3552.100 Renouvier, Charles. La nouvelle monadologie. Paris, 1899.
Phil 575.31 Renouvier, Charles. Le personnalisme suivi d'une étude sur la perception extrême. Paris, 1903.
Phil 2840.99.15 Renouvier, disciple et critique de Kant. (Verneaux, Roger.) Paris, 1945.
Phil 2840.83A Renouvier. (Archambault, P.) Paris, 1911.
Phil 2840.99 Renouvier. Thèse. (Verneaux, Roger.) Paris, 1944.
Phil 8672.13 Rensi, G. Apologia dell'ateismo. Roma, 1925.
Phil 8418.10 Rensi, G. La scepsi estetica. Bologna, 1919.
Phil 4215.3.30 Rensi, G. Le antinomie dello spirito. Piacenza, 1910.
Phil 645.22.12 Rensi, Giuseppe. Apologia dello scetticismo. Roma, 1926.
Phil 8892.32.5 Rensi, Giuseppe. Critica dello morale. Catania, 1935.
Phil 4215.3.45 Rensi, Giuseppe. La filosofia dell'assurdo. Milano, 1937.
Phil 4215.3.33 Rensi, Giuseppe. La filosofia dell'autorita. Palermo, 1920.
Phil 4215.3.31 Rensi, Giuseppe. Formalismo e amoralismo giuridico. Verona, 1914.
Phil 4215.3.38 Rensi, Giuseppe. Il genio etico, ed altri saggi. Bari, 1912.
Phil 8892.32 Rensi, Giuseppe. Introduzione alla scepsi etica. Firenze, n.d.
Phil 4215.3.35 Rensi, Giuseppe. L'irrazionale, il lavoro, l'amore. Milano, 1923.
Phil 645.22 Rensi, Giuseppe. Lineamenti di filosofia scetica. Bologna, 1919.
Phil 645.22.2 Rensi, Giuseppe. Lineamenti di filosofia scetica. Bologna, 1921.
Phil 4215.3.32 Rensi, Giuseppe. Polemiche antidogmatiche. Bologna, 1920.
Phil 4215.3.40 Rensi, Giuseppe. Le ragioni dell'irrazionalismo. 2a ed. Napoli, 1933.
Phil 645.22.7 Rensi, Giuseppe. Lo scetticismo. Milano, 1926.
Phil 3837.20.5 Rensi, Giuseppe. Spinoza. 2. ed. Milano, 1944.
Phil 705.10 Rensi, Giuseppe. La trascendenza; studio sul problema morale. Torino, 1914.
Phil 2805.30.800 Rensi, Leopardi e Pascal. (Mignone, C.) Milano, 1954.
Phil 1540.32 Renucci, P. L'aventure de l'humanisme européen au moyen-âge. Clermont-Ferrand, 1953.
Phil 1504.10 Renz, O. Die Synteresis nach dem hl. Thomas von Aquin. v.10, pt.1-2. Münster, 1911.
Phil 27.4.5 Répertoire bibliographique de la philosophie. Louvain. 1,1949+ 21v.
Phil 7082.6 Répertoire des images et symboles oniriques rencontrés au cours des analyses psychothérapiques. (Arthurs, André.) Genève, 1967.
Phil 75.45 Répertoires d'incipit pour la littérature latine philosophique. (Pelzer, A.) Roma, 1951.
Phil 3960.1 Repertorium der Nederlanden wijsbegeerte. Amsterdam, 1948-3v.
Phil 6128.11.9 Reply to Bakewell. (Strong, C.A.) n.p., 1904.
Htn Phil 2115.73.5* Reply to the Lord Bishop of Worcester's answer to his letter. (Locke, J.) London, 1697.
Htn Phil 2115.73.7* Reply to the Lord Bishop of Worcester's answer to his second letter. (Locke, J.) London, 1699.
Phil 7054.117 A reply to Wm. T. Dwight, D.D., on spiritualism. (Woodman, J.C.) Portland, 1857.
Phil 2855.5.33 Réponse à Charles Renouvier au sujet de son appreciation de l'Esquisse d'une philosophie synthésiste. (Richard, C.) Paris, 1875.
Phil 8610.798.10 Réponse à divers contradicteurs sur la coéternelle existence de la matière. (Gradis, David.) Paris, 1798-99.
Phil 3480.120 Réponse á Eberhard. (Kant, Immanuel.) Paris, 1959.
Phil 1750.166.205 Réponse à Heidegger sur l'humanisme. (Castanos, Stelios.) Paris, 1966.
Phil 4115.96 Réponse à un article. (Gioberti, V.) Bruxelles, 1844.
Phil 6679.2 Reponse au discours. (Janin de Combe Blanche, J.) Genève, 1784.
Phil 2805.101 Réponse aux lettres provinciales. (Daniel, Gabriel.) Amsterdam, 1697.
Phil 2805.101.5 Réponse aux lettres provinciales. (Daniel, Gabriel.) Bruxelles, 1698.
Phil 2805.101.8 Réponse aux lettres provinciales. (Daniel, Gabriel.) La Haye, 1716.

Htn Phil 2733.57* Réponse du Père Malebranche à la troisième lettre de Mr. Arnauld. (Malebranche, Nicolas.) Amsterdam, 1704.
Phil 177.12 Réponses aux questions de philosophie. (Charma, Antoine.) Paris, 1841.
Phil 9495.37 Report...Je. 1917 to Jl. 1919. (Young Women's Christian Association, United States. National Board. War Council Work. Social Morality Committee.) N.Y.? 1919?
Phil 8505.1 Report...National Liberal League. Boston, 1876.
Phil 59.8 Report. (Tavistock Institute of Human Relations, London.) 1963+
Phil 30.7 Report. (University of Southern California. Psychological Laboratory.) Los Angeles. 1,1952+
Phil 62.7 Report. (Western Behavioral Sciences Institute, La Jolla, California.) La Jolla, California. 3-22
Phil 5643.94 Report of a joint discussion on vision. (Physical Society of London.) London, 1933.
Phil 9495.23 Report of sex education sessions. (International Congress on School Hygiene, 4th, Buffalo, 1913.) N.Y., 1913.
Phil 6111.52 Report of the Boston mental hygiene survey, 1930. (Boston Mental Hygiene Survey.) Boston, 1930.
Phil 52.7.15 Report of the Boston Mental Hygiene Survey. (Massachusetts. Society for Mental Hygiene.) Boston.
Phil 6750.16 Report of the commission. (Pennsylvania. Commission on Segregation, Care and Treatment of the Feebleminded and Epileptic Persons.) Harrisburg, 1913.
Phil 9230.2 Report of the committee on betting and gambling. (Convocation of the Province of York.) London, 1890.
Phil 150.20 Report of the committee on definitions of the American Philosophical Association. N.Y., 1911.
Phil 5645.6.5 Report of the examination of school children for color blindness. (Jeffries, B.J.) Boston, 1880.
Phil 8662.5.5 The report of the four nights' public discussion...on the truth of Christianity. (Holyoake, George Jacob.) London, 1850.
Phil 6750.262 Report of the mission to Denmark and Sweden. (United States. President's Panel on Mental Retardation.) Washington, D.C., 1962.
Phil 6750.2 Report of the proceedings...of idiotry. (Colquhoun, L.) Edinburgh, 1837.
Phil 6750.263 Report of the task force education and rehabilitation. (United States. Presdent's Panel on Mental Retardation.) Washington, D.C., 1963.
Phil 6675.4 Report on experiments on animal magnetism. (Académie des Sciences, Paris.) Edinburgh, 1833.
Phil 55.10 Report on five years of activities. (Parapsychology Foundation.) N.Y., 1959.
Phil 7069.09.5A Report on Mrs. Piper's Hodgson-control. (James, William.) n.p., 1909.
Phil 7068.73.10 Report on spiritualism of the committee of the London Dialectical Society. (London Dialectical Society.) London, 1873.
Phil 6677.3A Report on the magnetical experiments. (Husson, H.M.) Boston, 1836.
Phil 6945.11.10 Report to accompany Bill S44; include memorial of Miss D.L. Dix, January 23, 1848. (United States. Congress. Senate. Commission on Public Lands.) Washington, 1854.
Phil 6750.3 Report to the legislature. (Howe, S.G.) Boston, 1847.
Phil 6750.3.5 Report to the legistature of Massachusetts upon idiocy. (Howe, S.G.) Boston, 1848.
Phil 10.86F Reports. (Aabo, Finland. Yliopisto. Institute of Psychology.) Turku.
Phil 5240.52 Reports. (American Psychological Association. Project on Scientific Information. Exchange in Psychology.) Washington, 1963- 3v.
Phil 6945.11.5 Pamphlet vol. Reports of asylums...with mention of Miss Dix. 5 pam.
Phil 9045.18 Reports of lecture on morality. (Fox, William J.) London, 1836.
Phil 9045.18.5 Reports of lectures delivered. (Fox, William J.) London, 1838.
Phil 8612.22 Reports of lectures delivered at the chapel So. Place, Finsburg. Nos. 9,10,12. (Fox, W.J.) London, 1838.
Phil 9245.117 Reports on happiness. (Bradburn, Norman Marshall.) Chicago, 1965.
Phil 5585.63 La représentation. (Cresson, A.) Paris, 1936.
Phil 8440.5 Representation and meaning in the visual arts. (Hermeren, Göran.) Lund, 1969.
Phil 5232.8 Representative psychologists. (Westerhof, A.C.) Union Bridge, Md., 1938.
Phil 8418.4 The representative significance of form. (Raymond, G.L.) N.Y., 1900.
Phil 8418.4.2 The representative significance of form. 2. ed. (Raymond, G.L.) N.Y., 1909.
Phil 6312.1.7 Repressed emotions. (Coriat, I.H.) N.Y., 1920.
Phil 5258.106 La répression mentale. (Sollier, Paul.) Paris, 1930.
Phil 5258.8 Reproduction, Gefühl und Wille. (Schubert-Soldern, R. von.) Leipzig, 1887.
Phil 5027.3.5 Rescher, N. The development of Arabic logic. Pittsburgh, 1964.
Phil 5057.41 Rescher, N. Introduction to logic. N.Y., 1964.
Phil 5027.3 Rescher, N. Studies in the history of Arabic logic. Pittsburgh, 1963.
Phil 9550.24 Rescher, Nicholas. Distributive justice; a constructive critique of the utilitarian theory of distribution. Indianapolis, 1966.
Phil 165.432 Rescher, Nicholas. Essays in philosophical analysis. Pittsburg, 1969.
Phil 5115.10 Rescher, Nicholas. Hypothetical reasoning. Amsterdam, 1964.
Phil 735.268 Rescher, Nicholas. Introduction to value theory. Englewood Cliffs, N.J., 1969.
Phil 5190.42 Rescher, Nicholas. The logic of commands. London, 1966.
Phil 3552.454 Rescher, Nicholas. The philosophy of Leibniz. Englewood Cliffs, N.J., 1967.
Phil 1020.62 Rescher, Nicholas. Studies in Arabic philosophy. Pittsburgh, 1967[1968]
Phil 5066.316.5 Rescher, Nicholas. Temporal logic. Wien, 1971.
Phil 5066.316 Rescher, Nicholas. Topics in philosophical logic. Dordrecht, Holland, 1968.
Phil 6420.2 Research and experiment in Stuttering. (Beech, H.R.) Oxford, 1966.
Phil 5870.75 Research at the Hampstead Child-Therapy Clinic and other papers, 1956-1965. (Freud, Anna.) London, 1970.
Phil 5068.11 A research for the consequences of the Vienna circle philosophy for ethics. Proefschrift. (Zuurdeeg, Willem Frederik.) Utrecht, 1946.
Phil 5590.457 Research in clinical assessment. (Megargee, Edwin I.) N.Y., 1966.

Phil 6953.15   Research in methods of adjustment. (Dunlap, K.) Berkeley, 1941.

Phil 6980.466   Research in psychotherapy. 1. ed. (Meltzoff, Julian.) N.Y., 1970.

Phil 6135.5   A research in report on mental hygiene, brain, exercises, sanitation and foods. (Zitex, Edward.) New Orleans, La., 1935.

Phil 5520.490   Research in verbal behavior and some neurophysiological implications. Papers presented at a conference in New York, 1965. N.Y., 1967.

Phil 6140.6   Research Seminar on the Evaluation of Community Mental Health Programs. Community mental health; an international perspective. San Francisco, 1968.

Phil 5645.8.5   Researches in colour vision. (Abney, W. de W.) London, 1913.

Phil 7068.74.26   Researches in the phenomena of spiritualism. (Crookes, W.) London, 1874.

Phil 7068.74.26.5   Researches in the phenomena of spiritualism. (Crookes, W.) London, 1874.

Phil 7060.108   Researches in the phenomenena of spiritualism. (Crookes, William.) London, 1874.

Phil 6687.1.3   Researches on magnetism, electricity. (Reichenback, C.) London, 1850.

Phil 730.30   Resemblance and identity. (Butchvarov, Panayot.) Bloomington, 1966.

Phil 6980.760   Residential treatment centers for emotional disturbed children. (United States. Children's Bureau.) Washington, 1953.

Phil 8880.1.4   Resolves. (Feltham, O.) Cambridge, 1832.
Htn   Phil 8880.1*   Resolves. (Feltham, O.) London, 1636.
Htn   Phil 8880.1.12*   Resolves. (Feltham, O.) London, 1670.
  Phil 8880.1.2   Resolves. (Feltham, O.) London, 1806.
Htn   Phil 8880.1.3.2*   Resolves. (Feltham, O.) London, 1840.
  Phil 8880.1.3   Resolves. (Feltham, O.) London, 1840.
  Phil 8880.1.7   Resolves. (Feltham, O.) London, 1904.
Htn   Phil 8800.6*   Resolves. (Feltham, Owen.) London, 1661.
Htn   Phil 8800.6.2*   Resolves. (Feltham, Owen.) London, 1677.
Htn   Phil 8800.6.5*   Resolves. (Feltham, Owen.) London, 1696.
Htn   Phil 2005.4.30F*   Resolves: Divine, moral, political. (Felltham, Owen.) London, 1677.
Htn   Phil 8880.1.8*   Resolves. 2nd ed. (Feltham, O.) London, 1628. 2 pam.
Htn   Phil 8880.1.9*   Resolves. 3rd ed. (Feltham, O.) London, 1628.
Htn   Phil 8880.1.10*   Resolves. 4th ed. (Feltham, O.) London, 1631.
Htn   Phil 8880.1.11*   Resolves. 5th ed. (Feltham, O.) London, 1634.
  Phil 5251.41.15A   Resolving social conflicts. 1st ed. (Lewin, Kurt.) N.Y., 1948.

Phil 8587.44.5   The resources of religion. (Harkness, George E.) N.Y., 1936.

Phil 9470.10   Responsabilità e comunità umana. (Semerari, Giuseppe.) Manduria, 1960.

Phil 6957.5   La responsabilité. (Hamon, A.) Lyon, 1897.
Htn   Phil 2520.146*   Response au livre qui a pour titre P. Danielis Huetii. (Regis, P.S.) Paris, 1691.

Phil 5592.75   Response set as a measure of personality. (Frederiksen, Norman Oliver.) Princeton, 1958.

Phil 5722.32.5   Responses to material presented during various levels of sleep. (Simon, C.W.) Santa Monica, 1954.

Phil 2750.11.87   La responsibilité de l'artiste. (Maritain, Jacques.) Paris, 1961.

Phil 5756.16   Responsibility. (Glover, Jonathan.) London, 1970.
Phil 9470.8   Responsibility. (Sears, L.) N.Y., 1932.
Phil 9470.12   Responsibility and practical freedom. (Roberts, Moira.) Cambridge, Eng., 1965.

Phil 6962.2   Responsibility in mental disease. (Maudsley, H.) N.Y., 1874.

Phil 8959.6   Responsibility in modern religious ethics. (Jonsen, Albert R.) Washington, 1968.

Phil 2750.11.86   The responsibility of the artist. (Maritain, Jacques.) N.Y., 1960.

Phil 3640.296   Responso heroico. (Garcia Barcena, R.) La Habana, 1943.
Phil 4710.50.35   Respublikans'ka Naukova Konferentsiia za Aktual'nykh Pytan' Istorii Filosofii na Ukraïni, Kiev, 1965. Z istorii filosofii na Ukraïni. Kyïv, 1967.

Phil 3850.18.35   Ressentiment. (Scheler, Max.) N.Y., 1961.
Phil 2138.175   Restaino, Franco. J.S. Mill e la cultura filosofica britannica. Firenze, 1968.

Phil 3160.3.84   La restauration de l'a priori kantien par H. Cohen. (Rosenzweig, L.) Paris, 1927.

Phil 5272.10   Restle, Frank. Introduction to mathematical psychology. Reading, Mass., 1970.

Phil 5352.15   Restle, Frank. Psychology of judgment and choice. N.Y., 1961.

Phil 7069.67.55   The restless ghosts of Ladye Place, and other true hauntings. (Ludlam, Harry.) London, 1967.

Phil 192.79   Restrepo, D. Nociones de alta critica. Manziales, 1937.
Phil 672.210   Restrepo, F. Entre el tiempo y la eternidad. Bogotá, 1960.

Phil 5057.15   Restrepo-Hernandez, J. Lecciones de lógica dictadas en el Colegio. 2nd ed. Bogota, 1914.

Phil 3625.1.133   Die Resultate der Jacobischen und Mendelssohnschen Philosophie. (Wizenmann, T.) Leipzig, 1786.

Phil 349.26   Resultate des philosophischen Forschungen über...Erkenntnis. (Suabedissen, D.T.A.) Marburg, 1805.

Phil 5066.24.10   Results in non-classical propositional logic. (Segerberg, Krister.) Lund, 1968.

Phil 811.1   Résumé de l'histoire de la philosophie. (Laurent, P.M.) Paris, 1826.

Phil 5259.25   Resumen de psicología. (Trejos, J.) San José, 1929.
Phil 8410.6   Resumen de teoría general del arte. 1. ed. (Jordán de Urríes y Azara, José.) Madrid, 1933.

Phil 2270.75   Resumen sintético de los principios de la moral. (Spencer, Herbert.) Paris, 1910.

Phil 5248.2.25   Resumen sintético y brevisémo del sistema de psicología. (Gonzalez Velez, J.) Habana, 192-.

Phil 2750.20.50   Résumés de cours, Collège de France, 1952-1960. (Merleau-Ponty, Maurice.) Paris, 1968.

Htn   Phil 1850.75.10*   Resuscitatio, or Bringing into public light. (Bacon, Francis.) London, 1657.

Htn   Phil 1850.5.2F*   Resuscitatio. 2nd ed. (Bacon, Francis.) London, 1661.
  Phil 2493.84   Réthoré, François. Condillac. Paris, 1864.
  Phil 1890.85   Réthoré, François. Critique de la philosophie de Thomas Brown. Paris, 1863.

Phil 5190.4.5   Rethwisch, E. Der Begriff der Definition. Berlin, 1880.
Phil 2905.1.620   Rétif, André. Teilhard et l'évangélisation des temps nouveaux. Paris, 1970.

Phil 5645.45   Retinal structure and colour vision. (Wellmer, E.N.) Cambridge, Eng., 1946.

Phil 9400.16   The retirement handbook. 1st ed. (Buckley, J.C.) N.Y., 1953.

Phil 4260.98   La retorica et la poetica di G.B. Vico. (Sorrentino, A.) Torino, 1927.

Phil 1750.159   Retorno à vida (ensaios). (Rossi, Edmundo.) São Paulo, 1941.

Phil 1750.800   Le retour de tragique, essai. (Domenach, Jean Marie.) Paris, 1967.

Phil 298.5   Le retour éternel et la philosophie de la physique. (Rey, Abel.) Paris, 1927.

Phil 1812.10   Retreat from truth. (Mure, G.R.G.) Oxford, 1958.
Phil 623.40   The retreat to commitment. 1st ed. (Bartley, William W.) N.Y., 1962.

Phil 8680.5   Retreat to reality. (Zuver, Dudley.) N.Y., 1959.
VPhil 450.8   Retschlag, Max. Von der Urmaterie zum Urkraft-Elixier. Leipzig, 1926.

Phil 6854.10   Retterstøl, Nils. Selvmord. Oslo, 1970.
Phil 7054.175.15   The return of Arthur Conan Doyle. 2. ed. (Cooke, I.) Liss, 1963.

Phil 7069.30.9   The return of Captain W.G.R. Hinchliffe. (Hinchliffe, Emilie.) London, 1930.

Phil 1980.3.104   The return of Havelock Ellis, or Limbo or the dove? (Delisle, Françoise Roussel.) London, 1968.

Phil 8707.7.3   The return to faith. (Rice, William N.) N.Y., 1916.
Phil 8677.17   The return to God. (Walker, L.J.) London, 1933.
Phil 184.26.9   Return to philosophy. (Joad, C.E.M.) London, 1935.
Phil 184.26.12   Return to philosophy. (Joad, C.E.M.) N.Y., 1936.
Phil 630.49.10   The return to reason. (Wild, John.) Chicago, 1955.
Phil 5850.258.4   The return to religion. (Link, Henry C.) N.Y., 1937.
Phil 5440.23   Retzius, Gustaf. Om förvärfvade egenskapers ärftlighet. Stockholm, 1895.

Phil 2805.200   Reuchlin, H. Pascal's Leben und der Geist seiner Schriften. Stuttgart, 1840.

Phil 5257.64   Reuchlin, Maurice. Histoire de la psychologie. Paris, 1957.

Phil 5257.64.5   Reuchlin, Maurice. Les méthodes quantitatives en psychologie. Paris, 1962.

Phil 5856.10   Reuchlin, Maurice. La psychologie différentielle. Paris, 1969.

Phil 5360.32   Reumann, Kurt. Das antithetische Kamptbild. Inaug. Diss. Berlin, 1966.

Phil 70.81   Reunion de Aproximacion Filosofica Cuntifica. La materia. v.2. Zaragoza, 1961.

Phil 8638.2   Reunion in eternity. (Nicoll, N.R.) N.Y., 1919.
Phil 8707.2   Reusch, F.H. Nature and the Bible. Edinburgh, 1886. 2v.

Phil 8707.38   Reusch, Franz Heinrich. Die biblische Schöpfungsgesichte und ihr Verhältniss zu den Ergebnissen der Naturforschung. Bonn, 1877.

Phil 3850.1.80   Reuschle, C.G. Philosophie und Naturwiss...D.F. Strauss. Bonn, 1874.

Phil 8672.18.3   Reusner, M.A. Nuzhna li vera v Boga. 3. izd. Moskva, 1923.

Phil 192.118   Reuss, Materhus. Vorlesungen über die theoretische und praktische Philosophie. Bruxelles, 1968.

Phil 5590.490   Reuter, Jürgen Paul. Die Persönlichkeitsveränderung im Sinne der Deformierung noch schwerer Hungerdystrophie. Bonn, 1966.

Phil 5827.6   Reuter, Odo M. Die Seele der Tiere im Lichte der Forschung. Leipzig, 1908.

Phil 3450.33.20   Reuter, Otfried. Sittichkert und ethische Werterkenntnis nach D. von Hildebrand. Münster? 1966.

Phil 8707.13   Reuterdahl, A. The God of science. Minneapolis, 1928.
Phil 3837.35   Révah, J.S. Spinoza et le Dr. Juan de Prado. Paris, 1959.
Phil 176.87   Revaluations. (Benn, Alfred W.) London, 1909.
Phil 5400.26   Revault d'Allonnes, G. Les inclinations; leur role dans la psychologie des sentiments. Paris, 1907.

Phil 5627.12   Revault D'Allonnes, G. Psychologie d'une religion. Paris, 1908.

Phil 6967.6   Revault D'Allounes, G. Thèse pour le doctorat en médecine. Paris, 1971.

Phil 5440.30   Revda, A. Il destino delle dinastie. Torino, 1904.
Phil 8170.2   Reve, K. van het. Sovjet-annexatie der klassieken. Amsterdam, 1954.

Phil 7082.190   Le rêve, une porte sur le réel. (Teillard, Ania.) Paris, 1951.

Phil 7082.164   Le rêve. (Delage, Yves.) Paris, 1924.
Phil 7082.32.2   Le rêve. 2e éd. (Surbled, Georges.) Paris, 1898.
Phil 7082.64   Le rêve et la personnalité. (Combes, Marguerite.) Paris, 1932.

Phil 7084.4.15   Le rêve et la psychanalyse. (Laforgue, René.) Paris, 1926.

Phil 7082.22   Le rêve et les sociétés humaines. (Caillois, Roger.) Paris, 1967.

Phil 7084.48   Rêve et sexualité. (Becker, Raymond de.) Paris, 1965.
Phil 7082.172   Le rêve éveillé. (Daudet, Léon.) Paris, 1926.
Phil 192.64   Revel, Camille. Esquisse d'un essai sur les facultés humaines. Lyons, 1927.

Phil 9030.3   Revel, Camille. Le hasard. Paris, 1905.
Phil 270.57   Revel, Camille. Le hasard sa loi et ses conséquences dans les sciences et en philosophie. Paris, 1905.

Phil 817.30   Revel, Jean François. Histoire de la philosophie occidentale. Paris, 1968.

Phil 192.98   Revel, Jean Francois. Pourquoi des philosophes? Paris, 1957. 2v.

Phil 192.98.2   Revel, Jean Francois. Pourquoi des philosophes? Paris, 1964.

Phil 192.98.3   Revel, Jean Francois. Pourquoi des philosophes? Utrecht, 1965. 2v.

Phil 7054.87   The revelation...twenty-one days' entrancement. (Pierce, David.) Bangor, 1857.

Phil 8701.10   Revelation and science. (Leslie, John.) Aberdeen, 1921.
Phil 7054.75   A revelation from heaven. (Monroe, L.B.) Boston, 1851.
Phil 8674.8.15   The revelation of deity. (Turner, J.E.) London, 1931.
Phil 8701.23   La révélation primitive, et les données actuelles de la science. (Lemonnyer, Antoine.) Paris, 1914.

Phil 8697.21   Revelation through reason. (Harris, Errol E.) New Haven, 1958.

Phil 6060.10   Les révélations de l'écriture d'après un controle scientifique. (Binet, Alfred.) Paris, 1906.

Phil 7068.91.25   Revelations of a spirit medium. St. Paul, 1891.
Phil 7069.20.80   Revelations of Louise. (Crockett, Albert Stevens.) N.Y., 1920.

Phil 7059.5   Revelations of the great modern mystery planchette. Boston, 1868.

Phil 2070.82   Reverdin, H. La notion d'expérience d'après William James. Genève, 1913.

Phil 6967.8   Revere, John. Disputatio medica inauguralis de insania. Edinburgh, 1811.

Phil 3850.27.65.5   Reverence for life. (Schweitzer, A.) N.Y., 1969.

Phil 2855.10.30   Revertin, Henri. Les exigences de la vie de l'esprit. Neuchâtel, 1966.

Phil 7082.26   Les rêves. (Tissié, Philippe.) Paris, 1890.

Phil 7084.22   Les rêves et leur interpretation psychanalytique. (Allendy, René Félix.) Paris, 1926.

Phil 665.23   Révésy, Béla. Geschichte des Seelenbegriffes. Stuttgart, 1917.

Phil 5520.126   Révész, G. Thinking and speaking. Amsterdam, 1954.

Phil 5257.57   Révész, Géza. Die Bedeutung der Psychologie für die Wissenschaft. Bern, 1947.

Phil 5648.20   Révész, Géza. Die Formenwelt des Tastsinnes. Haag, 1938. 2v.

Phil 5425.84   Révész, Géza. Talent und Genie. Bern, 1952.

Phil 6327.25   Reviere, Joan. Developments in psycho-analysis. London, 1952.

Phil 8656.14.27   A review, giving the main ideas in E. Beecher's Conflict of ages. (Blain, Jacob.) Buffalo, 1856.

Phil 18.26   Review. (Institute of Applied Psychology.) N.Y. 1,1961+ 3v.

Phil 2225.5.95   Review: Collected papers of Charles Sanders Peirce. v.6. Scientific metaphysics. (Feuer, L.S.) Bruges, 1932.

Phil 1870.83   Review of Berkeley's theory of vision. (Bailey, S.) London, 1842.

Phil 8663.3.85   Review of Col. Ingersoll's attacks upon Christianity. (Bertron, Ottilie.) Philadelphia, 1889.

NEDL Phil 5754.1.25   Review of Edward's inquiry...freedom. (Tappan, H.P.) N.Y., 1839.

Phil 27.82   Review of existential psychology and psychiatry. Pittsburgh. 1,1961+ 6v.

Phil 2050.107   A review of Hume and Huxley on miracles. (Grimthorpe, E.B.) London, 1883.

Phil 7054.92   A review of J.B. Dods...theory of spiritual manifestations. (Courtney, W.S.) N.Y., 1855.

Phil 3489.8   Review of Kant's Critique of pure reason. Supplement to Theology and science of goverment. (Harris, John, of Montreal.) Montreal, 1874.

Phil 27.45   The review of metaphysics. New Haven. 1,1947+ 27v.

Phil 27.45.3   The review of metaphysics. Index, 1947-1967. New Haven, n.d.

Phil 5850.349.25   Review of P.M. Symonds' Diagnosing personality. (Allport, G.W.) Cambridge, Mass., 1932.

Phil 27.29   Review of philosophy and religion. Poona. 1-9,1930-1940 3v.

Phil 288.1.8   Review of rational cosmology. (Hickok, S.P.) n.p., 18-?

Phil 7054.61   A review of Rev. Charles Beecher's report. (Brittan, S.B.) N.Y., 1853.

Phil 8610.915   Review of the Bibles. (Coughlin, D.R.) East Aurora, N.Y., 1915.

Phil 7069.25.11   A review of the Margery case. (Prince, Walter Franklin.) Ithaca, 1926.

Htn Phil 2215.30*   A review of the principal questions and difficulties in morals. (Price, Richard.) London, 1758.

Phil 2215.30.2   A review of the principal questions and difficulties in morals. 2d ed. (Price, Richard.) London, 1769.

Phil 2215.30.3   A review of the principal questions in morals. 3d ed. (Price, Richard.) London, 1787.

Phil 7054.60.5   A review of the spiritual manifestations. (Beecher, Charles.) London, 1853.

Phil 7054.60.4   A review of the spiritual manifestations. (Beecher, Charles.) N.Y., 1853.

Phil 9150.29   A review of the systems of ethics founded on the theory of evolution. (Williams, C.M.) N.Y., 1893.

Phil 2035.80.20A   Review of the work of Mr. John Stuart Mill. (Grote, George.) London, 1868.

Phil 8705.1.5   A review of theoretical geology. (Paine, M.) N.Y., 1856.

Phil 8972.2.8   A review on the Calvinistic views of moral philosophy. (Dewey, Orville.) N.Y., 1835.

Phil 6317.52   Reviews of research in behavior pathology. (Holmes, David S.) N.Y., 1968.

Phil 3210.51   Revision der Hauptpunkte der Psychophysik. (Fechner, G.T.) Leipzig, 1882.

Phil 27.54   Revista brasileira de filosofia orgão oficial do Instituto Brasileiro de Filosofia. São Paulo. 1,1951+ 17v.

Phil 27.46   Revista cubana de filosofia. La Habana. 12,1959+

Phil 27.7   Revista de filosofia, cultura, ciencias, educacion. Buenos Aires. 1-30,1915-1929 24v.

Phil 27.58   Revista de filosofia. La Plata. 1,1950+ 5v.

Phil 27.42   Revista de filosofia. Madrid. 6,1947+ 18v.

Phil 27.72   Revista de filosofia. Santiago. 3,1955+ 4v.

Phil 27.70   Revista de filosofia de la Universidad de Costa Rica. San José. 1,1957+ 6v.

Phil 27.40   Revista de neuro-psiquíatría. Lima. 1-13,1938-1950 13v.

Phil 27.39   Revista de neurología e psiquiátria de São Paulo. São Paulo. 5-9,1939-1943 8v.

Phil 27.94   Revista de psicoanalisis, psiquiatria y psicologia. Mexico. 2,1968+

Phil 27.43   Revista de psicologia; general y aplicade. Madrid. 1,1946+ 15v.

Phil 27.80   Revista de psicologia. Bogota. 1,1956+ 5v.

Phil 27.31   Revista de psicologia i pedagogia. Barcelona. 3-5 3v.

Phil 27.74   Revista de psihologie. Bucuresti. 4,1958+ 13v.

Phil 27.36   Revista de psihologie. Cluj. 3-4,1940-1941 4v.

Phil 27.64   Revista dominicana de filosofia. Ciudad Trujillo. 1956-1957 2v.

Phil 27.50   Revista filosofica. Coimbra. 1-7,1951-1957 3v.

Phil 27.5   Revista filosofica. Pavia. 8

Phil 27.96   Revista latinoamericana de psicología. 1,1969+

Phil 27.84   Revista mexicana de psicologia. Guadalajara. 1963-1965+

Phil 27.66   Revista pernambucana de filosofia. Recife.

Phil 27.56   Revista portuguesa de filosofia. Braga. 1,1945+ 25v.

Phil 27.56.5   Revista portuguesa de filosofia. Suplemento bibliográfico. Braga. 1,1950+ 4v.

Phil 5627.72   The revival in the West. 4. ed. (Stead, W.T.) London, 19-

Phil 4843.4   The revival of Greek thought, 1620-1830. (Henderson, George Patrick.) Albany, 1970.

Phil 7084.2   The revival of interest in the dream. (Fliess, Robert.) N.Y., 1953.

Phil 2805.218A   The revival of Pascal. (Eastwood, D.M.) Oxford, 1936.

Phil 2005.9.30   The revival of realism. (Feibleman, James.) Chapel Hill, 1946.

Phil 1520.3.3   Revival of scholastic philosophy, XIX century. (Perrier, J.L.) N.Y., 1909.

Phil 1520.3   Revival of scholastic philosophy, XIX century. (Perrier, J.L.) N.Y., 1909.

Phil 2905.1.625   Revol, Enrique Luis. Símbolo y evolución humana. Cordoba, 1970.

Phil 8400.65.5   Revoliutsiia, prekrasnoe, chelovek. Moskva, 1968.

Phil 4761.5.80   Revoliutsionnyi prosvetitel' F.V. Karzhaviv. (Rabinovich, Valerii I.) Moskva, 1966.

Phil 315.6A   The revolt against dualism. (Lovejoy, A.O.) Chicago, 1930.

Phil 315.6.3   The revolt against dualism. (Lovejoy, A.O.) La Salle, Ill., 1955.

Phil 8589.14.12   The revolt against mechanism. (Jacks, L.P.) London, 1934.

Phil 8589.14.9   The revolt against mechanism. (Jacks, L.P.) N.Y., 1934.

Phil 1750.373   La revolución existencialista. (Astrada, C.) n.p., 1952.

Phil 2475.1.175   Une révolution dans la philosophie. 2e ed. (Grandjian, Frank.) Genève, 1916.

Phil 2477.15.120   La révolution de Gaston Bachelard en critique littéraire. (Therrien, Vincent.) Paris, 1970.

Phil 585.153   La révolution de l'homme au XXe siècle. (Leclerq, J.) Tournai, 1966.

Phil 8408.8   Revolution der Ästhetik als Einleitung zu einer Revolution der Wissenschaft. (Hart, Julius.) Berlin, 1909.

Phil 9070.117   Revolution der Satten. (Windisch, Konrad.) Wolfsburg, 1967.

Phil 6315.2.470   La révolution freudienne. (Fougeyrollas, Pierre.) Paris, 1970.

Phil 8835.6   The revolution in ethical theory. (Kerner, George.) N.Y., 1966.

Phil 1717.19A   The revolution in philosophy. London, 1956.

Phil 9075.60   La révolution originelle. (Chaperd, Marc.) Paris, 1958.

Phil 1750.6   La révolution philosophique. (Huet, F.) Paris, 1871.

Phil 1718.12   La revolution philosophique et la science. (Sageret, Jules.) Paris, 1924.

Phil 6315.2.380   La révolution psychanalytique. (Robert, Marthe.) Paris, 1964. 2v.

Phil 14.23   Révolution psychiatrique. Paris. 1948+ 33v.

Phil 14.23.2   Révolution psychiatrique. Tables des matieres. Paris. 1925+

Phil 9495.168.25   La révolution sexuelle. (Gagey, Roland.) Paris, 1968.

Phil 302.4   La révolution totale, en tout. (Valsardieu, Paul.) Paris, 1968- 2v.

Phil 3246.298.5   Revolution und Philosophie. (Buhr, Manfred.) Berlin, 1965.

Phil 27.27   Revue cosmique. Paris. 1-5,1901-1906 5v.

Phil 17.2   Revue de l'hypnotisme. Paris. 1-13 13y.

Phil 3425.304   Revue de Métaphysique et de Morale. Études sur Hegel. Paris, 1931.

Phil 70.1.4   Revue de metaphysique et de morale. (International Congress of Philosophy, 4th, Bologna, 1911.) Paris. 1911

Phil 27.3   Revue de metaphysique et de morale. Paris. 1+ 68v.

Phil 27.3.10   Revue de metaphysique et de morale. Table générale, 1893-1923. Paris, 1924.

Phil 9495.41   Revue de morale sociale. Paris. 1899-1903 4v.

Phil 27.41   Revue de psychologie. Montreal. 1946-1952

Phil 27.28   Revue de psychologie concrete. Paris. 1-2 2v.

Phil 27.20   Revue des études psychiques. Paris. 1-2

Phil 27.6   Revue des sciences psychologiques. Paris, n.d.

Phil 27.22   Revue d'histoire de la philosophie. Paris. 1,1927+ 32v.

Phil 27.88   Revue du monde invisible. Paris. 1-10,1898-1908 10v.

Phil 6315.2.250   Revue Francaise de Psychanalyse. Hommage à Sigmund Freud. Paris, 1956.

Phil 27.37   Revue internationale de philosophie. Bruxelles. 2,1939+ 22v.

Phil 27.15.5   La revue occidentale. Tables des matières, 1878-1889. Paris, 1888.

Phil 27.15   La revue occidentale-philosophique. Versailles. 1878-1914 42v.

Phil 27.1   Revue philosophique. Paris. 1+ 139v.

Htn Phil 27.1.5*   Revue philosophique. Tables 1876-1912. Paris, 1888- 4v.

NEDL Phil 27.1.10   Revue philosophique de la France et de l'étranger. Paris. 1-67,1876-1909 67v.

Phil 27.4   Revue philosophique de Louvain. Louvain. 1,1894+ 70v.

Phil 27.4.2   Revue philosophique de Louvain. Table, 1894-1913. Louvain, 1914.

Phil 27.38   La revue psychologique. Bruxelles. 1-7,1908-1914 3v.

Phil 27.30   Revue spirite. Paris. 1-9,1858-1866 9v.

Phil 27.8   Revue spiritualiste. Paris. 1-6 6v.

Phil 2905.1.225   Revue Teilhard de Chardin. Bruxelles. 1,1960+ 3v.

Phil 27.25   Revue théosophique. Paris. 1-2,1889-1890

Phil 27.86   Revue universitaire de science morale. Havre-lez-Mons. 1,1965+ 2v.

Phil 5535.28.5   Reward and punishment in human learning: elements of a behavior theory. (Nuttin, Jozef.) N.Y., 1968.

Phil 2450.82   Rex, Walter. Essays on Pierre Bayle and religious controversy. The Hague, 1965.

Phil 6060.24   Rexford, John. What handwriting indicates. N.Y., 1904.

Phil 5257.44   Rexroad, Carl N. General psychology for college students. N.Y., 1929.

Phil 5257.55   Rexroad, Carl N. Psychology and personality development. Boston, 1940.

Phil 5257.15   Rey, A. Leçons de psychologie et de philosophie. 3. éd. Paris, 1911.

Phil 192.25   Rey, A. Leçons élémentaire de psychologie et de philosophie. Paris, 1908.

Phil 192.25.9   Rey, A. Logique et morale. 4. ed. Paris, 1916.

Phil 1717.7   Rey, A. La philosophie moderne. Paris, 1908.

Phil 192.25.5   Rey, A. Les sciences philosophiques. 2. ed. Paris, 1911.

Phil 298.5   Rey, Abel. Le retour éternel et la philosophie de la physique. Paris, 1927.

Phil 5592.80   Rey, André. L'examen clinique en psychologie. Paris, 1958.

Phil 5272.16   Rey, André. Techniques inédites pour l'examen psychologique. Neuchâtel, 1967.

Phil 5545.238   Rey, André. Les troubles de la mémoire et leur examen psychométrique. Bruxelles, 1966.

Phil 1750.166.60   Rey, Gabriel. Humanisme et surhumanisme. Paris, 1951.

Phil 176.5.51   Rey, J. La philosophie de M. Balfour. Paris, 1897.

Phil 3640.850   Rey, Jean Michel. L'enjeu des signes; lecture de Nietzsche. Paris, 1971.

Phil 8642.9   Rey Altuna, Luis. La inmortalidad del alma a la luz de los filósofos. Madrid, 1959.

Phil 8842.5   Reybekiel, A. Das biologische Prinzip in den moralphilosophischen Anschauungen W. Rolph's, M. Guyau's und Fr. Nietzsches. Krakau, 1906.

Phil 5257.38   Reyburn, H.A. An introduction to psychology. Cape Town, 1924.

Phil 3425.124   Reyburn, Hugh A. The ethical theory of Hegel. Oxford, 1921.

Phil 3640.336 Reyburn, Hugh A. Nietzsche. London, 1948.
Phil 8892.86 Reyer, Wilhelm. Anthropologische Ethik. Köln, 1963.
Phil 583.2 Reyer, Wilhelm. Einführung in der Phänomenologie. Leipzig, 1926.
Phil 1020.4.30 Reyes, A. Averroes y Lulio. Caracas, 1940.
Phil 1020.4.31 Reyes, A. El racionalismo averroísta y el razonamiento luliano. Madrid, 1935.
Phil 817.6 Reyes Ruiz, Jesús Maria. Historia de la filosofia y terminología filosofica. 2. ed. Granada, 1910.
Phil 2855.6.25 Reymond, A. Philosophie spiritualiste. Lausanne, 1942. 2v.
Phil 5057.25 Reymond, Arnold. Les principes de la logique et la critique contemporaine. Paris, 1932.
Phil 5057.25.2 Reymond, Arnold. Les principes de la logique et la critique contemporaine. Paris, 1957.
Phil 2630.3.84 Reymond, M. La philosophie de Jean-Jacques Gourd. Chambéry, 1949.
Phil 6682.16 Reymond, Mine. Vve. Cours de magnétisme. Paris, 1886.
Phil 5870.120.5 Reymond-Rivier, Berthe. Le développement social de l'enfant et de l'adolescent. 5. ed. Bruxelles, 1965.
Phil 8597.8.2 Reynaud, J.E. Philosophie religieuse terre et ciel. Paris, 1858.
Phil 8597.8 Reynaud, J.E. Philosophie religiuse terre et ciel. Paris, 1854.
Phil 5330.26 Reynax. L'attention. Paris, 1930.
Phil 672.228 Reyner, John Hereward. God beyond time. London, 1965.
Phil 4363.2.82 Reynier, Frédéric. Étude sur la doctrine de Molinos. Thèse. Strasbourg, 1856.
Htn Phil 665.11* Reynolds, E. Treatise of the passions and faculties of the soule of men. London, 1640.
X Cg Phil 8418.24.5 Reynolds, J. Discourses. London, 1842.
Phil 8418.24 Reynolds, J. Discourses. London, 1884.
Phil 6967.2 Reynolds, J.R. The diagnosis of diseases. London, 1855.
Phil 3210.89 Rezazadeh-Schafagh, Sadeg. Mystische Motive in Fechners Philosophie. Inaug. Diss. Charlottenburg, 1928.
Phil 3805.250 Rezeptivität und Spontaneität. Inaug. Diss. (Groell, Johannes.) Münster? 1966?
Phil 5520.286 Reznikov, Lazar' O. Gnoseologicheskie voprosy semiotiki. Leningrad, 1964.
Phil 5520.285 Reznikov, Lazar' O. Poniatie i slovo. Leningrad, 1958.
Phil 3925.16.235 Rhees, Rush. Discussions of Wittgenstein. London, 1970.
Phil 2255.11 Rhees, Rush. Without answers. London, 1969.
Phil 6819.6 Rheingold, Joseph Cyrus. The fear of being a woman; a theory of maternal destructiveness. N.Y., 1964.
Phil 5790.2 Rheingold, Joseph Cyrus. The mother, anxiety, and death: the catastrophic death complex. London, 1967.
Phil 1619.5 Rhetoric and philosophy in Renaissance humanism. (Seigel, Jerrold Edward.) Princeton, 1968.
Phil 2805.428 The rhetoric of Pascal. (Topliss, Patricia.) Leicester, 1966.
Phil 8581.106A The rhetoric of religion. (Burke, K.) Boston, 1961.
Phil 5620.26 Rhétorique et philosophie pour une théorie de l'argumentation en philosophie. 1. ed. (Perelman, Chaim.) Paris, 1952.
Phil 1560.15 Le Rhin Mystique de Maitre Eckert à Thomas à Kempis. (Michelet, Marcel.) Paris, 1960.
Phil 8707.4 Rhind, W. The age of the earth. Edinburgh, 1838.
Phil 7069.34.25A Rhine, Joseph B. Extra-sensory perception. Boston, 1934.
Phil 7069.34.25.2A
Phil 7069.34.26 Rhine, Joseph B. Extra-sensory perception. Boston, 1935.
Phil 7069.37.5A Rhine, Joseph B. Extra-sensory perception. Boston, 1964.
Phil 7069.53 Rhine, Joseph B. New frontiers of the mind. N.Y., 1937.
Phil 7069.57.16 Rhine, Joseph B. New world of the mind. N.Y., 1953.
Rhine, Joseph B. Parapsychology, frontier science of the mind. 2. ed. Springfield, 1962.
Phil 7069.57.15 Rhine, Joseph B. Parapsychology. Springfield, Ill., 1957.
Phil 7069.65.15 Rhine, Joseph B. Parapsychology from Duke to FRNM. Durham, 1965.
Phil 7069.47.5A Rhine, Joseph B. The reach of the mind. N.Y., 1947.
Phil 7010.10 Rhine, Joseph Banks. Parapsychology today. 1. ed. N.Y., 1968-
Phil 7162.267.5 Rhine, Louisa E. ESP in life and lab. N.Y., 1967.
Phil 7069.61.10 Rhine, Louisa E. Hidden channels of the mind. N.Y., 1961.
Phil 720.5 Rhodes, D.P. Philosophy of change. N.Y., 1909.
Phil 5257.29 Rhodes, G. The mind at work. London, 1914.
Phil 57.14F Rhodes University, Grahamstown, South Africa. Department of Philosophy. Occasional papers. Grahamstown. 1,1965+
Phil 57.14 Rhodes University, Grahamstown, South Africa. Department of Philosophy. Philosophical papers. Grahamstown. 3,1967+
Phil 3549.8.30 Rhyghmen und Runen aus dem Nachlass. (Klages, Ludwig.) Leipzig, 1944.
Phil 5047.38 The rhyme of reason; a guide to accurate and mature thinking. (Holmes, R.W.) N.Y., 1939.
Phil 9495.164.10 Rhymes, D.A. No new morality. Indianapolis, Ind., 1964.
Phil 178.60 Rhythmic affinity, a philosophic hypothesis. (Dakin, John E.) N.Y., 1929.
Phil 575.29 Rhythmus, Religion, Persönlichkeit. (König, Karl.) Jena, 1908.
Phil 192.9 Riambourg, J.B. Oeuvres philosophiques. Paris, 1846. 3v.
Phil 1210.2 Riambourg, Jean B.C. L'école d'Athènes. Paris, 1829.
Phil 8672.24 Riazantsev, N.I. Chto takoe ateizm. Moskva, 1961.
Phil 9590.27 Riazantsev, N.I. Sushchestvet li sud'ba? Moskva, 1959.
Phil 8707.19 Riba Elichabe, R. La ciencia confirma a Cristo. Rosario, 1939.
Phil 4372.1.130 Riba y García, Carlos. Luis Vives y el pacifismo. Zaragoza, 1933.
Phil 4630.1.35 Ribbing, Sigurd. Eristiska blad. Upsala, 1852.
Phil 4630.1.31 Ribbing, Sigurd. Grundlinier till anthropololgien. 4. uppl. Upsala, 1870.
Phil 817.12 Ribbing, Sigurd. Grundlinier till philosophiens historia. Upsala, 1864.
Phil 7069.34.63 Ribbons of the sky. v.1-3. (Wells, Helen B.) N.Y., 1934-35.
Phil 2475.1.460 Ribeiro, Alvaro. Escritores doutrinados. Lisboa, 1965.
Phil 192.99 Ribeiro, Alvaro. Estudos gerais. Lisboa, 1961.
Phil 9035.15 Ribery, C. Essai de classification naturelle des caracteres. Paris, 1902.
Phil 5545.22.5 Ribot, T. Diseases of memory. N.Y., 1882.
Phil 5545.22.6 Ribot, T. Diseases of memory. N.Y., 1883.
Phil 7040.2.5 Ribot, T. Diseases of personality. Photoreproduction. N.Y., 1887.
Phil 5767.1.12 Ribot, T. The diseases of the will. Chicago, 1894.
Phil 5767.1.10 Ribot, T. The diseases of the will. 3. ed. Chicago, 1903.
Phil 5227.1.10 Ribot, T. English psychology. London, 1873.
Phil 5227.1.5 Ribot, T. English psychology. London, 1892.
Phil 5440.4.5 Ribot, T. Die Erblichkeit. Paris, 1897.
Phil 5440.4.3 Ribot, T. Die Erblichkeit. v.1-4. Leipzig, 1876.

Phil 5400.18.15 Ribot, T. Essai sur les passions. Paris, 1907.
Phil 5400.18.19 Ribot, T. Essai sur les passions. 4. éd. Paris, 1917.
Phil 5465.5 Ribot, T. Essai sur l'imagination créatrice. Paris, 1900.
Phil 5465.5.4 Ribot, T. Essai sur l'imagination créatrice. 4. éd. Paris, 1914.
Phil 5465.5.3 Ribot, T. Essai sur l'imagination créatrice. 6. éd. Paris, 1921.
Phil 5465.5.5 Ribot, T. Essay on the creative imagination. Chicago, 1906.
Phil 348.3 Ribot, T. L'évolution des idées générales. Paris, 1897.
Phil 348.3.4 Ribot, T. L'évolution des idées générales. Paris, 1915.
Phil 348.3.5 Ribot, T. Evolution of general ideas. Chicago, 1899.
Phil 5227.2.5 Ribot, T. German psychology of to-day. N.Y., 1886.
Phil 5227.2.6 Ribot, T. German psychology of to-day. N.Y., 1899.
Phil 5440.4.9 Ribot, T. L'hérédité psychologique. 2. éd. Paris, 1882.
Phil 5440.4.2 Ribot, T. Heredity. N.Y., 1891.
Phil 5400.18.9 Ribot, T. La logique des sentiments. 2. éd. Paris, 1907.
Phil 5400.18.12 Ribot, T. La logique des sentiments. 5. éd. Paris, 1920.
Phil 5545.22.2 Ribot, T. Les maladies de la mémoire. Paris, 1881.
Phil 5545.22 Ribot, T. Les maladies de la mémoire. Paris, 1881.
Phil 5767.1 Ribot, T. Les maladies de la volonté. Paris, 1883.
Phil 3808.94 Ribot, T. La philosophie de Schopenhauer. Paris, 1874.
Phil 3808.94.10 Ribot, T. La philosophie de Schopenhauer. 12. éd. Paris, 1909.
Phil 5400.18.25 Ribot, T. Problèmes de psychologie affective. Paris, 1910.
Phil 5227.2 Ribot, T. La psychologie allemande contemporaine. Paris, 1879.
Phil 5227.2.3 Ribot, T. La psychologie allemande contemporaine. 2. éd. Paris, 1885.
Phil 5227.1 Ribot, T. La psychologie anglaise contemporaine. Paris, 1870.
Phil 5330.4.6 Ribot, T. Psychologie de l'attention. Paris, 1889.
Phil 5330.4.15 Ribot, T. Die Psychologie der Aufmerksamkeit. 9 Aufl. Leipzig, 1908.
Phil 5400.18.6 Ribot, T. Psychologie der Gefühle. Altenburg, 1903.
Phil 5400.18.4 Ribot, T. La psychologie des sentiments. Paris, 1896.
Phil 5400.18.5 Ribot, T. La psychologie des sentiments. 16. éd. Paris, 1939.
Phil 5330.4.7 Ribot, T. The psychology of attention. Chicago, 1890.
Phil 5330.4.5 Ribot, T. Psychology of attention. N.Y., 1889.
Phil 5400.18 Ribot, T. The psychology of the emotions. London, 1897.
Phil 5330.4.10 Ribot, T. Uppmärksamhetens psykologi. Stockholm, 1891.
Phil 5545.22.10 Ribot, T. Viljans sjukdomar. 6. uppl. Stockholm, 1890.
Phil 6327.46.10 Ribot, Théodule. The diseases of personality. Chicago, 1891.
Phil 6327.46.14 Ribot, Théodule. The diseases of personality. 4th ed. Chicago, 1906.
Phil 6327.46 Ribot, Théodule. Les maladies de la personnalité. Paris, 1885.
Phil 6327.46.7 Ribot, Théodule. Les maladies de la personnalité. 7. éd. Paris, 1897.
Phil 6327.46.20 Ribot, Théodule. Le malattie della personalità. Milano, 1923.
Phil 6327.46.18 Ribot, Théodule. Personlighetens sjukdomar. Stockholm, 1892.
Phil 2855.2.81 Ribot, Théodule. Théodule Ribot; choix de textes. Paris, 1913.
Phil 5649.11.3 Ribot, Théodule. La vie inconsciente et les mouvements. 3. éd. Paris, 1914.
Phil 6687.9 Ricard, J.J.A. Letters d'un magnétiseur. Paris, 1843.
Phil 400.37 Ricardon, A. De l'idéal. Étude philosophique. Paris, 1890.
Phil 3837.6 Ricardou, A. De hrimauae mentis aeternitate apud Spinoza. Lutet, 1890.
Phil 4080.3.485 Ricci, Angelo. Benedetto Croce. Pôrto Alegre, 1966.
Phil 4265.4.85 Ricci, Umberto. Necrologio di Giovanni Vailati. Roma, 1909.
Phil 2115.164 Ricci Garotti, Loris. Locke e i suoi problemi. Urbino, 1964.
Phil 2750.11.215 Riccio, Franco. Maritain umano e metafisico. Trapani, 1968.
Phil 8672.20 Ricciotti, G. Dio nella ricerca umana. 3. ed. Roma, 1954.
Phil 3837.14 Ricco, Cesare. Le dottrine giuridiche...di Spinoza e Hobbes. Giovinazzo, 1884.
Phil 192.83 Rice, Cale Y. A new approach to philosophy. Lebanon, Tennessee, 1943.
Phil 9513.40 Rice, Charles E. The vanishing right to live. 1st ed. Garden City, N.Y., 1969.
Phil 9530.17 Rice, Elwood E. Rice leaders of the world association, its inspiration, realization and objects. N.Y., 1914.
Phil 1618.5 Rice, Eugene Franklin. The Renaissance idea of wisdom. Cambridge, 1958.
Phil 6060.25.10 Rice, L.G. (Mrs.). Practical graphology. Chicago, 1910.
Phil 6060.25 Rice, L.G. (Mrs.). Who is your mate? N.Y., 1930.
Phil 298.22 Rice, Laban Lucy. The universe, its origin, nature and destiny. N.Y., 1951.
Phil 9240.13 Rice, P.B. On the knowledge of good and evil. N.Y., 1955.
Phil 8707.7 Rice, William N. Christian faith in an age of science. N.Y., 1903.
Phil 8707.7.5 Rice, William N. The poet of science and other addresses. N.Y., 1919.
Phil 8707.7.3 Rice, William N. The return to faith. N.Y., 1916.
Phil 8707.7.9 Rice, William N. Science and religion. Cincinnati, 1925.
Phil 9530.17 Rice leaders of the world association, its inspiration, realization and objects. (Rice, Elwood E.) N.Y., 1914.
Phil 4070.7.30 La ricerca della realta. (Banfi, Antonio.) Firenze, 1959. 2v.
Phil 70.60 La ricerca filodofica. (Istituto di Studi Filosofici Serione di Torino.) Roma, 1941.
Phil 1717.20 La ricerca filosofia nella coscienza delle nuove generazioni. Bologna, 1957.
Phil 4073.97.5 Ricerche Campanelliane. (Firpo, Luigi.) Firenze, 1947.
Phil 4170.3.84 Ricerche e documenti Desanctisiani. Dal carteggio inedito di A.C. de Meis. (Croce, B.) Napoli, 1915.
Phil 6115.25 Ricerche ergografiche nella donna. (Ferrari, G.C.) Reggio Emilia, 1898.
Phil 41.10 Ricerche filosofiche. (Bologna. Universita. Instituto di Filosofia. Sgione Teoretica.) 1,1959+ 5v.
Phil 176.180 Ricerche filosofiche. (Bosco, Giovanni.) Napoli, 1953.
Phil 27.34 Ricerche filosofiche. Messina. 1-9,1931-1939 4v.
Phil 27.34.5 Ricerche filosofiche. Index to 1-10 (1931-1940). Messina, n.d.
Phil 3800.340.20 Ricerche filosofiche su...libertá umana. (Schelling, F.W.J. von.) Lanciano, 1910.
Phil 3425.530 Ricerche hegeliane. (Fazio Allmayer, Vito.) Firenze, 1959.

Phil 8403.37 Ricerche per un'estetica del contenuto. (Carbonara, C.) Napoli, 1960.

Phil 45.1 Ricerche psicologia. (Laboratorio di Psicologia Sperimentale, Florence. Istituto di Studi Superiori.) Firenze. 1-2,1905-1907

Phil 1195.16 Ricerche sul linguaggio e sulla logica del sofista. (Zadro, Attilio.) Padova, 1961.

Phil 623.50 Ricerche sul razionalismo della prassi. (Vasa, Andrea.) Firenze, 1957.

Phil 4265.3.33 Ricerche sulla scienza speculativa e esperimentale. (Vera, A.) Parigi, 1864.

Phil 343.65 Ricerche sulla struttura della conoscenza formale. (Moscato, Alberto.) Milano, 1962.

Phil 8084.2F Ricerche sulla teorica delle arti figurative nella riforma cattolica. (Prodi, Paolo.) Roma, 1962.

Phil 3425.714 Ricerche sull'estetica di Hegel. (Brissoni, Armando.) Padova, 1968.

Phil 2050.45 Ricerche sull'intelletto umano e sui principii della morale. (Hume, David.) Bari, 1910.

Phil 2050.45.5 Ricerche sull'intelletto umano e sui principii della morale. 2a ed. (Hume, David.) Bari, 1927.

Phil 192.24 Richard, A. Souvenirs...d'un penseur moderne. Genève, 1905.

Phil 2855.5.31 Richard, C. Esquisse d'une philosophie synthésiste. Paris, 1875.

Phil 298.1 Richard, C. Les lois de Dieu. Paris, 1862.

Phil 2855.5.33 Richard, C. Réponse à Charles Renouvier au sujet de son appreciation de l'Esquisse d'une philosophie synthésiste. Paris, 1875.

Phil 1750.136 Richard, Christian. Le mouvement humaniste en Amerique. Paris, 1934.

Phil 1750.136.5 Richard, Christian. Le mouvement humaniste en Amérique et les courants de pensée similaire en France. Thèse. Paris, 1934.

Phil 365.7 Richard, G. L'idée d'evolution. Paris, 1903.

Phil 5590.90 Richard, G. La psychanalyse de l'homme normal. Lausanne, 1951.

Phil 8672.12 Richard, Gaston. L'athéisme dogmatique en sociologie religieuse. Strasbourg, 1923.

Phil 8842.9 Richard, Gaston. L'évolution des moeurs. Paris, 1925.

Phil 7069.65.40 Richard, Hermann. La tradition ésotérique et la science. Paris, 1965.

Phil 1522.4 Richard, J. Introduction à l'étude et à l'enseignement de la scolastique. Paris, 1913.

Phil 192.46 Richard, R.P. Le probabilisme moral et la philosophie. Paris, 1922.

Phil 175.12.9 Richard Avenarius. (Ewald, Oskar.) Berlin, 1905.

Phil 331.2.8 Richard Avenarius' Biomechanische Grundlegung. (Carstanjen, F.) München, 1894.

Phil 1928.80 Richard Cumberland...englischen Ethik. (Spaulding, F.E.) Leipzig, 1894.

Phil 179.24.2 Richard Kane looks at life. (Edman, Irwin.) Boston, 1926.

Phil 179.24 Richard Kane looks at life. (Edman, Irwin.) Boston, 1926.

Phil 8411.7 Richard Payne Knight et le pittoresque essai sur une phase esthétique. (Mayoux, J.J.) Paris, 1932.

Phil 8892.19 Richards, C.H.B. Springs of action. N.Y., 1863.

Phil 8892.68 Richards, David A.J. A theory of reasons for action. Oxford, 1971.

Phil 5520.145.10 Richards, Ivor Armstrong. Design for escape; world education through modern media. 1. ed. N.Y., 1968.

Phil 5520.145.15 Richards, Ivor Armstrong. Interpretation in teaching. N.Y., 1938.

Phil 5520.145 Richards, Ivor Armstrong. Speculative instruments. Chicago, 1955.

Phil 5520.145.5 Richards, Ivor Armstrong. So much nearer; essays toward a world English. 1. ed. N.Y., 1968.

Phil 7054.126 Richards, L.S. The beginning of man and what becomes of him. Boston, 1815.

Phil 192.20 Richards, L.S. New propositions in...philosophy. Plymouth, 1903.

Phil 5545.150 Richards, Lysander. The analysis and cause of existence of memory and The analysis and cause of unconsciousness and sleep. pt.1-2. n.p., 1920.

Phil 1750.162 Richards, P.S. Humanism. London, 1934.

Phil 8672.11 Richards, William. Reflections on French atheism. 2. ed. Lynn, n.d.

Phil 5465.182 Richardson, Alan. Mental imagery. London, 1969.

Phil 5465.182.1 Richardson, Alan. Mental imagery. N.Y., 1969.

Phil 192.36.10 Richardson, C.A. Spiritual pluralism and recent philosophy. Cambridge, 1919.

Phil 192.36 Richardson, C.A. Spiritual pluralism and recent philosophy. Cambridge, 1919.

Phil 192.36.5 Richardson, C.A. The supremacy of spirit. London, 1922.

Phil 4752.2.185 Richardson, David B. Berdyaev's philosophy of history. The Hague, 1968.

Phil 5827.5 Richardson, F. A study of sensory control in the rat. n.p., 1909.

Phil 5841.10 Richardson, Herbert Warren. Nun, witch, playmate; the Americanization of sex. 1st ed. N.Y., 1971.

Phil 7069.02.17 Richardson, J.E. The great psychological crime. 11th ed. Chicago, 1912.

Phil 7069.06.35 Richardson, J.E. The great work. 12. ed. Chicago, 1911.

Phil 7069.25.10 Richardson, Mark Wyman. Margery, Harvard veritas. Boston, 1925.

Phil 7069.25.9A Richardson, Mark Wyman. Margery - Harvard - Veritas; a study in psychics. Boston, 1925.

Phil 7069.28.10 Richardson, Mark Wyman. The thumbprint and cross correspondence experiments made with the medium Margery during 1927-1928. n.p., 1928.

Phil 7082.124 Richardson, Phelps. A book on the interpretation of dreams. Worcester, 1904-05.

Phil 8597.46 Richardson, Robert D. Christian belief and practice. London, 1940.

Phil 3450.19.280 Richardson, W.J. Heidegger: through phenomenology. The Hague, 1963.

Phil 8610.940.5 Richberg, Donald. G. Hovah explains. Washington, 1940.

Phil 5257.23 Riche, A. Essai de psychologie; sur le cerveau. Paris, 1881.

Phil 6619.4.2 Richer, Paul. Études cliniques sur la grande hystérie ou hystéro-épilepsie. 2. ed. Paris, 1885.

Phil 8878.52 The richer life. (Dyer, W.A.) Garden City, 1911.

Phil 8050.91 Richerche di estetica e il guidizio stoico. (Fazio-Allmayer, Bruna.) Bologna, 1968.

Phil 4170.7 Richerche di psichiatria...dedicate al...E. Morselli. Milano, 1907.

Phil 5585.275 Richerche sperimentali sulla percezione. Trieste, 1968.

Phil 3425.180 Richert, Hans. Hegels Religionsphilosophie. Bromberg, 1900.

Phil 3808.119 Richert, Hans. Schopenhauer; seine Persönlichkeit. 3. Aufl. Leipzig, 1916.

Phil 900.13 The richest vein. (Eaton, Gai.) London, 1949.

Phil 7060.126 Richert, C. Experimentelle Studien. Stuttgart, 1891.

Phil 5257.6.5 Richet, Charles. Essai de psychologie général. 10. éd. Paris, 1919.

Phil 5257.6 Richet, Charles. L'homme et l'intelligence. Paris, 1884.

Phil 192.60.5 Richet, Charles. L'homme impuissant. Paris, 1927.

Phil 5390.6 Richet, Charles. L'homme stupide. Paris, 1919.

Phil 192.60.10 Richet, Charles. The impotence of man. Boston, 1929.

Phil 5257.6.10 Richet, Charles. L'intelligence et l'homme. Paris, 1927.

Phil 5635.31 Richet, Charles. Recherches experimentales et cliniques sur la sensibilité. Paris, 1877.

Phil 7069.23.15 Richet, Charles. Thirty years of psychical research. N.Y., 1923.

Phil 7069.23.16 Richet, Charles. Traité de métaphysique. 2. ed. Paris, 1923.

Phil 7069.22.20 Richet, Charles R. Traité de métapsychique. Paris, 1922.

Phil 3195.6.125 Richey, H.G. Die Überwindung der Subjektivität in der empirischen Philosophie Diltheys und Deweys. Göttingen, 1935.

Phil 3910.81 Richler, H. Über Christian Wolffs Ontologie. Leipzig, 1910.

Phil 18.7.11 Richman, John. Development...psycho-analytical theory of psychosis, 1893-1926. London, 1928.

Phil 7060.102.9 Richmond, Almon B. What I saw at Cassadaga lake: Seybert Commission report. Boston, 1888.

Phil 7069.15.50 Richmond, Cora L. My experiences while out of my body and my return after many days. Boston, 1915.

Phil 7069.15.53 Richmond, Cora L. Psychosophy. Chicago, 1915.

Phil 7054.176 Richmond, Cora L. Spiritual sermons [delivered in 1886-1889]. n.p., n.d.

Phil 8642.8 Richmond, I. Archaeology. London, 1950.

Phil 7069.39.50 Richmond, K. Evidence of identity. London, 1939.

Phil 575.7 Richmond, W. Essay on personality as a philosophical principle. London, 1900.

Phil 8597.28 Richmond, W. Philosophy and the Christian experience. Oxford, 1922.

Phil 5257.49 Richmond, W.V. Personality: its development and hygiene. N.Y., 1937.

Phil 7069.38.50 Richmond, Z. Evidence of purpose. London, 1939.

Phil 5057.21 Richter, A. Grundlegung der philosophischen Wissenschaften und Elemente der Logik. 1888.

Phil 3640.164 Richter, Claire. Nietzsche et les théories biologiques contemporaines. 2. éd. Paris, 1911.

Phil 5257.40 Richter, Conrad. Human vibrations. Harrisburg, 1925.

Phil 5257.40.5 Richter, Conrad. Principles in bio-physics. Harrisburg, 1925.

Phil 5545.227 Richter, Derek. Aspects of learning and memory. N.Y., 1966.

Phil 8448.15 Richter, G. Erbauliches, Belehrendes, wie auch Vergnügliches kitsch Lexion. Gütersloh, 1970.

Phil 298.8 Richter, G. Die Philosophie der Eimmaligkeit. Wien, 1928-32. 3v.

Phil 3837.7 Richter, G.T. Spinozas philosophische Terminologie. Leipzig, 1913.

Phil 192.49 Richter, H. Anrede bey Eröffnung von Vorlesungen über Metaphysik. Leipzig, 1823.

Phil 5057.5 Richter, Heinrich. Über den Gegenstand und den Umfang der Logik. Leipzig, 1825.

Phil 5871.72 Richter, Horst Eberhard. Eltern, Kind und Neurose. 2. Aufl. Stuttgart, 1967.

Phil 6687.2 Richter, J.A.L. Betrachtungen und der animal Magnetismus. Leipzig, 1817.

Phil 8642.1 Richter, J.P.F. Das Kampaner Thal. Erfurt, 1797.

Phil 3625.1.180 Richter, Johann Andreas Lebrecht. Moses Mendelssohn als Mensch. Dessau, 1829.

Phil 8520.15 Richter, Johannes. Die Religionsphilosophie der fichteschen Schule. Berlin, 1931.

Phil 3552.328 Richter, L. Leibniz und sein Russland. Berlin, 1946.

Phil 2520.285 Richter, L. René Descartes. Hamburg, 1942.

Phil 2880.8.282 Richter, Liselotte. Jean-Paul Sartre. N.Y., 1970.

Phil 3625.1.165 Richter, Liselotte. Philosophie der Dicht Kunst. Berlin, 1948.

Phil 2020.88 Richter, M. The politics of conscience. Cambridge, 1964.

Phil 2020.89 Richter, M. The politics of conscience. London, 1964.

Phil 3499.7 Richter, Otto. Kants Auffassung des Verhaltnisses von Glaüben und Wissen. Lauban, 1905.

Phil 3640.93.2 Richter, R. Friedrich Nietzsche. 3. Aufl. Leipzig, 1917.

Phil 8597.31 Richter, R. Religionsphilosophie. Leipzig, 1912.

Phil 192.37.10 Richter, Raoul. Dialoge über Religionsphilosophie. Leipzig, 1911.

Phil 192.37.3 Richter, Raoul. Einführung in die Philosophie. 3e Aufl. Leipzig, 1913.

Phil 192.37 Richter, Raoul. Einführung in die Philosophie. 4e Aufl. Leipzig, 1913.

Phil 192.37.5 Richter, Raoul. Essays. Leipzig, 1913.

Phil 3808.163 Richter, Raoul. Schopenhauer's Verhältnis zu Kant in seinen Grundzügen. Leipzig, 1893.

Phil 645.9 Richter, Raoul. Der Skeptizismus in der Philosophie. Leipzig, 1904-08.

Phil 3837.17 Richter, Raoul. Der Willensbegriff in der Lehre Spinoza's. Leipzig, 1898.

Phil 75.86 Richter, Richard. Humdert Jahre philosophische Bibliothek 1868-1968. Hamburg, 1968.

Phil 5374.28 Richter, Rudolf. Herbart'sch und Bergmann'sche Problem des Bewusstseins. Inaug. Diss. Greifswald, 1883?

Phil 5066.257 Richter, Vladimir. Untersuchungen zur operativen Logik der Gegenwart. Freiburg, 1965.

Phil 3640.225 Richtlinien christlicher Apologetik wider Nietzsche. (Simon, Theodor.) Berlin, 1917.

Phil 3903.3.113 Richtscheid, H. Das Problem des philosophischen Skeptizismus. Diss. Düsseldorf, 1935.

Phil 3790.30 Richtscheid, Hans. Existenz in dieser Zeit. München, 1965.

Phil 3790.30.5 Richtscheid, Hans. Helle Nächte; drei Stücke Existenzphilosophie. München, 1968.

Phil 5767.2.3A Rickaby, Joseph. Free will and four English philosophers. London, 1906.

Phil 1535.6.14 Rickaby, Joseph. Moral philosophy. 4th ed. London, 1919.

Phil 1522.3.3 Rickaby, Joseph. Scholasticism. N.Y., 1908.

Phil 1522.3 Rickaby, Joseph. Scholasticism. London, 1908.

Phil 8610.917 Ricker, M.M. I am not afraid, are you? East Aurora, N.Y., 1917.

Phil 8610.916 Ricker, M.M. I don't know, do you? East Aurora, N.Y., 1916.

Phil 5593.60.5 Rickers-Ovsiankiua, Maria A. Rorschach psychology. N.Y., 1960.

Phil 192.21.15　Rickert, H. Allgemeine Grundlegung der Philosophie. Tübingen, 1921.

Phil 192.21　Rickert, H. Der Gegenstand der Erkenntniss. Freiburg, 1892.

Phil 192.21.2　Rickert, H. Der Gegenstand der Erkenntniss. Tübingen, 1904.

Phil 192.21.3　Rickert, H. Der Gegenstand der Erkenntniss. 3. Aufl. Tübingen, 1915.

Phil 192.21.3.6　Rickert, H. Der Gegenstand der Erkenntniss. 6. Aufl. Tübingen, 1928.

Phil 348.9　Rickert, H. Der Gegenstand der Erkenntnistheorie. 4. und 5. Aufl. Tübingen, 1921.

Phil 192.21.20　Rickert, H. Grundprobleme der Philosophie. Tübingen, 1934.

Phil 3499.14　Rickert, H. Kant als Philosoph der Modernen. Tübingen, 1924.

Phil 192.21.5　Rickert, H. Philosophie: ihr Wesen, ihre Probleme. Leipzig, 1912.

Phil 1750.122.2　Rickert, H. Die Philosophie des Lebens. Tübingen, 1922.

Phil 3925.6.90　Rickert, H. Wilhelm Windelband. Tübingen, 1915.

Phil 5190.4　Rickert, H. Zur Lehre von der Definition. 2e Aufl. Tübingen, 1915.

Phil 5190.4.2　Rickert, H. Zur Lehre von der Definition. 3. Aufl. Tübingen, 1929.

Phil 192.21.10　Pamphlet vol. Rickert, H. Zur Lehre von der Definition. 15 pam.

Phil 6327.11　Rickman, J. Index psychoanalyticus, 1893-1926. London, 1928.

Phil 6327.11.5　Rickman, J. Selected contributions to psychoanalysis. London, 1957.

Phil 210.55　Ricoeur, Paul. Le conflit des interprétations; essais d'herméneutique. Paris, 1969.

Phil 6315.2.365　Ricoeur, Paul. De l'interprétation. Paris, 1965.

Phil 2750.19.115　Ricoeur, Paul. Entretiens Paul Ricoeur, Gabriel Marcel. Paris, 1968.

Phil 5767.11.10　Ricoeur, Paul. Freedom and nature. Evanston, Ill., 1966.

Phil 6315.2.444　Ricoeur, Paul. Freud and philosophy. New Haven, 1970.

Phil 2750.13.85　Ricoeur, Paul. Gabriel Marcel et Karl Jaspers. Paris, 1948.

Phil 3450.11.370　Ricoeur, Paul. Husserl; an analysis of his phenomenology. Evanston, 1967.

Phil 5767.11A　Ricoeur, Paul. Philosophie de la volonté. Photoreproduction. Paris, 1950. 2v.

Phil 5767.11.5　Ricoeur, Paul. Philosophy of the will. v.2, pt. 1. Chicago, 1965-

Phil 2070.144　Riconda, G. La filosofia di William James. Torino, 1962.

Phil 3808.240　Riconda, Giuseppe. Schopenhauer interprete dell'occidente. Milano, 1969.

Phil 193.181　Riconda, Giuseppe. Ugo Spirito. Torino, 1956.

Phil 4160.1.85　Ricordi autobiografici. (Labanca, Baldassare.) Agnone, 1913.

Phil 348.6　Riddell, Newton N. Science of creation. Des Moines, Iowa, 192-.

Phil 8597.9　Riddle, A.G. Alcastor. n.p., 1883.

Phil 197.59　Riddle of being. (Wells, Gabriel.) N.Y., 1934.

Phil 5628.55.21　The riddle of Konnersreuth; a psychological and religious study. (Siwek, Paul.) Dublin, 1954.

Phil 5252.18.38　The riddle of life. (McDougall, William.) London, 1938.

Phil 8696.15　The riddle of nature. (Gaulter, A.) London, 1929.

Phil 575.12　Riddle of personality. (Bruce, H.A.) N.Y., 1908.

Phil 575.12.2　Riddle of personality. (Bruce, H.A.) N.Y., 1915.

Phil 575.59　The riddle of personality: mechanism or mystery? (McBride, Peter.) London, 1926.

Phil 7069.27.33　The riddle of spiritualism. (Palmer, E.C.) London, 1927.

Phil 510.1.9　The riddle of the universe; a review. (Scarrett, W.R.) n.p., 1902.

Phil 180.2　The riddle of the universe. (Fawcett, E.D.) London, 1893.

Phil 510.1.7.5　The riddle of the universe. (Haeckel, Ernst.) London, 1925.

Phil 510.1.6A　The riddle of the universe. (Haeckel, Ernst.) N.Y., 1900.

Phil 510.131　The riddle of the universe scientifically interpreted. (Brooks, H.J.) n.p., 1924.

Phil 193.9.2　Riddles of the Sphinx. (Schiller, F.C.S.) London, 1894.

Phil 193.9.3　Riddles of the Sphinx. (Schiller, F.C.S.) London, 1910.

Phil 192.94　Rideau, E. Paganisme ou christianisme. Tournai, 1953.

Phil 2475.1.238.15　Rideau, Émile. Descartes, Pascal, Bergson. Paris, 1937.

Phil 2475.1.237　Rideau, Émile. Le dieu de Bergson. Paris, 1932.

Phil 2475.1.236　Rideau, Émile. Le dieu de Bergson. Thèse. Paris, 1932.

Phil 2905.1.365　Rideau, Émile. La pensée du Père Teilhard de Chardin. Paris, 1965.

Phil 2475.1.238　Rideau, Émile. Les rapports de la matière et de l'esprit dans le bergsonisme. Paris, 1932.

Phil 2475.1.238.5　Rideau, Émile. Les rapports de la matière et de l'esprit dans le bergsonisme. Thèse. Paris, 1932.

Phil 2905.1.500　Rideau, Émile. Teilhard, oui ou non? Paris, 1967.

Phil 2905.1.366　Rideau, Émile. Teilhard de Chardin; a guide to his thought. London, 1967.

Phil 6946.1.10　Ridenour, Nina. Mental health in the United States. Cambridge, 1961.

Phil 7069.09.20　Rider, Fremont. Are the dead alive? N.Y., 1909.

Phil 6360.5　Rie, Herbert E. Perspectives in child psychopathology. Chicago, 1971.

Phil 3850.32.85　Rieber, Arnulf. Vom Positivismus zum Universalismus. Berlin, 1971.

Phil 5057.19　Rieber, Charles H. Footnotes to formal logic. Berkeley, 1916.

Phil 3017.4　Riecke, H. Der Rassegedanke und die neuere Philosophie. Leipzig, 1935.

Phil 3425.618　Riedel, Manfred. Theorie und Praxis im Denken Hegels. Stuttgart, 1965.

Phil 585.418　Riedel, Maximilian. Der Mensch und das Ganze. München, 1969.

Phil 3499.3　Riedel, O.J. Die monadologischen...Bestimmungen...Kant's. Hamburg, 1884.

Phil 298.12　Rieder, Albert. Die Pole der Gesamtnatur. Pfaffenhofen an der Ilm, 1959.

Phil 5875.125　Rieder, Oskar. Die Entwicklung des kindlichen Fragens. München, 1968.

Phil 75.33　Riedl, J.O. A catalogue of Renaissance philosophers. Milwaukee, 1940.

Phil 585.315　Riedweg, Franz. Konservative Evolution. München, 1968.

Phil 6315.2.240　Rieff, Philip. Freud; the mind of the moralist. N.Y., 1959.

Phil 585.172　Rieff, Philip. The triumph of the therapeutic. 1st ed. N.Y., 1966.

Phil 6687.3　Rieger, C. Der Hypnotismus. Jena, 1884.

Phil 5767.4　Rieger, Conrad. Experimentelle Untersuchungen. Jena, 1885.

Phil 6127.17　Rieger, Conrad. Über Apparate in dem Hirn. Jena, 1909.

Phil 8892.20　Riego, Julio del. Nociones fundamentales de ética ó filosofía moral. Madrid, 1903.

Phil 4065.89　Riehl, A. Giordano Bruno. Edinburgh, 1905.

Phil 4065.89.20　Riehl, A. Giordano Bruno. Leipzig, 1889.

Phil 4065.89.5　Riehl, A. Giordano Bruno. 2e, Aufl. Leipzig, 1900.

Phil 3640.118.6　Riehl, Alois. Friedrich Nietzsche. 6e Aufl. Stuttgart, 1920.

Phil 3640.118.7　Riehl, Alois. Friedrich Nietzsche. 7e Aufl. Stuttgart, 1920.

Phil 3640.118A　Riehl, Alois. Friedrich Nietzsche der Künstler und der Denker. Stuttgart, 1897.

Phil 3640.118.2　Riehl, Alois. Friedrich Nietzsche der Künstler und der Denker. 2e Aufl. Stuttgart, 1898.

Phil 3791.40　Riehl, Alois. Führende Denker und Forscher. Leipzig, n.d.

Phil 1717.5.9　Riehl, Alois. Inleiding tot de hedendaagsche wijsbegeerte. Zutphen, 1918.

Phil 3791.36　Riehl, Alois. Introduction to theory of science and metaphysics. London, 1894.

Phil 3791.06　Riehl, Alois. Moral und Dogma. n.p., 1871-92. 5 pam.

Phil 1717.5.2　Riehl, Alois. Philosophie der Gegenwart. 2e Aufl. Leipzig, 1904.

Phil 3791.35.2A　Riehl, Alois. Der philosophische Kritcismus. 2e Aufl. Leipzig, 1908.

Phil 3791.35　Riehl, Alois. Der philosophischeKriticismus. v.1-2. Leipzig, 1876-1887.

Phil 3791.35.3　Riehl, Alois. Der philosophische Kritizismus. Leipzig, 1924-1926. 3v.

Phil 3791.75　Riehl, Alois. Philosophische Studien aus 4 Jahrzehnten. Leipzig, 1925.

Phil 3791.45　Riehl, Alois. Realistische Grundzüge. Graz, 1870.

Phil 3791.30　Riehl, Alois. Uber Begriff und Form der Philosophie. Berlin, 1872.

Phil 3791.50　Riehl, Alois. Zur Einführung in der Philosophie des Gegenwart. Leipzig, 1903.

Phil 1717.5.4　Riehl, Alois. Zur Einführung in die Philosophie der Gegenwart. 4. Aufl. Leipzig, 1913.

Phil 1717.5.5　Riehl, Alois. Zur Einführung in die Philosophie der Gegenwart. 5e Aufl. Leipzig, 1919.

Phil 1618.2　Riekel, August. Die Philosophie der Renaissance. München, 1925.

Phil 3790.4.79　Pamphlet box. Riekert, Heinrich.

Phil 817.23　Riel, Hans. Urwissen. 2. Aufl. Wien, 1956.

Phil 3925.16.240　Rielkopf, Charles F. Strict finitism. The Hague, 1970.

Phil 5401.47　Riemann, Fritz. Grundformen der Angst und die Antinomien des Lebens. München, 1961.

Phil 6315.2.190　Riemann, Fritz. Lebendige Psychoanalyse. München, 1956.

Phil 5593.66.20　Riemsdijk, Jan van. Geschiedenis en perspectieven van de Rorschach. Proefschrift. Utrecht, 1966.

Phil 960.282　Riepe, Dale Maurice. The philosophy of India and its impact on American thought. Springfield, 1970.

Phil 3640.775　Ries, Wiebrecht. Grundzüge des Nietzsche-Verständnisses in der Deutung seiner Philosophie. Maulburg, 1967?

Phil 6980.644　Riese, Hertha. Heal the hurt child. Chicago, 1962.

Phil 6965.3.95　Riese, Walter. The legacy of Philippe Pinel. N.Y., 1969.

Phil 5400.174　Riese, Walther. La théorie des passions à la lumière de la pensée médicale du XVIIe siècle. N.Y., 1965.

Phil 5827.11　Riess, Bernard F. Limits of learning ability in the white rat and the guinea pig. Diss. Worcester, Mass., 1934.

Phil 3790.22　Riessen, Hendrick van. Mens en werk. Amsterdam, 1962.

Phil 3790.22.5　Riessen, Hendrick van. Op wijsgerige wegen. Wageningen, 1963.

Phil 6327.36A　Riessman, Frank. Mental health of the poor. London, 1964.

Phil 348.17　Riet, G. van. L'épistémologie thomiste. Louvain, 1946.

Phil 348.17.5　Riet, G. van. Problèmes d'épistémologie. Louvain, 1960.

Phil 348.24　Riet, G. van. Thomistic epistemology. St. Louis, 1963. 2v.

Phil 8597.66　Riet, Georges van. Philosophie et religion. Louvain, 1970.

Phil 3837.18　Rietz, J.E. De Spinozismi fonte orientali. Diss. Lundae, 1839.

Phil 3790.15.30　Riezler, K. Man, mutable and immutable. Chicago, 1950.

Phil 5767.6　Riezler, Kurt. Gestalt und Gesetz. München, 1924.

Phil 2490.172　Riezu, J. Sozialmoral. München, 1961.

Phil 5871.65　Rifbjerg, Sofie. Psykologisk iagttagelse af børn. København, 1966.

Phil 3450.19.385　Rifga, Fuad. Studien zur Ästhetik Martin Heideggers und Oskar Beckers. Inaug. Diss. Tübingen, 1965.

Phil 8092.14　Il rifiuto del mondo nell'arte comtemporanea. (Bianco, Giovanni A.) Bari, 1964.

Phil 5625.85　I riflessi orientative nella studio delle attività mentali. (Tullio, P.) Bologna, 1938.

Phil 5625.69　I riflessi vascolari nelle membra e nel cervello dell'uomo. (Patrizi, M.L.) Reggio-Emilia, 1897.

Phil 8887.65　Riflessioni per la vita morale civile. (Mancini, F.O.) Parma, 1706.

Phil 1740.24　Riflessioni su filosofia e cultura. (Raschini, Maria A.) Milano, 1968.

Phil 192.85.10　Riflessioni su temi filosofici fondamentali. (Raeymaeker, Louis de.) Milano, 1958.

Phil 1506.8　Riflessioni sulla scolastica. (Bruni, Gerardo.) Roma, 1907.

Phil 2520.352　Riforma cattolica e filosofia moderna. (Noce, Augusto del.) Bologna, 1965.

Phil 3425.209　La riforma della dialettica Hegeliana. (Gentile, G.) Messina, 1913.

Phil 3425.209.5　La riforma della dialettica Hegeliana. 2a ed. (Gentile, G.) Messina, 1923.

Phil 187.82　Rifts in the universe. (Moore, J.S.) New Haven, 1927.

Phil 7054.30　Rifts in the veil. London, 1878.

Phil 4368.1.80　Rigau, P. La obra del filósofo español Diego Ruiz. Paris, 1913.

Phil 8707.14　Rigdon, Jonathan. Science and religion as they look to a layman. Danville, Ind., 1928.

Phil 8892.51　Rigerus, Johannes. Ethicorum liber. v.1-2. n.p., 16- ?

Phil 4195.40　Rigg, J.M. Giovanni Pico della Mirandola: his life. London, 1890.

Phil 6127.18　Riggs, A.F. Intelligent living. Garden City, 1929.

Phil 6127.18.10　Riggs, A.F. Just nerves. Boston, 1922.

Phil 6127.18.12　Riggs, A.F. Talks to patients. n.p., 1924-27.

Phil 4080.3.137　Righi, Gaetano. Il Croce interprete del Vico. Bologna, 1931.

Phil 194.42　Right; a study in physical and moral order. (Tilby, Aubry W.) London, 1933.

Phil 8880.49　Right and reason. (Fagathey, Austin.) St. Louis, 1953.

Phil 8880.49.2 — Right and reason. 2nd ed. (Fagathey, Austin.) St. Louis, 1959.

Phil 8892.46 — The right and the good. (Ross, W.D.) Oxford, 1930.

Phil 8897.88 — Right and wrong; a philosophical dialogue between father and son. (Weiss, Paul.) N.Y., 1967.

Phil 3850.5.15 — Right and wrong. (Spir, Afrikan.) Edinburgh, 1954.

Phil 5242.14.12 — Right and wrong thinking. (Crane, A.M.) Boston, 1914.

Phil 6132.3 — The right hand. Left handedness. (Wilson, D.) London, 1891.

Phil 8882.26.5 — Right living as a fine art. (Hillis, N.D.) N.Y., 1899.

Phil 9177.4 — The right relationship between parents and children. (Rowntree, Constance M.) Bannisdale, 19- ?

Phil 8960.7 — The right road. (Kramer, J.W.) N.Y., 1891.

Phil 5041.40.20 — Right thinking. 3rd ed. (Burtt, Edwin Arthur.) N.Y., 1946.

Phil 9245.49 — The right to be happy. (Russell, Dora.) N.Y., 1927.

Phil 8597.17 — Right to believe. (Rowland, E.H.) Boston, 1909.

Phil 5465.184 — The right to create. 1. ed. (Groch, Judith.) Boston, 1970.

Phil 6116.6 — Righthandedness and lefthandedness. (Gould, G.M.) Philadelphia, 1908.

Phil 9560.44 — Rightness and goodness. (Johnson, Oliver A.) The Hague, 1959.

Phil 9070.70 — Rights and right conduct. (Melden, Abraham.) Oxford, 1959.

Phil 5257.36 — Rignano, E. Come funziona la nostra intelligenza. Bologna, 1922.

Phil 8892.45 — Rignano, E. Il fine dell'uomo. Bologna, 1928.

Phil 192.61 — Pamphlet vol. Rignano, E. Das biologische Gedächtnis. 10 pam.

Phil 5620.9 — Rignano, Eugenio. Psychologie du raisonnement. Paris, 1920.

Phil 5620.9.7 — Rignano, Eugenio. Psychology of reasoning. N.Y., 1927.

Phil 8597.27 — Rignano, Eugenio. Religione, materialismo, socialismo. Bologna, 1920.

Phil 3499.31 — Rigobello, A. I limiti del trascendentale in Kant. Milano, 1963.

Phil 1830.40 — Rigobello, Armando. La filosofia americana contemporanea. Torino, 1960.

Phil 8670.9 — Rigou, Arthur C. The problem of theism. London, 1908.

Phil 978.49.810 — Rihonët-Coroze, S. Rudolf Steiner. Paris, 1951.

Phil 5027.2 — Rijh, Lambertus. Logica modernorum. Assen, 1962. 3v.

Phil 3120.40.45 — Het rijk van den geest. (Bierens de Haan, J.D.) Zeist, 1938.

Phil 3846.10 — Rijnsburg, Netherlands. Spinozahuis. Mededeslingen. Leiden. 1,1934+ 3v.

Phil 5400.55 — Rikimaru, J. Emotion and endocrine activities. n.p., 1924.

Phil 1817.3A — Riley, I.W. American philosophy. N.Y., 1907.

Phil 1817.3.8 — Riley, I.W. American thought. Gloucester, 1959.

Phil 1817.3.5 — Riley, I.W. American thought. N.Y., 1915.

Phil 1817.3.7 — Riley, I.W. American thought. 2nd ed. N.Y., 1923.

Phil 1817.3.5.5 — Riley, I.W. Le génie américain. Paris, 1921.

Phil 525.69 — Riley, I.W. The meaning of mysticism. N.Y., 1930.

Phil 1817.3.9 — Riley, I.W. La philosophie française en Amérique. Paris, 1919.

Phil 1817.9 — Riley, I.W. La philsophie française en Amérique. Paris, n.d.

Phil 8842.7 — Riley, Isaac. Men and morals. Garden City, 1929.

Phil 8610.918 — Riley, Isaac W. Early free thinking societies in America. N.Y., 1918.

Phil 5350.5.10 — Riley, Matilda White. Aging and society. N.Y., 1968. 2v.

Phil 8707.11.2 — Riley, W.B. Inspiration or evolution. 2. ed. Cleveland, 1926.

Phil 4115.94 — Rinaldi, R. Gioberti e il problema religioso del risorgimento. Firenze, 1929.

Phil 6327.6 — Rinaldo, Joel. Psychoanalysis of the "reformer". N.Y., 1921.

Phil 8980.213.5 — Die Rind dir andere neben Dir. (Bittighoefer, Bernd.) Berlin, 1965.

Phil 298.3 — Rindell, E. Framställning af teorierna om det kosmiska före Sölger och Hegel. Helsingfors, 1885.

Phil 4580.81.5 — Rindom, E. Harald Høffding. Kjøbenhavn, 1918.

Phil 4580.81 — Rindom, E. Samtaler med Harald Høffding, 1909-1918. København, 1918.

Phil 192.100 — Rinerso, Emmanuele. Metafisica e scientismo. Napoli, 1957.

Phil 8892.50 — Rines, George E. Getting the most out of life. Boston, 1935.

Phil 6967.16 — Ringel, Erwin. Einführung in die Grundprobleme der Neurose. Wien, 1959.

Phil 7150.50 — Ringel, Erwin. Neue Untersuchungen zum Selbstmordproblem. Wien, 1961.

Phil 190.54.10 — Ringen der Gegenwart. (Przywara, Erich.) Augsburg, 1929. 2v.

Phil 5257.82 — Ringness, Thomas A. Psychology in theory and practice. Boston, 1959.

Phil 3499.26 — Rink, Friedrich T. Ansichten aus Immanuel Kant's Leben. Königsberg, 1805.

Phil 3499.26.5 — Rink, Friedrich T. Mancherley zur Geschichte der metacritischen Invasion. Bruxelles, 1969.

Phil 8709.10 — Il rinnovamento...tomistico e la scienza. (Talamo, S.) Roma, 1927.

Phil 4210.24.5 — Il rinnovamento della filosofia in Italia. (Rosmini-Serbati, Antonio.) Milano, 1836. 3 pam.

Phil 5628.55.25 — Rinser, Luise. Die Wahrheit über Konnersreuth. Einsiedeln, 1954.

Phil 3415.102 — Rintelen, F.J. von. Pessimistische Religionsphilosophie der Gegenwart. München, 1924.

Phil 817.18 — Rintelen, F.J. von. Philosophia perennis. Regensburg, 1930. 2v.

Phil 735.100 — Rintelen, F.J. von. Der Wertgedanke in der europäischen Geistesentwicklung. Halle, 1932.

Phil 192.67.22 — Rintelen, Fritz J. von. Der Aufstieg im Geiste. 2. Aufl. Frankfurt, 1968.

Phil 192.67.15 — Rintelen, Fritz J. von. Beyond existentialism. London, 1961.

Phil 192.67.10 — Rintelen, Fritz J. von. Der europäische Mensch. Wien, 1957.

Phil 192.67 — Rintelen, Fritz J. von. Philosophia perennis. Regensburg, 1930. 2v.

Phil 192.67.5 — Rintelen, Fritz J. von. Philosophie der Endlichkeit. Meisenheim, 1951.

Phil 3017.10 — Rintelen, Fritz-Joachim von. Contemporary German philosophy and its background. Bonn, 1970.

Phil 293.22 — Das Rinzen der alten Stoff-Form-Metaphysik mit der heutigen Stoff-Physik. (Mitterer, Albert.) Innsbruck, 1935.

Phil 4979.41.30 — Rio, Manuel. La liberté; choix, amour, création. Paris, 1961.

Phil 57.10 — Rio de Janeiro. Universidade do Brasil. Instituto de Psicologia. Annuario.

Phil 57.12 — Rio de Janeiro. Universidade do Brasil. Instituto de Psicologia. Boletim; revista de estudos psicológicos. 7,1957+ 2v.

Phil 5057.6 — Rion, J. Gemeinfassliche Darstellung der Denklehre. Reutlingen, 1844.

Phil 196.29.5 — Rionas y byondas. (Vincenzi, M.) San José, 1921.

Phil 1145.94 — Riondato, E. Ethos. Padova, 1961.

Phil 4372.1.93 — Ríos Sarmiento, Juan. Juan Luis Vives. 1. ed. Madrid, 1940.

Phil 2417.2A — Ripley, G. Philosophical miscellanies...Cousin, Jouffray. Boston, 1838. 2v.

Phil 2475.1.69.7 — Le rire. (Bergson, Henri.) Genève, 1945.

Phil 2475.1.69.5 — Le rire. (Bergson, Henri.) Paris, 1928.

Phil 5525.16 — Le rire. (Philbert, Louis.) Paris, 1883.

NEDL Phil 5525.11.10 — Le rire. 5. éd. (Bergson, Henri.) Paris, 1908.

Phil 2475.1.69 — Le rire. 57. éd. (Bergson, Henri.) Paris, 1941.

Phil 5525.52 — Le rire et le risible. 1. éd. (Victoroff, D.) Paris, 1953.

Phil 5525.21 — Le rire et les exhilarants. (Raulin, J.M.) Paris, 1900.

Phil 5525.27 — Le rire et l'origine des idées. (Talhouet, J. de.) Rennes, 1923.

Phil 585.169 — La riscoperta del sacro. (Morra, Gianfranco.) Bologna, 1964.

Phil 8602.55 — The rise and fall of the individual. (Witcutt, W.P.) N.Y., 1958.

Phil 8592.32 — The rise of modern religous ideas. (McGiffert, A.C.) N.Y., 1922.

Phil 1717.17 — The rise of scientific philosophy. (Reichenbach, H.) Berkeley, 1951.

Phil 4012.9 — Riserve su l'umanesimo. (Montanari, Fausto.) Milano, 1943.

Phil 5790.40 — Risikoverhalten als Persönlichkeitsmerkmal. (Klebelsberg, Dieter von.) Bern, 1969.

Phil 5627.134.50F — Rising tide. Chicago, 1938.

Phil 270.75 — Risk and gambling. (Cohen, John.) London, 1956.

Phil 1750.250 — Riskante philosophie. (Peursen, C.A. van.) Amsterdam, 1948.

NEDL Phil 5525.11.5 — Il riso, saggio sul significato del comico. (Bergson, Henri.) Bari, 1916.

Phil 5525.65.5 — Il riso e l'arte del ridere. (Ruvo, Vincenzo de.) Bari, 1965.

Phil 5525.46 — Il riso in psicologia. (Senise, T.) Napoli, 1950.

Phil 4011.3 — Il risorgimento filosofica in Italia. (Librizzi, C.) Padova, 1952. 2v.

Phil 4015.1 — Il risorgimento filosofico in Italia. (Puglia, F.) Napoli, 1891.

Phil 4210.129.5 — Risposta ad alcuni appunti...sul libro A. Rosmini ed i neoscolastici. (Petri, Giuseppe.) Torino 1879.

Phil 4210.92.15 — Risposta agli attachi di G. di Cavour. (Gioberti, Vincenzo.) Torino, 1848.

Phil 4210.116.10 — Risposta 1a al padre Cornoldi in difesa delle nozioni di ontologia. (Buroni, Giuseppe.) Torino, 1878.

Phil 9070.113 — Risque et prudence. (Brihat, Denise.) Paris, 1966.

Phil 5003.12 — Risse, Wilhelm. Bibliographia logica. Hildesheim, 1965.

Phil 5027.4 — Risse, Wilhelm. Die Logik der Neuzeit. Stuttgart, 1964- 2v.

Phil 1170.18 — Rist, John M. Eros and Psyche. Toronto, 1964.

Phil 1200.70 — Rist, John Michael. Stoic philosophy. London, 1969.

Phil 1817.10 — Ritchie, A.D. British philosophers. London, 1950.

Phil 2255.6 — Ritchie, Arthur D. Essays in philosophy and other pieces. London, 1948.

Phil 5257.48 — Ritchie, Arthur D. The natural history of mind. London, 1936.

Phil 1870.160 — Ritchie, Arthur David. George Berkeley, a reappraisal. Manchester, 1967.

Phil 192.10A — Ritchie, D.G. Darwin and Hegel. London, 1893.

Phil 192.10.5 — Ritchie, D.G. Philosophical studies. London, 1905.

Phil 575.5 — Ritchie, E. The problem of personality. Ithaca, N.Y., 1889.

Phil 2050.86 — Ritchie, T.E. Account of life...D. Hume. London, 1807.

Phil 5257.16 — Rith, L. L'intelligence. Thèse. Paris, 1912.

Phil 2805.187 — Un ritratto immaginario di Pascal. (Neri, F.) Torino, 1921.

Phil 735.15 — Ritschel, Otto. Über Wethurtheile. Freiburg, 1895.

Phil 3805.185 — Ritschl, Alfrecht. Schleiermachers Reden über die Religion und ihre Nachwirkungen auf die evangelische Kirche Deutschlands. Bonn, 1874.

Phil 2150.6.82F — Ritschl, Otto. Die Causalbetrachtung in den Geisteswissenschaften. Bonn, 1901.

Phil 3640.178.5 — Ritschl, Otto. Nietzsches Welt und Lebensanschauung. Freiburg, 1897.

Phil 3640.178 — Ritschl, Otto. Nietzsches Welt und Lebensanschauung. 2. Aufl. Leipzig, 1899.

Phil 5057.18 — Ritschl, Otto. Program zur Feier des Gedächtnisses. Bonn, n.d.

Phil 3805.159 — Ritschl, Otto. Schleiermacher's Stellung zum Christentum. Gotha, 1888.

Phil 3425.702 — Ritta, Joachim. Metaphysik und Politik. Frankfurt, 1969.

Phil 3640.270.90 — Ritteleyer, F. Friedrich Nietzsche und das Erkenntnisproblem. Leipzig, 1903.

Phil 3640.271 — Rittelmeyer, F. Friedrich Nietzsche und die Religion. Ulm, 1904.

Phil 974.3.51 — Rittelmeyer, F. Rudolf Steiner enters my life. London, 1929.

Phil 974.3.50 — Rittelmeyer, F. Von der Theosophie Rudolf Steiners. Nürnberg, 1919.

Phil 1522.1 — Ritter, A.H. Die christliche Philosophie. Göttingen, 1858-9.

Phil 817.2 — Ritter, A.H. Geschichte der Philosophie. Hamburg, 1829-45. 12v.

Phil 817.2.1 — Ritter, A.H. Geschichte der Philosophie. v.1-4. Hamburg, 1929-53.

Phil 817.2.4 — Ritter, A.H. Geschichte der Philosophie. 2e Aufl. Hamburg, 1836-53. 12v.

Phil 1522.1.5 — Ritter, A.H. Histoire de la philosophie chretienne. Paris, 1843-4. 2v.

Phil 1717.2 — Ritter, A.H. Histoire de la philosophie moderne. Paris, 1861. 3v.

Phil 3017.2 — Ritter, A.H. Versuch zur neueste deutsche Philosophie...Kant. Braunschweig, 1853.

Phil 817.2.2 — Ritter, A.H. Zusätze und Verbesserungen. Hamburg, 1838.

Phil 8892.30 — Ritter, Eli F. Moral law and civil law; parts of the same thing. N.Y., 1896.

Phil 8892.30.2   Ritter, Eli F. Moral law and civil law; parts of the same thing. Westerville, Ohio, 1910.
Phil 1540.41   Ritter, Gerhard. Via Antique und via Moderna auf den deutschen Universitaeten des XV Jahrhunderts. Darmstadt, 1963.
Phil 8620.10   Ritter, H. Über das Böse und seine Folgen. Cotha, 1869.
Phil 8620.10.5   Ritter, H. Über das Böse und seine Folgen. Kiel, 1839.
Phil 8672.3   Ritter, H. Über die Erkenntniss Gottes in der Welt. Hamburg, 1836.
Phil 1020.16   Ritter, H. Über unsere Kenntniss der arabischen Philosophie. Göttingen, 1844.
Phil 5057.12   Ritter, Heinrich. Abriss der philosophischen Logik. Berlin, 1824.
Phil 5057.12.4   Ritter, Heinrich. Abriss der philosophischen Logik. 2. Aufl. Berlin, 1829.
Phil 192.12.7   Ritter, Heinrich. Encyklopädie der philosophischen Wissenschaften. Göttingen, 1862-1864. 3v.
Phil 1122.2.10   Ritter, Heinrich. Geschichte der jonischen Philosophie. Berlin, 1821.
Phil 1122.2   Ritter, Heinrich. Histoire de la philosophie ancienne. Paris, 1835-36. 4v.
Phil 1122.3.17   Ritter, Heinrich. Historia philosophiae graecae. Gotha, 1898.
Phil 1122.3.25   Ritter, Heinrich. Historia philosophiae graecae. 9th ed. Gotha, 1913.
Phil 1122.3.27   Ritter, Heinrich. Historia philosophiae graecae. 10 ed. Gotha, 1934.
Phil 1122.3.9   Ritter, Heinrich. Historia philosophiae graecae et romanae. Gotha, 1864.
Phil 1122.3.11   Ritter, Heinrich. Historia philosophiae graecae et romanae. 5. ed. Gotha, 1875.
Phil 1122.3.12   Ritter, Heinrich. Historia philosophiae graecae et romanae. 6. ed. Gotha, 1878.
Phil 1122.3.13   Ritter, Heinrich. Historia philosophiae graecae et romanae. 7.ed. Gotha, 1888.
Phil 1122.3.5   Ritter, Heinrich. Historia philosophiae graeco-romanae. Gotha, 1857.
Phil 1122.3   Ritter, Heinrich. Historia philosophiae graeco-romanae. Hamburg, 1838.
Phil 1122.2.5   Ritter, Heinrich. History of ancient philosophy. Oxford, 1838-46. 4v.
Phil 1122.2.6   Ritter, Heinrich. History of ancient philosophy. Oxford, 1838-46. 4v.
Phil 192.12.5   Ritter, Heinrich. Kleine philosophische Schriften. v.1-3. Kiel, 1839-1840.
Phil 192.12.15   Ritter, Heinrich. Philosophische Paradoxa. Leipzig, 1867.
Phil 192.12   Ritter, Heinrich. System der Logik und der Metaphysik. Göttingen, 1856. 2v.
Phil 850.18   Ritter, Heinrich. Über die Unanationslehre im Übergange aus der Alterlhümlichen in die christlicheDenkeweise. Göttingen, 1847.
Phil 8642.5.5   Ritter, Heinrich. Unsterblichkeit. Leipzig, 1866.
Phil 2520.265   Ritter, Heinrich. Welcher Einfluss hat die Philosophie des Cartesius auf die Ausbildung der des Spinoza Gehabt. Leipzig, 1817.
Phil 3625.1.135   Ritter, I.H. Mendelssohn und Lessing. 2e Aufl. Berlin, 1886.
Phil 8892.29.7   Ritter, P.H. Ethische fragmenten. 7. druk. Haarlem, 1924.
Phil 8892.29.15   Ritter, P.H. Etiske fragmenter. København, 1896.
Phil 3552.116   Ritter, P.H. De monadenleer van Leibniz. Leiden, 1882.
Phil 5643.46   Ritter, Sarah M. The vertical-horizontal illusion. Princeton, 1917.
Phil 8892.31   Ritter, T.H. Lifvets konst. Stockholm, 1906.
Phil 9150.28   Ritter, William E. The natural history of our conduct. N.Y., 1927.
Phil 8820.5   Ritterliches Tugendsystem. (Eifler, Günter.) Darmstadt, 1970.
Phil 7068.74.40   Ritti, A. Théorie psychologique de l'hallucination Paris, 1874.
Phil 8672.30   Ritti, Jean Marie Paul. De la notion de Dieu d'après la méthode sentimentale. Paris, 1930.
Phil 6327.12.5   Ritual; psycho-analytical studies. (Reik, Theodor.) London, 1931.
Phil 6327.12.7   Ritual; psycho-analytical studies. (Reik, Theodor.) N.Y., 1958.
Phil 5627.185   The ritual of higher magic. (Morrish, Furze.) London, 1947?
Phil 2477.6.122   Ritz, Maria. Le problème de l'être dans l'ontologie de Maurice Blondel. Fribourg, 1958.
Phil 3246.258   Ritzel, W.W. Fichtes Religionsphilosophie. Stuttgart, 1956.
Phil 165.380   Ritzel, Wolfgang. Rationalität, Phänomenalität, Individualität. Bonn, 1966.
Phil 1750.840   Riu, Federico. Ontología del siglo XX: Husserl. Caracas, 1966.
Phil 8597.54   Riva, C. Pensiero e coerenza cristiana. Brescia, 1963.
Phil 4210.166   Riva, Clemente. Antonio Rosmini nel primo centenario della morte. Firenze, 1958.
Phil 7054.37.30   Rivail, H.L.D. El cielo y el infierno. 4. ed. Barcelona, 1871.
Phil 7054.37.25   Rivail, H.L.D. El evangelio segun el espiritismo. Barcelona, 1875.
Phil 7054.37.33   Rivail, H.L.D. El génesis, los milagros. Barcelona, 1871.
Phil 7054.37.35   Rivail, H.L.D. El génesis. San Martin de Provensals, 1887.
Phil 7054.37   Rivail, H.L.D. Le livre des esprits. Paris, 1857.
Phil 7054.37.15   Rivail, H.L.D. Le livre des esprits. 15. ed . Paris, 1866.
Phil 7054.37.40   Rivail, H.L.D. Spiritizm v samom prostom ego vyrazhenii. Leiptsig, 1864.
Phil 7068.93.10   Rivail, H.L.D. Spiritualist philosophy. Boston, 1893.
Phil 300.10   Rival theories of cosmology. (Third Programme.) London, 1960.
Phil 4372.1.84   Rivari, Enrico. La sapienza psicologica e pedagogica di Giovanni L. Vives. Bologna, 1922.
Phil 8892.52   Rivarol, E.F. de. Encyclopédie morale. Paris, 1803.
Phil 1122.8   Rivaud, Albert. Les grands couvants de la pensée antique. Paris, 1929.
Phil 817.21   Rivaud, Albert. Histoire de la philosophie. Paris, 1948-3v.
Phil 817.21.2   Rivaud, Albert. Histoire de la philosophie. 2. ed. Paris, 1960.
Phil 3837.9   Rivaud, Albert. Les notions d'essence...de Spinoza. Paris, 1906.
Phil 1122.7   Rivaud, Albert. Le problème du devenir et la notion de la matière dans la philosophie grecque depuis les origines jusqu'à Theophraste. Paris, 1906.

Phil 4752.2.180   La rivelazione della libertà. (Zoppo, Franco.) Firenze, 1966.
Phil 8582.39   Rivelazione e filosofia. (Cordovani, M.) Milano, n.d.
Phil 348.15   Riveline, M. Essai sur le problème le plus général, action et logique. Thèse. Paris, 1939.
Phil 2255.1.120   Riverro, Emmanuele. Il pensiero di Bertrand Russell. Napoli, 1958.
Phil 6327.5A   Rivers, W.H.R. Instinct and the unconscious. Cambridge, Eng., 1920.
Phil 6327.5.5   Rivers, W.H.R. Instinct and the unconscious. 2. ed. Cambridge, Eng., 1924.
Phil 6327.5.15   Rivers, W.H.R. L'instinct et l'inconscient. Paris, 1926.
Phil 6127.14   Rivers, W.H.R. Mind and medicine. 2d ed. Manchester, 1920.
Phil 7084.26   Rivers, William Halse Rivers. Conflict and dream. London, 1923.
Phil 7084.28   Rivers, William Halse Rivers. Dreams and primitive culture. Manchester, 1917-18.
Phil 817.26   Riverso, E. Il pensiero occidentale. v.1-3. Napoli, 1964.
Phil 1828.8   Riverso, Emanuele. La filosofia analitica in Inghilterra. Roma, 1969.
Phil 3925.16.180   Riverso, Emanuele. Il pensiero di Ludovico Wittgenstein. Napoli, 1965?
Phil 5520.397   Riverso, Emmanuele. La costruzione interpretative del mondo analizzata dal l'epistenrologia genetica. Napoli, 1956.
Phil 8430.28   Riverso, M. L'esperienza estetica e la vita del fanciullo. Napoli, 1958.
Phil 720.62   Rivetti Barbo, Francesca. L'antinomia del mentitore nel pensiero contemporaneo da Peirce a Tarski. Milano, 1961.
Phil 192.78.5   Rivier, W. Les deux chemins. Bruxelles, 1951.
Phil 192.78   Rivier, W. Le problème de la vie. Paris, 1937.
Phil 192.102   Rivier, William. Le pouvoir de l'esprit. Neuchâtel, 1957.
Phil 2905.1.530   Rivière, Claude. En Chine avec Teilhard. Paris, 1968.
Phil 400.72   La rivincita dell'idealismo. (Corti, Settimio.) Rieti, 1920.
Phil 27.78   Rivista di filosofia. Torino. 3,1910+ 47v.
Phil 27.21   Rivista di filosofia e scienze affini. Padova. 1899-1908 10v.
Phil 27.12   Rivista di filosofia neo-scolastica. Firenze. 1,1909+ 57v.
NEDL Phil 27.2   Rivista di filosofia scientifica. Milano, 1881-1891. 10v.
Phil 27.11   Rivista di psicologia. Bologna. 1,1905+ 46v.
Phil 27.11.5   Rivista di psicologia. Indice generale, 1905-1936. Bologna, n.d. 2v.
Phil 27.62   Rivista di psicologia della scrittura. Milano. 1,1955+ 7v.
Phil 27.44   Rivista di storia della filosofia. Milano. 1,1946+ 23v.
Phil 4080.3.415   Rivista di studi crociani. Napoli. 1,1964+
Phil 27.19   Rivista di studi psichici. Padova. 1-4,1895-1898 3v.
Phil 4260.97   Rivista internationale di filosofia del diritto. Per il secondo centenario della "Scienza nuova" di Vico. Roma, 1925.
Phil 27.13   Rivista italiana di filosofia. Roma. 1,1886+ 13v.
Phil 27.35   Rivista rosminiana. Torino. 1,1906+ 46v.
Phil 27.14   Rivista trimestrale di studi filosofici. Perugia. 1-4,1920-1923 3v.
Phil 2750.22.115   La rivoluzione cristiana. (Campanini, Giorgio.) Brescia, 1968.
Phil 7054.89   A rivulet from the ocean of truth. (Adams, J.S.) Boston, 1854.
Phil 2255.1.180   Rizzacasa, Aurelio. Il pacifismo nella dottrina politico-pedagogica di Bertrand Russell. Bologna, 1969.
Phil 8672.28   Rizzacasa, Aurelio. Il problema di Dio nella filosofia occidentale. Viterbo, 1969?
Phil 348.19   Rizzi, Erminio. L'esperienza e la sua possibilita. Padova, 1958.
Phil 348.19.10   Rizzi, Erminio. Il progresso delle conoscenze umane. Padova, 1967.
Phil 2905.1.540   Rizzo, Enrico. La problematica di Teilhard de Chardin. Bologna, 1965.
Phil 4265.2.96   Rizzo, R. Teocrazia e neo-cattaluisimo nel risorgimento. Palermo, 1938.
Phil 5827.9   Rizzolo, Attilio. Études expérimentales sur l'exitabilité de l'écorce cérébrale du chien. Thèse. Paris, 1928.
Phil 3819.35.30A   The road to inner freedom. (Spinoza, Benedictus de.) N.Y., 1957.
Htn Phil 192.82*   Roas, A. Den amsteldamsen diogenes. Utrecht, 1684.
Phil 6329.22   Roazen, Paul. Brother animal; the story of Freud and Tausk. 1st ed. N.Y., 1969.
Phil 6315.2.390   Roazen, Paul. Freud; political and social thought. 1. ed. N.Y., 1968.
Phil 5850.326.12   Roback, A.A. Aspects of applied psychology and crime. Cambridge, 1964.
Phil 5257.28   Roback, A.A. Behaviorism and psychology. Cambridge, 1935.
Phil 5257.28.30   Roback, A.A. Behaviorism at twenty-five. Cambridge, Mass., 1937.
Phil 9035.45.5   Roback, A.A. A bibliography of character. Cambridge, Mass., 1927.
Phil 575.57   Roback, A.A. Character and inhibition. n.p., 1925.
Phil 5850.326.5F   Roback, A.A. Course in business psychology assignment. v.1-8. n.p., n.d.
Phil 6315.2.185   Roback, A.A. Freudiana. Cambridge, Mass., 1957.
Phil 6315.2.107   Roback, A.A. Freudiana. n.p., n.d. 3 pam.
Phil 5850.326.9   Roback, A.A. Getting more out of life. n.p., 1937.
Phil 5420.5.5   Roback, A.A. Getting rid of self-consciousness. n.p., 1934.
Phil 5227.6   Roback, A.A. History of American psychology. N.Y., 1951.
Phil 5227.6.2   Roback, A.A. History of American psychology. N.Y., 1964.
Phil 5227.6.10   Roback, A.A. History of psychology and psychiatry. N.Y., 1961.
Phil 9530.38.50   Roback, A.A. I am winning friends. Cambridge, 1938.
Phil 5850.326   Roback, A.A. The moral issues involved in applied psychology. n.p., 1917.
Phil 575.57.10   Roback, A.A. Personality, the crux of social intercourse. Cambridge, Mass., 1931.
Phil 575.57.11   Roback, A.A. Personality. London, 1931.
Phil 5590.50   Roback, A.A. Personality in theory and practice. Cambridge, Mass., 1950.
Phil 5257.28.9   Roback, A.A. Popular psychology. Cambridge, 1928.
Phil 5257.28.35   Roback, A.A. Present day psychology. N.Y., 1955.
Phil 9035.45.4   Roback, A.A. Psicologia del caracter. Traduccion de Santo Rubiano. Madrid, 192-?
Phil 5257.28.5   Roback, A.A. Psychology. Rahway, 1923.
Phil 9035.45   Roback, A.A. The psychology of character. London, 1927.
Phil 9035.45.2   Roback, A.A. The psychology of character. N.Y., 1927.
Phil 9035.45.3   Roback, A.A. The psychology of character. N.Y., 1928.

Phil 9035.45.10	Roback, A.A. The psychology of character. 3. ed. Cambridge, Mass., 1952.
Phil 5257.28.10	Roback, A.A. The psychology of common sense. Cambridge, 1939.
Phil 5627.29	Roback, A.A. The psychology of confession. Montreal, 1917.
Phil 5257.28.15	Roback, A.A. Psychorama; a mental outlook and analysis. Cambridge, 1942.
Phil 5420.5	Roback, A.A. Self-consciousness and its treatment. Cambridge, 1933.
Phil 5420.5.10	Roback, A.A. Self-consciousness self-treated. Cambridge, 1936.
Htn Phil 8892.38F*	Roback, A.A. The status of ethics. n.p., 1914.
Phil 5420.5.11	Roback, A.A. Varför hämmar jag mig själo? Stockholm, 1939.
Phil 5257.28.25	Pamphlet box. Roback, A.A.
Phil 5780.8	Roback, Abraham A. The interference of will-impulses. Lancaster, Pa., 1918.
Phil 7082.72.10	Roback, Abraham Aaron. The meaning of dreams. n.p., 193-
Phil 5590.458	Robaye, Francine. Niveaux d'aspiration et d'expectation. Paris, 1957.
Phil 6947.1.10	Robb, Barbara. Sans everything; a case to answer. London, 1967.
Phil 4114.81	Pamphlet vol. Robba, R. Commemorazione di A. Genovesi. 2 pam.
Phil 3450.11.340	Robberechts, L. Husserl. Paris, 1964.
Phil 1135.170	Robbers, Joannes Henricus. Antieke wijsgerige opvattingen in het christelijk denkleven. Roermond, 1959.
Phil 5066.300	Robbin, Joel W. Mathematical logic; a first course. N.Y., 1969.
Phil 7069.09.40	Robbins, A.M. Both sides of the veil. Boston, 1909.
Phil 7060.91	Robbins, Anne M. Both sides of the veil. Boston, 1911.
Phil 9560.13	Robbins, C. Force of right purpose. Boston, 1859.
Phil 1865.194	Robbins, Lionel. Bentham in the twentieth century. London, 1965.
Phil 6420.20	Robbins, Samuel D. Stammering and its treatment. Boston, 1926.
Phil 2730.91	Robef, E. Leibniz et Maine de Biran. Thèse. Paris, 1925.
Phil 192.55	Robef, Euthyme. De l'analyse réflexive. Thèse. Paris, 1925.
NEDL Phil 2045.81	Roberstson, G.C. Hobbes. Philadelphia, 1886.
Phil 8892.21	Robert, A. Leçons de morale. Quebec, 1915.
Phil 817.5	Robert, A.A. Histoire de la philosophie. Québec, 1912.
Phil 5057.22	Robert, Arthur. Leçons de logique. Québec 1914.
Phil 5257.19	Robert, Arthur. Leçons de psychologie. Québec, 1915.
Phil 5257.19.3	Robert, Arthur. Leçons de psychologie. 3. éd. Québec, 1921.
Phil 9070.15	Robert, B.R. The glorious game. N.Y., 1929.
Phil 974.2.30	Robert, C.E.B. The mysterious Madame Helena P. Blavatsky. N.Y., 1931.
Phil 645.4	Robert, Louis. De la certitude et des formes recontes du scepticisme. Paris, 1880.
Phil 2493.85	Robert, Louis. Les théories logiques de Condillac. Thèse. Paris, 1869.
Phil 8707.27	Robert, M.D. Approche contemporaine d'une affirmation de Dieu. Bruges, 1962.
Phil 6315.2.382	Robert, Marthe. The psychoanalytic revolution. London, 1966.
Phil 6315.2.380	Robert, Marthe. La révolution psychanalytique. Paris, 1964. 2v.
Phil 8663.3.100	Robert G. Ingersoll; a checklist. 1. ed. (Stein, Gordon.) Kent, Ohio? 1969.
Phil 4060.1.81	Roberto Ardigo, l'uomo e l'umanista. (Marchesini, G.) Firenze, 1922.
Phil 4060.1.93	Roberto Ardigo. (Tarozzi, Giuseppe.) Roma, 1928.
Phil 1750.475	Roberts, D.C. Existentialism and religious belief. N.Y., 1959.
Phil 7069.61.15	Roberts, D.O. Elizabethan episode. London, 1961.
Phil 8892.49	Roberts, G.L. The domain of utilitarian ethics. Philadelphia, 1903.
Phil 8610.900.5	Roberts, G.L. Rational agnosticism. n.p., n.d.
Phil 630.27	Roberts, George L. Objective reality. London, 1925.
Phil 6327.13	Roberts, Harry. The troubled mind. N.Y., 1939.
Phil 1817.20	Roberts, James Deotis. From Puritanism to Platonism in seventeenth century England. The Hague, 1968.
Phil 1717.14	Roberts, Michael. The modern mind. London, 1937.
Phil 9470.12	Roberts, Moira. Responsibility and practical freedom. Cambridge, Eng., 1965.
Phil 7069.48.12	Roberts, Ursula. Mary Baker Eddy, her communications from beyond the grave to Harold Horwood. London, 1964.
Phil 7069.20.370	Roberts, W. Adair. A spiritual interpretation of some psychic happenings. London, 1932.
Phil 8430.23	Robertson, A. Contrasts: the arts and religion. London, 1947.
Phil 8672.4	Robertson, A. The laws of thought. London, 1865.
Phil 192.74	Robertson, A. Philosophers on holiday. London, 1933.
Phil 623.28	Robertson, A. Rationalism in theory and practice. London, 1954.
Phil 8842.11	Robertson, Archibald M.A. Morals in world history. London, 1945.
Phil 192.13	Robertson, G.C. Elements of general philosophy. London, 1896.
Phil 5257.7	Robertson, G.C. Elements of psychology. London, 1896.
Phil 192.13.5	Robertson, G.C. Philosophical remains. London, 1894.
Phil 2045.81.4	Robertson, George Croan. Hobbes. St. Clair Shores, Michigan, 1970.
Phil 7069.17.40	Robertson, Helen F. The letters of a woman who wa. Minneapolis, 1917.
Phil 9075.7	Robertson, J.D. Conscience. London, 1894.
Phil 192.77	Robertson, J.M. Explorations. London, 1923.
Phil 8610.929	Robertson, J.M. A history of freethought in the nineteenth century. London, 1929.
Phil 8610.929.5	Robertson, J.M. A history of freethought in the nineteenth century. N.Y., 1930. 2v.
Phil 8610.929.9	Robertson, J.M. A history of freethought in the nineteenth century. 4. ed. London, 1936. 2v.
Phil 1817.4	Robertson, J.M. Pioneer humanists. London, 1907.
Phil 623.4	Robertson, J.M. Rationalism. London, 1912.
Phil 8610.899	Robertson, J.M. A short history of freethought, ancient and modern. London, 1899.
Phil 8610.899.5	Robertson, J.M. A short history of freethought, ancient and modern. 2. ed. London, 1906. 2v.
Phil 8842.4	Robertson, J.M. A short history of morals. London, 1920.
Phil 192.77.5	Robertson, J.M. Spoken essays. London, 1925.
Phil 7069.20.290	Robertson, Mabel N. "The other side of God's door". London, 1920.
Phil 645.29	Roberty, E. de. Agnosticisme. 2e éd. Paris, 1893.
Phil 817.10	Roberty, E. de. L'ancienne et la nouvelle philosophie. Paris, 1887.
Phil 8892.4	Roberty, E. de. Constitution de l'éthique. Paris, 1900.
Phil 8892.4.10	Roberty, E. de. L'éthique. Le bien et le mal. Paris, 1896.
Phil 8892.4.5	Roberty, E. de. L'éthique. Les fondements de l'éthique. 2. ed. Paris, 1899.
Phil 1750.5	Roberty, E. de. La philosophie du siècle. Paris, 1891.
Phil 192.31	Roberty, E. de. Recherche de l'unité. Paris, 1893.
Phil 6668.3	Robiano, Comte de. Neururgie oder der thierische Magnetismus. Stuttgart, 1849.
Htn Phil 9495.35*	Robie, W.F. Rational sex ethics. Boston, 1916.
Phil 1145.82	Robin, L. La morale antique. Paris, 1938.
Phil 1122.6.5	Robin, Léon. Greek thought. N.Y., 1928.
Phil 1122.6.3	Robin, Léon. La pensée grecque et les origines de l'esprit scientifique. Paris, 1928.
Phil 1122.6.4	Robin, Léon. La pensée grecque et les origines de l'esprit scientifique. Paris, 1948.
Phil 1122.6.10	Robin, Léon. La pensee hellenique des origines a epicule questions de methode. 1.ed. Paris, 1942.
Phil 1190.15	Robin, Léon. Pyrrkon et le scepticisme grec. 1. éd. Paris, 1944.
Phil 1930.8.90	Robin George Collingwood, 1889-1943. (McCallum, R.B.) London, 1943.
Phil 1930.8.95	Robin George Collingwood, 1889-1943. (Tomlin, E.W.F.) London, 1953.
Phil 3552.461	Robinet, André. Leibniz und Wir. Göttingen, 1967.
Phil 2733.120	Robinet, Andre. Système et existence dans l'oeuvre de Malebranche. Paris, 1965.
Phil 600.36	Robinet, E. Den positiva filosofien i sammandrag. Stockholm, 1889.
Phil 2490.85	Robinet, J.F. Notice sur l'oeuvre et sur la vie d'Auguste Comte. Paris, 1860.
Phil 2855.7.30	Robinet, Jean Baptiste René. De la nature. Amsterdam, 1761.
Phil 2855.7.32	Robinet, Jean Baptiste René. De la nature. v.1-2. Amsterdam, 1763.
Phil 5066.90	Robinson, A. Complete theories. Amsterdam, 1956.
Phil 5252.18.65	Robinson, A.L. William McDougall, M.B., D.S.C., F.R.S.: a bibliography. Durham, 1943.
Phil 5057.13	Robinson, A.T. The applications of logic. N.Y., 1912.
Phil 8597.42	Robinson, D.F. In search of a religion. Chester, 1938.
Phil 1717.11	Robinson, D.S. Anthology of recent philosophy. N.Y., 1929.
Phil 1717.11.5	Robinson, D.S. Anthology of recent philosophy. N.Y., 1931.
Phil 1717.11.20	Robinson, D.S. Crucial issues in philosophy. Boston, 1955.
Phil 5057.20.7	Robinson, D.S. Illustrations of the methods of reasoning. N.Y., 1927.
Phil 1717.11.15	Robinson, D.S. An introduction to living philosophy. N.Y., 1932.
Phil 5057.20	Robinson, D.S. The principles of reasoning. N.Y., 1924.
Phil 5057.20.2	Robinson, D.S. The principles of reasoning. 2nd ed. N.Y., 1930.
Phil 5057.20.5	Robinson, D.S. The principles of reasoning. 3rd ed. N.Y., 1949.
Phil 1830.51	Robinson, D.S. The story of Scottish philosophy. 1st ed. N.Y., 1961.
Phil 2250.116	Robinson, Daniel Sommer. Royce and Hocking: American idealists. Boston, 1968.
Phil 8597.15	Robinson, E.K. The religion of nature. London, 1906.
Phil 5325.26	Robinson, E.S. Association theory today. N.Y., 1932.
Phil 5257.27.10	Robinson, E.S. Man as psychology sees him. N.Y., 1934.
Phil 5257.27.6	Robinson, E.S. Practical psychology; human nature in everyday life. N.Y., 1927.
Phil 5257.27	Robinson, E.S. Readings in general psychology. Chicago, 1923.
Phil 5257.27.3	Robinson, E.S. Readings in general psychology. Chicago, 1929.
Phil 7054.80	Robinson, J.H. The religion of manhood. Boston, 1854.
Phil 3450.19.270A	Robinson, J.M.C. The later Heidegger and theology. N.Y., 1963.
Phil 8642.10	Robinson, John Arthur Thomas. In the end, God. 1. ed. N.Y., 1968.
Phil 8597.55	Robinson, John Arthur Thomas. The new reformation? London, 1965.
Phil 3837.11	Robinson, L. Metafizika Spinozy. Sankt Peterburg, 1913.
Phil 3837.15	Robinson, Lewis. Kommentar zu Spinozas Ethik. v.1-2. Leipzig, 1928.
Phil 6327.21.90	Robinson, Paul Arnold. The Freudian left: Wilhelm Reich, Geza Roheim, Albert Marcuse. 1st ed. N.Y., 1969.
Phil 8672.25	Robinson, R. An atheist's values. Oxford, 1964.
Phil 5190.4.25	Robinson, R. Definition. Oxford, 1950.
Phil 5827.5.2	Robinson, R. (Mrs.). A study of sensory control in the rat. Lancaster, Pa., 1909.
Phil 1122.20	Robinson, Richard. Essays in Greek philosophy. Oxford, 1969.
Phil 5062.30.15	Robinson, Richard. The province of logic; an interpretation of certain parts of Cook Wilson's "Statement and inference". London, 1931.
Phil 1905.11.80	Robinson, Sanford. John Bascom, prophet. N.Y., 1922.
Phil 6952.18.25	Robinson, Victor. The Don Quixote of psychiatry. N.Y., 1919.
Phil 7068.98.15	Robinson, William E. Spirit state writing and kindred phenomena. N.Y., 1898.
Phil 5066.288	Robison, Gerson B. An introduction to mathematical logic. Englewood Cliffs, 1969.
Phil 4318.4	Robledo, Maria N. El mundo clásico en el pensamiento español contemporáneo. Madrid, 1965.
Phil 8597.10	Robles, M. Bigotry, superstition, hypocrasy...Atheism. London, 1742.
Phil 4959.240	Robles, Oswaldo. Filósofos mexicanos del siglo XVI. Mexico, 1950.
Phil 3850.27.93	Robock, A.A. The Albert Schweitzer jubilee book. Cambridge, 1945.
Phil 3850.27.94	Robock, A.A. In Albert Schweitzer's realms. Cambridge, 1962.
Phil 2855.2.82	Robot, Théodule. Théodule Ribot; choix de textes. Paris, 1917?
Phil 5241.170	Robots, men, and minds; psychology in the modern world. (Bertalanffy, Ludwig von.) N.Y., 1967.
Phil 7069.27.20	Robotton. Realms of light and healing. London, 1927.
Phil 2138.155	Robson, John Mercel. The improvement of mankind; the social and political thought of John Stuart Mill. Toronto, 1968.

Phil 2138.155.1   Robson, John Mercel. The improvement of mankind; the social and political thought of John Stuart Mill. Toronto, 1968.

Phil 8597.48   Rocafuerte, Vicente. Ensayo sobre tolerencia religiosa. 2. ed. México, 1831.

Phil 4478.1.30   Rocha, Germano da Costa. Nova filosofia cristã. Lisboa, 1961?

Phil 6687.6   Rochas, d'Aiglun, A. L'extériorisation de la sensibilité. 6e éd. Paris, 1909.

Phil 6687.6.2   Rochas d'Aiglun, A. L'extériorisation de la sensibilité. 2e éd. Paris, 1895.

Phil 6687.6.9   Rochas d'Aiglun, A. de. Les forces non définies. Paris, 1887.

Phil 7052.8   Rochas d'Aiglun, Albert de. L'extériorisation de la motricité. Paris, 1896.

Phil 9070.41   Roche, A. Knots and crosses. Dublin, 1943.
Phil 8892.55   Roche, J. Le gouvernement de soi. Paris, 1938.
Phil 192.90   Roche, Jean. Discussions metaphysiques. Paris, 1950.
Phil 817.24   Rochedieu, Edmond. La pensée occidentale face à la sagesse de l'orient. Paris, 1963.

Phil 5627.262   Rochedieu, Edmond. Personnalité et vie religieuse chez l'adolescent. Neuchâtel, 1962.

Phil 5403.10   Rochlin, Gregory. Griefs and discontents. London, 1965.
Phil 5400.172   Rochlin, Gregory. Griefs and discontents. 1. ed. Boston, 1965.

Phil 8418.43   Rochlitz, Manfred. Einige philosophische und informationstheoretische Aspekte der moralisch-ästhetischen Verhaltensdetermination der Persönlichkeit. Diss. Leipzig? 1967?

Phil 6327.35   Rochman, S. Critical essays on psychoanalysis. N.Y., 1963.

Phil 2520.204   Rochon, Antoine. Lettre d'un philosophie à un cartesien de ses amis. Paris, 1672.

Phil 2610.86   Rochot, Bernard. Les travaux de Gassendi sur Épicure. Paris, 1944.

Phil 2610.87   Rochot, Bernard. Les travaux de Gassendi sur Épicure et sur l'atomisme. Thèse. Paris, 1944.

Phil 8082.2   Rocio, Montano. L'estetica del rinascimento e del Barocco. Napoli, 1962.

Phil 5643.138   Rock, Irvin. The nature of perceptual adaptation. N.Y., 1966.

Phil 9347.7   Rocks and shoals. (Hepworth, G.) Boston, 1870.
Phil 27.77   Rocznjk woknej myśli. Warszawa. 1961+
Phil 8842.1   Rod, E. Les idées morales du temps present. Paris, 1891.
Phil 3850.27.180   Rode, Ebbe. Møde med Albert Schweitzer. København, 1959.
Phil 8610.881.25   Rodenhausen, C. Christenthum ist Heidenthum. Hamburg, 1881.

Phil 8707.15   Rodger, James George. Passages from the scientist's Bible. Washington, 1931.

Phil 3808.140   Rodhe, J. Schopenhauers filosofiska grundtankar i systematisk framställning och Kritisk belysning. Lund, 1888.

Phil 735.113   Rodhe, S.E. Über die Möglichkeit einer Werteinteilung. Lund, 1937.

Phil 3195.6.200   Rodi, Frithjof. Morphologie und Hermeneutik. Stuttgart, 1969.

Phil 396.16   Rodi, Frithjof. Provokation, Affirmation. Das Dilemma des kritischen Humanismus. Stuttgart, 1970.

Phil 5170.4   Rodier, G. De vi propria syllogismi. Thesis. v.1-2. Parisiis, 1891.

Phil 1122.5   Rodier, Georges. Etudes de philosophie grecque. Paris, 1926.

VPhil 5057.43   Rodin, Davor. Aspekti odnosa izmedju Hegelove i Marxove dijalektike. Beograd, 1967.

Phil 310.788   Rodin, Davor. Dijalektika gradjanskog drustva. Beograd, 1971.

Phil 4829.749.30   Rodin, Davor. Metafizika i ćudoredje. Zagreb, 1971.
Phil 2733.117   Rodis-Lewis, G. Nicolas Malebranche. Paris, 1963.
Phil 2520.275.10   Rodis-Lewis, Geneviève. Descartes et le rationalisme. Paris, 1966.

Phil 2520.275   Rodis-Lewis, Geneviève. La morale de Descartes. 1. ed. Paris, 1957.

Phil 2520.276   Rodis-Lewis, Geneviève. La morale de Descartes. 3e ed. Paris, 1970.

Phil 1200.72   Rodis-Lewis, Geneviève. La morale stoïcienne. Paris, 1970.

Phil 3705.3.95   Rodnyi, Naum I. Vil'gel'm Ostval'd. Moskva, 1969.
Phil 4170.16   Rodolfo Mondolfo. v.1-2. (Pró Diego F.) Buenos Aires, 1967-68.

Phil 4170.16.5   Rodolfo Mondolfo nella vita e nel pensiero socialista. (Bassi, Enrico.) Bologna, 1968.

Phil 815.20   Rodovani, Umberto Antonio. Sommario di storia della filosofia, con particolare riguardo ai problemi morali e religiosi. Roma, 1966. 3v.

Phil 2475.1.209   Rodrigues, G. Bergsonisme et moralité. Paris, 1921.
Phil 8892.17   Rodrigues, G. Le problème de l'action. Paris, 1909.
Phil 2520.159   Rodrigues, G. Quid de mundi externi existentia...Cartesius. Thesis. Lutetiae Parisiorum, 1903.

Phil 600.19   Rodrigues, Gustave. L'idée de relation. Paris, 1904.
Phil 8892.59   Rodriguez, G.H. Etica y jurisprudencia. Mexico, 1947.
Phil 4363.1.80   Rodriguez, J.I. Vida del Doctor José Manuel Mestre. Habana, 1909.

Phil 4983.5.90   Rodriguez, José Ignacio. Vida del presbítero don Félix Varela. N.Y., 1878.

Phil 4368.2.90   Rodríguez Acala, Hugo. Francisco Romero, 1891: vija y obra. Mexico, 1954.

Phil 4368.2.85   Rodriguez Acala, Hugo. Mision y pensamiento de Francisco Romero. 1. ed. Mexico, 1959.

Phil 3640.170   Rodriguez Aniceto, N. Maquiarelo y Nietzsche. Madrid, 1919.

Phil 4318.2   Rodriguez Aranda, Luis. El desarrollo de la razón en la cultura española. Madrid, 1962.

Phil 4979.10.30   Rodríguez Delgado, Rafael. Introducción a una filosofía de la era atómica. Habana, 1950.

Phil 6687.14   Rodriquez, Rafael E. Psicoterapia por medio de la hipnosis. Montevideo, 1944.

Phil 5238.90   Roe, Anne. Behavior and evolution. New Haven, 1958.
Phil 5425.88   Roe, Anne. The making of a scientist. N.Y., 1953.
Phil 3837.2   Roe, E.D. The probability; a critique of Spinoza's demonstration. Andover, 1894.

Phil 2725.2.115   Roe, William. Lamennais and England. Oxford, 1966.
Phil 5875.10   Roecker, Doris. Sprachfreie Kategorisierung bei Kleinkindern. Diss. Tübingen, 1965.

Phil 2520.347   Roed, Wolfgang. Descartes. München, 1964.
Phil 2050.195   Rödder, Paul. Über Hume's Erkenntnistheorie. Gollnow, 1909.

Phil 3499.20   Roeder, E. De voce "a priori" in philosophia Kantii. Diss. Bonnae, 1866.

Phil 3120.55.90   Roeder von Diersburg, Egenolf. Zur Ontologie und Logik offener Systeme. Hamburg, 1967.

Phil 5330.9   Roehrich, E. L'attention spontanée et volontaire. Paris, 1907.

Phil 3837.40   Roehrich, Welfried. Staat der Freiheit. Darmstadt, 1969.
Phil 575.200   Roem, H.A.C. Structuurphenomenologische systematisering van het menszijn door centraalstelling van de vrijheidsbeleving. 's-Gravenhage, 1952.

Phil 3270.7.80   Römer, Alfred. Der Gottesbegriff Franks. Inaug. Diss. Halle, 1912.

Phil 3640.168   Römer, H. Nietzsche. Leipzig, 1921. 2v.
Phil 1350.13.5   Römische Wertbegriffe. (Oppormann, Hans.) Darmstadt, 1967.

Phil 1750.742   Roesch, E.J. The totalitarian threat. N.Y., 1963.
Phil 3640.570.5   Roeschl, Herbert. Nietzsche. Paris, 1960.
Phil 3640.570   Roeschl, Herbert. Nietzsche et la solitude. Manosque, 1958.

NEDL Phil 5257.8   Röse, F. Die Psychologie. Göttingen, 1856.
Phil 1717.9   Rösener, Karl. Moderne Propheten. München, 1907.
Phil 5057.7   Rösling, C.L. Die Lehren der reinen Logik. Ulm, 1826.
Phil 5628.55.30   Roessler, Max. Therese Neumann von Konnersreuth. Wurzburg, 1963.

Phil 850.3   Röth, E. Geschichte unserer abendländischen Philosophie. Mannheim, 1862. 2v.

Phil 5850.328   Roethlisberger, F.J. Training for human relations. Boston, 1954.

Phil 8597.50   Roetschi, R. Humanität und Idealismus. Bern, 1943.
Phil 5525.15   Roetschi, Robert. Der ästhetische Wert des Komischen und das Wesen des Humors. Bern, 1915.

Phil 3499.21   Röver, G. Zur Lehre vom Raum...Lehre Kants. Oldenburg, 1923.

Phil 5421.20.30   Rof Carballo, Juan. Violincía y ternura. Madrid, 1967.
Phil 5257.41   Roffenstein, G. Das Problem des psychologischen Verstehens. Stuttgart, 1926.

Phil 2750.20.90   Rofinet, A. Merleau-Ponty. Paris, 1963.
Phil 3640.545   Rogachev, B. Fr. Nitsshe. Parizh, 1909.
Phil 310.663   Rogachev, Petr M. Natsii - narod - chelovechestvo. Moskva, 1967.

Phil 8080.17   Roger Fry and other essays. (Hannay, Howard.) London, 1937.

Phil 8597.40   Rogeri, G. Iddio, l'uomo e la religione. Revere, 1887.
Phil 8418.7   Rogerio Sanchez, J. Estética general. Madrid, 1907.
Phil 1717.4   Rogers, A.K. A brief introduction to modern philosophy. N.Y., 1899.

Phil 1817.5.3   Rogers, A.K. English and American philosophy since 1800. N.Y., 1923.

Phil 8892.25.15   Rogers, A.K. Ethics and moral tolerance. N.Y., 1934.
Phil 8842.6   Rogers, A.K. Morals in review. N.Y., 1927.
Phil 6127.8.5   Rogers, A.K. Parallelism of mind and body. Chicago, 1899.
Phil 6127.8   Rogers, A.K. Parallelism of mind and body. Chicago, 1899.
Phil 8597.16   Rogers, A.K. The religious conception of the world. N.Y., 1907.

Phil 817.4   Rogers, A.K. A student's history of philosophy. N.Y., 1901.

Phil 817.4.15   Rogers, A.K. A student's history of philosophy. N.Y., 1923.

Phil 817.4.20A   Rogers, A.K. A student's history of philosophy. 3d ed. N.Y., 1932.

Phil 8892.25   Rogers, A.K. The theory of ethics. N.Y., 1922.
Phil 348.8   Rogers, A.K. What is truth? New Haven, 1923.
Phil 5585.49   Rogers, Anna Sophie. An analytic study of visual perceptions. Thesis. Worcester, Mass., 1917.

Phil 8642.3   Rogers, C.F. Immortality. London, 1930?
Phil 6967.18.2   Rogers, C.R. Psychothérapie et relations humaines. Louvain, 1965. 2v.

Phil 6127.22   Rogers, Carl R. Counseling and psychotherapy; newer concepts in practice. Boston, 1942.

Phil 6127.22.10A   Rogers, Carl R. Counseling with returned servicemen. 1. ed. N.Y., 1946.

Phil 6327.28   Rogers, Carl Ransom. Client-centered therapy. Boston, 1951.

Phil 5535.34   Rogers, Carl Ransom. Freedom to learn. Columbus, Ohio, 1969.

Phil 6980.650.35   Rogers, Carl Ransom. On becoming a person. Boston, 1961.
Phil 6980.650.40   Rogers, Carl Ransom. Psychothérapie et relations humaines. Louvain, 1962. 2v.

Phil 5870.70   Rogers, Dorothy. Issues in child psychology. Belmont, 1969.

Phil 7054.140   Rogers, E.C. Philosophy of mysterious agents. Boston, 1853.

Phil 8642.6   Rogers, E.H. National life in the spirit world. Chelsea? 1891.

Phil 8597.11.8   Rogers, H. A defence of the eclipse of faith. Boston, 1856.

Phil 8597.11.7   Rogers, H. A defence of the eclipse of faith. London, 1854.

Phil 8597.11.4   Rogers, H. The eclipse of faith. 8. ed. Boston, 1863.
Phil 8597.11.15   Rogers, H. Reason and faith. Boston, 1853.
Phil 8597.11.12   Rogers, H. Reason and faith. London, 1850.
Phil 978.51   Rogers, L.W. Elementary theosophy. 2d ed. Chicago, 1923.
Phil 978.51.3   Rogers, L.W. Elementary theosophy. 3rd ed. Chicago, 1929.
Phil 978.51.5   Rogers, L.W. Reincarnation, and other lectures. Chicago, 1925.

Phil 7082.82.2   Rogers, Louis William. Dreams and premonitions. 2d ed. Chicago, 1923.

Phil 5257.32   Rogers, M.C. Adenoids and diseased tonsils; their effect on general intelligence. N.Y., 1922.

Phil 9035.105   Rogers, Raymond. Coming into existence. Cleveland, 1967.
Phil 705.30   Rogers, W.C. Transcendentalism truly remarkable. Boston, 1947.

Phil 8581.10.5   Roget, P.M. Bridgewater treatises [5]. Animal, vegetable physiology. Philadelphia, 1836. 2v.

Phil 192.92   Rogge, E. Axiomatik alles möglichen Philosophierens. Meisenheim, 1950.

Phil 5780.20   Rogge, Oetje G. Why men confess. N.Y., 1959.
Phil 8418.14   Rogger, K. Essai sur la valeur expressive de l'art. Dijon, 1929.

Phil 4080.3.472   Roggerone, Giuseppe A. Benedetto Croce e la fondazione del concetto di libertà. Milano, 1966.

Phil 4080.3.535   Roggerone, Giuseppe A. Prospettive crociane. Lecce, 1968.
Phil 2070.162   Roggerone, Giuseppe Agostino. James e la crisi della coscienza contemporanea. 2. ed. Milano, 1964.

Phil 2725.13.85   Roggerone, Giuseppe Agostino. La via nuova di Lequier. Milano, 1968.

Phil 6967.21   Rogler, Lloyd H. Trapped: families and schizophrenia. N.Y., 1965.

Phil 1750.366   Rognoni, L. L'espressionismo. Torino, 1953.

Phil 5545.228 — Rogovin, Mikhail S. Filosofskie problemy teorii pamiati. Moskva, 1966.

Phil 6980.650 — Rogow, Arnold A. The psychiatrists. N.Y., 1970.

Phil 9558.5 — Rogues de Fursac, J. L'avarice. Paris, 1911.

Phil 6967.11.15 — Rogues de Fursac, J. Manual of psychiatry. 3. ed. N.Y., 1913.

Phil 6327.3 — Rogues de Fursac, J. Manuel de psychiatrie. Paris, 1917.

Phil 6967.11.6 — Rogues de Fursac, J. Manuel de psychiatrie. 6. éd. Paris, 1923.

Phil 192.62 — Roguin, Ernest. Sociologie; partie de philosophie. Lausanne, 1928-1929. 3v.

Phil 5592.150 — Rohde, Amanda R. The sentence completion method. N.Y., 1957.

Phil 3640.535 — Rohde, Erwin. Afterphilologie. Leipzig, 1872.

Phil 5585.53 — Rohde, F. Sinneswahrnehmungen und Sinnestäuschungen. Braunsberg, 1877.

Phil 8672.22 — Rohde, Hubert. Mensch ohne Gott. Freiburg, 1961.

Phil 6480.194 — Roheim, Geza. The gates of the dream. N.Y., 1952.

Phil 6327.18 — Roheim, Geza. The origin and function of culture. N.Y., 1943.

Phil 6327.24 — Rohitsek, A. Der Katillon. Zürich, 1925.

Phil 5628.51.10 — Rohling, August. Louise Lateau: her stigmas and ecstasy. N.Y., 1879.

Phil 8842.10 — Rohmer, J. La finalité morale. Paris, 1939.

Phil 8842.10.5 — Rohmer, J. La finalité morale chez les théologiens de Saint Augustin à Duns Scot. Thèse. Paris, 1938.

Phil 1504.11.5 — Rohner, A. Das Schöpfungsproblem bei Moses Maimonides. v.11, pt.5. Münster, 1913.

Phil 5767.15 — Rohner, Peter. Das Phänomen des Wollens. Bern, 1964.

Phil 6127.3 — Rohon, J.V. Bau und Verrichtung des Gehirns. Heidelburg, 1887.

Phil 575.65 — Rohracher, H. Persönlichkeit und Schicksal. Wien, 1926.

Phil 5257.58.5 — Rohracher, Hubert. Einführung in die Psychologie. 2. Aufl. Wien, 1947.

Phil 5257.58.6 — Rohracher, Hubert. Einführung in die Psychologie. 6. Aufl. Wien, 1958.

Phil 8707.34 — Rohrbach, Hans. Naturwissenschaft, Weltbild, Glaube. Wuppertal, 1967.

Phil 5257.66 — Rohrbach, M.A. La pensée vivante; réales et techniques de la pensée créatrice. Paris, 1959.

Phil 676.2 — Rohrbach, Marc Adrien. L'éveil spirituel, accomplissement personnel par la pensée créatrice. Paris, 1969.

Phil 192.54 — Rohrbaugh, L.G. The energy concept. Iowa City?, 1922.

Phil 192.54.5 — Rohrbaugh, L.G. A natural approach to philosophy. N.Y., 1934.

Phil 5627.104 — Rohrbaugh, L.G. The science of religion: an introduction. N.Y., 1927.

Phil 310.736 — Rohrmoser, Günter. Das Elend der kritischen Theorie. Theodor W. Adorno, Herbert Marcuse, Jürgen Habermas. Freiburg, 1970.

Phil 8597.64 — Rohrmoser, Günter. Emanzipation und Freiheit. München, 1970.

Phil 3425.764 — Rohrmoser, Günter. Theologie et aliénation dans la pensée du jeune Hegel. Paris, 1970.

Phil 4960.265 — Roig, Arturo Andres. Los krausistas argentinos. Puebla, Mexico, 1969.

Phil 192.104 — Roig Gironella, J. Estudios de metafisica. Barcelona, 1959.

Phil 1717.16 — Roig Gironella, J. Filosofía y razón. Madrid, 1948.

Phil 192.65 — Roisel, Godefroy De. La substance; essai de philosophie rationnelle. Paris, 1881.

Phil 4365.1.80 — Rojo Perez, E. La ciencia de la cultura, teoría histórologica de Eugenio d'Ors. Barcelona, 1963.

Phil 6967.19 — Rokeach, M. The three Christs of Ypsilanti. N.Y., 1964.

Phil 5627.268.18 — Rokeach, Milton. Beliefs, attitudes and values; a theory of organization and change. San Francisco, 1970.

Phil 5335.6 — Rokeach, Milton. The open and closed mind. N.Y., 1960.

Phil 8673.34 — Rol' estestvornaniia v razvitii ateisticheskogo miroponimaniia. (Ivanov, Ivan G.) Moskva, 1969.

Phil 8171.200 — Rol' khudozhestvennogo naslediia v esteticheskom vospitanii. (Kazykhanova, Batish R.) Alma-ata, 1967.

Phil 349.45 — Rol' modelei v poznanii. (Shtoff, V.A.) Leningrad, 1963.

Phil 575.253.5 — Rol' truda v razvitii lichnosti v usloviiakh stroitelstva kommunizma. (Kalinin, Ananii I.) Cheboksary, 1969.

Phil 192.81 — Rolbiecki, J.J. Prospects of philosophy. N.Y., 1939.

Phil 5722.23.2 — Le rôle de l'inconscient dans l'invention scientifique. Thèse. (Montmasson, J.M.) Bourg, 1928.

Phil 2070.134 — Le rôle des images dans la pensée de William James. Thèse. (Cornesse, Marie.) Grenoble, 1933.

Phil 1182.10 — Le rôle du pythagorisme dans l'évolution des idées. (Brunschvicg, Léon.) Paris, 1937.

Phil 5052.42 — Le rôle médiateur de la logique. (Meyer, H.) Assen, 1956.

Phil 2270.74.25 — Le rôle moral de la bienfaisance. (Spencer, Herbert.) Paris, 1895.

Phil 5819.3 — The role of instinct in social psychology. (Josey, Charles C.) N.Y., 1921.

Phil 8707.24 — The role of knowledge in western religion. (Randall, John Herman.) Boston, 1958.

Phil 5402.27 — The role of pleasure in behavior. (Heath, R.G.) N.Y., 1964.

Phil 2130.80 — The role of reason in religion: a study of Henry Mansel. (Freeman, Kenneth D.) The Hague, 1969.

Phil 8430.37 — The role of the creative arts in comtemporary society. (Mumford, L.) Durham, 1958.

Phil 9575.15 — The role of wealth in society. (Masani, Rustom Pestonji.) Bombay, 1956.

Phil 5335.4 — Role playing, reward, and attitude change. (Elms, Alan C.) N.Y., 1969.

Phil 6980.794 — Role relations in the mental health professions. (Zander, A.F.) Ann Arbor, 1957.

Phil 8587.26.80 — Rolffs, Ernst. Harnack's Wesen des Christentums und die religiösen Strömmungen der Gegenwart. Leipzig, 1902.

Phil 8892.42 — Rolffs, Ernst. Politische Ethik und ethische Weltanschauung. Liepzig, 1923.

Phil 3705.3.90 — Rolla, A. La filosofia energetica. Torino, 1907.

Phil 8140.3 — Rolla, Alfredo. Storia delle idee estetiche in Italia. Torino, 1905.

Phil 3552.306 — Rolland, E. Le déterminisme monadique. Paris, 1935.

Phil 3552.306.5 — Rolland, E. Le déterminisme monadique. Thèse. Paris, 1935.

Phil 2475.1.261 — Rolland, E. Le finalité morale dans le Bergsonisme. Paris, 1937.

Phil 365.53 — Rolle, Friedrich. Der Mensch, seine Abstammung und Gesittung. Frankfurt, 1866.

Phil 3120.22.80 — Die Rolle der Erotik in der männlichen Gesellschaft. (Thies, Heinz.) Baum, 193-.

Phil 735.278 — Die Rolle der Werte im Leben. Festschrift für Johannes Hessen zu seinen 80. Geburtstag. Köln, 1969.

Phil 8620.42 — Die Rolle des Bösen. (Steinhausen, H.) Stockholm, 1939.

Phil 1750.115.115 — Rollin, France. La phénoménologie au départ, Husserl, Heidagger, Gaboriau. Paris, 1967.

Phil 9160.1 — The Rollo code of morals. (Abbott, Jacob.) Boston, 1841.

Phil 3425.680 — Rollwage, Jürgen. Das Modalproblem und die historische Handlung. München, 1969.

Phil 1135.210 — Roloff, Dietrich. Gottähnlichkeit, Vergöttlichung und Erhöhung zu seligem Leben. Berlin, 1970.

Phil 8892.3 — Rolph, W.H. Biologische Probleme. Leipzig, 1882.

Phil 8892.3.3 — Rolph, W.H. Biologische Probleme. 2. Aufl. Leipzig, 1884.

Phil 8967.1.85 — Roltzmann, H.J. R. Rothe's speculatives System. Freiburg, 1899.

Phil 6990.22 — Romagne, M. l'abbe de. Dictionnaire historique des miracles. Paris, 1824.

Phil 8842.8 — Romagnosi, G.D. L'antica morale filosofia. Prato, 1838.

Phil 4215.1.30 — Romagnosi, G.D. Opere di Romagnosi. Milano, 1957.

Phil 4215.1.25 — Romagnosi, G.D. Opuscoli filosofici. Lanciano, 1923.

Phil 5057.27 — Romagnosi, G.D. Vedute fondamentali sull'arte logica. Roma, 1936.

Phil 4215.1.78 — Pamphlet vol. Romagnosi, G.D. 8 pam.

Phil 4215.1.79 — Pamphlet box. Romagnosi, G.D.

Phil 5643.109 — Romains, Jules. Eyeless sight, a study of extra-retinal vision and the paroptic sense. N.Y., 1924.

Phil 585.162 — Román, Julián. El hombre como síntesis del universo. 1. ed. Rosario, 1951.

Phil 6060.70 — Roman, Klara Goldzieher. Encyclopedia of the written word. N.Y., 1968.

Htn Phil 7069.29.20* — The Roman Catholic church, a rejoinder (to Herbert Thurston). (Doyle, Arthur Conan.) London, 1929.

Phil 1300.15 — The Roman mind. (Clarke, M.L.) Cambridge, Mass., 1956.

Phil 1300.10A — The Roman mind. (Clarke, M.L.) London, 1956.

Phil 1350.8 — Roman stoicism. (Arnold, E.V.) Cambridge, 1911.

Phil 4961.45.3 — Romanell, P. La formación de la mentalidad mexicana. México, 1954.

Phil 4959.225 — Romanell, Patrick. La formación de la mentalidad mexicana. 1. ed. México, 1954.

Phil 1817.12 — Romanell, Patrick. Toward a critical naturalism. N.Y., 1958.

Phil 4120.4.87 — Romanelli, P. Gentile. N.Y., 1938.

Phil 5827.1.13 — Romanes, G.J. Animal intelligence. N.Y., 1888.

Phil 5827.1.28 — Romanes, G.J. Die geistige Entwicklung im Tierreich. Leipzig, 1885.

Phil 5827.1 — Romanes, G.J. Mental evolution in animals. London, 1883.

Phil 5827.1.3A — Romanes, G.J. Mental evolution in animals. N.Y., 1884.

Phil 5827.1.6 — Romanes, G.J. Mental evolution in man, origin of human faculty. N.Y., 1889.

Phil 5827.1.5 — Romanes, G.J. Mental evolution in men. London, 1888.

Phil 510.2 — Romanes, G.J. Mind and motion and monism. N.Y., 1895.

Phil 8597.12.5 — Romanes, G.J. Thoughts on religion. Chicago, 1895.

Phil 8597.12.8 — Romanes, G.J. Thoughts on religion. Chicago, 1898.

Phil 8597.12 — Romanes, G.J. Thoughts on religion. London, 1895.

Phil 8672.5 — Romanes, J. A candid examination of theism. London, 1878.

Htn Phil 2055.3.30* — The Romanes lecture 1893. (Huxley, Thomas H.) London, 1893.

Phil 8597.13 — Romang, J.P. Über Wichtigere Fragen der Religion. Heidelberg, 1870.

Phil 5767.2 — Romang, T.P. Über Willensfreiheit und Determinismus. Bern, 1835.

Phil 3450.19.495 — Romano, Bruno. Tecnica e giustizia nel pensiero di Martin Heidegger. Milano, 1969.

Phil 4170.10.90 — Romano, F. Il pensiero filosofico di Piero Martinetti. Padova, 1959.

Phil 4070.1.93 — Romano, P. Ausonio Franchi. Savona, 1896.

Phil 4080.8.80 — Romano, Pietro. La filosofia di Augusto Conti. Genova, 1895.

Phil 3499.40 — Romano, Vincenzo. Kant; il problema della conoscenza. Napoli, 1965.

Phil 4080.3.93 — Romano Palazzo, F. Influssi del pensiero Kantiano vell Croce. Bari, 1938.

Phil 8672.26 — Romanov, Aleksandr A. Dorogami zemli. Moskva, 1965.

VPhil 2475.1.470 — Romanowski, Henryk. Nowa filozofja. Lublin, 1929.

Phil 8090.2 — The romantic idealism of art, 1800-1848. (Zabel, M.D.) Chicago, 1938.

Phil 978.95 — Romanticism comes of age. 1st American ed. (Barfield, Owen.) Middletown, Conn., 1967[1966]

Phil 4374.5.80 — El romanticismo filosófico observaciones a la weltanschauung de Joaquin Xirau. (Larroya, Francisco.) Mexico, 1941.

Phil 3017.6 — Romantická věda. (Rádl, E.) V Praze, 1918.

Phil 8110.16 — Romantische Asthetik. Habilitationsschrift. (Mainusch, Herbert.) Bad Homburg, 1969.

Phil 5215.4 — Romantische Einflüsse in der Geschichte der Psychologie. (Farbstein, Wolf.) Zürich, 1953.

Phil 5041.45 — Romantische oder klassische Logik? (Behn, Siegfried.) Münster, 1925.

Phil 5258.7.80 — Romantische Sehnsucht und Kosmogonie. (Elschenbroich, Adalbert.) Tübingen, 1971.

Phil 282.17 — Romantiske Naturphilosophie. (Bernoulli, C.) Jena, 1926.

Phil 8120.12 — Le romantisme et le goût esthétique du XVIIIe siècle. (Simches, S.O.) Paris, 1964.

Phil 8589.9 — Romantisme et religion. (Joussain, André.) Paris, 1910.

Phil 2725.2.97 — Le romantisme social de Lamennais. Thèse. (Poisson, Jacques.) Paris, 1931.

Phil 176.55 — Un romantisme utilitaire. (Berthelot, René.) Paris, 1911. 3v.

Phil 4080.3.165 — Romarell, Patrick. Croce versus Gentile. N.Y., 1946.

Phil 585.185 — Rombach, Heinrich. Die Frage nach dem Menschen. Freiburg, 1966.

Phil 192.115 — Rombach, Heinrich. Die Gegenwart der Philosophie. Freiburg, 1966.

Phil 192.115.5 — Rombach, Heinrich. Substanz, System, Struktur. Freiburg, 1965. 2v.

Htn Phil 5545.52* — Romberch, J. Congestorium artificiose. Venetijs, 1533.

Phil 6967.12 — Romberg, M.H. Manual of the nervous diseases. London, 1853. 2v.

Phil 8597.34 — Romberg, P.A. Filosofi och religion. Karlskrona, 1881.

Phil 2733.116 — Rome, B.K. The philosophy of Malebranche. Chicago, 1963.

Phil 1760.20 — Rome, Sydney C. Philosophical interrogations. 1. ed. N.Y., 1964.

Phil 57.2 — Rome. Pontificia Universitas Gregoriana. Textus et documenta. Series philosophica. Romae. 1-14,1932-1938 13v.

Phil 57.3 — Rome. Rome Universita. Istituto di Psicologia Sperimentale. Contributi psicologia dell' Instituto. Roma. 1-6,1910-1933 6v.

Phil 57.1 — Rome. Universita. Scuola di Filosofia. Pabblicazioni. Roma. 1-17 14v.

Phil 2905.1.345   Rome et Teilhard de Chardin. (Philippe de la Trinité, Father.) Paris, 1964.

Htn   Phil 8892.40.5*   Romei, A. The courtiers academie. London, 1598.

Htn   Phil 8892.40*   Romei, A. Discori...in sette giornate. Verona, 1586.

Phil 5057.30.5   Romer, Francisco Argentine. Lógica y nóciones de teoria del concimiento. 5. ed. Buenos Aires, 1942.

Phil 575.136   Romero, F.A. Filosofía de la persona y otros ensayos de filosofía. Buenos Aires, 1944.

Phil 4972.5.55   Romero, Francisco. Alejandro Korn. Buenos Aires, 1940.

Phil 4972.5.56   Romero, Francisco. Alejandro Korn. Buenos Aires, 1956.

Phil 4972.5.53   Romero, Francisco. Alejandro Korn. La Plata, 1938.

Phil 4979.15.30   Romero, Francisco. La estructura de la historia de la filosofía y otros ensayos. Buenos Aires, 1967.

Phil 4368.2.33   Romero, Francisco. Filosofía contemporanea estudios y notas. Buenos Aires, 1941.

Phil 4368.2.35   Romero, Francisco. Filosofía contemporanea estudios y notas. 2. ed. Buenos Aires, 1944.

Phil 4368.2.60   Romero, Francisco. Filósofos y problemas. 2. ed. Buenos Aires, 1957.

Phil 4368.2.40   Romero, Francisco. Ideas y figuras. 2. ed. Buenos Aires, 1958.

Phil 4368.2.50   Romero, Francisco. Ortega y Gasset y el problema de la jefatura espiritual. Buenos Aires, 1960.

Phil 4368.2.55   Romero, Francisco. Relaciones de la filosofía: la filosofía y el filósofo. Buenos Aires, 1958.

Phil 4957.35   Romero, Francisco. Sobre la filosofía en América. Buenos Aires, 1952.

Phil 4368.2.45   Romero, Francisco. Teoría del hombre. Buenos Aires, 1952.

Phil 4368.2.47   Romero, Francisco. Theory of man. Berkeley, 1964.

Phil 5057.30   Romero, Francisco Argentine. Lógica y nóciones de teoria del concimiento. 2. ed. Buenos Aires, 1939.

Phil 4979.65.30   Romero, Sylvio. Obra filosófica. Rio de Janeiro, 1969.

Phil 4960.645   Roméro, Sylvio. A philosophia no Brasil. Pôrto Alegre, 1878.

Phil 5520.535A   Rommetreit, Ragnar. Words, meanings, and messages. N.Y., 1968.

Phil 5585.200   Rommetveit, R. Selectivity, intuition and halo effects in social perception. Oslo, 1960.

Phil 7082.102   Romsche, Heinrich. Unsere Träume und Traumzustände. Stuttgart, 1926.

Phil 3499.6.18   Romundt, H. Antäus. Leipzig, 1882.

Phil 3499.6.5   Romundt, H. Die drei Fragen Kants. Berlin, 1887.

Phil 3499.6.20   Romundt, H. Grundlegung zur Reform der Philosophie. Berlin, 1885.

Phil 3499.6.13   Romundt, H. Kants Kritik der reinen Vernunft Abgekürzt auf Grund ihrer Entstehungsgeschichte. Gotha, 1905.

Phil 3499.6   Romundt, H. Kants philosophische Religionslehre. Gotha, 1902.

Phil 3499.6.9   Romundt, H. Ein neuer Paulus. Berlin, 1886.

Phil 3499.6.15   Romundt, H. Der Professorenkant. Gotha, 1906.

Phil 817.27   Roncuzzi, Alfredo. Origini del pensiero europeo. Milano, 1964.

Phil 817.27.5   Roncuzzi, Alfredo. Umane certezze; il libro della verità ragionata. Roma, 1966.

Phil 5190.5   Rondelet, A. Théorie logique des propositions modales. Paris, 1861.

Phil 3425.626   Rondet, Henri. Hegelianisme et christianisme. Paris, 1965.

Phil 3903.5.40   Rondom de leegte. (Verhoeven, Cornelius W.M.) Utrecht, 1967.

Phil 1182.45   Rongier, Louis. La religion astrale des pythagoriciens. Paris, 1959.

Phil 4356.1.80   Ronilla y San Martin, A. Fernando de Córdoba. Madrid, 1911.

Phil 2805.410   Ronnet, G. Pascal et l'homme moderne. Paris, 1963.

Phil 2515.6.5   Rons, Ivo. Introduction au socialisme rationnel de Colins. Neuchâtel, 1968.

Phil 6117.47   Roon, K. The new way to relax. N.Y., 1949.

Phil 3499.24   Roos, Andreas Praeses. Dissertatio philosophica de summo bono secundum decreta philosophiae criticae. Lundae, 1799.

Phil 3640.307   Roos, Carl Nissen. Nietzsche und das Labyrinth. Copenhagen, 1940.

Phil 8892.15.2   Roosevelt, T. Applied ethics being one of the Wm.B. Noble lectures for 1910. Cambridge, 1911.

Phil 8892.15   Roosevelt, T. Applied ethics being one of the Wm.B. Noble lectures for 1910. Cambridge, 1911.

Phil 2750.20.85   Roosfen, S. De idee der zelfvervramding. Delft, 1963.

Phil 5421.20.75   Roots of aggression. 1. ed. (Berkowitz, Leonard.) N.Y., 1969.

Phil 2475.1.274   Roots of Bergson's philosophy. (Scharfstein, B.A.) N.Y., 1943.

Phil 5548.5.5   The roots of consciousness. (McClelland, D.C.) Princeton, N.J., 1964.

Phil 6310.4.9   Roots of crime. (Alexander, Franz G.) N.Y., 1935.

Phil 5871.60   The roots of individuality. (Escalona, Sibylle Korsch.) Chicago, 1968.

Phil 6980.36   Roots of modern psychiatry. (Altschule, Mark David.) N.Y., 1957.

Phil 6980.36.2   Roots of modern psychiatry. 2. ed. (Altschule, Mark David.) N.Y., 1965.

Phil 2175.3.30   The roots of our learning. (Neilson, Francis.) N.Y., 1947.

Phil 176.14.5   The roots of reality. (Bax, E.B.) London, 1907.

Phil 8581.52   The roots of religion in the human soul. (Baillie, John.) London, 1926.

Phil 348.16   Roque Pascual, R. Logical analysis of fictionalism with respect to the theory of truth. Chicago, Ill., 1940.

Phil 8707.36   Roqueplo, Philippe. La foi d'un mal-eroyant ou mentalité scientifique et vie de foi. Paris, 1969.

Phil 3425.114   Roques, P. Hegel; sa vie et ses oeuvres. Paris, 1912.

Htn   Phil 5827.2*   Rorario, G. Quôd animalia bruta ratione utantur meliùs homine. Paris, 1648.

Phil 2530.82   Roretz, Karl. Diderots Weltanschauung. Wien, 1914.

Phil 192.58   Roretz, Karl. Die Metaphysik: eine fiktion. Wien, 1927.

Phil 3499.16   Roretz, Karl. Zur Analyse von Kants Philosoph des organischen. Wien, 1922.

Phil 5767.8   Roretz, Karl von. Der Zweckbegriff im psychologischen und erkenntnistheoretischen Denken. Leipzig, 1910.

Phil 5593.10   Rorschach, Hermann. Gesammelte Aufsätze. Bern, 1965.

Phil 5593.66.5   Rorschach-Bibliographie, 1921-1964. (Lang, Alfred.) Bern, 1966.

Phil 5593.45.20   The Rorschach in practice. (Alcock, T.) Philadelphia, 1964[1963]

Phil 5593.53   Rorschach interpretation. (Phillips, L.) N.Y., 1953.

Phil 5593.45.5   Rorschach psychology. (Maslow, Paul.) Brooklyn, 1945.

Phil 5593.60.5   Rorschach psychology. (Rickers-Ovsiankiua, Maria A.) N.Y., 1960.

Phil 5593.54.10   Rorschach responses in old age. 1. ed. (Ames, Louise Bates.) N.Y., 1954.

Phil 5593.62   Rorschach science; readings in theory and method. (Hirt, Michael.) N.Y., 1962.

Phil 5593.69   The Rorschach system. (Exner, John E.) N.Y., 1969.

Phil 5593.42.5   The Rorschach technique; a manual for a projective method of personality diagnosis. (Klopfer, Bruno.) Yonkers-on-Hudson, 1942.

Phil 5593.1   Pamphlet box. Rorschach test.

Phil 27.60   Rorschachiana Sonderhefte der schweizerischen Zeithschrift für Psychologie. Bern. 2-5

Phil 5520.463   Rorty, Richard. The linguistic turn; recent essays in philosophical method. Chicago, 1967.

Phil 192.76   Rosa, Gabriele. Le meraviglio del mondo. Milano, 1851.

Phil 2115.200   Rosa, Pasquale. Il pensiero filosofico e pedagogico di G. Locke. Napoli, 1965.

Phil 7069.60.25   Rosa dos ventos; artigos e palestras. (Abreu Filho, Julio.) São Paulo, 1960.

Phil 8612.60   Rosa Lee; motivation and the crisis of dying. (Zinker, Joseph Chaim.) Painesville, Ohio, 1966.

Phil 3450.19.545   Rosales, Alberto. Transzendenz und Differenz. Den Haag, 1970.

Phil 672.8   Rosanes, J. Über die neuesten Untersuchungen in Betreff unserer Anschauung vom Raume. Breslau, 1871.

Phil 6980.652.8   Rosanoff, A.J. Manuel of psychiatry. 6. ed. N.Y., 1927.

Phil 8892.82   Roscam Abbing, Pieter Johan. Om de mens. Leiden, 1968.

Phil 5880.5   Roscam Abbing, Pieter Johan. Volwassenheid. Hilversum, 1968.

Phil 8892.77   Roschacher, E. Das Recht und die Rechtssätze. Winterthur, 1963.

Phil 5425.21   Roscoe, T.G. Mental and physical decadence. London, 1914.

Phil 1075.1.5   Rose, Valentin. Leben des Heiligen David von Thessalonilke. Berlin, 1887.

Phil 2115.128   Rosell, Anton. Betraktelse af Lockes. Upsala, 1857.

Phil 8610.896.5   Roselli, G. Confutazione degli argomenti teologici. Foggia, 1896.

Phil 6159.15   Roseman, Bernard. The peyote story. Hollywood, Calif., 1966.

Phil 6967.25   Rosen, George. Madness in society. London, 1968.

Phil 3790.8.82   Rosén, Hugo. Föhållandet mellan moral och religion...den Ritschelska skolan. Lund, 1919.

Phil 3640.217   Rosen, Hugo. Livsproblemet hos Nietzsche. Stockholm, 1923.

Phil 535.45   Rosen, Stanley. Nihilism: a philosophical essay. New Haven, 1969.

Phil 192.96   Rosenberg, Max. Introduction to philosophy. N.Y., 1955.

Phil 5520.431   Rosenberg, Sheldon. Directions in psycholinguistics. N.Y., 1965.

Phil 8870.30   Rosenberg, Stuart E. A humane society. Toronto, 1962.

Phil 5421.25.65   Rosenberg, Stuart E. More loves than one. N.Y., 1963.

Phil 6420.8   Rosenberg, William L. Stuttering, its cause and remedy. Cleveland, 19- ?

Phil 5066.42   Rosenbloom, P.C. The elements of mathematical logic. 1st ed. N.Y., 1965.

Phil 3120.30.195   Rosenblueth, Pinchas Erich. Martin Buber: sein Denken und Wirken. Hannover, 1968.

Phil 6327.37.1   Rosenfeld, Herbert A. Psychotic states. N.Y., 1966.

Phil 3552.264   Rosenfeld, J. Die doppelte Wahrheit...Leibniz und Hurne. Diss. Bern, 1912.

Phil 5841.22   Rosenfels, Paul. Love and power. N.Y., 1966.

Phil 1930.10.85   Rosenfield, Leonora. Portrait of a philosopher. N.Y., 1962.

Phil 2417.4A   Rosenfield, Leonora D.C. From beast-machine to man-machine. N.Y., 1941.

Phil 2417.4.5   Rosenfield, Leonora D.C. From beast-machine to man-machine. N.Y., 1968.

Phil 3640.262   Rosengarth, W. Nietzsche and George. Leipzig, 1934.

Phil 3790.5.31   Rosenkrantz, Wilhelm. Die Wissenschaft des Wissens und Begründung der besonderer Wissenschaften durch die allgemeine Wissenschaft. v.1-2. München, 1866-68.

Phil 3837.3   Rosenkrantz, C. De Spinozae philosophia dissertatio. Halae, 1828.

Phil 3801.749.2   Rosenkranz, J.K.F. Schelling Vorlesungen. Danzig, 1843.

Htn   Phil 3801.749*   Rosenkranz, J.K.F. Schelling Vorlesungen. Danzig, 1843.

Htn   Phil 3801.749.6*   Rosenkranz, J.K.F. Über Schelling und Hegel. Königsberg, 1843. 2 pam.

Htn   Phil 3801.749.5*   Rosenkranz, J.K.F. Über Schelling und Hegel. Königsberg, 1843.

Phil 8418.11   Rosenkranz, K. Asthetik des Hässlichen. Königsberg, 1853.

Phil 3425.91.5   Rosenkranz, K. Apologie Hegel's gegen Dr. R. Haym. Berlin, 1858.

Phil 3425.91.7   Rosenkranz, K. Aus Hegels Leben. Leipzig, 1845.

Phil 3425.91.19   Rosenkranz, K. Erläuterungen zu Hegel's Encyklopädie der philosophischen Wissenschaften. Leipzig, 1920.

Phil 3425.91.10   Rosenkranz, K. Georg Wilhelm F. Hegel's Leben. Berlin, 1844.

Phil 3425.91.35   Rosenkranz, K. Hegel; Sendschreiben an...Carl Friedrich Bachmann. Königsberg, 1843.

Phil 3425.91.13A   Rosenkranz, K. Hegel als deutscher Nationalphilosoph. Leipzig, 1870.

Phil 3425.91.15   Rosenkranz, K. Hegel as national philosopher of Germany. St.Louis, 1874.

Phil 3425.91.22   Rosenkranz, K. Hegel's Naturphilosophie. Berlin, 1868.

Phil 3425.91   Rosenkranz, K. Kritische Erläuterungen des Hegel's...Systems. Königsberg, 1840.

Phil 8685.18   Rosenkranz, K. Die Naturreligion. Iserlohn, 1831.

Phil 3017.3   Rosenkranz, K. Neue Studien: IV Geschichte deutschen Philosophie. v.1-2. Leipzig, 1878. 3v.

Phil 3425.91.40   Rosenkranz, K. Über Schelling und Hegel. Königsberg, 1843.

Phil 3780.36   Rosenkranz, Karl. Epilegomena...Wissenschaft der logischen Idee. Königsberg, 1862.

Phil 3195.4.81   Rosenkranz, Karl. Erinnerungen an Karl Daub. Berlin, 1837.

Phil 3805.175   Rosenkranz, Karl. Kritik der Schleiermacherschen Glaubenslehre. Königsberg, 1836.

Phil 3780.79   Rosenkranz, Karl. Meine Reform der hegelschen Philosophie. Königsberg, 1852.

Phil 5057.24   Rosenkranz, Karl. Die Modification in des Logik. Leipzig, 1846.

Phil 3780.37   Rosenkranz, Karl. Psychologie oder die Wissenschaft vom subjectiven Geist. Königsberg, 1837.

Phil 3780.30   Rosenkranz, Karl. Studien. v.1-5. Berlin, 1839-48. 4v.

Phil 3780.38   Rosenkranz, Karl. System der Wissenschaft. Königsberg, 1850.

Phil 3780.35.2   Rosenkranz, Karl. Wissenschaft der logischen Idee. Königsberg, 1858-59. 2v.

Phil 3780.35 — Rosenkranz, Karl. Wissenschaft der logischen Idee. v.1-2. Königsberg, 1858-59.

Phil 6687.8 — Rosenmüller, J.G. Lettre à la société exegétique...magnétisme animal. Leipzig, 1788.

Phil 3565.114 — Rosenquist, G.G. Lotzes religionsfilosofi. Helsingfors, 1889.

Phil 3890.1.115 — Rosensbock, G.G. F.A. Trendelenburg. Carbondale, 1964.

Phil 5599.39.10 — Rosenstiel, Lutz von. Zur Validität von Formdeutverfahren. München, 1967.

Phil 3790.20.10 — Rosenstock, Eugen. Ja und Nein. Heidelberg, 1968.

Phil 3790.20.5 — Rosenstock, Eugen. Die Sprache des Menschengeschlechts. Heidelberg, 1963-64. 2v.

Phil 3790.20 — Rosenstock, Eugen. Zurück in das Wagnis der Sprache. Berlin, 1957.

Phil 6967.22 — Rosenthal, David. The Genain quadruplets. N.Y., 1963.

Phil 7069.49.12 — Rosenthal, Eric. They walk by night; true South African ghost stories and tales of the supernormal. Cape Town, 1965.

Phil 1030.5A — Rosenthal, Franz. Knowledge triumphant; the concept of knowledge in medieval Islam. Leiden, 1970.

Phil 683.2 — Rosenthal, Klaus. Die Überwindung des Subjekt-Objekt-Denkens als philosophisches und theologisches Problem. Göttingen, 1970.

Phil 510.132 — Rosenthal, L.A. Die monistische Philosophie. Berlin, 1880.

Phil 5270.18 — Rosenthal, Robert. Artifact in behavioral research. N.Y., 1969.

Phil 5279.10 — Rosenthal, Robert. Experimenter effects in behavioral research. N.Y., 1966.

Phil 3425.241 — Rosenzweig, Franz. Hegel und der Staat. v.1-2. Aalen, 1962.

Phil 3160.3.84 — Rosenzweig, L. La restauration de l'a priori kantien par H. Cohen. Paris, 1927.

Phil 6127.20 — Rosett, J. Intercortical systems. N.Y., 1933.

Phil 5257.51 — Rosett, Joshua. The mechanism of thought. N.Y., 1939.

Phil 1750.166.105 — Roshwald, M. Humanism in practice. London, 1955.

Phil 3499.27 — Rosikat, K.A. Kants Kritik der reinen Vernunft. Königsberg, 1901.

Phil 9560.19 — Rosini, G. Introduzione alle virtù. Firenze, 1810.

Phil 5500.9 — Rosinski, A. Das Urteil und die Lehre vom synthetischen Charakter desselben. Leipzig, 1889.

Phil 5257.80 — Roskam, Edwarda Elias Charles Iben. Metric analysis of ordinal data in psychology. Proefschrift. Voorschoten, 1968.

Phil 298.2 — Rosley, Carl. Das Körpergesetz. San Francisco, 19- .

Phil 298.2.10 — Rosley, Carl. Life's reality. Hayward, 1932.

Phil 5257.50 — Rosling, B. Some aspects of psychology. London, 1936.

Phil 3160.3.89 — Rosmarin, T.W. (Mrs.). Religion of reason. N.Y., 1936.

Phil 4210.91 — Rosmini, a Christian philosopher. 2. ed. (Jarvis, Stephen E.) Market Weighton, 1888.

Phil 4210.193 — Rosmini. (Brunello, B.) Bologna, 1963.

Phil 4210.106 — Rosmini. (Dyroff, Adolf.) Mainz, 1906.

Phil 4210.165 — Rosmini. (Leetham, C.R.) London, 1957.

Phil 4210.108.5 — Rosmini. (Palhoriès, F.) Paris, 1908.

Phil 4210.140.5 — Rosmini. Roma, 1943.

Phil 4210.149 — Rosmini. 2a ed. (Morando, Dante.) Brescia, 1945.

Phil 4210.240 — Rosmini antiromantico. (Cristaldi, Mariano.) Catania, 1967.

Phil 4210.117 — Rosmini e Gioberti. (Gentile, G.) Pisa, 1898.

Phil 4115.99 — Rosmini e Gioberti. (Gentile, G.) Pisa, 1898.

Phil 4210.117.2 — Rosmini e Gioberti. 2. ed. (Gentile, G.) Firenze, 1955.

Phil 4210.153 — Rosmini e Gioia. (Donati, B.) Firenze, 1949.

Phil 4210.255 — Rosmini e il Rosminianesimo nel veneto. Padova, 1970.

Phil 4210.81.8 — Rosmini e Kant. (Nardi, P. de.) Forli, 1902.

Phil 4210.85 — Rosmini e Spencer. (Vidari, G.) Milano, 1899.

Phil 4210.140 — Rosmini nell'ultima critica di Ausonio Franchi. (Bozzetti, Giuseppe.) Firenze, 1917.

Phil 4210.185 — Rosmini on human rights. (Emery, Cuthbert Joseph.) London, 1957.

Phil 4115.80 — Rosmini-Serbati, A. Vincenzo Gioberti. Lucca, 1853.

Phil 4115.80.5 — Rosmini-Serbati, A. Vincenzo Gioberti e il panteismo. Milano, 1847.

Phil 4115.80.10 — Rosmini-Serbati, A. Vincenzo Gioberti e il panteismo. Napoli, 1847.

Phil 4210.11 — Rosmini-Serbati, Antonio. Anthologie philosophique. Lyon, 1954.

Phil 4210.14 — Rosmini-Serbati, Antonio. Antologia pedagogica. 1. ed. Brescia, 1955.

Phil 4210.26 — Rosmini-Serbati, Antonio. Antropologia. Novara, 1847.

Phil 4210.15 — Rosmini-Serbati, Antonio. Breve esposizione della filosofia di Melchiorre Gioja. Milano, 1840. 8 pam.

Phil 1717.18 — Rosmini-Serbati, Antonio. Breve schizzo dei sistemi di filosofia moderna e del proprio sistema. Napoli, 1952.

Phil 1717.18.4 — Rosmini-Serbati, Antonio. Breve schizzo dei sistemi di filosofia moderna e del proprio sistema. 4e ed. Firenze, 1964.

Phil 4210.35 — Rosmini-Serbati, Antonio. Compendio di etica e breve storia di essa. Roma, 1907.

Phil 4210.75 — Rosmini-Serbati, Antonio. Epistolario. pt.1, v.1-2. Torino, 1857. 2v.

Phil 4210.38 — Rosmini-Serbati, Antonio. Esposizione del sistema morale dell'autore e compendio di etica. Mozara, 1952.

Phil 4210.21 — Rosmini-Serbati, Antonio. Filosofia del diritto. Napoli, 1856. 2v.

Phil 4210.76 — Rosmini-Serbati, Antonio. Giovane età e primi studi di Antonio Rosmini-Serbati. Italia, 1860.

Phil 4210.72 — Rosmini-Serbati, Antonio. Il giovane Rosmini. Urbino, 1963.

Phil 4210.57 — Rosmini-Serbati, Antonio. Gnoseologia. Messina, 1953.

Phil 4210.22.5 — Rosmini-Serbati, Antonio. Ideologia (Nuovo saggio sull'origine delle idee). Torino, 1851-53. 3v.

Phil 4210.20 — Rosmini-Serbati, Antonio. Introduzione alla filosofia. Casalle, 1850.

Phil 4210.20.10 — Rosmini-Serbati, Antonio. Introduzione alla filosofia. v.1-4. Torino, 1924-25. 2v.

Phil 4210.74 — Rosmini-Serbati, Antonio. Leitsätze für Christen von Antonio Rosmini. Einsiedeln, 1964.

Phil 4210.62 — Rosmini-Serbati, Antonio. Letteratura e arti belle. pt.1-2. Intra, 1870-73.

Phil 4210.23 — Rosmini-Serbati, Antonio. Logica. Intra, 1867.

Phil 4210.23.2 — Rosmini-Serbati, Antonio. Logica. Torino, 1853.

Phil 4210.22 — Rosmini-Serbati, Antonio. Nouovo saggio sull'origine delle idee. Milano, 1836-37. 3v.

Phil 4210.22.10 — Rosmini-Serbati, Antonio. Nuovo saggio sull'origine delle idee. 3. ed. Bari, 1948.

Phil 4210.10 — Rosmini-Serbati, Antonio. Opere. v.1, 9-10, 11-12, 15. Napoli, 1842-47. 4v.

Phil 4210.8 — Rosmini-Serbati, Antonio. Opere edite e inedite. v.5, 11-14, 20, 27-30. Milano, 1837. 10v.

Phil 4210.12 — Rosmini-Serbati, Antonio. Opere edite e inedite. Roma, 1934-63. 42v.

Phil 4210.45 — Rosmini-Serbati, Antonio. Opuscali morali. Milano, 1841.

Phil 4210.50 — Rosmini-Serbati, Antonio. The origin of ideas. London, 1883-84. 3v.

Phil 4210.68 — Rosmini-Serbati, Antonio. Il pensiero giuridico e politico di Antonio Rosmini. Firenze, 1962.

Phil 4210.5 — Rosmini-Serbati, Antonio. Per Antonio Rosmini nel 1o centenario dalla sua nascita. Milano, 1897. 2v.

Phil 4210.41 — Rosmini-Serbati, Antonio. The philosophical system. London, 1882.

Phil 4210.40 — Rosmini-Serbati, Antonio. Philosophisches System. Regensburg, 1879.

Phil 8892.70 — Rosmini-Serbati, Antonio. Principi della scienza morale. Roma, 1959.

Phil 4210.30 — Rosmini-Serbati, Antonio. Principi della scienza morale. Torino, 1928.

Phil 4210.29 — Rosmini-Serbati, Antonio. Il principio della morale. Bari, 1924.

Phil 4210.27 — Rosmini-Serbati, Antonio. Psicologia. v.1-2. Napoli, 1858.

Phil 4210.60 — Rosmini-Serbati, Antonio. Psychology. London, 1886-88. 3v.

Phil 4210.42 — Rosmini-Serbati, Antonio. Il razionalismo. Prato, 1882.

Phil 4210.24.5 — Rosmini-Serbati, Antonio. Il rinnovamento della filosofia in Italia. Milano, 1836. 3 pam.

Phil 4210.70 — Rosmini-Serbati, Antonio. Saggio storico critico sulle categorie e la dialettica. v.1-2. Torino, 1885.

Phil 4210.73 — Rosmini-Serbati, Antonio. Saggio sui divertimenti publici. Roma, 1964.

Phil 4210.69 — Rosmini-Serbati, Antonio. Saggio sul comunismo e socialismo. Pescara, 1964.

Phil 4210.41.20 — Rosmini-Serbati, Antonio. Sistema filosofico. Torino, 1924.

Phil 4210.41.30 — Rosmini-Serbati, Antonio. Il sistema filosofico. Torino, 1951.

Phil 4210.67 — Rosmini-Serbati, Antonio. La societa teocratico. Brescia, 1963.

Phil 4210.32 — Rosmini-Serbati, Antonio. Storia comparativa e critica dei sistemi intorno al principio della morale, a cura di C. Caviglione. Pt. 1. Torino, 1928.

Phil 4210.25.20 — Rosmini-Serbati, Antonio. Sul principio: Pa legge dubia non obliga. Milano, 1851.

Phil 4210.28 — Rosmini-Serbati, Antonio. Teosofia. Torino, 1859-74. 2v.

Phil 4210.25 — Rosmini-Serbati, Antonio. Trattato della coscienza morale. Milano, 1844.

Phil 4210.79 — Pamphlet vol. Rosmini-Serbati, Antonio. 37 pam.

Phil 4210.112 — Il Rosmini vero. (Caviglione, C.) Voghera, 1912.

Phil 4210.65 — Rosmini-Werbati, Antonio. Quaranta proposizioni attribute ad A. Rosmini. Milano, 1889.

Phil 4210.119 — Il rosminiamismo. (Cornoldi, G.M.) Roma, 1881.

Phil 4210.185.5 — The Rosminians. (Emery, Cuthbert Joseph.) London, 1960.

Phil 4210.89 — Rosmini's contribution to ethical philosophy. (Bruno, J.F.) N.Y., 1916.

Phil 5190.45 — Rosnow, Ralph L. Experiments in persuasion. N.Y., 1967.

Phil 510.28 — Rosny, J.H. Le pluralisme. Paris, 1909.

Phil 5700.2 — Rosolato, Guy. Essais sur le symbolique. Paris, 1969.

Htn — Phil 8628.3.3* — Ross, Alexander. Philosophical touchstone. London, 1645.

Phil 8892.80 — Ross, Alf. Directives and norms. London, 1968.

Phil 9513.3 — Ross, E.A. Sin and society. Boston, 1907.

Phil 3499.32 — Ross, H.D. Kant's ethical theory. Oxford, 1954.

Phil 348.25 — Ross, Jacob Joshua. The appeal to the given. London, 1970.

Phil 8597.49 — Ross, John Elliot. Truths to live by. N.Y., 1929.

Phil 1885.88 — Ross, R.G. Scepticism and dogma; a study in philosophy of F.H. Bradley. N.Y., 1940.

Phil 9120.185 — Ross, Ralph Gilbert. Obligation; a social theory. Ann Arbor, 1970.

Phil 6967.7 — Ross, T.A. The common neuroses, their treatment by psychotherapy. London, 1923.

Phil 6327.17.5 — Ross, Thomas Arthur. The common neuroses. 2. ed. London, 1942.

Phil 6327.17.15 — Ross, Thomas Arthur. An enquiry into prognosis in the neuroses. Cambridge, Eng., 1936.

Phil 6327.17.10 — Ross, Thomas Arthur. Lectures on war neuroses. London, 1941.

Phil 8707.20 — Ross, W.D. Foundations of ethics. Oxford, 1939.

Phil 2150.12.80 — Ross, W.D. John Henry Muirhead. London, 1940?

Phil 8892.46 — Ross, W.D. The right and the good. Oxford, 1930.

Phil 9070.50 — Ross, William. It's up to you A way to a better life. N.Y., 1950.

Phil 2050.213.5 — Ross, William G. Human nature and utility in Hume's social philosophy. Thesis. Garden City, N.Y., 1942.

Phil 2050.213 — Ross, William W.G. Human nature and utility in Hume's social philosophy. Garden City, N.Y., 1942.

Htn — Phil 2045.87* — Rosse, A. Leviathan drawn out with a hook. London, 1653.

Phil 5645.54 — Rosseau, René L. Les couleurs. Paris, 1959.

Phil 5066.50.5 — Rosser, J.B. Logic for mathematicians. N.Y., 1953.

Phil 5066.50 — Rosser, J.B. Many-valued logics. Amsterdam, 1952.

Phil 3808.246 — Rosset, Clément. L'esthetique de Schopenhauer. Paris, 1969.

Phil 2855.9.35 — Rosset, Clément. Lettre sur les chimpanzés. Paris, 1966.

Phil 2855.9.30 — Rosset, Clément. Le monde et ses remèdes. Paris, 1964.

Phil 192.108 — Rosset, Clément. La philosophie tragique. Paris, 1960.

Phil 1750.159 — Rossi, Edmundo. Retorno à vida (ensaios). São Paulo, 1941.

Phil 5520.581 — Rossi, Eduard. Das menschliche Begreifen und seine Grenzen. Bonn, 1968.

Phil 645.10 — Rossi, G. Agrippa di Nettesheym e la direzione scettica. Torino, 1906.

Phil 492.10 — Rossi, M.M. Alle fonti del deismo e del materialismo moderno. Firenze, 1942.

Phil 192.56 — Rossi, M.M. Per una concezione attivistica della filosofia. Bologna, 1921.

Phil 4073.88 — Rossi, M.M. T. Campanella metafisico. Firenze, 1923.

Phil 3425.740 — Rossi, Mario. Da Hegel a Marx. Milano, 1970- 2v.

Phil 4017.5.5 — Rossi, Mario. Sviluppi dello hegelismo in Italia. Torino, 1962.

Phil 4017.5 — Rossi, Mario. Sviluppi dello hegelismo in Italia. Torino, 1957.

Phil 1630.23 — Rossi, P. I filosofi e le machine, 1400-1700. Milano, 1962.

Phil 1717.26 — Rossi, Paolo. Aspetti della rivoluzione scientifica. Napoli, 1971.

Phil 5545.210 — Rossi, Paolo. Clavis universalis. Milano, 1960.

Phil 1850.147.5   Rossi, Paolo. Francesco Bacone, dalla magia alla scienza. Bari, 1957.

Phil 1850.147.10   Rossi, Paolo. Francis Baconi from magic to science. London, 1968.

Phil 1850.147   Rossi, Paolo. L'interpretazione baconiana delle janole antiche. Roma, 1953.

Phil 1630.23.5   Rossi, Paolo. Philosophy, technology, and the arts in the early modern era. N.Y., 1970.

Phil 4260.175   Rossi, Paolo. Le sterminate antichità. Studi vichiani. Pisa, 1969.

Phil 2417.5   Rossi, Pietro. Gli illuministi francesi. Torino, 1962.

Phil 1740.22   Rossi, Pietro. Lo storicismo contemporaneo. Torino, 1968.

Phil 2150.17.90   Rossi-Landi, Ferruccio. Charles Morris. 1st ed. Roma, 1953.

Phil 1817.15   Rossi Landi, Ferruccio. Il pensiero americano contemporaneo. Milano, 1958. 2v.

Phil 5520.427   Rossi-Landi, Ferruccio. Significato comunicazioni e parlare comune. Padova, 1961.

Phil 6687.11   Rossi-Pagnoni, F. Quelques essais de médiumnité hypnotique. Paris, 1889.

Phil 192.73   Rossignoli, Giovanni. Primi passi nello studio della metafisica. 8a ed. Torino, 1932.

Phil 7150.23   Rost, Hans. Bibliographie des Selbstmords. Augsburg, 1927.

Phil 2730.93   Rostan, E. La religion de Maine de Biran. Thèse. Paris, 1890.

Phil 6967.14.5   Rostan, L. Untersuchungen über die Erweichung des Gehirns. 2. Aufl. Leipzig, 1824.

Phil 8892.7   Rosteri, P.L. Sentenze e massime morali. London, 1842.

Phil 7069.64   Rosterna från rymden. (Juegenson, F.) Stockholm, 1964.

Phil 57.5   Rostock. Universitat. Gesammelte Dissertations. Rostock.

Phil 5257.42   Rostohar, M. Studie z vyvojové psychologie. Brno, 1928.

VPhil 5257.76   Rostohar, Mihajlo. Psihologija. Ljubljana, 1966.

Phil 310.633   Rostov on the Don, Russia. Gosudarstvennyi Pedagogicheskii. Institut Kafedra Filosofii. Voprosy dialekticheskogo i istoricheskogo materializma. Rostov-na-Donn, 1966.

Phil 310.616   Rostov on the Don, Russia. Universitet. Kafedra Dialektichnskogo i Estoricheskogo Materializma. Nekotorye voprosy istoricheskogo materializma. Rostov-na-Donn, 1962.

Phil 4777.282.10   Roszkowski, Antonio. Poględy spofeczne i ekonomiczne Augusta Cieszkowskiego. Poznań, 1923.

Phil 337.23   Rot' praktiki v protsesse poznaniia. (Goidukov, I.G.) Moskva, 1964.

Phil 4110.5.80   Rota Ghibandi, Silvia. Giuseppe Ferrari. L'evoluzione del suo pensiero (1838-1860). Firenze, 1969.

Phil 1750.751   Rotenstreich, N. Humanism in the contemporary era. The Hague, 1963.

Phil 2255.9   Rotenstreich, N. Spirit and man. the Hague, 1963.

Phil 3499.34   Rotenstreich, Nathan. Experience and its systematization; studies in Kant. The Hague, 1965.

Phil 8707.25   Roth, A. Stiinta si religie. Bucaresti, 1960.

Phil 3450.11.250   Roth, Alois. Edmund Husserls ethische Untersuchungen. Den Haag, 1960.

Phil 900.3   Roth, E. Geschichte und abendländischen Philosophie. Mannheim, 1846.

Phil 5590.474   Roth, Erwin. Einstellung als Determination individuellen Verhaltens. Habilitationsschrift. Göttingen, 1967.

Phil 8597.44   Roth, J. Der antichrist. Amsterdam, 1934.

Phil 2070.164   Roth, John K. Freedom and the moral life. Philadelphia, 1969.

Phil 2520.86.5   Roth, Leon. Descartes' discourse on method. Oxford, 1937.

Phil 8892.41   Roth, Leon. The science of morals; an essay in method. London, 1928.

Phil 3837.12.7   Roth, Leon. Spinoza, Descartes and Maimonides. N.Y., 1963.

Phil 3837.12A   Roth, Leon. Spinoza, Descartes and Maimonides. Oxford, 1924.

Phil 3837.12.5   Roth, Leon. Spinoza. London, 1929.

Phil 298.14   Roth, Samuel. The peep-hole of the present. N.Y., 1945.

Phil 192.72.5   Rothacker, E. Einleitung in die Geistwissenschaften. 2e Aufl. Tübingen, 1930.

Phil 3790.24   Rothacker, E. Heitere Erinnerungen. Frankfurt, 1963.

Phil 575.93   Rothacker, E. Die Schichten der Persönlichkeit. Leipzig, 1938.

Phil 575.93.15   Rothacker, E. Die Schichten der Persönlichkeit. 4e Aufl. Bonn, 1948.

Phil 420.4   Rothacker, Erich. Intuition und Begriff. Bonn, 1963.

Phil 585.160   Rothacker, Erich. Philosophische Anthropologie. Bonn, 1964.

Phil 585.160.5   Rothacker, Erich. Zur Genealogie des menschlichen Bewusstseins. Bonn, 1966.

Phil 8967.1   Rothe, R. Theologische Ethik. Wittenberg, 1845-48. 3v.

NEDL   Phil 8967.1   Rothe, R. Theologische Ethik. Wittenberg, 1845-48. 3v.

Phil 8967.1.3   Rothe, R. Theologische Ethik. Wittenberg, 1869-71. 5v.

Phil 8967.1.10   Rothe, R. Uebersicht der theologischen Ethik. Bremen, 1895.

Phil 817.16   Rothenbücher, A. Geschichte der Philosophie. Berlin, 1904.

Phil 3790.32   Rothert, Helmut. Welt, All, Einheit. München, 1969.

Phil 2725.35.95   Rothkopf, Wolfgang. Der Einfluss Kants auf die Erkenntnismetaphysik. München, 1960.

Phil 2250.88   Rothman, W. Josiah Royces Versuch einer Synthese von Pragmatismus und Objektivität. Inaug. Diss. Jena, 1926.

Phil 2250.88.2   Rothman, W. Josiah Royces Versuch einer Synthese von Pragmatismus und Objektivität. Jena, 1926.

Phil 3625.1.117   Rothman, W. Mendelssohn's character and philosophy of religion. n.p., 1929.

Htn   Phil 6045.95*   Rothmann, J. Chiromantie. Erphordiae, 1595.

Phil 192.66   Rothschild, R. The destiny of modern thought. N.Y., 1930.

Phil 735.105   Rothschild, R. Reality and illusion. N.Y., 1934.

Phil 8892.88   Rotter, Hans. Strukturen sittlichen Handelns. Mainz, 1970.

Phil 5850.328.10   Rotter, Julian. Social learning and clinical psychology. Englewood Cliffs, N.J., 1958.

Phil 6980.653   Rotthaus, Erich. Das sittliche, eine Kraft des menschlichen Unbewussten. Stuttgart, 1949.

Phil 8707.29   Rotureau, G. Conscience religieuse et mentalité technique. Paris, 1962.

Phil 8418.25   Rouart, Eugène. L'artiste et la société. Paris, 1902.

Phil 7054.101   Rouband, F. La danse des tables. Paris, 1853.

Phil 1750.753   Roubiczek, P. Existentialism; for and against. Cambridge, 1964.

Phil 8892.84   Roubiczek, Paul. Ethical values in the age of science. Cambridge, Eng., 1969.

Phil 5257.60   Roubiczek, Paul. Thinking in opposites. London, 1952.

Phil 1717.24   Rouche, Gerhard Albin. The philosophy of actuality. Fort Hare, 1963.

Phil 8620.43.7   Rougemont, Denis de. The devil's share. 2. ed. N.Y., 1945.

Phil 8620.43   Rougemont, Denis de. La part du diable. N.Y., 1942.

Phil 8620.43.3   Rougemont, Denis de. La part du diable. N.Y., 1944.

Phil 9513.6   Rouger, G. Spécialisation et évolution. Paris, 1935.

Phil 4368.3.5   Rouges, Alberto. Obras completas. Tucumán, 1960.

Phil 1522.5.5   Rougier, Louis. Histoire d'une faillite philosophique: la scolastique. Paris, 1966.

Phil 192.106   Rougier, Louis. La metaphysique et le langage. Paris, 1960.

Phil 348.7.3   Rougier, Louis. Les paralogismes du rationalisme. Thèse. Paris, 1920.

Phil 1522.5   Rougier, Louis. La scolastique et le thomisme. Paris, 1925.

Phil 5125.14   Rougier, Louis. La structure des théories déductives. Paris, 1921.

Phil 348.7.5   Rougier, Louis A.P. Traité de la connaissance. Paris, 1955.

Phil 623.14   Roulleaux Dugage, G. Théorie des principes de l'absolu. Paris, 1909.

Phil 6687.7   Roullier, A. Exposition physiologique des phénomènes du magnétisme animal. Paris, 1817.

Phil 165.373   Rouner, Leroy S. Philosophy, religion, and the coming world civilization. The Hague, 1966.

Phil 2055.7.85   Rouner, Leroy S. Within human experience; the philosophy of William Ernest Hocking. Cambridge, 1969.

Phil 3195.6.111   Roura-Parella, J. El mundo histórico social. México, 1948.

Phil 192.45   Roure, L. Doctrines et problèmes. Paris, 1900.

Phil 5057.34   Roure, Marie Louise. Logique et métalogique. Paris, 1957.

Phil 4352.1.82   Roure, Narciso. Las ideas de Balmes. Madrid, 1910.

Phil 4352.1.80   Roure, Narciso. La vida y las obras de Balmes. Madrid, 1910.

Phil 5421.30.5   Rourke, Byron P. Explorations in the psychology of stress and anxiety. Don Mills, Ontario, 1969.

Htn   Phil 2855.4.30*   Rousseau, J.J. Principes du droit politique. Amsterdam, 1762.

Phil 1750.141.7A   Rousseau, Kant, Goethe; two essays. (Cassirer, Ernst.) Princeton, 1947.

Phil 585.216   Rousseaus, Herders und Kants Theorie vom Zukunftsideal der Menschheitsgeschichte. Inaug. Diss. (Plantiko, Otto.) Greifswald, 1895.

Phil 8418.12   Roussel-Despierres, F. L'idéal esthétique. Paris, 1904.

Phil 530.40.15   Rousselot, P. Los místicos españoles. Barcelona, 1907. 2v.

Phil 530.40.5   Rousselot, P. Les mystiques espagnols. Paris, 1869.

Phil 1504.6.6   Rousselot, P. Pour l'histoire du problème. v.6. pt.6. Münster, 1908.

Phil 1522.2   Rousselot, X. Etudes sur la philosophie...moyen âge. Paris, 1840-42. 3v.

Phil 3499.36   Rousset, Bernard. La doctrine Kantienne de l'objectivité, l'autonomie comme devoir et devenir. Paris, 1967.

Phil 3837.16   Rousset, Bernard. La perspective finale de l'éthique et le problème de la coherence du Spinozisme. Paris, 1968.

Phil 192.32   Roustan, D. Leçons de philosophie. Paris, 1912.

Phil 2490.94   Rouvre, C. de. L'amoureuse histoire d'Auguste Comte et de C. de Vaux. Paris, 1917.

Phil 2490.94.10   Rouvre, C. de. Auguste Comte et le catholicisme. Paris, 1928.

Phil 5645.47   Rouwer, B. Colors and their characters. The Hague, 1949.

Phil 348.12   Roux, Antoine. Le problème de la connaissance. Paris, 1930.

Phil 8418.19   Roux, J. Le sentiment de la beauté; étude de psychologie. Paris, 1908.

Phil 2805.175   Roux, Marie. Pascal en Poitou et les Poitevins. Paris, 1919.

Phil 6687.12   Rouxel. Histoire et philosophie du magnétisme. Paris, 1895. 2v.

Phil 7028.4   Rouxel. Rapports du magnétisme et du spiritisme. Paris, 1892.

Phil 2880.8.265   Rovatti, Pier Aldo. Che cosa ha veramente detto Sartre. Roma, 1969.

Phil 4210.154   Rovea, G. Filosofia e religione in Antonio Rosmini. Domodossola, 1951.

Phil 2750.11.180   Rover, Thomas Dominic. The poetics of Maritain. Washington, 1965.

Phil 4210.135   Rovereto. Comitato Centrale per la Commemorazione di A. Rosmini. Commemorazione del primo centenario dalla nascita di A. Rosmini. Milano, 1897.

Phil 8642.7   Rovighi, S.V. L'immortalità dell'anima nei maestri francescani del secolo XIII. Milano, 1936.

Phil 3837.4   Rovijen, A.J.L. van. Inventaire de livrés de B. Spinoza. La Haye, 1888.

Phil 8967.2   Row, C.A. The moral teaching of the New Testament. London, 1873.

Phil 5780.3   Rowe, E.C. Voluntary movement. n.p., 1910.

Phil 8892.6   Rowe, E.S. Friendship in death. London, 1733-34.

Htn   Phil 8892.6.3*   Rowe, E.S. Friendship in death. N.Y., 1795.

Htn   Phil 8892.6.5*   Rowe, E.S. Friendship in death. New Haven, 1802.

Htn   Phil 8892.6.2*   Rowe, E.S. Friendship in death. Philadelphia, 1805.

Phil 7069.23.17   Rowe, Lucien. Le spiritisme d'aujourd'hui et d'hier. 2. ed. Paris, 1923.

Phil 3499.4   Rowland, D. Essay...unsolved ethical questions in Kant's. London, 1871.

Phil 8597.17   Rowland, E.H. Right to believe. Boston, 1909.

Phil 5520.26   Rowland, Eleanor H. The psychological experiences connected with the different parts of speech. Lancaster, 1907.

Phil 8707.22   Rowland, J. One man's mind. London, 1952.

Phil 9357.4.2   Rowland, James. Ruin and restoration. Albany, 1860.

Phil 9357.4   Rowland, James. Ruin and restoration. Albany, 1862.

Phil 9415.10   Rowley, Harold H. Submission in suffering. Cardiff, 1942.

Phil 5827.10   Rowley, Jean B. Discrimination limens of pattern and size in the goldfish, Carassius auratus. Thesis. Worcester, Mass., 1934.

Phil 9177.4   Rowntree, Constance M. The right relationship between parents and children. Bannisdale, 19- ?

Phil 6536.14   Rows, R.G. Epilepsy, a functional mental illness. N.Y., 1926.

Phil 960.255   Roy, Ellen (Gottschalk). In man's own image. 1. ed. Calcutta, 1948.

Phil 492.5   Roy, M.N. Materialism. 2nd ed. Calcutta, 1951.

Phil 4872.247.30   Roy, Manendra Nath. Reason, romanticism and revolution. Calcutta, 1952-55. 2v.

Phil 8663.3.96   Royal Bob. 1. ed. (Cramer, C.H.) Indianapolis, 1952.

Phil 27.92 | Royal Institute of Philosophy. Lectures. London. 1,1966+ 3v.

Phil 4752.2.75 | Royaume de l'esprit et royaume de César. (Berdiaev, Nikolai Aleksandrovich.) Neuchâtel, 1951.

Phil 8672.6 | Royce, J. The conception of God. Berkeley, 1895.
Phil 8672.6.5 | Royce, J. The conception of God. N.Y., 1894.
Phil 8672.6.4A | Royce, J. The conception of God. N.Y., 1898.
Phil 8672.6.6 | Royce, J. The conception of God. N.Y., 1902.
Phil 8633.1.4 | Royce, J. The conception of immortality. Boston, 1900.
Phil 3017.5 | Royce, J. Lectures on modern idealism. New Haven, 1964.
Phil 8892.12.9 | Royce, J. The philosophy of loyalty. N.Y., 1908.
Phil 8892.12.4 | Royce, J. The philosophy of loyalty. N.Y., 1908.
Phil 8892.12.10 | Royce, J. The philosophy of loyalty. N.Y., 1908.
Phil 8892.12.15A | Royce, J. The philosophy of loyalty. N.Y., 1920.
Phil 8892.12.20A | Royce, J. The philosophy of loyalty. N.Y., 1924.
Phil 5057.8 | Royce, J. Primer of logical analysis. San Francisco, 1881.
Phil 8892.12.5A | Royce, J. Race questions, provincialism and other American problems. N.Y., 1908.
Phil 1717.3A | Royce, J. Spirit of modern philosophy. Boston, 1892.
Phil 1717.3.5A | Royce, J. Spirit of modern philosophy. Boston, 1893.
Phil 1717.3.8 | Royce, J. The spirit of modern philosophy. Boston, 1896.
Phil 1717.3.20 | Royce, J. The spirit of modern philosophy. N.Y., 1955.
Phil 2250.15 | Royce, Josiah. The basic writings of Josiah Royce. Chicago, 1969. 2v.
Phil 2250.51 | Royce, Josiah. La filosofia della fedeltá. Bari, 1911.
Phil 2250.55 | Royce, Josiah. Fugitive essays. Cambridge, 1920.
Phil 2270.94A | Royce, Josiah. Herbert Spencer; an estimate and review. N.Y., 1904.
Htn Phil 2250.30* | Royce, Josiah. The intention of the Prometheus Bound of Aeschylus. Thesis. Berkeley, 1875.
Phil 2250.45A | Royce, Josiah. Lectures on modern idealism. New Haven, 1919.
Phil 2250.45.5 | Royce, Josiah. Lectures on modern idealism. New Haven, 1923.
Phil 2250.25 | Royce, Josiah. Letters. Chicago, 1970.
Phil 5257.11.15 | Royce, Josiah. Lineamenti di psicologia. Bari, 1928.
Phil 2250.10 | Royce, Josiah. Logical essays. Dubuque, Iowa, 1951.
Phil 2250.43.5 | Royce, Josiah. Il mondo e l'individuo. Bari, 1913-14. 4v.
Phil 5257.11A | Royce, Josiah. Outlines of psychology. N.Y., 1903.
Phil 5257.11.5 | Royce, Josiah. Outlines of psychology. N.Y., 1906.
Phil 5257.11.3 | Royce, Josiah. Outlines of psychology. N.Y., 1908.
Phil 2250.70 | Royce, Josiah. The philosophy of Josiah Royce. N.Y., 1971.
Htn Phil 2250.35* | Royce, Josiah. Primer of logical analysis. San Francisco, 1881.
Phil 8597.20A | Royce, Josiah. The problem of Christianity. N.Y., 1913. 2v.
Phil 8597.20.2 | Royce, Josiah. The problem of Christianity. N.Y., 1914.
Htn Phil 192.16.5* | Royce, Josiah. Religious aspect of philosophy. Boston, 1885.
NEDL Phil 192.16A | Royce, Josiah. Religious aspect of philosophy. Boston, 1885. (Changed to KD 55178)
Phil 2250.62 | Royce, Josiah. The religious philosophy of Josiah Royce. Syracuse, 1952.
Phil 2250.60 | Royce, Josiah. The social philosophy of Josiah Royce. Syracuse, 1950.
Phil 8597.20.10 | Royce, Josiah. The sources of religious insight. Edinburgh, 1912.
Phil 8597.19A | Royce, Josiah. The sources of religious insight. N.Y., 1912.
Phil 192.16.15A | Royce, Josiah. The sources of religious insight. N.Y., 1912.
Phil 2250.65 | Royce, Josiah. Studies of good and evil. Hamden, 1898.
Phil 192.16.7A | Royce, Josiah. Studies of good and evil. N.Y., 1898.
Phil 8597.20.5 | Royce, Josiah. What is vital in Christianity? N.Y., 1909.
Phil 192.16.18A | Royce, Josiah. William James and other essays on the philosophy of life. N.Y., 1911.
Phil 192.16.10A | Royce, Josiah. The world and the individual. N.Y., 1900-1901. 2v.
Phil 192.16.11A | Royce, Josiah. The world and the individual. N.Y., 1901. 2v.
Phil 192.16.10.5A | Royce, Josiah. The world and the individual. N.Y., 1923-1927. 2v.
Phil 2250.116 | Royce and Hocking: American idealists. (Robinson, Daniel Sommer.) Boston, 1968.
Phil 2250.100A | Royce on the human self. (Catton, J.B.) Cambridge, 1954.
Phil 2250.94.5 | Royce's metaphysics. (Marcel, Gabriel.) Chicago, 1956.
Phil 2250.96 | Royce's social infinite. (Smith, J.E.) N.Y., 1950.
Phil 2250.105A | Royce's synoptic vision. (Loewenberg, J.) n.p., 1955.
Phil 9495.123 | Royden, A.M. Sex and common-sense. N.Y., 1922.
Phil 8892.23 | Royer, Clémence. Le bien et la loi morale; éthique. Paris, 1881.
Phil 2855.1.31 | Royer-Tollard. Les fragments philosophiques. Paris, 1913.
Phil 8892.74 | Roys, F.X. Ethica et jus naturae in usum auditorum. Viennae, 1755.
Phil 5425.65 | Royse, Noble K. A study of genius. Chicago, 1890.
Phil 9357.2 | Rozan, C. Le jeune homme. Paris, 1878.
Phil 310.1.5 | Rozanov, Iakov S. Filosofsko-sotsiologicheskaia literartura marksizma za 1917-1927. Moskva, 1928.
Phil 310.1.5.5 | Rozanov, Iakov S. Istoricheskii materializm. Kiev, 1925.
Phil 192.17 | Rozaven, J.L. Examen d'un ouvrage intitulé. Avignon, 1831.
Phil 3808.233 | Rozdroza pesymizmu. Wyd. 1. (Garewicz, Jan.) Wrocław, 1965.
Phil 5649.44 | Roze, Nina A. Psikhomotorika vzroslogo cheloveka. Leningrad, 1970.
Phil 4768.1.5 | Rozental', M.M. Chto takoe marksistskaia teoriia poznaniia. Moskva, 1955.
Phil 310.3.8 | Rozental', M.M. Kategorien der materialistischen Dialektik. Berlin, 1959.
Phil 310.3.5 | Rozental', M.M. Kategorii materialisti cheskoi dialektiki. Moskva, 1956.
Phil 4768.1 | Rozental', M.M. Materialisticheskaia dialektika. Moskva, 1937.
Phil 5057.38 | Rozental', M.M. Prenlsipy dialekticheskoi logiki. Moskva, 1960.
Phil 348.22 | Rozental, M.M. Qué es la teoria Marxista del conocimiento. Santiago, 1962.
Phil 310.290 | Rozental', Mark M. Kniga dlia chteniia po marksistsko filosofii.
Phil 102.5.14 | Rozental, Mark Moiseevich. A dictionary of philosophy. Moscow, 1967.
Phil 102.5.7 | Rozental, Mark Moiseevich. Filosofskii slovar'. Moskva, 1963.
Phil 102.5.8 | Rozental, Mark Moiseevich. Filosofskii slovar'. Izd. 2. Moskva, 1963.

Phil 102.5.10 | Rozental, Mark Moiseevich. Filozoficky slovnik. Bratislava, 1965.
Phil 102.5.1 | Rozental, Mark Moiseevich. Handbook of philosophy. N.Y., 1949.
Phil 102.5 | Rozental, Mark Moiseevich. Kratkii filosofskii slovar'. Moskva, 1939.
Phil 102.5.2 | Rozental, Mark Moiseevich. Kratkii filosofskii slovar'. Moskva, 1940.
Phil 102.5.3 | Rozental', Mark Moiseevich. Kratkii filosofskii slovar'. Izd. 3. Moskva, 1951.
Phil 102.5.5 | Rozental', Mark Moiseevich. Kratkii filosofskii slovar'. Izd. 4. Leningrad, 1954.
Phil 102.5.12 | Rozental, Mark Moiseevich. Petit dictionnaire philosophique. Moscow, 1955.
Phil 310.673 | Rozhim, Vasilii P. Voprosy filosofii i sotsiologii v reskeniiekh XXIII s'ezda KPSS. Leningrad, 1968.
Phil 310.3.10 | Rozhin, V.P. Marksistsko-leninskaia dialektika. Leningrad, 1957.
Phil 310.3.12 | Rozhin, V.P. Predmet i struktura marksistsko-leninskoi filosofii. Leningrad, 1958.
Phil 5360.19 | Rozov, Mikhail A. Nauchnaia abstraktsiia i ee vidy. Novosibirsk, 1965.
Phil 194.41 | Rozprawy i artykuly filozoficzne. (Twardowski, Kazimierz.) Livów, 1927.
Phil 165.349 | Rozprawy logiczne. Warszawa, 1964.
Phil 2520.351 | Rozsnyai, Ervin. Etudes sur Descartes. Budapest, 1964.
Phil 4710.50.45 | Rozvytok filosofii v Ukrainskii RSR. Kyïv, 1968.
Phil 4783.1 | Rozvytok materialistychnoi filosofii na Ukrainii. (Ostrianyn, Danylo Kh.) Kyiv, 1971.
Phil 5520.11 | Rozwadowski, J. von. Wortbildung und Wortbedeutung. Heidelberg, 1904.
Phil 8125.26 | Rozwáj myśli. (Morawski, Stefan.) Warszawa, 1957.
Phil 4803.500.20 | Rozwazania wokól Hegla. (Kroński, Tadeusz.) Warszawa, 1960.
Phil 585.191.5 | Rozwój nowożytnej filozofii człowieka. (Suchodolski, Bogdan.) Warszawa, 1967.
VPhil 585.191.5 | Rozwój nowożytnej filozofii człowieka. (Suchodolski, Bogdan.) Warszawa, 1967.
Phil 5761.8.5 | Rozwójpotęgi woli przez psychofizyczne ćiviczenia. (Lutosławski, W.) Warszawa, 1910.
Phil 4352.1.95 | Ruano y Corbo, J.M. Balmes apologista. Santiago, 1911.
Phil 960.170 | Ruben, Walter. Geschichte der indischen Philosophie. Berlin, 1954.
Phil 6127.4 | Rubenstein, S. Zur Natur der Bewegungen. Leipzig, 1890.
Phil 4357.14.80 | Rubert Candau, José María. El conocimiento de Dios en la filosofía de Guillermo Rubió. Madrid, 1952?
Phil 4357.9 | Rubert Candau, José Maria. El siglo XIV. Madrid, 1952.
Phil 192.110 | Rubert Condan, José Marin. Fenomenologia de la accion del hombre. Madrid, 1961.
Phil 8418.40 | Rubert de Ventós, Xavier. Teoría de la sensibilidad. 1. ed. Barcelona, 1969.
Phil 8892.72 | Rubert y Candau, José M. Fundamento constitutivo de la moral. Madrid, 1956.
Phil 4630.6.30 | Rubin, E. Af efterladte papirer. København, 1956.
Phil 5827.12 | Rubin, E. Mennesker og Høns. København, 1937.
Phil 4585.9.81 | Rubin, E. En ung dansk filosof. København, 1920.
Phil 5643.68.5 | Rubin, Edgar. Synsoplevedefigurer. København, 1915.
Phil 5643.68 | Rubin, Edgar. Visuell wahrgenommene figuren. København, 1921.
Phil 5535.14 | Rubin, Frederick. Current research in hypnopaedia; a symposium of selected literature. London, 1968.
Phil 930.76 | Rubin, Vitalii A. Ideologiia i kul'tura Drevnego Kitaia. Moskva, 1970.
Phil 1930.8.125 | Rubinoff, Lionel. Collingwood and the reform of metaphysics; a study in the philosophy of mind. Toronto, 1970.
Phil 4768.2.5 | Rubinshtein, Sergei L. Bytie i soznanie o meste psikhologii. Moskva, 1957.
Phil 5257.68 | Rubinshtein, Sergei L. Grundlagen der allgemeinen Psychologie. Berlin, 1958.
Phil 4769.6.83.5 | Rubinshtein, Sergei L. I.M. Sechenov. Moskva, 1957.
Phil 4768.2.7 | Rubinshtein, Sergei L. O myshlenii i putiakh ego issledovaniia. Moskva, 1958.
Phil 4768.2.9 | Rubinshtein, Sergei L. Printsipy i puti razvitiia psikhologii. Moskva, 1959.
Phil 4768.2.6 | Rubinshtein, Sergei L. Sein und Bewusstsein. 4. Aufl. Berlin, 1966.
Phil 5640.21 | Rubinstein, S. Aus der Innenwelt. Leipzig, 1888.
Phil 5257.10 | Rubinstein, Susanna. Psychologisch-ästhetische Essays. Heidelberg, 1877-88. 2v.
Phil 5057.36 | Ruby, Lionel. The art of making sense. London, 1956.
Phil 5257.53 | Ruch, F.L. Psychology and life. Chicago, 1937.
Phil 27.24 | Ruch filosofický. Praze. 1-12,1920-1939 4v.
Phil 27.76 | Ruch filozoficzny. Toruń. 18,1958+ 8v.
Phil 1817.22 | Rucker, Darnell. The Chicago pragmatists. Minneapolis, 1969.
Phil 510.5 | Ruckhaber, Erich. Des Daseins und Denkens Mechanik und Metamechanik. Hirschberg, 1910.
Phil 510.5.15 | Ruckhaber, Erich. Der Mechanismus des menschlichen Denkens. Brackwede, 1911.
Phil 5257.34 | Ruckmick, C.A. The brevity book on psychology. Chicago, 1920.
Phil 102.4 | Ruckmick, C.A. German-English dictionary of psychological terms. Iowa City, 1928.
Phil 5257.34.5 | Ruckmick, C.A. The mental life. N.Y., 1928.
Phil 5400.90 | Ruckmick, C.A. The psychology of feeling and emotion. 1st ed. N.Y., 1936.
Phil 930.25 | Rudd, H.F. Chinese moral sentiments before Confucius. Diss. Chicago? 1915?
Phil 930.25.2 | Rudd, H.F. Chinese social organs. Chicago, 1928.
Phil 9357.7 | Rudd, John C. A series of discourses...to young men. 2d ed. Auburn, 1831.
Phil 5257.35 | Ruddell, G.A.R. Some things that matter. London, 1922.
Phil 8707.3 | Rudder, W. The mutual relations of natural science and theology. Philadelphia, 1869.
Phil 7069.30.26 | Rudi Schneider; a scientific example of his mediumship. (Price, Harry.) London, 1930.
Phil 1750.148 | Rudiger, H. Wesen und Wandlung des Humanismus. Hamburg, 1937.
Phil 5258.20 | Rudimentary psychology. (Steele, G.M.) Boston, 1890.
Phil 5938.13 | Rudiments of metal philosophy and phrenological chart. (Stevens, Enos.) Lampeter, Pa., 1839.
Phil 9200.3 | Rudin, Josef. Fanaticismus. Olten, 1965.
Phil 8597.43 | Rudin, W. Om det personligas betydelse. Upsala, 1885?
Phil 192.53 | Rudin, W. Tillvarons problem. Stockholm, 1905.
Phil 817.25 | Rudmanśki, S. Z dziejów filozofii. Warszawa, 1959.
Phil 179.3.20 | Rudolf Eucken; ein Geistesbild. (Eucken, R.) Berlin, 1927?

Author and Title Listing

Phil 179.3.76   Rudolf Eucken, his life, work and travels. (Eucken, R.) London, 1921.

Phil 179.3.99   Rudolf Eucken; his philosophy. (Booth, Meyrick.) London, 1914.

Phil 179.3.114   Rudolf Eucken. (Jones, Abel John.) London, 1913.

Phil 179.3.84   Rudolf Eucken. (Kappstein, T.) Berlin, 1909.

Phil 179.3.90   Rudolf Euckens Bedeutung für das modern Christentum. (Kesseler, K.) Bunzlau, 1912.

Phil 179.3.81.7   Rudolf Euckens Kampf um einen neuen Idealismus. (Boutroux, Émile.) Leipzig, 1911.

Phil 179.3.86   Rudolf Euckens noologische Methode. (Kade, Richard.) Leipzig, 1912.

Phil 179.3.109   Rudolf Euckens Philosophie und das Bildungsproblem. (Braun, Otto.) Leipzig, 1909.

Phil 179.3.82   Rudolf Eucken's philosophy of life. (Gibson, W.R.B.) London, 1907.

Phil 179.3.105   Rudolf Euckens Theologie. (Höhlmann, Hans.) Berlin, 1903.

Phil 179.3.81.5   Rudolf Euckens Welt- und Lebensanschauung. 2. Aufl. (Siebert, Otto.) Langensalza, 1911.

Phil 179.3.81   Rudolf Euckens Werk. (Kessler, K.) Bunzlau, 1911.

Phil 3450.9.30   Rudolf Maria Holzapfel. (Astrov, V.) Jena, 1928.

Phil 3450.9.85   Rudolf Maria Holzapfel. Basel, 1930.

Phil 8594.16.80   Rudolf Otto's Bedeutung für die Religionswissenschaft und die Theologie. (Benz, Ernst.) Leiden, 1971.

Phil 3745.8.10   Rudolf Pannwitz. (Jäckle, E.) Hamburg, 1937.

Phil 974.3.135   Rudolf Steiner, das literarische und künstlerische Werk. (Rudolf Steiner-Nachlassverwaltung.) Dornach, 1961.

Phil 974.3.112   Rudolf Steiner, der grosse Unbekannte. (Poepping, Fred.) Wien, 1960.

Phil 970.16   Pamphlet vol. Rudolf Steiner. 2 pam.

Phil 974.3.126   Rudolf Steiner. (Bock, Emil.) Stuttgart, 1961.

Phil 974.3.175   Rudolf Steiner. (Petersen, Klaus.) Berlin, 1968.

Phil 978.49.810   Rudolf Steiner. (Rihonët-Coroze, S.) Paris, 1951.

Phil 974.3.140   Rudolf Steiner. (Sunden, Hjalmar.) Stockholm, 1962.

Phil 974.3.124   Rudolf Steiner. (Zeylmans von Emmichoven, F.W.) Zeist, 1960.

Phil 974.3.20   Rudolf Steiner: ein kämpfer Gegen seine Zeit. (Boldt, Ernst.) München, 1923.

Phil 978.49.860   Rudolf Steiner education. (Edmunds, L.F.) London, 1962.

Phil 974.3.51   Rudolf Steiner enters my life. (Rittelmeyer, F.) London, 1929.

Phil 974.3.155   Rudolf Steiner i gete v mirovozzrenii sovremennosti. (Bugaev, Boris N.) Moskva, 1917.

Phil 974.3.150   Rudolf Steiner im Geistesgang des Abendlandes. (Hiebel, Friedrich.) Bern, 1965.

Phil 978.49.270   Rudolf Steiner in der Waldorfschule. 1. Aufl. (Steiner, R.) Stuttgart, 1958.

Phil 978.49.875   Rudolf Steiner-Nachlassverwaltung. Nachrichten mit Veröffentlichungen aus dem Archiv. Dornach. 5-11

Phil 974.3.135   Rudolf Steiner-Nachlassverwaltung. Rudolf Steiner, das literarische und künstlerische Werk. Dornach, 1961.

Phil 978.49.220   Rudolf Steiner über Schauspielkunst (eine Fragenbeantwortung). (Steiner, R.) Dornach, 1939.

Phil 5768.10.35   Rudolf Steiner über seine "Philosophie der Freiheit". (Steiner, Rudolf.) Stuttgart, 1966.

Phil 978.49.835   Rudolf Steiner und Brunn am Gebirge bei Wien. (Muellner, L.) Wien, 1960.

Phil 974.3.25   Rudolf Steiner und das Epigonenturn. (Boldt, Ernst.) München, 1923.

Phil 974.3.170   Rudolf Steiner und die heutige Welt. (Abendroth, Walter.) München, 1969.

Phil 974.3.60   Rudolf Steiner und die Religion. (Geyer, C.K.L.) München, n.d.

Phil 974.3.130   Rudolf Steiner wie ich ihn Sah und Erlebte. (Hahn, Herbert.) Stuttgart, 1961.

Phil 974.3.91   Rudolf Steiners Anthroposophie in Weltanschauungskampfe der Gegenwart. 8. Aufsätze. (Lauer, Hans E.) Basel, 1927.

Phil 974.3.90   Rudolf Steiner's Lebenswerk. (Lauer, Hans E.) Basel, 1926.

Phil 974.3.128   Rudolf Steiners musikalische Inpulse. (Baltz, Karl von.) Dornach, 1961.

Phil 974.3.65   Rudolf Steiners Weltanschauung und ihre Gegner. 3. Aufl. (Lévy, Eugène.) Berlin, 1926?

Phil 6000.3   Rudolph, H. Der Ausdruck der Gemütsbewegungen. Dresden, 1903. 2v.

Phil 978.69   Rudolph, Hermann. Theosophischer Kulturbücher. Leipzig, 1932-33.

Phil 5257.71   Rudolph, Rigmor. Er jeg nig? Traek of Jeg'ets psykologi. Kjøbenhavn, 1960.

Phil 745.8   Rudy, Hirsch. Die Entwicklung der vitalistischen Naturphilosophie im 20. Jahrhundert. Inaug. Diss. Charlottenburg, 1927.

Phil 6132.11   Die Rückenmarksnewen über ihre Segmentbezüge. (Wichmann, R.) Berlin, 1900.

Phil 3801.319   Die Rückwendung zum Mythos. (Dekker, Gerbrand J.) München, 1930.

Phil 5643.34   Ruediger, W.C. The field of distinct vision. n.p., 1907.

Phil 6127.15.5   Rüdinger, N. Ein Beitrag zur Anatomie des Sprach-Centrums. Stuttgart, 1882.

Phil 6127.15   Rüdinger, N. Über die Wage und Ziele. München, 1893.

Phil 5257.26.2   Rüegg, H.R. Grundriss der Seelenlehre. 2. Aufl. Bern, 1864.

Phil 5257.26.8   Rüegg, H.R. Lehrbuch der Psychologie. 3. Aufl. Bern, 1876.

Phil 1540.25   Rüegg, Walter. Cicero und der Humanismus; formale Untersuchungen über Petrarca und Erasmus. Zürich, 1946.

Phil 8418.22   Ruefenacht, E. Lebensstufe und Kunstwerk, ihre Symbolik und ihre Foringesetze. 1. Aufl. Zürich, 1960.

Phil 8430.27   Ruefenacht, E. Mächte der Gestaltung; vom künstlerischen, philosophischen und religiösen Sein. Zürich, 1957.

Phil 8892.28   Rueff, Jacques. Des sciences physiques aux sciences morales. Paris, 1922.

Phil 8707.32   Rueff, Jacques. Les Dieux et les rois, regards sur le pouvoir créateur. Paris, 1967.

Phil 1122.9.5   Rüfner, Vinzenz. Grundbegriffe griechischen Wissenschaftslehre. 2. Aufl. Bamberg, 1947.

Phil 6327.22   Rühle, Alice G. Freud und Adler. Dresden, 1924.

Phil 5871.105.2   Ruehle, Otto. Zur Psychologie des proletarischen Kindes. 2. Aufl. Frankfurt, 1970.

Phil 9455.17   Rühlmann, Paul. Kulturpropaganda. Charlottenburg, 1919.

Phil 9450.4   Ruemelin, G. Politics, and the moral law. N.Y., 1901.

Phil 192.30   Rümelin, G. Reden und Aufsätze. Freiburg, 1881. 3v.

Phil 192.30.5   Rümelin, G. Reden und aufsätze. Freiburg, 1881. 2v.

Phil 3790.3.80   Pamphlet box. Rümelin, Gustav von.

Phil 5627.205   Ruemke, H.C. The psychology of unbelief. London, 1952.

Phil 3790.34   Ruemke, Henricus Cornelius. Levenstijdperken van de naan. Amsterdam, 1968.

Phil 5767.9   Ruesch, Arnold. Die Unfreiheit des Willens. Darmstadt, 1925.

Phil 6967.15   Ruesch, Jurgen. Chronic disease and psychological individualism. N.Y., 1946.

Phil 665.61   Rüsche, Franz. Das Seelenpneuma. Paderborn, 1933.

Phil 8597.45   Rüssel, H.W. Gestalt eines christlichen Humanismus. Amsterdam, 1940.

Phil 3499.28   Rüther, R. Kant und Antikant. Paderborn, 1921.

Phil 8590.44   Der Ruf des Steuermanns. (Kamlah, Wilhelm.) Stuttgart, 1954.

Phil 3246.225   Ruf zur Tat; Johann Gottlieb Fichte. 1. Aufl. (Boettger, Fritz.) Berlin, 1956.

Phil 3246.74   Rufe an die deutsche Nation. (Fichte, Johann Gottlieb.) Berlin, 1943.

Phil 192.18   Ruge, Arnold. Anekdota. Zürich, 1843. 2v.

Phil 192.43   Ruge, Arnold. Einführung in die Philosophie. Leipzig, 1914.

Phil 5062.18.3   Ruge, Arnold. Encyclopädie der philosophischen Wissenschaften in Verbindung mit W. Windelband. Pt.1. Logik. Photoreproduction. Tübingen, 1912.

Phil 5062.18   Ruge, Arnold. Logic. London, 1913.

Phil 3499.11   Ruge, Arnold. Das Problem der Freiheit in Kants Erkenntnistheorie. Leipzig, 1910.

Phil 3925.6.92   Ruge, Arnold. Wilhelm Windelband. Leipzig, 1917.

Phil 5257.13   Ruger, Henry A. Psychology of efficiency. N.Y., 1910.

Phil 1717.8.15   Ruggiero, G. de. Filosofi del novecento. Bari, 1934.

Phil 1717.8.20   Ruggiero, G. de. Filosofi del novecento. 3e ed. Bari, 1946.

Phil 1717.8   Ruggiero, G. de. La filosofia contemporanea. Bari, 1912.

Phil 1717.8.2   Ruggiero, G. de. La filosofia contemporanea. 2a ed. Bari, 1920. 2v.

Phil 1717.8.3   Ruggiero, G. de. La filosofia contemporanea. 3a ed. Bari, 1929. 2v.

Phil 1717.8.5A   Ruggiero, G. de. Modern philosophy. London, 1921.

Phil 1717.8.10   Ruggiero, G. de. Philosophische Strömungen des zivanzigsten Jahrhunderts. Köln, 1949.

Phil 817.8.15   Ruggiero, Guido de. Breve storia della filosofia ad uso delle scuole. Bari, 1955. 3v.

Phil 4215.8.32   Ruggiero, Guido de. L'esistenzialismo. 1. ed. Bari, 1943.

Phil 4215.8.30   Ruggiero, Guido de. Existentialism. London, 1946.

Phil 4215.8.34   Ruggiero, Guido de. Existentialism: disintegration of man's soul. N.Y., 1948.

Phil 4215.8.35   Ruggiero, Guido de. Myths and ideals. London, 1946.

Phil 4215.8.21   Ruggiero, Guido de. Scritti politici, 1912-26. Bologna, 1963.

Phil 817.8.9   Ruggiero, Guido de. Sommario di storia della filosofia. Bari, 1927.

Phil 817.8.5   Ruggiero, Guido de. Storia della filosofia. pt. 1 (v.1-2), pt. 2 (v.1-3), pt. 3 (v.1-2), pt. 4 (v.1-5). Bari, 1934-48. 12v.

Phil 817.8   Ruggiero, Guido de. Storia della filosofia. v.1-2,4 (pt. 1.) Bari, 1918- 12v.

Phil 6945.12   Ruggles, A.H. Mental health. Baltimore, 1934.

Phil 530.20.115   Ruh, Kurt. Altdeutsche und altniederländische Mystik. Darmstadt, 1964.

Phil 2475.1.132   Ruhe, A. Henri Bergson, an account of his life. London, 1914.

Phil 2475.1.133   Ruhe, A. Henri Bergson. Stockholm, 1914.

Phil 5227.4   Ruin, Hans. Erlebnis und Wissen. Helsingfors, 1921.

Phil 4630.4.40   Ruin, Waldemar. Kulturen och tiden. Helsingfors, 1920.

Phil 4630.4.30   Ruin, Waldemar. Kunskap och ideal. Helsingfors, 1886.

Phil 9357.4.2   Ruin and restoration. (Rowland, James.) Albany, 1860.

Phil 9357.4   Ruin and restoration. (Rowland, James.) Albany, 1862.

Phil 3499.9   Ruisch, Arnold. Freiheit Unstirblichkeit und Gott. Leipzig, 1913.

Phil 5590.432   Ruitenbeek, H.M. The individual and the crowd. N.Y., 1964.

Phil 6327.34   Ruitenbeek, H.M. Psychoanalysis and existential philosophy. N.Y., 1962.

Phil 6327.32   Ruitenbeek, H.M. Psychoanalysis and social science. N.Y., 1962.

Phil 5465.143   Ruitenbeek, Hendrik M. The creative imagination. Chicago, 1965.

Phil 6315.2.375   Ruitenbeek, Hendrik Marinus. Freud and America. N.Y., 1966.

Phil 6315.2.370   Ruitenbeek, Hendrik Marinus. Heirs to Freud. N.Y., 1966.

Phil 4368.1.79   Pamphlet box. Ruiz, D.

Phil 8892.43   Ruiz Gómez, J.E. El nuevo mundo moral ó La nueva vida del hombre. Madrid, 1892.

Phil 6967.13   Ruiz Maya, M. Psiquiatria penal y civil. Madrid, 1931.

Phil 720.32   Ruja, H. A critique of the postulational theory of the a priori. Diss. Princeton, 1940.

Phil 5625.75.7   Rukopisnye materialy I.P. Pavlova. (Akademiia Nauk SSSR. Arkhiv.) Moskva, 1949.

Phil 810.7   Rukovet filosofie. (Kratochvii, J.) Brno, 1939.

Phil 3640.680   Rukser, Udo. Nietzsche in der Hispania; ein Beitrag zur hispanischen Kultur- und Geistesgeschichte. Bern, 1962.

Phil 8837.12   Rule and end in morals. (Muirhead, J.H.) London, 1932.

Phil 8892.10   The rule of life. Springfield, 1800.

Phil 8879.40   Rules, roles, and relations. (Emmet, Dorothy Mary.) N.Y., 1966.

Phil 8956.2   Ruling ideas of the present age. (Gladden, Washington.) Boston, 1895.

Phil 3095.82   Ruman, Albert. Die Aesthetik Alex Gottlieb Baumgartens. Halle, 1928.

Phil 5068.54.5   Ruml, Vladimir. Der logische Positivismus. (Übersetzung aus den Techechischen.) Berlin, 1965.

Phil 5068.54   Ruml, Vladimir. Základné otázky filosofie logického pozitivismu. Praha, 1962.

Phil 2270.139   Rumney, J. Herbert Spencer's sociology. London, 1934.

Phil 5465.41   Rumpf-Thevenot, Theodor Richard. Phantasie - ewiger Born. Zürich, 1943.

Phil 5520.685   Rundle, Clement William Kennedy. A critique of linguistic philosophy. Oxford, 1970.

Phil 102.6A   Runes, D.D. the dictionary of philosophy. N.Y., 1942.

Phil 102.6.5   Runes, D.D. Dictionary of thought. N.Y., 1959.

Phil 165.26   Runes, D.D. Treasury of philosophy. N.Y., 1955.

Phil 817.28F   Runes, Dagobert. Pictorial history of philosophy. N.Y., 1965.

Phil 2255.7.15   Runes, Dagobert D. A book of contemplation. N.Y., 1957.

Phil 5039.4   Runes, Dagobert D. Classics in logic. N.Y., 1962.

Phil 2255.7.20   Runes, Dagobert D. Letters to my God. N.Y., 1958.

Phil 2255.7   Runes, Dagobert D. Letters to my son. N.Y., 1949.

Phil 2255.7.3   Runes, Dagobert D. Letters to my teacher. N.Y., 1961.

Phil 2255.7.5   Runes, Dagobert D. Of God, the devil and the Jews. N.Y., 1952.

Phil 2255.7.10   Runes, Dagobert D. On the nature of man. N.Y., 1956.
Phil 1740.4   Runes, Dagobert D. Twentieth century philosophy; living schools of thought. N.Y., 1943.
Phil 8586.36.60   Runte, H. Glaube und Geschichte. Festschrift für Friedrich Gogarten. Giessen, 1948.
Phil 8672.7   Runze, G. Der ontologische Gottesbeweis. Halle, 1882.
Phil 3805.179   Runze, G. Schleiermacher's Glaubenslehre in ihrer Abhängigkeit von seiner Philosophie. Berlin, 1877.
Phil 8597.24   Runze, Georg. Katechismus der Religionsphilosophie. Leipzig, 1901.
Phil 192.38   Runze, Georg. Metaphysik. Leipzig, 1905.
Phil 5627.27.15   Runze, George. Essays zur Religionspsychologie. Berlin, 1913.
Phil 3499.12   Runze, Max. Kant's Bedeutung auf Grund der Entwicklungsgeschichte Seiner Philosophie. Berlin, 1881.
Phil 3499.12.5   Runze, Max. Kant's Kritikan Humes Skepticismus. Berlin, 1880.
Phil 5257.43   Rupp, Hans. Probleme und Apparate zur experimentellen Pädagogik und Jugendpsychologie. Leipzig, 1919.
Phil 9050.1   Rural philosophy. (Bates, E.) London, 1803.
Phil 9050.1.2   Rural philosophy. (Bates, E.) London, 1804.
Phil 9050.1.3   Rural philosophy. (Bates, E.) Philadelphia, 1807.
Phil 310.647   Rus, Vojan. Dialektika človcka, misli in sveta. Ljubljana, 1967.
Phil 9450.61   Rus, Vojan. Kultura, politika in morala. Maribor, 1969.
VPhil 310.647.10   Rus, Vojan. Sodobna filosofija med dialektiko in metafiziko. Ljubljana, 1968.
Phil 8418.35   Ruschioni, Ada. Lineamenti di una storia della poetica e dell'estetica. Milano, 1966.
Phil 310.686   Rusev, Pancho. Teoriiata na otrazhenieto v domarksovata filosofiia. Sofiia, 1968.
Phil 6967.3.2   Rush, B. Medical inquiries...diseases...mind. Philadelphia, 1830.
Phil 6967.3.5   Rush, B. Medical inquiries...diseases...mind. 5. ed. Philadelphia, 1835.
Phil 8892.8.2   Rush, Benjamin. An inquiry into the influence of physical causes upon the moral faculty. Philadelphia, 1839.
Phil 8892.8   Rush, Benjamin. An oration...enquiry into the influence of physical causes upon the moral faculty. Philadelphia, 1786.
Phil 8892.36   Rush, Jacob. Charges, and extracts of charges on moral and religious subjects. Philadelphia, 1803.
Phil 1817.2   Rusk, Robert R. Pragmatische und humanistische Strömung. Jena, 1906.
Phil 8418.13   Ruskin, J. Frondes agrestes. N.Y., 1875.
Phil 7069.11.70   Russel, Fox. Hugsíminn. Reykjavik, 1911.
Phil 6127.28   Russel, Roger. Frontiers in physiological psychology. N.Y., 1966.
Phil 5627.134.12   Russell, A.J. One thing I know. N.Y., 1933.
Phil 5627.134.4   Russell, Arthur J. For sinners only. N.Y., 1932.
Phil 192.28.21A   Russell, B. A free man's worship. 2d ed. Portland, 1927.
Phil 672.16   Russell, B. Is position in time or space absolute or relative? London, 1901.
Phil 192.28.8.5   Russell, B. Méthode scientifique en philosophie. Paris, 1929.
Phil 192.28.19   Russell, B. Mysticism and logic. N.Y., 1929.
Phil 192.28.17   Russell, B. Mysticism and logic and other essays. London, 1919.
Phil 192.28.9   Russell, B. Our knowledge of the external world. Chicago, 1914.
Phil 192.28.20.2   Russell, B. An outline of philosophy. London, 1956.
Phil 192.28.5A   Russell, B. Philosophical essays. London, 1910.
Phil 192.28.6   Russell, B. Philosophical essays. N.Y., 1967.
Phil 2475.1.129   Russell, B. The philosophy of Bergson. Cambridge, 1914.
Phil 192.28.4   Russell, B. Die Probleme der Philosophie. Erlangen, 1926.
Phil 192.28.3   Russell, B. Les problèmes de la philosophie. Paris, 1923.
Phil 192.28   Russell, B. The problems of philosophy. London, 1912.
Phil 192.28.2A   Russell, B. The problems of philosophy. N.Y., 1912.
Phil 192.28.8   Russell, B. Scientific method in philosophy. Oxford, 1913.
Phil 192.28.14   Russell, B. Unser Wissen von der Aussenwelt. Leipzig, 1926.
Phil 9245.43.2   Russell, B.A.W. The conquest of happiness. London, 1930.
Phil 9245.43A   Russell, B.A.W. The conquest of happiness. N.Y., 1930.
Phil 9245.43.1   Russell, B.A.W. The conquest of happiness. N.Y., 1930.
Phil 645.30   Russell, B.A.W. Sceptical essays. N.Y., 1928.
Phil 817.19.5   Russell, B.R. History of Western philosophy. London, 1947.
Phil 817.19.4   Russell, B.R. A history of Western philosophy. N.Y., 1945.
Phil 817.19.4   Russell, B.R. Wisdom of the West. Garden City, 1959.
Phil 5257.25.5   Russell, Bertrand Russell. Analyse de l'esprit. Paris, 1926.
Phil 5257.25   Russell, Bertrand Russell. The analysis of mind. London, 1921.
Phil 5257.25.2   Russell, Bertrand Russell. The analysis of mind. London, 1924.
Phil 2255.1.38   Russell, Bertrand Russell. The art of philosophizing. N.Y., 1968.
Phil 2255.1.15   Russell, Bertrand Russell. The autobiography of Bertrand Russell, 1872-1914. 1st American ed. Boston, 1967. 3v.
Phil 2255.1.52   Russell, Bertrand Russell. Basic writings, 1903-1959. N.Y., 1961.
Phil 2255.1.58A   Russell, Bertrand Russell. Bertrand Russell speaks his mind. 1st ed. Cleveland, 1960.
Phil 2255.1.63   Russell, Bertrand Russell. Common sense and nuclear warfare. London, 1959.
Phil 3552.104.2   Russell, Bertrand Russell. A critical exposition of the philosophy of Leibniz. 2d ed. London, 1967.
Phil 2255.1.64   Russell, Bertrand Russell. Dear Bertrand Russell: a selection of his correspondence with the general public, 1950-1968. London, 1969.
Phil 2255.1.131   Russell, Bertrand Russell. A detailed catalogue of the archives of Bertrand Russell. London, 1967.
Phil 2255.1.65   Russell, Bertrand Russell. Dictionary of mind, matter and morals. N.Y., 1952.
Phil 2255.1.48   Russell, Bertrand Russell. Essays in skepticism. N.Y., 1962.
Phil 2255.1.73   Russell, Bertrand Russell. Fact and fiction. London, 1961.
Phil 2255.1.20   Russell, Bertrand Russell. La filosofía en el siglo XX y otros ensayos. Montevideo, 1962.
Phil 2255.1.77   Russell, Bertrand Russell. The future of science. N.Y., 1959.
Phil 2255.1.76   Russell, Bertrand Russell. The good citizen's alphabet. London, 1953.
Phil 2255.1.68   Russell, Bertrand Russell. Has man a future? London, 1961.

Phil 2255.1.45   Russell, Bertrand Russell. Human knowledge; its scope and limits. London, 1948.
Phil 8892.62   Russell, Bertrand Russell. Human society in ethics and politics. London, 1954.
Phil 8892.62.5   Russell, Bertrand Russell. Human society in ethics and politics. N.Y., 1955.
Phil 5068.7.4   Russell, Bertrand Russell. An inquiry into meaning and truth. London, 1951.
Phil 5068.7.6   Russell, Bertrand Russell. An inquiry into meaning and truth. London, 1966.
Phil 2255.1.36   Russell, Bertrand Russell. Let the people think. 2nd ed. London, 1961.
Phil 2255.1.75   Russell, Bertrand Russell. Logic and knowledge. London, 1956.
Phil 2255.1.32   Russell, Bertrand Russell. My philosophical development. London, 1959.
Phil 2255.1.60   Russell, Bertrand Russell. New hopes for a changing world. London, 1951.
Phil 2255.1.61   Russell, Bertrand Russell. New hopes for a changing world. N.Y., 1951.
Phil 2255.1.30A   Russell, Bertrand Russell. Philosophy. N.Y., 1927.
Phil 2255.1.40   Russell, Bertrand Russell. Philosophy and politics. London, 1947.
Phil 2255.1.43   Russell, Bertrand Russell. Political ideals. N.Y., 1963.
Phil 2255.1.78   Russell, Bertrand Russell. Portraits from memory. London, 1956.
Phil 8610.927.10   Russell, Bertrand Russell. Pourquoi je ne suis pas chrétien. Paris, 1964.
Phil 2255.1.74A   Russell, Bertrand Russell. Power; a new social analysis. N.Y., 1969.
Phil 8707.16.5   Russell, Bertrand Russell. Religion and science. London, 1968.
Phil 2255.1.10A   Russell, Bertrand Russell. Selected papers. N.Y., 1927.
Phil 2255.1.79   Russell, Bertrand Russell. Understanding history. N.Y., 1957.
Phil 2255.1.50   Russell, Bertrand Russell. Unpopular essays. London, 1950.
Phil 2255.1.51   Russell, Bertrand Russell. Unpopular essays. N.Y., 1950.
Phil 8892.37   Russell, Bertrand Russell. What I believe. London, 1925.
Phil 8892.37.3   Russell, Bertrand Russell. What I believe. N.Y., 1925.
Phil 8892.37.10   Russell, Bertrand Russell. What I believe. N.Y., 1928.
Phil 8610.927.7   Russell, Bertrand Russell. Why I am not a Christian. Girard, Kansas, 1929.
Phil 8610.927.8   Russell, Bertrand Russell. Why I am not a Christian. N.Y., 1957.
Phil 2255.1.72   Russell, Bertrand Russell. The will to doubt. N.Y., 1958.
Phil 2255.1.55   Russell, Bertrand Russell. The wit and wisdom. Boston, 1951.
Phil 510.147   Russell, C.W. Mind: creative and dynamic. N.Y., 1932.
Phil 5421.20.55   Russell, Claire. Violence, monkeys, and man. London, 1968.
Phil 9245.49   Russell, Dora. The right to be happy. N.Y., 1927.
Phil 8707.10   Russell, H.N. Fate and freedom. New Haven, 1927.
Phil 5057.11   Russell, J.E. An elementary logic. N.Y., 1906.
Phil 192.29A   Russell, J.E. A first course in philosophy. N.Y., 1913.
Phil 5257.47   Russell, J.T. Applicability of the probable error formulae to psychological data. Diss. Chicago, 1934.
Phil 5057.14   Russell, L.J. An introduction to logic. London, 1914.
Phil 3850.27.103   Russell, L.M. The path to reconstruction...Albert Schweitzer's philosophy of civilization. London, 1941.
Phil 3850.27.103.5   Russell, L.M. The path to reconstruction. London, 1943.
Phil 1717.12   Russell, Leonard. An introduction to philosophy. London, 1929.
Phil 5850.330   Russell, W.L. Peace and power within. Houston, Texas, 1951.
Phil 5850.330.5   Russell, W.L. Peace and power within. N.Y., 1954.
Phil 5548.150   Russell, Wallace Addison. Milestones in motivation; contributions to the psychology of drive and purpose. N.Y., 1970.
Phil 2255.1.175   Russell: the journal of the Bertrand Russell Archives. Hamilton, Ont. 1,1971+
Phil 2255.1.170   Russell and Moore: the analytical heritage. (Ayer, Alfred Jules.) Cambridge, 1971.
Phil 2255.1.185   Russell remembered. (Crawshay-Williams, Rupert.) London, 1970.
Phil 8418.16   Russi, Antonio. L'arte et le arti. Pisa, 1960.
Phil 1717.22   Russia, 1917. Ministerstvo vysshego Obrazovaniia. Kritika sovremennoi burzhuaznoi ideologi. Petrozavodsk, 1963.
Phil 8980.787.20   Russia (1917-). Upravlenie Prepodavaniia Obshchestvennykh Nauk. Marksistskaia etika; khrestomatiia. Moskva, 1961.
RRC Phil 310.12   Russia (1917-). Upravlenie Prepodavatel'skogo Obshchestvennogo Nauk. Programma kursa dialekticheskogo i istoricheskogo materializma dlia vyshego uchebrogo zaved. Moskva, 1954.
Phil 310.12.15   Russia (1917-). Upravlenie Prepodavatel'skogo Obshchestvennogo Nauk. Programma kursa dialekticheskogo i istoricheskogo materializma. Moskva, 1957.
Phil 5204.16   Russian-English glossary of psychiatric terms. (Telberg, Ina.) N.Y., 1964.
Phil 4710.142   Russian philosophical terminology. (Ballestrem, Karl G.) Dordrecht, 1964.
Phil 4710.96   Pamphlet vol. Russian philosophy. 7 pam.
Phil 4710.144   Russian philosophy. 1. ed. (Edie, James M.) Chicago, 1965. 3v.
Phil 4710.70.15   Russian thinkers and Europe. (Zen'kovskii, V.V.) Ann Arbor, 1953.
Phil 4710.158   Die russiche Weltanschauung. 1. Aufl. (Frank, Semen L.) Darmstadt, 1967.
Phil 2805.255   Russier, Jeanne. La foi selon Pascal. v.1-2. Thèse. Paris, 1949.
Phil 2520.290   Russier, Jeanne. Sagesse cartésienne et religion. Paris, 1958.
Phil 4710.6   Russische Denker. (Schultze, B.) Wien, 1950.
Phil 4710.15   Der russische Idealismus der 30er Jahre und seine Überwindung. Inaug. Diss. (Billig, Joseph.) Berlin, 1930.
Phil 530.70.5   Russische Mystik. (Walter, R. von.) Düsseldorf, 1957.
Phil 4710.20.5   Russische Philosophie. (Radloff, E. von.) Bredau, 1925.
Phil 4710.37   Russische Religionsphilosophen. (Bubnov, Nikolai M.) Heidelberg, 1956.
Phil 4710.168   Russkaia filosofiia XI-XIX vekov. (Galaktionov, Anatolii A.) Leningrad, 1970.
Phil 4752.2.35   Russkaia ideia. (Berdiaev, Nikolai Aleksandrovich.) Parizh, 1946.
Phil 4769.1.122   Russkaia ideia. (Solov'ev, V.S.) Moskva, 1911.

Phil 4710.84 — Russkaia materialisticheskaia filosofiia XVIII-IX vekov i ee istoricheskoe znachenie. (Shchipanov, I.Ia.) Moskva, 1953.

Phil 4710.82 — Russkaia progressivnaia filosficheskaia mysl' XIX veka. (Vasetskii, G.S.) Moskva, 1959.

Phil 4710.70 — Russkie mysliteli i Evropa. (Zen'kovskii, V.V.) Paris, 1926.

Phil 4710.70.2 — Russkie mysliteli i Evropa. Izd. 2. (Zen'kovskii, V.V.) Paris, 1955.

Phil 4710.146 — Russkie prosvetiteli, ot Radishcheva do dekabristov. (Shchipanov, I.Ia.) Moskva, 1966. 2v.

Phil 310.380 · — Russkie uchenye v bor'be protiv idealizma i metafiziki vozzrenii v estestvoznanii. (Akademiia Nauk SSSR. Kafedra Filosofii.) Moskva, 1961.

Phil 2905.1.220 — Russo, F. Essais sur Teilhard de Chardin. Paris, 1962.
Phil 493.7 — Russo, F. Science et matérialisme. Paris, 1962.
Phil 8418.15 — Russo, S. Arte e libertá e altri saggi. Padova, 1960.
Phil 8707.30 — Rust, Eric C. Science and faith. N.Y., 1967.
Htn — Phil 8597.14* — Rust, G. A discourse...reason in matters of religion. London, 1683.

Phil 8418.8.5 — Rusu, Liviu. Essai sur la création artistique. Paris, 1935.

Phil 8418.8 — Rusu, Liviu. Essai sur la création artistique comme révélation du sens de l'éxistence. Paris, 1935.

Phil 4265.1.35 — Rutenburg, V.I. Velikii ital'ianskii ateist Vanini. Moskva, 1959.

Phil 8892.11 — Rutherforth, T. An essay on the nature and obligations of virtue. Cambridge, 1744.

Phil 3850.18.220 — Rutishauser, Bruno. Max Schelers Phänomenologie des Fühlens. Bern, 1969.

Phil 310.175 — Rutkevich, M.N. Dialekticheskii materializm. Moskva, 1959.

Phil 8980.759 — Rutkovs'kyi, Borys O. Katehoriia dovir'ia v marksysts'kii etytsi. Kyiv, 1970.

Phil 7069.23.19 — Rutot, A. Le mécanisme de la survie. Paris, 1923.
Phil 5520.220 — Rutt, Theodor. Vom Wesen der Sprache. Ratingen, 1957.
Phil 5643.85 — Rutten, F.J.T. Psychologie der waarneming. Diss. Nijmegen, 1929.

Phil 5330.34 — Rutten, Josephus W.H.M. Attentiviteit als psychodiagnosticum. Proefschrift. Maastricht, 1964.

Phil 5257.33 — Ruttmann, W.J. Die Hauptergebnisse der modernen Psychologie. Leipzig, 1914.

Phil 6027.2 — Rutz, Ottmar. Vom Ausdruck des Menschen. Celle, 1925.
Phil 8418.30.2 — Ruvo, Vincenzo de. Il bello. 2. ed. Napoli, 1965.
Phil 630.60 — Ruvo, Vincenzo de. Introduzione al realismo critico. Padova, 1964.

Phil 3499.42 — Ruvo, Vincenzo de. Il pensiero filosofico di Kant, ovvero problemi di critica Kantiana. Paris, 1969.

Phil 720.98 — Ruvo, Vincenzo de. Il problema della verità da Spinoza a Hume. Padova, 1970.

Phil 5525.65.5 — Ruvo, Vincenzo de. Il riso e l'arte del ridere. Bari, 1965.

Phil 8892.57 — Ruvo, Vincenzo de. I valori morali. Bari, 1942.
Phil 8892.57.2 — Ruvo, Vincenzo de. I valori morali. 2. ed. Padora, 1970.
Phil 192.69 — Ruyer, R. Esquisse d'une philosophie de structure. Paris, 1930.

Phil 192.69.2 — Ruyer, R. Esquisse d'une philosophie de structure. Thèse. Paris, 1930.

Phil 2515.4.94 — Ruyer, R. L'humanité de l'avenir, d'après Cournot. Paris, 1930.

Phil 2515.4.95 — Ruyer, R. L'humanité de l'avenir, d'après Cournot. Thèse secondaire. Paris, 1930.

Phil 8735.24 — Ruyer, R. Néo-finalisme. 1. éd. Paris, 1952.
Phil 735.132 — Ruyer, R. Philosophie de la valeur. Paris, 1952.
Phil 5374.60 — Ruyer, Raymond. La conscience et le corps. Paris, 1937.
Phil 8597.62 — Ruyer, Raymond. Dieu des religions, dieu de la science. Paris, 1970.

Phil 5500.1 — Ruyssen, T. Essai sur l'évolution psychologique du jugement. Nimes, 1904.

Phil 3808.112 — Ruyssen, T. Les grands philosophes; Schopenhauer. Paris, 1911.

Phil 3499.5 — Ruyssen, T. Kant. Paris, 1900.
Phil 3499.5.5 — Ruyssen, T. Quid de natura...senserit Kantius. Nemausi, 1903.

Phil 2138.165 — Ryan, Alan. John Stuart Mill. N.Y., 1970.
Phil 817.20 — Ryan, Arthur H. Perennial philosophers. Dublin, 1946.
Phil 978.5.810 — Ryan, C.J. H.P. Blavatsky and the theosophical movement. Point Loma, Calif., 1937.

Phil 192.50 — Ryan, J.H. An introduction to philosophy. N.Y., 1924.
Phil 1522.6 — Ryan, J.K. Basic principles and problems of philosophy. Washington, 1939.

Phil 165.21 — Ryan, J.K. Philosophical studies in honor of the very Reverend Ignatius Smith. Westminster, Maryland, 1952.

Phil 9495.167 — Ryan, Mary Perkins. Love and sexuality. 1st ed. N.Y., 1967.

Phil 5548.140 — Ryan, Thomas Arthur. Intentional behavior; an approach to human motivation. N.Y., 1970.

Phil 6980.661 — Rycroft, Charles. Imagination and reality; psycho-analytical essays, 1951-1961. London, 1968.

Phil 6327.21.100 — Rycroft, Charles. Wilhelm Reich. N.Y., 1972.
Phil 5272.14 — Rydberg, Sven. Bias in prediction; on correction methods. Uppsala, 1963.

Phil 4630.5.2 — Rydberg, V. Filosofiska föreläsningar. Stockholm, 1900-01. 4v.

Phil 3552.111.15 — Rydberg, Viktor. Leibniz' Theodicee. Leipzig, 1903.
Phil 4630.3.39 — Rydelius, Anders. Aphorismi philosophici de moderamine libertatis philosophicae. Diss. Lundini, 1726.

Phil 4630.3.37 — Rydelius, Anders. Dissertatio metaphysica de novis...axiomatibus...Leibnitus et Volfius. Lundini, 1725.

Phil 4630.3.44 — Rydelius, Anders. Dissertatio philosophica, fidelem praeceptorem...privatum adumbrans. Diss. Lundini, 1726.

Phil 4630.3.42 — Rydelius, Anders. Dissertatio philosophica, gradualis de tempore. Diss. Lundini, 1726.

Phil 4630.3.46 — Rydelius, Anders. Dissertatio philosophica de vera rationis humanae definitione. Diss. Lund, 1727.

Phil 4630.3.35 — Rydelius, Anders. Dissertatio philosophica mepi...seu de excessu subtilitatis in philosophicae. Lund, 1726.

Phil 4630.3.31 — Rydelius, Anders. Förnufts-öfningar. Linköping, 1737.
Phil 4508.10 — Ryding, Erik. Den svenska filosofins historia. Stockholm, 1959.

Phil 8892.9 — Ryland, F. Ethics. London, 1893.
Phil 5257.22.3 — Ryland, F. Psychology. 7. ed. London, 1897.
Phil 192.34 — Ryland, F. Questions on psychology, metaphysics, and ethics. London, 1887.

Phil 5257.22.5 — Ryland, F. The story of thought and feeling. London, 1900.

Phil 5257.54 — Ryland, F. A student's handbook of psychology and ethics. London, 1885.

Phil 6327.23 — Rylander, G. Personality changes after operations on the frontal lobes. Copenhagen, 1939.

Phil 5190.28.2 — Ryle, G. Dilemmas. Cambridge, Eng., 1962.
Phil 6127.26 — Ryle, Gilbert. The concept of mind. London, 1949.
Phil 6127.26.5 — Ryle, Gilbert. The concept of mind. London, 1963.
Phil 5257.70 — Ryle, Gilbert. A puzzling element in the notion of thinking. London, 1958.

Phil 5257.70.5 — Ryle, Gilbert. A rational animal. London, 1962.
Phil 2255.12 — Ryle. London, 1971.
Phil 8892.27 — Ryner, J.H. Le subjectivisme. Paris, 1923.
Phil 9245.53 — Le rythme de la vie, le bonheur. (Somer, Marcelle de.) Gand, 1933.

Phil 186.147 — Rythmologie universelle et métaphysique de l'harmonie. (Lamouche, André.) Paris, 1966. 2v.

Phil 7028.2 — Rýzl, Milan. Parapsychology. N.Y., 1970.
Phil 4795.4 — Rzaev, Agababa. Peredovaia politicheskaia mysl' Rossii i Azerbaidzhana XIX vekai ikh vzaimosviazi. Baku, 1967.

VPhil 3925.16.155 — Rzeczy i fakty. (Wolniewicz, Bogusław.) Warszawa, 1968.
Phil 3808.117 — Rzewuski, S. L'optimisme de Schopenhauer. Paris, 1908.
Phil 4768.5 — S.L. Rubinstein and the philosophical foundations of Soviet psychology. (Payne, T.R.) Dordrecht, 1968.

Phil 4756.1.46 — S nami Bog; tri razmyshleniia. (Frank, Semen L.) Paris, 1964.

Phil 4600.4.80 — Så minns Bengt Lidforss. (Geijerstam, G.L. af.) Stockholm, 1945.

Phil 6328.60 — Saada, Denise. L'héritage de Freud. Paris, 1966.
Phil 3940.3.30 — Saager, Q. Der Winterthurer Naturphilosoph J.H. Ziegler. Winterthur, 1930.

Phil 3160.5.81 — Saal, Ernst. Hans Cornelius Erkenntnistheorie im Verhältnis zu der Kants. Diss. Giessen, 1919.

Phil 7082.126.1 — Saalfeld, Adam Friedrich William. Philosophical discourse on the nature of dreams. London, 1764.

Phil 3552.420 — Saame, Otto. Der Satz vom Gound bei Leibniz. Mainz, 1961.
Phil 8419.52 — Saarinen, E. Search for form. N.Y., 1948.
Phil 5058.90 — Saarnio, Uuno. Logikens Uppkomst och Väsen. Helsingfors, 1957.

Phil 5058.92 — Saarnio, Uuno. Ord och Mängd. Helsingfors, 1960.
Phil 8612.33 — Saat und Ernte. (Bürgel, B.H.) Berlin, 1942.
Phil 4260.131 — Sabarini, Raniero. Il tempo in G.B. Vico. Milano, 1954.
Phil 3838.11 — Sabatier, A. de Castres. Apologie de Spinoza et du s'isme. Altona, 1805.

Phil 8643.20.3 — Sabatier, Armand. Essai sur l'immortalité au point de vue du naturalisme évolutionniste. 3. éd. Paris, 1911.

Phil 8598.24.2 — Sabatier, Auguste. Esquisse d'une philosophie de la religion. Paris, 1897.

Phil 8598.24.3 — Sabatier, Auguste. Esquisse d'une philosophie de la religion d'après la psychologie et l'histoire. 10. éd. Paris, 1937.

Phil 8598.24.7 — Sabatier, Auguste. Outlines of a philosophy of religion. N.Y., 1902.

Phil 8598.24.9 — Sabatier, Auguste. Philosophie de l'effort. Paris, 1908.
Phil 4980.1.30 — Sabato, Ernesto R. Hombres y engranajes. Buenos Aires, 1951.

Phil 585.152 — Saber-se entendre. (Muñoz Espinalt, Carlos.) Barcelona, 1961.

Phil 809.6 — Saber y dialectia. (Jasinowski, Bogumil.) Santiago, 1957.
Phil 2050.272 — Sabetti, Alfredo. David Hume, filosofo della religione. Napoli, 1965.

Phil 3425.708 — Sabetti, Alfredo. Hegel e il problema della filosofia come storia. Napoli, 1967.

Phil 310.594 — Sabetti, Alfredo. Sulla fondazione del materialismo storico. Firenze, 1969.

Phil 4260.38 — Sabiduría primitiva de los italianos. (Vico, G.B.) Buenos Aires, 1939.

Phil 177.40 — Sabine, George H. Philosophical essays in honor of J.E. Creighton. N.Y., 1917.

Phil 8708.27 — Sabine, P.E. Atoms, men and God. N.Y., 1953.
Phil 7069.51.15 — Sabine, Waldo. Second sight in daily life. London, 1951.
Phil 8419.65 — Šabouk, Sáva. Jazyk umění. Praha, 1969.
Phil 2515.2.81 — Sabrié, J.B. De l'humanisme au rationalisme. Pierre Charron. Paris, 1913.

Phil 585.60 — Sabuco de Nantes Barrera, O. Nueva filosofía de la naturaleza del hombre. Madrid, 1728.

Phil 8419.2 — Sacchetti, E. Che cos è l'arte. Firenze, 1961.
Phil 8673.9 — Sacchi, Gaetano. Esistenza di Dio. Roma, 1919.
Phil 2270.132 — Sacerdote, S. La vita di H. Spencer, ed "I primi principii". Torino, 1907.

Phil 3195.9.77 — Sache, Leben, und Feinde. 2. Aufl. (Dühring, E.) Leipzig, 1903.

Phil 4225.4 — Sacheli, C.A. Atto e valore. Firenze, 1938.
Phil 325.3 — Sacheli, C.A. Fenomenismo. Genova, 1925.
Phil 8893.99 — Sacheli, C.A. Ragion pratica. Firenze, 1938.
Phil 3195.10.113 — Sacher, Heinz. Vergleich zwischen Rehmkes und Drieschs Philosophie. Inaug. Diss. Dresden, 1933.

Phil 5710.20 — Sacherl, Karl. Die Pedanterie. Göttingen, 1957.
Phil 3494.45.10 — Sachindsco zu Kants Kritik der reinen Vernunft. (Martin, Gottfried.) Berlin, 1967.

Phil 3640.436 — Sachlicher Vorbericht zur Gesamtausgabe der Werke Friedrich Nietzsches. (Mette, H.J.) n.p., 193-?

Phil 3450.48.80 — Sachlichkeit und Bildung; kritische Studie...Hans-Eduard Hengstenberg. (Bittner, Gerhard.) München? 1965?

Phil 6315.2.127A — Sacho, H. Freud, master and friend. Cambridge, Mass., 1944.

Phil 5585.45 — Sachs, H. Die Entstehung der Raumvorstellung. Breslau, 1897.

Phil 6328.25.5 — Sachs, Hanns. The creative unconscious. Cambridge, 1942.
Phil 6328.25 — Sachs, Hanns. Gemeinsame Tagträume. Leipzig, 1924.
Phil 6328.42 — Sachs, Hanns. Masks of love and life. London, 1957.
Phil 5850.331 — Sachs, Hildegard. Zur Organisation der Eignungspsychologie. Leipzig, 1920.

Phil 6328.17 — Sachs, Wulf. Psychoanalysis. London, 1934.
Phil 299.30 — Sachsse, Hans. Naturerkenntnis und Wirklichkeit. Braunschweig, 1967.

Phil 510.3 — Sack, J. Monistische Gottes und Weltanschauung. Leipzig, 1899.

Phil 5409.7 — Sack, Max. Die Verzweiflung: eine Untersuchung ihres Wesens und ihrer Entstehung. Inaug. Diss. Kallmünz, 1930.

Phil 4769.1.95 — Sacke, G. W.S. Solowjews Geschichtsphilosophie. Berlin, 1929.

Phil 1905.13 — A sacramental universe. (Bowman, A.A.) Princeton, 1939.
Phil 2515.14 — Le sacre de la liberté. (Cordonnier, P.) Paris, 1958.
Phil 8430.44 — Sacred and profane beauty. (Leeuw, G. van der.) N.Y., 1963. 10v.

Phil 8708.6 — Sacred geology. London, 1847.
Phil 8709.14.10 — The sacred history of the world. (Turner, Sharon.) N.Y., 1835-36. 2v.

Phil 8709.14.8 — The sacred history of the world. (Turner, Sharon.) N.Y., 1835-39. 3v.

Phil 8709.14.6   The sacred history of the world. v.1. (Turner, Sharon.) N.Y., 1832.

Phil 8709.14.5   The sacred history of the world. 3. ed. (Turner, Sharon.) London, 1833. 2v.

Phil 7069.59   The sacred mushroom. (Puharich, A.) Garden City, 1959.

Phil 8583.8.2   Sacred philosophy. v.3. (Duncan, H.) Boston, 1839?

Phil 8583.8   Sacred philosophy of the Seasons. (Duncan, H.) Boston, 1839. 2v.

Phil 8691.8.9   The sacred theory of the earth. (Burnet, Thomas.) Glasgow, 1753. 2v.

Phil 8691.8.4   The sacred theory of the earth. (Burnet, Thomas.) London, 1719. 2v.

Phil 8691.8.7   The sacred theory of the earth. (Burnet, Thomas.) London, 1722-26. 2v.

Phil 8691.8.15   The sacred theory of the earth. (Burnet, Thomas.) London, 1965.

Phil 8691.8.12   The sacred theory of the earth. 7. ed. (Burnet, Thomas.) London, 1759. 2v.

Phil 4073.66   I sacri segni, inediti. (Campanella, Tommaso.) Roma, 1965. 6v.

Phil 3450.19.210   Sacristán Luzón, Manuel. Las ideas gnoseologicas de Heidegger. Barcelona, 1959.

Phil 9005.2   Sacy, M.L. de. Traité de la gloire. La Haye, 1745.

Phil 5500.30   Sadacca, Robert. Dimensions of response consistency in paired comparisons. Princeton, 1962.

Phil 8591.14   Sadd, G.T. The philosophy of religion. N.Y., 1905. 2v.

Phil 910.2   Saddhatissa, Hammalaiva. Buddhist ethics: essence of Buddhism. London, 1970.

Phil 8408.30.5   Sádecký, Z. O některých otázkách estetiky Otakara Hostinskéko. Praha, 1956.

Phil 5650.22.10   Sader, Manfred. Lautheit und Lärn. Göttingen, 1966.

Phil 7085.10   Sadger, Isidor. Sleep walking and moon walking. N.Y., 1920.

Phil 7085.10.1   Sadger, Isidor. Über Nachtwandeln und Mondsucht. Nendeln, 1970.

Phil 6128.79   Sadhu, Mouni. Ways to self-realization. N.Y., 1962.

Phil 193.101   Sadler, G.T. A new world by a new vision. London, 1925. 2 pam.

Phil 665.68   Sadler, W.S. The evolution of the soul. Chicago? 1941.

Phil 5722.26   Sadler, W.S. The mind at mischief. N.Y., 1929.

Phil 5421.25.20   Sadler, William Alan. Existence and love. N.Y., 1969.

Phil 6128.42   Sadler, William S. The truth about mind cure. Chicago, 1928.

Phil 193.164   Sadoleto, J. Elogia della sapienza. Napoli, 1950.

Phil 349.90   Sadovskii, Grigorii I. Leninskaia kontseptsiia poniatiia i evoliutsiia poniatiia "vid". Minsk, 1970.

Phil 3450.19.275   Sadzik, J. Esthétique de Martin Heidegger. Paris, 1963.

Phil 8725.6   Säkularisierung. (Luebbe, Hermann.) Freiburg, 1965.

Phil 3480.19.12   Sämmtliche Kleine Schriften. (Kant, Immanuel.) Königsberg, 1797. 3v.

Phil 3819.11   Sämmtliche philosophische Werke. (Spinoza, Benedictus de.) Berlin, 1869-71. 2v.

Phil 3090.10   Sämmtliche Werke. (Baader, Franz von.) Leipzig, 1851-60. 16v.

Phil 3235.10   Sämmtliche Werke. (Feuerbach, Ludwig.) Leipzig, 1846-90. 10v.

Phil 3246.10   Sämmtliche Werke. (Fichte, Johann Gottlieb.) Berlin, 1845-46. 8v.

Phil 3246.11   Sämmtliche Werke. (Fichte, Johann Gottlieb.) Berlin, 1845-46. 11v.

Phil 3246.18   Sämmtliche Werke. (Fichte, Johann Gottlieb.) Leipzig, 1924. 8v.

Phil 3428.10   Sämmtliche Werke. (Herbart, J.F.) Leipzig, 1850-52. 12v.

Phil 3480.12   Sämmtliche Werke. (Kant, Immanuel.) Leipzig, 1838-40. 12v.

Phil 3480.13A   Sämmtliche Werke. (Kant, Immanuel.) Leipzig, 1867-68. 8v.

Phil 3625.1.5   Sämmtliche Werke. (Mendelssohn, Moses.) Wien, 1838. 3v.

Phil 3805.10   Sämmtliche Werke. (Schleiermacher, Friedrich.) Berlin, 1826-64. 29v.

Phil 3808.10   Sämmtliche Werke. (Schopenhauer, Arthur.) Leipzig, 1873-77. 6v.

Phil 3808.12   Sämmtliche Werke. (Schopenhauer, Arthur.) Leipzig, 1891. 6v.

Phil 3808.18   Sämmtliche Werke. (Schopenhauer, Arthur.) Leipzig, 1919. 2v.

Phil 3808.19   Sämmtliche Werke. (Schopenhauer, Arthur.) Leipzig, 1937-41. 7v.

Phil 3819.11.2   Sämmtliche Werke. (Spinoza, Benedictus de.) Leipzig, 1914-22. 3v.

Phil 3549.8.5   Sämmtliche Werke. Supplement. (Klages, Ludwig.) Bonn, 1966.

Htn Phil 3800.30.5*   Sämmtliche Werke. v.1. pt.1-10, v.2. pt.1-4. (Schelling, F.W.J. von.) Stuttgart, 1856-61. 14v.

Phil 3808.13   Sämmtliche Werke. v.1-6,9-11,13-16. (Schopenhauer, Arthur.) München, 1911-42. 13v.

Phil 3110.11   Sämmtliche Werke. v.1-7. (Böhme, J.) Leipzig, 1860. 6v.

Phil 3110.11.2   Sämmtliche Werke. v.1-7. (Böhme, J.) Leipzig, 1922. 6v.

Phil 3235.74   Sämmtliche Werke. v.1-13. (Feuerbach, Ludwig.) Stuttgart, 1964. 10v.

Phil 3428.11   Sämmtliche Werke. v.1-19. (Herbart, J.F.) Langensalza, 1887-1912. 14v.

Phil 3805.12   Sämmtliche Werke. 2. Aufl. (Schleiermacher, Friedrich.) Berlin, 1884.

Phil 3808.15   Sämmtliche Werke. 2. Aufl. (Schopenhauer, Arthur.) Leipzig, 1877. 6v.

Phil 3808.15.7   Sämmtliche Werke. 2. Aufl. (Schopenhauer, Arthur.) Leipzig, 1908. 6v.

Phil 3808.17   Sämmtliche Werke in fünf Bänden. (Schopenhauer, Arthur.) Leipzig, 1919. 5v.

Phil 3110.13   Sämtliche Schriften. (Böhme, J.) Stuttgart, 1942. 10v.

Phil 3195.3   Sämtliche Schriften. (Dietzgen, Joseph.) Wiesbaden, 1911. 3v.

Phil 3200.17   Sämtliche Schriften in Einzelausgaben. (Edelmann, Johann Christian.) Stuttgart, 1970. 5v.

Phil 3552.12   Sämtliche Schriften und Briefe. v.1, pt.1-8. (Leibniz, Gottfried Wilhelm.) Darmstadt, 1923-50. 8v.

Phil 3425.12   Sämtliche Werke. (Hegel, Georg Wilhelm Friedrich.) Stuttgart, 1927-40. 19v.

Phil 3640.17.12   Sämtliche Werke. (Nietzsche, Friedrich.) Stuttgart, 1964-65. 12v.

Phil 3549.8.2   Sämtliche Werke. v.1,2,6-8. (Klages, Ludwig.) Bonn, 1964. 5v.

Phil 3800.30A   Sämtliche Werke. v.1. pt.1-10, v.2. pt.1-4. (Schelling, F.W.J. von.) Stuttgart, 1856-61. 14v.

Phil 3480.16   Sämtliche Werke. v.1-9 und Ergänzungsband. 10. Aufl. (Kant, Immanuel.) Leipzig, 1913. 10v.

Phil 3500.26   Sänger, E.A. Kants Lehre vom Glauben. Leipzig, 1903.

Phil 3090.22   Sätze ans der erotischen Philosophie und andere Schriften. (Baader, Franz von.) Frankfurt, 1966.

Phil 3245.32   Sätze zur Vorschule der Theologie. (Fichte, Immanuel Hermann.) Stuttgart, 1826.

Phil 3850.27.160   Safari of discovery. (Phillips, Herbert M.) N.Y., 1958.

Phil 6122.59   Safeguarding mental health. (McCarthy, R.C.) N.Y., 1937.

Phil 1718.42   Saffet, Mehmet. Muasir Aurupa felsefesi. Ankara, 1933.

Phil 299.10   Sagaret, Jules. Le système du monde des chaldéens à Newton. 2. éd. Paris, 1913.

Phil 4352.1.107   Sagarra y de Castellarnau, Fernando. Encrucijada. Barcelona, 1957.

Phil 193.124   Sagcret, Emile. Essais de philosophie synthetique. Paris, 1928.

Phil 7069.29.105   Sage, Michel. Frú Piper og Ensk-Vestraena Salarransóknarfjelagid Reykjavik, 1929.

Phil 6688.6   Sage, X.L. Hypnotism as it is. N.Y., 1897.

Phil 6688.6.2   Sage, X.L. Hypnotism as it is. Rochester, 1899.

Phil 6100.17   Sager, O. Recherches sur la somatotopie sensitive dans le thalamus des singes. Harlem, 1933.

Phil 270.52   Sageret, Jules. Le lasard et la destinée. Paris, 1927.

Phil 1718.12   Sageret, Jules. La revolution philosophique et la science. Paris, 1924.

Phil 525.27   Sageret, Jules. La vague mystique. Paris, 1920.

Phil 820.2   Sages and schoolmen. (Ussher, Arland.) Dublin, 1967.

Phil 8598.104   Sagesse. Bruges, 1951.

Phil 2520.185   La sagesse cartésienne et la doctrine de la science. (Segond, J.) Paris, 1932.

Phil 2520.290   Sagesse cartésienne et religion. (Russier, Jeanne.) Paris, 1958.

Htn Phil 2515.2.35*   La sagesse de Charron. (Charron, P.) Paris, 1672.

Phil 190.106   Sagesse et illusions de la philosophie. (Piaget, Jean.) Paris, 1965.

Phil 193.232   Saggi. (Salvucci, P.) Urbino, 1963.

Phil 181.45   Saggi critici. Ser. I. (Gentile, Giovanni.) Napoli, 1921.

Phil 8952.13   Saggi di analisi dell'atto morale. (Cattani de Menasce, Giovanni.) Roma, 1957.

Phil 4070.1.50   Saggi di critica e polemica per Ausonio Franchi (pseud.). (Bonavino, Cristoforo.) Milano, 1871-72. 3v.

Phil 8420.18   Saggi di estetica e metafisica. (Tari, Antonio.) Bari, 1911.

Phil 8894.22   Saggi di etica. (Trivero, Camillo.) Milano, 1917.

Phil 8877.49   Saggi di etica e di diritto. Ser. 1-2,3-5. (Castellotti, G. de.) Ascoli Piceno, 1903-06. 2v.

Phil 8825.10   Saggi di etica e di filosofia del diritto. (Attisam, Adelchi.) Napoli, 1970.

Phil 4225.2.31   Saggi di filosofia. (Sarlo, Francesco de.) Torino, 1896-97. 2v.

Phil 3850.5.9   Saggi di filosofia critica. (Spir, Afrikan.) Firenze, 1939.

Phil 4265.5.30   Saggi di filosofia sociale e giuridica. (Vanni, Icilio.) Bologna, 1906-11. 2v.

NEDL Phil 8880.15   Saggi di morale. v.1-2. (Franklin, B.) Volterre, 1834.

Phil 4260.147   Saggi di poetica vichiana. (Lanza, Franco.) Varese, 1961.

Phil 4110.2.31   Saggi di psicologia e di logica. (Florenzi Waddington, Marianna.) Firenze, 1864.

Phil 165.454   Saggi e ricerche su Alessandro di Afrodisia, Avicenna, Miceli, Brentano, Jaspers, Ingarden, Carr. (Giacon, Carlo.) Padova, 1970.

Phil 1506.11   Saggi e studi di filosofia medievale. (Bertala, E.) Padova, 1951.

Phil 4060.3.30   Saggi filosofici. (Allievo, G.) Milano, 1866.

Phil 176.46   Saggi filosofici. (Benvenuti, F.) Firenze, 1863.

Phil 177.35   Saggi filosofici. (Croce, Benedetto.) Bari, 1910-52. 14v.

Phil 4135.1   Saggi filosofici. (Iaja, Donato.) Napoli, 1886.

Phil 4265.3.39   Saggi filosofici. (Vera, A.) Napoli, 1883.

Phil 4080.3.22   Saggi filosofici. v. 1,3-5,11. (Croce, Benedetto.) Bari, 1948-54. 5v.

Phil 3552.79.30   Saggi filosofici e lettere. (Leibniz, Gottfried Wilhelm.) Bari, 1963.

Phil 4235.11.30   Saggi filosofici vari. (Tradu, L.) Padova, 1960.

Phil 2045.93   Saggi per la storia della morale utilitaria. (Mandolfo, R.) Verona, 1903-04.

Phil 187.42   Saggi per la storia della morale utilitaria. (Mondolfo, Rodolfo.) Verona, 1903. 2 pam.

Phil 2070.55   Saggi pragmatisti. (James, William.) Lanciano, 1919.

Phil 3826.14   Saggi su Spinoza. (Garulli, Enrico.) Urbino, 1958.

Phil 1106.18   Saggi sul pensiero antico. (Bertozzi, A.) Padova, 1960.

Phil 4200.1.90   Saggi sul pensiero inedito di Pietri Pomponazzi. (Poppi, Antonio.) Padova, 1970.

Phil 1506.12   Saggi sulla filosofia medievale. (Bonafede, Giulio.) Torino, 1951.

Phil 4013.2   Saggi sull'aristotelismo padovana dal secolo XIV al XVI. (Nardi, Bruno.) Firenze, 1958.

Phil 3195.6.120   Saggi sullo storicismo tedesco. (Negri, Antonio.) Milano, 1959.

Phil 1714.5   Saggi varii di filosofia moderna e contemporanea. (Orsi, Domenico d'.) Padova, 1962.

Phil 4260.124.5   Saggi vichiani. (Nicolini, F.) Napoli, 1955.

Phil 181.15   Saggio...della scienza umana. (Grazia, V. de.) Napoli, 1839.

Phil 4080.10.35   Saggio circa la ragione logica di tutte le cose (Pasaelogices specimen). v.1-5. (Ceretti, Pietro.) Torino, 1888-1905. 7v.

Phil 3484.15   Saggio Culle contraddizioni di Emanuele Kant. (Cavicchi, G. de.) Catania, 1929.

Phil 194.38   Saggio dei principali sistemi. (Traina, T.) Palermo, 1880.

Phil 4080.10.80   Il saggio di panlogica ovvero l'enciclopedia filosofica. (Ercole, P. d'.) Torino, 1911.

Phil 2523.31.2   Saggio di un trattato di morale. (Compagnoni, G.) Milano, 1816.

Phil 4011.1   Saggio di una bibliografia filosofia italiana. (Levi, A.) Bologna, 1906.

Phil 176.141   Saggio di una metafisica dell'esperienza. (Bontadini, G.) Milano, 1938.

Phil 177.86   Saggio di una sistema di filosofia busato sulla suggestione. (Camera, Ugo.) Aquila, 1920.

Phil 8893.46   Saggio di uno studio sui sentimenti morali. (Salvadori, Guglielmo.) Firenze, 1903.

Phil 4112.35   Saggio filosofico. v.1-6. 1a ed. (Galluppi, Pasquale.) Milano, 1846-47. 3v.

Phil 8419.13   Saggio sopra la bellezza. (Spalletti, G.) Firenze, 1933.

Phil 4210.70   Saggio storico critico sulle categorie e la dialettica. v.1-2. (Rosmini-Serbati, Antonio.) Torino, 1885.

Phil 4080.3.145   Saggio su Benedetto Croce. (Molina, G.) Genova, 1928.

Phil 1850.129   Saggio su Francesco Bacon. (Ossi, M.M.) Napoli, 1935.

Phil 1850.124   Saggio su Francesco Bacone. (Fazio-Allmayer, V.) Palermo, 1928.

Phil 4215.1.100   Saggio su G.D. Romagnosi. (Martino, R. de.) Napoli, 1887.

Phil 4070.2.80   Saggio su la filosofia di Francesco Bonatelli. (Cheula, Pietro.) Milano, 1934.

Phil 4210.138   Saggio su Rosmini il mondo delle idee. (Capone-Braga, G.) Milano, 1914.

Phil 4210.73   Saggio sui divertimenti publici. (Rosmini-Serbati, Antonio.) Roma, 1964.

Phil 270.85   Saggio sui rapporti fra ubertà e causalità. (Gennaro, Guiseppe de.) Padova, 1958.

Phil 4210.69   Saggio sul comunismo e socialismo. (Rosmini-Serbati, Antonio.) Pescara, 1964.

Phil 705.46   Saggio sul trascendente e sul trascendentale. (Fieschi, Andrea.) Padova, 1958.

Phil 181.57.5   Saggio sulla dialettica della realta spirituale. (Galli, Gallo.) Milano, 1933.

Phil 4112.85   Saggio sulla filosofia del Galluppi. (Tranfo, C.T.) Napoli, 1902.

Phil 4110.2.35   Saggio sulla filosofia dello spirito. (Florenzi Waddington, Marianna.) Firenze, 1867.

Phil 5465.4.5   Saggio sulla immaginazione. (Ambrosi, L.) Roma, 1892.

Phil 303.11   Saggio sulla natura. (Waddington, M.F.) Firenze, 1866.

Phil 5242.45   Saggio sulla natura dell'uomo. (Chiavacci, G.) Firenze, 1936.

Phil 187.45   Saggio sulla naturale unità del pensiero. (Marchesini, G.) Firenze, 1895.

Phil 5243.49   Saggio sulla psicologia contemporanea. (Devoto, Andrea.) Firenze, 1959.

Phil 8598.71   Saggio sulla religione in generale. Torino, 1866.

Phil 180.88   Saggio sulla struttura della metafisica. (Faggiotto, Pietro.) Padova, 1965.

Phil 2045.106   Saggio sulle idee morali e politiche di T. Hobbes. (Tarantino, G.) Napoli, 1900.

Phil 3425.109.10   Saggio sullo Hegel. (Croce, B.) Bari, 1913.

Phil 5258.1   Sagra, R. de la. L'âme. Paris, 1868.

Phil 5258.94   Sahai, Mahajot. A new primer of psychology. London, 1928.

Phil 8843.18   Sahakian, W. Systems of ethics and value theory. N.Y., 1963.

Phil 5238.224   Sahakian, William S. History of psychology. Itasca, Ill., 1968.

Phil 8598.140   Sahakian, William S. Philosophies of religion. Cambridge, 1965.

Phil 5535.50   Sahakian, William S. Psychology of learning. Chicago, 1970.

Phil 6980.666   Sahakian, William S. Psychotherapy and counselling; studies in technique. Chicago, 1969.

Phil 3500.102   Saher, Hans. Kants Weg vom Krieg zum Frieden. München, 1968-

Phil 8598.138.1   Saher, Purvezji Jamshedji. Easten wisdom and Western thought. London, 1969.

Phil 8598.138.5   Saher, Purvezji Jamshedji. Evolution und Gottesidee. Ratigen, 1967.

Phil 8598.138   Saher, Purvezji Jamshedji. Indische Weisheit und das Abendland. Meisenheim, 1965.

Phil 3425.252   Sahlin, C. Yngve. Har Hegel öfvervunnit dualismen? Upsala, 1851.

Phil 3500.18   Sahlin, C.Y. Kants, Schleiermacher's och Bostroms etiska. Upsala, 1877.

Phil 3246.189   Sahlin, Enar. Johann Gottlieb Fichtes idealism. Upsala, 1888.

Phil 4515.87.2   Sahlin, K.Y. Om menistrarne i den konstitutionela monarkien enligt Boströms statslära. Upsala, 1877.

Phil 4515.87   Sahlin, K.Y. Om ministrarne i den konstitutionela monarkien enligt Boströms statslära. Upsala, 1877.

Phil 8893.77   Sahlin, Karl Y. Om vilkoren för möjligheten al praktisk philosophi. Lund, 1855.

Phil 1718.26   Sahm, August. Jaspers als Blickpunkt für neue Einsichten. Worms am Rhein, 1952.

Phil 5590.550   Şahsiyet. 2. b. (Ozgü, Halis.) Istanbul, 1969.

Phil 5258.2   Sailer, J.D.M. Vernunftlehre für Menschen, wie sie sind. München, 1785.

Phil 4872.109.80   Sailley, Robert. Crî Aurobindo, philosophe du yoga intégral. Paris, 1970.

Phil 6968.15   Sailo, Francesco. La patologia mentale im rapporto. Milano, 1908.

Phil 4080.3.230   Sainati, V. L'estetica di Benedetto Croce. Firenze, 1953.

Phil 193.129.5   Sainsbury, Geoffrey. The theory of polarity. London, 1931.

Phil 1850.155   Saint Albans, England. City Council. Catalogue of exhibition organized by the St. Albans City Council in the Council Chamber. St. Albans, 1961.

Phil 8969.1   Saint Ambroise et la morale chrétienne au IV siècle. (Thamin, R.) Paris, 1895.

Phil 58.9   St. Andrews University. Publications of the departments of philosophy and divinity. Glasgow, 1911.

Phil 5853.6   Saint-Arnaud, Yves. La consultation pastorale d'orientation Rogérienne. Paris, 1969.

Phil 8636.6   Saint Athanase, ou Traité de la nature. (Le Long, Jean.) Middelburg, 1645.

Phil 2725.60   Saint-Aubin et son oeuvre. (Tedeschi, Paul.) Paris, 1968.

Phil 7069.55.20   Saint-Clair, Simone. The heart aflame. London, 1955.

Phil 665.64   St. Cyr, E. The essay: let us think it over. 12th ed. Chicago, 1936.

Phil 2805.98   St. Cyres, S.H.N. Pascal. London, 1909.

Phil 2805.98.10   St. Cyres, S.H.N. Pascal. N.Y., 1910.

Phil 6048.97.13   Saint-Germain, C. de. Practical palmistry illustrated. Chicago, 1897.

Phil 6048.97.9   Saint-Germain, C. de. The practice of palmistry. Chicago, 1897. 2v.

Phil 6048.99.5   St. Hill, K. The grammar of palmistry. Philadelphia, 19-

Phil 6053.6   St. Hill, Katharine. Hands of celebrities. Westminster, 1889?

Phil 193.1   Saint-Hyacinth, T. Recherches philosophiques. Rotterdam, 1743.

Phil 9358.9   Saint-Jacques, F. Lettres à Claude. Québec, 1916.

Phil 2477.6.155   Saint-Jean, Raymond. L'apologétique philosophique. Paris, 1966.

Phil 2477.6.165   Saint-Jean, Raymond. Genèse de l'action; Blondel, 1882-1893. Bruges, 1965.

Phil 9358.10   St. Lambert, J.F. de. Principes des moeurs chez toutes les nations. Paris, 1798. 3v.

Phil 28.1   The Saint Louis magnet. v.1-2. St. Louis, 1845.

Phil 1815.1   The Saint Louis movement in philosophy. (Perry, C.M.) Norman, 1930.

Phil 2880.1.79   Saint-Martin, L.C. La correspondance inédite de L.C. Saint-Martin dit le philosophe inconnu et Kirchberger. Amsterdam, 1862.

Htn   Phil 2880.1.33*   Saint-Martin, L.C. Des erreurs et de la vérité. Edimbourg, 1775.

Phil 2880.1.30   Saint-Martin, L.C. Des erreurs et de la vérité. Edimbourg, 1782.

Phil 2880.1.55   Saint-Martin, L.C. Der Dienst desGeist-Menschen. Münster, 1858.

Phil 2880.1.60   Saint-Martin, L.C. Ecce homo. Lyon, 1959.

Phil 2880.1.42   Saint-Martin, L.C. L'homme de désir. Londres, 1808.

Htn   Phil 2880.1.40*   Saint-Martin, L.C. L'homme de désir. Lyon, 1790.

Phil 2880.1.35   Saint-Martin, L.C. Irrtümer und Wahrheit. Stuttgart, 1925. 2v.

Phil 2880.1.65   Saint-Martin, L.C. Mon portrait historique et philosophique. Paris, 1961.

Phil 2880.1.25   Saint-Martin, L.C. NachgelasseneWerke. Münster, 1833.

Phil 2880.1.45   Saint-Martin, L.C. Tableau naturel des rapports qui existent entre Dieu, l'homme et l'univers. Paris, 1900.

Phil 2880.1.47   Saint-Martin, L.C. Tableau naturel des rapports qui existent entre Dieu, l'homme et l'univers. Rochefort-sur-Mer, 1946.

Htn   Phil 2880.1.50*   Saint-Martin, L.C. Vom Geist und Wesen der Dinge. v.1-2. Leipzig, 1812.

Phil 2880.1.82.5   Saint-Martin; the French mystic. (Waite, Arthur E.) London, 1922.

Phil 2880.1.87   Saint-Martin. 2. ed. (Matter, Jacques.) Paris, 1862.

Phil 5258.90   Saint-Paul, G. Thèmes psychologiques. Paris, 1926.

Phil 5520.30   Saint-Paul, Georges. Le langage intérieur et les paraphasies. Paris, 1904.

Phil 1865.177   Saint Paul vindicated, being Part I of a reply...not Paul, but Jesus. (Wells, D.B.) Cambridge, 1824.

Phil 8598.1   Saint Pierre, J.H.B. de. Vindication of divine providence. Worcester, 1797.

Phil 6990.3.38   Saint-Pierre, M. de. Bernadette and Lourdes. N.Y., 1954.

Phil 5374.46   Saint Prix, J. de. La conscience comme principe spirituel. Paris, 1927.

Phil 8598.69   Saint René-Taillandier, R.G.E. Histoire et philosophie religieuse. Paris, 1859.

Phil 2400.3   Saint-Simonisme-Positivisme. (Avezac-Lavigne, C.) Paris, 1905.

Phil 6990.3.88   Sainte Bernadette. (Guynot, Ernest.) Paris, 1959.

Phil 6990.3.70   Sainte Bernadette Soubirous. (Trouch, F.) Lyon, 1953.

Phil 1750.382   La sainte famille existentialiste. (Mougin, Henri.) Paris, 1947.

Phil 623.7.5   Saintes, A. Critical history of rationalism in Germany. 2nd ed. London, 1849.

Phil 3838.1   Saintes, A. Histoire...ouvrages de B. de Spinoza. Paris, 1842.

Phil 623.7   Saintes, A. Histoire critique du rationalisme en Allemagne. Paris, 1841.

Phil 3500.1   Saintes, A. Histoire de la vie et de la philosophie de Kant. Paris, 1844.

Phil 5627.176   La sainteté. 1. éd. (Festugière, André M.J.) Paris, 1942.

Phil 2805.112.5   La sainteté de Pascal. (Stewart, Hugh F.) Paris, 1919.

Phil 5627.32   Saints, initiés et possédés modernes. (Finot, Jean.) Paris, 1918.

Phil 6990.12.5   Saintyves, P. Le discernement du miracle. Paris, 1909.

Phil 6990.12   Saintyves, P. La simulation du merveilleux. Paris, 1912.

Phil 4352.1.145   Sainz de Robles, Federico Carlos. Jaime Balmes; estudio y antologia. Madrid, 1964.

Phil 530.40.55   Sainz Rodriguez, P. Espiritualidad española. Madrid, 1961.

Phil 8120.13   Saisselin, Rémy Gilbert. Taste in eighteenth century France. Syracuse, 1965.

Phil 8598.2   Saisset, E. Essais sur la philosophie et la religion. Paris, 1845.

Phil 645.5   Saisset, E. Le scepticisme. Paris, 1865.

Phil 5258.3   Saisset, E.E. L'âme et la vie. Paris, 1864.

Phil 193.3   Saisset, E.E. Critique...de la philosophie. Paris, 1865.

Phil 8673.1   Saisset, E.E. Essai de philosophie religieuse. Paris, 1859.

Phil 8673.1.5   Saisset, E.E. Essay on religious philosophy. Edinburgh, 1863. 2v.

Phil 193.3.5   Saisset, E.E. Mélanges d'histoire, de morale. Paris, 1859.

Phil 2915.80   Saisset, E.E. Renaissance du Voltairianisme. Paris, 1845.

Phil 3838.10   Saisset, Émile. Introduction critique aux oeuvres de Spinoza. Paris, 1860.

Phil 2520.97   Saisset, Émile. Précurseurs et disciples de Descartes. Paris, 1862.

Phil 2520.97.3   Saisset, Émile. Précurseurs et disciples de Descartes. Paris, 1862.

Phil 2475.1.139   Sait, Una B. Ethical implications of Bergson's philosophy. N.Y., 1914.

Phil 8419.33   Saitschick, R. Kunstschöpfer und Kunstschaffen. Marburg, 1957.

Phil 193.91.2   Saitschick, R. Der Mensch und sein Ziel. 2. Aufl. München, 1922.

Phil 193.121   Saitta, G. Filosofia italiana e umanesimo. Venezia, 1928.

Phil 1195.9   Saitta, G. L'illuminismo della sofistica greca. Milano, 1938.

Phil 4018.5   Saitta, G. Il pensiero italiano nell'umanesimo e nel Rinascimento. Bologna, 1949. 3v.

Phil 4018.5.2   Saitta, G. Il pensiero italiano nell'umanesimo e nel Rinascimento. 2. ed. Firenze, 1961. 3v.

Phil 8673.18   Saitta, G. Il problema di Dio e la filosofia della immanenza. Bologna, 1953.

Phil 4110.1.80   Saitta, Giuseppe. La filosofia di Marsilio Ficino. Messina, 1923.

Phil 1523.6.5   Saitta, Giuseppe. Le origine del neo-tomismo. Bari, 1912.

Phil 4115.85   Saitta, Giuseppe. Il pensiero di Vincenzo Gioberti. Messina, 1917.

Phil 4115.85.2   Saitta, Giuseppe. Il pensiero di Vincenzo Gioberti. 2a ed. Firenze, 1927.

Phil 1523.6   Saitta, Giuseppe. La scolastica del secolo XVI e la politica dei Gesuiti. Torino, 1911.

Phil 4352.1.165   Sáiz Barberá, Juan. Pensamiento histórico cristiano. 1. ed. Madrid, 1967.

Phil 8170.3   Sakharova, E.M. Osnovy marksistsko-leninskoi estetiki. Moskva, 1961.

Phil 2128.83   Sakmann, Paul. Bernard de Mandeville und die Bienenfabel. Freiburg, 1897.

Phil 1818.9 — Sakmann, Paul. Die Denker und Kämpfer der englischen Aufklärung. Stuttgart, 1946.

Phil 3805.181 — Die Sakramentstheorie Schleiermachers und ihre Weiterbildung innerhalb der kritischen Theologie des 19. Jahrhunderts. Inaug. Diss. (Graeber, Martin.) Wuppertal, 1937.

Phil 5545.269 — Salaman, Esther Polianowsky. A collection of moments; a study of involuntary memories. N.Y., 1972.

Phil 6060.8 — Salamanea, F. de. The philosophy of handwriting. London, 1879.

Phil 400.4.15 — Salamonowiez, L. Die Ethik des Positivismus nach Ernst Laas. Inaug. Diss. Dortmund, 1935.

Phil 2225.5.175 — Salanitro, Niccolò. Peirce e i problemi dell'interpretazione. Roma, 1969.

Phil 193.103 — Salat, J. Ueber den Geist der Philosophie. München, 1803.

Phil 3801.763.7 — Salat, Jacob. Schelling in München. pt.1-2. Heidelberg, 1845.

Htn Phil 3801.763.10* — Salat, Jacob. Schelling und Hegel. Heidelberg, 1842.

Phil 8893.83.15 — Salat, Jakob. Auch die Aufklärung hat ihre Gefahren. München, 1801.

Phil 8893.83.15.5 — Salat, Jakob. Auch ein paar Worte über die Fräge.

Htn Phil 3801.763* — Salat, Jakob. Erläuterung einiger Hauptpunkt der Philosophie. Landshut, 1812.

Phil 8893.83.10 — Salat, Jakob. Grundlinien der Moralphilosophie. München, 1827.

Phil 8893.83.25 — Salat, Jakob. Die literarische Stellung des Protestanten zu dem Katholiken. Laudshut, 1831.

Phil 8893.83 — Salat, Jakob. Die Moralphilosophie. 3. Aufl. München, 1821.

Phil 8893.83.16 — Salat, Jakob. Die Philosophie mit obskuranten und Sophisten in Kampfe. Nachtrag: Auch die Aufklärung. Ulm, 1802.

Htn Phil 3801.763.5* — Salat, Jakob. Schelling in München. pt.I. Freiburg, 1837.

Phil 8893.83.20 — Salat, Jakob. Winke über das Verhältniss der intellektuellen und der verfeinernden Kultur zur Sittlichen. München, 1802.

Phil 4957.65 — Salazar, Bondy Augusto. Existe una filosofía de nuestra América? 1. ed. México, 1968[1969]

Phil 4961.605 — Salazar Bondy, Augusto. La filosofía en el Perú. Wáshington, 1955.

Phil 4961.605.5 — Salazar Bondy, Augusto. História de las ideas en el Perú contemporáneo. Lima, 1965.

Phil 193.238 — Salazar Bondy, Augusto. Iniciación filosofía. Lima, 1964.

Phil 193.258 — Salazar Bondy, Augusto. Irrealidad e idealidad. 1. ed. Lima, 1958.

Phil 5590.508 — Salber, Wilhelm. Charakterentwicklung. Wuppertal, 1969.

Phil 5258.152.10 — Salber, Wilhelm. Morphologie des seelischen Geschehens. Ratingen, 1965.

Phil 5258.152 — Salber, Wilhelm. Der psychische Gegenstand. Bonn, 1959.

Phil 6060.72 — Salberg, Renée de. Nouvelle graphologie pratique. Paris, 1967?

Htn Phil 3801.764* — Saldanha, J.C. de S. de B.D. de. Concordancia das sciencas naturaes. Vienna, 1845.

Phil 3425.246 — Salditt, Maria. Hegels Shakespeare-Interpretation. Berlin, 1927.

Phil 6128.14 — Saleeby, C.W. Worry; the disease of the age. N.Y., 1907.

Phil 3500.114 — Salem, Joseph. Immanuel Kants Lehre und ihre Auswirkungen. Gelsenkirchen-Buer, 1969.

Phil 7054.43.3A — The Salem seer. (Bartlett, G.C.) N.Y., n.d.

Phil 7054.43 — The Salem seer. (Bartlett, G.C.) N.Y., 1891.

Phil 5411.12 — Salgado, Enrique. Radiografía del odio. Madrid, 1969.

Phil 1020.8.15 — Saliba, D. Etude sur la métaphysique d'Avicenne. Paris, 1926.

Phil 1020.8.16 — Saliba, D. Etude sur la métaphysique d'Avicenne. Thèse. Paris, 1926.

Htn Phil 193.149* — Salicino, A. In lode della filosofia. Fiorenza, 1569.

Phil 8430.26 — Salicrú Puigvert, C. Moray y arte. Barcelona, 1960.

Phil 3640.550 — Salin, Edgar. Vom deutschen Verhängnis. Hamburg, 1959.

Phil 8419.35A — Salinger, H. Über das Schöne als Sinnbild und Wegweisung. Köln, 1960.

Phil 365.45 — Salis Goulart, J. O sentido da evolução. Porto Allegre, 1937.

Phil 3640.210 — Salis-Marschlins, M. von. Philosoph und Edelmensch. Leipzig, 1897.

Phil 8419.6F — Salisbury, Edward. Principles of domestic taste. New Haven, 1877.

Phil 3500.45 — Salits, Peter. Darstellung und Kritik des Kantischen Lehre von der Willensfreiheit. Rostock, 1898.

Phil 8893.70 — Sallwürk, E v. Ethik in entwickelnder Darstellung. Langensalza, 1920.

Phil 5258.49 — Sallwürk, Ernst von. Die Seele des Menschen. Karlsruhe, 1918.

Phil 7069.39.52 — Salminen, I. Essence of life in psychic phenomena. Brooklyn, 1938.

Phil 2050.215 — Salmon, C.V. The central problem of David Hume's philosophy. Halle , 1929.

Phil 9240.12 — Salmon, E.G. The good in existential metaphysics. Milwaukee, 1953.

Phil 5058.94 — Salmon, W. Logic. Englewood, 1963.

Phil 2880.2.92 — Salmona, Bruno. Il pensiero di Charles Secrétan. Milano, 1968.

Phil 3500.93 — Salmony, H.A. Kants Schrift. Zürich, 1962.

Phil 349.30 — Salomaa, J.E. The category of relation. Helsinki, 1929.

Phil 1818.6 — Salomaa, J.E. Idealismus undRealismus in der englischen Philosophie der Gegenwart. Helsinki, 1929.

Phil 3808.182 — Salomaa, J.E. Schopenhauer ja von Hartmann. Turku, 1918.

Phil 735.96 — Salomaa, J.E. Studien zur Wertphilosophie. Helsinki, 1930.

Phil 1050.4.5 — Salomo ben Gabirol. (Dukes, L.) Hannover, 1860.

Phil 525.20.5 — Salomon, Gotfried. Beitrag zur Problematik von Mystik und Glaube. Strassburg, 1916.

Phil 2885.100 — Salomon, Michel. H. Taine. Paris, 1908.

Phil 3850.54 — Salomon Ludwig Steinheim zum Gedenken. (Steinheim, Salomon Ludwig.) Leiden, 1966.

Phil 3850.54.80 — Salomon Ludwig Steinheims "Offenbarung nach dem Lehrbegriff der Synagoge". (Andorn, Hans.) Berlin, 1930.

Phil 3625.5.86 — Salomon Maimon. (Bitte, I.H.) Berlin, 1876.

Phil 3625.5.78.10 — Salomon Maimon. (Maimon, Salomon.) Boston, 1888.

Phil 3625.5.89 — Salomon Maimon und der kritischen Idealismus. (Zubersky, A.) Leipzig, 1925.

Phil 3625.5.91 — Salomon Maimons erkenntnistheoretische Verbesserungveruche der Kantischen Philosophie. Inaug. Diss. (Moeltzner, A.) Greifswald, 1889.

Phil 4060.1.100 — Saloni, Alfredo. Il positivismo e Roberto Ardigò. Roma, 1969.

Phil 6688.29 — Salter, Andrew. What is hypnosis. N.Y., 1944.

Phil 8615.1.20 — Salter, W.M. Christmas from an ethical standpoint. Chicago, 1888.

Phil 8615.1 — Salter, W.M. Ethical religion. Boston, 1889.

Phil 8615.1.3 — Salter, W.M. Ethical religion. London, 1905.

Phil 193.4 — Salter, W.M. First steps in philosophy. Chicago, 1892.

Phil 8615.1.15 — Salter, W.M. Moral aspiration and song. Philadelphia, 1905.

Phil 8615.1.7 — Salter, W.M. On a foundation for religion. Boston, 1879. 17 pam.

Phil 8615.1.5 — Salter, W.M. Der Religion der Moral. Leipzig, 1885.

Phil 8893.1A — Salter, W.M. What can ethics do for us? Chicago, 1891.

Phil 7069.61.20 — Salter, William Henry. Zoar, or The evidence of psychical research concerning survival. London, 1961.

Phil 3640.116A — Salter, William M. Nietzsche the thinker; a study. N.Y., 1917.

Phil 3640.116.2 — Salter, William M. Nietzsche the thinker; a study. N.Y., 1968.

Phil 9430.10.10 — Saltus, Edgar. The anatomy of negation. N.Y., 1925?

Phil 9430.10.4 — Saltus, Edgar. The philosophy of disenchantment. N.Y., 1885.

Phil 2493.86 — Saltykow, W. Die Philosophie Condillacs. Inaug.-Diss. Bern, 1901.

Phil 5535.54 — Saltz, Eli. The cognitive bases of human learning. Homewood, 1971.

Phil 8893.96 — Saltzmann, C.G. Elements of morality. Baltimore, 1811.

Phil 5627.130 — Salut par la foi et conversion brusque. (Swarts, G.) Paris, 1931.

Phil 5627.130.2 — Salut par la foi et conversion brusque. Thèse. (Swarts, G.) Paris, 1931.

Phil 5240.40 — La salute del pensiero "I libro d'oro". (Anile, Antonio.) Bari, 1922.

Phil 2270.104 — Salvadori, Guglielmo. L'etica evoluzionista...di Herbert Spencer. Torino, 1903.

Phil 8893.46 — Salvadori, Guglielmo. Saggio di uno studio sui sentimenti morali. Firenze, 1903.

Phil 2880.8.136 — Salvan, Jacques L. To be and not to be. Detroit, 1962.

Phil 1750.795 — Salvan, Jacques León. The scandalous ghost; Sartre's existentialism as related to vitalism, humanism, mysticism, Marxism. Detroit, 1967.

Phil 5258.208 — Salvat, Henri. L'intelligence; mythes et réalités. Paris, 1969.

Phil 8605.5 — Salvation by laughter. (Zuver, Dudley.) N.Y., 1933.

Phil 4170.9.90 — Salvatore Mancino e l'ecletticismo in Sicilia. (Giovanni, V. di.) Palermo, 1867.

Htn Phil 4065.01* — Salvestrini, V. Bibliografia delle opere di Giordano Bruno. Pisa, 1926.

Phil 4065.02 — Salvestrini, V. Bibliografia di Giordano Bruno. 2. ed. Firenze, 1958.

Phil 2477.6.110 — Salvo, Franco. La logica della vita morale in Maurice Blondel. Palermo, 1942.

Phil 193.232 — Salvucci, P. Saggi. Urbino, 1963.

Phil 3500.75 — Salvucci, Pasquale. La dottrina Kantiana dello schematismo transcendentale. Urbino, 1957.

Phil 3500.80 — Salvucci, Pasquale. Grandi interpreti di Kant. Urbino, 1958.

Phil 2493.94 — Salvucci, Pasquale. Linguaggio e mondo umano in Condillac. Urbino, 1957.

Phil 5768.6 — Salzbrunner, B. Das Gesetz der Freiheit. Ein Beiträg zur Reinigung der Volksreligion. Nürnberg, 1869.

Phil 396.20 — Salzburger Humanismusgespräch. Die erschreckende Zivilisation. Wien, 1970.

Phil 28.52 — Salzburger Jahrbuch für Philosophie und Psychologie. Salzburg. 1,1957+ 8v.

Phil 1135.85.16 — Salzi, Pierre. La genèse de la sensation...chez Protagoras, Platon et Aristote. Thèse. Paris, 1934.

Phil 1135.85.15 — Salzi, Pierre. La genèse de la sensation...chez Protagoras. Paris, 1934.

Phil 5635.36.5 — Salzi, Pierre. La sensation, étude de sa genèse et de son rôle dans la connaissance. Thèse. Paris, 1934.

Phil 5635.36 — Salzi, Pierre. La sensation. Paris, 1934.

Phil 6328.54 — Salzman, Leon. Modern concepts of psychoanalysis. N.Y., 1962.

Phil 7069.05.12 — Samband vidframlida menn. (Kvaran, E.H.) Reykjavik, 1905.

Phil 8893.105 — Sambarino, Mario. Investigaciones sobre la estructura aporético-dialéctica. Montevideo, 1959-60.

Phil 310.606 — Samek, Antonín. Filosofie a politika. Praha, 1963.

Phil 5400.97 — De samenhang tussen psycho-galvanische reflex en grondeigenschappen van het temperament. Proefschrift. (Vleugel, E.S.) Groningen, 1939.

Phil 960.4 — Die Samkhya - Philosophie. (Garbe, R.) Leipzig, 1894.

Phil 4520.2.3 — Samlade skrifter. (Biberg, N.F.) Upsala, 1828-30. 3v.

Phil 4575.10 — Samlade skrifter. (Höijer, B.C.H.) Stockholm, 1825-27. 5v.

Phil 189.4.2 — Samlede og efterladte skrifter. v.1-3, 4-6, 7-9. (Oersted, H.C.) Kjøbenhavn, 1851-1852. 3v.

Phil 4540.5 — Samlede skrifter. 3. udg. (Feilberg, Ludvig.) Kjøbenhavn, 1949- 2v.

Phil 3910.84 — Sammlung Auszüge der sämmtlichen Wegen der Wolffischen Philosophie. Pt.1-2. (Ludovici, Karl G.) Leipzig, 1737-38.

Phil 3745.2.31 — Sammlung der Schriften welche den logischen calcul Herrn Prof. Ploucquets Betreffen, mit neuen Zusäben, Frankfurt und Leipzig, 1766. (Ploucquet, Gottfried.) Stuttgart, 1970.

Htn Phil 3480.19.20* — Sammlung einiger bisher unbekannt gebliebener kleiner Schriften. (Kant, Immanuel.) Königsberg, 1800.

Phil 6315.2.20.7 — Sammlung kleiner Schriften. 3. Aufl. 1e, 2e Folge. (Freud, Sigmund.) Leipzig, 1920-21. 2v.

Htn Phil 6315.2.20* — Sammlung kleiner Schriften zur Neurosenlehre. 2e, 4e, 5e Folge. (Freud, Sigmund.) Leipzig, 1909-22. 3v.

Phil 6315.2.20.5 — Sammlung kleiner Schriften zur Neurosenlehre aus den Jahren 1893-1906. 2. Aufl. 1e, 2e Folge. (Freud, Sigmund.) Leipzig, 1911-21. 2v.

Phil 28.2 — Sammlung physiologischer Abhandlungen. (Preyer, W.) Jena, 1877. 2v.

Phil 5252.27 — Sammlung von populär- wissenschaftlichen Vorträgen über den bau und die leistungen des gehirns. (Meynert, T.) Wien, 1892.

Phil 8581.69.7 — Samopoznanie: opyt filosofskoi avtobiografii. (Berdiaev, N.A.) Parizh, 1949.

Phil 4803.522.35 — Samowładztwo rozumu i objawy filozofii słowiańskiej. (Libelt, Karol.) Warszawa, 1967.

Phil 2750.11.160 — Sampaio, L.F.A. L'intuition dans la philosophie de Jacques Maritain. Paris, 1963.

Phil 4462.3 — Sampaio Bruno. (Serrão, Joel.) Lisboa, 1958.

Phil 3585.30.10   Sampaio Ferraz, Torcio. Die Zweidimensionalität des Rechts als Voraussetzung für den Methodendualismus von Emil Lask. Meisenheim am Glan, 1970.

Phil 7060.63   Sampford ghost. (Colton, C.) Tiverton, 1810.

Phil 7068.10   Sampford ghost. (Colton, C.C.) Tiverton, 1810.

Phil 182.101.20   Sampson, A.H. The philosophy of John Scott Haldane. Philadelphia, 1938.

Phil 8708.12   Sampson, H.E. Progressive creation. London, 1909. 2v.

Phil 8708.12.5   Sampson, H.E. Theou sophia...divine mysteries. London, 1918.

Phil 3500.44   Samsom, A. Kants kennis der grieksche Philosophie. Thesis. Alphen aan den Rijn, 1927.

Phil 8843.3   Samson, G.W. Outlines of the history of ethics. Washington, 1861.

Phil 7054.33   Samson, G.W. The physical in spiritualism. Philadelphia, 1880.

Phil 7054.33.7   Samson, G.W. Spiritualism tested. Boston, 1860.

Phil 7054.33.5   Samson, G.W. "To daemoion" or The spiritual medium. Boston, 1852.

Phil 4580.81   Samtaler med Harald Høffding, 1909-1918. (Rindom, E.) København, 1918.

Phil 299.25   Samtonge, F. Sumina cosmologiae. Montreal, 1941.

Phil 8620.39   Samuel, H. The tree of good and evil. London, 1933.

Phil 8893.89   Samuel, Herbert. Practical ethics. London, 1935.

Phil 193.132.10   Samuel, Herbert S. Creative man. Oxford, 1947.

Phil 193.132.15   Samuel, Herbert S. In search of reality. Oxford, 1957.

Phil 193.132   Samuel, Herbert S. Philosophy and the ordinary man. London, 1932.

Phil 8708.34   Samuel, Herbert S. A threefold cord. London, 1961.

Phil 3450.18.110   Samuel, O. A foundation of ontology. N.Y., 1953.

Phil 193.170   Samuel, Otto. Die Ontologie der Kultur. Berlin, 1956.

Phil 1915.78   Pamphlet box. Samuel Clarke.

Phil 4570.1.85   Samuel Grubbe; en studie i transcendental religionsfilosofi. (Cuelberg, John.) Upsala, 1926.

Phil 4570.1.81   Samuel Grubbe's skönhetslära. Akademisk afhandling. (Schéele, Frans von.) Upsala, 1885.

Phil 4979.5.80   Samuel Ramos. (Hernández Luna, Juan.) México, 1956.

Phil 8597.3.18   Samuel Reimarus zur Religion. (Schettler, R.) Leipzig, 1904.

Phil 672.202   Samuells, Roberto. La dialéctica del espacio. Madrid, 1952.

Phil 3625.1.44   Samuels, M. Memoirs of Moses Mendelssohn. London, 1825.

Phil 3625.1.45   Samuels, M. Memoirs of Moses Mendelssohn. 2. ed. London, 1827.

Phil 8673.2   Samuelson, J. Views of the deity. London, 1871.

Phil 4570.3.31   Samvetet. (Geijer, R.) Stockholm, 1905.

Phil 176.93   Samvetet i forhallaude till natur. (Bexell, Carl E.) Jönköping, 1840.

Phil 9075.73.2   Samvetets uppkomst. 2. Uppl. (Wermlund, Sven.) Stockholm, 1966.

Phil 4635.2.31   Samvittighedslivet. (Starcke, C.N.) København, 1894-97.

Phil 812.19   San Anselmo y el insensato. (Marias Aguilera, J.) Madrid, 1944.

Phil 6980.668   San Francisco, Department of Public Health. An experiment in the psychiatric treatment of promiscuous girls. San Francisco, 1945.

NEDL Phil 58.17   San Miguel, Buenos Aires. Facultades de Filosofía y Teología. Biblioteca. San Miguel.

Phil 5425.38   Sanborn, K.A. The vanity and insanity of genius. N.Y., 1886.

Phil 1750.825   Sanborn, Patricia F. Existentialism. N.Y., 1968.

Phil 4369.2.86   Sanches, Francisco. Opera philosophica. Coimbra, 1955.

Phil 193.48   Sanchez, C.L. Estudios de la filosofia. Buenos Aires, 1894.

Phil 645.35   Sánchez, Francisco. Que nada se sabe. Buenos Aires, 1944.

Phil 645.35.5   Sánchez, Francisco. Que nada se sabe. Madrid, 1926.

Phil 4958.505   Sánchez, Juan Francisco. El pensamiento filosófico en Santo Domingo. Ciudad Trujillo, 1956?

Phil 4363.2.85   Sanchez-Castañer, Francisco. Miguel de Molinos en Valencia y Roma, nuevos datas biográficos. Valencia, 1965.

Phil 4957.20.5   Sanchez Reulet, Aníbal. Contemporary Latin-American philosophy. New Mexico, 1954.

Phil 4957.20   Sánchez Reulet, Aníbal. La filosofía latinoamericana contemporanea. Washington, 1949.

Phil 4980.41   Sánchez Reulet, Aníbal. Raíz y destino de la filosofía. Tucumán, 1942.

Phil 1865.171   Sánchez-Rivera de la Lastra, Juan. El utilitarismo; estudio de las doctrinas de Jeremías Bentham. Madrid, 1922.

Phil 3640.122   Sánchez Torres, E. Nietzsche, Emerson, Tolstoy. Barcelona, 1902.

Phil 4372.1.110   Sancipriano, M. Il pensiero ssicologico e morale di G.L. Vives. Firenze, 1958.

Phil 3450.11.336   Sancipriano, Mario. L'ethos di Husserl. Torino, 1967.

Phil 3450.11.335   Sancipriano, Mario. Il logos di Husserl. Torino, 1962.

Phil 193.5.3   Sanctis, F. de. La scienza e la vita. Napoli, 1872.

Phil 193.5   Sanctis, F. de. La scienza e la vita. Philadelphia, 1884.

Phil 5627.107   Sanctis, S. de. Religious conversion. London, 1927.

Phil 6028.5   Sanctis, Sante de. Die Mimik des Denkens. Halle, 1906.

Phil 5258.140   Sanctis, Sante de. Psicologia sperimental. Roma, 1929-30. 2v.

Phil 7082.86   Sanctis, Sante de. I sogni. Torino, 1899.

Phil 6619.4.5   Sanctis, Sante de. I sogni e il sonno nell'isterismo e nella epilessia. Roma, 1896.

Phil 3705.2.80   Sandberg, A.J. Het stelsel der ervaring van Mr. C.W. Opzoomer. Zeist, 1865.

Phil 3801.765   Sandberg, Sven. Några anteckningar om Schellings philosophi. Lund, 1856.

Phil 6688.8.2   Sandby, G. Mesmerism and its opponents. London, 1844.

Phil 6688.8   Sandby, G. Mesmerism and its opponents. 2. ed. London, 1848.

Phil 5870.20   Sandels, Stina. Utvecklingsykologiska beteendestudier hos barn i aldern 1 1/2 - 8 1/2 år. Thesis. Uppsala, 1956.

Phil 5258.192   Sander, F. Ganzheitspsychologie::Grundlagen. München, 1962.

Phil 672.153   Sander, Franz. Die Entwicklung der Raumtheorien in der 2. Hälfte des 17. Jahrhunderts. Inaug.-Diss. Halle, 1931.

Phil 3850.60   Sander, Heinrich. Von der Güte und Weisheit Gottes in der Natur. Carlsruhe, 1780.

Phil 3500.67   Sander, J. Die Begründung der Notwehr in der Philosophie von Kant und Hegel. Bleicherode, 1939.

Phil 5643.168   Sanders, Andries Frans. The selective process in the functional visual field. Assen, 1963.

Phil 8598.94   Sanders, B.G. Christianity after Freud. London, 1949.

Phil 9178.1   Sanders, C.E. The little family. v.1-2. Haverhill, n.d.

Phil 8598.45.5   Sanders, Frederic W. A reasonable religion (Religio doctoris). Boston, 1913?

Phil 8598.45   Sanders, Frederic W. Religio doctoris; meditations upon life and thought. Boston, 1913.

Phil 9590.29   Sanders, Willy. Glück. Köln, 1965.

Phil 9150.14   Sanderson, J.R. The relation of evolutionry theory to ethical problem. Toronto, 1912.

Phil 8968.8   Sanderson, R. Christian ethics. London, 1833.

Phil 5058.1   Sandersono, R. Logicae artis compend. Oxoniae, 1741.

Phil 3801.768   Sandkuehler, Hans-Jörg. Freiheit und Wirklichkeit. Frankfurt, 1968.

Phil 3801.768.10   Sandkuehler, Hans-Jörg. Friedrich Wilhelm Joseph Schelling. Stuttgart, 1970.

Phil 5520.119   Sandman, M. Subject and predicate. Edinburgh, 1954.

Phil 3200.13   Sandmann, P. Das Weltproblem bei Ferdinand Ebner. München, 1962.

Phil 6328.6   Sando, I.J. Abnormal behavior. N.Y., 1923.

Phil 8893.2   Sandona, G. Della filosofia morale. Firenze, 1847. 2v.

Phil 1718.40   Sándor, Pál. A filozófia is közügy! Tanulmányok. Budapest, 1968.

Phil 5028.3   Sándor, Pál. Histoire de la dialectique. Paris, 1947.

VPhil 310.708.2   Sándor, Pál. A történelmi materializmus története. 2. kiad. Budapest, 1945.

Phil 5647.7   Sandovici, Constantin. Les sensations de température. Thèse. Montpellier, 1936.

Phil 6980.372   Sandspiel. (Kalff, Dora M.) Zürich, 1966.

Phil 8893.74   Sandström, A. Modern; romantik och etik. Stockholm, 1898.

Phil 103.5   Sandström, C.I. Psykologisk ordbak. 2. uppl. Stockholm, 1951.

Phil 5585.345   Sandstroem, Carl Ivar. Iakttagelse och upplevelse. Stockholm, 1969.

Phil 8419.60   Sandstroem, Sven. Konstforskning. Stockholm, 1965.

Phil 6328.23   Sandström, T. Ist die aggressivität ein übel? Stockholm, 1939.

Phil 3640.716   Sandvoss, E. Sokrates und Nietzsche. Leiden, 1966.

Phil 5252.60.12   Sane psychology. 2d ed. (McDowall, R.J.S.) London, 1944.

Phil 3475.3.250   Saner, Hans. Karl Jaspers in Selbstzeugnissen und Bilddokumenten. Reinbek, 1970.

Phil 5258.4.3   Sanford, E.C. Course in experimental psychology. Boston, 1894.

Phil 5258.4   Sanford, E.C. Course in experimental psychology. Boston, 1895.

Phil 5258.4.4   Sanford, E.C. Course in experimental psychology. Boston, 1901.

Phil 349.33   Sanford, H.W. Concerning knowledge. N.Y., 1935. 2v.

Phil 8708.19   Sanford, Hugh W. Science and faith, or The spiritual side of science. N.Y., 1930. 2v.

Phil 7082.42   Sanford, John A. Dreams; God's forgotten language. Philadelphia, 1968.

Phil 5590.518   Sanford, Nevitt. Issues in personality theory. 1. ed. San Francisco, 1970.

Phil 575.250   Sanford, Nevitt. Self and society. 1st ed. n.p., 1966.

Phil 5627.134.70   Sangster, W.E. God does guide us. N.Y., 1934.

Phil 6976.17   Sanity, madness and family: families of schizophrenics. 2. ed. (Laing, Ronald David.) London, 1970.

Phil 5401.36   Sanity. 1st ed. (Woodworth, H.M.) Victoria, B.C., 1958.

Phil 6962.4   Sanity and insanity. (Mercier, C.A.) London, 1890.

Phil 6961.6.2   Sanity of mind. (Lincoln, D.F.) N.Y., 1901.

Phil 6128.22   Sankey, Dora J. Bible authority for metaphysical healing. Boston, 1912.

Phil 5627.50   Sankey-Jones, N.E. Bibliography of Theodore Schroeder on the psychology of religion. Cos Cob, Conn., 1934.

Phil 3808.125   Sannders, T.B. Schopenhauer; a lecture. London, 1901.

Phil 3018.17   Sannwald, A. Der Begriff der Dialektik und die Anthropologie. München, 1931.

Phil 4620.3.5   Sannyall. (Péturss, Helgi.) Reykjavík, 1943.

Phil 6947.1.10   Sans everything; a case to answer. (Robb, Barbara.) London, 1967.

Phil 5028.1   Sanseverino, G. Philosophia Christiana cum antiqua et nova comparata. Neapoli, 1862-66. 3v.

Phil 5228.4   Sanseverino, G. Philosophia christianacum antigua et nova comparata. Neapoli, 1862-66. 3v.

Phil 504.4   Sansgruber, Kurt. Einflüsse der Naturwissenschaften auf unser Weltbild. Brigenz, 1962.

Phil 5440.5   Sanson, A. L'hérédité. Paris, 1893.

Phil 5627.257.10   Sanson, Henri. Spiritualité de la vie active. Le Puy, 1957.

Phil 8419.27   Santangelo, P.E. Discorso sull'arte. Milano, 1956.

Phil 4482.2.80   Sant'Anna, Dionisio. Teólogo laico. Seara Nova, 1961.

Phil 2280.5.145   Santayana, art, and aesthetics. (Ashmore, Jerome.) Cleveland, 1966.

Phil 193.49.12   Santayana, G. The birth of reason and other essays. N.Y., 1968.

Phil 193.49.18.5   Santayana, G. Character and opinion in the United States. Garden City, 1956.

Phil 193.49.15   Santayana, G. Character and opinion in the United States. N.Y., 1920.

Phil 193.49.16   Santayana, G. Character and opinion in the United States. N.Y., 1921.

Phil 193.49.18   Santayana, G. Character and opinion in the United States. N.Y., 1934.

Phil 193.49.25.5   Santayana, G. Diálogos en el limbo. Buenos Aires, 1941.

Phil 193.49.25   Santayana, G. Dialogues in limbo. N.Y., 1925.

Phil 193.49.25.15   Santayana, G. Dialogues in limbo. N.Y., 1926.

Phil 193.49.25.10A   Santayana, G. Dialogues in limbo. N.Y., 1948.

Phil 3018.7.7   Santayana, G. Egotism in German philosophy. N.Y., 1940.

Phil 3018.7A   Santayana, G. Egotism in German philosophy. Photoreproduction. London, 1916?

Phil 3018.7.9   Santayana, G. L'erreur de la philosophie allemande. Paris, 1917.

Phil 3838.4   Santayana, G. The ethical doctrine of Spinoza. Cambridge, 1886.

Phil 193.49.41   Santayana, G. The genteel tradition; nine essays. Cambridge, 1967.

Phil 193.49.40A   Santayana, G. The genteel tradition at bay. N.Y., 1931.

Phil 193.49A   Santayana, G. Life of reason. N.Y., 1905. 5v.

Phil 193.49.1   Santayana, G. Life of reason. N.Y., 1906. 5v.

Phil 193.49.3   Santayana, G. The life of reason. v.1,3-5. N.Y., 1924-1925. 4v.

Phil 193.49.2   Santayana, G. The life of reason. v.2-3. N.Y., 1921. 2v.

Phil 193.49.4   Santayana, G. The life of reason. v.3. N.Y., n.d.

Phil 193.49.20   Santayana, G. Little essays drawn from writings of George Santayana. N.Y., 1920.

Phil 193.49.23   Santayana, G. Little essays drawn from writings of George Santayana. N.Y., 1924.

Phil 193.49.45A   Santayana, G. Obiter dicta. N.Y., 1936.

Phil 193.49.19 Santayana, G. Il pensiero americano e altri saggi. Milano, 1939.

Phil 193.49.9 Santayana, G. Philosophical opinion in America. London, 1918. 2v.

Phil 193.49.50 Santayana, G. The philosophy of Santayana; selections. N.Y., 1936.

Phil 193.49.30 Santayana, G. Platonism and the spiritual life. N.Y., 1927.

Phil 193.49.35 Santayana, G. The realm of essence: book first of Realms of being. London, 1928.

Phil 193.49.37 Santayana, G. The realm of matter. Book second of Realms of being. N.Y., 1930.

Phil 193.49.39.8A Santayana, G. The realm of spirit. N.Y., 1940.

Phil 193.49.38 Santayana, G. The realm of truth. N.Y., 1938.

Phil 645.25.2 Santayana, G. Scepticism and animal faith. London, 1923.

Phil 645.25A Santayana, G. Scepticism and animal faith. N.Y., 1923.

Phil 8419.40.5 Santayana, G. The sense of beauty, being the outlines of aesthetic theory. N.Y., 1898.

Phil 8419.40 Santayana, G. The sense of beauty, being the outlines of aesthetic theory. N.Y., 1955.

Phil 8419.40.6A Santayana, G. The sense of beauty. N.Y., 1896. 3v.

Phil 193.49.60 Santayana, G. Vagabond scholar. N.Y., 1962.

Phil 193.49.5 Santayana, G. Winds of doctrine. London, 1913.

Phil 193.49.8 Santayana, G. Winds of doctrine. N.Y., 1957.

Phil 193.49.7 Santayana, G. Winds of doctrine. Studies in contemporary opinion. N.Y., 1926.

Phil 193.49.65 Santayana, G. The wisdom of George Santayana. 2d. ed. N.Y., 1964.

Phil 2280.5.30 Santayana, George. Animal faith and spiritual life. N.Y., 1967.

Phil 1818.7 Santayana, George. The genteel tradition in American philosophy...public address...1911. Berkeley, 1911.

Phil 2280.5.84 Santayana, George. The idler and his works. N.Y., 1957.

Phil 2280.5.88 Santayana, George. The life of reason. N.Y., 1954.

Phil 3565.132 Santayana, George. Lotze's system of philosophy. Bloomington, 1971.

Phil 2280.5.87 Santayana, George. Persons and places. London, 1944.

Phil 2280.5.85A Santayana, George. Persons and places. v.1,3. N.Y., 1944-53. 2v.

Phil 2280.5.25 Santayana, George. The philosophy of Santayana. N.Y., 1953.

Phil 2280.5.91 Santayana, George. Physical order and moral liberty. Nashville, 1969.

Phil 2280.5.79.5 Santayana, George. Selected critical writing. Cambridge, Eng., 1968. 2v.

Phil 1750.142 Santayana, George. Some turns of thought in modern philosophy. Cambridge, Eng., 1933.

Phil 1750.142.2 Santayana, George. Some turns of thought in modern philosophy. N.Y., 1933.

Phil 2270.123 Santayana, George. The unknowable; Herbert Spencer lecture. Oxford, 1923.

Phil 2280.5.7 Santayana, George. The works of George Santayana. N.Y., 1936-40. 14v.

Phil 2280.5.125 Santayana: the later years. (Cory, D.) N.Y., 1963.

Phil 2280.5.109 Santayana and the sense of beauty. (Arnett, W.E.) Bloomington, Ind., 1955.

Phil 2280.5.130A Santayana's aesthetics; a critical introduction. (Singer, Irving.) Cambridge, 1957.

Phil 2280.5.99 Santayana's debt to New England. (MacCampbell, D.) n.p., 1935.

Phil 4073.87 Sante Felici, G. Die religionsphilosophischen Grundanschauungen des Thomas Campanella. Inaug. Diss. Halle, 1887.

Phil 3500.94 Santeler, J. Die Grundlegung der Menschenwürde bei I. Kant. Innsbruck, 1962.

Phil 6980.668.10 Santer-Weststrate, Henrietta Cornelia. Gedragstherapie in het bijzonder de methode van wedenkerige remming. Assen, 1964.

Phil 176.57.2 Santi, solitari e filosofi. 2nd ed. (Barzellotti, G.) Bologna, 1886.

Phil 8419.61 Santinello, Giovanni. Estetica della forma. Padova, 1962.

Phil 3500.96 Santinello, Giovanni. Metafisica e critica in Kant. Bologna, 1965.

Phil 1750.166.290 Santinello, Giovanni. Studi sull'Umanesimo europeo. Padova, 1969.

Phil 5828.1 Santlus, J.C. Zur Psychologie der menschlichen Triebe. Neuwied, 1864.

Phil 4170.3.82 Un santo nel secolo XIX: A.C. de Meis. (Amante, B.) Lanciano, 1920.

Phil 5520.575 Santoni, Ronald E. Religious language and problem of religious knowledge. Bloomington, 1968.

Phil 4479.2.30 Santos, Delfin. Meditação sobre a cultura. Lisboa, 1946.

Phil 4018.8 Santucci, Antonio. Esistenzialismo e filosofia italiana. Bologna, 1959.

Phil 4018.8.5 Santucci, Antonio. Il pragmatismo in Italia. Bologna, 1963.

Phil 2050.282 Santucci, Antonio. Sistema e ricerca in David Hume. Bari, 1969.

Phil 530.40.45 Santullano, Luis. Místicos españoles. Madrid, 1934.

Phil 4372.1.125 Sanz, Victor. Vigencia actual de Luis Vives. Montevideo, 1967.

Phil 193.46 Sanz del Rio, D.J. Analisis del pensamiento racional. Madrid, 1877.

Phil 4369.7 Sanz del Rio, Julián. Cartas ineditas. Madrid, 1873?

Phil 4369.7.3 Sanz del Rio, Julián. Sanz del Río, 1814-1869. Madrid, 1969.

Phil 4369.7.3 Sanz del Río, 1814-1869. (Sanz del Rio, Julián.) Madrid, 1969.

Phil 4369.7.5 Sanz del Rio. (Manrique, Gervasio.) Madrid, 1935.

Phil 3640.289 Sanz y Escartin, Eduardo. Federico Nietzsche y el anarquismo intelectual. Madrid, 1898.

Phil 28.20 São Paulo (City). Universidade. Faculdade de Filosofia, Ciencias e Letras. Filosofia. São Paulo. 5

Phil 58.19 São Paulo Brazil (City). Universidade. Faculdade de Filosofia, Ciencias e Letras. Psicologia. 4-7 2v.

Phil 28.50 Sapientia; revista tomista de filosofía. La Plata. 1,1946+ 22v.

Phil 28.72 Sapienza. Napoli. 18,1965+ 6v.

Phil 4372.1.84 La sapienza psicologica e pedagogica di Giovanni L. Vives. (Rivari, Enrico.) Bologna, 1922.

Phil 6128.18 Sapolini, G. Un tredicesimo nervo craniale. Milano, 1881.

Phil 5520.365 Saporta, Sol. Psycholinguistics. N.Y., 1961.

Phil 5590.445 Sappenfield, Bert Reese. Personality dynamics. N.Y., 1961.

Phil 299.14 Sapper, Karl. Das Element der Wirklichkeit und die Welt der Erfahrung. München, 1924.

Phil 4872.242.1030 The Sār Bachan; an abstract of the teachings of Swamiji Maharaj. 4th ed. (Radhas Vamidayal.) Beas, 195-?

Phil 310.535 Sarab'ianov, V.N. Dialekticheskii i istoricheskii materializm. Moskva, 1934.

Phil 4065.122 Saracista, M. La filosofia di Giordano Bruno nei suoi motivi plotiniani. Firenze, 1935.

Phil 3450.11.495 Saraiva, Maria Manuela. L'imagination selon Husserl. La Haye, 1970.

Phil 5402.28 Sarano, Jacques. La douleur. Paris, 1965.

Phil 5590.410 Sarason, Irwin G. Contemporary research in personality. Princeton, 1962.

Phil 5590.468 Sarason, Irwin G. Personality. N.Y., 1966.

Phil 5593.54.15 Sarason, S.B. The clinical interaction (with specific reference to Rorschach). N.Y., 1954.

Phil 6328.35 Sarason, S.B. Psychological problems in mental deficiency. N.Y., 1949.

Phil 6328.35.5 Sarason, S.B. Psychological problems in mental deficiency. 3d ed. N.Y., 1959.

Phil 4065.160 Saraw, Julie. Der Einfluss Plotins auf Giordano Brunos Degli eroici furori. Borna-Leipzig, 1916.

Phil 6328.52 Sarbin, T.R. Studies in behavior pathology. N.Y., 1961.

Phil 5258.175 Sarbin, Theodore. Clinical inference and cognitive theory. N.Y., 1960.

Phil 1718.46 Šarčević, Abdulah. Iskon i smisao. Sarajevo, 1971.

Phil 4260.101 Sarchi, Carlo. Della dottrina di B. Spinoza e di G.B. Vico. Milano, 1877.

Phil 3500.42 Sarchi, Charles. Examen de la doctrine de Kant. Paris, 1872.

Phil 5627.107.15 Sargant, W.W. Battle for the mind. Melbourne, 1957.

Phil 7054.34.5 Sargent, Epes. Planchette; or, The despair of science. Boston, 1869.

Phil 7054.34.10 Sargent, Epes. The proof palpable of immortality. 3. ed. Boston, 1881.

Phil 7054.34.8 Sargent, Epes. The proof palpable of immortalty. Boston, 1875.

Phil 7054.34 Sargent, Epes. The scientific basis of spiritualism. Boston, 1880.

Phil 7068.91.10 Sargent, Epes. The scientific basis of spiritualism. 6th ed. Boston, 1891.

Phil 5058.2.2 Sargent, J. The method to science. London, 1696.

Phil 193.6 Sargent, J. Transnatural philosophy, or Metaphysics. London, 1700.

X Cg Phil 9358.1 Sargent, J.A. Letters from a mother...daughter. Boston, n.d.

Phil 8893.91 Sargent, Porter E. The new immoralities. Boston, 1935.

Phil 2725.35.85 Sargi, Bechara. La participation à l'être. Paris, 1957.

Phil 8980.770 Sarich, A.L. Obshchie metody nravstvennogo vospitaniia. Moskva, 1956.

Phil 6128.33 Sarjant, L.G. Is the mind a coherer? London, 1912.

Phil 4120.4.83 Sarlo, F. de. Gentile e Croce. Firenze, 1925.

Phil 193.122 Sarlo, F. de. Introduzione alla filosofia. Milano, 1928.

Phil 4210.90 Sarlo, Francesco de. Le basi della psicologia e della biologia secondo il Rosmini. Roma, 1893.

Phil 665.57 Sarlo, Francesco de. Il concetto dell'anima nella psicologia contemporanea. Firenze, 1900.

Phil 1718.6 Sarlo, Francesco de. Filosofi del tempo nostro. Firenze, 1916.

Phil 5258.44.5 Sarlo, Francesco de. Idati della esperienza psichica. Firenze, 1903.

Phil 5258.44 Sarlo, Francesco de. Psicologia e filosophia. Firenze, 1918. 2v.

Phil 4225.2.31 Sarlo, Francesco de. Saggi di filosofia. Torino, 1896-97. 2v.

Phil 8893.43.5 Sarlo, Francisco de. L'altività pratica e la coscienza morale. Firenze, 1907.

Phil 8893.43.10 Sarlo, Francisco de. Metafisica, scienza e moralità. Roma, 1898.

Phil 8893.43 Sarlo, Francisco de. Principii di scienza etica. Milano, 1907.

Phil 5590.418 Sarnoff, Irving. Personality, dynamics and development. N.Y., 1962.

Phil 9150.24 Sarolea, Charles. La liberté et le déterminisme rapports avec la théorie de l'évolution. Thèse. Bruxelles, 1893.

Phil 9410.9 Sarrazin, N.J. Le véritable optimisme. Nancy, 19- ?

Phil 6688.25 Sarrazin de Montferrier, A.A.V. Der principes et des procédés du magnetisme animal. Paris, 1819. 2v.

Phil 6128.75 Sartakov, S.V. Krasota truda. Moskva, 1961.

Phil 4225.77.30 Sarti, Sergio. L'azione creatice di Sergio Sarti. Brescia, 1959.

Phil 349.70 Sarti, Sergio. Io cogitante ed io problematico. Brescia, 1962.

Phil 3500.28 Sartiaux, F. Morale Kantienne et morale humaine. Paris, 1917.

Htn Phil 1930.1.30* Sartor Resartus. (Carlyle, Thomas.) Boston, 1836.

Phil 4080.3.295 Sartori, G. Croce etico-politico e filosofo. Firenze, 1956.

Phil 4080.3.525 Sartori, Giovanni. Stato e politica nel pensiero di Benedetto Croce. Napoli, 1966.

Phil 5768.14 Sartorius, E. Die Lutherische Lehre vom Unvermögen des Freyen Willens zur Höheren. Göttingen, 1821.

Phil 2880.8.88 Sartre, est-il un possédé? (Boutang, P.) Paris, 1947.

Phil 2880.8.88.5 Sartre, est-il un possédé? (Boutang, P.) Paris, 1950.

Phil 2880.8.116.2 Sartre, his philosophy and existential psychoanalysis. 2.ed. (Stern, Alfred.) N.Y., 1967.

Phil 5465.35.10 Sartre, Jean P. L'imaginaire. Paris, 1940.

Phil 5465.35.5 Sartre, Jean P. L'imagination; psychologie. Paris, 1940.

Phil 5465.35.15 Sartre, Jean P. Imagination. Ann Arbor, 1962[1960]

Phil 5465.35 Sartre, Jean P. L'imagination. Paris, 1936.

Phil 2880.8.56.3A Sartre, Jean Paul. Being and nothingness. N.Y., 1956.

Phil 2880.8.56.2 Sartre, Jean Paul. Being and nothingness. N.Y., 1965.

Phil 2880.8.70 Sartre, Jean Paul. The communists and peace, with a reply to Claude Lefort. N.Y., 1968.

Phil 2880.8.57A Sartre, Jean Paul. Critique de la raison dialectique. Paris, 1960.

Phil 2880.8.46 Sartre, Jean Paul. The emotions, outline of a theory. N.Y., 1948.

Phil 2880.8.44 Sartre, Jean Paul. Esquisse d'une théorie des émotions. Paris, 1939.

Phil 2880.8.45 Sartre, Jean Paul. Esquisse d'une théorie des émotions. Paris, 1963.

Phil 2880.8.35 Sartre, Jean Paul. Essays in aesthetics. N.Y., 1963.

Phil 2880.8.55 Sartre, Jean Paul. L'être et le néant. Paris, 1943[1946].

Phil 2880.8.60 Sartre, Jean Paul. Existential psychoanalysis. N.Y., 1953.

Phil 2880.8.42A Sartre, Jean Paul. Existentialism. N.Y., 1947.

Phil 2880.8.65 Sartre, Jean Paul. Existentialism and human emotions. N.Y., 1957.

Phil 2880.8.41.2   Sartre, Jean Paul. Existentialism and humanism.
                     London, 1960.
Phil 2880.8.41.3   Sartre, Jean Paul. Existentialism and humanism.
                     London, 1965.
Phil 2880.8.40A   Sartre, Jean Paul. L'existentialisme est un humanisme. 5.
                     ed. Paris, 1946.
Phil 2880.8.43   Sartre, Jean Paul. Ist der Existentialismus ein
                     Humanismus? Zürich, 1947.
Phil 2880.8.58   Sartre, Jean Paul. Marxismus und Existentialismus.
                     Reinbeck, 1964.
Phil 2880.8.20A   Sartre, Jean Paul. The philosophy of Jean Paul Sartre.
                     N.Y., 1965.
Phil 2880.8.30   Sartre, Jean Paul. The psychology of imagination.
                     N.Y., 1948.
Phil 2880.8.33   Sartre, Jean Paul. The psychology of imagination.
                     N.Y., 1961.
Phil 2880.8.52   Sartre, Jean Paul. Search for a method. 1st American ed.
                     N.Y., 1963.
Phil 2880.8.62   Sartre, Jean Paul. Das Sein und das Nichts.
                     Hamburg, 1952.
Phil 5400.202   Sartre, Jean-Paul. Sketch for a theory of the emotions.
                     London, 1962.
Phil 2880.8.64.5   Sartre, Jean Paul. La transcendance de l'égo.
                     Paris, 1965.
Phil 2880.8.64A   Sartre, Jean-Paul. The transcendence of the ego.
                     N.Y., 1957.
Phil 2880.8.155   Sartre, ou La théologie de l'absurde. (Jolivet, Régis.)
                     Paris, 1965.
Phil 2880.8.245   Sartre; the radical conversion. (Sheridan, James Francis.)
                     Athens, Ohio, 1969.
Phil 2880.8.116   Sartre. (Stern, Alfred.) N.Y., 1953.
Phil 2880.8.101   Sartre: a philosophic study. (Manser, Anthony Richards.)
                     London, 1966.
Phil 2880.8.154   Sartre: the theology of the absurd. (Jolivet, Régis.)
                     Westminster, 1967.
Phil 2880.8.250   Sartre and the artist. (Bauer, George Howard.)
                     Chicago, 1969.
Phil 2880.8.92   Sartre contre l'homme. (Henri-Hoyen, E.) Genève, 1947.
Phil 2880.8.305   Sartre e il comunismo. (Fé, Franco.) Firenze, 1970.
Phil 2880.8.300   Sartre e la dialettica. (Pagano, Giacoma Maria.)
                     Napoli, 1970.
Phil 2880.8.165   Sartre et la réalité humaine. (Audry, Colette.)
                     Paris, 1966.
Phil 2880.8.210   Sartre il marxismo. 1. ed. (Chiodi, Pietro.)
                     Milano, 1965.
Phil 2880.8.230   Sartre y los prolegómenos a la antropología. (Herra,
                     Rafael Angel.) Ciudad Universitaria, 1968.
Phil 2880.8.124   Sartre y su existencialismo. 2. ed. (Quiles, Ismael.)
                     Buenos Aires, 1952.
Phil 2880.8.160   Sartres Sozialphilosophie. (Hartmann, Klaus.)
                     Berlin, 1966.
Phil 75.90   Sarva-darsana-sangraha; a bibliographical guide to the
                     global history of philosophy. (Plott, John C.)
                     Leiden, 1969.
Phil 5850.332F   Sasha, A.W. Condensed outline of "The laws of life".
                     Oakland, Cal., 1932.
Phil 3425.604   Sass, H.M. Untersuchungen zur Religionsphilosophie.
                     Münster, 1963.
Phil 3450.19.455   Sass, Hans-Martin. Heidegger-Bibliographie. Meisenheim am
                     Glan, 1968.
Phil 2520.343   Sassen, F. Descartes. Den Haag, 1963.
Phil 1718.20   Sassen, F. Geschiedenis van de wijshegeerte der
                     negentiende eeuw. Antwerpen, 1934.
Phil 3960.16.5   Sassen, Ferdinand. Geschiedenis van de wijsbegeerte in
                     Nederland tot het einde der negentiende eeuw.
                     Amsterdam, 1959.
Phil 3960.16   Sassen, Ferdinand. De wijsbegeerte der middeleeuvren in de
                     Nederlanden. Lochen, 1944.
Phil 1523.20   Sassen, Ferdinand. Wijsgerig denken in de middeleeuwen.
                     Haarlem, 1965.
Phil 3960.16.13   Sassen, Ferdinand. Wijsgerig leven in Nederland in de
                     twintigste eeuw. 3. druk. Amsterdam, 1960.
Phil 260.1.5   Sasswitz, K. Atomistik und Kriticismus.
                     Braunschweig, 1878.
Phil 260.1   Sasswitz, K. Geschichte de Atomistik. Hamburg, 1890.
                     2v.
Phil 7060.149   Satan et la magie de nos jours. (Duroy de Bruignac, A.)
                     Paris, 1864.
Phil 8620.60   Satan in the Old Testament. (Kluger, Rivkah Schärf.)
                     Evanston, 1967.
Phil 4372.1.39   Satellitium animi. (Vives, Juan Luis.) Wien, 1883.
Phil 8893.135   Sathaye, S.G. A philosophy of living. N.Y., 1963.
Phil 165.110   Satin, J.H. Ideas in context. Boston, 1958.
Phil 3450.29.20   Satire und Polemik. (Haecker, Theodor.) München, 1961.
Phil 2705.83   Die Satiren des Herrn Maschine. (Bergmann, Ernst.)
                     Leipzig, 1913.
Phil 6688.17   Satow, Louis. Hypnotism and suggestion. London, 1923.
Phil 4515.30.2   Satser om lag och lagstiftning med tillägg och anmärkningar
                     å nyo utgifne. 2e uppl. (Boström, C.J.) Upsala, 1871.
Phil 3195.2.80   Sattel, G. Martin Deutinger als Ethiker. Paderborn, 1908.
Phil 3195.2.79   Sattel, G. Martin Deutingers Gotteslehre.
                     Regensburg, 1905.
Phil 8598.38   Satterlee, Henry Y. A creedless Gospel and the Gospel
                     creed. N.Y., 1895.
Phil 3120.8.135   Satue, A.A. La doctrina de la intencionalidad en Franz
                     Brentano. Barcelona, 1961.
Phil 5590.576   Satura, Vladimir. Struktur und Genese der Person.
                     Innsbrück, 1970.
Phil 9352.13   The Saturday letters. (Manchester, R.E.) Cuyahoga
                     Falls, 1937.
Phil 9352.13.5   The Saturday letters. (Manchester, R.E.) Cuyahoga
                     Falls, 1938.
Phil 9070.12   The Saturday letters. (Manchester, R.E.) Cuyahooga
                     Falls, 1941.
Phil 8893.76   Saturday Review. Studies in conduct. London, 1867.
Phil 5710.22   Saturn and melancholy. (Klibansky, R.) London, 1964.
Phil 8893.142   Satyananda, Swami. World ethics. Calcutta, 1967.
Phil 193.237*   Satyananda, Swami. World philosophy. Calcutta, 1959-1963.
                     3v.
Phil 3552.420   Der Satz vom Gound bei Leibniz. (Saame, Otto.)
                     Mainz, 1961.
Phil 3450.19.75   Der Satz vom Grund. (Heidegger, Martin.)
                     Pfullingen, 1957.
Phil 5042.26   Der Satz vom Widerspruch. (Conze, E.) Hamburg, 1931.
Phil 5051.11   Der Satz vom Widerspruch. (Lasson, Adolf.) Halle, 1885.
Phil 5125.5   Der Satz von Grunde als Prinzip der Schliessens. (Erhardt,
                     F.) Halle, 1891.
Phil 6060.18.15   Saudek, R. Experimentelle Graphologie. Berlin, 1929.

Phil 6060.18.10   Saudek, R. Experiments with handwriting. London, 1928.
Phil 6060.18   Saudek, R. The psychology of handwriting. London, 1925.
Phil 6060.18.20   Saudek, R. Schrift und Mensch. Berlin, 1928.
VPhil 6060.78   Saudek, Robert. What your handwriting shows.
                     London, 1932.
Phil 3018.38   Sauer, Ernst Friedrich. Deutsche Philosophen: von Eckhart
                     his Heidegger. Göttingen, 1968.
Phil 193.104.2   Sauer, W. Philosophie der Zukunft. 2e Aufl.
                     Stuttgart, 1926.
Phil 193.104   Sauer, W. Philosophie der Zukunft eine Grundlegung der
                     Kultur. Stuttgart, 1923.
Phil 349.19   Sauerbeck, E. Vom Wesen der Wissenschaft. Leipzig, 1914.
Phil 5402.26.2   Sauerbruch, F. Wesen und Bedeutung des Schmerzes. 2. Aufl.
                     Frankfurt, 1961.
Phil 5590.420   Saul, Leon J. Emotional maturity. Philadelphia, 1960.
Phil 5412.10   Saul, Leon Joseph. The hostile mind. N.Y., 1956.
Phil 510.10   Saulze, J.B. Le monisme matérialiste. Paris, 1911.
Phil 6990.42   Saunders, E. Lourdes. N.Y., 1940.
Phil 5374.50.15   Saunders, H.S. The higher consciousness. Toronto, 1924.
Phil 5520.491   Saunders, John Turk. The private language problem.
                     N.Y., 1967.
Phil 8843.13   Saunders, K.J. The ideals of East and West. Cambridge,
                     Eng., 1934.
Phil 8843.13.2   Saunders, K.J. The ideals of East and West. N.Y., 1934.
Htn Phil 5938.11F* Saunders, R. Saunders physiognomie. 2nd ed.
                     London, 1670-71.
Phil 7069.27.23   Saunders, R.H. Healing through spirit agency.
                     London, 1927.
Phil 6128.44   Saunders, R.H. Health; its recovery and maintanance, by
                     Abduhl Latif. London, 1928.
Htn Phil 5938.11F* Saunders physiognomie. 2nd ed. (Saunders, R.)
                     London, 1670-71.
Phil 705.51   Saur, Karl. Transzendenz als Wirklichkeit. Hamburg, 1965.
Phil 6968.1   Saury, H. Étude clinique sur la folie héréditaire.
                     Paris, 1886.
Phil 665.82   Sausgruber, Kurt. Atom und Seele. Freiburg, 1958.
Phil 3090.86   Sauter, J. Baader und Kant. Jena, 1928.
Phil 193.241   Sauvage, Micheline. L'aventure philosophique.
                     Paris, 1966.
Phil 2880.6   Sauvage-Jousse, P. Le métaverbe. Paris, 1928.
Phil 8673.10   Savage, M.J. Belief in God. 2. ed. Boston, 1881.
Phil 8708.1   Savage, M.J. Evolution and religion. Philadelphia, 1886.
Phil 8643.11   Savage, M.J. Life beyond death. N.Y., 1899.
Phil 8893.31.5   Savage, M.J. The morals of evolution. Boston, 1881.
Phil 8598.23   Savage, M.J. Passing and permanent in religion.
                     N.Y., 1901.
Phil 7069.02.20   Savage, Minot J. Can telepathy explain? N.Y., 1902.
Phil 7068.93.15   Savage, Minot J. Psychics; facts and theories.
                     Boston, 1893.
Phil 6854.16   The savage god: a study of suicide. (Alvarez, Alfred.)
                     London, 1972.
Phil 192.23   Les savants et la philosophie. (Rageot, G.) Paris, 1908.
Phil 1818.12   Savelle, Max. The colonial origins of American thought.
                     Princeton, 1964.
Phil 811.4   Savérien, A. Histoire des progrès de l'esprit humain dans
                     les sciences et dans les arts que en dépendent.
                     Paris, 1777.
Phil 2520.151   Savérien, Alexandre. Vita di Renato Cartesio.
                     Venezia, 1774.
Phil 5400.61   Savescu, Michael. Die Gefühlslehre in der neuesten
                     französischen Psychology. Leipzig, 1900.
Phil 8980.770.5   Savez Komunista Srbije. Univerzitetski Komitet. O
                     sociajalističkom moralu. Beograd, 1964.
Phil 5520.624   Savigny, Eike von. Die Philosophie der normalen Sprache.
                     Frankfurt, 1969.
Phil 7060.37.15   Savile, B.W. Apparitions; a narrative of facts. 2. ed.
                     London, 1880.
Phil 5871.35   Savioz, Esther. Die Anfänge der Geschwisterbeziehung.
                     Bern, 1968.
Phil 2465.90   Savioz, R. La philosophie de Charles Bonnet de Genève.
                     Thèse. 1e éd. Paris, 1948. 4v.
Phil 974.3.160   Savitch, Marie. Marie Steiner von Sivers, Mitarbeiterin
                     von Rudolf Steiner. Dornach, 1965.
Phil 5853.4   Savoir communiquer. (Gauguelin, François.) Paris, 1970.
Phil 3640.630   Savounet, Marie. Nietzsche et DuBos. Paris, 1960.
Phil 28.88   Savremene filozofske teme. Beograd. 1966-1969// 2v.
Phil 3552.352   Saw, R.L. Leibniz. Harmondsworth, Eng., 1954.
Phil 1718.24   Sawicki, F. Lebensanschauungen moderner Denker.
                     Paderborn, 1949-1952. 2v.
Phil 5590.23.2   Sawicki, Franz. Das Ideal der Persönlichkeit. 2. Aufl.
                     Paderborn, 1922.
Phil 818.9   Sawicki, Franz. Lebensanschauungen Alter und neuer Denker.
                     Paderborn, 1923. 3v.
Phil 9010.2   Sawyer, F.W. A plea for amusements. N.Y., 1847.
Phil 9010.2.2   Sawyer, F.W. A plea for amusements. N.Y., 1847.
Phil 7080.19   Sawyer, James. Insomnia: its causes and cure.
                     Birmingham, 1904.
Phil 5258.87   Saxby, I.B. The psychology of the thinker. London, 1926.
Phil 1885.95   Saxena, Sushil Kumar. Studies in the metaphysics of
                     Bradley. N.Y., 1967.
Phil 8893.75   Say, J.B. Olbie, ou Essai sur les moyens de reformer.
                     Paris, 1799-1800.
Phil 8886.86.5   Saydah, J. Roger. The ethical theory of Clarence Irving
                     Lewis. Athens, Ohio, 1969.
Phil 8598.82   Sayers, Dorothy L. The mind of the maker. London, 1941.
Phil 8598.82.5   Sayers, Dorothy L. The mind of the maker. N.Y., 1941.
Phil 8876.14.2   The sayings of the wise. (Baldwin, W.) London, 1908.
Phil 1153.15   Sayre, Farrand. The Greek cynics. Baltimore, 1948.
Phil 4756.1.49   Sbornik pamiati Semena L. Franka. (Zen'kovskii, V.V.)
                     Miunkhen, 1954.
Phil 4756.5.30   Sbornik sochinenii. v.1-2. (Giliarov-Platonov, N.P.)
                     Moskva, 1899-1900.
Phil 4762.1.35   Sbornik zadach po logike. (Losskii, Nikolai Onufrievich.)
                     Praga, 1924.
Phil 4809.498.80   Sboruiik ku poctě Frantiska Krejciho. (Šimsa, Jaroslav.)
                     Praha, 1929.
Htn Phil 176.123.5* Scala naturale. (Maffei, G.C.) Venice, 1573.
Htn Phil 8880.7*   A scale of first principles. (Fleming, C.) London, 1755.
Phil 194.30.80   Scalero, L. Adriano Tilgher. Padova, 1962.
Phil 2905.1.440   Scaltriti, Giacinto. Teilhard de Chardin tra il mito e
                     l'eresia. Roma, 1964.
Phil 1750.795   The scandalous ghost; Sartre's existentialism as related to
                     vitalism, humanism, mysticism, Marxism. (Salvan, Jacques
                     León.) Detroit, 1967.
Phil 28.60   The Scandinavian journal of psychology. Stockholm.
                     1,1960+ 10v.
Phil 28.6   Scandinavian scientific review. Kristiania. 1-3,1922-1924
                     2v.

Phil 2477.6.170 — Scannone, Juan Carlos. Sein und Inkarnation. Diss. Freiburg, 1968.

Phil 9240.24 — Scarcity and evil. (Walsh, V.C.) Englewood Cliffs, N.J., 1961.

Phil 5401.52 — Scared to death; an examination of fear. (Barker, John Charles.) London, 1968.

Phil 193.168 — Scarlata, G.P. Lineamenti di metalogica. Padova, 1951.

Phil 510.1.9 — Scarrett, W.R. The riddle of the universe; a review. n.p., 1902.

Phil 8402.9 — The scenery-shower, with word-paintings of the beautiful. (Burton, W.) Boston, 1844.

Phil 7054.116.5 — Scenes in the spirit world. (Tuttle, H.) N.Y., 1855.

Phil 5592.40 — Der Scenotest. (Engels, Helma.) Münster, 1957.

Phil 8418.10 — La scepsi estetica. (Rensi, G.) Bologna, 1919.

Phil 4215.3.83 — La scepsi etica di Giuseppe Rensi. (Nonis, Piero.) Roma, 1957.

Htn Phil 2030.1.30* — Scepsis scientifica. (Glanvill, Joseph.) London, 1665.

Phil 645.2.5 — Scepsis scientifica: or, Confest ignorance, the way to science. (Glanvill, J.) London, 1885.

Phil 645.28 — Sceptica. (Levi, Adolfo.) Torino, 1921.

Phil 645.30 — Sceptical essays. (Russell, B.A.W.) N.Y., 1928.

Phil 1802.4 — Sceptical examination of contemporary British philosophy. (Coates, A.) London, 1929.

Phil 645.55 — Scepticism. (Naess, Arne.) London, 1968[1969]

Phil 645.25.2 — Scepticism and animal faith. (Santayana, G.) London, 1923.

Phil 645.25A — Scepticism and animal faith. (Santayana, G.) N.Y., 1923.

Phil 645.31.5A — Scepticism and construction. (Campbell, Charles A.) London, 1931.

Phil 1885.88 — Scepticism and dogma; a study in philosophy of F.H. Bradley. (Ross, R.G.) N.Y., 1940.

Phil 6112.44 — Scepticism and the first person. (Coval, Samuel Charles.) London, 1966.

Phil 3494.3 — Le scepticisme...Scepticisme de Kant. (Maurial, É.) Montpellier, 1856.

Phil 3494.3.2 — Le scepticisme...Scepticisme de Kant. Supplément. (Maurial, É.) Paris, 1857.

Phil 645.5 — Le scepticisme. (Saisset, E.) Paris, 1865.

Phil 645.39 — Scepticismul grec și filosofia indiană. (Frenkian, Aram M.) Bucuresti, 1957.

Phil 1190.6.5 — Les sceptiques grecs. (Brochard, Victor.) Paris, 1959.

Phil 1190.25 — Les sceptiques grecs. (Dumont, Jean-Paul.) Paris, 1966.

Phil 2428.15 — Sceptiques ou libertins de la première moitié du XVIIe siècle. (Denis, Jacques.) Genève, 1970.

Phil 6128.1 — Scervini, P. Anatomia dei centri nervosi. Napoli, 1892.

Phil 645.22.7 — Lo scetticismo. (Rensi, Giuseppe.) Milano, 1926.

Phil 2651.85 — Scetticismo cristiano. (Sciacca, Giuseppe Maria.) Palermo, 1968.

Phil 4215.3.85 — Scetticismo e misticismo nel pensiero di Giuseppe Rensi. (Morra, Gianfranco.) Siracuse, 1958.

Phil 2610.110 — Scetticismo ed empirismo. (Gregory, Tullio.) Bari, 1961.

Phil 1190.22 — Lo scetticismo greco. (Pra, Mario dal.) Milano, 1950.

Phil 3890.10.110 — Schaaf, J.J. Geschichte und Begriff. Tübingen, 1946.

Phil 349.18 — Schaaf, Juliis Jakob. Über Wissen und Selbstbewisstsein. Stuttgart, 1947.

Phil 6315.19.20 — Schaar, John H. Escape from authority. N.Y., 1961.

Phil 6315.19.5 — Schaar, John H. The fear of freedom. London, 1942.

Phil 1718.17 — Schaarschmidt, C. Der Entwicklungsgang der neueren Speculation. Bonn, 1857.

Phil 3890.11 — Schabad, M. Die Wiederenteleskung des ich in der Metaphysik Teichmüllers. Basel, 1940.

Phil 3640.160 — Schacht, W. Nietzsche. Bern, 1901.

Phil 5593.66 — Schachtel, Ernest G. Experiential foundations of Rorschach's test. N.Y., 1966.

Phil 5590.280.5 — Schachtel, Ernest G. Metamorphosis. London, 1963.

Phil 5590.280 — Schachtel, Ernest G. Metamorphosis. N.Y., 1959.

Phil 8612.51 — Schachtel, H.J. The shadowed valley. N.Y., 1962.

Phil 6028.3 — Schack, S. Physiognomische Studien. Jena, 1881.

Phil 6028.3.2 — Schack, S. Physiognomische Studien. 2e Aufl. Jena, 1890.

Phil 6028.3.10 — Schack, S. La physionomie chez l'homme. Paris, 1887.

Phil 3246.96 — Schad, Johann B. Gemeinfassliche Darstellung des Fichteschen Systems und der daraus. Erfurt, 1800-02. 3v.

Phil 5058.3 — Schaden, E.A. System der Positiven Logik. Erlangen, 1841.

Phil 3492.3 — Der Schädel Immanuel Kant's. (Küpffer, C.) Braunschweig, 1881?

Phil 9430.11 — Schädelin, K.F.E. Der moderne Pessimismus. Bern, 1878.

Phil 3120.30.135 — Schaeder, Grete. Martin Buber, hebräischer Humanismus. Gottingen, 1966.

Phil 2490.119 — Schaefer, Albert. Die Moralphilosophie Auguste Comte's Versuch einer Darstellung und Kritik. Basel, 1906.

Phil 2050.240 — Schaefer, Alfred. Erkenntnis. Berlin, 1960?

Phil 6968.13 — Schaefer, H. Allgemeine Gerichtliche Psychiatrie. Berlin, 1910.

Phil 5649.8.5 — Schäfer, Karl. Die Erklärung der Bewegungsempfindungen. Inaug. Diss. Jena, 1889.

Phil 3500.100 — Schäfer, Lothar. Kants Metaphysik der Natur. Berlin, 1966.

Phil 5520.700 — Schaefer, Wolfgang von. Was geht uns Noah an? München, 1968.

Phil 3246.222 — Schäffer, W.F. Uber des Herrn Professor Fichte Appellation an das Publikum. Gotha, 1799.

Phil 3500.116 — Schaeffer, Wilhelm Friedrich. Inconsequenzen, und auffallende Widersprüche in der Kantischen Philosophie. Dessau, 1792. Bruxelles, 1969.

Phil 193.240 — Schaeffler, Richard. Wege zu einer Ersten Philosophie. Frankfurt, 1964.

Phil 3018.30 — Schäpferische deutsche Philosophie. (Scifert, F.) Köhn, 1944.

Phil 3552.27 — Schäpferische Vernunft. (Leibniz, Gottfried Wilhelm.) Marbrug, 1951.

Phil 165.347 — Schäpferisches Leben. (Gerner-Beuerle, M.) München, 1964.

Phil 6319.1.57 — Schär, Hans. Religion and the cure of souls in Jung's psychology. N.Y., 1950.

Phil 6319.1.184 — Schär, Hans. Religion und Seele in der Psychologie C.G. Jung. Zürich, 1946.

Phil 720.92 — Schär, Hans. Was ist Wahrheit? Eine theologisch-psychologische Untersuchung. Zürich, 1970.

Phil 5710.15 — Schaer, K.F. Charakter, Blutgruppe und Konstitution. Zürich, 1941.

Phil 2115.155 — Schärer, E. John Locke. Leipzig, 1860.

Phil 1123.13 — Schaerer, René. Le heros, le sage et l'événement dans l'humanisme grec. Paris, 1964.

Phil 1123.13.10 — Schaerer, René. L'homme antique et la structure du monde interieur d'Homère à Socrate. Paris, 1958.

Phil 1123.13.5 — Schaerer, René. L'homme devant ses choix dans la tradition grecque. Louvain, 1965.

Phil 9495.169 — Schaetzing, Eberhard. Schön wieder ein Aufklärungsbuch? Hamburg, 1969.

Phil 185.48.25 — Schafberger, F. Kritik der Schrift Darstellung des Wesens der Philosophie. Nürnberg, 1813.

Phil 5520.325.1 — Schaff, Adam. Einführung in die Semantik. Frankfurt, 1969.

Phil 5520.325.7 — Schaff, Adam. Essays über die Philosophie der Sprache. Frankfurt, 1968.

Phil 310.445.15 — Schaff, Adam. Filozofia człowieka. 3. Wyd. Warszawa, 1965.

Phil 310.445.5 — Schaff, Adam. Filozofiia człowiekas. 2. Wyd. Warszawa, 1962.

Phil 5520.325.2 — Schaff, Adam. Introduction to semantics. N.Y., 1962.

Phil 5520.325.3 — Schaff, Adam. Język a poznanie. Warszawa, 1964.

Phil 5520.325.10 — Schaff, Adam. Language et connaissance. Paris, 1969.

Phil 310.445 — Schaff, Adam. Marksizm i egzystencjalizm. Warszawa, 1961.

Phil 310.445.10 — Schaff, Adam. Marx oder Sartre? Wien, 1964.

Phil 310.447 — Schaff, Adam. Marxisme et existentialisme. Paris, 1962.

Phil 310.445.4 — Schaff, Adam. A philosophy of man. London, 1963.

Phil 8980.792 — Schaff, Adam. Spór o zagadnienie moralności. Warszawa, 1958.

Phil 5520.325.5 — Schaff, Adam. Szkice z filozofii języka. Warszawa, 1967.

Phil 5520.325 — Schaff, Adam. Wstęp do semantyki. Warszawa, 1960.

Phil 310.280 — Schaff, Adam. Wstęp do teorii marksizmu. Warszawa, 1948.

Phil 310.135 — Schaff, Adam. Z zagadnień marksistowskiej teorii prawdy. Warszawa, 1959.

Phil 310.14A — Schaff, Adam. Zu einigen Fragen der marxistischen Theorie der Wahrheit. 1. Aufl. Berlin, 1954.

Phil 6688.1 — Schaffer, K. Suggestion und Reflex. Jena, 1895.

Htn Phil 3801.776* — Schaffroth, J.A.G. Blicke auf die Schellingsch-Jacobi'sche Streitsache. Stuttgart, 1812.

Phil 3500.2 — Schaller, J. Darstellung Kantscher Philosophie. Halle, 1846.

Phil 1718.3 — Schaller, J. Geschichte der Naturphilosophie, Bacon. pt.1-2. Leipzig, 1841-6.

Phil 6128.2 — Schaller, J. Leib und Seele. Weimar, 1858.

Phil 6128.2.2 — Schaller, J. Leib und Seele. 2. Aufl. Weimar, 1856.

Phil 3018.12 — Schaller, J. Die Philosophie unserer Zeit. Leipzig, 1837.

Phil 5258.5 — Schaller, J. Das Seelenleben des Menschen. Weimar, 1860.

Phil 3235.113 — Schaller, Julius. Darstellung und Kritik der Philosophie Ludwig Feuerbach's. Leipzig, 1847.

Phil 3805.157 — Schaller, Julius. Vorlesungen über Schleiermacher. Halle, 1844.

Phil 75.8 — Schaller, Karl A. Handbuch der klassischen philosophischen Literatur. Halle, 1816.

Phil 8062.9 — Schaper, Eva. Prelude to aesthetics. London, 1968.

Phil 5585.44.2 — Schapp, W. Beiträge zur Phänomenologie der Wahrnehmung. Erlangen, 1925.

Phil 5585.44 — Schapp, W. Beiträge zur Phänomenologie der Wahrnehmung. Halle, 1910.

Phil 193.215 — Schapp, Wilhelm. Philosophie der Geschichten. Leer, 1959.

Phil 9178.10 — Schapp, Wilhelm. Zur Metaphysik des Muttertums. Den Haag, 1965.

Phil 6315.2.442 — Scharfenberg, Joachim. Sigmund Freud und sein Religionskritik als Herausforderung für den christlichen Glauben. Göttingen, 1968.

Phil 2475.1.274 — Scharfstein, B.A. Roots of Bergson's philosophy. N.Y., 1943.

Phil 8968.10 — Scharling, C. Henrik. Christliche Sittenlehre nach evangesischluthericher Auffassung. Bremen, 1892.

Phil 8419.4 — Schasler, Max. Asthetik, Grundzüge der Wissenschaft des Schönen und der Kunst. Leipzig, 1886. 2v.

Phil 3235.83 — Schat Petersen, L.W. Ludwig Feuerbach og kristendommen. København, 1883.

Phil 3838.17 — Schaub, E.L. Spinoza, the man and his thought. Chicago, 1933.

Phil 9245.56 — Schauffler, Robert H. The joyful heart. Boston, 1914.

Phil 3246.223 — Schaumann, J.C.G. Erklärung über Fichte's Appellation. Giessen, 1799.

Phil 8598.3 — Schaumann, J.C.G. Philosophie der Religion. Halle, 1793.

Phil 705.70 — Schaumann, Johann Christian Gottlieb. Uber die transcendentale Asthetik. Bruxelles, 1968.

Phil 3850.62 — Schaumann, Johann Christian Gottlieb. Versuch eines neuen Systems des natürlichen Rechts. Bruxelles, 1969.

Phil 185.40.10 — Schaumann, Otto. Die Triebrichtungen des Gewissens. Frankfurt, 1969.

Phil 3460.82 — Schaumburg, E. Jacobis Garten zu Pempelfort. Aachen, 1873.

Phil 2493.88 — Schaupp, Zora. The naturalism of Condillac. Lincoln, 1926.

Phil 2493.88.2 — Schaupp, Zora. The naturalism of Condillac. Diss. n.p., 1925.

Phil 193.233 — Schazmann, P.E. Siegende Geduld. Bern, 1963.

Phil 1504.13 — Schedler, M. Die Philosophie des Macrobius. v.13, pt.1. Münster, 1916.

Phil 5625.97 — Schedules of reinforcement. (Ferster, Charles B.) N.Y., 1957.

Phil 4635.4.31 — Schéele, Frans von. Filosofiens uppgift. Upsala, 1899.

Phil 4635.4.33 — Schéele, Frans von. Filosofiska studier. Första samlingen. Stockholm, 1899.

Phil 5258.72.5 — Scheele, Frans von. Lärobok i psykologi. Stockholm, 1899.

Phil 5258.72 — Scheele, Frans von. Det mänskliga själslifvet. Stockholm, 1896.

Phil 4570.1.81 — Schéele, Frans von. Samuel Grubbe's skönhetslära. Akademisk afhandling. Upsala, 1885.

Phil 3195.12.90 — Scheele, Fritz. Hugo Dinglers philosophisches System. Inaug. Diss. Corbach, 1933.

Phil 623.18 — Scheele, K.H.G. von. Rationalismens förberedelser. Upsala, 1868.

Phil 5258.108 — Scheerer, M. Die Lehre von der Gestalt. Berlin, 1931.

Phil 3808.108.5 — Scheffer, Wessel. Arthur Schopenhauer; de philosophie. Leiden, 1870.

Phil 9430.23 — Scheffer, Wessel. Het wijsgeerig pessimisme van den jongstentijd. Leiden, 1875.

Phil 6128.27 — Scheffler, H. Körper und Geist. Braunschweig, 1862.

Phil 193.45 — Scheffler, H. Die Naturgesetze. v.1-4 and Supplement 1-3. Leipzig, 1876-1883. 7v.

Phil 299.11 — Scheffler, Hermann. Die Grundlagen des Weltsystems. Braunschweig, 1898.

Phil 299.11.5 — Scheffler, Hermann. Realität und Ideelität ferner Naturkraft und Schöpfungskraft. Braunschweig, 1897.

Phil 720.84 — Scheffler, Israel. Science and subjectivity. Indianapolis, 1967.

Phil 8419.8 — Scheffler, K. Form als Schicksa. 2. Aufl. Erlenbach, 1943.

Phil 5425.78 — Scheffler, K. Lebensbild des Talents. Berlin, 1948.

Phil 5627.270.10 — Scheibe, Karl Edward. Beliefs and values. N.Y., 1970.

Phil 665.22 — Scheibler, Christoph. Liber de anima. Francofurti, 1665.

Htn Phil 193.7* Scheiblero, C. Philosophia compendiosa. Oxoniae, 1639.
Htn Phil 193.7.2* Scheiblero, C. Philosophia compendiosa. Oxoniae, 1639.
Phil 6128.35 Scheidemacher, C.B. Das Seelenleben und die Behirnthatigkeit. Regensburg, 1876.
Phil 5258.122 Scheidemann, N.V. Lecture demonstrations for general psychology. Chicago, 1939.
Phil 5258.101 Scheidemann, Norma Valentine. Experiments in general psychology. Chicago, 1929.
Phil 3838.5 Scheidemantel, H. Die Grundprobleme der Ethik Spinoza's. Leipzig, 1898.
Phil 6328.33A Scheidlinger, S. Psychoanalysis and group behavior. 1st ed. N.Y., 1952.
Phil 5258.109 Schein, Josef. Zentralistische Organisation und Seelenleben. München, 1931. 2v.
Phil 5643.12 Die Schein-Bewegungen. (Hoppe, J.F.) Würzburg, 1879.
Phil 510.1.31 Scheinchristentum und Haeckels Welträtsel. Inaug. Diss. (Müller, D.A.) Gotha, 1901.
Phil 5871.5 Scheinfeld, Amram. Twins and supertwins. Philadelphia, 1967.
Phil 333.12.5A Scheinprobleme in der Philosophie. (Carnap, Rudolf.) Berlin, 1928.
Phil 5828.2 Scheitlin, P. Versuch einer vollständigen Thierseelenkunde. Stuttgart, 1840. 2v.
Phil 6980.674 Schelder, Paul. Psychotherapy. N.Y., 1951.
Phil 3850.18.15 Scheler, Max. Abhandlungen und Aufsätze. Leipzig, 1915. 2v.
Phil 3850.18.10 Scheler, Max. Bildung und Wissen. Frankfurt, 1947.
Phil 8893.86.5 Scheler, Max. Der formalismus in der Ethik und die materiale Wertethik. 2. Aufl. Halle, 1921.
Phil 349.24 Scheler, Max. Die Formen des Wissens und die Bildung. Bonn, 1925.
Phil 735.18.5 Scheler, Max. L'homme du ressentiment. Paris, 1933.
Phil 3850.18.30A Scheler, Max. Liebe und Erkenntnis. Bern, 1955.
Phil 3850.18.5 Scheler, Max. Mensch und Geschichte. Zürich, 1929.
Phil 5415.7.9 Scheler, Max. The nature of sympathy. Hamden, 1970.
Phil 3850.18.45 Scheler, Max. On the eternal in man. N.Y., 1960.
Phil 3850.18.40 Scheler, Max. Philosophical perspectives. Boston, 1958.
Phil 3850.18.20A Scheler, Max. Philosophische Weltanschauung. Bern, 1954.
Phil 193.127 Scheler, Max. Philosophische Weltanschauung. Bonn, 1929.
Phil 3850.18.35 Scheler, Max. Ressentiment. N.Y., 1961.
Phil 8598.46.2 Scheler, Max. Vom Ewigen im Menschen. 2e Aufl. Leipzig, 1923. 2v.
Phil 735.18.2 Scheler, Max. Vom Umsturz der Werte. 2e Aufl. Leipzig, 1919. 2v.
Phil 3850.18.25 Scheler, Max. Vom Umsturz der Werte. 4. Aufl. v.2,3,5,6,8,10. Bern, 1955. 7v.
Phil 5415.7 Scheler, Max. Wesen und Formen der Sympathie. Bonn, 1923.
Phil 349.24.5 Scheler, Max. Die Wissensformen und die Gesellschaft. Leipzig, 1926.
Phil 5415.7.5 Scheler, Max. Zur Phänomenologie und Theorie der Sympathiegefühle. Halle, 1913.
Phil 3850.18.195 Scheler's phenomenology of community. (Ranly, Ernest W.) The Hague, 1966.
Phil 3310.6.90 Schelle, K.G. Briefe über Garve's Schriften und Philosophie. Leipzig, 1800.
Phil 2418.2 Schelle, Meta. Studien zum französischen Pyrrhomismus. Inaug. Diss. Göttingen, 1930.
Phil 530.20.45 Schellenberg, E.L. Die deutsche Mystik. Berlin, 1919.
Phil 3800.59 Schelling, F.W.J. von. Darlegung des wahren Verhältnisses der Naturphilosophie zu der verbesserten Fichte'schenLehre. n.p., n.d. 4 pam.
Htn Phil 3801.185* Schelling, der Philosoph in Christo. Berlin, 1842.
Phil 3800.387 Schelling, F.W.J. von. The ages of the world. N.Y., 1942.
Phil 3800.387.5 Schelling, F.W.J. von. The ages of the world. N.Y., 1942.
Htn Phil 3800.51* Schelling, F.W.J. von. Anthologie aus Schelling's Werken. Berlin, 1844.
Htn Phil 3800.100* Schelling, F.W.J. von. Antiquissimi de prima malorum humanorum origine. Tubingae, 1792.
Phil 3800.720 Schelling, F.W.J. von. Aus Schellings Leben. In briefe. v.1, 2-3. Leipzig, 1869-70. 2v.
Phil 3800.135 Schelling, F.W.J. von. Briefe über Dogmatismus und Kritizismus. Leipzig, 1914.
Phil 3800.730 Schelling, F.W.J. von. Briefe und Dokumente. Bonn, 1962.
Phil 3800.722 Schelling, F.W.J. von. Briefwechsel mit Niethammer von seiner Berufung nach Jena. Leipzig, 1913.
Htn Phil 3800.200* Schelling, F.W.J. von. Bruno. Berlin, 1802.
Phil 3800.200.7 Schelling, F.W.J. von. Bruno. Hamburg, 1954.
Phil 3800.200.17 Schelling, F.W.J. von. Bruno. Leipzig, 1928.
Phil 3800.200.20 Schelling, F.W.J. von. Bruno. Paris, 1845.
Htn Phil 3800.200.5* Schelling, F.W.J. von. Bruno. Reutlingen, 1834.
Phil 3800.200.30 Schelling, F.W.J. von. Bruno. Torino, 1906.
Phil 3800.200.11A Schelling, F.W.J. von. Bruno. 2. Aufl. Berlin, 1842.
Htn Phil 3800.200.10* Schelling, F.W.J. von. Bruno. 2e Aufl. Berlin, 1842.
Phil 3800.390.10 Schelling, F.W.J. von. Clara. München, 1948.
Htn Phil 3800.390* Schelling, F.W.J. von. Clara. Stuttgart, 1862.
Htn Phil 3800.390.5* Schelling, F.W.J. von. Clara. 2e Aufl. Stuttgart, 1865.
Htn Phil 3800.230*A Schelling, F.W.J. von. Darlegung der wahren Verhältnisses der Naturphilosophie. Tübingen, 1806.
Htn Phil 3800.260* Schelling, F.W.J. von. Denkmal der Schrift von den göttlichen Dingen des Herrn F.H. Jacobi. Tübingen, 1812.
Phil 3800.33 Schelling, F.W.J. von. Écrits philosophiques. Paris, 1847.
Htn Phil 3800.33.2* Schelling, F.W.J. von. Écrits philosophiques. Paris, 1847.
Htn Phil 3800.170.5* Schelling, F.W.J. von. Einleitung zu seinem Entwurf eines Systems der Naturphilosophie. Jena, 1799. 2 pam.
Htn Phil 3800.170* Schelling, F.W.J. von. Einleitung zu seinem Entwurf eines Systems der Naturphilosophie. Jena, 1799.
Phil 3800.170.10 Schelling, F.W.J. von. Einleitung zu seinem Entwurf eines Systems der Naturphilosophie. Leipzig, 1911.
Htn Phil 3800.380*A Schelling, F.W.J. von. Erste Vorlesung in Berlin, 15 nov. 1841. Stuttgart, 1841.
Htn Phil 3800.160*A Schelling, F.W.J. von. Erster Entwurf eines Systems der Naturphilosophie. Jena, 1799.
Phil 3800.195.5 Schelling, F.W.J. von. Esposizione del mio sistema filosofico. Bari, 1923.
Phil 3800.67 Schelling, F.W.J. von. Gedichte. Jena, 1917.
Phil 3800.61A Schelling, F.W.J. von. Gedichte und poetische Ubersetzungen. Leipzig, 1913.
Phil 3800.140.2 Schelling, F.W.J. von. Ideen zu einer Philosophie der Natur. v.1-2. Leipzig, 1797.
Htn Phil 3800.140* Schelling, F.W.J. von. Ideen zu einer Philosophie der Natur. v.1-2. Leipzig, 1797.
Htn Phil 3800.140.5*A Schelling, F.W.J. von. Ideen zu einer Philosophie der Natur. 2e Aufl. Landshut, 1803.
Phil 3800.386.2 Schelling, F.W.J. von. Münchener Vorlesungen. Leipzig, 1902.
Phil 3801.959.2 Schelling, F.W.J. von. Der neue Reineke Fuchs in acht philosophischen Fabeln. Stuttgart, 1844.
Htn Phil 3801.959* Schelling, F.W.J. von. Der neue Reineke Fuchs in acht philosophischen Fabeln. Stuttgart, 1844.
Phil 3800.340.25 Schelling, F.W.J. von. Of human freedom. Chicago, 1936.
Phil 3800.65 Schelling, F.W.J. von. Philosophie. Berlin, 1918?
Phil 3800.280 Schelling, F.W.J. von. Philosophie der Mythologie. Darmstadt, 1957. 2v.
Htn Phil 3800.220* Schelling, F.W.J. von. Philosophie und Religion. Tübingen, 1804.
Htn Phil 3800.50*A Schelling, F.W.J. von. Philosophische Schriften. Landshut, 1809.
Htn Phil 3800.340* Schelling, F.W.J. von. Philosophische Untersuchungen über das Wesen der menschlichen Freiheit. Reutlingen, 1834.
Htn Phil 3800.310* Schelling, F.W.J. von. Rede an die Studierenden der Ludwig-Maximilians-Universität...29 dec. 1830. München, 1831.
Htn Phil 3800.250.5* Schelling, F.W.J. von. Rede über das Verhältniss der bildenden Künste zu der Natur. Upsala, 1818.
Htn Phil 3800.290* Schelling, F.W.J. von. Rede zum siebzigsten in öffentlicher Sitzung gefeyerten Jahrestag der K. Akademie der Wissenschaften. München, 1829.
Htn Phil 3800.320* Schelling, F.W.J. von. Rede zum zwei und Siebzigsten...Jahrestag der k. Academie der Wissenschaften. München, 1831.
Htn Phil 3800.350* Schelling, F.W.J. von. Rede zum 75. Jahrestag der k. Academie der Wissenschaften. München, 1834.
Phil 3800.340.20 Schelling, F.W.J. von. Ricerche filosofiche su...libertá umana. Lanciano, 1910.
Htn Phil 3800.30.5* Schelling, F.W.J. von. Sämmtliche Werke. v.1. pt.1-10, v.2. pt.1-4. Stuttgart, 1856-61. 14v.
Phil 3800.30A Schelling, F.W.J. von. Sämtliche Werke. v.1. pt.1-10, v.2. pt.1-4. Stuttgart, 1856-61. 14v.
Phil 3800.735 Schelling, F.W.J. von. Schelling und Cotta. Stuttgart, 1965.
Phil 3800.32 Schelling, F.W.J. von. Schellings Werke. München, 1927-28. 5v.
Phil 3800.32.3 Schelling, F.W.J. von. Schellings Werke. München, 1943. 6v.
Phil 3800.57 Schelling, F.W.J. von. Schöpferisches Handeln. Herausgegeben und Eingeleitet von Emil Fuchs. Jena, 1907.
Phil 3800.63 Schelling, F.W.J. von. Shellings Schriften zur Gesellschaftsphilosophie. Jena, 1926.
Phil 3800.180.15 Schelling, F.W.J. von. Sistema dell'idealismo trancendentale. Bari, 1908.
Phil 3800.210.15 Schelling, F.W.J. von. Studium generale. Stuttgart, 1954.
Phil 3800.180.7 Schelling, F.W.J. von. System des transscendentalen Idealismus. Hamburg, 1957.
Htn Phil 3800.180.5* Schelling, F.W.J. von. System des transscendentalen Idealismus. Tübingen, 1800.
Htn Phil 3800.180* Schelling, F.W.J. von. System des transscendentalen Idealismus. Tübingen, 1800.
Phil 3800.180.10 Schelling, F.W.J. von. Système de l'idéalisme trancendental. Paris, 1812.
NEDL Phil 3800.250.50 Schelling, F.W.J. von. The philosophy of art. London, 1845.
Htn Phil 3800.250* Schelling, F.W.J. von. Über das Verhältniss der bildenden Künste zu der Natur. München, 1807.
Htn Phil 3800.250.15* Schelling, F.W.J. von. Über das Verhältniss der bildenden Künste zu der Natur. Berlin, 1843.
Phil 3800.250.20 Schelling, F.W.J. von. Über das Verhältniss der bildenden Künste zu der Natur. Marbach, 1954.
Htn Phil 3800.240* Schelling, F.W.J. von. Über das Verhältniss der Realen und Idealen in der Natur. Hamburg, 1806.
Htn Phil 3800.250.10* Schelling, F.W.J. von. Über das Verhätniss der bildenden Künste zu der Natur. Wien, 1825.
Phil 3800.340.5 Schelling, F.W.J. von. Über das Wesen der menschlichen Freiheit. Leipzig, 1911.
Htn Phil 3800.270.1* Schelling, F.W.J. von. Über die Gottheiten von Samothrace. Stuttgart, 1815.
Htn Phil 3800.270.5* Schelling, F.W.J. von. Über die Gottheiten von Samothrace. Stuttgart, 1815.
Htn Phil 3800.270* Schelling, F.W.J. von. Über die Gottheiten von Samothrace. Stuttgart, 1815.
Htn Phil 3800.190* Schelling, F.W.J. von. Über die jenaische allgemeine Literaturzeitung. Jena, 1800.
Htn Phil 3800.190.2* Schelling, F.W.J. von. Über die jenaische allgemeine Literaturzeitung. Jena, 1800. 3 pam.
Htn Phil 3800.120* Schelling, F.W.J. von. Über die Möglichkeit einer Form der Philosophie überhaupt. Tübingen, 1795.
Htn Phil 3800.120.5* Schelling, F.W.J. von. Über die Moglichkeit einer Form der Philosophie überhaupt. Tubingen, 1795.
Htn Phil 3800.330* Schelling, F.W.J. von. Über Faradays neueste EntdIckung. München, 1832.
Htn Phil 3800.105* Schelling, F.W.J. von. Über Mythen. Leipzig, 1793.
Htn Phil 3800.130* Schelling, F.W.J. von. Vom ich als Princip der Philosophie. Tübingen, 1795.
Htn Phil 3800.150* Schelling, F.W.J. von. Von der Weltseele. Hamburg, 1798.
Htn Phil 3800.150.3* Schelling, F.W.J. von. Von der Weltseele. 2e Aufl. Hamburg, 1806.
Htn Phil 3800.150.6*A Schelling, F.W.J. von. Von der Weltseele. 3e Aufl. Hamburg, 1809.
Phil 3800.150.2 Schelling, F.W.J. von. Von der Weltseele. 3e Aufl. Hamburg, 1809.
Htn Phil 3800.210* Schelling, F.W.J. von. Vorlesungen über die Methode des academische Studium. Tübingen, 1803.
Htn Phil 3800.210.5* Schelling, F.W.J. von. Vorlesungen über die Methode des academische Studium. 2e Ausg. Stuttgart, 1813.
Htn Phil 3800.210.10* Schelling, F.W.J. von. Vorlesungen über die Methode des academische Studium. 3e Ausg. Stuttgart, 1830.
Htn Phil 3800.385.5* Schelling, F.W.J. von. Vorwort zu H. Steffens Nachgelassenen Schriften. Berlin, 1846.
Phil 3800.387.10 Schelling, F.W.J. von. Die Weltalter; Fragmente. München, 1946.
Phil 3800.340.1 Schelling, F.W.J. von. Das Wesen der menschlichen Freiheit. 1. Aufl. Düsseldorf, 1950.
Phil 3800.386.5 Schelling, F.W.J. von. Zur Geschichte der neueren Philosophie; Münchener Vorlesungen. Stuttgart, 1955.
Htn Phil 3800.300* Schelling, F.W.J. von. Zur öffentlichen Sitzung der k. Academie der Wissenschaften am Vorabend des Ludwigs-Tages 1829. München, 1829.
Htn Phil 140.1* Pamphlet vol. Schelling, Fichte and Garnier. 4 pam.
Htn Phil 3801.546* Schelling, Hegel, Cousin und Krug. (Marbach, G.O.) Leipzig, 1835.
Phil 3801.222 Schelling, Hegel, Fechner en de nieuwere theosophie. (Bolland, G.J.P.L.) Leiden, 1910.
Phil 3801.544.2 Schelling, ou La philosophie de la nature. (Matter, Jacques.) Paris, 1845.

Htn Phil 3801.544* Schelling, ou La philosophie de la nature. (Matter, Jacques.) Paris, 1845.
Phil 3801.320.10 Schelling; zwei Reden. (Dempf, Alois.) München, 1955.
Phil 3801.203 Schelling. (Benz, Ernst.) Zürich, 1955.
Phil 3801.232 Schelling. (Bréhier, Emile.) Paris, 1912.
Phil 3801.465.10 Schelling. (Jaspers, Karl.) München, 1955.
Phil 3801.529 Schelling. (Losacco, Michele.) Milano, 1914?
Phil 3801.895A Schelling. (Zeltner, Hermann.) Stuttgart, 1954.
Phil 3800.36 Schelling. F.W.J. von. Schelling als persönlichkeit Briefe, Reden, Aufsätze. Leipzig, 1908.
Phil 3801.837.15 Schelling: une philosophie en devenir. (Tilliette, Xavier.) Paris, 1970. 2v.
Phil 3801.465.15 Schelling. v.2. (Jaehnig, Dieter.) Pfullingen, 1966.
Phil 3800.36 Schelling als persönlichkeit Briefe, Reden, Aufsätze. (Schelling. F.W.J. von.) Leipzig, 1908.
Htn Phil 3800.5* Pamphlet box. Schelling bibliography.
Phil 3801.775.10 Schelling et la réalité finie. (Schlanger, Judith E.) Paris, 1966.
Htn Phil 3801.763.5* Schelling in München. pt.I. (Salat, Jakob.) Freiburg, 1837.
Phil 3801.763.7 Schelling in München. pt.1-2. (Salat, Jacob.) Heidelberg, 1845.
Htn Phil 3801.872* Schelling oder Hegel oder Keiner von Beyden? (Vogel, Emil F.) Leipzig, 1843.
Phil 3801.496.5 Schelling-Studien. (Ko Ktanck, Anton Mirko.) München, 1965.
Phil 3800.735 Schelling und Cotta. (Schelling, F.W.J. von.) Stuttgart, 1965.
Htn Phil 3801.612* Schelling und der Philosophie des Romantik. (Noack, Ludwig.) Berlin, 1859. 2v.
Phil 3801.612.2 Schelling und der Philosophie des Romantik. v.1-2. (Noack, Ludwig.) Berlin, 1859.
Phil 3801.982 Schelling und die Offerbarung. Leipzig, 1842.
Phil 3801.491 Schelling und die romantische Schule. (Knittermeyer, H.) München, 1929.
Htn Phil 3801.564* Schelling und die Theologie. Berlin, 1845.
Phil 3801.564.2 Schelling und die Theologie. Berlin, 1845.
Htn Phil 3801.498* Schelling und Hegel. (Krug, W.T.) Leipzig, 1835.
Htn Phil 3801.570*A Schelling und Hegel. (Michelet, Carl L.) Berlin, 1839.
Phil 3801.570.2 Schelling und Hegel. (Michelet, Carl L.) Berlin, 1839.
Htn Phil 3801.763.10* Schelling und Hegel. (Salat, Jacob.) Heidelberg, 1842.
Htn Phil 3801.846* Schelling und Hegel. (Trahndorff, Karl F.E.) Berlin, 1842.
Phil 3800.725 Schelling und Swedenborg. (Horn, F.) Zürich, 1954.
Phil 3801.749.2 Schelling Vorlesungen. (Rosenkranz, J.K.F.) Danzig, 1843.
Htn Phil 3801.749* Schelling Vorlesungen. (Rosenkranz, J.K.F.) Danzig, 1843.
Phil 3425.260 Schelling-Wollny, Kurt. Hegels Wissenschaft von der Wirklichkeit und ihre Quellen. München, 1929.
Phil 3801.437 Die Schellingische Gottes- und Freiheits - Lehre. (Groos, Friedrich.) Tübingen, 1819.
Htn Phil 3801.773* Schelling's alte und neue Philosophie. (Schwarz, J.L.) Berlin, 1844.
Phil 3801.451 Schellings Entwicklungslehre dargestellt. (Heussler, Hans.) Frankfurt, 1882.
Phil 3801.493 Schellings erste münchner Vorlesung. Inaug. Diss. (Koktanek, A.M.) München, 1959.
Phil 3801.472 Schellings Frauen: Caroline und Pauline. (Kahr-Wallerstein, C.) Bern, 1959.
Phil 3801.499 Schellings Gedichte und dichtischer Pläne. (Kunz, Hans.) Zürich, 1955.
Htn Phil 3801.197.30*A Schelling's Geistesentwicklung in Ihrem inneren Zusammenhang. (Beckers, Hubert.) München, 1875.
Phil 3801.233.8 Schellings geistige Wandlungen in den Jahren 1800-1810. (Braun, Otto.) Leipzig, 1906.
Phil 3801.233.5 Schellings geistige Wandlungen in den Jahren 1800-1810. Inaug. Diss. (Braun, Otto.) Leipzig, 1906.
Phil 3801.565 Schellings Geschichtsphilosophie in den Jahren 1799-1804. (Mehlis, Georg.) Heidelberg, 1906.
Phil 3801.774.10 Schellings Gesetz der Polarität. (Schneiter, Rudolf.) Winterthur, 1968.
Phil 3801.448 Schellings Lehre von den Letzten Dingen. (Heinrich, W.) Salzburg, 1955.
Phil 3801.879 Schellings Lehre von der Zeit. (Wieland, W.) Heidelberg, 1956.
Htn Phil 3801.697* Schellings nachgelassene Werke. (Planck, Adolf.) Erlangen, 1858.
Htn Phil 3801.979* Schellings Offenbarungsphilosophie. Drei Briefe. Berlin, 1843.
Htn Phil 3801.896* Schelling's Philosophie der Kunst. (Zimmermann, R.) Wien, 1875.
Phil 3801.410 Schelling's Philosophie der Weltalter. (Fuhrmans, H.) Düsseldorf, 1954.
Phil 3801.464 Schellings politische Anschauungen. (Jäger, G.) Berlin, 1939.
Htn Phil 3801.446* Schelling's positive Philosophie. (Hartmann, K.R.E. von.) Berlin, 1869.
Phil 3801.446.2 Schelling's positive Philosophie. (Hartmann, K.R.E. von.) Berlin, 1869.
Phil 3801.406 Schelling's positive Philosophie. Pt.1-3. (Frantz, Constantin.) Cöthen, 1879-80.
Htn Phil 3801.743* Schellings religiongeschichtliche Ansicht. Berlin, 1841.
Htn Phil 3801.801*A Schellings religionsgechichtliche Ansicht. Berlin, 1841.
Phil 3801.496 Schellings Seinslehre und Kierkegaard. (Koktanek, A.M.) München, 1962.
Phil 3801.874.2A Schelling's transcendental idealism. (Watson, John.) Chicago, 1882.
Htn Phil 3801.874* Schelling's transcendental idealism. (Watson, John.) Chicago, 1882.
Phil 3801.874.5 Schelling's transcendental idealism. 2nd ed. (Watson, John.) Chicago, 1892.
Phil 3801.780 Schellings und Hegels schwäbische Geistesahnen. (Schneider, R.) Würzburg, 1938.
Htn Phil 3801.772* Schelling's und Hegel's Verhältniss zur Naturwissenschaft. (Schleiden, M.J.) Leipzig, 1844.
Htn Phil 3801.405* Schelling's Vorlesungen in Berlin. (Frauenstädt, J.) Berlin, 1842.
Phil 3801.405.5 Schelling's Vorlesungen in Berlin. (Frauenstädt, J.) Berlin, 1842.
Phil 3800.32 Schellings Werke. (Schelling, F.W.J. von.) München, 1927-28. 5v.
Phil 3800.32.3 Schellings Werke. (Schelling, F.W.J. von.) München, 1943. 6v.
Htn Phil 3801.494* Schellingslehre. (Köppen, Friedrich.) Hamburg, 1803.
Phil 3801.494.2 Schellingslehre. (Köppen, Friedrich.) Hamburg, 1803.
Phil 270.11 Schellwein, R. Das Gesets der Causalität in der Natur. Berlin, 1876.
Phil 1718.2 Schellwien, R. Der Geist der neueren Philosophie. Leipzig, 1895.
Phil 5768.20 Schellwien, R. Der Wille, die Lebensgrundmacht. Berlin, 1879.
Phil 5768.20.15 Schellwien, R. Wille und Erkenntnis. Hamburg, 1899.
Phil 6315.2.103 Schelts van Kloosterhuis, E. Freud as ethnoloog. Proefschrift. Amsterdam, 1933.
Phil 7060.39 Schelwig, Samuel. De apparitionibus. Lipziae, 1709.
Phil 6110.12 Schema des Faserverlaufes im menschlichen Gehirn und Rückenmark. (Aeby, C.T.) Bern, 1883.
Phil 4803.435.30 Schemaly i człowiek. (Grzegorczyk, Andrzej.) Kraków, 1963.
Phil 5649.24 Le schematisme, psychologie de l'action. (Bujeau, L.V.) Paris, 1941.
Phil 1930.5.51 The scheme of literal prophecy considered. (Collins, Anthony.) London, 1727.
Htn Phil 1930.5.50* The scheme of literal prophecy considered. (Collins, Anthony.) London, 1727.
Phil 193.102 Schenach, G. Metaphysik. Innsbruck, 1856.
Phil 5645.25 Schenck, F. Über die physiologischen Grundlagen des Farbensinns. Marburg, 1906.
Phil 7080.41 Schenk, Paul. Versuch einer psychologischen Theorie des Schlafes. Inaug. Diss. Leipzig, 1928.
Phil 3805.176 Schenkel, D. Friedrich Schleiermacher, ein Lebens- und Charakterbild. Elberfeld, 1868.
Phil 282.4.9 Schenker, M. C. Batteux von seine nachahmungs Theorie in Deutsch. Leipzig, 1909.
Phil 8677.6 Scheping en voorzienigheid. (Weener, J.) Utrecht, 1899.
Phil 6128.76 Scher, Jordan. Theories of the mind. N.Y., 1962.
Phil 930.39.5 Scherbatskii, F.I. Teoriia poznaniia i logika po ucheniu pozdreishikh buddistov. Sankt Peterburg, 1903-09. 2v.
Phil 3790.1.90 Scherer, C.C. Der biologisch-psychologische Gottesbeweis bei Herman S. Reimarus. Würzburg, 1899.
Phil 3790.1.93 Scherer, C.C. Das Tier in der Philosophie des H.S. Reimarus. Diss. Würzburg, 1898.
Phil 3500.3 Scherer, G. Kritik über Kant's Subjektivität und Apriorität des Raumes und der Zeit. Frankfurt, 1871.
Phil 3450.11.390 Schérer, René. La phénoménologie des "Recherches logiques" de Husserl. Paris, 1967.
Phil 5520.515 Schérer, René. Structure et fondement de la communication humaine, essai critique sur les théories contemporaines de la communication. Thèse. Paris, 1965.
Phil 3552.474 Schering, Ernst. Leibniz und die Versöhnung der Konfessionen. Stuttgart, 1966.
Phil 5258.117 Schering, W.M. Zuschauen oder Handeln? Leipzig, 1937.
Phil 6060.76 Schermann, Rafael. Die Schrift lügt nicht! Berlin, 1929.
Phil 5627.87.2 Scherr, J. Die Gekreuzigte. 2. Aufl. Leipzig, 1874.
Phil 3850.55 Scherrer, Eduard. Wissenschaftslehre. Bern, 1968.
Phil 7082.134 Scheruer, Karl Albert. Das Leben des Traums. Berlin, 1861.
Phil 283.5 Schets eener kritische geschiedenis van het begrip natuurwet. (Clay, J.) Leiden, 1915.
Phil 5590.4 Schettler, C.H. Problems of personality traits. Chicago, 1940.
Phil 8597.3.18 Schettler, R. Samuel Reimarus zur Religion. Leipzig, 1904.
Phil 3640.278 Scheuffler, G. Friedrich Nietzsche im Dritten Reich. Erfurt, 1933.
Phil 2880.13.100 Scheurer, Pierre. An interior metaphysics. Weston, Mass., 1966.
Phil 5938.9 Scheve, G. Phrenologische Bilder. Leipzig, 1874.
Phil 3640.224 Schian, Martin. Friedrich Nietzsche und das Christentum drei Vorträge. Görlitz, 1902.
Phil 476.6 Schiarimenti sulla controversia fra spiritualismo e materialismo. (Bertini, G.M.) Torino, 1870.
Phil 4065.85 Schiattarella, R. La dottrina di Giordano Bruno. Palermo, 1888.
Phil 193.109 Schiattarella, R. Note e problemi di filosofia contemporanea. Palermo, 1891.
Phil 2520.380 Schiavo, Mario. Il problema etico in Cartesio. Rome, 1948?
Phil 845.4 Schiavone, Michel. Problemi ed aspetti dell'Umanesimo. Milano, 1969.
Phil 4110.11.30 Schiavone, Michelle. Problemi filosofia in Marsilio Ficino. Milano, 1951.
Phil 575.93 Die Schichten der Persönlichkeit. (Rothacker, E.) Leipzig, 1938.
Phil 575.93.15 Die Schichten der Persönlichkeit. 4e Aufl. (Rothacker, E.) Bonn, 1948.
Phil 818.32 Das Schicksal der Metaphysik von Thomas zu Heidegger. (Siewerth, G.) Einsiedeln, 1959.
Phil 5590.195 Schicksal und Charakter. (Ninck, M.) Wien, 1956.
Phil 3475.3.25 Schicksal und Wille. (Jaspers, Karl.) München, 1967.
Phil 6315.2.315 Die Schicksale Sigmund Freuds und J. Breners. (Koenig, K.) Stuttgart, 1962.
Phil 978.49.830 Schicksalswege zu Rudolf Steiner. 2. Aufl. (Peoppig, Fred.) Stuttgart, 1955.
Phil 3640.709 Schieder, Theodor. Nietzsche und Bismarck. Krefeld, 1963.
Phil 6128.37 Schiff, M. Leziomi di fisiologia sperimentale sul sistema nervoso. 2. ed. Firenze, 1873.
Phil 8708.40 Schiffers, Norbert. Fragen der Physik an die Theologie. 1. Aufl. Düsseldorf, 1968.
Phil 193.8 Schildener, H. Progress der Weltgeschichte. Greifswald, 1854.
Phil 5190.24 Schilder, Klaas. Zur Begriffsgeschichte des "Paradoxon". Inaug. Diss. Kampen, 1933.
Phil 6328.10.20 Schilder, Paul. Entwurf zu einer Psychiatrie auf psychoanalysischer Grundlage. Leipzig, 1925.
Phil 299.21 Schilder, Paul. Gedanken zur Naturphilosophie. Wien, 1928.
Phil 6328.10.30 Schilder, Paul. Goals and desires of man, a psychological survey of life. N.Y., 1942.
Phil 6328.10.40 Schilder, Paul. The image and appearance of the human body. N.Y., 1950.
Phil 6328.10.21 Schilder, Paul. Introduction to a psychoanalytic psychiatry. N.Y., 1928.
Phil 6328.10.10 Schilder, Paul. Das Körperschema...Bewusstsein des eigenen Körpers. Berlin, 1923.
Phil 6688.18 Schilder, Paul. Lehrbuch der Hypnose. Wien, 1926.
Phil 5258.124.5 Schilder, Paul. Medical psychology. N.Y., 1953.
Phil 5258.124 Schilder, Paul. Mind: perception and thought in their constructive aspects. N.Y., 1942.
Phil 6328.10 Schilder, Paul. Seele und Leben. Berlin, 1923.
Phil 6688.19 Schilder, Paul. Über das Wesen derHypnose. 2. Aufl. Berlin, 1922.
Phil 193.169 Schilfgaarde, P. von. Over de wijsgeerige verwondering. Assen, 1948.
Phil 5828.19 Schiller, C.H. Instinctive behavior. N.Y., 1957.

Phil 193.9.13   Schiller, F.C.S. Études sur l'humanisme. Paris, 1909.
Phil 5058.24   Schiller, F.C.S. Formal logic. London, 1912.
Phil 193.9.5A   Schiller, F.C.S. Humanism philosophical essays. London, 1903.
Phil 193.9.6   Schiller, F.C.S. Humanism philosophical essays. 2. ed. London, 1912.
Phil 193.9.15   Schiller, F.C.S. Humanismus...pragmatische Philosophie. Leipzig, 1911.
Phil 2280.7.35   Schiller, F.C.S. Humanistic pragmatism. N.Y., 1966.
Phil 5058.24.10   Schiller, F.C.S. Logic for use. London, 1929.
Phil 193.9.25   Schiller, F.C.S. Must philosophers disagree? London, 1934.
Phil 2280.7.30   Schiller, F.C.S. Our human truths. N.Y., 1939.
Phil 5070.16   Schiller, F.C.S. Problems of belief. London, 1924.
Phil 5070.16.5   Schiller, F.C.S. Problems of belief. N.Y., 1924.
Phil 193.9.2   Schiller, F.C.S. Riddles of the Sphinx. London, 1894.
Phil 193.9.3   Schiller, F.C.S. Riddles of the Sphinx. London, 1910.
Phil 193.9.9   Schiller, F.C.S. Studies in humanism. London, 1907.
Phil 193.9.18   Pamphlet box. Schiller, F.C.S.
Phil 5520.584   Schiller, Jerome Paul. I.A. Richard's theory of literature. New Haven, 1969.
Phil 5228.12   Schiller, P. von. Aufgabe der Psychologie. Wien, 1948.
Phil 8520.14   Schillers Theodizee bis zum Beginn der Kantischen Studien. (Wolff, Karl.) Leipzig, 1909.
Phil 493.4   Schilling, G. Beiträge zur Geschichte und Kritik des Materialismus. Leipzig, 1867.
Phil 3500.58   Schilling, Georg. Kants Lebenswerk als Gabe und Aufgabe. Detmold, 1924.
Phil 5258.61.3   Schilling, Gustav, of Giessen. Lehrbuch der Psychologie. Langensalza, 1913.
Phil 8708.36   Schilling, Harold K. Science and religion. N.Y., 1962.
Phil 818.24.10   Schilling, Kurt. Einfuhrung in die Geschichte der Philosophie. Heidelberg, 1949.
Phil 818.24A   Schilling, Kurt. Geschichte der Philosophie. München, 1943-44. 2v.
Phil 818.24.5   Schilling, Kurt. Geschichte der Philosophie. München, 1951. 2v.
Phil 3801.775   Schilling, Kurt. Natur und Wahrheit; Untersuchungen über Entstehung...der Schellingschen Systems. München, 1934.
Phil 818.37   Schilling, Kurt. Weltgeschichte der Philosophie. Berlin, 1964.
Phil 8968.13   Schilling, Otto. Apologie der katholischen Moral. Paderborn, 1936.
Phil 3235.117   Schilling, Werner. Feuerbach und die Religion. München, 1957.
Phil 8419.53   Schillinger, J. The mathematical basis of the arts. N.Y., 1948.
Phil 3500.63   Schilpp, P.A. Kant's pre-critical ethics. Evanston, 1938.
Phil 3500.63.2   Schilpp, P.A. Kant's pre-critical ethics. 2d ed. Evanstown, 1960.
Phil 3475.3.140   Schilpp, P.A. Karl Jaspers. Stuttgart, 1957.
Phil 187.59.80   Schilpp, P.A. The philosophy of G.E. Moore. Evanston, 1942.
Phil 187.59.82   Schilpp, P.A. The philosophy of G.E. Moore. 2. ed. N.Y., 1952.
Phil 2280.5.106.2   Schilpp, P.A. The philosophy of George Santayana. 2nd ed. N.Y., 1951.
Phil 1955.6.101   Schilpp, P.A. The philosophy of John Dewey. Evanston, 1939.
Phil 1955.6.102   Schilpp, P.A. The philosophy of John Dewey. 2d ed. N.Y., 1951.
Phil 3475.3.140.5   Schilpp, P.A. The philosophy of Karl Jaspers. 1st ed. N.Y., 1957.
Phil 2280.5.106   Schilpp, P.A. The philosophy of Santayana. Evanston, 1940.
Phil 1905.22.79   Schilpp, Paul. The philosophy of C.D. Broad. N.Y., 1959.
Phil 3160.12.7   Schilpp, Paul. The philosophy of Ernst Cassirer. N.Y., 1958.
Phil 1930.18.80   Schilpp, Paul. The philosophy of Rudolf Carnap. La Salle, 1887.
Phil 2340.10.101A   Schilpp, Paul A. The philosophy of Alfred North Whitehead. Evanston, 1941.
Phil 2340.10.127   Schilpp, Paul A. The philosophy of Alfred North Whitehead. 2nd ed. N.Y., 1951.
Phil 2255.1.100   Schilpp, Paul A. The philosophy of Bertrand Russell. Evanston, Ill., 1944.
Phil 2255.1.102   Schilpp, Paul A. The philosophy of Bertrand Russell. Evanston, Ill., 1946.
Phil 2255.1.103   Schilpp, Paul A. The philosophy of Bertrand Russell. N.Y., 1951.
Phil 2120.4.95   Schilpp, Paul A. The philosophy of C.I. Lewis. 1. ed. Facsimile. La Salle, 1968.
Phil 4872.242.80   Schilpp, Paul A. The philosophy of Sarvepalli Radhakrishnan. N.Y., 1952.
Phil 3120.30.150   Schilpp, Paul Arthur. The philosophy of Martin Buber. 1st ed. La Salle, 1967.
Phil 8419.32   Schimmelpenninck, Mary Anne. The principles of beauty as manifested in nature, art, and human character. London, 1859.
Phil 5258.65   Schindler, Ferdinand. Lehrbuch der Psychologie. Troppau, 1913.
Phil 3246.300   Schindler, I.M.T. Reflexion und Bildung in Fichte Wissenschaftslehre. Bonn, 1962.
Phil 3246.300.1   Schindler, I.M.T. Reflexion und Bildung in Fichtes Wissenschaftslehre von 1794. 1. Aufl. Düsseldorf, 1966.
Phil 5421.20.115   Schindler, Sepp. Aggressionshandlungen Jugendlicher. Wien, 1969.
Phil 5058.47.5   Schingnitz, Werner. Mensch und Begriff. Leipzig, 1935.
Phil 5058.47   Schingnitz, Werner. Prolegomenon zu einer Logik als Lehre von der Vergegrifflichten Gegenständlichkeit. Leipzig, 1931.
Phil 193.80   Schinz, Albert. Anti-pragmatism. Boston, 1909.
Phil 600.27   Schinz, Max. Die Anfänge des französischen Positivismus. Teil I. Strassburg, 1914.
Phil 3890.6.83   Schinz, Max. Die Moralphilosophie von Tetens. Leipzig, 1906.
Phil 8598.27   Schinz, Max. Wahrheit der Religion nach den neuesten Vertretern der Religionsphilosophie. Zürich, 1908.
Phil 4580.82   Schiodte, C. Betmaerkninger om den Høffdingske filosofi. København, 1900.
Phil 5058.75   Schipper, Edith Watson. Principles of applied logic. Dubuque, 1956.
Phil 3801.777   Schirnhafer, R. von. Vergleich zwischen den Lehren Schelling's und Spinoza's. Zürich, 1884.
Phil 2428.20   Schiwy, Günther. Der französische Strukturalismus. Reinbek, 1970.
Phil 6976.25   Le schizo et les langues. (Wolfson, Louis.) Paris, 1970.

Phil 6322.22   Der schizoid-dämonische Charakter. (Mauerhofer, Hugo.) Leipzig, 1930.
Phil 6956.17   Schizoid phenomena, object relations and the self. (Guntrip, Henry James Samuel.) London, 1968.
Phil 6976.20   Schizophasie in linguistischer Deutung. (Flegel, Horst.) Berlin, 1965.
Phil 6955.15   Das schizophrene Denken. (Frostig, Jakób.) Leipzig, 1929.
Phil 6954.7   Schizophrenia, the Cinderella of psychiatry. (Ellery, Reginald S.) Sidney, 1941.
Phil 6954.7.5   Schizophrenia, the Cinderella of psychiatry. (Ellery, Reginald S.) Sydney, 1944.
Phil 6322.42A   Schizophrenia, 1677. (Macalpine, Ida.) London, 1956.
Phil 6961.13   Schizophrenia. (Lundholm, Helge.) Durham, N.C., 1932.
Phil 6950.10   Schizophrenia. (Symposium on Schizophrenia.) N.Y., 1959.
Phil 6968.34   Schizophrenia as human process. (Sullivan, Harry Stack.) N.Y., 1962.
Phil 6976.5   Schizophrenia in psychoanalytic office practice. (Society of Medical Psychoanalysts.) N.Y., 1957.
Phil 28.83   The schizophrenic syndrome. N.Y. 1,1971+
Phil 6951.30   Schizophrenie. (Binswanger, Ludwig.) Pfullingen, 1957.
Phil 6961.17   The schizophreniform states. (Langfeldt, G.) Copenhagen, 1939.
Phil 3484.24.10   Schizzo storico della esegesi e critica kantiana. (Campo, M.) Varese, 1959.
Phil 5258.89.5   Schjelderup, H. Psychologie. Berlin, 1928.
Phil 5258.89   Schjelderup, H. Referat av H. Schjelderups forelaesninger over psykologi. Oslo, 192-.
Phil 1718.9.5   Schjelderup, Harald K. Filosofiens historie. Oslo, 1925.
Phil 1718.9.10   Schjelderup, Harald K. Geschichte der philosophischen Ideen von der Renaissance bis zur Gegenwart. Berlin, 1929.
Phil 1718.9   Schjelderup, Harald K. Hauptlinien der Entwicklung der Philosophie von mitte des 19. Jahrhunderts bis zur Gegenwart. n.p., n.d.
Phil 7069.62.30   Schjelderup, Harald Krabbe. Det skjulte menneske. Köbenhavn, 1962.
Phil 5627.116   Schjelderup, K. von. Die Askese; eine religionspsychologische Untersuchung. Berlin, 1928.
Phil 193.151   Schjoth, Emil. Gegenstands und verhältenislehre. Oslo, 1938.
Phil 6328.56   Schläfer-Wolfram, E. Und du wirst Getrieben. Berlin, 1933.
Phil 575.27   Schlaf, Johannes. Das absolute Individuum. Berlin, 1910.
Phil 3640.195   Schlaf, Johannes. Der "Fall" Nietzsche. Leipzig, 1907.
Phil 2885.105   Schlaf, Johannes. Kritik der Taineschen Kunsttheorie. Wien, 1906.
Phil 3640.195.5   Schlaf, Johannes. Die Kritik und mein "Fall Nietzsche". Leipzig, 1907.
Phil 7080.15   Die Schlaf- und Traumzustände der menschlichen Seele. (Spitta, H.) Tübingen, 1878.
Phil 7080.15.2   Die Schlaf- und Traumzustände der menschlichen Seele. 2. Aufl. (Spitta, H.) Tübingen, 1882.
Phil 7080.32   Der Schlaf nach seinerBedeutung. (Michaelis, A.O.) Leipzig, 1894.
Phil 7082.68   Der Schlaf und das Traumleben. (Brander, Robert.) Leipzig, 1884.
NEDL Phil 7080.11   Schlaf und Traum. (Radestock, P.) Leipzig, 1879.
Phil 3500.15   Schlaff, O. Kant's Lehre vom Genie. Göttingen, 1901.
Phil 8583.28.15   Schlagberger, Frans Xavier. Die Geschichts- und Kulturphilosophie Christopher Dawson. München, 1965?
Phil 3801.775.10   Schlanger, Judith E. Schelling et la réalité finie. Paris, 1966.
Phil 3425.366   Schlawin, H. Die Dialektik im System Hegels. Inaug. Diss. Bern, 1953.
Phil 3640.409   Schlechta, Karl. Der Fall Nietzsche. München, 1958.
Phil 3640.409.2   Schlechta, Karl. Der Fall Nietzsche. München, 1959.
Phil 3640.408   Schlechta, Karl. Nietzsches grosser Mittag. Frankfurt, 1954.
Phil 5414.40   Schlederer, Franz. Schuld, Reue und Krankheit. München, 1970.
Phil 2262.97   Schlegel, D.B. Shaftesbury and the French deists. Chapel Hill, 1956.
Phil 5374.25   Schlegel, Emil. Das Bewusstsein. Stuttgart, 1891.
Htn Phil 193.10.3*   Schlegel, Friedrich von. Die drey ersten Vorlesungen über die Philosophie des Lebens. Wien, 1827.
Htn Phil 3850.10.30*   Schlegel, Friedrich von. Die drey ersten Vorlesungen über die Philosophie des Lebens. Wien, 1827.
Phil 3850.10.50   Schlegel, Friedrich von. Lifrets philosophie. Stockholm, 1834.
Phil 193.10.15   Schlegel, Friedrich von. Neve philosophische Schriften. Frankfurt, 1935.
Phil 193.10.9   Schlegel, Friedrich von. Philosophie de la vie. Paris, 1838.
Htn Phil 193.10.10*   Schlegel, Friedrich von. Philosophie des Lebens. Wien, 1828.
Htn Phil 193.10*   Schlegel, Friedrich von. Philosophische Vorlesungen. Bonn, 1836-37. 2v.
Phil 193.10.6   Schlegel, Friedrich von. Philosophy of life. London, 1847.
Phil 193.10.7   Schlegel, Friedrich von. Philosophy of life. N.Y., 1848.
Phil 672.218   Schlegel, R. Time and the physical world. East Lansing? 1961.
Phil 9495.170.15   Schlegelberger, Bruno. Vor- und ausserehelicher Geschlechtsverkehr. Remscheid, 1970.
Phil 665.69   Schleich, C.L. Von der Seele. Berlin, 1921.
Phil 665.69.5   Schleich, C.L. Die Wunder der Seele. Berlin, 1940.
Phil 8643.27   Schleich, Carl L. Bewusstsein und Unsterblichkeit. Berlin, 1922.
Phil 8612.24   Schleich, Carl L. Das Problem des Todes. Berlin, 1921.
Phil 6615.16   Schleich, Carl Ludwig. Gedankenmacht und Hysterie. Berlin, 1922.
Phil 5258.85   Schleich, Carl Ludwig. Das ich und die Dämonien. Berlin, 1924.
Phil 5258.85.5   Schleich, Carl Ludwig. Jaget och demonierna. Stockholm, 1925.
Phil 5258.85.15   Schleich, Carl Ludwig. Von Schaltwerk der Gedanken. 47. bis 49. Aufl. Berlin, 1926.
Htn Phil 3801.772*   Schleiden, M.J. Schelling's und Hegel's Verhältniss zur Naturwissenschaft. Leipzig, 1844.
Phil 5258.206   Schleiden, Matthias Jacob. Zur Theorie des Erkennens durch den Gesichtssinn. Leipzig, 1861.
Phil 193.141   Schleier, S.T. An analysis of man and his philosophy. St. Louis, 1920.
Phil 3805.55   Schleiermacher, Friedrich. Asthetik. Berlin, 1931.
Phil 3805.75   Schleiermacher, Friedrich. Aus Schleiermacher's Leben. Berlin, 1860. 2v.
Phil 3805.33.20   Schleiermacher, Friedrich. Brief outline of the study of theology. Edinburgh, 1850.
Phil 3805.76   Schleiermacher, Friedrich. Briefe. Berlin, 1923.

Phil 3805.78   Schleiermacher, Friedrich. Briefwechsel mit J.C. Gass. Berlin, 1852.

Phil 3805.76.9   Schleiermacher, Friedrich. Briefwechsel mit seiner Braut. 2. Aufl. Gotha, 1920.

Phil 3805.32.15   Schleiermacher, Friedrich. Der christliche Glaube; nach den Grundsätzen. Berlin, 1960. 2v.

Phil 3805.32   Schleiermacher, Friedrich. Der christliche Glaube. Bd.1-2. Reutlingen, 1828.

Phil 3805.32.5   Schleiermacher, Friedrich. Der christliche Glaube. 2. Aufl. Berlin, 1830-31. 2v.

Phil 3805.32.10   Schleiermacher, Friedrich. Der christliche Glaube. 5. Aufl. Berlin, 1861. 2v.

Phil 3805.22   Schleiermacher, Friedrich. Dialektik. Berlin, 1903.

Phil 3805.37   Schleiermacher, Friedrich. Entwurf eines Systems der Sittenlehre. Berlin, 1835.

Phil 3805.20   Schleiermacher, Friedrich. Friedrich Schleiermacher. Langensalza, 1912.

Phil 3805.35   Schleiermacher, Friedrich. Grundlinien eines Kritik...Sittenlehre. Berlin, 1803.

Phil 3805.36.5   Schleiermacher, Friedrich. Grundriss der philosophischen Ethik. Berlin, 1841.

Phil 3805.36   Schleiermacher, Friedrich. Grundriss der philosophischen Ethik. Leipzig, 1911.

Phil 3805.25   Schleiermacher, Friedrich. Ideen, Reflexionen und Betrachtungen aus Schleiermachers Werken. Berlin, 1854.

Phil 3805.18   Schleiermacher, Friedrich. Kleine Schriften und Predigten. Berlin, 1969-70. 3v.

Phil 3805.33.10   Schleiermacher, Friedrich. Kurze Darstellung des theologischen Studiums. Berlin, 1811.

Phil 3805.40   Schleiermacher, Friedrich. Monologen. Berlin, 1800.

Phil 3805.41   Schleiermacher, Friedrich. Monologen. Berlin, 1868.

Phil 3805.45   Schleiermacher, Friedrich. Monologen nebst den Vorarbeiten. 2. Aufl. Leipzig, 1914.

Phil 3805.31.6   Schleiermacher, Friedrich. On religion. N.Y., 1955.

Phil 3805.31.5   Schleiermacher, Friedrich. On religion. N.Y., 1958.

Phil 3805.93   Schleiermacher, Friedrich. Philosophische Sittenlehre. Berlin, 1870.

Phil 3805.29   Schleiermacher, Friedrich. Ein poetischer Brief Schlesiermachers. Halle, 1917.

Phil 3805.34.10   Schleiermacher, Friedrich. Räthsel und Charaden. Berlin, 1874.

Phil 3805.10   Schleiermacher, Friedrich. Sämmtliche Werke. Berlin, 1826-64. 29v.

Phil 3805.12   Schleiermacher, Friedrich. Sämmtliche Werke. 2. Aufl. Berlin, 1884.

Phil 3805.76.5   Schleiermacher, Friedrich. Schleiermacher als Mensch...Briefe. Gotha, 1922. 2v.

Phil 3805.49   Schleiermacher, Friedrich. Soliloquies. Chicago, 1926.

Htn   Phil 3805.30*   Schleiermacher, Friedrich. Über die Religion. Berlin, 1799.

Phil 3805.30.2   Schleiermacher, Friedrich. Über die Religion. Berlin, 1806.

Phil 3805.30.3   Schleiermacher, Friedrich. Über die Religion. Berlin, 1821.

Phil 3805.30.4   Schleiermacher, Friedrich. Über die Religion. Berlin, 1831.

Phil 3805.30.10   Schleiermacher, Friedrich. Über die Religion. Berlin, 191-.

Phil 3805.30.12   Schleiermacher, Friedrich. Über die Religion. Hamburg, 1958.

Phil 3805.30.5   Schleiermacher, Friedrich. Über die Religion. Leipzig, 1868-69.

Phil 3805.30.12.6   Schleiermacher, Friedrich. Über die Religion. 6. Aufl. Göttingen, 1967.

Htn   Phil 3805.34*   Schleiermacher, Friedrich. Über Offenbarung und Mythologie. Berlin, 1799.

Phil 3805.50.15   Schleiermacher, Friedrich. Die Weihnachtsfeier. Basel, 1954.

Phil 3805.50.5   Schleiermacher, Friedrich. Die Weihnachtsfeier. Halle, 1806.

Phil 3805.50   Schleiermacher, Friedrich. Die Weihnachtsfeier. Leipzig, 1908.

Phil 3805.50.10   Schleiermacher, Friedrich. Die Weihnachtsfeier. 3. Ausg. Berlin, 1837.

Phil 3805.17   Schleiermacher, Friedrich. Werke. Berlin, 1924.

Phil 3805.15   Schleiermacher, Friedrich. Werke. Leipzig, 1910-11. 4v.

Phil 3805.97   Schleiermacher, personal and speculative. (Munro, R.) Paisley, 1903.

Phil 3805.153   Schleiermacher. (Dentice di Accadia, Cecilia.) Milano, 1918.

Phil 3805.205   Schleiermacher. (Luetgert, Wilhelm.) Berlin, 1934.

Phil 3805.188   Schleiermacher. (Neumann, J.) Berlin, 1936.

Phil 3805.155   Schleiermacher. (Selbie, W.B.) London, 1913.

Phil 3805.76.5   Schleiermacher als Mensch...Briefe. (Schleiermacher, Friedrich.) Gotha, 1922. 2v.

Phil 3805.177   Schleiermacher and religious education. (Osborn, A.R.) London, 1934.

Phil 3805.230   Schleiermacher filosofo dell'interpretazione. (Vattimo, Gianni.) Milano, 1968.

Phil 3805.171   Schleiermacher in der Geschichte der Staatsides. (Müsebeck, Ernst.) Berlin, 1927.

Phil 3805.172   Schleiermacher in der Zeit seines Werdens. (Wehrung, Georg.) Gütersloh, 1927.

Phil 3805.33   Schleiermacher Kurze Darstellung des theologischen Studiums. Leipzig, 1910.

Phil 3805.222   Schleiermacher on Christ and religion. (Niebuhr, Richard R.) N.Y., 1964.

Phil 3805.156   Schleiermacher und die Gegenwart. (Völter, Hans.) Heilbronn, 1919.

Phil 3805.178   Schleiermacher und seine Lieben. (Herz, Henriette de Lemos.) Magdeburg, 1910.

Phil 3805.87   Schleiermachers. (Fischer, M.) Berlin, 1899.

Phil 3805.155.7   Schleiermachers Asthetizismus in Theorie und Praxis wahrend der Jahre 1796 bis 1802. (Stammer, Martin O.) Leipzig, 1913.

Phil 3805.221   Schleiermachers christliche Sittenlehre, im Zusammenhang seines philosophisch-theologischen Systems. (Birkner, Hans J.) Berlin, 1964.

Phil 3805.235   Schleiermachers Christusglaube drei Studien. 1. Aufl. (Hirsch, Emanuel.) Gütasloh, 1968.

Phil 3805.95   Schleiermachers Entwurf einer Kritik der bisherigen Sittenlehre dargestellt. (Uhlhorn, Otto.) Oldenburg, 1894. 2v.

Phil 3805.30.15   Schleiermachers Glaubenslehre. Leipzig, 1910.

Phil 3805.179   Schleiermacher's Glaubenslehre in ihrer Abhängigkeit von seiner Philosophie. (Runze, G.) Berlin, 1877.

Phil 3805.30.20   Schleiermacher's handschriftlichen Anmerkungen zur I. Theil der Glaubenslehre. (Thönes, C.) Berlin, 1873.

Phil 3805.200   Schleiermachers Lehrjahre. (Meisner, Heinrich.) Berlin, 1934.

Phil 3805.155.5   Schleiermachers Psychologie. (Siegmund-Schultze, F.) Tübingen, 1913.

Phil 3805.185   Schleiermachers Reden über die Religion und ihre Nachwirkungen auf die evangelische Kirche Deutschlands. (Ritschl, Alfrecht.) Bonn, 1874.

Phil 3805.167   Schleiermachers Reden und Kants Predigten. (Kügelgen, C. von.) Leipzig, 1901.

Phil 3805.160   Schleiermachers religionsbegrepp. Thesis. (Lindroth, H.) Uppsala, 1926.

Phil 3805.92   Schleiermacher's Religionsbegriff. (Schürer, Emil.) Leipzig, 1868.

Phil 3805.88   Schleiermachers Religionsbegriff und religiöse Stellung zur Zeit der ersten Ausgabe der Reden, 1799-1806. Inaug. Diss. (Fuchs, Emil.) Giessen, 1900.

Phil 3805.103   Schleiermachers Religionsphilosophie. (Thilo, C.A.) Langensalza, 1906.

Phil 3805.100   Schleiermachers Sittenlehre ausführlich. (Vorlander, Franz.) Marburg, 1851.

Phil 3805.159   Schleiermacher's Stellung zum Christentum. (Ritschl, Otto.) Gotha, 1888.

Phil 3805.180   Schleiermachers System der Ästhetik. (Odebrecht, Rudolf.) Berlin, 1932.

Phil 3805.83   Schleiermachers Theologie. v.1-2. (Bender, W.) Nördlingen, 1876-78.

Phil 3805.173.5   Schleiermachers völkische Botschaft. (Ungern-Sternberg, Arthur Freiherr von.) Gotha, 1933.

Phil 3805.94   Schleiermachers Wirksamkeit als Prediger. (Schweizer, A.) Halle, 1834.

Phil 585.416   Schleissheimer, Bernhard. Der Mensch als Wissender und Glaubender. Inaug. Diss. Wien, 1970.

Phil 3585.12.85   Schlemper, Hans Otto. Reflexion und Geseteltungswille. Ratingen, 1964.

Phil 8583.28   Schlesinger, Bruno P. Christopher Dawson and the modern political crisis. Notre Dame, 1949.

Phil 299.1   Schlesinger, J. Die Entstehung der physischen...Welt. Wien, 1882.

Phil 8598.115   Schlesinger, Ruth. Probleme seines religiösen Apriori. Berlin, 1959.

Phil 8598.135.15   Schlette, Heinz Robert. Aporie und Glaube. München, 1970.

Phil 8598.135.10   Schlette, Heinz Robert. Philosophie, Theologie, Ideologie. Köln, 1968.

Phil 8598.135   Schlette, Heinz Robert. Die Religionen als Thema der Theologie. Freiburg, 1963.

Phil 8598.135.5   Schlette, Heinz Robert. Towards a theology of religions. Freiburg, 1966.

Phil 3850.29.20   Schlich, M. Gesemmelte Aufsätze, 1926-1936. Wien, 1938.

Phil 3460.87   Schlichtegroll, A.H.F. Friedrich Heinrich Jacobi. München, 1819.

Phil 3850.29.30   Schlick, M. Gesetz, Kausalität und Wahrscheinlichkeit. Wien, 1948[1938]

Phil 349.9   Schlick, Moritz. Allgemeine Erkenntnislehre. Berlin, 1918.

Phil 8893.84   Schlick, Moritz. Fragen der Ethik. Wien, 1930.

Phil 8893.84.8A   Schlick, Moritz. Problems of ethics. N.Y., 1962.

Phil 349.9.10   Schlick, Moritz. Sur le fondement de la connaissance. Paris, 1935.

Phil 5058.4   Schlötel, W. Die Logik. Göttingen, 1854.

Phil 525.155   Schloetermann, Heinz. Mystik in den Religionen der Völker. München, 1958.

Phil 2262.89   Schlosser, J.G. Über Schaftsbury von der Tugend. Basel, 1785.

NEDL   Phil 8882.7   Der Schlüssel zu Himmel und Hölle. (Heinroth, J.C.A.) Leipzig, 1839.

Phil 3500.22   Der Schlüssel zum objektiven Erkennen. (Seydel, R.) Halle, 1889.

Phil 3838.12   Schlüter, C.B. Die Lehre des Spinoza. Münster, 1836.

Phil 3808.104   Schlüter, R. Schopenhauers Philosophie. Leipzig, 1900.

Phil 818.17   Schlunk, M. Die Weltanschauung von den Griechen bis zu Hegel. Hamburg, 1921.

Phil 3790.4.81   Schlunke, Otto. Die Lehre vom Bewusstsein bei Heinrich Rickert. Inaug. Diss. Leipzig, 1911.

Phil 3850.31   Schmalenbach, H. Geist und Sein. Basel, 1939.

Phil 3500.41   Schmalenbach, H. Die Kantische Philosophie und die Religion. Göttingen, 1926.

Phil 3500.41.10   Schmalenbach, H. Kants Religion. Berlin, 1929.

Phil 3552.260   Schmalenbach, H. Leibniz. München, 1921.

Phil 9495.130   Schmalhausen, S.D. Why we misbehave. Garden City, N.Y., 1928.

Phil 9495.130.7   Schmalhausen, S.D. Why we misbehave. N.Y., 1929.

Phil 3425.475   Schmandt, Jürgen. Hegel Ethik aus dem Geist der Religion. Bonn, 1957.

Phil 5828.9   Schmarda, L.K. Andeutungen aus dem Seelenleben der Thiere. Wien, 1846.

Phil 3552.118   Schmarsow, A. Justus-Georgius Schottelius i. Leibniz und Schottelius. Strassburg, 1877.

Phil 5585.105   Schmeidler, G. ESP and personality patterns. New Haven, 1958.

Phil 7160.5   Schmeidler, Gertrude R. Extra-sensory perception. N.Y., 1969.

Phil 1123.11   Schmekel, A. Forschungen. Berlin, 1938.

Phil 1200.7   Schmekel, A. Die Philosophie der mittleren Stoa. Berlin, 1892.

Phil 193.153   Schmick, J.H. Geist oder Stoff? Leipzig, 1889.

Phil 3425.123   Schmid, Aloys. Entwicklungsgeschichte der Hegel'schen Logik. Regensburg, 1858.

Phil 165.5   Schmid, Bastian. Philosophisches Lesebuch zum Gebrauch an höheren Schulen und zum Selbststudium. Leipzig, 1906.

Phil 5828.16.5   Schmid, Bastian. Das Tier in seinen Spielen. Leipzig, 1919.

Phil 5828.16   Schmid, Bastian. Das Tier und Wir. Leipzig, 1916.

Phil 2725.2.130   Schmid, Beat. L'espérance et l'itinéraire de la certitude chez Lamennais. Berne, 1970.

Phil 5258.82   Schmid, C.C.E. Empirische Psychologie. Jena, 1791.

Phil 8893.61.5   Schmid, C.C.E. Versuch einer Moralphilosophie. Jena, 1790.

Phil 8893.61   Schmid, C.C.E. Versuch einer Moralphilosophie. 2. Ausg. Jena, 1792.

Phil 3460.86A   Schmid, F.A. Friedrich Heinrich Jacobi. Heidelberg, 1908.

Phil 193.11   Schmid, F.X. Entwurf eines Systems der Philosophie. v.1-3. Wien, 1863-1868. 2v.

Phil 8893.29   Schmid, G.L. Traités sur divers sujets. n.p., 1760.

Phil 193.12   Schmid, J.H. Vorlesungen...Wesen der Philosophie. Stuttgart, 1836.

Phil 3500.4.5   Schmid, K.C.E. Critik der reinen Vernunft. Jena, 1784.

Phil 3500.4   Schmid, K.C.E. Wörterbuch zum leichtern Gebrauch der Kantischen Schriften. Jena, 1788.

Phil 3500.4.3   Schmid, K.C.E. Wörterbuch zum leichtern Gebrauch der Kantischen Schriften. 3. Ausg. Jena, 1795.

Phil 193.13   Schmid, L. Grundzüge der Einleitung in die Philosophie. Giessen, 1860.

Phil 2520.162   Schmid, Paul J. Die Prinzipien der menschischen Erkenntniss nach Descartes. Leipzig, 187-?

Phil 559.2   Schmida-Wöllersdorfer, Susanna. Perspektiven des Seins. München, 1968. 2v.

Phil 3475.3.125   Schmidhauser, N. Allgemeine Wahrheit und existentielle Wahrheit. Bonn, 1953.

Phil 7140.8.5   Schmidkung, Hans. Psychologie der Suggestion. Stuttgart, 1892.

Htn   Phil 3801.774*   Schmidt, A. Beleuchtung der neuen Schellingschen Lehre. Berlin, 1843.

Phil 978.88   Schmidt, A.N. Iz rukopisei Anny Nikolaevny Shmidt. Moskva, 1916.

Phil 525.14   Schmidt, C. Les libertins spirituels. Bale, 1876.

Phil 3425.360   Schmidt, E. Hegels Lehre von Gott. Gütersloh, 1952.

Phil 5258.43   Schmidt, E. Zum Begriff und Sitz der Seele. Freiburg, 1897.

Phil 818.12   Schmidt, Edward. Umrisse zur Geschichte der Philosophie. Berlin, 1839.

Phil 3246.234   Schmidt, Erich. Fichtes Reden an die deutsche Nation. Berlin, 1908.

Phil 400.42   Schmidt, F.J. Der philosophische Sinn. Göttingen, 1912.

Phil 400.22   Schmidt, F.J. Zur Wiedergeburt des Idealismus. Leipzig, 1908.

Phil 9530.8   Schmidt, F.L. An object in life. N.Y., 1889.

Phil 349.35   Schmidt, Franz. Kleine Logik der Geisteswissenschaften. München, 1938.

Phil 193.175   Schmidt, Franz. Ordnungslehre. München, 1956.

Phil 5520.465   Schmidt, Franz. Zeichen und Wirklichkeit. Stuttgart, 1966.

Phil 3425.562   Schmidt, G. Hegel in Nürnberg. Tübingen, 1960.

Phil 2520.355   Schmidt, Gerhart. Aufklärung und Metaphysik. Die Neubegründung des Wissens durch Descartes. Tübingen, 1965.

Phil 3500.36   Schmidt, H. Immanuel Kants Leben. Halle, 1858.

Phil 3425.601   Schmidt, H. Verheissung und Schrecken der Freiheit. Stuttgart, 1964.

Phil 5066.160   Schmidt, H.A. Mathematische Gesetze der Logik. Berlin, 1960.

Phil 1750.11   Schmidt, H.J. Geschichte der Romantik...philosophische Geschichte. Leipzig, 1850. 2v.

Phil 8598.77   Schmidt, H.W. Zeit und Ewigkeit. Gutersloh, 1927.

Phil 103.3   Schmidt, Heinrich. Philosophisches Wörterbuch. Leipzig, 1912.

Phil 103.3.30   Schmidt, Heinrich. Philosophisches Wörterbuch. N.Y., 1945.

Phil 103.3.25   Schmidt, Heinrich. Philosophisches Wörterbuch. Stuttgart, 1943.

Phil 103.3.20   Schmidt, Heinrich. Philosophisches Wörterbuch. 9. Aufl. Leipzig, 1934.

Phil 103.3.30.5   Schmidt, Heinrich. Philosophisches Wörterbuch. 11. Aufl. Stuttgart, 1951.

Phil 103.3.30.10   Schmidt, Heinrich. Philosophisches Wörterbuch. 13. Aufl. Stuttgart, 1955.

Phil 103.3.31   Schmidt, Heinrich. Philosophisches Wörterbuch. 14. Aufl. Stuttgart, 1957.

Phil 510.1.39   Schmidt, Heinrich. Was wir Ernst Haeckel Verdanken. Leipzig, 1914. 2v.

Phil 2070.143   Schmidt, Hermann. Der Begriff der Erfahrungskontinuität bei William James. Heidelberg, 1959.

Phil 3850.25.80   Schmidt, Hugo. Die Lehre von der psychologischen Kausalität in der Philosophie Ludwig Strümpells. Inaug. Diss. Leipzig, 1907.

Phil 3552.93   Schmidt, J. Leibnitz und Baumgarten. Halle, 1875.

Phil 974.3.55   Schmidt, J.W. Recht und Unrecht der Anthroposophie. Göttingen, 1922.

Phil 8598.86   Schmidt, K. From science to God. 1. ed. N.Y., 1944.

Phil 3500.16   Schmidt, Karl. Beiträge zur Entwicklung der Kant'schen Ethik. Inaug. Diss. Marburg, 1900.

Phil 3500.16.5   Schmidt, Karl. Beiträge zur Entwicklung der Kant'schen Ethik. Inaug. Diss. Marburg, 1900.

Phil 193.146   Schmidt, Karl. The creative I and the Divine. N.Y., 1937.

Phil 493.12   Schmidt, Karl. Zur Überwindung des wissenschaftlichen Materialismus. Basel, 1968.

Phil 9070.67   Schmidt, Karl Otto. Wunder der Lebenskunst. Büdingen, 1959.

Phil 1145.18   Schmidt, L. Die Ethik der alten Griechen. Berlin, 1882.

Phil 1145.18.1   Schmidt, L. Hé éthiké tón archaión Hellénón. Athenas, 1901.

Phil 3415.85   Schmidt, O. Die naturwissenschaftlichen Grundlagen der Philosophie des Unbewussten. Leipzig, 1877.

Phil 2885.90   Schmidt, O.A. Hippolyte Taines Theorie. Halle, 1936.

Phil 5465.48   Schmidt, Otto. Zur revision der Eidetek. Marburg, 1933.

Phil 3640.855   Schmidt, Otto Ernst. Nietzsche der falsche Prophet. Leipzig, 1914.

Phil 3805.162   Schmidt, P. Spinoza und Schleiermacher. Berlin, 1868.

Phil 2340.10.200   Schmidt, Paul Frederic. Perception and cosmology in Whitehead's philosophy. New Brunswick, 1967.

Phil 3925.11.50   Schmidt, R.H. Peter Wust. Saarbrücken, 1954.

Phil 5520.580.5   Schmidt, Siegfried J. Bedeutung und Begriff. N.Y., 1969.

Phil 5520.580   Schmidt, Siegfried J. Die Beschreibung des Zusammenhangs von Sprache und Denken in der Sprachphilosophie von Locke bis Wittgenstein. n.p., 1965.

Phil 8419.67   Schmidt, Siegfried Josef. Asthetische Prozesse. Köln, 1971.

Phil 1750.860   Schmidt, Siegfried Josef. Sprache und Denken als sprachphilosophisches Problem von Locke bis Wittgenstein. Den Haag, 1968[1969].

Phil 5643.180   Schmidt, Udo. Figurale Nachwirkungen auf Kinästhetischen Gebeit bei Lageveränderung von Objekt und tastender Hand. Frankfurt, 1970.

Phil 9075.23   Schmidt, W. Das Gewissen. Leipzig, 1889.

Phil 1350.10   Schmidt, W.A. Geschichte der Denk- und Glaubensfreiheit. Berlin, 1847.

Phil 3425.318   Schmidt, Werner. Hegel und die Idee der Volksordnung. Leipzig, 1944.

Phil 665.24   Schmidt, Wilhelm. Der Kampf um die Seele. Gütersloh, 1909.

Phil 6315.2.86   Schmidt, Wilhelm. Der Ödipus-Komplex der Freudschen Psychoanalyse. Berlin, 1929.

Phil 8673.7   Schmidt, Wilhelm. L'origine de l'idée de Dieu. pt.1. Paris, 1910.

Phil 5520.18.5   Schmidt, William A. An experienced study in the psychology of reading. Theses. Chicago, 1917.

Phil 2520.115   Schmidt aus Schwarzenberg, X. René Descartes und seine Reform der Philosophie. Nördlingen, 1859.

Phil 3450.11.80   Schmidt Degener, H. Proeve eener ver gelijkende studie over Plato en Husserl. Groningen, 1924.

Phil 3425.224   Schmidt-Japing, J.W. Die Bedeutung der person Jesu...Hegel. Göttingen, 1924.

Phil 3500.5.30   Schmidt-Phiseldek, C. Briefe ästhelischen Inhalts. Altona, 1797.

Phil 3500.5   Schmidt-Phiseldek, C. Criticae ratien. Purae expositio systematica. Hafniae, 1796.

Phil 3246.247   Schmidt-Warneck, J. von. Die Sociologie Fichte's. Berlin, 1884.

Phil 6128.82   Schmidtke, Heinz. Die Ermüdung; Symptome, Theorien, Messversache. Bern, 1965.

Phil 8419.16   Schmied, W. Das Poetische in der Kunst. Nürnberg, 1960.

Phil 5258.38.5   Schmied-Kowarzik, W. Umriss einer neuen analytischen Psychologie. 2. Aufl. Teil I. Leipzig, 1928.

Phil 5258.38   Schmied-Kowarzik, W. Umrisz einer neuen analytischen Psychologie. Leipzig, 1912.

Phil 5520.38   Schmieder, A. Anregungen zur psychologischen Betrachtung der Sprache. Langensalza, 1902.

Phil 193.111   Schmieder, J. Einführung in System und Geschichte der Philosophie. Leipzig, 1921.

Phil 1050.19   Schmiedl, A. Studien über jüdische, Insonders jüdisch-arabische Religionsphilosophie. Wien, 1969.

Phil 4196.80   Schmitt, Charles B. Gianfrancesco Pico della Mirandola, 1469-1533. The Hague, 1967.

Phil 3425.117   Schmitt, E.H. Das Geheimniss der hegelschen Dialektik. Halle, 1888.

Phil 193.77   Schmitt, Eugen H. Kritik der Philosophie. Leipzig, 1908.

Phil 5258.196   Schmitt, Friedrich. ABC des Helfens. Stuttgart, 1965.

Phil 3450.19.445   Schmitt, Richard. Martin Heidegger on being human. N.Y., 1969.

Phil 1750.115.160   Schmitz, Hermann. Subjektivität; Beiträge zur Phänomenologie und Logik. Bonn, 1968.

Phil 193.247   Schmitz, Hermann. System der Philosophie. v.1-3. Pt.1-2. Bonn, 1964. 5v.

Phil 8735.50   Schmitz, Josef. Disput über das teleologische Denken. Mainz, 1960.

Phil 3428.164   Schmitz, Josef Nikolaus. Herbart Bibliographie, 1842-1963. Weinheim, 1964.

Phil 1925.82   Schmitz, Kurt J. Cudworth und der Platonismus. Diss. Bonn, 1919.

Phil 6328.12   Schmitz, O.A.H. Psychoanalyse und Yoga. Darmstadt, 1923.

Phil 510.152   Schmitz, Oscar A.H. Die Weltanschauung des Halbgebildeten. München, 1914.

Phil 193.82   Schmitz-Dumont, A. Natur Philosophie als exakte Wissenschaft. Leipzig, 1895.

Phil 349.5   Schmitz-Dumont, O. Die mathematischen Elemente der Erkenntnisstheorie. Berlin, 1878.

Phil 2905.1.495   Schmitz-Moormann, Karl. Das Weltbild Teilhard de Chardins. Köln, 1966.

Phil 8893.145   Schmoebz, Franz Martin. Das Naturgesetz und seine dynamische Kraft. Freiburg, 1959.

Phil 5628.52.5   Schmöger, Karl Erhard. Leben der Gottseligen Anna Katharina Emmerich. Freiburg, 1885.

Phil 1020.1   Schmölders, A. Essai...Ecoles philosophiques chez les Arabes. Paris, 1882.

Phil 9450.60   Schmölz, Franz Martin. Chance und Dilemma der politischen Ethik. Köln, 1966.

Phil 3552.275   Schmoger, F. Leibniz in seiner Stellung zur tellurischen Physik. München, 1901.

Phil 3838.22   Schmoldt, H. Der Spinozastreit. Inaug. Diss. Würzburg, 1938.

Phil 8673.30   Schmucker, Josef. Die primären Quellen des Gottesglaubens. Freiburg, 1967.

Phil 3500.88   Schmucker, Josef. Das Problem der Kontingenz der Welt. Freiburg, 1969.

Phil 5258.6   Schmucker, S.S. Psychology. N.Y., 1842.

Phil 5643.90   Schmülling, Wilhelm. Aufdeckung latenter eidetischer Anlagen und des integrierton Typus mit der Intermittenz-Methode. Inaug. Diss. Marburg, 1927.

Phil 2675.6.80   Schmugge, Ludwig. Johannes von Jandun. Stuttgart, 1966.

Phil 600.64   Schnaedelbach, Herbert. Erfahrung, Begründung und Reflexion. 1. Aufl. Frankfurt, 1971.

Phil 525.238   Schnapper, Edith B. The inward Odyssey. London, 1965.

Phil 3450.29.85   Schnarwiler, W. Theodor Haeckers christliches Menschenbild. Frankfurt, 1962.

Phil 193.119   Schnass, F. Einführung in die Philosophie. Osterwieck, 1928.

Phil 6906.5   Schneck, Jerome M. A history of psychiatry. Springfield, Ill., 1960.

Phil 3800.12   Schneeberger, G. Friederich Wilhelm Joseph von Schelling. Bern, 1954.

Phil 3450.19.245   Schneeberger, Guido. Nachlese zu Heidegger. Bern, 1962.

Phil 5625.106   Schneersohn, Fischel. Der Weg zum Menschen. Berlin, 1928.

Phil 6060.84   Schneevoigt, Ihno. Die graphologische Intelligenzdiagnose. Bonn, 1968.

Phil 2138.170   Schneewind, Jerome B. Mill, a collection of critical essays. Notre Dame, 1969.

Phil 5270.20   Schneewind, Klaus Alfred. Methodisches Denken in der Psychologie. Bern, 1969.

Phil 299.9   Schnehen, W. Energetische Weltanschauung? Leipzig, 1908.

Phil 3415.109   Schnehen, W. von. Eduard von Hartmann. Stuttgart, 1929.

Phil 3500.71   Schneiberger, Guido. Kants Konzeption der Modalbegriffe. Basel, 1952.

Phil 672.30   Schneid, Mathias. Die philosophische Lehre von Zeit und Raum. Mainz, 1886.

Phil 1535.34   Schneid, Mathias. Spezielle Metaphysik im Geiste des Heil. Paderborn, 1890-92. 2v.

Phil 6060.5   Schneidemühl, Georg. Handschrift und Charakter. Leipzig, 1911.

Phil 6060.5.2   Schneidemühl, Georg. Die Handschriftenbeurteilung. 2e Aufl. Leipzig, 1918.

Phil 1504.17.4   Schneider, A. Die abendländische Spekulation. v.17, pt.4. Münster, 1915.

Phil 1504.4.5A   Schneider, A. Die Psychologie Alberts des Grossen. v.4, pt.5-6. v.1 rejected 1971. Münster, 1906.

Phil 193.76   Schneider, Albert. Wirklichkeiten. Strassburg, 1910.

Phil 1523.8   Schneider, Artur. Die Erkenntnislehre bei Beginn der Scholastik. Fulda, 1921.

Phil 1535.16   Schneider, C.M. Das Wissen Gottes. v.1-4. Regensburg, 1884-86. 3v.

Phil 6968.23   Schneider, Carl. Die Psychologie der Schizophrenen und ihre Bedeutung für die Klinik der Schizophrenie. Leipzig, 1930.

Phil 8419.11   Schneider, E. Aesthetic motive. N.Y., 1939.

Phil 5627.82   Schneider, E. Les raisons du coeur. Paris, 1907.

Phil 193.190   Schneider, Erich. Auch ein Weg zur Philosophie. Berlin, 1947.

Phil 1718.27   Schneider, F. Philosophie der Gegenwart. München, 1953.

Phil 349.42   Schneider, Friedrich. Die haupt Probleme der Erkenntnistheorie. München, 1959.

Phil 349.42.5   Schneider, Friedrich. Kennen und Erkennen. 2. Aufl. Bonn, 1967.

Phil 9420.4   Schneider, G.H. Freud und Leid des Menschengeschlechte. Stuttgart, 1883.

Phil 5768.1   Schneider, G.H. Der menschliche Wille. Berlin, 1882.

Phil 5828.3   Schneider, G.H. Der thierische Will. Leipzig, 1880.

Phil 5635.21   Schneider, G.H. Über die Empfindung der Ruhe. Zürich, 1876.

Phil 193.99   Schneider, H. Metaphysik als exakte Wissenschaft. Pt.1-3. Leipzig, 1919-1921.

Phil 1818.8   Schneider, H.W. A history of American philosophy. N.Y., 1946.

Phil 1818.8.2   Schneider, H.W. A history of American philosophy. 2nd ed. N.Y., 1963.

Phil 8598.78   Schneider, H.W. Meditations in season on the elements of Christian philosophy. N.Y., 1938.

Phil 8893.48   Schneider, H.W. Science and social progress. Lancaster, Pa., 1920.

Phil 630.57   Schneider, H.W. Sources of contemporary philosophical realism in America. Indianapolis, 1964.

Phil 9450.28   Schneider, H.W. Three dimensions of public morality. Bloomington, Ind., 1956.

Phil 8893.110   Schneider, Herbert W. Morals for mankind. Columbia, 1960.

Phil 193.236   Schneider, Herbert Wallace. Ways of being. N.Y., 1962.

Phil 5828.6.5   Schneider, K.C. Tierpsychologisches Praktikum. Leipzig, 1912.

Phil 5828.6   Schneider, K.C. Vorlesungen über Tierpsychologie. Leipzig, 1909.

Phil 299.13   Schneider, K.C. Die Welt wie sie Jetzt ist und wie sie sein Wird. Wien, 1917.

Phil 3120.8.94   Schneider, Karl. Zur Kritik der Urteilslehre Franz Brentanos. Heidelberg, 1915.

Phil 6328.14.2   Schneider, Kurt. Die psychopathischen Personlichkeiten. 2. Aufl. Leipzig, 1928.

Phil 8643.1   Schneider, L. Die Unsterblichkeitsidee im Glauben. Regensburg, 1870.

Phil 8598.136   Schneider, Louis. Religion, culture and society. N.Y., 1964.

Phil 3790.4.82   Schneider, Max. Die erkenntnistheoretischen Grundlagen in Rickerts Lehre von der Transzendenz. Inaug. Diss. Dresden, 1918.

Phil 3500.6   Schneider, O. Die psychologische Entwickelung des Apriori...Kants Kritik der reinen Vernunft. Bonn, 1883.

Phil 3018.22   Schneider, P. Deutschen Philosophen des 19. Jahrhunderts. Berlin, 1927.

Phil 193.244   Schneider, Peter K. Die Begründung der Wissenschaften durch Philosophie und Kybernetik. Stuttgart, 1966.

Phil 705.62   Schneider, Peter K. Die Wissenschaftsbegrundende Funktion der Transzendent alphilosophie. Freiburg, 1965.

Phil 3801.780   Schneider, R. Schellings und Hegels schwäbische Geistesahnen. Würzburg, 1938.

Phil 1980.4.30   Schneider, R.E. Positivism in the United States. Rosario, 1946.

Phil 8417.3.15   Schneider, René. L'esthétique classique chez Quatremère. Paris, 1910.

Phil 8417.3.20   Schneider, René. Quatremère de Quincy et son intervention dans les arts, 1788-1830. Paris, 1910.

Phil 3850.14.85   Schneider, Theodor. Teleologie als theologische Kategorie bei Herman Schell. Essen, 1966.

Phil 6980.674.10   Schneider, Ulment Victor. Music and medicine; inaugural lecture. Johannesburg, 1964. 2v.

Phil 3808.173   Schneider, W. Schopenhauer. Vienna, 1937.

Phil 8893.47.2   Schneider, Wilhelm. Göttliche Weltordnung und religionslose Sittlichkeit. Paderborn, 1909.

Phil 7060.101   Schneider, Wilhelm. Der neuere Geisterglaube. Paderborn, 1882.

Phil 8419.51   Schneiderfranken, J.A. Aus Meiner Malerwerkstatt. Basel, 1932.

Phil 8419.54   Schneiderfranken, J.A. Das Reich der Kunst. Basel, 1933.

VPhil 9070.130   Schneiderfranken, Joseph Anton. Der Weg meiner Schüler. Basel, 1932.

Phil 5400.164   Schneiders, A.A. The anarchy of feeling. N.Y., 1963.

Phil 6128.77   Schneiders, Alexander A. Personality dynamics and mental health. N.Y., 1965.

Phil 3475.3.210   Schneiders, Werner. Karl Jaspers in der Kritik. Bonn, 1965.

Phil 3890.8.115   Schneiders, Werner. Recht. Münster, 1961.

Phil 299.20   Schneidewin, M. Die Unendlichkeit der Welt. Berlin, 1900.

Phil 193.96   Schneidkunz, H. Philosophische Propädeutik in neuster Literatur. Halle, 1917.

Phil 3801.774.10   Schneiter, Rudolf. Schellings Gesetz der Polarität. Winterthur, 1968.

Phil 6328.15   Schnell, János. Eredmények a magyar kiaérleti gyógypedagógiai és orvosi psychologia. Budapest, 1929.

Phil 3552.442   Schnelle, H. Zeichensysteme zur wissenschaftlichen Darstellung. Stuttgart, 1962.

Phil 3850.32.80   Schneller, Martin. Zurischen Romantik und Faschismus. 1. Aufl. Stuttgart, 1970.

Phil 6328.34   Schnetze-Niemann, M. Schöpferische Gestaltung aus dem Unbewussten. München, 1953.

Htn   Phil 6100.10*   Schnitte durch das centrale Nervensystem des Menschen. (Kronthal, P.) Berlin, 1892.

Phil 818.27   Schnittkind, H.T. Living biographies of great philosophers. Garden City, 1941.

Phil 3850.40   Schnitzler, Otto. Von der Feststellung. Bonn, 1953.

Phil 525.103   Schnur, H.C. Mystic rebels. N.Y., 1949.

Phil 2045.133   Schnur, R. Individualismus und Absolutismus. Berlin, 1963.

Phil 193.79   Schnyder, Otto. Philosophische Reden. Zürich, 1916.

Phil 730.15   Schobinger, J.P. Vom Sein der Universalien. Winterthur, 1958.

Phil 3018.35   Schoch, Otto D. Der Völherbundsgedanke zur Zeit. Zürich, 1960.

Phil 8673.13   Schock, Adolph. The problem of God's identity in cosmic change. Chicago, 1932.

Phil 5058.98   Schock, Rolf. Logics without existence assumptions. Uppsala, 1968.

Phil 3018.18   Schod, J.B. Geschichte der Philosophie unserer Zeit. Jena, 1800.

Phil 193.14   Schoebel, C. Philosophie de la raison pure. Paris, 1865.

Phil 3640.374   Schoeck, H. Nietzsches Philosophie. Tübingen, 1948.

Phil 5413.16.5   Schoeck, Helmut. Envy; a theory of social behaviour. London, 1969.

Phil 5413.16   Schoeck, Helmut. Der Neid. Freiburg, 1966.

Phil 8416.31   Schöhiedszon en levensvijsheid. (Pierson, A.) Arnhem, 1886.

Phil 3428.158   Schoel, A. Johann Friedrich Herbart's philosophische Lehre von der Religion. Dresden, 1884.

Phil 299.12   Schoeler, H. von. Kritik der wissenschaftlichen Erkenntnis. Leipzig, 1898.

Phil 510.18   Schoeler, Heinrich von. Probleme. Leipzig, 1900.

Phil 3500.77   Schoeler, Wilhelm. Die transzendentale Einheit der Apperzeption von Immanuel Kant. Bern, 1958.

Phil 5520.55   Schölkopf, H. Sinn; eine philosophische Untersuchung. Inaug. Diss. Metzingen, 1931.

Phil 8598.134   Schoell, F. Heimkehr Gottes in seine Wirklichkeit. Erbstetten, 1962.

Phil 8893.120   Schoellgen, W. Konkrete Ethik. Düsseldorf, 1961.

Phil 3565.86   Schoen, H. La métaphysique de Hermann Lotze. Paris, 1902.

Phil 3500.7   Schön, L.F. Philosophie transcendentale...Kant. Paris, 1831.

Phil 5258.102A   Schoen, M. Human nature; a first book in psychology. N.Y., 1930.

Phil 8419.45   Schoen, Max. Art and beauty. N.Y., 1932.

Phil 9495.169   Schön wieder ein Aufklärungsbuch? (Schaetzing, Eberhard.) Hamburg, 1969.

Phil 6315.2.430   Schoenan, Walter. Sigmund Freuds Prosa. Stuttgart, 1968.

Phil 5645.65   Schoenborn-Buchheim, Elisabeth. Experimentelle Untersuchungen den Eindruckscharakter von Einzelfarben. Freiburg, 1963?

Phil 299.26   Schöndorfer, Ulrich A. Philosophie des Materie. 1. Aufl. Graz, 1954.

Phil 3500.40   Schöndorffer, O. Kants Leben und Lehre. Leipzig, 1924.

Phil 5893.2   Schoene, Wolfgang. Über die Psychoanalyse in der Ethnologie. Dortmund, 1966.

Phil 8405.5   Das Schöne. (Eleutheropoulos, Abroelas.) Berlin, 1905.

Phil 8060.6   Das schöne als Weltanschauung. (Standinger, J.) Wien, 1948.

Phil 8422.7.10   Das Schöne und die Kunst. (Vischer, F.T.) Stuttgart, 1898.

Phil 6045.19   Ein schönes Büchlin der kunst Chiromantia dess Wolgelrten Magistri Andree Corvi von Mivandula. (Corvi, Andreas.) Strassburg, 1964.

Phil 8408.11   Schönheit; ein Versuch. (Haecker, T.) Leipzig, 1936.

Phil 8408.10   Schönheit; ein Versuch. 3. Aufl. (Haecker, T.) München, 1953.

Phil 181.59   Schönheit, Güte, Zweck. 1. Teil: Kant und Schopenhauer. (Germer, Hugo.) Berlin, 1908.

Phil 8407.18.5   Die Schönheit. (Gleichen-Russwurm, A.) Stuttgart, 1916?

Phil 8423.28   Die Schönheit und das Böse. (Wiegand, Anke.) München, 1967.

Phil 2038.81   Schoenlank, B. Hartley und Priestley. Photoreproduction. Halle, 1882.

Phil 165.393   Schoenman, Ralph. Bertrand Russell, philosopher of the century. London, 1967.

Phil 6109.4   Schoenpflug, Wolfgang. Methoden der Aktivierungsforschung. Bern, 1969.

Phil 6315.2.160   Schoenwald, R.L. Freud. 1st ed. N.Y., 1956.

Phil 8612.42   Schoepf, Bernhard. Das Tötungsrecht bei den frühchristlichen Schriftstellern. Regensburg, 1958.

Phil 177.104   Das Schöpferische. (Cysarz, Herbert.) Halle, 1943.

Phil 2475.1.73   Schöpferische Entwicklung. (Bergson, Henri.) Jena, 1921.

Phil 341.14   Schöpferische Erkenntnis. (Keyserling, H. Graf von.) Darmstadt, 1922.

Phil 5465.121   Schöpferische Freiheit. 2. Aufl. (Metzger, Wolfgang.) Frankfurt, 1962.

Phil 6328.34   Schöpferische Gestaltung aus dem Unbewussten. (Schnetze-Niemann, M.) München, 1953.

Phil 180.34   Schöpferische Indifferenz. (Friedlaender, S.) München, 1918.

Phil 5590.305   Der schöpferische Mensch. (Neumann, Erich.) Zürich, 1959.

Phil 5520.275   Schöpferische Sprache und Rhythmus. (Mayer, Felix.) Berlin, 1959.

Phil 3800.57   Schöpferisches Handeln. Herausgegeben und Eingeleitet von Emil Fuchs. (Schelling, F.W.J. von.) Jena, 1907.

Phil 978.49.745   Die Schöpfung der Welt und des Menschen. (Steiner, R.) Dornach, 1969.

Phil 287.1   Schöpfung and Chaos. (Gunkel, H.) Göttingen, 1895.

Phil 193.120   Schöpfung und Mensch. Hamburg, 1871.

Phil 400.76   Der Schöpfungsgang des Geistes. Theil I. (Spann, Othmar.) Jena, 1928.

Phil 400.76.2   Der Schöpfungsgang des Geistes. 2. Aufl. (Spann, Othmar.) Graz, 1969.

Phil 365.58   Schöpfungsglaube und Endzeiterwartung. (Benz, Ernst.) München, 1965.

Phil 1504.11.5   Das Schöpfungsproblem bei Moses Maimonides. v.11, pt.5. (Rohner, A.) Münster, 1913.

Phil 585.90   Schoeps, H.J. Was ist der Mensch? Göttingen, 1960.

Phil 5593.54.20   Schofer, Roy. Psychoanalytic interpretation in Rorschach testing. N.Y., 1954.

Phil 2490.87   Schoff, W.F. A neglected chapter in the life of Comte. Philadelphia, 1896.

Phil 6128.15.3   Schofield, A.T. The force of mind. N.Y., 1903.

Phil 7069.20.298   Schofield, A.T. Modern spiritism. London, 1920.

Phil 5722.16   Schofield, A.T. The unconscious mind. London, 1898.

Phil 5722.16.2   Schofield, A.T. The unconscious mind. 2. ed. London, 1899.

Phil 6980.674.25   Schofield, William. Psychotherapy. Englewood Cliffs, N.J., 1964.

Phil 9490.2   The scholar in politics. (Olney, R.) Philadelphia, 1896.

Phil 1540.8   The scholastic theory of the species sensibilis. (Knappe, O.F.) Washington, 1915.

Phil 1520.5.10   Scholasticism. (Pieper, Josef.) N.Y., 1960.

Phil 1522.3.3   Scholasticism. (Rickaby, Joseph.) N.Y., 1908.

Phil 1522.3   Scholasticism. (Rickaby, Joseph.) London, 1908.

Phil 2750.11.76   Scholasticism and politics. (Maritain, Jacques.) N.Y., 1940.

Phil 1527.1.9   Scholasticism old and new. (Wulf, M. de.) Dublin, 1910.

Phil 1527.1.9.5   Scholasticism old and new. (Wulf, M. de.) N.Y., 1907.

Phil 1540.60   Scholastick Lexicon. (Axters, Stephanus.) Antwerpen, 1937.

Phil 1507.8   Scholastico ratione historico-critica instaurada. (Congressus Scholasticus Internationalis, Rome.) Romae, 1951.

Phil 1510.10   Scholastik, Barock exakte Wissenschaften. (Fleckenskein, J.O.) Einsiedeln, 1949.

Phil 1520.5.5   Scholastik. (Pieper, Josef.) München, 1960.

Phil 1527.2   Die Scholastik des späteren Mittelalters. (Werner, Karl.) Wien, 1881. 4v.

Phil 640.2   Die Scholastiker. (Wichmann, Ottomar.) München, 1921.

Htn   Phil 1845.2.30*   The scholemaster. (Ascham, Roger.) London, 1571.

Phil 308.4 Scholes, Robert E. The philosopher critic. Tulsa, Okla., 1970.

Phil 9075.94 Scholl, Robert. Das Gewissen des Kindes. 2. Aufl. Stuttgart, 1970.

Phil 5768.2 Scholten, J.H. Der freie Wille. Berlin, 1874.

Phil 818.10 Scholten, J.H. Kortfattet fremstilling ad filosofiens historie. 3. Opl. Kjøbenhavn, 1886.

Phil 818.10.5 Scholten, J.H. Manuel d'histoire comparée de la philosophie et de la religion. Paris, 1861.

Phil 2805.355 Scholtens, M. Études médico-psychologiques sur Pascal. Haarlem, 1958.

Phil 5593.65.5 Scholtz, Walter. Zur Frage der Persönlichkeitsveränderung nach stereotaktischen Operationen. Inaug. Diss. Freiburg, 1965?

Phil 6328.3 Scholz, F. Die Diätetik des Geistes. Leipzig, 1887.
Phil 7080.47 Scholz, F. Sleep and dreams. N.Y., 1893.
Phil 2520.233 Scholz, H. Descartes. Münster, 1951.
Phil 5066.185 Scholz, H. Grundzüge der mathematischen Logik. Berlin, 1961.

Phil 193.225 Scholz, H. Mathesis Universalis. Stuttgart, 1961.
Phil 193.225.7 Scholz, H. Metaphysik als strenge Wissenschaft. 2. Aufl. Darmstadt, 1965.

Phil 8598.50 Scholz, H. Die Religionsphilosophie des Als-Ob. Leipzig, 1921.

Phil 5190.4.20 Scholz, H. Die sogenannten Definitionen durch Abstraktion. Leipzig, 1935.

Phil 5028.2.10 Scholz, Heinrch. Concise history of logic. N.Y., 1961.
Phil 5028.2 Scholz, Heinrich. Geschichte der Logik. Berlin, 1931.
Phil 3625.1.125 Scholz, Heinrich. Die Hauptschriften zum pantheismus Streit. Berlin, 1916.

Phil 530.20.65 Scholz, W. von. Deutsche Mystiker. Berlin, 1927.
Phil 270.58 Scholz, W. von. Der Zufall. Stuttgart, 1924.

Phil 974.3.75 Schomerus, H.W. Die Anthroposophie Steiners und Indien. Leipzig, 1922.

Phil 5360.24 Schon, Donald A. Displacement of concepts. London, 1963.
Phil 2262.88 Schonfeld, V. Die Ethik Shaftesburys. Diss. Budapest, 1920.

Phil 2520.150 Schoock, Martin. Admiranda methodus novae philosophiae Renati des Cartes. Waesberge, 1643.

Phil 9340.4 The school-boy. (Abbott, John S.) Boston, 1839.
Phil 28.22 School case work manuels. Stanford.
Phil 9160.2.5 The school-girl. (Abbott, Jacob.) Boston, 1840.
Phil 8875.24 The school of life. (Alger, W.R.) Boston, 1881.
Phil 6322.35 Schools of psychoanalytic thought. (Munroe, R.L.) N.Y., 1955.

Phil 5238.236 Schools of psychology. N.Y., 1969.
Phil 8673.26 Schoonbrood, C.A. Wijsgerige teksten over het absolute. Arnhem, 1967.

Phil 3120.11.94 Het schoone en de kunst of de naaste en onmiddellijke zelfbevrediging van absolute geestelijkheid in het kort besproken. (Bolland, G.J.P.J.) Amsterdam, 1906.

Phil 3808.125 Schopenhauer; a lecture. (Sannders, T.B.) London, 1901.
Phil 3808.62.5 Schopenhauer, Arthur. Aforismi sulla saggezza della vita. Torino, 1923.

Phil 3808.25.7 Schopenhauer, Arthur. Aphorismen zur Lebensweisheit. Leipzig, 1920.

Phil 3808.25.5 Schopenhauer, Arthur. Aphorismen zur Lebensweisheit. Stuttgart, 1924.

Phil 3808.30 Schopenhauer, Arthur. Art of controversy. London, 1896.
Phil 3808.28 Schopenhauer, Arthur. Art of literature. London, 1891.
Phil 3808.76.50 Schopenhauer, Arthur. Arthur Schopenhauer; Mensch und Philosoph in seinen Briefen. Wiesbaden, 1960.

Phil 3808.24.14 Schopenhauer, Arthur. Arthur Schopenhauer. n.p., n.d.
Phil 3808.20 Schopenhauer, Arthur. Aus A. Schopenhauer's handschriftlichen Nachlass. Leipzig, 1864.

Phil 3808.71 Schopenhauer, Arthur. The basis of morality. London, 1903.

Phil 3808.71.2 Schopenhauer, Arthur. The basis of morality. 2nd ed. London, 1915.

Htn Phil 3808.70* Schopenhauer, Arthur. Die beiden Grundprobleme der Ethik. Frankfurt, 1841.

Phil 3808.70.10 Schopenhauer, Arthur. Die beiden Grundprobleme der Ethik. Leipzig, 1860.

Phil 3808.70.12A Schopenhauer, Arthur. Die beiden Grundprobleme der Ethik. Leipzig, 1881.

Phil 3808.70.5 Schopenhauer, Arthur. Die beiden Grundprobleme der Ethik. 5. Aufl. Leipzig, 1908.

Phil 3808.24.17 Schopenhauer, Arthur. Das Bild des Menschen in Schopenhauers Philosophie. Berlin, 1932.

Phil 3808.76.15 Schopenhauer, Arthur. Briefe. Leipzig, 1893.
Phil 3808.76 Schopenhauer, Arthur. Brieftasche, 1822-1823. Berlin, n.d.

Phil 3808.76.20 Schopenhauer, Arthur. Briefwechsel und andere Dokumente; Ausgewählt und Herausgegeben von Mar Brahn. Leipzig, 1911.

Phil 3808.43 Schopenhauer, Arthur. Complete essays. v.1-7. N.Y., 1942.
Phil 3808.25.30 Schopenhauer, Arthur. Counsels and maxims. London, 1890.
Phil 3808.26 Schopenhauer, Arthur. Counsels and maxims. London, 1891.
Phil 3808.50 Schopenhauer, Arthur. De la guadruple racine du principe de la raison suffisante. Paris, 1882.

Phil 3808.75.5 Schopenhauer, Arthur. Écrivains et style. Paris, 1905.
Phil 3808.47 Schopenhauer, Arthur. Das Erwacher aus dem Leben- Fraum. Pfullingen, 1961.

Phil 3808.68 Schopenhauer, Arthur. Essai sur le Libre Arbitre. Paris, 1877.

Phil 3808.68.5 Schopenhauer, Arthur. Essai sur le Libre Arbitre. 13. éd. Paris, 1925.

Phil 3808.61.5 Schopenhauer, Arthur. Essays and aphorisms. Harmondsworth, Eng., 1970.

Phil 3808.61 Schopenhauer, Arthur. Essays from the Parerga and Paralipomena. London, 1951?

Phil 3808.44 Schopenhauer, Arthur. The essays of Arthur Schopenhauer. N.Y., n.d.

Phil 3808.69.3 Schopenhauer, Arthur. Le fondement de la morale. 3. éd. Paris, 1888.

Phil 3808.69.8 Schopenhauer, Arthur. Le fondement de la morale. 11. éd. Paris, 1925.

Phil 3808.60.40 Schopenhauer, Arthur. Frammenti di storia della filosofia. Milano, 1926?

Phil 3808.75.10 Schopenhauer, Arthur. Gedanken über Schriftstellerei und ahnliche Gegenslande. Dortmund, 1943.

Phil 3808.23.5 Schopenhauer, Arthur. Der handschriftliche Nachlass. v.1-3,5. Frankfurt, 1966. 4v.

Phil 3808.23 Schopenhauer, Arthur. Handschriftlicher Nachlass. Leipzig, 1895.

Htn Phil 3808.59* Schopenhauer, Arthur. Kan menneskets frie villie bevises af dets selvebevidsthed. Trodhjem, 1840.

Phil 3808.72 Schopenhauer, Arthur. Lebensweisheit. Berlin, 1943.

Phil 3808.21 Schopenhauer, Arthur. Lichtstrahlen aus seinen Werken. Leipzig, 1867.

Phil 3808.176 Schopenhauer, Arthur. Living thoughts presented by Thomas Mann. N.Y., 1939.

Phil 3808.35.28 Schopenhauer, Arthur. Le monde comme volonté et comme représentation. 8. éd. v.3. Paris, 1913.

Phil 3808.38.5 Schopenhauer, Arthur. Il mondo come volontà e rappresentazione. 2. ed. Bari, 1920-21. 2v.

Phil 3808.62 Schopenhauer, Arthur. Morale e religione. Torino, 1921.
Phil 3808.31.5 Schopenhauer, Arthur. On human nature; essays. London, 1957.

Phil 3808.31.2 Schopenhauer, Arthur. On human nature. London, 1897.
Phil 3808.51.7 Schopenhauer, Arthur. On the fourfold root of the principle of sufficient reason. London, 1903.

Phil 3808.51.6 Schopenhauer, Arthur. On the fourfold root of the principle of sufficient reason and on the will in nature; two essays. London, 1891.

Phil 3808.63.20 Schopenhauer, Arthur. Parapsychologische Schriften. Basel, 1961.

Phil 3808.60.8 Schopenhauer, Arthur. Parerga en Paralipomena. Amsterdam, 1908. 2v.

Phil 3808.60.30 Schopenhauer, Arthur. Parerga et Paralipomena: fragments sur l'histoire de la philosophie. Paris, 1912.

Phil 3808.60 Schopenhauer, Arthur. Parerga und Paralipomena. Berlin, 1862.

Phil 3808.60.2 Schopenhauer, Arthur. Parerga und Paralipomena. v.1-2. Berlin, 1851.

Phil 3808.29.25 Schopenhauer, Arthur. La pensée de Schopenhauer. Paris, 1918.

Phil 3808.55 Schopenhauer, Arthur. Pensées et fragments. 9. éd. Paris, 1889.

Phil 3808.55.11 Schopenhauer, Arthur. Pensées et fragments. 25. éd. Paris, 1911.

Phil 3808.24.15 Schopenhauer, Arthur. Die Persönlichkeit und das Werk. Leipzig, 1925.

Phil 3808.60.10 Schopenhauer, Arthur. Philosophie et philosophes. 2. éd. Paris, 19- .

Phil 3808.20.10 Schopenhauer, Arthur. Philosophische Aphorismen. Leipzig, 1924.

Phil 3808.53 Schopenhauer, Arthur. Philosophische Meschenkunde. Stuttgart, 1957.

Phil 3808.60.50 Schopenhauer, Arthur. The philosophy of Schopenhauer. N.Y., 1956.

Phil 3808.78 Schopenhauer, Arthur. Reisetagebücher aus den Jahren 1803-1804. Leipzig, 1923.

Phil 3808.27 Schopenhauer, Arthur. Religion: a dialogue. London, 1890.
Phil 3808.10 Schopenhauer, Arthur. Sämmtliche Werke. Leipzig, 1873-77. 6v.

Phil 3808.12 Schopenhauer, Arthur. Sämmtliche Werke. Leipzig, 1891. 6v.

Phil 3808.18 Schopenhauer, Arthur. Sämmtliche Werke. Leipzig, 1919. 2v.

Phil 3808.19 Schopenhauer, Arthur. Sämmtliche Werke. Leipzig, 1937-41. 7v.

Phil 3808.13 Schopenhauer, Arthur. Sämmtliche Werke. v.1-6,9-11,13-16. München, 1911-42. 13v.

Phil 3808.15 Schopenhauer, Arthur. Sämmtliche Werke. 2. Aufl. Leipzig, 1877. 6v.

Phil 3808.15.7 Schopenhauer, Arthur. Sämmtliche Werke. 2. Aufl. Leipzig, 1908. 6v.

Phil 3808.17 Schopenhauer, Arthur. Sämmtliche Werke in fünf Bänden. Leipzig, 1919. 5v.

Phil 3808.76.40 Schopenhauer, Arthur. Schopenhauer-Brevier. Wiesbaden, 1955.

Phil 3808.77 Schopenhauer, Arthur. Schopenhauer et ses disciples. Paris, 1920.

Phil 3808.76.30 Schopenhauer, Arthur. Schopenhauer und Brockhaus. Leipzig, 1926.

Phil 3808.26.50 Schopenhauer, Arthur. Schopenhauer und Schleiermacher über die Lebensalter. Leipzig, 1925?

Phil 3808.45.15 Schopenhauer, Arthur. Selected essays. London, 1926.
Phil 3808.45 Schopenhauer, Arthur. Selected essays. Milwaukee, 1881.
Phil 3808.45.20 Schopenhauer, Arthur. Selections. N.Y., 1956.
Phil 3808.29.5 Schopenhauer, Arthur. Studies in pessimism. London, 1891.
Phil 3808.29.10 Schopenhauer, Arthur. Studies in pessimism. London, 1923.
Phil 3808.51.5 Schopenhauer, Arthur. Two essays. London, 1889[1888]
Htn Phil 3808.63* Schopenhauer, Arthur. Über das Sehn und die Farben. Leipzig, 1816.

Phil 3808.63.10 Schopenhauer, Arthur. Über das Sehn und die Farben. 3. Aufl. Leipzig, 1870.

Phil 3808.24.20 Schopenhauer, Arthur. Über den Satz vom Grunde. Leipzig, 1891.

Htn Phil 3808.65* Schopenhauer, Arthur. Über den Willen in der Natur. Frankfurt, 1836.

Htn Phil 3808.65.5* Schopenhauer, Arthur. Über den Willen in der Natur. Frankfurt, 1854.

Phil 3808.65.2 Schopenhauer, Arthur. Über den Willen in der Natur. Leipzig, 1867.

Htn Phil 3808.48* Schopenhauer, Arthur. Über die vierfache Wurzel des Satzes vom zureichen den Grunde. 2. Aufl. Frankfurt, 1847.

Phil 3808.49 Schopenhauer, Arthur. Über die vierfache Wurzel des Satzes vom zureichen den Grunde. 3. Aufl. Leipzig, 1864.

Phil 3808.49.5 Schopenhauer, Arthur. Über die vierfache Wurzel des Satzes vom zureichen den Grunde. 4. Aufl. Leipzig, 1875.

Phil 3808.49.10 Schopenhauer, Arthur. Über die vierfache Wurzel des Satzes vom zureichen den Grunde. Hamburg, 1957.

Phil 3808.75 Schopenhauer, Arthur. Über Schriftstellerei und Stil. Leipzig, 1913.

Phil 3808.24 Schopenhauer, Arthur. Über Urtheil, Kritik, Beifall, Ruhm, Warheit und Irrthum. Leipzig, 1891.

Phil 3808.29.15 Schopenhauer, Arthur. Uren met Schopenhauer. Baarn, 1916.
Phil 3808.37 Schopenhauer, Arthur. De vier hocksteenen der Wereld en harr Bouwmeester. v.1-2. 's-Gravenhage, 1893.

Phil 3808.65.30 Schopenhauer, Arthur. La volontà nella natura. Milano, 1927.

Phil 3808.73 Schopenhauer, Arthur. Die wahren Güter des Lebens. München, 194-?

Phil 3808.35.10 Schopenhauer, Arthur. Die Welt als Wille und Vorstellung. Berlin, 1930.

Phil 3808.35.3 Schopenhauer, Arthur. Die Welt als Wille und Vorstellung. Halle, 1891? 2v.

Htn Phil 3808.33* Schopenhauer, Arthur. Die Welt als Wille und Vorstellung. Leipzig, 1819.

Htn Phil 3808.35* Schopenhauer, Arthur. Die Welt als Wille und Vorstellung. Leipzig, 1859. 2v.

Phil 3808.35.2.3 Schopenhauer, Arthur. Die Welt als Wille und Vorstellung. Leipzig, 1873. 2 pam.

Phil 3808.35.2 Schopenhauer, Arthur. Die Welt als Wille und Vorstellung. Leipzig, 1873. 2v.

Phil 3808.35.5 Schopenhauer, Arthur. Die Welt als Wille und Vorstellung. München, 1912-13. 2v.

Phil 3808.35.6 Schopenhauer, Arthur. Die Welt als Wille und Vorstellung. Stuttgart, 19- ? 2v.

Phil 3808.35.4 Schopenhauer, Arthur. Die Welt als Wille und Vorstellung. 5. Aufl. Leipzig, 1879. 2v.

Phil 3808.11.2 Schopenhauer, Arthur. Werke. Leipzig, 1891. 2v.

Phil 3808.11 Schopenhauer, Arthur. Werke. 2. Aufl. Leipzig, 1891. 2v.

Phil 3808.25.25 Schopenhauer, Arthur. The wisdom of life. London, 1963.

Phil 3808.22.15 Schopenhauer, Arthur. The wisdom of Schopenhauer. London, 1911.

Phil 3808.22.20 Schopenhauer, Arthur. Works. Abridged. N.Y., 1931.

Phil 3808.22.3 Schopenhauer, Arthur. The works of Schopenhauer, abridged. Garden City, 1928.

Phil 3808.22 Schopenhauer, Arthur. The works of Schopenhauer, abridged. N.Y., 1928.

NEDL Phil 3808.36.2 Schopenhauer, Arthur. The world as will and idea. Boston, 1883-86. 3v.

Phil 3808.36.10 Schopenhauer, Arthur. The world as will and idea. London, 19- . 3v.

Phil 3808.36.10.3 Schopenhauer, Arthur. The world as will and idea. London, 1906-09. 3v.

Phil 3808.36.5 Schopenhauer, Arthur. The world as will and idea. v.2. London, 1896.

Phil 3808.36.10.5 Schopenhauer, Arthur. The world as will and idea. 7th ed. London, 19- . 3v.

Phil 3808.36.10.10 Schopenhauer, Arthur. The world as will and representation. Indian Hills, Colo., 1958. 2v.

Phil 3808.74 Schopenhauer, Arthur. Zur Ästhetik der Poesie, Musik und der bildend en Künste. Leipzig, n.d.

Phil 3808.164.5 Schopenhauer, his life and philosophy. (Zimmern, Helen.) London, 1932.

Phil 3808.138 Schopenhauer; pessimisme-athéisme. Thèse. (Calas, T.) Montauban, 1909.

Phil 3808.161 Schopenhauer; pessimist and pagan. (McGill, Vivian J.) N.Y., 1931.

Phil 3808.119 Schopenhauer; seine Persönlichkeit. 3. Aufl. (Richert, Hans.) Leipzig, 1916.

Phil 3808.159 Schopenhauer, seine Persönlichkeit in seinen Werken. Bd.II. (Friedlander, Salomo.) Stuttgart, 1907.

Phil 3808.236 Schopenhauer, waarheid en dwaling. (Hoyack, Louis.) Deventer, 1968.

Phil 3808.179 Schopenhauer, Wagner, Nietzsche. (Lessing, Theodor.) München, 1906.

Phil 3808.153 Schopenhauer. (Beer, Margrieta.) London, 1914.

Phil 3808.172 Schopenhauer. (Bierens de Haan, J.D.) 's Gravenhage, 1933.

Phil 3808.188 Schopenhauer. (Borch, Rudolf.) Boston, 1941.

Phil 3808.184.3 Schopenhauer. (Cresson, André.) Paris, 1947.

Phil 3808.180 Schopenhauer. (Doring, W.O.) Zürich, 1919.

Phil 3808.107.10 Schopenhauer. (Grisebach, Eduard.) Berlin, 1905.

Phil 3808.114.15 Schopenhauer. (Hasse, Heinrich.) München, 1926.

Phil 3808.87 Schopenhauer. (Hecker, M.F.) Köln, 1897.

Phil 3808.169.5 Schopenhauer. (Hübscher, Arthur.) Stuttgart, 1952.

Phil 3808.92 Schopenhauer. (Lehmann, R.) Berlin, 1894.

Phil 3808.174A Schopenhauer. (Mann, Thomas.) Stockholm, 1938.

Phil 3808.175 Schopenhauer. (Mignosi, P.) Brescia, 1934.

Phil 3808.173 Schopenhauer. (Schneider, W.) Vienna, 1937.

Phil 3808.244 Schopenhauer. (Sørensen, Villy.) København, 1969.

Phil 3808.205 Schopenhauer. (Terzi, Carlo.) Romae, 1955.

Phil 3808.110 Schopenhauer. (Whittaker, T.) London, 1909.

Phil 3808.131 Schopenhauer. (Zini, Zino.) Milano, 1923.

Phil 3808.118 Schopenhauer. Thèse. (Dueros, Louis.) Paris, 1883.

Phil 3808.250 Schopenhauer. Wyd. 1. (Garewicz, Jan.) Warszawa, 1970.

Phil 3808.116.3 Schopenhauer. 3. éd. (Bossert, Adolphe.) Paris, 1912.

Phil 3808.107 Schopenhauer - Bibliothek. (Baer, J.) Frankfurt, 1905.

Phil 3808.124 Schopenhauer - Gesellschaft. Jahrbuch der...Gesellschaft. Kiel. 1912-1969+ 48v.

Phil 3808.135 Schopenhauer als erbe Kants in der philosophischen Seelenanalyse. (Frost, Walter.) Bonn, 1918.

Phil 3808.200 Schopenhauer als Erlebnis. (Zint, Hans.) München, 1954.

Phil 3808.192 Schopenhauer als Erzieher. (Nietzsche, F.W.) Leipzig, 1931.

Phil 3808.116.10 Schopenhauer als Mensch und Philosoph. (Bossert, Adolphe.) Dresden, 1905.

Phil 3808.85.15 Schopenhauer als Philosoph der Tragödie. (Reich, Emil.) Wien, 1888.

Phil 3808.97 Schopenhauer als Scholastiker. (Venetianer, M.) Berlin, 1873.

Phil 3808.196 Schopenhauer als Verbilder. (Keyserling, H.) Leipzig, 1910.

Phil 3808.238 Schopenhauer as transmitter of buddhist ideas. (Dauer, Dorothoa W.) Berne, 1967.

Phil 3808.156 Schopenhauer-Bilder, Grundlagen einer Ikonographie. (Gebhardt, Carl.) Frankfurt, 1913.

Phil 3808.242 Schopenhauer-Bildnisse. (Hübscher, Arthur.) Frankfurt, 1968.

Phil 3808.76.40 Schopenhauer-Brevier. (Schopenhauer, Arthur.) Wiesbaden, 1955.

Phil 9430.31 Schopenhauer-Darwin, Pessimismus oder Optimismus? (Weng, Gustav.) Berlin, 1911.

Phil 4210.128 Lo Schopenhauer e il Rosmini. (Paoli, A.) Roma, 1878.

Phil 3808.114.10 Schopenhauer Erkenntnislehre. (Hasse, Heinrich.) Leipzig, 1913.

Phil 3808.77 Schopenhauer et ses disciples. (Schopenhauer, Arthur.) Paris, 1920.

Phil 3808.212 Schopenhauer ethik. (Holn, Søren.) Kjøbenhavn, 1932.

Phil 3808.120 Lo Schopenhauer i il Rosmini. (Paoli, Alessandro.) Roma, 1878.

Phil 3808.240 Schopenhauer interprete dell'occidente. (Riconda, Giuseppe.) Milano, 1969.

Phil 3808.182 Schopenhauer ja von Hartmann. (Salomaa, J.E.) Turku, 1918.

Phil 3808.83 Schopenhauer-Lexikon. (Frauenstädt, C.M.J.) Leipzig, 1871. 2v.

Htn Phil 3808.83.1* Schopenhauer-Lexikon. (Frauenstädt, C.M.J.) Leipzig, 1871. 2v.

Phil 3808.90.1 Die Schopenhauer-Literatur. (Laban, Ferdinand.) N.Y., 1970.

Phil 3808.231 Schopenhauer pädagogische. (Arnold, Otto.) Leipzig, 1906.

Phil 3808.207 Schopenhauer ueber die Thiere und den Tierschutz. (Guetzlaff, Victor.) Berlin, 1879.

Phil 3808.76.30 Schopenhauer und Brockhaus. (Schopenhauer, Arthur.) Leipzig, 1926.

Phil 3808.115 Schopenhauer und Chamfort. (Anspach, F.W.) Göttingen, 1914.

Phil 3808.157 Schopenhauer und der Animismus. (Kaplan, Leo.) Leipzig, 1925.

Phil 3808.122 Schopenhauer und die Entwickelung der monistischen Weltanschauung. (Lehman, Rudolf.) Berlin, 1892.

Phil 3808.141 Schopenhauer und die Juden. (Groener, M.) München, 1920.

Phil 9430.17 Schopenhauer und Naturgeschichte des Pessimismus. (Paulsen, F.) Berlin, 1900.

Phil 3808.108 Schopenhauer und Nietzsche. (Simmel, G.) Leipzig, 1907.

Phil 3808.108.3 Schopenhauer und Nietzsche. 3. Aufl. (Simmel, G.) München, 1923.

Phil 3808.26.50 Schopenhauer und Schleiermacher über die Lebensalter. (Schopenhauer, Arthur.) Leipzig, 1925?

Phil 3808.86.10 Schopenhauer und seine Freunde. (Gwinner, W.) Leipzig, 1863.

Phil 3808.184 Schopenhauers a vie, son oeuvre. (Cresson, André.) Paris, 1946.

Phil 3501.4 Schopenhauer's criticism of Kant's Theory of experience. (Tsanoff, P.A.) N.Y., 1911.

Phil 3808.101 Schopenhauer's doctrine of the Thing-in-itself. (Colvin, S.S.) Providence, 1897.

Phil 3808.89 Schopenhauer's Erlösungslehre. (Koeber, R. von.) Leipzig, 1881?

Phil 3808.123 Schopenhauers Ethik im Verhaltnis zu seiner Erkenntnislehre und Metaphysik. (Damm, Oscar.) Annaberg, 1898.

Phil 3808.140 Schopenhauers filosofiska grundtankar i systematisk framställning och Kritisk belysning. (Rodhe, J.) Lund, 1888.

Phil 3808.86.5 Schopenhauer's Leben. (Gwinner, W.) Leipzig, 1878.

Phil 3808.86.7 Schopenhauer's Leben. (Gwinner, W.) Leipzig, 1910.

Phil 3808.165 Schopenhauers Lehre von der menschlichen Freiheit in ihrer Beziehung zu Kant und Schelling. Inaug. Diss. (Wyczołkowska, A.) Wien, 1893.

Phil 3808.104 Schopenhauers Philosophie. (Schlüter, R.) Leipzig, 1900.

Phil 3808.113.5 Schopenhauers Rechts- und Staatslehre. (Warschauer, Erich.) Kattowitz, 1911.

Phil 3808.88 Schopenhauers-Register. (Hertslet, M.L.) Leipzig, 1890.

Phil 3808.114.12 Schopenhauers Religionsphilosophie und ihre Bedeutung für die Gegenwart. (Hasse, Heinrich.) Frankfurt, 1924.

Phil 3808.132 Schopenhauers Seelenwanderungslehre. (Flink, Carl G.) Berlin, 1906.

Phil 3808.105 Schopenhauer's system...philosophical significance. (Caldwell, W.) Edinburgh, 1896.

Phil 3808.163 Schopenhauer's Verhältnis zu Kant in seinen Grundzügen. (Richter, Raoul.) Leipzig, 1893.

Phil 2750.11.235 Schopferische Erkenntnis. (Bauer, Hans Ludwig.) München, 1968.

Phil 4580.113 Schott, Georg. Harald Høffding, als Religionsphilosoph. München, 1913.

Phil 4580.113.3 Schott, Georg. Harald Høffding als Religionsphilosoph. Inaug. Diss. München, 1913.

Phil 8610.925.30 Schott, Walter E. The immaculate deception. Sausahto, Calif., 1925.

Phil 7069.09.2 Der Schotte Home. (Bormann, W.) Leipzig, 1909.

Phil 6128.65 Schottlaender, Felix. Das ich und seine Welt. Stuttgart, 1959.

Phil 9560.42 Schottlaender, Rudolf. Theorie des Vertrauens. Berlin, 1957.

Phil 6968.25 Schou, H.J. Religiøsitet og sygelige sindstilstande. 3. udg. København, 1928.

Phil 5420.15 Schouten, Jan. De verlegenheid. Proefschrift. Groningen, 1935.

Phil 5650.43 Schouteu, Jan F. Five articles on the perception of sound, 1938-1940. Eindhoven, 1960.

Phil 5500.2.5 Schrader, E. Die bewusste Beziehung. Leipzig, 1893.

Phil 5500.2 Schrader, E. Elemente der Psychologie des Urteils. Leipzig, 1905.

Phil 960.10.5 Schrader, F.O. Über den Stand der indischen Philosophie zur Zeit Mahávíras und Buddhas. Inaug. Diss. Strassburg, 1902.

Phil 1750.172 Schrader, George Alfred. Existential philosophers. N.Y., 1967.

Phil 3425.728 Schrader-Klebert, Karin. Das Problem des Anfangs in Hegels Philosophie. Wien, 1969.

Phil 8586.36.50 Schräter, Fritz. Glaube und Geschichte bei Friedrich Gogarten und Wilhelm Hermann. Inaug. Diss. Kothenanhalt, 1932?

Phil 1750.665 Schrag, C.O. Existence and freedom. Evanston, Ill., 1961.

Phil 349.65 Schrag, Calvin Orville. Experience and being. Evanston, Ill., 1969.

Phil 3475.3.245 Schrag, Oswald O. Existence, existenz, and transcendence. Pittsburgh, 1971.

Phil 3018.16 Schram, J. Beitrag zur Geschichte der Philosophie. Bonn, 1836.

Phil 3850.33 Schramm, A. Philosophische Studien zum Begriff der Entscheidung. Inaug. Diss. Berlin, 1940.

Phil 6968.2 Schramm, F. Über die Zweifelsucht und Berührungsangst. Berlin, 1888.

Phil 3500.62 Schramm, G. Kant's kategorischen Imperativ nach seiner Genesis und Bedeutung für die Wissenschaft. Bamberg, 1873.

Phil 4265.1.83 Schramm, J.M. De vita et scriptis...Julii Caesaris Vanini. 2. ed. Ciistrini, 1715.

Phil 6968.32 Schreben, Daniel P. Memoirs of my nervous illness. London, 1955.

Phil 6128.28 Schreber, D.G.M. Das Buch der Erziehung an Leib und Seele. 2. ed. Leipzig, 1882.

Phil 6327.12.30 Der Schrecken und andere psychoanalytische Studien. (Reik, Theodor.) Wien, 1929.

Phil 2475.1.213 Schrecker, P. Henri Bergsons Philosophie der Persönlichkeit. München, 1912.

Phil 3552.307A Schrecker, Paul. Leibniz; ses idées sur l'organisation des relations internationales. London, 1937.

Phil 5625.99 Das Schreckverhalten des Menschen. (Wieser, S.) Bern, 1961.

Htn Phil 3625.1.40* Schreiben an den Herrn Diaconus Lavater. (Mendelssohn, Moses.) Berlin, 1770-87. 3 pam.

Phil 3500.46 Schreiber, C. Kant und die Gottesbeweise. Dresden, 1922.

Phil 6990.39 Schreiber, G. Deutsche Mirakelbücher. Dusseldorf, 1938.

Phil 5548.25 Schreier, F.T. Human motivation. Glencoe, Ill., 1957.

Phil 3450.20.10 Schreiher, H.W. Joseph Hillebraud. Diss. Giessen, 1937.

Phil 8598.43 Schrempf, C. Gegen den Strom. Stuttgart, 1922. 5v.

Phil 8893.95.5 Schrempf, C. Die Grundlage der Ethik. Stuttgart, 1936.

Phil 3640.248 Schrempf, Christof. Friedrich Nietzsche. Stuttgart, 1922.

Phil 3850.44.3 Schrempf, Christof. Gesammelte Werke. Stuttgart, 1930-40.

Phil 7140.8 Schrenck-Notzing, Albert. Die Suggestions-Therapie. Stuttgart, 1892.

Phil 6688.22   Schrenck von Notzing, A. Ein Beitrag zur therapeutischen Verwerthung des Hypnotismus. n.p., 1888-97. 18 pam.

Phil 6688.9   Schrenck von Notzing, A.P. Die Traumtänzerin Magdeleine G. Stuttgart, 1904.

Phil 7069.24.44   Schrenck von Notzing, Albert. Experimente der Fernbewegung. Stuttgart, 1924.

Phil 7069.14.58   Schrenck von Notzing, Albert. Die Kampf und die Materialisationsphänomene. München, 1914.

Phil 7069.14.60   Schrenck von Notzing, Albert. Materialisationsphaenomene. München, 1914.

Phil 7069.14.61   Schrenck von Notzing, Albert. Materialisationsphaenomene. 2. ed. München, 1923.

Phil 7069.20.303   Schrenck von Notzing, Albert. Phenomena of materialisation; a contribution to the investigation of mediumistic telepastics. London, 1920.

Phil 7069.20.301   Schrenck von Notzing, Albert. Physikalische Phaenomene des Mediumismus. München, 1920.

Phil 978.49.920   Schrey, Helmut. Waldorfpädagogik. Bad Godesberg, 1968.

Phil 525.111   Schreyer, L. Die Vallendeten. Heidelberg, 1949.

Phil 6060.76   Die Schrift lügt nicht! (Schermann, Rafael.) Berlin, 1929.

Phil 6060.18.20   Schrift und Mensch. (Saudek, R.) Berlin, 1928.

Phil 3925.16.52   Schriften...Beiheft. (Wittgenstein, Ludwig.) Frankfurt, 1960.

Phil 3090.23   Schriften. (Baader, Franz von.) Leipzig, 1921.

Phil 3110.28.2   Schriften. (Böhme, J.) Leipzig, 1920.

Phil 3110.12   Schriften. (Böhme, J.) Leipzig, 1938.

Phil 8610.922   Die Schriften. (Costa, U. da.) Amsterdam, 1922.

Phil 3195.3.35   Schriften. (Dietzgen, Joseph.) Berlin, 1962.

Phil 3460.21   Schriften. (Jacobi, F.H.) Berlin, 1926.

Phil 3625.24   Schriften. (Müller, Adam H.) Neuwield, 1967. 2v.

Phil 3925.16.50A   Schriften. (Wittgenstein, Ludwig.) Frankfurt, 1960-64. 2v.

Phil 28.12   Schriften aus dem Euckenkreis. Langensalza. 1-31,1909-1929 2v.

Phil 288.17   Schriften aus dem Nachlass. (Hoenigswald, Richard.) Stuttgart, 1957- 8v.

Phil 6315.2.58   Schriften aus dem Nachlass 1892-1938. (Freud, Sigmund.) London, 1941.

Phil 46.1   Schriften der Gesellschaft für psychologischer Forschung. Leipzig. 1

Phil 46.1.2   Schriften der Gesellschaft für psychologischer Forschung. Leipzig. 2

Phil 46.1.3   Schriften der Gesellschaft für psychologischer Forschung. Leipzig. 3-4

Phil 46.1.5   Schriften der Gesellschaft für psychologischer Forschung. Leipzig. 5

Phil 46.1.6   Schriften der Gesellschaft für psychologischer Forschung. Leipzig. 6

Phil 46.1.7   Schriften der Gesellschaft für psychologischer Forschung. Leipzig. 7-8

Phil 46.1.9   Schriften der Gesellschaft für psychologischer Forschung. Leipzig. 9-10

Phil 46.1.11   Schriften der Gesellschaft für psychologischer Forschung. Leipzig. 11

Phil 46.1.12   Schriften der Gesellschaft für psychologischer Forschung. Leipzig. 12

Phil 46.1.13   Schriften der Gesellschaft für psychologischer Forschung. Leipzig. 13-14

Phil 46.1.15   Schriften der Gesellschaft für psychologischer Forschung. Leipzig. 15

Phil 46.1.16   Schriften der Gesellschaft für psychologischer Forschung. Leipzig. 16

Phil 46.1.17   Schriften der Gesellschaft für psychologischer Forschung. Leipzig. 17

Phil 46.1.18   Schriften der Gesellschaft für psychologischer Forschung. Leipzig. 18-20

Phil 3110.28   Schriften Jakob Böhme. (Böhme, J.) Leipzig, 1923.

Phil 3120.30.60   Die Schriften über das dialogische Prinzip. (Buber, Martin.) Heidelberg, 1954.

Phil 3246.320   Die Schriften zu Johann Gottlieb Fichtes Atheismus-Streit. (Boeckelmann, Frank.) München, 1969.

Phil 3246.99.5   Die Schriften zu Johann Gottlieb Fichte's Atheismusstreit. (Lindau, Hans.) München, 1912.

Phil 8411.28.5   Schriften zur Asthetik. (Kuhn, Helmut.) München, 1966.

Phil 338.12   Schriften zur Erkenntnistheorie. (Helmholtz, H.) Berlin, 1921.

Phil 3090.24   Schriften zur Gesellschaftsphilosophie. (Baader, Franz von.) Jena, 1925.

Phil 3425.19   Schriften zur Gesellschaftsphilosophie. (Hegel, Georg Wilhelm Friedrich.) Jena, 1927.

Phil 8406.28   Schriften zur Kunst. (Fiedler, Konrad.) München, 1971. 2v.

Phil 3480.28.17   Schriften zur Naturphilosophie. 3. Aufl. (Kant, Immanuel.) Leipzig, 1922. 3v.

Phil 3160.15.10   Schriften zur Philosophie. (Conrad-Martius, Hedwig.) München, 1963-64. 3v.

Phil 3625.1.25   Schriften zur Philosophie. (Mendelssohn, Moses.) Leipzig, 1880.

Phil 3625.13.19   Schriften zur Philosophie. (Müller, Aloys.) Bonn, 1967. 2v.

Phil 28.13   Schriften zur Philosophie der Neuzeit. Augsburg. 1-2,1928-1931 2v.

Phil 177.28.10   Schriften zur Philosophie und Zeitgeschichte. (Cohens, Hermann.) Berlin, 1928. 2v.

Phil 3425.41   Schriften zur Politik und Rechtsphilosophie. (Hegel, Georg Wilhelm Friedrich.) Leipzig, 1913.

Phil 28.5   Schriften zur Psychologie der Berufseignung. Leipzig. 1918-1933 36v.

Phil 5360.20   Schroder, Harold M. Human information processing. N.Y., 1967.

Phil 5642.22   Schroder, Ludwig. Sinne und Sinnesverknüpfungen. Heidelberg, 1969.

Phil 5066.16   Schröber, Karl. Ein allgemeiner Kalkülbegriff. Leipzig, 1941.

Phil 3565.125   Schröder, Arthur. Geschichtsphilosophie bei Lotze. Diss. Leipzig, 1896.

Phil 3850.21.91   Schroeder, B. Leopold Schmid's Leben und Denken. Leipzig, 1871.

Phil 3801.777.25   Schröder, C.M. Das Verhältnis von Heidentum und Christentum in Schellings Philosophie der Mythologie und Offenbarung. München, 1936.

Phil 5058.5.9A   Schröder, E. Abriss der Algebra der Logik. Leipzig, 1909. 2v.

Phil 5058.5   Schröder, E. Der Operationskries der Logikkalkuls. Leipzig, 1877.

Phil 5058.5.5   Schröder, E. Vorlesungen über der Algebra der Logik. Leipzig, 1891-95. 4v.

Phil 1750.858   Schröder, Erich Christian. Abschied von der Metaphysik? Beiträge zu einer Philosophie der Endlichkeit. Trier, 1969.

Phil 5258.110   Schröder, Paul. Stimmungen und Verstimmungen. Leipzig, 1930.

Phil 5627.39   Schroeder, Theodore. Erotogenesis of religion. N.Y., 1916.

Phil 5627.40   Schroeder, Theodore. Erotogenesis of religion. St. Louis, 1913.

Phil 5258.199   Schroeder, Theodore. An evolutionary psychologist. Berkeley Heights, N.J., 1965.

Phil 5627.38   Pamphlet box. Schroeder, Theodore.

NEDL Phil 6128.26.5   Schroeder van der Kolk, J.L.C. On the minute structure and functions of the spinal cord. London, 1859.

Phil 6128.26   Schroeder van der Kolk, J.L.C. Seele und Leib in Wechselbeziehung zu Einander. Braunschweig, 1865.

Phil 6968.20   Schroeder van der Kolk, J.L.K. The pathology and therapeutics of mental diseases. London, 1870.

Phil 1135.166   Schroedinger, E. Nature and the Greeks. Cambridge, Eng., 1954.

Phil 6128.59.5   Schroedinger, Erwin. Geist und Materie. Braunschweig, 1959.

Phil 193.230   Schroedinger, Erwin. Meine Weltansicht. Hamburg, 1961.

Phil 6128.59   Schroedinger, Erwin. Mind and matter. Cambridge, Eng., 1958.

Phil 193.230.3   Schroedinger, Erwin. My view of the world. Cambridge, 1964.

Phil 3018.21   Schroeter, R. Geschichte und Geschichtlichkeit in der deutschen Philosophie der Gegenwart. Inaug. Diss. Kölm am Rhein, 1937.

Phil 193.156   Schubart, W. Geistige Wandlung. Luzern, 1940.

Phil 193.15   Schubert, G. von. Ansichten von der Nachseite der Naturwissenschaft. Dresden, 1840.

Phil 193.15.3   Schubert, G. von. Vermischte Schriften. Erlangen, 1857-1860. 2v.

Phil 3850.6.79   Schubert, G.H. Der Erwerb aus...Leben: eine Selbstbiographie. Erlangen, 1854-56. 3v.

Phil 3850.6.75   Schubert, G.H. Gotthilf Heinrich Schubert in seinen Briefen. Stuttgart, 1918.

Phil 5258.7.3   Schubert, G.H. von. Altes und Neues aus dem Gebiet der innren Seelenkunde. Leipzig, 1817.

Phil 5258.7   Schubert, G.H. von. Altes und Neues aus dem Gebiet der innren Seelenkunde. Leipzig, 1825-44. 5v.

Phil 5258.7.5   Schubert, G.H. von. Die Geschichte der Seele. Stuttgart, 1833.

Phil 5258.7.6   Schubert, G.H. von. Die Geschichte der Seele. Stuttgart, 1850. 2v.

Phil 6968.3   Schubert, G.H. von. Die Krankheiten, Störungen, menschlichen Seele. Stuttgart, 1845.

Phil 5258.7.10   Schubert, G.H. von. Lehrbuch der Menschen- und Seelenkunde. Erlangen, 1838.

Phil 7082.4.5   Schubert, Gotthilf Heinrich von. Die Symbolik des Traumes. Heidelberg, 1968.

Phil 7082.4.3   Schubert, Gotthilf Heinrich von. Die Symbolik des Traumes. 3. Aufl. Leipzig, 1840.

Phil 2266.81   Schubert, Johannes. Adam Smith's Moralphilosophie. Leipzig, 1890.

Phil 349.1   Schubert-Soldern, R. von. Grundlagen einer Erkenntnisstheorie. Leipzig, 1884.

Phil 8893.42   Schubert-Soldern, R. von. Grundlagen zu einer Ethik. Leipzig, 1887.

Phil 5258.8   Schubert-Soldern, R. von. Reproduction, Gefühl und Wille. Leipzig, 1887.

Phil 193.16   Schubert-Soldern, R. von. Über Transcendenz der Objects und Subjects. Leipzig, 1882.

Phil 5768.12   Schuch, Hermann. Kant, Schopenhauer, Ihering. München, 1907.

Phil 5258.50.5   Schuchter, Josef. Empirische Psychologie. Brixen, 1897.

Phil 5258.50   Schuchter, Josef. Kurzgefaszte empirische Psychologie. Wien, 1902.

Phil 6968.4   Schüle, H. Handbuch der Geisteskrankheiten. Leipzig, 1880.

Phil 6968.4.3   Schüle, H. Klinische Psychiatrie. 3. Aufl. Leipzig, 1886.

Phil 5203.34   Schueling, H. Bibliographie der psychologischen Literatur des 16. Jahrhunderts. Hildesheim, 1967.

Phil 5374.245.2   Schueling, Hermann. Denkstil. Beschreibung und Deutung der Denkformen. 2. Aufl. Düsseldorf, 1967.

Phil 210.74   Schueling, Hermann. Die Geschichte der axiomatischen Methode im 16. und Beginnenden 17. Jahrhundert. Hildesheim, 1969.

Phil 8698.15   Schueppe, Otto. Gott sprach-es-ward. Bern, 1970.

Phil 3805.92   Schürer, Emil. Schleiermacher's Religionsbegriff. Leipzig, 1868.

Phil 6060.12.55   Schuerer, Wilhelm. Hestia, 1960-61...Ludwig Klages. Bonn, 1960.

Phil 440.12   Schuette, Hermann Günther. Freiheit ist anders. München, 1970.

Phil 8673.16   Schütz, A. Gott in der Geschichte. Salzburg, 1936.

Phil 193.114   Schütz, C.G. Einleitung in die speculative Philosophie. Lemgo, 1776.

Htn Phil 3801.778*   Schütz, C.G. Vertheidigung gegen Herren Professor Schellings...Erläuterungen. Jena, 1800. 4v.

Phil 3625.1.90   Schütz, F.W. von. Leben und Meinungen M. Mendelssohn. Hamburg, 1787.

Phil 193.85   Schütz, Ludwig. Einleitung in die Philosophie. Paderborn, 1879.

Phil 3415.100   Schüz, A. Philosophie und Christentum. Stuttgart, 1884.

Phil 3246.302   Schuffenhauer, H. Die Padagogik Johann Gottlieb Fichtes. Berlin, 1963.

Phil 3805.195   Schuffenhauer, Heinz. Der fortschrittliche Gehalt der Pädagogik Schleiermachers. Berlin, 1956.

Phil 1850.143   Schuhl, P. La pensée de Lord Bacon. Paris, 1949.

Phil 5465.138   Schuhl, P.M. Imaginer et réaliser. Paris, 1963.

Phil 5170.12   Schuhl, Pierre M. Le dominateur el les possibles. 1. éd. Paris, 1960.

Phil 1123.9   Schuhl, Pierre Maxime. Essai sur la formation de la pensée grecque. Paris, 1934.

Phil 1123.9.10   Schuhl, Pierre Maxime. Essai sur la formation de la pensée grecque. 2. ed. Paris, 1949.

Phil 3246.315   Schuhmann, Karl. Die Grundlage der Wissenschaftslehre in ihrem Umrisse. Den Haag, 1968[1969]

Phil 5414.40   Schuld, Reue und Krankheit. (Schlederer, Franz.) München, 1970.

Phil 1750.33   Schuld ist Schicksal. (Stackelberg, J. von.) München, 1948.

Phil 3120.30.64   Schuld und Schuldgefühle. (Buber, Martin.) Heidelberg, 1958.

Phil 525.65 — Der Schuldbegriff bei den Mystikern der Reformationszeit. (Ihringer, Bernhard.) Bern, 1912.

Phil 3475.3.35 — Die Schuldfrage. 2. Aufl. (Jaspers, Karl.) Zürich, 1946.

Phil 3450.19.114 — Het schuldprableem ein die existentiephilosophie van Martin Heidegger. (Graaff, F. de.) 's Gravenhage, 1951.

Phil 5520.56.10 — Schule der Abstraktion und der Dialektik. (Jordan, Leo.) München, 1932.

Phil 180.37 — Schule der Philosophie. (Feldmann, J.) Paderborn, 1925.

Phil 1195.10 — Die Schule von Gaza. (Seitz, K.) Heidelberg, 1892.

Phil 8050.40 — Schulemann, G. Asthetik. Breslau, 1930.

Phil 1504.13.5 — Schulemann, G. Das Kausalprinzip. v.13, pt.5. Münster, 1915.

Phil 9528.5 — Schulfeierstunden. (Oppermann, W.) Leipzig, 1923.

Phil 3425.480 — Schulin, Ernst. Die weltgeschichtliche Erfassung des Orients bei Hegel und Ranke. Göttingen, 1958.

Phil 9530.62 — Schuller, Robert. Move ahead with possibility thinking. 1. ed. Garden City, 1967.

Phil 7140.128 — Schulmedizin und Wunderkuren. (Arnold, Hans.) Leipzig, 1892.

Phil 7069.66.40 — Schult, Arthur. Vom übersinnlichen Wesen des Menschen. Bietigheim, 1966.

Phil 193.94 — Schulte-Tigges, A. Philosophische Propadeutik. n.p., n.d. 3 pam.

Phil 3500.51 — Schultheis, P. Kant's Lehre vom radicalen Bösen. Diss. Leipzig, 1873.

Phil 6046.91 — Schulty, Christoph. Dissertatio academica, de chiromantiae vanitate. Regiomonti, 1691?

Phil 5228.18 — Schultz, Duane P. A history of modern psychology. N.Y., 1969.

Phil 5640.137 — Schultz, Duane P. Sensory restriction. N.Y., 1965.

Phil 5828.8 — Schultz, F. Vergleichende Seelenkunde. Leipzig, 1892-97. 2v.

Phil 5258.200 — Schultz, Hans Jürgen. Was weiss man von der Seele? Stuttgart, 1967.

Phil 5258.78 — Schultz, J. Briefe über genetische Psychologie. Berlin, 1902.

Phil 349.14 — Schultz, J. Die drei Welten der Erkenntnistheorie. Göttingen, 1907.

Phil 193.105 — Schultz, J. Die Philosophie am Scheidewege. Leipzig, 1922.

Phil 3500.52.5 — Schultz, John. Ensayo de una clara exposición del contenido a la critica de la razón pura. Cordoba, 1942.

Phil 3500.52 — Schultz, John. Prüfung der Kantischen Critik der reinen Vernunft. v.1-2. Königsberg, 1789-92.

Phil 5190.3 — Schultz, Julius. Psychologie der Axiome. Göttingen, 1899.

Phil 349.20 — Schultz, Julius. Die Maschinen-Theorie des Lebens. Göttingen, 1909.

Phil 349.20.5 — Schultz, Julius. Die Maschinen-Theorie des Lebens. 2. Aufl. Leipzig, 1929.

Phil 3500.55 — Schultz, Martin. Kants Religion innerhalb der Grenzen der blossen Vernunft. Königsberg, 1927.

Phil 5258.60 — Schultz, Paul. Gehirn und Seele. Leipzig, 1906.

Phil 343.4.9 — Schultz, R. Die Machsche Erkenntnistheorie. Berlin, n.d.

Phil 3425.296 — Schultz, Werner. Die Grundprinzipien der Religionsphilosophie Hegels und der Theologie Schleiermachers. Berlin, 1937.

Phil 6328.13 — Schultz-Hencke, Harald. Enführung in die Psychoanalyse. Jena, 1927.

Phil 7084.12.1 — Schultz-Hencke, Harald. Lehrbuch der Traumanalyse. 1. Aufl. Stuttgart, 1968.

Phil 5258.10 — Schultz-Schultzenstein, K.H. Die Bildung der menschlichen Geistes. Berlin, 1855.

Phil 5258.10.25 — Schultz-Schultzenstein, K.H. Naturstudium und Kultur. Berlin, 1866.

Phil 672.138 — Schultze, A. Ist die Welt vierdimensional? Leipzig, 1922.

Phil 4710.6 — Schultze, B. Russische Denker. Wien, 1950.

Phil 5649.10 — Schultze, Ernst. Über die Umwandlung willkürlicher Bewegungen in unwillkürliche. Leipzig, 1898.

Phil 7054.131 — Schultze, F. Die Grundgedanken des Spiritismus und die Kritik derselben. Leipzig, 1883.

Phil 3500.29 — Schultze, F. Kant und Darwin. Jena, 1875.

Phil 193.17 — Schultze, F. Philosophie der Naturwissenschaft. Leipzig, 1881.

Phil 5258.28 — Schultze, F. Psychologie der Naturvölker. Leipzig, 1900.

Phil 125.3 — Schultze, F. Stammbaum der Philosophie. Jena, 1890.

Phil 1619.2 — Schultze, Fritz. Geschichte der Philosophie der Renaissance. Jena, 1874.

Phil 5058.32 — Schultze, Fritz. Grundlinien der Logik in schematischer Darstellung. Leipzig, 1902.

Phil 6315.2.83 — Schultze, J.H. Sigmund Freud's Sexualpsychoanalyse. Berlin, 1917.

Phil 2050.202 — Schultze, W.F. Hume und Kant über den Causalbegriff. Inaug. Diss. Rostock, 1870.

Phil 5190.25 — Schultzer, B. Observation and protocolstatement. Copenhagen, 1938.

Phil 705.24 — Schultzer, Bent. Transcendence and the logical difficulties of transcendence; a logical analysis. Copenhagen, 1935.

Phil 5258.42 — Schulz, B. Psychologische Wanderungen auf Seitenwegen. Jena, 1913.

Phil 575.28 — Schulz, Bernhard. Das Bewusstseinsproblem. Wiesbaden, 1964.

Phil 3500.92 — Schulz, H. Innerer Sinn und Erkenntnis in der Kantischen Philosophie. Düsseldorf, 1962.

Phil 5627.261.5 — Schulz, Johannes Josef. Bionome Geschlechtsentfaltung. München, 1961.

Phil 3246.301 — Schulz, W. Johann Gottlieb Fichte. Pfullingen, 1962.

Phil 193.177 — Schulz, Walter. Der Gott der neuzeitlichen Metaphysik. Pfullingen, 1957.

Phil 3801.775.20 — Schulz, Walter. Die Vollendung des deutschen Idealismus in der Spätphilosophie Schellings. Stuttgart, 1955.

Phil 3925.16.165 — Schulz, Walter. Wittgenstein; die Negation der Philosophie. Pfullingen, 1967.

Phil 8598.120 — Schulz-Angern, Karl Friedrich. Ewiges-Vergängliches. Berlin, 1958.

Phil 1123.1 — Schulze, E. Übersicht über die griechische Philosophie. Leipzig, 1886.

Phil 5058.100 — Schulze, Ernst. Grundriss der Logik und Übersicht über die Griechische Philosophie für die prima der Gymnasien. Leipzig, 1886.

Phil 3640.540 — Schulze, Friedrich. Der junge Nietzsche in den Jahren. Leipzig, 1941.

Phil 3850.13.35 — Schulze, G.E. Aenesidemus. Berlin, 1911.

Phil 3850.13.33 — Schulze, G.E. Aenesidemus öder über die Fundamenta. Helmstadt, 1792.

Phil 3850.13.31 — Schulze, G.E. Encyclopaedie der philosophischen Wissenschaften. Göttingen, 1823.

Phil 3850.13.32 — Schulze, G.E. Encyklopaedie der philosophischen Wissenschaften. Göttingen, 1824.

Phil 3850.13.25 — Schulze, G.E. Grundriss der philosophischen Wissenschaften und Zerbst. Wittenberg, 1788-90. 2v.

Phil 3850.13.55 — Schulze, G.E. Grundsätze der allgemeinen Logik. Göttingen, 1831.

Phil 3850.13.30 — Schulze, G.E. Kritik der theoritischen Philosophie. Hamburg, 1801. 2v.

Phil 3850.13.60 — Schulze, G.E. Leitfaden der Entwickelung der philosophischen Prinzipien. Göttingen, 1813.

Phil 8893.88 — Schulze, G.E. Philosophische Tugendlehre. Göttingen, 1817.

Phil 3850.13.40 — Schulze, G.E. Psychische Anthropologie. Göttingen, 1816.

Phil 3850.13.41 — Schulze, G.E. Psychische Anthropologie. Göttingen, 1826.

Phil 3850.13.42 — Schulze, G.E. Psychische Anthropologie. 2. Aufl. Göttingen, 1819.

Phil 3850.13.27 — Schulze, G.E. Über den höchsten Zweck des Studiums der Philosophie. Leipzig, 1789.

Phil 3552.248 — Schulze, G.E. Über die Entdeckung, dass Leibnitz ein Katholik gewesen sey. Göttingen, 1827.

Phil 3850.13.70 — Schulze, G.E. Ueber die Menschliche Erkenntnis. Göttingen, 1832.

Phil 3500.56 — Schulze, Gottlob E. Einige Bemerkungen über Kants philosophische Religionslehre. Kiel, 1795.

Phil 6329.18 — Schulze, H. Der progressiv, domesticierte Mensch und seine Neurosen. München, 1964.

Phil 3500.14 — Schulze, J. Erläuterungen...Kant Critik der reinen Vernunft. Frankfurt, 1791.

Phil 3500.14.2 — Schulze, J. Erläuterungen...Kant Critik der reinen Vernunft. Königsberg, 1784.

Phil 8893.69 — Schulze, K.E. Ethik der Dekadenz. Leipzig, 1925.

Phil 5258.96.5 — Schulze, Rudolf. Die moderne Seelenlehre; Begabungsforschung und Berufsberatung. 3. Aufl. Leipzig, 1921.

Phil 8598.90.5 — Schulze-Gaevernitz, G. Zur Wiedergeburt des Abendlandes. 2. Aufl. Berlin, 1934.

Phil 8419.15 — Schulze-Soelde, W. Das Gesetz der Schönheit. Darmstadt, 1925.

Phil 8419.29 — Schumacher, F. Die Sprache der Kunst. Stuttgart, 1942.

Phil 8708.32 — Schumann, F.K. Überwindung des Säkularismus in der Wissenschaft. Gladbeck, 195-.

Phil 3915.80 — Schumann, H. Wundts Lehre vom Willen. Leipzig, 1912.

Phil 6849.2 — Schumann, Hans Joachim von. Liebesunfähigkeit bie Frauen und ihre Behandlung. München, 1969.

Phil 7084.42 — Schumann, Hans Joachim von. Träume der Blinden vom Standpunkt der Phänomenologie. Basel, 1959.

Phil 2630.2.127 — Schumm, Felix. Jean Marie Guyaus Religionsphilosophie. Tübingen, 1913.

Phil 349.27 — Schunck, Karl. Verstehen und Einsehen. Halle an der Saale, 1926.

Phil 8598.110.5 — Schuon, Frithjof. Gnosis. London, 1959.

Phil 8598.110.20 — Schuon, Frithjof. Language of the self. Madras, 1959.

Phil 8598.110 — Schuon, Frithjof. Sentien de gnose. Paris, 1957.

Phil 8598.110.10 — Schuon, Frithjof. Spiritual perspectives and human facts. London, 1954.

Phil 8598.110.15A — Schuon, Frithjof. Stations of wisdom. London, 1961.

Phil 8598.110.25 — Schuon, Frithjof. Transcendent unity of religions. N.Y., 1953.

Phil 5058.7 — Schuppe, W. Erkenntnisstheoretische Logik. Bonn, 1878.

Phil 349.10.5A — Schuppe, W. Grundriss der Erkenntnistheorie und Logik. Berlin, 1894.

Phil 349.10 — Schuppe, W. Grundriss der Erkenntnistheorie und Logik. 2. Aufl. Berlin, 1910.

Phil 8893.3 — Schuppe, W. Grundzüge der Ethik und Rechtsphilosophie. Breslau, 1881.

Phil 5058.7.5 — Schuppe, W. Das menschliche Denken. Berlin, 1870.

Phil 6128.80 — Schur, Max. The id and the regulatory principles of mental functioning. London, 1967.

Phil 8610.896 — Schurman, J.G. Agnosticism and religion. N.Y., 1896.

Phil 9150.3 — Schurman, J.G. The ethical import of Darwinism. N.Y., 1887.

Phil 9150.3.2 — Schurman, J.G. The ethical import of Darwinism. N.Y., 1888.

Phil 3500.8 — Schurman, J.G. Kantian ethics. London, 1881.

Phil 5722.2 — Schuster, P.R. Gibtesunbewusste und vererbte Vorstellungen? Leipzig, 1879.

Phil 3903.1.86 — Schuster, Willy. Zwischen Philosophie und Kunst, Johannes Volkelt zum 100 Lehrsemester. Leipzig, 1926.

Phil 2280.21.5 — Schutz, Alfred. Collected papers. The Hague, 1962. 3v.

Phil 1750.115.205 — Schutz, Alfred. On phenomenology and social relations. Chicago, 1970.

Phil 1750.115.80 — Schutz, Alfred. The phenomenology of the social world. Evanston, Ill., 1967.

Phil 2280.21.10 — Schutz, Alfred. Reflections on the problem of relevance. New Haven, 1970.

Phil 8643.2 — Schutz, L. Vernunf-Beweis...Unsterblichkeit der menschlichen Seele. Paderborn, 1874.

Phil 5400.21 — Schutz, L.H. Die Lehre von den Leidenschaften. Hagen, 1901.

Phil 5403.12 — Schutz, William Carl. Joy; expanding human awareness. N.Y., 1968.

Phil 7054.51.10 — Die Schutzgeister. (Werner, H.) Stuttgart, 1839.

Phil 3100.43 — Schutzschrift für meine Grundlegung zur Physik der Sitten. (Beneke, F.E.) Leipzig, 1823.

Phil 193.62 — Schuyler, A. Critical history of philosophical theories. Boston, n.d.

Phil 5058.8 — Schuyler, A. The principles of logic. Cincinnatti, n.d.

Phil 3500.17.15 — Schwab, J.C. Bemerkungen unter den Kantischen Begriff...metaphysischen Rechtslehre. Bruxelles, 1968.

Htn   Phil 3500.17.10* — Schwab, J.C. Neun Gespräche zwischen Christian Wolff. Berlin, 1798.

Phil 3018.1 — Schwab, J.C. Preisschriften...Metaphysik séet Leibnitz. Berlin, 1796.

Phil 3500.17.20 — Schwab, J.C. Über die Wahrheit der Kantischen Philosophie...Aushung dieser Philosophie. Berlin, 1803.

Htn   Phil 3500.17* — Schwab, J.C. Vergleichung des Kantischen Moralprinzips. Berlin, 1800.

Phil 3500.110 — Schwab, Johann Christoph. Sendschreiben an einen Recensenten in der Gothaischen gelehrten Zeitung über die gerichtlichen Eyd. v.1-2. Bruxelles, 1968.

Phil 8673.5 — Schwab, L.H. The kingdom of God. N.Y., 1967.

Phil 3625.1.109 — Schwab, Moise. Mendelssohn, sa vie et ses oeuvres. Paris, 1868.

Phil 3246.83 — Schwabe, G. Fichtes und Schopenhauer's Lehre von Willen. Jena, 1887.

Phil 4210.114 — Schwaiger, Georg. Die Lehre vom sentimento fondamentale bei Rosmini nach ihrer Anlage. Inaug. Diss. Fulda, 1914.

Phil 8893.62 — Schwalb, Carl J. Ethische und philosophische Betrachtungen auf empirischer Grundlage. Zürich, 1897.

Phil 3450.19.345 — Schwan, Alexander. Politische Philosophie im Denken Heideggers. Köln, 1965.

Phil 3500.106 — Schwartlaender, Johannes. Der Mensch ist Person. Stuttgart, 1968.

Phil 5401.24 — Schwartz, C. Neurotic anxiety. N.Y., 1954.

Phil 5850.335.10 — Schwartz, David J. The magic of psychic power. West Nyack, N.Y., 1965.

Phil 1145.87 — Schwartz, E. Ethik der Griechen. Stuttgart, 1951.

Phil 8881.26.28 — Schwartz, E.J. M. Guyaus Moral. Inaug. Diss. Strassburg, 1909.

Phil 4065.123 — Schwartz, M. Giordano Bruno. Erfurt, 1939.

Phil 5768.17 — Schwartzkopff, P. Die Freiheit des Willens als Grundlage der Sittlichkeit. Leipzig, 1885.

Phil 349.12.5 — Schwartzkopff, P. Was ist Denken? Wernigerode, 1906.

Phil 349.12 — Schwartzkopff, P. Das Wesen der Erkenntnis. Heidelberg, 1909.

Phil 5402.14 — Schwarz, Balduin. Untersuchungen zur Psychologie des Weinens. Inaug. Diss. München, 1928.

Phil 349.37 — Schwarz, Baldwin. Der Irrtum in der Philosophie. Münster, 1934.

Phil 3450.33.8 — Schwarz, Baldwin. The human person and the world of values. N.Y., 1960.

Phil 8598.5 — Schwarz, C.H.W. Das Wesen der Religion. Halle, 1847.

Phil 3018.15 — Schwarz, H. Deutsche systematische Philosophie nach ihren Gestaltern. Berlin, 1931-34. 2v.

Phil 3246.207 — Schwarz, H. Einführung in Fichtes Reden an die deutsche Nation. 2. Aufl. Langensalza, 1925.

Phil 9245.15 — Schwarz, H. Glück und Sittlichkeit. Halle, 1902.

Phil 8643.9 — Schwarz, H. Der Gottesgedanke in der Geschichte der Philosophie. Heidelberg, 1913.

Phil 193.68 — Schwarz, H. Grundfragen der Weltanschauung. 2e Aufl. Leipzig, 1912.

Phil 2520.98 — Schwarz, H. Die Lehre von den Sinnesqualitäten...Descartes. Halle, 1894.

Phil 3552.94 — Schwarz, H. Die Leibniz'sche Philosophie. Jena, 1888.

Phil 5768.5 — Schwarz, H. Psychologie des Willens. Leipzig, 1900.

Phil 5585.10.5 — Schwarz, H. Umwälzung der Wahrnehmungshypothesen. Leipzig, 1895.

Phil 5585.10 — Schwarz, H. Das Wahrnehmungsproblem. Leipzig, 1892.

Phil 3415.86 — Schwarz, H. Das Ziel der religiösen und wissenschaftlichen Gährung nachgewiesen Hartmann's Pessimismus. Berlin, 1875.

Phil 525.66 — Schwarz, Hermann. Auf Wegen der Mystik. Erfurt, 1924.

Phil 8893.39.10 — Schwarz, Hermann. Ethik. Breslau, 1925.

Phil 3246.176 — Schwarz, Hermann. Fichte und Wir. Osterwieck, 1917.

Phil 8893.39.5 — Schwarz, Hermann. Grundzüge der Ethik. Leipzig, 1896.

Phil 3018.24 — Schwarz, Hermann. Grundzüge einer Geschichte der artdeutschen Philosophie. Berlin, 1937.

Phil 8893.39 — Schwarz, Hermann. Das sittliche Leben, eine Ethik auf psychologische Grundlage. Berlin, 1901.

Phil 8598.44 — Schwarz, Hermann. Das Ungegebene; eine Religions- und Wertphilosophie. Tübingen, 1921.

Phil 630.16 — Schwarz, Hermann. Was will der kritische Realismus? Leipzig, 1894.

Htn Phil 3801.773* — Schwarz, J.L. Schelling's alte und neue Philosophie. Berlin, 1844.

Phil 3425.298 — Schwarz, Justus. Hegels philosophische Entwicklung. Frankfurt, 1938.

Phil 8893.93 — Schwarz, O.L. Unconventional ethics. Washington, 1936.

Phil 585.255 — Schwarz, Richard. Menschliche Existenz und moderne Welt. Ein internationales Symposon zum Selbstverständnis des heutigen Menschen. Berlin, 1967. 2v.

Phil 2880.8.290 — Schwarz, Theodor. Jean-Paul Sartres "Kritik der dialektischen Vernunft". Berlin, 1967.

Phil 6328.31 — Schwarz, Theodor. Zur Kritik der Psychoanalyse. Zürich, 1947.

Phil 972.16 — Schwarz, W. Hoffnung in Wichts. München, 1961.

Phil 3500.54 — Schwarz, W. Immanuel Kant als Pädagoge. Langensalza, 1915.

Phil 5258.21 — Schweden, P. Über elementarische psychische Prozesse. Berlin, 1894.

Phil 1123.2 — Schwegler, A. Geschichte der griechischen Philosophie. Tübingen, 1859.

Phil 818.15 — Schwegler, A. Grunddragen af filosofiens historia. Örebro, 1856.

Phil 818.1 — Schwegler, F.C.A. Geschichte der Philosophie. Stuttgart, 1870.

Phil 818.1.3.3 — Schwegler, F.C.A. Geschichte der Philosophie. Stuttgart, 1882.

Phil 818.1.3 — Schwegler, F.C.A. Geschichte der Philosophie. 8e Aufl. Stuttgart, 1873.

Phil 818.1.4 — Schwegler, F.C.A. Geschichte der Philosophie. 13. Aufl. Stuttgart, 1885.

Phil 818.1.4.5 — Schwegler, F.C.A. Geschichte der Philosophie. 14. Aufl. Stuttgart, 1887.

NEDL Phil 818.1.7 — Schwegler, F.C.A. Handbook of the history of philosophy. Edinburgh, 1867.

Phil 818.1.8 — Schwegler, F.C.A. Handbook of the history of philosophy. 2d ed. Edinburgh, 1868.

Phil 818.1.12 — Schwegler, F.C.A. Handbook of the history of philosophy. 5th ed. N.Y., 1873.

Phil 818.1.16 — Schwegler, F.C.A. Handbook of the history of philosophy. 9th ed. Edinburgh, 1884.

Phil 818.1.5 — Schwegler, F.C.A. History of philosophy in epitome. N.Y., 1856.

Phil 818.1.6.5 — Schwegler, F.C.A. History of philosophy in epitome. N.Y., 1864.

Phil 3890.6.85 — Schweig, Helmut. Die Psychologie des Enkennens bei Bonnet und Tetens. Trier, 1921.

Phil 3850.27.40 — Schweitzer, A. Albert Schweitzers Leben und Denken. N.Y., 1949.

Phil 3850.27.55 — Schweitzer, A. The animal world of Albert Schweitzer. Boston, 1950.

Phil 3850.27.21 — Schweitzer, A. An anthology. N.Y., 1947.

Phil 3850.27.45 — Schweitzer, A. Das Christentum und die Welterligionen. München, 1949.

Phil 3850.27.50 — Schweitzer, A. Denken und Fat. Hamburg, 1950.

Phil 3850.27.75 — Schweitzer, A. Die Lehre von der Ehrfurcht vor dem Leben. München, 1966.

Phil 3850.27.35 — Schweitzer, A. Memoirs of childhood and youth. 1st American ed. N.Y., 1949.

Phil 3850.27.65.5 — Schweitzer, A. Reverence for life. N.Y., 1969.

Phil 3850.27.65 — Schweitzer, A. Strassburger Predigten. München, 1966.

Phil 3850.27.23 — Schweitzer, A. Vom Lich in Uns. Stuttgart, 1947.

Phil 3850.27.30 — Schweitzer, A. Waffen des Lichts. 1. Aufl. Heilbronn, 1940.

Phil 3850.27.230.5 — Schweitzer; a biography. 1st ed. (Marshall, George N.) Garden City, 1971.

Phil 3500.34 — Schweitzer, Albert. Die Religionsphilosophie Kants. Freiburg, 1899.

Phil 3850.27.127 — Schweitzer tel qu'il fut. (Babel, Henry.) Boudry-Neuchâtel, 1966.

Phil 3805.94 — Schweizer, A. Schleiermachers Wirksamkeit als Prediger. Halle, 1834.

Phil 193.113 — Schweizer, Robert. Der charakterwolle und der begriffliche Gegenstand. Leipzig, 1927.

Phil 8423.8.25 — Schweizer, V. Ludolf Wienbarg als jungdeutscher Ästhetiker und Kunstkritiker. Leipzig, 1896.

Phil 5258.86 — Schweizer, Walter. Erklären und Verstehen in der Psychologie. Bern, 1924.

Phil 5525.64.5 — Schweizer, Werner R. Der Witz. Bern, 1964.

Phil 28.23 — Schweizerische philosophische Gesellschaft. Jahrbuch. Basel. 1,1941+ 28v.

Phil 28.23.10 — Schweizerische philosophische Gesellschaft. Jahrbuch. Beihefte. Basel. 1,1943+ 11v.

Phil 5850.335 — Schweizerische Stiftung für Angewandte Psychologie. Angewandte Psychologie in der Schweiz. Bern, 1959.

Phil 28.39 — Schweizerische Zeitschrift für Psychologie und ihre Anwendungen. Bern. 1,1942+ 17v.

Phil 978.49.45 — Die Schwelle der geistigen Welt. 10. Aufl. (Steiner, R.) Berlin, 1921.

Phil 8968.11 — Schwellenbach, R. Die Erneuerung des Abendlandes. Berlin, 1922.

Phil 5251.41.85 — Schwermer, Josef. Die experimentelle Willenspsychologie Kurt Lewin. Meisenheim, 1966.

Phil 3640.45 — Schwert des Geistes. (Nietzsche, Friedrich.) Stuttgart, 1941.

Phil 5640.31 — Schwertschlager, J. Die Sinneserkenntnis. München, 1924.

Phil 5440.32.5 — Schwesinger, G. Heredity and environment. N.Y., 1933.

Phil 2477.1.139 — Schyns, M. La philosophie d'Emile Boutroux. Paris, 1924.

Phil 2651.85 — Sciacca, Giuseppe Maria. Scetticismo cristiano. Palermo, 1968.

Phil 3500.95 — Sciacca, Guiseppe M. L'idea della libertà. Palermo, 1963.

Phil 2477.6.145 — Sciacca, M.E. Dialogo con M. Blondel. Milano, 1962.

Phil 2240.85 — Sciacca, M.F. La filosofia di Tomaso Reid. Napoli, 1935.

Phil 2240.85.3 — Sciacca, M.F. La filosofia di Tommaso Reid. 3a ed. Milano, 1963.

Phil 4210.190 — Sciacca, M.F. La filosofia morale di Antonio Rosmini. 3a ed. Milano, 1958.

Phil 4210.190.5 — Sciacca, M.F. Interpretarioni rosminiane. Milano, 1958.

Phil 2805.400 — Sciacca, M.F. Pascal. 3. ed. Milan, 1962.

Phil 4018.6.5 — Sciacca, M.F. Il pensiero italiano nell'età del Risorgimento. 2. ed. Milano, 1963.

Phil 4018.7 — Sciacca, M.F. La philosophie italienne contemporaine. Lyon, 1953.

Phil 4018.6 — Sciacca, M.F. Il secolo XX. Milano, 1947. 2v.

Phil 818.21 — Sciacca, M.F. Studi sulla filosofia medioevale e moderna. Napoli, 1935.

Phil 4170.10.80 — Sciacca, Michele F. Martinetti. Brescia, 1943.

Phil 1123.10 — Sciacca, Michele F. Studi sulla filosofia antica. Napoli, 1935.

Phil 4225.8.37 — Sciacca, Michele Federico. Akt und Sein. 4. Aufl. Freiburg, 1964.

Phil 4225.8.36 — Sciacca, Michele Federico. Atto ed essere. 2. ed. Milano, 1958.

Phil 4225.8.67.2 — Sciacca, Michele Federico. La chiesane la civiltà moderna. 2. ed. Milano, 1969.

Phil 4225.8.42 — Sciacca, Michele Federico. La clessidra. 3. ed. Milano, 1960.

Phil 4225.8.38 — Sciacca, Michele Federico. Come si vince a Waterloo. Milano, 1957.

Phil 4225.8.52 — Sciacca, Michele Federico. Cosi mi parlano le cose muti. Milano, 1962.

Phil 4225.8.70 — Sciacca, Michele Federico. Dallo spiritualismo critico allo spiritualismo cristiano, 1939-1951. Milano, 1965. 2v.

Phil 4225.8.50 — Sciacca, Michele Federico. Dull'attualismo. Milano, 1961.

Phil 4225.8.58 — Sciacca, Michele Federico. Filosofia e antifilosofia. Milano, 1968.

Phil 4225.8.46 — Sciacca, Michele Federico. Filosofia e metafisica. v.1-2. 2. ed. Milano, 1962.

Phil 4225.8.32 — Sciacca, Michele Federico. La filosofia oggi. 3. ed. Milano, 1958. 2v.

Phil 4225.8.48 — Sciacca, Michele Federico. Gliarieti contro la verticale. Milano, 1969.

Phil 1718.29.5 — Sciacca, Michele Federico. Les grands courants de la pensée modiale contemporaine. v.1-3. Milan, 1958- 6v.

Phil 4225.8.44 — Sciacca, Michele Federico. In spirito e verità. 4. ed. Milano, 1960.

Phil 4225.8.30 — Sciacca, Michele Federico. L'interiorità oggetiva. Milano, 1958.

Phil 4225.8.68 — Sciacca, Michele Federico. Lettere dalla campagna, e scritti affini. 2. ed. Milano, 1966.

Phil 4225.8.65 — Sciacca, Michele Federico. La libertà e il tempo. Milano, 1965.

Phil 4225.8.34.2 — Sciacca, Michele Federico. Morte e immortalità. 2. ed. Milano, 1962.

Phil 4225.8.34 — Sciacca, Michele Federico. Morte ed immortalità. Milano, 1959.

Phil 4225.8.2 — Sciacca, Michele Federico. Opere complete. Milano, 1952-56. 7v.

Phil 4225.8.62 — Sciacca, Michele Federico. L'oscuramento dell'intelligenza. Milano, 1970.

Phil 1718.29 — Sciacca, Michele Federico. Il pensiero moderno. Brescia, 1949.

Phil 1718.29.10 — Sciacca, Michele Federico. Philosophical trends in the contemporary world. Notre Dame, 1964.

Phil 4225.8.60 — Sciacca, Michele Federico. Il problema di Dio e della religione nella filosofia attuale. 4. ed. Milano, 1964.

Phil 4225.8.55 — Sciacca, Michele Federico. Studi sulla filosofia moderna. 3. ed. Milano, 1964.

Phil 4225.8.40 — Sciacca, Michele Federico. L'uomo. 2. ed. Milano, 1958.

Phil 4260.195 — Sciacca, Michele Federico. Verità e storia in Vico. Roma, 1968.

Phil 8691.27 — Science, Christianity and truth. (Baker, Albert E.) London, 1943.

Phil 186.65.30 — Science, esthétique, métaphysique. (Lavelle, Louis.) Paris, 1967.

Phil 8709.11 — Science, evolution, religion. (Thallackson, E.) Boston, 1927.

Phil 165.369 — Science, folklore, and philosophy. N.Y., 1966.

Phil 70.30 — Science, language and human rights. Philadelphia, 1952.

Phil 349.44 — Science, perception, and reality. (Sellars, W.) London, 1963.

Phil 7069.67.40 — Science, philosophy and E.S.P. (McCreery, Charles.) London, 1967.

Phil 176.9 — Science, philosophy and religion. (Bascom, J.) N.Y., 1871.

Phil 8707.21 — Science, religion, and the future. (Raven, C.E.) Cambridge, Eng., 1943.

Phil 8703.2 — Science, religion and reality. (Needham, Joseph.) N.Y., 1928.

Phil 3120.15.40 — Science, spirit, superstition; a new enquiry into human thought. (Brunner, Constantin.) Toronto, 1968.

Phil 5262.57.5 — Science, synthesis and sanity. (Williamson, George Scott.) Chicago, 1966.

Phil 5262.57 — Science, synthesis and sanity. (Williamson, George Scott.) London, 1965.

Phil 3120.32.21 — Science a road to wisdom: collected philosophical studies. (Beth, Evert Willem.) Dordrecht, 1968.

Phil 8705.2 — Science a witness for the Bible. (Pendleton, W.N.) Philadelphia, 1860.

Phil 7069.05.10 — Science and a future life. (Hyslop, James Hervey.) Boston, 1905.

Phil 7069.10.5 — Science and a future life. 5. ed. (Hyslop, James Hervey.) Boston, 1910.

Phil 2905.1.63 — Science and Christ. (Teilhard de Chardin, Pierre.) London, 1968.

Phil 8692.20A — Science and Christian belief. (Coulson, C.A.) Chapel Hill, 1955.

Phil 8697.5.15 — Science and Christian tradition; essays. (Huxley, T.H.) N.Y., 1898.

Phil 8697.5.20 — Science and Christian tradition; essays. (Huxley, T.H.) N.Y., 1913.

Phil 8735.23 — Science and cosmic purpose. 1. ed. Thesis. (Van Nuys, K.) N.Y., 1949.

Phil 187.123 — Science and criticism. (Muller, H.J.) New Haven, 1943.

Phil 8882.55 — Science and ethics. (Haldane, J.B.S.) London, 1928.

Phil 9590.18 — Science and ethics. (Waddington, C.H.) London, 1942.

Phil 8702.30 — Science and faith, co-existence or synthesis? (Muller, C.) Louvain, 1962.

Phil 8708.19 — Science and faith, or The spiritual side of science. (Sanford, Hugh W.) N.Y., 1930. 2v.

Phil 8691.26 — Science and faith. (Bragg, W.) London, 1941.

Phil 8707.30 — Science and faith. (Rust, Eric C.) N.Y., 1967.

Phil 8709.3 — Science and faith. (Topinard, P.) Chicago, 1899.

Phil 2905.1.173 — Science and faith in Teilhard de Chardin. (Cuénot, Claude.) London, 1967.

Phil 8691.22 — Science and God. (Bavink, B.) London, 1933.

Phil 5258.120.8 — Science and human behavior. (Skinner, Burrhus F.) Cambridge, Mass.? 1951.

Phil 5258.120.10 — Science and human behavior. (Skinner, Burrhus F.) N.Y., 1953.

Phil 5258.120.12 — Science and human behavior. (Skinner, Burrhus F.) N.Y., 1958.

Phil 5258.120.13 — Science and human behavior. (Skinner, Burrhus F.) N.Y., 1964.

Phil 585.148 — Science and human perspectives. (Tsanoff, Radoslav.) London, 1963.

Phil 5115.4.6 — Science and hypothesis. (Poincaré, Henri.) London, 1905.

Phil 5115.4.7 — Science and hypothesis. (Poincaré, Henri.) London, 1914.

Phil 5115.4.5 — Science and hypothesis. (Poincaré, Henri.) N.Y., 1905.

Phil 600.51 — Science and idealism. (Cornforth, M.) N.Y., 1947.

Phil 400.19 — Science and idealism. (Münsterberg, H.) Boston, 1906.

Htn Phil 3625.10.35* — Science and idealism. (Münsterberg, H.) Boston, 1906.

Phil 8691.13 — Science and immortality. (Borrows, Samuel Jure.) Boston, 1903.

Phil 8701.4 — Science and immortality. (Lodge, Oliver Joseph.) N.Y., 1908.

Phil 8701.4.2 — Science and immortality. (Lodge, Oliver Joseph.) N.Y., 1914.

Phil 8633.1.6.5 — Science and immortality. (Osler, W.) Boston, 1904.

Phil 182.101.10 — Science and life. (Haldane, John Burdon Sanderson.) London, 1968.

Phil 450.2 — Science and man; the philoosophy of scientific humanism. (Clements, Tad S.) Springfield, Illinois, 1968.

Phil 5241.167 — Science and man. (Brain, Walter.) London, 1966.

Phil 5241.97.5 — Science and man's behavior. (Burrow, Trigant.) N.Y., 1953.

Phil 3500.112 — Science and metaphysics; variations on Kantian themes. (Sellars, Wilfrid.) London, 1968.

Phil 5628.51.5 — Science and miracle. Louise Lateau ou la stigmatisée belge. (Bourneville, Désiré Magloire.) Paris, 1875.

Phil 510.148 — Science and monism. (Wightman, W.P.D.) London, 1934.

Phil 5241.28.17 — Science and personality. (Brown, W.) New Haven, 1929.

Phil 176.56.7 — Science and philosophy and other essays. (Bosanquet, B.) London, 1927.

Phil 7069.38.60 — Science and psychical phenomena. (Tyrrell, G.N.M.) London, 1938.

Phil 28.62 — Science and psycholoanalysis. N.Y. 1,1958+ 13v.

Phil 8708.20 — Science and religion; a symposium. N.Y., 1931.

Phil 8709.17 — Science and religion; being the Morse lecture for 1924. (Thomson, J.A.) N.Y., 1925.

Phil 8700.1 — Science and religion, rational and superrational. (Keyser, C.J.) New Haven, 1914.

Phil 8698.10 — Science and religion. (Ikeda, Daisaku.) Tokyo, 1965.

Phil 8707.7.9 — Science and religion. (Rice, William N.) Cincinnati, 1925.

Phil 8708.36 — Science and religion. (Schilling, Harold K.) N.Y., 1962.

Phil 8708.24 — Science and religion. London, 1931.

Phil 8707.14 — Science and religion as they look to a layman. (Rigdon, Jonathan.) Danville, Ind., 1928.

Phil 8705.20 — Science and religion for modern man. (Perlman, Robert Odehyah.) Jerusalem, 1964.

Phil 8712.27 — Science and religion in American thought. (White, E.A.) Stanford, 1952.

Phil 8691.6.5 — Science and religion in contemporary philosophy. (Boutroux, E.) London, 1909.

Phil 8700.14.5 — Science and religion in Elizabethan England. (Kocher, Paul Harold.) N.Y., 1969.

Phil 8700.14 — Science and religion in Elizabethan England. (Kocher, Paul Harold.) San Marino, Calif., 1955.

Phil 8697.15 — Science and revelation. (Hayden, W.B.) Boston, 1852.

Phil 8712.23 — Science and revelation. (Walker, L.J.) London, 1932.

Phil 8712.6 — Science and revelation. (Wright, T.S.) Bellefontaine, 1878.

Phil 8708.38 — Science and revelation: a series of lectures. Belfast, 1875.

Phil 5520.96.10 — Science and sanity. (Korzybski, Alfred.) Lakeville, Conn., 1958.

Phil 6536.9 — Science and seizures. (Lennox, W.G.) N.Y., 1941.

Phil 190.15.5 — Science and sentiment. (Porter, N.) N.Y., 1882.

Phil 8893.48 — Science and social progress. (Schneider, H.W.) Lancaster, Pa., 1920.

Phil 720.84 — Science and subjectivity. (Scheffler, Israel.) Indianapolis, 1967.

Phil 193.37.2 — Science and superstition. (Stevens, Samuel Eugene.) N.Y., 1913.

Phil 8701.2.7 — Science and the bible, a review of the Six days of creation. (Dana, J.D.) Andover, 1856.

Phil 7069.67.25 — Science and the E.S.P. (Smythies, John Raymond.) London, 1967.

Phil 8950.5 — Science and the gospel. (Anglican and International Christian Moral Science Association, L.) London, 1870.

Phil 8697.17 — Science and the idea of God. (Hocking, W.E.) Chapel Hill, 1944.

Phil 2200.5A — Science and the moral life. (Otto, Max Carl.) N.Y., 1949.

Phil 8707.12 — Science and the religious life. (Rahn, Carl.) New Haven, 1928.

Phil 8701.16 — Science and the supernatural; a correspondence between Arnold Lunn and J.B.S. Haldane. (Lunn, Arnold.) N.Y., 1935.

Phil 8694.4A — Science and the unseen world. (Eddington, Arthur.) N.Y., 1929.

Phil 8694.4.5 — Science and the unseen world. (Eddington, Arthur.) N.Y., 1930.

Phil 8712.15 — Science and theology. (Westaway, F.W.) London, 1920.

Phil 8698.1 — Science and ultimate truth. (Inge, W.P.) London, 1926.

Phil 2750.11.57.5 — Science and wisdom. (Maritain, Jacques.) N.Y., 1940.

Phil 600.7.3 — La science au point de vue philosophique. (Littré, Émile.) Paris, 1873.

Phil 2840.50 — Science de la morale. (Renouvier, C.B.) Paris, 1869. 2v.

Phil 2840.50.5 — Science de la morale. (Renouvier, C.B.) Paris, 1908. 2v.

Phil 182.25 — La science de l'esprit. (Huet, F.) Paris, 1864. 2v.

Phil 186.9 — La science de l'invisible. (Lévêque, J.C.) Paris, 1865.

Phil 5850.127 — La science des caractères. (Band, Francis.) Paris, 1944.

Phil 5400.39.3 — La science des émotions. (Bhagavan, Das.) Bruxelles, 1921.

Phil 8876.51.13 — La science des faits moraux. (Bayet, Albert.) Paris, 1925.

Phil 8412.5 — La science du beau, ses principes, ses applications et son histoire. 2. éd. (Lévêque, C.) Paris, 1872. 2v.

Phil 8881.3 — Science du bien et du mal. (Géhant, J.B.V.) Paris, 1848. 2v.

Phil 9245.29 — La science du bonheur. (Lescoeur, Louis.) Paris, 1873.

Phil 2750.26.30 — Science du bonheur. (Mathieu, Guy.) Paris, 1957.

Phil 9035.63 — La science du caractère. (Boven, William.) Neuchâtel, 1931.

Phil 8583.31 — La science du Christ et de l'homme. (Dutoit-Mombrini, P.) n.p., 1810. 3v.

Phil 4075.45.15 — La science du monde. 4e éd. (Cardano, Girolamo.) Paris, 1661.

Phil 185.8 — La science du vrai. (Koenig, E.) Paris, 1844.

Phil 8702.36 — Science et foi chrétienne. (Mairlot, Édouard.) Bruxelles, 1968.

Phil 2477.13 — Science et humanisme. (Bréhier, Émile.) Paris, 1947.

Phil 9075.8 — La science et la conscience. (Vacherot, E.) Paris, 1870.

Phil 8691.16 — La science et la religion. (Broglie, Paul.) Paris, 1885.

Phil 600.33 — La science et l'esprit positif chez les penseurs contemporains. (Boll, Marcel.) Paris, 1921.

Phil 5115.4 — La science et l'hypothèse. (Poincaré, Henri.) Paris, 1903.

Phil 645.15 — Science et libre pensée. 2e éd. (Berthelot, M.) Paris, 1905.

Phil 493.7 — Science et matérialisme. (Russo, F.) Paris, 1962.

Phil 2520.229.5 — Science et métaphysique chez Descartes. (Alquié, F.) Paris, 1965.

Phil 8887.73 — Science et morale. (Michaud, Félix.) Paris, 1941.

Phil 176.33.5 — Science et nature. v.1-2. (Büchner, L.) Paris, 1866.

Phil 178.82 — Science et nescience. (Diéguez, Manuel de.) Paris, 1970.

Phil 2750.10.95 — Science et philosophie d'après la doctrine de Emile Meyerson. (Sée, Henri.) Paris, 1932.

Phil 2730.30 — Science et psychologie. (Maine de Biran, Pierre.) Paris, 1887.

NEDL Phil 8691.6.1 — Science et religion. (Boutroux, E.) Paris, 1908.

Phil 2750.11.57 — Science et sagesse. (Maritain, Jacques.) Paris, 1935.

Phil 8689.105 — Science et théologie: méthode et langage. Paris, 1970.

Phil 3015.1 — Science française, scolastique allemande. (Papillault, G.) Paris, 1917.

Phil 7069.45.65 — Science from the unseen. (Jordan, Alfred McKay, (Mrs.).) N.Y., 1945.

Phil 8690.6 — Science in defense of liberal religion. (Anderson, Paul R.) N.Y., 1933.

Phil 8702.16A — Science in search of God. (Mather, K.F.) N.Y., 1928.

Phil 8702.16.2 — Science in search of God. (Mather, K.F.) N.Y., 1928.

Phil 8695.10 — Science in theology: sermons. (Farrar, Adam Storey.) Philadelphia, 1860.

Phil 1511.5 — Science moderne et philosophie médiévale. (Gorce, M.M.) Paris, 1938.

Phil 8876.81 — La science morale. (Bellaigue, A.) Paris, 1904.

NEDL Phil 4260.35.9 — La science nouvelle. (Vico, G.B.) Bari, 1911-16. 3v.

Phil 4260.35.5 — La science nouvelle. (Vico, G.B.) Paris, 1844.

Phil 8404.5 — The science of aesthetics. (Day, Henry.) New Haven, 1872.

Phil 8430.17 — The science of beauty, as developed in nature. (Hay, D.R.) Edinburgh, 1856.

Phil 575.51.15 — The science of character. (Klages, Ludwig.) London, 1929.

Phil 298.6 — Science of creation. (Riddell, Newton N.) Des Moines, Iowa, 192-.

Phil 7082.14 — The science of dreams. 1st ed. (Diamond, Edwin.) Garden City, 1962.

Phil 3246.72.5 — Science of ethics...based on Science of knowledge. (Fichte, Johann Gottlieb.) London, 1897.

Phil 8877.55 — The science of ethics. (Cronin, Michael.) Dublin, 1909.

NEDL Phil 8893.23.2 — The science of ethics. (Stephen, L.) N.Y., 1882.

Phil 8877.55.2 — The science of ethics. 2nd ed. (Cronin, Michael.) Dublin, 1920-22. 2v.

Phil 3850.64 — The science of freedom; an essay in applied philosophy. (Stern-Mitcherlich, Axel Ludwig.) London, 1969.

Phil 5825.3 — The science of human behavior. (Parmelee, M.) N.Y., 1913.

Phil 5262.41 — Science of human behavior. (Wait, W.T.) N.Y., 1938.

Phil 5255.50 — The science of human nature. (Pyle, William H.) Boston, 1917.

Phil 2490.103 — The science of individuality. Thesis. (DeGrange, McQuilkin.) Lyon, 1923.

X Cg Phil 3246.58.2 — Science of knowledge. (Fichte, Johann Gottlieb.) Philadelphia, 1868.

Phil 6310.1.20   The science of living. (Adler, A.) Garden City, N.Y., 1929.
Phil 6310.1.21   The science of living. (Adler, A.) N.Y., 1929.
Phil 5042.11   The science of logic. (Coffey, P.) London, 1912. 2v.
Phil 3425.34.31A   Science of logic. (Hegel, Georg Wilhelm Friedrich.) London, 1951. 2v.
Phil 3425.34.29   Science of logic. (Hegel, Georg Wilhelm Friedrich.) London, 1961. 2v.
Phil 3425.34.30   Science of logic. (Hegel, Georg Wilhelm Friedrich.) N.Y., 1929.
Phil 5052.35   The science of logic. (Mahan, Asa.) N.Y., 1857.
Phil 5241.7.2   The science of mind. (Bascom, J.) N.Y., 1881.
Phil 181.28   Science of minds. (Godlover, H.B.) n.p., n.d.
Phil 8892.41   The science of morals; an essay in method. (Roth, Leon.) London, 1928.
X Cg   Phil 6049.05   The science of palmistry. (Lawrence, E.) London, 1905.
Phil 7011.2.2   The science of psychic phenomena. 2. ed. (Abhedânanda, Swami.) Calcutta, 1966.
Phil 5262.36   The science of psychology. (Wheeler, R.H.) N.Y., 1929.
Phil 5262.36.2   The science of psychology. (Wheeler, R.H.) N.Y., 1940.
Phil 5627.104   The science of religion: an introduction. (Rohrbaugh, L.G.) N.Y., 1927.
X Cg   Phil 3246.60   Science of rights. (Fichte, Johann Gottlieb.) London, 1889.
X Cg   Phil 3246.60.5   Science of rights. (Fichte, Johann Gottlieb.) Philadelphia, 1869.
Phil 3246.60.5   Science of rights. (Fichte, Johann Gottlieb.) Philadelphia, 1869.
Phil 6677.14   The science of seership. (Hodson, Geoffrey.) Philadelphia, 1930.
Phil 7069.45.20   The science of spirit healing. (Edwards, H.J.) London, 1945.
Phil 7054.170   The science of spirit return. (Dawburn, Charles.) Springfield, Mass., 188-.
Phil 5400.39   The science of the emotions. (Bhagavan, Das.) London, 1900.
Phil 5400.39.9   The science of the emotions. 3rd ed. (Bhagavan, Das.) Adyar, 1924.
Phil 665.63   The science of the soul. (Clymer, R.S.) Quakertown, 1922.
Phil 5044.3.4   The science of thought. (Everett, C.C.) Boston, 1882.
Phil 5520.3   Science of thought. (Müller, F.M.) London, 1887.
Phil 28.45   Science of thought. Tokyo.
Phil 5044.3.5   The science of thought. Rev. ed. (Everett, C.C.) Boston, 1890.
Phil 5520.3.5   Science of thought. v.2. (Müller, F.M.) N.Y., 1887.
Phil 186.10   La science positive. (Liard, L.) Paris, 1879.
Phil 186.10.5   La science positive. 5. ed. (Liard, L.) Paris, 1905.
Phil 3425.656   La science universelle ou la logique de Hegel. (Fleishmann, Eugène.) Paris, 1968.
Phil 1930.12.32   Science versus idealism. (Cornforth, Maurice Campbell.) N.Y., 1962.
Phil 177.115   Science versus philosophy. (Connally, F.G.) N.Y., 1957.
Phil 7054.164   Science vs. modern spiritualism. (Gasparin, Agénov.) N.Y., 1857. 2v.
Phil 182.101   The sciences and philosophy. (Haldane, J.S.) London, 1928.
Phil 1750.115.125   Les sciences de l'homme et la phénoménologie. (Merleau-Ponty, Maurice.) Paris, 1965.
Phil 5090.8   Les sciences et la méthode reconstructives. (Dellepiane, A.) Paris, 1915.
Phil 187.10   Les sciences et la philosophie. (Martin, T.H.) Paris, 1869.
Phil 70.18.10   Les sciences et la sagesse. (Congrès des Sociétés de Philosophie de Langue Française, 5th, Bordeaux, 1950.) Paris. 1950
Phil 180.13   Les sciences humaines: la philosophie. (Funck-Brentano, T.) Paris, 1868.
Phil 181.136   Sciences humaines et philosophie. (Goldmann, Lucien.) Paris, 1966.
Phil 7069.59.30   Les sciences occultes ne sont pas des sciences. (Imbert-Nergal, R.) Paris, 1959.
Phil 190.15   Sciences of nature vs. sciences of man. (Porter, N.) N.Y., 1871.
Phil 5275.15   The sciences of the artificial. (Simon, Herbert Alexander.) Cambridge, 1969.
Phil 192.25.5   Les sciences philosophiques. 2. ed. (Rey, A.) Paris, 1911.
Phil 7069.18.140   Sciens, (pseud.) How to speak with the dead. N.Y., 1918.
Phil 8699.1   The scientifc eye of faith. (Jones, Richard U.) Boston, 1935.
Phil 8655.5.5   Scientifc theism. 2. ed. (Abbot, F.E.) Boston, 1886.
Phil 8691.24.2   Scientifc theory and religion. (Barnes, E.W.) N.Y., 1934.
Phil 5590.446   The scientific analysis of personality. (Cattell, Raymond.) Chicago, 1966.
Phil 177.65   The scientific approach to philosophy. (Carr, H.W.) London, 1924.
Phil 8712.5.9   Scientific aspects of Christian evidences. (Wright, George F.) N.Y., 1898.
Phil 2218.47   A scientific autobiography of Joseph Priestley, 1733-1804. (Priestley, Joseph.) Cambridge, 1966.
Phil 5927.2   Scientific basis of education demonstrated. (Hecker, J.) N.Y., 1867.
Phil 8592.16.2   The scientific basis of faith. (Murphy, J.J.) London, 1873.
Phil 8877.75   The scientific basis of morals, and other essays. (Clifford, William K.) N.Y., 1884.
Phil 7054.34   The scientific basis of spiritualism. (Sargent, Epes.) Boston, 1880.
Phil 7068.91.10   The scientific basis of spiritualism. 6th ed. (Sargent, Epes.) Boston, 1891.
Phil 735.195   Scientific Conference on New Knowledge...1st. New knowledge in human values. N.Y., 1959.
Phil 5465.136   Scientific creativity. (Taylor, C.W.) N.Y., 1963.
Phil 8632.1.12   A scientific demonstration...future life. 12th ed. (Hudson, T.J.) Chicago, 1922.
Phil 7082.100   The scientific dream book and dictionary of dream symbols. (Westerfield, Jonathan B.) N.Y., 1932.
Phil 5220.5   The scientific evolution of psychology. (Kantor, J.R.) Chicago, 1963. 2v.
Phil 175.16   Scientific fact and metaphysical reality. (Arnold, R.B.) London, 1904.
Phil 5520.112   A scientific foundation of philosophy. (Haerber, W.L.) Los Angeles, 1952.
Phil 5520.112.1   A scientific foundation of philosophy. (Haerber, W.L.) Los Angeles, 1960.
Phil 400.46   Scientific idealism. (Kingsland, William.) London, 1909.
Phil 5762.36   Scientific indeterminism and human freedom. (Margenau, Henry.) Latrobe, Pa., 1968.

Phil 6111.18   Scientific mental healing. (Bruce, H.A.) Boston, 1911.
Phil 8413.7   Scientific method in aesthetics. (Munro, Thomas.) N.Y., 1928.
Phil 192.28.8   Scientific method in philosophy. (Russell, B.) Oxford, 1913.
Phil 5270.22   Scientific method in psychology. (Brown, Clarence William.) N.Y., 1955.
Phil 5850.306   Scientific mind training. (Pelman Institute of America.) N.Y., 1924.
Phil 5850.306.5   Scientific mind training. (Pelman Institute of America.) N.Y., 1927.
Phil 182.47   Scientific occultism. (Hatch, D.P.) Los Angeles, 1905.
Phil 510.1.50   The scientific origins of National Socialism: Social Darwinism in Ernst Haeckel and the German Monist League. (Gasman, Daniel.) London, 1971.
Phil 331.1   Scientific philosophy. (Abbot, F.E.) London, 1882.
Phil 5238.205   Scientific psychology: principles and approaches. (Wolman, Benjamin B.) N.Y., 1965.
Phil 5250.60   Scientific psychology and naive psychology. (Kremers, Johan.) Nijmegen, 1960.
Phil 8594.5.5   Scientific religion. (Oliphant, L.) Buffalo, 1889.
Phil 8594.5.2   Scientific religion. 2. ed. (Oliphant, L.) Edinburgh, 1888.
Phil 6671.27   A scientific report on the search for Bridey Murphy. (Kline, M.V.) N.Y., 1956.
Phil 182.33.2   Scientific romances. (Hinton, C.H.) London, 1886.
Phil 182.33   Scientific romances. Nos. 1-5,7-8. (Hinton, C.H.) London, 1884-1888. 7v.
Phil 8655.5   Scientific theism. (Abbot, F.E.) Boston, 1885.
Phil 8691.24   Scientific theory and religion. (Barnes, E.W.) Cambridge, Eng., 1933.
Phil 2520.237   The scientific work of René Descartes. (Scott, J.F.) London, 1952.
Phil 8692.28   The scientist and the supernatural: a systematic examination of the relation between Christianity and humanism. (Clark, Cecil Henry Douglas.) London, 1966.
Phil 8709.22   A scientist who believes in God. (Temperley, H.N.V.) London, 1961.
Phil 8702.20   A scientist's approach to religion. (Miller, C.W.) N.Y., 1947.
Phil 188.14.5   Scientologie. (Nordenholz, A.) München, 1934.
Phil 188.14.7   Scientologie. (Nordenholz, A.) München, 1937.
Phil 6317.32.5   Scientology. (Hubbard, L. Ron.) London, 1956.
Phil 4120.8.30   La scienza. (Guzzo, Augusto.) Torino, 1955.
Phil 8708.44   Scienza e fede e il liro preteso conflitto. (Semeria, Giovanni.) Roma, 1903.
Phil 193.140   Scienza e filosofia. (Spirito, Ugo.) Firenze, 1933.
Phil 4065.150   Scienza e filosofia in Giordano Bruno. (Giusso, Lorenzo.) Napoli, 1955.
Phil 193.5.3   La scienza e la vita. (Sanctis, F. de.) Napoli, 1872.
Phil 193.5   La scienza e la vita. (Sanctis, F. de.) Philadelphia, 1884.
Phil 349.52   Scienza e methologia; saggi de epistemologia. (Selvaggi, Filippo.) Roma, 1962.
Phil 196.8.7   Scienza e opinioni. (Varisco, B.) Roma, 1901.
Phil 623.19   Scienza e razionalismo. (Enriques, F.) Bologna, n.d.
Phil 8696.10.5   Scienza ed apologetica. (Gemelli, Agostino.) Milano, 1920.
Phil 4260.35.32   Scienza nuova...a cura di G. Flores d'Arcais. 2. ed. (Vico, G.B.) Padova, 1939.
Phil 4260.35.33   Scienza nuova...a cura di G. Flores d'Arcais. 3. ed. (Vico, G.B.) Padova, 1943.
Phil 4260.28   La scienza nuova e opere scelte di Giambattista Vico. (Vico, G.B.) Torino, 1952.
Phil 8890.32   Scienze ausiliarie della morale. (Pascot, Giovanni.) Udine, 1903.
Phil 585.70.10   Scienze umane e antropologia filosofica. (Cantoni, Remo.) Milano, 1966.
Phil 3018.30   Scifert, F. Schäpferische deutsche Philosophie. Köhn, 1944.
Phil 2477.6.95   Scivittaro, F. L'azione e il pensiero. Roma, 1936.
Phil 5620.34   Scivoletto, Angelo. Il segno della ragione. Padova, 1963.
Phil 6688.23.2   Scobardi, R.P. Rapport confidentiel sur le magnétisme animal. 2. éd. Paris, 1839.
Phil 665.49   Scofield, A. Insights and heresies. Boston, 1913.
Phil 1523.6   La scolastica del secolo XVI e la politica dei Gesuiti. (Saitta, Giuseppe.) Torino, 1911.
Phil 1522.5   La scolastique et le thomisme. (Rougier, Louis.) Paris, 1925.
Phil 1517.4   La scolastique et les traditions franciscaines. (Martigné, P. de.) Paris, 1888.
Phil 1133.23   Scoon, Robert. Greek philosophy before Plato. Princeton, 1928.
Phil 5058.25   The scope of formal logic. (Shearman, A.T.) London, 1911.
Phil 6310.4.30   The scope of psychoanalysis. (Alexander, Franz G.) N.Y., 1961.
Phil 8708.31   Scopes, John Thomas. Center of the storm. N.Y., 1967.
Phil 8622.88   Scoppio, Domenico. Fede e verità nel Cristianesimo contemporaneo. Bari, 1968.
Phil 6688.14   Scoresby, William. Zoistic magnetism. London, 1849.
Phil 5548.70   Scoring human motives. (Dollard, John.) New Haven, 1959.
Phil 8598.26   Scot, David. Discourses on...subjects of natural and revealed religion. Edinburgh, 1825.
Phil 8968.12   Scott, Charles A.A. New Testament ethics. Cambridge, Eng., 1930.
Phil 6128.84   Scott, Donald Fletcher. The psychology of work. London, 1970.
Phil 193.19   Scott, J. McD. Theories and criticisms. Halifax, 1883.
Phil 2520.237   Scott, J.F. The scientific work of René Descartes. London, 1952.
Phil 5828.20   Scott, J.P. Animal behavior. Garden City, 1963.
Phil 5421.20   Scott, John Paul. Aggression. Chicago, 1958.
Phil 3500.38   Scott, John W. Kant on the moral life. London, 1924.
Phil 5258.12   Scott, R.E. Elements of intellectual philosophy. Edinburgh 1805.
Phil 270.12   Scott, R.E. Inquiry into limits...nature of causation. Edinburgh, 1810.
Phil 9050.2   Scott, Rev. Dr. A lecture...on the influences of great cities. San Francisco, 1854.
Htn   Phil 8595.16.20*   Scott, Thomas. Treatises on various theological subjects. Middletown, Conn., 1815.
Phil 8595.16.21   Scott, Thomas. Treatises on various theological subjects. Middletown, Conn., 1824. 5v.
Htn   Phil 8595.16.19*   Scott, Thomas. Vindication of divine inspiration. London, 1797.
Phil 5938.1   Scott, W. The harmony of phrenology with scripture. Edinburgh, 1837.

Phil 5610.1.15 Scott, W.D. The psychology of public speaking. N.Y., 1926.
Phil 5610.1 Scott, W.D. The psychology of public speaking. Philadelphia, 1907.
Htn Phil 9358.5* Scott, William. An essay of drapery. London, 1635.
Phil 5258.187 Scott, William. Introduction to psychological research. N.Y., 1962.
Phil 2053.80 Scott, William Robert. Francis Hutcheson, his life, teaching and position in the history of philosophy. Cambridge, 1900.
Phil 2053.80.2 Scott, William Robert. Francis Hutcheson, his life, teaching and position in the history of philosophy. N.Y., 1966.
NEDL Phil 1925.81 Scott, William Robert. Introduction to Cudworth's treatise...with life. London, 1891.
Phil 8843.6 Scotti, Giulio. La metafisica nella morale moderna. Milano, 1903.
Phil 1828.14 Scottish common sense in America, 1768-1850. Thesis. (Petersen, Richard J.) Ann Arbor, 1972.
Phil 193.20 Scottish metaphysics. Edinburgh, 1887.
Phil 1811.1 Scottish philosophy. (Laurie, H.) Glasgow, 1902.
Phil 1812.1 The Scottish philosophy. (McCosh, J.) N.Y., 1875.
Phil 1818.1 Scottish philosophy. (Seth, A.) Edinburgh, 1885.
Phil 1818.1.5 Scottish philosophy. 3e ed. (Seth, A.) Edinburgh, 1899.
Phil 1806.10 The Scottish philosophy of common sense. (Grave, Selwyn A.) Oxford, 1960.
Phil 8610.871 Pamphlet vol. Scott's tracts. v.1. 21 pam.
Phil 8610.871.2 Pamphlet vol. Scott's tracts. v.2. 7 pam.
Phil 8610.871.4 Pamphlet vol. Scott's tracts. v.4. 28 pam.
Phil 8610.871.5 Pamphlet vol. Scott's tracts. v.5. 21 pam.
Phil 8610.871.6 Pamphlet vol. Scott's tracts. v.6. 25 pam.
Phil 8610.871.7 Pamphlet vol. Scott's tracts. v.7. 8 pam.
Phil 8610.871.8 Pamphlet vol. Scott's tracts. v.8. 19 pam.
Phil 8610.871.9 Pamphlet vol. Scott's tracts. v.9. 20 pam.
Phil 8610.871.10 Pamphlet vol. Scott's tracts. v.10. 21 pam.
Phil 8610.871.11 Pamphlet vol. Scott's tracts. v.11. 16 pam.
Phil 8610.871.12 Pamphlet vol. Scott's tracts. v.12. 18 pam.
Phil 8591.44.5A The screwtape letters. (Lewis, Clive Staples.) N.Y., 1943.
Phil 8591.44.8 The screwtape letters. (Lewis, Clive Staples.) N.Y., 1969.
Phil 8591.44.6 The screwtape letters and Screwtape proposes a toast. (Lewis, Clive Staples.) London, 1961.
Phil 7054.156 The scribe of a soul. (Von Ravens, Clara I.) Seattle, 1901.
Phil 813.6 Scrieri inedite. (Negulescu, P.P.) Bucuresti, 1969.
Phil 3450.11.245 Scrimieri, G. Problemi di logica. Bari, 1959.
Phil 1850.30 Scripta in naturali...philosophia. (Bacon, Francis.) Amsterdam, 1653.
Phil 5811.9 Scriptural and philosophical arguments. (Buchan, P.) Peterhead, 1824.
Phil 5425.11 Scripture, E.W. Arithmetical prodigies. Worcester, 1891.
Phil 5258.13.10 Scripture, E.W. The new psychology. London, 1897.
Phil 5258.13.15 Scripture, E.W. The new psychology. London, 1901.
Phil 5258.13 Scripture, E.W. Problem of psychology. London, 1891.
Phil 5258.13.5 Scripture, E.W. Thinking, feeling, doing. Meadville, 1895.
Phil 5258.13.6 Scripture, E.W. Thinking, feeling, doing. N.Y., 1907. 2v.
Phil 5325.9 Scripture, E.W. Über der associativen Verlauf der Vorstellungen. Leipzig, 1891.
Phil 5325.9.5 Scripture, E.W. Vorstellung und Gefühl. Leipzig, 1891.
Phil 1915.61 The scripture-doctrine of the Trinity. (Clarke, Samuel.) London, 1712.
Phil 1915.61.2 The scripture-doctrine of the Trinity. 2d ed. (Clarke, Samuel.) London, 1719.
Phil 1915.61.3 The scripture-doctrine of the Trinity. 3d ed. (Clarke, Samuel.) London, 1732.
Htn Phil 8636.9* Scripture revelations of the life of man after death. 3. ed. (Lyttelton, W.H.) London, 1876.
Phil 4160.66.12 Scritti; saggi. v.10-13. (Lombardi, Franco.) Firenze, 1965- 4v.
Phil 4160.66.12.2 Scritti; saggi. v.11- 2. ed. (Lombardi, Franco.) Firenze, 1970-
Phil 4080.20.30 Scritti. (Cairola, G.) Torino, 1954.
Phil 4080.18.5 Scritti. (Calogero, Guido.) Firenze, 1960. 2v.
Phil 4160.66.14 Scritti. Opere. (Lombardi, Franco.) Firenze, 1963- 6v.
Phil 4265.4.5F Scritti (1863-1909). (Vailati, G.) Leipzig, 1911.
Phil 8401.25.5 Scritti di estetica. (Antoni, Carlo.) Napoli, 1968.
Phil 8407.28 Scritti di estetica. (Gargiulo, A.) Firenze, 1952.
Phil 5238.6 Scritti di psicologia raccolti in onore di Federico Kiesow. Torino, 1933.
Phil 8408.24 Scritti e frammenti di estetica. (Hamann, J.G.) Roma, 1938.
Phil 2115.61 Scritti editi e inediti sulla tolleranza. (Locke, J.) Torino, 1961.
Phil 4225.23.30 Scritti filosofica. (Stellini, J.) Milano, 1942.
Phil 4070.4.30 Scritti filosofici. (Bertini, Giovanni M.) Milano, 1942.
Phil 180.41.10 Scritti filosofici. (Ferro, A.A.) Milano, 1932.
Phil 4225.1 Scritti filosofici. (Spaventa, Bertrando.) Napoli, 1900.
Phil 190.29 Scritti filosofici et letterari. (Politeo, Giorgio.) Bologna, 1919.
Phil 4225.1.21 Scritti inediti e rari, 1840-1880. (Spaventa, Bertrando.) Padova, 1966.
Phil 3480.28.25 Scritti minori. (Kant, Immanuel.) Bari, 1923.
Phil 4215.8.21 Scritti politici, 1912-26. (Ruggiero, Guido de.) Bologna, 1963.
Phil 4060.10.30 Scritti scelti. (Abbagnano, Nicola.) Torino, 1967.
Phil 4115.20 Scritti scelti. (Gioberti, V.) Torino, 1954.
Phil 4060.1.25 Scritti vari. (Ardigo, Roberto.) Firenze, 1920.
Phil 181.45.30 Scritti vari. (Gentile, Giovanni.) Lanciano, 1920-1926. 5v.
Phil 4260.23 Scritti vari e pagine sparse. (Vico, G.B.) Bari, 1940.
Phil 181.68 Scritti varii di filosofia e letteratura. (Gatti, Stanislao.) Napoli, 1861. 2v.
Phil 4005.2.5 Scritti varii di letteratura, filosofia e critica. (Fiorentino, F.) Napoli, 1876.
Phil 180.29 Scritti varj. v.1-3. (Ferrari, Giuseppe M.) Roma, 1899-1927. 3v.
Phil 4260.85.25 Scrocca, A. Giambattista Vico nella critica di Benedetto Croce. Napoli, 1919.
Phil 8598.51 Scudder, D. The passion for reality. N.Y., 1910.
Phil 8599.21.90 Scudder, D.L. Tennant's philosophical theology. New Haven, 1740.
Phil 8968.5 Scullard, H.H. Early Christian ethics in the West. London, 1907.
Htn Phil 8893.4* Sculteti, A. Ethicorum. Argentinae, 1614.
X Cg Phil 6028.4.5 Scuola di fisionomia, chiromantia. (Spadon, N.) Macerata, 1654.
Htn Phil 5765.1.5* Se l'huomo diventa buono o cattivo volontariamente. (Porzio, S.) Fiorenza, 1551.
Phil 3525.95 Se opone El Krausismo a la fé católica? (Fernandez Valbuena, Ramiro.) Badajoz, 1882[1883]
Phil 6122.8.5 Se sia l'anima o il cervello che pente e pensa. Firenze, 1881.
Phil 9070.45 Se suffire à soi-même. (Spezzafumo de Faucamberge, S.) Paris, 1941.
Phil 6328.18.10 Seabury, David. Adventures in self discovery. N.Y., 1938.
Phil 6128.46.7 Seabury, David. Growing into life. N.Y., 1928.
Phil 6128.46.12 Seabury, David. Help yourself to happiness. N.Y., 1937.
Phil 6128.46 Seabury, David. How to worry successfully. Boston, 1936.
Phil 5850.337 Seabury, David. Unmasking our minds. N.Y., 1924.
Phil 5850.337.9 Seabury, David. Unmasking our minds. N.Y., 1929.
Phil 6328.18 Seabury, David. What makes us seem so queer? N.Y., 1934.
Phil 9358.17 Seabury, Samuel. Self government and the power of an ideal. n.p., 1931.
Phil 8893.33 Séailles, G. Les affirmations de la conscience moderne. Paris, 1903.
Phil 8419.44 Séailles, G. Essai sur le génie dans l'art. Paris, 1883.
Phil 2840.81 Séailles, G. Philosophie de Charles Renouvier. Paris, 1905.
Phil 2725.11.81A Séailles, G. La philosophie de Jules Lachelier. Paris, 1920.
Phil 193.112 Seailles, G. La philosophie du travail. Paris, 1923.
Phil 9560.33 The seamless robe; the religion of loving kindness. (Cleghorn, S.N.) N.Y., 1945.
Phil 5465.188 The seamless web; language thinking. (Burnshaw, Stanley.) N.Y., 1970.
Phil 7060.74 Une séance de spiritisme. (Boucher, G.) Niort, 1908.
Phil 978.59.14 The search. (Krishnamurti, J.) N.Y., 1927.
Phil 978.59.15 The search. (Krishnamurti, J.) N.Y., 1927[1928]
Htn Phil 8624.2* A search after souls. (Layton, Henry.) n.p., 1706.
Htn Phil 2733.31* Search after truth. (Malebranche, Nicolas.) London, 1694-95. 2v.
Phil 8582.36 A search after ultimate truth. (Crane, A.M.) Boston, 1910.
Phil 2880.8.52 Search for a method. 1st American ed. (Sartre, Jean Paul.) N.Y., 1963.
Phil 8885.38 The search for a way of life. (Kresge, E.E.) N.Y., 1950.
Phil 1750.720 The search for being. (Wilde, Jean T.) N.Y., 1962.
Phil 6671.28.6 The search for Bridey Murphy. (Bernstein, Morey.) Garden City, N.Y., 1965.
Phil 6671.28 The search for Bridey Murphy. (Bernstein, Morey.) London, 1956.
Phil 6671.28.5 The search for Bridey Murphy. 1. ed. (Bernstein, Morey.) Garden City, N.Y., 1956.
Phil 8419.52 Search for form. (Saarinen, E.) N.Y., 1948.
Phil 8971.8 The search for human values. (Van der Poel, Cornelius J.) N.Y., 1971.
Phil 575.260 A search for identity. (Merchant, Francis.) Salem, 1967.
Phil 2225.14 A search for knowledge. (Pearson, A.N.) Melbourne, 1889.
Phil 5241.97.15 A search for man's sanity. (Burrow, Trigant.) N.Y., 1958.
Phil 6980.759 The search for meaning. (Ungersma, Aaron J.) Philadelphia, 1961.
Phil 2280.23.30 The search for meaning: philosophical vistas. (Stern, Alfred.) Memphis, 1971.
Phil 1750.805 The search for meaningful existence. (Ketcham, Charles Brown.) N.Y., 1968.
Phil 735.205 The search for values. (Coleburt, Russell.) London, 1960.
Phil 5241.10 A search of truth. (Beasley, F.) Philadelphia, 1822.
Phil 6327.12.36 The search within; the inner experience of a psychoanalyst. (Reik, Theodor.) N.Y., 1968.
Phil 6327.12.35 The search within. (Reik, Theodor.) N.Y., 1956.
Phil 8708.25 The searchers. (Strömberg, G.) Philadelphia, 1948.
Phil 1127.5A The searching mind of Greece. (Warbeke, John M.) N.Y., 1930.
Htn Phil 7069.02.30* Searching the truth. N.Y., 1902.
Phil 9513.5 Searchlights. (Coleman, George William.) Boston, 1910.
Phil 193.57A Searle, A. Essays I-XXX. Cambridge, 1910.
Phil 6968.35 Searles, Harold F. Collected papers on schizophrenia and related subjects. London, 1965.
Phil 5058.53A Searles, Herbert L. Logic and scientific methods. N.Y., 1948.
Phil 5058.53.5 Searles, Herbert L. Logic and scientific methods. 2. ed. N.Y., 1956.
Phil 5627.35 Sears, Annie L. The drama of the spiritual life. N.Y., 1915.
Phil 9470.8 Sears, L. Responsibility. N.Y., 1932.
Phil 6315.2.122 Sears, R.R. Survey of objective studies of psychoanalytic concepts. N.Y., 1942.
Phil 5258.34.4 Seashore, C.E. Elementary experiments in psychology. N.Y., 1909.
Phil 5258.34.13 Seashore, C.E. Introduction to psychology. N.Y., 1923.
Phil 5258.34.10 Seashore, C.E. Psychology in daily life. N.Y., 1928.
Phil 5258.143 Seashore, R.H. Fields of psychology. N.Y., 1942.
Phil 8969.15 The seasons of life. (Tournier, Paul.) Richmond, Va., 1970[1963]
Phil 3850.27.16 Seaver, George. Albert Schweitzer; the man and his mind. 6th ed. London, 1969.
Phil 3850.27.110.2 Seaver, George. Albert Schweitzer. Boston, 1951.
Phil 3850.27.109 Seaver, George. Albert Schweitzer. London, 1947.
Phil 3850.27.108 Seaver, George. Albert Schweitzer: revolutionary christian. N.Y., 1944.
Phil 3850.27.110 Seaver, George. Albert Schweitzer. 4th ed. London, 1951.
Phil 4752.2.95 Seaver, George. Nicolas Berdyaev. London, 1950.
Phil 8893.98 Seaverns, A.S. Thoughts for the thoughtful. N.Y., 1893.
Phil 8419.36 Sébag, Henri. Anatomie de l'âme; essai de psych-esthétique. Paris, 1952. 3v.
Phil 6990.21.5 Sebastian, L. Fürst Alexander von Hohenlohe-Schillings. Inaug. Diss. Kempten, 1918.
Phil 4356.2.81 Sebastian Fox Morzillo und seine erkenntnistheoretische Stellung zur Naturphilosophie. Inaug. Diss. (Lueben, Robert.) Bonn, 1911.
Phil 3255.92 Sebastian Franck. (Peuckert, W.C.) München, 1943.
Phil 3255.87 Sebastian Franck von deutsche Geschichtsschreibung. (Bischof, Hermann.) Tübingen, 1857.
Phil 3255.80.5 Sebastian Francks lateinische Paraphrase der deutschen Theologie und seine hollandische erhaltenen Traktate. (Hegler, Alfred.) Tübingen, 1901.
Phil 3255.85 Sebastian Frank von Wörd der Schwarmgeist. (Hase, Karl A.) Leipzig, 1869.
Phil 3255.90 Sebastien Franck. (Koyré, Alexandre.) Paris, 1932.
Phil 2520.2 Sebba, G. Bibliographia cartesiana. The Hague, 1964.

Phil 2520.300   Sebba, Gregor. Descartes and his philosophy. Athens, Ga., 1959.
VPhil 1153.20   Sebestyén, Károly. A einikusok. Budapest, 1902.
Htn   Phil 4369.1.30*   Sebon, Raymond. La theologie naturelle. 2. ed. Paris, 1640.
Phil 4809.796.1   Sebrané spisy. (Smetana, Augustin.) Praha, 1960- 2v.
Phil 8416.40   Secesija. (Pilar, Ivo.) Zagreb, 1898.
Phil 5520.13   Sechehaye, C.A. Programme et méthodes de la linguistique théorique. Paris, 1908.
Phil 6328.46   Sechehaye, Marguerte Albert. Diagnosties psychologiques. Berne, 1949.
Phil 5585.67   Sechenov, I.M. Elementy mysli. Moskva, 1943.
Phil 5585.67.5   Sechenov, I.M. Izbrannye filosofskie i psikhologicheskie proizvedeniia. Moskva, 1947.
Phil 5258.165   Sechenov, Ivan M. Oeuvres philosophiques et psychologiques choisies. Moscou, 1957.
Phil 5258.165.10   Sechenov, Ivan M. Selected works. Moscow, 1935.
Phil 5520.19   Sechrist, F.K. The psychology of unconventional language. n.p., n.d.
Phil 1707.8   Die sechs grossen Themen der abendländischen Metaphysik. (Heimsoeth, H.) Berlin, 1922.
Phil 1707.8.3   Die sechs grossen Themen der abendländischen Metaphysik. 3e Aufl. (Heimsoeth, H.) Stuttgart, 1954?
X Cg   Phil 180.21   Sechs philosophische Vorträge. 2. Ausg. (Fortlage, Karl.) Jena, 1872.
Phil 8876.11   Sechs Vorträge aus dem Gebiete der praktischen Philosophie. (Baumann, Julius.) Leipzig, 1874.
Phil 3552.78.10   Sechzehn ungedruckte Briefe. (Leibniz, Gottfried Wilhelm.) Zürich, 1844.
Phil 4002.8   Il secolo XV. (Carbonara, Cleto.) Milano, 1943.
Phil 4018.6   Il secolo XX. (Sciacca, M.F.) Milano, 1947. 2v.
Phil 2262.39A   Second characters. (Shaftesbury, A.A.C.) Cambridge, 1914.
Phil 9495.24   Second communication. (New York. Homeopathic Medical Society. Communication on Public Education.) Albany? 1905.
Phil 8878.10   A second essay...execution...laws against immorality. (Disney, J.) London, 1710.
Phil 6672.1   Second half-yearly report. (Calcutta Mesmeric Hospital.) London, 1850.
Phil 8592.30   A second letter to professor Goldwin Smith. (Mansel, H.L.) Oxford, 1862.
Phil 6323.24   The second look: the reconstruction of personal history in psychiatry and psychoanalysis. (Novey, Samuel.) Baltimore, 1968.
Htn   Phil 1850.5.5F*   The second part of the Resuscitatio. (Bacon, Francis.) London, 1670.
Phil 672.223   Le second principe de la science du temps. (Costa de Beauregard, Olivier.) Paris, 1963.
Phil 7069.51.15   Second sight in daily life. (Sabine, Waldo.) London, 1951.
Htn   Phil 665.3*   Second thoughts concerning human souls. (Coward, William.) London, 1704.
Phil 9240.6.5   Second thoughts in moral philosophy. (Ewing, Alfred C.) London, 1959.
Htn   Phil 2115.127*   A second vindication of Mr. Locke. (Perronet, Vincent.) London, 1738.
Phil 5590.455   Le secret d'après une conférence donnée à Athènes en la Salle de la Société d'Archéologie le 12 mai 1963. (Tournier, Paul.) Genève, 1963.
Phil 978.71   Le secret de l'absolu. (Coulomb, E.J.) Paris, 1892.
Phil 181.120   Le secret de l'être. (Gaigneron, L. de.) Paris, 1955.
Phil 978.5.9   The secret doctrine. v.1-2. (Blavatsky, H.P.) Point Loma, Calif., 1925. 4v.
Phil 978.5.6   The secret doctrine. v.3. (Blavatsky, H.P.) London, 1888-97.
Phil 6116.3   The secret of a clear head. (Granville, J.M.) Salem, 1879.
NEDL   Phil 5545.11   Secret of a good memory. (Granville, J.M.) Boston, 1887.
Phil 5545.11.5   Secret of a good memory. (Granville, J.M.) n.p., 1906.
Phil 8878.27   The secret of character building. (DeMotte, J.B.) Chicago, 1893.
Phil 5330.28   The secret of concentration. 1st. ed. (Knowlson, T.S.) N.Y., 1931.
Phil 9245.31   The secret of happiness. (Holmes, E.) London, 1919.
Phil 3425.94   The secret of Hegel. (Stirling, J.H.) London, 1865. 2v.
Phil 5525.37   Secret of laughter. (Ludovici, A.M.) London, 1932.
Phil 6990.3.43   The secret of Lourdes. (Martin, Stuart.) London, 1926.
Phil 5545.161   The secret of memory. (Segno, A.V.) Los Angeles, 1906.
Phil 2805.112.7   The secret of Pascal. (Stewart, Hugh F.) Cambridge, Eng., 1941.
Phil 575.23   Secret of personality. (Ladd, George T.) N.Y., 1918.
Phil 6321.17   Secret of self-help in psychiatric aftercare. v.1-3. (Low, A.A.) Chicago, 1943.
Phil 6327.12.45   The secret self. (Reik, Theodor.) N.Y., 1953.
Phil 6324.1   The secret springs. (O'Higgins, H.) N.Y., 1920.
Phil 6320.9.5   Secret ways of the mind. (Kranefeldt, W.M.) N.Y., 1932.
Phil 193.21   Secrétan, C. La philosophie de la liberté. Paris, 1849. 2v.
Phil 193.21.2   Secrétan, C. La philosophie de la liberté. 2e ed. Paris, 1866.
Phil 3552.95   Secrétan, C. La philosophie de Leibnitz. Genève, 1840.
Phil 193.21.5   Secrétan, C. Préis élémentaire de philosophie. Lausanne, 1868.
Phil 8893.5.5   Secrétan, C. Le principe de la morale. Lausanne, 1883.
Phil 8598.40   Secretan, Charles. Recherches de la méthode qui conduit à la vérité sur nos plus grands intérêts. Neuchâtel, 1857.
Phil 2880.2.80   Secrétan, L. Charles Secrétan: sa vie et son oeuvre. Lausanne, 1911.
Phil 7082.122   El secreto de los sueños. (Meseguer, Pedro.) Madrid, 1956.
Phil 5590.455.1   Secrets. (Tournier, Paul.) Richmond, 1968.
Phil 7060.65   Secrets of the invisible world disclos'd. (Moreton, A.) London, 1735.
Phil 7060.65.5   Secrets of the invisible world disclos'd. (Moreton, A.) London, 1740.
Phil 7060.64.5   The secrets of the invisible world laid open. (Defoe, D.) London, 1770.
Phil 190.44   Section I. Auto-philosophy founded on the straight and the curve; the 4 and the 9 of Pythagoras. (Page, Harvey L.) San Antonio, 1927.
Phil 2402.8   Secular religions in France, 1815-1870. (Charlton, D.G.) London, 1963.
Phil 8610.917.10   Secular Society, Ltd. A fight for right. London, 1917.
X Cg   Phil 8610.875.20   The secular song and hymn book. (National Secular Society.) London, 1875?
Phil 8725.1   Secularism; its progress and morals. (Bonham, J.) N.Y., 1894.

Phil 8662.5   Secularism, scepticism and atheism. (Holyoake, George Jacob.) London, 1870.
Phil 8865.636   Secularism and materialism in modern India. (Tiwari, Brij Gopal.) Delhi, 1964?
Phil 8962.7   Sedeläran i sammandrag. (Moren, Thorbjörn.) Stockholm, 1823.
Phil 9255.17   Sedgewick, Garrett G. Of irony, especially in drama. Toronto, 1935.
Phil 9255.17.5   Sedgewick, Garrett G. Of irony, especially in drama. Toronto, 1948.
Phil 8598.6.10   Sedgwick, Adam. A discourse on the studies of the university. N.Y., 1969.
Phil 8598.6   Sedgwick, Adam. A discourse on the studies of the university of Cambridge. Cambridge, 1850.
Phil 8598.6.2   Sedgwick, Adam. A discourse on the studies of the university of Cambridge. 2. ed. Cambridge, 1834.
Phil 8598.6.4   Sedgwick, Adam. A discourse on the studies of the university of Cambridge. 3. ed. Cambridge, 1834.
Htn   Phil 9358.2.5*   Sedgwick, C. Means and ends, or Self-training. Boston, 1839.
Phil 9358.2   Sedgwick, C. Talks with my pupils. N.Y., n.d.
Phil 8893.6   Sedgwick, C.M. A short essay to do good. Stockbridge, 1828.
Phil 1158.27   Sedgwick, H.D. Art of happiness. Indianapolis, 1933.
Phil 193.75   Sedgwick, W. Man and his future. Philadelphia, 1913.
Phil 8708.11   Sedgwick, William. Man's position in the universe. London, 1902.
Phil 3425.198   Sedlák, F. A holiday with a Hegelian. London, 1911.
Phil 310.672   Sedlák, Jaromír. Marxisticko-leninská teorie tžíd a třídního boje. Vyd. 1. Praha, 1959.
Phil 2750.10.95   Sée, Henri. Science et philosophie d'après la doctrine de Emile Meyerson. Paris, 1932.
Phil 8643.6   Seebach, E. Die Lehre von der bedingten Unsterblichkeit in ihren Entstehung geschichtlichen Entwickelung. Krefeld, 1898.
Phil 2295.87   Seeber, Anna. John Toland als politischer Schriftsteller. Inaug. Diss. Schramberg, 1933.
Phil 8643.25.4   Seeberg, R. Ewiges Leben. Leipzig, 1920.
Phil 3425.570   Seeberger, W. Hegel, oder die Entwicklung. Stuttgart, 1961.
Phil 3450.11.300   Seebohm, W.T. Die Bedingungen der Möglichkeit der Transzendentalphilosophie. Bonn, 1961.
Phil 8886.11   Seed-grain for thought and discussion. (Lowell, A.C. (Mrs.).) Boston, 1856. 2v.
Phil 5643.130   Seeing, knowing, and believing. (Soltis, Jonas Francis.) Reading, Mass., 1966.
Phil 334.12   Seeing and knowing. (Dretske, Fred I.) London, 1969.
Phil 5643.41   Seeing and thinking. (Clifford, W.K.) London, 1879.
Phil 8590.10.5   Seeing life whole; a Christian philosophy of life. (King, Henry C.) N.Y., 1923.
Phil 8643.31   Seek paradise. (Litwell, Constance.) London, 1948.
Phil 1350.9.2   Seekers after God. (Farrar, F.W.) London, 1868.
Phil 1350.9.5   Seekers after God. (Farrar, F.W.) London, 1891.
Phil 1350.9   Seekers after God. (Farrar, F.W.) Philadelphia, 1868.
Phil 665.98   Seele, Entwicklung, Leben. Bern, 1966.
Phil 5246.14.10   Die Seele, ihr Verhältnis zum Bewusstsein. (Geyser, J.) Leipzig, 1914.
Phil 6111.57   Die Seele. 3. Aufl. (Bier, A.) München, 1939.
Phil 6117.41   Seele als Ausserung. (Helwig, Paul.) Leipzig, 1936.
Phil 5827.6   Die Seele der Tiere im Lichte der Forschung. (Reuter, Odo M.) Leipzig, 1908.
Phil 5252.38.15   Die Seele des Alltags. 2. Aufl. (Müller-Freienfels, R.) Berlin, 1925.
Phil 5255.8.15   Die Seele des Menschen. (Pfänder, A.) Halle, 1933.
Phil 5257.3.5   Die Seele des Menschen. (Rehmke, J.) Leipzig, 1902.
Phil 5258.49   Die Seele des Menschen. (Sallwürk, Ernst von.) Karlsruhe, 1918.
Phil 5816.6   Die Seele des Tieres. (Gesellschaft für Tierpsychologie.) Berlin, 1916.
Phil 665.104   Die Seele-Grenzbegriff der Naturwissenschaft und Theologie. (Heimann, Hans.) Bern, 1966.
Phil 5250.4   Die Seele im Lichte des Monismus. (Kroell, H.) Strassburg, 1902.
Phil 665.54   Die Seele indischer und hellenischer Philosophie in den Gespenstern moderner Geisterseherei. (Bastian, Adolf.) Berlin, 1886.
Phil 665.80   Seele und Beseeltes. (Strasser, Stephan.) Wien, 1955.
Phil 9075.31   Die Seele und das Gewissens. (Anderson, Louis F.) Leipzig, 1929.
Phil 665.77   Seele und Geist. (Gindl, I.) Wien, 1955.
Phil 5255.4.5   Seele und Geist. (Plank, K.C.) Leipzig, 1871.
Phil 5250.9   Die Seele und ihre Thätigkeiten. 2. Aufl. (Körner, F.) Leipzig, 1890.
Phil 6328.10   Seele und Leben. (Schilder, Paul.) Berlin, 1923.
Phil 6128.26   Seele und Leib in Wechselbeziehung zu Einander. (Schroeder van der Kolk, J.L.C.) Braunschweig, 1865.
Phil 6972.13   Seele und Seelenkrankheit. (Wildermuth, H.) Berlin, 1926.
Phil 3090.65   Seele und Welt. (Baader, Franz von.) Berlin, 1928.
Phil 665.30   Seele und Welt. (Joël, Karl.) Jena, 1912.
Phil 978.49.55   Der Seelen Erwachen. (Steiner, R.) Bern, 1922.
Phil 292.3   Seelen und Ziele. Beiträge zum Weltverständnis. (Lassivitz, Kurd.) Leipzig, 1908.
Phil 6328.2.45   Der Seelenarzt. (Stekel, Wilhelm.) Leipzig, 1933.
Phil 5252.55   Der Seelenbegriff in der modernen Psychologie. (Meier, M.) München, n.d.
Phil 5643.42   Die Seelenblindheit als Herderscheinung. (Wilbrand, H.) Wiesbaden, 1887.
Phil 3245.43   Die Seelenfortdauer und die Weltstellung des Menschen. (Fichte, Immanuel Hermann.) Leipzig, 1867.
Phil 665.56   Die Seelenfrage. (Flügel, O.) Cöthen, 1878.
Phil 665.60   Seelenglaube und Psychologie. (Rank, Otto.) Leipzig, 1930.
Phil 5241.37   Die Seelenkunde des Menschen als eine Erfahrungswissenschaft. (Benedikt, M.) Leipzig, 1895.
Phil 5819.5   Das Seelenleben der Fische. (Jarmer, Karl.) München, 1928.
Phil 5828.10   Seelenleben der Tiere. (Skowronnek, Fritz.) Berlin, 1911.
Phil 5815.3   Das Seelenleben der Tiere. 3e Aufl. (Fluegel, Otto.) Langensalza, 1897.
Phil 5258.5   Das Seelenleben des Menschen. (Schaller, J.) Weimar, 1860.
Phil 6128.35   Das Seelenleben und die Behirnthatigkeit. (Scheidemacher, C.B.) Regensburg, 1876.
Phil 5238.95   Seelenleben und Menschenbild. (Däumling, Adolf.) München, 1957.
Phil 5251.8   Seelenlebens. (Lipps, T.) Bonn, 1883.
Phil 6951.14   Die Seelenleiden der Nervösen. 2. und 3. Aufl. (Bergmann, W.) Freiburg, 1922.

Phil 665.7 — Seelenmacht; Abriss einer zeitgemässen Weltanschauung. (Lutosławski, W.) Leipzig, 1899.
Phil 665.61 — Das Seelenpneuma. (Rüsche, Franz.) Paderborn, 1933.
Phil 6319.1.37 — Seelenprobleme der Gegenwart. (Jung, C.G.) Zürich, 1932.
Phil 6980.335 — Seelenspiegel des Kindes. (Graber, Gustav.) Zürich, 1946.
Phil 5247.21 — Die Seelentheorie und die Gesetze. 2. Aufl. (Hanspaul, F.) Berlin, 1901.
Phil 8635.9 — Die Seelenwaage. (Kretzenbacher, Leopold.) Klagenfurt, 1958.
Phil 1135.101 — Die Seelenwanderung bei Griechen und Römern. Inaug. Diss. (Stettner, Walter.) Stuttgart, 1930.
Phil 8598.7.3 — Seeley, R. Natural religion. Boston, 1882.
Phil 8598.7 — Seeley, R. Natural religion. London, 1882.
Phil 7140.116.75 — Seeling, Otto. Der Couéismus. Diss. Giessen, 1926.
Phil 5627.94 — Der seelische Aufbau des religiösen Erlebens. (Girgensohn, K.) Leipzig, 1921.
Phil 5627.94.5 — Der seelische Aufbau des religiösen Erlebens. 2. Aufl. (Girgensohn, K.) Gütersloh, 1930.
Phil 5250.30 — Der seelische Konflikt; Psychologie und existentiale Bedeutung. (Krauss, S.) Stuttgart, 1933.
Phil 6309.6 — Seelische Störungen. Frankfurt am Main, 1969.
Phil 6122.61 — Seelischer Gesundheitschutz. (Meng, H.) Basel, 1939.
Phil 5465.70 — Seelisches Leben und schöpferische Leistung. (Zwicker, Heinz.) Bern, 1954.
Phil 493.6.15 — Seely, Charles Sherlock. The essentials of modern materialism. N.Y., 1969.
Phil 493.6.5 — Seely, Charles Sherlock. Modern materialism. N.Y., 1960.
Phil 493.6 — Seely, Charles Sherlock. Philosophy and the ideological conflict. N.Y., 1953.
Phil 493.6.10 — Seely, Charles Sherlock. The philosophy of science. N.Y., 1964.
Phil 9120.2 — Seelye, J.H. Duty. Boston, 1891.
Phil 8590.10.15 — Seeming unreality of the spiritual life. (King, Henry C.) N.Y., 1911.
Phil 6680.1.5 — The Seeress of Prevorst. (Kerner, J.) N.Y., 1855.
Phil 7054.167 — Seers of the ages, embracing spiritualism. (Peebles, J.M.) Boston, 1869.
Phil 6687.5 — Seership. The magnetic mirror. (Randolph, P.B.) Toledo, 1875.
Phil 530.20.75 — Seesholtz, A.G. Friends of God. N.Y., 1934.
Phil 6320.11.80 — Segal, H. Introduction to the work of M. Klein. N.Y., 1964.
Phil 193.98 — Segal, Hyman. The law of struggle. N.Y., 1918.
Phil 5643.134 — Segall, Marshall H. The influence of culture on visual perception. Indianapolis, 1966.
Phil 193.136 — Segall-Socolin, I. Zur Verjüngung der Philosophie. 1e Reihe. Berlin, 1893.
Phil 5066.24.10 — Segerberg, Krister. Results in non-classical propositional logic. Lund, 1968.
Phil 5520.390 — Segerstedt, T. Torgnysson. Die Macht des Wortes. Zürich, 1946.
Phil 8598.49 — Segerstedt, T.K. Gammal och my religiositet. Stockholm, 1915.
Phil 8598.49.5 — Segerstedt, T.K. Det religiösa sanningsproblemet. Stockholm, 1912.
Phil 1885.85 — Segerstedt, T.K. Value and reality in Bradley's philosophy. Lund, 1934.
Phil 1818.10 — Segerstedt, T.T. The problem of knowledge in Scottish philosophy. Lund, 1935.
Phil 8725.8 — El seglarismo y su integridad. (Alvarez, Lili.) Madrid, 1959.
Phil 6968.5.15 — Séglas, J. Le délire des négations. Paris, 189-.
Phil 6968.5.5 — Séglas, J. Des troubles du langage...aliénés. Paris, 1892.
Phil 6968.5.10 — Séglas, J. Leçons cliniques sur les maladies. Paris, 1895.
Phil 6968.5 — Séglas, J. Paranoia, systematized delusions. N.Y., 1888.
Htn — Phil 6025.8* — I segni de la natura ne l'huomo. (Pellegrini, A.) Venetia, 1569.
Phil 6688.21 — Segnitz, F.L. Specimen inaugurale medicum de electricitate. Jenae, 1790.
Phil 6128.41 — Segno, A.V. The law of mentalism. 26th ed. Los Angeles, 1902.
Phil 5545.161 — Segno, A.V. The secret of memory. Los Angeles, 1906.
Phil 5520.411 — Il segno dalla fino al cinema. (Bottotini, Gianfranco.) Milano, 1963.
Phil 5620.34 — Il segno della ragione. (Scivoletto, Angelo.) Padova, 1963.
Phil 2418.3 — Segond, J. Art et science dans la philosophie française contemporaine. Paris, 1936.
Phil 2515.4.90 — Segond, J. Cournot et la psychologie vitaliste. Thèse. Paris, 1910.
Phil 5258.64 — Segond, J. Intuition et anité. Paris, 1919.
Phil 5627.19 — Segond, J. La prière-étude de psychologie religieuse. Paris, 1911.
Phil 2520.185 — Segond, J. La sagesse cartésienne et la doctrine de la science. Paris, 1932.
Phil 3838.18 — Segond, J. La vie de Benoit de Spinoza. Paris, 1933.
Phil 270.55 — Segond, J.L.P. Hasard et contingence. Paris, 1938.
Phil 270.56 — Segond, J.L.P. Logique du pari. Paris, 1938.
Phil 5258.107 — Segond, Joseph. Traité de psychologie. Paris, 1930.
Phil 2475.1.89 — Segoud, J. L'intuition Bergsonienne. Paris, 1913.
Phil 5425.48 — Segoud, Joseph. Le problème du génie. Paris, 1930.
Phil 6688.15.2 — Ségouin, A. Les mystéres de la magie ou les secrets du magnetisme. 2e éd. Paris, 1853.
Phil 4319.2 — Segovia Canosa, R. Tres salvaciones del siglo XVIII español. Xalapa, 1960.
Phil 6750.7.10 — Seguin, E. Idiocy. Albany, 1907.
Phil 6750.7 — Seguin, E. Idiocy and its treatment. N.Y., 1866.
Phil 6750.7.5 — Seguin, E. New facts and remarks concerning idiocy. N.Y., 1870.
Phil 6945.9 — Seguin, E.C. Lunacy reform. v.1-4. N.Y., 1879-
Phil 2493.30.3 — Segunda edición de la Lógica puesta. (Condillac, Étienne Bonnot.) Madrid, 1800.
Phil 7069.34.47.2 — La segunda parte que ha dado el regentador del mondo solar, para que los lectores lo leau que va siquiendo su lectura. (Vilanova, Maria.) Barcelona, 1934.
Phil 4752.2.130 — Segundo, J.L. Berdiaeff. Paris, 1963.
Phil 6680.1.6 — Die Seherin von Prevorst. (Kerner, J.) Leipzig, 18-.
Htn — Phil 6680.1* — Die Seherin von Prevorst. (Kerner, J.) Stuttgart, 1829. 2v.
Phil 6680.1.25 — Die Seherin von Prevorst. (Kretschmar, F.) Weinsberg, 1892.
Phil 6680.1.4.5 — Die Seherin von Prevorst. 2. Aufl. (Kerner, J.) Stuttgart, 1892.
Phil 6680.1.4 — Die Seherin von Prevorst. 4. Aufl. (Kerner, J.) Stuttgart, 1746.

Phil 3450.28.20 — Die Sehnsucht nach dem ganz Anderen. (Horkheimer, Max.) Hamburg, 1970.
Phil 5643.57 — Der Sehraum auf grund der Erfahrung. (Daublebsky, Storneck von.) Leipzig, 1907.
Phil 3425.344 — Sehring, L. Hegel. Berlin, 1908.
Phil 4012.1.5 — Sei lettere...intorno al libro filosofia antica italiana. (Mamiani di Rovere, T.) Parigi, 1838.
Phil 4012.1.7 — Sei lettere...intorno al libro filosofia antica italiana. 2. ed. (Mamiani di Rovere, T.) Firenze, 1842.
Phil 3018.5 — Seibert, C. Geschichte der neueren deutschen Philosophie. Gottingen, 1898.
Phil 3018.5.3 — Seibert, C. Geschichte der neueren deutschen Philosophie. 2e Aufl. Gottingen, 1905.
Phil 3565.120 — Seibert, F. Lotze als Anthropologe. Wiesbaden, 1900.
Phil 5374.156 — Seidel, A. Bewusstsein als Verhangnis. Bonn, 1927.
Phil 3890.6.86 — Seidel, A. Tetens Einfluss auf die kritische Philosophie Kants. Inaug. Diss. Würzburg, 1901.
Phil 8893.71 — Seidel, A. Wegweiser zum moralischen Handeln. Leipzig, 1914.
Phil 3450.19.310 — Seidel, G.J. Martin Heidegger and the pre-Socratics. Lincoln, 1964.
Phil 559.4 — Seidel, George Joseph. Being nothing and God; a philosophy of appearance. Assen, 1970.
Phil 5465.146 — Seidel, George Joseph. The crisis of creativity. Notre Dame, 1966.
Phil 3790.4.95 — Seidel, Hermann. Wert und Wirklichkeit in der Philosophie Heinrich Rickerts. Bonn, 1968.
Phil 400.47 — Seidenberger, J.B. Grundlinien idealer Weltanschauung. Braunschweig, 1902.
Phil 3120.2.120 — Seidlerová, I. Politické a pociálné názory Bernard Bolzano. Praha, 1963.
Phil 8673.36 — Seidlitz, Carl Siegmund von. Briefe über Gott und Unsterblichkeit. Bruxelles, 1968.
Phil 6980.679 — Seidmann, Peter. Der Weg der Tiefenpsychologie in geistesgeschichtlicher Perspektive. Zürich, 1959.
Phil 3160.11.10 — Das seiende Sein. (Cysarz, Herbert.) Wien, 1948.
Phil 5722.40 — Seifert, F. Tiefenpsychologie. Düsseldorf, 1955.
Phil 6328.59 — Seifert, Friedrich. Bilder und Urbilder; Erscheinungsformen des Arrhetypus. München, 1965.
Phil 5228.5 — Seifert, Friedrich. Die Wissenschaft von Menschen in der Gegenwart. Leipzig, 1930.
Phil 3850.47 — Seifert, Hans. Heinrich Scholz. Münster, 1958.
Phil 5358.2 — Seifert, Karl Heinz. Grundformen und theoretische Perspektiven psychologischer Kompensation. Meisenheim, 1969.
Phil 8669.3.29 — Seifert, P. Die Religionsphilosophie bei Rudolf Otto. Inaug. Diss. Dusseldorf, 1936.
Phil 1619.5 — Seigel, Jerrold Edward. Rhetoric and philosophy in Renaissance humanism. Princeton, 1968.
Phil 193.235 — Seijas, Rodolfo. Carta a Sartre, y otros ensayos. Buenos Aires, 1962.
Phil 3120.7.81 — Seiling, Max. Mäinlander, ein neuer Messias. München, 1888.
Phil 3808.113 — Seillière, E. Arthur Schopenhauer. Paris, 1911.
Phil 2490.112 — Seillière, E. Auguste Comte. Paris, 1924.
Phil 2475.1.179 — Seillière, E. L'avenir de la philosophie Bergsonienne. Paris, 1917.
Phil 3018.13 — Seillière, E. Morales et religions nouvelles en Allemagne. Paris, 1927.
Phil 525.8.5 — Seillière, E. Mysticisme et domination. Paris, 1913.
Phil 525.8 — Seillière, E. Les mystiques du néo-romantisme. Paris, 1911.
Phil 525.8.9 — Seillière, E. Le péril mystique dans l'inspiration des démocraties contemporaines. Paris, 1918.
Phil 3450.19.295 — Sein, Mensch und Tod. (Demske, James M.) Freiburg, 1963.
Phil 3160.15 — Das Sein. (Conrad-Martius, Hedwig.) München, 1957.
Phil 180.70.10 — Sein. (Fink, Eugen.) Den Haag, 1958.
Phil 176.185 — Das Sein der Dinge. (Barth, Heinrich.) Wien, 1956.
Phil 3450.16.15 — Sein Leben in seiner Briefen. (Wahl, Jean A.) Frankfurt, 1938.
Phil 3110.26 — Sein Leben und seine theosophischen Werke. (Böhme, J.) Stuttgart, 1885.
Phil 7150.52 — Sein oder Nichtsein. (Siegmund, Georg.) Trier, 1961.
Phil 4768.2.6 — Sein und Bewusstsein. 4. Aufl. (Rubinshtein, Sergei L.) Berlin, 1966.
Phil 3549.21 — Das Sein und das Gute. (Kuhn, H.) München, 1962.
Phil 2880.8.62 — Das Sein und das Nichts. (Sartre, Jean Paul.) Hamburg, 1952.
Phil 185.63 — Sein und Denken. (König, J.) Halle, 1937.
Phil 176.20 — Sein und Erkennen. (Bergmann, J.) Berlin, 1880.
Phil 8980.29.3 — Sein und Ethos. (Engelhardt, Paulus.) Mainz, 1963.
Phil 1750.552.15 — Sein und Existenz. (Lotz, Johannes Baptist.) Freiburg, 1965.
Phil 3450.19.240 — Sein und Existenz. (Noller, Gerhard.) München, 1962.
Phil 193.125 — Sein und Gegenstand. (Söhngen, G.) Münster, 1930.
Phil 1707.15 — Sein und Gewissen. (Hollenbach, J.M.) Baden-Baden, 1954.
Phil 2477.6.170 — Sein und Inkarnation. Diss. (Scannone, Juan Carlos.) Freiburg, 1968.
Phil 8697.19 — Sein und Ursprünglichkeit. (Hengstenberg, Hans E.) München, 1958.
Phil 8879.27 — Sein und Wollen. (Erismann, T.) Wien, 1953.
Phil 3450.19.30 — Sein und Zeit. 7e Aufl. (Heidegger, Martin.) Tübingen, 1953.
Phil 3450.19.30.10 — Sein und Zeit. 10e Aufl. (Heidegger, Martin.) Tübingen, 1963.
Phil 3450.19.116 — Die Seinsfrage bei Martin Heidegger. (Fritz, E.) Stuttgart, 1950.
Phil 400.108 — Seinsordnung und Gehalt der Idealitäten. (Janssen, O.) Meisenheim/Glan, 1950.
Phil 8411.21 — Die Seinssymbolik des Schönen und die Kunst. (Kuznitzky, G.) Berlin, 1932.
Phil 525.15 — Seisdedos Sanz, J. Principios fundamentales de la mistica. v.1-2,3. Madrid, 1919. 2v.
Phil 9035.62 — Seiterich, Eugen. Die logische Struktur des Typusbegriffes. Inaug. Diss. Freiburg, 1930.
Phil 530.20.80 — Seitz, Jasy. Der Traktat des "unbekannten deutschen Mystikers" bei Greith. Leipzig, 1936.
Phil 1195.10 — Seitz, K. Die Schule von Gaza. Heidelberg, 1892.
Phil 8598.74 — Sekendorf, V.L. von. Christen-Staat. Leipzig, 1716.
Phil 5627.113.95 — Selbie, W.B. Psychology of religion. Oxford, 1924.
Phil 8598.63 — Selbie, W.B. Religion and life. Cambridge, 1930.
Phil 3805.155 — Selbie, W.B. Schleiermacher. London, 1913.
Phil 818.40 — Selbmann, Fritz. Wahrheit und Wirklichkeit. Dresden, 1947.
Phil 6111.24.5 — Die Selbständigkeit des sympathischen Nervensystems. (Bidder, Friedrich.) Leipzig, 1842.

	Phil 5244.10.10	Selbstbeobachtung und Experiment in der Psychologie. (Elsenhans, Theodor.) Freiburg, 1897.
	Phil 6032.2	Selbstbeurteilung und Frembdeurteilung im wissentlichen und Unwissentlichen Versuch. Inaug. Diss. (Wolff, Werner.) Berlin, 1932.
	Phil 3092.1	Selbstbiographie undAntrittsrede. (Bachofen, J.J.) Halle, 1927.
	Phil 8586.19	Selbstbwusstsein und Willensfreiheit. (Grane, Georg.) Berlin, 1904.
	Phil 6315.2.72	Selbstdarstellung. (Freud, Sigmund.) London, 1946.
	Phil 185.60.10	Selbstdarstellung. (Kraus, O.) Leipzig, 1929.
	Phil 6315.2.72.5	Selbstdarstellung. 2. Aufl. (Freud, Sigmund.) Wien, 1936.
	Phil 5255.48	Selbsterfahrung. (Pulver, Max.) Zürich, 1941.
	Phil 343.14.10	Selbsterkenntnis. (Meurer, W.) Berlin, 1931.
	Phil 3585.12	Die Selbsterkenntnis des Menschen. (Litt, Theodor.) Leipzig, 1938.
	Phil 3585.12.5	Die Selbsterkenntnis des Menschen. 2. Aufl. (Litt, Theodor.) Hamburg, 1948.
	Phil 6329.12.5.2	Selbsterlösung. 1. und 2. Aufl. (Turel, Adrien.) Berlin, 1919.
	Phil 3585.12.90	Das Selbsterständnis der Pädagogik Theodor Litts. (Lassahn, Rudolf.) Wuppertal, 1968.
	Phil 6310.1.104	Selbsterziehung der charakters; Alfred Adler zum 60. geburtstage. Leipzig, 1930.
	Phil 180.66	Die Selbstgestaltung des Lebendigen. (Friederichs, K.) München, 1955.
	Phil 3450.24	Das Selbsthewusstwerden des Geistes. (Hessing, Jacob.) Stuttgart, 1936.
	Phil 178.68	Selbstkritik der Philosophie und vergleichende Philosophiegeschitte im Umriss. (Dempf, Alois.) Wien, 1947.
	Phil 7150.36	Selbstmörder. (Szittya, E.) Leipzig, 1925.
	Phil 7150.61	Selbstmord. (Balluseck, Lothar von.) Bad Godesberg, 1965.
	Phil 7150.51	Der Selbstmord. (Fuellkrug, Gerhard.) Schwerin, 1919.
	Phil 7150.2	Der Selbstmord. (Geiger, K.A.) Augsburg, 1888.
	Phil 6854.6	Der Selbstmord als sociale Massenerscheinung des modernen Civilisation. (Masaryk, Tomáš Gottigue.) Wien, 1881.
	Phil 7150.80	Selbstmordversuche bei Kindern und Jugendlichen. (Haffter, Carl.) Basel, 1966.
	Phil 348.10	Das Selbstopfer der Erkenntnis. (Reisner, E.) München, 1927.
	Phil 585.214	Selbstschöpfung oder Selbstintegration des Menschen. (Maaz, Wilhelm.) Münster, 1967.
	Phil 4260.205	Selbstverständnis und Menschenbild in den Selbstdarstellungen Giambattista Vicos und Pietro Giannones. Thesis. (Daus, Hans-Jürgen.) Genève, 1962.
	Phil 6319.1.245	Selbstverwirklichung. (Kaune, Fritz Jürgen.) München, 1967.
	Phil 185.41	Die Selbstverwirklichung des Geistes. (Kroner, Richard.) Tübingen, 1928.
	Phil 8660.20	Der Selbstwiderspruch des philosophischen Atheismus. (Fuerstenberg, E.) Regensburg, 1960.
	Phil 3415.61	Die Selbstzersetzung des Christenthums. 2. Aufl. (Hartmann, Eduard von.) Berlin, 1874.
	Phil 8843.2.2	Selby-Bigge, L.A. British moralists. v.1-2. Indianapolis, 1964.
	Phil 8843.2	Selby-Bigge, L.A. British moralists. v.1-2. Oxford, 1897.
	Phil 6128.4	Select discourses on the functions of the nervous system. (Smith, J.A.) N.Y., 1840.
	Phil 2270.20	Select works. (Spencer, Herbert.) N.Y., 1886.
	Phil 2120.10.20	Selected addresses. (Lindsay, A.D.L.) Cumberland, 1957.
	Phil 6327.11.5	Selected contributions to psychoanalysis. (Rickman, J.) London, 1957.
	Phil 2280.5.79.5	Selected critical writing. (Santayana, George.) Cambridge, Eng., 1968. 2v.
	Phil 3808.45.15	Selected essays. (Schopenhauer, Arthur.) London, 1926.
	Phil 3808.45	Selected essays. (Schopenhauer, Arthur.) Milwaukee, 1881.
	Phil 97.6	Selected glossary of philosophical terms. (Means, B.W.) Hartford, Connecticut, 1943.
	Phil 2070.75.10	Selected letters. (James, William.) N.Y., 1961.
	Phil 3640.78	Selected letters. (Nietzsche, Friedrich.) London, 1921.
	Phil 3640.78.5	Selected letters of Friedrich Nietzsche. (Nietzsche, Friedrich.) Chicago, 1969.
	Phil 8587.32.85	Selected letters 1896-1924. (Hügel, Friedrich von.) London, 1928.
	Phil 5066.276	Selected logic papers. (Quine, Willard van Orman.) N.Y., 1966.
	Phil 2255.1.10A	Selected papers. (Russell, Bertrand Russell.) N.Y., 1927.
X Cg	Phil 6315.2.19	Selected papers on hysteria and other psychoneuroses. (Freud, Sigmund.) N.Y., 1912.
	Phil 184.3.34A	Selected papers on philosophy. (James, W.) London, 1927.
	Phil 184.3.34.5	Selected papers on philosophy. (James, W.) London, 1929.
	Phil 6316.12.10	Selected papers on psycho-analysis. (Glover, Edward.) London, 1956- 2v.
	Phil 2530.20	Selected philosophical writings. (Diderot, Denis.) Cambridge, Eng., 1953.
	Phil 3480.130	Selected pre-critical writings and correspondence. (Kant, Immanuel.) Manchester, 1968.
	Phil 5876.10.10	Selected problems of adolescence; with special emphasis on group formation. (Deutsch, Thelene.) N.Y., 1967.
	Phil 9035.88	Selected readings in character education. (Troth, D.C.) Boston, 1930.
	Phil 5203.11	Selected reference list. (Harvard University. Psychology Library.) Cambridge, 1936.
	Phil 165.366	Selected studies. (Tamás, György.) Budapest, 1965.
	Phil 5051.28.10	Selected works. (Lukasiewicz, Jan.) Amsterdam, 1970.
	Phil 5625.75.15	Selected works. (Pavlov, Ivan P.) Moscow, 1955.
	Phil 5258.165.10	Selected works. (Sechenov, Ivan M.) Moscow, 1935.
	Phil 5058.104	Selected works in logic. (Skolem, Thoralf.) Oslo, 1970.
	Phil 75.13.9	Selected works on history of philosophy in English language. (Rand, Benjamin.) Boston, 1906.
	Phil 2150.15.20	Selected writings. (Mead, George Herbert.) Indianapolis, 1964.
	Phil 185.59.5	Selected writings in philosophy. N.Y., 1939.
	Phil 3850.27.155	A selection of writings of and about Albert Schweitzer. (Kirschner, Carol F.) Boston, 1958.
	Phil 3480.25.20A	Selectiones. (Kant, Immanuel.) N.Y., 1929.
	Phil 1870.20A	Selections. (Berkeley, G.) Oxford, 1874.
	Phil 2520.29A	Selections. (Descartes, René.) N.Y., 1927.
	Phil 3425.28	Selections. (Hegel, Georg Wilhelm Friedrich.) N.Y., 1929.
	Phil 2045.26	Selections. (Hobbes, Thomas.) N.Y., 1930.
	Phil 2050.23	Selections. (Hume, David.) N.Y., 1927.
	Phil 2050.23.2	Selections. (Hume, David.) N.Y., 1955.
	Phil 3552.36	Selections. (Leibniz, Gottfried Wilhelm.) N.Y., 1951.
	Phil 2115.26	Selections. (Locke, J.) Chicago, 1928.
	Phil 3808.45.20	Selections. (Schopenhauer, Arthur.) N.Y., 1956.
	Phil 1870.20.3	Selections (Fraser). 3rd ed. (Berkeley, G.) Oxford, 1884.
	Phil 1870.20.4	Selections annotated. 5th ed. (Berkeley, G.) Oxford, 1899.
	Phil 165.4	Selections from Hellenistic philosophy. (Clark, G.H.) N.Y., 1940.
	Phil 2218.55	Selections from his writings. (Priestley, Joseph.) University Park, 1962.
	Phil 2055.2.20	Selections from manuscripts. (Hinton, James.) London, 1870. 4v.
	Phil 1560.10	Selections from medieval philosophers. (McKeon, Richard P.) N.Y., 1929-1930. 2v.
	Phil 55.6	Selections from the papers of the society. (Thasmatological Society.) Oxford 1,1882
	Phil 5922.5	Selections from the Phrenological Journal. (Cox, R.) Edinburgh, 1836.
	Phil 1830.2	Selections from the Scottish philosophy of common sense. (Johnston, George A.) Chicago, 1915.
	Phil 4260.08	A selective bibliography of Vico scholarship, 1948-68. (Gianturco, Elio.) Firenze, 1968.
	Phil 5643.174	Selective history of theories of visual perception: 1650-1950. (Pastore, Nicholas.) N.Y., 1971.
	Phil 5643.168	The selective process in the functional visual field. (Sanders, Andries Frans.) Assen, 1963.
	Phil 5585.200	Selectivity, intuition and halo effects in social perception. (Rommetveit, R.) Oslo, 1960.
	Phil 9450.35	Selekman, Sylvia Kopald. Power and morality in a business society. N.Y., 1956.
	Phil 75.68	Selektiv bibliografi i teoretisk filosofi. (Berg, Jan.) Stockholm, 1960.
	Phil 5590.512	Self; an introduction to philosophical psychology. (Myers, Gerald E.) N.Y., 1969.
	Phil 165.255	Self, religion and metaphysics. (Myers, G.E.) N.Y., 1961.
	Phil 2150.15.86	Self, society, existence. (Pfuetze, P.E.) N.Y., 1961.
	Phil 343.18	Self, thought and reality. (Mukerji, A.C.) Allahabad, 1933.
	Phil 5590.320	The self. (Moustakas, Clark E.) N.Y., 1956.
	Phil 5247.42A	The self: its body and freedom. (Hocking, W.E.) New Haven, 1928.
	Phil 6317.22.10A	Self-analysis. (Horney, Karen.) N.Y., 1942.
	Phil 960.163.10	Self and falsity in Advaita Vedanta. 1st ed. (Ray Chaudhuri, A.K.) Calcutta, 1955.
	Phil 3475.3.105	The self and its hazards...K. Jaspers. (Allen, L.) London, 1950.
	Phil 197.44	The self and its world. (Wilson, George A.) N.Y., 1926.
	Phil 190.26	Self and nature. (Parker, DeWitt H.) Cambridge, 1917.
	Phil 8882.33	Self and neighbor. (Hirst, E.W.) London, 1919.
	Phil 6961.19	The self and others. (Laing, Ronald David.) London, 1961.
	Phil 6961.19.2	Self and others. 2. ed. (Laing, Ronald David.) London, 1969.
	Phil 575.250	Self and society. 1st ed. (Sanford, Nevitt.) n.p., 1966.
	Phil 8878.54	The self and the ideal. (Das, Ras-Vihari.) Calcutta, 1935.
	Phil 6319.13	The self and the object world. (Jacobsen, Edith.) London, 1965.
	Phil 185.41.5	Self and world; the religious philosophy of Richard Kroner. (Skinner, J.E.) Philadelphia, 1963.
	Phil 575.165	The self as agent. (Macmurray, John.) London, 1957. 2v.
	Phil 5590.365	The self concept. (Wylie, R.C.) Lincoln, 1961.
	Phil 5420.5	Self-consciousness and its treatment. (Roback, A.A.) Cambridge, 1933.
	Phil 5374.2	Self-consciousness of noted persons. (Morrill, J.S.) Boston, 1887.
	Phil 5420.5.10	Self-consciousness self-treated. (Roback, A.A.) Cambridge, 1936.
	Phil 5590.22	Self-consistency; a theory of personality. (Lecky, Prescott.) N.Y., 1945.
	Phil 8884.4.5	Self-control, its kingship and majesty. (Jordan, W.G.) N.Y., 1905.
	Phil 8878.24.5	Self-control and how to secure it. (DuBois, P.) N.Y., 1909.
	Phil 8880.13	Self culture and perfection of character. (Fowler, O.S.) N.Y., 1856.
	Phil 5925.2.18	Self-culture and the perfection of character. (Fowler, O.S.) N.Y., 1868.
	Phil 5590.272	Self-deception. (Fingarette, Herbert.) London, 1969.
	Phil 8881.6	Self-education. (Gerando, J.M.) Boston, 1830.
	Phil 8881.6.2	Self-education. 2nd ed. (Gerando, J.M.) Boston, 1832.
	Phil 8881.6.4	Self-education. 3rd ed. (Gerando, J.M.) Boston, 1860.
	Phil 5590.465	Self-evaluation. (Diggory, James C.) N.Y., 1966.
	Phil 8661.15	The self-evolution of God and His creation of nature. (Graham, Bothwell.) Greenville, S.C., 1923.
	Phil 960.119	Self-expression and the Indian social problem. (Dass, Satya.) Lahore, 1937.
	Phil 9347.5	Self formation. 3d ed. (Hood, E.P.) London, 1878.
	Phil 9358.17	Self government and the power of an ideal. (Seabury, Samuel.) n.p., 1931.
	Phil 7140.120	Self healing by autosuggestion. (Dolonne, A.) London, 1923.
	Phil 6125.22	Self healing simplified. (Perin, George L.) N.Y., 1922.
	Phil 8893.14.7	Self-help. (Smiles, Samuel.) Chicago, 1890.
	Phil 8893.14.8.25	Self-help. (Smiles, Samuel.) London, 1958.
	Phil 8893.14.4	Self-help. (Smiles, Samuel.) N.Y., 1860.
NEDL	Phil 8893.14.8	Self-help. (Smiles, Samuel.) N.Y., 1870.
	Phil 8893.14.6.5	Self-help. (Smiles, Samuel.) N.Y., 1875.
	Phil 8893.14.8.20	Self-help. (Smiles, Samuel.) N.Y., 1915.
	Phil 6322.20	Self help for nervous women. (Mitchell, John K.) Philadelphia, 1909.
	Phil 960.246	The self in Indian philosophy. (Organ, T.W.) London, 1964.
	Phil 585.164	The self in philosophy. (Castell, Alburey.) N.Y., 1965.
	Phil 5240.34	The self in psychology. (Allen, A.H.B.) London, 1935.
	Phil 6315.54	The self in transformation. (Fingrette, H.) N.Y., 1963.
	Phil 8887.6	Self-knowledge. (Mason, J.) London, 1745.
	Phil 8887.6.2	Self-knowledge. (Mason, J.) London, 1753.
	Phil 8887.6.3	Self-knowledge. (Mason, J.) London, 1755.
	Phil 8887.6.4.5	Self-knowledge. (Mason, J.) London, 1794.
	Phil 8887.6.10	Self-knowledge. (Mason, J.) London, 1824.
	Phil 8887.6.5	Self-knowledge. (Mason, J.) Portland, 1807.
Htn	Phil 8887.6.4*	Self-knowledge. (Mason, J.) Worcester, Mass., 1789.
	Phil 575.245	Self-knowledge and self-identity. (Shoemaker, S.) Ithaca, 1963.
	VPhil 6060.30.5	Self-knowledge through handwriting. (Jacoby, Hans.) London, 1941.
	Phil 9530.3	The self-made man. (Cleveland, G.) N.Y., 1897.
	Phil 8882.24.8	Self-measurement. (Hyde, W. De W.) N.Y., 1912.
	Phil 8897.56	Self realization. (Wright, Henry W.) N.Y., 1913.
	Phil 8883.4	The self-seeker and his search. (Isbyam, I.C. (pseud.).) London, 1926.

Phil 9530.27   The self-starter. (Lyons, Albert E.) Boston, 1924.
Phil 8586.50   Self-transcendence. (Gregg, R.B.) London, 1956.
Phil 7140.116   Selfmastery through conscious autosuggestion. (Coué, Emile.) N.Y., 1922.
Phil 5421.20.60   Selg, Herbert. Diagnostik der Aggressivität. Habilitationsschrift. Göttingen, 1968.
Phil 2115.205   Seligen, Martin. The liberal politics of John Locke. London, 1968.
Phil 5258.146   Seliger, Josef. Das sociale Verhalten. Bern, 1903.
Phil 8893.130   Selivanov, F.A. Etika. Tomsk, 1961.
Phil 630.9   Sellars, R.W. Critical realism. N.Y., 1916.
Phil 5058.27   Sellars, R.W. Essentials of logic. Boston, 1917.
Phil 5058.27.5   Sellars, R.W. The essentials of logic. Boston, 1925.
Phil 5058.27.7   Sellars, R.W. The essentials of logic. Boston, 1945.
Phil 493.5   Sellars, R.W. Philosophy for the future. N.Y., 1949.
Phil 630.9.10   Sellars, R.W. The philosophy of physical realism. N.Y., 1932.
Phil 8598.35.15   Sellars, Roy W. Religion coming of age. N.Y., 1928.
Phil 193.66   Sellars, Roy Wood. Essentials of philosophy. N.Y., 1917.
Phil 193.66.5   Sellars, Roy Wood. Evolutionary naturalism. Chicago, 1922.
Phil 193.66.9   Sellars, Roy Wood. The principles and problems of philosophy. N.Y., 1926.
Phil 349.44   Sellars, W. Science, perception, and reality. London, 1963.
Phil 193.252   Sellars, Wilfrid. Philosophical perspectives. Springfield, 1967.
Phil 8870.38   Sellars, Wilfrid. Readings in ethical theory. N.Y., 1952.
Phil 3500.112   Sellars, Wilfrid. Science and metaphysics; variations on Kantian themes. London, 1968.
Phil 3850.70   Selle, Christian Gottlieb. Grundsätze der reinen Philosophie. Bruxelles, 1969.
Phil 8968.18   Sellers, James. Theological ethics. N.Y., 1966.
Phil 2805.440   Sellier, Philippe. Pascal et la liturgie. Paris, 1966.
Phil 2805.480   Sellier, Philippe. Pascal et Saint Augustin. Paris, 1970.
Phil 1135.23.15   Sellin, Ernst. Die Spuren griechischer Philosophie. 1e and 2e Aufl. Leipzig, 1905.
Phil 5850.338   Selling, L.S. Studies on the problem driver. Detroit, 1941.
Phil 705.27   Selling, M. Studien zur Geschichte der Transzendantalphilosophie. Inaug. Diss. Lund, 1938.
Phil 8598.96   Sellmair, Josef. Humanitas Christiana. München, 1950.
Phil 8598.96.5   Sellmair, Josef. Der Mensch in der Fragik. München, 1948.
Phil 6692.7   Selma, die jüdische Seherin. (Wiener, M.) Berlin, 1838.
Phil 1050.4.25   Sêlomó Ibn Gabirol como poeta y filósofo. (Millás y Vallicrosa, José María.) Madrid, 1945.
Phil 193.148.5   Selsam, H. Philosophy in revolution. N.Y., 1957.
Phil 193.148   Selsam, H. What is philosophy? N.Y., 1938.
Phil 193.148.3   Selsam, H. What is philosophy? N.Y., 1962.
Phil 8893.139   Selsam, Howard. Ethics and progress. N.Y., 1965.
Phil 2020.805   Selsam, Howard. T.H. Green. N.Y., 1930.
Phil 193.92   Seltmann, Otto. Das Urteil der Vernunft. Caliv, 1920.
Htn Phil 8893.73.5*   Selva, Lorenzo. Della metamorfosi...del virtuoso. Firenze, 1583.
Htn Phil 8893.73.10*   Selva, Lorenzo. Della metamorfosi...del virtuoso. Firenze, 1615.
Htn Phil 8893.73*   Selva, Lorenzo. Della metamorfosi...del virtuoso. Orvieto, 1582.
Phil 270.140   Selvaggi, Filippo. Causalità e indeterminismo. Roma, 1964.
Phil 349.52   Selvaggi, Filippo. Scienza e methologia; saggi de epistemologia. Roma, 1962.
Phil 6854.10   Selvmord. (Retterstøl, Nils.) Oslo, 1970.
Phil 3500.48   Selz, Otto. Kants Stellung in der Geistesgeschichte. Mannheim, 1924.
Phil 5258.59   Selz, Otto. Über die Gesetze des geordneten Denkverlaufs. Stuttgart, 1913. 2v.
Phil 5258.59.7   Selz, Otto. Über die Persönlichkeitstypen. Jena, 1924.
Phil 8968.22   Semaine des Intellectuels Catholiques, 1966. Morale humaine, morale chrétienne. Paris, 1966.
Phil 8968.22.5   Semaine des Intellectuels Catholiques, 1967. La violence. Roma, 1968.
Phil 720.78   Semaine des Intellectuels Catholiques, 1969. Chercher la vérité, 5-12 mars 1969. Paris, 1969.
Phil 9358.19   Semaines Sociales de France. 48th, Reims, 1961. La montée des jeunes dans la communauté des générations. Lyon, 1962.
Phil 6625.4   Semal. De la sensibilité générale et de ses altérations dans les affections mélancoliques. Paris, 1875.
Phil 70.50   Semana Española de Filosofía, 4th, Madrid, 1957. La forma. Madrid, 1959.
Phil 70.50.5   Semana Española de Filosofía. Ponencias y conferencias. Madrid, 1-9 4v.
Phil 5520.335.2A   Semantic analysis. (Ziff, Paul.) Ithaca, 1962.
Phil 5599.80   Semantic differential technique; a sourcebook. (Snider, James G.) Chicago, 1969.
Phil 5520.150   Semantica. (Archivo di Filosofia.) Roma, 1955.
Phil 5520.742   Semanticheskaia struktura slova. Moskva, 1971.
Phil 5520.435   Semantics. (Thurman, Kelly.) Boston, 1960.
Phil 346.19.5   Semantics and necessary truth. (Pap, Athur.) New Haven, 1958.
Phil 5520.135A   Semantics and the philosophy of language. (Linsky, Leonard.) Urbana, Ill., 1952.
Phil 5520.550   Semantik. (Levin, Poul.) København, 1968.
Phil 310.734   Semantik und dialektischer Materialismus; Darstellung und Analyse der modernen marxistisch-leninistischen Wissenschaftstheorie in der DDR. (Goerlich, Johann Wolfgang.) Berlin, 1969.
Phil 5520.752   Semantikk i teori og praksis. (Wormnaes, Odd.) Oslo, 1971.
Phil 5520.180   La sémantique. 1. éd. (Guiraud, P.) Paris, 1955.
Phil 5520.404   Semantischer Positivismus in den USA. (Neubert, Q.) Halle, 1962.
Phil 5066.320   Sembolik mantik. (Grünberg, Teo.) Istanbul, 1968.
Phil 8980.780.5   Semenov, Mikhail N. O moral'nom avtoritete. Alma-Ata, 1967.
Phil 3838.28   Semerari, G. Il problemi dello Spinozismo. Trani, 1952.
Phil 4080.17.15   Semerari, G. Storia e storicismo. Trani, 1953.
Phil 1718.37   Semerari, Giuseppe. Da Schelling a Merkau-Ponty. Bologna, 1962.
Phil 1718.44   Semerari, Giuseppe. Esperienze del pensiero moderno. Urbino, 1969.
Phil 3801.781   Semerari, Giuseppe. Interpretazione di Schelling. Napoli, 1958.
Phil 349.54   Semerari, Giuseppe. La lotta per la scienza. 1. ed. Milano, 1965.
Phil 9470.10   Semerari, Giuseppe. Responsabilità e comunità umana. Manduria, 1960.

Phil 8708.44   Semeria, Giovanni. Scienza e fede e il liro preteso conflitto. Roma, 1903.
Phil 6968.6   Sémérie, E. Des symptomes intellectuels de la folie. Paris, 1867.
Phil 3850.26.90   Semewald, L. Carl Christian Ehrhard Schmid und sein Verhältnis zu Fichte. Inaug. Diss. Leipzig, 1929.
Phil 6956.5.5   The semi-insane and semi-responsible. (Grasset, Joseph.) N.Y., 1907.
Phil 3903.3.109   Semifiktionen und Vollfiktionen in der Philosophie des Als Ob von H. Vaihinger. Inaug. Diss. (Willrodt, S.) Gräfenhainichen, 1933.
Phil 6968.39   Semiotic approaches to psychiatry. (Shands, Harley C.) The Hague, 1970.
Phil 5066.5   Semiotik; eine Theorie der Zeichengestalten als Grundlage für Untersuchungen von formalisierten Sprachen. (Hermes, H.) Leipzig, 1938.
Phil 5520.551   Semiotik. (Bense, Max.) Baden-Baden, 1967.
Phil 5520.577   Semiotika i ee osnovnye problemy. (Vetrov, Anatolii A.) Moskva, 1968.
Phil 5520.748   Semiotyka polska, 1894-1969. (Pelc, Jerzy.) Warszawa, 1971.
Phil 332.27   Eine Semiphilosophie im Grundriss Dargestellt. (Bechert, R.) München, 1941.
Phil 3310.4.80   Semmelink, J.H. Professor Dr. J.H. Gunning. Zeist, 1926.
Phil 8708.37   Semmelroth, O. Die Welt als Schöpfung. Frankfurt, 1962.
Phil 5640.22   Semon, R. Bewusstseinsvorgang und Gehirnprozess. Wiesbaden, 1920.
Phil 5545.54.10   Semon, R. The mneme. Leipzig, 1921.
Phil 5545.54   Semon, R. Die Mneme als erhaltendes Prinzip im Wechsel des organischen Gesehens. 3. Aufl. Leipzig, 1911.
Phil 5545.54.15   Semon, R. Mnemic psychology. N.Y., 1923.
Phil 5545.54.5   Semon, R. Die mnemischen Empfindungen. Leipzig, 1909.
Phil 8980.780   Semov, Mois I. Prichini za ostatutsite ot burzhoazniia moral v nasheto obshchestvo. Sofiia, 1965.
Phil 4195.85   Semprini, G. La filosofia di Pico della Mirandola. Milano, 1936.
Phil 4195.84   Semprini, G. Giovanni Pico della Mirandola. Todi, 1921.
Phil 4120.1.81   Semprini, G. Melchiorre Gioia e la sua dottrina politica. Genova, 1934.
Phil 103.4.5   Semprini, G. Nuovo dizionario di coltura filosofica e scientifica. Torino, 1952.
Phil 103.4   Semprini, G. Piccolo dizionario di coltura filosofica e scientifica. Milano, 1931.
Phil 5440.33   Sen Gupta, N. Heredity in mental traits. 1. ed. London, 1941.
Phil 8893.147   Sen Gupta, Santosh Chandra. Good, freewill and God. Calcutta, 1963.
Phil 8843.20   Sena, Cemil. Insanlar ve ahlâklar. Istanbul, 1970.
Phil 8893.30   Senac de Meilhan, G. Considérations sur l'esprit et les moeurs. London, 1787.
Phil 8893.30.3   Senac de Meilhan, G. Considérations sur l'esprit et les moeurs. Paris, 1905.
Phil 5635.39   La senation et l'image. Thèse. (Wolff, E.M.) Carcassonne, 1943.
Phil 5400.196   Senault, Jean Francois. De l'usage des passions. Paris, 1964.
Phil 8673.38   Sencer, Muammer. Allah neden var. Istanbul, 1970.
Phil 29.17   Sendai, Japan. University. Tohoku psychologica folia. Sendai. 4,1936+ 10v.
Phil 5520.441   Sendel, Bess Selher. The humanity of words. Cleveland, 1958.
Htn Phil 3801.471*   Sendschreiben an den...von Schelling. (Kapp, Christian.) n.p., 1830.
Phil 3500.110   Sendschreiben an einen Recensenten in der Gothaischen gelehrten Zeitung über den gerichtlichen Eyd. v.1-2. (Schwab, Johann Christoph.) Bruxelles, 1968.
Phil 623.6   Sendschreiben an einen Staatsmann über die Frage...Rationalismus. (Bretschneider, K.G.) Leipzig, 1830.
Phil 3778.36   Sendschreiben an J.C. Lavater und J.G. Fichte über den Glauben an Gott. (Reinhold, K.L.) Hamburg, 1799. 3 pam.
Phil 195.4   Die Sendung der Philosophie in unserer Zeit. (Utitz, Emil.) Leiden, 1935.
Phil 9590.32   Sendy, Jean. Les Dieux nous sont nées. Paris, 1966-
Phil 9590.32.5   Sendy, Jean. L'ère du verseau. Paris, 1970.
Phil 960.270   Seneviratne, M.J. On the nature of man and society, and other essays. 1st ed. Colombo, 1967.
Phil 349.2   Sengler, J. Erkenntnisslehre. Heidelberg, 1858.
Phil 3018.2   Sengler, J. Ueber das Wesen...Philosophie und Theologie in der gegenwärtigen Zeit...Religionsphilosophie. Heidelberg, 1837.
Phil 193.22   Sengler, J. Über das Wesen und speculativen Philosophie. Mainz, 1834.
Phil 5090.11   Sengupta, Pradip Kumar. Demonstration and logical truth. 1st ed. Calcutta, 1968.
Phil 7054.43.15   Senillosa, Felipe. Concordancia del espiritismo con la ciencia. v.1-2. Buenos Aires, 1891.
Phil 5525.46   Senise, T. Il riso in psicologia. Napoli, 1950.
Phil 600.34   Senna Freitas, J.J. de. A doutrina positivista. Póvoa de Varzim, n.d.
Phil 6990.3.33   Senna Freitas, José J. de. O milagre e a critica moderna on a immaculada conceição de Lourdes. Braga, 1873.
Phil 978.59.90   El Señor Krishnamurti. (Franceschi, G.J.) Buenos Aires, 1935.
Phil 5640.2.5   Les sens. 5e éd. (Bernstein, J.) Paris, 1893.
Phil 8592.81   Sens chrétien de l'homme. (Mouroux, Jean.) Paris, 1953.
Phil 2520.99   Le sens commun de M. Gerbet. (Jammes.) Paris, 1827.
Phil 4752.2.73   Le sens de la création. (Berdiaev, Nikolai Aleksandrovich.) Paris, 1955.
Phil 5651.7   Le sens de la direction et l'orientation lointaine chez l'homme. (Jaccard, Pierre.) Paris, 1932.
Phil 178.56   Le sens de la mêtaphysique. (Durand-Doat, J.) Paris, 1928.
Phil 178.56.2   Le sens de la métaphysique. Thèse. (Durand-Doat, J.) Paris, 1928.
Phil 8407.14.4   Le sens de l'art. 4. éd. (Gaultier, Paul.) Paris, 1911.
Phil 193.55   Le sens de l'existence. (Stein, Ludwig.) Paris, 1909.
Phil 338.18   Le sens du réel. (Hubert, René.) Paris, 1925.
Phil 3450.11.455   Le sens du temps et de la perception chez E. Husserl. (Granel, Gérard.) Paris, 1968.
Phil 2750.27.30   Sens et existence dans la philosophie de Maurice Merleau-Ponty. (Hyppolite, J.) Oxford, 1963.
Phil 2750.20.20   Sens et non-sens. (Merleau-Ponty, Maurice.) Paris, 1948.
Phil 5251.43   Le sens intime en psychologie. (Lévy, Albert.) Bruxelles, 1896.
Phil 5635.36.5   La sensation, étude de sa genèse et de son rôle dans la connaissance. Thèse. (Salzi, Pierre.) Paris, 1934.

Phil 5635.02   Pamphlet box. Sensation.
Phil 5635.36   La sensation. (Salzi, Piierre.) Paris, 1934.
Phil 5640.130.2   La sensation. 2. éd. (Piéron, Henri.) Paris, 1957.
Phil 5258.25.16   Sensation and intuition. 2d ed. (Sully, J.) London, 1880.
Phil 5640.39   Sensation and pain. (Taylor, C.F.) N.Y., 1881.
Phil 5585.180   Sensation and perception. (Hamlyn, David Walter.) N.Y., 1961.
Phil 5211.4.20   Sensation and perception in the history of experimental psychology. (Boring, E.G.) N.Y., 1942.
Phil 5635.32   Sensation and the sensory pathway. (Stopford, J.S.B.) London, 1930.
Phil 5635.11   Sensation et énergie. (Henry, Charles.) Paris, 1911.
Phil 5635.7   Sensation et mouvement. (Féré, C.) Paris, 1900.
Phil 331.30   Sensationalism and scientific explanation. (Alexander, Peter.) London, 1963.
Phil 1870.118   Sensationalism and theology in Berkeley's philosophy. Inaug. Diss. (Hedenius, Ingemar.) Uppsala, 1936.
Phil 5635.01   Pamphlet vol. Sensations. German dissertations. 2 pam.
Phil 5647.7   Les sensations de température. Thèse. (Sandovici, Constantin.) Montpellier, 1936.
Phil 5635.18   Les sensations internes. (Beaunis, H.) Paris, 1889.
Phil 9355.5   Sense. (Pomeroy, Marcus.) N.Y., 1871.
Phil 1905.22.80   Sense - perception and matter. (Lean, Martin.) London, 1953.
Phil 9070.150   Sense and delusion. (Dilman, Ilhman.) London, 1971.
Phil 2750.20.24   Sense and non-sense. (Merleau-Ponty, Maurice.) Evanston, 1964.
Phil 5244.30   Sense and nonsense in psychology. (Eysenck, H.J.) Harmondsworth, Middlesex, 1957.
Phil 8598.143   Sense and nonsense in religion. (Stenson, Sten H.) Nashville, 1969.
Phil 7069.50   The sense and nonsense of prophecy. (Garrett, Eileen Jeanette Lyttle.) N.Y., 1950.
Phil 5520.488   Sense and sense development. (Waldron, R.A.) London, 1967.
Phil 331.29   Sense and sensibilia. (Austin, J.L.) Oxford, 1962.
Phil 5520.2   Sense and sound. (Gaskell, J.) Philadelphia, 1854.
Phil 8419.40.5   The sense of beauty, being the outlines of aesthetic theory. (Santayana, G.) N.Y., 1898.
Phil 8419.40   The sense of beauty, being the outlines of aesthetic theory. (Santayana, G.) N.Y., 1955.
Phil 8419.40.6A   The sense of beauty. (Santayana, G.) N.Y., 1896. 3v.
Phil 199.2   The sense of community. (Younghusband, F.) London, 1916.
Phil 2070.07   The sense of dizziness in deaf-mutes. (James, William.) n.p., 1882-1911. 11 pam.
Phil 5649.16   The sense of effort. (Waller, A.D.) n.p., 1891?
Phil 5525.20A   The sense of humor. (Eastman, Max.) N.Y., 1921.
Phil 5525.20.5   The sense of humor. (Eastman, Max.) N.Y., 1922.
Phil 8633.1.24   The sense of immortality. (Cabot, Philip.) Cambridge, 1924.
Phil 5653.5   The sense of taste. (Hollingworth, H.L.) N.Y., 1917.
Phil 410.9   The sense of the infinite. (Kuhns, Levi O.) N.Y., 1908.
Phil 8581.52.30   The sense of the presence of God. (Baillie, John.) London, 1962.
Phil 486.9   Sense without matter, or Direct perception. (Luce, A.A.) Edinburgh, 1954.
Phil 806.25   Sensei e soluzzi della filosofia europea. (Galli, Dario.) Bologna, 1959.
Phil 5241.2.20   The senses and the intellect. (Bain, A.) London, 1855.
Phil 5241.2.22   The senses and the intellect. (Bain, A.) N.Y., 1879.
Phil 5241.2.21   The senses and the intellect. 2. ed. (Bain, S.) London, 1864.
Phil 5241.2.21.5   The senses and the intellect. 3. ed. (Bain, A.) N.Y., 1872.
Phil 5241.2.27   The senses and the intellect. 4th ed. (Bain, A.) N.Y., 1894.
Phil 5585.243   The senses considered as perceptual systems. (Gibson, James Jerome.) Boston, 1966.
Phil 5640.144   The senses of animals and men. (Milne, Lorus J.) N.Y., 1962.
Htn   Phil 8893.66*   Sensi, Lodovico. La historia dell'huomo. Perugia, 1577.
Phil 5400.132   La sensibilité. (Michaud, H.) Lyon, 1954?
Phil 1706.1.43   La sensibilité métaphysique. 3e éd. (Gaultier, Jules de.) Paris, 1924.
Phil 5648.19   Les sensibilités cutanées. v.1-3. (Piéron, Henri.) Paris, 1928-32.
Phil 2268.3.100   Sensism, the philosophy of the West. (Smith, Charles.) N.Y., 1956. 2v.
Phil 6960.7   Der sensitive Beziehungwahn. (Kretschmer, E.) Berlin, 1918.
Phil 6687.1.6   Der sensitive Mensch. (Reichenback, C.) Leipzig, 1910. 2v.
Phil 5421.15.25   Sensitivity to people. (Smith, Henry Clay.) N.Y., 1966.
Phil 585.265   Il senso del fondamento. (Masullo, Aldo.) Napoli, 1967.
Phil 8673.32   Il senso dell'ateismo contemporaneo. Bologna, 1967.
Phil 4080.25   Senso e natura. (Cini, Giovanni.) Firenze, 1959?
Phil 70.22.10   Senso e valore del discorso metafisico. (Centro di Studi Filosofici di Gallarate.) Padova, 1966.
Phil 5643.58   Die sensorielle Theorie der optischen Raumempfindung. (Kolbenheyer, E.G.) Leipzig, 1905.
Htn   Phil 6103.8*   Die sensorischen Functionen des Rückenmarks. (Pflüger, E.) Berlin, 1853. 5 pam.
Phil 5490.5   Sensory, intellectual and mystical intuition. v.1-2. (Losskii, Nikolai O.) n.p., n.d.
Phil 5640.30   The sensory basis and structure of knowledge. (Watt, Henry J.) London, 1925.
Phil 5640.133   Sensory communication...Symposium...July 19-Aug. 1, 1959, M.I.T. (Symposium on Principles of Sensory Communication.) Cambridge, 1962.
Phil 5640.136   Sensory deprivation. (Symposium on Sensory Deprivation.) Cambridge, 1961.
Phil 5640.136.15   Sensory deprivation: fifteen years of research. (Zuber, John Peter.) N.Y., 1969.
Phil 5635.48   Sensory experience. (Christman, Raymond John.) Scranton, 1971.
Phil 5640.140   Sensory inhibition. (Békésy, Georg von.) Princeton, 1967.
Phil 5640.137   Sensory restriction. (Schultz, Duane P.) N.Y., 1965.
Htn   Phil 2262.62*   Sensus communis. (Shaftesbury, A.A.C.) London, 1709.
Phil 5592.150   The sentence completion method. (Rohde, Amanda R.) N.Y., 1957.
Phil 1504.7.2   Sententiae divinitatis. Ein Sentanzenbuch der gilbertschen Schule. v.7, pt.2-3. (Geyer, B.) Münster, 1909.
Phil 8892.7   Sentenze e massime morali. (Rosteri, P.L.) London, 1842.
Phil 365.45   O sentido da evolução. (Salis Goulart, J.) Porto Allegre, 1937.
Phil 1750.778   Sentido de la filosofía contemporánea. (Nuño Montes, Juan Antonio.) Caracas, 1965.

Phil 8403.17   El sentido del dolor en el arte. (Cabrisas y Madero.) La Habana, 1937.
Phil 3450.11.120   Sentido del movimiento. (Miro Quesada, F.) Lima, 1941.
Phil 1750.772   El sentido existencial de la política. (Bustos, Ismael.) Santiago de Chile, 1956.
Phil 8598.110   Sentien de gnose. (Schuon, Frithjof.) Paris, 1957.
Phil 8418.19   Le sentiment de la beauté; étude de psychologie. (Roux, J.) Paris, 1908.
Phil 5246.7   Le sentiment et la pensée. (Godfernaux, A.) Paris, 1894.
Phil 5246.7.3   Le sentiment et la pensée. 3. éd. (Godfernaux, A.) Paris, 1907.
Phil 2070.51   Sentiment of rationality. (James, William.) Aberdeen, 18-
Phil 2070.09   The sentiment of rationality. (James, William.) n.p., 1879-1907. 8 pam.
Phil 2070.51.5   Sentiment of rationality. (James, William.) N.Y., 1905.
Phil 8595.18   Le sentiment religieux, base logique de la morale? (Perovsky-Petrovo, Solovovo.) Paris, 1913.
Phil 5627.34   Le sentiment religieux. (Perrier, Louis.) Paris, 1912.
Phil 8600.2   Le sentiment religieux à l'heure actuelle. (Union de Libres Penseurs et à Libres Croyants pour la Culture Morale.) Paris, 1919.
Phil 5627.7.5   Sentiment religieux et sentiment moral. (Bois, Henri.) Paris, 1903.
Phil 525.85   Der sentimentale Mensch. (Wieser, Max.) Gotha, 1924.
Phil 525.85.2   Der sentimentale Mensch gesehen aus der Welt. (Wieser, Max.) Gotha, 1924.
Phil 5871.110   I sentimenti del fanciullo nell'ambito familiare. (Cacciagierra, Francesco.) Milano, 1968.
Phil 6328.9   Les sentiments, les passions et la folie explications des phénomènes de la pensée et des sensations. (Simonin, A.H.) Paris, 1885.
Phil 177.68.15   Sentiments, pasiions et signes. 2e éd. (Chartier, Émile.) Paris, 1935.
Phil 5400.136   Les sentiments. 4. ed. (Maisonneuve, Jean.) Paris, 1957.
Phil 5400.136.5   Les sentiments. 5. ed. (Maisonneuve, Jean.) Paris, 1960.
Phil 6310.1.95   Les sentiments d'infériorité. (Oliver Brachfield, F.) Genève, 1945.
Phil 8887.71.10   Sentiments et coutumes. 56. ed. (Maurois, André.) Paris, 1934.
Phil 5249.20   Les sentiments et l'intelligence. (Joussain, A.) Paris, 1930.
Phil 5400.53   Les sentiments généraux. (Cartault, A.) Paris, 1912.
Phil 1718.19   Sentit i valor de la nova filosofia. (Serra, Hunter J.) Barcelona, 1934.
Phil 3500.21.15   Sentroul, C. Kant et Aristote. 2. éd. Louvain, 1913.
Phil 3500.21.5   Sentroul, C. Kant und Aristoteles. n.p., 1911.
Phil 3500.21   Sentroul, C. L'objet de la métaphysique selon Kant. Louvain, 1905.
Phil 5374.235.10   A separate reality; further conversations with Don Juan. (Castaneda, Carlos.) N.Y., 1971.
Phil 3450.19.140   Sepich, Juan R. La filosofía de Ser y tiempo de M. Heidegger. Buenos Aires, 1954.
Phil 2750.11.74   Sept leçons sur l'être. (Maritain, Jacques.) Paris, 1934?
Phil 5170.1   Sept lois fondamentales de la théorie des égalités logiques. (Poretsky, P.) Kazan, 1899.
Phil 4803.454.21   Sept manuscrits inédits, écrits de 1803 à 1806. (Hoene-Wroński, Józef Maria.) Paris, 1879.
Phil 177.80   Les septèmes philosophiques. (Cresson, André.) Paris, 1929.
Phil 3838.23   Septimana Spinozana. (Societas Spinoza.) Hagae, 1933.
Htn   Phil 5768.9*   Sepulveda, J.G. De fato i libris arbitrio libero tres. Roma, 1526.
Phil 8592.4.5   Sequel to the inquiry, what is revelation? (Maurice, F.D.) Cambridge, 1860.
Phil 4962.20   El ser del hombre. (Arroyave Calle, J.C.) Medellín, 1952.
Phil 3450.19.315   El ser en la filosofía de Heidegger. (Echauri, Raúl.) Rosario, 1964.
Phil 8612.56.5   El ser la muerte. (Ferrater Mora, José.) Madrid, 1962.
Phil 4356.3.5   El ser y el sentido. (Ferrater Mora, José.) Madrid, 1967.
Phil 189.31   El ser y la accion en la dimension humana. (Ortuzar Arriaga, M.) Madrid, 1961.
Phil 8893.63   Sera, G. Sulle tracce della vita. Roma, 1907.
Phil 8419.68   Séran de la Tour. L'art de sentir et de juger en matière de goût. v.1-2. Genève, 1970.
Phil 2630.7.95   Sérant, Paul. René Guenon. Paris, 1953.
Phil 5628.11.6   Seraph among angels; the life of St. Mary Magadalene de' Pazzi. (Mary Minima, Sister.) Chicago, 1958.
Phil 3850.10.80   Serch, Paul. Friedrich Schlegels Philosophie Anschauungen in ihrer Entwicklung und systematischen Ausgestaltung. Berlin, 1905.
Phil 5258.197   Serebriakoff, Victor. I.Q.: a Mensa analysis and history. London, 1966.
Phil 5058.110   Serebriannikov, Oleg F. Evristicheskie printsipy i logicheskie ischisleniia. Moskva, 1970.
Phil 1730.10   Seredi, P. Lajos. Az ismeret eredetének kérdése a XVII és XVIII szazad filozofiai küzdelmeiben Kantig. Eperjes, 1889.
Htn   Phil 2115.85*   Sergeant, J. Solid philosophy asserted. London, 1697.
Phil 7069.36.15   Sergeant, P.W. Historic British ghosts. London, 1936.
Phil 5258.70.5   Sergi, G. L'origine dei fenomeni psichici e il loro significato biologico. 2. ed. Torino, 1904.
Phil 5258.70   Sergi, G. La psychologie physiologique. Paris, 1888.
Phil 5585.9   Sergi, G. Teoria fisiologica della percezione. Milano, 1881.
Phil 5645.23   Sergi, Giuseppe. Fisiologia e psicologia del colore. Milano, 1881.
Phil 2520.214   Sergio, Antonio. Cartesianismo ideal e cartesianismo real. Lisboa, 1937.
Phil 5400.49   Sergio, Antonio. Da natureza da affecção. Rio de Janeiro, 1913.
Phil 672.136.15   The serial universe. (Dunne, John W.) N.Y., 1938.
Phil 5238.180   Serie geestelijke volksgezondheid. (Katholieke Centrale Vereniging voor Geestelijke Volksgezondheid.) 20-42 6v.
Phil 9357.7   A series of discourses...to young men. 2d ed. (Rudd, John C.) Auburn, 1831.
Phil 8692.5.12   Series of discourses on the Christian revelation, viewed in connexion with modern astronomy. (Chalmers, Thomas.) N.Y., 18- .
Phil 8692.5.3   Series of discourses on the Christian revelation, viewed in connexion with modern astronomy. (Chalmers, Thomas.) N.Y., 1817.
Phil 8692.5.7   Series of discourses on the Christian revelation, viewed in connexion with modern astronomy. (Chalmers, Thomas.) Hartford, 1818.

Phil 8692.5.5 Series of discourses on the Christian revelation, viewed in connexion with modern astronomy. (Chalmers, Thomas.) N.Y., 1818. 2 pam.

Phil 8692.5.15 Series of discourses on the Christian revelation, viewed in connexion with modern astronomy. 12th ed. (Chalmers, Thomas.) Glasgow, 1834.

Phil 6100.1 A series of engravings...brain...in man. (Mayo, H.) London, 1827.

Phil 960.33 A series of lessons on the inner teachings of the philosophies and religions of India. (Atkinson, W.W.) Chicago, 1908.

Phil 7069.00.32 A series of meditations on the ethical and physical relation of spirit to the human organism. (Gaffield, E.C.) Syracuse,.N.Y., 1900.

Phil 5645.46 The series of plates designed as tests for colour-blindness. 8. ed. (Ishihara, S.) Tokyo, 1939.

Phil 8882.2A A series of popular essays. (Hamilton, E.) Boston, 1817. 2v.

Phil 2475.1.214 Serini, P. Bergson e lo spiritualismo. Genova, 1923.

Phil 5440.19 Sériot, Pauline. Effets nocifs du croisement des races sur la formation du caractère. Thèse. Paris, 1918.

Htn Phil 9010.14* A serious address. (Mather, Cotton.) Boston, 1726.

Htn Phil 2120.2.30* A serious call to a devout and holy life. (Law, William.) London, 1729.

Phil 8598.8 Serious thoughts...Brougham's discourse of natural theology. London, 1836-31. 2 pam.

Phil 2280.6.87 A sermon, memorial of the Rev. Charles W. Shields. (Potter, H.C.) Princeton, N.J., 1905.

Phil 8581.18.7 A sermon containing some reflections upon Mr. Balguy's essay on moral goodness. (Silvester, Tipping.) London, 1734.

Phil 8893.38 A sermon preach'd at Faringdon...opening a charity school. (Stockwell, Joseph.) Oxford, 1717.

Phil 1925.65 A sermon preached before the House of Commons, March 31, 1647. (Cudworth, R.) N.Y., 1930.

Phil 1850.59.50 Sermones fideles, ethici, politici, o economici, sive interiora rerum. (Bacon, Francis.) Lugdunum Batavorum, 1659.

Htn Phil 1850.60* Sermones fidelis. (Bacon, Francis.) Amsterdam, 1662.

Phil 1900.60.15 Sermons. (Butler, Joseph.) Cambridge, 1827.

Phil 8598.12 Sermons and speeches. (Smith, Goldwin.) N.Y., 1861.

Phil 1900.76 Sermons I, II, III upon human nature. (Butler, Joseph.) Edinburgh, 1888.

Phil 8702.2 Sermons in stones. (McCausland, D.) London, 1873.

Phil 8595.1.6 Sermons of Theism, Atheism, and the popular theology. (Parker, T.) Boston, 1853.

Phil 8595.1.7 Sermons of Theism, Atheism, and the popular theology. (Parker, T.) Boston, 1856.

Phil 9510.4 Sermons on evil-speaking. (Barrow, I.) N.Y., 1887.

Phil 1915.20 Sermons on several subjects and occasions. 8th ed. (Clarke, Samuel.) London, 1756. 8v.

Phil 8676.3.5 Sermons preached at St. George's Hall, Laugham Place. (Voysey, C.) London, 1872-77. 4v.

Phil 6128.16 Sermyn, W.C. de. Contribution à l'étude de certaines facultés cérébrales méconnues. Sawsanne, 1910.

Phil 4210.134 Sernagiotto, L. Antonio Rosmini all'estero. Venezia, 1889.

Phil 9120.8 Sérol, Maurice. Le besoin et la devoir religieux. Paris, 1908.

Phil 1718.21 Séronya, Henri. Initiation à la philosophie contemporaine. Paris, 1933.

Phil 1750.530 Sérouya, Henri. Les philosophies de l'existence. Paris, 1957.

Phil 3838.19 Sérouya, Henri. Spinoza. Paris, 1933.

Phil 293.28 The serpent and the satellite. (Morin, J.A.) N.Y., 1953.

Phil 1718.19 Serra, Hunter J. Sentit i valor de la nova filosofia. Barcelona, 1934.

Phil 818.22 Serra Hunter, J. Figures i perspectives de la història del pensamiento. Barcelona, 1935.

Phil 8598.139 Serrand, A.Z. Evolution technique et théologies. Paris, 1965.

Phil 7055.205 Serrano, Geraldo. Arigó, desafio à ciência. Rio de Janeiro, 1967.

Phil 818.23 Serrano, J. História de filosofia; ou Pensamento filosófico através dos séculos. Rio de Janeiro, 1944.

Phil 525.99 Serrano Plaja, A. Los místicos. Buenos Aires, 1943.

Phil 4462.3 Serrão, Joel. Sampaio Bruno. Lisboa, 1958.

Phil 1540.13 Serras, Pereira, M. A tese escolastica do composto humano. Diss. Coimbra, 1923.

Phil 6319.1.225 Serreano, Miguel. C.G. Jung and Hermann Hesse. London, 1966.

Phil 3425.587 Serreau, R. Hegel et l'hégélianisme. Paris, 1962.

Phil 3552.482 Serres, Michel. Le système de Leibniz et ses modèles mathématiques. Paris, 1968.

Phil 2520.79.10 Serrurier, C. Descartes. Paris, 1951.

Phil 2520.177 Serrurier, C. Descartes leer en leven. 's-Gravenhage, 1930.

Phil 3500.59 Serrus, C. L'esthétique transcendantale et la science moderne. Paris, 1930.

Phil 5058.51 Serrus, Charles. Essai sur la signification de la logique. Paris, 1939.

Phil 5520.61.10 Serrus, Charles. La langue, le sens, la pensée. Paris, 1941.

Phil 2520.188 Serrus, Charles. La méthode de Descartes et son application à la métaphysique. Paris, 1933.

Phil 2520.188.5 Serrus, Charles. La méthode de Descartes et son application à la métaphysique. Thèse. Paris, 1933.

Phil 5520.61 Serrus, Charles. Le parallélisme logico-grammatical. Thèse. Paris, 1933.

Phil 9240.8 Sertellanges, A.G. Le problème du mal. Paris, 1948-1951. 2v.

Phil 2475.1.272 Sertillanges, A.G. Henri Bergson et le catholicisme. Paris, 1941.

Phil 2477.9.85 Sertillanges, A.G. La philosophie de Claude Bernard. Paris, 1944.

Phil 8673.21 Sertillanges, Antonio Gilbert. Dieu ou rien? Paris, 1965.

Phil 8520.37 Sertillanges, R.P. Le christianisme et les philosophies. Paris, 1939-41. 2v.

Phil 1695.25 Servadio, E. La psicoanalisi. Torino, 1963. 3v.

Phil 6688.28 Servan, J.M.A. Questions adressées. Padova, 1784.

Phil 8592.19 The service of man. (Morison, J.C.) London, 1887.

Phil 3245.88 Serwe, Arthur. Die Raum- und Zeitlehre Immanuel Hermann Fichtes. Saarbrücken, 1959.

Phil 28.18 Sesamums. N.Y. 1937-1946 7v.

Phil 193.133 Seshagiri Row, T.V. New light on fundamental problems. Mylapore, Madras, 1932.

VPhil 310.648 Šešić, Bogdan. Dijalektički materijalizam. 2. Izd. Beograd, 1967.

Phil 270.130 Šešić, Bogdan. Nužnost i sloboda. Beograd, 1963.

Phil 2655.3.100 Sesmat, A. Dialectique. Paris, 1955.

Phil 5058.57 Sesmat, A. Logique. Paris, 1950.

Phil 2050.259 Sesonske, Alexander. Human understanding: studies in the philosophy of David Hume. Belmont, Calif., 1965.

Phil 2520.358.4 Sesonske, Alexander. Meta-meditations; studies in Descartes. Belmont, Calif., 1967[1965].

Phil 8400.43 Sesonske, Alexander. What is art? N.Y., 1965.

Phil 9495.160.5 Sesso e cività. 2. ed. (Marchi, L. de.) Bari, 1960.

Phil 8419.55 Sesti, Luigi. Quattro dialoghi sull'arte. Milano, 1963.

Phil 8894.17.4 Set synliga i samklang med det o synliga. (Trine, Ralph W.) Stockholm, 1910.

Phil 8893.58 Seta, Ugo della. Filosofia morale. Roma, 1917-19. 2v.

Phil 8893.58.10 Seta, Ugo della. I valori morali. 3. ed. Roma, 1925.

Phil 5258.15 Setchénov, J. Études psychologiques. Paris, 1884.

Phil 3018.4 Seth, A. Developmnt from Kant to Hegel. London, 1882.

Phil 3425.92A Seth, A. Hegelianism and personality. Edinburgh, 1887.

Phil 3425.92.2 Seth, A. Hegelianism and personality. 2d ed. Edinburgh, 1893.

Phil 1818.1 Seth, A. Scottish philosophy. Edinburgh, 1885.

Phil 1818.1.5 Seth, A. Scottish philosophy. 3e ed. Edinburgh, 1899.

Phil 8673.17 Seth, A. Two lectures on theism delivered on the occasion of the sesquicentennial celebration of Princeton University. N.Y., 1897.

Phil 1818.3.5 Seth, J. English philosophers and schools of philosophy. London, 1925.

Phil 8893.8.15 Seth, J. Essays in ethics and religion with other papers. Edinburgh, 1926.

Phil 5768.3 Seth, J. Freedom as an ethical postulate. Edinburgh, 1891.

Phil 8893.8 Seth, J. A study of ethical principles. Edinburgh, 1894.

Phil 8893.8.2 Seth, J. A study of ethical principles. 5th ed. N.Y., 1899.

Phil 8893.8.3 Seth, J. A study of ethical principles. 8. ed. N.Y., 1905.

Phil 8893.8.5 Seth, J. A study of ethical principles. 12. ed. N.Y., 1911.

Phil 8893.8.10 Seth, J. A study of ethical principles. 17. ed. N.Y., 1926.

Phil 1718.8 Seth, Pringle-Pattison Andrew. The present position of the phisophical sciences. Edinburgh, 1891.

Phil 193.23 Seth Pringle-Pattison, A. Essays in philosophical criticism. London, 1883.

Phil 8643.22 Seth Pringle-Pattison, A. The idea of immortality. Oxford, 1922.

Phil 193.23.5 Seth Pringle-Pattison, A. Man's place in the cosmos. N.Y., 1897.

Phil 193.23.7 Seth Pringle-Pattison, A. Man's place in the cosmos. 2d ed. Edinburgh, 1902.

Phil 193.23.9 Seth Pringle-Pattison, A. The philosophical radicals and other essays. Edinburgh, 1907.

Phil 630.41 Seth Pringle Pattison, Andrew. The Balfour lectures on realism. Edinburgh, 1933.

Phil 8598.62 Seth Pringle-Pattison, Andrew. Studies in the philosophy of religion. Oxford, 1930.

Phil 2280.8.95 Seth Pringle-Pattison, Andrew. Testimonials in favor of Andrew Seth. Photoreproduction. Edinburgh, 1891.

Phil 8595.17 Seth Prugle Pattison, A. The idea of God. Aberdeen, 1917.

Phil 4756.2.31 Setniskii, N.A. Kapitalisticheskii stroi v izobrazhenii N.F. Fedorova. Kharbin, 1926. 2 pam.

Phil 4769.5 Setnitskii, N.A. O konechnom ideale. Kharbin, 1932.

Phil 5066.232.20 Sets, models and recursion theory. (Leicester, England. University. Summer School in Mathematical Logic.) Amsterdam, 1967.

Phil 4195.32 Le sette sposizioni. (Pico della Mirandola, Giovanni.) Pescia, 1555.

Phil 4080.3.90 Settimelli, Emilio. La critica di Benedetto Croce. Bologna, 1912.

Phil 8893.55.2 Seu, Mohit C. The elements of moral philosophy. 2. ed. London, 1913.

Htn Phil 3801.779* Seuberg, J.A. Ob Schelling? ob Schmitt? Mainz, 1845.

Phil 5520.716 Seuphor, Michel. Le don de la parole. Saint-Aguilin-de-Pacy, 1970.

Phil 2418.4 Sève, L. La philosophie françise contemporaine et sa genèse de 1789 à nos jours. Paris, 1962.

Phil 1721.9 The seven against man. (Vieteck, George S.) Scotch Plains, N.J., 1941.

Phil 6121.18 Seven essays on the subject of your practical forces on the subject of practical occultism. (Loomis, E.) Chicago, 1897.

Phil 7085.3 Seven lectures on somnambulism. (Wienholt, A.) Edinburgh, 1845.

Phil 600.49 Seven lectures on the doctrine of positivism...May, June and July, 1879. (Kainer, J.) London, 1880.

Phil 978.6.60 The seven principles of man. (Besant, Annie.) London, 1892.

Phil 978.6.61 The seven principles of man. (Besant, Annie.) London, 1892.

Phil 978.6.61.5 The seven principles of man. 15th ed. (Besant, Annie.) London, 189-?

Phil 5217.5 Seven psychologies. (Heidbreder, Edna.) N.Y., 1961.

Phil 7069.18.50 The seven purposes. (Cameron, Margaret.) N.Y., 1918.

Phil 1821.10 Seven sages. 1st ed. (Van Wesep, Hendrikus.) N.Y., 1960.

Phil 8876.9.5 Seven seventy seven sensations. (Basford, J.L.) Boston, 1897.

Phil 585.412 Seventeen problems of man and society. 1. ed. (Borsodi, Ralph.) Anand, 1968.

Phil 1730.36 Seventeenth-century metaphysics. (Leyden, Wolfgang von.) N.Y., 1968.

Phil 8589.11 The seventh seal. (Jeanette, Agnes.) Philadelphia, 1920.

Phil 18.1.5 Seventy-five year index. (International journal of ethics.) Chicago, 1890. 2v.

Phil 9400.3 Seventy years young. (Bishop, E.M.) N.Y., 1907.

Phil 4769.1.82A Severac, B. Vladimir Soloviev. Paris, n.d.

Phil 2494.82A Séverac, J.B. Condorcet. Paris, n.d.

Phil 2636.81 Séverac, J.B. Helvétius. Paris, n.d.

Htn Phil 9358.7.5* Several discourses and characters. (Shannon, F.) London, 1689.

Htn Phil 8951.6* Several miscellaneous and mighty cases of conscience. (Barlow, Thomas.) London, 1692.

Phil 8419.38 Severgnini, D. La inevitabile illusione; rilievi modali dell'estetica. Torino, 1960.

Phil 4225.7 Severgnini, D. L'interiorità teologica dello storicismo. Roma, 1940. 3v.

Phil 4260.137 Severgnini, Dante. Studi vichiani. Milano, 1954-56. 2v.

Phil 3838.6 Severijn, Johannes. Spinoza en de gereformeerde theologie zijner dagen. Utrecht, 1919.

Phil 3246.294   Severino, Emanuele. Per un innovamento nella interpretazione della filosofia Fichtiana. Brescia, 1968.

Phil 4225.90.30   Severino, Emanuele. Studi di filosofia della prassi. Milano, 1962.

Phil 8893.40   Severn, Elizabeth. The psychology of behavior. N.Y., 1917.

Phil 5938.12   Severn, J.M. Life story and experiences of a phrenologist. Brighton, Eng., 1929.

Phil 672.147   Sevin, Emile. Le temps absolu et l'espace à quatre dimensions. Paris, 1928.

Phil 8980.782   Sevrikov, Konstantin I. Prostye istiny. Moskva, 1969.

Phil 8893.7   Sewall, F. The new ethics. N.Y., 1881.

Phil 193.24   Sewall, F. The new metaphysics. London, 1888.

Phil 5938.2.2   Sewall, T. An examination of phrenology. Boston, 1839.

Phil 5938.2   Sewall, T. An examination of phrenology. Washington, 1837.

Phil 5585.57   Seward, John P. The effect of practice on the visual perception of form. N.Y., 1931.

Phil 5525.35   Seward, Samuel S. The paradox of the ludicrous. Stanford, 1930.

Phil 6128.39   Seward, T.F. The Don't Worry movement. N.Y., 1898.

Phil 8419.17   Sewell, Arthur. The physiology of beauty. London, 1931.

Htn   Phil 7069.20.300*   Sewell, May Wright. Neither dead nor sleeping. Indianapolis, 1920.

Phil 7069.20.300   Sewell, May Wright. Neither dead nor sleeping. Indianapolis, 1920.

Phil 8968.1   Sewell, W. Christian morals. London, 1841.

Phil 9495.166.5   Sex, love and the life of the spirit. (Aquinas Institute of Philosophy and Theology. Institute of Spiritual Theology.) Chicago, 1966.

Phil 9495.155   Sex, sin and sanity. (Langdon Davies, J.) London, 1954.

Phil 3905.31   Sex and character. (Weininger, Otto.) London, 1906.

Phil 3905.30.15   Sex and character. Photoreproduction. (Weininger, Otto.) London, 1910.

Phil 9495.123   Sex and common-sense. (Royden, A.M.) N.Y., 1922.

Phil 5590.496   Sex and gender; on the development of masculinity and feminity. (Stoller, Robert J.) London, 1968.

Phil 9495.139   Sex and life. (Galloway, T.W.) N.Y., 1920.

Phil 9495.166   Sex and morality: a report to the British Council of Churches. (British Council of Churches.) London, 1966.

Phil 9495.154   Sex and morality. 1st ed. (Kardiner, A.) Indianapolis, Ind., 1954.

Phil 9495.135.5   Sex habits. (Buschke, A.) N.Y., 1933.

Phil 9495.155.15   Sex in Christianity and psychoanalysis. (Cole, William G.) N.Y., 1955.

Phil 6315.1.10   Sex in psychoanalysis. (Ferenczi, Sandor.) N.Y., 1950.

Phil 5841.01   Pamphlet box. Sex psychology.

Phil 3110.27.10   Sex puncta theosophica. (Böhme, J.) Leipzig, 1921.

Phil 5841.6   Sex roles and social structure. (Holter, Harriet.) Oslo, 1970.

X Cg   Phil 9495.127.15   The sex side of life; an explanation for young people. (Dennett, M.W. (Mrs.).) Astoria, 1928.

Phil 3415.45   The sexes compared and other essays. (Hartmann, Eduard von.) London, 1895.

Phil 9495.10   Sexology as philosophy of life. (Willard, E.O.G. (Mrs.).) Chicago, 1867.

Htn   Phil 3801.198*   Sextus oder über die absolute Erkenntniss von Schelling. (Berg, Franz.) Würzburg, 1804.

X Cg   Phil 9495.125   The sexual life of our time. (Bloch, Iwan.) London, 1910?

Phil 9495.165   Sexual morality. (Acland, Richard.) London, 1965.

Phil 6327.21.41   The sexual revolution. (Reich, Wilhelm.) N.Y., 1971.

Phil 5925.3.25   Sexual science; including manhood, womanhood and their mutual interrelations. (Fowler, O.S.) Philadelphia, 1870.

Phil 9495.130.10   Sexualethik. (Kolnai, Aurel.) Paderborn, 1930.

Phil 9495.169.5   Sexualethik. (Trillhaas, Wolfgang.) Göttingen, 1969.

Phil 5841.18.10   Sexualität und Schuldgefühl. (Rank, Otto.) Leipzig, 1926.

Phil 9495.163.5   Sexualité et limitation des naissances. Paris, 1963.

Phil 5841.8   Sexualité humaine. Paris, 1970.

Phil 5875.155   Sexuality and aggression in maturation: new facets. London, 1969.

Phil 9495.168.10   Sexuality and moral responsibility. (O'Neil, Robert P.) Washington, 1968.

Phil 5925.3.15   Sexuality restored. (Fowler, O.S.) Boston, 1870.

Phil 5841.14   Sexualleben und Nervenleiden. (Loewenfeld, Leopold.) Wiesbaden, 1906.

Phil 9495.43   Sexuelle Ethik. (Forel, Auguste.) München, 1908.

Phil 6327.21.40   Die sexuelle Revolution. (Reich, Wilhelm.) Frankfurt am Main, 1970.

Phil 8893.9   Seydel, R. Ethik. Leipzig, 1874.

Phil 5058.9   Seydel, R. Logik. Leipzig, 1866.

Phil 3500.22   Seydel, R. Der Schlüssel zum objektiven Erkennen. Halle, 1889.

Phil 3925.3.80   Seydel, Rudolf. Christian Hermann Weisse. Leipzig, 1866.

Phil 8598.39   Seydel, Rudolf. Religionsphilosophie im Umriss. Freiburg, 1893.

Phil 1050.4.9   Seyerlen, R. Die gegenseitigen Bezeihungen. Jena, 1899.

Phil 2725.1.80   Seyfarth, H. Louis de la Forge. Jena, 1887.

Phil 5643.28   Seyfert, R. Über die Auffassung einfachster Raumformen. Leipzig, 1902.

Phil 6128.58A   Seyle, Hans. The stress of life. N.Y., 1956.

Phil 9178.5   Seymour, A. Home, the basis of the state. Boston, 1869.

Phil 7069.44.30   Seymour, C.J. Curiosities of psychical research. London, 1944.

Phil 7069.40.10   Seymour, C.J. This spiritualism. London, 1940.

Phil 7060.110   Seymour, S.J.D. True Irish ghost stories. Dublin, 1914.

Phil 7069.26.30   Seymour, S.J.D. True Irish ghost stories. 2. ed. Dublin, 1926.

Phil 530.20.120   Seyppel, Joachim Hans. Texte deutscher Mystik des 16. Jahrhunderts. Göttingen, 1963.

Phil 3425.281   Sfard, D. Du role de l'idée de contradiction chez Hegel. Thèse. Nancy, 1931.

Phil 5228.3   Sganzini, Carlo. Die Fortschritte der Völkerpsychologie. Bern, 1913.

Phil 5325.14   Sganzini, Carlo. Neuere Einsichten...Ideenassoziationen. Bern, 1918.

Phil 193.152.5   Sganzini, Carlo. Ursprung und Wirklichkeit. Bern, 1951.

Phil 4080.3.180   Sgoi, Carmelo. Benedetto Croce. Messina, 1947.

Phil 4115.87   Sgroi, Carmelo. L'estetica e la critica letteraria in V. Gioberti. Firenze, 1921.

Phil 8140.2   Sgroi, Carmelo. Gli studi estetici in Italia nel primo trantennio dell'900. Firenze, 1932.

Phil 28.47   Sguardi su la filosofia contemporanea. Torino. 1-20 7v.

Phil 960.8   Shaddarcaneshu on religionsstudie. (Valentin, O.) Stockholm, 1899.

Phil 8591.23   The shadow Christ. (Lee, Gerald S.) N.Y., 1896.

Phil 7069.46.5   The shadow of destiny. (Cannon, A.) London, 1946?

Phil 7069.08.20   The shadow world. (Garland, Hamlin.) N.Y., 1908.

Phil 8612.51   The shadowed valley. (Schachtel, H.J.) N.Y., 1962.

Phil 8881.36   Shadows and realities. (Gehring, Albert.) Cleveland, 1912.

Phil 8708.13   Shafer, Robert. Christianity and naturalism. New Haven, 1926.

Phil 585.340   Shaffer, Jerome A. Philosophy of mind. Englewood Cliffs, N.J., 1968.

Phil 6128.49   Shaffer, Laurance F. Psychology of adjustment. Boston, 1936.

Phil 6128.49.2   Shaffer, Laurance F. The psychology of adjustment. 2d ed. Boston, 1956.

Phil 2262.57   Shaftesbury, A.A.C. Ein Brief über den Enthusiasmus. Die Moralisten, eine philosophische Rhapsodie. Leipzig, 1909.

Phil 2262.33   Shaftesbury, A.A.C. Characteristicks. Basel, 1790. 3v.

Htn   Phil 2262.45*   Shaftesbury, A.A.C. Characteristicks. Leipzig, 1768.

Htn   Phil 2262.29*   Shaftesbury, A.A.C. Characteristicks. London, 1711. 3v.

Phil 2262.30   Shaftesbury, A.A.C. Characteristicks. London, 1723. 3v.

Phil 2262.30.7   Shaftesbury, A.A.C. Characteristicks. London, 1732. 3v.

Htn   Phil 2262.32.5*   Shaftesbury, A.A.C. Characteristicks. London, 1749. 3v.

Phil 2262.35.3A   Shaftesbury, A.A.C. Characteristicks. N.Y., 1900. 2v.

Phil 2262.34   Shaftesbury, A.A.C. Characteristicks. v.1. London, 1870.

Phil 2262.30.3   Shaftesbury, A.A.C. Characteristicks. v.2,3. London, 1727. 2v.

Phil 2262.30.2   Shaftesbury, A.A.C. Characteristicks. v.3. London, 17- .

Htn   Phil 2262.29.5*   Shaftesbury, A.A.C. Characteristicks. 2nd ed. London, 1714. 3v.

Phil 2262.30.4   Shaftesbury, A.A.C. Characteristicks. 4th ed. n.p., 1727. 3v.

Htn   Phil 2262.30.5*   Shaftesbury, A.A.C. Characteristicks. 5th ed. Birmingham, 1773. 3v.

Phil 2262.31.2   Shaftesbury, A.A.C. Characteristicks. 5th ed. London, 1732. 3v.

Phil 2262.32   Shaftesbury, A.A.C. Characteristicks. 6th ed. London, 1737. 3v.

Phil 2262.35.4   Shaftesbury, A.A.C. Characteristics of men, manners, opinions, times. Gloucester, Mass., 1963. 2v.

Phil 2262.35.5   Shaftesbury, A.A.C. Characteristics of men. v.1-2. Indianapolis, 1964.

Htn   Phil 2262.76*   Shaftesbury, A.A.C. Letter concerning enthusiasm. London, 1708-09. 4 pam.

Phil 2262.59A   Shaftesbury, A.A.C. Letter concerning enthusiasm. Paris, 1930.

Phil 2262.75   Shaftesbury, A.A.C. Letters. London, 1750.

Phil 2262.55   Shaftesbury, A.A.C. Lettres sur l'enthousiasme de milord Shaftesbury. London, 1761.

Phil 2262.77   Shaftesbury, A.A.C. Life. Unpublished letters. London, 1900.

Phil 2262.50   Shaftesbury, A.A.C. Die Moralisten, eine philosophische Rhapsodie. Jena, 1910.

Phil 2262.51   Shaftesbury, A.A.C. Moralisterna, en filosofisk rhapsodi. Stockholm, 1926.

Htn   Phil 2262.49*   Shaftesbury, A.A.C. The moralists. London, 1709.

Phil 2262.2   Shaftesbury, A.A.C. Les oeuvres. v.1-3. Genève, 1769.

Phil 2262.60.2   Shaftesbury, A.A.C. Religion und Tugend. Leipzig, 1905.

Phil 2262.39A   Shaftesbury, A.A.C. Second characters. Cambridge, 1914.

Htn   Phil 2262.62*   Shaftesbury, A.A.C. Sensus communis. London, 1709.

Phil 2262.63   Shaftesbury, A.A.C. Soliloquy. London, 1710.

Htn   Phil 2262.63*   Shaftesbury, A.A.C. Soliloquy. Photoreproduction. London, 1710.

Phil 2262.60   Shaftesbury, A.A.C. Untersuchung über die Tugend. Leipzig, 1905.

Phil 2262.90   Shaftesbury; etica e religione, la morale del sentimento. (Bandini, L.) Bari, 1930.

Phil 2262.81A   Shaftesbury and Hutcheson. (Fowler, T.) London, 1882.

Phil 2262.81.5A   Shaftesbury and Hutcheson. (Fowler, T.) N.Y., 1883.

Phil 2262.97   Shaftesbury and the French deists. (Schlegel, D.B.) Chapel Hill, 1956.

Phil 2262.84   Shaftesbury und das deutsche Geistesleben. (Weiser, C.F.) Leipzig, 1916.

Phil 2262.99   Shaftesbury und seine Bedeutung für die englische Literatur des 18. Jhs. (Wolff, Erwin.) Tübingen, 1960.

Phil 2262.86   Shaftesbury's dygdelära. (Waern, L.M.) Upsala, 1875.

Phil 2262.91   Shaftesbury's ethical principle of adaptation to universal harmony. (Lyons, Alexander.) N.Y., 1909?

Phil 2262.78.5   Shaftesburys Optimismus und sein Verhältnis zum Leibnizschen. Inaug. Diss. (Bacharach, A.) Thann, 1912.

Phil 2050.221   Shaftesbury's und Hutcheson's Verhältnis zu Hume. Inaug. Diss. (Martin, John J.) Halle, 1905.

Phil 193.143   Shah, R.V. Pourings of a struggling soul. Ahmedabad, 1932.

Phil 2340.10.115   Shahan, E.P. Whitehead's theory of experience. N.Y., 1950.

Phil 193.137   Shahani, R.G. The coming of Karuna. London, 1934.

Phil 1865.200   el Shakankiri, Mohamed Abd el-Hadi. La philosophie juridique de Jeremy Bentham. Paris, 1970.

Phil 525.242   Shakhnovich, Mikhail. Sovremennaia mistika v svete nauki. Leningrad, 1965.

VPhil 7072.21   Shakhnovich, Mikhail I. Primety v svete nauki. 2. izd. Leningrad, 1969.

Phil 310.3.15   Shakhparonov, M.I. Dialekticheskii materializm i nekotorye problemy fiziki i khimii. Moskva, 1958.

Phil 8708.2.7   Shaler, N.S. The interpretation of nature. 2. ed. Boston, 1893.

Phil 193.51   Shaler, S.P. The masters of fate...the power of the will. N.Y., 1906.

Phil 1535.30   Shallo, Michael. Lessons in scholastic philosophy. Philadelphia, 1916.

Phil 197.60   Shallows and deeps. (Weir, Archibald.) Oxford, 1934.

Phil 1930.8.115   Shalom, Albert. R.G. Collingwood, philosophie et historien. Paris, 1967.

Phil 5414.15A   Shame and guilt. (Piers, Gerhart.) Springfield, Ill., 1953.

Phil 6945.30   The shame of the States. 1. ed. (Deutsch, Albert.) N.Y., 1948.

Phil 8419.62   Shamota, Mykolaz. O svobode tvorchestva. Moskva, 1966.

Phil 8660.2.10   Shanahan, E.T. John Fiske on the idea of God. Washington, 1897.

Phil 960.5   Shand, A.F. The foundations of character. London, 1914.

Phil 9035.21   Shand, A.F. The foundations of character. London, 1920.

Phil 9035.21.2   (blank)

Phil 5258.170   Shands, Harley. Thinking and psychotherapy. Cambridge, 1960.

Phil 6968.39   Shands, Harley C. Semiotic approaches to psychiatry. The Hague, 1970.

Phil 5520.760   Shands, Harley Cecil. The war with words, structure and transcendence. The Hague, 1971.

Phil 6990.3.29   Shanley, W.J. The story of Lourdes. Hartford, 1908.

Phil 349.17   Shann, George. The evolution of knowledge. London, 1922.

Htn   Phil 9358.7*   Shannon, F. Discourses...useful for vain modish ladies and their gallants. London, 1696.

Htn   Phil 9358.7.5*   Shannon, F. Several discourses and characters. London, 1689.

Htn   Phil 8893.64*   Shannon, F.B. Moral essays and discourses upon several subjects. London, 1690.

Phil 8411.2   The shape of time; remarks on the history of things. (Kubler, George.) New Haven, 1962.

Phil 6980.635.5   The shaping of psychiatry by war. (Rees, J.R.) London, 1945.

Phil 6968.37   Shapiro, David. Neurotic styles. N.Y., 1965.

Phil 1523.14   Shapiro, Herman. Medieval philosophy. N.Y., 1964.

Phil 299.27   Shapley, Harlow. Of stars and men. Boston, 1958.

Phil 299.27.5   Shapley, Harlow. Of stars and men. Boston, 1964.

Phil 5249.2.85   Shargha, I.K. Examination of Prof. W. James' psychology. London, 1909.

Phil 1020.46   Sharif, M.M. A history of Muslim philosophy. Wiesbaden, 1963. 2v.

Phil 8980.785   Shariia, P.A. O nekotorykh voprosakh kommunisticheskoi morali. Moskva, 1951.

Phil 960.175.5   Sharma, C. A critical survey of Indian philosophy. London, 1960.

Phil 960.175   Sharma, C. Indian philosophy. Banaras, 1952.

Phil 960.274   Sharma, Dhirendra. The differentiation theory of meaning in Indian logic. The Hague, 1969.

Phil 8865.636.5   Sharma, Ishwar Chandra. Ethical philosophies of India. London, 1965.

Phil 1900.100   Sharma, Sukhde. Ethics of Butler and the philosophy of action in Bhogavadgita according to Madhusudana Sarasvati. Varanasi, 1961.

Phil 6968.28   Sharp, A.A. Dynamic era of court psychiatry, 1914-44. Chicago, 1944.

Phil 8893.10.5   Sharp, F.C. The aesthetic element in morality. N.Y., 1893.

Phil 8893.10   Sharp, F.C. Das aesthetische Element in der Moral. Berlin, 1892.

Phil 8893.10.15   Sharp, F.C. Ethics. N.Y., 1928.

Phil 5500.13   Sharp, F.C. Goodwill and ill will. Chicago, 1950.

Phil 9075.12   Sharp, F.C. Study of influence, of custom on world judgment. Madison, 1908.

Phil 8893.10.10   Sharp, F.C. A study of the influence of custom. Madison, Wis., 1908.

Phil 525.51.2   Sharpe, A.B. Mysticism: its true nature and value. London, 1910?

Phil 193.97   Sharpe, A.B. The spectrum of truth. London, 1908.

Phil 6328.32   Sharpe, E.F. Collected papers on psycho-analysis. London, 1950.

Phil 7084.4.5   Sharpe, Ella Freeman. Dream analysis: a practical handbook for psycho-analysts. London, 1937.

Phil 2138.153   Sharpless, F. Parvin. The literary criticism of J.S. Mill. The Hague, 1967.

Phil 3500.85   Shashkevich, P.D. Teoriia poznaniia I. Kanta. Moskva, 1960.

Phil 960.41   Shastri, P.D. The essentials of Eastern philosophy. N.Y., 1928.

Phil 960.25   Shastri, Prabhu D. The conception of freedom in Hegel, Berigson and Indian philosophy. Calcutta, 1914.

Phil 5258.95   Shastri, Prabhu D. Elementary psychology. Calcutta, 1928.

Phil 3838.21   Shauki, Alexander. An introduction to Spinoza's Ethic. London, 1938.

Phil 193.64   Shaw, C.G. The ego and its place in the world. N.Y., 1913.

Phil 193.64.9   Shaw, C.G. The ground and goal of human life. N.Y., 1919.

Phil 193.64.5   Shaw, C.G. The value and dignity of human life. Boston, 1911.

Phil 5058.48   Shaw, Charles G. Logic in theory and practice. N.Y., 1935.

Phil 8598.30   Shaw, Charles G. The precinct of religion in culture of humanity. London, 1908.

Phil 5850.340   Shaw, Charles G. Short talks on psychology. N.Y., 1920.

Phil 8643.15   Shaw, Fred G. Our future existence. London, 1912.

Phil 4809.779.80   Shaw, Nellie. A Czech philosopher on the Cotswolds...Francis Sedlák. London, 1940.

Phil 8419.47   Shaw, T.L. Art reconstructed, a new theory of aesthetics. Boston, 1937.

Phil 4752.1.35   Shcheglov, A.V. Bor'ba Lenina protiv Bogdanovskoi revizii marksizma. Moskva, 1937.

Phil 310.782   Shchekina, Liubov' I. Poniatiia "dvizhenie" i razvitie i ikhvol' v izuchsnii fizicheskikh protsessov. Moskva, 1970.

Phil 8980.785.20   Shcherbak, F.N. Nravstvennyi oblik razvedchikov budushchego. Leningrad, 1961.

Phil 960.39   Shcherbatskii, F.I. Erkenntnistheorie und Logik. München, 1924.

Phil 960.39.10   Shcherbatskii, F.I. Teoriia poznaniia i logika po ucheniiu pozdneishikh buddistov. Sankt Peterburg, 1903-09. 2v.

Phil 960.39.5   Shcherbatskii, F.I. La théorie de la connaissance. Paris, 1926.

Phil 3500.103   Shcherbina, A.M. Uchenie Kanta o veshchi vě sebe. n.p., n.d.

Phil 4710.100   Shchipanov, I.Ia. Protiv sovremennykh fal'sifikatorov istorii russkoi filosofii. Moskva, 1960.

Phil 4710.84   Shchipanov, I.Ia. Russkaia materialisticheskaia filosofiia XVIII-IX vekov i ee istoricheskoe znachenie. Moskva, 1953.

Phil 4710.146   Shchipanov, I.Ia. Russkie prosvetiteli, ot Radishcheva do dekabristov. Moskva, 1966. 2v.

Phil 7076.5   She wears a crown of thorns; Marie Rose Perron, 1902-1936. (Boyer, Onesimas Alfred.) N.Y., 1951.

Phil 2050.100   Shearer, Edna Aston. Hume's place in ethics. Diss. Bryn Mawr, 1915.

Phil 9358.6   Shearer, W.J. Morals and manners. N.Y., 1904.

Phil 5058.25   Shearman, A.T. The scope of formal logic. London, 1911.

Phil 193.86   Shearon, William. The hypothesis of the universality of life. St. Louis, 1922.

Phil 8598.34   Shebbeare, Charles J. Challenge of the universe. London, 1918.

Phil 8598.34.5   Shebbeare, Charles J. The design argument reconsidered. London, 1923.

Phil 8598.34.6   Shebbeare, Charles J. The design argument reconsidered. London, 1923.

Phil 5058.10   Shedden, T. The elements of logic. London, 1864.

Phil 8673.11   Sheen, F.J. God and intelligence in modern philosophy. London, 1925.

Phil 8598.98   Sheen, Fulton John. Philosophy of religion. Dublin, 1952.

Phil 5150.1   Sheffer, H.M. General theory of notational relativity. Cambridge, 1921.

Phil 5150.1.5   Sheffer, H.M. Notational relativity. n.p., 1926?

Phil 5520.20   Sheffield, A.D. Grammar and thinking. N.Y., 1912.

Phil 6750.17   Sheffield, Herman B. The backward baby. N.Y., 1915.

Phil 1020.50   Sheikh, M. Saeed. Studies in Muslim philosophy. 1st ed. Lahore, 1962.

Phil 4710.156   Shein, Louis J. Readings in Russian philosophical thought. The Hague, 1968.

Phil 5485.6   Sheinin, Iulian M. Integral'nyi intelleks. Moskva, 1970.

Phil 5545.99   Shekhter, Mark S. Psikhologicheskie problemy uznavaniia. Moskva, 1967.

Phil 8673.27   Shekhterman, Efim I. Vera ili zhanie. Alme-Ata, 1967.

Phil 7054.61.9   The Shekinah. N.Y., 1853. 3v.

Phil 8598.84   Sheldon, Henry Clay. The essentials of Christianity. N.Y., 1922.

Phil 193.70.5   Sheldon, W.H. America's progressive philosophy. New Haven, 1942.

Phil 818.29   Sheldon, W.H. God and polarity; a synthesis of philosophies. New Haven, 1954.

Phil 1750.158   Sheldon, W.H. Process and polarity. N.Y., 1944.

Phil 5258.121A   Sheldon, W.H. Psychology and the promethean will. N.Y., 1936.

Phil 193.70   Sheldon, W.H. Strife of systems and productive duality. Cambridge, 1918.

Phil 8615.2.7   Sheldon, Walter L. Ethical culture; its threefold attitude. St. Louis, Mo? 188-?

Phil 8615.2   Sheldon, Walter L. An ethical movement. N.Y., 1896.

Phil 8615.17   Sheldon, Walter L. Ethics and the belief in a God. St. Louis, 1892.

Phil 8615.2.3   Sheldon, Walter L. The meaning of the ethical movement, fifth anniversary address. St. Louis, 1891.

Phil 6688.24   Sheldon, William. The millennium: the goodtime coming. Springfield, 1862.

Phil 5590.8   Sheldon, William H. The varieties of temperament; a psychology of constitutional differences. N.Y., 1942.

Phil 7054.11   Shelhamer, M.F. Life and labor in the spirit world. Boston, 1885.

Phil 3800.63   Shellings Schriften zur Gesellschaftsphilosophie. (Schelling, F.W.J. von.) Jena, 1926.

Phil 7080.24   Shepard, J.F. The circulation and sleep. Text and atlas. N.Y., 1914. 2v.

Phil 6980.685   Shepard, Martin. Games analysts play. N.Y., 1970.

Phil 6985.15   Shepard, Martin. Marathon 16. N.Y., 1970.

Phil 8434.6   Shepard, Paul. Man in the landescape. N.Y., 1967.

Phil 5828.15   Shepherd, James. Instinct. Kirkcaldy, 1884.

Phil 270.13   Shepherd, M. Essays...doctrine of causation. London, 1827.

Phil 5045.19.5   The shepherd's logic. (Fraunce, Abraham.) Menston, 1969.

Phil 3838.32   Shepo, Elias. The strange death of Barukh Spinoza. Cambridge, 1952.

Phil 6128.24   Sheppard, E.E. The thinking universe. Los Angeles, 1915.

Phil 2270.150   Shepperson, J. A comparative study of St. Thomas Aquinas and Herbert Spencer. Diss. Pittsburgh, 1923.

Phil 310.617   Sheptulin, Aleksandr P. Dialekticheskii materializm. Moskva, 1965.

Phil 310.617.5   Sheptulin, Aleksandr P. Osnovnye zakony dialektiki. Moskva, 1966.

Phil 310.617.10   Sheptulin, Aleksandr P. Sistema kategorii dialektiki. Moskva, 1967.

Phil 310.570   Sheputo, L.L. Voprosy dialekticheskogo materializma i meditsina. v.2. Moskva, 1963.

Phil 2340.10.185   Sherburne, Donald W. A key to Whitehead's Process and realty. N.Y., 1966.

Phil 2340.10.160   Sherburne, Donald W. A Whiteheadian aesthetic. New Haven, 1961.

Phil 9513.14   Sheremetev, Vl.Vl. Dukh vremeni. Shankai, 1937.

Phil 2880.8.245   Sheridan, James Francis. Sartre; the radical conversion. Athens, Ohio, 1969.

Phil 5500.22   Sherif, Muzafer. Social judgment. New Haven, 1961.

Phil 8843.12   Sheriff, W.S. Religion and ethics. Thesis. Philadelphia, 1933.

Phil 6750.11   Sherlock, E.B. Feeble minded, guide to study. London, 1911.

Phil 8893.68   Sherman, C.L. The moral self: an introduction to the science of ethics. Boston, 1927.

Phil 6990.65   Sherman, Harold Morrow. Wonder healers of the Philippines. London, 1967.

Phil 6128.25   Sherman, J.C. The stunted saplings. Boston, 1911.

Phil 5258.123   Sherman, M. Basic problems of behavior. N.Y., 1941.

Phil 7054.168   Sherman, M.L. The gospel of nature. Chicago, 1877.

Phil 5258.134   Sherman, Mandel. Intelligence and its deviations. N.Y., 1945.

Phil 6805.4   Sherman, Mandel. Mental conflicts and personality. N.Y., 1938.

Phil 6328.58   Sherman, Murray Herbert. Psychoanalysis in America. Springfield, 1966.

Phil 9530.46   Sherman, Ray W. If you want to get ahead. Boston, 1934.

Phil 3450.19.520   Sherover, Charles M. Heidegger, Kant and time. Bloomington, 1971.

Phil 5722.83   Sheroziia, Apollon E. K probleme soznaniia i bessoznatel'nogo psikhicheskogo. v.1-. Tbilisi, 1969.

Phil 4791.8   Sheroziia, Apollon Epifonovich. Filosofskaia mysl' v Gruzii v pervoi chetverti XX veka. Tbilisi, 1963.

Phil 7069.27.38   Sherrill, E.P. The mechanism of death. Boston, 1927.

Phil 6128.13.8   Sherrington, C.S. The integrative action of the nervous system. Cambridge, Eng., 1948.

Phil 6128.13   Sherrington, C.S. The integrative action of the nervous system. N.Y., 1906.

Phil 6128.13.7A   Sherrington, C.S. The integrative action of the nervous system. New Haven, 1926.

Phil 6128.13.10   Sherrington, C.S. Man on his nature. Cambridge, Eng., 1946.

Phil 6128.13.9A   Sherrington, C.S. Man on his nature. Cambridge, 1940.

Phil 6128.13.11   Sherrington, C.S. Man on his nature. N.Y., 1941.

Phil 7069.45.10   Sherwood, Jane. The country beyond; a study of survival and rebirth. London, 1945.

Phil 9178.8   Sherwood, M.E.W. Amenities of home. N.Y., 1881.

Phil 2805.207   Shestor, Lev. La nuit de Gethsémani. Paris, 1923.

Phil 8598.79.5.10   Shestov, L. Afiny i Ierusalim. Parizh, 1951.

Phil 193.134.10   Shestov, L. Apotheoz pespohveiossiti. Sankt Peterburg, 1905.

Phil 8598.79.5   Shestov, L. Athènes et Jerusalem. Paris, 1938.

Phil 8598.79.5.15   Shestov, L. Athens and Jerusalem. Athens, 1966.

Phil 193.134.5   Shestov, L. In job's balances. London, 1932.

Phil 193.134   Shestov, L. Na vesakh Iova. Parizh, 1929.

Phil 4769.7.33   Shestov, Lev. Potestas clavium. Athens, Ohio, 1968.

Phil 4769.7.32   Shestov, Lev. Potestas clavium. München, 1926.

Phil 193.260   Shibles, Warren. Philosophical pictures. Dubuque, 1969.
Phil 3925.16.280   Shibles, Warren. Wittgenstein; language and philosophy. Dubuque, Iowa, 1969.
Phil 193.25.3   Shields, C.W. The final philosophy. N.Y., 1877.
Phil 193.25.4   Shields, C.W. Philosophia ultima. N.Y., 1888-1889. 3v.
Phil 193.25   Shields, C.W. Philosophia ultima. Philadelphia, 1861.
Phil 3549.2.94   Shilpnagel, U. Graf Edward von Keyserling und seine pisches Werk. Inaug. Diss. Rostock, 1926.
Phil 510.1.45   Shiltov., A. Ernst Gekkel' pered sudom logiki. Khar'kov, 1907.
Phil 8702.2.5   Shinar. (McCausland, D.) London, 1867.
Phil 7069.41.6   The shining brother. (Temple, Laurence.) London, 1941.
Phil 3425.597   Shinkaruk, V.I. Logika dialektika i teoriia poznaniia Gegelia. Kiev, 1964.
Phil 6128.47.7   Shinn, F.S. (Mrs.). The game of life and how to play it. 7th ed. N.Y., 1927.
Phil 8708.14A   Shipley, Maynard. The war on modern science. N.Y., 1927.
Phil 5238.155   Shipley, T. Classics in psychology. N.Y., 1961.
Phil 8893.137   Shirk, Evelyn Urban. The ethical dimension. N.Y., 1965.
Phil 7072.3   Shirley, Ralph. The mystery of the human double. N.Y., 1965.
Phil 525.25   Shirley, Ralph. Occultists and mystics of all ages. London, 1920.
Phil 310.350   Shirokanov, D.I. Dialektika neobkhodimosti i sluchainosti. Minsk, 1960.
Phil 5075.7   Shirokanov, Imitri I. Vzaimosviaz' kategorii dialektiki. Minsk, 1969.
Phil 5058.96   Shirwood, William. William of Sherwood's introduction to logic. Minneapolis, 1966.
Phil 5058.96.5   Shirwood, William. William of Sherwood's treatise on syncategorematic words. Minneapolis, 1968.
Phil 9590.25.5   Shishkin, A.F. Die bürgerliche Moralinwaffe der imperialistischen Reaktion. Berlin, 1952.
Phil 9590.25   Shishkin, A.F. Burzhuaznaia moral' - oruzhie imperialisticheskoi reaktsii. Moskva, 1951.
Phil 8843.16   Shishkin, A.F. Iz istorii eticheskikh uchenii. Moskva, 1964.
Phil 8980.787.25   Shishkin, Aleksandr F. Dvadtsatyi vek i moral'nye tsennosti chelovechestva. Moskva, 1968.
Phil 8980.787.5   Shishkin, Aleksandr F. Die Grundlagen der kommunistischen Moral. Berlin, 1958.
Phil 8980.787   Shishkin, Aleksandr F. Osnovy kommunisticheskoi morali. Moskva, 1955.
Phil 8980.787.15   Shishkin, Aleksandr F. Osnovy marksistskoi etiki. Moskva, 1961.
Phil 8419.14   Shishkov, G. Erschopfte Kunst oder Kunstformalismus? Schlehdorf, 1952.
Phil 310.675   Shliakhtenko, Sergei G. Kategorii kachestva i kolichestva. Leningrad, 1968.
Phil 7150.38   Shneidman, Edwin S. Clues to suicide. N.Y., 1957.
Phil 7150.38.5   Shneidman, Edwin S. Essays in self-destruction. N.Y., 1967.
Phil 6854.4   Shneidman, Edwin S. The psychology of suicide. N.Y., 1970.
Phil 1930.15.30   The shocky existence. (Creegon, R.F.) Cambridge, 1954.
Phil 575.245   Shoemaker, S. Self-knowledge and self-identity. Ithaca, 1963.
Phil 8598.85   Shoemaker, S.M. The church can save the world. N.Y., 1938.
Phil 5627.134.65   Shoemaker, S.M. The conversion of the church. N.Y., 1932.
Phil 5066.263   Shoenfield, Joseph R. Mathematical logic. Reading, Mass., 1967.
Phil 6128.83   Shontz, Frank C. Perceptual and cognitive aspects of body experience. N.Y., 1969.
Phil 6688.30   Shor, Ronald E. The nature of hypnosis. N.Y., 1965.
Phil 6140.10   Shore, Milton F. Mental health and the community; problems, programs and strategies. N.Y., 1969.
Phil 5374.215   Shorokhova, E.V. Problema soznaniia v filosofii i estestvoznanii. Moskva, 1961.
Phil 5258.198   Shorokhova, Ekaterina V. Issledovaniia myshleniia v sovetskoi psikhologii. Moskva, 1966.
Htn   Phil 8666.4*   A short and easie method with the deists. 8. ed. v.1-3. (Leslie, Charles.) London, 1723.
Phil 974.4.20   A short biography of Annie Besant. (Jinarajadasa, C.) Adyar, Madras, 1932.
Phil 2205.82   A short commentary, with strictures on certain parts of the moral writings of Dr. Paley and Mr. Gisborne. (Croft, G.) Birmingham, 1797.
Phil 3486.9.6A   A short commentary on Kant's Critique of pure reason. (Ewing, Alfred Cyril.) Chicago, 1970.
Phil 5056.1.10A   A short course in logic. (Quine, Willard Van Orman.) Cambridge, 1946.
Phil 8893.6   A short essay to do good. (Sedgwick, C.M.) Stockbridge, 1828.
Phil 197.40   Short essays in constructive philosophy. (Wordsworth, J.C.) London, 1911.
Phil 5217.7   A short history of British psychology, 1840-1940. (Hearnshaw, L.S.) London, 1964.
Phil 815.6A   Short history of Celtic philosophy. (Pim, Herbert M.) Dundalk, 1920.
Phil 930.54   A short history of Chinese philosophy. (Hou, Wai-lu.) Peking, 1959.
Phil 8837.17   A short history of ethics. (MacIntyre, Alasdair C.) N.Y., 1966.
Phil 1750.187   A short history of existentialism. (Wahl, Jean André.) N.Y., 1949.
Phil 8610.899   A short history of freethought, ancient and modern. (Robertson, J.M.) London, 1899.
Phil 8610.899.5   A short history of freethought, ancient and modern. 2. ed. (Robertson, J.M.) London, 1906. 2v.
Phil 1117.1.2   Short history of Greek philosophy. (Marshall, John.) London, 1891.
Phil 1117.1.3   Short history of Greek philosophy. (Marshall, John.) London, 1898.
Phil 5010.1   A short history of logic. (Adamson, R.) Edinburgh, 1911.
Phil 1527.4   A short history of medieval philosophy. (Weinberg, J.R.) Princeton, 1964.
Phil 8842.4   A short history of morals. (Robertson, J.M.) London, 1920.
Phil 800.2   A short history of philosophy. (Alexander, A.B.D.) Glasgow, 1907.
Phil 819.11   A short history of philosophy. (Thonnard, F.J.) Paris, 1955.
Phil 800.2.3   A short history of philosophy. 3. ed. (Alexander, A.B.D.) Glasgow, 1922.
Phil 6980.419   A short history of psychiatric achievement. (Lewis, Nolan don Carpentier.) N.Y., 1941.

Phil 6980.14.102   A short history of psychiatry. (Ackerknecht, E.H.) N.Y., 1959.
Phil 6332.15   A short history of psychotherapy in theory and practice. (Walker, Nigel.) London, 1957.
Phil 1507.5   A short history of western philosophy in middle ages. (Curtis, S.J.) London, 1950.
X Cg   Phil 2053.41.2   A short introduction to moral philosophy. v.1,2-3. (Hutcheson, F.) Glasgow, 1764. 2v.
Htn   Phil 2053.41*   A short introduction to moral philosophy. v.1-3. (Hutcheson, F.) Glasgow, 1753.
Phil 5390.8   A short introduction to the history of human stupidity. (Pitkin, Walter B.) N.Y., 1932.
Phil 5049.14   A short introduction to the study of logic. (Johnstone, Lawrence.) London, 1887.
Phil 978.56   Short lessons in theosophy. (Clark, S.C.) Boston, 1892.
Phil 5832.13   A short outline of comparative psychology. (Warden, C.J.) N.Y., 1927.
Phil 9343.9   Short patent sermons. (Paige, Elbridge G.) N.Y., 1845.
Phil 5627.105   A short psychology of religion. (Jordan, G.J.) N.Y., 1927.
Phil 8656.14.25   A short review of Edward Beecher's work on the conflict of ages. 2. ed. (King, Thomas S.) Boston, 1854.
Phil 9035.44   Short studies in character. (Bryant, S.W.) London, 1894.
Phil 5850.340   Short talks on psychology. (Shaw, Charles G.) N.Y., 1920.
Phil 177.56   Short talks upon philosophy. (Cunynghame, H.) London, 1923.
Phil 7061.10   Short title catalogue of works...from c.1450 to 1929. (National Laboratory of Psychical Research, London.) London, 1929.
Phil 3819.38.6   Short treatise on God, man and his well-being. (Spinoza, Benedictus de.) N.Y., 1963.
Phil 665.46   A short view of great questions. (Smith, O.J.) N.Y., 1899.
Phil 8598.31   Shotwell, James T. The religious revolution of to-day. Boston, 1913.
Phil 5465.204   Shouksmith, George. Intelligence, creativity and cognitive style. London, 1970.
Phil 193.44   Shoup, F.A. Mechanism and personality. Boston, 1891.
Phil 7069.35.15   Show me the way; spirit counsels for right living. (Herodius (pseud.).) Boston, 1935.
Phil 4769.4.10   Shpet, Gustav. Esteticheskie fragmenti. Pts.1-3. Peterburg, 1923.
Phil 4769.4.15   Shpet, Gustav. Iavlenie i smysl. Moskva, 1914.
Phil 4769.4.5   Shpet, Gustav. Ocherk razvitiia russkoi filosofii. Petrograd, 1922.
Phil 4073.115   Shtekli, Al'fred E. Kampanella. Izd. 3. Moskva, 1966.
Phil 349.45   Shtoff, V.A. Rol' modelei v poznanii. Leningrad, 1963.
Phil 8419.63   Shudria, Kateyna P. Estetychnyi ideal myttsia. Kyïv, 1967.
Phil 5828.17   Shuey, A.M. The limits of learning ability in kittens. Worcester, 1931.
Phil 5592.45   Shuey, Audrey Mary. The testing of Negro intelligence. Lynchburg, 1958.
Phil 5592.45.2   Shuey, Audrey Mary. The testing of Negro intelligence. 2. ed. N.Y., 1966.
Phil 7054.103   Shufeldt, G.A., Jr. History of the Chicago artesian well. Chicago, 1867. 2 pam.
Phil 193.205   Shul'gyn, O. L'histoire el la vie. Paris, 1957.
Phil 8598.73   Shumaker, E.E. God and man. N.Y., 1909.
Phil 380.6   Shumilin, A.T. Problemy struktuny i soderzhaniia protsessa poznaniia. Moskva, 1969.
Phil 5620.33   Shurter, Robert. Critical thinking. N.Y., 1966.
Phil 5938.3   Shurtleff, N.R. An epitome of phrenology. Boston, 1835.
Phil 9070.9   Shurtleft, A.D.K. Lighted candles. Boston, 1939.
Phil 193.26   Shute, M. A discourse on truth. London, 1877.
Phil 8893.127.5   Shvartsman, Klara Aronovna. Ethik ohme Moral. Berlin, 1967.
Phil 8893.127   Shvartsman, Klara Aronvna. Etika...bez morali. Moskva, 1964.
Phil 8893.125   Shvartsman, Klara Aronvna. Kritika sovremennykh burzhuaznykh filosofsko-esteticheskikh system. Moskva, 1966.
Phil 3850.27.265   Shveitser. (Nosik, Boris M.) Moskva, 1971.
Phil 5068.57   Shvyrev, Vladimir S. Neopozitivizm i problemy empiricheskogo oboshovaniia nauki. Moskva, 1966.
Phil 5270.3.1   Shwayder, David S. The stratification of behaviour. London, 1965.
Phil 5270.3   Shwayder, David S. The stratification of behaviour. N.Y., 1965.
Phil 8893.138   Sibben, Frederik Christian. Moralphilosophie. Kjobenhavn, 1878.
Phil 5258.77.5   Sibbern, F.C. Loeren om de menneskelige Folelser. Kjøbenhavn, 1885.
Phil 5058.37.5   Sibbern, F.C. Logik sem taenkelaere. 2. udg. Kjøbenhavn, 1835.
Phil 8598.76   Sibbern, F.C. Meddelelser af indholdet af et skrivt fra aaret. v.1-2. Kjøbenhavn, 1858-72.
Phil 4635.8.31   Sibbern, F.C. Om philosophiens begreb. Kjøbenhavn, 1843.
Phil 5258.77   Sibbern, F.C. Psychologie, indledet ved almindelig biologie, i sammentroengt fremstelling. Kjøbenhavn, 1856.
Phil 4635.8.33   Sibbern, F.C. Speculativ kosmologie med grundlag. Kjøbenhavn, 1846.
Phil 5058.37   Sibbern, F.C. Taenkelaere eller logik i sammentraengt fremstilling. 3. udg. Kjøbenhavn, 1866.
Phil 1200.26   Sibbern, G. Den stoiske og epikuraeiske moral. Kjøbenhavn, 1853.
Phil 8893.87   Sibecas, S. Factores morales. Habana, 1926.
Phil 5871.95   The sibling. (Sutton-Smith, Brian.) N.Y., 1970.
Phil 9495.131   Sicard de Plauzales, J. La fonction sexuelle au point de vue de l'éthique et de l'hygiène sociales. Paris, 1908.
Phil 5520.345   Das Sichbeswien auf Wörber. (Weyers, Gertrud.) Köln, 1958.
Phil 4225.3.89   Sichirollo, G. La mia conversione dal Rosmini a S. Tommaso. Padova, 1887.
Phil 310.645   Sichirollo, Livio. Dialejesta-Dialektik voy Homer bis Aristoteles. Hildesheim, 1966.
Phil 5058.85   Sichirollo, Livio. Logica e dialettica. Milano, 1957.
Phil 5258.16   Siciliani, P. Prolégomènes a la psychogénie moderne. Paris, 1880.
Phil 4018.1   Siciliani, P. Sul rinnovamento della filosofia positiva in Italia. Firenze, 1871.
Phil 9500.3   Sick-room thoughts and gleanings. (Anderson, Maggie P.) Saint John, N.B., 1897.
Phil 6128.56   Siddall, R.B. Towards understanding our minds. N.Y., 1951.
Phil 5520.594   Siddiqi, J.A. Experimentelle Untersuchungen über den Zusammenhang von Sprachgestalt und Bedeutung. Meisenheim, 1969.

Phil 8631.4   Side-lights on immortality. (Gilbert, L.) London, 1903.
Phil 299.19   Sidereal evolution, or, A new cosmology. Boston, 1889.
Phil 4520.8.44   Sidraed (Bjarnason, Ágúst.) Reykjavik, 1924.
Phil 3500.19   Sidgwich, H. Lectures on the philosophy of Kant. London, 1905.
Phil 5058.22.19   Sidgwick, A. The application of logic. London, 1910.
Phil 5058.22.9   Sidgwick, A. Distinction and the criticism of beliefs. London, 1892.
Phil 5058.22.5   Sidgwick, A. Elementary logic. Cambridge, 1914.
Phil 5100.2A   Sidgwick, A. Fallacies. N.Y., 1884.
Phil 2280.1.80   Sidgwick, A. Henry Sidgwick. London, 1906.
Phil 5058.22.15   Sidgwick, A. The process of argument. London, 1893.
Phil 5058.22   Sidgwick, A. The use of words in reasoning. London, 1901.
Phil 7069.62.10   Sidgwick, Eleanor Mildred. Phantasms of the living. N.Y., 1962.
Phil 8893.11.22   Sidgwick, H. Die Methoden der Ethick. v.1-2. Leipzig, 1909.
Phil 8893.11   Sidgwick, H. The methods of ethics. London, 1874.
Phil 8893.11.2   Sidgwick, H. The methods of ethics. London, 1874.
Phil 8893.11.15   Sidgwick, H. The methods of ethics. London, 1922.
Phil 8893.11.10   Sidgwick, H. The methods of ethics. Supplement to 1. ed. Photoreproduction. London, 1877.
Phil 8893.11.6   Sidgwick, H. The methods of ethics. 6. ed. London, 1801.
Phil 8893.11.17   Sidgwick, H. The methods of ethics. 7. ed. London, 1930.
Phil 193.47   Sidgwick, H. Philosophy, its scope and relations. Photoreproduction. London, 1902.
Phil 8615.4   Sidgwick, H. Practical ethics. London, 1898.
Phil 8843.1.5   Sidgwick, Henry. Lectures on the ethics of T.H. Green. London, 1902.
Htn   Phil 2280.1.30*   Sidgwick, Henry. The methods of ethics. London, 1874.
Phil 8843.1.7   Sidgwick, Henry. Outlines of history of ethics for English readers. Boston, 1960.
Phil 193.47.2   Sidgwick, Henry. Philosophy; its scope and relations. N.Y., 1968.
Phil 8843.1.10   Sidgwick, Henry. Prime livee di una storia della morale. Torino, 1922.
Phil 5525.12   Sidis, B. The psychology of laughter. N.Y., 1913.
Phil 5525.12.3   Sidis, B. The psychology of laughter. N.Y., 1919.
Phil 7140.2A   Sidis, B. The psychology of suggestion. N.Y., 1898.
Phil 6968.12.7   Sidis, Boris. The causation and treatment of psychopathic diseases. Boston, 1916.
Phil 6968.12.15   Sidis, Boris. An inquiry into the nature of hallucination. n.p., 1904-12. 10 pam.
Phil 7042.6A   Sidis, Boris. Multiple personality: an experimental investigation. N.Y., 1905.
Phil 6968.12.9   Sidis, Boris. Nervous ills; their cause and cure. Boston, 1922.
Phil 6968.12   Sidis, Boris. Psychopathological researches. N.Y., 1902.
Phil 6968.12.5   Sidis, Boris. Symptomatology, psychognosis, and diagnosis of psychopathic diseases. Boston, 1914.
Phil 299.15   Sidis, W.G. The animate and the inanimate. Boston, 1925.
Htn   Phil 2280.4.30F*   Sidney, Algernon. Discourses concerning government. London, 1698.
Phil 165.412   Sidney Hook and contemporary world; essay on the pragmatie intelligence. N.Y., 1968.
Phil 8968.20   Sidorov, D.I. Khristianstvo i pravstvennost'. Moskva, 1962.
Phil 5270.4   Sidowski, Joseph B. Experimental methods and instrumentation in psychology. N.Y., 1966.
Phil 5228.1.5   Siebeck, H. Beiträge...Psychologie. Giessen, 1891.
Phil 5228.1   Siebeck, H. Geschichte der Psychologie. Gotha, 1880-84.
Phil 5228.1.2   Siebeck, H. Geschichte der psychologie. v.1-2. Amsterdam, 1961.
Phil 8419.10   Siebeck, H. Das Wesen der ästhetischen Anschauung. Berlin, 1875.
Phil 8598.9   Siebeck, Hermann. Lehrbuch der Religionsphilosophie. Freiburg, 1893.
Phil 8598.9.5   Siebeck, Hermann. Zur Religionsphilosophie. Tübingen, 1907.
Phil 3018.25   Siebecke, H. Ernte deutscher Humanitat. 2. Aufl. Bad Nauheim, 1952.
Phil 9200.2.5   Sieben Kapitel aus der Geschichte des Schreckens. (Heer, Friedrich.) Zürich, 1957.
Phil 3640.303   Sieben Thesen wider den Nietzsche-Geist. (Zickendraht, Karl.) Basel, 193-.
Phil 525.160   Der siebenfarbige Bogen auf den Spuren der grossen Mystiker. (Graef, Hilda Charlotte.) Frankfurt, 1959.
Phil 7082.150   Siebenthal, Walter von. Die Wissenschaft vom Traum, Ergebnisse und Probleme. Berlin, 1953.
Phil 1750.310   Siebers, G. Die Krisis des Existentialismus. Hamburg, 1949.
Phil 8550.388   Siebert, Otto. Die Religionsphilosophie in Deutschland in ihren gegenwärtigen Hauptvertretern. Langensalza, 1906.
Phil 179.3.81.5   Siebert, Otto. Rudolf Euckens Welt- und Lebensanschauung. 2. Aufl. Langensalza, 1911.
Phil 818.7.3   Siebert, Otto. Was jeder Gebildete aus der Geschichte. 3e Aufl. Langensalza, 1912.
Htn   Phil 8595.15.28*   La siècle de la raison. (Paine, Thomas.) Paris, 1794.
Phil 8595.15.30   Siècle de la raison. pt.2. (Paine, Thomas.) Paris, 1795-96.
Phil 3808.167   Siedel, K.G. Die Lehre von der Freiheit bei Kant und Schopenhauer. Inaug. Diss. Erlangen, 1888.
Phil 8407.18   Sieg der Freude. (Gleichen-Russwurm, A.) Stuttgart, 1913.
Phil 5520.78   Der Sieg des Denkens. (Beyer, Alfred.) Berlin, 192-.
Phil 3018.6   Siegel, C. Geschichte der deutschen Naturphilosophie. Leipzig, 1913.
Phil 3791.125   Siegel, Carl. Alois Riehl. Graz, 1932.
Phil 5585.20   Siegel, Carl. Entwickelung der Raumvorstellung. Leipzig, 1899.
Phil 3425.280   Siegel, Carl. Georg Wilhelm Freidrich Hegel. Graz, 1931.
Phil 193.110   Siegel, Carl. Grundprobleme der Philosophie. Wien, 1925.
Phil 3640.274   Siegel, Carl. Nietzsches Zarathustra; Gehalt und Gestalt. München, 1938.
Phil 349.15   Siegel, Carl. Zur Psychologie und Theorie der Erkenntnis. Leipzig, 1903.
Phil 5500.34   Siegel, S. Decision and choice. N.Y., 1964.
Phil 5352.18   Siegel, Sidney. Choice, strategy and utility. N.Y., 1964.
Phil 193.233   Siegende Geduld. (Schazmann, P.E.) Bern, 1963.
Phil 9420.10   Siegfried, R. Lettres et discours sur les passions. Paris, 1925.
Phil 3090.89   Siegl, Josef. Franz von Baader. München, 1957.
Phil 5627.236.2   Siegmend, Georg. Psychologie des Gottesglaubens auf Grund literarischer Selbstzeugnisse. 2. Aufl. Münster, 1965.
Phil 3640.430   Siegmund, G. Nietzsche der Atheist und Anti-christ. 4e Aufl. Paderborn, 1946.
Phil 585.5   Siegmund, Georg. Der Mensch in seinem Dasein. Freiburg, 1953.

Phil 3640.713   Siegmund, Georg. Nietzsches Kunde vom Tode Gottes. Berlin, 1964.
Phil 7150.52   Siegmund, Georg. Sein oder Nichtsein. Trier, 1961.
Phil 3805.155.5   Siegmund-Schultze, F. Schleiermachers Psychologie. Tübingen, 1913.
Phil 193.248   Siegwalt, Gérard. Nature et histoire; leur réalité et leur vérité. Leiden, 1965.
Phil 5545.34   Siehl, A. Zum Studium der Merkfähigkeit. Berlin, 1902.
Phil 3500.53   Siehr, Carl. Kant und das freie Wort und Gerechtigkeit und...bei Kant. Königsberg, 1927.
Phil 5257.72   Sielutieteen oppikirja. (Rein, Thiodolf.) Helsingissa, 1884.
Phil 7082.88   Siemens, Otto. Wissenschaftliche Traum de Terei. Leipzig, 1919?
Phil 2750.22.105   Siena, Primo. Il profeta della chiesa proletaria. Torino, 1965.
Phil 3425.768   Siep, Ludwig. Hegels Fichtekritik und die Wissenschaftslehre von 1804. Freiburg, 1970.
Phil 5258.83   Sièrebois, R.P. Psychologie réaliste. Paris, 1876.
Phil 806.37   Siete modelos de filosofar. (García Bacca, Juan David.) Venezuela, 1963.
Phil 6060.45   Sievers, A. Gestaltwandel und Gestaltzerfall. Bonn, 1962.
Phil 3085.5.80   Sieverth, Gustav. Andre's Philosophie des Lebens. Salzburg, 1959.
Phil 818.32.5   Siewerth, G. Grunfragen der Philosophie in Horizont der Seinsdifferenz. Düsseldorf, 1963.
Phil 818.32   Siewerth, G. Das Schicksal der Metaphysik von Thomas zu Heidegger. Einsiedeln, 1959.
Phil 9240.15   Siewerth, Gustav. Die Freiheit und das Gute. Freiburg, 1959.
Phil 193.220   Siewerth, Gustav. Ontologie du langage. Bruges, 1958.
Phil 5520.403   Siewerth, Gustav. Philosophie der Sprache. Einsiedeln, 1962.
Phil 9245.7   Sigaud de la Fond, J.R. L'école du bonheur. Paris, 1785.
Phil 5875.30.5   Sigel, Irving Edward. Logical thinking in children; research based on Piaget's theory. N.Y., 1968.
Phil 193.161   Siger de Brabant. Question sur la metaphysique. Louvain, 1948.
Phil 7069.15.60   Sigfússon, S. Dulsýnir. Reykjavik, 1915.
Phil 5258.210   Sighele, Scipio. Mentre il secolo muore. Milano, 1899.
Phil 9045.21   Sighele, Scipio. Morale privata e morale politica. Milano, 1913.
Phil 5643.15   Sight. (Le Conte, J.) N.Y., 1881.
Phil 5643.24   Sight and hearing. (Clark, J.H.) N.Y., 1856.
Phil 8407.31.5   Sight and insight, a prediction of new perceptions in art. (Guggenheimer, R.H.) N.Y., 1945.
Phil 1870.82A   Sight and touch...Berkeleian theory. (Abbot, T.K.) London, 1864.
Phil 5643.1   Sight and touch. (Abbott, T.K.) London, 1864.
Phil 7052.10   Sights and sounds. (Spicer, Henry.) London, 1853.
Phil 5590.400   Sigl-Kiener, I. Uber die individuelle Konfiguration des Leitbildes. München, 1960.
Phil 4357.9   El siglo XIV. (Rubert Candau, José Maria.) Madrid, 1952.
Phil 6315.2.335   Sigmund Freud, a short biography. (Costigan, Giovanni.) N.Y., 1965.
Phil 6315.2.136   Sigmund Freud; an introduction. (Hollitscher, W.) London, 1947.
Phil 6315.2.138   Sigmund Freud; an introduction. (Hollitscher, W.) N.Y., 1947.
Phil 6315.2.200   Sigmund Freud; homenaje. (Casa de la Cultura Ecuatoriana.) Cuenca, 1956.
Phil 6315.2.345   Sigmund Freud. (Bayen, Jeanne Françoise.) Paris, 1964.
Phil 6315.2.225A   Sigmund Freud. (Binswanger, Ludwig.) N.Y., 1957.
Phil 6315.2.300   Sigmund Freud. (Choisy, Maryse.) N.Y., 1963.
Phil 6315.2.96   Sigmund Freud. (Delgado, H.) Lima, 1926.
Phil 6315.2.85   Sigmund Freud. (Hermann, István.) Budapest, 1964.
Phil 6315.2.180   Sigmund Freud. (Marcuse, L.) Hamburg, 1956.
Phil 6315.2.170   Sigmund Freud. (Mette, Alexander.) Berlin, 1956.
Phil 6315.2.87   Sigmund Freud. (Wittels, Fritz.) N.Y., 1924.
Phil 6315.2.146   Sigmund Freud. (Zilboorg, G.) N.Y., 1951.
Phil 6315.2.112   Sigmund Freud. Photoreproduction. (Bartlett, Francis H.) London, 1938.
Phil 6315.2.170.3   Sigmund Freud. 3. Aufl. (Mette, Alexandre.) Berlin, 1958.
Phil 6315.2.230   Sigmund Freud and the Jewish mystical tradition. (Bakan, David.) Princeton, N.J., 1958.
Phil 6315.2.290F   Sigmund Freud in Übersetzungen. (Bentz, Hans Willi.) Frankfurt, 1961.
Phil 6315.2.480   Sigmund Freud und die Religion. (Birk, Kasimir.) Münsterschwarzach, 1970.
Phil 6315.2.383   Sigmund Freud und die Wiener Universität. (Eissler, Kurt Robert.) Bern, 1966.
Phil 6315.2.442   Sigmund Freud und sein Religionskritik als Herausforderung für den christlichen Glauben. (Scharfenberg, Joachim.) Göttingen, 1968.
Phil 6315.2.265   Sigmund Freuds akademische Laufbahn im. (Gicklhorn, Josef.) Wien, 1960.
Phil 6315.2.235A   Sigmund Freud's mission. 1st ed. (Fromm, Erich.) N.Y., 1959.
Phil 6315.2.148   Sigmund Freuds neurologische Schriften. (Spehlmann, Rainer.) Berlin, 1953.
Phil 6315.2.430   Sigmund Freuds Prosa. (Schoenan, Walter.) Stuttgart, 1968.
Phil 6315.2.83   Sigmund Freud's Sexualpsychoanalyse. (Schultze, J.H.) Berlin, 1917.
Phil 3235.114   Sigmund Freuds und Ludwig Feuerbachs Religionskritik. Inaug. Diss. (Weser, H.A.) Bettrop, 1936.
Phil 5585.250   Sigmund the unserene. (Bailey, Percival.) Springfield, Ill., 1965.
Phil 5625.107   Signal detection theory and psychophysics. (Green, David Marvin.) N.Y., 1966.
Phil 3110.37.4   Signal i uslovnyi refleks. (Abramian, Lev.) Erevan, 1961.
Phil 3110.37.5   The signature of all things, with other writings. (Böhme, J.) London, 1926.
Phil 2750.20.30   The signature of all things, with other writings. (Böhme, J.) London, 1934.
Phil 8581.108   Signes. (Merleau-Ponty, Maurice.) Paris, 1960.
Phil 8423.18   Les signes de crédibilité de la révélation chrétienne. (Broglie, Guy de.) Paris, 1964.
Phil 3120.23.81   The significance of art. (Wembridge, Eleanor Harris Rowland.) Boston, 1913.
Phil 4752.2.145   The significance of Clemens Baeumker in neo-scholastic philosophy. (Bogdanski, A.A.) Milwaukee, 1942.
Phil 2070.135   The significance of eschatology in the thoughts of Nicolas Berdiaev. (Calian, Carnegie Samuel.) Leiden, 1965.
Phil 575.73   The significance of James' essay. Thesis. (Lapan, A.) N.Y., 1936.
  The significance of personality. (Vaughan, Richard M.) N.Y., 1930.

Phil 8620.54   The significance of Satan. (Ling, Trevor.) London, 1961.

Phil 8897.98   The significance of sense. (Wertheimer, Roger.) Ithaca, 1972.

Phil 3823.16   The significance of Spinoza's first kind of knowledge. (Deugd, Cornelis de.) Assen, 1966.

Phil 6972.15   The significance of the physical constitution in mental disease. (Wertheimer, F.I.) Baltimore, 1926.

Phil 5520.417   Signification and significance. (Morric, C.W.) Cambridge, 1964.

Phil 2445.5.35   Signification de la philosophie. (Alquié, Ferdinand.) Paris, 1971.

Phil 2750.11.68   La signification de l'athéisme contemporain. (Maritain, Jacques.) Paris, 1949.

Phil 5585.64   La signification du sensible. (Nogué, Jean.) Paris, 1936.

Phil 5585.64.5   La signification du sensible. Thèse. (Nogué, Jean.) Paris, 1936.

Phil 5520.427   Significato comunicazioni e parlare comune. (Rossi-Landi, Ferruccio.) Padova, 1961.

Phil 8444.2   Il significato del tragico. (Cantoni, Remo.) Milano, 1970.

Phil 1200.67.2   Il significato della logica stoica. 2. edizione riveduta. (Mignucci, Mario.) Bologna, 1967.

Phil 4260.132   Il significato morale dell'estetica vichiana. (Banchetti, Silvestro.) Milano, 1957.

Phil 3552.288   Il significato storico di Leibniz. (Olgiati, Francesco.) Milano, 1929.

Phil 5520.23.5   Significs and language. (Welby, Victoria.) London, 1911.

Phil 4120.4.135   Signorini, Alberto. Il giovane Gentile e Marx. Milano, 1966.

Phil 103.1   Signorrello, N. Lexicon peripateticum philosophico theologicum. Neapoli, 1872.

Phil 193.139   Signpost (pseud.). In tune with the universe. London, 1932.

Phil 5520.84A   Signs, language and behavior. (Morris, Charles W.) N.Y., 1946.

Phil 2750.20.32   Signs. (Merleau-Ponty, Maurice.) Evanston, 1964.

Phil 7060.84   Signs before death. (Welby, H.) London, 1825.

Phil 7060.85   Signs before death. London, 1875.

Phil 6125.14   Signs of sanity and the principles of mental hygiene. (Paton, Stewart.) N.Y., 1922.

Phil 7054.100   The signs of the times. (Coggshall, W.T.) Cincinnati, 1851.

Phil 8598.83.10   Signs of these times. (Sperry, Willard L.) Garden City, N.Y., 1929.

Phil 3552.256   Sigorgne, P. Institutions léibnitiennes. Lyon, 1768.

Phil 9178.2.2   Sigourney, L.H. Letters to mothers. Hartford, 1838.

Phil 9178.2   Sigourney, L.H. Letters to mothers. N.Y., 1839.

Phil 6985.5   Sigrell, B. Group psychotherapy. Stockholm, 1968.

Phil 2218.87   Sigsbee, Ray A. Das philosophische System Joseph Priestleys. Heidelberg, 1912.

Phil 1200.67   Il siguificato della logica stoica. (Mignucci, Mario.) Bologna, 1965.

Phil 6049.40   Sigurdson, J.S. Hördin min og höndin jn. Reykjavík, 1940.

Phil 7069.24.33   Sigurgeirsson, Oddur. Andatrúin. Reykjavik, 1924.

Phil 5115.2   Sigwart, C. Beigefügt sind Beiträge zur Lehre vom hypothetischen Urtheile. Tübingen, 1871.

Phil 4065.117   Sigwart, C. Die Lebensgeschichte Giordano Bruno's. Tübingen, 1880.

Phil 8893.12   Sigwart, C. Vorfragen der Ethik. Freiburg, 1886.

Phil 193.27   Sigwart, Christoph von. Kleine Schriften. Freiburg, 1881. 2v.

Phil 3838.16   Sigwart, Christoph von. Spinoza's neuentdeckter Tractat von Gott. Gotha, 1866.

Phil 818.8   Sigwart, H.C.W. Geschichte der Philosophie. v.1-3. Stuttgart, 1844.

Phil 193.28   Sigwart, H.C.W. Handbuch der theoretischen Philosophie. Tübingen, 1820.

Phil 5058.11   Sigwart, H.C.W. Handbuch zu Vorlesungen über Logik. Tübingen, 1835.

Phil 5058.13.15   Sigwart, H.C.W. Die Impersonalien. Freiburg, 1888.

Phil 5058.13   Sigwart, H.C.W. Logic. 2nd ed. London, 1895. 2v.

Phil 5058.13.5   Sigwart, H.C.W. Logic. 5e aufl. Tübingen, 1924. 2v.

Phil 5058.12.2   Sigwart, H.C.W. Logik. Freiberg, 1889-1893. 2v.

Phil 5058.12   Sigwart, H.C.W. Logik. Tübingen, 1873-78. 2v.

Phil 818.8.5   Sigwart, H.C.W. Die Propädeutik der Geschichte. Tübingen, 1840.

Phil 3838.2   Sigwart, H.C.W. Der Spinozismus. Tübingen, 1839.

Phil 193.27.5   Sigwart, H.C.W. Vermischte philosophische Abhandlungen. Tübingen, 1831.

Phil 1135.76   Sikes, E.E. The anthropology of the Greeks. London, 1914.

Phil 8612.47   Sikken, Willem. Midden in het leven. Kampen, 1960.

Phil 9065.2   Sikken, William. Het compromis als zedelijk vraagstuk. Academie proefachaft. Assen, 193-.

Phil 3838.26   Sikkes, J.W.T.E. Spinoza. Den Haag, 1946.

Phil 818.41.3   Sikora, Adam. Spotkania z filozofia. 3. Wyd. Warszawa, 1970.

Phil 349.48   Sikora, Joseph John. The Christian intellect and the mystery of being. The Hague, 1966.

Phil 2280.18.5   Sikora, Joseph John. Inquiry into being. Chicago, 1965.

Phil 8430.77   Sikors'kyi, Qurii P. Estetychna tsinnist' tekhniky. Kyïv, 1970.

Phil 6328.5.5   Silberer, Herbert. Probleme der Mystik und ihrer Symbolik. Wien, 1914.

Phil 6328.5   Silberer, Herbert. Problems of mysticism and its symbolism. N.Y., 1917.

Phil 6328.5.10   Silberer, Herbert. Der Zufall und die Kaboldstreiche. Bern, 1921.

Phil 3552.238   Silberstein, Adela. Leibniz' Apriorismus. Weimar, 1902.

Phil 270.42   Silberstein, L. Causality. London, 1933.

Phil 299.2   Silberstein, S.J. Disclosures of the universal mysteries. N.Y., 1896.

Phil 960.180   Silburn, Lilian. Instant et cause. Paris, 1955.

Phil 8419.30   Silcock, Arnold. A background for beauty. London, 1951.

Phil 8598.80   Silen, S. Den kristna människouppfattningen. Stockholm, 1938.

Phil 623.48   El silencio de Dios. (Gambra Ciudad, Rafael.) Madrid, 1968.

Phil 5871.100   The silent majority; families of emotionally healthy college students. (Westley, William A.) San Francisco, 1970.

Phil 7069.60.20   The silent road in the light of personal experience. (Pole, W.T.) London, 1960.

Phil 525.31   The silent voice. 2d ser. London, 1916.

Phil 349.25   Silfverberg, K.W. Der Wirklichkeitsdualismus. Helsingfors, 1912.

Phil 310.603   Silipo, Luigi. Il materialismo dialettico e storico. Padova, 1962.

Phil 299.3   Siljeström, P.A. Tretten aftnar hos en spiritist. Stockholm, 1886.

Phil 1870.132   Sillem, E.A. George Berkeley and the proofs for the existence of God. London, 1957.

Phil 3110.178   Sillig, J.F. Jakob Böhme. Perna, 1801.

Phil 8708.21   Silliman, B. Suggestions relative to the philosophy of geology. New Haven, 1839.

Phil 5170.3   Sillogismo e proporzione. (Pastore, A.) Milano, 1910.

Phil 193.131   Sills, Milton. Values; a philosophy of human needs. Chicago, 1932.

Phil 5170.11   Silogistica judecaţilor de predicaţie. (Ţuţugan, F.) Bucuresti, 1957.

Phil 585.224   Silva, Antonio da. Filosofia social. Évora, 1966.

Phil 4980.52.30   Silva, Vicente Ferreira da. Obras completas. São Paulo, 1964. 2v.

Phil 8893.56   Silva Cordeira, J.A. da. A crise em seus aspectos morals. Coimbra, 1896.

Phil 4980.3   Silva Mello, Antonio da. Man; his life, his education, his happiness. N.Y., 1956.

Phil 7069.50.6   Silva Mello, Antonio da. Mysteries and realities of this world and the next. London, 1960.

Phil 585.175   Silva Mello, Antonio da. A superioridade do homen tropical. Rio de Janeiro, 1965.

Phil 193.185.5   Silva-Tarouca, Amadeo. Aufsätze zur Sozialphilosophie. Wien, 1970.

Phil 5421.10.10   Silva-Tarouca, Amadeo. Die Logik der Angst. Innsbrucke, 1953.

Phil 1718.30   Silva-Tarouca, Amadeo. Philosophie im Mittelpunkt. Graz, 1957.

Phil 193.185   Silva Tarouca, Amadeo. Totale Philosophie und Wirklichkeit. Freiburg, 1937.

Phil 8598.68   Silver, Abba H. Religion in a changing world. N.Y., 1930.

Phil 70.8.5F   Silver jubilee commemoration volume. (Indian Philosophical Congress.) Madras, 1950. 2v.

Phil 6128.57A   Silverberg, W.V. Childhood experience and personal destiny. N.Y., 1952.

Phil 193.147.5   Silverman, H.L. Philosophy and its significance in contemporary civilization. Boston, 1946.

Phil 193.147   Silverman, H.L. Random thoughts; liberalism in life and philosophy. N.Y., 1936. 2v.

Phil 6328.64   Silverman, Samuel. Psychologic cues in forecasting physical illness. N.Y., 1970.

Phil 8581.18.7   Silvester, Tipping. A sermon containing some reflections upon Mr. Balguy's essay on moral goodness. London, 1734.

Phil 585.226   Silvestre, Georges. L'harmonie vitale; à temps nouveau, philosophie nouvelle. Paris, 1964.

Phil 4466.1.80   Silvestre Pinheiro Ferreira. (Louzada de Magalhaes, J.J.) Bonn, 1881.

Phil 4235.10.80   Silvestro da Valsanzibio. Vita e dottrina di Laetano di Thiene. 2. ed. Padova, 1949.

Phil 5068.20   Simàn, B. Der logische Positivismus und das Existenzproblem der höheren Ideen. Tel-Aviv, 1950.

Phil 310.536   Simard, E. Communisme et science. Québec, 1963.

Phil 1523.10   Simard, G. Les maîtres chrétiens de nos pensées et de nos vies. Ottawa, 1941.

Phil 9240.2.5   Simard, Georges. Maux présents et foi chrétienne. 2. éd. Montréal, 1941.

Phil 8419.21   Simat, Zarko. Sotto il velame; aspetti psicologici dell'arte. 1.ed. Roma, 1959.

Phil 4170.6.35   Il simbolismo nella conoscenza. (Marchesini, G.) Torino, 1901.

Phil 8404.3.15   Simbolo. (Dorfles, Gillo.) Torino, 1962.

Phil 8407.48   Simbolo e schema. (Giorgi, Rubina.) Padova, 1968.

Phil 2905.1.625   Símbolo y evolución humana. (Revol, Enrique Luis.) Cordoba, 1970.

Phil 8120.12   Simches, S.O. Le romantisme et le goût esthétique du XVIIIe siècle. Paris, 1964.

Phil 8893.13   Simcox, E. Natural law. London, 1877.

Phil 5938.4   Simesen, R.J. Om den nöiagtige bestemmelse. Kjöbenhavn, 1846.

Phil 8691.3   Similarities of physical and religious knowledge. (Bixby, J.T.) N.Y., 1876.

Phil 2555.11.71   Similitude et dépassement. (Dupréel, Eugène.) Paris, 1968.

Phil 8893.41   Simmel, G. Einleitung in die Moralwissenschaft. Berlin, 1892-93. 2v.

Phil 193.59.25A   Simmel, G. Fragmente und Aufsätze. München, 1923.

Phil 193.59.2.3A   Simmel, G. Hauptprobleme der Philosophie. Leipzig, 1910.

Phil 193.59.2A   Simmel, G. Hauptprobleme der Philosophie. Leipzig, 1911.

Phil 193.59.3   Simmel, G. Hauptprobleme der Philosophie. 7. Aufl. Berlin, 1950.

Phil 3500.20.2   Simmel, G. Kant: sechzehn Vorlesungen. Leipzig, 1904.

Phil 3500.20   Simmel, G. Kant: sechzehn Vorlesungen. Leipzig, 1905.

Phil 3500.20.3   Simmel, G. Kant: sechzehn Vorlesungen. 3. Aufl. München, 1913.

Phil 3500.20.4   Simmel, G. Kant: sechzehn Vorlesungen. 4. Aufl. München, 1918.

Phil 3500.20.6   Simmel, G. Kant: sechzehn Vorlesungen. 5. Aufl. München, 1921.

Phil 3500.20.5   Simmel, G. Kant und Goethe. Berlin, 1906.

Phil 193.59.20A   Simmel, G. Der Konflikt der modernen Kultur. 2. Aufl. München, 1921.

Phil 193.59.15   Simmel, G. Lebensanschauung; vier...Kapitel. München, 1918.

Phil 193.59.5   Simmel, G. Philosophische Kultur. Leipzig, 1911.

Phil 193.59.30   Simmel, G. Die Probleme der Geschichtsphilosophie. n.p., 1892-1909. 9 pam.

Phil 8598.33.3   Simmel, G. Die Religion. Frankfurt, 1906.

Phil 8598.33   Simmel, G. Die Religion. 2. Aufl. Frankfurt, 1912.

Phil 3808.108   Simmel, G. Schopenhauer und Nietzsche. Leipzig, 1907.

Phil 3808.108.3   Simmel, G. Schopenhauer und Nietzsche. 3. Aufl. München, 1923.

Phil 3500.20.15   Simmel, G. Das Wesen der Materie nach Kants physischer Monadologie. Inaug. Diss. Berlin, 1881.

Phil 3850.16.31   Simmel, Georg. Brüche und Tür. Stuttgart, 1957.

Phil 3850.16.41   Simmel, Georg. The conflict in modern culture and other essays. N.Y., 1968.

Phil 3850.16.21   Simmel, Georg. Georg Simmel, 1858-1918. Columbus, 1959.

Phil 3850.16.45   Simmel, Georg. Das individuelle Gesetz. Frankfurt, 1968.

Phil 8419.23   Simmel, Georg. Zur Philosophie der Kunst. Potsdam, 1922.

Phil 3850.16.85   Simmels Religionstheorie. (Knevels, Wilhelm.) Leipzig, 1920.

Phil 6128.45   Simmons, D.A. Cosmicology. N.Y., 1931?

Phil 6028.1   Simms, J. Human faces. N.Y., 1887.

Phil 6028.1.5   Simms, J. Physiognomy illustrated. N.Y., 1887.

Phil 9290.10 Simnett, William E. Leisure, how to enjoy it. London, 1946.
Phil 5258.190 Simões, M.B. Pora uma psicologia na premeira pessoa. Lisboa, 1961.
Phil 5238.40 Simon, Brian. Psychology in the Soviet Union. Stanford, Calif., 1957.
Phil 5722.32 Simon, C.W. Considerations for research in a sleep-learning program. Santa Monica, 1954.
Phil 5722.32.2 Simon, C.W. Considerations for research in a sleep-learning program. Santa Monica, 1954.
Phil 5722.32.10 Simon, C.W. The EEG. Santa Monica, 1955.
Phil 5722.32.5 Simon, C.W. Responses to material presented during various levels of sleep. Santa Monica, 1954.
Phil 7069.23.20 Simon, Gustave. Chez Victor Hugo. Les tables tournantes de Jersey. Paris, 1923.
Phil 1200.56 Simon, Heinrich. Die alte Stoa und ihr Naturbegriff. Berlin, 1956.
Phil 5275.15 Simon, Herbert Alexander. The sciences of the artificial. Cambridge, 1969.
Phil 9120.3 Simon, J. Le devoir. Paris, 1854.
Phil 9120.3.2 Simon, J. Le devoir. Paris, 1855.
Phil 1135.15 Simon, J. Études sur la Théodicée de Platon. Paris, 1840.
Phil 1150.2 Simon, J. Histoire de l'ecole d'Alexandrie. Paris, 1845. 2v.
Phil 8598.10.5 Simon, J. Natural religion. London, 1857.
Phil 8598.10 Simon, J. La religion naturelle. 3. éd. Paris, 1857.
Phil 5520.590 Simon, Josef. Sprache und Raum. Berlin, 1969.
Phil 4815.790.30 Simòn, Józsaf Sándor. A spekulativ termeszettudomány alapgondolatai mint az egységes érzet filozofia rendszere. Budapest, 1904.
Phil 5258.132 Simon, M. Tratado de psicología. Lima, 1944. 2v.
Phil 705.55 Simon, Myron. Transcendentalism and its legacy. Ann Arbor, 1966.
Phil 7054.186 Simon, Otto J. The message of Anne Simon. Boston, 1920.
Phil 2418.1 Simon, Paul M. Der Pragmatisme in der modernen französischen Philosophie. Paderborn, 1920.
Phil 7082.152.2 Simon, Paul Max. Le monde des rêves. 2. éd. Paris, 1888.
Phil 9070.116 Simon, Pierre Henri. Pour un garçon de vingt ans, essai. Paris, 1967.
Phil 3565.106 Simon, Theodor. Leib und Seele bei Fechner und Lotze als vertretern Zweier massgebenden Weltanschauungen. Göttingen, 1894.
Phil 3640.225 Simon, Theodor. Richtlinien christlicher Apologetik wider Nietzsche. Berlin, 1917.
Phil 9240.34 Simon, Ulrich Ernest. A theology of Auschwitz. London, 1967.
Phil 9450.22 Simon, Yves. Community of the free. N.Y., 1947.
Phil 5768.22 Simon, Yves. Freedom of choice. N.Y., 1969.
Phil 8893.136 Simon, Yves. The tradition of natural law. N.Y., 1965.
Phil 1750.450.5 Simona, Maria. La notion de liberte dans l'existentialisme positif de Nicola Abbagnano. Fribourg, 1962.
Phil 7082.45 Símonardottir, Helga. Draumur. Reykjavík, 1916.
Phil 1750.157 Simond, D. Antipolitique. Lausanne, 1941.
Phil 408.2 Simondon, Gilbert. L'individuation à la lumière des notions de forme et d'information. Thèse. Paris, 1964.
Phil 1630.22 Simone, F. La reductio artium ad Sacram scripturam. Torino, 1959?
Phil 4080.5.90 Simone Corleo. (Carlo, E. di.) Palermo, 1924.
Phil 2805.340 Simonetti, Maria. Studi Pascaliani. Roma, 1957?
Phil 4018.4 Simoni, M. Il nuovo spiritualismo in Italia. Napoli, 1936.
Phil 6128.62 Simonian, G.A. Soderzhanie i sushchnost' antagonizma mezhdu fizicheskim i umstvennym trudom. Baku, 1958.
Phil 5258.17 Simonin, A. Traité de psychologie. Paris, 1876.
Phil 493.1 Simonin, A.H. Le matérialisme de masque. Paris, 1878.
Phil 6328.9 Simonin, A.H. Les sentiments, les passions et la folie explications des phénomènes de la pensée et des sensations. Paris, 1885.
Phil 5520.330 Simonis, Hans. Die Sprachphilosophie O.F. Guppe's und G. Gerber's. Bonn, 1959.
Phil 5400.162 Simonov, P.V. Metod K.S. Stanislavskogo i fiziologiia emotsii. Moskva, 1962.
VPhil 3552.476 Simonovits, Istvánné. A dialektika Leibniz filozófiá. Budapest, 1965.
Phil 3552.476.5 Simonovits, Istvánné. Dialektisches Denken in der Philosophie von Gottfried Wilhelm Leibniz. Budapest, 1968.
Phil 8893.140 Simonsen, Andreas. Erkendelse og lidenskab. København, 1966.
Phil 2750.11.130 Simonson, V.L. L'esthétique de Jacques Maritain. Copenhagen, 1956.
Phil 8708.30 Simonsson, Tord. Face to face with Darwinism. Lund, 1958.
Phil 9182.4.10 The simple life. (Wagner, Charles.) N.Y., 1904.
Phil 9182.4.9 The simple life. (Wagner, Charles.) N.Y., 1904.
Phil 3640.825 Simpozium na temu Niče i Marksizam, Belgrade, 1968. Niče i marksizam. Beograd, 1969.
Phil 310.752 Simpozium po Dialekticheskoi Logike, Alma-Ata, 1968. Aktual'nye problemy dialekticheskoi logiki. Alma-Ata, 1971.
Phil 310.778 Simpozium po Teme Ob"ektivnye Zakony Istorii i Nauchnoe Rukovodstov Obshchestvom, Moscow, 1967. Ob"ektirnye zako istorii i nauchnoe rukovodstov obshchestvom. Moskva, 1970.
Phil 8980.790 Simpozium Posviashchennyi 100-letiiu so Dnia Rozhdeniia V.I. Lenina, Novosibirsk? 1968? Problemy kategorii marksistsko-leninskoi etiki. Novosibirsk, 1968.
Phil 7082.146 Simpson, David. A discourse on dreams and night-visions. Macclesfield, 1791.
Phil 8643.23 Simpson, J.Y. Man and the attainment of immortality. 2. ed. London, 1923.
Phil 8708.10.5 Simpson, James Y. Landmarks in the struggle between science and religion. N.Y., 1925?
Phil 8708.10.9 Simpson, James Y. Nature. New Haven, 1929.
Phil 8708.10 Simpson, James Y. The spiritual interpretation of nature. 2. ed. London, 1912.
Phil 4809.498.80 Šimsa, Jaroslav. Sboruiík ku poctě Frantiska Krejciho. Praha, 1929.
Phil 6128.19 Simson, T. An inquiry how far the vital and animal actions of the more perfect animals can be accounted for independent of the brain. Edinburgh, 1752.
Phil 6958.2 Simulación de la locura. 8. ed. (Ingenieros, José.) Buenos Aires, 1918.
Phil 4970.1.30 La simulación en la lucha por la vída. (Ingenieros, José.) Valencia, 191-?
Phil 5425.20 Los simuladores del talento. (Ramos Mejia, J.M.) Barcelona, n.d.
Phil 6990.12 La simulation du merveilleux. (Saintyves, P.) Paris, 1912.
Phil 6980.102.5 A simulation of the initial psychiatric interview. (Bellman, Richard.) Santa Monica, Calif., 1966.
Phil 5643.27 Der simultane Farben- und Helligkeitskontrast. (Kohler, J.) Leipzig, 1903.
Phil 9070.108 Sin, sex and self control. 1st ed. (Peale, Norman Vincent.) Garden City, 1965.
Phil 9513.3 Sin and society. (Ross, E.A.) Boston, 1907.
Phil 6311.13 Sin and the new psychology. (Barbour, C.E.) London, 1931.
Phil 9558.12 The sin of sloth. (Wenzel, Siegfried.) Chapel Hill, 1967.
Phil 2805.490 Sina, Mario. L'anti-Pascal di Voltaire. Milano, 1970.
Phil 2280.1.86 Sinclair, A.G. Der Utilitarismus bei Sidgwick...Spencer. Heidelberg, 1907.
Phil 400.33 Sinclair, May. A defence of idealism. N.Y., 1917.
Phil 400.33.5 Sinclair, May. The new idealism. N.Y., 1922.
Phil 8893.91.90 Sinclair, Upton. The book of life. Chicago, 1921.
Phil 8893.92A Sinclair, Upton. The book of life. 4th ed. v.1-2. Long Beach, 1926.
Phil 7069.30.30 Sinclair, Upton B. Mental radio. N.Y., 1930.
Phil 7069.30.30.2 Sinclair, Upton B. Mental radio. N.Y., 1930.
Phil 349.40 Sinclair, W.A. The conditions of knowing. London, 1951.
Phil 193.158 Sinclair, W.A. An introduction to philosophy. London, 1944.
Phil 5058.50 Sinclair, W.A. The traditional formal logic. London, 1937.
Phil 5520.504 Sinclair-de Zwart, Hermina. Acquisition du langage et développement de la pensée, sous-systèmes, et opérations concrètes. Paris, 1967.
Phil 3552.268 Sind es Vorzugsweise speculative oder naturwissenschaftliche Gründe. (Reinhardt, Arthur.) Jena, 1873.
Phil 288.6 Sind Naturgesetze Veränderlich? (Hartmann, L.) Halle, 1926.
Phil 8419.50.5 Šindelář, Dušan. Estetické vnémáné. Praha, 1961.
Phil 8419.50 Šindelář, Dušan. Smysl věcí. Praha, 1963.
Phil 8419.50.10 Šindelář, Dušan. Tržiště estetiky. Vyd. 1. Praha, 1969.
VPhil 585.192 Šindelář, Jan. Co řeší filosofická antropologie. Vyd. 1. Praha, 1966.
Phil 7069.27.27 Sinel, J. The sixth sense. London, 1927.
Phil 8884.12 The sinfulness of little sins. 5th ed. (Jackson, John.) London, 1851.
Phil 2280.5.161 Singer, Beth J. The rational society; a critical study of Santayana's social thought. Cleveland, 1970.
Phil 8708.18 Singer, Charles. Religion and science considered in their historical relations. N.Y., 1929.
Phil 4065.127 Singer, D. (Waley). Giordano Bruno. N.Y., 1950.
Phil 193.145 Singer, E.A. On the contented life. N.Y., 1936.
Phil 2280.17.80 Singer, Edgar. Experience and reflection. Philadelphia, 1959.
Phil 5258.91 Singer, Edgar A. Mind as behavior and studies in empirical idealism. Columbus, Ohio, 1924.
Phil 193.95 Singer, Edgar A. Modern thinkers and present problems. N.Y., 1923.
Phil 2280.5.130A Singer, Irving. Santayana's aesthetics; a critical introduction. Cambridge, 1957.
Phil 315.12 Singer, Kent. The idea of conflict. Melbourne, 1949.
Phil 8893.115A Singer, M.G. Generalization in ethics. 1. ed. N.Y., 1961.
Phil 728.5 Singevin, Charles. Essai sur l'un. Thèse. Paris, 1969.
Phil 8625.4 The single eye. (Arjuna.) N.Y., 1921.
Phil 9349.3 Singles from life's gathering. (Jacks, William.) Glasgow, 1902.
Phil 1750.115.145 Sinha, Debabrata. Studies in phenomenology. The Hague, 1969.
Phil 5228.6 Sinha, Jadunath. Indian psychology; perception. London, 1934.
Phil 5228.6.5 Sinha, Jadunath. Indian psychology. Calcutta, 1958.
Phil 193.179 Sinha, Jadunath. Introduction to philosophy. 2d. ed. Calcutta, 1957.
Phil 960.148 Sinha, Judunath. Indian realism. London, 1938.
Phil 1750.115.165 Sini, Carlo. La fenomenologia. 1. ed. Milano, 1965.
Phil 1750.115.140 Sini, Carlo. Introduzione alla fenomenologia come scienza. Milano, 1965.
Phil 2340.10.220 Sini, Carlo. Whitehead e la funzione della filosofia. Vicenza, 1965.
Phil 193.89 Sinibaldi, T. Elementos de philosophia. 3a ed. Coimbra, 1906. 2v.
Phil 5400.204 Sinirlenmeden yaşayeniz. (Dermon, Emiir.) Izmir, 1970.
Phil 9560.56 Sinko, Tadeuz. Od filantropii do human i humanizmu. 2. wyd. Warszawa, 1960.
Phil 5520.55 Sinn; eine philosophische Untersuchung. Inaug. Diss. (Schölkopf, H.) Metzingen, 1931.
Phil 177.43 DerSinn der gegenwärtigen Kultur. (Cohn, Jonas.) Leipzig, 1914.
Phil 193.55.3 Der Sinn des Daseins. (Stein, Ludwig.) Tübingen, 1904.
Phil 6310.1.38 Der Sinn des Lebens. (Adler, A.) Wien, 1933.
Phil 1750.799 Der Sinn heutigen Philosophierens. (Kanz, Heinrich.) Ratingen, 1967.
Phil 5640.132 Sinn und Geist. (Juritsch, M.) Freiburg, 1961.
Phil 182.91.5 Sinn und Geschichte. (Hofmann, P.) München, 1937.
Phil 187.125 Sinn und Gesetze des Lebens. (Märker, F.) Berlin, 1938.
Phil 165.215 Sinn und Sein. (Wisser, Richard.) Tubingen, 1960.
Phil 822.22 Sinn und Teilhabe. (Weier, Winfried.) Salzburg, 1970.
Phil 5520.62 Sinn und Unsinn. (Blumenfeld, W.) München, 1933.
Phil 179.3.25 Der Sinn und Wert des Lebens. (Eucken, R.) Leipzig, 1910.
Phil 179.3.27 Sinn und Wert des Lebens. 3rd ed. (Eucken, R.) Leipzig, 1913.
Phil 179.3.27.3 Der Sinn und Wert des Lebens. 6. Aufl. (Eucken, R.) Leipzig, 1918.
Phil 8897.57 Der Sinn und Zweck des Lebens. (Wintzer, Wilhelm.) Stuttgart, 1922.
Phil 5640.125 Die Sinne des Menschen. 3. Aufl. (Kreibig, Josef K.) Leipzig, 1917.
Phil 5810.3.3 Die Sinne und das geistige Leben der Thiere. (Avebury, John L.) Leipzig, 1889.
Phil 5642.22 Sinne und Sinnesverknüpfungen. (Schroder, Ludwig.) Heidelberg, 1969.
Phil 6834.5 Sinnerfülltes Anders-sein. (Bovet, Théodore.) Tübingen, 1959.
Phil 5460.7 Die Sinnesdelirien. (Kraft-Ebing, R.) Erlangen, 1864.
Phil 5640.31 Die Sinneserkenntnis. (Schwertschlager, J.) München, 1924.
Phil 5640.125.5 Sinnesphysiologische Untersuchungen. (Pikler, Gyula.) Leipzig, 1917.
Phil 5460.3 Die Sinnestäuschungen. (Mayer, A.) Wien, 1869.
Phil 5585.1 Die Sinneswahrnehmung. (Böhmer, H.) Erlangen, 1868.
Phil 5585.53 Sinneswahrnehmungen und Sinnestäuschungen. (Rohde, F.) Braunsberg, 1877.
Phil 978.9.25 Sinnett, A.P. Collected fruits of occult teaching. London, 1919.
Phil 978.9.8 Sinnett, A.P. Esoteric Buddhism. Boston, 1885.
Phil 978.9.8.5 Sinnett, A.P. Esoteric Buddhism. 3d ed. Boston, 1886.

Phil 978.9.3 Sinnett, A.P. Esoteric Buddhism. 3rd ed. London, 1884.
Phil 978.9.7 Sinnett, A.P. Esoteric Buddhism. 5th ed. London, 1885.
Phil 978.9.9 Sinnett, A.P. Esoteric Buddhism. 6th ed. Boston, 1896.
Phil 978.9.18 Sinnett, A.P. The growth of the soul. 2nd ed. London, 1905.
NEDL Phil 978.5.800 Sinnett, A.P. Incidents in the life of Madame Blavatsky. London, 1886.
Phil 978.9.10 Sinnett, A.P. The occult world. Boston, 1882.
Phil 6688.2 Sinnett, A.P. The relationale of mesmerism. Boston, 1892.
Phil 978.65 Sinnett, Patience E. The purpose of theosophy. London, 1885.
Phil 3850.27.106.10 Sinngeburg des Lebens. (Grabs, R.) Hamburg, 1950.
Phil 1135.190 Sinnige, Theo G. Matter and infinity in the Presocratic school and Plato. Assen, 1968.
Phil 3915.67 Sinnliche und übersinnliche Welt. (Wundt, Wilhelm.) Leipzig, 1914.
Phil 5635.30 Die sinnlichen Gefühle des Menschen. (Heilig, G.) Jena, 1919.
Phil 8140.8 Sinnonini, Augusto. Storia dei movimenti estetici nella cultura italiana. Firenze, 1968.
Phil 8708.28 Sinnott, Edmund Ware. Matter. 1. ed. N.Y., 1957.
Phil 8708.26 Sinnott, Edmund Ware. Two roads to truth. N.Y., 1953.
Phil 3270.11.31 Sinnvolle Odyssee. (Friedmann, H.) München, 1950.
Phil 802.1 Sinossi della storia di filosofia. (Cicchitti-Suriani, F.) Torino, 1886.
Phil 8708.28.2 Sinott, Edmund Ware. Matter, mind and man. N.Y., 1962.
Phil 5416.2 The sins of bias. (Loeb, Robert H.) N.Y., 1970.
Phil 8700.9 Sins of science. (Klyce, S.) Boston, 1925.
Phil 8643.3.10 Sintenis, F. Elpizon, oder Über meine Fortdauer im Tode. 3. Aufl. Köln, 1811. 6v.
Phil 8643.3 Sintenis, F. Immortality or annihilation? London, 1827.
Phil 190.114 Sinteses e hipóteses de ser-humano. (Pacini, Dante.) Rio de Janeiro, 1967.
Phil 191.3 Sintesi di un sistema filosofica. (Quarto Di Palo, A.) Roma, 1935.
Phil 4353.15 Sintesis de su obra filosofica: antroposofica y metafisica de la presencia. (Caba, Pedro.) Mexico, 1959.
Phil 1850.137.5 Sir Francis Bacon. (Green, Adwin W.) N.Y., 1966.
Phil 1850.137 Sir Francis Bacon. (Green, Adwin W.) Syracuse, N.Y., 1948.
Phil 2035.87 Sir W. Hamilton. (Sterling, J.H.) London, 1865.
Htn Phil 8591.17.8* Sir Walter Rawleigh's ghost. (Lessius, Leonardus.) London, 1651.
Phil 2035.85 Sir William Hamilton. English philosopher. (Monck, W.H.S.) London, 1881.
Phil 2035.88.3 Sir William Hamilton: the man and his philosophy. (Veitch, J.) London, 1883.
Phil 8610.899.30 Sirai and Olympus. N.Y., 1899.
Phil 960.256 Sircar, Mahendranath. Eastern lights; a brief account of some phases of life, thought and mysticism in India. Calcutta, 1935.
Phil 3450.18.195 Sirchia, Francesco. Nicolai Hartmann dal neokantismo all ontologia. Milano, 1969.
Phil 5828.18 Sire, Marcel. L'intelligence des animaux. Paris, 1954.
Phil 1870.65.15 Siris. (Berkeley, G.) Leipzig, 1915.
Phil 1870.66.5 La siris. (Berkeley, G.) Paris, 1920.
Htn Phil 1870.65* Siris: a chain of...reflexions. (Berkeley, G.) Dublin, 1744.
Phil 2520.167 Sirven, J. Les années d'apprentissage de Descartes (1596-1628). Albi, 1928.
Phil 2520.167.2 Sirven, J. Les années d'apprentissage de Descartes (1596-1628). v.1-2. Thèse. Albi, 1928.
Phil 9035.24 Sisson, E.O. The essentials of character. N.Y., 1915.
Phil 1715.18 Sistem i egzistencija. (Pejović, Danilo.) Zagreb, 1970.
Phil 1865.191 Sistema de la ciencia social. (Nuñez, T.) Salamanca, 1820.
Phil 4080.5.32 Il sistema della filosofia universale. (Corleo, Simone.) Roma, 1879.
Phil 3800.180.15 Sistema dell'idealismo trancendentale. (Schelling, F.W.J. von.) Bari, 1908.
Phil 5046.11 Sistema di logica come teoria del conscere. (Gentile, G.) Pisa, 1917.
Phil 3552.131 Il sistema die Leibniz. (Carlotti, G.) Messina, 1923.
Phil 2050.282 Sistema e ricerca in David Hume. (Santucci, Antonio.) Bari, 1969.
Phil 4210.41.20 Sistema filosofico. (Rosmini-Serbati, Antonio.) Torino, 1924.
Phil 4210.41.30 Il sistema filosofico. (Rosmini-Serbati, Antonio.) Torino, 1951.
Phil 4210.155 Il sistema filosofico di Antonio Rosmini. 2a ed. (Esposito, G.) Milano, 1933.
Phil 4120.2.92 Il sistema filosofico di Cosmo Guastella. (Albeggiani, F.) Firenze, 1927.
Phil 4265.3.85 Il sistema filosofico di Hegel...sulla pena di morte di A. Vera. (Longoni, L.) Milano, 1863.
Phil 2250.89 Il sistema filosofico di Josiah Royce. (Albeggiani, F.) Palermo, 1930.
Phil 4115.82 Il sistema filosofico di V. Gioberti. (Zarelli, T.) Paris, 1848.
Phil 3425.505 Sistema i metod filosofii Gegelia. (Bakradze, K.S.) Tbilisi, 1958.
Phil 310.617.10 Sistema kategorii dialektiki. (Sheptulin, Aleksandr P.) Moskva, 1958.
Phil 4351.6.85 Sistematización de lo personal y lo sobrenatural. (Barreiro Gomez, José.) Lugo, 1969.
Phil 4352.1.150 Sistematizacion del pensamiento de Balmes en orden a la filosofia de la historia. (Feliu Egidio, Vicente.) Madrid, 1952.
Phil 5520.712 I sistemi di segni e lo strutturalismo sovietico. (Faccani, Remo.) Milano, 1969.
Phil 310.759 Sistemno-strukturnyi analiz osnovnykh kategorii dialektilu. (Zel'kina, Ol'ga S.) Saratov, 1971.
Phil 2855.7.35 Sitkovskii, E. Filosofiia Zh. B. Robine, ocherk iz istorii frantsuzskogo materializma XVIII v. Moskva, 1936.
Phil 8897.47 Sitte, Recht und Morale. (Weigelin, Ernst.) Berlin, 1919.
Phil 8894.19 Die Sitte. (Tönnies, Ferdinand.) Frankfurt, 1909.
Phil 8893.50 Das Sittengesetz. 2. Aufl. (Staudinger, Franz.) Berlin, 1897.
Phil 8887.53.10 Sittenlehre. (Messer, A.) Leipzig, 1920.
Phil 3819.30.50 Sittenlehre. (Spinoza, Benedictus de.) Frankfurt, 1744.
Phil 8879.21 Sittenlehre der Vernunft. (Eberhard, J.A.) Berlin, 1786.
Phil 2520.132 Die Sittenlehre des Descartes. (Hunze, Max.) Leipzig, 1872.
Phil 3450.33.20 Sittichkert und ethische Werterkenntnis nach D. von Hildebrand. (Reuter, Otfried.) Münster? 1966.
Phil 7069.63.10 Sittings with Eussapia Palladino and other studies. (Feilding, Everard.) New Hyde Park, 1963.
Phil 6980.653 Das sittliche, eine Kraft des menschlichen Unbewussten. (Rotthaus, Erich.) Stuttgart, 1949.
Phil 2270.112 Die sittliche Erziehung nach Herbert Spencer. (Geraskoff, Michael.) Zürich, 1912.
Phil 8885.22 Sittliche fragen. (Kittel, Rudolf.) Stuttgart, 1885.
Phil 8957.12.5 Sittliche Grundhaltungen. (Hildebrand, D. von.) Mainz, 1954.
Phil 3488.12 Das sittliche Handeln nach Kants Ethik. (Gneisse, Karl.) Colmar, 1895.
Phil 8893.39 Das sittliche Leben, eine Ethik auf psychologische Grundlage. (Schwarz, Hermann.) Berlin, 1901.
Phil 8880.33 Das sittliche Leben. (Frauenstädt, Julius.) Leipzig, 1866.
Phil 8885.11 Sittliche Lebens anschauungen der Gegenwart. 2. Aufl. (Kirn, O.) Leipzig, 1911.
Phil 8831.6 Der sittliche Mensch. (Gent, W.) Meisenheim, 1950.
Phil 9120.9 Die sittliche Pflicht. (Wendt, Hans H.) Göttingen, 1916.
Phil 8878.47 Die sittliche Tat. (Driesch, Hans.) Leipzig, 1927.
Phil 8877.61 Die sittliche Weltordnung. (Christ, Paul.) Leiden, 1894.
Phil 8894.21 Die sittliche Weltordnung. (Traub, Friedrich.) Freiburg, 1892.
Phil 8900.3 Die sittliche Weltordnung. (Zweifel, Hans.) München, 1875.
Phil 8893.53.7 Die sittlichen Forderungen und die Frage ihrer Gultigkeit. (Störring, Gustav.) Leipzig, 1919.
Phil 3425.362 Die sittlichen Grundlagen des Denkens. (Flügge, J.) Hamburg, 1953.
Phil 1145.22 Sittlichen Ideen der Griechen. (Kühn, O.) Leipzig, 1888.
Phil 8900.1 Sittliches Sein und sittliches Werden. 2. Aufl. (Zeigler, T.) Strassburg, 1890.
Phil 8893.82 Die sittlichkei Verbindung mit der Glükseligkeit einzelner Menschen und gauzer Staaten. (Snell, C.W.) Frankfurt, 1790.
Phil 3485.13 Sittlichkeit, Staat und Recht bei Kant. (Dünnhaupt, Rudolf.) Berlin, 1927.
Phil 2630.2.35 Sittlichkeit ohne Pflicht. (Guyau, J.M.) Leipzig, 1909.
Phil 9150.6 Sittlichkeit und Darwinismus. (Carneri, B.) Wien, 1871.
Phil 8879.17 Die Sittlichkeit und der philosophische Sittlichkeitswahn. (Eleutheropoulos, A.) Berlin, 1899.
Phil 3905.82 Die Sittlichkeitsmetaphysik Otto Weiningers. (Biró, Paul.) Wien, 1927.
Phil 3905.82.2 Die Sittlichkeitsmetaphysik Otto Weiningers. Diss. (Biró, Paul.) Wien, 1927.
Phil 28.30 Situation; contributions to phenomenological psychology and psychopathology. Utrecht. 1
Phil 8955.8 Situation ethics. (Fletcher, Joseph Francis.) Philadelphia, 1966.
Phil 8955.8.80 The situation ethics debate. (Cox, Harvey G.) Philadelphia, 1968.
Phil 8952.25 Situationism and the new morality. (Cunningham, Robert L.) N.Y., 1970.
Phil 7069.40.7 Sitwell, S. Poltergeists. London, 1940.
Phil 1750.85 Siu, Ralph G.H. The Tao of science. Cambridge, Mass., 1957.
Phil 8419.31 Siunerberg, K.A. Iskusstvo i narod; sbornik. Peterburg, 1922.
Phil 310.125 Siusiukalov, B.I. Osnovnye zotkony materialisticheskoi dialektiki. Moskva, 1958.
Phil 672.163 Sivadjian, J. Le temps. Paris, 1938.
Phil 672.163.5 Sivadjian, J. Le temps. Paris, 1938. 6v.
Phil 9045.20 Siveking, Gustav A. Rede über einige Hauptregeln zum wohlthätigen Einwirken auf das Zeitalter. Hamburg, 1814.
Phil 3838.15 Siwek, Paul. L'ame et le corps d'après Spinoza. Paris, 1930.
Phil 3838.15.10 Siwek, Paul. An coeur du Spinozisme. Paris, 1952.
Phil 8643.32 Siwek, Paul. The enigma of the hereafter. N.Y., 1952.
Phil 5628.55.21 Siwek, Paul. The riddle of Konnersreuth; a psychological and religious study. Dublin, 1954.
Phil 3838.15.5 Siwek, Paul. Spinoza et le panthéisme religieux. Paris, 1937.
Phil 3838.15.7 Siwek, Paul. Spinoza et le panthéisme religieux. Paris, 1950.
Phil 600.7.105 Six, J.F. Littré devant Dieu. Paris, 1962.
Phil 8701.2.2 Six days of creation. 2nd ed. (Lewis, Tayler.) Schenectady, 1855.
Phil 8708.29 Six days or forever? (Ginger, Ray.) Boston, 1958.
Phil 5865.5.6 Six études de psychologie. (Piaget, Jean.) Genève, 1964.
Phil 1750.362 Six existentialist thinkers. (Blackham, H.J.) London, 1952.
Phil 5640.7 The six gateways of knowledge. (Thomson, W.) N.Y., 1884.
Phil 130.10 Six great thinkers. (De Selincourt, Audrey.) London, 1958.
Phil 6673.3 Six lectures on philosophy of mesmerism. (Dods, J.B.) Boston, 1843.
Phil 8610.898 Six lectures on the nature of knowledge, free enquiry, the more important divisions and essentials of knowledge, religion, morals, opinions. (D'Arusmont, Frances Wright.) London, 1898.
Phil 2490.76 Six lettres inédites à Romeo Pouzin. (Comte, Auguste.) Paris, 1914.
Htn Phil 2520.52.15* Six metaphysical meditations. (Descartes, René.) London, 1680.
Phil 2402.9 Six philosophes français du XVIIIe siècle. (Callot, E.) Annecy, 1963.
Phil 5865.5.7 Six psychological studies. (Piaget, Jean.) N.Y., 1967.
Phil 1812.4 Six radical thinkers. (MacCunn, J.) London, 1907.
Phil 1812.4.5 Six radical thinkers. (MacCunn, J.) London, 1910.
Phil 1812.4.10 Six radical thinkers. (MacCunn, J.) N.Y., 1964.
Phil 9245.45 Six roads to happiness. (Lush, Samuel Beryl.) N.Y., 1930.
Phil 8581.105 Six secular philosophers. 1. ed. (Beck, Lewis W.) N.Y., 1960.
Phil 1900.75 Six sermons on moral subjects. (Butler, Joseph.) Cambridge, 1849.
Phil 960.7 The six systems of Indian philosophy. (Muller, F.M.) N.Y., 1899.
Phil 960.220 The six systems of Indian philosophy. (Rajadhyaksha, N.D.) Bombay, 1959.
Phil 5252.68.5 Six theories of mind. (Morris, Charles W.) Chicago, 1959.
Phil 3110.27 Six theosophic points, and other writings. (Böhme, J.) London, 1919.
Phil 7069.59.5 The sixth sense. (Heywood, Rosalind.) London, 1959.
Phil 7069.27.27 The sixth sense. (Sinel, J.) London, 1927.
Phil 5272.11 Sixtl, Friedrich. Messmethoden der Psychologie. Weinheim, 1967.
NEDL Phil 5938.10 Sizer, N. Heads and faces. N.Y., 1890.
Phil 5938.10.5 Sizer, Nelson. Forty years in phrenology. N.Y., 1891.
Phil 5938.10.10 Sizer, Nelson. How to teach according to temperament and mental development. N.Y., 1877.

Phil 188.15   Sjaele-og taenkelaere i almenfattelig. 4e udg. (Nielsen, F.K.) Kjøbenhavn, 1882.

Phil 665.48.5   Själen och hennes historia. (Stosch, George.) Stockholm, 1908.

Phil 7054.188   Sjaelens gaade. (Eriksen, R.) Kristiania, 1893.

Phil 8581.24.18   Själslifvet. (Brierley, J.) Stockholm, 1904.

Phil 6317.12   Själslifvets underjordiska verld. (Herrlin, Axel.) Malmo, 1901.

Phil 5249.2.20   Sjalslifrets. (James, William.) Uppsala, 1898.

Phil 8882.90   Sjn studier i praktish filosof. (Hedenius, Ingemar.) Uppsala, 1968.

Phil 5058.34   Sjoberg, Gustaf. Lärobok i logik af Gustaf Sjöberg och Gustaf Klingberg. Stockholm, 1887.

Phil 6328.1   Sjobring, H. Den individual psykologiska frage ställningen inom psykistrien. Uppsala, 1913.

Phil 3552.284   Sjöberg, Gustaf M. Historisk öfversigt af den på monadlären grundade metafysikens utveckling. Upsala, 1868.

Phil 5258.160   Sjöbring, Henrik. Struktur och utveckling. Lund, 1958.

Phil 4635.6.30   Sjöholm, L.A. Det historiska sammanhanget mellan Humes skepticism och Kants kriticism. Upsala, 1869.

Phil 5039.16   Sju filosofiska studier, tillägnade Anders Wedberg. Stockholm, 1963.

NEDL Phil 176.51.25   Den skabende udvikling. (Bergson, H.) Kobenhavn, 1914.

Phil 5258.113.5   Skaggs, E.B. A textbook of experimental and theoretical psychology. Boston, 1935.

Phil 5477.5   Skaggs, Ernest B. Major forms of inhibition in man. Chicago, 1931.

Phil 8893.72   Skala, Richard. Der Stachel der Ethik. Wien, 1927.

Phil 4800.22.10   Skarbek, Janusz. Koncepcja nauki w pozytywizmie polskim. Wrocław, 1968.

Phil 5228.14   Skard, Ase Gruda. Psykologi og psykologar i Norge. Oslo, 1959.

Phil 4800.22   Skarga, Barbara. Naroziny pozytywizmu polskiego, 1831-1864. Warszawa, 1964.

VPhil 2490.176   Skarga, Barbara. Ortodoksja i rewizja w pozytywizmie francuskim. Warszawa, 1967.

Phil 5871.2   Skasa-Weiss, Eugen. Mütter-Schicksal grosser Söhne. Oldenburg, 1966.

Htn Phil 5246.16*   Skeleton project of a science of psychology. (Gurley, R.R.) n.p., n.d.

Htn Phil 5246.16.2*   Skeleton project of a science of psychology. (Gurley, R.R.) n.p., n.d.

Phil 3801.495   Skellighios iti oligha tina peri ton vion ke tis filosofias aftou. (Kotzias, Nikolaos.) Athena, 1855.

Phil 1850.133   Skemp, A.R. Francis Bacon. London, 1912.

Phil 645.23   Die Skepsis in Philosophie und Wissenschaft. (Hönigswald, Richard.) Göttingen, 1914.

Phil 5520.21.15   Skepsis und Mystik. (Landauer, Gustav.) Berlin, 1903.

Phil 8610.856   The skeptical era in modern history. (Post, T.M.) N.Y., 1856.

Phil 8610.882   Skepticism and divine relation. (Ellis, John.) N.Y., 1882.

Phil 645.27   Skepticismen. (Starcke, C.N.) Kjøbenhavn, 1890.

Phil 8610.895   The skeptics defense against all Christian or other priests. (Landers, C.M.) Rochester, 1895.

NEDL Phil 2414.1   The skeptics of the French renaissance. (Owen, J.) London, 1893.

Phil 4014.1   Skeptics of the Italian Renaissance. Photoreproduction. (Owen, J.) London, 1893.

Phil 1190.6   Les skeptiques grecs. (Brochard, Victor.) Paris, 1887.

Phil 3494.55   Skeptische Methode im Blick auf Kant. (Marguard, Odo.) Freiburg, 1958.

Phil 645.9   Der Skeptizismus in der Philosophie. (Richter, Raoul.) Leipzig, 1904-08.

Phil 978.97   Skerst, Herman von. Der unbekannte Gott. Stuttgart, 1967.

Phil 813.2.3   A sketch...development of philosophical thought. (Noire, L.) London, 1908.

Phil 5400.202   Sketch for a theory of the emotions. (Sartre, Jean-Paul.) London, 1962.

Phil 193.71   Sketch of a new theory of man. Vivey, 1819.

Phil 187.3   Sketch of a philosophy. v.1-4. (Macvicar, J.G.) London, 1868-1874.

Phil 1890.30.7   Sketch of a system of human mind. (Brown, T.) Edinburgh, 1820.

Phil 1117.2.7   A sketch of ancient philosophy. (Mayor, J.B.) Cambridge, Eng., 1889.

Phil 1117.2A   Sketch of ancient philosophy. (Mayor, J.B.) Cambridge, 1881.

Phil 1117.2.5   Sketch of ancient philosophy. (Mayor, J.B.) Cambridge, 1885.

Phil 1512.12   A sketch of mediaeval philosophy. (Hawkins, D.J.B.) London, 1946.

Phil 8881.26.5   A sketch of morality. (Guyau, M.) London, 1898.

Phil 815.5   Sketch of philosophical systems. (Perry, Rufus L.) n.p., n.d.

Phil 5211.2.5   Sketch of the history of psychology. (Baldwin, J.M.) Lancaster, 1905.

Phil 9179.6   Sketches from the notebook of Laurie Todd on marriage. (Thorburn, Grant.) N.Y., 1847.

Phil 5921.4   Sketches of Buchanan's discoveries in neurology. (Buchanan, J.R.) Louisville, 1842.

Phil 8610.851   Sketches of modern irreligion and infidelity. (Wright, B.W.) London, 1851.

Phil 3012.4   Sketches of modern philosophy. (Murdock, J.) Hartford, 1842.

Phil 7060.17   Sketches of the philosophy of apparitions. (Hibbert, S.) Edinburgh, 1824.

Phil 7060.17.2   Sketches of the philosophy of apparitions. (Hibbert, S.) London, 1825.

Phil 8887.19   Sketches of the philosophy of morals. (Morgan, T.C.) London, 1822.

Phil 270.46   Skilvierwski, S.L. Kausalität. Paderborn, 1930.

Phil 5648.2   The skin considered as an organ of sensation. (Lemon, J.S.) Gardner, Mass., 1896.

Phil 5625.120   Skinner, B.F. Contingencies of reinforcement. N.Y., 1969.

Phil 5258.120   Skinner, Burrhus F. Behavior of organisms. N.Y., 1938.

Phil 5258.120.20A   Skinner, Burrhus F. Beyond freedom and dignity. 1st ed. N.Y., 1971.

Phil 5258.155A   Skinner, Burrhus F. Cumulative record. N.Y., 1959.

Phil 5258.155.5A   Skinner, Burrhus F. Cumulative record. N.Y., 1961.

Phil 5258.120.8   Skinner, Burrhus F. Science and human behavior. Cambridge, Mass.? 1951.

Phil 5258.120.10   Skinner, Burrhus F. Science and human behavior. N.Y., 1953.

Phil 5258.120.12   Skinner, Burrhus F. Science and human behavior. N.Y., 1958.

Phil 5258.120.13   Skinner, Burrhus F. Science and human behavior. N.Y., 1964.

Phil 5258.120.15   Skinner, Burrhus F. Verbal behavior. N.Y., 1957.

Phil 9240.3   Skinner, Clarence R. Human nature, or The nature of evil. Boston, 1939.

Phil 185.41.5   Skinner, J.E. Self and world; the religious philosophy of Richard Kroner. Philadelphia, 1963.

Phil 3450.19.390   Skirbekk, Gunnar. Dei filosofiske vilkår for sanning. Oslo, 1966.

Phil 531.8   Skjeroheim, Hans. Objectivism and the study of man. Oslo, 1959.

Phil 4635.10.30   Skjervheim, Hans. Vitskapen om mennesket ogden filosofiske refleksjon. Oslo, 1964.

Phil 7069.62.30   Det skjulte menneske. (Schjelderup, Harald Krabbe.) København, 1962.

Phil 4769.1.101   Skobtsov, E. Mirosozertsanie Vl. Solov'eva. Paris, 1929.

Phil 5058.104   Skolem, Thoralf. Selected works in logic. Oslo, 1970.

Phil 4800.28   Skolimowski, Henryk. Polish analytical philosophy. London, 1967.

Phil 4803.794.30   Skolimowski, Henryk. Polski Marksizm. Londyn, 1969.

Phil 1135.200   Skovgaard Jensen, Søren. Dualism and demonology. Thesis. København, 1966.

Phil 5828.10   Skowronnek, Fritz. Seelenleben der Tiere. Berlin, 1911.

Phil 5640.32   Skramlik, E. von. Handbuch der Physiologie der niederen Sinne. Leipzig, 1926.

Phil 3120.8.89   Skrbensky, L.H. Franz Brentano als Religionsphilosophie. Zürich, 1937.

Phil 4520.6.2   Skrifter. (Björklund, G.) Upsala, 1924.

Phil 4525.2.5   Skrifter. (Claeson, Krist.) Stockholm, 1860. 2v.

Phil 4600.6.2   Skrifter. (Lagerwall, A.) Göteborg, 1921.

Phil 4655.1.2   Skrifter. (Wikner, Pontus.) Stockholm, 1920-27. 12v.

Phil 4515.10   Skrifter af C.J. Boström utgifna af H. Edfeldt. v.1-3. (Boström, C.J.) Upsala, 1883-1901. 2v.

Phil 349.6   Skrochowski, F. Human knowledge. Cnacow, 1893.

Phil 8420.21   Skupienie i marzenie. (Tatarkiewicz, W.) Kraków, 1951.

Phil 4769.10   Skvortsov, Lev V. Obretaet li metafizika vtoroe dykhanie. Moskva, 1966.

Phil 8598.67.5   Skvortsov-Stepanov, I.I. Izbra mye ateisticheskie proizve - deniia. Moskva, 1959.

Phil 5058.102   Skyrms, Brian. Choice and chance; an introduction to inductive logic. Belmont, Calif., 1968.

Phil 5190.24.10   Slaatte, Howard Alexander. The pertinence of the paradox. N.Y., 1968.

Phil 8598.11   Slack, David B. The celestial magnet. Providence, R.I., 1820-21. 2 pam.

Phil 8598.70   Slack, Robert. Old truths and modern progress. London, 1856.

Phil 5938.5   Slade, J. Colloquies. Imaginary conversations between a phrenologist and the shade of Dugald Stewart. London, 1838.

Phil 6328.7   Slade, T. Kenrick. Our phantastic emotions. London, 1923.

Phil 6328.28   Sladen, F.J. Psychiatry and the war. 1st ed. Baltimore, 1943.

Phil 5520.380   Slama-Cazacu, T. Langage et contexte. 's-Gravenhage, 1961.

Phil 8643.13   Slater, J.R. Living for the future. Boston, 1916.

Phil 8643.12   Slattery, C.L. The gift of immortality. Boston, 1916.

Phil 8968.14   Slattery, M. Thy kingdom come...but not now. N.Y., 1938.

Phil 8419.70   Slattery, Mary Francis. Hazard, form, and value. Detroit, 1971.

Phil 8643.134.35   Slattery, Sarah L. A year with the Oxford Group. Cambridge, 193-?

Phil 176.138.15   Slavery and freedom. (Berdiaev, Nikolai A.) London, 1943.

Phil 176.138.16   Slavery and freedom. (Berdiaev, Nikolai A.) N.Y., 1944.

Phil 4769.1.90   Slavianofil'stvo i natsionalizm; otvet k Solov'evy. (Kireev, A.A.) Petrograd, 1905.

Phil 8550.508   Slavonic religious philosophy. (Lossky, Nikolai O.) n.p., n.d.

Phil 5258.203   Slavskaia, Kseniia A. Mysl' v deistvii. Moskva, 1968.

Phil 7140.140   Slavson, S.R. An introduction to group therapy. N.Y., 1943.

Phil 7140.140.6   Slavson, S.R. An introduction to group therapy. N.Y., 1954.

Phil 7080.58   Sleep, dreams, and arousal. (Murray, Edward.) N.Y., 1965.

Phil 7080.13   Sleep, its physiology, pathology, hygiene and psychology. (Manaceine, M. de.) London, 1897.

Phil 7080.3   Sleep. (Fosgate, B.) N.Y., 1850.

Phil 7080.56   Sleep. (Luce, Gay Gaer.) N.Y., 1966.

Phil 7080.47   Sleep and dreams. (Scholz, F.) N.Y., 1893.

NEDL Phil 7080.5.2   Sleep and its derangements. (Hammond, W.A.) Philadelphia, 1869.

Phil 7080.26   Sleep and sleeplessness. (Bruce, H.A.) Boston, 1915.

Phil 7080.4   Sleep and sleeplessness. (Granville, J.M.) Boston, 1881.

Phil 7085.10   Sleep walking and moon walking. (Sadger, Isidor.) N.Y., 1920.

Phil 6672.14A   Sleeping through space. 1st ed. (Cannon, A.) N.Y., 1939.

Phil 8599.19.5   Sleigh, R.S. The sufficiency of Christianity and Ernst Troeltsch. London, 1923.

Phil 193.72.5   Slesser, Henry H. The judicial office and other matters. London, 1943.

Phil 193.72   Slesser, Henry H. The nature of being...essay in ontology. London, 1919.

Phil 1523.11   Slesser, Henry H. Order and disorder; a study of mediaeval principles. London, 1945.

Phil 5645.30   Sloan, Louise L. The effect of intensity of light...eye and size...on the visibility curve. Diss. n.p., 1926?

Phil 5237.512   Slobin, Dan Isaac. Handbook of Soviet psychology. White Plains, N.Y., 1966.

Phil 5520.736   Slobin, Dan Isaac. Psycholinguistics. Glenview, Ill., 1971.

Phil 575.292   Slobodianuz, Sergei S. Lichnost' llaaz asennost! Moskva, 1971.

Phil 3640.640   Slobodskoi, I. Fridrikh Nitsche. Sankt Peterburg, 1905.

Phil 5627.91   Slocum, Phebe B. Akin. Witnessing. Brattleboro, 1899.

Phil 4195.89   Sloek, Johannes. Tradition og nybrud. København, 1957.

Phil 5768.13   Slosson, P.W. Fated or free? Boston, 1914.

Phil 645.60   Slote, Michael A. Reason and scepticism. London, 1970.

Phil 3001.7   Slotemaker de Bruine, N.A.C. Eschatologie en Historie. Wageningen, 1925.

Phil 8980.795   Slovak, Emil. Desat prikazani. Bratislava, 1968.

Phil 8980.3   Slovar po etike. Izd. 2. (Drobnitskii, Oleg G.) Moskva, 1970.

Phil 5867.5   Slovenko, Ralph. Motivations in play, games and sports. Springfield, 1967.

Phil 130.11F   Słownik filozofów. Warszawa, 1966.

Phil 5828.21   Sluchin, Wladyslaw. Imprinting and early learning. Chicago, 1965.

Phil 5535.44   Sluckin, Wladyslaw. Early learning in man and animal. London, 1970.

Phil 6328.66   Small, Saul Mouchly. Symptoms of personality disorder. N.Y., 1944.
Phil 6968.24   Small, Victor R. I knew 3000 lunatics. N.Y., 1935.
Phil 5062.7   Smart, B.H. Easy lessons on reasoning. Boston, 1857.
Phil 5062.6.55 Smart, B.H. A letter to Dr. Whately. London, 1852.
Phil 5520.47   Smart, B.H. Thought and language: an essay on...Locke's philosophy. London, 1855.
Phil 193.29   Smart, Benjamin Humphrey. Beginnings of a new school of metaphysics. London, 1839.
Phil 8968.9   Smart, G.T. Studies in conduct. N.Y., 1909.
Phil 5058.41   Smart, Harold R. The philosophical presuppositions of mathematical logic. Thesis. N.Y., 1925.
Phil 818.34   Smart, Hawed. Philosophy and its history. La Salle, 1962.
Phil 193.231.2 Smart, J. Philosophy and and scientific realism. N.Y., 1963.
Phil 193.231   Smart, J. Philosophy and scientific realism. London, 1963.
Phil 672.229   Smart, John Jamieson Carswell. Problems of space and time. N.Y., 1964.
Phil 960.249   Smart, Ninian. Doctrine and argument in Indian philosophy. London, 1964.
Phil 8598.131   Smart, Ninian. Historical selections in the philosophy of religion. London, 1962.
Phil 5090.6   Smedley, E.A. Treatise on moral evidence. Cambridge, 1850.
Phil 5545.189   Smedslund, Jan. Multiple-probability learning. Oslo, 1955.
Phil 6128.10   Smee, Alfred. Elements of electrobiology. London, 1849.
Phil 6128.10.3 Smee, Alfred. Principle of the human mind, deduced from physical laws. N.Y., 1850.
Phil 6128.10.2 Smee, Alfred. Principle of the human mind, sequel to elements of electrobiology. London, 1849.
Phil 3640.311   Smelik, Evert Louis. Vergelden en wergeven. Thesis. 's-Gravenhage, 1943.
Phil 5590.426   Smelser, Neil Joseph. Personality and social systems. N.Y., 1963.
Phil 5590.426.2 Smelser, Neil Joseph. Personality and social systems. 2. ed. N.Y., 1970.
Phil 5520.710   Smerud, Warren B. Can there be a private language? The Hague, 1970.
Phil 4873.10   Smet, Richard V. de. Philosophical activity in Pakistan. Lahore, 1961.
Phil 4809.796.1 Smetana, Augustin. Şebrané spisy. Praha, 1960- 2v.
Phil 4809.796.36 Smetana, Augustin. Uvahy o budoncnosti lidstva. Praha, 1903.
Phil 4809.796.30 Smetana, Augustin. Vznik a zánik ducha. Praha, 1923.
Phil 5058.39   Smiglecki, Marcin. Logica Martini. Oxonii, 1658.
VPhil 9245.125 The smile. (Curry, Samuel Silas.) Boston, 1915.
Phil 9035.7.13 Smiles, S. El carácter; version española. Paris, 1892.
Phil 9035.7.5   Smiles, S. Character. Chicago, 1890.
Phil 9035.7   Smiles, S. Character. N.Y., 1880?
Phil 9120.4.13 Smiles, S. El deber; versión española. Paris, 1898.
Phil 9120.4.5   Smiles, S. Duty. Chicago, 1890.
Phil 9120.4.3   Smiles, S. Duty. London, 1880.
Phil 9120.4   Smiles, S. Duty. N.Y., 1881.
Phil 8893.14.15 Smiles, Samuel. The art of living. Boston, 1887.
Phil 8893.14.9 Smiles, Samuel. Ayúdate! Self-help. 5. ed. Paris, 1900.
Phil 8893.14.3 Smiles, Samuel. Life and labour. Chicago, 1891.
Phil 8893.14   Smiles, Samuel. Life and labour. London, 1887.
Phil 8893.14.2 Smiles, Samuel. Life and labour. N.Y., 1888.
Phil 8893.14.7 Smiles, Samuel. Self-help. Chicago, 1890.
Phil 8893.14.8.25 Smiles, Samuel. Self-help. London, 1958.
Phil 8893.14.4 Smiles, Samuel. Self-help. N.Y., 1860.
NEDL Phil 8893.14.8 Smiles, Samuel. Self-help. N.Y., 1870.
Phil 8893.14.6.5 Smiles, Samuel. Self-help. N.Y., 1875.
Phil 8893.14.8.20 Smiles, Samuel. Self-help. N.Y., 1915.
Phil 8893.14.13 Smiles, Samuel. Thrift. Chicago, 1890.
Phil 8893.14.11 Smiles, Samuel. Thrift. Toronto, 1876.
Phil 5870.30   Smirnoff, Victor. La psychanalyse de l'enfant. Paris, 1966.
Phil 5545.225   Smirnov, Anatolii A. Problemy psikhologii pamiati. Moskva, 1966.
Phil 5585.85   Smirnov, M.T. Protsess poznaniia v obuchenii. Moskva, 1956.
VPhil 175.66   Smisao i vrednost eqzistencije. (Atanasijević, Ksenija.) Beograd, 1968.
Phil 3903.3.80 Smit, H.W.V.D.V. Hans Vaihinger en de als-ob-philosophie. Baarn, 1925.
Phil 3500.65A   Smith, A.H. Kantian studies. Oxford, 1947.
Phil 349.38   Smith, A.H. A treatise on knowledge. Oxford, 1943.
Phil 9150.8   Smith, A.W. A new theory of evolution. N.Y., 1901.
Phil 8598.75   Smith, Abbot Edes. Philosophy of life; with an appendix on the Bible. Norwood, 1938.
Phil 2266.35   Smith, Adam. A dissertation on the origin of languages. Tübingen, 1970.
Phil 2266.50   Smith, Adam. The early writings of Adam Smith. N.Y., 1967.
Phil 2266.30.5 Smith, Adam. Essay on philosophical subjects. Basil, 1799.
Phil 2266.30.10 Smith, Adam. Essays; philosophical and literary. London, 1880?
Phil 2266.30   Smith, Adam. Essays. London, 1795.
Phil 2266.30.50A Smith, Adam. Essays on I. Moral sentiment; II. Astronomical inquiries. London, 1869.
Htn Phil 2266.68* Smith, Adam. An inquiry into the nature and causes of the wealth of nations. London, 1776. 2v.
Phil 2266.70   Smith, Adam. An inquiry into the nature and causes of the wealth of nations. London, 1796. 3v.
Phil 2266.43.5 Smith, Adam. La métaphysique de l'âme. Paris, 1764. 2v.
Phil 2266.20   Smith, Adam. Moral and political philosophy. N.Y., 1948.
Phil 2266.42   Smith, Adam. Theorie der ethischen Gefühle. Leipzig, 1926. 2v.
Phil 2266.42.5 Smith, Adam. Theorie der sittlichen Gefühle. Leipzig, 1791-95. 2v.
Phil 2266.43   Smith, Adam. Théorie des sentiments moraux. Paris, 1830. 2v.
Htn Phil 2266.36* Smith, Adam. The theory of moral sentiments. London, 1759.
Phil 2266.41.5 Smith, Adam. The theory of moral sentiments. N.Y., 1966.
Phil 2266.41.10 Smith, Adam. The theory of moral sentiments. New Rochelle, 1969.
Phil 2266.41.2 Smith, Adam. The theory of moral sentiments. Philadelphia, 1817.
Phil 2266.41   Smith, Adam. The theory of moral sentiments. v.1-2. Boston, 1817.
Phil 2266.37   Smith, Adam. The theory of moral sentiments. 2nd ed. London, 1761.

Phil 2266.38   Smith, Adam. The theory of moral sentiments. 7th ed. London, 1792. 2v.
Phil 6060.23   Smith, Albert J. Applied graphology. N.Y., 1920.
Phil 8893.15   Smith, Alexander. The philosophy of morals. London, 1835. 2v.
Phil 5545.224   Smith, Brian. Memory. London, 1966.
Phil 2418.6   Smith, C. Contemporary French philosophy. N.Y., 1964.
Phil 2268.3.100 Smith, Charles. Sensism, the philosophy of the West. N.Y., 1956. 2v.
Phil 9178.3   Smith, D.D. Lectures on domestic duties. Portland, 1837.
Phil 5545.30   Smith, D.T. The philosophy of memory. Louisville, Ky., 1899.
Phil 5535.3   Smith, David D. Mammalian learning and behavior. Philadelphia, 1965.
Phil 2636.91   Smith, David Warner. Helvetius; a study in persecution. Oxford, 1965.
Phil 5850.340.50 Smith, E.D. Psychology for executives. N.Y., 1928.
Phil 5828.7   Smith, E.M. The investigation of mind in animals. Cambridge, 1915.
Phil 5828.7.2   Smith, E.M. The investigation of mind in animals. 2. ed. Cambridge, 1923.
Phil 9400.20   Smith, E.S. The dynamics of aging. 1st ed. N.Y., 1956.
Phil 8893.97   Smith, F.B. Men wanted. N.Y., 1911.
Phil 5465.214   Smith, Frederick Madison. The higher powers of man. Thesis. Lamoni, Ia., 1918.
Phil 5258.185   Smith, Frederick Viggers. The explanation of human behavior. London, 1951.
Phil 8968.16   Smith, G.B. Social idealism and the changing theology. N.Y., 1913.
Phil 5058.21   Smith, G.H. Logic. N.Y., 1901.
Phil 9070.3   Smith, G.W. Constructive human relationship. Kutztown, Pa., 1940.
Phil 9330.1   Smith, Garnet. The melancholy of Stephen Allard. N.Y., 1895.
Phil 720.45   Smith, Gerard. The truth that frees. Milwaukee, 1956.
Phil 8598.36   Pamphlet box. Smith, Gerrit. Pamphlets on religion.
Phil 8598.12.15 Smith, Goldwin. Guesses at the riddle of existence. N.Y., 1897.
Phil 8598.12.5 Smith, Goldwin. Inquest of light. N.Y., 1906.
Phil 8598.12.9 Smith, Goldwin. No refuge but in truth. N.Y., 1909.
Phil 8598.12.3 Smith, Goldwin. Rational religion. Oxford, 1861.
Phil 8598.12   Smith, Goldwin. Sermons and speeches. N.Y., 1861.
Phil 3838.3   Smith, H. Spinoza...environment. Cincinnatti, 1886.
Phil 193.108   Smith, H.B. The collective mind. Columbus, 1924.
Phil 5058.28.5 Smith, Henry B. A first book in logic. N.Y., 1922.
Phil 5058.28.17 Smith, Henry B. Foundations of formal logic. Philadelphia, 1922.
Phil 5058.28.21 Smith, Henry B. How the mind falls into error. N.Y., 1923.
Phil 5058.28.15 Smith, Henry B. Letters on logic, to a young man. Philadelphia, 1920.
Phil 5058.28.9 Smith, Henry B. Non-Aristotelian logic. Philadelphia, 1919.
Phil 5058.28   Smith, Henry B. A primer of logic. Pulaski, 1917.
Phil 5058.28.28 Smith, Henry B. Symbolic logic: method and development. N.Y., 1927.
Phil 5058.28.18 Smith, Henry B. A system of formal logic. Ann Arbor, 1925.
Phil 5058.28.19 Smith, Henry B. A system of formal logic. pt.1. Columbus, 1926.
Phil 5421.15.25 Smith, Henry Clay. Sensitivity to people. N.Y., 1966.
Phil 7069.19.200 Smith, Hester T. Voices from the void. N.Y., 1919.
Phil 5520.452   Smith, Huston. Condemned to meaning. 1. ed. N.Y., 1965.
Phil 5585.230   Smith, Ian Macfarlane. Spatial ability. 1. ed. San Diego, Calif., 1964.
Phil 8893.36   Smith, J.A. Knowing and acting. Oxford, 1910.
Phil 6128.4   Smith, J.A. Select discourses on the functions of the nervous system. N.Y., 1840.
Phil 5058.14   Smith, J.C. Culmination of the science of logic. Brooklyn, 1888.
Phil 6328.22   Smith, J.C. Psykiatriske forelaesninger. København, 1939.
Phil 8598.130   Smith, J.E. Reason and God. New Haven, 1961.
Phil 2250.96   Smith, J.E. Royce's social infinite. N.Y., 1950.
Phil 1818.11   Smith, J.E. The spirit of American philosophy. N.Y., 1963.
Phil 6128.3   Smith, J.M. A discourse on the influence of diseases on the intellectual and moral powers. N.Y., 1848.
Phil 193.172   Smith, J.W. Theme for reason. Princeton, 1957.
Phil 8598.137   Smith, John E. Philosophy of religion. N.Y., 1965.
Phil 8598.141   Smith, John Edwin. Religion and empiricism. Milwaukee, 1967.
Htn Phil 2268.1.30* Smith, Joseph. The book of Mormon. Palmyra, 1830.
Phil 5585.212   Smith, Karl. Perception and motion; analysis of space-structured behavior. Philadelphia, 1962.
Phil 5374.280   Smith, Kendon Rasey. Behavior and conscious experience. Athens, 1969.
Phil 5590.210.2 Smith, M.B. Opinions and personality. N.Y., 1964.
Phil 1020.7.10 Smith, Margaret. Al-Ghazáli, the mystic. London, 1944.
Phil 525.72   Smith, Margaret. Studies in early mysticism in the Near and Middle East. London, 1931.
Phil 5850.341.5 Smith, May. Handbook of industrial psychology. N.Y., 1944.
Phil 5850.341   Smith, May. An introduction to industrial psychology. London, 1943.
Phil 3500.27   Smith, N.K. Commentary to Kant's Critique of pure reason. London, 1918.
Phil 8673.12   Smith, N.K. Is divine existence credible? London, 1931.
Phil 2115.144   Smith, N.K. John Locke, 1632-1704. Manchester, 1933.
Phil 2520.119.5 Smith, N.K. New studies in the philosophy of Descartes. London, 1952.
Phil 2050.210   Smith, N.K. The philosophy of David Hume. London, 1941.
NEDL Phil 2520.119A Smith, N.K. Studies in the Cartesian philosophy. N.Y., 1902.
Phil 2520.119.2 Smith, N.K. Studies in the Cartesian philosophy. N.Y., 1962.
Phil 8708.22   Smith, Nathan A. Through science to God. N.Y., 1936.
Phil 3500.60.5A Smith, Norman K. A commentary to Kant's "Critique of pure reason". 2d ed. London, 1923.
Phil 349.28A   Smith, Norman K. Prolegomena to idealist theory of knowledge. London, 1924.
Phil 8643.24   Smith, O. Tho material, why not immortal? Boston, 1921.
Phil 665.46   Smith, O.J. A short view of great questions. N.Y., 1899.
Phil 8708.17   Smith, Orlando Jay. Balance the fundamental verity. Boston, 1904.
Phil 6049.01   Smith, R.C. Cheirosophy, the hand. London, 1901.
Phil 6990.62   Smith, Robert D. Comparative miracles. St. Louis, 1965.
Phil 3120.30.145 Smith, Ronald Gregor. Martin Buber. Richmond, 1967.
Phil 6968.14   Smith, S. Who is insane? N.Y., 1916.

Phil 9358.3   Smith, S.R. Words to young gentlemen and ladies. Boston, n.d.

Htn Phil 5058.15*   Smith, Samuel. Aditis at logicam. Oxoniae, 1656-1657.
Htn Phil 5058.15.3*   Smith, Samuel. Aditus ad logicam. Oxoniae, 1634.
Phil 5258.66.3   Smith, Stevenson. Chapters in general psychology. Seattle, 1921.
Phil 5258.66.2   Smith, Stevenson. General psychology. N.Y., 1927.
Phil 7055.341   Smith, Susy. Confessions of a psychic. N.Y., 1971.
Phil 7072.5   Smith, Susy. The enigma of out-of-body travel. N.Y., 1965.
Phil 7055.256   Smith, Susy. The mediumship of Mrs. Leonard. New Hyde Park, N.Y., 1964.
Phil 8893.16.5   Smith, Sydney. Elementary sketches of moral philosophy. N.Y., 1850.
Phil 9075.36   Smith, T.V. Beyond conscience. N.Y., 1934.
Phil 645.33   Smith, T.V. Creative sceptics. Chicago, 1934.
Phil 165.1   Smith, T.V. From Descartes to Kant. Chicago, 1940.
Phil 1123.8   Smith, T.V. Philosophers in Hades. Chicago, Ill., 1932.
Phil 193.123   Smith, Thomas V. Essays in philosophy by 17 Ph.D.'s of University of Chicago. Chicago, 1929.
Phil 193.123.5   Smith, Thomas V. The philosophic way of life. Chicago, 1929.
Phil 193.123.8   Smith, Thomas V. The philosophic way of life in America. 2d. ed. N.Y., 1943.
Phil 9540.8   Smith, Thomas Vernor. The ethics of compromise and the art of containment. Boston, 1956.
Phil 1718.23   Smith, V.E. Idea man of today. Milwaukee, 1950.
Phil 3246.84   Smith, W. Memoir. Boston, 1846.
Phil 8598.133   Smith, W.C. The meaning and end of religion. N.Y., 1963.
Phil 672.121   Smith, W.W. A theory of the mechanism of survival; the fourth dimension. London, 1920.
Phil 349.11   Smith, Walter. Methods of knowledge. N.Y., 1899.
Phil 7069.20.310   Smith, Walter W. The foundations of spiritualism. N.Y., 1920.
Phil 4120.4.140   Smith, William Aloysius. Giovanni Gentile on the existence of God. Louvain, 1970.
Phil 8843.14   Smith, Wilson. Professors and public ethics. Ithaca, N.Y., 1956.
Phil 8110.12   Smith,A.C. Theories of the nature and standard of taste in England, 1700-1790. Chicago, 1937.
Phil 58.12   Smith College. William Allen Neilson Research Laboratory. Studies in psychology. Northampton.
Phil 3450.27.80   Smits, Everard J.F. Herders humaniteitsphilosophie. Assen, 1939.
Phil 3850.20.84   Smits, J.P. Filosofies opooedkundige sketse. Amsterdam, 1929.
Phil 5592.175   Smits, Willem C.M. Onderzoek naar de kleurintentionaliteit. Nijmegen, 1964.
Phil 5645.60   Smits, Willem Canisius Maria. Symboliek van de kleut. Amsterdam, 1967.
Phil 8583.9.5   The smoke and the flame. (Dole, Charles F.) Boston, 1892.
Phil 5627.268.5   Smolenaars, A.J. Kerkelijkheid en persoonlijkheidskenmerken in twee Zuiderzeepolders. Amsterdam, 1968.
Phil 2905.1.267   Smulders, P.F. Theologie und Evolution. Essen, 1963.
Phil 2905.1.265   Smulders, P.F. Het visioen van Teilhard de Chardin. Brugge, 1962.
Phil 2905.1.266   Smulders, P.F. La vision de Teilhard de Chardin. Paris, 1964.
Phil 365.19A   Smuts, J.C. Holism and evolution. N.Y., 1926.
Phil 818.39   Smuts, Johannes Petrus. Kruispaaie van die filosofie. Kaapstad, 1968.
Phil 8980.546   Smysl lidského života. (Machovec, Milan.) Praha, 1965.
Phil 282.8   Smysl tvorchestva. (Berdiaev, N.) Moskva, 1916.
Phil 8419.50   Smysl věcí. (Šindelář, Dušan.) Praha, 1963.
Phil 286.8   Smysl zhizni. (Frank, S.L.) Paris, 1925.
Phil 300.4   Smysl' zhizni. (Trubetskoi, E.N.) Berlin, 1922.
Phil 818.2   Smyth, C.B. Christian metaphysics. London, 1851.
Phil 8643.19   Smyth, John P. The gospel of the hereafter. N.Y., 1910.
Phil 8643.19.10   Smyth, John P. The gospel of the hereafter. N.Y., 1930.
Phil 8968.4   Smyth, N. Christian ethics. N.Y., 1892.
Phil 8643.30   Smyth, Newman. Modern belief in immortality. N.Y., 1910.
Phil 8708.8   Smyth, Newman. Through science to faith. N.Y., 1902.
Phil 5585.81   Smythies, J.R. Analysis of perception. London, 1956.
Phil 6128.78   Smythies, John Raymond. Brain and mind. London, 1965.
Phil 7069.67.25   Smythies, John Raymond. Science and the E.S.P. London, 1967.
Phil 8598.53   Snaith, John. The philosophy of spirit. London, 1914.
Phil 8843.11   Sneath, E.H. Evolution of ethics...in great religions. New Haven, 1927.
Phil 8893.82   Snell, C.W. Die sittlichkei Verbindung mit der Glükseligkeit einzelner Menschen und gauzer Staaten. Frankfurt, 1790.
Phil 3500.91   Snell, Christian. Lehrbuch der Kritik des Geschmach. Leipzig, 1795.
Phil 3500.35   Snell, E.W.D. Darstellung und Erläuterung I. Kant Critik. v.1-2. Mannheim, 1791.
Phil 5058.42   Snell, F.W.D. Erste Grundlinien der Logik oder Verstandeslehre. Gieosen, 1828.
Phil 3500.35.5   Snell, F.W.D. Menon oder Versuch in Gesprächen. Mannheim, 1789.
Phil 3500.35.7   Snell, F.W.D. Menon oder Versuch in Gesprächen. 2. Aufl. Mannheim, 1796.
Phil 299.18   Snell, Karl. Philosophische Betrachtungen der Natur. Dresden, 1839.
Phil 8598.13   Snell, M.M. One hundred theses, foundations of human knowledge. Washington, 1891.
Phil 818.16   Snell, P.L. Kurzer Abriss der Geschichte der Philosophie. Giessen, 1819. 2v.
Phil 193.117   Snellman, J.W. Philosophisk elementar-curs. 1. Psychologi; 2. Logik; 3. Rättslära. Stockholm, 1837-1840. 3 pam.
Phil 2050.251   Snethlage, J.L. David Hume. Den Haag, 1963.
Phil 4803.799.2   Śniadecki, Jan. Dzieła. v.1-7. Warszawa, 1837-39. 3v.
Phil 4803.799.25   Śniadecki, Jan. Korespondencja Jana Śniadeckiego; listy z Krakowa. Krakow, 1932-54. 2v.
Phil 4803.799.23   Śniadecki, Jan. Pisma filozoficzne. Warszawa, 1958. 2v.
Phil 4803.799.22   Śniadecki, Jan. Pisma pedagogiczne. Wrocław, 1961.
Phil 4803.799.20   Śniadecki, Jan. Pisma rozmaite. Wilno, 1818-22. 4v.
Phil 4803.799.21   Śniadecki, Jan. Wybor pism naukowych. Warszawa, 1954.
Phil 1123.4   Snider, D.J. Ancient European philosophy...Greek. St. Louis, Mo., 1903.
Phil 5258.19.5   Snider, D.J. Feeling psychologically treated. St.Louis, 1905.
Phil 5258.19   Snider, D.J. Psychology and the psychosis. St.Louis, 1896.

Phil 193.73.5   Snider, Denton J. The biocomos...life psychologically ordered. St. Louis, 1911.
Phil 193.73   Snider, Denton J. Cosmos and diacosmos...nature psychologically treated. St. Louis, 1909.
Phil 1718.5   Snider, Denton J. Modern European philosophy. Saint Louis, 1904.
Phil 5768.16   Snider, Denton J. The will and its world. St. Louis, 1899.
Phil 5599.80   Snider, James G. Semantic differential technique; a sourcebook. Chicago, 1969.
Phil 5425.31   Snille och sjalssjukdom. (Herrlin, Axel.) Lund, 1903.
Phil 7069.27.60   Snipes, Joseph F. Fifty years in psychic research. Boston, 1927.
Phil 9558.27   Le snobisme. (DuPuy de Clinchamps, Philippe.) Paris, 1964.
Phil 5258.71   Snow, Adolph J. Problems in psychology. N.Y., 1923.
Phil 8598.14   Snow, G.D. A theologico-political treatise. London, 1874.
Phil 7054.104   Snow, H. Spirit-intercourse containing incidents of personal experience. Boston, 1853.
Phil 8643.14.5   Snowden, J.F. Can we believed in immortality. N.Y., 1919.
Phil 8708.16   Snowden, J.H. Old faith and new knowledge. N.Y., 1928.
Phil 193.56   Snowden, J.H. The world a spiritual system. N.Y., 1910.
Phil 299.7.5   Snyder, C. The world machine...cosmic mechanism. N.Y., 1907.
Phil 6128.32   Snyder, John Jacob. How to obtain happiness and health. Chicago, 1905.
Phil 6980.699   Snyder, William U. The psychotherapy relationship. N.Y., 1961.
Phil 5520.145.5   So much nearer; essays toward a world English. 1. ed. (Richards, Ivor Armstrong.) N.Y., 1968.
Phil 7069.19.210   "So saith the spirit." London, 1919.
Phil 7069.47.15   Soal, Samuel G. The experimental situation in psychical research. London, 1947.
Phil 7069.59.10   Soal, Samuel G. The mind readers. London, 1959.
Phil 7069.54.5   Soal, Samuel G. Modern experiments in telepathy. New Haven, 1954.
Phil 818.35   Soares, L.R. Quatro meditacões sobre o filósofo. Porto, 1963.
Phil 3640.730   Sobejano, Gónzalo. Nietzsche en España. Madrid, 1967.
Phil 8892.1   Sober thoughts on staple themes. (Randolph, R.) Philadelphia, 1889.
Phil 8419.34   Sobeski, M. Myśl a marmur, i inne szkice estetyczne. Wyd. 1. Warszawa, 1959.
Phil 5648.3   Sobeski, M. Über Täuschungen des Tastsinns. Breslau, 1903.
Phil 3425.613   Sobotka, Milan. Die idealistische Dialektik der Praxis bei Hegel. Praha, 1965.
Phil 4770.1   Sobranie sochinenii. v.1-2,5-6. (Trubetskoi, S.N.) Moskva, 1907. 4v.
Phil 1111.5   Sobre estetica griega. (Garcia Bacca, J.D.) Mexico, 1943.
Phil 3450.19.335   Sobre Heidegger. (Fraga, Gustavo de.) Coimbra, 1965.
Phil 4351.2   Sobre la cultura. (Arias, Alejandro C.) Montevideo, 1943.
Phil 4957.35   Sobre la filosofía en América. (Romero, Francisco.) Buenos Aires, 1952.
Phil 3480.125   Sochineniia. (Kant, Immanuel.) Moskva, 1963. 6v.
Phil 8703.1   Sociabilidade natural do homem. (Netto. F.J.) Povoa de Varzim, 1914.
Phil 5241.3.5A   Social and ethical interpretations. Mental development. (Baldwin, J.M.) N.Y., 1897.
Phil 5241.3.6   Social and ethical interpretations. Mental development. (Baldwin, J.M.) N.Y., 1902.
Phil 5241.3.6.10   Social and ethical interpretations. Mental development. 5. ed. (Baldwin, J.M.) N.Y., 1913.
Phil 2750.11.78   The social and political philosophy of Jacques Maritain. (Maritain, Jacques.) N.Y., 1955.
Phil 2005.11   The social and political thought of Adam Ferguson. (Kettler, David.) Columbus, 1965.
Phil 9362.17   Social and religious problems and young people. (Weston, S.A.) N.Y., 1934.
Phil 8951.15   Social aspects of Christian morality. (Bruce, William S.) London, 1905.
Phil 6128.55   Social aspects of mental hygiene. New Haven, 1925.
Phil 5374.45.2   The social basis of consciousness. (Burrow, Trigant.) N.Y., 1927.
Phil 6322.32   Social change and scientific progress. (Menninger, W.C.) Portland, 1951.
Phil 6957.25   Social class and mental illness. (Hollingshead, A. de B.) N.Y., 1958.
Phil 5875.65.5   Social class language and communication. (Brandis, Walter.) London, 1970.
Phil 2150.15.107   The social concepts of George Herbert Mead. (Tremmel, William C.) Emporia, 1927.
Phil 2150.15.105   The social concepts of George Herbert Mead. (Tremmel, William C.) Emporia, 1957.
Phil 193.126   The social contract of the universe. (Stone, Charles G.) London, 1930.
Phil 9400.15   Social contribution by the aging. (American Academy of Political and Social Science, Philadelphia.) Philadelphia, 1952.
Phil 6750.223   Social control of the feebleminded. (Davies, S.P.) N.Y., 1923.
Phil 6750.223.10   Social control of the mentally deficient. (Davies, S.P.) N.Y., 1930.
Phil 5592.70   The social desirability variable in personality assessment and research. (Edwards, A.L.) N.Y., 1957.
Phil 8889.8.5   Social determinants of moral ideas. (Ossowska, Maria.) Philadelphia, 1970.
Phil 5649.42   Social dimensions of physical activity. (Cratty, Bryant J.) Englewood Cliffs, 1967.
Phil 2150.15.100   The social dynamics of George H. Mead. (Natanson, M.) Washington, 1956.
Phil 9495.22   The social emergency. (Foster, W.T.) Boston, 1914.
Phil 8897.34   Social environment and moral progress. (Wallace, A.R.) N.Y., 1913.
Phil 6959.9   The social epidemiology of mental disorders. (Jaco, E.G.) N.Y., 1960.
Phil 9513.4   Social equilibrium. (Batchelor, George.) Boston, 1887.
Phil 8887.75   Social ethics; natural law in the modern world. (Messner, J.) St. Louis, 1949.
Phil 9513.18   Social ethics. (Hanis, Robert T.) Philadelphia, 1962.
Phil 8900.1.5   Social ethics. (Zeigler, T.) London, 1892.
Phil 9495.5   Social evil in university life. (Willson, R.N.) N.Y., 1904.
Phil 8520.11   The social evolution of religion. (Cooke, George W.) Boston, 1920.
Phil 5467.8   Social facilitation and imitative behavior. (Miami. University. Symposium on Social Behavior, 1st, 1967.) Boston, 1968.

Phil 575.99 Social forces in personality stunting. (Kamiat, A.H.) Cambridge, 1933.
Phil 7150.95 Social forces in urban suicide. (Maris, Ronald W.) Homewood, 1969.
Phil 8589.18 Social functions of religion. (James, E.O.) Nashville, 1940.
Phil 8968.16 Social idealism and the changing theology. (Smith, G.B.) N.Y., 1913.
Phil 6310.1.22 Social interest. (Adler, A.) London, 1938.
Phil 5500.22 Social judgment. (Sherif, Muzafer.) New Haven, 1961.
Phil 5850.328.10 Social learning and clinical psychology. (Rotter, Julian.) Englewood Cliffs, N.J., 1958.
Phil 5252.78A Social learning and imitation. (Miller, N.E.) New Haven, 1941.
Phil 5252.78.5 Social learning and imitation. (Miller, N.E.) New Haven, 1953.
Phil 5590.427 Social learning and personality development. (Bandura, A.) N.Y., 1963.
Phil 7150.64 The social meanings of suicide. (Douglas, Jack D.) Princeton, 1967.
Phil 8887.10 Social morality. (Maurice, F.D.) London, 1869.
Phil 5245.82 The social nature of psychological research. (Friedman, Neil.) N.Y., 1967.
Phil 1718.22A Social philosophies of an age of crisis. (Sorokin, P.) Boston, 1950.
Phil 2490.98A The social philosophy...of Comte. 2nd ed. (Caird, Edward.) Glasgow, 1893.
Phil 585.135.2 Social philosophy. (Plattel, Martinus Gulielmus.) Pittsburgh, 1965.
Phil 2490.98.1 The social philosophy and religion of Comte. (Caird, Edward.) Glasgow, 1885.
Phil 1807.6 Social philosophy and the social mind. (Holmes, E.C.) N.Y., 1942.
Phil 1807.5A Social philosophy and the social mind. Thesis. (Holmes, E.C.) N.Y., 1942.
Phil 1812.14 The social philosophy of English idealism. (Milne, A.J.M.) London, 1962.
Phil 4120.4.89 The social philosophy of Giovanni Gentile. (Harris, Henry S.) Urbana, 1960.
Phil 5819.3.5 The social philosophy of instinct. (Josey, Charles C.) N.Y., 1922.
Phil 2250.60 The social philosophy of Josiah Royce. (Royce, Josiah.) Syracuse, 1950.
Phil 6319.11 Social psychiatry. (Jones, Maxwell.) London, 1952.
Phil 5257.52 Social psychology. (Reinbardt, J.M.) Chicago, 1938.
Phil 2150.15.96 The social psychology of George Herbert Mead. (Meltzer, Bernard.) Kalamazoo, Michigan, 1964.
Phil 2150.15.95 The social psychology of George Herbert Meal. (Mead, G.H.) Chicago, 1956.
Phil 5270.30 The social psychology of psychological research. (Miller, Arthur G.) N.Y., 1971.
Phil 5627.262.5 The social psychology of religious experience. (Hopkins, Pryns.) N.Y., 1962.
Phil 8893.23.5 Social rights and duties. (Stephen, L.) London, 1896. 2v.
Phil 6980.606 Social science and psychotherapy for children. (Pollak, Otto.) N.Y., 1952.
Phil 5520.428A Social Science Research Committee on Linguistics and Psychology. Psycholinguistics; a survey of theory and research problems. Bloomington, 1965.
Phil 2270.55.3 Social statics. (Spencer, Herbert.) London, 1851.
Phil 2270.55.2 Social statics. (Spencer, Herbert.) London, 1851.
Htn Phil 2270.55.1* Social statics. (Spencer, Herbert.) London, 1851.
Phil 2270.55 Social statics. (Spencer, Herbert.) London, 1851.
Phil 2270.55.4 Social statics. (Spencer, Herbert.) N.Y., 1865.
Phil 2270.55.7.5 Social statics. (Spencer, Herbert.) N.Y., 1872.
Phil 2270.55.8 Social statics. (Spencer, Herbert.) N.Y., 1882.
Phil 2270.55.9 Social statics. (Spencer, Herbert.) N.Y., 1886.
NEDL Phil 2270.56.5 Social statics. (Spencer, Herbert.) N.Y., 1893.
Phil 2270.56.6 Social statics. (Spencer, Herbert.) N.Y., 1897.
Phil 2270.56.7 Social statics. (Spencer, Herbert.) N.Y., 1904.
Phil 2270.56.10 Social statics. (Spencer, Herbert.) N.Y., 1954.
Phil 5590.375 Social structure and personality. (Cohen, Yehudi A.) N.Y., 1961.
Phil 575.246 Social structure and personality. (Parsons, Talcott.) N.Y., 1964.
Phil 735.126 The social structure of values. (Mukerjee, Radhakamal.) London, 1950.
Phil 735.126.2 The social structure of values. 2nd ed. (Mukerjee, Radhakamal.) New Delhi, 1965.
Phil 5252.12.29 Social studies of today. (Münsterberg, H.) London, 1913.
Phil 8587.47 Social substance of religion. (Heard, Gerald.) London, 1931.
Phil 6980.712.100 The social theories of Harry Stack Sullivan. (Blisten, D.R.) N.Y., 1953.
Phil 1865.81 Het sociale utilisme van Bentham. (Greyvenstein, J.H.J.A.) Utrecht, 1911.
Phil 5258.146 Das sociale Verhalten. (Seliger, Josef.) Bern, 1903.
Phil 585.135 Sociale wijsbegeerte. v.1-2. (Plattel, Martinus Gulielmus.) Utrecht, 1960-64.
Phil 2648.31.15 Sociales System oder Naturliche Principien der Moral und der Politik. (Holbach, Paul Henri T.) Leipzig, 1898.
Phil 4582.4.49 Socialfilosofiska uppsatser. (Hägerström, Axel.) Stockholm, 1966.
Phil 8657.20 Socialism, atheism and Christianity. (Cohen, Chapman.) London, 1908.
Phil 2750.22.130 Le socialisme d'Emmanuel Mounier. (Barlow, Michel.) Toulouse, 1971.
Phil 2725.4.89 Le socialisme romantique. (Evans, David O.) Paris, 1948.
Phil 1695.29 Socialist humanism. 1st ed. (Fromm, Erich.) Garden City, N.Y., 1965.
Phil 2648.80 Socialiste-révolution au commencement du XVIII siècle. (Petifils, E.) Paris, 1908.
Phil 4582.4.40 De socialistiska idéernas historia. (Hägerström, Axel.) Stockholm, 1946.
Phil 5415.5 Sociality and sympathy. (Jones, J.W.L.) N.Y., 1903.
Phil 8877.36 The socialized conscience. (Coffin, J.H.) Baltimore, 1913.
Phil 28.25 Sociatry; journal of group and intergroup theory. Beacon, N.Y. 2,1948+ 15v.
Phil 165.135 Sociedad Cubana de Filosofía. Conversaciones filosóficas interamericanas. Habana, 1955.
Phil 7068.83.12 Sociedad de Estudios Espiritistas de Key West. Contestación a los detractores del espiritismo. Key West, 1883.
Phil 58.16 Sociedade Brasileira de Filosofía. Anais. Rio de Janeiro. 1-8,1939-1945+
Phil 585.174 Società e cultura. (Cantoni, Remo.) Milano, 1964.

Phil 3850.18.180 Società e cultura nel pensiero di Max Scheler. (Filippone, Vincenzo.) Milano, 1964. 2v.
Phil 70.72 Società Filosofica Italiana. Veritá e libertá di Guzzo. Palumbo, 1960.
Phil 1830.45 Società Filosofica Romana. La filosofia contemporanea in U.S.A. Roma, 1958.
Phil 1740.26 La società fuori tutela. (Calabró, Gaetano.) Napoli, 1970.
Phil 193.166 Società Italiana di Metapsichica. Oltre i cinque sensi. Torino? 1952.
Phil 6315.19.35 La società malata. (Catemario, A.) Napoli, 1962.
Phil 58.10.3 Società per gliStudi Filosofici, Palermo. Bibliotheca Filosofica. Annuario. Palermo, 1912.
Phil 4210.235 Società religiosa e società civile in Rosmini. (Traniello, Francesco.) Bologna, 1966.
Phil 4210.67 La società teocratico. (Rosmini-Serbati, Antonio.) Brescia, 1963.
Phil 3838.23 Societas Spinoza. Septimana Spinozana. Hagae, 1933.
Phil 58.15 Société Belge de Philosophie. Archives. Bruxelles. 1-5,1928-1933
Phil 8592.122.10 Société des Etudes Robespierristes. Études sur le curé Meslier. Paris, 1966.
Phil 58.6 Société Française de Philosophie. Bulletin, 1901-1914. Paris. 1,1901+ 33v.
Phil 3640.698 Société Française d'Études Nietzschéennes. Bulletin. Paris.
Phil 3640.394A Société Française d'Études Nietzschéennes. Nietzsche. Paris, 1950.
Phil 6688.27 Société Harmonique des Amis-Reunis de Strasbourg. Exposé de différentes cures. Strasbourg, 1786.
Phil 58.20 Société Internationale pour l'Étude de la Philosophie Mediévale. Bulletin. Louvain. 1,1959+ 4v.
Phil 8697.20 Society, evolution and revelation. (Hanaghan, J.) Dublin, 1957.
Phil 70.94.10 Society, revolution and reform; proceedings. (Oberlin Colloquium in Philosophy.) Cleveland, 1971.
Phil 8589.5.10A Society, the redeemed form of man. (James, H.) Boston, 1879.
Phil 333.16 Society and knowledge. 1st ed. (Childe, Vere G.) N.Y., 1956.
Phil 62.1 Society for Philosophical Inquiry, Washington, D.C. Memoirs. Lancaster, Pa. 1-4,1893-1927+
Phil 58.4 Society for Psychical Research, London. Combined index. London, 1904. 3v.
Phil 58.1 Society for Psychical Research, London. Journal. London. 1,1884+ 36v.
Phil 7061.5 Society for Psychical Research, London. Library catalogue of the Society for Psychical Research. Glasgow, 1927.
Phil 58.2.5 Society for Psychical Research, London. Presidential addresses, 1882-1911. Glasgow, 1912.
Phil 58.2 Society for Psychical Research, London. Proceedings. London. 1-49,1882-1952 43v.
Phil 58.2.3 Society for Psychical Research, London. Proceedings. v.1, pt.2-3. London, 1883.
Phil 7069.01 Pamphlet box. The Society for Psychical Research.
Phil 58.5 Pamphlet box. Society for psychical research.
Phil 9380.5A Society for the Psychological Study of Social Issues. Civilian morale. N.Y., 1942.
Phil 5258.118 Society of Applied Psychology. Psychology and achievement. San Francisco, 1914.
Phil 8615.3 Society of Ethical Propagandists. Ethics and religion. London, 1900.
Phil 6949.366 Society of Medical Psycho-Analysts. The etiology of neuroses. Palo Alto, Calif., 1966.
Phil 6976.5 Society of Medical Psychoanalysts. Schizophrenia in psychoanalytic office practice. N.Y., 1957.
Phil 299.16 Society of Universal Science. Belmont, Mass. The system of the universe. Belmont, 1924.
Phil 5590.439 Sociocultural foundations of personality. (Ullman, Albert Daniel.) Boston, 1965.
Phil 8855.2 Sociogenese en evolutie van het probleem der seksuele propaedeuse tussen de 16 en de 18 de eeuw. (Ussel, Jozef Maria Willem van.) Gent, 1967. 2v.
Phil 4352.1.130 La sociologia de Jaime Balmes. (Auhofer, H.J.) Madrid, 1959.
Phil 402.18 Sociologia dell'ideologia. (Leonardi, Franco.) Catania, 1966.
Phil 5421.20.5 A sociological contribution to the understanding of aggression and its treatment. (Folkard, M.S.) Coulsdon, 1961.
Phil 192.62 Sociologie; partie de philosophie. (Roguin, Ernest.) Lausanne, 1928-1929. 3v.
Phil 2490.140 La sociologie d'Auguste Comte. (Lacroix, Jean.) Paris, 1956.
Phil 2490.140.5 La sociologie d'Auguste Comte. 2. éd. (Lacroix, Jean.) Paris, 1961.
Phil 2490.184 Sociologie de Comte. (Arnaud, Pierre.) Paris, 1969.
Phil 3246.247 Die Sociologie Fichte's. (Schmidt-Warneck, J. von.) Berlin, 1884.
Phil 6903.5 The sociology and anthropology of mental illness, a reference guide. (Driver, Edwin D.) Amherst, 1965.
Phil 2055.5.95 Sociology and philosophy. (Hobhouse, Leonard Trelawney.) Cambridge, 1966.
Phil 1812.16 Sociology and pragmatism. (Mills, Charles W.) N.Y., 1964.
Phil 6112.37 Sociology and the field of mental health. (Clausen, John A.) N.Y., 1956.
Phil 8612.84 Sociology of death; an analysis of death-related behavior. (Vernon, Glenn M.) N.Y., 1970.
Phil 349.41.2 The sociology of knowledge. (Stark, Werner.) Glencoe, 1958.
Phil 349.41 The sociology of knowledge. (Stark, Werner.) London, 1958.
Phil 349.41.3 The sociology of knowledge. (Stark, Werner.) London, 1960.
Phil 5590.175 Sociology of personality functioning. (Hawthorn, H.B.) Sioux City, Iowa, 1955.
Phil 8582.66 The sociology of religious belonging. (Carrier, Hervé.) N.Y., 1965.
Phil 4803.108.90 Socjologia Edwarda Abramowskiego. (Krawczyk, Zbigniew.) Warszawa, 1965.
Phil 8889.8 Socjologia moralności. (Ossowska, Maria.) Warszawa, 1963.
Phil 8889.8.2 Socjologia moralności 2. wyd. (Ossowska, Maria.) Warszawa, 1969.
Phil 8893.81 Sockman, R.W. Morals of tomorrow. N.Y., 1931.
Phil 3235.126 Sockrinemia. (Feuerbach, Ludwig.) Moskva, 1923.
Phil 5826.5 Socrate e le bestie. (Quarelli, Elena.) Cuneo, 1958.
Phil 5242.32 Socrates, or The emancipation of mankind. (Carlill, H.F.) London, 1927.

Phil 665.86 — Socrates and the animals. (Quarelli, Elena.) London, 1960.

Phil 1130.6 — Socrates and the Socratic schools. (Zeller, Eduard.) London, 1868.

Phil 1130.6.5 — Socrates and the Socratic schools. (Zeller, Eduard.) London, 1877.

Phil 1130.6.8 — Socrates and the Socratic schools. 3rd ed. (Zeller, Eduard.) London, 1885.

Phil 3640.58.7 — Socrates und die griechische Tragödie. (Nietzsche, Friedrich.) München, 1933.

Phil 28.41 — The socratic; contemporary philosophy and christian faith. Oxford. 5

Phil 188.9.10 — Socratic method and critical philosophy. (Nelson, L.) New Haven, 1949.

Phil 182.15 — Die Socratic Schule. v.1-2. (Heusde, P.W.) Erlangen, 1838.

Phil 3450.13.32 — De Socratische school of Wijsgeerte. (Heusde, P.W.) Utrecht, 1834. 2v.

Phil 1750.166.70 — Sodalitas Erasmiana. Il valore universale dell'umanesimo. Napoli, 1950.

Phil 5374.195 — Sodan, Guenter. Über den Gebrauch des Ausdrücke "Intention". Berlin, 1958.

Phil 6105.233 — Soddy, Kenneth. Identity. Mental health and value systems. London, 1961.

Phil 8422.4.5 — Soderzhanie i forma v iskusstve. (Vanslov, V.V.) Moskva, 1956.

Phil 6128.62 — Soderzhanie i sushchnost' antagonizma mezhdu fizicheskim i umstvennym trudom. (Simonian, G.A.) Baku, 1958.

Phil 8411.24 — Soderzhanie odforma v proizvedeniiakh iskusstva. (Kaloshin, F.I.) Leningrad, 1953.

VPhil 310.647.10 — Sodobna filosofija med dialektiko in metafiziko. (Rus, Vojan.) Ljubljana, 1968.

Phil 8968.8.20 — Soe, N.H.Christliche Ethik. München, 1949.

Phil 5828.13 — Söderhjelm, H. Instinkterna och det mänskliga känslolivet. Helsingfors, 1913.

Phil 5870.17 — Söderling, Bertil. Barn av samma stam. Stockholm, 1967.

Phil 5520.461 — Soehingen, Gottlieb. Analogie und Metapher. Freiburg, 1962.

Phil 193.125.5 — Söhngen, G. Philosophische Einübung in die Theologie. Freiburg, 1955.

Phil 193.125 — Söhngen, G. Sein und Gegenstand. Münster, 1930.

Phil 6128.43 — Sömmerring, S.T. Über das Organ der Seele. Königsberg, 1796.

Phil 3640.697 — Sørensen, V. Friedrich Nietzsche. København, 1963.

Phil 3808.244 — Sørensen, Villy. Schopenhauer. København, 1969.

Phil 2805.90.15 — Soeurs de grands hommes: J. Pascal. (Giraud, V.) Paris, 1926.

Phil 4710.66 — Sofiia; problemy dukhovnoi kul'tury i religioznoi filosofii. (Berdiaev, N.A.) Paris, 1967.

Phil 4120.3.32 — Sofismi e buon senso, serati campestri. 2. ed. (Giovanni, V. di.) Palermo, 1873.

Phil 1195.13 — Sofisti. (Untersteiner, M.) Firenze, 1949-62. 2v.

Phil 5421.20.20 — Das sogenannte Böse. 2. Aufl. (Lorenz, Konrad Zacharias.) Wien, 1964.

Phil 5831.2 — Die sogenannte Hypnose der Thiere. (Verworn, M.) Jena, 1898.

Phil 5190.4.20 — Die sogenannten Definitionen durch Abstraktion. (Scholz, H.) Leipzig, 1935.

Phil 6675.8 — Der sogenante Lebensmagnetismus oder Hypnotismus. (Fischer, E.L.) Mainz, 1883.

Phil 720.96 — Soggettività e intersoggettività. Padova, 1969.

Phil 8050.23 — Soggettività e oggettività del bello. (Trudu,, Luciano.) Padova, 1962.

Phil 6480.192 — I sogni. (Mozzuchelli, M.) Milano, 1954.

Phil 7082.86 — I sogni. (Sanctis, Sante de.) Torino, 1899.

Phil 6619.4.5 — I sogni e il sonno nell'isterismo e nella epilessia. (Sanctis, Sante de.) Roma, 1896.

Phil 7082.198 — Il sogno e le civiltà umane. Bari, 1966.

Phil 1750.115.135 — Il sogno finito. (Forni, Guglielmo.) Bologna, 1967.

Phil 7082.56 — Sögur af ymsu tagi. (Austmann, S.J.) Winnipeg, 1915.

Phil 2490.170 — Sokoloff, Boris. The "mad" philosopher. 1st ed. N.Y., 1961.

Phil 8419.64 — Sokolov, Aleksandr N. Teoriia stilia. Moskva, 1968.

Phil 5258.204 — Sokolov, Aleksandr N. Vnutrenniaia rech' i myshlenie. Moskva, 1968.

Phil 8980.801 — Sokolov, Andrei V. Filosofiia bor'by. Moskva, 1909.

Phil 5585.225 — Sokolov, E.N. Perception and the conditioned reflex. Oxford, 1963.

Phil 5237.516.10 — Sokolov, Mikhail V. Iz istorii russkoi psikhologii. Moskva, 1961.

Phil 5237.516.5 — Sokolov, Mikhail V. Ocherki istorii psikhologicheskikh vozznenii v Rossii v XI-XVIII vekakh. Moskva, 1963.

Phil 8525.20 — Sokolov, Nikolai P. Istoriia svobodo mysliia i ateizma v Evrope. Moskva, 1966.

Phil 3838.30 — Sokolov, V.V. Filosofiia Spinozy i sovremennost'. Moskva, 1964.

Phil 3450.11.345 — Sokolowski, Robert. The formation of Husserl's concept of constitution. The Hague, 1964.

Phil 5828.11.5 — Sokolowsky, A. Aus dem Seelenleben höherer Tiere. Leipzig, 1910.

Phil 5828.11 — Sokolowsky, A. Beobachtungen über die Psyche. Frankfurt, 1908.

Phil 3823.1 — Der Sokrates der Neuzeit...Spinoza's. (Dessauer, M.) Cöthen, 1877.

Phil 1750.127 — Sokrates im achtzehnten Jahrhundert. (Boehm, Benno.) Leipzig, 1929.

Phil 1750.127.2 — Sokrates im achtzehnten Jahrhundert. (Boehm, Benno.) Leipzig, 1929.

Phil 8735.30 — Sokrates und der Engel. (Wasmuth, E.) Olten, 1948.

Phil 3640.716 — Sokrates und Nietzsche. (Sandvoss, E.) Leiden, 1966.

Phil 1133.16.5 — Die Sokratiker. (Nestle, W.) Jena, 1922.

Phil 2905.1.480 — Solages, Bruno de. Teilhard de Chardin, témoignage et étude sur le développement de la pensée. Toulouse, 1967.

Phil 4352.1.135 — Solaguren, Celestino. Metodalogía filosófica de Balmes. Madrid, 1961.

Phil 4319.1 — Solana, Marcial. Los grandes escolásticos espanoles de los siglos XVI y XVII. Madrid, 1928.

Phil 4319.1.5 — Solana, Marcial. Historia de la filosofía española. Madrid, 1940-41. 3v.

Phil 4210.198 — Solari, Gioele. Studi rosminiani. Milano, 1957.

Phil 310.632 — Soldatov, Vasyl' I. Problema vzaiemovidnoshennia svitohliadu i metodu v dialektychnomu materializmi. Kyiv, 1966.

Phil 600.60 — Soler, Ricaurte. El positivismo argentino. Panamá, 1959.

Phil 3450.19.170 — Soler Grimma, Francisco. El origen de la obra de arte y la verdad en Heidegger. Bogota, 1953.

Phil 4362.10 — Soler Puigoriol, Pedro. El hombre, ser indigente: el pensamiento antropológico de Pedro Lain Entralgo. Madrid, 1966.

Phil 3850.22.93 — Solger; esthétique et philosophie de la présence. Thèse. (Boucher, Maurice K.N.F.) Paris, 1934.

Phil 5590.335 — Solger, Friedrich. Das überpersönliche Leben. Berlin, 1959.

Phil 8419.43 — Solger, K.W.F. Erwin; vier Gespräche über das Schöne une die Kunst. Berlin, 1815. 2v.

Phil 8419.43.2 — Solger, K.W.F. Erwin. München, 1971.

Phil 8419.7 — Solger, K.W.F. K.W.F. Solger's Vorlesungen über Ästhetik. Leipzig, 1829.

Phil 193.30 — Solger, K.W.F. Philosophische Gespräche. Berlin, 1817.

Phil 8419.43.80 — Solgers Lehre vom Schönen in ihrem Verhältnis zur Kunstlehre. (Grunert, B.) Marburg, 1960.

Phil 3850.22.90 — Solgers Philosophie der ironischen Dialektik. (Heller, Joseph E.) Berlin, 1928.

Phil 3850.22.90.2 — Solgers Philosophie der ironischen Dialektik. Diss. (Heller, Joseph E.) Berlin, 1928.

Phil 4065.115 — Soliani, B. La filosofia di Giordano Bruno. Firenze, 1930.

Htn Phil 2115.85* — Solid philosophy asserted. (Sergeant, J.) London, 1697.
Phil 6159.5

Phil 3805.49 — Soliloquies. (Schleiermacher, Friedrich.) Chicago, 1926.
Phil 2262.63 — Soliloquy. (Shaftesbury, A.A.C.) London, 1710.
Htn Phil 2262.63* — Soliloquy. Photoreproduction. (Shaftesbury, A.A.C.) London, 1710.

Phil 735.270 — Solimini, Maria. Genealogia e scienza dei valori. Manduria, 1968.

Phil 400.115 — Il solipsismo. (Archivio di Filosofia.) Padova, 1950.
Phil 4200.4.35 — Il solipsismo. (Pastore, A.) Torino, 1924.
Phil 9515.3.5 — Solitude. (Zimmermann, J.G.) Dublin, 1800.
Phil 9515.3.6.5 — Solitude. (Zimmermann, J.G.) London, 1800.
NEDL Phil 9515.3.6 — Solitude. (Zimmermann, J.G.) London, 1800-02.
Phil 9515.3.9 — Solitude. (Zimmermann, J.G.) N.Y., 1813.
Phil 9515.3.8 — Solitude. v.1-2. (Zimmermann, J.G.) Exeter, 1836.
Htn Phil 9515.3.7.2* — Solitude. 1st ed. (Zimmermann, J.G.) N.Y., 1801.
Htn Phil 9515.3.7* — Solitude. 1st ed. (Zimmermann, J.G.) N.Y., 1801.
Phil 9515.3.3 — Solitude. 2d ed. (Zimmermann, J.G.) London, 1792.
Phil 176.138.5 — Solitude and society. (Berdiaev, Nikolai A.) London, 1938.

Phil 176.138.8 — Solitude and society. (Berdiaev, Nikolai A.) London, 1947.

Htn Phil 9515.1* — Solitude and society contrasted. (Burges, T.) Providence, 1797.

Phil 2445.5.30 — Solitude de la raison. (Alguié, Ferdinand.) Paris, 1966.

Phil 9515.2 — The solitudes of nature and of man. 4. ed. (Alger, W.R.) Boston, 1867.

Phil 9515.2.5 — Solitudes of nature and of man. 5th ed. (Alger, W.R.) Boston, 1867.

Phil 3425.718 — Soll, Ivan. An introduction to Hegel's metaphysics. Chicago, 1969.

Phil 5585.150 — Solley, Charles. Development of the perceptual world. N.Y., 1960.

Phil 5070.8 — Sollier, P. Le doute. Paris, 1909.
Phil 5400.23 — Sollier, P. Le mécanisme des émotions. Paris, 1905.
Phil 7069.03.25 — Sollier, P. Les phénomènes d'autoscopie. Paris, 1903.
Phil 5545.31 — Sollier, P. La problème de la mémoire. Paris, 1900.
Phil 6750.8 — Sollier, P. Psychologie de l'idiot. Paris, 1891.
Phil 5545.31.5 — Sollier, P. Les troubles de la mémoire. Paris, 1901.
Phil 5325.7 — Sollier, Paul. Essai sur l'association. Paris, 1907.
Phil 9075.21 — Sollier, Paul. Morale et moralité. Paris, 1912.
Phil 5850.342 — Sollier, Paul. La psychotechnique. Bruxelles, 1935.
Phil 5258.106 — Sollier, Paul. La répression mentale. Paris, 1930.
Phil 5768.18 — Solly, J.R. Free will and determinism. London, 1922.
Phil 5768.16 — Solly, T. A syllabus of logic. Cambridge, 1839.
Phil 5768.11 — Solly, Thomas. The will divine and human. Cambridge, 1856.

Phil 3110.192 — Solms-Rödelheim, Günther. Die Grundvorstellungen Jacob Böhme. München, 1960.

Phil 6158.5 — Solomon, David. LSD: the consciousness-expanding drug. N.Y., 1964.

Phil 2475.1.81 — Solomon, J. Bergson. London, 1911.
Phil 1050.4.17 — Solomon Ibn-Gabirol. La fuente de la vída. Madrid, 1901.
Phil 1050.13 — Solomon Pappenheim on time and space and his relation to Locke and Kant. (Wolfson, Harry A.) Vienna, 1927.

Phil 4769.1.108 — Solove'ev, V.S. I fondamenti spirituali della vita. Bologna, 1922.

Phil 978.14 — Solovef, V.S. Nodern priestess of Isis. London, 1895.
Phil 1750.784 — Solov'ev, Erikh I. Ekzistentsializm i naunchnoe poznanie. Moskva, 1966.

Phil 3640.711 — Solov'ev, Evgenii A. Nitsshe. Sankt Peterburg, 1902.
Phil 4769.1.10 — Solov'ev, V.S. Ausgewählte Werke. Jena, 1914-16. 2v.

Phil 4769.1.75 — Solov'ev, V.S. Crise de la philosophie occidentale. Paris, 1947.

Phil 4769.1.81 — Solov'ev, V.S. La grande controverse et la politique chrétienne. Paris, 1953.

Phil 4769.1.45 — Solov'ev, V.S. Kritika otvlechennykh nachal. Moskva, 1880.

Phil 4769.1.70 — Solov'ev, V.S. The meaning of love. London, 1945.
Phil 4769.1.130 — Solov'ev, V.S. O khristianskom edinstve. Briussell, 1967.
Phil 4769.1.50 — Solov'ev, V.S. De onda. Tre samtal. Stockholm, 1918.
Phil 4769.1.85 — Solov'ev, V.S. Pis'ma. Sankt Peterburg, 1908-09.
Phil 4769.1.122 — Solov'ev, V.S. Russkaia ideia. Moskva, 1911.
Phil 4769.1.60 — Solov'ev, V.S. A Solovyov anthology. London, 1950.
Phil 4769.1.78 — Solov'ev, V.S. Tri razgovora. N'iu-Iork, 1954.
Phil 4769.1.120 — Solov'ev, V.S. Tri rechi v pamiat' Dostoevskogo. Berlin, 1925.
Phil 4769.1.40 — Solov'ev, V.S. Werke. v.2,3,6,7. Freiburg, 1953. 4v.
Phil 4769.1.80 — Pamphlet box. Solov'ev, V.S.
Phil 8893.45 — Solov'ev, Vladimir. The justification of the good. N.Y., 1918.

Phil 8598.88.2 — Solov'ev, Vladimir Sergeevich. Lectures on Godmanhood. London, 1948.

Phil 4769.1.102 — Solovjev und der Protestantismus. (Müller, Ludolf.) Freiburg, 1951.

Phil 4769.1.112 — Solovyev. (Munzer, Egbert.) London, 1956.
Phil 4769.1.60 — A Solovyov anthology. (Solov'ev, V.S.) London, 1950.
Phil 4769.1.94 — Solowiew. (Bayer, J.J.M.) Den Haag, 1964.
Phil 4769.1.96 — Solowiew. (Lange, H.M.) Mainz, 1923.
Phil 2805.202.1 — Soltau, R.H. Pascal: the man and the message. Westport, 1970.

Phil 5643.130 — Soltis, Jonas Francis. Seeing, knowing, and believing. Reading, Mass., 1966.

Phil 5066.28.5 — Soluable cases of the decision problem. (Ackermann, W.) Amsterdam, 1954.

Phil 7069.30.14 La solution du mystère de la mort. (Matla, J.L.W.P.) La Haye, 1930.
Phil 3484.25 La soluzione kantiana. (Cavagna, G.B.) Bologna, 1962.
Phil 7085.4 Somanmbulism and cramp. (Reichenbacn, C.A.) N.Y., 1860.
Phil 974.2 Some account of my intercourse with Mme. Blavatsky. (Coulomb, E.) London, 1885.
Phil 7068.92.45 Some account of the vampires of onset, past and present. Boston, 1892.
Phil 6325.1.17 Some applications of psychoanalysis. (Pfister, Oskar.) London, 1923.
Phil 5257.50 Some aspects of psychology. (Rosling, B.) London, 1936.
Phil 5627.1.10 Some aspects of religious growth. (Starbuck, E.D.) n.p., 1897.
Phil 3640.260 Some aspects of the life and work of Nietzsche. (Knight, A.H.J.) Cambridge, 1933.
Phil 8626.12 Some assurances of immortality. (Berry, J.B.N.) N.Y., 1909.
Phil 338.7 Some cardinal points in knowledge. (Hodgson, S.H.) London, n.d.
Htn Phil 8691.5* Some considerations about the reconcileablness of reason and religion. (Boyle, R.) London, 1675.
Phil 8620.34 Some difficulties proposed for solution. (Worcester, Noah.) Newbury-Port, 1786.
Phil 531.6 Some dilemmas of naturalism. (Dennes, William R.) N.Y., 1960.
Phil 8592.21.5 Some dogmas of religion. (McTaggart, J.M.E.) London, 1930.
Phil 8591.7 Some elements of religion. (Liddon, H.P.) London, 1872.
Phil 8591.7.10 Some elements of religion. 10. ed. (Liddon, H.P.) London, 1894.
Phil 8595.26 Some enquiries, chiefly related to spiritual beings. (Perronet, V.) London, 1740.
Phil 525.55.10 Some exponents of mystical religion. (Jones, Rufus M.) N.Y., 1930.
Phil 2115.74.50 Some familiar letters between Mr. Locke and his friends. (Locke, J.) London, 1708.
Phil 3842.13.5 Some guiding principles in determining Spinoza's mediaeval sources. (Wolfson, H.A.) Philadelphia, 1937.
Phil 7060.92.5 Some haunted houses. (O'Donnell, Elliot.) London, 1908.
Phil 5052.40 Some hints on arguing. (Marriott, J.W.O.E.D.) London, 1948.
Phil 6321.1 Some illustrative clinic cases. Thesis. (Lattimore, E.L.) Menasha, 1916.
Phil 1707.3 Some influences in modern philosophic thought. (Hadley, A.T.) New Haven, 1913.
Phil 7069.35.52 Some laws of materialization. Dictated by John King. (Wells, Helen B.) N.Y., 1935.
Phil 4365.2.41 Some lessons in metaphysics. 1st ed. (Ortega y Gasset, José.) N.Y., 1969.
Phil 8587.32.87 Some letters. (Hügel, Friedrich von.) London, 1925.
Phil 2150.18.30 Some main problems of philosophy. (Moore, George Edward.) London, 1953.
Phil 7069.30.1 Some modern mediums. (Besterman, T.) London, 1930.
Phil 8667.19 Some modern non-intellectual approaches to God. (McAuliffe, A.T.) Washington, D.C., 1934.
Phil 6316.9 Some neurological and psychological aspects of shock. Thesis. (Gard, W.L.) n.p., 1908.
Phil 5625.87 Some notes for simple Pavlovian learning. (Householder, A.S.) Santa Monica, 1951.
Phil 2675.2.80 Some notes on the psychology of Pierre Janet. (Mayo, Elton.) Cambridge, 1948.
Phil 5274.12 Some observations on factor analysis. (Harmon, Harry Horace.) Santa Monica, 1955.
Htn Phil 2045.103* Some opinions of Mr. Hobbs. (Eachard, John.) London, 1673.
Phil 1135.102 Some phases...Post-Aristotelian period. (Sunne, D.G.) Chicago, 1911.
Phil 1750.2 Some phases of modern philosophy. (Price, E.K.) Philadelphia, 1872. 2 pam.
Phil 5241.32 Some phases of the psychology of puzzle learning. (Ballard, J.H.) N.Y., 1915.
Phil 6972.6 Some points connected with the questions of responsibility as it relates to the partially insane. (Wright, T.L.) n.p., 18- .
Phil 8884.22 Some problems of ethics. (Joseph, H.W.B.) Oxford, 1931.
Phil 190.21 Some problems of existence. (Pearson, N.) London, 1907.
Phil 978.6.35 Some problems of life. 2nd ed. (Besant, Annie.) London, 1904.
Phil 175.3 Some problems of philosophy. (Alexander, A.) N.Y., 1886.
Phil 184.3.27A Some problems of philosophy. (James, W.) N.Y., 1911.
Phil 184.3.28 Some problems of philosophy. (James, W.) N.Y., 1911.
Phil 5400.77 Some prominent characteristics of human nature and a new conception of God. (Begtrup, Julius.) London, 1929.
Phil 5875.90 Some psychological aspects of the chorcatiform syndrome: development of the intelligence. (Nooteboom, Wilhelmina E.) Assen, 1967.
Phil 7069.25.12 Some recent personal experiences with Margery. (Tillyard, R.J.) N.Y., 1926.
Phil 2750.11.51 Some reflections on culture and literature. (Maritain, Jacques.) Chicago, 1933.
Phil 5520.507 Some relations between perception, speech and thought. Proefschrift. (Verhaar, John W.M.) Assen, 1963.
Phil 181.37.2 Some religious implications of pragmatism. (Geiger, Joseph R.) Chicago, 1919.
Phil 7076.2.2 Some remarkable passages in the life of Dr. George de Benneville. (Benneville, George de.) Germantown, Pa., 1870.
Phil 194.27 Some remarks on the axioms and postulates of athetic philosophy. (Tarner, George E.) Cambridge, 1922.
Phil 6132.26 Some social aspects of mental hygiene. (Williams, Frankwood Earl.) Philadelphia, 1930.
Phil 8876.50 Some suggestions in ethics. (Bosanquet, B.) London, 1918.
Phil 5257.35 Some things that matter. (Ruddell, G.A.R.) London, 1922.
Phil 8670.11 Some thoughts about God. (Pounder, R.M.) Toronto, 1923.
Htn Phil 2115.71* Some thoughts concerning education. (Locke, J.) London, 1693.
Phil 1750.142 Some turns of thought in modern philosophy. (Santayana, George.) Cambridge, Eng., 1933.
Phil 1750.142.2 Some turns of thought in modern philosophy. (Santayana, George.) N.Y., 1933.
Phil 6980.263 Some uncommon psychiatric syndromes. (Enoch, M. David.) Bristol, 1967.
Phil 978.5.85 Some unpublished letters. (Blavatsky, H.P.) London, 1929.
Phil 672.23 Some views of the time problem. Diss. (VanRiper, B.W.) Menasha, 1916.
Phil 5238.177 Some views on Soviet psychology. (Bauer, Raymond A.) Washington, 1962.

Phil 9245.53 Somer, Marcelle de. Le rythme de la vie, le bonheur. Gand, 1933.
Phil 8610.872 Somerset, Edward Adolphhus. Christian theology and modern scepticism. London, 1872.
Phil 8610.872.2 Somerset, Edward Adolphhus. Christian theology and modern scepticism. N.Y., 1872.
Phil 9178.6.5 Somerville, E. A birthday present. Boston, 1803.
Phil 9178.6.6 Somerville, E. A birthday present. Boston, 1805.
Phil 1955.6.240 Somjee, Abdulkarim Husseinbhay. The political theory of John Dewey. N.Y., 1968.
Phil 75.11 Sommaire idéologique. (Louvain. Université Catholique. Institut Supérieur de Philosophie.) Bruxelles. 1-20,1895-1914 4v.
Phil 4065.125 Il sommario del processo di Giordano Bruno. Citta del Vaticano, 1942.
Phil 815.2 Sommario della storia di filosofia. (Pompa, R.P.) Napoli, 1865.
Phil 196.8.15 Sommario di filosofia. (Varisco, B.) Roma, 1928.
Phil 815.20 Sommario di storia della filosofia, con particolare riguardo ai problemi morali e religiosi. (Rodovani, Umberto Antonio.) Roma, 1966. 3v.
Phil 817.8.9 Sommario di storia della filosofia. (Ruggiero, Guido de.) Bari, 1927.
Phil 819.8.5 Sommario di storia della filosofia. (Troilo, E.) Milano, 1929.
Phil 8586.30 Sommario d'un filosofia della religione. (Gentile, P.) Bari, 1923.
Phil 2725.37.30 La somme et le reste. (Lefebvre, Henri.) Paris, 1959. 2v.
Phil 7080.42 Le sommeil. (Lhermitte, J.J.) Paris, 1931.
Phil 7080.27 Le sommeil et les rêves. (Delboeuf, Joseph.) Paris, 1885.
Phil 7080.9 Le sommeil et les rêves. (Maury, L.F.A.) Paris, 1861.
Phil 7080.9.3 Le sommeil et les rêves. (Maury, L.F.A.) Paris, 1865.
Phil 7080.28 Le sommeil et les rêves. (Vaschide, Nicolas.) Paris, 1914.
Phil 7080.8 Le sommeil et l'insomnie. (Marvaud, J.L.A.) Paris, 1881.
Phil 7080.12 Le sommeil normal. (Yung, E.) Paris, 1883.
Phil 6681.4.5 Le sommeil provoqué et les etats analogues. (Liébeault, A.A.) Paris, 1889.
Phil 2475.1.253 Sommer, Erika. Bergson's Einfluss auf die französische Schriftsprache. Inaug. Diss. München, 1935.
Phil 5440.20 Sommer, Georg. Geistige Veranlagung und Vererbung. Leipzig, 1916.
Phil 6128.34 Sommer, George. Leib und Seele in ihrem verhältnis Zueinander. Leipzig, 1920.
Phil 5768.15 Sommer, H. Über das Wesen und die Bedeutung. Berlin, 1885.
Phil 3915.82 Sommer, Hugo. Individualismus oder Evolutionismus? Berlin, 1887.
Phil 9430.24.2 Sommer, Hugo. Der Pessimismus und der Sittenlehre. Berlin, 1883.
Phil 5228.2 Sommer, R. Grundzüge einer Geschichte der deutschen Psychologie. Würzburg, 1892.
Phil 2115.136 Sommer, R. Locke's Verhältnis zu Descartes. Diss. Berlin, 1887.
Phil 5828.14 Sommer, R. Tierpsychologie. Leipzig, 1925.
Phil 6968.22 Sommer, Robert. Lehrbuch der psychopathologischen untersuchungs Methoden. Berlin, 1899.
Phil 960.152 Sommerfeld, S. Indienschau und Indiendeutung romantischer Philosophen. Zürich, 1943.
Phil 3585.30.5 Sommerhäuser, Hanspeter. Emil Lask in der Auseinander-Setzung mit Heinrich Rickert. Berlin, 1965.
Phil 3808.95 Sommerlad, F. Darstellung und Kritik. Offenbach, 1895.
Phil 4170.14 I sommi problemi. (Mazzilli, Stefano.) Padova, 1963. 2v.
Phil 7085.8 Les somnambules extra-lucides. (Perry, L. de.) Paris, 1897.
Phil 6677.11.2 Somnolism and psycheism. 2d ed. (Haddock, J.W.) London, 1851.
Phil 5425.58 Somogyi, J. Begabung im Lichte der Eugenik. Leipzig, 1936.
Phil 193.135 Somogyi, Jozsef. As ideák problémája. Budapest, 1931.
Phil 2750.11.140 Son oeuvre philosophique. (Maritain, Jacques.) Paris, 1949?
Phil 3640.254 Son of the morning; a portrait of F. Nietzsche. (O'Brien, Edward J.) N.Y., 1932.
Phil 6968.21 Sondén, Tarsten. A study of somatic conditions in manic-depressive psychosis. Inaug. Diss. Uppsala, 1927.
Phil 4369.5 Sondereguér, Pedro. El enigma de la realidad. Buenos Aires, 1941.
Phil 978.59.8 The song of life. (Krishnamurti, J.) Ommen, 1931.
Phil 7069.29.40 The song of Sano Tarot. (Fullwood, A.M.) N.Y., 1929.
Phil 8885.32 Song of the optimist. (Kramer, Morris.) N.Y., 1926.
Phil 7069.34.55 The song of the seven seas. (Wells, Helen B.) N.Y., 1934.
Phil 2750.11.72.5 Le songe de Descartes. (Maritain, Jacques.) Paris, 1932.
Phil 2750.11.91 Le songe de Descartes. (Maritain, Jacques.) Paris, 1965.
Phil 7082.178 Les songes. (Becker, Raymond de.) Paris, 1958.
Phil 187.19 Les songes physiques. (Moreau de St. Elier, L.) Amsterdam, 1781.
Phil 4060.2.83 Sonne, I. Intorno alla vita di Leone Ebreo. Firenze, 1934.
Phil 7080.43 Il sonne e la vigilia. (Zambeccari, G.) Firenze, 1928.
Phil 1750.610 Sonnemann, Ulrich. Existence and therapy. N.Y., 1954.
Phil 6060.40.5 Sonnemann, Ulrich. Handwriting analysis. N.Y., 1953.
Phil 6060.40.10 Sonnemann, Ulrich. Handwriting analysis as a psychodiagnostic tool. N.Y., 1964.
Phil 585.270 Sonnemann, Ulrich. Negative Anthropologie. Reinbeck bei Hamburg, 1969.
Phil 5850.343 Sonnet, André. Lerne menschen Kennen und Behandeln. Freiburg, 1959.
Phil 7069.59.25 Sonnet, Andre. Der Mensch ist voller Geheimnisse. Berlin, 1959.
Phil 3640.460 Sonns, Stefan. Das Gewissen in der Philosophie Nietzsches. Winterthur, 1955.
Phil 2750.19.85 Sonsbeeck, Dawiet van. Het zijn als mysterie in de ervaring en het denken van Gabriel Marcel. Bilthoven, 1966.
Phil 193.256 Sontag, Frederick. The existentialist prolegomena. Chicago, 1969.
Phil 5039.32 Sootnoshenie istorii i logiki nauki. Dnepropetrovsk, 1970.
Phil 310.85 Sootnoshenie kategorii istoricheskögo materializma. (Tugarinov, V.P.) Leningrad, 1958.
Phil 310.23 Sootnoshenii kategorii dialekticheskoi marksizma. (Tuzarinov, V.P.) Leningrad, 1956.
Phil 28.15 Sophia. Palermo. 15,1947+ 32v.
Phil 3200.15 Sophia und Logos oder die Philosophie der Wiederherstellung. (Eberz, Otfried.) München, 1967.

Phil 5520.94 — Sophie, oder Über die Sprache. (Wasmuth, E.) Berlin, 1943.

Phil 1195.4 — Die Sophisten und die Sophistik nach den angaben Plato's. (Wecklein, N.) Wurzburg, 1866.

Phil 1195.11 — Les sophistes. (Dupréel, E.) Neuchâtel, 1949.

Phil 1750.14.10 — Les sophistes et la critique. (Gratry, A.J.A.) Paris, 1864.

Phil 1195.15 — Les sophistes et le droit. (Periphanakes, K.) Athènes, 1953.

Phil 1750.15 — Les sophistes grecs...et contemporains. (Funck-Brentano, T.) Paris, 1879.

Phil 178.16.5 — La sophistique contemporaine. (Dumesni, G.) Paris, 1912.

Phil 812.9.9 — La sophistique étude de philosophie comparée. n.p., 1916.

Phil 1195.13.3 — The sophists. (Untersteiner, M.) Oxford, 1954.

Phil 176.125 — Sophylus oder Sittlichkeit und Natur. (Bardili, C.G.) Stuttgart, 1794.

Phil 8643.8 — Sopote, M. Grades of life. Letters on immortality. Oxford, 1909.

Phil 193.61 — Sopote, M. Mind and brain with other studies. Oxford, n.d.

Phil 6680.1.30 — Sopp, Erich. Auf den Spuren der Seheim. Sersheim, 1953.

Phil 2050.106 — Sopper, A.J. David Hume's kenleer en ethiek. Leiden, 1907.

Phil 4080.7.31 — Sopra alcune quistioni...della filosofeia. (Colecchi, O.) Napoli, 1843.

Phil 4285.1.95 — Sopra Giacomo Zabarella. (Labanca, B.) Napoli, 1878.

Phil 6327.1 — Sorcellerie, magnètisme, morphinisme. (Regnard, P.) Paris, 1887.

Phil 4115.100 — Sordi, Serafino. I misteri di Demofilo. Milano, 1850. 3 pam.

Phil 8120.2 — Soreil, A. Introduction à l'histoire de l'esthétique. Bruxelles, 1930.

Phil 8120.3 — Soreil, A. Introduction à l'histoire de l'esthétique française. Bruxelles, 1955.

Phil 5828.12 — Sorel, C.L.F. De l'intelligence chez l'animal. Paris, 19-

Phil 8598.65.5 — Sorel, G. La religione d'oggi. Lanciani, 1911.

Phil 193.93.10 — Sorel, Georges. D'Aristote à Marx. Paris, 1935.

Phil 193.93.2 — Sorel, Georges. De l'utilité du pragmatisme. 2e ed. Paris, 1928.

Phil 630.13.7 — Sorely, W. R. Moral values and the idea of God. 2nd ed. N.Y., 1921.

Phil 175.29 — Le sorgenti irrazionali del pensiero. (Abbagnano, N.) Genova, 1923.

Phil 5258.125.5 — Soria, T.D. Psicología. 4. ed. México, 1940.

Phil 2340.6.90 — Sorley, W.R. James Ward, 1843-1925. London, 192-.

Phil 8893.37 — Sorley, W.R. The moral life and moral worth. Cambridge, Eng., 1911.

Phil 630.13 — Sorley, W.R. Moral values and the idea of God. Cambridge, 1918.

Phil 9150.4 — Sorley, W.R. On the ethics of naturalism. London, 1885.

Phil 9150.4.3 — Sorley, W.R. On the ethics of naturalism. 2. ed. London, 1904.

Phil 8843.5 — Sorley, W.R. Recent tendencies in ethics. Edinburgh, 1904.

Phil 1818.5 — Sorley, William R. A history of English philosophy. Cambridge, Eng., 1920.

Phil 1818.5.5 — Sorley, William R. A history of English philosophy. N.Y., 1921.

Phil 5592.125 — Sormani, Jacques. Contribution à l'étude pratique. Marseille, 1958.

Phil 3500.32 — Sornmerlath, Ernst. Kants Lehre vom Intelligiblencharakter. Leipzig, 1917.

Phil 187.28.25 — Sorok let iskaniia ratsional'nago mirovozzreniia. (Mechnikov, I.I.) Moskva, 1913.

Phil 8980.802 — Sorokin, K.F. Za leninskii stil' v rabote. Kiev, 1960.

Phil 1718.22A — Sorokin, P. Social philosophies of an age of crisis. Boston, 1950.

Phil 9495.156A — Sorokin, P.A. The American sex revolution. Boston, 1956.

Phil 8893.103A — Sorokin, Pitirim Aleksandrovich. Altruistic love. Boston, 1950.

Phil 8893.103.2 — Sorokin, Pitirim Aleksandrovich. Altruistic love. N.Y., 1969.

Phil 8893.104 — Sorokin, Pitirim Aleksandrovich. Explorations in altruistic love and behavior. Boston, 1950.

Phil 8893.104.3 — Sorokin, Pitirim Aleksandrovich. Explorations in altruistic love and behavior. N.Y., 1970.

Phil 8893.104.5 — Sorokin, Pitirim Aleksandrovich. Forms and techniques of altruistic and spiritual growth. Boston, 1954.

Phil 8893.104.6 — Sorokin, Pitirim Aleksandrovich. Forms and techniques of altruistic and spiritual growth. Boston, 1954. N.Y., 1971.

Phil 4260.98 — Sorrentino, A. La retorica et la poetica di G.B. Vico. Torino, 1927.

Phil 1850.97 — Sortain, J. The life of Francis Lord Bacon. London, n.d.

Phil 818.14 — Sortais, G. Histoire de la philosophie ancienne. Paris, 1912.

Phil 193.54 — Sortais, G. Traité de philosophie. Paris, 1906-1907. 3v.

Phil 1718.10 — Sortais, Gaston. La philosophie moderne. Paris, 1921-22.

Phil 4260.102 — La sorte di G.B. Vico e le polemiche...della fine del XVII alla metà del XVIII secolo. (Cotugno, R.) Bari, 1914.

Phil 630.62 — Sosa López, Emilio. Fronteras de lo real. Córdoba, Argentina, 1965.

Phil 3270.1.82 — Sosnoioski, M.E.V. Kuno Fischer. Breslau, n.d.

Htn Phil 293.4* — Sostanza et forma del mondo. (Memma, G.M.) Venice, 1545. 4v.

Phil 2880.8.170 — Sotelo, Ignacio. Das Problem der dialektischen Vernunft bei Jean Paul Sartre. Köln, 1965.

Phil 5520.596 — Sotnikian, Pogos A. Osnovnye problemy iazyka i myshleniia. Erevan, 1968.

Phil 4369.3 — Soto, Juan B. La tragedia del pensamiento. Rio Piedras, 1937.

Phil 1504.8.4 — Soto, P.B. Petri Compostellani. v.8, pt.4. Münster, 1912.

Phil 8019.15 — Sotsialisticheskii realizm i problemy estetiki. Moskva. 1,1967+

Phil 8950.7 — Sotsialistychnyi humanizm i khrystianskyi bubov do blyzhiv'oho. (Antnenko, V.H.) Kyïv, 1961.

Phil 5590.562 — Sotsializm i lichnost'. Volgograd, 1970.

Phil 8599.38 — Sotsial'naia religiia. (Tarasov, A.A.) Miunkhen, 1959.

Phil 5590.486 — Sotsial'naia sreda i soznanie lichnosti. (Bueva, Liudmila P.) Moskva, 1968.

Phil 5590.563 — Sotsial'naia vol' i aktivnost' lichnosti. (Anufriev, Evgenii A.) Moskva, 1971.

Phil 182.138 — Sotsial'ne seredovishche ta istoriko-filosofs'kyi protses. (Hors'kyï, Vilen S.) Kyïv, 1969.

Phil 8598.125 — Sotsial'nye i gnoseologicheskie korni religii. (Sukhov, Andrei D.) Moskva, 1961.

Phil 8430.85 — Sotsiologiia iskusstva. (Novozhilova, Larisa I.) Leningrad, 1968.

Phil 575.261 — Sotsiologiia lichnosti. (Koy, Igor' S.) Moskva, 1967.

Phil 8419.21 — Sotto il velame; aspetti psicologici dell'arte. 1.ed. (Simat, Zarko.) Roma, 1959.

Phil 4710.25 — Současná filosofie u Slovanů. (Pelikán, Ferdinand.) Praha, 1932.

Phil 2905.1.470 — Soucy, Claude. Pensée logique et pensée politique chez Teilhard de Chardin. Paris, 1967.

Phil 6968.19 — Souhard, E.E. The kingdom of evils. N.Y., 1922.

Phil 6110.6 — The soul, a study of past and present beliefs. (Arnett, L.D.) n.p., 1904.

Phil 665.19 — The soul; its organ and development. (Corey, J.W.) Los Angeles, 1913.

Phil 8593.2.9 — Soul, its sorrows and its aspirations. 3. ed. (Newman, F.W.) London, 1852.

Phil 8593.2.5 — The soul. (Newman, F.W.) London, 1849.

Phil 8593.2.6 — The soul. (Newman, F.W.) London, 1853.

Phil 8593.2.8 — The soul. (Newman, F.W.) London, 1858.

Phil 665.71 — The soul. (Syme, David.) London, 1903.

Phil 525.93 — The soul afire. (Reinhold, Hans.) N.Y., 1944.

Phil 525.93.5 — The soul afire. (Reinhold, Hans.) N.Y., 1960.

Phil 6114.5.8 — Soul and body. (Evans, W.F.) Boston, 1876.

Phil 5241.81 — The soul and its mechanism (the problem of psychology). (Bailey, A.A. (Mrs.).) N.Y., 1930.

Phil 177.88 — Soul and matter. (Castaner, C.) London, 1933.

Phil 5627.260 — Soul and psyche. (White, Victor.) London, 1960.

Phil 665.53 — The soul comes back. (Coffin, Joseph H.) N.Y., 1929.

Phil 665.80.5 — The soul in metaphysical and empirical psychology. (Strasser, Stephan.) Pittsburgh, 1957.

Phil 189.4.12 — The soul in nature. (Oersted, H.C.) London, 1852.

Phil 6112.10 — The soul of man. (Carus, P.) Chicago, 1891.

Phil 299.24 — The soul of the universe. (Strömberg, G.) Philadelphia, 1940.

Phil 299.24.2 — The soul of the universe. 2. ed. (Strömberg, G.) Philadelphia, 1948.

Phil 7059.7 — The soul of things. (Denton, William.) Boston, 1863.

Phil 665.45 — Soul shapes. London, 1890.

Phil 665.44 — Souls. (Aber, Mary R.A.) Chicago, 1893.

Phil 5627.15.3 — Souls in action. (Begbie, H.) N.Y., 1911.

Phil 5627.108.15 — The soul's sincere desire. (Clark, Glenn.) Boston, 1926.

Phil 5247.5 — Sound mind. (Haslam, J.) London, 1819.

Phil 336.10 — Sound thinking. (Fireman, Peter.) N.Y., 1947.

Phil 1106.1A — Source book in ancient philosophy. (Bakewell, C.M.) N.Y., 1907.

Phil 1106.1.5 — Source book in ancient philosophy. (Bakewell, C.M.) N.Y., 1907.

Phil 1106.1.7 — Source book in ancient philosphy. (Bakewell, C.M.) N.Y., 1940.

Phil 5238.204 — A source book in history of psychology. (Hernnstein, Richard J.) Cambridge, 1965.

Phil 5244.22.5 — A source book of Gestalt. (Ellis, Willis D.) London, 1950.

Phil 735.190 — La source des valeurs. (Pucelle, Jean.) Lyon, 1957. 3v.

Phil 1127.6 — La source grecque. (Weil, S.) Paris, 1953.

Phil 9346.5 — Les sources. v.1-2. (Gratry, A.J.) Paris, 1862-69.

Phil 9346.5.5 — Les sources. 16. éd. (Gratry, A.J.) Paris, 1921.

Phil 8406.2 — Les sources de la création artistique. (Fuerstenberg, Hans.) Monaco, 1962.

Phil 8889.1.10 — Les sources de la paix intellectuelle. 7. ed. (Ollé-Laprune, L.) Paris, 1916.

Phil 623.23.5 — Les sources et le développement du rationalisme dans la littérature française de la Renaissance. (Busson, Henri.) Paris, 1922.

Phil 623.23 — Les sources et le développement du rationalisme dans la littérature française de la Renaissance. Thèse. (Busson, Henri.) Paris, 1922.

Phil 2401.3.15A — Les sources et les courants de la philosophie contemporaine en France. (Benrubi, Isaac.) Paris, 1933. 2v.

Phil 1511.3.15 — Les sources gréco-arabes de l'augustinisme avicennisant. (Gilson, Etienne.) Paris, 1930.

Phil 2115.105 — Les sources médiévales de la philosophie de Locke. (Krakowski, E.) Paris, 1915.

Phil 2115.106 — Les sources médiévales de la philosophie de Locke. Thèse. (Krakowski, E.) Paris, 1915.

Phil 8847.14 — Les sources mystiques des concepts moraux de l'occident. (Winkler, Paul.) Paris, 1957.

Phil 630.57 — Sources of contemporary philosophical realism in America. (Schneider, H.W.) Indianapolis, 1964.

Phil 5610.2 — Sources of effectiveness in public speaking. (Neil, C.E.) Philadelphia, 1920.

Phil 960.18.5 — Sources of Hindu dharma in its socio-religious aspects. (Altekar, A.S.) Chicago, 1917.

Phil 960.17.40 — Sources of Hindu dharma in its socio-religious aspects. (Altekar, A.S.) Shalapur, 1952?

Phil 5838.266 — The sources of instinctive life, and A theory of mental functioning. (Palmeri, R.) N.Y., 1966.

Phil 8597.20.10 — The sources of religious insight. (Royce, Josiah.) Edinburgh, 1912.

Phil 8597.19A — The sources of religious insight. (Royce, Josiah.) N.Y., 1912.

Phil 192.16.15A — The sources of religious insight. (Royce, Josiah.) N.Y., 1912.

Phil 735.180 — The sources of value. (Pepper, Stephen C.) Berkeley, 1958.

Phil 8832.7 — The sources of western culture. (Harkness, G.E.) London, 1955.

Phil 5400.59.2 — Souriau, E. L'abstraction sentimentale. Paris, 1925.

Phil 5400.59 — Souriau, E. L'abstraction sentimentale. Thèse. Paris, 1925.

Phil 5400.59.5 — Souriau, E. L'abstraction sentimentale. 2. ed. Paris, 1951.

Phil 2880.7 — Souriau, E. Avoir une âme. Paris, 1938.

Phil 1750.435 — Souriau, E. L'ombre de Dieum. 1e éd. Paris, 1955.

Phil 8893.65 — Souriau, M. La fonction pratique de la finalité. Paris, 1925.

Phil 8893.65.2 — Souriau, M. La fonction pratique de la finalité. Thèse. Paris, 1925.

Phil 530.15.9 — Souriau, M. Le mysticisme en Normandie au XVIIe siècle. Paris, 1923.

Phil 5465.17 — Souriau, Paul. L'imagination de l'artiste. Paris, 1901.

Phil 8419.48 — Souriau, E. L'avenir de l'esthétique essai sur l'objet d'une science naissante. Paris, 1929.

Phil 8430.42.1 — Souriau, Etienne. La correspondance des arts, éléments d'esthétique comparée. Paris, 1969.

Phil 8430.42 — Souriau, Etienne. La correspondance des arts. Paris, 1947.

Phil 193.159A   Souriau, Étienne. Les différents modes d'éxistence. Paris, 1943.

Phil 5258.88   Souriau, Étienne. Pensée vivante et perfection formelle. Thèse. Paris, 1925.

Phil 5258.88.5   Souriau, Étienne. Pensée vivante et perfection formelle. 2. éd. Paris, 1952.

Phil 2805.87   Souriau, M. Pascal. Paris, 1898.

Phil 672.162   Souriau, Michel. Le temps. Paris, 1937.

Phil 7140.1   Souriau, P. La suggestion dans l'art. Paris, 1893.

Phil 9245.20   Souriau, Paul. Les conditions du bonheur. Paris, 1908.

Phil 5645.19   Souriau, Paul. L'esthétique de la lumière. Paris, 1913.

Phil 5649.8   Souriau, Paul. L'esthétique du mouvement. Paris, 1889.

Phil 5525.5   La sourire. (Dumas, G.) Paris, 1906.

Phil 6116.5.85   Soury, Jules. Les fonctions du cerveau, doctrines de F. Goltz. Paris, 1866.

Phil 6128.21   Soury, Jules. Histoire des doctrines...les fonctions du cerveau. Paris, 1891.

Phil 299.8   Soury, Jules. Philosophie naturelle. Paris, 1882.

Phil 6128.21.5   Soury, Jules. Le système nerveux centrale. Paris, 1899. 2v.

Phil 6688.26   Sousselier, de la Tour. L'âmi de la nature, ou Manière de traiter les maladies. Dijon, 1784.

Phil 7106.4   South, Thomas. Early magnetism in its higher relations to humanity. London, 1846.

Phil 28.78   South African journal of philosophy. Rondebosch. 1,1964+ 2v.

Phil 28.92   South African journal of psychology. Johannesburg. 1,1970+

Phil 58.18   South African Psychological Association. Proceedings. 1,1950+

Phil 3549.2.30.2   South American meditations. 1st ed. (Keyserling, Hermann.) N.Y., 1932.

Phil 28.68   The southern journal of philosophy. Memphis, Tenn. 3,1965+ 4v.

Phil 28.37   Southern philosopher. Chapel Hill. 5-6,1956-1957

Phil 128.86   Southwestern journal of philosophy. Norman, Okla. 1,1970+

Phil 28.86   Southwestern journal of philosophy. Norman. 1,1970+

Phil 9358.12   Southwick, Solomon. Five lessons for young men. Albany, 1837.

Phil 5545.192   Le souvenir. 2. éd. (Bridoux, André.) Paris, 1956.

Phil 192.24   Souvenirs...d'un penseur moderne. (Richard, A.) Genève, 1905.

Phil 2725.14.90   Souvenirs concernant Jules Lagneau. 2. éd. (Chartier, Émile.) Paris, 1925.

Phil 2725.14.93   Souvenirs concernant Jules Lagneau. 5e éd. (Chartier, Émile.) Paris, 1925.

Phil 2630.1.79   Souvenirs de ma jeunesse. 5e ed. (Gratry, Auguste.) Paris, 1897.

Phil 8583.1   Souvenirs de vingt ans d'enseignement. (Damiron, J.P.) Paris, 1859.

Phil 2475.1.280   Souvenirs sur Henri Bergson. (Benrubi, Isaak.) Neuchâtel, 1942.

Phil 3500.43   Souviau, M. Le jugement réfléchissant dans la philosophie critique de Kant. Paris, 1926.

Phil 3500.43.2   Souviau, M. Le jugement réfléchissant dans la philosophie critique de Kant. Thèse. Paris, 1926.

Phil 4960.620   Souza, Remy de. Vocação filosófica do Brasil. Salvador, 1960.

Phil 1750.785   Soveral, Eduardo S. O método fenomenológico; estudo para a determinação do seu valor filosófico. Porto, 1965.

Phil 8661.6   The sovereignty of God. (Vance, J.G.) Oxford, 1934.

Phil 8620.62.5   The sovereignty of good. (Murdoch, Iris.) London, 1970.

Phil 8620.62   The sovereignty of good over other concepts. (Murdoch, Iris.) London, 1967.

Phil 310.623   Soveshchanie po Sovremennym Problemam Materialisticheskoi Dialektiki. Materialy. Moskva, 1966. 4v.

Phil 8980.787.10   Soveshchanie po Voprosam Marksistko-Leninskoi Etiki, Leningrad, 1959. Voprosy marksistsko-leninskoi etiki. Moskva, 1960.

Phil 4710.170   Sovetskaia filosofskaia nauka i ee problemy. (Okulov, Aleksandr F.) Moskva, 1970.

Phil 8980.320A   Soviet ethics and morality. (De George, Richard T.) Ann Arbor, 1969.

Phil 28.80   Soviet neurology and psychiatry. White Plains, N.Y. 1,1968+ 2v.

Phil 4710.110.5   Soviet philosophy; a general introduction to contemporary Soviet thought. (Blakeley, Thomas J.) Dordrecht, 1964.

Phil 6332.14   Soviet psychiatry. (Wartis, Joseph.) Baltimore, 1950.

Phil 5203.35   Soviet psychology; a continuing bibliography. North Hollywood, Calif. 1,1950+

Phil 5328.24.5   Soviet psychology. N.Y., 1961.

Phil 28.67   Soviet psychology. White Plains, N.Y. 5,1966+ 3v.

Phil 28.66   Soviet psychology and psychiatry. N.Y. 1-4,1962-1966// 4v.

Phil 4710.110   Soviet scholasticism. (Blakeley, Thomas J.) Dordrecht, 1961.

Phil 28.64   Soviet studies in philosophy. N.Y. 3,1964+ 4v.

Phil 4710.110.10   Soviet theory of knowledge. (Blakeley, Thomas J.) Dordrecht, 1964.

Phil 8170.2   Sovjet-annexatie der klassieken. (Reve, K. van het.) Amsterdam, 1954.

Phil 5520.444   Sovremennaia angliiskaia lingvisticheskaia filosofiia. (Begiashvili, Archil.) Tbilisi, 1965.

Phil 585.375   Sovremennaia "Anlosofskaia antropoligiia". (Antonovich, Ivan I.) Minsk, 1970.

Phil 1804.5   Sovremennaia burzhuaznaia filosofiia SShA. (Ermolenko, Dimitrii V.) Moskva, 1965.

Phil 1810.6   Sovremennaia burzhuaznaia filosofiia SShA. (Kopnin, Pavel V.) Kiev, 1966.

Phil 5222.10   Sovremennaia curzhuazhaia psikhologiia. (Manswrov, N.S.) Moskva, 1962.

Phil 8220.5   Sovremennaia estetika v SShA. (Zemlianova, L.M.) Moskva, 1962.

Phil 1700.10   Sovremennaia filosofiia i sotsiologiia v stranakh Zapadnoi Evropy i Ameriki. (Akademiia Nauk SSSR. Institut Filosofii.) Moskva, 1964.

Phil 900.27   Sovremennaia filosofskaia i sotsiologicheskaia mysl' stran vostoka. (Krikorian, Sergei.) Moskva, 1965.

Phil 525.242   Sovremennaia mistika v svete nauki. (Shakhnovich, Mikhail.) Leningrad, 1965.

Phil 5210.10   Sovremennaia psikhologiia v kapitalisticheskikh stranakh. (Akademiia Nauk SSSR. Institut Filosofii.) Moskva, 1963.

Phil 400.121.5   Sovremennia idealisticheskaia gnoseologiia. (Kursanov, Georgii A.) Moskva, 1968.

Phil 8700.16   Sovremennoe bogoslov'e i nauka. (Kryvelev, I.A.) Moskva, 1959.

Phil 8400.40   Sovremennoe iskusstvoznanie za rubezhom; ocherki. (Akademiia Nauk SSSR. Institut Istorii Iskusstv.) Moskva, 1964.

Phil 349.92   Sovremennye problemy seorii poznaniia dialekticheskogo materializma. Moskva, 1970. 2v.

Phil 1695.20   Sovremennye religioznye filosofskie techeniia kapitalisticheskikh stran. (Akademiia Nauk SSR. Institut Filosofii.) Moskva, 1962.

Phil 1750.560.30   Sovremennyi ekzistensializm. (Oizerman, Teodor I.) Moskva, 1966.

Phil 400.121   Sovremennyi ob"ektivnyi idealizm. (Kursanov, Georgii A.) Moskva, 1966.

Phil 5068.48   Sovremennyi pozitivizm. (Narskii, I.S.) Moskva, 1960.

Phil 400.120   Sovremennyi sub"ektivnyi idealizm. (Baskin, M.P.) Moskva, 1957.

Phil 9045.11   Sowdon, A.J.C. Political duties. Boston, 1878.

Phil 8897.29.8   Sowing and reaping. (Washington, B.T.) Boston, 1900.

Phil 4710.155   Die sowjetische Erkenntnismetaphysik und ihr Verhältnis zu Hegel. (Ballestrem, Karl G.) Dordrecht, 1968.

Phil 4710.152   Die Sowjetphilosophie. (Goerdt, Wilhelm.) Basel, 1967.

Phil 5467.10   Soziale Aktivierung. (Lueck, Helmut E.) Köln, 1969.

Phil 978.49.415   Die soziale Grundforderung unserer Zeit in gländerter Zeitlage. (Steiner, R.) Dornach, 1963.

Phil 9513.8   Das Soziale im Leben und im Denken. (Wiese, Leopold von.) Köln, 1956.

Phil 5535.24   Soziales Lernen; das Problem der Lertheorien in der Sozialpsychologie. (Marnet, Otto.) Zürich, 1968.

Phil 9513.19   Sozialethik. (Berg, Ludwig.) München, 1959.

Phil 2138.147   Die Sozialethik des John Stuart Mill. (Ludwig, M.) Zürich, 1963.

Phil 9513.44   Sozialethik im Umbruch der Gesellschaft. Göttingen, 1969.

Phil 6360.8   Sozialisationsbedingungen der öffentlichen Erziehung. 1. Aufl. (Eckensberger, Diethild.) Frankfurt am Main, 1971.

Phil 8430.86   Sozialistischer Realismus-Positionen, Probleme, Perspektiven. 1. Aufl. (Pracht, Erwin.) Berlin, 1970.

Phil 1540.17A   Die Sozialmetaphysik der Scholastik. (Winter, E.K.) Leipzig, 1929.

Phil 2490.172   Sozialmoral. (Riezu, J.) München, 1961.

Phil 5763.2   Sozialpädagogik. Theorie der Willenserziehung. 3. Aufl. (Natorp, Paul.) Stuttgart, 1909.

Phil 5763.2.5   Sozialpädagogik. Theorie der Willenserziehung. 6. Aufl. (Natorp, Paul.) Stuttgart, 1925.

Phil 3425.690   Die Sozialphilosophie Hegels als Heilslehre und Herrschaftsideologie. (Topitsch, Ernst.) Neuwied, 1967.

Phil 3890.10.130   Die Sozialphilosophie von Ernst Troeltsch. (Kasch, W.F.) Tübingen, 1963.

Phil 5590.572.4   Sozialpsychologische Grundlagen der Persönlichrechtsformung. 4. Aufl. (Hiebsch, Hans.) Berlin, 1969.

Phil 1721.4   Soziologie der Freiheit. (Veit, Otto.) Frankfurt a.M., 1957.

Phil 9415.5   Soziologie der Leiden. (Mueller-Lyer, Franz.) München, 1914.

Phil 6951.32   Soziologie des maladies mentales. (Bastide, Roger.) Paris, 1965.

Phil 3492.35   Die soziologischen Gedanken Kants in Zusammenhang seiner Philosophie. (Kress, Rudolf.) Berlin, 1929.

Phil 5374.276   Soznanie i obshchenie. Frunze, 1968.

Phil 4065.40   Spaccio de la bestia trionfante. (Bruno, Giordano.) Roma, 1888.

Phil 4065.45   Spaccio della bestia trionfante. v.1-2. (Bruno, Giordano.) Lanciano, 1920.

Phil 293.31   Space, time, and creation. (Munitz, Milton Karl.) Glencoe, 1957.

Phil 672.120   Space, time and deity. (Alexander, S.) London, 1920. 2v.

Phil 672.174   Space, time and life; and, What is time? v.1-2. (Goeje, C.H. de.) Leiden, 1949.

Phil 8691.31   Space age to Christianity. (Bayne, Stephen.) N.Y., 1963.

Phil 672.17   Space and geometry. (Mach, E.) Chicago, 1906.

Phil 672.20   Space and personality. (Allan, A.) Edinburgh, 1913.

Phil 303.14   Space and spirit. (Whittaker, E.) London, 1946.

Phil 672.134.5   Space and time. (Benedicks, Carl.) London, 1924.

Phil 672.252   Space and time. (Swinburne, Richard.) London, 1968.

Phil 5643.17   Space and vision. (Monck, W.H.S.) Dublin, 1872.

X Cg   Phil 6028.4.5   Spadon, N. Scuola di fisionomia, chiromantica. Macerata, 1654.

Phil 6028.4   Spadon, N. Studio di curiosita. Venetia, 1663.

Phil 8665.5   Späte Vergeltung aus der Geschichte der Theodicee. (Klostermann, E.) Strassburg, 1916.

Phil 3940.2.30   Spätlese eigener Hand. (Ziegler, L.) München, 1953.

Phil 5258.92.2   Spaier, A. La pensée concrète. Thèse. Paris, 1927.

Phil 4319.3   Spain. Filosofía española y portuguesa de 1500 a 1650. Madrid, 1948.

Phil 7150.47   Spain. Instituto Nacional de Estadística. El suicidio en España durante medio siglo. Madrid, 1959.

Phil 193.150.5   Spakovski, A. Chelo-vecheskoe "ia" i kul'tura. Novyi Sad, 1936.

Phil 193.150   Spakovski, A. Das menschliche Ich und die Kultur; der psychische Dynamismus und seine Gestabtung der Welt. Novi Sad, 1939.

Phil 193.150.10   Spakovski, A. Razreshenie sud'by chelovecheskoi. Novyi Sad, 1934.

Phil 384.5   Spakovski, Anatol. Freedom, determinism, indeterminism. The Hague, 1963.

Phil 4829.803.20   Spakovski, Anatol. Kleinere philosophische Schriften. Velika Kikinda, 1938.

Phil 9590.40   Spalding, Baird Thomas. Life and teaching of the masters of the Far East. Los Angeles, California, 1944. 5v.

Phil 193.88   Spalding, K.J. Desire and reason. London, 1922.

Phil 8598.106   Spalding, K.J. Essays on the evolution of religion. Oxford, 1954.

Phil 193.88.5   Spalding, K.J. Talks on philosophy. Oxford, 1931.

Phil 5058.17   Spalding, W. An introduction to logical science. Edinburgh, 1857.

Phil 8599.19.107   Spaleck, G. Religionssoziologische Grundbegriffe bei Troeltsch. Bleichersde, 1937.

Phil 9590.8   Spallazani, L. The devil laughs. Boston, 1937.

Phil 8419.13   Spalletti, G. Saggio sopra la bellezza. Firenze, 1933.

Phil 5246.25.80   Spaltro, Enzo. Agostino Gemelli e la psicologia del lavoro in Italia. Milano, 1966.

Phil 530.20.35   Spamer, Adolf. Uber die Zersetzung und Vererbung in den deutschen Mystikertexten. Diss. Giessen, 1910.

Phil 5258.46   Spamer, K. Physiologie der Seele. Stuttgart, 1877.

Phil 6128.36   Spamer, Karl. Physiologie der Seele. Stuttgart, 1877.

Phil 4065.98.5   Spampanato, V. Documenti della vita di Giordano Bruno. Firenze, 1933.

Author and Title Listing

Phil 4065.98 Spampanato, V. Vita di Giordano Bruno. v.1-2. Messina, 1921.
Phil 3011.5 Spanisch-Jesuisitische und Deutsch-Lutherische Metaphysik des 17. Jahrhunderts. (Lewalter, E.) Hamburg, 1935.
Phil 530.40.50 Spanische Mystik. (Behn, Irene.) Düsseldorf, 1957.
Phil 530.40.25 Spanish mysticism. (Peers, E.A.) London, 1924.
Phil 193.163 Spann, O. Philosophenspiegel. 2. Aufl. Wien, 1950.
Phil 8598.92.2 Spann, Othhmar. Religionsphilosophie auf geschichtlicher Grundlage. 2. Aufl. Graz, 1970.
Phil 3850.32.10 Spann, Othmar. Erkenne dich Selbst. Jena, 1935.
Phil 3850.32.10.2 Spann, Othmar. Erkenne dich Selbst. 2. Aufl. Graz, 1968.
Phil 5058.80 Spann, Othmar. Gangheitliche Logik. v.1-2. Salzburg, 1957.
Phil 5058.82 Spann, Othmar. Ganzheitliche Logik. 2. Aufl. Graz, 1971.
Phil 3850.32.24 Spann, Othmar. Gespräch über Unsterblichkeit; Betrachtungen zweier Krieger im Felde. Graz, 1965.
Phil 3850.66 Spann, Othmar. Kämpfende Wissenschaft. 2. Aufl. Graz, 1969.
Phil 5075.3 Spann, Othmar. Kategorienlehre. Jena, 1924.
Phil 5075.3.3 Spann, Othmar. Kategorienlehre. 3. Aufl. Graz, 1969.
Phil 3850.32.20 Spann, Othmar. Naturphilosophie. Jena, 1937.
Phil 3850.32.22 Spann, Othmar. Naturphilosophie. 2. Aufl. Graz, 1963.
Phil 193.163.3 Spann, Othmar. Philosophenspiegel; die Hauptlehren der Philosophie begrifflich und geschichtlich dargestellt. 3. Aufl. Graz, 1970.
Phil 3850.37 Spann, Othmar. Das philosophische Gesamtinerk im Auszug. Wien, 1950.
Phil 8598.92 Spann, Othmar. Religions-Philosophie auf geschichtlicher Grundlage. Wien, 1947.
Phil 400.76 Spann, Othmar. Der Schöpfungsgang des Geistes. Theil I. Jena, 1928.
Phil 400.76.2 Spann, Othmar. Der Schöpfungsgang des Geistes. 2. Aufl. Graz, 1969.
Phil 193.152 Spanzini, Carlo. Philosophie und Pädagogik. Bern, 1936.
Phil 8876.9 Sparks from the philosophers stone. (Basford, J.L.) London, 1882.
Phil 5627.107.10 The sparrow hath found herself a house. (Collins, Joyce.) Dublin, 1943.
Phil 8843.15 Sparshott, F.E. An enquiry into goodness. Chicago, 1958.
Phil 8419.56 Sparshott, F.E. The structure of aesthetics. Toronto, 1963.
Phil 5520.726 Spasov, Dobrin I. Filosofiia na lingvistikata sreshchu lingvisticheskata filosofiia. Sofiia, 1970.
Phil 299.28 Spathellenistische Berichte über Welt. (Spoerri, Walter.) Basel, 1959.
Phil 5585.230 Spatial ability. 1. ed. (Smith, Ian Macfarlane.) San Diego, Calif., 1964.
Phil 630.42 Spaulding, E.G. The new rationalism. N.Y., 1918.
Phil 8708.15 Spaulding, E.G. What am I? N.Y., 1928.
Phil 630.42.15 Spaulding, E.G. A world of chance. N.Y., 1936.
Phil 1928.80 Spaulding, F.E. Richard Cumberland...englischen Ethik. Leipzig, 1894.
Phil 4115.91.2 Spaventa, B. La filosofia di Gioberti. Napoli, 1870.
Phil 4115.91 Spaventa, B. La filosofia di Gioberti. v.1. Napoli, 1863.
Phil 3425.282F Spaventa, B. Le prime categorie della logica di Hegel; memoria. Napoli, 1864.
Phil 3425.282.5F Spaventa, B. Studii sull'etica hegeliana; memoria. Napoli, 1869.
Phil 4018.2.10 Spaventa, Bertrando. La Circolarità del pensiero europeo. Palermo, 1964.
Phil 4018.2 Spaventa, Bertrando. La filosofia italiana. Bari, 1908.
Phil 4018.2.5 Spaventa, Bertrando. La filosofia italiana. 3. ed. Bari, 1926.
Phil 4225.1.32 Spaventa, Bertrando. Logica e metafisica. Bari, 1911.
Phil 4225.1.40 Spaventa, Bertrando. Principii di etica. Napoli, 1904.
Phil 4225.1.52 Spaventa, Bertrando. Prolusione e introduzione alle lezioni di filosofia nella Università di Napoli. 2a ed. Napoli, 1886.
Phil 4225.1 Spaventa, Bertrando. Scritti filosofici. Napoli, 1900.
Phil 4225.1.21 Spaventa, Bertrando. Scritti inediti e rari, 1840-1880. Padova, 1966.
Phil 8643.38 Spazier, Karl. Antiphädon. Berlin, 1961.
Phil 7060.79 Spaziergänge eines Wahrheitssuchers. (Ludwig, W.) Leipzig, 1899.
Phil 3493.30 Spazio e materia in Kant. (Luperini, Cesuce.) Firenze, 1961.
Phil 2905.1.455 Speaight, Robert. Teilhard de Chardin: a biography. London, 1967.
Phil 2905.1.456 Speaight, Robert. Teilhard de Chardin: re-mythologization. Chicago, 1970.
Phil 5520.486 Speaker's meaning. 1. ed. (Barfield, Owen.) Middletown, 1967.
Phil 5520.110.5 Speaking (La parole). (Gusdorf, George.) Evanston, Ill., 1965.
Phil 5628.5 Speaking with tongues, historically and psychologically considered. (Cutten, George Barton.) New Haven, 1927.
Phil 5258.68.5A Spearman, C. The abilities of man; their nature and measurement. N.Y., 1927.
Phil 5258.68.10 Spearman, C. Human ability. London, 1950.
Phil 5258.68 Spearman, C. The nature of "intelligence" and the principles of cognition. London, 1923.
Phil 5258.68.2 Spearman, C. The nature of "intelligence" and the principles of cognition. London, 1927.
Phil 5648.5 Spearman, C. Normaltäuschungen in der Lagewahrnehmung. Leipzig, 1905.
Phil 5228.8 Spearman, C. Psychology down the ages. London, 1937. 2v.
Phil 5465.31.5 Spearman, Charles. Creative mind. Cambridge, Eng., 1931.
Phil 5465.31 Spearman, Charles. Creative mind. London, 1930.
Phil 28.13.20 Specchio umano. Napoli.
Phil 193.246 Specht, Ernst K. Sprache und Sein. Berlin, 1967.
Phil 3925.16.195 Specht, Ernst Konrad. The foundations of Wittgenstein's late philosophy. Manchester, 1969.
Phil 525.44 Specht, G. Die Mystik im Irrsinn. Wiesbaden, 1891.
Phil 3665.5.95 Specht, Minna. Leonard Nelson zum Gedächtnis. Frankfurt, 1953.
Phil 2520.360 Specht, Rainer. Commercium mentis et corporis. Stuttgart, 1966.
Phil 978.29 Special teachings from the arcane science. (Farnsworth, E.C.) Portland, Maine, 1913.
Phil 9513.6 Spécialisation et évolution. (Rouger, G.) Paris, 1935.
Phil 1540.84 La species medievale e i prodromi del fenomenismo moderno. (Prezioso, Faustino Antonio.) Padova, 1963.
Phil 5645.21 The specific brightness of colors. (Lucky, Bertha.) Lincoln, 1916.
Phil 5640.6.25 Die specifischen Sinnesenergien nach John Müller. (Brühl, P.N.) Fulda, 1915.
Phil 2115.139 Specimen academicum. (Mellring, J.G.) Upsaliae, 1792.
Phil 5042.6 Specimen artes ratiocinandi. v.1-3. (Cuffelaer, A.J.) Hamburgi, 1684.
Phil 6688.21 Specimen inaugurale medicum de electricitate. (Segnitz, F.L.) Jenae, 1790.
Htn Phil 2050.96* Specimen of the Scots Review. n.p., 1774.
Phil 2520.35.2 Specimina philosophiae. (Descartes, René.) Amsterdam, 1656.
Phil 4582.6.35 Speciminis academici. (Hermansson, J.) Upsaliae, 1733.
Phil 3745.5.90 Speck, Johannes. Friedrich Paulsen, sein Leben und sein Werk. Langensalza, 1926.
Phil 8673.8 Specker, Gideon. Versuch eines neuen Gottesbegriffs. Stuttgart, 1902.
Phil 2050.183 Speckmann, A. Über Hume's metaphysische Skepsis. Bonn, 1877.
Phil 7068.36.20 The spectre. (Ottway, T.) London, 1836.
Phil 7060.3 Spectriana. Paris, 1817.
Phil 7060.120 Spectrologia, h. e. Discursus ut plurimum philosophicus de spectris. (Decker, Johann H.) Hamburgi, 1690.
Phil 5645.29 Spectropia. 3. ed. (Brown, J.H.) London, 1864.
Phil 181.63.5 Het spectrum der philosophie in de 20e eeuw. (Goedewaagen, T.) Leiden, 1933.
Phil 193.97 The spectrum of truth. (Sharpe, A.B.) London, 1908.
Phil 5238.206 Spectrum Psychologiae, ein Freundesgabe. (Frey-Wehrlin, Caspar J.) Zürich, 1965.
Phil 810.11 Speculation and revelation in the history of philosophy. (Kroner, Richard.) London, 1952.
Phil 2120.9.30 A speculation in reality. (Laucks, I.F.) N.Y., 1953.
Phil 2055.15.37 Speculations; essays on humanism and the philosophy of art. (Hulme, Thomas E.) London, 1965.
Phil 2055.15.34A Speculations; essays on humanism and the philosophy of art. (Hulme, Thomas E.) N.Y., 1924.
Phil 2055.15.35 Speculations. 2nd ed. (Hulme, Thomas E.) London, 1958.
Phil 4635.8.33 Speculativ kosmologie med grundlag. (Sibbern, F.C.) Kjøbenhavn, 1846.
Phil 585.290 Speculative Anthropologie. (Werner, Karl.) Frankfurt, 1967.
Phil 1714.1 Speculative Entwicklung...neueren Philosophie. (Oischinger, J.N.P.) Schaffhaussen, 1853-4. 2v.
Phil 5761.15 Die speculative Idee der Freiheit. (Loewe, Johann H.) Prag, 1890.
Phil 5520.145 Speculative instruments. (Richards, Ivor Armstrong.) Chicago, 1955.
Phil 850.4 Die speculative Lehre vom Menschen. (Stöcke, A.) Würzburg, 1858-59. 2v.
Phil 3245.60 Die speculative Theologie der Allgemeine Religionslehre. (Fichte, Immanuel Hermann.) Heidelberg, 1846.
Phil 3010.1 Die speculativen Systeme seit Kant. (Kirchner, C.K.) Leipzig, 1860.
Phil 4514.1.80 Den specultiva philosophen Johann Jacob Borelius Calmar. (Boström, C.J.) Upsala, 1860.
Phil 177.85.5 Speculum mentis. (Collingwood, R.G.) Oxford, 1924.
Htn Phil 8800.3* Speculum morale. (Vincent de Beauvais.) Venetiis, 1493.
Phil 6025.10 Speculum physionomicum. (Petit-Douxciel, A.) Langres, 1648.
Phil 8598.60 Speculum religionis, being essays, presented to C.G. Montefiore. Oxford, 1929.
Phil 4225.5.2 Spedalieri, Nicola. De diritti dell'uomo libri 6. Assisi, 1791.
Phil 4170.7.48 Lo Spedalieri. (Mamiani della Rovere, Terenzio.) Roma, 1894.
Phil 1850.17 Spedding, James. The collection of books used by James Spedding as his working library in preparing his...works of Sir F. Bacon. London, 19- ?
Phil 8893.18 Speece, C. The mountaineer. Staunton, 1823.
Phil 5520.45 Speech; its function and development. (Laguna, Grace A. de.) New Haven, 1927.
Phil 6125.28 Speech and brain-mechanisms. (Penfield, Wilder.) N.J., 1959.
Phil 6400.25 Speech and voice. (Hein, Leopold.) London, 1942.
Phil 5650.52 The speech chain; the physics and biology of spoken language. (Denes, Peter B.) Baltimore? 1968.
Phil 6400.30.2 Speech disorders; aphasia, apraxia and agnosia. 2d ed. (Brain, Walter Russell.) London, 1965.
Phil 6420.6 Speech hesitation. (Thorpe, Eliza Jane Ellery.) N.Y., 1900.
Phil 6945.16 Speech on the veto message of the President on the bill for the benefit of the indigent insane. (Clayton, J.M.) Washington, 1854.
Phil 6400.33 Speech pathology. (Travis, Lee E.) N.Y., 1931.
Phil 960.14.5 Speeches and writings of the Karma philosophy. (Gandhi, V.R.) Bombay, 1913.
Phil 6328.27 Speer, Ernst. Die Liebesfähigkeit. 2e Aufl. München, 1937.
Phil 9450.40 Speer, James. For what purpose? Washington, 1960.
Phil 7069.27.25 Speer, W.H. Companions still. London, 1927?
Phil 6315.2.148 Spehlmann, Rainer. Sigmund Freuds neurologische Schriften. Berlin, 1953.
Phil 2733.89 Spehner, Edmund. Malebranches Lehre von der Erkenntnis in psychologischer Hinsicht. Inaug.-Diss. Borna, 1915.
Phil 9495.169.10 Speicher, Günter. Die grossen Tabus. Düsseldorf, 1969.
Phil 7150.100 Speijer, Nico. Het zelfmoordvraagstuk. Arnhem, 1969.
Phil 193.165 Speiser, A. Elemente der Philosophie und der Mathematik. Basel, 1952.
Phil 3850.42 Speiser, Andreas. Die geistige Arbeit. Basel, 1955.
Phil 5203.7 Spek, J. van der. Literatuurlijsten en atlas. Groningen, 1927.
Phil 4769.3 Spektorskii, E. Khristianstvo i kul'tura. Sankt Peterburg, 1925.
Phil 623.20 Spekulation und Philosophie. v.1-2. (Wolf, Hermann.) Berlin, 1878.
Phil 4815.790.30 A spekulativ termeszettudomány alapgondolatai mint az egységes érzet filozofia rendszere. (Simòn, József Sándor.) Budapest, 1904.
Phil 1020.18.10 Die spekulative und positive Theologie des Islam. (Horten, M.) Hildesheim, 1967.
Phil 3850.18.200 Spekulativer und Phänomenologischer. (Haskamp, Reinhold J.) Freiburg, 1966.
Phil 8419.26.1 Spence, Joseph. Crito, or A dialogue on beauty. Edinburgh, 1885.
Phil 8419.26 Spence, Joseph. Crito, or A dialogue on beauty. Edinburgh, 1885.
Phil 5625.92 Spence, K.W. Behavior theory and conditioning. New Haven, 1956.
Phil 5258.195 Spence, Kenneth Wartenbee. Behavior theory and learning; selected papers. Englewood Cliffs, 1960.
Phil 8598.29 Spencer, F.A.M. The meaning of Christianity. 2. ed. London, 1914.
Phil 5627.134.60 Spencer, F.A.M. The meaning of the groups. London, 1934.

Phil 8643.29   Spencer, Frederick A.M. The future life. 1. ed. London, 1935.

Phil 2138.86   Spencer, H. John Stuart Mill. Boston, 1873.

Phil 2270.79.10   Spencer, Herbert. Eine Autobiographie. Stuttgart, 1905. 2v.

Phil 2270.79A   Spencer, Herbert. An autobiography. N.Y., 1904. 2v.

Phil 2270.74.20   Spencer, Herbert. Les bases de la morale évolutionniste. 8e éd. Paris, 1905.

Phil 2270.76.5   Spencer, Herbert. Le basi della morale. 3a ed. Piacenza, 1920.

Phil 2270.60.10   Spencer, Herbert. Classification des sciences. Paris, 1888.

Phil 2490.86   Spencer, Herbert. The classification of the sciences...philosophy of M. Comte. London, 1871.

Htn   Phil 2270.60*   Spencer, Herbert. The classification of the sciences. London, 1864.

Phil 2270.60.3   Spencer, Herbert. The classification of the sciences. N.Y., 1864.

Phil 2270.77.10   Spencer, Herbert. The coming slavery and other essays. N.Y., 1888.

Phil 2270.74.5   Spencer, Herbert. Data of ethics. London, 1879.

Phil 2270.30.5   Spencer, Herbert. Data of ethics. London, 1887.

Phil 2270.74.1.5   Spencer, Herbert. Data of ethics. N.Y., 1879.

Phil 2270.74   Spencer, Herbert. Data of ethics. N.Y., 1879.

Phil 2270.74.4   Spencer, Herbert. Data of ethics. N.Y., 1883.

Phil 2270.74.12   Spencer, Herbert. Data of ethics. N.Y., 189-?

Phil 2270.77   Spencer, Herbert. Data of ethics. Pt. IV. Justice. N.Y., 1891.

Phil 2270.74.7   Spencer, Herbert. Data of ethics. 3rd ed. London, 1881.

Phil 2270.35   Spencer, Herbert. Epitome of the synthetic philosophy. N.Y., 1889.

Phil 2270.35.2   Spencer, Herbert. Epitome of the synthetic philosophy. N.Y., 1895.

Phil 2270.40.30   Spencer, Herbert. Essais de morale, de science et d'esthétique. 5e éd. Paris, 1904.

Phil 2270.40   Spencer, Herbert. Essays. London, 1858.

Phil 2270.40.2   Spencer, Herbert. Essays. N.Y., 1865.

Phil 2270.40.3.5   Spencer, Herbert. Essays. N.Y., 1868.

Phil 2270.40.3   Spencer, Herbert. Essays. N.Y., 1871.

Phil 2270.40.4   Spencer, Herbert. Essays. N.Y., 1874.

Phil 2270.40.5   Spencer, Herbert. Essays. N.Y., 1891. 3v.

Phil 2270.40.8   Spencer, Herbert. Essays. N.Y., 1896. 3v.

X Cg   Phil 2270.39   Spencer, Herbert. Essays. v.1. N.Y., 1868.

Phil 2270.39   Spencer, Herbert. Essays. v.2,3. London, 1868. 2v.

Phil 2270.40.35A   Spencer, Herbert. Essays on education and kindred subjects. London, 1910.

Phil 2270.72   Spencer, Herbert. L'evoluzione del pensiero. Milano, 1909. 2v.

Phil 2270.76   Spencer, Herbert. L'evoluzione morale. Milano, 1909.

Phil 2270.41.6   Spencer, Herbert. Facts and comments. N.Y., 1902.

Phil 2270.41.5   Spencer, Herbert. Facts and comments. N.Y., 1902.

Phil 2270.41   Spencer, Herbert. Facts and comments. N.Y., 1902.

Phil 2270.41.9   Spencer, Herbert. Faits et commentaires. 2e éd. Paris, 1904.

Phil 2270.45.2   Spencer, Herbert. First principles. London, 1862.

Htn   Phil 2270.45.2.5*   Spencer, Herbert. First principles. London, 1862.

Phil 2270.45   Spencer, Herbert. First principles. London, 1862.

Htn   Phil 2270.45.1*   Spencer, Herbert. First principles. London, 1862.

Phil 2270.30   Spencer, Herbert. First principles. London, 1870.

Phil 2270.45.7   Spencer, Herbert. First principles. N.Y., n.d.

Phil 2270.45.3   Spencer, Herbert. First principles. N.Y., 1864.

Phil 2270.45.3.10   Spencer, Herbert. First principles. N.Y., 1865.

Phil 2270.45.3.15   Spencer, Herbert. First principles. N.Y., 1866.

Phil 2270.45.4   Spencer, Herbert. First principles. N.Y., 1873.

Phil 2270.45.4.7   Spencer, Herbert. First principles. N.Y., 188-?

Phil 2270.45.4.10   Spencer, Herbert. First principles. N.Y., 188-?

Phil 2270.45.17   Spencer, Herbert. First principles. N.Y., 188-.

Phil 2270.45.5   Spencer, Herbert. First principles. N.Y., 1886.

Phil 2270.45.15   Spencer, Herbert. First principles. N.Y., 1892.

Phil 2270.45.25   Spencer, Herbert. First principles. N.Y., 1894.

Phil 2270.45.27   Spencer, Herbert. First principles. N.Y., 1896.

Phil 2270.45.9   Spencer, Herbert. First principles. N.Y., 1900.

Phil 2270.45.30   Spencer, Herbert. First principles. N.Y., 1958.

Phil 2270.45.14   Spencer, Herbert. First principles. 4th ed. N.Y., 1885.

Phil 2270.65   Spencer, Herbert. Illustrations of universal progress. N.Y., 1864.

Phil 2270.74.35   Spencer, Herbert. La morale des différents peuples et la morale personnelle. Paris, 1896.

Phil 2270.45.50   Spencer, Herbert. Les premiers principes. Paris, 1871.

Phil 2270.30.2   Spencer, Herbert. Principles of biology. London, 1864-67. 2v.

Phil 2270.73   Spencer, Herbert. Principles of ethics. N.Y., 1892-93. 2v.

Phil 2270.73.3   Spencer, Herbert. Principles of ethics. N.Y., 1895.

Phil 2270.73.4   Spencer, Herbert. Principles of ethics. N.Y., 1895-96. 2v.

Phil 2270.73.5   Spencer, Herbert. Principles of ethics. N.Y., 1899.

Phil 2270.70   Spencer, Herbert. Principles of psychology. London, 1855.

Phil 2270.70.2   Spencer, Herbert. Principles of psychology. London, 1855.

Phil 2270.30.3   Spencer, Herbert. Principles of psychology. London, 1870-72. 2v.

Phil 2270.70.5   Spencer, Herbert. Principles of psychology. London, 1881. 2v.

Phil 2270.70.4.15   Spencer, Herbert. Principles of psychology. N.Y., 1878. 2v.

Phil 2270.70.10   Spencer, Herbert. Principles of psychology. N.Y., 1894. 2v.

Phil 2270.70.12   Spencer, Herbert. Principles of psychology. N.Y., 1895. 2v.

Phil 2270.70.14   Spencer, Herbert. Principles of psychology. N.Y., 1901. 2v.

Phil 2270.70.15   Spencer, Herbert. Principles of psychology. N.Y., 1926.

Phil 2270.74.30   Spencer, Herbert. Qu'est-ce que la morale? Paris, 1909.

Phil 2270.50.2   Spencer, Herbert. Recent discussions in science. N.Y., 1871.

Phil 2270.50   Spencer, Herbert. Recent discussions in science. N.Y., 1873.

Phil 2270.77.20   Spencer, Herbert. A rejoinder to Professor Weismann. London, 1893?

Phil 2270.75   Spencer, Herbert. Resumen sintético de los principios de la moral. Paris, 1910.

Phil 2270.74.25   Spencer, Herbert. Le rôle moral de la bienfaisance. Paris, 1895.

Phil 2270.20   Spencer, Herbert. Select works. N.Y., 1886.

Htn   Phil 2270.55.1*   Spencer, Herbert. Social statics. London, 1851.

Phil 2270.55.3   Spencer, Herbert. Social statics. London, 1851.

Phil 2270.55.2   Spencer, Herbert. Social statics. London, 1851.

Phil 2270.55   Spencer, Herbert. Social statics. London, 1851.

Phil 2270.55.4   Spencer, Herbert. Social statics. N.Y., 1865.

Phil 2270.55.7.5   Spencer, Herbert. Social statics. N.Y., 1872.

Phil 2270.55.8   Spencer, Herbert. Social statics. N.Y., 1882.

Phil 2270.55.9   Spencer, Herbert. Social statics. N.Y., 1886.

NEDL   Phil 2270.56.5   Spencer, Herbert. Social statics. N.Y., 1893.

Phil 2270.56.6   Spencer, Herbert. Social statics. N.Y., 1897.

Phil 2270.56.7   Spencer, Herbert. Social statics. N.Y., 1904.

Phil 2270.56.10   Spencer, Herbert. Social statics. N.Y., 1954.

Phil 2270.31.2   Spencer, Herbert. System der synthetischen Philosophie: Biologie. Stuttgart, 1876-77. 2v.

Phil 2270.31.5   Spencer, Herbert. System der synthetischen Philosophie: Ethik. Stuttgart, 1879-95. 2v.

Phil 2270.31   Spencer, Herbert. System der Synthetischen Philosophie: Grundlagen. Stuttgart, 1875.

Phil 2270.31.3   Spencer, Herbert. System der synthetischen Philosophie: Psychologie. Stuttgart, 1882-86. 2v.

Phil 2270.31.4   Spencer, Herbert. System der synthetischen Philosophie: Sociologie. Stuttgart, 1877-97. 4v.

Phil 2270.71.10   Spencer, Herbert. Uppfostran i intellektuelt, moraliskt och fysiskt afseende. 2a uppl. Stockholm, 1890.

Phil 2270.43   Spencer, Herbert. Various fragments. N.Y., 1898.

Phil 2270.67.5   Spencer, Herbert. What knowledge is of most worth. N.Y., 1884.

Phil 5058.106.1   Spencer, Thomas. The art of logic. 1628. Facsimile. Menston, Eng., 1970.

Phil 5258.100   Spencer, Willard Wylie. Our knowledge of other minds. New Haven, 1930.

Phil 2270.91A   Spencer and Spencerism. (Macpherson, H.) N.Y., 1900.

Phil 2270.92   Spencer et le principe de la morale. (Dubois, J.) Paris, 1899.

Phil 2270.105   Spencer's Ansicht über das Verhältnis der Religion zur Wissenschaft. (Spicker, Gideon.) Münster, 1889.

Phil 6315.2.330   Spengler, Ernst. Das Gewissen bei Freud und Jung. Zürich, 1964.

Phil 3850.53   Spengler, Oswald. Urfragen. München, 1965.

Phil 8423.16.80   Spengler, Walter Eckehart. Der Begriff des Schönen bei Winckelmann. Göppingen, 1970.

Phil 1718.28   Spenlé, J.E. Les grands maîtres de l'humanisme européen. Paris, 1952.

Phil 3018.19   Spenlé, J.E. La pensée allemande de Luther à Nietzsche. Paris, 1934.

Phil 8637.14   La speranza nell immortalità. (Mazzantini, C.) Torino, n.d.

Phil 6328.24   Sperber, Alice. Über die seelischen Ursachen des Alterns, der Jugendlichkeit und der Schönheit. Leipzig, 1925.

Phil 5528.2   Sperisen, Walter. Arbeitsschen, eine psychologischpädagogische Studie. Bern, 1946.

Phil 6310.1.110   Sperker, Manès. Alfred Adler oder das Elénd der Psychologie. 1. Aufl. Wien, 1970.

Phil 9495.3.2   Sperry, L.B. Confidential talks with young men. N.Y., 1892.

Phil 8598.83   Sperry, Willard L. The disciplines of liberty. New Haven, 1921.

Phil 8598.83.5A   Sperry, Willard L. The disciplines of liberty. New Haven, 1923.

Phil 8598.83.10   Sperry, Willard L. Signs of these times. Garden City, N.Y., 1929.

X Cg   Phil 9590.14   Spetien Montero y Austri, P.A. Meximas de buena educación. México, 1828.

Phil 8408.39   Spetsyfichni osoblynosti zmistu i formy v mystetstvi. (Havryliuk, P.J.) Kyïv, 1963.

Phil 8171.300   Spetsyfika mystetstva. (Ivan'o Ivan V.) Kyïv, 1970.

Phil 2225.6.80   Spettmann, P.H. Die Psychologie des Johannes Pecham. Inaug. Diss. Münster, 1919.

Phil 978.30   Speyer, J.S. Die indische Theosophie. Leipzig, 1914.

Phil 978.30.5   Speyer, J.S. De indische theosophie en hare beteekenis voor ons. Leiden, 1910.

Phil 5520.542   Spezielle Erkenntnistheorie. 2. Aufl. (Klaus, Georg.) Berlin, 1966.

Phil 1535.34   Spezielle Metaphysik im Geiste des Heil. (Schneid, Mathias.) Paderborn, 1890-92. 2v.

Phil 9070.45   Spezzafumo de Faucamberge, S. Se suffire à soi-même. Paris, 1941.

Phil 8407.7   La sphère de beauté, lois d'évolution. (Griveau, Maurice.) Paris, 1901.

Phil 5047.10   Sphere of science. (Hoffman, F.S.) N.Y., 1898.

Phil 978.6.70   The sphinx of theosophy. (Besant, Annie.) London, 189-?

Phil 182.29.10   Sphinx philosophica. (Heidfeld, J.) Herbornae Nassoviorum, 1600.

Phil 7052.10.2   Spicer, Henry. Facts and fantasies, a sequel to Sights and sounds. London, 1853.

Phil 7052.10   Spicer, Henry. Sights and sounds. London, 1853.

Phil 349.3   Spicer, G. Kant, Hume und Berkeley. Berlin, 1875.

Phil 2262.83   Spicer, G. Die Philosophie des Grafen von Shaftesbury. Freiburg, 1872.

Phil 3500.9   Spicker, G. Über das Verhältniss...Kantische. Berlin, 1874.

Phil 193.65.5   Spicker, Gideon. Der Kampf zweier Weltanschauungen. Stuttgart, 1898.

Phil 2270.105   Spicker, Gideon. Spencer's Ansicht über das Verhältniss der Religion zur Wissenschaft. Münster, 1889.

Phil 193.65   Spicker, Gideon. Die Ursachen des Verfalls der Philosophie in alter und neuer Zeit. Leipzig, 1892.

Phil 585.325   Spicker, Stuart F. The philosophy of the body. Chicago, 1970.

Phil 3903.3.92   Spickerbaum, P. Das Vaihingersche Als-Ob und die Methode der Formensprache in Religion und Theologie. München, 1922.

Phil 3778.94   Spickhoff, K. Die Vorstellung in der Polemik zwischen Reinhold. München, 1961.

Phil 4115.83   Spiegazione analitica della formola ideale di V. Gioberti. (Morkos, D.) Torino, 1865.

Phil 5548.45   Spiegel, Berut. Werbepsychologische Untersuchungsmethoden. Berlin, 1958.

Phil 3805.226   Spiegel, Yorick. Theologie der bürgerlichen Gesellschaft. München, 1968.

Phil 9400.18   Spiegel des Altes. (Heller, Edward.) Affoltern, 1956.

Phil 3745.10.5   Spiegelberg, H. Alexander Pfänders phänomenologie. Den Haag, 1963.

Phil 735.112   Spiegelberg, H. Antirelativismus. Zürich, 1935.

Phil 1750.115.50   Spiegelberg, Herbert. The phenomenological movement. Hague, 1960. 2v.

Phil 1050.3   Spiegler, J.S. Geschichte der Philosophie des Judenthums. Leipzig, 1890.

Phil 8643.17   Spiegler, Julius. Die Unsterblichkeit der Seele. 3. Aufl. Leipzig, 1909.

Author and Title Listing

	Phil 5643.172	Spiekers, Rudolf. Über die optische Unterscheidbarkeit einfacher Zeichen. Thesis. Meisenheim am Glan, 1969.
	Phil 186.50.2	Spiel und Widerspiel. 2. Ausg. (Ludowici, A.) München, 1917.
	Phil 5816.3.5	Die Spiele der Menschen. (Groos, K.) Jena, 1899.
	Phil 5816.3	Die Spiele der Thiere. (Groos, K.) Jena, 1896.
	Phil 2490.107	Spielfogel, R. Comte's moralphilosophische Methode. Zürich, 1909.
	Phil 8413.44	Spielräume. (Malecki, Herbert.) Frankfurt, 1969.
	Phil 1750.353	Spier, J.M. Calvinisme en existentie-philosophie. Kampen, 1951.
	Phil 1750.353.5	Spier, J.M. Christianity and existentialism. Philadelphia, 1953.
	Phil 193.210	Spier, Johannes. Van Thales tot sartre. Kampen, 1959.
	Phil 8599.19.90	Spiess, Emil. Die Religionstheorie von Ernst Troeltsch. Paderborn, 1927.
	Phil 3890.9.95	Spiess, Emil Jakob. Ignoz Paul Vital Troxler. Bern, 1967.
	Phil 5722.28	Spiess, Emil Jakob. Rätsel der Seele. Olten, 1946.
	Phil 5643.125	Spigel, Irwin Myron. Readings in the study of visually perceived movement. N.Y., 1965.
	Phil 8615.12	Spiller, G. The ethical movement in Great Britain. London, 1934.
	Phil 5258.30.3	Spiller, G. The mind of man. "Ethical series." London, 1902.
	Phil 7082.90	Spiller, Gustav. A contribution towards a science of dreams. London, 1934.
	Phil 299.17	Spiller, P. Die Urkraft des Weltalls. Berlin, 1876.
	Phil 9070.24	Spillman, Harry Collins. Personality. N.Y., 1919.
	Phil 5440.9.5	Spillman, W.J. "Mental and moral heredity in royalty" - Woods. Lancaster, 1909.
	Phil 6118.4	Spina bifida and cranium bifidum. (Ingraham, F.D.) Boston, 1944.
	Phil 3640.180	Spindler, Josef. Nietzsches Persönlichkeit und Lehre. Stuttgart, 1913.
	Phil 2418.7	Spink, John Stephenson. French free-thought from Gassendi to Voltaire. London, 1960.
	Phil 4752.2.85	Spinka, M. Nicholas Berdyaev. Philadelphia, 1950.
	Phil 6128.38.2	Spinney, W.A. Health through self-control in thinking, breathing, eating. Boston, 1907.
	Phil 8893.35	Spínola, R. Moral razonada. Guatemala, 1900.
	Phil 3850.27.190	Spinosa, Antonio. Dottor Schweitzer e dintorni. Roma, 1960.
	Phil 3842.11	Spinoza; a life of reason. (Wolfson, Abraham.) N.Y., 1932.
	Phil 3842.11.2	Spinoza; a life of reason. 2nd ed. (Wolfson, Abraham.) N.Y., 1969.
	Phil 3820.4.5	Spinoza; an address...tercentenary...birth. (Alexander, Samuel.) Manchester, 1933.
	Phil 2520.163.5	Spinoza, B. de. Descartes' Prinzipien der Philosophie. Leipzig, 1922.
Htn	Phil 2520.163.20*	Spinoza, B. de. Renati des Cartes principiorum philosophial pars I, et II. Amstelodami, 1663.
Htn	Phil 2520.163.15*	Spinoza, B. de. Renatus des Cartes beginzelen der wijsbegeerte. Amsterdam, 1664.
	Phil 3819.45.9	Spinoza, Benedictus de. Abhandlung über die Verbesserung des Verstandes. 4. Aufl. Leipzig, 1922.
	Phil 3819.58	Spinoza, Benedictus de. Adnotationes ad tractatum theologico politicum. Hagae, 1802.
	Phil 3819.10.14	Spinoza, Benedictus de. Benedictus de Spinoza's Sämmtliche Werke. Stuttgart, 1871. 2v.
	Phil 3819.57.25	Spinoza, Benedictus de. Bogoslovsko-politicheskii traktat. Moskva, 1935.
	Phil 3819.70	Spinoza, Benedictus de. Briefwechsel; Einleitung. Leipzig, 1876.
	Phil 3819.70.5	Spinoza, Benedictus de. Briefwechsel; Übertragen und mit Einleitung. Leipzig, 1914.
	Phil 3819.73	Spinoza, Benedictus de. Der Briefwechsel Spinozas. Halle, 1919. 2v.
	Phil 3819.72	Spinoza, Benedictus de. Briefwechsel und andere Dokumente. Leipzig, 1916.
	Phil 3819.72.5	Spinoza, Benedictus de. Briefwechsel und andere Dokumente. Leipzig, 1923.
	Phil 3819.74	Spinoza, Benedictus de. Brieven,,,vertoog over het zuivere denken. Amsterdam, 1897.
	Phil 3819.14.10	Spinoza, Benedictus de. Chief works. N.Y, 1955[1951] 2v.
	Phil 3819.14.5	Spinoza, Benedictus de. Chief works. v.2. London, 1919.
	Phil 3819.76	Spinoza, Benedictus de. The correspondence of Spinoza. London, 1928.
	Phil 3819.60	Spinoza, Benedictus de. Dio. Lanciano, 1911.
	Phil 3819.43	Spinoza, Benedictus de. Das Endliche und Unendliche. Wiesbaden, 1947.
	Phil 3819.31.9	Spinoza, Benedictus de. Ethic demonstrated in geometrical order. London, 1927.
	Phil 3819.31.6	Spinoza, Benedictus de. Ethic demonstrated in geometrical order. N.Y., 1894.
	Phil 3819.36.33	Spinoza, Benedictus de. Ethica, ordine geometrico demonstrata. Hagae, 1914.
	Phil 3819.33.10	Spinoza, Benedictus de. Ethica. Amsterdam, 19- .
	Phil 3819.36.60	Spinoza, Benedictus de. Ethica. München, 1919.
	Phil 3819.36	Spinoza, Benedictus de. Ethica. 's Gravenhage, 1895.
	Phil 3819.36.5	Spinoza, Benedictus de. Ethica op meelkundige wijze uiteengezet. 3. druk. Amsterdam, 1923.
	Phil 3819.36.31	Spinoza, Benedictus de. Ethica ordine geometrico demonstrata. Hagae, 1905.
	Phil 3819.32	Spinoza, Benedictus de. Ethics, demonstrated after the methods of geometers. N.Y., 1888.
	Phil 3819.35.25A	Spinoza, Benedictus de. Ethics. N.Y., 1949.
	Phil 3819.35.26	Spinoza, Benedictus de. Ethics and De intellectus emendatione. London, 1922.
	Phil 3819.45.7A	Spinoza, Benedictus de. Ethics and "De intellectus emendatione". London, 1930.
	Phil 3819.30.5	Spinoza, Benedictus de. Ethik. Berlin, 1868. 2 pam.
	Phil 3819.30	Spinoza, Benedictus de. Die Ethik. Leipzig, 1875.
	Phil 3819.30.25	Spinoza, Benedictus de. Die Ethik. Leipzig, 1910.
	Phil 3819.30.30	Spinoza, Benedictus de. Die Ethik. 7. Aufl. Leipzig, 192-?
	Phil 3819.30.35	Spinoza, Benedictus de. Die Ethik. 10. Aufl. Leipzig, 1922.
	Phil 3819.31	Spinoza, Benedictus de. Ethik demonstrated in geometrical order. London, 1883.
	Phil 3819.30.55	Spinoza, Benedictus de. Die Ethik nach geometrischer Methode dargestellt. Hamburg, 1955.
	Phil 3819.30.29	Spinoza, Benedictus de. Ethik nebst Briefen Welche sich auf die Gegenstände der Ethik. Bd.1. Berlin, 1812.
	Phil 3819.33	Spinoza, Benedictus de. Éthique. Paris, 1907.
	Phil 3819.33.5	Spinoza, Benedictus de. Éthique. Paris, 1908.
	Phil 3819.33.3	Spinoza, Benedictus de. Éthique. Paris, 1908.
	Phil 3819.33.20	Spinoza, Benedictus de. Éthique. Paris, 1961.
	Phil 3819.33.15	Spinoza, Benedictus de. Éthique démontrée suivant l'ordre géométrique et divisée en cinq parties. v.1-2. Paris, 1953.
	Phil 3819.36.35	Spinoza, Benedictus de. Etica...testo latino. Bari, 1915.
	Phil 3819.36.70	Spinoza, Benedictus de. Etica. Madrid, 1940.
	Phil 3819.36.30	Spinoza, Benedictus de. L'etica. Milano, 1913.
	Phil 3819.36.20	Spinoza, Benedictus de. L'etica. Milano, 1914.
	Phil 3819.36.40	Spinoza, Benedictus de. Etica. Milano, 1939.
	Phil 3819.36.25	Spinoza, Benedictus de. Etica. Pt.1-2. Firenze, 1924.
	Phil 3819.33.25	Spinoza, Benedictus de. L'étique. Paris, 1930. 2v.
	Phil 3819.38	Spinoza, Benedictus de. God, man, and human welfare. Chicago, 1909.
	Phil 3819.39.10	Spinoza, Benedictus de. How to improve your mind. N.Y., 1956.
	Phil 3819.39.5	Spinoza, Benedictus de. Improvement of the understanding. N.Y., 1901.
	Phil 3819.39	Spinoza, Benedictus de. Improvement of the understanding. Washington, 1901.
	Phil 3819.40	Spinoza, Benedictus de. Korte verhandeling van God. Amsterdam, 1869.
	Phil 3819.41.15	Spinoza, Benedictus de. Kurze Abhandlung von Gott dem Menschen und seinen Glück. Leipzig, 1922.
	Phil 3819.41	Spinoza, Benedictus de. Kurzer Tractat von Gott. Freiburg, 1881.
	Phil 3819.77	Spinoza, Benedictus de. Lettere. Lanciano, 1938. 2v.
	Phil 3819.63	Spinoza, Benedictus de. Letters to friend and foe. N.Y., 1966.
	Phil 3819.71	Spinoza, Benedictus de. Lettres inédites en français. Paris, 1884.
	Phil 3819.29.30	Spinoza, Benedictus de. The living thoughts of Spinoza. N.Y., 1939.
Htn	Phil 3819.73.10F*	Spinoza, Benedictus de. Nachbildung der im Jahre 1902 noch Erhaltenen...Briefe. Haag, 1903.
	Phil 3819.12	Spinoza, Benedictus de. Oeuvres. Paris, 1842.
	Phil 3819.12.2	Spinoza, Benedictus de. Oeuvres. Paris, 1861.
	Phil 3819.12.3	Spinoza, Benedictus de. Oeuvres. Paris, 1872. 3v.
	Phil 3819.12.4	Spinoza, Benedictus de. Oeuvres complètes. Paris, 1954.
	Phil 3819.15	Spinoza, Benedictus de. Oeuvres de Spinoza. Paris, 1914. 2v.
	Phil 3819.39.7	Spinoza, Benedictus de. On the improvement of the understanding. N.Y., 1958.
	Phil 3819.10.10	Spinoza, Benedictus de. Opera, im Auftrag der Heidelberg Akademie der Wissenschaften Herausgegeben. Heidelberg, 1925. 4v.
	Phil 3819.10.2	Spinoza, Benedictus de. Opera philosophische omnia. v.3. Stuttgardiae, 1830.
Htn	Phil 3819.10.11*	Spinoza, Benedictus de. Opera posthuma. Pt.2. Amstelodami, 1677.
	Phil 3819.10	Spinoza, Benedictus de. Opera quae supersunt omnia. Ienae, 1802. 2v.
	Phil 3819.10.3	Spinoza, Benedictus de. Opera quae supersunt omnia. Lipsiae, 1843-46. 3v.
	Phil 3819.10.4	Spinoza, Benedictus de. Opera quae supersunt omnia supplementum. Amstelodami, 1862.
	Phil 3819.10.8	Spinoza, Benedictus de. Opera quotquot reperta sunt. Hagae, 1882-83. 2v.
	Phil 3819.10.9	Spinoza, Benedictus de. Opera quotquot reperta sunt. 2. ed. Hagae, 1895-96. 3v.
	Phil 3819.10.9.3	Spinoza, Benedictus de. Opera quotquot reperta sunt. 3. ed. v.1-4. Hagae, 1913-14. 2v.
	Phil 3819.35.3	Spinoza, Benedictus de. Philosophy of Spinoza. N.Y., 1892.
	Phil 3819.35	Spinoza, Benedictus de. Philosophy of Spinoza. N.Y., 1894.
	Phil 3819.29A	Spinoza, Benedictus de. The philosophy of Spinoza. N.Y., 1927.
	Phil 3819.57.15A	Spinoza, Benedictus de. The political works. Oxford, 1958.
	Phil 3819.25	Spinoza, Benedictus de. Renati des Cartes et Benedicti de Spinoza praecipua opera. Lipsiae, 1843.
	Phil 3819.35.30A	Spinoza, Benedictus de. The road to inner freedom. N.Y., 1957.
	Phil 3819.11	Spinoza, Benedictus de. Sämmtliche philosophische Werke. Berlin, 1869-71. 2v.
	Phil 3819.11.2	Spinoza, Benedictus de. Sämmtliche Werke. Leipzig, 1914-22. 3v.
	Phil 3819.38.6	Spinoza, Benedictus de. Short treatise on God, man and his well-being. N.Y., 1963.
	Phil 3819.30.50	Spinoza, Benedictus de. Sittenlehre. Frankfurt, 1744.
	Phil 3819.57	Spinoza, Benedictus de. theologisch-politischer Traktat. 4. Aufl. Leipzig, 1922.
	Phil 3819.29.40	Spinoza, Benedictus de. Spinoza dictionary. N.Y., 1951.
	Phil 3819.57.20	Spinoza, Benedictus de. Spinoza on freedom of thought. Montreal, 1962.
	Phil 3819.38.5	Spinoza, Benedictus de. Spinoza's short treatise on God, man and his well-being. London, 1910.
	Phil 3819.38.3	Spinoza, Benedictus de. Spinoza's short treatise on God, man and human welfare. Chicago, 1909.
NEDL	Phil 3819.18	Spinoza, Benedictus de. Spisy filosofické. Prag, 1932.
	Phil 3819.61	Spinoza, Benedictus de. Stelkonstige reeckening van den regenboog. Leiden, 1884.
	Phil 3819.57.5	Spinoza, Benedictus de. Der theologisch-politische Traktat. 2. Aufl. Leipzig, 1910.
	Phil 3819.37	Spinoza, Benedictus de. Tractatus de Deo et homine eiusque felicitate lineamenta atque adnotationes ad tractatum theologico politicum. Halae, 1852.
	Phil 3819.59	Spinoza, Benedictus de. Tractatus politicus. Lanciano, 1915.
	Phil 3819.45	Spinoza, Benedictus de. Tractus De intellectus emendatione. N.Y., 1895.
	Phil 3819.45.15	Spinoza, Benedictus de. Traité de la réforme de l'ertendement. Paris, 1937.
	Phil 3819.59.5	Spinoza, Benedictus de. Trattato politico. Torino, 1958.
	Phil 3819.50	Spinoza, Benedictus de. A treatise partly theological, and partly political. London, 1689.
	Phil 3819.20	Spinoza, Benedictus de. Die Unvollendeten lateinischen Abhandlungen. Heidelberg, 1892.
	Phil 3819.27	Spinoza, Benedictus de. Uren met Spinoza. 2. druk. Baarn, 1917.
	Phil 3819.28	Spinoza, Benedictus de. Von den festen und ewigen Dingen. Heidelberg, 1925.
	Phil 3830.10	Spinoza; Bildnis eines geistigen Helden. (Kayser, Rudolf.) Wien, 1932.
	Phil 3837.8.5	Spinoza; conference tenue à La Haye. (Renan, Ernest.) Paris, 1877.
	Phil 3841.4	Spinoza, de mensch, het leven en het werk. (Vloemans, Antoon.) 's Gravenhage, 1931.

Phil 3837.12.7   Spinoza, Descartes and Maimonides. (Roth, Leon.) N.Y., 1963.

Phil 3837.12A   Spinoza, Descartes and Maimonides. (Roth, Leon.) Oxford, 1924.

Phil 3832.10.15   Spinoza, een levensbeeld. (Meijer, W.) Amsterdam, 1915.

Phil 3820.1.8   Spinoza; ein Denkerleben. (Auerbach, B.) Berlin, 1911.

Phil 3832.5.5   Spinoza; eine Umriss seine Lebens und Wirkens. (Mauthner, Fritz.) Dresden, 1921.

Phil 3830.2   Spinoza, essays by Land, Fischer, Vloten, and Renan. (Knight, E.) London, 1882.

Phil 3821.3.3   Spinoza, et ses contemporaines. 3. éd. (Brunschvicg, L.) Paris, 1923.

Phil 3835.2   Spinoza, handbook to the Ethics. (Picton, Allanson.) London, 1907.

Phil 3835.1.16.2   Spinoza; his life and philosophy. 2nd ed. (Pollock, F.) N.Y., 1966.

Phil 3018.8   Spinoza, Jacobi, Lessing. (Stockum, T.C.) Groningen, 1916.

Phil 3819.75   Spinoza, Lebensbeschreibung und Gespräche. (Gebhardt, Carl.) Leipzig, 1914.

Phil 3823.8   Spinoza, liberator of God and man, 1632-1932. (De Casseres, B.) N.Y., 1932.

Phil 3841.5   Spinoza, mercator en autodidactus. (Vaz Dias, A.M.) 's Gravenhage, 1932.

Phil 3832.20   Spinoza; présentation, choix et traduction des textes. 2. éd. (Misrahi, Robert.) Paris, 1966.

Phil 3837.8   Spinoza; Rede...gehalten im Haag. (Renan, Ernest.) Leipzig, 1877.

Phil 3825.4   Spinoza, sein Leben und seine Lehre. (Freudenthal, J.) Stuttgart, 1904.

Phil 3830.8   Spinoza, sein Leben und seine Lehre. (Klaar, Alfred.) Berlin, 1926.

Phil 3830.9   Spinoza, the biosopher. (Kettner, F.) N.Y., 1932.

Phil 3838.17   Spinoza, the man and his thought. (Schaub, E.L.) Chicago, 1933.

Phil 3831.17   Spinoza, the young thinker who destroyed the past. (Levin, Dan.) N.Y., 1970.

Phil 3819.57   Spinoza; theologisch-politischer Traktat. 4. Aufl. (Spinoza, Benedictus de.) Leipzig, 1922.

Phil 3826.11   Spinoza; vier Reden. (Gebhardt, Carl.) Heidelberg, 1927.

Phil 3842.8.5   Spinoza, 1632-1677. (Wolf, Abraham.) Amsterdam, 1950.

Phil 3838.3   Spinoza...environment. (Smith, H.) Cincinnatti, 1886.

Phil 3820.5   Spinoza. (Alexander, B.) München, 1923.

Phil 3820.7   Spinoza. (Amzalak, M.B.) Lisboa, 1927.

Phil 3820.6   Spinoza. (Appuhn, C.) Paris, 1927.

Phil 3820.1   Spinoza. (Auerbach, B.) Mannheim, 1854.

Phil 3821.27   Spinoza. (Baer, Joseph.) Frankfurt, 191-?

Phil 3821.26   Spinoza. (Belen'kii, M.S.) Moskva, 1964.

Phil 3821.10   Spinoza. (Bohin, Vilhelm.) Berlin, 1894.

Phil 3821.13   Spinoza. (Bolland, G.J.P.J.) Leiden, 1899.

Phil 3822.1.10   Spinoza. (Caird, John.) Edinburgh, 1902.

Phil 3822.1   Spinoza. (Caird, John.) Philadelphia, 1888.

Phil 3822.10   Spinoza. (Cresson, André.) Paris, 1940.

Phil 3823.11   Spinoza. (Dujovne, Leon.) Buenos Aires, 1941-45. 4v.

Phil 3823.7   Spinoza. (Dumrath, O.H.) Stockholm, 1908.

Phil 3825.8.5   Spinoza. (Francès, Madeleine.) Paris, 1937.

Phil 3826.15   Spinoza. (Gallicet Calvetti, Carla.) Milano, 1968.

Phil 3827.9   Spinoza. (Hamphire, S.) Harmondsworth, 1951.

Phil 3827.9.3   Spinoza. (Hamphire, S.) London, 1956.

Phil 3827.15.5   Spinoza. (Hubbeling, H.G.) Baarn, 1966.

Phil 3830.10.5   Spinoza. (Kayser, Rudolf.) N.Y., 1946.

Phil 3831.13   Spinoza. (Lehmans, J.B.) Würzburg, 1864.

Phil 3831.3   Spinoza. (Linde, A. van der.) Göttingen, 1862.

Phil 3832.5   Spinoza. (Mauthner, Fritz.) Berlin, 1906.

Phil 3835.1.15   Spinoza. (Pollock, F.) London, 1935.

Phil 3837.12.5   Spinoza. (Roth, Leon.) London, 1929.

Phil 3838.19   Spinoza. (Sérouya, Henri.) Paris, 1933.

Phil 3838.26   Spinoza. (Sikkes, J.W.T.E.) Den Haag, 1946.

Phil 3838.34   Spinoza. (Stybe, Svend Erik.) København, 1969.

Phil 3841.1.10   Spinoza. (Vloten, J. van.) 's Gravenhage, 1880.

Phil 3842.10   Spinoza. (Wijck, J. van.) Groningen, 1877.

Phil 3825.4.2   Spinoza: Leben und Lehre. 2. Aufl. v.1-2. (Freudenthal, J.) Heidelberg, 1927.

Phil 3826.10   Spinoza. 2. Aufl. (Bolin, Wilhelm.) Darmstadt, 1927.

Phil 3821.3   Spinoza. 2. éd. (Brunschvicg, L.) Paris, 1894.

Phil 3837.20.5   Spinoza. 2. ed. (Rensi, Giuseppe.) Milano, 1944.

Phil 3835.1.2   Spinoza. 2nd ed. (Pollock, F.) London, 1899.

Phil 3822.10.4   Spinoza. 4. éd. (Cresson, André.) Paris, 1959.

Phil 3822.6.5   Spinoza. 5. éd. (Chartier, Emile A.) Paris, 19- .

Phil 3832.5.7   Spinoza. 16. Aufl. (Mauthner, Fritz.) Dresden, 1922.

Phil 3839.1   Spinoza als Metaphysiker. (Thomas, K.) Königsberg, 1840.

Phil 3827.16   Spinoza als uitgangspant. (Hoyack, Louis.) Deventer, 1965.

Phil 3832.13   Spinoza and Buddha. (Melames, S.M.) Chicago, Ill., 1933.

Phil 3835.4.2   Spinoza and religion. (Powell, E.E.) Chicago, 1906.

Phil 3842.13.10   Spinoza and religion. (Wolfson, H.A.) N.Y., 1950.

Phil 3842.13.12   Spinoza and religion. (Wolfson, H.A.) N.Y., 1950.

Phil 3827.14   Spinoza and the idea of freedom. (Hampshire, Stuart.) London, 1960.

Phil 3825.10   Spinoza and The use of liberalism. (Feuer, L.S.) Boston, 1958.

Phil 3820.4   Spinoza and time. (Alexander, Samuel.) London, 1921.

Phil 3837.10   Spinoza as educator. (Rabenort, W.L.) N.Y., 1911.

Phil 3823.5.5   Spinoza aus den Tagen Spinozas. (Dunin-Borkowski, Stanislaus von.) Münster, 1933. 3v.

Phil 3819.5   A Spinoza bibliography, particularly on the period 1940-1967. (Wetlesen, Jon.) Oslo, 1968.

Phil 3834.3   The Spinoza bibliography. (Oko, Adolph S.) Boston, 1964.

Phil 3825.8   Spinoza dans les pays Néerlandais. (Francès, Madeleine.) Paris, 1937.

Phil 3841.6   Spinoza d'après les livres de la bibliothèque. (Vulliaud, P.) Paris, 1934.

Phil 3819.29.40   Spinoza dictionary. (Spinoza, Benedictus de.) N.Y., 1951.

Phil 3827.8.5   Spinoza dreihundert Jahre Ewigkeit. (Hessing, Siegfried.) Den Haag, 1962.

Phil 3832.14   Spinoza e due antecedenti italiani dello Spinozismo. (Meli, Fausto.) Firenze, 1934.

Phil 3821.30   Spinoza e il suo tempo. (Bonfi, Antonio.) Firenze, 1969.

Phil 3838.6   Spinoza en de gereformeerde theologie zijner dagen. (Severijn, Johannes.) Utrecht, 1919.

Phil 3826.5   Spinoza en de idee der personlijkleid. 1. druk. (Gunning, J.H.) Baarn, 1919.

Phil 3821.7.7   Spinoza en de vrijheid. (Betz, H.J.) 's Gravenhage, 1877.

Phil 3821.7.5   Spinoza en Kant. (Betz, H.J.) 's Gravenhage, 1883.

Phil 3832.3   Spinoza en zijn kring. (Meinsma, K.O.) 's Gravenhage, 1896.

Phil 3835.3   Spinoza et la liberté des hommes. (Préposiet, Jean.) Paris, 1967.

Phil 3833.1   Spinoza et la naturalisme contemporain. (Nourrisson, J.F.) Paris, 1866.

Phil 3841.7   Spinoza et la pensée française avant la révolution. (Vernière, P.) Paris, 1954. 2v.

Phil 3841.7.2   Spinoza et la pensée française avant la révolution. Thèse. (Vernière, P.) Paris, 1954. 2v.

Phil 3821.12   Spinoza et la philosophie moderne. (Bellangé, C.) Paris, 1912.

Phil 3837.35   Spinoza et le Dr. Juan de Prado. (Révah, J.S.) Paris, 1959.

Phil 3838.15.5   Spinoza et le panthéisme religieux. (Siwek, Paul.) Paris, 1937.

Phil 3838.15.7   Spinoza et le panthéisme religieux. (Siwek, Paul.) Paris, 1950.

Phil 3823.18.1   Spinoza et le problème de l'expression. (Deleuze, Gilles.) Paris, 1968.

Phil 3831.18   Spinoza et le problème du salut. (Lacroix, Jean.) Paris, 1970.

Phil 3832.26   Spinoza et le spinozisme. 1. éd. (Moreau, Joseph.) Paris, 1971.

Phil 3845.3.10   Spinoza et l'interpretation de l'écriture. (Zac, Sylvain.) Paris, 1965.

Phil 3827.8   Spinoza-Festschrift. (Hessing, Siegfried ed.) Heidelberg, 1933.

Phil 3821.11   Spinoza Gegen Kant und die Sache der geistigen Wahrheit. (Brunner, Constantin.) Berlin, 1910.

Phil 3425.310   The Spinoza-Hegel paradox. (Myers, Henry Alonzo.) Ithaca, 1944.

Phil 3820.3   Spinoza im Porträt. (Altkircli, Ernst.) Jena, 1913.

Phil 3826.4   Spinoza in Deutschland. Gekrönte Preisschrift. (Grunwald, Max.) Berlin, 1897.

Phil 3830.12   Spinoza in Soviet philosophy. (Kline, G.L.) London, 1952.

Phil 3832.16   Spinoza nel terzo centenario della sua nascita. (Milan. Universita Cattolica del Sacro Cuore-Facolta di Filosofia.) Milano, 1934.

Phil 3819.57.20   Spinoza on freedom of thought. (Spinoza, Benedictus de.) Montreal, 1962.

Phil 3837.19   Spinoza on God. (Ratner, J.) N.Y., 1930.

Phil 3838.14   Spinoza Redivivus: eine Fibel für Anfanger. Berlin, 1917.

Phil 3839.2   Spinoza systema philosophicum adumbratum. (Thomas, C.) Borussorum, n.d.

Phil 3823.1.5   Spinoza und Hobbes. (Dessauer, M.) Breslau, 1868.

Phil 3826.1   Spinoza und Hobbes. (Gaspary, A.) Berlin, 1873.

Phil 3827.5   Spinoza und Leibniz. (Helfferich, A.) Hamburg, 1846.

Phil 3822.2.5   Spinoza und Schleiermacher. (Camerer, T.) Stuttgart, 1903.

Phil 3805.162   Spinoza und Schleiermacher. (Schmidt, P.) Berlin, 1868.

Phil 3808.162   Spinoza und Schopenhauer. (Rappaport, S.) Berlin, 1899.

Phil 3832.3.15   Spinoza und sein Kreis. (Meinsma, K.O.) Berlin, 1909.

Phil 3821.24   Spinoza y el panteismo. (Brandt, C.) Buenos Aires, 1941.

Phil 3832.10   Spinozana 1897-1922. (Meijer, W.) Heidelberg, 1922.

Phil 3830.5   Spinoza's Ansicht über den Zweckbegriff. (Kratz, H.) Newied, 1871.

Phil 3838.7   Spinoza's beoordeeling en invloed in duitschland van 1677 tob 1750. (Stockum, T.C. van.) Groningen, 1916.

Phil 3838.31   Spinoza's critique of religion. (Stranso, Leo.) N.Y., 1965.

Phil 3821.1   Spinoza's Entwicklungsgang. (Baltzer, A.) Kiel, 1888.

Phil 3821.5   Spinoza's Erkenntnisslehre. (Berendt, M.) Berlin, 1881.

Phil 3841.2   Spinozas erkjendelsestheori. (Vold, J.M.) Kristiania, 1888.

Phil 3821.14   Spinozas Erste Einwirkungen auf Deutschland. (Bäck, Leo.) Berlin, 1895.

Phil 3827.3.7   Spinozas ethica, analyse og karakteristik. (Høffding, H.) Heidelberg, 1924.

Phil 3827.3.5   Spinozas ethica, analyse og karakteristik. (Høffding, H.) København, 1918.

Phil 3842.14   Spinozas Ethik. (Wolff, Hans M.) München, 1958.

Phil 3830.4   Spinoza's Ethik gegenüber der Erfahrung. (Kniat, Joseph.) Posen, 1888.

Phil 3834.1   Spinoza's Leben und Lehre. (Orelli, J.C. von.) Aurau, 1843.

Phil 3827.10   Spinoza's Lehre vom Verhältniss der Substanz zu ihren Bestimmtheiten Dargestellt. (Hebler, Carl.) Bern, 1850.

Phil 3826.9   Spinoza's Lehren von der Ewigkeit und Unsterblichkeit. (Grzymisch, S.) Breslau, 1898.

Phil 3827.3   Spinozas liv og laere. (Høffding, H.) København, 1877.

Phil 3822.12   Spinoza's metaphysics. (Curley, E.M.) Cambridge, 1969.

Phil 3827.15   Spinoza's methodology. (Hubbeling, H.G.) Assen, 1964.

Phil 3838.16   Spinozas neuentdeckter Tractat von Gott. (Sigwart, Christoph von.) Gotha, 1866.

Phil 3837.7   Spinozas philosophische Terminologie. (Richter, G.T.) Leipzig, 1913.

Phil 3823.3   Spinoza's political and ethical philosophy. (Duff, R.A.) Glasgow, 1903.

Phil 3826.3   Spinoza's Psychologie der Affekte mit Rücksicht auf Descartes. (Gordon, A.) Breslau, 1874.

Phil 3835.9   Spinozas Rationalismus und Erkenntnislehre im Lichte. (Pasig, Walter.) Leipzig, 1892.

Phil 3819.38.5   Spinoza's short treatise on God, man and his well-being. (Spinoza, Benedictus de.) London, 1910.

Phil 3819.38.3   Spinoza's short treatise on God, man and human welfare. (Spinoza, Benedictus de.) Chicago, 1909.

Phil 3827.4   Spinoza's Staatslehre. (Horn, J.F.) Dessau, 1851.

Phil 3821.15   Spinoza's System der Philosophie. (Brasch, Moritz.) Berlin, 1870.

Phil 3829.2   Spinoza's theologisch-politischer Traktat. (Joel, Manuel.) Breslau, 1870.

Phil 3835.8   Spinoza's theory of knowledge. (Parkinson, G.H.R.) Oxford, 1854.

Phil 3829.1.7   Spinoza's Tractus. (Joachim, H.H.) Oxford, 1940.

Phil 3831.10   Spinoza's wijsbegeerte. (Lotsij, M.C.L.) Utrecht, 1888-?

Phil 3838.22   Der Spinozastreit. Inaug. Diss. (Schmoldt, H.) Würzburg, 1938.

Phil 3838.13   Spinozastudien. (Stumpf, K.) Berlin, 1919.

Phil 3823.6   Le spinozisme. (Delblos, Victor.) Paris, 1916.

Phil 3826.6   Spinozismus. (Gans, M.E.) Wien, 1907.

Phil 3838.2   Der Spinozismus. (Sigwart, H.C.W.) Tübingen, 1839.

Phil 3846.5   Spinozistisch Bulletin. Zeist. 1-2,1938-1940

Phil 3246.196   Spinozistisch Bulletin. Zeist. 1-2,1938-1940

Phil 8893.19   Spir, A. Johann Gottlieb Fichte nach seinen Briefen. Leipzig, 1879.

Htn   Phil 193.31.5*   Spir, A. Moralität und Religion. Leipzig, 1874.

Phil 193.31.6   Spir, A. von. Denken und Wirklichkeit. Leipzig, 1877. 2v.

Phil 193.31   Spir, A. von. Denken und Wirklichkeit. v.1-2. Leipzig, 1873.

  Spir, A. von. Denken und Wirklichkeit. v.1-4. Leipzig, 1884-1885. 3v.

Phil 193.31.7   Spir, A. von. Denken und Wirklichkeit. 4e aufl. Leipzig, 1908.

Phil 193.31.15   Spir, A. von. Esquisses de philosophie critique. Paris, 1887.

Phil 193.31.16   Spir, A. von. Esquisses de philosophie critique. Paris, 1930.

Phil 193.31.9   Spir, A. von. Forschung nach der Gewissheit. Leipzig, 1869.

Phil 193.31.8   Spir, A. von. Moralität und Religion. 4e aufl. Leipzig, 1909.

Phil 193.31.17   Spir, A. von. Philosophische Essays. Stuttgart, 18- .

Phil 193.31.13   Spir, A. von. Vorschlag an die Freunde einer vernünftigen Lebensführung. Leipzig, 1869.

Phil 193.31.2   Pamphlet box. Spir, A. von. Pamphlets.

Phil 3850.5.100   Spir, Afrikan. Lettres inédites au professeur. Neuchâtel, 1948.

Phil 3850.5.8   Spir, Afrikan. Paroles d'un sage. Paris, 1938.

Phil 3850.5.15   Spir, Afrikan. Right and wrong. Edinburgh, 1954.

Phil 3850.5.9   Spir, Afrikan. Saggi di filosofia critica. Firenze, 1939.

Phil 5643.127   The spiral after-effect. (Holland, Harry C.) Oxford, 1965.

Phil 2255.9   Spirit and man. (Rotenstreich, N.) The Hague, 1963.

Phil 179.38A   Spirit and nature. (Eranos-Jahrbuch.) N.Y., 1954.

Phil 8406.20   The spirit and substance of art. (Flaccus, L.W.) N.Y., 1926.

Phil 8406.20.5   The spirit and substance of art. (Flaccus, L.W.) N.Y., 1931.

Phil 8406.20.8   The spirit and substance of art. (Flaccus, L.W.) N.Y., 1941.

Phil 8406.20.9   The spirit and substance of art. (Flaccus, L.W.) N.Y., 1947.

Phil 7069.19.165   Spirit experiences. (Mercier, C.A.) London, 1919.

Phil 7054.68   The spirit home: a closet companion. (Gleason, S.W.) Boston, 1852.

Phil 7054.8.5   Spirit identity. (Moses, William S.) London, 1879.

Phil 7069.16.65   Spirit intercourse. 5th ed. (McKenzie, J.H.) London, 1916.

Phil 7054.104   Spirit-intercourse containing incidents of personal experience. (Snow, H.) Boston, 1853.

Phil 7054.120   The spirit land. (Emmons, S.B.) Philadelphia, 1857.

Phil 7054.146   Spirit life of Theodore Parker. (Ramsdell, Elizabeth.) Boston, 1870.

Phil 7054.146.5   Spirit life of Theodore Parker. (Ramsdell, Sarah.) Boston, 1876.

Phil 7054.92.5   Spirit manifestations. (Dods, John B.) N.Y., 1854.

Phil 7054.167.10   Spirit mates, their origin and destiny. (Peebles, J.M.) Battle Creek, 1909.

Phil 7069.19.50   Spirit messages. (Corson, Hiram.) Boston, 1919.

Phil 1818.11   The spirit of American philosophy. (Smith, J.E.) N.Y., 1963.

Phil 8416.30   The spirit of beauty; essays, scientific and aesthetic. (Parker, H.W.) N.Y., 1888.

Phil 930.29.10   The spirit of Chinese philosophy. (Fung, Yu-lan.) London, 1941.

Phil 585.10   The spirit of man. 1st ed. (Burnett, Whit.) N.Y., 1958.

Phil 1511.3.13.5A   The spirit of mediaeval philosophy. (Gilson, Etienne.) N.Y., 1940.

Phil 1717.3A   Spirit of modern philosophy. (Royce, J.) Boston, 1892.

Phil 1717.3.5A   Spirit of modern philosophy. (Royce, J.) Boston, 1893.

Phil 1717.3.8   The spirit of modern philosophy. (Royce, J.) Boston, 1896.

Phil 1717.3.20   The spirit of modern philosophy. (Royce, J.) N.Y., 1955.

Phil 2138.25   The spirit of the age. (Mill, John S.) Chicago, 1942.

Phil 960.15A   The spirit of the East contracted with spirit of the West. (Rāmanāthan, P.) N.Y., 1906.

Phil 192.40   The spirit of the new philosophy. (Randall, J.H.) London, 1919.

Phil 178.12.37   The spirit of the new thought. (Dresser, H.W.) N.Y., 1917.

Phil 9540.12   The spirit of tolerance. (Moore, Katharine.) London, 1964.

Phil 818.25   The spirit of Western philosophy. 1st ed. (Stallknecht, N.P.) N.Y., 1950.

Phil 7072.6.10   Spirit photography. (Morse, James Johnson.) Manchester, 1909.

Phil 7069.14.40   Spirit-psychometry and trance communications by unseen agencies. (D'Aute-Hooper, T.) London, 1914.

Phil 7054.57.5   The spirit-rapper, an autobiography. (Brownson, O.A.) Detroit, 1884.

Phil 7054.57   The spirit-rapper. (Brownson, O.A.) Boston, 1854.

Phil 7054.38   Spirit rapping in England and America. London, 1853.

Phil 7054.23.5   Spirit-rapping unveiled. (Mattison, H.) N.Y., 1855.

Phil 7054.23.3   Spirit rapping unveiled. (Mattison, H.) N.Y., 1953.

Phil 7068.98.15   Spirit state writing and kindred phenomena. (Robinson, William E.) N.Y., 1898.

Phil 7068.94.45   Spirit teachings. (Moses, W.S.) London, 1894.

Phil 7054.150   Spirit voices. (Henck, E.C.) Philadelphia, 1853.

Phil 7068.87.10   Spirit workers in the home circle. (Theobald, Morell.) London, 1887.

Phil 7069.04.10   Spiritism, hypnotism and telepathy. 2. ed. (Bell, Clark.) N.Y., 1904.

Phil 7068.88   Pamphlet vol. Spiritism, psychical research. 9 pam.

Phil 7068.99.60   Pamphlet vol. Spiritism, psychical research. 6 pam.

Phil 7069.26.85   Pamphlet vol. Spiritism, psychical research. 6 pam.

Phil 7054.32   Spiritism; the keystone of Christianity. (Clerk, A.M.) London, 1894.

Phil 7050.8   Pamphlet vol. Spiritism. 13 pam.

Htn   Phil 7050.4*   Pamphlet vol. Spiritism. 7 pam.

Htn   Phil 7050.5*   Pamphlet vol. Spiritism. 8 pam.

Htn   Phil 7050.6*   Pamphlet vol. Spiritism. 18 pam.

Htn   Phil 7050.3PF*   Pamphlet box. Spiritism. Newspaper clippings.

Phil 7069.47.40   Spiritism. 1. ed. (Estabrooks, George Hoben.) N.Y., 1947.

Htn   Phil 7050.12*   Pamphlet vol. Spiritism. 1852-1868.

Phil 7069.11.20   Spiritism and psychology. (Flournoy, Theodore.) N.Y., 1911.

Phil 7060.144   Spiritism and religion. Diss. (Liljencrants, Johan.) Lynchburg, Va., 1918.

Phil 7069.20.140   Spiritism and the fallen angels in the light of the Old and New Testaments. (Gray, James M.) N.Y., 1920.

Phil 7069.19.110   Spiritism in the light of the faith. (Hardy, Thomas J.) London, 1919.

Phil 7054.39   Le spiritisme. (Gibier, P.) Paris, 1887.

Phil 7069.59.35   Le spiritisme. 2. ed. (Castellan, Yvonne.) Paris, 1959.

Phil 7069.22.3   Le spiritisme dans l'église. (Chevreuil, L.) Paris, 1922.

Phil 7069.23.17   Le spiritisme d'aujourd'hui et d'hier. 2. ed. (Rowe, Lucien.) Paris, 1923.

Phil 7069.04.35   Le spiritisme devant la science. (Grasset, J.) Montpellier, 1904.

Phil 7069.36.7   Le spiritisme en face de l'historie. (Glardon, R.) Lausanne, 1936.

Phil 7054.128.5   Lo spiritismo e la scienza di Ateo e Trinacrio. Trecastagne, 1902.

Phil 7054.177   Lo spiritismo nella unianità. (Bonfiglioli, Casimiro.) Bologna, 1888.

Phil 7060.103   Der Spiritismus. (Hartmann, K.R.E. von.) Leipzig, 1885.

Phil 7069.25.20   Der Spiritismus. (Moll, A.) Stuttgart, 1925.

Phil 3915.06   Der Spiritismus. (Wundt, Wilhelm.) Leipzig, 1879-1913. 7 pam.

Phil 7069.21.33   Spiritismus und experimental-psychologie. (Flournoy, Theodor.) Leipzig, 1921.

Phil 7054.37.40   Spiritizm v samom prostom ego vyrazhenii. (Rivail, H.L.D.) Leiptsig, 1864.

Phil 193.87   Spirito, U. Il pragmatismo nella filosofia contemporanea. Firenze, 1921.

Phil 4080.3.135   Spirito, Ugo. Benedetto Croce. Roma, 1929.

Phil 8419.57   Spirito, Ugo. Critica dell'estetica. Firenze, 1964.

Phil 4225.15.40   Spirito, Ugo. Dal mito alla scienza. Firenze, 1966.

Phil 4120.4.130   Spirito, Ugo. Giovanni Gentile. Firenze, 1969.

Phil 177.105.30   Spirito, Ugo. Ideale del dialogo o ideale della scienza? Roma, 1966.

Phil 400.77   Spirito, Ugo. L'idealismo italiano e i suoi critici. Firenze, 1930.

Phil 4120.4.110   Spirito, Ugo. Note sur pensiero di Giovanni Gentile. Firenze, 1954.

Phil 4018.3   Spirito, Ugo. Il nuovo idealismo italiano. Roma, 1923.

Phil 1750.166.195   Spirito, Ugo. Nuovo umanesimo. Roma, 1964.

Phil 193.140   Spirito, Ugo. Scienza e filosofia. Firenze, 1933.

Phil 165.362   Spirito, Ugo. Storia antologica dei problemi filosofici. Firenze, 1965. 7v.

Phil 4225.15.30   Spirito, Ugo. La vita come arte. Firenze, 1941.

Phil 8735.22   Lo spirito assoluto. (Cogni, G.) Firenze, 1937.

Phil 188.26   Spirito del tempo e costume speculativo. (Negri, Antimo.) Firenze, 1962.

Phil 194.31.5   Lo spirito della filosofia. (Troilo, Erminis.) Citta di Castello, 1925.

Phil 181.57   Spirito e realta. (Galli, Gallo.) Milano, 1927.

Phil 4060.1.82   Lo spirito evangelico di Roberto Ardigo. (Marchesini, G.) Bologna, 1919.

Phil 6111.66   Spirits in rebellion. (Braden, C.S.) Dallas, 1963.

Phil 7054.17   The spirits tried. (Pridham, A.) London, 1874.

Phil 7069.29.80   The spiritual adventures of a business man. 2. ed. (Purchas, T.A.R.) London, 1930.

Phil 7059.12.9   The spiritual Alps and how we ascend them. 5th ed. (Hull, Moses.) Chicago, 1895.

Phil 7069.27.55   Spiritual America. (Wells, H.B.) Boston, 1927.

Phil 7061.15   Spiritual and Ethical Society, N.Y. Publications. N.Y., 19- .

Phil 7069.29.90   Spiritual and Ethical Society, New York. How do the dead communicate. n.p., 1929.

Phil 8589.6   Spiritual ascent of man. (Jones, William T.) N.Y., 1917.

Phil 8586.49   The spiritual basis of democracy. (Gillett, H.T.) Oxford, 1952.

Phil 7068.95   Spiritual Christianity revealed by occultism. (Tindall, A.F.) London, 189-.

Phil 7054.77F   A spiritual communicating diagram. (Kidder, L.) n.p., n.d.

Phil 7054.28   Spiritual communications. (Kiddle, H.) Boston, 1879.

Phil 8598.22   Spiritual consciousness. (Sprague, F.H.) Wollaston, 1898.

Phil 7054.143   The "spiritual" delusion. (Lum, Dyer D.) Philadelphia, 1873.

Phil 7069.61.5   Spiritual dimensions. (Teillard, A.) London, 1961.

Phil 8693.7   Spiritual evolution. (Deyo, M.L.) Binghamton, N.Y., 1913.

Phil 7054.85   Spiritual experience. (Platt, L.L.) New Haven, 1852. 2 pam.

Phil 7054.141.5   Spiritual experiences. (Cooper, Robert.) London, 1867.

Phil 8592.36   Spiritual gravity of the cosmist. (Moore, Willis L.) Pasadena, 1926.

Htn   Phil 4363.2.30*   The spiritual guide. (Molinos, M. de.) Venice, 1688.

Phil 4363.2.36   The spiritual guide of Michael de Molinos. (Molinos, M. de.) London, 191-?

Phil 4363.2.35   The spiritual guide of Michael de Molinos. (Molinos, M. de.) Philadelphia, 1897.

Phil 6312.15   Spiritual healing. (Geikie Cobb, W.J.) London, 1914.

Phil 8708.10   The spiritual interpretation of nature. 2. ed. (Simpson, James Y.) London, 1912.

Phil 7069.20.370   A spiritual interpretation of some psychic happenings. (Roberts, W. Adair.) London, 1932.

Phil 5627.26   The spiritual life; studies in the science of religion. (Coe, George A.) Chicago, 1914.

Phil 5627.26.2   The spiritual life; studies in the science of religion. (Coe, George A.) N.Y., 1900.

Phil 8581.86   The spiritual life. (Brightman, E.S.) N.Y., 1942.

Phil 5627.60.20   The spiritual life. (Underhill, E.) N.Y., 1937.

Phil 8599.29   The spiritual life. 2. ed. (Tanquerey, A.) Tournai, 1932.

Phil 7069.00.10   Spiritual manifestations. (Cooper, William Earnshaw.) Exeter, 19- .

Phil 8615.9.2   The spiritual nature of man. (Coit, Stanton.) Bayswater, 1910.

Phil 7054.10   Spiritual or magnetic forces. 2. ed. (Holland, C.) N.Y., 1882.

Phil 179.3.61   The spiritual outlook of Europe today. (Eucken, R.) London, 1922.

Phil 8598.110.10   Spiritual perspectives and human facts. (Schuon, Frithjof.) London, 1954.

Phil 181.16   Spiritual philosophy. (Green, Joseph Henry.) London, 1865.

Phil 7054.109   The spiritual philosophy vs. diabolism. (King, M.M.) Boston, 1871.

Phil 192.36.10   Spiritual pluralism and recent philosophy. (Richardson, C.A.) Cambridge, 1919.

Phil 192.36   Spiritual pluralism and recent philosophy. (Richardson, C.A.) Cambridge, 1919.

Phil 7069.19.215   Spiritual reconstruction. N.Y., 1919.

Phil 8581.80   Spiritual religion. (Baillie, James.) London, 1940.

Phil 7054.129   Spiritual science, universal religion. (Wright, Alfred A.) N.Y., 1917.

Phil 7054.176   Spiritual sermons [delivered in 1886-1889]. (Richmond, Cora L.) n.p., n.d.

Phil 7054.4.15   The spiritual significance. (Whiting, Lilian.) Boston, 1900.

Phil 7069.34.9   A spiritual spiritualism. (Clark, R.P.) London, 1934.

Phil 7059.16   Spiritual teacher. (Ambler, R.P.) N.Y., 1852.

Phil 7054.61.8   Spiritual telegraph. The telegraph papers. N.Y., 1853. 8v.

Phil 7054.147   The spiritual telegraphic opposition line. (Campbell, Z.) Springfield, 1853.

Phil 6112.19 Spiritual therapeutics. (Colville, W.W.J.) Chicago, 1890.
Phil 7069.24.31 The spiritual universe. (Murray, O.) London, 1924.
Phil 8630.9 Spiritual values and eternal life. (Fosdick, H.E.)
Cambridge, 1927.
Phil 7054.41 Spiritual vampirism. (Webber, C.W.) Philadelphia, 1853.
Phil 7054.98.3 Spiritualism, a satanic delusion. (Ramsey, William.)
Peace Dale, R.I., 1856.
Phil 7054.98 Spiritualism, a satanic delusion. (Ramsey, William.)
Rochester, N.Y., 1857.
Phil 7069.20.61 Spiritualism, its present-day meaning. (Carter, Huntly.)
Philadelphia, 1920.
Phil 7054.97 Pamphlet vol. Spiritualism. 6 pam.
Phil 7069.00.1 Pamphlet box. Spiritualism.
Phil 7069.00.2 Pamphlet vol. Spiritualism. 4 pam.
Phil 7069.46.15 Spiritualism. (Desmond, Shaw.) London, 1946?
Phil 7054.52 Spiritualism. (Edmonds, J.W.) N.Y., 1855. 2v.
Phil 7054.132 Spiritualism. (Hill, J. Arthu.) N.Y., 1919.
Phil 7069.20.180 Spiritualism. (Kernahan, Coulson.) N.Y., 1920.
Phil 7069.20.220 Spiritualism. (McCabe, J.) N.Y., 1920.
Phil 7069.66.35 Spiritualism: a critical survey. (Edmunds, Simeon.)
London, 1966.
Phil 7054.52.4 Spiritualism. 4th ed. (Edmonds, J W.) N.Y., 1853.
Phil 7054.184 Spiritualism among civilised and savage races. (Lawrence,
E.) London, 1921.
Phil 7054.151 Spiritualism and necromancy. (Morrison, A.B.)
Cincinnati, 1873.
Phil 7054.154 Spiritualism and other signs. London, n.d.
Phil 7069.44.20 Spiritualism and religion. (Butterworth, G.W.)
London, 1944.
Phil 7069.17.31 Spiritualism and Sir Oliver Lodge. (Mercier, Charles A.)
London, 1917.
Phil 7069.69.5 Spiritualism and society. (Nelson, Geoffrey K.)
London, 1969.
Phil 7069.20.82 Spiritualism and the new psychology. (Culpin, Millais.)
London, 1920.
Phil 7060.107 Spiritualism answered by science. (Cox, E.W.)
London, 1871.
Phil 7068.71.2 Spiritualism answered by science. (Cox, E.W.) N.Y., 1872.
Phil 7069.44.40 Spiritualism as spiritualists have written of it.
(O'Neill, Herbert V.) London, 1944.
Phil 7069.28.95 Spiritualism explained. (Whitehead, George.)
London, 1928.
Phil 7054.137.5 Spiritualism explained. 2. ed. (Tiffany, Joel.)
N.Y., 1856.
Phil 7069.31.10 Spiritualism for the enquirer. (Hunt, H. Ernest.)
London, 1931.
Phil 7069.31.8 Spiritualism in the light of occult science. (Firth,
Violet M.) London, 1931.
Phil 7054.33.7 Spiritualism tested. (Samson, G.W.) Boston, 1860.
Phil 7060.109 Spiritualism tested by science. (Johnson, Samuel.) New
Haven, 1858.
Phil 7054.171 Spiritualism unveiled. (Grant, Miles.) Boston, 1866.
Phil 7054.139 Spiritualism versus Christianity. (Daniels, J.W.)
N.Y., 1856.
Phil 7054.90.5 Spiritualisme; faits curieux. (Auguez, Paul.)
Paris, 1858.
Phil 186.1 Le spiritualisme. (Landon, E.) Paris, 1872.
Phil 7069.66.15 Le spiritualisme athée. (Lance, Pierre.) Paris, 1966.
Phil 2405.2.3 Spiritualisme et libéralisme. (Ferraz, Marin.)
Paris, 1887.
Phil 8685.7 Spiritualisme et panthéisme. (Martha-Beker, F.)
Paris, 1867.
Phil 2725.25.90 Le spiritualisme existentiel de René LeSenne. (Paumen,
Jean.) Paris, 1949.
Phil 4073.120 Lo spiritualismo di Tommasco Campanella. (Femiano,
Salvatore Beniamino.) Napoli, 1965. 2v.
Phil 4011.3.5 Lo spiritualismo religioso nell'età del Risorgimento
italiano. (Librizzi, C.) Catania, 1955.
Phil 7068.84.15 Der Spiritualismus und die Urssenschaft. 2. Aufl.
(Crookes, William.) Leipzig, 1884.
NEDL Phil 28.4 Spiritualist newspaper. London. 1869-1882 12v.
Phil 7068.93.10 Spiritualist philosophy. (Rivail, H.L.D.) Boston, 1893.
Phil 28.3 Le spiritualiste de la Nouvelle Orleans. Nouvelle
Orleans, 1857.
Phil 7069.62.5 The spiritualists; story of F. Cook and Wm. Crookes.
(Hall, Trevor.) London, 1962.
Phil 3552.303 La spiritualitá dell'essere e Leibniz. (Barié, G.E.)
Padova, 1933.
Phil 2475.1.485 La spiritualité de Bergson. (Violette, René.)
Toulouse, 1968.
Phil 486.25 Spiritualité de la matière. (Linssen, Robert.)
Paris, 1966.
Phil 5627.257.10 Spiritualité de la vie active. (Sanson, Henri.) Le
Puy, 1957.
Phil 530.50.10 La spiritualité des Pays-Bas. (Arters, Stephanus.)
Louvain, 1948.
Phil 8626.10 Spiritualité et immortalité. (Bernies, V.) Paris, 1901.
Phil 978.49.620 Die spirituellen Hintergründe der äusseren Welt. (Steiner,
R.) Dornach, 1966.
Phil 5520.250 Spirkin, A.G. Myshlenie i iazyk. Moskva, 1958.
Phil 5374.205 Spirkin, A.G. Proiskhozhdenie soznaniia. Moskva, 1960.
Phil 310.751.6 Spirkin, Aleksandr G. The basic principles of dialectical
and historical materialism. Moscow, 1971.
Phil 310.751 Spirkin, Aleksandr G. Teoriia, preobrasui ushchaia mir.
Moskva, 1969.
Phil 400.128 Spisani, Franco. Natura e spírito nell'idealismo attuale.
Milano, 1968?
Phil 5066.304 Spisani, Franco. Neutralizzazione dello spazio per
sintesiproduttiva. 2. ed. Milano, 1968.
Phil 5069.2 Spisoni, Franco. Logica ed esperienza. Milano, 1967.
NEDL Phil 3819.18 Spisy filosofické. (Spinoza, Benedictus de.) Prag, 1932.
Phil 8643.7 Spitta, H. Mein Recht auf Leben. Tübingen, 1900.
Phil 7080.11 Spitta, H. Die Schlaf- und Traumzustände der menschlichen
Seele. Tübingen, 1878.
Phil 7080.15.2 Spitta, H. Die Schlaf- und Traumzustände der menschlichen
Seele. 2. Aufl. Tübingen, 1882.
Phil 5780.7 Spitta, H. Die Willensbestimmungen und ihr Verhältniss zu
den Impulsiven. Tübingen, 1881.
Phil 5258.45 Spitta, Heinrich. Einleitung in die Psychologie als
Wissenschaft. Freiburg, 1886.
Phil 5258.45.5 Spitta, Heinrich. Die psychologische Forschung und ihre
Aufgabe in der Gegenwart. Freiburg, 1889.
Phil 3640.219 Spitteler, Carl. Meine Beziehungen zu Nietzsche.
München, 1908.
Phil 5402.20 Spitz, C. Zur Psychologie des Weinens. Inaug. Diss.
Zeulenroda, 1935.
Phil 6328.48 Spitz, René. A genetic field theory of ego formation.
N.Y., 1959.

Phil 3625.8.85 Spitzer, David. Darstellung und Kritik der
Thierpsychologie Georg Friedrich Meier's. Inaug. Diss.
Györ 1903.
Phil 299.5 Spitzer, H. Über Ursprung...des Hylozoismus. Graz, 1881.
Phil 8050.59 Spitzer, H. Kritische studien zur Asthetik der
Gegenwart. Wien, 1897.
Phil 3018.11 Spitzer, Hugo. Nominalismus und Realismus in der neuesten
deutschen Philosophie. Leipzig, 1876.
Phil 193.81 Spitzer, Hugo. Ueber das Verhältnis der Philosophie.
Leipzig, 1883.
Phil 6968.7 Spitzka, E.C. Insanity, its classification. N.Y., 1887.
Phil 7069.35.25 Spivey, T.S. The awakening of the sixth sense; a look into
the great unknown. Shawneetown, Ill., 1935.
Phil 7069.03.45 Spivey, T.S. Lavius Egyptus. Cincinnati, 1903. 2v.
Phil 310.575 Spizkin, A.G. Kurs marksistskoi filosofii. Moskva, 1963.
Phil 8876.42 The splendor of the human body. (Brent, C.H.) N.Y., 1904.
Phil 3425.623 Splett, Jörg. Die Trinitätslehre G.W.F. Hegels.
Freiburg, 1965.
Htn Phil 7068.99* Spoer, Adela Goodrich-Freer. Essays in psychical research.
London, 1899.
Phil 7068.99.20 Spoer, Adela Goodrich-Freer. Essays in psychical research.
2. ed. London, 1899.
Phil 8050.60 Spoerri, T. Die Struktur der Existenz. Zürich, 1951.
Phil 2805.300 Spoerri, T. Der verborgene Pascal. Hamburg, 1955.
Phil 5520.459 Spoerri, Theodor. Sprachphänomene und Psychose.
Basel, 1964.
Phil 1750.380 Spoerri, Theophil F. Die Herausforderung des
Existenzialismus. Hamburg, 1954.
Phil 299.28 Spoerri, Walter. Spathellenistische Berichte über Welt.
Basel, 1959.
Phil 192.77.5 Spoken essays. (Robertson, J.M.) London, 1925.
Phil 1750.166.153 Spongano, Raffaele. Due saggi sull'umanesimo.
Firenze, 1964.
Phil 4570.4.81 Spongberg, V.H. The philosophy of Erik Gustaf Geijer.
Rock Island, 1945.
Phil 6028.6 Spontane, Ciro. La metoposcopia, overo comensuratione
delle linea della fronte. Venetia, 1626.
Phil 5762.28 Spontaneität und Gesetzlichkeit. (Mueller, Heinz Alfred.)
Bonn, 1967.
Phil 7054.128 "Spookland", a record of research. (Henry, T.S.)
Chicago, 1902.
Phil 1900.94 Spooner, W.A. Bishop Butler. London, 1901.
Phil 4803.462.1 Spór o istnienie świata. (Ingarden, Roman.)
Kraków, 1947-48. 2v.
Phil 4803.462.2 Spór o istnienie świata. Wyd. 2. (Ingarden, Roman.)
Warszawa, 1960-61. 2v.
Phil 4803.320.30 Spór o metafizyke. (Dembowski, Bronisław.)
Warszawa, 1969.
Phil 8980.792 Spór o zagadnienie moralności. (Schaff, Adam.)
Warszawa, 1958.
Phil 8980.572.5 Sporiu. (Mikhalevich, Aleksandr Vl.) Moskva, 1968.
Phil 818.41.3 Spotkania z filozofia. 3. Wyd. (Sikora, Adam.)
Warszawa, 1970.
Phil 6980.704 Spotnitz, Hyman. The couch and the circle. N.Y., 1961.
Phil 8419.29 Die Sprache der Kunst. (Schumacher, F.) Stuttgart, 1942.
Phil 5592.115 Die Sprache der Zeichnung. (Biedma, Carlos.) Bern, 1959.
Phil 3790.20.5 Die Sprache des Menschengeschlechts. (Rosenstock, Eugen.)
Heidelberg, 1963-64. 2v.
Phil 7082.38 Die Sprache des Traumes. (Stekel, Wilhelm.)
Wiesbaden, 1911.
Phil 7082.38.2 Die Sprache des Traumes. 2e Aufl. (Stekel, Wilhelm.)
München, 1922.
Phil 7082.38.3 Die Sprache des Traumes. 3e Aufl. (Stekel, Wilhelm.)
München, 1927.
Phil 3425.588 Die Sprache in der Philosophie Hegels. (Lauener, H.)
Berlin, 1962.
Phil 5520.425 Sprache und Bewusstsein. (Liebrucks, Bruno.)
Frankfurt, 1964. 5v.
Phil 1750.860 Sprache und Denken als sprachphilosophisches Problem von
Locke bis Wittgenstein. (Schmidt, Siegfried Josef.) Den
Haag, 1968[1969].
Phil 5055.38 Sprache und Logik. (Patzig, Günther.) Göttingen, 1970.
Phil 8593.24 Sprache und Offenbarung. (Noack, H.) Gütersloh, 1960.
Phil 5520.590 Sprache und Raum. (Simon, Josef.) Berlin, 1969.
Phil 193.246 Sprache und Sein. (Specht, Ernst K.) Berlin, 1967.
Phil 3640.615 Sprache und Stil von Nietzsches Zarathustra. (Morawa,
Hans.) München, 1958.
Phil 5875.10 Sprachfreie Kategorisierung bei Kleinkindern. Diss.
(Roecker, Doris.) Tübingen, 1965.
Phil 3915.75 Sprachgeschichte und Sprachpsychologie. (Wundt, Wilhelm.)
Leipzig, 1901.
Phil 978.49.145 Sprachgestaltung und dramatische Kunst. (Steiner, R.)
Dornach, 1926.
Phil 978.49.145.3 Sprachgestaltung und dramatische Kunst. 3. Aufl. (Steiner,
R.) Dornach, 1969.
Phil 3640.392 Die Sprachkunst Friedrich Nietzsches in Also sprach
Zarathustra. (Vitens, Siegfried.) Bremen, 1951.
Phil 5520.422 Die sprachlichen Grundlagen der Philosophie. (Jánoska, G.)
Graz, 1962.
Phil 5520.498 Sprachlicher Ausdrucksgehalt und akustische Struktur.
(Hoeffe, Wilhelm Laziar.) Ratingen bei Düsseldorf, 1966.
Phil 6400.35 Sprachpflege kurs für Schwerhörige und Ertaubte. (Heese,
Gerhard.) Berlin, 1963.
Phil 5520.459 Sprachphänomene und Psychose. (Spoerri, Theodor.)
Basel, 1964.
Phil 5520.405 Sprachphilosophie der Gegenwart. (Wein, Hermann.) Den
Haag, 1963.
Phil 5520.330 Die Sprachphilosophie O.F. Guppe's und G. Gerber's.
(Simonis, A.) Bonn, 1959.
Phil 7069.67.15 Spraggett, Allen. The unexplained. N.Y., 1967.
Phil 8598.22 Sprague, F.H. Spiritual consciousness. Wollaston, 1898.
Phil 8893.20 Sprague, W.B. Letters on practical subjects.
Hartford, 1822.
Phil 9358.8.2 Sprague, W.B. Letters to young men. 2d ed. Albany, 1845.
Phil 5258.74.5 Spranger, Eduard. Gedanken zur Daseinsgestaltung.
München, 1954.
Phil 3850.46.1 Spranger, Eduard. Gesammelte Schriften. v.1-3,8.
Tübingen, 1969- 4v.
Phil 5258.74.4 Spranger, Eduard. Lebensformen; geisteswissenschaftliche
Psychologie und Ethik der Personlichkeit. 4. Aufl.
Halle, 1924.
Phil 5258.74.9A Spranger, Eduard. Types of men. Halle, 1928.
Phil 3195.6.83A Spranger, Eduard. Wilhelm Dilthey. Berlin, 1912.
Phil 4803.497.35 Sprawność i błąd. (Kotarbiński, Tabeusz.) Warszawa, 1956.
Phil 3195.17.30 Sprechen. (Diez, Max.) Berlin, 1934.
Phil 5590.255 Spreither, Franz. Verwirklichen. Konstanz, 1958.
Phil 5590.255.2 Spreither, Franz. Verwirklichende Vern-Zentrierung. 2.
Aufl. Konstanz, 1959.

Phil 1523.16 — Sprengard, Karl Anton. Systematisch-historische Untersuchungen zur Philosophie des XIV. Jahrhunderts. Bonn, 196-.

Phil 3120.11.98 — Spreuken. (Bolland, G.J.P.J.) 's Gravenhage, 1962.

Htn Phil 9358.11* — Sprigg, William. Philosophicall essayes...advises to ladyes. London, 1657.

Phil 4080.3.210 — Sprigge, Cecil Jackson Squire. Benedetto Croce. Cambridge, Eng., 1952.

Phil 4080.3.211 — Sprigge, Cecil Jackson Squire. Benedetto Croce. New Haven, 1952.

Phil 5070.32 — Sprigge, Timothy Lauro Squire. Facts, words, and beliefs. N.Y., 1970.

Phil 2630.6.85 — Spring, Gerald M. Man's invincible surmise; a personal interpretation of Bovarysm. N.Y., 1968.

Phil 978.49.140 — Spring, H.P. Essays on human science. Winter Park, 1943.

Phil 3425.275 — Springer, Anton T.H. Die Hegel'sche Geschichtsanschauung. Tübingen, 1848.

Phil 3475.3.110 — Springer, J.L. Existentiele metaphysica. Assen, 1951.

Phil 8892.19 — Springs of action. (Richards, C.H.B.) N.Y., 1863.

Phil 9150.2 — The springs of conduct. (Morgan, C.L.) London, 1885.

Phil 6980.776 — The springs of creativity. (Westman, H.) N.Y., 1961.

Phil 5259.21 — The springs of human action. (Thomson, M.K.) N.Y., 1927.

Phil 5525.34 — The springs of laughter. (Kimmins, G.W.) London, 1928.

Phil 5258.116 — Sprott, W.J.H. General psychology. London, 1937.

Phil 5258.116.5 — Sprott, W.J.H. Psychology for everyone. London, 1937.

Phil 5480.2 — Spruijt, C.B. Proeve van eene geschiedenis van de leer der aangeboren begrippen. Leiden, 1879.

Phil 8708.42.5 — Spülbeck, Otto. Grenzfragen zwischen Naturwissenschaft und Glaube. München, 1970.

Phil 8708.42 — Spülbeck, Otto. Zur Begegnung von Naturwissenschaft und Theologie. Einsiedeln, 1969.

Phil 7060.156 — Spuk. (Moser, F.) Baden bei Zürich, 1950.

Phil 7069.17.31.15 — Der Spuk. 2. Aufl. (Piper, Otto.) München, 1922.

Phil 7069.22.11 — Spuk und Geistererscheinungen oder was sonst? 2. Aufl. (Grabinski, B.) Hildesheim, 1922.

Phil 7060.46 — Spuls-Geschichten. (Puls, G.) Berlin, n.d.

Phil 8876.84 — Spunti di dottrina etica. (Bonatelli, Paolo.) Bologna, 1928.

Phil 176.69.10 — Spuren. (Bloch, Ernst.) Berlin, 1930.

Phil 176.69.12 — Spuren. (Bloch, Ernst.) Berlin, 1960.

Phil 176.69.12.5 — Spuren. 5. Aufl. (Bloch, Ernst.) Frankfurt, 1967.

Phil 1135.23.15 — Die Spuren griechischer Philosophie. 1e and 2e Aufl. (Sellin, Ernst.) Leipzig, 1905.

Phil 9400.1 — Spurinna...comforts of old age. (Bernard, T.) London, 1816.

Phil 6128.5 — Spurzheim, J.K. The anatomy of the brain. London, 1826.

Phil 6968.8 — Spurzheim, J.K. Beobashtungen über den Wahnsinn. Hamburg, 1818.

Phil 8893.21.3 — Spurzheim, J.K. The natural laws of man. N.Y., 1849.

Phil 6968.8.6 — Spurzheim, J.K. Observations...mind...insanity. Boston, 1833.

Phil 6968.8.5 — Spurzheim, J.K. Observations...mind...insanity. London, 1817.

Phil 8893.21 — Spurzheim, J.K. Philosophical catechism...natural laws of man. Boston, 1832.

Phil 8893.21.2 — Spurzheim, J.K. Philosophical catechism...natural laws of man. Boston, 1835.

Phil 5938.6 — Spurzheim, Johann Gaspar. Outlines of phrenology. Boston, 1832.

Phil 5938.6.2 — Spurzheim, Johann Gaspar. Outlines of phrenology. 2nd ed. Boston, 1833.

Phil 5938.6.5 — Spurzheim, Johann Gaspar. Outlines of phrenology. 3rd ed. Boston, 1834.

Phil 5938.6.3 — Spurzheim, Johann Gaspar. Outlines of phrenology. 3rd ed. Boston, 1834.

Phil 5938.6.43 — Spurzheim, Johann Gaspar. Philosophical catechism of the natural laws of man. Boston, 1833.

Phil 5938.6.30 — Spurzheim, Johann Gaspar. Phrenology, in connection with the study of physiognomy. Boston, 1833.

Phil 5938.6.11 — Spurzheim, Johann Gaspar. Phrenology. Boston, 1834. 2v.

Phil 5938.6.23 — Spurzheim, Johann Gaspar. Phrenology. London, 1825?

Phil 5938.6.24 — Spurzheim, Johann Gaspar. Phrenology. pt.1. London, 1826.

Phil 5938.6.10 — Spurzheim, Johann Gaspar. Phrenology. v.1-2. Boston, 1832.

Phil 5938.6.12 — Spurzheim, Johann Gaspar. Phrenology. 5th American ed. Boston, 1838.

Phil 5938.6.18 — Spurzheim, Johann Gaspar. A view of the philosophical principles of phrenology. 3rd ed. London, 18- .

Phil 8673.20 — Sputnik ateista. 2. izd. Moskva, 1961.

Phil 4073.122 — Squillace, Mario. La vita eroica di Tommaso Campanella. Roma, 1967.

Phil 1020.39 — Srednevekovaia filosofiia narodov Blizhnego i Srednego Vostoka. (Krikorian, Sergei.) Moskva, 1966.

Phil 735.122 — Sreenivasa Iyengar, K.R. The metaphysics of value. Mysore, 1942.

Phil 4870.14 — Srivastava, Rama Shanker. Contemporary Indian philosophy. Delhi, 1965.

Phil 3120.8.150 — Srzednicki, Jan. Franz Brentano's analysis of truth. The Hague, 1965.

Phil 8673.4 — Staab, K. Die Gottesbeweise. Paderborn, 1909.

Phil 5258.62 — Staak, Hermann. Aufbau der höheren geistigen Entwicklung. Rostock, 1921.

Phil 5258.62.15 — Pamphlet box. Staak, Hermann.

Phil 193.243 — Staal, J.F. Euclides en Panini. Amsterdam, 1963.

Phil 3425.76 — Der Staat. (Hegel, Georg Wilhelm Friedrich.) Leipzig, 1924.

Phil 3837.40 — Staat der Freiheit. (Roehrich, Welfried.) Darmstadt, 1969.

Phil 1504.19 — Der Staat in seinen Beziehungen zur sittlichen. v.19, pt.1. (Müller, W.) Münster, 1966.

Phil 3808.119.5 — Staat und Recht bei Schopenhauer. (Pfordten, T. von der.) München, 1916.

Phil 5258.194 — Staats, A.W. Complex human behavior. N.Y., 1964.

Phil 3552.385 — Das Staatsdenken bei Leibniz. (Herrmann, Karl.) Bonn, 1958.

Phil 3246.224 — Die Staatsidee des Rationalismus...und die Staatsphilosophie Fichte's. (Walz, G.A.) Berlin, 1928.

Phil 3425.101 — De staatsleer van Hegel. (Kredenburch, W.C.A.) Utrecht, 1931.

Htn Phil 3246.77* — Staatslehre. (Fichte, Johann Gottlieb.) Berlin, 1820.

Phil 3493.3 — Die Staatslehre auf Kantischer Grundlage. (Lefkovits, M.) Bern, 1899.

Phil 4769.1.97 — Die Staatslehre W. Solowjews. (Ambrozaitis, K.) Paderborn, 1927.

Phil 3805.164 — Die Staatsphilosophie Schleiermachers. (Holstein, Günther.) Bonn, 1923.

Phil 3528.80 — Die staatswissenschaftlichen Anschauungen und die politisch-publizistische Tätigkeit des Nachkantianers Wilhelm Traugott Krug. Inaug. Diss. (Fiedler, A.) Dresden, 1933.

Phil 9530.20 — Stability, an indispensable element of usefulness and greatness. (Wyckoff, Isaac N.) Albany, 1840.

Phil 5590.578.1 — Stability and change in human characteristics. (Bloom, Benjamin Samuel.) N.Y., 1966.

Phil 3425.199A — Stace, N.J. The philosophy of Hegel. London, 1924.

Phil 1123.5 — Stace, W.T. Critical history of Greek philosophy. London, 1920.

Phil 8419.28 — Stace, W.T. The meaning of beauty, a theory of aesthetics. London, 1929.

Phil 193.154 — Stace, W.T. The nature of the world; an essay in phenomenalist metaphysics. Princeton, 1940.

Phil 8598.100 — Stace, W.T. Religion and the modern mind. 1. ed. Philadelphia, 1952.

Phil 349.32 — Stace, W.T. Theory of knowledge and existence. Oxford, 1932.

Phil 525.205 — Stace, Walter T. Mysticism and philosophy. 1st ed. Philadelphia, 1960.

Phil 5548.40 — Stacey, Chalmers L. Understanding human motivation. Cleveland, 1958.

Phil 8893.72 — Der Stachel der Ethik. (Skala, Richard.) Wien, 1927.

Phil 349.46 — Stachowiak, Herbert. Denken und Erkennen im kybernetischen Modell. Wien, 1965.

Phil 1135.240 — Stachowiak, Herbert. Rationalismus im Ursprung. Wien, 1971.

Phil 6322.1 — Stachyologie, weitere vermischte Aufsätze. (Möbius, P.J.) Leipzig, 1909.

Phil 1870.180 — Stack, George J. Berkeley's analysis of preception. The Hague, 1970.

Phil 1750.33 — Stackelberg, Jo. von. Schuld ist Schicksal. München, 1948.

Phil 1523.7 — Stadelmann, R. Vom Geist des ausgehenden Mittelalters. Halle, 1929.

Phil 5870.28 — Stades et concept de stade de développement de l'enfant dans la psychologie contemporaine. (Tran-Thong.) Paris, 1967.

Phil 349.13.2 — Stadler, A. Die Grundbegriffe der Erkenntnis. Leipzig, 1913.

Phil 349.13 — Stadler, A. Grundbegriffe der Erkenntnis. Leipzig, 1918.

Phil 3500.10.15 — Stadler, A. Die Grundsätze der reinen Erkenntnisstheorie in der Kantischen Philosophie. Leipzig, 1876.

Phil 3500.10.5 — Stadler, A. Kant akademische Vorlesungen. Leipzig, 1912.

Phil 3500.10 — Stadler, A. Kant's Teleologie. Berlin, 1874.

Phil 3500.10.10 — Stadler, A. Kants Theorie der Materie. Leipzig, 1883.

Phil 5058.29 — Stadler, A. Logik. Leipzig, 1912.

Phil 5258.58 — Stadler, August. Einleitung in die Psychologie. Leipzig, 1918.

Phil 2270.118.10 — Stadler, August. Herbert Spencer; Zürcher Rathaus-Vortrag gehalten am 6. dezember 1906. Zürich, 1907.

Phil 2270.118.2 — Stadler, August. Herbert Spencer. Spencers Ethik. Leipzig, 1913.

Phil 2270.118 — Stadler, August. Herbert Spencer. Spencers Ethik. Leipzig, 1918.

Phil 1504.15 — Stadler, H.J. Albertus Magnus. v.15,16. Münster, 1916. 2v.

Phil 3625.1.190 — Stadler, Károly. Mendelssohn Mózes, a zsidó Sokrates. Szekesfehérvárott, 1895.

Phil 9255.25 — Staecker, Karlheinz. Ironie und Ironiker. Diss. Mainz? 1963.

Phil 3850.15.31 — Staegmann, B.A. von. Die Theorie des Bewusstseyns im Wesen. Berlin, 1864.

Phil 3018.9 — Stählin, Leonhard. Kant, Lotze, and Ritschl. Edinburgh, 1889.

Phil 3018.9.5 — Stählin, Leonhard. Kant, Lotze, and Ritschl. Leipzig, 1889.

Phil 8893.90 — Staehr, V. von. Logische Struktur des emotionalen Ich. Diss. Saalfeld, 1934.

Htn Phil 5400.4.2* — Stael-Holstein, Anne Louise G. De l'influence des passions. Lausanne, 1796.

Phil 5400.4 — Stael-Holstein, Anne Louise G. Treatise on the influence of the passions. London, 1798.

Phil 818.28 — Staerig, H.J. Kleine Weltgeschichte der Philosophie. 3. Aufl. Stuttgart, 1953.

Phil 8598.15 — Stäudlin, C.F. Beiträge zur Philosophie und Geschichte der Religion und Sittenlehre überhaupt und verschiedenen Glaubensarten und kirchen Insbesondere. Lübeck, 1797-98. 4v.

Phil 8968.2 — Stäudlin, C.F. Geschichte der christlichen Moral. Göttingen, 1808.

Phil 645.6 — Stäudlin, C.F. Geschichte und Geist des Skepticismus. Leipzig, 1794.

Phil 8968.2.5 — Stäudlin, C.F. Neues Lehrbuch der Moral. Göttingen, 1813.

Phil 6990.3.105 — Stafford, Ann (pseud.). Bernadette and Lourdes. London, 1967.

Phil 5685.5 — The stage fright. (Kielblock, A.) Boston, 1891.

Phil 5401.16 — Stage fright and what to do about it. (Watkins, D.E.) Boston, 1940.

Phil 6681.13 — Stage hypnotism. (Leonidas (pseud.).) Chicago, 1901.

Phil 5258.145.2 — Stager, Ross. Psychology. Instructor's manual. 1st ed. N.Y., 1952.

Phil 2880.8.128 — Stages on Sartre's way. (Champigny, Robert.) Bloomington, 1959.

Phil 8088.6 — Stagione ragioni nell'estetica del settecento. (Assunto, Rosario.) Milano, 1967.

Phil 575.98 — Stagner, R. Psychology of personality. N.Y., 1937.

Phil 5258.145 — Stagner, Ross. Psychology. 1st ed. N.Y., 1952.

Phil 5066.155 — Stahl, Gerold. Introduccion a la logica simbolica. Santiago, Chile, 1956.

Htn Phil 193.32* — Stahli, D. Axiomata philosophica. London, 1651.

Phil 193.32.3 — Stahli, D. Metaphysicae. Bredae, 1650.

Phil 3246.211 — Stahr, Adolf. Fichte, der Held unter der deutschen Denkern. Berlin, 1862.

Phil 3801.806 — Staiger, Emil. Der Geist der Liebe und das Schicksal. Frauenfeld, 1935.

Phil 6688.16 — Staite, Opie. Mesmerism, or The new school of arts. London, 1844.

Phil 3805.255 — Stalder, Robert. Grundlinien der Theologie Schleiermachers. Wiesbaden, 1969.

Phil 5627.28 — Stalker, James. Christian psychology. 3. ed. N.Y., 1914.

Phil 9495.1.8 — Stall, Sylvanus. What a young boy ought to know. Philadelphia, 1897.

Phil 3850.52.40 — Stallaert, L. Onze nonger naar oprechtheid. Brugge, 1958.

Phil 3850.52.35 — Stallaert, L. Peilingen. Rotterdam, 1956. 3v.

Phil 3850.52.30 — Stallaert, L. Voor alleenstaanden. Rotterdam, 1958.

Phil 7069.30.32 — Stallard, C.L. Beyond our ken. London, 1930.

Phil 2475.1.243 — Stallknecht, N.P. Bergson's idea of creation. Princeton, N.J., 1934?

Phil 818.25 — Stallknecht, N.P. The spirit of Western philosophy. 1st ed. N.Y., 1950.

Phil 299.22 — Stallknecht, N.P. Studies in the philosophy of creation. Princeton, 1934.

NEDL Phil 299.4.2 — Stallo, J.B. Concepts and theories of modern physics. N.Y., 1882.

Phil 6128.81 — Stalpers, Jacobus Antonius. Zelfbehoud, aanpassing en cultuur. Arnhem, 1964.

Phil 3640.600 — Stambaugh, Joan. Untersuchungen zum Problem der Zeit bei Nietzsche. Den Haag, 1959.

Phil 3270.8.80 — Stamm, E. Konstantin Frantz' Jugendjahre und erste Schriften. Heidelberg, 1907.

Phil 125.3 — Stammbaum der Philosophie. (Schultze, F.) Jena, 1890.

Phil 3805.155.7 — Stammer, Martin O. Schleiermachers Asthetizismus in Theorie und Praxis wahrend der Jahre 1796 bis 1802. Leipzig, 1913.

Phil 6420.24 — Stammering; a psychoanalytic interpretation. (Coriat, Isador H.) N.Y., 1928.

Phil 6420.16.9 — Stammering; its cause and correction. (Bogue, Benjamin N.) Indianapolis, 1939.

Phil 6420.16.5 — Stammering; its cause and cure. (Bogue, Benjamin N.) Indianapolis, 1926.

Phil 6420.01 — Pamphlet box. Stammering.

Phil 6420.26 — Stammering. (Fogerty, Elsie.) N.Y., 1930.

Phil 6420.12.5 — Stammering and allied disorders. (Blumel, Charles Sidney.) N.Y., 1935.

Phil 6420.12 — Stammering and cognate defects of speech. (Bluemel, Charles Sidney.) N.Y., 1913. 2v.

Phil 6420.20 — Stammering and its treatment. (Robbins, Samuel D.) Boston, 1926.

Phil 2128.84 — Stammler, B. Mandevilles Bienenfabel. Berlin, 1918.

Phil 5058.43 — Stammler, G. Begriff, Urteil, Schluss. Halle, 1928.

Phil 3552.289 — Stammler, G. Leibniz. München, 1930.

Phil 5768.19 — Stammler, Gerhard. Notwendigkeit in Natur- und Kulturwissenschaft. Halle, 1926.

Phil 28.8 — The standard. N.Y. 2,1915+ 26v.

Phil 6315.2.3.10A — The standard edition of the complete psychological works. v.1-20,22-23. (Freud, Sigmund.) London, 1953-64. 22v.

Phil 720.33.5 — The standardization of error. (Stefansson, V.) London, 1928.

Phil 720.33 — The standardization of error. (Stefansson, V.) N.Y., 1927.

Phil 9450.7 — Standards of public morality. (Hadley, A.T.) N.Y., 1907.

Phil 9070.22 — Standing up to life. (Cole, Walton E.) Boston, 1943.

Phil 8598.144 — Standinger, Hugo. Gott: Fehlanzeige? Tries, 1968.

Phil 8060.6 — Standinger, J. Das schöne als Weltanschauung. Wien, 1948.

Phil 6692.10.5 — Stanford hypnotic suseptibility scale. (Weitzenhoffer, André M.) Palo Alto, 1959.

Phil 28.35 — Stanford University. Department of Psychology. Technical report. 1-9,1953-1955 3v.

Phil 2636.83 — Stanganelli, Irma. La teoria pedagogica di Helvetius. Napoli, 1919.

Phil 8419.9 — Stange, Alfred. Die Welt als Gestalt. Köln, 1952.

Phil 8598.55.2 — Stange, Carl. Christentum und moderne Weltanschauung. Leipzig, 1913-14. 2v.

Phil 3500.33.6A — Stange, Carl. Die Ethik Kants zur Einführung in die Kritik der praktischen Vernunft. Leipzig, 1920.

Phil 3500.33.4 — Stange, Carl. Der Gedankengang der Kritik der reinen Vernunft. Leipzig, 1920.

Phil 8893.51 — Stange, Karl. Einleitung in die Ethik. Leipzig, 1901.

Phil 5585.238 — Staniland, Alan Charles. Patterns of redundancy. Cambridge, Eng., 1966.

Phil 5238.213 — Stanje i perspective jugoslovenske psihologije. (Vdruženje Psihologa Jugoslavije.) Beograd, 1965.

Phil 5258.99 — Stanley, H.M. An outline sketch. Chicago, 1899.

Phil 5400.11 — Stanley, Hiram Miner. Studies in the evolutionary psychology of feeling. London, 1895.

Phil 1123.3.4 — Stanley, T. Historia philosophiae. Lipsiae, 1711.

Phil 1123.3.5 — Stanley, T. Historia philosophiae. Lipsiae, 1743.

Htn Phil 1123.3* — Stanley, T. History of philosophy. London, 1687.

Phil 1123.3.3 — Stanley, T. History of philosophy. London, 1701.

Phil 1123.3.1 — Stanley, T. History of philosophy. v.1-3. London, 1656-60. 2v.

Htn Phil 1123.3.2* — Stanley, T. History of philosophy. v.1-3. London, 1656-60. 2v.

Phil 8643.16 — Stanley, T.P. The gift of immortality. Collingswood, 1919.

Phil 5066.242 — Stanovlenie idei matematischeskoi logiki. (Stiazhkin, Nikolai Ivanovich.) Moskva, 1964.

Phil 8610.913.10 — Stansbury, H. In quest of truth. London, 1917.

Phil 6945.45 — Stanton, Alfred Hodgin. The mental hospital. N.Y., 1954.

Phil 8643.21 — Stanton, H.C. The starry universe the Christian's future empire. N.Y., 1909.

Phil 6028.2 — Stanton, M.O. A system...physiognomy. Philadelphia, 1890. 2v.

Phil 8893.34 — Stanton, S.B. The essential life. N.Y., 1908.

Phil 8893.34.10 — Stanton, S.B. The hidden happiness. N.Y., 1917.

Phil 8598.28 — Stapfer, P. L'inquiétude religieuse du temps présent. Paris, 1912.

Phil 1850.115 — Stapfer, P. Qualis sapientae antiquae laudator qualis interpres Franciscus Baconus exstiterit. Paris, 1870.

Phil 193.74 — Stapfer, Paul. Questions esthétiques et religeuses. Paris, 1906.

Phil 193.157 — Stapledon, Olaf. Philosophy and living. v.1-2. Harmondsworth, Eng., 1939.

Phil 8893.79 — Stapledon, W.O. A modern theory of ethics. London, 1929.

Phil 672.14.5 — The star and the earth. 7th ed. London, 1861.

Phil 978.59.25 — Star bulletin. Ommen. 1929-1933 4v.

Phil 978.78.5 — Star habits and orbits. (Plummer, L.G.) Covina, Calif., 1944.

Phil 3790.1.100 — Starauss, D.F. Herman S. Reimarus und seine Schitzschrift für die vernünftigen Verehrer Gottes. Leipzig, 1862.

Phil 5627.1 — Starbuck, E.D. The psychology of religion. London, 1899.

NEDL Phil 5627.1 — Starbuck, E.D. The psychology of religion. London, 1899.

Phil 5627.1.10 — Starbuck, E.D. Some aspects of religious growth. n.p., 1897.

Phil 5627.1.5 — Starbuck, E.D. A study of conversion. n.p., 189-?

Phil 5650.14 — Starch, D. Perimetry of the localization of sound. Pt.1-2. Thesis. n.p., 1906.

Phil 5258.115 — Starch, Daniel. Controlling human behavior. N.Y., 1936.

Phil 1730.2 — Starck, Johann G. Der Triumph der Philosophie im Achtzehnten Jahrhunderts. Germantown, 1804. 2v.

Phil 3838.9 — Starcke, C.N. Baruch de Spinoza. Kjøbenhavn, 1923.

Phil 5258.76.10 — Starcke, C.N. Kritiken af min psychologi svar til mine kritikere. Kjøbenhavn, 1916.

Phil 3235.111 — Starcke, C.N. L. Feuerbach; en monografi. Kjøbenhavn, 1883.

Phil 4635.2.34F — Starcke, C.N. Den menneskelige tänkning. Kopenhagen, 1916.

Phil 5258.76.3 — Starcke, C.N. Psychologi. 3. udg. Kjøbenhavn, 1923.

Phil 2520.156 — Starcke, C.N. René Descartes. Kjøbenhavn, 1919.

Phil 4635.2.31 — Starcke, C.N. Samvittighedslivet. København, 1894-97.

Phil 645.27 — Starcke, C.N. Skepticismen. Kjøbenhavn, 1890.

Phil 818.2.5 — Starcke, C.N. Types af den filosofiske bankings historie. Kjøbenhavn, 1918.

Phil 5058.36 — Starcke, Carl N. Formel logik, grundlag for forelaesninger. 2. udg. Kjøbenhavn, 1922.

Phil 3235.88 — Starcke, Carl N. Ludwig Feuerbach. Stuttgart, 1885.

Phil 9070.122 — Starcke, Walter. The ultimate revolution. 1st ed. N.Y., 1969.

Phil 4635.2.92 — Starckes forsvar, metoder og resultater. (Naesgaard, S.) København, 1917.

Phil 8430.49 — Stardelov, Georgi. Esci. Skopje, 1958.

Phil 1750.385 — Staritz, Ekkehart. Vom Schein zum Sein. Bonn, 1953.

Phil 2305.6.30 — Stark, Franz. Das Problem der moralischen Rechtfertigung bei S.E. Toulmin. München, 1964.

Phil 349.41.2 — Stark, Werner. The sociology of knowledge. Glencoe, 1958.

Phil 349.41 — Stark, Werner. The sociology of knowledge. London, 1958.

Phil 349.41.3 — Stark, Werner. The sociology of knowledge. London, 1960.

Phil 4635.2.33 — Starke, C.N. Etikens teoretiske grundlag. Kjøbenhavn, 1889.

Phil 4635.2.90 — Starkes psykologi. (Naesgaard, S.) København, 1916.

Phil 5401.58 — Starnberger Gespräche. Aspekte der Angst. Stuttgart, 1965.

Phil 6328.19.5 — Starr, Moses A. Familiar forms of nervous disease. 2d ed. N.Y., 1891.

Phil 6128.30 — Starrett, D.W. The last lap. Boston, 1915.

Phil 9358.15.5 — Starrett, H.E. (Mrs.). The charm of fine manners. Philadelphia, 1921.

Phil 8643.21 — The starry universe the Christian's future empire. (Stanton, H.C.) N.Y., 1909.

Phil 8708.7 — The stars and the angels. London, 1858.

Phil 672.14.7 — The stars and the earth. Boston, 1849.

Phil 672.14 — The stars and the earth. 4th ed. London, 1850.

Phil 672.14.9 — The stars and the earth. 5th American ed. Boston, 1882.

Phil 7069.46 — The stars are still there. 1. ed. (White, Stewart E.) N.Y., 1946.

Phil 7054.53 — Startling facts in modern spiritualism. (Wolfe, N.B.) Cincinnati, 1874.

Phil 4582.4.38 — Stat och rätt. (Hägerström, Axel.) Upsala, 1904.

Phil 332.24 — The state of public knowledge. (Barlow, K.E.) London, 1946.

Phil 5062.30.1 — Statement and inference. (Wilson, John Cook.) Oxford, 1969. 2v.

Phil 5068.84 — Statera, Gianni. Logica, linguaggio e sociologia. Torino, 1967.

Phil 8598.16 — Statham, F. From old to new. London, 1872.

Phil 8401.23.5 — Stat'i ob estetike. (Adamian, Arshag.) Erevan, 1967.

Phil 8401.23 — Stat'i ob iskusstve. (Adamian, Arshag.) Moskva, 1961.

Phil 8403.12.10 — Stat'i po estetike. (Chernyshevskii, N.G.) Moskva, 1938.

Phil 7069.13.40 — Station, Horace C. Telepathy of the celestial world. N.Y., 1913.

Phil 7069.32.13 — Station Astral. (Drouet, Bessie Clarke.) N.Y., 1932.

Phil 8598.110.15A — Stations of wisdom. (Schuon, Frithjof.) London, 1961.

Phil 5244.25.2 — Statistical analysis. (Edwards, Allen L.) N.Y., 1958.

Phil 5244.25 — Statistical analysis for students in psychology and education. (Edwards, Allen L.) N.Y., 1946.

Phil 5145.2 — Statistical and inductive probabilities. (Leblanc, Hugues.) Englewood Cliffs, 1962.

Phil 5249.25 — Statistical estimation in factor analysis. (Joereskog, K.G.) Stockholm, 1963.

Phil 5244.25.5 — Statistical methods for the behavioral sciences. (Edwards, Allen L.) N.Y., 1964.

Phil 5545.16 — Statistical study of memory. (Jastrow, J.) N.Y., 1891.

Phil 5247.76 — Statistics for psychologists. (Hays, W.) N.Y., 1963.

Phil 5910.3 — Statistics of phrenology. (Watson, H.C.) London, 1836-1837. 2 pam.

Phil 7150.14 — Statistik des Selbstmordes im Königreich Sachsen. (Kürten, O.) Leipzig, 1913.

Phil 4080.3.525 — Stato e politica nel pensiero di Benedetto Croce. (Sartori, Giovanni.) Napoli, 1966.

Phil 3585.13.30 — Statt Heiligenschein oder Hexenzeichen mein Leben. v.2- (Ludendurff, Mathilde.) München, 193- 5v.

Phil 3500.57.10 — Stattler, B. Anti-Kant. München, 1788. 2v.

Phil 3500.57 — Stattler, B. Kurzer Entwurf der unausstehlichen Ungereimtheiten der Kantischen Philosophie. n.p., 1791.

Phil 3500.57.5 — Stattler, B. Wahres Verhaltniss der Kantischen Philosophie. München, 1794.

Phil 6675.1A — Statu volism. (Fahnestock, W.B.) Chicago, 1871.

Phil 7150.55 — Status integration and suicide. (Gibbs, J.P.) Eugene, Oreg., 1964.

Htn Phil 8892.38F* — The status of ethics. (Roback, A.A.) n.p., 1914.

Phil 630.30 — The status of values in new realism. (Evans, Daniel L.) Columbus, 1923.

Phil 860.2.2 — Staudacher, Willibald. Die Trennung von Himmel und Erde; ein vorgriechischer Schöpfungsmythus bei Hesiod und den Orphikern. 2. Aufl. Darmstadt, 1968.

Phil 3850.18.205 — Staude, John Raphael. Max Scheler, 1874-1928; an intellectual portrait. N.Y., 1967.

Phil 3425.93 — Staudenmaier, F. Darstellung und Kritik des Hegelschen Systems. Mainz, 1844.

Phil 3850.8.81 — Staudenmaier's Wissenschaftliche Leistung. (Michelis, F.) Freiburg, 1877.

Phil 8893.50 — Staudinger, Franz. Das Sittengesetz. 2. Aufl. Berlin, 1897.

Phil 8893.50.5 — Staudinger, Franz. Wirtschaftliche Grundlagen der Moral. Darmstadt, 1907.

Phil 8643.40 — Staudinger, Josef. Die letzte Zeit. Innsbruck, 1955.

Phil 9220.1 — Staudlin, C.F. Geschichte der Vorst...Freundschaft. Hannover, 1826.

Phil 623.12 — Staudlin, C.F. Geschichte des Naturalismus. Göttingen, 1826.

Phil 575.155 — Stauenhagen, K. Person und Persönlichkeit. Göttingen, 1957.

Phil 3110.195 — Staurt, J.J. Sunrise to eternity. Philadelphia, 1957.

Phil 8420.17 — Stavba a báseň; uménídues a zítra. (Teige, Karel.) Praha, 1927.

Phil 3500.69 — Stavenhagen, F. Kant und Königsberg. Gottingen, 1949.

Phil 3640.700A — Stavrou, C.N. Whitman and Nietzsche. Chapel Hill, 1964.

Phil 5627.72 — Stead, W.T. The revival in the West. 4. ed. London, 19- .

Phil 7054.22.5 — Stead, William T. After death; a personal narrative. N.Y., 1914.

Phil 7054.22 Stead, William T. After death or Letters from Julia. 3. ed. Chicago, 1910.
Phil 7060.254 Stead, William T. Real ghost stories. N.Y., 1921.
Phil 7069.63.5 Stearn, J. The door to the future. Garden City, 1963.
Phil 7069.69.20 Stearn, Jess. Adventures into the psychic. N.Y., 1969.
Phil 6112.40.5 Stearn, Jess. Edgar Cayce, the sleeping prophet. Garden City, 1967.
Phil 9560.8 Stearne, J. De obstinatione. Dublin, 1672.
Phil 3450.3.90 Stearne, John. Adriani Heereboordi. Dublinii, 1660.
Phil 9358.14 Stearns, Alfred E. The challenge of youth. Boston, 1923.
Phil 9358.14.5 Stearns, Alfred E. To him that overcometh. Boston, 1935.
Phil 6968.9 Stearns, H.P. Lectures on mental disease. Philadelphia, 1893.
Phil 8893.101 Stebbing, L.S. Ideals and illusions. London, 1941.
Phil 193.63 Stebbing, L.S. Pragmatism and French voluntarism. Cambridge, 1914.
Phil 5058.46.15 Stebbing, Lizzie S. Logic in practice. London, 1934.
Phil 5058.46.30 Stebbing, Lizzie S. Logic in practice. 4. ed. London, 1954.
Phil 5058.46.10A Stebbing, Lizzie S. Logical positivism and analysis. London, 1933.
Phil 5058.46.25 Stebbing, Lizzie S. A modern elementary logic. London, 1943.
Phil 5058.46 Stebbing, Lizzie S. A modern introduction to logic. London, 1930.
Phil 5058.46.3 Stebbing, Lizzie S. A modern introduction to logic. 2. ed. N.Y., 1933.
Phil 5058.46.7 Stebbing, Lizzie S. A modern introduction to logic. 7. ed. London, 1961.
Phil 5058.46.20 Stebbing, Lizzie S. Thinking to some purpose. Harmondsworth, 1939.
Phil 2138.88 Stebbing, W. Analysis of Mr. Miil's system of logic. London, 1875.
Phil 3585.1.45F Steck, Max. Bibliographia Lambertiana. Berlin, 1943.
Phil 3500.39 Steckelmacher, M. Die formale Logik Kant's in ihren Beziehungen zur Transcendentalen. Breslau, 1879.
Phil 8598.81 Steckelmacher, M. Die Gottesidee der Offenbarung. Mannheim, 1890.
Phil 6968.11 Stedman, H.R. Case of moral insanity. Boston, 1904.
Phil 193.144 Steeksma, J. Philosophical inquiry. London, 1935.
Phil 9178.4 Steel, D. A system of moral philosophy. Boston, 1847.
Phil 5467.1 Steel, R. Imitation or mimetic force. London, 1900.
Phil 5258.20 Steele, G.M. Rudimentary psychology. Boston, 1890.
Phil 9245.40 Steele, Mary D. A happy life. Dayton, Ohio, 1895.
Phil 4610.9.85 Steen, H. Problemet om tro og viden. Kjøbenhavn, 1813.
Phil 1523.12.10 Steenberghen, F. Aristotle in the West. Louvain, 1955.
Phil 1523.12 Steenberghen, F. Atistote en Occident. Louvain, 1946.
Phil 1523.12.15 Steenberghen, F. Directives pour la confection d'une monographie. Louvain, 1961.
Phil 193.162 Steenberghen, F. Ontologie. Louvain, 1946.
Phil 1523.12.5 Steenberghen, F. Philosophie des Mittelalters. Bern, 1950.
Phil 6128.60 Steenberghen, F. van. Psychology, morality and education. London, 1958.
Phil 818.36 Steenberghen, Ferdinand van. Histoire de la philosophie. Louvain, 1964.
Phil 8673.19 Steenberghen, Fernand van. Dieu caché. Louvain, 1961.
Phil 349.39.5 Steenberghen, Fernand van. Épistémologie. 2e éd. Louvain, 1947.
Phil 349.39.6 Steenberghen, Fernand van. Épistémologie. 3e éd. Louvain, 1956.
Phil 349.39.4 Steenberghen, Fernand van. Épistémologie. 4e éd. Paris, 1965.
Phil 8673.23 Steenberghen, Fernand van. Hidden God; how do we know that God exists? Saint Louis, 1966.
Phil 1540.35.5 Steenberghen, Fernand van. La philosophie au XIIE siècle. Louvain, 1966.
Phil 8633.1.42 Steere, Douglas. V. Death's illumination of life. Cambridge, 1942.
NEDL Phil 1850.101 Steeves, G.W. Francis Bacon, a sketch of his life. London, 1910.
Phil 6968.36 Stefan, Gregory. In search of sanity. New Hyde Park, 1966.
Phil 4803.755.80 Stefan Rudnianskii. (Kliauchenia, Aliaksandr S.) Minsk, 1968.
Phil 193.155 Stefanesco, Marin. Le problème de la méthode. Paris, 1938.
Phil 315.3 Stefanescu, M. Le dualisme logique. Paris, 1915.
Phil 3500.25 Stefanescu, M. Essai sur le rapport entre le dualisme. Paris, 1915.
Phil 1750.357 Stefanini, L. Esistenzialismo ateo et esistenzialismo teistro. Padova, 1952.
Phil 5590.160 Stefanini, L. Metafisica della persona. Padova, 1950.
Phil 1123.12 Stefanini, L. Il preimoginisimo dei Greci. Padova, 1953.
Phil 8843.10 Stefanini, L. Il problema morale nello stoicismo e nel cristianesimo. Torino, 1926.
Phil 4225.9 Stefanini, Luigi. Metafisica della forma. Padova, 1949.
Phil 193.183 Stefanini, Luigi. Metafisica dell'arte e altri saggi. Padova, 1948.
Phil 574.4 Stefanini, Luigi. Personalismo filosofico. Brescia, 1962.
Phil 8419.18 Stefanini, Luigi. Trattato di estetica. Brescia, 1955-
Phil 3808.198 Stefano Escher dal, Anna. La filosofia di Arturo Schopenhauer. Padova, 1958.
Phil 3195.6.150 Stefanovies, T. Dilthey; una filosofia de la vida. Montevideo, 1961.
Phil 3801.807 Stefansky, Georg. Das hellenisch-deutsche Weltbild. Bonn, 1925.
Phil 720.33.5 Stefansson, V. The standardization of error. London, 1928.
Phil 720.33 Stefansson, V. The standardization of error. N.Y., 1927.
Phil 7085.9 Steffanius, J.J. Dissertatio medica inauguralis de somnambulis. Basileae, 1701.
Phil 978.49.820 Steffen, A. Begegnungen mit Rudolf Steiner. Dornach, 1955.
Phil 974.3.83 Steffen, Albert. Auf Geisteswegen. Dornach, 1942.
Phil 974.3.80 Steffen, Albert. Begegnungen mit Rudolf Steiner. Zürich, 1926.
Phil 978.49.880 Steffen, Albert. Gegenwartsaufgaben der Menschheit. Schweiz, 1966.
Phil 193.34.3 Steffens, H. Anthropologie. Breslau, 1822. 2v.
Phil 8598.58.5 Steffens, H. Christliche Religionsphilosophie. Pt.1-2. Breslau, 1839. 2v.
Phil 193.34 Steffens, H. Grundzüge der philosophischen Naturwissenschaft. Berlin, 1806.
Phil 193.34.5 Steffens, H. Henrik Steffens indledning til forelaesninger in Kobenhavn 1803. Kobenhavn, 1905.
Phil 8598.58 Steffens, H. Von der falschen Theologie und der wahren Glauben. Breslau, 1823.

Htn Phil 3800.385* Steffens, Henrik. Nachgelassene Schriften...Vorwort von Schelling. Berlin, 1846.
Phil 3415.99 Steffes, J.P. Eduard von Hartmanns Religionsphilosophie des Unbewuszten. Mergentheim, 1921?
Phil 8598.52 Steffes, J.P. Religionsphilosophie. München, 1925.
Phil 2880.8.104 Stefoni, M. La libertà esistenziale in Jean Paul Sartre. Milano, 1949.
Phil 400.83 Stefunini, L. Idealismo cristiano. Padova, 1931?
Phil 8598.47 Stegenga, P. Twijfel als psychological verschijnsel in het religieuse leven. Amsterdam, 1924.
Phil 1718.25 Stegmüller, W. Hauptströmungen der Gegenwartphilosophie. Wien, 1952.
Phil 1718.25.2 Stegmüller, W. Hauptströmungen der Gegenwartphilosophie. 2. Aufl. Stuttgart, 1960.
Phil 1718.25.1 Stegmüller, W. Main currents in contemporary German, British, and American philosophy. Bloomington, 1970.
Phil 5520.210 Stegmüller, W. Das Wahrheitsproblem und die Idee der Semantik. Wien, 1957.
Phil 349.94 Stegmueller, Wolfgang. Aufsätze zur Wissenschaftstheorie. Darmstadt, 1970.
Phil 1740.16.4 Stegmüller, Wolfgang. Hauptströmungen der Gegenwartsphilosophie. 4. Aufl. Stuttgart, 1969.
Phil 3850.72.2 Stegmueller, Wolfgang. Metaphysik, Skepsis, Wissenschaft. 2. Aufl. Berlin, 1969.
Phil 582.2 Stegmueller, Wolfgang. Der Phänomenalismus und seine Schwierigkeiten. Darmstadt, 1969.
Phil 3500.23 Stehr, H. Über Immanuel Kant. Leipzig, 1896.
Phil 8890.54 Steht uns der Himmel offen. (Pons, Walter.) Wiesbaden, 1960.
Phil 8890.54.2 Steht uns der Himmel offen. 2. Aufl. (Pons, Walter.) Wiesbaden, 1960.
Phil 5635.38 Steige, R. Gefühl und Affekt. Inaug. Diss. Breslau? 1937.
Phil 2150.22.115 Steigerwald, Robert Reinhold. Herbert Marcuses dritter Weg. Köln, 1969.
Phil 3195.6.81 Stein, Arthur. Der Begriff des Geistes bei Dilthey. Bern, 1913.
Phil 3195.6.84 Stein, Arthur. Der Begriff des Verstehens bei Dilthey. 2. Aufl. Tübingen, 1926.
Phil 5421.15.12 Stein, Edith. On the problem of empathy. 2d ed. The Hague, 1970.
Phil 8893.60 Stein, F.J. Historisch-kritische Darstellung der pathologischen Moralprincipien. Wien, 1871.
Phil 8663.3.100 Stein, Gordon. Robert G. Ingersoll; a checklist. 1. ed. Kent, Ohio? 1969.
Phil 4065.84 Stein, H. von. Giordano Bruno, Gedanken über seine Lehre. Leipzig, 1900.
Phil 8419.42 Stein, H. von. Vorlesungen über Ästhetik. Stuttgart, 1897.
Phil 349.16 Stein, Heinrich. Ueber Wahrnehmung. Berlin, 1877.
Phil 2418.5 Stein, Jay W. The mind and the sword. N.Y., 1961.
Phil 315.2 Stein, L. Dualismus oder Monismus. Berlin, 1909.
Phil 3552.96 Stein, L. Leibniz und Spinoza. Berlin, 1890.
Phil 8419.12.5 Stein, Leo. The ABC of aesthetics. N.Y., 1927.
Phil 8419.12 Stein, Leo. Appreciation: painting, poetry and prose. N.Y., 1947.
Phil 5520.98 Stein, Leopold. The infancy of speech and the speech of infancy. London, 1949.
Phil 9430.32 Stein, Ludwig. Evolution and optimism. N.Y., 1926.
Phil 3640.300 Stein, Ludwig. Friedrich Nietzsches Weltanschauung und ihre Gefahren. Berlin, 1893.
Phil 1718.7.5 Stein, Ludwig. Philosophical currents of the present day. Calcutta, 1918-19. 2v.
Phil 1718.7 Stein, Ludwig. Philosophische Strömungen der Gegenwart. Stuttgart, 1908.
Phil 193.55 Stein, Ludwig. Le sens de l'existence. Paris, 1909.
Phil 193.55.3 Stein, Ludwig. Der Sinn des Daseins. Tübingen, 1904.
Phil 193.55.9 Stein, Ludwig. Die Willensfreiheit...bei den jüdischen philosophen des Mittelalters. n.p., 1882-1908. 9 pam.
Phil 5401.38 Stein, Maurice R. Identity and anxiety. Glencoe, 1960.
Phil 5401.38.2 Stein, Maurice R. Identity and anxiety. Glencoe, 1962.
Phil 6980.707 Stein, Morris. Contemporary psychotherapies. N.Y., 1961.
Phil 5465.100 Stein, Morris. Creativity and the individual. Glencoe, 1960.
Phil 5465.100.2 Stein, Morris. Creativity and the individual. Glencoe, 1964.
Phil 978.82 Stein, W.J. Weltgeschichte im Lichte des heiligen Gral. Stuttgart, 1928.
Phil 6688.4 Steinbeck, F.A. Der Dichter ein Seher. Leipzig, 1856.
Phil 3246.231 Steinbeck, W. Das Bild des Menschen in der Philosophie Fichtes. München, 1939.
Phil 2225.2.85 Steinberg, Ira Sherman. Ralph Barton Perry on education for democracy. Columbus, 1970.
Phil 3805.169 Steinberg, Julius. Liebe und Ehe in Schleiermachers Kreis. Dresden, 1921.
Phil 193.167 Steinberg, W. Grundfragen des menschlichen Seins. München, 1953.
Phil 5585.31 Steinberg, Wilhelm. Die Raumwahrnehmung der Blinden. München, 1920.
Phil 6021.2.85 Steinbrucker, C. Lavaters physiognomische...Kunst. Berlin, 1915.
Phil 1750.265 Steinbüchel, T. Existenzialismus und christliche Ethos. Heidelberg, 1948.
Phil 3425.284 Steinbüchel, T. Das Grundproblem der hegelschen Philosophie. Bonn, 1933.
Phil 8968.15 Steinbüchel, T. Zerfall des christlichen Ethos im XIX. Jahrhundert. Frankfurt, 1951.
Phil 1504.11 Steinbüchel, T. Der Zweckgedanke in der Philosophie. v.11, pt.1-2. Münster, 1912.
Phil 3640.815 Steinbuechel, Theodor. Nietzsche; eine christliche Besinnung. Photoreproduction. Stuttgart, 1946.
Phil 3200.14.80 Steinbuechel, Theodor. Der Umbruch des Denkens. Darmstadt, 1966.
Phil 1540.34 Steinbueckel, T. Vom Menschenbild des christlichen Mittelalters. Basel, 1953.
Phil 450.10 Steiner, Hans Friedrich. Marxiaten-Lennisten über den Sinn des Lebens. Essen, 1970.
Phil 5628.55.35 Steiner, Johannes. Therese Neumann von Konnersreuth. München, 1963.
Phil 9590.23 Steiner, L.R. (Mrs.). Where do people take their troubles? Boston, 1945.
Phil 974.3.119 Steiner, M. Erinnerungen. v.1-2. Dornach, 1949.
Phil 978.49.895 Steiner, Marie von Sivers. Gesammelte Schriften. Dornach, 1967.
Phil 978.49.165 Steiner, R. Alte Mythen und ihre Bedeutung. Dornach, 1937.
Phil 978.49.375 Steiner, R. Alte und neue Einweihungsmethoden. Dornach, 1967.
Phil 978.49.697 Steiner, R. Anthroposophie. 3. Aufl. Dornach, 1968.

Phil 978.49.465   Steiner, R. Anthroposophie, Psychosophie, Pneumatosophie. Dornach, 1965.

Phil 978.49.767   Steiner, R. Anthroposophie. 2. Aufl. Dornach, 1970.

Phil 978.49.650   Steiner, R. Anthroposophische Gemeinschaftsbildung. Dornach, 1965.

Phil 978.49.130   Steiner, R. Anthroposophy. n.p., n.d. 5 pam.

Phil 978.49.720   Steiner, R. Anweisungen für eine esoterische Schulung: aus den Inhalten der Esoterischen Schule. Dornach, 1968.

Phil 978.49.125   Steiner, R. Art in the light of mystery wisdom. N.Y., 1935.

Phil 978.49.40   Steiner, R. Die Aufgabe der Geisteswissenschaft und deren Bau in Dornach. Berlin, 1921.

Phil 978.49.410   Steiner, R. Aus dem mitteleuropäschen Geisteleben.

Phil 978.49.692.4   Steiner, R. Aus der Akasha-Chronik. 4. Aufl. Dornach, 1969.

Phil 978.49.694   Steiner, R. Aus der Akasha-Forschung: Das Fünfte Evangelium. Dornach, 1963.

Phil 978.49.300   Steiner, R. Aus Schicksals fragender Zeit. Dornach, 1959.

Phil 3160.2.87   Steiner, R. Bartholomäus Carneri, der Ethiker des Darwinismus. Dresden, 1900.

Phil 978.49.729   Steiner, R. Die Beantwortung von Welt- und Lebensfragen durch Anthroposophie. Dornach, 1970.

Phil 978.49.170   Steiner, R. Bedeutsames aus dem äusseren Geistesleben um die Mitte des XIX Jahrhunderts. Dornach, 1939.

Phil 978.49.260   Steiner, R. Die Bedeutung der Anthroposophie im Geistesleben der Gegenwart. Dornach, 1957.

Phil 978.49.690   Steiner, R. Biographien und biographische Skizzen, 1894-1905. 1. Aufl. Dornach, 1967.

Phil 978.49.645   Steiner, R. Briefwechel und Dokumente, 1901-1925. 1. Aufl. Dornach, 1967.

Phil 978.49.180   Steiner, R. Charakteristisches zur Kennzeichnung der gegenwart Wirklichkeits-Entfremdung. Dornach, 1939.

Phil 978.49.700   Steiner, R. Christ and the spiritual world. London, 1963.

Phil 978.49.525   Steiner, R. Das christliche Mysterium. Dornach, 1968.

Phil 978.49.320   Steiner, R. Christus und die menschliche Seele. Dornach, 1960.

Phil 978.49.490   Steiner, R. Des Prinzip der spirituellen Ökonomie im Zusammenhang mit Wiederverkörperungsfragen; 22 Vorträge. Dornach, 1965.

Phil 978.49.240   Steiner, R. Drama und Dichtung im Bewusstseins-Umschwung der Neuzeit. Dornach, 1956.

Phil 978.49.715   Steiner, R. Durch den Geist zur Wirklichkeits-Erkenntnis der Menschenrätsel. Dornach, 1965- 6v.

Phil 978.49.100   Steiner, R. The East in the light of the West. London, 1922.

Phil 818.20.5   Steiner, R. Gli enigmi della filosofia. Milano, 1935.

Phil 978.49.735   Steiner, R. Entwürfe, Fragmente und Paralipomenn zu den vier Mysteriendramen: Die Pforte der Einwiehung. Dornach, 1969.

Phil 978.49.572   Steiner, R. Erdensterben und Weltenleben und anthroposophisdie Lebensgaben. 2. Aufl. Dornach, 1967.

Phil 978.49.670   Steiner, R. Erdenwissen und Himmelserkenntnis. Dornach, 1966.

Phil 978.49.470   Steiner, R. Das Ereignis der Christuserscheinung in der ätherischen Welt. Dornach, 1965.

Phil 978.49.330   Steiner, R. Ergebnisse der Geistesforschung. Dornach, 1960.

Phil 978.49.460   Steiner, R. Die Erkenntnis der Seele und des Geistes. Dornach, 1965.

Phil 978.49.285   Steiner, R. Die Erneuerung der pödagogisch-didaktischen Kunst. Dornach, 1958.

Phil 978.49.679   Steiner, R. Erziehungskunst; Methodisch-Didaktisches. 4. Aufl. Dornach, 1966. 2v.

Phil 978.49.95   Steiner, R. Esquisse d'une cosmogonie psychologique, d'après des conférences faites à Paris en 1906. Paris, 1928.

Phil 978.49.115   Steiner, R. Eurhythmy as visible song. London, 1932.

Phil 978.49.120   Steiner, R. Eurhythmy as visible speech. London, 1931.

Phil 978.49.117   Steiner, R. Eurythmie als sichtbarer Gesang. 1. Aufl. Dornach, 1956.

Phil 978.49.400   Steiner, R. Das Ewige in der Menschenseele. Dornach, 1962.

Phil 978.49.383   Steiner, R. Exkurse in das Gebiet des Markus-Evangeliums. Dornach, 1963.

Phil 978.49.25   Steiner, R. The gates of knowledge. Chicago, Ill., 1922.

Phil 978.49.510   Steiner, R. Gegensätze in der Menschheitsentwickelung; 11 Vorträge. Dornach, 1967.

Phil 978.49.740   Steiner, R. Das Geheimnis der Trinität. Dornach, 1970.

Phil 978.49.540   Steiner, R. Das Geheimnis des Todes; Wesen und Bedeutung Mitteleuropas und die europäischen Volksgeister. Dornach, 1967.

Phil 978.49.370   Steiner, R. Geist und Stoff, Leben und Tod. Dornach, 1961.

Phil 978.49.530   Steiner, R. Geisteswissenschaft als Erkenntuis der Grundimpulse sozialer Gestaltung. Dornach, 1967.

Phil 978.49.305   Steiner, R. Geisteswissenschaft als Lebensgut. Dornach, 1959.

Phil 978.49.230   Steiner, R. Geisteswissenschaft und die Lebensforderungen der Gegenwart. pt.1-8. Dornach, 1950. 2v.

Phil 978.49.625   Steiner, R. Geisteswissenschaftliche Grundlage zum Gedeihen der Landwirtschaft; landwirtschaftlicher Kursus. 4. Aufl. Dornach, 1963.

Phil 978.49.30   Steiner, R. Die geistige Führung des Menschen und der Menschheit. Dornach, 1925.

Phil 978.49.655   Steiner, R. Die geistige und soziale Wandlungen in der Menschheitsentwickelung; achtzehn Vorträge. Dornach, 1966.

Phil 978.49.535   Steiner, R. Die geistige Vereinigung der Menschheit durch den Christus-Impuls. 1. Aufl. Dornach, 1968.

Phil 978.49.420   Steiner, R. Geistige Wirkenskräfte. Dornach, 1964.

Phil 978.49.152   Steiner, R. Gesammelte Aufsätze zur Kultur- und Zeitgeschichte, 1887-1901. Dornach, 1966.

Phil 978.49.705   Steiner, R. Die Geschichte der Menschheit und die Weltanschauungen der Kulturvölker. Dornach, 1968.

Phil 978.49.210   Steiner, R. Die Geschichte des Hypnotismus und des Somnambulismus. Basel, 1941.

Phil 978.49.215   Steiner, R. Die Geschichte des Spiritismus. Basel, 1941.

Phil 978.49.160   Steiner, R. Geschichtliche Notwendigkeit und Freiheit. Dornach, 1939.

Phil 978.49.162   Steiner, R. Geschichtliche Notwendigkeit und Freiheit. 2. Aufl. Dornach, 1966.

Phil 978.49.440   Steiner, R. Gesteswissenschaftliche Behandlung. Dornach, 1964.

Phil 978.49.778   Steiner, R. Die gesunde Entwickelung des Leiblich-Physischen als Grundlage der freien Entfaltung des Seelison-Geistigen. 3. Aufl. Dornach, 1969.

Phil 978.49.198   Steiner, R. Der Goetheanismus ein Umwandlungsimpuls und Auferstehungsgedanke: Menschwissenschaft und Sozialwissenschaft. Dornach, 1967.

Phil 978.49.335   Steiner, R. Der goetheanumgedanke Insnitten der Kulturkreis der Gegenwart. Dornach, 1961.

Phil 978.49.195   Steiner, R. Goethes Geistesart in unseren Schicksalsschweren tagen und die deutsche Kultur. Dornach, 1930.

Phil 978.49.759   Steiner, R. Grenzen der Naturerkenntnis. 4. Aufl. Dornach, 1969.

Phil 349.4   Steiner, R. Die Grundfrage der Erkenntnisstheorie. n.p., 1891.

Phil 978.49.665   Steiner, R. Die Grundimpulse des weltgeschichtlichen Werdens der Menschheit. 2. Aufl. Dornach, 1965.

Phil 978.49.785.3   Steiner, R. Die Grundsteinlegung der Allgemeinen Anthroposophischen Gesellschaft. 3. Aufl. Dornach, 1969.

Phil 978.49.483   Steiner, R. Heileurythmie; acht Vorträge. 3. Aufl. Dornach, 1966.

Phil 978.49.760   Steiner, R. Heilfaktoren für den sozialen Organismus. 1. Aufl. Dornach, 1969.

Phil 978.49.578   Steiner, R. Heilpädagogischer Kursus. 3. Aufl. Dornach, 1965.

Phil 978.49.50   Steiner, R. Der Hüter der Schwelle, Seelenvorgänge in scenischen Bildern. Berlin, 1922.

Phil 978.49.502   Steiner, R. Die Impulsiviue des weltgeschichtlichen Gescheheus durch geistige Mächte; sieben Vorträge. 2. Aufl. Dornach, 1966.

Phil 978.49.580   Steiner, R. Individuelle Geistwesen und ihr Wirken in der Seele des Menschen. Dornach, 1966.

Phil 978.49.75   Steiner, R. Das Initiaten-Bewusstsein. Dornach, 1927.

Phil 978.49.76   Steiner, R. Das Initiaten-Bewusstsein. Freiburg, 1955.

Phil 978.49.77   Steiner, R. Das Initiaten-Bewusstsein: die Wahren und die falschen Wege der geistigen Forschung. Dornach, 1969.

Phil 978.49.36   Steiner, R. Initiation and its results. N.Y., 1909.

Phil 978.49.445   Steiner, R. Initiationswissenschaft und Sternenerkenntnis. Dornach, 1964.

Phil 978.49.710   Steiner, R. Der innere Aspekt des sozialen Rätsels. Dornach, 1968.

Phil 978.49.590   Steiner, R. Der Jahres kreislauf als Atmungsvorgang der Erde und die vier grossen Festeszeiten. Dornach, 1966.

Phil 978.49.275   Steiner, R. Das Johannes-Evangelium. 7. Aufl. Dornach, 1955.

Phil 978.49.17   Steiner, R. Knowledge of the higher worlds. 3d English ed. London, 1937.

Phil 978.49.16   Steiner, R. Knowledge of the higher worlds and its attainment. N.Y., 193-?

Phil 978.49.615   Steiner, R. Die Konstitation der Allgemeinen anthroposophischen Gesellschaft und der freien Hochschule. Dornach, 1966.

Phil 978.49.155   Steiner, R. Kosmische und menschliche Geschichte. Dornach, 1933-34. 5v.

Phil 978.49.157   Steiner, R. Kosmische und menschliche Geschichte. Dornach, 1964. 4v.

Phil 978.49.143   Steiner, R. Die Kunst der Rezitation und Deklamation. 2. Aufl. Dornach, 1967.

Phil 978.49.610   Steiner, R. Kunst im Lichte der Mysterienweisheit. Dornach, 1966.

Phil 978.49.340   Steiner, R. Kunst und Kunsterkuntniss. Dornach, 1961.

Phil 978.49.640   Steiner, R. Lebendiges Naturerkennen. Dornach, 1964.

Phil 978.49.695   Steiner, R. Das Lukas-Evangelium. Ein Zyklus von zehn Vorträgen. 6. Aufl. Dornach, 1968.

Phil 978.49.310   Steiner, R. Luzifer-Gnosis, 1903-1908. Dornach, 1960.

Phil 978.49.295   Steiner, R. Major writings. 1. ed. Englewood, 1959- 6v.

Phil 978.49.350   Steiner, R. Makrokosmos und Mikrokosmos. Dornach, 1962.

Phil 978.49.325   Steiner, R. Das Markus-Evanqelium. Dornach, 1960.

Phil 978.49.245   Steiner, R. Der materialistische Erkenntnisimpuls und seine Bedeutung für die ganze Menscheitsentwicklung. Basel, 1953.

Phil 978.49.255   Steiner, R. Die materialistische Weltanschauung des neunzehnten Jahrhunderts. Basel, 1955.

Phil 978.49.545   Steiner, R. Meditative Betrachtungen und Anleitungen zur Vertiefung der Heilkunst. Dornach, 1967.

Phil 978.49.605   Steiner, R. Der Mensch in seinem Zusammenhange mit dem Kosmos. v.5-6,9. Dornach, 1967- 3v.

Phil 978.49.685   Steiner, R. Menschenfragen und Weltenantworten. 1. Aufl. Dornach, 1969.

Phil 978.49.390   Steiner, R. Menschengeschichte im Lichte der Geistesforschung. Berlin, 1962.

Phil 978.49.315   Steiner, R. Menschenschichsale und Völkerschicksale. Dornach, 1960.

Phil 978.49.408   Steiner, R. Menschenwesen, Menschenschicksal und Weltentwicklunz. 3. Aufl. Dornach, 1966.

Phil 978.49.278   Steiner, R. Menschheitsentwicklung und Christus-Erkenntnis. Dornach, 1967.

Phil 978.49.600   Steiner, R. Die menschliche Seele in ihrem Zusammenhang mit göttlich-geistigen Individualitäten. Dornach, 1966.

Phil 978.49.450   Steiner, R. Menschliche und menschheitliche Entwicklungswahrheiten. Dornach, 1964.

Phil 978.49.145.5   Steiner, R. Methodik und Wesen der Sprachgestaltung. Dornach, 1955.

Phil 978.49.360   Steiner, R. Methodische Grundlagen der Anthroposophie. Dornach, 1961.

Phil 978.49.175   Steiner, R. Mysterienstätten des Mittelalters. Dornach, 1932.

Phil 978.49.635   Steiner, R. Mysterienwahrheiten und Weihnachtsimpulse. Dornach, 1966.

Phil 525.56.5   Steiner, R. Mystics of the Renaissance. N.Y., 1911.

Phil 978.49.60   Steiner, R. Die Mystik im Aufgange des neuzeitlichen Geisteslebens und ihr Verhältnis zur modernen Weltanschauung. 2. Aufl. Stuttgart, 1924.

Phil 978.49.62   Steiner, R. Die Mystik im Aufgange des neuzeitlichen Geisteslebens und ihr Verhältnis zur modernen Weltanschauung. 3. Aufl. Stuttgart, 1924.

Phil 978.49.660   Steiner, R. Nationalökonomischer Kurs. 4. Aufl. Dornach, 1965.

Phil 978.49.552   Steiner, R. Natur und Menschin geisteswissenschaftlicher Betrachtung. 2. Aufl. Dornach, 1965.

Phil 978.49.730   Steiner, R. Die Naturwissenschaft und die weltgeschichtliche Entwicklung der Menschheit seit dem Altertum. Dornach, 1969.

Phil 978.49.782   Steiner, R. Die neue Geistigkeit und das Christus-Erlebnis des zwanzigsten Jahrhunderts. 2. Aufl. Dornach, 1970.

Phil 978.49.430   Steiner, R. Neugestaltung, des sozialen Organismus. Dornach, 1963.

Phil 978.49.185   Steiner, R. Die not Nach dem Christus. Dornach, 1942.

Phil 978.49.173   Steiner, R. Die okkulte Bewegung im Neunzehnten Jahrhundert und ihre Beiziehung zur Weltkultur. 3. Aufl. Dornach, 1969.

Phil 978.49.585   Steiner, R. Okkultes Lesen und okkultes Hören. 4. Aufl. Dornach, 1967.

Phil 978.49.19   Steiner, R. An outline of occult science. Chicago, Ill., 1922.

Phil 978.49.65   Steiner, R. Die Pforte der Einweihung (Initiation). Dornach, 1925.

Phil 978.49.680   Steiner, R. Die Philosophie des Thomas von Aquino. 3. Aufl. Dornach, 1967.

Phil 978.49.110   Steiner, R. Philosophy and anthroposophy. London, 1928.

Phil 978.49.560   Steiner, R. Physiologisch-therapeutisches auf Grundlage der Geisteswissenschaft and zur Therapie und Hygiene. Dornach, 1965.

Phil 978.49.770   Steiner, R. Die Polarität von Dauer und Entwickelung im Menschenleben. Dornach, 1968.

Phil 978.49.80   Steiner, R. Praktische Ausbildung des Denkens. Stuttgart, 1927.

Phil 978.49.135   Steiner, R. The problems of our time. London, 1934.

Phil 978.49.750.8   Steiner, R. Die Rätsel der Philosophie. 8. Aufl. Dornach, 1968.

Phil 978.49.270   Steiner, R. Rudolf Steiner in der Waldorfschule. 1. Aufl. Stuttgart, 1958.

Phil 978.49.220   Steiner, R. Rudolf Steiner über Schauspielkunst (eine Fragenbeantwortung). Dornach, 1939.

Phil 978.49.745   Steiner, R. Die Schöpfung der Welt und des Menschen. Dornach, 1969.

Phil 978.49.45   Steiner, R. Die Schwelle der geistigen Welt. 10. Aufl. Berlin, 1921.

Phil 978.49.55   Steiner, R. Der Seelen Erwachen. Berlin, 1922.

Phil 978.49.415   Steiner, R. Die soziale Grundforderung unserer Zeit in gländerter Zeitlage. Dornach, 1963.

Phil 978.49.620   Steiner, R. Die spirituellen Hintergründe der äusseren Welt. Dornach, 1966.

Phil 978.49.145   Steiner, R. Sprachgestaltung und dramatische Kunst. Dornach, 1926.

Phil 978.49.145.3   Steiner, R. Sprachgestaltung und dramatische Kunst. 3. Aufl. Dornach, 1969.

Phil 978.49   Steiner, R. Theosophie. Stuttgart, 1922.

Phil 978.49.7   Steiner, R. Theosophy. 18th ed. N.Y., 1910.

Phil 978.49.515   Steiner, R. Die tieferen Geheimnisse des Menschheitswerdens im Lichte der Evangelien. Dornach, 1966.

Phil 978.49.595   Steiner, R. Der Tod als Lebenswandlung. 1. Aufl. Dornach, 1969.

Phil 510.1.35   Steiner, R. Two essays on Haeckel. London, 19- .

Phil 978.49.696   Steiner, R. Die Verbindung zwischen Lebenden und Toten; acht Vorträge genalten im verschiedenen Stadten zwischen dem 16. Februar und 3. Dezember, 1916. 1. Aufl. Dornach, 1968.

Phil 978.49.523   Steiner, R. Das Verhältnis der Sternenwelt zum Menschen und des Menschen zur Steinenwelt. 3. Aufl. Dornach, 1966.

Phil 978.49.150   Steiner, R. Veröffentlichungen aus dem literarischen Frühwerk. Dornach, 1939-41. 4v.

Phil 978.49.265   Steiner, R. Vier Mysteriendramen. 2. Aufl. Dornach, 1956.

Phil 978.49.205   Steiner, R. Das volk Schillers und Fichtes. Dornach, 1930.

Phil 3018.14   Steiner, R. Vom Menschenrätsel. Berlin, 1918.

Phil 978.49.280   Steiner, R. Von der Initiatian. 3. Aufl. Dornach, 1959.

Phil 978.49.90   Steiner, R. Von Seelenrätseln. Berlin, 1921.

Phil 978.49.455   Steiner, R. Vorstufen zum Mysterium von Golgatha. Dornach, 1964.

Phil 978.49.70   Steiner, R. Wahrheit und Wissenschaft. Dornach, 1925.

Phil 978.49.727   Steiner, R. Wahrspruchworte: anthroposophischer Selenkalender. 2. Aufl. Dornach, 1969.

Phil 978.49.35   Steiner, R. The way of initiation. 1st American ed. N.Y., 1910.

Phil 978.49.225   Steiner, R. Welche Gesichtspunkte liegeni Errichtung der Waldorfschule zu Grunde? Dornach, 1932.

Phil 978.49.250   Steiner, R. Welt, Erde und Mensch. 2. Aufl. Freiburg, 1956.

Phil 978.49.190   Steiner, R. Das Weltbild des deutschen Idealismus. Dornach, 1930.

Phil 978.49.630   Steiner, R. Die Welträtsel und die Anthroposophie. 1. Aufl. Dornach, 1966.

Phil 978.49.85   Steiner, R. Wendepunkte des Geisteslebens. Dornach, 1927.

Phil 978.49.86   Steiner, R. Wendepunkte des Geisteslebens. 3. Aufl. Freiburg, 1954.

Phil 978.49.688   Steiner, R. Das Wesen des Musikaleschen und das Tonerlebnis im Menschen. 1. Aufl. Dornach, 1969.

Phil 978.49.699.2   Steiner, R. Wie Kann die Menschheit den Christus Wiedertinden? 2. Aufl. Dornach, 1968.

Phil 978.49.385   Steiner, R. Die Wissenschaft vom Werden des Menschen. Dornach, 1967.

Phil 978.49.425   Steiner, R. Der Zusammenhang des Menschen mit der elementaren Welt. Dornach, 1968.

Phil 978.49.235   Pamphlet vol. Steiner, R. 6 pam.

Phil 978.49.290   Pamphlet vol. Steiner, R. Lectures. 5 pam.

Phil 3640.675   Steiner, Rudolf. Friedrich Nietzsche, ein Kampfer gegen seine Zeit. Dornach, 1963.

Phil 3640.214   Steiner, Rudolf. Friedrich Nietzsche: ein Kämpfer gegen seiner Zeit. Weimar, 1895.

Phil 3640.214.2   Steiner, Rudolf. Friedrich Nietzsche: ein Kämpfer gegen seiner Zeit. 2e Aufl. Dornich, 1926.

Phil 5768.10.30   Steiner, Rudolf. Frihedens filosofi. København, 1924.

Phil 974.3.15   Steiner, Rudolf. From Luther to Steiner. London, 1923.

Phil 974.3.3   Steiner, Rudolf. Das Künstlerische in seiner Weltmission. Dornach, 1961.

Phil 974.3   Steiner, Rudolf. Mein Lebensgang. Geotheanum, 1925.

Phil 974.3.6   Steiner, Rudolf. Mein Legebensgang. Dornach, 1962.

Phil 974.3.8   Steiner, Rudolf. Die okkulten Grundlagen des Bhagavad Gita. 3. Aufl. Dornach, 1962.

Phil 5768.9.95   Steiner, Rudolf. Die Philosophie der Freiheit. Berlin, 1894.

Phil 5768.10.5   Steiner, Rudolf. Die Philosophie der Freiheit. Berlin, 1921.

Phil 5768.10   Steiner, Rudolf. The philosophy of freedom. London, 1916.

Phil 5768.10.3   Steiner, Rudolf. The philosophy of freedom. London, 1964.

Phil 1718.15.5   Steiner, Rudolf. Die Rätsel der Philosophie in ihrer Geschichte. Stuttgart, 1924-26. 2v.

Phil 5768.10.35   Steiner, Rudolf. Rudolf Steiner über seine "Philosophie der Freiheit". Stuttgart, 1966.

Phil 974.3.5   Steiner, Rudolf. The story of my life. London, 192-.

Phil 974.3.7   Steiner, Rudolf. The story of my life. London, 1928.

Phil 974.3.16   Steiner, Rudolf. Die Weihnachtstagung zur Begründung. 3. Aufl. Dornach, 1963.

Phil 1718.15   Steiner, Rudolf. Welt- und Lebensanschauungen im neunzehnten Jahrhundert. v.1-2. Berlin, 1901.

Phil 974.3.2   Steiner, Rudolf. Die Wirklichkeit der höheren Welten. Dornach, 1962.

Phil 5645.41   Steinfels, W. Farbe und Dasein. Jena, 1926.

Phil 3425.276   Steinhart, C. Hegel und sein Werk. Naumburg, 1841.

Phil 2490.175   Steinhauer, Margarete. Die politische Soziologie Auguste Comtes und ihre Differenz zur liberalen Gesellschaftstheorie Condorcets. Meisenheim, 1966.

Phil 8620.42   Steinhausen, H. Die Rolle des Bösen. Stockholm, 1939.

Phil 3850.54   Steinheim, Salomon Ludwig. Salomon Ludwig Steinheim zum Gedenken. Leiden, 1966.

Phil 1718.11   Steinilber, E. Essais critiques sur les idées philosophiques contemporaines. Paris, 1912.

Phil 3018.3   Steininger, F. Examen critique de la philosophie allemande. Trèves, 1841.

Phil 310.766.2   Steininger, Herbert. Dialektik, Wissenschaft und Waffe. 2. Aufl. Berlin, 1967.

Phil 3850.27.132   Steinitz, Benno. Albert Schweitzer. Wien, 1955.

Phil 5400.17   Steinitzer, M. Die menschlichen und tierischen Gemütsbewegungen. München, 1889.

Phil 1870.155   Steinkraus, Warren Edward. New studies in Berkeley's philosophy. N.Y., 1966.

Phil 8587.32.117   Steinmann, J. Friedrich von Hügel. Paris, 1962.

Phil 2805.406   Steinmann, J. Les trois nuits de Pascal. Paris, 1963.

Phil 2805.284.5   Steinmann, Jean. Pascal. London, 1965.

Phil 2805.284   Steinmann, Jean. Pascal. Paris, 1954.

Phil 2805.284.2   Steinmann, Jean. Pascal. Paris, 1962.

Phil 8643.18.2   Steinmann, Theophil. Der religiose Unsterblichkeitsglaube. 2. Aufl. Göttingen, 1912.

Phil 7069.59.50   Steinour, Harold Heiges. Exploring the unseen world. 1. ed. N.Y., 1959.

Phil 8893.22   Steinthal, H. Allgemeine Ethik. Berlin, 1885.

Phil 7080.51   Stekel, W. Der Wille zum Schlaf! Wiesbaden, 1915.

Phil 6328.2.31   Stekel, Wilhelm. Autobiography. N.Y., 1950.

Phil 6328.2.5   Stekel, Wilhelm. The beloved ego. London, 1921.

Phil 6968.17   Stekel, Wilhelm. Compulsion and doubt. N.Y., 1949.

Phil 6328.2.4A   Stekel, Wilhelm. Conditions of nervous anxiety. London, 1923.

Phil 6328.2.15   Stekel, Wilhelm. The depth of the soul. London, 1921.

Phil 6328.2.28   Stekel, Wilhelm. Erziehung derEltern. Wien, 1934.

Phil 7082.38.5   Stekel, Wilhelm. Fortschritte und Technik der Traumdeutung. Wien, 1935.

Phil 6328.2.10   Stekel, Wilhelm. Impulshandlungen. Berlin, 1922.

Phil 7082.38.6   Stekel, Wilhelm. The interpretation of dreams. N.Y., 1943. 2v.

Phil 6328.2.35   Stekel, Wilhelm. Das liebe Ich. Berlin, 1913.

Phil 6328.2   Stekel, Wilhelm. Nervöse Angstzustände und ihre Behandlung. Berlin, 1908.

Phil 6328.2.20   Stekel, Wilhelm. Peculiarities of behavior. N.Y., 1924. 2v.

Phil 6328.2.45   Stekel, Wilhelm. Der Seelenarzt. Leipzig, 1933.

Phil 7082.38   Stekel, Wilhelm. Die Sprache des Traumes. Wiesbaden, 1911.

Phil 7082.38.2   Stekel, Wilhelm. Die Sprache des Traumes. 2e Aufl. München, 1922.

Phil 7082.38.3   Stekel, Wilhelm. Die Sprache des Traumes. 3e Aufl. München, 1927.

Phil 6328.2.22   Stekel, Wilhelm. Technik der analytischen Psychotherapie. Bern, 1938.

Phil 6328.2.25   Stekel, Wilhelm. Technique of analytical psychotherapy. London, 1939.

Phil 7084.46   Stekel, Wilhelm. Die Träume der Dichter. Wiesbaden, 1912.

Phil 6328.2.17   Stekel, Wilhelm. Was im Grund der seele Ruht. 4e Aufl. Wien, 1909?

Phil 6328.2.40   Stekel, Wilhelm. Zwang und Zweifel. Berlin, 1927-28. 2v.

X Cg   Phil 7075.131   Stekel, William. Der Fetischismus dargestellt für Ärzte und Kriminalogen. Berlin, 1923.

Phil 3819.61   Stelkonstige reeckening van den regenboog. (Spinoza, Benedictus de.) Leiden, 1884.

Phil 7069.20.90   A stellar key to the summer land. 6th ed. (Davis, Andrew J.) Los Angeles, 1920.

Phil 5374.17.5   Die Stelle des Bewusstseins in der Natur. (Pikler, Gyula.) Leipzig, 1910.

Phil 4225.23.15   Stellini, J. Opera omnia. Patavii, 1778-79. 4v.

Phil 4225.23.30   Stellini, J. Scritti filosofica. Milano, 1942.

Phil 1504.3.3   Die Stellung. v.3, pt.3. (Wittmann, M.) Münster, 1900.

Phil 9420.13   Die Stellung der Liebe. (Plack, A.) Landshut, 1962.

Phil 8597.25   Die Stellung des Christentums zum Geschlechtsleben. (Rade, Martin.) Tübingen, 1911.

Phil 3140.85   Die Stellung des Johannes Clauberg in der Philosophie. Diss. (Weier, Winfred.) Mainz, 1960.

Phil 293.34   Die Stellung des Menschen im Kosmos. (Mueller, Aloys.) Bonn, 1948.

Phil 3494.22   Die Stellung des Substanzbegriffes. Inaug. Diss. (Manns, Richard.) Bonn, 1887.

Phil 2045.109   Die Stellung des Thomas Hobbes zu den politischen Parteien der grossen englischen Revolution. (Lips, Julius.) Leipzig, 1927.

Phil 3625.1.93   Die Stellung M. Mendelssohn's in der Geschichte der Asthitik. (Kanngiesser, G.) Frankfurt, 1868.

Phil 3805.245   Die Stellung und Bedeutung der Familie in der Pädagogik Schleiermachers. (Preuss, Eckhardt.) Münster? 1966?

Phil 5643.18   Stellwag, K. von C. Die Accommodationsfehler des Auges. n.p., 1855.

Phil 3705.2.80   Het stelsel der ervaring van Mr. C.W. Opzoomer. (Sandberg, A.J.) Zeist, 1865.

Phil 8968.17   Stelzenberger, J. Synerdesis. Paderborn, 1963.

Phil 3500.73   Stemberger, R. Immanuel Kant als Philosoph und Soziologe. Wien, 1953.

Phil 349.43   Stempkovskaia, V.I. O roli abstraktsnii v poznanii. Moskva, 1959.

Phil 8643.39   Stendahl, Krister. Immortality and resurrection. N.Y., 1965.

Phil 3925.16.90   Stenius, Erik. Wittgenstein's Tractatus. Ithaca, 1960.

Phil 8598.143   Stenson, Sten H. Sense and nonsense in religion. Nashville, 1969.

Phil 1750.552.20   Stenström, Thure. Existentialismen. Stockholm, 1966.

Phil 1123.7.5   Stenzel, Julius. Kleine Schriften zur griechischen Philosophie. 2. Aufl. Darmstadt, 1957.

Phil 1123.7   Stenzel, Julius. Metaphysik des Altertums. München, 1931.

Phil 3625.1.170   Step by step. (Isaacs, Abram Samuel.) Philadelphia, 1910.

Phil 7069.67.10   A step in the dark. (Lethbridge, Frances.) London, 1967.

Phil 8598.67   Stepanov, I. Mysli o religii. Moskva, 1922.

Phil 310.622   Stepanov, V.I. Dialekticheskii materializm kak metodologiia estestvennonauchnop poznaniia. Minsk, 1965.

Phil 5238.208   Stephanos. (Banks, Charlotte.) London, 1965.

Phil 960.118 Stephen, D.J. Studies in early Indian thought. Cambridge, 1918.

Phil 5258.97.5 Stephen, Henry. Elements of analytical psychology. 5th. ed. Calcutta, 1922.

Phil 2475.1.262 Stephen, Karin. The misuse of mind. N.Y., 1922.
Phil 2475.1.205 Stephen, Karin. The misuse of the mind. London, 1922.
Phil 6328.16 Stephen, Karin. Psychoanalysis and medicine. Cambridge, Eng., 1933.

NEDL Phil 193.35 Stephen, L. An agnostic's apology. London, 1893.
NEDL Phil 193.35.1 Stephen, L. An agnostic's apology. N.Y., 1893.
X Cg Phil 193.35.2 Stephen, L. An agnostic's apology. 2d ed. N.Y., 1903.
Phil 193.35.4 Stephen, L. An agnostic's apology and other essays. 2d ed. London, 1903.

NEDL Phil 8893.23.2 Stephen, L. The science of ethics. N.Y., 1882.
Phil 8893.23.5 Stephen, L. Social rights and duties. London, 1896. 2v.

Phil 1818.2.10A Stephen, Leslie. The English Utilitarians. London, 1950. 3v.
Phil 1818.2.6 Stephen, Leslie. The English Utilitarians. n.p., n.d.
Phil 1818.2.5 Stephen, Leslie. The English Utilitarians. v.2. London, 1900.

Phil 8610.873 Stephen, Leslie. Essays on freethinking and plain-speaking. London, 1873.
Phil 1818.2.8 Stephen, Leslie. History of English thought in the eighteenth century. v.2. London, 1927.
Phil 1818.2.7.5 Stephen, Leslie. History of English thought in the eighteenth century. v.2. 3rd ed. N.Y., 1902.
Phil 1818.2.4 Stephen, Leslie. History of English thought in the eighteenth century. 3rd ed. N.Y., 1949. 2v.
Phil 1818.2.15 Stephen, Leslie. History of English thought in the 18th century. N.Y., 1962. 2v.
Phil 1818.2 Stephen, Leslie. History of English thought in XVIIIth century. N.Y., 1876. 2v.
Phil 1818.2.3 Stephen, Leslie. History of English thought in XVIIIth century. 3rd ed. London, 1902.

Phil 2045.86.2 Stephen, Leslie. Hobbes. London, 1904.
Phil 2045.86 Stephen, Leslie. Hobbes. London, 1904.
Phil 187.32.90 Stephens, I.K. The hermit philosopher of Liendo. Dallas, 1951.
Phil 9178.7 Stephens, John. Advantages which man derives from woman. N.Y., 1815.

Htn Phil 8673.14* Stephens, William. An account of the growth of deism in England. London, 1696.
Phil 6688.10 Stephenson, Charles Y. (Mrs.). Clairvoyance and crystal gazing. London, 1918.
Phil 5594.153.2 Stephenson, William. The study of behavior. Chicago, 1964.

Phil 4873.5 Stepovniants, Marietta Tigranovna. Filosofiia i sotsiologiia v Pakistane. Moskva, 1967.
Phil 8882.12.9 Steps of life, further essays on happiness. (Hilty, K.) N.Y., 1907.

Phil 6328.21 Sterba, Richard. Handwörterbuch der Psychoanalyse. Wien, 1936-37.
Phil 6328.21.8 Sterba, Richard. Introduction to the psychoanalytic theory of the libido. 3d ed. N.Y., 1968.
Phil 2045.140 Der sterbliche Gott oder Leviathan gegen Behemoth. Thesis. (Braun, Dietrich.) Zürich, 1963.

Phil 5643.67 Stereoskopisches Sehen und Messen. (Dittler, Rudolf.) Leipzig, 1919.
Phil 3500.24 Stériad, A. L'interprétation de la doctrine de Kant. Paris, 1913.
Phil 3585.1.95 Sterkman, P. De plaats van J.H. Lambert...idealisme voor Kant. 's-Gravenhage, 1928.
Phil 2035.87 Sterling, J.H. Sir W. Hamilton. London, 1865.
Phil 4260.175 Le sterminate antichità. Studi vichiani. (Rossi, Paolo.) Pisa, 1969.

Phil 8598.41 Stern, Adolf. Die religiöse Stellung der vornehmsten Denker. Berlin, 1911.
Phil 3500.37 Stern, Albert. Über die Beziehungen Garve's zu Kant. Inaug. Diss. n.p., n.d.
Phil 720.25 Stern, Alfred. Die philosophischen Grundlagen von Wahrheit, Wirklichkeit, Wert. München, 1932.
Phil 2880.8.116.2 Stern, Alfred. Sartre, his philosophy and existential psychoanalysis. 2.ed. N.Y., 1967.
Phil 2880.8.116 Stern, Alfred. Sartre. N.Y., 1953.
Phil 2280.23.30 Stern, Alfred. The search for meaning: philosophical vistas. Memphis, 1971.
Phil 3838.20 Stern, Alfred. Über einen Bisher unbeachteten Brief Spinozas. Göttingen, 1872?

Phil 6968.26 Stern, Edith M. Mental illness. N.Y., 1942.
Phil 5590.245 Stern, Erich. Experimentelle Persönlichkeitsanalyse nach dem Murray-Test. 1. Aufl. Zürich, 1952.
Phil 6328.36 Stern, Erich. Handbuch der klinischen Psychologie. v.1-2. Zürich, 1954. 3v.
Phil 193.116 Stern, Erich. Zufall und Schicksal. Karlsruhe, 1926.
Phil 5590.310 Stern, George G. Methods in personality assessment. Glencoe, Ill., 1956.
Phil 349.29 Stern, Günther. Über das Haben. Bonn, 1928.
Phil 3808.136 Stern, I. Arthur Schopenhauer. Zürich, 1883.
Phil 3838.8 Stern, Jakob. Die Philosophie Spinoza's. 2. Aufl. Stuttgart, 1894.
Phil 3838.8.5 Stern, Jakob. Die Philosophie Spinoza's. 3. Aufl. Stuttgart, 1908.
Phil 5841.26 Stern, Karl. The flight from woman. N.Y., 1965.
Phil 5325.11 Stern, L.W. Analogie in volkstümlichen Denken. Berlin, 1893.
Phil 193.53 Stern, L.W. Person und Sache. Leipzig, 1906- 2v.
Phil 193.53.2 Stern, L.W. Person und Sache. Leipzig, 1923-1924. 3v.
Phil 5350.1 Stern, L.W. Psychologie der Veränderungsauffassung. Breslau, 1898.
Phil 193.53.5 Stern, L.W. Vorgedanken zur Weltanschauung. Leipzig, 1915.
Phil 5850.347 Stern, Louis W. Angewandte Psychologie. n.p., 1903. 2 pam.
Phil 5850.347.5 Stern, Louis W. Zur Psychologie der Aussage. Berlin, 1902.
Phil 8968.6 Stern, M.L. Monistische Ethik. Leipzig, 1911.
Phil 510.26 Stern, M.L. Philosophischer und naturwissenschaftlicher Monismus. Leipzig, 1885.
Phil 193.138.5 Stern, M.R. von. Das Welt-Vakuum. Linz, 1923.
Phil 193.138 Stern, M.R. von. Weltanschauung; Ergebnisse freien Denkens. Linz, 1921.
Phil 6060.88 Stern, Martin. Entwicklungshemmungen und Graphologie. Thesis. Zürich, 1934.
Phil 5258.37 Stern, N. Das Denken und sein Gegenstand. München, 1909.
Phil 193.67A Stern, Paul. Grundprobleme der Philosophie. Berlin, 1903.

Phil 5258.35.15 Stern, W. Allgemeine Psychologie auf personalistischer Grundlage. Haag, 1935.
Phil 5258.35.3 Stern, W. Die differentielle Psychologie. Leipzig, 1921.
Phil 5258.35 Stern, W. Die differentielle Psychologie. Leipzig, 1911.
Phil 5258.35.20 Stern, W. General psychology from the personalistic standpoint. N.Y., 1938.
Phil 5258.35.5 Stern, W. Die Psychologie und der Personalismus. Leipzig, 1917.
Phil 575.77 Stern, W. Studien zur Personwissenschaft. I. Leipzig, 1930.
Phil 5258.35.12 Stern, W. Über Psychologie der individuellen Differenzen. Leipzig, 1900.
Phil 8893.49 Stern, Wilhelm. Das Wesen des Mitleids. Berlin, 1903.
Phil 8643.26 Stern-Gwiazdowski, H. von. Leben wir nach unseren Tode weiter? Leipzig, 1896.
Phil 3850.64 Stern-Mitcherlich, Axel Ludwig. The science of freedom; an essay in applied philosophy. London, 1969.
Phil 5402.39 Sternbach, Richard A. Pain; a psychophysiological analysis. N.Y., 1968.
Phil 400.59 Sternberg, K. Idealismus und Kultur. Berlin, 1923.
Phil 193.78 Sternberg, Kurt. Einführung in die Philosophie vom Stand...Kritizismus. Leipzig, 1919.
Phil 193.78.5 Sternberg, Kurt. Der Kampf zwischen Pragmatismus und Idealismus in Philosophie und Weltkrieg. Berlin, 1917.
Phil 1135.28.20 Sternberg, Kurt. Das Problem des Ursprungs in der Philosophie des Altertums. Breslau, 1935.
Phil 3500.31 Sternberg, Kurt. Versuch einer Entwicklungsgeschichte des Kantischen...des Kriticismus. Berlin, 1909.
Phil 818.19 Sternberg, Kurt. Was Heisst und zu welchem Ende studiert man Philosophiegeschichte. Berlin, 1926.
Phil 299.32 Sterneder, Hans. Das kosmische Weltbild. Freiburg, 1969.
Phil 3270.12.90 Sternfeld, Robert. Frege's logical theory. Carbondale, 1966.
Phil 3425.308 Sterrett, James M. Studies in Hegel's philosophy of religion. N.Y., 1890.
Phil 5258.41 Sterrett, John D. The power of thought. N.Y., 1896.
Phil 2490.150 Sterzel, Georg Friedrick. A. Comte als Pädagog. Leipzig, 1886.
Phil 3552.286 Das Stetigkeitsgesetz bei Leibniz. Inaug. -Diss. (Wanke, Georg.) Kiel, 1892.
Phil 2070.91.2 Stettheimer, E. Die Urteilsfreiheit als Grundlage der Rechtfertigung des religiösen Glaubens. Inaug. Diss. Wittenburg, 1903.
Phil 2070.91 Stettheimer, E. Die Urteilsfreiheit als Grundlage der Rechtfertigung des religiösen Glaubens. Inaug. Diss. Wittenburg, 1903.
NEDL Phil 2070.91.5 Stettheimer, E. The will to believe as a basis for defense of religious faith. N.Y., 1907.
Phil 1135.33 Stettner, E. Antike Humanität in moderner Beleuchtung. Bieletz, 1912.
Phil 1135.101 Stettner, Walter. Die Seelenwanderung bei Griechen und Römern. Inaug. Diss. Stuttgart, 1934.
Phil 9065.3 Steubing, Hans. Der Kompromiss als ethisches Problem. Gütersloh, 1955.
Phil 193.36.5 Steudel, A. Das goldene ABC der Philosophie. Berlin, 1891.
Phil 193.36 Steudel, A. Philosophie im Umriss. Stuttgart, 1871-1884. 6v.
Phil 8893.52 Steudel, F. Alte und neue Tafeln. Berlin, 1912?
Phil 3195.6.103 Steuzel, J. Über Diltheys Verhaltnis zu Hegel. n.p., n.d.
Phil 7039.8 Stevens, E. Winchester. The Watseka wonder. Chicago, 1879.
Phil 7039.8.2 Stevens, E. Winchester. The Watseka wonder. Chicago, 1887.
Phil 672.25 Stevens, E.M. Psychology of space perception. New Orleans, 1915.
Phil 5938.13 Stevens, Enos. Rudiments of metal philosophy and phrenological chart. Lampeter, Pa., 1839.
Phil 5330.14 Stevens, H.C. Plethysmographic study of attention. n.p., 1905.
Phil 5374.284 Stevens, John O. Awareness: exploring, experimenting, experiencing. Lafayette, Calif., 1971.
Phil 493.2 Stevens, S.E. Philosophy of the great unconscious. Boston, 1908.
Phil 5238.18 Stevens, S.S. Handbook of experimental psychology. N.Y., 1951.
Phil 193.37.2 Stevens, Samuel Eugene. Science and superstition. N.Y., 1913.
Phil 5650.24 Stevens, Stanley S. Hearing; its psychology and physiology. N.Y., 1938.
Phil 7069.45.35 Stevens, William O. Unbidden guests, a book of real ghosts. N.Y., 1945.
Phil 7082.96 Stevens, William Oliver. The mystery of dreams. London, 1950.
Phil 8893.102 Stevenson, Charles Leslie. Ethics and language. New Haven, 1944.
Phil 8893.102.2 Stevenson, Charles Leslie. Ethics and language. New Haven, 1946.
Phil 8893.102.5 Stevenson, Charles Leslie. Ethics and language. New Haven, 1948.
Phil 8893.102.15 Stevenson, Charles Leslie. Facts and values. New Haven, 1963.
Phil 5710.6 Stevenson, J.G. Religion and temperament. London, 1913.
Phil 7054.13 Stevenson, William G. Does spiritualism transcend natural law? Poughkeepsie, 1880.
Phil 5710.9 Stewart, A. Our temperaments; their study and teaching. 2. ed. London, 1892.
Phil 5710.14 Stewart, A. Our temperaments. London, 1887.
Phil 8643.28.7 Stewart, Balfour. The unseen universe. 7. ed. London, 1878.
Phil 2275.50.10 Stewart, D. Anfangsgründe der Philosophie über die menschliche Seele. Berlin, 1794. 2v.
Phil 2275.11 Stewart, D. Collected works. v.1-4, 6-10, and supplement. Edinburgh, 1854-60. 10v.
X Cg Phil 2275.11 Stewart, D. Collected works. v.5. Edinburgh, 1854-60.
Phil 2275.12 Stewart, D. Collected works. 2nd ed. Edinburgh, 1877. 11v.
Phil 2275.80 Stewart, D. Élémens de la philosophie de l'esprit humain. Genève, 1808. 3v.
Phil 2275.34 Stewart, D. Elements of the philosophy of the human mind. Boston, 1814-27. 3v.
Phil 2275.50 Stewart, D. Elements of the philosophy of the human mind. Boston, 1854.
Phil 2275.50.2 Stewart, D. Elements of the philosophy of the human mind. Boston, 1855.
Phil 2275.37 Stewart, D. Elements of the philosophy of the human mind. Boston, 1866.

Author and Title Listing

Phil 2275.33 — Stewart, D. Elements of the philosophy of the human mind. Brattleborough, 1808.

Phil 2275.33.2 — Stewart, D. Elements of the philosophy of the human mind. Brattleborough, 1813.

Phil 2275.35 — Stewart, D. Elements of the philosophy of the human mind. Cambridge, 1829. 2v.

Phil 2275.30 — Stewart, D. Elements of the philosophy of the human mind. London, 1792.

Phil 2275.31.5 — Stewart, D. Elements of the philosophy of the human mind. London, 1802.

Phil 2275.36 — Stewart, D. Elements of the philosophy of the human mind. London, 1843.

Htn Phil 2275.34.6* — Stewart, D. Elements of the philosophy of the human mind. N.Y., 1818. 2v.

Phil 2275.34.5 — Stewart, D. Elements of the philosophy of the human mind. N.Y., 1818. 2v.

Phil 2275.31 — Stewart, D. Elements of the philosophy of the human mind. Philadelphia, 1793.

Phil 2275.34.15 — Stewart, D. Elements of the philosophy of the human mind. v.1-2. Albany, 1822.

Phil 2275.34.11 — Stewart, D. Elements of the philosophy of the human mind. v.1-2. Boston, 1821.

Phil 2275.35.2 — Stewart, D. Elements of the philosophy of the human mind. v.1-2. Cambridge, 1829.

Phil 2275.32 — Stewart, D. Elements of the philosophy of the human mind. v.2. Boston, 1814.

Phil 2275.60.10 — Stewart, D. Essais philosophique sur les systèmes de Locke, Berkeley. Paris, 1828.

Phil 2275.65 — Stewart, D. A general view of the progress of...philosophy. Boston, 1822.

Phil 2275.20 — Stewart, D. Oeuvres. Bruxelles, 1829. 5v.
Phil 2275.22 — Stewart, D. Oeuvres. Paris, 1829. 2v.
Phil 2275.70 — Stewart, D. Outlines of moral philosophy. Edinburgh, 1893.

Htn Phil 2275.59* — Stewart, D. Philosophical essays. Edinburgh, 1810.
Phil 2275.60 — Stewart, D. Philosophical essays. Philadelphia, 1811.
Phil 2275.40 — Stewart, D. Philosophie des facultés actives et morales de l'homme. v.1-2. Paris, n.d.

Phil 2275.39 — Stewart, D. Philosophy of the active and moral poweers. Cambridge, 1849.

Htn Phil 2275.38*A — Stewart, D. Philosophy of the active and moral powers. Boston, 1828. 2v.

Phil 2275.39.2 — Stewart, D. Philosophy of the active and moral powers. Boston, 1858.

Phil 2275.38.2 — Stewart, D. Philosophy of the active and moral powers. v.1-2. Boston, 1828.

Phil 2275.10 — Stewart, D. Works. Cambridge, 1829. 7v.
Phil 5421.15.20 — Stewart, David A. Money, power, and sex. N.Y., 1965.
Phil 5421.15 — Stewart, David A. Preface to empathy. N.Y., 1956.
Phil 3640.109 — Stewart, H.L. Nietzsche and the ideals of modern Germany. London, 1915.

Phil 193.60 — Stewart, H.L. Questions of the day in philosophy and psychology. London, 1912.

Phil 2805.112.10 — Stewart, Hugh F. Blaise Pascal. London, 1942.
Phil 2805.112.15 — Stewart, Hugh F. The heart of Pascal. Cambridge, 1945.
Phil 2805.112.5 — Stewart, Hugh F. La sainteté de Pascal. Paris, 1919.
Phil 2805.112.7 — Stewart, Hugh F. The secret of Pascal. Cambridge, Eng., 1941.

X Cg Phil 8893.24 — Stewart, J. The book of nature. London, n.d.
Phil 2050.252 — Stewart, J.B. The moral and political philosophy of David Hume. N.Y., 1963.

Phil 5754.1.27 — Stewart, J.G. Freedom of the will vindicated. Glasgow, 1876.

Phil 2475.1.82 — Stewart, J.W.K. A critical exposition of Bergson's philosophy. London, 1911.

Phil 6315.2.410 — Stewart, Walter A. Psychoanalysis; the first ten years. N.Y., 1967.

Phil 4215.1.82 — Stiattesi, Andrea. Notizia storica di Gian Domenico Romagnosi. Firenze, 1878.

Phil 5028.4 — Stiazhkin, N.I. Kratkii ochesk istorii obshchei i matematicheskoi logiki v Rossii. Moskva, 1962.

Phil 5066.242.5 — Stiazhkin, Nikolai Ivanovich. Formirovanre matematicheskoi logiki. Moskva, 1967.

Phil 5066.242.1 — Stiazhkin, Nikolai Ivanovich. History of mathematical logic from Leibniz to Peano. Cambridge, Mass., 1969.

Phil 5066.242 — Stiazhkin, Nikolai Ivanovich. Stanovlenie idei matematicheskoi logiki. Moskva, 1964.

Phil 5585.21 — Stiborius. Die Kategorien der sinnlichen Perception. Leipzig, 1890.

Phil 5520.730 — Stichl, Ulrich. Einführung in die allgemeine Semantik. Bern, 1970.

Phil 3085.7.35 — Stichworte. Kritische Modelle. (Adorno, Theodor W.) Frankfurt, 1969.

Phil 193.115 — Stickers, J. Die Wiedergeburt der systematischen Philosophie. Berlin, 1927.

Phil 575.138 — Stiefel, Kurt. Persönlichkeit und Form. Zürich, 1943.
Phil 974.3.121 — Stieglitz, K. von. Die Christosophie Rudolf Steiners. Witten, 1955.

Phil 8843.8 — Stieglitz, T. Über den Ursprung des Sittlichen und die Formen seiner Erscheinung. Wien, 1894.

Phil 493.10 — Stiehler, G. Beiträge zur Geschichte des vormarxistischen Materialismus. 1. Aufl. Berlin, 1961.

Phil 3425.596 — Stiehler, G. Die Dialektik in Hegels Phänomenologie des Geistes. Berlin, 1964.

Phil 310.665.5 — Stiehler, Gottfried. Dialektik und Praxis. Berlin, 1968.
Phil 310.665.2 — Stiehler, Gottfried. Der dialektische Widusprud. 2. Aufl. Berlin, 1960.

Phil 3425.545 — Stiehler, Gottfried. Hegel und der Marxismus über den Widerspruch. Berlin, 1960.

Phil 400.132 — Stiehler, Gottfried. Der Idealismus von Kant bis Hegel. Berlin, 1970.

Phil 3552.330 — Stieler, Georg. Gottfried Wilhelm Leibniz. Paderborn, 1950.

Phil 2733.93 — Stieler, Georg. Nikolaus Malebranche. Stuttgart, 1925.
Phil 3963.2 — Stien, Hendrik. Das Leib-Seele-Problem in der Philosophie Hollands im 19. und 20. Jahrhundert. Lengerich, 1937.

Phil 126.2 — Stier, J. Praecepta doctrinae logicae. London, 1671.
Phil 1845.3.110A — Stiernotte, A.P.N.F. God and space time. N.Y., 1954.
Phil 5628.50.20 — La stigmatisation, l'extase divine, et les miracles de Lourdes. (Imbert-Gourbeyre, Antoine.) Clermont-Ferrand, 1894. 2v.

Phil 5628.55 — Die Stigmatisierte Therese Neumann von Konnersreuth. (Gerlich, Fritz.) München, 1929. 2v.

Phil 5628.52 — Die Stigmatisirten des neunzehnten Jahrhunderts: Anna Katharina Emmerich, Maria von Mörl, Domenico Lazzari. Regensburg, 1877.

Phil 8707.25 — Stiinta si religie. (Roth, A.) Bucaresti, 1960.

Phil 8050.32 — Stilbegriffe und Stilphänomene. (Weisbach, Werner.) Wien, 1957.

Phil 4260.118.5.2 — Stile e umanità di Giambattista Vico. 2. ed. (Fubini, Mario.) Milano, 1965.

Phil 4260.118 — Stile i umanità di Giambattista Vico. (Fubini, Mario.) Bari, 1946.

Phil 6128.31.5 — Stiles, Percy G. The nervous system and its conservation. Philadelphia, 1915.

Phil 7082.98 — Stiles, Percy Goldthwait. Dreams. Cambridge, 1927.
Phil 5643.48 — Stilling, Jacob. Psychologie der Gesichtsvorstellung. Berlin, 1901.

Htn Phil 2115.83* — Stillingfleet, E. Answer to Mr. Locke's letter. London, 1697.

Htn Phil 2115.83.3* — Stillingfleet, E. Answer to Mr. Locke's second letter. London, 1698.

Phil 349.75 — Stillwater Conference on the Nature of Concepts, their Structure and Social Inter-relation, Oklahoma Agricultural and Mechanical College, 1950. The nature of concepts, their inter-relation and role in social structure. Stillwater, Oklahoma, 1950.

Phil 3246.220 — Eine Stimme aus dem Publikum über Gottes Sein und Wesen. (Grusber, J.G.) Leipzig, 1799.

Phil 6962.35 — Die Stimme der Neurose. (Moses, Paul Joseph.) Stuttgart, 1956.

Phil 3415.106.9 — Stimmen der Kritik über Eduard von Hartmanns Werke. (Haacke, Hermann.) Leipzig, 1904.

Phil 5258.110 — Stimmungen und Verstimmungen. (Schröder, Paul.) Leipzig, 1930.

Phil 5875.160 — Stimulation in early infancy. London, 1969.
Phil 5640.148 — Stimulus and sensation; readings in sensory psychology. (Cain, William S.) Boston, 1971.

Phil 5253.15 — Stimulus sampling theory. (Neimark, Edith.) San Francisco, 1967.

Phil 5520.72 — Stinchfield, S.M. The psychology of speech. Boston, 1928.
Phil 3246.237 — Stine, R.W. The doctrine of God in the philosophy of Fichte. Philadelphia, 1945.

Phil 3246.245 — Stiner, Rudolf. Fichtes Geist mitten unter uns. Dornach, 1933.

Phil 8893.25 — Stinson, J.H. Ethica. N.Y., 1860.
Phil 5058.26 — Stinson, J.H. Organon of science. Eureka, Calif., 1879.
Phil 9035.54 — Stipriaan Luiscius, J.M. van. Karakter. Haag, 1925.
Phil 7069.57.10 — Stirling, A.M.W.P. Ghosts vivisected. London, 1957.
Phil 2280.15.80 — Stirling, Amelia H. James Hutchinson Stirling, his life and work. London, 1912.

Phil 5075.1 — Stirling, J.H. The categories. Edinburgh, 1903.
Phil 3425.94 — Stirling, J.H. The secret of Hegel. London, 1865. 2v.

Phil 5258.47 — Stirling, James H. What is thought? Edinburgh, 1900.
Phil 3640.86 — Stirner et Nietzsche. (Levy, Albert.) Paris, 1904.
Phil 4635.7.9 — Stjernhjelm, Georg. Filosofiska fragment. v.1-2. Stockholm, 1924.

Phil 1200.42 — De stoa; een wereld-philosophie. (Jong, K.H.E.) Amsterdam, 1937.

Phil 1200.10 — Die Stoa. (Barth, P.) Stuttgart, 1903.
Phil 1200.44.2 — Die Stoa. 2. und 4. Aufl. (Pohlenz, Max.) Göttingen, 1970. 2v.

Phil 1200.10.6 — Die Stoa. 5. Aufl. (Barth, P.) Stuttgart, 1941.
Phil 1200.10.7 — Die Stoa. 6. Aufl. (Barth, P.) Stuttgart, 1946.
Phil 1200.44.5 — Stoa und Stoiker. (Pohlenz, Max.) Zürich, 1950.
Phil 7069.26.35 — Stobart, M.A. Torchbearers of spiritualism. N.Y., 1926.
Phil 3640.725 — Stobbe, Erhard. Nietzsches Lehre vom Verbrecher. Inaug. Diss. Marburg, 1964.

Phil 8893.94 — Stoce, W.J. The concept of morals. N.Y., 1937.
Phil 5535.2 — Stochastic models for learning. (Bush, Robert Ray.) N.Y., 1964.

Phil 1870.119 — Stock, J. An account of the life of George Berkeley. 2nd ed. Dublin, 1777.

Phil 1818.4 — Stock, Saint George. English thought for English thinkers. London, 1912.

Phil 1200.11 — Stock, St. George. Stoicism. London, 1908.
Phil 6980.710.63 — Stocker, Arnold. De la psychoanalyse à la psychosynthese. Paris, 1957.

X Cg Phil 9495.124.2 — Stockham, A.B. (Mrs.). Karezza, ethics of marriage. Chicago, 1898.

Phil 9495.124 — Stockham, A.B. (Mrs.). Karezza, ethics of marriage. Chicago, 1903.

Phil 103.7 — Stockhammer, Morris. Philosophisches Wörterbuch. Köln, 1967.

Phil 28.49 — Stockholm studies in philosophy. Stockholm. 2 2v.
Phil 193.130 — Stocks, J.L. The limits of purpose and other essays. London, 1932.

Phil 193.130.15 — Stocks, J.L. Morality and purpose. N.Y., 1969.
Phil 8598.72 — Stocks, J.L. On the nature and grounds of religious belief. London, 1934.

Phil 193.130.10 — Stocks, J.L. Reason and intuition and other essays. London, 1939.

Phil 193.130.5 — Stocks, J.L. Time; cause and eternity. London, 1938.
Phil 5865.178 — Stocks, John L. Jeremy Bentham (1748-1832). Manchester, 1933.

Phil 3018.8 — Stockum, T.C. Spinoza, Jacobi, Lessing. Groningen, 1916.
Phil 3838.7 — Stockum, T.C. van. Spinoza's beoordeeling en invloed in duitschland van 1677 tob 1750. Groningen, 1916.

Phil 8643.4 — Stockwell, C.T. The evolution of immortality. Chicago, 1887.

Phil 8893.38 — Stockwell, Joseph. A sermon preach'd at Faringdon...opening a charity school. Oxford, 1717.

Phil 5790.35.5 — Stoddard, Ellwyn R. Conceptual models of human behavior in disaster. El Paso, 1968.

Htn Phil 2280.3.30* — Stoddard, Solomon. An answer to some cases of conscience. Boston, 1722.

Phil 850.4 — Stöcke, A. Die speculative Lehre vom Menschen. Würzburg, 1858-59. 2v.

Phil 8125.14 — Stöcker, Helene. Zur Kunstanschauung des XVIII. Jahrhunderts. Berlin, 1904.

Phil 1718.1 — Stöckl, A. Geschichte der neueren Philosophie. Mainz, 1883. 2v.

Phil 1523.1 — Stöckl, A. Geschichte der Philosophie der Mittelalters. Mainz, 1864-6. 3v.

Phil 8419.37 — Stoeckl, A. Grundriss der Ästhetik. Mainz, 1871.
Phil 818.5A — Stöckl, A. Handbook of the history of philosophy. N.Y., 1911.

Phil 1535.11 — Stöckl, A. Lehrbuch der Philosophie. Mainz, 1876. 2v.

Phil 1535.11.8 — Stöckl, A. Lehrbuch der Philosophie. Mainz, 1905-12. 2v.

Phil 193.37.5 — Stöckl, Albert. Grundzüge der philosophie. 2e Aufl. v.1-2. Mainz, 1910.

Phil 5643.82   Stöhr, Adolf. Grundfragen der psychophysiologischen Optik. Leipzig, 1904.

Phil 5058.31.5   Stöhr, Adolf. Lehrbuch der Logik in psychologisierender Darstellung. Leipzig, 1910.

Phil 5058.31   Stöhr, Adolf. Leitfaden der Logik in psychologisierender Darstellung. 2e Aufl. Leipzig, 1915.

Phil 5258.63   Stöhr, Adolf. Psychologie. Wien, 1917.

Phil 5520.52   Stöhr, Adolf. Umriss einer Theorie der Namen. Leipzig, 1889.

Phil 5360.3   Stöhr, Adolf. Die Vieldeutigkeit des Urtheiles. Leipzig, 1895.

Phil 6028.8   Stoehr, Coelestinus. Phyisiognomik. Coburg, 1804. 2v.

Phil 5258.112   Stoelting, C.H., Co., Chicago. Psychology and physiology apparatus and supplies. Chicago, 1923.

Phil 5520.592   Stoep, F. van der. Taalanalise en taalevaluering as pedagogies-didaktiese diagnostiseungsmetode. Pretoria, 1965.

Phil 349.7   Störring, G. Einführung in die Erkenntnistheorie. Leipzig, 1909.

Phil 8598.56   Störring, G. Die Frage der Wahrheit der christlichen Religion. Leipzig, 1920.

Phil 735.108   Störring, G. Die moderne ethische Wertphilosophie. Leipzig, 1935.

Phil 5258.144   Störring, G. Psychologie. Leipzig, 1923.

Phil 5125.12   Störring, G. Das urteilende und schliessende Denken in kausaler Behandlung. Leipzig, 1926.

Phil 2138.106   Störring, G.W. John Stuart Mill's Theorie über den psychologischen Ursprung des Vulgärglaubens an die Aussenwelt. Inaug. Diss. Berlin, 1889.

Phil 3890.6.80   Störring, Gustav. Die Erkenntnistheorie von Tetens. Leipzig, 1901.

Phil 8893.53   Störring, Gustav. Ethische Grundfragen. Leipzig, 1906.

Phil 5058.30.10   Störring, Gustav. Experimentelle Untersuchungen über Einfache schlussprozesse. Leipzig, 1908.

Phil 8893.53.10   Störring, Gustav. Grundfragen der philosophischen Ethik. Meisenheim, 1967.

Phil 5058.30   Störring, Gustav. Logik. Leipzig, 1916.

Phil 8893.53.5   Störring, Gustav. Moralphilosophische Streitfragen. Leipzig, 1903.

Phil 5400.41   Störring, Gustav. Psychologie des menschlichen Gefühlslebens. Bonn, 1916.

Phil 8893.53.7   Störring, Gustav. Die sittlichen Forderungen und die Frage ihrer Gultigkeit. Leipzig, 1919.

Phil 5850.256   Størst unbytte af legemligt og aandeligt arbejde. (Lehmann, A.) København, 1919.

Phil 5520.27.2   Die Störungen der Sprache. (Kussmaul, A.) Leipzig, 1887.

Phil 5645.28   Die Störungen des Farbensinnes ihre klinische Bedeutung und ihre Diagnose. (Höllner, Hans.) Berlin, 1912.

Phil 5135.6   Stoetzel, Jean. Théorie des opinions. 1. éd. Paris, 1943.

Phil 6315.2.475   Stoev, Stoiu G. Froidizmat i preodoliavaneto ma v Bulgariia. Sofiia, 1969.

Phil 3705.7   Stoff und Leben. (Oberth, Hermann.) Remagen, 1959.

Phil 187.119   Stoic, Christian and humanist. (Murray, G.) London, 1940.

Phil 1200.76   Stoic and Epicurean. (Hicks, Robert Drew.) N.Y., 1962.

X Cg   Phil 1200.17   The stoic creed. (Davidson, W.L.) Edinburgh, 1907.

Phil 1200.17   The stoic creed. (Davidson, W.L.) Edinburgh, 1907.

Phil 1200.27.2   The stoic moralists, and the Christians in the first two centuries. 2d ed. (Jordan, T.) Dublin, 1884.

Phil 1200.15.7   The stoic philosophy. (Murray, G.) London, 1918.

Phil 1200.70   Stoic philosophy. (Rist, John Michael.) London, 1969.

Phil 1200.63   The Stoic theory of knowledge. (Watson, Gerard.) Belfast, 1966.

Phil 1200.24   Les stoïciens. (Lafon, R.) Paris, n.d.

Phil 1200.14.5   Stoïciens et sceptiques. (Bevan, E.R.) Paris, 1927.

Phil 1200.3   Stoicism. (Capes, W.W.) London, 1880.

Phil 1200.11   Stoicism. (Stock, St. George.) London, 1908.

Phil 1200.23   Stoicism and its influence. (Wenley, R.M.) Boston, 1924.

Phil 1200.60   Le stoïcisme. (Brun, Jean.) Paris, 1958.

Phil 1350.11   Le stoïcisme à Rome. (Montée, P.) Paris, 1865.

Phil 1200.20   Le stoïcisme et les stoïciens. (Avenel, J.) Paris, 1886.

Phil 1200.58   Stoïcisme et pedagogie. (Pire, Georges.) Liege, 1958.

Phil 1200.64   Le stoïcisme et son influence. (Bridoux, André.) Paris, 1966.

Phil 1200.25   Stoicos' Aéatheiae falso suspectos. (Karg, F.) Lipsiae, 1716.

Phil 1130.8A   The Stoics, Epicureans, and Sceptics. (Zeller, Eduard.) London, 1870.

Phil 1130.8.3   The Stoics, Epicureans, and Sceptics. (Zeller, Eduard.) London, 1880.

Phil 1130.8.5   The Stoics, Epicureans, and Sceptics. (Zeller, Eduard.) London, 1892.

Phil 1200.14   Stoics and sceptics. (Bevan, E.R.) Oxford, 1913.

Phil 3500.90   Stoikhammer, Morris. Kants Zurechnungsidee und Freiheitsantinomie. Köln, 1961.

Phil 1200.26   Den stoiske og epikuraeiske moral. (Sibbern, A.) Kjobenhavn, 1853.

Phil 4825.16   Stojković, Andrija B. Počeci filosofije Srba od Save do Dositeja na osnovama narodne mudrosti. Beograd, 1970.

Phil 9075.28   Stoker, H.G. Das Gewissen, Erscheinungsformen und Theorie. Bonn, 1925.

Phil 5421.20.145   Stokes, Allen W. Aggressive man and aggressive beast. Logan, 1968?

Phil 8708.4   Stokes, G.G. On the absence of real opposition between science and revelation. London, 1884?

Phil 720.2   Stokes, G.J. Objectivity of truth. London, 1884.

Phil 860.10   Stokes, Michael C. One and many in Presocratic philosophy. Washington, 1971.

Phil 5545.23   Stokes, W. Memory. London, 1888.

Phil 6990.3.95   Stolarek, Z. Gorod chudes svoimi i chuzhimi glazami. Moskva, 1961.

Phil 5425.80   Stolen fire. (Kenmare, D.) London, 1951.

Phil 6060.13   Stoll, Jakob. Zur Psychologie der Schreibfehler. Zürich, 1913.

Phil 2340.9.90   Stoll, Marion R. Whewell's philosophy of induction. Diss. Lancaster, Pa., 1929.

Phil 7140.3   Stoll, O. Suggestions und Hypnotismus...Volkerpsychologie. Leipzig, 1894.

Phil 5841.16   Stoll, Otto. Die Geschlechtsleben in der Völkerpsychologie. Leipzig, 1908.

Phil 3310.6.80   Stolleis, Michael. Die Moral in der Politik bei Christian Grane. Inaug. Diss. München, 1967.

Phil 6328.11   Stollenhoff, H. Kurzes Lehrbuch der Psychoanalyse. Stuttgart, 1926.

Phil 5590.496   Stoller, Robert J. Sex and gender; on the development of masculinity and feminity. London, 1968.

Phil 8419.22   Stolnitz, Jerome. Aesthetics and philosophy of art criticism. Boston, 1960.

Phil 8419.19   Stolovich, L.N. Predmet estetiki. Moskva, 1961.

Phil 8419.66   Stolovich, Leonid N. Kategoriia prekrasnogo i obshchestvennyi ideal. Moskva, 1969.

Phil 6328.26   Stolz, Karl R. The church and psychotherapy. N.Y., 1943.

Phil 1718.14   Stolzle, R. Das Problem des Lebens in der heutigen Philosophie. Paderborn, 1922.

Phil 632.10   Stommel, Joannes Antonius. L'unification du réel. Utrecht, 1964?

Phil 193.126   Stone, Charles G. The social contract of the universe. London, 1930.

Phil 5870.80.2   Stone, Lawrence Joseph. Childhood and adolescence. 2nd ed. N.Y., 1968.

Phil 6328.50   Stone, Leo. The psychoanalytic situation. N.Y., 1961.

Phil 8893.85   Stone, M.A. The philosophy of indifference. Providence, 1931.

Phil 665.32   Stone, M.M. A practical study of the soul. N.Y., 1901.

Phil 7069.64.10   Stone, W.C. The other side of the mind. Englewood Cliffs, 1964.

Phil 8419.46   Stone, W.F. Questions on the philosophy of art. London, 1897.

Phil 6688.5   Stone, W.L. Letter to Dr. Brigham on animal magnetism. N.Y., 1837.

Phil 7060.116   The stoneground ghost tales. (Batchel, R.) Cambridge, Eng., 1912.

Phil 720.10   Stoner, J.R. Logic and imagination in the perception of truth. N.Y., 1910.

Phil 5066.223   Stonert, H. Język i nauka. Warszawa, 1964.

Phil 6315.2.255   Stoodley, Bartlett. The concepts of Sigmund Freud. Glencoe, 1959.

Phil 8843.9   Stoops, J.D. Ideals of conduct. N.Y., 1926.

Phil 9178.9   Stopes, M.C.C. Radiant motherhood. N.Y., 1932.

Phil 5635.32   Stopford, J.S.B. Sensation and the sensory pathway. London, 1930.

Phil 4210.136   Stopppani, Pietro. Antonio Rosmini. Milano, 1905.

Phil 5058.44   Storchenau, S. Institutiones logicae. Venetiis, 1819.

Phil 193.38   Storchenau, S. Metaphysicae. v.1-4. Venice, 1819-1820. 2v.

Phil 4580.63   Den store humor. (Høffding, Harald.) Kjøbenhavn, 1916.

Phil 6968.10   Storer, H.R. The causation...reflex insanity in women. Boston, 1871.

Phil 9495.15.4   Storer, H.R. Is it D? A book for every man. Boston, 1867.

Phil 6990.3.40   Storer, M.L. (Mrs.). The story of a miracle at Lourdes, Aug., 1907. N.Y., 1908.

Phil 5649.5   Storey, Thomas Andrew. Studies in voluntary muscular contraction. Palo Alto, Calif., 1904.

Phil 165.362   Storia antologica dei problemi filosofici. (Spirito, Ugo.) Firenze, 1965. 7v.

Phil 4210.32   Storia comparativa e critica dei sistemi intorno al principio della morale, a cura di C. Caviglione. Pt. 1. (Rosmini-Serbati, Antonio.) Torino, 1928.

Phil 817.13   Storia critica delle categorie dai primordj della filosofia Greca sino ad Hagel. v.1-2. (Ragnisco, P.) Firenze, 1871.

Phil 8050.63   Storia degli orientamenti artistici. (Propris, A de.) Roma, 1953.

Phil 4002.4   Storia dei filosofi e dei matematici napolitani. v.1-3. (Colangelo, F.) Napoli, 1833-34.

Phil 8140.8   Storia dei movimenti estetici nella cultura italiana. (Sinnonini, Augusto.) Firenze, 1968.

Phil 402.8   Storia del concetto di ideologia. (Mongardini, Carlo.) Roma, 1968.

Phil 476.8   Storia del materialismo nei secoli XVI e XVII. v.1-2. (Banfi, A.) Milano, 1951-53.

Phil 806.18   Storia del pensiero filosofico. (Geymonat, Ludoviro.) Milano, 1955-56.

Phil 1133.32   Storia del pensiero presocratico. (Paci, Enzo.) Torino, 1957.

Phil 1350.14   Storia del pitagorismo nel mondo romano. (Ferrero, L.) Torino, 1955.

Phil 802.6   Storia della filosofia; lezioni. 6a ed. (Conti, Augusto.) Roma, 1908-09. 2v.

Phil 815.15   Storia della filosofia. (Fabro, C.) Roma, 1954.

Phil 806.14   Storia della filosofia. (Greca, Carlo.) Palermo, 1951.

Phil 811.16   Storia della filosofia. (Lamanna, E. Paolo.) Firenze, 1961. 6v.

Phil 818.18   Storia della filosofia. Milano. 1-3,1929-1930 2v.

Phil 818.18.5   Storia della filosofia. Milano. 1961 3v.

Phil 817.8.5   Storia della filosofia. pt. 1 (v.1-2), pt. 2 (v.1-3), pt. 3 (v.1-2), pt. 4 (v.1-5). (Ruggiero, Guido de.) Bari, 1934-48. 12v.

Phil 817.8.20   Storia della filosofia. v.1 (pt. 1-2), v.2 (pt. 1-3), v.3-10. (Guggiero, Guido de.) Bari, 1958. 13v.

Phil 817.8   Storia della filosofia. v.1-2,4 (pt. 1.) (Ruggiero, Guido de.) Bari, 1918- 2v.

Phil 800.16   Storia della filosofia. 2. ed. (Abbagnano, N.) Torino, 1963. 3v.

Phil 806.14.2   Storia della filosofia. 2. ed. (Greca, Carlo.) Firenze, 1956.

Phil 930.5   Storia della filosofia cinese antica. (Tucci, G.) Bologna, 1912.

Phil 801.26   Storia della filosofia e della scienza. (Beccari, Arturo.) Torino, 1928.

Phil 4006.3   Storia della filosofia in Sicilia. (Giovanni, V.) Palermo, 1873. 2v.

Phil 960.205   Storia della filosofia Indiana. (Tucci, Giuseppe.) Bari, 1957.

Phil 4006.5.60   Storia della filosofia italiana. (Garin, Eugenio.) Torino, 1966. 3v.

Phil 4012.12   Storia della filosofia italiana. (Marciano, Francesco.) Roma, 1959.

Phil 4006.2.8   Storia della filosofia italiani dal Genovesi al Galuppi. 2a ed. (Gentile, G.) Milano, 1930. 2v.

Phil 4015.2   Storia della filosofia italiano. (Piccoli, V.) Torino, 1924.

Phil 1506.12.5   Storia della filosofia medievale. 2. ed. (Bonafede, Giulio.) Roma, 1957.

Phil 1707.1.8   Storia della filosofia moderna. (Höffding, H.) Torino, 1913. 2v.

Phil 1701.12   Storia della filosofia moderna. pt.1. (Bertini, G. Maria.) Torino, 1881.

Phil 8836.4   La storia della filosofia morale; studio. (Lessona, Marco.) Torino, 1888.

Phil 1300.20   Storia della filosofia romana. (Levi, Adolfo.) Firenze, 1949.

Phil 1135.184.5   Storia della logica antica. (Calogero, Giudo.) Bari, 1967-

Phil 4210.133   La storia della questione rosminiana. (Bulgarini, G.B.) Milano, 1888.

Phil 1195.20   Storia della sofistica. (Levi, Adolfo.) Napoli, 1966.

Phil 8140.3　Storia delle idee estetiche in Italia. (Rolla, Alfredo.) Torino, 1905.

Phil 337.14　Storia delle scienze ed epistemologia. (Guia, Michele.) Torino, 1945.

Phil 8050.22　Storia dell'estetica per saggi. (Croce, Benedetto.) Bari, 1942.

Phil 9150.32　Storia dell'uomo avantie dopo Cristo. (Ferabino, Aldo.) Assisi, 1957.

Phil 4000.16　Storia e dialogo. (Alorpio, F. de.) Bologna, 1962.

Phil 4170.12　Storia e significato del superuomo. (Mei, F.) Milano, 1962.

Phil 2885.114　Storia e sociologia nell'opera di H. Taine. (Mongardini, Carlo.) Milano, 1965.

Phil 4080.17.15　Storia e storicismo. (Semerari, G.) Trani, 1953.

Phil 2050.68.25　Storia naturale della religione e saggio sul suicidio. (Hume, David.) Bari, 1928.

Phil 1740.22　Lo storicismo contemporaneo. (Rossi, Pietro.) Torino, 1968.

Phil 4260.153　Lo storicismo di G.B. Vico. (Manno, Ambrogio G.) Napoli, 1965.

Phil 4170.3.86　Storicismo e moderatismo nel pensiero politico di Angelo Camillo de Meis. (Negrelli, Giorgio.) Milano, 1968.

Phil 585.70.15　Storicismo e scienze dell'uomo. (Cantoni, Remo.) Milano, 1967.

Phil 8630.4.5　Stories of infinity. (Flammarion, C.) Boston, 1873.

Phil 9530.41　Storing up triple reserves. (Babson, Roger Ward.) N.Y., 1929.

Phil 4080.3.550　Storiografia e storia nel pensiero di Benedetto Croce. (Vitiello, Vincenzo.) Napoli, 1968.

Phil 1120.5　La storiografia filosofica antica. 1.ed. (Pra, Mario dal.) Milano, 1950.

Phil 5421.20.40　Storr, Anthony. Human aggression. 1. American ed. N.Y., 1968.

Phil 6980.709　Storr, Anthony. The integrity of the personality. N.Y., 1961.

Phil 3500.13　Storr, D.G.C. Bemerkungen über Kant's Philosophie Religion. Tübingen, 1794.

Phil 6968.16　Storring, Gustav. Vorlesungen über Psychopathologie. Leipzig, 1900.

Phil 9560.5　Storrs, R.S. Manliness in the scholar. N.Y., 1883.

Phil 8598.37　Storrs, Richard S. The recognition of the supernatural. N.Y., 1881.

Phil 525.4　Story, T. (pseud.). Substantialism, or Philosophy of knowledge. Boston, 1879.

Phil 6990.3.40　The story of a miracle at Lourdes, Aug., 1907. (Storer, M.L. (Mrs.).) N.Y., 1908.

Phil 960.276　The story of creation as seen by the seers. (Bhagavad Datta.) Delhi, 1968.

Phil 7106.5　The story of hypnotism. (Marks, Robert.) N.Y., 1947.

Phil 6990.3.29　The story of Lourdes. (Shanley, W.J.) Hartford, 1908.

Phil 5247.29　The story of man's mind. (Humphrey, G.) Boston, 1923.

Phil 5247.29.5　The story of man's mind. (Humphrey, G.) N.Y., 1932.

Phil 974.3.5　The story of my life. (Steiner, Rudolf.) London, 192-.

Phil 974.3.7　The story of my life. (Steiner, Rudolf.) London, 1928.

Phil 8712.5.18　Story of my life and work. (Wright, George F.) Oberlin, 1916.

Phil 525.240　The story of mysticism. 1st ed. (Graef, Hilda Charlotte.) Garden City, N.Y., 1965.

Phil 900.10　The story of Oriental philosophy. (Beck, Lily M.A.) N.Y., 1928.

Phil 803.6.25　The story of philosophy. (Durant, W.) Cambridge, 1927.
Phil 803.6.5A　The story of philosophy. (Durant, W.) N.Y., 1926.
Phil 803.6.18　The story of philosophy. (Durant, W.) N.Y., 1933.
Phil 803.6.19　The story of philosophy. (Durant, W.) N.Y., 1954.
Phil 5249.17　The story of psychology. (Jordan, G.J.) London, 1926.
Phil 8592.47　Story of religious controversy. (McCabe, Joseph.) Boston, 1929.

Phil 1830.51　The story of Scottish philosophy. 1st ed. (Robinson, D.S.) N.Y., 1961.

Phil 5241.3.28　The story of the mind. (Baldwin, J.M.) N.Y., 1898.
Phil 5241.3.24　The story of the mind. (Baldwin, J.M.) N.Y., 1901.
Phil 930.37　The story of the Monad. (Northern Pacific Railroad Company.) St. Paul, Minn., 1933.

Phil 5257.22.5　The story of thought and feeling. (Ryland, F.) London, 1900.

Phil 5374.69　Story sequence analysis. (Arnold, Magda.) N.Y., 1962.

Phil 665.48.5　Stosch, George. Själen och hennes historia. Stockholm, 1908.

Phil 4803.846.45　Stosunek filozofii do cybernetyki czyli sztuki rządzenia narodem. (Trentowski, Bronisław F.) Poznań, 1843.

Phil 2725.12.81　Stosz, Wilhelm. Le Sage als Vorkämpfer der Atomistik. Inaug. Diss. Halle, 1884.

Phil 5421.35.15　Stotland, Ezra. The psychology of hope. 1. ed. San Francisco, 1969.

Phil 6420.18　Das Stottern: assoziative Aphasie. (Froeschels, Emil.) Leipzig, 1925.

Phil 1190.30　Stough, Charlotte L. Greek skepticism; a study in epistemology. Berkeley, 1969.

Phil 9035.21.15　Stout, G.F. Alexander Faulkner Shand, 1858-1936. London, 1936?
Phil 5258.27.15　Stout, G.F. Analytic psychology. London, 1902. 2v.
Phil 5258.27.12　Stout, G.F. Analytic psychology. London, 1896. 2v.
Phil 193.128.10　Stout, G.F. God and nature. Cambridge, Eng., 1952.
Phil 5258.27.5　Stout, G.F. Groundwork of psychology. N.Y., 1903.
Phil 5258.27.6　Stout, G.F. Groundwork of psychology. 2d ed. London, 1927.
Phil 5258.27.2　Stout, G.F. A manual of psychology. N.Y., 1899.
Phil 5258.27　Stout, G.F. A manual of psychology. v.1-2. London, 1898-99.
Phil 5258.27.1　Stout, G.F. A manual of psychology. 2d ed. London, 1901.
Phil 5258.27.9　Stout, G.F. A manual of psychology. 3. ed. London, 1913.
Phil 5258.27.10　Stout, G.F. A manual of psychology. 4th ed. London, 1929.
Phil 193.128　Stout, G.F. Mind and matter. N.Y., 1931.
Phil 5258.27.25　Stout, G.F. Studies in philosophy and psychology. London, 1930.

Phil 3850.12.31　Stoy, Karl V. Philosophische Propädentik. Leipzig, 1869.

Phil 8598.61　Strachan, Robert H. The authority of Christian experience. London, 1929.

Phil 6328.30　Strachey, Alix. A new German-English psycho-analytical vocabulary. Baltimore, 1943.

Phil 193.40　Strada, G.J. de. Essai d'un ultimum organum. Paris, 1865. 2v.

Phil 1750.361　Straelen, H. van. Man the lonely. Tokyo, 1952.
Phil 5440.15　Strahan, S.A.K. Marriage and disease. London, 1892.
Phil 7150.3　Strahan, S.A.K. Suicide and insanity. London, 1893.
Phil 3552.293　Strahm, Hans. Die "Petites Perceptions" im System von Leibniz. Bern, 1930.

Phil 5059.20.2　Straight and crooked thinking. (Thouless, R.H.) N.Y., 1932.

Phil 8893.80　Strain, J. The postulates of the moral life. Cambridge, 1929.

Phil 8598.66　Strakhov, F.A. Voprosy zhizni. Christchurch, Hants, Eng., 1903.

Phil 4769.8.21　Strakhov, N.N. Filosofskie ocherki. Sankt Peterbrug, 1895.

Phil 4769.8.20　Strakhov, N.N. Mir kak tseloe. 2. izd. Sankt Peterburg, 1892.

Phil 974.3.120　Strakosch, A. Lebenswege mit Rudolf Steiner. Strasbourg, 1947.

Phil 5465.20　Strang, W. Imagination and fancy. London, 1913.
Phil 7009.145.1　A strange and seeing time. (Byrd, Elizabeth.) London, 1971.

Phil 3838.32　The strange death of Barukh Spinoza. (Shepo, Elias.) Cambridge, 1952.

Phil 7069.67.60　Strange dreams and their portents and other reflections (Lots-Poole, Marietta.) Brentwood, 1967.

Phil 7009.210　Strange experience; the autobiography of a hexenmeister. (Gandee, Lee R.) Englewood Cliffs, 1971.

Phil 7069.23.9　A strange manuscript. (Cavanagh, M.R.) N.Y., 1923.
Phil 7069.68.40　Strange things: the story of Fr. Allan McDonald, Ada Goodrich Freer, and the Society for Psychical Research's enquiry into Highland second sight. (Campbell, John Lorne.) London, 1968.

Phil 7054.144　Strange visitors. (Horn, Henry J.) N.Y., 1869.
Phil 7060.78　Stranger than fiction. (Lewes, M.L.) London., 1911.
Phil 2905.1.640　Straniero, Giorgio. L'ontologia fenomenologica di Teilhard de Chardin. Milano, 1969.

Phil 3838.31　Stranso, Leo. Spinoza's critique of religion. N.Y., 1965.
Phil 1750.736　Straser, S. Phenomenology and the human scientific ideal. Pittsburg, 1963.

Phil 3260.80　Strasosky, H. Jacob Friedrich Fries. Hamburg, 1891.
Phil 200.2.75　Strassburger Abhandlungen zur Philosophie E. Zeller zu 70n Geburtstage. Freiburg, 1884.

Phil 3850.27.65　Strassburger Predigten. (Schweitzer, A.) München, 1966.
Phil 5828.5　Strassen, O.Z. Die neuere Tierpsychologie. Leipzig, 1908.
Phil 3120.19.95　Strasser, Johano. Die Bedeutung des hypothetischen Imperativs in der Ethik Bruno Bauchs. Bonn, 1967.

Phil 1750.690　Strasser, S. Fenomenologie en emperische Menskunde. Arnhem, 1962.

Phil 5400.122　Strasser, S. Das Gemüt. Antwerpen, 1956.
Phil 585.230　Strasser, Stephan. Bouwstenen voor een filosofische anthropologie. Hilversum, 1965.

Phil 583.4　Strasser, Stephan. The idea of dialogal phenomenology. Pittsburgh, 1969.

Phil 665.80　Strasser, Stephan. Seele und Beseeltes. Wien, 1955.
Phil 665.80.5　Strasser, Stephan. The soul in metaphysical and empirical psychology. Pittsburgh, 1957.

Phil 665.80.10　Strasser, Stephan. Het zielsbegrip in de metaphysische en in de empirische psychologie. Leuven, 1950.

Phil 5258.84　Strasser, Vera. Psychologie der Zusammenhänge und Beziehungen. Berlin, 1921.

Phil 818.3　Straszewski, M. Dzieje filozofu w zarysie. Krakowie, 1894.

Phil 4803.810.30　Straszewski, Maurycy. Dzieje filozoficznej myśli polskiej w okresie porozbiorowym. Kraków, 1912.

Phil 4802.2　Straszewski, Maurycy. Polska filozofja narodowa, 15 wykładow. Krakow, 1921.

Phil 5850.385.40　Strategy in handling people. (Webb, Ewing T.) Chicago, 1931.

Phil 5270.3.1　The stratification of behaviour. (Shwayder, David S.) London, 1965.

Phil 5270.3　The stratification of behaviour. (Shwayder, David S.) N.Y., 1965.

Phil 6311.34.12　Stratiotikoi kai koinōnikoi polemoi. (Bonaparte, Marie.) Manchester, N.H., 1929.

Phil 5412.5　Stratton, G.M. Anger; its religious and moral significance. N.Y., 1923.

Phil 5258.29.5　Stratton, G.M. Experimental psychology. N.Y., 1914.
Phil 8643.5　Straub, J. The consolations of science. Chicago, 1884.
Phil 193.142.5　Straub, L.W. Aufsatzentürufe. 3e Aufl. Leipzig, 1897.
Phil 6978.5　Straub, Richard Ralph. A view of the levels of perceptual development in autistic syndromes. Academisch proefschrift. n.p., 1964.

Phil 8520.23　Straubinger, H. Die Religion und ihre Grundwahrheiten in der deutschen Philosophie seit Leibniz. Freiburg, 1919.

Phil 8598.102　Straubinger, H. Religionsphilosophie mit Theodizee. 2. Aufl. Freiburg, 1949.

Phil 3903.3.90　Strauch, W. Die Philosophie des "Als-Ob" und...Rechtswissenschaft. München, 1923.

Phil 6968.30　Straus, Erwin. On obsession, a clinical and methodological study. N.Y., 1948.

Phil 5258.114.10　Straus, Erwin. Phenomenological psychology. N.Y., 1966.
Phil 5258.114.5　Straus, Erwin. The primary world of senses. N.Y., 1963.
Phil 5258.114　Straus, Erwin. Vom Sinn der Sinne. Berlin, 1935.
Phil 7140.123　Straus, Erwin. Wesen und Vorgang der Suggestion. Berlin, 1925.

Phil 5465.134　Štraus, T. Umelecké myslenie. Bratislava, 1962.
Phil 8598.18　Straus-Durckheim, H.E. Théologie de la nature. Paris, 1852. 3v.

Phil 3850.1.30　Strauss, D.F. Der alte und der neue Glaube. Bonn, 1873. 2v.

Phil 3850.1.29　Strauss, D.F. Der alte und der neue Glaube. Leipzig, 1872.

Phil 3850.1.35　Strauss, D.F. Der alte und der neue Glaube. 2. Aufl. Bonn, 1881.

Phil 3850.1.45　Strauss, D.F. Essais d'histoire religieuse et mélanges littéraires. Paris, 1872.

Phil 3850.1.36　Strauss, D.F. The old faith and the new. London, 1873.
Phil 3850.1.37　Strauss, D.F. The old faith and the new. v.1-2. N.Y., 1873.

Phil 3850.1.43　Strauss, D.F. The opinions of Professor D.F. Strauss. London, 1844.

Phil 3850.1.75　Strauss, D.F. Der papier-Reisende. Weimar, 1907.
Phil 2915.81　Strauss, D.F. Voltaire. 4e Aufl. Bonn, 1877.
Phil 6980.710　Strauss, E.B. Psychiatry in the modern world. London, 1958.

Phil 5627.210　Strauss, H.A. Psychologie und astrologische Symbolis. Zürich, 1953.

Phil 1540.29　Strauss, Leo. Persecution and the art of writing. Glencoe, Ill., 1952. 2v.

Phil 2045.117　Strauss, Leo. The political philosophy of Hobbes. Oxford, 1936.

Phil 960.37　Strauss, Otto. Indische Philosophie. München, 1925.
Phil 3850.1.94　Strauss and Renan. (Zeller, Eduard.) London, 1866.
Phil 193.200　Strawson, P.F. Individuals. London, 1959.

Phil 5058.60   Strawson, P.F. Introduction to logic theory. London, 1952.

Phil 3500.98   Strawson, Peter Frederick. The bounds of sense: an essay on Kant's 'Critique of pure reason'. London, 1966.

Phil 5520.746   Strawson, Peter Frederick. Meaning and truth: an inaugural lecture delivered before the University of Oxford on 5 November 1969. Oxford, 1970.

Phil 165.420   Strawson, Peter Frederick. Studies in the philosophy of thought and action. London, 1968.

Phil 9358.16   Stray thoughts. (Strickland, C.J.) Charlotte, N.C., 1931.

Phil 9220.5.5   Streamer, Volney. In friendship's name. Chicago, 1891.

Phil 9220.5.6   Streamer, Volney. In friendship's name. 10th ed. N.Y., 1899.

Phil 9220.5.9   Streamer, Volney. In friendship's name. 14th ed. N.Y., 1904.

Phil 9220.5.11   Streamer, Volney. In friendship's name. 16th ed. N.Y., 1909.

Phil 9220.5   Streamer, Volney. What makes a friend? 9th ed. N.Y., 1904.

Phil 7069.34.35   Streamline (pseud.). Foretold; stories of modern second-sight. Stirling 1934.

Phil 632.8   Streatfeild, D. Persephone: a study of two worlds. London, 1959.

Phil 6028.7   Streble, Hermann. Analyse des Gebarens. Inaug. Diss. Berlin, 1934.

Phil 6128.50   Strecker, E.A. Beyond the clinical frontiers. N.Y., 1940.

Phil 6328.29   Strecker, E.A. Fundamentals of psychiatry. London, 1944.

Phil 6328.29.10   Strecker, E.A. Psychiatry in modern warfare. N.Y., 1945.

Phil 5258.104   Strecker, Edward A. Discovering ourselves. N.Y., 1931.

Phil 5258.104.5   Strecker, Edward A. Discovering ourselves. 2d ed. N.Y., 1943.

Phil 6805.8   Strecker, Edward Adam. Their mother's sons. Philadelphia, 1951.

Phil 3640.157   Strecker, Karl. Nietzsche und Strindberg. München, 1921.

Phil 3246.175   Strecker, Reinhard. Die Anfänge von Fichtes Staatsphilosophie. Leipzig, 1916.

Phil 3246.175.2   Strecker, Reinhard. Die Anfänge von Fichtes Staatsphilosophie. Leipzig, 1916.

Phil 3500.30   Strecker, Reinhard. Kants Ethik. Giessen, 1909.

Phil 2138.111   Street, Charles L. Individualism and individuality in the philosophy of John Stuart Mill. Milwaukee, 1926.

Phil 978.32.5   Street, J.C. The hidden way across the threshold. Boston, 1887.

Phil 5228.7   Streeter, B.H. The church and modern psychology. Evanston, Ill., 1934.

Phil 8673.15   Streeter, B.H. The God who speaks. N.Y., 1936.

Phil 8643.35   Streeter, B.H. Immortality. London, 1925.

Phil 8893.78   Streeter, Burnett. Moral adventure. N.Y., 1929.

Phil 8598.57.8   Streeter, Burnett. Reality; a new correlation of science and religion. N.Y., 1926.

Phil 8598.57   Streeter, Burnett. Reality; a new correlation of science and religion. N.Y., 1926.

Phil 8419.25   Streignart, Joseph. Trente-trois oeuvres d'art. v.1-2. Gembloux, 1953?

Htn   Phil 3480.86*   Der streit der Facultaeten. (Kant, Immanuel.) Königsberg, 1798.

Htn   Phil 3480.86.2*   Der streit der Facultaeten. (Kant, Immanuel.) Königsberg, 1798.

Phil 3480.86.10   Der Streit der Fakultäten. (Kant, Immanuel.) Hamburg, 1959.

Phil 3480.86.5   Der Streit der Fakultäten. (Kant, Immanuel.) Leipzig, 1922.

Phil 5055.11   Der streit der Psychologisten. (Palágyi, Melchior.) Leipzig, 1902.

Phil 4803.462.35   Der Streit um die Existenz der Welt. v.1-2. (Ingarden, Roman.) Tübingen, 1964-65. 3v.

Phil 3460.94   Streit um die göttlichen Dinge. (Weischedel, Wilhelm.) Darmstadt, 1967.

Phil 3425.645   Der Streit vom Hegel bei den Slawen; Symposium. (Polsko-Czechoslowacka Sesja Naukowa, Poświęcona Recepcji Filozofii Hegle w Krajach Słowianskich, Warsaw.) Prag, 1967.

Phil 3640.795   Der Streit um Nietzsches "Geburt der Tragödie". (Gruenter, Karlfried.) Hildersheim, 1969.

Phil 5754.3   Der Streit zwischen Erasmus und Luther über die Willensfreiheit. (Zickendraht, K.) Leipzig, 1909.

Phil 8712.21   Der Streit zwischen glauben. (Wittstein, T.) Hannover, 1884.

Phil 5465.27.5   Die Streitfrage zwischen Assoziation. (Jaensch, Erich.) Berlin, 1927.

Phil 3565.55   Streitschriften. (Lotze, Hermann.) Leipzig, 1857.

Phil 5258.142   Streletski, C. Clavier psychologigue. Paris, 1942.

Phil 2880.8.115   Streller, Justus. Jean Paul Sartre. N.Y., 1960.

Phil 2880.8.114   Streller, Justus. Zur Freiheit verurteilt. Hamburg, 1952.

Phil 4769.1.107   Strémooukhoff, D. Vladimir Soloviev et son oeuvre messianique. Paris, 1935.

Phil 4769.1.107.5   Strémooukhoff, D. Vladimir Soloviev et son oeuvre messianique. Thèse. Strasbourg, 1935.

Phil 5751.3   Strength of will. (Barrett, Edward Boyd.) N.Y., 1915.

Phil 6322.29.5   StrengtheningThe nerves. (MacFadden, B.) N.Y., 1928.

Phil 4210.88.5   Stresa, Italy. Istituto della Carità. Cenni biografici di Antonio Rosmini. Firenze, 1924.

Phil 4210.88.2   Stresa, Italy. Istituto della Carità. Cenni biografici di Antonio Rosmini. 2a ed. Milano, 1857.

Phil 6128.58A   The stress of life. (Seyle, Hans.) N.Y., 1956.

Phil 623.22   Strich, Walter. Der irrationale Mensch. Berlin, 1928.

Phil 735.4   Strich, Walter. Das Wertproblem in der Philosophie der Gegenwart. Berlin, 1909.

Phil 5374.5   Stricker, S. Studien über das Bewusstsein. Wien, 1879.

Phil 5258.23   Stricker, S. Studien über die Bewegungsvorstellungen. Wien, 1882.

Phil 5325.2.10   Stricker, Salomon. Studien über die Association der Vorstellungen. Wien, 1883.

Phil 9358.16   Strickland, C.J. Stray thoughts. Charlotte, N.C., 1931.

Phil 3925.16.240   Strict finitism. (Rielkopf, Charles F.) The Hague, 1970.

Phil 193.70   Strife of systems and productive duality. (Sheldon, W.H.) Cambridge, 1918.

Phil 3120.40.40   De strijd tusschen idealisme en naturalisme in de 19. eeuw. (Bierens de Haan, J.D.) Haarlem, 1929.

Phil 5275.5   Stríženec, Michal. Psychológia a kybernetika. Bratislava, 1966.

Htn   Phil 3585.1.50*   Strnadt, A. Gedanken über die schönen und soliden Wissenschaften. Dresden, 1794.

Phil 818.30   Strobach, W. Liebe zum Wissen. Wien, 1957.

Phil 3805.163   Strobel, Anton. Die Pädagogik und Philosophie Schleiermachers in ihren Bezienungen zu J.J. Tousseau. Inaug. Diss. n.p., 1927.

Htn   Phil 5058.23*   Strode, R. Consequentie. Venice, 1493.

Phil 182.87   Strödda afhandlingar öfver ämnen inom philosophiens gebiet. (Hammarsköld, L.) Mariefred, 1827.

Phil 3450.33.15   Stroeker, E. Zahl und Raum. Bonn, 1953.

Phil 8708.25   Strömberg, G. The searchers. Philadelphia, 1948.

Phil 299.24   Strömberg, G. The soul of the universe. Philadelphia, 1940.

Phil 299.24.2   Strömberg, G. The soul of the universe. 2. ed. Philadelphia, 1948.

Phil 6128.9   Strömberg, J.D. Undersökningar i läran om själ och kropp. Lund, 1897.

Phil 5058.55   Strogovich, M.S. Logika. Moskva, 1949.

Phil 476.3.53   Strohecker, J.R. Die freie Naturbetrachtung. Augsburg, 1869.

Phil 8586.36.65   Strohm, Theodor. Konservative politische Romantik. Berlin, 1961.

Phil 8586.36.66   Strohm, Theodor. Theologie im Schatten politischer Romantik. Mainz, 1970.

Phil 4805.25   Stroħs, Slavomil. Marxisticko-leninská filosofie v Ceskoslovensku mezi dvěma světovými válkami. Vyd. 1. Praha, 1962.

Phil 349.80   Stroll, Avrum. Epistemology; new essays in the theory of knowledge. N.Y., 1967.

Phil 1718.35   Strolz, Walter. Der vergessene Ursprung. Freiburg, 1959.

Phil 193.242   Strolz, Walter. Widerspruch und Hoffnung des Daseins. Frankfurt, 1965.

Phil 5058.108   Strombach, Werner. Die Gesetze unseres Denkens. München, 1970.

Phil 1718.38   Stromberg, Roland N. An intellectual history of modern Europe. N.Y., 1966.

Phil 5627.14.2   Strong, A.L. A consideration of prayer. Chicago, 1908.

Phil 5627.14   Strong, A.L. The psychology of prayer. Chicago, 1909.

Phil 193.83.5   Strong, C.A. A creed for sceptics. London, 1936.

Phil 6128.11.15   Strong, C.A. Essays on the natural origin of the mind. London, 1930.

Phil 6128.11.9   Strong, C.A. Reply to Bakewell. n.p., 1904.

Phil 349.21   Strong, C.A. A theory of knowledge. N.Y., 1923.

Phil 6128.11.2   Strong, C.A. Why the mind has a body. N.Y., 1903.

Phil 6128.11   Strong, C.A. Why the mind has a body. N.Y., 1903.

Phil 193.83   Strong, C.A. The wisdom of the beasts. Boston, 1922.

Phil 5374.21   Strong, Charles A. The origin of consciousness. London, 1918.

Phil 5330.27   Strong, E.K. Change of interest with age. Palo Alto, 1931.

Phil 9358.4   Strong, J. The times and young men. N.Y., 1901.

Phil 5627.248.1   The strong and weak. (Tournier, Paul.) Philadelphia, 1963.

Phil 3640.222   Stroux, Johannes. Nietzsches Professur in Basel. Jena, 1925.

Phil 2805.95   Strowski, F. Pascal et son temps. Paris, 1907-22. 3v.

Phil 2805.95.10A   Strowski, F. Les pensées de Pascal; étude et analyse. Paris, 1930.

Phil 3120.6.85   Struck, Gustav. Friedrich Bouterwek. Inaug. Diss. Rostock, 1919.

Phil 5243.55   The structural basis of behavior. (Deutsch, Jaroslav A.) Chicago, 1960.

Phil 5520.450   The structural basis of word association behavior. (Pollio, Howard R.) Paris, 1966.

Phil 5643.165   Structural information of visual pattern. (Leeuwerberg, Emanuel Laurens Jan.) The Hague, 1968.

Phil 5520.586   A structural inquiry into the symbolic representation of ideas. (Grava, Arnolds.) The Hague, 1969.

Phil 680.26   Structuralism: a reader. (Lane, Michael.) London, 1970.

Phil 680.30   Le structuralisme. (Millet, Louis.) Paris, 1970.

Phil 1750.830.8   Le structuralisme. 3e éd. (Piaget, Jean.) Paris, 1968.

Phil 680.20   Les structuralistes: les linguistes, Michel Foucault, Claude Lévi-Strauss, Jacques Lacan, Louis Althusser, les critiques littéraires. (Corvez, Maurice.) Paris, 1969.

Phil 5066.38A   Structure, method, and meaning. (Henle, Paul.) N.Y., 1951.

Phil 1750.115.37   La structure absolue; essai de phénoménologie génétique. (Abellio, Raymond.) Paris, 1965.

Phil 1750.767   Structure and development of phenomenal reality. (MacColl, Sylvia.) N.Y., 1965.

Phil 5520.429   Structure and direction in thinking. (Berlyne, Daniel E.) N.Y., 1965.

Phil 6980.775.50   The structure and dynamics of the human mind. (Weiss, Edward.) N.Y., 1960.

Phil 5252.16   Structure and growth of the mind. (Mitchell, W.) London, 1907.

Phil 6317.18.2   The structure and meaning of psychoanalysis as related to personality and behavior. (Healy, William.) N.Y., 1953.

Phil 181.74   Structure and reality. (Gotshalk, D.W.) N.Y., 1937.

Phil 5590.454   La structure de la personnalité. (Nuttin, Jozef.) Paris, 1965.

Phil 665.52   La structure de l'âme et l'expérience mystique. (Gardeil, A.) Paris, 1927. 2v.

Phil 5125.14   La structure des théories déductives. (Rougier, Louis.) Paris, 1921.

Phil 5252.85   La structure du comportement. 1. ed. (Merleau-Ponty, M.) Paris, 1942.

Phil 5252.85.5   La structure du comportement. 3. ed. (Merleau-Ponty, M.) Paris, 1955.

Phil 3450.18.123   La structure du monde réel d'apres Nicolai Hartmann. (Wahl, Jean André.) Paris, 1953.

Phil 8951.28   Structure et dimensions de la liberté. (Berthélemy, Jean.) Paris, 1966.

Phil 5520.515   Structure et fondement de la communication humaine, essai critique sur les théories contemporaines de la communication. Thèse. (Schérer, René.) Paris, 1965.

Phil 8400.54   Structure in art and in science. (Kepes, Gyorgy.) N.Y., 1965.

Phil 6750.265   The structure of abilities at lower levels of intelligence. (Keblon, Lars.) Stockholm, 1965.

Phil 8419.56   The structure of aesthetics. (Sparshott, F.E.) Toronto, 1963.

Phil 8690.2   The structure of animal life. (Agassiz, L.J.R.) N.Y., 1866.

Phil 1750.115.3A   The structure of appearance. (Goodman, Nelson.) Cambridge, 1951.

Phil 1750.115.2   The structure of appearance. (Goodman, Nelson.) Indianapolis, 1966.

Phil 5052.37   The structure of Aristotelian logic. (Miller, James N.) London, 1938.

Phil 5325.42   The structure of association in language and thought. (Deese, James.) Baltimore, 1966.

Phil 5252.85.10A   The structure of behavior. (Merleau-Ponty, M.) Boston, 1963.

Phil 585.140.5   The structure of evil. (Becker, Ernest.) N.Y., 1968.

Phil 5590.45.10   The structure of human personality. (Eysenck, Hans Jurgen.) London, 1953.

Phil 5590.45.13   The structure of human personality. 3. ed. (Eysenck, Hans Jurgen.) London, 1970.

Phil 6951.20   The structure of insanity. (Burrow, T.) London, 1932.

Phil 5520.420   The structure of language. (Fodor, J.A.) Englewood Cliffs, N.J., 1964.

Phil 186.120   The structure of metaphysics. (Lazerowitz, M.) London, 1955.

Phil 186.120.2   The structure of metaphysics. (Lazerowitz, M.) N.Y., 1955.

Phil 337.25   The structure of mind. (Grossmann, Reinhardt Siegbert.) Madison, 1965.

Phil 9380.6   The structure of morale. (MacCurdy, J.T.) Cambridge, Eng., 1943.

Phil 5251.28.7   The structure of our apprehension of reality. (Lambek, C.) Copenhagen, 1933.

Phil 9245.136   The structure of psychological well-being. (Bradburn, Norman Marshall.) Chicago, 1969.

Phil 5627.144.1   The structure of religious experience. (Macmurray, John.) Hamden, Conn., 1971.

Phil 6321.45   Structure of the ego. (Langstroth, Lovell.) Stanford, Calif., 1955.

Phil 336.7.5   The structure of thought. (Fischer, L.) London, 1930.

Phil 735.262   The structure of value; foundations of scientific axiology. (Hartman, Robert S.) Carbondale, 1967.

Phil 5465.105   Les structures anthropologiques de l'imaginaire. (Durand, G.) Grenoble, 1960.

Phil 5465.105.2   Les structures anthropologiques de l'imaginaire. 2. éd. (Durand, G.) Paris, 1963.

Phil 3425.675   Structures et mouvement dialectique dans la phenoménologie de l'esprit de Hegel. (Labarriere, Pierre Jean.) Paris, 1968.

Phil 5041.93   Structures intellectuelles. (Blanché, Robert.) Paris, 1966.

Phil 5585.140.5   Les structures rythmiques. Thèse. (Fraisse, Paul.) Bruxelles, 1956.

Phil 720.90   Structures subjectives du champ transcendantal. Thèse. (Lanteri-Laura, Georges.) Paris, 1968.

Phil 5374.270   Structuur en sanctie van het bewustzijn. Wassenaar, 1967.

Phil 3483.51   De structuur van het aesthetisch a priori bij Kant Proef. (Bartling, Dirk.) Assen, 1931.

Phil 575.200   Structuurphenomenologische systematisering van het menszijn door centraalstelling van de vrijheidsbeleving. (Roem, H.A.C.) 's-Gravenhage, 1952.

Phil 8893.32   Strümpell, L. Abhandlungen aus dem Gebiete der Ethik, der Staatswissenschaft, der Asthetik und der Theologie. Leipzig, 1895.

Phil 193.41   Strümpell, L. Die Einleitung in die Philosophie. Leipzig, 1886.

Phil 5058.18   Strümpell, L. Entwurf der Logik. Mitau, 1846.

Phil 1123.6   Strümpell, L. Die Geschichte der griechischen Philosophie zur Ubersicht. pts.1-2. Leipzig, 1854-61.

Phil 5058.18.5   Strümpell, L. Grundriss der Logik. Leipzig, 1881.

Phil 5258.22   Strümpell, L. Grundriss der Psychologie. Leipzig, 1884.

Phil 720.7   Strümpell, L. Die Unterschiede der Wahrneiten und der Irrthümer. Leipzig, 1897.

Phil 8893.32.5   Strümpell, L. Die Vorschule der Ethik. Mitau, 1844.

Phil 3018.10   Strümpell, Ludwig. Abhandlungen zur Geschichte de Metaphysik, Psychologie. Leipzig, 1896.

Phil 7082.162   Strümpell, Ludwig. Die Natur und Entstehung der Träume. Leipzig, 1874.

Phil 3428.97   Strümpell. Die Hauptpuncte der Herbartschen Metaphysik. Braunschweig, 1840.

Phil 1630.45   Struever, Nancy S. The language of history in the Renaissance. Princeton, N.J., 1970.

Phil 8640.4   The struggle for immortality. (Phelps, E.S.) Boston, 1889.

Phil 8092.15   Strujanja u savremenoj estetici. (Damnjanović, Milan.) Zagreb, 1966.

Phil 8050.60   Die Struktur der Existenz. (Spoerri, T.) Zürich, 1951.

Phil 176.124   Die Struktur der Ganzheiten. (Burkamp, Wilhelm.) Berlin, 1929.

Phil 306.1   Die Struktur der Materie und das Welträtsel. (Ziegler, Johann H.) Bern, 1908.

Phil 8408.54   Die Struktur des ästhetischen Urteils. (Hopf, Andreas.) München, 1968.

Phil 5066.306   Die Struktur formalisierter Sprachen. Darmstadt, 1965.

Phil 5258.160   Struktur och utveckling. (Sjöbring, Henrik.) Lund, 1958.

Phil 5651.8   Struktur-psychologische Untersuchungen über die Leistung des Zeitsinns. Inaug. Diss. (Oster, Wilhelm.) Würzburg, 1937.

Phil 5245.80   Struktur und Dynamik. (Fischel, Werner.) Bern, 1962.

Phil 5238.242   Struktur und Dynamik des menschlichen Verhaltens; zum Stand der modernen Psychologie. Stuttgart, 1970.

Phil 5590.576   Struktur und Genese der Person. (Satura, Vladimir.) Innsbrück, 1970.

Phil 5585.77   Struktur und Metrik figuraloptischer Wahrnehmung. (Rausch, E.) Frankfurt, 1952.

Phil 8870.40   Struktura morali. Sverdlovsk, 1970.

Phil 5520.704   Struktura myslitel'noi deiatel'nosti cheloveka. (Tikhomirov, Oleg K.) Moskva, 1969.

Phil 680.45   Strukturalismus a avantgarda. 1. vyd. (Chvotík, Květoslav.) Praha, 1970.

Phil 1750.830.5   Ştrukturalizam. Zagreb, 1970.

Phil 680.35   Ştrukturalizmus v slovenskej vede. (Popovič, Anton.) Martin, 1970.

Phil 5585.100   Strukturanalyse der binokularen Tiefenwahrnehmung. (Linschoten, J.) Groningen, 1956.

Phil 4812.457.31   Strukturation und Apperzeption des Konkreten. (Hrušovský, Igor.) Bratislava, 1966.

Phil 2490.173   Strukturbeziehungen Zwischen den Gesellschaftslehren Comtes und Heges. (Negt, Oskar.) Frankfurt a.M., 1964.

Phil 5850.226   Strukturen analiz na obshtestvenoto Suznanie. (Gurdev, Dinó.) Sofiia, 1970.

Phil 8897.94   Strukturen der Moral. (Wyss, Dieter.) Göttingen, 1968.

Phil 8897.94.2   Strukturen der Moral. 2. Aufl. (Wyss, Dieter.) Göttingen, 1970.

Phil 8892.88   Strukturen sittlichen Handelns. (Rotter, Hans.) Mainz, 1970.

Phil 5047.46   Die Strukturformen der Probleme. (Hartkopf, Werner.) Berlin, 1958.

Phil 291.16   Strukturnze urovni zhivoi materii. (Kremianskii, Viktor I.) Moskva, 1969.

Phil 3925.16.230   Strukur und Sprachspiel bei Wittgenstein. (Wuchteil, Kurt.) Frankfurt, 1969.

Phil 5828.4   Strumpell, L. Die Geisteskräfte der Menschen. Leipzig, 1878.

Phil 6980.710.80   Strupp, Hans Herman. Psychotherapy and the modification of abnormal behavior. N.Y., 1971.

Phil 2750.20.130   La struttura della percezione. (Brena, Gian Luigi.) Milano, 1969.

Phil 5520.660   La struttura dialogica del linguaggio. (Testa, Aldo.) Bologna, 1967.

Phil 176.226   Struttura e significato nella storia della filosofia. (Bartolone, Filippo.) Bologna, 1964.

Phil 2630.13.80   Lo strutturalismo dialettico di Lucien Goldmann. (Crispini, Franco.) Napoli, 1970.

Phil 680.40   Strutturalismo filosofico. (Centro di studi filosofici di gallarate.) Padova, 1970.

Phil 5520.565   La strutture assente. (Eco, Umberto.) Milano, 1968.

Phil 75.9   Struve, B.G. Bibliothecae philosphicae. Göttingen, 1740.

Phil 5938.8   Struve, Gustav von. Phrenologie in und ausserhalb Deutschland. Heidelberg, 1843.

Phil 5258.24   Struve, H. von. Zur Entstehung der Seele. Tübingen, 1862.

Phil 4800.2.2   Struve, Henryk. Historya logiki jako teoryi pozuania w Polsce. Wyd. 2. Warszawa, 1911.

Phil 3850.68   Struve, Wolfgang. Der andere Zug. Salzburg, 1969.

Phil 705.72   Struve, Wolfgang. Philosophie und Transzendenz. Freiburg, 1969.

Phil 2880.8.240   Struyker Boudier, C.E.M. Jean Paul Sartre. Tielt, 1967.

Phil 1123.16   Strycker, Emile de. Beknopte geschiedenis van de antieke filosofie. Antwerpen, 1967.

Phil 7067.00   Stryk, Johann S. Disputatio iuridica inauguralis de iure spectrorum...Andreas Becker. Halae Magdeburgicae, n.d.

Phil 7067.00.5   Stryk, Johann S. Disputatio iuridica inauguralis de iure spectrorum...Andreas Becker. Jenae, 1745.

Phil 5465.186   Strzalecki, Andrzej. Wybrane zagadnienia psychologii twórczości. Wyd. 1. Warszawa, 1969.

Phil 193.90   Stuart, (Mrs.). C. The threshold of the new. London, 1920.

Phil 575.97   Stuart, C. Achievement of personality. N.Y., 1938.

Phil 978.57   Stuart, C. A dialogue. n.p., 1901.

Phil 193.106   Stuart, H.W. The logic of self-realization. Berkeley, 1904.

Phil 735.13   Stuart, H.W. Valuation as a logical process. Thesis. Chicago, 1918.

Phil 8598.64   Stuart-Glennie, John S. In the morningland. London, 1873.

Phil 2138.92   Stuart Mill. (Archambault, P.) Paris, n.d.

Phil 2138.152   Stuart Mill ve Türkiyedeki tesirleri. (Findikoğlu, Z.F.) Istanbul, 1963.

Phil 2138.102   Stuart Mills etik. (Winslow, Christian.) København, 1909.

Phil 8419.20   Stubbe, Achilles. Het zien en genieten van schilderkunst. 4. druk. Hasselt, 1960.

Phil 193.42   Stuckenberg, J.H.W. Introduction to the study of philosophy. N.Y., 1888.

Phil 5261.9   Studenbilder der philosophischen Propadeutik. (Vogt, P.) Freiburg, 1909. 2v.

Phil 6118.6   The student and mental health. (International Conference on Student Mental Health.) London, 1959.

Phil 165.205   The student seeks an answer. (Clark, John A.) Waterville, Me., 1960.

Phil 8893.266   The student's companion. London, 1748.

Phil 89.3.10   A student's dictionary of psychological terms. 3rd ed. (English, Horace B.) Yellow Springs, Ohio, 1929.

Phil 5261.17.19   Student's guide for beginning the study of psychology. (Valentine, Willard Lee.) N.Y., 1935.

Phil 5865.5.35   A student's guide to Piaget. 1st ed. (Boyle, D.G.) Oxford, 1969.

X Cg   Phil 2138.37   The student's handbook...of Mill's...logic. (Mill, John S.) London, 1870.

Phil 2138.37.15   The student's handbook...of Mill's logic. (Mill, John S.) London, 1891.

Phil 5257.54   A student's handbook of psychology and ethics. (Ryland, F.) London, 1885.

Phil 817.4   A student's history of philosophy. (Rogers, A.K.) N.Y., 1901.

Phil 817.4.15   A student's history of philosophy. (Rogers, A.K.) N.Y., 1923.

Phil 817.4.20A   A student's history of philosophy. 3d ed. (Rogers, A.K.) N.Y., 1932.

Phil 1122.15   A student's key to ancient Greek thought. (Rauche, Gerhard Albin.) Fort Hare, 1966.

Phil 8881.12.5   Students manual of ethical philosophy. (Gizycki, G.) London, 1889.

Phil 5250.10   A student's manual of psychology. (Kirchner, F.) London, 1888.

Phil 8602.32   A student's philosophy of religion. (Wright, William K.) London, 1922.

Phil 181.65   Students' prolegomena to philosophy. (Granberry, John C.) Ann Arbor, 1931.

Phil 5421.30   Students under stress. (Mechanu, David.) N.Y., 1962.

Phil 165.444   Studenty - Oktiabriu. Moskva, 1968.

Phil 4073.90   Studi Campanelliani. (Mattei, R. de.) Firenze, 1934.

Phil 2520.221   Studi cartesiani. (Galli, Gallo.) Torino, 1943.

Phil 4080.3.141   Studi crociani. (Calogero, G.) Rieti, 1930.

Phil 8019.10   Studi di estetica. Bologna. 1,1965+

Phil 8050.55   Studi di estetica dell'irrazionale. (Gori, Gino.) Milano, 1921.

Phil 4225.90.30   Studi di filosofia della prassi. (Severino, Emanuele.) Milano, 1962.

Phil 8598.108   Studi di filosofia della religione. Roma, 1955.

Phil 165.322   Studi di filosofia e di storia della filosofia in onore di Francesco Olgiati. Milano, 1962.

Phil 1105.8   Studi di filosofia greca. (Alfieri, V.E.) Bari, 1950.

Phil 1518.2   Studi di filosofia medievale. (Nardi, Bruno.) Roma, 1960.

Phil 196.8.12   Studi di filosofia naturale. (Varisco, B.) Roma, 1903.

Phil 3925.16.305   Studi di logica e di filosofia della scienza. (Egidi, Rosaria.) Roma, 1971.

Phil 800.6   Studi di storia della filosofia. (Amato, F. d'.) Geneva, 1931.

Phil 28.27   Studi e recerche distoria della filosofia. Torino. 1-49 8v.

Phil 1505.7   Studi e ricerche di filosofia medievale. (Alessio, Franco Paolo.) Pavia, 1961.

Phil 8140.2   Gli studi estetici in Italia nel primo trantennio del'900. (Sgroi, Carmelo.) Firenze, 1932.

Phil 4115.28   Studi filologici. (Gioberti, V.) Torino, 1867.

Phil 4070.1.35   Studi filosofici e religiosi; del sentimento. 1. ed. (Bonavino, Cristoforo.) Torino, 1854.

Phil 4070.1.36   Studi filosofici e religiosi; del sentimento. 2. ed. (Bonavino, Cristoforo.) Torino, 1854.

Phil 333.9   Studi filosofici sulla cognizione. (Cosalini, Alessandro.) Roma, 1914.

Phil 165.464   Studi in memoria di Carlo Ascheri. Urbino, 1970.

Phil 165.460   Studi in onore di Antonio Corsano. Manduria, 1970.

Phil 4225.8.85 Studi in onore di M.F. Sciacca. (Antonelli, M.T.) Milano, 1959.
Phil 28.90 Studi internazionali di filosofia. Torino. 1,1969+
Phil 3475.3.170 Studi Jaspersiani. (Caracciolo, Alberto.) Milano, 1958.
Phil 3501.5 Studi Kantiani. (Tocco, Felice.) Milano, 1909.
Phil 3484.23 Studi kantiani sul trascendente. (Casula, Mario.) Milano, 1963.
Phil 4065.120 Studi letterari. Sugli eroici furori di G. Bruno. (Brambilla, E.) Milano, 1892.
Phil 9075.65 Studi nella coscienza etica e religiosa del seicento. (Crippa, Romeo.) Brescia, 1960. 3v.
Phil 2805.340 Studi Pascaliani. (Simonetti, Maria.) Roma, 1957?
Phil 4195.110 Studi pichiani; atti e memorie del Convegno di studi pichiani per il V centenario della nascita di Giovanni Pico della Mirandola, Mondena, Mirandola, 25-26 maggio, 1963. (Convegno di Studi Pichiani per il V Centenario della Nascita di Giovanni Pico della Mirandola.) Modena, 1965.
Phil 4210.180 Studi rosminiani. (Galli, Dario.) Padova, 1957.
Phil 4210.198 Studi rosminiani. (Solari, Gioele.) Milano, 1957.
Phil 2840.95 Studi storico-critici sulla filosofia di C. Renouvier. v.1-2. (Galli, Gallo.) Gubbio, 1933-35.
Phil 4080.1.85 Studi su Cesare Cremonini. (Del Torre, Maria A.) Padova, 1968.
Phil 4200.1.84 Studi su Pietro Pomponazzi. (Nardi, Bruno.) Firenze, 1965.
Phil 2880.8.200 Studi su Sartre. (Borrello, Oreste.) Bologna, 1964.
Phil 3837.30 Studi su Spinoza e Fichte. (Rava, Adolfo.) Milano, 1958.
Phil 3925.16.82 Studi su Wittgenstein. (Campanale, Domenico.) Bari, 1956.
Phil 4285.2.80 Studi sul pensiero di Giuseppe Zamboni. Milano, 1957.
Phil 1105.12 Studi sul pensiero greco. (Adorno, Francesco.) Firenze, 1966.
Phil 1540.50A Studi sul platonismo medievale. (Garin, Eugenio.) Firenze, 195⁹.
Phil 1200.50 Studi sul reostoicismo. (Agostino, V.) Torino, 1950.
Phil 4006.2.9 Studi sul rinascimento. (Gentile, G.) Firenze, 1923.
Phil 4006.2.10 Studi sul rinascimento. 2a ed. (Gentile, G.) Firenze, 1936.
Phil 1622.5 Studi sulla cultura del Rinascimento. (Vasoli, Cesare.) Manduria, 1968.
Phil 1123.10 Studi sulla filosofia antica. (Sciacca, Michele F.) Napoli, 1935.
Phil 4070.7.40 Studi sulla filosofia del novecento. (Banfi, Antonio.) Roma, 1965.
Phil 818.21 Studi sulla filosofia medioevale e moderna. (Sciacca, M.F.) Napoli, 1935.
Phil 4225.8.55 Studi sulla filosofia moderna. 3. ed. (Sciacca, Michele Federico.) Milano, 1964.
Phil 7069.37.50 Studi sulle precognizioni. (Vivante, Leone.) Firenze, 1937.
Phil 1750.340 Studi sull'esistenzialismo. 2. ed. (Pareyson, Luigi.) Firenze, 1950.
Phil 1730.20 Studi sull'illuminismo di G. Solinas. Firenze, 1966.
Phil 1350.7 Studi sullo stoicismo romano. (Gentile, G.) Trani, 1904.
Phil 1750.166.290 Studi sull'Umanesimo europeo. (Santinello, Giovanni.) Padova, 1969.
Phil 1602.2 Studi sull'Umanesimo. Secoli XIV-XVI. (Bonicatti, Maurizio.) Firenze, 1969.
Phil 4260.94.5 Studi vichiani. (Gentile, Giovanni.) Firenze, 1927.
Phil 4260.94 Studi vichiani. (Gentile, Giovanni.) Messina, 1915.
Phil 4260.137 Studi vichiani. (Severgnini, Dante.) Milano, 1954-56. 2v.
Phil 4260.170 Studi vichiani. Napoli. 1,1969+
Phil 28.17 Studia Anselmiana philosophica theologica edita a professoribus Instituti Pontificii S. Anselmi de Urbs. Roma. 1,1933+ 32v.
Phil 8019.5 Studia estetyczne. Warszawa. 2,1965+ 6v.
Phil 28.55 Studia filosoficzne. Warszawa. 1957-1964 20v.
Phil 28.56 Studia filozoficzne. Izbrannye stat'i. Warszawa. 1,1962+
Phil 3552.5 Studia Leibnitiana. Wiesbaden. 1,1969+
Phil 3552.6 Studia Leibnitiana. Supplementa. Wiesbaden. 1,1968+ 8v.
Phil 25.97 Studia logica. (Polska Akademia Nauk, Warsaw. Komitet filozoficzny.) 1-24 10v.
Phil 21.10 Studia logica. Warszawa. 1,1934
Phil 28.76 Studia metodologiczne. Poznań. 1,1965+ 3v.
Phil 28.58 Studia parapsychologica. Roma.
Phil 28.16 Studia philosophica; commentarii societates philosophiae polonorum. Leopoli. 3-4,1949-1950 2v.
Phil 28.70 Studia philosophica Gandensia. Gent. 1,1963+
Phil 28.11.20 Studia psychologica et paedagogica. Lund. 7-9,1955-1958 3v.
Phil 28.84 Studia psychologiczne. Wrocław. 4,1963+
Phil 1504.30 Studia scholastico-Scotistica. Romae. 1,1968+ 4v.
Phil 4800.12 Studia z dziejów polskiej myśli filozoficznej i naukowej. Wyd. 1. (Suchodolski, Bogdan.) Warszawa, 1959.
Phil 5520.724 Studia z dziejów semiotyki. Wrocław, 1971.
Phil 4803.462.5 Studia z estetyki. (Ingarden, Roman.) Warszawa, 1957-70. 3v.
Phil 8088.8 Studia z historii myśli estetycznej XVII:i XIX wieku. (Morawski, Stefan.) Warszawa, 1961.
Phil 4803.497.6 Studia z zakresu filozofii, etyki i nauk społecznych. (Kotarbiński, Tadeusz.) Wrocław, 1970.
Phil 3425.605 Studie k Hegel om pojetí historie. (Kudrna, J.) Praha, 1964.
Phil 4809.524.80 Studie o G.A. Lindnerovi. (Král, Josef.) Bratislava, 1930.
Phil 4805.20 Studie o současné české filosofii. (Popelová, Jiřina.) Praha, 1946.
Phil 5257.42 Studie z vyvoje psychologie. (Rostohar, M.) Brno, 1928.
Phil 486.10 Studie zur Geschichte des Materialismus im Mittelalter. (Ley, Hermann.) Berlin, 1957.
Phil 2045.88 Studien...über Ursprung des Sittlichen; Hobbes. (Jodl, F.) München, n.d.
Phil 178.24 Studien. (Daub, E.) Frankfurt, 1805. 6v.
Phil 2630.1.20 Studien. (Gratry, Auguste.) Regensburg, 1858-1859. 3v.
Phil 49.4 Studien. (Jung-Institut, Zürich.) Zürich. 1,1949+ 18v.
Phil 3780.30 Studien. v.1-5. (Rosenkranz, Karl.) Berlin, 1839-48. 4v.
Phil 3837.25 Studien über Causalität und Identität als Grundprincipie des Spinozismus. (Rackwitz, Max.) Halle, 1884.
Phil 5374.5 Studien über das Bewusstsein. (Stricker, S.) Wien, 1879.
Phil 2038.82 Studien über David Hartley. Inaug. Diss. (Heider, Maria.) Bergisch Gladbach, 1913.
Phil 5525.62 Studien über des Lachen. (Ramondt, Marie.) Groningen, 1962.

Phil 5325.2.10 Studien über die Association der Vorstellungen. (Stricker, Salomon.) Wien, 1883.
Phil 5258.23 Studien über die Bewegungsvorstellungen. (Stricker, S.) Wien, 1882.
Phil 1750.465 Studien über die Existenzphilosophie. (Mende, Georg.) Berlin, 1956.
Phil 187.28.4 Studien über die Natur des Menschen. (Mechnikov, I.I.) Leipzig, 1904.
Phil 2055.1.80 Studien über Henry Home. (Bühler, K.) Bonn, 1905.
Htn Phil 6720.6*A Studien über Hysterie. (Breuer, Josef.) Leipzig, 1895.
Htn Phil 6720.6.10* Studien über Hysterie. (Breuer, Josef.) Leipzig, 1909.
Phil 1050.19 Studien über jüdische, Insonders jüdisch-arabische Religionsphilosophie. (Schmiedl, A.) Wien, 1969.
Phil 6965.10 Studien über motorische Apraxie. (Pick, Arnold.) Leipzig, 1905.
Phil 5643.71 Studien über Wahrnehmungstauschungen. (Winkler, F.) Leipzig, 1915.
Phil 28.14 Studien und Bibliographien zur Gegenwartsphilosophie. Leipzig. 1-26,1932-1939 26v.
Phil 200.3.7 Studien und Kritiken zur Philosophie und Aesthetik. v.1-2. (Zimmermznn, R.) Wien, 1870.
Phil 8585.13.10 Studien und Kritiken zur Theologie und Philosophie. (Frauestädt, C.M.J.) Berlin, 1840.
Phil 6319.1.206 Studien zu C.G. Jungs Psychologie. (Wolff, Toni.) Zürich, 1959.
Phil 3500.105 Studien zu Kants philosophischer Entwicklung. Hildesheim, 1967.
Phil 178.43 Studien zu Methodenlehre und Erkenntnisskritik. (Dreyer, Friedrich.) Leipzig, 1895-1903.
Phil 1540.78 Studien zum Einfluss Senecas auf die Philosophie und Theologie des 12. Jahrhunderts. (Nothdurft, Kalus Dieter.) Leiden, 1963.
Phil 2418.2 Studien zum französischen Pyrrhomismus. Inaug. Diss. (Schelle, Meta.) Göttingen, 1930.
Phil 3494.46 Studien zum pflichtbegriff in Kants Kritischer Ethhik. (Maritz, M.) Lund, 1951.
Phil 8612.36 Studien zum Todesgedanken in der Alten Kirche. (Fischer, J.A.) München, 1954.
Phil 3450.19.385 Studien zur Asthetik Martin Heideggers und Oskar Beckers. Inaug. Diss. (Rifga, Fuad.) Tübingen, 1965.
Phil 6319.1.80 Studien zur analytischen Psychologie. (Jung-Institut, Zürich,) Zürich, 1955. 2v.
Phil 28.28 Studien zur diagnostischen Psychologie. Biel. 1-4+
Phil 3001.13 Studien zur dutschen Geistesgeschichte. (Baeumler, A.) Berlin, 1929.
Phil 960.136 Studien zur Eigenart indischen Denkens. (Heimann, B.) Tübingen, 1930.
Phil 978.49.855 Studien zur Einführung in die Mysteriendramen Rudolf Steiners. 2. Aufl. (Fels, Alice.) Dornach, 1961.
Phil 3246.94 Studien zur Entwicklungsgeschichte der Fichteschen Wissenschaftslehre. (Kabitz, Willy.) Berlin, 1902.
Phil 8881.80 Studien zur Ethik. (Gupta, Rajender Kumas.) Bonn, 1967.
Phil 5250.37.20 Studien zur experimentellen Psychologie. (Katz, David.) Basel, 1953.
Phil 3255.81 Studien zur geistesgeschichtlichen Stellung S. Francks. (Körner, Hermann.) Breslau, 1935.
Phil 1124.1 Studien zur Geschichte der Begriffe. (Teichmüller, G.) Berlin, 1874.
Phil 705.27 Studien zur Geschichte der Transzendantalphilosophie. Inaug. Diss. (Selling, M.) Lund, 1938.
Phil 8125.30 Studien zur Geschichte des deutschen Asthetik seit Kant. (Neudecher, Georg.) Wurzburg, 1878.
Phil 3255.94 Studien zur Geschichtsbibel Sebastian Francks. (Raeber, Kuno.) Basel, 1952.
Phil 3255.95 Studien zur Geschichtsbibel Sebastian Francks. Inaug. Diss. (Raeber, Kuno.) Basel, 1952.
Phil 5258.33 Studien zur Grundlegung der Psychologie. (Swoboda, H.) Leipzig, 1905.
Phil 3425.712 Studien zur Metaphysik Hegels. (Lakebrink, Bernhard.) Freiburg, 1969.
Phil 2520.153 Studien zur neueren Erkenntnistheorie. (Kastil, Alfred.) Halle, 1909.
Phil 575.77 Studien zur Personwissenschaft. I. (Stern, W.) Leipzig, 1930.
Phil 577.2 Studien zur Perspektivität. Thesis. (Boehm, Gottfried.) Heidelberg, 1969.
Phil 1750.115.70 Studien zur Phänomenologie, 1930-1939. (Fink, Eugen.) Den Haag, 1966.
Phil 6315.2.18 Studien zur Psychoanalyse der Neurosen aus den Jahren 1913-25. (Freud, Sigmund.) Wien, 1926.
Phil 8897.38.5 Studien zur Rechtsphilosophie. (Wallaschek, R.) Leipzig, 1889.
Phil 5627.135 Studien zur Religionspsychologie. (Wauer, G.A.) Plauen, 1909.
Phil 5520.502 Studien zur sprachkommunikativen Orientierung. Inaug. Diss. (Ulshoefer-Heinloth, Elisabeth.) Passau, 1964.
Phil 705.57 Studien zur Transzendentalphilosophie. (Brelage, Manfred.) Berlin, 1965.
Phil 735.14 Studien zur Wertaxiomatik. 2e Ausg. (Lessing, Theodor.) Leipzig, 1914.
Phil 735.96 Studien zur Wertphilosophie. (Salomaa, J.E.) Helsinki, 1929.
Phil 735.2A Studien zur Werttheorie. (Eisler, R.) Leipzig, 1902.
Phil 3246.335 Studien zur Wirkungsgeschichte Fichtes als Pädagoge Habilitationsschrift. (Lassahn, Rudolf.) Heidelberg, 1970.
Phil 28.82 Studien zur Wissenschaftstheorie. Meisenheim. 1,1968+ 2v.
Phil 3425.52 Studienausgabe. Ausgewählt. (Hegel, Georg Wilhelm Friedrich.) Frankfurt, 1968. 3v.
Phil 6315.2.40 Studienausgabe. v.1,4,6,8,10. (Freud, Sigmund.) Frankfurt, 1969. 6v.
Phil 3640.23 Studienausgabe in 4 Bänden. (Nietzsche, Friedrich.) Frankfurt, 1968. 4v.
Phil 28.32 Studiengesellschaft für praktische Psychologie. Jahrbuch. Lüneburg. 1953-1955 3v.
Phil 4600.8 Studier Aillägnade Efraim Liljequish. (Asfelin, G.) Lund, 1930. 2v.
Phil 2262.92 Studier i Shaftesburys filosofi. (Almer, T.) Lund, 1939.
Phil 5241.60 Studier i själstäkekonst. (Bjerre, Poul.) Stockholm 1914.
Phil 4600.2.36 Studier och meditationer. 4e uppl. (Larsson, Hans.) Lund, 1912.
Phil 3805.104 Studier öfver Schleiermachers uppfattning af det evangeliska skapelsebegreppet. (Alin, Folke.) Lund, 1909.
Phil 187.28.8 Studier öfver människans natur. (Mechnikov, I.I.) Stockholm, 1906.
Htn Phil 3801.539* Studier over Schelling. Thesis. (Lyng, Georg V.) Christiania, 1866.

Phil 2270.113   Studier over Spencer, Lotze og Grundtvig. (Nörregård, Jens.) København, 1890.

Phil 2035.86.30   Studier over W. Hamiltons filosofi. (Rasmussen, S.V.) København, 1921.

Phil 4582.4.100   Studier till Axel Hägerströms filosofi. (Marc-Wogan, Konrad.) Stockholm, 1968.

Phil 3501.6   Studier till uppkomsten av Kants. (Tegen, Einar.) Uppsala, 1918.

Phil 3450.4.80   Studier till Wilhelm Hermanns etik. (Engestrom, Sigfrid.) Uppsala, 1920.

Phil 8585.1   Studies...philosophy of religion and history. (Fairbairn, A.M.) London, 1877.

Phil 8585.1.2   Studies...philosophy of religion and history. 4. ed. (Fairbairn, A.M.) N.Y., 1876.

Phil 52.5   Studies. Philosophie and education series. (Missouri. University.) Columbia, 1911.

Phil 59.1.5   Studies. Philosophy. (Toronto. University.) Toronto. 1,1914

Phil 59.1   Studies. Psychological series. (Toronto. University.) Toronto. 1-5 3v.

Phil 5050.3   Studies and exercises in formal logic. (Keynes, J.N.) London, 1884.

Phil 5050.3.2   Studies and exercises in formal logic. 2nd ed. (Keynes, J.N.) London, 1887.

Phil 5050.3.5   Studies and exercises in formal logic. 4th ed. (Keynes, J.N.) London, 1928.

Phil 8581.22   Studies and speculation in natural history. (Blamires, W.L.) London, 1901.

Htn   Phil 6315.2.77*   Pamphlet vol. Studies by Freud. 3 pam.

Phil 18.9   Studies from the psychological laboratory of University of Illinois. (Illinois. University. Psychological laboratory.) Lancaster, Pa. 1,1909

Phil 8403.39.5   Studies in aesthetics. (Chaudhury, P.J.) Calcutta, 1964.

Phil 343.55   Studies in analogy. (McInerny, Ralph M.) The Hague, 1969.

Phil 6310.1.37   Studies in analytical psychology. (Adler, Gerhard.) London, 1948.

Phil 1020.62   Studies in Arabic philosophy. (Rescher, Nicholas.) Pittsburgh, 1967[1968]

Phil 5585.12   Studies in auditory and visual space perception. (Pierce, A.H.) N.Y., 1901.

Phil 6328.52   Studies in behavior pathology. (Sarbin, T.R.) N.Y., 1961.

Phil 2475.1.230   Studies in Bergson's philosophy. (Mitchell, A.) Lawrence, 1914-

Phil 48.1.10   Studies in character. (Iowa. University.) Iowa City. 1-4,1927-1931 2v.

Phil 9035.32   Studies in character. (Norton, Carol.) Boston, 1906.

Phil 8957.9.5   Studies in Christian love. (Hirst, E.W.) London, 1944.

Phil 8592.31   Studies in Christian philosophy. (Matthews, W.R.) London, 1921.

Phil 8581.37.5   Studies in Christianity. (Bowne, Borden P.) Boston, 1909.

Phil 5870.45   Studies in cognitive development. N.Y., 1969.

Phil 8403.39   Studies in comparative aesthetics. (Chaudhury, P.J.) Santiniketan, 1953.

Phil 8893.76   Studies in conduct. (Saturday Review.) London, 1867.

Phil 8968.9   Studies in conduct. (Smart, G.T.) N.Y., 1909.

Phil 182.49   Studies in contemporary metaphysics. (Hoernlé, R.F.A.) N.Y., 1920.

Phil 1050.14.3   Studies in Crescas. (Wolfson, Harry A.) N.Y., 1934.

Phil 9035.75   Studies in deceit. (Hartshore, H.) N.Y., 1928.

Phil 5049.5.2   Studies in deductive logic. (Jevons, W.S.) London, 1880.

Phil 7082.112.1   Studies in dreams. (Arnold-Forster, Mary Story-Maskelyne.) London, 1921.

Phil 7082.112   Studies in dreams. (Arnold-Forster, Mary Story-Maskelyne.) N.Y., 1921.

Phil 960.118   Studies in early Indian thought. (Stephen, D.J.) Cambridge, 1918.

Phil 525.72   Studies in early mysticism in the Near and Middle East. (Smith, Margaret.) London, 1931.

Phil 1845.15   Studies in empirical philosophy. (Anderson, John.) Sydney, 1962.

Phil 811.10   Studies in European philosophy. (Lindsay, James.) Edinburgh, 1909.

Phil 5649.19A   Studies in expressive movement. (Allport, G.W.) N.Y., 1933.

Phil 5400.120   Studies in feeling and desire. (Flugel, J.C.) London, 1955.

Phil 5520.748.2   Studies in functional logical semiotics of natural language. (Pelc, Jerzy.) The Hague, 1971.

Phil 176.44.5   Studies in general science. (Blackwell, A.B.) N.Y., 1869.

Phil 5425.74   Studies in genius. (Bowerman, Walter.) N.Y., 1947.

Phil 850.48   Studies in Greek philosophy. (Vogel, Cornelia Johanna de.) Assen, 1970.

Phil 3425.100.5A   Studies in Hegelian cosmology. (McTaggart, John McTaggart Ellis.) Cambridge, 1901.

Phil 3425.308   Studies in Hegel's philosophy of religion. (Sterrett, James M.) N.Y., 1890.

Phil 5425.86   Studies in hereditary ability. (Gun, W.T.J.) London, 1928.

Phil 6111.65   Studies in higher neurodynamics as related to problems of psychology. (Boiko, E.) Jerusalem, 1961.

Phil 5251.50   Studies in human behavior. (Lawrence, Merle.) Princeton, 1949.

Phil 5249.27   Studies in human development. (Jones, Harold Ellis.) N.Y., 1949.

Phil 176.78   Studies in human nature. (Baillie, J.B.) London, 1921.

Phil 193.9.9   Studies in humanism. (Schiller, F.C.S.) London, 1907.

Phil 6615.20.7   Studies in hysteria. (Breuer, Josef.) Boston, 1961.

Phil 49.2   Studies in linguistic psychology. (James Millikin University.) Decatur, Ill.

Phil 5055.1.5A   Studies in logic. (Pierce, C.S.) Boston, 1883.

Phil 5041.15.4   Studies in logic and probability. (Boole, George.) London, 1952.

Phil 5043.16A   Studies in logical theory. (Dewey, J.) Chicago, 1903.

Phil 5039.12   Studies in logical theory. Oxford, 1968.

Phil 5535.2.5   Studies in mathematical learning theory. (Bush, Robert Ray.) Stanford, 1959.

Phil 5238.197   Studies in mathematical psychology. (Atkinson, R.C.) Stanford, 1964.

Phil 1507.4   Studies in medieval thought. (Coulton, G.G.) London, 1940.

Phil 6750.222   Studies in mental deviations. (Porteus, S.D.) Vineland, 1922.

Phil 28.11   Studies in mental inefficiency. London. 1-12 3v.

Phil 186.120.5   Studies in metaphilosophy. (Lazerowitz, M.) London, 1964.

Phil 8870.32   Studies in moral philosophy. Oxford, 1968.

Phil 8882.40   Studies in moral science. (Hamilton, William E.) Chicago, 1916.

Phil 5520.407.5   Studies in multilingualism. Leiden, 1969.

Phil 5500.60   Studies in multiobjective decision models. (Johnsen, Erik.) Lund, 1968.

Phil 1020.50   Studies in Muslim philosophy. 1st ed. (Sheikh, M. Saeed.) Lahore, 1962.

Phil 525.55   Studies in mystical religion. (Jones, Rufus M.) London, 1919.

Phil 525.19   Studies in mysticism and certain aspects of the secret tradition. (Waite, A.E.) London, 1906.

Phil 6965.11   Studies in neurological diagnosis. (Putnam, J.J.) Boston, 1902.

Phil 6117.30   Studies in neurology. (Head, Henry.) London, 1920. 2v.

Phil 705.5.5A   Studies in New England transcendentalism. (Goddard, H.C.) N.Y., 1908.

Phil 705.5   Studies in New England transcendentalism. Thesis. (Goddard, H.C.) N.Y., 1908.

Phil 978.68.10   Studies in occult philosophy. (Purucker, G. de.) Covina, California, 1945.

Phil 978.5.30   Studies in occultism. 2nd ed. (Blavatsky, H.P.) Boston, 1897.

Phil 7060.99   Studies in outlying fields of psychic science. (Tuttle, H.) N.Y., 1889.

Phil 5590.7   Studies in personality. Contributions in honor of Lewis M. Terman. 1. ed. N.Y., 1942.

Phil 3808.29.5   Studies in pessimism. (Schopenhauer, Arthur.) London, 1891.

Phil 3808.29.10   Studies in pessimism. (Schopenhauer, Arthur.) London, 1923.

Phil 1750.115.145   Studies in phenomenology. (Sinha, Debabrata.) The Hague, 1969.

Phil 1750.773   Studies in phenomenology and psychology. (Gurwitsch, Aron.) Evanston, 1966.

Phil 494.1   Studies in philosophical naturalism. (Townsend, H.G.) Eugene, 1931.

Phil 165.240   Studies in philosophy. (Bergman, S.) Jerusalem, 1960.

Phil 1905.26   Studies in philosophy. (Boodin, J.E.) Los Angeles, 1957.

Phil 42.2   Studies in philosophy. (Cornell University.) N.Y. 1-17,1900-1925 3v.

Phil 177.23   Studies in philosophy. (Courtney, W.L.) London, 1882.

Phil 180.28.5   Studies in philosophy. (Field, G.C.) Bristol, 1935.

Phil 182.49.10.2   Studies in philosophy. (Hoernlé, R.F.A.) Cambridge, Mass., 1952.

Phil 182.49.10   Studies in philosophy. (Hoernlé, R.F.A.) London, 1952.

Phil 186.31   Studies in philosophy. (Lightfoot, John.) Edinburgh, 1888.

Phil 165.386   Studies in philosophy: British Academy lectures. (Findlay, John N.) London, 1966.

Phil 185.7.5   Studies in philosophy and literature. (Knight, W.) London, 1879.

Phil 5258.27.25   Studies in philosophy and psychology. (Stout, G.F.) London, 1930.

Phil 193.50   Studies in philosophy and psychology. Boston, 1906.

Phil 1930.10.35   Studies in philosophy and science. (Cohen, Morris R.) N.Y., 1949.

Phil 28.74   Studies in philosophy and the history of philosophy. Washington. 1,1961+ 4v.

Phil 5643.92   Studies in physiological optics, Dec. 1928-Oct. 1934. (Ferree, C.E.) Baltimore, 1934. 2v.

Phil 1133.52   Studies in presocratic philosophy. (Furley, David J.) London, 1970-

Phil 7068.97.10   Studies in psychical research. (Podmore, Frank.) London, 1897.

Phil 7068.97.11   Studies in psychical research. (Podmore, Frank.) N.Y., 1897.

Phil 6311.6.5   Studies in psychoanalysis, (Baudouin, C.) N.Y., 1922.

Phil 6311.6   Studies in psychoanalysis. (Baudouin, C.) London, 1922.

Phil 5244.20   Studies in psychology. (Elder, William.) London, 1927.

Phil 48.1   Studies in psychology. (Iowa. University.) Iowa City. 1-7,1897-1918 2v.

Phil 24.4   Studies in psychology. (Oregon. University.) Eugene. 1-3,1943-1959 3v.

Phil 24.5   Studies in psychology. (Oregon. University.) Eugene. 2,1955

Phil 58.12   Studies in psychology. (Smith College. William Allen Neilson Research Laboratory.) Northampton.

Phil 5259.5.28   Studies in psychology. Worcester, 1917.

Phil 42.8   Studies in psychology and psychiatry. (Catholic University of America.) Washington. 1,1927+ 9v.

Phil 5620.30   Studies in reason and faith. (Dar, B.A.) Lahore, 1957.

Phil 8092.7   Studies in recent aesthetic. (Gilbert, Katherine Everett.) Chapel Hill, 1927.

Phil 8585.17.5   Studies in religion. (Fiske, J.) Boston, 1902.

Phil 5635.17   Studies in rhythm. (Weidensall, C.J.) Cincinnati, 1916.

Phil 8712.5.5   Studies in science and religion. (Wright, George F.) Andover, 1882.

Phil 5420.16   Studies in self-confrontation. (Milsen, G.) Copenhagen, 1962.

Phil 5066.13   Studies in semantics. Cambridge, Mass. 1-2,1942-1943 2v.

Phil 58.21   Studies in Soviet thought. Dordrecht. 1,1961+ 8v.

Phil 177.40.5   Studies in speculative philosophy. (Creighton, J.E.) N.Y., 1925.

Phil 5145.3   Studies in subjective probability. (Kyburg, Henry E.) N.Y., 1964.

NEDL   Phil 2520.119A   Studies in the Cartesian philosophy. (Smith, N.K.) N.Y., 1902.

Phil 2520.119.2   Studies in the Cartesian philosophy. (Smith, N.K.) N.Y., 1902.

Phil 186.91   Studies in the dynamic coherence. (Lambek, C.) Copenhagen, 1938.

Phil 5400.84   Studies in the dynamics of behavior. (Lashley, K.S.) Chicago, 1932.

Phil 2050.190   Studies in the eighteenth-century background of Hume's empiricism. (Kuypers, M.S.) Minneapolis, 1930.

Phil 1822.5   Studies in the English outlook in the period between the world wars. (Weber, Conrad G.) Bern, 1945.

Phil 5400.11   Studies in the evolutionary psychology of feeling. (Stanley, Hiram Miner.) London, 1895.

Phil 3425.100.2   Studies in the Hegelian dialectic. 2. ed. (McTaggart, John McTaggart Ellis.) Cambridge, 1922.

Phil 3425.100.2.1   Studies in the Hegelian dialectic. 2. ed. (McTaggart, John McTaggart Ellis.) N.Y., 1964.

Phil 5027.3   Studies in the history of Arabic logic. (Rescher, N.) Pittsburgh, 1963.

Phil 42.1.5   Studies in the history of ideas. (Columbia College.) N.Y. 1-3,1918-1935 3v.

Phil 8602.18.5   Studies in the history of natural theology. (Webb, C.C.J.) Oxford, 1915.

Phil 978.63 — Studies in the lesser mysteries. (Powell, F.G.M.) London, 1913.

Phil 1885.95 — Studies in the metaphysics of Bradley. (Saxena, Sushil Kumar.) N.Y., 1967.

Phil 9035.76 — Studies in the nature of character. v.2. (Columbia University. Teachers College. Character Education Inquiry.) N.Y., 1929.

Phil 730.26 — Studies in the nature of universals. (Dar, B.A.) Lahore, 1958.

Phil 9035.77 — Studies in the organization of character. (Hartshore, H.) N.Y., 1930.

Phil 2225.5.85 — Studies in the philosophy of Charles Sanders Peirce. (Wiener, P.P.) Cambridge, Mass., 1952.

Phil 2225.5.120A — Studies in the philosophy of Charles Sanders Peirce. 2nd series. (Moore, Edward C.) Amherst, 1964.

Phil 299.22 — Studies in the philosophy of creation. (Stallknecht, N.P.) Princeton, 1934.

Phil 2050.176A — Studies in the philosophy of David Hume. (Hendel, C.W.) Princeton, 1925.

Phil 2150.18.105 — Studies in the philosophy of G.E. Moore. (Klemke, E.D.) Chicago, 1969.

Phil 3483.85 — Studies in the philosophy of Kant. 1st ed. (Beck, Lewis White.) Indianapolis, 1965.

Phil 8581.74 — Studies in the philosophy of religion. (Bowman, Archibald Allan.) London, 1938. 2v.

Phil 8586.10 — Studies in the philosophy of religion. (Galloway, G.) Edinburgh, 1904.

Phil 8598.62 — Studies in the philosophy of religion. (Seth Pringle-Pattison, Andrew.) Oxford, 1930.

Phil 165.420 — Studies in the philosophy of thought and action. (Strawson, Peter Frederick.) London, 1968.

Phil 3925.16.200 — Studies in the philosophy of Wittgenstein. (Winch, Peter.) N.Y., 1969.

Phil 5627.20.10 — Studies in the psychology of religious phenomena. (Leuba, J.H.) Worcester, 1896.

Phil 5590.12 — Studies in the relation of personality to field of work. Cambridge.

Phil 5465.52A — Studies in the theory of imagination. (Gordon, Kate.) Los Angeles, 1941.

Phil 349.85 — Studies in the theory of knowledge. Oxford, 1970.

Phil 197.13.3 — Studies in the thought world. (Wood, H.) Boston, 1896.

Phil 197.13.8 — Studies in the thought world. 8th ed. (Wood, H.) Boston, 1906.

Phil 8656.8 — Studies in theism. (Bowne, B.P.) N.Y., 1879.

Phil 190.18.5 — Studies in theory of knowledge. (Perry, R.B.) n.p., 1900-1910.

Phil 5520.634 — Studies in thought and language. (Cowan, Joseph Lloyd.) Tucson, 1970.

Phil 960.42 — Studies in Vedantism. (Krishnachandra, B.) Calcutta, 1909.

Phil 5649.5 — Studies in voluntary muscular contraction. (Storey, Thomas Andrew.) Palo Alto, Calif., 1904.

Phil 6319.1.15 — Studies in word association. (Jung, C.G.) London, 1918.

Phil 5822.9.10 — Studies of abnormal behavior in the rat. (Maier, Norman Raymond Frederick.) N.Y., 1939.

Phil 5400.92 — Studies of emotional reactions. (Landis, Carney.) n.p., 1924.

Phil 530.11.5 — Studies of English mystics. (Inge, William R.) London, 1907.

Phil 2250.65 — Studies of good and evil. (Royce, Josiah.) Hamden, 1898.

Phil 192.16.7A — Studies of good and evil. (Royce, Josiah.) N.Y., 1898.

Phil 9070.17 — Studies of man. (Ellis, William J.) London, 1874.

Phil 530.40.27 — Studies of the Spanish mystics. (Peers, E.A.) London, 1927-30. 2v.

Phil 530.40.27.5 — Studies of the Spanish mystics. 2nd ed. (Peers, E.A.) London, 1951-60. 3v.

Phil 5643.104A — Studies of visual fatigue. (McFarland, R.A.) Boston, 1942.

Phil 3270.12.95 — Studies on Gottlob Frege and Traditional philosophy. (Angehelli, Ignacio.) Dordrecht, 1967.

Phil 6615.20.5 — Studies on hysteria. (Breuer, Josef.) London, 1956.

Phil 6615.20.6 — Studies on hysteria. (Breuer, Josef.) N.Y., 1957.

Phil 3425.390.5 — Studies on Marx and Hegel. (Hyppolite, Jean.) N.Y., 1969.

Phil 5850.338 — Studies on the problem driver. (Selling, L.S.) Detroit, 1941.

Phil 51.3 — Studies psychology series. (Lehigh University.) Bethlehem, Pa.

Phil 1900.84 — Studies subsidiary to works of...Butler. (Gladstone, W.E.) Oxford, 1896.

Phil 8407.40 — Studii, statii, pisma i spomeni. (Gacher, Dmitrii I.) Sofiia, 1964.

Phil 5019.5 — Studii de logica. (Joja, A.) Bucuresti, 1960. 3v.

Phil 194.8.5 — Studii filosofici. (Tommaseo, N.) Lanciano, 1920.

Phil 194.8 — Studii filosofici. (Tommaseo, N.) Venezia, 1840. 2v.

Phil 3425.282.5F — Studii sull'etica hegeliana; memoria. (Spaventa, B.) Napoli, 1869.

Phil 8430.45.5 — Studije, eseji, kritike. (Vučković, Vojislav.) Beograd, 1958. 2v.

Phil 1540.23 — Lo studio della natura nell'umanesimo. (Bonfarri, G.) Mantova, 1937.

Phil 6028.4 — Studio di curiosita. (Spadon, N.) Venetia, 1663.

Phil 5245.48 — Lo studio psicologica dell'intelligenza e della matricità. (Falorni, M.L.) Firenze, 1952.

Phil 1865.180 — Studio sulla morale di Geremia Bentham. (Surra, G.) Torino, 1893.

Phil 3800.210.15 — Studium generale. (Schelling, F.W.J. von.) Stuttgart, 1954.

Phil 4803.896.230 — Studja nad filozofja wartosci. (Zňaniecki, Florian.) Warszawa, 1912.

Phil 672.21 — Study, E. Die realistische Weltansicht und die Lehre vom Raume. Braunschweig, 1914.

Phil 5625.80 — A study and analysis of the conditioned reflex. Diss. (Hamel, I.A.) Washington, 1918.

Phil 5252.41 — A study for the times. (McKim, William D.) N.Y., 1920.

Phil 349.58 — Study Group on the Unity of Knowledge. The anatomy of knowledge. Amherst, 1969.

Phil 8418.21 — A study in aesthetics. (Reid, L.A.) London, 1931.

Phil 978.6.45 — Study in consciousness. (Besant, Annie.) London, 1904.

Phil 8887.95 — A study in ethical theory. (Mackinnon, D.M.) London, 1957.

Phil 5465.6 — A study in imagination. (Brittain, H.L.) n.p., 1907.

Phil 5545.55 — Study in incidental memory. (Myers, G.C.) N.Y., 1913.

Phil 3485.14 — A study in Kant's aesthetics. Diss. (Dunham, B.) Lancaster, Pa., 1934.

Phil 5545.166 — A study in memorising various materials by the reconstruction method. (Gamble, E.A.M.) Lancaster, Pa., 1909.

Phil 5545.184 — A study in memory. (Furlong, E.J.) London, 1951.

Phil 8886.35 — A study in moral problems. (Laing, B.M.) London, 1922.

Phil 8886.45 — A study in moral theory. (Laird, John.) N.Y., 1926.

Phil 8883.2 — Study in psychology of ethics. (Irons, D.) Edinburgh, 1903.

Phil 5649.14 — A study in reaction time and movement. Diss. (Moore, T.V.) Washington, 1904.

Phil 630.22 — A study in realism. (Laird, John.) Cambridge, 1920.

Phil 735.93 — A study in the logic of value. (Clarke, Mary E.) London, 1929.

Phil 2475.1.157 — A study in the philosophy of Bergson. (Cunningham, G.W.) N.Y., 1916.

Phil 2733.103 — A study in the philosophy of Malebranche. (Church, Ralph W.) London, 1931.

Phil 575.68 — A study in the philosophy of personality. (Oakeley, Hilda D.) London, 1928.

Phil 5627.37 — A study in the psychology of ritualism. Diss. (Henke, Frederick G.) Chicago, 1910.

Phil 3925.16.275 — A study in Wittgenstein's Tractatus. (Maslow, Alexander.) Berkeley, 1961.

Phil 5594.153.2 — The study of behavior. (Stephenson, William.) Chicago, 1964.

Phil 5425.18.5A — A study of British genius. (Ellis, H.) Boston, 1926.

Phil 5425.18 — Study of British genius. (Ellis, H.) London, 1904.

Phil 5650.26 — A study of children's hearing as it relates to reading. Thesis. (Kennedy, Helen.) n.p., 1942.

Phil 5627.131 — A study of conversion. (Lang, Wyatt.) London, 1931.

Phil 5627.1.5 — A study of conversion. (Starbuck, E.D.) n.p., 189-?

Phil 5648.12 — A study of cutaneous after-sensations. (Hayes, M.H.S.) Chicago, 1912.

Phil 8612.5 — A study of death. (Alden, Henry M.) N.Y., 1895.

Phil 5645.43 — A study of discriminative serial action. Thesis. (Weaver, H.B.) Philadelphia, 1942.

Phil 8893.8 — A study of ethical principles. (Seth, J.) Edinburgh, 1894.

Phil 8893.8.2 — A study of ethical principles. 5th ed. (Seth, J.) N.Y., 1899.

Phil 8893.8.3 — A study of ethical principles. 8. ed. (Seth, J.) N.Y., 1905.

Phil 8893.8.5 — A study of ethical principles. 12. ed. (Seth, J.) N.Y., 1911.

Phil 8893.8.10 — A study of ethical principles. 17. ed. (Seth, J.) N.Y., 1926.

Phil 8878.11.7 — The study of ethics, a syllabus. Photoreproduction. (Dewey, John.) Ann Arbor, 1897.

Phil 5401.2 — Study of fears. (Hall, G.S.) Worcester, 1897.

Phil 3120.8.160 — A study of Franz Brentano; his psychological standpoint and his significance in the history of psychology. (Rancurello, Antos C.) N.Y., 1968.

Phil 3270.12.85 — A study of Frege. (Walker, J.P.B.) Oxford, 1965.

Phil 5425.65 — A study of genius. (Royce, Noble K.) Chicago, 1890.

Phil 1050.15.5 — A study of Gersonedes in his proper perspective. (Alderblum, N.H.H.) N.Y., 1926.

Phil 5590.42 — A study of greatness in men. (Larned, Josephus N.) Boston, 1911.

Phil 1117.7 — A study of Greek philosophy. (Mitchell, E.M. (Mrs.).) Chicago, 1891.

Phil 4757.2.95 — A study of Gurdjieff's teaching. (Walker, K.M.) London, 1957.

Phil 6119.7 — A study of handedness. (Jones, Wallace Franklin.) Vermillion, S.D., 1918.

Phil 3425.326A — A study of Hegel's logic. (Mure, G.R.G.) Oxford, 1950.

Phil 3450.11.191 — A study of Husserl's formal and transcendental logic. (Bachelard, Suzanne.) Evanston, 1968.

Phil 960.130 — A study of Indian philosophy. (Desia, Shantaram Anant.) Bombay, 1906.

Phil 9075.12 — Study of influence, of custom on world judgment. (Sharp, F.C.) Madison, 1908.

Phil 6980.485 — A study of interpersonal relations. (Mullahy, Patrick.) N.Y., 1957.

Phil 5413.14 — A study of jealousy as differentiated from envy. (Ankles, T.M.) Boston, 1939.

Phil 3504.22A — A study of Kant. (Ward, James.) Cambridge, Eng., 1922.

Phil 3483.22 — A study of Kant's psychology. (Buchner, E.F.) N.Y., 1893.

Phil 5238.186 — The study of lives; essays on personality in honour of Henry A. Murray. (White, R.W.) N.Y., 1963.

Phil 2115.145A — A study of Locke's theory of ideas. (Thompson, S.M.) Monmouth, Ill., 1934.

Phil 2115.124 — A study of Locke's theory of knowledge. (Gregory, Raymond.) Wilmington, Ohio, 1919.

Phil 2115.124.5 — A study of Locke's theory of knowledge. Thesis. (Gregory, Raymond.) Wilmington, Ohio, 1919.

Phil 346.20.5A — The study of man. (Polanyi, Michael.) London, 1959.

Phil 5545.35 — A study of memory. (Henderson, E.N.) n.p., n.d.

Phil 5241.63 — The study of mental science. (Brough, J.) London, 1903.

Phil 176.47A — Study of nature...with other essays. (Blewett, G.J.) Toronto, 1907.

Phil 190.16.2 — Study of origins. 2d ed. (Pressensé, E. de.) N.Y., 1885.

Phil 5817.11 — A study of perseverance reactions. (Hamilton, Gilbert V.) N.Y., 1916.

Phil 5590.165 — The study of personality. (Brand, Howard.) N.Y., 1954.

Phil 5590.500 — The study of personality. N.Y., 1968.

Phil 5251.6.4 — The study of psychology. (Lewes, G.H.) London, 1879.

Phil 1750.20 — Study of realistic movement in contemporary philosophy. (McClure, M.T.) Staunton, 1912.

Phil 8592.6.2 — Study of religion. (Martineau, James.) London, 1900. 2v.

Phil 8592.6 — Study of religion. (Martineau, James.) Oxford, 1888. 2v.

Phil 8592.6.3 — A study of religion. (Martineau, James.) Oxford, 1888. 2v.

Phil 8592.6.4 — A study of religion. 1. American ed. (Martineau, James.) Oxford, 1888. 2v.

Phil 8550.342 — Study of religious thought in England from 1850. (Webb, Clement C.J.) Oxford, 1933.

Phil 5545.61 — Study of retroactive inhibition. Thesis. (DeCamp, J.E.) Princeton, 1915.

Phil 5827.5 — A study of sensory control in the rat. (Richardson, F.) n.p., 1909.

Phil 5827.5.2 — A study of sensory control in the rat. (Robinson, R. (Mrs.).) Lancaster, Pa., 1909.

Phil 6968.21 — A study of somatic conditions in manic-depressive psychosis. Inaug. Diss. (Sondén, Tarsten.) Uppsala, 1927.

Phil 3832.1A — A study of Spinoza. (Martineau, J.) London, 1882.

Phil 5400.24 — Study of the affective qualities. (Hayes, Samuel P.) n.p., 1906.

Phil 1135.162 — A study of the doctrine of metempsychocis in Greece. Thesis. (Long, Herbert S.) Princeton, 1948.

Phil 3829.1.10   A study of the Ethics of Spinoza. (Joachim, H.H.) N.Y., 1964.

Phil 3829.1   A study of the Ethics of Spinoza. (Joachim, H.H.) Oxford, 1901.

Phil 8599.10   The study of the history and philosophy of religion. (Tyler, Charles Mellon.) Ithica, N.Y., 1891.

Phil 6032.6   The study of the human face. (Woolnoth, Thomas.) London, 1865.

Phil 8893.10.10   A study of the influence of custom. (Sharp, F.C.) Madison, Wis., 1908.

Phil 6750.224   A study of the major emotions in persons of defective intelligence. (Morrison, B.M.) Berkeley, 1924.

Phil 5246.29   A study of the relation of accuracy to speed. (Garrett, Henry E.) N.Y., 1922.

Phil 5440.29   A study of the resemblance of parents and children in general intelligence. Thesis. (Outhit, M.C.) N.Y., 1933.

Phil 5241.118   A study of thinking. (Bruner, J.S.) N.Y., 1956.

Phil 5590.437   Studying personality cross-culturally. (Kaplan, Bert.) N.Y., 1961.

Phil 575.230   Studying personality crossculturally. (Kaplan, Bert.) Evanston, Illinois, 1961.

Phil 5548.146   Stückmann, Günther. Der Berufserfolg als Motivationsphänomen. Berlin, 1968.

Phil 3500.12A   Stuelsenberg, J. Life of Immanuel Kant. London, 1882.

Phil 349.31   Stürmann, J.F. Untersuchungen über das Wesen der philosophischen Erkenntnis. Inaug. Diss. Münster in Westfalen, 1931.

Phil 193.254   Stuettgen, Albert. Offenheit und Perspektive. Warendorf, 1966.

Phil 735.120   Die Stufen der Erkenntnis. (Fiedler, K.) München, 1929.

Phil 5643.155   Stufen der ganzheitlichen Auffassung bei 2- bis 7 järigen Kindern. Thesis. (Kleinhans, Walter H.) Weinheim, 1966.

Phil 1135.245   Die Stufen der Liebe; Eros, Phila, Agape. 1. Aufl. (Lotz, Johannes Baptist.) Frankfurt, 1971.

Phil 575.76   Stufen der Personalität. (Ehrlich, Walter.) Halle, 1930.

Phil 3745.7   Die Stufen des Organischen und des Marisch; Einleitung in die philosophische Anthropologie. (Plessner, Helmuth.) Berlin, 1928.

Phil 176.158   Der Stufenbau der Welt. 1. Aufl. (Brunner, August.) München, 1950.

Phil 3425.208   Stuhrmann, J. Die Wurzeln der Hegelschen Logik bei Kant. Neustadt, 1887.

Phil 3018.36   Stuke, H. Philosophie der Tat. Stuttgart, 1963.

Phil 3910.132   Die Stuktur der Gotteserkenntnis. (Bissinger, Anton.) Bonn, 1970.

Htn   Phil 3200.1.35*   Stultitiae laus. (Erasmus, D.) Basiliae, 1676.

Phil 6128.12   Stumpf, C. Leib und Seele. Der Entwicklungs gedanke. Leipzig, 1903.

Phil 126.3   Stumpf, C. Tafeln zur Geschichte der Philosophie. Berlin, 1896.

Phil 126.3.2   Stumpf, C. Tafeln zur Geschichte der Philosophie. Berlin, 1900.

Phil 126.3.3   Stumpf, C. Tafeln zur Geschichte der Philosophie. Berlin, 1910.

Phil 126.3.4   Stumpf, C. Tafeln zur Geschichte der Philosophie. 4. Aufl. Berlin, 1928.

Phil 672.13   Stumpf, C. Über den psychologischen Ursprung der Raumvorstellung. Leipzig, 1873.

Phil 2070.120   Stumpf, Carl. William James nach seinen Briefen. Berlin, 1927.

Phil 2070.120.2A   Stumpf, Carl. William James nach seinen Briefen. Berlin, 1928.

Phil 7082.92   Stumpf, E.J.G. Der Traum und seine Dentung. Leipzig, 1899.

Phil 193.69.8   Stumpf, K. Gustav Engel...Klangfarbe. n.p., 1888-1915. 23 pam.

Phil 193.69   Stumpf, K. Philosophische Reden und Vorträge. Leipzig, 1910.

Phil 3838.13   Stumpf, K. Spinozastudien. Berlin, 1919.

Phil 1718.4   Stumpf, K. Die Wiedergeburt der Philosophie. Leipzig, 1908.

Phil 349.36   Stumpf, Karl. Erkenntnislehre. Bd. I-II. Leipzig, 1939-1940.

Phil 8893.67.5   Stumpf, Karl. Vom ethischen Skeptizismus; Rede. Berlin, 1908.

Phil 8893.67   Stumpf, Karl. Vom ethischen Skeptizismus. Leipzig, 1909.

Phil 3850.35   Stumpf, Karl. Zur Einteilung der Wissenschaften. Berlin, 1907.

Phil 3120.30.57   Die Stunde und die Erkenntnis. (Buber, Martin.) Berlin, 1936.

Phil 6128.25   The stunted saplings. (Sherman, J.C.) Boston, 1911.

Phil 299.6   Stunz, F. Naturbetrachtung und Naturkenntnis. Leipzig, 1904.

Phil 3425.230   Sturge, M.C. Opposite things. Bristol, 1927.

Phil 3500.49   Sturm, A. Kant, Schopenhauer, Nietzsche und deren...Gemüt. Langensalza, 1921.

Phil 3905.90   Sturm, Bruno. Gegen Weininger. Wien, 1912.

Phil 6688.12   Sturm, G. Mesmerismus und Hypnotismus. Leipzig, n.d.

Phil 8893.27   Sturman, E.A. Inaugural dissertation, moral philosophy. London, 1871.

Phil 8419.3   Sturmfels, W. Grundprobleme der Ästhetik. München, 1963.

Phil 400.13.5   Sturt, H. Idola theatri; a criticism of Oxford thought and thinkers. London, 1906.

Phil 400.13   Sturt, H. Personal idealism; philosophical essays of members of Oxford University. London, 1902.

Phil 8893.57   Sturt, Henry. Human value. Cambridge, 1923.

Phil 8893.57.10   Sturt, Henry. Moral experience, an outline of ethics for class-teaching. London, 1928.

Phil 5258.39   Sturt, Henry. Principles of understanding. Cambridge, 1915.

Phil 1850.127   Sturt, Mary. Francis Bacon; a biography. London, 1932.

Phil 672.133   Sturt, Mary. The psychology of time. London, 1925.

Phil 3488.22   Sturz der Metaphysik als Wissenschaft. (Gartelmann, Henri.) Berlin, 1893.

Phil 6420.42   Stuttering; a symposium. (Eisenson, John.) N.Y., 1958.

Phil 6420.8   Stuttering, its cause and remedy. (Rosenberg, William L.) Cleveland, 19- ?

Phil 6128.66   Stuttgart. Institut für Psychotherapie und Tiefenpsychologie. Felix Schottlaender zum Gedächnis. Stuttgart, 1959.

Phil 6128.70   Stuttgart. Institut für Psychotherapie und Tiefenpsychologie. Nervose. Stuttgart, 1960.

Phil 6328.38   Stuttgart. Institut für Psychotherapie und Tiefenpsychologie. Wiedergeburt des Einzelnen. Stuttgart, 1956.

Phil 5418.2   Stuttgarter Gemeinschaft "Arzt und Seelsorger". Einsamkeit in medizinisch-psychologischer, theologischer und soziologischer Sicht. Stuttgart, 1967.

Phil 365.66   Stuttgarter Gemeinschaft "Arzt und Seelsorger." Evolution; Fortschrittsglaube und Heilserwartung. Ein Tagungsbericht. Stuttgart, 1970.

Phil 5627.200   Stuxen des Gebets. (Amstutz, J.) Bern, 1954.

Phil 3838.34   Stybe, Svend Erik. Spinoza. København, 1969.

Phil 2490.117   Style, Jane M. Auguste Comte thinker and lover. London, 1928.

Phil 4513.4.39   Stylus character animi. (Asp, Matthia.) Upsaliae, 1732.

Phil 4070.1.45   Su la teoria del giudizio. (Bonavino, Cristoforo.) Milano, 1871. 2v.

Phil 3850.19.30   Suabedissen, D.T.A. Die Grundzüge der Metaphysik. Marburg, 1836.

Phil 3850.19.50   Suabedissen, D.T.A. Die Grundzüge der philosophischen Tugend- und Rechtslehre. Marburg, 1839.

Phil 349.26   Suabedissen, D.T.A. Resultate des philosophischen Forschungen über...Erkenntnis. Marburg, 1805.

Phil 5258.80   Suabedissen, D.T.A. Von dem Begriffe der Psychologie. Marburg, 1829.

Phil 3850.19.40   Suabedissen, D.T.A. Zur Einleitung in die Philosophie. Marburg, 1827.

Phil 960.27   Suali, Luigi. Introduzione allo studio della filosofia indiania. Pavia, 1913.

Phil 2805.222   Suarès, André. Puissances de Pascal. Paris, 1923.

Phil 978.59.97   Suares, Carlo. Krishnamurti. Paris, 1933.

Phil 5642.7   Suarez de Mendoza, Ferdinand. L'audition colorée. 2. éd. Paris, 1899.

Phil 5228.16   Suarez Soto, Vicente. Psicología abismal del mexicano. 2. ed. Puebla de Zaragoza, 1967.

Phil 4210.130   I suareziani e l'abate Rosmini. (Moglia, A.) Piacenza, 1882.

X Cg   Phil 4752.2.30   Sub specie aeternitatis. (Berdiaev, Nikolai Aleksandrovich.) Sankt Peterburg, 1907.

Phil 5170.14   Subbotin, Aleksandr L. Teoriia sillogistiki v sovremennoi formal'noi logike. Moskva, 1965.

Phil 5170.14.5   Subbotin, Aleksandr L. Traditsionnaia i sovremennaia formal'naia logika. Moskva, 1969.

Phil 9400.40   Subcommittee reports. (Pennsylvania. Governor's White House Conference Committee on Aging.) Harrisburg, 1960.

Phil 5722.5   Le subconscient normal. (Abramowski, Edouard.) Paris, 1914.

Phil 5722.15   The subconscious. (Jastrow, J.) Boston, 1906.

Phil 5520.478   The subconscious language. (Thass-Thienemann, Théodore.) N.Y., 1967.

Phil 5722.12   Subconscious phenomena. (Münsterberg, Hugo.) Boston, 1910.

Phil 5722.38.1   The subconscious self and its relation to education and health. (Waldstein, Louis.) N.Y., 1902.

Phil 5722.38.2   The subconscious self and its relation to education and health. (Waldstein, Louis.) N.Y., 1926.

Phil 310.687   Sub"ektivnyi faktor. (Chagin, Boris A.) Moskva, 1968.

Phil 5068.30   Sub"ektivnyi idealizm. (Baknadze, K.S.) Tbilisi, 1955.

Phil 341.44   Sub'ieks, ob'iekt i fizychne piznannia. (Kanak, Fedvi M.) Kyïv, 1970.

Phil 197.24   Subject and object. (Walter, Johnston E.) West Newton, Pa., 1915.

Phil 5520.119   Subject and predicate. (Sandman, M.) Edinburgh, 1954.

Phil 575.280   The subject of consciousness. (Evans, Cedric Oliver.) London, 1970.

Htn   Phil 2138.60*   The subjection of women. (Mill, John S.) London, 1869.

Phil 8583.3.5   The subjective difficulties in religion. (DeVere, Aubrey.) n.p., n.d.

Phil 3425.36   The subjective logic of Hegel. (Hegel, Georg Wilhelm Friedrich.) London, 1855.

Phil 8892.27   Le subjectivisme. (Ryner, J.H.) Paris, 1923.

Phil 3425.754   Subjekt; Versuch zur Ontologie bei Hegel. (Brockard, Hans.) München, 1970.

Phil 310.604   Subjekt a objekt. (Mužík, Josef.) Praha, 1964.

Phil 3425.334   Subjekt-Objekt; Erläuterungen zu Hegel. (Bloch, Ernst.) Berlin, 1951.

Phil 8407.17   Subjekt und Objekt des ästischen Aktes. (Gadmann, E.) Halle, 1904.

Phil 1512.9   Die subjektiven GrundlagenDer scholastischen Ethik. (Hochsteller, E.) Halle, 1915.

Phil 1750.115.160   Subjektivität; Beiträge zur Phänomenologie und Logik. (Schmitz, Hermann.) Bonn, 1968.

Phil 165.175.5   Subjektivität und Metaphysik. (Henrich, Dieter.) Frankfurt, 1966.

Phil 3425.564   Subjektivität und verden Glichung. (Rahrmoser, Günter.) Gütersloh, 1961.

Phil 8110.3   The sublime; a study of critical theories in 18th century England. (Monk, S.H.) Ann Arbor, 1960.

Phil 6990.41   The sublime shepherdess; the life of St. Bernadette of Lourdes. (Keyes, F.P.W. (Mrs.).) N.Y., 1940.

Phil 5695.2   Subliminal perception. (Dixon, Norman F.) London, 1971.

Phil 9415.10   Submission in suffering. (Rowley, Harold H.) Cardiff, 1942.

Phil 5058.33.4   Subrahmanyam, A. Logic, inductive and deductive. Madras, 1916.

Phil 192.65   La substance; essai de philosophie rationnelle. (Roisel, Godefroy de.) Paris, 1881.

Phil 333.5.8A   Substance and function and Einstein's theory of relativity. (Cassirer, Ernst.) N.Y., 1953.

Phil 8701.4.5   The substance of faith allied with science. (Lodge, Oliver Joseph.) London, 1915.

Phil 8701.4.4   The substance of faith allied with science. (Lodge, Oliver Joseph.) N.Y., 1907.

Phil 6125.25.5   The substance of mental health. (Preston, G.H.) London, 1944.

Phil 6125.25   The substance of mental health. (Preston, G.H.) N.Y., 1943.

Phil 510.1.7.10   The substance of the riddle of the universe. (Haeckel, Ernst.) N.Y., 1927.

Phil 333.5.5   Substansbegriff und Funktionsbegriff. (Cassirer, Ernst.) Berlin, 1910.

Phil 525.4   Substantialism, or Philosophy of knowledge. (Story, T. (pseud.).) Boston, 1879.

Phil 192.115.5   Substanz, System, Struktur. (Rombach, Heinrich.) Freiburg, 1965. 2v.

Phil 8610.958.5   Die Substanz des christlichen Glaubens, ihr Verlust und ihre Neugewinnung. (Buri, Fritz.) Tübingen, 1969.

Phil 1870.88   Substanz und Causalitat bei Berkeley. (Freedman, L.A.) Strassburg, 1902.

Phil 8408.21   Substanz und Thema in der Kunst. (Hirsch, W.) Amsterdam, 1961.

Phil 1750.16   Substanzbegriff in der neueren Philosophie. (Leschbrand, A.) Rostock, 1895.

Phil 3825.9 Der Substanzbegriff Spinozas neu und gegen die herrschenden Ansichten zu Gunsten des Philosophen erläutert. Inaug. Diss. (Friedrichs, Max.) Greifswald, 1896.

Phil 3280.87 Das Substanzproblem bei Arnold Geulincx. Inaug. Diss. (Nagel, Karl.) Köln, 1930.

Phil 1135.105 Das Substanzproblem in der griechischen Philosophie bis zur Blütezeit. (Bauch, B.) Heidelberg, 1910.

Phil 5049.7.5 The substitution of similars. (Jevons, W.S.) London, 1869.

Phil 665.18 Les substituts de l'âme. (Kostyleff, Nicolas.) Paris, 1906.

Phil 5590.34 Il substrato biologico della personalità. (Pastori, Giuseppina.) Brescia, 1945.

Phil 7060.26 Subversion of materialism. (Dennis, J.) Bath, n.d.
Phil 9530.01 Pamphlet box. Success.
Phil 9530.25.10 Success. (Marden, Orison S.) Boston, 1897.
Phil 9530.36.5 Success. 2. ed. (Beaverbrook, W.M.A.) London, 1921.
Phil 9530.11 Success and its conditions. (Whipple, E.P.) Boston, 1880.
Phil 9530.22 The success of defeat. (Babcock, M.D.) N.Y., 1905.
Phil 6315.2.114 The successful error; a critical study of Freudian psychoanalysis. (Allers, R.) N.Y., 1940.

Phil 9530.42 The successful man. (Ranson, J.C.) Richmond, 1887.
VPhil 585.191 Suchodolski, Bogdan. Narodziny nowożytnej filozofii człowieka. Warszawa, 1963.

VPhil 585.191.5 Suchodolski, Bogdan. Rozwój nowożytnej filozofii człowieka. Warszawa, 1967.

Phil 585.191.5 Suchodolski, Bogdan. Rozwój nowożytnej filozofii człowieka. Warszawa, 1967.

Phil 4800.12 Suchodolski, Bogdan. Studia z dziejów polskiej myśli filozoficznej i naukowej. Wyd. 1. Wrocław, 1959.

Phil 7067.48 Sucro, J.G. Widerlegung der Gedancken von Gespentern. Halle im Magdeburgischen, 1748.

Phil 8592.122.25 Sud'ba "Zaveshchaniia" zhana mel'e v XVIII veke. (Kucherenko, Gennadii S.) Moskva, 1968.

Phil 7069.26.40 Sudre, R. Introduction à la métapsychique humaine. Paris, 1926.

Phil 7069.60.5 Sudre, René. Treatise on parapsychology. London, 1960.
Phil 8407.35 Sudurzhanie i forma v izkustvoto. (Goranov, Krusto.) Sofiia, 1958.

Phil 3549.2.30 Südamerikanische Meditationen. (Keyserling, Hermann.) Stuttgart, 1932.

Phil 5545.92 Suellwold, F. Das umittelbare Behalten. Göttingen, 1964.
Phil 3805.223 Suenkel, Wolfgang. Friedrich Schleiermachers Begründung der Pädagogik als Wissenschaft. Düsseldorf, 1964.

Htn Phil 3801.812* Süskind, F.G. von. Prüfung der Schellingischen Lehren von Gott. Tübingen, 1812.

Phil 3805.184 Süskind, H. Der Einfluss Schellings auf die Entwicklung von Schleiermachers System. Tübingen, 1909.

Phil 8599.19.5 The sufficiency of Christianity and Ernst Troeltsch. (Sleigh, R.S.) London, 1923.

Phil 7140.4 La suggestibilité. (Binet, A.) Paris, 1900.
Phil 7140.133 Die Suggestion. (Pöll, Wilhelm.) München, 1951.
Phil 7140.115 Suggestion and autosuggestion. (Baudouin, C.) London, 1920.

Phil 7140.115.3 Suggestion and autosuggestion. (Baudouin, C.) London, 1921.

Phil 7140.115.5 Suggestion and autosuggestion. (Baudouin, C.) N.Y., 1921.
Phil 6680.7A Suggestion and hypnosis made practical. (Kahn, S.) Boston, 1945.

Phil 6671.19.3 Suggestion and mental analysis. 3. ed. (Brown, William.) London, 1923.

Phil 6119.5 Suggestion and psychotherapy. (Jacoby, G.W.) N.Y., 1912.
Phil 7140.1 La suggestion dans l'art. (Souriau, P.) Paris, 1893.
Phil 7140.115.20 Suggestion et autosuggestion. 5. ed. (Baudouin, C.) Neuchâtel, 1938.

Phil 7140.10 Suggestion instead of medicine. (Barrows, C.M.) Boston, 1900.

Phil 6671.8 La suggestion mentale. (Bourru, H.) Paris, 1887.
Phil 6945.2 Suggestion of the law of the lunacy. (Leech, J.) London, 1852.

Phil 7140.115.15 Suggestion und autosuggestion. (Baudouin, C.) Dresden, 1924.

Phil 6680.5.2 Suggestion und Hypnose. 2. Aufl. (Kauffmann, M.) Berlin, 1923.

Phil 6671.5.4 Die Suggestion und ihre Heilwirkung. (Bernheim, H.) Leipzig, 1888.

Phil 6688.1 Suggestion und Reflex. (Schaffer, K.) Jena, 1895.
Phil 6671.20 La suggestione e l'ipnosi come mezzi di analisi psichisa reale. (Benussi, V.) Bologna, 1925.

Phil 8740.1 Suggestions for a public religious service. London, 1876.
Phil 8708.21 Suggestions relative to the philosophy of geology. (Silliman, B.) New Haven, 1839.

Phil 7140.8 Die Suggestions-Therapie. (Schrenck-Notzing, Albert.) Stuttgart, 1892.

Phil 7140.3 Suggestions und Hypnotismus...Volkerpsychologie. (Stoll, O.) Leipzig, 1894.

Phil 8893.44 Sugimori, K. The principles of the moral empire. London, 1917.

Phil 960.9.5 Sugivra, Sadajiro. Hindu logic as preserved in China and Japan. Philadelphia, 1900.

Phil 6112.40 Sugrue, Thomas. There is a river; the story of Edgar Cayce. N.Y., 1959.

Phil 2880.8.270 Suhl, Benjamin. Jean-Paul Sartre: the philosopher as a literary critic. N.Y., 1970.

Phil 7150.32 Suicide, a social and historical study. (Fedden, Henry R.) London, 1938.

Phil 7150.27.20 Suicide; a study in sociology. (Durkheim, É.) Glencoe, 1962.

Phil 7150.11 Suicide, ou La mort volontaire. (Douay, Edmond.) Paris, 1870.

Phil 7150.01 Pamphlet box. Suicide.
Phil 7150.46 Le suicide. (Berdiaev, N.A.) Paris, 1953?
Phil 7150.29 Le suicide. (Blondel, Charles.) Strasbourg, 1933.
Phil 7150.24 Suicide. (Cavan, R.S.) Chicago, 1928.
Phil 6854.14 Suicide. (Choran, Jacques.) N.Y., 1972.
Phil 7150.53 Suicide. (Dublin, L.I.) N.Y., 1963.
Phil 7150.27.5 La suicide. (Durkheim, É.) Paris, 1930.
Phil 7150.27.15 Le suicide. (Durkheim, É.) Paris, 1960.
Phil 7150.40 Le suicide. (Meyuard, L.) Paris, 1958.
Phil 7150.9.5 Suicide. (Morsell, H.) N.Y., 1882.
Phil 7150.3 Suicide and insanity. (Strahan, S.A.K.) London, 1893.
Phil 7150.57 Suicide and Scandinavia. (Hendin, H.) N.Y., 1964.
Phil 6854.6.5 Suicide and the meanings of civilization. (Masaryk, Tomáš Gottigue.) Chicago, 1970.

Phil 7150.44 Le suicide ascétique. (Touraine, Yves.) Paris, 1960.
Phil 7150.21.2 Le suicide et la morale. Thèse. (Bayet, Albert.) Paris, 1922.

Phil 7150.63F Suicide in Durban. (Meer, Fatima.) Durban, 1964.

Phil 7150.22 The suicide problem in the United States. Diss. (Frenay, A.D.) Boston, 1927.

Phil 7150.25 Suicide problems. (Hoffman, F.L.) Newark, 1927.
Phil 7150.12 Les suicidés illustrés. (Dabadie, F.) Paris, 1859.
Phil 7150.65 Suicidio e tentato suicidio. (Centro Nazionale di Prevenzione e Difesa Sociale.) Milano, 1967.

Phil 7150.65.10 Suicidio e tentato suicidio in Italia. (Convegno di Studio su Suicidio eTentato Suicidio in Italia, Milan, 1967.) Milano, 1968.

Phil 7150.47 El suicidio en España durante medio siglo. (Spain. Instituto Nacional de Estadística.) Madrid, 1959.

Phil 7150.35 Il suicidio sotto l'aspetto fisiopatologico. (Palazzo, D.) Napoli, 1953.

Phil 7150.19 Los suicidios en Cataluña y en general en toda España. (Tapia, Ambrosios.) Barcelona, 1900.

Phil 176.200 Die Suingebung des Daseins. (Bauernfeind, Otto.) Meisenheim, 1957.

Htn Phil 8886.21.7* Suite de l'Académie française. (La Primaudaye, P. de.) Paris, 1580.

Phil 2880.1.90 Suite des erreurs et de la vérité. Salomonapolis, 1784.
Phil 349.61 Sukhotin, Anatoli K. Gnoselogicheskii analiz em kosti znaniia. Tomsk, 1968.

Phil 8598.125.5 Sukhov, Andrei D. Filosofskie problemy proiskhozhdeniia religii. Moskva, 1967.

Phil 8598.125 Sukhov, Andrei D. Sotsial'nye i gnoseologicheskie korni religii. Moskva, 1961.

Phil 494.6 Sul materialismo. (Timpanaro, Sebastiano.) Pisa, 1970.
Phil 190.20.3 Sul pragmatismo. (Papini, Giovanni.) Milano, 1913.
Phil 4210.25.20 Sul principio: Pa legge dubia non obliga. (Rosmini-Serbati, Antonio.) Milano, 1851.

Phil 4018.1 Sul rinnovamento della filosofia positiva in Italia. (Siciliani, P.) Firenze, 1871.

Phil 4210.87.5 Sul valore scientifico e sulle pratiche consequenze. (Avogadro della Motta, Emiliano.) Napoli, 1853.

Phil 8598.19 Sulivan, R.J. A view of nature. London, 1794. 6v.
Phil 177.9.5 Sull' uomo; pensieri. (Catara-Lettieri, Antonio.) Messina, 1869.

Phil 1117.10 Sulla cosmologia ionica da talete a eraclita. (Maddalena, Antonio.) Padova, 1940.

Phil 5190.65 Sulla dialettica dell'apriori. (Finazzo, Giancarlo.) Roma, 1966.

Phil 4210.77 Sulla difesa del...A. Rosmini-Serbai. Firenze, 1841.
Phil 3829.3.10 Sulla dottrina dello Spinoza. (Jacobi, F.E.) Bari, 1914.
Phil 583.10 Sulla fenomenologie e la rivelazione delle cose. (Colombo, Arrigo.) Bologna, 1968.

X Cg Phil 6116.2 Sulla fina anatomia degli organi centrali. (Golgi, C.) Napoli, 1886.

Phil 310.594 Sulla fondazione del materialismo storico. (Sabetti, Alfredo.) Firenze, 1962.

Phil 814.2.5 Sulla necessità della instaurazione. 2a ed. (Ondes Reggio, V.) Palermo, 1861.

Phil 293.19 Sulla proposizione il mondo va da se. (Momo, Giovanni.) Lucca, 1827.

Phil 4112.60 Sull'analisi e la sintesi. (Galluppi, Pasquale.) Firenze, 1935.

Phil 6952.3 Sulle alterazioni delle pupille nei pazzi. (Castiglioni, C.) Milano, 1863-65. 2 pam.

Phil 8893.63 Sulle tracce della vita. (Sera, L.G.) Roma, 1907.
Phil 4001.2 Sull'indole e le vicende della filosofia italiana. (Bertinaria, F.) Torino, 1846.

Phil 9070.90 Sullivan, Aloysius Michael. The three-dimensional man. N.Y., 1956.

Phil 5258.69 Sullivan, E.T. Mood in relation to performance. N.Y., 1922.

Phil 5258.40 Sullivan, H. Mediation; the function of thought. Andover, 1871.

Phil 6980.712.1 Sullivan, Harry Stack. Collected works. N.Y., 1965. 2v.

Phil 6980.712.10 Sullivan, Harry Stack. The fusion of psychiatry and social science. N.Y., 1964.

Phil 6980.712 Sullivan, Harry Stack. The interpersonal theory of psychiatry. 1. ed. N.Y., 1953. 4v.

Phil 6980.712.5 Sullivan, Harry Stack. The psychiatric interview. N.Y., 1954.

Phil 6968.34 Sullivan, Harry Stack. Schizophrenia as human process. N.Y., 1962.

Phil 585.155 Sullivan, L.H. Democracy: a man-search. Detroit, 1961.
Phil 2750.11.170 Sullivan, S.M. Maritain's theory of poetic intuition. Fribourg, 1964.

Phil 8893.28 Sullivan, W. The moral class book. Boston, 1831.
Phil 8893.28.3 Sullivan, W. The moral class book. Boston, 1833.
Phil 8893.28.8 Sullivan, W.R. Morality as a religion. London, 1898.
Phil 4006.3.12 Sullo stato attuale...filosofici in Sicilia. (Giovanni, V.) Palermo, 1854.

Htn Phil 4006.3.10* Sullo stato attuale...filosofici in Sicilia. (Giovanni, V.) Palermo, 1854.

Phil 5525.4 Sully, J. An essay on laughter. London, 1902.
Phil 5258.25.11 Sully, J. Human mind. N.Y., 1892. 2v.
Phil 5460.1.5 Sully, J. Die Illusionen. Leipzig, 1884.
Phil 5460.1.3 Sully, J. Illusions: a psychological study. N.Y., 1884.
Phil 5460.1.2 Sully, J. Illusions: a psychological study. pt.1-2. N.Y., 1884.

Phil 5258.25.4 Sully, J. Outlines of psychology. London, 1920.
Phil 5258.25.2 Sully, J. Outlines of psychology. N.Y., 1885.
Phil 5258.25.3.5 Sully, J. Outlines of psychology. N.Y., 1900.
Phil 5258.25.3 Sully, J. Outlines of psychology. 6th ed. London, 1889.
Phil 9430.12 Sully, J. Pessimism. London, 1877.
Phil 9430.12.2 Sully, J. Pessimism. 2. ed. N.Y., 1891.
Phil 5258.25.5 Sully, J. Sensation and intuition. 2d ed. London, 1880.
Phil 5258.25.5 Sully, J. Teacher's handbook of psychology. London, 1886.
Phil 5258.25.5.3 Sully, J. Teacher's handbook of psychology. N.Y., 1888.
Phil 5258.25.6 Sully, J. Teacher's handbook of psychology. N.Y., 1897.
Phil 5258.25.5.5 Sully, J. Teacher's handbook of psychology. 3d ed. N.Y., 1892.

Phil 2280.2.75 Sully, James. My life and friends. London, 1918.
Phil 8419.41 Sully Prudhomme, R.F.A. L'expression dans les beaux-arts. Paris, 1883.

Phil 8735.3 Sully-Prudhomme, René F.A. Le problème de causes finales. Paris, 1903.

Phil 2280.20.30 Sulzberger, Cyrus. My brother death. 1st ed. N.Y., 1961.
Phil 8593.16 Suma contra una nueva edad media. (Nuñez Regueiro, Manuel.) Rosario, 1938.

Phil 75.60 Sumarios y extractos de las tesis doctorales en las secciones de filosofía y pedagogía. (Madrid. Universidad. Facultad de Filosofía y Letras.) 1940-1950

Phil 299.25 Sumina cosmologiae. (Samtonge, F.) Montreal, 1941.
Phil 181.63 Summa contra metaphysicos. (Goedewaagen, T.) Utrecht, 1931.

Htn Phil 8890.7* Summa ethicae. (Pavonio, F.) Oxonii, 1633.

Phil 8953.6 Summa philosophiae christianae. v.7-8. (Donat, J.) Oeniponte, 1920-21.

Htn Phil 1535.4.5* Summa philosophiae quadripartita. (Eustachius a S. Paulo.) Cantabrigiae, 1640.

Htn Phil 1535.4.4* Summa philosophiae quadripartita. (Eustachius a S. Paulo.) Cantabrigiae, 1640.

Htn Phil 1535.4* Summa philosophiae quadripartita. (Eustachius a S. Paulo.) Cantabrigiae, 1698.

Phil 1535.12 Summa philosophica in usum scholarum. (Zigliara, F.T.M.) Lyon, 1884. 3v.

Phil 1535.12.5 Summa philosophica in usum scholarum. 15. ed. v.3. (Zigliara, F.T.M.) Paris, 1912.

Htn Phil 4950.1.30F* Summa theologica. (Thomas Aquinas, St.) Duaci, 1614.

Phil 1535.15.5 Summa totius philosophiae Aristotelicae. pt.1-2. (Bonaventura, St., Cardinal.) Romae, 1635. 2v.

Phil 8950.6.2 Summarium theologiae morales. (Arregui, Antonio M.) Bilbao, 1919.

Phil 8950.6 Summarium theologiae morales. (Arregui, Antonio M.) Bilbao, 1922.

Phil 3549.19 Summe der Filosofie. (Kaiser, Josef.) München, 1961.

Phil 8598.20 Summer, J.B. A treatise...records of the creation. London, 1816. 2v.

Phil 525.115 Summers, M. The physical phenomena of mysticism. N.Y., 1950.

Htn Phil 3552.58* Summi polyhistoris Godefridi Guilielmi Leibntii Protogaea. (Leibniz, Gottfried Wilhelm.) Goettingae, 1749.

Phil 5041.58 Summulae logicales. (Beth, Evert Willem.) Groningen, 1942.

Phil 5049.15 Summulae logicales. (Joannes XXI, Pope.) Venetiis, 1597.

Phil 8598.20.2 Sumner, J.B. A treatise...records of the creation. London, 1818. 2v.

Phil 1020.75 Sunar, Cavit. Islam felsefesi der'sleri. Ankara, 1967.

Phil 525.250 Sunar, Cavit. Mistisizmin ana hatlari. Ankara, 1966.

Phil 6328.55 Sundberg, N.D. Clinical psychology. N.Y., 1962.

Phil 5627.259.15 Sundén, Hjalmar. Religionen och rollerna. Stockholm, 1959.

Phil 974.3.140 Sunden, Hjalmar. Rudolf Steiner. Stockholm, 1962.

Phil 2475.1.298 Sundén, Hjalmar. La théorie bergsonienne de la religion. Thèse. Uppsala, 1940.

Phil 2475.1.298.5 Sundén, Jalmar. La théorie bergsonienne de la religion. Paris, 1947.

Phil 8592.6.6 Sunderland, J.T. James Martineau and his Great Book. Toronto, 1905.

Phil 7060.23 Sunderland, L. Book of human nature. N.Y. 1853.

Phil 7060.23.5 Sunderland, L. Book of psychology. N.Y. 1853.

Phil 5258.26 Sunderland, La Ray. Pathetism. Boston, 1847.

Phil 6688.11 Sunderland, La Roy. "Confessions of a magnetiser" exposed. Boston, 1845.

Phil 193.245 Suner, Soffet. Düsuncenin Tarihteki evrimi. Istanbul, 1967.

Phil 1135.102 Sunne, D.G. Some phases...Post-Aristotelian period. Chicago, 1911.

Phil 6128.40.6 Sunner, Paul. The brain and the mind. N.Y., 1926.

Phil 9500.4 The sunny side of shadow. (Benjamin, F.N. (Mrs.).) Boston, 1887.

Phil 3110.195 Sunrise to eternity. (Staurt, J.J.) Philadelphia, 1957.

Phil 4967.5.10 Supay; diálogos. (Francovich, Guillermo.) Sucre, 1939.

Phil 5850.348 Super, D.E. The psychology of careers. 1st ed. N.Y., 1957.

Phil 6315.2.440 Het super-ego. (Vansina, M.J.) Antwerpen, 1969.

Phil 7069.00.37 Super-physical projection. (Omni Victis (pseud.).) n.p., 19- ?

Phil 6311.26.5 The superego. (Bergler, Edmund.) N.Y., 1952.

Phil 585.175 A superioridade do homen tropical. (Silva Mello, Antonio da.) Rio de Janeiro, 1965.

Phil 6310.1.45 Superiority and social interest. (Adler, A.) Evanston, Ill., 1964.

Phil 7054.94 Supernal theology and life in the spheres. (Warren, O.G.) N.Y., 1852.

Phil 7068.91.15 The supernatural? (Weatherly, L.A.) Bristol, 1891.

Phil 2125.66 The supernatural in relation to the natural. (McCosh, James.) Cambridge, Eng., 1862.

Phil 7068.09 The supernatural magazine. Dublin, 1809.

Phil 8598.59.5 Supernatural religion. (Cassels, W.R.) London, 1874-77. 3v.

Phil 8598.59.10 Supernatural religion. (Cassels, W.R.) London, 1879. 3v.

Phil 8598.59 Supernatural religion. 5th ed. London, 1875. 2v.

Phil 5628.12 El supernaturalismo de Santa Teresa y la filosofía médica. (Perales y Gutiérrez, Arturo.) Madrid, 1894.

Phil 7069.23.11 Supernormal faculties in man. (Osty, Eugène.) London, 1923.

Phil 7069.22.40 Supernormale vermogens. (Tenhaeff, W.H.C.) Amsterdam, 1922.

Phil 186.48.5 Superpersonalism, the outer consciousness. (Lighthall, W.D.) Montreal, 1926.

Phil 8595.14.5 Superstition and common sense. (Piercy, B.H.) London, 1912.

Phil 6322.26 Superstition and society. (Money-Kyrle, R.E.) London, 1939.

Phil 176.139 Superuniversity studies. (Byers, R.P.) Boston, 1936.

Phil 8628.15 Supervivencia del hombre. (Delgado Varela, J.M.) Madrid, 1966.

Phil 5058.70.9 Suppes, Patrick. Introduction to logic. Princeton, N.J., 1966.

Phil 5058.70.10 Suppes, Patrick. Introduction to logic. Princeton, N.J., 1968.

Phil 4073.104.2 A supplement to the critical bibliography. (Grillo, F.) N.Y., 1957. 2v.

Phil 9343.2.3 A supplement to the first part of the G.I. (Darell, W.) London, 1708.

Phil 40.1.5 Supplementary volume. (Aristotelian Society.) London. 1,1918+ 43v.

Phil 19.11.5 Supplements. (Journal of psycho-asthetics.) Fairbault, 1911.

Phil 5922.4.51 The suppressed documents. (Combe, George.) Glasgow, 1836.

Phil 7054.172 Supramundane facts. (Nichols, T.L.) London, 1865.

Phil 7069.56.25 Supranormal ou surnaturel. (Omez; Réginald.) Paris, 1956.

Phil 8610.924 The supremacy of reason. (Reid, W.N.) London, 1924.

Phil 192.36.5 The supremacy of spirit. (Richardson, C.A.) London, 1922.

Phil 8590.9 The supremacy of the spiritual. (Knowles, E.R.) Boston, 1895.

Phil 8876.87 The supreme human tragedy and other essays. (Bullock, Arthur B.) London, 1920.

Phil 8677.20 The supreme identity. (Watts, A.W.) London, 1950.

Phil 720.3 The supreme law. (Tabor, J.A.) Colchester, 1879.

Phil 8882.56 The supreme law of the future man. 2nd ed. (Hochfelder, J.) N.Y., 1909.

Phil 9070.148 The supreme philosophy of man; the laws of life. (Montapert, Alfred Armand.) Englewood Cliffs, N.J., 1970.

Phil 7060.72.7 The supreme problem. (Raupert, J.G.) Buffalo, 1910.

Phil 187.79.2 Sur diverses questions se présentant dans l'étude du concept de réalité. (MacLeod, A.H.D.) Paris, 1927.

Phil 187.79 Sur diverses questions se présentant dans l'étude du concept de réalité. (MacLeod, A.H.D.) Paris, 1927.

Phil 5585.11.11F Sur la collection des sensations. (La Rive, Lucien de.) Genève, 1888.

Phil 150.5 Sur la critique et la fixation du langage philosophique. (Lalande, André.) Paris, 19- . 2 pam.

Phil 3090.35 Sur la notion du tems. (Baader, Franz von.) Munic, 1818.

Phil 2475.1.264 Sur la philosophie Bergsonienne. (Tonquédec, J.) Paris, 1936.

Phil 5812.12 Sur la psychologie animale. (Cuny, Hilaire.) Paris, 1966.

Phil 3625.1.147 Sur la réforme politique des Juifs. (Mirabeau, H.G.R.) Bruxelles, 1788.

Phil 190.58 Sur l'angoisse métaphysique; essai de philosophie. (Pirenne, H.E.) Bruxelles, 1934.

Phil 2905.1.25 Sur le bonheur. (Teilhard de Chardin, Pierre.) Paris, 1966.

Phil 5875.20 Sur le développement de la connaissance d'autrui. Thèse. (Lévy-Schoen, Ariane.) Paris, 1964.

Phil 349.9.10 Sur le fondement de la connaissance. (Schlick, Moritz.) Paris, 1935.

Phil 9245.10 Sur le plaisir. (Grasset, B.) Paris, 1954.

Phil 8520.39 Sur le problème religieux dans la première moitié du XVIIe siècle. (Adam, Antoine.) Oxford, 1959.

Phil 2475.1.191 Sur le succès du Bergsonisme. (Benda, Julien.) Paris, 1914.

Phil 600.18 Sur les chemins de la croyance. (Brunetière, F.) Paris, 1912.

Phil 410.90 Sur les confins du fini, métaphysique, physique, mathématiques et religion. (Chany, Robert de.) Paris, 1968.

Phil 8583.23 Sur les frontières de la foi. (Dugard, Marie.) Paris, 1928.

Phil 3625.1.145 Sur Moses Mendelssohn. (Mirabeau, H.G.R.) Leipzig, 1853.

Phil 3640.320 Sur Nietzsche. (Bataille, Georges.) Paris, 1945.

Phil 1930.8.100 Suranyi-Unger, Nora. Die politische Philosophie von R.G. Collingwood. München, 1960.

Phil 5768.8 Surbled, G. La volonté. 5. éd. Paris, n.d.

Phil 6128.29 Surbled, Georges. L'âme et le cerveau. 3. éd. Paris, 1908.

Phil 5258.98 Surbled, Georges. Éléments de psychologie. Paris, 1894.

Phil 5258.98.2 Surbled, Georges. Éléments de psychologie. 2e éd. Paris, 1894.

Phil 7082.32.2 Surbled, Georges. Le rêve. 2e éd. Paris, 1898.

Phil 177.8.5 The surd of metaphysics. (Carus, Paul.) Chicago, 1903.

Phil 9341.13.5 A sure guide to hell, in seven sections. (Bourn, Benjamin.) London, 1785.

Phil 8626.3 Le surnaturel. (Blanche, C.I.) Paris, 1872.

Phil 7069.22.10 Le surnaturel contemporain. (Godard, André.) Paris, 1922.

Phil 5627.169 Le surnaturel et les dieux d'après les maladies mentales. (Dumas, Georges.) Paris, 1946.

Phil 6327.12.15 Surprise and the psycho-analyst. (Reik, Theodor.) London, 1936.

Phil 7039.2.2 The surprising case of Rachel Baker who prays and preaches in her sleep. v.1-2. 2d ed. (Mais, Charles.) N.Y., 1814.

Phil 1865.180 Surra, G. Studio sulla morale di Geremia Bentham. Torino, 1893.

Phil 8092.11 Surrealism. (Duplessis, V.) N.Y., 1963.

Phil 2477.15.90 Surrealism and the literary imagination; a study of Breton and Bachelard. (Caws, Mary Ann.) The Hague, 1966.

Phil 5722.65 Surréalisme et psychologie. (Cazaux, Jean.) Paris, 1958.

Phil 8400.4.5 Surrealismo e simbolismo. (Archivio di Filosofia.) Padova, 1965.

Phil 8677.2 A survey...wisdom of God in the creation. (Wesley, J.) Bristol, 1770. 3v.

Phil 8836.2.15 A survey of English ethics. (Lecky, W.E.H.) London, 1903.

Phil 310.611 A survey of Marxism. (Gregor, A. James.) N.Y., 1965.

Phil 5066.214 A survey of mathematical logic. (Wang, Hao.) Peking, 1962.

Phil 5066.215 A survey of mathematical logic. (Wang, Hao.) Peking, 1963.

Phil 6315.2.122 Survey of objective studies of psychoanalytic concepts. (Sears, R.R.) N.Y., 1942.

Phil 8705.11 A survey of six days work of creation. (Parker, Benjamin.) London, 1745.

Phil 5051.10.2 A survey of symbolic logic. (Lewis, Clarence I.) Berkeley, 1918.

Phil 5051.10.14 A survey of symbolic logic. (Lewis, Clarence I.) N.Y., 1960.

Phil 5250.17.5 A survey of the science of psychology. (Kantor, J.R.) Bloomington, 1933.

Phil 8640.16 Survival and disembodied existence. (Penelhum, Terence.) London, 1970.

Phil 7069.66.30 Survival of death: for and against. (Beard, Paul.) London, 1966.

Phil 7069.10.19 The survival of man. (Lodge, Oliver Joseph.) N.Y., 1909.

Phil 7069.10.20 The survival of man. 3. ed. (Lodge, Oliver Joseph.) London, 1910.

Phil 7069.16.41 The survival of man. 7. ed. (Lodge, Oliver Joseph.) London, 1916.

Phil 7069.21.20 The survival of the soul and its evolution after death. (Cornillier, PE.) London, 1921.

Phil 7069.12.51 La survivance humaine. 3. ed. (Lodge, Oliver Joseph.) Paris, 1912.

Phil 103.6 Sury, Kurt F. von. Wörterbuch der Psychologie und ihrer Grenzgebiete. Basel, 1951.

Phil 103.6.2 Sury, Kurt F. von. Wörterbuch der Psychologie und ihrer Grenzgebiete. 2. Aufl. Basel, 1958.

Phil 5204.18.3 Sury, Kurt F. von. Wörterbuch der Psychologie und ihrer Gunzgebiete. 3. Aufl. Basel, 1967.

Phil 9590.27 Sushchestovet li sud'ba? (Riazantsev, N.I.) Moskva, 1959.

Phil 8951.8 Sushchestvennyia cherty pravoslavnago. (Babrovnitzki, I.) Elisavetgrad, 1897.

Phil 310.500 Sushchnost' i iavlenie. (Bogdanov, I.A.) Kiev, 1962.

Phil 3090.87 Susini, Eugene. Franz von Baader et le romantisme mystique. Thesis. Paris, 1942. 2v.

Phil 3090.87.5 Susini, Eugene. Franz von Baader et le romantisme mystique. v.2-3. Paris, 1942. 2v.

Phil 3195.6.135 Suter, Jean F. Philosophie et histoire chez W. Dilthey. Bale, 1960.

Phil 331.2.25 Suter, Jules. Die Philosophie von Richard Avenarius. Zurich, 1910.

Phil 5258.149   Suter, Jules. Psychologie; Grundlagen und Aufbau. Frauenfeld, 1942.

Phil 5330.23   Suter, Jules. Zur Theorie der Aufmerksamkeit. Zürich, 1914.

Phil 8843.4   Sutherland, A. The origin and growth of moral instinct. London, 1898. 2v.

Phil 5325.10   Sutherland, A.H. Critique of word association reactions; an experimental study. Menasha, Wisc., 1913.

Phil 5325.10.2   Sutherland, A.H. Critique of word association reactions. n.p., 191-.

Phil 6328.44   Sutherland, John D. Psycho-analysis and contemporary thought. London, 1958.

Phil 310.653   Sutlič, Vanja. Bit i suvremenost. Sarajevo, 1967.

Phil 5520.9.5   Sutro, Emil. The basic law of vocal utterance. N.Y., 1894.

Phil 5520.9.2   Sutro, Emil. Das Doppelwesen der Menschlichen Stimme. Berlin, 1902.

Phil 5520.9.9   Sutro, Emil. Das Doppelwesen in die Religion der Vernunft. Berlin, n.d.

Phil 5520.9.3   Sutro, Emil. Duality of thought and language. N.Y., 1904.

Phil 5520.9   Sutro, Emil. Duality of voice. N.Y., 1899.

Phil 5421.25.76   Suttie, Ian Dishart. The origins of love. N.Y., 1966.

Phil 5871.95   Sutton-Smith, Brian. The sibling. N.Y., 1970.

Phil 310.435   Suvorov, L.M. Bor'ba marksistsko-leninskoi filosofii v SSSR. Moskva, 1961.

VPhil 4012.13   Suvremena talijanska filozofija. (Mikecin, Vjekoslav.) Zagreb, 1966.

Phil 5203.20   Suvremenna materialisticheska psikhologiia. (Emanuilova, E.) Sofiia, 1959.

Phil 8865.660   Suyematsu, Kencho. The ethics of Japan. Washington, 1907.

Phil 5059.21   Suzhdenie i ego vidy. (Tavanets, P.V.) Moskva, 1953.

Phil 525.140   Suzuki, D.T. Mysticism. N.Y., 1957.

Phil 930.33   Suzuki, Daisetz T. A brief history of early Chinese philosophy. 2. ed. London, 1914.

Phil 5876.10.5   Svåra unga år. (Hertzman-Ericson, Merit.) Stockholm, 1967.

Phil 5592.202   Den svårfångade intelligensen. 2. uppl. (Gaestrin, Jan Emanuel.) Stockholm, 1968.

Phil 5640.136.5   Šváb, L. Bibliography of sensory deprivation and social isolation. Prague, 1966.

Phil 3552.135   Svahn, Oscar. Monadlärans uppkomst. Lund, 1863.

Phil 4582.4.83   Svar på kritik af ett kompétensutlåtande. (Leander, P.H.J.) Lund, 1898.

Phil 7080.40A   Svefn og draumar. (Thorlákson, Björg Caritas.) Reykjavík, 1926.

Phil 7082.60   Sveinsson, Ingimundur. 2 draumur. Reykjavík, 1914.

Phil 4080.3.370   Svenaeus, G. Methodologie et spéculation esthétique. Lund, 1961.

Phil 75.24   Svensk filosofi. (Vaunérus, Allen.) Stockholm, 1930.

Phil 4508.10   Den svenska filosofins historia. (Ryding, Erik.) Stockholm, 1959.

Phil 5460.4   Svenson, Frey. Vanföreställningarnas och sinnesvillornas psykologi. Stockholm, 1919.

Phil 493.3   Svenson, S.G. Betraktelseröfver den materialistiska och idealistiska verldsåsigten. Stockholm, 1871.

Phil 3915.158   Svensson, P.I.K. Kunskapsteoretiska studier med särskild hänsyn till Wundts åsikt. Lund, 1904.

Phil 3915.156   Svensson, P.I.K. Wundts etik, framställning och granskning. Lund, 1913.

Phil 8893.59   Svensson, P.K. Om autonoma och heteronoma moralprinciper. Lund, 1904.

Phil 8598.48   Svensson, P.K. Religionsfilosofi. Lund, 1904.

Phil 310.630   Sverdlin, Matvei A. Nekotorye voprosy istoricheskogo materializma i nauchnogo kommunizma. Volgograd, 1965.

Phil 525.234   Svet nezrimyi. Izd. 2. (Lodyzhenskii, M.V.) Petrograd, 1915.

Phil 4756.1.37   Svet vo t'me; opyt khristianskoi etikhi i sotsial'noi filosofii. (Frank, Semen L.) Parizh, 1949

Phil 8610.880.14   Světový kongres volné myšlenky v Praze 8,9,10,11 a 12 září 1907. Podrobná Zpráva. (Congrès Universel de la Libre Pensée, 14th, Prague, 1907.) Praha, 1908.

Phil 585.335   Sviaz' vremen. (Podol'nyi, Roman Grigor'evich.) Moskva, 1969.

Phil 310.754   Svidenskii, Vladimir I. Novye filosofskie aspekty elementno-strukturnykh otnoshenii. Leningrad, 1970.

Phil 672.195   Sviderskii, V.I. Filosofskoe znachenie prostranstvenno-vremennykh predstavlenii v fizike. Leningrad, 1956.

Phil 310.627   Sviderskii, Vladimir I. Nekotorye voprosy dialektiki izmeneniia i razvitiia. Moskva, 1965.

Phil 310.117   Sviderskii, Vladimir Io. O dialektike elementov i struktury v ob"ektivnom mire i v poznanii. Moskva, 1962.

Phil 310.118   Sviderskii, Vladimir Io. O nekotorykh formakh protivorechivosti v ob'ektivnom mire. Leningrad, 1968.

Phil 310.115   Sviderskii, Vladimir Io. Protivorechivost' dvizheniia i ee proiavleniia. Leningrad, 1959.

Phil 8581.54   Sviet nevechernii. (Bulgakov, S.) Moskva, 1917.

Phil 4017.5.5   Sviluppi dello hegelismo in Italia. (Rossi, Mario.) Torino, 1962.

Phil 4017.5   Sviluppi dello hegelismo in Italia. (Rossi, Mario.) Torino, 1957.

Phil 293.26   Lo sviluppo del mondo nelle principali teorie filosofiche. (Morelli, G.) Avellino, 1892.

Phil 4809.814.30   Sviták, Ivan. Lidský smysl kultury. Vyd. 1. Praha, 1968.

Phil 585.370   Sviták, Ivan. Man and his world; a Marxian view. N.Y., 1970.

Phil 193.118   Svoboda, A.V. Ideale Lebensziele. Leipzig, 1901. 2v.

Phil 665.17   Svoboda, A.V. Kritische Geschichte der Ideale. Leipzig, 1886.

Phil 310.250   Svoboda i neobkhodimost'. (Akhmedli, D.) Baku, 1960.

Phil 8401.34   Svoboda khudozhestvennogo tvorchestva. (Apresian, Zorii Grantovich.) Moskva, 1965.

Phil 4762.1.37   Svoboda voli. (Losskii, Nikolai Onufrievich.) Paris, n.d.

Phil 623.43   Svobodomyslie i ateizm v SShA, XVII-XIX vv. (Gol'dberg, N.M.) Leningrad, 1965.

Phil 29.26   Svokodna misel; glasilo Slovenske sekcye Svobodne misli. Praja, 1,1907+ 2v.

Phil 3801.194.5   Lo svolgimento del pensiero di Schelling. (Bausola, Adriano.) Milano, 1969.

Phil 5058.65   Swabey, M. Logic and nature. 2nd ed. N.Y., 1955.

Phil 5058.45   Swabey, Marie. Logic and nature. N.Y., 1930.

Phil 8843.17   Swabey, W.C. Ethical theory. N.Y., 1961.

Phil 349.34   Swabey, William C. Being and being known. N.Y., 1937.

Phil 7069.45.60   Swaffer, Hannen. My greatest story. London, 1945.

Phil 3245.83   Swahn, F.O.B. Kritiska anmärkningar vid I.H. Fichtes ethiska grundsatzer. Lund, 1856.

Phil 1135.130   Swain, Joseph W. The Hellenic origins of Christian asceticism. N.Y., 1916.

Phil 5125.38   Swain, Marshall. Induction, acceptance and rational belief. Dordrecht, 1970.

Phil 183.2   Swain school lectures. (Ingraham, A.) Chicago, 1903. 2v.

Phil 3110.165   Swainson, W.P. Jacob Boehme, the Teutonic philosopher. London, 1921.

Phil 6128.6   Swan, J. The brain in relation to the mind. London, 1854.

Phil 9358.18   Swan, John N. Four lives. Boston, 1935.

Phil 6128.20   Swan, Joseph. Observations on nervous system. London, 1822.

Phil 7074.16   Swan on a black sea: a study in automatic writing, the Cummins-Willet scripts. (Cummins, Geraldine Dorothy.) London, 1970.

VPhil 7069.68   Swanson, Mildred Burris. God bless U, daughter. Independance, 1968.

Phil 2520.78   Swarte, V. de. Descartes, directeur spirituel. Paris, 1904.

Phil 5627.130.10   Swarts, G. Le banc des pénitents. Paris, 1931.

Phil 5627.130.12   Swarts, G. Le banc des pénitents. Thèse. Paris, 1931.

Phil 5627.130   Swarts, G. Salut par la foi et conversion brusque. Paris, 1931.

Phil 5627.130.2   Swarts, G. Salut par la foi et conversion brusque. Thèse. Paris, 1931.

Phil 349.47   Swartz, Robert Jason. Perceiving, sensing, and knowing. 1. ed. Garden City, N.Y., 1965.

Phil 6128.13.12   Swazey, Judith Pound. Reflexes and motor integration; Sherrington's concept of integrative action. Cambridge, 1969.

Phil 6128.7   Swedenborg, E. The brain. London, 1882-87.

Phil 193.43.5   Swedenborg, E. Ontology. Boston, 1901.

Phil 193.43   Swedenborg, E. Ontology. Photoreproduction. Philadelphia, 1880.

Phil 410.4.5   Swedenborg, E. The philosophy of the infinite. Boston, 1848.

Htn   Phil 4635.1.30*   Swedenborg, E. Prodromus philosophiae. Dresdae, 1734.

Phil 6128.53   Swedenborg, Emanuel. Three transactions on the cerebrum; a posthumous work. V.1-2 and atlas. Philadelphia, 1938-40. 3v.

Phil 193.234   Sweeney, Leo. A metaphysics of authentic existentialism. Englewood Cliffs, N.J., 1965.

Phil 7054.5   Sweet, Elizabeth. The future life as described...by spirits. 4th ed. Boston, 1873.

Phil 9350.3.8   Sweet counsel. (Keddie, H.) Boston, 1866.

Phil 5525.61   Sweet madness. (Fry, W.F.) Palo Alto, 1963.

Phil 6128.8.3   Sweetser, W. Mental hygiene. N.Y., 1843.

Phil 6128.8   Sweetser, W. Mental hygiene. N.Y., 1850.

Phil 2280.13.30   Swenson, D. Kierkegaardian philosophy in the faith of a scholar. Philadelphia, 1949.

Phil 5627.83   Swetenham, L. Religious genius. London, 1905.

VPhil 3195.6.175   Swiatopogląd a zycie u Dilheya. (Kuderowicz, Zbigniew.) Warszawa, 1966.

Phil 4803.799.80   Świezawski, Leon. Jan Śniadecki, jego zycie i działalność naukowa. Petersburg, 1898.

Phil 818.38   Świeżawski, Stefan. Zagadnienie historii filozofii. Warszawa, 1966.

Phil 5258.105   Swift, Edgar J. The jungle of the mind. N.Y., 1931.

Phil 5850.349.50   Swift, Edgar J. Psychology and the day's work. N.Y., 1924.

Phil 5058.20   Swinburne, A.J. Picture logic. London, 1881.

Phil 672.252   Swinburne, Richard. Space and time. London, 1968.

Phil 6128.54   Swindle, Percy Ford. Quantum reactions and associations; a theory of physical and physiological units or quanta. Boston, 1922.

Phil 3500.108   Swing, Thomas K. Kant's transcendental logic. New Haven, 1969.

Phil 5627.56.5   Swisher, Walter. Religion and the new psychology. Boston, 1920.

Phil 349.23   Switalski, B.N. Probleme der Erkenntnis. v.1-2. Münster in Westfalen, 1923.

Phil 1504.3.6   Switalski, B.W. Des Chalcidius Kommentar zu Platos Timaeus. v.3, pt.6. Münster, 1902.

Phil 5058.38   Switalski, B.W. Vom Denken und Erkennen. Kempten, n.d.

Phil 2070.130   Switalski, B.W. Der Wahrheitsbegriff des Pragmatismus nach William James. Braunsberg, 1910.

Phil 3905.86   Swoboda, H. Otto Weiningers Tod. 2. Aufl. Wien, 1923.

Phil 5258.33   Swoboda, H. Studien zur Grundlegung der Psychologie. Leipzig, 1905.

Phil 6128.17.5   Swodenborgs konespondenslära. (Jonsson, Inge.) Stockholm, 1969.

Phil 400.31.10   Sydow, Eckhart von. Der Gedanke des Ideal-Reichs in der idealistischen Philosophie von Kant bis Hegel. Leipzig, 1914.

Phil 3850.48   Sydow, W. Das Geheimnis des ewigen Lebens und des jüngsten Tages. Berlin, 1960?

Phil 960.139   Syed, M.H. L'optimisme dans la pensée indienne. Thèse. n.p., 1932.

Phil 8598.21   Sykes, A.A. The principles and connexion of natural and revealed religion distinctly considered. London, 1740.

Phil 5258.180.5   Sykes, G. The hidden remnant. London, 1962.

Phil 5258.180   Sykes, G. The hidden remnant. 1. ed. N.Y., 1962.

Phil 2520.236   Sykes, L.C. A philosopher for the modern university. Leicester, 1951.

Phil 5242.40   Syllabus for the first course in experimental psychology. (Crawley, Sumner Lee.) N.Y., 1930.

Phil 5402.2   Syllabus of...lectures on the psychology of pain. (Gilman, B.T.) Worcester, Mass., 1893.

Phil 5043.5.5A   Syllabus of a proposed system of logic. (DeMorgan, Augustus.) London, 1860.

Phil 5058.16   A syllabus of logic. (Solly, T.) Cambridge, 1839.

Phil 5241.23   A syllabus of psychology. (Bawden, H.H.) Poughkeepsie, N.Y., 1902.

Phil 9560.52   Le syllogisme prudentiel. (Morisset, B.) Laval, 1961.

Phil 3100.70   Syllogismorum analyticorum origines et ordinem naturalem. (Beneke, F.E.) Berolini, 1839.

Phil 5170.10   Der Syllogismus. (Lebzeltern, G.) Graz, 1948.

Phil 175.17   The syllogistic philosophy. (Abbott, F.E.) Boston, 1906. 2v.

Htn   Phil 9173.2*   Sylva nuptialis. (Nevizanis, J. de.) n.p., 1602.

Htn   Phil 1850.71*   Sylva Sylvarum. (Bacon, Francis.) London, 1627.

Phil 4479.1.30   Sylvan, F. Filosofia e politica no destino de Portugal. Lisboa, 1963.

Phil 4635.3.31   Sylwan, O.C. Naturvetenskap eller .netafysik? Stockholm, 1881.

Phil 4635.3.33   Sylwan, O.C. Vetenskapens evangelium. Stockholm, 1879.

Phil 5520.75.10   Symbol, status. 1. ed. (Hayakawa, S.I.) N.Y., 1963.

Phil 180.64 — Symbol and metaphor in human experience. (Foss, Martin.) Princeton, N.J., 1949.
Phil 3160.12.10 — Symbol and reality. (Hamburg, C.H.) The Hague, 1956.
Phil 5520.414 — Symbol formation. (Werner, H.) N.Y., 1963.
Phil 5520.31 — Symbol in der Psychologie. (Häberlin, Paul.) Bern, 1916.
Phil 8890.6 — Symbolae ad systemata philosophiae moralis. (Paulsen, F.) Berolini, 1871.
Phil 165.190 — Le symbole. Paris, 1959.
Phil 6319.1.8.2 — Symbole der Wandlung. (Jung, C.G.) Zürich, 1952.
Phil 2630.7.39 — Symboles fondament aux de la science sacrée. (Guénon, René.) Paris, 1962.
Phil 5520.545 — Symbolic behavior. (Thass-Thienemann, Théodore.) N.Y., 1968.
Phil 5066.80 — Symbolic logic. (Berkeley, E.C.) N.Y., 1955.
Phil 5066.46 — Symbolic logic. (Fitch, F.B.) N.Y., 1952.
Phil 5066.200 — Symbolic logic. (Lee, Harold Newton.) N.Y., 1961.
Phil 5051.10.10 — Symbolic logic. (Lewis, Clarence I.) N.Y., 1932.
Phil 5061.1.6 — Symbolic logic. (Venn, J.) London, 1894.
Phil 5058.28.28 — Symbolic logic: method and development. (Smith, Henry B.) N.Y., 1927.
Phil 5043.8.7 — Symbolic logic. pt.1. 4th ed. (Dodgson, C.L.) London, 1897.
Phil 5066.54.2 — Symbolic logic. 2nd ed. (Copi, Irving M.) N.Y., 1965.
Phil 5051.10.12 — Symbolic logic. 2nd ed. (Lewis, Clarence I.) N.Y., 1959.
Phil 5052.12 — Symbolic logic and its applications. (MacColl, H.) London, 1906.
Phil 5066.233 — Symbolic logic and language. (Dickoff, James.) N.Y., 1965.
Phil 6332.45 — The symbolic quest. (Whitmont, Edward.) N.Y., 1969.
Phil 5645.60 — Symboliek van de kleut. (Smits, Willem Canisius Maria.) Amsterdam, 1967.
Phil 3903.5.45 — Symboliek van de voet. (Verhoeven, Cornelius W.M.) Assen, 1956.
Phil 6022.4 — Symbolik der Gesichtsformen. (Märker, Friedrich.) Erlenbach, 1933.
Phil 6060.29 — Symbolik der Handschrift. (Pulver, Max.) Zürich, 1931.
Phil 7082.4.5 — Die Symbolik des Traumes. (Schubert, Gotthilf Heinrich von.) Heidelberg, 1968.
Phil 7082.4.3 — Die Symbolik des Traumes. 3. Aufl. (Schubert, Gotthilf Heinrich von.) Leipzig, 1840.
Phil 353.9.2 — Symbolism: its meaning and effect. (Whitehead, A.N.) Cambridge, Eng., 1928.
Phil 353.9A — Symbolism: its meaning and effect. (Whitehead, A.N.) N.Y., 1927.
Phil 8581.72 — Symbolism and belief. (Bevan, E.R.) London, 1938.
Phil 335.2 — Symbolism and truth. (Eaton, R.M.) Cambridge, 1925.
Phil 5520.24 — Symbolism or mind matter, language as elements of thinking. (Haig, James.) Edinburgh, 1869.
Phil 2725.11.95 — Le symbolisme dans la philosophie. (Millet, Louis.) Paris, 1959.
Phil 348.18 — Symbolization and fictional reference. (Regnéll, Hans.) Lund, 1949.
Phil 3625.26 — Symbolos. (Müller, Max.) München, 1967.
Phil 70.92 — Symbols and values; an initial study. (Conference on Science, Philosophy and Religion.) N.Y., 1954.
Phil 8590.29 — The symbols of religious faith. (Kimpel, B.F.) N.Y., 1954.
Phil 6329.6 — Het symbool in de psychoanalyse. (Tuinstra, C.L.) Amsterdam, 1933.
Phil 665.71 — Syme, David. The soul. London, 1903.
Phil 9590.10 — Symes, (Mrs.) Character reading. Akron, O., 1903.
Phil 8419.24 — Symonds, J.A. The principles of beauty. London, 1857.
Htn — Phil 9495.36* — Symonds, J.A. A problem in modern ethics. London, 1896.
Phil 974.2.60 — Symonds, John. Madame Blavatsky. London, 1959.
Htn — Phil 1145.55* — Symonds, John A. A problem in Greek ethics. London, 1901.
Phil 5850.349 — Symonds, P.M. Diagnosing personality and conduct. N.Y., 1931.
Phil 5258.136A — Symonds, P.M. The dynamics of human adjustment. N.Y., 1946.
Phil 5258.136.5A — Symonds, P.M. The ego and the self. N.Y., 1951.
Phil 5415.10 — La sympathie. (Ochanine, D.) Paris, 1938.
Phil 5415.01 — Pamphlet box. Sympathy.
Phil 9070.146 — The sympathy of life. (Natesan, B.) Madras, 1967.
Phil 8587.15 — The sympathy of religions. (Higginson, T.W.) Boston, 1876.
Phil 8587.15.2 — The sympathy of religions. (Higginson, T.W.) Chicago, 1893.
Phil 70.26 — Symphilosophein. (Deutscher Kongress für Philosophie, 3rd, Brenen, 1950.) München. 1952
Phil 197.13 — The symphony of life. (Wood, H.) Boston, 1901.
Phil 70.100 — Symposia. 1. ed. (International Congress of Philosophy, 13th, México, 1963.) México. 1963
Phil 270.129 — Symposia on basic human values and causality. (Pakistan. Philosophical Congress, 7th, Dacca, Pakistan, 1960.) Lahore, 1960?
Phil 28.10 — Symposion; philosophische Zeitschrift für Forschung und Aussprache. Erlangen. 1-3
Phil 28.21 — Symposion. Freiburg. 1-4,1948-1955 4v.
Phil 70.65 — Symposium. (Group for the Advancement of Psychiatry.) N.Y. 1-7 2v.
Phil 70.3.71 — Symposium. (International Congress of Psychology, 18th, Moscow, 1966.) Moskva. 1966 19v.
Phil 70.85 — Symposium Iberoamericano de Filosofía. Primer Symposium Iberoamericano de Filosofía. Guatemala, 1961.
Phil 70.84 — Symposium Iberoamericano de Filosofía. Trabajos. Guatemala.
Phil 2340.10.93A — Symposium in honor of the 70th birthday of Alfred North Whitehead. Cambridge, 1932.
Phil 5500.42 — Symposium on Cognition, 1st, Pittsburgh, 1965. Problem solving: research, method and theory. N.Y., 1966.
Phil 5360.22 — Symposium on Cognition, 2d, Pittsburgh, 1966. Concepts and the structure of memory. N.Y., 1967.
Phil 5500.55 — Symposium on Cognition, 3rd, Carnegie Institute of Technology, 1967. Formal representation of human judgment. N.Y., 1968.
Phil 5400.165 — Symposium on Expression. Expression of the emotions in man. N.Y., 1963.
Phil 7069.56.10 — Symposium on extrasensory perception. (Ciba Foundation.) London, 1956.
Phil 6118.8 — Symposium on Interdisciplinary Research, University of Wisconsin. Biological and biochemical basis of behavior. Madison, Wis., 1958.
Phil 1845.16.5 — Symposium on J.L. Austin. (Fann, K.T.) London, 1969.
Phil 5548.15 — Symposium on motivation. (United States Research and Development Board. Committee on Human Resources.) Washington, 1953.
Phil 5590.431A — Symposium on Personality Change, University of Texas. Personality change. N.Y., 1964.

Phil 5640.133 — Symposium on Principles of Sensory Communication. Sensory communication...Symposium...July 19-Aug. 1, 1959, M.I.T. Cambridge, 1962.
Phil 5274.14 — Symposium on Psychological Factor Analysis, Uppsala University, 1953. Uppsala symposium on psychological factor analysis, 17-19 March 1953. Copenhagen, 1953.
Phil 5545.186 — Symposium on psychology of learning basic to military training problems. (United States Research and Development Board.) Washington, 1953.
Phil 6950.10 — Symposium on Schizophrenia. Schizophrenia. N.Y., 1959.
Phil 5640.136 — Symposium on Sensory Deprivation. Sensory deprivation. Cambridge, 1961.
Phil 1750.490 — Symposium sobre existencialismo. pts.1-7. (Universidad Nacional del Litoral. Santa Fé, Argentina. Instituto de Filosofía.) Rosario, 195-?
Phil 6968.12.5 — Symptomatology, psychognosis, and diagnosis of psychopathic diseases. (Sidis, Boris.) Boston, 1914.
Phil 6328.66 — Symptoms of personality disorder. (Small, Saul Mouchly.) N.Y., 1944.
Phil 5642.15 — The synaesthesia of a blind subject. (Wheeler, R.H.) Eugene, 1920.
Phil 6115.9 — Les synalgies et les synesthésies. (Fromentel, Henry de.) Paris, 1888.
Phil 8850.3 — Syneidesis-conscientia. (Zucker, Friedrich.) Jena, 1928.
Phil 8968.17 — Synerdesis. (Stelzenberger, J.) Paderborn, 1963.
Phil 4762.4.30 — La synergie spirituelle. (Lapshin, I.I.) Praha, 1935.
Phil 1135.179 — Syngeneia. (Des Places, E.) Paris, 1964.
Phil 182.26 — Synopsis metaphysicae. (Hutcheson, F.) Glasguae, 1756.
Phil 5924.1 — Synopsis of phrenology. (Ellis, G.W.) Boston, 1844.
Phil 40.1.3 — Synoptic index, 1900-49. (Aristotelian Society.) Oxford, 1949. v.
Phil 1930.16.30 — Synoptic naturalism. (Canger, Georg P.) Minneapolis, 1960.
Phil 815.33 — Synoptike historia tes philosophias. 3. ed. (Papalexandrou, K.) Athens, 1969.
Phil 5643.68.5 — Synsoplevedefigurer. (Rubin, Edgar.) København, 1915.
Phil 8610.828.5 — Syntagma of the evidences of the Christian religion. (Taylor, Robert.) Boston, 1828.
Phil 5520.695 — Syntaktische Faktoren im verbalen Lernen. (Wettler, Manfred.) Bern, 1970.
Phil 1504.10 — Die Synteresis nach dem hl. Thomas von Aquin. v.10, pt.1-2. (Renz, O.) Münster, 1911.
Phil 303.8 — La synthèse concrète. (Warrain, F.) Paris, 1910.
Phil 1701.7.5 — La synthèse des connaissances et l'histoire. Thèse. (Berr, Henri.) Paris, 1898.
Phil 335.2.34.14 — La synthèse mentale. (Dwelshauvers, George.) Paris, 1908.
Phil 2490.60 — Synthèse subjective. (Comte, Auguste.) Paris, 1856.
Phil 5245.18 — The synthesis of mind. (Ford, Corydon.) n.p., 1883-1893.
Phil 8700.12 — The synthesis of science and religion. (Kettner, F.) N.Y., 1939.
Phil 187.95 — Synthetic philosophy. (Manley, R.M.) Cleveland, Ohio, 1931.
Phil 5246.39 — A synthetic psychology. (Griffith, Percy.) London, 1927.
Phil 186.19 — Synthetica. (Laurie, S.S.) London, 1906. 2v.
Phil 8402.18 — Synthetische Kunstwissenschaft. (Balet, Leo.) Stuttgart? 1938.
Phil 4843.6 — Syntome historia tēs neoellenikēs philosophias. (Apostolopoulos, Ntimēs.) Athena? 1949.
Phil 5258.81 — Syrkin, N. Was muss man von der Psychologie wissen? Berlin, n.d.
Phil 6121.55 — System, structure, and experience. (Laszlo, Ervin.) N.Y., 1969.
Phil 6028.2 — A system...physiognomy. (Stanton, M.O.) Philadelphia, 1890. 2v.
Phil 178.37.15 — Das System... (Dingler, Hugo.) München, 1930.
Phil 8411.8 — System der Ästhetik. (Kahlert, August.) Leipzig, 1846.
Phil 8422.5 — System der Ästhetik. (Volkelt, J.) München, 1905-14. 3v.
Phil 8423.26.2 — System der Ästhetik als Wissenschaft von der Idee der Schönheit, reprografischer Nachdruck von 1830. (Weisse, Christian H.) Hildesheim, 1966.
Phil 8972.4 — System der christlichen Ethik. (Werner, Karl.) Regensburg, 1888. 2v.
Phil 8967.5.4 — System der christlichen Moral. (Reinhard, Franz V.) Wittenberg, 1802-05. 5v.
Phil 8967.5.10 — System der christlichen Moral. (Reinhard, Franz V.) Wittenberg, 1814-15. 5v.
Phil 2138.35.10 — System der deductiven und inductiven Logik. (Mill, John S.) Leipzig, 1872. 3 pam.
Phil 2138.35.8 — System der deductiven und inductiven Logik. 2e Aufl. (Mill, John S.) Braunschweig, 1862-63. 2v.
Phil 2138.35.6 — System der deductiven und inductiven Logik. 4e Aufl. v.1-2. (Mill, John S.) Braunschweig, 1877.
Phil 175.1 — System der Elementarphilosophie. (Abicht, J.H.) Erlangen, 1795.
Phil 3245.65 — System der Ethik. (Fichte, Immanuel Hermann.) Leipzig, 1850-51. 2v.
Phil 8885.1 — System der Ethik. (Kaulich, W.) Prag, 1877.
Phil 8887.129 — System der Ethik. (Margolius, Hans.) Freiburg, 1967.
Phil 8890.6.5 — System der Ethik. (Paulsen, F.) Berlin, 1889.
Phil 8890.6.6 — System der Ethik. (Paulsen, F.) Berlin, 1896-97. 2v.
Phil 8890.6.7 — System der Ethik. (Paulsen, F.) Stuttgart, 1903. 2v.
Phil 8890.6.5.8 — System der Ethik. 2. Aufl. (Paulsen, F.) Berlin, 1891.
Phil 8890.6.5.9 — System der Ethik. 3. Aufl. (Paulsen, F.) Berlin, 1894. 2v.
Phil 8890.6.8 — System der Ethik. 11. und 12. Aufl. (Paulsen, F.) Stuttgart, 1921. 2v.
Phil 5245.16.3 — System der gerichtlichen Psychologie. 3e Aufl. (Friedreich, J.B.) Regensburg, 1852.
Phil 8886.39 — System der gesammten Ethik. Band 1-2. (Landau, L.R.) Berlin, 1877-78.
Phil 197.1.7 — System der Idealphilosophie. (Wagner, J.) Leipzig, 1804.
Phil 181.13 — System der kritischen Philosophie. (Göring, C.) Leipzig, 1874. 2v.
Phil 3665.8.30 — System der kritischen Philosophie auf den Satz des Bewustseyns gegründet. (Neeb, Johann.) Bruxelles, 1968. 2v.
Phil 5041.1 — System der Logik. (Bachmann, C.F.) Leipzig, 1828.
Phil 3100.40 — System der Logik. (Beneke, F.E.) Berlin, 1842. 2v.
Phil 5044.2 — System der Logik. (Esser, Wilhelm.) Münster, 1830.
Phil 3260.49 — System der Logik. (Fries, J.F.) Heidelberg, 1811.
Phil 3260.50 — System der Logik. (Fries, J.F.) Heidelberg, 1837.
Phil 5047.31 — System der Logik. (Heilner, R.) Leipzig, 1897.
Phil 5060.1 — System der Logik. (Ueberweg, F.) Bonn, 1857.
Phil 3895.49 — System der Logik. (Ulrici, H.) Leipzig, 1852.
Phil 5057.1 — System der Logik. v.1-2. (Reichlin-Meldegg, K.A.F.) Wien, 1870.
Phil 3260.50.5 — System der Logik. 3e Aufl. (Fries, J.F.) Leipzig, 1914.

Phil 5060.1.6 System der Logik. 5e Aufl. (Ueberweg, F.) Bonn, 1882.
Phil 192.12 System der Logik und der Metaphysik. (Ritter, Heinrich.) Göttingen, 1856. 2v.
Phil 5045.6.2 System der Logik und Metaphysik oder Wissenschaftslehre. 2e Aufl. (Fischer, Kuno.) Heidelberg, 1865.
Phil 176.100 System der Metaphysik. (Braniss, C.J.) Breslau, 1834.
Phil 3260.30 System der Metaphysik. (Fries, J.F.) Heidelberg, 1824.
Phil 3310.3.31 System der Metaphysik. (George, L.) Berlin, 1844.
Phil 185.27 System der Metaphysik. (Kaulish, W.) Prag, 1874.
Phil 192.7.2 System der Metaphysik. (Reinhold, C.E.) Jena, 1854.
Phil 194.24 System der Metaphysik. (Thone, Johannes F.) Dresden, 1908.
Phil 3100.30 System der Metaphysik and Religionsphilosophie. (Beneke, F.E.) Berlin, 1840.
Phil 179.1 System der metaphysischen Grundbegriffe. (Engel, G.E.) Berlin, 1852.
Phil 8897.26 System der moralischen Bewusstseins. (Woltmann, L.) Düsseldorf, 1898.
Phil 8879.7 System der Moralphilosophie. (Eschenmayer, C.A.A.) Stuttgart, 1818.
Phil 3270.16.31 Das System der ontischen Kategorien. (Fechner, O.) Hildesheim, 1961.
Phil 3200.8.10 System der Philosophie. (Ehrlich, W.) Bad Ragaz, 1966.
Phil 3565.30 System der Philosophie. (Lotze, Hermann.) Leipzig, 1874-79. 2v.
Phil 3565.30.25 System der Philosophie. (Lotze, Hermann.) Leipzig, 1912. 2v.
Phil 187.14 Das System der Philosophie. (Michelet, K.L.) Berlin, 1876-1881. 5v.
Phil 187.70 System der Philosophie. (Müller, Josef.) Mainz, 1898.
Phil 3915.30 System der Philosophie. (Wundt, Wilhelm.) Leipzig, 1889.
Phil 192.63 System der Philosophie. v.1. (Reiser, Beat.) Einsiedeln, 1920.
Phil 193.247 System der Philosophie. v.1-3. Pt.1-2. (Schmitz, Hermann.) Bonn, 1964. 5v.
Phil 177.41 System der Philosophie. v.1-4. (Commer, E.) Münster, 1883.
Phil 3915.30.2 System der Philosophie. 2. Aufl. (Wundt, Wilhelm.) Leipzig, 1897.
Phil 3565.30.3A System der Philosophie. 2e Aufl. (Lotze, Hermann.) Leipzig, 1880-84. 2v.
Phil 3915.30.5 System der Philosophie. 3. Aufl. v.1-2. (Wundt, Wilhelm.) Leipzig, 1907.
Phil 3260.31 System der Philosophie als evidente Wissenschaft. (Fries, J.F.) Leipzig, 1804.
Phil 3415.70 System der Philosophie im Grundriss. (Hartmann, Eduard von.) Bad Sachsa, 1907-09. 8v.
Phil 180.12.5 System der Philosophie im Umriss. (Frohschammer, J.) München, 1892.
Phil 8888.6.2 System der philosophischen Ethik und Pädagogik. (Nelson, Leonard.) Göttingen, 1932.
Phil 8888.6.3 System der philosophischen Rechtslehre und Politik. (Nelson, Leonard.) Leipzig, 1924.
Phil 5058.3 System der Positiven Logik. (Schaden, E.A.) Erlangen, 1841.
Phil 3528.35.2 System der praktischen Philosophie. (Krug, Wilhelm Traugott.) Königsberg, 1830-38. 2v.
Phil 3528.35.5 System der praktischen Philosophie. (Krug, Wilhelm Traugott.) Wien, 1818.
Phil 3528.35 System der praktischen Philosophie. 2. Aufl. (Krug, Wilhelm Traugott.) Königsberg, 1817-19. 3v.
Phil 6113.10 System der Psychologie. (Dimmler, H.) München, n.d.
Phil 5245.9.5 System der Psychologie. (Fortlage, A.R.K.) Leipzig, 1855. 2v.
Phil 181.43 Das System der Seinsgebiete als Grundlage einer umfassenden Philosophie. (Geissler, Kurt.) Leipzig, 1919.
Htn Phil 3246.72* Das System der Sittenlehre. (Fichte, Johann Gottlieb.) Jena, 1798.
Phil 3525.70 System der Sittenlehre. Bd.1. (Krause, K.C.F.) Leipzig, 1810.
Phil 3246.72.3 Das System der Sittenlehre nach Prinzipien der Wissenschaftslehre, 1798. 2. Aufl. (Fichte, Johann Gottlieb.) Hamburg, 1969.
Phil 3246.72.2 Das System der Sittenlehre nach Prinzipien der Wissenschaftslehre. (Fichte, Johann Gottlieb.) Neuausgabe, 1963.
Phil 3425.68.5 System der Sittlichkeit. (Hegel, Georg Wilhelm Friedrich.) Osterwiech, 1893.
Phil 8877.53 System der speculativen Ethik. (Chalybäus, Heinrich.) Leipzig, 1850. v.
Phil 8897.54 System der speculativen Ethik. v.1-2. (Wirth, J.U.) Heilbronn, 1841-42.
Phil 1200.13 System der stoischen Philosophie. (Tiedemann, D.) Leipzig, 1776. 3v.
Phil 2270.31.2 System der synthetischen Philosophie: Biologie. (Spencer, Herbert.) Stuttgart, 1876-77. 2v.
Phil 2270.31.5 System der synthetischen Philosophie: Ethik. (Spencer, Herbert.) Stuttgart, 1879-95. 2v.
Phil 2270.31 System der Synthetischen Philosophie: Grundlagen. (Spencer, Herbert.) Stuttgart, 1875.
Phil 2270.31.3 System der synthetischen Philosophie: Psychologie. (Spencer, Herbert.) Stuttgart, 1882-86. 2v.
Phil 2270.31.4 System der synthetischen Philosophie: Sociologie. (Spencer, Herbert.) Stuttgart, 1877-97. 4v.
Phil 3552.69.30 System der Theologie. (Leibniz, Gottfried Wilhelm.) Mainz, 1820.
Phil 3528.30.2 System der theoretischen Philosophie. (Krug, Wilhelm Traugott.) Königsberg, 1806-18. 2v.
Phil 3528.30 System der theoretischen Philosophie. (Krug, Wilhelm Traugott.) Königsberg, 1823-33. 3v.
Phil 5066.28 Ein System der typenfreien Logik. Pt.1. (Ackermann, W.) Leipzig, 1941-
Phil 3549.7.90 Das System der Werte. (Port, Kurt.) München, 1929.
Phil 8879.12 System der Werttheorie. (Ehrenfels, C.) Leipzig, 1897.
Phil 5767.7 Das System der Willensbestimmungen. (Reiff, J.F.) Tübingen, 1842.
Phil 3425.72 System der Wissenschaft. (Hegel, Georg Wilhelm Friedrich.) Bamberg, 1807.
Phil 3780.38 System der Wissenschaft. (Rosenkranz, Karl.) Königsberg, 1850.
Phil 4195.81 Das System des Johannes Pico. (Dreydorff, Georg.) Warburg, 1858.
Phil 400.17 System des objectiven Idealismus. (Bergmann, J.) Marburg, 1903.
Phil 400.99.5 Das System des Panhumanismus. (Kränzlin, Gerhard.) Zürich, 1949.
Phil 3800.180.7 System des transscendentalen Idealismus. (Schelling, F.W.J. von.) Hamburg, 1957.

Htn Phil 3800.180* System des transscendentalen Idealismus. (Schelling, F.W.J. von.) Tübingen, 1800.
Htn Phil 3800.180.5* System des transscendentalen Idealismus. (Schelling, F.W.J. von.) Tübingen, 1800.
Phil 960.3 System des Vedânta. (Deussen, P.) Leipzig, 1883.
Phil 8955.2 System du christliche Sittlichkeit. (Frank, F.H.R.) Erlangen, 1884-87. 2v.
Phil 341.1 System einer Theorie der Grenzbegriffe. (Kerry, B.) Leipzig, 1890.
Phil 8410.5 A system of aesthetics. (Jacques, G.H.) Dublin, 1921-
Phil 5590.428 A system of characterology. (Boer, J. de.) Assen, 1963.
Phil 8953.5 System of Christian ethics. (Dorner, I.A.) N.Y., 1887.
Phil 8957.2 System of Christian ethics. (Harless, G.C.A.) Edinburgh, 1868.
Phil 8888.6.30 System of ethics. (Nelson, Leonard.) New Haven, 1956.
Phil 8890.6.9 System of ethics. (Paulsen, F.) N.Y., 1899.
Phil 8890.6.11 System of ethics. (Paulsen, F.) N.Y., 1899.
Phil 5058.28.18 A system of formal logic. (Smith, Henry B.) Ann Arbor, 1925.
Phil 5058.28.19 A system of formal logic. pt.1. (Smith, Henry B.) Columbus, 1926.
Phil 8885.16 A system of general ethics. (Keyser, Leander S.) Burlington, 1918.
Phil 5252.2 System of intellectual philosophy. (Mahan, A.) N.Y., 1847.
Phil 5052.1 A system of logic. (McGregor, P.) N.Y., 1862.
Htn Phil 2138.35.1* A system of logic. (Mill, John S.) London, 1843. 2v.
Phil 2138.35.4 A system of logic. (Mill, John S.) London, 1886.
Phil 2138.35.5 A system of logic. (Mill, John S.) London, 1896.
Phil 2138.35.5.3 A system of logic. (Mill, John S.) London, 1898.
Phil 2138.35.5.10 A system of logic. (Mill, John S.) London, 1911.
Phil 2138.35.20 A system of logic. (Mill, John S.) London, 1965.
NEDL Phil 2138.35.3 A system of logic. (Mill, John S.) N.Y., 1869.
Phil 5060.1.5 System of logic. (Ueberweg, F.) London, 1871.
NEDL Phil 2138.35.2 A system of logic. 3rd ed. (Mill, John S.) London, 1851. 2v.
Phil 2138.35.3.15A A system of logic. 8th ed. (Mill, John S.) London, 1872. 2v.
Phil 2138.35.3.19 A system of logic. 8th ed. (Mill, John S.) N.Y., 1874.
Phil 2138.35.3.23 A system of logic. 8th ed. (Mill, John S.) N.Y., 1881.
Phil 5056.1A A system of logistic. (Quine, Willard Van Orman.) Cambridge, 1934.
Phil 5252.2.5 System of mental philosophy. 4th ed. (Mahan, A.) Chicago, 1886.
Phil 180.17.2 A system of metaphysics. (Fullerton, G.S.) N.Y., 1914.
Phil 8881.21 A system of moral philosophy. (Grove, H.) London, 1749.
Phil 8881.21.4 A system of moral philosophy. (Grove, H.) London, 1755. 2v.
Phil 2053.30 System of moral philosophy. (Hutcheson, F.) Glasgow, 1755. 2v.
Htn Phil 2053.30.1* System of moral philosophy. (Hutcheson, F.) London, 1755. 2v.
Phil 9178.4 A system of moral philosophy. (Steel, D.) Boston, 1847.
Phil 8882.9.5 A system of moral science. (Hickok, L.P.) Boston, 1880.
Phil 8882.9 A system of moral science. (Hickok, L.P.) Schenectady, 1853.
Phil 8882.9.3 A system of moral science. 3rd ed. (Hickok, L.P.) N.Y., 1873.
Phil 8665.3 A system of natural theism. (Keyser, L.S.) Burlington, Ia., 1917.
Phil 2648.31 System of nature. (Holbach, Paul Henri T.) N.Y., 1835.
Phil 5922.3.7 A system of phrenology. (Combe, George.) Boston, 1835.
Phil 5922.3.3 A system of phrenology. (Combe, George.) Boston, 1838.
Phil 5922.3.5 A system of phrenology. (Combe, George.) N.Y., 1841.
Phil 5243.15 A system of psychology. (Dunlap, K.) N.Y., 1912.
Phil 5259.3 System of psychology. (Thompson, D.G.) London, 1884. 2v.
Phil 299.16 The system of the universe. (Society of Universal Science. Belmont, Mass.) Belmont, 1924.
Phil 960.3.3 System of the Vedânta. (Deussen, P.) Chicago, 1912.
Phil 3552.69 A system of theology. (Leibniz, Gottfried Wilhelm.) London, 1850.
Phil 486.7 System und Geschichte des Naturalismus. (Löwenthal, E.) Leipzig, 1863.
Phil 3425.223 System und Methode in Hegels Philosophie. (Heimann, B.) Leipzig, 1927.
Phil 8887.32 Systema ethicum. (Matthia, C.) Marpurgi, 1626.
Phil 8875.36 Systèma êthikès. (Androutsos, Chrêstos.) Athênai, 1925.
Phil 1925.50 Systema intellectuale. (Cudworth, R.) Lugduni Batavorum, 1773. 2v.
VPhil 1925.49F Systema intellectuale huius universi. (Cudworth, R.) Jenae, 1733.
Phil 5050.2.5 Systema logicae. (Keckermann, B.) Coloniae, 1611. 2 pam.
Htn Phil 5050.2* Systema logicae minus. (Keckermann, B.) Hanoviae, 1606.
Phil 197.41.5 Systema metaphysicum. v.1-4. (Wallerius, N.) Stockholmiae, 1750-1752. 7v.
Phil 185.15 Systema physicum. (Keckermann, B.) Hanoviae, 1623.
Phil 5000.2 Systema systematum. (Keckermann, B.) Hanoviae, 1613.
Phil 8884.2 Systematic morality. v.1-2. (Jevons, W.) London, 1827.
Phil 187.175 Systematic pluralism. (Myers, Henry.) Ithaca, 1961.
Phil 5259.5.50 Systematic psychology; prolegomena. (Titchener, E.B.) N.Y., 1929.
Phil 1523.16 Systematisch-historische Untersuchungen zur Philosophie des XIV. Jahrhunderts. (Sprengard, Karl Anton.) Bonn, 196-.
Phil 3488.20.5 Systematische Darstellung der Kantischen Vernunftkritik zum gebrauch akademischer Vorlesungen. (Goess, G.F.D.) Nürnberg, 1794.
Phil 3625.20.30 Systematische Philosophie. (Meyer, Hans.) Paderborn, 1955. 4v.
Phil 193.52 Systematische Philosophie. Berlin, 1907.
Phil 190.47 Systematische Philosophie in leichtfasslicher Darstellung. (Peiser, Fritz.) Berlin, 1923.
Phil 5260.8.5 Systematische Psychologie für Oberlyzeen und Seminare. (Ufer, Christian.) Leipzig, 1912.
Phil 5500.70 Systematische Tendenzen bei Persönlichkeitsbeurteilungen. (Cohen, Rudolf.) Bern, 1969.
Phil 3270.3.90 Systematische und kritische Darstellung der Psychologie Jakob Frohschammers. (Johann, F.) Würzburg, 1899.
Phil 3484.2.30 Die systematischen Begriffe. (Cohen, H.) Berlin, 1873.
Phil 3499.23 Systematisches Handlexikon zu Kants Kritik der reinen Vernunft. (Ratke, Heinrich.) Leipzig, 1929.
Phil 87.1 Systematisches Wörterbuch der Philosophie. (Clauberg, K.N.) Leipzig, 1923.
Phil 1845.3.90 Le système d'Alexander. (Devaux, P.) Paris, 1929.
Phil 2520.111 Le système de Descartes. (Hamelin, O.) Paris, 1911.

Phil 2520.111.2   Le système de Descartes. 2e éd. (Hamelin, O.) Paris, 1921.

Htn   Phil 2648.29*   Système de la nature. (Holbach, Paul Henri T.) London, 1770. 2v.

Htn   Phil 2648.30*   Système de la nature. (Holbach, Paul Henri T.) London, 1770. 2v.

Phil 2648.30.14   Système de la nature. (Holbach, Paul Henri T.) Londres, 1777.

Phil 2648.30.10   Système de la nature. (Holbach, Paul Henri T.) Paris, 1820. 2v.

Phil 2648.30.12   Système de la nature. (Holbach, Paul Henri T.) Paris, 1821. 2v.

Phil 182.59   Systéme de la nature. (Hugueny, Charles.) Nancy, 1890.

Phil 177.94   Systéme de la raison. 3e éd. (Carra, J.L.) Paris, 1791.

Phil 3552.261   Le système de Leibniz et le problème des rapports de la raison et de la foi. Thèse. (Ravier, E.) Caen, 1927.

Phil 3552.482   Le système de Leibniz et ses modèles mathématiques. (Serres, Michel.) Paris, 1968.

Phil 3800.180.10   Système de l'idéalisme trancendental. (Schelling, F.W.J. von.) Paris, 1812.

Phil 990.23   Systeme de philosophie dynamo synthetique. (Foroughi, A.H.) Paris, 1940. 2v.

Phil 2840.98   Le système de Renouvier. (Hamelin, Octave.) Paris, 1927.

Phil 8828.3   Systeme der moral. Bd. 1-3. (Dittrich, Ottmar.) Leipzig, 1923-26. 3v.

Phil 8403.23   Système des beaux-arts. (Chartier, Émile.) Paris, 1926.

Phil 299.10   Le système du monde des chaldéens à Newton. 2. éd. (Sageret, Jules.) Paris, 1913.

Phil 8886.2   Le système du monde moral. (Lambert, C.) Paris, 1862.

Phil 2733.120   Système et existence dans l'oeuvre de Malebranche. (Robinet, Andre.) Paris, 1965.

Phil 4818.298.80   Un système matérialiste métaphysique au XIXe siècle: la philosophie de Basile Conta. (Badareu, Dan.) Paris, 1924.

Phil 6128.21.5   Le système nerveux centrale. (Soury, Jules.) Paris, 1899. 2v.

Phil 2490.89   Le système psychologique d'Auguste Comte. (Georges, A.) Lyon, 1908.

Phil 2648.30.9   Système social. (Holbach, Paul Henri T.) London, 1773. 3v.

Phil 2648.30.8   Système social. (Holbach, Paul Henri T.) London, 1774.

Phil 2648.30.5   Système social. (Holbach, Paul Henri T.) Paris, 1795. 2v.

Phil 2648.30.7   Système social. v.1-2. (Holbach, Paul Henri T.) London, 1773.

Phil 1200.55   Le système stoïcien et l'idée de temps. (Goldschmidt, V.E.) Paris, 1953.

Phil 5374.190   Les systèmes de la vie. (Joussain, André.) Paris, 1958.

Phil 188.11   Les systèmes de philosophie. (Naville, Ernest.) Paris, 1909.

Phil 5055.9   Les systèmes logiques et la logistique. (Peslöuan, C.L. de.) Paris, 1909.

Phil 5252.152   Systems and theories in psychology. (Marx, M.H.) N.Y., 1963.

Phil 5212.20.2   Systems and theories of psychology. 2. ed. (Chaplin, James Patrik.) N.Y., 1968.

Phil 8843.18   Systems of ethics and value theory. (Sahakian, W.) N.Y., 1963.

Phil 5066.258   Systems of formal logic. (Hackstaff, L.H.) Dordrecht, 1966.

Phil 5414.25   Syyllisyydentuntoon vaikuttavista tekijöistä. (Airas, Erkki.) Helsinki, 1956.

Phil 310.620   Szabó, András. Man and law. Budapest, 1965.

Phil 6328.20   Szalai, Alex. Philosophische Grundprobleme der psychoanalytischen Psycholgie. Budapest, 1935.

Phil 6688.13   Szapary, Franz von. Magnétisme et magnétothérapie. Paris, 1853.

Phil 5402.23   Szasz, T.S. Pain and pleasure. N.Y., 1957.

Phil 6328.62.5   Szasz, Thomas Stephen. The ethics of psychoanalysis; the theory and method of autonomous psychotherapy. N.Y., 1965.

Phil 6328.62   Szasz, Thomas Stephen. Ideology and insanity. Garden City, 1970.

Phil 5258.193   Szasz, Thomas Stephen. Law, liberty and psychiatry. N.Y., 1963.

Phil 2475.1.259A   Szathmary, A. The aesthetic theory of Bergson. Cambridge, 1937.

Phil 6980.717.30   Szasz, Thomas Stephen. The manufacture of madness. 1ṣt ed. N.Y., 1970.

Phil 6980.717.25   Szasz, Thomas Stephen. The myth of mental illness. N.Y., 1961.

Phil 8610.958   Szczesny, Gerhard. Die Zukunft des Unglaubens. München, 1958.

Phil 3915.145   Szczurat, Vassil. Wundt's Apperzeptionstheorie. Brody, 1903.

Phil 4815.223.30   Szellemi haladásunk törvénye. (Bodnár, Zsigmond.) Budapest, 1892.

Phil 4065.178   Szemere, Samu. Giordano Bruno. Budapest, 1917.

Phil 5520.355   Szewczuk, W. Badania eksperymentalne nad rozumieniem zdán. Kraków, 1960.

Phil 2150.22.150   Szewczyk, Jan. Eros i rewolucja. Wyd. 1. Warszawa, 1971.

Phil 3450.11.220   Szilasi, Wilhelm. Einführung in die Phänomenologie Edmund Husserls. Tübingen, 1959.

Phil 193.160   Szilasi, Wilhelm. Macht und Ohnmacht des Geistes. Bern, 1946.

Phil 193.160.5   Szilasi, Wilhelm. Philosophie und Naturwissenschaft. Bern, 1961.

Phil 7150.36   Szittya, E. Selbstmörder. Leipzig, 1925.

Phil 4803.498.20   Szkice filozofczne. Wyd. 1. (Krajewski, Władysław.) Warszawa, 1963.

Phil 165.342   Szkice filozoficzne; Romanowi Ingardinowi w darze. Warszawa, 1964.

Phil 4803.497.420   Szkice filozoficzne. (Kozłowski, Władysław M.) Warszawa, 1900.

Phil 5520.325.5   Szkice z filozofii języka. (Schaff, Adam.) Warszawa, 1967.

Phil 4803.462.20   Szkice z filozofii literatury. (Ingarden, Roman.) Łódź, 1947.

VPhil 2280.5.150   Szmyd, Jan. Filozofia moralna Santayany. Wyd. 1. Warszawa, 1968.

Phil 5258.205   Szondi, Lipot. Freiheit und Zwang im Schicksal des Einzelnen. Bern, 1968.

Phil 6980.717   Szondi, Lipot. Heilweg der Tiefenpsychologie. Bern, 1956.

Phil 6328.40.5   Szondi, Lipot. Kain, Gestalten des Bösen. Bern, 1969.

Phil 6328.40   Szondi, Lipot. Triebpathologie. Bern, 1956. 2v.

Phil 28.43   Szondiana. Bern. 6-7 2v.

Phil 4813.10   Szontagh, Gusztav. Propylaeumok a' magyar philosophiákoz. Budán, 1839.

Phil 5545.222   Sztuka pamietania. (Gorczyński, S.) Warszawa, 1963.

Phil 672.225   Szumilewicz, Irena. O kierunku upływu czasu. Warszawa, 1964.

Phil 6328.57   Szumowski, W. Névroses et psychoses au moyen age et au début des temps modernes. Paris, 1939.

Phil 3195.16.80   Szylkarski, W. Jugendgeschichte Adolf Dyroffs. 2. Aufl. Bonn, 1948.

Phil 5400.60   Szymanski, J.S. Gefühl und Erkennen. Berlin, 1926.

Phil 5258.103   Szymanski, J.S. Psychologie vom Standpunkt der Abhängigkeit des Erkennens von den Lebensbedürfnissen. Leipzig, 1930.

Phil 193.262   Szymański, Jesy. Technika i mowa jako narsedsia pornania ludskiego. Pornań, 1971.

Phil 3018.40   Szyszkowka, Maria. Neokantyzm - filozofia społeczna wraz a filozofia prawa natury o zmilnnej treści. Wyd. 1. Warszawa, 1970.

Phil 4073.88   T. Campanella metafisico. (Rossi, M.M.) Firenze, 1923.

Phil 5592.176.5   T.A.T. and understanding people. (Kahn, Samuel.) N.Y., 1966.

Phil 2020.85   T.H. Green. (Selsam, Howard.) N.Y., 1930.

Phil 5520.592   Taalanalise en taalevaluering as pedagogies-didaktiese diagnostiseungsmetode. (Stoep, F. van der.) Pretoria, 1965.

Htn   Phil 1865.55*   Taber, H.M. Faith or fact. N.Y., 1897. A table of the springs of action. (Bentham, Jeremy.) London, 1815.

Phil 7050.11   Table qui douse et table qui répond. (Guillard, J.-C.A.) Paris, 1853. 3 pam.

Phil 2422.5   Tableau de la philosophie française. (Wahl, Jean A.) Paris, 1946.

Phil 2422.5.2   Tableau de la philosophie française. (Wahl, Jean A.) Paris, 1962.

Phil 8886.59   Tableau de l'inconstance et instabilité de toutes choses. (Lancre, P. de.) Paris, 1607.

Phil 813.1   Tableau des progrès de la pensée humaine. (Nourrisson, J.F.) Paris, 1858.

Phil 813.1.2   Tableau des progrès de la pensée humaine. (Nourrisson, J.F.) Paris, 1867.

Phil 813.1.7   Tableau des progrès de la pensée humaine. 7e éd. (Nourrisson, J.F.) Paris, 1886.

Htn   Phil 2648.56*   Tableau des saints. (Holbach, Paul Henri T.) Londres, 1770. 2v.

Phil 2419.3   Tableau des trois époques, ou Les philosophes. (Théard.) Paris, 1829.

Phil 2880.1.45   Tableau naturel des rapports qui existent entre Dieu, l'homme et l'univers. (Saint-Martin, L.C.) Paris, 1900.

Phil 2880.1.47   Tableau naturel des rapports qui existent entre Dieu, l'homme et l'univers. (Saint-Martin, L.C.) Rochefort-sur-Mer, 1946.

Phil 125.2   Tables of philosophy. (Rand, Benjamin.) Cambridge, 1882.

Phil 7054.61.3   The tables turned. (Brittan, Samuel B.) N.Y., 1854.

Phil 5238.191   Taboo topics. (Farberow, N.L.) N.Y., 1963.

Phil 720.3   Tabor, J.A. The supreme law. Colchester, 1879.

Phil 5390.10   Tabori, Paul. The natural science of stupidity. 1. ed. Philadelphia, 1959.

Phil 346.20.10   The tacet dimension. 1. ed. (Polanyi, Michael.) Garden City, N.Y., 1966.

Phil 5535.28   Tâche réussite et échec. (Nuttin, Jozef.) Louvain, 1953.

Phil 8663.3.90   Tactics of infidels. (Lambert, L.A.) Buffalo, 1887.

Phil 4235.5.30   Taddeo da Parma. Le quaestiones de anima de Taddeo da Parma. Milano, 1951.

Phil 4803.497.90   Tadeusz Kotarbiński. Wyd. 1. (Jawonski, Manek.) Warszawa, 1971.

Phil 5058.37   Taenkelaere eller logik i sammentraengt fremstilling. 3. udg. (Sibbern, F.C.) Kjøbenhavn, 1866.

Phil 5244.17   Taenkningens psychologiske utviklingsbetingelser. (Eriksen, R.) Kristiania, 1915.

Phil 8894.30   Taeusch, C.F. Professional and business ethics. N.Y., 1926.

Phil 645.32   Tafel, J.F.I. Geschichte und Kritik des Skepticismus und Irrationalismus. Tübingen, 1834.

Phil 5599.98   Der Tafeln-Z-Test für individuelle psychologische Prüfungen, ein abgekürztes Rorschach-Verfahren. (Zulliger, Hans.) Bern, 1954.

Phil 126.3   Tafeln zur Geschichte der Philosophie. (Stumpf, C.) Berlin, 1896.

Phil 126.3.2   Tafeln zur Geschichte der Philosophie. (Stumpf, C.) Berlin, 1900.

Phil 126.3.3   Tafeln zur Geschichte der Philosophie. (Stumpf, C.) Berlin, 1910.

Phil 126.3.4   Tafeln zur Geschichte der Philosophie. 4. Aufl. (Stumpf, C.) Berlin, 1928.

Phil 8599.31   Taft, Charles Phelps. Do we still need religion? N.Y., 1942.

Phil 194.17.5   Taft, Oren B. Evolution of idea; a thesis. Chicago, 1926.

Phil 194.17   Taft, Oren B. Hypothesis for a ceptacle theory. Chicago, 1900.

Phil 8420.11   Tafts, James. On the genesis of the aesthetic categories. Chicago, 1902.

Phil 3450.29.73   Tag- und Nachtbücher, 1939-1945. 3e Aufl. (Haecker, Theodor.) München, 1959.

Phil 3450.29.70   Tag- und Nachtbücher. (Haecker, Theodor.) München, 1947.

Phil 2115.86   Tagart, E. Locke's writings and philosophy. London, 1855.

Phil 5059.1   Tagart, Edward. Remarks on mathematical or demonstrative reasoning. London, 1837.

Phil 5252.38.10   Tagebuch eines Psychologen. (Müller-Freienfels, R.) Leipzig, 1931.

Phil 3195.5.81   Tagebücher...Bauernphilosophen. (Deubler, Konrad.) Leipzig, 1886. 2v.

Phil 3210.30A   Tagesansicht gegenüber der Nachtansicht. (Fechner, G.T.) Leipzig, 1879.

Phil 3210.30.5   Tagesansicht gegenüber der Nachtansicht. 3. Aufl. (Fechner, G.T.) Leipzig, 1919.

Phil 5585.125   Tagiuri, Renato. Person perception and interpersonal behavior. Stanford, 1958.

Phil 5585.125.3   Tagiuri, Renato. Person perception and interpersonal behavior. Stanford, 1965.

Phil 4370.5   Tagle, A. La experiencia humana. Buenos Aires, 1938.

Phil 4260.160   Tagliacozzo, Giorgio. Giambattista Vico. Baltimore, 1969.

Phil 8430.76   Tagliaferri, Aldo. L'estetica dell'oggettivo. Milano, 1968.

Phil 7060.1   Taillepied, F.N. Traité de l'apparition des esprits. Roven, 1602.

Phil 7069.33.43   Taillepied, N. A treatise of ghosts. London, 1933.

Phil 7060.1.5   Taillepied, Noël. Psichologie ou traité de l'apparition des esprits. Paris, 1588.

Phil 7060.143   Taillepied, Noël. Traicté de l'apparition des esprits. Paris, 1917.

Phil 2885.89 Taine; formation de sa pensée. (Chevrillon, A.) Paris, 1932.
Phil 8062.5 Taine, H.A. Philosophie de l'art en Grèce. Paris, 1869.
Phil 2138.87 Taine, H.A. Positivisme anglais. Paris, 1864.
Phil 2885.33 Taine, Hippolyte Adolphe. De l'ideal dans l'art. Paris, 1867.
NEDL Phil 2885.30 Taine, Hippolyte Adolphe. De l'intelligence. Paris, 1878. 2v.
Phil 2885.30.5 Taine, Hippolyte Adolphe. De l'intelligence. 2. éd. v.1-2. Paris, 1870. 2v.
Phil 2885.30.8 Taine, Hippolyte Adolphe. De l'intelligence. 13. éd. Paris, 1914. 2v.
Phil 2885.34.14 Taine, Hippolyte Adolphe. The ideal in art. N.Y., 1874.
Phil 2885.32 Taine, Hippolyte Adolphe. Lectures on art. 1st series. N.Y., 1875.
Phil 2885.32.5A Taine, Hippolyte Adolphe. Lectures on art. 2nd series. N.Y., 1889.
Phil 2885.34.16A Taine, Hippolyte Adolphe. Lectures on art. 3d ed. 1st series. N.Y., 1875. 2v.
NEDL Phil 2885.31.1 Taine, Hippolyte Adolphe. On Intelligence. N.Y., 1871.
Phil 2885.31.3 Taine, Hippolyte Adolphe. On intelligence. N.Y., 1875. 2v.
Phil 2885.31.6 Taine, Hippolyte Adolphe. On intelligence. N.Y., 1889. 2v.
Phil 2885.31 Taine, Hippolyte Adolphe. On intelligence. pt. 1-2. London, 1871.
Phil 2419.1.3 Taine, Hippolyte Adolphe. Les philosophes clasiques du XIXe siècle. Paris, 1868.
Phil 2419.1 Taine, Hippolyte Adolphe. Les philosophes français du XIXe siècle. Paris, 1857.
Phil 2419.1.2 Taine, Hippolyte Adolphe. Les philosophes français du XIXe siècle. Paris, 1860.
Phil 2419.1.2.5 Taine, Hippolyte Adolphe. Les philosophes français du XIXe siècle. Paris, 1966.
Phil 2885.34.5 Taine, Hippolyte Adolphe. Philosophie de l'art. Paris, 1865.
Phil 2885.34A Taine, Hippolyte Adolphe. Philosophie de l'art. Paris, 1881. 2v.
Phil 2885.34.8 Taine, Hippolyte Adolphe. Philosophie de l'art. 8. éd. Paris, 1895?
Phil 2885.34.12 Taine, Hippolyte Adolphe. The philosophy of art. Photoreproduction. London, 1867.
Phil 2885.34.10 Taine, Hippolyte Adolphe. The philosophy of art. Photoreproduction. 2. ed. N.Y., 1873.
Phil 2885.31.8 Taine, Hippolyte Adolphe. Der Verstand. v.1-2. Bonn, 1880.
Phil 2885.112 Taine. Wyd. 1. (Krzemień-Ojak, Sław.) Warszawa, 1966.
Phil 2885.84 Taine historien et sociologue. (Lacombe, Paul.) Paris, 1909.
Phil 6131.6 Tainstvennye iavleniia chelov psikhiki. (Vasil'ev, Leonid L.) Moskva, 1963.
Phil 6131.6.3 Tainstvennye iavleniia chelovecheskoi psikhiki. Izd. 3. (Vasil'ev, Leonid L.) Moskva, 1964.
Htn Phil 6045.83F* Taisnier, Joannes. Opus mathematicum cheiromantis. Coloniae, 1583.
Htn Phil 6045.62F* Taisnier, Joannes. Opus mathematicum octs libros complectens. Coloniae, 1562.
Phil 8674.1 Tait, J. Mind in matter. London, 1884.
Phil 8644.1.5 Tait, P.G. Paradoxical philosophy. London, 1879.
Phil 8644.1 Tait, P.G. The unseen universe. N.Y., 1875.
Phil 8644.1.2 Tait, P.G. The unseen universe. N.Y., 1875.
Phil 3839.5 Tak, W.G. van der. Bento de Spinoza. 's Gravenhage, 1928.
Phil 6125.26 Take it easy. (Pitkin, W.B.) N.Y., 1935.
Phil 6314.9 Take off your mask. (Eidelberg, L.) N.Y., 1948.
Phil 3501.22 Takeda, Sueo. Kant und das Problem der Analogie. Den Haag, 1969.
Phil 5627.96.5 Taking men alive. (Trumbull, Charles G.) N.Y., 1912.
Phil 5648.10 Die taktile Schätzung von Ausgefüllten und leeren Strecken. (Cook, H.D.) Leipzig, 1910.
Phil 4610.7.45 Tal och tankar. (Norström, V.) Stockholm, 1919.
Phil 8709.24 Talafous, Camillus D. Readings in science and spirit. Englewood Cliffs, N.J., 1966.
Phil 8709.10 Talamo, S. Il rinnovamento...tomistico e la scienza. Roma, 1927.
Phil 1540.47 Talamo, Salvatore. L'aristotelismo della scolastica nella storia. 3. ed. Siena, 1881.
Phil 3246.87.2 Talbot, E.B. Fundamental principle of Fichte's philosophy. N.Y., 1906.
Phil 3246.87 Talbot, E.B. Fundamental principle of Fichte's philosophy. Diss. N.Y., 1906.
Phil 5870.15 Talbot, Toby. The world of the child. Garden City, 1967.
Phil 6969.1 Talcott, S.H. Mental diseases...modern treatment. N.Y., 1901.
Phil 5465.208 Talejko, Eugeniusz. Zagadnienie psychologii twórezoju technivzncj. Poznań, 1971.
Phil 6329.22.5 Talent and genius. (Eissler, Kurt Robert.) N.Y., 1971.
Phil 9530.56 Talent and performance. (Ginzberg, Eli.) N.Y., 1964.
Phil 5425.96 Talent and society. Princeton, 1958.
Phil 5425.32 Das Talent und das Genie. (Rauschenberger, W.) Frankfurt, 1952.
Phil 5425.84 Talent und Genie. (Révész, Géza.) Bern, 1952.
Phil 7054.153.15 Tales of the horrible, or The book of spirits. London, 1837.
Phil 2905.1.100 Talhonët, Jean de. Le lyrisme et la mystique dans les oeuvres du Pierre Teilhard de Chardin. Paris, 1959.
Phil 5525.27 Talhouet, J. de. Le rire et l'origine des idées. Rennes, 1923.
Phil 8420.15 Talia, G.B. Principi di estetica. Venezia, 1827-28. 2v.
Phil 3120.8.126 Taljaard, J.A.L. Franz Brentano as wysgeer. Franeker, 1955.
Phil 408.4 Talking about particulars. (Meiland, Jack W.) London, 1970.
Phil 978.59.30 Talks, Ojai, California. (Krishnamurti, J.) Ojai, California, 1950.
Phil 978.59.70 Talks and dialogues, Saanen 1968. (Krishnamurti, J.) Wassenaar, 1970.
Phil 978.59.72 Talks and discussions at Brockwood Park, 1969. (Krishnamurti, J.) Wassenaar, 1970.
Phil 978.59.65 Talks in Europe, 1968. (Krishnamurti, J.) Wassenaar, 1920.
Phil 193.88.5 Talks on philosophy. (Spalding, K.J.) Oxford, 1931.
Phil 6111.41 Talks on psychotherapy. (Brown, William.) London, 1923.
Phil 8592.53 Talks on religion. (Mitchell, H.B.) N.Y., 1908.
Phil 6127.18.12 Talks to patients. (Riggs, A.F.) n.p., 1924-27.
Phil 9342.5 Talks to young men. (Collyer, R.) Boston, 1888.
Phil 978.59.74 Talks with American students, 1968. (Krishnamurti, J.) Wassenaar, 1970.

Phil 9352.10 Talks with my boys. (Mowry, William A.) Boston, 1885.
Phil 9352.10.5 Talks with my boys. 5th ed. (Mowry, William A.) N.Y., 1909.
Phil 9358.2 Talks with my pupils. (Sedgwick, C.) N.Y., n.d.
Phil 7069.31.37 Talks with spirit friends, bench and bar. London, 1931.
Phil 7069.30.13 Talks with the invisible. (Lovejoy, H.T.) Sunderland, 1930.
Phil 4370.15 Tallet, Jorge. The absolute being. N.Y., 1958.
Phil 6311.26 Talleyrand, Napoleon, Stendhal, Grabbe, psychoanalytisch-biographishe essays. (Bergler, Edmund.) Wien, 1935.
Phil 400.98 Tallon, H.J. Concept of self in British and American idealism. Washington, 1939.
Htn Phil 8883.1* Talmudic maxims. (Israel, L.S. d'.) Boston, 1848.
Phil 292.20 El tamaño del espacio. (Lugones, Leopoldo.) Buenos Aires, 1921.
Phil 5190.4.30 Tamás, György. Die wissenschaftliche Definition. Budapest, 1964.
Phil 165.366 Tamás, György. Selected studies. Budapest, 1965.
Phil 6689.11 Tamburini, A. Anleitung zur experimentellen Untersuchung des Hypnotismus. Wiesbaden, 1882-85.
Phil 3501.20 Taminiaux, Jacques. La nostalgie de la Grèce à l'aube de l'idéalisme allemand. La Haye, 1967.
Phil 5069.6 Tammelo, Ilmar. Outlines of modern legal logic. Wiesbaden, 1969.
Phil 8599.28 Tampoe, A.McG. Coomarasamy. Life negation; an Indian study of Christ. London, 19- .
Phil 194.54 Tanasescu, Horia. Existencialismo; pensamiento oriental y psicoanalisis. México, 1967.
Phil 8709.25 Tancher, Volodymyr K. Nauka oprovergaet religioznye dogmaty. Kiev, 1970.
Phil 4080.3.335 Tanga, Igino. L'esteticca di Benedetto Croce nella storia del pensiero e della letteratura. Roma, 1959.
Phil 6129.10 Taniguchi, Masaham. Recovery from all diseases. Tokyo, 1963.
Phil 2805.40.40 Tankar i religiösa frägor. 2. uppl. (Pascal, Blaise.) Stockholm, 1911.
Phil 4610.7.13 Tankar och forskningar. (Norström, V.) Stockholm, 1915.
Phil 4655.1.58 Tankar och frågor inför menniskones son. 4. uppl. (Wikner, Pontus.) Stockholm, 1893.
Phil 4610.7.10 Tankelinier. (Norström, V.) Stockholm, 1905.
Phil 4513.2.31 Tanker og syn En liden studie. (Aars, K.B.R.) Kristiania, 1894.
Phil 9400.45 Tanker til overvejelse for os aeldre. (Brøndsted, Holger Valdemar.) København, 1969.
Phil 4605.1.46 Tankeretninger i den nyere tid. 2 opl. (Monrad, M.J.) Christiania, 1884.
Phil 6315.2.81 Tannenbaum, S.A. The psychology of accidents and "symtomatic actions". N.Y., 1924.
Phil 2905.1.545 Tanner, Henri. Le grain de sénévé. De la science à la religion avec Teilhard de Chardin. Saint-Maurice, 1967.
Phil 8599.29 Tanquerey, A. The spiritual life. 2. ed. Tournai, 1932.
Phil 5259.13.15 Tansley, A.G. Mind and life. London, 1952.
Phil 5259.13.2 Tansley, A.G. The new psychology. London, 1920.
Phil 5259.13.10 Tansley, A.G. The new psychology. N.Y., 1924.
Phil 1750.85 The Tao of science. (Siu, Ralph G.H.) Cambridge, Mass., 1957.
Phil 7150.19 Tapia, Ambrosios. Los suicidios en Cataluña y en general en toda España. Barcelona, 1900.
Phil 7054.160 Tappan, Cora L.V. Discourses through the mediumship of Mrs. C. Tappan. London, 1875.
Phil 7054.160.5 Tappan, Cora L.V. What is the use of spiritualism? London, 1874.
Phil 5769.1.2 Tappan, H.P. Doctrine of the will. N.Y., 1840.
Phil 5769.1.5 Tappan, H.P. Doctrine of the will. N.Y., 1841.
Phil 5059.2 Tappan, H.P. Elements of logic. N.Y., 1844.
NEDL Phil 5754.1.25 Tappan, H.P. Review of Edward's inquiry...freedom. N.Y., 1839.
Phil 9530.29 Tapper, Thomas. Youth and opportunity. N.Y., 1912.
Phil 5259.18 Tapy, George H. Outline of psychology. Crawfordsville, 19- ?
Htn Phil 1870.96* Pamphlet vol. The tar water controversy. 15 pam.
Phil 6980.721 Tarachow, S. An introduction to psychotherapy. N.Y., 1963.
Phil 2115.135 Tarantino, G. Giovanni Locke. Milano, 1886.
Phil 2045.106 Tarantino, G. Saggio sulle idee morali e politiche di T. Hobbes. Napoli, 1900.
Phil 8894.18 Tarantino, Giuseppe. Il principio dell'ética e la crisi morale contemporanea; memoria. Napoli, 1904.
Phil 8894.18.5 Tarantino, Giuseppe. Il problema della morale di fronte al positivismo ed alla metafisica. Pisa, 1901.
Phil 8599.38 Tarasov, A.A. Sotsial'naia religiia. Miunkhen, 1959.
Phil 5380.3.3 Tarde, G. L'opinion et la foule. 3rd éd. Paris, 1910.
Phil 194.43 Tardé, G. L'opposition universelle. Paris, 1897.
Phil 5467.6 Tarde, Gabriel. Les lois de l'imitation; étude sociologique. 4. éd. Paris, 1904.
Phil 5407.5.2 Tardieu, E. L'ennui; étude psychologique. Paris, 1903.
Phil 6689.6.15 Tardy de Montravel, A.A. Essai sur la théorie du somnambulisme magnétique. Londres, 1787.
Phil 6689.6 Tardy de Montravel, A.A. Journal du traitement magnétique. London, 1786. 2 pam.
Phil 6689.6.3 Tardy de Montravel, A.A. Journal du traitement magnétique. Strasbourg, 1787.
Phil 8599.24 Tarenne, G. La théologie naturelle, histoire, philosophique, critique et morale, ou Les pensées d'un homme sur l'être-Suprême. Paris, 1800?
Phil 6969.7 Targowla, René. L'intuition délirante. Paris, 1931.
Phil 8420.18 Tari, Antonio. Saggi di estetica e metafisica. Bari, 1911.
Htn Phil 4200.3.30* Tariffa. (Pasi, Bartholomeo.) Vinetia, 1540.
Phil 6689.1 Tarkhanof, J.R. Hypnotisme, suggestion. Paris, 1891.
Phil 194.27 Tarner, George E. Some remarks on the axioms and postulates of athetic philosophy. Cambridge, 1922.
Phil 2070.112 Tarozzi, G. Compendio dei principii di psicologia. Milano, 1911.
Phil 5769.8 Tarozzi, G. La libertà umana e la critica del determinismo. Bologna, 1936.
Phil 5259.22 Tarozzi, G. Nozioni di psicologia. Bologna, 1925.
Phil 194.19.35 Tarozzi, Giuseppe. L'esistenza e l'anima. Bari, 1930.
Phil 194.19.30 Tarozzi, Giuseppe. L'idea di esistenza e la pensabilità del reale trascendente. Bologna, 1927.
Phil 194.19 Tarozzi, Giuseppe. Lezioni di filosofia. v.1-3. Torino, 1896-1898.
Phil 194.19.25 Tarozzi, Giuseppe. La racerca filosofica. Napoli, 1936.
Phil 4060.1.93 Tarozzi, Giuseppe. Roberto Ardigo. Roma, 1928.
Phil 705.8 Tarrida del Mármol, F. Problemas trascendentales. Paris, 1908.

Phil 8894.23 Tarrozzi, G. Filosofia morale e nozioni affini. Bologna, 1911.
Phil 8894.23.15 Tarrozzi, G. Idea di una scienza del bene. Firenze, 1901.
Phil 8894.23.5 Tarrozzi, G. La virtù contemporanea. Torino, 1900.
Phil 720.39 Tarski, Alfred. De Wahrheitsbegriff in der...Sprachen. Photostat. Leopoli, 1935.
Phil 5374.278 Tart, Charles T. Altered states of consciousness. N.Y., 1969.
Phil 8420.26 Tartalja, Ivo. Djure Daničića lekcije iz estetike. Beograd, 1968.
Phil 6689.9 Tartaruga, U. Aus dem Reiche der Hellsehwunders. Pfullingen, 1924.
Phil 9145.7.5 The Tartuffian age. (Montegazza, P.) Boston, 1890.
Phil 6329.15 Tashman, H.F. Today's neurotic family. N.Y., 1957.
Phil 5545.97 Task experience as a source of attitudes. (Breer, Paul E.) Homewood, 1965.
Phil 5545.248 Task interruption. (Bergon, Annie van.) Amsterdam, 1968.
Phil 5250.15.18 The task of Gestalt psychology. (Köhler, Wolfgang.) Princeton, 1969.
Phil 29.41 Tasmania. University. Hobart. Department of Psychology. Publication.
Phil 4363.3.95 Tassara y Sangian, Luz. Mañara. Sevilla, 1959.
Htn Phil 8612.23* Tasso, Ercole. Il confortatore. Bergamo, 1595.
Phil 194.28 Tassy, E. La philosophie constructive. Paris, 1921.
Phil 5259.20 Tassy, Edme. L'activité psychique. Paris, 1925.
Phil 8959.8 Tästa on kysymys. (Juva, Mikko.) Söderström, 1965.
Phil 8430.66 Taste and temperament. (Evans, Joan.) London, 1939.
Phil 8120.13 Taste in eighteenth century France. (Saisselin, Rémy Gilbert.) Syracuse, 1965.
Phil 5648.4 Tastsinn und Gemeingefühl. (Weber, E.H.) Leipzig, 1905.
Phil 3246.79.25 Tat und Freiheit, ein Fichtebuch. 3. Aufl. (Fichte, Johann Gottlieb.) Hamburg, 1922.
Phil 1400.5 Tatakes, B.N. Themata christianikės kai buzantinės philosophias. Athens, 1952.
Phil 819.9 Tatarkiewiaz, W. Historja filozafji. Lwów, 1931. 2v.
Phil 9245.115 Tatarkiewicz, W. A szczęsciu. Wyd. 3. Warszawa, 1962.
Phil 8420.21 Tatarkiewicz, W. Skupienie i marzenie. Kraków, 1951.
Phil 4803.822.30 Tatarkiewicz, Władysław. Droga do filozofii i inne rozprowy filozoficzne. Wyd. 1. v.1- Warszawa, 1971-
Phil 8050.26 Tatarkiewicz, Władysław. Historia estetyki. Wrocław, 1960. 2v.
Phil 8050.95 Tatarkiewicz, Wladyslaw. History of aesthetics. The Hague, 1970.
Phil 179.3.112 Die Tatwelt, Zeitschrift für Erneuerung des Geiteslebens. Berlin, 1927.
Phil 29.11 Die Tatwelt. Berlin. 7-17,1931-1941 5v.
Phil 3850.27.135 Tau, Max. Albert Schweitzer und der Friede. Hamburg, 1955.
Phil 270.44 Taube, M. Causation, freedom, and determinism. London, 1936.
Phil 5722.55 Tauber, Edward. Prelogical experience. N.Y., 1959.
Phil 9430.16 Taubert, A. Der Pessimismus. Berlin, 1873.
Phil 9035.100 Taulemonde, Jean. Les extériorises. Lyon, 1958[1959]
Htn Phil 3890.3.30F* Tauler, J. Des heilige Lerers Predigfast. Basel, 1621.
Phil 194.49 Taulmin, St. E. Metaphysical beliefs. London, 1957.
Phil 4060.5.80 Taura, Giacoma. La vita ed il pensiero di Andrea Anguilli. Milano, 1914.
Phil 4110.4.102 Tauro, G. Luigi Ferri. Roma, 1896.
Phil 350.3 Tauschinski, Hippolyt. Der Begriff. Wien, 1865.
Phil 4688.110.36 Tauta ir tautine ištikimybė. (Girnius, Juozas.) Chicago, 1961.
Phil 3425.34.32 Tavadze, I.K.V.I. Lenin o nauke logiki Gegelia. Tbilisi, 1959.
Phil 5059.21.6A Tavanets, P.V. Izbrannye trudy russkikh XIX v. Moskva, 1956.
Phil 5066.252 Tavanets, P.V. Logicheskaia struktura nauchnogo znaniia. Moskva, 1965.
Phil 5066.165 Tavanets, P.V. Primenie logiki v nauke i tekhnika. Moskva, 1960.
Phil 5059.21 Tavanets, P.V. Suzhdenie i ego vidy. Moskva, 1953.
Phil 5190.27 Tavanets, P.V. Voprosy teorii suzhdeniia. Moskva, 1955.
Phil 2750.13.80 Tavares, M. de la Salette. Aproximaçõa do pensamento concerto de Gabriel Marcel. Lisboa, 1948.
Phil 7150.13 Taverni, Romeo. Del suicidio massime In Italia nel quinquiennio 1866-70. Roma, 1873.
Phil 4170.7.98 Tavianini, U. Una polemica filosofica dell'1800. Padova, 1955.
Phil 6903.10 Tavistock Institute of Human Relations, London. Annotated list of publications, 1946-1970. London, 1970?
Phil 59.8 Tavistock Institute of Human Relations, London. Report. 1963+
Phil 59.8.5 Tavistock pamphlet. London. 1,1957+ 4v.
Phil 9179.1.2 Taylor, A. Hinton. Practical hints to young females. Boston, 1816.
Phil 9179.1 Taylor, A. Hinton. Practical hints to young females. London, 1815.
Phil 9179.1.5 Taylor, A. Hinton. Reciprocal duties of parents and children. Boston, 1825.
Phil 2050.184 Taylor, A.E. David Hume and the miraculous. Cambridge, Eng., 1927.
Htn Phil 194.11* Taylor, A.E. Elements of metaphysics. London, 1903.
Phil 194.11.25 Taylor, A.E. Philosophical studies. London, 1934.
Phil 8894.12 Taylor, A.E. The problem of conduct. London, 1901.
Phil 2045.89 Taylor, A.E. Thomas Hobbes. London, 1908.
Phil 1850.120 Taylor, Alfred. Francis Bacon. London, 1926?
Phil 8644.11 Taylor, Alfred E. The Christian hope of immortality. London, 1938.
Phil 8599.22 Taylor, Alfred E. Faith of a moralist. London, 1930. 2v.
Htn Phil 194.2* Taylor, B.S. Contemplatio philosophica. London, 1793.
Phil 194.1 Taylor, B.S. Helps to understanding of nature. Albion, 1889.
Phil 5640.39 Taylor, C.F. Sensation and pain. N.Y., 1881.
Phil 5465.139 Taylor, C.W. Creativity, progress and potential. N.Y., 1964.
Phil 5465.136 Taylor, C.W. Scientific creativity. N.Y., 1963.
Phil 5259.56 Taylor, Charles. The explanation of behavior. London, 1964.
Phil 8644.4 Taylor, D. The composition of matter and the evolution of the mind. London, 1912.
Phil 194.60 Taylor, Daniel Malcolm. Explanation and meaning. Cambridge, Eng., 1970.
Phil 6129.6 Taylor, E.W. The mental element in the treatment of disease. Boston, 1891.
Phil 6129.6.5 Taylor, E.W. Psychotherapy. Cambridge, 1926.
Htn Phil 3110.25*A Taylor, Edward. Jakob Böhme's theosophick philosophy. London, 1691.
Phil 5850.251 Taylor, F.K. The analysis of therapeutic groups. London, 1961.
Phil 8709.20 Taylor, F.S. Man and matter. N.Y., 1953?
Phil 6329.20 Taylor, Frederick K. Psychopathology. London, 1966.
Phil 8674.2 Taylor, G. The indications of the creator. N.Y., 1852.
Phil 8894.1 Taylor, H. Notes from life. Boston, 1853.
Phil 6316.8.25 Taylor, H.M. Life's unknown ruler...teaching of George Groddeck. London, 1935. 2v.
Phil 194.36.10 Taylor, H.O. Fact: the romance of mind. N.Y., 1932.
Phil 194.36.2 Taylor, H.O. Human values and verities. London, 1928.
Phil 194.36 Taylor, H.O. Human values and verities. N.Y., 1928.
Phil 194.36.3 Taylor, H.O. Human values and verities. Pt.I. N.Y., 1929.
Htn Phil 194.36.4* Taylor, H.O. Human values and verities. Pt.I. N.Y., 1929.
Phil 1524.2 Taylor, H.O. The mediaeval mind. London, 1911. 2v.
Phil 1524.2.15A Taylor, H.O. The mediaeval mind. 4th ed. Cambridge, Mass., 1949. 2v.
Phil 8430.24 Taylor, Harold. Art and the intellect. N.Y., 1960.
Phil 1750.22A Taylor, Henry O. Thought and expression in the 16th century. N.Y., 1920. 2v.
Phil 1750.22.5 Taylor, Henry O. Thought and expression in the 16th century. 2. ed. N.Y., 1930. 2v.
Phil 1750.22.10 Taylor, Henry O. Thought and expression in the 16th century. 2. ed. N.Y., 1959. 2v.
Phil 104.1 Taylor, I. Elements of thought. London, 1843.
Phil 104.1.5 Taylor, I. Elements of thought. London, 1863.
Phil 104.1.9 Taylor, I. Elements of thought. 2nd American ed. N.Y., 1851.
Phil 8599.30 Taylor, I. Essay on the application of abstract reasoning to the Christian doctrines. 1. American ed. Boston, 1832.
Phil 5405.5.2 Taylor, I. Natural history of enthusiasm. Boston, 1830.
Phil 5405.5.5 Taylor, I. Natural history of enthusiasm. London, 1830.
Phil 5405.5.3 Taylor, I. Natural history of enthusiasm. London, 1830.
Phil 5405.5.10 Taylor, I. Natural history of enthusiasm. 10th ed. London, 1845.
Phil 9179.9.4 Taylor, Isaac. Advice to the teens. Boston, 1820.
Phil 9200.1.5 Taylor, Isaac. Fanaticism. London, 1833.
Phil 9200.1.10 Taylor, Isaac. Fanaticism. London, 1853.
Phil 9200.1 Taylor, Isaac. Fanaticism. N.Y., 1834.
Phil 9470.4 Taylor, Isaac. Man responsible for his dispositions, opinions, and conduct. London, 1840.
Phil 8644.2 Taylor, Isaac. Physical theory of another life. N.Y., 1836.
Phil 8644.2.2 Taylor, Isaac. Physical theory of another life. 2. ed. N.Y., 1836.
Phil 8644.2.3 Taylor, Isaac. Physical theory of another life. 3. ed. London, 1847.
Phil 7060.11 Taylor, J. Apparitions. London, 1815.
Phil 5259.29 Taylor, J.G. Popular psychological fallacies. London, 1938.
Phil 5585.210 Taylor, James. The behavioral basis of perception. New Haven, 1962.
Phil 8894.2 Taylor, Jane. The contributions of Q.Q. Philadelphia, 1830.
Phil 8894.2.5 Taylor, Jane. The contributions of Q.Q. to a periodical work. 6. ed. London, 1831.
Phil 9220.3A Taylor, Jeremy. A discourse of friendship. Cedar Rapids, 1913.
Htn Phil 9220.3.5* Taylor, Jeremy. A discourse of the nature...of friendship. London, 1671. 2 pam.
Phil 1124.3 Taylor, M.E.J. Greek philosophy. London, 1924.
Phil 735.240 Taylor, Paul. Normative discourse. Englewood, 1961.
Phil 585.177 Taylor, Richard. Action and purpose. Englewood Cliffs, N.J., 1966.
Phil 8610.857 Taylor, Robert. The astronomico-theological lectures. Boston, 1857.
Phil 8610.831.3 Taylor, Robert. The devil's pulpit. Boston, 1866.
Phil 8610.831.20 Taylor, Robert. The devil's pulpit. London, 1882. 2v.
Phil 8610.831.5 Taylor, Robert. The devil's pulpit. v.1, no.1-15,17-23; v.2, no.1. London, 1879.
Phil 8610.829.5 Taylor, Robert. The diegesis. Boston, 1832.
Phil 8610.829.15 Taylor, Robert. The diegesis. Boston, 1873.
Phil 8610.829.10 Taylor, Robert. The diegesis. 3. ed. London, 1845.
Phil 8610.828.5 Taylor, Robert. Syntagma of the evidences of the Christian religion. Boston, 1828.
Phil 8610.859 Taylor, Robert. Who is the Holy Spirit? N.Y., 1859.
Phil 8709.13 Taylor, Robert O.P. Universe within us. N.Y., 1931.
Phil 3050.8 Taylor, Ronald Jack. The romantic tradition in Germany. London, 1970.
Phil 9035.9 Taylor, S. Character essential to success in life. Canandaigua, 1821.
Phil 7069.32.40 Taylor, Sarah E.L. Fox - Taylor automatic writing, 1869-1892. Minneapolis, 1932.
Phil 7069.32.45 Taylor, Sarah E.L. Fox - Taylor automatic writing, 1969-1892. Boston, 1936.
Phil 5259.2 Taylor, T. World of mind. N.Y., 1858.
Htn Phil 2305.1.35* Taylor, Thomas. The fable of Cupid and Psyche. London, 1795.
Phil 1124.4 Taylor, Thomas. Miscellanies in prose and verse. London, 1805.
Htn Phil 2305.1.30* Taylor, Thomas. The mystical initiations. London, 1787.
Phil 585.168 Taylor, Thomas. A vindication of the rights of brutes (1792). Gainesville, Fla., 1966.
Phil 1900.86 Taylor, W.E. Ethical and religious theories of Bishop Butler. Toronto, 1903.
Phil 6329.3 Taylor, W.S. Readings in abnormal psychology. N.Y., 1926.
Phil 6990.23 Taylor, William F. Miracles; their physical possibility. Liverpool, 1868.
Phil 7069.37.45 Taylor, William G.L. Immortality. Boston, 1937.
Phil 7069.33.46 Taylor, William G.L. Katie Fox, epochmaking medium. N.Y., 1933.
Phil 5059.14 Taylor, William J. Elementary logic. N.Y., 1909.
Phil 6325.8.80 Taylor, William Sentman. Morton Prince and abnormal psychology. N.Y., 1928.
Phil 2477.6.92 Taymans d'Eypernon, F. Le blondelisme. Louvain, 1933.
Phil 8434.5 Tea, Eva. Il corpo umano. Brescia, 1949.
Htn Phil 2225.7.30* The teacher. (Palmer, George H.) Boston, 1908.
Phil 5258.25.5 Teacher's handbook of psychology. (Sully, J.) London, 1886.
Phil 5258.25.5.3 Teacher's handbook of psychology. (Sully, J.) N.Y., 1888.
Phil 5258.25.6 Teacher's handbook of psychology. (Sully, J.) N.Y., 1897.
Phil 5258.25.5.5 Teacher's handbook of psychology. 3d ed. (Sully, J.) N.Y., 1892.
Phil 5262.10 The teacher's psychology. (Welch, A.S.) N.Y., 1889.
Phil 5850.264.25 The teaching of human relations. (Magoun, F.A.) Boston, 1959.
Phil 7054.166 Teachings...from the spirit world. (Longley, Mary.) Chicago, 1908.

Phil 5374.235.5 — The teachings of Don Juan; a yaqui way of knowledge. (Castaneda, Carlos.) Berkeley, 1968.

Phil 4757.2.105 — Teachings of Gurdjieff. (Nott, C.S.) London, 1961.

Phil 3501.15 — Teale, A.E. Kantian ethics. London, 1951.

Phil 4080.17.10 — Tebaldeschi, I. Il problema della natura nel pensiero di Pantaleo Carabellese. Roma, 1955.

Phil 1135.215 — Techne. 1. ed. (Isnardi Parente, Margherita.) Firenze, 1966.

Phil 28.35 — Technical report. (Stanford University. Department of Psychology.) 1-9,1953-1955 3v.

Phil 6328.2.22 — Technik der analyschen Psychotherapie. (Stekel, Wilhelm.) Bern, 1938.

Phil 6310.1.11 — Die Technik der Individual-Psychologie. Teil 1-2. (Adler, A.) München, 1928-30.

Phil 6327.4.9 — Technik der Psychoanalyse. (Rank, Otto.) Leipzig, 1926-31. 3v.

Phil 6332.12 — Die Technik der Psychoanalyse. (Wittels, Fritz.) München, 1926.

Phil 3450.19.82 — Die Technik und die Kehre. (Heidegger, Martin.) Pfullingen, 1962.

Phil 5627.245.1 — Technik und Glaube. (Tournier, Paul.) Basel, 1945.

Phil 400.130 — Technik und Idealismus. (Zschimmer, Eberhard.) Jena, 1920.

Phil 193.262 — Technika i mowa jako narsedsia pornania ludskiego. (Szymański, Jesy.) Pornań, 1971.

Phil 6316.27 — The technique and practice of psychoanalysis. (Greenson, Ralph R.) London, 1967.

Phil 8706.3 — La technique contre la foi? (Queffélec, H.) Paris, 1962.

Phil 5259.10 — Technique de psychologie experiment. (Toulouse.) Paris, 1911. 2v.

Phil 7069.59.45 — Technique et panthéon des mediums viêtnamiens. (Durand, M.) Paris, 1959.

Phil 5525.42.10 — Technique et psychologie du comique. Thèse. (Aubouin, Elie.) Marseille, 1948.

Phil 7069.17.45 — A technique for the experimental study of telepathy. (Troland, L.T.) Albany, N.Y., 1917.

Phil 6328.2.25 — Technique of analytical psychotherapy. (Stekel, Wilhelm.) London, 1939.

Phil 5041.39.2 — The technique of controversy. (Bogoslovsky, B.B.) London, 1928.

Phil 5041.39 — The technique of controversy. (Bogoslovsky, B.B.) N.Y., 1928.

Phil 9245.51 — Technique of happiness. (Patter, Charles F.) N.Y., 1935.

Phil 6316.12.5 — The technique of psycho-analysis. (Glover, Edward.) London, 1955.

Phil 6321.11.15 — Technique of psychoanalytic therapy. (Lorand, Sándor.) N.Y., 1946.

Phil 6980.780.15.2 — The technique of psychotherapy. 2. ed. (Wolberg, Lewis Robert.) N.Y., 1967. 2v.

Phil 6111.27.2 — The technique of rest. (Brackett, Anna C.) N.Y., 1893.

Phil 5545.220 — Techniques for efficient remembering. (Laird, Donald.) N.Y., 1960.

Phil 5272.16 — Techniques inédites pour l'examen psychologique. (Rey, André.) Neuchâtel, 1967.

Phil 5465.147 — The techniques of creative thinking. 1. ed. (Crawford, Robert Platt.) N.Y., 1954.

Phil 5066.251 — Techniques of deductive inference. (Leblanc, Hugues.) Englewood Cliffs, 1966.

Phil 5190.38 — Techniques of persuasion. (Brown, J.A.C.) Baltimore, 1963.

Phil 310.18 — Der technische Eros. (Hommes, Jakob.) Freiburg, 1955.

Phil 1750.295 — Technische Existenz, Essays. (Bence, Max.) Stuttgart, 1949.

Phil 6969.10 — Technisches Schaffen Geisteskranker. (Tramer, Moritz.) München, 1926.

Phil 1750.660 — Die Technisierung der Welt. (Meyer, H.J.) Tübingen, 1961.

Phil 5585.355 — Technology and perception. (Cappon, Daniel.) Springfield, 1971.

Phil 960.145 — Techoueyres, E. A la recherche de l'unité. Reims, 1934.

Phil 5190.80 — Técnica de la persuasión. (Morales Encina, Carlos.) Santiago de Chile, 1969.

Phil 5465.160 — La tecnica divina: el movimiento. (Patron Miranda, Joaquin R.) Campeche, 1945.

Phil 70.96 — Tecnica e casistica. (Archivio di Filosofia.) Padova, 1964.

Phil 3450.19.495 — Tecnica e giustizia nel pensiero di Martin Heidegger. (Romano, Bruno.) Milano, 1969.

Phil 177.138 — Un tecnico fra i filosofi. (Ceccato, Silvio.) Padova, 1964- 2v.

Phil 5421.25.50 — De tederheid. Gedachten over de liefde. (Lemaire, Ton.) Utrecht, 1968.

Phil 1819.7 — Tedeschi, Paul. Paradoxe de la pensée anglaise au XVIIe siècle. Paris, 1961.

Phil 2725.60 — Tedeschi, Paul. Saint-Aubin et son oeuvre. Paris, 1968.

Phil 8644.5 — Teed, Cyrus R. The immortal manhood. 2. ed. Estero, 1909.

Phil 5246.86 — The teenager and psychology. 1. ed. (Gelinas, Robert P.) N.Y., 1971.

Phil 5645.56 — Teevan, R.C. Color vision. Princeton, 1961.

Phil 5548.110 — Teevan, Richard Collier. Theories of motivation in learning. Princeton, 1964.

Phil 2050.197 — Tegen, Einar. Humes uppfattning av jagets identitet. Uppsala, 1932.

Phil 3501.6 — Tegen, Einar. Studier till uppkomsten av Kants. Uppsala, 1918.

Phil 194.18.5 — Teichmüller, G. Neue Grundlegung der Psychologie und Logik. Breslau, 1889.

Phil 1124.1.5 — Teichmüller, G. Neue Studien zur Geschichte der Begriffe. Gotha, 1876-1879. 2v.

Phil 1124.1 — Teichmüller, G. Studien zur Geschichte der Begriffe. Berlin, 1874.

Phil 8644.6.2 — Teichmüller, G. Über die Ansterblichkeit der Seele. 2. Aufl. Leipzig, 1879.

Phil 194.18 — Teichmüller, G. Die Wirkliche und die scheinbare Welt. Breslau, 1882.

Phil 8599.25 — Teichmüller, Gustav. G. Teichmüllers Philosophie des Christentums von E. Tennmann. Tartu, 1931.

Phil 8599.13 — Teichmüller, Gustav. Religionsphilosophie. Breslau, 1886.

Phil 8420.17 — Teige, Karel. Stavba a báseň; uměnídues a zítra. Praha, 1927.

Phil 2905.1.635 — Teiiardizm. (Babosov, Evgenii M.) Minsk, 1970.

Phil 2905.1.410 — Teilhard, missionnaire et apologiste. (Lubac, Henri de.) Toulouse, 1966.

Phil 2905.1.500 — Teilhard, oui ou non? (Rideau, Émile.) Paris, 1967.

Phil 2905.1.366 — Teilhard de Chardin; a guide to his thought. (Rideau, Émile.) London, 1967.

Phil 2905.1.520 — Teilhard de Chardin, père de l'Église ou pseudo-prophète? (Tilloy, Alain.) Saint Cénère, 1968.

Phil 2905.1.33 — Teilhard de Chardin, Pierre. Album. London, 1966.

Phil 2905.1.67 — Teilhard de Chardin, Pierre. Building the earth. London, 1965.

Phil 2905.1.65 — Teilhard de Chardin, Pierre. Building the earth. 1st American ed. Wilkes-Barre, Pa., 1965.

Phil 2905.1.15 — Teilhard de Chardin, Pierre. The divine milieu. 1st ed. N.Y., 1960.

Phil 2905.1.350 — Teilhard de Chardin, Pierre. Écrits du temps de la guerre, 1916-1919. Paris, 1965.

Phil 2905.1.50 — Teilhard de Chardin, Pierre. The future of man. London, 1964.

Phil 2905.1.48 — Teilhard de Chardin, Pierre. The future of man. 1st American ed. N.Y., 1964.

Phil 2905.1.35 — Teilhard de Chardin, Pierre. Genèse d'une pensée. Paris, 1961.

Phil 2905.1.18 — Teilhard de Chardin, Pierre. Human energy. London, 1969.

Phil 2905.1.42 — Teilhard de Chardin, Pierre. Hymn of the universe. London, 1965.

Phil 2905.1.40 — Teilhard de Chardin, Pierre. Hymne de l'universe. Paris, 1961.

Phil 2905.1.69 — Teilhard de Chardin, Pierre. Je m'explique. Paris, 1966.

Phil 2905.1.69.1 — Teilhard de Chardin, Pierre. Let me explain. London, 1970.

Phil 2905.1.30 — Teilhard de Chardin, Pierre. Letters from a traveler. London, 1962.

Phil 2905.1.60 — Teilhard de Chardin, Pierre. Letters from Egypt. N.Y., 1965.

Phil 2905.1.29.5 — Teilhard de Chardin, Pierre. Letters to Léontine Zanta. London, 1969.

Phil 2905.1.28 — Teilhard de Chardin, Pierre. Letters to two friends, 1926-1952. N.Y., 1968.

Phil 2905.1.29 — Teilhard de Chardin, Pierre. Lettres à Léontine Zanta. Bruges, 1965.

Phil 2905.1.55 — Teilhard de Chardin, Pierre. Lettres d'Egypte, 1905-1908. Aubier, 1963.

Phil 2905.1.73 — Teilhard de Chardin, Pierre. Lettres d'Hastings et de Paris, 1908-1914. Paris, 1965.

Phil 2905.1.36 — Teilhard de Chardin, Pierre. The making of a mind. London, 1965.

Phil 2905.1.70 — Teilhard de Chardin, Pierre. La messe sur le monde. Paris, 1965.

Phil 2905.1.7 — Teilhard de Chardin, Pierre. L'oeuvre scientifique. Olten, 1971.

Phil 2905.1.5 — Teilhard de Chardin, Pierre. Oeuvres. Paris, 1956-10v.

Phil 2905.1.10 — Teilhard de Chardin, Pierre. The phenomenon of man. N.Y., 1959.

Phil 2905.1.12 — Teilhard de Chardin, Pierre. The phenomonon of man. N.Y., 1965.

Phil 2905.1.45 — Teilhard de Chardin, Pierre. La place de l'homme dans la nature. Paris, 1962.

Phil 2905.1.63 — Teilhard de Chardin, Pierre. Science and Christ. London, 1968.

Phil 2905.1.25 — Teilhard de Chardin, Pierre. Sur le bonheur. Paris, 1966.

Phil 2905.1.27 — Teilhard de Chardin, Pierre. Writings in time of war. London, 1968.

Phil 2905.1.235 — Teilhard de Chardin, prophète d'un âge totalitaire. (Charbonneau, B.) Paris, 1963.

Phil 2905.1.610 — Teilhard de Chardin, su concepción de la historia. 1. ed. (Bravo, Francisco.) Barcelona, 1970.

Phil 2905.1.480 — Teilhard de Chardin, témoignage et étude sur le développement de la pensée. (Solages, Bruno de.) Toulouse, 1967.

Phil 2905.1.290 — Teilhard de Chardin. (Braybrook, N.) N.Y., 1964.

Phil 2905.1.300 — Teilhard de Chardin. (Carles, Jules.) Paris, 1964.

Phil 2905.1.96 — Teilhard de Chardin. (Chauchard, Paul.) Paris, 1964?

Phil 2905.1.172 — Teilhard de Chardin. (Cuénot, Claude.) London, 1965.

Phil 2905.1.170 — Teilhard de Chardin. (Cuénot, Claude.) Paris, 1962.

Phil 2905.1.115 — Teilhard de Chardin. (Delfgaauw, B.M.I.) Baarn, 1961.

Phil 2905.1.165 — Teilhard de Chardin. (Grenet, Paul.) Paris, 1961.

Phil 2905.1.110 — Teilhard de Chardin. (Kahane, E.) Paris, 1960.

Phil 2905.1.385 — Teilhard de Chardin. (Luyten, Norbert Alfons.) Fribourg, 1965.

Phil 2905.1.310 — Teilhard de Chardin. (Magloire, G.) Paris, 1964.

Phil 2905.1.355 — Teilhard de Chardin. (Martinazzo, Eusebio.) Romae, 1965.

Phil 2905.1.125 — Teilhard de Chardin. (Rabut, Oliver A.) N.Y., 1961.

Phil 2905.1.185 — Teilhard de Chardin. (Raven, Charles.) London, 1962.

Phil 2905.1.570 — Teilhard de Chardin. (Reinhard, Edmond.) Pähl, 1966.

Phil 2905.1.535 — Teilhard de Chardin. (Trinité, Phillipe de la.) Paris, 1968.

Phil 2905.1.257 — Teilhard de Chardin. (Viallet, François A.) Nurnberg, 1963. 2v.

Phil 2905.1.130 — Teilhard de Chardin. (Wildiers, N.M.) Paris, 1961.

Phil 2905.1.240 — Teilhard de Chardin. Paris, 1963?

Phil 2905.1.455 — Teilhard de Chardin: a biography. (Speaight, Robert.) London, 1967.

Phil 2905.1.456 — Teilhard de Chardin: re-mythologization. (Speaight, Robert.) Chicago, 1970.

Phil 2905.1.675 — Teilhard de Chardin als Christ und als Mensch. (Goerres, Ida F.C.) Wiesbaden, 1971.

Phil 2905.1.380 — Teilhard de Chardin and the mystery of Christ. (Mooney, Christopher F.) London, 1966.

Phil 2905.1.550 — Teilhard de Chardin e a convergência das civilizações e das ciências. Lisboa, 1964?

Phil 2905.1.196.5 — Teilhard de Chardin e il pensiero cattolico. (Cuénot, Claude.) Firenze, 1966.

Phil 2905.1.196 — Teilhard de Chardin et la pensée catholique: colloque de Venise sous les auspices de Pax Romana. (Cuénot, Claude.) Paris, 1965.

Phil 2905.1.590 — Teilhard de Chardin et la sainte èvolution. (Combes, André.) Paris, 1969.

Phil 2905.1.377 — Teilhard de Chardin et le mystère du Christ. (Mooney, Christopher F.) Paris, 1966.

Phil 2905.1.430 — Teilhard de Chardin et le socialisme. (Coffy, Robert.) Lyon, 1966.

Phil 2905.1.445 — Teilhard de Chardin et l'unité du genre humain. Lisboa, 1965.

Phil 2905.1.440 — Teilhard de Chardin tra il mito e l'eresia. (Scaltriti, Giacinto.) Roma, 1964.

Phil 2905.1.465 — Teilhard de Chardin's theology of the Christian in the world. (Faricy, Robert L.) N.Y., 1967.

Phil 2905.1.620 — Teilhard et l'évangélisation des temps nouveaux. (Rétif, André.) Paris, 1970.

Phil 2905.1.395 — Teilhard ou Marx? (Monestier, André.) Paris, 1965.

Phil 2905.1.605 — Teilhard reassessed: a symposium of critical studies in the thought of Père Teilhard de Chardin attempting an evaluation of his place in contemporary Christian thinking. London, 1970.

Phil 2905.1.490 The Teilhard review. London. 1,1966+
Phil 2905.1.475 Teilhard study library. London. 2,1967+ 4v.
Phil 2905.1.390 Teilhard und Solowjew. (Truhlar, Karel Vladimir.) Freiburg, 1966.
Phil 7069.61.5 Teillard, A. Spiritual dimensions. London, 1961.
Phil 7082.190.5 Teillard, Ania. Ce que disent les rêves. Paris, 1970.
Phil 6060.57.2 Teillard, Ania. Handschriftendeutung auf tiefenpsychologischen Grundlage. 2. Aufl. Bern, 1963.
Phil 7082.190 Teillard, Ania. Le rêve, une porte sur le réel. Paris, 1951.
Phil 7084.10 Teillard, Ania. Traumsymbolik. Zürich, 1944.
Phil 3246.18.5 Eine Teilsammlung mit der Einfuhrung. (Fichte, Johann Gottlieb.) Stuttgart, 1935.
Phil 5769.7 Teisen, N. Om viljens frihed. København, 1904.
Phil 2070.87 Teisen, N. William James' laere om retten til at tro. København, 1911.
Phil 8659.4 Il teismo filosofico cristiano. pt.1. (Ercole, P. d'.) Torino, 1884.
Phil 3475.3.240 Teken en motief der creatuur. (Mekkes, Johan Peter Albertus.) Amsterdam, 1965.
Phil 5274.3 Tekhnicheskaia psikhologiia. (Bobneva, Margarita I.) Moskva, 1966.
Phil 5204.16 Telberg, Ina. Russian-English glossary of psychiatric terms. N.Y., 1964.
Phil 2905.1.85 Teldy-Naim, Robert. Faut-il brûler Teilhard de Chardin? Paris, 1959.
Phil 7054.61.8 The telegraph papers. (Spiritual telegraph.) N.Y., 1853. 8v.
Phil 7054.61.7 The telegraph's answer. (Brittan, Samuel B.) N.Y., 1855.
Phil 8665.10 Teleologický, kosmologický, a etický důkaz existence Boha v neotomismu. Vyd. 1. (Krejčí, Jaroslav.) Praha, 1967.
Phil 3850.14.85 Teleologie als theologische Kategorie bei Herman Schell. (Schneider, Theodor.) Essen, 1966.
Phil 8667.12 Der teleologische Gottesbeweis und der Darwinismus. (Mayer, P.) Mainz, 1901.
Phil 8735.7 Die teleologische Mechanik der lebendigen Natur. 2. Aufl. (Pflüger, E.F.W.) Bonn, 1877.
Phil 3160.9.83 Das teleologische Prinzip bei Carl Gustav Carus. Inaug. Diss. (Langewisch, Eva.) Würzburg, 1927.
Phil 182.94.85 Teleologisches Denken. (Brandenstein, Béla.) Bonn, 1960.
Phil 182.94.12 Teleologisches Denken. (Hartmann, N.) Berlin, 1951.
Phil 1900.93 Teleology in the philosophy of Joseph Butler and Abraham Tucker. Thesis. (Harris, W.G.) Philadelphia, 1941.
Phil 7069.21.90 La télépathie, recherches experimentales. (Warcollier, R.) Paris, 1921.
Phil 7069.58.5 La télépathie. (Amadou, Robert.) Paris, 1958.
Phil 7069.22.14 Telepathie. (Hellberg, E.) Prien, 1922.
Phil 7069.30.7 Telepathie und Hellsehen. (Friedländer, A.A.) Stuttgart, 1930.
Phil 7060.255 Telepathie und Hellsehen. (Wasielewski, W.) Halle, 1922.
Phil 7069.45.45 Telepathy. 2. ed. (Carington, Whately.) London, 1945.
Phil 7069.25.25 Telepathy and clairvoyance. (Tischner, R.) London, 1925.
Phil 7069.47.20 Telepathy and medical psychology. (Ehrenwald, Jan.) London, 1947.
Phil 7069.52 Telepathy and spiritualism. (Hettinger, John.) N.Y., 1952.
Phil 7068.97.30 Telepathy and the subliminal self. (Mason, R.O.) N.Y., 1897.
Phil 7068.97.34 Telepathy and the subliminal self. (Mason, R.O.) N.Y., 1899.
Phil 7069.41.7 Telepathy in search of a lost faculty. (Garrett, Eileen Jeanette Lyttle.) N.Y., 1941.
Phil 7069.13.40 Telepathy of the celestial world. (Station, Horace C.) N.Y., 1913.
Phil 7060.44 La telepatia. (Ermacora, G.B.) Padova, 1898.
Phil 7069.12.98 Telepatia e sogno. (Zingaropoli, F.) Napoli, 1912.
Phil 7060.142 Telergy, the communion of souls. (Constable, Frank C.) London, 1918.
Phil 4235.1.99 Telesio, the first of the moderns. (Van Deusen, Neil C.) N.Y., 1932.
Phil 4235.1.30 Telesius, B. Consentini de rerum. Neapoli, 1570.
Phil 4235.1.35 Telesius, B. De rerum natura. Modena, 1910. 3v.
Phil 4235.1.40 Telesius, B. Varii de naturalibus rebus libelli. Hildesheim, 1971.
Phil 5421.20.125 Television and aggression. 1. ed. (Feshbach, Seymour.) San Francisco, 1971.
Phil 9065.5 Telifcilipin tenokurlan. (Ülken, Hilmi Ziyoi.) Istanbul, 1933.
Phil 5029.1 Tellbom, J.P. De progressibus desciplinae logicae. Diss. Upsaliae, 1830.
Phil 8709.15 Teller, Woolsey. The atheism of astronomy. N.Y., 1938.
Phil 8709.15.5 Teller, Woolsey. Essays of an atheist. N.Y., 1945.
Phil 293.8.4 Telliamed. (Maillet, Benoît de.) La Haye, 1755. 2v.
Phil 293.8.2 Telliamed. (Maillet, Benoît de.) La Haye, 1755. 2v.
Phil 293.8.6 Telliamed. (Maillet, Benoît de.) London, 1750.
Phil 293.8.8 Telliamed. (Maillet, Benoît de.) Urbana, 1968.
Htn Phil 293.8.15* Telliamed. The world explained. (Maillet, Benoît de.) Baltimore, 1797.
Phil 293.8 Telliamed. v.1-2. (Maillet, Benoît de.) Amsterdam, 1748.
Phil 2115.138 Tellkamp, A. Das Verhältnis John Locke's zur Scholastik. Münster, 1927.
Htn Phil 8691.8.5* Telluris theoria sacra. v.1-2. (Burnet, Thomas.) London, 1681-89.
Phil 4073.31 Telogia. (Campanella, Tommaso.) Milano, 1936.
Phil 29.49 Telos. Amherst, N.Y. 1,1968+ 2v.
Phil 8661.18 El tema de Dios en la filosofía existencial. (Gonzalez Alvarez, Angel.) Madrid, 1945.
Phil 187.139 El tema del hombre. (Marias Aquilera, J.) Madrid, 1943.
Phil 8585.47 Temas de mistica y religion. (Fatone, Vicente.) Bahía Blance, 1963.
Phil 181.85 Temas existenciales. (Guglielmini, H.) Buenos Aires, 1939.
Phil 4357.6.80 Temas filosoficos medievales. (Alonso, Manuel.) Comillas, 1959.
Phil 705.52 La tematica della trascendenza. (Giannini, Giorgio.) Roma, 1964.
Phil 400.134 La tematico religiosa nell idealismo attuale. (Fichera, Giuseppe.) Catania, 1969.
Phil 165.320 Temi e problemi di filosofia classica. Milano, 1960.
Phil 5710.11 Temperament, a survey of psychological theories. (Bloor, Constance.) London, 1928.
Phil 6980.732 Temperament and behavior disorders in children. (Thomas, Alexander.) N.Y., 1969.
Phil 9035.10 Tempérament et caractère. (Fouillée, A.) Paris, 1895.
Phil 9035.111 Temperament lichnosti i fiksiorovannaia ustanovka. (Norakidze, Vladimir G.) Tbilisi, 1970.
Phil 5710.7 Temperament und Charakter. (Ewald, G.) Berlin, 1924.
Phil 5710.12 Les tempéraments. (Allendy, R.) Paris, 1922.
Phil 5710.5.2 The temperaments. (Jaques, D.H.) N.Y., 1879.
Phil 6122.7.15 La température du cerveau, études thermometriques. (Mosso, A.) Turin, 1895.
Phil 8709.22 Temperley, H.N.V. A scientist who believes in God. London, 1961.
Phil 7069.41.6 Temple, Laurence. The shining brother. London, 1941.
Phil 8709.6 Temple, William. The faith and modern thought. London, 1913.
Phil 8599.17 Temple, William. Mens creatrix. v.1-2. London, 1917.
Phil 8599.17.10 Temple, William. Nature, man and God. London, 1935.
Phil 2725.38 Le temple et le Dieu. (Leyvraz, Jean Pierre.) Paris, 1960.
Phil 29.1 The temple of reason. N.Y., 1800.
Phil 9070.48 The temple of the spirit. (Meehan, Francis Joseph D.) N.Y., 1948.
Phil 185.13 The temple of truth. (Kaufmann, P.) Cincinnati, 1858.
Phil 5059.17 Templin, Olin. A guide to thinking; a beginner's book in logic. Garden City, N.Y., 1927.
Phil 672.197 Il tempo. (Archivio di Filosofia.) Padova, 1958.
Phil 5330.21 Il tempo di reazione semplice. (Patrizi, M.L.) Reggio-Emilia, 1897.
Phil 672.198 Tempo e eternità. (Archivio di Filosofia.) Padova, 1959.
Phil 672.199 Tempo e intenzionalità. (Archivio di Filosofia.) Padova, 1960.
Phil 2725.35.87 Il tempo e la libertà in L. Lavelle. (Beschin, Giuseppe.) Milano, 1964.
Phil 3450.19.485 Il tempo e quattro saggi su Heidegger. (Mazzantini, Carlo.) Parma, 1969.
Phil 1750.820 Tempo e relazione. (Paci, Enzo.) Milano, 1965.
Phil 672.264 Tempo e significato. (Jacobelli Isoldi, Angela Maria.) Roma, 1968.
Phil 4080.12.62 Il tempo esaurito. 2. ed. (Castelli, Enrico.) Milano, 1954.
Phil 4260.131 Il tempo in G.B. Vico. (Sabarini, Raniero.) Milano, 1954.
Phil 2020.87 The temporal and eternal in the philosophy of Thomas H. Green. Thesis. (McKirachan, John C.) Ann Arbor, 1941.
Phil 5066.316.5 Temporal logic. (Rescher, Nicholas.) Wien, 1971.
Phil 5520.442 Temporal sequence in the perception of speed. (Fay, Warren H.) The Hague, 1966.
Phil 4080.16 Temps, espace devenir, moi. (Consentino, A.) Paris, 1938.
Phil 672.240 Le temps, quatrième dimension de l'esprit. (Wallis, Robert.) Paris, 1966.
Phil 672.163.5 Le temps. (Sivadjian, J.) Paris, 1938. 6v.
Phil 672.163 Le temps. (Sivadjian, J.) Paris, 1938.
Phil 672.162 Le temps. (Souriau, Michel.) Paris, 1937.
Phil 672.147 Le temps absolu et l'espace à quatre dimensions. (Sevin, Emile.) Paris, 1928.
Phil 8886.84 Le temps dans la vie morale. (Lévy-Valensi, Eliane Amado.) Paris, 1968.
Phil 5585.141 Le temps dans la vie psychologique. (Lévy-Valensi, Elaine Amado.) Paris, 1965.
Phil 4320.10A Le temps et la mort dans la philosophie espagnole contemporaine. Toulouse, 1968.
Phil 672.250 Temps et langage. (Jacob, André.) Paris, 1967.
Phil 4080.12.50 Le temps Larcelant. (Castelli, Enrico.) Paris, 1952.
Phil 8520.80 Temps présent et religion. (Joussain, André.) Toulouse, 1967.
Phil 5585.340 Le temps psychologique. (Lévy, Jean Claude.) Paris, 1969.
Phil 8881.71 Temptation. (Gilbert, Headley B.) Dallas, Texas, 1949.
Phil 2515.10.5 The temptation to exist. (Cioran, Émile M.) Chicago, 1968.
Phil 3450.11.112 Temuralk, T. Über die Grenzen der Erkennbarkeit. Inaug. Diss. Berlin, 1937.
Phil 3450.11.110 Temuralk, T. Über die Grenzen der Erkennbarkeit bei Husserl und Scheler. Berlin, 1937.
Phil 1830.52 Ten contemporary thinkers. (Amend, V.E.) N.Y., 1964.
Phil 8877.74 Ten lessons in ethics. (Cushman, H.E.) Newton, 1924.
Phil 9350.2 Ten minute talks to boys. (Kittredge, H.C.) Concord, N.H., 1917.
Phil 7040.39 Ten studies into psychopathic personality. (Craft, Michael.) Bristol, 1965.
Phil 7082.44.1 Ten thousand dreams interpreted; or, What's in a dream. (Miller, Gustavus Hindman.) Chicago, 1931.
Phil 7069.65.10 Ten years of activities. (Parapsychology Foundation.) N.Y., 1965.
Phil 7054.65 Ten years with spiritual mediums. (Fairfield, F.G.) N.Y., 1875.
Phil 2480.81 Tencer, Marie. La psychophysiologie de Cabanis. Thèse. Toulouse, 1931.
Phil 3006.7.5 Les tendances actuelles de la philosophie allemande. (Gurvitch, G.) Paris, 1949.
Phil 3006.7 Les tendances actuelles de la philosophie allemande. Photoreproduction. (Gurvitch, G.) Paris, 1930.
Phil 5223.1 Tendences nouvelles dans la psychologie contemporaine. (Nuttin, Jozef.) Louvain, 1951.
Phil 4960.625 Tendências do pensamento estético contemporâneo no Brasil. (Vita, Luís Washington.) Rio de Janeiro, 1967.
Phil 7069.26.70 Tenhaeff, W.H.C. Beknopte Handleiding der psychical research. 's Gravenhage, 1926. 3v.
Phil 7069.33.45 Tenhaeff, W.H.C. Paragnosie en "Einfuehlen". Proefschrift. Bussum, N.H., 1933.
Phil 7069.22.40 Tenhaeff, W.H.C. Supernormale vermogens. Amsterdam, 1922.
Phil 7030.2 Tenhaeff, Wilhelm H.C. Parapsychologie. Antwerpen, 1968.
Htn Phil 2045.107* Tenison, Thomas. The creed of Mr. Hobbes examined. London, 1670.
Phil 2138.118 Tennant, C. Utilitarianism explained and exemplified in moral and political government. In answer to John Stuart Mill's utilitarianism. London, 1864.
Phil 6990.28 Tennant, F.R. Miracle and its philosophical presuppositions. Cambridge, 1925.
Phil 8599.21.5 Tennant, F.R. The nature of belief. London, 1943.
Phil 8599.21 Tennant, F.R. Philosophical theology. Cambridge, 1928-30. 2v.
Phil 8599.21.90 Tennant's philosophical theology. (Scudder, D.L.) New Haven, 1740.
Phil 819.1 Tennemann, W.G. Geschichte der Philosophie. v.1-11. Leipzig, 1798-1819. 12v.
Phil 819.1.3 Tennemann, W.G. Grundriss der Geschichte der Philosophie. Leipzig, 1820.
Phil 819.1.5 Tennemann, W.G. Grundriss der Geschichte der Philosophie. 5. Aufl. Leipzig, 1829.
Phil 819.1.13A Tennemann, W.G. Manual of the history of philosophy. London, 1852.
Phil 819.1.12 Tennemann, W.G. Manual of the history of philosophy. Oxford, 1832.

Phil 819.1.7   Tennemann, W.G. Manuel de l'histoire de la philosophie. Paris, 1829. 2v.

Phil 819.1.8   Tennemann, W.G. Manuel de l'historie de la philosophie. Paris, 1839. 2v.

Phil 8700.7   The Tennessee evolution case. (Keebler, R.S.) Memphis, 1925.

Phil 8969.2   Tenney, E.P. Jubilee essays. Boston, 1862.

Phil 9359.8   Tenow, Elsa. Kärlek och lycka af Elsa Törne, [Pseud.]. Stockholm, 1910.

Phil 5259.23   Ten Seldam, W.H. Psychologische hoofdstukken. Amsterdam, 1926.

Phil 8590.3   Tentamen theologiae dunatscopicae. (Kemp, J.T. van der.) Lugdunum Batavorum, 1775.

Phil 3552.63.20   Tentamina theodicaeae de bonitate Dei libertate hominis et origine mali. (Leibniz, Gottfried Wilhelm.) Francofurti, 1719.

Phil 3552.63.25   Tentamina theodicaeae de bonitate Dei libertate hominis et origine mali. (Leibniz, Gottfried Wilhelm.) Tubingae, 1771.

Phil 8622.20   La tentation de faire du bien. (Duméry, Henry.) Paris, 1957.

Phil 2515.10   La tentation d'exister. 2. éd. (Cioran, Émile M.) Paris, 1956.

Phil 5360.34   Tenzer, Oliver. Abstrakcia. 1. vyd. Bratislava, 1966.

Phil 4265.2.96   Teocrazia e neo-cattaluisimo nel risorgimento. (Rizzo, R.) Palermo, 1938.

Phil 4210.175   La teodicea sociale di Rosmini. (Piovani, Pietro.) Padova, 1957.

Phil 5628.55.11   Teodorowicz, Józef. Mystical phenomena in the life of Theresa Neumann. St. Louis, Mo., 1940.

Phil 282.23   Teogonie e cosmogonie. (Bianchi, Ugo.) Roma, 1960.

Phil 8951.29   Teologia moralna. Wyd. 2. (Borowski, A.) Lublin, 1960.

Phil 4112.90   La teologia razionale di P. Galluppi. (Cardone, Elsa.) Palmi, 1959.

Phil 4482.2.80   Teólogo laico. (Sant'Anna, Dionisio.) Seara Nova, 1961.

Phil 8092.4   Teoremi e problemi di estetica contemporanea. (Assunto, Rosario.) Milano, 1960.

Phil 310.747   Teoreticheskol nasledie V.I. Lenina i meditsina. Moskva, 1970.

Phil 5649.29   Teoretické a metodologické problémy výzkumů průběhu volních pohybu. (Brichcín, Milan.) Praha, 1966.

Phil 5870.10   Teoretisk barnpsykologi. (Gästrin, Jan Emanuel.) Stockholm, 1966.

Phil 185.85   Teoria analogii bytu. (Krąpiec, M.A.) Lublin, 1959.

Phil 8418.40   Teoría de la sensibilidad. 1. ed. (Rubert de Ventós, Xavier.) Barcelona, 1969.

Phil 735.220   Teoría de los valores y filosofía de la historia. (Dujoune, L.) Buenos Aires, 1959.

Phil 8964.2   Teoria degli atti umani. (Oddone, Andrea.) Milano, 1933.

Phil 177.136   Teoría del autodeísmo. (Cernuschi, Alberto.) Buenos Aires, 1962.

Phil 2805.350   La teoría del conocimiento en Pascal. (Perdomo, Garcia José.) Madrid, 1956.

Phil 2805.360   La teoría del conocimiento en Pascal. (Perdomo, Garcia José.) Madrid, 1956.

Phil 4368.2.45   Teoría del hombre. (Romero, Francisco.) Buenos Aires, 1952.

Phil 189.24   Teoría del nous. (Oribe, Emilio.) Buenos Aires, 1934.

Phil 189.24.5   Teoría del nous. (Oribe, Emilio.) Buenos Aires, 1944.

Phil 194.30   Teoria del pragmatismo trascendentale. (Tilgher, A.) Milano, 1915.

Phil 3903.1.91   La teoria della conoscenza in G. Volkelt. (Ferro, A.A.) Aosta, 1903.

Phil 2115.123   La teoria della conoscenza in Locke e Leibnitz. (Corti, S.) Siena, 1908.

Phil 5039.30   Teoria della demostrazione. (Centro di Studi Filosofici di Gallarate.) Padova, 1963.

Phil 3425.125   La teoria della libertà nella filosofia di Hegel. (Fazio-Allmayer, C.) Messina, 1920.

Phil 4210.113   La teoria della percezione intellettiva. (Carabellese, P.) Bari, 1907.

Phil 4080.3.461   La teoria della storia di Benedetto Croce. (Franchini, Raffaello.) Napoli, 1966.

Phil 8416.37   Teoria dell'arte d'avanguardia. (Poggioli, Renato.) Bologna, 1962.

Phil 8412.35   Teoria dell'arte e della critica. (Logroscimo, G.) Padova, 1962.

Phil 2050.201   La teoria delle passioni di Davide Hume. (Volpe, Galvano della.) Bologna, 1931.

Phil 9550.12   La teoria dell'utile. (Marchesini, G.) Milano, 1900.

Phil 175.26.5   La teoria di Einstein. (Aliotta, Antonio.) Palmero, 1922.

Phil 343.40   Teoria do conhecimento. (Martins, Diamantino.) Braga, 1957.

Phil 8581.90   Teoria do destino. (Bandeira de Mello, L.M.) Gazeta de Leopoldina, 1944.

Phil 4473.1.30   Teoria do ser e da verdade. (Marinho, José.) Lisboa, 1961.

Phil 5722.30   Teoria e practica del Mandala. (Tucci, Giuseppe.) Roma, 1949.

Phil 8050.84   Teoria e storia dell'estetica. (Miele, Franco.) Milano, 1965.

Phil 5585.9   Teoria fisiologica della percezione. (Sergi, G.) Milano, 1881.

Phil 181.45.9   Teoria generale dello spirito come atto puro. 2a ed. (Gentile, Giovanni.) Pisa, 1918.

Phil 181.45.11   Teoria generale dello spirito come atto puro. 3a ed. (Gentile, Giovanni.) Bari, 1920.

Phil 181.45.15   Teoria generale dello spirito come atto puro. 6a ed. (Gentile, Giovanni.) Firenze, 1944.

Phil 5039.8   Teoria i doświadczenie. (Poloka Akademia Nauk. Instytut Filozofii i Socjologii.) Warszawa, 1966.

Phil 2636.83   La teoria pedagogica di Helvetius. (Stanganelli, Irma.) Napoli, 1919.

Phil 341.30   Teoria poznania praktycznego. (Kalinowski, J.) Lublin, 1960.

Phil 1711.9   Teoría y realidad del otro. (Laín Entralgo, Pedro.) Madrid, 1961. 2v.

Phil 8886.73.10   Teoria y sociedad. (López Aranguren, José Luis.) Barcelona, 1970.

Phil 8407.42   Teorías estéticas. (Garcia Prado, Carlos,) Madrid, 1962.

Phil 6122.54   Teórica del sistema nervioso. (Mainini, Carlos.) n.p., 1901.

Phil 4115.50   Teorica del sovranaturale. (Gioberti, V.) Capolago, 1850. 2v.

Phil 4115.50.5   Teorica del sovranaturale. (Gioberti, V.) Venezia, 1850.

Phil 4115.42   La teorica delle mente umana. (Gioberti, V.) Milano, 1910.

Phil 2138.105   La teorica dell'individualismo secondo J.S. Mill. (Martinazzoli, A.L.) Milano, 1905.

Phil 2045.101   Le teorie di Hobbes e Spinoza. (Iodice, A.) Napoli, 1901.

Phil 5242.2   Le teorie nativistiche e genetiche della localizzazione spaziale. (Cesca, G.) Verona, 1883.

Phil 310.751   Teoriia, preobrasui ushchaia mir. (Spirkin, Aleksandr G.) Moskva, 1969.

Phil 5640.135   Teoriia oshchushchenii. (Anan'ev, B.G.) Leningrad, 1961.

Phil 5625.103   Teoriia otrazheniia i ee estestvenno-nauchnoe obosnovanie. (Medvedev, N.M.) Moskva, 1963.

Phil 310.130   Teoriia poznaniia dialekticheskogo materializma. (Presniakov, P.V.) Alma-Ata, 1959.

Phil 310.7.7   Teoriia poznaniia dialekticheskogo materializma. (Vostrikov, A.V.) Moskva, 1965.

Phil 3500.85   Teoriia poznaniia I. Kanta. (Shashkevich, P.D.) Moskva, 1960.

Phil 960.39.10   Teoriia poznaniia i logika po ucheniiu pozdneishikh buddistov. (Shcherbatskii, F.I.) Sankt Peterburg, 1903-09. 2v.

Phil 930.39.5   Teoriia poznaniia i logika po ucheniiu pozdreishikh buddistov. (Scherbatskii, F.I.) Sankt Peterburg, 1903-09. 2v.

Phil 350.6   Teoriia poznaniia i sovremennaia nauka. Moskva, 1967.

Phil 5520.315   Teoriia poznaniia obshchei semantiki. (Brutian, G.A.) Erevan, 1959.

Phil 5520.576   Teoriia rechevoi deiatel'nosti. Moskva, 1968.

Phil 5170.14   Teoriia sillogistiki v sovremennoi formal'noi logike. (Subbotin, Aleksandr L.) Moskva, 1965.

Phil 8419.64   Teoriia stilia. (Sokolov, Aleksandr N.) Moskva, 1968.

Phil 5170.13   Teoriia sylogizmu zdań asertorycznych u azystotelesa. (Korcik, Antoni.) Lublin, 1948.

Phil 310.20.5   Teoriiata na otrazhenieto i nashata suvremennost. (Pavlov, Todor D.) Sofiia, 1961.

Phil 310.686   Teoriiata na otrazhenieto v domarksovata filosofiia. (Rusev, Pancho.) Sofiia, 1968.

Phil 4210.28   Teosofia. (Rosmini-Serbati, Antonio.) Torino, 1859-74. 2v.

Phil 5259.50   Teplov, B.M. Problemy individual'nykh razlichii. Moskva, 1961.

NEDL Phil 5259.36   Teplov, B.M. Psikhologiia. Moskva, 1948.

Phil 6129.9   Tepp, Max. Vom Sinn des Körpers. Hamburg, 1919.

Phil 3120.40.80   Ter herdenling van Dr. J.D. Bierens de Haan. (Brahell Brujs, W.R. van.) Naarden, 1944.

Phil 9164.2   Tercero encontro Latino-Americano. (Encontro Latino Americano, 3d, Rio de Janeiro, 1963.) Rio de Janeiro, 1963.

Phil 8980.827   Terekhov, S.S. Za kommunisticheskuiu nravstvennost'. Leningrad, 1964.

Phil 310.146   Teriaev, G.V. Due fazy kommunisticheskogo obshchestva i zakonomernosti pererastatelnogo sotsializma v kommunizm. Moskva, 1962.

Phil 8879.56   Terkiye ilminin problemlen. (Egemen, Bedi Ziya.) Ankara, 1965.

Phil 575.160   Terlecki, Tymon. Krytyka personalistyczna. Londyn, 1957.

Phil 705.11   Der Terminus transszendental in seiner historischen Entwickelung bis zu Kant. Inaug. Diss. (Knittermeyer, Hinrich.) Marburg, 1920.

Phil 3925.16.270   Terms in their proportional contexts in Wittgenstein's Tractatus; an index. (Polochmann, George Kimball.) Carbondale, 1962.

Phil 2905.1.295   Terra, Helmut de. Memories of Teilhard de Chardin. London, 1964.

Phil 2905.1.296   Terra, Helmut de. Perspektiven Teilhard de Chardins. München, 1966.

Phil 29.47   Terra nova. München. 3-4 2v.

Phil 9560.7   Terraillon, E. L'honneur sentiment et principle moral. Paris, 1912.

Phil 3280.83   Terraillon, E. La morale de Geulincx. Paris, 1912.

Phil 5465.56.10   La terre et les rêveries de la volonté. (Bachelard, G.) Paris, 1948.

Phil 5465.56.30   La terre et les rêveries du repos. (Bachelard, G.) Paris, 1948.

Phil 8582.51.10   The terrible crystal; studies in Kierkegaard and modern Christianity. (Chaning-Pearce, Melville.) London, 1940.

Phil 7084.16   The terror-dream. (Green, George Henry.) London, 1927.

Phil 672.122.9   Tertium organum. (Uspenskii, P.D.) Berlin, 1931.

Phil 672.122.7   Tertium organum. (Uspenskii, P.D.) Rochester, 1920.

Phil 672.122   Tertium organum. 2nd American ed. (Uspenskii, P.D.) N.Y., 1922.

Phil 672.122.3   Tertium organum. 2nd American ed. (Uspenskii, P.D.) N.Y., 1923.

Phil 672.122.5   Tertium organum. 2nd American ed. (Uspenskii, P.D.) N.Y., 1923.

Phil 179.32   Tertium quid; ratiocination. (Elrick, C.F.) St. Louis, 1934.

Phil 7069.20.320   Tertium Quid (pseud.). The verdict:-? London, 1920.

Phil 5520.570   Terwilliger, Robert F. Meaning and mind. N.Y., 1968.

Phil 2805.390   Terzi, Carlo. Pascal. Bergamo, 1960.

Phil 3808.205   Terzi, Carlo. Schopenhauer. Romae, 1955.

Phil 1540.13   A tese escolastica do composto humano. Diss. (Serras, Pereira, M.) Coimbra, 1923.

Phil 140.17   Pamphlet vol. Tesi di filosofia e lettere. 8 pam.

Phil 7069.34.41   El tesoro de la ciencia eterna de Dios. (Vilanova, María.) Barcelona, 1933-34. 2v.

Phil 1750.55   Das Test der Seele. (Damur, Carl.) Bern, 1947.

Phil 5599.85.5   Le test des trois personnages. (Backes-Thomas, Madeleine.) Neuchâtel, 1969.

Phil 5545.51   Test of accuracy of testimony of by-standers. n.p., 1912.

Phil 7069.70   Test your E.S.P. (Ebon, Martin.) N.Y., 1970.

Phil 8420.19   Testa, Aldo. Filosofia dell'arte. Bologna, 1959.

Phil 1870.165   Testa, Aldo. Meditazioni su Berkeley. Bologna, 1965.

Phil 4073.116   Testa, Aldo. Meditazioni su Campanella. Bologna, 1965.

Phil 5520.660   Testa, Aldo. La struttura dialogica del linguaggio. Bologna, 1967.

Phil 4235.3.31   Testa, Alfonso. Della filosofia della mente. Piacenza, 1836.

Phil 5520.120   Testability and meaning. (Carnap, Rudolf.) New Haven, 1950.

Phil 8666.2   Testaceo-Theologia. (Lesser, F.C.) Leipzig, 1756.

Phil 9345.7   Testament, ou Conseils fideles d'un bon pere. (Fortin, P.) Leide, 1653.

Phil 2490.77   Testament. (Comte, Auguste.) Paris, 1884.

Phil 3808.190   Das Testament Arthur Schopenhauer. (Busch, Hugo.) Wiesbaden, 1888.

Phil 2490.77.2   Testament d'Auguste Comte, avec les documents qui s'y rapportent. (Comte, Auguste.) Paris, 1896.

Phil 8592.122.5   Le testament de Jean Meslier. (Meslier, Jean.) Amsterdam, 1864. 3v.

Author and Title Listing

Phil 3745.6.35 Testament eines Deutschen; Philosophie der Natur und Menschheit. 3e Ausg. (Planck, K.C.) Jena, 1925.

Phil 182.51 Testament philosophique...essai de synthése evolutioniste. (Horion, Charles.) Bruxelles, 1900.

Phil 2855.3.15 Testament philosophique et fragments. (Ravaisson-Mollien, Félix.) Paris, 1933.

Phil 9450.5 Testament politique et moral. (Ferencz II Rakoczi, Prince of Transylvania.) La Haye, 1751.

Phil 6689.4 Teste, A. A practical manual of animal magnetism. London, 1843.

Phil 194.33 Teste, Paulin. Le precurseur. Le Haye, 1912.

Phil 48.8 Testi e documenti. (Instituto di Studi Filosofici, Rome.) Firenze. 1,1949

Phil 4030.5 Testi umanistici inediti sul De anima. (Archivio di Filosofia.) Padova, 1951.

Phil 1630.5 Testi umanistici su l'ermetismo. (Archivio di Filosofia.) Roma, 1955.

Phil 5922.4.20 Testimonials. (Combe, George.) Edinburgh, 1836. 3 pam.

Phil 2280.8.95 Testimonials in favor of Andrew Seth. Photoreproduction. (Seth Pringle-Pattison, Andrew.) Edinburgh, 1891.

Phil 2150.8.80 Testimonials in favor of J.S. Mackenzie. Glasgow, 1888. 2 pam.

Phil 1845.4.90 Testimonials to his character. (Abbot, F.E.) Boston, 1879.

Phil 8586.3 The testimony of natural theology to Christianity. (Gisborne, T.) London, 1818.

Phil 9010.8 Testimony of Progressive Friends. Amusements. N.Y., 1856-59. 3 pam.

Phil 8595.11 The testimony of reason. (Phillips, S.L.) Washington, 1903.

Phil 8702.6 The testimony of the rocks. (Miller, H.) Boston, 1857.

Phil 5592.45 The testing of Negro intelligence. (Shuey, Audrey Mary.) Lynchburg, 1958.

Phil 5592.45.2 The testing of Negro intelligence. 2. ed. (Shuey, Audrey Mary.) N.Y., 1966.

Phil 5272.26.2 Tests and measurements. 2d ed. (Tyler, Leona Elizabeth.) Englewood Cliffs, 1971.

Phil 2125.35 The tests of the various kinds of truth. (McCosh, James.) N.Y., 1891.

Phil 6854.8 Tetaz, Numa. Du darfst Leben. Zürich, 1970.

Phil 5259.6 Tetens, J.N. Philosophische Versuche über die menschliche Natur. Leipzig, 1777. 2v.

Phil 5259.6.8 Tetens, J.N. Uber die allgemeine speculativische Philosophie. Berlin, 1913.

Phil 3890.6.86 Tetens Einfluss auf die kritische Philosophie Kants. Inaug. Diss. (Seidel, A.) Würzburg, 1932.

Phil 3425.301 Tetralogia Hegeliana. (Contri, S.) Bologna, 1938-39. 2v.

Phil 3195.10.130 Teufel, Herbert. Der Begriff des Werdens und der Entwicklung bei Driesch. München, 1960.

Phil 2115.131 Tex, Jan den. Locke en Spinoza over de tolerantie. Amsterdam, 1926.

Phil 59.4 Texas. Society of Mental Hygiene. Yearbook. Austin.

Phil 5242.4 Text-book in intellectual philosophy. (Champlin, J.T.) Boston, 1860.

Phil 3428.45 Text-book in psychology. (Herbart, J.F.) N.Y., 1891.

Phil 6321.25 Text book of abnormal psychology. (Landis, Carney.) N.Y., 1946.

Phil 5252.19 Text-book of experimental psychology. (Myers, C.S.) N.Y., 1909.

Phil 5252.19.3 Text-book of experimental psychology. 3d ed. (Myers, C.S.) Cambridge, 1925.

Phil 5252.19.2.5 A text book of experimental psychology with laboratory exercises. 2nd ed. pt.1. (Myers, C.S.) Cambridge, 1911.

Phil 5052.23 A text-book of inductive logic. (Mukerji, A.C.) Allahabad, 1919.

Phil 6962.4.4 A text-book of insanity. (Mercier, C.A.) London, 1902.

Phil 6962.4.5 A text-book of insanity. (Mercier, C.A.) London, 1914.

Phil 5043.19 A text-book of logic. (Davies, A.E.) Columbus, 1915.

Phil 6320.6.15 A text book of medical psychology. (Kretschmer, E.) London, 1934.

Phil 6961.10 A text-book of mental diseases. (Lewis, W.B.) Philadelphia, 1890.

Phil 6962.10 Text-book of psychiatry. (Mendel, Emanuel.) Philadelphia, 1907.

Phil 6957.17.20 A text-book of psychiatry for students and practitioners. (Henderson, D.K.) Oxford, 1947.

Phil 6957.17.5 A text-book of psychiatry for students and practitioners. 2. ed. (Henderson, D.K.) London, 1930.

Phil 6957.17.7 A text-book of psychiatry for students and practitioners. 3. ed. (Henderson, D.K.) London, 1933.

Phil 5255.9 A text book of psychology. (Putnam, Daniel.) N.Y., 1901.

Phil 5259.5.35 A text-book of psychology. (Titchener, E.B.) N.Y., 1924.

Phil 5259.5.37 A text-book of psychology. (Titchener, E.B.) N.Y., 1926.

Phil 5259.5.38 A text-book of psychology. (Titchener, E.B.) N.Y., 1928.

Phil 6313.10 Textbook of abnormal psychology. (Dorcus, Roy M.) Baltimore, 1934.

Phil 6313.10.2 Textbook of abnormal psychology. 2d ed. (Dorcus, Roy M.) Baltimore, 1944.

Phil 5258.113.5 A textbook of experimental and theoretical psychology. (Skaggs, E.B.) Boston, 1935.

Phil 5042.19 Textbook of logic. (Cunningham, H.E.) N.Y., 1924.

Phil 5047.37 A textbook of logic. (Hartman, S.J.) N.Y., 1936.

Phil 5062.22.12 Textbook of logic. (Wolf, Abraham.) N.Y., 1930.

Phil 5062.22.16 Textbook of logic. 2nd ed. (Wolf, Abraham.) London, 1961.

Phil 6951.11.5 Textbook of psychiatry. (Bleuler, E.) N.Y., 1924.

Phil 978.8.19 Textbook of theosophy. (Leadbeater, C.W.) Chicago, 1925.

Phil 530.20.95 Textbuch zur Mystik des deutschen Mittelalters. (Quint, Josef.) Halle, 1952.

Phil 530.20.120 Texte deutscher Mystik des 16. Jahrhunderts. (Seyppel, Joachim Hans.) Göttingen, 1963.

Phil 2805.30.3 Texte primitif des Lettres provinciales. (Pascal, Blaise.) Paris, 1867.

Phil 2648.20 Textes choisis. (Holbach, Paul Henri T.) Paris, 1957.

Phil 2705.20 Textes choisis. (La Mettrie, Julien Offray de.) Paris, 1954.

Phil 165.341 Textes choisis des auteurs philosophiques. v.2. (Cuvillier, A.) Paris, 1961.

Phil 2880.8.195 Textes de Jean Paul Sartre. (Jeason, Francis.) Paris, 1966.

Phil 5520.738 Textes et communications sur le thème: philosophie et langage, 24 avril, 1969. Photoreproduction. (Centre Regional de Documentation, Pedagogique de Poitiers.) Paris, 1969?

Phil 29.13 Textes et études d'histoire de la philosophie. Paris.

Phil 2805.27 Textes inédits. (Pascal, Blaise.) Bruges, 1962.

Phil 3552.72 Textes inédits d'après les manuscrits de la Bibliothèque provinciale. (Leibniz, Gottfried Wilhelm.) Paris, 1948. 2v.

Phil 525.135 Textes mystiques d'Orient et d'Occident. (Lemaître, S.) Paris, 1955.

Phil 2648.96 Textkritische Studien zum Werk Holbachs. (Besthern, Rudolf.) Berlin, 1969.

Phil 4960.615 Textos brasileiros de filosofía. Rio de Janeiro. 1-5,1957-1960// 4v.

Phil 4977.5 Textos filosóficos. (Pessoa, Fernando.) Lisboa, 1968. 2v.

Phil 6127.7.5 Textura del sistema nervioso del hombre y de los Vertebrados. V.1-2. (Ramón y Cajal, S.) Madrid, 1899. 3v.

Phil 57.2 Textus et documenta. Series philosophica. (Rome. Pontificia Universitas Gregoriana.) Romae. 1-14,1932-1938 13v.

Phil 3425.425 Teyssèdre, Bernard. L'asthétique de Hegel. Paris, 1958.

Phil 54.5 Tezisy dokladov, 29 iiunia -4 iiulia 1959 g. v.1-3. (Obshchestvo Psikhologov, Moscow, 1. S"ezd, 1959.) Moskva, 1959.

Phil 70.3.70 Tezisy soobshchenii. Abstracts of communications. (International Congress of Psychology, 18th, Moscow, 1966.) Moskva. 1966 3v.

Phil 7150.54 Thakur, Upendra. The history of suicide in India. 1st ed. Delhi, 1963.

Phil 5400.84.6 The thalamus and emotion. (Lashley, K.S.) Lancaster, 1938.

Phil 6969.6 Thalbitzer, S. Emotion and insanity. London, 1926.

Phil 802.21 Thales to Dewey. (Clark, Gordon Haddon.) Boston, 1957.

Phil 194.23 Thalheimer, A. The meaning of terms 'existence' and 'reality'. Princeton, 1920.

Phil 2305.5.30 Thalheimer, Alvin. Existential metaphysics. N.Y., 1960.

Phil 8709.11 Thallackson, E. Science, evolution, religion. Boston, 1927.

Phil 8844.1 Thamin, R. Extraits des moralistes. Paris, 1897.

Phil 8969.1 Thamin, R. Saint Ambroise et la morale chrétienne au IV siècle. Paris, 1895.

Phil 1200.19 Thamin, Raymond. Un problème moral dans l'antiquité. Paris, 1884.

Phil 7140.118.2 Thamiry, E. De l'influence: étude psychologique, métaphysique, pédagogique. Lille, 1922.

Phil 7140.118 Thamiry, E. De l'influence: étude psychologique. Thèse. Lille, 1921.

Phil 8632.16 Thanataphobia and immortality. (Hall, G.S.) n.p., 1915.

Phil 8612.21 Thanatos. (Lovatelli, E.) Roma, 1888.

Phil 400.91.25 Thanner, Ignaz. Der Transcendental-Idealismus. München, 1805.

Phil 55.6 Thasmatological Society. Selections from the papers of the society. Oxford 1,1882

Phil 5520.478 Thass-Thienemann, Théodore. The subconscious language. N.Y., 1967.

Phil 5520.545 Thass-Thienemann, Théodore. Symbolic behavior. N.Y., 1968.

Phil 182.63 That life is the origin and purpose of the universe. (Hallett, T.G.P.) London, 1916.

Phil 672.7 That space is necesary being. (Place, C.) London, 1728.

Phil 3640.810 Thatcher, David S. Nietzsche in England, 1890-1914. Toronto, 1970.

Htn Phil 3246.65* Die Thatsachen des Bewusstseyns. (Fichte, Johann Gottlieb.) Stuttgart, 1817.

Phil 5585.3 Thatsachen in der Wahrnehmung. (Helmholtz, Hermann van.) Berlin, 1879.

Phil 194.16.10 Thayer, H.D. The Herodian me. Atlantic City, 1930.

Phil 194.16 Thayer, H.D. Physio-Psychics. Philadelphia, 1914.

Phil 1955.6.120 Thayer, H.S. The logic of pragmatism. N.Y., 1952.

Phil 194.56 Thayer, Horace Standish. Meaning and action. Indianapolis, 1968.

Phil 9530.9 Thayer, W.M. Ethics of success. Boston, 1893.

Phil 9179.4 Thayer, W.M. Hints for the household. Photoreproduction. Boston, 1853.

Phil 9359.2 Thayer, W.M. Poor girl and true woman. Boston, 1859.

Phil 5260.9 The adjustment of personality. (United States. Department of Agriculture. Graduate School.) Washington, 1939.

Phil 8589.19.8 The Christ of the Mount. (Jones, E.S.) N.Y., 1935.

Phil 2138.113 The Examiner, London. John Stuart Mill. London, 1873.

Phil 17.1.5 The Hibbert journal. Index. v.1-10. Boston, 1902-1911.

Phil 3450.33.8 The human person and the world of values. (Schwarz, Baldwin.) N.Y., 1960.

Phil 19.41 The Japanese psychological research. Tokyo. 1,1954+ 5v.

NEDL Phil 3800.250.50 The philosophy of art. (Schelling, F.W.J. von.) London, 1845.

Phil 6315.2.45 The psychologie collective et analyse du moi. (Freud, Sigmund.) Paris, 1924.

Phil 5255.11 The psychology of belief in objective existence. pt.1. (Pikler, Gyula.) London, 1890.

Phil 3050.8 The romantic tradition in Germany. (Taylor, Ronald Jack.) London, 1970.

Phil 9495.68 The sexuality of nature. (Grindon, Leopold Hartley.) Boston, 1868.

Phil 3415.115 The unconcious and Eduard von Hartmann; a historico-critical monograph. (Darnoi, D.N.K.) The Hague, 1968.

Phil 2419.3 Théard. Tableau des trois époques, ou Les philosophes. Paris, 1829.

Phil 5722.45 Théâtre de veille et théâtre de songe. (Gonseth, J.P.) Neuchâtel, 1950.

Htn Phil 8870.7* Theatrum virtutis et honoris. (Pirckheimer, W.) Nürnberg, 1606.

Phil 2475.1.515 Theau, Jean. La critique bergsonienne du concept. Thèse. Toulouse, 1967.

Phil 3805.82 Theil. Friedrich Daniel Ernst Schleiermacher. Berlin, 1835.

Phil 3120.10.80 Theile, Günther. Philosophische Streifzüge an deutschen Hochschulen. Berlin, 1904.

Phil 1135.64 Theiler, W. Zur Geschichte der teleologischen Naturbetrachtung bis auf Aristoteles. Inaug. Diss. Zürich, 1924.

Phil 1135.64.5 Theiler, W. Zur Geschichte der teleologischen Naturbetrachtung bis auf Aristoteles. Zürich, 1925.

Phil 1170.24 Theiler, Willy. Forschungen zum Neuplatonismus. Berlin, 1966.

Phil 8599.52 Theill-Wunder, Hella. Die archaische Verborgenheit. München, 1970.

Phil 8969.16 Theiner, Johann. Die Entwicklung der Moraltheologie zur eigenständigen Disziplin. Regensburg, 1970.

Phil 8520.36 Theios. (Bieler, Ludwig.) Wien, 1935-36. 2v.

Phil 6805.8   Their mother's sons. (Strecker, Edward Adam.)
               Philadelphia, 1951.
Phil 3450.18.180   Theisen, Hans. Determination und Freiheit bei Nicolai
                   Hartmanns. Köln, 1962.
Phil 8656.8.7   Theism. (Bowne, B.P.) N.Y., 1902.
Phil 8669.1   Theism. (Orr, John.) London, 1857.
Phil 8599.7   Theism. (Tulloch, J.) Edinburgh, 1855.
Phil 8660.4   Theism. (Baird lectures for 1876). (Flint, R.)
                Edinburgh, 1877.
Phil 8660.4.4   Theism (Baird lectures for 1876). 10. ed. (Flint, R.)
                London, 1902.
Phil 8666.13   Theism and cosmology. (Laird, John.) London, 1940.
Phil 8586.62   Theism and empiricism. (Gibson, Alexander Boyce.)
                London, 1970.
Phil 8656.13   Theism and humanism. (Balfour, A.J.B.) N.Y., 1915.
Phil 8879.10.5 Theism and the Christian faith. (Everett, C.C.)
                N.Y., 1909.
Phil 8662.13   Theism and the modern mood. (Horton, Walter M.)
                N.Y., 1930.
Phil 8656.13.5 Theism and thought. (Balfour, A.J.B.) London, 1923.
Phil 8656.13.7 Theism and thought. (Balfour, A.J.B.) N.Y., 1924.
Phil 8676.3   Theism as a science of natural theology. (Voysey, C.)
                London, 1895.
Phil 8658.8   Theism as grounded in human nature. (Davidson, W.L.)
                London, 1893.
Phil 8661.12.5 Theism found wanting. (Godfrey, W.S.) London, 1920.
Phil 1905.12.90 The theism of Edgar S. Brightman. Diss. (McLarney, James
                J.) Washington, 1936.
Phil 8657.16   Theism or atheism. (Cohen, Chapman.) London, 1921.
Phil 8585.4   Le théisme. 2. éd. v.1-2. (Ferrières, C.E.) Paris, 1790.
Phil 8658.5   The theistic argument as affected by recent theories.
                (Diman, J.L.) Boston, 1881.
Phil 8657.4   The theistic conception of the world. (Cocker, B.F.)
                N.Y., 1875.
Phil 8674.5   Pamphlet box. Theistic Endeavour Society.
Phil 8659.5   Theistic monism. (Evans, Joseph.) London, 1928.
Phil 3245.45   Die theistische Weltansicht. (Fichte, Immanuel Hermann.)
                Leipzig, 1873.
Phil 1400.5   Themata christianikēs kai buzantinēs philosophias.
                (Tatakēs, B.N.) Athens, 1952.
Phil 5590.15   Thematic apperception test. (Murray, Henry A.) Cambridge,
                Mass., 1943. 2v.
Phil 5590.38   The thematic apperception test. (Tomkins, Silvan S.)
                N.Y., 1947.
Phil 193.172   Theme for reason. (Smith, J.W.) Princeton, 1957.
Phil 1701.23.3 Les thèmes actuels de la philosophie. (Bréhier, Émile.)
                Paris, 1954.
Phil 1701.23   Les thèmes actuels de la philosophie. 1. éd. (Bréhier,
                Émile.) Paris, 1951.
Phil 3640.510   Thèmes et structures dans l'oeuvre de Nietzsche.
                (Kremer-Marietti, Angèle.) Paris, 1957.
Phil 525.165   Thèmes et textes mystiques. (Gardet, Louis.) Paris, 1958.
Phil 2750.20.50.5 Themes from the lectures at the Collège de France,
                   1952-1960. (Merleau-Ponty, Maurice.) Evanston, 1970.
Phil 5249.31   Themes in speculative psychology. (Jordan, Nehemiah.)
                London, 1968.
Phil 5258.90   Thèmes psychologiques. (Saint-Paul, G.) Paris, 1926.
Phil 7068.87.10 Theobald, Morell. Spirit workers in the home circle.
                London, 1887.
Phil 3552.62   Theodicaea. (Leibniz, Gottfried Wilhelm.) Paris, 1726.
Phil 3310.5.30 Die Theodicee. (Gutberlet, C.) Münster, 1878.
Phil 3552.62.10 Théodicée. (Leibniz, Gottfried Wilhelm.) Hannover, 1744.
Htn Phil 3552.63*   Théodicée. (Leibniz, Gottfried Wilhelm.) Hannover, 1763.
Phil 3552.63.15 Die Theodicee. (Leibniz, Gottfried Wilhelm.)
                Leipzig, 1883. 2v.
Phil 8592.5   Théodicée. (Margerie, A. de.) Paris, 1865. 2v.
Phil 8592.8   Théodicée chrétienne. (Maret, H.L.C.) Paris, 1844.
Phil 8520.25   Die Theodicee im 18 Jahrhundert. (Lindau, Hans.)
                Leipzig, 1911.
Phil 8656.19   Theodicee of natuurlijke godsleer. 2. druk. (Beysens,
                J.T.) Bussum, 1919.
Phil 8620.1   A theodicy. (Bledsoe, A.T.) N.Y., 1856.
Phil 3552.63.10 Theodicy. (Leibniz, Gottfried Wilhelm.) New Haven, 1952.
Phil 3501.9   Theodor, J. Der Unendlichkeitsbegriff bei Kant und
                Aristoteles. Breslau, 1877.
Phil 2138.151   Theodor Gomperz and John Stuart Mill. (Weinberg,
                Adelaide.) Genève, 1963.
Phil 3450.29.80 Theodor Haecker. (Blessing, Eugen.) Nürnberg, 1959.
Phil 3450.29.85 Theodor Haeckers christliches Menschenbild. (Schnarwiler,
                W.) Frankfurt, 1962.
Phil 3585.14.20 Theodor Lessing. (Hieronimus, E.) Hannover, 1964.
Phil 3585.10.94 Theodor Lipps' neuere Urteilslehre. (Anschütz, G.)
                Leipzig, 1913.
Phil 3585.12.80 Theodor Litt. (Vogel, Paul.) Berlin, 1955.
Phil 2605.3.40 Theodore Flournoy, 1854-1920. Genève, 1928.
Phil 2672.80   Théodore Jouffroy. (Ollé-Laprune, L.) Paris, 1899.
Phil 2672.90   Théodore Jouffroy: sa vie et ses écrits. (Tissot, J.)
                Paris, 1876.
Phil 1504.12.5 Theodoricus Teutonicus de Vriberg De iride et radialibus
                impressionibus. v.12, pt.5-6. (Würschmidt, J.)
                Münster, 1914.
Phil 2855.2.81 Théodule Ribot; choix de textes. (Ribot, Théodule.)
                Paris, 1913.
Phil 2855.2.82 Théodule Ribot; choix de textes. (Robot, Théodule.)
                Paris, 1917?
Phil 2855.2.95 Théodule Ribots Psychologie. (Krauss, S.) Jena, 1905.
Htn Phil 3585.4.30*   Theologia Deütsch. (Luther, Martin.) n.p., 1519.
Phil 8961.11   Theologia moralis. (Lehmkuhl, A.) Freiburg, 1888. 2v.
Phil 8958.9   Theologia moralis. 5. ed. (Iorio, Tommaso Angelo.)
                Neapolis, 1960-64. 3v.
Phil 2205.31   Theologia naturale. (Paley, W.) Roma, 1808.
Phil 3910.50   Theologia naturalis. (Wolff, Christian von.)
                Francofurti, 1736-41. 2v.
Phil 3910.50.5 Theologia naturalis. (Wolff, Christian von.)
                Veronae, 1738. 2v.
Phil 177.25.30 Theologia naturalis thetico-polemica. (Canz, Israel
                Gottlieb.) Dresdae, 1742.
Htn Phil 4934.2.30*   Theologia vivificans. (Dionysius Areopagita.)
                Argētine, 1502.
Phil 8610.870.10   Theological essays. (Bradlaugh, Charles.) London, 1883.
Phil 8968.18   Theological ethics. (Sellers, James.) N.Y., 1966.
Phil 8602.75   Theological explanation. (Woods, George.) Welwyn, 1958.
Phil 8962.20   The theological frontier of ethics. (Maclagan, W.G.)
                N.Y., 1961.
Phil 8595.15.3.5   The theological works. (Paine, Thomas.) Boston, 1834.
Phil 8595.15.4 Theological works. (Paine, Thomas.) Boston, 1859.
Phil 8595.15.4.3   Theological works. (Paine, Thomas.) Chicago, 19- ?
Phil 8595.15.4.10 Theological works. (Paine, Thomas.) London, 1819.
Phil 8595.15.2 Theological works. (Paine, Thomas.) London, 1824.
Phil 8595.15.2.5   The theological works. (Paine, Thomas.) London, 1827.
Phil 8598.14   A theologico-political treatise. (Snow, G.D.)
                London, 1874.
Phil 8622.78   Theologie aus Glaubenserfahrung. (Duss-von Werdt, Josef.)
                Zürich, 1969.
Phil 8598.18   Théologie de la nature. (Straus-Durckheim, H.E.)
                Paris, 1852. 3v.
Phil 8601.3   Théologie de la religion naturelle. (Vidal, F.)
                Paris, 1859.
Phil 3805.226   Theologie der bürgerlichen Gesellschaft. (Spiegel,
                Yorick.) München, 1968.
Phil 1114.10   Die Theologie der Frühen griechischen Denker. (Jaeger,
                Werner W.) Stuttgart, 1953.
Phil 8666.2.5   Theologie des insects. (Lesser, F.C.) La Hague, 1742.
Phil 3552.119   Die Theologie des Leibniz. (Pichler, A.) München, 1869.
                2v.
Phil 3425.764   Theologie et aliénation dans la pensée du jeune Hegel.
                (Rohrmoser, Günter.) Paris, 1970.
Phil 8740.10   Théologie et histoire de la spiritualité. (Gilson,
                Étienne.) Paris, 1943.
Phil 8586.36.66 Theologie im Schatten politischer Romantik. (Strohm,
                Theodor.) Mainz, 1970.
Phil 8599.24   La théologie naturelle, histoire, philosophique, critique
                et morale, ou Les pensées d'un homme sur l'être-Suprême.
                (Tarenne, G.) Paris, 1800?
Phil 8661.20   Théologie naturelle, ou théodicée. (Grison, M.)
                Paris, 1959.
Htn Phil 4369.1.30*   La théologie naturelle. 2. ed. (Sebon, Raymond.)
                Paris, 1640.
Phil 1516.2   La théologie scolastique. (Ligeard, H.) Paris, 1908.
Phil 3425.615   Theologie und Aufklärung. (Krueger, H.J.)
                Stuttgart, 1966.
Phil 2905.1.267 Theologie und Evolution. (Smulders, P.F.) Essen, 1963.
Phil 1504.11.3 Theologie und Wissenschaft nach de Lehre. v.11, pt.3-4.
                (Krebs, E.) Münster, 1912.
Phil 3819.57.5 Der theologisch-politische Traktat. 2. Aufl. (Spinoza,
                Benedictus de.) Leipzig, 1910.
Phil 8590.37   Theologische Anthropologie; die biblische Sicht des
                Menschen und der Mensch der Gegenwart. (Koehler, Hans.)
                München, 1967.
Phil 8590.23   Theologische Anthropologie im Abriss. (Kuhlmann, G.)
                Tübingen, 1935.
NEDL Phil 8967.1   Theologische Ethik. (Rothe, R.) Wittenberg, 1845-48.
                3v.
Phil 8967.1   Theologische Ethik. (Rothe, R.) Wittenberg, 1845-48.
                3v.
Phil 8967.1.3   Theologische Ethik. (Rothe, R.) Wittenberg, 1869-71.
                5v.
Phil 8969.4   Theologische Ethik. v.1-3. (Thielicke, Helmut.)
                Tübingen, 1951. 4v.
Phil 3425.61   Theologische Judenschriften. (Hegel, Georg Wilhelm
                Friedrich.) Tübingen, 1907.
Phil 1730.6   Die theologische und philosophische Aufklärung des
                achtzshuten und neunzehuten Jahrhunderts. (Erdmann, Karl.)
                Leipzig, 1849.
Phil 8595.15.4.5   Theologische Werke. v.1-4,6. (Paine, Thomas.)
                Philadelphia, 1851.
Phil 3801.485   Die theologischen Grundlagen von Schellings Philosophie der
                Freiheit. (Kile, Frederick O.) Leiden, 1965.
Phil 1135.18   Die theologischen Lehren der griechischen Denker.
                (Krische, A.B.) Göttingen, 1840.
Phil 3552.69.20 Theologisches System. (Leibniz, Gottfried Wilhelm.)
                Tübingen, 1860.
Phil 5627.270   Theology after Freud; an interpretive inquiry. (Homans,
                Peter.) Indianapolis, 1970.
Phil 8525.5   Theology and meaning: a critique of metatheological
                scepticism. (Heimbeck, Raeburne Seeley.) Stanford, 1969.
Phil 8878.4A   Theology and morality. (Davies, J.L.) London, 1873.
Phil 8592.48.3 Theology as an empirical science. (Macintosh, D.C.)
                N.Y., 1919.
Phil 8697.7   Theology in an age of science. (Hodgson, Leonard.)
                Oxford, 1944.
Phil 9240.34   A theology of Auschwitz. (Simon, Ulrich Ernest.)
                London, 1967.
Phil 8583.9   Theology of civilization. (Dole, Charles F.) N.Y., 1899.
Phil 1114.5.2   The theology of the early Greek philosophers. (Jaeger,
                Werner W.) London, 1968.
Phil 1114.5   The theology of the early Greek philosophers. (Jaeger,
                Werner W.) Oxford, 1947.
Phil 8592.35   The theology of the real. (Milburn, R.G.) London, 1925.
Phil 2750.11.73 Théonas. 2. éd. (Maritain, Jacques.) Paris, 1925.
Phil 5259.14   Theone, Alois S. Die Mechanik der Seelenlebens.
                Bonn, 1911.
Phil 8590.17   Theophilosophie. (Kreiss.) Berlin, 1880.
Phil 4515.90   Theorell, Sven L. Betraktelser i samhällslären med
                granskning af Boströmska statsläräns grundinier.
                Stockholm, 1860.
Phil 5066.11.35 A theorem on parametric Boolean functions. (Quine, Willard
                van Orman.) Santa Monica, 1949.
Phil 7069.09.70 Theorem or teleology of spiritualism. (Wiltse, May B.)
                New-Rockford, N. Dak., 1909.
Phil 5374.161   Théorème de la connaissance. (Paliard, J.) Paris, 1938.
Phil 5262.30   A theoretical basis of human behavior. (Weiss, Albert P.)
                Columbus, 1925.
Phil 5262.30.5 A theoretical basis of human behavior. 2d ed. (Weiss,
                Albert P.) Columbus, 1929.
Phil 8896.18   Theoretical ethics. (Valentine, M.) Chicago, 1897.
Phil 5238.175   Theoretical foundations of psychology. (Nelson, Harry.)
                Princeton, 1959.
Phil 5251.34.10 Theoretical psychology. (Lindworsky, J.) St. Louis, 1932.
Phil 5520.499   Der theoretische Bedeutungbegriff. Inaug. Diss. (Brandt,
                Elmar.) München, 1964.
Phil 3428.93   Die theoretische Philosophie Herbarts und seiner Schule.
                (Langenbeck, H.) Berlin, 1867.
Phil 5251.34.3 Theoretische Psychologie im Umriss. 3. Aufl. (Lindworsky,
                J.) Leipzig, 1926.
Phil 5241.71   Eine theoretische und experimentelle Untersuchung über den
                psychologischen der Klarheit. Diss. (Britz, Carl August.)
                Saarlouis, 1913.
Phil 1885.84   Der theoretische Weg Bradley's. (Chappuis, A.)
                Paris, 1933.
Phil 29.27   Theoria. Göteborg. 1,1935+ 19v.
Phil 1122.10   Theoria. Theoretische und praktische Lebensauffassung im
                philosophischen Denken der Antike. (Redlow, Götz.)
                Berlin, 1966.
Phil 8416.8.5   Theoria dell'arte; saggi di estetica. (Pareyson, Luigi.)
                Milano, 1965.

Phil 2475.1.298.5   La théorie bergsonienne de la religion. (Sundén, Jalmar.) Paris, 1947.

Phil 2475.1.298   La théorie bergsonienne de la religion. Thèse. (Sundén, Hjalmar.) Uppsala, 1940.

Phil 3480.71.21   Theorie de Kant sur la religion dans limites. (Kant, Immanuel.) Paris, 1842.

Phil 960.39.5   La théorie de la connaissance. (Shcherbatskii, F.I.) Paris, 1926.

Phil 630.23.10   La théorie de la connaissance chez les néo-réalistes anglais. (Kremer, René.) Louvain, 1928.

Phil 2730.99.5   La théorie de la connaissance chez Maine de Biran. 2e éd. (Vancourt, Raymond.) Paris, 1944.

Phil 2733.102   La théorie de la connaissance dans la philosophie de Malebranche. (Bridet, L.) Paris, 1929.

Phil 2733.102.5   La théorie de la connaissance dans la philosophie de Malebranche. Thèse. (Bridet, L.) Paris, 1929.

Phil 5545.12   Théorie de la mémoire. (Gratacap, A.) Montpellier, 1866.

Phil 176.26   Theorie de la raison impersonnelle. (Bouillier, F.) Paris, 1844.

Phil 2270.107   La théorie de la religion chez Spencer et ses sources. Thèse. (Absi, Marcelle.) Beyrouth, 1952.

Phil 3246.46   La théorie de la science expose de 1804. Thèse. (Fichte, Johann Gottlieb.) Paris, 1967.

Phil 2725.30.80   Théorie de la vérité chez Edouard LeRoy. (Miranda, Maria do Carmo Tavares de.) Paris, 1957.

Phil 9560.26   Théorie de l'ambition. (Herault de Séchelles, M.J.) Paris, 1802.

Phil 6110.8   Théorie de l'âme humaine. (Alaux, J.E.) Paris, 1896.

Phil 2070.49   La théorie de l'émotion. 5e éd. (James, William.) Paris, 1917.

Phil 3425.106   La théorie de l'état dans Hegel. (Lévy-Bruhl, L.) Paris, 1889.

Phil 1540.21   La théorie de l'idée suivant l'école thomiste. Thèse. (Garin, Pierre.) Bruges, 1932.

Phil 8430.3   Théorie de l'information et perception esthétique. (Moles, Abraham A.) Paris, 1958.

Phil 3450.11.97   La théorie de l'institution dans la phénoménologie de Husserl. (Levinas, Emmanuel.) Paris, 1930.

Phil 3450.11.98   La théorie de l'institution dans la phénoménologie de Husserl. Thèse. (Levinas, Emmanuel.) Paris, 1930.

Phil 3808.126.2   La theorie de l'intelligence chez Schopenhauer. (Medilch, P.) Paris, 1923.

Phil 5262.51   Theorie der Begabung. 2. Aufl. (Wenzl, Aloys.) Heidelberg, 1957.

Phil 5042.18   Theorie der Dialektik. (Cohn, Jonas.) Leipzig, 1923.

Phil 5045.11   Die Theorie der diskursiven Erkenntnis. (Frey, T.) Dorpat, 1929.

Phil 5640.125.10   Theorie der Empfindungsqualität als Abbildes des Reizes. (Pikler, Gyula.) Leipzig, 1922.

Phil 5640.125.9   Theorie der Empfindungsstärke und Insbesondere des Weberschen Gesetzes. (Pikler, Gyula.) Leipzig, 1920.

Phil 2266.42   Theorie der ethischen Gefühle. (Smith, Adam.) Leipzig, 1926. 2v.

Htn   Phil 7060.10.7*   Theorie der Geister-Kunde. (Jung Stilling, J.H.) Nürnberg, 1808 .

Phil 185.56   Theorie der Geisteswerthe. (Kniepf, Albert.) Leipzig, 1892.

Phil 5245.20   Theorie der Gesichtswahrnehmung. (Fischer, E.L.) Mainz, 1891.

Phil 5125.1   Die Theorie der Induction. (Apelt, E.F.) Leipzig, 1854.

Phil 5640.125.8   Theorie der Konsonanz und Dissonanz. (Pikler, Gyula.) Leipzig, 1919.

Phil 6310.1.15   Die Theorie der Organminderwertigkeit. (Adler, A.) Leipzig, 1908.

Phil 5850.214   Theorie der Psychotechnik: Grundzüge der praktischen Psychologie. (Giese, Fritz.) Braunschweig, 1925.

Htn   Phil 3480.72.5*   Theorie der Reinmoralischen Religion. (Kant, Immanuel.) Elberfeld, 1798.

Htn   Phil 3480.72*   Theorie der Reinmoralischen Religion. (Kant, Immanuel.) Riga, 1796.

Phil 2266.42.5   Theorie der sittlichen Gefühle. (Smith, Adam.) Leipzig, 1791-95. 2v.

Phil 3310.15   Theorie der Willensfreiheit und frühe philosophische Schriften. (Gehlen, Arnold.) Neuvied, 1965.

Phil 5756.13   Theorie der Willensfreiheit. (Gehlen, A.) Berlin, 1933.

Phil 3850.15.31   Die Theorie des Bewusstseyns im Wesen. (Staegmann, B.A. von.) Berlin, 1864.

Phil 3450.18.120   La théorie des catégories fondamentales dans Nicolai Hartmann. (Wahl, Jean André.) Paris, 1954.

Phil 5360.7   Théorie des concepts. (Peillaude, E.) Paris, n.d.

Phil 5640.125.15   Theorie des Gedächtnisses. (Pikler, Gyula.) Leipzig, 1926.

Phil 8404.13.5   Theorie des Gefühls zur Begrundung des Ästhetik. (Diez, Max.) Stuttgart, 1892.

Phil 3504.12.5   Theorie des Gegenstandes...bei I. Kant. (Wernieke, A.) Braunschweig, 1904.

Phil 5403.2   Die Theorie des Glücks. (Piderit, Theodor.) Leipzig, 1867.

Phil 2733.87   La théorie des idées dans la philosophie de Malebranche. (Gaonach, J.M.) Brest, 1908.

Phil 1200.18   La théorie des incorporels dans l'ancien stoïcisme. Thèse. (Bréhier, Émile.) Paris, 1908.

Phil 1200.18.5   La théorie des incorporels dans l'ancien stoïcisme. 2e éd. (Bréhier, Émile.) Paris, 1928.

Phil 192.7   Theorie des menschlichen Erkenntnissvermögens. (Reinhold, C.E.) Gotha, 1832-1835. 2v.

Phil 2885.82   Die Theorie des Milieu. (Dutoit, E.) Bern, 1899.

Phil 5066.250   Théorie des modèles en logique mathématique. (Daigneault, Aubert.) Montréal, 1963.

Phil 180.38   Theorie des objektiven Geistes. (Freyer, Hans.) Leipzig, 1923.

Phil 180.38.5   Theorie des objektiven Geistes. 3. Aufl. (Freyer, Hans.) Leipzig, 1934.

Phil 5135.6   Théorie des opinions. 1. éd. (Stoetzel, Jean.) Paris, 1943.

Phil 8620.52   La théorie des oppositions et la théologie du péché, au XIIIe siècle. (Gillen, Louis Bertrand.) Paris, 1937.

Phil 9420.6   Théorie des passions. (Carrau, L.) Strasbourg, 1870.

Phil 5400.174   La théorie des passions à la lumière de la pensée médicale du XVIIe siècle. (Riese, Walther.) N.Y., 1965.

Phil 8837.14   La théorie des passions du P. Senault et la morale chrétienne en France au XVIIe siècle. Thèse. (Miloyévitch, Voukossava.) Paris, 1934.

Phil 1865.43   Theorie des peines et des récompenses. v.1-2. (Bentham, Jeremy.) London, 1811.

Phil 623.14   Théorie des principes de l'absolu. (Roulleaux Dugage, G.) Paris, 1909.

Phil 2520.180   La théorie des sciences chez Descartes d'après sa géométrie. Thèse. (Mitrovitch, R.) Paris, 192-?

Phil 5402.4   Theorie des sentimens agreables. (Levesque de Pouilly, L.J.) Paris, 1748.

Phil 5402.4.2   Theorie des sentimens agreables. (Levesque de Pouilly, L.J.) Paris, 1774.

Phil 2266.43   Théorie des sentiments moraux. (Smith, Adam.) Paris, 1830. 2v.

Phil 9560.42   Theorie des Vertrauens. (Schottlaender, Rudolf.) Berlin, 1957.

Phil 5585.38   Theorie des Vorstellungsverlaufs. (Müller, Günter.) Mannheim, 1925.

Phil 1020.12   La théorie d'Ibn Rochd. (Gauthier, L.) Paris, 1909.

Phil 1750.70   Théorie du champ de la conscience. (Gurwitsch, Aron.) Paris, 1957.

Phil 2475.1.231   La théorie du comique de M.H. Bergson. (Laurila, K.S.) Helsinki, 1929.

Phil 2490.118   La théorie du savoir dans la philosophie d'Auguste Comte. (Uta, Michel.) Paris, 1928.

Phil 2490.118.5   La théorie du savoir dans la philosophie d'Auguste Comte. Thèse. (Uta, Michel.) Bourg, 1928.

Phil 5722.29   La théorie du subconscient de Morton Prince. (Casey, D.M.) Paris, 1945.

Phil 2150.22.130   La théorie et la pratique, dialogue imaginaire mais non tout à fait apocryphe entre Herbert Marcuse et Henri Lefebvre. (Delbo, Charlotte.) Paris, 1969.

Phil 3497.24   Théorie et praxis dans la pensée morale et politique de Kant et de Fichte en 1793. (Philonenko, Alexis.) Paris, 1968.

Phil 5635.2   Théorie générale de la sensibilité. (Delboeuf, J.R.L.) Bruxelles, 1876.

Phil 735.150   Théorie générale de la valeur et ses applications en esthétique et en économie. (Glansdorff, Maxime.) Bruxelles, 1954.

Phil 4112.81   La theorie idéologique de Galluppi. (Palhoriès, F.) Paris, 1909.

Phil 5190.5   Théorie logique des propositions modales. (Rondelet, A.) Paris, 1861.

Phil 5057.26.2   La théorie marxiste de la connaissance. (Raphael, Max.) Paris, 1937.

Phil 337.16   La théorie matérialiste de la connaissance. 1. ed. (Garaudy, R.) Paris, 1953.

Phil 284.4.2   La theorie physique, son objet, sa structure. 2. éd. (Duhem, P.) Paris, 1914.

Phil 284.4   La theorie physique. (Duhem, P.) Paris, 1906.

Phil 672.232   La theorie physique et la notion de temps. (Costa de Beauregard, Olivier.) Bordeaux, 1963.

Phil 672.3   Théorie psychologique de l'espace. (Dunan, C.) Paris, 1895.

Phil 7068.74.40   Théorie psychologique de l'hallucination (Ritti, A.) Paris, 1874.

Phil 5402.1   Théorie scientifique de la sensibilité. (Dumont, L.) Paris, 1875.

Phil 5247.80   Theorie und Experiment in der Psychologie. (Holzkamp, Klaus.) Berlin, 1964.

Phil 3480.26.10   Theorie und praxis. (Kant, Immanuel.) Leipzig, 1913.

Phil 3425.622   Theorie und Praxis. System theoretische Betrachtungen zu Hegel und Marx. (Benner, Dietrich.) Wien, 1966.

Phil 3425.618   Theorie und Praxis im Denken Hegels. (Riedel, Manfred.) Stuttgart, 1965.

Phil 187.44   Theories about the truth of things. (Mann, William E.) Franklin, Mass., 1919.

Phil 193.19   Theories and criticisms. (Scott, J. McD.) Halifax, 1883.

Phil 5125.13   Les théories de l'induction et de l'expérimentation. (Lalande, André.) Paris, 1929.

Phil 8125.37.5   Les théories esthétiques en Allemagne de Baumgarten à Kant. (Nivelle, A.) Paris, 1955.

Phil 5252.155   Theories in contemporary psychology. (Marx, Melvin Herman.) N.Y., 1965.

Phil 5062.20.10   Theories in logic. (Windelband, W.) N.Y., 1961.

Phil 2493.85   Les théories logiques de Condillac. Thèse. (Robert, Louis.) Paris, 1869.

Phil 5421.10.45   Theories of anxiety. (Fischer, William Frank.) N.Y., 1970.

Phil 5645.1   Theories of color-perception. (Burnett, S.M.) Philadelphia, 1884.

Phil 5650.32   Theories of hearing. (Kostelijk, P.J.) Leiden, 1950.

Phil 331.34   Theories of knowledge. (Ackermann, Robert John.) N.Y., 1965.

Phil 345.5   Theories of knowledge. (O'Neill, Reginald.) Englewood Cliffs, N.J., 1960.

Phil 5535.10.3   Theories of learning. 3. ed. (Hilgard, Ernest Ropiequet.) N.Y., 1966.

Phil 505.5.1   Theories of macrocosms and microcosms in the history of philosophy. (Conger, George Perrigo.) N.Y., 1967.

Phil 5545.156   Theories of memory. (Edgell, Beatrice.) Oxford, 1924.

Phil 5548.95.4   Theories of motivation; a comparative study. 4. ed. (Madsen, Kaj Berg.) Kent, Ohio, 1968.

Phil 5548.95   Theories of motivation. (Madsen, Kaj Berg.) Copenhagen, 1959.

Phil 5548.110   Theories of motivation in learning. (Teevan, Richard Collier.) Princeton, 1964.

Phil 5655.15   Theories of odor and odor measurement. (NATO Advanced Study Institute on Theories of Odor and Odor Measurement, Istanbul, 1966.) Bebek, Istanbul, 1966.

Phil 5585.78   Theories of perception and the concept of structure. (Allport, F.H.) N.Y., 1955.

Phil 5590.215   Theories of personality. (Hall, Calvin S.) N.Y., 1957.

Phil 5590.215.2   Theories of personality. (Hall, Calvin S.) N.Y., 1965.

Phil 5590.215.2.2   Theories of personality. 2. ed. (Hall, Calvin S.) N.Y., 1970.

Phil 5627.154   Theories of religious experience. Thesis. (Moore, J.M.) N.Y., 1938.

Phil 6976.10   Theories of schizophrenia. (Buss, Arnold H.) N.Y., 1969.

Phil 5640.40   Theories of sensation. (Rawdon-Smith, A.F.) Cambridge, 1938.

Phil 6128.76   Theories of the mind. (Scher, Jordan.) N.Y., 1962.

Phil 8110.12   Theories of the nature and standard of taste in England, 1700-1790. (Smith,A.C.) Chicago, 1937.

Phil 665.33   Theories of the transmigration of souls. (Gibbons, J.) London, 1907.

Phil 525.83   Theory and art of mysticism. (Mukerjee, R.) London, 1937.

Phil 5850.356   Theory and methods of scaling. (Torgerson, Warren S.) N.Y., 1958.

Phil 6985.30   Theory and practice of family psychiatry. (Howells, John Gwilym.) N.Y., 1971.

Phil 6673.16.5   The theory and practice of human magnetism. (Durville, H.) Chicago, 1900.

Phil 6980.734 The theory and practice of psychiatry. (Redlich, Fredrick.) N.Y., 1966.

Phil 5722.30.5 The theory and practice of the Mandala. (Tucci, Giuseppe.) London, 1961.

Phil 5722.30.6 The theory and practice of the Mandala. (Tucci, Giuseppe.) London, 1969.

Phil 5870.107 Theory and problems of child development. 2nd ed. (Ausubel, David Paul.) N.Y., 1970.

Htn Phil 2175.2.30* The theory and regulation of love. (Norris, John.) Oxford, 1688.

Phil 5592.176 Theory and research in projective techniques, emphasizing the TAT. (Murstein, Bernard.) N.Y., 1965.

Phil 8402.39.5 Theory and taste. (Brunius, Teddy.) Uppsala, 1969.

Htn Phil 6953.2* Theory concerning the nature of insanity. (DeRenne, G.W.J.) Wormsloe, 1847.

Phil 8897.37 Theory of abstract ethics. (Whittaker, Thomas.) Cambridge, 1916.

Phil 5548.108 A theory of achievement motivation. (Atkinson, John W.) N.Y., 1966.

Htn Phil 5769.6.5* Theory of agency...an essay on moral freedom. Boston, 1771.

Phil 5769.6 Theory of agency...an essay on moral freedom. Boston, 1771.

Phil 5402.4.5 Theory of agreeable sensations. (Levesque de Pouilly, L.J.) Boston, 1812.

Phil 8415.4 Theory of beauty; an introduction to aesthetics. (Osborne, .H.) N.Y., 1953.

Phil 8403.13.5 The theory of beauty. (Canitt, Edgar.) London, 1914.

Phil 8877.68.15 The theory of beauty. (Carritt, Edgar F.) London, 1962.

Phil 283.15 The theory of celestial influence. (Collin, R.) London, 1954.

Phil 5325.30A A theory of cognitive dissonance. (Festinger, Leon.) Evanston, Ill., 1957.

Phil 5325.40F The theory of cognitive dissonance. (Jordan, Nehemiah.) Washington, 1964.

Phil 5645.4.8 Theory of colours. (Goethe, J.W. von.) London, 1840.

Phil 8875.4 A theory of conduct. (Alexander, A.) N.Y., 1890.

Phil 302.1 Theory of cosmic reason. (Vinogradoff, I.) n.p., n.d.

Phil 5272.4 A theory of data. (Coombs, Clyde.) N.Y., 1967.

Phil 5125.27A Theory of deduction. Pts.1-4. (Quine, Willard van Orman.) Cambridge, 1948.

Phil 1955.6.225 The theory of democratic education; a critical exposition of John Dewey's philosophy of education. (Banerjee, Gour Moham.) Calcutta, 1961.

Phil 630.29.5 A theory of direct realism and the relation of realism to idealism. (Turner, J.E.) N.Y., 1925.

Phil 7082.136 The theory of dreams: in which an inquiry is made into the powers and faculties of the human mind. v.1-2. (Gray, Robert.) London, 1808.

Phil 8892.25 The theory of ethics. (Rogers, A.K.) N.Y., 1922.

Phil 8587.11 The theory of evolution of living things. (Henslow, G.) London, 1873.

Phil 8420.16 A theory of fine art. (Torrey, J.) N.Y., 1874.

Phil 9560.32.5 Theory of games. (Braithwaite, R.B.) Cambridge, Eng., 1963.

Phil 9560.32 Theory of games as a tool for the moral philosopher. (Braithwaite, R.B.) Cambridge, Eng., 1955.

Phil 8892.13 The theory of good and evil. (Rashdall, Hastings.) Oxford, 1907. 2v.

Phil 8892.13.4 The theory of good and evil. 2. ed. (Rashdall, Hastings.) London, 1948. 2v.

Phil 8892.13.2 The theory of good and evil. 2. ed. (Rashdall, Hastings.) Oxford, 1924. 2v.

Phil 2150.18.95 The theory of goodness in the writings of George Edward Moore, 1873-1958. (Hund, William Byrne.) Notre Dame, Ind., 1964.

Phil 5650.40 Theory of hearing. (Wever, Ernest.) N.Y., 1957.

Phil 5246.84 A theory of human action. (Goldman, Alvin I.) Englewood Cliffs, N.J., 1970.

Phil 5465.32 The theory of imagination in classical and mediaeval thought. (Bundy, Murray W.) Urbana, 1927.

Phil 5125.8 The theory of inference. (Hughes, Henry.) London, 1894.

Phil 1885.92 The theory of judgment in the philosophies of F.H. Bradley and John Cook Wilson. (Ahmed, M.) Dacca, 1955.

Phil 333.26 The theory of knowledge. (Cornforth, Maurice Campbell.) N.Y., 1955.

Phil 338.1 Theory of knowledge. (Hobhouse, L.T.) London, 1896.

Phil 2050.59.30 Theory of knowledge. (Hume, David.) Edinburgh, 1951.

Phil 349.21 A theory of knowledge. (Strong, C.A.) N.Y., 1923.

Phil 353.19 Theory of knowledge. (Woozley, A.) London, 1949.

Phil 349.32 Theory of knowledge and existence. (Stace, W.T.) Oxford, 1932.

Phil 2255.1.135* The theory of knowledge of Bertrand Russell. (Chisholm, John Edward.) Rome, 1967.

Phil 4260.165 The theory of knowledge of Giambattista Vico. (Manson, Richard.) Hamden, Conn., 1969.

Phil 5525.36 A theory of laughter. (Menon, V.K.K.) London, 1931.

Phil 5060.6 The theory of logic. (Ushenko, A.P.) N.Y., 1936.

Phil 4368.2.47 Theory of man. (Romero, Francisco.) Berkeley, 1964.

Phil 5520.640 Theory of meaning. (Lehrer, Adrienne.) Englewood Cliffs, N.J., 1970.

Phil 5272.18 Theory of measurement. (Pfanzogl, Johann.) Würzburg, 1968.

Phil 5252.20 A theory of mind. (March, J.L.) N.Y., 1908.

Phil 181.45.5 The theory of mind as pure act. (Gentile, Giovanni.) London, 1922.

Htn Phil 510.127 A theory of monads. (Carr, H. Wildon.) London, 1922.

Htn Phil 2266.36* The theory of moral sentiments. (Smith, Adam.) London, 1759.

Phil 2266.41.5 The theory of moral sentiments. (Smith, Adam.) N.Y., 1966.

Phil 2266.41.10 The theory of moral sentiments. (Smith, Adam.) New Rochelle, 1969.

Phil 2266.41.2 The theory of moral sentiments. (Smith, Adam.) Philadelphia, 1817.

Phil 2266.41 The theory of moral sentiments. v.1-2. (Smith, Adam.) Boston, 1817.

Phil 2266.37 The theory of moral sentiments. 2nd ed. (Smith, Adam.) London, 1761.

Phil 2266.38 The theory of moral sentiments. 7th ed. (Smith, Adam.) London, 1792. 2v.

Phil 8877.68 Theory of morals. (Carritt, Edgar F.) London, 1928.

Phil 8882.10 Theory of morals. (Hildreth, R.) Boston, 1844.

Phil 2268.55.5 Theory of morals. (Janet, Paul A.R.) N.Y., 1883.

Phil 8894.34 Theory of morals. (Timur, Mohammed.) London, 1956.

Phil 189.30 Theory of order. (Oliver, W.D.) Yellow Springs, Ohio, 1951.

Phil 5640.146 A theory of perception. (Pitcher, George Willard.) Princeton, N.J., 1971.

Phil 7060.10 Theory of pneumatology. (Jung Stilling, J.H.) London, 1834.

Phil 193.129.5 The theory of polarity. (Sainsbury, Geoffrey.) London, 1931.

Phil 2050.59.35 Theory of politics. (Hume, David.) Edinburgh, 1951.

Phil 343.35 The theory of practical reason. (Murphy, Arthur Edward.) La Salle, Ill., 1964[1965]

Phil 8882.14 The theory of practice. (Hodgson, S.H.) London, 1870. 2v.

Phil 2115.154 The theory of private property in John Locke's political philosophy. (Czajkowski, C.J.) Notre Dame, 1941.

Phil 5243.13 The theory of psychical dispositions. (Dubray, C.A.) Washington, 1905.

Phil 6319.1 The theory of psychoanalysis. (Jung, C.G.) N.Y., 1915.

Phil 6322.32.5 Theory of psychoanalytic technique. (Menningen, Karl Augustus.) N.Y., 1958.

Phil 5751.21 A theory of psychological reactance. (Brehm, Jack Williams.) N.Y., 1966.

Phil 186.16.5 Theory of reality. (Ladd, G.T.) N.Y., 1899.

Phil 5041.2.5 The theory of reasoning. (Bailey, Samuel.) London, 1851.

Phil 5041.2 The theory of reasoning. (Bailey, Samuel.) London, 1852.

Phil 8892.68 A theory of reasons for action. (Richards, David A.J.) Oxford, 1971.

Phil 8594.4 The theory of religion. (Orr, J.) London, 1762.

Phil 3425.71.5 Theory of right, duties, and religion. (Hegel, Georg Wilhelm Friedrich.) Ann Arbor, 1892.

Phil 5643.7 A theory of sight, or How we see. (Goblet, H.F.) London, 1869.

Phil 7150.70 Theory of suicide. (Farber, Maurice.) N.Y., 1968.

Phil 8416.37.5 The theory of the avant-garde. (Poggioli, Renato.) Cambridge, 1968.

Phil 8712.9 Theory of the earth, from its original. (Whiston, W.) London, 1755.

Htn Phil 8691.8F* The theory of the earth. v.1-4. (Burnet, Thomas.) London, 1684-90.

Htn Phil 8691.8.2F* The theory of the earth. 2. ed. (Burnet, Thomas.) London, 1690-91. 4 pam.

Phil 2038.50 Theory of the human mind. (Hartley, D.) London, 1775.

Phil 6116.1 Theory of the influence exerted by the mind over the body. (Glen, J.) London, 1855.

Phil 672.121 A theory of the mechanism of survival; the fourth dimension. (Smith, W.W.) London, 1920.

Phil 288.2 Theory of the universe. (Hutchins, S.) N.Y., 1868.

Phil 5043.2 The theory of thought. (Davis, N.K.) N.Y., 1880.

Phil 332.2 Theory of thought and knowledge. (Bowne, B.P.) N.Y., 1897.

Phil 730.5 The theory of universals. (Aaron, Richard Ithamar.) Oxford, 1952.

Phil 730.5.2 The Theory of universals. 2nd ed. (Aaron, Richard Ithamar.) London, 1967.

Phil 735.117 A theory of value. (Reid, John R.) N.Y., 1938.

Phil 1870.60.2 The theory of vision vindicated. (Berkeley, G.) Cambridge, 1860.

Phil 5525.9 Theory of wit and humor. (Fleet, F.R.) London, 1890.

Phil 29.43 Theosofia. Amsterdam. 63,1962+ 9v.

Phil 29.7 The theosophical forum. N.Y. 1-10,1889-1905 16v.

Phil 29.7.5 The theosophical forum. Point Loma, Calif.

Phil 978.5.28A The theosophical glossary. (Blavatsky, H.P.) London, 1892.

Phil 978.42 Theosophical manuals. v.1-18. Point Loma, 1910. 4v.

Phil 29.9 The theosophical messenger. Los Angeles. 6-15,1918-1928 3v.

Phil 978.19 Theosophical miscellanies. v.1-2. (Iyer, S.S.) Calcutta, 1883.

Phil 978.73 The theosophical movement, 1875-1925. N.Y., 1925.

Phil 29.5.10 The theosophical movement. Bombay. 9-16,1938-1945 7v.

NEDL Phil 29.3 Theosophical path. Point Loma, Calif. 1-36,1911-1929 30v.

NEDL Phil 29.2 Theosophical quarterly. N.Y. 1-35,1906-1938 27v.

Phil 29.8 Theosophical siftings. London. 1-7,1888-1895 7v.

Phil 974.2.25 The theosophical society and H.P.B. Three articles. (Besant, A.) London, 1891?

Phil 59.3 Theosophical Society in America. Annual convention. N.Y. 5-7,1891-1893

Phil 59.3.6 Theosophical Society in America. Oriental Department. Pamphlet. N.Y. 1891-1897 2v.

Phil 971.8 La théosophie. (Lantier, Jacques.) Paris, 1970.

Phil 978.49 Theosophie. (Steiner, R.) Stuttgart, 1922.

Phil 8582.52 Théosophie ou science de Dieu. (Coqueret, H.) Paris, 1803.

Phil 978.24.5 Theosophie und Anthroposophie. (Bruhn, Wilhelm.) Leipzig, 1921.

Phil 978.24 Theosophie und Theologie. (Bruhn, Wilhelm.) Glückstadt, 1907.

Phil 1135.14 Theosophies of Plato, Aristotle and Plotinus. (Wa Saïd, Dibinga.) N.Y., 1970.

Phil 978.58 Die theosophische Bewegung. (Frohnmeyer, L.J.) Stuttgart, 1920.

Phil 978.69 Theosophischer Kulturbücher. (Rudolph, Hermann.) Leipzig, 1932-33.

Phil 971.5.5 Le theosophise; histoire d'une pseudo-religion. 2. ed. (Guénon, R.) Paris, 1929.

NEDL Phil 29.5 The theosophist. Madras. 1-30 8v.

Phil 978.16.5 Theosophy; the path ofthe mystic. 2d ed. (Tingley, K.A. (Mrs.).) Point Loma, Calif., 1922.

Phil 978.67 Theosophy. (Kuhn, Alvin Boyd.) N.Y., 1930.

Phil 978.72.5 Theosophy. (Ljumgström, O.) n.p., n.d. 6 pam.

NEDL Phil 25.15 Theosophy. N.Y. 11-17,1896-1903 7v.

NEDL Phil 29.4 Theosophy. San Francisco. 1-15,1920-1927 15v.

Phil 978.49.7 Theosophy. 18th ed. (Steiner, R.) N.Y., 1910.

Phil 978.33 Theosophy and modern socialism. (Brailsford-Bright, J.) London, 1889.

Phil 978.6.40 Theosophy and new psychology. (Besant, Annie.) London, 1904.

Phil 978.48 Theosophy and the higher life. London, 1880.

Phil 978.6.88 Theosophy and the theosophical society. (Besant, Annie.) Adyar, 1913.

Phil 978.52 Theosophy in outline. (Willis, F.M.) Girard, 1923.

Phil 8520.2 Theosophy or psychological religion. (Müller, F.M.) London, 1893.

Phil 978.31 Theosophy Publishing Company. The pitt and marrow of some sacred writings. N.Y., 1899.

Phil 978.60.15 Theosophy simplified. 3d ed. (Cooper, I.S.) Hollywood, 1919.

Phil 978.26 Theosophy Society in America. A primer of theosophy. Chicago, 1909.

Phil 978.53 Theosophy unveiled. (Murdoch, J.) Madras, 1885.
Phil 8708.12.5 Theou sophia...divine mysteries. (Sampson, H.E.)
 London, 1918.
Phil 5650.2 þer die funktionelle Prüfung des menschlichen Gehörorgans.
 (Bezold, Friedrich.) Wiesbaden, 1897.
Phil 6325.15 Therapeutic advances in psychiatry. (Pennsylvania.
 University. Bicentennial Conference.) Philadelphia, 1941.
Phil 6684.2.3 Therapeutic value of suggestion. (Osgood, H.)
 Boston, 1890.
Phil 6681.4.10 Thérapeutique suggestive, son mécanisme, propriétés du
 sommeil provoqué. (Liébeault, A.A.) Paris, 1891.
Phil 6315.2.460 Therapie der Menscheit. (Herwig, Hedda Juliane.)
 München, 1969.
Phil 6985.35 Therapy with families of sexually acting-out girls.
 N.Y., 1971.
Phil 7069.49.5 There is a psychic world. (Westwood, Horace.) N.Y., 1947.
Phil 6112.40 There is a river; the story of Edgar Cayce. (Sugrue,
 Thomas.) N.Y., 1959.
Phil 1200.36 Thereianos. Dianeamma Stoikės philesophks.
 Tergeoiė, 1892.
Phil 5628.55.6 Therese Neumann; a stigmatist of our days. (Lama,
 Friedrich.) Milwaukee, 1929.
Phil 5628.55.30 Therese Neumann von Konnersreuth. (Roessler, Max.)
 Wurzburg, 1963.
Phil 5628.55.35 Therese Neumann von Konnersreuth. (Steiner, Johannes.)
 München, 1963.
Phil 2905.1.145 Thérines, Jacques de. Quodlibets. Paris, 1958.
Phil 2477.15.120 Therrien, Vincent. La révolution de Gaston Bachelard en
 critique littéraire. Paris, 1970.
Phil 9179.5 Théry, A.F. Conseils aux mères. Paris, 1859. 2v.
Phil 821.7 Die These der Metaphysik. (Vollrath, Ernst.)
 Wuppertal, 1969.
Phil 6967.6 Thèse pour le doctorat en médecine. (Revault D'Allounes,
 G.) Paris, 1971.
Phil 9070.5 These three alone. (Wilson, F.T.) N.Y., 1940.
Phil 2520.189 Thèses cartésiennes et thèses thomistes. Thèse. (Garin,
 Pierre.) Bruges, 193-.
Phil 8656.7 Theses theologicae de atheismo. (Buddeus, J.F.) Traiecti
 ad Rhenum, 1737.
Phil 25.129 Thessalonike-Panepistémion. Philosophike-Schole
 Episticoniki epetires. 1,1927+ 10v.
Phil 5867.15 Thetmark, J.C. Barnesprog. København, 1964.
Phil 3425.772 Theunissen, Michael. Hegels Lehre vom absoluten Geist als
 theologisch-politischer Traktat. Berlin, 1970.
Phil 194.47 Thévenaz, P. L'homme et sa raison. Neuchâtel, 1956.
 2v.
Phil 8599.42 Thévenaz, Pierre. La condition de la raison philosophique.
 Neuchâtel, 1960.
Phil 1750.115.62 Thevenaz, Pierre. De Husserl à Merleau-Ponty.
 Neuchâtel, 1966.
Phil 1750.115.60 Thevenaz, Pierre. What is phenomenology? Chicago, 1967.
Phil 8591.44.35 They asked for a paper. (Lewis, Clive Staples.)
 London, 1962.
Phil 8632.7 They do not die. (Hall, Charles A.) London, 1918.
Phil 8644.12.5 They live and are not far away. (Turk, Morris H.)
 N.Y., 1923.
Phil 3850.27.105 They thought he was mad; Albert Schweitzer. (Henrich, R.)
 N.Y., 1940.
Phil 7069.49.12 They walk by night; true South African ghost stories and
 tales of the supernormal. (Rosenthal, Eric.) Cape
 Town, 1965.
Phil 2730.102 Thibaud, Marguerite. L'effort chez Maine de Biran et
 Bergson. Thèse. Grenoble, 1939.
Phil 3640.351 Thibon, G. Nietzsche; ou Le declin de l'espirit. 13e éd.
 Lyon, 1948.
Phil 8969.5 Thibon, G. What God has joined together. Chicago, 1952.
Phil 7069.20.330 Thiébault, Jules. The vanished friend. N.Y., 1920.
Phil 5190.20 Thiede, J. Über die Negation, den Widerspruch und den
 Gegensatz. Inaug.-Diss. Berlin, 1883.
Phil 194.46 Thiel, M. Versuch einer Ontologie der Persönlichkeit.
 Berlin, 1950.
Phil 5059.16 Thiele, G. Grundriss der Logik und Metaphysik.
 Halle, 1878.
Phil 3501.1 Thiele, G. Kant's intellektuelle Anschauung. Halle, 1876.
Phil 3501.1.5 Thiele, G. Die Philosophie Immanuel Kant. Halle, 1882.
Phil 8430.79 Thiele, Joachim. Verfahren der statistischen Asthetik.
 Hamburg, 1966.
Phil 9495.164 Thielicke, H. The ethics of sex. 1st ed. N.Y., 1964.
Phil 8599.26 Thielicke, H. Geschichte und Existenz. Gütersloh, 1935.
Phil 535.16 Thielicke, H. Nihilism, its origin and nature, with a
 Christian answer. 1st ed. N.Y., 1961.
Phil 535.15 Thielicke, H. Der Nihilismus. Tübingen, 1950.
Phil 8430.41 Thielicke, H. Das Verhältnis zwischen demethischen und dem
 ästhetischen. Leipzig, 1932.
Phil 8969.10 Thielicke, Helmut. Die Atomwaffe als Frage an die
 christliche Ethik. Tübingen, 1958.
Phil 8969.4 Thielicke, Helmut. Theologische Ethik. v.1-3.
 Tübingen, 1951. 4v.
Phil 8110.4 Thielke, K.L.F. Literatur- und Kunstkritik in ihren
 Wechselbeziehung. Halle, 1935.
Phil 3565.122 Thieme, K. Glaube und Wissen bei Lotze. Leipzig, 1888.
Phil 130.8 Thieme, Karl. Philosophenbilden. Basel, 1964.
Phil 5817.4 Thier-Psychologie. (Hoffman, S.) Stuttgart, 1881.
Phil 6685.3 Der thierische magnetismus. (Petri, J.G.) Tlmenau, 1824.
Phil 5828.3 Der thierische Will. (Schneider, G.H.) Leipzig, 1880.
Phil 5814.2 Die Thierischen Gesellschaften; eine vergleichend-
 psychologische Üntersuchung. 2. Aufl. (Espinas, Alfred.)
 Braunschweig, 1879.
Phil 9010.28 Thiers, Jean B. Traité des jeux et des divertissements.
 Paris, 1686.
Phil 485.1.5 Thierseele und Menschengeist. (Körner, F.) Leipzig, 1872.
Phil 5829.6 Thierseelen-Kunde auf thatsachen Begrundet.
 Berlin, 1804-05. 2v.
Phil 3120.22.80 Thies, Heinz. Die Rolle der Erotik in der männlichen
 Gesellschaft. Baum, 193-.
Phil 8894.3 Thiess, J.O. Vorlesungen über die Moral.
 Leipzig, 1801-03. 2v.
Phil 7040.29 Thigpen, C.H. The three faces of Eve. N.Y., 1957.
Phil 3019.5 Thijssen-Schoute, Caroline Louise. Uit de Republiek der
 Letteren. 's-Gravenhage, 1967[1968]
Phil 819.7.2A Thilly, F. A history of philosophy. N.Y., 1914.
Phil 819.7.5 Thilly, F. A history of philosophy. N.Y., 1955.
Phil 819.7.7 Thilly, F. A history of philosophy. 3. ed. N.Y., 1957.
Phil 8894.11.5 Thilly, F. Introduction to ethics. N.Y., 1913.
Phil 3640.114 Thilly, F. Philosophy of Friedrich Nietzsche.
 Photoreproduction. N.Y., 1905.
Phil 3552.227 Thilly, Frank. Leibnizens Streit gegen Locke.
 Heidelberg, 1891.

Phil 1719.1 Thilo, C.A. Kurze pragmatische Geschichte der neueren
 Philosophie. Göthen, 1874.
Phil 3805.103 Thilo, C.A. Schleiermachers Religionsphilosophie.
 Langensalza, 1906.
Phil 3808.96 Thilo, C.A. Uber Schopenhauer's ethischen Atheism.
 Leipzig, 1868.
Phil 5190.94 Thilo, Ingmar. Vom Fragen. Inaug. Diss. München, 1969.
Phil 5585.216 Thinès, G. Contribution à la théorie de la causalité
 perceptive. Louvain, 1962.
Phil 5259.60 Thines, Georges. La problématique de la psychologie. La
 Haye, 1968.
Phil 5829.14 Thinès, Georges. Psychologie des animaux.
 Bruxelles, 1966.
Phil 189.11 Things and ideals. (Otto, M.C.) N.Y., 1924.
Phil 8581.14 Things divine and supernatural. (Browne, Peter.)
 London, 1733.
Phil 7069.44.10 Things I can't explain. (Moore, M.G.) London, 1944.
Phil 1905.11.78 Things learned by living. (Bascom, John.) N.Y., 1913.
Phil 8405.10 The things which are seen. (Edwards, A.T.) London, 1947.
Phil 7069.21.37 Think on these things. (Green, H.L.) Pasadena, 1921.
Phil 5246.58 Thinkers at work. (Gibson, A.B.) London, 1946.
Phil 2150.24.30 Thinker's handbook. (Mika, Lumir Victor.) Columbia,
 Mo., 1947.
Phil 5258.13.5 Thinking, feeling, doing. (Scripture, E.W.)
 Meadville, 1895.
Phil 5258.13.6 Thinking, feeling, doing. (Scripture, E.W.) N.Y., 1907.
 2v.
Phil 5520.205 Thinking. (Bartlett, F.C.) London, 1958.
Phil 802.18 Thinking. (Casey, F.) London, 1922.
Phil 5251.42 Thinking. (Levy, Hyman.) London, 1936.
Phil 5238.202 Thinking. (Mandler, J.M.) N.Y., 1964.
Phil 5250.22 Thinking about thinking. (Keyser, C.J.) N.Y., 1926.
Phil 5227.8.10 Thinking about thinking. (Reeves, Joan Wynn.)
 London, 1965.
Phil 5520.165 Thinking about thinking. (Wolfard, M.R.) N.Y., 1955.
Phil 5520.111A Thinking and experience. (Price, H.H.) Cambridge,
 Mass., 1953.
Phil 5264.4 Thinking and perceiving. (Yolton, J.W.) Lasalle,
 Ill., 1962.
Phil 5258.170 Thinking and psychotherapy. (Shands, Harley.)
 Cambridge, 1960.
Phil 346.14 Thinking and representation. (Price, Henry H.)
 London, 1946.
Phil 5520.126 Thinking and speaking. (Révész, G.) Amsterdam, 1954.
Phil 735.128 Thinking and valuing. (McCracken, D.J.) London, 1950.
Phil 5247.81 The thinking animal. (Hunt, Morton M.) Boston, 1964.
Phil 5044.9 Thinking clearly. (Emmet, Eric Revell.) N.Y., 1962.
Phil 5135.4 Thinking for ourselves. v.1-2. (Coleridge, J.D.)
 London, 1890.
Phil 5257.60 Thinking in opposites. (Roubiczek, Paul.) London, 1952.
Phil 5520.451 Thinking in structures. (Dienes, Zoltau Paul.)
 London, 1965.
Phil 5247.45.2 The thinking machine. 2. ed. (Herrick, C.J.)
 Chicago, 1929.
Phil 5047.42 Thinking things through. (Hepp, M.H.) N.Y., 1956.
Phil 5058.46.20 Thinking to some purpose. (Stebbing, Lizzie S.)
 Harmondsworth, 1939.
Phil 6128.24 The thinking universe. (Sheppard, E.E.) Los
 Angeles, 1915.
Phil 5360.17 Thinking with concepts. (Wilson, J.) Cambridge, 1963.
Phil 5650.45 Thinking without language. (Furth, Hans G.) N.Y., 1966.
Phil 7069.19.230 The thinning of the veil. (Wallace, Mary B.) N.Y., 1919.
Phil 2262.94 The third earl of Shaftesbury. (Brett, R.L.)
 London, 1951.
Htn Phil 2115.70.2* A third letter for toleration. (Locke, J.) London, 1692.
Phil 8882.58 The third morality. (Heard, G.) London, 1937.
Phil 300.10 Third Programme. Rival theories of cosmology.
 London, 1960.
Phil 7082.24.5 The third Reich of dreams. (Beradt, Charlotte.)
 Chicago, 1968.
Htn Phil 8886.21.12* The third volume of the French Academie. (La Primaudaye,
 P. de.) London, 1601.
Phil 9420.9 Thiroux d'Arconville, M. Des passions. Londres, 1764.
Phil 5259.38 Thirring, H. Homo sapiens. 2. Aufl. Wien, 1948.
Phil 59.2 Thirteen Club, New York. Annual report of the officers.
 N.Y. 4-11,1884-1893+ 2v.
Phil 2120.12.30 The thirteen pragmatisms. (Lovejoy, A.O.)
 Baltimore, 1963.
Phil 8610.876.10 Thirty discussions, Bible stories, essays and lectures.
 (Bennett, D.M.) N.Y., 1876.
Phil 7069.24.40 Thirty years among the dead. (Wickland, C.A.) Los
 Angeles, 1924.
Phil 5066.254 Thirty years of foundational studies. (Mostowski,
 Andrzej.) Oxford, 1966.
Phil 7069.23.15 Thirty years of psychical research. (Richet, Charles.)
 N.Y., 1923.
Phil 6329.17 This, Bernard. La psychanalyse. Paris, 1960.
Phil 9513.5.6 This business of living. (Coleman, George William.)
 Boston, 1936.
Phil 9513.5.5 This business of living. (Coleman, George William.)
 Boston, 1936.
Phil 9590.7 This Egyptian miracle. (Wood, F.H.) Philadelphia, 1939.
Phil 9070.55 This I believe. (Murrow, E.R.) N.Y., 1952. 2v.
Phil 9220.14 This is friendship. (Kennell, Earl.) N.Y., 1949.
Phil 525.200 This is it. (Watts, Alan W.) N.Y., 1960.
Phil 165.70 This is my philosophy. 1st ed. (Burnett, Whit.)
 N.Y., 1957.
Phil 7069.40.10 This spiritualism. (Seymour, C.J.) London, 1940.
Phil 6117.45.5 This thing called life. (Holmes, E.S.) N.Y., 1948.
Phil 8582.48 This world and the next. (Clark, E.H.) Boston, 1934.
Phil 8643.24 Tho material, why not immortal? (Smith, O.) Boston, 1921.
Phil 5262.29 Thobbing; a seat at the circus of the intellect. (Ward,
 Henshaw.) Indianapolis, 1926.
Phil 8430.40 Thode, H. Kundt und Sittlichkeit. Heidelberg, 1906.
Phil 5259.16.2 Thoden van Velzen, H. De wetenschap van ons geestelijk
 wezen. 2. druk. Amsterdam, 1894.
Phil 3120.11.80 Thodoroff, C. Julius Bahnsen und die Hauptprobleme seiner
 charakterologie. Erlangen, 1910.
Phil 3120.17.90 Thöne, Fritz. Erich Becher als Vertreter des Eudämonismus.
 Diss. Giessen, 1933.
Phil 3805.30.20 Thönes, C. Schleiermacher's handschriftlichen Anmerkungen
 zur I. Theil der Glaubenslehre. Berlin, 1873.
Phil 5590.492 Thomae, Hans. Das Idividuum und seine Welt.
 Göttingen, 1968.
Phil 5352.10 Thomae, Hans. Der Mensch in der Entscheidung.
 München, 1960.
Phil 5548.105 Thomae, Hans. Die Motivation menschlichen Handelns.
 Köln, 1965.

Phil 5590.492.5   Thomae, Hans. Vita humana. Frankfurt, 1969.
Phil 5259.31   Thomae, Hans. Das Wesen der menschlichen Antriebsstruktur.
                   Leipzig, 1944.
Htn Phil 2045.95*   Thomae Hobbes angli malmesburiensis vita. (Blackburne,
                   Richard.) Carolopoli, 1681.
Htn Phil 2045.97.5* Thomae Hobbes quadratura circuli. 2. ed. (Wallis, John.)
                   Oxoniae, 1669.
Htn Phil 2520.172* Thomas, A.L. Eloge de René Descartes. Paris, 1765.
                   2 pam.
Phil 2520.172.5   Thomas, A.L. Eulogy of Descartes. Cheltenham, 1826.
Phil 5590.430   Thomas, Alexander. Behavioral individuality in early
                   childhood. N.Y., 1963.
Phil 6980.732   Thomas, Alexander. Temperament and behavior disorders in
                   children. N.Y., 1969.
Phil 6129.5   Thomas, André. Localisations cérébelleuses. Paris, 1914.
Phil 3839.2   Thomas, C. Spinoza systema philosophicum adumbratum.
                   Borussorum, n.d.
Phil 7069.36.50   Thomas, C.D. An amazing experiment. London, 1936.
Phil 7069.38.59   Thomas, Charles D. Beyond life's sunset. London, 194-.
Phil 7069.38.58   Thomas, Charles D. In the dawn beyond death.
                   London, 1938?
Phil 7069.38.58.5 Thomas, Charles D. In the dawn beyond death.
                   London, 194-.
Phil 7069.28.70   Thomas, Charles D. Life beyond death, with evidence. 1st
                   ed. London, 1937.
Phil 194.35   Thomas, E.E. The ethical basis of reality. London, 1927.
Phil 8599.27   Thomas, E.E. The political aspects of religious
                   development. London, 1937.
Phil 1524.4   Thomas, Elliott C. History of the schoolmen.
                   London, 1941.
Phil 194.37.5   Thomas, Elyston. A view of all existence. London, 1936.
Phil 194.37   Thomas, Elyston. What existence means. London, 1928.
Phil 3565.109   Thomas, Evan E. Lotze's theory of reality. London, 1921.
Phil 5400.56   Thomas, Félix. L'éducation des sentiments. Paris, 1899.
Phil 5259.27   Thomas, Frank C. Ability and knowledge: the London school.
                   London, 1935.
Phil 8599.34.5   Thomas, George Finger. Philosophy and religious belief.
                   N.Y., 1970.
Phil 8599.36   Thomas, George Finger. Poetry, religion, and the spiritual
                   life. Houston, 1951.
Phil 8599.34   Thomas, George Finger. The vitality of the Christian
                   tradition. N.Y., 1944.
Phil 194.50   Thomas, H. Understanding the great philosophers. 1st ed.
                   Garden City, N.Y., 1962.
Phil 8709.16   Thomas, J.B. The old Bible and the new science. 2. ed.
                   N.Y., 1877.
Phil 8610.912   Thomas, J.C. The darkness, the dawn and the day.
                   London, 1912.
Phil 7069.37.12   Thomas, J.F. Beyond normal cognition. Boston, 1937.
Phil 3428.82   Thomas, K. Herbart, Spinoza, Kant. Langensalza, 1875.
Phil 3501.2   Thomas, K. Kant und Herbart. Berlin, 1840-69. 2 pam.
Phil 3839.1   Thomas, K. Spinoza als Metaphysiker. Königsberg, 1840.
Phil 7150.62   Thomas, Klaus. Handbuch der Selbstmordverhütung.
                   Stuttgart, 1964.
Phil 5780.15.20   Thomas, Klaus. Die künstlich gesteuerte Seele.
                   Stuttgart, 1970.
Phil 5829.9   Thomas, Maurice. L'instinct: théories - réalité.
                   Paris, 1929.
Phil 5829.9.5   Thomas, Maurice. La notion de l'instinct et ses bases
                   scientifiques. Paris, 1936.
Phil 1955.6.01   Thomas, Milton H. A bibliography of John Dewey.
                   N.Y., 1929.
Phil 1955.6.05A   Thomas, Milton H. Bibliography of John Dewey. 2d ed.
                   N.Y., 1939.
Phil 1955.6.2   Thomas, Milton H. John Dewey. Chicago, 1962.
Phil 6689.5   Thomas, Northcote W. Crystal gasping. London, 1905.
Phil 7069.05.20   Thomas, Northcote W. Thought transference. N.Y., 1905.
Phil 2725.4.81   Thomas, P. F. Pierre Leroux. Paris, 1904.
Phil 2610.81   Thomas, P. Felix. Philosophie de Gassendi. Paris, 1889.
Phil 194.25.5   Thomas, P.F. Cours de philosophie pour les classes de
                   philosophie A et B. 5e éd. Paris, 1921.
Phil 835.4   Thomas, Viktor. Das Erkenntnisproblem; ein
                   historischkritischer Versuch. Stuttgart, 1921.
Phil 8709.21   Thomas, W. On the resolution of science and faith.
                   N.Y., 1946.
Phil 194.22   Thomas, William C. Cosmic ethics. London, 1896.
Phil 8685.19   Thomas a Scrupulis. (Günther, A.) Wien, 1835.
Phil 1135.83   Thomas Aquinas, Sister. The pre-Socratic use of [Psyche].
                   Washington, 1915.
Htn Phil 4950.1.30F* Thomas Aquinas, St. Summa theologica. Duaci, 1614.
Phil 1504.5.2   Thomas Bradwardinus. v.5, pt.2. (Hahn S.) Münster, 1905.
Phil 1890.80   Thomas Browns Causationstheorie. (Woods, J.H.)
                   Leipzig, 1897.
Phil 4073.130   Thomas Campanella, 1568-1639. Milleciquecentoses
                   santotto-millescicentotrentanove. Napoli, 1969.
Phil 5465.218   Thomas de Saint-Laurent, Raymond de. L'imagination, son
                   importance, sa nature. Avignon, 1970.
Phil 2020.81   Thomas Hill Green und der Utilitarismus. (James, G.F.)
                   Halle, 1894.
Phil 2045.125   Thomas Hobbes. (Jessop, T.E.) London, 1960.
Phil 2045.89   Thomas Hobbes. (Taylor, A.E.) London, 1908.
Phil 2045.111   Thomas Hobbes: seine logische Problematik. (Moser, H.)
                   Bern, 1923.
Phil 2045.85.2   Thomas Hobbes. 2e Aufl. (Tönnies, F.) Osterwieck, 1912.
Phil 2045.85.3   Thomas Hobbes. 3e Aufl. (Tönnies, F.) Stuttgart, 1925.
Phil 2045.98   Thomas Hobbes as philosopher, publicist and man of letters.
                   (Catlin, George E.G.) Oxford, 1922.
Phil 2045.124   Thomas Hobbes et Jean-Jacques Rousseau. (Davy, G.)
                   Oxford, 1953.
Phil 2045.96   Thomas Hobbes' filosofi. (Larsen, Eduard.)
                   København, 1891.
Phil 2045.126   Thomas Hobbes' Leviathan. Proefschrift. (Konijnenburg,
                   Willem van.) Assen, 1945.
Phil 2045.108.5   Thomas Hobbes' mechanical conception of nature. (Brandt,
                   Frithiof.) Copenhagen, 1928.
Phil 2045.137   Thomas Hobbes und das Widerstandsrecht. (Mayer-Tasch,
                   Peter Cornelius.) Mainz? 1964.
Phil 2045.144   Thomas Hobbes und der Puritanismus. (Foester, Winfried.)
                   Berlin, 1969.
Phil 2240.81   Thomas Reid. (Fraser, A.C.) London, 1898.
Phil 3890.8.85   Thomasiana; Arbeiten aus dem Institut für Staats und
                   Rechtsgeschichte bei der Martin Luther. Universität
                   Halle-Wittenberg. Weimar. 1-4
Phil 7080.17   Thomasius, C. De jure circa somnum et somnia.
                   Regiomonti, 1712.
Phil 7060.134   Thomasius, C. Dissertatio iuridica de non rescindendo
                   contractu conductionis ob natura spectrorum. Halle, 1711.

Phil 3890.8.6   Thomasius, Christian. Allerhand bissher Publicirte Kleine
                   deutsche Schriften. Halle, 1701.
Phil 3890.8.40   Thomasius, Christian. Ausübung der Sittenlehre.
                   Hildesheim, 1968.
Phil 3890.8.45.1 Thomasius, Christian. Ausübung der Vernunftlehre.
                   Hildesheim, 1968.
Phil 3890.8.30.1 Thomasius, Christian. Einleitung zur Sittenlehre.
                   Hildesheim, 1968.
Phil 5059.24.2   Thomasius, Christian. Einleitung zur Vernunftlehre.
                   Hildesheim, 1968.
Phil 3890.8.120   Thomasius, Christian. Kleine deutsche Schriften.
                   Halle, 1894.
Phil 3890.8.35   Thomasius, Christian. Von der Artzeney widner die
                   Unvernunfftige Lieben und der zuvorher Nöthigen Erkäntniss
                   sein Sellst. Halle, 1696.
Phil 3890.8.30   Thomasius, Christian. Von der Kunst vernünftig und
                   tugendhafft zu Lieben als dem eintzigen Mittel zu einen
                   Glückselingen. Halle, 1692.
Htn Phil 1200.2* Thomasius, J. Exercitatio de stoica mundi exustione.
                   Leipzig, 1676.
Phil 8894.4   Thomassen, J.H. Das Evangelium der Wahrheit und Freiheit.
                   Leipzig, 1871.
Phil 1522.5.15   Thomisme et scolastique à propos de M. Rougier. 2e éd.
                   (Descoqs, P.) Paris, 1935.
Phil 1527.3   Der Thomismus. (Wyser, Paul.) Bern, 1951.
Phil 1750.782   The Thomist spectrum. (John, Helen James.) N.Y., 1966.
Phil 5217.1   The Thomistic concept of mental faculty. Diss. (Hart,
                   Charles A.) Washington, 1930.
Phil 348.24   Thomistic epistemology. (Riet, G. van.) St. Louis, 1963.
                   2v.
Phil 181.108   Thomistic philosophy. (Grenier, H.) Charlotte-town,
                   Canada, 1950. 4v.
Phil 3246.85.2   Thompson, A.B. Unity of Fichte's Doctrine of knowledge.
                   Boston, 1895.
Phil 2340.5.80   Thompson, C.G. The ethics of William Wollaston. Diss.
                   Boston, 1922.
Phil 7069.30.35   Thompson, C.J.S. Mystery and love of apparitions.
                   London, 1930.
Phil 6329.19   Thompson, Clara M. Interpersonal psychoanalysis.
                   N.Y., 1964.
Phil 8620.11   Thompson, D.G. The problem of evil. London, 1887.
Phil 5259.3   Thompson, D.G. System of psychology. London, 1884.
                   2v.
Phil 575.80   Thompson, Dow. A mind that was different. Wellston, 1932.
Phil 5440.6   Thompson, E. Rowell. Heredity. Boston, 1882.
Phil 2340.10.95   Thompson, E.J. An analysis of the thought of Alfred N.
                   Whitehead and William E. Hocking concerning good and evil.
                   Diss. Chicago, 1935.
Phil 5829.7   Thompson, E.L. An analysis of the learning process in the
                   snail. Cambridge, 1917.
Phil 5259.9   Thompson, H.B. The mental traits of sex. Chicago, 1903.
Phil 365.8   Thompson, H.C. New reading of evolution. Chicago, 1907.
Phil 575.6   Thompson, H.M. The world and the wrestlers. N.Y., 1895.
Phil 5627.81   Thompson, J.B. The other paraclete. n.p., 1897.
Phil 6129.4   Thompson, J.J. Mirage of the nervous system. n.p., 1914.
Phil 1200.16   Thompson, J.W. The last pagan. Chicago, 1917.
Phil 5545.24   Thompson, L. Influence of memory. Boston, 1840.
Phil 8599.18   Thompson, L. Buckland. Exact science of Christianity.
                   Garden City, N.Y., 1916.
Phil 7069.39.55   Thompson, L.S. Geometric telepathy. Los Angeles, 1939.
Phil 2225.5.98.5 Thompson, M.H. The pragmatic philosophy of C.S. Peirce.
                   Chicago, 1953.
Phil 2225.5.98   Thompson, M.H. The pragmatic philosophy of C.S. Peirce.
                   Part of thesis. Chicago, 1945.
Phil 8674.3   Thompson, R.A. Christian theism. N.Y., 1856.
Phil 8644.7   Thompson, R.J. The proofs of life after death.
                   Paris, 1906.
Phil 3640.378   Thompson, R.M. Nietzsche and Christian ethics.
                   London, 1951.
Phil 2115.145A   Thompson, S.M. A study of Locke's theory of ideas.
                   Monmouth, Ill., 1934.
Phil 2050.98   Thomsen, A. David Hume: sein Leben und seine Philosophie.
                   Berlin, 1912.
Phil 3425.126   Thomsen, A. Hegel. København, 1905.
Phil 5769.2   Thomsen, H. Die rechtliche Willens Bestimmung.
                   Kiel, 1882.
Phil 130.13   Thomsen, Henrik. Hvem taenkte hvad; filosofiens
                   hvem-hvad-hvor. København, 1961.
Phil 4582.7.90   Thomsen, O. F.G. Howitz, 1789-1826. København, 1924.
Phil 5520.295   Thomson, Robert. The psychology of thinking.
                   Harmondsworth, 1959.
Phil 2270.127A   Thomson, J.A. Herbert Spencer. London, 1906.
Phil 8709.17   Thomson, J.A. Science and religion; being the Morse
                   lecture for 1924. N.Y., 1925.
Phil 104.3   Thomson, J.R. A dictionary of philosophy in the words of
                   philosophers. 2nd ed. London, 1892.
Phil 9179.10   Thomson, John. The domestic circle. Edinburgh, n.d.
Phil 8870.18   Thomson, Judith J. Ethics. N.Y., 1968.
Phil 5259.21   Thomson, M.K. The springs of human action. N.Y., 1927.
Phil 8595.16.29   Thomson, Robert. Divine authority of the Bible.
                   Boston, 1807.
Phil 5229.2   Thomson, Robert. The Pelican history of psychology.
                   Harmondsworth, 1968.
Phil 8709.7   Thomson, S.H. Geology as an interpreter of scripture.
                   Cincinnati, 1858.
Phil 5059.4.2   Thomson, W. Outline of the necessary laws of thought.
                   Cambridge, 1859.
Phil 5059.4   Thomson, W. Outline of the necessary laws of thought.
                   London, 1849.
Phil 5059.4.3   Thomson, W. Outline of the necessary laws of thought.
                   N.Y., 1879.
Phil 5059.4.4   Thomson, W. Outline of the necessary laws of thought. 4th
                   ed. London, 1857.
Phil 5640.7   Thomson, W. The six gateways of knowledge. N.Y., 1884.
Phil 6129.1.4   Thomson, W.H. Brain and personality. N.Y., 1906.
Phil 6129.1.8   Thomson, W.H. Brain and personality. N.Y., 1914.
Phil 6129.1.4.2   Pamphlet box. Thomson, W.H. Letters.
Phil 3501.8   Thon, O. Die Grundprinzipien der Kantischen
                   Moralphilosophie. Berlin, 1895.
Phil 194.24   Thone, Johannes F. System der Metaphysik. Dresden, 1908.
Phil 819.11   Thonnard, F.J. A short history of philosophy.
                   Paris, 1955.
Phil 9179.6   Thorburn, Grant. Sketches from the notebook of Laurie Todd
                   on marriage. N.Y., 1847.
Phil 8420.12   Thorburn, J.M. Art and the unconscious; a psychological
                   approach to a problem of philosophy. London, 1925.
Phil 5829.8   Thorlakson, B.C. Le fondement physiologique des instincts
                   des systèmes nutritif. Thèse. Paris, 1926.

Author and Title Listing

Phil 7080.40A — Thorlákson, Björg Caritas. Svefn og draumar. Reykjavík, 1926.

Phil 7082.51 — Thorleifsdóttir, Elízabet. Draumur. Reykjavík, 1892.

Phil 7082.51.1 — Thorleifsdóttir, Elízabet. Draumur. Reykjavík, 1905.

Phil 1819.1 — Thormeyer, Paul. Die grossen englischen Philosophen, Locke, Berkeley, Hume. Leipzig, 1915.

Phil 5259.7.5 — Thorndike, E.L. The elements of psychology. N.Y., 1905.

Phil 5259.7.6 — Thorndike, E.L. The elements of psychology. 2d ed. N.Y., 1905.

Phil 5259.7.22 — Thorndike, E.L. Human nature and the social order. Cambridge, 1969.

Phil 5259.7.20 — Thorndike, E.L. Human nature and the social order. N.Y., 1940.

Phil 5259.7.3 — Thorndike, E.L. The human nature club. N.Y., 1900.

Phil 5259.7 — Thorndike, E.L. The human nature club. N.Y., 1901.

Phil 5259.7.30 — Thorndike, E.L. Man and his works. Cambridge, 1943.

Phil 5259.7.15 — Thorndike, E.L. The psychology of wants, interests and attitudes. N.Y., 1935.

Phil 5259.7.78 — Pamphlet vol. Thorndike, E.L. Papers. 1899-1908. 9 pam.

Phil 5259.7.76 — Pamphlet vol. Thorndike, E.L. Papers. 1900-1910. 17 pam.

Phil 5259.7.77 — Pamphlet vol. Thorndike, E.L. Papers. 1911-1921. 17 pam.

Phil 5627.165 — Thornhill, Alan. One fight more. London, 1943.

Phil 104.2.2 — Thornmeyer, P. Philosophisches Wörterbuch. 2. Aufl. Leipzig, 1920.

Phil 104.2.3 — Thornmeyer, P. Philosophisches Wörterbuch. 3e Aufl. Leipzig, 1922.

Phil 8674.11 — Thornton, L.S. The incarnate Lord. London, 1928.

Phil 194.4 — Thornton, W.T. Old-fashioned ethics. London, 1873.

Phil 2045.120 — Thorpe, C.D. The aesthetic theory of Thomas Hobbes. Ann Arbor, 1940.

Phil 6420.6 — Thorpe, Eliza Jane Ellery. Speech hesitation. N.Y., 1900.

Phil 2218.86A — Thorpe, J.E. Joseph Priestley. London, 1906.

Phil 575.96 — Thorpe, L.P. Psychological foundations of personality. N.Y., 1938.

Phil 6329.16 — Thorpe, Louis P. The psychology of abnormal behavior. N.Y., 1961.

Phil 5590.240 — Thorpe, Louis Peter. Personality. Princeton, 1958.

Phil 5829.11 — Thorpe, W.H. Learning and instinct in animals. London, 1956.

Phil 9050.5.5 — Thorsch, Berthold. Der Einzelne und die Gesellschaft. Dresden, 1907.

Phil 6132.7.10 — Those nerves. (Walton, G.L.) Philadelphia, 1909.

Phil 2150.13.6 — Thought, action and passion. (McKeon, Richard P.) Chicago, 1968.

Phil 1885.87 — Thought, existence and reality as viewed by F.H. Bradley and B. Bosanquet. (Gamertsfelder, W.S.) Columbus, 1920.

Phil 2055.10.30 — Thought and action. (Hampshire, Stuart.) London, 1959.

Phil 181.133 — Thought and change. (Gellner, Ernest.) Chicago, 1965.

Phil 2070.129.5A — The thought and character of William James. (Perry, R.B.) Boston, 1935. 2v.

Phil 2070.129.7A — The thought and character of William James. (Perry, R.B.) Cambridge, 1948.

Phil 1750.22A — Thought and expression in the 16th century. (Taylor, Henry O.) N.Y., 1920. 2v.

Phil 1750.22.5 — Thought and expression in the 16th century. 2. ed. (Taylor, Henry O.) N.Y., 1930. 2v.

Phil 1750.22.10 — Thought and expression in the 16th century. 2. ed. (Taylor, Henry O.) N.Y., 1959. 2v.

Phil 5520.47 — Thought and language: an essay on...Locke's philosophy. (Smart, B.H.) London, 1855.

Phil 400.95 — Thought and reality; Hegelianism and Advaita. (Raju, P.T.) London, 1937.

Phil 343.18.5 — Thought and reality. (Mukerji, A.C.) Allahabad, 1930.

Phil 5520.71 — Thought and speech. (Norris, Tom C.) London, 1938.

Phil 6125.18.5 — Thought and the brain. (Piéron, Henri.) London, 1927.

Phil 5041.29 — Thought and things. (Baldwin, J.M.) London, 1906-11. 3v.

Phil 187.147 — Thought and truth. (Maisels, Misha.) N.Y., 1956.

Phil 185.19 — A thought book on Socratic method. (Knowlson, T.S.) London, 1920?

Phil 5250.29 — Thought considered as action and the logical axioms. (Kozlowski, W.M.) N.Y., 1927.

Phil 5850.108 — Thought-control in everyday life. (Alexander, James.) N.Y., 1928.

Phil 7069.18.70 — Thought for help from those who know men's need. (Comstock, William C.) Boston, 1918.

Phil 7069.01.10 — Thought-force in business and everyday life. 2. ed. (Atkinson, W.W.) Chicago, 1901.

Phil 978.6.72 — Thought-forms. (Besant, Annie.) Wheaton, Ill., 1969.

Phil 2225.5.102 — The thought of C.S. Peirce. (Goudge, T.A.) Toronto, 1950.

Phil 2905.1.375 — The thought of Teilhard de Chardin. (Murray, Michael Hunt.) N.Y., 1966.

Phil 978.6.44A — Thought power; its control and culture. (Besant, Annie.) London, 1901.

Phil 978.6.43 — Thought power; its control and culture. (Besant, Annie.) London, 1906.

Phil 7068.88.10 — A thought-reader's thoughts. (Cumberland, Stuart.) London, 1888.

Phil 7060.30 — Thought-reading. (Blackburn, D.) London, 1884.

Phil 5780.22A — Thought reform and the psychology of totalism. (Lifton, Robert.) N.Y., 1961.

Phil 7069.46.25 — Thought transference. (Carington, Whately.) N.Y., 1946.

Phil 7069.05.20 — Thought transference. (Thomas, Northcote W.) N.Y., 1905.

Phil 7069.25.30 — Thought transference. (Wilson, T.S.) London, 1925..

Phil 1725.2 — The thoughtlessness of modern thought. (Zema, Demetrius.) N.Y., 1934.

Phil 187.118.5 — Thoughts, deeds and human happiness. (Monsarrat, K.W.) London, 1944.

Phil 8876.24 — Thoughts, feelings, and fancies. (Bovee, C.N.) N.Y., 1857.

X Cg   Phil 2805.41.15 — Thoughts, letters, and opuscules. (Pascal, Blaise.) N.Y., 1861.

Htn   Phil 2805.41* — Thoughts, meditations, and prayers, touching matters moral and divine. (Pascal, Blaise.) London, 1688.

Phil 180.89 — Thoughts about life. (Friedberg, Felix.) N.Y., 1954.

Phil 8897.13.10 — Thoughts and apophthegms. (Whately, R.) Philadelphia, 1856.

Phil 8662.8 — Thoughts concerning God and nature. (Hill, J.) London, 1755.

Phil 8893.98 — Thoughts for the thoughtful. (Seaverns, A.S.) N.Y., 1893.

Phil 178.64.6 — Thoughts for the times. (Dixon, W.M.) Glasgow, 1941.

Phil 178.64.5 — Thoughts for the times. (Dixon, W.M.) N.Y., 1941.

Phil 8587.10.10 — Thoughts in aid of faith. (Hennell, S.S.) London, 1860.

Phil 9342.13 — Thoughts in the forms of maxims. (Carlisle, Isabella (Byron) Howard.) London, 1790.

Phil 8693.6 — Thoughts of a catholic anatomist. (Dwight, T.) London, 1911.

Phil 2805.42.2 — The thoughts of Blaise Pascal. (Pascal, Blaise.) London, 1888.

Phil 2805.42.9 — The thoughts of Blaise Pascal. (Pascal, Blaise.) London, 1904.

Phil 9343.7.6 — Thoughts of busy girls. (Dodge, Grace H.) N.Y., 1892.

Phil 8627.9.5 — Thoughts of the spiritual. (Chambers, A.) London, 1905.

Phil 9070.14 — The thoughts of youth. (Dowry, S.S.) N.Y., 1932.

Phil 8633.1.36 — Thoughts on death and life. (Hocking, W.E.) N.Y., 1937.

Phil 5435.11 — Thoughts on habit and discipline. (Gurney, Joseph J.) Philadelphia, 1877.

Phil 8599.2 — Thoughts on life science. (Thring, E.) London, 1871.

Phil 8881.13A — Thoughts on man. (Godwin, W.) London, 1831.

Phil 9169.2 — Thoughts on marriage. (Jay, W.) Boston, 1833.

Phil 8897.5 — Thoughts on moral and spiritual culture. (Waterson, R.C.) Boston, 1844.

Phil 8581.65 — Thoughts on nature and religion. (Blair, P.) London, 1774.

Phil 8599.1 — Thoughts on recent scientifc conclusions. London, 1872.

Htn   Phil 2805.42.4* — Thoughts on religion. (Pascal, Blaise.) London, 1704.

NEDL   Phil 2805.42.7 — Thoughts on religion. (Pascal, Blaise.) London, 1825.

Phil 2805.42.3 — Thoughts on religion. (Pascal, Blaise.) London, 1836.

Phil 8597.12.5 — Thoughts on religion. (Romanes, G.J.) Chicago, 1895.

Phil 8597.12.8 — Thoughts on religion. (Romanes, G.J.) Chicago, 1898.

Phil 8597.12 — Thoughts on religion. (Romanes, G.J.) London, 1895.

Phil 8584.1 — Thoughts on religion and morality. (Eddy, J.) Providence, R.I., 1891.

Phil 2805.42.5 — Thoughts on religion and other curious subjects. (Pascal, Blaise.) London, 1749.

Phil 8586.7 — Thoughts on religion and philosophy. (Gresley, W.) London, 1875.

Phil 2805.40.25 — Thoughts on religion and philosophy. (Pascal, Blaise.) London, 1894.

Phil 197.27 — Thoughts on science, theology, and ethics. (Wilson, John.) London, 1885.

Phil 6129.2 — Thoughts on the mental functions. Edinburgh, 1843.

Phil 9165.4.2 — Thoughts on the times. (Foster, F.) London, 1779.

Phil 8674.10 — Thoughts on theism with suggestions towards a public religious service. London, 1880.

Phil 6120.6.5 — Thoughts on things psychic. (Kenilworth, W.W.) N.Y., 1911.

Phil 8695.3 — Thoughts on ultimate problems. 4. ed. (Frankland, F.W.) London, 1911.

Phil 5850.354.5 — Thouless, R.H. The control of the mind. London, 1928.

Pl. 5059.20.5 — Thouless, R.H. How to think straight. N.Y., 1939.

Pl. 5059.20.10 — Thouless, R.H. How to think straight. N.Y., 1941.

Pl. 5059.20.2 — Thouless, R.H. Straight and crooked thinking. N.Y., 1932.

Phil 5627.59 — Thouless, Robert H. An introduction to the psychology of religion. N.Y., 1923.

Phil 5627.59.5 — Thouless, Robert H. An introduction to the psychology of religion. 2. ed. Cambridge, Eng., 1928.

Phil 6689.8 — Thouret. Recherches et doutes sur le magnetisme animal. Paris, 1784.

Phil 630.1 — Thouverez, É. Le réalisme métaphysique. Paris, 1894.

Phil 8894.15 — Thouverez, Emile. Eléments de morale théoretique et pratique appliquée a la pédagogie. 2. éd. Paris, 1911.

Phil 2270.130 — Thouverez, Emile. Herbert Spencer. Paris, 1913.

Phil 8884.18.6 — Thrasymachus; or The future of morals. (Joad, Cyril E.M.) London, 1925.

Phil 8884.18.7 — Thrasymachus. (Joad, Cyril E.M.) N.Y., 1926.

Phil 4960.255 — Three Argentine thinkers. (Lipp, Solomon.) N.Y., 1969.

Phil 7054.40.5 — Three articles on modern spiritualism. (Hall, T.B.) Boston, 1863.

Phil 5241.24.5A — Three chapters on the nature of the mind. (Bosanquet, B.) London, 1923.

Phil 705.29 — Three Christian transcendentalists. (Wells, R.V.) N.Y., 1943.

Phil 6967.19 — The three Christs of Ypsilanti. (Rokeach, M.) N.Y., 1964.

Phil 5249.16 — Three conceptions of mind. (Jascalevich, A.A.) N.Y., 1926.

Phil 6315.2.75.14 — Three contributions to the theory of sex. 4th ed. (Freud, Sigmund.) N.Y., 1948.

Phil 193.107 — The three conventions; metaphysical dialogues, principia metaphysica, and commentary. N.Y., 1926.

Phil 1870.45.3 — Three dialogues...Hylas and Philonous. (Berkeley, G.) Chicago, 1901.

Htn   Phil 1870.45.1* — Three dialogues...Hylas and Philonous. (Berkeley, G.) London, 1713.

Phil 5751.16 — Three dialogues. (Barwis, J.) London, 1776.

Phil 9070.90 — The three-dimensional man. (Sullivan, Aloysius Michael.) N.Y., 1956.

Phil 9450.28 — Three dimensions of public morality. (Schneider, H.W.) Bloomington, Ind., 1956.

Htn   Phil 2610.35* — Three discourses of happiness, virtue and liberty. (Gassendi, P.) London, 1699.

Phil 9230.3.7 — Three dissertations on...gaming. (Hey, R.) Cambridge, 1812.

Htn   Phil 8434.2.5* — Three essays: on picturesque beauty. (Gilpin, W.) London, 1792.

Phil 3475.3.20 — Three essays. 1st ed. (Jaspers, Karl.) N.Y., 1964.

Phil 2138.45.10 — Three essays on religion. (Mill, John S.) London, 1925.

Phil 2138.45.2 — Three essays on religion. (Mill, John S.) N.Y., 1874.

X Cg   Phil 2138.45.5 — Three essays on religion. (Mill, John S.) N.Y., 1874.

Phil 6315.2.75.17 — Three essays on the theory of sexuality. (Freud, Sigmund.) London, 1962.

Phil 6315.2.75.15 — Three essays on the theory of sexuality. 1st English ed. (Freud, Sigmund.) London, 1949.

Phil 7040.29 — The three faces of Eve. (Thigpen, C.H.) N.Y., 1957.

Phil 7069.40.14 — Three famous occultists: Dr. John Dee. Photoreproducton. (Hort, Gertrude M.) Philadelphia, 1940.

Phil 7054.142 — A three-fold test of modern spiritualism. (Gordon, William R.) N.Y., 1856.

Phil 6949.363 — Three hundred years of psychiatry, 1535-1860; a history presented in selected English texts. (Hunter, Richard A.) London, 1963.

Phil 9530.36.8 — The three keys to success. (Beaverbrook, W.M.A.) N.Y., 1956.

Phil 8402.13 — Three lectures on aesthetic. (Bosanquet, B.) London, 1915.

Phil 960.7.5 — Three lectures on the Vedânta philosophy. (Muller, F.M.) London, 1894.

Phil 8877.72 — Three lords of destiny. (Crothers, S.McC.) Boston, 1913.

Phil 6314.10 — Three men. 1st ed. (Evans, Jean.) N.Y., 1954.

Htn   Phil 5055.1.9* — Three papers on logic. (Pierce, C.S.) n.p., 1867?

Phil 292.4 — Three papers reprinted. (Logan, J.D.) n.p., 1897-99.

Phil 165.290 — Three philosophers. (Anscombe, G.E.M.) Ithaca, N.Y., 1961.

Phil 8597.2 Three physico-theological discourses. (Ray, J.)
London, 1721.

Phil 2750.11.71.10
Three reformers: Luther, Descartes, Rousseau. (Maritain,
Jacques.) Paris, 1929?

Phil 9070.22.5 The three R's of religion. (Cole, Walton E.)
Boston, 1945.

Phil 8691.21 Three things that matter; religion, philosophy, science.
(Bond, Walter G.) London, 1931.

Phil 6112.12 Three thousand years of mental healing. (Cutter, G.B.)
N.Y., 1911.

Phil 8835.5 Three traditions of moral thought. (Krook, Dorothea.)
Cambridge, Eng., 1959.

Phil 6128.53 Three transactions on the cerebrum; a posthumous work.
V.1-2 and atlas. (Swedenborg, Emanuel.)
Philadelphia, 1938-40. 3v.

Htn Phil 9245.12 Three treatises. (Harris, J.) London, 1744.
Htn Phil 9245.12.2* Three treatises. (Harris, J.) London, 1765.
Phil 9245.12.2 Three treatises. (Harris, J.) London, 1765.
Phil 9245.12.3 Three treatises. (Harris, J.) London, 1772.
Htn Phil 6100.11* Three treatises. On the brain, the eye and the ear.
(Monro, A.) Edinburgh, 1797.

Phil 8615.21 Three types of practical ethical movements. (Jacobs, Leo.)
N.Y., 1922.

Phil 930.38 Three ways of thought in ancient China. (Waley, Arthur.)
London, 1939.

Phil 930.38.5 Three ways of thought in ancient China. (Waley, Arthur.)
London, 1953.

Phil 3850.27.150 The three worlds of Albert Schweitzer. (Payne, Robert.)
N.Y., 1957.

Phil 1145.95 The three worlds of man. (Barr, S.) Columbia, 1963.
Phil 8708.34 A threefold cord. (Samuel, Herbert S.) London, 1961.
Phil 978.55 The threefold path to peace. (Rees, J.R.) N.Y., 1904.
Phil 193.90 The threshold of the new. (Stuart, (Mrs.). C.)
London, 1920.

Phil 365.52 Thresholds of existence. (Ewing, Upton Clary.)
N.Y., 1956.

Phil 6317.50 Thresholds of initiation. 1. ed. (Henderson, Joseph.)
Middletown, 1967.

Phil 2120.15 Thrice-born. (Loewenberg, Jacob.) N.Y., 1968.
Phil 8893.14.13 Thrift. (Smiles, Samuel.) Chicago, 1890.
Phil 8893.14.11 Thrift. (Smiles, Samuel.) Toronto, 1876.
Phil 8592.70 The thrill of tradition. (Moffatt, J.) London, 1944.
Phil 6311.40 Thrills and regressions. (Balint, Michael.) London, 1959.
Phil 8599.2 Thring, E. Thoughts on life science. London, 1871.
Phil 9530.37 Through failure to success. (Alexander, James.)
N.Y., 1934.

Phil 7069.20.280 Through jewelled windows. (Raynor, Frank C.)
London, 1920.

Phil 8585.17 Through nature to God. (Fiske, J.) Boston, 1899.
Phil 8708.8 Through science to faith. (Smyth, Newman.) N.Y., 1902.
Phil 8708.22 Through science to faith. (Smith, Nathan A.) N.Y., 1936.
Phil 978.15.5 Through the gates of gold. (Cook, M.C.) Boston, 1901.
Phil 7069.35.56 Through the gates of time. v.1. (Wells, Helen B.)
N.Y., 1935.

Phil 6958.1.5 Through the ivory gate. (Ireland, W.W.) Edinburgh, 1889.
Phil 7069.20.210 Through the mists. (Lees, Robert James.) London, 1920.
Phil 8647.14 Through the psychic door. (Wood, Frederic Herbert.)
Houston, 1964?

Phil 8592.68 Through tragedy to triumph. (Mathews, B.) N.Y., 1939.
Htn Phil 3801.831* Thürmer, J. Versuch die Anhänger Hegel's und Schelling's.
Berlin, 1843.

Phil 6969.4 Thuillier-Landry, L. Études sur les délires d'évolution
démentielle précoce. Thèse. Paris, 1916.

Phil 525.73 Thulié, H. La mystique divine. Paris, 1912.
Phil 7069.28.10 The thumbprint and cross correspondence experiments made
with the medium Margery during 1927-1928. (Richardson,
Mark Wyman.) n.p., 1928.

Phil 530.11.18 Thune, Nils. The Behmenists and the Philadelphians.
Inaug.-Diss. Uppsala, 1948.

Phil 8633.1.47 Thurman, Howard. The negro spiritual speaks of life and
death. N.Y., 1947.

Phil 5520.435 Thurman, Kelly. Semantics. Boston, 1960.
Phil 5259.45 Thurner, Franz K. Kurzzeitige nacheffekte unserer
Wahrnehmungen. Berlin, 1961.

Phil 5620.5 Thurot, J.F. De l'entendement de la raison. Paris, 1830.
2v.

Phil 9359.3 Thurston, D. Letters from a father to a son.
Portland, 1858.

Phil 525.119 Thurston, H. The physical phenomena of mysticism.
Chicago, 1952.

Phil 7069.54 Thurston, Herbert. Ghosts and poltergeists.
Chicago, 1954.

Phil 7069.28.75 Thurston, Herbert. Modern spiritualism. St-Louis, 1928.
Phil 5585.68 Thurstone, L.L. A factorial study of perception.
Chicago, 1944.

Phil 5259.17 Thurstone, L.L. The nature of intelligence. London, 1924.
Phil 3640.40.2 Thus spake Zararhustra. (Nietzsche, Friedrich.)
N.Y., 1908.

Phil 3640.40.12 Thus spake Zarathustra. (Nietzsche, Friedrich.)
Chicago, 1957.

Phil 3640.40.10 Thus spake Zarathustra. (Nietzsche, Friedrich.)
London, 1958.

Phil 3640.40.5 Thus spake Zarathustra. (Nietzsche, Friedrich.)
N.Y., 1896.

Phil 3640.40.30 Thus spake Zarathustra. (Nietzsche, Friedrich.)
N.Y., 1936.

Phil 3640.40.3 Thus spake Zarathustra. 2d ed. (Nietzsche, Friedrich.)
N.Y., 1911.

Phil 8894.28 Thwing, C.F. The best life; an address. N.Y., 1898.
Phil 194.14 Thwing, E.P. Windows of character. N.Y., 1889.
Phil 8968.14 Thy kingdom come...but not now. (Slattery, M.)
N.Y., 1938.

Phil 7069.18.150 Thy son liveth. Boston, 1918.
Phil 7069.19.220 Thy son liveth. Boston, 1919.
Phil 6980.744 Thymotherapie. (Török, Stephan.) Göttingen, 1967.
Htn Phil 7060.7.5* Thyraeus, P. Loca infesta, hoc est, de infestes.
London, 1599.

Phil 7060.7 Thyraeus, Petrus. De apparitionibus spirituum tractatus
duo. Coloniae Agrippinae, 1600.

Phil 2270.115 Thyren, Johan. Kritisk framställning af Herbert Spencer's
"Principles of Psychology". Akademisk afhandling.
Lund, 1883.

Phil 1719.6 Thyssen, Johannes. Grundlinien eines realistischen Systems
der Philosophie. Bonn, 1966. 2v.

Phil 194.40 Thyssen, Johannes. Die philosophische Methode.
Halle, 1930.

Phil 350.8.2 Thyssen, Johannes. Der philosophische Relativismus. 2.
Aufl. Bonn, 1947.

Phil 1719.5 Thyssen, Johannes. Realismus und moderne Philosophie.
Bonn, 1959.

Phil 6750.269 Ti år med Erik; en mors beretning om sin hjerneskadede
sønn. (Heggland, Ruth.) Oslo, 1969.

Phil 6307.452 Ti ars andssvageforsorg, 1, oktober, 1969. (Denmark.
Statens Andssvageforsorg.) København, 1969.

Phil 5059.5 Tiberghein, G. Logique. Paris, 1865. 2v.
Phil 3525.23 Tiberghien, G. De la doctrine de Krause. Bruxelles, 1855.
Phil 8894.5.5 Tiberghien, G. Elementos de ética ó filosofía moral.
Madrid, 1873.

Phil 8894.5 Tiberghien, G. Éléments de morale universelle.
Bruxelles, 1879.

Phil 8894.5.10 Tiberghien, G. Esquisse de philosophie morale.
Bruxelles, 1854.

Phil 819.2 Tiberghien, G. Essai théorique et historique.
Bruxelles, 1844.

Phil 8599.3 Tiberghien, G. Estudios sobre religion. Madrid, 1873.
Phil 194.5 Tiberghien, G. Introduction a la philosophie.
Bruxelles, 1868.

Phil 6631.5 Der Tic. (Meige, Henry.) Leipzig, 1903.
Phil 5259.24.2 Tickell, Sydney. Psychology really simplified in terms of
machinery. Cirencester, 1927.

Phil 179.21 Tidens kurs. (Eriksen, Richard.) Kristiania, 1912.
Phil 8110.5 Tides in English taste (1619-1800); a background for the
study of literature. (Allen, B.S.) Cambridge,
Mass., 1937. 2v.

Phil 8887.4.13 Tides of the spirit. (Martineau, J.) Boston, 1905.
Phil 4513.1.42 Tidoreflexer; filosofiska uppsatser. (Ahlberg, A.)
Stockholm, 1926.

Phil 2475.1.223 Tids- och intuitionsproblemen i Bergson's filosofi. Thesis.
(Oxenstierna, G.) Uppsala, 1926.

Phil 819.3 Tiedemann, D. Geschichte der spekulativen Philosophie.
Marburg, 1791-97. 6v.

Phil 1124.2 Tiedemann, D. Griechenlands erste Philosophen.
Leipzig, 1780.

Phil 1200.13 Tiedemann, D. System der stoischen Philosophie.
Leipzig, 1776. 3v.

Phil 3890.16 Tiedemann, Dieterich. Idealistische Briefe Marburg.
Bruxelles, 1969.

Phil 8885.30 Die Tiefen der Seele. (Klug, J.) Paderborn, 1926.
Phil 5722.40 Tiefenpsychologie. (Seifert, F.) Düsseldorf, 1955.
Phil 6980.632 Tiefenpsychologie und Humanismus. (Rattner, Josef.)
Zürich, 1967.

Phil 8888.14 Tiefenpsychologie und neue Ethik. (Neumam, Erich.)
Zürich, 1949.

Phil 6060.31 Eine tiefenpsychologische Grundlage zur Klages'chen
Graphologie. (Margadant, S.V.) Amsterdam, 1938.

Phil 6332.22 Die tiefenpsychologischen Schulen von der Anfanger bis zur
Gegenwart. (Wyss, Dieter.) Göttingen, 1961.

Phil 978.49.515 Die tieferen Geheimnisse des Menschheitswerdens im Lichte
der Evangelien. (Steiner, R.) Dornach, 1966.

Phil 5059.19 Tieftrunk, J.H. Grundriss der Logik. Halle, 1801.
Phil 300.3 Tieftrunk, J.H. Das Weltall nach menschlicher Ansicht.
Halle, 1821.

Phil 8599.11 Tiele, C.P. Elements of the science of religion.
Edinburgh, 1897-99. 2v.

Phil 8599.11.5 Tiele, C.P. Grundzüge der Religionswissenschaft.
Tübingen, 1904.

Phil 8403.2 El tiempo en el arte. (Camón Aznar, J.) Madrid, 1958.
Phil 4363.7.15 El tiempo que ni vuelve ni tropieza. (Marias Aguilera,
Julián.) Barcelona, 1964.

Phil 672.208 El tiempo y el "hay". (Fernández Suárez, Alvaro.)
Madrid, 1955.

Phil 5243.5.50 El tiempo y la vida anímica normal. (Delgrado, Honario.)
Lima, 1944.

Phil 3565.108.5 Tienes, Alfred. Lotze's Gedanken zur den Principienfragen
der Ethik. Heidelberg, 1896.

Phil 5821.9 Tier- und Menschenverstand. (Langfeldt.) München, 1909.
Phil 3790.1.93 Das Tier in der Philosophie des H.S. Reimarus. Diss.
(Scherer, C.C.) Würzburg, 1898.

Phil 3808.166 Das Tier in der Philosophie Schopenhauer's. Inaug. Diss.
(Bamberger, Herz.) Wirzburg, 1897.

Phil 5828.16.5 Das Tier in seinen Spielen. (Schmid, Bastian.)
Leipzig, 1919.

Phil 5828.16 Das Tier und Wir. (Schmid, Bastian.) Leipzig, 1916.
Phil 5811.12.10 Tierfabeln und andere Irrtümer in der Tierkunde. 19. Aufl.
(Bauke, Leopold.) Stuttgart, 19- ?

Phil 5780.24 Tierkreis. v.1-2. (Julius, Fritz Hendrik.)
Freiburg, 1964-

Phil 4370.7 Tierno, G. E. Tradicíon y modernismo. Madrid, 1962.
Phil 1750.796 Tierno Galván, Enrique. Humanismo y sociedad. 1. ed.
Barcelona, 1964.

Phil 310.760 Tierno Galvan, Enrique. Razon mecanica y razon dialectica.
Madrid, 1969.

Phil 4981.41.100 Tierno Galvan, Enrique. La realidad como resultado. Rio
Piedras, 1966.

Phil 5828.14 Tierpsychologie. (Sommer, R.) Leipzig, 1925.
Phil 5817.13 Tierpsychologie vom Standpunkte des Biologen. (Hempelmann,
F.) Leipzig, 1926.

Phil 5835.3 Tierpsychologische Beiträge zur Psylogenese der
ich-über-ich-instanzen. (Zweig, Adam.) Bern, 1959.

Phil 5835.3.5 Tierpsychologische Beiträge zur Psylogenese der
ich-über-ich-instanzen. (Zweig, Adam.) Bern, 1959.

Phil 5811.18 Die tierpsychologische Forschung, ihre Ziele und Wege.
(Bierens de Haan, J.A.) Leipzig, 1935.

Phil 5828.6.5 Tierpsychologisches Praktikum. (Schneider, K.C.)
Leipzig, 1912.

Phil 3552.249 Die Tierseele in der leibnizschen Philosophie. (Ernst,
Charles.) Wiesbaden, 1918.

Phil 7140.11 Tietjens, E. Die Desuggestion; ihre Bedeutung und
Auswertung. Berlin, 1928.

Phil 7140.11.5 Tietjens, E. Desuggestion for the attainment of health.
London, 1931.

Phil 4668.123.30 Tieto on valtaa ja muita aatehistoriallisia esseitä.
(Hintikka, Kaarlo Jaakko Juhani.) Porvoo, 1969.

Phil 575.130 Tietzen, Hermann. Die menschliche Persönlichkeit in
Anlehnung an Zinzendorfsche Gedanken. Stuttgart, 1922.

Phil 7054.137 Tiffany, Joel. Lectures on spiritualism. Cleveland, 1851.
Phil 7054.137.3 Tiffany, Joel. Modern spiritualism compared with
Christianity. Warren, Ohio, 1855.

Phil 7054.137.5 Tiffany, Joel. Spiritualism explained. 2. ed. N.Y., 1856.
Phil 5259.30 Tiffin, J. The psychology of normal people. Boston, 1940.
Phil 5520.704 Tikhomirov, Oleg K. Struktura myslitel'noi deiatel'nosti
cheloveka. Moskva, 1969.

Phil 4650.1.45 Til det andliga lifvets filosofi. (Vannérus, Allen.)
Stockholm, 1910.

Phil 5374.30   Tilby, A Wyatt. The evolution of consciousness. London, 1922.

Phil 194.42   Tilby, Aubry W. Right; a study in physical and moral order. London, 1933.

Phil 7180.2   Tildragelser under ahnelser. (Frankenau, Rasmus.) Kjøbenhavn, 1804.

Phil 4019.1   Tilgher, A. Antologia dei filosofi italiani del dopoguerra. 2. ed. Modena, 1937.

Phil 8420.14.5   Tilgher, A. Estetica; teoria generale dell'attività artistica. Roma, 1931.

Phil 850.12   Tilgher, A. Filosofi antichi. Todi, 1921.
Phil 8894.27   Tilgher, A. Filosofia delle morali. Roma, 1937.
Phil 8420.14   Tilgher, A. Primi scritti de estetica. Roma, 1931.
Phil 1750.125   Tilgher, A. Relativisti contemporanei. Roma, 1923.
Phil 194.30   Tilgher, A. Teoria del pragmatismo trascendentale. Milano, 1915.

Phil 1735.10   Tilgher, Adriano. Filosofi e moralisti del novecento. Roma, 1932.

Phil 8420.28   Tilghman, Benjamin R. The expression of emotion in the visual arts: a philosophical inquiry. The Hague, 1970.

Phil 4515.84   Till Boströms teoretiska filosofi. (Vannérus, Allen.) Stockholm, 1897.

Phil 3483.23   Till Kants lära om tinget i och för sig. (Bensow, O.) Lund, 1896.

Phil 4650.1.31   Till kritiken af den religiösa kunskapen. (Vannérus, Allen.) Stockholm, 1902.

Phil 6110.13   Till nervsystems dynamik. (Abrutz, Sydney.) Stockholm, 1917.

Phil 5850.227.14   Tillämpad psykologi. 4. uppl. (Haernqvist, Kjell.) Stockholm, 1966.

Phil 8894.16   Tille, A. Von Darwin bis Nietzsche. Leipzig, 1895.
Phil 2270.151   Tillet, A.W. Herbert Spencer betrayed. London, 1939.
Phil 9530.10   Tilley, W.J. Masters of the situation. Chicago, 1887.
Phil 8969.11   Tillich, Paul. Morality and beyond. N.Y., 1963.
Phil 3801.837   Tillich, Paul. Die religionsgechichtliche Konstruktive in Schellings positiver Philosophie. Breslau, 1910.

Phil 8599.50   Tillich, Paul. What is religion? 1. ed. N.Y., 1969.
Phil 2750.19.105   Tilliette, X. Philosophes contemporains. Paris, 1962.
Phil 2725.13.98   Tilliette, Xavier. Jules Lequier. Paris, 1964.
Phil 3475.3.175   Tilliette, Xavier. Karl Jaspers. Paris, 1960.
Phil 2750.20.145   Tilliette, Xavier. Merleau-Ponty. Paris, 1970.
Phil 3801.837.15   Tilliette, Xavier. Schelling: une philosophie en devenir. Paris, 1970. 2v.

Phil 3501.18   Tilling, Christian Gottfried. Gedanken zur Prüfung von Kants...der Sitten, Leipzig, 1789. Bruxelles, 1968.

Phil 2905.1.520   Tilloy, Alain. Teilhard de Chardin, père de l'Eglise ou pseudo-prophète? Saint Cénére, 1968.

Phil 192.53   Tillvarons problem. (Rudin, W.) Stockholm, 1905.
Phil 7069.25.12   Tillyard, R.J. Some recent personal experiences with Margery. N.Y., 1926.

Phil 6124.4   Tilney, Frederick. The brain from ape to man. N.Y., 1928. 2v.

Phil 5259.32   Tilquin, A. Le behaviorisme. Thèse. Paris, 1942-45.
Phil 7060.89.5   Timbs, John. Mysteries of life, death and futurity. N.Y., 1863.

Phil 193.130.5   Time; cause and eternity. (Stocks, J.L.) London, 1938.
Phil 5585.325   Time, experience and behavior. (Orme, John Edward.) London, 1969.

Phil 672.240.2   Time, fourth dimension of the mind. 1st ed. (Wallis, Robert.) N.Y., 1968.

Phil 8703.2.10   Time: the refreshing river; essays and addresses, 1932-1942. (Needham, Joseph.) London, 1943.

Phil 672.233   Time and Eastern man. (Needham, Joseph.) London, 1965.
Phil 672.168   Time and eternity. (Coomaraswamy, A.) Ascona, 1947.
Phil 672.234   Time and eternity. (Hatano, Seiichi.) Tokyo? 1963.
Phil 2475.1.42   Time and free will; an essay on the immediate data of consciousness. (Bergson, Henri.) London, 1959.

Phil 2475.1.41   Time and free will; an essay on the immediate data of consciousness. (Bergson, Henri.) N.Y., 1960.

Phil 4260.129   Time and idea. (Caponigri, A.R.) London, 1953.
Phil 720.30   Time and its importance to modern thought. (Cleugh, M.F.) London, 1937.

Phil 5066.100   Time and modality. (Prior, Arthur Norman.) Oxford, 1957.
Phil 182.19.8   Time and space. A metaphysical essay. (Hodgson, S.H.) London, 1865.

Phil 672.218   Time and the physical world. (Schlegel, R.) East Lansing? 1961.

Phil 8592.65   Time and the timeless. (Murray, J.) London, 1942.
Phil 672.140   Time and Western man. (Lewis, Wyndham.) N.Y., 1928.
Phil 185.45   Time-binding; the general theory. (Korzybski, A.) N.Y., 1924. 2 pam.

Phil 672.222   Time devoured. (Parsons, E.) London, 1964.
Phil 1713.3   A time for truth. (Newman, J.) Dublin, 1955.
Phil 7069.47.10   Time is kind. (Pond, Mariam B.) N.Y., 1947.
Phil 8875.27.5   The time of our lives. 1st ed. (Adler, Mortimer Jerome.) N.Y., 1970.

Phil 5635.22   The time of perception as a measure of differences in sensations. (Henmon, V.A.C.) N.Y., 1906.

Phil 5640.11   Time of perception as a measure of differences in sensations. (Henmon, V.A.C.) N.Y., 1906.

Phil 8587.25   The time of transition. (Hyndman, F.A.) London, 1900.
Phil 9070.4   Time out to live. (Tomlison, W.W.) N.Y., 1939.
Phil 5585.02   Pamphlet vol. Time perception. 26 pam.
Phil 5249.6.10   The time-relations of mental phenomena. (Jastrow, J.) n.p. 1890-1912. 10 pam.

Phil 665.100   Timeless documents of the soul. Evanston, 1968.
Phil 525.101   The timeless moment. (Allen, Warner.) London, 1946.
Phil 8887.54   Timely lessons on today's living. (McNair, G.H.) Newport, Vt., 1922.

Phil 9358.4   The times and young men. (Strong, J.) N.Y., 1901.
Phil 177.50   Times garland of grace. (Chainey, George.) San Diego, 1918.

Phil 5401.3.5   Les timides dans la littérature et l'art. (Dugas, L.) Paris, 1925.

Phil 5401.3   La timidité. (Dugas, L.) Paris, 1910.
Phil 5401.18   La timidité constitutionnelle et ses formes passive et active. (Litwinski, Léon de.) Lisbonne, 1944.

Phil 8876.105   Timidity. (Blanchard, Mme.) N.Y., 1916.
Phil 5585.248   Timing in temporal tracking. Proefschrift. (Michon, John Albertus.) Assen, 1967.

Phil 494.6   Timpanaro, Sebastiano. Sul materialismo. Pisa, 1970.
Phil 8894.34   Timur, Mohammed. The theory of morals. London, 1956.
Phil 7054.29   Tindall, A.F. Occult revelations in prose and verse. London, n.d.

Phil 7068.95   Tindall, A.F. Spiritual Christianity revealed by occultism. London, 189-.

Htn   Phil 8599.4*   Tindall, M. Christianity as old as the creation. London, 1730. 2v.

Phil 8599.4.2   Tindall, M. Christianity as old as the creation. London, 1732.

Phil 978.16.13   Tingley, K.A. (Mrs.). The gods await. Point Loma, California, 1926.

Phil 974.2.15   Tingley, K.A. (Mrs.). Helena Petrovna Blavatsky. Point Loma, Calif., 1921.

Phil 978.16   Tingley, K.A. (Mrs.). The mysteries of the heart doctrine. Point Loma, Calif., 1902.

Phil 978.16.5   Tingley, K.A. (Mrs.). Theosophy; the path ofthe mystic. 2d ed. Point Loma, Calif., 1922.

Phil 1850.131   Tinivella, G. Baconee Locke. Milano, 1939.
Phil 3425.395   Tinivella, Giovanni. Critica dell'idea di progresso. Milano, 1955.

Phil 5252.154   Tipologicheskie issledovaniia po psikhologii lichnosti i po psikhologii truda. (Merlin, Vol'f S.) Perm', 1964.

Phil 287.6   Tipos historicos del filosofar físico. (Garcia Bacca, Juan D.) Tucuman, 1941.

Phil 7054.27.9   Tipping his tables. (Putnam, A.) Boston, 1873.
Phil 9035.101   Tipy kharaktera i fiksirovannaia ustanovka. (Norakidze, Vladimir.) Tbilisi, 1966.

Phil 186.99   Tipy mirovozzrenii. (Losskii, N.O.) Parizh, 1931.
Phil 3552.302   Tirtsch, Gergely. Leibniz erkolcatana. Balassagyarmat, 1898.

Phil 282.13   Tis filosofias i ipothesis ke i epitonvion ropi. (Boreas, Theophilos.) Athens, 1913.

Phil 7054.45.60   Tischner, R. Das medium D.D. Home. Leipzig, 1925.
Phil 7069.25.25   Tischner, R. Telepathy and clairvoyance. London, 1925.
Phil 6689.10   Tischner, Rudolf. Franz Anton Mesmer. München, 1928.
Phil 7068.66.80   Tissandier, J.B. Des sciences occultes et du spiritisme. Paris, 1866.

Phil 2730.85   Tisserand, Pierre. L'anthropologie de Maine de Biran. Paris, 1909.

Phil 3640.206   Tissi, Silvio. Nietzsche. Milano, 1926.
Phil 6329.5   Tissi, Silvio. La psicanalisi. Milano, 1929.
Phil 7082.26   Tissié, Philippe. Les rêves. Paris, 1890.
Phil 5259.4   Tissot, C.J. Anthropologie. Paris, 1843. 2v.
Phil 194.6   Tissot, C.J. Cours élémentaire de philosophie. Dijon, 1840.

Phil 194.6.2   Tissot, C.J. Cours élémentaire de philosophie. Paris, 1847.

Phil 5059.6   Tissot, C.J. Essai de logique objective. Paris, 1868.
Phil 819.4   Tissot, C.J. Histoire de la philosophie. Paris, 1840.
Phil 5829.1   Tissot, C.J. Psychologie comparée. Paris, 1878.
Phil 2672.90   Tissot, J. Théodore Jouffroy: sa vie et ses écrits. Paris, 1876.

Phil 8894.6.10   Tissot, Joseph. Décadence du sentiment moral et religieux. Paris, 1878.

Phil 8894.6   Tissot, Joseph. Éthique ou science des moeurs. Paris, 1840.

Phil 8894.6.5   Tissot, Joseph. Méditations morales. Paris, 1860.
Phil 8894.6.1   Tissot, Joseph. Principes de la morale. Paris, 1866.
Phil 5055.21.10   A tiszta logika alapkérdesei. (Madárászné Zsigmond Anna.) Budapest, 1965.

Phil 8980.838   Titarenko, Aleksandr I. Kriterii nravstvennogo progressa. Moskva, 1967.

Phil 9513.41   Titarenko, Aleksandr I. Nravstvennyi progress. Moskva, 1969.

Phil 310.456   Titarenko, Aleksandr I. Pragmatistskii lzhemarksizm filosofiia antikommunizme. Moskva, 1964.

Phil 310.455   Titarenko, Aleksandr I. Protiv fal'sifikatsii filosofii marksizma progmatistami SShA. Moskva, 1961.

Phil 5259.5.18   Titchener, E.B. A beginner's psychology. N.Y., 1916.
Phil 5259.5.19   Titchener, E.B. A beginner's psychology. N.Y., 1924.
Phil 5259.5.25   Titchener, E.B. Elementos de psicología. Paris, 1913.
Phil 5259.5.9   Titchener, E.B. Experimental psychology. v.1-2; v.2, pt.1. n.p., 1901-27. 5v.

Phil 5259.5.9.5   Titchener, E.B. Experimental psychology. v.1-2. N.Y., 1927. 4v.

Phil 5400.25   Titchener, E.B. Lectures on the elementary psychology of feeling and attention. N.Y., 1908.

Phil 5400.25.5   Titchener, E.B. Lectures on the elementary psychology of feeling and attention. N.Y., 1924.

NEDL   Phil 5259.5.10A   Titchener, E.B. Lectures on the experimental psychology of the thought-processes. N.Y., 1909.

Phil 5259.5.10.5   Titchener, E.B. Lectures on the experimental psychology of the thought-processes. N.Y., 1926.

Phil 5259.5.16   Titchener, E.B. Manuel de psychologie. Paris, 1922.
Phil 5259.5.5   Titchener, E.B. An outline of psychology. N.Y., 1897.
Phil 5259.5A   Titchener, E.B. A primer of psychology. N.Y., 1898.
Phil 5259.5.50   Titchener, E.B. Systematic psychology; prolegomena. N.Y., 1929.

Phil 5259.5.35   Titchener, E.B. A text-book of psychology. N.Y., 1924.
Phil 5259.5.37   Titchener, E.B. A text-book of psychology. N.Y., 1926.
Phil 5259.5.38   Titchener, E.B. A text-book of psychology. N.Y., 1928.
Phil 9359.6.5   Titcomb's letters to young people, single and married. 15th ed. (Holland, Josiah G.) N.Y., 1859.

Phil 9359.6.25   Titcomb's letters to young people. 50th ed. (Holland, Josiah G.) N.Y., 1884.

Phil 4120.3.90   Titoli del professore Vincenzo di Calabria. Palermo, 1870.
Phil 5520.426   Titone, Renzo. La psicolinguistica oggi. Zürich, 1964.
Phil 3501.12   Tittel, Gottlob August. Kantischen den Reformen oder Kategorien. Frankfurt, 1787.

Phil 194.32   Tittmann, F.W. Aphorismen zur Philosophie. Dresden, 1859.
Phil 8599.5   Tittmann, J.A.H. Uber Supranaturalismus. Leipzig, 1816.
Phil 8894.26   Titus, H.H. Ethics for today. Boston, 1936.
Phil 8894.26.5   Titus, H.H. What is mature morality. Boston, 1943.
Phil 270.144   Titze, Hans. Der Kausalbegriff in Philosophie und Physik. Meisenheima, 1964.

Phil 8865.636   Tiwari, Brij Gopal. Secularism and materialism in modern India. Delhi, 1964?

VPhil 9070.124   A tizparancsalat a közeletben. (Almásy, József.) Budapest, 1942.

Phil 8980.839   Tkachenko, Vera M. Vernost'. 2. izd. Moskva, 1965.
Phil 310.586   Tlustý, V. Dialektické rozpory a jejich zakonitosti. Praha, 1962.

Phil 672.224   Tlustý, Vojtěch. Prostor a čas. 2. vyd. Praha, 1963.
Phil 2880.8.136   To be and not to be. (Salvan, Jacques L.) Detroit, 1962.
Phil 575.258   To be or not to be...existential psychological perspectives on the self. Gainesville, 1967.

Phil 7054.33.5   "To daemoion" or The spiritual medium. (Samson, G.W.) Boston, 1852.

Phil 585.187   To deny our nothingness. (Friedman, Maurice Stanley.) N.Y., 1967.

Phil 5048.2   To essays om vor erkendelse. (Iversen, H.) Kjøbenhavn, 1918.

Phil 9347.3   To girls. A budget of letters. (Hersey, H.E.) Boston, 1901.

Phil 9358.14.5   To him that overcometh. (Stearns, Alfred E.) Boston, 1935.
Phil 7069.20.200   To walk with God. (Lane, Anne W.) N.Y., 1920.
Phil 9070.47.5   To whom it may concern. 2. ed. (Ashton, M.O.) Salt Lake City, 1946.
Phil 7069.20.232   To woman from Meslom. (McEvilly, Mary A.) N.Y., 1920.
Phil 8228.2   Tobias, José Antônio. História das idéias estéticas no Brasil. São Paulo, 1967.
Phil 194.7   Tobias, W. Grenzen der Philosophie. Berlin, 1875.
Phil 4065.96   Tocco, Felice. Giordano Bruno. Firenze, 1886.
Phil 3501.5   Tocco, Felice. Studi Kantiani. Milano, 1909.
Phil 5421.20.70   Toch, Hans. Violent men; an inquiry into the psychology of violence. Chicago, 1969.
Phil 5223.5   Tôche relussité et échec. (Nuttin, Jozef.) Bruxelles, 1953.
Phil 5545.264   Tocquet, Robert. La mémoire, comment l'acquérer, comment la conserver. Paris, 1968.
Phil 8612.40   Der Tod als Antwort auf das Leben. (Mangoldt, Ursula von.) München, 1957.
Phil 978.49.595   Der Tod als Lebenswandlung. 1. Aufl. (Steiner, R.) Dornach, 1969.
Phil 8612.58   Der Tod im Phänomen der Bildung und Erziehung. Thesis. (Zoepfl, Helmut.) München, 1963.
Phil 8612.68   Tod und Vusterblichkeit. (Pieper, Josef.) München, 1968.
Phil 9590.21   Today we think of our tomorrows. (Drummond, D.D.) Richmond, Va., 1945.
Phil 9070.2   Today you are a man. (Perley, R.N.) Omaha, 1940.
Phil 6329.15   Today's neurotic family. (Tashman, H.F.) N.Y., 1957.
Phil 9359.4   Todd, J. Hints addressed to the young men of the United States. 2d ed. Northampton, 1845.
Phil 9179.8   Todd, J. Nuts for boys to crack. N.Y., n.d.
Phil 8420.9   Todd, John. The arts, artists and thinkers. London, 1959.
Phil 9050.8   Todd, John. The moral influence, dangers and duties connected with great cities. Northampton, 1841.
Phil 400.116   Todd, William. Analytical solipsism. The Hague, 1968.
Phil 8612.76   Todesbilder in der modernen Gesellschaft. (Fuchs, Werner.) Frankfurt, 1969.
Phil 760.2   El todo y las partes; estudios de ontología formal. (González Asenjo, Florencio.) Madrid, 1962.
Phil 8599.37   Todoli, José. Filosofía de la religion. Madrid, 1955.
Phil 4983.9.30   Todología. (Vasconcelos, J.) México, 1952.
Phil 9035.45.20   Todoranu, D. O conceptie americana despre caracter. Cluj, 1933.
Phil 3483.29   Die Todtenfeyer Kant's. 1. Aufl. (Böckel, C.G.A.) Königsberg, 1804.
Phil 5850.143   Toegepaste psychologie. (Bromberg, R.) Leiden, 1926.
Phil 5850.161   Toegepaste psychologie. (Coetsier, Leo.) Gent, 1965.
Phil 5251.57   De toekomst der psychologie. (Leyden. Universiteit.) Leiden, 1960.
Phil 8599.6   Töllner, J.G. Beweis dass Gott die menschen bereits durch seine Offenbarung in der Natur zur seligkeit führt. Züllichau, 1766.
Phil 5829.5   Toenjes, H. Principles of animal understanding. N.Y., 1905.
Phil 2045.85   Tönnies, F. Hobbes Leben und Lehre. Stuttgart, 1896.
Phil 150.1   Tönnies, F. Philosophische Terminologie. Leipzig, 1906.
Phil 2045.85.2   Tönnies, F. Thomas Hobbes. 2e Aufl. Osterwieck, 1912.
Phil 2045.85.3   Tönnies, F. Thomas Hobbes. 3e Aufl. Stuttgart, 1925.
Phil 8894.19.5   Tönnies, Ferdinand. Custom. N.Y., 1961.
Phil 3640.249   Tönnies, Ferdinand. Der Nietzsche-Kultus; eine Kritik. Leipzig, 1897.
Phil 8894.19   Tönnies, Ferdinand. Die Sitte. Frankfurt, 1909.
Phil 5190.24.15   Toensma, E. The paradoxes. Assen, 1969.
Phil 5066.243   Toernelohm, Håkan. Information and confirmation. Göteborg, 1964.
Phil 8894.31   Törngren, P.H. Moralsjukdomen. Stockholm, 1940.
Phil 6980.744   Török, Stephan. Thymotherapie. Göttingen, 1967.
VPhil 310.708.2   A történelmi materializmus története. 2. kiad. (Sándor, Pál.) Budapest, 1945.
Phil 585.210   Toesca, Maurice. Voyage autour de l'homme et au-delà. Paris, 1967.
Phil 1750.166.215   Toesca, Pietro M. Verità e rivoluzione. Roma, 1965.
Phil 6060.74   Toetsing van grafologische uitspraken. (Jansen, Abraham.) Amsterdam, 1963.
Phil 8612.42   Das Tötungsrecht bei den frühchristlichen Schriftstellern. (Schoepf, Bernhard.) Regensburg, 1958.
Phil 5535.32   Toğrol, Beğlan. Duygusal anlam sistemlesi. Istanbul, 1967.
Phil 29.17   Tohoku psychologica folia. (Sendai, Japan. University.) Sendai. 4,1936+ 10v.
Phil 8599.48   Toinet, Paul. Existence chrétienne et philosophie. Paris, 1965.
Phil 3425.609   Het tolaliteitsbegrip bij Hegel en zijn voorgangers. (Dooren, Willem van.) Assen, 1965.
Phil 2295.36   Toland, John. Christianity not mysterious. Stuttgart, 1964.
Htn   Phil 2295.34*   Toland, John. Christianity not mysterious. v.1-3. London, 1696.
Htn   Phil 2295.35*   Toland, John. Christianity not mysterious. 2nd ed. London, 1696.
Phil 2295.10   Toland, John. Collection of several pieces. London, 1726. 2v.
Htn   Phil 2295.27*   Toland, John. Historical account of life. London, 1718-22. 3 pam.
Htn   Phil 2295.24*   Toland, John. Letters to Serena. London, 1704.
Htn   Phil 2295.65*   Toland, John. Lettres philosophiques. London, 1768.
Phil 2295.15   Toland, John. Miscellaneous works. London 1747. 2v.
Htn   Phil 2295.39*   Toland, John. Pantheisticon, sive formula celebrandae sodalitatis Socraticae. Cosmopoli, 1720.
Phil 2295.40.5   Toland, John. Das Pantheistikon. Leipzig, 1897.
Htn   Phil 2295.75*   Toland, John. Vindicius liberius. London, 1702.
Htn   Phil 2295.75.2*   Toland, John. Vindicius liberius. London, 1702.
Phil 9540.1.10   Tolerance. (Van Loon, H.W.) Garden City, 1927.
Phil 9540.1.5   Tolerance. (Van Loon, H.W.) N.Y., 1925.
Phil 9540.1   Tolerance. (Van Loon, H.W.) N.Y., 1939.
Phil 1750.116   Tolerance and revolution. (Marxist-Non-Marxist Humanist Dialogue, 2d, Herceg-Novi, 1969.) Beograd, 1970.
Phil 8581.27   Tolerance in religion; liberal thoughts of modern thinkers. (Biroth, H.) Rome, 1913.
Phil 9540.9   Toleranz eine Grundforderung geschichtlicher Existenz. (Freie Akademie Nüremberg.) Nürnberg, 1960.
Phil 3501.10   Toll, C.H. Die erste Antinomie Kants und der Pantheismus. Berlin, 1910.
Phil 8420.23   Tollemonde, G. de. Du juste milieu; traité général de philosophie et d'art. Paris, 1910.
Phil 300.15.5   Tollenaere, M. de. Le corps et le monde. Bruges, 1967.
Phil 300.15   Tollenaere, M. de. Lichaam en wereld. Brugge, 1967.

Phil 672.260   Tollenaere, M. de. Een philosophie van de tijd. Leuven, 1952.
Phil 3475.3.180   Tollhoetter, Bernhard. Erziehung und Selbstsein. Rätingen, 1966.
Phil 1150.12   Tollington, R.B. Alexandrine teaching on the universe. London, 1932.
Phil 5259.40.5   Tolman, Edward C. Behavior and psychological man. Berkeley, 1958.
Phil 5259.40A   Tolman, Edward C. Collected papers in psychology. Berkeley, 1951.
Phil 5829.10.2   Tolman, Edward C. Purposive behavior in animals and men. Berkeley, 1951.
Phil 5829.10   Tolman, Edward C. Purposive behavior in animals and men. N.Y., 1932.
Phil 2651.83   Tolmer, L. Pierre-Daniel Huet, 1630-1721. Bayeux, 1949.
Phil 8420.5   Tolstykh, V. Iskusstvo i moral'. Moskva, 1962.
Phil 8587.33   Tolv forebaesninger over tro og taenkning. (Horn, E.F.B.) Kristiania, 1896.
Phil 7053.344   Tom Corbett's stately ghosts of England. (Norman, Diana.) N.Y., 1970.
Phil 5259.55   Toman, Walter. Family constellation. N.Y., 1961.
Phil 5259.55.2   Toman, Walter. Family constellation. 2d ed. N.Y., 1969.
Phil 5548.75   Toman, Walter. An introduction to psychoanalytic theory of motivation. N.Y., 1960.
Phil 5548.75.5   Toman, Walter. Motivation, Persönlichkeit, Umwelt. Göttingen, 1968.
Phil 6980.398   Tomas de Aquino y la psicopatología. (Krapf, E. Eduardo.) Buenos Aires, 1943.
Phil 310.698   Tomášek, Ladislav. Marxisticka' dialektika a neotomizmus. Vyd. 1. Bratislava, 1967.
Phil 4073.102   Tomaso Campanella. (Jacabelli Isaldi, A.M.) Milano, 1953.
Phil 9245.19   Le tombeau des délices du monde. (Laserre, J.P. de.) Brusselles, 1632.
Phil 960.134   Tombleson, J.B. As above, so below. London, 1928.
Phil 8894.13   Tomkins, D.B. The individual and society. Thesis. Somerville, N.J., 1915.
Phil 5590.416   Tomkins, S.S. Affect, imagery, consciousness. N.Y., 1962. 2v.
Phil 1900.90   Tomkins, S.S. Conscience, self love and benevolence in the system of Bishop Butler. Thesis. Philadelphia, 1934.
Phil 6329.8   Tomkins, S.S. Contemporary psychopathology. Cambridge, 1943.
Phil 5590.39   Tomkins, Silvan S. Computer simulation of personality. N.Y., 1963.
Phil 5590.38   Tomkins, Silvan S. The thematic apperception test. N.Y., 1947.
Phil 5400.168   Tomkins, Silvan Solomon. Affect, cognition, and personality. N.Y., 1965.
Phil 194.45   Tomlin, E.W.F. The approach to metaphysics. London, 1947.
Phil 130.5   Tomlin, E.W.F. The great philosophers. London, 1949?
Phil 194.45.5   Tomlin, E.W.F. Living and knowing. London, 1955.
Phil 1930.8.95   Tomlin, E.W.F. Robin George Collingwood, 1889-1943. London, 1953.
Phil 9070.4   Tomlison, W.W. Time out to live. N.Y., 1939.
Phil 4210.93.15   Tommaséo, N. Antonio Rosmini. Domodossola, 1958.
Phil 9179.11   Tommaséo, N. Consigli ai giovani. Milano, 1869.
Phil 4210.93.10   Tommaséo, N. Esposizione sul sistema filosofico del nuovo saggio. Torino, 1840?
Phil 194.8.5   Tommaséo, N. Studii filosofici. Lanciano, 1920.
Phil 194.8   Tommaséo, N. Studii filosofici. Venezia, 1840. 2v.
Phil 4260.105   Tommaséo, Niccolo. G.B. Vico. Torino, 1930.
Phil 4073.20   Tommaso Campanella, poeta. (Campanella, Tommaso.) Salerno, 1957.
Phil 4073.128   Tommaso Campanella, poète. (Ducros, Franc.) Paris, 1969.
Phil 4073.124   Tommaso Campanella. (Bonansea, Bernardino M.) Washington, 1969.
Phil 4073.112   Tommaso Campanella. (Corpano, Antonio.) Bari, 1961.
Phil 4073.85   Tommaso Campanella. (Dentice di Accadia, C.) Firenze, 1921.
Phil 4073.99   Tommaso Campanella. (Orestano, F.) Roma, 1940.
Phil 4073.117   Tommaso Campanella. 1. ed. (Badaloni, Nicola.) Milano, 1965.
Phil 4073.95   Tommaso Campanella and his poetry. (Gardner, E.G.) Oxford, 1923.
Phil 4073.104   Tommaso Campanella in America. (Grillo, F.) N.Y., 1954.
Phil 4073.126   Tommaso Kampanella. (Gonfunkel', Aleksandrkh.) Moskva, 1969.
Phil 4215.2.86   Tommaso Rossi. (Giordano-Zocchi, V.) Napoli, 1866.
Phil 4215.2.83   Tommaso Rossi e Benedetto Spinoza, saggio storico-critico. (Ragnisco, P.) Salerno, 1873.
Phil 4215.2.81   Tommaso Rossi e la sua filosofia. (Ventura, L.) Genova, 1912.
Phil 350.5   Tomov, Kiril. Poznanie i praktika. Sofiia, 1960.
Phil 8708.29.5   Tompkins, Jerry R. D-days at Dayton. Baton Rouge, La., 1965.
Phil 5059.22   Toms, Eric. Being, negation, and logic. Oxford, 1962.
Phil 5066.256   Tondl, Ladislav. Problémy sémantiky. Praha, 1966.
Phil 1719.3   Tonelli, L. L'anima moderna, da Lessing a Nietzsche. Milano, 1925.
Phil 9179.3   Toner, J.M. Maternal instinct, or Love. Baltimore, 1864.
Phil 6122.4   Toner lectures, IX. Mental overwork. (Mills, C.K.) Washington, 1885.
Phil 194.20   Tongiorgi, Salvator. Institutiones philosophicae. Romae, 1861. 3v.
Phil 2905.2.30   Tonguèdec, J. La philosophie de la nature. v. 1-2. Paris, 1956. 4v.
Phil 9510.2   Tonna, C.E.B.P. Backbiting. N.Y., 1842. 2 pam.
Phil 2475.1.264   Tonquédec, J. Sur la philosophie Bergsonienne. Paris, 1936.
Phil 2477.6.80.5   Tonquédec, J. de. Deux études sur "La pensée de M. Blondel". Paris, 1936.
Phil 184.19.18   Tonquédec, J. de. L'existence d'après Karl Jaspers. Paris, 1945.
Phil 2477.6.80   Tonquedec, J. de. Immanence: essai critique sur le doctrine de M. Maurice Blondel. 2e éd. Paris, 1913.
Phil 720.13   Tonquédec, J. de. La notion de vérité dans la "philosophie nouvelle". Paris, 1908.
Phil 5059.13   Tookey, J.J. An elementary handbook of logic. N.Y., 1918.
Phil 2648.93   Topazio, V.W. D'Holbach's moral philosophy. Geneva, 1956.
Phil 5066.316   Topics in philosophical logic. (Rescher, Nicholas.) Dordrecht, Holland, 1968.
Phil 8582.22   Topics of the time. Questions of belief. (Coan, T.M.) N.Y., 1883.
Phil 8709.3   Topinard, P. Science and faith. Chicago, 1899.
Phil 6123.4   Topische Diagnostik der Gehirnkrankheiten. (Nothnagel, H.) Berlin, 1879.
Phil 194.58   Topitsch, Ernst. Mythos, Philosophie, Politik. Freiburg, 1969.

Author and Title Listing

Phil 3425.690 Topitsch, Ernst. Die Sozialphilosophie Hegels als Heilslehre und Herrschaftsideologie. Neuwied, 1967.
Phil 194.48 Topitsch, Ernst. Vom Ursprung und Ende der Metaphysik. Wien, 1958.
Phil 2805.428 Topliss, Patricia. The rhetoric of Pascal. Leicester, 1966.
Phil 5627.271.5 Topos und Typos; Motive und Strukturen religiösen Lebens. (Mensching, Gustav.) Bonn, 1971.
Phil 4080.3.490 Topuridze, Elena I. Estetika Benedetto Kroche. Tbilisi, 1967.
Phil 8587.72 Tor och roetande. (Hedenius, Ingemar.) Stockholm, 1949.
Phil 585.141 The torch of life. (Dubos, René Jules.) N.Y., 1962.
Phil 7069.26.35 Torchbearers of spiritualism. (Stobart, M.A.) N.Y., 1926.
Phil 4960.235 Torchia Estrada, Juan Carlos. La filosofía en la Argentina. Washington, 1961.
Phil 2880.8.205 Tordai, Záder. Existance et realité polémique avec certaines thèses fondamentales dé "L'être et le néant" de Sartre. Budapest, 1967.
Phil 5850.356 Torgerson, Warren S. Theory and methods of scaling. N.Y., 1958.
Phil 4635.9.30 Torgny Segershedt. (Grieg, Harald V.) Oslo, 1945.
Phil 4635.9.80 Torgny Segerstedt, 1876-1945. (Ancker, E.) Stockholm, 1962.
Phil 1750.864 Tormey, Alan. The concept of expression. Princeton, N.J., 1971.
Phil 194.51 Tornadas de filosofía, 21 al 26 de mayo de 1961. (Tucuman, Argentina.) Tucuman, 1961.
Phil 4370.10 Torner, F.M. Doña Oliva Sabuco de Nantes. Madrid, 1935.
Phil 2419.2 Tornezy, Albert. La légende des "philosophes". Paris, 1911.
Phil 8599.46 Toro, Antonio del. La crisis del pensamiento cristiano en el siglo XVI. Madrid, 1961.
Phil 59.1.5 Toronto. University. Studies. Philosophy. Toronto. 1,1914
Phil 59.1 Toronto. University. Studies. Psychological series. Toronto. 1-5 3v.
Phil 8420.24 Torossian, A. A guide to aesthetics. Stanford, 1937.
Phil 8709.26 Torrance, Thomas Forsyth. God and rationality. London, 1971.
Phil 4960.610 Torres, João Camillo de Oliveira. O positivismo no Brasil. Petropolis, 1943.
Phil 4960.610.2 Torres, João Camillo de Oliveira. O positivismo no Brasil. 2. ed. Rio de Janeiro, 1957.
Phil 6315.19.25 Torres, M. El irracionalismo en Erich Fromm. México, 1960.
Phil 8420.13.5 Torres-García, J. La recuperacion del objeto. v.1-2. Montevideo, 1965.
Phil 8420.13 Torres-García, J. Universalismo constructivo. Buenos Aires, 1944.
Phil 5259.28 Torrey, D.C. The normal person. Jaffrey, New Hampshire, 1927.
Phil 8599.14 Torrey, D.C. Protestant modernism. Boston, 1910.
Phil 8599.14.2 Torrey, D.C. Protestant modernism. N.Y., 1910.
Phil 8420.16 Torrey, J. A theory of fine art. N.Y., 1874.
Htn Phil 8894.25.5* Torrey, Jesse, Jr. The moral instructor. 2d ed. Albany, 1819.
Phil 2430.3 Torrey, Norman L. Les philosophes. N.Y., 1960.
Phil 5203.30 Törster Husén. Tryckataskrifter 1940-1965. (Kullman, Siv-Aino.) Stockholm, 1966.
Phil 3640.94 Tosi, T. F. Nietzsche, R. Wagner e la tragedie Greca. Firenze, 1905.
Phil 9550.6 Total utility and the economic judgment. (Parris, M.) Philadelphia, 1909.
Phil 3246.345 Die totale Freiheit. (Willms, Bernhard.) Köln, 1967.
Phil 193.185 Totale Philosophie und Wirklichkeit. (Silva Tarouca, Amadeo.) Freiburg, 1937.
Phil 4580.50 Der totalitätsbegriff. (Høffding, Harald.) Leipzig, 1917.
Phil 1750.742 The totalitarian threat. (Roesch, E.J.) N.Y., 1963.
Phil 2725.42 Totalité et l'infini. (Levinas, Emmanuel.) La Haye, 1961.
Phil 4580.40 Totalitet som kategori en erkendelsesteoretisk undersøgelse. (Høffding, Harald.) København, 1917.
Phil 2725.42.5 Totality and infinity. (Levinas, Emannuel.) Pittsburgh, Pennsylvania, 1969.
Phil 8709.18.5 Tóth, T. God's amazing world. N.Y., 1935.
Phil 75.52 Totok, Wilhelm. Bibliographischer Wegweiser der philosophischen Literatur. Frankfurt, 1959.
Phil 75.65 Totok, Wilhelm. Handbuch der Geschichte der Philosophie. v.2, pt.1. Frankfurt, 1964. 2v.
Phil 3552.452 Totok, Wilhelm. Leibniz. Hannover, 1966.
Phil 735.265 Totuus, arvo ja ihminen. (Krohn, Sven.) Porvoo, 1967.
Phil 2520.100 Touchard, G. La morale de Descartes. Paris, 1898.
Phil 8882.64 Touchstone for ethics. 1st ed. (Huxley, Thomas H.) N.Y., 1941.
Phil 3450.11.285 Toulemont, Renę L'essence de la société selon Husserl. Paris, 1962.
NEDL Phil 300.1 Toulmin, G.H. Eternity of the universe. Philadelphia, 1830.
Phil 8894.33 Toulmin, S. An examination of the place of reason in ethics. Cambridge, England, 1950.
Phil 5190.30 Toulmin, S.E. The uses of argument. Cambridge, Eng., 1958.
Phil 672.258.1 Toulmin, Stephen Edelston. The discovery of time. London, 1965.
Phil 672.258 Toulmin, Stephen Edelston. The discovery of time. N.Y., 1965.
Phil 5259.10 Toulouse. Technique de psychologie experiment. Paris, 1911. 2v.
Phil 194.15 Tounissoux, M. L'Abbé. L'homme dan sa triple vie. Paris, n.d.
Phil 6990.34.5 Touquédec, J. de. Introduction a l'étude du merveilleux et du miracle. 3. éd. Paris, 1923.
Phil 29.40 La Tour Saint Jacques. Paris. 1-16,1955-1958 4v.
Phil 29.40.3 La Tour Saint Jacques. Cahiers. Paris. 1,1960+ 3v.
Phil 5850.356.5 Touraine, Alain. La conscience ouvrière. Thèse. Paris, 1966.
Phil 7150.44 Touraine, Yves. Le suicide ascétique. Paris, 1960.
Phil 2520.168 Les tourbillons de Descartes et la science moderne. (Parenty, Henri.) Paris, 1903.
Phil 2805.241.5 Tourneur, Zacharie. Beauté poétique. Muln, 1933.
Phil 2805.241 Tourneur, Zacharie. Une vie avec Blaise Pascal. Paris, 1943.
Phil 5590.455.11 Tournier, Paul. The adventure of living. N.Y., 1965.
Phil 5590.455.6 Tournier, Paul. Escape from loneliness. Philadelphia, 1962.
Phil 5414.30 Tournier, Paul. Guilt and grace. London, 1962.
Phil 5627.266.20 Tournier, Paul. L'homme et son lieu. Psychologie et foi. Neuchâtel, 1966.
Phil 5790.50 Tournier, Paul. The meaning of gifts. Richmond, Va., 1970.
Phil 5590.548 Tournier, Paul. The meaning of persons. N.Y., 1957.
Phil 5627.245.2 Tournier, Paul. The person reborn. N.Y., 1966.
Phil 5627.266.21 Tournier, Paul. A place for you; psychology and religion. 1st U.S. ed. N.Y., 1968.
Phil 8969.15 Tournier, Paul. The seasons of life. Richmond, Va., 1970[1963]
Phil 5590.455 Tournier, Paul. Le secret d'après une conférence donnée à Athènes en la Salle de la Société d'Archéologie le 12 mai 1963. Genève, 1963.
Phil 5590.455.1 Tournier, Paul. Secrets. Richmond, 1968.
Phil 5627.248.1 Tournier, Paul. The strong and weak. Philadelphia, 1963.
Phil 5627.245.1 Tournier, Paul. Technik und Glaube. Basel, 1945.
Phil 5627.247.1 Tournier, Paul. The whole person in a broken world. N.Y., 1964.
Phil 2750.20.5 Touron del Pie, Eliseo. El mundo. Madrid, 1961.
Phil 194.39 Tourville, Henri. Precis de philosophie fondamentale d'apres la methode d'observation. Paris, 1928.
Htn Phil 8894.8.6* Toussaint, F.V. Eclaircissement sur les moeurs. Amsterdam, 1762.
Phil 8894.8.15 Toussaint, F.V. Manners. 2d ed. London, 1752.
Phil 8894.8.2 Toussaint, F.V. Les moeurs. Amsterdam, 1763.
Htn Phil 8894.8.5* Toussaint, F.V. Les moeurs. pt. 3. Amsterdam, 1748.
Htn Phil 8894.8.3* Toussaint, F.V. Les moeurs. pt.1-2,3. Aux Indes, 1749.
Htn Phil 8894.8* Toussaint, F.V. Les moeurs. 4th ed. n.p., 1749.
Phil 5829.3.4 Toussenel, A. L'esprit des bêtes; zoologie passionnelle. Paris, 1884.
Phil 5829.3.2 Toussenel, A. L'esprit des bêtes; zoologie passionnelle. 2. éd. Paris, 1855.
Phil 8962.22 Toward a Christian ethic. (Marck, Wilhelm Henricus Marie van der.) Westminster, 1967.
Phil 8957.13.15 Toward a Christian moral theology. (Haering, Bernhard.) Notre Dame, 1966.
Phil 5262.65 Toward a contemporary psychology of intuition. (Westcott, Malcolm Robert.) N.Y., 1968.
Phil 1817.12 Toward a critical naturalism. (Romanell, Patrick.) N.Y., 1958.
Phil 2225.9 Toward a dimensional realism. (Perry, C.M.) Norman, Okla., 1939.
Phil 5500.14 Toward a general theory of human judgment. (Buchler, J.) N.Y., 1951.
Phil 8962.32 Toward a new Catholic morality. (Milhaven, John Giles.) Garden City, 1970.
Phil 2150.19.30 Toward a perspective realism. (McGilvary, E.B.) LaSalle, Ill., 1956.
Phil 8401.40 Toward a psychology of art. (Arnheim, Rudolf.) Berkeley, 1967.
Phil 5548.100 Toward a psychology of being. (Maslow, Abraham Harold.) Princeton, 1962.
Phil 5548.100.2 Toward a psychology of being. 2. ed. (Maslow, Abraham Harold.) Princeton, 1968.
Phil 3024.5 Toward a reformed philosophy. (Young, William.) Grand Rapids, Mich., 1952.
Phil 5590.449 Toward a theory of personality development. (Kinsella, Noël A.) Fredericton, N.B., 1966.
Phil 5238.38A Toward a unified theory of human behavior. 1. ed. (Grinker, R.R.) N.Y., 1956.
Phil 5520.439 Toward an informal and creative conference method. (Keller, Benjamin.) Santa Monica, 1965.
Phil 8615.28 Toward common ground; the study of the ethical societies in the United States. (Radest, Howard B.) N.Y., 1969.
Phil 1722.9.5 Toward reunion in philosophy. (White, M.G.) Cambridge, 1956.
Phil 8413.7.5 Toward science in aesthetics. (Munro, Thomas.) N.Y., 1956.
Phil 5590.300 Toward understanding human personalities. (Leeper, Robert.) N.Y., 1959.
Phil 70.114 Toward unification in psychology. (Banff Conference on Theoretical Psychology, 1st, 1965.) Toronto, 1970.
Phil 5066.18 Towards a general logic of propositions. Thesis. (Churchman, C.W.) Philadelphia, 1942.
Phil 5465.36 Towards a law of creative thought. (Harding, R.E.M.) London, 1936.
Phil 6120.9 Towards a new era in healing. (Knapp, Sheldon.) London, 1926.
Phil 3195.6.160 Towards a phenomenological theory of literature. (Mueller-Vollmer, K.) The Hague, 1963.
Phil 8583.29.5 Towards a religious philosophy. (De Burgh, William George.) London, 1937.
Phil 8598.135.5 Towards a theology of religions. (Schlette, Heinz Robert.) Freiburg, 1966.
Phil 291.10 Towards a unified cosmology. (Kapp, Reginald O.) London, 1960.
Phil 8881.65 Towards an objective ethics. (Geiger, George R.) Yellow Springs, 1938.
Phil 6952.21.10 Towards mental health. (Campbell, C.M.) Cambridge, 1933.
Phil 8610.926 Towards the answer. (Freeman, C.R.B.) Derbyshire, 1926.
Phil 525.220 Towards the center. (Baloković, J.B.) N.Y., 1956.
Phil 6128.56 Towards understanding our minds. (Siddall, R.B.) N.Y., 1951.
Phil 1870.87 Tower, C.V. The relation of Berkeley's later to his early ideal. Ann Arbor, 1899.
Phil 4872.187.30 The towering wave. (Mallik, Basanta Kumar.) London, 1953.
Phil 2138.120 Towers, C.M.D. John Stuart Mill and the London and Westminster review. v.1-2. Boston, 1892.
Phil 6750.235 Town, C.H. Familial feeblemindedness. Buffalo, 1939.
Phil 6969.2 Town, C.H. The train of thought. Philadelphia, 1909.
Phil 6689.2 Townehend, C.H. Facts in mesmerism. Boston, 1841.
Phil 6689.2.2 Townehend, C.H. Facts in mesmerism. N.Y., 1841.
Phil 6689.2.5 Townehend, C.H. Mesmerism proved true. London, 1854.
Phil 9500.2 Townsend, F. Mutterings and musings of an invalid. N.Y., 1851.
Phil 1819.2 Townsend, H.G. Philosophical ideas in the United States. N.Y., 1934.
Phil 2020.83 Townsend, H.G. Principle of individuality in the philosophy of T.H. Green. Lancaster, 1914.
Phil 494.1 Townsend, H.G. Studies in philosophical naturalism. Eugene, 1931.
Phil 8709.1 Townsend, L.T. The Bible and other ancient literature in the nineteenth century. N.Y., 1888.
Phil 8709.1.5 Townsend, L.T. Credo. Boston, 1870.
Phil 9179.7 Townsend, S. A practical essay designed for general use. Boston, 1783.
Phil 1524.1 Townsend, W.J. The great schoolmen of the Middle Ages. London, 1881.
Phil 4019.10 Tozzi, Antonio. L'eredità del neo-idealismo italiana. Firenze, 1953.

Author and Title Listing

Phil 1750.166.117 Tra umanesimo e reforma. (Paparelli, Gioacchino.) Napoli, 1946.
Phil 3085.6.80 Traaf, B. Alardus Amstelredamus. Amsterdam, 1958.
Phil 70.84 Trabajos. (Symposium Iberoamericano de Filosofia.) Guatemala.
Phil 5259.11.5 Trabue, M.R. Measure your mind. Garden City, 1921.
Phil 5401.10 Le "trac" et la timidité. 2e éd. (Gratia, L.E.) Paris, 1926.
Phil 9430.2 La trace du pessimisme dans la société. (Bourchenin, D.) Paris, 1892.
Htn Phil 6672.11* Traces du magnétisme. (Cambry, Jacques.) La Haye, 1784. 2 pam.
Phil 342.11 Track af vor erkendelses psykologi. (Lambek, C.) København, 1925.
Phil 2520.61.5 Tractat von den Leidenschafften der Seele. (Descartes, René.) Franckfurth, 1723.
Phil 3819.37 Tractatus de Deo et homine eiusque felicitate lineamenta atque adnotationes ad tractatum theologico politicum. (Spinoza, Benedictus de.) Halae, 1852.
Phil 2520.34.5 Tractatus de homine et de formatione Foetus. (Descartes, René.) Amsterdam, 1677.
Phil 2520.13.15 Tractatus de homine et de formatione foetus. (Descartes, René.) Amsterdam, 1686.
Phil 8640.1.12 Tractatus de immortalitate animae. (Pomponazzi, P.) Haverford, Pa., 1938.
Htn Phil 8640.1* Tractatus de immortalitate animae. (Pomponazzi, P.) Paris, 1534.
Htn Phil 8640.1.15* Tractatus de immortalitate animae. (Pomponazzi, P.) Paris, 161-?
Phil 3824.1 Der Tractatus de Intellectus emendatione. (Elbogen, Ismar.) Breslau, 1898.
Phil 3824.1.5 Der Tractatus de Intellectus emendatione. Diss. (Elbogen, Ismar.) Breslau, 1898.
Phil 179.31 Tractatus de re logica. (Egaña, Juan.) Santiago, 1827.
Htn Phil 5041.23* Tractatus guidam logici. (Brerewood, E.) Oxoniae, 1631. 3 pam.
Phil 3925.16.41 Tractatus logico-philosophicus. (Wittgenstein, Ludwig.) London, 1922.
Phil 3925.16.45 Tractatus logico-philosophicus. (Wittgenstein, Ludwig.) London, 1960.
Phil 3925.16.47A Tractatus logico-philosophicus. (Wittgenstein, Ludwig.) London, 1961.
Phil 197.36.12A Tractatus logico-philosophicus. (Wittgenstein, Ludwig.) London, 1961.
Phil 3925.16.60 Tractatus logico-philosophicus. (Wittgenstein, Ludwig.) Milano, 1954.
Phil 3925.16.46 Tractatus logico-philosophicus. (Wittgenstein, Ludwig.) Paris, 1961.
Phil 3819.59 Tractatus politicus. (Spinoza, Benedictus de.) Lanciano, 1915.
Phil 8676.2 Tractatus theologicus dedeo. (Vorstius, Conrad.) Steinfursti, 1610. 2 pam.
Htn Phil 2045.31* Tracts. (Hobbes, Thomas.) London, 1678-82. 2 pam.
Htn Phil 2045.31.5* Tracts. (Hobbes, Thomas.) London, 1681.
Htn Phil 2045.32* Tracts. (Hobbes, Thomas.) London, 1682-84. 2 pam.
Phil 3819.45 Tractus De intellectus emendatione. (Spinoza, Benedictus de.) N.Y., 1895.
Phil 6536.8 Tracy, Edward A. The basis of epilepsy. Boston, 1930.
Phil 8701.15 The trade of scientific thought away from religious beliefs. (Ladd, H.O.) Boston, 1909.
Phil 4370.7 Tradicíon y modernismo. (Tierno, G. E.) Madrid, 1962.
Phil 1750.235 Tradition de l'existentialisme. (Benda, J.) Paris, 1947.
Phil 7069.65.40 La tradition ésotérique et la science. (Richard, Hermann.) Paris, 1965.
Phil 8893.136 The tradition of natural law. (Simon, Yves.) N.Y., 1965.
Phil 4195.89 Tradition og nybrud. (Sloek, Johannes.) København, 1957.
Phil 2419.4 La tradition philosophique et la pensée française. Paris, 1922.
Phil 8960.12 Tradition und Fortschritt in der Moraltheologie: die grundsätzliche Bedeutung der Kontroverse zwischen Jansenismus und Probabilismus. (Klomps, Heinrich.) Köln, 1963.
Phil 165.418 Tradition und Kritik. Stuttgart 1967.
Phil 346.30 Tradition und Transformation der Modalitat Habilitationschrift. (Pape, Ingetrud.) Hamburg, 1966-
Phil 8610.903.10 Tradition versus truth. (Hawley, J.S.) N.Y., 1903.
Phil 70.86 Traditional cultural values. (International Institute of Philosophy.) Mysore, 1959.
Phil 5058.50 The traditional formal logic. (Sinclair, W.A.) London, 1937.
Phil 8591.37 Le traditionalisme et le rationalisme. (Lupus, J.) Liége, 1858. 3v.
Phil 2405.2.2 Traditionalisme et ultramontanisme. 2e éd. (Ferraz, Marin.) Paris, 1880.
Phil 703.3 Traditionsfeindschaft und Traditionsgehundenheit. (Ehbinghaus, Julius.) Frankfurt, 1969.
Phil 5170.14.5 Traditsionnaia i sovremennaia formal'naia logika. (Subbotin, Aleksandr L.) Moskva, 1969.
Phil 1630.15 La tradizione aristotelica nel Rinascimento. (Kristeller, P.O.) Padova, 1962.
Phil 196.2.10 La tradizione e i semi-Pelagiani della filosofia. pt.1-2. (Ventura de Raulica, G.) Milano, 1857.
Phil 4006.8.30 La tradizione ermetica nella filosofia italiana. (Giusso, Lorenzo.) Roma, 1955?
Phil 4235.11.30 Tradu, L. Saggi filosofici vari. Padova, 1960.
Phil 5769.5 Traeger, L. Wille, Determinismus, Strafe. Berlin, 1895.
Phil 5628.50.25 Träger der Wundmale Christi. (Höcht, Johannes Maria.) Wiesbaden, 1951-52. 2v.
Phil 400.34 Die Träger des deutschen Idealismus. (Eucken, Rudolf.) Berlin, 1915.
Phil 3004.1.10 Die Träger des deutschen Idealismus. (Eucken, Rudolf.) Berlin, 1916.
Phil 5066.20 Traek af deduktionsteoriens Udvikling i den nyere Tid. (Jørgensen, J.) København, 1937.
Phil 7084.42 Träume der Blinden vom Standpunkt der Phänomenologie. (Schumann, Hans Joachim von.) Basel, 1959.
Phil 7084.46 Die Träume der Dichter. (Stekel, Wilhelm.) Wiesbaden, 1912.
Phil 7084.20 Das Träumen als Heilungsweg der Seele. (Bjerre, Paul.) Zürich, 1936.
Phil 7082.70 Das Träumende ich. (Hoche, Alfred.) Jena, 1927.
Phil 4957.40 La tragectoria del pensamiento filosófico en Latinoamérica. (Carrillo Narváez, Alfredo.) Quito, 1959.
Phil 4369.3 La tragedia del pensamiento. (Soto, Juan B.) Rio Piedras, 1937.
Phil 4974.50.2 Tragedia y realización del espíritu. 2. ed. (Molina, Enrique.) Santiago, 1953.
Phil 575.296 La tragédie cosmique de la conscience. (Karquel, André.) Paris, 1970.
Phil 5761.22 Tragediia svobody. (Levitskii, S.H.) Frankfurt, 1958.
Phil 2880.8.118 The tragic finale. (Desan, Wilfred.) Cambridge, Mass., 1954.
Phil 3640.490 The tragic philosopher. (Lea, F.A.) London, 1957.
Phil 4190.2.30 La tragicita del reale. (Ottaviano, Carmelo.) Padova, 1964.
Phil 4080.26 Tragico e senso comune. (Cantoni, Remo.) Cremona, 1963.
Phil 3850.16.112 Die Tragik in der Existenz des modernen Menschen bei Georg Simmel. (Bauer, Isidora.) Berlin, 1961.
Phil 3850.16.110 Die Tragik in der Existenz des modernen Menschen bei Georg Simmel. (Bauer, Isidora.) München, 1961.
Phil 822.6.2 Die Tragikomödie der Weisheit die Ergebnisse und der Geschichte des Philosophierens. (Wahle, R.) Wien, 1925.
Phil 176.3.9 Das tragische als Weltgesetz und der Humor. (Bahnsen, J.) Lauenburg, 1877.
Phil 176.3.10 Das tragische als Weltgesetz und der Humor. (Bahnsen, J.) Leipzig, 1931.
Phil 195.2.5 Das tragische Lebensgefühl. (Unamuno, M. de.) München, 1925.
Phil 3120.40.30 Het tragische schuld noodlot en bevrijding. (Bierens de Haan, J.D.) Leiden, 1933.
Phil 3925.12 Das Tragische und die Geschichte. (Weber, Alfred.) Hamburg, 1943.
Phil 176.116 Die Tragödie der Philosophie. (Bulgakov, S.N.) Darmstadt, 1927.
Phil 5425.100 Tragödie des Genius. (Kotsovsky, D.) München, 1959.
Phil 8969.3.5 Traherne, Thomas. Christian ethicks. Ithaca, 1968.
Phil 8969.3 Traherne, Thomas. Of magnanimity and charity. N.Y., 1942.
Phil 1828.10 Traherne and the seventeenth-century English platonists, 1900-1966. (Guffey, George Robert.) London, 1969.
Phil 1750.126.8 La trahison des clercs. (Benda, Julien.) Paris, 1958.
Phil 1750.126.8.2 La trahison des clercs. (Benda, Julien.) Paris, 1965.
Phil 8420.20 Trahndorff, K.F.E. Ästhetik, oder Lehre von der Weltauschauung und Kunst. v.1-2. Berlin, 1827.
Phil 3425.293 Trahndorff, K.F.E. Wie kann der Supernaturalismus sein Recht gegen Hegel's Religionsphilosophie behaupten? Berlin, 1840.
Htn Phil 3801.846* Trahndorff, Karl F.E. Schelling und Hegel. Berlin, 1842.
Phil 7060.143 Traicté de l'apparition des esprits. (Taillepied, Noël.) Paris, 1917.
Phil 6122.56 Train development. (Miller, A.G.) N.Y., 1909.
Phil 6969.2 The train of thought. (Town, C.H.) Philadelphia, 1909.
Phil 194.38 Traina, T. Saggio dei principali sistemi. Palermo, 1880.
Phil 2270.101 Traina, Tommaso. La morale di Herbert Spencer. Torino, 1881.
Phil 9490.8 The training for an effective life. (Eliot, C.W.) Boston, 1915.
Phil 5850.328 Training for human relations. (Roethlisberger, F.J.) Boston, 1954.
Phil 9035.36 The training of mind and will. (Jones, W. Tudor.) London, 1920.
Phil 5761.10.15 The training of the will. (Lindworsky, J.) Milwaukee, 1929.
Phil 9495.2 Training of the young in laws of sex. (Lyttelton, E.) London, 1900.
Phil 6961.5 Traité clinique et pratique des maladies mentales. (Luys, J.) Paris, 1881.
Phil 6115.24 Traite complet de l'anatomie, de la physiologie et de la pathologie du système nerveux. Pt.1. (Foville, A.) Paris, 1844.
Phil 6673.4.3 Traité complet de magnétisme animal. 5e éd. (Du Potet, J. de S.) Paris, 1894.
Phil 6060.1 Traite de graphologie. (Crepieux-Jamin, J.) Paris, 1885.
Phil 6060.20 Traité de graphologie scientifique. 2d ed. (Joire, Paul.) Paris, 1921.
Phil 348.7.5 Traité de la connaissance. (Rougier, Louis A.P.) Paris, 1955.
Phil 9005.2 Traité de la gloire. (Sacy, M.L. de.) La Haye, 1745.
Htn Phil 9162.2* Traité de la jalousie. (Courtin, A. de.) Paris, 1685.
Htn Phil 2733.55.5* Traité de la nature et de la grace. (Malebranche, Nicolas.) Amsterdam, 1680. 2 pam.
Phil 2733.67 Traité de la nature et de la grâce. (Malebranche, Nicolas.) Paris, 1958. 2v.
Phil 2733.55.10 Traité de la nature et de la grace. (Malebranche, Nicolas.) Rotterdam, 1712. 2 pam.
Phil 2050.60 Traité de la nature humaine. (Hume, David.) Paris, 1878.
Phil 3819.45.15 Traité de la réforme de l'ertendement. (Spinoza, Benedictus de.) Paris, 1937.
Phil 8876.155 Traite de l'action morale. (Bastide, Georges.) Paris, 1961. 2v.
Htn Phil 2733.65.1* Traité de l'amour de Dieu. (Malebranche, Nicolas.) Lyon, 1707.
Phil 2733.65 Traité de l'amour de Dieu. (Malebranche, Nicolas.) Paris, 1922.
Phil 7060.1 Traité de l'apparition des esprits. (Taillepied, F.N.) Roven, 1602.
Phil 5055.29 Traité de l'argumentation. v.1-2. (Perelman, Chaim.) Paris, 1958.
Phil 8656.7.10 Traité de l'athéisme et de la superstition. (Buddeus, J.F.) Amsterdam, 1740.
Phil 6121.20 Traité de l'esprit de l'homme. (La Forge, Louis de.) Amsterdam, n.d.
Phil 6121.20.5 Traité de l'esprit de l'homme. (La Forge, Louis de.) Genève, 1725.
Phil 6121.20.3 Traité de l'esprit de l'homme. (La Forge, Louis de.) Paris, 1666.
Phil 8881.72A Traité de l'existence morale. (Gusdorf, Georges.) Paris, 1949.
Phil 410.80 Le traité "De l'infini" de Jean Muir. (Major, John.) Paris, 1938.
Phil 5043.14 Traité de logique. (Duval-Jouve, J.) Paris, 1855.
Phil 5046.12.4 Traité de logique. (Goblot, Edmond.) Paris, 1922.
Phil 5066.36 Traité de logique. (Piaget, Jean.) Paris, 1949.
Phil 5059.18 Traité de logique formelle. (Tricot, Jules.) Paris, 1930.
Phil 6684.4 Traité de magnétisme. (Olivier, J.) Paris, 1854.
Phil 2915.51 Traité de métaphysique, 1734. (Voltaire, F.M.A. de.) Manchester, 1937.
Phil 181.114.5 Traité de métaphysique. (Gusdorf, G.) Paris, 1956.
Phil 197.72 Traité de métaphysique. (Wahl, J.A.) Paris, 1953.
Phil 7069.23.16 Traité de métaphysique. 2. ed. (Richet, Charles.) Paris, 1923.
Phil 7069.22.20 Traité de métapsychique. (Richet, Charles R.) Paris, 1922.
Phil 8878.50 Traité de morale. (Dupréel, Eugène.) Bruxelles, 1932. 2v.

Phil 8878.50.1   Traité de morale. (Dupréel, Eugène.) Bruxelles, 1967. 2v.

Htn   Phil 2733.50.3*   Traité de morale. (Malebranche, Nicolas.) Lyon, 1697. 2v.

Htn   Phil 2733.50*   Traité de morale. pt.1-2. (Malebranche, Nicolas.) Rotterdam, 1684.

Phil 8886.64   Traité de morale générale. 1. ed. (Le Senne, René.) Paris, 1942.

Phil 176.32   Traité de philosophie. (Buchez, P.T.B.) Paris, 1838. 3v.

Phil 181.69.5   Traité de philosophie. (Gorce, M.M.) Paris, 1938.

Phil 193.54   Traité de philosophie. (Sortais, G.) Paris, 1906-1907. 3v.

Phil 2750.7.35   Traité de philosophie psycho-physiologique. (Massias, Nicolas.) Paris, 1830.

Phil 1506.2.5   Traité de philosophie scolastique. (Blanc, Elie.) Lyon, 1909. 3v.

Phil 6323.21   Traité de psychanalyse. (Nacht, Sacha.) Paris, 1965.

Phil 5243.29   Traité de psychologie. (Dumas, George.) Paris, 1923. 2v.

Phil 5258.107   Traité de psychologie. (Segond, Joseph.) Paris, 1930.

Phil 5258.17   Traité de psychologie. (Simonin, A.) Paris, 1876.

Phil 5850.310   Traité de psychologie appliquée. (Piéron, Henri.) Paris, 1949- 7v.

Phil 5627.178   Traité de psychologie de la religion. (Berguer, Georges.) Lausanne, 1946.

Phil 5238.196   Traite de psychologie expérimentale. (Fraisse, Paul.) Paris, 1963. 9v.

Phil 5255.49   Traité de psychologie générale. 1st éd. v.1-2, pt.1-2. (Pradines, Maurice.) Paris, 1943-46. 3v.

Phil 2493.35   Traité des animaux. (Condillac, Étienne Bonnot.) Amsterdam, 1755.

Phil 2493.35.2   Traité des animaux. (Condillac, Étienne Bonnot.) Amsterdam, 1766.

Phil 190.46   Traité des antinomies. (Peladan, J.) Paris, 1901.

Phil 5246.2.10   Traite des facultés de l'âme. (Garnier, A.) Paris, 1865. 3v.

Phil 177.22   Traité des idées fondamentales. (Cournot, A.A.) Paris, 1861.

Phil 9010.28   Traité des jeux et des divertissements. (Thiers, Jean B.) Paris, 1686.

Phil 6951.8   Traité des maladies du cerveau. (Bayle, A.L.J.) Paris, 1826.

Phil 2520.61.19   Traité des passions. (Descartes, René.) Paris, 1928.

Phil 2520.61.20   Traité des passions suivi de la correspondance avec la princess Elisabeth. (Descartes, René.) Paris, 1965.

Phil 8959.3   Traité des restitutions des grands. (Joly, C.) Amsterdam, 1665.

Phil 5640.8.5   Traité des sens. (Le Cat, C.N.) Rouen, 1740.

Phil 2493.45.3   Traité des sensations. Première partie. Photoreproduction. (Condillac, Étienne Bonnot.) Paris, 1886.

Htn   Phil 2493.45*   Traité des sensations. v.1-2. (Condillac, Étienne Bonnot.) Londres, 1754.

Phil 2493.45.2   Traité des sensations. v.1-2. (Condillac, Étienne Bonnot.) Londres, 1788.

Phil 2493.51   Traité des sistèmes. (Condillac, Étienne Bonnot.) Amsterdam, 1771.

Phil 2493.50   Traité des sistèmes. (Condillac, Étienne Bonnot.) La Haye, 1749.

Htn   Phil 3839.6.10*   Traité des trois imposteurs. Amsterdam, 1777.

Phil 3839.6.5   Traité des trois imposteurs. Amsterdam? 1768?

Phil 3839.6.15   Traité des trois imposteurs. Luísse, 1793.

Phil 8402.8   Traité d'esthétique. (Bayer, Raymond.) Paris, 1956.

Phil 8402.61   Traité d'esthétique. (Berthelemy, J.) Paris, 1964.

Phil 8403.46   Traité du beau, où l'on montre en quoi consiste ce que l'on nomme ainsi, Amsterdam, 1715. (Crousaz, Jean Pierre de.) Genève, 1970.

Phil 9230.5   Traité du jeu. (Barbeyrac, J.) Amsterdam, 1737. 3v.

Phil 7085.7   Traité du somnambulisme. (Bertrand, A.) Paris, 1823.

Phil 8886.49   Traité élémentaire de métaphysique et de morale. (Lamblardie.) Brunswick, 1801.

Phil 2668.30   Traité élémentaire de philosophie. (Janet, Paul A.R.) Paris, 1880.

Phil 7060.5   Traité historique et dogmatique...apparitions. (Lenglet, Dufresnoy N.) Avignon, 1751. 2v.

Phil 6322.3   Traité international de psychologie pathologique. (Marie, Auguste.) Paris, 1910-12. 3v.

Phil 6965.3   Traité médico-philosophique sur l'aliénation mentale. (Pinel, Philippe.) Paris, 1809.

Phil 7120.2   Traité méthodique de magnétisme personnel. (Jagot, Paul Clément.) Paris, 1969.

Phil 2651.30   Traité philosophique de la faiblesse. (Huet, Pierre Daniel.) London, 1741.

Phil 1928.31   Traité philosophique des loix naturelles. (Cumberland, R.) Amsterdam, 1744.

Phil 7067.46.10   Traité sur les apparitions des esprits. (Calmet, Augustin.) Paris, 1751. 2v.

Htn   Phil 7067.46.10*   Traité sur les apparitions des esprits. (Calmet, Augustin.) Paris, 1751. 2v.

Htn   Phil 6673.19*   Traité théorique. (Doppet, F.A.) Turin, 1784.

Phil 5761.9.12   Le traitement moral. (Lévy, Paul Emile.) Paris, 1927.

Phil 8582.40   Traités de l'existence et des attributs de Dieu, des devoirs de la religion naturelle. (Clarke, M.) n.p., 1744. 3v.

Phil 8893.29   Traités sur divers sujets. (Schmid, G.L.) n.p., 1760.

Htn   Phil 2805.60*   Traitez de l'equilibre. (Pascal, Blaise.) Paris, 1663.

Htn   Phil 5751.11*   Traitez du libre-arbitre. (Bossuet, J.B.) Paris, 1731.

Phil 177.11   Traiti des extrêmes. (Changeux, P.J.) Amsterdam, 1767. 2v.

Phil 7150.59   Traitor within: our suicide problem. 1st ed. (Ellis, E.R.) Garden City, N.Y., 1961.

Phil 845.2   Die Trajödie des Humanismus. (Weinstock, Heinrich.) Heidelberg, 1953.

Phil 494.4   Trakhtenberg, I.V. Razvetie materializma i ego bor'ba protiv idealizma. Moskva, 1956.

Phil 1819.5   Trakhtenberg, O.V. Ocherki po istorii filosofii i sotsiologii Anglii XIX v. Moskva, 1959.

Phil 530.20.80   Der Traktat des "unbekannten deutschen Mystikers" bei Greith. (Seitz, Jasy.) Leipzig, 1936.

Phil 5250.79.4   Traktat o dobrej robocie. Wyd. 4. (Kotarbiński, Tadeusz.) Wrocław, 1965.

Phil 3120.22.40   Traktat über die Heilkunde. (Blüher, Hans.) Jena, 1928.

Phil 2050.60.28   Traktat über die menschliche Natur. (Hume, David.) Hamburg, 1895-1906. 2v.

Phil 2050.60.30   Traktat über die menschliche Natur. v.1-2. (Hume, David.) Leipzig, 1923.

Phil 185.100   Traktat über die Methode der Philosophie. (Kuhn, Helmut.) München, 1966.

Phil 4803.495.21   Traktat über die Sterblichkeit der Vernunft. (Kotakowski, Leszek.) München, 1967.

Phil 308.2   Traktat über kritische Vernunft. (Atbert, Hans.) Tübingen, 1968.

Phil 1524.5   Traktenberg, O.V. Ocherki po istorii zapadno-evropeiskoi Srednovekovoi filosofii. Moskva, 1957.

Phil 6329.10   Tramer, Moritz. Lehrbuch der allgemeinen Kinderpsychiatrie. Basel, 1945.

Phil 300.6   Tramer, Moritz. Philosophie des schöpferischen. Bern, 1957.

Phil 5590.464   Tramer, Moritz. Reifung und Formung von Persönlichkeiten. Erlenbach, 1965.

Phil 6969.10   Tramer, Moritz. Technisches Schaffen Geisteskranker. München, 1926.

Phil 1714.5.5   Il tramonto della filosofia moderna. (Orsi, Domenico d'.) Padova, 1962.

Phil 1714.5.8   Il tramonto della filosofia moderna. 3. ed. (Orsi, Domenico d'.) Padova, 1970.

Phil 3640.740   Tramonto della ragione. (Mei, Flavio.) Milano, 1967.

Phil 1750.115.35   Trân-Dúc-Thao. Phénoménologie et materialisme dialectique. Paris, 1951.

Phil 5870.28   Tran-Thong. Stades et concept de stade de développement de l'enfant dans la psychologie contemporaine. Paris, 1967.

Phil 7230.7   Trance and possession states. (Bucke (R.M.) Memorial Society for the Study of Religious Experience.) Montreal? 1968.

Phil 5811.7   Trance and trancoidal states in the lower animals. (Beard, G.M.) N.Y., 1881.

Phil 4112.85   Tranfo, C.T. Saggio sulla filosofia del Galluppi. Napoli, 1902.

Phil 3705.6.20   Trangott Konstanin Österreich. (Oesterreich, Trangott K.) Stuttgart, 1954.

Phil 4210.235   Traniello, Francesco. Società religiosa e società civile in Rosmini. Bologna, 1966.

Phil 6980.105.5   Transactional analysis in psychotherapy. (Berne, Eric.) N.Y., 1961.

Phil 53.2   Transactions, 1901. (National Association for Study of Epilepsy and Care and Treatment of Epileptics.) Buffalo, 1901.

Phil 2225.5.140   Transactions. (Charles S. Pierce Society.) Amherst. 1,1965+ 2v.

Phil 2880.8.64.5   La transcendance de l'égo. (Sartre, Jean Paul.) Paris, 1965.

Phil 705.24   Transcendence and the logical difficulties of transcendence; a logical analysis. (Schultzer, Bent.) Copenhagen, 1935.

Phil 8658.17.80   Transcendence de Dieu et création des valeurs. (Malevez, Léopold.) Paris, 1958.

Phil 2005.14   The transcendence of the cave. (Findlay, John N.) London, 1967.

Phil 2880.8.64A   The transcendence of the ego. (Sartre, Jean Paul.) N.Y., 1957.

Phil 8598.110.25   Transcendent unity of religions. (Schuon, Frithjof.) N.Y., 1953.

Phil 334.14.10   Transcendental criticism and Christian philosophy. (Bruemmer, Vincent.) Franeker, 1961.

Phil 400.91.25   Der Transcendental-Idealismus. (Thanner, Ignaz.) München, 1805.

Phil 400.91   Transcendental-Idealismus. (Wagner, G.F.) Ulm, 1934.

Phil 1750.107.2   The transcendental method. (Muck, Otto.) N.Y., 1968.

Phil 7060.97   Transcendental physics. (Zöllner, J.C.F.) London, 1880.

Phil 7060.97.3   Transcendental physics. 2. ed. (Zöllner, J.C.F.) Boston, 1881.

Phil 705.17   Transcendentale values. (Byers, R.P.) Boston, 1925.

Phil 3625.7.90   Die transcendentale Harmonie bei Ernst Marcus. (Gaquoin, Karl.) Wiesbaden, 1907.

Phil 7068.79   Die transcendentale Physik und die sogenannte Philosophie. (Zöllner, J.K.F.) Leipzig, 1879.

Phil 333.10   Transcendentale Systematik. Teil 1-2. (Cornelius, Hans.) München, 1916.

Phil 3450.11.430   De transcendentale vreemdeling. (Beerling, Reiner F.) Hilversum, 1965.

Htn   Phil 705.26*   Transcendentalism. (Greene, William B.) West Brookfield, 1849.

Phil 705.2   Transcendentalism. (Johnson, S.) n.p., n.d.

Phil 705.55   Transcendentalism and its legacy. (Simon, Myron.) Ann Arbor, 1966.

Phil 705.3.7A   Transcendentalism in New England, a history. (Frothingham, Octavius Brooks.) Gloucester, Mass., 1965.

Phil 705.4   Transcendentalism in New England. (Dall, C.H.) Boston, 1897.

Phil 705.3.5   Transcendentalism in New England. (Frothingham, Octavius Brooks.) Boston, 1903.

NEDL   Phil 705.3   Transcendentalism in New England. (Frothingham, Octavius Brooks.) N.Y., 1876.

Phil 705.30   Transcendentalism truly remarkable. (Rogers, W.C.) Boston, 1947.

Phil 705.35   The transcendentalist revolt against materialism. (Whicher, S.E.) Boston, 1949.

Phil 705.16   Die Transcendenz des erkennens. (Landmann, E.) Berlin, 1923.

Phil 29.45   Transcultural psychiatric research. Montreal. 1963+ 2v.

Phil 5545.62   Transfer effects of practice in cancellation tests. (Martin, M.A.) N.Y., 1915.

Phil 5832.10   Transfer of training in white rats upon various series of mazes. (Wiltbank, R.T.) Chicago, 1919.

Phil 6327.40   Transference and counter transference. (Racker, Heinrich.) London, 1968.

Phil 3549.10.35   Transfiguration. (Kassner, Rudolf.) Erlenbach, 1946.

Phil 5066.245   A transfinite type theory with type variables. (Andrews, Peter Bruce.) Amsterdam, 1965.

Phil 2401.10   Transformation de la philosophie française. (Bréhier, E.) Paris, 1950.

Phil 8957.12.10   Transformation in Christ. (Hildebrand, D. von.) Baltimore, 1960.

Phil 8190.2   The transformation of nature in art. (Coomaraswamy, Ananda.) Cambridge, Mass., 1934.

Phil 8697.18   The transformation of the scientific world view. (Heim, Karl.) N.Y., 1953.

Phil 8406.6F   Transformations; critical and speculative essays on art. (Fry, R.E.) N.Y., 1927.

Phil 5066.30   Transformations on lattices and structures of logic. (Kiss, Stephen A.) N.Y., 1947.

Phil 5400.45   Les transformations sociales des sentiments. (Paulhan, Frédéric.) Paris, 1920.

Phil 8695.8   Transformisme et christianisme. (Fargues, Paul.) Paris, 1909.

Phil 1955.4.87   Transition. (Durant, Will.) N.Y., 1927.

Phil 9550.7 Transition to an objective standard of social control. (Bernard, L.L.) Chicago, 1911.

Phil 175.15 Transitional eras in thought. (Armstrong, A.C.) N.Y., 1904.

Phil 3270.12.37 Translations from the philosophical writings. 2nd ed. (Frege, Gottlob.) Oxford, 1966.

Phil 3270.12.33 Translations from the philosophical writings of Gottlob Frege. (Frege, Gottlob.) Oxford, 1952.

Phil 3270.12.35 Translations from the philosophical writings of Gottlob Frege. (Frege, Gottlob.) Oxford, 1960.

Phil 8631.10 La transmigration des âmes. (Girard, Victor.) Paris, 1888.

Phil 1020.85 Le transmission de la philosophie grecque au monde arabe. (Badawi, Abdurrahman.) Paris, 1968.

Phil 6969.14 The transmission of schizophrenia: proceedings of the second research conference of the Foundations' Fund for Research in Psychiatry. Oxford, 1968.

Phil 193.6 Transnatural philosophy, or Metaphysicks. (Sargent, J.) London, 1700.

Phil 5590.568.1 The transparent self. (Jourard, Sidney Marshall.) N.Y., 1971.

Phil 8591.44.20 Transposition, and other addresses. (Lewis, Clive Staples.) London, 1949.

Phil 3493.10 Transscendentalfilosofiens problem och metod hos Kant. (Lagerwall, A.) Göteborg, 1904.

Phil 3246.187 Die Transscendentalphilosophie Fichte's und Schelling's. (Burman, E.O.) Upsala, 1891.

Phil 705.20 Das Transzendentale. Diss. (Leider, Kurt.) Königsberg, 1925.

Phil 3489.43 Transzendentale Dialektik. Ein Kommentar zu Kants Kritik der reinen Vernunft. (Heimsoeth, Heinz.) Berlin, 1966-4v.

Phil 3500.77 Die transzendentale Einheit der Apperzeption von Immanuel Kant. (Schoeler, Wilhelm.) Bern, 1958.

Phil 3488.43 Der transzendentale Existenzbeweis in Kants Kritischer Metaphysik der ausserbewussten Wirklichkeit. (Gersch, Walter.) Würzburg, 1938.

Phil 705.50 Transzendentale Logik. (Krings, Hermann.) München, 1964.

Phil 1750.107 Die transzendentale Methode in der scholastischen Philosophie der Gegenwart. (Muck, Otto.) Innsbruck, 1964.

Phil 705.64 Transzendentalphilosophie und Metaphysik. (Holz, Harald.) Mainz, 1966.

Phil 5238.212 Transzendenz als Erfahrung: Beitrag und Widerhall. Weilheim, 1966.

Phil 705.51 Transzendenz als Wirklichkeit. (Saur, Karl.) Hamburg, 1965.

Phil 3450.19.545 Transzendenz und Differenz. (Rosales, Alberto.) Den Haag, 1970.

Phil 8674.7 Trap, William M. Divine personality. Ann Arbor, 1925.

Phil 6967.21 Trapped: families and schizophrenia. (Rogler, Lloyd H.) N.Y., 1965.

Phil 705.10 La trascendenza; studio sul problema morale. (Rensi, Giuseppe.) Torino, 1914.

Phil 8411.33 Tratado de estetica. v.1- (Kupareo, Raimundo.) Santiago de Chile, 1964-

Phil 196.27 Tratado de metafisica. (Vasconcelos, J.) Mexico, 1929.

Phil 188.16 Tratado de metalogica. (Nuñez Requeiro, M.) Rosario, 1936.

Phil 5257.46 Tratado de psicología. (Radecki, Wacław.) Buenos Aires, 1933.

Phil 5258.132 Tratado de psicología. (Simon, M.) Lima, 1944. 2v.

Phil 5240.39.15 Tratado de psicología general. v.1-2, pt.1. 4a ed. (Agramonte y Richardo, R.) Habana, 1940.

Phil 5400.40 Tratado del alma. (Vives, Juan L.) Madrid, 1916.

Phil 5545.75 Tratado demnemonica. (Castillio, A.F. de.) Lisboa, 1851.

Phil 6952.28 Tratamiento social de los enfermos de la mente. (Caravedo, B.) Lima, 1943.

Phil 8419.18 Trattado di estetica. (Stefanini, Luigi.) Brescia, 1955-

Phil 6329.2.5 Il trattamento morale dello scrupole e dell'ossessione morbossa. (Turco, Natale.) Torino, 1919-20. 2v.

Phil 8890.3 Trattato de regimine rectoris. (Paolino.) Vienna, 1868.

Phil 9175.1 Trattato del governo della famiglia. (Pandolfini, A.) Milano, 1802.

Phil 9175.1.8 Trattato del governo della famiglia. (Pandolfini, A.) Milano, 1829.

Phil 4210.25 Trattato della coscienza morale. (Rosmini-Serbati, Antonio.) Milano, 1844.

Phil 5465.2 Trattato della forza della fantasia umana. (Muratori, L.A.) Napoli, 1783.

Phil 2050.60.5 Trattato della natura humana. (Hume, David.) Torino, 1924.

Phil 2493.45.20 Trattato delle sensazioni. (Condillac, Étienne Bonnot.) Bologna, 1927.

Phil 8420.22 Trattato d'estetica. (Treves, Marco.) Firenze, 1938.

Phil 3819.59.5 Trattato politico. (Spinoza, Benedictus de.) Torino, 1958.

Phil 9450.15 Trattato sulla unione della morale colla politica. Torino, 1846.

Phil 8640.1.5 Trattato sull'immortalità dell'anima. (Pomponazzi, P.) Roma, 1914.

Phil 6683.3 Trattato teorico-pratico sul magnetismo animale. (Nani, Giacomo D.) Torino, 1850.

Phil 8674.9 Trattner, Ernest R. The autobiography of God. N.Y., 1930.

Phil 1870.40.45 Tratto dei principii della cognoscenza umana e tre dialogui. (Berkeley, G.) Bari, 1923.

Phil 8894.21 Traub, Friedrich. Die sittliche Weltordnung. Freiburg, 1892.

Phil 3480.53.6 Träume eines Geistersehers. (Kant, Immanuel.) Leipzig, 1880?

Htn Phil 3480.53.5* Träume eines Geistersehers. (Kant, Immanuel.) Riga, 1766.

Phil 8612.80 Trauer und Trost. (Johann, Horst Theodor.) München, 1968.

Phil 7082.34 Traugott, Richard. Der Traum. Würzburg, 1913.

Phil 7082.116 Der Traum. (Henning, Hans.) Wiesbaden, 1914.

Phil 7082.34 Der Traum. (Traugott, Richard.) Würzburg, 1913.

Phil 7082.40 Der Traum als Welt. (Uslar, Detlev von.) Pfullingen, 1964.

Phil 7082.36 Die Traum-Phantasie. (Volkelt, Johannes.) Stuttgart, 1875.

Phil 7082.92 Der Traum und seine Dentung. (Stumpf, E.J.G.) Leipzig, 1899.

Phil 7084.6 Traum und Traumdeutung als medizinisch-naturwissenschaftliches Problem im Mittelalter. (Diepgen, Paul.) Berlin, 1912.

Phil 5590.115A Trauma, growth and personality. (Greenacre, P.) London, 1953.

Phil 6327.4.5A Das Trauma der Geburt. (Rank, Otto.) Leipzig, 1924. 2v.

Phil 6327.4.6A The trauma of birth. (Rank, Otto.) London, 1929.

Phil 6327.4.7 The trauma of birth. (Rank, Otto.) N.Y., 1952.

Phil 6400.34 Traumatic aphasia. (Luriia, Aleksandr Romanovich.) The Hague, 1970.

Phil 7082.8.14 Die Traumdeuting. 4. Aufl. (Freud, Sigmund.) Leipzig, 1914.

Htn Phil 6480.23* Die Traumdeutung. (Freud, Sigmund.) Leipzig, 1909.

Phil 7080.36 Das Traumleben und seine Deutung. (Pfaff, E.R.) Leipzig, 1868.

Phil 7082.106 Der Traumspiegel. (Lomer, Georg.) München, 1918.

Phil 7084.10 Traumsymbolik. (Teillard, Ania.) Zürich, 1944.

Phil 6688.9 Die Traumtänzerin Magdeleine G. (Schrenck von Notzing, A.P.) Stuttgart, 1904.

Phil 8599.35 Trautmann, O. Die wiederkehr Göttes. Stuttgart, 1950.

Phil 9430.13 Trautz, T. Der Pessimismus. Karlsruhe, 1876.

Phil 4060.10.80 Travaglia, Sandro. La nozione di possibilità nel pensiero di Nicola Abbagnano. Padova, 1969.

Phil 5765.2.10 Le travail intellectuel et la volonté. (Payot, Jules.) Paris, 1919.

Phil 5765.2.11 Le travail intellectuel et la volonté. (Payot, Jules.) Paris, 1920.

Phil 51.1.5 Travaux. (Louvain. Université. Laboratoire de Psychologie Experimentale.) Louvain.

Phil 2610.86 Les travaux de Gassendi sur Épicure. (Rochot, Bernard.) Paris, 1944.

Phil 2610.87 Les travaux de Gassendi sur Épicure et sur l'atomisme. Thèse. (Rochot, Bernard.) Paris, 1944.

Phil 70.16 Travaux du congrès international de philosophie. (Inter-American Congress of Philosophy, 1st, Port-au-Prince, 1944.) Port-au-Prince, 1947.

Phil 6116.25 Travaux neurologiques de guerre. (Guillain, Georges.) Paris, 1920.

Phil 3549.2.78 The travel diary of a philosopher. (Keyserling, Hermann.) London, 1925. 2v.

Phil 3549.2.78.2 The travel diary of a philosopher. (Keyserling, Hermann.) N.Y., 1925. 2v.

Phil 3549.2.78.5 The travel diary of a philosopher. (Keyserling, Hermann.) N.Y., 1929.

Phil 3425.580 Travis, Don Carlos. A Hegel symposium. Austin, 1962.

Phil 5769.3 Travis, H. Moral freedom reconciled with causation. London, 1865.

Phil 6129.8 Travis, L.E. Personal problems of everyday life. N.Y., 1941.

Phil 6400.33.5 Travis, Lee E. Handbook speech pathology. N.Y., 1957.

Phil 6400.33 Travis, Lee E. Speech pathology. N.Y., 1931.

Phil 1819.10 Trawick, Leonard Moses. Backgrounds of romanticism. Bloomington, 1967.

Phil 5270.8 Traxel, Werner. Über Gegenstand und Methode der Psychologie. Bern, 1968.

Phil 8120.11 Traz, Georges. De Diderot à Valéry. Paris, 1960.

Phil 8120.8 Traz, Georges de. Diderot à Valéry. Paris, 1926.

Phil 4080.18.80 Tre brevi studi: La conclusione della filosofia del conoscere di Guido Calogero. (Raggiunti, Renzo.) Firenze, 1946.

Phil 2138.45.20 Tre religions-filosofiska afhandlingar. (Mill, John S.) Stockholm, 1883.

Phil 4080.3.15 Tre saggi filosofici. (Croce, Benedetto.) Palermo, 1932.

Phil 6945.14 Treadway, Walter L. Mental hygiene with special reference to the migration of the people. Washington, 1925.

Phil 1750.126.6A The treason of the intellectuals. (Benda, Julien.) N.Y., 1928.

Phil 9070.62 A treasury of parables. (Bartek, Edward.) N.Y., 1959.

Phil 165.26 Treasury of philosophy. (Runes, D.D.) N.Y., 1955.

Phil 5752.5 A treatis of freewill. (Cudworth, R.) London, 1838.

Htn Phil 8632.13* A treatise, concerning the death and resurrection of our bodies. (Hoddesdon, H.) London, 1606.

Phil 5643.22 Treatise...nature, treatment, morbid sensibility...retina. (Dix, J.H.) Boston, 1849.

Htn Phil 1870.40.1* Treatise...principles of human knowledge. (Berkeley, G.) Dublin, 1710.

Htn Phil 1870.40.2* Treatise...principles of human knowledge. (Berkeley, G.) London, 1734.

Phil 1870.40.3 Treatise...principles of human knowledge. (Berkeley, G.) London, 1776.

Phil 8598.20 A treatise...records of the creation. (Summer, J.B.) London, 1816. 2v.

Phil 8598.20.2 A treatise...records of the creation. (Sumner, J.B.) London, 1818. 2v.

Htn Phil 2733.6.1F* Treatise...Search for truth. (Malebranche, Nicolas.) Oxford, 1694.

Phil 5160.1 A treatise...sufficient reason. (Fitzgerald, Penelope F.) London, 1887.

Htn Phil 9510.3* A treatise against detraction. (Le Mercier, A.) Boston, 1733.

Htn Phil 9359.7.5* A treatise against painting...of men and women. (Tuke, Thomas.) London, 1616.

Htn Phil 5405.6* A treatise concerning enthusiasme. 2. ed. (Casaubon, M.) London, 1656.

Htn Phil 8580.22.5* A treatise concerning religions. (Amyraut, M.) London, 1660.

Phil 1870.40.9 Treatise concerning the principles of human knowledge. (Berkeley, G.) Chicago, 1878.

Phil 1870.40.13 A treatise concerning the principles of human knowledge. (Berkeley, G.) Chicago, 1904.

Phil 1870.40.12 A treatise concerning the principles of human knowledge. (Berkeley, G.) Philadelphia, 1881.

Phil 8626.15.9 A treatise concerning the state of the departed souls. (Burnet, Thomas.) London, 1633.

Phil 8626.15.12 A treatise concerning the state of the departed souls. 2. ed. (Burnet, Thomas.) London, 1739.

Phil 5405.6.2 A treatise conserning enthusiasme (1655). 2. ed. (Casaubon, M.) Gainsville, 1970.

Htn Phil 6480.15* A treatise of dreams and visions. (Tryon, T.) London, 168-.

Phil 5049.18 A treatise of formal logic. (Jorgenson, J.) Copenhagen, 1931. 3v.

Phil 7069.33.43 A treatise of ghosts. (Taillepied, N.) London, 1933.

Phil 2050.59.4 A treatise of human nature. (Hume, David.) Harmondsworth, 1969.

Phil 2050.59.3 A treatise of human nature. (Hume, David.) Oxford, 1964.

Phil 2520.13.15.5 Treatise of man. (Descartes, René.) Cambridge, 1972.

Phil 6967.5.4 Treatise of medical jurisprudence of insanity. (Ray, Isaac.) Boston, 1838.

Phil 6625.6 A treatise of melancholie. (Bright, Timothy.) N.Y., 1940.

Htn Phil 9560.22* A treatise of moral and intellectual virtues. (Hartcliffe, John.) London, 1691.

Htn Phil 8890.1* A treatise of moral philosophy. (Palfreyman, T.) London?, 1564?

Htn	Phil 2733.50.5*	A treatise of morality. pt.1-2. (Malebranche, Nicolas.) London, 1699.
Htn	Phil 8876.14.8*	A treatise of morall philosophie. (Baldwin, W.) London, n.d.
Htn	Phil 8876.14.5*	A treatise of morall philosophie. (Baldwin, W.) London, 1640.
Htn	Phil 8876.14.3*	A treatise of morall phylosophye. (Baldwin, W.) London, n.d.
	Phil 2050.70	Treatise of morals. Photoreproduction. (Hume, David.) Boston, 1893.
	Phil 2733.55	A treatise of nature and grace. (Malebranche, Nicolas.) London, 1695. 2 pam.
Htn	Phil 7060.6.5*	Treatise of specters. (Le Loyer, P.) London, 1605.
Htn	Phil 1928.33*	A treatise of the laws of nature. (Cumberland, R.) London, 1727.
Htn	Phil 665.11*	Treatise of the passions and faculties of the soule of men. (Reynolds, E.) London, 1640.
	Phil 978.74.5	A treatise on cosmic fire. 2d ed. (Bailey, A.A. (Mrs.).) N.Y., 1930[1925]
	Phil 294.3	Treatise on cosmology. (Nichols, H.) Cambridge, 1904.
	Phil 300.2	Treatise on electrical theory and problem of universe. (Tunzelmann, G.W. de.) London, 1910.
	Phil 2050.51	Treatise on human nature. (Hume, David.) London, 1874. 2v.
	Phil 2050.53	Treatise on human nature. (Hume, David.) Oxford, 1888.
	Phil 2050.58	Treatise on human nature. (Hume, David.) Oxford, 1928.
	Phil 2050.52	Treatise on human nature. v.2. (Hume, David.) London, 1878.
	Phil 5125.21	A treatise on induction and probability. (Wright, G.H. von.) London, 1951.
	Phil 6965.3.5	Treatise on insanity. (Pinel, Philippe.) Sheffield, 1806.
	Phil 6965.4	Treatise on insanity and other disorders. (Prichard, J.C.) Philadelphia, 1837.
	Phil 6957.2.5	A treatise on insanity in its medical relations. (Hammond, W.A.) N.Y., 1891.
	Phil 349.38	A treatise on knowledge. (Smith, A.H.) Oxford, 1943.
	Phil 1880.46	Treatise on logic. (Bowen, F.) Cambridge, 1864.
	Phil 1880.46.4	Treatise on logic. 4th ed. (Bowen, F.) Cambridge, 1866.
	Phil 1880.46.8	Treatise on logic. 8th ed. (Bowen, F.) Boston, 1880.
	Phil 6951.31	A treatise on madness. (Battie, William.) London, 1962.
	Phil 2636.31.2	A treatise on man. (Helvétius, C.A.) London, 1810. 2v.
	Phil 2636.31	A treatise on man. (Helvétius, C.A.) London, 1877. 2v.
	Phil 6972.10.4	Treatise on mental unsoundness. 4. ed. (Wharton, F.) Philadelphia, 1882.
	Phil 187.2	Treatise on metaphysics. (MacMahon, J.H.) London, 1860.
	Phil 5090.6	Treatise on moral evidence. (Smedley, E.A.) Cambridge, 1850.
	Phil 6965.8	A treatise on nervous derangements. (Peters, John C.) N.Y., 1854.
	Phil 7069.60.5	Treatise on parapsychology. (Sudre, René.) London, 1960.
	Phil 5643.8.12	Treatise on physiological optics. (Helmholtz, H.) Rochester, N.Y., 1924-25. 3v.
	Phil 8837.13	Treatise on right and wrong. (Mencken, H.L.) N.Y., 1934.
	Phil 8887.6.6	A treatise on self-knowledge. (Mason, J.) Boston, 1809.
	Phil 8887.6.9	A treatise on self-knowledge. (Mason, J.) London, 1821.
	Phil 8887.6.7	A treatise on self-knowledge. (Mason, J.) Montpelier, 1813.
	Phil 8887.6.15	A treatise on self-knowledge. (Mason, J.) N.Y., 1943.
Htn	Phil 8887.6.6.5*	A treatise on self-knowledge. (Mason, J.) Newburyport, 1812.
	Phil 8887.6.9.5	A treatise on self-knowledge. 3. ed. (Mason, J.) Boston, 1822.
	Phil 8887.6.12	A treatise on self knowledge. 4th ed. (Mason, J.) Boston, 1826.
	Phil 6957.2.9	A treatise on the diseases of the nervous system. 6. ed. (Hammond, W.A.) N.Y., 1876.
	Phil 5400.4	Treatise on the influence of the passions. (Stael-Holstein, Anne Louise G.) London, 1798.
	Phil 6967.5.10	A treatise on the medical jurisprudence of insanity. (Ray, Isaac.) Cambridge, 1962.
	Phil 6967.5.5	Treatise on the medical jurisprudence of insanity. 2. ed. (Ray, Isaac.) Boston, 1844.
	Phil 6967.5.8	Treatise on the medical jurisprudence of insanity. 5. ed. (Ray, Isaac.) Boston, 1871.
	Phil 6965.2	Treatise on the more obscure affections of the brain. (Philip, A.P.W.) London, 1835.
	Phil 9420.2	A treatise on the passions and affections of the mind. v.2-5. v.1 lost. (Cogan, T.) London, 1813. 4v.
	Phil 1890.30.6	Treatise on the philosophy of human mind. (Brown, T.) Cambridge, 1827. 2v.
	Phil 7060.60	Treatise on the second sight. (M'Leod, D.) Edinburgh, 1763.
	Phil 978.74.15	A treatise on the seven rays. (Bailey, A.A. (Mrs.).) N.Y., 1936-42. 4v.
	Phil 960.149.5	A treatise on the Yoga philosophy. 3d ed. (Paul, N.C.) Bombay, 1888.
	Phil 8888.4.2	A treatise on virtue. (Nettleton, T.) Edinburgh, 1774.
NEDL	Phil 8888.4	A treatise on virtue. (Nettleton, T.) London, 1759.
	Phil 978.74.10	A treatise on white magic. (Bailey, A.A. (Mrs.).) N.Y., 1934.
	Phil 2515.2.42	A treatise on wisdom. (Charron, P.) N.Y., 1891.
	Phil 3819.50	A treatise partly theological, and partly political. (Spinoza, Benedictus de.) London, 1689.
	Phil 8580.6	A treatise upon theological subjects. (Andrews, W.S.) Cambridge, 1829.
Htn	Phil 8595.16.20*	Treatises on various theological subjects. (Scott, Thomas.) Middletown, Conn., 1815.
	Phil 8595.16.21	Treatises on various theological subjects. (Scott, Thomas.) Middletown, Conn., 1824. 5v.
	Phil 6750.1	Treatment, cure, cretins, idiots. (Brown, B.) Boston, 1847-62. 4 pam.
	Phil 6689.3.5	Treatment by hypnotism and suggestion. 6. ed. (Tuckey, C.L.) London, 1913.
	Phil 6331.4	Treatment of neurasthenia by teaching of brain control. (Vittoz, Roger.) London, 1911.
	Phil 6957.28	The treatment of schizophrenia. (Hinsie, Leland.) Baltimore, 1930.
	Phil 6980.424	Treatment of the child in emotional conflict. (Lippman, Hyman.) N.Y., 1956.
	Phil 6952.7	The treatment of the insane without mechanical restraints. (Conolly, John.) London, 1856.
	Phil 4967.20.20	Trechos escolhidos. (Farias Brito, Raymundo de.) Rio de Janeiro, 1967.
	Phil 6750.18	Tredgold, A.F. Mental deficiency (Amentia). N.Y., 1908.
	Phil 6750.18.5	Tredgold, A.F. Mental deficiency (Amentia). 2d ed. N.Y., 1914.
	Phil 6750.18.12	Tredgold, A.F. Mental deficiency (Amentia). 4.ed. N.Y., 1922.
	Phil 6750.18.15	Tredgold, A.F. Mental deficiency (Amentia). 5th ed. N.Y., 1929.
	Phil 6128.18	Un tredicesimo nervo craniale. (Sapolini, G.) Milano, 1881.
	Phil 8620.39	The tree of good and evil. (Samuel, H.) London, 1933.
	Phil 5592.5	The tree test. (Koch, Charles.) Bern, 1952.
	Phil 3925.8.81	Trefzger, Hermann. Der philosophische Entwicklungsgang von Joseph Weber. Freiburg, 1933.
	Phil 7060.117	Tregortha, John. News from the invisible world. Burslem, 1813.
	Phil 3890.14	Treher, W. Das Oknosprinzip. München, 1962.
	Phil 3425.710	Treher, Wolfgang. Hegels Geisteskrankheit. Emmendin, 1969.
	Phil 8980.566	Treiheit und Verantwortung. (Mende, Georg.) Berlin, 1958.
	Phil 6311.34.6	Treis dialexeis eisagōgēs eis tēn psychanalēse. (Bonaparte, Marie.) Athenai, 1950.
	Phil 5259.25.5	Trejos, J. Cuestiones de psicologiá racional. 2. ed. San José de Costa Rica, 1935.
	Phil 5259.25	Trejos, J. Resumen de psicología. San José, 1929.
	Phil 2150.15.107	Tremmel, William C. The social concepts of George Herbert Mead. Emporia, 1927.
	Phil 2150.15.105	Tremmel, William C. The social concepts of George Herbert Mead. Emporia, 1957.
Htn	Phil 9359.5*	Trenchfield, C. A cap of gray hairs for a green head. London, 1688.
	Phil 310.681	Trendafilov, Nikola. Za deistvieto na zakona za edinstvoto i borbata na protivopolozhnostite pri sotsializma. Sofiia, 1968.
	Phil 3890.1.75	Trendelenburg, A. Contribution to history of the word person. Chicago, 1910. 2 pam.
	Phil 3428.90F	Trendelenburg, A. Herbarts praktische Philosophie. Berlin, 1856.
	Phil 3890.1.30	Trendelenburg, A. Historische Beiträge zur Philosophie. Berlin, 1846-67. 3v.
	Phil 3487.1.10	Trendelenburg, A. Kuno Fischer und sein Kant. Leipzig, 1869.
	Phil 3425.270	Trendelenburg, A. Die logische Frage in Hegel's System. Leipzig, 1843.
	Phil 3890.1.42	Trendelenburg, A. Logische Untersuchungen. Berlin, 1840. 2v.
	Phil 3890.1.41	Trendelenburg, A. Logische Untersuchungen. 2. Aufl. Leipzig, 1862. 3v.
	Phil 3890.1.45A	Trendelenburg, A. Logische Untersuchungen. 3. Aufl. Leipzig, 1870. 2v.
	Phil 3428.90.5	Trendelenburg, A. Über Herbart's Metaphysik. Berlin, 1854.
	Phil 3246.193	Trendelenburg, A. Zur Erinnerung an Johann Gottlieb Fichte. Berlin, 1862.
	Phil 3890.1.110	Trendelenburg Bölcseleti rendszere tekintettie. (Gál, Keleman.) Kolozsvárt, 1895.
	Phil 5865.7	Trends and issues in developmental psychology. N.Y., 1969.
	Phil 6311.33	Trends in psycho-analysis. (Brierley, Marjorie Ellis.) London, 1951.
	Phil 4610.6.3	Trenne filosofiska uppsatser. Lund, 1878.
	Phil 4610.6.2	Trenne religiousfilosfiska uppsatser. 2. uppl. (Nyblaeus, Axel.) Lund, 1874.
	Phil 5790.2.20	Die Trennung der Liebenden. (Caruso, Igor A.) Bern, 1968.
	Phil 860.2.2	Die Trennung von Himmel und Erde; ein vorgriechischer Schöpfungsmythus bei Hesiod und den Orphikern. 2. Aufl. (Staudacher, Willibald.) Darmstadt, 1968.
	Phil 8419.25	Trente-trois oeuvres d'art. v.1-2. (Streignart, Joseph.) Gembloux, 1953?
	Phil 4803.846.30	Trentowski, Bronisław F. Grundlage der universellen Philosophie. Karlsruhe, 1837.
	Phil 4803.846.40	Trentowski, Bronisław F. Myślini czyli całokształt loiki narodowéj. Poznań, 1844. 2v.
	Phil 4803.846.45	Trentowski, Bronisław F. Stosunek filozofii do cybernetyki czyli sztuki rządzenia narodem. Poznań, 1843.
	Phil 4803.846.35	Trentowski, Bronisław F. Wizerunki duszy narodowej s końca ostatniego szesnastolecia. Paryż, 1847.
	Phil 3552.276	Trepte, Adolf. Die metaphysische Unvollkommenheit...bei Augustin und Leibniz. Inaug. Diss. Halle, 1889.
	Phil 8416.17	Tres aspectos de la cultura. (Pro, Diezo F.) Mendoza, 1942.
	Phil 8060.5	Las tres categorías estétecas de la cultura clásica. (O'Callaghan, J.) Madrid, 1960.
	Phil 8846.4	Tres éticas del siglo XX. (Vázquez, Francisco.) Madrid, 1970.
	Phil 8080.2	Tres ideales esteticos. (Oribe, Emilia.) Montevideo, 1958.
	Phil 4319.2	Tres salvaciones del siglo XVIII español. (Segovia Canosa, R.) Xalapa, 1960.
	Phil 4640.1.30	Treschow, N. Om den menneskelige natur. København, 1812.
	Phil 2477.6.140	Tresmontant, C. Introduction à la metaphysique de Maurice Blondel. Paris, 1963.
	Phil 8520.40	Tresmontant, C. Les origines de la philosophie chrétienne. Paris, 1962.
	Phil 8599.44.2	Tresmontant, Claude. Les idées maîtresses de la métaphysique chrétienne. Paris, 1962.
	Phil 8599.44	Tresmontant, Claude. La métaphysique du christianisme. Paris, 1961.
	Phil 8599.44.10	Tresmontant, Claude. La métaphysique du christianisme. Paris, 1964.
	Phil 8674.13	Tresmontant, Claude. Essai sur la connaissance de Dieu. Paris, 1959.
	Phil 2905.1.263	Tresmoutant, Claude. Introduccion al pensamiento de Teilhard de Chardin. 2. ed. Madrid, 1960.
	Phil 2905.1.260	Tresmoutant, Claude. Introduction à la pensée de Teilhard de Chardin. Paris, 1962.
	Phil 7069.31.40	Trespioli, Gino. "Ultrafamia", esegesi della fenomenologia intellettuale dello spiritismo moderno. Milano, 1931.
	Phil 2750.8.91	Tressan, Louis Elisabeth de la Vergne. Éloge de M. Moreau de Maupertuis. Nancy, 17- .
	Phil 299.3	Tretten aftnar hos en spiritist. (Siljeström, P.A.) Stockholm, 1886.
	Phil 9540.5	Trevelyan, G.M. De haeretico comburendo. Cambridge, Eng., 1914.
	Phil 8420.22	Treves, Marco. Trattato d'estetica. Firenze, 1938.
	Phil 2725.2.101	Treves, P. Lamennais. Milano, 1934.
	Phil 4073.86	Treves, Paulo. La filosofia politica di Tommaso Campanella. Bari, 1930.
	Phil 2475.1.405	Trevisan, A. Essai sur le problèmes. Fribourg, 1963.
	Phil 5780.12	Trey, M. de. Der Wille in der Handschrift. Bern, 1946.
	Phil 9450.57	Tri-ennial Congress of the International Union for the Protection of Public Morality, 3rd, London, 1961. International public morals. Rushden, 1961?

Phil 310.588 Tri iniciatívy v dejinách filozofie. (Hrušovský, I.) Bratislava, 1959.
Phil 4769.1.78 Tri razgovora. (Solov'ev, V.S.) N'iu-Iork, 1954.
Phil 4769.1.120 Tri rechi v pamiat' Dostoevskogo. (Solov'ev, V.S.) Berlin, 1925.
Phil 181.57.15 Tri studi di filosofia. (Galli, Gallo.) Torino, 1956.
Phil 29.35 Triades; revue trimestrielle de culture humaine. Paris. 1,1953+ 17v.
Phil 29.35.2 Triades; revue trimestrielle de culture humaine. Sommaires des numéros parus, 1953-1972. Paris, 1972.
Phil 2630.3.82 Trial, Louis. Jean-Jacques Gourd 1850-1909. Nimes, 1914.
Phil 6957.8 The trial of Ebenezer Haskell in lunacy. (Haskell, E.) Philadelphia, 1869.
Phil 7069.45.50 The trial of Mrs. Duncan. (Duncan, V.H.M.) London, 1945.
Phil 5922.6.8 Trials and triumphs of an orphan girl; biography. (Hammond, L.M. (Mrs.).) Cortland, N.Y., 1859.
Phil 5335.10 Triandis, Harry C. Attitude and attitude change. N.Y., 1971.
Phil 194.62 Trias, Eugenio. Metodologia del pensamiento mágico. Bercelona, 1970.
Phil 260.17 Triaspekta atomistiki. (Kedrov, Bonifatii M.) Moskva, 1969. 3v.
Phil 8525.10 Tribe, David H. One hundred years of freethought. London, 1967.
Phil 8586.45.5 Les tribulations de Sophie. (Gilson, Étienne.) Paris, 1967.
Phil 3850.27.240 A tribute on the ninetieth birthday of Albert Schweitzer. (Friends of Albert Schweitzer.) Boston, 1964.
Phil 6315.2.165 Tribute to Freud. (Aldington, H.D.) N.Y., 1956.
Htn Phil 6045.61.7* Tricasso, Patricio. La chiromance. Paris, 1583.
Htn Phil 6045.61.5* Tricasso, Patricio. La chiromance. Paris, 1583.
Htn Phil 6045.60* Tricasso, Patricio. Enarratio pulcherrima principiorum chyromantiae. Noribergae, 1560.
Phil 2520.205 Tricentenaire de la parution du discours de la méthode, 1637-1937. (Cercle Philosophique, Lorrain.) Metz, 1937.
Phil 2805.485F Tricentenaire du mémorial de Blaise Pascal, 23 Novembre 1654-1954. Paris, 1955.
Phil 5059.18 Tricot, Jules. Traité de logique formelle. Paris, 1930.
Phil 6329.1.8 Tridon, André. Easy lessons in psychoanalysis. N.Y., 1921.
Phil 6317.5 Tridon, André. Psychoanalysis, its history, theory and practice. N.Y., 1919.
Phil 6329.1.10 Tridon, André. Psychoanalysis; its history, theory and practice. N.Y., 1920.
Phil 6329.1.9 Tridon, André. Psychoanalysis; its history, theory and practice. N.Y., 1923.
Phil 7084.4.10 Tridon, André. Psychoanalysis, sleep and dreams. N.Y., 1921.
Phil 6329.1.3 Tridon, André. Psychoanalysis and behavior. N.Y., 1920.
Phil 6329.1.12 Tridon, André. Psychoanalysis and man's unconscious motives. N.Y., 1924.
Phil 3491.14 Trieb als sittliches Phänomen. (Jacobs, Wilhelm Gustav.) Bonn, 1967.
Phil 6060.29.15 Trieb und Verbrechen in der Handschrift. 2e Aufl. (Pulver, Max.) Zürich, 1934.
Phil 6328.40 Triebpathologie. (Szondi, Lipot.) Bern, 1956. 2v.
Phil 185.40.10 Die Triebrichtungen des Gewissens. (Schaumann, Otto.) Frankfurt, 1941.
Phil 5400.138 Triebwirkung des Films auf Jugendliche. (Bellingroth, Friedhelm.) Bern, 1958.
Phil 4080.3.498 Trieste. Università Facoltà di Lettere e Filosofia. Lezioni crociane. Trieste, 1967.
Phil 5059.8 Trieu, A.R.P.P.D. Manuductio ad logicam. Oxoniae, 1662.
Phil 5402.42 Trigg, Roger. Pain and emotion. Oxford, 1970.
Phil 1524.3 Trikál, Josef. Benezető a közepkori kereszteny hölcselet tortenelmehe. Budapest, 1913.
Phil 6060.36 Trillat, Raymond. Eléments de graphologie pratique. Paris, 1944.
Phil 5627.198 Trillhaas, W. Die innere Welt. 2. Aufl. München, 1955.
Phil 8969.18.3 Trillhaas, Wolfgang. Ethik. 3. Aufl. Berlin, 1970.
Phil 9495.169.5 Trillhaas, Wolfgang. Sexualethik. Göttingen, 1969.
Phil 6315.2.157A Trilling, L. Freud and the crisis of our culture. Boston, 1955.
Phil 3270.12.100 Trinchero, Mario. La filosofia dell'aritmetica di Gottlob Frege. Giappichelli, 1967.
Phil 8894.17.5 Trine, Ralph W. Auf dem Wege zur Wahrheit. Stuttgart, 1909.
Phil 8894.17.20 Trine, Ralph W. The greatest thing ever known. N.Y., 1898.
Phil 8894.17.3 Trine, Ralph W. In tune with the infinite. N.Y., 1897.
Phil 8894.17.15 Trine, Ralph W. On the open road. N.Y., 1908.
Phil 8894.17.4 Trine, Ralph W. Set synliga i samklang med det o synliga. Stockholm, 1910.
Htn Phil 8894.17.23* Trine, Ralph W. What all the world's a-seeking. Boston, 1897.
Phil 8894.17.22 Trine, Ralph W. What all the world's a-seeking. N.Y., 1896.
Phil 4362.2 La Trinidad, principio fundamental del universo. (Leret, Carlos.) Madrid, 1938.
Phil 3425.623 Die Trinitätslehre G.W.F. Hegels. (Splett, Jörg.) Freiburg, 1965.
Phil 2905.1.535 Trinité, Phillipe de la. Teilhard de Chardin. Paris, 1968.
Phil 3850.50 Trinitorische Anthropologie bei Franz Anton Staudenmaiet. (Huenermann, Peter.) Freiburg, 1962.
Phil 8610.759 Trinius, Johann Anton. Freydenker-Lexicon. Leipzig, 1759.
Phil 8610.759.5F Trinius, Johann Anton. Freydenker-Lexicon. Torino, 1966.
Phil 396.10 Trinkaus, Charles Edward. In our image and likeness; humanity and divinity in Italian humanist thought. London, 1970. 2v.
Phil 9245.55A Trinkhaus, C.E. Adversity's noblemen. N.Y., 1940.
Phil 5401.48 Triomphez de l'angoisse. (Réal, Pierre.) Verviers, 1963.
Phil 8966.2 Il triplice frutto della vita cristiana. (Quacquarelli, Antonio.) Roma, 1953.
Phil 5259.26 Tripp, Erich. Untersuchungen zur Rechtspsychologie des Individuums. Leipzig, 1931.
Phil 196.36.5 Tríptico de idéias. (Vita, Luis Washington.) São Paulo, 1967.
Phil 9490.9 Trisca, P.C. Die Pflichten der Intelligenten. Jena, 1911.
Phil 9520.3 La tristesse contemporaine. (Fierens-Gevaert, H.) Paris, 1899.
Phil 5403.6 La tristesse et la joie. (Dumas, G.) Paris, 1900.
Phil 1730.2 Der Triumph der Philosophie im Achtzehnten Jahrhunderts. (Starck, Johann G.) Germantown, 1804. 2v.
Phil 8691.19 The triumph of life. (Barry, W.) London, 1928.
Phil 3450.11.142.5A The triumph of subjectivity. (Lauer, Quentin.) N.Y., 1958.

Phil 7068.72 Triumph of the blessed sacrament or History of Nicola Aubry. (Müller, M.) Baltimore, 1872.
Phil 9355.6 The triumph of the man who acts. (Purinton, E.E.) N.Y., 1920.
Phil 585.172 The triumph of the therapeutic. 1st ed. (Rieff, Philip.) N.Y., 1966.
Phil 6317.28 The triumphant spirit. (Howe, Eric Graham.) London, 1943.
Phil 3501.7 Trivero, Camillo. Nuova critica della morale Kantiana. Milano, 1914.
Phil 8894.22 Trivero, Camillo. Saggi di etica. Milano, 1917.
Phil 8712.16 Tro och vebande. (Webber, G.P.) Stockholm, 1915. 3v.
Phil 4605.1.31 Tro og viden. (Monrad, M.J.) Kristiania, 1892.
Phil 9495.162.1 Trobisch, Walter. I loved a girl (including I loved a young man); young Africans speak. N.Y., 1965.
Phil 974.3.85 Tröger, Walter. Grundriss der Anthroposophie in engem Anschluss an die Schriften Dr. Rudolf Steiners. Breslau, 1921.
Phil 8701.3 Troels Lund, Troels Frederik. Himmelsbild und Weltanschauung. Leipzig, 1900.
Phil 8701.3.4 Troels Lund, Troels Frederik. Himmelsbild und Weltanschauung. 4. Aufl. Leipzig, 1913.
Phil 8701.3.6 Troels Lund, Troels Frederik. Himmelsbild und Weltanschauung. 5. Aufl. Leipzig, 1929.
Phil 600.39 Troeltsch, E. Die Dynamik der Geschichte nach der Geschichtsphilosophie des Positivismus. Berlin, 1919. 101v.
Phil 3501.11 Troeltsch, E. Das Historische in Kants Religionsphilosophie. Berlin, 1904.
Phil 8599.19.2 Troeltsch, Ernst. Die Absolutheit des Christentums. 2. Aufl. Tübingen, 1912.
Phil 8599.19.21 Troeltsch, Ernst. Christian thought, its history and application. London, 1923.
Phil 8599.19.20 Troeltsch, Ernst. Der Historismus und seine Überwindung; fünf Vorträge. Berlin, 1924.
Phil 8599.19.10 Troeltsch, Ernst. Psychologie und Erkenntnistheorie in der Religionswissenschaft. Tübingen, 1905.
Phil 8599.19.15 Troeltsch, Ernst. Zur religiösen Lage. 2. Aufl. Tübingen, 1922.
Phil 8599.19.100 Troeltsch und die Absolulheit des Christentums. Inaug. Diss. (Leidreiter, Erich.) Mahrungen, 1927.
Phil 7080.23 Trömmer, E. Das Problem des Schlafes. Wiesbaden, 1912.
Phil 6689.7.3 Trömner, Ernst. Hypnotismus und Suggestion. 3e Aufl. Leipzig, 1919.
Phil 3640.585 Troenle, Ludwig. Elitebildung durch agonale Auslese. Wien, 1958.
Phil 8090.4 Trofimov, P.S. Ocherki istorii marksistskoi estetiki. Moskva, 1963.
Phil 8050.86 Trofimov, Pavel S. Estetika i iskusstvo. Moskva, 1966.
Phil 8420.25 Trofimov, Pavel S. Estetika marksizma-leninizma. Moskva, 1964.
Phil 6329.7 Trog, H. Die Religionstheorie der Psychoanalyse. Diss. Hamburg, 1934.
Phil 3450.19.98 Trogische Existenz; zur Philosophie Martin Heideggers. (Delp, A.) Freiburg, 1935.
Phil 4235.1.90 Troilo, E. Bernardino Telesio. Modena, 1910.
Phil 3501.14 Troilo, E. Emmanuele Kant. Roma, 1924.
Phil 819.8 Troilo, E. Figure e studii de storia della filosofia. Roma, 1918.
Phil 525.5.15 Troilo, E. Il misticismo moderno. Torino, 1899.
Phil 600.35 Troilo, E. Il positivismo e i diritti dello spirito. Torino, 1912.
Phil 705.28 Troilo, E. La ragioni della trascendenza o del realismo assoluto. Venezia, 1936.
Phil 819.8.5 Troilo, E. Sommario di storia della filosofia. Milano, 1929.
Phil 4060.1.91 Troilo, Erminio. Ardigò. Milano, 1926.
Phil 4065.91 Troilo, Erminio. La filosofia di Giordano Bruno. Torino, 1904.
Phil 4065.91.5 Troilo, Erminio. Giordano Bruno. Roma, 1918.
Phil 194.31A Troilo, Erminis. Filosofia, vita e modernita. Roma, 1906.
Phil 194.31.5 Troilo, Erminis. Lo spirito della filosofia. Citta di Castello, 1925.
Phil 177.77 Trois conférences d'Oxford. (Chevalier, Jacques.) Paris, 1928.
Phil 177.77.5 Trois conférences d'Oxford. 2. ed. (Chevalier, Jacques.) Paris, 1933.
Phil 6990.3.80 Trois écrivains devant Lourdes. Paris, 1958.
Phil 6315.2.75.12 Trois essais sur la théorie de la sexualité. 51. éd. (Freud, Sigmund.) Paris, 1949.
Phil 6315.2.75.11 Trois essais sur la théorie de la sexualité. 23e éd. (Freud, Sigmund.) Paris, 1925.
Phil 2480.80 Trois études sur Cabanis. (Vermeil de Conchard, P.P.) Brive, 1914.
Phil 1701.22 Trois idoles romantique. (Benda, J.) Genève, 1948.
Htn Phil 2733.56* Trois lettres...la defense de Mr. Arnauld. (Malebranche, Nicolas.) Rotterdam, 1685.
Phil 4011.2 Trois novateurs. (Lenoir, E.) Paris, 1939.
Phil 2805.406 Les trois nuits de Pascal. (Steinmann, J.) Paris, 1963.
Phil 3480.18.16 Trois opuscules scientifiques. (Kant, Immanuel.) Mistral, 1914.
Phil 2805.249A Trois pensées inédites de Pascal. (Lafuma, Louis.) Paris, 1945.
Phil 2412.4.7 Trois réformateurs; Luther, Descartes, Rousseau. (Maritain, Jacques.) Paris, 1939.
Phil 2750.11.71A Trois réformateurs: Luther-Descartes-Rousseau. (Maritain, Jacques.) Paris, 1925.
Phil 2750.11.71.5 Trois réformateurs: Luther-Descartes-Rousseau. (Maritain, Jacques.) Paris, 1925. 2v.
Htn Phil 2515.2.45* Les trois veritez. 2e éd. (Charron, P.) Bordeaux, 1595.
Phil 186.7 Les trois voyageurs. (Lemoine, J.J.) Paris, 1819.
Phil 310.567 Troise, Emilio. Materialismo dialectico. Buenos Aires, 1938.
Phil 2750.13.95 Troisfontaines, R. De l'existence à l'être. Namur, 1953. 2v.
Phil 1750.263.5 Troisfontaines, R. Existentialism and Christian thought. London, 1950.
Phil 1750.263 Troisfontaines, R. Existentialisme et pensée chrétienne. 2e éd. Louvain, 1948.
Phil 2880.8.82 Troisfontaines, Roger. Le choix de Jean Paul Sartre. Paris, 1945.
Phil 2880.8.82.2 Troisfontaines, Roger. Le choix de Jean Paul Sartre. 2. éd. Paris, 1946.
Phil 2805.407 Le troisième centenaire de la mort de la Blaise Pascal. (Jacques, E.) Bruxelles, 1963.
Phil 2805.415 Troisième centenaire de la mort de Pascal. (Massis, Henri.) Paris, 1962.
Phil 4757.1.35 Troistvennyi obraz sovershenstva. (Gershenzon, M.O.) Moskva, 1918.

Author and Title Listing

Phil 3501.3 Troitzsch, J.G. Etwas über den Werth der kritischen Philosophie. Leipzig, 1780-1800. 3 pam.
Phil 194.13 Trojano, P.R. Le basi dell'umanismo. Torino, 1907.
Phil 8894.20 Trojano, Paolo R. Ethica. Napoli, 1897.
Phil 8894.20.10 Trojano, Paolo R. La filosofia morale. Torino, 1902.
Phil 5259.19.9 Troland, L.T. The fundamentals of human motivation. N.Y., 1928.
Phil 5259.19 Troland, L.T. The mystery of mind. N.Y., 1926.
Phil 5643.69 Troland, L.T. The present status of visual science. Washington, 1922.
Phil 5259.19.15A Troland, L.T. The principles of psychology. N.Y., 1929. 3v.
Phil 7069.17.45 Troland, L.T. A technique for the experimental study of telepathy. Albany, N.Y., 1917.
Phil 494.3 Tromp, Salco U. The religion of the modern scientist. Leiden, 1947.
Phil 3640.595.5 Tropami Zaratustry. (Oduev, S.F.) Moskva, 1971.
Phil 1190.5 Die Tropen der griechischen Skeptiker. (Pappenheim, E.) Berlin, 1885.
Phil 5421.15.35 Trost, Jan. Om bildandet av dyader. Uppsala, 1966.
Phil 9035.88 Troth, D.C. Selected readings in character education. Boston, 1930.
Phil 3450.19.350 Trotignon, Pierre. Heidegger. Paris, 1965.
Phil 2475.1.495 Trotignon, Pierre. L'idée de vie chez Bergson et la critique de la metaphysique. Paris, 1968.
Phil 2428.12 Trotignon, Pierre. Les philosophes français d'aujourd'hui. 2. éd. Paris, 1970.
Phil 3425.286 Trott zu Solz, A. v. Hegels Staatsphilosophie. Göttingen, 1932.
Phil 5380.5.15 Trotter, Wilfred. Instincts of the herd in peace and war. 3. ed. N.Y., 1941.
Phil 6311.23 The troubled mind. (Bluemel, C.S.) Baltimore, 1938.
Phil 6327.13 The troubled mind. (Roberts, Harry.) N.Y., 1939.
Phil 5545.31.5 Les troubles de la mémoire. (Sollier, P.) Paris, 1901.
Phil 5545.238 Les troubles de la mémoire et leur examen psychométrique. (Rey, André.) Bruxelles, 1966.
Phil 6990.3.70 Trouch, F. Sainte Bernadette Soubirous. Lyon, 1953.
Phil 8894.14 Troufleau, L. Morale pratique. 3e éd. Paris, 1913.
Phil 5627.128 Trout, David McC. Religious behavior. N.Y., 1931.
Phil 8599.15 Troward, T. The Doré lectures. N.Y., 1909.
Phil 8599.15.5 Troward, T. The Doré lectures. N.Y., 1919.
Phil 194.21.5 Troward, Thomas. The creative process in the individual. London, 1910.
Phil 194.21.2 Troward, Thomas. The Edinburgh lectures on mental science. N.Y., 1915.
Phil 194.21.3 Troward, Thomas. The Edinburgh lectures on mental science. 3d. ed. London, 1908.
Phil 194.21.7 Troward, Thomas. The law and the word. N.Y., 1919.
Phil 194.34.10 Troxler, I.P.V. Blicke in das Wesen des Menschen. Aarau, 1812.
Phil 3890.9.85 Troxler, I.P.V. Der Briefwechsel zwischen Ignoz Paul Vital Troxler. Aran, 1953.
Phil 5059.9 Troxler, I.P.V. Logik. Stuttgart, 1829-30. 3v.
Phil 194.34 Troxler, I.P.V. Naturlehre dis menschlichen Erkennens. Aarau, 1828.
Phil 3890.9.88 Troxler, I.P.V. Philosophische Enzyklopädie und Methodologie der Wissenschaften. Beromünster, 1956.
Phil 194.34.15 Troxler, I.P.V. Vorlesungen über Philosophie. Bern, 1835.
VPhil 585.261 Trstenjak, Anton. Hoja za človekom. Celje, 1968.
Phil 7069.19.152 Trú og sannanir. (Kvaran, E.H.) Reykjavik, 1919.
Phil 3501.13 Trubetskoi, E. Metafizika predpolozheniia poznaniia opyt preodolevaniia Kanta. Moskva, 1917.
Phil 300.4 Trubetskoi, E.N. Smysl' zhizni. Berlin, 1922.
Phil 1135.125 Trubetskoi, S. Metafizika v drevnei Gretsii. Moskva, 1890.
Phil 4770.1 Trubetskoi, S.N. Sobranie sochinenii. v.1-2,5-6. Moskva, 1907. 4v.
Phil 1135.81 Trubetskoi, S.N. Uchenie o Logose. Moskva, 1900.
Phil 1135.81.5 Trubetskoi, S.N. Uchenie o Logose. Moskva, 1906.
VPhil 8735.59 Trubnikov, Nikolai N. O kategoriiakh "tsel'", "sredstvo", "rezul'tat". Moskva, 1968.
Phil 1750.165 Truc, G. De J.P. Sartre à L. Lavelle. Paris, 1946.
Phil 819.10 Truc, Gonzague. Histoire de la philosophie. Paris, 1950.
Phil 8400.63 Trud i esteticheskoe vospitanie. Riga, 1969.
Phil 8980.604 Trud i moral' v sovetskom doshchestve. (Nesteroo, Vladimir G.) Moskva, 1969.
Phil 8980.564 Trudnaia kniga. (Medynskii, Grigorii A.) Moskva, 1964.
Phil 8050.23 Trudu,, Luciano. Soggettività e oggettività del bello. Padova, 1962.
Phil 8420.7 Trudu, Luciano. La legge del bello. Padova, 1962.
Phil 50.30 Trudy. (Ukrainskii. Psikhonevrologicheskii Institut, Kharkov.) Kharkov.
Phil 5059.10 True, C.K. The elements of logic. Boston, 1840.
Phil 194.12 True, H.B. How to obtain our own. N.Y., 1909.
Phil 7085.5 A true account of a natural sleep walker. (Levade, L.) Edinburgh, 1792.
Htn Phil 7066.72* A true and perfect account of a strange and dreadful apparition. (Pye, John.) London, 1672.
Phil 332.14.12 The true and the evident. (Brentano, Franz.) London, 1966.
Phil 720.43 The true and the valid. (Aaron, Richard Ithamar.) London, 1955.
Htn Phil 9359.9* The true conduct of persons of quality. London, 1694.
Phil 7060.75.5 True ghost stories. (Carrington, H.) N.Y., 1915.
Phil 2230.95 The true history of mental science. (Dresser, J.A.) Boston, 1899.
Phil 1925.31 The true intellectual system of the universe. (Cudworth, R.) Andover, 1837-38. 2v.
Htn Phil 1925.1.3* True intellectual system of the universe. (Cudworth, R.) London, 1678.
Htn Phil 1925.1.2* True intellectual system of the universe. (Cudworth, R.) London, 1678.
Phil 1925.1 True intellectual system of the universe. (Cudworth, R.) London, 1678.
Phil 1925.31.55 The true intellectual system of the universe. (Cudworth, R.) London, 1820. 4v.
Phil 1925.32 The true intellectual system of the universe. (Cudworth, R.) London, 1845. 3v.
Htn Phil 1925.30.2* The true intellectual system of the universe. 2d ed. (Cudworth, R.) London, 1743. 2v.
Phil 7060.110 True Irish ghost stories. (Seymour, S.J.D.) Dublin, 1914.
Phil 7069.26.30 True Irish ghost stories. 2. ed. (Seymour, S.J.D.) Dublin, 1926.
Phil 9560.2 True manliness. (Hughes, T.) Boston, 1880?
Phil 9354.2.5 True men as we need them. 4th ed. (O'Reilly, B.) N.Y., 1882.
Phil 510.158 A true monistic philosophy. (Waton, Harry.) N.Y., 1947-1955. 2v.
Phil 8957.12.7 True morality and its counterfeits. (Hildebrand, D. von.) N.Y., 1955.
Htn Phil 1850.62* True peace; or A moderate discourse. (Bacon, Francis.) London, 1663.
Phil 181.31 The true philosophy of mind. (Graham, C.) Louisville, 1869.
Phil 7084.30.2 A true relation of Mr. Justice Cook's passage by sea from Wexforel to Kinsaile, and of the great storm. 2d ed. (Cook, John.) London, 1652?
Htn Phil 6990.8* A true relation of the wonderful cure of Mary Maillard. (Maillard, Mary.) London, 1694.
Phil 9342.18 True womanhood. (Cunningham, W.) N.Y., 18- .
Phil 9349.2 True womanhood. (Johnson, F.) Cambridge, 1882.
Phil 6329.14 Trüb, Hans. Heilung aus der Begenung. Stuttgart, 1951.
Phil 8674.12 Trueblood, D.E. Knowledge of God. N.Y., 1939.
Phil 8599.33 Trueblood, D.E. The logic of belief. 1. ed. N.Y., 1942.
Phil 5627.155 Trueblood, D.E. The trustworthiness of religious experience. London, 1939.
Phil 7054.119 Truesdell, J.W. The bottom facts...science of spiritualism. N.Y., 1883.
Phil 7068.84 Truesdell, J.W. The bottom facts concerning the science of spiritualism. N.Y., 1884.
Phil 4769.1.105 Truhetskoĭ, E.N. Mirosozertsanie Vl.C. Solov'eva. v.1-2. Moskva, 1913.
Phil 2905.1.390 Truhlar, Karel Vladimir. Teilhard und Solowjew. Freiburg, 1966.
Phil 4210.141.5 Trullet, Angelo Parere intorno alle dottrine ed alle opere di Antonio Rosmini-Serbati. Modena, 1882.
Phil 2730.81 Truman, N.E. Maine de Biran's philosophy of will. N.Y., 1904.
Phil 5627.96.5 Trumbull, Charles G. Taking men alive. N.Y., 1912.
Phil 9220.11 Trumbull, H.C. Friendship the master-passion. Philadelphia, 1894.
Phil 8709.12 Trumbull, William. Evolution and religion. N.Y., 1907.
Phil 6129.7 Trumper, Henry. The message of mysticism in spiritual healing. London, 1933.
Phil 6420.22 Trumper, Max. A hemato-respiratory study of 101 consecutive cases of stammering. Thesis. Philadelphia, 1928.
Phil 5627.155 The trustworthiness of religious experience. (Trueblood, D.E.) London, 1939.
Phil 9558.11 Truth; an essay in moral reconstruction. (Walston, C.) Cambridge, 1919.
Phil 270.26.5 Truth, knowledge and causation. (Ducasse, Cuit J.) London, 1968.
Phil 720.76 Truth. (Pitcher, George Willard.) Englewood Cliffs, N.J., 1964.
Phil 9495.72 The truth about love. N.Y., 1872.
Phil 6128.42 The truth about mind cure. (Sadler, William S.) Chicago, 1928.
Phil 7069.16.10 The truth about our dead told by those who know. 1st ed. (Churchill, Lida A.) N.Y., 1916.
Phil 7069.18.40 The truth about spiritualism. (Bryan, William J.) N.Y., 1918.
Phil 8408.40 Truth and art. (Hofstsdter, Albert.) N.Y., 1965.
Phil 720.29 Truth and corrigibility. (Price, H.H.) Oxford, 1936.
Phil 5068.34 Truth and denotation. (Martin, R.M.) London, 1958.
Phil 190.17 Truth and error. (Powell, J.W.) Chicago, 1898.
Phil 2750.11.77 Truth and human fellowship. (Maritain, Jacques.) Princeton, 1957.
Phil 5520.195 Truth and meaning. (Greenwood, David.) N.Y., 1957.
Phil 332.5 Truth and reality. (Boodin, J.E.) N.Y., 1911.
Phil 6327.4.21A Truth and reality. (Rank, Otto.) N.Y., 1936.
Phil 4752.2.77A Truth and revelation. (Berdiaev, Nikolai Aleksandrovich.) London, 1953.
Phil 5049.20.3 Truth and symbol. (Jaspers, Karl.) N.Y., 1959.
Phil 8580.21 Truth and the faith. (Alexander, H.B.) N.Y., 1929.
Phil 5190.37 Truth-functional logic. (Faris, John A.) London, 1962.
Htn Phil 9355.2.9* The truth of our times. (Peacham, Henry.) London, 1638.
Phil 9355.2.10 The truth of our times. (Peacham, Henry.) N.Y., 1942.
Phil 8584.5.3 The truth of religion. (Eucken, Rudolf.) N.Y., 1911.
Phil 7069.20.170 The truth of spiritualism. (Humphreys, Eliza Margaret J.G.) Philadelphia, 1920.
Phil 187.44.5 The truth of things. (Mann, William E.) Boston, 1922.
Phil 720.6 Truth on trial. (Carus, P.) Chicago, 1910.
NEDL Phil 29.6 The truth promotor. v.1-3. London, 1849-55.
Phil 29.25 Truth-seeker, or Present eye. London. 1849
Phil 8610.876 Truth seeker tracts upon a variety of subjects by different authors. v.2-4. N.Y., 1876-77. 3v.
Phil 720.45 The truth that frees. (Smith, Gerard.) Milwaukee, 1956.
Phil 8697.25.2 Truths in tension. 1. ed. (Habgood, J.S.) N.Y., 1965.
Phil 7068.76.10 The truths of spiritualism. (Wilson, Ebenezer V.) Chicago, 1876.
Phil 7068.96.20 The truths of spiritualism. (Wilson, Ebenezer V.) Chicago, 1896.
Phil 8597.49 Truths to live by. (Ross, John Elliot.) N.Y., 1929.
Phil 182.55 The truths we live by. (Hudson, Jay W.) N.Y., 1921.
Phil 5190.35 Try abo chotyry zakony diialektyky. (Korchyns'ka, H.) Miunkhen, 1956.
Htn Phil 6480.15* Tryon, T. A treatise of dreams and visions. London, 168-.
Phil 4803.241.90 Trzebuchowski, Pavel. Filozofia pracy Stanisława Brzozowskiego. Wyd. 1. Warszawa, 1971.
Phil 8419.50.10 Tržiště estetiky. Vyd. 1. (Šindelář, Dušan.) Praha, 1969.
Phil 4757.5 Tsallaev, Khariton K. Filosofskie i obshchestvenno-politicheskie vozzreniia Afanasiia Gassieva. Ordzhonikidze, 1966.
Phil 3501.4 Tsanoff, P.A. Schopenhauer's criticism of Kant's Theory of experience. N.Y., 1911.
Phil 8844.4 Tsanoff, R.A. The moral ideals of our civilization. N.Y., 1942.
Phil 8620.37 Tsanoff, R.A. The nature of evil. N.Y., 1931.
Phil 8644.9 Tsanoff, R.A. The problem of immortality. N.Y., 1924.
Phil 8599.32 Tsanoff, R.A. Religious corssroads. N.Y., 1942.
Phil 585.148 Tsanoff, Radoslav. Science and human perspectives. London, 1963.
Phil 585.147 Tsanoff, Radoslav. Worlds to know. N.Y., 1962.
Phil 8894.32 Tsanoff, Radoslov A. Ethics. N.Y., 1947.
Phil 8894.32.5 Tsanoff, Radoslov A. Ethics. N.Y., 1955.
Phil 310.551 Tsaregorodtsev, Gennadi I. Dialekticheskii materializm i meditsina. Moskva, 1963.
Phil 310.551.2 Tsaregorodtsev, Gennadi I. Dialekticheskii materializm i meditsina. 2. Izd. Moskva, 1966.
Phil 4752.2.50 Tsarstvo dukha i tsarstvo kesaria. (Berdiaev, Nikolai Aleksandrovich.) Parizh, 1951.
Phil 1124.5 Tsatsos, K. He koinonikē filosofia tōn arkhaion Hellēnon. Athenai, 1938.
Phil 585.300 Tsatsos, Kōnstantinos. Aphorismoí kaí dialogismoí. v.1-2. Athens, 1965-68.

Phil 5643.8.30   Tscherning, M. Herman von Helmholtz und der Akkommodationstheorie. Leipzig, 1910.

Phil 3890.2.30   Tschirnhaus, E.W. von. Medicina mentis. Lipsiae, 1695.

Phil 3808.121   Tschofen, Johann. Die Philosophie Arthur Schopenhauers. München, 1879.

Phil 9560.9   Tschubrovitz, P. Die Entwicklung der Moraltugenden. Leipzig, 1911.

Phil 2419.5   Tsebenko, M.D. Der Atheismus der französischen Materialisten des 18. Jarhunderts. 1. Aufl. Berlin, 1956.

Phil 8414.5   Tsel ili samotselnost na izkustvoto. (Natev, A.) Sofiia, 1960.

Phil 179.16   Tsel tvorchestva. (Erberg, K.) Moskva, 1913.

Phil 8735.61   Tselesoobraznost' i tsel' v obshchestvennom razvitii. (Kazakevich, Tat'iana A.) Leningrad, 1969.

Phil 8980.850   Tselikova, Ol'ga P. Kommunisticheskii ideal i nravstvennoe razvitie lichnosti. Moskva, 1970.

Phil 8181.2   Tsenkov, Boris. Iz istoriiata na esteticheskata misul v Bulgariia. Sofiia, 1964.

Phil 4761.2.40   Tserkov', lichnost' i gosudarstvo. (Karsavin, L.P.) Parizh, 1927.

Phil 735.284   Tseunoi real'nye i mnimye. (Anisimov, Sergei F.) Moskva, 1970.

Phil 8897.40   Tsing Hua lectures on ethics. (Walcott, Gregory.) Boston, 1919.

Phil 1200.39   Tsirimbas, Antonios. Die Allgemeinen pädagogischen Gedanken der alten Stoa. Inaug. Diss. München, 1936.

Phil 4890.10   Tsuchida, Kyoson. Contemporary thought of Japan and China. London, 1927.

Phil 4890.10.2   Tsuchida, Kyoson. Contemporary thought of Japan and China. N.Y., 1927.

Phil 5645.49   Tsvetovoe zrenie. (Kravkou, S.V.) Moskva, 1951.

Phil 29.30   Tu sei me; filosofia dell'unicita. Milano. 1,1956+ 13v.

Phil 7069.35   Tubby, G.O. Psychics and mediums. Boston, 1935.

Phil 930.5   Tucci, G. Storia della filosofia cinese antica. Bologna, 1912.

Phil 960.205   Tucci, Giuseppe. Storia della filosofia Indiana. Bari, 1957.

Phil 5722.30   Tucci, Giuseppe. Teoria e practica del Mandala. Roma, 1949.

Phil 5722.30.5   Tucci, Giuseppe. The theory and practice of the Mandala. London, 1961.

Phil 5722.30.6   Tucci, Giuseppe. The theory and practice of the Mandala. London, 1969.

Phil 3565.129   Tuch, Ernst. Lotzes Stellung zum Occasionalismus. Berlin, 1897.

Phil 8693.20.15   Tuchel, K. Die Philosophie der Technik. Frankfurt, 1964.

Phil 2300.30.15   Tucker, Abraham. An abridgment of the Light of nature pursued. London, 1807.

Htn   Phil 2300.40*   Tucker, Abraham. Freewill, foreknowledge. v.1-2. London, 1763.

Phil 2300.30.5   Tucker, Abraham. Light of nature pursued. Cambridge, 1831. 4v.

Phil 2300.30.2   Tucker, Abraham. Light of nature pursued. London, 1768. 5v.

Phil 2300.30   Tucker, Abraham. Light of nature pursued. London, 1768-77. 7v.

Phil 2300.30.3   Tucker, Abraham. Light of nature pursued. London, 1805. 7v.

Phil 8644.8   Tucker, C.C. On the doctrine of personal identity. London, 1909.

Phil 8709.4   Tucker, G.M. A layman's apology. Boston, 1913.

Phil 9490.5   Tucker, W.J. Personal power counsels to college men. Boston, 1910.

Phil 9045.7   Tucker, W.J. Public mindedness, an aspect of citizenship. Concord, 1910.

Phil 7060.91.5   Tuckett, I.L. The evidence for the supernatural. London, 1911.

Phil 6689.3   Tuckey, C.L. Psycho-therapeutics. London, 1890.

Phil 6689.3.5   Tuckey, C.L. Treatment by hypnotism and suggestion. 6. ed. London, 1913.

Phil 194.51   Tucuman, Argentina. Tornadas de filosofia, 21 al 26 de mayo de 1961. Tucuman, 1961.

Phil 59.5   Tucumán. Universidad Nacional. Facultad de Filosofía y Letras. Cuadernos de filosofía. Tucumán. 1,1942+ 7v.

Phil 2070.136   A tudatalatti világ: William James lélektanában. (Biró, B.) Szeged, 1929.

Phil 5768.4   Tübingen, Germany. Universität. Verzeichnies der Doctoren: Begriff der Wollens...von C. Sigwart. Tübingen, 1879.

Phil 176.69.5   Tübinger Einleitung in die Philosophie. (Bloch, Ernst.) Berlin, 1923.

Phil 3120.55.55   Tübinger Einleitung in die Philosophie I. (Bloch, Ernst.) Frankfurt, 1963.

Phil 5425.15   Türck, H. Der geniale Mensch. Berlin, 1899.

Phil 5425.15.10   Türck, H. Der geniale Mensch. 8. Aufl. Berlin, 1917.

Phil 5425.15.15   Türck, H. Der geniale Mensch. 10. Aufl. Berlin, 1920?

Phil 3640.99   Türck, Hermann. Friedrich Nietzsche und seine philosophischen Irrewege. München, 1894.

Phil 3270.1.83   Türck, Hermann. Meine Erfahrungen mit Kuno Fischer. Jena, 1895.

Phil 8844.3   Tufts, J.H. The individual and his relation to society. N.Y., 1904.

Phil 310.85   Tugarinov, V.P. Sootnoshenie kategorii istorichesk0go materializma. Leningrad, 1958.

Phil 5374.282   Tugarinov, Vasilii P. Filosifiia soznaniia. Moskva, 1971.

Phil 8980.851.5   Tugarinov, Vasilii P. Lichnost' i obshchestvo. Moskva, 1965.

Phil 8980.851   Tugarinov, Vasilii P. O tsennostiakh zhizni i kul'tury. Leningrad, 1960.

Phil 3496.3   Der Tugendbegriff bei Kant. Inaug. Diss. (Orestano, F.) Palermo, 1901.

Phil 3450.11.405   Tugendhat, Ernst. Der Wahrheitsbegriff bei Husserl und Heidegger. Berlin, 1967.

Phil 3805.182   Die Tugendlehre Schleiermachers. (Kroker, P.) Erlangen, 1889.

Phil 3832.2   Die Tugendlehre Spinoza's. (Meyer, M.) Fleusburg, 1885.

Phil 8674.14   Tugov, Iu.M. Osnovy nauchnogo ateizma. Moskva, 1959.

Phil 6329.6   Tuinstra, C.L. Het symbool in de psychoanalyse. Amsterdam, 1933.

Phil 978.13   Tukarama Tatya. A guide to theosophy. Bombay, 1887.

Phil 6129.3.3   Tuke, D.H. Geist und Körper. Jena, 1888.

Phil 6129.3   Tuke, D.H. Illustration of the mind upon the body. London, 1872.

Phil 6129.3.2   Tuke, D.H. Illustration of the mind upon the body. 2d ed. Philadelphia, 1884.

Phil 6969.5   Tuke, Daniel H. Insanity in ancient and modern life. London, 1878.

Htn   Phil 9359.7*   Tuke, Thomas. A discourse against painting...of women. London, 1616.

Htn   Phil 9359.7.5*   Tuke, Thomas. A treatise against painting...of men and women. London, 1616.

Phil 8894.29   Tuker, M.A.R. Past and future of ethics. London, 1938.

Phil 5829.16   Tukh, Nina A. Predystoniia obshehestva. Leningrad, 1970.

Phil 29.20   Tulane studies in philosophy. New Orleans. 1,1952+ 6v.

Phil 310.265   Tulenov, Z. Zakon kak filosofskaia kategoriia. Alma-Ata, 1959.

Phil 8622.55   Tülilä, Osmo. Epäilyksistä uskoon. Helsinki, 1963.

Phil 5625.85   Tullio, P. I riflessi orientative nella studio delle attività mentali. Bologna, 1938.

Phil 5650.18   Tullio, Pietro. L'orecchio. Bologna, 1928.

Phil 2805.86   Tulloch, J. Pascal. Edinburgh, 1878.

Phil 2805.86.5   Tulloch, J. Pascal. Edinburgh, 1878.

Phil 8599.7   Tulloch, J. Theism. Edinburgh, 1855.

Phil 8599.12   Tulloch, John. Rational theology and Christian philosophy in England in the 17th century. Edinburgh, 1872. 2v.

Phil 1719.2   Tullock, J. Modern theories in philosophy and religion. Edinburgh, 1884.

Phil 8419.39.5   Tumarkin, Anna. Der Ästhetiker Johann G. Sulzer. Frauenfeld, 1933.

Phil 5259.15.10   Tumarkin, Anna. Die Methoden der psychologischen Forschung. Leipzig, 1929.

Phil 5259.15   Tumarkin, Anna. Prolegomena zu einer wissenschaftliche Psychologie. Leipzig, 1923.

Phil 2980.5   Tumarkin, Anna. Wesen und Werden der schweizerischen Philosophie. Frauenfeld, 1948.

Phil 8599.8   Tunstall, J. Lectures on natural and revealed religion. London, 1765.

Phil 300.2   Tunzelmann, G.W. de. Treatise on electrical theory and problem of universe. London, 1910.

Phil 8709.5   Tupper, Martin F. Probabilities; an aid to faith. N.Y., 1847.

Phil 4235.2.79   Pamphlet box. Turamini, Alessandro.

Phil 3235.87   Turban, Theodor. Das Wesen des Christentumes von Ludwig Feuerbach. Inaug. Diss. Karlsruhe, 1894.

Phil 5520.395   Turbayne, C.M. The myth of metaphor. New Haven, 1962.

Phil 2733.96   Turbiglio, S. Le antitesi...in specie nella dottrina...di Malebranche. Roma, 1877.

Phil 3839.4   Turbiglio, S. Benedetto Spinoza. v.3. Roma, 1874.

Phil 5425.15.27   Türck, H. The man of genius. London, 1923.

Phil 6329.2.5   Turco, Natale. Il trattamento morale dello scrupole e dell'ossessione morbossa. Torino, 1919-20. 2v.

Phil 6329.12   Turel, Adrien. Bachofen-Freud. Bern, 1939.

Phil 6329.12.5.2   Turel, Adrien. Selbsterlösung. 1. und 2. Aufl. Berlin, 1919.

Phil 3428.83   Turic, G. Der Entschluss im dem Herbarts Metaphysik. Langensalza, 1892.

Phil 8644.12.5   Turk, Morris H. They live and are not far away. N.Y., 1923.

Phil 8644.10   Turlot, F.C. Études sur la théorie de l'avenir. Paris, 1810. 2v.

Phil 4065.93   Turnbull, C. Life and teachings of Giordano Bruno, 1548-1600. San Diego, 1913.

Phil 8894.10   Turnbull, G. The principles of moral philosophy. London, 1740. 2v.

Phil 8844.2   Turner, Arthur T. A new morality. London, 1904.

Phil 8894.36   Turner, Dean. The autonomous man. St. Louis, 1970.

Phil 8644.3   Turner, F.H. Beside the new-made grave. Boston, 1906.

Phil 350.2   Turner, F.S. Knowledge, belief and certitude. London, 1900.

Phil 5769.4   Turner, G.L. Wish and will. London, 1880.

Phil 8599.23   Turner, J.E. Essentials in the development of religion. London, 1934.

Phil 2070.119   Turner, J.E. An examination of William James's philosophy. Oxford, 1919.

Phil 8674.8.7   Turner, J.E. The nature of deity; a sequel to Personality and reality. London, 1927.

Phil 8674.8   Turner, J.E. Personality and reality. N.Y., 1926.

Phil 8894.24   Turner, J.E. The philosophic basis of moral obligation; a study in ethics. London, 1924.

Phil 8674.8.15   Turner, J.E. The revelation of deity. London, 1931.

Phil 630.29.5   Turner, J.E. A theory of direct realism and the relation of realism to idealism. N.Y., 1925.

Phil 400.5.5   Turner, J.P. Idealistic beginnings in England. n.p., 1910.

Phil 6329.4   Turner, Julia. The psychology of self-consciousness. London, 1923.

Phil 8610.899.55   Turner, M.M. (Mrs.). The Bible God, Bible teachings. N.Y., 1899.

Phil 5259.58   Turner, Merle. Philosophy and the science of behavior. N.Y., 1967.

Phil 8709.14.10   Turner, Sharon. The sacred history of the world. N.Y., 1835-36. 2v.

Phil 8709.14.8   Turner, Sharon. The sacred history of the world. N.Y., 1835-39. 3v.

Phil 8709.14.6   Turner, Sharon. The sacred history of the world. v.1. N.Y., 1833.

Phil 8709.14.5   Turner, Sharon. The sacred history of the world. 3. ed. London, 1833. 2v.

Phil 819.5.2   Turner, W. History of philosophy. Boston, 1903.

Phil 819.5.7   Turner, W. History of philosophy. Boston, 1929.

Phil 5059.12   Turner, W. Lessons in logic. Washington, 1911.

Phil 3625.14.90   Turner, William D. Georg Elias Müller. Cambridge, 1928.

Phil 5059.11   Turrell, H.J. A manual of logic. London, 1870.

Phil 350.4   Turró, R. La base trofica de la intelegencia. Madrid, 1918.

Phil 194.26   Turró, R. Filosofia critica. 1a ed. Madrid, 1919.

Phil 5374.20   Turró, R. Origines de la connaissance. Paris, 1914.

Phil 8599.9   Turton, Thomas. Natural theology considered with reference to Lord Brougham's discourse on that subject. 2. ed. Cambridge, 1836.

Phil 8599.9.5   Turton, Thomas. Natural theology considered with reference to Lord Brougham's discourse on that subject. 2. ed. London, 1836.

Phil 7060.253   Turvey, Vincent N. The beginnings of seership. London, 1911.

Phil 3501.24   Tuschling, Burkhard. Metaphysische und transzendentale Dynamik in Kants opus postumum. Berlin, 1971.

Phil 8709.19   Tute, Richard C. After materialism - what? 1. ed. N.Y., 1945.

Phil 4260.17.5   Tutte le opere di Giambattista Vico. (Vico, G.B.) Milano, 1957.

Phil 7054.116.2   Tuttle, H. Arcana of nature. London, 1909.

Phil 7054.116.7   Tuttle, H. Arcana of spiritualism. Chicago, 1934.

Phil 7054.116.5   Tuttle, H. Scenes in the spirit world. N.Y., 1855.

Phil 7060.99 — Tuttle, H. Studies in outlying fields of psychic science. N.Y., 1889.

Phil 3195.6.205 — Tuttle, Howard Nelson. Wilhelm Dilthey's philosophy of historical understanding. Leiden, 1969.

Phil 7069.00.40 — Tuttle, Hudson. Arcana of spiritualism. Manchester, 1900.

Phil 8610.878.10 — Tuttle, Hudson. Career of religious ideas. N.Y., 1878.

Phil 8674.6 — Tuttle, Hudson. Evolution of the God and Christ ideas. Berlin, 1906.

Phil 7069.00.53 — Tuttle, Hudson. Mediumship and its laws. 3. ed. Chicago, 1900.

Phil 8709.8 — Tuttle, Hudson. Religion of man and ethics of science. Chicago, 1902.

Phil 4110.10.30 — Il tutto e il nulla. 1. ed. (Fabi, Bruno.) Milano, 1952.

Phil 5170.11 — Tuțugan, F. Silogistica judecaților de predicație. Bucuresti, 1957.

Phil 4773.5 — Tutundzhian, Ovsep. Psikhologicheskaja kontseptsiia Anri Vallona. Erevan, 1966.

Phil 2115.180 — Tuveson, E.L. The imagination as a means of grace. Berkeley, 1960.

Phil 5875.110.5 — Tuvo, Fulvio. Il disegno nella psicopatologia dell'età evolutiva. Trieste, 1966.

Phil 310.23 — Tuzarinov, V.P. Sootnoshenii kategorii dialekticheskoi marksizma. Leningrad, 1956.

Phil 300.13 — Tuzet, Hélène. Le cosmos et l'imagination. Paris, 1965.

Phil 4515.81 — Tvänne uppsatser om den Boströmska filosofien. (Nyblâeus, A.) Lund, 1885.

Phil 8674.16 — Tvethoworn, Illtyd. Absolute value: a study in Christian theism. London, 1970.

Phil 8170.5 — Tvorit' mir po zakonam krasoty. (Rappoport, S.Kh.) Moskva, 1962.

Phil 2050.187 — Tvrdý, Josef. Problém skutečnosti u Davida Huma. Brno, 1925.

Phil 2520.84.5 — Twardowski, K. Idee und Perception. Wien, 1892.

Phil 350.1 — Twardowski, K. Zur Lehre von Inhalt und Gegenstand. Wien, 1894.

Phil 194.41 — Twardowski, Kazimierz. Rozprawy i artykuły filozoficzne. Livów, 1927.

Phil 4803.854.20 — Twardowski, Kazimierz. Wybrane pisma filozoficzne. Warszawa, 1965.

Phil 7060.151.5 — Tweedale, C.L. Man's survival after death. 2. ed. London, 1920.

Phil 7069.40.8 — Tweedale, C.L. News from the next world. London, 1940.

Phil 7069.21.60 — Tweedale, Charles L. Man's survival after death. N.Y., 1921?

Phil 7060.151 — Tweedale, V.C. Ghosts I have seen. N.Y., 1919.

Phil 6969.12 — Tweedie, D.F. Logotherapy and the Christian faith. Grands Rapids, 1961.

Phil 190.60 — Tweeërlei subjectiviteit. (Poortman, J.J.) Haarlem, 1929.

Phil 1504.32 — Twelfth century logic. (Minio-Palvello, Lorenzo.) Roma, 1956- 2v.

Phil 8712.13.1 — Twelve lectures on the connexion between science and revealed religion. (Wiseman, N.P.S.) Andover, 1837.

Phil 8712.13.2 — Twelve lectures on the connexion between science and revealed religion. 2. ed. (Wiseman, N.P.S.) London, 1842.

Phil 8712.13.8 — Twelve lectures on the connexion between science and revealed religion. 4. ed. (Wiseman, N.P.S.) Baltimore, 1852. 2v.

Phil 7069.19.30 — Twelve lessons from the seven purposes. (Cameron, Margaret.) N.Y., 1919.

Phil 7054.56 — Twelve messages from the spirit. (Adams, John Quincy.) Boston, 1859.

Phil 6027.1.8 — The twelve qualities of mind...physiognomy. no. 11. (Redfield, J.W.) N.Y., 1850.

Phil 8587.41 — The twentieth century Christ. (Hatch, D.P.) Boston, 1906.

Phil 6051.18 — Twentieth century guide to palmistry. (Zancing, Julius.) Chicago, n.d.

Phil 1740.4 — Twentieth century philosophy; living schools of thought. (Runes, Dagobert D.) N.Y., 1943.

Phil 7159.8 — Twentieth century prophecy: Jeane Dixon, Edgar Cayce. (Bjornstad, James.) Minneapolis, 1969.

Phil 5247.61 — Twentieth century psychology. (Harriman, P.L.) N.Y., 1946.

Phil 8592.11 — Twentieth century religion. (Mills, B.F.) Boston, 1898.

Phil 8520.44 — Twentieth century religious thought. (Macquarrie, J.) London, 1963.

Phil 7069.19.240 — The twentieth plane. (Watson, Albert D.) Philadelphia, 1919.

Phil 1050.27.5 — Twenty centuries of Jewish thought. (Lichtigfeld, A.) London, 1937.

Phil 6990.3.42 — Twenty cures at Lourdes. (Grandmaison de Bruno, F.) St. Louis, 1912.

Phil 6951.5.12 — Twenty-five years of mental hygiene; a tribute to C.W. Beers. (Farrar, C.B.) n.p., 1933.

Phil 525.32 — Twenty minutes of reality. (Montague, M.P.) N.Y., 1917.

Phil 9347.13 — Twenty-one. (Harris, Erdman.) N.Y., 1931.

Phil 7068.94.25 — Twenty photographs of the risen dead. (Wilmot, T.S.) Lonon, 1894.

Phil 7060.92.41 — Twenty years' experience as a ghost hunter. (O'Donnell, Elliot.) London, 1916.

Phil 24.1.5 — Twenty Years of The Open Court. An index, 1887-1906. Chicago, 1907.

Phil 7069.08.45 — The twice-born. London, 1906.

Phil 5627.15 — Twice-born men, a clinic in regeneration. (Begbie, H.) N.Y., 1909.

Phil 8598.47 — Twijfel als psychologisch verschijnsel in het religieuse leven. (Stegenga, P.) Amsterdam, 1924.

Phil 8581.87 — The twilight of Christianity. (Barnes, H.E.) N.Y., 1929.

Phil 2750.11.45.5 — The twilight of civilization. (Maritain, Jacques.) N.Y., 1943.

Phil 8610.923.10 — The twilight of the gods. (McCabe, Joseph.) London, 1923.

Phil! 5871.5 — Twins and supertwins. (Scheinfeld, Amram.) Philadelphia, 1967.

Phil 5871.5.5 — The twins who found each other. (Lindeman, Bard.) N.Y., 1969.

Phil 7068.86.10F — Twixt two worlds. (Farmer, John S.) London, 1886.

Phil 2270.160 — Two (pseud.) Home life with Herbert Spencer. Bristol, 1906.

Phil 8595.16.27.7 — Two apologies, one for Christianity. (Watson, R.) London, 1818.

Phil 7054.91 — Two appeals to the leaders of spiritualism. (Parisi, G.) Florence, 1871.

Htn — Phil 1850.31* — The two books of proficience and advancement of learning. (Bacon, Francis.) London, 1605.

Htn — Phil 665.12.2* — Two choice and useful treatises: Lux orientalis and A discourse of truth, by Dr. Rust. (Glanvill, Joseph.) London, 1682.

Phil 8876.123 — Two concepts of liberty. (Berlin, Isaiah.) Oxford, 1958.

Phil 1905.30.30 — Two concepts of liberty. (Berlin, Isaiah.) Oxford, 1959.

Htn — Phil 5242.18.2* — Two discourses. 2. ed. (Charleton, Walter.) London, 1675.

Htn — Phil 5640.29* — Two dissertations concerning sense and the imagination. (Mayne, Zachary.) London, 1728.

Phil 8403.16 — Two essays. (Cameron, Charles.) London, 1835.

Phil 3808.51.5 — Two essays. (Schopenhauer, Arthur.) London, 1889[1888]

Phil 6319.1.13 — Two essays on analytical psychology. (Jung, C.G.) London, 1928.

Phil 6319.1.14 — Two essays on analytical psychology. (Jung, C.G.) N.Y., 1928.

Phil 510.1.35 — Two essays on Haeckel. (Steiner, R.) London, 19- .

Phil 5585.145 — The two faces of man. (Murloo, Abraham.) N.Y., 1954.

Phil 1870.86 — The two-hundredth birthday of Bishop George Berkeley. (Porter, N.) N.Y., 1885.

Phil 7059.12.5 — Two in one...spiritualism of the Bible settled. (Hull, Moses.) Chicago, 1895.

Phil 735.252 — Two kinds of values. (Loring, L.M.) London, 1966.

Phil 7054.86 — Two lectures on the present crisis. (Hatch, Cora L.V.) N.Y., 1860.

Phil 8673.17 — Two lectures on theism delivered on the occasion of the sesquicentennial celebration of Princeton University. (Seth, A.) N.Y., 1897.

Phil 5757.1.6 — Two letters on causation and freedom. (Hazard, R.G.) Boston, 1869.

Phil 5061.10 — Two logics. (Veatch, Henry B.) Evanston, 1969.

Phil 8961.12 — The two moralities: our duty to God and society. (Lindsay, A.D.) London, 1940.

Phil 720.26 — Two neglected aspects of the truth situation. Thesis. (Kearney, C.M.) Chicago, 1933.

Phil 384.30 — Two new studies in moral philosophy. (Ofstad, Harald.) Stockholm, 1967.

Phil 8593.19 — Two popular philosophic-scientific essays in the spirit of faith and religion. (Nass, R.B.) Brooklyn, N.Y., 1943.

Phil 8702.6.25 — The two records: The mosaic and the geological. (Miller, H.) Boston, 1854.

Phil 1607.10 — The two reformations in the 16th century. (Gelder, Herman Arend Enno van.) The Hague, 1961.

Phil 6120.11 — Two remarkable lectures. (Knowlton, C.) Boston, 1833.

Phil 8708.26 — Two roads to truth. (Sinnott, Edmund Ware.) N.Y., 1953.

Phil 4752.2.160 — Two Russian thinkers: essays in Berdyaev and Shestov. (Wernham, James C.S.) Toronto, 1968.

Htn — Phil 7150.20* — Two sermons on the atrocity of suicide. (Lathrop, Joseph.) Suffield, 1805.

Phil 2475.1.38.6 — The two sources of morality and religion. (Bergson, Henri.) N.Y., 1935.

Phil 8581.66.15 — The two sources of morality and religion. (Bergson, Henri.) N.Y., 1946.

Phil 2005.9.20 — The two story world. 1st ed. (Feibleman, James.) N.Y., 1966.

Phil 1158.38 — Two studies in the Greek atomists. (Furley, David J.) Princeton, N.J., 1967.

Phil 2115.21 — Two tracts on government. (Locke, J.) Cambridge, Eng., 1967.

Htn — Phil 8628.3.2F* — Two treatises...nature of bodies...nature of man's soul. (Digby, K.) Paris, 1644.

Htn — Phil 8628.3.4* — Two treatises. (Digby, K.) London, 1645. 2 pam.

Htn — Phil 8628.3* — Two treatises. (Digby, K.) London, 1658-57.

Htn — Phil 2115.74* — Two treatises of government. (Locke, J.) London, 1690.

Phil 3120.30.68A — Two types of faith. (Buber, Martin.) London, 1951.

Phil 7069.21.10 — The two worlds of attraction. (Abbott, Anne.) Boston, 1921.

Phil 5871.85 — Two worlds of childhood: U.S. and U.S.S.R. (Bronfenbrenner, Urie.) N.Y., 1970.

Phil 5465.115 — Twórczość a osobowość twórcy. (Naksianowicz-Gołaszewska, M.) Lublin, 1958.

Phil 29.28 — Tÿdschrift voor philosophie. Leuven. 1939+ 57v.

Phil 8674.4 — Tyerman, D. Essays on the wisdom of God. London, 1818.

Phil 8599.10.6 — Tyler, Charles Mellen. Bases of religious belief. N.Y., 1897.

Phil 8599.10 — Tyler, Charles Mellon. The study of the history and philosophy of religion. Ithica, N.Y., 1891.

Phil 365.37 — Tyler, J.M. The place of the church in evolution. Boston, 1914.

Phil 5259.34 — Tyler, Leona E. The psychology of human differences. N.Y., 1947.

Phil 5272.26.2 — Tyler, Leona Elizabeth. Tests and measurements. 2d ed. Englewood Cliffs, 1971.

Phil 5853.10.3 — Tyler, Leona Elizabeth. The work of the counselor. 3d ed. N.Y., 1969.

Phil 1850.89 — Tyler, S. Discourse of the Baconian philosophy. Frederick City, 1844.

Phil 1850.89.2 — Tyler, S. Discourse of the Baconian philosophy. Frederick City, 1846.

Phil 1850.89.3 — Tyler, S. Discourse of the Baconian philosophy. N.Y., 1850.

Phil 1850.89.5 — Tyler, S. Discourse of the Baconian philosophy. 3rd ed. Washington, 1877.

Phil 819.6 — Tyler, S. The progress of philosophy. Philadelphia, 1888.

Phil 8599.20.2 — Tyler, W.F. The dimensional idea as an aid to religion. London, 1907.

Phil 8599.20 — Tyler, W.F. The dimensional idea as an aid to religion. N.Y., 1910.

Phil 165.351 — Tymienicka, Anna Teresa. Contributions to logic and methodology in honor of J.M. Bochenski. Amsterdam, 1965.

Phil 4803.462.80 — Tymienicka, Anna Teresa. Essence et existence. Paris, 1957.

Phil 1750.101 — Tymienicka, Anna Teresa. Phenomenology and science in contemporary European thought. N.Y., 1962.

Phil 1750.101.5 — Tymienicka, Anna Teresa. Why is there something rather than nothing? Assen, 1966.

Phil 3552.447 — Tymierniecka, A.T. Leibniz' cosmological synthesis. Assen, 1966.

Phil 8709.2.4 — Tyndall, John. Address...before British association. N.Y., 1875.

Phil 8709.2 — Tyndall, John. Address. Cambridge, 1874. 2 pam.

Phil 8709.2.9 — Tyndall, John. Address. N.Y., 1874.

Htn — Phil 2305.2.30* — Tyndall, John. Address before...British association at Belfast. London, 1874.

Phil 8709.2.13 — Tyndall, John. Advancement of science. N.Y., 1874.

Phil 8709.2.14 — Tyndall, John. Advancement of science. N.Y., 1874.

Phil 5520.44 — Type crossings. (Drange, Theodore.) The Hague, 1966.

Phil 6022.4.10 — Typen; Grundlagen der Charakterkunde. (Märker, Friedrich.) Erlenbach, 1931.

Phil 8826.7 — Typen van zedelee. (Banning, Willem.) Haarlem, 1965.

Phil 3195.6.85 — Die Typenlehre Trendelenburgs und ihr Einfluss auf Dilthey. (Wach, Joachim.) Tübingen, 1926.

Phil 818.2.5 — Types af den filosofiske bankings historie. (Starcke, C.N.) København, 1918.

Phil 187.133   Types and problems of philosophy. (Mead, Hunter.) N.Y., 1946.

Phil 8402.16   Types of aesthetic judgment. (Bartlett, E.M.) London, 1937.

Phil 8887.4   Types of ethical theory. (Martineau, J.) Oxford, 1885.

Htn   Phil 2150.2.30*   Types of ethical theory. (Martineau, James.) Oxford, 1885. 2v.

Phil 8887.4.5   Types of ethical theory. v.1-2. 3. ed. (Martineau, J.) Oxford, 1891.

Phil 8887.4.3   Types of ethical theory. 2. ed. (Martineau, J.) Oxford, 1886. 2v.

Phil 8887.4.2   Types of ethical theory. 2. ed. (Martineau, J.) Oxford, 1886. 2v.

Phil 8887.4.10   Types of ethical theory. 3. ed. (Martineau, J.) Oxford, 1901. 2v.

Phil 420.2   Types of intuition. (Bahm, Archie J.) Albuquerque, 1960[1961]

Phil 1020.55   Types of Islamic thought in criticism and reconstruction. (Kamali, Sabin Ahmad.) Aligarh, 1963.

Phil 5258.74.9A   Types of men. (Spranger, Eduard.) Halle, 1928.

Phil 182.88A   Types of philosophy. (Hocking, W.E.) N.Y., 1929.

Phil 182.88.7A   Types of philosophy. (Hocking, W.E.) N.Y., 1939.

Phil 182.88.3   Types of philosophy. 3d ed. (Hocking, W.E.) N.Y., 1959.

Phil 8581.76   Types of religious philosophy. 1. ed. (Burtt, Edwin A.) N.Y., 1939.

Phil 186.156   Types of world views; an introduction to metaphysics. Typescript. (Losskii, N.O.) n.p., n.d.

Phil 2125.60   Typical forms and special ends in creation. (McCosh, James.) Edinburgh, 1857.

Phil 5050.8   Typical methods of thinking. (Kells, S.C.) N.Y., 1910.

Phil 8666.5   Typical modern conceptions of God. (Leighton, J.A.) N.Y., 1901.

Phil 5751.4   Typical recent conceptions of freedom. Thesis. (Bussey, Gertrude C.) Greenfield, 1917.

Phil 6315.60   Typologies of delinquency. (Ferdinand, Theodore N.) N.Y., 1966.

Phil 5247.52   Der Typus Begriff im Lichte der neuen Logik. (Hempel, Carl G.) Leiden, 1936.

Phil 5245.38   The tyranny of the mind. (Fuller, B.) London, 1935.

Phil 672.166   The tyranny of time. (Allen, Chalinder.) N.Y., 1947.

Phil 672.142.5   The tyranny of time. (Nordmann, Charles.) London, 1925.

Phil 5520.68.3   The tyranny of words. (Chase, Stuart.) N.Y., 1938.

Phil 5259.42   Tyrrell, G.N.M. Homo faber. London, 1952.

Phil 7069.38.60   Tyrrell, G.N.M. Science and psychical phenomena. London, 1938.

Phil 7069.42.10   Tyrrell, George N.M. Apparitions. London, 1942?

Phil 7069.42.12   Tyrrell, George N.M. Apparitions. London, 1953.

Phil 7069.47.30   Tyrrell, George N.M. The personality of man. W. Drayton, 1948.

Phil 4800.8   Tyszyński, Aleksander. Piérwsze zasady krytyki powszechnéj. v.1-2. Warszawa, 1870.

Phil 2805.251   Tytgat, J. Pascal. Gand, 1948.

Htn   Phil 8595.16.13*   Tytler, James. Paine's second part of The age of reason answered. Salem, 1796.

Phil 30.1.5   U.L.T. pamphlet. (United Lodge of Theosophists.) Bombay.

Phil 6946.42   U.S. President's Task Force on the Mentally Handicapped. Action against mental disability; the report. Washington, 1970.

Phil 2401.16   U istokov frantsuzskogo ateizma i materializma. (Boguslavskii, Veniamin M.) Moskva, 1964.

Phil 8430.90   U istokov sovetskoi khudozhestvennoi kritiki. (Pavlovskii, Boris V.) Leningrad, 1970.

Phil 8980.895   U istokov zhiznennogo puti. (Zemlianskii, D.S.) Moskva, 1962.

Phil 4803.462.10   U podsław sevrii poznania. Wyd. 1. (Ingarden, Roman.) Warszawa, 1971.

Phil 8415.2   U podstaw estetyki. Wyd. 3. (Ossowski, S.) Warszawa, 1958.

VPhil 3450.11.385   U podstaw fenomenologii Husserla. (Martel, Karol.) Warszawa, 1967.

Phil 8585.45   U tserkovnoi ogrady. (Fedorov, N.I.) Buenos Aires, 1955.

Phil 8615.18   U znaku preporoda. Odjek Vivodićevoj pokreta. (Petrović, E.) Sarajevo, 1928.

Phil 5060.5   Ubahgs, G.C. Logicae seu philosophiae rationalis elementa. 6. ed. Lovanii, 1860.

Phil 2070.85   Ubbink, J.G. Het pragmatisme van William James. Arnhem, 1912.

Phil 6319.1.36   Uber die Psychologie des Unbewussten. 5. Aufl. (Jung, C.G.) Zürich, 1943.

Phil 850.18   Uber die Unanationslehre im Übergange aus der Alterlhümlichen in die christliche Denkeweise. (Ritter, Heinrich.) Göttingen, 1847.

Phil 3002.6   Uber französische und deutsche Philosophie. (Cousin, Victor.) Stuttgart, 1834.

Phil 8418.2   Uber Naturschilderung. (Ratzel, Friedrich.) München, 1904.

Phil 3805.270   Der Ubergang. 1. Aufl. (Miller, Marlin E.) Gütersloh, 1970.

Phil 1123.1   Ubersicht über die griechische Philosophie. (Schulze, E.) Leipzig, 1886.

Phil 4753.1.35   Uchebnik logiki. (Chelpanov, G.) Kharbin, 1921.

Phil 3425.746   Uchenie Gegelia o gosudarstve i sovremennost. (Man'kovski, Boris S.) Moskva, 1970.

Phil 3425.554.5   Uchenie Gegelia o prave i gosudarstve i ego ugolovno-pravovaia teoriia. (Piontkovskii, A.A.) Moskva, 1963.

Phil 4769.6.83   Uchenie I.M. Sechenova ob obshchushchenii i myshlenii. (Budilova, E.A.) Moskva, 1924.

Phil 3500.103   Uchenie Kanta o veshchi vě sebe. (Shcherbina, A.M.) n.p., n.d.

Phil 5040.22.5   Uchenie logiki o dokazatel'stvi oprovrrzheniia. (Asmus, V.F.) Moskva, 1954.

Phil 310.779   Uchenie o dialektike v burzhnarnoi filosofii XX veka. (Kissel', Mikhail A.) Leningrad, 1970.

Phil 1135.81   Uchenie o Logose. (Trubetskoi, S.N.) Moskva, 1900.

Phil 1135.81.5   Uchenie o Logose. (Trubetskoi, S.N.) Moskva, 1906.

Phil 4791.4   Uchenie o prirode cheloveka v drevnei Gruzii. (Beritashvili, Ivan Solomonovich.) Tbilisi, 1961.

Phil 4710.78   Uchenie ob induktivnykh vyrodakh v istorii russkoi logiki. (Moskalenko, F.Ia.) Kiev, 1955.

Phil 310.275   Uchenie ob obshchestvennom soznanii v svete teorii poznaniia. (Gak, G.M.) Moskva, 1960.

Phil 3850.18.210   Uchiyam, Mivoru. Das Wertwidrige an der Ethik Max Schelers. Bonn, 1966.

Phil 5260.6   Ude, Johann. Einführung in die Psychologie. Graz, 1916.

Phil 365.14   Udkast til en sjaelelig bevaegelseslaere. (Lambek, C.) København, 1901-1906.

Phil 5052.11   Udsigt over den høiere logik. (Monrad, M.J.) Christiania, 1881.

Phil 5265.3F   Übbarkeit verschiedener Aufgaben. (Zapan, Georg.) München, 1932.

Phil 3890.6.84   Uebele, Wilhelm. Johann Nicolaus Tetens. Inaug. Diss. Berlin, 1911.

Htn   Phil 3495.1*   Über...kritischen Philosophie...Kant. (Nicolai, C.F.) Berlin, 1799.

Phil 5374.14   Über abstrahierende Apperception. (Mittenzwey, K.) Leipzig, 1907.

Phil 5360.1   Über abstraktion. (Maennel, B.) Gütersloh, 1890.

Phil 3528.50   Über altes und neues Christenthum. (Krug, Wilhelm Traugott.) Leipzig, 1836.

Phil 343.5.50   Über Annahmen; eine Streitschrift. (Kerler, D.H.) Ulm, 1910.

Phil 343.5   Über Annahmen. (Meinong, A.) Leipzig, 1902.

Phil 343.5.2   Über Annahmen. 2. Aufl. (Meinong, A.) Leipzig, 1910.

Phil 6127.17   Über Apparate in dem Hirn. (Rieger, Conrad.) Jena, 1909.

Phil 5374.7   Über Apperception. (Lange, K.M.) Plauen, 1879.

Phil 8412.19.15   Über Bedingungen der Kunstschönheit. (Lotze, Hermann.) Göttingen, 1847.

Phil 3791.30   Über Begriff und Form der Philosophie. (Riehl, Alois.) Berlin, 1872.

Phil 5635.1   Über Bewegungsempfindungen. (Delabarre, E.B.) Freiburg, 1891.

Phil 5593.63   Über Blutdeutungen im Rorschachschen Formdeutversuch. (Künsler, W.) Bern, 1963.

Phil 3270.6.80   Über Christian Gabriel Fischers vernünftige Gedanken von der Natur. Inaug. Diss. (Kurz, August.) Halle, 1908.

Phil 3910.81   Über Christian Wolffs Ontologie. (Richler, H.) Leipzig, 1910.

Phil 197.48.10   Über das aufschliessende Symbol. (Weinhandl, F.) Berlin, 1929.

Phil 9240.20   Über das Böse. (Welte, Bernhard.) Basel, 1959.

Phil 8620.10   Über das Böse und seine Folgen. (Ritter, H.) Cotha, 1869.

Phil 8620.10.5   Über das Böse und seine Folgen. (Ritter, H.) Kiel, 1839.

Phil 8656.20   Über das Daseyn Gottes in Beziehung auf Kantische und Mendelssonnsche Philosophie. (Bornträger, J.C.F.) Hannover, 1788.

Phil 5247.41   Über das Denken...Auschauung. (Hertz, Paul.) Berlin, 1923.

Phil 5242.19   Über das Denken. (Cohn, Max.) Berlin, 1910.

Phil 8422.7.15   Über das Erhabene und konische Einleitung. (Vischer, F.T.) Frankfurt, 1967.

Phil 3842.1   Über das Erste Buch der Ethik des Spinoza. (Weise, H.) Salzwede, 187-?

Phil 3507.2   Über das Fundament der Ethik. (Zango, F.) Leipzig, 1872.

Phil 3489.52   Über das Fundament der gesammten Philosophie des Herrn Kant. Halle, 1791. (Holst, Johann Ludolf.) Bruxelles, 1968.

Phil 3778.40   Über das fundament des philosophischen Wissens. (Reinhold, K.L.) Jena, 1791.

Phil 5831.1   Über das Fundamentalgesetz der Intelligenz im Thierreiche. (Vignoli, Tito.) Leipzig, 1879.

Phil 5545.5   Über das Gedächtnis. (Ebbinghaus, H.) Leipzig, 1885.

Phil 5545.37   Über das Gedächtnis. (Hering, Ewald.) Leipzig, 1905.

Phil 5400.200   Über das Gefühl. (Krueger, Felix.) Darmstadt, 1967.

Phil 5425.30   Über das Genie. (Wendel, Georg.) Strassburg, 1909.

Phil 349.29   Über das Haben. (Stern, Günther.) Bonn, 1928.

Phil 3210.42   Über das höchste Gut. (Fechner, G.T.) Leipzig, 1846.

Phil 3246.218   Über das idealistisch-atheistische System des Professor Fichte in Jena. (Heusinger, J.H.G.) Dresden, 1799.

Phil 3488.21   Ueber das Kantische Prinzip für die Naturgeschichte. (Gertanner, Christoph.) Göttingen, 1796.

Phil 5068.46   Über das Kriterium der Verifizierbarkeit. (Wilson, Max.) Berlin, 1959.

Phil 180.12.15   Über das Mysterium magnum des Daseins. (Frohschammer, J.) Leipzig, 1891.

Phil 6128.43   Über das Organ der Seele. (Sömmerring, S.T.) Königsberg, 1796.

Phil 1870.145   Über das Problem der Einheit un des Sinnes von Erscheinung bei Berkeley. (Rauschenberger, J.P.) Gernsbach, 1959.

Phil 3450.11.230   Über das Problem des Angangs der Philosophie im Spätwerk Edmund Husserl. (Kutschera, Franz.) München, 1960.

Htn   Phil 3480.70.80*   Ueber das radikale Böse in der menschlichen Natur. Pt. 1. (Kant, Immanuel.) n.p., 1792.

Phil 8876.86   Über das Richtige. (Bergmann, J.) Berlin, 1883.

Phil 6135.2   Über das Riechcentrum. (Zuckerkandl, E.) Stuttgart, 1887.

Phil 5643.4   Über das Schlussverfahren der Sehactes. (Classen, A.) Rostock, 1863.

Phil 8402.6   Über das Schöne. (Bergmann, J.) Berlin, 1887.

Phil 8419.35A   Über das Schöne als Sinnbild und Wegweisung. (Salinger, H.) Köln, 1960.

Phil 5825.1   Über das Seelenleben der Thiere. (Perty, J.A.M.) Leipzig, 1876.

Htn   Phil 3808.63*   Über das Sehn und die Farben. (Schopenhauer, Arthur.) Leipzig, 1816.

Phil 3808.63.10   Über das Sehn und die Farben. 3. Aufl. (Schopenhauer, Arthur.) Leipzig, 1870.

Phil 344.1   Über das sogenannte Erkenntnisproblem. (Nelson, L.) Göttingen, 1908.

Phil 8876.39   Über das Sollen und das Gute. (Bon, Fred.) Leipzig, 1898.

Phil 6400.12   Über das Sprachverständnis. (Pick, A.) Leipzig, 1909.

Phil 9035.52   Über das Studium der Individualität. (Lasurski, A.) Leipzig, 1912.

Phil 3508.4   Über das Studium der Kantischen Philosophie und ihren Werth. Bruxelles, 1968.

Phil 5049.20.10   Über das tragische. (Jaspers, Karl.) München, 1952.

Phil 2050.101.5   Über das Verhältnis der Geschichtsschreibung David Hume's zu seiner praktischen Philosophie. (Daiches, Sally.) Leipzig, 1903.

Phil 3552.257   Über das Verhältnis der leibnizischen Ethik zu Metaphysik und Theologie. Diss. (Nathan, Bernhard.) Jena, 1916.

Phil 193.81   Ueber das Verhältnis der Philosophie. (Spitzer, Hugo.) Leipzig, 1883.

Phil 8595.4.15   Über das Verhältnis der Religionsphilosophie. (Pfleiderer, O.) Berlin, 1906.

Phil 3499.25   Über das Verhältnis von Sittlichkeit und Religion bei Kant. (Reinhard, Walter.) Bern, 1927.

Phil 3500.9   Über das Verhältniss...Kantischen. (Spicker, G.) Berlin, 1874.

Htn   Phil 3800.250*   Über das Verhältniss der bildenden Künste zu der Natur. (Schelling, F.W.J. von.) München, 1807.

Htn   Phil 3800.250.15*   Über das Verhältniss der bildenden Künste zu der Natur. (Schelling, F.W.J. von.) Berlin, 1843.

Phil 3800.250.20   Über das Verhältniss der bildenden Künste zu der Natur. (Schelling, F.W.J. von.) Marbach, 1954.

	Phil 5585.14	Über das Verhältniss der Ebenmerk...Gebiet des Zeitsinns. (Wrinch, F.S.) Leipzig, 1902.
	Phil 2050.94	Über das Verhältniss der Hume'schen und Kantischen Erkenntnisstheorie. (Kühne, R.) Berlin, 1878.
Htn	Phil 3800.240*	Über das Verhältniss der Realen und Idealen in der Natur. (Schelling, F.W.J. von.) Hamburg, 1806.
	Phil 5325.15	Über das Verhalten der Reaktionszeit. (Jung, Carl G.) Leipzig, 1915.
	Phil 3090.40	Über das Verhalten des Wissens zum Glauben. (Baader, Franz von.) Münster, 1833.
Htn	Phil 3800.250.10*	Über das Verhältniss der bildenden Künste zu der Natur. (Schelling, F.W.J. von.) Wien, 1825.
	Phil 3018.2	Ueber das Wesen...Philosophie und Theologie in der gegenwärtigen Zeit...Religionsphilosophie. (Sengler, J.) Heidelberg, 1837.
	Phil 6688.19	Über das Wesen derHypnose. 2. Aufl. (Schilder, Paul.) Berlin, 1922.
	Phil 3800.340.5	Über das Wesen der menschlichen Freiheit. (Schelling, F.W.J. von.) Leipzig, 1911.
	Phil 197.56	Ueber das Wesen der Philosophie. (Wagner, J.J.) Bamberg, 1804.
	Phil 8876.58	Über das Wesen der Sittlichkeit. (Bender, Hedwig.) Halle, 1891.
	Phil 8402.53	Über das Wesen des Ästhetischen. (Bodensohn, A.) Frankfurt, 1961.
	Phil 4899.162.30	Über das Wesen und den Ursprung des Menschen. (Kaneko, Shōseki.) Osaka, 1932.
	Phil 8615.8.15	Über das Wesen und die Aufgabe der ethischen Gesellschaft. 2. Aufl. (Jodl, Friedrich.) Wien, 1903.
	Phil 5768.15	Über das Wesen und die Bedeutung. (Sommer, H.) Berlin, 1885.
	Phil 193.22	Über das Wesen und speculativen Philosophie. (Sengler, J.) Mainz, 1834.
	Phil 3850.1.95	Über David Friedrich Strauss. (Fischer, Kuno.) Heidelberg, 1908.
	Phil 9450.26	Über del Gerechtigkeit. (Pieper, J.) München, 1953.
	Phil 5232.1	Über den...psychologische Forschung. (Windelband, W.) Leipzig, 1876.
	Phil 8670.12.5	Über den Atheismus. (Platner, E.) Leipzig, 1783.
	Phil 5585.40.2	Über den Aufbau der Wahrnehmungswelt. 2. Aufl. (Jaeusch, Erich.) Leipzig, 1927-1931. 2v.
	Phil 6322.1.10	Über den Begriff der Hysterie und andere Vorwürfe vorwegend psychologischer Art. (Mobius, P.J.) Leipzig, 1894.
	Phil 400.1	Über den Begriff der Philosophie. (Fischer, Friedrich.) Tübingen, 1830.
	Phil 180.35	Über den Begriff der Philosophie. (Freytag, Willy.) Halle, 1904.
	Phil 8412.19.10	Über den Begriff der Schonhëit. (Lotze, Hermann.) Göttingen, 1845.
	Phil 1135.40	Über den Begriff der Ursache im der griechischen Philosophie. (Goring, C.) Leipzig, 1874.
Htn	Phil 3246.44*	Über den Begriff der Wissenschaftslehre. (Fichte, Johann Gottlieb.) Weimar, 1794.
	Phil 672.216	Über den Begriff der Zeit. (Kuemmel, F.) Tübingen, 1962.
	Phil 3090.30	Über den Begriff des Gut-Oderpositiv und der Richtgut-Oder-Negative-Gewordnen. (Baader, Franz von.) Luzern, 1829.
	Phil 8881.44	Über den Begriff des sittlichen Ideals. (Gomperz, Heinrich.) Bern, 1902.
	Phil 8957.7	Über den Begriffs der Mässigung. Inaug. Diss. (Hermanns, W.) Aachen, 1913.
	Phil 5875.120	Über den Egozentrismus des Kindes. (Aebli, Hans.) Stuttgart, 1968.
	Phil 5643.75	Über den Einfluss der Gesichtsschärfe. Inaug. Diss. (Pollak, G.F.X.) Dillingen, 1829.
	Phil 3428.155.5	Über den Einfluss der Tonlehre auf Herbart's Philosophie. (Zimmerman, R.) Wien, 1873.
	Phil 5465.25	Über den Einfluss des Gefühls auf die Thätigkeit der Phantasie. (Zeller, E.) Tübingen, 1900.
	Phil 3484.8	Über den Einfluss Kants auf die Theorie der Sinneswahrnehmung. (Classen, August.) Leipzig, 1886.
	Phil 5585.13	Über den Einfluss von Nebenreizen. (Pearce, H.J.) Leipzig, 1903.
	Phil 6323.2	Über den Einfluss von Rechtsansprüchen bei Neurosen. (Naegeli, Otto.) Leipzig, 1913.
	Phil 178.40	Über den Existenzialbegriff. (Dyroff, Adolf.) Freiburg im Breisgau, 1902.
	Phil 5374.195	Über den Gebrauch des Ausdrücke "Intention". (Sodan, Guenter.) Berlin, 1958.
	Phil 5057.5	Über den Gegenstand und den Umfang der Logik. (Richter, Heinrich.) Leipzig, 1825.
	Phil 3925.6.06	Ueber den Gegenwärtigen stand der Psychologie. (Windelband, W.) n.p., 1876-1914. 12 pam.
	Phil 3425.285	Über den gegenwärtigen Standpunct der philosophischen Wissenschaft. (Weisse, C.H.) Leipzig, 1829.
	Phil 193.103	Ueber den Geist der Philosophie. (Salat, J.) München, 1803.
	Phil 3246.53.10	Über den Gelehrten. (Fichte, Johann Gottlieb.) Berlin, 1956.
	Phil 3480.75.30	Über den Gemeinspruch: Das mag in der Theorie richtig sein taugt. (Kant, Immanuel.) Frankfurt, 1968.
Htn	Phil 3480.75.25*	Über den Gemeinspruch: Das mag in Theorie richtig sein taugt, aber nicht für die Praxis. (Kant, Immanuel.) Berlin, 1793. 2 pam.
	Phil 3480.75.20	Über den Gemeinspruch: Das mag in Theorie richtig sein taugt, aber nicht für die Praxis. (Kant, Immanuel.) Frankfurt, 1946.
	Phil 8408.15	Über den Geschmack. (Heimann, B.) Berlin, 1924.
	Phil 2270.88	Über den Gesetz der Entwicklung. (Fischer, E.L.) Würzburg, 1875.
	Phil 3246.192	Über den Gott des Herrn Professor Fichte. (Eberhard, J.A.) Halle, 1799.
	Phil 9558.48	Über den Hochmut. (Kraus, Annie.) Frankfurt, 1966.
	Phil 3850.13.27	Über den höchsten Zweck des Studiums der Philosophie. (Schulze, G.E.) Leipzig, 1789.
	Phil 1750.166.30	Über den Humanismus. (Heidegger, Martin.) Frankfurt, 1949.
	Phil 5761.2	Über den individuellen Beweis für die Freiheit. (Liebmann, O.) Stuttgart, 1866.
	Phil 720.67	Über den Irrtum. (Haensel, Carl.) Heidelberg, 1965.
	Phil 3487.8	Über den Kantischen Idealismus. (Freytag, Willy.) Leipzig, 1924.
	Phil 6122.7.9	Über den Kreislauf des Blutes. (Mosso, A.) Leipzig, 1881.
	Phil 5262.25	Über den Mechanismus des geistigen Lebens. (Wahle, Richard.) Wien, 1906.
	Phil 9513.12	Über den Menschen und seine Verhältnisse. (Fröhlich, C.W.) Berlin, 1960.
	Phil 2115.49.30	Über den menschlichen Verstand. (Locke, J.) Berlin, 1962. 2v.
	Phil 2115.49.15	Über den menschlichen Verstand. (Locke, J.) Leipzig, 1897. 2v.
	Phil 510.124	Über den modernen Monismus. (Erdmann, Benno.) Berlin, 1914.
	Phil 3504.41	Über den nachsten Zweck der Erziehung nach Kantischen Grunsätzen. (Weiller, K.) Regensburg, 1798.
	Phil 6110.10.10	Über den nervösen Charakter. (Adler, Alfred.) München, 1922.
	Phil 6110.10.11	Über den nervösen Charakter. 4. Aufl. (Adler, Alfred.) München, 1928.
Htn	Phil 3801.989*	Über den neuesten Idealismus der Herren Schelling und Hegel. München, 1803.
	Phil 9430.25	Über den Pessimismus und seine Wurzeln. (Wentscher, M.) Bonn, 1897.
	Phil 7060.22	Über den psychischen Mechanismus der Sinnestäuschungen. (Vulpius, W.) Jena, 1885.
	Phil 672.13	Über den psychologischen Ursprung der Raumvorstellung. (Stumpf, C.) Leipzig, 1873.
	Phil 6957.11	Über den Quärulantenwahnsinn. (Hitzig, E.) Leipzig, 1895.
	Phil 3808.24.20	Über den Satz vom Grunde. (Schopenhauer, Arthur.) Leipzig, 1891.
	Phil 5250.50	Über den Sinn und die Grenzen des psychologischen Erkennens. (Kunz, Hans.) Stuttgart, 1957.
	Phil 960.10.5	Über den Stand der indischen Philosophie zur Zeit Mahávíras und Buddhas. Inaug. Diss. (Schrader, F.O.) Strassburg, 1902.
	Phil 8602.24	Über den Tod und über den Glauben an Gott. (Wittels, Fritz.) Wien, 1914.
	Phil 7082.138	Über den Traum. (Vold, John Mourly.) Leipzig, 1910-1912. 2v.
	Phil 7082.8.2	Über den Traum. 2. Aufl. (Freud, Sigmund.) Wiesbaden, 1911.
Htn	Phil 6480.23.7*	Über den Traumdeutung. (Freud, Sigmund.) Wiesbaden, 1901.
	Phil 9513.2	Über den Umgang mit Menschen. Pt.1-3. (Knigge, A. von.) Hildburghausen, 1830.
	Phil 9513.2.5	Über den Umgang mit Menschen. 3. Aufl. pt.1-3. (Knigge, A. von.) Hannover, 1790.
	Phil 3246.73	Über den Unterschied des Geistes und des Buchstabens in der Philosophie. (Fichte, Johann Gottlieb.) Leipzig, 1924.
	Phil 346.9	Ueber den Ursprung der Begriffe. (Portius, K.N.) Leipzig, 1848.
Htn	Phil 3801.471.10*	Über den Ursprung der Menschen und Völker nach der mosaischen Genesis. (Kapp, Christian.) Nürnberg, 1829.
	Phil 8843.8	Über den Ursprung des Sittlichen und die Formen seiner Erscheinung. (Stieglitz, T.) Wien, 1894.
	Phil 332.16	Über den Ursprung unserer Erkenntniss. (Bendavid, L.) Berlin, 1802.
	Phil 9550.10	Über den Utilitarianismus. (Bergmann, Julius.) Marburg, 1883.
	Phil 5643.93	Über den Vergleich von Komplexen geometrischen Gebilde und tontfreier Farben. Inaug. Diss. (Nahm, E.) Frankfurt, 1930?
	Phil 6955.12	Über den Wahn. v.1-2. (Friedmann, M.) Wiesbaden, 1894.
	Phil 178.44.5	Über den Weg, zum Wissen und zur Gewissheit zu Gesangen. (Delff, Heinrich K.H.) Leipzig, 1882.
	Phil 6972.2.15	Über den wessenschaftlichen Standpunkt. (Wernicke, C.) Cassel, 1880.
Htn	Phil 3808.65*	Über den Willen in der Natur. (Schopenhauer, Arthur.) Frankfurt, 1836.
Htn	Phil 3808.65.5*	Über den Willen in der Natur. (Schopenhauer, Arthur.) Frankfurt, 1854.
	Phil 3808.65.2	Über den Willen in der Natur. (Schopenhauer, Arthur.) Leipzig, 1867.
	Phil 5750.3	Über den Willensakt und das Temperament. (Ach, Narziss.) Leipzig, 1910.
	Phil 5325.9	Über der associativen Verlauf der Vorstellungen. (Scripture, W.) Leipzig, 1891.
	Phil 3494.9	Über der Bedeutung v. Leibniz...für Kant. (Merren, R.) Leipzig, 1908.
Htn	Phil 3246.20*	Über der Begriff der Wissenschaftslehre. (Fichte, Johann Gottlieb.) Jena, 1798-1822. 4 pam.
	Phil 1750.17	Über den Einfluss der Epicureischen...Philosophie des 16 und 17 Jahrhunderts. (Haas, A.) Berlin, 1896.
	Phil 8885.28	Über den ersten Grundsatz der Moralphilosophie. (Kiesewetter, J.G.C.) Berlin, 1790-1791. 2v.
	Phil 745.7.15	Über der grundsätzliche Unmöglichkeit einer "Vereinigung" von universeller Teleologie und Mechanismus. (Driesch, H.) Heidelberg, 1914.
	Phil 3200.7	Über der Naturalismus. (Erdmann, J.E.) Halle, 1854.
Htn	Phil 3480.75*	Über des Ausgesetzte Preisfrage. (Kant, Immanuel.) Königsberg, 1803-04. 2 pam.
	Phil 3246.222	Über des Herrn Professor Fichte Appellation an das Publikum. (Schäffer, W.F.) Gotha, 1799.
	Phil 3820.2	Ueber die...Spinozischen Pantheismus. (Avenarius, R.) Leipzig, 1868.
	Phil 8412.18.5	Über die (Beson derheit) als Kategorie der Ästhetik. (Lukács, Georg.) Neuwied, 1967.
	Phil 2115.89A	Über die Abhängigkeit Locke's von Descartes. (Geil, Georg.) Strassburg, 188-.
	Phil 5052.10	Über die Algebra der Logik. v. 1-2. (Müller, E.) Leipzig, 1900-01.
	Phil 5259.6.8	Über die allgemeine speculativische Philosophie. (Tetens, J.N.) Berlin, 1913.
	Phil 6135.3	Über die allgemeinen Beziehungen. (Ziehen, Theodore.) Leipzig, 1902.
	Phil 5421.10.40	Über die Angst. (Hellner, Hans.) Stuttgart, 1969.
	Phil 3485.24	Über die Anlage. (Daxer, Georg.) Hamburg, 1897.
	Phil 5932.3	Über die Anlage zur Mathematik. (Möbius, P.J.) Leipzig, 1900.
	Phil 8644.6.2	Über die Ansterblichkeit der Seele. 2. Aufl. (Teichmüller, G.) Leipzig, 1879.
	Phil 400.31	Über die Antinomienlehre als Begründung des transzendentalen idealismus. Inaug. Diss. (Howaleivsky, M.) Göttingen, 1914.
	Phil 342.4	Über die apriorischen Elemente. (Levy, Heinrich.) Leipzig, 1914.
	Phil 5722.18.15	Über die Archetypen. (Jung, C.G.) Zürich, 1935.
	Phil 5643.28	Über die Auffassung einfachster Raumformen. (Seyfert, R.) Leipzig, 1902.
	Phil 3491.9	Ueber die Auffindung des Apriori. (Jacobson, Julius.) Berlin, 1876.
	Phil 286.6	Über die Aufgabe der Naturphilosophie. (Frohschammer, J.) München, 1861.
	Phil 490.2	Über die Bedeutung der Anthropologie. (Perty, M.) Bern, 1853.

Phil 3487.4   Ueber die Bedeutung der Einbildungskraft. (Frohschammer, J.) München, 1879.

Htn   Phil 3801.197.10*A   Über die Bedeutung des Schelling'schen Metaphysik. (Beckers, Hubert.) München, 1861.

Phil 3210.86   Über die Bedeutung von Fechners "Nanna". (Hollander, K. von.) Göttingen, 1908.

Htn   Phil 3801.391*   Über die Bedingungen eines spekulativen Theismus. (Fichte, I.H.) Elberfeld, 1835.

Phil 5250.18.10   Über die Beeinflussung einfacher psychischer Vorgänge durch einige Arzneimittel. (Kraepelin, Emil.) Jena, 1892.

Phil 8876.166   Über die Begründung der Ethik durch die Physik und andere Schriften. (Baader, Franz von.) Stuttgart, 1969.

Phil 9410.3   Über die Berechtigung des Optimismus. (Prantl, Carl von.) München, 1879.

Phil 3833.2   Ueber die bestimmende Ursache des Philosophirens. (Nossig, Alfred.) Stuttgart, 1895.

Phil 3246.53.5   Über die Bestimmung des Gelehrten. (Fichte, Johann Gottlieb.) Berlin, 1812.

Phil 8664.2   Über die Beweise für das Daseyn Gottes. (Jakob, L.H.) Liebau, 1798.

Phil 5520.40   Über die Bezeichnungen der sinnlichen Wahrnehmungen. (Bechtel, F.) Weimar, 1879.

Phil 3500.37   Über die Beziehungen Garve's zu Kant. Inaug. Diss. (Stern, Albert.) n.p., n.d.

Phil 5235.1   Über die Beziehungen zwischen Gehirn und Seelenleben. (Ziehen, T.) Leipzig, 1902.

Phil 340.4   Über die Beziehungen zwischen Kategorien und Urtheilsfarmen. Inaug. Diss. (Jacobson, J.) Königsberg, 1877.

Phil 900.5   Über die biblische Gnosis. (Horn, J.) Hannover, 1805.

Phil 3499.2.10   Über die bisherigen Schicksale der Kantischen Philosophie. (Reinhold, K.L.) Jena, 1789.

Htn   Phil 3480.89*   Über die Büchmacheren. (Kant, Immanuel.) Königsberg, 1798.

Phil 3120.61.30   Über die Charlatanerie der Gelehrten seit Menken. (Bueschel, Johann Gabriel Bernhard.) Leipzig, 1971.

Phil 3488.20   Ueber die Critik der reinen Vernunft. (Goess, G.F.D.) Erlangen, 1793.

Phil 5190.4.10   Über die Definition. 2. Aufl. (Dubislav, W.) Berlin, 1927.

Phil 5190.4.10.3   Über die Definition. 3. Aufl. (Dubislav, W.) Leipzig, 1931.

Phil 1135.17   Ueber die Denkweise der altesten Philosophen. (Fortlage, C.) München, 1829.

Phil 3425.247   Ueber die dialektische Methode. (Hartmann, E. v.) Berlin, 1868.

Phil 5246.62   Über die Dummheit. (Geyer, Horst.) Göttingen, 1954.

Phil 5390.4   Über die Dummheit. (Loewenfeld, Leopold.) Wiesbaden, 1909.

Phil 5390.12   Über die Dummheit. (Musil, Robert.) Wien, 1937.

Phil 3487.30   Über die Eigenschaft der Analysis und der analytischen Methode in der Philosophie. (Francke, Georg Samuel.) Bruxelles, 1968.

Phil 3915.36   Über die Einfluss der Philosophie. (Wundt, Wilhelm.) Leipzig, 1876.

Phil 185.80   Über die Einsamkeit. (Koelbel, Gerhard.) München, 1960.

Phil 9515.3   Über die Einsamkeit. (Zimmermann, J.G.) Leipzig, 1784-85. 4v.

Phil 187.146   Über die Einseitigkeit. (Meimberg, R.) Berlin, 1951.

Phil 3246.79.10   Über die Einzig mögliche Störung der akademischen Freiheit. (Fichte, Johann Gottlieb.) Heidelberg, 1905.

Phil 8060.7   Über die Empfindung der Naturschönheit bei den Alten. (Motz, H.) Leipzig, 1865.

Phil 5635.21   Über die Empfindung der Ruhe. (Schneider, G.H.) Zürich, 1876.

Phil 6319.1.7   Über die Energetik der Seele und andere psychologische Abhandlungen. (Jung, C.G.) Zürich, 1928.

Phil 3552.248   Über die Entdeckung, dass Leibnitz ein Katholik gewesen sey. (Schulze, G.E.) Göttingen, 1827.

Phil 5460.8   Über die Entstehung der Sinnestäuschung. (Leubuscher, R.) Berlin, 1852.

Phil 8592.37   Über die Entstehung religiöser Volksbegriffe. (Münzenberger, H.C.) Göttingen, 1791.

Phil 8050.34   Über die Entstehung und Entwicklung des Gefühls für das Romantische in der Natur. (Friedlaender, L.) Leipzig, 1873.

Phil 7060.12   Über die Entwickelung von Wahnideen. (Ackermann, G.) Weimar, 1892.

Phil 352.4   Ueber die Entwicklung der Erkenntniss. (Voit, Carl von.) München, 1878.

Phil 343.5.15   Über die Erfahrungsgrundlagen unseres Wissens. (Meinong, A.) Berlin, 1906.

Phil 5240.7.5   Über die Erforschung der Denkvorgänge. (Anschütz, Georg.) Osterwieck, 1912.

Phil 5545.71   Über die Erinnerung. (Uphues, Goswin K.) Leipzig, 1889.

Phil 346.4.5   Über die Erkennbarkeit. (Pichler, H.) Wien, 1909.

Phil 8672.3   Über die Erkenntniss Gottes in der Welt. (Ritter, H.) Hamburg, 1836.

Phil 5814.6   Über die Erregbarkeitsmessung. Inaug. Diss. (Eichler, Walter.) München, 1929.

Phil 5545.76   Über die erste Einzelerinnerung. (Kammel, W.) Leipzig, 1913.

Htn   Phil 6671.14*   Über die Extase oder das Verzücktseyn der magnetischen Schlafredner. (Baader, F.) Leipzig, 1817.

Phil 3480.22.5   Über die Form und die Prinzipien der Sinnen - und Geisteswelt. (Kant, Immanuel.) Hamburg, 1958.

Phil 9035.73   Über die Formkraft des Vorbildes für die Charakterprägung in der Reifezeit. Inaug. Diss. (Volkmann, E.) Würzburg, 1936.

Phil 3428.156   Über die Fortbildung der Philosophie durch Herbart. (Drobisch, M.W.) Leipzig, 1876.

Phil 3210.53   Über die Frage des Weber'schen Gesetzes. (Fechner, G.T.) Leipzig, 1884.

Phil 2138.40.13   Über die Freiheit. (Mill, John S.) Frankfurt, 1860. 4 pam.

Phil 3090.38   Über die Freiheit der Intelligenz. (Baader, Franz von.) München, 1826.

Phil 8695.9   Über die Freiheit der Wissenschaft. (Frohschammer, J.) München, 1861.

Phil 5755.1   Über die Freiheit des menschlichen Willens und die Einheit der Naturgesetze. (Fischer, J.C.) Leipzig, 1858.

Phil 9245.132   Über die Freude; zwei Betrachtungen. (Kramp, Willy.) Hamburg, 1968.

Phil 5046.23   Über die Funktion der Copula. (Grote, Albert.) Leipzig, 1935.

Phil 5374.275   Über die Funktion der Mobilität in der geistigen Entwicklung. (Moutada, Leo.) Stuttgart, 1968.

Phil 6122.11   Über die Funktionen der Grosshirnrinde. (Munk, H.) Berlin, 1881.

Phil 6122.11.2   Über die Funktionen der Grosshirnrinde. 2. Aufl. (Munk, H.) Berlin, 1890.

Phil 3005.3.7   Über die gegenwärtige Lage der deutschen Philosophie. (Falckenberg, Richard.) Leipzig, 1890.

Phil 8965.13.5   Über die Gerechtigkeit. 1. Aufl. (Pieper, Josef.) München, 1953.

Phil 5258.59   Über die Gesetze des geordneten Denkverlaufs. (Selz, Otto.) Stuttgart, 1913. 2v.

Phil 5325.25   Über die Geseze der Ideenassoziation. (Bardili, C.G.) Tübingen, 1796.

Phil 353.8   Ueber die Gewissheit der Erkenntniss. (Windelband, W.) Berlin, 1873.

Phil 1135.21   Über die Gottes Idee des Anagoras. (Hoffmann, F.) Wurzbrug, 1860.

Htn   Phil 3800.270*   Über die Gottheiten von Samothrace. (Schelling, F.W.J. von.) Stuttgart, 1815.

Htn   Phil 3800.270.1*   Über die Gottheiten von Samothrace. (Schelling, F.W.J. von.) Stuttgart, 1815.

Htn   Phil 3800.270.5*   Über die Gottheiten von Samothrace. (Schelling, F.W.J. von.) Stuttgart, 1815.

Phil 3450.11.112   Über die Grenzen der Erkennbarkeit. Inaug. Diss. (Temuralk, T.) Berlin, 1937.

Phil 3450.11.110   Über die Grenzen der Erkennbarkeit bei Husserl und Scheler. (Temuralk, T.) Berlin, 1937.

Phil 5255.29   Über die Grenzen der Tonwahrnehmung. (Preyer, W.) n.p., 1876-89. 9 pam.

Phil 5585.6   Über die Grenzen des Empfindungsvermögens und des Willens. (Preyer, W.) Bonn, 1868.

Phil 3665.2.31   Über die Grenzen zwischen Philosophie und Naturwissenschaften. (Naumann, M.E.A.) Leipzig, 1823.

Phil 8597.3.11   Über die Gründe der menschlichen Erkenntniss und der natürlichen Religion. (Remarus, Johann Albert Heinrich.) Bruxelles, 1968.

Phil 8597.3.10   Über die Grunde der menschlichen Erkenntniss und der natürlichen Religion. (Reimarus, Johann Albert Heinrich.) Hamburg, 1787.

Phil 334.2   Über die Grundlagen der Erkenntnis in der exacten Wissenschaften. (Du Bois-Reymond, P.) Tübingen, 1890.

Phil 3830.3   Über die Grundlagen der Lehre des Spinoza. (Kühnemann, E.) Halle, 1902.

Phil 210.60   Über die Grundlagen einer universalen Methode der Philosophie. (Hirsch, Wolfgang.) Bad Homburg, 1969.

Phil 575.8   Über die Grundvoraussetzungen und Consequenzen der individualistischen Weltanschauung. (Lutoslawski, W.) Helsingfors, 1898.

Phil 3415.108   Über die hartmannsche Philosophie des Unbewussten. (Ebbinghaus, Hermann.) Düsseldorf, 1873.

Phil 3425.111   Über die Hegel'sche Dialektik. (Reiff, F.) Tübingen, 1866.

Phil 3805.102   Über die Herkunft des Individualitäts - Gedankens bei Schleiermacher. (Eck, Samuel.) Giessen, 1908.

Phil 482.1   Über die Hypothese der Materie. (Heinroth, J.C.) Leipzig, 1828.

Phil 5590.400   Über die individuelle Konfiguration des Leitbildes. (Sigl-Kiener, I.) München, 1960.

Phil 5265.4   Über die Intelligenz und ihren Ort im Gefüge des Verhalttens. (Zürcher, W.) Bern, 1941.

Htn   Phil 3800.190*   Über die jenaische allgemeine Literaturzeitung. (Schelling, F.W.J. von.) Jena, 1800.

Htn   Phil 3800.190.2*   Über die jenaische allgemeine Literaturzeitung. (Schelling, F.W.J. von.) Jena, 1800. 3 pam.

Phil 3486.15   Über die Kantische Philosophie. (Ewald, J.L.) Berlin, 1790.

Phil 3504.4   Über die Kantischen Anschauungen. (Weishaupt, A.) Nürnberg, 1788.

Phil 2225.5.55.5   Über die Klarheit unserer Gedanken. (Peirce, C.S.) Frankfurt, 1968.

Phil 6963.3   Über die Knochenbrüche bei Geisteskranken. (Neumann, H.) Berlin, 1883.

Phil 5241.27   Über die körperlichen Äusserungen psychologischen Zustände. (Berger, H.) Jena, 1904. 2v.

Phil 5046.18   Über die kritische Logik. (Goesch, H.) Berlin, 1904.

Phil 3829.3   Über die Lehre des Spinoza. (Jacobi, F.E.) Breslau, 1789.

Phil 2520.61.7   Über die Leidenschaften der Seele. 3e Aufl. (Descartes, René.) Leipzig, 1911.

Phil 3905.35   Über die letzen Dinge. (Weininger, Otto.) Wien, 1904.

Phil 6963.5   Über die Localisation der Gehirnkrankheiten. (Nothnagel, H.) Wiesbaden, 1887.

Phil 5374.9.9   Über die materiellen Grundlagen der Bewusstseins-Erscheinungen. (Kries, Johannes.) Tübingen, 1901.

Phil 3850.13.70   Ueber die Menschliche Erkenntnis. (Schulze, G.E.) Göttingen, 1832.

Phil 5755.2A   Über die menschliche Freiheit. (Fischer, E.K.B.) Heidelberg, 1888.

Phil 2050.60.25   Über die menschliche Natur. Bd.2. (Hume, David.) Halle, 1791.

Phil 5756.7   Über die Menschlichefreiheit. (Göring, Carl.) Leipzig, 1876.

Phil 3210.70   Über die Methode der richtigen und falschen Fälle. (Fechner, G.T.) Leipzig, 1884.

Htn   Phil 3800.120*   Über die Möglichkeit einer Form der Philosophie überhaupt. (Schelling, F.W.J. von.) Tübingen, 1795.

Phil 735.113   Über die Möglichkeit einer Werteinteilung. (Rodhe, S.E.) Lund, 1937.

Phil 3120.31.30   Über die Möglichkeit systematischer Kulturphilosophie. (Boem, W.) Saale, 1927.

Htn   Phil 3800.120.5*   Über die Moglichkeit einer Form der Philosophie überhaupt. (Schelling, F.W.J. von.) Tübingen, 1795.

Phil 5190.20   Über die Negation, den Widerspruch und den Gegensatz. Inaug.-Diss. (Thiede, J.) Berlin, 1893.

Phil 974.3.165   Über die neu Mysteriendramen Rudolf Steiners. (Walther, Kurt.) Freiburg, 1966-67. 3v.

Phil 3428.160   Über die neuesten Darstellungen und Beurtheilungen der Herbart'schen Philosophie. (Hartenstein, G.) Leipzig, 1838.

Phil 672.8   Über die neuesten Untersuchungen in Betreff unserer Anschauung vom Raume. (Rosanes, J.) Breslau, 1871.

Phil 3494.66.2   Über die Nichtigkeit der Kantische Grundsätze in der Philosophie...Logik von Professor Kreil. Facsimile. (Miotti, Peter.) Bruxelles, 1968.

Phil 3090.64   Über die Nothwendigkeit einer Revision der Wissenschaft natürlicher. (Baader, Franz von.) Erlanzen, 1841.

Phil 5643.172   Über die optische Unterscheidbarkeit einfacher Zeichen. Thesis. (Spiekers, Rudolf.) Meisenheim am Glan, 1969.

Phil 3778.35   Über die Paradoxien der neuesten Philosophie. (Reinhold, K.L.) Hamburg, 1799.

Phil 5258.59.7   Über die Persönlichkeitstypen. (Selz, Otto.) Jena, 1924.

Htn Phil 7060.20*   Über die phantastischen Gesichteserscheinungen. (Müller, J.) Coblenz, 1826.

Phil 3210.34   Über die physikalische und philosophische Atomenlehre. (Fechner, G.T.) Leipzig, 1855.

Phil 5645.25   Über die physiologischen Grundlagen des Farbensinns. (Schenck, F.) Marburg, 1906.

Phil 1706.8   Über die Problematik der neueren Philosophie. Inaug. Diss. (Gause, Hermann.) Basel, 1928.

Phil 3625.5.30   Über die Progressen der Philosophie. (Maimon, Salomon.) Bruxelles, 1969.

Phil 5643.76   Über die pseudoskopische Ablenkung paralleler Linien. (Metz, Bernhard.) Marburg, 1882.

Phil 5893.2   Über die Psychoanalyse in der Ethnologie. (Schoene, Wolfgang.) Dortmund, 1966.

Phil 6959.8   Über die Psychologie der Dementia Praecox. (Jung, C.G.) Halle, 1907.

Phil 5413.5   Über die Psychologie der Eifersucht. (Friedmann, Max.) Wiesbaden, 1911.

Phil 6319.1.36.2   Über die Psychologie des Unbewussten. 7 Aufl. (Jung, C.G.) Zürich, 1960.

Phil 6315.2.325   Über die psychologischen Theorien Freuds und verwandte Anschauungen. (Kronfeld, A.) Leipzig, 1912.

Phil 5244.14   Über die Psychophysik. (Elsas, Adolf.) Marburg, 1886.

Phil 3450.18.190   Über die Raumlehre Nicolai Hartmanns und ihre Bezlehungen zur modernen Mathematik und Physik. (Koerschgen, Hans.) Köln, 1959?

Phil 2520.195   Über die Realitätstheorie Descartes'. Inaug.-Diss. (Molitor, Emil.) Mayen, 1935.

Phil 5821.8   Über die Reize des Spiels. (Lazarus, M.) Berlin, 1883.

Phil 672.33   Über die Relativität der Raum- und Zeitbestimmungen. (Phalén, Adolf K.) Uppsala, 1922.

Htn Phil 3805.30*   Über die Religion. (Schleiermacher, Friedrich.) Berlin, 1799.

Phil 3805.30.2   Über die Religion. (Schleiermacher, Friedrich.) Berlin, 1806.

Phil 3805.30.3   Über die Religion. (Schleiermacher, Friedrich.) Berlin, 1821.

Phil 3805.30.4   Über die Religion. (Schleiermacher, Friedrich.) Berlin, 1831.

Phil 3805.30.10   Über die Religion. (Schleiermacher, Friedrich.) Berlin, 191-.

Phil 3805.30.12   Über die Religion. (Schleiermacher, Friedrich.) Hamburg, 1958.

Phil 3805.30.5   Über die Religion. (Schleiermacher, Friedrich.) Leipzig, 1868-69.

Phil 8602.5   Über die Religion. (Wette, W.M.L. de.) Berlin, 1827.

Phil 3805.30.12.6   Über die Religion. 6. Aufl. (Schleiermacher, Friedrich.) Göttingen, 1967.

Phil 3210.45   Über die Seelenfrage. (Fechner, G.T.) Leipzig, 1861.

Phil 3210.45.10   Über die Seelenfrage. 2. Aufl. (Fechner, G.T.) Hamburg, 1907.

Phil 6328.24   Über die seelischen Ursachen des Alterns, der Jugendlichkeit und der Schönheit. (Sperber, Alice.) Leipzig, 1925.

Phil 8897.8.10   Ueber die Selbstkenntniss. (Weishaupt, A.) Regensburg, 1794.

Phil 3494.34   Über die settliche Natur und Bestimmung des Menschen. v.1-2. (Michaelis, C.F.) Leipzig, 1796-97.

Phil 8878.30   Über die sittliche Freiheit. (Dittes, F.) Leipzig, 1860.

Phil 8878.30.2   Über die sittliche Freiheit. 2e Aufl. (Dittes, F.) Leipzig, 1892.

Phil 9182.1.2   Über die Sozalen-Pflichten der Familie. 2. Aufl. (Weber, M.W.) Berlin, 1876.

Phil 339.1   Über die Stellung der Erkenntnistheorie im System der Philosophie. (Ingarden, Roman.) Halle an der Saale, 1926.

Phil 343.5.9   Über die Stellung der Gegenstand Theorie im System der Wissenschaften. (Meinong, A.) Leipzig, 1907.

Phil 5240.28   Über die Stellung der Psychologie im Stammbaum der Wissenschaften. (Ahlenstiehl, H.) Berlin, 1923.

Phil 5545.262   Über die strukturelle Eigenart und personate Bedeutsamkeit der Erinnerung. Inaug. Diss. (Urach, Elisabeth Furstin von.) Bamburg, 1965.

Phil 3552.295   Über die Theodicee des Leibniz. (Bussenius, Karl.) Halle, 1876.

Phil 705.70   Über die transcendentale Ästhetik. (Schaumann, Johann Christian Gottlieb.) Bruxelles, 1968.

Phil 7068.94.15   Über die Trugwahrnehmung. (Parish, Edmond.) Leipzig, 1894.

Phil 8886.26   Über die Tugenden und Laster...des Menschen. (Lawätz, H.W.) Flensburg, 1789-1792. 3v.

Phil 3110.43   Über die Umkehr und die Einsicht. (Böhme, J.) Wien, 1953.

Phil 5649.10   Über die Umwandlung willkürlicher Bewegungen in unwillkürliche. (Schultze, Ernst.) Leipzig, 1898.

Phil 7080.33   Über die Ursache des Schlafes. (Preyer, William.) Stuttgart, 1877.

Phil 9470.16   Über die Verantwortung. (Ingarden, Roman.) Stuttgart, 1970.

Phil 6116.5   Über die Verrichtungen. (Goltz, F.L.) Bonn, 1881.

Phil 178.35   Über die Verschiedenegrade. (Drossbach, M.) Berlin, 1873.

Phil 3808.49.10   Über die vierfache Wurzel des Satzes vom zureichen den Grunde. (Schopenhauer, Arthur.) Hamburg, 1957.

Htn Phil 3808.48*   Über die vierfache Wurzel des Satzes vom zureichen den Grunde. 2. Aufl. (Schopenhauer, Arthur.) Frankfurt, 1847.

Phil 3808.49   Über die vierfache Wurzel des Satzes vom zureichen den Grunde. 3. Aufl. (Schopenhauer, Arthur.) Leipzig, 1864.

Phil 3808.49.5   Über die vierfache Wurzel des Satzes vom zureichen den Grunde. 4. Aufl. (Schopenhauer, Arthur.) Leipzig, 1875.

Htn Phil 3801.876.40*   Über die von der neusten Philosophie. (Wegscheider, J.A.L.) Hamburg, 1804.

Phil 5831.4   Über die vorstellungen Deutiere. v.2. (Volkelt, Johannes.) Leipzig, 1914.

Phil 6127.15   Über die Wage und Ziele. (Rüdinger, N.) München, 1893.

Htn Phil 3801.197.25*   Über die Wahre und bleibende Bedeutung der Naturphilosophie Schelling's. (Beckers, Hubert.) München, 1864.

Phil 3500.17.20   Über die Wahrheit der Kantischen Philosophie...Ausehung dieser Philosophie. (Schwab, J.C.) Berlin, 1803.

Phil 5650.12   Über die Wahrnehmung. (Brücke, Ernst.) Wien, 1884.

Phil 6112.7   Über die Wechselwirkung zwischen Leib und Seele. (Cornelius, K.S.) Halle, 1875.

Phil 5757.4   Über die Willensfreiheit. (Huber, Johannes.) München, 1858.

Phil 5750.3.2   Über die Willenstätigkeit und das Denken. (Ach, Narziss.) Göttingen, 1905.

Phil 1850.41.7   Über die Würde und den Fortgang der Wissenschaften. (Bacon, Francis.) Darmstadt, 1966.

Phil 672.22.5   Über die Zeit; philosophische Untersuchung. (Eyfferth, Max.) Berlin, 1871.

Phil 530.20.35   Über die Zersetzung und Vererbung in den deutschen Mystikertexten. Diss. (Spamer, Adolf.) Giessen, 1910.

Phil 3120.8.40   Über die Zukunft der Philosophie. (Brentano, Franz.) Leipzig, 1929.

Phil 6060.60   Über die Zuverlässigkeit der Beschreibung von Sprechstimme und Handschrift. Inaug. Diss. (Broeren, Wilhelm.) n.p., 1964.

Phil 3808.137   Über die Zweck Mässigkeit in der Natur bei Schopenhauer. (Keutel, Otto.) Leipzig, 1897.

Phil 6968.2   Über die Zweifelsucht und Berührungsangst. (Schramm, F.) Berlin, 1888.

Phil 3195.6.103   Über Diltheys Verhaltnis zu Hegel. (Steuzel, J.) n.p., n.d.

Phil 5642.19   Über Doppelempfindung. Diss. (Ellinger, A.) Stuttgart, 1889.

Phil 5390.2.2   Über Dummheit. (Erdmann, Johann Eduard.) Berlin, 1866.

Htn Phil 3480.43*   Über eine Entdeckung, nach der alle neue Critik der reinen Vernunft. (Kant, Immanuel.) Königsberg, 1791-97. 2 pam.

Phil 3480.43.5   Über eine Entdeckung, nach der alle neue Critik der reinen Vernunft. (Kant, Immanuel.) Grätz, 1796. 2 pam.

Phil 3838.20   Über einen Bisher unbeachteten Brief Spinozas. (Stern, Alfred.) Göttingen, 1872?

Phil 575.69   Über Einzigkeit und Individualität. (Lehmann, G.) Leipzig, 1926.

Phil 186.58   Über Einzigkeit und Individualität. (Lehmann, Gerhard.) Leipzig, 1926.

Phil 5258.21   Über elementarische psychische Prozesse. (Schweden, P.) Berlin, 1894.

Phil 5250.13   Über Entwicklungspsychologie. (Krueger, Felix.) Leipzig, 1915.

Phil 3120.55.95   Über Ernst Bloch. Frankfurt, 1968.

Htn Phil 3800.330*   Über Faradays neueste Entdlckung. (Schelling, F.W.J. von.) München, 1832.

Phil 5046.26   Über formale Logik und Dialektik. (Gesellschaft für Deutsch-Ravjetische Freundschaft.) Berlin, 1954.

Phil 1850.104   Über Francis Bacons Formenlehre. (Natge, Hans.) Leipzig, 1891.

Htn Phil 3801.293*   Über französische und deutsche Philosophie...Nebst einer Beurtheilen den Vorrede des...Schelling. (Cousin, Victor.) Stuttgart, 1834.

Phil 5772.7   Über Freiheit des Willens. (Witte, J.H.) Bonn, 1882.

Phil 3245.40   Über Gegen satz Wendepunkt und Zeit. (Fichte, Immanuel Hermann.) Heidelberg, 1832.

Phil 5270.8   Über Gegenstand und Methode der Psychologie. (Traxel, Werner.) Bern, 1968.

Phil 8628.1.5   Über Geisternähe und Geisterwirkung oder über die Wahrscheinlichkeit das die Geister der Verstorbenen den Lebenden sowohl nahe seyn, als auch auf sie wirken können. (Dedekind, G.E.W.) Hannover, 1797.

Phil 5400.50.5   Über Gemüthsbewegungen. (Lange, C.G.) Leipzig, 1887.

Phil 5249.19   Über Gestaltpsychologie und Gestalttheorie. (Jaensch, Erich.) Langensalza, 1929.

Phil 5262.31.9   Über Gestalttheorie. (Wertheimer, M.) Erlangen, 1925.

Phil 9075.29   Über Gewissen und Gewissensbildung. (Wohlrabe, W.) Gotha, 1883.

Phil 5435.6   Über Gewohnheiten und Angewohnheiten. (Erdmann, J.E.) Berlin, 1858.

Phil 4260.88   Über Giambattista Vico als Geschichtsphilosophen und begründer der neueren italienischen Philosophie. (Werner, K.) Wien, 1877.

Phil 3494.25   Ueber Glauben und Wissen. Progr. (Markull, G.) Danzig, 1884.

Phil 175.6.9   Über Glauben und Wissen in der Philosophie. (Ancillon, F.) Berlin, 1824.

Phil 8591.10   Über Gott, Geist und Unsterblichkeit. (Löwenhardt, E.) Wolgast, 1875.

Phil 6012.7   Über Grund und Bedeutung der verschiedenen formenen der hand in verschiedenen Personen. (Carus, Karl G.) Berlin, 1927.

Phil 735.103   Über Grundbegriffe philosophischer Wertlehre. Inaug. Diss. (Müller, Max.) Freiburg, 1932.

Phil 3491.6   Über Grundlagen und Werth der Entdeckungen des Herrn Professor Kant. (Jenisch, D.) Berlin, 1796.

Phil 3903.3.99   Über H. Vaihingers "Philosophie des Als Ob". (Reininger, R.) Leipzig, 1912.

Phil 3425.91.30   Über Hegel's System und die Nothwendigkeit. (Bachmann, C.F.) Leipzig, 1833.

Phil 3428.96.4   Über Herbarts Lehre von der Stufen des Unterrichts. 4. Aufl. (Gleichmann, A.) Langensalza, 1904.

Phil 3428.90.5   Über Herbart's Metaphysik. (Trendelenburg, A.) Berlin, 1854.

Phil 2050.182   Über Hume's empirische Begründung der Moral. (Zimmermann, R.) Wien, 1884.

Phil 2050.195   Über Hume's Erkenntnistheorie. (Rödder, Paul.) Gollnow, 1909.

Phil 2050.180   Über Hume's Lehre von den Ideen. Inaug. Diss. (Long, William J.) Heidelberg, 1897.

Phil 2050.183   Über Hume's metaphysische Skepsis. (Speckmann, A.) Bonn, 1877.

Phil 6615.12   Über hysterie. (Kretschmer, Ernst.) Leipzig, 1923.

Phil 270.32   Über Identität und Kausalität. (Rauschenberger, W.) Leipzig, 1922.

Phil 3500.23   Über Immanuel Kant. (Stehr, H.) Leipzig, 1896.

Phil 3502.5   Ueber Immanuel Kant's philosophische Religionslehre. Augsburg? 1793.

Phil 575.61   Über Individualität in Natur- und Geisteswelt. (Haering, T.L.) Leipzig, 1926.

Phil 270.21   Über Inhalt und Geltung des Kausalgesetzes. (Erdmann, Benno.) Halle, 1905.

Phil 3482.1.5   Über Kant's Philosophie. (Adamson, R.) Leipzig, 1880.

Phil 3487.9   Ueber Kant's Princip der Ethik. (Frederichs, F.) Berlin, 1875.

Phil 3493.22   Über Kant's Principien der Ethik und Schopenhauer's Beurtheilung derselben. (Lehmann, Otto.) Greifswald, 1880.

Phil 3489.28   Über Kant's synthetische Urteile a priori. Pt.1-4. (Hacks, Jakob.) Kattowitz, 1895-99.

Phil 3494.35   Ueber Kant's Transscendentale Aesthetik. Diss. (Massonius, M.) Leipzig, 1890.

Phil 3495.14.5   Über Kant's Verdienste um das Interesse der philosophiren den Vernunft. 2. Aufl. (Neeb, Johann.) Frankfurt, 1795.

Phil 3507.4   Ueber Kant's Widerlegung des Idealismus von Berkeley. (Zimmerman, R.) Wien, 1871.

Phil 8980.5   Über Kommunistische Moral. Berlin, 1953.

Phil 284.2   Über Kraft und Bewegung. (Drossbach, M.) Halle, 1879.
Phil 3525.89   Über Krause's Philosophie. (Reiff, F.) n.p., n.d.
Phil 186.152   Über Leben, Lüge and Liebe. (Leist, Fritz.) Freiburg, 1966.
Phil 3552.313   Über Leibniz: Leibniz und seine Ideology. (Berse, Max.) Jena, 1946.
Phil 3090.28   Über Liebe. (Baader, Franz von.) München, 1953.
Phil 5643.78   Über Linien- und Flächenvergleichung. Inaug. Diss. (Leeser, Otto.) Leipzig, 1915.
Phil 3235.84.10   Über Ludwig Feuerbach's Briefwechsel und Nachlass. (Bolin, Wilhelm.) Helsingfors, 1877.
Phil 3925.16.205   Über Ludwig Wittgenstein. Frankfurt, 1968.
Phil 3428.65   Über meiner Streit met der Modephilosophie. (Herbart, J.F.) Königsberg, 1814.
Phil 6629.2   Über Melankolie. (Fawcett, Benjamin.) Leipzig, 1785.
Phil 3425.756   Über Methode und System bei Hegel. (Bloch, Ernst.) Frankfurt am Main, 1970.
Phil 343.5.25   Über Möglichkeit und Wahrscheinlichkeit. (Meinong, A.) Leipzig, 1915.
Phil 510.138   Über Monismus (Pantheismus). (Wirth, R.) Plauen, 1874.
Htn   Phil 3480.68*   Über moralische und politische Gegenstände. (Kant, Immanuel.) Frankfurt, 1795.
Phil 3625.1.96   Über Moses Mendelssohn's Jerusalem. (Zöllner, J.F.) Berlin, 1784.
Htn   Phil 3800.105*   Über Mythen. (Schelling, F.W.J. von.) Leipzig, 1793.
Phil 7085.10.1   Über Nachtwandeln und Mondsucht. (Sadger, Isidor.) Nendeln, 1970.
Phil 5640.28   Über Natur der Sinne. (Drbal, M.A.) Linz, 1860.
Phil 6117.37   Über nervöse Erkraukungen nach Eisenbahnunfällen. (Horn, Paul.) Bonn, 1913.
Htn   Phil 3805.34*   Über Offenbarung und Mythologie. (Schleiermacher, Friedrich.) Berlin, 1799.
Phil 5643.31   Über optische Täuschung. (Zehender, W.) Leipzig, 1902.
Htn   Phil 3480.74.7*   Über Pädagogik. (Kant, Immanuel.) Königsberg, 1803.
Htn   Phil 3480.74.5*   Über Pädagogik. (Kant, Immanuel.) Königsberg, 1803.
Phil 3480.74.15   Über Pädagogik. (Kant, Immanuel.) Leipzig, 1924.
Phil 3480.74   Über Pädagogik. 3. Aufl. (Kant, Immanuel.) Langensalza, 1901.
Phil 5465.29   Über Phantasie-Vorstellungen. (Ölzelt-Newin, A.) Graz, 1889.
Phil 3235.52   Über Philosophie und Christenthum. (Feuerbach, Ludwig.) Mannheim, 1839.
Phil 3270.4.30   Über Philosophie und Empirie in ihrem Verhältnisse zur positiven Rechtswissenschaft. (Feuerbach, P.J.A.) Landshut, 1804.
Phil 186.12.8   Über philosophische Tradition. (Liebmann, O.) Strassburg, 1883.
Phil 3428.63   Über philosophisches Studium. (Herbart, J.F.) Leipzig, 1873.
Phil 270.14   Über Physische und Psychische Kausalität. (Wentscher, M.) Leipzig, 1896.
Phil 3425.219   Über Princip und Methode der hegelschen Philosophie. (Ulrici, Hermann.) Halle, 1841.
Htn   Phil 5255.31.10   Über psychische Gesetzmässigkeit. (Pauli, R.) Jena, 1920.
Htn   Phil 6315.2.4.5*   Über Psychoanalyse. (Freud, Sigmund.) Leipzig, 1910.
Phil 6315.2.6.10   Über Psychoanalyse. 2e Aufl. (Freud, Sigmund.) Leipzig, 1912.
Phil 6315.2.4A   Über Psychoanalyse. 5e Aufl. (Freud, Sigmund.) Leipzig, 1920.
Phil 6315.2.6.5   Über Psychoanalyse. 6e Aufl. (Freud, Sigmund.) Leipzig, 1922.
Phil 6315.2.7   Über Psychoanalyse. 7e Aufl. (Freud, Sigmund.) Leipzig, 1924.
Phil 6315.2.7.5   Über Psychoanalyse. 9e Aufl. (Freud, Sigmund.) Wien, 1946.
Phil 5258.35.12   Über Psychologie der individuellen Differenzen. (Stern, W.) Leipzig, 1900.
Phil 6956.4   Über psychopatische Minderwertiguten. (Gross, Otto.) Wien, 1909.
Phil 672.152.5   Über Raum. (Jaffé, George.) Berlin, 1954.
Phil 3487.6   Ueber Raum und Caussalitat. (Feder, J.G.H.) Göttingen, 1787.
Phil 2138.46   Über Religion. (Mill, John S.) Berlin, 1875.
Phil 5257.18   Über respiratorische Affektsymptome. (Rehwoldt, F.) Leipzig, 1911.
Phil 5648.16   Über Reumwahrnehmungen im Gebiet des Tastsinnes. Inaug. Diss. (Judd, Charles H.) Leipzig, 1896.
Phil 2262.89   Über Schaftsbury von der Tugend. (Schlosser, J.G.) Basel, 1785.
Htn   Phil 3801.367   Über Schelling. (Erdmann, Johann E.) Halle, 1857.
Htn   Phil 3801.367.2*   Über Schelling. (Erdmann, Johann E.) Halle, 1857.
Htn   Phil 3801.749.5*   Über Schelling und Hegel. (Rosenkranz, J.K.F.) Königsberg, 1843.
Htn   Phil 3801.749.6*   Über Schelling und Hegel. (Rosenkranz, J.K.F.) Königsberg, 1843. 2 pam.
Phil 3425.91.40   Über Schelling und Hegel. (Rosenkranz, K.) Königsberg, 1843.
Phil 3805.91   Über Schleiermachers erkenntnisstheoretische Grundausicht. (Iuäbicker, R.) Berlin, 1871.
Phil 3805.158   Über Schleiermachers Glaubenslehre. (Braniss, C.J.) Berlin, 1824.
Phil 3808.102   Über Schopenhauer. (Möbius, P.J.) Leipzig, 1899.
Phil 3003.2   Ueber Schopenhauer zu Kant; ein Kleines Geschichtsbild. (Deutschthümler, W.) Wien, 1899.
Phil 3808.96   Über Schopenhauer's ethischen Atheism. (Thilo, C.A.) Leipzig, 1868.
Phil 3808.75   Über Schriftstellerei und Stil. (Schopenhauer, Arthur.) Leipzig, 1913.
Phil 3255.89   Über Sebastian Francks Erstlingsschrift. (Haggenmacher, O.) Zürich, 1892.
Phil 5246.40   Über Sinn und Sinngebilde. (Gomperz, H.) Tübingen, 1929.
Phil 5585.52   Über Sinneswahrnehmung und deren Entwicklung zur Intelligenz. (Böse, Karl G.) Braunschweig, 1872.
Phil 5400.46   Über sittliche Dispositionen. (Oelzelt-Newin, A.) Graz, 1892.
Phil 5643.47   Über subjektive optische Anschauungsbilder. (Urbantschitsch, V.) Leipzig, 1907.
Phil 8599.5   Über Supranaturalismus. (Tittmann, J.A.H.) Leipzig, 1816.
Phil 5585.138   Über systematische Fehler bei wiederholter Schätzung von Zeitintervallen. (Zoltobrocki, Josefa.) Frankfurt, 1965.
Phil 5251.10.9   Über Tact, Kunst, Freundschaft und Sitten. 3e Aufl. (Lazarus, M.) Berlin, 1896.
Phil 5648.3   Über Täuschungen des Tastsinns. (Sobeski, M.) Breslau, 1903.
Phil 8735.9   Über Teleologie des Geistes und über Teleologie überhaupt. (Prandtl, Antonin.) Leipzig, 1915.
Phil 3585.10.91   Über Theodor Lipps' Versuch einer Theorie des Willens. (Pikler, Julius.) Leipzig, 1908.

Phil 3502.6   Ueber Theorie und Praxis. Frankfurt, 1967.
Phil 5814.3   Über Tierpsychologie. (Edinger, Ludwig.) Leipzig, 1909.
Phil 5252.42.15   Über Tonverschmelzung. (Meyer, M.F.) n.p., 1898-1913. 20 pam.
Phil 193.16   Über Transcendenz der Objects und Subjects. (Schubert-Soldern, R. von.) Leipzig, 1882.
Phil 3428.155   Über Trendelenburg's Einwürfe gegen Herbarts praktische Ideen. (Zimmerman, R.) Wien, 1872.
Phil 5425.14   Über ungleiche Befähigung der verschiedenen Menschheitstämme. (Carus, Karl G.) Leipzig, 1849.
Phil 1020.16   Über unsere Kenntniss der arabischen Philosophie. (Ritter, H.) Göttingen, 1844.
Phil 5477.10   Über unterschiedliches Behalten eigener Leistungen. (Junker, Erika.) Frankfurt, 1960.
Phil 299.5   Über Ursprung...des Hylozoismus. (Spitzer, H.) Graz, 1881.
Phil 5090.9   Über Urteilswahrheit. (Meinhandl, F.) Leipzig, 1923.
Phil 3808.24   Über Urtheil, Kritik, Beifall, Ruhm, Warheit und Irrthum. (Schopenhauer, Arthur.) Leipzig, 1891.
Phil 5440.28.5   Über Vererbung psychischer Fähigkeiten. (Peters, Wilhelm.) Leipzig, 1915.
Phil 5545.163   Über Vorstellungs-Elemente und Aufmerksamkeit. (Fränkl, Ernst.) Augsburg, 1905.
Phil 349.16   Ueber Wahrnehmung. (Stein, Heinrich.) Berlin, 1877.
Phil 735.15   Über Wethurtheile. (Ritschel, Otto.) Freiburg, 1895.
Phil 8597.13   Über Wichtigere Fragen der Religion. (Romang, J.P.) Heidelberg, 1870.
Phil 5757.7   Über Willenseinheit bei Arbeitsgehmeinschaft. (Hilber, H. (pseud.).) Leipzig, 1914.
Phil 5772.5.2   Über Willensfreiheit. (Windelband, Wilhelm.) Tübingen, 1904.
Phil 5772.5   Über Willensfreiheit. 3. Aufl. (Windelband, Wilhelm.) Tübingen, 1918.
Phil 5767.2   Über Willensfreiheit und Determinismus. (Romang, T.P.) Bern, 1835.
Phil 3925.4.80   Über Wirblichkeit und Logik; eine kritische Darlegung der Lehre Richard Wahles. (Funker, F.) Cernauti, 1924.
Phil 497.2.5   Über Wissen und Glauben. (Wagner, R.) Göttingen, 1854.
Phil 349.18   Über Wissen und Selbstbewisstsein. (Schaaf, Juluis Jakob.) Stuttgart, 1947.
Phil 3791.31   Über wissenschaftliche und nichtwissenschaftliche Philosophie. (Eiehl, Alois.) Freiburg, 1883.
Phil 6990.47.5   Über Wunder. 2. Aufl. (Virchow, R.) Frankfurt, 1908.
Phil 821.2   Überblick über der Geschichte der Philosophie. (Vogel, August.) Leipzig, 1904-05. 2v.
Phil 5599.93   Übereinstimmungsvalidität des HAWE und Entwicklung einer reduzierten Testform. (Dahl, Gerhard.) Meisenheim am Glan, 1968.
Phil 1701.19   Der Übergang vom Feudalen zum bügerlichen Weltbild. (Borkenan, Franz.) Paris, 1934.
Phil 3552.334   Das übergegensätzliche Gezeigt am Kontinuitätsprinzip bei Leibniz. (Kanitz, H.J.) Hamburg, 1951.
Phil 3502.2   Ueberhorst, C. Kant's Lehre von dem Verhältnisse der Kategorien zu der Erfahrung. Göttingen, 1878.
Phil 5525.8   Ueberhorst, K. Das Komische. Leipzig, 1896-1900. 2v.
Phil 5643.49   Ueberhorst, Karl. Die Entslehung der Gesichtswahrnehmung. Göttingen, 1876.
Phil 8876.28   Überhumanes Leben. (Brandis, J.D.) Schleswig, 1825.
Phil 3085.9.30   Überlegungen; Vierzehn Essays. (Alff, Wilhelm.) Heidelberg, 1964.
Phil 5590.335   Das überpersönliche Leben. (Solger, Friedrich.) Berlin, 1959.
Phil 6327.12.13   Der überraschte Psychologie. (Reik, Theodor.) Leiden, 1935.
Phil 1701.2   Übersecht des Entwicklungsganges der Philosophie. (Braniss, C.J.) Breslau, 1842.
Phil 1120.2   Übersicht der griech-römischen Philosophie. (Prantl, K.) Stuttgart, 1854.
Phil 5627.160   Übersicht der Religionspsychologie. (Hellpach, W.) Leipzig, 1939.
Phil 8967.1.10   Uebersicht der theologischen Ethik. (Rothe, R.) Bremen, 1895.
Phil 8831.3   Übersicht der vornehmsten Principien der Sittenlehre. (Garve, Christian.) Breslau, 1798.
Phil 3525.81   Uebersichtliche Darstellung des Lebens und der Wissenschaftlehre K.C.F. Krause's. (Lindemann, H.S.) München, 1839.
Phil 7069.59.20   Übersinnliche Gaben. 1. Aufl. (Huber, Guido.) Zürich, 1959.
Phil 5590.450   Übertragungsphänomene bei verwahrlosten männlichen Jugendlichen. (Hiese, Manfred.) Erlangen, 1965.
Phil 1870.102   Ueberweg, F. Berkeley's Abhandlung über Principien der menschlichen Erkenntnis. Berlin, 1869.
Phil 3502.4   Ueberweg, F. De priore et posteriore forma Kantianae critices. Berolini, 1862.
Phil 820.1.7.7   Ueberweg, F. Grundriss der Geschichte der Philosophie. Basel, 1960.
Phil 820.1.1   Ueberweg, F. Grundriss der Geschichte der Philosophie. Berlin, 1894. 3v.
Phil 820.1.3   Ueberweg, F. Grundriss der Geschichte der Philosophie. Berlin, 1894-97. 5v.
Phil 820.1.2   Ueberweg, F. Grundriss der Geschichte der Philosophie. v.1-2,3. 7. Aufl. Berlin, 1886-88. 2v.
Phil 820.1.4   Ueberweg, F. Grundriss der Geschichte der Philosophie. v.1-2,4. 9. Aufl. Berlin, 1902. 3v.
Phil 820.1.6   Ueberweg, F. Grundriss der Geschichte der Philosophie. v.1-2. 6. ed. Berlin, 1880-1914.
Phil 820.01   Ueberweg, F. Grundriss der Geschichte der Philosophie. v.1-3. Berlin, 1863.
Phil 820.1   Ueberweg, F. Grundriss der Geschichte der Philosophie. v.1-3. Berlin, 1868-71. 2v.
Phil 820.1.6.5   Ueberweg, F. Grundriss der Geschichte der Philosophie. v.2. 10. ed. Berlin, 1915.
Phil 820.1.7   Ueberweg, F. Grundriss der Geschichte der Philosophie. v.2-4. 11. Aufl. Berlin, 1914-28. 3v.
Phil 820.01.3   Ueberweg, F. Grundriss der Geschichte der Philosophie. 3rd ed. Berlin, 1867.
Phil 820.1.2.5   Ueberweg, F. Grundriss der Geschichte der Philosophie. 5. Aufl. Berlin, 1880.
Phil 820.1.5   Ueberweg, F. Grundriss der Geschichte der Philosophie. 10. ed. Berlin, 1906. 4v.
Phil 820.1.7.5A   Ueberweg, F. Grundriss der Geschichte der Philosophie. 12. Aufl. Berlin, 1926-51. 5v.
Phil 820.1.14   Ueberweg, F. History of philosophy. London, 1874-75. 2v.
Phil 820.1.8A   Ueberweg, F. History of philosophy. N.Y., 1872-4. 2v.
Phil 820.1.10   Ueberweg, F. History of philosophy. N.Y., 1874. 2v.

Phil 5060.1 Ueberweg, F. System der Logik. Bonn, 1857.
Phil 5060.1.6 Ueberweg, F. System der Logik. 5e Aufl. Bonn, 1882.
Phil 5060.1.5 Ueberweg, F. System of logic. London, 1871.
Phil 8599.19.95 Das überweltliche Gut und die innerweltlichen Güter. Diss. (Fellner, Karl.) Leipzig, 1927.
Phil 705.66 Überweltliches Leben in der Welt. (Dürckheim-Montmartin, Karlfried.) Weilheim, 1968.
Phil 510.150 Überwindung der Materie. (Bräuer, E.W.) Leipzig, 1925.
Phil 3195.6.125 Die Überwindung der Subjektivität in der empirischen Philosophie Diltheys und Deweys. (Richey, H.G.) Göttingen, 1935.
Phil 1750.748 Die Überwindung des Expressionismus. (Utitz, Emil.) Stuttgart, 1927.
Phil 3745.12 Überwindung der Massenmenschen durch echte Philosophie. 1. Aufl. (Pfeil, Hans.) Graz, 1956.
Phil 478.4 Die Überwindung des Materialismus. (Driesch, Hans.) Zürich, 1935.
Phil 475.2 Die Überwindung des Materialismus. 3e Aufl. (Apel, Paul.) Berlin, 1921.
Phil 3808.150 Die Überwindung des Pessimismus. (Fahsel, H.) Freiburg, 1927.
Phil 8708.32 Überwindung des Säkularismus in der Wissenschaft. (Schumann, F.K.) Gladbeck, 195-.
Phil 3808.106 Die Überwindung des Schopenhauerschen Pessimismus durch F. Nietzsche. (Hauff, W.) Halle, 1904.
Phil 683.2 Die Überwindung des Subjekt-Objekt-Denkens als philosophisches und theologisches Problem. (Rosenthal, Klaus.) Göttingen, 1970.
Phil 489.1A Überwindung des wissenschaftlichen Materialismus. (Ostwald, W.) Leipzig, 1895.
Phil 5500.24 Überwindung von Vorurteilen. 2. Aufl. (Friedrich-Ebert-Stiftung.) Hannover, 1960.
Phil 4466.2.80 Uedelhofen, M. Die Logik Petrus Fonseca's mit Ausschluss des Sprachlogischen. Inaug. Diss. Bonn, 1914.
Phil 3450.11.90 Ueber die Phänomenologie Husserl. (Grunwaldt, H.H.) Berlin, 1927.
Phil 9065.5 Ülken, Hilmi Ziyoi. Telifçilipin tenokurlan. Istanbul, 1933.
Phil 195.10 Uemov, A.I. Veshchi, svoistva i otnosheniia. Moskva, 1963.
Phil 301.5 Uexkuell, T. von. Der Mensch und die Natur. Bern, 1953.
Phil 351.3 Uexküll, T. von. Wirklichkeit als Geheimmis und Auftrag. Bern, 1945.
Phil 5260.8.5 Ufer, Christian. Systematische Psychologie für Oberlyzeen und Seminare. Leipzig, 1912.
Phil 484.4 Uffe sjoel og legeme. (Juul, Jensen.) København, 1970.
Phil 5060.2 Ufford, H.G. Elementary treatise on logic. N.Y., 1823.
Phil 193.181 Ugo Spirito. (Riconda, Guiseppe.) Torino, 1956.
Phil 8600.6 Ugrinovich, Dimitrii M. Filosofskie problemy Kritiki religii. Moskva, 1965.
Phil 4810.4 Uher, Ján. Filozofia v boji o dněšok. Vyd. 1. Bratislava, 1961.
Phil 2050.236 Uhl, Josef. Humes Stellung in der englischen Philosophie. v.1-2. Prag, 1890-91.
Phil 5330.5 Uhl, L.L. Attention. Baltimore, 1890.
Phil 3805.95 Uhlhorn, Otto. Schleiermachers Entwurf einer Kritik der bisherigen Sittenlehre dargestellt. Oldenburg, 1894. 2v.
Phil 3494.28 Uiber die Falschheit und Gottlosigkeit des Kantischen System. (Miotti.) Augsburg, 1802.
Phil 3494.28.5 Uiber die Falschheit und Gottlosigkeit des Kantischen System. (Miotti.) Wien, 1801.
Phil 3019.5 Uit de Republiek der Letteren. (Thijssen-Schoute, Caroline Louise.) 's-Gravenhage, 1967[1968]
Phil 3425.515 Het uitgangspunt van Hegel's ontologie. (Kruithof, J.) Brugge, 1959.
Phil 4803.454.95 Ujejski, Józef. O cenę absolutu; rzecz o Hoene-Wroński. Warszawa, 1925.
Phil 50.30 Ukrainskii. Psikhonevrologicheskii Institut, Kharkov. Trudy. Kharkov.
Phil 4710.50.30 Ukrains'ko-bolgars'ki filosofs'ki zv'iazki. (Buchvarov, Mikhail D.) Kyïv, 1966.
Phil 310.690 Ukraintsev, Boris S. Otobrazhenie v nezhivoi prirode. Moskva, 1969.
Phil 1020.60.5 Ulken, H.Z. Islam duzancesi ve tarihteki yeri. Ankara, 1959.
Phil 1020.60 Ulken, H.Z. Islam felsefesi kouynoklou ve teni. Ankara, 1967.
Phil 351.7 Ülken, Hilmi Ziya. Bilgi ve değer. Ankara, 1965.
Phil 195.13 Ulken, Hilmi Zuja. Felsejeye gini. Ankara, 1957. 2 pam.
Phil 195.13.5 Ulken, Hilmi Zuja. Varlik ve olus. Ankara, 1968.
Phil 2150.22.145 Ulle, Dieter. E'rivoluzionaria la dottrina di Marcuse? Torino, 1969.
Phil 5230.1 Ullersperger, J.B. Die Geschichte der Psychologie und der Psychiatrik in Spanien. Würzburg, 1871.
Phil 5590.439 Ullman, Albert Daniel. Sociocultural foundations of personality. Boston, 1965.
Phil 6330.2 Ullmann, Leonard P. A psychological approach to abnormal behavior. Englewood, Cliffs, 1969.
Phil 1750.166.25 Ulmann, Andre. L'humanisme du 20e siècle. Paris, 1946.
Phil 720.86 Ulmer, Karl. Die Wissenschaften und die Wahrheit. Stuttgart, 1966.
Phil 270.61A Ul'mskaia noch': filosofi slucnaia. (Landau, M.A.) N'iu Iork, 1953.
VPhil 5125.34 Uloga indukcije u naučnom istraživanju. (Arandjelović, Jovan T.) Beograd, 1967.
Phil 8895.1 Uloth, L. Begriff, Wesen...Darstellung der Ethik. Göttingen, 18- .
Phil 195.9 Ulrich, Ferdinand. Homo Abyssus. Johannes, 1961.
Phil 5871.106 Ulrich, Ferdinand. Der Mensch als Anfang. Benziger, 1970.
Phil 672.27 Ulrich, Georg. Der Begriff des Raumes. Berlin, 1907.
Phil 351.2 Ulrich, Georg. Grundlegung des Systems aller möglichen Erfahrung. Berlin, 1896.
Phil 3895.50 Ulrici, H. Compendium der Logik. Leipzig, 1860.
Phil 3895.53 Ulrici, H. Compendium der Logik. 2. Aufl. Leipzig, 1872.
Phil 3895.30 Ulrici, H. Glauben und Wissen. Leipzig, 1858.
Phil 3895.35 Ulrici, H. Gott und der Mensch. Bd.1. Leipzig, 1873.
Phil 3895.35.2 Ulrici, H. Gott und der Mensch. 2. Aufl. Bd.1-2. Leipzig, 1874. 2v.
Phil 3895.40 Ulrici, H. Gott und die Natur. Leipzig, 1862.
Phil 3895.40.2 Ulrici, H. Gott und die Natur. Leipzig, 1875.
Phil 3895.40.5 Ulrici, H. Gott und die Natur. 2. Aufl. Leipzig, 1866.
Phil 3895.45 Ulrici, H. Das Grundprincip der Philosophie. Leipzig, 1845-46. 2v.
Phil 3850.1.83 Ulrici, H. Der Philosoph Strauss. Halle, 1873.
Phil 3895.49 Ulrici, H. System der Logik. Leipzig, 1852.
Phil 3425.219 Ulrici, Hermann. Über Princip und Methode der hegelschen Philosophie. Halle, 1841.

Phil 8421.2 Ulricus Engelberti, Argentinensis. Des Ulricus Engelberti von Strassburg O. Pr. (+1277) Abhandlung de Pulchro. München, 1926.
Phil 5520.502 Ulshoefer-Heinloth, Elisabeth. Studien zur sprachkommunikativen Orientierung. Inaug. Diss. Passau, 1964.
Phil 4070.1.60 Ultima critica. (Bonavino, Cristoforo.) Milano, 1889-93. 3v.
Phil 2840.70.5 As ultimas conversações. (Renouvier, C.B.) Coimbra, 1930.
Phil 8870.20 The ultimate defense. 1st ed. (Clair, F.F.) Rutland, 1959.
Phil 8879.10 The ultimate facts of ethics. (Everett, C.C.) Boston, 1887.
Phil 190.5 The ultimate generalization. (Peck, J.S.) N.Y., 1876.
Phil 1930.19.30 The ultimate reductibility of essence to existence in existential metaphysics. (Carlo, William E.) The Hague, 1966.
Phil 9070.122 The ultimate revolution. 1st ed. (Starcke, Walter.) N.Y., 1969.
Phil 735.78 Ultimate values in the light of contemporary thought. (Mackenzie, J.S.) London, 1924.
Phil 9430.7 The ultimatum of pessimism. (Barlow, J.W.) London, 1882.
Phil 1750.155 Ultimi contributi alla storia degli umanisti. pt.1-2. (Mercati, G.) Città del Vaticano, 1939.
Phil 177.35.40 Ultimi saggi. 2. ed. (Croce, Benedetto.) Bari, 1948.
Phil 3450.19.109 L'ultimo. 1e ed. (Chiodi, Pietro.) Torino, 1952.
Phil 3450.19.109.2
Phil 365.62 L'ultimo Heidegger. 2e ed. (Chiodi, Pietro.) Torino, 1960.
Phil 7069.40.4 Ultimo umanesimo. (Grillo, Ugo.) Bari, 1966.
Phil 7069.31.40 The ultra-perceptive faculty. (Hettinger, John.) London, 1940.
Phil 1133.47 "Ultrafamia", esegesi della fenomenologia intellettuale dello spiritismo moderno. (Trespioli, Gino.) Milano, 1931.
Phil 575.70 Um die Begriffswelt der Vorsokratiker. (Gadamer, Hans G.) Darmstadt, 1968.
Phil 310.661 Um die Persönlichkeit. Bd.1. (Prinzhorn, H.) Heidelberg, 1927.
Phil 3640.276 Um eine "dialektische Logik". (Huber, Eduard.) München, 1966.
Phil 817.27.5 Um Nietzsches Untergang; Beiträge zum Verständnis des Genies. (Cohn, Paul.) Hannover, 1931.
Phil 4006.5.37 Umane certezze; il libro della verità ragionata. (Roncuzzi, Alfredo.) Roma, 1966.
Phil 210.45 L'umanesimo italiano. (Garin, Eugenio.) Bari, 1952.
Phil 1630.10 Umanesimo e ermeneutica. Padova, 1963.
Phil 1750.166.75 Umanesimo e esoterismo. (Archivio di Filosofia.) Padova, 1960.
Phil 1507.6 Umanesimo e machiavellismo. Padova, 1949.
Phil 845.6 Umanesimo e scienza politica. (Congresso Internationale di Studi Umanistici, Rome.) Milano, 1951.
Phil 4260.110 Umanesimo moderno o tramonto dell'Umanesimo? (Pozzo, Gianni M.) Padova, 1970.
Phil 190.45 Umanesimo e religione in G.B. Vico. (Corsano, Antonio.) Bari, 1935.
Phil 1715.12 Umanismo antivitale. (Pagani, Silvio.) Milano, 1925.
Phil 8401.12 Umanismo logico. (Pepi, Sergio.) Roma, 1963.
Phil 8412.16 Umanità dell'arte. (Aranio, Ruiz.) Firenze, 1954.
Phil 585.70 L'umanità dell'arte. (La Via, Vincenzo.) Roma, 1924.
Phil 3415.35 Umano e disumani. 1. ed. (Cantoni, Remo.) Milano, 1958.
Phil 3415.35.2 Das Umbewusste...Physiologie. (Hartmann, Eduard von.) Berlin, 1872.
Phil 3200.14.80 Das Umbewusste...Physiologie. 2. Aufl. (Hartmann, Eduard von.) Berlin, 1877.
Phil 5465.134 Der Umbruch des Denkens. (Steinbuechel, Theodor.) Darmstadt, 1966.
Phil 8413.41 Umelecké myslenie. (Štraus, T.) Bratislava, 1962.
Phil 960.190A Umení, skutečnost, poznání. (Morkrejs, Antonín.) Praha, 1966.
  Umesha, Mishra. History of Indian philosophy. Allahabad, 1957.
Phil 8182.2 Umetnost i kriterijumi. (Lukić, Sveta.) Beograd, 1964.
Phil 8430.45 Umetnost i umetničko delo. (Vučković, Vojislav.) Beograd, 1962.
Phil 3549.10.50 Umgang der Jahre. (Kassner, Rudolf.) Erlenbach, 1949.
Phil 1750.369 Umgang mit Gätterbilden. (Huebner, F.M.) Frankfurt, 1950.
Phil 8590.34 Umgang mit Göttlichem. (Kerényi, Karoly.) Göttingen, 1955.
Phil 8590.34.2 Umgang mit Göttlichem. 2. Aufl. (Kerényi, Karoly.) Göttingen, 1961.
Phil 5545.92 Das umittelbare Behalten. (Suellwold, F.) Göttingen, 1964.
Phil 3000.2 Die Umkehr der Wissenschaft in Preussen. (Allihn, F.H.T.) Berlin, 1855.
Phil 4710.9 Die Umkehrung Hegels. (Wetter, G.A.) Köln, 1963.
Phil 3640.299 Umland, Karl. Nietzsches Würdigung des Menschen. Würzburg, 1964.
Phil 3450.19.320 L'umo e il mondo nella filosofia di M. Heidegger. (Finazzo, Giancarlo.) Roma, 1963.
Phil 8520.55 Die Umprägung der natürlichen Theologie in Religionsphilosophie. (Feiereis, Konrad.) Leipzig, 1965.
Phil 5258.38.5 Umriss einer analytischen Psychologie. 2. Aufl. Teil I. (Schmied-Kowarzik, W.) Leipzig, 1928.
Phil 5520.52 Umriss einer Theorie der Namen. (Stöhr, Adolf.) Leipzig, 1889.
Phil 818.12 Umrisse zur Geschichte der Philosophie. (Schmidt, Edward.) Berlin, 1839.
Phil 5044.1.6 Umrisse zur Psychologie des Denkens. 2e Aufl. (Erdmann, B.) Tübingen, 1908.
Phil 5258.38 Umrisz einer neuen analytischen Psychologie. (Schmied-Kowarzik, W.) Leipzig, 1912.
Phil 5585.10.5 Umwälzung der Wahrnehmungshypothesen. (Schwarz, H.) Leipzig, 1895.
Phil 3640.27.1 Umwertung aller Werte. (Nietzsche, Friedrich.) München, 1969. 2v.
Phil 8876.15 Un moraliste. (Bersot, D.P.E.) Paris, 1882.
Phil 175.39 Un testament philosophique. (Accambray, Leon.) Paris, 1937.
Phil 3640.17.2 Un zeitgemässe Betrachtungen. (Nietzsche, Friedrich.) Stuttgart, 1955.
Phil 177.132 Una filosofia da cultura. (Cruz Malpique, M.) Porto, 1962.
Phil 195.2.5 Unamuno, M. de. Das tragische Lebensgefühl. München, 1925.
Phil 1705.12 Unamuno, William James y Kirkegaard y otros ensayos. (Farré, Luis.) Buenos Aires, 1967.
Phil 1857.1 Unancestral voice. (Barfield, Owen.) London, 1965.

Phil 4365.2.40   Unas lecciones de metafísica. (Ortega y Gasset, José.) Madrid, 1966.

Phil 3450.18.140   Die Unbedingtheit des Sittlichen. (Baumgartner, Hans Michael.) München, 1962.

Phil 3030.6   Die unbefriedigte Aufklärung. (Oelmueller, W.) Frankfurt, 1969.

Htn   Phil 6315.2.64.1*   Das Unbehagen in der Kultur. (Freud, Sigmund.) Wien, 1930.

Phil 6315.2.64   Das Unbehagen in der Kultur. (Freud, Sigmund.) Wien, 1931.

Phil 978.97   Der unbekannte Gott. (Skerst, Herman von.) Stuttgart, 1967.

Phil 5251.52   Das unbekannte Ich. (Leithauser, J.C.) Berlin, 1955.

Phil 2805.277   Der unbekannte Pascal. (Nasmuth, E.) Regensburg, 1962.

Phil 5401.12   Das Unbekannte und die Angst. (Liebeck, O.) Leipzig, 1928.

Phil 8610.881   Unbelief in the eighteenth century as contrasted with its earlier and later history. (Cairns, John.) Edinburgh, 1881.

Phil 8610.964.5   The unbelievers. (Crekshut, A.O.J.) London, 1964.

Phil 6315.2.14   Die Unbewusste. (Freud, Sigmund.) Frankfurt, 1960.

Phil 3552.125   Das Unbewusste bei Leibniz...Theorien. (Ganz, Hans.) Zürich, 1917.

Phil 5722.19   Das unbewusste Denken. (Wenzl, Aloys.) Karlsruhe, 1927.

Phil 6319.1.35   Das Unbewusste im normalen und kranken. (Jung, C.G.) Zürich, 1926.

Phil 3415.88   Das Unbewusste und der Pessimismus. (Volkelt, J.) Berlin, 1873.

Phil 7069.45.35   Unbidden guests, a book of real ghosts. (Stevens, William O.) N.Y., 1945.

Phil 7069.27.18   Uncanny stories. (Daily News, London.) London, 1927.

Phil 5246.76A   Uncertainty and structure as psychological concepts. (Garner, W.R.) N.Y., 1962.

Phil 8582.53   The uncharted way. (Churchill, W.) Philadelphia, 1940.

Phil 9182.6   Uncle Henry's letters to the farm boy. 4. ed. (Wallace, Henry.) N.Y., 1906.

Phil 9175.5   Uncle Jerry's letters to young mothers. (Porter, Ann E.) Boston, 1854.

Phil 5940.1   Uncle Sam (pseud.) Uncle Sam's recommendation of phrenology. N.Y., 1842.

Phil 5940.1.3   Uncle Sam's letters on phrenology. N.Y., 1896.

Phil 5940.1   Uncle Sam's recommendation of phrenology. (Uncle Sam (pseud.).) N.Y., 1842.

Phil 5722.10   The unconscious. (Levine, I.) N.Y., 1923.

Phil 6325.8.5   The unconscious. (Prince, Morton.) N.Y., 1914.

Phil 6325.8.6   The unconscious. (Prince, Morton.) N.Y., 1916.

Phil 5722.21.9   The unconscious: a symposium. N.Y., 1927.

Phil 5722.22   The unconscious: a symposium. N.Y., 1928.

Phil 6325.8.7   The unconscious. 2d ed. (Prince, Morton.) N.Y., 1921.

Phil 6325.8.8   The unconscious. 2d ed. (Prince, Morton.) N.Y., 1929.

Phil 5722.42.2   The unconscious before Freud. (Whyte, Lancelot.) London, 1967.

Phil 5722.42   The unconscious before Freud. (Whyte, Lancelot.) N.Y., 1960.

Phil 6317.11.9   The unconscious in life and art. (Herbert, S.) London, 1932.

Htn   Phil 5545.4*   Unconscious memory. (Butler, S.) London, 1880.

Phil 5722.3A   Unconscious memory. (Butler, S.) N.Y., 1911.

Phil 6317.11   The unconscious mind. (Herbert, S.) London, 1923.

Phil 5722.16   The unconscious mind. (Schofield, A.T.) London, 1898.

Phil 5722.16.2   The unconscious mind. 2. ed. (Schofield, A.T.) London, 1899.

Phil 1870.125A   The unconscious origin of Berkeley's philosophy. (Wisdom, J.O.) London, 1953.

Phil 5722.25   Unconsciousness. (Miller, James G.) N.Y., 1942.

Phil 8893.93   Unconventional ethics. (Schwarz, O.L.) Washington, 1936.

Phil 6328.56   Und du wirst Getrieben. (Schläfer-Wolfram, E.) Berlin, 1933.

Phil 8580.29   Under the highest leadership. (Adam, J.D.) N.Y., 1918.

Phil 4600.2.38   Under världskrisen. (Larsson, Hans.) Stockholm, 1920.

Phil 1980.4.20A   Under whatever sky. (Edman, Irwin.) N.Y., 1951.

NEDL Phil 7054.7   Underhill, A. Leah. The missing link in modern spiritualism. N.Y., 1885.

Phil 5627.60.10   Underhill, E. The golden sequence. 2. ed. London, 1932.

Phil 5627.60.7   Underhill, E. The life of the spirit and the life of today. London, 1922.

Phil 5627.60.5   Underhill, E. The life of the spirit and the life of today. N.Y., 1926.

Phil 5627.60   Underhill, E. The life of the spirit and the life of today. 3d ed. London, 1923.

Phil 8600.3.5   Underhill, E. Man and the supernatural. London, 1927.

Phil 8600.3   Underhill, E. Man and the supernatural. N.Y., 1928.

Phil 5627.60.20   Underhill, E. The spiritual life. N.Y., 1937.

Phil 525.7.15   Underhill, Evelyn. Collected papers of Evelyn Underhill. London, 1946.

Phil 525.7.20   Underhill, Evelyn. Concerning the inner life, with The house of the soul. London, 1947.

Phil 525.7.7   Underhill, Evelyn. The essentials of mysticism and other essays. London, 1920.

Phil 525.7.10   Underhill, Evelyn. The mystic way. London, 1913.

Phil 525.7.1   Underhill, Evelyn. Mysticism. 3rd ed. N.Y., 1911.

Phil 525.7.2   Underhill, Evelyn. Mysticism. 4th ed. N.Y., 1912.

NEDL Phil 525.7.3   Underhill, Evelyn. Mysticism. 8th ed. N.Y., 1911.

Phil 525.7.5.3   Underhill, Evelyn. Practical mysticism; a little book for normal people. N.Y., 1915.

Phil 525.7.5   Underhill, Evelyn. Practical mysticism. London, 1914.

Phil 7069.28.100   Underhill, Margaret. Your infinite possibilities. London, 1928.

Phil 3489.12   Undersøgelser verdrørende grundlaget for Kants erkendelsesteori. (Hansen, Oscar.) København, 1892.

Phil 4582.4.31   Undersökning af den empiristiska etikens möjlighet. (Hägerström, Axel.) Upsala, 1895.

Phil 3483.38   Undersökning af läran om viljans frihet - Kants behandling af problemet. (Bolin, W.) Helsingfors, 1868.

Phil 5620.8   Undersökningar...problemräkningens förutsättningar och förlopp. (Jonsson, K.G.) Uppsala, 1919.

Phil 4655.1.64   Undersökningar angående den materialistiska verldsåskådningen. (Wikner, Pontus.) Stockholm, 1870.

Phil 6128.9   Undersökningar i läran om själ och kropp. (Strömberg, J.D.) Lund, 1897.

Phil 4655.1.43   Undersökningar om enhet och mängfald. (Wikner, Pontus.) Upsala, 1863.

Phil 6854.2   Understanding and preventing suicide. (Leonard, Calista V.) Springfield, Ill., 1967.

Phil 2255.1.79   Understanding history. (Russell, Bertrand Russell.) N.Y., 1957.

Phil 5548.40   Understanding human motivation. (Stacey, Chalmers L.) Cleveland, 1958.

Phil 9035.53.2A   Understanding human nature. (Adler, Alfred.) Garden City, N.Y., 1927.

Phil 9035.53   Understanding human nature. (Adler, Alfred.) N.Y., 1927.

Phil 9035.53.4   Understanding human nature. (Adler, Alfred.) N.Y., 1928.

Phil 9035.53.10   Understanding human nature. (Adler, Alfred.) N.Y., 1946.

Phil 3850.27.230   An understanding of Albert Schweitzer. (Marshall, George.) N.Y., 1966.

Phil 9590.11   The understanding of religion. (Brewster, E.T.) Boston, 1923.

Phil 6312.17   Understanding our behavior. 1st ed. (Crow, Lester D.) N.Y., 1956.

Phil 5243.33.3   Understanding ourselves. (Dearden, H.) N.Y., 1926.

Phil 5260.9.5   Understanding ourselves. (United States. Department of Agriculture. Graduate School.) Washington, 1938.

Phil 5066.318   Understanding symbolic logic. (Massey, Gerald J.) N.Y., 1970.

Phil 194.50   Understanding the great philosophers. 1st ed. (Thomas, H.) Garden City, N.Y., 1962.

Phil 2340.10.170   Understanding Whitehead. (Lowe, Victor A.) Baltimore, 1962.

Phil 5246.48   Understanding yourself, the mental hygiene of personality. (Groves, Ernest R.) N.Y., 1935.

Phil 5627.107.5   Underwood, A.C. Conversion: Christian and non-Christian. N.Y., 1925.

Phil 8610.878.15   Underwood, B.F. The Underwood-Marples debate. N.Y., 1878.

Phil 7068.96.15   Underwood, Sara A. Automatic or spirit writing, with other psychic experiences. Chicago, 1896.

Phil 8610.878.15   The Underwood-Marples debate. (Underwood, B.F.) N.Y., 1878.

Phil 6319.1.62.1   The undiscovered self. (Jung, C.G.) N.Y., 1958.

Phil 4301.1.5   Une lettre à Jacques Maritain. (Avelino, Andres.) Ciudad Trujillo, 1944.

Phil 1508.2.5   Das Unendliche in der mittelalterlichen Metaphysik und in der Kantschendialektik. (Dempf, Alois.) Münster, 1925.

Phil 525.82   Unendliche Sphäre und Allmittelpunkt. (Mahnke, D.) Halle, 1937.

Phil 299.20   Die Unendlichkeit der Welt. (Schneidewin, M.) Berlin, 1900.

Phil 3501.9   Der Unendlichkeitsbegriff bei Kant und Aristoteles. (Theodor, J.) Breslau, 1877.

Phil 7069.66.25   The unexplained; some strange cases in psychical research. (Mackenzie, Andrew.) London, 1966.

Phil 7069.67.15   The unexplained. (Spraggett, Allen.) N.Y., 1967.

Phil 8962.6   The unexplored self. (Montgomery, G.R.) N.Y., 1910.

Phil 5047.7   Unfangsgrunde der Logik. (Hoffbauer, J.C.) Halle, 1810.

Phil 978.74.40   Unfinished autobiography. (Bailey, A.A. (Mrs.).) N.Y., 1951.

Phil 7074.10   Unfinished symphonies; voices from the beyond. (Brown, Rosemary.) N.Y., 1971.

Phil 5238.201   Unfinished tasks in the behavioral sciences. (Abrams, A.) Baltimore, 1964.

Phil 5767.9   Die Unfreiheit des Willens. (Ruesch, Arnold.) Darmstadt, 1925.

Phil 4585.9.81   En ung dansk filosof. (Rubin, E.) Kjøbenhavn, 1920.

Phil 8598.44   Das Ungegebene; eine Religions- und Wertphilosophie. (Schwarz, Hermann.) Tübingen, 1921.

Phil 8402.56.5   Ungeborner der Ideen. (Bense, Max.) Köln, 1965.

Phil 3900.2   Unger, E. The imagination of reason. London, 1952.

Phil 3900.2.5   Unger, Erich. Das Lebendige und das Goettliche. Jerusalem, 1966.

Phil 8612.15   Unger, Rudolf. Herder, Novalis und Kleist. Frankfurt, 1922.

Phil 5258.22.5   Unger, Rudolf. Die kinderpsychologischen Bestrebungen L. Strümpells. Strassburg, 1912.

Phil 3195.6.86   Unger, Rudolf. Weltanschauung und Dichtung...Dilthey. Zürich, 1917.

Phil 3805.173   Ungern-Sternberg, Arthur Freiherr von. Freiheit und Wirklichkeit. Gotha, 1931.

Phil 3805.173.5   Ungern-Sternberg, Arthur Freiherr von. Schleiermachers völkische Botschaft. Gotha, 1933.

Phil 6980.759   Ungersma, Aaron J. The search for meaning. Philadelphia, 1961.

Phil 3925.11.70   Ungesichertheit und Wagnis. (Leenhouwen, Albinus.) Essen, 1964.

Phil 197.65   Ungewissheit und Wagnis. (Wust, Peter.) Salzburg, 1937.

Phil 7069.64.15   The unhappy medium. (Fornell, Earl W.) Austin, 1964.

Phil 6980.429.5   Die unheimlichen Moglichkeiten oder die Manipulierte Seele. (Loebsacu, T.) Düsseldorf, 1967.

Phil 7072.22   Unhorbares wird Hörbar. (Raudive, Konstantins.) Ramagen, 1968.

Phil 283.4   Unidad del universo. (Cuyás, F.G.) Habana, 1874.

Phil 632.10   L'unification du réel. (Stommel, Joannes Antonius.) Utrecht, 1964?

Phil 351.5   L'unification del sopere. Firenze, 1965.

Phil 2070.161   The unifying moment; the psychological philosophy of William James and Alfred North Whitehead. (Eisendrath, Craig Ralph.) Cambridge, 1971.

Phil 2750.20.55   L'union de l'âme et du corps chez Malebranche, Biran et Bergson. (Merleau-Ponty, Maurice.) Paris, 1968.

Phil 8600.2   Union de Libres Penseurs et de Libres Croyants pour la Culture Morale. Le sentiment religieux à l'heure actuelle. Paris, 1919.

Phil 5409.8   Union des Religieuses Enseignantes. L'éducation de l'espérance. Paris, 1959?

Phil 9450.32   Union Internationale d'Études Sociales. Code de morale politique. Bruxelles, 1957.

Phil 75.27   Union list of foreign serials cited in Psychological index, 1922. (National Research Council. Research Information Service.) Washington, 1925.

Phil 2725.14.85   Union pour l'Action Morale, Paris. Jules Lagneau. Paris, n.d.

Phil 177.65.5   The unique status of man. (Carr, H.W.) N.Y., 1928.

Phil 585.280   The uniqueness of man. (Nobel Conference, 4th, Gustavus Adolphus College.) Amsterdam, 1969.

Phil 5075.5   L'unità come categoria. (Moschetti, A.M.) Milano, 1952. 2v.

Phil 1730.32   L'unità de sapere nell'illuminismo. (Ponte Orvieto, Marina da.) Padova, 1968.

Phil 187.80   L'unita del mondo nel sistema del pensiero. (Maggiore, G.) Palermo, 1913.

Phil 3450.19.400   L'unità del pensiero in Martin Heidegger; una ontologia estetica. (Penzo, Giorgio.) Padova, 1965.

Phil 3425.641   L'unità del sapere in Hegel. (Chiereghin, Franco.) Padova, 1963.

Phil 3450.11.420   L'unità del sapere in Husserl. (Biral, Alessandro.) Padova, 1967.

Phil 5068.55   L'unità del sapere nel neopositivismo. (Ponte Orvieto, Marina da.) Padova, 1965.

Phil 4260.190 — L'unità e la religiosità del pensiero di Giambattista Vico. (Candela, Silvestro.) Napoli, 1969.
Phil 333.15 — L'unité de la connaissance humaine. (Coninces, A.) Bruges, 1943.
Phil 5270.24 — L'unité de la psychologie. 2. éd. (Lagache, Daniel.) Paris, 1969.
Phil 585.181 — Unité de l'homme. (Hartung, Henri.) Paris, 1963.
Phil 5255.66 — L'unité des science humaines. (Palmade, G.) Paris, 1961.
Phil 2725.45 — Unité et diversité. (Lévêque, R.) Paris, 1963.
Phil 180.55 — Unité et intelligibilité. (Fiszer, E.) Paris, 1936.
Phil 180.55.5 — Unité et intelligibilité. Thèse. (Fiszer, E.) Paris, 1936.
Phil 8876.53 — L'unité morale des religions. (Bonet-Maury, G.) Paris, 1913.
Phil 6962.18 — L'unité psychique et les troubles mentaux. (Mignard, Maurice.) Paris, 1928.
Phil 30.1.5 — United Lodge of Theosophists. U.L.T. pamphlet. Bombay.
Phil 6980.760 — United States. Children's Bureau. Residential treatment centers for emotional disturbed children. Washington, 1953.
Phil 5780.15.10 — United States. Congress. House. Communist psychological warfare. Washington, 1958.
Phil 6945.11.10 — United States. Congress. Senate. Commission on Public Lands. Report to accompany Bill S44; include memorial of Miss D.L. Dix, January 23, 1848. Washington, 1854.
Phil 5260.9 — United States. Department of Agriculture. Graduate School. The adjustment of personality. Washington, 1939.
Phil 5260.9.5 — United States. Department of Agriculture. Graduate School. Understanding ourselves. Washington, 1938.
Phil 9070.140 — United States. Department of the Army. Character guidance discussion topics; duty, honor, country. Washington. 1951+ 2v.
Phil 9400.17 — United States. Federal Security Agency. Committee on Aging and Geriatrics. Fact book on aging. Washington, D.C., 1952.
Phil 5406.2 — United States. National Institute of Child Health and Human Development. Perspectives on human deprivation: biological, psychological, and sociological. Washington, 1968.
Phil 5203.16 — United States. National Institute of Mental Health. Reference guide. Bethesda, Md.
Phil 6750.263 — United States. Presdent's Panel on Mental Retardation. Report of the task force education and rehabilitation. Washington, D.C., 1963.
Phil 6750.262 — United States. President's Panel on Mental Retardation. Report of the mission to Denmark and Sweden. Washington, D.C., 1962.
Phil 9495.120 — United States. Public Health Service. Fighting venereal diseases. Washington, 1920.
Phil 5545.186 — United States Research and Development Board. Symposium on psychology of learning basic to military training problems. Washington, 1953.
Phil 5548.15 — United States Research and Development Board. Committee on Human Resources. Symposium on motivation. Washington, 1953.
Phil 8740.5 — Unity in the spirit. (De Pierrefeu, Elsa (Tudor).) Rindge, N.H., 1955.
Phil 2490.80 — The unity of Comte's life and doctrine. (Bridges, J.H.) London, 1866.
Phil 3246.85.2 — Unity of Fichte's Doctrine of knowledge. (Thompson, A.B.) Boston, 1895.
Phil 342.20 — The unity of knowledge. (Leary, Lewis.) Garden City, N.Y., 1955.
Phil 333.14PF — The unity of knowledge and the organization of thought. (Custard, Harry L.) Washington, D.C., 1940.
Phil 177.6 — The unity of law. (Carey, H.C.) Philadelphia, 1872.
Phil 1135.182 — The unity of mankind in Greek thought. (Baldry, Harold Capame.) Cambridge, Eng., 1965.
Phil 497.6 — The unity of matter. (Wilson, A.S.) London, 1855.
Phil 8582.3.6 — The unity of nature. (Argyll, G.D.C.) London, 1884.
Phil 8582.3.7 — The unity of nature. (Argyll, G.D.C.) N.Y., 1884.
Phil 806.13.1 — The unity of philosophical experience. (Gilson, Etienne.) N.Y., 1937.
Phil 806.13.2 — The unity of philosophical experience. (Gilson, Etienne.) N.Y., 1946.
Phil 303.12.25 — The unity of the universe. (Lintz, E.J.) Fribourg, 1939.
Phil 8697.2 — The unity of truth in Christianity and evolution. (Hark, J.M.) N.Y., 1888.
Phil 5757.9 — The unity of will. (Hight, G.A.) London, 1906.
Phil 30.2F — The univercoelum and spiritual philosopher. N.Y. 2,1848
Phil 30.12 — Univers. Paris. 1,1964+
Phil 2475.1.294.6 — L'univers bergsonien. (Adolphe, Lydie.) Paris, 1955.
Phil 3552.358 — L'univers leibnizien. (Moreau, Joseph.) Paris, 1956.
Phil 176.91 — L'univers-organisme. (Bardonnet, L.) Paris, 1923. 4v.
Phil 2905.1.255 — L'univers personnel de Teilhard. (Viallet, François A.) Paris, 1955-61. 2v.
Phil 8890.34.5 — Universa philosophia de moribus. (Piccolomineus, F.) Francofurti, 1627.
Htn   Phil 8890.35F* — Universa philosophia de moribus. (Piccolomineus, F.) Venetiis, 1583.
Phil 6110.3.15 — The universal constant in living. (Alexander, F.M.) N.Y., 1941.
Phil 4260.133 — The universal humanity of Giambattista Vico. (Grimaldi, A.A.) N.Y., 1958.
Phil 7069.35.20 — Universal knowledge; the road home. (O'Hare, Elizabeth.) N.Y., 1935.
Phil 665.40 — The universal medium; a new interpretation of the soul. (Mackenzie, J.N. Landseer.) London, 1922.
Phil 8610.905 — A universal monistic alliance. (Haeckel, Ernst.) Los Angeles, 1905.
Phil 182.17.20 — Universal-philosophische Prolegomena. (Hillebrand, J.) Mainz, 1830.
Phil 1507.3 — Universal scholastic philosophy publicly defended. (Currie, F.J.) n.p., 1928.
Phil 184.36 — Universal tradition. v.6. (Johnson, E.V.) Alexandria, Va., 1932.
Phil 3585.11.30 — Der universale Humanismus. (Liebert, Arthur.) Zürich, 1946.
Phil 3903.3.110 — Universalis philosophiae. (Vossius, G.J.) Leiden, 1955.
Phil 8420.13 — Universalismo constructivo. (Torrés-García, J.) Buenos Aires, 1944.
Phil 1540.92 — Universalismus und Partikularismus in Mittelalter. (Koelner Mediaevistentagung.) Berlin, 1968.
Phil 3850.27.112 — Die Universalmenschen Goethe und Schweitzer. (Lind, Emil.) Neustadt, 1964.
Phil 3528.45 — Universalphilosophische Vorlesungen für Gebildete beiderlei Geschlechts. (Krug, Wilhelm Traugott.) Neustadt, 1831.

Phil 730.28 — Universals; a new look at an old problem. (Zabeeh, Farhang.) The Hague, 1966.
Phil 298.22 — The universe, its origin, nature and destiny. (Rice, Laban Lucy.) N.Y., 1951.
Phil 291.2F — Universe. (Klyce, Scudder.) Winchester, Mass., 1921.
Phil 200.11 — Universe and reality. (Zehnder, M.) Toronto, 1929.
Phil 188.20 — The universe and you. (Neal, H.H.) Laguna Beach, Calif., 1954.
Phil 282.21.5 — The universe at large. (Bondi, Hermann.) Garden City, 1960.
Phil 282.9 — L'universe-organisme. (Bardonnet, L.) Paris, 1912. 2v.
Phil 281.2 — Universe powers of nature revealed. (Atkinson, J.) London, 1856.
Phil 8709.13 — Universe within us. (Taylor, Robert O.P.) N.Y., 1931.
Phil 4972.5.60 — Universidad Nacional del Litoral. Alejandro Korn. Rosario, 1962.
Phil 30.9 — Universidad Nacional del Litoral. Santa Fe, Argentina. Instituto de Filosofía. Cuadernos filosóficos. Rosario.
Phil 1750.490 — Universidad Nacional del Litoral. Santa Fé, Argentina. Instituto de Filosofía. Symposium sobre existencialismo. pts.1-7. Rosario, 195-?
Phil 3450.26.10 — Universitas litterarum. (Hellpach, Willy.) Stuttgart, 1948.
Phil 6673.4.17 — L'université de Montpellier et le magnétisme animal. (Du Potet, J. de S.) Beziers, 1836.
Phil 42.11 — University of Colorado studies. Series in philosophy. (Colorado. University.) Boulder.
Phil 9035.37 — The university of hard knocks. (Parlette, R.A.) Chicago, 1917.
Phil 8965.2 — University of Pennsylvania. The Boardman Lectureship in Christian ethics. Philadelphia, 1900.
Phil 30.7 — University of Southern California. Psychological Laboratory. Report. Los Angeles. 1,1952+
Phil 70.105.5 — University of Western Ontario. Philosophy Colloquium. Fact and existence; proceedings of the University of Western Ontario philosophy colloquium, 1966. Toronto, 1969. 2v.
Phil 70.105 — University of Western Ontario. Philosophy Colloquium. Fact and existence; proceedings of the University of Western Ontario philosophy colloquium, 1966. Oxford, 1969.
Phil 185.33 — El universo, Dios y el hombre, ó Creador, creacion y criaturas. (Kaeppelin, E.R.) Paris, 1864.
Phil 585.179 — El universo está cerca. (Hidalgo, Alberto.) Buenos Aires, 1945.
Phil 8612.67 — Universum, döden och den logiska analysen. (Halldén, Sören.) Lund, 1967.
Phil 2270.123 — The unknowable; Herbert Spencer lecture. (Santayana, George.) Oxford, 1923.
Phil 8668.5 — The unknown god. (Noyes, A.) London, 1937.
Phil 5850.337 — Unmasking our minds. (Seabury, David.) N.Y., 1924.
Phil 5850.337.9 — Unmasking our minds. (Seabury, David.) N.Y., 1929.
Phil 8840.3 — Das Unmittelbare in der Philosophie der Moral. (Prell, H.H.) Amsterdam, 1941.
Phil 185.55.2 — Die Unmöglichkeit der Geisteswissenschaft. (Kraft, Julius.) Frankfurt, 1957.
Phil 185.55 — Die Unmöglichkeit der Geisteswissenschaft. (Kraft, Julius.) Leipzig, 1934.
Phil 7069.40.13 — The unobstructed universe. (White, S.E.) N.Y., 1940.
Phil 3502.3 — Unold, J. Die ethnologischen und anthropogeographischen...bei I. Kant und J.R. Forster. Leipzig, 1886.
Phil 8895.2 — Unold, J. Grundlegung für eine moderne praktisch-ethische Lebensanschauung. Leipzig, 1896.
Phil 510.16 — Unold, Johannes. Der Monismus und seine Ideale. Leipzig, 1908.
Phil 182.46 — Unorthodox conception of being. (Hermance, W.E.) N.Y., 1912.
Phil 5245.49 — Das unpersönliche Denken. (Feldkeller, P.) Berlin, 1949.
Phil 335.3 — Das unpersonale Erlebnis. (Ehrlich, Walter.) Halle, 1927.
Phil 2255.1.50 — Unpopular essays. (Russell, Bertrand Russell.) London, 1950.
Phil 2255.1.51 — Unpopular essays. (Russell, Bertrand Russell.) N.Y., 1950.
Phil 3640.77.5 — Unpublished letters. (Nietzsche, Friedrich.) N.Y., 1959.
Phil 978.36.5 — Unpublished writings. (Constant, L.) Calcutta, 1883.
Phil 1822.4A — The unrealists. (Wickham, H.) N.Y., 1930.
Phil 5790.45 — The unresponsive bystander: why doesn't he help? (Latané, Bibb.) N.Y., 1970.
Phil 3246.239 — Unruh, F.F. von. Johann Gottlieb Fichte. Stuttgart, 1942.
Phil 1750.395 — Die Unsachlichkeit der Existenzphilosophie. (Reidemeister, Kurt.) Berlin, 1954.
Phil 1750.395.2 — Die Unsachlichkeit der Existenzphilosophie. 2. Aufl. (Reidemeister, Kurt.) Berlin, 1970.
Phil 3640.17.10 — Die Unschuld des Werdens. v.1-2. (Nietzsche, Friedrich.) Leipzig, 1931.
Phil 497.5 — Unscientific materialism. (Wilder, S.H.) N.Y., 1881.
Phil 8644.1 — The unseen universe. (Tait, P.G.) N.Y., 1875.
Phil 8644.1.2 — The unseen universe. (Tait, P.G.) N.Y., 1875.
Phil 8643.28.7 — The unseen universe. 7. ed. (Stewart, Balfour.) London, 1878.
Phil 7060.88 — The unseen world: communications. London, 1847.
Phil 10.16 — The unseen world and other essays. (Fiske, J.) Boston, 1876.
Phil 3120.55.85 — Unseld, Siegfried. Ernst Bloch zu ehren. Frankfurt, 1965.
Phil 3120.15.31 — Unser Charakter, oder Ich bin der Richtige! (Brunner, Constantin.) Zürich, 1939.
Phil 178.75 — Unser Dasein. (Doeblin, Alfred.) Olten, 1964.
Phil 182.109 — Unser Glaube. (Huxley, A.) Stockholm, 1939.
Phil 7012.4 — Unser sechster Sinn. (Bender, Hans.) Stuttgart, 1971.
Phil 192.28.14 — Unser Wissen von der Aussenwelt. (Russell, B.) Leipzig, 1926.
Phil 5400.150 — Unsere Leidenschaften. 2. Aufl. (Muszynski, Franz.) Paderborn, 1926.
Phil 7082.102 — Unsere Träume und Traumzustände. (Romsche, Heinrich.) Stuttgart, 1926.
Phil 365.68 — Der unsichtbare Ursprung. Evolution als Nachvollzug. (Gebser, Hans.) Olten, 1970.
Phil 7072.10 — Unsought visitors; a book of visitations. v.1-2. (Mahony, Patrick.) N.Y., 1953. 2v.
Phil 3160.11.5 — Das Unsterbliche. (Cysarz, Herbert.) Halle, 1940.
Phil 3493.9 — Eine unsterbliche Entdeckung Kants. (Lind, Paul von.) Leipzig, 1898.
Phil 8642.5.5 — Unsterblichkeit. (Ritter, Heinrich.) Leipzig, 1866.
Phil 8647.12 — Unsterblichkeit. (Wenzl, Aloys.) Berlin, 1951.
Phil 8635.4 — Unsterblichkeit. 2. Aufl. (Keyserling, Hermann.) München, 1911.
Phil 8643.17 — Die Unsterblichkeit der Seele. 3. Aufl. (Spiegler, Julius.) Leipzig, 1909.

Phil 8635.3   Die Unsterblichkeitsbeweise. (Kaufmann, H.) Paderborn, 1912.

Phil 8625.3   Die Unsterblichkeitsfrage. (Andresen, Karl.) Leipzig, 1906.

Phil 8640.9   Die Unsterblichkeitsfrage. (Polak, M.S.) Amsterdam, 1857.

Phil 8632.21   Unsterblichkeitsglaube und Jenseitshoffnung in der Geschichte der Religionen. (Heiler, Friedrich.) München, 1950.

Phil 8643.1   Die Unsterblichkeitsidee im Glauben. (Schneider, L.) Regensburg, 1870.

Phil 3832.4   Die Unsterblichkeitslehre des Benedictus Spinoza. Inaug. Diss. (Matthes, Ewald.) Heidelberg, 1892.

Phil 8626.22   Die Unsterblichkeitslehre des israelitischen Volkes. (Brecher, G.) Leipzig, 1857.

Phil 3801.197.20   Die Unsterblichkeitslehre Schelling's im ganzen Zusammenhange ihrer Entwicklung. (Beckers, Hubert.) München, 1865.

Phil 8277.2   Das Unsterblichkeitsproblem in der abendländischen Philosophie. (Huonder, Quirin.) Stuttgart, 1970.

Phil 3246.80.5   Die Unsterblichkeitstheorie. (Melzer, Ernst.) Neisse, 1881.

Phil 2520.53.2   Unstersuchungen über die Grundlagen der Philosophie. 2e Aufl. (Descartes, René.) Heidelberg, 1884.

Phil 5722.14   Das Unterbewusstsein, eine Kritik. (Bumke, O.) Berlin, 1922.

Phil 5722.14.2   Das Unterbewusstsein, eine Kritik. 2. Aufl. (Bumke, O.) Berlin, 1926.

Phil 9162.6   Unterhaltungen zur Beförderung der häuslichen Glückseligkeit. (Cramer, W.M.A.) Berlin, 1781.

Phil 5811.12.5   Unterscheidet das tier Mann und Frau? (Bauke, Leopold.) Berlin, 1908.

Phil 3160.3.87   Die Unterscheidung von Mythos und Religion hei Hermann Cohen. Inaug. Diss. (Jospe, Alfred.) Oppeln, 1932.

Phil 2050.90   Der Unterschied der lehren Humes. (Brede, W.) Halle, 1896.

Phil 2050.214   Der Unterschied der Lehren Humes im Treatise und im Inquiry. (Brede, Wilhelm.) Halle, 1896.

Phil 720.7   Die Unterschiede der Wahrneiten und der Irrthümer. (Strümpell, L.) Leipzig, 1897.

Phil 343.10   Untersiechungen zur Frage die Differenz der Phänomenologie und des Kantianismus. (Metzger, Arnold.) Jena, 1915.

Phil 1195.13   Untersteiner, M. Sofisti. Firenze, 1949-62. 2v.
Phil 1195.13.3   Untersteiner, M. The sophists. Oxford, 1954.
Phil 5875.115   Untersuchung der Sympathieäbhangigkeit von Aussageleiustungen bei Kindern und Jugendlichen. (Gondolatsch, Karl Heinz.) Köln, 1958.

Htn   Phil 2050.42.12*   Eine Untersuchung über den menschlichen Verstand. (Hume, David.) Jena, 1793.

Phil 2050.42   Eine Untersuchung über den menschlichen Verstand. (Hume, David.) Leipzig, 1893.

Phil 2050.42.8   Eine Untersuchung über den menschlichen Verstand. 8e Aufl. (Hume, David.) Leipzig, 1920.

Htn   Phil 3480.42*   Untersuchung über die Deutlichkeit der Grundsätze der natürlichen Theologie und der Moral. (Kant, Immanuel.) Berlin, 1764. 2 pam.

Phil 2050.37.25   Eine Untersuchung über die Principien der Moral. (Hume, David.) Wien, 1883.

Phil 2050.69.30   Untersuchung über diePrinzipien der Moral. (Hume, David.) Leipzig, 1929.

Phil 2262.60   Untersuchung über die Tugend. (Shaftesbury, A.A.C.) Leipzig, 1905.

Phil 3495.6   Untersuchungen...Kantischen Erkenntnistheorie. (Nelson, Leonard.) Göttingen, 1909.

Phil 5648.22   Untersuchungen im haptischen Raum. Diss. (Betz, Dieter.) Hamburg, 1964.

Phil 6122.22   Untersuchungen Psychologie der Nervenfaser. (Meyer, G.H.) Tübingen, 1843.

Phil 342.2   Untersuchungen über Augustins Erkenntnistheorie. (Leder, H.) Warburg, 1901.

Phil 2138.84   Untersuchungen über das Causalproblem. (Kohn, Benno.) Wien, 1881.

Phil 9035.65   Untersuchungen über das charakterologische Rhythmusproblem. Inaug. Diss. (Aulich, Werner.) Halle, 1932.

Phil 410.75.5   Untersuchungen über das Endliche und das Unendliche. (Isenkrahe, Caspar.) Bonn, 1920. 3v.

Phil 6117.35   Untersuchungen über das Gehirn. (Hitzig, E.) Berlin, 1874.

Phil 6122.11.5   Untersuchungen über das Wesen. (Munk, H.) Leipzig, 1868.
Phil 349.31   Untersuchungen über das Wesen der philosophischen Erkenntnis. Inaug. Diss. (Stürmann, J.F.) Münster in Westfalen, 1931.

Phil 5545.33   Untersuchungen über den Einfluss der Geschwindigkeit des lauten Lesens. (Ogden, R.M.) Leipzig, 1903.

Phil 3425.243   Untersuchungen über den Freiheitsbegriff Hegels in seinen Jugendarbeiten. (Ephraim, F.) Berlin, 1928.

Phil 5066.48   Untersuchungen über den Modalkalkül. (Becker, O.) Meinsenheim/Glan, 1952.

Phil 3552.266   Untersuchungen über den Substansbegriff bei Leibniz. Inaug.-Diss. (Ohse, Jakob.) Dorpat, 1888.

Phil 5635.25   Untersuchungen über den Temperatursinn. Inaug. Diss. (Kessler, Jacob.) Bonn, 1884.

Phil 334.1   Untersuchungen über die Bedeutung der Denkform. (Dippe, A.) Jena, 1893.

Phil 6967.14.5   Untersuchungen über die Erweichung des Gehirns. 2. Aufl. (Rostan, L.) Leipzig, 1824.

Phil 6114.12.5   Untersuchungen über die Localisation der Functionen. (Exner, Sigmund.) Wien, 1881.

Phil 5643.2   Untersuchungen über die Sehthätigkeit. (Angelucci, A.) Giessen, 1890.

Phil 5640.9   Untersuchungen über die Sinneswahrnehmungen des neugeborenen Menschen. (Genzmer, A.O.H.) Halle, n.d.

Phil 5640.9.2   Untersuchungen über die Sinneswahrnehmungen des neugeborenen Menschen. (Genzmer, A.O.H.) Halle, 1882.

Phil 6111.24.9   Untersuchungen über die Textur des Rückenmarks. (Bidder, Friedrich.) Leipzig, 1857.

Phil 8882.102   Untersuchungen über die wichtigsten Gegenstände. (Hoffbauer, Johann C.) Dortmund, 1799-

Phil 3483.39   Untersuchungen über Kants Critik der practischen Vernunft. (Brastberger, G.U.) Tübingen, 1792.

Phil 3483.39.5   Untersuchungen über Kants Critik der reinen Vernunft. (Brastberger, G.U.) Halle, 1790.

Phil 6121.16   Untersuchungen über Leidenschaften und Gemüthsaffecten als Ursachen. (Lenhossék, Mihaly.) Pesth, 1804.

Phil 5247.4.10   Untersuchungen über Psychologie. (Hartsen, F.A.) Leipzig, 1869.

Phil 210.20   Untersuchungen zu einer Hermeneutischen Logik. 2. Aufl. (Lipps, Hans.) Frankfurt, 1959.

Phil 1750.115.185   Untersuchungen zu einer realistischen Grundlegung der phänomenologischen Wesensschau. (Ehel, Gerhard.) München, 1965.

Phil 1170.22   Untersuchungen zu Gebet und Gottesverehrung der Neuplatoniker. (Esser, Hans Peter.) Köln, 1967.

Phil 3482.2.20   Untersuchungen zu Kants Physicher Geographie. (Adickes, E.) Tübingen, 1911.

Phil 1540.22   Untersuchungen zu Prinzipien Fragen der scholastischen Erkenntnistheorie. (Orth, Albert.) Bahenhausen, 1933.

Phil 860.8   Untersuchungen zum Begriff des Gottgeziemenden in der Antike. (Dreyer, Oskar.) Hildesheim, 1970.

Phil 3640.600   Untersuchungen zum Problem der Zeit bei Nietzsche. (Stambaugh, Joan.) Den Haag, 1959.

Phil 8661.22   Untersuchungen zum Problem des Atheismus. (Gent, Werner.) Hildesheim, 1964.

Phil 3640.710   Untersuchungen zum Problem des Übermenschen bei Friedrich Nietzsche. (Brassard, Werner à.) Freiburg, 1962.

Phil 3488.36   Untersuchungen zum Verhältnis von Recht und Sittlichkeit. (Goessl, Max.) München, 1941.

Phil 3450.19.200   Untersuchungen zur Denhart Martin Heideggers. (Huebener, Wolfgang.) Berlin, 1960.

Phil 5043.35   Untersuchungen zur dialogischen Deutung der Logik. Diss. (Drieschner, Rudolf.) Hambrig, 1966.

Phil 735.88   Untersuchungen zur Entstehung der Wertproblems in der Philosophie des 19. Jahrhunderts. (Bamberger, F.) Halle, 1924.

Phil 5585.15   Untersuchungen zur Gegenstandstheorie und Psychologie. (Meinong, A.) Leipzig, 1904.

Phil 3850.18.170   Untersuchungen zur Kantkritik Max Schelers. (Heidemann, I.) Köln? 1955.

Phil 5360.2   Untersuchungen zur Lehre vom Begriff. Inaug. Diss. (Heinrich, E.) Göttingen, 1910.

Phil 5050.9   Untersuchungen zur Logik Gegenwart. (Koppelmann, W.) Berlin, 1913-18. 2v.

Phil 3915.44   Untersuchungen zur Mechanik der Nerven. v.1-2. (Wundt, Wilhelm.) Erlangen, 1871-76.

Phil 185.102   Untersuchungen zur Möglichkeit Habilitationsschrift. (Kreiser, Lothar.) Leipzig?, 1967?

Phil 8409.2   Untersuchungen zur Ontologie der Kunst. (Ingarden, R.) Tübingen, 1962.

Phil 5066.257   Untersuchungen zur operativen Logik der Gegenwart. (Richter, Vladimir.) Freiburg, 1965.

Phil 5867.20   Untersuchungen zur Periodik im Spielverhalten 6-10 jähriger Kinder. (Gilles, Brigitte.) Bonn, 1965.

Phil 342.12   Untersuchungen zur Phänomenologie der Erkenntnis. v.1-2. (Lipps, Hans.) Bonn, 1927-28.

Phil 1135.30   Untersuchungen zur Philosophie der Griechen. (Liebeck, H.) Halle, 1873.

Phil 1135.31   Untersuchungen zur Philosophie der Griechen. 2nd ed. (Liebeck, H.) Freiburg, 1888.

Phil 5520.505   Untersuchungen zur Problematik der sogenannten synthetischen Sätze apriori. (Delius, Harald.) Göttingen, 1963.

Phil 30.5   Untersuchungen zur Psychologie, Philosophie und Pädagogik. Göttingen.

Phil 5402.14   Untersuchungen zur Psychologie des Weinens. Inaug. Diss. (Schwarz, Balduin.) München, 1928.

Phil 3494.38   Untersuchungen zur Raumlehre Kants. Inaug. Diss. (Marc-Wogau, K.) Lund, 1932.

Phil 5259.26   Untersuchungen zur Rechtspsychologie des Individuums. (Tripp, Erich.) Leipzig, 1931.

Phil 3425.604   Untersuchungen zur Religionsphilosophie. (Sass, H.M.) Münster, 1963.

Phil 5635.37   Untersuchungen zur Sinnespsychologie. (Brentano, Franz.) Leipzig, 1907.

Phil 3494.37   Untersuchungen zur Sitten - und Rechtslehre Kants und Fichtes. (Metzger, Wilhelm.) Heidelberg, 1912.

Phil 3493.48   Untersuchungen zur Sprache von Kants Kritik der reinen Vernunft. (Lauter, Josef.) Köln, 1966.

Phil 5500.12   Untersuchungen zur Theorie der unendlichen Urteils. (Gordin, Jakob.) Berlin, 1929.

Phil 5272.22   Untersuchungen zur Theorie psychologischen Messens. (Kristof, Walter.) Meisenheim, 1969.

Phil 735.115   Untersuchungen zur Werttheorie und Theodizee. (Katkov, Georg.) Brünn, 1937.

Phil 341.25   Untersuchuugen über den grundsatzlichen Auspruch der Wahrnehmung. (Krausser, Peter.) Meisenheim am Glan, 1959.

Phil 6685.1   Untersungen und der Lebensmagnetismus. (Passavant, J.K.) Frankfurt, 1821.

Phil 3925.11.60   Unterwegs zur Heimat. (Wust, Peter.) Münster, 1956.
Phil 3450.19.57   Unterwegs zur Sprache. (Heidegger, Martin.) Pfullingen, 1959.

Phil 6117.32   The untroubled mind. (Hall, H.J.) Boston, 1915.
Phil 195.12   Unurn, George. What I believe. London, 1966.
Phil 978.77.1   Unveiled mysteries. 2d ed. (King, G.R.) Chicago, 1935.
Phil 7054.84   The unveiling: or What I think of spiritualism. (Randolph, P.B.) Newburyport, 1860.

Phil 2050.77A   Unveröffentlichte Briefe David Humes. (Hume, David.) Leipzig, 1929.

Phil 3819.20   Die Unvollendeten lateinischen Abhandlungen. (Spinoza, Benedictus de.) Heidelberg, 1882.

Phil 480.4   Die Unwahrheit des Sensualismus und Materialismus. (Fischer, K.P.) Erlangen, 1853.

Phil 9182.2.5   The unwelcome child. (Wright, H.C.) Boston, 1860.
Phil 8890.25   Unwritten laws of active careers. (Pitcairn, E.H.) London, 1899.

Phil 3640.64.5   Unzeigemässe Betrachtungen. (Nietzsche, Friedrich.) Leipzig, 189-?

Phil 3640.11.5   Unzeitgemässe Betrachtungen. (Nietzsche, Friedrich.) Leipzig, 189-?

Phil 5627.264.15   Das Unzerstörbare. (Müller-Eckhard, Hans.) Stuttgart, 1964.

Phil 1725.1   Uomini e dottrine. (Zuccante, Giuseppe.) Torino, 1926.
Phil 8605.3.5   L'uomo. (Zacchi, P.A.) Roma, 1921. 2v.
Phil 4225.8.40   L'uomo. 2. ed. (Sciacca, Michele Federico.) Milano, 1958.
Phil 1620.5   L'uomo antico nel pensiero del Rinascimento. (Joffanin, Giuseppe.) Bologna, 1957.

Phil 4070.7.60   L'uomo copernicano. (Banfi, Antonio.) Milano, 1965.
Phil 5425.4   L'uomo di genio. (Lombroso, C.) Torino, 1894.
Phil 4225.8.110   L'uomo e il suo destino. (Giannuzzi, Eugenio.) Cosenza, 1968.

Phil 310.163.5   L'uomo e la storia. (Vranicki, Predrag.) Roma, 1968.
Phil 8881.60   L'uomo e le scienze morali. (Gabelli, Aristide.) Torino.

Phil 200.5   L'uomo e l'infinito. (Zucca, Antioco.) Roma, 1906.
Phil 3487.29   L'uomo nella storia in Kant. (Fazio-Allmayer, Bruna.) Bologna, 1968.

Phil 4120.9.35   L'uomo nell'assoluto. (Galli, Gallo.) Torino, 1965.

Phil 180.42 — L'uomo:saggio popolare. (Falco, Francesco.) Piacenza, 1870.

Phil 9550.17 — Upartiskhet og utilitarisme. (Ofstad, Harald.) Stockholm, 1962.

Phil 8710.1 — Upham, F.W. The debate between the church and science. Andover, 1860.

Phil 5260.1 — Upham, T.C. Elements of intellectual philosophy. Portland, 1827.

Phil 5260.1.5 — Upham, T.C. Elements of mental philosophy. N.Y., 1841.
Phil 5260.1.8 — Upham, T.C. Elements of mental philosophy. N.Y., 1857.
Phil 5260.1.9 — Upham, T.C. Elements of mental philosophy. N.Y., 1859.
Phil 5260.1.2 — Upham, T.C. Elements of mental philosophy. Portland, 1831. 2v.

Phil 5260.1.4 — Upham, T.C. Elements of mental philosophy. 3. ed. Portland, 1839. 2v.

Phil 5260.1.3 — Upham, T.C. Mental philosophy. N.Y., 1869. 2v.
Phil 5260.1.15 — Upham, T.C. Mental philosophy. v.2. N.Y., 1875.

Phil 5627.90 — Upham, Thomas C. Principles of the interior or hidden life. London, 1874.

Phil 5770.1 — Uphan, T.C. A philosophical and practical treatise on the will. Portland, 1834.

Phil 5060.3.5 — Uphues, G. Erkenntniskritische Logik. Halle, 1909.
Phil 5260.5 — Uphues, G. Erkenntniskritische Psychologie. Halle, 1909.
Phil 5060.3 — Uphues, G. Zur Krisis in der Logik. Berlin, 1903.
Phil 351.1.5 — Uphues, G.K. Geschichte der Philosophie als Erkenntniskritik. Halle, 1909.

Phil 3502.1 — Uphues, G.K. Kant und seine Vorgänger. Berlin, 1906.
Phil 351.1 — Uphues, G.K. Psychologie des Erkennens I. Leipzig, 1893.
Phil 5585.11 — Uphues, G.K. Wohrnehmung und Empfindung. Leipzig, 1888.
Phil 5374.29 — Uphues, Goswin. Vom Bewusstsein. Osterwieck, 1904.
Phil 5545.71 — Uphues, Goswin K. Über die Erinnerung. Leipzig, 1889.
Phil 5060.3.10 — Uphues, Karl. Grundlagen der Logik. Breslau, 1883.

Phil 7069.55.25 — Upper purgatory. (Bodin, Edward Longstreet.) Daytona Beach, Fla., 1955.

Phil 2270.71.10 — Uppfostran i intellektuelt, moraliskt och fysiskt afseende. 2a uppl. (Spencer, Herbert.) Stockholm, 1890.

Phil 5251.20.20 — Uppfostran till arbete. (Lehmann, Alfred.) Stockholm, 1920.

Phil 4520.8.46 — Upphaf kristninnar og...Jesús Kristur. (Bjarnason, Ágúst.) Reykjavík, 1904.

Phil 5330.4.10 — Uppmärksamhetens psykologi. (Ribot, T.) Stockholm, 1891.
Phil 5330.32 — Uppmärksamhetsförloppens psykologi. Akademisk avhandling. (Käellén, Elov.) Göttesburg, 1949.

Phil 5274.14 — Uppsala symposium on psychological factor analysis, 17-19 March 1953. (Symposium on Psychological Factor Analysis, Uppsala University, 1953.) Copenhagen, 1953.

Phil 4655.1.70 — Uppsatser i religiösa ämnen. (Wikner, Pontus.) Stockholm, 1871.

Phil 4630.2.31 — Uppsatser och tal. (Rein, T.) Helsingfors, 1903.
Phil 5520.376 — Upton, Albert. Creative analysis. Whittier, Calif., 1961.
Phil 5520.375 — Upton, Albert. Design for thinking. Stanford, 1961.
Phil 5520.374 — Upton, Albert. Design for thinking. Whittier, Calif., 1948.

Phil 8600.1 — Upton, C.B. Lectures on the bases of religious belief. London, 1894.

Phil 8592.6.15 — Upton, Charles B. Doctor Martineau's philosophy; a survey. London, 1905.

Phil 400.24 — Upward, A. The new world. N.Y., 1910.
Phil 7069.06.13 — Ur dularheimum. (Jónsson, G.) Reykjavik, 1906.
Phil 1505.4 — Ur medeltidens tankevärld. (Aspelin, Gunnar.) Stockholm, 1959.

Phil 342.9 — Ur världoförklaringarnas och kunskapsteoriernas urkunder. (Liljeckrantz, B.) Stockholm, 1921.

Phil 5545.262 — Urach, Elisabeth Furstin von. Über die strukturelle Eigenart und personate Bedeutsamkeit der Erinnerung. Inaug. Diss. Bamburg, 1965.

Phil 3552.246 — Urbach, B. Leibnizens Rechtfertigung des Uebels. Prag, 1901.

Htn Phil 5260.4* — Pamphlet vol. Urban, F.M. L'analyse des sphygmogrammes. 1906-1913. 14 pam.

Phil 5404.1 — Urban, J. L'epithymologie. Paris, 1939.
Phil 630.50 — Urban, W.M. Beyond realism and idealism. London, 1949.
Phil 8895.3 — Urban, W.M. Fundamentals of ethics. N.Y., 1930.
Phil 8600.5 — Urban, W.M. Humanity and deity. London, 1951.
Phil 735.10.5 — Urban, W.M. The intelligible world. London, 1929.
Phil 735.10 — Urban, W.M. Valuation: its nature and laws. London, 1909.
Phil 6980.760.10 — Urban challenges to psychiatry. 1. ed. Boston, 1969.
Phil 4825.18 — Urbancic, Juan. Poglavitne ideje slovenskih filozofov med sholastiko in neosholako. Ljubljana, 1971.

Phil 3450.17.92 — Urbanowski, J. Georg von Hertlings Gesellschaftslehre. Inaug. Diss. Battrop, 1936.

Phil 6330.1 — Urbantschitsch, R. Psycho-analysis for all. London, 1928.
Phil 5643.47 — Urbantschitsch, V. Über subjektive optische Anschauungsbilder. Leipzig, 1907.

Phil 3525.50 — Das Urbild der Menschheit. (Krause, K.C.F.) Göttingen, 1851.

Phil 3120.30.30 — Urdistanz und Beziehung. (Buber, Martin.) Heidelberg, 1951.

Phil 5627.121 — Uren, A.R. Recent religious psychology. Edinburgh, 1928.
Phil 3808.29.15 — Uren met Schopenhauer. (Schopenhauer, Arthur.) Baarn, 1916.
Phil 3819.27 — Uren met Spinoza. 2. druk. (Spinoza, Benedictus de.) Baarn, 1917.
Phil 8050.73 — Uren van schoonheid. (Nauwelaerts, M.A.M.E.) Antwerpen, 1960.

Phil 2045.116 — Die Urform der "Computatio sive logica" des Hobbes. (Brockdorff, Cay von.) Kiel, 1934.
Phil 3850.53 — Urfragen. (Spengler, Oswald.) München, 1965.
Phil 178.53 — Urgesetze des Lebens. (Delius, Rudolf von.) Darmstadt, 1922.

Phil 177.2.5 — Urgesetzlehre der wahren Guten und Schöne. (Calker, F.) Berlin, 1820.

Phil 299.17 — Die Urkraft des Weltalls. (Spiller, P.) Berlin, 1876.
Phil 195.5 — Urmeneta, F. de. Nuevos ensayos de critica filosofica. Barcelona, 1953.

Phil 4352.1.105 — Urmeneta, F. de. Principios de filosofia de la historia. Madrid, 1952.

Phil 972.22 — Der Urmensch und der Mensch der Zukunft. (Wehr, Gerhard.) Freiburg, 1964.

Phil 105.5 — Urmson, J.O. The concise encyclopaedia of Western philosophy and philosophers. London, 1960.

Phil 1720.5 — Urmson, J.O. Philosophical analysis. Oxford, 1956.
Phil 5360.27 — Urovni logicheskogo protsessa i osnovnye napravleniia ikh issledovaniia. (Borisov, Vadim N.) Novosibirsk, 1967.

Phil 8661.8.80 — Urquhart, James. William Honyman Gillespie. Edinburgh, 1902.

Phil 8685.15 — Urquhart, W.S. Pantheism, and the value of life. Thesis. London, 1919.

Phil 1535.24 — Urráburu, J.J. Institutiones philosophicae. Vallistoleli, 1891-1908. 8v.

Phil 177.8.9 — Ursache Grund und Zweck. (Carus, Paul.) Dresden, 1883.
Phil 270.22 — Ursache und Bedingung. (Heim, Karl.) Leipzig, 1913.
Phil 8735.56 — Die Ursachen aller geschaffenen Dinge. (Meyers, A.M.) Limburg, 1963?

Phil 193.65 — Die Ursachen des Verfalls der Philosophie in alter und neuer Zeit. (Spicker, Gideon.) Leipzig, 1892.

Phil 1135.194 — Ursprongsbild und Schöpfertat. (Landmann, Michael.) München, 1966.

Phil 5871.112.2 — Ursprung, Einheit und Zwiespalt der Seele. (Graber, Gustav Hans.) München, 1970.

Phil 8826.1 — Ursprung...Sittlichkeit. (Becker, J.H.) Leipzig, 1888.
Phil 1111.9 — Der Ursprung der griechischen Philosophie von Hesiod bis Parmenides. (Gigon, Olof.) Berlin, 1945.

Phil 8892.44 — Der Ursprung der moralischen Empfindungen. (Rée, Paul.) Chemnitz, 1877.

Phil 1135.62 — Der Ursprung der Naturphilosophie aus dem Geiste der Mystik. (Joël, Kar.) Basel, 1903.

Phil 525.39 — Der Ursprung der Naturphilosophie aus dem Geiste der Mystik. (Joël, Karl.) Jena, 1906.

Phil 8582.32 — Ursprung der Religion und des Gottesglaubens. (Cunow, Heinrich.) Berlin, 1913.

Phil 8887.36 — Der Ursprung der Sittlichkeit. (Münsterberg, H.) Freiburg, 1889.

Phil 5620.2 — Der Ursprung der Vernunft. (Keller, J.) Heidelberg, 1884.
Phil 3450.19.63 — Der Ursprung des Kunstwerkes. (Heidegger, Martin.) Stuttgart, 1960.

Phil 184.53 — Ursprung und Arten des realen Seins. (Jancke, Rudolf.) Bern, 1963.

Phil 7082.144 — Ursprung und Sinn der Träume. (Andreas-Friedrich, Ruth.) Zürich, 1958.

Phil 193.152.5 — Ursprung und Wirklichkeit. (Sganzini, Carlo.) Bern, 1951.
Phil 4650.1.56 — Ursprungens filosofi. (Vannérus, Allen.) Stockholm, 1925.
Phil 5374.163 — Ursprungsgeschichte des Bewusstseins. 1. Aufl. (Neumann, E.) Zürich, 1949.

Phil 2520.106 — Das Urteil bei Descartes. (Christiansen, B.) Hanau, 1902.
Phil 193.92 — Das Urteil der Vernunft. (Seltmann, Otto.) Caliv, 1920.
Phil 3585.28.10 — Das Urteil und das Sein. (Lotz, Johannes Baptist.) München, 1957.

Phil 5500.9 — Das Urteil und die Lehre vom synthetischen Charakter desselben. (Rosinski, A.) Leipzig, 1889.

Phil 3489.7 — Urteile und Kategorien; eine Studie zu Kants Logik. (Hauck, P.) Strassburg, 1903.

Phil 5125.12 — Das urteilende und schliessende Denken in kausaler Behandlung. (Störring, G.) Leipzig, 1926.

Phil 2070.91 — Die Urteilsfreiheit als Grundlage der Rechtfertigung des religiösen Glaubens. Inaug. Diss. (Stettheimer, E.) Wittenburg, 1903.

Phil 2070.91.2 — Die Urteilsfreiheit als Grundlage der Rechtfertigung des religiösen Glaubens. Inaug. Diss. (Stettheimer, E.) Wittenburg, 1903.

Phil 5500.3 — Die Urtheilsfunction. (Jerusalem, W.) Wien, 1895.
Phil 195.3 — Urtin, Henri. Vers une science du réel. Paris, 1930.
Phil 2520.295 — Urvagi do medytacji metafizycznych René Descartes. (Wolzogen, J.L.) Warszawa, 1959.

Phil 3195.14.34 — Urwelt, Sage und Menschheit, eine naturhistori-metaphysische Studie. 4. Aufl. (Dacqué, Edgar.) München, 1927.

Phil 8895.4 — Urwick, Edward. The values of life. Toronto, 1948.
Phil 2420.1 — Urwin, Kenneth. A century for freedom; a survey of the French philosophers. London, 1946.

Phil 817.23 — Urwissen. 2. Aufl. (Riel, Hans.) Wien, 1956.
Phil 4260.148 — Uscatescu, George. Juan Batista Vico y el mundo histórico. 1. ed. Madrid, 1956.

Phil 6130.1 — Uschakoff, J. Das Lokalisationsgesetz. Helsingfors, 1900.
Phil 6130.1.2 — Uschakoff, J. Das Lokalisationsgesetz. Leipzig, 1900.
Phil 5520.493 — The use of lateral thinking. (De Bono, Edward.) London, 1969.

Phil 8886.12.5 — The use of life. (Avebury, John Lubbock.) N.Y., 1900.
Phil 9070.56 — The use of life. 1st ed. (Kates, J.W.) N.Y., 1953.
Phil 187.63.12 — The use of philosophy. (Muirhead, J.H.) Cambridge, 1929.
Htn Phil 2340.4.30* — The use of reason. (Wilson, Thomas.) n.p., 1553.
Phil 7054.64 — The use of spiritualism? (Hall, S.C.) Glasgow, 1876.
Phil 5500.41 — A use of sumulation for the study of future values. (Helmer, Olaf.) Santa Monica, 1966.

Phil 6122.5 — The use of the body in relation to the mind. (Moore, G.) N.Y., 1847.

Htn Phil 1850.59* — The use of the law. (Bacon, Francis.) London, 1629.
Phil 8881.55 — The use of the margin. (Griggs, Edward H.) N.Y., 1907.
Phil 9290.4 — The use of the radio in leisure time. (Bryson, Lyman.) N.Y., 1935?

Phil 6110.3.10 — The use of the self. (Alexander, F.M.) N.Y., 1932.
Phil 9530.54 — The use of time. 3. ed. (Lebhar, G.M.) N.Y., 1958.
Phil 5058.22 — The use of words in reasoning. (Sidgwick, A.) London, 1901.

Phil 4829.860.2 — Ušeničnik, Aleš. Izbrani spisi. Ljubljana, 1939-41. 10v.

Phil 5190.30 — The uses of argument. (Toulmin, S.E.) Cambridge, Eng., 1958.

Phil 1980.4.25 — The uses of philosophy. (Edman, Irwin.) N.Y., 1955.
Phil 343.22 — The uses of reason. (Murphy, A.E.) N.Y., 1943.
Phil 8421.4 — Ushenko, A.P. Dynamics of art. Indiana, 1953.
Phil 5520.215 — Ushenko, A.P. The field theory of meaning. Ann Arbor, 1958.

Phil 2310.1.30 — Ushenko, A.P. Power and events. Princeton, 1946.
Phil 5060.6.7 — Ushenko, A.P. The problems. Princeton, 1941.
Phil 5060.6.5 — Ushenko, A.P. The problems of logic. London, 1941.
Phil 5060.6 — Ushenko, A.P. The theory of logic. N.Y., 1936.
Phil 8600.4 — Usher, E.P. The Greek gospel; an interpretation of the coming faith. Grafton, Mass., 1909.

Phil 8421.3 — Usher, James. Clio, or A discourse on taste. 2. ed. London, 1769.

Phil 860.6 — Ushida, Noriko. Étude comparative de la psychologie d'Aristote, d'Avicenne et de St.Thomas d'Aquin. Tokyo, 1968.

Phil 4668.40.30 — Uskonnonfilosofian käsitteestä ja metoodista. (Castrén, Zacharias.) Helsingissä, 1899.

Phil 585.408 — Uskutečnění současného člověka. 1. vyd. (Hermach, Yiří.) Praha, 1969.

Phil 7082.40 — Uslar, Detlev von. Der Traum als Welt. Pfullingen, 1964.
Phil 5585.335 — Uslar, Detlev von. Die Wirklichkeit des Psychischen. Pfullingen, 1969.

Phil 8886.69 — Usloviia absoliutnogo dobra. (Losskii, N.O.) Parizh, 1949.

Phil 310.10 — Usloviia materialicheskoi zhizni obshchestva. (Fedoseev, P.N.) Moskva, 1954.

Phil 4769.1.86 — Usnadse, D. von. Wladimir Ssolowiow. Halle, 1909.

Phil 4803.570.80   Usovicz, Aleksandr. Ksiądz Konstanty Michalski, 1879-1947. Wyd. 1. Kraków, 1949.

Phil 8709.23   Uspekhi sovremennoi nauki i religiia. (Akademiia Nauk SSSR. Institut Filosofii.) Moskva, 1961.

Phil 4771.3A   Uspenskii, P.D. The fourth way. 1st American ed. N.Y., 1957.

Phil 4771.1A   Uspenskii, P.D. In search of the miraculous. 1. ed. N.Y., 1949.

Phil 4771.5.2   Uspenskii, P.D. A new model of the universe. 2d ed. N.Y., 1956.

Phil 672.122.9   Uspenskii, P.D. Tertium organum. Berlin, 1931.
Phil 672.122.7   Uspenskii, P.D. Tertium organum. Rochester, 1920.
Phil 672.122   Uspenskii, P.D. Tertium organum. 2nd American ed. N.Y., 1922.
Phil 672.122.3   Uspenskii, P.D. Tertium organum. 2nd American ed. N.Y., 1923.
Phil 672.122.5   Uspenskii, P.D. Tertium organum. 2nd American ed. N.Y., 1930.

Phil 8855.2   Ussel, Jozef Maria Willem van. Sociogenese en evolutie van het probleem der seksuele propaedeuse tussen de 16 en 18 de eeuw. Gent, 1967. 2v.

Phil 1750.26   Ussher, A. Journey through dread. N.Y., 1955.
Phil 820.2   Ussher, Arland. Sages and schoolmen. Dublin, 1967.
Phil 8050.67   Ut pictura poesis; a historical investigation. (Howard, W.G.) Cambridge, 1909.

Phil 2490.118.10   Uta, Michel. La loi des trois etats dans la philosophie d'Auguste Comte. Bourg, 1928.
Phil 2490.118   Uta, Michel. La théorie du savoir dans la philosophie d'Auguste Comte. Paris, 1928.
Phil 2490.118.5   Uta, Michel. La théorie du savoir dans la philosophie d'Auguste Comte. Thèse. Bourg, 1928.

Phil 5465.141   Utah Creativity Research Conference. Proceedings of the fifth conference, 1964. N.Y., n.d. 2v.
Phil 4809.393.330   Útěcha z ontologie. Vyd. 1. (Fišer, zbyněk.) Praha, 1967.
Phil 2150.6.83   Utgångspunkterna för Münsterbergs värdelära. (Aspelin, G.) Lund, 1929.

Phil 9070.13.5   La utilidad de la honradez. (Pereira Alves, A.) Buenos Aires, 1942.

Phil 5592.15   Utilisation du dessin comme test psychologique chez les enfants. 3. éd. (Cotte, S.) Marseille, 1951.

Phil 8886.33   L'utilità e il senso morale. (Lessona, Marco.) Torino, 1886.

Phil 9550.15A   Utilitarianism. (Bentham, J.) London, 1890.
Phil 2138.50.21   Utilitarianism. (Mill, John S.) Belmont, Calif., 1969.
Phil 2138.50.8   Utilitarianism. (Mill, John S.) Chicago, 1906.
Htn   Phil 2138.50.4*   Utilitarianism. (Mill, John S.) London, 1863.
Phil 2138.50.20   Utilitarianism. (Mill, John S.) N.Y., 1953.
Phil 2138.50.5   Utilitarianism. 4th ed. (Mill, John S.) London, 1871.
Phil 2138.50.6   Utilitarianism. 12th ed. (Mill, John S.) London, 1895.
Phil 2138.118   Utilitarianism explained and exemplified in moral and political government. In answer to John Stuart Mill's utilitarianism. (Tennant, C.) London, 1864.
Phil 1865.192   The Utilitarians. Garden City, 1961.
Phil 2138.50.17   L'utilitarisme. (Mill, John S.) Paris, 1883.
Phil 1865.171   El utilitarismo; estudio de las doctrinas de Jeremías Bentham. (Sánchez-Rivera de la Lastra, Juan.) Madrid, 1922.

Phil 2280.1.86   Der Utilitarismus bei Sidgwick...Spencer. (Sinclair, A.G.) Heidelberg, 1907.

Phil 8050.77   Utitz, Emil. Aesthetik. Berlin, 1923.
Phil 8062.6   Utitz, Emil. Bemerkungen zur altgriechischen Kunsttheorie. Berlin, 1959.
Phil 9035.43   Utitz, Emil. Charakterologie. Charlottenburg, 1925.
Phil 8050.30   Utitz, Emil. Geschichte der Ästhetik. Berlin, 1932.
Phil 5645.22   Utitz, Emil. Grundzüge der ästhetischen Farbenlehre. Stuttgart, 1908.
Phil 5467.3   Utitz, Emil. Psychologie der Simulation. Stuttgart, 1918.
Phil 195.4   Utitz, Emil. Die Sendung der Philosophie in unserer Zeit. Leiden, 1935.
Phil 1750.748   Utitz, Emil. Die Überwindung des Expressionismus. Stuttgart, 1927.

Phil 4600.4.36   Utkast och silhuetter. Malmö, 1909.
Phil 185.32   Utkast til en systematisk afhandling i theoretiska och practiska philosophien. (Kolmark P.) Stockholm, 1799.

Phil 8956.9   Utkast till en undersökning af religionen. (Göransson, N.J.) Sköfde, 1899.
Phil 8980.861   Utkin, S.S. Ocherki po marksistsko-leninskoi etike. Moskva, 1962.

Phil 1730.31   Utopia and reform in the enlightenment. (Venturi, Franco.) Cambridge, Eng., 1971.
Phil 2050.267   L'utopia controllata. (Molinari, Ernesto.) Milano, 1964.
Phil 1730.30   Utopia e riforma nell'iluminismo. (Venturi, Franco.) Torino, 1970.
Phil 6158.40   Utopiates; the use and users of LSD-25. (Blum, Richard H.) N.Y., 1966.
Phil 1750.845   Utopie, Eschatologie, Geschichtsteleologie. (Kamlah, Wilhelm.) Mannheim, 1969.
Phil 2494.81   L'Utopie de Condorcet. (Gillet, M.) Paris, 1883.
Phil 2150.22.85   Utopie und Anarchismus; zur Kritik der kritischen Theorie H. Marcuses. (Holz, Hans Heinz.) Köln, 1968.
Phil 3120.55.105   Utopie und Ideologie. (Kraenzle, Karl.) Bern, 1970.
Phil 2411.8   Les utopies prérévolutionnaires et la philosophie du XVIIIe siècle. (LeFlamanc, Auguste.) Brest, 1933.
Phil 195.8   Utrecht. Rijks Universiteit. Utrechts Universiteits fonds. Leven en dood. Haarlem, 1961.
Phil 60.2   Utrecht. Rijksuniversiteit. Psychologisch Laboratorium. Mededeelingen. Utrecht. 1-7,1924-1933 3v.
Phil 5870.20   Utvecklingsykologiska beteendestudier hos barn i aldern 1 1/2 - 8 1/2 år. Thesis. (Sandels, Stina.) Uppsala, 1956.
Phil 8905.10   Utz, Arthur Fridolin. Ethik und Politik. Stuttgart, 1970.
Phil 4809.796.36   Úvahy o budoucnosti lidstva. (Smetana, Augustin.) Praha, 1903.
Phil 4809.727.30   Úvahy vědecké a filosofické. (Rádl, Emanuel.) Praha, 1906.
Phil 310.590   Uvarov, A.I. Leninskii printsip ob"ektivnosti v poznanii. Tomsk, 1963.
Phil 5260.10   Uznadze, Dmitrii N. Eksperimental'nye osnovy psikhologii ustanovki. Tbilisi, 1961.
Phil 5260.10.5   Uznadze, Dmitrii N. Psikhologicheskie issledovaniia. Moskva, 1966.
Phil 8980.896.5   Uznaiu cheloveka. (Ziuziukin, Ivan I.) Mosva, 1970.
Phil 310.798   V.I. Lenin i aktual'nye problemy filosofii. (Mitin, Mark B.) Moskva, 1971.
Phil 310.718   V.I. Lenin i dialekticheskoe ponimanie otritsaniia. (Bagirov, Z.N.) Baku, 1969.
Phil 4720.7   V.I. Lenin i istoriia filosofii narodov SSSR. Moskva, 1970.

Phil 310.777   V.I. Lenin i metodologicheskie voprosy sovremennoi nauki. Kiev, 1971.
Phil 310.527   V.I. Lenin i nekotorye voprosy nauchnogo predvideniia v obshchestvennom zhizni. (Vasil'ev, Iu. Al.) Minsk, 1962.
Phil 342.28   V.I. Lenin i sovremennye problemy teorii poznaniia. (Levin, Grigorii Aronovich.) Minsk, 1970. 9v.
Phil 8980.486   V.I. Lenin i voprosy etiki. (Kiselev, Askol'd A.) L'vov, 1969.
Phil 310.685   V.I. Lenin o nauchnom poniatii materii. (Arkhiptsev, Fedor T.) Moskva, 1957.
Phil 310.55   V chem sostoit osnovnoi vopros filosofii. (Kutasov, D.A.) Moskva, 1958.
Phil 292.11   V poiskakh istiny. (Lavrov, A.S.) Paris, 1940.
Phil 8980.712.20   V sem'e; vzaimnoe uvazhenie, zabota o detiakh. (Protopopova, A.N.) Moskva, 1962.
Phil 5640.17.5   Le va del l'anima. (Aitken, E.H.) Torino, 1913.
Phil 7069.34.43   Va siguiendo la tercera parte de el radio de luz del regentador del mundo solar. (Vilanova, María.) Barcelona, 1934. 8 pam.
Phil 5040.13   Vårt tankelif. (Almquist, S.) Stockholm, 1906.
Phil 8885.11.5   Vårtids etiska Lifsåskådningar. (Kirn, O.) Stockholm, 1909.
Phil 4225.1.85   Vacca, Giuseppe. Politica e filosofia in Bertrando Spaventa. Bari, 1967.
Phil 196.1.5   Vacherot, E. Essais de philosophie critique. Paris, 1864.
Phil 1150.3   Vacherot, E. Histoire critique de l'ecole d'Alexandrie. Paris, 1846-51. 3v.
Phil 196.1   Vacherot, E. La métaphysique. Paris, 1858. 2v.
Phil 196.1.2   Vacherot, E. La métaphysique et de science. 2d ed. Paris, 1863.
Phil 196.1.8   Vacherot, E. Le nouveau spiritualisme. Paris, 1884.
Phil 8601.1   Vacherot, E. La religion. Paris, 1869.
Phil 9075.8   Vacherot, E. La science et la conscience. Paris, 1870.
Phil 5620.11   Vacherot, Etienne. De rationis autoritate. Cadomi, 1836.
Phil 4260.89   Vadalà-Papale, G. Dati psicologici nella dottrina giuridica. Roma, 1889.
Phil 402.6   Världsbilder och livsidal. (Aspelin, Gunnar.) Lund, 1968.
Phil 801.19   Världsförklaringar och lifsåskådningar. (Barr, Knut.) Stockholm, 1910.
Phil 510.1.4   Världsgåtorna. (Haeckel, Ernst.) Stockholm, 1905.
Phil 8581.24.20   Värt gemensamma lif. (Brierley, J.) Stockholm, 1907.
Phil 9010.24   Vaes, Lachlan. Amusements and the Christian life. Philadelphia, 1884.
Phil 960.144   Väth, Alfons. Im Kampfe mit der Zauberwelt des Hinduismus. Berlin, 1928.
Phil 193.49.60   Vagabond scholar. (Santayana, G.) N.Y., 1962.
Phil 8615.5.4   Vägen till målet. (Adler, Felix.) Stockholm, 1925.
Phil 3640.726   Vaglia, Anna Teresa. Nietzsche e la letteratura francese. Brescia, 1967.
Phil 8980.866   Vagovič, Stefano. Etica comunista. Roma, 1959.
Phil 8980.866.5   Vagovič, Stefano. L'etica comunista. Roma, 1966.
Phil 525.27   La vague mystique. (Sageret, Jules.) Paris, 1920.
Phil 8725.5   Vahanian, G. The death of God. N.Y., 1961.
Phil 3503.1   Vaihinger, H. Commentar zu Kants Kritik der reinen Vernunft. Stuttgart, 1881. 2v.
Phil 3415.87   Vaihinger, H. Hartmann, Dühring und Lange. Faerlohn, 1876.
Phil 3503.1.2   Vaihinger, H. Kommentar zu Kants Kritik der reinen Vernunft. 2. Aufl. Stuttgart, 1922. 2v.
Phil 3503.1.5   Vaihinger, H. Zu Kants Gedächtnis. Berlin, 1904.
Phil 3903.3.50   Vaihinger, Hans. Der Atheismusstreit gegen die Philosophie des Als Ob. Berlin, 1916.
Phil 3640.244   Vaihinger, Hans. Nietzsche als Philosoph. Berlin, 1902.
Phil 3640.126.4   Vaihinger, Hans. Nietzsche als Philosoph. 4e Aufl. Berlin, 1916.
Phil 3903.3.30   Vaihinger, Hans. Die Philosophie des Als Ob. Berlin, 1911.
Phil 3903.3.34   Vaihinger, Hans. Die Philosophie des Als Ob. 2. Aufl. Leipzig, 1924.
Phil 3903.3.33   Vaihinger, Hans. Die Philosophie des Als Ob. 3. Aufl. Leipzig, 1918.
Phil 3903.3.43   Vaihinger, Hans. The philosophy of "As if"; a system of the theoretical, practical and religious fictions of mankind. 2. ed. London, 1968.
Phil 3903.3.40   Vaihinger, Hans. The philosophy of "As if". London, 1924.
Phil 3903.3.92   Das Vaihingersche Als-Ob und die Methode der Formensprache in Religion und Theologie. (Spickerbaum, P.) München, 1922.
Phil 5627.148   The vaiidity of religious experience. (Knudson, A.C.) N.Y., 1937.
Phil 5520.42   Vailati, G. Alcune osservazioni sulle questioni di parole. Torino, 1899.
Phil 4265.4.10   Vailati, G. El metodo della filosofia. Bari, 1957.
Phil 4265.4.5F   Vailati, G. Scritti (1863-1909). Leipzig, 1911.
Phil 4021.1   Vailati, Giovanni. De quelques caractères du mouvement philosophique contemporain en Italie. Paris, 1907.
Phil 8422.18   Vaiman, Semen T. Marksistskaia estetika i problemy realizma. Moskva, 1964.
Phil 6990.37.5   Vains efforts de plusieurs évêques. (Le Quien de la Neufville, Charles Jacques.) Paris, 1830.
Phil 1526.3   Vaintrob, M. Istoriia srednevekovoi filosofii. Riga, 1929.
Phil 165.368   Vaira. Budapest, 1930.
Phil 353.32   Vakhtomin, N.K. O roli kategorii sushchnost' i iavlenie v poznanii. Moskov, 1963.
Phil 352.12   Vakhtomin, Nikolai K. Zakony dialektiki, zakony poznaniia. Moskva, 1966.
Phil 4570.2.6   Valda skrifter. (v.1-2. (Genberg, P.) Stockholm, 1878.
Phil 5261.7   Valdarnini, Angelo. Elementi scientifici di psicologia e logica. 3-4. ed. pt.1-2. Torino, 1915.
Phil 5261.23   Valdefievre. P. La psychologie du poéte. Paris, 1933.
Phil 8422.6   Valdes Rodriguez, Manuel. Relaciones entre lo bueno, lo bello y lo verdadero. Tesis, 1888.
Phil 4363.3.110   Valdes y Mañara. (Gestoso y Pérez, José.) Sevilla, 1890.
Phil 7069.28.90   Valdry, Luma. Living secrets. London, 1928.
Phil 9361.2   Valenca, Francisco P. de. Instrucçam. Lisboa, 1745. 3 pam.
Phil 2805.196   Valensin, A. A la suite de Pascal. Saint-Felicien-en-Vivarais, 1926.
Phil 196.20   Valensin, A. A travers la métaphysique. Paris, 1925.
Phil 2805.196.5   Valensin, A. Balthazar. Paris, 1934.
Phil 2805.196.7   Valensin, A. Balthazar. Paris, 1954.
Phil 2477.6.99   Valensin, A. Maurice Blondel. 2e éd. Paris, 1934.
Phil 2920.3.30   Valensin, Auguste. Auguste Valensin. Paris, 1961.
Phil 2920.3.32   Valensin, Auguste. Regards. Paris, 1955-56. 3v.
Phil 6131.2   Valentin, G.G. Versuch einer physiologischen Pathologie der Nerven. Leipzig, 1864.

Phil 960.8   Valentin, O. Shaddarcaneshu en religionsstudie. Stockholm, 1899.

Phil 6331.1   Valentine, C.W. Dreams and the unconscious; an introduction to the study of psycho-analysis. London, 1921.

Phil 6331.1.5   Valentine, C.W. The new psychology of the unconscious. London, 1932.

Phil 8896.18   Valentine, M. Theoretical ethics. Chicago, 1897.

Phil 575.62   Valentine, P.F. The psychology of personality. N.Y., 1927.

Phil 5261.17.25   Valentine, Willard Lee. Experimental foundations of general psychology. N.Y., 1938.

Phil 5261.17.26   Valentine, Willard Lee. Experimental foundations of general psychology. N.Y., 1946.

Phil 5261.17.10   Valentine, Willard Lee. Psychology laboratory manual. N.Y., 1932.

Phil 5261.17.12   Valentine, Willard Lee. Psychology laboratory manual. N.Y., 1933.

Phil 5261.17   Valentine, Willard Lee. Readings in experimental psychology. 1. ed. N.Y., 1931.

Phil 5261.17.19   Valentine, Willard Lee. Student's guide for beginning the study of psychology. N.Y., 1935.

Phil 3503.35.4   Valentiner, Theodor. Kant und seine Lehre. Eine Einführung in die kritische Philosophie. 4. Aufl. Stuttgart, 1969.

Phil 2421.7   Valentini, Francesco. La filosofia francese contemporanea. 1a ed. Milano, 1958.

Phil 1750.744.5   Valenze esistenziali del cristianesimo. (Bartolone, Filippo.) Messina, 1968.

Phil 2775.5.80   Valenziano, Crispino. Introduzione alla filosofia dell' amore di Maurice Nédoncelle. Roma, 1965.

Phil 2475.1.292   Valery, Paul. Henri Bergson. Paris, 1945.

Phil 4680.312   Valeskalns, Peteris. Ocherk razvitiia progressivnoi filosofskoi iobshchestvenno-politicheskoi mysli v Latvii. Riga, 1967.

Phil 3903.3.97   Valeton, Matthée. De "Als ob" philosophie en het psychisch monisme. Amsterdam, 1923.

Phil 735.109   Valeur. (Bènèzè, Georges.) Paris, 1936.

Phil 735.109.5   Valeur. Thèse. (Bènèzè, Georges.) Paris, 1936.

Phil 735.185   La valeur. 1. ed. (Césari, Paul.) Paris, 1957.

Phil 2725.35.90   La valeur dans la philosophie de Louis Lavelle. (Piersol, Wesley.) Paris, 1959.

Phil 9075.35   Valeur et signification de la mauvais conscience. Thèse. (Jankélévitch, Vladimir.) Paris, 1933.

Phil 70.25   Valeur philosophique de la psychologie. (Centre International de Synthése, Paris.) Paris, 1951.

Phil 8597.53   Valeur spirituelle du profane. (Rabut, Olivier A.) Paris, 1963.

Phil 5241.65   Les valeurs affectives et l'exercice discursif de la pensée. (Bertrand-Barraud, D.) Paris, 1924.

Phil 5241.65.5   Les valeurs affectives et l'exercice discursif de la pensée. Thèse. (Bertrand-Barraud, D.) Paris, 1924.

Phil 5062.39   Valid thinking. 1st ed. (Wheelwright, P.E.) N.Y., 1962.

Phil 8581.58   The validity of the religious experience. (Barrow, George A.) Boston, 1917.

Phil 8951.24.5   Valken, L. Der Glaube bei Emil Brunner. Freiburg, 1947.

Htn   Phil 5771.2.5*   Valla, Lorenzo. De libero arbitrio. Basileae, 1518.

Phil 5771.2   Valla, Lorenzo. De libero arbitrio. Firenze, 1934.

VPhil 5627.215.15   A vallás lelektana, irta Czakó Ambró. (Czakó, Ambrosius.) Pécs, 1915.

Phil 7069.66.45   Vallberg, Viktor. Den kära okunnigheten, eller, Den fördolda kunskapen. Stockholm, 1966.

Phil 365.17   Valle, G. La psicogenesi della coscienza. Milano, 1905.

Phil 525.111   Die Vallendeten. (Schreyer, L.) Heidelberg, 1949.

Phil 1540.70   Vallese, Giulia. Da Dante ad Erasmo. Napoli, 1962.

Phil 821.3   Vallet, P. Histoire de la philosophie. 3e ed. Paris, 1886.

Phil 1535.35   Vallet, Pa. Praelectiones philosophicae. Parisiis, 1878-9. 2v.

Phil 735.11   Valli, Luigi. Il valore supremo. Genova, 1913.

Phil 8896.7   Vallier, C.A. De l'intention morale. Paris, 1883.

Phil 3552.116.5   Vallier, Charles A. De possibilibus apud Leibnitium. Thesis. Burdigalae, 1882.

Phil 2920.2.30   Vallin, Georges. Être et individualite. Paris, 1959.

Phil 2920.2.35   Vallin, Georges. La perspective métaphysique. Paris, 1958.

Phil 8601.4   Vallis, R. Die Naturgeschichte der Göttes. Leipzig, 1875.

Phil 978.49.890   Vallmer, Georg. Die Begegnung Max Heindel mit Rudolf Steiner. Darmstadt, 1965.

Phil 3503.6   Vallois, M. La formation de l'influence Kantienne en France. Paris, 1925?

Phil 3503.6.5   Vallois, M. La formation de l'influence Kantienne en France. Thèse. Paris, 1924.

Phil 4752.2.110   Vallon, Michell A. An apostle of freedom. N.Y., 1960.

Phil 720.65   El valor de la verdad y otros estudios. (García López, Jesús.) Madrid, 1965.

Phil 400.57   Il valore degl'ideali. (Giuliano, B.) Torino, 1916.

Phil 8735.40   Il valore del fine nel mondo. (Fondazione Giorgio Cini, Venice. Centro di Cultura e Civiltà.) Firenze, 1955.

Phil 4160.5.230   Valore e religione nell'orizzonte esistenziale. (Lazzarini, Renato.) Padova, 1965.

Phil 8402.59   Il valore estetico. (Battaglia, F.) Brescia, 1963.

Phil 4060.1.87   Il valore scientifico del positivismo di Roberto Ardigò. (Zamboni, G.) Verona, 1921.

Phil 735.11   Il valore supremo. (Valli, Luigi.) Genova, 1913.

Phil 1750.166.70   Il valore universale dell'umanesimo. (Sodalitas Erasmiana.) Napoli, 1950.

Phil 4972.6.30   Valores do espirito; ensaios. (Kelly, Celso.) Rio de Janeiro, 195-?

Phil 5590.1   Los valores psicologicos de la personalidad. (Abaunza, A.) Mexico, 1940.

Phil 1750.670   Valori, Paolo. Il metodo fenomenologico e la fondazione della filosofia. Roma, 1959.

Phil 8892.57   I valori morali. (Ruvo, Vincenzo de.) Bari, 1942.

Phil 8892.57.2   I valori morali. 2. ed. (Ruvo, Vincenzo de.) Padora, 1970.

Phil 8893.58.10   I valori morali. 3. ed. (Seta, Ugo della.) Roma, 1925.

Phil 192.57.5   Valori spirituali e realtà. (Renda, Antonio.) Messina, 1930.

Phil 8889.3   I valori umani. (Orestano, F.) Milan, 1907.

Phil 2805.231.5   Valot, Stephen. Regardons vivre Blaise Pascal. 2. éd. Paris, 1945.

Phil 302.4   Valsardieu, Paul. La révolution totale, en tout. Paris, 1968- 2v.

Phil 735.10   Valuation: its nature and laws. (Urban, W.M.) London, 1909.

Phil 735.13   Valuation as a logical process. Thesis. (Stuart, H.W.) Chicago, 1918.

Phil 735.124A   Value; a cooperative inquiry. (Lepley, Ray.) N.Y., 1949-50.

Phil 575.18.5   Value and destiny of the individual. (Bosanquet, B.) London, 1913.

Phil 193.64.5   The value and dignity of human life. (Shaw, C.G.) Boston, 1911.

Phil 735.110   Value and ethical objectivity. (Jury, G.S.) London, 1937.

Phil 735.107   Value and existence. (Losskii, Nikolai O.) London, 1935.

Phil 585.165   Value and existence. (Patka, Frederick.) N.Y., 1964.

Phil 1885.85   Value and reality in Bradley's philosophy. (Segerstedt, T.K.) Lund, 1934.

Phil 735.140   The value judgement. (Lamont, W.D.) Edinburgh, 1955.

Phil 8887.30.5   "The value of this earthly life": a reply. (Aveling, E.B.) London, 1879.

Phil 5352.16   The value of unchosen alternatives. (Downs, A.) Santa Monica, 1964.

Phil 8602.13   The value religious facts. (Woods, J.H.) N.Y., 1899.

Phil 735.95   Value theory andCriticism. Thesis. (Pell, Orlie A.H.) N.Y., 1930.

Phil 735.266   Value theory and the behavioral sciences. (Handy, Rollo.) Springfield, Ill., 1969.

Phil 193.131   Values; a philosophy of human needs. (Sills, Milton.) Chicago, 1932.

Phil 8887.136   Values and conduct. (Margolis, Joseph Zalman.) Oxford, 1971.

Phil 8886.86   Values and imperatives. (Lewis, Clarence I.) Stanford, Calif., 1969.

Phil 8880.50   Values and intentions. (Findlay, John Niemayer.) London, 1961.

Phil 735.91.10   Values and reality. (Ward, Leo Richard.) N.Y., 1935.

Phil 8875.34   Values as integrating forces in personality society and culture. (Alisjahbana, Sutan Takdir.) Kuala Lumpur, 1966.

Phil 735.77   Values immediate and contributory and their interrelation. (Picard, Maurice.) N.Y., 1920.

Phil 2225.5.40   Values in a universe of chance. (Peirce, C.S.) Stanford, 1958.

Phil 9120.170   The values of life. (Barker, E.) Glasgow, 1939.

Phil 735.99   The values of life. (Ennismore, R.G.) London, 1931.

Phil 8895.4   The values of life. (Urwick, Edward.) Toronto, 1948.

Phil 75.14   Valverde Téllez, E. Bibliografía. México, 1907.

Htn   Phil 7065.09*   Van Arnolt Boschmä und Herich syme alde vader. Collen, 1509.

Phil 3280.30   Van de Hooft-Deuchden. (Geulincx, A.) Antwerp, 1895.

Phil 1707.28   Van Hegel zu Heidegger. (Huebscher, Arthur.) Stuttgart, 1961.

Phil 193.210   Van Thales tot sartre. (Spier, Johannes.) Kampen, 1959.

Phil 3640.79.20   Van vornehmen Menschen. (Nietzsche, Friedrich.) Klosterberg, 1945.

Phil 1801.2   Van Becelaere, L. La philosophie en Amériqe depuis les origine jusqu'à nos jours, 1607-1900. N.Y., 1904.

Phil 5627.196   Van Buskirk, J.D. Religion, healing and health. N.Y., 1952.

Phil 9035.50   Vance, J.G. A mirror of personality. London, 1927.

Phil 8676.4   Vance, J.G. The sovereignty of God. Oxford, 1934.

Phil 630.10   Vance, John G. Reality and truth. London, 1917.

Phil 4818.410.80   Vance, Wilson. René Fülöp-Miller's search for reality. London, 1930.

Phil 1750.35   Vancourt, R. La phénoménologie et la foi. Tournai, 1953.

Phil 196.32   Vancourt, R. La philosophie et sa structure. v.1,3. Paris, 1953. 2v.

Phil 8601.17   Vancourt, Raymond. Pensée moderne et philosophie chrétienne. Paris, 1957.

Phil 3425.607   Vancourt, Raymond. La pensée religieuse de Hegel. Paris, 1965.

Phil 2730.99.5   Vancourt, Raymond. La théorie de la connaissance chez Maine de Biran. 2e éd. Paris, 1944.

Phil 8971.4   Vandenbroucke, Francois. La morale monastique du XIe au XVIe siècle. Louvain, 1966.

Phil 6322.41   Vandendriessche, Gaston. The parapraxis in the Haizmann case of Sigmund Freud. Louvain, 1955.

Phil 6331.10   Vandendriessche, Gaston. The parapraxis in the Haizmann case of Sigmund Freud. Louvain, 1965.

Phil 2750.2.80   Van der Elst, Robert. Michelet, naturaliste. Paris, 1914.

Phil 7069.61.35   Van der Huok, P. Psychic. Indianapolis, 1961.

Phil 8971.8   Van der Poel, Cornelius J. The search for human values. N.Y., 1971.

Phil 9558.41   Van der Schaar, P.J. Dynamik der Pseudologie. München, 1964.

Phil 1885.97   Vander Veer, Garrett L. Bradley's metaphysics and the self. New Haven, 1970.

Phil 6331.6   Van der Veldt, J.H. Psychiatry and Catholicism. 1st ed. N.Y., 1952.

Phil 6331.6.2   Van der Veldt, J.H. Psychiatry and Catholicism. 2nd ed. N.Y., 1957.

Phil 4235.1.99   Van Deusen, Neil C. Telesio, the first of the moderns. N.Y., 1932.

Phil 8971.1   Van Dyke, Henry. The gospel for a world of sin. N.Y., 1899.

Phil 8434.3.5   Van Dyke, J.C. Nature for its own sake. 5th ed. N.Y., 1908.

Phil 5460.4   Vanföreställningarnas och sinnesvillornas psykologi. (Svenson, Frey.) Stockholm, 1919.

Phil 5066.259.5   Van Heijenoort, Jean. Frege und Gödel; two fundamental texts in mathematical logic. Cambridge, 1970.

Phil 5066.259   Van Heijenoort, Jean. From Frege to Gödel; a source book in mathematical logic, 1879-1931. Cambridge, 1967.

Htn   Phil 4265.1.30*   Vanini, Lucilio, afterwards Giulio Cesare. De admirandis naturae reginae deaeque mortalium arcanis. Lutetieae, 1616.

Phil 4265.1.15   Vanini, Lucilio, afterwards Giulio Cesare. Oeuvres philosophiques. Paris, 1842.

Phil 4265.1.18   Vanini, Lucilio, afterwards Giulio Cesare. Opere. Lecce, 1912. 2v.

Phil 4265.1.20   Vanini, Lucilio, afterwards Giulio Cesare. Le opere di Giulio Cesare Vanini e le loro fonti. Milano, 1933-34. 2v.

Htn   Phil 8676.1*   Vanino, G.C. Amphitheatrum. Lugdunum, 1615.

Phil 7069.20.330   The vanished friend. (Thiébault, Jules.) N.Y., 1920.

Phil 9513.40   The vanishing right to live. 1st ed. (Rice, Charles E.) Garden City, N.Y., 1969.

Phil 5425.38   The vanity and insanity of genius. (Sanborn, K.A.) N.Y., 1886.

Phil 8875.3.5   The vanity of arts and sciences. (Agrippa von Nettesheim, Heinrich Cornelius.) London, 1676.

Htn   Phil 337.4*   The vanity of dogmatizing. (Glanvill, Joseph.) London, 1661. 2 pam.

Phil 337.4.5   The vanity of dogmatizing. (Glanvill, Joseph.) N.Y., 1931.

Phil 337.4.6 — The vanity of dogmatizing. Facsimile reprints of the London editions of 1661, 1665 and 1676. (Glanvill, Joseph.) Brighton, 1970.
Phil 6131.7 — Van Kaam, Adrian. Existential foundations and psychology. Pittsburgh, 1966.
Phil 1811.5 — Van Leeuwen, H.G. The problem of certainty in English thought. The Hague, 1963.
Phil 9540.1.10 — Van Loon, H.W. Tolerance. Garden City, 1927.
Phil 9540.1.5 — Van Loon, H.W. Tolerance. N.Y., 1925.
Phil 9540.1 — Van Loon, H.W. Tolerance. N.Y., 1939.
Phil 8971.2.5 — Vann, Gerald. Morals and man. N.Y., 1960.
Phil 8601.12 — Vann, Gerald. On being human; St. Thomas and Mr. Aldous Huxley. N.Y., 1934.
Phil 8971.2 — Vann, Gerald. The water and the fire. London, 1953.
Phil 5261.11 — Vannérus, A. Om psykisk energi. Stockholm, 1896.
Phil 5261.12 — Vannérus, A. De psykologiska vetenskapernas system. Stockholm, 1907.
Phil 4650.1.33 — Vannérus, Allen. Ateism contra teism. Stockholm, 1903.
Phil 4650.1.70 — Vannérus, Allen. Den empiriska naturuppfattningen. 2. ed. Stockholm, 1913.
Phil 4650.1.69 — Vannérus, Allen. Etiska tankegångar. Stockholm, 1922.
Phil 4650.1.51 — Vannérus, Allen. Filosofiska konturer. Göteborg, 1902.
Phil 4582.4.90 — Vannérus, Allen. Hägerströmstudier. Stockholm, 1930.
Phil 4650.1.35 — Vannérus, Allen. Kulturidealism. Stockholm, 1903.
Phil 4650.1.39 — Vannérus, Allen. Kunskapslära. Stockholm, 1905.
Phil 4650.1.37 — Vannérus, Allen. Lära och lif. Stockholm, 1904.
Phil 4650.1.43 — Vannérus, Allen. Logik och vetenskapslära. Stockholm, 1918.
Phil 4650.1.59 — Vannérus, Allen. Materiens värld. Stockholm, 1925.
Phil 4650.1.53 — Vannérus, Allen. Metafysik. Lund, 1914.
Phil 4650.1.47 — Vannérus, Allen. Om erfarenheten ett kunskapsteoretiskt studieförsök. Akademisk afhandling. Stockholm, 1890.
Phil 4650.1.45 — Vannérus, Allen. Til det andliga lifvets filosofi. Stockholm, 1910.
Phil 4515.84 — Vannérus, Allen. Till Boströms teoretiska filosofi. Stockholm, 1897.
Phil 4650.1.31 — Vannérus, Allen. Till kritiken af den religiösa kunskapen. Stockholm, 1902.
Phil 4650.1.56 — Vannérus, Allen. Ursprungens filosofi. Stockholm, 1925.
Phil 4650.1.40 — Vannérus, Allen. Vetenskapernas system. Stockholm, 1892.
Phil 4650.1.41 — Vannérus, Allen. Vetenskapssystematik. Stockholm, 1907.
Phil 3915.105 — Vannérus, Allen. Vid studiet af Wundts psykologi. Stockholm, 1896.
Phil 4650.1.48 — Vannérus, Allen. Det yttersta tankegångar. Stockholm, 1924.
Phil 3915.105.5 — Vannérus, Allen. Zur Kritik des Seelenbegriffs. n.p., n.d.
Phil 4265.5.30 — Vanni, Icilio. Saggi di filosofia sociale e giuridica. Bologna, 1906-11. 2v.
Phil 4021.2 — Vanni Ronighi, S. Il problema morale nella filosofia italiana dell prima metà de secolo XIX. Milano, 1951.
Phil 3450.19.106 — Vanni Rovighi, S. Heidegger. Brescia, 1945.
Phil 3503.10 — Vanni Rovighi, Sofia. Introduzione allo studio di Kant. Como, 1945.
Phil 5261.6 — Van Norden, Charles. The psychic factor; outline of psychology. N.Y., 1894.
Phil 196.5.3F — Van Nostrand, J.J. Prefatory lessons in a mechanical philosophy. Chicago, 1907.
Phil 196.5 — Van Nostrand, J.J. Prefatory lessons in a mechanical philosophy. Chicago, 1907.
Phil 8735.23 — Van Nuys, K. Science and cosmic purpose. 1. ed. Thesis. N.Y., 1949.
Phil 196.40 — Van Nuys, Kevin. Is reality meaningful? Static contradictions and dynamic resolutions between facts and value. N.Y., 1966.
Phil 2475.1.210 — Van Paassen, C.R. De antithesen in de philosophie van Henri Bergson. Haarlem, 1923.
Phil 5771.1 — Van Peyma, P.W. The why of the will. Boston, 1910.
Phil 672.23 — VanRiper, B.W. Some views of the time problem. Diss. Menasha, 1916.
Phil 2805.305 — Vansina, Dirk. Pascal. Bussum, 1954.
Phil 6315.2.440 — Vansina, M.J. Het super-ego. Antwerpen, 1969.
Phil 8422.4 — Vanslov, V.V. Problema prekrasnogo. Moskva, 1957.
Phil 8422.4.5 — Vanslov, V.V. Soderzhanie i forma v iskusstve. Moskva, 1956.
Phil 530.20.40 — Vansteenberghe, E. Autour de la docte ignorance. Munster en Westphalie, 1914?
Phil 1504.14.2 — Vansteenberghe, E. Autour de la "Docte Ignorance." v.14, pt.2-4. Münster, 1915.
Phil 1504.8.6 — Vansteenberghe, E. Le "de Ignota Litteratura." v.8, pt.6-7. Münster, 1910.
Phil 6331.5 — Van Teslaar, J.S. An outline of psychoanalysis. N.Y., 1925.
Phil 8897.43 — Van Wesep, H.B. The control of ideals. N.Y., 1920.
Phil 1821.10 — Van Wesep, Hendrikus. Seven sages. 1st ed. N.Y., 1960.
Phil 8591.75 — Vapaamielisyys. (Laurila, K.S.) Helsingissä, 1912.
Phil 5040.23 — Voprosy logiki. (Akademiia Nauk SSSR. Institut Filosofii.) Moskva, 1955.
Phil 8601.16 — Varadachari, K. Idea of God. Tirupati, 1950.
Phil 4120.6.95 — Varano, F.S. Vincenzo de Grazia. Napoli, 1931.
Phil 5115.1.5 — Varano, Francesco S. L'ipotesi nella filosofia di Ernesto Naville. Gubbio, 1931.
Phil 196.6 — Varas, J. Miguel y Marin. Elementos de ideolojia. Santiago de Chile, 1830.
Phil 4080.6.80 — Varchi, B. Vita di Francesco Cattani da Diacceto. Ancona, 1843.
Phil 352.11 — Vardapetian, K. O nekotorykh osnovnykh voprosakh marks - leninskoi gnoseologii. Erevan, 1963.
Phil 9045.9 — Varela, Alfredo. Patria! Livro da Mocidade. Rio de Janeiro, 1900.
Phil 196.28 — Varela, F. Lecciones de filosofía. Havana, 1940.
Phil 4983.5.22 — Varela, Félix. Cartas a Elpidio (Selección). Habana, 1960.
Phil 4983.5.85 — Varela, Félix. Cartas a Elpidio sobre la impiedad. v.1-2. Habana, 1944.
Phil 4983.5.20 — Varela, Félix. Lecciones de filosofía. 5. ed. Habana, 1961. 2v.
Phil 4983.5.6 — Varela, Félix. Miscelanea filosófica. Habana, 1944.
Phil 4260.152 — Varela Domínguez de Ghiolai, Delfina. Filosofía argentina: Vico en los escritos de Sarmiento. Buenos Aires, 1950.
Phil 4960.260 — Varela Dominguez de Ghioldi, Delfina. Filosofía argentina; los ideólogos. Buenos Aires, 1938.
Phil 5261.8.5 — Varendonck, J. L'évolution des facultés conscientes. Thèse. Gand, 1921.
Phil 5261.8.8 — Varendonck, J. The evolution of the concious faculties. N.Y., 1923.
Phil 5261.8 — Varendonck, J. La psychologie du témoinage. Gand, 1914.
Phil 7225.2A — Varendonck, Julien. The psychology of day-dreams. London, 1921.
Phil 5420.5.11 — Varför hämmar jag mig själo? (Roback, A.A.) Stockholm, 1939.
Phil 352.9 — Varga, A. von. Einführung in die Erkenntnislehre. München, 1953.
Phil 3503.20 — Varga, Alexander von. Macht und Ohnmacht der Vernunft. Zur Einführung in die Philosophie Kants. München, 1967.
Phil 185.7.9 — Varia; studies on problems of philosophy and ethics. (Knight, W.) London, 1901.
Phil 5047.48 — Variabilität und Disziplinierung des Denkens. (Hampel, Hans-Jürgen.) München, 1967.
Phil 5599.39 — Die Variablen der Holtzman Inkblot Technique in ihrer Beziehung zur Introversion und Extraversion. (Zeppelin, Ilka Sigried von.) Bern, 1966.
Phil 4356.3.10 — Variaciones sobre el espíritu. (Ferrater Mora, José.) Buenos Aires, 1945.
Phil 5593.51 — De varianten der intentionaliteit bij de Rorschachtest. (Kijm, J.M.) Nijmegen, 1951.
Phil 1106.15 — Varias lectiones ex historia philosophiae antiquae. (Bakhuizen Van Den Brink, R.C.) Lugduni-Batavorum, 1842.
Phil 1702.9 — Variazioni sulla storia della filosofia moderna. (Campo, M.) Brescia, 1946.
Phil 5627.6.14 — La varie forme della coscienza religiosa. (James, William.) n.p., n.d.
Phil 190.16.10 — Variétés morales et politiques. (Pressensé, E. de.) Paris, 1885.
Phil 2630.9 — Variétés philosophiques. (Gex, Maurice.) Lausanne, 1948.
Phil 178.39 — Variétés philosophiques. 2e éd. (Durand, J.P.) Paris, 1900.
Phil 5627.156 — Varieties of Christian experience. (Norborg, S.) Minneapolis, 1938.
Phil 2055.7.10 — Varieties of educational experience. (Hocking, William E.) Madison, N.H., 1952. 2v.
Phil 165.90 — Varieties of experience. (Levi, A.W.) N.Y., 1957.
Phil 9240.31 — The varieties of goodness. (Wright, Georg.) London, 1963.
Phil 9240.31.5 — The varieties of goodness. (Wright, Georg.) N.Y., 1963.
Phil 735.160 — Varieties of human value. (Morris, C.W.) Chicago, 1956.
Phil 525.237 — Varieties of mystic experience, an anthology and interpretation. 1st ed. (O'Brien, E.) N.Y., 1964.
Phil 6155.6 — The varieties of psychedelic experience. 1st ed. (Masters, Robert E.L.) N.Y., 1966.
Phil 5627.6.3 — Varieties of religious experience. (James, William.) London, 1915.
Phil 5627.6.5.16 — Varieties of religious experience. (James, William.) London, 1960.
Phil 5627.6.2.4 — Varieties of religious experience. (James, William.) N.Y., 1902.
Phil 5627.6.2.5 — Varieties of religious experience. (James, William.) N.Y., 1902.
Htn Phil 5627.6.2* — Varieties of religious experience. (James, William.) N.Y., 1902.
Htn Phil 5627.6.1* — Varieties of religious experience. (James, William.) N.Y., 1902.
NEDL Phil 5627.6.5 — Varieties of religious experience. (James, William.) N.Y., 1903.
Phil 5627.6.5.10 — Varieties of religious experience. (James, William.) N.Y., 1904.
Phil 5627.6.4A — Varieties of religious experience. (James, William.) N.Y., 1928.
Phil 5627.6.5.15 — Varieties of religious experience. (James, William.) N.Y., 1936.
Phil 5590.8 — The varieties of temperament; a psychology of constitutional differences. (Sheldon, William H.) N.Y., 1942.
Phil 6131.1 — Varigny, H.C. de. Recherches expérimentales sur l'excitabilité électrique. Paris, 1884.
Phil 4235.1.40 — Varii de naturalibus rebus libelli. (Telesius, B.) Hildesheim, 1971.
Phil 6615.4 — Various forms of functional paralysis. (Bastian, Henry Charlton.) London, 1893.
Phil 2270.43 — Various fragments. (Spencer, Herbert.) N.Y., 1898.
Phil 8897.2 — Various prospects of mankind. (Wallace, R.) London, 1761.
Phil 196.8.3 — Varisco, B. La conoscenza. Pavia, 1904.
Phil 196.8 — Varisco, B. The great problems. London, 1914.
Phil 196.8.20 — Varisco, B. Lines de filosofia critica. 2a ed. Roma, 1931.
Phil 196.8.7 — Varisco, B. Scienza e opinioni. Roma, 1901.
Phil 196.8.15 — Varisco, B. Sommario di filosofia. Roma, 1928.
Phil 196.8.12 — Varisco, B. Studi di filosofia naturale. Roma, 1903.
Phil 195.13.5 — Varlik ve olus. (Ulken, Hilmi Zuja.) Ankara, 1968.
Phil 196.11 — Varnbüler, Theodore. Acht Aufsätze zur Apologie der menschlichen Vernunft. Leipzig, 1878.
Phil 196.11.9 — Varnbüler, Theodore. Die Lehre vom Sein. Leipzig, 1883.
Phil 196.11.5 — Varnbüler, Theodore. Der Organismus der Allvernunft und das Leben der Menschheit in Ihm. Prag, 1891.
Phil 2490.120 — Varney, M.M. L'influence des femmes sur Auguste Comte. Thèse. Paris, 1931.
Phil 5261.21 — Varnuar, W.C. Psychology in everyday life. N.Y., 1938.
Phil 8896.6 — Varona, E.J. Conferencias sobre el fundamento de la moral. N.Y., 1913.
Phil 5061.2 — Varona, E.J. Nociones de lógica. Habana, 1902.
Phil 4983.8.6 — Varona, Enrique. Conferencias filosóficas. Ser.1, 3. Habana, 1880. 2v.
Phil 5261.5 — Varona, Enrique José. Conferencias filosoficas. Havana, 1888.
Phil 5261.5.5 — Varona, Enrique José. Curso de psicologia. Fascimile 2. Havana, 1906.
Phil 585.397 — Váross, Marian. Estetično, umenie a človek. Bratislava, 1969.
Phil 4810.6 — Várossová, Elena. Kapitoly z dejín slovenskej filozofie. Bratislava, 1957.
Phil 4810.6.5 — Várossová, Elena. Prehl'ad dejín slovenskej filozofie. Bratislava, 1965.
Phil 821.5 — Varsencelos, Jóse. Historia del pensamiento filosofico. Mexico, 1937.
Phil 2520.239 — Vartanian, A. Diderot and Descartes. Princeton, 1953.
Phil 5261.16 — Varvaro, P. L'intelligenza. Palermo, 1927.
Htn Phil 196.21* — Varvaro, Paolo. Introduzione alla filosofia. Palermo, 1925.
Phil 3503.25 — Vas, Harmen de. Kant als theoloog. Baarn, 1968.
Phil 623.50 — Vasa, Andrea. Ricerche sul razionalismo della prassi. Firenze, 1957.
Phil 6053.10 — Vaschide, Nicolas. Essai sur la psychologie de la main. Paris, 1909.
Phil 7082.148 — Vaschide, Nicolas. La psychologie du rêve au point de une médical. Paris, 1902.
Phil 7080.28 — Vaschide, Nicolas. Le sommeil et les rêves. Paris, 1914.

Phil 8896.19   Vasconcelos, J. Etica. 2. ed. Mexico, 1939.
Phil 196.27.5   Vasconcelos, J. Manual de filosofía. Mexico, 1940.
Phil 4983.9.30   Vasconcelos, J. Todología. México, 1952.
Phil 196.27   Vasconcelos, J. Tratado de metafisica. Mexico, 1929.
Phil 8422.10   Vascoucelos, J. Estética. 2. ed. México, 1936.
Phil 4710.82   Vasetskii, G.S. Russkaia progressivnaia filosficheskaia mysl' XIX veka. Moskva, 1959.
X Cg   Phil 2138.95   Vasey, George. Individual liberty, legal, moral, and licentious. 2nd ed. London, 1877.
Phil 5525.19.2   Vasey, George. The philosophy of laughter and smiling. 2. ed. London, 1877.
Phil 310.527   Vasil'ev, Iu. Al. V.I. Lenin i nekotorye voprosy nauchnogo predvideniia v obshchestvennom zhizni. Minsk, 1962.
Phil 7069.62.20   Vasil'ev, L.L. Vnushenie na rasstoianii. Moskva, 1962.
Phil 6131.6.5   Vasil'ev, Leonid L. Mysterious phenomena of the human psyche. New Hyde Park, N.Y., 1965.
Phil 6131.6   Vasil'ev, Leonid L. Tainstvennye iavleniia chelov psikhiki. Moskva, 1963.
Phil 6131.6.3   Vasil'ev, Leonid L. Tainstvennye iavleniia chelovecheskoi psikhiki. Izd. 3. Moskva, 1964.
Phil 1630.35   Vasoli, Cesare. La dialettica e la retorica dell'Umanesimo. Milano, 1968.
Phil 1622.5   Vasoli, Cesare. Studi sulla cultura del Rinascimento. Manduria, 1968.
Phil 187.93.30   Vassallo, Angel. Cuatro lecciones sobre metafísica. Buenos Aires, 1938.
Phil 196.29.3   Vassallo, Angel. Elogio de la vigilia. Buenos Aires, 1939.
Phil 196.29   Vassallo, Angel. Nuevos prolegómenos a la metafisica. Buenos Aires, 1938.
Phil 5401.20F   Vassos, John. Phobia. N.Y., 1931.
Phil 575.294   Västerlandet inför personlighetstanken. (Petander, Karl.) Uppsala, 1969.
Phil 5871.10   Das Vaterbild den Tocher. Diss. (Erni, Margrit.) n.p., 1965.
Phil 9342.17.5   Vaterlicher Rath für meine Tochter. 2. Aufl. (Campe, J.H.) Tübingen, 1789.
Htn   Phil 2925.2.35*   Vattel, Emmerich. The law of nations. v.1-2. London, 1760[1759].
Phil 3640.750   Vattimo, Gianni. Ipostesi su Nietzsche. Torino, 1967.
Phil 8601.20   Vattimo, Gianni. Poesia e ontologia. Milano, 1967.
Phil 3805.230   Vattimo, Gianni. Schleiermacher filosofo dell'interpretazione. Milano, 1968.
Phil 735.79.1   Vaucher, G. Le langage affectif et les jugements de valeur. Paris, 1925.
Phil 735.79   Vaucher, G. Le langage affectif et les jugements de valeur. Thèse. Paris, 1925.
Phil 525.9   Vaughan, R.A. Hours with the mystics. London, 1856. 2v.
Phil 525.9.2   Vaughan, R.A. Hours with the mystics. 2nd ed. London, 1860. 2v.
Phil 575.73   Vaughan, Richard M. The significance of personality. N.Y., 1930.
Phil 5261.15.10   Vaughan, W.F. General psychology. Garden City, 1936.
Phil 5261.15.25   Vaughan, W.F. General psychology. 1st ed. N.Y., 1939.
Phil 5261.15   Vaughan, W.F. The lure of superiority. N.Y., 1928.
Phil 5261.20   Vaughn, J. Positive versus negative instruction. N.Y., 1928.
Phil 75.24   Vaunérus, Allen. Svensk filosofi. Stockholm, 1930.
Phil 5068.98   Vax, Louis. L'empirisme logique. Paris, 1970.
Phil 196.13   Vaz, F.M. Estudos philosóphicos. Porto, 1897. 2v.
Phil 3841.5   Vaz Dias, A.M. Spinoza, mercator en autodidactus. 's Gravenhage, 1932.
Phil 5261.4   Vaz Ferreira, C. Ideas y observaciones. Montevideo, 1905.
Phil 9490.15   Vaz Ferreira, C. Moral para intelectuales. La Plata, 1957.
Phil 5771.4   Vaz Ferreira, C. Los problemas de la libertad y los del determinismo. Buenos Aires, 1957.
Phil 4983.1.30   Vaz Ferreira, Carlos. Fermentario. Buenos Aires, 1940.
Phil 4983.1.32   Vaz Ferreira, Carlos. Fermentario. Montevideo, 1953.
Phil 5061.4.5   Vaz Ferreira, Carlos. Lógica viva. Montevideo, 1920.
Phil 5061.4.15   Vaz Ferreira, Carlos. Lógica viva (adaptación prática y didáctica). Buenos Aires, 1945.
Phil 4983.1.5   Vaz Ferreira, Carlos. Obras. v.1-25. Montevideo, 1957. 20v.
Phil 4983.1.80   Vaz Ferreira. 1. ed. (Arias, Alejandro.) México, 1948.
Phil 4960.272   Vazela Dominiguez de Ghioldi, Delfina. Para la historia de las ideas argentinas. 1. ed. Buenos Aires, 1952.
Phil 8846.4   Vázquez, Francisco. Tres éticas del siglo XX. Madrid, 1970.
Phil 4960.240   Vázquez, Juan Adolfo. Antología filosófica argentina del siglo XX. Buenos Aires, 1965.
Phil 196.42   Vazquez, Juan Adolfo. Que es la ontologia. Buenos Aires, 1964.
Phil 9035.92   Vbbink, G. Karakterkundig woordenbock des Nederlands taal. Baarn, 1951.
Phil 5238.213   Vdruženje Psihologa Jugoslavije. Stanje i perspektive jugoslovenske psihologije. Beograd, 1965.
Phil 196.24   Veale, César. Mas espiritu, meuos materia. Buenos Aires, 1931.
Phil 8896.21   Veatch, Henry B. Rational man; a modern interpretation. Bloomington, 1962.
Phil 630.53   Veatch, Henry B. Realism and nominalism revisited. Milwaukee, 1954.
Phil 5061.10   Veatch, Henry B. Two logics. Evanston, 1969.
Phil 3503.30   Veca, Salvatore. Fondazione e modalita in Kant. Milano, 1969.
Phil 3425.465   Vecchi, Giovanni. L'estetica di Hegel. Milano, 1956.
Phil 8896.10   Vecchia, Paolo. Elementi di morale e cenni di economia politica. 8. ed. Torino, 1917?
Phil 8884.15   Il vecchio e il nuovo problema della morale. (Juvalta, E.) Bologna, 1914.
Phil 4170.3.80   Vecchio-Veneziani, Augusta del. La vita e l'opere di A.C. de Meis. Bologna, 1921.
Phil 3808.252   Vecchiotti, Icilio. La dottrina di Schopenhauer. Roma, 1969.
Phil 3460.90   Vecchiotti, Icilio. Premessa a Jacobi. 1. ed. Roma, 1959.
Phil 4710.18   Vechnoe v russkoi filosofii. (Vysheslavtsev, B.P.) N.Y., 1955.
Phil 4580.32   Ved aarhundredeskiftet. (Høffding, Harald.) København, 1901.
Phil 4809.497.30   Věda a duch. (Kozák, Jan Blahoslav.) Praha, 1938.
Phil 1750.290   Vedaldi, A. Essere gli altri. 1. ed. Torino, 1948.
Phil 960.3.15   Vedânta, Platon und Kant. 2. Aufl. (Deussen, P.) Wien, 1917.
Phil 960.128.10   The Vedânta according to Samkara and Rāmānuja. (Radhakrishnan, S.) London, 1928.

Phil 960.3.19   Vedânta und Platonismus im Lichte der kantischen Philosophie. (Deussen, P.) Berlin, 1922.
Phil 8422.12   Vedel, V. Liv og kunst. København, 1949. 2v.
Phil 5780.14   Vedenov, A.V. Vospitanie voli u rebenka v sem'e. Moskva, 1952.
Phil 960.195   Vedic religion and philosophy. (Prabhavananda, Swami.) Madras, 1950.
Phil 4065.180   Védrine, Hélène. La conception de la nature chez Giordano Bruno. Paris, 1967.
Phil 5057.27   Vedute fondamentali sull'arte logica. (Romagnosi, G.D.) Roma, 1936.
Phil 3890.1.80   Veeck, O. Darstellung...Trendelenburgs. Gotha, 1888.
Phil 3705.2.85   Veer, Hendrik. Mr. C.W. Opzoomer als wijsgeer. Assen, 1961.
Phil 3705.2.86   Veer, Hendrik. Mr. C.W. Opzoomer als wijsgeer. Assen, 1961.
Phil 8982.2   Vega, Rafael de la. Marxismus und Ethik. 1. Aufl. Frankfurt am Main, 1970.
Phil 4772.1   Veideman, A. Opravdanie zla. Riga, 1939.
Phil 8601.11   Veiga, Antonio D.A. Lei das contrastes. Porto, 1928.
Phil 5425.70   Veiga Azvedo, A.V. O problema do génio; ensaio para uma tesse de redução. Lisboa, 1944.
Phil 7072.6.5   The veil lifted; modern developments of spirit photography. (Glendinning, Andrew.) London, 1894.
Phil 400.6   The veil of Isis...essays on idealism. (Webb, J.E.) Dublin, 1885.
Phil 7067.04   Der Veilfoermige Hintzelmann. Göttingen, 1965.
Phil 200.19   Los veinte lemas que le cultivado en los cincuenta. (Zaragüela Bengoechea, J.) Madrid, 1958.
Phil 1721.4   Veit, Otto. Soziologie der Freiheit. Frankfurt a.M., 1957.
Phil 2035.88   Veitch, J. Hamilton. Philadelphia, 1882.
Phil 2035.88.5   Veitch, J. Memoir of William Hamilton. Edinburgh, 1869.
Phil 2035.88.3   Veitch, J. Sir William Hamilton: the man and his philosophy. London, 1883.
Phil 196.12.5   Veitch, John. Dualism and monism. Edinburg, 1895.
Phil 5061.3   Veitch, John. Institutes of logic. Edinburgh, 1885.
Phil 196.12   Veitch, John. Knowing and being. Edinburg, 1889.
Phil 6615.22   Veith, Ilza. Hysteria; the history of a disease. Chicago, 1965.
Phil 8430.48   Vek nauki i iskusstvo. (Eremeev, Arkadii F.) Moskva, 1965.
Phil 2399.1   Vek Prosveshcheniia. Moskva, 1970.
Phil 5585.232   Vekker, Lev M. Vospriiatie i osnovy ego modelirovaniia. Leningrad, 1964.
Phil 5435.12   Veldt, Jacobus van der. L'apprentissage du mouvement et l'automatisme. Louvain, 1928.
Phil 1721.7.5   Vélez Correa, Jaime. Filosofía moderna y contemporanea. Madrid, 1965.
Phil 1721.7   Vélez Correa, Jaime. Historia de la filosofía moderna y contemporánea. Bogotá, 1959.
Phil 4769.1.135   Velichko, Vasilii L. Vladimir Solov'ev. Sankt Peterburg, 1902.
Phil 310.4   Velikaia sila idei lenimizma; sbornik statei. Moskva, 1950.
Phil 4265.1.35   Velikii ital'ianskii ateist Vanini. (Rutenburg, V.I.) Moskva, 1959.
Phil 8696.22   Velikii konflikt. (Gurev, Grigorii.) Moskva, 1965.
Phil 525.79   Vellani, Giovanni E. La mistica dell'avenire. Modena, 1936.
Phil 1721.3   Veloso, A. Nos encruzilhada do pensamento. Porto, 1956.
Phil 9240.30   Veloso, Agostinho. O homem em face da dor. Lisboa, 1961.
Phil 8876.150   Venatio hominum. (Bersandius, J.) Francofonte, 1677.
Phil 9230.7   Venault de charmilly. Letter...to Lieutenant General B. Tarleton. London, 1810.
Phil 8422.9   Vendéen, E. Principes du beau. Paris, 1912.
Phil 196.9   Venetianer, M. Der allgeist. Grundzüge des Panpsychismus. Berlin, 1874.
Phil 3808.97   Venetianer, M. Schopenhauer als Scholastiker. Berlin, 1873.
Phil 5061.1.9   Venn, J. The logic of chance. London, 1866.
Phil 5061.1.8   Venn, J. The logic of chance. London, 1876.
Phil 5061.1.11   Venn, J. The logic of chance. London, 1888.
X Cg   Phil 5061.1.11   Venn, J. The logic of chance. London, 1888.
Phil 5070.2   Venn, J. On some of the characteristics of belief; scientific and religious. London, 1870.
Phil 5061.1   Venn, J. Principles of empirical or inductive logic. London, 1889.
Phil 5061.1.2   Venn, J. Principles of empirical or inductive logic. London, 1907.
Phil 5061.1.6   Venn, J. Symbolic logic. London, 1894.
Phil 3552.472   Vennelusch, Joachim. Gottfried Wilhelm Leibniz; philosopher and politician in the service of a universal culture. Bad Godesberg, 1966.
Phil 6315.2.275   Vennes, Gaston. Inconscient freudien et problèmes de liberté. Trois Rivières, 1960.
Phil 6947.1940   Venray, Netherlands. Psychiatrisch Ziekenhuis Sint Anna. Een halve eeuw. Venray, 1961?
Phil 3480.80.50   Vens la paix perpetuelle. 1. éd. (Kant, Immanuel.) Paris, 1958.
Phil 5520.487   Ventler, Zeno. Linguistics in philosophy. Ithaca, 1967.
Phil 4265.2.32   Ventura. De methodo philosphandi. Romae, 1828.
Phil 4215.2.81   Ventura, L. Tommaso Rossi e la sua filosofia. Genova, 1912.
Phil 4265.2.30   Ventura da Raulica, G. Della vera e della falsa filosofia. Napoli, 1854.
Phil 2520.125   Ventura da Raulica, G. Essai sur l'origine des idées...sur le carthésianisme. Paris, 1853.
Phil 4265.2.10   Ventura da Raulica, G. Opere. v.1-13. Napoli, 1856-64. 11v.
Phil 196.2   Ventura da Raulica, G. La philosophie chrétienne. Paris, 1861. 3v.
Phil 196.2.5   Ventura da Raulica, G. La raison philosophique et la raison catholique. Paris, 1854-1864. 4v.
Phil 196.2.10   Ventura da Raulica, G. La tradizione e i semi-Pelagiani della filosofia. pt.1-2. Milano, 1857.
Phil 7069.64.35   Venture inward. (Cayce, Hugh Lynn.) N.Y., 1964.
Phil 4757.2.90   Venture with ideas. (Walker, K.M.) London, 1951.
Phil 1730.31   Venturi, Franco. Utopia and reform in the enlightenment. Cambridge, Eng., 1971.
Phil 1730.30   Venturi, Franco. Utopia e riforma nell'iluminismo. Torino, 1970.
Phil 6830.4   Venturi, Silvio. Li digenerazioni psico-sessuali. Torino, 1892.
Phil 3503.3   Venturini, Karl. Geist der kritischen Philosophie. Altona, 1796-97. 2v.
Phil 194.13.25   Venturini, M. La filosofia dell'umanesimo di P.R. Trojano, 1863-1909. Torino, 1919.

Phil 672.176   Venturini, Saul. Chiacchierata sul concetto di spazio. Milano, 1951.

Phil 5425.107   Venzmer, Gerhard. Genius und Wahn. Stuttgart, 1964.

Phil 978.43   Ver-Planck, J.C. (Mrs.). The wonder-light, true philosophy for children. N.Y., 1890.

Phil 3425.95.8   Véra, A. Essais de philosophie hégélienne. Paris, 1864.

Phil 3425.95.12   Véra, A. L'hégélianisme et la philosophie. Paris, 1861.

Phil 4265.3.32   Vera, A. In inquiry into speculative and experimental science. London, 1856.

Phil 3425.95   Véra, A. Introduction à la philosophie de Hegel. Paris, 1845-55. 3 pam.

Phil 3425.95.15   Véra, A. Introduction à la philosophie de Hegel. 2. éd. Paris, 1864.

Phil 4265.3.30   Vera, A. Introduction to speculative logic and philosophy. St. Louis, 1873.

Phil 4265.3.37   Vera, A. Mélanges philosophiques. Paris, 1862.

Phil 3425.95.4   Véra, A. Philosophie de l'esprit. Paris, 1867-69. 2v.

Phil 4265.3.35   Vera, A. Problema dell'assoluto. v.1-4. Napoli, 1872-82.

Phil 4265.3.45   Vera, A. Prolusioni alla storia della filosofia. Milano, 1861.

Phil 4265.3.33   Vera, A. Ricerche sulla scienza speculativa e esperimentale. Parigi, 1864.

Phil 4265.3.39   Vera, A. Saggi filosofici. Napoli, 1883.

Phil 8698.5   Vera i znanie; o Boge, religii. (Irkolin, N.E.) Muinkhen, 1961.

Phil 8673.27   Vera ili zhanie. (Shekhterman, Efim I.) Alme-Ata, 1967.

Phil 8403.14   Il vera interiore. (Ciaccio, G.) Sarzana, 1921.

Phil 7082.104.4   La vera spiegazione numerica dei sogni. 4a ed. Palermo, 1886.

Phil 5625.79   Veraguth, Otto. Das psychogalvanische Reflexphänomen. Berlin, 1909.

Phil 1750.815   Verantwortung im Wondel der Zeit. (Wisser, Richard.) Mainz, 1967.

Phil 5258.120.15   Verbal behavior. (Skinner, Burrhus F.) N.Y., 1957.

Phil 5520.690   Verbal conditioning and behavior. 1. ed. (Das Jagannath, Prasad.) Oxford, 1969.

Phil 5545.252   Verbal learning and memory; selected readings. (Postman, Leo Joseph.) Baltimore, 1970.

Phil 6331.3   Verband der Vereine Katholischer Akademiker, Kevalaer. Religion und Seelenleiden. v. 1,2,3,6. Düsseldorf, 1926. 4v.

Phil 7069.20.115   Verbatim report of a public debate on "The truth of spiritualism" between A.C. Dolye and Joseph McCabe. (Doyle, Arthur Conan.) London, 1920.

Phil 850.19   Verbeke, G. L'évolution de la doctriné du pneuma. Paris, 1945.

Phil 5040.17.5   Verbesserte Logik. (Abicht, Johann H.) Fürth, 1802.

Phil 310.609   Verbin, Andrei. Mesto istoricheskogo materializma v sisteme nauk. Moskva, 1965.

Phil 75.72   Verbinc, Franc. Filozofski tokovi na Slovenskem. Ljubljana, 1966.

Phil 75.72.5   Verbinc, Franc. Filozofski tokovi na Slovenskem. Ljubljana, 1970.

Phil 5520.92   Die Verbindlichkeit der Sprache. (Lipps, Hans.) Frankfurt, 1944.

Phil 978.49.696   Die Verbindung zwischen Lebenden und Toten; acht Vorträge genalten im verschieden Stadten zwischen dem 16. Februar und 3. Dezember, 1916. 1. Aufl. (Steiner, R.) Dornach, 1968.

Phil 176.115.2   De verborgen harmonie. 2e druk. (Bierens de Haan, J.D.) Amsterdam, 1918.

Phil 2805.300   Der verborgene Pascal. (Spoerri, T.) Hamburg, 1955.

Phil 3640.330   Verbrechen und Strafe bei Friedrich Nietzsche. (Heinze, Kurt.) Berlin, 1939.

Phil 630.28   Verda, Mary. New realism in the light of scholasticism. N.Y., 1926.

Phil 720.31   La verdad, la ciencia y la filosofía. (Belgodere, F.J.A.) México, 1939.

Phil 187.89   La verdadera legitimidad y el verdadero liberalismo. (Muzquiz, J.M.) Habana, 1886.

Phil 196.18   Verdensbetragtning, Sokrates og fantasi. (Vold, J.M.) Kristiania, 1889.

Phil 3425.269   Der verderbliche Einfluss der Hegelschen Philosophie. (Allihn, F.H.T.) Leipzig, 1852.

Phil 7069.20.320   The verdict:-? (Tertium Quid (pseud.).) London, 1920.

Phil 2835.87   Verdonk, Johannes Jacobus. Petrus Ramus en de wiskunde. Assen, 1966.

Phil 6131.5   Vere, James A. Physical and moral enquiry. London, 1778.

Phil 3504.33   Die Vereinigung von Kant und Marx. (Wagner, Walther.) Langensalza, 1921.

Phil 2421.10   Vereker, Charles. Eighteenth-century optimism. Liverpool, 1967.

Phil 5440.28   Die Vererbung geistiger Eigenschaften und die psychische Constitution. (Peters, Wjlhelm.) Jena, 1925.

Phil 8430.79   Verfahren der statistischen Asthetik. (Thiele, Joachim.) Hamburg, 1966.

Phil 3425.55   Die Verfassung des deutschen Reichs. (Hegel, Georg Wilhelm Friedrich.) Stuttgart, 1935.

Phil 3585.14.5   Die verfluchte Kultur. (Lessing, Theodor.) München, 1921.

Phil 5401.40   Verfolgung und Angst in ihren leib-seelischen Auswirkungen. (March, Hans.) Stuttgart, 1960.

Phil 3120.55.35   Verfremdungen. (Bloch, Ernst.) Frankfurt, 1962. 2v.

Phil 2733.121   Verga, Leonardo. La filosofia morale di Malebranche. Milano, 1964.

Phil 3640.311   Vergelden en wergeven. Thesis. (Smelik, Evert Louis.) 's-Gravenhage, 1943.

Phil 525.52   Le verger, le temple et la cellule. (Oulmont, Charles.) Paris, 1912.

Phil 1718.35   Der vergessene Ursprung. (Strolz, Walter.) Freiburg, 1959.

Phil 176.115.15   Vergezichten. Studies. (Bierens de Haan, J.D.) Amsterdam, 1921.

Phil 3450.29.75   Vergil. Schönheit Metaphysik des Fühlens. (Haecker, Theodor.) München, 1967.

Phil 3801.777   Vergleich zwischen den Lehren Schelling's und Spinoza's. (Schirnhafer, R. von.) Zürich, 1889.

Phil 3246.221   Vergleich zwischen Fichtens System. (Keyserlingk, H.W.E. von.) Königsberg, 1817.

Phil 3195.10.113   Vergleich zwischen Rehmkes und Drieschs Philosophie. Inaug. Diss. (Sacher, Heinz.) Dresden, 1933.

Phil 5357.1   Vergleichen und die Relationserkenntnis. (Brunswig, A.) Leipzig, 1910.

Htn   Phil 3801.392*   Vergleichende Darstellung der philosophen Systeme von Kant, Fichte, Schelling. (Fick, Georg Karl.) Heilbronn, 1825.

Phil 5812.5   Vergleichende Psychologie. (Carus, Carl Gustav.) Wien, 1866.

Phil 5828.8   Vergleichende Seelenkunde. (Schultz, F.) Leipzig, 1892-97. 2v.

Phil 5832.3   Vergleichende Studien über das Seelenleben der Ameisen und der höheren Thiere. (Wasmann, E.) Freiburg, 1897.

Phil 1106.14   Vergleichung der griechischen Philosophie mit der Neuern. (Büsching, A.F.) Berlin, 1785.

Phil 2733.97   Vergleichung der Philosophie des Malebranche und Spinoza. (Glaser, J.C.) Berlin, 1846.

Htn   Phil 3500.17*   Vergleichung des Kantischen Moralprinzips. (Schwab, J.C.) Berlin, 1800.

Phil 5402.1.3   Vergnügen und Schmerz. (Dumont, L.) Leipzig, 1876.

Phil 5627.266.5   Vergote, Antoine. Psychologie religieuse. Bruxelles, 1966.

Phil 5627.266.6   Vergote, Antoine. The religious man. Dublin, 1969.

Phil 5520.507   Verhaar, John W.M. Some relations between perception, speech and thought. Proefschrift. Assen, 1963.

Phil 3640.176   Das Verhältnis der Erkenntnis zum Unendlichkeit der Welt bei Nietzsche. (Hocks, Erich.) Leipzig, 1914.

Phil 2020.135   Das Verhältnis der Ethik T.H. Greens zu Derjenigen Kants. Inaug. Diss. (Günther, Oskar.) Dresden, 1915.

Phil 5045.13   Das Verhältnis der Kategorienlehre zur formalen Logik. (Fechner, Oskar.) Rostock, 1927.

Phil 187.66   Das Verhältnis der Philosophie zu den Einzel-Wissenschaften. (Moog, Willy.) Halle, 1919.

Phil 978.49.523   Das Verhältnis der Sternenwelt zum Menschen und des Menschen zur Steinenwelt. 3. Aufl. (Steiner, R.) Dornach, 1966.

Phil 3425.283   Das Verhältnis des jungen Hegel zu Kant. (Wacker, Herbert.) Berlin, 1932.

Phil 2115.138   Das Verhältnis John Locke's zur Scholastik. (Tellkamp, A.) Münster, 1927.

Phil 2250.110   Das Verhältnis von Einzelperson und Gemeinschaft nach Josiah Royce. (Humbach, K.T.) Heidelberg, 1962.

Phil 3850.18.90   Das Verhältnis von Ethik und Ästhetik bei Max Scheler. Diss. (Kürth, Herbert.) Leipzig, 1929.

Phil 3850.8.85   Das Verhältnis von Glauben und Wissen in der Theologie Franr Anton Staudenmaiers. (Weindel, Phil.) Düsseldorf, 1940.

Phil 3801.777.25   Das Verhältnis von Heidentum und Christentum in Schellings Philosophie der Mythologie und Offenbarung. (Schröder, C.M.) München, 1936.

Phil 2045.91   Das Verhältnis von Sittengesetz...bei Hobbes. (Messer, W.A.) Mainz, 1893.

Phil 3450.11.360   Das Verhältnis von Theorie und Praxis...Husserls. (Petersen, Uwe.) Heidelburg, 1964.

Phil 5190.2   Das Verhältnis von Urteil und Satz. (Kramp, Leo.) Bonn, 1916.

Phil 8430.41   Das verhältnis zwischen demethischen und dem ästhetischen. (Thielicke, H.) Leipzig, 1932.

Phil 9558.3   Verhältniss der öffentlichen Meinung zu Wahrheit und Lüge. (Ellinger, G.) Berlin, 1884.

Phil 3100.53   Das Verhältniss von Seele und Leib. (Beneke, F.E.) Göttingen, 1826.

Phil 1145.102   Das Verhängnis der Übel im Weltbild griechischer Denker. (Reinicke, Hans.) Berlin, 1969.

Phil 5279.5   Verhalten und Interaktion. (Malewski, Andrzej.) Tübingen, 1967.

Phil 5250.86   Verhaltensforschung im Rahmen der Wissenschaften vom Menschen. (Keiter, Friedrich.) Göttingen, 1969.

Phil 6980.776.10   Das verhaltensgestörte Kind. 1. Aufl. (Werner, Reiner.) Berlin, 1967.

Phil 5284.2   Verhaltenstheorie und Verhaltensmodifikation. (Kaminski, Gerhard.) Stuttgart, 1970.

Phil 3504.10   Verhaltnis des Beiden ersten Auflagen der Kritik der reinen Vernunft Zueinander. Inaug. Diss. (Wolf, Johannes.) Halle, 1905.

Phil 3552.272   Das Verhaltnis des Korperlichen zum Geistigen und die Entwicklung des Geistigen bei Leibniz. (Jaenicke, Kurt.) Cöthen, 1913.

Phil 11.1   Verhandlungen. v.1-21. (Philosophische Gesellschaft zu Berlin.) Leipzig, 1875-82. 2v.

Phil 3778.39   Verhandlungen über die Grundbegriffe und Grundsätze der Moralität. (Reinhold, K.L.) Lübeck, 1798.

Phil 70.15   Verhandlungsbericht. (Kongress für Synthetische Lebensforschung.) Prag, 1937.

Phil 3425.601   Verheissung und Schrecken der Freiheit. (Schmidt, H.) Stuttgart, 1964.

Phil 3903.5.35   Verhoeven, Cornelius W.M. Het grote gebeuren. Utrecht, 1966.

Phil 3903.5.30   Verhoeven, Cornelius W.M. Inleiding tot de verwondering. Utrecht, 1967.

Phil 3903.5.40   Verhoeven, Cornelius W.M. Rondom de leegte. Utrecht, 1967.

Phil 3903.5.45   Verhoeven, Cornelius W.M. Symboliek van de voet. Assen, 1956.

Phil 3903.5.31   Verhoeven, Cornelius Wilhelmus Maria. The philosophy of wonder. N.Y., 1972.

Phil 3120.8.155   De verhouting van de psycologie tot de wijsbegeerte in der leer van Brentano. (Dix, Petrus Gerandus.) n.p., 1966.

Phil 189.16.5   Verità dimostrate. (Orestano, F.) Napoli, 1934.

Phil 70.72   Veritá e libertá di Guzzo. (Societá Filosofica Italiana.) Palumbo, 1960.

Phil 720.12   Verità e realtà. (Bonucci, A.) Modena, 1911.

Phil 400.67   Verità e realtà: apologia dell'idealismo. (Guzzo, Augusto.) Torino, 1925.

Phil 1750.166.215   Verità e rivoluzione. (Toesca, Pietro M.) Roma, 1965.

Phil 4260.195   Verità e storia in Vico. (Sciacca, Michele Federico.) Roma, 1968.

Phil 9410.9   Le véritable optimisme. (Sarrazin, N.J.) Nancy, 18- ?

Phil 200.5.5   Le veritable role de l'homme dans l'universe. (Zucca, Antioco.) Paris, 19- ?

Phil 165.15   Veritati. (Falkenhahn, W.) München, 1949.

Phil 720.72   La verité. (Congrès des Sociétés de Philosophie de Langue Française, 12th, Brussels et Louvain, 1964.) Louvain, 1964-65. 2v.

Phil 2805.256   Vérité de Pascal. (Journet, C.) St. Maurice, 1951.

Phil 6990.1   La verité des miracles. (Carre, L.B.) n.p., 1737-41. 2v.

Phil 6990.1.2   La verité des miracles. (Carré, L.B.) Utrecht, 1737-41.

Phil 6682.20   La vérité du magnétisme, prouvée par les faits. (Mercier, A.D.) Paris, 1829.

Phil 8586.55   Vérité et religion; essai le problème. (Guerin, Pierre.) Paris, 1962.

Phil 8583.27   Vérité et révélation. (Draghicesco, D.) Paris, 1934. 2v.

Phil 5627.117   Verkappte Religionen. (Bry, Carl Christian.) Gotha, 1925.

Phil 3195.19.30   Verkenningen in de wijsbegeerte. (Dooyeweerd, H.) Amsterdam, 1962.

Phil 186.55.5 Verklighetsproblemet i den antika filosofien. (Liljekrantz, B.) Göteborg, 1915.

Htn Phil 3480.54* Verkündigung des nahen Abschlusses eines Traktats zum ewigen Frieden in der Philosophie. (Kant, Immanuel.) Ulm, 1798.

Phil 5831.6 Verlaine, Louis. L'âme des bêtes. Paris, 1931.

Phil 5831.6.5 Verlaine, Louis. Histoire naturelle de la connaissance chez le singe inférieur; le concret. Paris, 1935-36. 3v.

Phil 3625.1.163 Verland der vereine für Jüdische Geschichte und Literatur in Deutschland. Gedenkbuch für Moses Mendelssohn. Berlin, 1929.

Phil 8125.16 Das Verlangen nach einer neuen deutschen Kunst. (Volbehr, Theodor.) Leipzig, 1901.

Phil 3415.39 Verldsprocessens väsen eller det omedvetnas filosofi. (Hartmann, Eduard von.) Stockholm, 1877-78.

Phil 805.14 Verleden en toehomst van de filosofie. (Flam, Leopold.) Amsterdam, 1962.

Phil 5420.15 De verlegenheid. Proefschrift. (Schouten, Jan.) Groningen, 1935.

Phil 3195.14.40 Das verlorene Paradies. 4. Aufl. (Dacqué, Edgar.) München, 1953.

Phil 5261.10.2 Verluys, J. Beginselen der Zielkunde. 2e. Druk. Amsterdam, 1899.

Phil 3640.27 Das Vermächtnis Friedrich Nietzsches. (Nietzsche, Friedrich.) Salzburg, 1940.

Phil 9353.2 Vermaechtniss an Helene von ihrem Vater. (Niemeyer, J.F.) Bremen, 1794.

Htn Phil 3585.4.32* Vermanug an die Geistlichen. (Luther, Martin.) Wittemberg, 1531.

Phil 2480.80 Vermeil de Conchard, P.P. Trois études sur Cabanis. Brive, 1914.

Phil 6325.1.40 Vermeintliche Nullen und angebliche Musterkinder. (Pfister, Oskar.) Bern, 1921.

Phil 8896.13 Vermilye, T.E. An introductory address to the course of lectures before the young men's Association for Mutual Improvement in the city of Albany. Albany, 1837.

Phil 179.22 Vermischte Aufsätze. (Erdmann, J.E.) Leipzig, 1846.

Phil 6322.1.5 Vermischte Aufsätze. (Mobius, P.J.) Leipzig, 1898.

Phil 193.27.5 Vermischte philosophische Abhandlungen. (Sigwart, H.C.W.) Tübingen, 1831.

Phil 182.14.5 Vermischte philosophische Schriften. (Hemsterhuis, F.) Leipzig, 1782. 3v.

Phil 1117.3.10 Vermischte philosophische Schriften. (Meiners, C.) Leipzig, 1775. 3v.

Phil 8887.63 Vermischte Schriften, oder philosophischen Gedanken. 2. Aufl. (Mutschelle, S.) München, 1799. 4v.

Phil 3480.18 Vermischte Schriften. (Kant, Immanuel.) Halle, 1799-1807. 4v.

Phil 3480.18.7 Vermischte Schriften. (Kant, Immanuel.) Leipzig, 1912.

Phil 3480.18.9 Vermischte Schriften. (Kant, Immanuel.) Leipzig, 1922.

Phil 193.15.3 Vermischte Schriften. (Schubert, G. von.) Erlangen, 1857-1860. 2v.

Phil 3925.15 Vermischte Schriften. (Wendel, G.) Berlin, 1912.

Phil 3480.18.5 Vermischte Schriften und Briefwechsel. (Kant, Immanuel.) Berlin, 1873.

Phil 3450.19.380 Vermittlung und Kehre. (Pugliese, Orlando.) Freiburg, 1965.

Phil 1750.301 Verneaux, R. Leçons sur l'existentialisme. 4e éd. Paris, 1964.

Phil 1750.300 Verneaux, R. Leçons sur l'existentialisme et ses formes principales. Paris, 1949.

Phil 2840.99.20 Verneaux, Roger. Esquisse d'une théorie de la connaissance. Paris, 1954.

Phil 1721.6 Verneaux, Roger. Histoire de la philosophie moderne. Paris, 1958.

Phil 2840.99.10 Verneaux, Roger. L'idealisme de Renouvier. Paris, 1945.

Phil 2840.99.5 Verneaux, Roger. L'idealisme de Renouvier. Thèse. Paris, 1943.

Phil 2840.99.15 Verneaux, Roger. Renouvier, disciple et critique de Kant. Paris, 1945.

Phil 2840.99 Verneaux, Roger. Renouvier. Thèse. Paris, 1944.

Phil 4482.1.90 Vernei a filosofia portuguesa. (Andrade, Antonio Alberto de.) Braga, 1946.

Phil 4482.1.100 Vernei e a cultura do seu tempo. (Andrade, António Alberto de.) Coimbra, 1966.

Phil 3625.8.60 Vernenftlehre. 2e Aufl. (Meier, Georg Friedrich.) Halle, 1762.

Phil 2905.1.285 Vernet, M. La grande illusion de Teilhard de Chardin. Paris, 1964.

Phil 8896.22 Vernet, Maurice. L'homme, maître de sa destinée. Paris, 1956.

Phil 2905.1.425 Vernet, Maurice. Vernet contre Teilhard de Chardin. Paris, 1965.

Phil 2905.1.425 Vernet contre Teilhard de Chardin. (Vernet, Maurice.) Paris, 1965.

Phil 5545.50.5 Verneuil, Henri. La mémoire au point de vue physiologique. Paris, 1888.

Phil 5628.10 Vernier, André. L'extase et la personalité. Thèse. Montauban, 1901.

Phil 5400.3 Vernier, I. Caractère des passions. Paris, 1807. 2v.

Phil 3841.7 Vernière, P. Spinoza et la pensée française avant la révolution. Paris, 1954. 2v.

Phil 3841.7.2 Vernière, P. Spinoza et la pensée française avant la révolution. Thèse. Paris, 1954. 2v.

Phil 3195.19.35 Vernieuwing en bezinning. 2. druk. (Dooyeweerd, H.) Zutphen, 1963.

Phil 8612.84 Vernon, Glenn M. Sociology of death; an analysis of death-related behavior. N.Y., 1970.

Phil 5585.61 Vernon, M.D. Visual perception. Cambridge, Eng., 1937.

Phil 5585.213 Vernon, Magdalen. The psychology of perception. Harmondsworth, 1962.

Phil 5548.130 Vernon, Magdalen Dorothea. Human motivation. London, 1969.

Phil 5465.200 Vernon, Philip Ewart. Creativity: selected readings. Harmondsworth, 1970.

Phil 5871.45 Vernon, Philip Ewart. Intelligence and cultural environment. London, 1969.

Phil 8980.839 Vernost'. 2. izd. (Tkachenko, Vera M.) Moskva, 1965.

Phil 3483.65 Vernünftiger Wille und gläubige Liebe. (Ballauff, Theodor.) Meisenheim, 1957.

Phil 8643.2 Vernunf-Beweis...Unsterblichkeit der menschlichen Seele. (Schutz, L.) Paderborn, 1874.

Phil 3910.45 Vernünfftige Gedancken. (Wolff, Christian von.) Halle, 1749-53.

Phil 3910.72.15 Vernünfftige Gedancken von dem Absichten. (Wolff, Christian von.) Magdeburgischen, 1752.

Phil 3910.73.15 Vernünfftige Gedancken von dem Gebrauche. (Wolff, Christian von.) Magdeburgischen, 1753.

Phil 3910.68.6 Vernünfftige Gedancken von dem gesellschafftlichen. 6. Aufl. (Wolff, Christian von.) Franckfurt, 1747.

Phil 3910.70.5 Vernünfftige Gedancken von dem Würckungen der Natur. 5. Aufl. (Wolff, Christian von.) Halle, 1746.

Phil 3910.59.15 Vernünfftige Gedancken von der Menschen. (Wolff, Christian von.) Magdeburgischen, 1752.

Phil 3910.59.5 Vernünfftige Gedancken von der Menschen. 2. Aufl. (Wolff, Christian von.) Halle, 1723.

Phil 3910.57.15 Vernünfftige Gedancken von Gott. (Wolff, Christian von.) Halle, 1752-40. 2v.

Phil 3910.57 Vernünfftige Gedancken von Gott. 7. Aufl. (Wolff, Christian von.) Frankfurt, 1735.

Phil 3665.3.31 Vernunft gegen Vernunft. Frankfurt, 1797. (Neeb, Johann.) Bruxelles, 1969.

Phil 3425.40.10 Die Vernunft in der Geschichte. (Hegel, Georg Wilhelm Friedrich.) Hamburg, 1955.

Phil 3460.92 Vernunft und Erkenntnis. (Baum, Guenther.) Bonn, 1969.

Phil 184.19.15 Vernunft und Existenz. (Jaspers, K.) Groningen, 1935.

Phil 3475.3.55 Vernunft und Existenz. (Jaspers, Karl.) Bremen, 1949.

Phil 3475.3.55.5 Vernunft und Existenz. (Jaspers, Karl.) München, 1960.

Phil 5520.512 Vernunft und Sprache. (Kamrath, Gerhard.) Heidelberg, 1964.

Phil 187.186 Vernunft und Welt. (Marx, Werner.) The Hague, 1970.

Phil 3475.3.60 Vernunft und Widervernunft. (Jaspers, Karl.) München, 1950.

Phil 8581.56 Der Vernunftcharakter der Religion. (Bruhn, Wilhelm.) Leipzig, 1921.

Phil 3910.56 Der Vernunftigen Gedancken von Gott. 2. Aufl. Pt.2. (Wolff, Christian von.) Franckfurt, 1733.

Phil 5258.2 Vernunftlehre für Menschen, wie sie sind. (Sailer, J.D.M.) München, 1785.

Phil 3552.67.20 Vernunftprinzipien der Natur und der Gnade. (Leibniz, Gottfried Wilhelm.) Hamburg, 1956.

Phil 5057.2 Die Vernunstlehre. (Reimarus, H.S.) Hamburg, 1790.

Phil 3245.20 Vernuschte Schriften zur Philosophie, Theologie und Ethik. (Fichte, Immanuel Hermann.) Leipzig, 1869. 2v.

Phil 177.19.10 Il vero nell'ordine o Ondologia e logica. 2a ed. (Conti, Augusto.) Firenze, 1891. 2v.

Phil 2480.88 Vero rapporto del fisico e del morale dell'uomo. (Bigoni, Angelo.) Padova, 1813.

Phil 3425.79.50 Veroeffentlichungen. (Internationales Hegelbund.) Tübingen. v.1,1931 2v.

Phil 61.1.5 Veröffentlichungen. (Vienna. Universität. Philosophische Gesellschaft.) Leipzig, 1893- 3v.

Phil 978.49.150 Veröffentlichungen aus dem literarischen Frühwerk. (Steiner, R.) Dornach, 1939-41. 4v.

Phil 341.38 Veroiatnoe i dostovernoe znanie. (Kevorkian, Hamlet.) Erevan, 1965.

Phil 4683.55.31 Vērojumi un pārdomas par cilvēku un gara kultūru. (Dāle, Pauls.) Chicago, 1952.

Phil 8422.14A Véron, Eugène. Aesthetics. London, 1879.

Phil 8896.9 Véron, Eugène. La morale. Paris, 1884.

Phil 3503.15 Verondini, Enrico. La filosofia morale di Emanuele Kant. Bologna, 1966.

Phil 4210.230 Verondini, Enrico. Leffere sulla spiritualitá rosminiana. Milano, 1966.

Phil 7080.34 Veronese, F. Versuch einer Physiologie des Schlafes und des Traumes. Leipzig, 1910.

Phil 8896.8 Verplanck, G.C. The influence of moral causes upon opinion. N.Y., 1834.

Phil 1955.6.135 Verra, Valerio. Naturalismo umanistico e sperimentale di John Dewey. Torino, 1950.

Phil 8676.5 Verret, Michel. Les marxistes et la religion. Paris, 1961.

Phil 8676.5.3 Verret, Michel. Les marxistes et la religion. 3. éd. Paris, 1966.

Phil 3450.19.155 Vers la fin de l'ontologie. (Wahl, Jean A.) Paris, 1956.

Phil 800.15 Vers la pensée planétaire. (Axelos, Kostas.) Paris, 1964.

Phil 1722.7 Vers le concret; études d'histoire de la philosophie contemporaine. (Wahl, Jean.) Paris, 1932.

Phil 400.48 Vers le positivisme absolu par l'idéalisme. (Weber, Louis.) Paris, 1903.

Phil 400.89.9 Vers l'immanence intégrale. Thèse. (Etcheverry, A.) Paris, 1934.

Phil 2477.6.85 Vers un realisme integral...Blondel. (Archambault, P.) Paris, 1928.

Phil 8430.16 Vers une conscience plastique; la forme et l'histoire. (Gleizes, A.) Paris, 1932.

Phil 293.23 Vers une cosmologie. (Minkowski, E.) Paris, 1936.

Phil 2750.20.150 Vers une nouvelle philosophie transcendantale. (Geraets, Théodore F.) La Haye, 1971.

Phil 1750.560.35 Vers une pensée méditerranéenne. v.1-4. (Habachi, René.) Beyrouth, 1956- 2v.

Phil 575.140.5 Vers une philosophie de l'amour et de la personne. (Nédoncelle, Maurice.) Aubier, 1957.

Phil 187.115 Vers une philosophie de l'esprit ou de la totalité. (Milville, H.L.) Lausanne, 1937.

Phil 2725.14.95 Vers une philosophie réflexive. (Madinier, G.) Neuchâtel, 1960.

Phil 195.3 Vers une science du réel. (Urtin, Henri.) Paris, 1930.

Phil 3808.91 Die verschiedenartigen Elemente der Schopenhauer'schen Willenslehre. (Lehmann, E.) Strassburg, 1889.

Phil 5402.40 Het verschijnsel pijn. Proefschrift. (Metz, Willem.) Haarlem, 1964.

Htn Phil 3625.10.30* Verse; von Hugo Terberg. (Münsterberg, H.) Grossenhain, 1897.

Phil 3450.19.325 Versényi, Laszlo. Heidegger, being and truth. New Haven, 1965.

Phil 2520.209 Versfeld, M. An essay on the metaphysics of Descartes. London, 1940.

Phil 672.262 Versfeld, Marthinus. Wat is kontemporêr? Johannesburg, 1966.

Phil 665.84 Versiones españolas de animus y anima. (Morreale de Castro, Margherita.) Granada? 1957.

Phil 5645.52 Verslag. (Nederlandse. Kleurendag?) Den Haag. 6-11

Phil 3120.11.93 Verslag van de rede. (Bolland, G.J.P.J.) Leiden, 1906.

Phil 4080.23 Verso il trascendimento. (Cinato, Dante.) Palmi, 1959.

Phil 8581.45 Verso la luce. (Buonaiuti, Ernesto.) Foligno, 1924.

Phil 525.68 Verso una nuova mistica. (Manacarda, A.) Bologna, 1922.

Phil 6400.4 Versprechen und Verlesen. (Meringer, R.) Stuttgart, 1895.

Phil 3549.24 Verspreide Geschriften. (Kuypers, Karel.) Assen, 1968. 2v.

Phil 3195.20.30 Verspreide opstellen. (Duynstee, Willem Jacob A.J.) Roermond, 1963.

Phil 180.43 Verständigung als philosophisches Problem. (Feldkeller, Paul.) Erfurt, 1928.

Phil 665.65 Das Verständnis der Seele im Christentum und in der psychologischen Literatur der Gegenwart. Inaug. Diss. (Neuburger, E.) Tübingen, 1937.

Phil 2885.31.8 Der Verstand. v.1-2. (Taine, Hippolyte Adolphe.) Bonn, 1880.

Phil 332.26 Das Verstechen. (Bollnou, Atto.) Mainz, 1949.

Phil 335.3.10 Das Verstehen. (Ehrlich, Walter.) Zürich, 1939.

Phil 1750.124 Das Verstehen. (Wach, Joachim.) Tübingen, 1926-33. 3v.

Phil 5055.5.5 Verstehen und Beurtheilen. (Prantl, C.) München, 1877.

Phil 5246.60 Verstehen und Einfühlen. (Gruhle, H.W.) Berlin, 1953.

Phil 349.27 Verstehen und Einsehen. (Schunck, Karl.) Halle an der Saale, 1926.

Phil 1695.35 Verstehen und Vertranen. Otto Friedrich Bollnow zum 65. Geburtstag. Stuttgart, 1968.

Phil 5246.60.5 Verstehende Psychologie. 2. Aufl. (Gruhle, H.W.) Stuttgart, 1956.

Phil 6980.768 Verster, Justus. Psychische bijwerkings verschijnselen van moltergan. Assen, 1967.

Phil 3504.35 Versuch, die harten Urtheile über der Kantische Philosophie zu Mildern. (Weber, Joseph.) Wirzburg, 1793.

Phil 1704.1 Versuch...Geschichte der neuern Philosophie. (Erdmann, J.E.) Riga, 1834-53. 6v.

Phil 1704.1.5 Versuch...Geschichte der neuern Philosophie. Faksimile. (Erdmann, J.E.) Stuttgart, 1932-33. 10v.

Phil 3497.3.15 Versuch...Kantischen Erkenntnisstheorie. (Paulsen, Friedrich.) Leipzig, 1875.

Htn Phil 3480.84.3* Versuch den Begriff der negativen Grössen in die Weltweisheit einzuführen. (Kant, Immanuel.) Königsberg, 1763.

Phil 3480.84 Versuch den Begriff der negativen Grössen in die Weltweisheit einzuführen. (Kant, Immanuel.) Grätz, 1797.

Phil 6674.2 Versuch der scheinbare Magie der thierischen Magnetismus. (Eschenmayer, C.A.) Stuttgart, 1816.

Htn Phil 3801.831* Versuch die Anhänger Hegel's und Schelling's. (Thürmer, J.) Berlin, 1843.

Phil 3492.34.2 Versuch einer...Darstellung der wichtigsten Wahrheiten der kritischen Philosophie. (Kiesewetter, J.G.K.C.) Berlin, 1803. 2v.

Phil 3492.34 Versuch einer...Darstellung der wichtigsten Wahrheiten der neuern Philosophie. (Kiesewetter, J.G.K.C.) Berlin, 1795.

Phil 3625.8.52 Versuch einer Allegemeinen Auslegungskunst. (Meier, Georg Friedrich.) Dusseldorf, 1965.

Phil 5057.3 Versuch einer Begründung und neuen Darstellung der logischen Formen. (Reinhold, Ernest.) Leipzig, 1819.

Htn Phil 3246.30* Versuch einer Critik aller Offenbarung. (Fichte, Johann Gottlieb.) Königsberg, 1792.

Htn Phil 3246.30.5* Versuch einer Critik aller Offenbarung. (Fichte, Johann Gottlieb.) Königsberg, 1793.

Phil 1900.87 Versuch einer Darstellung der Ethik Joseph Butlers. Inaug. Diss. (Ayer, Joseph Cullen.) Leipzig, 1893.

Phil 6319.1.70 Versuch einer Darstellung der psycho analytischen Theorie. (Jung, C.G.) Leipzig, 1913.

Phil 6680.6.3 Versuch einer Darstellung dis animalischen Magnetismus. (Kluge, C.A.F.) Berlin, 1818.

Phil 3450.11.100 Versuch einer Darstellung und Beurteilung der Grundlagen der Philosophie E. Husserls. Inaug. Diss. (Bannes, Joachim.) Breslau, 1930.

Phil 3450.11.99 Versuch einer Darstellung und Beurteilung der Grundlagen der Philosophie E. Husserls. (Bannes, Joachim.) Breslau, 1930.

Phil 5635.23 Versuch einer einheitlichen Lehre von der Gefühlin. (Nitsche, Adolf.) Innsbruck, 1886.

Phil 3500.31 Versuch einer Entwicklungsgeschichte des Kantischen...des Kriticismus. (Sternberg, Kurt.) Berlin, 1909.

Phil 3625.8.35 Versuch einer Erklärung des Nachtwandelns. (Meier, Georg Friedrich.) Halle, 1758.

Phil 6315.1.7 Versuch einer Genitaltheorie. (Ferenczi, Sandor.) Leipzig, 1924.

Phil 8402.45 Versuch einer Geschmackslehre. (Bendavid, L.) Berlin, 1799.

Phil 3487.18 Versuch einer historisch-kritischen Darstellung. (Flügge, C.W.) Hannover, 1796-98. 2v.

Phil 5757.11 Versuch einer Lösung des Willensproblems. Inaug. Diss. (Heinzel, G.) Breslau, n.d.

Phil 8893.61.5 Versuch einer Moralphilosophie. (Schmid, C.C.E.) Jena, 1790.

Phil 8893.61 Versuch einer Moralphilosophie. 2. Ausg. (Schmid, C.C.E.) Jena, 1792.

Phil 3625.5.34 Versuch einer neuen Logik, oder Theorie. (Maimon, Salomon.) Berlin, 1794.

Phil 3625.5.35 Versuch einer neuen Logik, oder Theorie. (Maimon, Salomon.) Berlin, 1912.

Phil 1870.60.15 Versuch einer neuen Theorie der Gesichtswahrnehmung. (Berkeley, G.) Leipzig, 1912.

Phil 5257.5 Versuch einer neuen Theorie des menschlichen Vorstellungs-Vermögens. (Reinhold, K.L.) Prag, 1789.

Phil 194.46 Versuch einer Ontologie der Persönlichkeit. (Thiel, M.) Berlin, 1950.

Phil 7080.34 Versuch einer Physiologie des Schlafes und des Traumes. (Veronese, F.) Leipzig, 1910.

Phil 6131.2 Versuch einer physiologischen Pathologie der Nerven. (Valentin, G.G.) Leipzig, 1864.

Phil 8411.14 Versuch einer Psychologie der Kunst. (Kaplan, Leo.) Baden-Baden, 1930.

Phil 7080.41 Versuch einer psychologischen Theorie des Schlafes. Inaug. Diss. (Schenk, Paul.) Leipzig, 1928.

Phil 3494.32 Versuch einer solchen fasslichen Darstellung der Kantischen Philosophie. (Mutschelle, S.) München, 1803. 2v.

Phil 8412.8 Versuch einer Stellungnahme zu den Hauptfragen der Kunstphilosophie. (Laurila, K.S.) Helsingfors, 1903.

Phil 2477.7.81 Versuch einer systematischen Darstellung der Philosophie des C. Bovillus. (Dippel, Joseph.) Würzburg, 1865.

Phil 341.4 Versuch einer systematischen Enzyklopädie. (Krug, W.T.) Whittenberg, 1796.

Phil 5853.2 Versuch einer theoretischen Grundlegung des Beratungsprozesses. Habilitationsschrift. (Hruschka, Erna.) Meisenheim am Glan, 1969.

Phil 5500.8 Versuch einer Theorie der Existentialurteile. (Cornelius, Hans.) München, 1894.

Phil 5627.18A Versuch einer Theorie des religiösen Wahnsinns. (Ideler, K.W.) Halle, 1848-50. 2v.

Phil 5500.4 Versuch einer Theorie von Urteil und Begriff. (Pfordten, O.F. von.) Heidelberg, 1906.

Phil 5828.2 Versuch einer vollständigen Thierseelenkunde. (Scheitlin, P.) Stuttgart, 1840. 2v.

Phil 5249.10.5 Versuch einer wissenschaftlichen Begründung der Psychologie. (Jessen, Peter.) Berlin, 1855.

Phil 8673.8 Versuch eines neuen Gottesbegriffs. (Specker, Gideon.) Stuttgart, 1902.

Phil 3850.62 Versuch eines neuen Systems des natürlichen Rechts. (Schaumann, Johann Christian Gottlieb.) Bruxelles, 1969.

Phil 8401.2.10 Versuch über Alison's Ästhetik, Darstellung und Kritik. (Fedeles, Constantin.) München, 1911.

Phil 5402.18 Versuch über das Vergnügen. (Bendavid, L.) Wien, 1794.

Phil 9470.5 Versuch über das Wesen der Verantwortung. Inaug. Diss. (Wieschedel, W.) Heppenheim, 1932.

Phil 8408.34 Versuch über den Geschmach und die ursachen seiner Verschiednheit. (Herz, Marcus.) Leipzig, 1776.

Phil 2115.49.13 Versuch über den menschlichen Verstand. (Locke, J.) Berlin, 1872-73. 2v.

Phil 2115.49.10 Versuch über den menschlichen Verstand. (Locke, J.) Jena, 1795. 3v.

Phil 2115.49 Versuch über den menschlichen Verstand. (Locke, J.) Leipzig, 1913. 2v.

Phil 6957.16 Versuch über den Schwindel. (Herz, M.) Berlin, 1786.

Phil 5465.190 Versuch über die Einbildungskraft. (Maass, Johann Gebhard Ehrenreich.) Bruxelles, 1969.

Phil 332.14 Versuch über die Erkenntnis. (Brentano, Franz.) Leipzig, 1925.

Phil 332.14.2 Versuch über die Erkenntnis. 2. Aufl. (Brentano, Franz.) Hamburg, 1970.

Phil 5400.87 Versuch über die Leidenschaften. (Maas, J.G.E.) Halle, 1805-07. 2v.

Phil 5240.25.20 Versuch über die Natur der speculativen Vernunft zur Prüfung des Kantischen Systems. (Abel, Jakob Friedrich von.) Frankfurt, 1787.

Phil 5240.25.10 Versuch über die Seelenstärke. (Abel, Jacob Friedrich von.) Tübingen, 1804.

Phil 5068.90 Versuch über die sicherste und leichteste Anwendung der Analysis in den philosophischen Wissenschaften (Leipzig). (Hoffbauer, Johann Christoph.) Bruxelles, 1968.

Phil 332.40 Versuch über die ursprünglichen Grundlagen des menschlichen Denkens und die davon Abhängigen Schranken unserer Erkenntniss. (Born, Friedrich Gottlab.) Bruxelles, 1969.

Phil 5400.78 Versuch über Fühlen und Wollen. (Volkelt, J.) München, 1930.

Htn Phil 2115.49.5* Versuch vom menschlichen Verstand. (Locke, J.) Altenburg, 1757.

Phil 3017.2 Versuch zur neueste deutsche Philosophie...Kant. (Ritter, A.H.) Braunschweig, 1853.

Phil 6959.11 Ein Versuch zur quantitativen Analyse des gruppenpsychotherapeutischen Prozesses mit schizophrenen Patienten. (Jensen, Susanne.) Bonn, 1965.

Phil 5545.157 Versuche über das Gedächtnis. Inaug. Diss. (Loewenton, E.) Dorpat, 1893.

Phil 5650.1 Versuche über das Unterscheidungsvermögen des Hörsinnes für Zeitgrössen. Inaug. Diss. (Höring, Adolf.) Tübingen, 1864.

Phil 2055.1.35 Versuche über die ersten Gründe der Sittlichkeit. (Homes, Henry.) Braunschweig, 1768.

Phil 1120.1 Versuche zur Aufklärung der Philosophie des ältesten Alterthums. (Plessing, F.V.L.) Leipzig, 1788-90. 3v.

Phil 5050.7 Versuchplanmässiger und Naturgemässer unmittelbarer Denkübungen. (Krause, K.H.) Halle, 1844. 3v.

Phil 1750.166.17 Verteidigung des Humanismus. 2. Aufl. (Bottai, Giuseppe.) Berlin, 1942.

Phil 190.80.25 Verteidigungsrede für die Philosophie. (Pieper, Josef.) München, 1966.

Phil 3625.8.65 Vertheidigung der christlichen Religion. 2e Aufl. (Meier, Georg Friedrich.) Halle, 1749.

Phil 7067.48.10 Vertheidigung der Gedanken von Gespenstern. (Meier, George F.) Halle im Magdeburgischen, 1748.

Htn Phil 3801.778* Vertheidigung gegen Herren Professor Schellings...Erläuterungen. (Schütz, C.G.) Jena, 1800. 4v.

Phil 3504.2 Vertheidigung Kants Gegen Fries. (Wangenheim, F.) Berlin, 1876.

Phil 6990.27 Vertheidigungsschrift. (Blumhardt, C.G.) Reutlingen, 1850.

Phil 5643.46 The vertical-horizontal illusion. (Ritter, Sarah M.) Princeton, 1917.

Phil 179.3.91 Die Vertiefung der kantischen Religions-Philosophie. (Kesseler, K.) Bunzlau, 1908.

Phil 9560.31 Vertu. (Baurmann, W.) Berlin, 1939.

Phil 8881.72.5 La vertu de force. 1. éd. (Gusdorf, Georges.) Paris, 1957.

Phil 9361.3.6 Vertua-Gentile, Anna. Come devo compotarmi? 6. ed. Milano, 1909.

Phil 9035.20 Die Verwahrlosung der modernen Charakters. (Vogler, M.) Leipzig, 1884.

Phil 5870.117 Das verwaiste Kind der Natur. 2. Aufl. (Nitschke, Alfred.) Tübingen, 1968.

Phil 3552.89 Die Verwandtschaft Leibizens mit Thomas von Aquino. (Koppehl, H.) Jena, 1892.

Phil 3890.2.80 Verweyen, J. Ehrenfried Walther von Tschirnhaus. Bonn, 1905.

Phil 3640.525 Verweyen, J. Wagner und Nietzsche. Stuttgart, 1926.

Phil 575.127 Verweyen, J.M. Der Edelmensch und seine Werte. 2e Aufl. München, 1922.

Phil 196.16 Verweyen, J.M. Philosophie des Möglichen. Leipzig, 1913.

Phil 1540.11 Verweyen, Johannes. Das Problem der Willensfreiheit. Heidelberg, 1909.

Phil 1526.2 Verweyen, Johannes M. Die Philosophie der Mittelalters. 2e Aufl. Berlin, 1926.

Phil 1526.1 Verweyen, Johannes M. Philosophie und Theologie im Mittelalter. Bonn, 1911.

Phil 5590.255 Verwirklichen. (Spreither, Franz.) Konstanz, 1958.

Phil 5590.255.2 Verwirklichende Vern-Zentrierung. 2. Aufl. (Spreither, Franz.) Konstanz, 1959.

Phil 352.5.2 Verworm, Max. Die Frage nach den Grenzen der Erkenntnis. 2. Aufl. Jena, 1917.

Phil 6131.3.5 Verworn, M. Die Entwicklung des menschlichen Geistes. Jena, 1910.

Phil 5651.2 Verworn, M. Gleichgewicht und Otolithenorgan. Bonn, 1891.

Phil 6131.3 Verworn, M. Die Mechanik des Geisteslebens. Leipzig, 1910.

Phil 196.4 Verworn, M. Naturwissenschaft und Weltanschauung. 2e Aufl. Leipzig, 1904.

Phil 5831.2 Verworn, M. Die sogenannte Hypnose der Thiere. Jena, 1898.

Phil 270.28 Verworn, Max. Kausale und konditionale Weltanschauung. 2. aufl. Jena, 1918.

Phil 8601.2 Véry, P. Philosophie de la religion (Éléments). Paris, 1858.

Phil 6313.17   Very peculiar people. (Dignwall, E.J.) London, 1950.

Phil 3745.21   Verzamelde werken. (Polak, Leo.) Amsterdam, 1947.

Phil 5768.4   Verzeichnies der Doctoren: Begriff der Wollens...von C. Sigwart. (Tübingen, Germany. Universität.) Tübingen, 1879.

Phil 3110.78   Verzeichnis von Jakob Böhme-Handschreften. (Buddecke, W.) Göttingen, 1934.

Phil 3508.2   Verzeichniss der Bücher des Verstorben Professor Johann Friedrich Gensichen. Königsberg, 1808.

Phil 3280.81   Verzeichniss der Doctoren. (Pfleiderer, E.) Tübingen, 1882.

Phil 5409.7   Die Verzweiflung: eine Untersuchung ihres Wesens und ihrer Entstehung. Inaug. Diss. (Sack, Max.) Kallmünz, 1930.

Phil 3549.8.145   Das verzwistete Ich-Ludwig Klages und sein philosophisches Hauptwerk Der Geist als Widersacher der Seele. (Mueller, Roland.) Bern, 1971.

Phil 6131.10   Vesey, Godfrey Norman A. The embodied mind. London, 1965.

Phil 195.10   Veshchi, svoistva i otnosheniia. (Uemov, A.I.) Moskva, 1963.

Phil 8896.14   Vesper, Noël. Anticipations à une morale du risque. Paris, 1914.

Phil 9350.1   Vesper talks to girls. (Knott, Laura A.) Boston, 1916.

Phil 9167.6   Vesta; kleine Schriften zur Philosophie des Lebens. v.1-5. (Heydenreich, K.H.) Leizpig, 1798-1803. 4v.

Phil 5401.54   Vestdijk, Simon. Het wezen van de angst. Amsterdam, 1968.

Phil 189.1   Vestiges of civilization. (O'Connell, J.) N.Y., 1851.

Phil 4520.8.38   Vesturlönd. (Bjarnason, Agúst.) Reykjavík, 1915.

Phil 801.27.15   Vesturlönd. (Bjarnason, A.) Reykjavik, 1815.

Phil 4635.3.33   Vetenskapens evangelium. (Sylwan, O.C.) Stockholm, 1879.

Phil 4650.1.40   Vetenskapernas system. (Vannérus, Allen.) Stockholm, 1892.

Phil 342.8   Vetenskapliga vanföreställningars. (Lagerborg, R.) Helsingfors, 1920.

Phil 4650.1.41   Vetenskapssystematik. (Vannérus, Allen.) Stockholm, 1907.

Phil 1135.56   Veterum de Elementis Placita. (Lwellengrebel, J.G.H.) Rhenum, 1844.

Phil 5520.577   Vetrov, Anatolii A. Semiotika i ee osnovnye problemy. Moskva, 1968.

Phil 735.87   Vetter, A. Kritik des Gefühls. Prien, 1923.

Phil 3640.199   Vetter, A. Nietzsche. München, 1926.

Phil 5261.22   Vetter, A. Wirklichkeit des Menschlichen. Freiburg, 1960.

Phil 6060.92   Vetter, August. Die Zeichensprache von Schrift und Traum. Freiburg, 1970.

Phil 5627.259.5   Vetter, George. Magic and religion. London, 1959.

Phil 6400.36   Vetter, Harold J. Language behavior and psychopathology. Chicago, 1969.

Phil 6971.5   Vetter, Harold T. Language behavior in schizophrenia. Springfield, Ill., 1968.

Htn   Phil 3110.169*   Vetterling, H. The illuminate of Görlitz, or Jakob Böhme's (1575-1624) life and philosophy. Leipzig, 1923.

Phil 4080.3.225   Vettori, V. Benedetto Croce e gli studi contemporanei d'estetica e storia. Firenze, 1952.

Phil 4120.4.105   Vettori, V. Giovanni Gentile. Firenze, 1954.

Phil 196.25   Veuthy, L. La pensée contemporaine. Paris, 1938.

Phil 8581.24.25   Vi och världsalltet. (Brierley, J.) Stockholm, 1903.

Phil 1540.41   Via Antigue und via Moderna auf den deutschen Universitaeten des XV Jahrhunderts. (Ritter, Gerhard.) Darmstadt, 1963.

Phil 2725.13.85   La via nuova di Lequier. (Roggerone, Giuseppe Agostino.) Milano, 1968.

Phil 3549.2.100   El viajero y una de sus sombras; Keyserling en mis memorias. (Ocampo, Victoria.) Buenos Aires, 1951.

Phil 302.2   Vial, L.C.E. L'amour dans l'univers. Paris, 1896.

Phil 6990.6   Vialard, Felix. Recueil des pieces...sur les miracles. Nancy, 1735.

Phil 2045.118   Vialatoux, J. La cité de Hobbes. Paris, 1935.

Phil 352.6   Vialatoux, J. Le discours et l'intuition. Paris, 1930.

Phil 196.30   Vialatoux, J. L'intention philosophique. 1. ed. Paris, 1932.

Phil 3503.12   Vialatoux, J. La morale de Kant. 1. éd. Paris, 1956.

Phil 196.26   Vialle, L. Defense de la vie. Paris, 1938.

Phil 5261.19   Vialle, L. Le désir du néant. Paris, 1933.

Phil 5261.19.5   Vialle, L. Le désir du néant. Thèse. Paris, 1932.

Phil 196.26.5   Vialle, L. Introduction a la vie imparfaite. 1. ed. Paris, 1947.

Phil 3640.256   Vialle, Louis. Détresses de Nietzsche. Paris, 1932.

Phil 3640.256.5   Vialle, Louis. Détresses de Nietzsche. Thèse. Paris, 1932.

Phil 2905.1.257   Viallet, François A. Teilhard de Chardin. Nurnberg, 1963. 2v.

Phil 2905.1.255   Viallet, François A. L'univers personnel de Teilhard. Paris, 1955-61. 2v.

Phil 8430.57   Vian, Boris. En avant la zizique...et par ici les gros sous. Paris, 1966.

Phil 6331.8   Viane, Andre. Psychologie van het onheilsvoorspellen. Gent, 1963.

Phil 2115.195   Viano, Carlo A. John Locke. Torino, 1960.

Phil 2115.185   Viano, Carlo A. John Locke. Torino, 1960.

Phil 6331.7   Viard, Marcel. Le noeu suprême de Socrate. Paris, 1953.

Phil 8610.871.25   Viardot, L. Libre examen. 5. éd. Paris, 1877.

Phil 5838.259   Viaud, Gaston. Les instincts. Paris, 1949.

Htn   Phil 2128.82*   Vice and luxury publick mischiefs. (Dennis, John.) London, 1724.

Phil 9558.7   Vice unmasked; an essay. (Grayson, P.W.) N.Y., 1830.

Phil 9558.01   Pamphlet box. Vices.

Phil 8407.44   Vicissitudes de l'esthétique et révolutions du gout. (Grenier, Jean.) Paris, 1966.

Phil 4260.25.5   Vico, d'après la traduction de Michelet. (Vico, G.B.) Paris, 1927.

Phil 4260.17.16   Vico, G.B. Autobiografia. 1. ed. Torino, 1965.

Phil 4260.17.15   Vico, G.B. Autobiografia e scienza nuova. Torino, 1932.

Phil 4260.17.7   Vico, G.B. The autobiography of Giambattista Vico. Ithaca, 1944.

Phil 4260.30   Vico, G.B. La difesa dell'umanesimo. Firenze, 1958.

Phil 4260.27   Vico, G.B. L'estetica di G.B. Vico allraverso la scienza nuova e gli scritti minari. Napoli, 1926.

Phil 4260.41   Vico, G.B. L'ideale educativo. Napoli, 1954.

Phil 4260.37   Vico, G.B. Die neue Wissenschaft über die gemeinschaftliche Natur der Völker. Munchen, 1924.

Phil 4260.37.1   Vico, G.B. Die neue Wissenschaft über die gemeinschaftliche Natur der Völker. Hamburg, 1966.

Phil 4260.34   Vico, G.B. The new science of Giambattista Vico. Ithaca, 1948.

Phil 4260.34.2A   Vico, G.B. The new science of Giambattista Vico. Ithaca, 1968.

Phil 4260.25   Vico, G.B. Oeuvres. Paris, 1835. 2v.

Phil 4260.17   Vico, G.B. Opere. Bari, 1914. 6v.

Phil 4260.16   Vico, G.B. Opere. Milano, 1953.

Phil 4260.17.10   Vico, G.B. Opere. Milano, 1959.

Phil 4260.12   Vico, G.B. Opere. v.1-4. Napoli, 1840-41. 5v.

Phil 4260.15   Vico, G.B. Opere. v.1-6. Milano, 1854- 3v.

Phil 4260.31   Vico, G.B. Il pensiero di Giambattista Vico. Torino, 1959.

Phil 4260.36.5   Vico, G.B. Principes de la philosophie de l'histoire. Bruxelles, 1835.

Phil 4260.36A   Vico, G.B. Principes de la philosophie de l'histoire. Paris, 1827.

Htn   Phil 4260.33*   Vico, G.B. Principi di scienza nuova. v.1-2. Napoli, 1744.

Phil 4260.35.20   Vico, G.B. Principi di una scienza nuova. Milano, 1903.

Phil 4260.35   Vico, G.B. Principi di una scienza nuova. Napoli, 1826.

Phil 4260.38   Vico, G.B. Sabiduría primitiva de los italianos. Buenos Aires, 1939.

NEDL   Phil 4260.35.9   Vico, G.B. La science nouvelle. Bari, 1911-16. 3v.

Phil 4260.35.5   Vico, G.B. La science nouvelle. Paris, 1844.

Phil 4260.35.32   Vico, G.B. Scienza nuova...a cura di G. Flores d'Arcais. 2. ed. Padova, 1939.

Phil 4260.35.33   Vico, G.B. Scienza nuova...a cura di G. Flores d'Arcais. 3. ed. Padova, 1943.

Phil 4260.28   Vico, G.B. La scienza nuova e opere scelte di Giambattista Vico. Torino, 1952.

Phil 4260.23   Vico, G.B. Scritti vari e pagine sparse. Bari, 1940.

Phil 4260.17.5   Vico, G.B. Tutte le opere di Giambattista Vico. Milano, 1957.

Phil 4260.25.5   Vico, G.B. Vico, d'après la traduction de Michelet. Paris, 1927.

Phil 4260.39   Vico, G.B. Vom Wesen und Weg der geistigen Bildung. Godesberg, 1947.

Phil 4260.79   Pamphlet box. Vico, G.B.

Phil 4260.44   Vico, Giovanni Battista. De antiquissima Italorum sapientia. Roma, 1969.

Phil 4260.92   Vico, Hamann und Herder. Inaug. Diss. (Gemmingen, Otto.) Borna, 1918.

Phil 4260.82   Vico. (Flint, R.) Philadelphia, 1884.

Phil 4260.81.5   Vico et l'Italie. (Ferrari, G.) Paris, 1839.

Phil 4260.180   Vico nel risorgimento. (Brancato, Francesco.) Palermo, 1969.

Phil 4260.155   Vico storico. (Nicolini, F.) Napoli, 1967.

Phil 4260.122   Vico y Herder. (Buenos Aires. Universidad Nacional.) Buenos Aires, 1948.

Phil 9010.22   Victims of amusements. (Clark, Martha.) Philadelphia, n.d.

Phil 5525.30   Victor, C.R. Der Humor und seine Begründung. Bremen, 1925.

Phil 2496.79.10   Victor Cousin. (Ody, Hermann.) Saarbrücken, 1953.

Phil 2496.84   Victor Cousin et son oeuvre. (Janet, Paul.) Paris, 1885.

Phil 5525.40   Victoria, Marcos. Ensayo preliminar sobre lo cómico. Buenos Aires, 1941.

Phil 61.5   Victoria College, Wellington, New Zealand. Department of Psychology. Publications in psychology. 5+ 5v.

Phil 8836.2.20   A Victorian historian. (Lecky, W.E.H.) London, 1947.

Phil 178.12.39   The victorious faith, moral ideals in war time. (Dresser, H.W.) N.Y., 1917.

Phil 5525.52   Victoroff, D. Le rire et le risible. 1. éd. Paris, 1953.

Phil 2150.15.90   Victoroff, David. G.H. Mead, sociologue et philosophe. 1. ed. Paris, 1953.

Phil 8582.33.5   The victory of will. (Charbonnel, Victor.) Boston, 1907.

Phil 5401.16.5   Victory over fear. (Dollard, John.) N.Y., 1942.

Phil 3915.105   Vid studiet af Wundts psykologi. (Vannérus, Allen.) Stockholm, 1896.

Phil 4352.1.120   Vida de Balmes. (Garcia de Los Santos, B.) Madrid, 1848.

Phil 4363.1.80   Vida del Doctor José Manuel Mestre. (Rodriguez, J.I.) Habana, 1909.

Phil 4983.5.90   Vida del presbítero don Félix Varela. (Rodriguez, José Ignacio.) N.Y., 1878.

Phil 8416.36   Vida e morte das formas. (Pereira, M.A.) Lisboa, 1962.

Phil 8636.5.5   A vida futura; conferencias. (Lescoeur, Louis.) Lisboa, 1877.

Phil 4352.1.80   La vida y las obras de Balmes. (Roure, Narciso.) Madrid, 1910.

Phil 4974.65   Vida y obra del maestro Enrique Molina. (Bazán, Armando.) Santiago, 1954.

Phil 4357.2.80   Vida y obras de Don Francisco Giner de los Rios. 1. ed. (Navarro, Martin.) Mexico, 1945.

Phil 193.49.80   Vida y pensamiento de Jorge Santayana. (Farré, Luis.) Madrid, 1953.

Phil 4962.5.5   Vida y sentido. (Abad Carretero, Luis.) México, 1960.

Phil 8601.3   Vidal, F. Théologie de la religion naturelle. Paris, 1859.

Phil 4210.85   Vidari, G. Rosmini e Spencer. Milano, 1899.

Phil 8896.4.3   Vidari, Giovanni. Elementi di etica. 3. ed. Milano, 1911.

Phil 8896.4.4   Vidari, Giovanni. Elementi di etica. 4. ed. Milano, 1917.

Phil 8896.4.5   Vidari, Giovanni. Elementi di etica. 5. ed. Milano, 1922.

Phil 8846.3   Vidari, Giovanni. L'individualismo nelle dottrine morali del secolo XIX. Milano, 1909.

Phil 8896.4.9   Vidari, Giovanni. Problemi generali di etica. Milano, 1901.

Phil 4322.1   Vidart, Louis. La filosofía española. Madrid, 1866.

Phil 5640.139   Vidchuttia i diisnist'. (Mykytenko, Danylo A.) Kyïv, 1966.

Phil 410.82   Viderskii, Vladimir I. Konechnoe i beskonechnoe. Moskva, 1966.

Phil 2733.92   Vidgrain, J. Le Christianisme dans la philosophie de Malebranche. Paris, n.d.

Phil 2733.90   Vidgrain, Joseph. Le christianisme dans la philosophie de Malebranche. Thèse. Paris, 1923.

Phil 2733.78   Vidgrain, Joseph. Fragments philosophiques inédits et correspondance. Thèse. Caen, 1923.

Phil 2733.78.2   Vidgrain, Joseph. Malebranche. Paris, n.d.

Phil 2905.1.555   Vidoni, Egidio. L'individuo e il collettivo nella durata secondo Pierre Teilhard de Chardin. Milano, 1966[1965].

Phil 960.11   Vidyabhusana, Satis Chandra. History...mediaeval school of Indian logic. Calcutta, 1909.

Phil 960.11.5   Vidyabhusana, Satis Chandra. A history of Indian logic. Calcutta, 1921.

Phil 70.18.15   La vie, la pensée. (Congrès des Sociétés de Philosophie de Langue Française, 7th, Grenoblé, 1954.) Paris, 1954

Phil 5400.109   La vie affective. 1. éd. (Dumas, G.) Paris, 1948.

Phil 2805.241   Une vie avec Blaise Pascal. (Tourneur, Zacharie.) Paris, 1943.

Phil 4210.83.3   Vie d'Antonio Rosmini-Serbati. (Lockhart, W.) Paris, 1889.

Phil 3822.4   La vie de Benoit de Spinoza. (Colerus, Johannes.) La Haye, 1706.

Phil 3838.18   La vie de Benoit de Spinoza. (Segond, J.) Paris, 1933.

Phil 3640.77.20 La vie de Friedrich Nietzsche d'après sa correspondance. (Nietzsche, Friedrich.) Paris, 1932.
Phil 4260.116 Vie de J.B. Vico. (Chaix-Ruy, Jules.) Gap, 1943.
Phil 2750.8.85 Vie de Maupertuis. (De la Beaumelle, Laurent A.) Paris, 1856.
Htn Phil 2520.81.2* La vie de Monsieur Des-Cartes. (Baillet, A.) Paris, 1691. 2v.
Phil 2520.81 La vie de Monsieur Des-Cartes. (Baillet, A.) Paris, 1691.
Htn Phil 2520.81.5* La vie de Monsieur Des-Cartes. (Baillet, A.) Paris, 1692.
Phil 2520.81.6 La vie de Monsieur Des-Cartes. (Baillet, A.) Paris, 1706.
Phil 2520.81.15 Vie de Monsieur Descartes. (Baillet, A.) Paris, 1946.
Phil 2610.83 Vie de Pierre Gassendi. (Bougerel, J.) Paris, 1737.
Phil 333.19 Le vie del sapere. (Cortesi, Luigi.) Milano, 1959.
Phil 5871.25 La vie des enfants en collectivité. (Ziv, Avner.) Paris, 1965.
Phil 8406.18.5 Vie des formes. 3. ed. (Focillon, Henri.) Paris, 1947.
Phil 5070.14 La vie des vérités. (Le Bon, Gustave.) Paris, 1917.
Phil 2733.80 La vie du R.P. Malebranche, Bibliothèque Oratorienne. (André, Y.M.) Paris, 1886.
Phil 2475.1.307 Vie et conscience de la vie. Thèse. (Delhomme, J.) Paris, 1954.
Phil 293.32 Vie et cosmos. (Morin, Gérard.) Paris, 1962.
Phil 176.38 La vie et la pensée. (Burnouf, E.L.) Paris, 1886.
Phil 5255.22 La vie et la pensée. (Pioger, J.) Paris, 1893.
Phil 2905.1.80 Vie et l'âme de Teilhard de Chardin. (Cristiani, Léon.) Paris, 1957.
Phil 4265.1.84 Vie et les sentimens de Lucilio Vanini. Rotterdam, 1717.
Phil 2490.114 La vie et l'oeuvre de A.C. et de Pierre Laffitte. (Hillemand, C.) Paris, 1908.
Phil 6327.21.95 La vie et l'oeuvre der docteur Wilhelm Reich. (Cattier, Michel.) Lausanne, 1969.
Phil 6321.60 Vie et mort en psychanalyse. (Laplanche, Jean.) Paris, 1970.
Phil 6685.14 Vie et paroles du maitre. (Philippe, Anthelme Philippe.) Lyon, 1959.
Phil 8629.1 La vie éternelle. (Enfantin, B.P.) Paris, 1861.
Phil 8637.1 La vie future. (Martin, T.H.) Paris, 1870.
Phil 8632.12 La vie future et la science moderne. (Hirn, G.A.) Colmar, 1890.
Phil 2805.90.9 La vie héroique de Blaise Pascal. 15. éd. (Giraud, V.) Paris, 1923.
Phil 8961.4 La vie heureuse, ou L'homme content. (La Serre.) Paris, 1693.
Phil 5242.7 La vie inconsciente. (Colsenet, E.) Paris, 1880.
Phil 5649.11.3 La vie inconsciente et les mouvements. 3. éd. (Ribot, Théodule.) Paris, 1914.
Phil 8877.79 La vie morale et l'audelà. (Chevalier, J.) Paris, 1938.
Phil 1706.1.35 La vie mystique de la nature. (Gaultier, Jules de.) Paris, 1924.
Phil 575.72 La vie personnelle. (Bazaillas, Albert.) Paris, 1904.
Phil 5811.5.20 La vie psychique des bêtes. (Büchner, L.) Paris, 1881.
Phil 2520.121.5 La vie raisonnable de Descartes. (Dimier, Louis.) Paris, 1926.
Phil 8965.25 La vie selon l'Esprit, condition du chrétien. (Potterie, I. de.) Paris, 1965.
Phil 9182.4.6 La vie simple. 2. éd. (Wagner, Charles.) Paris, 1895.
Phil 2630.7.98 La vie simple de René Guenon. (Chacornac, Paul.) Paris, 1958.
Phil 2725.2.99 La vie tragique de Lamennais. (Giraud, Victor.) Paris, 1933.
Phil 5400.169 Vieira, Manuel. Emoções e felicidade. Lisboa, 1964.
Phil 5520.270 Vieira de Almeida, F. Aspectos de filosofia da linguagem. Coimbra, 1959.
Phil 8422.3 Vieira de Almeida, F. Fifosofia da arte; ensaio. Coimbra, 1942.
Phil 4482.1.97 Vieira de Almeida, Francisco. Pontos de referência. Lisboa, 1961.
Phil 8691.14 La vieja ortodoxia y la ciencia moderna. (Borrero Echeverria, E.) Habana, 1879.
Phil 5360.3 Die Vieldeutigkeit des Urtheiles. (Stöhr, Adolf.) Leipzig, 1895.
Phil 61.1.5 Vienna. Universität. Philosophische Gesellschaft. Veröffentlichungen. Leipzig, 1893- 3v.
Phil 61.1 Vienna. Universität. Philosophische Gesellschaft. WissenschaftlicheBeilage. Leipzig, 1902-1915. 2v.
Phil 8583.45.2 Vier Bücher von der religiösen Erkenntniss. (Denzinger, Heinrich.) Frankfurt, 1967. 2v.
Phil 1750.163 VierGestalten aus den Zeitalter des Humanismus. (Drewinc, H.) Saint Gallen, 1946.
Phil 3808.37 De vier hocksteenen der Wereld en harr Bouwmeester. v.1-2. (Schopenhauer, Arthur.) 's-Gravenhage, 1893.
Phil 1740.20 Vier Kritiken. Heidegger, Sartre, Adorno, Lukács. (Beyer, Wilhelm Raimund.) Köln, 1970.
Phil 8897.72 Vier moralisten. (Wijnaendts Francken, C.J.) Amsterdam, 1946.
Phil 978.49.265 Vier Mysteriendramen. 2. Aufl. (Steiner, R.) Dornach, 1956.
Phil 3120.8.32 Die vier Phasen der Philosophie und ihr augenblicklicher Stand. (Brentano, Franz.) Leipzig, 1926.
Phil 6315.2.65 Vier psychoanalytische Krankengeschichten. (Freud, Sigmund.) Wien, 1932.
Phil 5245.9.15 Vier psychologische Vorträge. (Fortlage, A.R.K.) Jena, 1874.
Phil 3549.15.80 Vier Schriften des Herrn Professor Kappes. Pt.1-2. (Adickes, Erich.) Berlin, 1903.
Phil 3120.3.30 Vierfältigkeit in Logik und Welt oder die vier Bücher vom Sinn des Ganzen. (Barnick, Johannes.) Berlin, 1969.
Phil 8965.13.15.5 Das Viergespann: Klugheit, Gerechtigkeit, Tapferkeit, Mass. (Pieper, Josef.) München, 1964.
Phil 315.5 Vierkandt, A. Der Dualismus mi modernen Weltbild. 2. Aufl. Berlin, 1923.
Phil 5585.1.5 Vierordt, Karl. Der Zeitsinn nach Versuchen. Tübingen, 1868.
Phil 31.2 Vierteljahrsschrift für Psychiatrie. Neuwied. 1-2,1867-1869 2v.
Phil 31.1 Vierteljahrsschrift für Wissen Philosophie. Leipzig. 1-40 38v.
Phil 31.1.5 Vierteljahrsschrift für Wissen Philosophie. Generalregister zu Jahrgang, I-XXX. Leipzig, 1908.
Phil 1158.9 Les vies d'Epicure de Platon et de Pythagore. (Combes, M.) Amsterdam, 1752.
Phil 815.9 Vies et doctrines des grands philosophes à travers les âges. (Palhariés, F.) Paris, 1928. 3v.
Phil 1721.9 Vieteck, George S. The seven against man. Scotch Plains, N.J., 1941.
Phil 8896.5 Vietinghoff, Jeanne de. La liberté intérieure. Paris, 1912.

Phil 5440.17 View at the foundatiuons...of character. (Fernald, W.M.) Boston, 1865.
Phil 194.37.5 A view of all existence. (Thomas, Elyston.) London, 1936.
Phil 8663.3.89 View of Lambert's "Notes on Ingersoll." (Lucas, H.M.) N.Y., 1909.
Phil 8598.19 A view of nature. (Sulivan, R.J.) London, 1794. 6v.
Phil 7060.8 View of the invisible world. London, 1752.
Phil 6978.5 A view of the levels of perceptual development in autistic syndromes. Academisch proefschrift. (Straub, Richard Ralph.) n.p., 1964.
Phil 5938.6.18 A view of the philosophical principles of phrenology. 3rd ed. (Spurzheim, Johann Gaspar.) London, 18- .
Phil 8520.5 A view of the principal deistical writers. (Leland, J.) London, 1754-56. 3v.
Htn Phil 8520.5.3* A view of the principal deistical writers. (Leland, J.) London, 1757. 2v.
Phil 8520.5.2 A view of the principal deistical writers. (Leland, J.) London, 1954.
Phil 8520.5.3.10 A view of the principal deistical writers. 5. ed. (Leland, J.) London, 1766. 2v.
Phil 8520.5.4 A view of the principal deistical writers. 5. ed. (Leland, J.) London, 1798. 2v.
Phil 6135.9 Viewpoint on mental health; transcripts, 1963-1965. (Ziskind, Robert.) N.Y., 1967.
Phil 8593.6 Views of religion. (Noyes, R.K.) Boston, 1906.
Phil 8673.2 Views of the deity. (Samuelson, J.) London, 1871.
Phil 4372.1.125 Vigencia actual de Luis Vives. (Sanz, Victor.) Montevideo, 1967.
Phil 5330.31 Vigilance. (Buckner, D.) Los Angeles, 1963.
Phil 5330.42.5 Vigilance and attention; a signal detection approach. (Mackworth, Jane F.) Harmondsworth, 1970.
Phil 5330.42 Vigilance and habituation: a new psychological approach. (Mackworth, Jane F.) Harmondsworth, 1969.
Phil 1526.4 Vignaux, Paul. Le pensée au moyen âge. Paris, 1938.
Phil 1526.4.5 Vignaux, Paul. Philosophie au moyen-âge. Paris, 1958.
Phil 1526.4.10 Vignaux, Paul. Philosophy in the Middle Ages. N.Y., 1959.
Phil 5261.2 Vignoli, T. Myth and science. N.Y., 1882.
Phil 5261.2.5 Vignoli, T. Peregrinazioni psicologiche. Milano, 1895.
Phil 5831.1.3 Vignoli, Tito. Della legge fondamentale dell'intelligenza nell regno animali. Milano, 1877.
Phil 1721.2 Vignoli, Tito. L'era nuova del pensiero. Milano, 1885.
Phil 8601.8 Vignoli, Tito. Mito e scienza saggio. Milano, 1879.
Phil 5831.1 Vignoli, Tito. Über das Fundamentalgesetz der Intelligenz im Thierreiche. Leipzig, 1879.
Phil 8711.2 Vignon, Paul. Au sauffle de l'esprit créatur. Paris, 1946.
Phil 2053.90 Vigone, L. L'etica del senso morale in Francis Hutcheson. Milano, 1954.
Phil 2905.1.280 Vigorelli, G. Il gesuita proibito. Milano, 1963.
Phil 7140.119 Vigouroux, A. Le contagion mentale. Paris, 1905.
Phil 291.14 A világ fejlödése az atom szemléletében. (Kiss, Elek.) Kolozsvár, 1946.
Phil 8696.28 Vilagegyetem es a lélek világa. (Giesswein, Sándor.) Budapest, 1913.
Phil 7069.34.45 Vilanova, María. Un drama del espacio. Año 1932. Dictado por el espiritu de Blasco Ibáñez. Barcelona, 1934.
Phil 7069.34.47 Vilanova, María. El regentador del mundo solar os da un radio de luz...julio de 1934. Barcelona, 1934.
Phil 7069.34.47.2 Vilanova, Maria. La segunda parte que ha dado el regentador del mondo solar, para que los lectores lo leau que va siquiendo su lectura. Barcelona, 1934.
Phil 7069.34.41 Vilanova, María. El tesoro de la ciencia eterna de Dios. Barcelona, 1933-34. 2v.
Phil 7069.34.43 Vilanova, María. Va siguiendo la tercera parte de el radio de luz del regentador del mundo solar. Barcelona, 1934. 8 pam.
Phil 6990.35 Vilar, Albert. Réflexions sur le miracle et les lois naturelles. Clamecy, 1934.
Phil 5520.407 Vildomec, V. Multilingualism. Leyden, 1963.
Phil 8601.6 Vilenkin, N.M. Religiia budushchago. Sankt Peterburg, 1905.
Phil 3705.3.95 Vil'gel'm Ostval'd. (Rodnyi, Naum I.) Moskva, 1969.
Phil 8586.64.80 Vilhelm Grønbech. En indføring. (Mitchell, Phillip Marshall.) København, 1970.
Phil 5761.11 Viljan. (Landquist, J.) Stockholm, 1908.
Phil 184.3.7.30 Viljan till tro och andra essayer. (James, W.) Stockholm, 1908.
Phil 4600.2.34 Viljans frihet. (Larsson, Hans.) Lund, 1899.
Phil 4600.2.35 Viljans frihet. (Larsson, Hans.) Lund, 1910.
Phil 5750.4 Viljans frihet från transcendental-filosofiens ståndpunkt. (Ahlberg, Alf.) Stockholm, 1915.
Phil 5545.22.10 Viljans sjukdomar. 6. uppl. (Ribot, T.) Stockholm, 1890.
Phil 5261.3.5 Villa, G. Contemporary psychology. London, 1903.
Phil 5261.3.12 Villa, G. Enleitung in die Psychologie der Gegenwart. Leipzig, 1902.
Phil 5261.3.9 Villa, G. La psicologia contemporanea. Milano, 1911.
Phil 5261.3 Villa, G. La psicologia contemporanea. Torino, 1899.
Phil 400.20.5 Villa, Guido. L'idealismo moderno. Torino, 1905. 2v.
Phil 4357.2.85 Villalopos, José. El pensamiento filsofico de Giner. Sevilla, 1969.
Phil 8620.16 Villaume, P. Von dem Ursprung und der Absichten des Übels. Leipzig, 1784. 3v.
Phil 4983.41 Villegas, Abelardo. La filosofía de lo mexicano. México, 1960.
Phil 4959.235 Villegas, Abelardo. La filosofía en la história política de México. 1. ed. México, 1966.
Phil 4957.55 Villegas, Abelardo. Panorama de la filosofía iberoamericana actual. Buenos Aires, 1963.
Phil 3503.2 Villers, C. Philosophie de Kant. v.1-2. Metz, 1801.
Phil 6971.4 Villey, G. La psychiatrie et les sciences de l'homme. Paris, 1938.
Phil 9558.4 Villiers, Pierre. Reflexions sur les défauts d'autruy. Paris, 1690.
Phil 196.35 Villoro, Luis. Paginas filosofias. Mexico, 1962.
Phil 5520.107 Vinacke, W.E. The psychology of thinking. 1. ed. N.Y., 1952.
Phil 1500.3 Vinas, M. de. Philosophia scholastica. Genuae, 1709. 3v.
Phil 4080.3.315 Vinceguerra, Mario. Croce. Napoli, 1957.
Phil 8896.1 Vincent, G.G. The appendix to volumes I. and II. of the moral system, or Law of human nature. London, 1850.
Phil 5374.170 Vincent, M. L'image dynamique. Paris, 1955.
Phil 9010.21 Vincent, Marvin. Amusement. Troy, 1867.
Phil 352.7 Vincent, Maxime. La vision interne. Paris, 1933.
Phil 6691.1 Vincent, R.H. Elements of hypnotism. London, 1893.
Phil 5831.3 Vincent, S.B. The function of the vibrissae in the behavior of the white rat. Chicago, 1912.

Phil 9361.1 — Vincent. Les caracteres de l'honneste homme et de l'homme chrestien. Paris, 1690.

Htn Phil 8800.3* — Vincent de Beauvais. Speculum morale. Venetiis, 1493.

Phil 2520.127 — Vincentius, Joannes. Discussio perysatitica. Tolosae, 1677.

Phil 3640.702 — Vincenzi, M. El caso Nietzsche. San Juan, 1963.

Phil 196.29.5 — Vincenzi, M. Rionas y byondas. San José, 1921.

Phil 196.22 — Vincenzi, Moises. Mi segunda dimension. San José, 1928.

Phil 4120.6.95 — Vincenzo de Grazia. (Varano, F.S.) Napoli, 1931.

Phil 4115.105 — Vincenzo Gioberti, critico letterario. (Fusco, Maria.) Catania, 1940.

Phil 4115.86 — Vincenzo Gioberti. (Piccoli, Valentino.) Roma, 1923.

Phil 4115.80 — Vincenzo Gioberti. (Rosmini-Serbati, A.) Lucca, 1853.

Phil 4115.80.5 — Vincenzo Gioberti e il panteismo. (Rosmini-Serbati, A.) Milano, 1847.

Phil 4115.80.10 — Vincenzo Gioberti e il panteismo. (Rosmini-Serbati, A.) Napoli, 1847.

Phil 6980.770 — Vinchon, Jean. La magie du dession. Paris, 1959.

Phil 6691.2 — Vinchon, Jean. Mesmer et son secret. Paris, 1936.

Phil 3552.309 — Le "vinculum substantiale" chez Leibniz. (Boehm, A.) Paris, 1938.

Htn Phil 8595.16.19* — Vindication of divine inspiration. (Scott, Thomas.) London, 1797.

Phil 8598.1 — Vindication of divine providence. (Saint Pierre, J.H.B. de.) Worcester, 1797.

Phil 2205.81 — A vindication of Dr. Paley's theory of morals. (Wainewright, L.) London, 1830.

Htn Phil 2115.126* — A vindication of Mr. Locke. (Perronet, Vincent.) London, 1736.

Phil 5942.2 — A vindication of phrenology. (Williams, N.M.) London, 1894.

Phil 8595.16.3 — A vindication of the age of reason, by Thomas Paine. (Dutton, Thomas.) London, 1795.

Phil 8693.3 — A vindication of the divine authority. (Dove, J.) n.p., 1888.

Phil 585.168 — A vindication of the rights of brutes (1792). (Taylor, Thomas.) Gainesville, Fla., 1966.

Phil 8691.7 — Vindiciae geologicae. (Buckland, William.) Oxford, 1820.

Htn Phil 665.50* — Vindiciae mentis. (E., T.) London, 1702.

Htn Phil 2295.75* — Vindicius liberius. (Toland, John.) London, 1702.

Htn Phil 2295.75.2* — Vindicius liberius. (Toland, John.) London, 1702.

Phil 2805.91.2 — Vinet, A. Études sur Blaise Pascal. Lausanne, 1936.

Phil 2805.91.1 — Vinet, A. Études sur Blaise Pascal. Paris, 1848.

Phil 2805.91 — Vinet, A. Etudes sur Blaise Pascal. Paris, 1856.

Phil 8896.12 — Vinet, Alexandre. Essais de philosophie morale et de moral e religieuse. Paris, 1837.

Phil 525.260 — Vinkenoog, Simon. Weergaloos. Hilversum, 1968.

Phil 302.1 — Vinogradoff, I. Theory of cosmic reason. n.p., n.d.

Phil 4080.3.355 — Viola, Italo. Problemi di critica crociana. Milano, 1960.

Phil 5421.20.55 — Violence, monkeys, and man. (Russell, Claire.) London, 1968.

Phil 8954.10 — Violence. (Ellul, Jacques.) N.Y., 1969.

Phil 5421.20.70 — Violent men; an inquiry into the psychology of violence. (Toch, Hans.) Chicago, 1969.

Phil 8968.22.5 — La violenza. (Semaine des Intellectuels Catholiques, 1967.) Roma, 1968.

Phil 8971.6 — La violenza die cristiani. Assisi, 1969.

Phil 2475.1.485 — Violette, René. La spiritualité de Bergson. Toulouse, 1968.

Phil 5421.20.30 — Violincía y ternura. (Rof Carballo, Juan.) Madrid, 1967.

Phil 2750.11.150 — Viotto, Piero. Jacques Maritain. Brescia, 1957.

Phil 2750.11.150.3 — Viotto, Piero. Jacques Maritain. 3. ed. Brescia, 1965.

Phil 4983.74.31 — Virasoro, M.A. Desesperación y rebeldía en la conciencia contemporánea. Bahia Blanca, 1959.

Phil 585.105 — Virasoro, M.A. Filosofía de la existencia y antropología filosófica. 1. ed. Bahía Blanca, 1960.

Phil 585.159 — Virasoro, M.A. Para una nueva idea del hombre y de la antropología filosófica. Tucuman, 1963.

Phil 1750.494 — Virasoro, Rafael. Existencialismo y moral. Argentina, 1957.

Phil 1750.495 — Virasoro, Rafael. Introducción al estudio de la fenomenologia de Husserl. Rosario, 195-?

Phil 6990.47.5 — Virchow, R. Über Wunder. 2. Aufl. Frankfurt, 1908.

Phil 8896.16 — Virey, J.J. L'art de perfectionner l'homme. Paris, 1808. 2v.

Phil 6750.12 — Virginia. State Board of Charities and Corrections. Mental defectives in Virginia. Richmond, 1915.

Phil 1200.52 — Virieux, A. La logique et l'épistémalogie des stoïciens. Lausanne, 1950.

Phil 9495.35.15 — The virile powers of superb manhood. (Macfadden, B.A.) London, 1896.

Phil 8894.23.5 — La virtù contemporanea. (Tarrozzi, G.) Torino, 1900.

Phil 1350.13 — Virtù romana. (Calderini, A.) Milano, 1936.

Phil 4472.1.30 — Virtudes e defeitas dos homens. (Lapas de Gusmão.) Lisboa, 1957.

Phil 2255.10.30 — The virtue of selfishness; a new concept of egoism. (Rand, Ayn.) N.Y., 1965.

Htn Phil 9560.24* — Virtutes et vitia. (Pasquali, C.) Parisiis, 1615.

Phil 6013.3 — Le visage de l'homme. (Denis, Robert.) Paris, 1961.

Phil 6012.8 — Visages et caractères. (Corman, Louis.) Paris, 1961.

Phil 8422.7.5 — Vischer, F.T. Asthetik; oder, Wissenschaft des Schönen. München, 1922-23. 6v.

Phil 8422.7A — Vischer, F.T. Asthetik. Reutlingen, 1846-57. 3v.

Phil 8422.7.2 — Vischer, F.T. Asthetik Vollständiges, Inhaltsverzeichniss, Namen und Sachregister. Stuttgart, 1858.

Phil 8422.7.10 — Vischer, F.T. Das Schöne und die Kunst. Stuttgart, 1898.

Phil 8422.7.15 — Vischer, F.T. Über das Erhabene und konische Einleitung. Frankfurt, 1967.

Phil 8422.16 — Vischer, R. Drei Schriften zum ästhetischen Formproblem. Halle, 1927.

Phil 2750.20.45 — The visible and the invisible. (Merleau-Ponty, Maurice.) Evanston, 1968.

Phil 2750.20.40A — Le visible et l'invisible. (Merleau-Ponty, Maurice.) Paris, 1964.

Phil 2905.1.265 — Het visioen van Teilhard de Chardin. (Smulders, P.F.) Brugge, 1962.

Phil 7069.38.65 — Vision, being the continuation of "Reality" and "Dedication". (Parkman, Frances.) Boston, 1938.

Phil 5643.103 — Vision. (Bartley, S. Howard.) N.Y., 1941.

Phil 5643.30 — La vision. (Nuel, J.P.) Paris, 1904.

Phil 5640.10 — Vision: color, sense and hearing. (Williams, C.H.) Chicago, 1902.

Phil 1830.12 — Vision and action. (Ratner, Sidney.) New Brunswick, N.J., 1953.

Phil 2905.1.266 — La vision de Teilhard de Chardin. (Smulders, P.F.) Paris, 1964.

Phil 5643.123 — La vision en lumière intermittente. (Piéron, Henri.) Paris, 1961.

Phil 2733.130 — The vision in God; Malebranche's scholastic sources. (Gonnell, Desmond.) Louvain, 1967.

Phil 8092.9 — Vision in motion. (Moholy-Nagy, L.) Chicago, 1956.

Phil 352.7 — La vision interne. (Vincent, Maxime.) Paris, 1933.

Phil 4235.1.95 — La visione della vita...Telesio. (Zavattari, E.) Torino, 1923.

Phil 7060.16 — Visions: study of false sight. (Clarke, E.H.) Boston, 1878.

Phil 6954.1.5 — A visit to thirteen asylums...insane, Europe. (Earle, P.) Philadelphia, 1841.

Phil 7067.91 — Visits from the world of spirits. London, 1791.

Phil 310.615 — Vislobokov, Aleksei Dmitrievich. O dialektike protsessa poznaniia prirody i kibernetika. Moskva, 1965.

Phil 20.8 — Visnyk. Seriia filosofii. (Kiev. Universitet.) Kiev. 1,1967+

Phil 7069.59.15 — Visser, B.J.J. Parapsychologie, paragnosie. Roermond, 1959.

Phil 5261.14 — Visser, H.L.A. Collectief-psychologische omtrekken. Haarlem, 1920.

Phil 3640.259 — Visser, H.L.A. Nietzsche de goede Europeaan. Zutphen, 1933.

Phil 821.4 — Visser, S. Zoekers naar wijsheid. Goes, 1938.

Phil 5643.33.2 — A visual illusion of motion during eye closure. (Carr, Harvey.) Lancaster, 1906.

Phil 5643.105 — Visual mechanisms. (Kluver, H.) Lancaster, 1942.

Phil 5585.65 — A visual motor gestalt test. (Bender, L.) N.Y., 1938.

Phil 176.145 — Visual outline of philosophy. (Bentley, J.E.) N.Y., 1939.

Phil 5585.330 — Visual pattern recognition. (Dodwell, P.C.) N.Y., 1970.

Phil 5585.61 — Visual perception. (Vernon, M.D.) Cambridge, Eng., 1937.

Phil 5585.205.5 — Visual perception: the nineteenth century. (Dember, William Norton.) N.Y., 1964.

Phil 5585.190.5 — Visual space perception. (Ittelson, William H.) N.Y., 1960.

Phil 8401.40.10 — Visual thinking. (Arnheim, Rudolf.) Berkeley, 1969.

Phil 5643.68 — Visuell wahrgenommene figuren. (Rubin, Edgar.) København, 1921.

Phil 5643.115 — Der visuelle Mensch. (Kiefer, Theodor.) München, 1956.

Phil 4960.625.5 — Vita, Luís Washington. Antologia do pensamento social e político no Brasil, seleção e notas. São Paulo, 1968.

Phil 4960.625.15 — Vita, Luís Washington. A filosofia contemporânea em São Paulo nos seus textos. São Paulo, 1969.

Phil 196.36.10 — Vita, Luis Washington. Introdução à filosofia. São Paulo, 1964.

Phil 821.6 — Vita, Luís Washington. Monólogos e diálogos. São Paulo, 1964.

Phil 4960.625.10 — Vita, Luis Washington. Panorama da filosofia no Brasil. Pôrto Alegre, 1969.

Phil 196.36 — Vita, Luis Washington. Que é filosofia. São Paulo, 1965.

Phil 4960.625 — Vita, Luis Washington. Tendências do pensamento estético contemporâneo no Brasil. Rio de Janeiro, 1967.

Phil 196.36.5 — Vita, Luis Washington. Tríptico de idéias. São Paulo, 1967.

Htn Phil 2045.30* — Vita. (Hobbes, Thomas.) Carolopoli, 1680-8-? 4 pam.

Htn Phil 2045.30.2* — Vita. (Hobbes, Thomas.) Carolopoli, 1681.

Phil 4060.9.35 — Vita can Giovanni Amendola. (Amendola, Evakühn.) Firenze, 1960.

Phil 4073.68 — Vita Christi. (Campanella, Tommaso.) Roma, 1962. 2v.

Phil 5628.13 — Vita Christiane Stumbelensis edibit Johannes Paukon. (Petrus de Dacia.) Gotoburgi, 1896.

Phil 4225.15.30 — La vita come arte. (Spirito, Ugo.) Firenze, 1941.

Phil 3552.294.5 — Vita del Signore Barone Goffredo G. di Leibnitz. (Lamprecht, J.F.) Roma, 1787.

Phil 5627.260.5 — La vita della religion e nella storia delle religioni. (Graneris, Giuseppe.) Torino, 1960.

Phil 8402.24 — Vita dell'arte. (Banfi, Antonio.) Milano, 1947.

Phil 8406.18 — Vita delle forme, di Henri Focillon. (Focillon, Henri.) Padova, 1945.

Phil 4080.9.35 — La vita dello spirito. (Carlini, Armando.) Firenze, 1921.

Phil 4210.107 — Vita di Antonio Rosmini scritta da un sacerdote dell'istituto della carità. (Pagani, G.B.) Rovereto, 1959. 2v.

Phil 4080.6.80 — Vita di Francesco Cattani da Diacceto. (Varchi, B.) Ancona, 1843.

Phil 7069.07.32 — La vita di Gesù. 2. ed. Roma, 1907.

Phil 4065.98 — Vita di Giordano Bruno. v.1-2. (Spampanato, V.) Messina, 1921.

Phil 4075.79.10 — Vita di Girolamo Cardano. (Cardano, Girolamo.) Milano, 1821.

Phil 2520.151 — Vita di Renato Cartesio. (Savérien, Alexandre.) Venezia, 1811.

Phil 530.20.110 — Vita Dorotheae Montoviensis. (Marienwerder, Johannes.) Graz, 1964.

Phil 4235.10.80 — Vita e dottrina di Laetano di Thiene. 2. ed. (Silvestro da Valsanzibio.) Padova, 1949.

Phil 3808.112.9 — La vita e il pensiero di Arturo Schopenhauer. (Covotti, Aurelio.) Milano, 1910.

Phil 4060.1.83 — La vita e il pensiero di Roberto Ardigo. (Marchesini, G.) Milano, 1907.

Phil 8612.11.2 — La vita e la morte. 2. ed. (Aurelj, T.) Roma, 1904.

Phil 4170.3.80 — La vita e l'opere di A.C. de Meis. (Vecchio-Veneziani, Augusta del.) Bologna, 1921.

Phil 4060.5.80 — La vita ed il pensiero di Andrea Anguilli. (Taura, Giacoma.) Milano, 1914.

Phil 4073.122 — La vita eroica di Tommaso Campanella. (Squillace, Mario.) Roma, 1967.

Phil 8417.2 — La vita estetica, e lo sviluppo della coscienza. (Quadri, G.) Firenze, 1953.

Phil 5590.492.5 — Vita humana. (Thomae, Hans.) Frankfurt, 1969.

Phil 31.7 — Vita humana. Basel. 1,1958+ 6v.

Phil 31.7.4 — Vita humana. Bibliotheca. 3,1965+

Htn Phil 1106.5.6* — Vita omnium philosophorum et poetarum. (Burley, W.) n.p., n.d.

Phil 4080.26.10 — La vita quotidiana. (Cantoni, Remo.) Milano, 1966.

Phil 6816.10.2 — Vita segreta del complesso d'inferiorita. 2. ed. (Natale, Nicola G.) Bologna, 1961.

Phil 4073.80 — Vita T. Campanella. (Cyprian, E.) Amstelodami, 1722.

Phil 3000.1.2 — Vitae germanorum philosophorum. (Adam, M.) Franefort, 1663.

Phil 3000.1 — Vitae germanorum superiori. (Adam, M.) Franefort, 1615.

Phil 6322.19.15 — The vital balance. (Menninger, Karl Augustus.) N.Y., 1963.

Phil 7054.173.10 — The vital choice, Endor or Calvary. (Forster, David.) London, 1919.

Phil 190.51 — Vital lies. (Paget, Violet.) London, 1912. 2v.

Phil 6671.1 — Vital magnetism. (Babbitt, E.D.) N.Y., n.d.

Phil 7069.19.93 — The vital message. (Doyle, Arthur Conan.) London, 1919.

Phil 7069.19.92 The vital message. (Doyle, Arthur Conan.) N.Y., 1919.
Phil 8604.2 Vital religion. (Younghusband, F.E.) London, 1940.
Phil 7069.60.15 The vital sense. (Heine, Hilda G.) London, 1960.
Phil 3552.450 Vitale, Ignazio. L'armonia prestabilita in Leibniz. Padova, 1959.
Phil 9035.59.30 Vitale Dialektik. (Künkel, Fritz.) Leizpig, 1929.
Phil 4610.7.87 Vitalis Norström. (Liljedal, E.) Stockholm, 1917-18. 2v.
Phil 745.9 Vitalism and mechanism. (Neal, Herbert V.) Lancaster, Pa., 1934.
Phil 3850.2.80A Le vitalisme et l'animisme de Stahl. (Lemoine, A.) Paris, 1864.
Phil 745.6.7 Il vitalismo. (Driesch, H.) Milano, 1911. 2v.
Phil 3415.94 Der Vitalismus Eduard von Hartmanns und seine philosophischen Grundlagen. Inaug. Diss. (Krüger, Gustav.) Schwerin, 1911.
Phil 745.3 Vitalismus und Mechanismus. (Bunge, Gustav von.) Leipzig, 1886.
Phil 8594.6 La vitalite chrétiene. (Ollé-Laprune, L.) Paris, 1914.
Phil 187.32.5 Vitality and organization of protoplasm. (Montgomery, E.) Austin, Texas, 1904.
Phil 8599.34 The vitality of the Christian tradition. (Thomas, George Finger.) N.Y., 1944.
Phil 3640.392 Vitens, Siegfried. Die Sprachkunst Friedrich Nietzsches in Also sprach Zarathustra. Bremen, 1951.
Phil 4080.3.550 Vitiello, Vincenzo. Storiografia e storia nel pensiero di Benedetto Croce. Napoli, 1968.
Phil 3503.13 Vitier, M. Kant. La Habana, 1958.
Phil 1821.15 Vitoux, Pierre. Hisotire des idées en Grande-Bretagne. Paris, 1969.
Phil 4635.10.30 Vitskapen om mennesket ogden filosofiske refleksjon. (Skjervheim, Hans.) Oslo, 1964.
Phil 6331.4.5 Vittoz, Roger. Le docteur Roger Vittoz et l'angoisse de l'homme moderne. Paris, 1965.
Phil 6331.4 Vittoz, Roger. Treatment of neurasthenia by teaching of brain control. London, 1911.
Phil 4655.1.18 Vittra skrifter. 3. uppl. (Wikner, Pontus.) Stockholm, 1894.
Phil 196.19 Vivante, L. Della intelligenza nell'espressione. Roma, 1922.
Phil 8896.11 Vivante, Lello. Principii di etica. Roma, 1920.
Phil 4265.1.40 Vivante, Leone. Elementi di una filosofia della potenzialità. Firenze, 1953.
Phil 196.19.5 Vivante, Leone. Intelligence in expression. London, 1925.
Phil 6331.2 Vivante, Leone. Note sopra la originalitá del pensiero. Roma, 1924?
Phil 6331.2.3 Vivante, Leone. Note sopra la originalità del pensiero. Roma, 1925.
Phil 6331.2.5 Vivante, Leone. Notes on the originality of thought. London, 1927.
Phil 4265.1.41 Vivante, Leone. A philosophy of potentiality. London, 1955.
Phil 7069.37.50 Vivante, Leone. Studi sulle precognizioni. Firenze, 1937.
Phil 5771.3 Vivanti, L. Il concetto della indeterminazione. Firenze, 1938.
Phil 31.10 Vivarium. 1,1963+ 2v.
Phil 8896.20 Vivas, E. The moral life and the ethical life. Chicago, 1950.
Phil 8400.30A Vivas, Eliseo. The problems of aesthetics. N.Y., 1953.
Phil 5400.40 Vives, Juan L. Tratado del alma. Madrid, 1916.
NEDL Phil 4372.1.35 Vives, Juan Luis. Causas de la decadencia de las artes. Buenos Aires, 1948.
Phil 4372.1.40 Vives, Juan Luis. De anima et vita. Torino, 1959.
Htn Phil 8896.3* Vives, Juan Luis. De disciplinis. Lugdunum Batavorum, 1636.
Phil 4372.1.45 Vives, Juan Luis. De veritate fidei christianae libri quinque. Lupluni, 1551.
Htn Phil 4372.1.31* Vives, Juan Luis. I.L. Vivis Valentini, de disciplinis libri XII. Batavorum Lugduni, 1636.
Phil 8896.3.5 Vives, Juan Luis. Introducción á la sabiduria. Valencia, 1779.
Phil 4372.1.1A Vives, Juan Luis. Obras completas. Madrid, 1947-48. 2v.
Phil 4372.1.36 Vives, Juan Luis. Obras sociales y políticas. Madrid, 1960.
Phil 4372.1.5 Vives, Juan Luis. Opera omnia. London, 1964. 8v.
Phil 4372.1.39 Vives, Juan Luis. Satellitium animi. Wien, 1883.
Phil 8896.3.10 Vives, Juan Luis. Vives' introduction to wisdom. N.Y., 1968.
Phil 4372.1.79 Pamphlet box. Vives, Juan Luis.
Phil 4372.1.105 Vives. (Manzoni, Bruno.) Lugano, 1960.
Phil 4372.1.95 Vives. (Paris. Bibliotheque Nationale.) Paris, 1942.
Phil 4372.1.100 Vivés. Paris, 1951.
Phil 8896.3.10 Vives' introduction to wisdom. (Vives, Juan Luis.) N.Y., 1968.
Phil 8050.69 Vlaanderen, Andre. Het zien van kunst en de kunst van het zien. Amsterdam, 1952.
Phil 3246.241 Vlachos, G. Fédéralisme et raison d'état dans la pensée internationale de Fichte. Paris, 1948.
Phil 3246.241.5 Vlachos, G. Fédéralisme et raison d'état dans la pensée internationale de Fichte. Thèse. Paris, 1948.
Phil 3503.14 Vlachos, G. La pensée politique de Kant. Paris, 1962.
Phil 2050.232 Vlachos, Georges. Essai sur la politique de Hume. Athènes, 1955.
Phil 2675.4.10 Vladimir Jankélévitch, ou De l'Effectivité. (Jankélévitch, Vladimir.) Paris, 1969.
Phil 4769.1.103 Vladimir Solov'ev; zhizn' i uchenie. (Mochul'skiĭ, K.) Paris, 1936.
Phil 4769.1.110 Vladimir Solov'ev; zhizn' i uchenie. (Radlov, E.L.) Sankt Peterburg, 1913.
Phil 4769.1.135 Vladimir Solov'ev. (Velichko, Vasilii L.) Sankt Peterburg, 1902.
Phil 4769.1.104 Vladimir Solov'ev. 2. izd. (Mochul'skiĭ, K.) Parizh, 1951.
Phil 4769.1.140 Vladimir Solov'ev und Max Scheler. (Dahm, Helmut.) München, 1971.
Phil 4769.1.82A Vladimir Soloviev. (Severac, B.) Paris, n.d.
Phil 4769.1.107 Vladimir Soloviev et son oeuvre messianique. (Strémoookhoff, D.) Paris, 1935.
Phil 4769.1.107.5 Vladimir Soloviev et son oeuvre messianique. Thèse. (Strémoukhoff, D.) Strasbourg, 1935.
Phil 4769.1.91 Vladimire Solov'eve. Moskva, 1911.
Phil 3503.9 Vleeschauwer, H.J. La déduction transcendentale dans l'oeuvre de Kant. v.1-2,3. Antwerp, 1934-36. 2v.
Phil 3503.9.10 Vleeschauwer, H.J. Development of Kantian thought. London, 1962.

Phil 5400.97 Vleugel, E.S. De samenhang tussen psycho-galvanische reflex en grondeigenschappen van het temperament. Proefschrift. Groningen, 1939.
Phil 2805.391 Vloemans, A. Pascal. Den Haag, 1962.
Phil 1721.5 Vloemans, Antoon. Europa in de spiegel. Den Haag, 1957.
Phil 3841.4 Vloemans, Antoon. Spinoza, de mensch, het leven en het werk. 's Gravenhage, 1931.
Phil 1133.39 Vlolmans, A. De voorsokratici. Den Haag, 1961.
Phil 3841.1.2 Vloten, J. van. Baruck d'Espinoza. Amsterdam, 1865.
Phil 3841.1.15 Vloten, J. van. Benedictus de Spinoza. 2. Aufl. Schiedam, 1871.
Phil 3841.1.10 Vloten, J. van. Spinoza. 's Gravenhage, 1880.
Phil 7069.62.20 Vnushenie na rasstoianii. (Vasil'ev, L.L.) Moskva, 1962.
Phil 5258.204 Vnutrenniaia rech' i myshlenie. (Sokolov, Aleksandr N.) Moskva, 1968.
Phil 150.10 Vocabolarietto di termini filosofici. (Mateucci, Arturo.) Milano, 1925.
Phil 94.2 Vocabulaire de la philosophie. 4. ed. (Jolivet, Régis.) Lyon, 1957.
Phil 5204.12.2 Vocabulaire de la psychologie. 2. éd. (Piéron, Henri.) Paris, 1957.
Phil 5204.12.3 Vocabulaire de la psychologie. 3. éd. (Piéron, Henri.) Paris, 1963.
Phil 2805.261 Le vocabulaire de Pascal. (Jungo, Michel.) Paris, 1950.
Phil 100.2 Vocabulaire de philosophie. (Piquet, Jean Claude.) Paris, 1960.
Phil 2905.1.680 Le vocabulaire de Teilhard de Chardin. (Deckers, Marie Christine.) Gembloux, 1968.
Phil 91.3 Le vocabulaire philosophique. (Goblot, E.) Paris, 1901.
Phil 96.3 Vocabulaire technique et critique de la philosophie. (Lalande, A.) Paris, 1926. 2v.
Phil 96.4.8 Vocabulaire technique et critique de la philosophie. (Lalande, A.) Paris, 1960.
Phil 96.4 Vocabulaire technique et critique de la philosophie. 4. ed. (Lalande, A.) Paris, 1932. 3v.
Phil 186.125 Vocabulaire technique et critique de la philosophie. 6. ed. (Lalande, André.) Paris, 1951.
Phil 87.4 Vocabulario filosófico. (Cantoro, Umberto.) Bologna, 1955.
Phil 96.6 Vocabulario filosófico. (Lopes de Mattos, Carlos.) Sao Paulo, 1957.
Phil 110.5 Vocabulario filosófico. (Zaragueta Bengoechea, Juan.) Madrid, 1955.
Phil 90.1.3 Vocabulary of philosophy. (Fleming, William.) London, 1857.
Phil 90.1 Vocabulary of philosophy. (Fleming, William.) London, 1858.
Phil 90.1.4 Vocabulary of philosophy. 4th ed. (Fleming, William.) N.Y., 1887.
Phil 95.3 Vocabulary of the philosophical sciences. (Krauth, C.P.) N.Y., 1878.
Phil 4960.620 Vocação filosófica do Brasil. (Souza, Remy de.) Salvador, 1960.
Phil 2475.1.380 La vocation de Bergson. (Guitton, Jean.) Paris, 1960.
Phil 2520.255 La vocation de Descartes. v.1-3. (Lefèvre, Roger.) Paris, 1956-1957. 2v.
Phil 2477.6.175 La vocation de la liberté. (Parys, Jean M. van.) Paris, 1968.
Phil 2725.35.110 La vocation de la liberté chez Louis Lavelle. (Hardy, Gilbert G.) Paris, 1968.
Phil 2733.94.7 La vocation de Malebranche. (Gouhier, Henri.) Paris, 1926.
Phil 3246.68.3 Vocation of man. (Fichte, Johann Gottlieb.) Chicago, 1906.
Phil 3246.68 Vocation of man. (Fichte, Johann Gottlieb.) London, 1848.
Phil 3246.68.15 The vocation of man. (Fichte, Johann Gottlieb.) N.Y., 1956.
Phil 8897.59 Vocational guidance. (Wilson, M.H.) Boston, 1916.
Phil 5850.230.11 Vocational psychology and character analysis. (Hollingworth, H.L.) N.Y., 1931.
Phil 2725.2.75 Una voce di prigione. (Lamennais, F.R. de.) Genova, 1850.
Phil 9430.21 Vögele, Albert. Der Pessimismus und das Tragische in Kunst und Leben. Freiburg, 1910.
Phil 8601.13A Voegelin, Eric. Die politischen religionen. Stockholm, 1939.
Phil 3018.35 Der Völherbundsgedanke zur Zeit. (Schoch, Otto D.) Zürich, 1960.
Phil 1135.176 Voelke, Andre J. Les rapports avec Autrui dans la philosophie grecque d'Aristole à Panetius. Paris, 1961.
Phil 3915.70 Völkerpsychologie. (Wundt, Wilhelm.) Leipzig, 1900- 5v.
Phil 3915.70.2 Völkerpsychologie. 2nd ed. (Wundt, Wilhelm.) Leipzig, 1908-20. 12v.
Phil 3805.156 Völter, Hans. Schleiermacher und die Gegenwart. Heilbronn, 1919.
Phil 196.34 Vogel, Arthur A. Reality. London, 1959.
Phil 196.14 Vogel, August. Die höchsten FragenBeleuchtet von den grössten Denkern der Neuzeit. Berlin, 1896-
Phil 821.2 Vogel, August. Uberblick über der Geschichte der Philosophie. Leipzig, 1904-05. 2v.
Phil 1126.2 Vogel, C. Greek philosophy. Leiden, 1950. 3v.
Phil 5261.18 Vogel, C.L. Psychology and the Franciscan school. N.Y., 1932.
Phil 1750.166.230 Vogel, Cornelia Johanna de. Het humanisme en zijn historische achtergrond. Assen, 1968.
Phil 850.48 Vogel, Cornelia Johanna de. Studies in Greek philosophy. Assen, 1970.
Htn Phil 3801.872* Vogel, Emil F. Schelling oder Hegel oder Keiner von Beyden? Leipzig, 1843.
Phil 8430.35 Vogel, Heinrich. Der Christ und das Schöne. 1. Aufl. Berlin, 1955.
Phil 3640.720 Vogel, Martin. Apollinisch und Dionysisch; Geschichte eines genialen Irrtums. Regensburg, 1966.
Phil 3585.12.80 Vogel, Paul. Theodor Litt. Berlin, 1955.
Phil 8601.7 Vogel, W. La religion de l'évolutionisme. Bruxelles, 1912.
Phil 8601.15 Vogeler, H. Friede. Bremen, 1922.
Phil 3805.190 Vogelsang, A.A. De preeken von Schleiermacher Praefschrift. Leiden, 1916.
Phil 3450.19.90 Vogl, A. Das Problem des Selhstseins bei Heidegger und Kierkegaard. Diss. Giessen, 1936.
Phil 9035.20 Vogler, M. Die Verwahrlosung der modernen Charakters. Leipzig, 1884.
NEDL Phil 497.2.9 Vogt, C. Köhlerglaube und Wissenschaft...Wagner. Giessen, 1856.
Phil 3503.7 Vogt, Carl. Darstellung und Beurtheilung der Kant'schen und Hegel'schen Christologie. Marburg, 1878.

Phil 9075.25   Vogt, Fritz. Das Wesen des Gewissens. Inaug. Diss. Greifswald, 1908.

Phil 6536.7   Vogt, Heinrich. Die Epilepsie im Kindesalter mit besonderer Berücksichtigung erzieherischer, unterrichtlicher und forensischer Fragen. Berlin, 1910.

Phil 5261.9   Vogt, P. Studenbilder der philosophischen Propadeutik. Freiburg, 1909. 2v.

Phil 1821.5   Vogt, P.B. From John Stuart Mill to William James. Washington, 1914.

Phil 8422.11   Vogt, T. Form und Gehalt in der Ästhetik. Wien, 1865.

Htn   Phil 2520.88.5*   Voiage du monde de Descartes. (Daniel, Gabriel.) Paris, 1690.

Phil 2520.88.7   Voiage du monde de Descartes. (Daniel, Gabriel.) Paris, 1691.

Phil 5520.30.5   Voice, speech, thinking. 2. ed. (Fruttchey, Frank.) Detroit, Mich., 1920.

Phil 7069.26.10   The voice. (Halford, J.) London, 1926.

Phil 6111.37   The voice eternal. 2nd ed. (Boyd, T.P.) San Francisco, 1912-14.

Phil 978.28   The voice of Isis. (Curtiss, H.A.) Los Angeles, 1912.

Phil 6962.35.1   The voice of neurosis. (Moses, Paul Joseph.) N.Y., 1954.

Phil 186.20   The voice of the machines. (Lee, G.S.) Northampton, 1906.

Phil 978.5.13   The voice of the silence. (Blavatsky, H.P.) N.Y., 1889.

Phil 978.5.12   The voice of the silence. (Blavatsky, H.P.) N.Y., 1889.

Phil 978.5.22   The voice of the silence. (Blavatsky, H.P.) Peking, 1927.

Phil 978.5.20   The voice of the silence. 4th ed. (Blavatsky, H.P.) Point Loma, 1920.

Phil 978.5.15   The voice of the silence. 5th ed. (Blavatsky, H.P.) London, 1896.

Phil 978.5.18   The voice of the silence. 6th ed. (Blavatsky, H.P.) London, 1903.

Phil 9340.3   Voice to youth. (Austin, J.M.) N.Y., 1847.

Phil 7069.31.5   The voice triumphant, the revelations of a medium. (Cook, Ellen A.P.) N.Y., 1931.

Phil 7069.13.30   The voices. (Moore, William U.) London, 1913.

Phil 7054.67   Voices from spirit-land. (White, N.F.) N.Y., 1854.

Phil 6327.12.50   Voices from the inaudible. (Reik, Theodor.) N.Y., 1964.

Phil 7069.12.10   Voices from the open door. (Fish, Dean.) Cleveland, 1912.

Phil 7069.19.200   Voices from the void. (Smith, Hester T.) N.Y., 1919.

Phil 178.12.14   Voices of freedom. (Dresser, H.W.) N.Y., 1899.

Phil 178.12.12   Voices of hope. (Dresser, H.W.) Boston, 1898.

Phil 8413.34   The voices of silence. (Malraux, Q.) Garden City, 1935.

Phil 672.231   The voices of time. (Fraser, Julius Thomas.) N.Y., 1966.

Phil 9070.60   La voie du bonheur. (Arnoux, André.) Paris, 1957.

Phil 9430.27   Voigt, G. Der moderne Pessimismus. Heilbronn, 1884.

Phil 8050.61   Voigtländer, E. Zur Gesetzlichkeit der abendländischen Kunst. Bonn, 1921.

Phil 5061.6.5   Voishvillo, Evgenii K. Poniatie. Moskva, 1967.

Phil 5061.6   Voishvillo, Evgenii K. Predmet i znachenie logiki. Moskva, 1960.

Phil 6971.3   Voisin, A. Lecons cliniques...maladies mentales. Paris, 1883.

Phil 6971.2   Voisin, F. Des causes...maladies mentales. Paris, 1826.

Phil 6750.9   Voisin, J. L'idiotie. Paris, 1893.

Phil 2477.15.110   Voisin, Marcel. Bachelard. Bruxelles, 1967.

Phil 352.4   Voit, Carl von. Ueber die Entwicklung der Erkenntniss. München, 1878.

Phil 310.520   Voitko, V.I. Dialekticheskii i istoricheskii materializm. Kiev, 1962.

Phil 2725.2.76   Une voix de prison. (Lamennais, F.R. de.) Paris, 1954.

Phil 3450.11.400   La voix et le phénomène, introduction au problème du signe dans la phénoménologie de Husserl. (Derride, Jacques.) Paris, 1967.

Phil 8980.872   Vokrug tebia, khoroshie liudi. Moskva, 1961.

Phil 3808.181   La "Volanta" in Arturo Schopenhauer. (Bonanno, S.) Torino, 1903.

Phil 106.1.13   Volataire, Francois Marie Arouet de. Dictionnaire philosophique. Paris, 1961.

Phil 2125.81   Volbeda, S. De intuitieve philosophie van James McCosh. Grand Rapids, n.d.

Phil 8422.2   Volbehr, Theodor. Gibt es Kunstgesetze. Esslingen, 1906.

Phil 8125.16   Volbehr, Theodor. Das Verlangen nach einer neuen deutschen Kunst. Leipzig, 1901.

Phil 3841.2   Vold, J.M. Spinozas erkjendelsestheori. Kristiania, 1888.

Phil 196.18   Vold, J.M. Verdensbetragtning, Sokrates og fantasi. Kristiania, 1889.

Phil 3492.2.55   Vold, John M. Albrecht Krause's Darstellung der Kantischen Raumtheorie und der Kantischen Lehre. Cristiania, 1885.

Phil 7082.138   Vold, John Mourly. Uber den Traum. Leipzig, 1910-1912. 2v.

Phil 7069.19.225   Vold, Karl. Andatrú vorra tíma. Reykjavik, 1919.

Phil 8422.17   Volek, Jaroslav. O předmětu a metodě estetáky a obecne teorie umění. Praha, 1963.

Phil 8422.17.5   Volek, Jaroslav. Základy obecné teorie umění. Praha, 1968.

Phil 5761.8   Volenté et liberté! (Lutoslawski, W.) Paris, 1913.

Phil 9560.27.5   Volgarizzamento della forma di onesta vita. (Martinus, Dumiensis.) Napoli, 1863.

Phil 2421.5   Volgin, V.P. Razvitie obshchestvennoi mysli vo Frantsii v XVIII veke. Moskva, 1958.

Phil 978.49.205   Das volk Schillers und Fichtes. (Steiner, R.) Dornach, 1930.

Phil 3808.103   Volkelt, J. Arthur Schopenhauer. Stuttgart, 1901.

Phil 352.1   Volkelt, J. Erfahrung und Denken. Hamburg, 1886.

Phil 352.1.2   Volkelt, J. Erfahrung und Denken. Aufl. 2. Leipzig, 1924.

Phil 352.1.15   Volkelt, J. Gewissheit und Wahrheit. München, 1918.

Phil 352.1.5   Volkelt, J. Die quellen der menschlichen Gewissheit. München, 1906.

Phil 8422.5   Volkelt, J. System der Ästhetik. München, 1905-14. 3v.

Phil 3415.88   Volkelt, J. Das Unbewusste und der Pessimismus. Berlin, 1873.

Phil 5400.78   Volkelt, J. Versuch über Fühlen und Wollen. München, 1930.

Phil 8422.15   Volkelt, Johannes. Das ästhetische Bewusstsein. Photoreproduction. München, 1920.

Phil 8422.15.5   Volkelt, Johannes. Asthetische Zeitfragen. München, 1895.

Phil 3503.5   Volkelt, Johannes. Immanuel Kant's Erkenntnisstheorie nach ihren Grundprincipien Analysirt. Leipzig, 1879.

Phil 3503.5.10   Volkelt, Johannes. Kant als Philosoph des Unbedingten. Erfurt, 1924.

Phil 3503.5.5   Volkelt, Johannes. Kant's kategorischer Imperativ. Wien, 1875.

Phil 672.135   Volkelt, Johannes. Phänomenologie und Metaphysik der Zeit. München, 1925.

Phil 575.67   Volkelt, Johannes. Das Problem der Individualität. München, 1928.

Phil 7082.36   Volkelt, Johannes. Die Traum-Phantasie. Stuttgart, 1875.

Phil 5831.4   Volkelt, Johannes. Über die vorstellungen Deutiere. v.2. Leipzig, 1914.

Phil 3120.30.22A   Volker, Staaten und Zion. (Buber, Martin.) Berlin, 1917.

Phil 1721.1   Volkett, J. Vorträge zur Einführung in die Philosophie der Gegenwart. Photoreproduction. München, 1892.

Phil 9035.73   Volkmann, E. Uber die Formkraft des Vorbildes für die Charakterprägung in der Reifezeit. Inaug. Diss. Würzburg, 1936.

Phil 352.3   Volkmann, P. Erkenntnistheoretische Grundzüge der Naturwissenschaften. Leipzig, 1896.

Phil 352.3.5   Volkmann, P. Erkenntnistheoretische Grundzüge der Naturwissenschaften. Leipzig, 1910.

Phil 496.1   Volkmann, P. Die materialistische Epoche des neunzehnten Jahrhunderts. Leipzig, 1909.

Phil 510.20.5   Volkmann, Paul. Die Eigenart der Natur und der Eigensinn des Monismus. Leipzig, 1910.

Phil 510.20   Volkmann, Paul. Fähigkeiten der Naturwissenschaften und Monismus der Gegenwart. Leipzig, 1909.

Phil 5261.1   Volkmann, W. Lehrbuch der Psychologie. Göthen, 1875-76. 2v.

Phil 5261.1.3   Volkmann, W. Lehrbuch der Psychologie. Göthen, 1884-8. 2v.

Phil 5261.1.2   Volkmann, W. Lehrbuch der Psychologie. v.1-2. Göthen, 1884-85.

Phil 3640.755   Volkmann-Schluck, Karl Heinz. Leben und Denken. Frankfurt, 1968.

Phil 3801.872.25   Volkmann-Schluck, Karl Heinz. Mythos und Logos. Berlin, 1969.

Phil 5585.73   Volkov, N.N. Vospriiatie predmeta i risunka. Moskva, 1950.

Phil 9150.34   Volkova, Emma V. Determinatsaia evoliutsionnogo professor. Minsk, 1971.

Phil 9250.34   Volkova, Emma V. Determinatsiia evoliutsionnogo protsessa. Minsk, 1971.

Phil 3195.3.84   Volkova, V.V. Iosif Ditsgen. Moskva, 1961.

Phil 3640.19   Volks-Nietzsche. (Nietzsche, Friedrich.) Berlin, 1931. 4v.

Phil 2725.2.52.5   Das Volksbuch von Félicité de Lamennais. (Lamennais, F.R. de.) Leipzig, 1905.

Phil 3425.116.5   Der Volksgeist bei Hegel. (Brie, S.) Berlin, 1909.

Phil 5262.44   Volkskunde und Psychologie; eine Einführung. (Weiser-Aall, Lily.) Berlin, 1937.

Phil 7060.45.5   Volkspsychologie. (Kleinpaul, R.) Berlin, 1914.

Phil 821.1.10   Volkstümliche Geschichte der Philosophie. 3. Aufl. (Vorländer, K.) Berlin, 1923.

Phil 3801.775.20   Die Vollendung des deutschen Idealismus in der Spätphilosophie Schellings. (Schulz, Walter.) Stuttgart, 1955.

Phil 5031.1   Vollenhoven, D.H.T. De noodzakelijkheid eener christelijke logica. Amsterdam, 1932.

Phil 3110.177   Der Vollkommene Mensch nach Böhme. (Benz, E.) Stuttgart, 1937.

Phil 821.7   Vollrath, Ernst. Die These der Metaphysik. Wuppertal, 1969.

Phil 180.33.10   Das Vollwirkliche und das Als-ob. (Fischer, Ludwig.) Berlin, 1921.

Phil 6980.772   Volmat, R. L'art pyschopathologique. Paris, 1956.

Phil 31.4   Volná myslenka. Praha. 1-7 4v.

Phil 8980.602   Volneniia, radosti, nadezoidy. (Nemtsov, V.I.) Moskva, 1961.

Phil 8896.17   Volney, C.F.C. The law of nature, or Principles of morality. Philadelphia, 1796.

Phil 8896.17.5   Volney, C.F.C. La loi naturelle. Paris, 1934.

Phil 5762.8   La volontà. (Marucci, Achille.) Roma, 1903.

Phil 3808.65.30   La volontà nella natura. (Schopenhauer, Arthur.) Milano, 1927.

Phil 5768.8   La volonté. 5. éd. (Surbled, G.) Paris, n.d.

Phil 184.3.7.15   La volonté de croire. (James, W.) Paris, 1920.

Phil 8582.33.2   La volonté de vivre. 2. éd. (Charbonnel, Victor.) Paris, 1898.

Phil 510.128   Volonté e conscience. (Frutiger, P.) Genève, 1920.

Phil 2733.115   La volonté selon Malebranche. (Drefus, Ginette.) Paris, 1958.

Phil 8407.22   Volontés de l'art moderne. (Goudal, Jean.) Paris, 1927.

Phil 310.614   Volovik, L.A. Istina v marksistskoi i domarksovoi filosofii. Moskva, 1965.

Phil 8422.13   Volpe, G. della. Fondamenti di una filosofia dell'espressione. Bologna, 1936.

Phil 5061.5   Volpe, G. della. Logica come scienza positiva. Messina, 1950.

Phil 5061.5.2   Volpe, G. della. Logica come scienza positiva. 2. ed. Messina, 1956.

Phil 402.10   Volpe, Galvano della. Critica dell'ideologia contemporanea. Roma, 1967.

Phil 2050.216   Volpe, Galvano della. Hume, o Il genio dell'empirismo. Firenze, 1939.

Phil 4120.4.80   Volpe, Galvano della. L'idealismo dell'atto e il problema delle categorie. Bologna, 1924.

Phil 2050.201   Volpe, Galvano della. La teoria delle passioni di Davide Hume. Bologna, 1931.

Phil 3425.255   Volpe, Galvano di. Hegel romantico e mistico (1793-1800). Firenze, 1929.

Phil 8090.8   Volpe, Galvo della. Crisi dell'estetica romantica. Roma, 1963.

Phil 3450.11.375   Voltaggio, Franco. Fondamenti della logica di Husserl. Milano, 1965.

Phil 2915.33   Voltaire, F.M.A. de. The ignorant philosopher. Glasgow, 1767.

Phil 2915.35   Voltaire, F.M.A. de. The ignorant philosopher. London, 1779.

Phil 2915.31   Voltaire, F.M.A. de. The ignorant philosopher. N.Y., 185-?

Htn   Phil 2915.74*   Voltaire, F.M.A. de. Lettre philosophique. Berlin, 1774.

Phil 2915.75   Voltaire, F.M.A. de. Lettres philosophiques. Paris, 1909. 2v.

Phil 2915.75.2   Voltaire, F.M.A. de. Lettres philosophiques. Paris, 1918.

Htn   Phil 2915.30*   Voltaire, F.M.A. de. Le philosophe ignorant. n.p., 1766.

Phil 2915.70   Voltaire, F.M.A. de. Philosophical dictionary of M. de Voltaire. N.Y., 1830.

Phil 2915.40   Voltaire, F.M.A. de. La philosophie. Paris, 1848.

Htn   Phil 2915.42*   Voltaire, F.M.A. de. Recueil necessaire. Leipsik, 1765[1766].

Phil 2915.51   Voltaire, F.M.A. de. Traité de métaphysique, 1734. Manchester, 1937.

Phil 106.1.25   Voltaire, Francois Marie Arouet de. Aus dem philosophischen Wörterbuch. Frankfurt, 1967.

Htn   Phil 106.1.3*   Voltaire, Francois Marie Arouet de. Dictionnaire philosophique. London, 1765.

Htn Phil 106.1.2* Voltaire, Francois Marie Arouet de. Dictionnaire philosophique. Londres, 1765.

Htn Phil 106.1* Voltaire, Francois Marie Arouet de. Dictionnaire philosophique. n.p., 1765.

Phil 106.1.4 Voltaire, Francois Marie Arouet de. Dictionnaire philosophique. Paris, 1816. 14v.

Phil 106.1.5 Voltaire, Francois Marie Arouet de. Dictionnaire philosophique. Paris, 1935-36. 2v.

Phil 106.1.10 Voltaire, Francois Marie Arouet de. Dictionnaire philosophique. Paris, 1954.

Phil 106.1.30 Voltaire, Francois Marie Arouet de. Dictionnaire philosophique. Paris, 1967.

Phil 106.1.12 Voltaire, Francois Marie Arouet de. Dictionnaire philosophique. 6. ed. Londres, 1767. 2v.

Phil 106.1.7 Voltaire, Francois Marie Arouet de. A philosophical dictionary. London, 1824. 6v.

Phil 106.1.20 Voltaire, Francois Marie Arouet de. Philosophical dictionary. N.Y., 1969. 2v.

Phil 106.1.6 Voltaire, Francois Marie Arouet de. The philosophical dictionary. v.1-2. London, 1819.

Phil 106.1.15 Voltaire, Francois Marie Arouet de. Voltaire's philosophical dictionary. N.Y., 193-.

Phil 2915.81 Voltaire. 4e Aufl. (Strauss, D.F.) Bonn, 1877.

Phil 106.1.15 Voltaire's philosophical dictionary. (Voltaire, Francois Marie Arouet de.) N.Y., 193-.

Phil 8846.1 Voltz, H. Die Ethik als Wissenschaft. Strassburg, 1886.

Phil 5585.155 Voluminalfigurale faenomener. (Johansen, Martin.) København, 1959.

Phil 5400.22 Volumpulscurven bei Gefühlen und Affecten. (Gent, W.) Leipzig, 1903.

Phil 5811.17 La voluntad en los microorganismos. (Brenes Mesén, Roberto.) Costa Rica, 1905.

Phil 3010.10 Der Voluntarismus. (Knauer, Rudolf.) Berlin, 1907.

Phil 5649.7 Voluntary isolation of control in a natural muscle group. Diss. (Barnes, J.C.) Princeton, 1916.

Phil 5780.3 Voluntary movement. (Rowe, E.C.) n.p., 1910.

Phil 6840.2 La volupté dans la souffrance. (Gagey, Roland.) Paris, 1970?

Phil 8896.2A Voluseno, F. De animi tranquillitate dialogus. Edinburg, 1751.

Phil 1135.20 Volution of theology in Greek philosophers. (Caird, Edward.) Glasgow, 1904. 2v.

Phil 5880.5 Volwassenheid. (Roscam Abbing, Pieter Johan.) Hilversum, 1968.

Phil 3552.99 Volz, L. Die Erkenntnisstheorien bei Leibniz und Kant. Rostock, 1895.

Phil 3120.25 Vom Adel des Geistes; gesammelte Reden. (Bohnenblust, Gottfried.) Zürich, 1943.

Phil 6027.2 Vom Ausdruck des Menschen. (Rutz, Ottmar.) Celle, 1925.

Phil 9346.11 Vom Baume der Erkenntnis. (Gizycki, Paul von.) Berlin, 1897.

Phil 5374.14.9 Vom Bewusstsein. (Hoffmann, Alfred.) Leipzig, 1907.

Phil 5374.29 Vom Bewusstsein. (Uphues, Goswin.) Osterwieck, 1904.

Phil 5374.27 Vom Bewusstsein in Zustanden sogennanten Bewusstlosigkeit. (Koch, Julius L.A.) Stuttgart, 1877.

Phil 8612.28 Vom Bild und Sinn des Todes. (Husemann, F.) Dresden, 1938.

Phil 8612.28.5 Vom Bild und Sinn des Todes. 2. Aufl. (Husemann, F.) Stuttgart, 1954.

Phil 806.15 Vom Brahma zur Existenz. 2. Aufl. (Gabriel, Leo.) Wien, 1954.

Phil 8656.21 Vom Dasein Gottes. (Brentano, Franz.) Leipzig, 1929.

Phil 5040.17 Vom dem Nutzen und der Einrichtung eines zu logischen uebingen Bestimmten Collegimus. (Abicht, Johann H.) Leipzig, 1790.

Phil 5058.38 Vom Denken und Erkennen. (Switalski, B.W.) Kempten, n.d.

Phil 3640.550 Vom deutschen Verhängnis. (Salin, Edgar.) Hamburg, 1959.

Phil 5243.25 Vom Diesseits der Seele. (Dessoir, Max.) Leipzig, 1923.

Phil 3110.36.30 Vom dreifachen Leben des Menschen. (Böhme, J.) Hamburg, 1924.

Phil 3120.15.50 Vom Einsiedler Constantin Brunner. (Brunner, Constantin.) Potsdam, 1924.

Phil 4803.462.55 Vom Erkennen des literarischen Kunstwerks. (Ingarden, Roman.) Tübingen, 1968.

Phil 8893.67.5 Vom ethischen Skeptizismus; Rede. (Stumpf, Karl.) Berlin, 1908.

Phil 8893.67 Vom ethischen Skeptizismus. (Stumpf, Karl.) Leipzig, 1909.

Phil 8598.46.2 Vom Ewigen im Menschen. 2e Aufl. (Scheler, Max.) Leipzig, 1923. 2v.

Phil 5190.94 Vom Fragen. Inaug. Diss. (Thilo, Ingmar.) München, 1969.

Phil 5761.12 Vom Fühlen, Wollen und Denken. (Lipps, Theodor.) Leipzig, 1902.

Phil 5761.12.3 Vom Fühlen, Wollen und Denken. 3. Aufl. (Lipps, Theodor.) Leipzig, 1926.

Phil 3625.4.30 Vom Gebeimnis des Lebens. (Müller, J.) Stuttgart, 1953. 3v.

Phil 1523.7 Vom Geist des ausgehenden Mittelalters. (Stadelmann, R.) Halle, 1929.

Htn Phil 972.18 Vom Geist des Nordens. (Maendl, Hans.) Stuttgart, 1966.

Htn Phil 2880.1.50* Vom Geist und Wesen der Dinge. v.1-2. (Saint-Martin, L.C.) Leipzig, 1812.

Phil 176.110.5 Vom geistigen Leben und Schaffen. (Becker, Carl.) Berlin, 1912.

Phil 9075.80 Vom Gesetz zum Gewissen. (Ziegler, Josef Georg.) Freiburg, 1968.

Phil 3450.11.460 Vom Gesichtspunkt des Phänomenologie. (Boehm, Rudolf.) Den Haag, 1968[1969]

Phil 5265.5 Vom Gleichgewicht der Seele. (Zippert, Erwin.) Ulm, 1958.

Phil 5421.5 Vom Heimweh. (Ernst, F.) Zürich, 1949.

Htn Phil 3800.130* Vom ich als Princip der Philosophie. (Schelling, F.W.J. von.) Tübingen, 1795.

Phil 6313.4.3 Vom Jenseits der Seele. 3. Aufl. (Dessoir, Max.) Stuttgart, 1919.

Phil 8612.13 Vom Leben und Sterben. 3. Aufl. (Müller, J.) München, 1913.

Phil 5815.10.2 Vom Leben zum Erleben. 2. Aufl. (Fischel, Werner.) München, 1967.

Phil 3195.6.115 Vom Leben zur Wahrheit. (Hoefer, Josef.) Freiburg, 1936.

Phil 3110.42 Vom Lebendigen Glauben. (Böhme, J.) Gütersloh, 1960.

Phil 3195.6.109 Vom Lebens- und Gedankenkreis Wilhelm Diltheys. (Misch, Georg.) Frankfurt, 1947.

NEDL Phil 184.16.5 Vom Lebenswege. (Jodl, F.) Stuttgart, 1916-1917. 2v.

Phil 3850.27.23 Vom Lich in Uns. (Schweitzer, A.) Stuttgart, 1947.

Phil 1540.34 Vom Menschenbild des christlichen Mittelalters. (Steinbueckel, T.) Basel, 1953.

Phil 3018.14 Vom Menschenrätsel. (Steiner, R.) Berlin, 1918.

Phil 5241.120 Vom menschlichen Denken. (Brecht, F.J.) Heidelberg, 1955.

Phil 5420.20 Vom menschlichen Selbst. Stuttgart, 1965.

Phil 2115.49.8 Vom menschlichen Verstande. (Locke, J.) Mannheim, 1791.

Phil 8430.68 Vom Musikalisch-Schönen. 16. Aufl. (Hanslick, Eduard.) Wiesbaden, 1966.

Phil 1135.94 Vom mythos zum logos. (Doerfler, Josef.) Freistadt, 1914.

Phil 6335.5 Vom Nervensystem. 3. Aufl. (Zander, R.) Leipzig, 1918.

Phil 3640.63.10 Vom Nietzen un Nachteil der Historie für das Leben. (Nietzsche, Friedrich.) Leipzig, 1931.

Phil 3850.32.85 Vom Positivismus zum Universalismus. (Rieber, Arnulf.) Berlin, 1971.

Phil 5247.37.10 Vom Problem des Rhythmus. (Hönigswald, R.) Leipzig, 1926.

Phil 1750.385 Vom Schein zum Sein. (Staritz, Ekkehart.) Bonn, 1953.

Phil 8411.26 Vom Schönen und seiner Wahrheit. (Koebner, R.) Berlin, 1957.

Phil 730.15 Vom Sein der Universalien. (Schobinger, J.P.) Winterthur, 1958.

Phil 185.21.2 Vom Sein und von der Seele. 2. Aufl. (Kinkel, Walter.) Giessen, 1914.

Phil 665.25 Vom Selbstbewusstsein. (Christiansen, Broder.) Berlin, 1912.

Phil 7150.33 Vom Selbstmorde. (Less, G.) Göttingen, 1786.

Phil 3195.14.50 Vom Sinn der Erkenntnis. (Dacqué, Edgar.) München, 1932.

Phil 3090.24.10 Vom Sinn der Gesellschaft. (Baader, Franz von.) Köln, 1966.

Phil 3120.45.30 Vom Sinn der Philosophie und ihrer Geschichte. (Brandenstein, Béla.) Bonn, 1957.

Phil 3549.17 Vom Sinn der Selbsterkenntnis. (Kanthack, Katharina.) Berlin, 1958.

Phil 5258.114 Vom Sinn der Sinne. (Straus, Erwin.) Berlin, 1935.

Phil 6129.9 Vom Sinn des Körpers. (Tepp, Max.) Hamburg, 1919.

Phil 3549.8.40 Vom Sinn des Lebens. (Klages, Ludwig.) Jena, 1943.

Phil 8612.49 Vom Sinn des Todes. (Wasmuth, E.) Heidelberg, 1959.

Phil 3640.237 Vom Sinn des Tragischen bei Nietzsche. (Hirschhorn, S.) Freiburg, 1930.

Phil 5241.17.20 Vom sinnlichen und noetischen Bewusstsein. (Brentano, Franz.) Leipzig, 1928.

Phil 8876.162 Vom sittlichen Bewusstsein. (Blumenfeld, Walter.) Bonn, 1968.

Phil 5811.19.12 Vom Spielraum der Freiheit. 2. Aufl. (Bally, Gustav.) Basel, 1966.

Phil 182.57 Vom Strome des Seins. (Haacke, Wilhelm.) Leipzig, 1905.

Phil 8612.32 Vom Tod; essay. (Ziegler, L.) Leipzig, 1937.

Phil 7082.176 Vom Traumbewusstsein. (Klages, Ludwig.) Hamburg, 1952.

Phil 7069.66.40 Vom übersinnlichen Wesen des Menschen. (Schult, Arthur.) Bietigheim, 1966.

Phil 3110.55.25 Vom übersinylichen Leben. (Böhme, J.) Hamburg, 1954.

Phil 187.135.5 Vom überzeitlichen in der Zeit. (Medicus, Fritz.) Zürich, 1954.

Phil 5590.285 Vom Umgang mit sich Selbst. (Hylander, Ernst.) München, 1958.

Phil 735.18.2 Vom Umsturz der Werte. 2e Aufl. (Scheler, Max.) Leipzig, 1919. 2v.

Phil 3850.18.25 Vom Umsturz der Werte. 4. Aufl. v.2,3,5,6,8,10. (Scheler, Max.) Bern, 1955. 7v.

Phil 346.1 Vom Ursprung der Menschlichen Erkenntnis. (Proelss, K.R.) Leipzig, 1879.

Phil 8876.41.9 Vom Ursprung sittlicher Erkenntnis. (Brentano, Franz.) Hamburg, 1955.

Phil 8876.41.6 Vom Ursprung sittlicher Erkenntnis. (Brentano, Franz.) Leipzig, 1889.

Phil 8876.41.7A Vom Ursprung sittlicher Erkenntnis. 2e Aufl. (Brentano, Franz.) Leipzig, 1921.

Phil 194.48 Vom Ursprung und Ende der Metaphysik. (Topitsch, Ernst.) Wien, 1958.

Phil 165.35.5 Vom Ursprung und Sinn des philosophischen Fragens. (Wagner, Johannes.) Braunschweig, 1954.

Phil 5811.19 Vom Ursprung und von den Grenzen der Freiheit. (Bally, Gustav.) Basel, 1945.

Phil 5545.78 Vom Vergessen. (Erdmann, E.J.E.T.) Berlin, 1869.

Phil 3246.171 Vom Werden dreier Denker. (Fuchs, Emil.) Tübingen, 1914.

Phil 5520.220 Vom Wesen der Sprache. (Rutt, Theodor.) Ratingen, 1957.

Phil 3450.19.59.1 Vom Wesen der Wahrheit. (Heidegger, Martin.) Frankfurt, 1949.

Phil 3450.19.60 Vom Wesen der Wahrheit. 3e Aufl. (Heidegger, Martin.) Frankfurt, 1954.

Phil 349.19 Vom Wesen der Wissenschaft. (Sauerbeck, E.) Leipzig, 1914.

Phil 5374.44.2 Vom Wesen des Bewusstseins. 2e Aufl. (Klages, Ludwig.) Leipzig, 1926.

Phil 5374.44.5 Vom Wesen des Bewusstseins. 4. Aufl. (Klages, Ludwig.) München, 1955.

Phil 5425.112 Vom Wesen des genialen Menschen. (Kuhn-Foelix, August.) Zürich, 1968.

Phil 3450.19.55A Vom Wesen des Grundes. 4e Aufl. (Heidegger, Martin.) Frankfurt, 1955.

Phil 182.106.5 Vom Wesen des Menschen; Natur und Geist. 3. Aufl. (Huch, Ricarda.) Prein, 1922.

Phil 184.31 Vom Wesen des Pluralismus. (Jakowenko, B.) Bonn, 1928.

Phil 5585.66 Vom Wesen des Rhythmus. (Klages, L.) Kampen auf Sylt, 1934.

Phil 3001.15 Vom Wesen deutscher Denker. (Bense, M.) München, 1938.

Phil 3549.18 Vom Wesen und Ursprung der Dummheit. (Kraus, Annie.) Köln, 1961.

Phil 4260.39 Vom Wesen und Weg der geistigen Bildung. (Vico, G.B.) Godesberg, 1947.

Phil 6111.88 Vom Zauberkult zur Psychoanalyse. (Baumer, Franz.) München, 1970.

Phil 3120.15.95 Von Constantin Brunner und seinem Werk. Berlin, 1927.

Phil 3006.10 Von Cusanus bis Marx. (Gropp, Rugard Otto.) Leipzig, 1965.

Phil 8894.16 Von Darwin bis Nietzsche. (Tille, A.) Leipzig, 1895.

Phil 281.20 Von dem ätherischen Raume. (Adams, George.) Stuttgart, 1964.

Phil 5258.80 Von dem Begriffe der Psychologie. (Suabedissen, D.T.A.) Marburg, 1829.

Phil 8597.3.21 Von dem daseyn Gottes und der menschlichen Seele. (Reimarus, Johann Albert Heinrich.) Hamburg, 1781.

Phil 3480.88 Von dem ersten Grunde des Unterschiedes der Gegenden im Raume. (Kant, Immanuel.) Steglitz, 1768[1920]

Htn Phil 1106.5* Von den Leben, sitten und freyen Sprüchen der alten Philosophie. (Burley, W.) Ausburg, 1519.

Phil 8620.16 Von dem Ursprung und den Absichten des Ubels. (Villaume, P.) Leipzig, 1784. 3v.

Phil 8597.3.13 Von dem Zwecke Jesu und seiner Jünger. (Reimarus, H.S.) Berlin, 1784.

Phil 8597.3.12 Von dem Zwecke Jesu und seiner Jünger. (Reimarus, H.S.) Braunschweig, 1778.

Phil 332.20A | Von den Begriffen, den Urteilen und der Wahrheit. (Bon, F.) Leipzig, 1913.

Phil 8631.1 | Von den Beweisen für die Unsterblichkeit der Menschlichen Seele. (Göschel, C.F.) Berlin, 1835.

Phil 3819.28 | Von den festen und ewigen Dingen. (Spinoza, Benedictus de.) Heidelberg, 1925.

Phil 6954.3.10 | Von den Geisteskrankheiten. (Esquirol, Etienne.) Bern, 1968.

Phil 3460.30.2 | Von den göttlichen Dingen und ihrer Offenbarung. (Jacobi, F.H.) Leipzig, 1822.

Phil 7080.14 | Von den Träumen und Nachtwandlern. (Hennings, Justus Christian.) Weimar, 1784.

Phil 6319.1.76 | Von den Wurzeln des Bewusstsens. (Jung, C.G.) Zürich, 1954.

Phil 5025.2 | Von der Analogie zum Syllogismus. (Platzeck, E.W.) Paderborn, 1954.

Phil 3890.8.35 | Von der Artzeney widner die Unvernunfftige Lieben und der zuvorher Nöthigen Erkäntniss sein Sellst. (Thomasius, Christian.) Halle, 1696.

Phil 182.146 | Von der Aufgabe der Philosophie und dem Wesen des Philosophen; zwei Vorlesungen. (Hessen, Johannes.) Heidelberg, 1947.

Phil 8876.91.5 | Von der Bestimmung des Menschen. (Berdiaev, N.A.) Bern, 1935.

Phil 8598.58 | Von der falschen Theologie und der wahren Glauben. (Steffens, H.) Breslau, 1823.

Phil 3850.40 | Von der Feststellung. (Schnitzler, Otto.) Bonn, 1953.

Phil 8412.10.5 | Von der Form des ästhetischen Apperception. (Lipps, Theodor.) Halle, 1902.

Phil 3110.41 | Von den Genaden-Wahl. (Böhme, J.) Amsterdam, 1682.

Phil 3850.60 | Von der Güte und Weisheit Gottes in der Natur. (Sander, Heinrich.) Carlsruhe, 1780.

Phil 978.49.280 | Von der Initiatian. 3. Aufl. (Steiner, R.) Dornach, 1959.

Phil 5241.17.13A | Von der Klassifikation der psychischen Phänomene. (Brentano, Franz.) Leipzig, 1911.

VPhil 9590.34 | Von der Krankheit und Genesung des Seienden, oder Der zweite Sündenfall. (Bergel, Bernard.) Tel-Aviv, 1966.

Phil 3890.8.30 | Von der Kunst vernünftig und tugendhafft zu Lieben als dem eintzigen Mittel zu einen Glückselingen. (Thomasius, Christian.) Halle, 1692.

Phil 3480.85.6.10 | Von der Macht des Gemüths durch den blossen Vorsatz seiner krankhaften Gefühle Meister zu seyn. (Kant, Immanuel.) Königsberg, 1798?

Htn   Phil 3480.85.5* | Von der Macht des Gemüths durch den blossen Vorsatz seiner krankhaften Gefühle Meister zu seyn. (Kant, Immanuel.) Jena, 1798.

Htn   Phil 3480.85.6* | Von der Macht des Gemüths durch den blossen Vorsatz seiner krankhaften Gefühle Meister zu seyn. (Kant, Immanuel.) Jena, 1798.

Phil 3480.85.7 | Von der Macht des Gemüths durch den blossen Vorsatz seiner krankhaften Gefühle Meister zu seyn. (Kant, Immanuel.) Frankfurt, 1800.

Phil 3480.85.9 | Von der Macht des Gemüths durch den blossen Vorsatz seiner krankhaften Gefühle Meister zu seyn. 2. Aufl. (Kant, Immanuel.) Leipzig, 1824.

Phil 3480.85.6.15 | Von der Macht des Gemüths durch den blossen Vorsatz seiner krankhaften Gefühle Meister zu seyn. (Kant, Immanuel.) Leipzig, 1824?

Phil 3480.85.10 | Von der Macht des Gemüths durch den blossen Vorsatz seiner krankhaften Gefühle Meister zu seyn. 3. Aufl. (Kant, Immanuel.) Leipzig, 1836.

Phil 3480.85.11 | Von der Macht des Gemüths durch den blossen Vorsatz seiner krankhaften Gefühle Meister zu seyn. 6. Aufl. (Kant, Immanuel.) Leipzig, 1852.

Phil 3480.85.20 | Von der Macht des Gemüths durch den blossen Vorsatz seiner krankhaften Gefühle Meister zu seyn. (Kant, Immanuel.) Heidelberg, 1924.

Phil 3005.9 | Von der Materialität des Seele. (Finger, Otto.) Berlin, 1961.

Phil 8402.8.5 | Von der Methode der Ästhetik. (Bayer, Raymond.) Darmstadt, 1960.

Phil 8584.9 | Von der Möglichkeit und der Notwendigkeit der reinen Religion. (Eberhardt, Paul.) Gotha, 1916.

Phil 303.20.1 | Von der Natur der Dinge. Mit einer physiognomischen Kupfertafel. Leipzig, 1803. (Wagner, Johann Jacob.) Bruxelles, 1968.

Phil 8050.56 | Von der Notwendigkeit der Kunst. (Fischer, Ernest.) Dresden, 1959.

Phil 3850.18.160 | Von der Ohnmacht des Geistes. (Lenk, Kurt.) Tübingen, 1959.

Phil 186.93 | Von der Pflicht der Philosophie in unserer Zeit. (Liebert, A.) Zürich, 1938.

Phil 5311.2.5 | Von der Psychoanalyse zur Psychosynthese. (Bjerre, P.) Halle, 1925.

Phil 6311.2.5 | Von der Psychoanalyse zur Psychosynthese. (Bjerre, P.) Halle, 1925.

Phil 195.6 | Von der Sache der Philosophie. (Gulmer, Karl.) Freiburg, 1959.

Phil 665.69 | Von der Seele. (Schleich, C.L.) Berlin, 1921.

Phil 177.69 | Von der Selbstoffenbarung des göttlichen Lebens. (Coellen, L.) Darmstadt, 1924.

Phil 974.3.50 | Von der Theosophie Rudolf Steiners. (Rittelmeyer, F.) Nürnberg, 1919.

VPhil 450.8 | Von der Urmaterie zum Urkraft-Elixier. (Retschlag, Max.) Leipzig, 1926.

Phil 4065.50.2 | Von der Ursache, dem Princip und dem Einen. 2. Ausg. (Bruno, Giordano.) Heidelberg, 1889.

Htn   Phil 3480.75.15* | Von der verschiedenen Racen der Menschen. (Kant, Immanuel.) Königsberg, 1775.

Phil 5049.20 | Von der Wahrheit. (Jaspers, Karl.) München, 1947.

Phil 197.73 | Von der Wahrheit der Philosophie. (Wasmuth, E.) Köln, 1952.

Htn   Phil 3800.150* | Von der Weltseele. (Schelling, F.W.J. von.) Hamburg, 1798.

Htn   Phil 3800.150.3* | Von der Weltseele. 2e Aufl. (Schelling, F.W.J. von.) Hamburg, 1806.

Htn   Phil 3800.150.6*A | Von der Weltseele. 3e Aufl. (Schelling, F.W.J. von.) Hamburg, 1809.

Phil 3800.150.2 | Von der Weltseele. 3e Aufl. (Schelling, F.W.J. von.) Hamburg, 1809.

Phil 8581.69.10 | Von der Würde des Christentums und der Unwürde der Christen. 4. Aufl. (Berdiajew, N.A.) Luzern, 1937.

Phil 3480.97 | Von der Würde des Menschen. (Kant, Immanuel.) Leipzig, 1944.

Phil 3195.6.31 | Von deutscher Dichtung und Musik. (Dilthey, Wilhelm.) Leipzig, 1933.

Phil 3195.6.31.2 | Von deutscher Dichtung und Musik. 2. Aufl. (Dilthey, Wilhelm.) Stuttgart, 1957.

Htn   Phil 3801.407.10* | Von deutscher Philosophie...ein Votum für F.H. Jacobi gegen...Schelling. (Fries, Jakob F.) Heidelberg, 1812.

Phil 179.3.125 | Von deutscher Philosophie des Lebens. (Oldendorff, Paul.) Langensalza, 1916.

Phil 6313.25 | Von Freud zu Frankel. (Dienelt, Karl.) Wien, 1967.

Phil 3487.7 | Von G.E. Schulze zu A. Schopenhauer. Diss. (Feder, Ernst.) Aarau, 1901.

Phil 8423.15 | Von Geschmack und seinen Wandlungen. (Weisbach, W.) Basel, 1947.

Phil 7060.66 | Von Gespenstergeschichten. (Diederich, Benno.) Leipzig, 1903.

Phil 3011.8A | Von Hegel bis Nietzsche. (Loewith, Karl.) Zürich, 1941.

Phil 8587.32.95 | Von Hügel and the supernatural. (Dakiri, A.H., Jr.) London, 1934.

Phil 3010.5 | Von Husserl zu Heidegger. (Kraft, J.) Leipzig, 1932.

Phil 3010.5.2 | Von Husserl zur Heidegger. 2. Aufl. (Kraft, J.) Frankfurt, 1957.

Phil 3010.3 | Von Kant bis Hegel. (Kroner, R.) Tübingen, 1921-24. 2v.

Phil 3010.3.2 | Von Kant bis Hegel. v.1-2. (Kroner, R.) Tübingen, 1961.

Phil 8406.14.5 | Von Kunst und Kennerschaft. (Friedländer, Max J.) Zürich, 1946.

Phil 8050.74 | Von Kunst und Künstlern. (Melchers, H.) München, 1953.

Phil 810.9 | Von Lao-Tse zu Sartre. (Kropp, Gerhard.) Berlin, 1953.

Phil 974.3.11 | Von Luther bis Steiner. (Boldt, Ernst.) München, 1921.

Phil 3640.50 | Von neuen Freiheiten des Geistes. 1. Aufl. (Nietzsche, Friedrich.) München, 1943.

Phil 3640.695 | Von Nietzsche zu Pannwitz. (Hess, K.) Lagnau, 1963.

Phil 807.9.2 | Von Plotin zu Goethe. (Hasse, Karl P.) Jena, 1912.

Phil 807.9 | Von Plotin zu Goethe. (Hasse, Karl P.) Leipzig, 1909.

Phil 5258.85.15 | Von Schaltwerk der Gedanken. 47. bis 49. Aufl. (Schleich, Carl Ludwig.) Berlin, 1926.

Phil 3801.125 | Von Schelling's nya lära. (Afzelius, F.G.) Upsala, 1843.

Phil 3805.260 | Von Schleiermacher zu Marx. (Fuchs, Emil.) Berlin, 1969.

Phil 978.49.90 | Von Seelenrätseln. (Steiner, R.) Berlin, 1921.

Phil 3090.39 | Von Segen und Fluch der Creatur. (Baader, Franz von.) Strassburg, 1826.

Phil 3850.27.120 | Von Sinn des Lebens. (Lotar, Peter.) Strasbourg, 1951.

Phil 811.12 | Von Thales bis Heidegger. (Ludat-Deniselle, A.) Ratingen, 1952.

Phil 806.7 | Von Thales bis Steiner. (Gleich, S. von.) Stuttgart, 1920.

Phil 1750.29 | Von Ursprung und Grenzen der Geisteswissenschaften und Naturwissenschaften. (Grassi, E.) Bern, 1950.

Phil 6131.4 | Von Boeckmann P. Nerve force. N.Y., 1919.

Phil 341.18 | Vonden Grenzen des Wissens. (Kurth, R.) München, 1953.

Phil 3549.2.92 | Vondran, Hugo. Kritik der Philosophie des Grafen H. Keyserling. Diss. Erlangen, 1927.

Phil 7054.156 | Von Ravens, Clara I. The scribe of a soul. Seattle, 1901.

Phil 5548.148 | Vontobel, Jacques. Leistungsbedürfnis und soziale Umwelt. Bern, 1970.

Phil 3483.87 | Voobrazhenie i teoriia poznaniia. (Borodai, I.M.) Moskva, 1966.

Phil 3850.52.30 | Voor alleenstaanden. (Stallaert, L.) Rotterdam, 1958.

Phil 1133.39 | De voorsokratici. (Vlolmans, A.) Den Haag, 1961.

Phil 310.582 | Voprosy dialektichskogo materializma; k lektsiiam. (Gurvich, S.S.) Kiev, 1964.

Phil 310.633 | Voprosy dialekticheskogo materializma. (Rostov on the Don, Russia. Gosudarstvennyi Pedagogicheskii. Institut Kafedra Filosofii.) Rostov-na-Donn, 1966.

Phil 310.195 | Voprosy dialekticheskogo materializma. (Akademiia Nauk SSSR. Institut Filosofii.) Moskva, 1963.

Phil 310.570 | Voprosy dialekticheskogo materializma i meditsina. v.2. (Sheputo, L.L.) Moskva, 1963.

Phil 31.17 | Voprosy dialektiki i logiki. Leningrad. 1,1964+

Phil 8400.6 | Voprosy estetiki. Moscow, 1958- 8v.

Phil 8022.5 | Voprosy estetiki [sbornik statei]. Saratov. 1,1963+

Phil 31.5 | Voprosy estetiki. Moskva. 1947+ 15v.

Phil 310.724 | Voprosy filosofii. Novosibirsk, 1968.

Phil 31.12 | Voprosy filosofii i psikhologii. Leningrad. 1,1965+

Phil 31.3 | Voprosy filosofii i psikhologiia. Moskva. 1-28,1890-1917 29v.

Phil 31.14 | Voprosy filosofii i sotsiologii. Leningrad. 1,1969+

Phil 310.673 | Voprosy filosofii i sotsiologii v reskeniiekh XXIII s'ezda KPSS. (Rozhim, Vasilii P.) Leningrad, 1968.

Phil 31.16 | Voprosy gnoseologii, logiki i metodologii nauchnogo issledovaniia. Leningrad. 1,1969+

Phil 310.706 | Voprosy istoricheskogo materializma i kritika nekototorykh kontseptsii burzhnaznoi sotsiologii. Moskva, 1969.

Phil 310.591 | Voprosy istoricheskogo materializma i nauchnogo kommunizma. (Moscow. Institut Povyshennoi Kvalifikatsii Prepodovatelei Obshchestvennykh Nauk. Kafedra Dialekticheskogo i Istoricheskogo Materializma.) Moskva, 1964.

Phil 5500.15 | Voprosy klassifikatsii suzhdenii. (Drozdov, A.V.) Leningrad, 1956.

Phil 8980.581 | Voprosy marksistko-leninskoi etiki. (Moscow. Akademiia Obshchestvennykh Nauk.) Moskva, 1962.

Phil 8980.872.10 | Voprosy marksistko-leninskoi etiki i kommunisticheskogo vospitaniia. Sverdlovsk, 1970.

Phil 8400.10 | Voprosy marksistko-leninskoi estetiki. (Akademiia Nauk SSSR. Institut Filosofii.) Moskva, 1956.

Phil 8980.787.10 | Voprosy marksistko-leninskoi etiki. (Soveshchanie po Voprosam Marksistko-Leninskoi Etiki, Leningrad, 1959.) Moskva, 1960.

Phil 310.666 | Voprosy marksistsko-leninskoi istorii filosofii. Deroslavl', 1967.

Phil 310.465 | Voprosy marksistsko-leninskoi sotsiologii. (Leningrad. Universitet. Filosofskii Fakultet.) Leningrad, 1962.

Phil 310.12.20 | Voprosy metodiki prepodavaniia marksistsko-leninskoi filosofii v vazakh. Moskva. 2,1967+

Phil 310.684 | Voprosy na istoricheskiia materializam. Sofiia. 1,1969+

Phil 8676.7 | Voprosy nauchnogo ateizma. Moskva. 1,1966+ 12v.

Phil 5238.221 | Voprosy psikhologii. (Nauchnaia Sessiia Posviashchennaia 50-Letiiu Velikoi Oktiabr'skoi Sotsialisticheskoi Revoliutsii, Sverdlovsk, 1967.) Sverdlovsk, 1967.

Phil 5238.178 | Voprosy psikhologii. (Novosibirsk. Gosudartvennyi Pedagogicheskii Institut.) Omsk, 1965.

Phil 31.6 | Voprosy psikhologii. Moskva. 1955+ 27v.

Phil 5590.441 | Voprosy psikhologii kharaktera. (Levitov, Nikolai D.) Moskva, 1952.

Phil 5590.385 | Voprosy psikhologii lichnosti. (Ignat'ev, E.I.) Moskva, 1960.

Phil 4710.150 | Voprosy psikhologii myshleniia v trudakh klassikov russkoi filosofii XIX v. (Zimin, Petr P.) Tashkent, 1966.

Phil 31.15 | Voprosy psikhologii vnimaniia. Saratov. 1,1969+

Phil 310.640 Voprosy teoreticheskogo nasledstva V.I. Lenina. (Krasnoiarsk, Siberia (City). Gosudarstvennyi Pedagogicheskii Institut. Kafedra Filosofii.) Krasnoiarsk, 1966.

Phil 8400.66 Voprosy esteticheskogo vospitaniia. Moskva, 1970.
Phil 8170.10 Voprosy teorii i istorii esteiki. (Asmus, Valenti F.) Moskva, 1968.
Phil 4710.115 Voprosy teorii poniatiia. (Chupakhin, I.Ia.) Leningrad, 1961.
Phil 352.13 Voprosy teorii poznaniia. Moskva, 1969.
Phil 352.10 Voprosy teorii poznaniia. Perm, 1961.
Phil 341.36 Voprosy teorii poznaniia dialekticheskogo materializma. (Khaskhachikh, Fedor I.) Moskva, 1967.
Phil 331.21 Voprosy teorii poznaniia i logiki. (Akadamiia Nauk SSSR. Kafedra Filosofii.) Moskva, 1960.
Phil 5190.27 Voprosy suzhdeniia. (Tavanets, P.V.) Moskva, 1955.
Phil 4756.5.31 Voprosy very i tserkvi. (Giliarov-Platonov, N.P.) Moskva, 1905.
Phil 8980.496.5 Voprosy vospitaniia trudiashchikhsia v dukhe kommunisticheskoi nravstvennosti. (Kosolapov, S.M.) Moskva, 1961.
Phil 8400.53 Voprosy zarubezhnoi literatury i estetiki. Moskva, 1967.
Phil 8598.66 Voprosy zhizni. (Strakhov, F.A.) Christchurch, Hants, Eng., 1903.
Phil 5360.14 Vopsosy abstraktsii i obrazovanie poniatiia. (Gorskii, D.P.) Moskva, 1961.
Phil 3450.11.105 Die Vor- phänomenologische philosophie Edmund Husserls. Inaug. Diss. (Illemann, U.) n.p., 1932.
Phil 9495.170.15 Vor- und ausserehelicher Geschlechtsverkehr. (Schlegelberger, Bruno.) Remscheid, 1970.
Phil 4655.2.30 Vor tids determinisme. (Wildhagen, A.) Kristiania, 1887.
Phil 9075.88 Das Vor-Urteil des Gewissens. (Baumhauer, Otto.) Limburg, 1970.
Phil 333.8 Voraussetzungen und Ziele des Erkennens. (Cohn, Jonas.) Leipzig, 1908.
Phil 1817.7 Die voraussetzungen Welche den empiresmus Lockis. Inaug.-Diss. (Raffel, J.) Berlin, 1887?
Phil 5627.9 Vorbrodt, G. Beiträge zur religiösen Psychologie. Leipzig, 1904.
Phil 3565.116 Vorbrodt, G. Principien der Ethick und Religionsphilosophie Lotzes. Dessau, 1891.
Phil 5070.15 Vorbrodt, Gustav. Psychologie des Glaubens. Göttingen, 1895.
Phil 8893.12 Vorfragen der Ethik. (Sigwart, C.) Freiburg, 1886.
Phil 190.37 Vorfragen der Naturphilosophie. (Pfordten, Otto.) Heidelberg, 1907.
Phil 630.36 Vorfragen der Wirklichkeitsphilosophie. (Jaensch, Erich.) Leipzig, 1931.
Phil 193.53.5 Vorgedanken zur Weltanschauung. (Stern, L.W.) Leipzig, 1915.
Phil 1519.1 Vorgeschichte und Jugend der mittelalterlichen Scholastek. (Overbeck, Franz.) Basel, 1917.
Phil 3090.80.15 Vorhalle zur speculativen Lehre F. Baader's. (Hoffmann, F.) Aschaffenburg, 1836.
Phil 8125.6 Vorholz, Gerhard. Der Begriff des Tragischen. Halle, 1932.
Phil 8846.2 Vorländer, F. Geschichte der philosophischen Moral. Marburg, 1855.
Phil 5261.13 Vorländer, F. Grundlinien einer organische Wissenschafte der menschlichen Seele. Berlin, 1841.
Phil 352.2 Vorlaender, F. Wissenschaft der Erkenntniss. Leipzig, 1847.
Phil 821.1.3 Vorländer, K. Geschichte der Philosophie. Leipzig, 1911. 2v.
Phil 821.1.15 Vorländer, K. Geschichte der Philosophie. Leipzig, 1964. 4v.
Phil 821.1 Vorländer, K. Geschichte der Philosophie. v.1-2. Leipzig, 1903.
Phil 821.1.6 Vorländer, K. Geschichte der Philosophie. 6. Aufl. Leipzig, 1921.
Phil 821.1.7 Vorländer, K. Geschichte der Philosophie. 7. Aufl. Leipzig, 1927. 2v.
Phil 821.1.9 Vorländer, K. Geschichte der Philosophie. 9. Aufl. Hamburg, 1949-55. 2v.
Phil 3503.4.15 Vorländer, K. Immanuel Kant. Leipzig, 1924. 2v.
Phil 3503.4.25 Vorländer, K. Immanuel Kant und sein Einfluss auf der deutsche Denken. 2. Aufl. Bielefeld, 1922.
Phil 3503.4 Vorländer, K. Immanuel Kant's Leben. Leipzig, 1911.
Phil 3503.4.2 Vorländer, K. Immanuel Kants Leben. 2. Aufl. Leipzig, 1921.
Phil 3503.4.5 Vorländer, K. Kant, Schiller, Goethe. Leipzig, 1907.
Phil 3503.4.10 Vorländer, K. Kant als Deutscher. Darmstadt, 1919.
Phil 3503.4.6 Vorländer, K. Kant-Schiller-Goethe. 2. Aufl. Leipzig, 1923.
Phil 3503.4.30 Vorländer, K. Kant und der Sozialismus unter besonderer Verücksichtigung der neuesten theoretischen Bewegung innerhalb des Marxismus. Berlin, 1900.
Phil 3503.4.3 Vorländer, K. Die Kantische Begründung der Moralprinzips. Solingen, 1923.
Phil 821.1.10 Vorländer, K. Volkstümliche Geschichte der Philosophie. 3. Aufl. Berlin, 1923.
Phil 2421.1 Vorländer, Karl. Französische Philosophie. Breslau, 1923.
Htn Phil 3801.669.10* Vorläufige Appellation...Contra das Philosophie...Schelling. (Paulus, H.E.G.) Darmstadt, 1843.
Phil 7060.106 Vorläuser des Spiritismus. (Aksakov, Aleksandr N.) Leipzig, 1898.
Phil 3805.100 Vorlander, Franz. Schleiermachers Sittenlehre ausführlich. Marburg, 1851.
Phil 3480.41 Eine Vorlesung Kants über Ethik. (Kant, Immanuel.) Berlin, 1924.
Phil 3480.41.2 Eine Vorlesung Kants über Ethik. 2. Aufl. (Kant, Immanuel.) Berlin, 1925.
Phil 3525.65 Vorlesung über psychische Anthropologie. (Krause, K.C.F.) Leipzig, 1905.
Phil 3090.37 Vorlesungen...über religiöse Philosophie. (Baader, Franz von.) München, 1827.
Phil 193.12 Vorlesungen...Wesen der Philosophie. (Schmid, J.H.) Stuttgart, 1836.
Phil 3480.41.10 Vorlesungen. (Kant, Immanuel.) Berlin, 1961.
Phil 3489.10 Vorlesungen Kants über Metaphysik aus drei Semestern. (Heinze, Max.) Leipzig, 1894.
Phil 3480.59.25 Vorlesungen Kants über Metaphysik aus drei Semestern. (Kant, Immanuel.) Leipzig, 1894.
Phil 8411.20.5 Vorlesungen über Ästhetik. (Kainz, F.) Detroit, 1962.
Phil 8411.20 Vorlesungen über Ästhetik. (Kainz, F.) Wien, 1948.
Phil 8419.42 Vorlesungen über Ästhetik. (Stein, H. von.) Stuttgart, 1897.

Phil 8426.5 Vorlesungen über Ästhetik. (Ziehen, T.) Halle, 1923-25. 2v.
Phil 3525.40 Vorlesungen über das System der Philosophie. (Krause, K.C.F.) Göttingen, 1828.
Phil 3235.55 Vorlesungen über das Wesen der Religion nebst Zusätzen und Anmerkungen. (Feuerbach, Ludwig.) Stuttgart, 1908.
Phil 5058.5.5 Vorlesungen über der Algebra der Logik. (Schröder, E.) Leipzig, 1891-95. 4v.
Phil 3483.33.5 Vorlesungen über der Critik der practischen Vernunft. (Bendavid, L.) Wien, 1796.
Phil 3483.33.10 Vorlesungen über der Critik der reinen Vernunft. (Bendavid, L.) Wien, 1795.
Phil 3483.33 Vorlesungen über der Critik des Urtheilskraft. (Bendavid, L.) Wien, 1796.
Phil 3504.34 Vorlesungen über der Kantische Philosophie. (Will, G.A.) Altdorf, 1788.
Htn Phil 3480.73.5* Vorlesungen über der philosophische Religionslehre. (Kant, Immanuel.) Leipzig, 1794-1817. 2 pam.
Phil 3480.73 Vorlesungen über der philosophische Religionslehre. (Kant, Immanuel.) Leipzig, 1830.
Phil 5625.75.25 Vorlesungen über die Arbeit der Grosshirnhemisphären. (Pavlov, Ivan P.) Lenogiz, 1932.
Phil 807.2.20 Vorlesungen über die Beweise vom Dasein Gottes. (Hegel, Georg Wilhelm Friedrich.) Leipzig, 1930.
Phil 807.2.20 Vorlesungen über die Geschichte der Philosophie. (Hegel, G.W.F.) Leiden, 1908.
Phil 807.2.27 Vorlesungen über die Geschichte der Philosophie. (Hegel, G.W.F.) Leipzig, 1938.
Phil 3915.55.12 Vorlesungen über die Menschen- und Thierseele. (Wundt, Wilhelm.) Hamburg, 1906. 2v.
Phil 3915.55 Vorlesungen über die Menschen- und Thierseele. (Wundt, Wilhelm.) Leipzig, 1863. 2v.
Htn Phil 3915.55.8 Vorlesungen über die Menschen- und Thierseele. 2. Aufl. (Wundt, Wilhelm.) Hamburg, 1892. 2v.
Htn Phil 3480.59.20* Vorlesungen über die Metaphysik. (Kant, Immanuel.) Erfurt, 1821.
Phil 3480.59.21 Vorlesungen über die Metaphysik. 2. Aufl. (Kant, Immanuel.) Rosswein, 1924.
Htn Phil 3800.210* Vorlesungen über die Methode des academische Studium. (Schelling, F.W.J. von.) Tübingen, 1803.
Htn Phil 3800.210.5* Vorlesungen über die Methode des academische Studium. 2e Ausg. (Schelling, F.W.J. von.) Stuttgart, 1813.
Htn Phil 3800.210.10* Vorlesungen über die Methode des academische Studium. 3e Ausg. (Schelling, F.W.J. von.) Stuttgart, 1830.
Phil 8894.3 Vorlesungen über die Moral. (Thiess, J.O.) Leipzig, 1801-03. 2v.
Phil 3425.40.6 Vorlesungen über die Philosophie der Geschichte. (Hegel, Georg Wilhelm Friedrich.) Leipzig, 1907.
Phil 3425.60.10 Vorlesungen über die Philosophie der Religion. (Hegel, Georg Wilhelm Friedrich.) Berlin, 1840. 2v.
Phil 3425.60.15 Vorlesungen über die Philosophie der Religion. (Hegel, Georg Wilhelm Friedrich.) Leiden, 1901. 2v.
Phil 3425.60.16 Vorlesungen über die Philosophie der Religion. (Hegel, Georg Wilhelm Friedrich.) Leipzig, 1944-
Phil 3425.60.12 Vorlesungen über die Philosophie der Religion. (Hegel, Georg Wilhelm Friedrich.) Hamburg, 1966. 2v.
Phil 3425.40.11 Vorlesungen über die Philosophie der Weltgeschichte. (Hegel, Georg Wilhelm Friedrich.) Leipzig, 1944. 4v.
X Cg Phil 3425.40.7 Vorlesungen über die Philosophie der Weltgeschichte. v.2-5. (Hegel, Georg Wilhelm Friedrich.) Leipzig, 1920. 4v.
Phil 8897.12 Vorlesungen über die Sittenlehre. v. 1-2. (Wette, W.M.L. de.) Berlin, 1823-24.
Phil 192.118 Vorlesungen über die theoretische und praktische Philosophie. (Reuss, Materhus.) Bruxelles, 1968.
Phil 8963.2 Vorlesungen über Geschichte der christlichen Ethik. (Neander, A.) Berlin, 1864.
Phil 5050.12 Vorlesungen über Logik. (Kulpe, Oswald.) Leipzig, 1923.
Phil 176.20.5 Vorlesungen über Metaphysik. (Bergmann, J.) Berlin, 1886.
Phil 295.09 Vorlesungen über Naturphilosophie. (Ostwald, W.) Leipzig, 1902.
Phil 295.1 Vorlesungen über Naturphilosophie. 2. Aufl. (Ostwald. W.) Leipzig, 1902.
Phil 8685.17 Vorlesungen über Pantheismus und Theismus. (Weissenborn, G.) Marburg, 1859.
Phil 194.34.15 Vorlesungen über Philosophie. (Troxler, I.P.V.) Bern, 1835.
Phil 188.12.9 Vorlesungen über praktische Philosophie. (Natorp, Paul.) Erlangen, 1925.
Phil 5242.1 Vorlesungen über Psychologie. (Carus, C.G.) Leipzig, 1831.
Phil 5242.53.2 Vorlesungen über Psychologie. (Carus, K.G.) Darmstadt, 1958.
Phil 5242.53 Vorlesungen über Psychologie. (Carus, K.G.) Erlerbach, 193-?
Phil 5243.22 Vorlesungen über Psychologie. (Dressler, Max.) Heidelberg, 1900.
Phil 5250.2.8 Vorlesungen über Psychologie. (Külpe, Oswald.) Leipzig, 1920.
Phil 5250.2.9 Vorlesungen über Psychologie. 2. Aufl. (Külpe, Oswald.) Leipzig, 1922.
Phil 6968.16 Vorlesungen über Psychopathologie. (Storring, Gustav.) Leipzig, 1900.
Phil 3805.157 Vorlesungen über Schleiermacher. (Schaller, Julius.) Halle, 1844.
Phil 3805.86 Vorlesungen über Schleiermacher's Dialektik und Dogmatik. v.1-2. (Weissenborn, G.) Leipzig, 1847-49.
Phil 3090.41 Vorlesungen über speculative Dogmatik. pt. 1-5. (Baader, Franz von.) Stuttgart, 1828-38.
Phil 5828.6 Vorlesungen über Tierpsychologie. (Schneider, K.C.) Leipzig, 1909.
Phil 1707.4A Vorlesungen und der Geschichte der Philosophie. (Hegel, E.W.F.) Berlin, 1840. 3v.
Phil 6315.2.9.10 Vorlesungen zur Einführung. 2. Aufl. (Freud, Sigmund.) Leipzig, 1918.
Phil 6315.2.10.10 Vorlesungen zur Einführung in die Psychoanalyse. (Freud, Sigmund.) Berlin, 1933.
Phil 6315.2.10A Vorlesungen zur Einführung in die Psychoanalyse. 2. Aufl. (Freud, Sigmund.) Leipzig, 1922.
Phil 6315.2.10.5A Vorlesungen zur Einführung in die Psychoanalyse. 4. Aufl. (Freud, Sigmund.) Leipzig, 1922.
Phil 8597.3.4 Die Vornehmstenwahrheiten der natürlichen Religion. 4. Aufl. (Reimarus, H.S.) Hamburg, 1772.
Phil 8597.3.3 Die Vornehmstenwahrheiten der natürlichen Religion. 3. Aufl. (Reimarus, H.S.) Hamburg, 1766.
Phil 310.425 Vorob'ev, L.V. Osnovnye kategorii i zakony materialisticheskoi dialektiki. Moskva, 1962.
Phil 310.5.3 Vorob'ev, M.F. Zakon otritsaniia otritsaniia. Moskva, 1958.

Phil 8676.6   Voronitsyn, I.P. Istoriia ateizma. 3. izd. Moskva, 1930.
Phil 5425.63   Voronoff, Serge. Du crétin au génie. N.Y., 1941.
Phil 5761.14   Vorsatz Wille und Bedürfnis. (Lewin, Kurt.) Berlin, 1926.
Phil 193.31.13   Vorschlag an die Freunde einer vernünftigen Lebensführung.
     (Spir, A. von.) Leipzig, 1869.
Phil 8725.16   Das Vorschreiten der Säkularisierung. (Werhahn, Hans.)
     Bonn, 1969.
Phil 8050.50   Vorschule der Ästhetik. (Egger, Alais.) Wien, 1872.
Phil 3210.63   Vorschule der Aesthetik. v.1-2. (Fechner, G.T.)
     Leipzig, 1876.
Phil 5775.51.30   Vorschule der Charakterkunde. 2e Aufl. (Klages, Ludwig.)
     Leipzig, 1937.
Phil 8893.32.5   Die Vorschule der Ethik. (Strümpell, L.) Mitau, 1844.
Phil 5046.15   Vorschule der Logik. (Gross, Peter.) Berlin, 1890.
Phil 186.59   Vorschule der Metaphysik. (Lehmann, Gerhard.)
     Berlin, 1927.
Phil 180.45   Vorschule der Philosophie. (Fritzsche, A.R.)
     Leipzig, 1906.
Phil 9400.7   Vorse, M.H. (Mrs.). Autobiography of an elderly woman.
     Boston, 1911.
Phil 1133.19A   Die Vorsokratiker. (Kafka, Gustav.) München, 1921.
Phil 1133.16   Die Vorsokratiker. (Nestle, W.) Auschauungen, 1908.
Phil 1133.18   Die vorsokratische Philosophie. (Goebel, Karl.)
     Bonn, 1910.
Phil 1133.15   Die vorsokratische Philosophie der Griechen. (Byk, S.A.)
     Leipzig, 1876-77. 2v.
Phil 3778.94   Die Vorstellung in der Polemik zwischen Reinhold.
     (Spickhoff, K.) München, 1961.
Phil 5241.83   Vorstellung und Denken. (Barthel, Ernst.) München, 1931.
Phil 5325.9.5   Vorstellung und Gefühl. (Scripture, E.W.) Leipzig, 1891.
Phil 281.4   Die Vorstellung von Weltebäude im Wandel du Zeit.
     (Bamberger, L.) Leipzig, 1908.
Phil 5816.4   Die Vorstellungen der Tiere. (Graeser, Kurt.)
     Berlin, 1906.
Phil 5757.6   Vorstellungs- und Willentheorie. (Henle, Rudolf.)
     Leipzig, 1910.
Phil 5325.16   Die Vorstellungsreihe. (Burchhardt, F.) Meissen, 1888.
Phil 5585.4   Die Vorstellungsreihen. (Lukens, H.T.) Gütersloh, 1892.
Phil 8676.2   Vorstius, Conrad. Tractatus theologicus dedeo.
     Steinfursti, 1610. 2 pam.
Phil 184.28   Vorstudien zur Metaphysik. (Janssen, O.) Halle, 1921.
     2v.
Phil 3640.58   Vorstufen der Geburt der Tragödie aus dem Geiste der Musik.
     (Nietzsche, Friedrich.) Leipzig, 1926-28. 3v.
Phil 978.49.455   Vorstufen zum Mysterium von Golgatha. (Steiner, R.)
     Dornach, 1964.
Phil 3640.121.15   Vorträge über Nietzsche. (Horneffer, Ernst.)
     Berlin, 1903.
Phil 3640.121.10   Vorträge über Nietzsche. (Horneffer, Ernst.)
     Berlin, 1906.
Phil 200.2.5   Vorträge und Abhandlungen geschichtlichen Inhalts.
     (Zeller, E.) Leipzig, 1865.
Phil 200.2.6   Vorträge und Abhandlungen Geschichtlichen Inhalts. 1. Aufl.
     (Zeller, E.) Leipzig, 1875.
Phil 200.2.7   Vorträge und Abhandlungen Geschichtlichen Inhalts. 2. Aufl.
     (Zeller, E.) Leipzig, 1877.
Phil 200.2.8   Vorträge und Abhandlungen Geschichtlichen Inhalts. 3. Aufl.
     (Zeller, E.) Leipzig, 1884.
Phil 3450.19.70   Vorträge und Anpätze. (Heidegger, Martin.)
     Pfullingen, 1954.
Phil 1721.1   Vorträge zur Einführung in der Philosophie der Gegenwart.
     Photoreproduction. (Volkert, J.) München, 1892.
Phil 5250.28   Vorträge zur Einführung in die Psychologie. (Kleinpeter,
     H.) Leipzig, 1914.
Phil 182.12.6   Die Vorurtheile des gemeinen Verstandes. (Hellenbach,
     L.B.) Wien, 1880.
Phil 3492.27   Vorwärts zu Kant! (Kremer, Josef.) Erfurt, 1924.
Phil 960.120   Vorwissenschaftliche Wissenschaft die Weltanschauung der
     Brahamana. (Oldenberg, Hermann.) Göttingen, 1919.
Htn   Phil 3800.385.5*   Vorwort zu H. Steffens Nachgelassenen Schriften.
     (Schelling, F.W.J. von.) Berlin, 1846.
Htn   Phil 3480.19.15*   Vorzügliche Kleine Schriften und Aufsätze. Bd.1-2. (Kant,
     Immanuel.) Leipzig, 1833.
Phil 3480.19.16   Vorzügliche Kleine Schriften und Aufsätze. v.1-2. (Kant,
     Immanuel.) Quedlinburg, 1838.
Phil 735.9   Vos, H. von de. Werte und Bewertungen in der
     Denkevolution. Berlin, 1909.
Phil 1126.3   Vos, Harmen de. Inleiding tot de wijsbegeerte van de
     Grieken en de Romeinen. Nijkerk, 1963.
Phil 8980.10   Vospitanie kommunistecheskoi morali u shkol nikov. Izd. 2.
     (Boldyrev, N.I.) Moskva, 1964.
Phil 8980.697   Vospitanie kommunisticheskoi soznatel'nosti. (Platonov,
     Rostislav P.) Minsk, 1970.
Phil 5780.14   Vospitanie voli u rebenka v sem'e. (Vedenov, A.V.)
     Moskva, 1952.
Phil 4762.1.36   Vospominaniia. (Losskii, Nikolai Onufrievich.)
     München, 1968.
Phil 5625.75.105   Vospominaniia o I.P. Pavlove. (Orbeli, Leon A.)
     Leningrad, 1966.
Phil 5585.232   Vospriiatie i osnovy ego modelirovaniia. (Vekker, Lev M.)
     Leningrad, 1964.
Phil 5135.7   Vospriiatie i ustanovka. (Bzhalava, Iosif T.)
     Tbilisi, 1965.
Phil 5585.73   Vospriiatie predmeta i risunka. (Volkov, N.N.)
     Moskva, 1950.
Phil 5585.311   Vospriiatie prostranstva i vremeni. (International
     Congress of Psychology, 18th, Moscow, 1966.)
     Leningrad, 1969.
Phil 3903.3.110   Vossius, G.J. Universalis philosophiae. Leiden, 1955.
Phil 3503.8   Vosters, J. La doctrine du droit de Kant.
     Bruxelles, 1920.
Phil 310.7.5   Vostrikov, A.V. Marksistskii filosofskii materializm.
     Moskva, 1954.
Phil 310.7.7   Vostrikov, A.V. Teoriia poznaniia dialekticheskogo
     materializma. Moskva, 1965.
Phil 3450.19.420   Vottimo, Gianni. Arte e verità nel pensiero di Martin
     Heidegger. Torino, 1966.
Phil 5231.5   Voutsinas, Dimitri. Documentation sur la psychologie
     française. v.1-6. Paris, 1958- 5v.
Phil 2730.112   Voutsinas, Dimitri. La psychologie de Maine de Biran,
     1766-1824. Paris, 1964.
Phil 196.23   Vowinckel, E. Metaphysik des Ich. Berlin, 1924.
Phil 3805.101   Vowinckel, Ernst. Religion und Religionen bei
     Schleiermacher und Hegel. Erlangen, 1896.
Phil 200.17   Vox Zenanias. (Zafiropulo, Jean.) Paris, 1958.
Phil 585.210   Voyage autour de l'homme et au-delà. (Toesca, Maurice.)
     Paris, 1967.

Phil 2520.88   Voyage du monde de Descartes...Suite du voyage du monde de
     Descartes. (Daniel, Gabriel.) Amsterdam, 1713.
Phil 2520.88.2   Voyage du monde de Descartes. (Daniel, Gabriel.)
     Paris, 1702.
Phil 2520.88.9   Voyage du monde de Descartes. (Daniel, Gabriel.)
     Paris, 1703.
Phil 2520.88.10   Voyage du monde de Descartes. v.1-2. (Daniel, Gabriel.)
     Amsterdam, 1706.
Phil 6990.3.65   The voyage to Lourdes. 1. ed. (Carrel, A.) N.Y., 1950.
Htn   Phil 2520.88.20*   Voyage to the world of Cartesius. (Daniel, Gabriel.)
     London, 1694.
Phil 7055.173   Un voyant au XXe siècle: Dieudonné. (Leroy, Roger.)
     Paris, 1965.
Phil 7068.96.40   La voyante de la rue de Paradis. (Mery, Gaston.)
     Paris, 1896.
Phil 8601.9   Voysey, C. Religion for all mankind. London, 1903.
Phil 8676.3.5   Voysey, C. Sermons preached at St. George's Hall, Laugham
     Place. London, 1872-77. 4v.
Phil 8676.3   Voysey, C. Theism as a science of natural theology.
     London, 1895.
Phil 8676.3.80   Pamphlet box. Voysey, Charles.
Phil 8676.3.85   Pamphlet box. Voysey establishment fund publications.
Phil 8877.67   La voz de la virtud. (Campos Gimenez, J.) Habana, 1868.
Phil 5265.7   Vozniknovenie abstraktnogo myshleniia. (Zhdanov, D.A.)
     Khar'kov, 1969.
Phil 310.21   Vozniknoveniie marksizma, revoliutsionnyi perevorst v
     filosofii. (Ivanov, A.I.) Moskva, 1956.
Phil 3450.19.415   De vraag naar her transcendentale. (Duintjer, Otto D.)
     Leiden, 1966.
Phil 5772.11   Het vraagstuk vanden vrijen wil. (Wijnaendts Francken,
     C.J.) Haarlem, 1912.
Phil 8691.28   Het vraagteken achter de horizon van ons Leven. (Broekman,
     R.W.) Assen, 1957.
Phil 2636.44   Le vrai sens du système de la nature. (Helvétius, C.A.)
     Londres, 1774.
Phil 2555.1.86   Le vrai système. (Deschamps, L.M.) Genève, 1963.
Phil 2555.1.85   Le vrai système. (Deschamps, L.M.) Paris, 1939.
Phil 2805.278   Le vrai visage de Blaise Pascal. (Moussalli, U.)
     Paris, 1952.
Phil 9075.2   La vraie conscience. (Bouillier, F.C.) Paris, 1882.
Phil 8876.52   La vraie morale basée sur l'étude de la nature. 3. ed.
     (Berge, Vincent.) Paris, 1913.
Phil 2805.100   La vraie religion selon Pascal. (Prudhomme, S.)
     Paris, 1905.
Phil 2675.3.30   La vraie vérité, alibi. (Jeanson, Francis.) Paris, 1954.
Phil 180.24   Les vraies bases de la philosophie. 3e éd. (Faug,
     Balthasar.) Paris, 1887.
VPhil 310.163   Vranicki, Predrag. Covjek i historija. Sarajevo, 1966.
Phil 310.160   Vranicki, Predrag. Dijalektički i istorijski
     materijalizam i odabrani tekstovi. Zagred, 1958.
Phil 310.163.5   Vranicki, Predrag. L'uomo e la storia. Roma, 1968.
Phil 5066.150   Vredenie v matematicheskuiu logiku. (Popov, A.I.)
     Leningrad, 1959.
Phil 8958.6   Vremia very. (Ioann, Bishop of San Francisco.)
     N'iu-Iork, 1954.
Phil 5325.37   De vrienden van mijn vrienden. (Jaspars, Joseph Maria
     Franciscus.) Leiden, 1967.
Phil 352.8.5.3   Vries, Joseph de. Critica. 3. ed. recognita et aucto.
     Barcinone, 1964.
Phil 352.8   Vries, Joseph de. Denken und Sein. Freiburg, 1937.
Phil 310.80   Vries, Joseph de. Die Erkenntnistheorie des dialektischen
     Materialismus. München, 1958.
Phil 5061.8   Vries, Joseph de. Logica, cui praemittitur.
     Friburgi, 1952.
Phil 315.19   Vries, Joseph de. Materie und Geist. München, 1970.
Phil 196.44   Vries, Joseph de. Philosophie im Grundriss.
     Würzburg, 1969.
Phil 3841.8   Vries, Theun de. Baruch de Spinoza in Selbstzeugnissen und
     Bilddokumenten. Reinbek, 1970.
Phil 5760.13   Vrije wil of determinisme. (Kohnstamm, Philipp A.)
     Haarlem, 1947.
Phil 440.14   Vrijheid, Horizon der Geschiedenis. (Nauta, Lolle Wibe.)
     Nijkerk, 1966.
Phil 5751.6   Het vrijheidsbegrip. (Brulez, Lucien.) 's
     Gravenhage, 1947.
Phil 8601.10   Vrooman, H. Religion rationalized. Philadelphia, 1910.
Phil 2520.395   Vrooman, Jack Rochford. René Descartes; a biography.
     N.Y., 1970.
Phil 4825.1   Vrtačiā, Ludvík. Einführung in den Jugoslawischen
     Marxismus-Leninismus; Organisation und Bibliographie.
     Dordrecht, 1963.
Phil 8594.2.15   De vrucht der godsdienst. 3. druk. (Opzoomer, C.W.)
     Amsterdam, 1868.
Phil 8404.16   Všeobecna aesthetika. (Durdík. Josef.) Praha, 1875.
Phil 310.584   Vserossiiskii Seminar pre Poda Vatelei po Voprosam Sovet
     Estestvozaniia. Dialekticheskii materializm i sovremennoe
     estestvoznanie. Moskva, 1964.
Phil 70.34   Vsesoiuznoe Soveshchanie po Voprosam Psikhologii, 2nd,
     Moskva, 1953. Doklady na soveshchanii po voprosam
     psikhologii 3-8 iiulia 1953 g. Moskva, 1954.
Phil 8980.872.5   Vstupaia v zhizn'. Moskva, 1967.
Phil 2750.22.125   Vu Duy Tu. Individualisme, collectivisme, personnalisme
     dans l'oeuvre d'Emmanuel Mounier. Bonn, 1962.
Phil 8430.45.5   Vučković, Vojislav. Studije, eseji, kritike.
     Beograd, 1968. 2v.
Phil 8430.45   Vučković, Vojislav. Umetnost i umetničko delo.
     Beograd, 1962.
Phil 7060.141   La vue à distance...des cas de psychométrie. (Duchâtel,
     Edmond.) Paris, 1910.
Phil 5831.5   Vues sur la psychologie animale. Paris, 1930.
Phil 705.39   Vuillemin, Jules. L'héritage Kantien et la révolution
     copernicienne. Paris, 1954.
Phil 2255.1.145   Vuillemin, Jules. Leçons sur la première philosophie de
     Russell. Paris, 1968.
Phil 254.2   Vuillemin, Jules. La logique et le monde sensible.
     Paris, 1971.
Phil 2520.310   Vuillemin, Jules. Mathématiques et métaphysique de
     Descartes. Paris, 1960.
Phil 3503.11   Vuillemin, Jules. Physique et métaphysique Kantiennes. 1.
     éd. Paris, 1955.
Phil 3841.6   Vulliaud, P. Spinoza d'après les livres de la
     bibliothèque. Paris, 1934.
Phil 5875.60   Vulnerable children; three studies of children in conflict.
     (Burton, Lindy.) Reinbek, 1968.
Phil 7060.22   Vulpius, W. Über den psychischen Mechanismus der
     Sinnestäuschungen. Jena, 1885.
Phil 5245.60   Vultos e problemas. (Furtado, Diogo.) Coimbra, 1957.

Phil 165.295 Vuprosi na dialekticheskiia materializum i na chastnite kauki. (Bulgarska Akademiia na Naukite, Sofia.) Sofiia, 1961.

Phil 5643.136 Vurpillot, Eliane. L'organisation perceptive: son rôle dans l'évolution des illusion optico-géométrique. Paris, 1963.

Phil 310.4.10 Vvedemie v filosofii dialekticheskogo materializma. (Deborin, A.M.) Moskva, 1922.

Phil 9590.17 Vvedenie v biosofiia. (Krol', L.I.) Kaunas, 1937.

Phil 8402.63 Vvedenie v estetiku. (Borev, Iurii B.) Moskva, 1965.

Phil 4753.1.30 Vvedenie v filosofiiu. (Chelpanov, G.) Riga, 1923.

Phil 4756.1.30 Vvedenie v filosofiiu. (Frank, Semen L.) Berlin, 1923.

Phil 4762.1.30 Vvedenie v filosofiiu. (Losskii, Nikolai Onufrievich.) Petrograd, 1918.

VPhil 185.99 Vvedenie v filosofiiu. Izd. 7. (Kudriavtsev-Platonov, Viktor D.) Sergiev Posad, 1908.

Phil 5050.26 Vvedenie v logiku. (Kondakov, Nikolai I.) Moskva, 1967.

Phil 310.639 Vvedenie v marksistskuiu gnoseologiiu. (Kopnin, Pavel V.) Kiev, 1966.

Phil 4772.10.5 Vvedenskii, A.I. Filosofskie ocherki. Praga, 1924.

Phil 4772.10 Vvedenskii, A.I. Logika, kak chast' teorii poznaniia. 2. izd. Sankt Peterburg, 1912.

X Cg Phil 4952.1.5 Vvedenskii, A.I. Psikhologiia bez vsiakoi metafiziki. Petrograd, 1915.

Phil 4757.3.20 Vvedenskii, Aleksei I. Protoierei Feodor Aleksandrovich Golubinski. Sergiev, 1898.

Phil 5722.72 Vvod i zakreplenre informatsii v pamiati cheloveka vo vremia estestvennogo sna. (Blyznychenko, Leonid A.) Kiev, 1966.

Phil 3450.19.74.1 Vycinas, V. Earth and gods. The Hague, 1961.

Phil 821.1.20 Vycinas, Vincent. Greatness and philosophy. The Hague, 1966.

Phil 6111.16.20 Vydaiushchiisia russkii uchenyi V.M. Bekhterev. (Dmitriev, V.D.) Cheboksary, 1960.

Phil 4710.18 Vysheslavtser, B.P. Vechnoe v russkoi filosofii. N.Y., 1955.

Phil 3246.236 Vysheslavtsev, B. Etika Fikhte. Moskva, 1914.

Phil 8896.15 Vysheslavtsev, V. Etika preobrazhennago erosa. Paris, 1931.

Phil 800.12.10 Vystuplenie na diskussii po knige G.F. Aleksandrova. "Istoriia zapnoevropeiskoi filosofii". (Zhdanov, A.A.) Moskva, 1947.

Phil 2421.2 Vyverberg, H.S. Historical pessimism in the French enlightenment. Cambridge, 1958.

Phil 5520.756 Vzaimootnoshenie iazyka i myshleniia. (Panfilov, Vladimir Z.) Moskva, 1971.

Phil 5075.7 Vzaimosviaz' kategorii dialektiki. (Shirokanov, Imitri I.) Minsk, 1969.

Phil 4809.796.30 Vznik a zánik ducha. (Smetana, Augustin.) Praha, 1923.

Phil 3195.6.130 W. Dilthey y el problema del mundo historico. (Diaz de Cerio Ruiz, Franco.) Barcelona, 1959.

Phil 3850.7.81 W. Schuppe and the immanent philosophy. (Pelazza, Aurelio.) London, 1915.

Phil 2005.3.80 W.E. Ford: a biography. (Beresford, J.D.) London, 1917.

Phil 2005.3.81 W.E. Ford: a biography. (Beresford, J.D.) N.Y., 1917.

Phil 4769.1.95 W.S. Solowjews Geschichtsphilosophie. (Sacke, G.) Berlin, 1929.

Phil 8622.84 W co wierze. Wol. 1. (Dobraczyński, Jan.) Warszawa, 1970.

Phil 1135.14 Wa Saïd, Dibinga. Theosophies of Plato, Aristotle and Plotinus. N.Y., 1970.

Phil 1750.166.140 Waarde van de mens en menselijke waardigheid. (Frerichs, J.G.) Zaandam, 1960.

Phil 189.15.5 De waarheid en hare kenbronnen. (Opzoomer, C.W.) Amsterdam, 1859.

Phil 2070.83 Waarheidstheorie van William James. (Brugmans, H.J.F.W.) Groningen, 1913.

Phil 5585.35 De waarnemingstijd. Proefschrift. (Hazelhoff, F.F.) Groningen, 1923.

Phil 8612.35 Wach, Joachim. Das Problem des Todes in der Philosophie unserer Zeit. Tübingen, 1934.

Phil 3195.6.85 Wach, Joachim. Die Typenlehre Trendelenburgs und ihr Einfluss auf Dilthey. Tübingen, 1926.

Phil 1750.124 Wach, Joachim. Das Verstehen. Tübingen, 1926-33. 3v.

Phil 3120.30.205 Wachinger, Lorenz. Der Glaubensbegriff Martin Bubers. 1. kaufl. München, 1970.

Phil 978.64 Wachsmuth, G. Die ätherischen Bildekräfte in Kosmos, Erde und Mensch. Dornach, 1926.

Phil 974.3.116 Wachsmuth, G. Bibliographie der Werke Rudolf Steiners in die Geburt. Dornach, 1942.

Phil 974.3.115 Wachsmuth, G. Die Geburt der Geisteswissenschaft. Dornach, 1941.

Phil 974.3.117 Wachsmuth, G. Goethe in unserer Zeit. Dornach, 1949.

Phil 978.64.5 Wachsmuth, G. Werdegang der Menschlheit. Dornach, 1953.

Phil 3425.283 Wacker, Herbert. Das Verhältnis des jungen Hegel zu Kant. Berlin, 1932.

Phil 5262.26 Wada, Tomi. An experimental study of hunger in its relation to activity. N.Y., 1922.

Phil 5062.1.5 Waddington, C. De l'utilité des études logiques. Paris, 1851.

Phil 5062.1 Waddington, C. Essais de logique. Paris, 1857.

Phil 2835.81 Waddington, C. Ramue (Pierre de la Ramée). Paris, 1855.

Phil 9150.33 Waddington, C.H. The ethical animal. London, 1960.

Phil 9590.18 Waddington, C.H. Science and ethics. London, 1942.

Phil 9075.9 Waddington, C.T. Dieu et la conscience. Paris, 1870.

Phil 5262.22 Waddington, Charles. L'âme humaine. 2. série. Paris, 1862.

Phil 5262.22.2 Waddington, Charles. De l'âme humaine. 2. série. Paris, 1862.

Phil 1127.4 Waddington, Charles. La philosophie ancienne et la critique historique. Paris, 1904.

Phil 1822.1 Waddington, M. The development of British thought. Toronto, 1919.

Phil 303.11 Waddington, M.F. Saggio sulla natura. Firenze, 1866.

Phil 6990.11 Waddle, C.W. Miracles of healing. n.p., 1909.

Phil 7069.43.15 Wade, A.M. Evidences of immortality. N.Y., 1943.

Phil 2422.3 Wade, Ira O. The Clandestine organization and diffusion of philosophic ideas in France from 1700 to 1750. Princeton, 1938.

Phil 197.62 Wade, Joseph M. A few texts. Wise to the wise. Boston, 1892.

Phil 5062.27 Wadstein, E.A. "Moralens matematik". Stockholm, 1888.

Phil 5780.15.15 Waechter, Michael. Hjärntvätt. Stockholm, 1965.

Phil 822.3 Wägner, S. Filosofiens historia i sammandrag. Lund, 1914.

Phil 6332.18 Waelder, Robert. Basic theory of psychoanalysis. N.Y., 1960.

Phil 8423.9 Waelhem, M. de. Quelques réflexions sur la conception du beau. Paris, 1958.

Phil 3450.19.96.12 Waelhens, A. de. Chemins et impusses de l'ontologie Heideggerienne. Louvain, 1953.

Phil 3450.19.96 Waelhens, A. de. La filosofía de Martin Heidegger. Madrid, 1945.

Phil 3450.11.145 Waelhens, A. de. Phénoménologie et vérité. Paris, 1953.

Phil 2750.20 Waelhens, A. de. Un philosophie de l'ambiguité. Louvain, 1951.

Phil 3450.19.96.10 Waelhens, A. de. La philosophie de Martin Heidegger. 3e éd. Louvain, 1948.

Phil 1722.12 Waelkens, Alphonse de. Existence et signification. Louvain, 1958.

Phil 1722.12.5 Waelkens, Alphonse de. La philosophie et les experiences naturelles. La Haye, 1961.

Phil 303.10 Wälte, Théodore. Philosophie d'un ignorant. Genève, 1914.

Phil 4655.3.33 Waerland, Are. Idealism och materialism. Uppsala, 1924.

Phil 4655.3.30 Waerland, Are. Materie eller ande? 3. uppl. Uppsala, 1919.

Phil 2262.86 Waern, A.M. Shaftesbury's dygdelära. Upsala, 1875.

Phil 3160.9.87 Wäsche, E. Carl Gustav Carus und die romantische Weltanschauung. Dusseldorf, 1933.

Phil 3195.6.140 Waesimann, A. Dilthey o la lírica del historicismo. Tucumán, 1959.

Phil 8423.14 Waetzoldt, W. Das Kunstwerk als Organismus. Leipzig, 1905.

Phil 3850.27.30 Waffen des Lichts. 1. Aufl. (Schweitzer, A.) Heilbronn, 1940.

Phil 5262.56 Waffenschmidt, Walter. Denkformen und Denktechnik. Meisenheim, 1961.

Phil 7054.49.4 Waggoner, J.H. The nature and tendency of modern spiritualism. 4. ed. Battle creek. Mich., 1872.

Phil 8602.37 Waggoner, John G. The beautiful sunset of life. Boston, 1928.

Phil 9362.16.6 Wagner, C. Jeunesse. 8e ed. Paris, 1893.

Phil 9362.16.5 Wagner, C. Youth. N.Y., 1893.

Phil 9182.4 Wagner, Charles. Auprès du foyer. Paris, 1898.

Phil 9182.4.15 Wagner, Charles. The better way. N.Y., 1903.

Phil 9182.4.5 Wagner, Charles. By the fireside. N.Y., 1904.

Phil 9182.4.9 Wagner, Charles. The simple life. N.Y., 1904.

Phil 9182.4.10 Wagner, Charles. The simple life. N.Y., 1904.

Phil 9182.4.6 Wagner, Charles. La vie simple. 2. éd. Paris, 1895.

Phil 9182.4.12 Wagner, Charles. Why appeal to America. N.Y., 1905.

Phil 3808.111 Wagner, G.F. Encyclopädisches Register...Schopenhauer. Karlsruhe, 1909.

Phil 400.91 Wagner, G.F. Transcendental-Idealismus. Ulm, 1934.

Phil 5520.500 Wagner, Geoffrey A. On the wisdom of words. Princeton, 1968.

Phil 5070.20 Wagner, Hans. Elements des Glaubens. Inaug. Diss. München, 193-.

Phil 197.80 Wagner, Hans. Philosophie und Reflexion. München, 1959.

Phil 197.1.5 Wagner, J. Erläuterungen zur Organon der menschlichen Erkenntnis. Ulm, 1854.

Phil 197.1 Wagner, J. Organon der menschlichen Erkenntniss. Ulm, 1851.

Phil 197.1.15 Wagner, J. Praktische Philosophie enthaltend Religionslehre. Ulm, 1857.

Phil 197.1.10 Wagner, J. Religion, Wissenschaft, Kunst und Staat in ihren Gegenseitigen Verhältnissen. Erlangen, 1819.

Phil 197.1.7 Wagner, J. System der Idealphilosophie. Leipzig, 1804.

Phil 353.30 Wagner, J. Was Kann ich Wissen? 2. Aufl. Braunschweig, 1962.

Phil 8870.16 Wagner, J. Was soll ich tun? Braunschweig, 1953.

Phil 497.1 Wagner, J.A. Naturwissenschaft und Bibel. Stuttgart, 1855.

Phil 197.56 Wagner, J.J. Ueber das Wesen der Philosophie. Bamberg, 1804.

Phil 6132.12 Wagner, J.R. Neurologische Untersuchungen. Göttingen, 1854.

Phil 303.20.1 Wagner, Johann Jacob. Von der Natur der Dinge. Mit einer physiognomischen Kupfertafel. Leipzig, 1803. Bruxelles, 1968.

Phil 165.35.5 Wagner, Johannes. Vom Ursprung und Sinn des philosophischen Fragens. Braunschweig, 1954.

Phil 165.35 Wagner, Johannes. Was ist der Mensch? 2. Aufl. Braunschweig, 1954.

Phil 5262.1 Wagner, M. Beyträge zur philosophischen Anthropologie. Wien, 1794-96. 2v.

Phil 497.2 Wagner, R. Menschenschöpfung und Seelensubstanz. Göttingen, 1854.

Phil 497.2.5 Wagner, R. Über Wissen und Glauben. Göttingen, 1854.

Phil 510.1.22 Wagner, Richard. Aether und Wille. Leipzig, 1901.

Phil 3504.33 Wagner, Walther. Die Vereinigung von Kant und Marx. Langensalza, 1921.

Phil 3450.19.91 Wagner de Peyna, A. de. La ontologia fundamental de Heidegger. Buenos Aires, 1939.

Phil 3450.19.104 Wagner de Reyna, A. La ontologia fundamental de Heidegger. Buenos Aires, 1939.

Phil 3640.525 Wagner und Nietzsche. (Verweyen, J.) Stuttgart, 1926.

Phil 3640.88.9 Wagner und Nietzsche zur zeit Freundschaft. (Förster-Nietzsche, E.) München, 1915.

Phil 705.33 Wahl, J. Existence humaine et transcendance. Neuchâtel, 1944.

Phil 3640.611 Wahl, J.A. L'avant dernière pensée de Nietzsche. Paris, 1961.

Phil 3450.19.305 Wahl, J.A. Mots, mythes et réalité dans la philosophie de Heidegger. Paris, 1961.

Phil 3640.610 Wahl, J.A. La pensée philosophique de Nietzsche. Paris, 1959.

Phil 197.72 Wahl, J.A. Traité de métaphysique. Paris, 1953.

Phil 2520.137 Wahl, Jean. Du rôle de l'idée de l'instant dans la philosophie de Descartes. Paris, 1920.

Phil 510.126 Wahl, Jean. Les philosophies pluralistes. Paris, 1920.

Phil 510.126.3 Wahl, Jean. Les philosophies pluralistes. Thèse. Paris, 1920.

Phil 510.126.9 Wahl, Jean. The pluralist philosophies of England and America. London, 1925.

Phil 1722.7 Wahl, Jean. Vers le concret; études d'histoire de la philosophie contemporaine. Paris, 1932.

Phil 3425.257.10 Wahl, Jean A. Commentaires de la logique de Hegel. Paris, 1959.

Phil 2422.5.5 Wahl, Jean A. Französische Philosophie. 1e Aufl. Säkingen, 1948.

Phil 3425.257 Wahl, Jean A. La malheur de la conscience dans la philosophie de Hegel. Paris, 1929.

Phil 822.13 Wahl, Jean A. The philosopher's way. N.Y., 1948.

Phil 3450.16.15 Wahl, Jean A. Sein Leben in seiner Briefen. Frankfurt, 1938.

Phil 2422.5 Wahl, Jean A. Tableau de la philosophie française. Paris, 1946.
Phil 2422.5.2 Wahl, Jean A. Tableau de la philosophie française. Paris, 1962.
Phil 3450.19.155 Wahl, Jean A. Vers la fin de l'ontologie. Paris, 1956.
Phil 2475.1.445 Wahl, Jean André. Bergson. Paris, 1965.
Phil 1750.188 Wahl, Jean André. Esquisse pour une histoire de l'existentialisme. Paris, 1949.
Phil 2940.2.30 Wahl, Jean André. L'expérience métaphysique. Paris, 1965.
Phil 1750.185 Wahl, Jean André. Petite histoire de "l'existentialisme". Paris, 1947.
Phil 1750.189 Wahl, Jean André. Les philosophies de l'existence. Paris, 1954.
Phil 1750.189.5 Wahl, Jean André. Philosophies of existence: an introduction to the basic thought of Kierkegaard. London, 1969.
Phil 1750.187 Wahl, Jean André. A short history of existentialism. N.Y., 1949.
Phil 3450.18.123 Wahl, Jean André. La structure du monde réel d'apres Nicolai Hartmann. Paris, 1953.
Phil 3450.18.120 Wahl, Jean André. La théorie des catégories fondamentales dans Nicolai Hartmann. Paris, 1954.
Phil 8423.25 Wahl, Marcelle. Création picturale et ordre cérébral. Paris, 1964.
Phil 3640.264 Wahle, Aloys. Der weltanschauliche Gehalt von Nietzsches Dichtungen. Inaug. Diss. Dillingen, 1933.
Phil 3450.11.202 Wahle, Jean A. Husserl. Paris, 1961.
Phil 3450.11.200 Wahle, Jean A. Husserl. v.1-2. Paris, 1958.
Phil 3450.11.205 Wahle, Jean A. L'ouvrage posthume de Husserl. Paris, 1957. 2v.
Phil 197.26 Wahle, R. Das Ganze der Philosophie und ihr Ende. Wien, 1896.
Phil 6132.22 Wahle, R. Gehirn und Bewusstsein. Wien, 1884.
Phil 822.6.5 Wahle, R. Geschichtlicher Überblick über die Entwicklung der Philosophie bis zu ihrer letzten Phase. Wien, 1895.
Phil 3842.3 Wahle, R. Kurze Erklarung Ethic von Spinoza. Wien, 1899.
Phil 822.6.2 Wahle, R. Die Tragikomödie der Weisheit die Ergebnisse und der Geschichte des Philosophierens. Wien, 1925.
Phil 9035.55 Wahle, Richard. Entstehung der Charakters. München, 1928.
Phil 5262.25 Wahle, Richard. Über den Mechanismus des geistigen Lebens. Wien, 1906.
Phil 5762.6 Die Wahlfreiheit des Willens in ihrer Nichtigkeit. (Meyer, W.) Gotha, 1886.
Phil 6951.30.5 Wahn; Beiträge zu seiner phanomenologischen und daseinsanalytischen Erforschung. (Binswanger, Ludwig.) Pfullingen, 1965.
Phil 7140.110 Wahn und Irrtum im Leben der Völker. (Gaupp, Robert.) Tübingen, 1916.
Phil 6961.18 Der Wahnsinn. (Leibbrand, Werner.) Freiburg, 1961.
Phil 6322.13.5 Wahnsinniger oder Prophet? (Muralt, Alexander von.) Zürich, 1946.
Phil 510.15 Die wahre Einheit von Religion und Wissenschaft. (Ziegler, J.H.) Zürich, 1904.
Phil 8972.6 Wahre Philosophie des praktischen Christenthums. Frankfurt, 1782.
Phil 8590.24A Wahre und falsche Reform. (Keppler, P.W. von.) Freiburg, 1903.
Phil 2515.2.50 Die wahre Weisheit. v.2. (Charron, P.) München, 1779.
Phil 5374.67 Das wahre Wesen und Wirken des Bewusstseins in seiner normalen und anormalen Erscheinung. (Lang, Ernst Hildegard.) München, 1960.
Phil 1135.115 Das Wahreitsproblem in der griechischen Philosophie. (Herbertz, R.) Berlin, 1913.
Phil 3808.73 Die wahren Güter des Lebens. (Schopenhauer, Arthur.) München, 194-?
Phil 3500.57.5 Wahres Verhaltniss der Kantischen Philosophie. (Stattler, B.) München, 1794.
Phil 3475.3.74 Wahrheit, Freiheit und Friede. (Jaspers, Karl.) München, 1958.
Phil 165.446 Wahrheit, Wert und Sein; Festgabe für Dietrich von Hildebrand zum 80. Geburtstag. Regensburg, 1970.
Phil 720.21 Wahrheit, Wert und Wirklichkeit. (Bauch, Bruno.) Leipzig, 1923.
Phil 720.37 Wahrheit. (Balthaser, Hans.) Einsiedeln, 1947.
Phil 978.90 Die Wahrheit als Gesamtanfang aller Weltansichten. (Gleich, Sigismund.) Stuttgart, 1957.
Phil 720.46 Die Wahrheit als metaphysisches Problem. (Raab, Elmar F.X.) Dillingen, 1959.
Phil 3625.2 Wahrheit aus meinem Leben. (Michelet, K.L.) Berlin, 1884.
Phil 1520.5 Wahrheit der Dinge. (Pieper, Josef.) München, 1947.
Phil 8598.27 Wahrheit der Religion nach den neuesten Vertretern der Religionsphilosophie. (Schinz, Max.) Zürich, 1908.
Phil 8590.27.10 Die Wahrheit in dem von J. von Kuhn in Tübingen. (Clemens, Franz J.) Münster, 1860.
Phil 2475.1.158 Die Wahrheit über Bergson. (Brockdorff, Cary.) Berlin, 1916.
Phil 510.1.33 Die Wahrheit über Ernst Haeckel und seine "Welträtsel". (Dennert, E.) Halle, 1920.
Phil 5628.55.25 Die Wahrheit über Konnersreuth. (Rinser, Luise.) Einsiedeln, 1954.
Phil 3415.97 Wahrheit und Dichtung in den Hauptlehren Eduard von Hartmann's. (Kurt, N.) Leipzig, 1894.
Phil 332.14.11 Wahrheit und Evidenz. (Brentano, Franz.) Hamburg, 1962.
Phil 332.14.10 Wahrheit und Evidenz. (Brentano, Franz.) Leipzig, 1930.
Phil 3120.8.87 Wahrheit und Evidenz bei Franz Brentano. Inaug. Diss. (Hauber, V.) Stuttgart, 1936.
Phil 3450.19.56 Wahrheit und Geschichtlichkeit. (Weplinger, F.) Freiburg, 1961.
Phil 176.151 Wahrheit und Ideologie. (Barth, Hans.) Zürich, 1945.
Phil 176.151.2 Wahrheit und Ideologie. 2. Aufl. (Barth, Hans.) Erlenbach, 1961.
Phil 210.31 Wahrheit und Methode. (Gadamer, Hans Georg.) Tübingen, 1960.
Phil 6325.1.5 Wahrheit und Schönheit in der Psychoanalyse. (Pfister, Oskar.) Zürich, 1918.
Phil 3552.410 Wahrheit und Schöpfung. (Wildermuth, A.) Winterthur, 1960.
Phil 3120.45.35 Wahrheit und Wirklichkeit. (Brandenstein, Béla.) Meisenheim, 1965.
Phil 6327.4.19 Wahrheit und Wirklichkeit. (Rank, Otto.) Leipzig, 1929.
Phil 818.40 Wahrheit und Wirklichkeit. (Selbmann, Fritz.) Dresden, 1947.
Phil 630.6.5 Wahrheit und Wirklichkeit; Untersuchungen zum realistischen Wahrheitsproblem. (Müller, Aloys.) Bonn, 1913.
Phil 181.50 Wahrheit und Wirklichkeiten. (Grisebach, E.) Halle, 1919.
Phil 3475.3.37 Wahrheit und Wissenschaft. (Jaspers, Karl.) München, 1960.
Phil 978.49.70 Wahrheit und Wissenschaft. (Steiner, R.) Dornach, 1925.

Phil 3120.2.82 Das Wahrheits Problem. Inaug. Diss. (Gotthardt, J.) Trier, 1918.
Phil 3450.11.405 Der Wahrheitsbegriff bei Husserl und Heidegger. (Tugendhat, Ernst.) Berlin, 1967.
Phil 2070.130 Der Wahrheitsbegriff des Pragmatismus nach William James. (Switalski, B.W.) Braunsberg, 1910.
Phil 3120.2.90 Der Wahrheitsbegriff in der Lehre. Inaug. Diss. (Wiegand, H.) Alfeld Leine, 1928.
Phil 8584.5.15 Der Wahrheitsgehalt der Religion. (Eucken, Rudolf.) Leipzig, 1901.
Phil 8584.5.14 Der Wahrheitsgehalt der Religion. (Eucken, Rudolf.) Leipzig, 1901.
Phil 8584.5.15.4 Der Wahrheitsgehalt der Religion. 4. Aufl. (Eucken, Rudolf.) Berlin, 1927.
Phil 5520.210 Das Wahrheitsproblem und die Idee der Semantik. (Stegmüller, W.) Wien, 1957.
Phil 8712.20 Wahrmund, L. Katholische Weltanschauung und freie Wissenschaft. München, 1908.
Phil 5648.6 Wahrnehmbarkeit plötzlicher Drückveranderungen. (Kobylecki, S) Leipzig, 1905.
Phil 5360.26 Wahrnehmen, Beobachten, Konstituieren. (Reenpää, Yrjö.) Frankfurt, 1967.
Phil 5585.59 Wahrnehmung und Gegenstandswelt. (Brunswick, E.) Leipzig, 1934.
Phil 5585.235 Wahrnehmung und mnemische Verarbeitung wertbetonter Reihen. (Weber, Klaus.) Stuttgart, 1964?
Phil 8592.9 Wahrnehmungen einer Seherin. v.1-2. (Meyer, J.F. von.) Hamburg, 1827-28.
Phil 5585.42 Wahrnehmungslehre. (Palágyi, M.) Leipzig, 1925.
Phil 5585.10 Das Wahrnehmungsproblem. (Schwarz, H.) Leipzig, 1892.
Phil 6021.1 Wahrsagekunst aus der menschlichen Gestalt. (Landsberg, I.) Berlin, 1895.
Phil 8749.49.727 Wahrspruchworte: anthroposophischer Selenkalender. 2. Aufl. (Steiner, R.) Dornach, 1969.
Phil 9560.7.13 Die Wahrung der Ehre und die sittliche Tat. (Weidauer, F.) Leipzig, 1936.
Phil 2205.81 Wainewright, L. A vindication of Dr. Paley's theory of morals. London, 1830.
Phil 197.92 Wainwright, Donald S. Existentialist essays. N.Y., 1965.
Phil 3890.10.120 Waismann, A. Ernst Troeltsch o el drama del historicismo. Cordoba, 1955.
Phil 3925.18.30 Waismann, Friedrich. How I see philosophy. N.Y., 1968.
Phil 5068.56 Waismann, Friedrich. The principles of linguistic philosophy. London, 1965.
Phil 3925.16.140 Waismann, Friedrich. Wittgenstein und der Wiener Kreis. Oxford, 1967.
Phil 5262.41 Wait, W.T. Science of human behavior. N.Y., 1938.
Phil 525.19 Waite, A.E. Studies in mysticism and certain aspects of the secret tradition. London, 1906.
Phil 2880.1.82 Waite, Arthur E. The life of Louis C. de Saint-Martin. London, 1901.
Phil 2880.1.82.5 Waite, Arthur E. Saint-Martin; the French mystic. London, 1922.
Phil 5062.26 Waite, Dorothy J. First lessons in logic. London, 1923.
Phil 5062.2 Waitz, F.H.W. Die Hauptlehren der Logic. Erfurt, 1840.
Phil 5262.2 Waitz, T. Grundlegung der Psychologie. Hamburg, 1846.
Phil 5262.2.5 Waitz, T. Lehrbuch der Psychologie. Braunschweig, 1849.
Phil 196.5.7 Wake, C.S. Explanation of Van Nostrand's theory of the mental constitution. Chicago, 1892.
Phil 8847.2 Wake, Charles S. The evolution of morality. London, 1878. 2v.
Phil 5465.57.10 Wake up your mind. (Osborn, A.F.) N.Y., 1952.
Phil 8595.16.7 Wakefield, Gilbert. An examination of the age or reason. 2. ed. London, 1794.
Phil 9362.18.5 Wakefield, P. Bell (Mrs.). Leisure hours. 3d ed. London, 1798-1801. 2v.
Phil 510.7 Wakeman, T.B. Addresses...at and in reference to the 1st Monist congress. Cos Cob, 1913.
Phil 6122.96.2 The waking brain. 2. ed. (Magnun, Horace.) Springfield, Ill., 1963.
Phil 197.95 Wal, Goossen Albertus van der. Wereldbeschouwelijk denken als filosofisch probleem. Den Haag, 1968.
Phil 1145.81 Wal, L.G. Het objectiviteitsbeginsel in de oudste Grieksche ethiek. Groningen, 1934.
Phil 5645.50 Wal, T.O. Proeve ener practische kleurenpsychologie. Amsterdam, 1954.
Phil 7069.24.35 Walbrook, L. The case of Lester Coltman. London, 1924.
Phil 5062.32 Walcott, G.D. An elementary logic. N.Y., 1931.
Phil 8677.7 Walcott, G.D. Kantian and Lutheran elements in Ritschls' conception of God. N.Y., 1904.
Phil 8897.40 Walcott, Gregory. Tsing Hua lectures on ethics. Boston, 1919.
Phil 197.33 Waldeck, Oscar. Zur Analyse der aesthetischen Substanz. Dresden, 1909.
Phil 6032.5 Waldemar, Charles. Lavater, der Menschenkenner. 1. Aufl. Zürich, 1960.
Phil 3425.658 Waldemar, George. Présence de l'esthetique de Hegel. Paris, 1967.
Phil 3450.11.510 Waldenfels, Bernhard. Das Zwischenreich des Dialogs. Den Haag, 1971.
Phil 6319.1.186 Walder, P. Mensch und Welt bei C.G. Jung. Zürich, 1951.
Phil 8602.80 Waldmann, Günter. Christliches Glauben und christliche Glaubenslogik. Tübingen, 1968.
Phil 978.49.920 Waldorfpädagogik. (Schrey, Helmut.) Bad Godesberg, 1968.
Phil 5520.488 Waldron, R.A. Sense and sense development. London, 1967.
Phil 3120.2.99 Waldschmitt, L. Bolzano's Begründung des objektivismus in der theoretischen und praktischen Philosophie. Giessen, 1937.
Phil 5400.12 Waldstein, C. Balance of emotion and intellect. London, 1878.
Phil 5722.38.1 Waldstein, Louis. The subconscious self and its relation to education and health. N.Y., 1902.
Phil 5722.38.2 Waldstein, Louis. The subconscious self and its relation to education and health. N.Y., 1926.
Phil 197.94 Walendy, Udo. Die Weltanschauung des Wissens. 1. Aufl. Vlotho, 1969. 2v.
Htn Phil 8972.7* Wales, Ebenezer. Counsels and directions of Ebenezer Wales to his children. Boston, 1813.
Phil 930.38 Waley, Arthur. Three ways of thought in ancient China. London, 1939.
Phil 930.38.5 Waley, Arthur. Three ways of thought in ancient China. London, 1953.
Phil 197.55 Walfenden, J.F. The approach to philosophy. London, 1932.
Phil 4710.125 Walicki, Andrzej. Filozofia i myśl społeczna rosyjska, 1825-1861. Warzawa, 1961.
Phil 5440.11 Walker, Alexander. Intermarriage. N.Y., 1839.
Htn Phil 5440.11.2* Walker, Alexander. Intermarriage. N.Y., 1839.

Phil 9495.168.5 — Walker, Brooks R. The new immorality. 1st ed. Garden City, 1968.
Phil 735.75 — Walker, Cyril T.H. The construction of the world. Oxford, 1919.
Phil 8647.13 — Walker, Daniel P. The decline of hell. London, 1964.
Phil 978.38 — Walker, E.D. Reincarnation. Boston, 1888.
Phil 978.38.5 — Walker, E.D. Reincarnation. Point Loma, Calif., 1923.
Phil 9230.10A — Walker, Gilbert. A manifest detection of the most vyle and detestable use of dice play. London, 1850.
Phil 3270.12.85 — Walker, J.P.B. A study of Frege. Oxford, 1965.
Phil 8972.3 — Walker, James. Government of the thoughts. Boston, 1899.
Phil 9558.40 — Walker, James L. The philosophy of egoism. Denver, 1905.
Phil 8602.42 — Walker, Joseph. Humanism as a way of life. N.Y., 1932.
Phil 4757.2.97 — Walker, K.M. The making of man. London, 1963.
Phil 8602.50 — Walker, K.M. Meaning and purpose. London, 1944.
Phil 4757.2.95 — Walker, K.M. A study of Gurdjieff's teaching. London, 1957.
Phil 4757.2.90 — Walker, K.M. Venture with ideas. London, 1951.
Phil 5262.43.5 — Walker, Kenneth M. The circle of life. London, 1942.
Phil 5262.43 — Walker, Kenneth M. Diagnosis of man. London, 1942.
Phil 7162.261.1 — Walker, Kenneth M. The extra-sensory mind. N.Y., 1965.
Phil 8677.17 — Walker, L.J. The return to God. London, 1933.
Phil 8712.23 — Walker, L.J. Science and revelation. London, 1932.
Phil 6332.15 — Walker, Nigel. A short history of psychotherapy in theory and practice. London, 1957.
Htn Phil 2340.2.80* — Walker, O. Proposed for the press. Boston, 1757.
Phil 8897.1.5 — Walker, S. Familiar introduction to the knowledge of ourselves. London, 1761.
Phil 8897.1 — Walker, S. Reformation of manners. London, 1711.
Phil 400.44 — Walker, W. Idealism. London, 1919.
Phil 8696.8 — Walks in the regions of science and faith. (Goodwin, H.) London, 1883.
Phil 7060.104.5 — Wallace, A.R. A defense of modern spiritualism. Boston, 1874.
Phil 7060.104.9 — Wallace, A.R. If a man die shall he live again? San Francisco, 1888.
Phil 7060.104 — Wallace, A.R. On miracles and modern spiritualism. London, 1875.
Phil 8897.34 — Wallace, A.R. Social environment and moral progress. N.Y., 1913.
Phil 7068.96.10 — Wallace, Alfred R. Miracles and modern spiritualism. London, 1896.
Phil 5590.395 — Wallace, Anthony F.C. Culture and personality. N.Y., 1961.
Phil 8870.34 — Wallace, Gerald. The definition of morality. London, 1970.
Phil 9182.6 — Wallace, Henry. Uncle Henry's letters to the farm boy. 4. ed. N.Y., 1906.
Phil 1850.162 — Wallace, Karl Richards. Francis Bacon on the nature of man. Urbana, 1967.
Phil 7069.19.230 — Wallace, Mary B. The thinning of the veil. N.Y., 1919.
Phil 8897.2 — Wallace, R. Various prospects of mankind. London, 1761.
Phil 8581.13.16 — Wallace, T. Additional observations...natural theology by H. Lord Brougham. Dublin, 1835.
Phil 8581.13.15 — Wallace, T. Observations...natural theology by H. Lord Brougham. London, 1835.
Phil 1158.6 — Wallace, W. Epicureanism. London, 1880.
Phil 8602.14 — Wallace, W. Lectures and essays on natural theology and ethics. Oxford, 1898.
Phil 3808.100A — Wallace, W. Life of Arthur Schopenhauer. London, 1890.
Phil 3808.100.5 — Wallace, W. Life of Arthur Schopenhauer. N.Y., 1890.
Phil 3425.96A — Wallace, W. Prolegomena to Hegel's philosophy. Oxford, 1894.
Phil 3504.1 — Wallace, William. Kant. Edinburgh, 1882.
Phil 3504.1.20 — Wallace, William. Kant. Edinburgh, 1886.
Phil 3504.1.10 — Wallace, William. Kant. Edinburgh, 1902.
Phil 3504.1.15 — Wallace, William. Kant. Edinburgh, 1911.
Phil 3504.1.3 — Wallace, William. Kant. Philadelphia, 1882.
Phil 8110.6 — Wallace, H.B. Die Kritik der rationalen Ästhetik in England im achtzehnten Jahrhundert. Jena, 1912.
Phil 5062.36 — Wallas, G. The art of thought. London, 1926.
Phil 5850.385 — Wallas, Graham. The art of thought. N.Y., 1926.
Phil 8897.38 — Wallaschek, R. Ideen zur praktischen Philosophie. Tübingen, 1886.
Phil 6972.9 — Wallaschek, R. Psychologie und Pathologie der Vorstellung. Leipzig, 1905.
Phil 8897.38.5 — Wallaschek, R. Studien zur Rechtsphilosophie. Leipzig, 1889.
Phil 3504.29 — Wallenberg, G. Kants Zeitlehre. Berlin, 1896.
Phil 2050.234 — Wallenfels, Walter. Die Rechtsphilosophie David Humes. Göttingen, 1928.
Phil 5062.25 — Waller, A.D. A contribution to the psychology of logic. London, 1912.
Phil 5649.16 — Waller, A.D. The sense of effort. n.p., 1891?
Phil 197.41 — Wallerius, N. Compendium metaphysicae. Stockholmiae, 1755.
Phil 197.41.5 — Wallerius, N. Systema metaphysicum. v.1-4. Stockholmiae, 1750-1752. 2v.
Phil 5525.31 — Wallerstein, M. Eine Arbeit über das Lachen und des Komische. Wien, 1925.
Phil 6132.34 — Wallin, J.E.W. Minor mental maladjustments in normal people. Durham, N.C., 1939.
Phil 6332.10 — Wallin, John E.W. Personality maladjustments and mental hygiene. 1st ed. N.Y., 1935.
Phil 6750.25 — Wallin, John E.W. Problems of subnormality. Yonkers-on-Hudson, 1917.
Phil 5592.100 — Wallis, Ingeborg. Formen und Ausprägung der seelischen Nachreifung. Berlin, 1959.
Phil 5062.3 — Wallis, J. Institutio logicae. Oxonii, 1715.
Htn Phil 2045.97* — Wallis, John. Hobbius Heauton-timorumenos. Oxford, 1662.
Htn Phil 2045.97.5* — Wallis, John. Thomae Hobbes quadratura circuli. 2. ed. Oxoniae, 1669.
Phil 8602.20 — Wallis, Louis. Egoism. Chicago, 1905.
VPhil 8423.27 — Wallis, Mieczysław. Przeżycie i wartość. Wyd. 1. Kraków, 1968.
Phil 672.240 — Wallis, Robert. Le temps, quatrième dimension de l'esprit. Paris, 1966.
Phil 672.240.2 — Wallis, Robert. Time, fourth dimension of the mind. 1st ed. N.Y., 1968.
Phil 3246.214 — Wallner, Nico. Fichte als politischer Denker. Halle, 1926.
Phil 5545.91 — Wallon, H. Les mécanismes de la mémoire en rapport avec ses objects. Paris, 1951.
Phil 6332.8 — Wallon, H. Psychologie pathologique. Paris, 1926.
Phil 5590.536.4 — Wallon, Henri. Les origines du caractère chez l'enfant. 4. éd. Paris, 1970.
Phil 5850.385.15 — Wallon, Henri. Principes de psychologie appliquée. Paris, 1930.

Phil 2496.82 — Wallon, J. Du livre de M. Cousin. Paris, 1854.
Phil 353.29 — Wallraff, C.F. Philosophical theory and psychological fact. Tucson, 1961.
Phil 8677.15 — Walmarans, H.P. Die mens naar die beeld van God. Purmerend, 1932.
Phil 7059.10 — Walrath, M.E. History of the earth's formation. N.Y., 1868.
Phil 5832.5 — Walse, C.S. Chapters on man...comparative psychology. London, 1868.
Phil 5262.23 — Walsemann, Hermann. Methodisches Lehrbuch der Psychologie. Potsdam, 1905.
Phil 8423.10 — Walsh, Dorothy. The objectivity of the judgment of aesthetic value. Lancaster, 1936.
Phil 1750.156 — Walsh, Gerald G. Medieval humanism. N.Y., 1942.
Phil 8712.11 — Walsh, J.J. The popes and science. N.Y., 1911.
Phil 8712.11.2 — Walsh, J.J. The popes and science. N.Y., 1915.
Phil 6132.15 — Walsh, J.J. Psychotherapy. London, 1912.
NEDL Phil 8897.67 — Walsh, Robert. Didactics. Philadelphia, 1836. 2v.
Phil 9240.24 — Walsh, V.C. Scarcity and evil. Englewood Cliffs, N.J., 1961.
Phil 5850.385.19 — Walsh, W.S. Making our minds behave. N.Y., 1935.
Phil 5401.7 — Walsh, W.S. The mastery of fear. N.Y., 1924.
Phil 8602.41 — Walsh, Walter. The world rebuilt. London, 1917.
Phil 3504.52 — Walsh, William Henry. Kant's moral theology. London, 1963.
Phil 353.18.5 — Walsh, William Henry. Reason and experience. Oxford, 1963.
Phil 6480.125 — Walsh, William S. The psychology of dreams. N.Y., 1920.
Phil 822.10 — Walshe, Thomas J. The quest of reality. London, 1933.
Phil 8430.25 — Walston, C. Harmonism and conscious evolution. London, 1922.
Phil 9558.11 — Walston, C. Truth; an essay in moral reconstruction. Cambridge, 1919.
Phil 8972.5 — Walter, Franz. Der Leib und sein Recht im Christentum. Donauwörth, 1910.
Phil 3625.1.129 — Walter, Hermann. Moses Mendelssohn, critic and philosopher. N.Y., 1930.
Phil 1135.90 — Walter, J. Die Lehre von der praktischen Vernunft. Jena, 1874.
Phil 672.9.5 — Walter, J.E. Nature and cognition of space and time. W. Newton, Pa., 1914.
Phil 672.9 — Walter, J.E. Perception of space and matter. Boston, 1879.
Phil 353.1 — Walter, J.E. The Principles of knowledge. West Newton, Pa., 1901. 2v.
Phil 197.24 — Walter, Johnston E. Subject and object. West Newton, Pa., 1916.
Phil 8062.4 — Walter, Julius. Die Geschichte der Ästhetik im Altertum. Leipzig, 1893.
Phil 530.70.5 — Walter, R. von. Russische Mystik. Düsseldorf, 1957.
Phil 5460.13 — Walter, W.G. The neurophysiological aspects of hallucinations and illusory experience. London, 1960.
Phil 7069.35.75 — Walter Franklin Prince, a tribute to his memory. Boston, 1935.
Phil 8677.12.2 — Walter von Walthoffen, Hippolyt. Die Gottesidee in religiöser und spekulativer Richtung. Wien, 1904.
Phil 9420.7 — Walters, H.G. The wisdom of passion. Boston, 1901.
Phil 6132.13 — Walters, J.G. Plates of the thoracic and abdominal nerves. London, 1804.
Phil 5520.460 — Walters, Theodore W. The Georgetown bibliography of studies contributing to the psycholinguistics of language learning. Washington, 1965.
Phil 525.123.2 — Walther, G. Phänomenologie der Mystik. 2. Aufl. Olten, 1955.
Phil 974.3.165 — Walther, Kurt. Über die neu Mysteriendramen Rudolf Steiners. Freiburg, 1966-67. 3v.
Phil 2520.335 — Waltheunis, O. De mens Descartes. Brussel, 1960.
Phil 197.29 — Walthoffen, H. Walter von. Lebensphilosophie und Lebenskunst. Wien, 1907.
Phil 9495.143 — Walton, A.H. New vistas...religion, sex and morals. London, 1943.
Phil 525.16.9 — Walton, C. Notes and materials for an adequate biography of...William Law. London, 1854.
Phil 6132.7.15 — Walton, G.L. Calm yourself. Boston, 1913.
Phil 6132.7.6 — Walton, G.L. Peg along. Philadelphia, 1915.
Phil 6132.7.10 — Walton, G.L. Those nerves. Philadelphia, 1909.
Phil 6132.7 — Walton, G.L. Why worry? Philadelphia, 1908.
Phil 6132.7.2 — Walton, G.L. Why worry? 2d ed. Philadelphia, 1919.
Phil 3246.224 — Walz, G.A. Die Staatsidee des Rationalismus...und die Staatsphilosophie Fichte's. Berlin, 1928.
Phil 1020.44 — Walzer, Richard. Greek into Arabic. Cambridge, 1962. 2v.
Phil 1020.44.2 — Walzer, Richard. Greek into Arabic. Oxford, 1962.
Phil 8125.4 — Der Wandel des deutschen Naturgefühls. (Flemming, Willi.) Halle, 1931.
Phil 8956.26.2 — Wandelbares und Unwandelbares in der Moraltheologie. 2. Aufl. (Gruendel, Johannes.) Düsseldorf, 1971.
Phil 3120.30.160 — The wanderer and the way. (Oliver, Roy.) Ithaca, N.Y., 1968.
Phil 7054.3 — A wanderer in the spirit lands. (Farnese, A.) Chicago, 1901.
Phil 3640.37 — Der Wanderer und sein Schatten. (Nietzsche, Friedrich.) Chemnitz, 1880.
Phil 7054.175.10 — The wanderings of a spiritualist. (Doyle, Arthur Conan.) London, 1921.
Phil 7054.175.11 — The wanderings of a spiritualist. (Doyle, Arthur Conan.) N.Y., 1921.
Phil 3549.10.40 — Wandlung. (Kassner, Rudolf.) Zürich, 1946.
Phil 1200.9 — Die Wandlung der stoischen Lehre. (Werzstein, Otto Heinrich Robert.) Newstrelitz, 1892.
Phil 450.12 — Wandlung der Welt durch Wandlung des Bewusstseins. (Braun-Urban, Heiner.) München, 1969.
Phil 8587.68 — Die Wandlung im naturwissenschaftlicher Weltbild. 2. Aufl. (Heins, Karl.) Hamburg, 1951.
Phil 6615.18 — Die Wandlungen des Psychogenie- Begriffs. Inaug. Diss. (Buess, Heinrich.) Hölstein, 1940.
Phil 1706.3 — Wandlungen in der Philosophie der Gegenwerk. (Goldstein, J.) Leipzig, 1911.
Phil 6319.1.7.9 — Wandlungen und Symbole der Libido. (Jung, C.G.) Leipzig, 1912.
Phil 6319.1.8 — Wandlungen und Symbole der Libido. 2. Aufl. (Jung, C.G.) Leipzig, 1925.
Phil 3549.8.110 — Wandrey, Conrad. Ludwig Klages und seine Lebensphilosophie. Leipzig, 1933.
Phil 5401.22 — Wandruszka von Wanstetten, M.W. Angst und Mut. Stuttgart, 1950.
Phil 3100.82 — Wandschneider, A. Die Metaphysik Benekes. Berlin, 1903.

Phil 5400.82 — Wang, Ging Hsi. Galvanic skin reflex and the measurement of emotions. Canton, China, 1930?

Phil 5066.214 — Wang, Hao. A survey of mathematical logic. Peking, 1962.

Phil 5066.215 — Wang, Hao. A survey of mathematical logic. Peking, 1963.

Phil 2840.96 — Wang, Tsun-Sheng. Le phénoménisme de Charles Renouvier. Thèse. Lyon, 1935.

Phil 3504.2 — Wangenheim, F. Vertheidigung Kants Gegen Fries. Berlin, 1876.

Phil 53.5 — Wangh, Martin. Fruition of an eden...in honor of the fiftieth anniversary of the New York Psychoanalytics Society. N.Y., 1962.

Phil 2340.22.30 — Wank, Martin. The real world. N.Y., 1970.

Phil 6332.34 — Wanke, Georg. Psychoanalyse: Geschichte, Wesen. 2. Aufl. Halle, 1926.

Phil 3552.286 — Wanke, Georg. Das Stetigkeitsgesetz bei Leibniz. Inaug. -Diss. Kiel, 1892.

Phil 1145.96 — Wankel, H. Kalos Kai Agaltos. Frankfurt, 1961.

Phil 5238.198 — Wann, T.W. Behaviorism and phenomenology. Chicago, 1964.

Phil 9558.10.20 — The wanton nymph. (Payne, R.) London, 1951.

Phil 5585.160 — Wapner, Seymour. Perceptual development. Worcester, Mass., 1957.

Phil 6311.23.5 — War, politics, and insanity. (Bluemel, C.S.) Denver, 1948.

Phil 2490.145 — War and industrial society. (Aron, Raymond.) London, 1958.

Phil 7069.15.10 — War letters from the living dead man. (Barker, Elsa.) N.Y., 1915.

Phil 6956.13 — War neuroses in North Africa. (Grinker, Roy.) N.Y., 1943.

Phil 8708.14A — The war on modern science. (Shipley, Maynard.) N.Y., 1927.

Phil 5520.760 — The war with words, structure and transcendence. (Shands, Harley Cecil.) The Hague, 1971.

Phil 8961.7 — The war within. (Le Bosquet, John E.) Boulder, Col., 1911.

Phil 1127.5A — Warbeke, John M. The searching mind of Greece. N.Y., 1930.

Phil 7069.48 — Warcollier, R. Mind to mind. N.Y., 1948.

Phil 7069.21.90 — Warcollier, R. La télépathie, recherches experimentales. Paris, 1921.

Phil 7069.38.5A — Warcollur, R. Experimental telepathy. Boston, 1939.

Phil 3552.109 — Ward, A.W. Leibniz as a politician. Manchester, 1911.

Phil 1722.6 — Ward, Charles H. Builders of delusion. Indianapolis, 1931.

Phil 8602.1.5 — Ward, D.J.H. The biography of God as men have told it. Denver, 1924?

Phil 8602.1 — Ward, D.J.H. How religion arises. Boston, 1888.

Phil 5545.25 — Ward, G.W. Dates by name. Baltimore, 1892.

Phil 8972.11 — Ward, H.F. Which way religion? N.Y., 1931.

Phil 5262.29 — Ward, Henshaw. Thobbing; a seat at the circus of the intellect. Indianapolis, 1926.

Phil 5262.19.5 — Ward, J. Naturalism and agnosticism. 4th ed. London, 1915.

Phil 197.45 — Ward, James. Essays in philosophy. Cambridge, Eng., 1927.

Phil 3504.22.5 — Ward, James. Immanuel Kant. London, 1923.

Phil 8610.899.15 — Ward, James. Naturalism and agnosticism. London, 1899. 2v.

Phil 8610.899.17 — Ward, James. Naturalism and agnosticism. v.1. v.2 lost. N.Y., 1899.

Phil 5262.19 — Ward, James. Psychological principles. Cambridge, 1918.

Phil 5262.19.3A — Ward, James. Psychological principles. 2d ed. Cambridge, Eng., 1920.

Phil 8677.8 — Ward, James. The realm of ends, or Pluralism and theism. Cambridge, 1911.

Phil 8677.8.2 — Ward, James. The realm of ends, or Pluralism and theism. 2. ed. Cambridge, 1912.

Phil 8677.8.3 — Ward, James. The realm of ends, or Pluralism and theism. 3. ed. Cambridge, 1920.

Phil 3504.22A — Ward, James. A study of Kant. Cambridge, Eng., 1922.

Phil 8735.52 — Ward, L.R. God and world order. Saint Louis, 1961.

Phil 735.91.5 — Ward, Leo Richard. Philosophy of value. Diss. N.Y., 1930.

Phil 735.91.10 — Ward, Leo Richard. Values and reality. N.Y., 1935.

Phil 5460.12 — Ward, R.H. A drug-taker's notes. London, 1957.

Htn Phil 8602.2* — Ward, S. A philosophical essay. Oxford, 1667.

Phil 8847.3 — Ward, Stephen. Ethics. London, 1924.

Phil 8897.41 — Ward, Stephen. The ways of life. London, 1920.

Phil 8897.41.3 — Ward, Stephen. The ways of life. N.Y., 1920.

Phil 600.9 — Ward, W. The clothes of religion. London, n.d.

Phil 8677.1 — Ward, W.G. Essays on the philosophy of theism. London, 1884. 2v.

Phil 5070.3 — Ward, Wilfred. The wish to believe. Photoreproduction. London, 1885.

Phil 3504.20 — Warda, Arthur. Die Druckschriften Immanuel Kants. Wiesbaden, 1919.

Phil 3504.20.5 — Warda, Arthur. Immanuel Kants Bücher. Berlin, 1922.

Phil 3504.20.9 — Warda, Arthur. Immanuel Kants Cetzte Ehrung. Königsberg, 1924.

Phil 5832.13.10 — Warden, C.J. Animal motivation. N.Y., 1931.

Phil 5832.13.15 — Warden, C.J. Comparative psychology. N.Y., 1935-40. 3v.

Phil 5832.13 — Warden, C.J. A short outline of comparative psychology. N.Y., 1927.

Phil 5262.3 — Warden, R.B. Familiar forensic view of man and law. Columbus, 1860.

Phil 8972.2 — Wardlaw, R. Christian ethics. London, 1833.

Phil 8972.2.2 — Wardlaw, R. Christian ethics. N.Y., 1835.

Phil 1722.4.5 — Wardwell, R.J. Contemporary philosophy. London, 1913.

Phil 8602.3.2 — Ware, H. An inquiry...religion. Cambridge, 1842. 2v.

Phil 8602.3 — Ware, H. An inquiry...religion. Cambridge, 1842. 2v.

Phil 6692.1 — Ware, J. Animal magnetism. n.p., 1851.

Phil 9495.20.2 — Ware, J. Hints to young men. Boston, 1879.

Phil 9182.3 — Ware, J.F.W. Home life: what it is, and what it needs. Boston, 1864.

Phil 9035.8.2 — Ware, M.G. Chandler. The elements of character. Boston, 1854.

Phil 8647.11 — Ware, Mary G.C. Death and life. Boston, 1864.

Phil 1712.19 — The warfare of democratic ideals. (Myers, Francis M.) Yellow Springs, Ohio, 1956.

Htn Phil 2340.3.30* — Waring, Robert. Amoris effigies. 4th ed. London, 1671.

Htn Phil 2340.3.31* — Waring, Robert. The picture of love. 4th ed .v.1-2. London, 1744.

Phil 5628.51 — Warlomont, Évariste. Louise Lateau. Bruxelles, 1875.

Phil 1870.126 — Warnock, G.J. Berkeley. London, 1953.

Phil 2805.115 — Warmuth, K. Das religiös-ethische Ideal Pascals. Leipzig, 1901.

Phil 6032.1 — Warner, F. Physical expression its modes. N.Y., 1886.

Phil 9972.12 — Warner, F.E. Future of man. London, 1944.

Htn Phil 9390.10* — A warning to sinners. London, 1660.

Phil 7069.27.17 — Warnings from beyond. (Daily News, London.) London, 1927.

Phil 1822.7 — Warnock, G.J. English philosophy since 1900. London, 1958.

Phil 8897.90 — Warnock, Geoffrey James. Contemporary moral philosophy. N.Y., 1967.

Phil 8897.90.5 — Warnock, Geoffrey James. The object of morality. London, 1971.

Phil 8847.15 — Warnock, Mary. Ethics since 1900. London, 1960.

Phil 8847.15.2 — Warnock, Mary. Ethics since 1900. 2nd ed. London, 1966.

Phil 1750.552.25 — Warnock, Mary. Existentialism. London, 1970.

Phil 2880.8.220 — Warnock, Mary. Existentialist ethics. London, 1967.

Htn Phil 3585.4.34* — Warnung. (Luther, Martin.) Nürnberg, 1556.

Phil 5585.265 — Warr, Peter Bryan. The perception of people and events. London, 1968.

Phil 2655.2.85 — Warrain, F. L'oeuvre psychobiophysique. Paris, 1931.

Phil 2655.2.86 — Warrain, F. L'oeuvre psychobiophysique. 2 ed. Paris, 1938.

Phil 303.8 — Warrain, F. La synthèse concrète. Paris, 1910.

Phil 4803.454.91 — Warrain, Francis. Wiązanie metafizyczme sporządzone według prawa stworzenia Hoene-Wrońskiego. Warszawa, 1928.

Phil 1822.3 — Warren, Austin. The Concord school of philosophy. n.p., 1929.

Phil 2075.6.90A — Warren, Austin. The elder Henry James. N.Y., 1934.

Htn Phil 665.5* — Warren, E. No praeexistence. London, 1667.

Phil 5262.20.5 — Warren, H.C. Elements of human psychology. Boston, 1922.

Phil 5262.20.7 — Warren, H.C. Elements of human psychology. Boston, 1930.

Phil 5262.20 — Warren, H.C. Human psychology. Boston, 1919.

Phil 5262.20.9 — Warren, H.C. Précis de psychologie. Paris, 1923.

Phil 5325.17 — Warren, Howard C. A history of the association psychology. N.Y., 1921.

Phil 5325.17.2 — Warren, Howard C. A history of the association psychology. Diss. Baltimore, 1921.

Phil 5207.10 — Warren, Howard Crosby. Dictionary of psychology. N.Y., 1934.

Phil 5942.3F — Warren, J.C. The collection of the Boston Phrenological Society, a retrospect. N.Y., 1921.

Phil 9495.4.5 — Warren, M.A. Almost fourteen. N.Y., 1897.

Phil 7054.94 — Warren, O.G. Supernal theology and life in the spheres. N.Y., 1852.

Phil 303.13 — Warren, W.F. The earliest cosmologies. N.Y., 1909.

Phil 8647.3 — Warren, William F. Religions of the world and the world religion. N.Y., 1911.

Phil 2045.130 — Warrender, H. The political philosophy of Hobbes. Oxford, 1957.

Phil 8712.22 — Warring, C.B. The mosaic account of creation. N.Y., 1875.

Phil 8062.2 — Warry, John Gibson. Greek aesthetic theory...in...Plato and Aristotle. London, 1962.

Phil 176.147 — Wars of families of minds. (Bryan, W.L.) New Haven, 1940.

Phil 1801.8A — The wars of truth. (Baker, H.C.) Cambridge, 1952.

Phil 1722.13 — Warsaw. Univerystet. Główne zagadnienia i kierunki filozofii. v.1-2. 2. Wyd. Warszawa, 1960.

Phil 3808.113.5 — Warschauer, Rechts. Schopenhauers Rechts- und Staatslehre. Kattowitz, 1911.

Phil 3565.131 — Wartenberg, Mscislaw. Das problem des Wirkens und die monistische Weltanschauung. Leipzig, 1900.

Phil 497.8 — Wartenberg, Mzcislaw. Das idealistische Argument in der Kritik des Materialismus. Leipzig, 1904.

Phil 6980.419.5 — Wartime psychiatry; a compendium. (Lewis, Nolan don Carpentier.) N.Y., 1954.

Phil 6332.14 — Wartis, Joseph. Soviet psychiatry. Baltimore, 1950.

Phil 615.1 — Wartość i fakt. Wyd. 1. (Buozyńska, Hanna.) Warszawa, 1970.

Phil 270.27 — Warum Fragen die menschen Warum? (Heuer, W.) Heidelberg, 1921.

Phil 8610.870 — Was, H. Geschichidenis van het scepticisme der zeventiende eeuw in de voornaamste europeesche staten. 1e aflevering. Utrecht, 1870.

Phil 9450.62 — Was des Kaisers ist. 1. Aufl. (Hauser, Richard.) Frankfurt, 1968.

Phil 6060.12.30 — Was die Graphologie nicht kann. (Klages, Ludwig.) Zürich, 1949.

Phil 1145.66 — Was die Wahrheit war für die Griechen. (Hirzel, R.) Jena, 1905.

Phil 200.3.12 — Was Erwarten wir von der Philosophie? (Zimmermann, R.) Prag, 1852.

Phil 3120.8.30 — Was für ein Philosoph manchmal Epoche macht. (Brentano, Franz.) Wien, 1876.

Phil 5520.700 — Was geht uns Noah an? (Schaefer, Wolfgang von.) München, 1968.

Phil 190.80.10 — Was heisst akademisch? (Pieper, Josef.) München, 1952.

Phil 3450.19.35A — Was heisst Denken? (Heidegger, Martin.) Tübingen, 1954.

Phil 179.5 — Was heisst Philosophie? (Eichbaum-Lange, W.) Leipzig, 1902.

Phil 190.80.15 — Was heisst philosophieren? 3. Aufl. (Pieper, Josef.) München, 1959.

Phil 187.48 — Was heisst Philosophiren und was 1st Philosophie? (Mirbt, Ernst.) Jena, 1839.

Phil 818.19 — Was Heisst und zu welchem Ende studiert man Philosophiegeschichte. (Sternberg, Kurt.) Berlin, 1926.

Phil 6328.2.17 — Was im Grund der seele Ruht. 4e. Aufl. (Stekel, Wilhelm.) Wien, 1909?

Phil 8408.32 — Was ist Ästhetisch? (Herzog, J.A.) Leipzig, 1900.

Phil 9035.51 — Was ist Charakter und wie Kann er durch die Erziehung gebildet? (Hagemann, C.L.A.) Dorpat, 1881.

Phil 3450.19.65 — Was ist das - die Philosophie? (Heidegger, Martin.) Pfullingen, 1956.

Phil 3450.19.67 — Was ist das- die Philosophie? 2. Aufl. (Heidegger, Martin.) Pfullingen, 1960.

Phil 349.12.5 — Was ist Denken? (Schwartzkopff, P.) Wernigerode, 1906.

Phil 310.405 — Was ist der dialektische Materialismus? (Gropp, R.O.) München, 1960.

Phil 3450.29.7 — Was ist der Mensch? (Haecker, Theodor.) München, 1965.

Phil 585.90 — Was ist der Mensch? (Schoeps, H.J.) Göttingen, 1960.

Phil 585.260 — Was ist der Mensch? Die Anthropologie der Gegenwart im Lichte der Theologie. (Pannenberg, Wolfhart.) Göttingen, 1962.

Phil 585.260.3 — Was ist der Mensch? Die Anthropologie der Gegenwart in Lichte der Theologie. 3e Aufl. (Pannenberg, Wolfhart.) Göttingen, 1968.

Phil 165.35 — Was ist der Mensch? 2. Aufl. (Wagner, Johannes.) Braunschweig, 1954.

Phil 3450.29.5 — Was ist der Mensch? 2e Aufl. (Haecker, Theodor.) Leipzig, 1934.

Phil 5635.33 — Was ist Empfindung? (Besser, L.) Bonn, 1881.

Phil 8670.18 — Was ist Gott; cinc Summula. (Przywara, Erich.) Nürnberg, 1953.

Phil 176.80 — Was ist Individualismus? (Burckhardt, Georg E.) Leipzig, 1913.

Phil 2880.8.157 — Was ist Literatur? (Kohut, Karl.) Marburg, 1965.

Author and Title Listing

Phil 182.93.5 — Was ist Metaphysik? (Heidegger, M.) Bonn, 1931.
Phil 3450.19.25 — Was ist Metaphysik? (Heidegger, Martin.) Bonn, 1929.
Phil 3450.19.10 — Was ist Metaphysik? 4e Aufl. (Heidegger, Martin.) Frankfort, 1943.
Phil 3450.19.10.2 — Was ist Metaphysik? 7e Aufl. (Heidegger, Martin.) Frankfort, 1955.
Phil 3450.11.130 — Was ist Phänomenologie. 1. Aufl. (Reinach, Adolf.) München, 1951.
Phil 3120.2.45 — Was ist Philosophie? (Bolzano, Bernard.) Amsterdam, 1969.
Phil 5585.217 — Was ist richtiges Sehen mit Umkehrbillen. (Kottenhoff, H.) Meisenheim am Glan, 1961.
Phil 8413.24 — Was ist Schön? Eine ästhetische Studie. (Moerth, L.) München, 1913?
Phil 3487.32 — Was ist uns Kant? (Falkenfeld, Hellmuth.) Weimar, 1924.
Phil 720.92 — Was ist Wahrheit? Eine theologisch-psychologische Untersuchung. (Schär, Hans.) Zürich, 1970.
Phil 720.35 — Was ist Wahrheit in Wirklichkeit? (Grisebach, Eberhard.) Bern, 1941.
Phil 818.7.3 — Was jeder Gebildete aus der Geschichte. 3e Aufl. (Siebert, Otto.) Langensalza, 1912.
Phil 353.30 — Was Kann ich Wissen? 2. Aufl. (Wagner, J.) Braunschweig, 1962.
Phil 3640.696 — Das was kommt gesehen von Nietzsche und Hölderlin. (Broecker, W.) Pfullingen, 1963.
Phil 5258.81 — Was muss man von der Psychologie wissen? (Syrkin, N.) Berlin, n.d.
Phil 3640.386 — Was Muss man von Nietzsche Wissen? (Diefke, Max.) Berlin, 1903.
Phil 7069.67.50.2 — Was niemand glauben will. (Andreas, Peter.) Berlin, 1967.
Phil 974.2.20 — Was she a charlatan? (Kingsland, W.) London, 1927.
Phil 8870.16 — Was soll ich tun? (Wagner, J.) Braunschweig, 1953.
Phil 3497.3.23 — Was uns Kant sein kann? (Paulsen, Friedrich.) Leipzig, 1881.
Phil 5258.200 — Was weiss man von der Seele? (Schultz, Hans Jürgen.) Stuttgart, 1967.
Phil 630.16 — Was will der kritische Realismus? (Schwarz, Hermann.) Leipzig, 1894.
Phil 510.1.39 — Was wir Ernst Haeckel Verdanken. (Schmidt, Heinrich.) Leipzig, 1914. 2v.
Phil 3640.380 — Was zu Kommen hat. (Brunngraber, Rudolf.) Wien, 1947.
Phil 9560.50 — Wasen und Wandel der Tugenden. (Bollnow, O.F.) Frankfurt, 1958.
Phil 5832.8 — Washburn, M.F. The animal mind. N.Y., 1908.
Phil 5832.8.5 — Washburn, M.F. The animal mind. 2. ed. N.Y., 1917.
Phil 5832.8.7 — Washburn, M.F. The animal mind. 3. ed. N.Y., 1926.
Phil 5780.6 — Washburn, M.F. Movement and mental imagery. Boston, 1916.
Phil 9035.12 — Washington, B.S. Character building. N.Y., 1902.
Phil 8897.29A — Washington, B.T. Putting the most into life. N.Y., 1906.
Phil 8897.29.8 — Washington, B.T. Sowing and reaping. Boston, 1900.
Phil 3504.45 — Washington, W.M. The formal and material elements of Kant's ethics. N.Y., 1898.
Phil 3504.31 — Wasianski, E.A.C. Immanuel Kant. Upsala, 1810.
Phil 3504.31.5 — Wasianski, E.A.C. Immanuel Kant in seinen letzen Lebensjahren. Königsberg, 1804.
Phil 3504.31.10 — Wasianski, E.A.C. Immanuel Kant in seinen letzen Lebensjahren. Zürich, 1945.
Phil 7060.255 — Wasielewski, W. Telepathie und Hellsehen. Halle, 1922.
Phil 4800.18 — Wasik, Wiktor. Historia filozofii polskiej. Warszawa, 1958-66. 2v.
Phil 5832.3.4 — Wasmann, E. Instinct und Intelligenz im Thierreich. Freiburg, 1899.
Phil 5832.3.9 — Wasmann, E. Menschen und Tierseele. Köln, 1906.
Phil 5832.3.13 — Wasmann, E. Menschen und Tierseele. 5. Aufl. Köln, 1910.
Phil 5832.3 — Wasmann, E. Vergleichende Studien über das Seelenleben der Ameisen und der höheren Thiere. Freiburg, 1897.
Phil 510.141 — Wasmann, Erich. Entwicklungstheorie und Monismus. Innsbruck, 1910.
Phil 8735.30 — Wasmuth, E. Sokrates und der Engel. Olten, 1948.
Phil 5520.94 — Wasmuth, E. Sophie, oder Über die Sprache. Berlin, 1943.
Phil 8612.49 — Wasmuth, E. Vom Sinn des Todes. Heidelberg, 1959.
Phil 197.73 — Wasmuth, E. Von der Wahrheit der Philosophie. Köln, 1952.
Phil 5500.18 — Wasserman, Paul. Decision-making. Ithaca, 1958.
Phil 7069.23.25 — Wasylewski, S. Pod urokiem zaświatów. Lwów, 1923.
Phil 5590.355 — Waszhewitz, B. Fundamente der Persönlichkeitspsychologie. München, 1960.
Phil 1750.195 — Wat is existentialisme? (Delfgaauw, B.M.I.) Amsterdam, 1948.
Phil 672.262 — Wat is kontemporêr? (Versfeld, Marthinus.) Johannesburg, 1966.
Phil 7068.97.22 — Watch Tower Bible and Tract Society. What say the scriptures about spiritualism? Brooklyn, 1897.
Phil 7068.97.20 — Watch Tower Bible and Tract Society. What say the scriptures about spiritualism? Allegheny, Pa., 1897.
Phil 8971.2 — The water and the fire. (Vann, Gerald.) London, 1953.
Htn Phil 9362.12* — Waterhoues, E. The gentleman's monitor. London, 1665.
Phil 8602.16 — Waterhouse, E.S. Modern theories of religion. London, 1910.
Phil 8602.16.5 — Waterhouse, E.S. The philosophical approach to religion. London, 1933.
Phil 5627.62 — Waterhouse, E.S. The philosophy of religious experience. Thesis. London, 1923.
Phil 5627.62.10 — Waterhouse, E.S. Psychology and religion. London, 1930.
Phil 9530.24 — Waterman, Nixon. Boy wanted. Chicago., 1906.
Phil 9362.13 — Waterman, Nixon. The girl wanted. Chicago, 1910.
Phil 8897.4.2 — Waters, R. Culture by self-help in a literary, an academic or an oratorical career. N.Y., 1909.
Phil 8897.4 — Waters, R. Intellectual pursuits. N.Y., 1892.
Phil 5832.20 — Waters, Rolland. Principles of comparative psychology. N.Y., 1960.
Phil 4075.81 — Waters, W.G. Jerome Cardan. London, 1898.
Phil 8897.5 — Waterson, R.C. Thoughts on moral and spiritual culture. Boston, 1844.
Phil 315.17 — Waterston, G.C. Order and counter-order. N.Y., 1966.
Phil 197.61.15 — Watkin, E.I. Men and tendencies. London, 1937.
Phil 197.61 — Watkin, E.I. A philosophy of form. London, 1935.
Phil 197.61.10 — Watkin, E.I. A philosophy of form. London, 1950.
Phil 525.26 — Watkin, Edward Ingram. The philosophy of mysticism. London, 1920.
Phil 5401.16 — Watkins, D.E. Stage fright and what to do about it. Boston, 1940.
Phil 2045.135 — Watkins, J.W.N. Hobbes' system of ideas; a study in the political significance of philosophical theories. London, 1965.
Phil 2255.1.160 — Watling, John. Bertrand Russell. Edinburgh, 1970.
Phil 2340.15.30 — Watmough, J.R. Cambridge conversations. Cambridge, 1949.
Phil 3842.12 — Waton, Harry. The kabbalah and Spinoza's philosophy. N.Y., 1931-32. 2v.

Phil 510.158 — Waton, Harry. A true monistic philosophy. N.Y., 1947-1955. 2v.
Phil 7039.8 — The Watseka wonder. (Stevens, E. Winchester.) Chicago, 1879.
Phil 7039.8.2 — The Watseka wonder. (Stevens, E. Winchester.) Chicago, 1887.
Phil 8602.22 — Watson, A.C. The logic of religion. Diss. Chicago, 1918.
Phil 7069.19.240 — Watson, Albert D. The twentieth plane. Philadelphia, 1919.
Phil 4372.1.115 — Watson, Foster. Les relacions de Juan Luis Vives amb els Anglesos i amb l'Angleterra. Barcelona, 1918.
Phil 1200.63 — Watson, Gerard. The Stoic theory of knowledge. Belfast, 1966.
Phil 5910.3 — Watson, H.C. Statistics of phrenology. London, 1836-1837. 2 pam.
Phil 400.7 — Watson, J. Christianity and idealism. N.Y., 1897.
Phil 400.7.2 — Watson, J. Christianity and idealism. N.Y., 1897.
Phil 197.2 — Watson, J. Comte, Mill, and Spencer, an outline of philosophy. Glasgow, 1895.
Phil 9245.14 — Watson, J. Hedonistic theories. Glasgow, 1895.
Phil 8602.15.9 — Watson, J. The interpretation of religious experience. Glasgow, 1912. 2v.
Phil 3504.3A — Watson, J. Kant and his English critics. N.Y., 1881.
Phil 197.2.2 — Watson, J. Outline of philosophy with notes. 2d ed. Glasgow, 1898.
Phil 8602.15 — Watson, J. The philosophical basis of religion. Glasgow, 1907.
Phil 3504.3.5 — Watson, J. The philosophy of Kant explained. Glasgow, 1908.
Phil 8897.27 — Watson, John. The homely virtues. N.Y., 1902.
Htn Phil 3801.874* — Watson, John. Schelling's transcendental idealism. Chicago, 1882.
Phil 3801.874.2A — Watson, John. Schelling's transcendental idealism. Chicago, 1882.
Phil 3801.874.5 — Watson, John. Schelling's transcendental idealism. 2nd ed. Chicago, 1892.
Phil 5832.7.5 — Watson, John B. Animal education; an experimental study on the psychological development of the white rat. Chicago, 1903.
Phil 5262.21.15 — Watson, John B. The battle of behaviorism. London, 1928.
Phil 5832.9 — Watson, John B. Behavior. N.Y., 1914.
Phil 5832.9.2A — Watson, John B. Behavior. N.Y., 1914.
Phil 5262.21.6 — Watson, John B. Behaviorism. N.Y., 1925.
Phil 5262.21.5 — Watson, John B. Behaviorism. N.Y., 1925.
Phil 5262.21.7 — Watson, John B. Behaviorism. N.Y., 1930.
Phil 5832.9.5 — Watson, John B. Kinaesthetic and organic sensations. Lancaster, 1907.
Phil 5262.21.2 — Watson, John B. Psychology from the standpoint of a behaviorist. 2d ed. Philadelphia, 1924.
Phil 5262.21.3 — Watson, John B. Psychology from the standpoint of a behaviorist. 3d ed. Philadelphia, 1929.
Phil 5262.21.10A — Watson, John B. The ways of behaviorism. 1st ed. N.Y., 1928.
Phil 5832.1 — Watson, John S. The reasoning power in animals. London, 1867.
Phil 5832.1.4 — Watson, John S. The reasoning power in animals. 2. ed. London, 1870.
Phil 8595.16.27.10 — Watson, R. Apologies for Christianity and the Bible. London, 1824.
Htn Phil 8595.16.24* — Watson, R. An apology for Christianity. Philadelphia, 1796.
Htn Phil 8595.16.27.3* — Watson, R. Apology for Christianity. 1st American ed. Providence, 1794.
Phil 8595.16.24.2 — Watson, R. An apology for Christianity. 2. ed. Cambridge, 1777.
Phil 8595.16.23 — Watson, R. An apology for the Bible. Cambridge, 1828.
Phil 8595.16.26.5 — Watson, R. An apology for the Bible. London, 1796.
Htn Phil 8595.16.27* — Watson, R. An apology for the Bible. N.Y., 1796.
Phil 8595.16.28.5 — Watson, R. An apology for the Bible. N.Y., 1835. 8 pam.
Phil 8595.16.27.25 — Watson, R. An apology for the Bible. Nashville, 1855.
Phil 8595.16.27.5 — Watson, R. Apology for the Bible. 2. ed. Philadelphia, 1796.
Htn Phil 8595.16.25* — Watson, R. Christian panoply. Sheperdstown, 1797. 2 pam.
Phil 8595.16.27.7 — Watson, R. Two apologies, one for Christianity. London, 1818.
Phil 8595.16.27.8 — Watson, R. Watson refuted: being an answer to the apology for the Bible. London, 1819.
Phil 2520.349 — Watson, Richard A. The downfall of Cartesianism, 1673-1712. The Hague, 1966.
Phil 5232.10 — Watson, Robert Irving. The great psychologists. Philadelphia, 1963.
Phil 5232.10.2 — Watson, Robert Irving. The great psychologists from Aristotle to Freud. 2. ed. Philadelphia, 1968.
Phil 8595.16.27.8 — Watson refuted: being an answer to the apology for the Bible. (Watson, R.) London, 1819.
Phil 5545.48 — Watt, H.J. Economy and training of memory. N.Y., 1911.
Phil 5262.8 — Watt, H.J. Experimentelle...Theorie des Denkens. Leipzig, 1904.
Phil 5262.8.5 — Watt, H.J. Psychology. A lecture. London, 1913.
Phil 5650.9A — Watt, Henry J. Psychology of sound. Cambridge, 1917.
Phil 5640.30 — Watt, Henry J. The sensory basis and structure of knowledge. London, 1925.
Phil 197.49 — Wattjes, J.G. Practische wijsbegeerte. 2e druk. Delft, 1926.
Phil 197.90 — Watts, A.W. Psychotherapy. N.Y., 1961.
Phil 8677.20 — Watts, A.W. The supreme identity. London, 1950.
Phil 9362.19 — Watts, Alan W. Nature, man and woman. N.Y., 1958.
Phil 525.200 — Watts, Alan W. This is it. N.Y., 1960.
Phil 8602.53 — Watts, Alan W. The wisdom of insecurity. N.Y., 1951.
Phil 575.278 — Watts, Alan Wilson. The book; on the taboo against knowing who you are. N.Y., 1966.
Phil 9070.144 — Watts, Alan Wilson. Does it matter? N.Y., 1970.
Phil 6332.4.3 — Watts, Frank. Abnormal psychology and its educational applications. London, 1921.
NEDL Phil 5400.5 — Watts, I. The doctrine of the passions. London, 1751.
Htn Phil 5400.5.6* — Watts, I. The doctrine of the passions. Trenton, n.d.
NEDL Phil 5062.4.11 — Watts, S. Logic. Edinburgh, 1807.
Phil 5062.4.25 — Watts, S. Logic. London, 17- .
NEDL Phil 5062.4.9 — Watts, S. Logic. London, 1802.
Phil 5062.4.11.5 — Watts, S. Logic. London, 1813.
Htn Phil 5062.4.10* — Watts, S. Logic. 3rd American ed. Exeter, 1806.
Htn Phil 5062.4.12* — Watts, S. Logic. 6th American ed. Boston, 1819.

Htn Phil 5062.4.2* — Watts, S. Logick. London, 1725.
NEDL Phil 5062.4.6 — Watts, S. Logick. London, 1786.
NEDL Phil 5062.4.8.5 — Watts, S. Logick. London, 1801.
Htn Phil 5062.4.8* — Watts, S. Logick. 2nd American ed. Newburyport, 1796.
NEDL Phil 5062.4.3 — Watts, S. Logick. 6th ed. London, 1736.
Phil 5062.4.3.5 — Watts, S. Logick. 8th ed. London, 1745.
NEDL Phil 5062.4.4 — Watts, S. Logick. 9th ed. London, 1751.
NEDL Phil 5062.4.5 — Watts, S. Logick. 10th ed. London, 1755.
Phil 5062.4.5.2 — Watts, S. Logick. 12th ed. London, 1763.
Htn Phil 5062.4.7* — Watts, S. Logick. 16th ed. Philadelphia, 1789.
Htn Phil 197.3* — Watts, T. Philosophical essays. London, 1733.
Phil 640.4 — Watzlaurk, Joseph. Leo XIII and the new scholasticism. Cebu City, 1966.
Phil 2340.14.30 — Wauchope, Oswald S. Deviation into sense. London, 1948.
Phil 5627.135 — Wauer, G.A. Studien zur Religionspsychologie. Plauen, 1909.
Phil 1050.14.5 — Waxman, Meyer. The philosophy of Don Hasdai Crescas. N.Y., 1920.
Phil 9070.85 — Way, Joseph. Happiness for you now. 2d ed. Adyar, 1959.
Phil 6310.1.98 — Way, Lewis M. Alfred Adler. Harmondsworth, 1956.
Phil 6113.13.3 — The way, the truth and the life...Christian theosophy. 3d ed. (Dewey, J.H.) NY., 1888.
Phil 2005.9.34 — The way of a man. (Feibleman, James.) N.Y., 1969.
Phil 1750.166.235 — The way of humanism, East and West. (Mukerjee, Radhakamal.) Bombay, 1968.
Phil 978.49.35 — The way of initiation. 1st American ed. (Steiner, R.) N.Y., 1910.
Phil 9490.10 — A way of life. (Osler, W.) London, 1918.
Phil 9425.5 — The way of peace. (Ironside, Henry A.) N.Y., 1940.
Phil 583.16 — The way of phenomenology. (Zaner, Richard M.) N.Y., 1970.
Phil 197.75 — The way of philosophy. (Wheelwright, Philip.) N.Y., 1960.
Phil 3120.30.20 — The way of response. (Buber, Martin.) N.Y., 1966.
Phil 3475.3.65 — Way of wisdom. (Jaspers, Karl.) New Haven, 1951.
Phil 8610.890.42 — The way out of agnosticism, or The philosophy of free religion. 2. ed. (Abbot, Francis Ellingwood.) Ann Arbor, 1962.
Phil 8580.1 — The way out of agnosticism. (Abbot, F.E.) Boston, 1890.
Phil 3110.55.5 — The way to Christ. 1st ed. (Böhme, J.) N.Y., 1947.
Phil 3110.55.15 — The way to Christ discovered. (Böhme, J.) Manchester, 1752.
X Cg Phil 3110.55.20 — The way to Christ discovered. (Böhme, J.) N.Y., 1850. (Changed to XM 710, 1971)
Phil 5850.258.5 — The way to security. (Link, Henry C.) Garden City, 1951.
Phil 9530.5.2 — The way to wealth. (Franklin, B.) N.Y., 1848.
Htn Phil 9530.5* — The way to wealth. (Franklin, B.) Paris, 1795.
Phil 3246.50.5 — The way toward the blessed life. (Fichte, Johann Gottlieb.) London, 1849.
Phil 5262.4 — Wayland, F. Elements of intellectual philosophy. Boston, 1854.
Phil 5262.4.9 — Wayland, F. Elements of intellectual philosophy. N.Y., 1865.
Phil 8897.6 — Wayland, F. Elements of moral science. Boston, 1835.
Phil 8897.6.3 — Wayland, F. The elements of moral science. Boston, 1838.
Phil 8897.6.5 — Wayland, F. The elements of moral science. Boston, 1859.
Phil 8897.6.7 — Wayland, F. The elements of moral science. Boston, 1872.
Phil 8897.6.15 — Wayland, F. The elements of moral science. Cambridge, Mass., 1963.
Phil 8897.6.2 — Wayland, F. The elements of moral science. N.Y., 1835.
Phil 8897.6.20 — Wayland, F. The elements of moral science. Rangoon, 1885.
Phil 8897.6.10 — Wayland, F. The elements of moral science. Abridged. Boston, 1848.
Phil 9470.1 — Wayland, F. The limitations of human responsibility. Boston, 1838.
Phil 9470.1.2 — Wayland, F. The limitations of human responsibility. N.Y., 1838.
Phil 8712.05 — Wayland, Francis. A discourse delivered at...dedication of...the chapel. Providence, 1835.
Phil 8622.4 — Waylen, B. Creators of the modern spirit. N.Y., 1951.
Phil 6132.25 — Waylen, H. An apostle of healing...Pastor Richard Howton. London, 1928.
Phil 70.102 — Wayne State University. Symposium in the Philosophy of Mind, 1962. Intentionality, minds, and pereception. Detroit, 1967.
Phil 5262.21.10A — The ways of behaviorism. 1st ed. (Watson, John B.) N.Y., 1928.
Phil 193.236 — Ways of being. (Schneider, Herbert Wallace.) N.Y., 1962.
Phil 1701.26 — The ways of enjoyment. (Birro, Cela.) N.Y., 1957.
Phil 5374.260 — Ways of growth. (Otto, Herbert Arthur.) N.Y., 1968.
Phil 343.13A — The ways of knowing. (Montague, William P.) London, 1925.
Phil 348.20 — Ways of knowledge and experience. (Reid, L.A.) London, 1961.
Phil 8897.41 — The ways of life. (Ward, Stephen.) London, 1920.
Phil 8897.41.3 — The ways of life. (Ward, Stephen.) N.Y., 1920.
Phil 5066.11.45 — The ways of paradox. (Quine, Willard van Orman.) N.Y., 1966.
Phil 2750.10.111 — The ways of reason; a critical study of the ideas of Emile Meyerson. (LaLumia, Joseph.) N.Y., 1966.
Phil 5240.23 — The ways of the mind. (Adams, H.F.) N.Y., 1925.
Phil 8587.6.5 — Ways of the spirit. (Hedge, F.H.) Boston, 1877.
Phil 5755.15.1 — The ways of the will. (Farber, Leslie H.) N.Y., 1966.
Phil 187.33.10 — The ways of things: a philosophy of knowledge, nature, and value. (Montague, W.P.) N.Y., 1940.
Phil 6128.79 — Ways to self-realization. (Sadhu, Mouni.) N.Y., 1962.
Phil 7069.31.6 — We are here. (Dahl, Ludwig.) London, 1931.
Phil 9575.4 — Wealth and worth. (Hensel, W.U.) South Bethlehem, Pa., 1907.
Phil 6113.3.5 — Weather influences. (Dexter, E.G.) N.Y., 1904.
Phil 9495.133.10 — Weatherhead, L.D. Mastery of sex through psychology and religion. N.Y., 1934.
Phil 9495.133.5 — Weatherhead, L.D. Mastery of sex through psychology and religion. 2d ed. London, 1931.
Phil 5262.45.10 — Weatherhead, L.D. Psychology and life. N.Y., 1940.
Phil 7068.91.15 — Weatherly, L.A. The supernatural? Bristol, 1891.
Phil 6132.9 — Weaver, E.E. Mind and health. N.Y., 1913.
Phil 8712.1 — Weaver, G.O. Moses and modern science. Cincinnati, 1872.
Phil 9182.1 — Weaver, G.S. The Christian household. Boston, 1856.
Phil 9362.1 — Weaver, G.S. Hopes and helps for the young. N.Y., 1855.
Phil 5942.1 — Weaver, G.S. Lectures on mental science. N.Y., 1852.
Phil 5942.1.5 — Weaver, G.S. Lectures on mental science according to the philosophy of phrenology. N.Y., 1852.
Phil 5645.43 — Weaver, H.B. A study of discriminative serial action. Thesis. Philadelphia, 1942.
Phil 266.2 — The web of belief. (Quine, Willard Van Orman.) N.Y., 1970.
Phil 5520.106.5 — Het web van menselijke en sociale relaties. (Meerloo, A.M.) Den Haag, 1962.
Phil 575.52.7 — Webb, C.C.J. Divine personality and human life. London, 1920.

Phil 575.52 — Webb, C.C.J. God and personality. Aberdeen, 1919.
Phil 8602.18 — Webb, C.C.J. Group theories of religion and the individual. London, 1916.
Phil 1722.3 — Webb, C.C.J. A history of philosophy. London, 1915.
Phil 8602.18.15 — Webb, C.C.J. Natural and comparative religion. Oxford, 1912.
Phil 575.52.15 — Webb, C.C.J. Our knowledge of one another. London, 1930.
Phil 8602.18.20 — Webb, C.C.J. Philosophy and the Christian religion. Oxford, 1920.
Phil 8602.18.7 — Webb, C.C.J. Problems in the relations of God and man. London, 1915.
Phil 8602.39 — Webb, c.C.J. Religion and the thought of today. London, 1929.
Phil 8602.18.5 — Webb, C.C.J. Studies in the history of natural theology. Oxford, 1915.
Phil 8972.8 — Webb, C.J. The contribution of Christianity to ethics. Calcutta, 1932.
Phil 822.12 — Webb, Clement C.J. A history of philosophy. N.Y., 1915.
Phil 3504.30 — Webb, Clement C.J. Kant's philosophy of religion. Oxford, 1926.
Phil 5627.172 — Webb, Clement C.J. Religious experience; a public lecture. London, 1945.
Phil 8550.342 — Webb, Clement C.J. A study of religious thought in England from 1850. Oxford, 1933.
Phil 400.6 — Webb, Ewing T. Strategy in handling people. Chicago, 1931.
Phil 2115.87 — Webb, J.E. The veil of Isis...essays on idealism. Dublin, 1885.
Phil 5262.54 — Webb, T.E. Intellectualism of Locke. London, 1857.
Phil 7054.41 — Webb, W.B. The profession of psychology. N.Y., 1962.
Phil 8712.16 — Webber, C.W. Spiritual vampirism. Philadelphia, 1853.
Phil 822.1 — Webber, G.P. Tro och vebande. Stockholm, 1915. 3v.
Phil 822.1.2 — Weber, A. Histoire de la philosophie européenne. Paris, 1872.
Phil 822.1.4 — Weber, A. Histoire de la philosophie européenne. Paris, 1886.
Phil 822.1.3 — Weber, A. Histoire de la philosophie européenne. Paris, 1957. 3v.
Weber, A. Histoire de la philosophie européenne. 9e éd. Paris, 1925.
Phil 822.1.5 — Weber, A. History of philosophy. N.Y., 1896.
Phil 822.1.12 — Weber, A. History of philosophy. N.Y., 1909.
Phil 822.1.14 — Weber, A. History of philosophy. N.Y., 1912.
Phil 822.1.15A — Weber, A. History of philosophy. N.Y., 1925.
Phil 497.4 — Weber, A. Die neueste Vergötterung des Stoffs. Giessen, 1858.
Phil 3100.85 — Weber, Adalbert. Kritik der Psychologie von Beneke. Inaug-Diss. Weimar, 1872.
Phil 3801.876.30 — Weber, Alfred. Examen critique de la philosophie religieuse se Schelling. Thèse. Strasbourg, 1860.
Phil 1722.11 — Weber, Alfred. Histoire de la philosophie européenne. Paris, 1957.
Phil 3925.12 — Weber, Alfred. Das Tragische und die Geschichte. Hamburg, 1943.
Phil 3415.95 — Weber, Alfred. Wille zum Leben oder Wille zum Guten? Strassburg, 1882.
Phil 5585.46 — Weber, Christian. The concept of duration as key to the logical forms of reason. Thesis. Lincoln, 1925.
Phil 1822.5 — Weber, Conrad G. Studies in the English outlook in the period between the world wars. Bern, 1945.
Phil 5648.4 — Weber, E.H. Tastsinn und Gemeingefühl. Leipzig, 1905.
Phil 3640.91 — Weber, Ernst. Die pädogogischen Gedanken...jungen Nietzsche. Leipzig, 1907.
Phil 6032.8 — Weber, F. Aptitudes et caractère par la physiognomonie. Genève, 1970.
Phil 2555.6.90 — Weber, Georg. Die Philosophie Debrye's. Inaug.-Diss. Augsburg, 1926.
Phil 197.15 — Weber, H.B. von. Kleine Philosophie und politische Schriften. Stuttgart, 1839.
Phil 8602.44 — Weber, H.E. Das Geisteserbe der Gegenwart und die Theologie. Leipzig, 1925.
Phil 1527.5 — Weber, Hans Emil. Der Einfluss der protestantischen Schulphilosophie auf die orthodox-lutherische Dogmatik. Darmstadt, 1969.
Phil 3504.19 — Weber, Heinrich. Hamann und Kant. München, 1904.
Phil 8423.2 — Weber, J. Paul. La psychologie de l'art. Paris, 1961.
Phil 9070.105 — Weber, Johann Adam. Annulus memoriae ex dictaminibus ethicis et politicis. Salisburgi, 1679.
Phil 3504.35 — Weber, Joseph. Versuch, die harten Urtheile über der Kantische Philosophie zu Mildern. Wirzburg, 1793.
Phil 5585.235 — Weber, Klaus. Wahrnehmung und mnemische Verarbeitung wertbetonter Reihen. Stuttgart, 1964?
Phil 9182.8 — Weber, L.M. Mysterium magnum. Freiburg, 1963.
Phil 400.48 — Weber, Louis. Vers le positivisme absolu par l'idéalisme. Paris, 1903.
Phil 9182.1.2 — Weber, M.W. Über die Sozalen-Pflichten der Familie. 2. Aufl. Berlin, 1886.
Phil 197.54 — Weber, Maximilian. Kritik der Weltanschauungen. Langensalza, 1926.
Phil 2270.138 — Weber, Reinhard H. Die Philosophie von Herbert Spencer. Darmstadt, 1892.
Phil 5643.133 — Weber, Renate. Experimentelle Untersuchung über die anschauliche Grösse. Inaug. Diss. Tübingen? 1963?
Phil 3022.1 — Weber, T. Die Geschichte der neueren deutschen Philosophie. v.1-3. Münster, 1873.
Phil 197.30 — Weber, Theodor. Metaphysik. v.1-2. Gotha, 1888-1891.
Phil 5850.385.60 — Weber, Wilhelm. Die praktische Psychologie im Wirtschaftsleben. Leipzig, 1927.
Phil 4363.9 — Weber, Wilhelm. Wirtschaftethik am Vorabend des Liberalismus. Münster, 1959.
Phil 5640.34 — Das Webersche Gesetz und die psychische Relativatät. (Grotenfelt, A.) Helsingfors, 1888.
Phil 197.35 — Webster, Florence. The nature of life. N.Y., 1922.
Phil 6114.10 — Die Wechselwirkung zwischen Leib und Seele. (Erhardt, Franz.) Leipzig, 1897.
Phil 5400.64 — Wechsler, David. The measurement of emotional reactions. N.Y., 1925.
Phil 6980.775 — Wechsler, Israel S. The neurologist's point of view. N.Y., 1945.
Phil 6972.16 — Wechsler, Israel S. The neuroses. Philadelphia, 1929.
Phil 6906.35 — Wechsler, James Arthur. In a darkness. 1. ed. N.Y., 1972.
Phil 3415.91 — Weckesser, A. Der empirische Pessimismus. Bonn, 1885.
Phil 1195.4 — Wecklein, N. Die Sophisten und die Sophistik nach den angaben Plato's. Wurzburg, 1866.
Phil 8847.12 — Wedar, S. Duty and utility. Lund, 1952.
Phil 4515.101 — Wedberg, A. Den logiska strukturen hos Boströms filosofi. Uppsala, 1937.

Phil 197.85   Wedberg, Anders. Filosofins historia. Stockholm, 1958.
                   3v.
Phil 4655.4.30   Wedberg, Anders. Philosophical papers. Stockholm, 1968-
Phil 5241.92.15   Wedell, C.H. Handbook in psychology, to accompany Boring's
                   Psychology. N.Y., 1936.
Phil 3488.4.30   Weder Kant noch Goethe. (Goldschmidt, L.) Gotha, 1920.
Phil 6132.38   Wedge, Bryant M. Psychosocial problems of college men.
                   New Haven, 1958.
Phil 5725.2   Wedgwood, H. On development of the understanding.
                   London, 1848.
Phil 8897.7   Wedgwood, J. The moral ideal. London, 1888.
Phil 8897.7.2   Wedgwood, J. The moral ideal. London, 1889.
Phil 6100.15   Weed, L.H. Reconstruction of the nuclear masses in the
                   lower portion of the human brain-stem. Washington, 1914.
Phil 1900.85   Weeda, W.H. Joseph Butler als zedekundige. Utrecht, 1899.
Phil 2340.16.30   Weems, B.F. Challenge eternal. N.Y., 1936.
Phil 8677.6   Weener, J. Scheping en voorzienigheid. Utrecht, 1899.
Phil 525.260   Weergaloos. (Vinkenoog, Simon.) Hilversum, 1968.
Phil 9400.25   Der Weg, ins Altern. (Pax, Schweyerische
                   Lebensmensecherungsgesellschaft, Basel.) Basel, 1958.
Phil 8586.40   Der Weg Aufwärts. (Gröbner, Wolfgang.) Wien, 1935.
Phil 3450.11.129   Der Weg der Phäramenologie. (Landgrabe, Ludwig.)
                   Gütersloh, 1963.
Phil 6980.679   Der Weg der Tiefenpsychologie in geistesgeschichtlicher
                   Perspektive. (Seidmann, Peter.) Zürich, 1959.
Phil 8876.95   Der Weg des Menschen. (Baumgarten, Arthur.)
                   Tübingen, 1933.
Phil 812.10   Der Weg in die Philosophie. (Misch, Georg.)
                   Leipzig, 1926.
Phil 812.10.5   Der Weg in die Philosophie. 2. Aufl. (Misch, Georg.)
                   München, 1950.
VPhil 9070.130   Der Weg meiner Schüler. (Schneiderfranken, Joseph Anton.)
                   Basel, 1932.
Phil 176.115.35   De weg tot het inzicht. (Bierens de Haan, J.D.)
                   Amsterdam, 1920.
Phil 5625.106   Der Weg zum Menschen. (Schneersohn, Fischel.)
                   Berlin, 1928.
Phil 8430.36   Der Weg zum Mythos. (Michel, E.) Jena, 1919.
Phil 974.5   Der Weg zum Selbst. (Zimmer, Heinrich.) Zürich, 1944.
Phil 974.5.6   Der Weg zum Selbst. (Zimmer, Heinrich.) Zürich, 1954.
Phil 182.99   Der Weg zum Sinn des Seins. (Höcksmann, F.X.) Wien, 1933.
Phil 6319.1.183.10
                   Der Weg zur Individuation. (Jacobi, Jolan.) Zürich, 1965.
Phil 185.39   Ein Weg zur Metaphysik. (Kynast, R.) Leipzig, 1927.
Phil 182.129   Ein Weg zur Philosophie. (Hildebrandt, K.) Bonn, 1962.
Phil 3549.2.25   Der Weg zur Vollendung. (Keyserling, Hermann.) Darmstadt.
                   1-20,1924-1932 2v.
Phil 480.7   Der Weg zur Wirklichkeit. (Franck, Otto.) Leipzig, 1928.
Phil 665.110   Wege der Seele. (Queis, Karl.) Wien, 1968.
Phil 3925.11.20   Wege einer Freundschaft. (Wust, Peter.) Heidelberg, 1951.
Phil 185.60   Wege und Abwege der Philosophie. (Kraus, O.) Prag, 1934.
Phil 978.91   Wege und Irrwege in die geistige Welt. (Husemann, F.)
                   Stuttgart, 1962.
Phil 193.240   Wege zu einer Ersten Philosophie. (Schaeffler, Richard.)
                   Frankfurt, 1964.
Phil 7069.62.25   Wege Zum Licht; Erlebnisse und Gespräche mit mystikern.
                   (Koernev, E.M.) Garmisch-Partenkirchen, 1962.
Phil 8587.12   Wege zum Monotheismus. (Hehn, Johannes.) Würzburg, 1913.
Phil 5811.15.15   Wege zum Verständnis der Tiere. (Buytendijk, Frederik
                   Jacobus Johannes.) Zürich, 1940?
Phil 182.120   Wege zur Klarheit. (Heyde, Johannes.) Berlin, 1960.
Phil 2520.385   Wegelingh, William. Cartesiaanse uitzichten.
                   Lochem, 1966.
Phil 8520.16   Wegener, R. Das Problem der Theodicee. Halle, 1909.
Phil 3450.19.74   Wegmarken. (Heidegger, Martin.) Frankfurt, 1967.
Phil 7067.47   Wegner, George W. Philosophische Abhandlung von
                   Gespenstern. Berlin, 1747.
Phil 3504.26   Wegner, Gustav. Kantlexikon. Berlin, 1893.
Phil 2050.199   Wegrich, Arno. Die Geschichtsauffassung David Hume's im
                   Rahmen seines philosophischen Systems. Inaug. Diss.
                   Köln, 1926.
Htn Phil 3801.876.40*
                   Wegscheider, J.A.L. Über die von der neusten Philosophie.
                   Hamburg, 1804.
Phil 75.3   Wegweiser. (Freude, C.G.A.) Ebersbach, 1858. 2v.
Phil 8893.71   Wegweiser zum moralischen Handeln. (Seidel, A.)
                   Leipzig, 1914.
Phil 3120.55.40   Wegzeichen der Hoffnung. (Bloch, Ernst.) Frankfurt, 1967.
Phil 197.43   Wehnert, B. Wissenschaft, Philosophie, Kunst und Religion.
                   Dortmund, 1910.
Phil 5850.385.87   Wehowski, D. Ein allgemeines Modell für die Skalierung von
                   Meinungen. Münster? 1961.
Phil 6319.1.265   Wehr, Gerhard. C.G. Jung in Selbstzeugnissen und
                   Bilddokumenten. Reinbek, 1969.
Phil 3120.30.190   Wehr, Gerhard. Martin Buber in Selbstzeugnissen und
                   Bilddokumenten. Reinbek, 1969.
Phil 6319.1.266   Wehr, Gerhard. Portrait of Jung; an illustrated biography.
                   N.Y., 1971.
Phil 972.22   Wehr, Gerhard. Der Urmensch und der Mensch der Zukunft.
                   Freiburg, 1964.
Phil 1145.79   Wehrli, Fritz. Lade biosas. Studien zur ältesten Ethik bei
                   den Griechen. Leipzig, 1931.
Phil 3805.172   Wehrung, Georg. Schleiermacher in der Zeit seines Werdens.
                   Gütersloh, 1927.
Phil 960.230   Wei-uri-wei (pseud.). Why Lazarus laughed. London, 1960.
Phil 3640.163.7   Weichelt, Hans. Nietzsche der Philosoph des Heroismus.
                   Leipzig, 1924.
Phil 3640.163.2   Weichelt, Hans. Zarathustrakommentar. 2. Aufl.
                   Leipzig, 1922.
Phil 353.14   Weidauer, F. Objektivität, voraussetzungslose Wissenschaft
                   und wissenschaftliche Wahrheit. Leipzig, 1935.
Phil 9560.7.13   Weidauer, F. Die Wahrung der Ehre und die sittliche Tat.
                   Leipzig, 1936.
Phil 665.59.5   Weidenbach, H. Die Mechanik der Seele. 3e Aufl.
                   Mannheim, 1931.
Phil 5772.12   Weidenbach, Oswald. Ethos contra Logos. München, 1948.
Phil 197.32   Weidenbach, Oswald. Mensch und Wirklichkeit.
                   Giessen, 1907.
Phil 197.32.5   Weidenbach, Oswald. Weltanschauung aus dem Geiste der
                   Kritizismus. München, 1923.
Phil 5635.17   Weidensall, C.J. Studies in rhythm. Cincinnati, 1916.
Phil 5645.34   Weidlich, Karl. Farben und Farben-Empfindung.
                   Stettin, 1930.
Phil 5645.34.3   Weidlich, Karl. Farben und Farben-Empfindung.
                   Stettin, 1933.
Phil 3140.85   Weier, Winfred. Die Stellung des Johannes Clauberg in der
                   Philosophie. Diss. Mainz, 1960.
Phil 822.22   Weier, Winfried. Sinn und Teilhabe. Salzburg, 1970.

Phil 5649.21   Weigand, E. Analyse der Handgeschicklichkeit. Inaug. Diss.
                   Würzburg, 1936.
Phil 3640.175   Weigand, Wilhelm. Friedrich Nietzsche. München, 1893.
Phil 353.27   Weigel, Gustave. Knowledge. Englewood Cliffs, N.J., 1961.
Phil 8897.47.5   Weigelin, Ernst. Einführung in die Moral- und
                   Rechtsphilosophie. Leipzig, 1827.
Phil 8897.47   Weigelin, Ernst. Sitte, Recht und Morale. Berlin, 1919.
Phil 1722.1   Weigelt, G. Zur Geschichte der neueren Philosophie.
                   Hamburg, 1855.
Phil 6332.50   Weigert, C. Edith. The courage to love. New Haven, 1970.
Phil 8591.44.25   The weight of glory. (Lewis, Clive Staples.) N.Y., 1949.
Phil 3805.50.15   Die Weihnachtsfeier. (Schleiermacher, Friedrich.)
                   Basel, 1954.
Phil 3805.50.5   Die Weihnachtsfeier. (Schleiermacher, Friedrich.)
                   Halle, 1806.
Phil 3805.50   Die Weihnachtsfeier. (Schleiermacher, Friedrich.)
                   Leipzig, 1908.
Phil 3805.50.10   Die Weihnachtsfeier. 3. Ausg. (Schleiermacher, Friedrich.)
                   Berlin, 1837.
Phil 974.3.16   Die Weihnachtstagung zur Begründung. 3. Aufl. (Steiner,
                   Rudolf.) Dornach, 1963.
Phil 2940.3.20   Weil, Éric. Essais et conférences. Paris, 1970.
                   2v.
Phil 3425.340.1   Weil, Eric. Hegel et l'état. Paris, 1950.
Phil 3425.340   Weil, Eric. Hegel et l'état. Thèse. Paris, 1950.
Phil 197.71   Weil, Eric. Logique de la philosophie. Paris, 1950.
Phil 8897.83   Weil, Eric. Philosophie morale. Paris, 1961.
Phil 3504.50.2   Weil, Eric. Problemes kantiens. 2. éd. Paris, 1970.
Phil 3504.50   Weil, Eric. Problems kantiens. Paris, 1963.
Phil 1050.15   Weil, Isidore. Philosophie religieuse de Léi-ben-Gerson.
                   Paris, 1868.
Phil 5062.35   Weil, R. The art of practical thinking. N.Y., 1940.
Phil 1127.6   Weil, S. La source grecque. Paris, 1953.
Phil 7054.48   Weil, Samuel. The religion of the future. Boston, 1894.
Phil 8897.76   Weil, Simone. L'enracinement. 3. éd. Paris, 1949.
Phil 8897.76.5   Weil, Simone. The need for roots. N.Y., 1952.
Phil 8712.35   Weil, Simone. On science, necessity, and the love of God.
                   London, 1968.
Phil 5520.25.1   Weiler, Gershon. Mauthner's Critique of language.
                   Cambridge, Eng., 1970.
Phil 8677.11   Weill, Alexandre. L'athéisme déraciné de la
                   science...démocratie. Paris, 1878.
Phil 8677.11.10   Weill, Alexandre. Gesetze und Mysterien der Liebe. 1.
                   Aufl. Berlin, 1895.
Phil 8677.11.5   Weill, Alexandre. Lois et mystères de la création.
                   Paris, 1896.
Phil 3504.41   Weiller, K. Über den nachsten Zweck der Erziehung nach
                   Kantischen Grunsätzen. Regensburg, 1798.
Htn Phil 3801.875* Weiller, K. von. Über der Geist der allerneuesten Philosophie
                   der Herren Schelling, Hegel. v.1-2. München, 1803-05.
Phil 5850.385.30   Weimer, H. Fehlerbehandlung und Fehlerbewertung.
                   Leipzig, 1926.
Phil 5850.385.28   Weimer, H. Psychologie der Fehler. 2e Aufl.
                   Leipzig, 1929.
Phil 585.120.10   Wein, Hermann. Kentaurische Philosophie; Vorträge und
                   Abhandlungen. München, 1968.
Phil 585.170   Wein, Hermann. Philosophie als Erfahrungswissenschaft.
                   Den Haag, 1965.
Phil 353.20   Wein, Hermann. Das Problem des Relativismus.
                   Berlin, 1950.
Phil 3425.415   Wein, Hermann. Realdialektik. München, 1957.
Phil 5520.405   Wein, Hermann. Sprachphilosophie der Gegenwart. Den
                   Haag, 1963.
Phil 303.18   Wein, Hermann. Zugang zu philosophischen Kosmologie.
                   München, 1954.
Phil 2138.151   Weinberg, Adelaide. Theodor Gomperz and John Stuart Mill.
                   Genève, 1963.
Phil 3625.3.88   Weinberg, Carlton Berenda. Mach's empirio-pragmatism in
                   physical science. N.Y., 1937.
Phil 5520.300   Weinberg, Harry. Levels of knowing and existence.
                   N.Y., 1959.
Phil 6332.31   Weinberg, Henry. Case book in abnormal psychology.
                   N.Y., 1964.
Phil 5465.75   Weinberg, J.R. Die Dynamik des schoepferischen Akts.
                   Göttingen, 1954.
Phil 600.47   Weinberg, J.R. An examination of logical positivism.
                   London, 1936.
Phil 1527.4   Weinberg, J.R. A short history of medieval philosophy.
                   Princeton, 1964.
Phil 5032.1   Weinberg, Julius Rudolph. Abstraction, relation, and
                   induction. Madison, 1965.
Phil 5360.36   Weinberg, Julius Rudolph. Ideas and concepts.
                   Milwaukee, 1970.
Phil 353.12   Weinberg, Siegfried. Erkenntnistheorie. Berlin, 1930.
Phil 3850.8.85   Weindel, Phil. Das Verhältnis von Glauben und Wissen in
                   der Theologie Franr Anton Staudenmaiers. Düsseldorf, 1940.
Phil 5068.56.10   Weingartner, Paul. Deskription, Analytizität und Existenz.
                   Salzburg, 1966.
Phil 3850.16.115   Weingartner, R.H. Experience and culture; the philosophy
                   of G. Simmel. Middletown, 1962.
Phil 197.48   Weinhandl, F. Einführung in das moderne philosophische
                   Denken. Gotha-Stuttgart, 1924.
Phil 5262.40   Weinhandl, F. Die Gestaltanalyse. Erfurt, 1927.
Phil 353.4   Weinhandl, F. Die Methode der Gestaltanalyse.
                   Leipzig, 1923.
Phil 197.48.10   Weinhandl, F. Über das aufschliessende Symbol.
                   Berlin, 1929.
Phil 5238.145   Weinhandl, Ferdinand. Gestalthaftes Sehen...zum
                   hundertjahrigen Geburtstag von Christian von Ehrenfels.
                   Darmstadt, 1960.
Phil 9362.15.5   Weininger, Otto. Gedanken über Geschlechtsprobleme.
                   Berlin, 1922.
Phil 3905.30.10   Weininger, Otto. Geschlecht und Charakter. Berlin, 1932.
Phil 3905.30   Weininger, Otto. Geschlecht und Charakter. Wien, 1903.
Phil 3905.30.3   Weininger, Otto. Geschlecht und Charakter. 3. Aufl.
                   Wien, 1904.
Phil 3905.31   Weininger, Otto. Sex and character. London, 1906.
Phil 3905.30.15   Weininger, Otto. Sex and character. Photoreproduction.
                   London, 1910.
Phil 3905.35   Weininger, Otto. Über die letzten Dinge. Wien, 1904.
Phil 5545.172   Weinland, J.D. Improving the memory for faces and names.
                   Boston, 1934.
Phil 353.10   Weinmann, R. Philosophie, Welt und Wirklichkeit.
                   München, 1922.
Phil 353.16   Weinschenk, C. Das Wirklichkeitsproblem der
                   Erkenntnistheorie. Leipzig, 1936.
Phil 6332.24   Weinschenk, Curt. Die erbliche Lese- rechtssch
                   Reiheschwäche. Bern, 1962.

Phil 5062.16 — Weinstein, B. Die philosophische Grundlagen der Wissenschaften. Leipzig, 1906.
Phil 6980.775.20 — Weinstein, E.A. Cultural aspects of delusion. N.Y., 1962.
Phil 845.2.5 — Weinstock, Heinrich. Realer Humanismus. Heidelberg, 1955.
Phil 845.2 — Weinstock, Heinrich. Die Trajödie des Humanismus. Heidelberg, 1953.
Phil 3450.17.90 — Weinzierl, H. Zur Entwicklungsgeschichte der neuern katholischen Philosophie...Hertlings. Inaug. Diss. Reimlingen, 1928.
Phil 5374.54 — Weir, A. Light, a philosophy of consciousness. Oxford, 1932.
Phil 3504.36 — Weir, Archibald. The critical philosophy of Kant. London, 1881.
Phil 197.60 — Weir, Archibald. Shallows and deeps. Oxford, 1934.
Phil 5832.6 — Weir, J. The dawn of reason. N.Y., 1899.
Phil 6332.1.2 — Weir, J. The psychical correlation of religious emotion and sexual desire. 2d ed. Louisville, Ky., 1897.
Htn   Phil 6332.1* — Weir, J. The psychical correlation of religious emotion and sexual desire. 2d ed. Louisville, Ky., 1897.
Phil 8647.9 — Weir, J.F. Human destiny in the light of revelation. Boston, 1903.
Phil 1210.16F — Weis, Georg. Nexus philosophiae theorico-politécae pecipatentica. Prague, 1670.
Phil 497.3 — Weis, L. Anti-Materialismus. v.1-2, 3. Berlin, 1871-73. 2v.
Phil 3504.28 — Weis, Ludwig. Kant: Naturgesetze, Natur- und Gotteserkennen. Berlin, 1903.
Phil 8423.15 — Weisbach, W. Von Geschmack und seinen Wandlungen. Basel, 1947.
Phil 8050.32 — Weisbach, Werner. Stilbegriffe und Stilphänomene. Wien, 1957.
Phil 3246.232 — Weischedel, W. Der Aufbruch der Freiheit. Leipzig, 1939.
Phil 3460.94.5 — Weischedel, Wilhelm. Jacobi und Schelling. Darmstadt, 1969.
Phil 3925.2.95 — Weischedel, Wilhelm. Philosophische Grunzgänge. Stuttgart, 1967.
Phil 3460.94 — Weischedel, Wilhelm. Streit um die göttlichen Dinge. Darmstadt, 1967.
Phil 3842.1 — Weise, H. Über das Erste Buch der Ethik des Spinoza. Salzwede, 187-?
Phil 2340.10.235 — Weisenbeck, Jude D. Alfred North Whitehead's philosophy of values. Thesis. Waukesha, Wisconsin, 1969.
Phil 6400.16 — Weisenburg, T. Aphasia. N.Y., 1935.
Phil 353.6 — Weisengrün, P. Das Problem. Leipzig, 1892.
Phil 2262.84 — Weiser, C.F. Shaftesbury und das deutsche Geistesleben. Leipzig, 1916.
Phil 5262.44 — Weiser-Aall, Lily. Volkskunde und Psychologie; eine Einführung. Berlin, 1937.
Phil 165.165 — Ein Weiser lebt unter uns. (Edel, Reiner F.) Marburg, 1958.
Phil 8897.8 — Weishaupt, A. Die Leuchte des Diogenes. Regensburg, 1804.
Phil 3504.4 — Weishaupt, A. Uber die Kantischen Anschauungen. Nürnberg, 1788.
Phil 8897.8.10 — Weishaupt, A. Ueber die Selbstkenntniss. Regensburg, 1794.
Phil 3504.4.10 — Weishaupt, A. Zweifel über die Kantischen Begriffe von Zeit und Raum. Nürnberg, 1788.
Phil 822.20 — Weishedel, Wilhelm. Die philosophische Hintertreppe. München, 1966.
Phil 3925.2.90 — Weishedel, Wilhelm. Wirklichkeit und Wirklichkeiten. Berlin, 1960.
Phil 3450.25.10 — Die Weisheit der Langenweile. (Hiller, Kurt.) Leipzig, 1913.
Phil 188.21 — Weisheit der Welt. (Natzmer, G. von.) Berlin, 1954.
Phil 1182.52 — Weisheit und Wissenschaft. (Burkert, Walter.) Nürnberg, 1962.
Phil 6332.32 — Weisman, A.D. The existential core of psychoanalysis. Boston, 1965.
Phil 5262.30 — Weiss, Albert P. A theoretical basis of human behavior. Columbus, 1925.
Phil 5262.30.5 — Weiss, Albert P. A theoretical basis of human behavior. 2d ed. Columbus, 1929.
Phil 3890.1.84 — Weiss, Antonia R. Friedrich Adolf Trendelenburg. Kallmünz, 1960.
Phil 8897.50.2 — Weiss, Berthold. Die ethische Aufgabe des Menschen. Berlin, 1893.
Phil 510.19.2 — Weiss, Bruno. Monismus, Monistenbund, Radikalismus und Christentum. 2e Aufl. Breme, 1908.
Phil 6980.775.50 — Weiss, Edward. The structure and dynamics of the human mind. N.Y., 1960.
Phil 8897.9 — Weiss, F.R. de. Principes philosophiques. Bruxelles, 1832. 2v.
Phil 3425.704 — Weiss, Frederich Gustav. Hegel's critique of Aristotle's philosophy of mind. The Hague, 1969.
Phil 3260.152 — Weiss, Georg. Fries' Lehre von Ahndung in Ästhetik. Göttingen, 1912.
Phil 7081.2 — Weiss, Harry Bischoff. Oneirocritica Americana. N.Y., 1944.
Phil 8602.4 — Weiss, J. American religion. Boston, 1871.
Phil 8647.1 — Weiss, J. The immortal life. Boston, 1880.
Phil 8602.78 — Weiss, P. The God we seek. Carbondale, 1964.
Phil 2340.11.40 — Weiss, Paul. Man's freedom. New Haven, 1950.
Phil 2340.11.50 — Weiss, Paul. Modes of being. New Haven, 1956. 2v.
Phil 2340.11.30 — Weiss, Paul. Nature and man. N.Y., 1947.
Phil 8423.11 — Weiss, Paul. Nine basic arts. Carbondale, 1961.
Phil 2340.11.60 — Weiss, Paul. Philosophy in process. Carbondale, 1963-64. 5v.
Phil 5003.6A — Weiss, Paul. A preliminary draft of a bibliography of contributions to modern logic. Supplement. n.p., n.d.
Phil 2340.11 — Weiss, Paul. Reality. Princeton, 1938.
Phil 2340.11.55 — Weiss, Paul. Religion and art. Milwaukee, 1963.
Phil 8897.88 — Weiss, Paul. Right and wrong; a philosophical dialogue between father and son. N.Y., 1967.
Phil 8897.74 — Weiss, Richard. World without frontiers. Sydney, 1950.
Phil 3640.625 — Weiss, Tomasz. Fryderyk Nietzsche w piśmiennictwie polskim lat 1890-1914. Wrocław, 1961.
Phil 3110.190 — Weiss, Victor. Die Gnosis Jakob Böhmes. Zürich, 1955.
Phil 6315.2.385 — Weiss-Rosmarin, Trude. The Hebrew Moses; an answer to Sigmund Freud. N.Y., 1939.
Phil 5062.28 — Weissborn, G. _Logik und Metaphysik. Halle, 1850.
Phil 3425.285 — Weisse, C.H. Über den gegenwärtigen Standpunct der philosophischen Wissenschaft. Leipzig, 1829.
Phil 8423.26.2 — Weisse, Christian H. System der Ästhetik als Wissenschaft von der Idee der Schönheit, reprografischer Nachdruck von 1830. Hildesheim, 1966.
Phil 3925.3.31 — Weisse, Christian Hermann. Grundzüge der Metaphysik. Hamburg, 1835.

Phil 3925.3.50 — Weisse, Christian Hermann. Kleine Schriften zur Aesthetik und ästhetischen Kritik. Leipzig, 1867.
Phil 3925.3.52 — Weisse, Christian Hermann. Kleine Schriften zur Ästhetik und ästhetischen Kritik. Hildesheim, 1966.
Phil 3925.3.35 — Weisse, Christian Hermann. Philosophische Dogmatik oder Philosophie des Christenthums. Leipzig, 1855-62. 3v.
Phil 3925.3.45 — Weisse, Christian Hermann. Das philosophische Problem der Gegenwart. Leipzig, 1842.
Phil 3925.3.40 — Weisse, Christian Hermann. Psychologie und Unsterblichkeitslehre. Leipzig, 1869.
Phil 8685.17 — Weissenborn, G. Vorlesungen über Pantheismus und Theismus. Marburg, 1859.
Phil 3805.86 — Weissenborn, G. Vorlesungen über Schleiermacher's Dialektik und Dogmatik. v.1-2. Leipzig, 1847-49.
Phil 3925.5.80 — Weissenborns Stellung zum Theismus. Inaug. Diss. (Goldstandt, H.) Würzburg, 1917.
Phil 3504.40 — Weissfeld, M. Kants Gesellschaftslehre. Bern, 1907.
Phil 3504.60 — Weisskopf, Traugott. Immanuel Kant und die Pädagogik. Zürich, 1970.
Phil 353.34 — Weissman, David J. Dispositional properties. Carbondale, 1965.
Phil 1135.50 — Weisz, C.O.M. Metaphysische Theorie der griechischen Philosophie. Rostock, 1873.
Phil 3486.14.10 — Die Weiterbildung der Kant'schen Aprioritätslehre bis zur Gegenwart. Inaug. Diss. (Eisler, Rudolf.) Leipzig, 1895.
Phil 930.7.50 — Weitere Verbesserungen zu Forke's Geschichte der chineschen Philosophie. (Zach, E. von.) Batavia, 1938.
Phil 8423.22 — Weitz, M. Philosophy of the arts. Cambridge, 1950.
Phil 8400.31 — Weitz, M. Problems in aesthetics. N.Y., 1959.
Phil 672.129 — Weitzenböck, R. Over de vierde dimensie. Groningen, 1923.
Phil 6692.10 — Weitzenhoffer, André M. Hypnotism. N.Y., 1953.
Phil 6692.10.5 — Weitzenhoffer, André M. Stanford hypnotic suseptibility scale. Palo Alto, 1959.
Phil 5262.48.20 — Weizsäcker, Viktor. Gestalt und Zeit. 2. Aufl. Göttingen, 1960.
Phil 5262.48.5 — Weizsäcker, Viktor. Der Gestaltkreis. 3. Aufl. Stuttgart, 1947.
Phil 7060.89 — Welby, H. Mysteries of life, death and futurity. London, 1861.
Phil 7060.84 — Welby, H. Signs before death. London, 1825.
Phil 5520.23.5 — Welby, Victoria. Significs and language. London, 1911.
Phil 5520.23 — Welby, Victoria. What is meaning. London, 1903.
Phil 8602.38 — Welby-Gregory, Victoria. Echoes of larger life. London, 1929.
Phil 8602.38.10 — Welby-Gregory, Victoria. Other dimensions. London, 1931.
Phil 5262.10 — Welch, A.S. The teacher's psychology. N.Y., 1889.
Phil 3450.11.101 — Welch, E.P. Edmund Husserl's phenomenology. Los Angeles, 1939.
Phil 3450.11.116 — Welch, E.P. Philosophy of Edmund Husserl...development of his phenomenology. N.Y., 1941.
Phil 5465.34 — Welch, Livingston. Imagination and human nature. London, 1935.
Phil 978.49.225 — Welche Gesichtspunkte liegeni Errichtung der Waldorfschule zu Grunde? (Steiner, R.) Dornach, 1932.
Phil 2520.265 — Welcher Einfluss hat die Philosophie des Cartesius auf die Ausbildung der des Spinoza Gehabt. (Ritter, Heinrich.) Leipzig, 1817.
Phil 5262.34 — Weld, Harry P. Psychology as science, its problems and points of view. London, 1928.
Phil 5262.34.2 — Weld, Harry P. Psychology as science, its problems and points of view. N.Y., 1928.
Phil 5590.470 — Weldes, Göran. Psykologi och mentalhygien. Lund, 1969.
Phil 3504.44.5 — Weldon, Thomas D. Critique of pure reason. 2nd ed. Oxford, 1958.
Phil 3504.44 — Weldon, Thomas D. Introduction to Kant's Critique of pure reason. Oxford, 1945.
Phil 7055.156 — Weldon, Warren. A happy medium: the life of Caroline Randolph Chapman. Englewood Cliffs, 1970.
Phil 1850.109 — Welhelmy, Gerrit. De vita et philosophia F. Baconi. Groningae, 1843.
Phil 3640.560 — Welke, Bernhard. Nietzsches Atheismus und das Christentum. Darmstadt, 1958.
Phil 6960.16 — Die wellanscharlie Orienterung der Schizophrenen. (Kreitler, Hans.) München, 1965.
Phil 5262.49 — Wellek, A. Ganzheitspsychologie und Strukturtheorie. Bern, 1955.
Phil 5286.7 — Wellek, Albert. Ganzheitspsychologie und Strukturtheorie. 2. Aufl. Bern, 1969. 4v.
Phil 5203.25 — Wellek, Albert. Gesamtverzeichnis der deutsparchigen psychologischen Literatur der Jahre 1942 bis 1960. Göttingen, 1965.
Phil 5262.4.50 — Wellek, Albert. Der Kückfall in die Methodenkrise der Psychologie. Göttingen, 1959.
Phil 5250.13.87 — Wellek, Albert. Das Problem des seeleschen Seins. 2. Aufl. Meisenheim, 1953.
Phil 5250.13.85 — Wellek, Albert. Die Wiederherstellung der Seelenwissenschaft im Lebenswerk Felix Kruegers. Hamburg, 1950.
Phil 3504.38A — Wellek, René. Immanuel Kant in England, 1793-1838. Princeton, 1931.
Phil 5247.75 — Das Wellengesetz unseres Lebens. (Hellpach, W.) Hamburg, 1941.
Phil 260.3 — Welling, J.C. Atomic philosophy. Washington, 1884.
Phil 8897.73.5 — Wellman, Carl. Challenge and response. Carbondale, 1971.
Phil 8897.73 — Wellman, Carl. The language of ethics. Cambridge, 1961.
Phil 2225.16.80 — Wellmer, Albrecht. Methodologie als Erkenntnistheorie. Frankfurt, 1967.
Phil 5645.45 — Wellmer, E.N. Retinal structure and colour vision. Cambridge, Eng., 1946.
Phil 1865.177 — Wells, D.B. Saint Paul vindicated, being Part I of a reply...not Paul, but Jesus. Cambridge, 1824.
Phil 6132.18 — Wells, D.W. Psychology applied to medicine. Philadelphia, 1907.
Phil 5650.4 — Wells, F.L. Linguistic lapses. N.Y., 1906.
Phil 6332.2.7 — Wells, F.L. Mental adjustments. N.Y., 1920.
Phil 6332.2.9 — Wells, F.L. Mental adjustments. N.Y., 1922.
Phil 5262.33 — Pamphlet vol. Wells, F.L. A statistical study of literary merit. 1907-16. 37 pam.
Phil 6972.11 — Pamphlet box. Wells, F.L. Minor writings.
Phil 5402.12 — Wells, Frederic L. Pleasure and behavior. N.Y., 1924.
Phil 6972.19.5 — Wells, Frederick L. Mental examiners handbook. 2. ed. N.Y., 1945.
Phil 5640.15 — Wells, G.R. Influence of stimulus...duration on reaction time. Princeton, 1913.
Phil 197.59 — Wells, Gabriel. Riddle of the body. N.Y., 1934.
Phil 7069.27.55 — Wells, H.B. Spiritual America. Boston, 1927.
Phil 197.16.4 — Wells, H.G. First and last things. London, 1918.
Phil 197.16 — Wells, H.G. First and last things. N.Y., 1908.

	Phil 8677.9.5	Wells, H.G. God the invisible king. London, 1917.
	Phil 8677.9	Wells, H.G. God the invisible king. N.Y., 1917.
	Phil 5232.9	Wells, H.K. Pavlov and Freud. N.Y., 1956. 2v.
	Phil 197.74	Wells, H.K. Pragmatism. N.Y., 1954.
	Phil 6332.30	Wells, Harry K. The failure of psychoanalysis. N.Y., 1963.
	Phil 2340.10.110	Wells, Harry K. Process and unreality. N.Y., 1950.
	Phil 7069.30.45	Wells, Helen. The hidden path. Floral Park, N.Y., 1930. 4 pam.
	Phil 7069.34.62	Wells, Helen B. As in a mirror. N.Y., 1934. 2 pam.
	Phil 7069.33.54	Wells, Helen B. Collection mimeographs. N.Y., 1933. 8 pam.
	Phil 7069.33.52	Wells, Helen B. Flower-life in ethic. N.Y., 1933. 2 pam.
	Phil 7069.30.46F	Wells, Helen B. The hidden path. v.2. N.Y., 1934.
	Phil 7069.34.60	Wells, Helen B. The intelligence of the spaces. N.Y., 1934.
	Phil 7069.35.50	Wells, Helen B. Key to the spaces...dictated by A.P. Mathewson. N.Y., 1935.
	Phil 7069.31.50	Wells, Helen B. Law governing mediumship. N.Y., 1931.
	Phil 7069.33.50	Wells, Helen B. Lessons in etheric and electric vibratory law. N.Y., 1933. 6 pam.
	Phil 7069.35.51F	Wells, Helen B. Linking the spaces. N.Y., 1935. 2 pam.
	Phil 7069.35.60	Wells, Helen B. The progressive Pllgrim's progress. N.Y., 1935.
	Phil 7069.34.50	Wells, Helen B. Pythagoras speaks. N.Y., 1934.
	Phil 7069.34.63	Wells, Helen B. Ribbons of the sky. v.1-3. N.Y., 1934-35.
	Phil 7069.35.52	Wells, Helen B. Some laws of materialization. Dictated by John King. N.Y., 1935.
	Phil 7069.34.55	Wells, Helen B. The song of the seven seas. N.Y., 1934.
	Phil 7069.35.56	Wells, Helen B. Through the gates of time. v.1. N.Y., 1935.
	Phil 7069.35.54	Wells, Helen B. "Whom the gods love". Dictated by Ernest Wells. N.Y., 1935.
	Phil 7069.35.45	Pamphlet box. Wells, Helen B. Psychic books.
	Phil 8897.10	Wells, K.G. Lessons in ethics. pt.1. Boston, 1882.
	Phil 5627.88	Wells, Mary. Memoir of Mrs. Joanna Turner. 1. American ed. N.Y., 1827.
	Phil 705.29	Wells, R.V. Three Christian transcendentalists. N.Y., 1943.
	Phil 5627.57	Wells, W.R. The biological foundations of belief. Boston, 1921.
	Phil 6132.32	Welsh, F.G. (Mrs.). Can we live forever? Chicago, 1938.
	Phil 1135.178	Welskopf, E.C. Probleme der Musse im alten Hellas. Berlin, 1962.
	Phil 3790.32	Welt, All, Einheit. (Rothert, Helmut.) München, 1969.
	Phil 978.49.250	Welt, Erde und Mensch. 2. Aufl. (Steiner, R.) Freiburg, 1956.
	Phil 3450.11.150	Welt. (Brand, Gerd.) Den Haag, 1955.
	Phil 291.4	Welt - Leben - Seele. (Kassowitz, Max.) Wien, 1908.
	Phil 3900.1.80	Welt- und Lebensanschauung Friedrich Ueberwegs. (Brasch, M.) Leipzig, 1889.
	Phil 1718.15	Welt- und Lebensanschauungen im neunzehnten Jahrhundert. v.1-2. (Steiner, Rudolf.) Berlin, 1901.
	Phil 176.10.10	Welt- und Lebensansichte in Ihren. (Baumann, Julius J.) Gotha, 1906.
	Phil 197.51	Welt- und libenanschauungen Hevoorgegangen aus Religion, Philosophie und Naturerkenntnis. (Wienstein, M.B.) Leipzig, 1910.
	Phil 9290.2	Die Welt als Arbeit. (Nagel, O.) Stuttgart, 1909.
	Phil 188.4	Die Welt als Entwicklung des Geistes. (Noire, L.) Leipzig, 1874.
	Phil 306.5	Die Welt als Fühlen. (Zirm, E.K.) Leipzig, 1937.
	Phil 8419.9	Die Welt als Gestalt. (Stange, Alfred.) Köln, 1952.
	Phil 188.14	Welt als Individuation. (Nordenholz, A.) Leipzig, 1927.
	Phil 8708.37	Die Welt als Schöpfung. (Semmelroth, O.) Frankfurt, 1962.
	Phil 176.121	Die Welt als Spannung und Rhythmus. (Barthel, Ernst.) Leipzig, 1928.
	Phil 176.114	Die Welt als Subjekt-Objekt. (Bauer, G.F.) Berlin, 1923.
	Phil 192.33.5	Die Welt als Tat. 3e Aufl. (Reinke, J.) Berlin, 1903.
	Phil 192.33	Die Welt als That. (Reinke, J.) Berlin, 1899.
	Phil 3270.2.31	Die Welt als Vorstellung. (Fick, Adolf.) Würzburg, 1870.
	Phil 348.4.5	Die Welt als Wahrnehmung und Begriff. (Rehmke, J.) Berlin, 1880.
	Phil 3808.35.10	Die Welt als Wille und Vorstellung. (Schopenhauer, Arthur.) Berlin, 1930.
	Phil 3808.35.3	Die Welt als Wille und Vorstellung. (Schopenhauer, Arthur.) Halle, 1891? 2v.
Htn	Phil 3808.33*	Die Welt als Wille und Vorstellung. (Schopenhauer, Arthur.) Leipzig, 1819.
Htn	Phil 3808.35*	Die Welt als Wille und Vorstellung. (Schopenhauer, Arthur.) Leipzig, 1859. 2v.
	Phil 3808.35.2.3	Die Welt als Wille und Vorstellung. (Schopenhauer, Arthur.) Leipzig, 1873. 2 pam.
	Phil 3808.35.2	Die Welt als Wille und Vorstellung. (Schopenhauer, Arthur.) Leipzig, 1873. 2v.
	Phil 3808.35.5	Die Welt als Wille und Vorstellung. (Schopenhauer, Arthur.) München, 1912-13. 2v.
	Phil 3808.35.6	Die Welt als Wille und Vorstellung. (Schopenhauer, Arthur.) Stuttgart, 19- ? 2v.
	Phil 3808.35.4	Die Welt als Wille und Vorstellung. 5. Aufl. (Schopenhauer, Arthur.) Leipzig, 1879. 2v.
	Phil 178.49	Die Welt als Wille zum Selbst. (Dressler, Max.) Seidelberg, 1904.
	Phil 400.61	Die Welt der Formen. (Friedmann, H.) Berlin, 1925.
	Phil 400.61.5	Die Welt der Formen. 2e Aufl. (Friedmann, H.) München, 1930.
	Phil 6319.1.78	Welt der Psyche. (Jung, C.G.) Zürich, 1954.
	Phil 298.20	Die Welt in der Sicht der wissenschaftlichen Vernunft. (Rademaker, Hans.) Bonn, 1965.
	Phil 3625.13.34	Welt und Mensch in ihrem irrealen Aufbau. 4. Aufl. (Müller, Aloys.) Leiden, 1951.
	Phil 193.138.5	Das Welt-Vakuum. (Stern, M.R. von.) Linz, 1923.
	Phil 299.13	Die Welt wie sie Jetzt ist und wie sie sein Wird. (Schneider, K.C.) Wien, 1917.
	Phil 300.3	Das Weltall nach menschlicher Ansicht. (Tieftrunk, J.H.) Halle, 1821.
	Phil 3800.387.10	Die Weltalter; Fragmente. (Schelling, F.W.J. von.) München, 1946.
	Phil 3640.264	Der weltanschauliche Gehalt von Nietzsches Dichtungen. Inaug. Diss. (Wahle, Aloys.) Dillingen, 1933.
	Phil 3850.18.108	Der weltanschauliche Hintergrund der materialen Wertethik Max Schelers. Diss. (Frick, Paul.) Stuttgart, 1933.
	Phil 8050.48	Weltanschaungsprobleme und Lebenssysteme in der Kunst der Vergangenheit. (Burger, Fritz.) München, 1918.
	Phil 193.138	Weltanschauung; Ergebnisse freien Denkens. (Stern, M.R. von.) Linz, 1921.
	Phil 801.25	Weltanschauung. (Bergmann, E.) Breslau, 1926. 2v.
	Phil 303.7	Weltanschauung. Philosophie und Religion. Berlin, 1911.
	Phil 176.90	Die Weltanschauung als Erlebnis. Heft 3-4. (Brausewetter, A.) Leipzig, 1920. 2v.
	Phil 197.32.5	Weltanschauung aus dem Geiste der Kritizismus. (Weidenbach, Oswald.) München, 1923.
	Phil 400.49.10	Die Weltanschauung des absoluten Idealismus. (Kröger, Otto.) Harz, 1909.
	Phil 510.152	Die Weltanschauung des Halbgebildeten. (Schmitz, Oscar A.H.) München, 1914.
	Phil 282.18	Die Weltanschauung des modernen Menschen. (Bürgel, B.H.) Berlin, 1932.
	Phil 284.11	Die Weltanschauung des modernen Naturforschers. (Dennert, E.) Stuttgart, 1907.
	Phil 182.54	Die Weltanschauung des Naturforschers. (Hallier, Ernst.) Jena, 1875.
	Phil 197.94	Die Weltanschauung des Wissens. 1. Aufl. (Walendy, Udo.) Vlotho, 1969. 2v.
	Phil 3625.3.91	Die Weltanschauung eines modernen Naturforschers. (Beer, Theodor.) Dresden, 1903.
	Phil 3090.88	Die Weltanschauung Franz von Baaders in ihrem Gegensatz zu Kant. (Klamroth, Erich.) Berlin, 1965.
	Phil 3640.187	Die Weltanschauung Friedrich Nietzsches. (Kaatz, Hugo.) Dresden, 1892.
	Phil 3210.85	Die Weltanschauung G.T. Fechners. (Adolph, H.) Stuttgart, 1923.
	Phil 181.72	Weltanschauung Ideologie. (Gessen, S.I.) Praha, 1934.
	Phil 5592.192	Weltanschauung in psychologischer Sicht. (Busemann, Adolf.) München, 1967.
	Phil 3824.2.5	Die Weltanschauung Spinozas. (Erhardt, Franz.) Stuttgart, 1928.
	Phil 3842.5	Die Weltanschauung Spinozas. Bd.1. (Wenzel, Alfred.) Leipzig, 1907.
	Phil 3195.6.86	Weltanschauung und Dichtung...Dilthey. (Unger, Rudolf.) Zürich, 1917.
	Phil 3270.3.93	Weltanschauung und Menschenleben...Jakob Frohschammer's. (Reich, Edward.) Grossenhain, 1884.
	Phil 818.17	Die Weltanschauung von den Griechen bis zu Hegel. (Schlunk, M.) Hamburg, 1921.
	Phil 185.11	Die Weltanschauungen. (Kym, A.L.) Zürich, 1854.
	Phil 1701.9.5	Die Weltanschauungen der grossen Philosophie der Neuzeit. 6e Aufl. (Busse, Ludwig.) Leipzig, 1917.
	Phil 3552.88	Die Weltanschauungen Leibnitz' und Schopenhauer's, ihre Gründe und ihre Berechtigung. (Jellinek, G.) Wien, 1872.
	Phil 3808.139	Die Weltanschauungen Leibnitz und Schopenhauer's ihre Gründe und ihre Berechtigung. (Jellinck, G.) Wien, 1872.
	Phil 291.3	Weltanschauungen und Welterkenntnis. (Kern, Berthold.) Berlin, 1911.
	Phil 187.46	Weltanschauungsfragen. (Menzer, Paul.) Stuttgart, 1918.
	Phil 185.26	Weltanschauungsfragen. 2e Aufl. (Koppelmann, W.) Berlin, 1922.
	Phil 176.80.10	Weltanschauungskrisis. v.1-2. (Burckhardt, Georg E.) Leipzig, 1925-26.
	Phil 287.3	Weltanschauungslehre. (Gomperz, Heinrich.) Jena, 1905-08. 2v.
	Phil 8592.85	Weltanschauungsprobleme der Gegenwart. 1. Aufl. (Meyer, Hans.) Recklinghausen, 1956.
	Phil 1722.5.2	Die Weltanschuungen der Gegenwart. 2e Aufl. (Wenzig, Carl.) Leipzig, 1919.
	Phil 4060.1.80	Die Weltauschauung Roberto Ardigo. (Bluwstein, J.) Leipzig, 1911.
	Phil 9070.75	Weltbewältigung. (Mueller-Eckhard, Hans.) Stuttgart, 1959.
	Phil 338.4.5	Das Weltbild der Zukunst. (Heim, Karl.) Berlin, 1904.
	Phil 978.49.190	Das Weltbild des deutschen Idealismus. (Steiner, R.) Dornach, 1930.
	Phil 813.5	Das Weltbild des Menschen. (Natzner, Gert von.) Berlin, 1962.
	Phil 3415.92	Das Weltbild Hartmanns. (Ziegler, Leopold.) Leipzig, 1910.
	Phil 2905.1.495	Das Weltbild Teilhard de Chardins. (Schmitz-Moormann, Karl.) Köln, 1966.
	Phil 3585.13.90	Die Weltdeutung Mathilde Ludendorffs. (Kurth, Hans.) München, 1932.
	Phil 3475.3.165	Welte, Bernard. La foi philosophique chez Jaspers et Saint Thomas d'Aquin. Bruges, 1958.
	Phil 384.15	Welte, Bernhard. Determination und Freiheit. 1. Aufl. Frankfurt, 1969.
	Phil 410.84	Welte, Bernhard. Im Spielfeld von Endlichkeit und Unendlichkeit. Frankfurt, 1967.
	Phil 9240.20	Welte, Bernhard. Über das Böse. Basel, 1959.
	Phil 3808.99	Weltelend und Weltschmerz. (Meyer, J.B.) Bonn, 1872.
	Phil 290.2.3	Das Weltgeheimnis. (Jellinek, K.) Stuttgart, 1922.
	Phil 306.3	Weltentstehung in Sage und Wissenschaft. (Ziegler, Konrat.) Leipzig, 1925.
	Phil 978.49.850	Weltenville und Menschenziele in der Geschichte. (Haeusler, Friedrich.) Dornach, 1961.
	Phil 6834.3	Welter, Ernst Günther. Bibliographie Freundschaftseros; einschliesslich Homoerotik, Homosexualität und der verwandten und vergleichenden Gebiete. Frankfurt, 1964.
	Phil 5520.600	Welterfahrung in der Sprache. Freiburg, 1968-
	Phil 3705.4	Welterlebnis. (Odebrecht, R.) Berlin, 1938.
	Phil 2805.450	Weltflucht und Politik. (Goldmann, Lucien.) Neuwied, 1967.
	Phil 282.7.11	Weltgebäude, Weltgesetze, Weltentwicklung. (Becher, Erich.) Berlin, 1915.
	Phil 186.87	Weltgeschehen und Welterkenntnis. (Lindemann, H.A.) Baden, 1914.
	Phil 818.37	Weltgeschichte der Philosophie. (Schilling, Kurt.) Berlin, 1964.
	Phil 6055.2.2	Weltgeschichte graphologisch Gesehen. (Mueller, Alfred Eugen.) Köln, 1965.
	Phil 978.82	Weltgeschichte im Lichte des heiligen Gral. (Stein, W.J.) Stuttgart, 1928.
	Phil 978.49.900	Die Weltgeschichte und das Menschen-Ish. (Gabert, Erich.) Stuttgart, 1967.
	Phil 3425.480	Die weltgeschichtliche Erfassung des Orients bei Hegel und Ranke. (Schulin, Ernst.) Göttingen, 1958.
	Phil 176.63	Weltharmonie monistische Betrachtungen. (Bertz, Eduard.) Dresden, 1908.
	Phil 343.12	Der welthistorische Prozess als die unzige Grundlage der Philosophie. (Mayer, J.V.) Freiburg, 1857.
	Phil 181.36	Das Weltleben oder die Metaphysik. (Grassmann, R.) Stettin, 1881.
	Phil 5062.17.8	Welton, James. Groundwork of logic. London, 1921.
	Phil 5062.17	Welton, James. An intermediate logic. London, 1911.
	Phil 5062.17.5	Welton, James. Intermediate logic. 4th ed. London, 1938.

Phil 1703.7 — Weltordnung und Heilsgeschichte. (Dempf, Alois.) Einsiedeln, 1958.

Phil 3200.13 — Das Weltproblem bei Ferdinand Ebner. (Sandmann, P.) München, 1962.

Phil 600.16 — Das Weltproblem vom positivistischen Standpunkte aus. (Petzoldt, Joseph.) Leipzig, 1906.

Phil 296.7.2 — Das Weltproblem vom Standpunkte. 2. Aufl. (Petzoldt, J.) Leipzig, 1912.

Phil 510.1.3 — Die Welträthsel. (Haeckel, Ernst.) Bonn, 1903.
Phil 510.1.2.5 — Die Welträthsel. (Haeckel, Ernst.) Stuttgart, 1899.
Phil 510.1.3.5 — Die Welträthsel. (Haeckel, Ernst.) Stuttgart, 1903.
Phil 510.1.2.4 — Die Welträthsel. 6e Aufl. (Haeckel, Ernst.) Bonn, 1901.
Phil 510.1.2 — Die Welträthsel. 7e Aufl. (Haeckel, Ernst.) Bonn, 1901.
Phil 510.1.2.6 — Die Welträtsel; gemeinverständliche Studien über monistische Philosophie. (Haeckel, Ernst.) Berlin, 1961.

Phil 978.49.630 — Die Welträtsel und die Anthroposophie. 1. Aufl. (Steiner, R.) Dornach, 1966.

Phil 3552.38 — Welträtsel und Lebensharmonie. (Leibniz, Gottfried Wilhelm.) Wiesbaden, 1949.

Phil 177.52 — Das Weltstreben. (Candidus, L.) München, 1913.
Phil 306.3.5 — Weltuntergang in Sage und Wissenschaft. (Ziegler, Konrat.) Leipzig, 1921.

Phil 185.25 — Weltweisheit. v.1-3. (Kralik, R.) Wien, 1896.
Phil 185.34 — Weltwille und Wertwille. (Kerler, D.H.) Leipzig, 1925.
Phil 185.25.5 — Weltwissenschaft. (Kralik, R.) Wien, 1896.
Phil 176.12 — Die Weltzellen. (Baumgärtner, H.) Leipzig, 1875.
Phil 6750.231 — Wembridge, Eleanor H.R. Life among the lowbrows. Boston, 1931.

Phil 8423.18 — Wembridge, Eleanor Harris Rowland. The significance of art. Boston, 1913.

Phil 353.23 — Wemme, G. Das Geheimnis der Gegensätze. Krailling, 1960.
Phil 6332.26 — Wenar, Charks. Origins of psychosomatic and emotional disturbances. N.Y., 1962.

Phil 3925.15 — Wendel, G. Vermischte Schriften. Berlin, 1912.
Phil 353.13 — Wendel, Georg. Kritik des Erkennens. Bonn, 1914.
Phil 5425.30 — Wendel, Georg. Über das Genie. Strassburg, 1909.
Phil 3504.47 — Wendel, J.A. Grundzüge und Kritik der Philosophien Kant's. Coburg, 1810.

Phil 5535.52 — Wendeler, Jürgen. Elementare Lernprinzipien; Darstellung und Modifikation von Postulaten der Hull'schen Theorie. Weinheim, 1967.

Htn — Phil 5062.5* — Wendelin, M.F. Logicae institutiones. Amstelrodami, 1654.
Phil 197.21 — Wendelino, M.F. Philosophia moralis. v.2. n.p., n.d.
Htn — Phil 3801.876* — Wendell, Johann A. Grundzüge und Kritik der Philosophien Kant's, Fichte's und Schelling's. 2. Aufl. (Coburg, 1824.

Phil 1735.2 — Wendepunkt der Philosophie im neunzehnten Jahrhundert. (Gruppe, Otto F.) Berlin, 1834.

Phil 978.49.85 — Wendepunkte des Geisteslebens. (Steiner, R.) Dornach, 1927.

Phil 978.49.86 — Wendepunkte des Geisteslebens. 3. Aufl. (Steiner, R.) Freiburg, 1954.

Phil 9450.64 — Wendland, Heinz Dietrich. Politik und Ethik. Darmstadt, 1969.

Phil 510.144 — Wendland, J. Monismus in alter und neuer Zeit. Basel, 1908.

Phil 3805.96 — Wendland, J. Die Religiöse Entwicklung Schleiermachers. Tübingen, 1915.

Phil 1127.1 — Wendland, Paul. Beiträge zur Geschichte der griechischen Philosophie. Berlin, 1895.

Phil 6692.6.5 — Wendler, C.A. De magnetismi animalis efficacia rite diiudicanda. Lipsiae, 1818.

Phil 6692.6 — Wendler, C.A. De magnetismi animali. Diss. Lipsiae, 1805.
Phil 3552.280 — Wendt, Emil. Die Entwickelung der leibnizschen Monadenlehre bis zum Jahre 1695. Inaug. Diss. Berlin, 1885.

Phil 5625.81 — Wendt, George R. An analytical study of the conditioned knee-jerk. N.Y., 1930.

Phil 9120.9 — Wendt, Hans H. Die sittliche Pflicht. Göttingen, 1916.
Phil 1145.41 — Wendt, M. Geschichte der griechischen Ethik. Leipzig, 1908. 2v.

Phil 1145.40 — Wendt, M. Der Intellektualismus in der griechischen Ethik. Leipzig, 1907.

Phil 9430.31 — Weng, Gustav. Schopenhauer-Darwin, Pessimismus oder Optimismus? Berlin, 1911.

Phil 3425.271 — Wenke, Hans. Hegels Theorie des objektiven Geistes. Halle, 1927.

Phil 3504.7.15 — Wenley, R.M. Kant and his philosophical revolution. Edinburgh, 1910.

Phil 2150.1.80 — Wenley, R.M. Life and work of George Sylvester Morris. N.Y., 1917.

Phil 8712.10 — Wenley, R.M. Modern thought and crisis in belief. N.Y., 1909.

Phil 3504.7 — Wenley, R.M. An outline introduction of Kant's Critique of pure reason. N.Y., 1897.

Phil 3504.7.5 — Wenley, R.M. An outline introduction of Kant's Critique of pure reason. N.Y., 1907.

Phil 1200.23 — Wenley, R.M. Stoicism and its influence. Boston, 1924.
Phil 3425.217 — Wennerberg, G. Num recte et vere de Spinozismo judicavit Hegelius? Upsaliae, 1848.

Phil 1822.2 — Wentscher, E. Englische Philosophie. Leipzig, 1924.
Phil 8897.35 — Wentscher, E. Grundzüge der Ethik. Leipzig, 1913.
Phil 3565.123 — Wentscher, E. Das Kausalproblem in Lotzes Philosophie. Halle, 1903.

Phil 270.41 — Wentscher, E.S. Geschichte des Kausalproblems in der neueren Philosophie. Leipzig, 1921.

Phil 2138.108 — Wentscher, Ela. Das Problem des Empirismus, dargestellt an John Stuart Mill. Bonn, 1922.

Phil 8897.30 — Wentscher, M. Ethik. Leipzig, 1902.
Phil 3565.89.5 — Wentscher, M. Fechner und Lotze. München, 1925.
Phil 3565.89 — Wentscher, M. Hermann Lotze. Heidelberg, 1913.
Phil 9430.25 — Wentscher, M. Über den Pessimismus und seine Wurzeln. Bonn, 1897.

Phil 270.14 — Wentscher, M. Über Physische und Psychische Kausalität. Leipzig, 1896.

Phil 8847.5 — Wentscher, Max. Geschichte der Ethik. Berlin, 1931.
Phil 197.14.5 — Wentscher, Max. Metaphysik. Berlin, 1928.
Phil 5643.88 — Wentworth, H.A. A quantitative study of achromatic and chromatic sensitivity from censes to periphery of the visual field. Diss. Princeton, 1930.

Phil 5262.28 — Wentzke, J.A. Compendium der Psychologie und Logik. Leipzig, 1868.

Phil 530.20.93 — Wentzlaff-Eggebert, F.W. Deutsche Mystik zwischen Mittelalter und Neuzeit. 2. Aufl. Tübingen, 1947.

Phil 530.20.93.3 — Wentzlaff-Eggebert, F.W. Deutsche Mystik zwischen Mittelalter und Neuzeit. 3. Aufl. Berlin, 1969.

Phil 3842.5 — Wenzel, Alfred. Die Weltanschauung Spinozas. Bd.1. Leipzig, 1907.

Phil 2050.270 — Wenzel, Leonhard. David Humes politische Philosophie in ihrem Zusammenhang mit seiner gesamten Lehre. Inaug. Diss. Koln? 1959.

Phil 3310.1.135 — Wenzel, Paul. Das wissenschaftliche Anliger des Güntherianismus. Essen, 1961.

Phil 9558.12 — Wenzel, Siegfried. The sin of sloth. Chapel Hill, 1967.
Phil 1722.5.2 — Wenzig, Carl. Die Weltanschuungen der Gegenwart. 2e Aufl. Leipzig, 1919.

Phil 3195.10.120 — Wenzl, Aloys. Hans Driesch. Basel, 1951.
Phil 6132.29 — Wenzl, Aloys. Das Leib-Seele-Problem. Leipzig, 1933.
Phil 197.63.7 — Wenzl, Aloys. Metaphysik als Weg von den Grenzen der Wissenschaft au die Grenzen der Religion. 2. Aufl. Graz, 1956.

Phil 197.63.5 — Wenzl, Aloys. Philosophie als Weg von den Grenzen der Wissenschaft au die Grenzen der Religion. Leipzig, 1939.

Phil 5262.51 — Wenzl, Aloys. Theorie der Begabung. 2. Aufl. Heidelberg, 1957.

Phil 5722.19 — Wenzl, Aloys. Das unbewusste Denken. Karlsruhe, 1927.
Phil 8647.12 — Wenzl, Aloys. Unsterblichkeit. Berlin, 1951.
Phil 197.63 — Wenzl, Aloys. Wissenschaft und Weltanschauung. Leipzig, 1936.

Phil 197.63.3 — Wenzl, Aloys. Wissenschaft und Weltanschauung. 2. Aufl. Hamburg, 1949.

Phil 5262.12 — Wenzlaff, G.G. The mental man. N.Y., 1909.
Phil 6972.1 — Wepferi, J.J. Observationes...affectibus capitis. Scaphusii, 1727.

Phil 3450.19.56 — Weplinger, F. Wahrheit und Geschichtlichkeit. Freiburg, 1961.

Phil 5590.434 — Wepman, J.M. The concepts of personality. London, 1964.
Phil 6400.19 — Wepman, J.M. Recovery from aphasia. N.Y., 1951.
Phil 3549.10.60 — Wer indische Gedanke. 2. Aufl. (Kassner, Rudolf.) Leipzig, 1921.

Phil 1850.93 — Wer Schrieb das "Norum Organon" von Francis Bacon. (Reichel, E.) Stuttgart, 1886.

Phil 5548.45 — Werbepsychologische Untersuchungsmethoden. (Spiegel, Berut.) Berlin, 1958.

Phil 3552.102 — Werckmeister, Walther. Der leibnizsche Substanzbegriff. Halle, 1899.

Phil 978.64.5 — Werdegang der Menschheit. (Wachsmuth, G.) Dornach, 1953.
Phil 5374.52 — Werden, Sein und Erscheinungsweise des Bewusstseins. (Jaesche, E.) Heidelberg, 1887.

Phil 5865.4 — Das Werden der Person. (Bollinger, Heinz.) München, 1967.
Phil 9035.61.12 — Das Werden der settlichen Person. 4. Aufl. (Allers, Rudolf.) Freiburg, 1935.

NEDL Phil 281.4.9 — Werden der Welten. (Auerbach, Felix.) Leipzig, 1913.
Phil 974.3.95 — Werden und Wesen der Anthroposophie. (Hauer, J.W.) Stuttgart, 1923.

Phil 3425.590 — Werden zu Sich. (Guzzoni, Ute.) Freiburg, 1963.
Phil 3640.77.7 — Der werdende Nietzsche. (Nietzsche, Friedrich.) München, 1924.

Htn — Phil 3110.80* — Werdenhagen, I.G. Psychologia. Amsterdam, 1632.
Phil 3425.309 — Werder, K. Logik. Als Commentar und Ergänzung zu Hegels Wissenschaft der Logik. Berlin, 1841.

Phil 2905.1.105 — Het wereldbeeld van Pierre Teilhard de Chardin. 2. druk. (Wildiers, N.M.) Antwerpen, 1960.

Phil 197.95 — Wereldbeschouwelijk denken als filosofisch probleem. (Wal, Goossen Albertus van der.) Den Haag, 1968.

Phil 5627.113 — Wereldbeschouwing en Godsdienstig bewustzyn. (Wijnaendts Francken, C.J.) Haarlem, 1923.

Phil 176.115.45 — Wereldorde engeesteleven. 2e Aufl. (Bierens de Haan, J.D.) Amsterdam, 1922.

Phil 510.1.8 — Die wereldraadselen. (Haeckel, Ernst.) Baarn, 1913.
Phil 8677.18 — Werfel, Franz. Können wir ohne Gottesglauben Leben? Berlin, 1932.

Phil 8602.51 — Werfel, Franz. Zwischen Oben und Unten. Stockholm, 1946.
Phil 575.270 — Werff, Jacobus Johannes van der. Zelbeelden zelfideaal. Assen, 1965.

Phil 8725.16 — Werhahn, Hans. Das Vorschreiten der Säkularisierung. Bonn, 1969.

Phil 4655.1.84 — Werin, A. Pontus Wikner. Lund, 1937.
Phil 1701.30 — Das Werk der Freiheit. (Berlinger, Rudolph.) Frankfurt, 1959.

Phil 575.30 — Werk und Persönlichkeit. (Platzhoff-Lejeune, E.) Minden, 1903.

Phil 3475.3.23 — Werk und Wirkung. (Jaspers, Karl.) München, 1963.
Phil 3120.30.15 — Werke. (Fichte, Johann Gottlieb.) Leipzig, 1911. 6v.
X Cg Phil 3246.17 — Werke. (Hegel, Georg Wilhelm Friedrich.) Berlin, 1832-45. 14v.
Phil 3425.8 — Werke. (Hegel, Georg Wilhelm Friedrich.) Berlin, 1832-87. 19v.

Phil 3425.10 — Werke. (Hegel, Georg Wilhelm Friedrich.) Berlin, 1835-45. 20v.

Phil 3425.9 — Werke. (Hegel, Georg Wilhelm Friedrich.) Leipzig, 1909.
Phil 3425.11 — Werke. (Jacobi, F.H.) Leipzig, 1812-25. 7v.
Phil 3460.10 — Werke. (Kant, Immanuel.) Leipzig, 1838-39. 10v.
Phil 3480.11 — Werke. (Leibniz, Gottfried Wilhelm.) Stuttgart, 1949.
Phil 3552.24.20 — Werke. (Nietzsche, Friedrich.) Leipzig, 1895-1926. 19v.
Phil 3640.10.2 — Werke. (Nietzsche, Friedrich.) Leipzig, 1896-1926. 20v.

Phil 3640.10A — Werke. (Nietzsche, Friedrich.) Leipzig, 1906-09. 11v.
Phil 3640.11.10A — Werke. (Nietzsche, Friedrich.) Leipzig, 1930. 2v.
Phil 3640.20 — Werke. (Nietzsche, Friedrich.) München, 1954-56. 3v.
Phil 3640.14.15A —

Phil 3640.14.10 — Werke. (Nietzsche, Friedrich.) Salzburg, 1952. 2v.
Phil 3805.17 — Werke. (Schleiermacher, Friedrich.) Berlin, 1924.
Phil 3805.15 — Werke. (Schleiermacher, Friedrich.) Leipzig, 1910-11. 4v.

Phil 3808.11.2 — Werke. (Schopenhauer, Arthur.) Leipzig, 1891. 2v.
Phil 3640.10.5 — Werke. Kritische Gesamtausgabe. (Nietzsche, Friedrich.) Berlin, 1967. 9v.

Phil 3425.13.5 — Werke. v.1-2,4-20. (Hegel, Georg Wilhelm Friedrich.) Frankfurt, 1969- 21v.

Phil 3480.15 — Werke. v.1-7,9,11. (Kant, Immanuel.) Berlin, 1912. 9v.

Phil 3640.17 — Werke. v.1-11. (Nietzsche, Friedrich.) Leipzig, 1931-59. 12v.

Phil 4769.1.40 — Werke. v.2,3,6,7. (Solov'ev, V.S.) Freiburg, 1953. 4v.

X Cg Phil 3480.15 — Werke. v.8,10. (Kant, Immanuel.) Berlin, 1912. 2v.
Phil 3808.11 — Werke. 2. Aufl. (Schopenhauer, Arthur.) Leipzig, 1891. 2v.

Phil 3480.16.25 — Werke in acht Büchern. v.1-4,5-8. (Kant, Immanuel.) Berlin, 1921. 2v.

Phil 8423.16.10 — Werke in einem Band. (Winckelmann, Johann Joachim.) Berlin, 1969.

Phil 3640.13   Werke und Briefe. (Nietzsche, Friedrich.) München, 1933-49. 5v.

Phil 3640.14   Werke und Briefe. (Nietzsche, Friedrich.) München, 1938-42. 4v.

Phil 3120.22.20   Werke und Tage. (Blüher, Hans.) München, 1953.

Phil 3552.13   Die Werke von Leibniz gemäss seinem handschriftlichen Nachlasse in der Königlichen Bibliothek zu Hannover. (Leibniz, Gottfried Wilhelm.) Hannover, 1864-84. 11v.

Phil 1822.6   Werkmeister, W.H. A history of philosophical ideas in America. N.Y., 1949.

Phil 5062.37   Wérkmeister, W.H. An introduction to critical thinking. Lincoln, Neb., 1948.

Phil 735.263   Werkmeister, William H. Man and his values. Lincoln, 1967.

Phil 9075.73.2   Wermlund, Sven. Samvetets uppkomst. 2. Uppl. Stockholm, 1966.

Phil 8423.3   Wernaer, R.M. Das ästhetische Symbol. Leipzig, 1907.

Phil 8423.17   Werner, Alfred. Impressionismus und Expressionismus. Leipzig, 1917.

Phil 8897.39   Werner, Charles. Études de philosophie morale. Genève, 1917.

Phil 1127.5.3   Werner, Charles. La philosophie grecque. Paris, 1938.

Phil 1722.10   Werner, Charles. La philosophie moderne. Paris, 1954.

Phil 7054.51.5   Werner, H. Guardian spirits. N.Y., 1964.

Phil 7054.51.10   Werner, H. Die Schutzgeister. Stuttgart, 1839.

Phil 5520.410   Werner, H. Symbol formation. N.Y., 1963.

Phil 5832.15A   Werner, Heinz. Comparative psychology of mental development. N.Y., 1940.

Phil 5832.15.5   Werner, Heinz. Comparative psychology of mental development. N.Y., 1948.

Phil 5832.15.10   Werner, Heinz. Comparative psychology of mental development. N.Y., 1957.

Phil 5832.15.12   Werner, Heinz. Comparative psychology of mental development. N.Y., 1966.

Phil 5262.32   Werner, Heinz. Einführung in die Entwicklungspsychologie. Leipzig, 1926.

Phil 5262.32.5   Werner, Heinz. Einführung in die Entwicklungspsychologie. 3. Aufl. München, 1953.

Phil 5262.32.6   Werner, Heinz. Einführung in die Entwicklungspsychologie. 4. Aufl. München, 1959.

Phil 5520.57   Werner, Heinz. Grundfragen der Sprachphysiognomik. Leipzig, 1932.

Phil 3425.97   Werner, J. Hegels Offenbarungsbegriff. Leipzig, 1887.

Phil 4022.1.5   Werner, K. Die cartesische-malebranche'sche Philosophie in Italien. Pt.1-2. Wien, 1883.

Phil 4260.87.5   Werner, K. Emerico Amari in seinern Verhaltniss zu G.B. Vico. Wien, 1880.

Phil 1500.1   Werner, K. Die Entwicklung der mittelalterlicher Psychologie. Wien, 1876.

Phil 4260.87   Werner, K. Giambattista Vico als Philosophie und Gelehrterforscher. Wien, 1881.

Phil 197.5   Werner, K. Grundlinien de Philosophie. Regensburg, 1855.

Phil 4022.1   Werner, K. Die italienische Philosophie. v. 1-5. Wien, 1884-86. 2v.

Phil 4260.88   Werner, K. Über Giambattista Vico als Geschichtsphilosophen und begründer der neueren italienischen Philosophie. Wien, 1877.

Phil 4210.125.10F   Werner, Karl. A. Rosmini's Stellung in der Geschichte der neueren Philosophie. Wien, 1884.

Phil 1020.4.25   Werner, Karl. Der Averroismus in der christlich-peripatetischen Psychologie des späteren Mittelalters. Wien, 1881.

Phil 4210.125   Werner, Karl. Die italien Philosophie. Wien, 1884.

Phil 3504.21F   Werner, Karl. Kant in Italien. Wien, 1881.

Phil 1540.9   Werner, Karl. Die nominalisirende Psychologie der Scholastik des späteren Mittelalters. Wien, 1882.

Phil 1527.2   Werner, Karl. Die Scholastik des späteren Mittelalters. Wien, 1881. 4v.

Phil 585.290   Werner, Karl. Speculative Anthropologie. Frankfurt, 1967.

Phil 8972.4   Werner, Karl. System der christlichen Ethik. Regensburg, 1888. 2v.

Phil 8602.43   Werner, Max. Das Christentum und die monistische Religion. Berlin, 1908.

Phil 6980.776.10   Werner, Reiner. Das verhaltensgestörte Kind. 1. Aufl. Berlin, 1967.

Phil 5772.8   Werner, S. Das Problem von der menschlichen Willensfreiheit. Berlin, 1914.

Phil 7069.18.159   Werner-Hagen. Gedankenlesen und Hellsehen. Berlin, 1918.

Phil 4752.2.160   Wernham, James C.S. Two Russian thinkers: essays in Berdyaev and Shestov. Toronto, 1968.

Phil 3552.97   Wernick, G. Der Begriff der Materie bei Leibniz. Jena, 1893.

Phil 5066.17   Wernick, William. Complete sets of logical functions. Thesis. N.Y., 1942.

Phil 3110.90   Wernicke, A. Meister Jacob Böhme. Braunschweig, 1898.

Phil 6400.6   Wernicke, C. Der aphasische Symptomencomplex. Photoreproduction. Breslau, 1874.

Phil 6972.2.5   Wernicke, C. Gesammelte Aufsätze und kritische Riferate. Berlin, 1893.

Phil 6972.2.10   Wernicke, C. Grundriss der Psychiatrie in klinischen Vorlesungen. v.1-2. Leipzig, 1894.

Phil 6972.2   Wernicke, C. Lehrbuch der Gehirnkrankheiten. v.1-2. Kassel, 1881.

Phil 6972.2.15   Wernicke, C. Über den wessenschaftlichen Standpunkt. Cassel, 1880.

Phil 3504.12.10   Wernieke, A. Die Begründung des deutschen Idealismus durch I. Kant. Braunschweig, 1910.

Phil 3504.12   Wernieke, A. Kant und kein Ende? 2. Aufl. Braunschweig, 1907.

Phil 3504.12.15   Wernieke, A. Kants kritischer Werdegang. Braunschweig, 1911.

Phil 3504.12.5   Wernieke, A. Theorie des Gegenstandes...bei I. Kant. Braunschweig, 1904.

Phil 735.84   Wert. (Heyde, Johannes E.) Erfurt, 1926.

Phil 735.80   Wert Begriff und Wertphilosophie. (Wiederhold, K.) Berlin, 1920.

Phil 9430.26   Der Wert des Lebens. (Goldschmidt, Kurt Walter.) Berlin, 1908.

NEDL Phil 735.83   Der Wert des Zwecklosen. (Goldstein, M.) Dresden, 1920.

Phil 3790.4.95   Wert und Wirklichkeit in der Philosophie Heinrich Rickerts. (Seidel, Hermann.) Bonn, 1968.

Phil 3805.187   Wertanalysen zu Schleiermachers. Diss. (Bredow, G.) Würzburg, 1959.

Phil 735.9   Werte und Bewertungen in der Denkevolution. (Vos, H. von de.) Berlin, 1909.

Phil 3450.33.2   Die Wertethik bei Dietrick von Hildebrand. (Hildebrand, Christa.) Düsseldorf, 1959.

Phil 8881.66   Wertethik oder religiöse Sittlichkeit? (Groos, R.) München, 1933.

Phil 5590.516   Die Wertfunktion des Menschen. (Gschwind, Martin.) Mainz, 1969.

Phil 735.100   Der Wertgedanke in der europäischen Geistesentwicklung. (Rintelen, F.J. von.) Halle, 1932.

Phil 8583.7   Der Werth des Lebens. (Dühring, E.K.) Leipzig, 1881.

Phil 8583.7.3   Der Werth des Lebens. 6. Aufl. (Dühring, E.K.) Leipzig, 1902.

Phil 6132.36   Wertham, F. The brain as an organ. N.Y., 1934.

Phil 6972.15   Wertheimer, F.I. The significance of the physical constitution in mental disease. Baltimore, 1926.

Phil 5262.31   Wertheimer, M. Drei Abhandlungen zur Gestalttheorie. Erlangen, 1925.

Phil 5262.31.15   Wertheimer, M. Gestalt theory. N.Y., 1944.
Phil 5262.31.26   Wertheimer, M. Productive thinking. London, 1961.
Phil 5262.31.25A   Wertheimer, M. Productive thinking. N.Y., 1959. 2v.
Phil 5262.31.9   Wertheimer, M. Über Gestalttheorie. Erlangen, 1925.
Phil 5262.31.5   Pamphlet vol. Wertheimer, M. Psychologische Tatbestandsdiagnostik. 1904-1912. 4 pam.

Phil 8897.98   Wertheimer, Roger. The significance of sense. Ithaca, 1972.

Phil 5255.33   Die Wertheimer-Koffka-Köhlersche Gestalttheorie und das Gestaltproblem. (Petermann, B.) Leipzig, 1929.

Phil 5225.2   Die Wertheimer-Koffka-Köhlersche Gestalttheorie und das Gestaltproblem systematische und kritisch Dargestellt. (Petermann, Bruno.) Leipzig, 1928.

Phil 303.2   Werther, C.A. Die Kräfte der unorganischen Natur. Dessau, 1852.

Phil 3450.33.12   Wertobjektivität und Realitätserfahrung. (Maliandi, Ricardo G.) Bonn, 1966.

Phil 8892.56   Wertphilosophie und Ethik. (Reininger, Robert.) Leipzig, 1939.

Phil 8892.56.5   Wertphilosophie und Ethik. 3. Aufl. (Reininger, Robert.) Wien, 1947.

Phil 735.4   Das Wertproblem in der Philosophie der Gegenwart. (Strich, Walter.) Berlin, 1909.

Phil 735.98   Wertrecht und Wertmacht. (Bommersheim, Paul.) Berlin, 1931.

Phil 735.116   Die Werttheorien; Geschichte und Kritik. (Kraus, O.) Brünn, 1937.

Phil 3850.18.210   Das Wertwidrige in der Ethik Max Schelers. (Uchiyam, Mivoru.) Bonn, 1966.

Phil 735.101   Wertwissenschaft. (Cohn, Jonas.) Stuttgart, 1932.
Phil 1200.9   Werzstein, Otto Heinrich Robert. Die Wandlung der stoichen Lehre. Newstrelitz, 1892.

Phil 7080.46   Weschcke, Charles. Overcoming sleeplessness. St. Paul, 1935.

Phil 8419.10   Das Wesen der ästhetischen Anschauung. (Siebeck, H.) Berlin, 1875.

Phil 349.12   Das Wesen der Erkenntnis. (Schwartzkopff, P.) Heidelberg, 1909.

Phil 9255.15   Das Wesen der Ironie. (Jancke, Rudolf.) Leipzig, 1929.
Phil 8412.31   Das Wesen der Kunst. (Lange, K. von.) Berlin, 1901. 2v.

Phil 8412.22   Das Wesen der Kunst. (Lange, K. von.) Berlin, 1907.
Phil 3640.500   Das Wesen der Kunst im Denken Nietzsches. (Diem, Gudrun.) Schorndorf, 1953.

Phil 3195.2.90   Das Wesen der Kunst in der$Ästhetik Martin Deutingers. (Henckmann, Wolfhart.) München, 1966.

Phil 3500.20.15   Das Wesen der Materie nach Kants physische Monadologie. Inaug. Diss. (Simmel, G.) Berlin, 1881.

Phil 5259.31   Das Wesen der menschlichen Antriebsstruktur. (Thomae, Hans.) Leipzig, 1944.

Phil 3800.340.1   Das Wesen der menschlichen Freiheit. 1. Aufl. (Schelling, F.W.J. von.) Düsseldorf, 1950.

Phil 3195.3.33   Das Wesen der menschlichen Kopfarbeit. (Dietzgen, Joseph.) Berlin, 1955.

Phil 525.15.15   Das Wesen der Persönlichkeit. (Hasse, Karl P.) Meerane, 1913.

Phil 6960.6   Das Wesen der psychiatrischen Erkenn. (Kronfeld, Arthur.) Berlin, 1920.

Phil 8584.5   Das Wesen der Religion, philosophisch Betrachtet. (Eucken, Rudolf.) Leipzig, 1901.

Phil 8581.6   Das Wesen der Religion. (Bender, W.) Bonn, 1886.
Phil 3235.55.5   Das Wesen der Religion. (Feuerbach, Ludwig.) Leipzig, 1908.

Phil 8597.6   Das Wesen der Religion. (Reinhold, E.) Jena, 1846.
Phil 8598.5   Das Wesen der Religion. (Schwarz, C.H.W.) Halle, 1847.
Phil 8581.6.4   Das Wesen der Religion. 4. Aufl. (Bender, W.) Bonn, 1888.
Phil 6967.20   Das Wesen der schizophrenen Reaktion. (Rattner, Josef.) München, 1963.

Phil 8408.17   Das Wesen der Schönheit. (Heller, R.) Wein, 1936.
Phil 5262.18   Das Wesen der Seele und die Natur der geistigen Vorgänge im Lichte. (Witte, J.H.) Halle-Saale, 1888.

Phil 5400.128   Das Wesen der Stimmungen. 3. Aufl. (Bollnow, O.F.) Frankfurt, 1956.

Phil 7082.76   Das Wesen der Träume. (Cohen, G.) Dresden, 1925.
Phil 182.84   Das Wesen der Welt. (Hellmund, H.) Zürich, 1920.
Phil 5080.2   Das Wesen des Begriffs und des Begreifens. (Dubs, Arthur.) Halle, 1911.

Phil 3235.45.2   Das Wesen des Christenthums. (Feuerbach, Ludwig.) Leipzig, 1841.

Phil 3235.45.6   Das Wesen des Christenthums. (Feuerbach, Ludwig.) Leipzig, 1909.

Phil 3235.45   Das Wesen des Christenthums. (Feuerbach, Ludwig.) Stuttgart, 1903.

Phil 3235.87   Das Wesen des Christenttumes von Ludwig Feuerbach. Inaug. Diss. (Turban, Theodor.) Karlsruhe, 1894.

Phil 8587.26.3   Das Wesen des Christentums. (Harnack, Adolf.) Leipzig, 1903.

Phil 8582.31   Das Wesen des Christentums. 3. Aufl. (Cremer, Herman.) Gütersloh, 1902.

Phil 8587.26   Das Wesen des Christentums. 4. Aufl. (Harnack, Adolf.) Leipzig, 1901.

Phil 5062.31   Das Wesen des Denkens. (Wrzecionko, R.) Wien, 1896.
Phil 5425.29.3   Das Wesen des Genies. (Gerhardi, Karl A.) Jauer, 1908.
Phil 9075.25   Das Wesen des Gewissens. Inaug. Diss. (Vogt, Fritz.) Greifswald, 1908.

Phil 5525.10   Das Wesen des Humors. (Backhaus, W.E.) Leipzig, n.d.
Phil 5585.7.5   Das Wesen des menschlichen Verstandus und Bewusstseins. (Rau, A.) München, 1910.

Phil 8893.49   Das Wesen des Mitleids. (Stern, Wilhelm.) Berlin, 1903.
Phil 978.49.688   Das Wesen des Musikaleschen und das Tonerlebnis im Menschen. 1. Aufl. (Steiner, R.) Dornach, 1969.

Phil 332.3   Das Wesen des Wissens. (Brodbick, A.) Stuttgart, 1884.
Phil 5402.26.2   Wesen und Bedeutung des Schmerzes. 2. Aufl. (Sauerbruch, F.) Frankfurt, 1961.

Phil 8050.90 — Wesen und Bestand ästhetischer Bildung in Geschichte und Begenwart. (Gehrig, Hans.) Zürich, 1964.

Phil 181.66 — Das Wesen und der Wert des Seins. (Grünhut, Ladislaus.) Leipzig, 1931.

Phil 5047.35.5 — Wesen und Formen der Dialektik. (Heiss, Robert.) Köln, 1952.

Phil 5415.7 — Wesen und Formen der Sympathie. (Scheler, Max.) Bonn, 1923.

Phil 334.6 — Wesen und Geschichte der Erkenntnistheorie. (Dürr, Karl.) Zürich, 1924.

Phil 5811.15.20 — Wesen und Sinn des Spiels. (Buytendijk, Frederik Jacobus Johannes.) Berlin, 1933.

Phil 1135.100 — Wesen und Ursprung der Lehre von der Präexistenz der Seele und von der Seelenwanderung in der griechischen Philosophie. (Laudowicz, Felix.) Berlin, 1898.

Phil 7140.123 — Wesen und Vorgang der Suggestion. (Straus, Erwin.) Berlin, 1925.

Phil 8591.12.5 — Wesen und Wahrheit der Religion. (Lang, Albert.) München, 1957.

Phil 1750.148 — Wesen und Wandlung des Humanismus. (Rudiger, H.) Hamburg, 1937.

Phil 2980.5 — Wesen und Werden der schweizerischen Philosophie. (Tumarkin, Anna.) Frauenfeld, 1948.

Phil 176.104 — Wesen und Wert. (Beck, Maximillian.) Berlin, 1925. 2v.

Phil 190.65 — Wesen und Wesenserkenntnis. (Pöll, Wilhelm.) München, 1936.

Phil 8411.28 — WesenUnd Wirken des Kunstwerks. (Kuhn, Helmut.) München, 1960.

Phil 165.120 — Wesen und Wirklichkeit des Menschen. (Ziegler, Klaus.) Göttingen, 1957.

Phil 3160.12.30 — Wesen und Wirkung des Symbolbegriffs. (Cassirer, Ernst.) Oxford, 1956.

Phil 3640.440 — Das Wesen von Friedrich Nietzsches Idealismus. (Noll, Baldwin.) Köln, 1940.

Phil 672.161 — Die wesenhafte oder absolute Realität des Raumes. (Wiessner, Alexander.) Leipzig, 1877.

Phil 293.22.5 — Wesensartwandel und Artensystem der physikalischen Körperwelt. (Mittere, Albert.) Bressanone, 1936. 3v.

Phil 3235.114 — Weser, H.A. Sigmund Freuds und Ludwig Feuerbachs Religionskritik. Inaug. Diss. Bettrop, 1936.

Phil 6692.9 — Wesermann, N.M. Der Magnetismus und die allgemeine Weltsprache. Creveld, 1822.

Phil 8677.2 — Wesley, J. A survey...wisdom of God in the creation. Bristol, 1770. 3v.

Phil 5062.24 — Wesley, John. A compendium of logic. 2nd ed. London, 1756.

Phil 5125.30 — Wesleyan Conference on Induction. Induction: some current issues. 1st ed. Middleton, 1963.

Phil 3504.15 — Wesselsky, Anton. Forberg und Kant. Leipzig, 1913.

Phil 5043.18.10 — Wessen und Denken. (Driesch, H.) Leipzig, 1922.

Phil 8712.12 — Wessenberg, J.G. von. Die falsche Wissenschaft. Stuttgart, 1844.

Phil 6972.18 — West, Charles. On some disorders. Philadelphia, 1871.

Phil 7069.54.10 — West, D.J. Psychical research today. London, 1954.

Phil 974.4.10 — West, G. Mrs. Annie Besant. London, 1927.

Phil 822.1.30 — West, H.F. Rebel thought. Boston, 1953.

Htn Phil 9362.2* — West, J. (Mrs.). Letters to a young lady. N.Y., 1806.

Htn Phil 9362.2.2* — West, J. (Mrs.). Letters to a young man. Charlestown, 1803.

Phil 1135.225 — West, M.L. Early Greek philosophy and the Orient. Oxford, 1971.

Phil 5850.385.65 — West, P.V. Psychology for religious and social workers. N.Y., 1930.

Htn Phil 5754.1.22* — West, Samuel. Essay on moral agency...remarks on Dana's Examination. New Haven, 1772.

Htn Phil 5754.1.23* — West, Samuel. Essay on moral agency...remarks on Dana's Examination. Salem, 1794.

Phil 5754.1.31 — West, Samuel. Essays on liberty and necessity. Boston, 1793.

Phil 5754.1.33 — West, Samuel. Essays on liberty and necessity. New Bedford, 1795.

Phil 822.11 — Westaway, F.W. Obsessions and convictions of the human intellect. London, 1938.

Phil 8712.15 — Westaway, F.W. Science and theology. London, 1920.

Phil 5262.65 — Westcott, Malcolm Robert. Toward a contemporary psychology of intuition. N.Y., 1968.

Phil 7082.100 — Westerfield, Jonathan B. The scientific dream-book and dictionary of dream symbols. N.Y., 1932.

Phil 5232.8 — Westerhof, A.C. Representative psychologists. Union Bridge, Md., 1938.

Phil 8897.69 — Westermarck, E. Christianity and morals. N.Y., 1939.

Phil 8897.28.15 — Westermarck, E. Ethical relativity. N.Y., 1932.

Phil 8897.28.5 — Westermarck, E. Moralens uppkomst och utveckling. Stockholm, 1916.

Phil 8897.28.3 — Westermarck, E. The origin and development...moral ideas. London, 1908-12. 2v.

Phil 8897.28 — Westermarck, E. The origin and development...moral ideas. 2nd ed. London, 1906-17. 2v.

Phil 8897.28.20 — Westermarck, E. The origin and development of the moral ideas. 2nd ed. London, 1924-26.

Phil 62.7 — Western Behavioral Sciences Institute, La Jolla, California. Report. La Jolla, California. 3-22

Phil 1701.40 — The Western intellectual tradition. (Bronowski, Jacob.) N.Y., 1960.

Phil 6310.4.25 — The western mind in transition. (Alexander, Franz G.) N.Y., 1960.

Phil 525.262 — The Western mystical tradition. (Katsaros, Thomas.) New Haven, 1969-

Phil 525.35 — Western mysticism. (Butler, Cuthbert.) London, 1922.

Phil 525.35.8 — Western mysticism: the teaching of Augustine, Gregory and Bernard. 3rd ed. (Butler, Cuthbert.) London, 1967.

Phil 525.35.5 — Western mysticism. 2d ed. (Butler, Cuthbert.) London, 1927.

Phil 62.3 — Western Philosophical Association. Proceedings. 1-2,1901-1902

Phil 32.9 — The Western psychologist. Alberta. 1,1969+

Phil 32.9.5 — The Western psychologist. Monograph series. Alberta. 1,1969+

Phil 5252.160 — Western psychology. (Murphy, Gardner.) N.Y., 1969.

Phil 6319.12 — Western psychotherapy and Hindu-Sādhanā. (Jacob, Hans.) London, 1961.

Phil 5871.100 — Westley, William A. The silent majority; families of emotionally healthy college students. San Francisco, 1970.

Phil 4870.18 — Westlicher Wissensdrang-Indische Weisheit. (Gessler, Clara.) Zürich, 1970.

Phil 6980.776 — Westman, H. The springs of creativity. N.Y., 1961.

Phil 9362.17 — Weston, S.A. Social and religious problems and young people. N.Y., 1934.

Phil 5850.385.70 — Weston, Sidney A. Finding your way in life. N.Y., 1942.

Phil 7069.49.5 — Westwood, Horace. There is a psychic world. N.Y., 1947.

Phil 5259.16.2 — De wetenschap van ons geestelijk wezen. 2. druk. (Thoden van Velzen, H.) Amsterdam, 1894.

Phil 3903.4.80 — Wetenschappelijke bijdragen door leerigen van D.H.M. Vollenhoveu. (Zuidema, Sytse Uebe.) Franeker, 1951.

Phil 8870.36 — Wetenschappelijke moraalstudie. Ledeberg, 1966.

Phil 8586.36.70 — Weth, Rudolf. Gott in Jesus; der Ansatz der Christologie Friedrich Gogartens. München, 1968.

Phil 3819.5 — Wetlesen, Jon. A Spinoza bibliography, particularly on the period 1940-1967. Oslo, 1968.

Phil 8897.12.5A — Wette, W.M.L. de. Human life; or Practical ethics. Boston, 1842. 2v.

Phil 8897.12.9 — Wette, W.M.L. de. Human life; or Practical ethics. Boston, 1856. 2v.

Phil 8602.5 — Wette, W.M.L. de. Über die Religion. Berlin, 1827.

Phil 8897.12 — Wette, W.M.L. de. Vorlesungen über die Sittenlehre. v. 1-2. Berlin, 1823-24.

Phil 4710.9 — Wetter, G.A. Die Umkehrung Hegels. Köln, 1963.

Phil 197.53 — Wetterburg, Jacobue. Dissertatio philosophica. Lundae, 1789.

Phil 6692.3 — Wetterstrand, O.G. Hypnotism and its application to practical medecine. N.Y., 1899.

Phil 5520.695 — Wettler, Manfred. Syntaktische Faktoren im verbalen Lernen. Bern, 1970.

Phil 3842.9 — Wetzel, Paul. Der Zweckbegriff bei Spinoza. Thesis. Leipzig, 1873.

Phil 5650.40 — Wever, Ernest. Theory of hearing. N.Y., 1957.

Phil 1200.35 — Wevers, Friedrich. Quid Paulus, quid stoici de virtute docuerint. Meursae, 1876? 3 pam.

Phil 3450.11.450 — Wewel, Meinolf. Die Konstitution des transzendenten Etevas im Vollzug des Sehens. Düsseldorf, 1968.

Phil 5262.35 — Wexberg, Erwin. Individual psychology. N.Y., 1929.

Phil 5262.35.5 — Wexberg, Erwin. Individualpsychologie. 2. Aufl. Leipzig, 1931.

Phil 9495.132 — Wexberg, Erwin. The psychology of sex. N.Y., 1931.

Phil 5054.2.2 — Het weyen der kennis. 2e druk. (Opyoomer, C.W.) Amsterdam, 1867.

Phil 525.180 — Weyergans, Franz. Mystiques parmi nous. Paris, 1959.

Phil 5520.345 — Weyers, Gertrud. Das Sichbeswien auf Wörber. Köln, 1958.

Phil 7082.28 — Weygandt, Wilhelm. Entstehung der Träume. Leipzig, 1893.

Phil 8712.19 — Weygoldt, G.P. Darwinismus, Religion, Sittlichkeit. Leiden, 1878.

Phil 9430.14 — Weygoldt, G.P. Kritik des philosophischen Pessimismus der neuesten Zeit. Leiden, 1875.

Phil 353.15 — Weyl, H. Mind and nature. Philadelphia, 1934.

Phil 3640.442 — Weyland, M. Una nueva imagen del hombre a través de Nietzsche y Freud. Buenos Aires, 1953.

Phil 8416.35 — Het wezen der kunst. (Piccardt, K.L.) Amsterdam, 1937.

Phil 5401.54 — Het wezen van de angst. (Vestdijk, Simon.) Amsterdam, 1968.

Phil 9240.9 — Whale, J.S. The Christian answers to the problem of evil. 2. ed. London, 1948.

Phil 6972.10.4 — Wharton, F. Treatise on mental unsoundness. 4. ed. Philadelphia, 1882.

Phil 8585.25 — What a man told his son. (Furman, R.T.) N.Y., 1924.

Phil 9495.1.8 — What a young boy ought to know. (Stall, Sylvanus.) Philadelphia, 1897.

Htn Phil 8894.17.23* — What all the world's a-seeking. (Trine, Ralph W.) Boston, 1897.

Phil 8894.17.22 — What all the world's a-seeking. (Trine, Ralph W.) N.Y., 1896.

Phil 8708.15 — What am I? (Spaulding, E.G.) N.Y., 1928.

Phil 7082.130 — What are dreams? N.Y., 1900.

Phil 8893.1A — What can ethics do for us? (Salter, W.M.) Chicago, 1891.

Phil 720.9 — What can I know? (Ladd, G.T.) N.Y., 1914.

Phil 8697.13 — What dare I think? (Huxley, Julian S.) London, 1931.

Phil 8697.13.5 — What dare I think? (Huxley, Julian S.) N.Y., 1931.

Phil 8602.49 — What do Christians believe? (Wheeler, F.) London, 1944.

Phil 6060.33 — What does your handwriting reveal? (Olyanova, N.) N.Y., 1929.

Phil 7082.66 — What dreams mean to you. (Cutting, Mary Stewart.) London, 1928.

Phil 194.37 — What existence means. (Thomas, Elyston.) London, 1928.

Phil 8969.5 — What God has joined together. (Thibon, G.) Chicago, 1952.

Phil 6060.24 — What handwriting indicates. (Rexford, John.) N.Y., 1904.

Phil 6060.42 — What handwriting tells about yourself. (Bunker, M.N.) Cleveland, 1951.

Phil 8615.14.15 — What human life is for. (Martin, Alfred W.) n.p., 19- .

Phil 8892.37 — What I believe. (Russell, Bertrand Russell.) London, 1925.

Phil 8892.37.3 — What I believe. (Russell, Bertrand Russell.) N.Y., 1925.

Phil 8892.37.10 — What I believe. (Russell, Bertrand Russell.) N.Y., 1928.

Phil 195.12 — What I believe. (Unurn, George.) London, 1966.

Phil 8610.964.10 — What I believe. v.1-2. (Mason, Gabriel Richard.) N.Y., 1964?

Phil 7060.102.9 — What I saw at Cassadaga lake: Seybert Commission report. (Richmond, Almon B.) Boston, 1888.

Phil 8965.7 — What is a Christian? (Powell, John W.) N.Y., 1915.

Phil 165.310 — What is a man. (Lucas, Eric.) London, 1962.

Phil 3489.27.20 — What is a thing? (Heidegger, Martin.) Chicago, 1968.

Phil 8412.27 — What is art? (Little, J.S.) London, 1884.

Phil 8400.43 — What is art? (Sesonske, Alexander.) N.Y., 1965.

Phil 8403.13.10 — What is beauty. (Canitt, Edger.) Oxford, 1932.

Phil 3450.19.36 — What is called thinking? (Heidegger, Martin.) N.Y., 1968.

Phil 8587.26.12 — What is Christianity? (Harnack, Adolf.) London, 1901.

Phil 8587.26.16 — What is Christianity? 2. ed. (Harnack, Adolf.) N.Y., 1903.

Phil 8587.26.13 — What is Christianity? 2. ed. (Harnack, Adolf.) N.Y., 1904.

Phil 1750.167 — What is existentialism? (Barrett, William.) N.Y., 1947.

Phil 1750.167.2 — What is existentialism? (Barrett, William.) N.Y., 1947.

Phil 1750.167.3A — What is existentialism? (Barrett, William.) N.Y., 1964.

Phil 5245.40 — What is Gestalt-theory. Diss. (Focht, Mildred.) N.Y., 1935.

Phil 6688.29 — What is hypnosis. (Salter, Andrew.) N.Y., 1944.

Phil 346.38 — What is knowledge? (Pears, David Francis.) N.Y., 1971.

Phil 3425.109.14A — What is living and what is dead of the philosophy of Hegel. (Croce, B.) London, 1915.

Phil 8894.26.5 — What is mature morality. (Titus, H.H.) N.Y., 1943.

Phil 5520.23 — What is meaning. (Welby, Victoria.) London, 1903.

Phil 6692.2.2 — What is mesmerism? 2nd ed. London, 1862.

Phil 8897.64 — What is morality? (Whitehead, George.) London, 1925.

Phil 525.34 — What is mysticism. (Addison, C.M.) N.Y., 1923.

Phil 525.247 — What is mysticism? (Knowles, David.) London, 1967.

Phil 1750.115.60 — What is phenomenology? (Thevenaz, Pierre.) Chicago, 1967.

Phil 3450.19.65.2 What is philosophy? (Heidegger, Martin.) N.Y., 1958.
Phil 182.62 What is philosophy? (Holmes, Edmond.) London, 1905.
Phil 185.104 What is philosophy? (Koerner, Stephan.) London, 1969.
Phil 193.148 What is philosophy? (Selsam, H.) N.Y., 1938.
Phil 193.148.3 What is philosophy? (Selsam, H.) N.Y., 1962.
Phil 190.23 What is pragmatism. (Pratt, J.B.) N.Y., 1909.
Phil 5247.31.5 What is psychology? (Hayward, C.W.) N.Y., 1923.
Phil 5262.47 What is psychology? (Wolff, W.) N.Y., 1947.
Htn Phil 8589.4* What is reality? (Johnson, F.H.) Boston, 1891.
Phil 8595.13 What is religion. (Pritchett, H.S.) Boston, 1906.
Phil 8599.50 What is religion? 1. ed. (Tillich, Paul.) N.Y., 1969.
Phil 5255.41 What is the mind? (Patrick, G.T.W.) N.Y., 1929.
Phil 5627.134.10 What is the Oxford Group? N.Y., 1933.
Phil 7054.160.5 What is the use of spiritualism? (Tappan, Cora L.V.) London, 1874.
Phil 7069.19.155 What is this spiritualism? (Leaf, Horace.) N.Y., 1919.
Phil 5258.47 What is thought? (Stirling, James H.) Edinburgh, 1900.
Phil 720.1.2 What is truth? (Argyll, G.D.C.) N.Y., 1889.
Phil 720.1 What is truth? (Campbell, G.D.) Edinburgh, 1889.
Phil 348.8 What is truth? (Rogers, A.K.) New Haven, 1923.
Phil 735.242 What is value? (Frondizi, R.) La Salle, 1963.
Phil 735.130A What is value? (Hall, Everett W.) London, 1952.
Phil 8597.20.5 What is vital in Christianity? (Royce, Josiah.) N.Y., 1909.
Phil 9351.16.2 What is worth while? (Lindsay, A.R.B.) N.Y., 1893.
Phil 9341.9.20 What is your name? (Brown, C.R.) New Haven, 1931.
Phil 6112.26.5 What it is that heals. (Cheney, A.C.P. (Mrs.).) London, 1912.
Phil 2270.67.5 What knowledge is of most worth. (Spencer, Herbert.) N.Y., 1884.
Phil 6310.1.36 What life should mean to you. (Adler, A.) Boston, 1931.
Phil 6310.1.35 What life should mean to you. (Adler, A.) N.Y., 1931.
Phil 9220.5 What makes a friend? 9th ed. (Streamer, Volney.) N.Y., 1904.
Phil 6328.18 What makes us seem so queer? (Seabury, David.) N.Y., 1934.
Phil 8881.18 What makes us unhappy? (Gross, J.B.) Philadelphia, 1882.
Phil 2055.7.5 What man can make of man. (Hocking, William E.) N.Y., 1942.
Phil 5240.36.5 What man has made of man. (Adler, M.J.) N.Y., 1938.
Phil 8827.5 What men live by. (Cabot, R.C.) Boston, 1914.
Phil 8877.65.8 What men live by. (Cabot, Richard C.) Boston, 1914.
Phil 9150.12 What nature is. (Franklin, C.K.) Boston, 1911.
Phil 3640.110 What Nietzsche taught. (Wright, Willard H.) N.Y., 1915.
Phil 9343.6 What now? (Deems, C.F.) N.Y., 1852.
Phil 9120.7 What ought I to do? (Ladd, G.T.) N.Y., 1915.
Phil 5590.21A What people are. (Heath, C.W.) Cambridge, Mass., 1945.
Phil 186.68 What philosophy is. (Larrabee, Harold A.) N.Y., 1928.
Phil 8581.62 What religion is. (Bosanquet, Bernard.) London, 1920.
Phil 8587.49 What religion is and does. (Houf, Horace T.) N.Y., 1935.
Phil 7068.97.22 What say the scriptures about spiritualism? (Watch Tower Bible and Tract Society.) Brooklyn, 1897.
Phil 7068.97.20 What say the scriptures about spiritualism? (Watch Tower Bible and Tract Society.) Allegheny, Pa., 1897.
Phil 6122.52 What shall make us whole? (Merriman, H.B. (Mrs.).) Boston, 1888.
Phil 5070.9 What should I believe? (Ladd, G.T.) London, 1915.
Phil 8660.16 What the great philosophers thought about God. (Fishler, Max.) Los Angeles, 1958.
Phil 5203.10 What to read on psychology. (Hawes, M.) Chicago, 1942.
Phil 8878.51.8 What we live by. (Dimnet, Ernest.) London, 1932.
Phil 8878.51.5 What we live by. (Dimnet, Ernest.) N.Y., 1932.
Phil 9560.28 What word will you choose? (Heron, Grace.) Chicago, 1932.
Phil 8610.890.30 What would follow on the effacement of Christianity. (Holyoake, G.J.) Buffalo, 1890.
VPhil 6060.78 What your handwriting shows. (Saudek, Robert.) London, 1932.
Phil 5262.5 Whately, R. Introductory lessons on mind. Boston, 1859.
Phil 5262.5.2 Whately, R. Introductory lessons on mind. London, 1859.
Phil 8897.13 Whately, R. Introductory lessons on morals. Cambridge, 1856.
Phil 8897.13.3 Whately, R. Introductory lessons on morals. Cambridge, 1860.
Phil 8897.13.5 Whately, R. Introductory lessons on morals. London, 1855.
Phil 8897.13.10 Whately, R. Thoughts and apophthegms. Philadelphia, 1856.
Phil 5062.6.7.5 Whately, Richard. Elements of logic. Boston, 1852.
Phil 5062.6.8.5 Whately, Richard. Elements of logic. Boston, 1859.
Phil 5062.6 Whately, Richard. Elements of logic. London, 1829.
Phil 5062.6.5 Whately, Richard. Elements of logic. London, 1840.
Phil 5062.6.6 Whately, Richard. Elements of logic. London, 1844.
Phil 5062.6.2 Whately, Richard. Elements of logic. N.Y., 1832.
Phil 5062.6.3.5 Whately, Richard. Elements of logic. N.Y., 1836.
Phil 5062.6.7.7 Whately, Richard. Logic. 2nd ed. London, 1852.
Phil 9240.28 Whatever is, is right. 2d ed. (Child, A. Bemis.) Boston, 1861.
NEDL Phil 181.150 What's it all about and what am I? (Gregg, Richard B.) N.Y., 1968.
Phil 181.150.5 What's it all about and what am I? 1. Indian ed. (Gregg, Richard B.) Ahmedabad, 1967.
Phil 197.98 Wheatley, Jon. Prolegomena to philosophy. Belmont, Calif., 1970.
Phil 5772.1 Whedon, D.D. Freedom of the will. N.Y., 1864.
Phil 8633.1.3 Wheeler, B.I. Dionysos and immortality. Boston, 1898.
Phil 5374.15 Wheeler, C.K. The autobiography of the I or ego. Boston, 1903.
Phil 3504.11 Wheeler, C.K. Critique of pure Kant. Boston, 1911.
Phil 197.17 Wheeler, C.K. Hundredth century philosophy. Boston, 1906.
VPhil 5850.386.10 Wheeler, Elmer. Word magic; tested answers to 100 everyday situations. N.Y., 1939.
Phil 8602.49 Wheeler, F. What do Christians believe? London, 1944.
Phil 8610.892 Wheeler, J.M. Bible studies. London, 1892.
Phil 8610.889.15 Wheeler, Joseph Mazzini. A bibliographical dictionary of freethinkers of all ages and nations. London, 1889.
Phil 5262.36.10 Wheeler, R.H. Laws of human nature. N.Y., 1932.
Phil 5262.36.5 Wheeler, R.H. Readings in psychology. N.Y., 1930.
Phil 5262.36 Wheeler, R.H. The science of psychology. N.Y., 1929.
Phil 5262.36.2 Wheeler, R.H. The science of psychology. N.Y., 1940.
Phil 5642.15 Wheeler, R.H. The synaesthesia of a blind subject. Eugene, 1920.
Phil 9035.94 Wheelis, Allen. The quest for identity. 1st ed. N.Y., 1958.
Phil 8897.65 Wheelwright, P. A critical introduction to ethics. Garden City, N.Y., 1935.
Phil 8897.65.5 Wheelwright, P. A critical introduction to ethics. N.Y., 1949.
Phil 5062.39 Wheelwright, P.E. Valid thinking. 1st ed. N.Y., 1962.
Phil 197.75 Wheelwright, Philip. The way of philosophy. N.Y., 1960.
Phil 5520.124A Wheelwright, Phillip Ellis. The burning fountain. Bloomington, 1954.
Phil 5520.124.2 Wheelwright, Phillip Ellis. The burning fountain. Bloomington, 1964.
Phil 5520.124.3 Wheelwright, Phillip Ellis. The burning fountain. Bloomington, 1968.
Phil 8897.63.5 When a man comes to himself. (Wilson, Woodrow.) N.Y., 1915.
Phil 8897.25 When to say no. London, n.d.
Phil 8593.4.10 Whence, what, where? (Nichols, J.R.) Boston, 1886.
Phil 175.33 Whence, whither, and why? (Arch, Robert.) London, 1926.
Phil 8696.18 Whence? Whither? Why? (Gaskell, A. (Mrs.).) N.Y., 1939.
Phil 8691.17 Whence comes man; from nature or from God? (Bell, A.J.) London, 1888.
Phil 8701.12 Whence comest thou? Whither goest thou? (Luckey, L.W.A.) Boston, 1927.
Phil 8647.10 Where are the dead? London, 1928.
Phil 7054.19 Where are the dead? or Spiritualism explained. (Fritz, (pseud.).) Manchester, 1873.
Phil 9590.23 Where do people take their troubles? (Steiner, L.R. (Mrs.).) Boston, 1945.
Phil 8885.35 Where dwells the soul serene. 3rd ed. (Kirkham, S.D.) San Francisco, 1907.
Phil 8581.39 Where knowledge fails. (Barnes, Earl.) N.Y., 1907.
Phil 978.75 Where theosophy and science meet. (Kauga, D.D.) Adyar, 1938.
Phil 7069.14.30 Where two worlds meet. (Cooper, William E.) London, 1914.
Phil 8897.14.1 Whewell, W. Elements of morality. N.Y., 185-? 2v.
Phil 8897.14.2 Whewell, W. Elements of morality. N.Y., 1854. 2v.
NEDL Phil 8897.14.5 Whewell, W. Elements of morality. 4th ed. Cambridge, 1864.
Phil 8847.1 Whewell, W. History of moral philosophy in England. London, 1852.
Phil 8897.14.9 Whewell, W. Lectures on systematic morality. London, 1846.
Phil 5062.8 Whewell, W. Novum organon renovatum. London, 1858.
Phil 5125.4 Whewell, W. Of induction. London, 1849.
Phil 8602.6 Whewell, W. Of the plurality of worlds. London, 1853.
Phil 8897.14.16 Whewell, W. On the foundations of morals. Cambridge, n.d.
Phil 8897.14.15 Whewell, W. On the foundations of morals. N.Y., 1839.
Phil 197.6.5 Whewell, W. On the philosophy of discovery. London, 1860.
Phil 8602.6.2 Whewell, W. The plurality of worlds. Boston, 1854.
Phil 8602.6.3 Whewell, W. The plurality of worlds. Boston, 1855.
Phil 8677.3 Whewell, William. Astronomy and general physics, considered with reference to natural theology. London, 1833.
Phil 8677.3.2 Whewell, William. Astronomy and general physics, considered with reference to natural theology. London, 1834.
Phil 8677.3.3 Whewell, William. Astronomy and general physics, considered with reference to natural theology. N.Y., 1841.
Phil 8677.3.6 Whewell, William. Astronomy and general physics, considered with reference to natural theology. 7. ed. London, 1852.
Phil 2340.9.90 Whewell's philosophy of induction. Diss. (Stoll, Marion R.) Lancaster, Pa., 1929.
Phil 7059.12.15 Which: spiritualism or Christianity? (Hull, Moses.) N.Y., 1873.
Phil 8972.11 Which way religion? (Ward, H.F.) N.Y., 1931.
Phil 705.35 Whicher, G.F. The transcendentalist revolt against materialism. Boston, 1949.
Phil 9530.11 Whipple, E.P. Success and its conditions. Boston, 1880.
Phil 5262.13 Whipple, G.M. Manual of mental and physical tests. Baltimore, 1910.
Phil 5262.13.2 Whipple, G.M. Manual of mental and physical tests. Pt. 1-2. Baltimore, 1914-15. 2v.
Phil 6132.6 Whipple, L.E. Mental healing. N.Y., 1907.
Phil 6132.6.5 Whipple, L.E. The philosophy of mental healing. N.Y., 1893.
Phil 6132.6.10 Whipple, L.E. Practical health. N.Y., 1907.
Phil 8677.4 Whish, J.C. The first cause. London, 1855.
Phil 1915.80 Whiston, W. Historical memoires of...Dr. S. Clarke. London, 1730.
Phil 8712.9 Whiston, W. Theory of the earth, from its original. London, 1755.
Phil 1850.157 Whitaker, Virgil Keeble. Francis Bacon's intellectual milieu. Los Angeles, 1962.
Phil 197.39 Whitby, C.J. The open secret. London, 1912.
Phil 9035.68 Whitby, Charles J. The logic of human character. London, 1905.
Phil 9035.68.5 Whitby, Charles J. Makers of man, a study of human initiative. London, 1911.
Phil 8897.15 Whitby, D. Ethices compendium. London, 1713.
Phil 6972.8 White, A.D. New chapters in the warfare of science. v.1-2. N.Y., 1889.
Phil 8897.49 White, A.K. The moral self; its nature and development. London, 1923.
Phil 187.59.85 White, Alan R. G.E. Moore. Oxford, 1958.
Phil 8712.3.15 White, Andrew Dickson. Histoire de la lutte entre la science et la théologie. Paris, 1899.
Phil 8712.3.5 White, Andrew Dickson. History of the warfare of science with theology in Christendem. N.Y., 1896. 2v.
NEDL Phil 8712.3.9 White, Andrew Dickson. History of the warfare of science with theology in Christendem. N.Y., 1901. 2v.
Phil 8712.3.10 White, Andrew Dickson. History of the warfare of science with theology in Christendem. N.Y., 1910. 2v.
Phil 8712.3.11 White, Andrew Dickson. History of the warfare of science with theology in Christendem. N.Y., 1920. 2v.
Phil 8712.3.12 White, Andrew Dickson. A history of the warfare of science with theology in Christendem. N.Y., 1965.
Phil 8712.3.4 White, Andrew Dickson. New chapters in the warfare of science. (Geology). N.Y., 1888.
Phil 8712.3.3 White, Andrew Dickson. New chapters in the warfare of science. (Meteorology). N.Y., 1887.
Phil 8712.27 White, E.A. Science and religion in American thought. Stanford, 1952.
Phil 6132.24 White, H.P. The philosophy of health. no.1-3. Kalamazoo, Mich., 1901.
Phil 6972.12 White, H.W. Demonism verified and analyzed. Shanghai, 1922.
Phil 1722.9 White, M.G. The age of analysis. Boston, 1955.
Phil 1722.9.5 White, M.G. Toward reunion in philosophy. Cambridge, 1956.
Phil 7069.17.50 White, Mary Blount. Letters from Harry and Helen. N.Y., 1917.
Phil 2340.17.30 White, Morton Gabriel. Religion, politics, and the higher learning. Cambridge, 1959.
Phil 7054.67 White, N.F. Voices from spirit-land. N.Y., 1854.

Phil 5238.186   White, R.W. The study of lives; essays on personality in honour of Henry A. Murray. N.Y., 1963.

Phil 2422.8   White, Reginald James. The anti-philosophers; a study of philosophers in eighteenth century France. London, 1970.

Phil 6332.19   White, Robert. The abnormal personality. 2. ed. N.Y., 1956.

Phil 6332.19.3   White, Robert. The abnormal personality. 3d ed. N.Y., 1964.

Phil 5262.46.01   Pamphlet box. White, Robert W.

Phil 5590.292   White, Robert Winthrop. Lives in progress. 2. ed. N.Y., 1966.

Phil 197.68   White, S.E. Anchors to windward. N.Y., 1943.

Phil 7069.40.13   White, S.E. The unobstructed universe. N.Y., 1940.

Phil 7069.47   White, S.E. With folded wings. 1. ed. N.Y., 1947.

Phil 1955.6.109   White, Stephen. S. A comparison of the philosophies of F.C.S. Schiller and John Dewey. Thesis. Chicago, 1940.

Phil 7069.46   White, Stewart E. The stars are still there. 1. ed. N.Y., 1946.

Phil 303.5   White, T. De mundo dialogi tres quibus. Paris, 1642.

Phil 5627.260   White, Victor. Soul and psyche. London, 1960.

Phil 5850.385.86   White, Wendell. Psychology in living. 3rd ed. N.Y., 1955.

Phil 5850.385.80   White, Wendell. The psychology of dealing with people. N.Y., 1936.

Phil 5850.385.82   White, Wendell. The psychology of dealing with people. N.Y., 1941.

Phil 5850.385.85   White, Wendell. The psychology of making life interesting. N.Y., 1939.

Phil 9035.23   White, William A. Mechanisms of character formation. N.Y., 1916.

Phil 6972.14.25   White, William Alanson. Essays in psychopathology. N.Y., 1925.

Phil 6972.14.20   White, William Alanson. Foundations of psychiatry. N.Y., 1921.

Phil 6132.43   White, William Alanson. An introduction to the study of the mind. Washington, 1924.

Phil 6972.14.30   White, William Alanson. Lectures in psychiatry. N.Y., 1928.

Phil 6972.14.13   White, William Alanson. Outlines of psychiatry. 13. ed. Washington, 1932.

Phil 6972.14.50   White, William Alanson. William Alanson White, the autobiography of a purpose. Garden City, 1938.

Phil 978.62   The white brother; an occult autobiography. (Juste, Michael.) London, 192-?

Phil 822.8A   Whitehead, A.N. Adventures of ideas. N.Y., 1933.

Phil 8602.33A   Whitehead, A.N. Religion in the making. N.Y., 1926.

Phil 8602.33.2   Whitehead, A.N. Religion in the making. N.Y., 1926.

Phil 8602.33.5   Whitehead, A.N. Religion in the making. N.Y., 1927.

Phil 8602.33.10   Whitehead, A.N. Religion in the making. N.Y., 1960[1954]

Phil 353.9.2   Whitehead, A.N. Symbolism: its meaning and effect. Cambridge, Eng., 1928.

Phil 353.9A   Whitehead, A.N. Symbolism: its meaning and effect. N.Y., 1927.

Phil 303.12.6   Whitehead, Alfred N. Process and reality; an essay in cosmology. N.Y., 1941.

Phil 303.12   Whitehead, Alfred N. Process and reality. Cambridge, Eng., 1929.

Phil 303.12.3   Whitehead, Alfred N. Process and reality. N.Y., 1929.

Phil 303.12.5   Whitehead, Alfred N. Process and reality. N.Y., 1930.

Phil 2340.10.25   Whitehead, Alfred North. Alfred North Whitehead; an anthology. N.Y., 1953.

Phil 2340.10.26   Whitehead, Alfred North. Alfred North Whitehead. N.Y., 1961.

Phil 2340.10.40   Whitehead, Alfred North. Alfred North Whitehead. 1st ed. N.Y., 1961.

Phil 2340.10.28   Whitehead, Alfred North. American essays in social philosophy. N.Y., 1959.

Phil 2340.10.35A   Whitehead, Alfred North. Dialogues of Alfred North Whitehead. 1st ed. Boston, 1954.

Phil 2340.10.96A   Whitehead, Alfred North. Essays in science and philosophy. N.Y., 1947.

Phil 2340.10.96.2   Whitehead, Alfred North. Essays in science and philosophy. N.Y., 1948.

Phil 2340.10.98A   Whitehead, Alfred North. Modes of thought. N.Y., 1938.

Phil 2340.10.98.5   Whitehead, Alfred North. Modes of thought. N.Y., 1956.

Phil 2340.10.30A   Whitehead, Alfred North. Wit and wisdom. Boston, 1947.

Phil 8677.16   Whitehead, George. The case against theism. London, 1922.

Phil 6332.9.15   Whitehead, George. Gods, devils, and men. London, 1928.

Phil 6332.9   Whitehead, George. Psycho-analysis and art. London, 1930.

Phil 5627.140   Whitehead, George. Religion and woman. London, 1928.

Phil 7069.28.95   Whitehead, George. Spiritualism explained. London, 1928.

Phil 8897.64   Whitehead, George. What is morality? London, 1925.

Phil 2340.10.120A   Whitehead and the modern world. (Lowe, Victor A.) Boston, 1950.

Phil 2340.10.220   Whitehead e la funzione della filosofia. (Sini, Carlo.) Vicenza, 1965.

Phil 2340.10.210   Whitehead en de wereld. Proefschrift. (Adhin, Herman S.) Delft, 1963.

Phil 2340.10.190   Whitehead on education. (Dunkel, Harold Baker.) Columbus, 1965.

Phil 2340.10.160   A Whiteheadian aesthetic. (Sherburne, Donald W.) New Haven, 1961.

Phil 2340.10.145   Whitehead's metaphysics. (Leclerc, Ivor.) London, 1958.

Phil 2340.10.205   Whitehead's metaphysics. (Pols, Edward.) Carbondale, 1967.

Phil 2340.10.135   Whitehead's philosophical development. (Lawrence, N.M.) Berkeley, 1956.

Phil 2340.10.130.5   Whitehead's philosophy of civilization. (Johnson, A.H.) Boston, 1958.

Phil 2340.10.90A   Whitehead's philosophy of organism. (Emmet, Dorothy M.) London, 1932.

Phil 2340.10.165   Whitehead's philosophy of science. (Palter, Robert M.) Chicago, 1960.

Phil 2340.10.115   Whitehead's theory of experience. (Shahan, E.P.) N.Y., 1950.

Phil 2340.10.100   Whitehead's theory of knowledge. (Blyth, J.W.) Providence, R.I., 1941.

Phil 2340.10.130   Whitehead's theory of reality. (Johnson, A.H.) Boston, 1952.

Phil 8712.30   Whitehouse, Walter. Order, goodness, glory. London, 1960.

Phil 8847.17   Whiteley, Charles Henry. The permissive morality. London, 1964.

Phil 8587.56   Whither Christianity. (Hough, Lynn Harold.) N.Y., 1929.

Phil 2255.5   Whither humanity; the philosophy of a doctor. (Reid, James K.) London, 1945.

Phil 7054.4.9   Whiting, Lilian. After her death. Boston, 1898.

Phil 7069.18.160   Whiting, Lilian. After her death. Boston, 1918.

Phil 7054.4.15   Whiting, Lilian. The spiritual significance. Boston, 1900.

Phil 8897.62.3   Whiting, Lilian. The world beautiful. Boston, 1897.

Phil 8897.62.5   Whiting, Lilian. The world beautiful. 3rd ser. Boston, 1898.

Phil 5262.62   Whitla, Dean. Handbook of measurement and assessment in behavioral sciences. Reading, 1968.

Phil 9362.3   Whitman, J. Young lady's aid. Portland, 1845.

Phil 9362.3.2   Whitman, J. Young lady's aid. 2d ed. Portland, 1839.

Phil 9362.3.5   Whitman, J. Young man's assistant. Portland, 1838.

Phil 3640.700A   Whitman and Nietzsche. (Stavrou, C.N.) Chapel Hill, 1964.

Phil 6332.45   Whitmont, Edward. The symbolic quest. N.Y., 1969.

Phil 3504.14   Whitney, G.J. An introduction to Kant's critical philosophy. N.Y., 1914.

Phil 3504.43   Whitney, G.T. The heritage of Kant. Princeton, 1939.

Phil 8897.66   Whitney, R.E. Morality in the making. N.Y., 1929.

Phil 672.212   Whitrow, G.J. The natural philosophy of time. London, 1961.

Phil 303.14   Whittaker, E. Space and spirit. London, 1946.

Phil 1135.205   Whittaker, John. God, time, being; studies in the transcendental tradition in Greek philosophy. Thesis. Bergen, 1970.

Phil 2490.90   Whittaker, T. Comte and Mill. London, 1908.

Phil 197.19   Whittaker, T. Essays and notices: philosophical and psychological. London, 1895.

Phil 197.19.10   Whittaker, T. Prolegomena to a new metaphysic. Cambridge, Eng., 1931.

Phil 5620.16   Whittaker, T. Reason. Cambridge, Eng., 1934.

Phil 3808.110   Whittaker, T. Schopenhauer. London, 1909.

Phil 1170.5.3   Whittaker, Thomas. Neo-Platonists. Photoreproduction. 2nd ed. Cambridge, 1928.

Phil 1170.5.5   Whittaker, Thomas. The Neo-Platonists. 4th ed. Olm, 1961.

NEDL Phil 1170.5   Whittaker, Thomas. Neo-Platonists::Study in history of Hellenism. Cambridge, 1901.

Phil 8897.37   Whittaker, Thomas. Theory of abstract ethics. Cambridge, 1916.

Phil 6980.777   Whittington, H.G. Psychiatry on the college campus. N.Y., 1963.

Phil 6972.17   Whitwell, James Richard. Historical notes on psychiatry. Photoreproduction. Philadelphia, 1937.

Phil 6968.14   Who is insane? (Smith, S.) N.Y., 1916.

Phil 585.182   Who is man? (Heschel, Abraham Joshua.) Stanford, Calif., 1965.

Phil 8610.859   Who is the Holy Spirit? (Taylor, Robert.) N.Y., 1859.

Phil 3640.98.9   Who is to be master of the world? (Ludovici, Anthony M.) Edinburgh, 1914.

Phil 6060.25   Who is your mate? (Rice, L.G. (Mrs.) N.Y., 1930.

Phil 978.49.200   Who was Rudolf Steiner? (Freeman, Arnold.) Sheffield, 1944.

Phil 8580.3.25   Who wrote "Ethan Allen's Bible"? (Anderson, George P.) n.p., 1937.

Phil 974.2.40   Who wrote the Mahatma letters? (Hare, H.E.) London, 1936.

Phil 974.2.44   Who wrote the Mahatma letters? Answered. (Hudson, Irene B.) Victoria, 1936.

Phil 974.2.42   Who wrote the March-hare attack on the Mahatma letters? (Cox, H.R.W.) Victoria, 1936.

Htn Phil 1845.1.35F*   The whole duty of man. (Allestree, Richard.) London, 1725.

Phil 9362.4   Whole duty of woman. (Kendrick, William.) Walpole, 1797.

Phil 9362.4.6   The whole duty of woman. n.p., 1821.

Phil 5241.108   The whole man. (Bittle, Alestine N.C.) Milwaukee, 1945.

Phil 5627.247.1   The whole person in a broken world. (Tournier, Paul.) N.Y., 1964.

Phil 1900.15   Whole works. (Butler, Joseph.) London, 1847.

Phil 1900.19   Whole works. (Butler, Joseph.) London, 1900. 2v.

Phil 7069.35.54   "Whom the gods love". Dictated by Ernest Wells. (Wells, Helen B.) N.Y., 1935.

Phil 9495.127   Who's obscene? (Dennett, M.W. (Mrs.).) N.Y., 1930.

Phil 8583.33.15   Whose son is Christ? (Delitzsch, Friedrich.) Boston, 1908.

Phil 9182.4.12   Why appeal to America. (Wagner, Charles.) N.Y., 1905.

Phil 5401.11   Why be afraid? (Mones, L.) Boston, 1931.

Phil 6311.20.5   Why be shy? (Bisch, L.E.) N.Y., 1941.

Phil 8662.5.10   Why do the clergy avoid discussion? (Holyoake, George Jacob.) London, 1852.

Phil 8612.10   Why do we die? (Mercer, Edward.) London, 1919.

Phil 8610.893   Why don't he lend a hand? (Putnam, J.P.) N.Y., 1893.

Phil 9415.12   Why good people suffer. (Wilds, Louis T.) Richmond, Va., 1944.

Phil 8610.927.7   Why I am not a Christian. (Russell, Bertrand Russell.) Girard, Kansas, 1929.

Phil 8610.927.8   Why I am not a Christian. (Russell, Bertrand Russell.) N.Y., 1957.

Phil 8620.44.5   Why I am satisfied; an open letter to Prof. C.E.M. Joad. (Headlam, A.C.) Oxford, 1944.

Phil 978.6.4   Why I became a theosophist. (Besant, Annie.) N.Y., 1890.

Phil 978.6.5   Why I became a theosophist. (Besant, Annie.) N.Y., 1891.

Phil 9435.2   Why I believe in poverty. (Bok, Edward.) Boston, 1915.

Phil 5627.134.45   Why I believe in the Oxford Group. 3. ed. (Winslow, J.C.) London, 1934.

Phil 8669.4   Why I know there is a God. 1. ed. (Oursler, F.) Garden City, N.Y., 1950.

Phil 8610.925   Why I quit going to church. (Hughes, R.) N.Y., 1925.

Phil 1750.101.5   Why is there something rather than nothing? (Tymieniecka, Anna Teresa.) Assen, 1966.

Phil 960.230   Why Lazarus laughed. (Wei-uri-wei (pseud.).) London, 1960.

Phil 5780.20   Why men confess. (Rogge, Oetje G.) N.Y., 1959.

Phil 6315.20   Why men fail. (Fishbein, M.) N.Y., 1928.

Phil 6125.24.4   Why not try God? (Pickford, Mary.) N.Y., 1934.

Phil 5242.52   The "why" of man's experience. (Cantrie, H.) N.Y., 1950.

Phil 5771.1   The why of the will. (Van Peyma, P.W.) Boston, 1910.

Phil 7068.95.20   Why she became a spiritualist. 3. ed. (Judson, Abby A.) Cincinnati, 1895.

Phil 6128.11   Why the mind has a body. (Strong, C.A.) N.Y., 1903.

Phil 6128.11.2   Why the mind has a body. (Strong, C.A.) N.Y., 1903.

Phil 6322.24   Why we do it? (Mason, E.C.) St. Louis, 1937.

Phil 9075.34   Why we do right. (Gorham, C.T.) London, 1924.

Phil 9495.130   Why we misbehave. (Schmalhausen, S.D.) Garden City, N.Y., 1928.

Phil 9495.130.7   Why we misbehave. (Schmalhausen, S.D.) N.Y., 1929.

Phil 6132.7   Why worry? (Walton, G.L.) Philadelphia, 1908.

Phil 6132.7.2   Why worry? 2d ed. (Walton, G.L.) Philadelphia, 1919.

Phil 7069.31.32   Whymant, A.N.J. Psychic adventures in New York. Boston, 1931.

Phil 8620.40   Whyte, A.G. The natural history of evil. London, 1920.

Phil 8610.913.20   Whyte, A.G. The religion of the open mind. London, 1913.

Phil 5722.42.2   Whyte, Lancelot. The unconscious before Freud. London, 1967.
Phil 5722.42   Whyte, Lancelot. The unconscious before Freud. N.Y., 1960.
Phil 380.2.5A   Whyte, Lancelot L. Accent on form. N.Y., 1954.
Phil 380.2.10   Whyte, Lancelot L. Aspects of form. London, 1951.
Phil 260.13   Whyte, Laucelot Law. Essay on atomism. 1st ed. Middletown, Conn., 1961.
Phil 7059.21   Whytt, James. Disembodied spirits. London, 1840.
Phil 5465.166   Wiart, Claude. Expression picturale et psychopathologie. Paris, 1967.
Phil 8897.17   Wiart, E. Du principe de la morale. Paris, 1862.
Phil 4803.454.91   Wiązanie metafizyczme sporządzone według prawa stworzenia Hoene-Wrońskiego. (Warrain, Francis.) Warszawa, 1928.
Phil 3504.27   Wichmann, G. Platon und Kant. Berlin, 1920.
Phil 5772.9   Wichmann, O. Wille und Freiheit. München, 1922.
Phil 640.2   Wichmann, Ottomar. Die Scholastiker. München, 1921.
Phil 6132.11   Wichmann, R. Die Rückenmarksnewen über ihre Segmentbezüge. Berlin, 1900.
Phil 3100.84   Die wichtigsten Grundlehren und Vorzüge der Psychologie Dr. Beneke's. (Freimuth, F.W.) Bautzen, 1845.
Phil 197.18   Die Wichtigsten philosophischen Fachausdrücke in historischer Anordnung. (Willmann, O.) Kempten, 1909.
Phil 9390.9   The wickedness of a disregard of oaths. London, 1723.
Phil 3504.48   Wickenhagen, Ernst. Die Logik bei Kant. Inaug. Diss. Jena, 1869.
Phil 5232.11   Wickert, F.R. Readings in African psychology. East Lansing, 1967.
Phil 3805.89   Wickert, R. Die Pädagogik Schleiermachers. Leipzig, 1907.
Phil 6332.11.5   Wickes, F.G. The inner world of choice. N.Y., 1963.
Phil 6332.11   Wickes, F.G. Inner world of man. N.Y., 1938.
Phil 5232.4   Wickham, H. The misbehaviorists. N.Y., 1928.
Phil 1822.4A   Wickham, H. The unrealists. N.Y., 1930.
Phil 7069.24.40   Wickland, C.A. Thirty years among the dead. Los Angeles, 1924.
Phil 9070.54   Wicks, R.R. The reason for living. N.Y., 1934.
Phil 9182.7   Wicks, Robert R. One operation and another. N.Y., 1939.
Phil 4065.104   Wickström, V.H. Giordano Brunos metafysik. Lund, 1883.
Phil 7060.151.20   Wickwar, J.W. The ghost world. London, 1919.
Phil 7084.14.8   Wickwar, John William. Dreams: what they are and what they mean. 3d ed. London, 1918.
Phil 2648.92   Wickwar, William H. Baron d'Holbach; a prelude to the French Revolution. London, 1935.
Phil 5535.18   Wictorin, Mauritz. Bidrag till zäknefärdighetens psykologi akademisk. Göteborg, 1952.
Phil 197.31   Widemann, P.H. Erkennen und Sein, Losung des Problems. Karlsruhe, 1885.
Phil 7069.40.15   Widening horizons. (Palmstierna, E.K.) London, 1940.
Phil 5870.110   The widening world of childhood. (Murphy, Lois Barclay.) N.Y., 1962.
Phil 1750.363   Wider den Existentialismus. (Haefliger, J.) Bern, 1949.
Phil 310.738   Wider die Fälscher der Geschichte. (Anders, Georg.) München, 1958.
Htn   Phil 3829.3.20*   Wider Mendelssohns Beschuldigungen Betreffend die Briefe über die Lehre des Spinoza. (Jacobi, F.E.) Leipzig, 1786.
Phil 7067.48   Widerlegung der Gedancken von Gespentern. (Sucro, J.G.) Halle im Magdeburgischen, 1748.
Phil 5047.44   Widerspiegelung und Begriff. (Horn, Heinz.) Berlin, 1958.
Phil 5041.27   Der Widerspruch im Wessen und Wesen der Welt. (Bahnsen, J.) Berlin, 1880-82. 2v.
Phil 193.242   Widerspruch und Hoffnung des Daseins. (Strolz, Walter.) Frankfurt, 1965.
Phil 8592.118   Widerspruch und Zuversicht. (Mainberger, G.) Olten, 1967.
Phil 4710.3   Das Widerspruchsprinzie in der neueren sowjetischen Philosophie. (Lobkowicz, Nikolaus.) Reidel, 1959.
Phil 1020.17.5   Die Widersprüche der Philosophie nach al Gozzali und ihr Ausgleich durch Ibn Rosd. (Boer, Tjitze de.) Strassburg, 1894.
Phil 5822.4.10   Widersprüche in der menschlichen Existenz. (Messner, J.) Innsbruck, 1952.
Phil 3528.55.2   Der Widerstreit der Vernunft mit sich Selbst in der Versöhnungslehre. (Krug, Wilhelm Traugott.) Bruxelles, 1968.
Phil 8972.9   Widgery, A.G. Christian ethics in history and modern life. N.Y., 1940.
Phil 197.38   Widgery, A.G. Outlines of a philosophy of life. London, 1923.
Phil 197.38.5   Widgery, A.G. A philosopher's pilgrimage. N.Y., 1961.
Phil 3246.296   Widmann, J. Analyse der formalen Strukturen des transzendentalen Wissens in Johann Gottlieb Fichtes. München? 1961.
Phil 3246.188   Widmark, Elof. Historisk øfversigt af Fichtes naturrält och Babergs outik deraf. Upsala, 1854.
Phil 2750.19.130   Widmer, Charles. Gabriel Marcel et le théisme existentiel. Paris, 1971.
Phil 8602.40   Widney, J.P. The faith that has come to me. Los Angeles, 1932.
Phil 7060.54   The widow's mite and other psychic phenomena. (Funk, Isaac Kaufmann.) N.Y., 1904.
Phil 6311.2.10   Wie deine Seele geheilt wird. (Bjerre, P.) Halle, 1925.
Phil 7054.14   Wie errichtet und leitet man spiritistische Zirkel in der Familie? (Arnold, H.) Leipzig, 1894.
Phil 5068.40   Wie fördert man heute die empirische Bewegung? (Naese, Arne.) Oslo, 1956.
Phil 176.3.7   Wie Wurde was ich Ward. (Bahnsen, J.) Leipzig, 1931.
Phil 176.3.5   Wie ich Wurde was ich Ward. (Bahnsen, J.) München, 1905.
Phil 3925.7.85   Wie ich zur Philosophie und Psychologie Ram. (Wirth, Wilhelm.) Leipzig, 1931.
Phil 8879.38   Wie ist Ethik als Wissenschaft möglich? (Eichhorn, Wolfgang.) Berlin, 1965.
Phil 186.35.5   Wie ist kritische Philosophie überhaupt möglich? (Liebert, Arthur.) Leipzig, 1919.
Phil 186.35.7   Wie ist kritische Philosophie überhaupt möglich? (Liebert, Arthur.) Leipzig, 1923.
Phil 3425.293   Wie kann der Supernaturalismus sein Recht gegen Hegel's Religionsphilosophie behaupten? (Trahndorff, K.F.E.) Berlin, 1840.
Phil 978.49.699.2   Wie Kann die Menschheit den Christus Wiedertinden? 2. Aufl. (Steiner, R.) Dornach, 1968.
Phil 6060.54   Wie man Menschen beurteilt. (Fervers, Hans.) Neuwied, 1929.
Phil 6327.12.25   Wie man psychologe wird. (Reik, Theodor.) Leipzig, 1927.
Phil 9530.48   Wie Rationalisiert man sein Leben. (Friedländer, Max.) Zürich, 1943?
Phil 3640.452   Wie was Nietzsche? (Flam, Leopold.) Antwerpen, 1960.
Phil 8630.10   Wie wird's sein? (Franck, K.) Halle, 1901.
Phil 5545.185   Wieck, H.H. Zur Psychologie und Psychopathologie der Erinnerungen. Stuttgart, 1955.

Phil 8423.12   Wieckberg, W. Grundwissenschaftliche Unterlage der Kunstwissenschaft. Charlottenburg, 1922.
Phil 3552.438   Wiedeburg, P.H. Der junge Leibniz das Keich und Europa. Wiesbaden, 1962. 3v.
Phil 7080.53   Wiedemann, Fritz. Müde Menschen. Heidenheim, 1953.
Phil 3890.11   Die Wiederenteleskung des ich in der Metaphysik Teichmüllers. (Schabad, M.) Basel, 1940.
Phil 3549.2.52   Wiedergeburt. (Keyserling, Hermann.) Darmstadt, 1927.
Phil 835.2   Die Wiedergeburt der Erkenntnis in der Entwicklungsgeschichte. (Lauer, Hans Erhard.) Freiburg, 1946.
Phil 1718.4   Die Wiedergeburt der Philosophie. (Stumpf, K.) Leipzig, 1908.
Phil 3120.22.35   Die Wiedergeburt der platonischen Akademie. (Blüher, Hans.) Jena, 1920. 4 pam.
Phil 193.115   Die Wiedergeburt der systematischen Philosophie. (Stickers, J.) Berlin, 1927.
Phil 6328.38   Wiedergeburt des Einzelnen. (Stuttgart. Institut für Psychotherapie und Tiefenpsychologie.) Stuttgart, 1956.
Phil 5250.13.85   Die Wiederherstellung der Seelenwissenschaft im Lebenswerk Felix Kruegers. (Wellek, Albert.) Hamburg, 1950.
Phil 735.80   Wiederhold, K. Wert Begriff und Wertphilosophie. Berlin, 1920.
Phil 8599.35   Die wiederkehr Göttes. (Trautmann, O.) Stuttgart, 1950.
Phil 8897.60   Wiedling, Hans. Die Wirklichkeit der Ethik. Leipzig, 1931.
Phil 353.33   Wiedmann, Franz. Das Problem der Gewissheit. Eine erkenntnismetaphysische Studie. München, 1966.
Phil 178.36   Wieg zur Metaphysik als exakten Wissenschaft. (Dilles, Ludwig.) Stuttgart, 1903-06. 2v.
Phil 8423.28   Wiegand, Anke. Die Schönheit und das Böse. München, 1967.
Phil 3120.2.90   Wiegand, H. Der Wahrheitsbegriff in der Lehre. Inaug. Diss. Alfeld Leine, 1928.
Phil 3460.89   Wiegand, Wilhelm. Zur Erinnerung an den Denker F.H. Jacobi und seine Weltansicht. Worms, 1863?
Phil 3504.42   Wiegershausen, H. Aenesidem-Schulze, der Gegner Kants. Inaug. Diss. Münster, 1910.
Phil 3801.879   Wieland, W. Schellings Lehre von der Zeit. Heidelberg, 1956.
Phil 197.50   Wielenga, B. In de school ijer wysbegeerte. Amsterdam, 1924.
Phil 8520.28A   Wieman, H.N. American philosophies of religion. Chicago, 1936.
Phil 8847.10   Wieman, H.N. The directive in history. Boston, 1949.
Phil 8712.17   Wieman, H.N. Religious experience and scientific method. N.Y., 1926.
Phil 8602.35.10   Wieman, Henry Nelson. Religious inquiry; some explorations. Boston, 1968.
Phil 8602.35   Wieman, Henry Nelson. The wrestle of religion with truth. N.Y., 1927.
Phil 3640.655   Wien, Hermann. Positives antichristentum. Den Haag, 1962.
Phil 8423.8.2   Wienbarg, Ludolf. Asthetische Feldzüge. Berlin, 1964.
Phil 8423.8   Wienbarg, Ludolf. Asthetische Feldzüge. 2. Aufl. Hamburg, 1919.
Phil 8599.19.105   Wieneke, Friedrich. Die Entwicklung des philosophischen Gottesbegriffs bei Ernst Troeltsch. Inaug. Diss. Berlin, 1929.
Phil 8602.31   Wienel, H. Die Wirkungen Des Geistes und der Glister. Freiburg, 1899.
Phil 6692.7   Wiener, M. Selma, die jüdische Seherin. Berlin, 1838.
Phil 5520.530   Wiener, Morton. Language within language; immediacy, a channel in verbal communication. N.Y., 1968.
Phil 365.50A   Wiener, P.P. Evolution and the founders of pragmatism. Cambridge, 1949.
Phil 2225.5.85   Wiener, P.P. Studies in the philosophy of Charles Sanders Peirce. Cambridge, Mass., 1952.
Phil 62.5   Wiener, P.V. Minutes of the Vienna Psychoanalytic Society. N.Y., 1962- 2v.
Phil 32.6   Wiener Archiv für Psychologie, Psychiatrie und Neurologie. Wien. 1-6,1951-1956 4v.
Phil 5068.65   Der Wiener Denkstil: Mach, Carnap. (Kyserling, Arnold.) Graz, 1965.
Phil 32.8   Wiener Jahrbuch für Philosophie. Wien. 1,1968+ 3v.
Phil 5068.16A   Der Wiener Kreis. (Kraft, Viktor.) Wien, 1950.
Phil 5068.16.2   Der Wiener Kreis. Der Ursprung des Neopositivismus. Ein Kapitel der jüngsten Philosophiegeschichte. 2. Aufl. (Kraft, Viktor.) Wien, 1968.
Htn   Phil 62.4*   Wiener psychoanalytisches Verein. Wiesbaden.
Phil 32.4   Wiener Zeitschrift für Philosophie, Psychologie, Pädagogik. Wien. 1,1947+ 5v.
Phil 32.4.5   Wiener Zeitschrift für Philosophie, Psychologie, Pädagogik. Beiheft. Wien. 1+
Phil 7085.3   Wienholt, A. Seven lectures on somnambulism. Edinburgh, 1845.
Phil 197.51   Wienstein, M.B. Welt- und libenanschauungen Hevoorgegangen aus Religion, Philosophie und Naturerkenntnis. Leipzig, 1910.
Htn   Phil 5412.3*   Wier, Johann. Ioannis VVieri De ira morbo. Basileae, 1577.
Phil 1200.41   Wiersma, W. Peri telous. Groningen, 1937.
Phil 5520.615   Wierzbicka, Anna. Dociekania semantyczne. Wrocław, 1969.
Phil 5520.616   Wierzbicka, Anna. Kocha, lubi, szanuje. Wyd. 1. Warszawa, 1971.
Phil 974.3.119.5   Wiesberger, Halla. Aus dem Leben von Marie Steiner von Silvers. Dornach, 1956.
Phil 9470.5   Wieschedel, W. Versuch über das Wesen der Verantwortung. Inaug. Diss. Heppenheim, 1932.
Phil 5772.2.4   Wiese, L. Die Bildung des Willens. Berlin, 1879.
Phil 9513.7   Wiese, Leopold von. Ethik in der Schauweise der Wissenschaften. Bern, 1947.
Phil 9513.7.2   Wiese, Leopold von. Ethik in der Schauweise der Wissenschaften. 2. Aufl. Bern, 1960.
Phil 2270.165   Wiese, Leopold von. Herbert Spencers Einführung in die Soziologie. Köln, 1960.
Phil 9513.8   Wiese, Leopold von. Das Soziale im Leben und im Denken. Köln, 1956.
Phil 6332.55   Wiesenhuetter, Eckhart. Grundbegriffe der Tiefenpsychologie. Darmstadt, 1969.
Phil 3504.24.2   Wieser, F. Kant-Festschrift zu Kants 200. Geburstag am April 1924. 2. Aufl. Berlin, 1924.
Phil 3504.24   Wieser, F. Kant-Festschrift zu Kants 200. Geburstag am 22 April 1924. Berlin, 1924.
Phil 525.85   Wieser, Max. Der sentimentale Mensch. Gotha, 1924.
Phil 525.85.2   Wieser, Max. Der sentimentale Mensch gesehen aus der Welt. Gotha, 1924.
Phil 6060.90   Wieser, Roda. Grundriss der Graphologie. München, 1969.
Phil 5625.99   Wieser, S. Das Schreckverhalten des Menschen. Bern, 1961.

Phil 3549.10.80   Wieser, T. Die Einbildungskraft bei Rudolf Kassner. Zürich, 1949.

Phil 5772.10   Wiesner, Johann. Die Freihert des menschlichen Willens. Wien, 1920.

Phil 672.161   Wiessner, Alexander. Die wesenhafte oder absolute Realität des Raumes. Leipzig, 1877.

Phil 6972.3   Wigan, A.L. A new view of insanity. The duality of the mind. London, 1844.

Phil 3925.17.25   Wigeroma, Baltus. Wordende waarheid. 's Gravenhage, 1959.
Phil 3120.13.90   Wigersma, I.B. Bolland. Amsterdam, 1927.
Phil 5850.386.5   Wiggam, A.E. The marks of a clear mind. N.Y., 1933.
Phil 8897.46.5   Wiggam, A.E. The new decalogue of science. Garden City, 1925.

Phil 8897.46   Wiggam, A.E. The new decalogue of science. Indianapolis, 1923.

Phil 5262.42   Wiggam, Albert E. Exploring your mind with the psychologists. Indianapolis, 1928.

Phil 8897.55   Wiggin, F.A. Cubes and spheres in human life. Boston, 1899.

Phil 274.2   Wiggins, David. Identity and spatio-temporal continuity. Oxford, 1967.

Phil 510.148   Wightman, W.P.D. Science and monism. London, 1934.
Phil 1850.108   Wigston, William F. The Columbus of literature. Chicago, 1892.

Phil 353.5   Wijck, B.H.C.K. van der. De oorsprong en de grenzen der kennis. 2e Druk. Groningen, 1863.

Phil 3842.10   Wijck, J. van. Spinoza. Groningen, 1877.
Phil 2050.179   Wijnaendts Francken, C.J. David Hume. Haarlem, 1907.
Phil 8897.53   Wijnaendts Francken, C.J. Ethische stundien. Haarlem, 1903.

Phil 2422.2   Wijnaendts Francken, C.J. Fransche moralisten. Haarlem, 1904.

Phil 8897.72   Wijnaendts Francken, C.J. Vier moralisten. Amsterdam, 1946.

Phil 5772.11   Wijnaendts Francken, C.J. Het vraagstuk vanden vrijen wil. Haarlem, 1912.

Phil 5627.113   Wijnaendts Francken, C.J. Wereldbeschouwing en Godsdienstig bewustzyn. Haarlem, 1923.

Phil 7082.59   Wijnaendtsfrancken, Cornelis Johannes. Die psychologie van het droomen. Haarlem, 1907.

Phil 9400.35   Wijngaarden, H.M. Hoofdproblemen der volwassenheid. Utrecht, 1957.

Phil 197.7   Wijnperse, D. Institutiones metaphysicae. Lugdunum Batavorum, 1770.

Phil 5062.9   Wijnperse, D. van de. Institutiones logicae. Groningae, 1767.

Phil 189.15   De wijsbegeerte, den mensch met zich zelvon verzoenende. (Opzoomer, C.W.) Leiden, 1846.

Phil 140.55   Pamphlet vol. Wijsbegeerte. 4 pam.
Phil 3960.16   De wijsbegeerte der middeleeuvren in de Nederlanden. (Sassen, Ferdinand.) Lochen, 1944.

Phil 3745.16   Wijsbegeerte en anthropologie. (Popma, Klaas.) Amsterdam, 1963.

Phil 3960.12   De wijsbegeerte in de Nederlanden. (Land, Jan P.N.) 's Gravenhage, 1899.

Phil 1020.17   De wijsbegeerte in den Islam. (Boer, Tjitze de.) Haarlem, 1921.

Phil 1750.585   Wijsbegeerte in verval. (Piccardt, Karel.) Amsterdam, 1959.

Phil 585.66   Wijsbegeerte van de ontmoeting. (Kwant, Remy C.) Utrecht, 1959.

Phil 8581.55   Wijsbegeerte van den godsdienst bewerkt naar dictaten. (Bolland, G.J.P.J.) Amsterdam, 1923.

Phil 1740.8   De wijsbegeerts va di 20. eeuw. (Delfgaauw, Bernardus M.I.) Baarn, 1957.

Phil 9430.23   Het wijsgeerig pessimisme van den jongstentijd. (Scheffer, Wessel.) Leiden, 1875.

Phil 3005.10   Wijsgeren in Nederland. (Faber, W.) Nijkerk, 1954.
Phil 1523.20   Wijsgerig denken in de middeleeuwen. (Sassen, Ferdinand.) Haarlem, 1965.

Phil 3160.9.90   Het wijsgerig en psychological denken van Carl Gustav Carus in het licht van zijn Godsbeschouwing. (Bakker, Reinout.) Assen, 1954.

Phil 3960.16.13   Wijsgerig leven in Nederland in de twintigste eeuw. 3. druk. (Sassen, Ferdinand.) Amsterdam, 1960.

Phil 3007.14   Het wijsgerig onderwijs aan het gymnasium illustre. (Haan, A.A.M. de.) Harderwijk, 1960.

Phil 32.7   Wijsgerig perspectief op maatschappij en wetenschap. Amsterdam. 2,1961+   8v.

Phil 8673.26   Wijsgerige teksten over het absolute. (Schoonbrood, C.A.) Arnhem, 1967.

Phil 3960.20   Wijsgerin in Nederland. (Faber, W.) Nijkork, 1954.
Phil 5272.7   Wike, Edward L. Data analysis. Chicago, 1971.
Phil 4515.98   Wikner, P. Om den svenske tänkaren Boström. Göteborg, 1888.

Phil 4655.1.25   Wikner, Pontus. Anteckningar till filosofiens historia efter P. Wikners kollegium af K.S. Upsala, 18- .

Phil 822.7   Wikner, Pontus. Filosofiens historia efter Pontus Wikner's kollegium. Rock Island, Ill., 1896.

Phil 4655.1.48   Wikner, Pontus. "Gud är kärleken." 2. uppl. Stockholm, 1895.

Phil 4655.1.53   Wikner, Pontus. Hvad vi behöfva. Upsala, 1865.
Phil 4655.1.72   Wikner, Pontus. I mensklighetens lifsfrågor. Stockholm, 1889.   2v.

Phil 4655.1.52   Wikner, Pontus. Kan philosophien bringa någon välsignelse ät mensklighten? 2. uppl. Upsala, 1864.

Phil 4655.1.35   Wikner, Pontus. Kultur och filosofi i deras förhällande till hvarandra. Stockholm, 1869.

Phil 4655.1.45   Wikner, Pontus. Lärobok i anthropologien. Upsala, 1870.
Phil 4655.1.50   Wikner, Pontus. Några drag af kulturens offerväsen. Upsala, 1880.

Phil 4655.1.55   Wikner, Pontus. Narkissos-sagan och platonismen. Upsala, 1880.

Phil 4655.1.67   Wikner, Pontus. Naturens förbannelse. Upsala, 1866.
Phil 4655.1.40   Wikner, Pontus. Öppet sändebref till teologisk tidskrift. Upsala, 1881.

Phil 4655.1.38   Wikner, Pontus. Om auktoritet och sjelfständighet. Upsala, 1872.

Phil 4655.1.30   Wikner, Pontus. Om egenskapen och närgränsande tankeföremäl. Upsala, 1880.

Phil 4655.1.62   Wikner, Pontus. Promotionspredikan. Upsala, 1872.
Phil 4655.1.2   Wikner, Pontus. Skrifter. Stockholm, 1920-27.   12v.
Phil 4655.1.58   Wikner, Pontus. Tankar och frågor inför mennishones son. 4. uppl. Stockholm, 1893.

Phil 4655.1.64   Wikner, Pontus. Undersökningar angående den materialistiska verldsåskådningen. Stockholm, 1870.

Phil 4655.1.43   Wikner, Pontus. Undersökningar om enhet och mängfald. Upsala, 1863.

Phil 4655.1.70   Wikner, Pontus. Uppsatser i religiösa ämnen. Stockholm, 1871.

Phil 4655.1.18   Wikner, Pontus. Vittra skrifter. 3. uppl. Stockholm, 1894.

Phil 2050.278   Wilbanks, Jan. Hume's theory of imagination. The Hague, 1968.

Phil 8897.36   Wilbois, J. Devoir et durée. Paris, 1912.
Phil 5643.42   Wilbrand, H. Die Seelenblindheit als Herderscheinung. Wiesbaden, 1887.

Phil 5238.22   Wilbur, G.B. Psychoanalysis and culture. N.Y., 1951.
Phil 5170.7   Wilcox, Stanley. The destructive hypothetical syllogism in Greek logic and in Attic oratory. n.p., 1938.

Phil 3801.878   Wild, Christoph. Reflexion und Erfahrung. Freiburg, 1968.
Phil 1750.400A   Wild, John. The challenge of existentialism. Bloomington, 1955.

Phil 1750.738   Wild, John. Existence and the world of freedom. Englewood, 1963.

Phil 1870.117A   Wild, John. George Berkeley. Cambridge, 1936.
Phil 8602.60   Wild, John. Human freedom and social order. Darban, N.C., 1959.

Phil 630.49   Wild, John. Introduction to realistic philosophy. N.Y., 1948.

Phil 2070.158   Wild, John. The radical empiricism of William James. 1st ed. Garden City, N.Y., 1969.

Phil 630.49.10   Wild, John. The return to reason. Chicago, 1955.
Phil 5262.39A   Wild, K.W. Intuition. Cambridge, Eng., 1938.
Phil 6316.8.30   The wild analyst. (Grossman, Carl M.) N.Y., 1965.
Phil 5374.232   Wildangel, G. Beiträge zur Grundlegung der Elementaranalytik des Bewusstseins. Köln, 1962.

Phil 193.30.80   Wildbalz, A. Der philosophische Dialog als literarisches Kunstwerk. Bern, 1952.

Phil 575.205   Wilde, Arie de. De persoon. Assen, 1951.
Phil 4065.97   Wilde, Georg. Giordano Bruno's Philosophie in den Hauptbegriffen Materie und Form. Breslau, 1901.

Phil 5535.16   Wilde, Henricus Andreas Maria. Coalitie formatie in triades. Rotterdam, 1968.

Phil 1750.720   Wilde, Jean T. The search for being. N.Y., 1962.
Phil 6132.27   Wilder, Alexander. Mind, thought and cerebration. n.p., 188-?

Phil 497.5   Wilder, S.H. Unscientific materialism. N.Y., 1881.
Phil 3552.410   Wildermuth, A. Wahrheit und Schöpfung. Winterthur, 1960.
Phil 5672.13   Wildermuth, H. Seele und Seelenkrankheit. Berlin, 1926.
Phil 4655.2.30   Wildhagen, A. Vor tids determinisme. Kristiania, 1887.
Phil 2905.1.130.5   Wildiers, N.M. An introduction to Teilhard de Chardin. 1st American ed. N.Y., 1968.

Phil 2905.1.130   Wildiers, N.M. Teilhard de Chardin. Paris, 1961.
Phil 2905.1.105   Wildiers, N.M. Het wereldbeeld van Pierre Teilhard de Chardin. 2. druk. Antwerpen, 1960.

Phil 9415.12   Wilds, Louis T. Why good people suffer. Richmond, Va., 1944.

Phil 6132.31   Wile, Ira S. Handedness, right and left. Boston, 1934.
Phil 8602.45   Wiley, H.O. Christian theology. Kansas City, 1940-41. 2v.

Phil 3640.694   Wilhelm, J. Friedrich Nietzsche und der französische Geist. Hamburg, 1939.

Phil 930.35   Wilhelm, R. Chinesische Philosophie. Breslau, 1929.
Phil 8125.34   Wilhelm, Richard. Friedrich Justus Riedel. Heidelberg, 1933.

Phil 3195.6.155   Wilhelm Dilthey. (Diwald, Hellmut.) Göttingen, 1963.
Phil 3195.6.94   Wilhelm Dilthey. (Hodges, Herbert A.) London, 1944.
Phil 3195.6.83A   Wilhelm Dilthey. (Spranger, Eduard.) Berlin, 1912.
Phil 3195.6.97   Wilhelm Dilthey und das Problem der dichterischen Phantasie. Inaug. Diss. (Nicolai, Heinz.) München, 1934.

Phil 3195.6.99   Wilhelm Diltheys Methode der Lebensphilosophie. (Katsube, Kenzo.) Hiroschima, 1931.

Phil 3195.6.205   Wilhelm Dilthey's philosophy of historical understanding. (Tuttle, Howard Nelson.) Leiden, 1969.

Phil 3450.4.85   Wilhelm Herrmann im kampf Gegen die positivistische Lebensanschauung. (Redeker, Martin.) Gotha, 1928.

Phil 3475.2.90   Wilhelm Jerusalem; sein Leben und Werken. (Eckstein, W.) Wien, 1935.

Phil 3120.68.79   Wilhelm Raimund Beyer, eine Bibliographie. (Buhr, Manfred.) Wien, 1967.

Phil 6327.21.26   Wilhelm Reich, biographical material. v.1. (Reich, Wilhelm.) Rangeley, Me., 1953-

Phil 6327.21.25   Wilhelm Reich, biographical material. v.2. (Reich, Wilhelm.) Rangeley, Me., 1953-

Phil 6327.21.85   Wilhelm Reich. (Reich, Ilse Ollendorff.) N.Y., 1969.
Phil 6327.21.100   Wilhelm Reich. (Rycroft, Charles.) N.Y., 1972.
Phil 2190.10   Wilhelm von Ockham. (Martin, G.) Berlin, 1949.
Phil 3925.6.90   Wilhelm Windelband. (Rickert, H.) Tübingen, 1915.
Phil 3925.6.92   Wilhelm Windelband. (Ruge, Arnold.) Leipzig, 1917.
Phil 3915.85   Wilhelm Wundt. (König, Edmund.) Stuttgart, 1901.
Phil 3915.85.5   Wilhelm Wundt als Psycholog und als Philosoph. (König, Edmund.) Stuttgart, 1902.

Phil 3915.161   Wilhelm Wundt und seine Zeit. (Petersen, Peter.) Stuttgart, 1925.

Phil 8419.39   Wili, Hans. Johann G. Sulzer; Personlichkeit und Kunstphilosophie. St. Gallen, 1945.

Phil 735.85   Wilken, F. Grundzüge einer personalistischen Werttheorie. Jena, 1924.

Phil 8897.52   Wilkens, C. Etisk vurdering. København, 1916.
Phil 8897.52.5   Wilkens, C. Livets grundvardier. København, 1909.
Phil 8423.13   Wilkens, Claudius. Aesthetik i ómrids. Kjøbenhavn, 1888.
Phil 353.11   Wilkens, Claudius. Erkjendelsens problem. København, 1875.

Phil 978.12   The Wilkesbarre letters on theosophy. (Fullerton, Alex.) N.Y., n.d.

Phil 9070.28   Wilkins, Ernest Hatch. Living in crisis. Boston, 1937.
Phil 7069.23.21   Wilkins, H.J. A further criticism of the psychical claims concerning Glastonbury Abbey. Bristol, 1923.

Htn   Phil 8602.7*   Wilkins, J. Of the principles and duties of natural religion. London, 1698-99.

Htn   Phil 8602.7.2*   Wilkins, J. Of the principles and duties of natural religion. London, 1710.

Phil 5650.15   Wilkinson, G. The mechanism of the cochlea. London, 1924.
Phil 8887.4.18   Wilkinson, J.J. James Martineaus Ethik...Kritik. Inaug. Diss. Leipzig, 1898.

Phil 8088.4   Will, F. Intelligible beauty in aesthetic though. Tübingen, 1958.

Phil 2496.88   Will, Frederic. Flumen historicum: Victor Cousin's aesthetic and its sources. Chapel Hill, 1965.

Phil 3504.34   Will, G.A. Vorlesungen über die Kantische Philosophie. Altdorf, 1788.

Phil 8740.3   Will, Robert. Le culte. Thèse. Strasbourg, 1925.
Phil 5768.16   The will and its world. (Snider, Denton J.) St. Louis, 1899.

Phil 5768.11   The will divine and human. (Solly, Thomas.) Cambridge, 1856.

Phil 7069.14.20   Will higher of God and free will of life. (Comstock, William C.) Boston, 1914.

Phil 5751.19   Will in Western thought. (Bourke, Vernon.) N.Y., 1964.

Phil 5765.2.20   Will-power and work. 2. ed. (Payot, Jules.) N.Y., 1921.

Phil 6327.4.32   Will therapy and truth and reality. (Rank, Otto.) N.Y., 1936.

Phil 6327.4.30   Will therapy and truth and reality. (Rank, Otto.) N.Y., 1945.

Phil 6327.4.33   Will therapy and truth and reality. (Rank, Otto.) N.Y., 1950.

Phil 5760.8   The will to be free. (Knox, Howard V.) London, 1928.

Phil 6125.17.5   The will to be well. 5th ed. (Patterson, C.B.) N.Y., 1906.

Phil 185.23   The will to beauty. (Kanovitch, A.) N.Y., 1922.

Phil 185.23.2   The will to beauty. (Kanovitch, A.) N.Y., 1923.

Phil 184.3.6   The will to believe. (James, W.) London, 1937.

Phil 184.3   The will to believe and other essays. (James, W.) N.Y., 1897.

Phil 184.3.3.10   The will to believe and other essays in popular philosophy. (James, W.) London, 1905.

Phil 184.3.3.15   The will to believe and other essays in popular philosophy. (James, W.) London, 1912.

Phil 184.3.3.5A   The will to believe and other essays in popular philosophy. (James, W.) N.Y., 1898.

Phil 184.3.3.7   The will to believe and other essays in popular philosophy. (James, W.) N.Y., 1899.

Phil 184.3.3   The will to believe and other essays in popular philosophy. (James, W.) N.Y., 1899.

Phil 184.3.5   The will to believe and other essays in popular philosophy. (James, W.) N.Y., 1927.

Phil 184.3.4.5   The will to believe and other essays in popular philosophy. 1st ed. (James, W.) N.Y., 1923.

NEDL Phil 2070.91.5   The will to believe as a basis for defense of religious faith. (Stettheimer, E.) N.Y., 1907.

Phil 645.8   The will to doubt. (Lloyd, A.H.) London, 1907.

Phil 2255.1.72   The will to doubt. (Russell, Bertrand Russell.) N.Y., 1958.

Phil 3640.115   The will to freedom. (Figgis, J.N.) N.Y., 1917.

Phil 187.88   The will to function. (Meek, Charles.) Bisley, 1929.

Phil 6117.48   The will to line. (Hutschnecker, A.A.) London, 1952.

Phil 5241.82   The will to live. (Badley, John H.) London, 1931.

Phil 3640.51.10   The will to power. (Nietzsche, Friedrich.) N.Y., 1967.

Phil 3640.51.11   The will to power. (Nietzsche, Friedrich.) N.Y., 1968.

Phil 9035.81   The will to win. (Boston.) Boston, 1938.

Phil 353.25   Willam, Franz. Aristotelische Erkenntnislehre bei Whately und Newman. Freiburg, 1960.

Phil 9495.10   Willard, E.O.G. (Mrs.). Sexology as philosophy of life. Chicago, 1867.

Phil 2422.6   Willard, Nedd. Le génie et la folie au dix-huitième siècle. Paris, 1963.

Phil 3552.103   Willareth, O. Die Lehre vom Uebel. Strassburg, 1898.

Phil 8620.19   Willcox, I.L. The psychological aspect of...sin and salvation. Oxford, 1910.

Phil 5062.34   Willcox, J.M. Elementary philosophy. Philadelphia, 1875.

Phil 2045.82   Wille, B. Der Phänomenalismus des T. Hobbes. Kiel, 1888.

Phil 303.9.3   Wille, Bruno. Das Lebendige all; idealistische Weltanschauung. Hamburg, 1905.

Phil 197.34.10   Wille, Bruno. Materie nie ohne Geist. Berlin, 1901.

Phil 197.34   Wille, Bruno. Philosophie der Befreiung. Berlin, 1894.

Phil 5769.5   Wille, Determinismus, Strafe. (Traeger, L.) Berlin, 1895.

Phil 5768.20   Der Wille, die Lebensgrundmacht. (Schellwien, R.) Berlin, 1879.

Phil 5761.10   Der Wille, seine Erscheinung und seine Beherrschung. (Lindworsky, J.) Leipzig, 1919.

Phil 5761.10.2   Der Wille, seine Erscheinung und seine Beherrschung. 2. Aufl. (Lindworsky, J.) Leipzig, 1921.

Phil 5759.3   Der Wille. (Joss, Hermann.) Bern, 1921.

Phil 5768.20.15   Wille und Erkenntnis. (Schellwien, R.) Hamburg, 1899.

Phil 5772.9   Wille und Freiheit. (Wichmann, O.) München, 1922.

Phil 5755.10   Wille und Vernunft. (Fröschels, E.) Leipzig, 1925.

Phil 5755.8   Der Wille zu höheren Einheit. (Froehlich, Joseph Anselm.) Heidelberg, 1905.

Phil 5751.14   Der Wille zum Geist. (Benda, Clemens E.) Berlin, 1932.

Phil 184.3.7.25   Der Wille zum Glauben. (James, W.) Stuttgart, 1899.

Phil 3415.95   Wille zum Leben oder Wille zum Guten? (Weber, Alfred.) Strassburg, 1882.

Phil 7080.51   Der Wille zum Schlaf! (Stekel, W.) Wiesbaden, 1915.

Phil 187.62   Der Wille zur Ewigkeit. (Mahnke, J.) Halle, 1917.

Phil 3640.51   Der Wille zur Macht. (Nietzsche, Friedrich.) Stuttgart, 1952.

Phil 3640.17.9   Der Wille zur Macht. (Nietzsche, Friedrich.) Stuttgart, 1959.

Phil 400.21.5   Willems, C. Die Erkenntnislehre des modernen Idealismus. Trier, 1906.

Phil 3504.25.5   Willems, C. Kant's Erkenntnislehre. Trier, 1919.

Phil 3504.25   Willems, C. Kant's Sittenlehre. Trier, 1919.

Phil 3837.17   Der Willensbegriff in der Lehre Spinoza's. (Richter, Raoul.) Leipzig, 1898.

Phil 5780.7   Die Willensbestimmungen und ihr Verhältniss zu den Impulsiven. (Spitta, H.) Tübingen, 1881.

Phil 5765.7   Willensfreiheit, moral und strafrecht. (Peterson, Julius.) München, 1905.

Phil 5750.001   Die Willensfreiheit; zur Bibliographie. (Fellin, J.) Graz, 1928.

Phil 5764.3   Willensfreiheit, Zurechnung, und Verantwortung. (Offner, Max.) Leipzig, 1904.

Phil 193.55.9   Die Willensfreiheit...bei den jüdischen philosophen des Mittelalters. (Stein, Ludwig.) n.p., 1902-1908. 9 pam.

Phil 5751.5   Die Willensfreiheit. (Bolliger, Adolf.) Berlin, 1903.

Phil 5756.5   Die Willensfreiheit. (Günther, Carl.) Berlin, 1909.

Phil 5765.5   Die Willensfreiheit. (Pfister, Oskar.) Berlin, 1904.

Phil 5762.12.5   Die Willensfreiheit des Menschen. (Mach, F.J.) Paderborn, 1894.

Phil 5760.6   Die Willensfreiheit und die innere Verantwortlichkeit. (Kneib, Philipp.) Mainz, 1898.

Phil 3832.8   Willensfreiheit und Erziehungsmöglichkeit Spinoza. Diss. (Mänoloff, P.) Bern, 1904.

Phil 5756.6.2   Die Willensfreiheit und ihre Gegner. 2. Aufl. (Gutberlet, C.) Fulda, 1907.

Phil 5755.12   Willensfreiheit und Verantwortlichkeit. (Fernkorn, C.M.) Greifswald, 1927.

Phil 5762.3   Die Willenshandlung. (Münsterberg, H.) Freiburg, 1888.

Phil 190.10   Willenswelt und Weltwille. (Peters, C.) Leipzig, 1883.

Phil 5767.3   Die Willensfreiheit. (Rehmke, Johanes.) Leipzig, 1911.

Phil 5760.3   Die Willensprobleme. (Kurt, H.) Weimar, 1902.

Phil 8865.342.5   Willey, Basil. The English moralists. London, 1964.

Phil 8897.92   William, Bernard Arthur Owen. Morality and the emotions: an inaugural lecture. London, 1966.

Phil 6972.14.50   William Alanson White, the autobiography of a purpose. (White, William Alanson.) Garden City, 1938.

Phil 5032.5   William Heytesbury. (Wilson, Curtis.) Madison, 1956.

Phil 8661.8.80   William Honyman Gillespie. (Urquhart, James.) Edinburgh, 1920.

Phil 2070.155A   William James; a biography. (Allen, Gay Wilson.) N.Y., 1967.

Phil 2070.139   William James, the man and the thinker. (Wisconsin. University.) Madison, 1942.

Phil 2070.141   William James; the message of a modern mind. (Morris, Lloyd R.) N.Y., 1950.

Phil 2070.141.5   William James; the message of a modern mind. (Morris, Lloyd R.) N.Y., 1969.

Phil 2070.155.1   William James. (Allen, Gay Wilson.) Minneapolis, 1970.

Phil 2070.111.5   William James. (Boutroux, E.) Leipzig, 1912.

Phil 2070.111A   William James. (Boutroux, E.) Paris, 1911.

Phil 2070.150.5A   William James. (Brennan, Bernard P.) N.Y., 1968.

Phil 2070.142   William James. (Compton, C.H.) N.Y., 1957.

Phil 2070.54   William James. (James, William.) Harmondsworth, 1950.

Phil 2070.152   William James. (Moore, Edward Carter.) N.Y., 1966.

Phil 2070.129   William James. (Perry, R.B.) Boston? 1910.

Phil 2070.140   William James. (Piane, A.L. delle.) Montevideo, 1943.

Phil 2070.137   William James. (Raback, A.A.) Cambridge, 1942.

Phil 2070.76   William James: extraits de sa correspondance. (James, William.) Paris, 1924.

Phil 2070.128   William James. Thèse. (Blau, Théodore.) Paris, 1933.

Phil 2070.159   William James: unfinished business. Washington, 1969.

Phil 2070.147   William James. 2d ed. (Boutroux, Emile.) N.Y., 1912.

Phil 5627.6.20A   William James als Religionsphilosoph. (Busch, K.A.) Göttingen, 1911.

Phil 2070.82.8   William James and American ideals. (Brett, George Sidney.) Toronto? 1937.

Phil 2070.81A   William James and Henri Bergson. (Kallen, H.M.) Chicago, 1914.

Phil 192.16.18A   William James and other essays on the philosophy of life. (Royce, Josiah.) N.Y., 1911.

Phil 5249.2.81.5   William James and phenomenology. (Wilshire, Bruce.) Bloomington, 1968.

Phil 2070.132   William James Bergsonien. (Delattre, F.) Paris, 192-.

Phil 2070.131   William James et le pragmatisme religieux. (Maire, Gilbert.) Paris, 1933.

Phil 2070.93   William James' filosofi. (Kortsen, K.K.) København, n.d.

Phil 2070.87   William James' laere om retten til at tro. (Teisen, N.) København, 1911.

Phil 2070.120   William James nach seinen Briefen. (Stumpf, Carl.) Berlin, 1927.

Phil 2070.120.2A   William James nach seinen Briefen. (Stumpf, Carl.) Berlin, 1928.

Phil 2070.92.5   William James og det religiøse. (Hansen, V.) København, 1936.

Phil 2070.92   William James og hans breve. (Hansen, V.) Stockholm, 1922.

Phil 2070.20   William James on psychical research. (James, William.) N.Y., 1960.

Phil 2070.76.11   A William James reader. (James, William.) Boston, 1972.

Phil 7055.251   William King's profession. (Drage, Charles.) London, 1960.

Phil 5252.18.65   William McDougall, M.B., D.S.C., F.R.S.: a bibliography. (Robinson, A.L.) Durham, 1943.

Phil 7069.67.65   William McDougall: explorer of the mind. (McDougall, William.) N.Y., 1967.

Phil 5058.96   William of Sherwood's introduction to logic. (Shirwood, William.) Minneapolis, 1966.

Phil 5058.96.5   William of Sherwood's treatise on syncategorematic words. (Shirwood, William.) Minneapolis, 1968.

Phil 1822.8   Williams, Bernard. British analytical philosophy. London, 1966.

Phil 5640.10   Williams, C.H. Vision: color, sense and hearing. Chicago, 1902.

Phil 197.25.5   Williams, C.L. As if; a philosophical phantasy. San Francisco, 1914.

Phil 197.25   Williams, C.L. Creative involution. N.Y., 1916.

Phil 197.25.7   Williams, C.L. The passing of evolution. Berkeley, 1912.

Phil 9150.29   Williams, C.M. A review of the systems of ethics founded on the theory of evolution. N.Y., 1893.

Phil 8677.19   Williams, Charles. He came down from heaven. London, 1938.

Phil 5125.19.5A   Williams, Donald C. The ground of induction. N.Y., 1963.

Phil 325.12   Williams, Donald Cary. Principles of empirical realism. Springfield, Ill., 1966.

Phil 5401.8   Williams, E.H. Our fear complexes. London, 1924.

Phil 6332.3   Williams, Edward H. Increasing your mental efficiency. N.Y., 1929.

Phil 6132.26   Williams, Frankwood Earl. Some social aspects of mental hygiene. Philadelphia, 1930.

Phil 8897.78   Williams, G. Humanistic ethics. N.Y., 1951.

Phil 974.2.55A   Williams, G.M. Priestess of the occult, Madame Blavatsky. N.Y., 1946.

Phil 7069.20.340   Williams, Gail. Fear not the crossing. N.Y., 1920.

Phil 585.360   Williams, Gershom Antonio. The measure of a man. 1st ed. Toronto, 1970.

Phil 974.4.15   Williams, Gertrude M. The passionate pilgrim. London, 1932.

Phil 974.4.13   Williams, Gertrude M. The passionate pilgrim. N.Y., 1931.

Phil 5062.29   Williams, Henry H. The evaluation of logic. Chapel Hill, 1925.

Phil 5062.29.5   Williams, Henry H. Logic for living. N.Y., 1951.

Phil 5722.78   Williams, John K. The knack of using your subconscious mind. Scarsdale, N.Y., 1952.

Phil 1750.759   Williams, John Rodman. Contemporary existentialism and Christian faith. Englewood Cliffs, N.J., 1965.

Phil 5942.2   Williams, N.M. A vindication of phrenology. London, 1894.

Phil 9400.41   Williams, R.H. Processes of aging. N.Y., 1963. 2v.

Phil 5886.10   Williams, Richard Hays. Lives through the years. 1st ed. N.Y., 1965.

Phil 6132.37   Williams, Roger J. The human frontier. N.Y., 1946.

Phil 5590.488   Williams, Roger J. You are extraordinary. N.Y., 1967.

Phil 5062.19   Williams, S. Principles of logic. London, n.d.

Phil 6332.6   Williams, T.A. Dreads and besetting fears. Boston, 1923.

Phil 3504.55   Williams, T.C. The concept of the categorical imperative. Oxford, 1968.

Htn Phil 2225.3.80*   Williams, Thomas. The age of infidelity...answer to the second part of The age of reason. Philadelphia, 1796.

Phil 3640.396   Williams, W.D. Nietzsche and the French. Oxford, 1952.

Phil 5627.124.20   Williamson, G. Inside Buchmanism. London, 1954.

Phil 9495.155.10   Williamson, Geoffrey. Morality fair. London, 1955.

Phil 5262.57.5 Williamson, George Scott. Science, synthesis and sanity. Chicago, 1966.

Phil 5262.57 Williamson, George Scott. Science, synthesis and sanity. London, 1965.

Phil 7054.58 Williamson, M.J. Modern diabolism; commonly called modern spiritualism. N.Y., 1873.

Phil 3504.5 Willich, A.F.M. Elements of the critical philosophy...Kant. London, 1798.

Phil 3805.161 Willich, E. von. Aus Schleiermacher's Hause: Jugender'en seiner Stiefsohnes. Berlin, 1909.

Phil 8647.8 Willink, Arthur. The world of the unseen. N.Y., 1893.

Phil 8677.14 Willink, M.D.R. The holy and the living God. London, 1931.

Phil 978.52 Willis, F.M. Theosophy in outline. Girard, 1923.

Phil 3842.2 Willis, R. Benedict de Spinoza. London, 1870.

Htn Phil 5262.16* Willis, T. De anima Brutorum. Oxonii, 1672.

Phil 8712.26 Williston, A.L. Beyond the horizon of science. Boston, 1944.

Phil 3022.2 Willm, J. Histoire de la philosophie allemande. Paris, 1846-49. 4v.

Phil 6132.8 Willman, R. Errors of mind healing. St. Joseph, 1909.

Phil 197.18.10 Willmann, O. Aus der Werkstatt der philosophia perennis. Freiburg, 1912.

Phil 400.11 Willmann, O. Geschichte des Idealismus. Braunschweig, 1894-1897. 3v.

Phil 197.18.5 Willmann, O. Philosophische Propädeutik. Freiburg, 1912-1914. 3v.

Phil 197.18 Willmann, O. Die Wichtigsten philosophischen Fachausdrücke in historischer Anordnung. Kempten, 1909.

Phil 2045.150 Willms, Bernard. Die Antwort des Leviathan; Thomas Hobbes' politische Theorie. Neuwied, 1970.

Phil 3246.345 Willms, Bernhard. Die totale Freiheit. Köln, 1967.

Phil 1504.4 Willner, H. Des Adelard von Bath Traktat. v.4, pt.1. Münster, 1903.

Phil 3903.3.109 Willrodt, S. Semifiktionen und Vollfiktionen in der Philosophie des Als Ob von H. Vaihinger. Inaug. Diss. Gräfenhainichen, 1933.

Phil 7060.113 Willson, Beckles. Occultism and common sense. London, 1908.

Phil 7069.09.30 Willson, Beckles. Occultism and common-sense. N.Y., 1908?

Phil 9495.5 Willson, R.N. Social evil in university life. N.Y., 1904.

Phil 5360.5 Willwoll, A. Begriffsbildung: eine psychologische Untersuchung. Leipzig, 1926.

Phil 5262.60 Willwoll, Alexander. Psychologia metaphysica, in Usum scholarum. Friburgi, 1952.

Phil 3640.82.15 Willy, Rudolf. Friedrich Nietzsche. Zürich, 1904.

Phil 197.28 Willy, Rudolf. Die Gesamterfahrung vom Gesichtspunkt des Primörmonismus. Zürich, 1908.

Phil 2475.1.225 Wilm, E.C. Henri Bergson. N.Y., 1914.

Phil 3504.23A Wilm, E.C. Immanuel Kant. New Haven, 1925.

Phil 8602.17 Wilm, Emil Carl. Problem of religion. Boston, 1912.

Phil 3504.39 Wilmans, C.A. Dissertatio philosophica de similitudine. Halis Saxonum, 1797.

Phil 6132.16 Wilmans, Helen. Back numbers Wilmans express, condensed. n.p., 18- ?

VPhil 978.116 Wilmar, F.H.J. Kinderkrankheinten im Lichte der Anthroposphie. Zeist, 1966.

Phil 7068.94.25 Wilmot, T.S. Twenty photographs of the risen dead. Lonon, 1894.

Phil 5850.387.5 Wilner, D.M. Human relations in interracial housing. Minneapolis, 1955.

Phil 5249.2.81.5 Wilshire, Bruce. William James and phenomenology. Bloomington, 1968.

Phil 6132.10 Wilson, A. Brain and body: the nervous system. 2d ed. London, 1900.

Phil 497.6 Wilson, A.S. The unity of matter. London, 1855.

Phil 9362.14 Wilson, Calvin D. Making the most of ourselves. Chicago, 1909.

Phil 1750.775 Wilson, Colin. Introduction to the new existentialism. London, 1966.

Phil 8602.52 Wilson, Colin. Religion and the rebel. London, 1957.

Phil 5032.5 Wilson, Curtis. William Heytesbury. Madison, 1956.

Phil 6132.3 Wilson, D. The right hand. Left handedness. London, 1891.

Phil 8602.26 Wilson, D.A. The faith of all sensible people. London, 1913.

Phil 7068.76.10 Wilson, Ebenezer V. The truths of spiritualism. Chicago, 1876.

Phil 7068.96.20 Wilson, Ebenezer V. The truths of spiritualism. Chicago, 1896.

Phil 197.42.3 Wilson, F.B. Man limitless. 3d. ed. N.Y., 1905.

Phil 9070.5 Wilson, F.T. These three alone. N.Y., 1940.

Phil 6132.28 Wilson, Floyd B. Paths to power. N.Y., 1901.

Phil 5640.4 Wilson, G. Five gateways of knowledge. Philadelphia, 1857.

Phil 5640.4.7 Wilson, G. The five gateways of knowledge. 7th ed. London, 1881.

Phil 8602.8 Wilson, G. Religio chemici. London, 1862.

Phil 197.44.5 Wilson, George A. Reckoning with life. New Haven, 1942.

Phil 197.44 Wilson, George A. The self and its world. N.Y., 1926.

Phil 6132.19 Wilson, H.B. Does Christ still heal? N.Y., 1917.

Phil 8602.65 Wilson, J. Philosophy and religion. London, 1961.

Phil 5360.17 Wilson, J. Thinking with concepts. Cambridge, 1963.

Phil 365.28 Wilson, J.C. On an evolutionist theory of axioms. Oxford, 1912.

Phil 8612.6 Wilson, J.K. Death; the meaning and result. N.Y., 1901.

Phil 5520.160 Wilson, John. Language and the pursuit of truth. Cambridge, Eng., 1956.

Phil 8897.80 Wilson, John. Reason and morals. Cambridge, Eng., 1961.

Phil 197.27 Wilson, John. Thoughts on science, theology, and ethics. London, 1885.

Phil 5062.30.1 Wilson, John Cook. Statement and inference. Oxford, 1969. 2v.

Phil 9070.10 Wilson, M. Make up your mind. N.Y., 1940.

Phil 8897.59 Wilson, M.H. Vocational guidance. Boston, 1916.

Phil 9513.16 Wilson, Matthew Hale. An inductive study of standards of right. Boston, 1916.

Phil 5068.46 Wilson, Max. Über das Kriterium der Verifizierbarkeit. Berlin, 1959.

Phil 5520.290 Wilson, Neil. The concept of language. Toronto, Canada, 1959.

Phil 7054.74 Wilson, R.P. Discourses from the spirit-world. N.Y., 1855.

Phil 8712.25 Wilson, Robert M. The witness of science. 1. ed. London, 1942.

Phil 9495.5.6 Wilson, Robert N. The American boy and the social evil. Philadelphia, 1905.

Phil 7069.25.30 Wilson, T.S. Thought transference. London, 1925..

Htn Phil 2340.4.30* Wilson, Thomas. The use of reason. n.p., 1553.

Phil 9070.34.5 Wilson, W. On being human. N.Y., 1916.

Phil 5062.11 Wilson, W.D. Elementary treatise on logic. N.Y., 1856.

Phil 197.8.5 Wilson, W.D. Five questions in psychology and metaphysics. N.Y., 1877.

Phil 8602.9 Wilson, W.D. The foundations of religious belief. N.Y., 1883.

Phil 197.8 Wilson, W.D. Introduction to metaphysics. Ithaca, 1872.

Phil 5832.2 Wilson, W.D. Lectures...psychology: thought, action. Ithaca, 1871.

Phil 5062.11.5 Wilson, W.D. Logic. Ithaca, N.Y., 1872.

Phil 5520.28 Wilson, William D. The influence of language on thought. Albany, 1879.

Phil 8897.63.5 Wilson, Woodrow. When a man comes to himself. N.Y., 1915.

Phil 5832.10 Wiltbank, R.T. Transfer of training in white rats upon various series of mazes. Chicago, 1919.

Phil 7069.09.70 Wiltse, May B. Theorem or teleology of spiritualism. New-Rockford, N. Dak., 1909.

Phil 5832.16 Wimersama Greidanus, H.T. van. De hormische psychologie van den mensch. Leiden, 1946.

Phil 5590.532 Wimersma Greidanus, H.T. Instinct en karakter proeve eener characterologie op instinct-psychologischen grondalag. Proefschrift. Zeist, 1933.

Phil 3925.10 Wimmer, H.A. Neue Dialoge; zwischen Hylas und Philoneris. Heidelberg, 1938.

Phil 8602.28 Wimmer, Richard. Hrad är sanning? Stockholm, 1894.

Phil 8602.28.5 Wimmer, Richard. Im Kampf um die Weltanschauung. 3. und 4. Aufl. Freiburg, 1888.

Phil 3022.5 Wimmershoff, H. Die Lehre von Sündenfall in der Philosophie Schellings. Inaug. Diss. Selingen, 1934.

Phil 6132.20 Winbigler, C.F. Handbook of instructions for healing and helping others. Los Angeles, 1918.

Phil 8897.96 Winch, Peter. Moral integrity: inaugural lecture in the Chair of Philosophy delivered at King's College, London, 9 May 1968. Oxford, 1968.

Phil 3925.16.200 Winch, Peter. Studies in the philosophy of Wittgenstein. N.Y., 1969.

Phil 6332.28 Winch, R.F. Identification and its familial determinants. Indianapolis, 1962.

Phil 8712.24 Winchell, A. Reconciliation of science and religion. N.Y., 1877.

Htn Phil 8595.16.11* Winchester, E. A defence of revelation. N.Y., 1796.

Phil 6319.1.210 Winckel, Erna van de. De l'inconscient à Dieu. Paris, 1959.

Phil 8423.16.15 Winckelmann, Johann Joachim. Gedanken über die Nachamung der griechischen Werke in der Malerei und Bildhauerkunst. Stuttgart, 1969.

Phil 8423.16 Winckelmann, Johann Joachim. Johann Winckelmann, G. Ephraim Lessing klassische Schönheit. Jena, 1906.

Phil 8423.16.5 Winckelmann, Johann Joachim. Kleine Schriften, Vorreden, Entwürfe. Berlin, 1968.

Phil 8423.16.10 Winckelmann, Johann Joachim. Werke in einem Band. Berlin, 1969.

Phil 575.256 Winckelmans de Cléty, Charles. The world of persons. Thesis. London, 1967.

Phil 8423.24 Wind, Edgar. Art and anarchy, and other essays. London, 1963.

Phil 197.9.13A Windelband, W. Einleitung in der Philosophie. Tübingen, 1914.

Phil 197.9.14A Windelband, W. Einleitung in der Philosophie. 2. Aufl. Tübingen, 1920.

Phil 3425.110 Windelband, W. Die Erneuerung des Hegelianismus. Heidelberg, 1910.

Phil 1127.2.9 Windelband, W. Geschichte der alten Philosophie. Nördlingen, 1888.

Phil 1722.2A Windelband, W. Die Geschichte der neueren Philosophie. Leipzig, 1878-80. 2v.

Phil 822.2A Windelband, W. Geschichte der Philosophie. Freiburg, 1892.

Phil 1127.2 Windelband, W. History of ancient philosophy. N.Y., 1899.

Phil 1127.2.5 Windelband, W. History of ancient philosophy. N.Y., 1901.

Phil 1127.2.7 Windelband, W. History of ancient philosophy. N.Y., 1956.

Phil 822.2.11 Windelband, W. History of philosophy. 2. ed. N.Y., 1901.

Phil 197.9.7 Windelband, W. Die Hypothese des Unbewussten.

Phil 3504.18 Windelband, W. Immanuel Kant und seine Weltanschauung. Heidelberg, 1904.

Phil 197.9.15 Windelband, W. Introduction to philosophy. London, 1921.

Phil 3270.1.80 Windelband, W. Kuno Fischer Gedächtnisrede. Heidelberg, 1907.

Phil 822.2.4.5 Windelband, W. Lehrbuch der Geschichte der Philosophie. Genf, 1945?

Phil 822.2.4 Windelband, W. Lehrbuch der Geschichte der Philosophie. Tübingen, 1935.

Phil 822.2.4.7 Windelband, W. Lehrbuch der Geschichte der Philosophie. Tübingen, 1957.

Phil 822.2.3 Windelband, W. Lehrbuch der Geschichte der Philosophie. 3. Aufl. Tübingen, 1903.

Phil 270.53 Windelband, W. Die Lehren vom Zufall. Berlin, 1870.

Phil 1722.2.5 Windelband, W. Die Philosophie im Beginn des Zwanzigsten. Heidelberg, 1904.

Phil 1722.2.7 Windelband, W. Die Philosophie im Beginn des Zwanzigsten. Jahrhunderts. 2e Aufl. Heidelberg, 1907.

Phil 1722.2.8 Windelband, W. Die Philosophie im Beginn des zwanzigsten Jahrhunderts. Heidelberg, 1907.

Phil 197.9A Windelband, W. Präludien. Freiburg, 1884.

Phil 197.9.3A Windelband, W. Präludien. 3. ed. Tübingen, 1907.

Phil 197.9.4 Windelband, W. Präludier. Stockholm, 1915.

Phil 5062.20 Windelband, W. Die Prinzipien der Logik. Tübingen, 1913.

Phil 5062.20.10 Windelband, W. Theories in logic. N.Y., 1961.

Phil 5232.1 Windelband, W. Uber den...psychologische Forschung. Leipzig, 1876.

Phil 3925.6.06 Windelband, W. Ueber den Gegenwärtigen stand der Psychologie. n.p., 1876-1914. 12 pam.

Phil 353.8 Windelband, W. Ueber die Gewissheit der Erkenntniss. Berlin, 1873.

Phil 5772.5.2 Windelband, Wilhelm. Über Willensfreiheit. Tübingen, 1904.

Phil 5772.5 Windelband, Wilhelm. Über Willensfreiheit. 3. Aufl. Tübingen, 1918.

Phil 197.69 Winderlich, R. Das Ding. Karlsruhe, 1924.

Phil 9070.117 Windisch, Konrad. Revolution der Satten. Wolfsburg, 1967.

Phil 3120.8.130 Windischer, Johannes. Franz Brentano und die Scholastik. Innsbruck, 1936.

Phil 900.1 Windischmann, C.J.H. von. Die Philosophie im Fortgang. v.1-4. Bonn, 1827-34. 3v.

Phil 3022.3.15 Windlband, Wilhelm. Die Blüthezeit der deutschen Philosophie. Leipzig, 1880.

Phil 3022.3.2   Windlband, Wilhelm. Die Philosophie im deutschen Geistesleben des 19. Jahrhunderts. Tübingen, 1909.

Phil 3022.3   Windlband, Wilhelm. Die Philosophie im deutschen Geistesleben des 19. Jahrhunderts. 2e Aufl. Tübingen, 1909.

Phil 3022.3.3   Windlband, Wilhelm. Die Philosophie im deutschen Geistesleben des 19. Jahrhunderts. 3. Aufl. Tübingen, 1927.

Phil 7069.69   Window to the past. (Holzer, Hans W.) Garden City, 1969.
Phil 194.14   Windows of character. (Thwing, E.P.) N.Y., 1889.
Phil 193.49.5   Winds of doctrine. (Santayana, G.) London, 1913.
Phil 193.49.8   Winds of doctrine. (Santayana, G.) N.Y., 1957.
Phil 193.49.7   Winds of doctrine. Studies in contemporary opinion. (Santayana, G.) N.Y., 1926.

Phil 2280.7.85   Winetrout, Kenneth. F.C.S. Schiller and the dimensions of pragmatism. Columbus, 1967.

Phil 8893.83.20   Winke über das Verhältniss der intellektuellen und der verfeinernden Kultur zur Sittlichen. (Salat, Jakob.) München, 1802.

Phil 5832.25   Winkelstraeter, K.H. Das Betteln der Zoo-Tiere. Bern, 1960.

Phil 6400.24   Winkler, Carl. Abnormal speech. Orange, Conn., 1932.
Phil 5643.71   Winkler, F. Studien über Wahrnehmungstauschungen. Leipzig, 1915.

Phil 585.55   Winkler, Franz E. Man: the bridge. N.Y., 1960.
Phil 6132.21   Winkler, H. Die Monotonie der Arbeit. Leipzig, 1922.
Phil 6132.35   Winkler, J.K. Mind explorers. N.Y., 1939.
Phil 8847.14   Winkler, Paul. Les sources mystiques des concepts moraux de l'occident. Paris, 1957.

Phil 5520.103   Winkler, R. Kritik der Wissenschaft. Wien, 1950.
Phil 8602.36   Winkler, R. Phänomenologie und Religion. Tübingen, 1921.
Phil 1830.15   Winn, R.B. American philosophy. N.Y., 1955.
Phil 107.5   Winn, R.B. A concise dictionary of existentialism. N.Y., 1960.

Phil 70.80   Winn, R.B. Psychotherapy in the Soviet Union. N.Y., 1961.
Phil 6332.40   Winnicott, Donald Woods. The maturational processes and the facilitating environment. London, 1965.

Phil 8640.5   Winning of immortality. (Palmer, Fred.) London, 1910.
Phil 5850.250   The winning of wealth. (Kandhi, S.) Boston, 1932.
Phil 1830.25   Winny, James. The frame of order. London, 1957.
Phil 303.4   Winslow, C.F. Cosmography. Boston, 1853.
Phil 2138.102   Winslow, Christian. Stuart Mills etik. København, 1909.
Phil 6972.5   Winslow, E. On obscure diseases of the brain. London, 1860.

Phil 7150.5   Winslow, F. Anatomy of suicide. London, 1840.
Phil 6972.4   Winslow, F. The case of Luigi Buranelli. London, 1855.
Phil 6972.5.2   Winslow, F. On obscure diseases of the brain. Philadelphia, 1860.

Phil 6972.4.5   Winslow, F. The plea of insanity in criminal cases. Boston, 1843.

Phil 5262.6   Winslow, H. Elements of intellectual philosophy. Boston, 1850.

Phil 5262.6.3   Winslow, H. Elements of intellectual philosophy. Boston, 1856.

Phil 8897.19   Winslow, H. Elements of moral philosophy. N.Y., 1856.
Phil 5262.6.10   Winslow, H. Intellectual philosophy. 8th ed. Boston, 1863.

Phil 9362.6   Winslow, H. Young man's aid. Boston, 1837.
Phil 9362.6.2   Winslow, H. Young man's aid. Boston, 1839.
Phil 5627.134.45   Winslow, J.C. Why I believe in the Oxford Group. 3. ed. London, 1934.

Phil 8897.61   Winsor, F. The art of behaviour. Boston, 1932.
Phil 3120.2.98   Winter, E. Bernard Bolzano und sein Kreis. Leipzig, 1933.
Phil 3120.2.98.5   Winter, E. Der Bolzanoprozess. Brünn, 1944.
Phil 3120.8.100   Winter, E. Fanz Brentanos Ringen um eine neue Gottessicht. Brünn, 1941.

Phil 3120.2.96   Winter, E. Leben und Geistige. Halle, 1949.
Phil 3120.2.97   Winter, E. Religion und Offenbarung in der Religionsphilosophie Bernard Bolzanos. Breslau, 1932.

Phil 1540.17A   Winter, E.K. Die Sozialmetaphysik der Scholastik. Leipzig, 1929.

Phil 3890.2.85   Winter, Eduard. E.W. von Tschirnhaus. Berlin, 1960.
Phil 1730.18   Winter, Eduard. Frühaufklärung; der Kampf Gegen den Konfessionalismus in Mittel- und Osteuropa und die deutsch-slawische Begegnung. Berlin, 1966.

Phil 8847.4   Winter, F.J. Der Individualismus. Leipzig, 1880.
Phil 2115.119   Winter, Hermann. Darlegung und Kritik der Lokeschen Lehre vom empirischen Ursprung der sittlichen Grundsätze. Inaug.-Diss. Bonn, 1883.

Phil 197.10   Winter, N. Pan-Gnosticism. N.Y., 1895.
Phil 6060.52   Wintermantel, F. Bibliographia graphologica. Stuttgart, 1958.

Phil 8897.70   Winternitz, M. Religion und Moral. Prag, 1922.
Phil 3940.3.30   Der Winterthurer Naturphilosoph J.H. Ziegler. (Saager, Q.) Winterthur, 1930.

Phil 1750.787   Wintrebert, Paul Marie Joseph. L'existense délivrée de l'existentialisme. Paris, 1965.

Phil 3805.240   Wintsch, Hans Ulrich. Religiosität und Bildung. Thesis. Zürich, 1967.

Phil 3235.85   Wintzer, Wilhelm. Die natürliche Sittenlehre Ludwig Feuerbachs. Leipzig, 1898.

Phil 8897.57   Wintzer, Wilhelm. Der Sinn und Zweck des Lebens. Stuttgart, 1922.

Phil 8612.88   Wiplinger, Fridolin. Der personal verstandene Tod. Freiburg, 1970.

Phil 1560.18   Wippel, John F. Medieval philosophy: from St. Augustine to Nicolas of Cusa. N.Y., 1969.

Phil 974.3.122.2   Wir Erlebten Rudolf Steiner. 2. Aufl. (Krueck, M.J.) Stuttgart, 1957.

Phil 6327.12.20   Wir Freud-Schüler. (Reik, Theodor.) Leiden, 1936.
Phil 179.22.10   Wir leben Nicht auf der Erde. (Erdmann, J.E.) Berlin, 1852-71. 5 pam.

Phil 8632.17   Wir sollen nicht sterben. (Hardenberg, H.) Darmstadt, 1920.

Phil 8625.3.15   Wir werden wieder geboren. (Andresen, Karl.) Hamburg, 1894.

Phil 185.22   Die Wirchlichkeit und ihre Erkenntnis. (Koch, J.L.A.) Göppingen, 1886.

Phil 3504.6   Wirgman, T. Kants works and life. n.p., n.d.
Phil 3504.6.2   Wirgman, T. Principles Kantesian...philosophy. London, 1824.

Htn   Phil 3504.6.3*   Wirgman, T. Principles Kantesian...philosophy. 2d ed. London, 1832.

Phil 194.18   Die Wirkliche und die scheinbare Welt. (Teichmüller, G.) Breslau, 1882.

Phil 181.77   Wirklicher und unwirklicher Geist. (Gehlen, A.) Leipzig, 1931.

Phil 180.33.5   Wirklichkeit, Wahrheit und Wissen. (Fischer, Ludwig.) Berlin, 1919.

Phil 187.81   Wirklichkeit. (Mossig, T.) Leipzig, 1927.
Phil 3160.13   Wirklichkeit als Aufgabe. (Cohn, Jonas.) Stuttgart, 1955.
Phil 351.3   Wirklichkeit als Geheimnis und Auftrag. (Uexküll, T. von.) Bern, 1945.

Phil 8897.60   Die Wirklichkeit der Ethik. (Wiedling, Hans.) Leipzig, 1931.

Phil 974.3.2   Die Wirklichkeit der höheren Welten. (Steiner, Rudolf.) Dornach, 1962.

Phil 585.250   Wirklichkeit der Mitte. Beiträge zu einer Strukturanthropologie. Freiburg, 1968.

Phil 181.75   Die Wirklichkeit der Wissenschaften und die Metaphysik. (Geiger, M.) Bonn, 1930.

Phil 3585.17   Die Wirklichkeit des Menschen. (Lipps, Hans.) Frankfurt, 1954.

Phil 5261.22   Wirklichkeit des Menschlichen. (Vetter, A.) Freiburg, 1960.

Phil 5585.335   Die Wirklichkeit des Psychischen. (Uslar, Detlev von.) Pfullingen, 1969.

Phil 6319.1.45   Wirklichkeit des Seele. (Jung, C.G.) Zürich, 1934.
Phil 190.80.20   Die Wirklichkeit und das Gute. 6. Aufl. (Pieper, Josef.) München, 1956.

Phil 9075.84   Wirklichkeit und Mass des Menschen. (Flither, Andreas.) München, 1967.

Phil 3120.20   Wirklichkeit und Sinn. v.1-2. (Burkamp, Wilhelm.) Berlin, 1938.

Phil 3120.15.97   Wirklichkeit und Wahrheit des Denkens. (Bickel, Lothar.) Zürich, 1953.

Phil 3925.2.90   Wirklichkeit und Wirklichkeiten. (Weishedel, Wilhelm.) Berlin, 1906.

Phil 193.76   Wirklichkeiten. (Schneider, Albert.) Strassburg, 1910.
Phil 349.25   Der Wirklichkeitsdualismus. (Silfverberg, K.W.) Helsingfors, 1912.

Phil 178.22.4   Wirklichkeitslehre. (Driesch, H.) Leipzig, 1922.
Phil 178.22.4.5   Wirklichkeitslehre. 3e Aufl. (Driesch, H.) Leipzig, 1930.
Phil 353.16   Das Wirklichkeitsproblem der Erkenntnistheorie. (Weinschenk, C.) Leipzig, 1936.

Phil 632.15   Das Wirklichkeitsverständnis der Gegenwart. Salzburg, 1970.

Phil 5650.3   Die Wirkung akustischer Sinnesreize auf Puls und Athmung. (Mentz, P.) Leipzig, 1895.

Phil 8602.31   Die Wirkungen Des Geistes und der Glister. (Wienel, H.) Freiburg, 1899.

Phil 8897.48   Wirpel, Aaron. Observations of a progressive religionist. Cleveland, 1923.

Phil 3450.18.185   Wirth, I. Realismus und Apriorismus in Nicolai Hartmanns Erkenntnistheorie. Berlin, 1965.

Phil 8897.54   Wirth, J.U. System der speculative Ethik. v.1-2. Heilbronn, 1841-42.

Phil 510.138   Wirth, R. Uber Monismus (Pantheismus). Plauen, 1874.
Phil 5262.14   Wirth, W. Psychophysik. Leipzig, 1912.
Phil 5374.162   Wirth, Wilhelm. Die experimentelle analyse der Bewusstseinsphänomenma. Brauschweig, 1908.

Phil 3925.7.85   Wirth, Wilhelm. Wie ich zur Philosophie und Psychologie Ram. Leipzig, 1931.

Phil 5643.83   Wirth, Wilhelm. Zur psychophysischen Analyse der repsoldschen Mikrometerrigistrierung von Sterndurchgängen. Leipzig, 1915.

Phil 197.46   Wirth, William. Zur Orientierung der Philosophie am Bewusstseinsbegriff. München, 1919.

Phil 4363.9   Wirtschaftethik am Vorabend des Liberalismus. (Weber, Wilhelm.) Münster, 1959.

Phil 8893.50.5   Wirtschaftliche Grundlagen der Moral. (Staudinger, Franz.) Darmstadt, 1907.

Phil 2070.139   Wisconsin. University. William James, the man and the thinker. Madison, 1942.

Phil 1870.125A   Wisdom, J.O. The unconscious origin of Berkeley's philosophy. London, 1953.

Phil 2340.19.30   Wisdom, John. The metamorphosis of metaphysics. London, 1961?

Phil 353.21.5   Wisdom, John. Other minds. Berkeley, 1968.
Phil 353.21   Wisdom, John. Other minds. Oxford, 1952.
Phil 353.31   Wisdom, John. Paradox and discovery. N.Y., 1965.
Phil 197.93   Wisdom, John. Philosophy and psychoanalysis. Oxford, 1964.

Phil 193.128.85   Wisdom, John. Problems of mind and matter. Cambridge, Eng., 1934.

Phil 6952.29   Wisdom, madness, and folly. (Custance, J.) N.Y., 1952.
Phil 5245.46   Wisdom and responsibility. (Fales, Walter.) Princeton, 1946.

Phil 8881.69   Wisdom in conduct. (Garnett, C.B.) N.Y., 1940.
Phil 165.367   Wisdom in depth. (Daues, Vincent F.) Milwaukee, 1966.

Htn   Phil 9362.8*   Wisdom in miniature. Worcester, 1796.
Phil 193.49.65   The wisdom of George Santayana. 2d. ed. (Santayana, G.) N.Y., 1964.

Htn   Phil 8672.2.5*   The wisdom of God manifested in the works of the creation. (Ray, J.) London, 1691.

Htn   Phil 8672.2.3*A   The wisdom of God manifested in the works of the creation. v.1-2. (Ray, J.) London, 1704.

Htn   Phil 8672.2*   The wisdom of God manifested in the works of the creation. v.1-2. (Ray, J.) London, 1714.

Phil 8672.2.2   The wisdom of God manifested in the works of the creation. v.1-2. (Ray, J.) London, 1717.

Phil 8602.53   The wisdom of insecurity. (Watts, Alan W.) N.Y., 1958.
Phil 8876.92   The wisdom of Lang-Sin. (Barclay, Thomas.) N.Y., 1963.
Phil 3808.25.25   The wisdom of life. (Schopenhauer, Arthur.) London, 1963.
Phil 9420.7   The wisdom of passion. (Walters, H.G.) Boston, 1901.
Phil 3425.27A   The wisdom of religion of a German philosopher. (Hegel, Georg Wilhelm Friedrich.) London, 1897.

Phil 3808.22.15   The wisdom of Schopenhauer. (Schopenhauer, Arthur.) London, 1911.

Phil 7069.16.20   Wisdom of the ages. 2. ed. (Fuller, George A.) Boston, 1916.

Phil 193.83   Wisdom of the beasts. (Strong, C.A.) Boston, 1922.
Phil 817.19.4   Wisdom of the West. (Russell, B.R.) Garden City, 1959.
Htn   Phil 8882.7.25*   Wisdomes tripos. (Herle, Charles.) London, 1655.
Htn   Phil 8882.8*   Wisdom's tripos. (Herle, Charles.) London, 1670.
X Cg   Phil 9182.5   Wise, D. Bridal greetings: a marriage gift. N.Y., 1852.
Phil 9362.5   Wise, D. Young lady's counsellor. N.Y., 1852.
Phil 9362.5.2   Wise, D. Young man's counsellor. N.Y., 1852.
Phil 9540.2   Wise, J.W. From bigotry to brotherhood. N.Y., 1953?
Phil 8677.5   Wise, Thomas. A confutation of the reason and philosophy of atheism. London, 1706. 2v.

Htn   Phil 1850.61*   A wise and moderate discourse concerning church affaires. (Bacon, Francis.) n.p., 1641.

Phil 6111.15   Wise-Kunst. (Björnson, B.) N.Y., 1909.
Phil 8697.14   Wise men worship. 1. ed. (Hill, Mabel.) N.Y., 1931.

Phil 8064.2 — Wiseman, N. On the perception of natural beauty by the ancients and moderns. London, 1856.

Phil 8712.13.1 — Wiseman, N.P.S. Twelve lectures on the connexion between science and revealed religion. Andover, 1837.

Phil 8712.13.2 — Wiseman, N.P.S. Twelve lectures on the connexion between science and revealed religion. 2. ed. London, 1842.

Phil 8712.13.8 — Wiseman, N.P.S. Twelve lectures on the connexion between science and revealed religion. 4. ed. Baltimore, 1852. 2v.

Phil 5262.70 — Wiseman, Stephen. Intelligence and ability. Baltimore, 1967.

Phil 3640.406 — Wiser, Edwin. Nietzsche als Prophet und das Geheimnis des Übermenschen. Affaltern, 1953.

Phil 5769.4 — Wish and will. (Turner, G.L.) London, 1880.

Phil 5249.6.20 — Wish and wisdom. (Jastrow, J.) N.Y., 1935.

Phil 5070.3 — The wish to believe. Photoreproduction. (Ward, Wilfred.) London, 1885.

Phil 8602.29 — Wishart, A.W. Primary facts in religious thought. Chicago, 1905.

Phil 176.109 — Wiskunde, waarheid, werkkeijkheid. (Brouwer, L.E.J.) Gröningen, 1919.

Phil 5066.85 — Wiskundig Genootschap. Amsterdam. Mathematical interpretation of formal systems. Amsterdam, 1955.

Phil 1195.19 — Wiśniewski, Bohdan. L'influence des sophistes sur Aristote, Epicur, stoiciens et sceptiques. Wrocław, 1966.

Phil 2138.112 — Wisniewski, J. Etude historique et critique de la théorie de la perception extérieure chez John Stuart Mill. Thèse. Paris, 1925.

Phil 3260.32 — Wissen, Glaube und Ahndung. (Fries, J.F.) Jena, 1805.

Phil 8591.65 — Wissen, Glaube und Skepsis. (Loewith, Karl.) Göttingen, 1956.

Phil 1535.16 — Das Wissen Gottes. v.1-4. (Schneider, C.M.) Regensburg, 1884-86. 3v.

Phil 8590.11.2 — Wissen und Glauben. 2. Aufl. (Kneib, Philipp.) Mainz, 1905.

Phil 8586.26 — Wissen und Glauben. 2e Aufl. (Güttler, C.) München, 1904.

Phil 165.40.5 — Wissen und Hoffen. (Bloch, Ernest.) Berlin, 1955.

Phil 332.6 — Der Wissensbegriff. (Baumann, J.) Heidelberg, 1908.

Phil 186.60.10 — Wissenschaft, Bildung, Weltanschauung. (Litt, Theodor.) Leipzig, 1928.

Phil 197.43 — Wissenschaft, Philosophie, Kunst und Religion. (Wehnert, B.) Dortmund, 1910.

Phil 720.55 — Wissenschaft, Wahrheit, Existenz. (Kamlah, Wilhelm.) Stuttgart, 1960.

Phil 345.2 — Die Wissenschaft. (Ostwald, N.) Leipzig, 1911.

Phil 338.42 — Wissenschaft als Handlung. (Holzkamp, Klaus.) Berlin, 1968.

Phil 705.31 — Wissenschaft als Philosophie. (Ezilasi, Wilhelm.) Zürich, 1945.

Phil 3549.8.85 — Die Wissenschaft am Scheidewege von Leben und Geist. (Klages, Ludwig.) Leipzig, 1932.

Phil 8704.3 — Wissenschaft contra Gottesglauben. (Ostwald, Wilhelm.) Leipzig, 1960.

Phil 352.2 — Wissenschaft der Erkenntniss. (Vorlaender, F.) Leipzig, 1847.

Phil 3425.29.12 — Wissenschaft der Logik. (Hegel, Georg Wilhelm Friedrich.) Göttingen, 1966-

Phil 3425.34 — Wissenschaft der Logik. (Hegel, Georg Wilhelm Friedrich.) Leipzig, 1923. 2v.

Phil 3425.29.10 — Wissenschaft der Logik. (Hegel, Georg Wilhelm Friedrich.) Leipzig, 1948.

Htn — Phil 3425.29* — Wissenschaft der Logik. (Hegel, Georg Wilhelm Friedrich.) Nürnberg, 1912. 3v.

Phil 3780.35.2 — Wissenschaft der logischen Idee. (Rosenkranz, Karl.) Königsberg, 1858-59. 2v.

Phil 3780.35 — Wissenschaft der logischen Idee. v.1-2. (Rosenkranz, Karl.) Königsberg, 1858-59.

Phil 5850.130 — Wissenschaft der Menschenbehandlung. (Beuesch, H.) Heidelberg, 1958.

Phil 180.6.7 — Die Wissenschaft der Metaphysik im Grundrisse. (Fischer, K.P.) Stuttgart, 1834.

Phil 176.22 — Wissenschaft des Geistes. (Biederman, G.) Leipzig, 1858.

Phil 3790.5.31 — Die Wissenschaft des Wissens und Begründung der besonderer Wissenschaften durch die allgemeine Wissenschaft. v.1-2. (Rosenkrantz, Wilhelm.) München, 1866-68.

Phil 310.200 — Wissenschaft im Kollektiv. (Meurers, Joseph.) München, 1959.

Phil 310.613 — Die Wissenschaft im Lichte des Marxismus. Zürich, 1937.

Phil 186.39 — Wissenschaft und Metaphysik. (Liard, Louis.) Leipzig, 1911.

Phil 182.43 — Wissenschaft und Philosophie. (Häberlin, Paul.) Basel, 1910.

Phil 8694.1 — Wissenschaft und Religion. (Eucken, R.) München, 1906.

Phil 8691.6.10 — Wissenschaft und Religion in der Philosophie unserer Zeit. (Boutroux, E.) Leipzig, 1910.

Phil 3120.2.40 — Wissenschaft und Religion in Vormärz. (Bolzano, Bernard.) Berlin, 1965.

Phil 3270.11 — Wissenschaft und Symbol. (Friedmann, H.) München, 1949.

Phil 197.63 — Wissenschaft und Weltanschauung. (Wenzl, Aloys.) Leipzig, 1936.

Phil 197.63.3 — Wissenschaft und Weltanschauung. 2. Aufl. (Wenzl, Aloys.) Hamburg, 1949.

Phil 1135.188 — Wissenschaft und Weltansehauung in der Antike. (Kroeber, Günter.) Berlin, 1966.

Phil 336.3 — Wissenschaft und Wirklichkeit. (Frischeisen-Köhler, Max.) Leipzig, 1912.

Phil 32.3 — Wissenschaft und Zeitgeist. Leipzig. 1-10,1935-1938

Phil 7082.150 — Die Wissenschaft vom Traum, Ergebnisse und Probleme. (Siebenthal, Walter von.) Berlin, 1953.

Phil 978.49.385 — Die Wissenschaft vom Werden des Menschen. (Steiner, R.) Dornach, 1967.

Phil 5228.5 — Die Wissenschaft von Menschen in der Gegenwart. (Seifert, Friedrich.) Leipzig, 1930.

Phil 720.86 — Die Wissenschaften und die Wahrheit. (Ulmer, Karl.) Stuttgart, 1966.

Phil 3310.1.135 — Das wissenschaftliche Anliger des Güntherianismus. (Wenzel, Paul.) Essen, 1961.

Phil 61.1 — WissenschaftlicheBeilage. (Vienna. Universität. Philosophische Gesellschaft.) Leipzig, 1902-1915. 2v.

Phil 3210.75 — Wissenschaftliche Briefe. (Fechner, G.T.) Hamburg, 1890.

Phil 5190.4.30 — Die wissenschaftliche Definition. (Tamás, György.) Budapest, 1964.

Phil 6114.11.10 — Wissenschaftliche Hypothesen über Leib und Seele. (Erdmann, B.) Köln, 1907.

Phil 6114.6 — Wissenschaftliche Hypothesen über Leib und Seele. (Erdmann, B.) Köln, 1908.

Phil 575.12.5 — Die wissenschaftliche Selbsterkenntnis. (Brockdorff, Cay.) Stuttgart, 1908.

Phil 7082.88 — Wissenschaftliche Traum de Terei. (Siemens, Otto.) Leipzig, 1919?

Phil 8702.15 — Eine wissenschaftliche Wellanschauung auf religiöser Grundlage. (Mikos, J.) Leipzig, 1895.

Phil 705.62 — Die Wissenschaftsbegrundende Funktion der Transzendent alphilosophie. (Schneider, Peter K.) Freiburg, 1965.

Phil 5041.47.5 — Wissenschaftslehre. (Balzano, Bernard.) Leipzig, 1929-31. 4v.

Phil 3850.55 — Wissenschaftslehre. (Scherrer, Eduard.) Bern, 1968.

Phil 3246.44.10 — Wissenschaftslehre 1804. (Fichte, Johann Gottlieb.) Frankfurt, 1966.

Phil 335.11 — Wissenschaftstheorie. v.2. (Essler, Wilhelm Karl.) Freiburg, 1971.

Phil 349.24.5 — Die Wissensformen und die Gesellschaft. (Scheler, Max.) Leipzig, 1926.

Phil 165.215 — Wisser, Richard. Sinn und Sein. Tubingen, 1960.

Phil 1750.815 — Wisser, Richard. Verantwortung im Wondel der Zeit. Mainz, 1967.

Phil 4803.879.06 — Wiszniewski, Michal. Charaktery rozumów ludzkich. Warszawa, 1876. 2 pam.

Phil 5520.458 — Wit, Gerard Antonius de. A psychological study of symbolism in word association and symbolic meaning of words. Eindhoven, 1962.

Phil 5525.6.5A — Wit and its relation to the unconscious. (Freud, Sigmund.) N.Y., 1916.

Phil 2255.1.55 — The wit and wisdom. (Russell, Bertrand Russell.) Boston, 1951.

Phil 2340.10.30A — Wit and wisdom. (Whitehead, Alfred North.) Boston, 1947.

Phil 1955.6.40A — The wit and wisdom of J. Dewey. (Dewey, John.) Boston, 1949.

Phil 5262.11 — Witasek, S. Grundlinien der Psychologie. Leipzig, 1908.

Phil 8423.4 — Witasek, Stephan. Grundzüge der allgemeinen Asthetik. Leipzig, 1904.

Phil 5643.55 — Witasek, Stephan. Psychologie der Raumwahrnehmung des Auges. Heidelberg, 1910.

Phil 8602.55 — Witcutt, W.P. The rise and fall of the individual. N.Y., 1958.

Phil 1504.3.2 — Witelo. v.3, pt.2. (Baeumker, C.) Münster, 1908.

Phil 8110.2 — With eyes of the past. (Ladd, H.A.) N.Y., 1928.

Phil 7069.47 — With folded wings. 1. ed. (White, S.E.) N.Y., 1947.

Phil 525.75 — With the door open, my experience. (Anker-Larsen, Johannes.) N.Y., 1931.

Phil 8897.20 — Witherspoon, J. Lectures on moral philosophy. Philadelphia, 1822.

Phil 8897.20.5 — Witherspoon, J. Lectures on moral philosophy. Princeton, 1912.

Phil 5262.55 — Within, Herman A. Psychological differentiation. N.Y., 1962.

Phil 2055.7.85 — Within human experience; the philosophy of William Ernest Hocking. (Rouner, Leroy S.) Cambridge, 1969.

Phil 5440.14 — Withington, C.F. Consanguineous marriages; their effect upon offspring. Boston, 1885.

Phil 2255.11 — Without answers. (Rhees, Rush.) London, 1969.

Phil 8656.1 — Without faith, without God. (Barclay, J.) London, 1836.

Phil 8610.883 — Without God. (Greg, Percy.) London, 1883.

Phil 6980.779 — Witmer, Helen L. Psychiatric interviews with children. N.Y., 1946.

Phil 5262.17.2 — Witmer, L. Analytical psychology. Boston, 1902.

Phil 6325.16 — The Witmer cylinder test. (Paschal, Franklin C.) Hershey, Pa., 1918.

Phil 525.225 — Witness. (Bennett, John G.) London, 1962.

Phil 7069.20.272 — The witness. (Platts, J.) London, 1920.

Htn — Phil 2020.32* — The witness of God and faith. (Green, T.H.) London, 1886.

Phil 8712.25 — The witness of science. 1. ed. (Wilson, Robert M.) London, 1942.

Phil 8582.25 — A witness testifies. (Carson, Capshaw, (pseud.).) Chicago, 1918.

Phil 7069.35.65 — A witness through the centuries. (Hegy, Reginald.) N.Y., 1935.

Phil 8631.3 — The witness to immortality. (Gordon, G.A.) Boston, 1900.

Phil 5627.91 — Witnessing. (Slocum, Phebe B. Akin.) Brattleboro, 1899.

Htn — Phil 8876.19.3* — Wits commonwealth. (Bodenham, John.) London, 1722.

Htn — Phil 8887.13* — Wits commonwealth. pt. 2. (Meres, F.) London, 1634.

Phil 3450.11.260 — Witschel, Guenter. Edmund Husserls Lehre von den sekundaren Qualitäten. Bonn, 1961.

Phil 310.325 — Witt-Hansen, J. Historical materialism. Copenhagen, 1960.

Phil 3504.8 — Witte, J.H. Beiträge zum Verständnis Kant's. Berlin, 1874.

Phil 8897.45 — Witte, J.H. Grundzüge der Sittenlehre. Bonn, 1882.

Phil 3504.8.5 — Witte, J.H. Kantischer Kriticismus Gegenüber unkritischen Dilettantismus. Bonn, 1885.

Phil 5772.7 — Witte, J.H. Über Freiheit des Willens. Bonn, 1882.

Phil 5262.18 — Witte, J.H. Das Wesen der Seele und die Natur der geistigen Vorgänge im Lichte. Halle-Saale, 1888.

Phil 353.7 — Witte, J.H. Zur Erkenntnistheorie und Ethik. Berlin, 1877.

Phil 6315.2.88.3 — Wittels, Fritz. Freud and his time. N.Y., 1931.

Phil 6315.2.88 — Wittels, Fritz. Freud and his time. N.Y., 1931.

Phil 6315.2.87 — Wittels, Fritz. Sigmund Freud. N.Y., 1924.

Phil 6332.12 — Wittels, Fritz. Die Technik der Psychoanalyse. München, 1926.

Phil 8602.24 — Wittels, Fritz. Über den Tod und über den Glauben an Gott. Wien, 1914.

Phil 3504.13 — Witter, C.E. Pragmatic elements in Kant's philosophy. Chicago, 1913.

Phil 3925.16.165 — Wittgenstein; die Negation der Philosophie. (Schulz, Walter.) Pfullingen, 1967.

Phil 3925.16.280 — Wittgenstein; language and philosophy. (Shibles, Warren.) Dubuque, Iowa, 1969.

Phil 3925.16.250 — Wittgenstein; l'ontologia inibita. (Cristaldi, Mariano.) Bologna, 1970.

Phil 3925.16.25 — Wittgenstein, Ludwig. Lectures and conversations on asthetics. Berkeley, 1966.

Phil 3925.16.15A — Wittgenstein, Ludwig. Notebooks. Oxford, 1961. 2v.

Phil 3925.16.35A — Wittgenstein, Ludwig. On certainty. Oxford, 1969.

Phil 3925.16.2 — Wittgenstein, Ludwig. Philosophical investigations. N.Y., 1953.

Phil 3925.16 — Wittgenstein, Ludwig. Philosophical investigations. Oxford, 1953.

Phil 3925.16.3 — Wittgenstein, Ludwig. Philosophical investigations. 3rd ed. N.Y., 1968[1958]

Phil 3925.16.3.2 — Wittgenstein, Ludwig. Philosophical investigations. 3rd ed. Oxford, 1968.

Phil 3925.16.3.1 — Wittgenstein, Ludwig. Philosophical investigations. 3rd ed. Oxford, 1968.

Phil 3925.16.20 — Wittgenstein, Ludwig. Philosophische Bemerkungen; aus dem Nachlass. Oxford, 1964.

Phil 3925.16.10   Wittgenstein, Ludwig. Preliminary studies for the "Philosophical investigations" generally known as the Blue and Brown books. Oxford, 1958.

Phil 3925.16.12   Wittgenstein, Ludwig. Preliminary studies for the "Philosophical investigations" generally known as the Blue and Brown books. 2nd ed. Oxford, 1969.

Phil 3925.16.4   Wittgenstein, Ludwig. Remarks on the foundations of mathematics. Oxford, 1956.

Phil 3925.16.5   Wittgenstein, Ludwig. Remarks on the foundations of mathematics. Oxford, 1964.

Phil 3925.16.52   Wittgenstein, Ludwig. Schriften...Beiheft. Frankfurt, 1960.

Phil 3925.16.50A   Wittgenstein, Ludwig. Schriften. Frankfurt, 1960-64. 2v.

Phil 3925.16.41   Wittgenstein, Ludwig. Tractatus logico-philosophicus. London, 1922.

Phil 3925.16.45   Wittgenstein, Ludwig. Tractatus logico-philosophicus. London, 1960.

Phil 3925.16.47A   Wittgenstein, Ludwig. Tractatus logico-philosophicus. London, 1961.

Phil 197.36.12A   Wittgenstein, Ludwig. Tractatus logico-philosophicus. London, 1961.

Phil 3925.16.60   Wittgenstein, Ludwig. Tractatus logico-philosophicus. Milano, 1954.

Phil 3925.16.46   Wittgenstein, Ludwig. Tractatus logico-philosophicus. Paris, 1961.

Phil 3925.16.30   Wittgenstein, Ludwig. Zettel. Oxford, 1967.

Phil 3925.16.120   Wittgenstein: the philosophical investigation. 1st ed. (Pitcher, George Willard.) Garden City, N.Y., 1966.

Phil 3925.16.290   Wittgenstein - the early philosophy. (Finch, Henry Leroy.) N.Y., 1971.

Phil 3925.16.93   Wittgenstein and modern philosophy. (Hartnack, Justus.) Garden City, 1965.

Phil 3925.16.88   Wittgenstein and the cult of language. (Hawkins, Dennis John Bernard.) London, 1957.

Phil 3925.16.150   Wittgenstein and the problem of other minds. (Morick, Harold.) N.Y., 1967.

Phil 3925.16.255   Wittgenstein e la filosofia. (Novielli, Valeria.) Bari, 1969.

Phil 3925.16.175.2   Wittgenstein in de mode en karze mier niet. 2. druk. (Hermans, Willem Frederich.) Amsterdam, 1967.

Phil 3925.16.80   Wittgenstein inedito. (Barone, Francesco.) Torino, 1953.

Phil 3925.16.220   Wittgenstein or religionen. (Glebe Møller, Jens.) København, 1969.

Phil 3925.16.140   Wittgenstein und der Wiener Kreis. (Waismann, Friedrich.) Oxford, 1967.

Phil 3925.16.92   Wittgenstein und die Moderne Philosophie. (Hartnack, Justus.) Stuttgart, 1962.

Phil 3925.16.210   Wittgenstein's conception of philosophy. (Fann, K.T.) Oxford, 1969.

Phil 3925.16.130   Wittgenstein's definition of meaning as use. (Hallett, Garth.) N.Y., 1967.

Phil 3925.16.100   Wittgenstein's logical atomism. (Griffin, J.P.) Oxford, 1964.

Phil 3925.16.190   Wittgenstein's Tractatus, a preliminary. (Ganguly, Sachindranath.) Santiniketan, 1968.

Phil 3925.16.90   Wittgenstein's Tractatus. (Stenius, Erik.) Ithaca, 1960.

Phil 8897.32.5   Wittman, M. Ethik. München, 1923.

Phil 8897.32   Wittman, M. Die Grundfragen der Ethik. Kempten, 1909.

Phil 735.243   Wittmann, M. Die moderne Wertethik. Münster, 1940.

Phil 1504.3.3   Wittmann, M. Die Stellung. v.3, pt.3. Münster, 1906.

Phil 1504.5   Wittmann, M. Zur Stellung Avencebrolis. v.5, pt.1. Münster, 1906.

Phil 3850.18.80   Wittmann, Michael. Max Scheler als Ethiker. Düsseldorf, 1923.

Phil 8712.21   Wittstein, T. Der Streit zwischen glauben. Hannover, 1884.

Phil 3925.16.285   A Wittgenstein workbook. (Leeds, England. University. Department of Philosophy.) Berkeley, 1970.

Phil 5262.66   Witvrouw, Marcel. Le comportement humain. Bruxelles, 1966.

Phil 8897.82   Witwicki, W. Pogadanki obczajowe. Warszawa, 1960.

Phil 5262.38   Witwicki, W. Psychologja. v.1-2. Lwów, 1930.

Phil 5627.174   Witwicki, Władisław. La foi des éclairés. Paris, 1939.

Phil 5525.64.5   Der Witz. (Schweizer, Werner R.) Bern, 1964.

Htn   Phil 5525.6*   Der Witz und seine Beziehung zum Unbewussten. (Freud, Sigmund.) Leipzig, 1905.

Phil 5525.6.3   Der Witz und seine Beziehung zum Unbewussten. 2. Aufl. (Freud, Sigmund.) Leipzig, 1912.

Phil 4260.113   Witzemann, Walter. Politischer Aktivismus und sozialer Mythos. Berlin, 1935.

Phil 9164.1.2   The wives of England. (Ellis, S. Stickney.) N.Y., 1843.

Phil 9164.1   The wives of England. (Ellis, S. Stickney.) N.Y., 1843.

Phil 8423.6   Wize, K.F. Abriss einer Wissenschaftslehre der Ästhetik. Berlin, 1909.

Phil 3625.1.133   Wizenmann, T. Die Resultate der Jacobischen und Mendelssohnschen Philosophie. Leipzig, 1786.

Phil 4803.846.35   Wizerunki duszy narodowej s końca ostatniego szesnastolecia. (Trentowski, Bronisław F.) Paryż, 1847.

Phil 4769.9.21   Wladimir Sergejewitsch Solowjew. (Maday, J.) Düsseldorf, 1961.

Phil 4769.1.86   Wladimir Ssolowiow. (Usnadse, D. von.) Halle, 1909.

Phil 4803.497.480   Władysław Mieczysław Kozłowski, 1858-1935. (Gawecki, Bolesław J.) Wrocław, 1961.

Phil 3625.3.89   Wlassak, R. Ernst Mach: Gedächtnisrede. Leipzig, 1917.

Phil 5545.223   Włodarski, Z. Pamięc jako właściowość poszczególnych analizatorów. Warszawa, 1964.

Phil 3475.3.72   Wo stehen wir heute. (Jaspers, Karl.) Olten, 1961.

Phil 8602.34.10   Wobbermin, G. The nature of religion. N.Y., 1933.

Phil 8520.24   Wobbermin, G. Religions Philosophie. Berlin, 1924.

Phil 8602.34   Wobbermin, G. Zwei akademische Vorlesungen über Grundprobleme der systematischen Theologie. Berlin, 1899.

Phil 510.1.25   Wobbermin, Georg. Ernst Haeckel im Kampf gegen die christliche Weltanschauung. Leipzig, 1906.

Phil 510.24   Wobbermin, Georg. Monismus und Monotheismus. Tübingen, 1911.

Phil 8677.10   Wobbermin, George. Christian belief in God. New Haven, 1918.

Phil 353.2   Wodehouse, H. The presentation of reality. Cambridge, 1910.

Phil 5772.6   Wodehouse, Helen. The logic of will. London, 1908.

Phil 8602.77   Woelber, Hans I. Religion ohne Entscheidung. 2. Aufl. Göttingen, 1960.

Phil 585.142   Wölcker, Joannes. Amussis vitae humanae. Olomucii, 1698.

Phil 8423.23   Woelflin, H. Das Erklären von Kunstwerken. Köln, 1940.

Phil 6132.14   Wörner, Ernst. Biblische Anthropologie. Stuttgart, 1887.

Phil 3480.105   Wörte Kants. (Kant, Immanuel.) Minden, 1911.

Phil 89.1   Wörterbuch der Philosophie Begriffe und aus Drücke. (Eisler, R.) Berlin, 1899.

Phil 89.1.4   Wörterbuch der Philosophie Begriffe und aus Drücke. 4. Aufl. (Eisler, R.) Berlin, 1927-29. 3v.

Phil 92.4   Wörterbuch der philosophischen Begriffe. (Hoffmeister, J.) Hamburg, 1955.

Phil 95.1.5   Wörterbuch der philosophischen Begriffe. (Kirchner, Friedrich.) Leipzig, 1944.

Phil 89.1.8   Wörterbuch der philosophischen Begriffe. 4. Aufl. (Eisler, Rudolf.) Berlin, 1927-30. 3v.

Phil 95.1.3   Wörterbuch der philosophischen Grundbegriffe. (Kirchner, Friedrich.) Heidelberg, 1886.

Phil 95.1   Wörterbuch der philosophischen Grundbegriffe. (Kirchner, Friedrich.) Heidelberg, 1890.

Phil 97.3   Wörterbuch der Philosphie. (Mauthner, F.) München, 1910. 2v.

Phil 103.6   Wörterbuch der Psychologie und ihrer Grenzgebiete. (Sury, Kurt F. von.) Basel, 1951.

Phil 103.6.2   Wörterbuch der Psychologie und ihrer Grenzgebiete. 2. Aufl. (Sury, Kurt F. von.) Basel, 1958.

Phil 5204.18.3   Wörterbuch der Psychologie und ihrer Gunzgebiete. 3. Aufl. (Sury, Kurt F. von.) Basel, 1967.

Phil 3500.4   Wörterbuch zum leichtern Gebrauch der Kantischen Schriften. (Schmid, K.C.E.) Jena, 1788.

Phil 3500.4.3   Wörterbuch zum leichtern Gebrauch der Kantischen Schriften. 3. Ausg. (Schmid, K.C.E.) Jena, 1795.

Phil 8897.44   Woffny, F. Leitfaden der Moral. 2. Aufl. Leipzig, 1903.

Phil 3425.742   Wofford Symposium on Hegel and the Philosophy of Religion, Wofford College, 1968. Hegel and the philosophy of religion; the Wofford Symposium. The Hague, 1970.

Phil 3246.260   Wohin, gehen wir? (Fischer, F.) Langensalza, 1931.

Phil 197.72.10   Wohl, J.A. Essence et phénomènes. Paris, 1958.

Phil 197.72.5   Wohl, J.A. Un renouvellement de la métaphysique. Est-il possible? Paris, 1957.

Phil 6332.7   Wohlgemuth, A. A critical examination of psycho-analysis. N.Y., 1923.

Phil 9075.29   Wohlrabe, W. Über Gewissen und Gewissensbildung. Gotha, 1883.

Phil 3504.17   Wohlrabe, Wilhelm. Kant's Lehre vom Gewissen. Halle, 1888.

Phil 5585.11   Wohrnehmung und Empfindung. (Uphues, G.K.) Leipzig, 1888.

Phil 8897.21   Woillez, C.T.R. Les médecins moralistes. Paris, 1862.

Phil 600.52   Wojénski, T. Publicystyka okvesu pozytywizmu. Wrocław, 1953.

Phil 9495.160   Wojtyka, Karol. Miłość i odpowiedzialność. Lublin, 1960.

Phil 3850.18.165   Wojtyta, K.B. Ocena mózliwósci zbudowania etybi chresc. Lublin, 1959.

Phil 5772.4   Wolański, L.T. Die Lehre von der Willensfreiheit des Menschen. Münster, 1868.

Phil 6332.13   Wolberg, Lewis R. Hypoanalysis. N.Y., 1945.

Phil 5590.522   Wolberg, Lewis Robert. The dynamics of personality. N.Y., 1970.

Phil 6332.33   Wolberg, Lewis Robert. Psychotherapy and the behavoral sciences. N.Y., 1966.

Phil 6980.780.15.2   Wolberg, Lewis Robert. The technique of psychotherapy. 2. ed. N.Y., 1967. 2v.

Phil 3640.108   Wolf, A. The philosophy of Nietzsche. London, 1915.

Phil 5062.22.9   Wolf, Abraham. Essentials of logic. London, 1926.

Phil 5062.22   Wolf, Abraham. Exercises in logic and scientific method. London, 1919.

Phil 5062.22.5   Wolf, Abraham. The existential import of categorical predication. Cambridge, 1905.

Phil 3842.8   Wolf, Abraham. The oldest biography of Spinoza. London, 1927.

Phil 3842.8.5   Wolf, Abraham. Spinoza, 1632-1677. Amsterdam, 1950.

Phil 5062.22.12   Wolf, Abraham. Textbook of logic. N.Y., 1930.

Phil 5062.22.16   Wolf, Abraham. Textbook of logic. 2nd ed. London, 1961.

Phil 2045.148   Wolf, Friedrich Otto. Die neue Wissenschaft des Thomas Hobbes. Stuttgart, 1969.

Phil 575.54   Wolf, H. De persoonlijkheidsidee bij meisterl Ekhart, Leibniz en Goethe. Amsterdam, 1920.

Phil 623.20   Wolf, Hermann. Spekulation und Philosophie. v.1-2. Berlin, 1878.

Phil 9495.142   Wolf, J. Die neue Sexualmoral und das Geburtenproblem unserer Tage. Jena, 1928.

Phil 3504.10   Wolf, Johannes. Verhaltnis des Beiden ersten Auflagen der Kritik der reinen Vernunft Zueinander. Inaug. Diss. Halle, 1905.

Phil 3425.540   Wolf, Kurt. Die Religionsphilosophie des Jüngen Hegel. München, 1960.

Phil 3850.4.81   Wolf, L. John Michael Sailer's Lehre vom Menschen. Diss. Giessen, 1937.

Phil 1150.9   Wolf, S. Hypatia, die Philosophin von Alexandria. Vienna, 1879.

Phil 5520.165   Wolfard, M.R. Thinking about thinking. N.Y., 1955.

Phil 6669.11   Wolfe, Bernard. Hypnotism comes of age. 1st ed. Indianapolis, 1948.

Phil 7054.53   Wolfe, N.B. Startling facts in modern spiritualism. Cincinnati, 1874.

Phil 6420.30   Wolfe, Paul J. A home study course in the correction of stuttering and stammering. n.p., 1932.

Phil 9070.6   Wolfe, W.B. How to be happy though human. N.Y., 1931.

Phil 6972.20   Wolfe, Walter Béran. Nervous breakdown; its cause and cure. N.Y., 1933.

Phil 5525.48   Wolfenstein, M. Children's humor. Glencoe, Ill., 1954.

Phil 5262.50   Wolfenstein, M. Disaster, a psychological essay. Glencoe, Ill., 1957.

Phil 6692.5   Wolff, C. Hipnotisms teatral. Barcelona, 19- .

Phil 6049.42.8A   Wolff, C. The human hand. N.Y., 1943.

Phil 2340.20.30   Wolff, Charlotte. On the way to myself: communications to a friend. London, 1969.

Phil 3910.75   Wolff, Christian von. Briefe...aus 1719-1753. St. Petersburg, 1860.

Phil 3910.58   Wolff, Christian von. Cosmologia generalis methodo scientifica. Francofurti, 1737.

Phil 3910.76   Wolff, Christian von. Eigene Lebensbeschreibung. Leipzig, 1841.

Phil 3910.10   Wolff, Christian von. Gesammelte kleine Philosophie Schrifften. Magdeburg, 1736-40. 6v.

Phil 3910.12   Wolff, Christian von. Gesammelte Werke. Hildesheim, 1962-22v.

Phil 3910.66   Wolff, Christian von. Logic. London, 1770.

Htn   Phil 3910.34*   Wolff, Christian von. Meinung von dem Wesen der Seele. Leipzig, 1727.

Phil 3910.60   Wolff, Christian von. Oeconomica. Halae, 1754.

Phil 3910.55   Wolff, Christian von. Philosophia moralis suie ethica. Halae, 1750-53. 5v.

Phil 3910.54 — Wolff, Christian von. Philosophia practica. Francofurti, 1738-39. 2v.

Phil 3910.54.5 — Wolff, Christian von. Philosophia practica. Veronae, 1739-42. 2v.

Phil 3910.29 — Wolff, Christian von. Philosophia prima. Francofurti, 1730.

Phil 3910.30 — Wolff, Christian von. Philosophia prima suie ontologia. Francofurti, 1736.

Phil 3910.2 — Wolff, Christian von. Philosophia rationalis suie logica. Helmstadia, 1746.

Phil 3910.1 — Wolff, Christian von. Philosophia rationalis suie logica. Veronae, 1735.

Phil 3910.35 — Wolff, Christian von. Psychologia empirica. Francofurti, 1732.

Phil 3910.35.5F — Wolff, Christian von. Psychologia empirica. Veronae, 1736.

Htn Phil 3910.40* — Wolff, Christian von. Psychologia rationalis. Francofurti, 1734.

Phil 3910.40.5 — Wolff, Christian von. Psychologia rationalis. Veronae, 1737.

Phil 3910.50 — Wolff, Christian von. Theologia naturalis. Francofurti, 1736-41. 2v.

Phil 3910.50.5 — Wolff, Christian von. Theologia naturalis. Veronae, 1738. 2v.

Phil 3910.45 — Wolff, Christian von. Vernunfftige Gedancken. Halle, 1749-53.

Phil 3910.72.15 — Wolff, Christian von. Vernunfftige Gedancken von dem Absichten. Magdebürgischen, 1752.

Phil 3910.73.15 — Wolff, Christian von. Vernunfftige Gedancken von dem Gebrauche. Magdebürgischen, 1753.

Phil 3910.68.6 — Wolff, Christian von. Vernunfftige Gedancken von dem gesellschafftlichen. 6. Aufl. Franckfurt, 1747.

Phil 3910.70.5 — Wolff, Christian von. Vernunfftige Gedancken von dem Würckungen der Natur. 5. Aufl. Halle, 1746.

Phil 3910.59.15 — Wolff, Christian von. Vernunfftige Gedancken von der Menschen. Magdebürgischen, 1752.

Phil 3910.59.5 — Wolff, Christian von. Vernunfftige Gedancken von der Menschen. 2. Aufl. Halle, 1723.

Phil 3910.57.15 — Wolff, Christian von. Vernunfftige Gedancken von Gott. Halle, 1752-40. 2v.

Phil 3910.57 — Wolff, Christian von. Vernunfftige Gedancken von Gott. 7. Aufl. Frankfurt, 1735.

Phil 3910.56 — Wolff, Christian von. Der Vernunftigen Gedancken von Gott. 2. Aufl. Pt.2. Franckfurt, 1733.

Phil 3910.25 — Wolff, Christian von. Wolffsche Begriffsbestimmungen. Leipzig, 1910.

Phil 2725.1.81 — Wolff, E. De la Forges Psychologie. Jena, 1893.

Phil 1850.102 — Wolff, E. Francis Bacon und seine Quellen. Berlin, 1910. 2v.

Phil 3504.46 — Wolff, E.M. Étude du role de l'imagination dans la conaissance chez Kant. Thèse. Carcassonne, 1943.

Phil 5635.39 — Wolff, E.M. La senation et l'image. Thèse. Carcassonne, 1943.

Phil 9035.98 — Wolff, Edgar Maurice. Le individualisme radical fondé sur la caractérologie. Paris, 1955.

Phil 2262.99 — Wolff, Erwin. Shaftesbury und seine Bedeutung für die englische Literatur des 18. Jhs. Tübingen, 1960.

Phil 197.58 — Wolff, Gustav. Sein und Erkennen. München, 1933.

Phil 5832.11 — Wolff, Gustav. Zur Psychologie des Erkennens. Leipzig, 1897.

Phil 8897.33 — Wolff, H. Handbuch der Ethik. Leipzig, n.d.

Phil 303.6 — Wolff, H. Kosmos die Weltentwickelung. Leipzig, 1890.

Phil 3808.230 — Wolff, H.M. Arthur Schopenhauer. Bern, 1960.

Phil 3640.455A — Wolff, H.M. Friedrich Nietzsche. Bern, 1956.

Phil 3842.14 — Wolff, Hans M. Spinozas Ethik. München, 1958.

Phil 9035.33 — Wolff, Hermann. Gemüth und Charakter sechs Vorträge. Leipzig, 1882.

Phil 5062.23 — Wolff, Hermann. Logik und Sprachphilosophie. Berlin, 1880.

Phil 5062.23.5 — Wolff, Hermann. Logik und Sprachphilosophie. Leipzig, 1883.

Phil 3504.16.5 — Wolff, Hermann. Die metaphysische Grundanschauung Kants. Leipzig, 1870.

Phil 3504.16 — Wolff, Hermann. Neue Kritik der reinen Vernunft. Leipzig, 1897.

Phil 197.11 — Wolff, Hermann. Zusammenhang unserer Vorstellungen. Leipzig, n.d.

Phil 5374.11.3 — Wolff, J. Das Bewusstsein und sein Object. Berlin, 1889.

Phil 6332.16 — Wolff, Konrad. Psychologie und Sittlichkeit. Stuttgart, 1958.

Phil 3425.730 — Wolff, Kurt Heinrich. Hingebung und Begriff. Neuwied, 1968.

Phil 822.5 — Wolff, M. Bidrag till filosofiens historia. Stockholm, 1882.

Phil 3485.28 — Wolff, Robert. Kant; a collection of critical essays. 1st ed. Notre Dame, 1967.

Phil 9540.10 — Wolff, Robert Paul. A critique of pure tolerance. Boston, 1965.

Phil 3504.53 — Wolff, Robert Paul. Kant's theory of mental activity. Cambridge, 1963. 2v.

Phil 165.456 — Wolff, Robert Paul. Philosophy. Englewood Cliffs, 1971.

Phil 5871.75 — Wolff, Sula. Children under stress. London, 1969.

Phil 6319.1.206 — Wolff, Toni. Studien zu C.G. Jungs Psychologie. Zürich, 1959.

Phil 575.115 — Wolff, W. The expression of personality. N.Y., 1943.

Phil 5262.47 — Wolff, W. What is psychology? N.Y., 1947.

Phil 6060.44 — Wolff, Wermer. Diagrams of the unconscious. N.Y., 1948.

Phil 6032.2 — Wolff, Werner. Selbstbeurteilung und Fremdbeurteilung im wissentlichen und Unwissentlichen Versuch. Inaug. Diss. Berlin, 1932.

Phil 3915.01 — Wolff's Werk: ein Verzeichnis seiner sämtlichen Schriften. (Wundt, E.W.) München, 1927.

Phil 3910.25 — Wolffsche Begriffsbestimmungen. (Wolff, Christian von.) Leipzig, 1910.

Phil 5425.110 — Wolfle, Dael Lee. The discovery of talent. Cambridge, 1969.

Phil 6332.5 — Wolfram, E. Gegen Psycho-Analyse. Leipzig, 1918.

Phil 3842.11 — Wolfson, Abraham. Spinoza; a life of reason. N.Y., 1932.

Phil 3842.11.2 — Wolfson, Abraham. Spinoza; a life of reason. 2nd ed. N.Y., 1969.

Phil 1020.20 — Wolfson, H.A. The amphibolous terms in Aristotle. Cambridge, Mass., 1938.

Phil 8602.46 — Wolfson, H.A. The double faith theory in Clement, Saadia, Averroes and St. Thomas. Philadelphia, 1942.

Phil 5232.6 — Wolfson, H.A. The internal senses in Latin, Arabic, and Hebrew philosophic texts. Cambridge, 1935.

Phil 8677.21 — Wolfson, H.A. The Muslim attributes and the Christian trinity. Cambridge, Mass., 1956.

Phil 3842.13A — Wolfson, H.A. The philosophy of Spinoza. Cambridge, 1934. 2v.

Phil 3842.13.2 — Wolfson, H.A. The philosophy of Spinoza. v.1-2. N.Y., 1958.

Phil 8602.46.5A — Wolfson, H.A. Religious philosophy. Cambridge, 1961.

Phil 3842.13.5 — Wolfson, H.A. Some guiding principles in determining Spinoza's mediaeval sources. Philadelphia, 1937.

Phil 3842.13.10 — Wolfson, H.A. Spinoza and religion. N.Y., 1950.

Phil 3842.13.12 — Wolfson, H.A. Spinoza and religion. N.Y., 1950.

Phil 1050.12.3 — Wolfson, Harry A. The amphibolous terms in Aristotle. Cambridge, Mass., 1938.

Phil 1050.12.5 — Wolfson, Harry A. The classification of sciences on mediaeval Jewish philosophy. Chicago, 1925.

Phil 1050.14.2 — Wolfson, Harry A. Crescas on problem of divine attributes. Philadelphia, 1916.

Phil 1050.22 — Wolfson, Harry A. Isaac Israeli on the internal senses. N.Y., 1935.

Phil 1050.12 — Wolfson, Harry A. Maimonides and Halevi. Philadelphia, 1912.

Phil 1050.14 — Wolfson, Harry A. Note on Crescas's definition of time. Philadelphia, 1919.

Phil 1050.13 — Wolfson, Harry A. Solomon Pappenheim on time and space and his relation to Locke and Kant. Vienna, 1927.

Phil 1050.14.3 — Wolfson, Harry A. Studies in Crescas. N.Y., 1934.

Phil 6976.25 — Wolfson, Louis. Le schizo et les langues. Paris, 1970.

Phil 8602.11.8 — Wollaston, W. Ebauche de la religion naturelle...avec un supplément. La Haye, 1756. 3v.

Htn Phil 8602.11.2.5* — Wollaston, W. The religion of nature delineated. London, 1724.

Phil 8602.11 — Wollaston, W. The religion of nature delineated. London, 1724.

Htn Phil 8602.11.7* — Wollaston, W. The religion of nature delineated. London, 1725.

Htn Phil 8602.11.3* — Wollaston, W. The religion of nature delineated. London, 1726.

Htn Phil 8602.11.4* — Wollaston, W. The religion of nature delineated. London, 1738.

Phil 8602.11.5 — Wollaston, W. The religion of nature delineated. London, 1759.

Htn Phil 2340.5.30* — Wollaston, William. The religion of nature. London, 1725.

Phil 5755.20.2 — Wollen; eine königliche Kunst. 2. und 3. Aufl. (Fassbender, Martin.) Freiburg, 1916.

Phil 5548.144 — Wollen und Wert. (Keiler, Peter.) Berlin, 1970.

Phil 6520.7 — Wollersheim, T. Das Leben der ekstatischen und stigmatischen Christina von Stommeln. Köln, 1859.

Phil 8520.14 — Wolff, Karl. Schillers Theodizee bis zum Beginn der Kantischen Studien. Leipzig, 1909.

Phil 9425.10 — Wollgast, Siegfried. Zur Friedensidee in der Reformationszeit. Berlin, 1968.

Phil 1885.93 — Wollheim, Richard. F.H. Bradley. Harmondsworth, 1960[1959]

Phil 1885.93.2 — Wollheim, Richard. F.H. Bradley. 2d ed. Harmondsworth, 1969.

Phil 6060.12.50 — Wollnik, H. Probleme der Graphologie. Inaug. Diss. Leipzig, 1933.

Phil 5262.24 — Wollny, F. Grundriss der Psychologie. Leipzig, 1887.

Phil 5232.2 — Wollny, F. Historisch-psychologischer Tractat. Leipzig, 1892.

Phil 497.9.2 — Wollny, F. Der Materialismus im Verhältnis zu Religion und Moral. 2e Aufl. Leipzig, 1902.

Phil 5262.53 — Wolman, Benjamin B. Contemporary theories and systems in psychology. N.Y., 1960.

Phil 5232.12 — Wolman, Benjamin B. Historical roots of contemporary psychology. N.Y., 1968.

Phil 5238.205 — Wolman, Benjamin B. Scientific psychology: principles and approaches. N.Y., 1965.

VPhil 3925.16.155 — Wolniewicz, Bogustaw. Rzeczy i fakty. Warszawa, 1968.

Phil 6980.780.10 — Wolpe, Joseph. Behavior therapy techniques. Oxford, 1967.

Phil 6980.780.5 — Wolpe, Joseph. The conditioning therapies. N.Y., 1964.

Phil 6980.780.20 — Wolpe, Joseph. The practice of behavior therapy. 1. ed. N.Y., 1970.

Phil 6980.780 — Wolpe, Joseph. Psychotherapy by reciprocal inhibition. Stanford, 1958.

Phil 5627.134.57 — Wolrige Gordon, Anne. Peter Howard: life and letters. London, 1969.

Phil 1955.6.115 — Wolstein, B. Experience and valuation. Thesis. N.Y., 1949.

Phil 6332.23 — Wolstein, B. Irrational despair. N.Y., 1962.

Phil 197.70 — Woltereck, Richard. Ontologie des Lebendigen. Stuttgart, 1940.

Phil 5640.36 — Wolters, A.W.P. The evidence of our senses. London, 1933.

Phil 730.36 — Wolterstorff, Nicholas Paul. On universals. Chicago, 1970.

NEDL Phil 497.7 — Woltmann, L. Der historische Materialismus. Düsseldorf, 1900.

Phil 8897.26 — Woltmann, L. System der moralischen Bewusstseins. Düsseldorf, 1898.

Phil 2520.295 — Wolzogen, H.L. Urvagi do medytacji metafizycznych René Descartés. Warszawa, 1959.

Phil 9344.3.7 — The woman of England. (Ellis, S.S.) N.Y., 1843.

Phil 9362.9 — Woman's worth; or Hints to raise the female character. N.Y., 1844.

Phil 8879.3.2 — The women of England. v.1-2. (Ellis, S.S.) Philadelphia, 1839.

Phil 8879.3 — The women of England. v.1-4. (Ellis, S.S.) N.Y., 1843.

Phil 6990.65 — Wonder healers of the Philippines. (Sherman, Harold Morrow.) London, 1967.

Phil 978.43 — The wonder-light, true philosophy for children. (Ver-Planck, J.C. (Mrs.).) N.Y., 1890.

Phil 6990.26.5 — Wonderful works of God. Fall River, Mass., 1877.

Phil 6990.26 — Wonderful works of God. Irvington, N.J., 1858.

Phil 510.1.15 — The wonders of life. (Haeckel, Ernst.) N.Y., 1905.

Phil 6121.15 — The wonders of life. (Lyon, I.L.R.) N.Y., 1910.

Phil 930.40 — Wong, Gung-Hsing. The Chinese mind. N.Y., 1946.

Phil 5402.10 — Die Wonne des Leids. 2e Aufl. (Zimmermann, O.) Leipzig, 1885.

Phil 8712.18 — Wood, A. In pursuit of truth. London, 1927.

Phil 2255.1.118 — Wood, Alan. Bertrand Russell. London, 1957.

Phil 3504.58 — Wood, Allen W. Kant's moral religion. Ithaca, 1970.

Phil 7082.84 — Wood, Clement. Dreams. N.Y., 1931.

Phil 7069.40.17 — Wood, E.C. The "how" of divine revelation. Camden, N.J., 1940.

Phil 9590.7 — Wood, H. This Egyptian miracle. Philadelphia, 1939.

Phil 8647.14 — Wood, Frederic Herbert. Through the psychic door. Houston, 1964?

NEDL Phil 6132.33 — Wood, H. Brain-work. Philadelphia, 1880.

Phil 197.13.15 — Wood, H. The new thought simplified. Boston, 1903.

Phil 197.13.3 — Wood, H. Studies in the thought world. Boston, 1896.

Phil 197.13.8   Wood, H. Studies in the thought world. 8th ed. Boston, 1906.
Phil 197.13   Wood, H. The symphony of life. Boston, 1901.
Phil 9375.6   Wood, H.A.W. Money hunger. N.Y., 1908.
Phil 6132.2   Wood, H.C. Brain-work and overwork. Philadelphia, 1885.
Phil 8602.30.3   Wood, Henry. God's image in man. Boston, 1892.
Phil 6132.17.9   Wood, Henry. Ideal suggestion through mental photography. 9. ed. Boston, 1899.
Phil 8602.30   Wood, Henry. Life more abundant. Boston, 1905.
Phil 6132.17.15   Wood, Henry. The new old healing. Boston, 1908.
Phil 8610.955   Wood, Herbert. Belief and unbelief since 1850. Cambridge, 1955.
Phil 8602.27.10   Wood, Herbert G. Christianity and the nature of history. Cambridge, Eng., 1934.
Phil 8602.27   Wood, Herbert G. Living issues in religious thought. London, 1924.
Phil 5832.4   Wood, J.G. Man and beast, here and hereafter. N.Y., n.d.
Phil 8712.32   Wood, John Karl. The nature of conflicts between science and religion. Logan, 1962.
Phil 353.17   Wood, L. The analysis of knowledge. London, 1940.
Phil 3120.30.180   Wood, Robert E. Martin Buber's ontology. Evanston, 1969.
Phil 8897.31   Wood, W. Ideals of life - symposium on the coming man. N.Y., 1892.
Phil 197.23.15   Woodbridge, F.J.E. An essay on nature. N.Y., 1940.
Phil 197.23   Woodbridge, F.J.E. Metaphysics. N.Y., 1908.
Phil 197.23.10   Woodbridge, F.J.E. Nature and mind. N.Y., 1937.
Phil 197.23.5   Woodbridge, F.J.E. The realm of mind. N.Y., 1926.
Phil 8712.14   Woodburne, A.S. The relation between religion and science. Chicago, 1920.
Phil 9362.10   Woodbury, A. Plain words to young men. Concord, 1858.
Phil 7054.117   Woodman, J.C. A reply to Wm. T. Dwight, D.D., on spiritualism. Portland, 1857.
Phil 960.125   Woodroffe, J.G. The world as power, power as life. Madras, 1922.
Phil 960.127   Woodroffe, J.G. The world as power; power as mind. Madras, 1922.
Phil 960.124   Woodroffe, J.G. The world as power reality. Madras, 1921.
Phil 5330.24   Woodrow, H. The measurement of attention. Princeton, 1914.
Phil 5635.9   Woodrow, H. Quantitative study of rhythm. N.Y., 1909.
Phil 8712.4.5   Woodrow, J. Evolution. Columbia, S.C., 1884.
Phil 8712.4   Woodrow, J. An examination of certain recent assaults on physical science. Columbia, S.C., 1873-74.
Phil 9495.25   Woodruff, C.S. Legalized prostitution. Boston, 1862.
Phil 8647.6   Woodruff, J.L.M. The king's garden. N.Y., 1902.
Phil 197.66   Woods, A. The great quest. n.p., n.d.
Phil 197.57   Woods, Elizabeth R. Music and meaning. Cambridge, 1932.
Phil 5440.9   Woods, F.A. Mental and moral heredity in royalty. N.Y., 1906.
Phil 5440.9.25   Pamphlet box. Woods, F.A. Heredity, minor publications.
Phil 8602.75   Woods, George. Theological explanation. Welwyn, 1958.
Phil 8647.2   Woods, J.H. Practice and science of religion. London, 1906.
Phil 1890.80   Woods, J.H. Thomas Browns Causationstheorie. Leipzig, 1897.
Phil 8602.13   Woods, J.H. The value religious facts. N.Y., 1899.
Phil 7055.386   Woods, Margaret. Mosaic; a psychic autobiography. London, 1968.
Phil 7082.156   Woods, Ralph Louis. The world of dreams. N.Y., 1947.
Phil 2138.140   Woods, Thomas. Poetry and philosophy. London, 1961.
Htn   Phil 8897.22*   Woodward, Josiah. An account of the societies for reformation of manners. London, 1699.
Phil 5401.36   Woodworth, H.M. Sanity. 1st ed. Victoria, B.C., 1958.
Phil 5520.99   Woodworth, Hugh. The nature and technique of understanding. Vancouver, B.C., 1949.
Phil 5262.9.30   Woodworth, R.S. Adjustment and mastery. Baltimore, 1933.
Phil 5232.5A   Woodworth, R.S. Contemporary schools of psychology. N.Y., 1931.
Phil 5232.5.10   Woodworth, R.S. Contemporary schools of psychology. N.Y., 1936.
Phil 5232.5.15A   Woodworth, R.S. Contemporary schools of psychology. N.Y., 1948.
Phil 5232.5.17   Woodworth, R.S. Contemporary schools of psychology. 3. ed. N.Y., 1967.
Phil 5262.9.35   Woodworth, R.S. Experimental psychology. N.Y., 1938.
Phil 5262.9.40   Woodworth, R.S. Experimental psychology. N.Y., 1950.
Phil 5262.9.42   Woodworth, R.S. Experimental psychology. N.Y., 1954.
Phil 5262.9.43   Woodworth, R.S. Experimental psychology. N.Y., 1965.
Phil 5649.6   Woodworth, R.S. Le mouvement. Paris, 1903.
Phil 5262.9   Woodworth, R.S. Psychology. N.Y., 1908.
Phil 5262.9.10   Woodworth, R.S. Psychology. N.Y., 1924.
Phil 5262.9.15   Woodworth, R.S. Psychology. N.Y., 1929.
Phil 5262.9.20   Woodworth, R.S. Psychology. 3d ed. N.Y., 1935.
Phil 5262.9.25   Woodworth, R.S. Psychology. 4th ed. N.Y., 1940.
Phil 6132.41   Wooldridge, Dean E. The machinery of the brain. N.Y., 1963.
Phil 6132.41.5   Wooldridge, Dean E. Mechanical man. N.Y., 1968.
Htn   Phil 665.6*   Woolnor, H. The extraction of man's soul. London, 1655.
Phil 6032.6   Woolnoth, Thomas. The study of the human face. London, 1865.
Phil 5585.51   Wooster, Margaret. Certain factors in the development of a new spatial co-ordination. Thesis. Princeton, 1923.
Phil 353.19   Woozley, A. Theory of knowledge. London, 1949.
Phil 2115.100.5   Worcester, E.E. The religious opinions of John Locke. Geneva, N.Y., 1889.
Phil 2115.100   Worcester, E.E. The religious opinions of John Locke. Thesis. Geneva, N.Y., 1889.
Phil 6132.4.13   Worcester, Elwood. Body, mind and spirit. Boston, 1931.
Phil 6132.4.7   Worcester, Elwood. Christian religion as a healing power. N.Y., 1809.
Phil 6132.4.20   Worcester, Elwood. Making life better. N.Y., 1933.
Phil 6132.4   Worcester, Elwood. Religion and medicine. N.Y., 1908.
Phil 8620.34   Worcester, Noah. Some difficulties proposed for solution. Newbury-Port, 1786.
NEDL   Phil 32.1   The word. N.Y. 9-25,1909-1917 17v.
Phil 5066.11.40A   Word and object. (Quine, Willard van Orman.) Cambridge, 1960.
Phil 6325.22   The word as a physiological and therapeutic factor. (Platonov, K.I.) Moscow, 1959.
Phil 5325.44   Word association. (Cramer, Phede.) N.Y., 1968.
VPhil 5850.386.10   Word magic; tested answers to 100 everyday situations. (Wheeler, Elmer.) N.Y., 1939.
Phil 8693.11   The word of God to be studied with his works. (Doane, George W.) Burlington, 1839.
Phil 7069.28.16   A word of warning. (Doyle, Arthur Conan.) London, 1928.
Phil 9161.4   A word to parents. (Bulkeley, H.W.) Philadelphia, 1858?
Phil 8880.16.5   A word to women. (Fry, Caroline.) Philadelphia, 1840.
Phil 180.51   A wordbook of metaphysics. (Felkin, F.W.) London, 1932.

Phil 3925.17.25   Wordende waarheid. (Wigeroma, Baltus.) 's Gravenhage, 1959.
Phil 310.701   Wording en ontbinding van de filosofie. (Flam, Léopold.) Amsterdam, 1969.
Phil 5520.535A   Words, meanings, and messages. (Rommetreit, Ragnar.) N.Y., 1968.
Phil 5066.11.80   Words and objections. N.Y., 1969.
Phil 5520.225   Words and things. (Brown, Roger William.) Glencoe, Ill., 1958.
Phil 5520.225.2   Words and things. (Brown, Roger William.) N.Y., 1958.
Phil 5068.42   Words and things. (Gellner, Ernest.) London, 1959.
Phil 2725.2.49   The words of a believer. (Lamenais, F.R. de.) London, 1834.
Phil 9358.3   Words to young gentlemen and ladies. (Smith, S.R.) Boston, n.d.
Phil 197.40.5   Wordsworth, J.C. Adventures in philosophy. N.Y., 1926.
Phil 197.40   Wordsworth, J.C. Short essays in constructive philosophy. London, 1911.
Phil 3480.83   Worin besteht der Fortschritt zum bessern im Menschengeschlecht? (Kant, Immanuel.) Wiesbaden, 1917.
Phil 9290.6   Work and education. (Donohue, John W.) Chicago, 1959.
Phil 8876.43   Work and habits. (Beveridge, Ernest.) Philadelphia, 1908.
Phil 5790.25   Work and human behavior. 1. ed. (Neff, Walter Scott.) N.Y., 1968.
Phil 8416.9   The work of art. (Pepper, Stephen.) Indiana, 1955.
Phil 5853.10.3   The work of the counselor. 3d ed. (Tyler, Leona Elizabeth.) N.Y., 1969.
Phil 5625.75.30   The work of the digestive glands. (Pavlov, Ivan P.) London, 1910.
Phil 972.9   The work of the masters. (Lazenby, C.) London, 1917.
Htn   Phil 2150.5.10*   Workes. (More, Thomas.) London, 1557.
Phil 8581.88   A working faith. (Brown, C.R.) Chapel Hill, 1926.
VPhil 1850.1.15F   Works. (Bacon, Francis.) London, 1740. 4v.
VPhil 1850.2F   Works. (Bacon, Francis.) London, 1753. 3v.
VPhil 1850.2.1F   Works. (Bacon, Francis.) London, 1765. 5v.
Phil 1850.2.2F   Works. (Bacon, Francis.) London, 1778. 5v.
Phil 1850.11   Works. (Bacon, Francis.) London, 1802-7. 12v.
Phil 1850.2.5   Works. (Bacon, Francis.) London, 1803. 10v.
Phil 1850.12.5   Works. (Bacon, Francis.) London, 1818. 12v.
Phil 1850.12.20   Works. (Bacon, Francis.) London, 1824. 10v.
Phil 1850.15.5   Works. (Bacon, Francis.) London, 1870-72. 7v.
Phil 1865.10   Works. (Bentham, Jeremy.) Edinburgh, 1843. 11v.
Phil 1870.10   Works. (Berkeley, G.) London, 1820. 3v.
Phil 1870.11.5   Works. (Berkeley, G.) London, 1853. 2v.
Phil 1870.10.5   Works. (Berkeley, G.) London, 1908. 3v.
Phil 1870.17   Works. (Berkeley, G.) London, 1948-53. 9v.
Phil 1870.12A   Works. (Berkeley, G.) Oxford, 1871. 4v.
Phil 1870.13A   Works. (Berkeley, G.) Oxford, 1901.
Phil 3110.22   Works. (Böhme, J.) Glasgow, 1886.
Htn   Phil 3110.10.2*   Works. (Böhme, J.) London, 1764- 4v.
Phil 1900.9   Works. (Butler, Joseph.) Edinburgh, 1804. 2v.
Phil 1900.10   Works. (Butler, Joseph.) Oxford, 1807. 2v.
Phil 1900.9.5   Works. (Butler, Joseph.) Oxford, 1844. 2v.
Phil 1900.9.9   Works. (Butler, Joseph.) Oxford, 1849-50. 2v.
Phil 1900.11   Works. (Butler, Joseph.) Oxford, 1896. 2v.
Htn   Phil 1915.10.2F*   Works. (Clarke, Samuel.) London, 1738. 2v.
VPhil 1915.10F   Works. (Clarke, Samuel.) London, 1738. 4v.
Phil 1915.12F   Works. (Clarke, Samuel.) London, 1742. 3v.
Phil 8877.13   Works. (Cockburn, C.) London, 1751. 2v.
Phil 8583.4.5.-.9   Works. (Dick, T.) Philadelphia, 1836. 5v.
Phil 8663.3.3   The works. (Ingersoll, Robert G.) N.Y., 1900-02. 12v.
Phil 2115.1.6F   Works. (Locke, J.) London, 1659. 3v.
Phil 2115.10   Works. (Locke, J.) London, 1801. 10v.
Phil 2115.10.5A   Works. (Locke, J.) London, 1812. 10v.
Phil 2115.11   Works. (Locke, J.) London, 1823. 10v.
Phil 2115.12   Works. (Locke, J.) London, 1854. 2v.
Phil 2115.13   Works. (Locke, J.) London, 1876.
Phil 2115.11.2   Works. (Locke, J.) London, 1893. 10v.
Phil 2205.10   Works. (Paley, W.) Boston, 1810-12. 5v.
Phil 2205.11.5   Works. (Paley, W.) Cambridge, 1830. 6v.
Phil 2205.12   Works. (Paley, W.) Edinburgh, 1833.
Phil 2205.13   Works. (Paley, W.) London, 1823. 5v.
Phil 2205.11   Works. (Paley, W.) London, 1825. 5v.
Phil 2205.13.15   Works. (Paley, W.) London, 1838. 4v.
Phil 2205.15   Works. (Paley, W.) London, 1851.
Phil 2205.14   Works. (Paley, W.) Philadelphia, 1850.
Phil 2240.10   Works. (Reid, Thomas.) Charlestown, 1813-15. 4v.
Phil 2240.14   Works. (Reid, Thomas.) Edinburgh, 1853. 2v.
Phil 2240.12   Works. (Reid, Thomas.) N.Y., 1822. 3v.
Phil 2275.10   Works. (Stewart, D.) Cambridge, 1829. 7v.
Phil 3808.22.20   Works. Abridged. (Schopenhauer, Arthur.) N.Y., 1931.
Phil 1850.15.3   Works. Faksimile-Neudruck. (Bacon, Francis.) Stuttgart, 1963. 14v.
Phil 2020.10   Works. v.1,3. (Green, T.H.) London, 1886-88. 2v.
Phil 2205.10.5   Works. v.1,3-5. (Paley, W.) Boston, 1812. 4v.
Phil 1850.15.2   Works. v.1,3-15. (Bacon, Francis.) Paris, 1860-65. 14v.
Phil 1900.9.2   Works. v.1-2. (Butler, Joseph.) Cambridge, 1827.
Phil 8583.4.15   Works. v.1-4. (Dick, T.) Hartford, 1839.
Phil 1850.14   Works. v.1-7, 9-14. (Bacon, Francis.) London, 1857-74. 13v.
Phil 1850.15A   Works. v.1-8, 10-15. (Bacon, Francis.) Boston, 1861-64. 14v.
Phil 1850.13   Works. v.1-16. (Bacon, Francis.) London, 1825-34. 17v.
Phil 1850.12   Works. v.2. (Bacon, Francis.) London, 1815.
Phil 2115.1   Works. 1st ed. v.1,3. (Locke, J.) London, 1714. 2v.
VPhil 2115.1.1   Works. 2nd ed. v.1,3. (Locke, J.) London, 1722. 3v.
VPhil 2115.1.2   Works. 3rd ed. (Locke, J.) London, 1727. 3v.
VPhil 2115.1.3   Works. 4th ed. v.1,3. (Locke, J.) London, 1740. 2v.
Phil 2115.1.3   Works. 4th ed. v.2. (Locke, J.) London, 1740.
VPhil 2115.1.5F   Works. 6th ed. (Locke, J.) London, 1759. 3v.
Phil 2115.1.8F   Works. 8th ed. (Locke, J.) London, 1777. 4v.
Phil 8887.38.5   Works and days. (Mabie, H.W.) N.Y., 1902.
Htn   Phil 2045.4*   Works in Latin. (Hobbes, Thomas.) Amsterdam, 1668-70.
Phil 2280.5.7   The works of George Santayana. (Santayana, George.) N.Y., 1936-40. 14v.
Phil 1865.12   The works of Jeremy Bentham. (Bentham, Jeremy.) N.Y., 1962. 11v.
Phil 1850.21   The works of Lord Bacon. (Bacon, Francis.) London, 1838. 2v.
Phil 3808.22.3   The works of Schopenhauer, abridged. (Schopenhauer, Arthur.) Garden City, 1928.
Phil 3808.22   The works of Schopenhauer, abridged. (Schopenhauer, Arthur.) N.Y., 1928.
Phil 5465.50   The works of the mind. (Chicago. University. Committee on Social Thought.) Chicago, 1947.

Author and Title Listing

Phil 8583.4.16 — The works of Thomas Dick. (Dick, T.) Hartford, 1851.

X Cg Phil 2020.15A — Works of Thomas H. Green. (Green, T.H.) London, 1906. 3v.

Phil 9380.7 — Worksheets on morale. (Harvard University. Department of Psychology.) Cambridge, 1943.

Phil 193.56 — The world a spiritual system. (Snowden, J.H.) N.Y., 1910.

Phil 8660.14 — The world and God. (Farmer, H.H.) London, 1935.

Phil 8656.25 — The world and God. Thesis. (Box, Hubert S.) London, 1934.

Phil 192.16.10A — The world and the individual. (Royce, Josiah.) N.Y., 1900-1901. 2v.

Phil 192.16.11A — The world and the individual. (Royce, Josiah.) N.Y., 1901. 2v.

Phil 192.16.10.5A — The world and the individual. (Royce, Josiah.) N.Y., 1923-1927. 2v.

Phil 575.6 — The world and the wrestlers. (Thompson, H.M.) N.Y., 1895.

Phil 186.64 — The world as an organic whole. (Losskii, N.O.) London, 1928.

Phil 180.2.5 — World as imagination. Series 1-2. (Fawcett, E.D.) London, 1916-1921. 2v.

Phil 960.125 — The world as power, power as life. (Woodroffe, J.G.) Madras, 1922.

Phil 960.127 — The world as power; power as mind. (Woodroffe, J.G.) Madras, 1922.

Phil 960.124 — The world as power reality. (Woodroffe, J.G.) Madras, 1921.

Phil 8413.29 — The world as the spectacle, an aesthetic view of philosophy. (Mueller, A.E.) N.Y., 1944.

NEDL Phil 3808.36.2 — The world as will and idea. (Schopenhauer, Arthur.) Boston, 1883-86. 3v.

Phil 3808.36.10 — The world as will and idea. (Schopenhauer, Arthur.) London, 19- . 3v.

Phil 3808.36.10.3 — The world as will and idea. (Schopenhauer, Arthur.) London, 1906-09. 3v.

Phil 3808.36.5 — The world as will and idea. v.2. (Schopenhauer, Arthur.) London, 1896.

Phil 3808.36.10.5 — The world as will and idea. 7th ed. (Schopenhauer, Arthur.) London, 19- . 3v.

Phil 3808.36.10.10 — The world as will and representation. (Schopenhauer, Arthur.) Indian Hills, Colo., 1958. 2v.

Phil 8897.62.3 — The world beautiful. (Whiting, Lilian.) Boston, 1897.

Phil 8897.62.5 — The world beautiful. 3rd ser. (Whiting, Lilian.) Boston, 1898.

Phil 7077.2 — A world beyond. (Montgomery, Ruth Shick.) N.Y., 1971.

Phil 8637.12 — The world beyond. (Moore, Justin H.) N.Y., 1920.

Phil 8691.25 — The world breath. (Beckett, Lucile C.) London, 1935.

Phil 178.47 — World cognition. (Danmar, W.) N.Y., 1923.

Phil 930.7 — The world conception of the Chinese. (Forke, A.) London, 1925.

Phil 8893.142 — World ethics. (Satyananda, Swami.) Calcutta, 1967.

Phil 6105.314 — World Federation for Mental Health. Population and mental health. Berne, 1964.

Phil 190.69 — World hypotheses; a study of evidence. (Pepper, Stephen C.) Berkeley, 1942.

Phil 2225.11.5 — World hypotheses. (Pepper, Stephen Coburn.) Berkeley, 1957.

Phil 3549.2.79.2 — The world in the making. (Keyserling, Hermann.) London, 1927.

Phil 3549.2.79 — The world in the making. (Keyserling, Hermann.) N.Y., 1927.

Phil 5590.55 — World invisible. (Kenmare, D.) London, 1949.

Phil 299.7.5 — The world machine...cosmic mechanism. (Snyder, C.) N.Y., 1907.

Phil 3850.27.128 — The world of Albert Schweitzer. (Anderson, E.) N.Y., 1955.

Phil 630.42.15 — A world of chance. (Spaulding, E.G.) N.Y., 1936.

Phil 2475.1.66 — The world of dreams. (Bergson, Henri.) N.Y., 1958.

Phil 7082.160 — The world of dreams. (Ellis, Havelock.) Boston, 1911.

Phil 7082.156 — The world of dreams. (Woods, Ralph Louis.) N.Y., 1947.

Phil 8692.9 — The world of matter and its testimony. (Christmas, H.) London, 1848.

Phil 5259.2 — World of mind. (Taylor, T.) N.Y., 1858.

Phil 575.256 — The world of persons. Thesis. (Winckelmans de Cléty, Charles.) London, 1967.

Phil 165.388 — The world of philosophy. (Iadir, C.A.) Lahore, 1965.

Phil 6321.50 — The world of psychoanalysis. (Levitas, G.B.) N.Y., 1965.

Phil 9560.10.20 — The world of silence. (Picard, Max.) London, 1948.

Phil 665.41 — The world of souls. (Lutosławski, W.) London, 1924.

Phil 7055.338 — The world of Ted Serios. (Eisenbud, Jule.) N.Y., 1967.

Phil 2905.1.205 — The world of Teilhard. (Francoeur, Robert.) Baltimore, 1961.

Phil 5870.15 — The world of the child. (Talbot, Toby.) Garden City, 1967.

Phil 8647.8 — The world of the unseen. (Willink, Arthur.) N.Y., 1893.

Phil 6685.2 — World of wonders. (Peabody, J.R.) Boston, 1838.

Phil 165.415 — World perspectives in philosophy, religion and culture. Patna, 1968.

Phil 2255.4.5 — World philosophy. (Reiser, Oliver L.) Pittsburgh, 1948.

Phil 193.237 — World philosophy. (Satyananda, Swami.) Calcutta, 1959-1963. 3v.

Phil 187.41 — The world process. (Malter, Mrs. M.P.) Fresno, Cal., 1914.

Phil 5627.134.56 — The world rebuilt...Frank Buchman. (Howard, Peter.) London, 1951.

Phil 5627.134.56.5 — The world rebuilt. (Howard, Peter.) N.Y., 1952.

Phil 8602.41 — The world rebuilt. (Walsh, Walter.) London, 1917.

Phil 8585.19.5 — The world soul. (Fielding-Hall, H.) N.Y., 1913.

Phil 8587.19 — The world unmasked. (Huber, M.) London, 1736.

Phil 182.24 — World unmasked. (Huber, M.) London, 1736.

Phil 182.24.2 — World unmasked. (Huber, M.) London, 1786.

Phil 8876.48 — World views and their ethical implications. (Benedict, W.R.) Cincinnati, 1902.

Phil 286.4 — The world we live in. (Fullerton, G.S.) N.Y., 1912.

Phil 197.67 — World Wide Revival Prayer Movement. Preparing the way. Atlantic City, 1941.

Phil 181.61 — The world without and the world within. (Geddes, Patrick.) Bournville, 1905.

Phil 8705.18 — World without end. (Pilkington, Roger.) London, 1961.

Phil 8897.74 — World without frontiers. (Weiss, Richard.) Sydney, 1950.

Phil 1857.2 — Worlds apart; a dialogue of the 1960's. 1st American ed. (Barfield, Owen.) Middletown, Conn., 1964.

Phil 7069.48.5 — Worlds beyond. (Keith, C.C.) Hastings, Neb., 1948.

Phil 8595.35 — The world's crisis and faiths. (Palmstierna, E.K.) London, 1942.

Phil 510.129 — The world's desires. (Ashcroft, E.A.) London, 1905.

Phil 7140.116.15 — The world's greatest power. pt.3-6. (Coué, Émile.) London, 192-. 2 pam.

Phil 281.4.5A — World's in the making. (Arrhenius, S.) London, 1908.

Phil 8591.44.30 — The world's last night. 1. ed. (Lewis, Clive Staples.) N.Y., 1960.

Phil 165.375 — The worlds of existentialism. (Friedman, Maurice Stanley.) N.Y., 1964.

Phil 585.147 — Worlds to know. (Tsanoff, Radoslav.) N.Y., 1962.

Phil 8597.38.15 — The world's unborn soul. (Radhakrishnan, S.) Oxford, 1936.

Phil 5520.752 — Wormnaes, Odd. Semantikk i teori og praksis. Oslo, 1971.

Phil 5421.25.70 — Worms, Jeannine. D'une malédiction. Paris, 1963.

Phil 1504.3.4 — Worms, M. Die Lehre von der Anfangslosigkeit. v.3, pt.4. Münster, 1900.

Phil 197.47 — Worms, René. Éléments de philosophie scientifique et...morale. Paris, 1891.

Phil 3842.6 — Worms, René. La morale de Spinoza. Paris, 1892.

Phil 7069.70.5 — Worrall, Ambrose A. Explore your psychic world. N.Y., 1970.

Phil 6132.42 — Worrall, Ambrose A. The gift of healing. 1st ed. N.Y., 1965.

Phil 497.10.5 — Worrall, R. L. The outlook of science. 2nd ed. N.Y., 1946.

Phil 8423.21 — Worringer, W. Abstraktion und Einfühlung. München, 1959.

Phil 6128.14 — Worry; the disease of the age. (Saleeby, C.W.) N.Y., 1907.

Phil 7054.50.2 — The worship of Satan in modern France. (Lillie, Arthur.) London, 1896.

Phil 510.130 — Worsley, A. Concepts of monism. London, 1907.

Phil 9347.9 — The worst boys in town. (Hill, James L.) Boston, 1919.

Phil 525.13 — Ein Wort...über die Mystik in der Theologie. (Reischle, Max.) Freiburg, 1886.

Phil 530.20.67 — Das Wort "Grund" in der Sprache der deutschen Mystik des 14. und 15. Jahrhunderts. Inaug.-Diss. (Kunisch, H.) Osnabrück, 1929.

Phil 5520.11 — Wortbildung und Wortbedeutung. (Rozwadowski, J. von.) Heidelberg, 1904.

Phil 2725.2.43 — Worte eines Gläubigen. (Lamennais, F.R. de.) Hamburg, 1834.

Phil 5204.22.2 — Worterbuch der Psychologie. 2. Aufl. (Zeddies, Adolf.) Dortmund, 1948.

Phil 7069.16.60 — Worth, Patience. Patience Worth; a psychic mystery. N.Y., 1916.

Phil 9375.2 — Worth and wealth. (Hunt, F.) N.Y., 1857.

Phil 8885.25 — Worth lectures. (Kane, Robert.) London, 1920.

Phil 9355.2 — The worth of a penny. (Peacham, Henry.) London, 1667.

Phil 6315.2.152 — Wortis, J. Fragments of an analysis with Freud. N.Y., 1954.

Phil 5525.63 — Worüber lachen wir? (Hirsch, Wolfgang.) Heidelberg, 1963.

Phil 3246.90 — Wotschke, Theodor. Fichte und Erigena. Halle, 1896.

Phil 5232.3 — Wray, W.J. The new psychology and the gospel. London, 1926.

Phil 197.37 — Wrench, G.T. The grammar of life. London, 1908.

Phil 6536.6 — Wreschner, A. Psychologische Untersuchungen an Normalen, Schwachbegabten und Epileptikern. Leipzig, 1927.

Phil 5400.80 — Wreschner, Arthur. Das Gefühl. Leipzig, 1931.

Phil 8602.35 — The wrestle of religion with truth. (Wieman, Henry Nelson.) N.Y., 1927.

Phil 197.20 — Wright, A.L. Modernism according to the law of sensual impression. Albany, 1910.

Phil 7054.129 — Wright, Alfred A. Spiritual science, universal religion. N.Y., 1917.

Phil 6132.40 — Wright, B.A. Physical disability; a psychological approach. N.Y., 1960.

Phil 8610.851 — Wright, B.W. Sketches of modern irreligion and infidelity. London, 1851.

Phil 197.12.5A — Wright, C. Letters. Cambridge, 1877.

Phil 197.12A — Wright, C. Philosophical discussions. N.Y., 1877.

Phil 2340.18.30 — Wright, Chauncey. Philosophical writings. N.Y., 1958.

Phil 8897.24 — Wright, F. Course of popular lectures. N.Y., 1829.

Phil 8897.24.5 — Wright, F. Course of popular lectures. v.2. Philadelphia, 1836.

Phil 5170.9 — Wright, G.H. Form and content in logic. Cambridge, 1949.

Phil 5066.44 — Wright, G.H. van. An essay in modal logic. Amsterdam, 1951.

Phil 8897.84 — Wright, G.H. von. The logic of preference, an essay. Edinburgh, 1963.

Phil 5125.21.5 — Wright, G.H. von. The logical problem of induction. 2nd ed. N.Y., 1957.

Phil 5125.21.7 — Wright, G.H. von. The logical problem of induction. 2nd ed. Oxford, 1957.

Phil 5062.38 — Wright, G.H. von. Logical studies. London, 1957.

Phil 8897.85 — Wright, G.H. von. Norm and action. London, 1963.

Phil 5125.21 — Wright, G.H. von. A treatise on induction and probability. London, 1951.

Phil 9240.31 — Wright, Georg. The varieties of goodness. London, 1963.

Phil 9240.31.5 — Wright, Georg. The varieties of goodness. N.Y., 1963.

Phil 7069.20.350 — Wright, George E. The church and psychical research. London, 1920.

Phil 7069.20.352 — Wright, George E. Practical views on psychic phenomena. N.Y., 1920.

Phil 8712.5 — Wright, George F. Recent works bearing on the relation of science to religion. New Haven, 1877-78. 2 pam.

Phil 8712.5.9 — Wright, George F. Scientific aspects of Christian evidences. N.Y., 1898.

Phil 8712.5.18 — Wright, George F. Story of my life and work. Oberlin, 1916.

Phil 8712.5.5 — Wright, George F. Studies in science and religion. Andover, 1882.

X Cg Phil 9182.2 — Wright, H.C. A kiss for a blow. Boston, 1858. (Changed to XP 9413)

Phil 8602.12 — Wright, H.C. The living present and the dead past. Boston, 1865.

Phil 9182.2.5 — Wright, H.C. The unwelcome child. Boston, 1860.

Phil 8602.19 — Wright, H.W. Faith justified by progress. N.Y., 1916.

Phil 8897.56 — Wright, Henry W. Self realization. N.Y., 1913.

Phil 9070.95 — Wright, L.B. Advise to a son. Ithaca, N.Y., 1962.

Phil 9455.12 — Wright, Quincy. Public opinion and world politics. Chicago, 1933.

Phil 8602.47.5 — Wright, Ronald S. Asking them questions. Second series. London, 1938.

Phil 8602.47.10 — Wright, Ronald S. Asking why. London, 1939.

Phil 8897.23.3 — Wright, T. A good life. Boston, 1837.

Phil 8647.4 — Wright, T.F. Life eternal. Boston, 1885.

Phil 6972.6 — Wright, T.L. Some points connected with the questions of responsibility as it relates to the partially insane. n.p., 18- .

Phil 8712.6 — Wright, T.S. Science and revelation. Bellefontaine, 1878.

Htn Phil 5400.10.2* — Wright, Thomas. The passions of the minde in generall. London, 1604.

Htn Phil 5400.10* Wright, Thomas. The passions of the minde in generall. London, 1604.

Htn Phil 5400.10.5* Wright, Thomas. The passions of the minde in generall. London, 1630.

Phil 8423.5 Wright, W.H. The creative will, studies in the philosophy and syntax of aesthetics. N.Y., 1916.

Phil 9245.17 Wright, W.K. Ethical significances of pleasure. Chicago, 1906.

Phil 1722.8 Wright, W.K. A history of modern philosophy. N.Y., 1941.

Phil 3640.110 Wright, Willard H. What Nietzsche taught. N.Y., 1915.

Phil 8897.58 Wright, William K. General introduction to ethics. N.Y., 1929.

Phil 8602.32 Wright, William K. A student's philosophy of religion. London, 1922.

Phil 7069.23.45 Wright A.A. Momentous memoirs. Boston, 1923.

Phil 270.148 Wright Georg Henrik van. Explanation and understanding. Ithaca, N.Y., 1971.

Phil 5585.14 Wrinch, F.S. Über das Verhältniss der Ebenmerk...Gebiet des Zeitsinns. Leipzig, 1902.

Phil 3120.30.7 Writings. (Buber, Martin.) N.Y., 1958.

Phil 978.49.825 The writings and lectures of Rudolf Steiner. (Allen, P.M.) N.Y., 1956.

Phil 2905.1.27 Writings in time of war. (Teilhard de Chardin, Pierre.) London, 1968.

Phil 6315.17.14 Writings of Anna Freud. v.2,4-6. (Freud, Anna.) N.Y., 1967. 4v.

Phil 8705.13 The writings of Ivan Panin. (Panin, Ivan.) New Haven, 1918.

Phil 2070.23 The writings of William James; a comprehensive edition. (James, William.) N.Y., 1967.

Phil 2050.78.5 Writings on economics. (Hume, David.) Madison, 1955.

Phil 2218.60 Writings on philosophy, science and politics. 1st ed. (Priestley, Joseph.) N.Y., 1965.

Phil 4803.454.79.5 Wroński i o Wrońskim; katalog. (Gawecki, Bolesław J.) Warszawa, 1958.

Phil 32.5 Wronskiana. Warszawa. 1939

Phil 3842.7 Wrzecionko, R. Der Grundganke der Ethik des Spinoza. Wien, 1894.

Phil 5062.31 Wrzecionko, R. Das Wesen des Denkens. Wien, 1896.

Phil 575.290 Współczesne problemy filosofii aechniki. (Ban'ka, Józef.) Poznań, 1971.

Phil 5590.526 Wstęp do nauki o osobowości. (Pieter, Józef.) Katowice, 1969.

Phil 5400.81 Wstęp do nauki prawa i moralności. (Petrażycki, L.) Warszawa, 1930.

Phil 5520.325 Wstęp do semantyki. (Schaff, Adam.) Warszawa, 1960.

Phil 5590.556 Wstęp do seorii osobowości. Wyd. 1. (Zawadski, Bohdan.) Warszawa, 1970.

Phil 310.280 Wstęp do teorii marksizmu. (Schaff, Adam.) Warszawa, 1948.

Phil 3310.19.80 Wucherer-Huldenfeld, Karl. Die Gegensatzphilosophie Romano Guardinis in ihren Grundlagen und Folgerungen. Wien, 1968.

Phil 3925.16.230 Wuchteil, Kurt. Strukur und Sprachspiel bei Wittgenstein. Frankfurt, 1969.

Phil 2045.155 Wudel, Witold. Filozofia strachu i nadziei. Wyd. 1. Warszawa, 1971.

Phil 8660.8.5 Wüchner, J.G. Frohschammers Stellung zum Theismus. Paderborn, 1913.

Phil 5643.19 Wüllner, F.H.A. Einleitung in die Dioptrik des Auges. Leipzig, 1866.

Phil 2053.125 Eine Würdigung der ethik Hutchesons. Inaug.-Diss. (Rampendahl, R.) Leipzig, 1892.

Phil 1504.12.5 Würschmidt, J. Theodoricus Teutonicus de Vriberg De iride et radialibus impressionibus. v.12, pt.5-6. Münster, 1914.

Phil 3640.191 Würzbach, F. Dionysos. 2e Aufl. München, 1922.

Phil 3640.388 Würzbach, F. Nietzsche. Berlin, 1942.

Phil 978.100 Wulf, Berthold. Athen und Ephesus. Freiburg, 1965.

Phil 5262.68 Wulf, Berthold. Idee und Denken. Stuttgart, 1964.

Phil 822.18.9 Wulf, M. Précis d'histoire de la philosophie. 9. ed. Louvain, 1950.

Phil 1527.1.8 Wulf, M. de. Geschichte der mittelalterlichen Philosophie. Tübingen, 1913.

Phil 2422.1 Wulf, M. de. Histoire de la philosophie en Belgique. Bruxelles, 1910.

Phil 1527.1 Wulf, M. de. Histoire de la philosophie médiévale. Louvain, 1900.

Phil 1527.1.6 Wulf, M. de. Histoire de la philosophie médiévale. 4e éd. Louvain, 1912.

Phil 1527.1.6.5 Wulf, M. de. Histoire de la philosophie médiévale. 5e éd. Louvain, 1924-25. 2v.

Phil 1527.1.6.7A Wulf, M. de. Histoire de la philosophie médiévale. 6e éd. Louvain, 1934-47. 3v.

Phil 1527.1.5.20 Wulf, M. de. History of mediaeval philosophy. N.Y., 1952.

Phil 1527.1.5.9 Wulf, M. de. History of medieval philosophy. London, 1926. 2v.

Phil 1527.1.5A Wulf, M. de. History of medieval philosophy. 3. ed. London, 1909.

Phil 1527.1.10 Wulf, M. de. An introduction to scholastic philosophy. N.Y., 1956.

Phil 1527.1.17 Wulf, M. de. Mediaeval philosophy illustrated from the system of Thomas Aquinas. Cambridge. 1922.

Phil 8423.7 Wulf, M. de. L'oeuvre d'art et la beauté. Louvain, 1920.

Phil 1527.1.15 Wulf, M. de. Philosophy and civilization in the Middle Ages. Princeton, 1922.

Phil 1527.1.16 Wulf, M. de. Philosophy and civilization in the Middle Ages. Princeton, 1922-24.

Phil 1527.1.9 Wulf, M. de. Scholasticism old and new. Dublin, 1910.

Phil 1527.1.9.5 Wulf, M. de. Scholasticism old and new. N.Y., 1907.

Phil 7069.22.91 Wulff, E. Okkultismus. Dresden, 1922.

Phil 7140.121.5 Das Wunder der Autosuggestion. (Gulat-Wellenburg.) Kempten im Allgäu, 1925.

Phil 9070.67 Wunder der Lebenskunst. (Schmidt, Karl Otto.) Büdingen, 1959.

Phil 665.69.5 Die Wunder der Seele. (Schleich, C.L.) Berlin, 1940.

Phil 8660.12 Das Wunder und die Erkennbarkeit Gottes. (Flügel, Otto.) Langensalza, 1869.

Phil 7069.05.35 Wunder und Wissenschaft. (Hennig, R.) Hamburg, 1905.

Phil 7069.24.29 Wunderbare Tatsachen aus dem Reich des Übersinnlichen. (Kemmerich, M.) Kempten im Allgäu, 1924.

Phil 3085.5.31 Wunderbare Wirklichkeit. (Andre, H.) Salzburg, 1955.

Phil 5627.66 Wunderle, G. Einführung in die moderne Religionspsychologie. Kempten, 1923.

Phil 8602.23 Wunderle, Georg. Grundzüge der Religionsphilosophie. Paderborn, 1918.

Phil 3235.130 Das Wunderverstaendnis Ludwig Feuerbaches in religionsphanomenologischer Sicht. (Klimkeit, Hans-Joachim.) Bonn, 1965.

Phil 5628.53 Die Wundmale des heiligen Franziskus von Assisi. (Merkt, Josef.) Leipzig, 1910.

Phil 3915.01 Wundt, E.W. Wolff's Werk: ein Verzeichnis seiner sämtlichen Schriften. München, 1927.

Phil 3425.330 Wundt, M. Hegels Logik. Köln, 1949.

Phil 3246.212.5 Wundt, Max. Fichte-Forschungen. Stuttgart, 1929.

Phil 822.9 Wundt, Max. Geschichte der Metaphysik. Berlin, 1931.

Phil 1127.3 Wundt, Max. Griechische Weltanschauung. Leipzig, 1910.

Phil 3246.212 Wundt, Max. Johann Gottlieb Fichte. Stuttgart, 1927.

Phil 3504.32 Wundt, Max. Kant als Metaphysiker. Stuttgart, 1924.

Phil 3022.6 Wundt, Max. Die Wurzeln der deutschen Philosophie in Staam und Vasse. Berlin, 1944.

Phil 3210.82 Wundt, W. Gustav Theodor Fechner. Leipzig, 1901.

Phil 3915.52 Wundt, Wilhelm. Beiträge zur Theorie der Sinneswahrnehm. Leipzig, 1862.

Phil 3915.3 Wundt, Wilhelm. Collected papers; articles. n.p., n.d.

Phil 3915.48 Wundt, Wilhelm. Einführung in die Psychologie. Leipzig, 1911.

Phil 3915.35 Wundt, Wilhelm. Einleitung in die Philosophie. Leipzig, 1902.

Phil 3915.59.3 Wundt, Wilhelm. Elemente der Völkerpsychologie. 2. Aufl. Leipzig, 1913.

Phil 3915.46 Wundt, Wilhelm. Éléments de psychologie physiologique. Paris, 1886. 2v.

Phil 3915.59 Wundt, Wilhelm. Elements of folk psychology. London, 1916.

Phil 3915.77.50 Wundt, Wilhelm. Erlebtes und Erkanntes. Stuttgart, 1920.

Phil 3915.78 Wundt, Wilhelm. Erlebtes und Erkanntes. 2. Aufl. Stuttgart, 1921.

Phil 3915.76.3 Wundt, Wilhelm. Essays. Leipzig, 1885.

Phil 3915.76 Wundt, Wilhelm. Essays. Leipzig, 1885.

Phil 3915.65.5 Wundt, Wilhelm. Ethik. London, 1897-1901. 3v.

Phil 3915.65 Wundt, Wilhelm. Ethik. Stuttgart, 1886.

Phil 3915.65.10 Wundt, Wilhelm. Ethik. 4. Aufl. Stuttgart, 1912. 3v.

Phil 3552.125.9 Wundt, Wilhelm. Gottfried Wilhelm Leibnitz. Gestorben 1716. Stuttgart, 1916.

Phil 3915.66.2 Wundt, Wilhelm. Griechische Weltanschauung. 2. Aufl. Leipzig, 1917.

Phil 3915.47.7 Wundt, Wilhelm. Grundriss des Psychologie. Leipzig, 1896.

Phil 3915.47.4 Wundt, Wilhelm. Grundriss des Psychologie. 2. Aufl. Leipzig, 1897.

Phil 3915.47.10 Wundt, Wilhelm. Grundriss des Psychologie. 4. Aufl. Leipzig, 1901.

Phil 3915.47.5 Wundt, Wilhelm. Grundriss des Psychologie. 7. Aufl. Leipzig, 1905.

Phil 3915.47.9 Wundt, Wilhelm. Grundriss des Psychologie. 9. Aufl. Leipzig, 1909.

Phil 3915.45 Wundt, Wilhelm. Grundzüge der physiologischen Psychologie. Leipzig, 1874.

Phil 3915.45.3 Wundt, Wilhelm. Grundzüge der physiologischen Psychologie. Leipzig, 1887- 2v.

Phil 3915.45.2 Wundt, Wilhelm. Grundzüge der physiologischen Psychologie. v.1-2. Leipzig, 1880.

Phil 3915.45.4 Wundt, Wilhelm. Grundzüge der physiologischen Psychologie. 4. Aufl. Leipzig, 1893. 2v.

Phil 3915.45.5 Wundt, Wilhelm. Grundzüge der physiologischen Psychologie. 5. Aufl. Leipzig, 1902. 3v.

Phil 3915.45.6 Wundt, Wilhelm. Grundzüge der physiologischen Psychologie. 6. Aufl. Leipzig, 1910. 3v.

Phil 3915.43 Wundt, Wilhelm. Hypnotismus und Suggestion. Leipzig, 1892.

Phil 3915.49A Wundt, Wilhelm. Introduction to psychology. London, 1912.

Phil 3915.8 Wundt, Wilhelm. Kleine Schriften. Leipzig, 1910-11. 2v.

Phil 3915.55.5A Wundt, Wilhelm. Lectures on human and animal psychology. London, 1894.

Phil 3915.55.7 Wundt, Wilhelm. Lectures on human and animal psychology. London, 1896.

Phil 3915.47.25 Wundt, Wilhelm. Leerboek der zielkunde. Amsterdam, 1898?

Phil 3915.53 Wundt, Wilhelm. Die Lehre von der Muskelbewegung. Braunschweig, 1858.

Phil 3552.125.5 Wundt, Wilhelm. Leibniz, zu seinen Zweihundertzahrigen. Leipzig, 1917.

Phil 3915.40 Wundt, Wilhelm. Logik. Stuttgart, 1880-83. 2v.

Phil 3915.40.2 Wundt, Wilhelm. Logik. Stuttgart, 1893-95. 3v.

Phil 3915.40.3 Wundt, Wilhelm. Logik. 3. Aufl. Stuttgart, 1906-08. 3v.

Phil 3915.40.4 Wundt, Wilhelm. Logik. 4. Aufl. Stuttgart, 1919-21. 3v.

Phil 3915.71.2 Wundt, Wilhelm. Nationen und ihre Philosophie. Leipzig, 1915.

Phil 3915.71 Wundt, Wilhelm. Die Nationen und ihre Philosophie. Leipzig, 1916.

Phil 3915.50 Wundt, Wilhelm. Naturwissenschaft und Psychologie. Leipzig, 1903.

Phil 3915.47 Wundt, Wilhelm. Outlines of psychology. Leipzig, 1897.

Phil 3915.47.2 Wundt, Wilhelm. Outlines of psychology. Leipzig, 1902.

Phil 3915.47.3 Wundt, Wilhelm. Outlines of psychology. 3rd ed. Leipzig, 1907.

Phil 3915.38 Wundt, Wilhelm. Philosophie und Psychologie. Leipzig, 1902.

Phil 3915.69 Wundt, Wilhelm. Die physikalischen Axiome und ihre Beziehung zum Causal Princip. Erlangen, 1866.

Phil 3915.46.6 Wundt, Wilhelm. Principles of physiological psychology. London, 1904.

Phil 3915.69.5 Wundt, Wilhelm. Die Prinzipien der mechanischen Naturlehre. Stuttgart, 1910.

Phil 3915.59.7 Wundt, Wilhelm. Probleme der Völkerpsychologie. 2. Aufl. Stuttgart, 1921.

Phil 3915.60 Wundt, Wilhelm. Die Psychologie im Kampf ums Dasein. Leipzig, 1913.

Phil 3915.56.2 Wundt, Wilhelm. Reden und Aufsätze. 2. Aufl. Leipzig, 1914.

Phil 3915.67 Wundt, Wilhelm. Sinnliche und übersinnliche Welt. Leipzig, 1914.

Phil 3915.06 Wundt, Wilhelm. Der Spiritismus. Leipzig, 1879-1913. 7 pam.

Phil 3915.75 Wundt, Wilhelm. Sprachgeschichte und Sprachpsychologie. Leipzig, 1901.

Phil 3915.30 Wundt, Wilhelm. System der Philosophie. Leipzig, 1889.

Phil 3915.30.2 Wundt, Wilhelm. System der Philosophie. 2. Aufl. Leipzig, 1897.

Phil 3915.30.5 Wundt, Wilhelm. System der Philosophie. 3. Aufl. v.1-2. Leipzig, 1907.

Phil 3915.36 Wundt, Wilhelm. Über die Einfluss der Philosophie. Leipzig, 1876.

Phil 3915.44 Wundt, Wilhelm. Untersuchungen zur Mechanik der Nerven. v.1-2. Erlangen, 1871-76.

Phil 3915.70 — Wundt, Wilhelm. Völkerpsychologie. Leipzig, 1900-5v.

Phil 3915.70.2 — Wundt, Wilhelm. Völkerpsychologie. 2nd ed. Leipzig, 1908-20. 12v.

Phil 3915.55.12 — Wundt, Wilhelm. Vorlesungen über die Menschen- und Thierseele. Hamburg, 1906. 2v.

Phil 3915.55 — Wundt, Wilhelm. Vorlesungen über die Menschen- und Thierseele. Leipzig, 1863. 2v.

Phil 3915.55.8 — Wundt, Wilhelm. Vorlesungen über die Menschen- und Thierseele. 2. Aufl. Hamburg, 1892. 2v.

Phil 3915.70.10 — Wundt, Wilhelm. Die Zukunft der Kultur. Leipzig, 1920.

Phil 3915.6 — Wundt, Wilhelm. Zur Psychologie und Ethik. Leipzig, 1911.

Phil 3915.145 — Wundt's Apperzeptionstheorie. (Szczurat, Vassil.) Brody, 1903.

Phil 3915.156 — Wundts etik, framställning och granskning. (Svensson, P.I.K.) Lund, 1913.

Phil 3915.80 — Wundts Lehre vom Willen. (Schumann, H.) Leipzig, 1912.

Phil 9070.102 — Wunsch und Pflicht im Auflau des menschlichen Lebens. (Brunswik, E.) Wien, 1937.

Phil 4815.672.80 — Wurmb, Albert. Darstellung und Kritik der logischen Grundbegriffe der Naturphilosophie Melchior Palagyis. Weisswasser, 1931.

Phil 3022.6 — Die Wurzeln der deutschen Philosophie in Staam und Vasse. (Wundt, Max.) Berlin, 1944.

Phil 3425.208 — Die Wurzeln der Hegelschen Logik bei Kant. (Stuhrmann, J.) Neustadt, 1887.

Phil 3808.146 — Die Wurzeln des Frauenhasses bei Arthur Schopenhauer. (Eichler, Oskar.) Bonn, 1926.

Phil 3022.4 — Wust, Peter. Die Auferstehung Metaphysik. Leipzig, 1920.

Phil 3925.11.28 — Wust, Peter. Brief und Aufsätze. Münster, 1958.

Phil 3925.11.25 — Wust, Peter. Briefe an Freunde. Münster, 1955.

Phil 3925.11.26 — Wust, Peter. Briefe an Freunde. 2. Aufl. Münster, 1956.

Phil 197.65.5 — Wust, Peter. Die Dialelitik des Geistes. Augsburg, 1928.

Phil 3022.4.5 — Wust, Peter. Gesammelte Werke. Münster, 1963. 10v.

Phil 3925.11.30 — Wust, Peter. Gestalten und Gedanken. 4. Aufl. München, 1950.

Phil 3925.11.40 — Wust, Peter. Im Sinnkreis des Ewigen. 1. Aufl. Graz, 1954.

Phil 197.65.10 — Wust, Peter. Der Mensch und die Philosophie. 2. Aufl. Münster, 1947.

Phil 197.65 — Wust, Peter. Ungewissheit und Wagnis. Salzburg, 1937.

Phil 3925.11.60 — Wust, Peter. Unterwegs zur Heimat. Münster, 1958.

Phil 3925.11.20 — Wust, Peter. Wege einer Freundschaft. Heidelberg, 1951.

Phil 303.3 — Wuttke, A. Abhandlung über die Cosmogonie. Haag, 1850.

Phil 8972.1.5 — Wuttke, K.F.A. Christian ethics. Boston, 1873. 2v.

Phil 8972.1 — Wuttke, K.F.A. Handbuch der christlichen Sittenlehre. Leipzig, 1874-75. 2v.

Phil 5400.88 — Wyatt, H.G. The art of feeling. Boston, 1932.

Phil 5262.37 — Wyatt, Horace G. Psychology of intelligence and will. London, 1930.

Phil 4803.497.25 — Wybór pism. (Kotarbiński, Tadeusz.) Warszawa, 1957-58. 2v.

Phil 4803.799.21 — Wybor pism naukowych. (Śniadecki, Jan.) Warszawa, 1954.

Phil 5190.92 — Wybramec-Skardowska, Urszula. Z badań nad seoria zdań odrzuconyeh. Opole, 1969.

Phil 4803.854.20 — Wybrane pisma filozoficzne. (Twardowski, Kazimierz.) Warszawa, 1965.

Phil 5465.186 — Wybrane zagadnienia psychologii twórczości. Wyd. 1. (Strzałecki, Andrzej.) Warszawa, 1969.

Phil 9530.20 — Wyckoff, Isaac N. Stability, an indispensable element of usefulness and greatness. Albany, 1840.

Phil 3808.165 — Wyczołkowska, A. Schopenhauers Lehre von der menschlichen Freiheit in ihrer Beziehung zu Kant und Schelling. Inaug. Diss. Wien, 1893.

Phil 3640.173 — Wyck, B.H.C.K. Friedrich Nietzsche. Baarn, 1920.

Phil 186.73.10 — Wykłady jagiellońskie. (Lutosławski, W.) Kraków, 1901-1902. 2v.

Phil 4803.497.40 — Wykłady z dziejów logiki. (Kotarbiński, Tadeusz.) Łódź, 1957.

Phil 5640.5 — Wyld, R.S. Physics and philosophy of the senses. London, 1875.

Phil 9362.20 — Wylie, Max. Career girl, watch your step N.Y., 1964.

Phil 2340.13.30 — Wylie, Philip. An essay on morals. N.Y., 1947.

Phil 5590.365 — Wylie, R.C. The self concept. Lincoln, 1961.

Phil 9495.128 — Wylm, Antoine. La morale sexuelle. Paris, 1907.

Phil 5832.14 — Wyman, Eva May. On instinct and intelligence. Thesis. Philadelphia, 1931.

Phil 197.52 — Wynaendts Franchen, C.J. Inleiding tot de wijsbegeerte. Haarlem, 1905.

Phil 107.1 — Wynaendts Francken, C.J. Kort woordenboek van wijsgeerige kunstlermen. Haarlem 1925.

Phil 353.3 — Wyneken, Ernst. Das Ding an Sich und das Naturgesetz der Seele. Heidelberg, 1901.

Phil 8897.42 — Wyneken, Ernst F. Das Naturgestz der Seele und...Freiheit. Heidelberg, 1906.

Phil 8677.13 — Wyneken, G.A. Amor dei intellectualis. Greifswald, 1898.

Phil 3504.37 — Wyneken, G.A. Hegels Kritik Kants. Greifswald, 1898.

Phil 3504.37.5 — Wyneken, G.A. Hegels Kritik Kants. Inaug. Diss. Greifswald, 1898.

Phil 8423.19F — Wyneken, Karl. Der Aufbau der form beim natürlichen Werden und kunstlerischen Schoffen. Atlas. Freiburg, 1903-

Phil 8423.19 — Wyneken, Karl. Der Aufbau der Form beim naturlichen Werden und kunstlerischen Schoffen. Freiburg, 1903- 2v.

Phil 8602.70 — Wynne-Tyson, Esmé. The philosophy of compassion. London, 1962.

Phil 6972.7 — Wynter, A. The borderlands of insanity. N.Y., 1875.

Phil 6972.7.2 — Wynter, A. The borderlands of insanity (with 5 new chpaters). London, 1877.

Phil 62.2 — Wyoming. University. Department of Psychology. Bulletin. 2. ed. no.1-3. Laramie, Wyoming, 1919-

Phil 6332.20 — Wyrsch, J. Gesellschaft, Kultur und psychische Störung. Stuttgart, 1960.

Phil 8972.10 — Wyse, Alexander. Moral and social questions arranged for high school religious discussion groups and study clubs. Paterson, 1943.

Phil 1527.3 — Wyser, Paul. Der Thomismus. Bern, 1951.

Phil 176.115.8 — Wysgeerige studies. (Bierens de Haan, J.D.) 's-Gravenhage, 1904.

Phil 6332.22.2 — Wyss, Dieter. Depth psychology, a critical history. N.Y., 1966.

Phil 8897.94 — Wyss, Dieter. Strukturen der Moral. Göttingen, 1968.

Phil 8897.94.2 — Wyss, Dieter. Strukturen der Moral. 2. Aufl. Göttingen, 1970.

Phil 6332.22 — Wyss, Dieter. Die tiefenpsychologischen Schulen von der Anfanger bis zur Gegenwart. Göttingen, 1961.

Phil 5062.14 — Wyttenback, D. Praecepta philosophiae logicae. Hallae, 1820.

Phil 7230.2 — X+Y=Z, or The sleeping preacher. (Mitchell, G.W.) N.Y., 1877.

Phil 5253.11 — The X of psychology. (Mason, Phillips.) Cambridge, 1940.

Phil 349.22 — Xenia Czernowiciensia. (Czernovitz. Gymnasium.) Czernowitz, 1900.

Phil 3235.136 — Xhaufflaire, Marcel. Feuerbach et la théologie de la sécularisation. Paris, 1970.

Phil 3450.11.113 — Xirau, J. La filosofía de Husserl. Buenos Aires, 1941.

Phil 4374.5.30 — Xirau, Joaquín. Lo fugaz y lo eterno. Mexico, 1942.

Phil 4374.5.20 — Xirau, Joaquín. Obras. 1. ed. Mexico, 1963.

Phil 525.266 — Xirau, Ramón. Palabra y silencio. 1. ed. México, 1968.

Phil 8610.880.18 — XVIII. Světový kongres volné myšlenky v Praze od 5-9 září, 1920. Přípravy. (Congrès Universel de la Libre Pensée, 18th, Prague, 1920.) Praha, 1920?

Phil 1915.25 — XVIII sermons. 3rd ed. (Clarke, Samuel.) London, 1734.

Phil 2475.1.245 — Y a-t-il deux sources de la religion et de la morale? (Loisy, Alfred.) Paris, 1933.

Phil 8962.24 — Y a-t-il une éthique sociale chrétienne? (Manaranche, André.) Paris, 1969.

Phil 8631.6 — Y a-t-il une vie future? (Giraudet, Jules.) Paris, 1864.

Phil 64.1 — Yale Psychological Studies. The psychological review and studies from Yale psychological laboratory. v.1., no.1-2 and supplement. New Haven, n.d. 3v.

Phil 9341.9.5 — Yale talks. (Brown, C.R.) New Haven, 1919.

Phil 5190.10.26 — Yale University. Institute of Human Relations. The order of presentation in persuasion. New Haven, 1961.

Phil 4325.2 — Yamuni, Tabush. Concepts e imágenes en pensadores. México, 1951.

Phil 930.52 — Yang, Jung-kuo. Istoriia drevnekitaiskoi ideologii. Moskva, 1957.

Phil 2840.94 — Yang, Pao-San. La psychologie de l'intelligence chez Renouvier. Thèse. Paris, 1930.

Phil 6334.10A — Yankelovich, Daniel. Ego and instinct; the psychoanalytic view of human nature. N.Y., 1970.

Phil 8669.8 — Yaroslavl', Russia (City). Gosudarstvennyi Pedagogicheskii Institut. Kafedra Filosofii. Osnovy nauchnogo ateizma. Iaroslavl', 1963.

Phil 5850.391 — Yates, Dorothy H. Psychological racketeers. Boston, 1932.

Phil 4065.173 — Yates, F.A. Giordano Bruno. London, 1964.

Phil 5545.95 — Yates, Frances Amelia. The art of memory. London, 1966.

Phil 630.58 — Den ydre verdens eksistens. (Hartnach, Justice.) København, 1964.

Phil 6844.2 — A year among the girls. (Raynor, Darrell G.) N.Y., 1966.

Phil 8615.6 — Year book. (New York Society for Ethical Culture.) N.Y. 1905

Phil 34.3 — Year book of neurology, psychiatry and endocrinology. Chicago, 1943.

Phil 5627.134.35 — A year with the Oxford Group. (Slattery, Sarah L.) Cambridge, 193-?

Phil 59.4 — Yearbook. (Texas. Society of Mental Hygiene.) Austin.

Phil 5330.25 — Yeh, Ling. La psychologie de l'intérêt. Thèse. Lyon, 1929.

Phil 8649.1.2 — Yeiser, J.O. Evolution proving immortality. Omaha, 1917.

Phil 8649.1 — Yeiser, J.O. Immortality established through science. Omaha, n.d.

Phil 5627.122 — Yellowlees, David. Psychology's defence of the faith. London, 1930.

Phil 6334.5 — Yellowlees, H. A manuel of psychotherapy. London, 1923.

Phil 199.3 — Yerington, William. Emerson and beyond. Columbus, Ohio, 1929.

Phil 5834.1.13 — Yerkes, R.M. Chimpanzee intelligence. Baltimore, 1925.

Phil 5834.1.25 — Yerkes, R.M. Chimpanzees; a laboratory colony. New Haven, 1943.

Phil 5834.1 — Yerkes, R.M. The dancing mouse. N.Y., 1907.

Phil 5264.2.2 — Yerkes, R.M. Introduction to psychology. N.Y., 1911.

Phil 5834.1.9A — Yerkes, R.M. Mental life of monkeys and apes. Cambridge, 1916.

Phil 5834.1.5 — Yerkes, R.M. Methods of studying vision in animals. Cambridge, n.d.

Phil 5834.1.15 — Yerkes, R.M. The mind of a gorilla. Worcester, Mass., 1926.

Phil 5834.1.20 — Yerkes, R.M. Reaction of entomostraca to...light. n.p., 1899-1916. 44 pam.

Phil 6694.1 — Yeshilian, M.A. Hypnotism and telepathy. N.Y., 1917.

Phil 960.38 — Yevtić, Paul. Karma and reincarnation in Hindu. Thesis. London, 1927.

Phil 6134.2 — Yoakum, C.S. Experimental study of fatique. Chicago, 1909.

Phil 6134.3A — Yogananda, Swami. Descriptive outline. 9th ed. Los Angeles, 1928.

Phil 5264.4 — Yolton, J.W. Thinking and perceiving. Lasalle, Ill., 1962.

Phil 2115.210 — Yolton, John W. John Locke: problems and perspectives. London, 1969.

Phil 2115.163 — Yolton, John W. John Locke and the way of ideas. London, 1969.

Phil 2115.225 — Yolton, John W. Locke and the compass of human understanding; a selective commentary on the Essay. Cambridge, Eng., 1970.

Phil 5520.506 — Yolton, John W. Metaphysical analysis. Toronto, 1967.

Phil 3935.1.30 — Yorck von Wartenburg, Paul. Bewusstseinsstellung und Geschichte. Tübingen, 1956.

Phil 7140.122 — Yoritomo-Tashi. Influence; how to exert it. N.Y., 1916.

Phil 8714.1 — Yorke, J.F. Notes on evolution and Christianity. N.Y., 1883.

Phil 5590.488 — You are extraordinary. (Williams, Roger J.) N.Y., 1967.

Phil 9070.107 — You are not the target. (Huxley, Laura.) N.Y., 1965.

Phil 6113.27 — You can have it, personality. (Dyer, V.A.) Long Beach, 1937.

Phil 7080.49.5 — You can sleep well. (Jacobson, Edmund.) N.Y., 1938.

Phil 6119.10.5 — You must relax. (Jacobson, Edmund.) N.Y., 1934.

Phil 6134.1 — Youmans, E.L. Observations on scientific study of human nature. N.Y., 1867.

Phil 199.1 — Young, A. The fractional family. N.Y., 1864.

Phil 8425.2 — Young, E. Art: its constitution and capacities. Bristol, 1854.

Phil 199.4 — Young, E.L. A philosophy of reality. Manchester, 1930.

Phil 8589.5.30 — Young, F.H. The philosophy of Henry James, Sr. N.Y., 1951.

Phil 5774.1 — Young, G.P. The ethics of freedom. Toronto, 1911.

Phil 5264.1 — Young, J. Lectures on intellectual philosophy. Glasgow, 1835.

Phil 8620.12 — Young, J. The mystery; or evil and God. Philadelphia, 1856.

Phil 8604.1.2 — Young, J. The providence of reason: criticism. London, 1860.

Phil 8604.1 — Young, J. The providence of reason: criticism. N.Y., 1860.

Author and Title Listing

Phil 6134.4A Young, J.Z. Doubt and certainty in science. Oxford, 1951.
Phil 5545.232 Young, John Zachary. The memory system of the brain. Berkeley, 1966.
Phil 5590.2 Young, Kimball. Personality and problems of adjustment. N.Y., 1941.
Phil 5590.2.1 Young, Kimball. Personality and problems of adjustment. N.Y., 1941.
Phil 5264.3 Young, P.T. Motivation of behavior. N.Y., 1936.
Phil 5264.3.5 Young, P.T. Motivation of behavior. N.Y., 1950.
Phil 6694.2 Young, Paul C. An experimental study of mental and physical functions in the normal and hypnotic states. Thesis. n.p., 1923.
Phil 6694.2.5 Young, Paul C. An experimental study of mental and physical functions in the normal and hypnotic states. Ithaca, 1925.
Phil 5400.101 Young, Paul T. Emotion in man and animal. N.Y., 1943.
Phil 5548.90 Young, Paul Thomas. Motivation and emotion. N.Y., 1961.
Phil 2255.3 Young, Robert F. A Bohemian philosopher at Oxford in the 17th century. London, 1925.
Phil 5234.2 Young, Robert Maxwell. Mind, brain and adaptation in the nineteenth century. Oxford, 1970.
Phil 9070.25 Young, Vashni. A fortune to share. Indianapolis, 1931.
Phil 5374.244 Young, Warren R. L.S.D. on campus. N.Y., 1966.
Phil 3024.5 Young, William. Toward a reformed philosophy. Grand Rapids, Mich., 1952.
Phil 9184.1 The young bride at home. (More, H.) Boston, 1836.
Phil 9352.4 Young gentleman and lady's monitor. (Moore, J.H.) London, 1794.
Phil 3425.722 The young Hegelians. (Brazill, William J.) New Haven, 1970.
NEDL Phil 9160.3 The young husband. (Alcott, W.A.) Boston, 1839.
Phil 9364.5 The young husband's book. Philadelphia, 1839.
Phil 9362.3 Young lady's aid. (Whitman, J.) Portland, 1845.
Phil 9362.3.2 Young lady's aid. 2d ed. (Whitman, J.) Portland, 1839.
Phil 9342.14 The young lady's companion. (Coxe, Margaret.) Columbus, 1839.
Phil 9362.5 Young lady's counsellor. (Wise, D.) N.Y., 1852.
Phil 9345.9 The young lady's friend. (Farrar, Eliza W.) Boston, 1837.
Phil 9342.3A Young lady's friend. (Farrar, Eliza W.R.) Boston, 1836.
Phil 9364.1 Young lady's own book. Philadelphia, 1832.
Phil 9364.1.3 Young lady's own book. Philadelphia, 1842.
Phil 9364.3 Young lady's Sunday book. Philadelphia, 1834.
Phil 9352.5.4 The young maiden. (Muzzey, A.B.) Boston, 1840.
Phil 9352.5.5 The young maiden. (Muzzey, A.B.) Boston, 1841.
Phil 9352.5.6 The young maiden. (Muzzey, A.B.) London, 1843.
Htn Phil 9345.6* The young man. (Fergurson, F.) Nashua, N.H., 1848.
Phil 9341.16 The young man and the world. (Beveridge, Albert J.) N.Y., 1906.
Phil 9349.1 Young man from home. (James, J.A.) N.Y., 1839.
Phil 9341.9 The young man's affairs. (Brown, C.R.) N.Y., 1909.
Phil 9362.6 Young man's aid. (Winslow, H.) Boston, 1837.
Phil 9362.6.2 Young man's aid. (Winslow, H.) Boston, 1839.
Phil 9362.3.5 Young man's assistant. (Whitman, J.) Portland, 1838.
Phil 9362.5.2 Young man's counsellor. (Wise, D.) N.Y., 1852.
Phil 9352.5.10 Young man's friend. (Muzzey, A.B.) Boston, 1836.
Phil 9352.5.11 Young man's friend. (Muzzey, A.B.) Boston, 1838.
Phil 9364.2.6 Young man's own book. Philadelphia, 1833.
Phil 9341.10A The young men of America. (Batchelder, S.) N.Y., 1858.
Phil 9375.3.2 The young merchant. 2d ed. (Pomeroy, R.W.) Boston, 1840.
Phil 3640.88.6 The young Nietzsche. (Förster-Nietzsche, E.) London, 1912.
Phil 3640.684 Young Nietzsche and the Wagnerian experience. (Love, F.R.) Chapel Hill, 1963.
Phil 9160.3.7 The young wife. (Alcott, W.A.) Boston, 1837.
Phil 9340.2.5 Young woman's guide to excellence. (Alcott, William Alex.) Boston, 1847.
Phil 9495.37 Young Women's Christian Association, United States. National Board. War Council Work. Social Morality Committee. Report...Je. 1917 to Jl. 1919. N.Y.? 1919?
X Cg Phil 6694.3 Younger, D. Full, concise instructions in mesmerism. 3. ed. London, 1887.
Phil 199.2 Younghusband, F. The sense of community. London, 1916.
Phil 305.1 Younghusband, F.E. The living universe. N.Y., 1933.
Phil 525.87.5 Younghusband, F.E. Modern mystics. 1st ed. N.Y., 1935.
Phil 8604.2 Younghusband, F.E. Vital religion. London, 1940.
Phil 6111.44.5 Your brain and its story. (Berry, Richard J.A.) London, 1939.
Phil 5465.57 Your creative power. (Osborn, A.F.) N.Y., 1951.
Phil 5421.25.30 Your fear of love. (Hodge, Marshall B.) Garden City, 1967.
Phil 6121.30 Your forces and how to use them. (Larson, Christian I.) N.Y., 1912.
Phil 6122.23 Your forces and how to use them. (Mulford, P.) N.Y., 1904. 2v.
Phil 6122.23.1 Your forces and how to use them. (Mulford, Prntice.) N.Y., 1888-92. 6v.
Phil 6049.42 Your hand tells all; a manual of simplified palmistry. (Jennings, Alice D.) N.Y., 1942.
Phil 7069.28.100 Your infinite possibilities. (Underhill, Margaret.) London, 1928.
Phil 6121.29 Your mental health. (Liber, B.) N.Y., 1940.
Phil 5240.22 Your mind and how to use it. (Atkinson, William W.) Holyoke, Mass., 1911.
Phil 6125.23 Your mind and you. (Pratt, George K.) N.Y., 1924.
NEDL Phil 6125.23.5 Your mind and you. (Pratt, George K.) N.Y., 1924.
Phil 5400.103 Your nerves. (Bisch, L.E.) N.Y., 1945.
Phil 5590.140 Your personality. (Case, V.S.) N.Y., 1946.
Phil 7069.20.53A Your psychic powers and how to develop them. (Carrington, Hereward.) N.Y., 1920.
Phil 7069.68.15 Your psychic powers and immortality. (Appleman, John A.) N.Y., 1968.
Phil 7069.32.20 Your psychic self. (Breitfield, R.) N.Y., 1932.
Phil 5627.270.5 Your religion: neurotic or healthy? 1st ed. (Anderson, George Christian.) Garden City, 1970.
Phil 9362.16.5 Youth. (Wagner, C.) N.Y., 1893.
Phil 9530.29 Youth and opportunity. (Tapper, Thomas.) N.Y., 1912.
Phil 9400.8 The youth of old age. (Brigham, H.) Boston, 1934.
Phil 9070.26 Youth points the way. (Fairbanks, Douglas.) N.Y., 1924.
Phil 9364.4 The youth's guide. Worcester, 1836.
Phil 4650.1.48 Det yttersta tankegångar. (Vannérus, Allen.) Stockholm, 1924.
Phil 7080.12 Yung, E. Le sommeil normal. Paris, 1883.
Phil 199.5 Yura, T. Geisteswissenschaft und Willensgesetz. Berlin, 1931.
Phil 4803.462.60 Z badań nad folozofią współczesną. (Ingarden, Roman.)
Phil 5190.92 Z badań nad seoria zdań odrzuconeyh. (Wybramec-Skardowska, Urszula.) Opole, 1969.

Phil 4800.24 Z dziejów filosofii na Uniwersytecie Krakowskim w XV wieku. (Kuksewicz, Zdzisław.) Wrocław, 1965.
Phil 817.25 Z dziejów filozofii. (Rudmański, S.) Warzawa, 1959.
Phil 4777.894 Z dziejów polskiej myśli filozoficznej i społecznej. Warszawa, 1956- 3v.
Phil 4710.50.50 Z istorii filosofii i sotsiolohii na Ukraïni. Kyïv, 1968.
Phil 4710.50.35 Z istorii filosofii na Ukraïni. (Respublikans'ka Naukova Konferentsiia za Aktual'nykh Pytan' Istorii Filosofii na Ukraïni, Kiev, 1965.) Kyïv, 1967.
Phil 4710.50.5 Z istorii filosofs'koi dumki na Ukraini. (Akademiia Nauk URSR, Kiev. Instytut Filosofii.) Kyïv, 1962.
Phil 4710.50.15 Z istorii filosofs'koi dumky na Ukraini. (Ievdokymenko, V.I.) Kyïv, 1965.
Phil 310.440 Z minulosti a sučasnosti filozofi. (Hrušovský, I.) Bratislava, 1961.
VPhil 185.108 Z teorii i metodologii metafizyki. Wyd. 1. (Kamiński, Stanisław.) Lublin, 1962.
Phil 310.135 Z zagadnień marksistowskiej teorii prawdy. (Schaff, Adam.) Warszawa, 1959.
Phil 310.681 Za deistvieto na zakona za edinstvoto i borbata na protivopolozhnostite pri sotsializma. (Trendafilov, Nikola.) Sofiia, 1968.
Phil 8980.827 Za kommunisticheskuiu nravstvennost'. (Terekhov, S.S.) Leningrad, 1964.
Phil 8980.802 Za leninskii stil' v rabote. (Sorokin, K.F.) Kiev, 1960.
Phil 6315.2.295 Za porogom soznaniia; kriticheskii ocherk freidizma. (Mikhailov, Feliks T.) Moskva, 1961.
Phil 4822.6 Za religiozno-idealisticheskata sŭshtnost na bŭlgarskata burzhoazno filosofiia. (Penev, Mikho.) Sofiia, 1964.
Phil 5000.4F Zabarella, Giacomo. Opera logica. 16a ed. Tarvisii, 1604.
Htn Phil 1535.14* Zabarella, J. De rebus naturalibus. Coloniae, 1597.
Phil 2050.238 Zabeeh, F. Hume, precursor of modern empiricism. The Hague, 1960.
Phil 730.28 Zabeeh, Farhang. Universals; a new look at an old problem. The Hague, 1966.
Phil 8090.2 Zabel, M.D. The romantic idealism of art, 1800-1848. Chicago, 1938.
Phil 3845.3.5 Zac, Sylvain. L'idée de vie dans la philosophie de Spinoza. Paris, 1963.
Phil 3845.3 Zac, Sylvain. La morale de Spinoza. Paris, 1959.
Phil 3845.3.2 Zac, Sylvain. La morale de Spinoza. 2. éd. Paris, 1966.
Phil 3845.3.10 Zac, Sylvain. Spinoza et l'interpretation de l'écriture. Paris, 1965.
Phil 4080.3.127 Zacchi, Angelo. Il nuovo idealismo italiano di Benedetto Croce. 2a ed. Roma, 1925.
Phil 8605.3.5 Zacchi, P.A. L'uomo. Roma, 1921. 2v.
Phil 930.7.55 Zach, E. von. Einige Verbesserungen zu Forke's Geschichte der chinesischen Philosophie. Batavia, 1939.
Phil 930.7.50 Zach, E. von. Weitere Verbesserungen zu Forke's Geschichte der chinesischen Philosophie. Batavia, 1938.
Phil 8400.32 Zadachi i metody izucheniia iskusstv. (Leningrad. Gosudarstvennyi Institut Istorii Iskusstv.) Peterburg, 1924.
Phil 2725.2.125 Zadei, Guido. Il pensiero socio-politico di Lamennais. Napoli, 1969.
Phil 1195.16 Zadro, Attilio. Ricerche sul linguaggio e sulla logica del sofista. Padova, 1961.
Phil 525.210 Zaehner, R.C. Hindu and Muslim mysticism. London, 1960.
Phil 200.9 Zafiropulo, J. La philosophie effective. Paris, 1931.
Phil 200.17.5 Zafiropulo, Jean. Appollon et Dionysos. Paris, 1961.
Phil 200.17 Zafiropulo, Jean. Vox Zenanias. Paris, 1958.
Phil 270.150 Zagadka budushchego. (Komarov, Viktor N.) Moskva, 1971.
Phil 5585.234 Zagadka chelovecheskogo Ia. (Mikhailov, Feliks T.) Moskva, 1964.
Phil 4803.130.30 Zagadnienia i Kierunki filozofii. (Ajdukiewicz, Kazimierz.) W Krakowie, 1949.
VPhil 5250.81 Zagadnienia psychologii myślenia. Wyd. 1. (Kozielecki, Józef.) Warszawa, 1966.
Phil 5257.30 Zagadnienia psychologji. (Radziwillowicz, P.) Kraków, 1911?
Phil 818.38 Zagadnienia historii filozofii. (Swieżawski, Stefan.) Warszawa, 1966.
Phil 5465.208 Zagadnienie psychologii twórezoju technivzncj. (Talejko, Eugeniusz.) Poznań, 1971.
Phil 6975.5.2 Zaglul, Antonio. Mis quinientos locos; memorias del director de un manicomio. 2. ed. Santo Domingo, 1966.
Phil 35.50 Zagreb. Univerzitet. Psihologijski Institut. Acta Instituti psychologici Universitatis Zagra iensis. 1,1964+
Phil 5403.4.10 Zahada štěsti. (Lindner, Gustav.) Praha, 1931.
Phil 3549.10.55 Zahl und Gesichte. (Kassner, Rudolf.) Wiesbaden, 1956.
Phil 3450.33.15 Zahl und Raum. (Stroeker, E.) Bonn, 1953.
Phil 8715.1 Zahm, John Augustine. Bible, science and faith. Baltimore, 1895.
Phil 8715.1.10 Zahm, John Augustine. The Catholic church and modern science. Notre Dame, Ind., 1886.
Phil 3640.370 Zahn, L. Friedrich Nietzsche. Düsseldorf, 1950.
Phil 4809.894.1 Zahradmk, Vincenc. Filosofické spisy. Praha, 1907-18. 3v.
Phil 5068.100 Zaichenko, Georgii A. K voprosu o kritike sovremennogo angliiskogo pozitivizma. Khar'kov, 1961.
Phil 310.655 Zajačeranovič, Gligorije. Analiza i sinteza u okviru dijalektike Hegela i Marksa. Beograd, 1966.
Phil 310.655.5 Zajačeranovič, Gligorije. Dijalektika ljudskog sveta. Novi Sad, 1969.
Phil 5835.10 Zajonc, Robert Boleslaw. Animal social psychology. N.Y., 1969.
Phil 310.355 Zakharov, F.I. Dialekticheskii materializm i nekotorye voprosy darvinizma. Moskva, 1961.
Phil 25.144 Zakład historii filozofii staroźytnej i srednoiwiecznej materiały i studia. (Polska Akademia Nauk.) Wrocław. 3-11,1964-1969//
Phil 5068.54 Základní otázky filosofie logického pozitivismu. (Ruml, Vladimir.) Praha, 1962.
Phil 5066.262 Základy infinitezimálnej logiky a jej axiómy. (Ciger, Juraj.) Bratislava, 1949.
Phil 8422.17.5 Základy obecné teorie umění. (Volek, Jaroslav.) Praha, 1968.
Phil 5250.25 Základy vědeckého systému psychologie. (Krejči, F.V.) Praha, 1929.
Phil 8414.13 Základy vědy o umění, se zvláštním zřením k vědeckému studiu hudby. (Novak, Mirko.) Praha, 1928.
Phil 310.662 Zakon edinstva i bor'by protivopolozhnostei. (Dudel', Savva N.) Moskva, 1967.
Phil 5068.96 Zakon edinstva i bor'by protivopolzhnostei. (Reintel'dt, Boris K.) Ioshkar-Ola, 1969.
Phil 5041.89 Zakon iskheichennogo tret'ego. (Babaiants, M.S.) Moskva, 1962.

Phil 310.265 Zakon kak filosofskaia kategoriia. (Tulenov, Z.) Alma-Ata, 1959.

Phil 310.5.3 Zakon otritsaniia otritsaniia. (Vorob'ev, M.F.) Moskva, 1958.

Phil 4803.454.80 Zakon tvoreniia. (Gennadii, abbot.) Buenos Aires, 1956.

Phil 352.12 Zakony dialektiki, zakony poznaniia. (Vakhtomin, Nikolai K.) Moskva, 1966.

Phil 310.65 Zakony materialisticheskoi dialektiki. (Dudel, S.P.) Moskva, 1958.

Phil 310.510 Zakony myshleniia. (Akademiia Nauk SSSR. Institut Filosofii.) Moskva, 1962.

Phil 5040.28 Zakony myshleniia v formal'noi i dialketicheskoi logike. (Astat'ev, Vsevdod K.) L'vov, 1968.

Phil 337.38 Zakony v sisteme naukhnogo znaniia. (Golovanov, Viacheslaw N.) Moskva, 1970.

Phil 3507.7 Zallinger, J.A. Disquisitionum philosophiae Kantianae. v.1-2. Augustae Vindelicorum, 1799.

Phil 35.18 Zalmoxis. Paris.

Phil 7080.43 Zambeccari, G. Il sonne e la vigilia. Firenze, 1928.

Phil 4060.1.87 Zamboni, G. Il valore scientifico del positivismo di Roberto Ardigö. Verona, 1921.

Phil 4326.1 Zambrano, M. Pensamiento y poesía en la vida española. México, 1939.

Phil 4376.2 Zambrano, Maria. España, sueño y verdad. Barcelona, 1965.

Phil 4987.53.30 Zambrano, María. Hacia un saber sobre el alma. Buenos Aires, 1950.

Phil 8520.42 Zampetti, Pier L. Il problema della giustizia nel protestantesimo tedesco contemporaneo. Milano, 1962.

Phil 4080.3.129 Zanacchi, G. L'intuizione di Benedetto Croce. Palermo, 1925.

Phil 6051.18 Zancing, Julius. Twentieth century guide to palmistry. Chicago, n.d.

Phil 6980.794 Zander, A.F. Role relations in the mental health professions. Ann Arbor, 1957.

Phil 6335.5 Zander, R. Vom Nervensystem. 3. Aufl. Leipzig, 1918.

Phil 6135.8 Zaneiwski, R. Les théories des milieux et la pédagogie mesologique. Tournai, 1952.

Phil 1750.102 Zaner, R.M. The problem of embodiment. The Hague, 1964.

Phil 583.16 Zaner, Richard M. The way of phenomenology. N.Y., 1970.

Phil 8850.2 Zangenberg, Therese. Aesthetische Gesichtspunkte in der englischen Ethik des 18. Jahrhunderts. Langensalza, 1918.

Phil 3507.2 Zango, F. Über das Fundament der Ethik. Leipzig, 1872.

Phil 2262.95 Zani, Lucio. L'etica di Lord Shaftesbury. Milano, 1954.

Phil 200.20 Zanstra, H. The construction of reality; lectures on the philosophy on science. N.Y., 1962.

Phil 1630.2 Zanta, Léontine. La renaissance du stoicisme au XVIe siècle. Paris, 1914.

Phil 900.25 Západ a východ; filosofia úvahy z cest. (Rádl, Emanuel.) Praze, 1925.

Phil 5265.3F Zapan, Georg. Übbarkeit verschiedener Aufgaben. München, 1932.

Phil 8980.873 Zapovedi tvoei zhizni. Moskva, 1963.

Phil 200.19 Zaragüela Bengoechea, J. Los veinte lemas que el cultivado en los cincuenta. Madrid, 1958.

Phil 1530.10 Zaragüeta Bengoechea, Juan. Una introducción moderna a la filosofía escolástica. Granada, 1946.

Phil 110.5 Zaragueta Bengoechea, Juan. Vocabulario filosófico. Madrid, 1955.

Phil 3640.302 Zarathustra-Commentar. (Naumann, Gustav.) Leipzig, 1899-1901. 4v.

Phil 3640.87.7 Zarathustra-Predigten. (Kalthoff, A.) Jena, 1908.

Phil 3640.163.2 Zarathustrakommentar. 2. Aufl. (Weichelt, Hans.) Leipzig, 1922.

Phil 200.7 Zarcone, O. Il genio dell'uomo. 2a ed. Palermo, 1850.

Phil 3625.1.150 Zarek, O. Moses Mendelssohn. Amsterdam, 1936.

Phil 4115.82 Zarelli, T. Il sistema filosofico di V. Gioberti. Paris, 1848.

Phil 8587.32.109 Zari, A. Frederico von Hügel. Pinerolo, 1935.

Phil 930.67 Zarozhdenie obshchestvenno-politicheskoi i filosofskoi mysli v kitae. (Bykov, Fedor S.) Moskva, 1966.

Phil 8715.2 Zart, G. Bibel und Naturwissenschaft. Berlin, 1878.

Phil 3025.1 Zart, G. Einfluss der englischen Philosophen...deutschen Philosophen. Berlin, 1881.

VPhil 1135.191 Zarys driejów mysli politycznej staroźytnosii. Wyd. 1. (Kornatowski, Wiktor.) Warsawa, 1968.

Phil 811.17 Zarys historii filozofii. (Legowicz, J.) Warszawa, 1964.

Phil 807.17.2 Zarys historii filozofii sredniowiecznej. (Heinrich, W.) Warszawa, 1963.

Phil 807.17 Zarys historji filozofji. (Heinrich, W.) Warszawa, 1925-30.

Phil 181.152 Zašto. (Grlić, Danko.) Zagreb, 1968.

Phil 4803.592.30 Zatracone ściezki, zagubione sľady. Wyd. 1. (Mysľakowski, Zygmunt.) Warszawa, 1967.

Phil 4235.1.95 Zavattari, E. La visione della vita...Telesio. Torino, 1923.

Phil 5590.556 Zawadski, Bohdan. Wstęp do seorii osobowosci. Wyd. 1. Warszawa, 1970.

Phil 672.160 Zawirski, Zygmunt. L'évolution de la notion du temps. Cracovie, 1936.

Phil 3120.8.140 Zawischa, E. Das Rätsel und sein Meister Franz Brentano. n.p., 1961.

Phil 3549.28.30 Zaworte, Neimworte, Aphorismen. 1. Aufl. (Kudszus, Hans.) Frankfurt, 1970.

Phil 575.147.80 Zaza, N. Étude critique de la notion d'engagement chez E. Mounier. Genève, 1955.

Phil 5592.140 Zazzo, René. Manuel pour l'examen psychologique de l'enfant. Neuchâtel, 1960.

Phil 1825.2 Zazzo, René. Psychologues et psychologies et psychologies d'Amérique. Paris, 1942.

Phil 5400.107 Zazzo, Revné. Le devenir de l'intelligence. Paris, 1946.

Phil 3450.9.80 Zbinden, H. Ein Künder neuer Lebenswege...R.M. Holzapfel. Jena, 1923.

Phil 8900.9 Zdotusskii, Igor P. Faust i fiziki. Moskva, 1968.

Phil 9430.36 Zdziechowski, M. Pessymizm romantyzm a podstawy chrześcijańitwa. v.1-2. Krakow, 1915.

Phil 4957.50 Zea, Leopoldo. América como conciencia. México, 1953.

Phil 4957.805 Zea, Leopoldo. Antología de la filosofía americana contemporánea. México, 1968.

Phil 1750.774 Zea, Leopoldo. La cultura y el hombre de nuestros días. México, 1959.

Phil 825.5 Zea, Leopoldo. Ensayos sobre filosofía en la historia. Mexico, 1948.

Phil 4957.810 Zea, Leopoldo. La filosofía americana como filosofia sin más. 1. ed. México, 1969.

Phil 4959.230.10 Zea, Leopoldo. La filosofía como compromiso, y otros ensayos. 1. ed. México, 1952.

Phil 4959.230.5 Zea, Leopoldo. La filosofía en México. v.1-2. Mexico, 1955.

Phil 4959.230.2 Zea, Leopoldo. El positivismo en México. 2. ed. México, 1953.

Phil 4829.867.80 Zečević, Seraphinus. Francisci Veber theoria de persona; internum drama philosophi sloveni. Montréal, 1954.

Phil 5204.22.2 Zeddies, Adolf. Worterbuch der Psychologie. 2. Aufl. Dortmund, 1948.

Phil 8877.84 Zedekunst. (Coornhert, D.V.) Leiden, 1942.

Phil 7150.10 De zedelijke waardeering den zelfmoord. (Hertog, Mattheus M.) 's Gravenhage, 1913.

Phil 8882.44 Zedenleer. (Hoekstra, S.) Amsterdam, 1894. 3v.

Phil 3120.24.80 Zee, Teartse van der. Eat oer it libben fan Prof. Dr. Tj. de Boer, 1866-1942. Ljouwert, 1965.

Phil 9290.3 Zeemans handboek. (Martinet, J.F.) Amsterdam, 1781.

Phil 5643.31 Zehender, W. Über optische Täuschung. Leipzig, 1902.

Phil 2880.8.185 Zehm, Günter Albrecht. Historische Vernunft und direkte Aktion. Stuttgart, 1964.

Phil 3705.1.80 Zehme, Berthold. Jakob Hermann Abereit. Inaug. Diss. Lindau, 1920.

Phil 306.2.2 Zehnder, Ludwig. Das Leben im Weltall. Tübingen, 1910.

Phil 200.11 Zehnder, M. Universe and reality. Toronto, 1929.

Phil 337.12 Zeichen, das Fundamente des Wissens. (Gätschenberger, R.) Stuttgart, 1932.

Phil 6049.61 Zeichen des Schicksals im Bild der Hand. (Mangoldt, Ursula von.) Olten, 1961.

Phil 5520.465 Zeichen und Wirklichkeit. (Schmidt, Franz.) Stuttgart, 1966.

Phil 6060.92 Die Zeichensprache von Schrift und Traum. (Vetter, August.) Freiburg, 1970.

Phil 3552.442 Zeichensysteme zur wissenschaftlichen Darstellung. (Schnelle, H.) Stuttgart, 1962.

Phil 6980.365 Zeichnungen und Gemälde der Geisteskranken. (Jakab, Irene.) Budapest, 1956.

Phil 6335.20 Zeigarnik, B.V. Patologiia myshleniia. Moskva, 1962.

Phil 8900.1 Zeigler, T. Sittliches Sein und sittliches Werden. 2. Aufl. Strassburg, 1890.

Phil 8900.1.5 Zeigler, T. Social ethics. London, 1892.

Phil 3120.2.125 Zeil, Wilhelm. Bolzano und die Sorben. Bautzen, 1967.

Phil 8426.2 Zeising, Adolf. Asthetische Forschungen. Frankfurt, 1855.

Phil 5066.75 Zeisler, E.B. Foundations of logic and math. 1. ed. Chicago, 1955- 3v.

Phil 672.178 Die Zeit. 1. Aufl. (Conrad-Martius, H.) München, 1954.

Phil 8876.64 Zeit- und Lebensfragen aus dem Gebiete der Moral. (Biedermann, Karl.) Breslau, 1899.

Phil 3494.19.10 Die Zeit- und Raumlehre Kants. (Marcus, Ernst.) München, 1927.

Phil 8575.16 Die Zeit Jesu. Freiburg, 1970.

Phil 8598.77 Zeit und Ewigkeit. (Schmidt, H.W.) Gutersloh, 1927.

Phil 1504.17 Zeit und Ewigkeit nach Thomas von Aquino. v.17, pt.1. (Beemelmans, F.) Münster, 1914.

Phil 2475.1.75 Zeit und Freiheit. (Bergson, Henri.) Jena, 1920.

Phil 6317.36 Die Zeit und ihre Neurose.ien, 1956 (Hoff, Hans.)

Phil 672.227 Zeit und Zeiten. (Nebel, Gerhard.) Stuttgart, 1965.

Phil 8520.65 Das Zeitalter der Ausklärung. (Philipp, Wolfgang.) Bremen, 1963.

Phil 3640.422 Zeitalter der Feste. (Noll, B.) Bonn, 1947.

Phil 672.146 Zeitbezug und Sprache. (Kaschmieder, E.) Berlin, 1929.

Phil 1707.26 Der Zeitgeist. (Herzberg, G.) Meisenheim, 1960.

Htn Phil 6315.2.76* Zeitgemässes über Krieg und Tod. (Freud, Sigmund.) Leipzig, 1924.

Phil 3640.65 Zeitgemässes und Unzeitgemässes. (Nietzsche, Friedrich.) Frankfurt, 1956.

Phil 5041.63 Die zeitgenossischen Denkmethoden. (Bochenski, I. Mario.) München, 1954.

Phil 5041.87 Die zeitgenossischen Denkmethoden. 2. Aufl. (Bocheński, Innocentius M.) Bern, 1959.

Phil 2885.110 Zeitler, Julius. Die Kunstphilosophie von H.A. Taine. Leipzig, 1901.

Phil 3640.81 Zeitler, Julius. Nietzsches Asthetik. Leipzig, 1900.

Phil 186.42 Zeitliches und Zeitloses. (Lasson, Adolf.) Leipzig, 1890.

Phil 35.7 Zeitschrift für angewandte Psychologie. Leipzig. 1-66,1908-1944 54v.

Phil 35.7.5 Zeitschrift für angewandte Psychologie. Beihefte. Leipzig. 1-93,1911-1948 24v.

Phil 35.30 Zeitschrift für diagnostische Psychologie und Persönlichkeitsforschung. Bern. 2-6,1954-1958 5v.

Phil 35.30.2 Zeitschrift für diagnostische Psychologie und Persönlichkeitsforschung. Beiheft. n.p., n.d.

Phil 35.9.5 Zeitschrift für die gesamte Neurologie und Psychiatrie. Berlin, 1910.

Phil 35.9 Zeitschrift für die gesamte Neurologie und Psychiatrie. Berlin, 1910.

Phil 35.13 Zeitschrift für exacte Philosophie. Leipzig. 1-20,1861-1896 15v.

Phil 35.25 Zeitschrift für experimentelle und angewandte Psychologie. Göttingen. 1,1853+ 14v.

Phil 35.17 Zeitschrift für Hypnotismus, Psychotherapie. Leipzig. 1-10,1892-1902 10v.

Phil 18.8 Zeitschrift für individual Psychologie. Continued as internationale Zeitschrift für individual Psychologie. Leipzig. 1-20,1914-1951 14v.

Phil 35.15 Zeitschrift für Menschenkunde. Heidelberg. 3-14,1927-1939 8v.

Phil 35.35 Zeitschrift für Parapsychologie und Grenzgebiete der Psychologie. Bern. 1,1957+ 7v.

Phil 35.8 Zeitschrift für Patho-Psychology. Leipzig. 1-2,1912-1914 2v.

Phil 35.1 Zeitschrift für Philosophie. Bonn. 1-165 77v.

Phil 35.12 Zeitschrift für Philosophie und Pädogogik. Langensalza. 1895-1914 21v.

Phil 35.1.2 Zeitschrift für Philosophie und philosophische Kritik. Engänzungsheft. Leipzig. 1-2,1909-1910 2v.

Phil 35.1.5 Zeitschrift für Philosophie und philosophische Kritik. Register. Leipzig. 1914

Phil 35.1.15 Zeitschrift für Philosophie und philosophische Kritik. Verzeichniss der Abhundlungen. Leipzig. 1892

Phil 3245.25 Zeitschrift für Philosophie und speculative Theologie. (Fichte, Immanuel Hermann.) Bonn, 1937-56. 8v.

Phil 35.19 Zeitschrift für philosophische Forschung. Reutlingen. 1,1946+ 23v.

Phil 35.19.3 Zeitschrift für philosophische Forschung. Beihefte. Meisenheim. 1,1951+ 15v.

Phil 35.19.2 Zeitschrift für philosophische Forschung. Sach-, Namen und Autoren Register. 1,1946+ 2v.

Phil 35.19.5 Zeitschrift für philosophische Forschung. Sonderheft. Wurzach.

Phil 35.5 Zeitschrift für positivistische Philosophie. Berlin. 1-2,1913-1914 2v.

Phil 35.20 Zeitschrift für Psychoanalyse. Berlin. 1949-1950

Phil 35.6.5 — Zeitschrift für Psychologie. Leipzig. 1-24 13v.
Phil 35.6.2 — Zeitschrift für Psychologie. Leipzig. 40-175 86v.
Phil 35.6.2.5 — Zeitschrift für Psychologie. Register, 51-150. Leipzig, 1918-1943. 4v.
Phil 35.6 — Zeitschrift für Psychologie und Philosophie der Sinnesorgane. Leipzig. 1-40 40v.
Phil 35.16 — Zeitschrift für Psychotherapie. Stuttgart. 1-8,1909-1924 8v.
Phil 35.3 — Zeitschrift für Religionspsychologie. Halle. 1-6 6v.
Phil 65.1 — Zeitschrift für sexual Wissenschaft. Bonn. 1-9 3v.
Phil 35.6.3 — Zeitschrift für Sinnesphysiologie. Leipzig. 41-70 20v.
Phil 35.4 — Zeitschrift für Timmanante Philosophie. Berlin, 1896-99. 4v.
Phil 5585.1.5 — Der Zeitsinn nach Versuchen. (Vierordt, Karl.) Tübingen, 1868.
Phil 4967.5.80 — Zelada C., Alberto. El pensamiento de Guillermo Francovich. Sucre, 1966.
Phil 575.270 — Zelbeelden zelfideaal. (Werff, Jacobus Johannes van der.) Assen, 1965.
Phil 8426.11 — Zelenov, L.A. Protsess esteticheskogo otrazheniia. Moskva, 1969.
Phil 310.670 — Zelený, Jindřich. O historickén materialismu. Vyd. 1. V Praze, 1960.
Phil 6128.81 — Zelfbehoud, aanpassing en cultuur. (Stalpers, Jacobus Antonius.) Arnhem, 1964.
Phil 5590.502 — Zelfbeoordelingen. (Aarts, Josephus Franciscus Maria Carolus.) Tilburg, 1964.
Phil 7150.100 — Het zelfmoordvraagstuk. (Speijer, Nico.) Arnhem, 1969.
Phil 3270.17.45 — Zelfvervreemding en zelfzijn. (Flam, Leopold.) Amsterdam, 1966.
Phil 4809.895.11 — Pamphlet vol. Želivan, Pavel. Původ vesmíru; and Původ života. 2 pam.
Phil 310.759 — Zel'kina, Ol'ga S. Sistemno-strukturnyi analiz osnovnykh kategorii dialektilu. Saratov, 1970.
Phil 3245.80 — Zeller, E. Antwort an...Dr. Immanuel Hermann Fichte. Berlin, 1876.
Phil 200.2.15 — Zeller, E. E. Zellers kleine Schriften, unter Mitwirking. Berlin, 1910. 3v.
Phil 200.2 — Zeller, E. Philosophische Aufsätze. Leipzig, 1887.
Phil 5465.25 — Zeller, E. Über den Einfluss des Gefühls auf die Thätigkeit der Phantasie. Tübingen, 1900.
Phil 200.2.5 — Zeller, E. Vorträge und Abhandlungen geschichtlichen Inhalts. Leipzig, 1865.
Phil 200.2.6 — Zeller, E. Vorträge und Abhandlungen Geschichtlichen Inhalts. 1. Aufl. Leipzig, 1875.
Phil 200.2.7 — Zeller, E. Vorträge und Abhandlungen Geschichtlichen Inhalts. 2. Aufl. Leipzig, 1877.
Phil 200.2.8 — Zeller, E. Vorträge und Abhandlungen Geschichtlichen Inhalts. 3. Aufl. Leipzig, 1884.
Phil 3850.1.93 — Zeller, Eduard. David Friedrich Strauss. London, 1874.
Phil 3850.1.91 — Zeller, Eduard. David Friedrich Strauss. 2. Aufl. Bonn, 1874.
Phil 3940.1.85 — Zeller, Eduard. Erinnerungen eines Neunzigjährigen. Stuttgart, 1908.
Phil 1130.2.17 — Zeller, Eduard. La filosofia dei Greci nel suo sviluppo storico. Firenze, 193-. 2v.
Phil 3025.2 — Zeller, Eduard. Geschichte der deutschen Philosophie. München, 1873.
Phil 3025.2.2 — Zeller, Eduard. Geschichte der deutschen Philosophie seit Liebniz. 2. Aufl. München, 1875.
Phil 1130.3 — Zeller, Eduard. Grundriss der Geschichte der griechischen Philosophie. Leipzig, 1883.
Phil 1130.6.9 — Zeller, Eduard. Grundriss der Geschichte der griechischen Philosophie. Leipzig, 1911.
Phil 1130.3.8 — Zeller, Eduard. Grundriss der Geschichte der griechischen Philosophie. 8th ed. Leipzig, 1907.
Phil 1130.3.9 — Zeller, Eduard. Grundriss der Geschichte der griechischen Philosophie. 9th ed. Leipzig, 1909.
Phil 1130.3.13 — Zeller, Eduard. Grundriss der Geschichte der griechischen Philosophie. 13e Aufl. Leipzig, 1928.
Phil 1135.5 — Zeller, Eduard. A history of eclecticism in Greek philosophy. London, 1883.
Phil 1130.9 — Zeller, Eduard. History of eclecticism in Greek philosophy. London, 1883.
Phil 1130.4A — Zeller, Eduard. History of Greek philosophy. London, 1881. 1v.
Phil 1130.5.2 — Zeller, Eduard. Outlines of history of Greek philosophy. London, 1886.
Phil 1130.5.5 — Zeller, Eduard. Outlines of history of Greek philosophy. London, 1895.
Phil 1130.5.9 — Zeller, Eduard. Outlines of history of Greek philosophy. London, 1922.
Phil 1130.5 — Zeller, Eduard. Outlines of history of Greek philosophy. N.Y., 1886.
Phil 1130.5.4 — Zeller, Eduard. Outlines of history of Greek philosophy. N.Y., 1889.
Phil 1130.5.3 — Zeller, Eduard. Outlines of history of Greek philosophy. N.Y., 1890.
Phil 1130.5.17 — Zeller, Eduard. Outlines of history of Greek philosophy. 13th ed. London, 1931.
Phil 1130.5.15 — Zeller, Eduard. Outlines of history of Greek philosophy. 13th ed. London, 1931.
Phil 1130.2 — Zeller, Eduard. Die Philosophie der Griechen. Leipzig, 1869-79. 3v.
Phil 1130.1 — Zeller, Eduard. Die Philosophie der Griechen. Tubingen, 1856-68. 5v.
Phil 1130.2.6 — Zeller, Eduard. Die Philosophie der Griechen. Register. Leipzig, 1882.
Phil 1130.2.11 — Zeller, Eduard. Die Philosophie der Griechen. v. 1,3-6. Leipzig, 1892. 5v.
Phil 1130.2.5 — Zeller, Eduard. Die Philosophie der Griechen. v. 1-2,4-5. Leipzig, 1876-81. 4v.
Phil 1130.2.9 — Zeller, Eduard. Die Philosophie der Griechen. v.2. Leipzig, 1892.
Phil 1130.2.15 — Zeller, Eduard. Die Philosophie der Griechen. 6e Aufl. Leipzig, 1919-23. 6v.
Phil 1130.7 — Zeller, Eduard. Plato and the older academy. Leipzig, 1876.
Phil 1130.7.5 — Zeller, Eduard. Plato and the older academy. London, 1888.
Phil 1130.6 — Zeller, Eduard. Socrates and the Socratic schools. London, 1868.
Phil 1130.6.5 — Zeller, Eduard. Socrates and the Socratic schools. London, 1877.
Phil 1130.6.8 — Zeller, Eduard. Socrates and the Socratic schools. 3rd ed. London, 1885.

Phil 1130.8A — Zeller, Eduard. The Stoics, Epicureans, and Sceptics. London, 1870.
Phil 1130.8.3 — Zeller, Eduard. The Stoics, Epicureans, and Sceptics. London, 1880.
Phil 1130.8.5 — Zeller, Eduard. The Stoics, Epicureans, and Sceptics. London, 1892.
Phil 3850.1.94 — Zeller, Eduard. Strauss and Renan. London, 1866.
Phil 3801.895A — Zeltner, Hermann. Schelling. Stuttgart, 1954.
Phil 1725.2 — Zema, Demetrius. The thoughtlessness of modern thought. N.Y., 1934.
Phil 8220.5 — Zemlianova, L.M. Sovremennaia estetika v SShA. Moskva, 1966.
Phil 8980.895 — Zemlianskii, D.S. U istokov zhiznennogo puti. Moskva, 1962.
Phil 930.68 — Zempliner, Artur. Cínská filosofie v novověké evropské filosofii. Praha, 1966.
Phil 1800.6 — Zen and American thought. (Ames, Van Meter.) Honolulu, 1962.
Phil 5650.54 — Zenatti, Arlette. Le développement génétique de la perception musicale. Paris, 1969.
Phil 3210.40 — Zend-Avesta. (Fechner, G.T.) Hamburg, 1906.
Phil 200.4 — Zenetti, Jacob. Einfluss der Philosophie auf das Leben. München, 1829.
Phil 930.27 — Zenker, E.V. Geschichte der chinesischen Philosophie. Reichenberg, 1926-27. 2v.
Phil 8605.8 — Zen'kovskii, V.V. Apologetika. 2. izd. Parizhe, 195-? 3 pam.
Phil 8900.7 — Zen'kovskii, V.V. Dar svobody. Paris, 193-?
Phil 4710.85.5 — Zen'kovskii, V.V. A history of Russian philosophy. N.Y., 1953. 2v.
Phil 4710.85 — Zen'kovskii, V.V. Istoriia russkoi filosofii. Paris, 1949. 2v.
Phil 9495.155.5 — Zenkovskii, V.V. Na poroge zrelosti. 2. izd. Parizh, 1955.
Phil 4710.36 — Zen'kovskii, V.V. O mnimom materializme russkoi nauki i filosofii. Miunkhen, 1956.
Phil 8605.10 — Zen'kovskii, V.V. Osnovy khristianskoi filosofii. Frankfurt, 1960.
Phil 4710.70.10 — Zen'kovskii, V.V. Pravoslavie i kul'tura. Berlin, 1923.
Phil 4710.70.15 — Zen'kovskii, V.V. Russian thinkers and Europe. Ann Arbor, 1953.
Phil 4710.70 — Zen'kovskii, V.V. Russkie mysliteli i Evropa. Paris, 1926.
Phil 4710.70.2 — Zen'kovskii, V.V. Russkie mysliteli i Evropa. Izd. 2. Paris, 1955.
Phil 4756.1.49 — Zen'kovskii, V.V. Sbornik pamiati Semena L. Franka. Miunkhen, 1954.
Phil 5090.3.80 — Zeno, Father. John Henry Newman. Leiden, 1957.
Phil 35.11 — Zentralblatt für Psychoanalyse. Wiesbaden. 1-4,1910-1914 4v.
Phil 35.10 — Zentralblatt für Psychologie und...Pädagogik. Würzberg. 1914-1915
Phil 5258.109 — Zentralistische Organisation und Seelenleben. (Schein, Josef.) München, 1931. 2v.
Phil 5599.39 — Zeppelin, Ilka Sigried von. Die Variablen der Holtzman Inkblot Technique in ihrer Beziehung zur Introversion und Extraversion. Bern, 1966.
Phil 4025.5 — Zeppi, Stelio. Il problema del dialogo nel pensiero italiano contemporaneo. Firenze, 1960.
Phil 9245.27 — Zerbst, Max. Die Philosophie der Freude. Leipzig, 191-.
Phil 4025.1 — Zerella, F. L'eclettisma francese e la cultura filosofica meridionale. 1. ed. Roma, 1953.
Phil 4825.14 — Zeremski, Sava D. Essays aus der südslawischen Philosophie. Novisad, 1939.
Phil 8968.15 — Zerfall des christlichen Ethos im XIX. Jahrhundert. (Steinbüchel, T.) Frankfurt, 1951.
Phil 8408.29 — Zergliederung der Schönheit, die schwankendenBegriffe von dem geschmack Festzusetzen. (Hogarth, William.) Berlin, 1754.
Phil 200.15.5 — Zerle, Herbert. Die Kunst des Kritisieren. Berlin, 1957.
Phil 180.2.15 — The Zermatt dialogues. (Fawcett, E.D.) London, 1931.
Phil 3011.6 — Die Zerstörung der Vernunft. (Lukács, G.) Berlin, 1954.
Htn Phil 3480.19.5* — Zerstreute Aufsätze. (Kant, Immanuel.) Frankfurt, 1793.
Phil 341.37 — Der zerstückelte Gott. (Klein, Martin.) München, 1967.
Phil 5252.5 — Zetemata dianoetika. (Martin, T.) Liverpool, 1821.
Phil 8605.4 — Zethraeus, A.G. Isätalät-ordens (sanningssökarnes) vishetslära. Stockholm, 1900.
Phil 3925.16.30 — Zettel. (Wittgenstein, Ludwig.) Oxford, 1967.
Phil 6315.62 — Zetzel, Elizabeth R. The capacity for emotional growth. London, 1970.
Phil 974.3.124 — Zeylmans von Emmichoven, F.W. Rudolf Steiner. Zeist, 1960.
Phil 2880.8.255 — Zhan-Pol Sartr i ekzistentsializm. (Kuznetsov, Vitalii N.) Moskva, 1969.
Phil 5235.2 — Zharikbaev, Kubigul B. Razvitie psikhologicheskoi mysli v Kazakhstane (so vtoroi poloviny XIXlveka i do nashikh dnei . Alma-Ata, 1968.
Phil 4751.1.30 — Zhazhda podlinnago Bytiia. (Arsen'ev, N.S.) Berlin, n.d.
Phil 800.12.10 — Zhdanov, A.A. Vystuplenie na diskussii po knige G.F. Aleksandrova. "Istoriia zapnoevropeiskoi filosofii". Moskva, 1947.
Phil 5265.7 — Zhdanov, D.A. Vozniknovenie abstraktnogo myshleniia. Khar'kov, 1969.
Phil 5520.416 — Zhinkin, N.I. Myshlenie i rech'. Moskva, 1963.
Phil 4756.1.33 — Zhivoe znanie. (Frank, Semen L.) Berlin, 1923.
Phil 6680.8 — Zhivotnyi magnitizm. (Kluge, C.) Sankt Peterberg, 1818.
Phil 4765.1 — Zhizn' i smert'; sbornik pamiatniki N.E. Osipova. (Bem, A.L.) Praga, 1936.
Phil 8980.895.5 — Zhuravkov, M.G. Moral'nyi oblik sovetskogo rabochego. Moskva, 1966.
Phil 8980.895.10 — Zhuravkov, M.G. Nravstvennye printsipy stroitelia kommunizma. Moskva, 1965.
Phil 4805.15 — Zich, Otakar. Lidová přislovi s logického hlediska. Praha, 1956.
Phil 3507.3 — Zickendraht, K. Kants Gedanken über Krieg und Frieden. Tübingen, 1922.
Phil 5754.3 — Zickendraht, K. Der Streit zwischen Erasmus und Luther über die Willensfreiheit. Leipzig, 1909.
Phil 3640.303 — Zickendraht, Karl. Sieben Thesen wider den Nietzsche-Geist. Basel, 193-.
Phil 3428.86 — Ziechner, A. Herbarts Ästhetik. n.p., n.d.
Phil 3507.6 — Ziegeler, E. Kants Sittenlehre in gemeinverständlicher Darstellung. Leipzig, 1919.
Phil 8426.3 — Ziegenfuss, W. Die phänomenologische Ästhetik nach Grundsätzen und bisherigen Ergebnissen kritisch Dargestellt. Borna, 1927.

Phil 8735.20.5 — Ziegenhagen, F.H. Lehre vom richtigen Verhältniss zu den Schöpfungswerken und die durch öffentliche Einführung derselben allein zu bewürkende allgemeine Menschenbeglückung. Braunschweig, 1799.

Phil 5835.1.3 — Ziegler, H.E. Der Begriff des Instinktes einst und jetzt. 3. Aufl. Jena, 1920.

Phil 5525.33 — Ziegler, J. Das Komische. Leipzig, 1900.

Phil 510.15 — Ziegler, J.H. Die wahre Einheit von Religion und Wissenschaft. Zürich, 1904.

Phil 306.1 — Ziegler, Johann H. Die Struktur der Materie und das Welträtsel. Bern, 1908.

Phil 9075.80 — Ziegler, Josef Georg. Vom Gesetz zum Gewissen. Freiburg, 1968.

Phil 165.120 — Ziegler, Klaus. Wesen und Wirklichkeit des Menschen. Göttingen, 1957.

Phil 306.3 — Ziegler, Konrat. Weltentstehung in Sage und Wissenschaft. Leipzig, 1925.

Phil 306.3.5 — Ziegler, Konrat. Weltuntergang in Sage und Wissenschaft. Leipzig, 1921.

Phil 3940.2.45 — Ziegler, L. Briefe, 1901-1958. München, 1963.
Phil 3940.2.40 — Ziegler, L. Dienst an der Welt. Darmstadt, 1925.
Phil 200.6.3 — Ziegler, L. Gestaltwandel der Götter. 3. Aufl. Darmstadt, 1922. 2v.

Phil 3940.2.35 — Ziegler, L. Das Lehrgespräch vom Allgemeinen Menschen in Lieben Abenden. Hamburg, 1956.

Phil 3940.2.30 — Ziegler, L. Spätlese eigener Hand. München, 1953.
Phil 8612.32 — Ziegler, L. Vom Tod; essay. Leipzig, 1937.
Phil 623.15 — Ziegler, Leopold. Der abendländische Rationalismus. Jena, 1905.

Phil 3415.92 — Ziegler, Leopold. Das Weltbild Hartmanns. Leipzig, 1910.
Phil 3850.1.87 — Ziegler, T. David Friedrich Strauss. Strassburg, 1908. 2v.

Phil 1145.76 — Ziegler, T. Die Ethik der Griechen und Römer. Bonn, 1886.
Phil 5400.75 — Ziegler, T. Das Gefühl. Stuttgart, 1893.
Phil 5400.75.5 — Ziegler, T. Das Gefühl. 5e Aufl. Berlin, 1912.
Phil 8850.1 — Ziegler, T. Geschichte der Ethik. Bonn, 1881-86. 2v.
Phil 3640.89 — Ziegler, Theobald. Friedrich Nietzsche. Berlin, 1900.
Phil 356.1.5 — Ziehen, T. Erkenntnistheorie...Grundlage. Jena, 1913.
Phil 5545.41 — Ziehen, T. Das Gedächtnis. Berlin, 1908.
Phil 306.4 — Ziehen, T. Grundlagen der Naturphilosophie. Leipzig, 1922.

Phil 6975.1 — Ziehen, T. Psychiatrie. Berlin, 1894.
Phil 356.1 — Ziehen, T. Psychophysiologische Erkenntnistheorie. Jena, 1898.

Phil 5235.1 — Ziehen, T. Über die Beziehungen zwischen Gehirn und Seelenleben. Leipzig, 1902.

Phil 8426.5 — Ziehen, T. Vorlesungen über Ästhetik. Halle, 1923-25. 2v.

Phil 356.1.10 — Ziehen, T. Zum gegenwärtigen Stand der Erkenntnistheorie. Wiesbaden, 1914.

Phil 5265.1.15 — Ziehen, Theodor. Allgemeine Psychologie. Berlin, 1923.
Phil 5265.1.9 — Ziehen, Theodor. Die Grundlagen der Psychologie. v.1-2. Leipzig, 1915.

Phil 5265.1.6 — Ziehen, Theodor. Introduction to physiological psychology. London, 1895.

Phil 5265.1.5 — Ziehen, Theodor. Introduction to physiological psychology. n.p., 1892.

Phil 5265.1 — Ziehen, Theodor. Leitfaden der physiologischen Psychologie. Jena, 1891.

Phil 5265.1.3 — Ziehen, Theodor. Leitfaden der physiologischen Psychologie. Jena, 1908.

Phil 5265.1.2 — Ziehen, Theodor. Leitfaden der physiologischen Psychologie. 3. Aufl. Jena, 1896.

Phil 5265.1.4 — Ziehen, Theodor. Leitfaden der physiologischen Psychologie. 5. Aufl. Jena, 1900.

Phil 5265.1.4.2 — Ziehen, Theodor. Leitfaden der physiologischen Psychologie. 7. Aufl. Jena, 1906.

Phil 5265.1.4.3 — Ziehen, Theodor. Leitfaden der physiologischen Psychologie. 10. Aufl. Jena, 1914.

Phil 5265.1.4.5 — Ziehen, Theodor. Leitfaden der physiologischen Psychologie. 12. Aufl. Jena, 1924.

Phil 6135.3 — Ziehen, Theodore. Über die allgemeinen Beziehungen. Leipzig, 1902.

Phil 3415.86 — Das Ziel des religiösen und wissenschaftlichen Gährung nachgewiesen Hartmann's Pessimismus. (Schwarz, H.) Berlin, 1875.

Phil 284.4.7 — Ziel und Struktur der physikalischen Theorien. (Duhem, P.) Leipzig, 1908.

Phil 298.7 — Ziele und Wege der heutigen Naturphilosophie. (Reichenbach, Hans.) Leipzig, 1931.

Phil 4803.454.85 — Zieleńczyk, Adam. Hoene-Wroński. Warszawa, 1930-?
Phil 525.24 — Zieliński, C. Der Begriff der Mystik. Jena, 1913.
Phil 665.80.10 — Het zielsbegrip in de metaphysische en in de empirische psychologie. (Strasser, Stephan.) Leuven, 1950.

Phil 8900.10 — Ziemba, Zdzisław. Logika deontyczna jako formalizacja rozumowań normalywnych. Wyd. 1. Warszawa, 1969.

Phil 8419.20 — Het zien en genieten van schilderkunst. 4. druk. (Stubbe, Achilles.) Hasselt, 1960.

Phil 8406.11 — Zien en verstaan. (Feltkamp, W.C.) Amsterdam, 1946.
Phil 8050.69 — Het zien van kunst en de kunst van het zien. (Vlaanderen, Andre.) Amsterdam, 1952.

Phil 8426.7 — Ziff, Paul. Philosophic turnings. Ithaca, N.Y., 1966.
Phil 5520.335.2A — Ziff, Paul. Semantic analysis. Ithaca, 1962.
Phil 1535.12 — Zigliara, F.T.M. Summa philosophica in usum scholarum. Lyon, 1884. 3v.

Phil 1535.12.5 — Zigliara, F.T.M. Summa philosophica in usum scholarum. 15. ed. v.3. Paris, 1912.

Phil 310.642 — Ziherl, Boris. Dijalektički i istoriski materijalizam. 2. Izd. Beograd, 1964.

Phil 2750.19.85 — Het zijn als mysterie in de ervaring en het denken van Gabriel Marcel. (Sonsbeeck, Dawiet van.) Bilthoven, 1966.

Phil 3195.10.110 — Zilberis, B. Kant und die Philosophie Drieschs. Inaug. Diss. Vilkaviskis, 1932.

Phil 6315.2.146.5 — Zilboorg, G. Freud - 1956. N.Y., 1956.
Phil 6695.1 — Zilboorg, G. A history of medical psychology. N.Y., 1941.
Phil 6315.2.146 — Zilboorg, G. Sigmund Freud. N.Y., 1951.
Phil 6335.15 — Zilboorg, Gregory. Mind, medicine and man. N.Y., 1943.
Phil 6335.15.5 — Zilboorg, Gregory. Psychoanalysis and religion. N.Y., 1962.

Phil 7150.42 — Zilfmoord. (Kruijt, Cornuijtus Simon.) Assen, 1960.
Phil 7054.31 — Zillah, the child medium. N.Y., 1857.
Phil 8900.4 — Ziller, T. Allgemeine philosophische Ethik. Langensalza, 1880.

Phil 1540.38 — Zilli, José B. Introducción a la psicología de los conimbricenses. Bonn, 1961.

Phil 356.2 — Zilsel, Edgar. Das Anwendungsproblem. Leipzig, 1916.
Phil 5425.39 — Zilsel, Edgar. Die Entstehung des Geniebegriffes. Tübingen, 1926.

Phil 575.56 — Zilsel, Edgar. Die Geniereligion. Wien, 1918.
Phil 5325.48 — Zimbardo, Philip G. The cognitive control of motivation: the consequences of choice and dissonance. Glenville, Ill., 1969.

Phil 4710.150 — Zimin, Petr P. Voprosy psikhologii myshleniia v trudakh klassikov russkoi filosofii XIX v. Tashkent, 1966.
Phil 4060.2.82 — Zimmels, B. Leo Hebraeus, ein jüdischer Philosoph. Breslau, 1886.

Phil 3246.89 — Zimmer, F. Johann Gottlieb Fichte's Religionsphilosophie. Berlin, 1878.

Phil 3450.6.80 — Zimmer, Friedrich. Grundriss der Philosophie nach Friedrich Harms. Tübingen, 1902.

Phil 960.164.5 — Zimmer, H.R. Philosophie und Religion Indiens. Zürich, 1961.

Phil 960.164 — Zimmer, H.R. Philosophies of India. N.Y., 1951.
Phil 974.5 — Zimmer, Heinrich. Der Weg zum Selbst. Zürich, 1944.
Phil 974.5.6 — Zimmer, Heinrich. Der Weg zum Selbst. Zürich, 1954.
Phil 8689.100 — Zimmerman, Paul A. Darwin, evolution, and creation. Saint Louis, 1959.

Phil 3507.4.5 — Zimmerman, R. Kant und die positive Philosophie. Wien, 1874.

Phil 3428.155.15 — Zimmerman, R. Leibnitz und Herbart. Wien, 1849.
Phil 3428.155.10 — Zimmerman, R. Perioden in Herbart's philosophischen Geistesgang. Wien, 1876.

Phil 200.3.5 — Zimmerman, R. Philosophische Propaedeutik. Wien, 1867.
Phil 3428.155.5 — Zimmerman, R. Über den Einfluss der Tonlehre auf Herbart's Philosophie. Wien, 1873.

Phil 3507.4 — Zimmerman, R. Über Kant's Widerlegung des Idealismus von Berkeley. Wien, 1871.

Phil 3428.155 — Zimmerman, R. Über Trendelenburg's Einwürfe gegen Herbarts praktische Ideen. Wien, 1872.

Phil 1540.87 — Zimmermann, Albert. Ontologie oder Metaphysik? Die Diskussion über den Gegenstand der Metaphysik im 13. und 14. Jahrhundert. Habilitationschrift. Leiden, 1965[1966].

Phil 3507.8 — Zimmermann, Heinz. Der Befreier; eine Begegnung mit Kant. München, 1930.

Phil 3120.2.115 — Zimmermann, J. Krug und Bolzano. Sulzbach, 1837.
Phil 9515.3.5 — Zimmermann, J.G. Solitude. Dublin, 1800.
Phil 9515.3.6.5 — Zimmermann, J.G. Solitude. London, 1800.
NEDL Phil 9515.3.6 — Zimmermann, J.G. Solitude. London, 1800-02.
Phil 9515.3.9 — Zimmermann, J.G. Solitude. N.Y., 1813.
Phil 9515.3.8 — Zimmermann, J.G. Solitude. v.1-2. Exeter, 1836.
Htn Phil 9515.3.7.2* — Zimmermann, J.G. Solitude. 1st ed. N.Y., 1801.
Htn Phil 9515.3.7* — Zimmermann, J.G. Solitude. 1st ed. N.Y., 1801.
Phil 9515.3.3 — Zimmermann, J.G. Solitude. 2d ed. London, 1792.
Phil 9515.3 — Zimmermann, J.G. Über die Einsamkeit. Leipzig, 1784-85. 4v.

Phil 200.8 — Zimmermann, K. Die Gemeinschaft der Einsamen. Jena, 1919.
Phil 5402.10 — Zimmermann, O. Die Wonne des Leids. 2e Aufl. Leipzig, 1885.

Phil 8426.4 — Zimmermann, R. Ästhetik. Wien, 1858-65. 2v.
Phil 200.3 — Zimmermann, R. Anthroposophie. Wien, 1882.
Phil 3552.292 — Zimmermann, R. Das Rechtsprinzip bei Leibnitz. Wien, 1852.

Htn Phil 3801.896* — Zimmermann, R. Schelling's Philosophie der Kunst. Wien, 1875.

Phil 2050.182 — Zimmermann, R. Über Hume's empirische Begründung der Moral. Wien, 1884.

Phil 200.3.12 — Zimmermann, R. Was Erwarten wir von der Philosophie? Prag, 1852.

Phil 4829.896.30 — Zimmermann, Stjepan. Religija i život. Zagreb, 1938.
Phil 200.3.7 — Zimmermnn, R. Studien und Kritiken zur Philosophie und Aesthetik. v.1-2. Wien, 1870.

Phil 3808.98 — Zimmern, H. Arthur Schopenhauer. London, 1876.
Phil 3808.164.5 — Zimmern, Helen. Schopenhauer, his life and philosophy. London, 1932.

Phil 5265.6 — Zimny, George. Method in experimental psychology. N.Y., 1961.

Phil 3120.40.35 — De zin van het komische. (Bierens de Haan, J.D.) Leiden, 1930.

Phil 5643.178 — Zinchenko, Vladimir P. Formirovanie zritel'nogo obraza. Moskva, 1969.

Phil 7069.12.98 — Zingaropoli, F. Telepatia e sogno. Napoli, 1912.
Phil 672.131 — Zini, Zino. La doppia maschera dell'universo. Milano, 1914.

Phil 8900.2 — Zini, Zino. Il pentimento e la morale ascentica. Torino, 1902.

Phil 3808.131 — Zini, Zino. Schopenhauer. Milano, 1923.
Phil 8900.8 — Zink, Sidney. The concepts of ethics. N.Y., 1962.
Phil 8612.60 — Zinker, Joseph Chaim. Rosa Lee; motivation and the crisis of dying. Painesville, Ohio, 1966.

Phil 356.5.3 — Zinkernagel, Peter. Conditions for description. London, 1962.

Phil 356.5 — Zinkernagel, Peter. Omverdens problemet. København, 1957.
Phil 8900.5 — Zinninger, E.D. Ethical philosophy and civilization. Los Angeles, 1935.

Phil 5066.170 — Zinov'ev, Aleksandr A. Filosofskie problemy mnogoznachnoi logiki. Moskva, 1960.
Phil 5066.172 — Zinov'ev, Aleksandr A. Kompleksnaia logika. Moskva, 1970.
Phil 5066.212 — Zinov'ev, Aleksandr A. Logika nauki. Moskva, 1971.
Phil 5066.210 — Zinov'ev, Aleksandr A. Logika vyskazyvanii i teoriia vyvoda. Moskva, 1962.

Phil 5066.211 — Zinov'ev, Aleksandr A. Osnovy logicheskoi teorii nauchnykh znanii. Moskva, 1967.

Phil 5066.171 — Zinov'ev, Aleksandr A. Philosophical problems. Dordrecht, 1973.

Phil 3808.200 — Zint, Hans. Schopenhauer als Erlebnis. München, 1954.
Phil 1750.747 — Zinzen, A. Die ontologische Betrachtungsweise. Meisenheim, 1963.

Phil 5520.65 — Zipf, G.K. The psycho-biology of language. Boston, 1935.
Phil 530.20.77 — Zippel, W. Die Mystiker und die deutsche Gesellschaft des 13. und 14. Jahrhunderts. Inaug.-Diss. Düren, 1935.

Phil 5265.5 — Zippert, Erwin. Vom Gleichgewicht der Seele. Ulm, 1958.
Phil 306.5 — Zirm, E.K. Die Welt als Fühlen. Leipzig, 1937.
Phil 3460.80 — Zirngiebl, E. F.H. Jacobis Seben, Dichten und Denken. Wien, 1867.

Phil 3450.5.80 — Zirngiebl, Eberhard. Johannes Huber. Gotha, 1881.
Phil 6035.1 — Zirwes, Ernest. Gesichtsausdruck und Wertraum. Inaug. Diss. Würzburg, 1935.

Phil 8426.8 — Zis', Avner Ia. Iskusstvo i estetika. Moskva, 1967.
Phil 6135.9 — Ziskind, Robert. Viewpoint on mental health; transcripts, 1963-1965. N.Y., 1967.

Phil 6135.5 — Zitex, Edward. A research in report on mental hygiene, brain, exercises, sanitation and foods. New Orleans, La., 1935.

Phil 8980.896.5 — Ziuziukin, Ivan I. Uznaiu cheloveka. Mosva, 1970.
Phil 5871.25 — Ziv, Avner. La vie des enfants en collectivité. Paris, 1965.

Phil 735.274 — Životić, Miladin. Čovek i vrednost. Beograd, 1969.
VPhil 1750.797 — Životić, Miladin. Pragmatizam i savremena filozofija. Beograd, 1966.
VPhil 8404.24 — Životot i umetnosta. (Dimitrov, D.N.) Skopje, 1967.
Phil 4803.555.32 — Złoty dar człowieka. Wyd. 2. (Mankowski, Mieczysław.) Kraków, 1912.
Phil 3640.714 — Zmierzch mies zczaństwa. (Kuczyński, Janusz.) Warszawa, 1967.
Phil 4688.110.34 — Žmogus de Dievo. (Girnius, Juozas.) Chicago? 1964.
Phil 5520.424 — Znaczenie słowa w języku naturalnym. (Grodziński, Eugeniusz.) Warszawa, 1964.
Phil 4803.896.20 — Znamierowski, Czesław Stanisław. Oceny i normy. Warszawa, 1957.
Phil 4803.896.235 — Znaniecki, Florian. Humanizm i poznanie. Warszawa, 1912.
Phil 4803.896.230 — Znaniecki, Florian. Studja nad filozofja wartosci. Warszawa, 1912.
Phil 5535.12 — Znaniia, myshlenie i umstvennoe razvitie. (Ponomarev, Iakov A.) Moskva, 1967.
Phil 338.43 — Znannia i peretvorennia diistnosti. (Hubenko, Volodymer I.) Kyiv, 1968.
Phil 7069.61.20 — Zoar, or The evidence of psychical research concerning survival. (Salter, William Henry.) London, 1961.
Phil 3640.123 — Zoccoli, Ettore G. Federico Nietzsche. Modena, 1898.
Phil 200.13 — Zocher, R. Die philosophische Grundlehre. Tübingen, 1939.
Phil 3450.11.102 — Zocher, Rudolf. Husserls Phänomenologie und Schuppes Logik. München, 1932.
Phil 3507.10 — Zocher, Rudolf. Kants Grundlehre. Erlangen, 1959.
Phil 356.3 — Zocher, Rudolf. Die objektive Geltung Slogik und der Immanenzge Danke. Tübingen, 1925.
Phil 8715.4 — Zocher, Rudolf. Philosophie in Begegnung mit Religion und Wissenschaft. München, 1955.
Phil 821.4 — Zoekers naar wijsheid. (Visser, S.) Goes, 1938.
Phil 3625.1.96 — Zöllner, J.F. Über Moses Mendelssohn's Jerusalem. Berlin, 1784.
Phil 8715.3 — Zöllner, J.F.K. Naturwissenschaft und christliche Offenbarung. Leipzig, 1881.
Phil 7068.79 — Zöllner, J.K.F. Die transcendentale Physik und die sogenannte Philosophie. Leipzig, 1879.
Phil 7068.87.20 — Zöllner. (Massey, C.C.) London, 1887.
Phil 6520.7.9 — Zoepf, L. Die Mystikerin Margaretha Ebner. Leipzig, 1914.
Phil 8612.58.1 — Zoepfl, Helmut. Bildung und Erziehung angesichts der Endlichkeit des Menschen. Donauwörth, 1967.
Phil 8612.58 — Zoepfl, Helmut. Der Tod im Phänomen der Bildung und Erziehung. Thesis. München, 1963.
Phil 35.2 — The zoist. London, 1848. 2v.
Phil 6688.14 — Zoistic magnetism. (Scoresby, William.) London, 1849.
Phil 665.102 — Zolla, Elémire. Le potenze dell'anima. Milano, 1968.
Phil 7060.97 — Zöllner, J.C.F. Transcendental physics. London, 1880.
Phil 7060.97.3 — Zöllner, J.C.F. Transcendental physics. 2. ed. Boston, 1881.
Phil 4210.197 — Zolo, Danilo. Il personalismo rosminiano. Brescia, 1963.
Phil 6319.8 — Zolowicz, E. Die Persönlichkeitsanalyse. Leipzig, 1926.
Phil 5585.138 — Zoltobrocki, Josefa. Über systematische Fehler bei wiederholter Schätzung von Zeitintervallen. Frankfurt, 1965.
NEDL Phil 177.32 — Zoltowski, A. Graf August Cieszkowski's "Philosophie der Tat". Posen, 1904.
Phil 3425.127 — Zółtowski, A. Metoda Hegla i zasady filosofii spekulatywej. Krakow, 1910.
Phil 70.118 — Zonal'naia Konferentsiia Psikhologov Pribaltki, 5th, Tartu, Kääriku, 1968. Materialy V Zonal'noi Konferentsii Psikhologov Pribaltiki. Tartu, 1968.
Phil 4710.149 — Zonal'naia Nauchnaia Konferentsiia po Filosofskim Naukam, 2d, Perm', 1965. Materialy. Perm', 1965.
Phil 1812.5 — Het zondebegrip in de engelsche evolutionislische wijsbegeerte. (Merwe, A.J. van der.) Utrecht, 1925.
Phil 8050.68 — Zonta, Giuseppe. Manualetto d'estetica. Torino, 1925.
Phil 4752.2.180 — Zoppo, Franco. La rivelazione della libertà. Firenze, 1966.
Phil 8605.2.5 — Zoppola, G. A vapore. Firenze, 1914.
Phil 8605.2 — Zoppola, G. Il pensiero religioso. Lugano, 1911. 2 pam.
Phil 7003.5 — Zorab, George. Bibliography of parapsychology. N.Y., 1957.
Phil 5590.544 — Zorzumiite samykh sebe. (Kucher, Volodymyr.) Kanada, 1969.
Phil 8426.6 — Zotov, Ivan A. Priroda prekrasnogo. Moskva, 1965.
Phil 5620.18 — Zoul, L. On the origin of reason. N.Y., 1938.
Phil 8605.15 — Žrvotić, Milad. Aktuelni problemi odnosa prema religiji. Beograd, 1961.
Phil 400.130 — Zschimmer, Eberhard. Technik und Idealismus. Jena, 1920.
Phil 338.32 — Zu einem Prinzip der Messung. (Husser, Friedrich F.) Meisenhem am Glan, 1960.
Phil 310.14A — Zu einigen Fragen der marxistischen Theorie der Wahrheit. 1. Aufl. (Schaff, Adam.) Berlin, 1954.
Phil 3246.210 — Zu Fichte's Gedächtniss. (Bayer, Karl.) Ansbach, 1835.
Phil 3246.97 — Zu Fichtes Lehre von Nicht- ich. (Bensow, Oscar.) Bern, 1898.
Phil 310.50.5 — Zu Fragen der Geschichte der Philosophie und des dialektischen Materialismus. (Gropp, Rugard Otto.) Berlin, 1959.
Phil 3425.267 — Zu Georg Wilhelm Friedrich Hegels 100. Todestag (am 14 november 1931). Berlin, 1931.
Phil 3503.1.5 — Zu Kants Gedächtnis. (Vaihinger, H.) Berlin, 1904.
Phil 3487.11 — Zu Kants Rechtsphilosophie. (Fricker, K.V.) Lipsiae, 1885.
Phil 5640.136.15 — Zuber, John Peter. Sensory deprivation: fifteen years of research. N.Y., 1969.
Phil 3625.5.89 — Zubersky, A. Salomon Maimon und der kritischen Idealismus. Leipzig, 1925.
Phil 4987.89.20 — Zubiri, Xavier. Estudios filosóficos. Madrid, 1963.
Phil 4987.89.30 — Zubiri, Xavier. Naturaleza, historia, Dios. Buenos Aires, 1948.
Phil 260.15 — Zubor, Vasilii P. Razvitie atomisticheskikh predstavlenii do nachala XIX veka. Moskva, 1965.
Phil 8650.1 — Zucca, A. Essere e non essere. Roma, 1920.
Phil 200.5.10 — Zucca, Antioco. I rapporti fra l'individuo e l'universo. Padova, 1937.
Phil 200.5 — Zucca, Antioco. L'uomo e l'infinito. Roma, 1906.
Phil 200.5.5 — Zucca, Antioco. Le veritable role de l'homme dans l'universe. Paris, 19- ?
Phil 2138.89.5 — Zuccante, G. Giovanni Stuart Mill e l'utilitarismo. Firenze, 1922.
Phil 2138.89F — Zuccante, G. La morale utilitaria dello Stuart Mill. Milano, 1899.
Phil 3808.158 — Zuccante, G. Osservazioni critiche alla filosofia di Arturo Schopenhauer. Milano, 1929.
Phil 1725.1 — Zuccante, Giuseppe. Uomini e dottrine. Torino, 1926.

Phil 825.10 — Zucchi, Hernan. Estudios de filosofía antigua y moderna. Tucumán, 1956[1957]
Phil 4210.121F — Zucchi, N. Parole dette da N. Zucchi per l'inaugurazione del monumento ad Antonio Rosmini in Milano. n.p., 1896.
Htn Phil 8900.6* — Zuccolo, G. I discorsi mi quali si tratta della nobilità. Venetia, 1575.
Phil 9560.15 — Zuccolo, L. Nobilita commune, et heroica penser nuova é curiosa. Venetia, 1625.
Phil 3850.16.105 — Zuch des Dankes an G. Simmel. (Gassen, Kurt.) Berlin, 1958.
Phil 8850.3 — Zucker, Friedrich. Syneidesis-conscientia. Jena, 1928.
Phil 6135.2 — Zuckerkandl, E. Über das Riechcentrum. Stuttgart, 1887.
Phil 3425.670 — Zuefle, Manfred. Prosa der Welt: die Sprache Hegels. Einsiedeln, 1968.
Phil 5265.4 — Zürcher, W. Über die Intelligenz und ihren Ort im Gefüge des Verhalttens. Bern, 1941.
Phil 5835.2 — Zürn, Friedrich A. Die intellectuellen Eigenschaften der Pferde. Stuttgart, 1899.
Phil 3808.112.15 — Züruck zu Schopenhauer. (Kusten, Wallebald.) Berlin, 1910.
Phil 5592.172 — Zuest, R. Das Dorfspiel. Bern, 1963.
Phil 4720.5 — Zuev, Ivan E. Ob"ektivnoe i sub"ektivnoe v poznanii i prakticheskoi deiatel'nosti. Moskva, 1969.
Phil 270.58 — Der Zufall. (Scholz, W. von.) Stuttgart, 1924.
Phil 6328.5.10 — Der Zufall und die Kaboldstreiche. (Silberer, Herbert.) Bern, 1921.
Phil 193.116 — Zufall und Schicksal. (Stern, Erich.) Karlsruhe, 1926.
Phil 8407.23 — Zugänge zur Asthetik. (Geiger, M.) Leipzig, 1928.
Phil 303.18 — Zugang zu philosophischen Kosmologie. (Wein, Hermann.) München, 1954.
Phil 294.8 — Zugang zur Wicklichkeit. (Nickel, E.J.) Freiburg, 1963.
Phil 75.54 — Zugange zur Philosophie. (Emunds, Heinz.) Köln, 1959.
Phil 186.50.20 — Zugleich. (Ludowici, A.) München, 1933.
Phil 5065.1A — Zuhen, Theodor. Lehrbuch der Logik. Bonn, 1920.
Phil 1750.166.125 — Zuidema, S.U. Baanbrekers van het humanisme. Franeker, 1959.
Phil 3903.4.80 — Zuidema, Sytse Uebe. Wetenschappelijke bijdragen door leerigen van D.H.M. Vollenhoveu. Franeker, 1951.
Phil 5241.182 — De zuilen van het Panthéon en andere studies. (Berg, Jan Hendrik van den.) Nijkerk, 1969.
Phil 3120.11.92 — Zuivere rede. (Bolland, G.J.P.J.) Leiden, 1904.
Phil 6135.1 — Zukrigl, J. Kritische Untersuchung über das Wesen der vernünstigen Geist-Seele. Regensburg, 1854.
Phil 3915.70.10 — Die Zukunft der Kultur. (Wundt, Wilhelm.) Leipzig, 1920.
Phil 8610.958 — Die Zukunft des Unglaubens. (Szczesny, Gerhard.) München, 1958.
Htn 6315.2.61* — Die Zukunft einer Illusion. (Freud, Sigmund.) Wien, 1927.
Phil 325.1 — Zulänglichkeit des Empirismus...Philosophie. (Hoppe, R.) Berlin, 1852.
Phil 3845.1 — Zulawski, J. Problem der Kausalität bei Spinoza. Bern, 1899.
Phil 1825.1 — Zulen, P.S. Del neohegelianismo al neorealismo. Lima, 1924.
Phil 2475.1.200 — Zulen, P.S. La filosofía de lo inexpresable. Lima, 1920.
Phil 5873.4 — Zulliger, Hans. Die Angst unserer Kinder. Frankfurt, 1969.
Phil 5592.50 — Zulliger, Hans. Der Diapositiv-Z-Test. Bern, 1955?
Phil 5870.55 — Zulliger, Hans. Das Kind in der Entwicklung. Bern, 1969.
Phil 5593.66.10 — Zulliger, Hans. Praxis des Zulliger-Tafeln- und Diapositiv-Tests und ausgewählte Aufsätze. Bern, 1966.
Phil 5599.98 — Zulliger, Hans. Der Tafeln-Z-Test für individuelle psychologische Prüfungen, ein abgekürztes Rorschach-Verfahren. Bern, 1954.
Phil 5599.98.5 — Zulliger, Hans. The Zulliger individual and group test. N.Y., 1969.
Phil 5599.98.5 — The Zulliger individual and group test. (Zulliger, Hans.) N.Y., 1969.
Phil 3900.1.81 — Zum Andenken an Friedrich Ueberweg. (Dilthey, W.) n.p., n.d.
Phil 5258.43 — Zum Begriff und Sitz der Seele. (Schmidt, E.) Freiburg, 1897.
Phil 3845.25 — Zum Charakter Spinozas. 2. Aufl. Halle, 1919.
Phil 270.33 — Zum Erweise des allgischen Kausalgesetzes. (Meinong, A.) Wien, 1918.
Phil 3480.79.10 — Zum ewigen Frieden. (Kant, Immanuel.) Berlin, 1917.
Htn Phil 3480.79* — Zum ewigen Frieden. (Kant, Immanuel.) Königsberg, 1795.
Htn Phil 3480.79.3* — Zum ewigen Frieden. (Kant, Immanuel.) Königsberg, 1795. 2 pam.
Htn Phil 3480.79.4* — Zum ewigen Frieden. (Kant, Immanuel.) Königsberg, 1796.
Phil 3480.79.7 — Zum ewigen Frieden. (Kant, Immanuel.) Leipzig, 1881?
Phil 3480.79.12 — Zum ewigen Frieden. 2. Aufl. (Kant, Immanuel.) Leipzig, 1919.
Phil 8092.8 — Zum Felde, A. Estetica del novecientos. Buenos Aires, 1928?
Phil 8715.5 — Zum Felde, Alberto. Croisto y nosotros. Montevideo, 1959.
Phil 8887.115 — Zum Formalismus in der neueren Ethik. (Molitor, Arnulf.) Wien, 1960.
Phil 3850.1.84 — Zum Gedächtnis an David Friedrich Strauss. (Kuenkler, Heinrich.) Wiesbaden, 1898.
Phil 356.1.10 — Zum gegenwärtigen Stand der Erkenntnistheorie. (Ziehen, T.) Wiesbaden, 1914.
Phil 180.62 — Zum Geisteskampf der Gegenwart. (Fischer, E.) Basel, 1941.
Phil 294.7 — Zum Gültigkeitsbereich der Naturgesetze. (Nernst, Walther.) Berlin, 1921.
Phil 6325.1.30 — Zum Kampf um die Psychoanalyse. (Pfister, Oskar.) Wien, 1920.
Phil 3640.182 — Zum Nietzsche-Verständnis. (Kämpfer, Hartfried.) Celle, 1919.
Phil 3425.332 — Zum Problem der hegelschen Dialectik. (Dürr, Agnes.) Berlin, 1938.
Phil 182.94 — Zum Problem der Realitätsgegebenheit. (Hartmann, N.) Berlin, 1931.
Phil 5649.25 — Zum Problem der Sensumotorik. (Kohl, Kurt.) Frankfurt, 1956.
Phil 720.94 — Zum Problem der Voraussetzungslosigkeit und Objektivität in der Wissenschaft. Photoreproduction. (Hennemann, Gerhard.) Bonn, 1947.
Phil 260.12 — Zum Problem des Infinitesimalen bei den antiken Atomisten. (Mau, Jergen.) Berlin, 1957.
Phil 8402.37 — Zum Problem des Typischen in der Kunst. (Besenbruch, Walter.) Weimar
Phil 3640.384.5 — Zum Stil des Zarathustra. (Landmann, M.) n.p., 1944.
Phil 6122.3 — Zum streit über Leib und Seele. (Meyer, J.B.) Hamburg, 1856.
Phil 5545.34 — Zum Studium der Merkfähigkeit. (Siehl, A.) Berlin, 1902.
Phil 3625.1.121 — Zum sweihundertjährigen Geburtstag Moses Mendelssohns; vier Abhandlungen. (Freudenthal, M.) Berlin, 1929.

Phil 176.3.3 — Zum Verhältniss Zwischen Wille und Motiv. (Bahnsen, J.) Lauenburg, 1870.

Phil 3496.6 — Zum Willinsproblem bei Kant und Reinhold. (Olivier, Paul.) Berlin, 1941.

Phil 3640.400 — Zum 50. Todestag Friedrich Nietzsches. (Gerbes, Hans E.) n.p., 195-.

Phil 3585.2.80 — Zum 70. Geburtstag Otto Liebmanns festschrift Kantstudien. Berlin, 1910.

Phil 6319.1.85 — Zum 85. Geburtstag von Professor Dr. Carl Gustav Jung. (Read, Herbert.) Zürich, 1960.

Phil 9070.39 — Zúñiga, Pallais M. Golpes en cantera reflexiva. San José, 1931.

Phil 4987.60.61 — Zunino Dubois, J.C. Entre robles y tilos. La Plata, 1962.

Phil 3808.74 — Zur Ästhetik der Poesie, Musik und der bildend en Künste. (Schopenhauer, Arthur.) Leipzig, n.d.

Phil 197.33 — Zur Analyse der aesthetischen Substanz. (Waldeck, Oscar.) Dresden, 1900.

Phil 5252.62 — Zur Analyse der Unterschiedsempfindlichkeit. (Martin, L.J.) Leipzig, 1899.

Phil 5250.7 — Zur Analyse der Vorstellungen und ihre Gesetze. (Koffka, K.) Leipzig, 1912.

Phil 5374.33 — Zur Analyse der Apperceptions begriffes. (Kodis, J.) Berlin, 1893.

Phil 3499.16 — Zur Analyse von Kants Philosoph des organischen. (Roretz, Karl.) Wien, 1922.

Phil 186.12 — Zur Analysis der Wirklichkeit. (Liebmann, O.) Strassburg, 1876.

Htn Phil 6400.3* — Zur Auffassung der Aphasien. (Freud, S.) Leipzig, 1891.

Phil 6060.50 — Zur Ausdruckslehre und Charaklerkunde. (Klages, Ludwig.) Heidelberg, 1927.

Phil 8708.42 — Zur Begegnung mit Naturwissenschaft und Theologie. (Spülbeck, Otto.) Einsiedeln, 1969.

Phil 5190.24 — Zur Begriffsgeschichte des "Paradoxon". Inaug. Diss. (Schilder, Klaas.) Kampen, 1933.

Phil 8885.34 — Zur Biologie der Ethik. (Kant, Otto.) Wien, 1932.

Phil 3552.259 — Zur Chronologie der leibnizischen Abhandlung "De vera methodo philosphiae et theologiae". (Kolls.) Schönberg, 1906.

Phil 6115.11.2 — Zur Diätetik der Seele. (Feuchtersleben, E.F.V.) Hamburg, 1880.

Phil 6115.11 — Zur Diätetik der Seele. (Feuchtersleben, E.F.V.) Wien, 1867.

Phil 6115.11.6 — Zur Diätetik der Seele. 2. Aufl. (Feuchtersleben, E.F.V.) Halle, 1893.

Phil 6115.11.4 — Zur Diätetik der Seele. 9. Aufl. (Feuchtersleben, E.F.V.) Wien, 1852.

Phil 3425.122 — Zur Dialektik des Bewusstseins nach Hegel. (Purpus, Wilhelm.) Berlin, 1908.

Phil 9245.8.5 — Zur Ehrenrettung des Eudämonismus. (Pfleiderer, E.) Tübingen, 1879.

Phil 3552.290 — Zur Ehrenrettung von Leibniz. (Klopp, O.) Berlin, 1878.

Phil 3791.50 — Zur Einführung in der Philosophie des Gegenwart. (Riehl, Alois.) Leipzig, 1903.

Phil 1717.5.4 — Zur Einführung in die Philosophie der Gegenwart. 4. Aufl. (Riehl, Alois.) Leipzig, 1913.

Phil 1717.5.5 — Zur Einführung in die Philosophie der Gegenwart. 5e Aufl. (Riehl, Alois.) Leipzig, 1919.

Phil 3850.19.40 — Zur Einleitung in die Philosophie. (Suabedissen, D.T.A.) Marburg, 1827.

Phil 3850.35 — Zur Einteilung der Wissenschaften. (Stumpf, Karl.) Berlin, 1907.

Phil 5258.24 — Zur Entstehung der Seele. (Struve, H. von.) Tübingen, 1862.

Phil 3552.262 — Zur Entwickelungsgeschichte der leibnitzschen Monadenlehre. Diss. (Auerbach, S.) Dessau, 1884.

Phil 3450.17.90 — Zur Entwicklungsgeschichte der neuern katholischen Philosophie...Hertlings. Inaug. Diss. (Weinzierl, H.) Reimlingen, 1928.

Phil 3460.89 — Zur Erinnerung an den Denker F.H. Jacobi und seine Weltansicht. (Wiegand, Wilhelm.) Worms, 1863?

Phil 3890.1.81 — Zur Erinnerung an Friedrich Adolf Trendelenburg. (Bonitz, Hermann.) Boston, 1872.

Phil 3640.412 — Zur Erinnerung an Friedrich Nietzsche. Leipzig, 190-?

Phil 3492.41 — Zur Erinnerung an Immanuel Kant. (Königsberg Universität.) Halle, 1904.

Phil 3246.193 — Zur Erinnerung an Johann Gottlieb Fichte. (Trendelenburg, A.) Berlin, 1862.

Phil 3525.87 — Zur Erinnerung an K.C.F. Krause. (Eucken, Rudolf.) Leipzig, 1881.

Phil 3425.278 — Zur Erinnerungen an Georg W.F. Hegel. (Harms, F.) Berlin, 1871.

Phil 3120.18.90 — Zur Erkenntnislehre Jakob Sigismund Becko. (Reiser, Joseph.) München, 1934.

Phil 5057.26 — Zur Erkenntnistheorie der konkreten Dialektik. (Raphael, Max.) Paris, 1934.

Phil 353.7 — Zur Erkenntnistheorie und Ethik. (Witte, J.H.) Berlin, 1877.

Phil 8881.41 — Zur Ethik des Gesamtwellens. (Goldscheid, Rudolf.) Leipzig, 1902.

Phil 8890.6.15 — Zur Ethik und Politik. (Paulsen, F.) Berlin, 19- . 2v.

Phil 8890.6.17 — Zur Ethik und Politik. (Paulsen, F.) Berlin, 19- ? 2v.

Phil 8890.6.12 — Zur Ethik und Politik. v.1-2. (Paulsen, F.) Berlin, n.d.

Phil 8876.107.5 — Zur ethischen Lebensgestaltung. (Börner, W.) Wien, 1937?

Phil 8826.4 — Zur ethnischen Ethik. (Bastian, Adolf.) Berlin, 1889.

X Cg Phil 5645.4 — Zur Farbenlehre. (Goethe, J.W. von.) Tübingen, 1810. 3v.

Htn Phil 5645.4.2* — Zur Farbenlehre. (Goethe, J.W. von.) Tübingen, 1810. 2v.

Phil 8960.1 — Zur Feier des Reformationsfestes. (Kirn, Otto.) Leipzig, 1906.

Phil 6959.5 — Zur Frage der Dementia Praecox. (Jahrmärker, M.) Halle, 1903.

Phil 5593.65.5 — Zur Frage der Persönlichkeitsveränderung nach stereotaktischen Operationen. Inaug. Diss. (Scholtz, Walter.) Freiburg, 1965?

Phil 3425.306 — Zur Frage nach dem Ursprung des dialektischen Denkens bei Hegel. Inaug. Diss. (Axmann, Walter.) Würzburg, 1939.

Phil 5593.68 — Zur Frage nach quantitativer und qualitativer Änderungen nach Rorschach-Kategorien im Schulalter. (Matejek, Georg.) Weinheim, 1968.

Phil 2880.8.114 — Zur Freiheit verurteilt. (Streller, Justus.) Hamburg, 1952.

Phil 3450.18.100 — Zur Freiheitslehre von Nicolai Hartmann. Inaug. Diss. (Daehler, J.) Freiburg, 1952.

Phil 9425.10 — Zur Friedensidee in der Reformationszeit. (Wollgast, Siegfried.) Berlin, 1968.

Phil 3640.34.5 — Zur Genealogie der Moral. (Nietzsche, Friedrich.) Leipzig, 193-.

Phil 585.160.5 — Zur Genealogie des menschlichen Bewusstseins. (Rothacker, Erich.) Bonn, 1966.

Phil 337.1 — Zur Geschichte der Erkenntnis Problems. (Grimm, E.) Leipzig, n.d.

Phil 5757.2 — Zur Geschichte der Lehre von der Freiheit des menschlichen Willens. (Heman, C.F.) Leipzig, 1887.

Phil 5014.1.5 — Zur Geschichte der Logik. (Enriques, Federigo.) Leipzig, 1927.

Phil 3800.386.5 — Zur Geschichte der neueren Philosophie; Münchener Vorlesungen. (Schelling, F.W.J. von.) Stuttgart, 1955.

Phil 1722.1 — Zur Geschichte der neueren Philosophie. (Weigelt, G.) Hamburg, 1855.

Phil 812.16 — Zur Geschichte der Philosophie. (Mehring, Franz.) Berlin, 1931?

Htn Phil 6315.2.3* — Zur Geschichte der psychoanalytischen Bewegung. Leipzig, 1924.

Phil 1135.64.5 — Zur Geschichte der teleologischen Naturbetrachtung bis auf Aristoteles. (Theiler, W.) Zürich, 1925.

Phil 1135.64 — Zur Geschichte der teleologischen Naturbetrachtung bis auf Aristoteles. Inaug. Diss. (Theiler, W.) Zürich, 1924.

Phil 1714.6 — Zur Geschichte der vormarxschen Philosophie. (Oizerman, Teodor I.) Berlin, 1960.

Phil 5425.13.15 — Zur Geschichte der Wissenschaften und der Gelehrten. (Candolle, A. de.) Leipzig, 1911.

Phil 5400.44 — Zur Geschichte des Achtungsbegriffes und zur Theorie der sittlichen Gefühle. Inaug. Diss. (Gurewitsch, Aron.) Würzburg, 1897.

Phil 1506.1 — Zur Geschichte des Nominalis von Roscellin. (Barach, C.S.) Wien, 1866.

Phil 3415.66 — Zur Geschichte und Begründung des Pessimismus. (Hartmann, Eduard von.) Berlin, 1880.

Htn Phil 3585.3.30* — Zur Geschichte und Literatur. (Lessing, G.E.) Braunschweig, 1777.

Phil 8050.61 — Zur Gesetzlichkeit der abendländischen Kunst. (Voigtländer, E.) Bonn, 1921.

Phil 9550.3.5 — Zur Grundlegung der allgemeinen Werth-Theorie. (Meinong, A.) Graz, 1923.

Phil 5052.21 — Zur Grundlegung der Logik. (Matičević, Stephan.) Wien, 1909.

Phil 182.94.15 — Zur Grundlegung der Ontologie. (Hartmann, N.) Berlin, 1935.

Phil 3425.584.5 — Zur Grundlegung der polytechnischen Bildung durch Hegel und Marx. (Reining, Richard.) Braunschweig, 1967.

Phil 5252.30 — Zur Grundlegung der Psychophysik. 2. Ausg. (Müller, G.E.) Berlin, 1879.

Phil 5545.68 — Zur Grundlegung einer Lehre von der Erinnerung. (Gallinger, A.) Halle, 1914.

Phil 3090.82 — Zur hundertjährigen Geburtsfeier Franz von Baaders. (Fischer, K.P.) Erlangen, 1865.

Phil 705.54 — Zur Idee der Transzendentalphilosophie. (Lauth, Reinhard.) München, 1965.

Phil 3487.28 — Zur Interpretation der Kantischen Ethik im Lichte der Achtung. Inaug. Diss. (Falaturi, Abdal-Jawad.) Bonn, 1965.

Phil 3493.12 — Zur Kantfeier der Albertina. (Ludwich, A.) Regimontii, 1889.

Phil 176.153 — Zur Klärung der Begriffe. 1. Aufl. (Burgmüller, H.) München, 1947.

Phil 5060.3 — Zur Krisis in der Logik. (Uphues, G.) Berlin, 1903.

Phil 8026.5 — Zur Kritik der bürgerlichen Ideologie. Berlin. 1,1971+

Phil 8591.65.5 — Zur Kritik der Christlichen Uberlieferung. (Loewith, Karl.) Stuttgart, 1966.

Phil 1711.1.5 — Zur Kritik der Gegenwart. (Liehert, A.) Langensalza, 1927.

Phil 3625.3.83 — Zur Kritik der Machschen Philosophie. (Hönigswald, R.) Berlin, 1903.

Phil 6328.31 — Zur Kritik der Psychoanalyse. (Schwarz, Theodor.) Zürich, 1947.

Phil 5205.34 — Zur Kritik der Psychologie. (Hildebrant, R.) Marburg, 1946. 4 pam.

Htn Phil 3801.545* — Zur Kritik der Schellingschen Offenbarungsphilosophie. (Marheineke, P.) Berlin, 1843.

Phil 3120.8.94 — Zur Kritik der Urteilslehre Franz Brentanos. (Schneider, Karl.) Heidelberg, 1915.

Phil 3915.105.5 — Zur Kritik des Seelenbegriffs. (Vannérus, Allen.) n.p., n.d.

Phil 3499.33 — Zur Kritik des Sowjetismus am Kritizismus Kants. (Reinig, Richard.) Ratingen, 1964.

Phil 8125.14 — Zur Kunstanschauung des XVIII. Jahrhunderts. (Stöcker, Helene.) Berlin, 1904.

Phil 9035.17 — Zur Lehre vom Gemüt. (Rehmeké, J.) Leipzig, 1911.

Phil 5643.11.5 — Zur Lehre vom Lichtsinne. (Hering, E.) Wien, 1878.

Phil 3499.21 — Zur Lehre vom Raum...Lehre Kants. (Röver, G.) Oldenburg, 1923.

Phil 6111.24 — Zur Lehre von dem Verhältniss der Ganglienkörper zu den Nervenfasern. (Bidder, Friedrich.) Leipzig, 1847.

Phil 5190.4 — Zur Lehre von der Definition. 2e Aufl. (Rickert, H.) Tübingen, 1915.

Phil 5190.4.2 — Zur Lehre von der Definition. 3. Aufl. (Rickert, H.) Tübingen, 1929.

Phil 5115.8 — Zur Lehre von der Hypothesenbildung. (Hillebrand, F.) Wien, 1896.

Phil 350.1 — Zur Lehre von Inhalt und Gegenstand. (Twardowski, K.) Wien, 1894.

Phil 176.81 — Zur Lösung des metaphysischen Problems. (Bender, Hedwig.) Berlin, 1886.

Phil 5055.18 — Zur Logik der Gemeinschaft. (Pichler, Hans.) Tübingen, 1924.

Phil 3160.12.42 — Zur Logik der Kulturwissenschaften. 2. Aufl. (Cassirer, Ernst.) Darmstadt, 1961.

Phil 5052.32 — Zur Logik des Konkreten Begriffs. (Manheim, Ernst.) München, 1930.

Phil 2115.108 — Zur Logik Lockes. (Martinak, E.) Graz, 1887.

Phil 3480.24 — Zur Logik und Metaphysik. 2. Aufl. (Kant, Immanuel.) Leipzig, 1921. 4v.

Phil 5041.12 — Zur logischen Frage. (Biedermann, Gustav.) Prag, 1870.

Phil 6122.44 — Zur Mechanik des Gehirnbaues. (Meynert, T.) Wien, 1874.

Phil 3790.2.30.8 — Zur Mechanik des Geistes. 8e und 9e Aufl. (Rathenau, W.) Berlin, 1918.

Phil 3450.11.160 — Zur Metakritik der Erkenntnistheorie. (Adorno, T.W.) Stuttgart, 1970.

Phil 9178.10 — Zur Metaphysik des Muttertums. (Schapp, Wilhelm.) Den Haag, 1965.

Phil 6127.4 — Zur Natur der Bewegungen. (Rubenstein, S.) Leipzig, 1890.

Phil 5810.6 — Zur nichteuklidischen Struktur des Phänomenalen Raumes. (Allesch, G.J. von.) Jena, 1931.

Htn Phil 3800.300* Zur öffentlichen Sitzung der k. Academie der Wissenschaften am Vorabend des Ludwigs-Tages 1829. (Schelling, F.W.J. von.) München, 1829.

Phil 5875.25 Zur Ontogenese des sittlichen Urteils in besonderer Antinüpfung und die einschlägige Theorie Piaget's. Inaug. Diss. (Pongratz, Josa Maria.) Heidelberg? 1964.

Phil 3120.55.90 Zur Ontologie und Logik offener Systeme. (Roeder von Diersburg, Egenolf.) Hamburg, 1967.

Phil 180.70 Zur ontologischen Frühgeschichte von Raum, Zeit, Bewegung. (Fink, Eugen.) Den Haag, 1957.

Phil 5850.331 Zur Organisation der Eignungspsychologie. (Sachs, Hildegard.) Leipzig, 1920.

Phil 197.46 Zur Orientierung der Philosophie am Bewusstseinsbegriff. (Wirth, William.) München, 1919.

Phil 5460.2 Zur Phänomenologie der Täuschungen. Inaug. Diss. (Leyendecker, Herbert.) Halle, 1913.

Phil 5460.2.3 Zur Phänomenologie der Täuschungen. 1. Teil. (Leyendecker, Herbert.) Halle, 1913.

Phil 5374.245.10 Zur Phänomenologie des Bewusstseinsstroms. (Gorsen, Peter.) Bonn, 1966.

Phil 5070.17 Zur Phänomenologie des Glaubens. Inaug. Diss. (Mertens, Paul.) Fulda, 1927.

Phil 735.260 Zur Phänomenologie des Werterlebens. (Bruederlin, Kurt.) Winterthur, 1962.

Phil 5520.73 Zur Phänomenologie und Analyse des Ausdrucks. (Kunz, H.) Basel, 1934.

Phil 5415.7.5 Zur Phänomenologie und Theorie der Sympathiegefühle. (Scheler, Max.) Halle, 1913.

Phil 8585.26 Zur philosophie der Christentums. (Flügel, O.) Langensalza, 1899.

Phil 200.12 Zur Philosophie der Gegenwart. Prag, 1934.

Phil 8419.23 Zur Philosophie der Kunst. (Simmel, Georg.) Potsdam, 1922.

Phil 3935.1.80 Zur Philosophie des Grafen Paul Vorck von Wartenburg. (Gruender, Karl Fried.) Göttingen, 1970.

Phil 5250.13.25 Zur Philosophie und Psychologie der Ganzheit. (Krueger, Felix.) Berlin, 1953.

Phil 6112.22 Zur Physiologie des Gehirnes. (Christiani, A.) Berlin, 1885.

Phil 5247.62 Zur Prinzipienfrage der Psychologie. (Heinrich, W.) Zürich, 1899.

Phil 336.17 Zur Prinzipienlehre der Auschauung. (Flach, W.) Hamburg, 1963.

Phil 310.612 Zur Problematik der materialistische Dialektischen. (Goerlich, J.) Berlin, 1965.

Phil 5247.23.25 Zur Propädeutik-Frage. (Höfler, Alois.) Wien, 1884.
Phil 6327.10 Zur psychoanalyse. 2. Aufl. (Raimann, Emil.) Berlin, 1925.

Phil 70.23 Zur Psychoanalyse der Kriegsneurosen. Leipzig, 1919.
Phil 5520.22 Zur Psychologie der Aussage. (Gmelin, J.G.) Hannover, 1909.

Phil 5850.347.5 Zur Psychologie der Aussage. (Stern, Louis W.) Berlin, 1902.

Phil 181.42 Zur Psychologie der Begriffsmetaphysik. (Gans, Max E.) Wien, 1914.

Phil 6327.38 Zur Psychologie der falschen Anschuldigung und falschen Selbstbezichtigung. (Reich-Dörr, Marta.) Hamburg, 1962.

Phil 5252.52 Zur Psychologie der Gegenwart. (Meyer, Hans.) Köln, 1909.
Phil 7140.124 Zur Psychologie der Hypnose und der Suggestion. (Friedrichs, T.) Stuttgart, 1922.

Phil 5828.1 Zur Psychologie der menschlichen Triebe. (Santlus, J.C.) Neuwied, 1864.

Phil 5590.472 Zur Psychologie der Persönlichkeit. (Petrilowitsch, Nikolaus.) Darmstadt, 1967.

Phil 182.79A Zur Psychologie der Philosophie und der Philosophen. (Herzberg, Alex.) Leipzig, 1926.

Phil 6060.13 Zur Psychologie der Schreibfehler. (Stoll, Jakob.) Zürich, 1913.

Phil 5241.49 Zur Psychologie der Zukunft. (Bleibtreu, K.) Leipzig, 1890.

Phil 5832.11 Zur Psychologie des Erkennens. (Wolff, Gustav.) Leipzig, 1897.

Phil 5870.25 Zur Psychologie des Kindes. (Hetzer, Hildegard.) Darmstadt, 1967.

Phil 5255.19 Zur Psychologie des philosophischen Denkens. (Pfister, O.) Bern, 1923.

Phil 5243.68.2 Zur Psychologie des Produktiven Denkens. 2e Neudruck. (Duncker, Karl.) Berlin, 1966.

Phil 5871.105.2 Zur Psychologie des proletarischen Kindes. 2. Aufl. (Ruehle, Otto.) Frankfurt, 1970.

Phil 6060.6 Zur Psychologie des Schreibens. (Preyer, William.) Hamburg, 1895.

Phil 6060.6.3 Zur Psychologie des Schreibens. (Preyer, William.) Leipzig, 1919.

Phil 5252.40 Zur Psychologie des Verstehens wissenschaftlicher Texte. Inaug. Diss. (Martin, Otto.) Freiburg, 1914.

Phil 5402.20 Zur Psychologie des Weinens. Inaug. Diss. (Spitz, C.) Zeulenroda, 1935.

Phil 3915.6 Zur Psychologie und Ethik. (Wundt, Wilhelm.) Leipzig, 1911.

Phil 735.104 Zur Psychologie und Metaphysik des Wert-Erlebens. (Groos, Karl.) Berlin, 1932.

Htn Phil 6319.1.25* Zur Psychologie und Pathologie sogenannter occulter Phänomene. Inaug. Diss. (Jung, C.G.) Leipzig, 1902.

Phil 5545.185 Zur Psychologie und Psychopathologie der Erinnerungen. (Wieck, H.H.) Stuttgart, 1955.

Phil 349.15 Zur Psychologie und Theorie der Erkenntnis. (Siegel, Carl.) Leipzig, 1903.

Phil 175.22 Zur psychologischen Analyse der Welt. (Aars, K.B.R.) Leipzig, 1900.

Phil 5643.80 Zur Psychophysik des Lichtsinns. (Neiglick, H.) Leipzig, 1887.

Phil 5643.83 Zur psychophysischen Analyse der repsoldschen Mikrometerrigistrierung von Sterndurchgängen. (Wirth, Wilhelm.) Leipzig, 1915.

Phil 8599.19.15 Zur religiösen Lage. 2. Aufl. (Troeltsch, Ernst.) Tübingen, 1922.

Phil 8598.9.5 Zur Religionsphilosophie. (Siebeck, Hermann.) Tübingen, 1907.

Phil 5627.261 Zur Rettung des Menschlichen in unserer Zeit. (Bitter, W.) Stuttgart, 1961.

Phil 5465.48 Zur revision der Eidetek. (Schmidt, Otto.) Marburg, 1933.
Phil 3450.19.58 Zur Sache des Denkens. (Heidegger, Martin.) Tübingen, 1969.

Phil 179.3.45 Zur Sammlung der Geistert. (Eucken, R.) Leipzig, 1914.
Phil 3245.33 Zur Seelenfrage. (Fichte, Immanuel Hermann.) Leipzig, 1859.

Phil 5252.56 Zur Seelenfrage. (Mayer, A.) Mainz, 1866.

Phil 3450.19.45 Zur Seinsfrage. (Heidegger, Martin.) Frankfurt, 1956.
Phil 1504.5 Zur Stellung Avencebrolis. v.5, pt.1. (Wittmann, M.) Münster, 1906.

Phil 331.2.10 Zur Terminalfunktion. (Avenarius, R.) Berlin, 1913.
Phil 8612.54.5 Zur Theologie des Todes. 5. Aufl. (Rahnez, Karl.) Freiburg, 1958.

Phil 5190.22 Zur Theorie der Analogie und des sogenannten Analogieschlusses. Diss. (Hänssler, Ernst H.) Basel, 1927.

Phil 5330.2 Zur Theorie der Aufmerksamkeit. (Kohn, H.E.) Halle, 1894.
Phil 5330.23 Zur Theorie der Aufmerksamkeit. (Suter, Jules.) Zürich, 1914.

Phil 4200.2.20 Zur Theorie der humanistischen Geschichtschreibung. (Lamprecht, F.) Zürich, 1950.

Phil 6117.23 Zur Theorie der Nerventhätigkeit. (Hering, Ewald.) Leipzig, 1899.

Phil 610.2 Zur Theorie der Praxis. (Engelhardt, Paulus.) Mainz, 1970.

Phil 3195.10.105 Zur Theorie der Setzung und des setzungshaften Wissens bei Driesch. (Gehlen, Arnold.) Leipzig, 1927.

Phil 3195.10.95 Zur Theorie der Setzung und des setzungshaften Wissens bei Driesch. Inaug. Diss. (Gehlen, Arnold.) Leipzig, 1927.

Phil 5330.3 Zur Theorie der sinnlichen Aufmerksamkeit. (Müller, G.E.) Leipzig, 1874?

Phil 3450.11.330 Zur Theorie der Sprache bei E. Husserl. (Huelsmann, H.) München, 1964.

Phil 6112.7.5 Zur Theorie der Wechselwirkung zwischen Leib und Seele. (Cornelius, K.S.) Halle, 1880.

Phil 5258.206 Zur Theorie des Erkennens durch den Gesichtssinn. (Schleiden, Matthias Jacob.) Leipzig, 1861.

Phil 9075.26 Zur Theorie des Gewissens. Inaug. Diss. (Pauly, Karl.) Greifswald, 1913.

Phil 8125.32 Zur Theorie des Schönen. (Begennu, Siegfried.) Berlin, 1956.

Phil 1865.151A Zur Theorie des Wertes. (Kraus, Oskar.) Halle, 1901.
Phil 1750.500 Zur transzendentalen Phänomenologie. (Funke, Gerhard.) Bonn, 1957.

Phil 493.12 Zur Überwindung des wissenschaftlichen Materialismus. (Schmidt, Karl.) Basel, 1968.

Phil 5599.39.10 Zur Validität von Formdeutverfahren. (Rosenstiel, Lutz von.) München, 1967.

Phil 5643.53 Zur vergleichenden Physiologie des Gesichtssinnes. (Raehlman, E.) Jena, 1907.

Phil 193.136 Zur Verjüngung der Philosophie. 1e Reihe. (Segall-Socolin, I.) Berlin, 1893.

Phil 8875.7 Zur Vermittlung der Extreme. (Ancillon, J.P.F.) Berlin, 1831-38. 2v.

Phil 8583.33 Zur Weiterbildung der Religion. (Delitzsch, Friedrich.) Stuttgart, 1908.

Phil 5585.320 Zur Wesenlehre des psychischen Lebens und Erlebens. (Conrad, Theodor.) Den Haag, 1968.

Phil 310.30 Zur Widerlegung des dialektische und historische Materialismus. 5. Aufl. (Andreas, Theodor.) n.p., 1954.

Phil 3488.4 Zur Wiedererweckung Kantischer Lehre. (Goldschmidt, L.) Gotha, 1910.

Phil 8598.90.5 Zur Wiedergeburt des Abendlandes. 2. Aufl. (Schulze-Gaevernitz, G.) Berlin, 1934.

Phil 400.22 Zur Wiedergeburt des Idealismus. (Schmidt, F.J.) Leipzig, 1908.

Phil 3090.80.10 Zur Würdigung des Vorurthelie über der Lehre Baaders. (Hoffmann, F.) Leipzig, 1855.

Phil 5590.476 Zurabashvili, Avlipii. Problemy psikhologii i patopsikholozii lichnosti. Tbilisi, 1968.

Phil 5590.477 Zurabashvili, Avlippi. Aktual'nye problemy persondogii i klinicheskoi psikhiatrii. Tbilisi, 1970.

Phil 6962.2.3 Die Zurechnungsfähigkeit der Geisteskranken. (Maudsley, H.) Leipzig, 1875.

Phil 3850.32.80 Zurischen Romantik und Faschismus. 1. Aufl. (Schneller, Martin.) Stuttgart, 1970.

Phil 3120.4.80 Zurschen Orthodoxie und Aufklärung. (Liebing, H.) Tubingen, 1961.

Phil 3790.20 Zurück in das Wagnis der Sprache. (Rosenstock, Eugen.) Berlin, 1957.

Phil 400.75 Zurück zum Idealismus. (Hartmann, Alma von.) Berlin, 1902.

Phil 817.2.2 Zusätze und Verbesserungen. (Ritter, A.H.) Hamburg, 1838.
Phil 178.37.5 Der Zusammenbruch der Wissenschaft und der Primat der philosophie. (Dingler, Hugo.) München, 1926.

Phil 178.37.7 Der Zusammenbruch der Wissenschaft und der Primat der Philosophie. 2e Aufl. (Dingler, Hugo.) München, 1931.

Phil 177.30 Zusammenhang der Dinge. (Caspari, Otto.) Breslau, 1881.
Phil 3565.74 Der Zusammenhang der Dinge. (Lotze, Hermann.) Berlin, 191-?

Phil 978.49.425 Der Zusammenhang des Menschen mit der elementarischen Welt. (Steiner, R.) Dornach, 1968.

Phil 197.11 Zusammenhang unserer Vorstellungen. (Wolff, Hermann.) Leipzig, n.d.

Phil 5258.117 Zuschauen oder Handeln? (Schering, W.M.) Leipzig, 1937.
Phil 8605.7 Zuurdeeg, Willem. An analytical philosophy of religion. N.Y., 1958.

Phil 5068.11 Zuurdeeg, Willem Frederik. A research for the consequences of the Vienna circle philosophy for ethics. Proefschrift. Utrecht, 1946.

Phil 8680.5 Zuver, Dudley. Retreat to reality. N.Y., 1959.
Phil 8605.5 Zuver, Dudley. Salvation by laughter. N.Y., 1933.
Phil 5585.285 Zwaan, Evert Joost. Links en rechts in waarneming en beleving. Proefschrift. Utrecht, 1965.

Phil 5655.7 Zwaardemaker, H. L'odorat. Paris, 1925.
Phil 5265.2 Zwanenburg, S. Inleiding tot de psychologie. Utrecht, 1926.

Phil 6328.2.40 Zwang und Zweifel. (Stekel, Wilhelm.) Berlin, 1927-28. 2v.

Phil 5643.16 Zwangsmässige Lichtemfindungen. (Bleuler, E.) Leipzig, 1881.

Phil 3507.5.2 Zwanziger, J.C. Commentar über Kant's Kritik der reinen Vernunft. Leipzig, 1792.

Phil 3507.5 Zwanziger, J.C. Commentar über Kant's Kritik der reinen Vernunft. Leipzig, 1794.

Phil 3940.4 Zwanziger, Johann Christian. Die Religion des Philosoph und sein Glaubenskenntniss. Bruxelles, 1968.

Phil 270.146 Zwart, P.J. Causaliteit. Assen, 1967[1968]
Phil 8735.8 Der Zweck; seine Bedeutung für Natur und Geist. (Eisler, Rudolf.) Berlin, 1914.

Phil 3486.7 Der Zweckbegriff bei Kant. (Ernst, W.) Halle, 1909.
Phil 3842.9 Der Zweckbegriff bei Spinoza. Thesis. (Wetzel, Paul.) Leipzig, 1873.

Phil 5767.8	Der Zweckbegriff im psychologischen und erkenntnistheoretischen Denken. (Roretz, Karl von.) Leipzig, 1910.
Phil 1504.11	Der Zweckgedanke in der Philosophie. v.11, pt.1-2. (Steinbüchel, T.) Münster, 1912.
Phil 2115.74.10	Zwei Abhandlungen über Regierung. (Locke, J.) Halle, 1906.
Phil 8602.34	Zwei akademische Vorlesungen über Grundprobleme der systematischen Theologie. (Wobbermin, G.) Berlin, 1899.
Phil 5757.1.7	Zwei Briefe über Verursachung und Freiheit im Wollen Gerichtet. (Hazard, R.G.) N.Y., 1875.
Phil 672.152	Zwei Dialoge über Raum und Zeit. (Jaffé, George.) Leipzig, 1931.
Phil 3120.30.47	Zwei Glaubensweisen. (Buber, Martin.) Zürich, 1950.
Phil 3625.18.30	Zwei Grundprobleme der scholastischen Naturphilosophie. 2. Aufl. (Maier, A.) Roma, 1951.
Phil 3808.134	Zwei Individualisten der Schopenhauer'schen Schule. (Plumacher, G.) Wien, 1881.
Phil 3480.110	Zwei Schriften über die Grundlegenden der Naturwissenschaften. (Kant, Immanuel.) Berlin, 1920.
Phil 1712.27	Zwei Untersuchungen zur nachscholastischen Philosophie. 2e Aufl. (Maier, Anneliese.) Roma, 1968.
Phil 5255.11.5	Zwei Vorträge über dynamische Psychologie. (Pikler, Gyula.) Leipzig, 1908.
Phil 284.6.5	Zwei Vorträge zur Naturphilosophie. (Driesch, Hans.) Leipzig, 1910.
Phil 8586.27	Die zwei Wege im religiösen Denken. (Grimm, E.) Göttingen, 1922.
Phil 3585.30.10	Die Zweidimensionalität des Rechts als Voraussetzung für den Methodendualismus von Emil Lask. (Sampaio Ferraz, Torcio.) Meisenheim am Glan, 1970.
Phil 5585.19	Zweierlei Denken. (Büttner, A.) Leipzig, 1910.
Phil 8605.1	Zweifel, H. Die gesetze Göttes. München, 1876.
Phil 8900.3	Zweifel, Hans. Die sittliche Weltordnung. München, 1875.
Phil 3504.4.10	Zweifel über die Kantischen Begriffe von Zeit und Raum. (Weishaupt, A.) Nürnberg, 1788.
Phil 5070.24	Der Zweifel und seine Grenzen. (Lindner, Herbert.) Berlin, 1966.
Phil 5649.38	Zweig, Adam. Grundzüge einer tensor-algebraischen Psycho-Dynamik. v.1-2. Zürich, 1965.
Phil 5835.3.5	Zweig, Adam. Tierpsychologische Beiträge zur Psylogenese der ich-über-ich-instanzen. Bern, 1959.
Phil 5835.3	Zweig, Adam. Tierpsychologische Beiträge zur Psylogenese der ich-über-ich-instanzen. Bern, 1959.
Phil 3845.4	Zweig, Arnold. Baruch Spinoza. Darmstadt, 1968.
Phil 5421.25.40	Zweig, Paul. The heresy of self-love. N.Y., 1968.
Phil 6335.10	Zweig, S. Die heilung durch den Geist; Mesmer, Mary Baker, Eddy, Freud. Wien, 1936.
Phil 6135.4.5A	Zweig, Stefan. Mental healers. N.Y., 1932.
Phil 1750.552	Zweiheit, Bezug und Vermittlung. (Blankart, Franz André.) Zürich, 1966.
Phil 8975.1	Zwicker, Heinz. Reich Gottes. Bern, 1948.
Phil 5465.70	Zwicker, Heinz. Seelisches Leben und schöpferische Leistung. Bern, 1954.
Phil 1750.367	Zwiespältiges Dosein. (Hommes, Jakob.) Freiburg, 1953.
Phil 3120.30.155	Zwiesprache mit Martin Buber. (Ben-Chorin, Schalom.) München, 1966.
Phil 3507.12	Zwingelberg, Hans Willi. Kants Ethik und das Problem der Einheit von Freiheit und Gesetz. Thesis. Bonn, 1969.
Phil 3507.9.5	Zwingmann, H. Kant. Berlin, 1924.
Phil 3507.9	Zwingmann, H. Kants Staatstheorie. München, 19- ?
Phil 185.66	Zwischen Dekadenz und Erneuerung. (Krueger, H.) Frankfurt, 1953.
Phil 182.85	Zwischen Dichtung und Philosophie. (Hartmann, Alma.) Berlin, 1912.
Phil 3120.30.77	Zwischen Gesellschaft und Staat. (Buber, Martin.) Heidelberg, 1952.
Phil 8602.51	Zwischen Oben und Unten. (Werfel, Franz.) Stockholm, 1946.
Phil 3425.380	Zwischen Phänomenologie und Logik. (Beyer, W.R.) Frankfurt, 1955.
Phil 190.82A	Zwischen Philosophie und Gesellschaft. (Plessner, H.) Bern, 1953.
Phil 3903.1.86	Zwischen Philosophie und Kunst, Johannes Volkelt zum 100 Lehrsemester. (Schuster, Willy.) Leipzig, 1926.
Phil 293.30	Zwischen Philosophie und Mechanik. (Maier, Anneliese.) Roma, 1958.
Phil 3640.410	Zwischen Seligkeit und Verdamnis. (Lotz, J.B.) Frankfurt, 1953.
Phil 3450.26	Zwischen Wittenberg und Rom. (Hellpach, Willy.) Berlin, 1931.
Phil 3450.11.510	Das Zwischenreich des Dialogs. (Waldenfels, Bernhard.) Den Haag, 1971.
Phil 3480.68.5	Zwo Abhandlungen über moralische Gegenstände. 2. Aufl. (Kant, Immanuel.) Königsberg, 1796.
Phil 8408.9	Zwölf Briefe eines ästhetischen Ketzer's. 2. Aufl. (Hillebrand, K.) Berlin, 1874.
Phil 978.49.805.5	Die zwölf Sumie des Menschen. (Lauer, H.E.) Basel, 1953.
Phil 5870.40	Die zwölf wichtigsten Jahre des Lebens. (Pfahler, Gerhard.) München, 1967.
Phil 1750.104	Zybura, John. S. Present-day thinkers and the new scholasticism. Saint Louis, 1926.
Phil 4803.502.20	Żyć i filozofować. Wyd. 1. (Kuczyński, Janusz.) Warszawa, 1969.
Phil 35.40	Zygon. Chicago. 1,1966+ 4v.
Phil 35.40.2	Zygon. Authors and titles, v. 1-5 (1966-1970). Chicago, 1971.
Phil 630.54	Zykmund, V. Co je realismus? Praha, 1957.
Phil 8426.9	Zykmund, Václav. K základní otázce estetiky. Praha, 1957.
Phil 7069.20.360	Zymonidas, Allessandro. The problems of mediumship. London, 1920.
Phil 9558.10	Zyromski, Ernest. L'orgueil humain. 2. éd. Paris, 1905.
Phil 7082.60	2 draumur. (Sveinsson, Ingimundur.) Reykjavík, 1914.
Phil 5594.154	Der 7-Quadrate-Test. (Hector, H.) Paderborn, 1954.
Phil 182.144	100 soruda felsefe el kilabi. (Hilv, Selhattin.) Istanbul, 1970.